PRESENTED

TO

BY

ON

YOUR WORD IS A LAMP TO MY FEET
AND A LIGHT FOR MY PATH.

PSALM 119:105

PROMISE KEEPERS

MEN'S STUDY BIBLE

NEW INTERNATIONAL VERSION

Zondervan Publishing House
Grand Rapids, Michigan 49530, U.S.A.

Requests for information should be addressed to
The Zondervan Corporation
Grand Rapids, Michigan, 49530

Library of Congress Catalog Card Number 97-060280
Published by Zondervan Publishing House
Grand Rapids, Michigan, 49530, U.S.A.
http://www.zondervan.com

Find out more about Promise Keepers at
http://www.promisekeepers.org

Printed in the United States of America

97 98 99 00 01 02 6 5 4 3 2 1

RRD

TO THE READER

The wonderful Word of God is indeed the proper food for our spirit. This eternal bread will forever bring revelation of the person, presence and power of our Heavenly Father.

It has been my privilege over years of Biblical study to find that the best commentary on Scripture is Scripture itself. I hope this will be your experience as well. May you read with utter enthusiasm, unfolding insight and continual joy. As you read, may the results of this delightful experience transform you into channels of blessing.

I pray as you read and grow in *God's* grace that you will master the techniques of spiritual discipline, communion and persistence, and that your faith grows and prevails. As you seek God according to Jeremiah 29:13, "You will seek me and find me when you seek me with all your heart," you will realize that this search must occur in all areas of life—spiritual, intellectual, emotional and physical.

May this book be the tool for the making of a *godly* man (marked by *humility, repentance, devotion, purity, reconciliation, servanthood* and *perseverance*). I pray that it will also be the tool to break down walls, as you receive God's direction and wisdom for your life, and that God's Spirit will strike a revival in your heart to be truly reconciled to Him, to your families and ultimately to all of your brothers in Christ.

I pray that this Bible will kindle a fire within you to reach out to people who are different from yourself. As you learn from men and women who are different, you will begin to break down the walls that separate you. For, "The LORD does not look at the things man looks at. Man looks at the outward appearance, but the LORD looks at the heart" (1 Samuel 16:7). By hungering for God's Word and will, we *will* let the walls fall down.

Finally, I pray that His grace, goodness and glory will fill your life to overflowing, causing you to embrace each new day in the joy and awe of being a son of the Living God.

Bishop Phillip Porter
Pastor, All Nations Pentecostal Center Church of God in Christ
Chairman of the Board, Promise Keepers

CONTENTS

THE OLD TESTAMENT

THE NEW TESTAMENT

CHARACTER PROFILES

BOOKS IN ALPHABETICAL ORDER

The books of the New Testament are in *italic*.

ABBREVIATIONS

The following abbreviations are used in the center-column cross-reference system included in this Bible; the abbreviations are also used in the *Index to Subjects* and the *NIV Concordance* at the back of this Bible.

Genesis	Ge
Exodus	Ex
Leviticus	Lev
Numbers	Nu
Deuteronomy	Dt
Joshua	Jos
Judges	Jdg
Ruth	Ru
1 Samuel	1Sa
2 Samuel	2Sa
1 Kings	1Ki
2 Kings	2Ki
1 Chronicles	1Ch
2 Chronicles	2Ch
Ezra	Ezr
Nehemiah	Neh
Esther	Est
Job	Job
Psalms	Ps
Proverbs	Pr
Ecclesiastes	Ecc
Song of Songs	SS
Isaiah	Isa
Jeremiah	Jer
Lamentations	La
Ezekiel	Eze
Daniel	Da
Hosea	Hos
Joel	Joel
Amos	Am
Obadiah	Ob
Jonah	Jnh
Micah	Mic
Nahum	Na
Habakkuk	Hab
Zephaniah	Zep
Haggai	Hag
Zechariah	Zec
Malachi	Mal
Matthew	Mt
Mark	Mk
Luke	Lk
John	Jn
Acts	Ac
Romans	Ro
1 Corinthians	1Co
2 Corinthians	2Co
Galatians	Gal
Ephesians	Eph
Philippians	Php
Colossians	Col
1 Thessalonians	1Th
1 Thessalonians	2Th
1 Timothy	1Ti
2 Timothy	2Ti
Titus	Tit
Philemon	Phm
Hebrews	Heb
James	Jas
1 Peter	1Pe
2 Peter	2Pe
1 John	1Jn
2 John	2Jn
3 John	3Jn
Jude	Jude
Revelation	Rev

INTRODUCTION
TO THE PROMISE KEEPERS MEN'S STUDY BIBLE

Godliness. Brotherhood. Faithfulness. Servanthood. Honor. Unity. Mission. These words describe the issues that you need to address as you seek to become a godly man. Helping men to address these issues effectively has been the primary goal of Promise Keepers since it was founded in 1991. For millions of men, the Scripture-based Seven Promises of a Promise Keeper (featured on page xviii) have organized and summarized the crucial areas of life in which they need God's guidance and perspective. They can serve the same function for you too as you use this Bible, which features notes and references that are organized around the Seven Promises.

What Is Promise Keepers All About?

Before you go any further in this introduction, please take a moment to read the Promise Keepers Statement of Faith, beginning on page xv. In this statement you will catch the true heart of Promise Keepers and God's movement among men today. You will find that our ministry to men is centered on nothing other than the Word of God, the single most important document in the history of humankind. Through this document, God speaks to his people and draws them closer to himself.

Features of The Promise Keepers Men's Study Bible

The primary feature of this Bible is the Word of God itself. As you seek to become a godly man, God's Spirit will guide and direct you through what he says in his Word. This Bible contains the popular New International Version text.

A letter from Bishop Phillip Porter welcomes you to *The Promise Keepers Men's Study Bible*. The Promise Keepers Statement of Faith and the Seven Promises of a Promise Keeper (and its accompanying two-track reading plan) are provided to give you an organized study approach for addressing the vital issues in your life. And whether you exploring God's call on your life for the very first time or have been a Christian for a lifetime, the article titled Man to Man About Being a Son of God is for you.

Other features that will help you as you read through this Bible are complete introductions for each of the Bible's 66 books; 334 brief in-text notes and 78 more in-depth articles on various passages, each of which is tied to one of the Seven Promises and linked with other notes throughout the Bible; 45 character profiles that show men and women of integrity (or those who lacked integrity); a side-column reference system that traces the Seven Promises through the Bible; and a center-column cross-reference system. Finally, this Bible contains a PromiseFinder index, a Subject Index and an NIV Concordance to enhance your study as you search through God's Word.

How to Use The Promise Keepers Men's Study Bible

The many features included in *The Promise Keepers Men's Study Bible* make it a wonderful tool for helping you gain confidence and competence in the seven areas of life that you need to address as you seek, through the power of the Holy Spirit, to become a godly man. Each feature is explained below.

THE SEVEN PROMISES READING TRACKS

Included in this Bible are two separate suggested reading tracks. Track One traces the Seven Promises throughout Scripture; Track Two links the in-text notes together. Each of these tracks provides you with a way to study each of the Seven Promises throughout Scripture, but is not meant to limit your study. The features of this Bible have been designed to be used profitably no matter what method of study you choose.

Side References: Track One

Since God's Word is the single most important factor in shaping a godly man's life, this Bible includes a side-column reference system that allows you to follow the Seven Promises throughout Scripture without any further in-text comment. By each reference you will find a small box, as follows: 1 →PG. 31 The number inside the box indicates which promise the passage reflects, and a bracket indicates the range of the appropriate passage. Below the box is an arrow with a page reference that tells you where the next passage on that promise is located. Another icon has been added to this reference system as well: This small rainbow indicates that the passage is one of God's promises to his people. A complete index of all of these "God's Promises" highlights is located within the PromiseFinder Index on page 1437.

In-Text Notes: Track Two

Each of the hundreds of in-text notes in this Bible is tied one of the Seven Promises, and each is linked to other notes on the same promise by means of a small statement at the bottom of the note. The numerical icon that appears in the upper right-hand corner of each in-text note PROMISE 1 gives you an instant idea of which area of life the note addresses. While most of those icons are numerical, you'll notice that two others appear throughout the text: (God's Promises) is intended to inspire you as you see how God can work in a man's life; **PE** (Promise Enabler) spans the Seven Promises with principles that will enlighten you as you consider each of these seven areas in your life.

BOOK INTRODUCTIONS

Complete introductions for each of the Bible's 66 books provide practical information about each book's background and place in the biblical narrative. They include timelines, overviews, and other visuals that provide at-a-glance information for those who want a thumbnail sketch of the book's contents, but also provide an in-depth study for the reader who is looking for a wider-ranging background introduction to a particular book.

CHARACTER PROFILES

Character profiles are included in this Bible to give you a perspective on how different individuals in the Bible lived their lives as godly men and women. As you study the lives of these individuals, you'll see that each one was undeniably human, just like you. Consider how each one followed God's call on his or her life, where he or she stumbled, and how God responded to each individual. You'll probably notice that these character profiles are not set off with promise icons, as are other in-text notes. Their stories reflect the fact that the Seven Promises often overlap, as happens in real life. For a complete index of these 45 character profiles, see page viii.

CROSS-REFERENCE SYSTEM

To further enhance this Bible's study potential, the NIV center-column cross-reference system has been included. The cross references link words or phrases in the NIV text with counterpart Biblical references. The raised letters indicating these cross references are set in a light italic typeface to distinguish them from the NIV text note letters, which use a bold roman typeface. When a single word is addressed by both, the roman NIV text note comes first (see, for example, the word "Jesus" in Matthew 1:21).

The lists of references are in Biblical order with one exception: If reference is made to a verse within the same chapter, that verse (indicated by "ver") is listed first.

In the Old Testament some references are marked with an asterisk (*), which means that the Old Testament verse or phrase is quoted in the New Testament (see, for example, Genesis 1:3). The corresponding information is provided in the New Testament by the NIV text note (see 2 Corinthians 4:6).

PARALLEL PASSAGES

When two or more passages of Scripture are nearly identical or deal with the same event, this "parallel" is noted under the sectional headings in the Bible text. *The Promise Keepers Men's Study Bible* employs this feature only in the four Gospels (Matthew, Mark, Luke and John).

INDEXES

The "PromiseFinder Index" on page 1437 includes a complete record of the Scripture address and page number for each reference to the Seven Promises within the pages of this Bible. Promise Enabler notes and God's Promises locations are also included to provide you with a complete, quick-reference guide to the in-text notes and side-column references that are highlighted throughout the text. This index is designed to enhance your study if you choose to study any or all of the Seven Promises through the Biblical narrative from Genesis to Revelation. The Index to Subjects on page 1455 contains references to key Biblical information on important topics.

DICTIONARY OF NIV TERMS

A dictionary has also been included in the back of this Bible. It is intended to give you a better understanding of many of the names, words, phrases and place names found in the NIV text. The dictionary begins on page 1445.

CONCORDANCE

The concordance on page 1473 will help you find Bible verses quickly and easily. By looking up key words, you can find verses for which you remember a word or two but not their location. For example, to find where the Bible has the statement, "Your word is a lamp to my feet and a light for my path," you could look up "word," "lamp," "feet," "light" or "path" and find the verse's location at Psalm 119:105.

All of these features combine to make *The Promise Keepers Men's Study Bible* a practical and useful resource to help you in your lifelong journey toward becoming a godly man. May God bless you as you seek to become a man who honors his God and his brothers, who is faithful to his commitments and to personal purity, who desires to be a servant to God and to others, who honors his pastor and contributes to the work of the church, who works toward unity in the body of Christ, and who follows God's call to influence his world for the sake of God's kingdom.

PROMISE KEEPERS STATEMENT OF FAITH

1. We believe that there is one God[1] eternally existing[2] in three persons: The Father, the Son, and the Holy Spirit[3].

[1]Deuteronomy 6:4:	Hear, O Israel: The Lord our God, the Lord is one.
1 Corinthians 8:4:	So then, about eating food sacrificed to idols: We know that an idol is nothing at all in the world and there is no God but one.
[2]Psalm 90:2:	From everlasting to everlasting, you are God.
1 Timothy 1:17:	Now to the King eternal, immortal, invisible, the only God, be honor and glory for ever and ever. Amen.
[3]Matthew 28:19:	Therefore go and make disciples of all nations, baptizing them in the name of the Father and of the Son and of the Holy Spirit.
2 Corinthians 13:14:	May the grace of the Lord Jesus Christ, and the love of God, and the fellowship of the Holy Spirit, be with you all.

2. We believe that the Bible is God's written revelation to man[1] and that it is verbally inspired[2], authoritative[3], and without error in the original manuscripts[4].

[1]2 Peter 1:20–21:	Above all, you must understand that no prophecy of Scripture came about by the prophet's own interpretation. For prophecy never had its origin in the will of man, but men spoke from God as they were carried along by the Holy Spirit.
[2]2 Timothy 3:16:	All Scripture is God-breathed and is useful for teaching, rebuking, correcting, and training in righteousness.
[3]Revelation 22:18–19:	I warn everyone who hears the words of the prophecy of this book: If anyone adds anything to them, God will add to him the plagues described in this book. And if anyone takes words away from this book of prophecy, God will take away from him his share in the tree of life and in the holy city, which are described in this book.
[4]John 17:17:	Sanctify them by the truth; your word is truth.
Matthew 5:17–18:	Do not think that I have come to abolish the Law or the Prophets; I have not come to abolish them but to fulfill them. I tell you the truth, until heaven and earth disappear, not the smallest letter, not the least stroke of a pen, will by any means disappear from the Law until everything is accomplished.

3. We believe in the deity of Jesus Christ[1], His virgin birth[2], sinless life[3], miracles[4], death on the cross to provide for our redemption[5], bodily resurrection and ascension into heaven[6], present ministry of intercession for us[7], and His return to earth in power and glory[8].

[1]John 1:1:	In the beginning was the Word, and the Word was with God, and the Word was God.
Colossians 2:9:	For in Christ all the fullness of the Deity lives in bodily form.
[2]Matthew 1:23:	The virgin will be with child and will give birth to a son, and they will call him Immanuel—which means, "God with us."

[3]Hebrews 4:15:	For we do not have a high priest who is unable to sympathize with our weaknesses, but we have one who has been tempted in every way, just as we are—yet was without sin.
[4]Acts 2:22–23:	Men of Israel, listen to this: Jesus of Nazareth was a man accredited by God to you by miracles, wonders and signs, which God did among you through him, as you yourselves know. This man was handed over to you by God's set purpose and foreknowledge; and you, with the help of wicked men, put him to death by nailing him to the cross.
[5]1 Peter 3:18:	For Christ died for sins once for all, the righteous for the unrighteous, to bring you to God. He was put to death in the body but made alive by the Spirit.
1 John 1:7:	The blood of Jesus, his Son, purifies us from all sin.
[6]1 Corinthians 15:4:	. . . that he was buried, that he was raised on the third day according to the Scriptures.
Mark 16:19:	After the Lord Jesus had spoken to them, he was received up into heaven, and sat down at the right hand of God.
[7]Hebrews 7:25:	Therefore he is able to save completely those who come to God through him, because he always lives to intercede for them.
[8]Matthew 24:30:	At that time the sign of the Son of Man will appear in the sky, and all the nations of the earth will mourn. They will see the Son of Man coming on the clouds of the sky, with power and great glory.

4. We believe in the personality[1] and deity[2] of the Holy Spirit, that He performs the miracle of new birth in an unbeliever[3] and indwells believers[4], enabling them to live a godly life[5].

[1]1 Corinthians 2:10–11:	. . . but God has revealed it to us by his Spirit. The Spirit searches all things, even the deep things of God. For who among men knows the thoughts of a man except the man's spirit within him? In the same way no one knows the thoughts of God except the Spirit of God.
1 Corinthians 12:11:	All these are the work of one and the same Spirit, and he gives them to each one, just as he determines.
Ephesians 4:30:	And do not grieve the Holy Spirit of God.
[2]Acts 5:3–4:	Then Peter said, "Ananias, how is it that Satan has so filled your heart that you have lied to the Holy Spirit? . . . You have not lied to men but to God."
[3]Titus 3:5:	. . . he saved us, not because of righteous things we had done, but because of his mercy. He saved us through the washing of rebirth and renewal by the Holy Spirit.
[4]1 Corinthians 6:19:	Do you not know that your body is a temple of the Holy Spirit, who is in you, whom you have received from God? You are not your own.
[5]Ephesians 5:18:	. . . be filled with the Spirit.
Galatians 5:16:	So I say, live by the Spirit, and you will not gratify the desires of the sinful nature.
Galatians 5:22–23:	But the fruit of the Spirit is love, joy, peace, patience, kindness, goodness, faithfulness, gentleness, self-control.

5. We believe that man was created in the image of God[1], but because of sin[2], was alienated from God[3]. Only through faith[4], trusting in Christ alone[5] for salvation which was made possible by His death[6] and resurrection[7], can that alienation be removed.

[1]Genesis 1:27:	So God created man in his own image, in the image of God he created him; male and female he created them.
[2]1 John 3:4:	Everyone who sins breaks the law; in fact, sin is lawlessness.
Romans 3:23:	. . . for all have sinned and fall short of the glory of God.
[3]Romans 6:23:	For the wages of sin is death.
Isaiah 59:2:	But your iniquities have separated you from your God; your sins have hidden his face from you, so that he will not hear.
[4]Ephesians 2:8–9:	For it is by grace you have been saved, through faith—and this not from yourselves, it is the gift of God—not by works, so that no one can boast.
Philippians 3:9:	. . . and be found in him, not having a righteousness of my own that comes from the law, but that which is through faith in Christ—the righteousness that comes from God and is by faith.
Romans 3:28:	For we maintain that a man is justified by faith apart from observing the law.
[5]John 14:6:	Jesus answered, "I am the way and the truth and the life. No one comes to the Father except through me."
Acts 4:12:	Salvation is found in no one else, for there is no other name under heaven given to men by which we must be saved.
1 John 5:11–12:	And this is the testimony: God has given us eternal life, and this life is in his Son. He who has the Son has life; he who does not have the Son of God does not have life.
[6]Romans 3:24:	. . . and are justified freely by his grace through the redemption that came by Christ Jesus.
Romans 5:8:	But God demonstrates his own love for us, in this: While we were still sinners, Christ died for us.
John 3:16:	For God so loved the world, that he gave his one and only Son, that whoever believes in him shall not perish but have eternal life.
Ephesians 1:7:	In him we have redemption through his blood, the forgiveness of sins, in accordance with the riches of God's grace.
[7]1 Corinthians 15:3–8:	For what I received I passed on to you as of first importance: that Christ died for our sins according to the Scriptures, and that he appeared to Peter, and then to the Twelve. After that, he appeared to more than five hundred of the brothers at the same time, most of whom are still living, though some have fallen asleep. Then he appeared to James, then to all the apostles, and last of all he appeared to me also, as to one abnormally born.

THE SEVEN PROMISES OF A PROMISE KEEPER

Promise One

A Promise Keeper is committed to honor Jesus Christ through worship, prayer and obedience to God's Word in the power of the Holy Spirit.

CORE ISSUE: Intimacy with God

KEY PASSAGE: Psalm 73:25

Promise Two

A Promise Keeper is committed to pursue vital relationships with a few other men, understanding that he needs brothers to help him keep his promises.

CORE ISSUE: Brotherhood

KEY PASSAGE: Hebrews 3:12–13

Promise Three

A Promise Keeper is committed to practice spiritual, moral, ethical and sexual purity.

CORE ISSUE: Faithfulness

KEY PASSAGE: 1 Corinthians 4:2

Promise Four

A Promise Keeper is committed to building strong marriages and families through love, protection and Biblical values.

CORE ISSUE: Servanthood

KEY PASSAGE: Matthew 20:27

Promise Five

A Promise Keeper is committed to support the mission of the church by honoring and praying for his pastor, and by actively giving his time and resources.

CORE ISSUE: Honor

KEY PASSAGE: 1 Thessalonians 5:12–13

Promise Six

A Promise Keeper is committed to reach beyond any racial and denominational barriers to demonstrate the power of Biblical unity.

CORE ISSUE: Unity

KEY PASSAGE: John 17:20–23

Promise Seven

A Promise Keeper is committed to influence his world, being obedient to the Great Commandment and the Great Commission.

CORE ISSUE: Mission

KEY PASSAGES: Mark 12:30–31; Matthew 28:19–20

THE SEVEN PROMISES OF A PROMISE KEEPER
READING PLAN

The purpose of this reading plan is to enrich your study by helping you to follow any or all of the Seven Promises throughout Scripture. This plan has two tracks:

TRACK ONE

The first track traces the Seven Promises within Scripture passages throughout the Bible, allowing God's Word to speak clearly and richly on each promise. Each chain of promises is tagged with a small promise number icon, and can be found in the side-column reference system contained on the pages of this Bible. You'll also notice a small rainbow icon in the side margins; those indicate God's Promises to his people throughout Scripture.

TRACK TWO

The second track brings the reader through the Scriptures with commentary on each of the seven promises as they relate to particular passages. Each one of these in-text notes uses an icon in the upper right-hand corner of the note to show which promise is being discussed. Short statements at the bottom of the note direct the reader to the next in-text note that applies that promise to a portion of Scripture.

PROMISE 1

Track One *begins on page 17 and includes 177 references.*
Track Two *begins on page 9 and includes 137 references.*

PROMISE 2

Track One *begins on page 9 and includes 73 references.*
Track Two *begins on page 71 and includes 22 references.*

PROMISE 3

Track One *begins on page 50 and includes 143 references.*
Track Two *begins on page 50 and includes 69 references.*

PROMISE 4

Track One *begins on page 4 and includes 77 references.*
Track Two *begins on page 5 and includes 29 references.*

PROMISE 5

Track One *begins on page 106 and includes 68 references.*
Track Two *begins on page 57 and includes 27 references.*

PROMISE 6

Track One *begins on page 20 and includes 58 references.*
Track Two *begins on page 16 and includes 42 references.*

PROMISE 7

Track One *begins on page 24 and includes 122 references.*
Track Two *begins on page 4 and includes 51 references.*

MAN TO MAN
ABOUT BEING A SON OF GOD

A man's relationship with his father is basic. The benefit of a strong, affirming bond with "Dad" is powerful.

On the other hand, the pain of a lost or nonexistent relationship with a father can last a lifetime. Insecurity and crippled relationships with others are often traced back to what wasn't gained from a loving, accepting father.

God Loves His Sons

God's love is strong, fatherly and complete. Men from all over the country are beginning to understand this relationship for the very first time.

Many of us, some for years, have been trying to gain God's approval by performance—doing good things. But it is impossible to live like God's sons before we're in a relationship with him. A wall of separation has come between God and man. Instead of a relationship, we find a barrier.

But there is good news!

Reconciliation Is Through Christ

Do you need to be reconciled? Jesus has broken down the wall that separated us from our Father God. Reconciliation is now possible. If you are not in a family relationship with God as a son to his Father, this is your primary need.

Here are some questions you may have:

"If God made me, why would I need to be reconciled?"

"What happened to the original relationship?"

"If I choose to stay the way I am, what are the consequences?"

Keep reading to find the answers to these and other questions. This invitation is for you, whether your background is religious on nonreligious. If you feel you are distanced from God and his acceptance, realize that an eternal and life-giving relationship with God is available to you.

What We Lost: A Relationship

Adam, the father of the human race, made a terrible choice. We, his sons, live in the aftermath of his failure. It started with an act of disobedience. He willingly joined his wife in doubting God's word and ignoring God's instructions. Their response was not according to God's design, and resulted in their being expelled from God's presence.

The result? Man's relationship with God was broken. In the process, the man failed his wife. From then on, they experienced times of contention in their relationship. And as if that wasn't bad enough, the man lost his job and was kicked off the family farm. He found some temporary jobs until he could get back with his Father, but this work was cursed from the start and resulted in pain and difficulty. His family relationships went from bad to worse. One of his sons even killed another! (You can read about this in Genesis 2—4.)

We have inherited a diseased spiritual DNA. It's no wonder we find failure and sin in our lives today. It is by our choices that we continue to exist outside of a relationship with God.

This leaves us without the bonds of communion with our Father that all of us are meant to have. The ties have been cut. This alienation is described in the New Testament as being "separate from Christ . . . without hope and without God in the world" (Ephesians 2:12).

Most men understand accountability and consequences. If we die still alienated from God, we will experience the horrible reality of his judgment that man's rebel spirit has merited—eternal separation from God.

What We Need: A Restored Relationship

Jesus Christ is the only One able to restore the relationship we lost. Because we are spiritually dead in our sins and God is alive in his perfection, we must be made alive to be able to have a relationship with him.

There is another obstacle to becoming a son of God. Men tend to be "fix it myself" people. We admit we're weak in establishing relationships. We admit we're far from perfect. We are, in fact, sinners. The problem is that our theme song is, "I did it my way."

When we do it our way, we remain isolated because of our own sins. We separate ourselves not only from God, but also from right relationships with our families and others. But we can't be "do-it-our-selfers" when it comes to our relationship with God. We can't fix what's wrong by our own efforts.

How Can the Relationship Be Restored?

Why do we need Jesus? Because, on his cross, Jesus broke down the walls of isolation that sin had built. Jesus came to earth as God in human form, took our place of judgment for sin and put us in his place as a son of God.

Now we know why we can't just do a little better ourselves: "For it is by grace you have been saved, through faith—and this not from yourselves, it is the gift of God—not by works, so that no one can boast" (Ephesians 2:8–9).

This is what a lot of men miss! A relationship with God is a gift. We don't earn it. We can't buy it. We can't boast or feel a sense of accomplishment about achieving it. God gives us this gift out of love for us and a desire to be in relationship with his people.

But a gift must be received: "To all who received him, to those who believed in his name, he gave the right to become children of God" (John 1:12). Don't be too proud to admit you need God's new life within you. This is God's way—through Jesus, the gift.

If you would like to accept this gift—eternal life in relationship with God—Jesus Christ has secured it for you. You can simply tell God. It's not these exact words, but the attitude of your heart that matters.

Pray This Prayer to Accept or Reaffirm Your Acceptance of Christ:

Father, I've come home. Please make me your son. I turn from my sin. I accept your forgiveness made possible through Jesus Christ by his death and resurrection. I place my faith and trust in Jesus Christ alone. I receive him as my Savior and Lord. I want to follow and serve you. Let today be the beginning of my new journey as your son and a member of your family. You have always kept your promises. Help me to keep my promises, too. In Jesus' name. Amen.

ACKNOWLEDGMENTS

Promise Keepers gives thanks to God for his grace and guidance in the development and production of this project. The Promise Keepers review board aided in the development and completion of this project, and also reviewed all of the in-text notes you'll see in the pages of this Bible. The board consisted of Dr. Rod Cooper, Jim Gordon, Tracey Lawrence, Dr. Gary Oliver, Pete Richardson, Dan Schaffer, Pastor Dale Schlafer, Dr. Glenn Wagner and Pastor Raleigh Washington. Mary Guenther was in charge of project and editorial management for Promise Keepers, and Michael Vander Klipp was the project editor at Zondervan Publishing House.

The above individuals would also like to thank the following team of authors for their thoughtful and insightful contributions to this project:

Dr. Kenneth Boa

Dr. Kenneth Boa is engaged in a ministry of relational evangelism and discipleship, teaching, writing and speaking. Dr. Boa is the president of Reflections Ministries, an organization that seeks to provide safe places for people to consider the claims of Christ and to help them mature and bear fruit in their relationship with him. His publications include *Cults, World Religions, and the Occult; I'm Glad You Asked; Talk Thru the Bible; Visual Survey of the Bible; Drawing Near; Face to Face: Praying the Scriptures for Intimate Worship; Face to Face: Praying the Scriptures for Spiritual Growth;* and *Simple Prayers.* He is also a contributing editor to *The Open Bible.* Dr. Boa wrote all of the Bible book introductions for this project.

Dr. Sid Buzzell

Dr. Sid Buzzell is the Dean of Biblical and Theological Studies at Colorado Christian University. He also has an active conference speaking ministry. Before going to CCU, he served as a seminary professor and administrator. He has also planted and pastored two thriving churches. Dr. Buzzell wrote the majority of the Old Testament notes, as well as many of the character profiles, for this project.

Dr. Gene A. Getz

Dr. Gene A. Getz is currently senior pastor at Fellowship Bible Church North in Plano, Texas. Since becoming involved in church planting following professorships at both Moody Bible Institute and Dallas Theological Seminary, Gene has often specialized in teaching and writing about what the Bible says regarding character. *The Measure of a Man,* published by Regal Books, is still a best seller. More recently, Gene has written the popular *Men of Character Series* published by Broadman & Holman, sharing "principles to live by" that emerge from the lives of Old Testament greats such as Abraham, Moses, Joshua, Jacob, Joseph, Samuel, David, Elijah and Nehemiah. His expertise in this area led him to produce the majority of the character profiles for this project. Dr. Getz hosts "Renewal," a daily radio program heard throughout the country.

Bill Perkins

Bill Perkins is senior pastor at South Hills Community Church in Portland, Oregon. He co-authored *The Journey: A Bible for Seeking God and Understanding Life,* and has written numerous books, including *When Good Men are Tempted, Kids in Sports,* and *Fatal Attractions: Overcoming Our Secret Addictions.* Bill has appeared on nationally broadcast television and radio shows and spoken to men's groups across the United States. He also conducts business seminars aimed at helping companies develop leadership, teamwork and customer service. He contributed to the notes in the Old Testament, and wrote all of the New Testament notes for this project.

PREFACE
TO THE NIV

THE NEW INTERNATIONAL VERSION is a completely new translation of the Holy Bible made by over a hundred scholars working directly from the best available Hebrew, Aramaic and Greek texts. It had its beginning in 1965 when, after several years of exploratory study by committees from the Christian Reformed Church and the National Association of Evangelicals, a group of scholars met at Palos Heights, Illinois, and concurred in the need for a new translation of the Bible in contemporary English. This group, though not made up of official church representatives, was transdenominational. Its conclusion was endorsed by a large number of leaders from many denominations who met in Chicago in 1966.

Responsibility for the new version was delegated by the Palos Heights group to a self-governing body of fifteen, the Committee on Bible Translation, composed for the most part of biblical scholars from colleges, universities and seminaries. In 1967 the New York Bible Society (now the International Bible Society) generously undertook the financial sponsorship of the project—a sponsorship that made it possible to enlist the help of many distinguished scholars. The fact that participants from the United States, Great Britain, Canada, Australia and New Zealand worked together gave the project its international scope. That they were from many denominations—including Anglican, Assemblies of God, Baptist, Brethren, Christian Reformed, Church of Christ, Evangelical Free, Lutheran, Mennonite, Methodist, Nazarene, Presbyterian, Wesleyan and other churches—helped to safeguard the translation from sectarian bias.

How it was made helps to give the New International Version its distinctiveness. The translation of each book was assigned to a team of scholars. Next, one of the Intermediate Editorial Committees revised the initial translation, with constant reference to the Hebrew, Aramaic or Greek. Their work then went to one of the General Editorial Committees, which checked it in detail and made another thorough revision. This revision in turn was carefully reviewed by the Committee on Bible Translation, which made further changes and then released the final version for publication. In this way the entire Bible underwent three revisions, during each of which the translation was examined for its faithfulness to the original languages and for its English style.

All this involved many thousands of hours of research and discussion regarding the meaning of the texts and the precise way of putting them into English. It may well be that no other translation has been made by a more thorough process of review and revision from committee to committee than this one.

From the beginning of the project, the Committee on Bible Translation held to certain goals for the New International Version: that it would be an accurate translation and one that would have clarity and literary quality and so prove suitable for public and private reading, teaching, preaching, memorizing and liturgical use. The Committee also sought to preserve some measure of continuity with the long tradition of translating the Scriptures into English.

In working toward these goals, the translators were united in their commitment to the authority and infallibility of the Bible as God's Word in written form. They believe that it contains the divine answer to the deepest needs of humanity, that it sheds unique light on our path in a dark world, and that it sets forth the way to our eternal well-being.

The first concern of the translators has been the accuracy of the translation and its fidelity to the thought of the biblical writers. They have weighed the significance of the lexical and grammatical details of the Hebrew, Aramaic and Greek texts. At the same time, they have striven for more than a word-for-word translation. Because thought patterns and syntax differ from language to language, faithful communication of the meaning of the writers of the Bible demands frequent modifications in sentence structure and constant regard for the contextual meanings of words.

A sensitive feeling for style does not always accompany scholarship. Accordingly the Committee on Bible Translation submitted the developing version to a number of stylistic consultants. Two of them read every book of both Old and New Testaments twice—once before and once after the last major revision—and made invaluable suggestions. Samples of the translation were tested for clarity and ease of reading by various kinds of people—young and old, highly educated and less well educated, ministers and laymen.

Concern for clear and natural English—that the New International Version should be idiomatic but not idiosyncratic, contemporary but not dated—motivated the translators and consultants. At the same time, they tried to reflect the differing styles of the biblical writers. In view of the international use of English, the translators sought to avoid obvious Americanisms on the one hand and obvious Anglicisms on the other. A British edition reflects the comparatively few differences of significant idiom and of spelling.

As for the traditional pronouns "thou," "thee" and "thine" in reference to the Deity, the translators judged that to use these archaisms (along with the old verb forms such as "doest," "wouldest" and "hadst") would violate accuracy in translation. Neither Hebrew, Aramaic nor Greek uses special pronouns for the persons of the Godhead. A present-day translation is not enhanced by forms that in the time of the King James Version were used in everyday speech, whether referring to God or man.

For the Old Testament the standard Hebrew text, the Masoretic Text as published in the latest editions of *Biblia Hebraica,* was used throughout. The Dead Sea Scrolls contain material bearing on an earlier stage of the Hebrew text. They were consulted, as were the Samaritan Pentateuch and the ancient scribal traditions relating to textual changes. Sometimes a variant Hebrew reading in the margin of the Masoretic Text was followed instead of the text itself. Such instances, being variants within the Masoretic tradition, are not specified by footnotes. In rare cases, words in the consonantal text were divided differently from the way they appear in the Masoretic Text. Footnotes indicate this. The translators also consulted the more important early versions—the Septuagint; Aquila, Symmachus and Theodotion; the Vulgate; the Syriac Peshitta; the Targums; and for the Psalms the *Juxta Hebraica* of Jerome. Readings from these versions were occasionally followed where the Masoretic Text seemed doubtful and where accepted principles of textual criticism showed that one or more of these textual witnesses appeared to provide the correct reading. Such instances are footnoted. Sometimes vowel letters and vowel signs did not, in the judgment of the translators, represent the correct vowels for the original consonantal text. Accordingly some words were read with a different set of vowels. These instances are usually not indicated by footnotes.

The Greek text used in translating the New Testament was an eclectic one. No other piece of ancient literature has such an abundance of manuscript witnesses as does the New Testament. Where existing manuscripts differ, the translators made their choice of readings according to accepted principles of New Testament textual criticism. Footnotes call attention to places where there was uncertainty about what the original text was. The best current printed texts of the Greek New Testament were used.

There is a sense in which the work of translation is never wholly finished. This applies to all great literature and uniquely so to the Bible. In 1973 the New Testament in the New International Version was published. Since then, suggestions for corrections and revisions have been received from various sources. The Committee on Bible Translation carefully considered the suggestions and adopted a number of them. These were incorporated in the first printing of the entire Bible in 1978. Additional revisions were made by the Committee on Bible Translation in 1983 and appear in printings after that date.

As in other ancient documents, the precise meaning of the biblical texts is sometimes uncertain. This is more often the case with the Hebrew and Aramaic texts than with the Greek text. Although archaeological and linguistic discoveries in this century aid in understanding difficult passages, some uncertainties remain. The more significant of these have been called to the reader's attention in the footnotes.

In regard to the divine name *YHWH,* commonly referred to as the *Tetragrammaton,* the translators adopted the device used in most English versions of rendering that name as "LORD" in capital letters to distinguish it from *Adonai,* another Hebrew word rendered "Lord," for which small letters are used. Wherever the two names stand together in the Old Testament as a compound name of God, they are rendered "Sovereign LORD."

Because for most readers today the phrases "the LORD of hosts" and "God of hosts" have little meaning, this version renders them "the LORD Almighty" and "God Almighty." These renderings convey the sense of the Hebrew, namely, "he who is sovereign over all the 'hosts' (powers) in heaven and on earth, especially over the 'hosts' (armies) of Israel." For readers unacquainted with Hebrew this does not make clear the distinction between *Sabaoth* ("hosts" or "Almighty") and *Shaddai* (which can also be translated "Almighty"), but the latter occurs infrequently and is always footnoted. When *Adonai* and *YHWH Sabaoth* occur together, they are rendered "the Lord, the LORD Almighty."

As for other proper nouns, the familiar spellings of the King James Version are generally retained. Names traditionally spelled with "ch," except where it is final, are usually spelled in this translation with "k" or "c," since the biblical languages do not have the sound that "ch" frequently indicates in English—for example, in *chant.* For well-known names such as Zechariah, however, the traditional spelling has been retained. Variation in the spelling of names in the original languages has usually not been indicated. Where a person or place has two or more different names in the Hebrew, Aramaic or Greek texts, the more familiar one has generally been used, with footnotes where needed.

To achieve clarity the translators sometimes supplied words not in the original texts but required by the context. If there was uncertainty about such material, it is enclosed in brackets. Also for the sake of clarity or style, nouns, including some proper nouns, are sometimes substituted for pronouns, and vice versa. And though the Hebrew writers often shifted back and forth between first, second and third personal pronouns without change of antecedent, this translation often makes them uniform, in accordance with English style and without the use of footnotes.

Poetical passages are printed as poetry, that is, with indentation of lines with separate stanzas. These are generally designed to reflect the structure of Hebrew poetry. This poetry is normally characterized by parallelism in balanced lines. Most of the poetry in the Bible is in the Old Testament, and scholars differ regarding the scansion of Hebrew lines. The translators determined the stanza divisions for the most part by analysis of the subject matter. The stanzas therefore serve as poetic paragraphs.

As an aid to the reader, italicized sectional headings are inserted in most of the books. They are not to be regarded as part of the NIV text, are not for oral reading, and are not intended to dictate the interpretation of the sections they head.

The footnotes in this version are of several kinds, most of which need no explanation. Those giving alternative translations begin with "Or" and generally introduce the alternative with the last word preceding it in the text, except when it is a single-word alternative; in poetry quoted in a footnote a slant mark indicates a line division. Footnotes introduced by "Or" do not have uniform significance. In some cases two possible translations were considered to have about equal validity. In other cases, though the translators were convinced that the translation in the text was correct, they judged that another interpretation was possible and of sufficient importance to be represented in a footnote.

In the New Testament, footnotes that refer to uncertainty regarding the original text are introduced by "Some manuscripts" or similar expressions. In the Old Testament, evidence for the reading chosen is given first and evidence for the alternative is added after a semicolon (for example: Septuagint; Hebrew *father*). In such notes the term "Hebrew" refers to the Masoretic Text.

It should be noted that minerals, flora and fauna, architectural details, articles of clothing and jewelry, musical instruments and other articles cannot always be identified with precision. Also measures of capacity in the biblical period are particularly uncertain (see the table of weights and measures following the text).

Like all translations of the Bible, made as they are by imperfect man, this one undoubtedly falls short of its goals. Yet we are grateful to God for the extent to which he has enabled us to realize these goals and for the strength he has given us and our colleagues to complete our task. We offer this version of the Bible to him in whose name and for whose glory it has been made. We pray that it will lead many into a better understanding of the Holy Scriptures and a fuller knowledge of Jesus Christ the incarnate Word, of whom the Scriptures so faithfully testify.

The Committee on Bible Translation

June 1978
(Revised August 1983)

Names of the translators and editors may be secured
from the International Bible Society,
translation sponsors of the New International Version,
1820 Jet Stream Drive, Colorado Springs, Colorado
80921-3696 U.S.A.

OLD TESTAMENT

GENESIS

AT A GLANCE

Key Principle: God calls us away from bondage to sin into a covenant relationship with him in which we are justified by faith in his promises.
Author: Moses
Time and Place: 4000+(??) B.C. to 1804 B.C. / From Ur to Haran to Canaan to Egypt
Key Verses: 1:1; 3:15; 12:1–3

BENEFIT

As the book of beginnings, Genesis gives us God's perspective on the beginning of several key Biblical issues such as creation, marriage, sin, sacrifice and Hebrew history. It also offers rich character studies of Abraham, Isaac, Jacob and Joseph that yield timeless principles for living.

SETTING

Genesis was probably written by Moses after Israel's exodus from Egypt. His first readers were the people of Israel, who needed a perspective on what God was doing with them and how his work in their lives related to his promises. This book spans an unknown number of years in chapters 1—11 as it moves through the four foundational (and undated) events of creation, the fall, the flood and the spread of the nations. Genesis chapters 12—50 survey the lives of the patriarchs Abraham, Isaac, Jacob and Joseph and move from Ur to Haran to Canaan and finally to Egypt, where Joseph's story ends.

TIME LINE

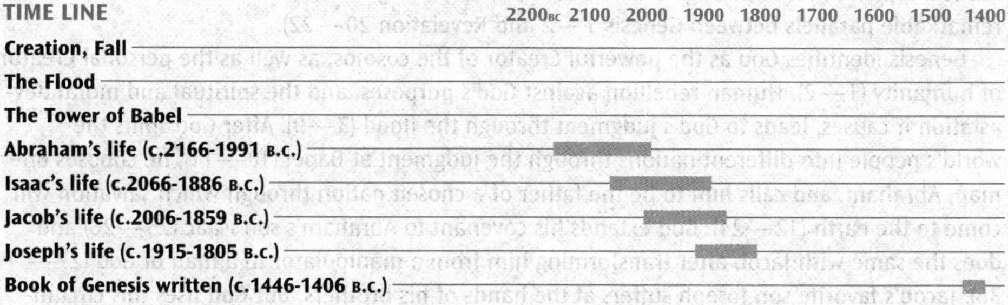

THEME AND PURPOSE

The theme of Genesis is the origin of the Hebrew people, through whom God would ultimately bless all the nations of the earth. Genesis surveys the origin of the human race, but the bulk of the book focuses on the lives of Abraham and his descendants. This book lays the foundation for the redemptive history that is further developed in the other four books of the Pentateuch (the first five books of the Bible). Genesis records how God chose the people of Israel—beginning with the divine call and covenant with Abraham—and demonstrates God's faithfulness in spite of his children's disobedience.

UNIQUE CONTRIBUTION

Genesis lays the foundation for the rest of the Bible by recording the beginning of the universe, the human race, marriage, sin, sacrifice, the family, human government, the nations and

Hebrew history. It covers more time and geography than all the rest of the Bible's books, and answers questions of origin and purpose that would otherwise have been completely mysterious. It not only introduces the Pentateuch and the rest of the Bible, but it also provides the seeds of the great doctrines of the Bible about God, human nature and justification by faith (Abraham).

LINKS TO THE NEW TESTAMENT

Several characters in Genesis prefigure Christ. Just as God created Adam without sin as the head of the old creation, so Jesus, the second Adam, was born without sin as the head of the new creation. As with Cain, Jesus' sacrificial offering was acceptable to God. Melchizedek ("king of righteousness") offered bread and wine and "like the Son of God he remains a priest forever" (Hebrews 7:3). Joseph's story is like Jesus' in that his brothers hated him, rejected him as a ruler, conspired against him and sold him for silver. As with Christ, Joseph was lifted up to a glorious (but earthly) position after his innocent suffering.

OVERVIEW

FOCUS	Four Key Events				Four Key People			
REFERENCE	1 2	3 5	6 9	10 11	12 24	25 26	27 36	37 50
TOPICS	Creation	Fall	Flood	Nations	Abraham	Isaac	Jacob	Joseph
	Foundation of the Hebrew Race				Foundation of the Hebrew Race			
	Primeval History				Patriarchal History			
LOCATION	Eden to Ur to Haran				Haran to Canaan			Egypt
TIME	2,000+ Years				About 286 Years			

Genesis anticipates the plot of the Bible in germinal form and contains the roots of every key Biblical topic. It moves through a whole series of beginnings but has no finality (notice the remarkable parallels between Genesis 1—2 and Revelation 20—22).

Genesis identifies God as the powerful Creator of the cosmos, as well as the personal Creator of humanity (1—2). Human rebellion against God's purposes, and the spiritual and moral devastation it causes, leads to God's judgment through the flood (3—9). After God splits the world's people into different nations through the judgment at Babel (10—11), he chooses one man, Abraham, and calls him to be the father of a chosen nation through which salvation will come to the earth (12—24). God extends his covenant to Abraham's son Isaac (25—26) and does the same with Jacob after transforming him from a manipulator to a man of God (27—36). Jacob's favorite son Joseph suffers at the hands of his brothers, but God uses this circumstance to bring him to Egypt. There Joseph rises to a position of great power and delivers his family from famine by bringing them into the land of Goshen in Egypt.

GENESIS

The Beginning

1 In the beginning[a] God created
the heavens and the earth.[b] 2Now
the earth was[a] formless and empty,[c] darkness was over the surface of the deep, and the Spirit of
God[d] was hovering over the waters.

3And God said,[e] "Let there be light,"
and there was light.[f] 4God saw
that the light was good, and he
separated the light from the darkness. 5God called the light "day,"
and the darkness he called
"night."[g] And there was evening,
and there was morning—the first
day.
6And God said, "Let there be an expanse[h] between the waters to
separate water from water." 7So
God made the expanse and separated the water under the expanse
from the water above it.[i] And it
was so. 8God called the expanse
"sky." And there was evening, and
there was morning—the second
day.
9And God said, "Let the water under
the sky be gathered to one place,[j]
and let dry ground appear." And
it was so. 10God called the dry
ground "land," and the gathered
waters he called "seas." And God
saw that it was good.
11Then God said, "Let the land
produce vegetation:[k] seed-bearing plants and trees on the
land that bear fruit with seed in it,
according to their various kinds."
And it was so. 12The land produced vegetation: plants bearing
seed according to their kinds and
trees bearing fruit with seed in it
according to their kinds. And God
saw that it was good. 13And there
was evening, and there was
morning—the third day.
14And God said, "Let there be lights[l]
in the expanse of the sky to separate the day from the night, and let
them serve as signs[m] to mark seasons[n] and days and years, 15and
let them be lights in the expanse of
the sky to give light on the earth."
And it was so. 16God made two
great lights—the greater light to
govern[o] the day and the lesser
light to govern[p] the night. He also
made the stars.[q] 17God set them
in the expanse of the sky to give
light on the earth, 18to govern the
day and the night,[r] and to separate light from darkness. And God
saw that it was good. 19And there
was evening, and there was
morning—the fourth day.
20And God said, "Let the water teem
with living creatures, and let birds
fly above the earth across the expanse of the sky." 21So God created the great creatures of the sea
and every living and moving thing
with which the water teems,[s] according to their kinds, and every
winged bird according to its kind.
And God saw that it was good.
22God blessed them and said, "Be
fruitful and increase in number
and fill the water in the seas, and
let the birds increase on the
earth."[t] 23And there was evening,
and there was morning—the fifth
day.
24And God said, "Let the land produce
living creatures according to their
kinds: livestock, creatures that
move along the ground, and wild
animals, each according to its
kind." And it was so. 25God made
the wild animals[u] according to
their kinds, the livestock according to their kinds, and all the creatures that move along the ground
according to their kinds. And God
saw that it was good.
26Then God said, "Let us[v]
make man in our image,[w] in our
likeness, and let them rule[x] over
the fish of the sea and the birds of
the air, over the livestock, over all
the earth,[b] and over all the creatures that move along the
ground."

27So God created man in his own
image,[y]
in the image of God he created
him;
male and female[z] he created
them.

28God blessed them and said to
them, "Be fruitful and increase in
number; fill the earth[a] and subdue it. Rule over the fish of the sea
and the birds of the air and over
every living creature that moves
on the ground."

1:1 [a]Jn 1:1-2 [b]Job 38:4; Ps 90:2; Isa 42:5; 44:24; 45:12,18; Ac 17:24; Heb 11:3; Rev 4:11
1:2 [c]Jer 4:23 [d]Ps 104:30
1:3 [e]Ps 33:6,9; 148:5; Heb 11:3 [f]2Co 4:6*
1:5 [g]Ps 74:16
1:6 [h]Jer 10:12
1:7 [i]Job 38:8-11, 16; Ps 148:4
1:9 [j]Job 38:8-11; Ps 104:6-9; Pr 8:29; Jer 5:22; 2Pe 3:5
1:11 [k]Ps 65:9-13; 104:14
1:14 [l]Ps 74:16 [m]Jer 10:2 [n]Ps 104:19
1:16 [o]Ps 136:8 [p]Ps 136:9 [q]Job 38:7, 31-32; Ps 8:3; Isa 40:26
1:18 [r]Jer 33:20,25
1:21 [s]Ps 104:25-26
1:22 [t]ver 28; Ge 8:17
1:25 [u]Jer 27:5
1:26 [v]Ps 100:3 [w]Ge 9:6; Jas 3:9 [x]Ps 8:6-8
1:27 [y]1Co 11:7 [z]Ge 5:2; Mt 19:4*; Mk 10:6*
1:28 [a]Ge 9:1,7; Lev 26:9

[a]2 Or possibly *became* [b]26 Hebrew; Syriac *all the wild animals*

29Then God said, "I give you every seed-bearing plant on the face of the whole earth and every tree that has fruit with seed in it. They will be yours for food.[b] 30And to all the beasts of the earth and all the birds of the air and all the creatures that move on the ground—everything that has the breath of life in it—I give every green plant for food.[c]" And it was so.

31God saw all that he had made,[d] and it was very good.[e] And there was evening, and there was morning—the sixth day.

2 Thus the heavens and the earth were completed in all their vast array.

2By the seventh day God had finished the work he had been doing; so on the seventh day he rested[a] from all his work.[f] 3And God blessed the seventh day and made it holy,[g] because on it he rested from all the work of creating that he had done.

Adam and Eve

4This is the account of the heavens and the earth when they were created.

When the LORD God made the earth and the heavens— 5and no shrub of the field had yet appeared on the earth[b] and no plant of the field had yet sprung up,[h] for the LORD God had not sent rain on the earth[b][i] and there was no man to work the ground, 6but streams[c] came up from the earth and watered the whole surface of the ground— 7the LORD God formed the man[d] from the dust[j] of the ground[k] and breathed into his nostrils the breath[l] of life,[m] and the man became a living being.[n]

8Now the LORD God had planted a garden in the east, in Eden;[o] and there he put the man he had formed. 9And the LORD God made all kinds of trees grow out of the ground—trees that were pleasing to the eye and good for food. In the middle of the garden were the tree of life[p] and the tree of the knowledge of good and evil.[q]

10A river watering the garden flowed from Eden; from there it was separated into four headwaters. 11The name of the first is the Pishon; it winds through the entire land of Havilah, where there is gold. 12(The gold of that land is good; aromatic resin[e] and onyx are also there.) 13The name of the second river is the Gihon; it winds through the entire land of Cush.[f] 14The name of the third river is the Tigris;[r] it runs along the east side of Asshur. And the fourth river is the Euphrates.

15The LORD God took the man and put him in the Garden of Eden to work it and take care of it. 16And the LORD God commanded the man, "You are free to eat from any tree in the garden; 17but you must not eat from the tree of the knowledge of good and evil, for when you eat of it you will surely die."[s]

4 →PG. 5

18The LORD God said, "It is not good for the man to be alone. I will make a helper suitable for him."[t]

19Now the LORD God had formed out of the ground all the beasts of the field[u] and all the birds of the air. He brought them to the man to see what he would name them; and whatever the man called each living creature,[v] that was its name. 20So the man gave names to all the livestock, the birds of the air and all the beasts of the field.

But for Adam[g] no suitable helper was found. 21So the LORD God caused the man to fall into a deep sleep; and while he was sleeping, he took one of

1:26–30

PROMISE 7

MADE IN GOD'S IMAGE

Your understanding of two truths in this paragraph will determine the course of your life. First, you are created in God's image. While no summary statement can capture the enormity of this fact, it at least means that we are created to be in relationship with God. Second, God made us responsible for the earth. No matter what a man's role or title or position in life, each of us is created in God's image and each is responsible to protect and nurture what God created.

Take a few minutes and read Psalm 8 as your prayer of gratitude for how God created you. You were created a noble creature and given a high calling. So was every other human being.

How, then, should we respond to God? To other humans created in his image? To all he created and placed under our care? In this book, you'll find out all you need to know. Read this Bible as God's instruction manual to those he created to be in relationship with him and appointed as caretakers of his creation.

For the next Promise 7 reading go to page 6.

1:29 [b]Ps 104:14
1:30 [c]Ps 104:14,27; 145:15
1:31 [d]Ps 104:24 [e]1Ti 4:4
2:2 [f]Ex 20:11; 31:17; Heb 4:4*
2:3 [g]Lev 23:3; Isa 58:13
2:5 [h]Ge 1:11 [i]Ps 65:9-10
2:7 [j]Ge 3:19 [k]Ps 103:14 [l]Job 33:4 [m]Ac 17:25 [n]1Co 15:45*
2:8 [o]Ge 3:23,24; Isa 51:3
2:9 [p]Ge 3:22,24; Rev 2:7; 22:2,14,19 [q]Eze 47:12
2:14 [r]Da 10:4
2:17 [s]Dt 30:15,19; Ro 5:12; 6:23; Jas 1:15
2:18 [t]1Co 11:9
2:19 [u]Ps 8:7 [v]Ge 1:24

a *2* Or *ceased*; also in verse 3 **b** *5* Or *land*; also in verse 6 **c** *6* Or *mist* **d** *7* The Hebrew for *man (adam)* sounds like and may be related to the Hebrew for *ground (adamah)*; it is also the name *Adam* (see Gen. 2:20). **e** *12* Or *good; pearls* **f** *13* Possibly southeast Mesopotamia **g** *20* Or *the man*

the man's ribs[a] and closed up the
4 →PG. 24
place with flesh. 22Then the LORD God
made a woman from the rib[b] [w] he had
taken out of the man, and he brought
her to the man.

23The man said,

"This is now bone of my bones
and flesh of my flesh;[x]
she shall be called 'woman,[c]'
for she was taken out of man."

24For this reason a man will leave his
father and mother and be united[y] to
his wife, and they will become one
flesh.[z]

25The man and his wife were both
naked,[a] and they felt no shame.

The Fall of Man

3 Now the serpent[b] was more crafty
than any of the wild animals the
LORD God had made. He said to the
woman, "Did God really say, 'You must
not eat from any tree in the garden'?"

2The woman said to the serpent,
"We may eat fruit from the trees in the
garden, 3but God did say, 'You must
not eat fruit from the tree that is in the
middle of the garden, and you must
not touch it, or you will die.' "

4"You will not surely die," the serpent said to the woman.[c] 5"For God
knows that when you eat of it your eyes
will be opened, and you will be like
God,[d] knowing good and evil."

6When the woman saw that the fruit
of the tree was good for food and pleasing to the eye, and also desirable[e] for
gaining wisdom, she took some and ate
it. She also gave some to her husband,
who was with her, and he ate it.[f]
7Then the eyes of both of them were
opened, and they realized they were
naked; so they sewed fig leaves together and made coverings for themselves.

8Then the man and his wife heard
the sound of the LORD God as he was
walking[g] in the garden in the cool of
the day, and they hid[h] from the LORD
God among the trees of the garden.
9But the LORD God called to the man,
"Where are you?"

10He answered, "I heard you in the
garden, and I was afraid because I was
naked; so I hid."

11And he said, "Who told you that
you were naked? Have you eaten from
the tree that I commanded you not to
eat from?"

12The man said, "The woman you
put here with me—she gave me some
fruit from the tree, and I ate it."

13Then the LORD God said to the
woman, "What is this you have done?"

The woman said, "The serpent deceived me,[i] and I ate."

14So the LORD God said to the serpent, "Because you have done this,

"Cursed[j] are you above all the
livestock
and all the wild animals!
You will crawl on your belly
and you will eat dust[k]
all the days of your life.
15And I will put enmity
between you and the woman,
and between your offspring[d] [l]
and hers;[m]
he will crush[e] your head,[n]
and you will strike his heel."

16To the woman he said,

"I will greatly increase your pains
in childbearing;
with pain you will give birth to
children.

2:18

PROMISE 4

NOT GOOD?

It was *not* good? Seven times in chapter 1 Moses wrote that when God saw what he created he said, "it was good." What, in God's creation, was *not* good? "For the man to be alone."

God created us to crave companionship—with him and with other humans. God created woman and instituted marriage as part of his plan to rectify what was not good in creation. Verse 24 is Moses' comment on this fact and it begins this way: "For this reason . . ." A man leaves his parent's care (grows up), unites with (makes a deep commitment to) his wife and becomes one flesh (forms an unbreakable bond) with her for *this* reason. What reason? God so ordered it.

Single men find legitimate ways to address isolation (1 Corinthians 7) and all men should cultivate strong friendships with other men. But when a man marries a woman he enters a unique, God-ordained relationship designed to address the loneliness and the needs of both people. Do you see—and treat your wife—as God's gift to you? Probe that opening phrase of verse 24: "For this reason." Then reread verses 18–23 and ask God to guide you in making your marriage conform to his reason for instituting it. Finally, read Ephesians 5:25–33 for additional insight on how a man is to relate to his wife.

For the next Promise 4 reading go to page 37.

2:22 w1Co 11:8,9,12
2:23 xGe 29:14; Eph 5:28-30
2:24 yMal 2:15 zMt 19:5*; Mk 10:7-8*; 1Co 6:16*; Eph 5:31*
2:25 aGe 3:7,10-11
3:1 b2Co 11:3; Rev 12:9; 20:2
3:4 cJn 8:44; 2Co 11:3
3:5 dIsa 14:14; Eze 28:2
3:6 eJas 1:14-15; 1Jn 2:16 f1Ti 2:14
3:8 gDt 23:14 hJob 31:33; Ps 139:7-12; Jer 23:24
3:13 i2Co 11:3; 1Ti 2:14
3:14 jDt 28:15-20 kIsa 65:25; Mic 7:17
3:15 lJn 8:44; Ac 13:10; 1Jn 3:8 mIsa 7:14; Mt 1:23; Rev 12:17 nRo 16:20; Heb 2:14

---

a21 Or *took part of the man's side* b22 Or *part* c23 The Hebrew for *woman* sounds like the Hebrew for *man.* d15 Or *seed* e15 Or *strike*

Your desire will be for your
husband,
and he will rule over you.[o]

17 To Adam he said, “Because you listened to your wife and ate from the
tree about which I commanded you,
‘You must not eat of it,’

“Cursed[p] is the ground because of
you;
through painful toil you will eat
of it
all the days of your life.[q]
18 It will produce thorns and thistles
for you,
and you will eat the plants of the
field.[r]
19 By the sweat of your brow
you will eat your food[s]
until you return to the ground,
since from it you were taken;
for dust you are
and to dust you will return.”[t]

20 Adam[a] named his wife Eve,[b] because she would become the mother of
all the living.

21 The LORD God made garments of
skin for Adam and his wife and clothed
them. 22 And the LORD God said, “The
man has now become like one of us,
knowing good and evil. He must not be
allowed to reach out his hand and take
also from the tree of life[u] and eat, and
live forever.” 23 So the LORD God banished him from the Garden of Eden[v]
to work the ground[w] from which he
had been taken. 24 After he drove the
man out, he placed on the east side[c]
of the Garden of Eden cherubim[x] and
a flaming sword[y] flashing back and
forth to guard the way to the tree of
life.[z]

3:16 [o] 1Co 11:3; Eph 5:22
3:17 [p] Ge 5:29; Ro 8:20-22 [q] Job 5:7; 14:1; Ecc 2:23
3:18 [r] Ps 104:14
3:19 [s] 2Th 3:10 [t] Ge 2:7; Ps 90:3; 104:29; Ecc 12:7
3:22 [u] Rev 22:14
3:23 [v] Ge 2:8 [w] Ge 4:2
3:24 [x] Ex 25:18-22 [y] Ps 104:4 [z] Ge 2:9
4:2 [a] Lk 11:51
4:3 [b] Nu 18:12
4:4 [c] Lev 3:16 [d] Ex 13:2,12 [e] Heb 11:4

Cain and Abel

4 Adam[a] lay with his wife Eve, and
she became pregnant and gave birth
to Cain.[d] She said, “With the help of
the LORD I have brought forth[e] a
man.” 2 Later she gave birth to his
brother Abel.[a]

Now Abel kept flocks, and Cain
worked the soil. 3 In the course of time
Cain brought some of the fruits of the
soil as an offering to the LORD.[b] 4 But
Abel brought fat portions[c] from some
of the firstborn of his flock.[d] The LORD
looked with favor on Abel and his offering,[e] 5 but on Cain and his offering he
did not look with favor. So Cain was
very angry, and his face was downcast.

[a] *20,1* Or *The man* [b] *20 Eve* probably means *living.* [c] *24* Or *placed in front* [d] *1 Cain* sounds like the Hebrew for *brought forth* or *acquired.* [e] *1* Or *have acquired*

3:1–24

PROMISE 7

THE FALL

In this passage we see that the prize of God’s creation quickly became the focus of Satan’s attack. Understanding Satan’s strategy is still important today, because he still attacks God’s people. Let’s take a look at his plan to ambush Adam and Eve.

First, Satan questioned Eve’s understanding of what God had said (v. 1). “Did God *really* say . . . ?” Second, Satan directly contradicted Eve’s response (v. 4). Notice that Satan didn’t debate God’s command until he first planted the seeds of doubt. Only then did he enter theological debate over Eve’s understanding of what God had said. By saying, “You will not surely die,” Satan tried to convince Eve that she misunderstood God. Third, Satan attacked Eve’s understanding of God’s character by implying that God had a selfish motive in telling Adam and Eve not to eat the forbidden fruit (v. 5).

So Satan’s attack began with planting doubts about understanding or interpreting God’s words, moved to theological debate about what God really meant, and finally focused those doubts on God’s character. With that accomplished, Satan’s work was nearly done. Human appetite, relieved of responsibility to God, took over.

Verse 6 explains why, in Eve’s mind, it made sense that what God forbade was, in fact, desirable. The fruit was good for food (practical and functional); pleasing to the eye (aesthetically desirable) and a source of wisdom (intellectually beneficial). Eve concluded that not only was it not bad to do what God had prohibited, it was actually good.

Notice how this passage contrasts with Jesus’ temptation as recorded in Matthew 4:1–11. While Eve was unsure of what God had said, Jesus based his whole defense against Satan on the clause, “It is written.” The issue centers right there. Read Matthew 4:1–11 and observe the use of this phrase (vv. 4, 7, 10). The outcome of Adam and Eve’s response to Satan (the fall of man) contrasted with the outcome of Jesus’ response (the redemption of man) is a powerful argument for knowing God’s Word.

The players have changed, but this battle is an ongoing part of the human story. Disobedience to God’s Word leads to death; obedience to God’s Word leads to life. You know the enemy’s strategy. You know how Jesus defeated him. You know the consequences of defeat and victory. The issue rests on your confidence when you say, “It is written!”

You can ward off Satan’s ambush attempts. Be an avid student of God and his Word.

For the next Promise 7 reading go to page 54.

ADAM

Master of the Blame Game

Adam and Eve were the first man and woman, the parents of us all, made directly by God's hand. The Lord created Adam first—"from the dust of the ground." He was special—and so are we—because God "breathed into his nostrils the breath of life, and the man became a living being" (Genesis 2:7). Adam was not just a "higher animal." He was a unique creation who reflected God's personality and character.

David captured this difference when he wrote that God created mankind "a little lower than the heavenly beings [literally, 'God himself'] and crowned him with glory and honor" (Psalm 8:5). That doesn't mean we are Godlike in terms of his all-encompassing wisdom and power. However, we are Godlike in terms of his ability to think, reason, and feel—and even to be creative.

The Perfect Woman

God placed Adam in the Garden of Eden to "work it and take care of it" (Genesis 2:15). Then God said, "It is not good for the man to be alone. I will make a helper suitable for him" (2:18). And so God created Eve from Adam's rib. Once and for all, Eve would be a part of Adam, not separate from him. Though she was uniquely female, Adam exclaimed, "This is now bone of my bones and flesh of my flesh" (2:23). She was the perfect woman.

Then God established a plan for men and women of all time. Today we call it marriage. The Lord said, "For this reason a man will leave his father and mother and be united to his wife, and they will become one flesh" (2:24).

Sin and Blame

Unfortunately, what God had created to be heaven on earth soon became a place of deterioration, pain, confusion, tension, and everything else in the world that creates unhappiness. In all of creation, God had made one tree off limits, the "tree of the knowledge of good and evil." If they ate from this tree, God said, Adam and Eve would "surely die" (2:17).

At that point, Satan entered the scene. Shrewd and conniving, he persuaded Eve to doubt God (3:1) and eat of the forbidden fruit. Eve then gave the fruit to Adam, who also ate. Instantly, Adam and Eve realized their sin and tried to hide from God.

What happened next set a pattern people have been following ever since that day. When the Lord challenged Adam's disobedience, he tried to lay the blame on someone else. He started by trying to pin it on Eve: "The woman . . . she gave me some fruit from the tree" (3:12). You can just picture him pointing an accusing finger at his wife. "Don't look at me! It was her fault!"

But Eve wasn't Adam's primary target. Notice this key phrase in Genesis 3:12: "The woman *you put here with me*—she gave me some fruit" (emphasis added). Adam's bottom-line excuse was that it was all *God's* fault! After all, God was the one who made this weak woman who couldn't hold up under Satan's temptation.

And what about Eve's excuse? When God questioned her, she took her husband's approach and tried to blame someone else for her disobedient choice: "The serpent deceived me, and I ate" (3:13). "It's all *his* fault," she was suggesting.

Obviously, God wasn't fooled. He knew Adam and Eve had both made their own deliberate decision to disobey his command. When the excuses were over, God stated the consequences of their fall. Eve would experience increased pain in bearing children, and a struggle in her relationship with Adam. Adam, too, suffered serious consequences, for the ground now was cursed and it would require great effort to provide for his family. To both, of course, came inevitable death. Finally, because of their sin, Adam and Even had to leave the paradise God had created for them, never to return (3:24).

Make no mistake about it, Adam and Eve—and each one of us as well—were personally responsible to God for their sin. Try as they might to pass it off to another, they found out the hard way that God calls each of us to account for our own actions.

Restoring God's Design

Ever since that day, and right up to the present, husbands and wives have tended to blame each other when decisions turn out to be bad ones. Knowing the Lord Jesus Christ personally as Savior, however, brings an element of restoration to our marriages. Though we'll always suffer the consequences of our first parents' sin, we can experience God's saving grace—not only in giving each of us eternal life when we believe in Christ, but also in enabling us as married couples to minimize the relational curse that fell on Adam and Eve.

Restoring and maintaining marriage isn't easy—it takes a lifetime of work. But with God's help, our marriages *can* provide the oneness and the mutual love, respect, and support that God intended from the beginning. To what extent are you drawing upon God's power through his indwelling Spirit as you relate to your wife?

—Dr. Gene Getz

6Then the LORD said to Cain, "Why
are you angry? Why is your face downcast? 7If you do what is right, will you
not be accepted? But if you do not do
what is right, sin is crouching at your
door;[f] it desires to have you, but you
must master it.[g]"
8Now Cain said to his brother Abel,
"Let's go out to the field."[a] And while
they were in the field, Cain attacked his
brother Abel and killed him.[h]
2 →PG. 20
9Then the LORD said to Cain, "Where
is your brother Abel?"
"I don't know," he replied. "Am I my
brother's keeper?"
10The LORD said, "What have you
done? Listen! Your brother's blood
cries out to me from the ground.[i]
11Now you are under a curse and driv-
en from the ground, which opened its
mouth to receive your brother's blood
from your hand. 12When you work the
ground, it will no longer yield its crops
for you. You will be a restless wanderer
on the earth."
13Cain said to the LORD, "My punishment is more than I can bear. 14Today
you are driving me from the land, and
I will be hidden from your presence;[j]
I will be a restless wanderer on the
earth, and whoever finds me will
kill me."[k]
15But the LORD said to him, "Not
so[b]; if anyone kills Cain[l], he will suffer vengeance seven times over.[m]"
Then the LORD put a mark on Cain so
that no one who found him would kill
him. 16So Cain went out from the
LORD's presence and lived in the land
of Nod,[c] east of Eden.[n]

17Cain lay with his wife, and she became pregnant and gave birth to
Enoch. Cain was then building a city,
and he named it after his son[o] Enoch.
18To Enoch was born Irad, and Irad
was the father of Mehujael, and Mehujael was the father of Methushael, and
Methushael was the father of Lamech.
19Lamech married two women, one
named Adah and the other Zillah.
20Adah gave birth to Jabal; he was the
father of those who live in tents and
raise livestock. 21His brother's name
was Jubal; he was the father of all who
play the harp and flute. 22Zillah also
had a son, Tubal-Cain, who forged all
kinds of tools out of[d] bronze and iron.
Tubal-Cain's sister was Naamah.
23Lamech said to his wives,

"Adah and Zillah, listen to me;
wives of Lamech, hear my words.
I have killed[e][p] a man for
wounding me,
a young man for injuring me.
24If Cain is avenged[q] seven times,[r]
then Lamech seventy-seven
times."

25Adam lay with his wife again, and
she gave birth to a son and named him
Seth,[f][s] saying, "God has granted me
another child in place of Abel, since
Cain killed him."[t] 26Seth also had a
son, and he named him Enosh.

4:7 [f]Nu 32:23 [g]Ro 6:16
4:8 [h]Mt 23:35; 1Jn 3:12
4:10 [i]Ge 9:5; Nu 35:33; Heb 12:24; Rev 6:9-10
4:14 [j]2Ki 17:18; Ps 51:11; 139:7-12; Jer 7:15; 52:3 [k]Ge 9:6; Nu 35:19,21, 27,33
4:15 [l]Eze 9:4,6 [m]ver 24; Ps 79:12
4:16 [n]Ge 2:8
4:17 [o]Ps 49:11
4:23 [p]Ex 20:13; Lev 19:18
4:24 [q]Dt 32:35 [r]ver 15
4:25 [s]Ge 5:3 [t]ver 8

[a]*8* Samaritan Pentateuch, Septuagint, Vulgate and Syriac; Masoretic Text does not have *"Let's go out to the field."* [b]*15* Septuagint, Vulgate and Syriac; Hebrew *Very well* [c]*16* *Nod* means *wandering* (see verses 12 and 14). [d]*22* Or *who instructed all who work in* [e]*23* Or *I will kill* [f]*25* *Seth* probably means *granted.*

4:1–8

PROMISE 1

MURDER ONE

As you read this story, you may be asking, "Why air the dirty linen?" Of all the events that occurred over the years between Genesis 3 and 4, God chose to tell this one. Why? Because it reveals vital truths about these beings whom God created in his image (1:26–30) and who chose to rebel (3:1–7). Cain, a son of Adam, turned an error into a disastrous sin because he responded to that error as a sinful man rather than as an image-bearer. After God corrected him (vv. 3–5), Cain "was very angry and. . . downcast." So God gave him another chance to adjust his attitude, another opportunity to learn how God wanted him to live. But instead of responding to God's correction, Cain murdered his brother out of a jealous rage.

This event warns us about sin's influence on the human condition. Two facts strike the observant reader: (1) the number of sins involved in this short account; (2) God's gracious attempts to help Cain correct his ways. Through many different stories with many different characters, the Bible repeats the kernel of this story over and over.

God gave Cain opportunities to live as God intended, and he offers us the same gift of his grace and forgiveness. Read John 3:16, where God succinctly presents this same offer to you. If you've already decided to accept this offer, contrast the results of Cain's rebellion against God with the hope you experience through new life in him.

Only God can change the disastrous results of sin on the human heart. Only he can counteract the rejection that Cain experienced and bring new life. And he is ready and willing to make that change in your life.

For the next Promise 1 reading go to page 10.

At that time men began to call on[a]
the name of the LORD.[u]

From Adam to Noah

5 This is the written account of
Adam's line.

When God created man, he made
him in the likeness of God.[v] 2He created them male and female[w] and
blessed them. And when they were created, he called them "man.[b]"
3When Adam had lived 130 years, he
had a son in his own likeness, in his
own image;[x] and he named him Seth.
4After Seth was born, Adam lived 800
years and had other sons and daughters. 5Altogether, Adam lived 930 years,
and then he died.[y]
6When Seth had lived 105 years, he
became the father[c] of Enosh. 7And after he became the father of Enosh, Seth
lived 807 years and had other sons and
daughters. 8Altogether, Seth lived 912
years, and then he died.
9When Enosh had lived 90 years, he
became the father of Kenan. 10And after he became the father of Kenan,
Enosh lived 815 years and had other
sons and daughters. 11Altogether,
Enosh lived 905 years, and then he
died.
12When Kenan had lived 70 years, he
became the father of Mahalalel. 13And
after he became the father of Mahalalel, Kenan lived 840 years and had other sons and daughters. 14Altogether,
Kenan lived 910 years, and then he
died.
15When Mahalalel had lived 65
years, he became the father of Jared.
16And after he became the father of Jared, Mahalalel lived 830 years and had
other sons and daughters. 17Altogether,
Mahalalel lived 895 years, and then he
died.
18When Jared had lived 162 years, he
became the father of Enoch.[z] 19And
after he became the father of Enoch,
Jared lived 800 years and had other
sons and daughters. 20Altogether, Jared
lived 962 years, and then he died.
21When Enoch had lived 65 years, he
became the father of Methuselah.
22And after he became the father of
Methuselah, Enoch walked with God[a]
300 years and had other sons and
daughters. 23Altogether, Enoch lived
365 years. 24Enoch walked with God;[b]
then he was no more, because God
took him away.[c]
25When Methuselah had lived 187
years, he became the father of Lamech.
26And after he became the father of Lamech, Methuselah lived 782 years and
had other sons and daughters. 27Alto-
gether, Methuselah lived 969 years,
and then he died.
28When Lamech had lived 182 years,
he had a son. 29He named him Noah[d]
and said, "He will comfort us in the
labor and painful toil of our hands
caused by the ground the LORD has
cursed.[d]" 30After Noah was born, Lamech lived 595 years and had other
sons and daughters. 31Altogether, Lamech lived 777 years, and then he died.
32After Noah was 500 years old, he
became the father of Shem, Ham and
Japheth.

The Flood

6 When men began to increase in
number on the earth[e] and daughters were born to them, 2the sons of
God saw that the daughters of men
were beautiful, and they married any of

4:26 [u]Ge 12:8; 1Ki 18:24; Ps 116:17; Joel 2:32; Zep 3:9; Ac 2:21; 1Co 1:2
5:1 [v]Ge 1:27; Eph 4:24; Col 3:10
5:2 [w]Ge 1:27; Mt 19:4; Mk 10:6; Gal 3:28
5:3 [x]Ge 1:26; 1Co 15:49
5:5 [y]Ge 3:19
5:18 [z]Jude 1:14
5:22 [a]ver 24; Ge 6:9; 17:1; 48:15; Mic 6:8; Mal 2:6
5:24 [b]ver 22 [c]2Ki 2:1,11; Heb 11:5
5:29 [d]Ge 3:17; Ro 8:20
6:1 [e]Ge 1:28

[a]26 Or *to proclaim* [b]2 Hebrew *adam*
[c]6 *Father* may mean *ancestor*; also in verses 7-26. [d]29 *Noah* sounds like the Hebrew for *comfort.*

6:1–22

PROMISE 1

CREATED FOR GOD'S PURPOSE

This story defies belief. In the first few verses we see how humans, those who had been created in God's image for the purpose of loving and serving God (1:26–30), turned against him. The sin described in Genesis 3 has been brought to its darkest point. Verses 5 through 7 detail God's perceptions at this point in time, outlining how far humans had fallen from his original intentions.

Then comes Noah, who sets a shining example for the rest of us. Despite the corrupting presence of sin in the world, Noah loved and pursued God (6:8–10). He defied the status quo and "found favor in the eyes of the LORD." And his actions in the next chapters bear out that fact.

These early chapters of Genesis present us with a choice. We can follow the distorted and destructive way of sin, or the noble way God intended for us by creating us in his image. The book you hold in your hands is God's invitation to follow his design. It contains instructions for how to do so. As you read it, understand the continual battle for your soul; a life-and-death struggle between sin's effects and God's gracious invitation. The accounts you'll read in this book aren't merely human interest stories. They are given to us to teach us about a fundamental choice we face every day: Sin's way of destruction or God's way of life. Choose carefully!

For the next Promise 1 reading go to page 11.

them they chose. 3Then the LORD said,
"My Spirit will not contend with[a] man
forever,[f] for he is mortal[b];[g] his days
will be a hundred and twenty years."
4The Nephilim[h] were on the earth
in those days—and also afterward—
when the sons of God went to the
daughters of men and had children by
them. They were the heroes of old,
men of renown.
5The LORD saw how great man's
wickedness on the earth had become,
and that every inclination of the
thoughts of his heart was only evil all
the time.[i] 6The LORD was grieved[j]
that he had made man on the earth,
and his heart was filled with pain. 7So
the LORD said, "I will wipe mankind,
whom I have created, from the face of
the earth—men and animals, and
creatures that move along the ground,
and birds of the air—for I am grieved
that I have made them." 8But Noah
found favor in the eyes of the LORD.[k]

9This is the account of Noah.

Noah was a righteous man, blameless among the people of his time,[l]
and he walked with God.[m] 10Noah had
three sons: Shem, Ham and Japheth.[n]
11Now the earth was corrupt in
God's sight and was full of violence.[o]
12God saw how corrupt the earth had
become, for all the people on earth had
corrupted their ways.[p] 13So God said
to Noah, "I am going to put an end to
all people, for the earth is filled with
violence because of them. I am surely
going to destroy both them and the
earth.[q] 14So make yourself an ark of
cypress[c] wood;[r] make rooms in it
and coat it with pitch[s] inside and out.
15This is how you are to build it: The
ark is to be 450 feet long, 75 feet wide
and 45 feet high.[d] 16Make a roof for
it and finish[e] the ark to within 18
inches[f] of the top. Put a door in the
side of the ark and make lower, middle
and upper decks. 17I am going to bring
floodwaters on the earth to destroy all
life under the heavens, every creature
that has the breath of life in it. Everything on earth will perish.[t] 18But I will
establish my covenant with you,[u] and
you will enter the ark[v]—you and your
sons and your wife and your sons'
wives with you. 19You are to bring into
the ark two of all living creatures, male
and female, to keep them alive with
you. 20Two[w] of every kind of bird, of
every kind of animal and of every kind
of creature that moves along the
ground will come to you to be kept
alive. 21You are to take every kind of
food that is to be eaten and store it
away as food for you and for them."
22Noah did everything just as God
commanded him.[x]

7 The LORD then said to Noah, "Go
into the ark, you and your whole
family,[y] because I have found you
righteous[z] in this generation. 2Take
with you seven[g] of every kind of
clean[a] animal, a male and its mate,
and two of every kind of unclean animal, a male and its mate, 3and also sev-
en of every kind of bird, male and female, to keep their various kinds alive
throughout the earth. 4Seven days
from now I will send rain on the earth
for forty days and forty nights, and I
will wipe from the face of the earth every living creature I have made."
5And Noah did all that the LORD
commanded him.[b]
6Noah was six hundred years old
when the floodwaters came on the
earth. 7And Noah and his sons and his
wife and his sons' wives entered the ark
to escape the waters of the flood. 8Pairs
of clean and unclean animals, of birds
and of all creatures that move along
the ground, 9male and female, came to
Noah and entered the ark, as God had
commanded Noah. 10And after the sev-
en days the floodwaters came on the
earth.
11In the six hundredth year of
Noah's life, on the seventeenth day of
the second month—on that day all the
springs of the great deep[c] burst forth,
and the floodgates of the heavens[d]
were opened. 12And rain fell on the
earth forty days and forty nights.[e]

6:3 [f]Isa 57:16 [g]Ps 78:39 **6:4** [h]Nu 13:33 **6:5** [i]Ge 8:21; Ps 14:1-3 **6:6** [j]1Sa 15:11,35; Isa 63:10 **6:8** [k]Ge 19:19; Ex 33:12,13,17; Lk 1:30; Ac 7:46 **6:9** [l]Ge 7:1; Eze 14:14,20; Heb 11:7; 2Pe 2:5 [m]Ge 5:22 **6:10** [n]Ge 5:32 **6:11** [o]Eze 7:23; 8:17 **6:12** [p]Ps 14:1-3 **6:13** [q]ver 17; Eze 7:2-3 **6:14** [r]Heb 11:7; 1Pe 3:20 [s]Ex 2:3 **6:17** [t]Ge 7:4,21-23; 2Pe 2:5 **6:18** [u]Ge 9:9-16 [v]Ge 7:1,7,13 **6:20** [w]Ge 7:15 **6:22** [x]Ge 7:5,9,16 **7:1** [y]Mt 24:38 [z]Ge 6:9; Eze 14:14 **7:2** [a]ver 8; Ge 8:20; Lev 10:10; 11:1-47 **7:5** [b]Ge 6:22 **7:11** [c]Eze 26:19 [d]Ge 8:2 **7:12** [e]ver 4

a3 Or *My spirit will not remain in* **b**3 Or *corrupt* **c**14 The meaning of the Hebrew for this word is uncertain. **d**15 Hebrew *300 cubits long, 50 cubits wide and 30 cubits high* (about 140 meters long, 23 meters wide and 13.5 meters high) **e**16 Or *Make an opening for light by finishing* **f**16 Hebrew *a cubit* (about 0.5 meter) **g**2 Or *seven pairs*; also in verse 3

6:22

PROMISE **1**

WHAT GOD WANTS

What a refreshing statement in this morally dry landscape! Noah did what God said. That is all God asks. As you read through the Bible—either from beginning to end or in sections—remember what it is: God's instruction manual for living a life that honors him. As you read the account of Noah, observe the results of not doing what God commands. Then contrast that with the outcome for this solitary individual whose testimony is summarized in this verse. Pray that it will be your testimony as you read and respond to "everything . . . God commanded."

For the next Promise 1 reading go to page 17.

NOAH

A Man Who Walked With God

God's attributes are easily traced throughout the stories in the Bible: He is merciful; he is faithful; he is just; he is holy. Yet God is richly complex. There is more to his character than we readily recognize. We come to know God in new ways when he reveals himself to us as we walk with him.

The Bible indicates that Noah knew a bit about God's character too. Though Noah did not have God's written Word as we know it today to lead him through challenging circumstances, Noah was able to take what he *did* know about God and walk with him.

In Noah's day, everyone had turned away from God. "The earth was corrupt in God's sight and was full of violence" (Genesis 6:11). The effects of sinfulness bombarded Noah's culture. Wickedness on the earth was so great, the Lord was grieved that he had ever made people.

Yet Noah was an exception. Noah lived a righteous life when everyone else had turned against God. And God approved of him. Noah was "blameless" and "righteous," setting his path apart from the rest of his culture. Noah proved that it is possible to "[walk] with God" (6:9) regardless of an evil society's influence.

A Walk With God Takes Work

When God commanded Noah to build the ark, Noah obeyed. We do not know if Noah was skilled in carpentry or if he had ever seen a boat. We do not know how difficult it may have been to corral "every wild animal according to its kind" (7: 14). Noah had many tasks to accomplish that were not glamorous or particularly edifying. But Noah had a profound desire to carry out what God had called him to do. He simply did as the Lord commanded and relied on God's blueprint to complete the task. His heart was not swayed toward the evils of the world, but remained steadfast toward God.

What a great tribute it would be for us to be known as people who walked with God! We, too, live in a decadent world. Evil is still in our midst. But, fortunately, we are not alone. We are surrounded by sincere brothers and sisters in Christ who, like Noah, are walking with God day by day.

Yet the walk is not an easy one. Temptations are everywhere. Ridicule and unbelief are common. This should not surprise us. Peter warned that "in the last days scoffers will come, scoffing and following their own evil desires" (2 Peter 3:3). Peter goes on to remind all of us—believers and nonbelievers—that in centuries past, the same thing happened. Many people probably scoffed at Noah. The coming destruction seemed impossible. As time passed and nothing happened, Noah's critics had more reasons to justify their unbelief.

But God's judgment did happen. God finally told Noah the rain would come in another seven days. In obedience to God, Noah collected his family and the animals and got on board the ark. And after the seven days, when the waters came, God himself "shut him in" (Genesis 7:16). Noah and his family and the animals sat safely inside the ark that Noah had obediently built, but it was too late for those on the outside. The rain fell on the earth for 40 days and 40 nights. The waters rose. Those on the outside entered a watery grave that was an entrance to an eternity without God. In a very tragic sense, humanity "missed the boat" and God started over with one man, his wife, their three sons and their wives.

Faithfully Stay on Board

Noah is listed in the book of Hebrews as one of the great Old Testament "Heroes of the Faith." After reminding us that it is impossible to please God without faith, the author of Hebrews cites Noah as a great example: "By faith Noah, when warned about things not yet seen, in holy fear built an ark to save his family" (Hebrews 11:7). Remember, Noah did not build the ark in one day. He got out of bed each morning ready to meet the challenges that each day presented. Because of his faith in God, he accomplished God's will for his family and for generations to come.

When we decide to walk with God, we may experience hardships and trials of many kinds. We cannot totally escape the consequences of living in a fallen, depraved world. Noah becomes our example when we feel we are sailing with God into these uncharted waters. As Noah lived a righteous and blameless life in the midst of his wicked world, so we must be faithful in our walk with God as we encounter daily challenges and temptations. Peter urges us to "make every effort to be found spotless, blameless and at peace with him" (2 Peter 3:14). In the power of God's Spirit, Noah did it. In the power of that same Spirit, so can we.

—Dr. Gene Getz

13 On that very day Noah and his sons, Shem, Ham and Japheth, together with his wife and the wives of his three sons, entered the ark. 14 They had with them every wild animal according to its kind, all livestock according to their kinds, every creature that moves along the ground according to its kind and every bird according to its kind, everything with wings. 15 Pairs of all creatures that have the breath of life in them came to Noah and entered the ark.[f] 16 The animals going in were male and female of every living thing, as God had commanded Noah. Then the LORD shut him in.

17 For forty days[g] the flood kept coming on the earth, and as the waters increased they lifted the ark high above the earth. 18 The waters rose and increased greatly on the earth, and the ark floated on the surface of the water. 19 They rose greatly on the earth, and all the high mountains under the entire heavens were covered.[h] 20 The waters rose and covered the mountains to a depth of more than twenty feet.[a,b] 21 Every living thing that moved on the earth perished—birds, livestock, wild animals, all the creatures that swarm over the earth, and all mankind.[i] 22 Everything on dry land that had the breath of life[j] in its nostrils died. 23 Every living thing on the face of the earth was wiped out; men and animals and the creatures that move along the ground and the birds of the air were wiped from the earth.[k] Only Noah was left, and those with him in the ark.[l]

24 The waters flooded the earth for a hundred and fifty days.[m]

8 But God remembered[n] Noah and all the wild animals and the livestock that were with him in the ark, and he sent a wind over the earth,[o] and the waters receded. 2 Now the springs of the deep and the floodgates of the heavens[p] had been closed, and the rain had stopped falling from the sky. 3 The water receded steadily from the earth. At the end of the hundred and fifty days the water had gone down, 4 and on the seventeenth day of the seventh month the ark came to rest on the mountains of Ararat. 5 The waters continued to recede until the tenth month, and on the first day of the tenth month the tops of the mountains became visible.

6 After forty days Noah opened the window he had made in the ark 7 and sent out a raven, and it kept flying back and forth until the water had dried up from the earth. 8 Then he sent out a dove to see if the water had receded from the surface of the ground. 9 But the dove could find no place to set its feet because there was water over all the surface of the earth; so it returned to Noah in the ark. He reached out his hand and took the dove and brought it back to himself in the ark. 10 He waited seven more days and again sent out the dove from the ark. 11 When the dove returned to him in the evening, there in its beak was a freshly plucked olive leaf! Then Noah knew that the water had receded from the earth. 12 He waited seven more days and sent the dove out again, but this time it did not return to him.

13 By the first day of the first month of Noah's six hundred and first year, the water had dried up from the earth. Noah then removed the covering from the ark and saw that the surface of the ground was dry. 14 By the twenty-seventh day of the second month the earth was completely dry.

15 Then God said to Noah, 16 "Come out of the ark, you and your wife and your sons and their wives.[q] 17 Bring out every kind of living creature that is with you—the birds, the animals, and all the creatures that move along the ground—so they can multiply on the earth and be fruitful and increase in number upon it."[r]

18 So Noah came out, together with his sons and his wife and his sons' wives. 19 All the animals and all the creatures that move along the ground and all the birds—everything that moves on the earth—came out of the ark, one kind after another.

20 Then Noah built an altar to the LORD[s] and, taking some of all the clean animals and clean[t] birds, he sacrificed burnt offerings[u] on it. 21 The LORD smelled the pleasing aroma[v] and said in his heart: "Never again will I curse the ground[w] because of man, even though[c] every inclination of his heart is evil from childhood.[x] And never again will I destroy all living creatures,[y] as I have done.

22 "As long as the earth endures,
seedtime and harvest,
cold and heat,
summer and winter,
day and night
will never cease."[z]

God's Covenant With Noah

9 Then God blessed Noah and his sons, saying to them, "Be fruitful and increase in number and fill the

7:15 [f]Ge 6:19
7:17 [g]ver 4
7:19 [h]Ps 104:6
7:21 [i]Ge 6:7,13
7:22 [j]Ge 1:30
7:23 [k]Mt 24:39; Lk 17:27; 1Pe 3:20; 2Pe 2:5 [l]Heb 11:7
7:24 [m]Ge 8:3
8:1 [n]Ge 9:15; 19:29; Ex 2:24; 1Sa 1:11,19 [o]Ex 14:21
8:2 [p]Ge 7:11
8:16 [q]Ge 7:13
8:17 [r]Ge 1:22
8:20 [s]Ge 12:7-8; 13:18; 22:9 [t]Ge 7:8; Lev 11:1-47 [u]Ge 22:2,13; Ex 10:25
8:21 [v]Lev 1:9,13; 2Co 2:15 [w]Ge 3:17 [x]Ge 6:5; Ps 51:5; Jer 17:9 [y]Ge 9:11,15; Isa 54:9
8:22 [z]Ge 1:14; Jer 33:20,25

a 20 Hebrew *fifteen cubits* (about 6.9 meters)
b 20 Or *rose more than twenty feet, and the mountains were covered*
c 21 Or *man, for*

earth.[a] 2The fear and dread of you will fall upon all the beasts of the earth and all the birds of the air, upon every creature that moves along the ground, and upon all the fish of the sea; they are given into your hands. 3Everything that lives and moves will be food for you.[b] Just as I gave you the green plants, I now give you everything.

4"But you must not eat meat that has its lifeblood still in it.[c] 5And for your lifeblood I will surely demand an accounting. I will demand an accounting from every animal.[d] And from each man, too, I will demand an accounting for the life of his fellow man.[e]

6"Whoever sheds the blood of man,
by man shall his blood be
shed;[f]
for in the image of God[g]
has God made man.

7As for you, be fruitful and increase in number; multiply on the earth and increase upon it."[h]

8Then God said to Noah and to his sons with him: 9"I now establish my covenant with you[i] and with your descendants after you 10and with every living creature that was with you—the birds, the livestock and all the wild animals, all those that came out of the ark with you—every living creature on earth. 11I establish my covenant[j] with you: Never again will all life be cut off by the waters of a flood; never again will there be a flood to destroy the earth.[k]"

12And God said, "This is the sign of the covenant[l] I am making between me and you and every living creature with you, a covenant for all generations to come: 13I have set my rainbow in the clouds, and it will be the sign of the covenant between me and the earth. 14Whenever I bring clouds over the earth and the rainbow appears in the clouds, 15I will remember my covenant[m] between me and you and all living creatures of every kind. Never again will the waters become a flood to destroy all life. 16Whenever the rainbow appears in the clouds, I will see it and remember the everlasting covenant[n] between God and all living creatures of every kind on the earth."

17So God said to Noah, "This is the sign of the covenant[o] I have established between me and all life on the earth."

The Sons of Noah

18The sons of Noah who came out of the ark were Shem, Ham and Japheth. (Ham was the father of Canaan.)[p] 19These were the three sons of Noah, and from them came the people who were scattered over the earth.[q]

20Noah, a man of the soil, proceeded[a] to plant a vineyard. 21When he drank some of its wine, he became drunk and lay uncovered inside his tent. 22Ham, the father of Canaan, saw his father's nakedness and told his two brothers outside. 23But Shem and Japheth took a garment and laid it across their shoulders; then they walked in backward and covered their father's nakedness. Their faces were turned the other way so that they would not see their father's nakedness.

24When Noah awoke from his wine and found out what his youngest son had done to him, 25he said,

"Cursed be Canaan![r]
The lowest of slaves
will he be to his brothers.[s]"

26He also said,

"Blessed be the LORD, the God of
Shem!
May Canaan be the slave of
Shem.[b]
27May God extend the territory of
Japheth[c];
may Japheth live in the tents of
Shem,
and may Canaan be his[d] slave."

28After the flood Noah lived 350 years. 29Altogether, Noah lived 950 years, and then he died.

The Table of Nations

10 This is the account[t] of Shem, Ham and Japheth, Noah's sons, who themselves had sons after the flood.

The Japhethites

2The sons[e] of Japheth:
Gomer,[u] Magog,[v] Madai, Javan, Tubal,[w] Meshech and Tiras.
3The sons of Gomer:
Ashkenaz,[x] Riphath and Togarmah.[y]
4The sons of Javan:
Elishah, Tarshish,[z] the Kittim and the Rodanim.[f] 5(From these the maritime peoples spread out into their territories by their clans within their na-

9:1 [a]Ge 1:22 **9:3** [b]Ge 1:29 **9:4** [c]Lev 3:17; 17:10-14; Dt 12:16, 23-25; 1Sa 14:33 **9:5** [d]Ex 21:28-32 [e]Ge 4:10 **9:6** [f]Ge 4:14; Ex 21:12,14; Lev 24:17; Mt 26:52 [g]Ge 1:26 **9:7** [h]Ge 1:22 **9:9** [i]Ge 6:18 **9:11** [j]ver 16; Isa 24:5 [k]Ge 8:21; Isa 54:9 **9:12** [l]ver 17; Ge 17:11 **9:15** [m]Ex 2:24; Lev 26:42,45; Dt 7:9; Eze 16:60 **9:16** [n]ver 11; Ge 17:7,13,19; 2Sa 7:13; 23:5 **9:17** [o]ver 12; Ge 17:11

9:18 [p]ver 25-27; Ge 10:6,15 **9:19** [q]Ge 10:32 **9:25** [r]ver 18 [s]Ge 25:23; Jos 9:23 **10:1** [t]Ge 2:4 **10:2** [u]Eze 38:6 [v]Eze 38:2; Rev 20:8 [w]Isa 66:19 **10:3** [x]Jer 51:27 [y]Eze 27:14; 38:6 **10:4** [z]Eze 27:12,25; Jnh 1:3

[a]20 Or *soil, was the first* [b]26 Or *be his slave* [c]27 *Japheth* sounds like the Hebrew for *extend.* [d]27 Or *their* [e]2 *Sons* may mean *descendants* or *successors* or *nations;* also in verses 3, 4, 6, 7, 20-23, 29 and 31. [f]4 Some manuscripts of the Masoretic Text and Samaritan Pentateuch (see also Septuagint and 1 Chron. 1:7); most manuscripts of the Masoretic Text *Dodanim*

tions, each with its own language.)

The Hamites

6 The sons of Ham:
Cush, Mizraim,[a] Put and Ca-
naan.[a]
7 The sons of Cush:
Seba, Havilah, Sabtah, Raa-
mah and Sabteca.
The sons of Raamah:
Sheba and Dedan.

8 Cush was the father[b] of Nimrod,
who grew to be a mighty warrior on the
earth. 9 He was a mighty hunter before
the LORD; that is why it is said, "Like
Nimrod, a mighty hunter before the
LORD." 10 The first centers of his kingdom were Babylon,[b] Erech, Akkad
and Calneh, in[c] Shinar.[d][c] 11 From
that land he went to Assyria,[d] where
he built Nineveh,[e] Rehoboth Ir,[e]
Calah 12 and Resen, which is between
Nineveh and Calah; that is the great
city.

13 Mizraim was the father of
the Ludites, Anamites, Lehabites, Naphtuhites, 14 Pathru-
sites, Casluhites (from whom
the Philistines[f] came) and
Caphtorites.
15 Canaan[g] was the father of
Sidon[h] his firstborn,[f] and of
the Hittites,[i] 16 Jebusites,[j] Amorites, Girgashites, 17 Hivites,
Arkites, Sinites, 18 Arvadites,
Zemarites and Hamathites.

Later the Canaanite[k] clans scattered 19 and the borders of Canaan[l]
reached from Sidon[m] toward Gerar as
far as Gaza, and then toward Sodom,
Gomorrah, Admah and Zeboiim, as far
as Lasha.
20 These are the sons of Ham by their
clans and languages, in their territories
and nations.

The Semites

21 Sons were also born to Shem,
whose older brother was[g] Japheth;
Shem was the ancestor of all the sons
of Eber.[n]
22 The sons of Shem:
Elam,[o] Asshur, Arphaxad,[p] Lud
and Aram.
23 The sons of Aram:
Uz,[q] Hul, Gether and Meshech.[h]
24 Arphaxad was the father of[i] Shelah,
and Shelah the father of
Eber.[r]
25 Two sons were born to Eber:
One was named Peleg,[j] because in his time the earth
was divided; his brother was
named Joktan.
26 Joktan was the father of
Almodad, Sheleph, Hazarmaveth, Jerah, 27 Hadoram, Uzal,
Diklah, 28 Obal, Abimael, Sheba, 29 Ophir, Havilah and Jobab. All these were sons of Joktan.

30 The region where they lived
stretched from Mesha toward Sephar,
in the eastern hill country.
31 These are the sons of Shem by
their clans and languages, in their territories and nations.

32 These are the clans of Noah's
sons,[s] according to their lines of descent, within their nations. From these
the nations spread out over the earth[t]
after the flood.

The Tower of Babel

11 Now the whole world had one language and a common speech. 2 As
men moved eastward,[k] they found a
plain in Shinar[d][u] and settled there.
3 They said to each other, "Come,
let's make bricks[v] and bake them
thoroughly." They used brick instead
of stone, and tar[w] for mortar. 4 Then
they said, "Come, let us build ourselves
a city, with a tower that reaches to the
heavens,[x] so that we may make a
name[y] for ourselves and not be scattered over the face of the whole
earth."[z]
5 But the LORD came down[a] to see
the city and the tower that the men
were building. 6 The LORD said, "If as
one people speaking the same language they have begun to do this, then
nothing they plan to do will be impossible for them. 7 Come, let us[b] go down
and confuse their language so they will
not understand each other."[c]
8 So the LORD scattered them from
there over all the earth,[d] and they
stopped building the city. 9 That is why
it was called Babel[l][e]—because there
the LORD confused the language of the
whole world. From there the LORD scat-

10:6 [a]ver 15; Ge 9:18
10:10 [b]Ge 11:9 [c]Ge 11:2
10:11 [d]Ps 83:8; Mic 5:6 [e]Jnh 1:2; 4:11; Na 1:1
10:14 [f]Ge 21:32,34; 26:1,8
10:15 [g]ver 6; Ge 9:18 [h]Eze 28:21 [i]Ge 23:3,20
10:16 [j]1Ch 11:4
10:18 [k]Ge 12:6; Ex 13:11
10:19 [l]Ge 11:31; 13:12; 17:8 [m]ver 15
10:21 [n]ver 24; Nu 24:24
10:22 [o]Jer 49:34 [p]Lk 3:36
10:23 [q]Job 1:1
10:24 [r]ver 21
10:32 [s]ver 1 [t]Ge 9:19
11:2 [u]Ge 10:10
11:3 [v]Ex 1:14 [w]Ge 14:10
11:4 [x]Dt 1:28; 9:1 [y]Ge 6:4 [z]Dt 4:27
11:5 [a]ver 7; Ge 18:21; Ex 3:8; 19:11, 18,20
11:7 [b]Ge 1:26 [c]Ge 42:23
11:8 [d]Ge 9:19; Lk 1:51
11:9 [e]Ge 10:10

[a] *6* That is, Egypt; also in verse 13 [b] *8 Father* may mean *ancestor* or *predecessor* or *founder*, also in verses 13, 15, 24 and 26. [c] *10* Or *Erech and Akkad—all of them in* [d] *10,2* That is, Babylonia [e] *11* Or *Nineveh with its city squares* [f] *15* Or *of the Sidonians, the foremost* [g] *21* Or *Shem, the older brother of* [h] *23* See Septuagint and 1 Chron. 1:17; Hebrew *Mash* [i] *24* Hebrew; Septuagint *father of Cainan, and Cainan was the father of* [j] *25 Peleg* means *division.* [k] *2* Or *from the east*; or *in the east* [l] *9* That is, Babylon; *Babel* sounds like the Hebrew for *confused.*

tered them over the face of the whole
earth.

From Shem to Abram

10 This is the account of Shem.

Two years after the flood, when
Shem was 100 years old, he became the
father[a] of Arphaxad. 11 And after he became the father of Arphaxad, Shem
lived 500 years and had other sons and
daughters.
12 When Arphaxad had lived 35 years,
he became the father of Shelah.[f]
13 And after he became the father of
Shelah, Arphaxad lived 403 years and
had other sons and daughters.[b]
14 When Shelah had lived 30 years, he
became the father of Eber. 15 And after
he became the father of Eber, Shelah
lived 403 years and had other sons and
daughters.
16 When Eber had lived 34 years, he
became the father of Peleg. 17 And after
he became the father of Peleg, Eber
lived 430 years and had other sons and
daughters.
18 When Peleg had lived 30 years, he
became the father of Reu. 19 And after
he became the father of Reu, Peleg
lived 209 years and had other sons and
daughters.
20 When Reu had lived 32 years, he
became the father of Serug.[g] 21 And after he became the father of Serug, Reu
lived 207 years and had other sons and
daughters.
22 When Serug had lived 30 years, he
became the father of Nahor. 23 And after he became the father of Nahor, Serug lived 200 years and had other sons
and daughters.
24 When Nahor had lived 29 years, he
became the father of Terah.[h] 25 And after he became the father of Terah, Nahor lived 119 years and had other sons
and daughters.
26 After Terah had lived 70 years, he
became the father of Abram,[i] Nahor[j] and Haran.

11:12 [f] Lk 3:35
11:20 [g] Lk 3:35
11:24 [h] Lk 3:34
11:26 [i] Lk 3:34 [j] Jos 24:2

[a] *10 Father* may mean *ancestor*; also in verses 11-25. [b] *12,13* Hebrew; Septuagint (see also Luke 3:35, 36 and note at Gen. 10:24) *35 years, he became the father of Cainan. 13 And after he became the father of Cainan, Arphaxad lived 430 years and had other sons and daughters, and then he died. When Cainan had lived 130 years, he became the father of Shelah. And after he became the father of Shelah, Cainan lived 330 years and had other sons and daughters*

11:1–8

PROMISE 6

BIBLICAL UNITY

Is God encouraging division among people in this story? Doesn't God want people to live in peace? God's design at Babel was not to divide people so they could live in suspicion and hatred and destroy each other. Those are our ideas, not his. What, then, was God doing?

God commanded Adam and Eve to fill the earth, to subdue it and rule over its creatures (1:28). He repeated this commission to Noah and his family after the flood (9:1–2). But as Noah's family grew, the members refused to accept their responsibility as God's stewards of the whole earth. One of their clear intentions in building this tower was that they "not be scattered over the face of the whole earth" (v. 4). Since they were working directly against God's purposes for humanity, God confused their language. The result was dramatic—and extremely effective. Moses reported, "So the LORD scattered them from there over all the earth" (v. 8).

God did intend to scatter people over the whole earth to care for his creation. He did not intend for us to be suspicious about or to discriminate against or to hate each other. Again, those were our ideas, a result of the sin in the hearts of men and women. We still foster suspicion, discrimination and hatred to this day, and they're no less acceptable in God's eyes now than they were then.

Jesus' teaching on the good Samaritan (Luke 10) shows us that God intends us to see as neighbors those whom we have turned into enemies. Ephesians 2 and Galatians 3:28 state that there is neither Jew nor Greek, male nor female, slave nor free person in the church of Christ—we are all one people, God's people. And one of the most powerful statements on reconciliation and unity between people in the church is in Ephesians 4:1–3, where Paul urges Christians to walk worthy of their calling. In verse 3 he states exactly what that means: "Make every effort to keep the unity of the Spirit through the bond of peace." Then in verses 4 through 6, he lists seven "ones" that we hold in common. Take a moment to read through that list.

Addressing the subject of unity in the Bible demands an illustrative rather than an exhaustive treatment. This brief insight can do little more than simply introduce this vast Biblical emphasis. Any attempt, however, to read Genesis 11 as an argument against reconciliation is an abuse of God's Word. The overwhelming emphasis on unity and reconciliation throughout the Bible is compelling. We have different languages and customs, but one Father and one Savior who died for us all. In the church we have but one calling, one that you can read about in Ephesians 4:1–7.

Be God's ambassador for unity. Be his apostle for reconciliation between Christian brothers and sisters. Be his evangelist for peace in Christ.

For the next Promise 6 reading go to page 43.

27This is the account of Terah.

Terah became the father of Abram,
Nahor and Haran. And Haran became
the father of Lot.[k] 28While his father
Terah was still alive, Haran died in Ur
of the Chaldeans,[l] in the land of his
birth. 29Abram and Nahor both married. The name of Abram's wife was
Sarai,[m] and the name of Nahor's wife
was Milcah;[n] she was the daughter of
Haran, the father of both Milcah and
Iscah. 30Now Sarai was barren; she had
no children.[o]

31Terah took his son Abram, his
grandson Lot son of Haran, and his
daughter-in-law Sarai, the wife of
his son Abram, and together they set
out from Ur of the Chaldeans[p] to go
to Canaan.[q] But when they came to
Haran, they settled there.

32Terah lived 205 years, and he died
in Haran.

The Call of Abram

1 →PG. 31

12 The LORD had said to Abram,
"Leave your country, your people
and your father's household and go to
the land I will show you.[r]

2"I will make you into a great
nation[s]
and I will bless you;[t]
I will make your name great,
and you will be a blessing.
3I will bless those who bless you,
and whoever curses you I will
curse;[u]
and all peoples on earth
will be blessed through you.[v]"

4So Abram left, as the LORD had told
him; and Lot went with him. Abram
was seventy-five years old when he set
out from Haran.[w] 5He took his wife
Sarai, his nephew Lot, all the possessions they had accumulated and the
people[x] they had acquired in Haran,
and they set out for the land of Canaan,
and they arrived there.

6Abram traveled through the land[y]
as far as the site of the great tree of
Moreh[z] at Shechem. At that time the
Canaanites[a] were in the land. 7The
LORD appeared to Abram[b] and said,
"To your offspring[a] I will give this
land."[c] So he built an altar there to the
LORD,[d] who had appeared to him.

8From there he went on toward the
hills east of Bethel[e] and pitched his
tent, with Bethel on the west and Ai on
the east. There he built an altar to the
LORD and called on the name of the
LORD. 9Then Abram set out and continued toward the Negev.[f]

Abram in Egypt

10Now there was a famine in the
land, and Abram went down to Egypt
to live there for a while because the
famine was severe. 11As he was about
to enter Egypt, he said to his wife Sarai,
"I know what a beautiful woman you
are. 12When the Egyptians see you,
they will say, 'This is his wife.' Then
they will kill me but will let you live.
13Say you are my sister,[g] so that I will
be treated well for your sake and my
life will be spared because of you."

14When Abram came to Egypt, the
Egyptians saw that she was a very
beautiful woman. 15And when Pharaoh's officials saw her, they praised her
to Pharaoh, and she was taken into his
palace. 16He treated Abram well for her
sake, and Abram acquired sheep and
cattle, male and female donkeys, menservants and maidservants, and camels.

17But the LORD inflicted serious diseases on Pharaoh and his household[h]
because of Abram's wife Sarai. 18So
Pharaoh summoned Abram. "What
have you done to me?"[i] he said. "Why
didn't you tell me she was your wife?
19Why did you say, 'She is my sister,' so
that I took her to be my wife? Now
then, here is your wife. Take her and
go!" 20Then Pharaoh gave orders about
Abram to his men, and they sent him

[a]7 Or *seed*

11:27 [k]ver 31; Ge 12:4; 14:12; 19:1; 2Pe 2:7
11:28 [l]ver 31; Ge 15:7
11:29 [m]Ge 17:15 [n]Ge 22:20
11:30 [o]Ge 16:1; 18:11
11:31 [p]Ge 15:7; Ne 9:7; Ac 7:4 [q]Ge 10:19
12:1 [r]Ac 7:3*; Heb 11:8
12:2 [s]Ge 15:5; 17:2, 4; 18:18; 22:17; Dt 26:5 [t]Ge 24:1,35
12:3 [u]Ge 27:29; Ex 23:22; Nu 24:9 [v]Ge 18:18; 22:18; 26:4; Ac 3:25; Gal 3:8*
12:4 [w]Ge 11:31
12:5 [x]Ge 14:14; 17:23
12:6 [y]Heb 11:9 [z]Ge 35:4; Dt 11:30 [a]Ge 10:18
12:7 [b]Ge 17:1; 18:1; Ex 6:3 [c]Ge 13:15,17; 15:18; 17:8; Ps 105:9-11 [d]Ge 13:4
12:8 [e]Ge 13:3
12:9 [f]Ge 13:1,3
12:13 [g]Ge 20:2; 26:7
12:17 [h]1Ch 16:21
12:18 [i]Ge 20:9; 26:10

12:1–3

PROMISE 1

GOD'S GENERATIONAL PROMISES

God remains forever true to his word, and this amazing passage is the acid test of that fact. These promises to Abraham set the stage for the rest of the Bible and salvation history. Amazingly, even though generation after generation of Abraham's descendants violated God's revealed will, he never withdrew his promises. God disciplined his people, sometimes severely, in an effort to protect them from their own destructive behavior, but still his promises were evident in each generation. And, century upon century, God was faithful to his promises all the way through to the life, death, and resurrection of Jesus Christ. When you read a warning or a promise in the Bible, remember the history of God's faithfulness. Believe it and act on it.

For the next Promise 1 reading go to page 23.

ABRAHAM

A Man Who Answered God's Call

A missionary was searching for a way to translate the word "obedience" to a native language. He was frustrated, because the language had no corresponding expression. One day he noticed a young boy calling his dog. The dog ran to the boy with all its might, every part of its body totally focused on its goal. Knowing that he had just witnessed a picture of obedience, the missionary excitedly went to an elder among the people and asked him to describe the dog's response.

The elder responded, "That dog has 'all ear' for his master."

Abraham was a man who had "all ear" for God. He is an example of someone who received a challenging call and, with God's help and grace, remained obedient to it all his life.

We're not told why God chose Abraham out of the mass of lost humanity for such a great calling. His call—as does our own—simply illustrates God's grace. But we do know that through God's call to Abraham, and Abraham's positive response, God initiated his redemptive plan to save a lost and sinful world from eternal damnation.

Called out of a Sinful World

Abraham certainly came from a sinful culture. He grew up in the city of Ur in Mesopotamia—a great commercial center numbering nearly 300,000 citizens. All those people, including Abraham's father, Terah, and their family, were idolaters. They kept and worshiped man-made gods who were, in fact, no gods at all.

After Abraham had married, Terah moved his family to the city of Haran, where he died. Then God called Abraham to make a radical and permanent change in his life.

God spoke directly to Abraham and told him he was to move away from his father's family "to the land I will show you" (Genesis 12:1). Abraham obeyed, "even though he did not know where he was going" (Hebrews 11:8). For his part, God promised Abraham lots of children and grandchildren (the people of Israel), even though Abraham and his wife, Sarah, were old by this time and she was barren. Most importantly, God promised Abraham that his offspring would be a special blessing to all nations of the earth. This promise included Jews and Gentiles, Africans and Caucasians, Asians and Aborigines, people who live in the east and people who live in the west—and every other place in the world. With this promise, God chose Abraham as the human channel who would bring Jesus Christ into the world to become the Savior of *all* who receive him by faith.

Stumbling Along the Way

Though Abraham followed God's call to a new land to establish a new nation, and though he's a model of faith for us in many ways, he also—as we do—stumbled from time to time. He didn't instantly become a mature man of God. For example, after he had been in Canaan—the land to which God led him—for some years and he still had no children, Genesis 16 tells us Abraham took matters into his own hands and tried to "help God out" by reverting to the pagan practice of producing an heir through a substitute woman.

On an earlier occasion, when he took his family to Egypt because of a famine in Canaan, he feared that the Egyptian men would kill him in order to take his beautiful wife. So Abraham lied about who she was, saying Sarah was his sister. He made Sarah do the same. As a result, Genesis 12 records that she was almost forced to commit adultery with the Pharaoh.

But even though he made mistakes, Abraham is for us an example of faith and obedience because he always responded positively to God's correction. When he "stumbled and fell," he picked himself up and moved on, never permanently turning back to his old way of life. At times, it was two steps forward and one step backward, but his direction was always heavenward. The author of Hebrews captured the essence of Abraham's walk with God: "By faith Abraham, when called to go to a place he would later receive as his inheritance, obeyed and went . . . For he was looking forward to the city with foundations, whose architect and builder is God" (Hebrews 11:8, 10).

Your Response to God's Call

Have you, as did Abraham, responded to God's call on your life? That means, first of all, have you become a Christian by putting your faith in the Lord Jesus Christ, realizing you can never live a good enough life to satisfy God's holiness? Second, are you walking by faith—following him day by day, even when you don't know exactly where your next step may lead and even when things aren't going the way you expect?

Abraham and Sarah demonstrate a great truth found in the book of Proverbs—a wonderful promise that applies to you no matter what your age, ethnic background, economic status, or geographic location: "Trust in the LORD with all your heart and lean not on your own understanding; in all your ways acknowledge him, and he will make your paths straight" (Proverbs 3:5–6).

—Dr. Gene Getz

on his way, with his wife and everything he had.

Abram and Lot Separate

13 So Abram went up from Egypt to the Negev,[j] with his wife and everything he had, and Lot went with him. 2Abram had become very wealthy in livestock and in silver and gold.

3From the Negev he went from place to place until he came to Bethel,[k] to the place between Bethel and Ai where his tent had been earlier 4and where he had first built an altar.[l] There Abram called on the name of the LORD.

5Now Lot, who was moving about with Abram, also had flocks and herds and tents. 6But the land could not support them while they stayed together, for their possessions were so great that they were not able to stay together.[m] 7And quarreling[n] arose between Abram's herdsmen and the herdsmen of Lot. The Canaanites and Perizzites were also living in the land[o] at that time.

6 →PG. 57

8So Abram said to Lot, "Let's not have any quarreling between you and me,[p] or between your herdsmen and mine, for we are brothers.[q] 9Is not the whole land before you? Let's part company. If you go to the left, I'll go to the right; if you go to the right, I'll go to the left."

10Lot looked up and saw that the whole plain of the Jordan was well watered, like the garden of the LORD,[r] like the land of Egypt, toward Zoar.[s] (This was before the LORD destroyed Sodom and Gomorrah.)[t] 11So Lot chose for himself the whole plain of the Jordan and set out toward the east. The two men parted company: 12Abram lived in the land of Canaan, while Lot lived among the cities of the plain[u] and pitched his tents near Sodom.[v] 13Now the men of Sodom were wicked and were sinning greatly against the LORD.[w]

14The LORD said to Abram after Lot had parted from him, "Lift up your eyes from where you are and look north and south, east and west.[x] 15All the land that you see I will give to you and your offspring[a] forever.[y] 16I will make your offspring like the dust of the earth, so that if anyone could count the dust, then your offspring could be counted. 17Go, walk through the length and breadth of the land,[z] for I am giving it to you."

18So Abram moved his tents and went to live near the great trees of Mamre[a] at Hebron,[b] where he built an altar to the LORD.[c]

Abram Rescues Lot

14 At this time Amraphel king of Shinar,[b][d] Arioch king of Ellasar, Kedorlaomer king of Elam and Tidal king of Goiim 2went to war against Bera king of Sodom, Birsha king of Gomorrah, Shinab king of Admah, Shemeber king of Zeboiim,[e] and the king of Bela (that is, Zoar).[f] 3All these latter kings joined forces in the Valley of Siddim (the Salt Sea[c][g]). 4For twelve years they had been subject to Kedorlaomer, but in the thirteenth year they rebelled.

5In the fourteenth year, Kedorlaomer and the kings allied with him went out and defeated the Rephaites[h] in Ashteroth Karnaim, the Zuzites in Ham, the Emites[i] in Shaveh Kiriathaim 6and the Horites[j] in the hill country of Seir,[k] as far as El Paran[l] near the desert. 7Then they turned back and went to En Mishpat (that is, Kadesh), and they conquered the whole territory of the Amalekites, as well as the Amorites who were living in Hazazon Tamar.[m]

8Then the king of Sodom, the king of Gomorrah,[n] the king of Admah, the king of Zeboiim[o] and the king of Bela (that is, Zoar) marched out and drew up their battle lines in the Valley of Siddim 9against Kedorlaomer king of Elam, Tidal king of Goiim, Amraphel king of Shinar and Arioch king of Ellasar—four kings against five. 10Now the Valley of Siddim was full of tar pits, and when the kings of Sodom and Gomorrah fled, some of the men fell into them and the rest fled to the hills.[p] 11The four kings seized all the goods of Sodom and Gomorrah and all their food; then they went away. 12They also carried off Abram's nephew Lot and his possessions, since he was living in Sodom.

2 →PG. 85

13One who had escaped came and reported this to Abram the Hebrew. Now Abram was living near the great trees of Mamre[q] the Amorite, a brother[d] of Eshcol and Aner, all of whom were allied with Abram. 14When Abram heard that his relative had been taken captive, he called out the 318 trained men born in his household[r] and went in pursuit as far as Dan.[s] 15During the night Abram divided his men to attack them and he routed them, pursuing them as far as Hobah, north of Damascus. 16He recovered all the goods and brought back his relative Lot and his possessions, together with the women and the other people.

13:1 [j]Ge 12:9
13:3 [k]Ge 12:8
13:4 [l]Ge 12:7
13:6 [m]Ge 36:7
13:7 [n]Ge 26:20,21 [o]Ge 12:6
13:8 [p]Pr 15:18; 20:3 [q]Ps 133:1
13:10 [r]Ge 2:8-10; Isa 51:3 [s]Ge 19:22,30 [t]Ge 14:8; 19:17-29
13:12 [u]Ge 19:17,25, 29 [v]Ge 14:12
13:13 [w]Ge 18:20; Eze 16:49-50; 2Pe 2:8
13:14 [x]Ge 28:14; Dt 3:27
13:15 [y]Ge 12:7; Gal 3:16*
13:17 [z]ver 15; Nu 13:17-25
13:18 [a]Ge 14:13,24; 18:1 [b]Ge 35:27 [c]Ge 8:20
14:1 [d]Ge 10:10
14:2 [e]Ge 10:19 [f]Ge 13:10
14:3 [g]Nu 34:3,12; Dt 3:17; Jos 3:16; 15:2,5
14:5 [h]Ge 15:20; Dt 2:11,20 [i]Dt 2:10
14:6 [j]Dt 2:12,22 [k]Dt 2:1,5,22 [l]Ge 21:21; Nu 10:12
14:7 [m]2Ch 20:2
14:8 [n]Ge 13:10; 19:17-29 [o]Dt 29:23
14:10 [p]Ge 19:17,30
14:13 [q]ver 24; Ge 13:18
14:14 [r]Ge 15:3 [s]Dt 34:1; Jdg 18:29

a 15 Or *seed*; also in verse 16 b 1 That is, Babylonia; also in verse 9 c 3 That is, the Dead Sea d 13 Or *a relative*; or *an ally*

17After Abram returned from defeating Kedorlaomer and the kings allied
with him, the king of Sodom came out
to meet him in the Valley of Shaveh
(that is, the King's Valley).[t]
18Then Melchizedek[u] king of Salem[a][v] brought out bread and wine.
He was priest of God Most High, 19and
he blessed Abram,[w] saying,

"Blessed be Abram by God Most
High,
Creator[b] of heaven and earth.[x]
20And blessed be[c] God Most High,[y]
who delivered your enemies into
your hand."

Then Abram gave him a tenth of everything.[z]
21The king of Sodom said to Abram,
"Give me the people and keep the
goods for yourself."
22But Abram said to the king of Sodom, "I have raised my hand[a] to the
LORD, God Most High, Creator of heav-
en and earth,[b] and have taken an oath
23that I will accept nothing belonging
to you,[c] not even a thread or the
thong of a sandal, so that you will never
be able to say, 'I made Abram rich.' 24I
will accept nothing but what my men
have eaten and the share that belongs
to the men who went with me—to
Aner, Eshcol and Mamre. Let them
have their share."

God's Covenant With Abram

15 After this, the word of the LORD
came to Abram[d] in a vision:

"Do not be afraid,[e] Abram.
I am your shield,[d][f]
your very great reward.[e]"

2But Abram said, "O Sovereign LORD,
what can you give me since I remain
childless[g] and the one who will inherit[f] my estate is Eliezer of Damascus?"
3And Abram said, "You have given me
no children; so a servant[h] in my
household will be my heir."
4Then the word of the LORD came to
him: "This man will not be your heir,
but a son coming from your own body
will be your heir.[i]" 5He took him outside and said, "Look up at the heavens
and count the stars[j]—if indeed you
can count them." Then he said to him,
"So shall your offspring be."[k]
6Abram believed the LORD, and he
credited it to him as righteousness.[l]
7He also said to him, "I am the LORD,
who brought you out of Ur of the Chaldeans to give you this land to take possession of it."
8But Abram said, "O Sovereign LORD,
how can I know[m] that I will gain possession of it?"
9So the LORD said to him, "Bring me
a heifer, a goat and a ram, each three
years old, along with a dove and a
young pigeon."
10Abram brought all these to him,
cut them in two and arranged the
halves opposite each other;[n] the
birds, however, he did not cut in half.[o]
11Then birds of prey came down on the
carcasses, but Abram drove them
away.
12As the sun was setting, Abram fell
into a deep sleep,[p] and a thick and
dreadful darkness came over him.
13Then the LORD said to him, "Know for
certain that your descendants will be
strangers in a country not their own,
and they will be enslaved[q] and mistreated four hundred years.[r] 14But I
will punish the nation they serve as
slaves, and afterward they will come
out[s] with great possessions.[t] 15You,
however, will go to your fathers in
peace and be buried at a good old
age.[u] 16In the fourth generation your
descendants will come back here, for
the sin of the Amorites[v] has not yet
reached its full measure."
17When the sun had set and darkness had fallen, a smoking firepot with
a blazing torch appeared and passed
between the pieces.[w] 18On that day
the LORD made a covenant with Abram
and said, "To your descendants I give
this land,[x] from the river[g] of Egypt[y]
to the great river, the Euphrates—
19the land of the Kenites, Kenizzites,
Kadmonites, 20Hittites, Perizzites,
Rephaites, 21Amorites, Canaanites, Girgashites and Jebusites."

Hagar and Ishmael

16 Now Sarai, Abram's wife, had
borne him no children.[z] But she
had an Egyptian maidservant[a] named
Hagar; 2so she said to Abram, "The
LORD has kept me from having children. Go, sleep with my maidservant;
perhaps I can build a family through
her."[b]
Abram agreed to what Sarai said. 3So
after Abram had been living in Canaan[c] ten years, Sarai his wife took
her Egyptian maidservant Hagar and
gave her to her husband to be his wife.
4He slept with Hagar, and she conceived.
When she knew she was pregnant,

14:17 t2Sa 18:18
14:18 uPs 110:4; Heb 5:6 vPs 76:2; Heb 7:2
14:19 wHeb 7:6 xver 22
14:20 yGe 24:27 zGe 28:22; Dt 26:12; Heb 7:4
14:22 aEx 6:8; Da 12:7; Rev 10:5-6 bver 19
14:23 c2Ki 5:16
15:1 dDa 10:1 eGe 21:17; 26:24; 46:3; 2Ki 6:16; Ps 27:1; Isa 41:10, 13-14 fDt 33:29; 2Sa 22:3,31; Ps 3:3
15:2 gAc 7:5
15:3 hGe 24:2,34
15:4 iGal 4:28
15:5 jPs 147:4; Jer 33:22 kGe 12:2; 22:17; Ex 32:13; Ro 4:18*; Heb 11:12
15:6 lPs 106:31; Ro 4:3*,20-24*; Gal 3:6*; Jas 2:23*
15:8 mLk 1:18
15:10 nver 17; Jer 34:18 oLev 1:17
15:12 pGe 2:21
15:13 qEx 1:11 rver 16; Ex 12:40; Ac 7:6,17
15:14 sAc 7:7* tEx 12:32-38
15:15 uGe 25:8
15:16 v1Ki 21:26
15:17 wver 10
15:18 xGe 12:7 yNu 34:5
16:1 zGe 11:30; Gal 4:24-25 aGe 21:9
16:2 bGe 30:3-4, 9-10
16:3 cGe 12:5

a18 That is, Jerusalem b19 Or *Possessor,* also in verse 22 c20 Or *And praise be to* d1 Or *sovereign* e1 Or *shield; / your reward will be very great* f2 The meaning of the Hebrew for this phrase is uncertain. g18 Or *Wadi*

she began to despise her mistress. **5**Then Sarai said to Abram, "You are responsible for the wrong I am suffering. I put my servant in your arms, and now that she knows she is pregnant, she despises me. May the LORD judge between you and me."[d]

6"Your servant is in your hands," Abram said. "Do with her whatever you think best." Then Sarai mistreated Hagar; so she fled from her.

7The angel of the LORD[e] found Hagar near a spring in the desert; it was the spring that is beside the road to Shur.[f] **8**And he said, "Hagar, servant of Sarai, where have you come from, and where are you going?"

"I'm running away from my mistress Sarai," she answered.

9Then the angel of the LORD told her, "Go back to your mistress and submit to her." **10**The angel added, "I will so increase your descendants that they will be too numerous to count."[g]

11The angel of the LORD also said to her:

"You are now with child
  and you will have a son.
You shall name him Ishmael,[a]
  for the LORD has heard of your
    misery.[h]
12He will be a wild donkey of a man;
  his hand will be against everyone
  and everyone's hand against
    him,
and he will live in hostility
  toward[b] all his brothers.[i]"

13She gave this name to the LORD who spoke to her: "You are the God who sees me," for she said, "I have now seen[c] the One who sees me."[j] **14**That is why the well was called Beer Lahai Roi[d]; it is still there, between Kadesh and Bered.

15So Hagar bore Abram a son,[k] and Abram gave the name Ishmael to the son she had borne. **16**Abram was eighty-six years old when Hagar bore him Ishmael.

The Covenant of Circumcision

17 When Abram was ninety-nine years old, the LORD appeared to him and said, "I am God Almighty[e];[l] walk before me and be blameless.[m] **2**I will confirm my covenant between me and you[n] and will greatly increase your numbers."

3Abram fell facedown, and God said to him, **4**"As for me, this is my covenant with you:[o] You will be the father of many nations.[p] **5**No longer will you be called Abram[f]; your name will be Abraham,[g][q] for I have made you a father of many nations.[r] **6**I will make you very fruitful;[s] I will make nations of you, and kings will come from you.[t] **7**I will establish my covenant as an everlasting covenant between me and you and your descendants after you for the generations to come, to be your God[u] and the God of your descendants after you.[v] **8**The whole land of Canaan,[w] where you are now an alien,[x] I will give as an everlasting possession to you and your descendants after you;[y] and I will be their God."

9Then God said to Abraham, "As for you, you must keep my covenant, you and your descendants after you for the generations to come. **10**This is my covenant with you and your descendants after you, the covenant you are to keep: Every male among you shall be circumcised.[z] **11**You are to undergo circumcision,[a] and it will be the sign of the covenant[b] between me and you. **12**For the generations to come every male among you who is eight days old must be circumcised,[c] including those born in your household or bought with money from a foreigner—those who are not your offspring. **13**Whether born in your household or bought with your money, they must be circumcised. My covenant in your flesh is to be an everlasting covenant. **14**Any uncircumcised male, who has not been circumcised in the flesh, will be cut off from his people;[d] he has broken my covenant."

15God also said to Abraham, "As for Sarai your wife, you are no longer to call her Sarai; her name will be Sarah. **16**I will bless her and will surely give you a son by her.[e] I will bless her so that she will be the mother of nations;[f] kings of peoples will come from her."

17Abraham fell facedown; he laughed[g] and said to himself, "Will a son be born to a man a hundred years old? Will Sarah bear a child at the age of ninety?" **18**And Abraham said to God, "If only Ishmael might live under your blessing!"

19Then God said, "Yes, but your wife Sarah will bear you a son,[h] and you will call him Isaac.[h] I will establish my covenant with him[i] as an everlasting covenant for his descendants after him. **20**And as for Ishmael, I have heard

16:5 [d]Ge 31:53
16:7 [e]Ge 21:17; 22:11,15; 31:11 [f]Ge 20:1
16:10 [g]Ge 13:16; 17:20
16:11 [h]Ex 2:24; 3:7,9
16:12 [i]Ge 25:18
16:13 [j]Ge 32:30
16:15 [k]Gal 4:22
17:1 [l]Ge 28:3; Ex 6:3 [m]Dt 18:13
17:2 [n]Ge 15:18
17:4 [o]Ge 15:18 [p]ver 16; Ge 12:2; 35:11; 48:19
17:5 [q]ver 15; Ne 9:7 [r]Ro 4:17*
17:6 [s]Ge 35:11 [t]Mt 1:6
17:7 [u]Ex 29:45,46 [v]Ro 9:8; Gal 3:16
17:8 [w]Ps 105:9,11 [x]Ge 23:4; 28:4; Ex 6:4 [y]Ge 12:7
17:10 [z]ver 23; Ge 21:4; Jn 7:22; Ac 7:8; Ro 4:11
17:11 [a]Ex 12:48; Dt 10:16 [b]Ro 4:11
17:12 [c]Lev 12:3; Lk 2:21
17:14 [d]Ex 4:24-26
17:16 [e]Ge 18:10 [f]Ge 35:11; Gal 4:31
17:17 [g]Ge 18:12; 21:6
17:19 [h]Ge 18:14; 21:2 [i]Ge 26:3

[a] *11 Ishmael* means *God hears.* [b] *12* Or *live to the east of* [c] *13* Or *seen the back of* [d] *14 Beer Lahai Roi* means *well of the Living One who sees me.* [e] *1* Hebrew *El-Shaddai* [f] *5 Abram* means *exalted father.* [g] *5 Abraham* means *father of many.* [h] *19 Isaac* means *he laughs.*

you: I will surely bless him; I will make
him fruitful and will greatly increase
his numbers.[j] He will be the father of
twelve rulers,[k] and I will make him
into a great nation.[l] 21But my covenant I will establish with Isaac, whom
Sarah will bear to you by this time next
year."[m] 22When he had finished speaking with Abraham, God went up from
him.
23On that very day Abraham took his
son Ishmael and all those born in his
household or bought with his money,
every male in his household, and circumcised them, as God told him.
24Abraham was ninety-nine years old
when he was circumcised,[n] 25and his
son Ishmael was thirteen; 26Abraham
and his son Ishmael were both circumcised on that same day. 27And every
male in Abraham's household, including those born in his household or
bought from a foreigner, was circumcised with him.

The Three Visitors

18 The LORD appeared to Abraham
near the great trees of Mamre[o]
while he was sitting at the entrance to
his tent in the heat of the day. 2Abra-
ham looked up and saw three men[p]
standing nearby. When he saw them,
he hurried from the entrance of his
tent to meet them and bowed low to
the ground.
3He said, "If I have found favor in
your eyes, my lord,[a] do not pass your
servant by. 4Let a little water be
brought, and then you may all wash
your feet[q] and rest under this tree.
5Let me get you something to eat,[r] so
you can be refreshed and then go on
your way—now that you have come to
your servant."
"Very well," they answered, "do as
you say."
6So Abraham hurried into the tent
to Sarah. "Quick," he said, "get three
seahs[b] of fine flour and knead it and
bake some bread."
7Then he ran to the herd and selected a choice, tender calf and gave it to a
servant, who hurried to prepare it. 8He
then brought some curds and milk and
the calf that had been prepared, and
set these before them.[s] While they
ate, he stood near them under a tree.
9"Where is your wife Sarah?" they
asked him.
"There, in the tent," he said.
10Then the LORD[c] said, "I will surely
return to you about this time next year,
and Sarah your wife will have a son."[t]
Now Sarah was listening at the entrance to the tent, which was behind
him. 11Abraham and Sarah were already old and well advanced in years,[u]
and Sarah was past the age of childbearing.[v] 12So Sarah laughed[w] to herself as she thought, "After I am worn
out and my master[d][x] is old, will I now
have this pleasure?"
13Then the LORD said to Abraham,
"Why did Sarah laugh and say, 'Will I
really have a child, now that I am old?'
14Is anything too hard for the LORD?[y]
I will return to you at the appointed
time next year and Sarah will have a
son."
15Sarah was afraid, so she lied and
said, "I did not laugh."
But he said, "Yes, you did laugh."

Abraham Pleads for Sodom

16When the men got up to leave,
they looked down toward Sodom, and
Abraham walked along with them to
see them on their way. 17Then the LORD
said, "Shall I hide from Abraham[z]
what I am about to do?[a] 18Abraham

17:15–22 PROMISE 1

HELPING GOD OUT?

This promise of a son came to Abraham and Sarah years after the original promise (12:2–3). For a quarter of a century this couple had waited patiently, until all hope of having a child seemed lost. Sarah, after all, was 90 years old; Abraham was 100. Following the legal standards of their culture, Abraham had a son through Hagar, Sarah's handmaid. God, it seemed, was off the hook (vv. 17–18). Abraham's alternative made sense.

But God responded in a way that defied logic. He reiterated his promise that Sarah would have this child in her old age. Chapter 21:1–7 records the miraculous fulfilling of God's original promise to Abraham. This was God's promise, fulfilled in God's time and in God's way. Abraham and Sarah's help was not needed.

Abraham and Sarah found out that there is no substitute for God's revealed will. They decided to take matters into their own hands when, humanly speaking, God's promises seemed impossible to fulfill. But God deals in the miraculous, and in this instance delighted in confounding human reason. Is there anything in your life that you have trouble trusting God for? Take a moment and pray for faith to trust God to act in his way and in his time.

For the next Promise 1 reading go to page 29.

17:20 [j]Ge 16:10 [k]Ge 25:12-16 [l]Ge 21:18 **17:21** [m]Ge 21:2 **17:24** [n]Ro 4:11 **18:1** [o]Ge 13:18; 14:13 **18:2** [p]ver 16,22; Ge 32:24; Jos 5:13; Jdg 13:6-11; Heb 13:2 **18:4** [q]Ge 19:2; 43:24 **18:5** [r]Jdg 13:15 **18:8** [s]Ge 19:3 **18:10** [t]Ro 9:9* **18:11** [u]Ge 17:17 [v]Ro 4:19 **18:12** [w]Ge 17:17; 21:6 [x]1Pe 3:6 **18:14** [y]Jer 32:17,27; Zec 8:6; Mt 19:26; Lk 1:37; Ro 4:21 **18:17** [z]Am 3:7 [a]Ge 19:24

[a] *3* Or *O Lord* [b] *6* That is, probably about 20 quarts (about 22 liters) [c] *10* Hebrew *Then he* [d] *12* Or *husband*

will surely become a great and powerful nation,[b] and all nations on earth will be blessed through him. **19**For I have chosen him, so that he will direct his children[c] and his household after him to keep the way of the LORD[d] by doing what is right and just, so that the LORD will bring about for Abraham what he has promised him."

4 →PG. 44

20Then the LORD said, "The outcry against Sodom and Gomorrah is so great and their sin so grievous **21**that I will go down[e] and see if what they have done is as bad as the outcry that has reached me. If not, I will know."

7 →PG. 131

22The men turned away and went toward Sodom,[f] but Abraham remained standing before the LORD.[a] **23**Then Abraham approached him and said: "Will you sweep away the righteous with the wicked?[g] **24**What if there are fifty righteous people in the city? Will you really sweep it away and not spare[b] the place for the sake of the fifty righteous people in it?[h] **25**Far be it from you to do such a thing—to kill the righteous with the wicked, treating the righteous and the wicked alike. Far be it from you! Will not the Judge[c] of all the earth do right?"[i]

26The LORD said, "If I find fifty righteous people in the city of Sodom, I will spare the whole place for their sake.[j]"

27Then Abraham spoke up again: "Now that I have been so bold as to speak to the Lord, though I am nothing but dust and ashes,[k] **28**what if the number of the righteous is five less than fifty? Will you destroy the whole city because of five people?"

"If I find forty-five there," he said, "I will not destroy it."

29Once again he spoke to him, "What if only forty are found there?"

He said, "For the sake of forty, I will not do it."

30Then he said, "May the Lord not be angry, but let me speak. What if only thirty can be found there?"

He answered, "I will not do it if I find thirty there."

31Abraham said, "Now that I have been so bold as to speak to the Lord, what if only twenty can be found there?"

He said, "For the sake of twenty, I will not destroy it."

32Then he said, "May the Lord not be angry, but let me speak just once more.[l] What if only ten can be found there?"

He answered, "For the sake of ten,[m] I will not destroy it."

33When the LORD had finished speaking with Abraham, he left, and Abraham returned home.

18:18 [b]Gal 3:8*
18:19 [c]Dt 4:9-10; 6:7 [d]Jos 24:15; Eph 6:4
18:21 [e]Ge 11:5
18:22 [f]Ge 19:1
18:23 [g]Nu 16:22
18:24 [h]Jer 5:1
18:25 [i]Job 8:3,20; Ps 58:11; 94:2; Isa 3:10-11; Ro 3:6
18:26 [j]Jer 5:1
18:27 [k]Ge 2:7; 3:19; Job 30:19; 42:6
18:32 [l]Jdg 6:39 [m]Jer 5:1

Sodom and Gomorrah Destroyed

19 The two angels arrived at Sodom[n] in the evening, and Lot was sitting in the gateway of the city.[o] When he saw them, he got up to meet them and bowed down with his face to the ground. **2**"My lords," he said, "please turn aside to your servant's house. You can wash your feet[p] and spend the night and then go on your way early in the morning."

"No," they answered, "we will spend the night in the square."

3But he insisted so strongly that they did go with him and entered his house. He prepared a meal for them, baking bread without yeast, and they ate.[q] **4**Before they had gone to bed, all the men from every part of the city of Sodom—both young and old—surrounded the house. **5**They called to Lot, "Where are the men who came to you tonight? Bring them out to us so that we can have sex with them."[r]

6Lot went outside to meet them[s] and shut the door behind him **7**and said, "No, my friends. Don't do this wicked thing. **8**Look, I have two daughters who have never slept with a man. Let me bring them out to you, and you can do what you like with them. But don't do anything to these men, for they have come under the protection of my roof."[t]

9"Get out of our way," they replied. And they said, "This fellow came here as an alien, and now he wants to play the judge![u] We'll treat you worse than them." They kept bringing pressure on Lot and moved forward to break down the door.

10But the men inside reached out and pulled Lot back into the house and shut the door. **11**Then they struck the men who were at the door of the house, young and old, with blindness[v] so that they could not find the door.

12The two men said to Lot, "Do you have anyone else here—sons-in-law, sons or daughters, or anyone else in the city who belongs to you?[w] Get them out of here, **13**because we are going to destroy this place. The outcry to the LORD against its people is so great that he has sent us to destroy it."[x]

14So Lot went out and spoke to his sons-in-law, who were pledged to marry[d] his daughters. He said, "Hurry and get out of this place, because the LORD is about to destroy the city![y]"

19:1 [n]Ge 18:22 [o]Ge 18:1
19:2 [p]Ge 18:4; Lk 7:44
19:3 [q]Ge 18:6
19:5 [r]Jdg 19:22; Isa 3:9; Ro 1:24-27
19:6 [s]Jdg 19:23
19:8 [t]Jdg 19:24
19:9 [u]Ex 2:14; Ac 7:27
19:11 [v]Dt 28:28-29; 2Ki 6:18; Ac 13:11
19:12 [w]Ge 7:1
19:13 [x]1Ch 21:15
19:14 [y]Nu 16:21

[a] *22* Masoretic Text; an ancient Hebrew scribal tradition *but the LORD remained standing before Abraham* [b] *24* Or *forgive;* also in verse 26
[c] *25* Or *Ruler* [d] *14* Or *were married to*

LOT

The Price of Selfishness

A certain missionary in the Philippines owned many books that she gladly loaned to others. But there were several books she selfishly hoarded in a footlocker under her bed. One night, the missionary heard a faint gnawing sound coming from her footlocker. To her dismay when she opened the lid, she found all the books she had selfishly hidden had been destroyed by termites. This missionary learned the hard way that what we give away we keep; what we hoard, we lose. The Bible gives a clear example of the price of selfishness in its story about a man named Lot.

When Abraham answered God's call to leave his country and move to the land of Canaan, Abraham's nephew "Lot went with him" (Genesis 12:4). Abraham and Lot both became rich men in this new land. Their flocks and herds grew so large that the land couldn't support both of them. This led to serious strife between their herdsmen.

Abraham revealed his unselfish heart when he said, "Let's not have any quarreling between you and me, or between your herdsmen and mine, for we are brothers. Is not the whole land before you? Let's part company" (13:8–9). Abraham was wise enough to know that, for the benefit of their relationship, the two of them had to move apart. He made Lot a magnanimous offer, "If you go to the left, I'll go to the right; if you go to the right, I'll go to the left" (13:9).

The moment Abraham gave Lot his choice, Lot's true character surfaced. He "looked up and saw that the whole plain of the Jordan was well watered, like the garden of the LORD" (13:10). Lot's wealth, combined with a selfish heart, made him vulnerable to becoming even more selfish. Wanting to keep the best pasture lands for himself, Lot chose to move toward the river, toward one of the most degenerate cities in the world at that time—Sodom.

A Disastrous Decision

If Lot was aware of the sinfulness of Sodom, it didn't deter him from making his selfish choice. Lot was motivated by *what he saw*: "Lot looked up" (13:10). Lot's eyes triggered selfish desires that caused him to forget or ignore everything his uncle Abraham had ever done for him. Lot may have rationalized his decision by thinking, *Uncle Abe has more than I have anyway; this will balance everything out. After all, he gave me my choice first.* Lot may have even thought, *That wicked city really needs a strong witness for the Lord. Who else is going to tell them about God?*

Whatever Lot's rationalizations, his decision was based on selfish desires. He didn't consult God. He didn't think long—if at all—about what consequences his decision might have on his uncle Abraham, his children or even himself. What he saw and wanted for himself spurred his choice. Without regard for anyone else, Lot selfishly made what would prove to be a disastrous decision.

Paying the Price

Genesis 19 records the terrible price that Lot and his family paid when they moved toward Sodom. Lot was subject to fierce harassment. He lost all influence over the young men engaged to his daughters. Eventually, Lot even lost the will to do what he knew was right.

Lot's wife, however, suffered the most tragic consequence of all. She developed such an attachment to Sodom she didn't want to leave it, even though she was warned that God was going to destroy the city. As God's angels forcibly led Lot's family to safety, Lot's wife disobeyed the angels' instructions and looked back as God "rained down burning sulfur" on the city (19:24). As a result of this sin, Lot's wife "became a pillar of salt" (19:26).

Learning From Lot's Mistake

Lot's selfish failings might make us wonder if Lot ever was a true follower of God. Peter answered this question in the affirmative when he used the word "righteous" three times to describe Lot in 2 Peter 2:7–8. Lot's selfish choice, however, led him down a path that resulted in disaster. When we, as God's children, make a habit of sin, we may not experience immediate judgment from God, but Lot's example proves we will eventually suffer the consequences of our sins.

Have problems arisen in your life because of your own selfish decisions? Confess your sins to God. Take responsibility for your actions. Do what you can to correct the problems. Then move forward, "forgetting what is behind and straining toward what is ahead" (Philippians 3:13), keeping your eyes on Jesus.

The steps Lot took toward personal disaster tempt us as well. What we see and the way we think affect the way we respond to every situation. We must remember Lot's example when we are tempted to rationalize selfish decisions. Instead, we must base our choices on Paul's words to the Philippians: "Finally, brothers, whatever is true, whatever is noble, whatever is right, whatever is pure, whatever is lovely, whatever is admirable—if anything is excellent or praiseworthy—think about such things" (Philippians 4:8).

—Dr. Gene Getz

But his sons-in-law thought he was joking.[z]

15With the coming of dawn, the angels urged Lot, saying, "Hurry! Take your wife and your two daughters who are here, or you will be swept away[a] when the city is punished.[b]"

16When he hesitated, the men grasped his hand and the hands of his wife and of his two daughters and led them safely out of the city, for the LORD was merciful to them. 17As soon as they had brought them out, one of them said, "Flee for your lives![c] Don't look back,[d] and don't stop anywhere in the plain! Flee to the mountains or you will be swept away!"

18But Lot said to them, "No, my lords,**[a]** please! 19Your**[b]** servant has found favor in your**[b]** eyes, and you**[b]** have shown great kindness to me in sparing my life. But I can't flee to the mountains; this disaster will overtake me, and I'll die. 20Look, here is a town near enough to run to, and it is small. Let me flee to it—it is very small, isn't it? Then my life will be spared."

21He said to him, "Very well, I will grant this request too; I will not overthrow the town you speak of. 22But flee there quickly, because I cannot do anything until you reach it." (That is why the town was called Zoar.**[c]**)

23By the time Lot reached Zoar, the sun had risen over the land. 24Then the LORD rained down burning sulfur on Sodom and Gomorrah[e]—from the LORD out of the heavens.[f] 25Thus he overthrew those cities and the entire plain, including all those living in the cities—and also the vegetation in the land.[g] 26But Lot's wife looked back,[h] and she became a pillar of salt.[i]

27Early the next morning Abraham got up and returned to the place where he had stood before the LORD.[j] 28He looked down toward Sodom and Gomorrah, toward all the land of the plain, and he saw dense smoke rising from the land, like smoke from a furnace.[k]

29So when God destroyed the cities of the plain, he remembered Abraham, and he brought Lot out of the catastrophe[l] that overthrew the cities where Lot had lived.

Lot and His Daughters

30Lot and his two daughters left Zoar and settled in the mountains,[m] for he was afraid to stay in Zoar. He and his two daughters lived in a cave. 31One day the older daughter said to the younger, "Our father is old, and there is no man around here to lie with us, as is the custom all over the earth. 32Let's get our father to drink wine and then lie with him and preserve our family line through our father."

33That night they got their father to drink wine, and the older daughter went in and lay with him. He was not aware of it when she lay down or when she got up.

34The next day the older daughter said to the younger, "Last night I lay with my father. Let's get him to drink wine again tonight, and you go in and lie with him so we can preserve our family line through our father." 35So they got their father to drink wine that night also, and the younger daughter went and lay with him. Again he was not aware of it when she lay down or when she got up.

36So both of Lot's daughters became pregnant by their father. 37The older daughter had a son, and she named him Moab**[d]**; he is the father of the Moabites[n] of today. 38The younger daughter also had a son, and she named him Ben-Ammi**[e]**; he is the father of the Ammonites[o] of today.

Abraham and Abimelech

20 Now Abraham moved on from there[p] into the region of the Negev and lived between Kadesh and Shur. For a while he stayed in Gerar,[q] 2and there Abraham said of his wife Sarah, "She is my sister.[r]" Then Abimelech king of Gerar sent for Sarah and took her.[s]

3But God came to Abimelech in a dream[t] one night and said to him, "You are as good as dead because of the woman you have taken; she is a married woman."[u]

4Now Abimelech had not gone near her, so he said, "Lord, will you destroy an innocent nation?[v] 5Did he not say to me, 'She is my sister,' and didn't she also say, 'He is my brother'? I have done this with a clear conscience and clean hands."

6Then God said to him in the dream, "Yes, I know you did this with a clear conscience, and so I have kept[w] you from sinning against me. That is why I did not let you touch her. 7Now return the man's wife, for he is a prophet, and he will pray for you[x] and you will live. But if you do not return her, you may be sure that you and all yours will die."

8Early the next morning Abimelech

19:14 [z]Ex 9:21; Lk 17:28
19:15 [a]Nu 16:26 [b]Rev 18:4
19:17 [c]Jer 48:6 [d]ver 26
19:24 [e]Dt 29:23; Isa 1:9; 13:19 [f]Lk 17:29; 2Pe 2:6; Jude 7
19:25 [g]Ps 107:34; Eze 16:48
19:26 [h]ver 17 [i]Lk 17:32
19:27 [j]Ge 18:22
19:28 [k]Rev 9:2; 18:9
19:29 [l]2Pe 2:7
19:30 [m]ver 19
19:37 [n]Dt 2:9
19:38 [o]Dt 2:19
20:1 [p]Ge 18:1 [q]Ge 26:1,6,17
20:2 [r]ver 12; Ge 12:13; 26:7 [s]Ge 12:15
20:3 [t]Job 33:15; Mt 27:19 [u]Ps 105:14
20:4 [v]Ge 18:25
20:6 [w]1Sa 25:26,34
20:7 [x]ver 17; 1Sa 7:5; Job 42:8

a *18* Or *No, Lord*; or *No, my lord* **b** *19* The Hebrew is singular. **c** *22* *Zoar* means *small.* **d** *37* *Moab* sounds like the Hebrew for *from father.* **e** *38* *Ben-Ammi* means *son of my people.*

summoned all his officials, and when
he told them all that had happened,
they were very much afraid. **9**Then
Abimelech called Abraham in and said,
"What have you done to us? How have
I wronged you that you have brought
such great guilt upon me and my kingdom? You have done things to me that
should not be done.[y]" **10**And Abimelech asked Abraham, "What was your
reason for doing this?"
11Abraham replied, "I said to myself,
'There is surely no fear of God[z] in this
place, and they will kill me because of
my wife.'[a] **12**Besides, she really is my
sister, the daughter of my father
though not of my mother; and she became my wife. **13**And when God had
me wander from my father's household, I said to her, 'This is how you can
show your love to me: Everywhere we
go, say of me, "He is my brother." ' "
14Then Abimelech brought sheep
and cattle and male and female slaves
and gave them to Abraham,[b] and he
returned Sarah his wife to him. **15**And
Abimelech said, "My land is before
you; live wherever you like."[c]
16To Sarah he said, "I am giving your
brother a thousand shekels[a] of silver.
This is to cover the offense against you
before all who are with you; you are
completely vindicated."
17Then Abraham prayed to God,[d]
and God healed Abimelech, his wife
and his slave girls so they could have
children again, **18**for the LORD had
closed up every womb in Abimelech's
household because of Abraham's wife
Sarah.[e]

The Birth of Isaac

21 Now the LORD was gracious to Sarah[f] as he had said, and the LORD
did for Sarah what he had promised.[g]
2Sarah became pregnant and bore a
son[h] to Abraham in his old age,[i] at
the very time God had promised him.
3Abraham gave the name Isaac[b][j] to
the son Sarah bore him. **4**When his son
Isaac was eight days old, Abraham circumcised him,[k] as God commanded
him. **5**Abraham was a hundred years
old when his son Isaac was born to
him.
6Sarah said, "God has brought me
laughter,[l] and everyone who hears
about this will laugh with me." **7**And
she added, "Who would have said to
Abraham that Sarah would nurse children? Yet I have borne him a son in his
old age."

Hagar and Ishmael Sent Away

8The child grew and was weaned,
and on the day Isaac was weaned Abraham held a great feast. **9**But Sarah saw
that the son whom Hagar the Egyptian
had borne to Abraham[m] was mocking,[n] **10**and she said to Abraham, "Get
rid of that slave woman and her son,
for that slave woman's son will never
share in the inheritance with my son
Isaac."[o]
11The matter distressed Abraham
greatly because it concerned his son.[p]
12But God said to him, "Do not be so
distressed about the boy and your
maidservant. Listen to whatever Sarah
tells you, because it is through Isaac
that your offspring[c] will be reckoned.[q] **13**I will make the son of the
maidservant into a nation[r] also, because he is your offspring."
14Early the next morning Abraham
took some food and a skin of water and
gave them to Hagar. He set them on
her shoulders and then sent her off
with the boy. She went on her way and
wandered in the desert of Beersheba.[s]
15When the water in the skin was
gone, she put the boy under one of the
bushes. **16**Then she went off and sat
down nearby, about a bowshot away,
for she thought, "I cannot watch the
boy die." And as she sat there nearby,
she[d] began to sob.
17God heard the boy crying,[t] and
the angel of God called to Hagar from
heaven and said to her, "What is the
matter, Hagar? Do not be afraid; God
has heard the boy crying as he lies
there. **18**Lift the boy up and take him by
the hand, for I will make him into a
great nation.[u]"
19Then God opened her eyes[v] and
she saw a well of water. So she went
and filled the skin with water and gave
the boy a drink.
20God was with the boy[w] as he grew
up. He lived in the desert and became
an archer. **21**While he was living in the
Desert of Paran, his mother got a wife
for him[x] from Egypt.

The Treaty at Beersheba

22At that time Abimelech and Phicol
the commander of his forces said to
Abraham, "God is with you in everything you do. **23**Now swear[y] to me
here before God that you will not deal
falsely with me or my children or my
descendants. Show to me and the
country where you are living as an
alien the same kindness I have shown
to you."

20:9 [y]Ge 12:18; 26:10; 34:7
20:11 [z]Ge 42:18; Ps 36:1 [a]Ge 12:12; 26:7
20:14 [b]Ge 12:16
20:15 [c]Ge 13:9
20:17 [d]Job 42:9
20:18 [e]Ge 12:17
21:1 [f]1Sa 2:21 [g]Ge 8:1; 17:16, 21; Gal 4:23
21:2 [h]Ge 17:19 [i]Gal 4:22; Heb 11:11
21:3 [j]Ge 17:19
21:4 [k]Ge 17:10,12; Ac 7:8
21:6 [l]Ge 17:17; Isa 54:1
21:9 [m]Ge 16:15 [n]Gal 4:29
21:10 [o]Gal 4:30*
21:11 [p]Ge 17:18
21:12 [q]Ro 9:7*; Heb 11:18*
21:13 [r]ver 18
21:14 [s]ver 31,32
21:17 [t]Ex 3:7
21:18 [u]ver 13
21:19 [v]Nu 22:31
21:20 [w]Ge 26:3,24; 28:15; 39:2,21, 23
21:21 [x]Ge 24:4,38
21:23 [y]ver 31; Jos 2:12

[a] *16* That is, about 25 pounds (about 11.5 kilograms) [b] *3* *Isaac* means *he laughs.* [c] *12* Or *seed* [d] *16* Hebrew; Septuagint *the child*

24 Abraham said, "I swear it."
25 Then Abraham complained to
Abimelech about a well of water that
Abimelech's servants had seized.[z]
26 But Abimelech said, "I don't know
who has done this. You did not tell me,
and I heard about it only today."
27 So Abraham brought sheep and
cattle and gave them to Abimelech,
and the two men made a treaty.[a]
28 Abraham set apart seven ewe lambs
from the flock, 29 and Abimelech asked
Abraham, "What is the meaning of
these seven ewe lambs you have set
apart by themselves?"
30 He replied, "Accept these seven
lambs from my hand as a witness[b]
that I dug this well."
31 So that place was called Beersheba,[a][c] because the two men swore an
oath there.
32 After the treaty had been made at
Beersheba, Abimelech and Phicol the
commander of his forces returned to
the land of the Philistines. 33 Abraham
planted a tamarisk tree in Beersheba,
and there he called upon the name of
the LORD,[d] the Eternal God.[e] 34 And
Abraham stayed in the land of the Philistines for a long time.

Abraham Tested

22 Some time later God tested[f]
Abraham. He said to him, "Abraham!"
"Here I am," he replied.
2 Then God said, "Take your son[g],
your only son, Isaac, whom you love,
and go to the region of Moriah.[h] Sacrifice him there as a burnt offering on
one of the mountains I will tell you
about."
3 Early the next morning Abraham
got up and saddled his donkey. He took
with him two of his servants and his
son Isaac. When he had cut enough
wood for the burnt offering, he set out
for the place God had told him about.
4 On the third day Abraham looked up
and saw the place in the distance. 5 He
said to his servants, "Stay here with the
donkey while I and the boy go over
there. We will worship and then we will
come back to you."
6 Abraham took the wood for the
burnt offering and placed it on his son
Isaac,[i] and he himself carried the fire
and the knife. As the two of them went
on together, 7 Isaac spoke up and said
to his father Abraham, "Father?"
"Yes, my son?" Abraham replied.
"The fire and wood are here," Isaac
said, "but where is the lamb[j] for the
burnt offering?"
8 Abraham answered, "God himself
will provide the lamb for the burnt offering, my son." And the two of them
went on together.
9 When they reached the place God
had told him about, Abraham built an

21:25 [z] Ge 26:15,18, 20-22
21:27 [a] Ge 26:28,31
21:30 [b] Ge 31:44,47, 48,50,52
21:31 [c] Ge 26:33
21:33 [d] Ge 4:26 [e] Dt 33:27
22:1 [f] Dt 8:2,16; Heb 11:17; Jas 1:12-13
22:2 [g] ver 12,16; Jn 3:16; Heb 11:17; 1Jn 4:9 [h] 2Ch 3:1
22:6 [i] Jn 19:17
22:7 [j] Lev 1:10

[a] 31 *Beersheba* can mean *well of seven* or *well of the oath.*

1 →PG. 46

22:1–19

PROMISE 1

PASSING GOD'S TEST

Does this story trouble you? After asking Abraham and Sarah to wait all those years and then miraculously giving them a son, God here asks Abraham to give Isaac back as a sacrifice. What was God thinking?

God had already shown Abraham that when his human logic disagreed with God's logic, he could trust God to be right. That's a tough lesson for many of us to absorb. And Abraham, had he cared to, could have argued from many positions that God had no business asking that he sacrifice Isaac. First, Isaac was the long-awaited fulfillment of God's promise! Second, God had clearly stated through Noah that shedding a man's blood was prohibited (9:5–6). Still, the text makes no reference to Abraham hesitating or debating. It simply records that he obeyed God (v. 3).

What's going on here? Read 22:1 and 12 again. While God knew he would not require Abraham to kill Isaac; Abraham didn't know that. This was God's test of Abraham's faith, of his ability to trust God when his reason ran out of reasons. James 2:20–24 teaches us that although Abraham claimed to have faith in God (Genesis 15:6), this act proved the veracity of his faith.

History records many stories of people who espouse faith but show little evidence of it. The converse is also true; many quiet people demonstrate heroic faith. God will, undoubtedly, never ask you to offer one of your children on an altar. But most men regularly confront the choice: "Do I believe this stuff or not?"

This story shows us that our actions really do reveal the truth about ourselves and the depth of our commitments. When your faith is tested, read Genesis 22:12 and translate it to fit your test. "Now I know that I, (Your name) do/do not fear God because I have/have not done what God asked me to."

This is a troubling story because Abraham was willing to offer his son as a sacrifice. It would be far more troubling if he had refused. As your story is being written, let it be a story of faith that works; a life that passes the test.

For the next Promise 1 reading go to page 70.

altar there and arranged the wood on
it. He bound his son Isaac and laid him
on the altar,[k] on top of the wood.
10Then he reached out his hand and
took the knife to slay his son. 11But the
angel of the LORD called out to him
from heaven, "Abraham! Abraham!"
"Here I am," he replied.
12"Do not lay a hand on the boy," he
said. "Do not do anything to him. Now
I know that you fear God,[l] because
you have not withheld from me your
son, your only son.[m]"
13Abraham looked up and there in a
thicket he saw a ram[a] caught by its
horns. He went over and took the ram
and sacrificed it as a burnt offering instead of his son.[n] 14So Abraham called
that place The LORD Will Provide. And
to this day it is said, "On the mountain
of the LORD it will be provided.[o]"
15The angel of the LORD called to
Abraham from heaven a second time
16and said, "I swear by myself,[p] declares the LORD, that because you have
done this and have not withheld your
son, your only son, 17I will surely bless
you and make your descendants[q] as
numerous as the stars in the sky[r] and
as the sand on the seashore.[s] Your
descendants will take possession of the
cities of their enemies,[t] 18and through
your offspring[b] all nations on earth
will be blessed,[u] because you have
obeyed me."[v]
19Then Abraham returned to his servants, and they set off together for Beersheba. And Abraham stayed in Beersheba.

Nahor's Sons

20Some time later Abraham was told,
"Milcah is also a mother; she has borne
sons to your brother Nahor:[w] 21Uz the
firstborn, Buz his brother, Kemuel (the
father of Aram), 22Kesed, Hazo, Pil-
dash, Jidlaph and Bethuel." 23Bethuel
became the father of Rebekah.[x] Milcah bore these eight sons to Abraham's
brother Nahor. 24His concubine,
whose name was Reumah, also had
sons: Tebah, Gaham, Tahash and Maacah.

The Death of Sarah

23 Sarah lived to be a hundred and
twenty-seven years old. 2She died
at Kiriath Arba[y] (that is, Hebron)[z] in
the land of Canaan, and Abraham went
to mourn for Sarah and to weep over
her.
3Then Abraham rose from beside his
dead wife and spoke to the Hittites.[c]
He said, 4"I am an alien and a stranger[a] among you. Sell me some property
for a burial site here so I can bury my
dead."
5The Hittites replied to Abraham,
6"Sir, listen to us. You are a mighty
prince[b] among us. Bury your dead in
the choicest of our tombs. None of us
will refuse you his tomb for burying
your dead."
7Then Abraham rose and bowed
down before the people of the land, the
Hittites. 8He said to them, "If you are
willing to let me bury my dead, then
listen to me and intercede with Ephron
son of Zohar[c] on my behalf 9so he will
sell me the cave of Machpelah, which
belongs to him and is at the end of his
field. Ask him to sell it to me for the full
price as a burial site among you."
10Ephron the Hittite was sitting
among his people and he replied to
Abraham in the hearing of all the Hittites who had come to the gate[d] of his
city. 11"No, my lord," he said. "Listen
to me; I give[d][e] you the field, and I
give[d] you the cave that is in it. I give[d]
it to you in the presence of my people.
Bury your dead."
12Again Abraham bowed down before the people of the land 13and he
said to Ephron in their hearing, "Listen
to me, if you will. I will pay the price of
the field. Accept it from me so I can
bury my dead there."
14Ephron answered Abraham,
15"Listen to me, my lord; the land is
worth four hundred shekels[e] of silver,[f] but what is that between me and
you? Bury your dead."
16Abraham agreed to Ephron's terms
and weighed out for him the price he
had named in the hearing of the Hittites: four hundred shekels of silver,[g]
according to the weight current among
the merchants.
17So Ephron's field in Machpelah
near Mamre[h]—both the field and the
cave in it, and all the trees within the
borders of the field—was deeded 18to
Abraham as his property in the presence of all the Hittites who had come
to the gate of the city. 19Afterward
Abraham buried his wife Sarah in the
cave in the field of Machpelah near
Mamre (which is at Hebron) in the
land of Canaan. 20So the field and the
cave in it were deeded[i] to Abraham
by the Hittites as a burial site.

22:9 [k]Heb 11:17-19; Jas 2:21
22:12 [l]1Sa 15:22; Jas 2:21-22 [m]ver 2; Jn 3:16
22:13 [n]Ro 8:32
22:14 [o]ver 8
22:16 [p]Lk 1:73; Heb 6:13
22:17 [q]Heb 6:14* [r]Ge 15:5 [s]Ge 26:24; 32:12 [t]Ge 24:60
22:18 [u]Ge 12:2,3; Ac 3:25*; Gal 3:8* [v]ver 10
22:20 [w]Ge 11:29
22:23 [x]Ge 24:15
23:2 [y]Jos 14:15 [z]ver 19; Ge 13:18
23:4 [a]Ge 17:8; 1Ch 29:15; Ps 105:12; Heb 11:9,13
23:6 [b]Ge 14:14-16; 24:35
23:8 [c]Ge 25:9
23:10 [d]Ge 34:20-24; Ru 4:4
23:11 [e]2Sa 24:23
23:15 [f]Eze 45:12
23:16 [g]Jer 32:9; Zec 11:12
23:17 [h]Ge 25:9; 49:30-32; 50:13; Ac 7:16
23:20 [i]Jer 32:10

a *13* Many manuscripts of the Masoretic Text, Samaritan Pentateuch, Septuagint and Syriac; most manuscripts of the Masoretic Text *a ram behind ⌞him⌟* **b** *18* Or *seed* **c** *3* Or *the sons of Heth*; also in verses 5, 7, 10, 16, 18 and 20 **d** *11* Or *sell* **e** *15* That is, about 10 pounds (about 4.5 kilograms)

Isaac and Rebekah

24 Abraham was now old and well advanced in years, and the LORD had blessed him in every way.[j] 2He said to the chief[a] servant in his household, the one in charge of all that he had,[k] "Put your hand under my thigh.[l] 3I want you to swear by the LORD, the God of heaven and the God of earth,[m] that you will not get a wife for my son[n] from the daughters of the Canaanites,[o] among whom I am living, 4but will go to my country and my own relatives[p] and get a wife for my son Isaac."

5The servant asked him, "What if the woman is unwilling to come back with me to this land? Shall I then take your son back to the country you came from?"

6"Make sure that you do not take my son back there," Abraham said. 7"The LORD, the God of heaven, who brought me out of my father's household and my native land and who spoke to me and promised me on oath, saying, 'To your offspring[b][q] I will give this land'[r]—he will send his angel before you[s] so that you can get a wife for my son from there. 8If the woman is unwilling to come back with you, then you will be released from this oath of mine. Only do not take my son back there." 9So the servant put his hand under the thigh[t] of his master Abraham and swore an oath to him concerning this matter.

10Then the servant took ten of his master's camels and left, taking with him all kinds of good things from his master. He set out for Aram Naharaim[c] and made his way to the town of Nahor. 11He had the camels kneel down near the well[u] outside the town; it was toward evening, the time the women go out to draw water.[v]

1 →PG. 46

12Then he prayed, "O LORD, God of my master Abraham,[w] give me success today, and show kindness to my master Abraham. 13See, I am standing beside this spring, and the daughters of the townspeople are coming out to draw water. 14May it be that when I say to a girl, 'Please let down your jar that I may have a drink,' and she says, 'Drink, and I'll water your camels too'—let her be the one you have chosen for your servant Isaac. By this I will know[x] that you have shown kindness to my master."

15Before he had finished praying,[y] Rebekah[z] came out with her jar on her shoulder. She was the daughter of Bethuel son of Milcah,[a] who was the wife of Abraham's brother Nahor.[b] 16The girl was very beautiful,[c] a virgin; no man had ever lain with her. She went down to the spring, filled her jar and came up again.

17The servant hurried to meet her and said, "Please give me a little water from your jar."

18"Drink,[d] my lord," she said, and quickly lowered the jar to her hands and gave him a drink.

19After she had given him a drink, she said, "I'll draw water for your camels too,[e] until they have finished drinking." 20So she quickly emptied her jar into the trough, ran back to the well to draw more water, and drew enough for all his camels. 21Without saying a word, the man watched her closely to learn whether or not the LORD had made his journey successful.[f]

22When the camels had finished drinking, the man took out a gold nose ring[g] weighing a beka[d] and two gold bracelets weighing ten shekels.[e] 23Then he asked, "Whose daughter are you? Please tell me, is there room in your father's house for us to spend the night?"

24She answered him, "I am the daughter of Bethuel, the son that Milcah bore to Nahor.[h]" 25And she added, "We have plenty of straw and fodder, as well as room for you to spend the night."

26Then the man bowed down and worshiped the LORD,[i] 27saying, "Praise be to the LORD,[j] the God of my master Abraham, who has not abandoned his kindness and faithfulness[k] to my master. As for me, the LORD has led me on the journey[l] to the house of my master's relatives."[m]

28The girl ran and told her mother's household about these things. 29Now Rebekah had a brother named Laban,[n] and he hurried out to the man at the spring. 30As soon as he had seen the nose ring, and the bracelets on his sister's arms, and had heard Rebekah tell what the man said to her, he went out to the man and found him standing by the camels near the spring. 31"Come, you who are blessed by the LORD,"[o] he said. "Why are you standing out here? I have prepared the house and a place for the camels."

32So the man went to the house, and the camels were unloaded. Straw and fodder were brought for the camels, and water for him and his men to wash their feet.[p] 33Then food was set before

24:1 [j]ver 35
24:2 [k]Ge 39:4-6 [l]ver 9; Ge 47:29
24:3 [m]Ge 14:19 [n]Ge 28:1; Dt 7:3 [o]Ge 10:15-19
24:4 [p]Ge 12:1; 28:2
24:7 [q]Gal 3:16* [r]Ge 12:7; 13:15 [s]Ex 23:20,23
24:9 [t]ver 2
24:11 [u]Ex 2:15 [v]ver 13; 1Sa 9:11
24:12 [w]ver 27,42,48; Ge 26:24; Ex 3:6,15,16
24:14 [x]Jdg 6:17,37
24:15 [y]ver 45 [z]Ge 22:23 [a]Ge 22:20 [b]Ge 11:29
24:16 [c]Ge 26:7
24:18 [d]ver 14
24:19 [e]ver 14
24:21 [f]ver 12
24:22 [g]ver 47
24:24 [h]ver 15
24:26 [i]ver 48,52; Ex 4:31
24:27 [j]Ex 18:10; Ru 4:14; 1Sa 25:32 [k]ver 49; Ge 32:10; Ps 98:3 [l]ver 21 [m]ver 12,48
24:29 [n]ver 4; Ge 29:5,12,13
24:31 [o]Ge 26:29; Ru 3:10; Ps 115:15
24:32 [p]Ge 43:24; Jdg 19:21

[a]*2* Or *oldest* [b]*7* Or *seed* [c]*10* That is, Northwest Mesopotamia [d]*22* That is, about 1/5 ounce (about 5.5 grams) [e]*22* That is, about 4 ounces (about 110 grams)

him, but he said, "I will not eat until I
have told you what I have to say."
"Then tell us," ⌞Laban⌟ said.
34So he said, "I am Abraham's servant. 35The LORD has blessed my master abundantly,[q] and he has become
wealthy. He has given him sheep and
cattle, silver and gold, menservants
and maidservants, and camels and
donkeys.[r] 36My master's wife Sarah
has borne him a son in her**a** old age,[s]
and he has given him everything he
owns.[t] 37And my master made me
swear an oath, and said, 'You must not
get a wife for my son from the daughters of the Canaanites, in whose land I
live,[u] 38but go to my father's family
and to my own clan, and get a wife for
my son.'[v]
39"Then I asked my master, 'What
if the woman will not come back
with me?'[w]
40"He replied, 'The LORD, before
whom I have walked, will send his angel with you[x] and make your journey
a success, so that you can get a wife for
my son from my own clan and from my
father's family. 41Then, when you go to
my clan, you will be released from my
oath even if they refuse to give her to
you—you will be released from my
oath.'[y]
42"When I came to the spring today,
I said, 'O LORD, God of my master
Abraham, if you will, please grant success[z] to the journey on which I have
come. 43See, I am standing beside this
spring;[a] if a maiden comes out to
draw water and I say to her, "Please let
me drink a little water from your jar,"[b]
44and if she says to me, "Drink, and I'll
draw water for your camels too," let her
be the one the LORD has chosen for my
master's son.'
45"Before I finished praying in my
heart,[c] Rebekah came out, with her
jar on her shoulder.[d] She went down
to the spring and drew water, and I said
to her, 'Please give me a drink.'[e]
46"She quickly lowered her jar from
her shoulder and said, 'Drink, and I'll
water your camels too.'[f] So I drank,
and she watered the camels also.
47"I asked her, 'Whose daughter are
you?'[g]
"She said, 'The daughter of Bethuel
son of Nahor, whom Milcah bore to
him.'[h]
"Then I put the ring in her nose and
the bracelets on her arms,[i] 48and I
bowed down and worshiped the
LORD.[j] I praised the LORD, the God of
my master Abraham, who had led me
on the right road to get the granddaughter of my master's brother for his
son.[k] 49Now if you will show kindness
and faithfulness[l] to my master, tell
me; and if not, tell me, so I may know
which way to turn."
50Laban and Bethuel answered,
"This is from the LORD;[m] we can say
nothing to you one way or the other.[n]
51Here is Rebekah; take her and go, and
let her become the wife of your master's son, as the LORD has directed."
52When Abraham's servant heard
what they said, he bowed down to the
ground before the LORD.[o] 53Then the
servant brought out gold and silver
jewelry and articles of clothing and
gave them to Rebekah; he also gave
costly gifts[p] to her brother and to her
mother. 54Then he and the men who
were with him ate and drank and spent
the night there.
When they got up the next morning,
he said, "Send me on my way[q] to my
master."
55But her brother and her mother replied, "Let the girl remain with us ten
days or so; then you**b** may go."
56But he said to them, "Do not detain me, now that the LORD has granted
success to my journey. Send me on my
way so I may go to my master."
57Then they said, "Let's call the girl
and ask her about it." 58So they called
Rebekah and asked her, "Will you go
with this man?"
"I will go," she said.
59So they sent their sister Rebekah
on her way, along with her nurse[r] and
Abraham's servant and his men. 60And
they blessed Rebekah and said to her,

"Our sister, may you increase
to thousands upon thousands;[s]
may your offspring possess
the gates of their enemies."[t]

61Then Rebekah and her maids got
ready and mounted their camels and
went back with the man. So the servant
took Rebekah and left.
62Now Isaac had come from Beer Lahai Roi,[u] for he was living in the Negev.[v] 63He went out to the field one
evening to meditate,**c**[w] and as he
looked up, he saw camels approaching.
64Rebekah also looked up and saw
Isaac. She got down from her camel
65and asked the servant, "Who is that
man in the field coming to meet us?"
"He is my master," the servant answered. So she took her veil and covered herself.
66Then the servant told Isaac all he
had done. 67Isaac brought her into the
tent of his mother Sarah, and he married Rebekah.[x] So she became his

24:35 [q]ver 1 [r]Ge 13:2
24:36 [s]Ge 21:2,10 [t]Ge 25:5
24:37 [u]ver 3
24:38 [v]ver 4
24:39 [w]ver 5
24:40 [x]ver 7
24:41 [y]ver 8
24:42 [z]ver 12
24:43 [a]ver 13 [b]ver 14
24:45 [c]1Sa 1:13 [d]ver 15 [e]ver 17
24:46 [f]ver 18-19
24:47 [g]ver 23 [h]ver 24 [i]Eze 16:11-12
24:48 [j]ver 26 [k]ver 27
24:49 [l]Ge 47:29; Jos 2:14
24:50 [m]Ps 118:23 [n]Ge 31:7,24, 29,42
24:52 [o]ver 26
24:53 [p]ver 10,22
24:54 [q]ver 56,59
24:59 [r]Ge 35:8
24:60 [s]Ge 17:16 [t]Ge 22:17
24:62 [u]Ge 16:14; 25:11 [v]Ge 20:1
24:63 [w]Ps 1:2; 77:12; 119:15,27,48, 97,148; 143:5; 145:5
24:67 [x]Ge 25:20

a *36* Or *his* **b** *55* Or *she* **c** *63* The meaning of the Hebrew for this word is uncertain.

wife, and he loved her;[y] and Isaac was comforted after his mother's death.[z]

The Death of Abraham

25 Abraham took[a] another wife, whose name was Keturah. 2She bore him Zimran, Jokshan, Medan, Midian, Ishbak and Shuah.[a] 3Jokshan was the father of Sheba and Dedan; the descendants of Dedan were the Asshurites, the Letushites and the Leummites. 4The sons of Midian were Ephah, Epher, Hanoch, Abida and Eldaah. All these were descendants of Keturah.

5Abraham left everything he owned to Isaac.[b] 6But while he was still living, he gave gifts to the sons of his concubines[c] and sent them away from his son Isaac[d] to the land of the east.

7Altogether, Abraham lived a hundred and seventy-five years. 8Then Abraham breathed his last and died at a good old age,[e] an old man and full of years; and he was gathered to his people.[f] 9His sons Isaac and Ishmael buried him[g] in the cave of Machpelah near Mamre, in the field of Ephron son of Zohar the Hittite,[h] 10the field Abraham had bought from the Hittites.[b][i] There Abraham was buried with his wife Sarah. 11After Abraham's death, God blessed his son Isaac, who then lived near Beer Lahai Roi.[j]

Ishmael's Sons

12This is the account of Abraham's son Ishmael, whom Sarah's maidservant, Hagar[k] the Egyptian, bore to Abraham.[l]

13These are the names of the sons of Ishmael, listed in the order of their birth: Nebaioth the firstborn of Ishmael, Kedar, Adbeel, Mibsam, 14Mishma, Dumah, Massa, 15Hadad, Tema, Jetur, Naphish and Kedemah. 16These were the sons of Ishmael, and these are the names of the twelve tribal rulers[m] according to their settlements and camps. 17Altogether, Ishmael lived a hundred and thirty-seven years. He breathed his last and died, and he was gathered to his people.[n] 18His descendants settled in the area from Havilah to Shur, near the border of Egypt, as you go toward Asshur. And they lived in hostility toward[c] all their brothers.[o]

Jacob and Esau

19This is the account of Abraham's son Isaac.

Abraham became the father of Isaac, 20and Isaac was forty years old[p] when he married Rebekah[q] daughter of Bethuel the Aramean from Paddan Aram[d] and sister of Laban[r] the Aramean.

21Isaac prayed to the LORD on behalf of his wife, because she was barren. The LORD answered his prayer,[s] and his wife Rebekah became pregnant. 22The babies jostled each other within her, and she said, "Why is this happening to me?" So she went to inquire of the LORD.[t]

23The LORD said to her,

"Two nations[u] are in your womb,
and two peoples from within you
will be separated;
one people will be stronger than
the other,
and the older will serve the
younger.[v]"

24When the time came for her to give birth, there were twin boys in her womb. 25The first to come out was red, and his whole body was like a hairy garment;[w] so they named him Esau.[e] 26After this, his brother came out, with his hand grasping Esau's heel;[x] so he was named Jacob.[f][y] Isaac was sixty years old when Rebekah gave birth to them.

27The boys grew up, and Esau became a skillful hunter, a man of the open country,[z] while Jacob was a quiet man, staying among the tents. 28Isaac, who had a taste for wild game,[a] loved Esau, but Rebekah loved Jacob.[b]

29Once when Jacob was cooking some stew, Esau came in from the open country, famished. 30He said to Jacob, "Quick, let me have some of that red stew! I'm famished!" (That is why he was also called Edom.[g])

31Jacob replied, "First sell me your birthright."

32"Look, I am about to die," Esau said. "What good is the birthright to me?"

33But Jacob said, "Swear to me first." So he swore an oath to him, selling his birthright[c] to Jacob.

34Then Jacob gave Esau some bread and some lentil stew. He ate and drank, and then got up and left.

So Esau despised his birthright.

24:67 [y]Ge 29:18,20 [z]Ge 23:1-2
25:2 [a]1Ch 1:32,33
25:5 [b]Ge 24:36
25:6 [c]Ge 22:24 [d]Ge 21:10,14
25:8 [e]Ge 15:15 [f]ver 17; Ge 35:29; 49:29,33
25:9 [g]Ge 35:29 [h]Ge 50:13
25:10 [i]Ge 23:16
25:11 [j]Ge 16:14
25:12 [k]Ge 16:1 [l]Ge 16:15
25:16 [m]Ge 17:20
25:17 [n]ver 8
25:18 [o]Ge 16:12
25:20 [p]ver 26; Ge 26:34 [q]Ge 24:67 [r]Ge 24:29
25:21 [s]1Ch 5:20; 2Ch 33:13; Ezr 8:23; Ps 127:3; Ro 9:10
25:22 [t]1Sa 9:9; 10:22
25:23 [u]Ge 17:4 [v]Ge 27:29,40; Mal 1:3; Ro 9:11-12*
25:25 [w]Ge 27:11
25:26 [x]Hos 12:3 [y]Ge 27:36
25:27 [z]Ge 27:3,5
25:28 [a]Ge 27: 19 [b]Ge 27:6
25:33 [c]Ge 27:36; Heb 12:16

[a] *1* Or *had taken* [b] *10* Or *the sons of Heth* [c] *18* Or *lived to the east of* [d] *20* That is, Northwest Mesopotamia [e] *25* *Esau* may mean *hairy*; he was also called Edom, which means *red.* [f] *26* *Jacob* means *he grasps the heel* (figuratively, *he deceives*). [g] *30* *Edom* means *red.*

JACOB

The Battle With a Willful Man

Jacob's story is a story of wills—Jacob's will, Rebekah's will, Isaac's will, Esau's will, and, ultimately God's will. Following the story of this crafty schemer is instructive for us all.

It all started simply enough. Esau, Jacob's twin brother, held the rights to their father's considerable fortune because he had been born first. Now Esau was a man's man—a hunter, a man of the field (Genesis 25:27). Esau lived by his brawn, which made him, to say the least, a bit short-sighted. To him, long-range planning extended only to his next meal. Jacob, on the other hand, lived by his brains. He lived by his wits. Esau had something that Jacob wanted, and Jacob would not be denied.

A Test of Wills

One day as Jacob was cooking some stew, Esau came in from hunting, famished, begging for food. Seeing his opportunity, Jacob agreed to feed him if Esau would sell Jacob his legal right to the family fortune. Amazingly, Esau agreed! Esau may have been a great hunter, but he was a lousy real estate speculator. "So Esau despised his birthright" (25:34). Jacob had won; he got the deed to the farm for the price of a bowl of soup.

Jacob's next target was his aged and feeble father, Isaac. In Jacob's time the final blessing from the father clinched the inheritance in the family. Jacob knew that Isaac was determined to bless Esau and give him the family fortune. In Isaac's mind, if he wanted Esau to have the blessing, Esau would have it.

What complicated Isaac's choice, however, was God's will in this matter. Years earlier, when Rebekah was pregnant with the twins, God had made it plain that "the older will serve the younger" (25:23). God said the blessing he had given to Abraham—who had passed it on to Isaac—should be passed on again to Jacob. Jacob was God's choice. Isaac, however, fully intended to ignore that bit of divine instruction. But Jacob, in partnership with his mother, Rebekah, had his eye on that blessing. It didn't matter that Isaac was old and blind and worthy of respect as Jacob's father. He had something Jacob wanted.

The Deceived

Like Esau, Isaac lived by his appetite, so as he prepared to bless Esau he sent his favorite son to bag some wild game. "Prepare me the kind of tasty food I like and bring it to me to eat, so that I may give you my blessing" (27:4). But while Esau was hunting, Rebekah and Jacob prepared a meal of goat meat flavored like wild game. Wearing a costume of goat hair and some of his brother's clothes, Jacob fooled old, blind Isaac and ended up with the blessing. Jacob's will prevailed once again.

When Esau came home with the venison and went in to get Isaac's blessing, Isaac had to tell his favorite son that he had mistakenly passed the blessing on and couldn't take it back. Now Esau had nothing. He had short-sightedly sold Jacob the family fortune for a bowl of stew, and old, blind Isaac had passed along his blessing for a plate of goat steaks. Outsmarted again, Esau resorted to what he did best: "Esau held a grudge against Jacob" (27:41). He wanted to murder his brother. So Jacob ran for his life.

God Deals With a Deceiver

God watched as this test of wills was played out. And while Jacob, Rebekah, Isaac, and Esau were perfectly happy to leave God out of the drama, God was never out of it. Make no mistake about it—whether in Jacob or Esau's life, or yours or mine, God is *never* out of the drama. And he was about to make a grand entrance.

As Jacob ran from Esau, God spoke to him in a dream, "I will give you and your descendants the land on which you are lying . . . I am with you and will watch over you wherever you go . . . I will not leave you until I have done what I have promised you" (28:13, 15). Jacob was impressed, but felt compelled to make a deal with God. As before, Jacob wanted to work on his own terms. In essence Jacob said, "*If* you will do all these things, *then* you can be my God."

Twenty years later, after an extended contest with another major-league schemer (28—31), Jacob finally turned back to his home territory. As he walked, God entered again in the form of an angel. Read Genesis 32 for an account of the strange wrestling match that ensued. Finally, after years of having his way, Jacob had to fight with his greatest enemy: his own willful, scheming heart.

All his life Jacob had suffered from the occupational hazard of the extremely gifted: the "Who needs God?" attitude. Up to this point God had been someone to bargain with, someone to use to his own advantage. Now Jacob engaged in a desperate, exhausting wrestling match between God and his own willful heart. When the dust settled, Jacob found that giving in to God's will was his only hope. Jacob limped away from the scene, carrying with him a physical reminder that God held the ultimate power in his life.

As Jacob fought against God, he learned that until he had fought life's issues through *with* God, he would never be a winner. No matter how smart, talented, driven, wealthy or powerful a man is, he must be defeated by God in the battle of the wills. God will only accept the number one position as absolute Lord of a man's life. The "Jacobs" of this world have to fight until they lose the battle of their wills—and lose them to God.

You can't fake this one. The only way out of the darkness of a willful heart is to face this battle of the wills with Almighty God and fight until you lose it. He must win if you are ever going to be a total man, a real winner.

—Dr. Sid Buzzell

Isaac and Abimelech

26 Now there was a famine in the
land[d]—besides the earlier famine
of Abraham's time—and Isaac went to
Abimelech king of the Philistines in
Gerar.[e] 2The LORD appeared[f] to
Isaac and said, "Do not go down to
Egypt; live in the land where I tell you
to live.[g] 3Stay in this land for a
while,[h] and I will be with you and will
bless you.[i] For to you and your
descendants I will give all these lands[j]
and will confirm the oath I swore to
your father Abraham. 4I will make your
descendants as numerous as the stars
in the sky[k] and will give them all these
lands, and through your offspring**[a]** all
nations on earth will be blessed,[l] 5be-
cause Abraham obeyed me[m] and kept
my requirements, my commands, my
decrees and my laws." 6So Isaac stayed
in Gerar.

7When the men of that place asked
him about his wife, he said, "She is my
sister,[n]" because he was afraid to say,
"She is my wife." He thought, "The
men of this place might kill me on account of Rebekah, because she is beautiful."

8When Isaac had been there a long
time, Abimelech king of the Philistines
looked down from a window and saw
Isaac caressing his wife Rebekah. 9So
Abimelech summoned Isaac and said,
"She is really your wife! Why did you
say, 'She is my sister'?"

Isaac answered him, "Because I
thought I might lose my life on account
of her."

10Then Abimelech said, "What is this
you have done to us?[o] One of the men
might well have slept with your wife,
and you would have brought guilt
upon us."

11So Abimelech gave orders to all the
people: "Anyone who molests[p] this
man or his wife shall surely be put to
death."

12Isaac planted crops in that land
and the same year reaped a hundred-
fold, because the LORD blessed him.[q]
13The man became rich, and his wealth
continued to grow until he became
very wealthy.[r] 14He had so many
flocks and herds and servants[s] that
the Philistines envied him.[t] 15So all
the wells[u] that his father's servants
had dug in the time of his father Abraham, the Philistines stopped up,[v] filling them with earth.

16Then Abimelech said to Isaac,
"Move away from us; you have become
too powerful for us.[w]"

17So Isaac moved away from there
and encamped in the Valley of Gerar
and settled there. 18Isaac reopened the
wells[x] that had been dug in the time
of his father Abraham, which the Philistines had stopped up after Abraham
died, and he gave them the same
names his father had given them.

19Isaac's servants dug in the valley
and discovered a well of fresh water
there. 20But the herdsmen of Gerar
quarreled with Isaac's herdsmen and
said, "The water is ours!"[y] So he
named the well Esek,**[b]** because they
disputed with him. 21Then they dug
another well, but they quarreled over
that one also; so he named it Sitnah.**[c]**
22He moved on from there and dug another well, and no one quarreled over
it. He named it Rehoboth,**[d]** saying,
"Now the LORD has given us room and
we will flourish[z] in the land."

23From there he went up to Beersheba. 24That night the LORD appeared to
him and said, "I am the God of your
father Abraham.[a] Do not be afraid,[b]
for I am with you; I will bless you and
will increase the number of your
descendants[c] for the sake of my servant Abraham."[d]

25Isaac built an altar[e] there and
called on the name of the LORD. There
he pitched his tent, and there his servants dug a well.

26Meanwhile, Abimelech had come
to him from Gerar, with Ahuzzath his
personal adviser and Phicol the commander of his forces.[f] 27Isaac asked
them, "Why have you come to me,
since you were hostile to me and sent
me away?[g]"

28They answered, "We saw clearly
that the LORD was with you;[h] so we
said, 'There ought to be a sworn agreement between us'—between us and
you. Let us make a treaty with you
29that you will do us no harm, just as
we did not molest you but always treated you well and sent you away in
peace. And now you are blessed by the
LORD."[i]

30Isaac then made a feast[j] for them,
and they ate and drank. 31Early the
next morning the men swore an oath[k]
to each other. Then Isaac sent them on
their way, and they left him in peace.

32That day Isaac's servants came
and told him about the well they had
dug. They said, "We've found water!"
33He called it Shibah,**[e]** and to this day
the name of the town has been Beersheba.**[f]**[l]

34When Esau was forty years old,[m]

26:1 [d]Ge 12:10 [e]Ge 20:1
26:2 [f]Ge 12:7; 17:1; 18:1 [g]Ge 12:1
26:3 [h]Ge 20:1; 28:15 [i]Ge 12:2; 22:16-18 [j]Ge 12:7; 13:15; 15:18
26:4 [k]Ge 15:5; 22:17; Ex 32:13 [l]Ge 12:3; 22:18; Gal 3:8
26:5 [m]Ge 22:16
26:7 [n]Ge 12:13; 20:2,12; Pr 29:25
26:10 [o]Ge 20:9
26:11 [p]Ps 105:15
26:12 [q]ver 3; Job 42:12
26:13 [r]Pr 10:22
26:14 [s]Ge 24:36 [t]Ge 37:11
26:15 [u]Ge 21:30 [v]Ge 21:25
26:16 [w]Ex 1:9
26:18 [x]Ge 21:30
26:20 [y]Ge 21:25
26:22 [z]Ge 17:6; Ex 1:7
26:24 [a]Ge 24:12; Ex 3:6 [b]Ge 15:1 [c]ver 4 [d]Ge 17:7
26:25 [e]Ge 12:7,8; 13:4,18; Ps 116:17
26:26 [f]Ge 21:22
26:27 [g]ver 16
26:28 [h]Ge 21:22
26:29 [i]Ge 24:31; Ps 115:15
26:30 [j]Ge 19:3
26:31 [k]Ge 21:31
26:33 [l]Ge 21:14
26:34 [m]Ge 25:20

a 4 Or *seed* **b** 20 *Esek* means *dispute.* **c** 21 *Sitnah* means *opposition.* **d** 22 *Rehoboth* means *room.* **e** 33 *Shibah* can mean *oath* or *seven.* **f** 33 *Beersheba* can mean *well of the oath* or *well of seven.*

he married Judith daughter of Beeri the
Hittite, and also Basemath daughter
of Elon the Hittite.[n] 35They were a
source of grief to Isaac and Rebekah.[o]

Jacob Gets Isaac's Blessing

27 When Isaac was old and his eyes
were so weak that he could no
longer see,[p] he called for Esau his older son[q] and said to him, "My son."
"Here I am," he answered.
2Isaac said, "I am now an old man
and don't know the day of my death.[r]
3Now then, get your weapons—your
quiver and bow—and go out to the
open country[s] to hunt some wild
game for me. 4Prepare me the kind of
tasty food I like and bring it to me to
eat, so that I may give you my blessing[t] before I die."
5Now Rebekah was listening as Isaac
spoke to his son Esau. When Esau left
for the open country to hunt game and
bring it back, 6Rebekah said to her son
Jacob,[u] "Look, I overheard your father
say to your brother Esau, 7'Bring me
some game and prepare me some tasty
food to eat, so that I may give you my
blessing in the presence of the LORD
before I die.' 8Now, my son, listen carefully and do what I tell you:[v] 9Go out
to the flock and bring me two choice
young goats, so I can prepare some
tasty food for your father, just the way
he likes it. 10Then take it to your father
to eat, so that he may give you his
blessing before he dies."
11Jacob said to Rebekah his mother,
"But my brother Esau is a hairy man,[w]
and I'm a man with smooth skin.
12What if my father touches me?[x] I
would appear to be tricking him and
would bring down a curse on myself
rather than a blessing."
13His mother said to him, "My son,
let the curse fall on me.[y] Just do what
I say;[z] go and get them for me."
14So he went and got them and
brought them to his mother, and she
prepared some tasty food, just the way
his father liked it. 15Then Rebekah took
the best clothes[a] of Esau her older
son, which she had in the house, and
put them on her younger son Jacob.
16She also covered his hands and the
smooth part of his neck with the goatskins. 17Then she handed to her son
Jacob the tasty food and the bread she
had made.
18He went to his father and said, "My
father."
"Yes, my son," he answered. "Who
is it?"
19Jacob said to his father, "I am Esau
your firstborn. I have done as you told
me. Please sit up and eat some of my
game so that you may give me your
blessing."[b]
20Isaac asked his son, "How did you
find it so quickly, my son?"
"The LORD your God gave me success,[c]" he replied.
21Then Isaac said to Jacob, "Come
near so I can touch you,[d] my son, to
know whether you really are my son
Esau or not."
22Jacob went close to his father
Isaac, who touched him and said, "The
voice is the voice of Jacob, but the
hands are the hands of Esau." 23He did
not recognize him, for his hands were
hairy like those of his brother Esau;[e]
so he blessed him. 24"Are you really my
son Esau?" he asked.
"I am," he replied.
25Then he said, "My son, bring me
some of your game to eat, so that I may
give you my blessing."[f]
Jacob brought it to him and he ate;
and he brought some wine and he
drank. 26Then his father Isaac said to
him, "Come here, my son, and
kiss me."
27So he went to him and kissed
him[g]. When Isaac caught the smell of
his clothes,[h] he blessed him and said,

27:1–45

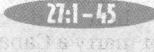

FAMILY MATTERS

PROMISE 4

This chapter is filled with lying, cheating, deception, and death threats—and these are the patriarchs? This is God's chosen family?!

Make a few notes here. First, in chapter 25:23 God told Rebekah that the older son (Esau) would serve the younger son (Jacob). So Jacob was the one God had chosen to receive the blessing of the covenant (Genesis 12:1–3). Second, in chapter 25:29–34 Esau despised his birthright. He gave up his legal place as firstborn son for a bowl of stew. Third, even though God wanted Jacob to receive the blessing, Isaac wanted Esau to have it (27:4). All the maneuverings of this chapter grew out of Rebekah and Jacob's attempts to fulfill God's wishes. They are both responsible for their actions, and for failing to believe God would accomplish his will without their deceit. But the frustration and turmoil in their home could have been avoided if Isaac had acted responsibly and had submitted his own desires to God's revealed will.

Does your relationship to God encourage or discourage godliness in your home? Watch yourself for a few weeks and ask what effect your actions have on your family's relationship with God.

For the next Promise 4 reading go to page 194.

26:34 [n]Ge 28:9; 36:2
26:35 [o]Ge 27:46
27:1 [p]Ge 48:10; 1Sa 3:2 [q]Ge 25:25
27:2 [r]Ge 47:29
27:3 [s]Ge 25:27
27:4 [t]ver 10,25,31; Ge 49:28; Dt 33:1; Heb 11:20
27:6 [u]Ge 25:28
27:8 [v]ver 13,43
27:11 [w]Ge 25:25
27:12 [x]ver 22
27:13 [y]Mt 27:25 [z]ver 8
27:15 [a]ver 27
27:19 [b]ver 4
27:20 [c]Ge 24:12
27:21 [d]ver 12
27:23 [e]ver 16
27:25 [f]ver 4
27:27 [g]Heb 11:20 [h]SS 4:11

"Ah, the smell of my son
is like the smell of a field
that the LORD has blessed.[i]
28May God give you of heaven's
dew[j]
and of earth's richness[k]—
an abundance of grain and new
wine.[l]
29May nations serve you
and peoples bow down to you.[m]
Be lord over your brothers,
and may the sons of your
mother bow down to you.[n]
May those who curse you be
cursed
and those who bless you be
blessed.[o]"

30After Isaac finished blessing him
and Jacob had scarcely left his father's
presence, his brother Esau came in
from hunting. 31He too prepared some
tasty food and brought it to his father.
Then he said to him, "My father, sit up
and eat some of my game, so that you
may give me your blessing."[p]
32His father Isaac asked him, "Who
are you?"[q]
"I am your son," he answered, "your
firstborn, Esau."
33Isaac trembled violently and said,
"Who was it, then, that hunted game
and brought it to me? I ate it just before
you came and I blessed him—and indeed he will be blessed![r]"
34When Esau heard his father's
words, he burst out with a loud and
bitter cry[s] and said to his father,
"Bless me—me too, my father!"
35But he said, "Your brother came
deceitfully[t] and took your blessing."
36Esau said, "Isn't he rightly named
Jacob**a**?[u] He has deceived me these
two times: He took my birthright,[v]
and now he's taken my blessing!" Then
he asked, "Haven't you reserved any
blessing for me?"
37Isaac answered Esau, "I have made
him lord over you and have made all
his relatives his servants, and I have
sustained him with grain and new
wine.[w] So what can I possibly do for
you, my son?"
38Esau said to his father, "Do you
have only one blessing, my father?
Bless me too, my father!" Then Esau
wept aloud.[x]
39His father Isaac answered him,

"Your dwelling will be
away from the earth's richness,
away from the dew[y] of heaven
above.
40You will live by the sword
and you will serve[z] your
brother.[a]
But when you grow restless,
you will throw his yoke
from off your neck.[b]"

Jacob Flees to Laban

41Esau held a grudge[c] against Jacob[d] because of the blessing his father
had given him. He said to himself,
"The days of mourning[e] for my father
are near; then I will kill my brother Jacob."[f]
42When Rebekah was told what her
older son Esau had said, she sent for
her younger son Jacob and said to him,
"Your brother Esau is consoling himself with the thought of killing you.
43Now then, my son, do what I say:[g]
Flee at once to my brother Laban[h] in
Haran.[i] 44Stay with him for a while[j]
until your brother's fury subsides.
45When your brother is no longer angry
with you and forgets what you did to
him,[k] I'll send word for you to come
back from there. Why should I lose
both of you in one day?"
46Then Rebekah said to Isaac, "I'm
disgusted with living because of these
Hittite women. If Jacob takes a wife
from among the women of this land,
from Hittite women like these, my life
will not be worth living."[l]
28 So Isaac called for Jacob and
blessed**b** him and commanded
him: "Do not marry a Canaanite woman.[m] 2Go at once to Paddan Aram,**c** to
the house of your mother's father Bethuel.[n] Take a wife for yourself there,
from among the daughters of Laban,
your mother's brother. 3May God Almighty**d**[o] bless you and make you
fruitful[p] and increase your numbers
until you become a community of peoples. 4May he give you and your
descendants the blessing given to
Abraham,[q] so that you may take possession of the land where you now live
as an alien,[r] the land God gave to
Abraham." 5Then Isaac sent Jacob on
his way, and he went to Paddan
Aram,[s] to Laban son of Bethuel the
Aramean, the brother of Rebekah,[t]
who was the mother of Jacob and Esau.
6Now Esau learned that Isaac had
blessed Jacob and had sent him to Paddan Aram to take a wife from there,
and that when he blessed him he commanded him, "Do not marry a Canaanite woman,"[u] 7and that Jacob had
obeyed his father and mother and had
gone to Paddan Aram. 8Esau then realized how displeasing the Canaanite
women[v] were to his father Isaac;[w]

a *36 Jacob* means *he grasps the heel* (figuratively, *he deceives*). **b** *1* Or *greeted* **c** *2* That is, Northwest Mesopotamia; also in verses 5, 6 and 7 **d** *3* Hebrew *El-Shaddai*

27:27 [i]Ps 65:9-13
27:28 [j]Dt 33:13 [k]ver 39 [l]Ge 45:18; Nu 18:12; Dt 33:28
27:29 [m]Isa 45:14,23; 49:7,23 [n]Ge 9:25; 25:23; 37:7 [o]Ge 12:3; Nu 24:9; Zep 2:8
27:31 [p]ver 4
27:32 [q]ver 18
27:33 [r]ver 29; Ge 28:3,4; Ro 11:29
27:34 [s]Heb 12:17
27:35 [t]Jer 9:4; 12:6
27:36 [u]Ge 25:26 [v]Ge 25:33
27:37 [w]ver 28
27:38 [x]Heb 12:17
27:39 [y]ver 28
27:40 [z]2Sa 8:14 [a]Ge 25:23 [b]2Ki 8:20-22
27:41 [c]Ge 37:4 [d]Ge 32:11 [e]Ge 50:4,10 [f]Ob 1:10
27:43 [g]ver 8 [h]Ge 24:29 [i]Ge 11:31
27:44 [j]Ge 31:38,41
27:45 [k]ver 35
27:46 [l]Ge 26:35
28:1 [m]Ge 24:3
28:2 [n]Ge 25:20
28:3 [o]Ge 17:1 [p]Ge 17:6
28:4 [q]Ge 12:2,3 [r]Ge 17:8
28:5 [s]Hos 12:12 [t]Ge 24:29
28:6 [u]ver 1
28:8 [v]Ge 24:3 [w]Ge 26:35

9so he went to Ishmael and married
Mahalath, the sister of Nebaioth[x] and
daughter of Ishmael son of Abraham,
in addition to the wives he already
had.[y]

Jacob's Dream at Bethel

10Jacob left Beersheba and set out
for Haran.[z] **11**When he reached a certain place, he stopped for the night because the sun had set. Taking one of
the stones there, he put it under his
head and lay down to sleep. **12**He had
a dream[a] in which he saw a stairway[a]
resting on the earth, with its top reaching to heaven, and the angels of God
were ascending and descending on
it.[b] **13**There above it[b] stood the
LORD,[c] and he said: "I am the LORD,
the God of your father Abraham and
the God of Isaac.[d] I will give you and
your descendants the land[e] on which
you are lying. **14**Your descendants will
be like the dust of the earth, and you[f]
will spread out to the west and to the
east, to the north and to the south.[g]
All peoples on earth will be blessed
through you and your offspring.[h] **15**I
am with you[i] and will watch over
you[j] wherever you go, and I will bring
you back to this land. I will not leave
you[k] until I have done what I have
promised you."[l]
16When Jacob awoke from his sleep,
he thought, "Surely the LORD is in this
place, and I was not aware of it." **17**He
was afraid and said, "How awesome is
this place![m] This is none other than
the house of God; this is the gate of
heaven."
18Early the next morning Jacob took
the stone he had placed under his head
and set it up as a pillar[n] and poured
oil on top of it.[o] **19**He called that place
Bethel,[c] though the city used to be
called Luz.[p]
20Then Jacob made a vow,[q] saying,
"If God will be with me and will watch
over me[r] on this journey I am taking
and will give me food to eat and clothes
to wear **21**so that I return safely[s] to my
father's house, then the LORD[d] will be
my God[t] **22**and[e] this stone that I have
set up as a pillar will be God's house,[u]
and of all that you give me I will give
you a tenth.[v]"

Jacob Arrives in Paddan Aram

29 Then Jacob continued on his journey and came to the land of the
eastern peoples.[w] **2**There he saw a well
in the field, with three flocks of sheep
lying near it because the flocks were
watered from that well. The stone over
the mouth of the well was large. **3**When
all the flocks were gathered there, the
shepherds would roll the stone away
from the well's mouth and water the
sheep. Then they would return the
stone to its place over the mouth of
the well.
4Jacob asked the shepherds, "My
brothers, where are you from?"
"We're from Haran,[x]" they replied.
5He said to them, "Do you know Laban, Nahor's grandson?"
"Yes, we know him," they answered.
6Then Jacob asked them, "Is he
well?"
"Yes, he is," they said, "and here
comes his daughter Rachel with the
sheep."
7"Look," he said, "the sun is still
high; it is not time for the flocks to be
gathered. Water the sheep and take
them back to pasture."
8"We can't," they replied, "until all
the flocks are gathered and the stone
has been rolled away from the mouth
of the well. Then we will water the
sheep."
9While he was still talking with them,
Rachel came with her father's sheep,[y]
for she was a shepherdess. **10**When Jacob saw Rachel daughter of Laban, his
mother's brother, and Laban's sheep,
he went over and rolled the stone away
from the mouth of the well and watered his uncle's sheep.[z] **11**Then Jacob
kissed Rachel and began to weep
aloud.[a] **12**He had told Rachel that he
was a relative[b] of her father and a son
of Rebekah. So she ran and told her
father.[c]
13As soon as Laban[d] heard the news
about Jacob, his sister's son, he hurried
to meet him. He embraced him and
kissed him and brought him to his
home, and there Jacob told him all
these things. **14**Then Laban said to him,
"You are my own flesh and blood."[e]

Jacob Marries Leah and Rachel

After Jacob had stayed with him for
a whole month, **15**Laban said to him,
"Just because you are a relative of
mine, should you work for me for nothing? Tell me what your wages
should be."
16Now Laban had two daughters; the
name of the older was Leah, and the
name of the younger was Rachel.
17Leah had weak[f] eyes, but Rachel
was lovely in form, and beautiful. **18**Jacob was in love with Rachel and said,

28:9 [x]Ge 25:13 [y]Ge 26:34
28:10 [z]Ge 11:31
28:12 [a]Ge 20:3 [b]Jn 1:51
28:13 [c]Ge 12:7; 35:7, 9; 48:3 [d]Ge 26:24 [e]Ge 13:15; 35:12
28:14 [f]Ge 26:4 [g]Ge 13:14 [h]Ge 12:3; 18:18; 22:18; Gal 3:8
28:15 [i]Ge 26:3; 48:21 [j]Nu 6:24; Ps 121:5,7-8 [k]Dt 31:6,8 [l]Nu 23:19
28:17 [m]Ex 3:5; Jos 5:15
28:18 [n]Ge 35:14 [o]Lev 8:11
28:19 [p]Jdg 1:23,26
28:20 [q]Ge 31:13; Jdg 11:30; 2Sa 15:8 [r]ver 15
28:21 [s]Jdg 11:31 [t]Dt 26:17
28:22 [u]Ge 35:7,14 [v]Ge 14:20; Lev 27:30
29:1 [w]Jdg 6:3,33
29:4 [x]Ge 28:10
29:9 [y]Ex 2:16
29:10 [z]Ex 2:17
29:11 [a]Ge 33:4
29:12 [b]Ge 13:8; 14:14,16 [c]Ge 24:28
29:13 [d]Ge 24:29
29:14 [e]Ge 2:23; Jdg 9:2; 2Sa 19:12-13

a *12* Or *ladder* **b** *13* Or *There beside him*
c *19* *Bethel* means *house of God.* **d** *20,21* Or *Since God . . . father's house, the LORD*
e *21,22* Or *house, and the LORD will be my God, 22then* **f** *17* Or *delicate*

"I'll work for you seven years in return
for your younger daughter Rachel."[f]
19 Laban said, "It's better that I give
her to you than to some other man.
Stay here with me." 20 So Jacob served
seven years to get Rachel, but they
seemed like only a few days to him because of his love for her.[g]
21 Then Jacob said to Laban, "Give
me my wife. My time is completed, and
I want to lie with her.[h]"
22 So Laban brought together all the
people of the place and gave a feast.[i]
23 But when evening came, he took his
daughter Leah and gave her to Jacob,
and Jacob lay with her. 24 And Laban
gave his servant girl Zilpah to his
daughter as her maidservant.
25 When morning came, there was
Leah! So Jacob said to Laban, "What is
this you have done to me?[j] I served
you for Rachel, didn't I? Why have you
deceived me?[k]"
26 Laban replied, "It is not our custom here to give the younger daughter
in marriage before the older one. 27 Finish this daughter's bridal week;[l] then
we will give you the younger one also,
in return for another seven years of
work."
28 And Jacob did so. He finished the
week with Leah, and then Laban gave
him his daughter Rachel to be his wife.
29 Laban gave his servant girl Bilhah[m]
to his daughter Rachel as her maidservant.[n] 30 Jacob lay with Rachel also,
and he loved Rachel more than Leah.[o]
And he worked for Laban another sev-
en years.[p]

Jacob's Children

31 When the LORD saw that Leah was
not loved,[q] he opened her womb,[r]
but Rachel was barren. 32 Leah became
pregnant and gave birth to a son. She
named him Reuben,[a] for she said, "It
is because the LORD has seen my misery.[s] Surely my husband will love me
now."
33 She conceived again, and when
she gave birth to a son she said, "Because the LORD heard that I am not
loved, he gave me this one too." So she
named him Simeon.[b][t]
34 Again she conceived, and when
she gave birth to a son she said, "Now
at last my husband will become attached to me,[u] because I have borne
him three sons." So he was named
Levi.[c][v]
35 She conceived again, and when
she gave birth to a son she said, "This
time I will praise the LORD." So she
named him Judah.[d][w] Then she
stopped having children.

30 When Rachel saw that she was not
bearing Jacob any children,[x] she
became jealous of her sister.[y] So she
said to Jacob, "Give me children, or I'll
die!"
2 Jacob became angry with her and
said, "Am I in the place of God, who
has kept you from having children?"[z]
3 Then she said, "Here is Bilhah, my
maidservant. Sleep with her so that she
can bear children for me and that
through her I too can build a family."[a]
4 So she gave him her servant Bilhah
as a wife.[b] Jacob slept with her,[c] 5 and
she became pregnant and bore him a
son. 6 Then Rachel said, "God has vindicated me;[d] he has listened to my
plea and given me a son." Because of
this she named him Dan.[e][e]
7 Rachel's servant Bilhah conceived
again and bore Jacob a second son.
8 Then Rachel said, "I have had a great
struggle with my sister, and I have
won."[f] So she named him Naphtali.[f][g]
9 When Leah saw that she had
stopped having children, she took her
maidservant Zilpah and gave her to Jacob as a wife.[h] 10 Leah's servant Zilpah
bore Jacob a son. 11 Then Leah said,
"What good fortune!"[g] So she named
him Gad.[h][i]
12 Leah's servant Zilpah bore Jacob
a second son. 13 Then Leah said,
"How happy I am! The women will
call me[j] happy."[k] So she named him
Asher.[i][l]
14 During wheat harvest, Reuben
went out into the fields and found
some mandrake plants,[m] which he
brought to his mother Leah. Rachel
said to Leah, "Please give me some of
your son's mandrakes."
15 But she said to her, "Wasn't it
enough[n] that you took away my husband? Will you take my son's mandrakes too?"
"Very well," Rachel said, "he can
sleep with you tonight in return for
your son's mandrakes."
16 So when Jacob came in from the
fields that evening, Leah went out to
meet him. "You must sleep with me,"
she said. "I have hired you with my
son's mandrakes." So he slept with her
that night.
17 God listened to Leah,[o] and she

29:18 f Hos 12:12
29:20 g SS 8:7; Hos 12:12
29:21 h Jdg 15:1
29:22 i Jdg 14:10; Jn 2:1-2
29:25 j Ge 12:18 k Ge 27:36
29:27 l Jdg 14:12
29:29 m Ge 30:3 n Ge 16:1
29:30 o ver 16 p Ge 31:41
29:31 q Dt 21:15-17 r Ge 11:30; 30:1; Ps 127:3
29:32 s Ge 16:11; 31:42; Ex 4:31; Dt 26:7; Ps 25:18
29:33 t Ge 34:25; 49:5
29:34 u Ge 30:20; 1Sa 1:2-4 v Ge 49:5-7
29:35 w Ge 49:8; Mt 1:2-3
30:1 x Ge 29:31; 1Sa 1:5-6 y Lev 18:18
30:2 z Ge 16:2; 20:18; 29:31
30:3 a Ge 16:2
30:4 b ver 9,18 c Ge 16:3-4
30:6 d Ps 35:24; 43:1; La 3:59 e Ge 49:16-17
30:8 f Hos 12:3-4 g Ge 49:21
30:9 h ver 4
30:11 i Ge 49:19
30:13 j Ps 127:3 k Pr 31:28; Lk 1:48 l Ge 49:20
30:14 m SS 7:13
30:15 n Nu 16:9,13
30:17 o Ge 25:21

a 32 *Reuben* sounds like the Hebrew for *he has seen my misery;* the name means *see, a son.*
b 33 *Simeon* probably means *one who hears.*
c 34 *Levi* sounds like and may be derived from the Hebrew for *attached.*
d 35 *Judah* sounds like and may be derived from the Hebrew for *praise.*
e 6 *Dan* here means *he has vindicated.*
f 8 *Naphtali* means *my struggle.*
g 11 Or *"A troop is coming!"*
h 11 *Gad* can mean *good fortune* or *a troop.*
i 13 *Asher* means *happy.*

became pregnant and bore Jacob a
fifth son. 18Then Leah said, "God has
rewarded me for giving my maidservant to my husband." So she named
him Issachar.[a][p]
19Leah conceived again and bore Jacob a sixth son. 20Then Leah said, "God
has presented me with a precious gift.
This time my husband will treat me
with honor, because I have borne him
six sons." So she named him Zebulun.[b][q]
21Some time later she gave birth to a
daughter and named her Dinah.
22Then God remembered Rachel;[r]
he listened to her and opened her
womb.[s] 23She became pregnant and
gave birth to a son[t] and said, "God
has taken away my disgrace."[u] 24She
named him Joseph,[c][v] and said, "May
the LORD add to me another son."[w]

Jacob's Flocks Increase

25After Rachel gave birth to Joseph,
Jacob said to Laban, "Send me on my
way[x] so I can go back to my own
homeland. 26Give me my wives and
children, for whom I have served
you,[y] and I will be on my way. You
know how much work I've done for
you."
27But Laban said to him, "If I have
found favor in your eyes, please stay. I
have learned by divination that[d] the
LORD has blessed me because of
you."[z] 28He added, "Name your
wages,[a] and I will pay them."
29Jacob said to him, "You know how
I have worked for you[b] and how your
livestock has fared under my care.[c]
30The little you had before I came has
increased greatly, and the LORD has
blessed you wherever I have been. But
now, when may I do something for my
own household?[d]"
31"What shall I give you?" he asked.
"Don't give me anything," Jacob replied. "But if you will do this one thing
for me, I will go on tending your flocks
and watching over them: 32Let me go
through all your flocks today and remove from them every speckled or
spotted sheep, every dark-colored
lamb and every spotted or speckled
goat.[e] They will be my wages. 33And
my honesty will testify for me in the
future, whenever you check on the
wages you have paid me. Any goat in
my possession that is not speckled or
spotted, or any lamb that is not dark-
colored, will be considered stolen."
34"Agreed," said Laban. "Let it be as
you have said." 35That same day he removed all the male goats that were
streaked or spotted, and all the speckled or spotted female goats (all that
had white on them) and all the dark-
colored lambs, and he placed them in
the care of his sons.[f] 36Then he put
a three-day journey between himself
and Jacob, while Jacob continued to
tend the rest of Laban's flocks.
37Jacob, however, took fresh-cut
branches from poplar, almond and
plane trees and made white stripes on
them by peeling the bark and exposing
the white inner wood of the branches.
38Then he placed the peeled branches
in all the watering troughs, so that they
would be directly in front of the flocks
when they came to drink. When the
flocks were in heat and came to drink,
39they mated in front of the branches.
And they bore young that were
streaked or speckled or spotted. 40Ja-
cob set apart the young of the flock by
themselves, but made the rest face the
streaked and dark-colored animals
that belonged to Laban. Thus he made
separate flocks for himself and did
not put them with Laban's animals.
41Whenever the stronger females were
in heat, Jacob would place the
branches in the troughs in front of the
animals so they would mate near
the branches, 42but if the animals were
weak, he would not place them there.
So the weak animals went to Laban
and the strong ones to Jacob. 43In this
way the man grew exceedingly prosperous and came to own large flocks,
and maidservants and menservants,
and camels and donkeys.[g]

Jacob Flees From Laban

31 Jacob heard that Laban's sons were
saying, "Jacob has taken everything
our father owned and has gained all
this wealth from what belonged to our
father." 2And Jacob noticed that Laban's attitude toward him was not
what it had been.
3Then the LORD said to Jacob, "Go
back[h] to the land of your fathers and
to your relatives, and I will be with
you."[i]
4So Jacob sent word to Rachel and
Leah to come out to the fields where
his flocks were. 5He said to them, "I see
that your father's attitude toward me is
not what it was before, but the God of
my father has been with me.[j] 6You
know that I've worked for your father
with all my strength,[k] 7yet your father
has cheated me by changing my wages
ten times.[l] However, God has not al-

30:18 p Ge 49:14 **30:20** q Ge 35:23; 49:13; Mt 4:13 **30:22** r Ge 8:1; 1Sa 1:19-20 s Ge 29:31 **30:23** t ver 6 u Isa 4:1; Lk 1:25 **30:24** v Ge 35:24; 37:2; 39:1; 49:22-26 w Ge 35:17 **30:25** x Ge 24:54 **30:26** y Ge 29:20,30; Hos 12:12 **30:27** z Ge 26:24; 39:3,5 **30:28** a Ge 29:15 **30:29** b Ge 31:6 c Ge 31:38-40 **30:30** d 1Ti 5:8 **30:32** e Ge 31:8,12 **30:35** f Ge 31:1 **30:43** g ver 30; Ge 12:16; 13:2; 24:35; 26:13-14 **31:3** h ver 13; Ge 32:9 i Ge 21:22; 26:3; 28:15 **31:5** j Ge 21:22; 26:3 **31:6** k Ge 30:29 **31:7** l ver 41; Job 19:3

a *18 Issachar* sounds like the Hebrew for *reward.*
b *20 Zebulun* probably means *honor.*
c *24 Joseph* means *may he add.* d *27* Or possibly *have become rich and*

lowed him to harm me.[m] **8**If he said,
'The speckled ones will be your wages,'
then all the flocks gave birth to speckled young; and if he said, 'The streaked
ones will be your wages,'[n] then all the
flocks bore streaked young. **9**So God
has taken away your father's livestock
and has given them to me.[o]
10"In breeding season I once had a
dream in which I looked up and saw
that the male goats mating with the
flock were streaked, speckled or spotted. **11**The angel of God[p] said to me in
the dream, 'Jacob.' I answered, 'Here I
am.' **12**And he said, 'Look up and see
that all the male goats mating with the
flock are streaked, speckled or spotted,
for I have seen all that Laban has been
doing to you.[q] **13**I am the God of Bethel,[r] where you anointed a pillar and
where you made a vow to me. Now
leave this land at once and go back to
your native land.[s]' "
14Then Rachel and Leah replied, "Do
we still have any share in the inheritance of our father's estate? **15**Does he
not regard us as foreigners? Not only
has he sold us, but he has used up what
was paid for us.[t] **16**Surely all the
wealth that God took away from our
father belongs to us and our children.
So do whatever God has told you."
17Then Jacob put his children and
his wives on camels, **18**and he drove all
his livestock ahead of him, along with
all the goods he had accumulated in
Paddan Aram,[a] to go to his father
Isaac[u] in the land of Canaan.[v]
19When Laban had gone to shear his
sheep, Rachel stole her father's household gods.[w] **20**Moreover, Jacob deceived[x] Laban the Aramean by not
telling him he was running away.[y]
21So he fled with all he had, and crossing the River,[b] he headed for the hill
country of Gilead.[z]

Laban Pursues Jacob

22On the third day Laban was told
that Jacob had fled. **23**Taking his relatives with him, he pursued Jacob for
seven days and caught up with him in
the hill country of Gilead. **24**Then God
came to Laban the Aramean in a dream
at night and said to him,[a] "Be careful
not to say anything to Jacob, either
good or bad."[b]
25Jacob had pitched his tent in the
hill country of Gilead when Laban
overtook him, and Laban and his relatives camped there too. **26**Then Laban
said to Jacob, "What have you done?
You've deceived me,[c] and you've carried off my daughters like captives in
war.[d] **27**Why did you run off secretly
and deceive me? Why didn't you tell
me, so I could send you away with joy
and singing to the music of tambourines[e] and harps?[f] **28**You didn't even
let me kiss my grandchildren and my
daughters good-by.[g] You have done
a foolish thing. **29**I have the power to
harm you;[h] but last night the God of
your father[i] said to me, 'Be careful
not to say anything to Jacob, either
good or bad.' **30**Now you have gone off
because you longed to return to your
father's house. But why did you steal
my gods?[j]"
31Jacob answered Laban, "I was
afraid, because I thought you would
take your daughters away from me by
force. **32**But if you find anyone who has
your gods, he shall not live.[k] In the
presence of our relatives, see for yourself whether there is anything of yours
here with me; and if so, take it." Now
Jacob did not know that Rachel had
stolen the gods.
33So Laban went into Jacob's tent
and into Leah's tent and into the tent
of the two maidservants, but he found
nothing. After he came out of Leah's
tent, he entered Rachel's tent. **34**Now
Rachel had taken the household gods
and put them inside her camel's saddle
and was sitting on them. Laban
searched[l] through everything in the
tent but found nothing.
35Rachel said to her father, "Don't be
angry, my lord, that I cannot stand up
in your presence;[m] I'm having my period." So he searched but could not
find the household gods.
36Jacob was angry and took Laban to
task. "What is my crime?" he asked Laban. "What sin have I committed that
you hunt me down? **37**Now that you
have searched through all my goods,
what have you found that belongs to
your household? Put it here in front of
your relatives[n] and mine, and let
them judge between the two of us.
38"I have been with you for twenty
years now. Your sheep and goats have
not miscarried, nor have I eaten rams
from your flocks. **39**I did not bring you
animals torn by wild beasts; I bore the
loss myself. And you demanded payment from me for whatever was stolen
by day or night.[o] **40**This was my situation: The heat consumed me in the
daytime and the cold at night, and
sleep fled from my eyes. **41**It was like
this for the twenty years I was in your
household. I worked for you fourteen
years for your two daughters[p] and six
years for your flocks, and you changed

31:7 [m]ver 52; Ps 37:28; 105:14
31:8 [n]Ge 30:32
31:9 [o]ver 1,16; Ge 30:42
31:11 [p]Ge 16:7; 48:16
31:12 [q]Ex 3:7
31:13 [r]Ge 28:10-22 [s]ver 3; Ge 32:9
31:15 [t]Ge 29:20
31:18 [u]Ge 35:27 [v]Ge 10:19
31:19 [w]ver 30,32, 34-35; Ge 35:2; Jdg 17:5; 1Sa 19:13; Hos 3:4
31:20 [x]Ge 27:36 [y]ver 27
31:21 [z]Ge 37:25
31:24 [a]Ge 20:3; Job 33:15 [b]Ge 24:50
31:26 [c]Ge 27:36 [d]1Sa 30:2-3
31:27 [e]Ex 15:20 [f]Ge 4:21
31:28 [g]ver 55
31:29 [h]ver 7 [i]ver 53
31:30 [j]ver 19; Jdg 18:24
31:32 [k]Ge 44:9
31:34 [l]ver 37; Ge 44:12
31:35 [m]Ex 20:12; Lev 19:3,32
31:37 [n]ver 23
31:39 [o]Ex 22:13
31:41 [p]Ge 29:30

a *18* That is, Northwest Mesopotamia
b *21* That is, the Euphrates

my wages ten times.[q] **42**If the God of
my father,[r] the God of Abraham and
the Fear of Isaac,[s] had not been with
me,[t] you would surely have sent me
away empty-handed. But God has seen
my hardship and the toil of my
hands,[u] and last night he rebuked
you."
43Laban answered Jacob, "The
women are my daughters, the children
are my children, and the flocks are my
flocks. All you see is mine. Yet what can
I do today about these daughters of
mine, or about the children they have
borne? **44**Come now, let's make a covenant,[v] you and I, and let it serve as a
witness between us."[w]
45So Jacob took a stone and set it up
as a pillar.[x] **46**He said to his relatives,
"Gather some stones." So they took
stones and piled them in a heap, and
they ate there by the heap. **47**Laban
called it Jegar Sahadutha,[a] and Jacob
called it Galeed.[b]
48Laban said, "This heap is a witness
between you and me today." That is
why it was called Galeed. **49**It was also
called Mizpah,[c][y] because he said,
"May the LORD keep watch between
you and me when we are away from
each other. **50**If you mistreat my
daughters or if you take any wives besides my daughters, even though no
one is with us, remember that God is a
witness[z] between you and me."

31:49

PROMISE **6**

GOD AS SURVEILLANCE CAMERA

The relationship between Jacob and Laban is tragic—and all too familiar. This verse essentially says, "I can't watch you all the time, so may God watch you when I can't." While many people mistakenly read this statement as a blessing, it is actually filled with skepticism and veiled accusation.

How sad that men's behavior breeds antagonism and mistrust. So many things drive us apart that we have to work overtime to build bridges. Although the suspicion and antagonism between these men had more than enough basis in behavior, the end result was still tragic. How much more tragic are the divisions between us that are based on tradition, race and other things. Only the power of God at work in men who love him can overcome the barriers that separate us. Do something today that actively builds a bridge to someone to whom you may not otherwise relate.

For the next Promise 6 reading go to page 62.

51Laban also said to Jacob, "Here is
this heap, and here is this pillar[a] I
have set up between you and me.
52This heap is a witness, and this pillar
is a witness,[b] that I will not go past
this heap to your side to harm you and
that you will not go past this heap and
pillar to my side to harm me.[c] **53**May
the God of Abraham[d] and the God of
Nahor, the God of their father, judge
between us."[e]
So Jacob took an oath[f] in the name
of the Fear of his father Isaac.[g] **54**He
offered a sacrifice there in the hill
country and invited his relatives to a
meal. After they had eaten, they spent
the night there.
55Early the next morning Laban
kissed his grandchildren and his
daughters[h] and blessed them. Then
he left and returned home.[i]

Jacob Prepares to Meet Esau

32 Jacob also went on his way, and
the angels of God[j] met him.
2When Jacob saw them, he said, "This
is the camp of God!"[k] So he named
that place Mahanaim.[d][l]
3Jacob sent messengers ahead of
him to his brother Esau[m] in the land of
Seir, the country of Edom.[n] **4**He instructed them: "This is what you are to
say to my master Esau: 'Your servant
Jacob says, I have been staying with
Laban and have remained there till
now. **5**I have cattle and donkeys, sheep
and goats, menservants and maidservants.[o] Now I am sending this message to my lord, that I may find favor in
your eyes.[p]' "
6When the messengers returned to
Jacob, they said, "We went to your
brother Esau, and now he is coming to
meet you, and four hundred men are
with him."[q]
7In great fear[r] and distress Jacob
divided the people who were with him
into two groups,[e] and the flocks and
herds and camels as well. **8**He thought,
"If Esau comes and attacks one
group,[f] the group[f] that is left may
escape."
9Then Jacob prayed, "O God of my
father Abraham, God of my father
Isaac,[s] O LORD, who said to me, 'Go
back to your country and your relatives, and I will make you prosper,'[t]
10I am unworthy of all the kindness
and faithfulness[u] you have shown
your servant. I had only my staff when

31:41 [q]ver 7
31:42 [r]ver 5; Ex 3:15; 1Ch 12:17 [s]ver 53; Isa 8:13 [t]Ps 124:1-2 [u]Ge 29:32
31:44 [v]Ge 21:27; 26:28 [w]Jos 24:27
31:45 [x]Ge 28:18
31:49 [y]Jdg 11:29; 1Sa 7:5-6
31:50 [z]Jer 29:23; 42:5
31:51 [a]Ge 28:18
31:52 [b]Ge 21:30 [c]ver 7; Ge 26:29
31:53 [d]Ge 28:13 [e]Ge 16:5 [f]Ge 21:23,27 [g]ver 42
31:55 [h]ver 28 [i]Ge 18:33; 30:25
32:1 [j]Ge 16:11; 2Ki 6:16-17; Ps 34:7; 91:11; Heb 1:14
32:2 [k]Ge 28:17 [l]2Sa 2:8,29
32:3 [m]Ge 27:41-42 [n]Ge 25:30; 36:8,9
32:5 [o]Ge 12:16; 30:43 [p]Ge 33:8,10,15
32:6 [q]Ge 33:1
32:7 [r]ver 11
32:9 [s]Ge 28:13; 31:42 [t]Ge 31:13
32:10 [u]Ge 24:27

[a] *47* The Aramaic *Jegar Sahadutha* means *witness heap.* [b] *47* The Hebrew *Galeed* means *witness heap.* [c] *49* *Mizpah* means *watchtower.* [d] *2* *Mahanaim* means *two camps.* [e] *7* Or *camps*; also in verse 10 [f] *8* Or *camp*

I crossed this Jordan, but now I have become two groups. **11**Save me, I pray, from the hand of my brother Esau, for I am afraid he will come and attack me,[v] and also the mothers with their children.[w] **12**But you have said, 'I will surely make you prosper and will make your descendants like the sand[x] of the sea, which cannot be counted.[y]' "

13He spent the night there, and from what he had with him he selected a gift[z] for his brother Esau: **14**two hundred female goats and twenty male goats, two hundred ewes and twenty rams, **15**thirty female camels with their young, forty cows and ten bulls, and twenty female donkeys and ten male donkeys. **16**He put them in the care of his servants, each herd by itself, and said to his servants, "Go ahead of me, and keep some space between the herds."

17He instructed the one in the lead: "When my brother Esau meets you and asks, 'To whom do you belong, and where are you going, and who owns all these animals in front of you?' **18**then you are to say, 'They belong to your servant[a] Jacob. They are a gift sent to my lord Esau, and he is coming behind us.' "

19He also instructed the second, the third and all the others who followed the herds: "You are to say the same thing to Esau when you meet him. **20**And be sure to say, 'Your servant Jacob is coming behind us.' " For he thought, "I will pacify him with these gifts I am sending on ahead; later, when I see him, perhaps he will receive me."[b] **21**So Jacob's gifts went on ahead of him, but he himself spent the night in the camp.

Jacob Wrestles With God

22That night Jacob got up and took his two wives, his two maidservants and his eleven sons and crossed the ford of the Jabbok.[c] **23**After he had sent them across the stream, he sent over all his possessions. **24**So Jacob was left alone, and a man[d] wrestled with him till daybreak. **25**When the man saw that he could not overpower him, he touched the socket of Jacob's hip[e] so that his hip was wrenched as he wrestled with the man. **26**Then the man said, "Let me go, for it is daybreak."

But Jacob replied, "I will not let you go unless you bless me."[f]

27The man asked him, "What is your name?"

"Jacob," he answered.

28Then the man said, "Your name will no longer be Jacob, but Israel,[a][g] because you have struggled with God and with men and have overcome."

29Jacob said, "Please tell me your name."[h]

But he replied, "Why do you ask my name?"[i] Then he blessed[j] him there.

30So Jacob called the place Peniel,[b] saying, "It is because I saw God face to face,[k] and yet my life was spared."

31The sun rose above him as he passed Peniel,[c] and he was limping because of his hip. **32**Therefore to this day the Israelites do not eat the tendon attached to the socket of the hip, because the socket of Jacob's hip was touched near the tendon.

Jacob Meets Esau

33 Jacob looked up and there was Esau, coming with his four hundred men;[l] so he divided the children among Leah, Rachel and the two maidservants. **2**He put the maidservants and their children in front, Leah and her children next, and Rachel and Joseph in the rear. **3**He himself went on ahead and bowed down to the ground[m] seven times as he approached his brother.

4But Esau ran to meet Jacob and embraced him; he threw his arms around his neck and kissed him. And they wept.[n] **5**Then Esau looked up and saw the women and children. "Who are these with you?" he asked.

Jacob answered, "They are the children God has graciously given your servant.[o]"

6Then the maidservants and their children approached and bowed down. **7**Next, Leah and her children came and bowed down. Last of all came Joseph and Rachel, and they too bowed down.

8Esau asked, "What do you mean by all these droves I met?"[p]

"To find favor in your eyes, my lord,"[q] he said.

9But Esau said, "I already have plenty, my brother. Keep what you have for yourself."

10"No, please!" said Jacob. "If I have found favor in your eyes, accept this gift from me. For to see your face is like seeing the face of God,[r] now that you have received me favorably.[s] **11**Please accept the present[t] that was brought to you, for God has been gracious to me[u] and I have all I need." And because Jacob insisted, Esau accepted it.

12Then Esau said, "Let us be on our way; I'll accompany you."

4 →PG. 60

13But Jacob said to him, "My lord

32:11 [v]Ps 59:2 [w]Ge 27:41
32:12 [x]Ge 22:17 [y]Ge 28:13-15; Hos 1:10; Ro 9:27
32:13 [z]Ge 43:11,15, 25,26; Pr 18:16
32:18 [a]Ge 18:3
32:20 [b]Ge 33:10; Pr 21:14
32:22 [c]Dt 2:37; 3:16; Jos 12:2
32:24 [d]Ge 18:2
32:25 [e]ver 32
32:26 [f]Hos 12:4
32:28 [g]Ge 17:5; 35:10; 1Ki 18:31
32:29 [h]Jdg 13:17 [i]Jdg 13:18 [j]Ge 35:9
32:30 [k]Ge 16:13; Ex 24:11; Nu 12:8; Jdg 6:22; 13:22
33:1 [l]Ge 32:6
33:3 [m]Ge 18:2; 42:6
33:4 [n]Ge 45:14-15
33:5 [o]Ge 48:9; Ps 127:3; Isa 8:18
33:8 [p]Ge 32:14-16 [q]Ge 24:9; 32:5
33:10 [r]Ge 16:13 [s]Ge 32:20
33:11 [t]1Sa 25:27 [u]Ge 30:43

a *28 Israel* means *he struggles with God.*
b *30 Peniel* means *face of God.*
c *31* Hebrew *Penuel,* a variant of *Peniel*

knows that the children are tender and that I must care for the ewes and cows that are nursing their young. If they are driven hard just one day, all the animals will die. 14So let my lord go on ahead of his servant, while I move along slowly at the pace of the droves before me and that of the children, until I come to my lord in Seir.[v]"

15Esau said, "Then let me leave some of my men with you."

"But why do that?" Jacob asked. "Just let me find favor in the eyes of my lord."[w]

16So that day Esau started on his way back to Seir. 17Jacob, however, went to Succoth,[x] where he built a place for himself and made shelters for his livestock. That is why the place is called Succoth.[a]

18After Jacob came from Paddan Aram,[b][y] he arrived safely at the[c] city of Shechem[z] in Canaan and camped within sight of the city. 19For a hundred pieces of silver,[d] he bought from the sons of Hamor, the father of Shechem,[a] the plot of ground[b] where he pitched his tent. 20There he set up an altar and called it El Elohe Israel.[e]

Dinah and the Shechemites

34 Now Dinah,[c] the daughter Leah had borne to Jacob, went out to visit the women of the land. 2When Shechem son of Hamor the Hivite, the ruler of that area, saw her, he took her and violated her. 3His heart was drawn to Dinah daughter of Jacob, and he loved the girl and spoke tenderly to her. 4And Shechem said to his father Hamor, "Get me this girl as my wife."

5When Jacob heard that his daughter Dinah had been defiled, his sons were in the fields with his livestock; so he kept quiet about it until they came home.

6Then Shechem's father Hamor went out to talk with Jacob.[d] 7Now Jacob's sons had come in from the fields as soon as they heard what had happened. They were filled with grief and fury, because Shechem had done a disgraceful thing in[f] Israel[e] by lying with Jacob's daughter—a thing that should not be done.[f]

8But Hamor said to them, "My son Shechem has his heart set on your daughter. Please give her to him as his wife. 9Intermarry with us; give us your daughters and take our daughters for yourselves. 10You can settle among us;[g] the land is open to you.[h] Live in it, trade[g] in it,[i] and acquire property in it."

11Then Shechem said to Dinah's father and brothers, "Let me find favor in your eyes, and I will give you whatever you ask. 12Make the price for the bride[j] and the gift I am to bring as great as you like, and I'll pay whatever you ask me. Only give me the girl as my wife."

13Because their sister Dinah had been defiled, Jacob's sons replied deceitfully as they spoke to Shechem and his father Hamor. 14They said to them, "We can't do such a thing; we can't give our sister to a man who is not circumcised.[k] That would be a disgrace to us. 15We will give our consent to you on one condition only: that you become like us by circumcising all your males.[l] 16Then we will give you our daughters and take your daughters for ourselves. We'll settle among you and become one people with you. 17But if you will not agree to be circumcised, we'll take our sister[h] and go."

18Their proposal seemed good to Hamor and his son Shechem. 19The young man, who was the most honored of all his father's household, lost no time in doing what they said, because he was delighted with Jacob's daughter.[m] 20So Hamor and his son Shechem went to the gate of their city[n] to speak to their fellow townsmen. 21"These men are friendly toward us," they said. "Let them live in our land and trade in it; the land has plenty of room for them. We can marry their daughters and they can marry ours. 22But the men will consent to live with us as one people only on the condition that our males be circumcised, as they themselves are. 23Won't their livestock, their property and all their other animals become ours? So let us give our consent to them, and they will settle among us."

24All the men who went out of the city gate[o] agreed with Hamor and his son Shechem, and every male in the city was circumcised.

25Three days later, while all of them were still in pain, two of Jacob's sons, Simeon and Levi, Dinah's brothers, took their swords[p] and attacked the unsuspecting city, killing every male.[q] 26They put Hamor and his son Shechem to the sword and took Dinah from Shechem's house and left. 27The sons of Jacob came upon the dead

33:14 [v]Ge 32:3
33:15 [w]Ge 34:11; 47:25; Ru 2:13
33:17 [x]Jos 13:27; Jdg 8:5,6,8,14, 14-16,15,16; Ps 60:6
33:18 [y]Ge 25:20; 28:2 [z]Jos 24:1; Jdg 9:1
33:19 [a]Jos 24:32 [b]Jn 4:5
34:1 [c]Ge 30:21
34:6 [d]Jdg 14:2-5
34:7 [e]Dt 22:21; Jdg 20:6; 2Sa 13:12 [f]Jos 7:15
34:10 [g]Ge 47:6,27 [h]Ge 13:9; 20:15 [i]Ge 42:34
34:12 [j]Ex 22:16; Dt 22:29; 1Sa 18:25
34:14 [k]Ge 17:14; Jdg 14:3
34:15 [l]Ex 12:48
34:19 [m]ver 3
34:20 [n]Ru 4:1; 2Sa 15:2
34:24 [o]Ge 23:10
34:25 [p]Ge 49:5 [q]Ge 49:7

[a] *17* *Succoth* means *shelters.* [b] *18* That is, Northwest Mesopotamia [c] *18* Or *arrived at Shalem, a* [d] *19* Hebrew *hundred kesitahs*; a kesitah was a unit of money of unknown weight and value. [e] *20* *El Elohe Israel* can mean *God, the God of Israel* or *mighty is the God of Israel.* [f] *7* Or *against* [g] *10* Or *move about freely*; also in verse 21 [h] *17* Hebrew *daughter*

bodies and looted the city where[a] their sister had been defiled. 28 They seized their flocks and herds and donkeys and everything else of theirs in the city and out in the fields. 29 They carried off all their wealth and all their women and children, taking as plunder everything in the houses.

30 Then Jacob said to Simeon and Levi, "You have brought trouble on me by making me a stench[r] to the Canaanites and Perizzites, the people living in this land.[s] We are few in number,[t] and if they join forces against me and attack me, I and my household will be destroyed."

31 But they replied, "Should he have treated our sister like a prostitute?"

Jacob Returns to Bethel

1 →PG. 82

35 Then God said to Jacob, "Go up to Bethel[u] and settle there, and build an altar there to God, who appeared to you when you were fleeing from your brother Esau."[v]

2 So Jacob said to his household[w] and to all who were with him, "Get rid of the foreign gods[x] you have with you, and purify yourselves and change your clothes.[y] 3 Then come, let us go up to Bethel, where I will build an altar to God, who answered me in the day of my distress[z] and who has been with me wherever I have gone.[a]" 4 So they gave Jacob all the foreign gods they had and the rings in their ears, and Jacob buried them under the oak at Shechem.[b] 5 Then they set out, and the terror of God[c] fell upon the towns all around them so that no one pursued them.

6 Jacob and all the people with him came to Luz[d] (that is, Bethel) in the land of Canaan. 7 There he built an altar, and he called the place El Bethel,[b] because it was there that God revealed himself to him[e] when he was fleeing from his brother.

8 Now Deborah, Rebekah's nurse,[f] died and was buried under the oak below Bethel. So it was named Allon Bacuth.[c]

9 After Jacob returned from Paddan Aram,[d] God appeared to him again and blessed him.[g] 10 God said to him, "Your name is Jacob,[e] but you will no longer be called Jacob; your name will be Israel.[f]"[h] So he named him Israel.

11 And God said to him, "I am God Almighty[g];[i] be fruitful and increase in number. A nation[j] and a community of nations will come from you, and kings will come from your body.[k] 12 The land I gave to Abraham and Isaac I also give to you, and I will give this land to your descendants after you.[l]"[m] 13 Then God went up from him[n] at the place where he had talked with him.

14 Jacob set up a stone pillar at the place where God had talked with him, and he poured out a drink offering on it; he also poured oil on it.[o] 15 Jacob called the place where God had talked with him Bethel.[h][p]

The Deaths of Rachel and Isaac

16 Then they moved on from Bethel. While they were still some distance from Ephrath, Rachel began to give birth and had great difficulty. 17 And as she was having great difficulty in childbirth, the midwife said to her, "Don't be afraid, for you have another son."[q] 18 As she breathed her last—for she was dying—she named her son Ben-Oni.[i] But his father named him Benjamin.[j]

19 So Rachel died and was buried on the way to Ephrath (that is, Bethlehem[r]). 20 Over her tomb Jacob set up a pillar, and to this day that pillar marks Rachel's tomb.[s]

21 Israel moved on again and pitched his tent beyond Migdal Eder. 22 While Israel was living in that region, Reuben went in and slept with his father's concubine[t] Bilhah,[u] and Israel heard of it.

Jacob had twelve sons:

23 The sons of Leah:
Reuben the firstborn[v] of Jacob,
Simeon, Levi, Judah,[w] Issachar and Zebulun.[x]

24 The sons of Rachel:
Joseph[y] and Benjamin.[z]

25 The sons of Rachel's maidservant Bilhah:
Dan and Naphtali.[a]

26 The sons of Leah's maidservant Zilpah:
Gad[b] and Asher.[c]

These were the sons of Jacob, who were born to him in Paddan Aram.

27 Jacob came home to his father Isaac in Mamre,[d] near Kiriath Arba[e] (that is, Hebron), where Abraham and Isaac had stayed. 28 Isaac lived a hundred and eighty years.[f] 29 Then he breathed his last and died and was

34:30 [r]Ex 5:21; 1Sa 13:4 [s]Ge 13:7 [t]Ge 46:27; 1Ch 16:19; Ps 105:12
35:1 [u]Ge 28:19 [v]Ge 27:43
35:2 [w]Ge 18:19; Jos 24:15 [x]Ge 31:19 [y]Ex 19:10,14
35:3 [z]Ge 32:7 [a]Ge 28:15, 20-22; 31:3,42
35:4 [b]Jos 24:25-26
35:5 [c]Ex 15:16; 23:27; Jos 2:9
35:6 [d]Ge 28:19; 48:3
35:7 [e]Ge 28:13
35:8 [f]Ge 24:59
35:9 [g]Ge 32:29
35:10 [h]Ge 17:5
35:11 [i]Ge 17:1; Ex 6:3 [j]Ge 28:3; 48:4 [k]Ge 17:6
35:12 [l]Ge 13:15; 28:13 [m]Ge 12:7; 26:3
35:13 [n]Ge 17:22
35:14 [o]Ge 28:18
35:15 [p]Ge 28:19
35:17 [q]Ge 30:24
35:19 [r]Ge 48:7; Ru 1:1,19; Mic 5:2; Mt 2:16
35:20 [s]1Sa 10:2
35:22 [t]Ge 49:4; 1Ch 5:1 [u]Ge 29:29; Lev 18:8
35:23 [v]Ge 46:8 [w]Ge 29:35 [x]Ge 30:20
35:24 [y]Ge 30:24 [z]ver 18
35:25 [a]Ge 30:8
35:26 [b]Ge 30:11 [c]Ge 30:13
35:27 [d]Ge 13:18; 18:1 [e]Jos 14:15
35:28 [f]Ge 25:7,20

[a]27 Or *because* [b]7 *El Bethel* means *God of Bethel.* [c]8 *Allon Bacuth* means *oak of weeping.* [d]9 That is, Northwest Mesopotamia; also in verse 26 [e]10 *Jacob* means *he grasps the heel* (figuratively, *he deceives*). [f]10 *Israel* means *he struggles with God.* [g]11 Hebrew *El-Shaddai* [h]15 *Bethel* means *house of God.* [i]18 *Ben-Oni* means *son of my trouble.* [j]18 *Benjamin* means *son of my right hand.*

gathered to his people,[g] old and full of years.[h] And his sons Esau and Jacob buried him.[i]

Esau's Descendants

36 This is the account of Esau (that is, Edom).[j]

2Esau took his wives from the women of Canaan:[k] Adah daughter of Elon the Hittite,[l] and Oholibamah daughter of Anah[m] and granddaughter of Zibeon the Hivite— 3also Basemath daughter of Ishmael and sister of Nebaioth.

4Adah bore Eliphaz to Esau, Basemath bore Reuel,[n] 5and Oholibamah bore Jeush, Jalam and Korah. These were the sons of Esau, who were born to him in Canaan.

6Esau took his wives and sons and daughters and all the members of his household, as well as his livestock and all his other animals and all the goods he had acquired in Canaan,[o] and moved to a land some distance from his brother Jacob. 7Their possessions were too great for them to remain together; the land where they were staying could not support them both because of their livestock.[p] 8So Esau[q] (that is, Edom) settled in the hill country of Seir.[r]

9This is the account of Esau the father of the Edomites in the hill country of Seir.

10These are the names of Esau's sons:
Eliphaz, the son of Esau's wife Adah, and Reuel, the son of Esau's wife Basemath.
11The sons of Eliphaz:[s]
Teman,[t] Omar, Zepho, Gatam and Kenaz.
12Esau's son Eliphaz also had a concubine named Timna, who bore him Amalek.[u] These were grandsons of Esau's wife Adah.[v]
13The sons of Reuel:
Nahath, Zerah, Shammah and Mizzah. These were grandsons of Esau's wife Basemath.
14The sons of Esau's wife Oholibamah daughter of Anah and granddaughter of Zibeon, whom she bore to Esau:
Jeush, Jalam and Korah.

15These were the chiefs[w] among Esau's descendants:

The sons of Eliphaz the firstborn of Esau:
Chiefs Teman,[x] Omar, Zepho, Kenaz, 16Korah,[a] Gatam and Amalek. These were the chiefs descended from Eliphaz in Edom; they were grandsons of Adah.[y]
17The sons of Esau's son Reuel:[z]
Chiefs Nahath, Zerah, Shammah and Mizzah. These were the chiefs descended from Reuel in Edom; they were grandsons of Esau's wife Basemath.
18The sons of Esau's wife Oholibamah:
Chiefs Jeush, Jalam and Korah. These were the chiefs descended from Esau's wife Oholibamah daughter of Anah.

19These were the sons of Esau (that is, Edom),[a] and these were their chiefs.

20These were the sons of Seir the Horite,[b] who were living in the region:
Lotan, Shobal, Zibeon, Anah, 21Dishon, Ezer and Dishan. These sons of Seir in Edom were Horite chiefs.
22The sons of Lotan:
Hori and Homam.[b] Timna was Lotan's sister.
23The sons of Shobal:
Alvan, Manahath, Ebal, Shepho and Onam.
24The sons of Zibeon:
Aiah and Anah. This is the Anah who discovered the hot springs[c] in the desert while he was grazing the donkeys of his father Zibeon.
25The children of Anah:
Dishon and Oholibamah daughter of Anah.
26The sons of Dishon[d]:
Hemdan, Eshban, Ithran and Keran.
27The sons of Ezer:
Bilhan, Zaavan and Akan.
28The sons of Dishan:
Uz and Aran.
29These were the Horite chiefs:
Lotan, Shobal, Zibeon, Anah, 30Dishon, Ezer and Dishan. These were the Horite chiefs, according to their divisions, in the land of Seir.

35:29 [g]Ge 25:8; 49:33 [h]Ge 15:15 [i]Ge 25:9
36:1 [j]Ge 25:30
36:2 [k]Ge 28:8-9 [l]Ge 26:34 [m]ver 25
36:4 [n]1Ch 1:35
36:6 [o]Ge 12:5
36:7 [p]Ge 13:6; 17:8; 28:4
36:8 [q]Dt 2:4 [r]Ge 32:3
36:11 [s]ver 15-16; Job 2:11 [t]Am 1:12; Hab 3:3
36:12 [u]Ex 17:8,16; Nu 24:20; 1Sa 15:2 [v]ver 16
36:15 [w]Ex 15:15 [x]Job 2:11
36:16 [y]ver 12
36:17 [z]1Ch 1:37
36:19 [a]Ge 25:30
36:20 [b]Ge 14:6; Dt 2:12,22; 1Ch 1:38

a *16* Masoretic Text; Samaritan Pentateuch (see also Gen. 36:11 and 1 Chron. 1:36) does not have *Korah.* **b** *22* Hebrew *Hemam,* a variant of *Homam* (see 1 Chron. 1:39) **c** *24* Vulgate; Syriac *discovered water;* the meaning of the Hebrew for this word is uncertain.
d *26* Hebrew *Dishan,* a variant of *Dishon*

The Rulers of Edom

31These were the kings who reigned
in Edom before any Israelite king[c]
reigned[a]:

32Bela son of Beor became king
of Edom. His city was named
Dinhabah.

33When Bela died, Jobab son of Zerah from Bozrah[d] succeeded
him as king.

34When Jobab died, Husham from
the land of the Temanites[e]
succeeded him as king.

35When Husham died, Hadad son
of Bedad, who defeated Midian in the country of Moab,[f]
succeeded him as king. His
city was named Avith.

36When Hadad died, Samlah from
Masrekah succeeded him as
king.

37When Samlah died, Shaul from
Rehoboth on the river[b] succeeded him as king.

38When Shaul died, Baal-Hanan
son of Acbor succeeded him as
king.

39When Baal-Hanan son of Acbor
died, Hadad[c] succeeded him
as king. His city was named
Pau, and his wife's name was
Mehetabel daughter of Ma-
tred, the daughter of Me-
Zahab.

40These were the chiefs descended
from Esau, by name, according to their
clans and regions:

Timna, Alvah, Jetheth, 41Ohol-
ibamah, Elah, Pinon, 42Kenaz,
Teman, Mibzar, 43Magdiel and
Iram. These were the chiefs of
Edom, according to their settlements in the land they occupied.

This was Esau the father of the
Edomites.

Joseph's Dreams

37 Jacob lived in the land where his
father had stayed,[g] the land of Canaan.[h]

2This is the account of Jacob.

Joseph, a young man of seventeen,
was tending the flocks[i] with his
brothers, the sons of Bilhah[j] and the
sons of Zilpah,[k] his father's wives, and
he brought their father a bad report[l]
about them.

3Now Israel loved Joseph more than
any of his other sons,[m] because he had
been born to him in his old age;[n] and
he made a richly ornamented[d] robe[o]
for him. 4When his brothers saw that
their father loved him more than any of
them, they hated him[p] and could not
speak a kind word to him.

5Joseph had a dream,[q] and when he
told it to his brothers, they hated him
all the more. 6He said to them, "Listen
to this dream I had: 7We were binding
sheaves of grain out in the field when
suddenly my sheaf rose and stood upright, while your sheaves gathered
around mine and bowed down to it."[r]

8His brothers said to him, "Do you
intend to reign over us? Will you actually rule us?"[s] And they hated him all
the more because of his dream and
what he had said.

9Then he had another dream, and he
told it to his brothers. "Listen," he said,
"I had another dream, and this time
the sun and moon and eleven stars
were bowing down to me."

10When he told his father as well as
his brothers,[t] his father rebuked him
and said, "What is this dream you had?
Will your mother and I and your brothers actually come and bow down to the
ground before you?"[u] 11His brothers
were jealous of him,[v] but his father
kept the matter in mind.[w]

Joseph Sold by His Brothers

12Now his brothers had gone to
graze their father's flocks near Shechem, 13and Israel said to Joseph, "As
you know, your brothers are grazing
the flocks near Shechem. Come, I am
going to send you to them."

"Very well," he replied.

14So he said to him, "Go and see if all
is well with your brothers and with the
flocks, and bring word back to me."
Then he sent him off from the Valley of
Hebron.[x]

When Joseph arrived at Shechem,
15a man found him wandering around
in the fields and asked him, "What are
you looking for?"

16He replied, "I'm looking for my
brothers. Can you tell me where they
are grazing their flocks?"

17"They have moved on from here,"
the man answered. "I heard them say,
'Let's go to Dothan.'"[y]

So Joseph went after his brothers
and found them near Dothan. 18But
they saw him in the distance, and before he reached them, they plotted to
kill him.[z]

36:31 [c]Ge 17:6; 1Ch 1:43
36:33 [d]Jer 49:13,22
36:34 [e]Eze 25:13
36:35 [f]Ge 19:37; Nu 22:1; Dt 1:5; Ru 1:1,6
37:1 [g]Ge 17:8 [h]Ge 10:19
37:2 [i]Ps 78:71 [j]Ge 35:25 [k]Ge 35:26 [l]1Sa 2:24
37:3 [m]Ge 25:28 [n]Ge 44:20 [o]2Sa 13:18-19
37:4 [p]Ge 27:41; 49:22-23; Ac 7:9
37:5 [q]Ge 20:3; 28:12
37:7 [r]Ge 42:6,9; 43:26,28; 44:14; 50:18
37:8 [s]Ge 49:26
37:10 [t]ver 5 [u]ver 7; Ge 27:29
37:11 [v]Ac 7:9 [w]Lk 2:19,51
37:14 [x]Ge 13:18; 35:27
37:17 [y]2Ki 6:13
37:18 [z]1Sa 19:1; Mk 14:1; Ac 23:12

[a]*31* Or *before an Israelite king reigned over them*
[b]*37* Possibly the Euphrates
[c]*39* Many manuscripts of the Masoretic Text, Samaritan Pentateuch and Syriac (see also 1 Chron. 1:50); most manuscripts of the Masoretic Text *Hadar*
[d]*3* The meaning of the Hebrew for *richly ornamented* is uncertain; also in verses 23 and 32.

19“Here comes that dreamer!” they
said to each other. 20“Come now, let’s
kill him and throw him into one of
these cisterns[a] and say that a ferocious animal devoured him. Then we’ll
see what comes of his dreams.”[b]

21When Reuben heard this, he tried
to rescue him from their hands. “Let’s
not take his life,” he said.[c] 22“Don’t
shed any blood. Throw him into this
cistern here in the desert, but don’t lay
a hand on him.” Reuben said this to
rescue him from them and take him
back to his father.

23So when Joseph came to his brothers, they stripped him of his robe—the
richly ornamented robe he was
wearing— 24and they took him and
threw him into the cistern.[d] Now the
cistern was empty; there was no water
in it.

25As they sat down to eat their meal,
they looked up and saw a caravan of
Ishmaelites coming from Gilead. Their
camels were loaded with spices, balm
and myrrh,[e] and they were on their
way to take them down to Egypt.[f]

26Judah said to his brothers, “What
will we gain if we kill our brother and
cover up his blood?[g] 27Come, let’s sell
him to the Ishmaelites and not lay our
hands on him; after all, he is our brother,[h] our own flesh and blood.” His
brothers agreed.

28So when the Midianite[i] merchants came by, his brothers pulled Joseph up out of the cistern and sold him
for twenty shekels[a] of silver to the Ishmaelites, who took him to Egypt.[j]

29When Reuben returned to the cistern and saw that Joseph was not there,
he tore his clothes.[k] 30He went back to
his brothers and said, “The boy isn’t
there! Where can I turn now?”[l]

31Then they got Joseph’s robe,[m]
slaughtered a goat and dipped the robe
in the blood. 32They took the ornamented robe back to their father and
said, “We found this. Examine it to see
whether it is your son’s robe.”

33He recognized it and said, “It is my
son’s robe! Some ferocious animal[n]
has devoured him. Joseph has surely
been torn to pieces.”[o]

34Then Jacob tore his clothes,[p] put
on sackcloth[q] and mourned for his
son many days.[r] 35All his sons and
daughters came to comfort him, but he
refused to be comforted. “No,” he said,
“in mourning will I go down to the
grave[b][s] to my son.” So his father
wept for him.

36Meanwhile, the Midianites[c] sold
Joseph in Egypt to Potiphar, one of
Pharaoh’s officials, the captain of the
guard.[t]

Judah and Tamar

38 At that time, Judah left his brothers
and went down to stay with a man
of Adullam named Hirah. 2There Judah
met the daughter of a Canaanite man
named Shua.[u] He married her and lay
with her; 3she became pregnant and
gave birth to a son, who was named
Er.[v] 4She conceived again and gave
birth to a son and named him Onan.
5She gave birth to still another son and
named him Shelah. It was at Kezib that
she gave birth to him.

6Judah got a wife for Er, his firstborn,
and her name was Tamar. 7But Er, Judah’s firstborn, was wicked in the
LORD’s sight; so the LORD put him to
death.[w]

8Then Judah said to Onan, “Lie with
your brother’s wife and fulfill your duty
to her as a brother-in-law to produce
offspring for your brother.”[x] 9But
Onan knew that the offspring would
not be his; so whenever he lay with his
brother’s wife, he spilled his semen on
the ground to keep from producing offspring for his brother. 10What he did
was wicked in the LORD’s sight; so he
put him to death also.[y]

11Judah then said to his daughter-
in-law Tamar, “Live as a widow in your
father’s house until my son Shelah
grows up.”[z] For he thought, “He may
die too, just like his brothers.” So Tamar went to live in her father’s house.

12After a long time Judah’s wife, the
daughter of Shua, died. When Judah
had recovered from his grief, he went
up to Timnah,[a] to the men who were
shearing his sheep, and his friend Hirah the Adullamite went with him.

13When Tamar was told, “Your
father-in-law is on his way to Timnah
to shear his sheep,” 14she took off her
widow’s clothes, covered herself with a
veil to disguise herself, and then sat
down at the entrance to Enaim, which
is on the road to Timnah. For she saw
that, though Shelah[b] had now grown
up, she had not been given to him as
his wife.

15When Judah saw her, he thought
she was a prostitute, for she had covered her face. 16Not realizing that she
was his daughter-in-law,[c] he went
over to her by the roadside and said,
“Come now, let me sleep with you.”

“And what will you give me to sleep
with you?” she asked.

17“I’ll send you a young goat[d] from
my flock,” he said.

37:20 [a]Jer 38:6,9 [b]Ge 50:20
37:21 [c]Ge 42:22
37:24 [d]Jer 41:7
37:25 [e]Ge 43:11 [f]ver 28
37:26 [g]ver 20; Ge 4:10
37:27 [h]Ge 42:21
37:28 [i]Ge 25:2; Jdg 6:1-3 [j]Ge 45:4-5; Ps 105:17; Ac 7:9
37:29 [k]ver 34; Ge 44:13; Job 1:20
37:30 [l]ver 22; Ge 42:13,36
37:31 [m]ver 3,23
37:33 [n]ver 20 [o]Ge 44:20,28
37:34 [p]ver 29 [q]2Sa 3:31 [r]Ge 50:3,10,11
37:35 [s]Ge 42:38; 44:22,29,31
37:36 [t]Ge 39:1
38:2 [u]1Ch 2:3
38:3 [v]ver 6; Ge 46:12; Nu 26:19
38:7 [w]ver 10; Ge 46:12; 1Ch 2:3
38:8 [x]Dt 25:5-6; Mt 22:24-28
38:10 [y]Ge 46:12; Dt 25:7-10
38:11 [z]Ru 1:13
38:12 [a]ver 14; Jos 15:10,57
38:14 [b]ver 11
38:16 [c]Lev 18:15; 20:12
38:17 [d]Eze 16:33

[a] *28* That is, about 8 ounces (about 0.2 kilogram)
[b] *35* Hebrew *Sheol*
[c] *36* Samaritan Pentateuch, Septuagint, Vulgate and Syriac (see also verse 28); Masoretic Text *Medanites*

"Will you give me something as a pledge[e] until you send it?" she asked.

18 He said, "What pledge should I give you?"

"Your seal[f] and its cord, and the staff in your hand," she answered. So he gave them to her and slept with her, and she became pregnant by him. 19 After she left, she took off her veil and put on her widow's clothes[g] again.

20 Meanwhile Judah sent the young goat by his friend the Adullamite in order to get his pledge back from the woman, but he did not find her. 21 He asked the men who lived there, "Where is the shrine prostitute[h] who was beside the road at Enaim?"

"There hasn't been any shrine prostitute here," they said.

22 So he went back to Judah and said, "I didn't find her. Besides, the men who lived there said, 'There hasn't been any shrine prostitute here.' "

23 Then Judah said, "Let her keep what she has, or we will become a laughingstock. After all, I did send her this young goat, but you didn't find her."

24 About three months later Judah was told, "Your daughter-in-law Tamar is guilty of prostitution, and as a result she is now pregnant."

Judah said, "Bring her out and have her burned to death!"[i]

25 As she was being brought out, she sent a message to her father-in-law. "I am pregnant by the man who owns these," she said. And she added, "See if you recognize whose seal and cord and staff these are."[j]

26 Judah recognized them and said, "She is more righteous than I,[k] since I wouldn't give her to my son Shelah.[l]" And he did not sleep with her again.

27 When the time came for her to give birth, there were twin boys in her womb.[m] 28 As she was giving birth, one of them put out his hand; so the midwife took a scarlet thread and tied it on his wrist and said, "This one came out first." 29 But when he drew back his hand, his brother came out, and she said, "So this is how you have broken out!" And he was named Perez.[a][n] 30 Then his brother, who had the scarlet thread on his wrist, came out and he was given the name Zerah.[b][o]

Joseph and Potiphar's Wife

39 Now Joseph had been taken down to Egypt. Potiphar, an Egyptian who was one of Pharaoh's officials, the captain of the guard,[p] bought him from the Ishmaelites who had taken him there.[q]

2 The LORD was with Joseph[r] and he prospered, and he lived in the house of his Egyptian master. 3 When his master saw that the LORD was with him[s] and that the LORD gave him success in everything he did,[t] 4 Joseph found favor in his eyes and became his attendant. Potiphar put him in charge of his household, and he entrusted to his care everything he owned.[u] 5 From the time he put him in charge of his household and of all that he owned, the LORD blessed the household of the Egyptian because of Joseph.[v] The blessing of the LORD was on everything Potiphar had, both in the house and in the field. 6 So he left in Joseph's care everything he had; with Joseph in charge, he did not concern himself with anything except the food he ate.

3 →PG. 120

Now Joseph was well-built and handsome,[w] 7 and after a while his master's wife took notice of Joseph and said, "Come to bed with me!"[x]

8 But he refused.[y] "With me in charge," he told her, "my master does not concern himself with anything in the house; everything he owns he has entrusted to my care. 9 No one is greater in this house than I am.[z] My master has withheld nothing from me except you, because you are his wife. How then could I do such a wicked thing and sin against God?"[a] 10 And though she spoke to Joseph day after day, he refused to go to bed with her or even be with her.

11 One day he went into the house to attend to his duties, and none of the

a 29 *Perez* means *breaking out.* b 30 *Zerah* can mean *scarlet* or *brightness.*

38:17 e ver 20 **38:18** f ver 25 **38:19** g ver 14 **38:21** h Lev 19:29; Hos 4:14 **38:24** i Lev 21:9; Dt 22:21,22 **38:25** j ver 18 **38:26** k 1Sa 24:17 l ver 11 **38:27** m Ge 25:24 **38:29** n Ge 46:12; Nu 26:20,21; Ru 4:12,18; 1Ch 2:4; Mt 1:3 **38:30** o 1Ch 2:4 **39:1** p Ge 37:36 q Ge 37:25; Ps 105:17

39:2 r Ge 21:20,22; Ac 7:9 **39:3** s Ge 21:22; 26:28 t Ps 1:3 **39:4** u ver 8,22; Ge 24:2 **39:5** v Ge 26:24; 30:27 **39:6** w 1Sa 16:12 **39:7** x 2Sa 13:11; Pr 7:15-18 **39:8** y Pr 6:23-24 **39:9** z Ge 41:33,40 a Ge 20:6; 42:18; 2Sa 12:13

39:6–10

PROMISE 3

FAITHFULNESS IS REWARDED

One statement, repeated twice in this context, explains Joseph's response to being tempted by Potiphar's wife. Verses 2 and 21 function like bookends to this story of Joseph's integrity: "The LORD was with Joseph."

Making a promise to maintain moral integrity is honorable; still, most of us wrestle with keeping this promise every day. Men, we cannot hope to live well without Joseph's guide to integrity. Begin every day with a couple of minutes of reflection on God's presence in your life. Ask him to be with you. Then when "Potiphar's wife"—in her many forms—comes to talk you out of your promises, focus on the fact that "the Lord is with you."

For the next Promise 3 reading go to page 103.

household servants was inside. 12She caught him by his cloak[b] and said, "Come to bed with me!" But he left his cloak in her hand and ran out of the house.

13When she saw that he had left his cloak in her hand and had run out of the house, 14she called her household servants. "Look," she said to them, "this Hebrew has been brought to us to make sport of us! He came in here to sleep with me, but I screamed.[c] 15When he heard me scream for help, he left his cloak beside me and ran out of the house."

16She kept his cloak beside her until his master came home. 17Then she told him this story:[d] "That Hebrew slave you brought us came to me to make sport of me. 18But as soon as I screamed for help, he left his cloak beside me and ran out of the house."

19When his master heard the story his wife told him, saying, "This is how your slave treated me," he burned with anger.[e] 20Joseph's master took him and put him in prison,[f] the place where the king's prisoners were confined.

But while Joseph was there in the prison, 21the LORD was with him; he showed him kindness and granted him favor in the eyes of the prison warden.[g] 22So the warden put Joseph in charge of all those held in the prison, and he was made responsible for all that was done there.[h] 23The warden paid no attention to anything under Joseph's care, because the LORD was with Joseph and gave him success in whatever he did.[i]

The Cupbearer and the Baker

40 Some time later, the cupbearer[j] and the baker of the king of Egypt offended their master, the king of Egypt. 2Pharaoh was angry[k] with his two officials, the chief cupbearer and the chief baker, 3and put them in custody in the house of the captain of the guard,[l] in the same prison where Joseph was confined. 4The captain of the guard assigned them to Joseph,[m] and he attended them.

After they had been in custody for some time, 5each of the two men—the cupbearer and the baker of the king of Egypt, who were being held in prison—had a dream the same night, and each dream had a meaning of its own.[n]

6When Joseph came to them the next morning, he saw that they were dejected. 7So he asked Pharaoh's officials who were in custody with him in his master's house, "Why are your faces so sad today?"[o]

8"We both had dreams," they answered, "but there is no one to interpret them."[p]

Then Joseph said to them, "Do not interpretations belong to God?[q] Tell me your dreams."

9So the chief cupbearer told Joseph his dream. He said to him, "In my dream I saw a vine in front of me, 10and on the vine were three branches. As soon as it budded, it blossomed, and its clusters ripened into grapes. 11Pharaoh's cup was in my hand, and I took the grapes, squeezed them into Pharaoh's cup and put the cup in his hand."

12"This is what it means,[r]" Joseph said to him. "The three branches are three days. 13Within three days Pharaoh will lift up your head and restore you to your position, and you will put Pharaoh's cup in his hand, just as you used to do when you were his cupbearer. 14But when all goes well with you, remember me[s] and show me kindness;[t] mention me to Pharaoh and get me out of this prison. 15For I was forcibly carried off from the land of the Hebrews,[u] and even here I have done nothing to deserve being put in a dungeon."

16When the chief baker saw that Joseph had given a favorable interpretation, he said to Joseph, "I too had a dream: On my head were three baskets of bread.**a** 17In the top basket were all kinds of baked goods for Pharaoh, but the birds were eating them out of the basket on my head."

18"This is what it means," Joseph said. "The three baskets are three days.[v] 19Within three days Pharaoh will lift off your head[w] and hang you on a tree.**b** And the birds will eat away your flesh."

20Now the third day was Pharaoh's birthday,[x] and he gave a feast for all his officials.[y] He lifted up the heads of the chief cupbearer and the chief baker in the presence of his officials: 21He restored the chief cupbearer to his position, so that he once again put the cup into Pharaoh's hand,[z] 22but he hanged**c** the chief baker,[a] just as Joseph had said to them in his interpretation.[b]

23The chief cupbearer, however, did not remember Joseph; he forgot him.[c]

Pharaoh's Dreams

41 When two full years had passed, Pharaoh had a dream:[d] He was

39:12 [b]Pr 7:13
39:14 [c]Dt 22:24,27
39:17 [d]Ex 23:1,7; Ps 101:5
39:19 [e]Pr 6:34
39:20 [f]Ge 40:3; Ps 105:18
39:21 [g]Ex 3:21
39:22 [h]ver 4
39:23 [i]ver 3
40:1 [j]Ne 1:11
40:2 [k]Pr 16:14,15
40:3 [l]Ge 39:20
40:4 [m]Ge 39:4
40:5 [n]Ge 41:11
40:7 [o]Ne 2:2
40:8 [p]Ge 41:8,15 [q]Ge 41:16; Da 2:22,28,47
40:12 [r]Ge 41:12,15, 25; Da 2:36; 4:19
40:14 [s]Lk 23:42 [t]Jos 2:12; 1Sa 20:14,42; 1Ki 2:7
40:15 [u]Ge 37:26-28
40:18 [v]ver 12
40:19 [w]ver 13
40:20 [x]Mt 14:6-10 [y]Mk 6:21
40:21 [z]ver 13
40:22 [a]ver 19 [b]Ps 105:19
40:23 [c]Job 19:14; Ecc 9:15
41:1 [d]Ge 20:3

a 16 Or *three wicker baskets* **b** 19 Or *and impale you on a pole* **c** 22 Or *impaled*

standing by the Nile, **2**when out of the river there came up seven cows, sleek and fat,[e] and they grazed among the reeds.[f] **3**After them, seven other cows, ugly and gaunt, came up out of the Nile and stood beside those on the riverbank. **4**And the cows that were ugly and gaunt ate up the seven sleek, fat cows. Then Pharaoh woke up.

5He fell asleep again and had a second dream: Seven heads of grain, healthy and good, were growing on a single stalk. **6**After them, seven other heads of grain sprouted—thin and scorched by the east wind. **7**The thin heads of grain swallowed up the seven healthy, full heads. Then Pharaoh woke up; it had been a dream.

8In the morning his mind was troubled,[g] so he sent for all the magicians[h] and wise men of Egypt. Pharaoh told them his dreams, but no one could interpret them for him.

9Then the chief cupbearer said to Pharaoh, "Today I am reminded of my shortcomings. **10**Pharaoh was once angry with his servants,[i] and he imprisoned me and the chief baker in the house of the captain of the guard.[j] **11**Each of us had a dream the same night, and each dream had a meaning of its own.[k] **12**Now a young Hebrew was there with us, a servant of the captain of the guard. We told him our dreams, and he interpreted them for us, giving each man the interpretation of his dream.[l] **13**And things turned out exactly as he interpreted them to us: I was restored to my position, and the other man was hanged.[a][m]"

14So Pharaoh sent for Joseph, and he was quickly brought from the dungeon.[n] When he had shaved and changed his clothes, he came before Pharaoh.

15Pharaoh said to Joseph, "I had a dream, and no one can interpret it. But I have heard it said of you that when you hear a dream you can interpret it."[o]

16"I cannot do it," Joseph replied to Pharaoh, "but God will give Pharaoh the answer he desires."[p]

17Then Pharaoh said to Joseph, "In my dream I was standing on the bank of the Nile, **18**when out of the river there came up seven cows, fat and sleek, and they grazed among the reeds. **19**After them, seven other cows came up—scrawny and very ugly and lean. I had never seen such ugly cows in all the land of Egypt. **20**The lean, ugly cows ate up the seven fat cows that came up first. **21**But even after they ate them, no one could tell that they had done so; they looked just as ugly as before. Then I woke up.

22"In my dreams I also saw seven heads of grain, full and good, growing on a single stalk. **23**After them, seven other heads sprouted—withered and thin and scorched by the east wind. **24**The thin heads of grain swallowed up the seven good heads. I told this to the magicians, but none could explain it to me.[q]"

25Then Joseph said to Pharaoh, "The dreams of Pharaoh are one and the same. God has revealed to Pharaoh what he is about to do.[r] **26**The seven good cows[s] are seven years, and the seven good heads of grain are seven years; it is one and the same dream. **27**The seven lean, ugly cows that came up afterward are seven years, and so are the seven worthless heads of grain scorched by the east wind: They are seven years of famine.[t]

28"It is just as I said to Pharaoh: God has shown Pharaoh what he is about to do. **29**Seven years of great abundance[u] are coming throughout the land of Egypt, **30**but seven years of famine[v] will follow them. Then all the abundance in Egypt will be forgotten, and the famine will ravage the land.[w] **31**The abundance in the land will not be remembered, because the famine that follows it will be so severe. **32**The reason the dream was given to Pharaoh in two forms is that the matter has been firmly decided[x] by God, and God will do it soon.

33"And now let Pharaoh look for a discerning and wise man[y] and put him in charge of the land of Egypt. **34**Let Pharaoh appoint commissioners over the land to take a fifth[z] of the harvest of Egypt during the seven years of abundance.[a] **35**They should collect all the food of these good years that are coming and store up the grain under the authority of Pharaoh, to be kept in the cities for food.[b] **36**This food should be held in reserve for the country, to be used during the seven years of famine that will come upon Egypt,[c] so that the country may not be ruined by the famine."

37The plan seemed good to Pharaoh and to all his officials.[d] **38**So Pharaoh asked them, "Can we find anyone like this man, one in whom is the spirit of God[b]?"[e]

39Then Pharaoh said to Joseph, "Since God has made all this known to you, there is no one so discerning and wise as you. **40**You shall be in charge of my palace, and all my people are to

41:2 [e]ver 26 [f]Isa 19:6 **41:8** [g]Da 2:1,3; 4:5,19 [h]Ex 7:11,22; Da 1:20; 2:2, 27; 4:7 **41:10** [i]Ge 40:2 [j]Ge 39:20 **41:11** [k]Ge 40:5 **41:12** [l]Ge 40:12 **41:13** [m]Ge 40:22 **41:14** [n]Ps 105:20; Da 2:25 **41:15** [o]Da 5:16 **41:16** [p]Ge 40:8; Da 2:30; Ac 3:12; 2Co 3:5 **41:24** [q]ver 8 **41:25** [r]Da 2:45 **41:26** [s]ver 2 **41:27** [t]Ge 12:10; 2Ki 8:1 **41:29** [u]ver 47 **41:30** [v]ver 54; Ge 47:13 [w]ver 56 **41:32** [x]Nu 23:19; Isa 46:10-11 **41:33** [y]ver 39 **41:34** [z]1Sa 8:15 [a]ver 48 **41:35** [b]ver 48 **41:36** [c]ver 56 **41:37** [d]Ge 45:16 **41:38** [e]Nu 27:18; Job 32:8; Da 4:8,8-9,18; 5:11,14

[a] 13 Or *impaled* [b] 38 Or *of the gods*

submit to your orders.[f] Only with respect to the throne will I be greater
than you."

Joseph in Charge of Egypt

41 So Pharaoh said to Joseph, "I hereby put you in charge of the whole land
of Egypt."[g] 42 Then Pharaoh took his
signet ring[h] from his finger and put it
on Joseph's finger. He dressed him
in robes of fine linen and put a gold
chain around his neck.[i] 43 He had him
ride in a chariot as his second-in-
command,[a] and men shouted before
him, "Make way[b]!"[j] Thus he put him
in charge of the whole land of Egypt.
44 Then Pharaoh said to Joseph, "I
am Pharaoh, but without your word no
one will lift hand or foot in all Egypt."[k]
45 Pharaoh gave Joseph the name
Zaphenath-Paneah and gave him Asenath daughter of Potiphera, priest of
On,[c] to be his wife.[l] And Joseph went
throughout the land of Egypt.
46 Joseph was thirty years old[m] when
he entered the service[n] of Pharaoh
king of Egypt. And Joseph went out
from Pharaoh's presence and traveled
throughout Egypt. 47 During the seven
years of abundance the land produced
plentifully. 48 Joseph collected all the
food produced in those seven years of
abundance in Egypt and stored it in the
cities. In each city he put the food
grown in the fields surrounding it. 49 Joseph stored up huge quantities of
grain, like the sand of the sea; it was so
much that he stopped keeping records
because it was beyond measure.
50 Before the years of famine came,
two sons were born to Joseph by Asenath daughter of Potiphera, priest of
On.[o] 51 Joseph named his firstborn[p]
Manasseh[d] and said, "It is because
God has made me forget all my trouble
and all my father's household." 52 The
second son he named Ephraim[e][q] and
said, "It is because God has made me
fruitful[r] in the land of my suffering."
53 The seven years of abundance in
Egypt came to an end, 54 and the seven
years of famine began,[s] just as Joseph
had said. There was famine in all the
other lands, but in the whole land of
Egypt there was food. 55 When all Egypt
began to feel the famine,[t] the people
cried to Pharaoh for food. Then Pharaoh told all the Egyptians, "Go to Joseph and do what he tells you."[u]
56 When the famine had spread over
the whole country, Joseph opened the
storehouses and sold grain to the Egyptians, for the famine[v] was severe
throughout Egypt. 57 And all the countries came to Egypt to buy grain from
Joseph,[w] because the famine was severe in all the world.

Joseph's Brothers Go to Egypt

42 When Jacob learned that there was
grain in Egypt,[x] he said to his
sons, "Why do you just keep looking at
each other?" 2 He continued, "I have
heard that there is grain in Egypt. Go
down there and buy some for us, so
that we may live and not die."[y]
3 Then ten of Joseph's brothers went
down to buy grain from Egypt. 4 But Jacob did not send Benjamin, Joseph's
brother, with the others, because he
was afraid that harm might come to
him.[z] 5 So Israel's sons were among
those who went to buy grain,[a] for the
famine was in the land of Canaan
also.[b]
6 Now Joseph was the governor of the
land,[c] the one who sold grain to all its
people. So when Joseph's brothers arrived, they bowed down to him with
their faces to the ground.[d] 7 As soon as
Joseph saw his brothers, he recognized
them, but he pretended to be a stranger and spoke harshly to them.[e]
"Where do you come from?" he asked.
"From the land of Canaan," they replied, "to buy food."
8 Although Joseph recognized his
brothers, they did not recognize him.[f]
9 Then he remembered his dreams[g]
about them and said to them, "You are
spies! You have come to see where our
land is unprotected."
10 "No, my lord," they answered.
"Your servants have come to buy food.
11 We are all the sons of one man. Your
servants are honest men, not spies."
12 "No!" he said to them. "You have
come to see where our land is unprotected."
13 But they replied, "Your servants
were twelve brothers, the sons of one
man, who lives in the land of Canaan.
The youngest is now with our father,
and one is no more."[h]
14 Joseph said to them, "It is just as I
told you: You are spies! 15 And this is
how you will be tested: As surely as
Pharaoh lives,[i] you will not leave this
place unless your youngest brother
comes here. 16 Send one of your number to get your brother; the rest of you
will be kept in prison, so that your
words may be tested to see if you are
telling the truth.[j] If you are not, then
as surely as Pharaoh lives, you are

41:40 [f] Ps 105:21-22; Ac 7:10
41:41 [g] Ge 42:6; Da 6:3
41:42 [h] Est 3:10 [i] Da 5:7,16,29
41:43 [j] Est 6:9
41:44 [k] Ps 105:22
41:45 [l] ver 50; Ge 46:20,27
41:46 [m] Ge 37:2 [n] 1Sa 16:21; Da 1:19
41:50 [o] Ge 46:20; 48:5
41:51 [p] Ge 48:14, 18,20
41:52 [q] Ge 48:1,5; 50:23 [r] Ge 17:6; 28:3; 49:22
41:54 [s] ver 30; Ps 105:11; Ac 7:11
41:55 [t] Dt 32:24 [u] ver 41
41:56 [v] Ge 12:10
41:57 [w] Ge 42:5; 47:15
42:1 [x] Ac 7:12
42:2 [y] Ge 43:8
42:4 [z] ver 38
42:5 [a] Ge 41:57 [b] Ge 12:10; Ac 7:11
42:6 [c] Ge 41:41 [d] Ge 37:7-10
42:7 [e] ver 30
42:8 [f] Ge 37:2
42:9 [g] Ge 37:7
42:13 [h] Ge 37:30,33; 44:20
42:15 [i] 1Sa 17:55
42:16 [j] ver 11

[a] *43* Or *in the chariot of his second-in-command;* or *in his second chariot* [b] *43* Or *Bow down*
[c] *45* That is, Heliopolis; also in verse 50
[d] *51* *Manasseh* sounds like and may be derived from the Hebrew for *forget.* [e] *52* *Ephraim* sounds like the Hebrew for *twice fruitful.*

spies!" 17And he put them all in custody[k] for three days.
18On the third day, Joseph said to
them, "Do this and you will live, for I
fear God:[l] 19If you are honest men, let
one of your brothers stay here in prison, while the rest of you go and take
grain back for your starving households. 20But you must bring your youngest brother to me,[m] so that your
words may be verified and that you
may not die." This they proceeded
to do.
21They said to one another, "Surely
we are being punished because of our
brother.[n] We saw how distressed he
was when he pleaded with us for his
life, but we would not listen; that's why
this distress[o] has come upon us."
22Reuben replied, "Didn't I tell you
not to sin against the boy?[p] But you
wouldn't listen! Now we must give an
accounting[q] for his blood."[r] 23They
did not realize that Joseph could understand them, since he was using an
interpreter.
24He turned away from them and
began to weep, but then turned back
and spoke to them again. He had Simeon taken from them and bound before
their eyes.[s]
25Joseph gave orders to fill their bags
with grain,[t] to put each man's silver
back in his sack,[u] and to give them
provisions for their journey.[v] After
this was done for them, 26they loaded
their grain on their donkeys and left.
27At the place where they stopped
for the night one of them opened his
sack to get feed for his donkey, and
he saw his silver in the mouth of his
sack.[w] 28"My silver has been returned," he said to his brothers. "Here
it is in my sack."
Their hearts sank and they turned to
each other trembling and said, "What
is this that God has done to us?"[x]
29When they came to their father Jacob in the land of Canaan, they told
him all that had happened to them.
They said, 30"The man who is lord over
the land spoke harshly to us[y] and
treated us as though we were spying on
the land. 31But we said to him, 'We are
honest men; we are not spies.[z] 32We
were twelve brothers, sons of one father. One is no more, and the youngest
is now with our father in Canaan.'
33"Then the man who is lord over
the land said to us, 'This is how I will
know whether you are honest men:
Leave one of your brothers here with
me, and take food for your starving
households and go.[a] 34But bring your
youngest brother to me so I will know
that you are not spies but honest men.
Then I will give your brother back to
you, and you can trade[a] in the
land.[b]' "
35As they were emptying their sacks,
there in each man's sack was his pouch
of silver! When they and their father
saw the money pouches, they were
frightened.[c] 36Their father Jacob said
to them, "You have deprived me of
my children. Joseph is no more and
Simeon is no more, and now you
want to take Benjamin.[d] Everything
is against me!"
37Then Reuben said to his father,
"You may put both of my sons to death
if I do not bring him back to you. Entrust him to my care, and I will bring
him back."
38But Jacob said, "My son will not go
down there with you; his brother is
dead[e] and he is the only one left. If
harm comes to him[f] on the journey
you are taking, you will bring my gray
head down to the grave[b][g] in sorrow.[h]"

The Second Journey to Egypt

43 Now the famine was still severe in
the land.[i] 2So when they had eat-
en all the grain they had brought from
Egypt, their father said to them, "Go
back and buy us a little more food."
3But Judah said to him, "The man
warned us solemnly, 'You will not see
my face again unless your brother is
with you.'[j] 4If you will send our brother along with us, we will go down and

[a] 34 Or *move about freely* [b] 38 Hebrew *Sheol*

42:21

PROMISE 7

BACK TO BASICS

This statement answers why Joseph acted so strangely toward his brothers. They came looking for food, but Joseph understood their most basic problem—they were guilty of a tragic sin. He eventually gave them food and a fertile place to live and grow their own food. He addressed their felt need. But throughout this story we see that Joseph was devoted to his brothers and helped them address life's deepest need: the need for reconciliation to their brother and to God.

Christian men live under the great commission to make disciples of all people (Matthew 28:19). Think over your key relationships with other men and women, and list some ways you can help them address their most basic need: to become one of Jesus' disciples.

For the next Promise 7 reading go to page 68.

42:17 [k]Ge 40:4
42:18 [l]Ge 20:11; Lev 25:43
42:20 [m]ver 15,34; Ge 43:5; 44:23
42:21 [n]Ge 37:26-28 [o]Hos 5:15
42:22 [p]Ge 37:21-22 [q]Ge 9:5 [r]1Ki 2:32; 2Ch 24:22; Ps 9:12
42:24 [s]ver 13; Ge 43:14,23; 45:14-15
42:25 [t]Ge 43:2 [u]Ge 44:1,8 [v]Ro 12:17, 20-21
42:27 [w]Ge 43:21-22
42:28 [x]Ge 43:23
42:30 [y]ver 7
42:31 [z]ver 11
42:33 [a]ver 19,20
42:34 [b]Ge 34:10
42:35 [c]Ge 43:12, 15,18
42:36 [d]Ge 43:14
42:38 [e] Ge 37:33 [f]ver 4 [g]Ge 37:35 [h]Ge 44:29,34
43:1 [i]Ge 12:10; 41:56-57
43:3 [j]Ge 42:15; 44:23

buy food for you. 5But if you will not send him, we will not go down, because the man said to us, 'You will not see my face again unless your brother is with you.[k]' "

6Israel asked, "Why did you bring this trouble on me by telling the man you had another brother?"

7They replied, "The man questioned us closely about ourselves and our family. 'Is your father still living?'[l] he asked us. 'Do you have another brother?'[m] We simply answered his questions. How were we to know he would say, 'Bring your brother down here'?"

8Then Judah said to Israel his father, "Send the boy along with me and we will go at once, so that we and you and our children may live and not die.[n] 9I myself will guarantee his safety; you can hold me personally responsible for him. If I do not bring him back to you and set him here before you, I will bear the blame before you all my life.[o] 10As it is, if we had not delayed, we could have gone and returned twice."

11Then their father Israel said to them, "If it must be, then do this: Put some of the best products of the land in your bags and take them down to the man as a gift[p]—a little balm[q] and a little honey, some spices[r] and myrrh, some pistachio nuts and almonds. 12Take double the amount of silver with you, for you must return the silver that was put back into the mouths of your sacks.[s] Perhaps it was a mistake. 13Take your brother also and go back to the man at once. 14And may God Almighty[a][t] grant you mercy before the man so that he will let your other brother and Benjamin come back with you.[u] As for me, if I am bereaved, I am bereaved."[v]

15So the men took the gifts and double the amount of silver, and Benjamin also. They hurried[w] down to Egypt and presented themselves[x] to Joseph. 16When Joseph saw Benjamin with them, he said to the steward of his house,[y] "Take these men to my house, slaughter an animal and prepare dinner;[z] they are to eat with me at noon."

17The man did as Joseph told him and took the men to Joseph's house. 18Now the men were frightened[a] when they were taken to his house. They thought, "We were brought here because of the silver that was put back into our sacks the first time. He wants to attack us and overpower us and seize us as slaves and take our donkeys."

19So they went up to Joseph's steward and spoke to him at the entrance to the house. 20"Please, sir," they said, "we came down here the first time to buy food.[b] 21But at the place where we stopped for the night we opened our sacks and each of us found his silver—the exact weight—in the mouth of his sack. So we have brought it back with us.[c] 22We have also brought additional silver with us to buy food. We don't know who put our silver in our sacks."

23"It's all right," he said. "Don't be afraid. Your God, the God of your father, has given you treasure in your sacks;[d] I received your silver." Then he brought Simeon out to them.[e]

24The steward took the men into Joseph's house,[f] gave them water to wash their feet[g] and provided fodder for their donkeys. 25They prepared their gifts for Joseph's arrival at noon, because they had heard that they were to eat there.

26When Joseph came home, they presented to him the gifts[h] they had brought into the house, and they bowed down before him to the ground.[i] 27He asked them how they were, and then he said, "How is your aged father you told me about? Is he still living?"[j]

28They replied, "Your servant our father is still alive and well." And they bowed low to pay him honor.[k]

29As he looked about and saw his brother Benjamin, his own mother's son, he asked, "Is this your youngest brother, the one you told me about?"[l] And he said, "God be gracious to you,[m] my son." 30Deeply moved[n] at the sight of his brother, Joseph hurried out and looked for a place to weep. He went into his private room and wept[o] there.

31After he had washed his face, he came out and, controlling himself,[p] said, "Serve the food."

32They served him by himself, the brothers by themselves, and the Egyptians who ate with him by themselves, because Egyptians could not eat with Hebrews,[q] for that is detestable to Egyptians.[r] 33The men had been seated before him in the order of their ages, from the firstborn to the youngest; and they looked at each other in astonishment. 34When portions were served to them from Joseph's table, Benjamin's portion was five times as much as anyone else's.[s] So they feasted and drank freely with him.

A Silver Cup in a Sack

44 Now Joseph gave these instructions to the steward of his house:

43:5 [k]Ge 42:15; 2Sa 3:13
43:7 [l]ver 27 [m]Ge 42:13
43:8 [n]Ge 42:2; Ps 33:18-19
43:9 [o]Ge 42:37; 44:32; Phm 1:18-19
43:11 [p]Ge 32:20; Pr 18:16 [q]Ge 37:25; Jer 8:22 [r]1Ki 10:2
43:12 [s]Ge 42:25
43:14 [t]Ge 17:1; 28:3; 35:11 [u]Ge 42:24 [v]Est 4:16
43:15 [w]Ge 45:9,13 [x]Ge 47:2,7
43:16 [y]Ge 44:1,4,12 [z]ver 31; Lk 15:23
43:18 [a]Ge 42:35
43:20 [b]Ge 42:3
43:21 [c]ver 15; Ge 42:27,35
43:23 [d]Ge 42:28 [e]Ge 42:24
43:24 [f]ver 16 [g]Ge 18:4; 24:32
43:26 [h]Mt 2:11 [i]Ge 37:7,10
43:27 [j]ver 7
43:28 [k]Ge 37:7
43:29 [l]Ge 42:13 [m]Nu 6:25; Ps 67:1
43:30 [n]Jn 11:33,38 [o]Ge 42:24; 45:2,14,15; 46:29
43:31 [p]Ge 45:1
43:32 [q]Gal 2:12 [r]Ge 46:34; Ex 8:26
43:34 [s]Ge 37:3; 45:22

[a] *14* Hebrew *El-Shaddai*

"Fill the men's sacks with as much
food as they can carry, and put each
man's silver in the mouth of his sack.[t]
2Then put my cup, the silver one, in the
mouth of the youngest one's sack,
along with the silver for his grain." And
he did as Joseph said.
3As morning dawned, the men were
sent on their way with their donkeys.
4They had not gone far from the city
when Joseph said to his steward, "Go
after those men at once, and when you
catch up with them, say to them, 'Why
have you repaid good with evil?[u] 5Isn't
this the cup my master drinks from and
also uses for divination?[v] This is a
wicked thing you have done.' "
6When he caught up with them, he
repeated these words to them. 7But
they said to him, "Why does my lord
say such things? Far be it from your
servants to do anything like that! 8We
even brought back to you from the
land of Canaan the silver we found inside the mouths of our sacks.[w] So why
would we steal silver or gold from your
master's house? 9If any of your servants is found to have it, he will die;[x]
and the rest of us will become my
lord's slaves."
10"Very well, then," he said, "let it be
as you say. Whoever is found to have it
will become my slave; the rest of you
will be free from blame."
11Each of them quickly lowered his
sack to the ground and opened it.
12Then the steward proceeded to
search, beginning with the oldest and
ending with the youngest. And the cup
was found in Benjamin's sack.[y] 13At
this, they tore their clothes.[z] Then
they all loaded their donkeys and returned to the city.
14Joseph was still in the house when
Judah and his brothers came in, and
they threw themselves to the ground
before him.[a] 15Joseph said to them,
"What is this you have done? Don't you
know that a man like me can find
things out by divination?[b]"
16"What can we say to my lord?" Judah replied. "What can we say? How
can we prove our innocence? God has
uncovered your servants' guilt. We are
now my lord's slaves[c]—we ourselves
and the one who was found to have the
cup.[d]"
17But Joseph said, "Far be it from me
to do such a thing! Only the man who
was found to have the cup will become
my slave. The rest of you, go back to
your father in peace."
18Then Judah went up to him and
said: "Please, my lord, let your servant
speak a word to my lord. Do not be
angry[e] with your servant, though you
are equal to Pharaoh himself. 19My lord
asked his servants, 'Do you have a father or a brother?'[f] 20And we answered, 'We have an aged father, and
there is a young son born to him in his
old age.[g] His brother is dead,[h] and he
is the only one of his mother's sons left,
and his father loves him.'[i]
21"Then you said to your servants,
'Bring him down to me so I can see him
for myself.'[j] 22And we said to my lord,
'The boy cannot leave his father; if he
leaves him, his father will die.'[k] 23But
you told your servants, 'Unless your
youngest brother comes down with
you, you will not see my face again.'[l]
24When we went back to your servant
my father, we told him what my lord
had said.
25"Then our father said, 'Go back
and buy a little more food.'[m] 26But we
said, 'We cannot go down. Only if our
youngest brother is with us will we go.
We cannot see the man's face unless
our youngest brother is with us.'
27"Your servant my father said to us,
'You know that my wife bore me two
sons.[n] 28One of them went away from
me, and I said, "He has surely been
torn to pieces."[o] And I have not seen
him since. 29If you take this one from
me too and harm comes to him, you
will bring my gray head down to the
grave[a] in misery.'[p]
30"So now, if the boy is not with us
when I go back to your servant my father and if my father, whose life is
closely bound up with the boy's life,[q]
31sees that the boy isn't there, he will
die. Your servants will bring the gray
head of our father down to the grave in
sorrow. 32Your servant guaranteed the
boy's safety to my father. I said, 'If I do
not bring him back to you, I will bear
the blame before you, my father, all my
life!'[r]
33"Now then, please let your servant
remain here as my lord's slave[s] in
place of the boy,[t] and let the boy return with his brothers. 34How can I go
back to my father if the boy is not with
me? No! Do not let me see the misery
that would come upon my father."[u]

Joseph Makes Himself Known

45 Then Joseph could no longer control himself[v] before all his attendants, and he cried out, "Have everyone leave my presence!" So there was
no one with Joseph when he made
himself known to his brothers. 2And he
wept[w] so loudly that the Egyptians

a 29 Hebrew *Sheol*; also in verse 31

44:1 t Ge 42:25
44:4 u Ps 35:12
44:5 v Ge 30:27; Dt 18:10-14
44:8 w Ge 42:25; 43:21
44:9 x Ge 31:32
44:12 y ver 2
44:13 z Ge 37:29; Nu 14:6; 2Sa 1:11
44:14 a Ge 37:7,10
44:15 b ver 5; Ge 30:27
44:16 c ver 9; Ge 43:18 d ver 2
44:18 e Ge 18:30; Ex 32:22
44:19 f Ge 43:7
44:20 g Ge 37:3 h Ge 37:33 i Ge 42:13
44:21 j Ge 42:15
44:22 k Ge 37:35
44:23 l Ge 43:5
44:25 m Ge 43:2
44:27 n Ge 46:19
44:28 o Ge 37:33
44:29 p Ge 42:38
44:30 q 1Sa 18:1
44:32 r Ge 43:9
44:33 s Ge 43:18 t Jn 15:13
44:34 u Est 8:6
45:1 v Ge 43:31
45:2 w Ge 29:11

heard him, and Pharaoh's household heard about it.[x]

6 →PG. 132

3Joseph said to his brothers, "I am Joseph! Is my father still living?"[y] But his brothers were not able to answer him,[z] because they were terrified at his presence.

4Then Joseph said to his brothers, "Come close to me." When they had done so, he said, "I am your brother Joseph, the one you sold into Egypt![a] 5And now, do not be distressed[b] and do not be angry with yourselves for selling me here,[c] because it was to save lives that God sent me ahead of you.[d] 6For two years now there has been famine in the land, and for the next five years there will not be plowing and reaping. 7But God sent me ahead of you to preserve for you a remnant[e] on earth and to save your lives by a great deliverance.[a][f]

8"So then, it was not you who sent me here, but God. He made me father[g] to Pharaoh, lord of his entire household and ruler of all Egypt.[h] 9Now hurry back to my father and say to him, 'This is what your son Joseph says: God has made me lord of all Egypt. Come down to me; don't delay.[i] 10You shall live in the region of Goshen[j] and be near me—you, your children and grandchildren, your flocks and herds, and all you have. 11I will provide for you there,[k] because five years of famine are still to come. Otherwise you and your household and all who belong to you will become destitute.'

12"You can see for yourselves, and so can my brother Benjamin, that it is really I who am speaking to you. 13Tell my father about all the honor accorded me in Egypt and about everything you have seen. And bring my father down here quickly.[l]"

14Then he threw his arms around his brother Benjamin and wept, and Benjamin embraced him, weeping. 15And he kissed[m] all his brothers and wept over them. Afterward his brothers talked with him.[n]

16When the news reached Pharaoh's palace that Joseph's brothers had come,[o] Pharaoh and all his officials were pleased. 17Pharaoh said to Joseph, "Tell your brothers, 'Do this: Load your animals and return to the land of Canaan, 18and bring your father and your families back to me. I will give you the best of the land of Egypt[p] and you can enjoy the fat of the land.'[q]

19"You are also directed to tell them, 'Do this: Take some carts[r] from Egypt for your children and your wives, and get your father and come. 20Never mind about your belongings, because the best of all Egypt will be yours.' "

21So the sons of Israel did this. Joseph gave them carts, as Pharaoh had commanded, and he also gave them provisions for their journey.[s] 22To each of them he gave new clothing, but to Benjamin he gave three hundred shekels[b] of silver and five sets of clothes.[t] 23And this is what he sent to his father: ten donkeys loaded with the best things of Egypt, and ten female donkeys loaded with grain and bread and other provisions for his journey. 24Then he sent his brothers away, and as they were leaving he said to them, "Don't quarrel on the way!"[u]

25So they went up out of Egypt and came to their father Jacob in the land of Canaan. 26They told him, "Joseph is still alive! In fact, he is ruler of all Egypt." Jacob was stunned; he did not believe them.[v] 27But when they told him everything Joseph had said to them, and when he saw the carts[w] Joseph had sent to carry him back, the spirit of their father Jacob revived. 28And Israel said, "I'm convinced! My son Joseph is still alive. I will go and see him before I die."

Jacob Goes to Egypt

46 So Israel set out with all that was his, and when he reached Beersheba,[x] he offered sacrifices to the God of his father Isaac.[y]

2And God spoke to Israel in a vision at night[z] and said, "Jacob! Jacob!"

[a]7 Or *save you as a great band of survivors*
[b]22 That is, about 7 1/2 pounds (about 3.5 kilograms)

45:2 [x]ver 16; Ge 46:29 **45:3** [y]Ac 7:13 [z]ver 15 **45:4** [a]Ge 37:28 **45:5** [b]Ge 42:21 [c]Ge 42:22 [d]ver 7-8; Ge 50:20; Ps 105:17 **45:7** [e]2Ki 19:4,30, 31; Isa 10:20, 21; 311:11,16; 46:3; Jer 6:9; 42:2; 50:20; Mic 4:7; Zep 2:7 [f]Ex 15:2; Est 4:14; Isa 25:9 **45:8** [g]Jdg 17:10 [h]Ge 41:41 **45:9** [i]Ge 43:10 **45:10** [j]Ge 46:28,34; 47:1 **45:11** [k]Ge 47:12

45:13 [l]Ac 7:14 **45:15** [m]Lk 15:20 [n]ver 3 **45:16** [o]Ac 7:13 **45:18** [p]Ge 27:28; 46:34; 47:6, 11,27; Nu 18:12,29 [q]Ps 37:19 **45:19** [r]Ge 46:5 **45:21** [s]Ge 42:25 **45:22** [t]Ge 37:3; 43:34 **45:24** [u]Ge 42:21-22 **45:26** [v]Ge 44:28 **45:27** [w]ver 19 **46:1** [x]Ge 21:14; 28:10 [y]Ge 26:24; 28:13; 31:42 **46:2** [z]Ge 15:1; Job 33:14-15

45:8

PROMISE 5

PROPER PERSPECTIVE

What a perspective! Joseph defined his whole life by the fact that God had placed him in his situation for ministry. Even though Joseph had experienced many tough times and had been in situations that would have made any man bitter, he chose to see these things as God's sovereign hand at work. Joseph believed that through these events God was placing him where he could best be used as God's instrument.

Think about the many roles that you fill in life—husband, father, employee, brother, son. God has placed you there to minister. Your church is his place of training; through its ministry and outreach, you can be a modern-day Joseph.

For the next Promise 5 reading go to page 72.

"Here I am,"[a] he replied.
3"I am God, the God of your father,"[b] he said. "Do not be afraid to go
down to Egypt, for I will make you into
a great nation[c] there.[d] 4I will go
down to Egypt with you, and I will
surely bring you back again.[e] And Joseph's own hand will close your
eyes.[f]"

5Then Jacob left Beersheba, and Israel's sons took their father Jacob and
their children and their wives in the
carts[g] that Pharaoh had sent to trans-
port him. 6They also took with them
their livestock and the possessions
they had acquired in Canaan, and Jacob and all his offspring went to
Egypt.[h] 7He took with him to Egypt
his sons and grandsons and his daughters and granddaughters—all his offspring.[i]

8These are the names of the sons of
Israel[j] (Jacob and his descendants)
who went to Egypt:

Reuben the firstborn of Jacob.
9The sons of Reuben:[k]
Hanoch, Pallu, Hezron and
Carmi.
10The sons of Simeon:[l]
Jemuel,[m] Jamin, Ohad, Jakin,
Zohar and Shaul the son of a
Canaanite woman.
11The sons of Levi:[n]
Gershon, Kohath and Merari.
12The sons of Judah:[o]
Er, Onan, Shelah, Perez and
Zerah (but Er and Onan had
died in the land of Canaan).
The sons of Perez:[p]
Hezron and Hamul.
13The sons of Issachar:[q]
Tola, Puah,[a][r] Jashub[b] and
Shimron.
14The sons of Zebulun:[s]
Sered, Elon and Jahleel.
15These were the sons Leah bore to
Jacob in Paddan Aram,[c] besides his
daughter Dinah. These sons and
daughters of his were thirty-three in
all.

16The sons of Gad:[t]
Zephon,[d][u] Haggi, Shuni, Ezbon, Eri, Arodi and Areli.
17The sons of Asher:[v]
Imnah, Ishvah, Ishvi and Beriah.
Their sister was Serah.
The sons of Beriah:
Heber and Malkiel.
18These were the children born to
Jacob by Zilpah,[w] whom Laban had
given to his daughter Leah[x]—sixteen
in all.

19The sons of Jacob's wife Rachel:
Joseph and Benjamin.[y] 20In
Egypt, Manasseh[z] and Ephraim[a] were born to Joseph by
Asenath daughter of Potiphera, priest of On.[e]
21The sons of Benjamin:[b]
Bela, Beker, Ashbel, Gera, Naaman, Ehi, Rosh, Muppim,
Huppim and Ard.
22These were the sons of Rachel who
were born to Jacob—fourteen in all.

23The son of Dan:
Hushim.
24The sons of Naphtali:
Jahziel, Guni, Jezer and Shillem.
25These were the sons born to Jacob
by Bilhah,[c] whom Laban had given to
his daughter Rachel[d]—seven in all.

26All those who went to Egypt with
Jacob—those who were his direct
descendants, not counting his sons'
wives—numbered sixty-six persons.[e]
27With the two sons[f] who had been
born to Joseph in Egypt, the members
of Jacob's family, which went to Egypt,
were seventy[g] in all.[f]

28Now Jacob sent Judah ahead of
him to Joseph to get directions to Goshen.[g] When they arrived in the region of Goshen, 29Joseph had his chariot made ready and went to Goshen to
meet his father Israel. As soon as Joseph appeared before him, he threw
his arms around his father[h] and wept
for a long time.[h]
30Israel said to Joseph, "Now I am
ready to die, since I have seen for myself that you are still alive."
31Then Joseph said to his brothers
and to his father's household, "I will go
up and speak to Pharaoh and will say
to him, 'My brothers and my father's
household, who were living in the land
of Canaan, have come to me.[i] 32The
men are shepherds; they tend livestock, and they have brought along
their flocks and herds and everything
they own.' 33When Pharaoh calls you in
and asks, 'What is your occupation?'[j]
34you should answer, 'Your servants
have tended livestock from our boy-
hood on, just as our fathers did.' Then
you will be allowed to settle in the re-

46:2 [a]Ge 22:1; 31:11 **46:3** [b]Ge 28:13 [c]Ge 12:2; Dt 26:5 [d]Ex 1:7 **46:4** [e]Ge 28:15; 48:21; Ex 3:8 [f]Ge 50:1,24 **46:5** [g]Ge 45:19 **46:6** [h]Dt 26:5; Jos 24:4; Ps 105:23; Isa 52:4; Ac 7:15 **46:7** [i]Ge 45:10 **46:8** [j]Ex 1:1; Nu 26:4 **46:9** [k]1Ch 5:3 **46:10** [l]Ge 29:33; Nu 26:14 [m]Ex 6:15 **46:11** [n]Ge 29:34; Nu 3:17 **46:12** [o]Ge 29:35 [p]1Ch 2:5; Mt 1:3 **46:13** [q]Ge 30:18 [r]1Ch 7:1 **46:14** [s]Ge 30:20 **46:16** [t]Ge 30:11 [u]Nu 26:15 **46:17** [v]Ge 30:13; 1Ch 7:30-31 **46:18** [w]Ge 30:10 [x]Ge 29:24

46:19 [y]Ge 44:27 **46:20** [z]Ge 41:51 [a]Ge 41:52 **46:21** [b]Nu 26:38-41; 1Ch 7:6-12; 8:1 **46:25** [c]Ge 30:8 [d]Ge 29:29 **46:26** [e]ver 5-7; Ex 1:5; Dt 10:22 **46:27** [f]Ac 7:14 **46:28** [g]Ge 45:10 **46:29** [h]Ge 45:14-15; Lk 15:20 **46:31** [i]Ge 47:1 **46:33** [j]Ge 47:3

a *13* Samaritan Pentateuch and Syriac (see also 1 Chron. 7:1); Masoretic Text *Puvah*
b *13* Samaritan Pentateuch and some Septuagint manuscripts (see also Num. 26:24 and 1 Chron. 7:1); Masoretic Text *Iob*
c *15* That is, Northwest Mesopotamia
d *16* Samaritan Pentateuch and Septuagint (see also Num. 26:15); Masoretic Text *Ziphion*
e *20* That is, Heliopolis
f *27* Hebrew; Septuagint *the nine children*
g *27* Hebrew (see also Exodus 1:5 and footnote); Septuagint (see also Acts 7:14) *seventy-five*
h *29* Hebrew *around him*

gion of Goshen,[k] for all shepherds are
detestable to the Egyptians.[l]"

47 Joseph went and told Pharaoh,
"My father and brothers, with their
flocks and herds and everything they
own, have come from the land of Canaan and are now in Goshen."[m] 2He
chose five of his brothers and presented them before Pharaoh.

3Pharaoh asked the brothers, "What
is your occupation?"[n]

"Your servants are shepherds," they
replied to Pharaoh, "just as our fathers
were." 4They also said to him, "We
have come to live here awhile,[o] because the famine is severe in Canaan[p]
and your servants' flocks have no pasture. So now, please let your servants
settle in Goshen."[q]

5Pharaoh said to Joseph, "Your father and your brothers have come to
you, 6and the land of Egypt is before
you; settle your father and your brothers in the best part of the land.[r] Let
them live in Goshen. And if you know
of any among them with special ability,[s] put them in charge of my own
livestock."

7Then Joseph brought his father Jacob in and presented him before Pharaoh. After Jacob blessed[a] Pharaoh,[t]
8Pharaoh asked him, "How old are
you?"

9And Jacob said to Pharaoh, "The
years of my pilgrimage are a hundred
and thirty.[u] My years have been few
and difficult,[v] and they do not equal
the years of the pilgrimage of my fathers.[w]" 10Then Jacob blessed[b] Pharaoh[x] and went out from his presence.

11So Joseph settled his father and his
brothers in Egypt and gave them property in the best part of the land, the
district of Rameses,[y] as Pharaoh directed. 12Joseph also provided his father and his brothers and all his father's household with food, according
to the number of their children.[z]

Joseph and the Famine

13There was no food, however, in the
whole region because the famine was
severe; both Egypt and Canaan wasted
away because of the famine.[a] 14Jo-
seph collected all the money that was
to be found in Egypt and Canaan in
payment for the grain they were buying, and he brought it to Pharaoh's palace.[b] 15When the money of the people
of Egypt and Canaan was gone, all
Egypt came to Joseph and said, "Give
us food. Why should we die before your
eyes?[c] Our money is used up."

16"Then bring your livestock," said
Joseph. "I will sell you food in exchange for your livestock, since your
money is gone." 17So they brought
their livestock to Joseph, and he gave
them food in exchange for their
horses,[d] their sheep and goats, their
cattle and donkeys. And he brought
them through that year with food in
exchange for all their livestock.

18When that year was over, they
came to him the following year and
said, "We cannot hide from our lord
the fact that since our money is gone
and our livestock belongs to you, there
is nothing left for our lord except our
bodies and our land. 19Why should we
perish before your eyes—we and our
land as well? Buy us and our land in
exchange for food, and we with our
land will be in bondage to Pharaoh.
Give us seed so that we may live and
not die, and that the land may not become desolate."

20So Joseph bought all the land in
Egypt for Pharaoh. The Egyptians, one
and all, sold their fields, because the
famine was too severe for them. The
land became Pharaoh's, 21and Joseph
reduced the people to servitude,[c]
from one end of Egypt to the other.
22However, he did not buy the land of
the priests, because they received a
regular allotment from Pharaoh and
had food enough from the allotment[e]
Pharaoh gave them. That is why they
did not sell their land.

23Joseph said to the people, "Now
that I have bought you and your land
today for Pharaoh, here is seed for you
so you can plant the ground. 24But
when the crop comes in, give a fifth[f]
of it to Pharaoh. The other four-fifths
you may keep as seed for the fields and
as food for yourselves and your households and your children."

25"You have saved our lives," they
said. "May we find favor in the eyes of
our lord;[g] we will be in bondage to
Pharaoh."

26So Joseph established it as a law
concerning land in Egypt—still in force
today—that a fifth of the produce belongs to Pharaoh. It was only the land
of the priests that did not become
Pharaoh's.[h]

27Now the Israelites settled in Egypt
in the region of Goshen. They acquired
property there and were fruitful and increased greatly in number.[i]

28Jacob lived in Egypt[j] seventeen
years, and the years of his life were a
hundred and forty-seven. 29When the

46:34 [k]Ge 45:10 [l]Ge 43:32; Ex 8:26
47:1 [m]Ge 46:31
47:3 [n]Ge 46:33
47:4 [o]Ge 15:13; Dt 26:5 [p]Ge 43:1 [q]Ge 46:34
47:6 [r]Ge 45:18 [s]Ex 18:21,25
47:7 [t]ver 10; 2Sa 14:22
47:9 [u]Ge 25:7 [v]Heb 11:9,13 [w]Ge 35:28
47:10 [x]ver 7
47:11 [y]Ex 1:11; 12:37
47:12 [z]Ge 45:11
47:13 [a]Ge 41:30; Ac 7:11
47:14 [b]Ge 41:56
47:15 [c]ver 19; Ex 16:3
47:17 [d]Ex 14:9
47:22 [e]Dt 14:28-29; Ezr 7:24
47:24 [f]Ge 41:34
47:25 [g]Ge 32:5
47:26 [h]ver 22
47:27 [i]Ge 17:6; 46:3; Ex 1:7
47:28 [j]Ps 105:23

[a] *7* Or *greeted* [b] *10* Or *said farewell to*
[c] *21* Samaritan Pentateuch and Septuagint (see also Vulgate); Masoretic Text *and he moved the people into the cities*

time drew near for Israel to die,[k] he called for his son Joseph and said to him, "If I have found favor in your eyes, put your hand under my thigh[l] and promise that you will show me kindness and faithfulness.[m] Do not bury me in Egypt, **30**but when I rest with my fathers, carry me out of Egypt and bury me where they are buried."[n]

"I will do as you say," he said.

31"Swear to me,"[o] he said. Then Joseph swore to him,[p] and Israel worshiped as he leaned on the top of his staff.[a][q]

Manasseh and Ephraim

48 Some time later Joseph was told, "Your father is ill." So he took his two sons Manasseh and Ephraim[r] along with him. **2**When Jacob was told, "Your son Joseph has come to you," Israel rallied his strength and sat up on the bed.

3Jacob said to Joseph, "God Almighty[b] appeared to me at Luz[s] in the land of Canaan, and there he blessed me[t] **4**and said to me, 'I am going to make you fruitful and will increase your numbers.[u] I will make you a community of peoples, and I will give this land as an everlasting possession to your descendants after you.'

5"Now then, your two sons born to you in Egypt[v] before I came to you here will be reckoned as mine; Ephraim and Manasseh will be mine,[w] just as Reuben and Simeon are mine. **6**Any children born to you after them will be yours; in the territory they inherit they will be reckoned under the names of their brothers. **7**As I was returning from Paddan,[c] to my sorrow Rachel died in the land of Canaan while we were still on the way, a little distance from Ephrath. So I buried her there beside the road to Ephrath" (that is, Bethlehem).[x]

8When Israel saw the sons of Joseph, he asked, "Who are these?"

4 →PG. 88

9"They are the sons God has given me here,"[y] Joseph said to his father.

Then Israel said, "Bring them to me so I may bless[z] them."

10Now Israel's eyes were failing because of old age, and he could hardly see.[a] So Joseph brought his sons close to him, and his father kissed them[b] and embraced them.

11Israel said to Joseph, "I never expected to see your face again, and now God has allowed me to see your children too."[c]

12Then Joseph removed them from Israel's knees and bowed down with his face to the ground. **13**And Joseph took both of them, Ephraim on his right toward Israel's left hand and Manasseh on his left toward Israel's right hand,[d] and brought them close to him. **14**But Israel reached out his right hand and put it on Ephraim's head, though he was the younger, and crossing his arms, he put his left hand on Manasseh's head, even though Manasseh was the firstborn.[e]

15Then he blessed[f] Joseph and said,

"May the God before whom my fathers
Abraham and Isaac walked,
the God who has been my shepherd[g]
all my life to this day,
16the Angel who has delivered me from all harm
—may he bless these boys.[h]
May they be called by my name
and the names of my fathers Abraham and Isaac,[i]
and may they increase greatly upon the earth."

17When Joseph saw his father placing his right hand on Ephraim's head[j] he was displeased; so he took hold of his father's hand to move it from Ephraim's head to Manasseh's head. **18**Joseph said to him, "No, my father, this one is the firstborn; put your right hand on his head."

19But his father refused and said, "I know, my son, I know. He too will become a people, and he too will become great.[k] Nevertheless, his younger brother will be greater than he,[l] and his descendants will become a group of nations." **20**He blessed them that day and said,

"In your[d] name will Israel pronounce this blessing:
'May God make you like Ephraim[m] and Manasseh.'[n]"

So he put Ephraim ahead of Manasseh.

21Then Israel said to Joseph, "I am about to die, but God will be with you[e][o] and take you[e] back to the land of your[e] fathers.[p] **22**And to you, as one who is over your brothers,[q] I give the ridge of land[f][r] I took from the Amorites with my sword and my bow."

47:29 [k]Dt 31:14 [l]Ge 24:2 [m]Ge 24:49
47:30 [n]Ge 49:29-32; 50:5,13; Ac 7:15-16
47:31 [o]Ge 21:23 [p]Ge 24:3 [q]Heb 11:21 *fn* 1Ki 1:47
48:1 [r]Ge 41:52
48:3 [s]Ge 28:19 [t]Ge 28:13; 35:9-12
48:4 [u]Ge 17:6
48:5 [v]Ge 41:50-52; 46:20 [w]1Ch 5:1; Jos 14:4
48:7 [x]Ge 35:19
48:9 [y]Ge 33:5 [z]Ge 27:4
48:10 [a]Ge 27:1 [b]Ge 27:27
48:11 [c]Ge 50:23; Ps 128:6
48:13 [d]Ps 110:1
48:14 [e]Ge 41:51
48:15 [f]Ge 17:1 [g]Ge 49:24
48:16 [h]Heb 11:21 [i]Ge 28:13
48:17 [j]ver 14
48:19 [k]Ge 17:20 [l]Ge 25:23
48:20 [m]Nu 2:18 [n]Nu 2:20; Ru 4:11
48:21 [o]Ge 26:3; 46:4 [p]Ge 28:13; 50:24
48:22 [q]Ge 37:8 [r]Jos 24:32; Jn 4:5

[a] *31* Or *Israel bowed down at the head of his bed* [b] *3* Hebrew *El-Shaddai* [c] *7* That is, Northwest Mesopotamia [d] *20* The Hebrew is singular. [e] *21* The Hebrew is plural. [f] *22* Or *And to you I give one portion more than to your brothers—the portion*

Jacob Blesses His Sons

49 Then Jacob called for his sons and
said: "Gather around so I can tell
you what will happen to you in days to
come.[s]

2"Assemble and listen, sons of
Jacob;
listen to your father Israel.[t]

3"Reuben, you are my firstborn,[u]
my might, the first sign of my
strength,[v]
excelling in honor, excelling in
power.
4Turbulent as the waters,[w] you will
no longer excel,
for you went up onto your
father's bed,
onto my couch and defiled it.[x]

5"Simeon and Levi are brothers—
their swords[a] are weapons of
violence.[y]
6Let me not enter their council,
let me not join their assembly,[z]
for they have killed men in their
anger[a]
and hamstrung oxen as they
pleased.
7Cursed be their anger, so fierce,
and their fury, so cruel!
I will scatter them in Jacob
and disperse them in Israel.[b]

8"Judah,[b] your brothers will praise
you;
your hand will be on the neck of
your enemies;
your father's sons will bow down
to you.[c]
9You are a lion's[d] cub, O Judah;[e]
you return from the prey, my
son.
Like a lion he crouches and lies
down,
like a lioness—who dares to
rouse him?
10The scepter will not depart from
Judah,[f]
nor the ruler's staff from
between his feet,
until he comes to whom it
belongs[c]
and the obedience of the nations
is his.[g]
11He will tether his donkey to a vine,
his colt to the choicest branch;
he will wash his garments in wine,
his robes in the blood of grapes.
12His eyes will be darker than wine,
his teeth whiter than milk.[d]

13"Zebulun[h] will live by the
seashore
and become a haven for ships;
his border will extend toward
Sidon.

14"Issachar[i] is a rawboned[e] donkey
lying down between two
saddlebags.[f]
15When he sees how good is his
resting place
and how pleasant is his land,
he will bend his shoulder to the
burden
and submit to forced labor.

16"Dan[g][j] will provide justice for his
people
as one of the tribes of Israel.
17Dan[k] will be a serpent by the
roadside,
a viper along the path,
that bites the horse's heels
so that its rider tumbles
backward.

18"I look for your deliverance,
O LORD.[l]

19"Gad[h][m] will be attacked by a
band of raiders,
but he will attack them at their
heels.

20"Asher's[n] food will be rich;
he will provide delicacies fit for a
king.

21"Naphtali[o] is a doe set free
that bears beautiful fawns.[i]

22"Joseph[p] is a fruitful vine,
a fruitful vine near a spring,
whose branches climb over a
wall.[j]
23With bitterness archers attacked
him;
they shot at him with hostility.[q]
24But his bow remained steady,
his strong arms[r] stayed[k]
limber,
because of the hand of the Mighty
One of Jacob,[s]
because of the Shepherd, the
Rock of Israel,[t]
25because of your father's God,[u]
who helps you,
because of the Almighty,[l] who
blesses you

49:1 [s]Nu 24:14; Jer 23:20 **49:2** [t]Ps 34:11 **49:3** [u]Ge 29:32 [v]Dt 21:17; Ps 78:51 **49:4** [w]Isa 57:20 [x]Ge 35:22; Dt 27:20 **49:5** [y]Ge 34:25; Pr 4:17 **49:6** [z]Pr 1:15; Eph 5:11 [a]Ge 34:26 **49:7** [b]Jos 19:1,9; 21:1-42 **49:8** [c]Dt 33:7; 1Ch 5:2 **49:9** [d]Nu 24:9; Eze 19:5; Mic 5:8 [e]Rev 5:5 **49:10** [f]Nu 24:17,19; Ps 60:7 [g]Ps 2:9; Isa 42:1,4 **49:13** [h]Ge 30:20; Dt 33:18-19; Jos 19:10-11 **49:14** [i]Ge 30:18 **49:16** [j]Ge 30:6; Dt 33:22; Jdg 18:26-27 **49:17** [k]Jdg 18:27 **49:18** [l]Ps 119:166, 174 **49:19** [m]Ge 30:11; Dt 33:20; 1Ch 5:18 **49:20** [n]Ge 30:13; Dt 33:24 **49:21** [o]Ge 30:8; Dt 33:23 **49:22** [p]Ge 30:24; Dt 33:13-17 **49:23** [q]Ge 37:24 **49:24** [r]Ps 18:34 [s]Ps 132:2,5; Isa 1:24; 41:10 [t]Isa 28:16 **49:25** [u]Ge 28:13

[a]*5* The meaning of the Hebrew for this word is uncertain. [b]*8* *Judah* sounds like and may be derived from the Hebrew for *praise.* [c]*10* Or *until Shiloh comes;* or *until he comes to whom tribute belongs* [d]*12* Or *will be dull from wine, / his teeth white from milk* [e]*14* Or *strong* [f]*14* Or *campfires* [g]*16* *Dan* here means *he provides justice.* [h]*19* *Gad* can mean *attack* and *band of raiders.* [i]*21* Or *free; / he utters beautiful words* [j]*22* Or *Joseph is a wild colt, / a wild colt near a spring, / a wild donkey on a terraced hill* [k]*23,24* Or *archers will attack . . . will shoot . . . will remain . . . will stay* [l]*25* Hebrew *Shaddai*

with blessings of the heavens
above,
blessings of the deep that lies
below,[v]
blessings of the breast and
womb.
26Your father's blessings are greater
than the blessings of the ancient
mountains,
than[a] the bounty of the age-old
hills.
Let all these rest on the head of
Joseph,
on the brow of the prince
among[b] his brothers.[w]

27"Benjamin[x] is a ravenous wolf;
in the morning he devours the
prey,
in the evening he divides the
plunder."

28All these are the twelve tribes of
Israel, and this is what their father said
to them when he blessed them, giving
each the blessing appropriate to him.

The Death of Jacob

29Then he gave them these instructions:[y] "I am about to be gathered to
my people.[z] Bury me with my fathers[a] in the cave in the field of
Ephron the Hittite, 30the cave in the
field of Machpelah,[b] near Mamre in
Canaan, which Abraham bought as a
burial place from Ephron the Hittite,
along with the field.[c] 31There Abraham[d] and his wife Sarah[e] were buried, there Isaac and his wife Rebekah[f]
were buried, and there I buried Leah.
32The field and the cave in it were
bought from the Hittites.[c]"

33When Jacob had finished giving instructions to his sons, he drew his feet
up into the bed, breathed his last and
was gathered to his people.[g]

50 Joseph threw himself upon his father and wept over him and kissed
him.[h] 2Then Joseph directed the physicians in his service to embalm his father Israel. So the physicians embalmed him,[i] 3taking a full forty days,
for that was the time required for em-
balming. And the Egyptians mourned
for him seventy days.[j]

4When the days of mourning had
passed, Joseph said to Pharaoh's court,
"If I have found favor in your eyes,
speak to Pharaoh for me. Tell him,
5'My father made me swear an oath[k]
and said, "I am about to die; bury me
in the tomb I dug for myself[l] in the
land of Canaan."[m] Now let me go up
and bury my father; then I will return.' "

6Pharaoh said, "Go up and bury your
father, as he made you swear to do."
7So Joseph went up to bury his father. All Pharaoh's officials accompanied him—the dignitaries of his court
and all the dignitaries of Egypt— 8be-
sides all the members of Joseph's
household and his brothers and those
belonging to his father's household.
Only their children and their flocks and
herds were left in Goshen. 9Chariots
and horsemen[d] also went up with
him. It was a very large company.

10When they reached the threshing
floor of Atad, near the Jordan, they lamented loudly and bitterly;[n] and
there Joseph observed a seven-day
period[o] of mourning for his father.
11When the Canaanites who lived there
saw the mourning at the threshing
floor of Atad, they said, "The Egyptians
are holding a solemn ceremony of
mourning." That is why that place near
the Jordan is called Abel Mizraim.[e]

12So Jacob's sons did as he had commanded them: 13They carried him to

[a] 26 Or *of my progenitors, / as great as*
[b] 26 Or *the one separated from*
[c] 32 Or *the sons of Heth*
[d] 9 Or *charioteers*
[e] 11 *Abel Mizraim* means *mourning of the Egyptians.*

49:25 [v]Ge 27:28
49:26 [w]Dt 33:15-16
49:27 [x]Ge 35:18; Jdg 20:12-13
49:29 [y]Ge 50:16 [z]Ge 25:8 [a]Ge 15:15; 47:30; 50:13
49:30 [b]Ge 23:9 [c]Ge 23:20
49:31 [d]Ge 25:9 [e]Ge 23:19 [f]Ge 35:29
49:33 [g]ver 29; Ge 25:8; Ac 7:15
50:1 [h]Ge 46:4
50:2 [i]ver 26; 2Ch 16:14
50:3 [j]Ge 37:34; Nu 20:29; Dt 34:8
50:5 [k]Ge 47:31 [l]2Ch 16:14; Isa 22:16 [m]Ge 47:31
50:10 [n]2Sa 1:17; Ac 8:2 [o]1Sa 31:13; Job 2:13

50:18–21

PROMISE 6

FORGIVE AND BE FORGIVEN

The Bible emphasizes forgiveness. God forgives us, and he demands that we forgive others. Joseph's amazing statement in this passage demonstrates that forgiveness. Nowhere in this story do we read Joseph saying "I forgive you," in so many words to his brothers, but throughout his story we find evidence that he did. And wouldn't all of us rather see forgiveness and not hear it, than hear it and not see it?

Only through forgiving others and accepting their forgiveness can we hope to function as genuine promise keepers. Only then will we be able to build true friendships that lead to accountability. Only then will we be able to reconcile ourselves to our brothers, our families, our pastors, and our God. Forgiving another person isn't easy; accepting forgiveness from someone else can be just as difficult. But you can start by taking a step in the right direction: List any wrongs that have been done to you, whether directly or indirectly, and ask God to empower you to forgive those people who have wronged you. Then make a conscious decision to live in the power and positivity of that forgiveness, knowing how much God has forgiven you.

For the next Promise 6 reading go to page 150.

JOSEPH

Why Retaliate When You Can Reconcile?

Joseph's brothers were terrified. By their calculation, it was payback time. In their jealousy, they had been mercilessly cruel to their brother Joseph; surely, he would want to retaliate now that their father Jacob was out of the way. To cover themselves, they fabricated a lie, telling Joseph their father had instructed him to forgive them. Like most bullies who use their power to oppress others, these guys thought that a person in Joseph's position would naturally use his power to his advantage.

But they were wrong. They had nothing to fear from Joseph. Their error was that they tried to predict Joseph's behavior by their view of how life worked. They had yet to grasp the simple, yet profound difference that set Joseph apart from them. They had yet to learn about the process of maturity and forgiveness that Joseph had undergone since that dark day when they sold him into slavery (37:27).

A Painful Past

What would you have done had you been in Joseph's sandals? Reflect for a minute on what he had experienced in his lifetime. When Joseph was a young boy, he had been Dad's favorite—and did he ever let his brothers know about it (37:4–11). In a jealous fit they threw him into a pit to die of exposure (37:24). While Joseph screamed for help, his brothers sat next to the pit and had lunch (37:25). Finally they discovered they could make a few shekels by selling Joseph, their younger brother, into slavery (37:26–28). These thugs had tried to destroy the destiny Joseph believed God had revealed to him in his dreams. They had broken their beloved father's heart by taking away the son he loved and enjoyed, depriving both father and son of years of a relationship that they could never recover.

When Joseph arrived in Egypt he had experienced further injustice, and learned some hard lessons. Although he tried to do what was right for Potiphar, his master, Joseph was framed by this man's wife and was thrown into prison (39:17–20). When Joseph helped the king's cupbearer get out of prison, he conveniently forgot about Joseph and left him to rot for two years. Had you been in Joseph's position, how would you have responded to such hardship?

A Powerful Perspective

Although he now had power to do whatever he wanted to whomever he wanted, Joseph had learned how to overcome the debilitating power of self-pity. Sure, he could have complained that life had been unfair, that he'd had a rotten childhood, that the circumstances of his life had ruined him. Instead, he chose to trust God and to live in line with God's will, no matter what. Joseph's supernatural perspective comes through clearly in Genesis 50:19–21. Of all we read about Joseph, this statement gives us the most insight into what made him tick. He said, simply, "I'm not God." Read this amazing statement in verses 19–21 and reflect on it for a moment. These words came about as the result of Joseph's long experience with hardship, forgiveness, and what he had found out about God's faithfulness.

Joseph wasn't any different than any other person. He wasn't some sort of super-spiritual guy who could shrug off his emotions at will. But he had allowed God to work in his life, to change and mold his attitudes toward his negative life experiences. It is enormously significant that Joseph treated the act of forgiveness as he did—as the natural result of God's work in his life, not as a begrudging, disciplined obedience to a difficult command. Joseph had experienced and learned and grown and seen. He had matured in his walk with God, and that maturity gave him the proper perspective at this point in his life.

Joseph's brothers lived in fear of Joseph's power because they couldn't imagine missing the opportunity to get even with someone who had hurt them. Joseph lived in the joy of his brother's company because he couldn't imagine any response but forgiveness and restoration. His brothers' thinking was driven by the human condition. Joseph's thinking was driven by a lifetime of learning the power of forgiveness through surrendering to God's will.

Forgiveness: God's Middle Name

Forgiveness is what God is all about. God is pleased to forgive the repentant sinner and receive him or her into his divine heart. We can't miss how much forgiveness is a part of his nature! Why would he not work that same desire into the life of one in whom his Spirit lives, such as Joseph? Or you?

Are you living with the pain of past betrayals and injustices? Have trusted people in your life "sold you out" and left you to rot? Have you ever been punished for doing the right thing? Forgiveness is difficult—make no mistake about that. But, through the power of God's forgiving Spirit, you can overcome the bitterness and pain that plague you. Many people choose to ignore God's promptings to forgive people who have wronged them, and live a life shackled to bitterness and regret instead of breaking those chains and living in the power of forgiveness.

You can choose to be like Joseph, who went to those who had wronged him and sought out reconciliation. You can choose to break the bonds of a painful past, and to address any future problem with the same perspective that Joseph had: "Am I in the place of God? You intended to harm me, but God intended it for good to accomplish what is now being done. . . " (50:19–20).

—Dr. Sid Buzzell

the land of Canaan and buried him in the cave in the field of Machpelah, near Mamre, which Abraham had bought as a burial place from Ephron the Hittite, along with the field.[p] 14After burying his father, Joseph returned to Egypt, together with his brothers and all the others who had gone with him to bury his father.

Joseph Reassures His Brothers

15When Joseph's brothers saw that their father was dead, they said, "What if Joseph holds a grudge against us and pays us back for all the wrongs we did to him?"[q] 16So they sent word to Joseph, saying, "Your father left these instructions before he died: 17'This is what you are to say to Joseph: I ask you to forgive your brothers the sins and the wrongs they committed in treating you so badly.' Now please forgive the sins of the servants of the God of your father." When their message came to him, Joseph wept.

18His brothers then came and threw themselves down before him.[r] "We are your slaves,"[s] they said.

19But Joseph said to them, "Don't be afraid. Am I in the place of God?[t] 20You intended to harm me,[u] but God intended[v] it for good[w] to accomplish what is now being done, the saving of many lives.[x] 21So then, don't be afraid. I will provide for you and your children.[y]" And he reassured them and spoke kindly to them.

The Death of Joseph

22Joseph stayed in Egypt, along with all his father's family. He lived a hundred and ten years[z] 23and saw the third generation[a] of Ephraim's children. Also the children of Makir[b] son of Manasseh were placed at birth on Joseph's knees.[a]

24Then Joseph said to his brothers, "I am about to die.[c] But God will surely come to your aid[d] and take you up out of this land to the land[e] he promised on oath to Abraham, Isaac and Jacob."[f] 25And Joseph made the sons of Israel swear an oath and said, "God will surely come to your aid, and then you must carry my bones up from this place."[g]

26So Joseph died at the age of a hundred and ten. And after they embalmed him,[h] he was placed in a coffin in Egypt.

50:13 [p]Ge 23:20; Ac 7:16
50:15 [q]Ge 37:28; 42:21-22
50:18 [r]Ge 37:7 [s]Ge 43:18
50:19 [t]Ro 12:19; Heb 10:30
50:20 [u]Ge 37:20 [v]Mic 4:11-12 [w]Ro 8:28 [x]Ge 45:5
50:21 [y]Ge 45:11; 47:12
50:22 [z]Ge 25:7; Jos 24:29
50:23 [a]Job 42:16 [b]Nu 32:39,40
50:24 [c]Ge 48:21 [d]Ex 3:16-17 [e]Ge 15:14 [f]Ge 12:7; 26:3; 28:13; 35:12
50:25 [g]Ge 47:29-30; Ex 13:19; Jos 24:32; Heb 11:22
50:26 [h]ver 2

a *23* That is, were counted as his

EXODUS

AT A GLANCE

Key Principle: As God's redeemed people, we are called to be set apart from the world's priorities and value systems and to be dedicated wholly to the Lord.
Author: Moses
Time and Place: 1446 B.C. or 1290 B.C. (late-date view) / From Egypt to Mount Sinai
Key Verses: 6:6; 19:5–6; 20:2

BENEFIT

This book vividly portrays the dramatic account of God's plan to redeem his people by raising up a deliverer (Moses), protecting the Israelites from the ten plagues, bringing them safely through the sea and providing for their needs in the wilderness.

SETTING

Assuming the 1446 B.C. date of the exodus rather than the 1290 B.C. late-date view, Moses composed this book and the rest of the Pentateuch (the first five books of the Bible) during the forty years of wilderness wanderings and possibly edited it in the plains of Moab before his death in 1405 B.C. Exodus begins with Joseph's generation (Jacob and his family came to Egypt c. 1875 B.C.) and ends as the people build the tabernacle in the wilderness. Jacob's family, the children of Israel, numbered only 70 when they went into Egypt, but over two million Israelites left Egypt four centuries later. Not counting women and children, 603,550 men twenty years old and older left Egypt with Moses (Numbers 2:32).

TIME LINE 2200BC 2100 2000 1900 1800 1700 1600 1500 1400

Moses' birth (c.1526 B.C.)
The plagues; The Passover (c.1446 B.C.)
The exodus (c.1446 B.C.)
Desert wanderings (c.1446-1406 B.C.)
The Ten Commandments (c.1445 B.C.)
Book of Exodus written (c.1440 B.C.)
Moses dies; Joshua becomes leader (c.1406 B.C.)
Israelites enter Canaan (c.1406 B.C.)

THEME AND PURPOSE

The theme of Exodus is God's redemption and deliverance of his people. This miraculous act is portrayed in the institution of the Passover sacrifice and the miraculous crossing of the Red Sea. This book was written to record the birth of Israel as a nation, to depict God's redemption of Israel in the first Passover, to give the early history of Moses as the Lord's chosen deliverer and leader, to portray God's providential care of the Israelites in the wilderness and to describe the components and construction of the tabernacle. Exodus also contrasts Yahweh with the false gods of Egypt and underscores the necessity of obedience to his divine mandates.

UNIQUE CONTRIBUTION

Exodus shows how Moses revealed God's laws and depicts the institution of Israel's priesthood, sanctuary and sacrificial system. The twin themes of the Passover and the exodus are foundational to the rest of the Old Testament, which refers to these events again and again. These saving acts of God are pivotal to the story of God's plan to bring salvation to the earth. Exodus also abounds in illustrations of the Messiah to come, including the Passover lamb, the structure of the tabernacle, the person of Moses, the seven feasts, the manna and the water and the high priest.

LINKS TO THE NEW TESTAMENT

Moses is an illustration of Christ in that he was a prophet, a priest and a king (Israel's ruler). As was Christ, Moses was endangered in infancy, he renounced his claim to power and wealth, he redeemed his people from bondage and he interceded for them to God. The Passover ceremony anticipated the redemptive work of Christ, our Passover Lamb who takes away the sins of the world (John 1:29, 36; 1 Corinthians 5:7). The exodus is related to our baptism into Christ's death and resurrection life in Romans 6:2–3 and 1 Corinthians 10:1–2. The manna and water are associated with Christ in John 6:31–63 and 1 Corinthians 10:3–4.

OVERVIEW

FOCUS	Bondage	Deliverance	Revelation
REFERENCE	1 — 6	7 — 18	19 — 40
TOPICS	Incubation of the Nation	Inception of the Nation	Infancy of the Nation
	Preparation	Redemption	Revelation
	People of God	Grace of God	Holiness of God
	Narration		Legislation
LOCATION	Egypt	Wilderness	Mt. Sinai
TIME	430 Years	2 Months	10 Months

Exodus begins by describing the plight of the children of Israel after four centuries of bondage in Egypt. When they cry to the God of their fathers, the Lord raises up Moses to deliver them from their oppressors and to prepare them for their journey into the wilderness (1—6). The ten plagues are God's indictment against the false gods of Egypt (7—10). The protection of the firstborn through the blood of Passover lambs (11—12) typifies the redemption of God's people. The miraculous Red Sea crossing (13—14) reveals God's power on behalf of the redeemed Israelites, and the preservation of Israel in the face of thirst, hunger and enemies (16—18) demonstrates God's providential care.

Having redeemed and protected his people, God prepares them to walk in holiness before him by establishing his covenant with them. Through Moses, the people receive the Ten Commandments and the book of the covenant (19—24) as well as detailed instructions concerning the construction of the tabernacle that will serve as Israel's central sanctuary (25—31). In spite of their idolatry and rebellion (32—33), God renews his covenant with the people and they build and consecrate the tabernacle (34—40).

EXODUS

The Israelites Oppressed

1 These are the names of the sons of Israel[a] who went to Egypt with Jacob, each with his family: 2Reuben, Simeon, Levi and Judah; 3Issachar, Zebulun and Benjamin; 4Dan and Naphtali; Gad and Asher. 5The descendants of Jacob numbered seventy[a] in all;[b] Joseph was already in Egypt.

6Now Joseph and all his brothers and all that generation died,[c] 7but the Israelites were fruitful and multiplied greatly and became exceedingly numerous,[d] so that the land was filled with them.

8Then a new king, who did not know about Joseph, came to power in Egypt. 9"Look," he said to his people, "the Israelites have become much too numerous[e] for us. 10Come, we must deal shrewdly[f] with them or they will become even more numerous and, if war breaks out, will join our enemies, fight against us and leave the country."[g]

11So they put slave masters[h] over them to oppress them with forced labor,[i] and they built Pithom and Rameses[j] as store cities[k] for Pharaoh. 12But the more they were oppressed, the more they multiplied and spread; so the Egyptians came to dread the Israelites 13and worked them ruthlessly.[l] 14They made their lives bitter with hard labor in brick and mortar and with all kinds of work in the fields; in all their hard labor the Egyptians used them ruthlessly.[m]

15The king of Egypt said to the Hebrew midwives, whose names were Shiphrah and Puah, 16"When you help the Hebrew women in childbirth and observe them on the delivery stool, if it is a boy, kill him; but if it is a girl, let her live." 17The midwives, however, feared[n] God and did not do what the king of Egypt had told them to do;[o] they let the boys live. 18Then the king of Egypt summoned the midwives and asked them, "Why have you done this? Why have you let the boys live?"

19The midwives answered Pharaoh, "Hebrew women are not like Egyptian women; they are vigorous and give birth before the midwives arrive."[p]

20So God was kind to the midwives[q] and the people increased and became even more numerous. 21And because the midwives feared God, he gave them families[r] of their own.

1:1 [a]Ge 46:8
1:5 [b]Ge 46:26
1:6 [c]Ge 50:26
1:7 [d]Ge 46:3; Dt 26:5; Ac 7:17
1:9 [e]Ps 105:24-25
1:10 [f]Ps 83:3 [g]Ac 7:17-19
1:11 [h]Ex 3:7 [i]Ge 15:13; Ex 2:11; 5:4; 6:6-7 [j]Ge 47:11 [k]1Ki 9:19; 2Ch 8:4
1:13 [l]Dt 4:20
1:14 [m]Ex 2:23; 6:9; Nu 20:15; Ps 81:6; Ac 7:19
1:17 [n]ver 21; Pr 16:6 [o]Da 3:16-18; Ac 4:18-20; 5:29
1:19 [p]Jos 2:4-6; 2Sa 17:20
1:20 [q]ver 12; Pr 11:18; Isa 3:10
1:21 [r]1Sa 2:35; 2Sa 7:11, 27-29; 1Ki 11:38
1:22 [s]Ac 7:19
2:1 [t]Ex 6:20; Nu 26:59
2:2 [u]Ac 7:20; Heb 11:23
2:4 [v]Ex 15:20; Nu 26:59
2:5 [w]Ex 7:15; 8:20

22Then Pharaoh gave this order to all his people: "Every boy that is born[b] you must throw into the Nile, but let every girl live."[s]

The Birth of Moses

2 Now a man of the house of Levi married a Levite woman,[t] 2and she became pregnant and gave birth to a son. When she saw that he was a fine child, she hid him for three months.[u] 3But when she could hide him no longer, she got a papyrus basket for him and coated it with tar and pitch. Then she placed the child in it and put it among the reeds along the bank of the Nile. 4His sister[v] stood at a distance to see what would happen to him.

5Then Pharaoh's daughter went down to the Nile to bathe, and her attendants were walking along the river bank.[w] She saw the basket among the reeds and sent her slave girl to get it. 6She opened it and saw the baby. He was crying, and she felt sorry for him. "This is one of the Hebrew babies," she said.

7Then his sister asked Pharaoh's daughter, "Shall I go and get one of the Hebrew women to nurse the baby for you?"

[a] *5* Masoretic Text (see also Gen. 46:27); Dead Sea Scrolls and Septuagint (see also Acts 7:14 and note at Gen. 46:27) *seventy-five*
[b] *22* Masoretic Text; Samaritan Pentateuch, Septuagint and Targums *born to the Hebrews*

1:15–17

PROMISE 7

ORDINARY PEOPLE

Who in the world were Shiphrah and Puah? No monuments are erected to their memory, but after all the monuments are destroyed, their names will endure in God's eternal Word. What did they do? They did what was right. These unsung heroes simply honored God in their positions as midwives.

You, too, can be known for your faithfulness to our Almighty God. These two women feared God and did what he wanted (v. 17). "So God was kind to the midwives" (v. 20). These were ordinary folks doing ordinary jobs with extraordinary commitment to God. While you live your normal, ordinary life like most of us, live it in fear of God and do what he says. That's all he asks.

For the next Promise 7 reading go to page 118.

8“Yes, go,” she answered. And the
girl went and got the baby’s mother.
9Pharaoh’s daughter said to her, “Take
this baby and nurse him for me, and I
will pay you.” So the woman took the
baby and nursed him. 10When the
child grew older, she took him to Pharaoh’s daughter and he became her son.
She named him Moses,[a] saying, “I
drew him out of the water.”

Moses Flees to Midian

11One day, after Moses had grown
up, he went out to where his own people[x] were and watched them at their
hard labor. He saw an Egyptian beating
a Hebrew, one of his own people.
12Glancing this way and that and seeing no one, he killed the Egyptian and
hid him in the sand. 13The next day he
went out and saw two Hebrews fighting. He asked the one in the wrong,
“Why are you hitting your fellow Hebrew?”[y]
14The man said, “Who made you ruler and judge over us?[z] Are you thinking of killing me as you killed the Egyptian?” Then Moses was afraid and
thought, “What I did must have become known.”
15When Pharaoh heard of this, he
tried to kill Moses, but Moses fled from
Pharaoh and went to live in Midian,[a]
where he sat down by a well. 16Now a
priest of Midian[b] had seven daughters, and they came to draw water[c]
and fill the troughs to water their father’s flock. 17Some shepherds came
along and drove them away, but Moses
got up and came to their rescue and
watered their flock.[d]
18When the girls returned to Reuel[e]
their father, he asked them, “Why have
you returned so early today?”
19They answered, “An Egyptian rescued us from the shepherds. He even
drew water for us and watered the
flock.”
20“And where is he?” he asked his
daughters. “Why did you leave him? Invite him to have something to eat.”[f]
21Moses agreed to stay with the man,
who gave his daughter Zipporah[g] to
Moses in marriage. 22Zipporah gave
birth to a son, and Moses named him
Gershom,[b] saying, “I have become an
alien[h] in a foreign land.”
23During that long period,[i] the king
of Egypt died. The Israelites groaned in
their slavery and cried out, and their
cry[j] for help because of their slavery
went up to God. 24God heard their
groaning and he remembered his covenant[k] with Abraham, with Isaac and
with Jacob. 25So God looked on the
Israelites and was concerned[l] about
them.

Moses and the Burning Bush

3 Now Moses was tending the flock of
Jethro[m] his father-in-law, the priest
of Midian, and he led the flock to the
far side of the desert and came to Horeb,[n] the mountain[o] of God. 2There
the angel of the LORD[p] appeared to
him in flames of fire from within a
bush.[q] Moses saw that though the
bush was on fire it did not burn up. 3So
Moses thought, “I will go over and see
this strange sight—why the bush does
not burn up.”
4When the LORD saw that he had
gone over to look, God called to him
from within the bush, “Moses! Moses!”
And Moses said, “Here I am.”
5“Do not come any closer,” God
said. “Take off your sandals, for the
place where you are standing is holy
ground.”[r] 6Then he said, “I am the
God of your father, the God of Abraham, the God of Isaac and the God of
Jacob.”[s] At this, Moses hid his face,
because he was afraid to look at God.
7The LORD said, “I have indeed seen
the misery of my people in Egypt. I
have heard them crying out because
of their slave drivers, and I am concerned[t] about their suffering. 8So I
have come down[u] to rescue them
from the hand of the Egyptians and to
bring them up out of that land into a
good and spacious land, a land flowing
with milk and honey[v]—the home of
the Canaanites, Hittites, Amorites, Perizzites, Hivites and Jebusites.[w] 9And
now the cry of the Israelites has
reached me, and I have seen the way
the Egyptians are oppressing[x] them.
10So now, go. I am sending you to Pharaoh to bring my people the Israelites
out of Egypt.”[y]
11But Moses said to God, “Who am
I,[z] that I should go to Pharaoh and
bring the Israelites out of Egypt?”
12And God said, “I will be with
you.[a] And this will be the sign to you
that it is I who have sent you: When
you have brought the people out of
Egypt, you[c] will worship God on this
mountain.”
13Moses said to God, “Suppose I go
to the Israelites and say to them, ‘The
God of your fathers has sent me to
you,’ and they ask me, ‘What is his
name?’ Then what shall I tell them?”
14God said to Moses, “I AM WHO I

2:11 [x]Ac 7:23; Heb 11:24-26
2:13 [y]Ac 7:26
2:14 [z]Ac 7:27*
2:15 [a]Ac 7:29; Heb 11:27
2:16 [b]Ex 3:1 [c]Ge 24:11
2:17 [d]Ge 29:10
2:18 [e]Nu 10:29
2:20 [f]Ge 31:54
2:21 [g]Ex 18:2
2:22 [h]Ex 18:3-4; Heb 11:13
2:23 [i]Ac 7:30 [j]Ex 3:7,9; Dt 26:7; Jas 5:4
2:24 [k]Ex 6:5; Ps 105:10,42
2:25 [l]Ex 3:7; 4:31
3:1 [m]Ex 2:18 [n]1Ki 19:8 [o]Ex 18:5
3:2 [p]Ge 16:7 [q]Dt 33:16; Mk 12:26; Ac 7:30
3:5 [r]Ge 28:17; Jos 5:15; Ac 7:33*
3:6 [s]Ex 4:5; Mt 22:32*; Mk 12:26*; Lk 20:37*; Ac 7:32*
3:7 [t]Ex 2:25
3:8 [u]Ge 50:24 [v]ver 17; Ex 13:5; Dt 1:25 [w]Ge 15:18-21
3:9 [x]Ex 1:14; 2:23
3:10 [y]Mic 6:4
3:11 [z]Ex 6:12,30; 1Sa 18:18
3:12 [a]Ge 31:3; Jos 1:5; Ro 8:31

a *10* *Moses* sounds like the Hebrew for *draw out.*
b *22* *Gershom* sounds like the Hebrew for *an alien there.*
c *12* The Hebrew is plural.

AM.[a] This is what you are to say to the
Israelites: 'I AM[b] has sent me to you.' "
15God also said to Moses, "Say to the
Israelites, 'The LORD,[b] the God of your
fathers—the God of Abraham, the God
of Isaac and the God of Jacob—has
sent me to you.' This is my name[c] forever, the name by which I am to be
remembered from generation to generation.
16"Go, assemble the elders[d] of Israel and say to them, 'The LORD, the God
of your fathers—the God of Abraham,
Isaac and Jacob—appeared to me and
said: I have watched over you and have
seen what has been done to you in
Egypt. 17And I have promised to bring
you up out of your misery in Egypt[e]
into the land of the Canaanites, Hittites, Amorites, Perizzites, Hivites and
Jebusites—a land flowing with milk
and honey.'
18"The elders of Israel will listen[f] to
you. Then you and the elders are to go
to the king of Egypt and say to him,
'The LORD, the God of the Hebrews, has
met with us. Let us take a three-day
journey into the desert to offer sacrifices[g] to the LORD our God.' 19But I
know that the king of Egypt will not let
you go unless a mighty hand[h] compels him. 20So I will stretch out my
hand[i] and strike the Egyptians with
all the wonders[j] that I will perform
among them. After that, he will let
you go.[k]

3:14–15

PROMISE 1

I AM

God had thrown Moses into the deep end of the pool. He was slated to face down Pharaoh. But first Moses had to convince a nation of slaves that he was going to deliver them.

"Now," Moses said, "Who should I say sent me to do this?" God's answer: "I AM." Tell them "I AM" has sent you. The eternal, unchanging God, the same God who guided and protected Abraham, Isaac and Jacob is sending you. As I was with them, so I will be with you.

Today, the great I AM adds to the three illustrations he gave Moses. "I am also the God of Moses, Joshua, David, Daniel, Paul and Peter. I am the God who raised my Son Jesus from the grave." When you go to your friends who are enslaved in sin and tell them you know how to deliver them, go as the representative of I AM. When you feel fear, as Moses did, go confidently. I AM has sent you. I AM has promised to be with you. I AM never changes.

For the next Promise 1 reading go to page 88.

21"And I will make the Egyptians favorably disposed[l] toward this people,
so that when you leave you will not go
empty-handed.[m] 22Every woman is to
ask her neighbor and any woman living
in her house for articles of silver and
gold[n] and for clothing, which you will
put on your sons and daughters. And
so you will plunder[o] the Egyptians."

Signs for Moses

4 Moses answered, "What if they do
not believe me or listen[p] to me and
say, 'The LORD did not appear to you'?"
2Then the LORD said to him, "What is
that in your hand?"
"A staff,"[q] he replied.
3The LORD said, "Throw it on the
ground."
Moses threw it on the ground and it
became a snake, and he ran from it.
4Then the LORD said to him, "Reach out
your hand and take it by the tail." So
Moses reached out and took hold of
the snake and it turned back into a staff
in his hand. 5"This," said the LORD, "is
so that they may believe[r] that the
LORD, the God of their fathers—the
God of Abraham, the God of Isaac and
the God of Jacob—has appeared to
you."
6Then the LORD said, "Put your hand
inside your cloak." So Moses put his
hand into his cloak, and when he took
it out, it was leprous,[c] like snow.[s]
7"Now put it back into your cloak,"
he said. So Moses put his hand back
into his cloak, and when he took it out,
it was restored,[t] like the rest of his
flesh.
8Then the LORD said, "If they do not
believe you or pay attention to the first
miraculous sign, they may believe the
second. 9But if they do not believe
these two signs or listen to you, take
some water from the Nile and pour it
on the dry ground. The water you take
from the river will become blood[u] on
the ground."
10Moses said to the LORD, "O Lord, I
have never been eloquent, neither in
the past nor since you have spoken to
your servant. I am slow of speech and
tongue."[v]
11The LORD said to him, "Who gave
man his mouth? Who makes him deaf
or mute? Who gives him sight or makes
him blind?[w] Is it not I, the LORD?
12Now go; I will help you speak and will
teach you what to say."[x]

3:14 [b]Ex 6:2-3; Jn 8:58; Heb 13:8
3:15 [c]Ps 135:13; Hos 12:5
3:16 [d]Ex 4:29
3:17 [e]Ge 15:16; Jos 24:11
3:18 [f]Ex 4:1,8,31 [g]Ex 5:1,3
3:19 [h]Ex 4:21; 5:2
3:20 [i]Ex 6:1,6; 9:15 [j]Dt 6:22; Ne 9:10; Ac 7:36 [k]Ex 12:31-33
3:21 [l]Ex 12:36 [m]Ps 105:37
3:22 [n]Ex 11:2 [o]Eze 39:10
4:1 [p]Ex 3:18; 6:30
4:2 [q]ver 17,20
4:5 [r]Ex 19:9
4:6 [s]Nu 12:10; 2Ki 5:1,27
4:7 [t]Nu 12:13-15; Dt 32:39; 2Ki 5:14; Mt 8:3
4:9 [u]Ex 7:17-21
4:10 [v]Ex 6:12; Jer 1:6
4:11 [w]Ps 94:9; Mt 11:5
4:12 [x]Isa 50:4; Jer 1:9; Mt 10:19-20; Mk 13:11; Lk 12:12; 21:14-15

a *14* Or *I WILL BE WHAT I WILL BE*
b *15* The Hebrew for *LORD* sounds like and may be derived from the Hebrew for *I AM* in verse 14.
c *6* The Hebrew word was used for various diseases affecting the skin—not necessarily leprosy.

13But Moses said, "O Lord, please send someone else to do it."

14Then the LORD's anger burned against Moses and he said, "What about your brother, Aaron the Levite? I know he can speak well. He is already on his way to meet[y] you, and his heart will be glad when he sees you. 15You shall speak to him and put words in his mouth;[z] I will help both of you speak and will teach you what to do. 16He will speak to the people for you, and it will be as if he were your mouth[a] and as if you were God to him. 17But take this staff[b] in your hand so you can perform miraculous signs[c] with it."

Moses Returns to Egypt

18Then Moses went back to Jethro his father-in-law and said to him, "Let me go back to my own people in Egypt to see if any of them are still alive."

Jethro said, "Go, and I wish you well."

19Now the LORD had said to Moses in Midian, "Go back to Egypt, for all the men who wanted to kill[d] you are dead.[e]" 20So Moses took his wife and sons, put them on a donkey and started back to Egypt. And he took the staff[f] of God in his hand.

21The LORD said to Moses, "When you return to Egypt, see that you perform before Pharaoh all the wonders[g] I have given you the power to do. But I will harden his heart[h] so that he will not let the people go. 22Then say to Pharaoh, 'This is what the LORD says: Israel is my firstborn son,[i] 23and I told you, "Let my son go,[j] so he may worship me." But you refused to let him go; so I will kill your firstborn son.' "[k]

24At a lodging place on the way, the LORD met ⌞Moses⌟[a] and was about to kill[l] him. 25But Zipporah took a flint knife, cut off her son's foreskin[m] and touched ⌞Moses'⌟ feet with it.[b] "Surely you are a bridegroom of blood to me," she said. 26So the LORD let him alone. (At that time she said "bridegroom of blood," referring to circumcision.)

27The LORD said to Aaron, "Go into the desert to meet Moses." So he met Moses at the mountain[n] of God and kissed[o] him. 28Then Moses told Aaron everything the LORD had sent him to say,[p] and also about all the miraculous signs he had commanded him to perform.

29Moses and Aaron brought together all the elders[q] of the Israelites, 30and Aaron told them everything the LORD had said to Moses. He also performed the signs before the people, 31and they believed.[r] And when they heard that the LORD was concerned[s] about them and had seen their misery, they bowed down and worshiped.

Bricks Without Straw

5 Afterward Moses and Aaron went to Pharaoh and said, "This is what the LORD, the God of Israel, says: 'Let my people go, so that they may hold a festival[t] to me in the desert.' "

2Pharaoh said, "Who is the LORD,[u] that I should obey him and let Israel go? I do not know the LORD and I will not let Israel go."[v]

3Then they said, "The God of the Hebrews has met with us. Now let us take a three-day journey into the desert to offer sacrifices to the LORD our God, or he may strike us with plagues[w] or with the sword."

4But the king of Egypt said, "Moses and Aaron, why are you taking the people away from their labor?[x] Get back to your work!" 5Then Pharaoh said, "Look, the people of the land are now numerous,[y] and you are stopping them from working."

6That same day Pharaoh gave this order to the slave drivers and foremen in charge of the people: 7"You are no longer to supply the people with straw for making bricks; let them go and gather their own straw. 8But require them to make the same number of bricks as before; don't reduce the quota. They are lazy; that is why they are crying out, 'Let us go and sacrifice to our God.' 9Make the work harder for

---

4:11–16

PROMISE 2

PICKING A PARTNER

Relationships are a vital part of life. But the relationship that we read about in this passage was based on dependency. Even though God's anger burned against Moses for making this request, he still got his wish. Aaron was recruited to do what Moses refused to do. Now turn to Exodus 32, where Aaron created a tragic situation for Moses.

This story holds a kernel of truth for us today. When building ministry or work partnerships, examine your motives carefully. Are you searching for a partner, or for a crutch? Note Moses' motives for teaming with Aaron and ask yourself what you are looking for from someone before you partner with that person in ministry, in friendship, or in some other sustained and dependent relationship.

For the next Promise 2 reading go to page 523.

4:14 [y]ver 27
4:15 [z]Nu 23:5,12,16
4:16 [a]Ex 7:1-2
4:17 [b]ver 2 [c]Ex 7:9-21
4:19 [d]Ex 2:15 [e]Ex 2:23
4:20 [f]Ex 17:9; Nu 20:8-9,11
4:21 [g]Ex 3:19,20 [h]Ex 7:3,13; 9:12,35; 14:4,8; Dt 2:30; Isa 63:17; Jn 12:40; Ro 9:18
4:22 [i]Isa 63:16; 64:8; Jer 31:9; Hos 11:1; Ro 9:4
4:23 [j]Ex 5:1; 7:16 [k]Ex 11:5; 12:12,29
4:24 [l]Nu 22:22
4:25 [m]Ge 17:14; Jos 5:2,3
4:27 [n]Ex 3:1 [o]ver 14
4:28 [p]ver 8-9,16
4:29 [q]Ex 3:16
4:31 [r]ver 8; Ex 3:18 [s]Ex 2:25
5:1 [t]Ex 3:18
5:2 [u]2Ki 18:35; Job 21:15 [v]Ex 3:19
5:3 [w]Ex 3:18
5:4 [x]Ex 1:11
5:5 [y]Ex 1:7,9

---

a 24 Or ⌞Moses' son⌟; Hebrew *him* b 25 Or *and drew near ⌞Moses'⌟ feet*

the men so that they keep working and
pay no attention to lies."
10Then the slave drivers and the
foremen went out and said to the people, "This is what Pharaoh says: 'I will
not give you any more straw. 11Go and
get your own straw wherever you can
find it, but your work will not be reduced at all.' " 12So the people scattered all over Egypt to gather stubble to
use for straw. 13The slave drivers kept
pressing them, saying, "Complete the
work required of you for each day, just
as when you had straw." 14The Israelite
foremen appointed by Pharaoh's slave
drivers were beaten[z] and were asked,
"Why didn't you meet your quota of
bricks yesterday or today, as before?"
15Then the Israelite foremen went
and appealed to Pharaoh: "Why have
you treated your servants this way?
16Your servants are given no straw, yet
we are told, 'Make bricks!' Your servants are being beaten, but the fault is
with your own people."
17Pharaoh said, "Lazy, that's what
you are—lazy![a] That is why you keep
saying, 'Let us go and sacrifice to the
LORD.' 18Now get to work. You will not
be given any straw, yet you must produce your full quota of bricks."
19The Israelite foremen realized they
were in trouble when they were told,
"You are not to reduce the number of
bricks required of you for each day."
20When they left Pharaoh, they found
Moses and Aaron waiting to meet
them, 21and they said, "May the LORD
look upon you and judge you! You have
made us a stench[b] to Pharaoh and his
officials and have put a sword in their
hand to kill us."[c]

God Promises Deliverance

22Moses returned to the LORD and
said, "O Lord, why have you brought
trouble upon this people?[d] Is this why
you sent me? 23Ever since I went to
Pharaoh to speak in your name, he has
brought trouble upon this people, and
you have not rescued[e] your people at
all."

6 Then the LORD said to Moses, "Now
you will see what I will do to Pharaoh: Because of my mighty hand[f] he
will let them go;[g] because of my
mighty hand he will drive them out of
his country."[h]
2God also said to Moses, "I am the
LORD. 3I appeared to Abraham, to Isaac
and to Jacob as God Almighty,[a][i] but
by my name[j] the LORD[b][k] I did not
make myself known to them.[c] 4I also
established my covenant[l] with them
to give them the land of Canaan, where
they lived as aliens.[m] 5Moreover, I
have heard the groaning[n] of the Israelites, whom the Egyptians are enslav-
ing, and I have remembered my covenant.
6"Therefore, say to the Israelites: 'I
am the LORD, and I will bring you out
from under the yoke of the Egyptians.
I will free you from being slaves to
them, and I will redeem[o] you with an
outstretched arm[p] and with mighty
acts of judgment. 7I will take you as my
own people, and I will be your God.[q]
Then you will know[r] that I am the
LORD your God, who brought you out
from under the yoke of the Egyptians.
8And I will bring you to the land[s] I
swore with uplifted hand[t] to give to
Abraham, to Isaac and to Jacob.[u] I will
give it to you as a possession. I am the
LORD.' "
9Moses reported this to the Israelites, but they did not listen to him because of their discouragement and cruel bondage.
10Then the LORD said to Moses,
11"Go, tell Pharaoh king of Egypt to let
the Israelites go out of his country."
12But Moses said to the LORD, "If the
Israelites will not listen to me, why

5:14 [z]Isa 10:24 **5:17** [a]ver 8 **5:21** [b]Ge 34:30 [c]Ex 14:11 **5:22** [d]Nu 11:11 **5:23** [e]Jer 4:10 **6:1** [f]Ex 3:19 [g]Ex 3:20 [h]Ex 12:31,33,39 **6:3** [i]Ge 17:1 [j]Ps 68:4; 83:18; Isa 52:6 [k]Ex 3:14 **6:4** [l]Ge 15:18 [m]Ge 28:4,13 **6:5** [n]Ex 2:23 **6:6** [o]Dt 7:8; 1Ch 17:21 [p]Dt 26:8 **6:7** [q]Dt 4:20; 2Sa 7:24 [r]Ex 16:12; Isa 41:20 **6:8** [s]Ge 15:18; 26:3 [t]Ge 14:22 [u]Ps 136:21-22

a *3* Hebrew *El-Shaddai* b *3* See note at Exodus 3:15. c *3* Or *Almighty, and by my name the LORD did I not let myself be known to them?*

6:6–8

PROMISE **5**

WE CAN BECAUSE OF I AM

Take a moment to count the "I am" and "I will" statements in this passage. Now think back to the people who heard these words from Moses. These Israelites had been born into slavery. Oppression was all they knew. Their ancestors for the previous 430 years had been slaves. They understood words like "I can't," "I won't," and "I don't" more than they understood these positive words. But God, through Moses, told these oppressed people, "I am" and "I will."

God's work often seems to limp along. Church members sometimes become overwhelmed with their situation and think in the negative: "We can't complete this building project"; "We won't reach our evangelism goals"; "We don't have what it takes to interest our young people in the things of the Lord." That's when we need to hear God say, "I am" and "I will." Be a voice of encouragement and hope in your church. Like Moses did, remind people that "God is" and "God will."

For the next Promise 5 reading go to page 79.

MOSES

The Man Who Met With God

Moses was a great man. There's no denying that. With God's help, he convinced a nation of slaves to escape their masters, travel across a barren desert with their children and animals, conquer the land they intended to live in and begin a new life there. Anyone who has tried to convince his kids to take out the trash or mow the lawn can understand the magnitude of Moses' task.

Moses' story is well known. He had to confront Pharaoh, one of the most powerful men on earth, and convince him to let God's people—all two million of them—go free. Threatening Pharaoh in his own house is not something a Midianite shepherd did every day of his life, but Moses told Pharaoh ten times that Egypt would suffer terrible consequences if he didn't free God's people. Moses was also the guy who had to take the heat from Pharaoh when God, true to his word, sent those ten terrible plagues.

Finally, Moses led the people out of Egypt. God allowed him to deliver Israel from Pharaoh's armies by parting the Red Sea. You would think that now, standing on the other side of the Red Sea, the worst of it would be over. Surely now, Moses would be established as Israel's leader under God's good hand.

Grumbling and Complaining

But life wasn't that simple for Moses. While God spoke with Moses and helped him lead the people toward their God-ordained destiny, Moses lived with some of the most intense opposition and unfair criticism recorded in the Bible. At Marah, the people griped that "they could not drink its water because it was bitter" (Exodus 15:23). Moses prayed and God miraculously sweetened the water so that all could drink. Then, "the whole community grumbled against Moses" (16:2) because they didn't like the food God provided. Moses prayed again and God provided meat and bread for everyone. At Rephidim the people "quarreled with Moses" (17:2) because there was no water. Once again, Moses prayed and God provided water for the people.

When the people of Israel finally arrived at Mount Sinai, God called Moses to come up the mountain and meet with him. Surely this would stop the complaints. Who could grumble at a man after he had spent time with God? Yet the Israelites complained as the days wore on that Moses had been gone too long from the camp.

Even Moses' sister and brother "began to talk against Moses" (Numbers 12:1). Miriam and Aaron challenged Moses' leadership, so God struck Miriam with leprosy. Moses prayed for her and God healed her.

This pattern of complaining, challenging and wailing continued throughout Moses' life. And Moses' response was consistent. Each time he heard the people's complaints, Moses prayed and God answered. God sometimes sent armies, threats of death, fire and poisonous snakes among the people because of their complaints against Moses. And each time, Moses' prayers spared the people from destruction.

How Does He Do It?

Two passages give us insight into what made this godly leader tick. Exodus 33:11 tells us that "the LORD would speak to Moses face to face, as a man speaks with his friend." Moses depended on God's presence and guidance. He could endure abuse from God's people because he knew he was God's man for the hour. Only a man who spends enough time with God to be sure he is doing what God wants him to do, will be this faithful when things really get tough.

We also read in Numbers 12:3 that "Moses was a very humble man, more humble than anyone else on the face of the earth." Moses' humility is amazing, considering the unique relationship he had with God. God describes the open, trusting nature of this relationship: "With him I speak face to face, clearly and not in riddles; he sees the form of the LORD" (12:8). How many men, knowing that they were so close to the all-powerful ruler of the universe, could still be humble?

Yet maybe—just maybe—that's the secret to it all. To be sure, Moses was a man's man. Who else could stand up to all that grief and still be such a powerful leader? But Moses also demonstrated, as do so many of God's heroes, that being a man's man begins by being secure in the fact that you are *God's* man. The more a man senses his approval before God, the less he needs to play the pride game. Humility begins by knowing the true source of affirmation and respect, by knowing God face to face, by being secure in God's presence and guidance. *—Dr. Sid Buzzell*

would Pharaoh listen to me, since I
speak with faltering lips[a]?"[v]

Family Record of Moses and Aaron

13 Now the LORD spoke to Moses and
Aaron about the Israelites and Pharaoh
king of Egypt, and he commanded
them to bring the Israelites out of
Egypt.

14 These were the heads of their
families[b]:[w]

The sons of Reuben the firstborn son of Israel were Hanoch
and Pallu, Hezron and Carmi.
These were the clans of Reuben.
15 The sons of Simeon[x] were
Jemuel, Jamin, Ohad, Jakin, Zohar
and Shaul the son of a Canaanite
woman. These were the clans of
Simeon.
16 These were the names of the
sons of Levi according to their
records: Gershon,[y] Kohath and
Merari.[z] Levi lived 137 years.
17 The sons of Gershon, by
clans, were Libni and Shimei.[a]
18 The sons of Kohath were Amram, Izhar, Hebron and Uzziel.[b]
Kohath lived 133 years.
19 The sons of Merari were Mahli and Mushi.[c]
These were the clans of Levi according to their records.
20 Amram married his father's
sister Jochebed, who bore him
Aaron and Moses.[d] Amram lived
137 years.
21 The sons of Izhar[e] were Korah, Nepheg and Zicri.
22 The sons of Uzziel were Mishael, Elzaphan[f] and Sithri.
23 Aaron married Elisheba,
daughter of Amminadab[g] and
sister of Nahshon, and she bore
him Nadab and Abihu,[h] Eleazar[i] and Ithamar.[j]
24 The sons of Korah[k] were Assir, Elkanah and Abiasaph. These
were the Korahite clans.
25 Eleazar son of Aaron married
one of the daughters of Putiel, and
she bore him Phinehas.[l]

These were the heads of the Levite families, clan by clan.

26 It was this same Aaron and Moses
to whom the LORD said, "Bring the Israelites out of Egypt by their divisions."[m]
27 They were the ones who spoke to
Pharaoh king of Egypt about bringing
the Israelites out of Egypt. It was the
same Moses and Aaron.

6:12 [v]ver 30; Ex 4:10; Jer 1:6
6:14 [w]Ge 46:9
6:15 [x]Ge 46:10; 1Ch 4:24
6:16 [y]Ge 46:11 [z]Nu 3:17
6:17 [a]1Ch 6:17
6:18 [b]1Ch 6:2,18
6:19 [c]Nu 1Ch 6:19; 23:21
6:20 [d]Ex 2:1-2; Nu 26:59
6:21 [e]1Ch 6:38
6:22 [f]Lev 10:4; Nu 3:30
6:23 [g]Ru 4:19,20 [h]Lev 10:1 [i]Nu 3:2,32 [j]Nu 26:60
6:24 [k]Nu 26:11
6:25 [l]Nu 25:7,11; Jos 24:33; Ps 106:30
6:26 [m]Ex 7:4; 12:17,41,51
6:29 [n]ver 11; Ex 7:2
6:30 [o]ver 12; Ex 4:10
7:1 [p]Ex 4:16
7:3 [q]Ex 4:21; 11:9
7:4 [r]Ex 11:9 [s]Ex 3:20; 6:6
7:5 [t]ver 17; Ex 8:19,22 [u]Ex 3:20
7:6 [v]ver 2
7:7 [w]Dt 31:2; 34:7; Ac 7:23,30
7:9 [x]Isa 7:11; Jn 2:18 [y]Ex 4:2-5
7:11 [z]Ge 41:8; 2Ti 3:8 [a]ver 22; Ex 8:7,18
7:13 [b]Ex 4:21
7:14 [c]Ex 8:15,32; 10:1,20,27

Aaron to Speak for Moses

28 Now when the LORD spoke to Moses in Egypt, 29 he said to him, "I am the
LORD.[n] Tell Pharaoh king of Egypt everything I tell you."
30 But Moses said to the LORD, "Since
I speak with faltering lips,[o] why would
Pharaoh listen to me?"

7 Then the LORD said to Moses, "See, I
have made you like God[p] to Pharaoh, and your brother Aaron will be
your prophet. 2 You are to say everything I command you, and your brother Aaron is to tell Pharaoh to let the
Israelites go out of his country. 3 But I
will harden Pharaoh's heart,[q] and
though I multiply my miraculous signs
and wonders in Egypt, 4 he will not listen[r] to you. Then I will lay my hand
on Egypt and with mighty acts of judgment[s] I will bring out my divisions,
my people the Israelites. 5 And the
Egyptians will know that I am the
LORD[t] when I stretch out my hand[u]
against Egypt and bring the Israelites
out of it."
6 Moses and Aaron did just as the
LORD commanded[v] them. 7 Moses was
eighty years old[w] and Aaron eighty-
three when they spoke to Pharaoh.

Aaron's Staff Becomes a Snake

8 The LORD said to Moses and Aaron,
9 "When Pharaoh says to you, 'Perform
a miracle,[x]' then say to Aaron, 'Take
your staff and throw it down before
Pharaoh,' and it will become a
snake."[y]
10 So Moses and Aaron went to Pharaoh and did just as the LORD commanded. Aaron threw his staff down in
front of Pharaoh and his officials, and
it became a snake. 11 Pharaoh then
summoned wise men and sorcerers,
and the Egyptian magicians[z] also did
the same things by their secret arts:[a]
12 Each one threw down his staff and it
became a snake. But Aaron's staff swallowed up their staffs. 13 Yet Pharaoh's
heart[b] became hard and he would not
listen to them, just as the LORD had
said.

The Plague of Blood

14 Then the LORD said to Moses,
"Pharaoh's heart is unyielding;[c] he refuses to let the people go. 15 Go to Pharaoh in the morning as he goes out to
the water. Wait on the bank of the Nile
to meet him, and take in your hand the
staff that was changed into a snake.

a *12* Hebrew *I am uncircumcised of lips*; also in verse 30 **b** *14* The Hebrew for *families* here and in verse 25 refers to units larger than clans.

16Then say to him, 'The LORD, the God
of the Hebrews, has sent me to say to
you: Let my people go, so that they
may worship[d] me in the desert. But
until now you have not listened. 17This
is what the LORD says: By this you will
know that I am the LORD:[e] With the
staff that is in my hand I will strike the
water of the Nile, and it will be changed
into blood.[f] 18The fish in the Nile will
die, and the river will stink; the Egyptians will not be able to drink its water.' "[g]

19The LORD said to Moses, "Tell Aaron, 'Take your staff and stretch out
your hand[h] over the waters of Egypt—
over the streams and canals, over the
ponds and all the reservoirs'—and
they will turn to blood. Blood will be
everywhere in Egypt, even in the wood-
en buckets and stone jars."

20Moses and Aaron did just as the
LORD had commanded. He raised his
staff in the presence of Pharaoh and his
officials and struck the water of the
Nile,[i] and all the water was changed
into blood.[j] 21The fish in the Nile
died, and the river smelled so bad that
the Egyptians could not drink its water.
Blood was everywhere in Egypt.

22But the Egyptian magicians did the
same things by their secret arts,[k] and
Pharaoh's heart became hard; he
would not listen to Moses and Aaron,
just as the LORD had said. 23Instead, he
turned and went into his palace, and
did not take even this to heart. 24And
all the Egyptians dug along the Nile to
get drinking water, because they could
not drink the water of the river.

The Plague of Frogs

25Seven days passed after the LORD
8 struck the Nile. 1Then the LORD said
to Moses, "Go to Pharaoh and say to
him, 'This is what the LORD says: Let
my people go, so that they may worship[l] me. 2If you refuse to let them go,
I will plague your whole country with
frogs. 3The Nile will teem with frogs.
They will come up into your palace and
your bedroom and onto your bed, into
the houses of your officials and on your
people,[m] and into your ovens and
kneading troughs. 4The frogs will go up
on you and your people and all your
officials.' "

5Then the LORD said to Moses, "Tell
Aaron, 'Stretch out your hand with
your staff[n] over the streams and canals and ponds, and make frogs come
up on the land of Egypt.' "

6So Aaron stretched out his hand
over the waters of Egypt, and the
frogs[o] came up and covered the land.

7:16 [d]Ex 3:18; 5:1,3
7:17 [e]Ex 5:2 [f]Ex 4:9; Rev 11:6; 16:4
7:18 [g]ver 21,24
7:19 [h]Ex 8:5-6,16; 9:22; 10:12,21; 14:21
7:20 [i]Ex 17:5 [j]Ps 78:44; 105:29
7:22 [k]ver 11
8:1 [l]Ex 3:12,18; 4:23
8:3 [m]Ex 10:6
8:5 [n]Ex 7:19
8:6 [o]Ps 78:45; 105:30
8:7 [p]Ex 7:11
8:8 [q]ver 28; Ex 9:28; 10:17 [r]ver 25
8:10 [s]Ex 9:14; Dt 4:35; 33:26; 2Sa 7:22; 1Ch 17:20; Ps 86:8; Isa 46:9; Jer 10:6
8:15 [t]Ex 7:14
8:17 [u]Ps 105:31
8:18 [v]Ex 9:11; Da 5:8 [w]Ex 7:11
8:19 [x]Ex 7:5; 10:7; Ps 8:3; Lk 11:20
8:20 [y]Ex 7:15; 9:13 [z]ver 1; Ex 3:18

7But the magicians did the same things
by their secret arts;[p] they also made
frogs come up on the land of Egypt.

8Pharaoh summoned Moses and
Aaron and said, "Pray[q] to the LORD to
take the frogs away from me and my
people, and I will let your people go to
offer sacrifices[r] to the LORD."

9Moses said to Pharaoh, "I leave to
you the honor of setting the time for
me to pray for you and your officials
and your people that you and your
houses may be rid of the frogs, except
for those that remain in the Nile."

10"Tomorrow," Pharaoh said.

Moses replied, "It will be as you say,
so that you may know there is no one
like the LORD our God.[s] 11The frogs
will leave you and your houses, your
officials and your people; they will remain only in the Nile."

12After Moses and Aaron left Pharaoh, Moses cried out to the LORD about
the frogs he had brought on Pharaoh.
13And the LORD did what Moses asked.
The frogs died in the houses, in the
courtyards and in the fields. 14They
were piled into heaps, and the land
reeked of them. 15But when Pharaoh
saw that there was relief, he hardened
his heart[t] and would not listen to Moses and Aaron, just as the LORD had
said.

The Plague of Gnats

16Then the LORD said to Moses, "Tell
Aaron, 'Stretch out your staff and strike
the dust of the ground,' and throughout the land of Egypt the dust will become gnats." 17They did this, and when
Aaron stretched out his hand with the
staff and struck the dust of the ground,
gnats[u] came upon men and animals.
All the dust throughout the land of
Egypt became gnats. 18But when the
magicians[v] tried to produce gnats by
their secret arts,[w] they could not. And
the gnats were on men and animals.

19The magicians said to Pharaoh,
"This is the finger[x] of God." But Pharaoh's heart was hard and he would not
listen, just as the LORD had said.

The Plague of Flies

20Then the LORD said to Moses, "Get
up early in the morning[y] and confront
Pharaoh as he goes to the water and
say to him, 'This is what the LORD says:
Let my people go, so that they may
worship[z] me. 21If you do not let my
people go, I will send swarms of flies on
you and your officials, on your people
and into your houses. The houses of
the Egyptians will be full of flies, and
even the ground where they are.

22 “ ‘But on that day I will deal differently with the land of Goshen, where my people live;[a] no swarms of flies will be there, so that you will know[b] that I, the LORD, am in this land. 23 I will make a distinction[a] between my people and your people. This miraculous sign will occur tomorrow.’ ”

24 And the LORD did this. Dense swarms of flies poured into Pharaoh’s palace and into the houses of his officials, and throughout Egypt the land was ruined by the flies.[c]

25 Then Pharaoh summoned[d] Moses and Aaron and said, “Go, sacrifice to your God here in the land.”

26 But Moses said, “That would not be right. The sacrifices we offer the LORD our God would be detestable to the Egyptians.[e] And if we offer sacrifices that are detestable in their eyes, will they not stone us? 27 We must take a three-day journey into the desert to offer sacrifices[f] to the LORD our God, as he commands us.”

28 Pharaoh said, “I will let you go to offer sacrifices to the LORD your God in the desert, but you must not go very far. Now pray[g] for me.”

29 Moses answered, “As soon as I leave you, I will pray to the LORD, and tomorrow the flies will leave Pharaoh and his officials and his people. Only be sure that Pharaoh does not act deceitfully[h] again by not letting the people go to offer sacrifices to the LORD.”

30 Then Moses left Pharaoh and prayed to the LORD,[i] 31 and the LORD did what Moses asked: The flies left Pharaoh and his officials and his people; not a fly remained. 32 But this time also Pharaoh hardened his heart[j] and would not let the people go.

The Plague on Livestock

9 Then the LORD said to Moses, “Go to Pharaoh and say to him, ‘This is what the LORD, the God of the Hebrews, says: “Let my people go, so that they may worship[k] me.” 2 If you refuse to let them go and continue to hold them back, 3 the hand[l] of the LORD will bring a terrible plague on your livestock in the field—on your horses and donkeys and camels and on your cattle and sheep and goats. 4 But the LORD will make a distinction between the livestock of Israel and that of Egypt,[m] so that no animal belonging to the Israelites will die.’ ”

5 The LORD set a time and said, “Tomorrow the LORD will do this in the land.” 6 And the next day the LORD did it: All the livestock[n] of the Egyptians died,[o] but not one animal belonging to the Israelites died. 7 Pharaoh sent men to investigate and found that not even one of the animals of the Israelites had died. Yet his heart was unyielding and he would not let the people go.[p]

The Plague of Boils

8 Then the LORD said to Moses and Aaron, “Take handfuls of soot from a furnace and have Moses toss it into the air in the presence of Pharaoh. 9 It will become fine dust over the whole land of Egypt, and festering boils[q] will break out on men and animals throughout the land.”

10 So they took soot from a furnace and stood before Pharaoh. Moses tossed it into the air, and festering boils broke out on men and animals. 11 The magicians[r] could not stand before Moses because of the boils that were on them and on all the Egyptians. 12 But the LORD hardened Pharaoh’s heart[s] and he would not listen to Moses and Aaron, just as the LORD had said to Moses.

The Plague of Hail

13 Then the LORD said to Moses, “Get up early in the morning, confront Pharaoh and say to him, ‘This is what the LORD, the God of the Hebrews, says: Let my people go, so that they may worship[t] me, 14 or this time I will send the full force of my plagues against you and against your officials and your people, so you may know[u] that there is no one like[v] me in all the earth. 15 For by now I could have stretched out my hand and struck you and your people[w] with a plague that would have wiped you off the earth. 16 But I have raised you up[b] for this very purpose,[x] that I might show you my power[y] and that my name might be proclaimed in all the earth. 17 You still set yourself against my people and will not let them go. 18 Therefore, at this time tomorrow I will send the worst hailstorm[z] that has ever fallen on Egypt, from the day it was founded till now.[a] 19 Give an order now to bring your livestock and everything you have in the field to a place of shelter, because the hail will fall on every man and animal that has not been brought in and is still out in the field, and they will die.’ ”

20 Those officials of Pharaoh who feared[b] the word of the LORD hurried to bring their slaves and their livestock inside. 21 But those who ignored the

8:22 [a] Ex 9:4,6,26; 10:23; 11:7 [b] Ex 7:5; 9:29
8:24 [c] Ps 78:45; 105:31
8:25 [d] ver 8; Ex 9:27
8:26 [e] Ge 43:32; 46:34
8:27 [f] Ex 3:18
8:28 [g] ver 8; Ex 9:28; 1Ki 13:6
8:29 [h] ver 15
8:30 [i] ver 12
8:32 [j] ver 8,15; Ex 4:21
9:1 [k] Ex 8:1
9:3 [l] Ex 7:4
9:4 [m] ver 26; Ex 8:22
9:6 [n] ver 19-21; Ex 11:5 [o] Ps 78:48-50
9:7 [p] Ex 7:14; 8:32
9:9 [q] Dt 28:27,35; Rev 16:2
9:11 [r] Ex 8:18
9:12 [s] Ex 4:21
9:13 [t] Ex 8:20
9:14 [u] Ex 8:10 [v] 2Sa 7:22; 1Ch 17:20; Ps 86:8; Isa 46:9; Jer 10:6
9:15 [w] Ex 3:20
9:16 [x] Pr 16:4 [y] Ro 9:17*
9:18 [z] ver 23 [a] ver 24
9:20 [b] Pr 13:13

a *23* Septuagint and Vulgate; Hebrew *will put a deliverance* **b** *16* Or *have spared you*

word of the LORD left their slaves and livestock in the field.

22Then the LORD said to Moses, "Stretch out your hand toward the sky so that hail will fall all over Egypt—on men and animals and on everything growing in the fields of Egypt." 23When Moses stretched out his staff toward the sky, the LORD sent thunder[c] and hail,[d] and lightning flashed down to the ground. So the LORD rained hail on the land of Egypt; 24hail fell and lightning flashed back and forth. It was the worst storm in all the land of Egypt since it had become a nation. 25Throughout Egypt hail struck everything in the fields—both men and animals; it beat down everything growing in the fields and stripped every tree.[e] 26The only place it did not hail was the land of Goshen,[f] where the Israelites were.[g]

27Then Pharaoh summoned Moses and Aaron. "This time I have sinned,"[h] he said to them. "The LORD is in the right,[i] and I and my people are in the wrong. 28Pray[j] to the LORD, for we have had enough thunder and hail. I will let you go;[k] you don't have to stay any longer."

29Moses replied, "When I have gone out of the city, I will spread out my hands[l] in prayer to the LORD. The thunder will stop and there will be no more hail, so you may know that the earth[m] is the LORD's. 30But I know that you and your officials still do not fear the LORD God."

31(The flax and barley[n] were destroyed, since the barley had headed and the flax was in bloom. 32The wheat and spelt, however, were not destroyed, because they ripen later.)

33Then Moses left Pharaoh and went out of the city. He spread out his hands toward the LORD; the thunder and hail stopped, and the rain no longer poured down on the land. 34When Pharaoh saw that the rain and hail and thunder had stopped, he sinned again: He and his officials hardened their hearts. 35So Pharaoh's heart[o] was hard and he would not let the Israelites go, just as the LORD had said through Moses.

The Plague of Locusts

10 Then the LORD said to Moses, "Go to Pharaoh, for I have hardened his heart[p] and the hearts of his officials so that I may perform these miraculous signs[q] of mine among them 2that you may tell your children[r] and grandchildren how I dealt harshly with the Egyptians and how I performed my signs among them, and that you may know that I am the LORD."

3So Moses and Aaron went to Pharaoh and said to him, "This is what the LORD, the God of the Hebrews, says: 'How long will you refuse to humble[s] yourself before me? Let my people go, so that they may worship me. 4If you refuse to let them go, I will bring locusts[t] into your country tomorrow. 5They will cover the face of the ground so that it cannot be seen. They will devour what little you have left[u] after the hail, including every tree that is growing in your fields. 6They will fill your houses and those of all your officials and all the Egyptians—something neither your fathers nor your forefathers have ever seen from the day they settled in this land till now.' " Then Moses turned and left Pharaoh.

7Pharaoh's officials said to him, "How long will this man be a snare[v] to us? Let the people go, so that they may worship the LORD their God. Do you not yet realize that Egypt is ruined?"[w]

8Then Moses and Aaron were brought back to Pharaoh. "Go, worship[x] the LORD your God," he said. "But just who will be going?"

9Moses answered, "We will go with our young and old, with our sons and daughters, and with our flocks and herds, because we are to celebrate a festival to the LORD."

10Pharaoh said, "The LORD be with you—if I let you go, along with your women and children! Clearly you are bent on evil.[a] 11No! Have only the men go; and worship the LORD, since that's what you have been asking for." Then Moses and Aaron were driven out of Pharaoh's presence.

12And the LORD said to Moses, "Stretch out your hand[y] over Egypt so that locusts will swarm over the land and devour everything growing in the fields, everything left by the hail."

13So Moses stretched out his staff over Egypt, and the LORD made an east wind blow across the land all that day and all that night. By morning the wind had brought the locusts;[z] 14they invaded all Egypt and settled down in every area of the country in great numbers. Never before had there been such a plague of locusts,[a] nor will there ever be again. 15They covered all the ground until it was black. They devoured[b] all that was left after the hail—everything growing in the fields and the fruit on the trees. Nothing green remained on tree or plant in all the land of Egypt.

9:23 [c]Ps 18:13 [d]Jos 10:11; Ps 78:47; 105:32; Isa 30:30; Eze 38:22; Rev 8:7; 16:21
9:25 [e]Ps 105:32-33
9:26 [f]ver 4 [g]Ex 8:22; 10:23; 11:7; 12:13
9:27 [h]Ex 10:16 [i]2Ch 12:6; Ps 129:4; La 1:18
9:28 [j]Ex 10:17 [k]Ex 8:8
9:29 [l]1Ki 8:22,38; Ps 143:6; Isa 1:15 [m]Ex 19:5; Ps 24:1; 1Co 10:26
9:31 [n]Ru 1:22; 2:23
9:35 [o]Ex 4:21
10:1 [p]Ex 4:21 [q]Ex 7:3
10:2 [r]Ex 12:26-27; 13:8,14; Dt 4:9; Ps 44:1; 78:4,5; Joel 1:3
10:3 [s]1Ki 21:29; Jas 4:10; 1Pe 5:6
10:4 [t]Rev 9:3
10:5 [u]Ex 9:32; Joel 1:4
10:7 [v]Ex 23:33; Jos 23:13; 1Sa 18:21; Ecc 7:26 [w]Ex 8:19
10:8 [x]Ex 8:8
10:12 [y]Ex 7:19
10:13 [z]Ps 105:34
10:14 [a]Ps 78:46; Joel 2:1-11,25
10:15 [b]ver 5; Ps 105:34-35

[a]*10* Or *Be careful, trouble is in store for you!*

16Pharaoh quickly summoned Moses and Aaron and said, "I have
sinned[c] against the LORD your God
and against you. 17Now forgive my sin
once more and pray[d] to the LORD your
God to take this deadly plague away
from me."
18Moses then left Pharaoh and
prayed to the LORD.[e] 19And the LORD
changed the wind to a very strong west
wind, which caught up the locusts and
carried them into the Red Sea.[a] Not
a locust was left anywhere in Egypt.
20But the LORD hardened Pharaoh's
heart,[f] and he would not let the Israelites go.

The Plague of Darkness

21Then the LORD said to Moses,
"Stretch out your hand toward the sky
so that darkness[g] will spread over
Egypt—darkness that can be felt." 22So
Moses stretched out his hand toward
the sky, and total darkness[h] covered
all Egypt for three days. 23No one could
see anyone else or leave his place for
three days. Yet all the Israelites had
light in the places where they lived.[i]
24Then Pharaoh summoned Moses
and said, "Go, worship the LORD. Even
your women and children[j] may go
with you; only leave your flocks and
herds behind."
25But Moses said, "You must allow
us to have sacrifices and burnt offerings to present to the LORD our God.
26Our livestock too must go with us;
not a hoof is to be left behind. We have
to use some of them in worshiping the
LORD our God, and until we get there
we will not know what we are to use to
worship the LORD."
27But the LORD hardened Pharaoh's
heart,[k] and he was not willing to let
them go. 28Pharaoh said to Moses, "Get
out of my sight! Make sure you do not
appear before me again! The day you
see my face you will die."
29"Just as you say," Moses replied, "I
will never appear[l] before you again."

The Plague on the Firstborn

11 Now the LORD had said to Moses, "I
will bring one more plague on Pharaoh and on Egypt. After that, he will let
you go from here, and when he does,
he will drive you out completely. 2Tell
the people that men and women alike
are to ask their neighbors for articles of
silver and gold."[m] 3(The LORD made
the Egyptians favorably disposed toward the people, and Moses himself
was highly regarded[n] in Egypt by
Pharaoh's officials and by the people.)
4So Moses said, "This is what the
LORD says: 'About midnight[o] I will go
throughout Egypt. 5Every firstborn[p]
son in Egypt will die, from the firstborn
son of Pharaoh, who sits on the throne,
to the firstborn son of the slave girl,
who is at her hand mill, and all the
firstborn of the cattle as well. 6There
will be loud wailing[q] throughout
Egypt—worse than there has ever been
or ever will be again. 7But among the
Israelites not a dog will bark at any
man or animal.' Then you will know
that the LORD makes a distinction[r] between Egypt and Israel. 8All these officials of yours will come to me, bowing
down before me and saying, 'Go,[s] you
and all the people who follow you!' After that I will leave." Then Moses, hot
with anger, left Pharaoh.
9The LORD had said to Moses, "Pharaoh will refuse to listen[t] to you—so
that my wonders may be multiplied in
Egypt." 10Moses and Aaron performed
all these wonders before Pharaoh, but
the LORD hardened Pharaoh's heart,[u]
and he would not let the Israelites go
out of his country.

The Passover

12 The LORD said to Moses and Aaron
in Egypt, 2"This month is to be for
you the first month,[v] the first month
of your year. 3Tell the whole community of Israel that on the tenth day of this
month each man is to take a lamb[b] for
his family, one for each household. 4If
any household is too small for a whole
lamb, they must share one with their
nearest neighbor, having taken into account the number of people there are.
You are to determine the amount of
lamb needed in accordance with what
each person will eat. 5The animals you
choose must be year-old males without defect,[w] and you may take them
from the sheep or the goats. 6Take care
of them until the fourteenth day of the
month,[x] when all the people of the
community of Israel must slaughter
them at twilight.[y] 7Then they are to
take some of the blood and put it on
the sides and tops of the doorframes of
the houses where they eat the lambs.
8That same night[z] they are to eat the
meat roasted[a] over the fire, along with
bitter herbs,[b] and bread made without yeast.[c] 9Do not eat the meat raw
or cooked in water, but roast it over the
fire—head, legs and inner parts. 10Do
not leave any of it till morning;[d] if
some is left till morning, you must
burn it. 11This is how you are to eat it:

10:16 [c]Ex 9:27 **10:17** [d]Ex 8:8 **10:18** [e]Ex 8:30 **10:20** [f]Ex 4:21; 11:10 **10:21** [g]Dt 28:29 **10:22** [h]Ps 105:28; Rev 16:10 **10:23** [i]Ex 8:22 **10:24** [j]ver 8-10 **10:27** [k]ver 20; Ex 4:21 **10:29** [l]Heb 11:27 **11:2** [m]Ex 3:21,22 **11:3** [n]Dt 34:11 **11:4** [o]Ex 12:29 **11:5** [p]Ex 4:23; Ps 78:51 **11:6** [q]Ex 12:30 **11:7** [r]Ex 8:22 **11:8** [s]Ex 12:31-33 **11:9** [t]Ex 7:4 **11:10** [u]Ex 4:21; 10:20,27 **12:2** [v]Ex 13:4; Dt 16:1 **12:5** [w]Lev 22:18-21; Heb 9:14 **12:6** [x]Lev 23:5; Nu 9:1-3,5,11 [y]Ex 16:12; Dt 16:4,6 **12:8** [z]Ex 34:25; Nu 9:12 [a]Dt 16:7 [b]Nu 9:11 [c]Dt 16:3-4; 1Co 5:8 **12:10** [d]Ex 23:18; 34:25

a *19* Hebrew *Yam Suph*; that is, Sea of Reeds
b *3* The Hebrew word can mean *lamb* or *kid*; also in verse 4.

with your cloak tucked into your belt,
your sandals on your feet and your staff
in your hand. Eat it in haste;[e] it is the
LORD's Passover.[f]
12"On that same night I will pass
through[g] Egypt and strike down every
firstborn—both men and animals—
and I will bring judgment on all the
gods[h] of Egypt. I am the LORD.[i] 13The
blood will be a sign for you on the
houses where you are; and when I see
the blood, I will pass over you. No destructive plague will touch you when I
strike Egypt.
14"This is a day you are to commemorate;[j] for the generations to come
you shall celebrate it as a festival to the
LORD—a lasting ordinance.[k] 15For
seven days you are to eat bread made
without yeast.[l] On the first day remove the yeast from your houses, for
whoever eats anything with yeast in it
from the first day through the seventh
must be cut off[m] from Israel. 16On the
first day hold a sacred assembly, and
another one on the seventh day. Do no
work at all on these days, except to prepare food for everyone to eat—that is
all you may do.
17"Celebrate the Feast of Unleavened Bread, because it was on this very
day that I brought your divisions out of
Egypt.[n] Celebrate this day as a lasting
ordinance for the generations to come.
18In the first month[o] you are to eat
bread made without yeast, from the
evening of the fourteenth day until the

12:11 [e]Dt 16:3 [f]ver 13,21,27,43; Dt 16:1
12:12 [g]Ex 11:4; Am 5:17 [h]Nu 33:4 [i]Ex 6:2
12:14 [j]Ex 13:9 [k]ver 17,24; Ex 13:5,10; 2Ki 23:21
12:15 [l]Ex 13:6-7; 23:15; 34:18; Lev 23:6; Dt 16:3 [m]Ge 17:14; Nu 9:13
12:17 [n]ver 41; Ex 13:3
12:18 [o]ver 2; Lev 23:5-8; Nu 28:16-25

12:1-30

PROMISE 5

PASSOVER

The event described in this chapter was significant enough that God specifically commanded the Israelites never to forget it. God felt that this was such an important moment that he changed Israel's calendar to commemorate it (v. 2). Although the Passover occurred in the seventh month of the calendar, God said, "This month is to be for you the first month, the first month of your year." The Passover symbolized a new beginning, a new way of life, a new identity for the descendants of Abraham. In fact, references to "the community of Israel" (vv. 3 and 6) appear here for the first time. Before this time the Israelites had been a disjointed collection of slaves in Egypt; now, through God's declaration, they had become a community.

God commanded that every household slaughter an unblemished lamb (vv. 5–6). Each family was to take some of the slain lamb's blood and paint it on the doorposts of their houses. Only then they could cook and eat the lamb as a feast. To our ears this directive may sound strange, but God had a reason for this ritual. God was to bring yet another plague on the Egyptians, one more devastating than the nine that had preceded it. The firstborn—both human and animal—of every house would be killed. Only houses with the lamb's blood around the door would be spared. By God's command, this plague of death would then "pass over" the house that had complied with his plan.

To make certain Israel never forgot this great act of salvation, God told them to commemorate the feast as a lasting ordinance. They were to celebrate it every year so their children would always remember how God had saved them from death. In fact, it was to be celebrated by every family in Israel at twilight on the same day. The simultaneous participation of every person in the "community of Israel" (v. 6) would unite the people around their worship of God.

The requirements for Passover strikingly symbolize Jesus' substitutionary death on Calvary. A few examples can bring the parallels into clearer focus. John the Baptist recognized Jesus as God's Lamb who had come to take away the world's sin (John 1:29). Peter added that Jesus was the "lamb without blemish or defect" (1 Peter 1:19). In 1 Corinthians 5:7, Paul wrote that "Christ, our Passover lamb, has been sacrificed." As the Passover lamb died to save the life of the firstborn, so also Jesus, God's own Passover lamb, gave his life so that his blood could cleanse us from all sin and save us from eternal spiritual death.

Jesus himself celebrated the Passover some 1400 years after the events described in this chapter. Growing up in a devout Jewish family, he would have celebrated this festival every year. In fact, Jesus participated in this Passover celebration with his disciples on the night before he was crucified. Paul recalls this evening celebration in 1 Corinthians 11:23–26. His account describes the ritual that Christ instituted on that Passover holiday—the Lord's Supper, the same holy communion that Christians all over the world celebrate today. Whenever Christians today take time to celebrate this supper, we commemorate Jesus' identity as the Lamb of God; and his death, the sacrificial act by which the world's sin was taken away (John 1:29).

A final resemblance; one too important to exclude in this brief discussion. The Passover was a new beginning for these Israelite slaves who were to become God's people. They had a new month to start a new year. Paul paralleled that thought when he informed us that "If anyone is in Christ, he is a new creation; the old has gone, the new has come" (2 Corinthians 5:17). Christ offers a new start, a new identity for those who will accept his death on their behalf. You, like the ancient Israelites, can break your enslavement to sin and become a member of God's eternal community.

For the next Promise 5 reading go to page 84.

evening of the twenty-first day. 19For
seven days no yeast is to be found in
your houses. And whoever eats anything with yeast in it must be cut off
from the community of Israel, whether
he is an alien or native-born. 20Eat
nothing made with yeast. Wherever
you live, you must eat unleavened
bread."

21Then Moses summoned all the elders of Israel and said to them, "Go at
once and select the animals for your
families and slaughter the Passover[p]
lamb. 22Take a bunch of hyssop, dip
it into the blood in the basin and put
some of the blood[q] on the top and on
both sides of the doorframe. Not one of
you shall go out the door of his house
until morning. 23When the LORD goes
through the land to strike down the
Egyptians, he will see the blood[r] on
the top and sides of the doorframe and
will pass over[s] that doorway, and he
will not permit the destroyer[t] to enter
your houses and strike you down.

24"Obey these instructions as a lasting ordinance for you and your descendants. 25When you enter the land that
the LORD will give you as he promised,
observe this ceremony. 26And when
your children[u] ask you, 'What does
this ceremony mean to you?' 27then tell
them, 'It is the Passover[v] sacrifice to
the LORD, who passed over the houses
of the Israelites in Egypt and spared
our homes when he struck down the
Egyptians.' " Then the people bowed
down and worshiped.[w] 28The Israelites did just what the LORD commanded Moses and Aaron.

29At midnight[x] the LORD struck
down all the firstborn[y] in Egypt, from
the firstborn of Pharaoh, who sat on
the throne, to the firstborn of the prisoner, who was in the dungeon, and the
firstborn of all the livestock[z] as well.
30Pharaoh and all his officials and all
the Egyptians got up during the night,
and there was loud wailing[a] in Egypt,
for there was not a house without
someone dead.

The Exodus

31During the night Pharaoh summoned Moses and Aaron and said,
"Up! Leave my people, you and the Israelites! Go, worship[b] the LORD as you
have requested. 32Take your flocks and
herds,[c] as you have said, and go. And
also bless me."

33The Egyptians urged the people to
hurry and leave[d] the country. "For
otherwise," they said, "we will all die!"
34So the people took their dough before the yeast was added, and carried it
on their shoulders in kneading troughs
wrapped in clothing. 35The Israelites
did as Moses instructed and asked the
Egyptians for articles of silver and
gold[e] and for clothing. 36The LORD
had made the Egyptians favorably disposed toward the people, and they
gave them what they asked for; so they
plundered[f] the Egyptians.

37The Israelites journeyed from
Rameses to Succoth.[g] There were
about six hundred thousand men[h] on
foot, besides women and children.
38Many other people[i] went up with
them, as well as large droves of livestock, both flocks and herds. 39With the
dough they had brought from Egypt,
they baked cakes of unleavened bread.
The dough was without yeast because
they had been driven out[j] of Egypt
and did not have time to prepare food
for themselves.

40Now the length of time the Israelite people lived in Egypt[a] was 430
years.[k] 41At the end of the 430 years,
to the very day, all the LORD's divisions[l] left Egypt.[m] 42Because the
LORD kept vigil that night to bring them
out of Egypt, on this night all the Israelites are to keep vigil to honor the LORD
for the generations to come.[n]

Passover Restrictions

43The LORD said to Moses and Aaron,
"These are the regulations for the Passover:[o]

"No foreigner[p] is to eat of it. 44Any
slave you have bought may eat of it
after you have circumcised[q] him,
45but a temporary resident and a hired
worker[r] may not eat of it.

46"It must be eaten inside one
house; take none of the meat outside
the house. Do not break any of the
bones.[s] 47The whole community of Israel must celebrate it.

48"An alien living among you who
wants to celebrate the LORD's Passover
must have all the males in his household circumcised; then he may take
part like one born in the land.[t] No
uncircumcised male may eat of it.
49The same law applies to the native-
born and to the alien[u] living among
you."

50All the Israelites did just what the
LORD had commanded Moses and Aaron. 51And on that very day the LORD
brought the Israelites out of Egypt by
their divisions.[v]

12:21 [p]ver 11; Mk 14:12-16
12:22 [q]ver 7; Heb 11:28
12:23 [r]Rev 7:3 [s]ver 13 [t]1Co 10:10; Heb 11:28
12:26 [u]Ex 10:2; 13:8, 14-15; Jos 4:6
12:27 [v]ver 11 [w]Ex 4:31
12:29 [x]Ex 11:4 [y]Ex 4:23; Ps 78:51 [z]Ex 9:6
12:30 [a]Ex 11:6
12:31 [b]Ex 8:8
12:32 [c]Ex 10:9,26
12:33 [d]Ps 105:38
12:35 [e]Ex 3:22
12:36 [f]Ex 3:22
12:37 [g]Nu 33:3-5 [h]Ex 38:26; Nu 1:46; 11:13,21
12:38 [i]Nu 11:4
12:39 [j]ver 31-33; Ex 6:1; 11:1
12:40 [k]Ge 15:13; Ac 7:6; Gal 3:17
12:41 [l]ver 17; Ex 6:26 [m]Ex 3:10
12:42 [n]Ex 13:10; Dt 16:1,6
12:43 [o]ver 11 [p]ver 48; Nu 9:14
12:44 [q]Ge 17:12-13
12:45 [r]Lev 22:10
12:46 [s]Nu 9:12; Jn 19:36*
12:48 [t]Nu 9:14
12:49 [u]Nu 15:15-16, 29; Gal 3:28
12:51 [v]ver 41; Ex 6:26

[a] *40* Masoretic Text; Samaritan Pentateuch and Septuagint *Egypt and Canaan*

Consecration of the Firstborn

13 The LORD said to Moses, 2"Consecrate to me every firstborn male.[w]
The first offspring of every womb
among the Israelites belongs to me,
whether man or animal."
3Then Moses said to the people,
"Commemorate this day, the day you
came out of Egypt, out of the land of
slavery, because the LORD brought you
out of it with a mighty hand.[x] Eat
nothing containing yeast.[y] 4Today, in
the month of Abib,[z] you are leaving.
5When the LORD brings you into the
land of the Canaanites, Hittites, Amorites, Hivites and Jebusites[a]—the land
he swore to your forefathers to give
you, a land flowing with milk and
honey—you are to observe this ceremony[b] in this month: 6For seven days
eat bread made without yeast and on
the seventh day hold a festival[c] to the
LORD. 7Eat unleavened bread during
those seven days; nothing with yeast in
it is to be seen among you, nor shall
any yeast be seen anywhere within
your borders. 8On that day tell your
son,[d] 'I do this because of what the
LORD did for me when I came out of
Egypt.' 9This observance will be for you
like a sign on your hand and a reminder on your forehead[e] that the law of
the LORD is to be on your lips. For the
LORD brought you out of Egypt with his
mighty hand. 10You must keep this ordinance[f] at the appointed time year
after year.
11"After the LORD brings you into the
land of the Canaanites and gives it to
you, as he promised on oath to you and
your forefathers, 12you are to give over
to the LORD the first offspring of every
womb. All the firstborn males of your
livestock belong to the LORD.[g] 13Re-
deem with a lamb every firstborn donkey, but if you do not redeem it, break
its neck.[h] Redeem every firstborn
among your sons.[i]
14"In days to come, when your son[j]
asks you, 'What does this mean?' say to
him, 'With a mighty hand the LORD
brought us out of Egypt, out of the land
of slavery.[k] 15When Pharaoh stubbornly refused to let us go, the LORD
killed every firstborn in Egypt, both
man and animal. This is why I sacrifice
to the LORD the first male offspring of
every womb and redeem each of my
firstborn sons.'[l] 16And it will be like a
sign on your hand and a symbol on
your forehead[m] that the LORD brought
us out of Egypt with his mighty hand."

Crossing the Sea

17When Pharaoh let the people go,
God did not lead them on the road
through the Philistine country, though
that was shorter. For God said, "If they
face war, they might change their
minds and return to Egypt."[n] 18So
God led[o] the people around by the
desert road toward the Red Sea.**[a]** The
Israelites went up out of Egypt armed
for battle.[p]
19Moses took the bones of Joseph[q]
with him because Joseph had made the
sons of Israel swear an oath. He had
said, "God will surely come to your aid,
and then you must carry my bones up
with you from this place."**[b]**[r]
20After leaving Succoth they camped
at Etham on the edge of the desert.[s]
21By day the LORD went ahead of them
in a pillar of cloud[t] to guide them on
their way and by night in a pillar of fire
to give them light, so that they could
travel by day or night. 22Neither the pillar of cloud by day nor the pillar of fire
by night left its place in front of the
people.
14 Then the LORD said to Moses, 2"Tell
the Israelites to turn back and encamp near Pi Hahiroth, between Migdol[u] and the sea. They are to encamp
by the sea, directly opposite Baal Zephon. 3Pharaoh will think, 'The Israelites are wandering around the land in
confusion, hemmed in by the desert.'
4And I will harden Pharaoh's heart,[v]
and he will pursue them. But I will gain
glory[w] for myself through Pharaoh
and all his army, and the Egyptians will
know that I am the LORD."[x] So the Israelites did this.
5When the king of Egypt was told
that the people had fled, Pharaoh and
his officials changed their minds about
them and said, "What have we done?
We have let the Israelites go and have
lost their services!" 6So he had his chariot made ready and took his army with
him. 7He took six hundred of the best
chariots, along with all the other chariots of Egypt, with officers over all
of them. 8The LORD hardened the
heart[y] of Pharaoh king of Egypt, so
that he pursued the Israelites, who
were marching out boldly.[z] 9The
Egyptians—all Pharaoh's horses and
chariots, horsemen**[c]** and troops—
pursued the Israelites and overtook[a]
them as they camped by the sea near Pi
Hahiroth, opposite Baal Zephon.
10As Pharaoh approached, the Israelites looked up, and there were the
Egyptians, marching after them. They
were terrified and cried[b] out to the

13:2 [w]ver 12,13,15; Ex 22:29; Nu 3:13; Dt 15:19; Lk 2:23*
13:3 [x]Ex 3:20; 6:1 [y]Ex 12:19
13:4 [z]Ex 12:2
13:5 [a]Ex 3:8 [b]Ex 12:25-26
13:6 [c]Ex 12:15-20
13:8 [d]ver 14; Ex 10:2; Ps 78:5-6
13:9 [e]ver 16; Dt 6:8; 11:18
13:10 [f]Ex 12:24-25
13:12 [g]Lev 27:26; Lk 2:23*
13:13 [h]Ex 34:20 [i]Nu 18:15
13:14 [j]Ex 10:2; 12:26-27; Dt 6:20 [k]ver 3,9
13:15 [l]Ex 12:29
13:16 [m]ver 9
13:17 [n]Ex 14:11; Nu 14:1-4; Dt 17:16
13:18 [o]Ps 136:16 [p]Jos 1:14
13:19 [q]Jos 24:32; Ac 7:16 [r]Ge 50:24-25
13:20 [s]Nu 33:6
13:21 [t]Ex 14:19,24; 33:9-10; Nu 9:16; Dt 1:33; Ne 9:12,19; Ps 78:14; 99:7; 105:39; Isa 4:5; 1Co 10:1
14:2 [u]Nu 33:7; Jer 44:1
14:4 [v]Ex 4:21 [w]Ro 9:17, 22-23 [x]Ex 7:5
14:8 [y]ver 4; Ex 11:10 [z]Nu 33:3; Ac 13:17
14:9 [a]Ex 15:9
14:10 [b]Jos 24:7; Ne 9:9; Ps 34:17

a *18* Hebrew *Yam Suph*; that is, Sea of Reeds
b *19* See Gen. 50:25.
c *9* Or *charioteers*; also in verses 17, 18, 23, 26 and 28

LORD. 11They said to Moses, "Was it because there were no graves in Egypt that you brought us to the desert to die?[c] What have you done to us by bringing us out of Egypt? 12Didn't we say to you in Egypt, 'Leave us alone; let us serve the Egyptians'? It would have been better for us to serve the Egyptians than to die in the desert!"

13Moses answered the people, "Do not be afraid.[d] Stand firm and you will see[e] the deliverance the LORD will bring you today. The Egyptians you see today you will never see[f] again. 14The LORD will fight[g] for you; you need only to be still."[h]

15Then the LORD said to Moses, "Why are you crying out to me? Tell the Israelites to move on. 16Raise your staff[i] and stretch out your hand over the sea to divide the water[j] so that the Israelites can go through the sea on dry ground. 17I will harden the hearts of the Egyptians so that they will go in after them.[k] And I will gain glory through Pharaoh and all his army, through his chariots and his horsemen. 18The Egyptians will know that I am the LORD when I gain glory through Pharaoh, his chariots and his horsemen."

19Then the angel of God, who had been traveling in front of Israel's army, withdrew and went behind them. The pillar of cloud[l] also moved from in front and stood behind them, 20coming between the armies of Egypt and Israel. Throughout the night the cloud brought darkness to the one side and light to the other side; so neither went near the other all night long.

21Then Moses stretched out his hand over the sea, and all that night the LORD drove the sea back with a strong east wind[m] and turned it into dry land. The waters were divided,[n] 22and the Israelites went through the sea on dry ground,[o] with a wall of water on their right and on their left.

23The Egyptians pursued them, and all Pharaoh's horses and chariots and horsemen followed them into the sea. 24During the last watch of the night the LORD looked down from the pillar of fire and cloud[p] at the Egyptian army and threw it into confusion. 25He made the wheels of their chariots come off**[a]** so that they had difficulty driving. And the Egyptians said, "Let's get away from the Israelites! The LORD is fighting[q] for them against Egypt."

26Then the LORD said to Moses, "Stretch out your hand over the sea so that the waters may flow back over the Egyptians and their chariots and horsemen." 27Moses stretched out his hand over the sea, and at daybreak the sea went back to its place.[r] The Egyptians were fleeing toward**[b]** it, and the LORD swept them into the sea.[s] 28The water flowed back and covered the chariots and horsemen—the entire army of Pharaoh that had followed the Israelites into the sea. Not one of them survived.

29But the Israelites went through the sea on dry ground,[t] with a wall of water on their right and on their left. 30That day the LORD saved[u] Israel from the hands of the Egyptians, and Israel saw the Egyptians lying dead on the shore. 31And when the Israelites saw the great power the LORD displayed against the Egyptians, the people feared the LORD and put their trust[v] in him and in Moses his servant.

The Song of Moses and Miriam

15 Then Moses and the Israelites sang this song[w] to the LORD:

"I will sing[x] to the LORD,
  for he is highly exalted.
The horse and its rider
  he has hurled into the sea.
2The LORD is my strength[y] and my song;
  he has become my salvation.[z]
He is my God,[a] and I will praise him,
  my father's God, and I will exalt[b] him.

1 →PG. 88

3The LORD is a warrior;[c]
  the LORD is his name.[d]
4Pharaoh's chariots and his army[e]
  he has hurled into the sea.
The best of Pharaoh's officers
  are drowned in the Red Sea.**[c]**
5The deep waters have covered them;
  they sank to the depths like a stone.[f]
6"Your right hand,[g] O LORD,
  was majestic in power.
Your right hand, O LORD,
  shattered the enemy.
7In the greatness of your majesty
  you threw down those who opposed you.
You unleashed your burning anger;[h]
  it consumed them like stubble.
8By the blast of your nostrils[i]
  the waters piled up.[j]
The surging waters stood firm like a wall;[k]
  the deep waters congealed in the heart of the sea.

a25 Or *He jammed the wheels of their chariots* (see Samaritan Pentateuch, Septuagint and Syriac) **b**27 Or *from* **c**4 Hebrew *Yam Suph*; that is, Sea of Reeds; also in verse 22

14:11 [c]Ps 106:7-8 **14:13** [d]Ge 15:1 [e]2Ch 20:17; Isa 41:10, 13-14 [f]ver 30 **14:14** [g]ver 25; Ex 15:3; Dt 1:30; 3:22; 2Ch 20:29 [h]Ps 37:7; 46:10; Isa 30:15 **14:16** [i]Ex 4:17; Nu 20:8-9,11 [j]Isa 10:26 **14:17** [k]ver 4 **14:19** [l]Ex 13:21 **14:21** [m]Ex 15:8 [n]Ps 74:13; 114:5; Isa 63:12 **14:22** [o]Ex 15:19; Ne 9:11; Ps 66:6; Heb 11:29 **14:24** [p]Ex 13:21 **14:25** [q]ver 14 **14:27** [r]Jos 4:18 [s]Ex 15:1,21; Ps 78:53; 106:11 **14:29** [t]ver 22 **14:30** [u]Ps 106:8,10, 21 **14:31** [v]Ps 106:12; Jn 2:11 **15:1** [w]Rev 15:3 [x]Ps 106:12 **15:2** [y]Ps 59:17 [z]Ps 18:2,46; Isa 12:2; Hab 3:18 [a]Ge 28:21 [b]Ex 3:6,15-16; Isa 25:1 **15:3** [c]Ex 14:14; Ps 24:8; Rev 19:11 [d]Ex 6:2-3,7-8; Ps 83:18 **15:4** [e]Ex 14:6-7 **15:5** [f]ver 10; Ne 9:11 **15:6** [g]Ps 118:15 **15:7** [h]Ps 78:49-50 **15:8** [i]Ex 14:21 [j]Ps 78:13 [k]Ex 14:22

9"The enemy boasted,
'I will pursue,[l] I will overtake them.
I will divide the spoils;[m]
I will gorge myself on them.
I will draw my sword
and my hand will destroy them.'
10But you blew with your breath,
and the sea covered them.
They sank like lead
in the mighty waters.[n]

11"Who among the gods is like you,[o] O LORD?
Who is like you—
majestic in holiness,[p]
awesome in glory,[q]
working wonders?
12You stretched out your right hand
and the earth swallowed them.
13"In your unfailing love you will lead[r]
the people you have redeemed.
In your strength you will guide them
to your holy dwelling.[s]
14The nations will hear and tremble;[t]
anguish will grip the people of Philistia.
15The chiefs[u] of Edom will be terrified,
the leaders of Moab will be seized with trembling,[v]
the people[a] of Canaan will melt[w] away;
16 terror[x] and dread will fall upon them.
By the power of your arm
they will be as still as a stone[y]—
until your people pass by, O LORD,
until the people you bought[b][z] pass by.
17You will bring them in and plant[a] them
on the mountain[b] of your inheritance—
the place, O LORD, you made for your dwelling,
the sanctuary, O Lord, your hands established.
18The LORD will reign
for ever and ever."

19When Pharaoh's horses, chariots
and horsemen[c] went into the sea,[c]
the LORD brought the waters of the sea
back over them, but the Israelites
walked through the sea on dry
ground.[d] 20Then Miriam[e] the prophetess,[f] Aaron's sister, took a tambourine in her hand, and all the women
followed her, with tambourines and
dancing.[g] 21Miriam sang to them:

"Sing to the LORD,
for he is highly exalted.
The horse and its rider
he has hurled into the sea."[h]

The Waters of Marah and Elim

22Then Moses led Israel from the
Red Sea and they went into the Desert
of Shur. For three days they traveled
in the desert without finding water.
23When they came to Marah, they
could not drink its water because it was
bitter. (That is why the place is called
Marah.[d][i]) 24So the people grumbled[j] against Moses, saying, "What
are we to drink?"

25Then Moses cried out[k] to the
LORD, and the LORD showed him a
piece of wood. He threw it into the water, and the water became sweet.

There the LORD made a decree and
a law for them, and there he tested[l]
them. 26He said, "If you listen carefully
to the voice of the LORD your God and
do what is right in his eyes, if you pay
attention to his commands and keep
all his decrees,[m] I will not bring on you
any of the diseases[n] I brought on the
Egyptians, for I am the LORD, who
heals[o] you."

27Then they came to Elim, where
there were twelve springs and seventy
palm trees, and they camped[p] there
near the water.

Manna and Quail

16 The whole Israelite community set
out from Elim and came to the
Desert of Sin,[q] which is between Elim
and Sinai, on the fifteenth day of the
second month after they had come out
of Egypt. 2In the desert the whole community grumbled[r] against Moses and
Aaron. 3The Israelites said to them, "If
only we had died by the LORD's hand in
Egypt![s] There we sat around pots of
meat and ate all the food[t] we wanted,
but you have brought us out into this
desert to starve this entire assembly to
death."

4Then the LORD said to Moses, "I will
rain down bread from heaven[u] for
you. The people are to go out each day
and gather enough for that day. In this
way I will test them and see whether
they will follow my instructions. 5On
the sixth day they are to prepare what
they bring in, and that is to be twice[v]
as much as they gather on the other
days."

6So Moses and Aaron said to all the
Israelites, "In the evening you will
know that it was the LORD who brought

15:9 [l]Ex 14:5-9 [m]Jdg 5:30; Isa 53:12
15:10 [n]ver 5; Ex 14:27-28
15:11 [o]Ex 8:10; Dt 3:24; Ps 77:13 [p]Isa 6:3; Rev 4:8 [q]Ps 8:1
15:13 [r]Ne 9:12; Ps 77:20 [s]Ps 78:54
15:14 [t]Dt 2:25
15:15 [u]Ge 36:15 [v]Nu 22:3 [w]Jos 5:1
15:16 [x]Ex 23:27; Jos 2:9 [y]1Sa 25:37 [z]Ps 74:2
15:17 [a]Ps 44:2 [b]Ps 78:54,68
15:19 [c]Ex 14:28 [d]Ex 14:22
15:20 [e]Nu 26:59 [f]Jdg 4:4 [g]Jdg 11:34; 1Sa 18:6; Ps 30:11; 150:4
15:21 [h]ver 1; Ex 14:27
15:23 [i]Nu 33:8
15:24 [j]Ex 14:12; 16:2
15:25 [k]Ex 14:10 [l]Jdg 3:4
15:26 [m]Dt 7:12 [n]Dt 28:27, 58-60 [o]Ex 23:25-26
15:27 [p]Nu 33:9
16:1 [q]Nu 33:11,12
16:2 [r]Ex 14:11; 15:24; 1Co 10:10
16:3 [s]Ex 17:3 [t]Nu 11:4,34
16:4 [u]Dt 8:3; Jn 6:31*
16:5 [v]ver 22

[a]*15* Or *rulers* [b]*16* Or *created* [c]*19* Or *charioteers* [d]*23* *Marah* means *bitter.*

you out of Egypt,[w] 7and in the morning you will see the glory[x] of the LORD, because he has heard your grumbling[y] against him. Who are we, that you should grumble against us?"[z] 8Moses also said, "You will know that it was the LORD when he gives you meat to eat in the evening and all the bread you want in the morning, because he has heard your grumbling against him. Who are we? You are not grumbling against us, but against the LORD."[a]

9Then Moses told Aaron, "Say to the entire Israelite community, 'Come before the LORD, for he has heard your grumbling.' "

10While Aaron was speaking to the whole Israelite community, they looked toward the desert, and there was the glory[b] of the LORD appearing in the cloud.[c]

11The LORD said to Moses, 12"I have heard the grumbling[d] of the Israelites. Tell them, 'At twilight you will eat meat, and in the morning you will be filled with bread. Then you will know that I am the LORD your God.' "

13That evening quail[e] came and covered the camp, and in the morning there was a layer of dew[f] around the camp. 14When the dew was gone, thin flakes like frost[g] on the ground appeared on the desert floor. 15When the Israelites saw it, they said to each other, "What is it?" For they did not know what it was.

Moses said to them, "It is the bread[h] the LORD has given you to eat. 16This is what the LORD has commanded: 'Each one is to gather as much as he needs. Take an omer[a][i] for each person you have in your tent.' "

17The Israelites did as they were told; some gathered much, some little. 18And when they measured it by the omer, he who gathered much did not have too much, and he who gathered little did not have too little.[j] Each one gathered as much as he needed.

19Then Moses said to them, "No one is to keep any of it until morning."[k]

20However, some of them paid no attention to Moses; they kept part of it until morning, but it was full of maggots and began to smell. So Moses was angry with them.

21Each morning everyone gathered as much as he needed, and when the sun grew hot, it melted away. 22On the sixth day, they gathered twice[l] as much—two omers[b] for each person—and the leaders of the community[m] came and reported this to Moses. 23He said to them, "This is what the LORD commanded: 'Tomorrow is to be a day of rest, a holy Sabbath[n] to the LORD. So bake what you want to bake and boil what you want to boil. Save whatever is left and keep it until morning.' "

24So they saved it until morning, as Moses commanded, and it did not stink or get maggots in it. 25"Eat it today," Moses said, "because today is a Sabbath to the LORD. You will not find any of it on the ground today. 26Six days you are to gather it, but on the seventh day, the Sabbath,[o] there will not be any."

27Nevertheless, some of the people went out on the seventh day to gather it, but they found none. 28Then the LORD said to Moses, "How long will you[c] refuse to keep my commands[p] and my instructions? 29Bear in mind that the LORD has given you the Sabbath; that is why on the sixth day he gives you bread for two days. Everyone is to stay where he is on the seventh day; no one is to go out." 30So the people rested on the seventh day.

31The people of Israel called the bread manna.[d][q] It was white like coriander seed and tasted like wafers made with honey. 32Moses said, "This is what the LORD has commanded: 'Take an omer of manna and keep it for the generations to come, so they can see the bread I gave you to eat in the desert when I brought you out of Egypt.' "

33So Moses said to Aaron, "Take a jar

16:6 [w]Ex 6:6 **16:7** [x]ver 10; Isa 35:2; 40:5 [y]ver 12; Nu 14:2,27,28 [z]Nu 16:11 **16:8** [a]1Sa 8:7; Ro 13:2 **16:10** [b]ver 7; Nu 16:19 [c]Ex 13:21; 1Ki 8:10 **16:12** [d]ver 7 **16:13** [e]Nu 11:31; Ps 78:27-28; 105:40 [f]Nu 11:9 **16:14** [g]ver 31; Nu 11:7-9; Ps 105:40 **16:15** [h]ver 4; Jn 6:31 **16:16** [i]ver 32,36 **16:18** [j]2Co 8:15* **16:19** [k]ver 23; Ex 12:10; 23:18 **16:22** [l]ver 5 [m]Ex 34:31 **16:23** [n]Ge 2:3; Ex 20:8; 23:12; Lev 23:3 **16:26** [o]Ex 20:9-10 **16:28** [p]2Ki 17:14; Ps 78:10; 106:13 **16:31** [q]Nu 11:7-9

a *16* That is, probably about 2 quarts (about 2 liters); also in verses 18, 32, 33 and 36
b *22* That is, probably about 4 quarts (about 4.5 liters) c *28* The Hebrew is plural.
d *31* *Manna* means *What is it?* (see verse 15).

16:1–3

PROMISE **5**

COMPLAINING IS DRAINING

Can anything be more disheartening than griping and complaining? One month—to the day—before the events of this passage, God had opened the Red Sea and delivered these same people from generations of slavery (which they had also griped and complained about). These were God's people, on their way to God's place, following God's chosen leader on God's path. And yet here we read that they were griping up a storm.

Just as Moses and Aaron needed people to encourage them in their mission, so also churches and pastors today need encouragers to balance the gripers. List five blessings from God on a piece of paper and thank God for them. Then either call or visit with someone in your church this week and focus on the positive.

For the next Promise 5 reading go to page 95.

and put an omer of manna[r] in it.
Then place it before the LORD to be
kept for the generations to come."
34 As the LORD commanded Moses,
Aaron put the manna in front of the
Testimony,[s] that it might be kept.
35 The Israelites ate manna[t] forty
years,[u] until they came to a land that
was settled; they ate manna until they
reached the border of Canaan.[v]
36 (An omer is one tenth of an
ephah.)

Water From the Rock

17 The whole Israelite community set
out from the Desert of Sin,[w] traveling from place to place as the LORD
commanded. They camped at Rephidim, but there was no water[x] for the
people to drink. 2 So they quarreled
with Moses and said, "Give us water[y]
to drink."
Moses replied, "Why do you quarrel
with me? Why do you put the LORD to
the test?"[z]
3 But the people were thirsty for water there, and they grumbled[a] against
Moses. They said, "Why did you bring
us up out of Egypt to make us and our
children and livestock die of thirst?"
4 Then Moses cried out to the LORD,
"What am I to do with these people?
They are almost ready to stone[b] me."
5 The LORD answered Moses, "Walk
on ahead of the people. Take with you
some of the elders of Israel and take in
your hand the staff with which you
struck the Nile,[c] and go. 6 I will stand
there before you by the rock at Horeb.
Strike the rock, and water[d] will come
out of it for the people to drink." So
Moses did this in the sight of the elders
of Israel. 7 And he called the place Massah[a] and Meribah[b][e] because the Israelites quarreled and because they
tested the LORD saying, "Is the LORD
among us or not?"

The Amalekites Defeated

8 The Amalekites[f] came and attacked the Israelites at Rephidim. 9 Moses said to Joshua, "Choose some of
our men and go out to fight the Amalekites. Tomorrow I will stand on top of
the hill with the staff[g] of God in my
hands."
2 →PG. 87
10 So Joshua fought the Amalekites as
Moses had ordered, and Moses, Aaron
and Hur[h] went to the top of the hill.
11 As long as Moses held up his hands,
the Israelites were winning,[i] but
whenever he lowered his hands, the
Amalekites were winning. 12 When Moses' hands grew tired, they took a stone
and put it under him and he sat on it.
Aaron and Hur held his hands up—
one on one side, one on the other—so
that his hands remained steady till
sunset. 13 So Joshua overcame the Amalekite army with the sword.
14 Then the LORD said to Moses,
"Write[j] this on a scroll as something
to be remembered and make sure that
Joshua hears it, because I will completely blot out the memory of Amalek[k] from under heaven."
15 Moses built an altar and called it
The LORD is my Banner. 16 He said, "For
hands were lifted up to the throne of
the LORD. The[c] LORD will be at war
against the Amalekites from generation
to generation."

Jethro Visits Moses

18 Now Jethro, the priest of Midian[l]
and father-in-law of Moses, heard
of everything God had done for Moses
and for his people Israel, and how the
LORD had brought Israel out of Egypt.
2 After Moses had sent away his wife
Zipporah,[m] his father-in-law Jethro
received her 3 and her two sons.[n] One
son was named Gershom,[d] for Moses
said, "I have become an alien in a foreign land";[o] 4 and the other was
named Eliezer,[e][p] for he said, "My father's God was my helper; he saved me
from the sword of Pharaoh."
5 Jethro, Moses' father-in-law, together with Moses' sons and wife,
came to him in the desert, where he
was camped near the mountain[q] of
God. 6 Jethro had sent word to him, "I,
your father-in-law Jethro, am coming
to you with your wife and her two
sons."
7 So Moses went out to meet his
father-in-law and bowed down[r] and
kissed[s] him. They greeted each other
and then went into the tent. 8 Moses
told his father-in-law about everything
the LORD had done to Pharaoh and the
Egyptians for Israel's sake and about all
the hardships they had met along the
way and how the LORD had saved[t]
them.
9 Jethro was delighted to hear about
all the good things the LORD had done
for Israel in rescuing them from the
hand of the Egyptians. 10 He said,
"Praise be to the LORD,[u] who rescued
you from the hand of the Egyptians
and of Pharaoh, and who rescued the
people from the hand of the Egyptians.
11 Now I know that the LORD is greater

16:33 [r]Heb 9:4
16:34 [s]Ex 25:16,21,22; 40:20; Nu 17:4,10
16:35 [t]Jn 6:31,49 [u]Ne 9:21 [v]Jos 5:12
17:1 [w]Ex 16:1 [x]Nu 33:14
17:2 [y]Nu 20:2 [z]Dt 6:16; Ps 78:18,41; 1Co 10:9
17:3 [a]Ex 15:24; 16:2-3
17:4 [b]Nu 14:10; 1Sa 30:6
17:5 [c]Ex 7:20
17:6 [d]Nu 20:11; Ps 114:8; 1Co 10:4
17:7 [e]Nu 20:13,24; Ps 81:7
17:8 [f]Ge 36:12; Dt 25:17-19
17:9 [g]Ex 4:17
17:10 [h]Ex 24:14
17:11 [i]Jas 5:16
17:14 [j]Ex 24:4; 34:27; Nu 33:2 [k]1Sa 15:3; 30:17-18
18:1 [l]Ex 2:16; 3:1
18:2 [m]Ex 2:21; 4:25
18:3 [n]Ex 4:20; Ac 7:29 [o]Ex 2:22
18:4 [p]1Ch 23:15
18:5 [q]Ex 3:1
18:7 [r]Ge 43:28 [s]Ge 29:13
18:8 [t]Ex 15:6,16; Ps 81:7
18:10 [u]Ge 14:20; Ps 68:19-20

[a] 7 *Massah* means *testing.* [b] 7 *Meribah* means *quarreling.* [c] 16 Or *"Because a hand was against the throne of the LORD, the* [d] 3 *Gershom* sounds like the Hebrew for *an alien there.* [e] 4 *Eliezer* means *my God is helper.*

JETHRO

A Man of Wisdom

Have you ever been so overwhelmed by the challenges in your life that it was hard for you to make time for even the most important things? If so, you're not alone. Even a great and godly leader like Moses found that 24 hours in a day simply weren't enough. Surprisingly, God brought a man who had spent most of his life in a pagan culture alongside Moses to help him solve his time-management problems.

Blind Spots

When Moses left Egypt at age 40 and went to live in the wilderness, Exodus 2 tells us that he married Zipporah, one of Jethro's seven daughters. Moses left Zipporah and their two sons with his father-in-law when he went back to Egypt to seek the Israelites' freedom. After Moses brought the Israelites out of Egypt he met Jethro once again—this time at the foot of Mount Sinai.

It was a grand reunion! After greeting one another, "Moses told his father-in-law about everything the LORD had done to Pharaoh and the Egyptians for Israel's sake . . . and how the LORD had saved them" (Exodus 18:8). Jethro was delighted and was now convinced that God was "greater than all other gods" (18:11). He verified his newfound faith by offering sacrifices to God (18:12).

A Source of Wisdom

Though up to this point Jethro had been a pagan priest, he had learned a great deal about leadership and how it works. Consequently, when Moses "took his seat to serve as judge for the people, and they stood around him from morning till evening" (18:13), Jethro was deeply concerned. He knew immediately that Moses couldn't possibly solve the problems of more than two million people, even if he didn't have other duties to attend to.

Jethro came straight to the point with Moses. "What you are doing is not good. You and these people who come to you will only wear yourselves out. The work is too heavy for you; you cannot handle it alone" (18:17–18). Then, advising Moses to first consult God about the matter, Jethro outlined his plan for helping Moses get control of his time and workload.

Jethro wisely advised Moses to establish two important priorities—to intercede for the people and to teach them God's will. And Jethro also urged Moses to delegate some of his other responsibilities to qualified men so he could concentrate on judging the most difficult cases. Jethro realized that men who were not capable or trustworthy or did not fear God would only make Moses' problems worse, so he strongly stressed the qualifications for Moses' subordinates.

With God's approval, Moses and the elders of Israel implemented Jethro's plan. And it worked! Moses was able to carry out all his duties without collapsing, and the people were happy. Their needs were being met. Jethro's advice was so good, in fact, that management consultants today still use Jethro's wisdom as a model for modern time management.

Our Need for a Jethro

Though Moses was wise and godly, he still had some "blind spots." He needed another man's perspective to help him see how to manage his time and responsibilities. And many times, so do we.

Remember that Jethro was a "new believer" who had had a lot of good leadership experience, even though it was in a "secular setting." That doesn't mean that all secular advice is good advice. But it *does* mean that "all truth is God's truth"—even if unbelievers have discovered it first. We need to be open to listening and learning from whomever God chooses to use in our lives.

Checking Our Own Priorities

Our vocational priorities may not be the same as those of Moses. However, we all need to make the best use of our time and make sure that we keep the important things in perspective. Jesus taught that all of us should "seek first his kingdom and his righteousness, and all these things will be given to [us] as well" (Matthew 6:33). If we were to examine our planning calendars for the last month, what conclusions would we draw about whether or not we have been seeking the things of God first?

If you, like Moses, need help in managing your time and priorities, perhaps you can delegate some of your load to others who are qualified to carry those responsibilities. Ask God to lead you to people who can help you in this crucial area. Are there any "Jethros" in your life you can listen to? Seek them out and prayerfully implement their wise words.

—*Dr. Gene Getz*

than all other gods,[v] for he did this to
those who had treated Israel arrogantly."[w] 12Then Jethro, Moses' father-in-
law, brought a burnt offering and other
sacrifices to God, and Aaron came with
all the elders of Israel to eat bread with
Moses' father-in-law in the presence[x]
of God.

13The next day Moses took his seat
to serve as judge for the people, and
they stood around him from morning
till evening. 14When his father-in-law
saw all that Moses was doing for the
people, he said, "What is this you are
doing for the people? Why do you
alone sit as judge, while all these people stand around you from morning till
evening?"

15Moses answered him, "Because
the people come to me to seek God's
will.[y] 16Whenever they have a dispute,
it is brought to me, and I decide between the parties and inform them of
God's decrees and laws."[z]

17Moses' father-in-law replied, "What
you are doing is not good. 18You
and these people who come to you will
only wear yourselves out. The work is
too heavy for you; you cannot handle it
alone.[a] 19Listen now to me and I will
give you some advice, and may God be
with you.[b] You must be the people's
representative before God and bring
their disputes[c] to him. 20Teach them
the decrees and laws,[d] and show them
the way to live[e] and the duties they
are to perform.[f] 21But select capable
men[g] from all the people—men who
fear God, trustworthy men who hate
dishonest gain[h]—and appoint them
as officials[i] over thousands, hundreds, fifties and tens. 22Have them
serve as judges for the people at all
times, but have them bring every difficult case[j] to you; the simple cases
they can decide themselves. That will
make your load lighter, because they
will share[k] it with you. 23If you do this
and God so commands, you will be
able to stand the strain, and all these
people will go home satisfied."

2 →PG. 176

24Moses listened to his father-in-
law and did everything he said. 25He
chose capable men from all Israel and
made them leaders of the people, officials over thousands, hundreds, fifties
and tens.[l] 26They served as judges for
the people at all times. The difficult
cases they brought to Moses, but the
simple ones they decided themselves.[m]

27Then Moses sent his father-in-law
on his way, and Jethro returned to his
own country.[n]

18:11 [v]Ex 12:12; 15:11; 2Ch 2:5 [w]Lk 1:51
18:12 [x]Dt 12:7
18:15 [y]Nu 9:6,8; Dt 17:8-13
18:16 [z]Lev 24:12
18:18 [a]Nu 11:11,14, 17
18:19 [b]Ex 3:12 [c]Nu 27:5
18:20 [d]Dt 5:1 [e]Ps 143:8 [f]Dt 1:18
18:21 [g]Ac 6:3 [h]Dt 16:19; Ps 15:5; Eze 18:8 [i]Dt 1:13,15; 2Ch 19:5-10
18:22 [j]Dt 1:17-18 [k]Nu 11:17
18:25 [l]Dt 1:13-15
18:26 [m]ver 22
18:27 [n]Nu 10:29-30

19:2 [o]Ex 17:1 [p]Ex 3:1
19:3 [q]Ex 3:4; Ac 7:38
19:4 [r]Dt 29:2 [s]Isa 63:9
19:5 [t]Ex 15:26 [u]Dt 5:2 [v]Dt 14:2; Ps 135:4 [w]Ex 9:29; Dt 10:14
19:6 [x]1Pe 2:5 [y]Dt 7:6; 26:19; Isa 62:12
19:8 [z]Ex 24:3,7; Dt 5:27
19:9 [a]ver 16; Ex 24:15-16 [b]Dt 4:12,36
19:10 [c]Lev 11:44; Heb 10:22 [d]Ge 35:2
19:11 [e]ver 16
19:13 [f]Heb 12:20*

At Mount Sinai

19 In the third month after the Israelites left Egypt—on the very day—
they came to the Desert of Sinai. 2After
they set out from Rephidim,[o] they entered the Desert of Sinai, and Israel
camped there in the desert in front of
the mountain.[p]

3Then Moses went up to God, and
the LORD called[q] to him from the
mountain and said, "This is what you
are to say to the house of Jacob and
what you are to tell the people of Israel:
4'You yourselves have seen what I did
to Egypt,[r] and how I carried you on
eagles' wings[s] and brought you to
myself. 5Now if you obey me fully[t]
and keep my covenant,[u] then out of
all nations you will be my treasured
possession.[v] Although the whole
earth[w] is mine, 6you[a] will be for me a
kingdom of priests[x] and a holy nation.'[y] These are the words you are to
speak to the Israelites."

7So Moses went back and summoned the elders of the people and set
before them all the words the LORD had
commanded him to speak. 8The people all responded together, "We will do
everything the LORD has said."[z] So
Moses brought their answer back to
the LORD.

9The LORD said to Moses, "I am going to come to you in a dense cloud,[a]
so that the people will hear me speaking[b] with you and will always put their
trust in you." Then Moses told the
LORD what the people had said.

10And the LORD said to Moses, "Go to
the people and consecrate[c] them today and tomorrow. Have them wash
their clothes[d] 11and be ready by the
third day,[e] because on that day the
LORD will come down on Mount Sinai
in the sight of all the people. 12Put limits for the people around the mountain
and tell them, 'Be careful that you do
not go up the mountain or touch the
foot of it. Whoever touches the mountain shall surely be put to death. 13He
shall surely be stoned[f] or shot with
arrows; not a hand is to be laid on him.
Whether man or animal, he shall not
be permitted to live.' Only when the
ram's horn sounds a long blast may
they go up to the mountain."

14After Moses had gone down the
mountain to the people, he consecrated them, and they washed their
clothes. 15Then he said to the people,
"Prepare yourselves for the third day.
Abstain from sexual relations."

[a]5,6 Or *possession, for the whole earth is mine.* 6*You*

16On the morning of the third day
there was thunder and lightning, with a
thick cloud over the mountain, and a
very loud trumpet blast.[g] Everyone in
the camp trembled.[h] 17Then Moses
led the people out of the camp to meet
with God, and they stood at the foot of
the mountain. 18Mount Sinai was covered with smoke,[i] because the LORD
descended on it in fire.[j] The smoke
billowed up from it like smoke from a
furnace,[k] the whole mountain[a] trembled[l] violently, 19and the sound of the
trumpet grew louder and louder. Then
Moses spoke and the voice[m] of God
answered[n] him.[b]

20The LORD descended to the top of
Mount Sinai and called Moses to the
top of the mountain. So Moses went up
21and the LORD said to him, "Go down
and warn the people so they do not
force their way through to see[o] the
LORD and many of them perish. 22Even
the priests, who approach[p] the LORD,
must consecrate themselves, or the
LORD will break out against them."[q]

23Moses said to the LORD, "The people cannot come up Mount Sinai, because you yourself warned us, 'Put limits[r] around the mountain and set it
apart as holy.' "

24The LORD replied, "Go down and
bring Aaron[s] up with you. But the
priests and the people must not force
their way through to come up to the
LORD, or he will break out against
them."

25So Moses went down to the people
and told them.

The Ten Commandments

1 →PG. 103

20 And God spoke all these words:

2"I am the LORD your God,
who brought you out of
Egypt, out of the land of
slavery.[t]
3"You shall have no other gods before[c] me.[u]
4"You shall not make for yourself
an idol[v] in the form of anything in heaven above or on
the earth beneath or in the
waters below. 5You shall not
bow down to them or wor-
ship[w] them; for I, the LORD
your God, am a jealous
God,[x] punishing the children for the sin of the fathers to the third and fourth
generation[y] of those who
hate me, 6but showing love
to a thousand[z] ⌞genera-
tions⌟ of those who love me
and keep my command-
ments.
7"You shall not misuse the name
of the LORD your God, for
the LORD will not hold anyone guiltless who misuses
his name.[a]
8"Remember the Sabbath[b] day
by keeping it holy. 9Six days
you shall labor and do all
your work,[c] 10but the seventh day is a Sabbath to the
LORD your God. On it you
shall not do any work, neither you, nor your son or
daughter, nor your manservant or maidservant, nor
your animals, nor the alien
within your gates. 11For in
six days the LORD made the
heavens and the earth, the
sea, and all that is in them,
but he rested[d] on the seventh day. Therefore the
LORD blessed the Sabbath
day and made it holy.
12"Honor your father and your 4 →PG. 192

19:16 [g]Heb 12:18-19; Rev 4:1 [h]Heb 12:21 19:18 [i]Ps 104:32 [j]Ex 3:2; 24:17; Dt 4:11; 2Ch 7:1; Ps 18:8; Heb 12:18 [k]Ge 19:28 [l]Jdg 5:5; Ps 68:8; Jer 4:24 19:19 [m]Ne 9:13 [n]Ps 81:7 19:21 [o]Ex 3:5; 1Sa 6:19 19:22 [p]Lev 10:3 [q]2Sa 6:7 19:23 [r]ver 12 19:24 [s]Ex 24:1,9 20:2 [t]Ex 13:3 20:3 [u]Dt 6:14; Jer 35:15 20:4 [v]Lev 26:1; Dt 4:15-19,23; 27:15 20:5 [w]Isa 44:15,17, 19 [x]Ex 34:14; Dt 4:24 [y]Nu 14:18; Jer 32:18 20:6 [z]Dt 7:9 20:7 [a]Lev 19:12; Mt 5:33 20:8 [b]Ex 31:13-16; Lev 26:2 20:9 [c]Ex 34:21; Lk 13:14 20:11 [d]Ge 2:2

a *18* Most Hebrew manuscripts; a few Hebrew manuscripts and Septuagint *all the people*
b *19* Or *and God answered him with thunder*
c *3* Or *besides*

20:1–17

PROMISE 1

GOD'S TOP TEN

To many people, these Ten Commandments ARE the Bible. Even some Christians believe that all of God's Word is summed up in these few rules and regulations. Some people who focus in this way on these commandments tend to think that, thousands of years ago, God determined what things we most enjoy and then made up rules to stop us from doing them.

Try this brief exercise. First, envision what your life would be like if you followed the first four commandments carefully (vv. 2–11). Then read the last six commands (vv. 12–17), asking for each: "What would my life be like if someone violated all six of these in relating to me?"

The Bible isn't about rules and restrictions, it is about living the highest possible quality of life. Be careful about reducing God's revelation to these Ten Commandments. Read through these few verses one more time, and notice God's concern for your protection and growth. Would you have a better life by violating or by keeping these commands? Would we have a better society if we all kept or if we all ignored these commands? What do your answers tell you about God's Word?

For the next Promise 1 reading go to page 102.

mother,[e] so that you may
live long in the land the
LORD your God is giving you.
13"You shall not murder.[f]
14"You shall not commit adultery.[g]
15"You shall not steal.[h]
16"You shall not give false testimony against your neighbor.[i]
17"You shall not covet[j] your
neighbor's house. You shall
not covet your neighbor's
wife, or his manservant or
maidservant, his ox or donkey, or anything that be-
longs to your neighbor."

18When the people saw the thunder
and lightning and heard the trumpet[k]
and saw the mountain in smoke, they
trembled with fear. They stayed at a
distance 19and said to Moses, "Speak to
us yourself and we will listen. But do
not have God speak to us or we will
die."[l]
20Moses said to the people, "Do not
be afraid. God has come to test you, so
that the fear[m] of God will be with you
to keep you from sinning."[n]
21The people remained at a distance,
while Moses approached the thick
darkness[o] where God was.

Idols and Altars

22Then the LORD said to Moses, "Tell
the Israelites this: 'You have seen for
yourselves that I have spoken to you
from heaven:[p] 23Do not make any
gods to be alongside me;[q] do not
make for yourselves gods of silver or
gods of gold.[r]
24" 'Make an altar of earth for me
and sacrifice on it your burnt offerings
and fellowship offerings,[a] your sheep
and goats and your cattle. Wherever I
cause my name[s] to be honored, I will
come to you and bless[t] you. 25If you
make an altar of stones for me, do not
build it with dressed stones, for you
will defile it if you use a tool[u] on it.
26And do not go up to my altar on
steps, lest your nakedness be exposed
on it.'

21 "These are the laws[v] you are to set
before them:

Hebrew Servants

2"If you buy a Hebrew servant, he is
to serve you for six years. But in the
seventh year, he shall go free,[w] without paying anything. 3If he comes
alone, he is to go free alone; but if he
has a wife when he comes, she is to go
with him. 4If his master gives him a
wife and she bears him sons or daughters, the woman and her children shall
belong to her master, and only the man
shall go free.
5"But if the servant declares, 'I love
my master and my wife and children
and do not want to go free,'[x] 6then
his master must take him before the
judges.[b][y] He shall take him to the
door or the doorpost and pierce his ear
with an awl. Then he will be his servant
for life.[z]
7"If a man sells his daughter as a servant, she is not to go free as menservants do. 8If she does not please the
master who has selected her for himself,[c] he must let her be redeemed. He
has no right to sell her to foreigners,
because he has broken faith with her.
9If he selects her for his son, he must
grant her the rights of a daughter. 10If
he marries another woman, he must
not deprive the first one of her food,
clothing and marital rights.[a] 11If he
does not provide her with these three
things, she is to go free, without any
payment of money.

Personal Injuries

12"Anyone who strikes a man and
kills him shall surely be put to death.[b]
13However, if he does not do it intentionally, but God lets it happen, he is to
flee to a place[c] I will designate. 14But
if a man schemes and kills another
man deliberately,[d] take him away
from my altar and put him to death.[e]
15"Anyone who attacks[d] his father
or his mother must be put to death.
16"Anyone who kidnaps another and
either sells[f] him or still has him when
he is caught must be put to death.[g]
17"Anyone who curses his father or
mother must be put to death.[h]
18"If men quarrel and one hits the
other with a stone or with his fist[e] and
he does not die but is confined to bed,
19the one who struck the blow will not
be held responsible if the other gets
up and walks around outside with his
staff; however, he must pay the injured
man for the loss of his time and see
that he is completely healed.
20"If a man beats his male or female
slave with a rod and the slave dies as
a direct result, he must be punished,
21but he is not to be punished if the
slave gets up after a day or two, since
the slave is his property.[i]
22"If men who are fighting hit a pregnant woman and she gives birth pre-
maturely[f] but there is no serious inju-

20:12 [e]Mt 15:4*; Mk 7:10*; Eph 6:2
20:13 [f]Mt 5:21*; Ro 13:9*
20:14 [g]Mt 19:18*
20:15 [h]Lev 19:11,13; Mt 19:18*
20:16 [i]Ex 23:1,7; Mt 19:18*
20:17 [j]Ro 7:7*; 13:9*; Eph 5:3
20:18 [k]Ex 19:16-19; Heb 12:18-19
20:19 [l]Dt 5:5,23-27; Gal 3:19
20:20 [m]Dt 4:10; Isa 8:13 [n]Pr 16:6
20:21 [o]Dt 5:22
20:22 [p]Ne 9:13
20:23 [q]ver 3 [r]Ex 32:4,8,31
20:24 [s]Dt 12:5; 16:6, 11; 2Ch 6:6 [t]Ge 12:2
20:25 [u]Dt 27:5-6
21:1 [v]Dt 4:14
21:2 [w]Jer 34:8,14
21:5 [x]Dt 15:16
21:6 [y]Ex 22:8-9 [z]Ne 5:5
21:10 [a]1Co 7:3-5
21:12 [b]Ge 9:6; Mt 26:52
21:13 [c]Nu 35:10-34; Dt 19:2-13; Jos 20:9; 1Sa 24:4,10,18
21:14 [d]Heb 10:26 [e]Dt 19:11-12; 1Ki 2:28-34
21:16 [f]Ge 37:28 [g]Ex 22:4; Dt 24:7
21:17 [h]Lev 20:9-10; Mt 15:4*; Mk 7:10*
21:21 [i]Lev 25:44-46

[a]24 Traditionally *peace offerings* [b]6 Or *before God* [c]8 Or *master so that he does not choose her* [d]15 Or *kills* [e]18 Or *with a tool*
[f]22 Or *she has a miscarriage*

ry, the offender must be fined whatever
the woman's husband demands[j] and
the court allows. 23 But if there is serious injury, you are to take life for life,[k]
24 eye for eye, tooth for tooth,[l] hand
for hand, foot for foot, 25 burn for burn,
wound for wound, bruise for bruise.
26 "If a man hits a manservant or
maidservant in the eye and destroys it,
he must let the servant go free to compensate for the eye. 27 And if he knocks
out the tooth of a manservant or maidservant, he must let the servant go free
to compensate for the tooth.
28 "If a bull gores a man or a woman
to death, the bull must be stoned to
death,[m] and its meat must not be eat-
en. But the owner of the bull will not be
held responsible. 29 If, however, the bull
has had the habit of goring and the
owner has been warned but has not
kept it penned up and it kills a man or
woman, the bull must be stoned and
the owner also must be put to death.
30 However, if payment is demanded of
him, he may redeem his life by paying
whatever is demanded.[n] 31 This law
also applies if the bull gores a son or
daughter. 32 If the bull gores a male or
female slave, the owner must pay thirty
shekels[a][o] of silver to the master of
the slave, and the bull must be stoned.
33 "If a man uncovers a pit or digs
one and fails to cover it and an ox or a
donkey falls into it, 34 the owner of the
pit must pay for the loss; he must pay
its owner, and the dead animal will be
his.
35 "If a man's bull injures the bull of
another and it dies, they are to sell the
live one and divide both the money
and the dead animal equally. 36 However, if it was known that the bull had the
habit of goring, yet the owner did not
keep it penned up, the owner must
pay, animal for animal, and the dead
animal will be his.

Protection of Property

22 "If a man steals an ox or a sheep
and slaughters it or sells it, he must
pay back[p] five head of cattle for the ox
and four sheep for the sheep.
2 "If a thief is caught breaking in[q]
and is struck so that he dies, the defender is not guilty of bloodshed;[r]
3 but if it happens[b] after sunrise, he is
guilty of bloodshed.
"A thief must certainly make restitution, but if he has nothing, he must be
sold[s] to pay for his theft.
4 "If the stolen animal is found alive
in his possession—whether ox or donkey or sheep—he must pay back double.[t]
5 "If a man grazes his livestock in a
field or vineyard and lets them stray
and they graze in another man's field,
he must make restitution from the best
of his own field or vineyard.
6 "If a fire breaks out and spreads
into thornbushes so that it burns
shocks of grain or standing grain or the
whole field, the one who started the
fire must make restitution.
7 "If a man gives his neighbor silver
or goods for safekeeping and they are
stolen from the neighbor's house, the
thief, if he is caught, must pay back
double.[u] 8 But if the thief is not found,
the owner of the house must appear
before the judges[c][v] to determine
whether he has laid his hands on the
other man's property. 9 In all cases of
illegal possession of an ox, a donkey,
a sheep, a garment, or any other lost
property about which somebody says,
'This is mine,' both parties are to bring
their cases before the judges.[w] The
one whom the judges declare[d] guilty
must pay back double to his neighbor.
10 "If a man gives a donkey, an ox, a
sheep or any other animal to his neighbor for safekeeping and it dies or is injured or is taken away while no one is
looking, 11 the issue between them will
be settled by the taking of an oath[x]
before the LORD that the neighbor did
not lay hands on the other person's
property. The owner is to accept this,
and no restitution is required. 12 But if
the animal was stolen from the neighbor, he must make restitution to the
owner. 13 If it was torn to pieces by a
wild animal, he shall bring in the remains as evidence and he will not be
required to pay for the torn animal.[y]
14 "If a man borrows an animal from
his neighbor and it is injured or dies
while the owner is not present, he must
make restitution. 15 But if the owner is
with the animal, the borrower will not
have to pay. If the animal was hired,
the money paid for the hire covers the
loss.

Social Responsibility

16 "If a man seduces a virgin[z] who is
not pledged to be married and sleeps
with her, he must pay the bride-price,
and she shall be his wife. 17 If her father
absolutely refuses to give her to him,
he must still pay the bride-price for virgins.
18 "Do not allow a sorceress[a] to live.
19 "Anyone who has sexual relations

21:22 [j] ver 30; Dt 22:18-19
21:23 [k] Lev 24:19; Dt 19:21
21:24 [l] Mt 5:38*
21:28 [m] ver 32; Ge 9:5
21:30 [n] ver 22; Nu 35:31
21:32 [o] Zec 11:12-13; Mt 26:15; 27:3,9
22:1 [p] 2Sa 12:6; Pr 6:31; Lk 19:8
22:2 [q] Mt 6:19-20; 24:43 [r] Nu 35:27
22:3 [s] Ex 21:2; Mt 18:25
22:4 [t] Ge 43:12
22:7 [u] ver 4
22:8 [v] Ex 21:6; Dt 17:8-9; 19:17
22:9 [w] ver 28; Dt 25:1
22:11 [x] Heb 6:16
22:13 [y] Ge 31:39
22:16 [z] Dt 22:28
22:18 [a] Lev 20:27; Dt 18:11; 1Sa 28:3

[a] *32* That is, about 12 ounces (about 0.3 kilogram) [b] *3* Or *if he strikes him* [c] *8* Or *before God*; also in verse 9 [d] *9* Or *whom God declares*

with an animal[b] must be put to death.

20"Whoever sacrifices to any god other than the LORD must be destroyed.[a][c]

21"Do not mistreat an alien[d] or oppress him, for you were aliens[e] in Egypt.

22"Do not take advantage of a widow or an orphan.[f] 23If you do and they cry out[g] to me, I will certainly hear their cry.[h] 24My anger will be aroused, and I will kill you with the sword; your wives will become widows and your children fatherless.[i]

25"If you lend money to one of my people among you who is needy, do not be like a moneylender; charge him no interest.[b][j] 26If you take your neighbor's cloak as a pledge,[k] return it to him by sunset, 27because his cloak is the only covering he has for his body. What else will he sleep in? When he cries out to me, I will hear, for I am compassionate.[l]

28"Do not blaspheme God[c][m] or curse the ruler of your people.[n]

29"Do not hold back offerings[o] from your granaries or your vats.[d]

"You must give me the firstborn of your sons.[p] 30Do the same with your cattle and your sheep.[q] Let them stay with their mothers for seven days, but give them to me on the eighth day.[r]

31"You are to be my holy people.[s] So do not eat the meat of an animal torn by wild beasts;[t] throw it to the dogs.

Laws of Justice and Mercy

23 "Do not spread false reports.[u] Do not help a wicked man by being a malicious witness.[v]

2"Do not follow the crowd in doing wrong. When you give testimony in a lawsuit, do not pervert justice[w] by siding with the crowd, 3and do not show favoritism to a poor man in his lawsuit.

4"If you come across your enemy's ox or donkey wandering off, be sure to take it back to him.[x] 5If you see the donkey[y] of someone who hates you fallen down under its load, do not leave it there; be sure you help him with it.

6"Do not deny justice[z] to your poor people in their lawsuits. 7Have nothing to do with a false charge[a] and do not put an innocent or honest person to death, for I will not acquit the guilty.

8"Do not accept a bribe,[b] for a bribe blinds those who see and twists the words of the righteous.

9"Do not oppress an alien;[c] you yourselves know how it feels to be aliens, because you were aliens in Egypt.

Sabbath Laws

10"For six years you are to sow your fields and harvest the crops, 11but during the seventh year let the land lie unplowed and unused. Then the poor among your people may get food from it, and the wild animals may eat what they leave. Do the same with your vineyard and your olive grove.

12"Six days do your work,[d] but on the seventh day do not work, so that your ox and your donkey may rest and the slave born in your household, and the alien as well, may be refreshed.

13"Be careful[e] to do everything I have said to you. Do not invoke the names of other gods; do not let them be heard on your lips.

The Three Annual Festivals

14"Three times[f] a year you are to celebrate a festival to me.

15"Celebrate the Feast of Unleavened Bread;[g] for seven days eat bread made without yeast, as I commanded you. Do this at the appointed time in the month of Abib, for in that month you came out of Egypt.

"No one is to appear before me empty-handed.[h]

16"Celebrate the Feast of Harvest with the firstfruits[i] of the crops you sow in your field.

"Celebrate the Feast of Ingathering at the end of the year, when you gather in your crops from the field.[j]

17"Three times[k] a year all the men are to appear before the Sovereign LORD.

18"Do not offer the blood of a sacrifice to me along with anything containing yeast.[l]

"The fat of my festival offerings must not be kept until morning.[m]

19"Bring the best of the firstfruits[n] of your soil to the house of the LORD your God.

"Do not cook a young goat in its mother's milk.[o]

God's Angel to Prepare the Way

20"See, I am sending an angel[p] ahead of you to guard you along the way and to bring you to the place I have prepared.[q] 21Pay attention to him and listen[r] to what he says. Do not rebel against him; he will not forgive your rebellion,[s] since my Name is in him. 22If you listen carefully to what

22:19 [b]Lev 18:23; Dt 27:21
22:20 [c]Dt 17:2-5
22:21 [d]Lev 19:33 [e]Dt 10:19
22:22 [f]Dt 24:6,10,12, 17
22:23 [g]Lk 18:7 [h]Dt 15:9; Ps 18:6
22:24 [i]Ps 69:24; 109:9
22:25 [j]Lev 25:35-37; Dt 23:20; Ps 15:5
22:26 [k]Dt 24:6
22:27 [l]Ex 34:6
22:28 [m]Lev 24:11,16 [n]Ecc 10:20; Ac 23:5*
22:29 [o]Ex 23:15,16, 19 [p]Ex 13:2
22:30 [q]Ex 13:12; Dt 15:19 [r]Lev 22:27
22:31 [s]Lev 19:2 [t]Eze 4:14
23:1 [u]Ex 20:16; Ps 101:5 [v]Ps 35:11; Ac 6:11
23:2 [w]Dt 16:19
23:4 [x]Dt 22:1-3
23:5 [y]Dt 22:4
23:6 [z]ver 2
23:7 [a]Eph 4:25
23:8 [b]Dt 10:17; 16:19; Pr 15:27
23:9 [c]Ex 22:21
23:12 [d]Ex 20:9
23:13 [e]1Ti 4:16
23:14 [f]Ex 34:23,24
23:15 [g]Ex 12:17 [h]Ex 34:20
23:16 [i]Ex 34:22 [j]Dt 16:13
23:17 [k]Dt 16:16
23:18 [l]Ex 34:25 [m]Dt 16:4
23:19 [n]Ex 22:29; Dt 26:2,10 [o]Dt 14:21
23:20 [p]Ex 14:19; 32:34 [q]Ex 15:17
23:21 [r]Nu 14:11; Dt 18:19 [s]Ps 78:8,40,56

[a]*20* The Hebrew term refers to the irrevocable giving over of things or persons to the LORD, often by totally destroying them. [b]*25* Or *excessive interest* [c]*28* Or *Do not revile the judges* [d]*29* The meaning of the Hebrew for this phrase is uncertain.

he says and do all that I say, I will be an enemy[t] to your enemies and will oppose those who oppose you. 23My angel will go ahead of you and bring you into the land of the Amorites, Hittites, Perizzites, Canaanites, Hivites and Jebusites,[u] and I will wipe them out. 24Do not bow down before their gods or worship[v] them or follow their practices.[w] You must demolish[x] them and break their sacred stones to pieces. 25Worship the LORD your God,[y] and his blessing[z] will be on your food and water. I will take away sickness[a] from among you, 26and none will miscarry or be barren[b] in your land. I will give you a full life span.[c]

27"I will send my terror[d] ahead of you and throw into confusion[e] every nation you encounter. I will make all your enemies turn their backs and run. 28I will send the hornet[f] ahead of you to drive the Hivites, Canaanites and Hittites out of your way. 29But I will not drive them out in a single year, because the land would become desolate and the wild animals[g] too numerous for you. 30Little by little I will drive them out before you, until you have increased enough to take possession of the land.

31"I will establish your borders from the Red Sea**a** to the Sea of the Philistines,**b** and from the desert to the River.**c**[h] I will hand over to you the people who live in the land and you will drive them out[i] before you. 32Do not make a covenant[j] with them or with their gods. 33Do not let them live in your land, or they will cause you to sin against me, because the worship of their gods will certainly be a snare[k] to you."

The Covenant Confirmed

24 Then he said to Moses, "Come up to the LORD, you and Aaron, Nadab and Abihu,[l] and seventy of the elders[m] of Israel. You are to worship at a distance, 2but Moses alone is to approach the LORD; the others must not come near. And the people may not come up with him."

3When Moses went and told the people all the LORD's words and laws, they responded with one voice, "Everything the LORD has said we will do."[n] 4Moses then wrote[o] down everything the LORD had said.

He got up early the next morning and built an altar at the foot of the mountain and set up twelve stone pillars[p] representing the twelve tribes of Israel. 5Then he sent young Israelite men, and they offered burnt offerings and sacrificed young bulls as fellowship offerings**d** to the LORD. 6Moses took half of the blood[q] and put it in bowls, and the other half he sprinkled on the altar. 7Then he took the Book of the Covenant[r] and read it to the people. They responded, "We will do everything the LORD has said; we will obey."

8Moses then took the blood, sprinkled it on the people and said, "This is the blood of the covenant[s] that the LORD has made with you in accordance with all these words."

9Moses and Aaron, Nadab and Abihu, and the seventy elders[t] of Israel went up 10and saw[u] the God of Israel. Under his feet was something like a pavement made of sapphire,**e**[v] clear as the sky[w] itself. 11But God did not raise his hand against these leaders of the Israelites; they saw[x] God, and they ate and drank.

12The LORD said to Moses, "Come up to me on the mountain and stay here, and I will give you the tablets of stone,[y] with the law and commands I have written for their instruction."

13Then Moses set out with Joshua[z] his aide, and Moses went up on the mountain[a] of God. 14He said to the elders, "Wait here for us until we come back to you. Aaron and Hur are with you, and anyone involved in a dispute can go to them."

15When Moses went up on the mountain, the cloud[b] covered it, 16and the glory[c] of the LORD settled on Mount Sinai. For six days the cloud covered the mountain, and on the seventh day the LORD called to Moses from within the cloud.[d] 17To the Israelites the glory of the LORD looked like a consuming fire[e] on top of the mountain. 18Then Moses entered the cloud as he went on up the mountain. And he stayed on the mountain forty[f] days and forty nights.[g]

Offerings for the Tabernacle

25 The LORD said to Moses, 2"Tell the Israelites to bring me an offering. You are to receive the offering for me from each man whose heart prompts[h] him to give. 3These are the offerings you are to receive from them: gold, silver and bronze; 4blue, purple and scarlet yarn and fine linen; goat hair; 5ram skins dyed red and hides of sea cows**f**; acacia wood; 6olive oil[i] for the light;

23:22 [t]Ge 12:3; Dt 30:7
23:23 [u]ver 20; Jos 24:8,11
23:24 [v]Ex 20:5 [w]Dt 12:30-31 [x]Ex 34:13; Nu 33:52
23:25 [y]Dt 6:13; Mt 4:10 [z]Dt 7:12-15; 28:1-14 [a]Ex 15:26
23:26 [b]Dt 7:14; Mal 3:11 [c]Job 5:26
23:27 [d]Ex 15:14; Dt 2:25 [e]Dt 7:23
23:28 [f]Dt 7:20; Jos 24:12
23:29 [g]Dt 7:22
23:31 [h]Ge 15:18 [i]Jos 21:44; 24:12,18
23:32 [j]Ex 34:12; Dt 7:2
23:33 [k]Dt 7:16; Ps 106:36
24:1 [l]Ex 6:23; Lev 10:1-2 [m]Nu 11:16
24:3 [n]Ex 19:8; Dt 5:27
24:4 [o]Dt 31:9 [p]Ge 28:18
24:6 [q]Heb 9:18
24:7 [r]Heb 9:19
24:8 [s]Heb 9:20*; 1Pe 1:2
24:9 [t]ver 1
24:10 [u]Mt 17:2; Jn 1:18; 6:46 [v]Eze 1:26 [w]Rev 4:3
24:11 [x]Ge 32:30; Ex 19:21
24:12 [y]Ex 32:15-16
24:13 [z]Ex 17:9 [a]Ex 3:1
24:15 [b]Ex 19:9
24:16 [c]Ex 16:10 [d]Ps 99:7
24:17 [e]Ex 3:2; Dt 4:36; Heb 12:18,29
24:18 [f]Dt 9:9 [g]Ex 34:28
25:2 [h]Ex 35:21; 1Ch 29:5,7,9; Ezr 2:68; 2Co 8:11-12; 9:7
25:6 [i]Ex 27:20; 30:22-32

a *31* Hebrew *Yam Suph*; that is, Sea of Reeds **b** *31* That is, the Mediterranean **c** *31* That is, the Euphrates **d** *5* Traditionally *peace offerings* **e** *10* Or *lapis lazuli* **f** *5* That is, dugongs

spices for the anointing oil and for the fragrant incense; 7and onyx stones and other gems to be mounted on the ephod[j] and breastpiece.[k]

8"Then have them make a sanctuary[l] for me, and I will dwell[m] among them. 9Make this tabernacle and all its furnishings exactly like the pattern[n] I will show you.

The Ark

10"Have them make a chest[o] of acacia wood—two and a half cubits long, a cubit and a half wide, and a cubit and a half high.[a] 11Overlay it with pure gold, both inside and out, and make a gold molding around it. 12Cast four gold rings for it and fasten them to its four feet, with two rings on one side and two rings on the other. 13Then make poles of acacia wood and overlay them with gold. 14Insert the poles into the rings on the sides of the chest to carry it. 15The poles are to remain in the rings of this ark; they are not to be removed.[p] 16Then put in the ark the Testimony,[q] which I will give you.

17"Make an atonement cover[b][r] of pure gold—two and a half cubits long and a cubit and a half wide.[c] 18And make two cherubim out of hammered gold at the ends of the cover. 19Make one cherub on one end and the second cherub on the other; make the cherubim of one piece with the cover, at the two ends. 20The cherubim are to have their wings spread upward, overshadowing[s] the cover with them. The cherubim are to face each other, looking toward the cover. 21Place the cover on top of the ark[t] and put in the ark the Testimony,[u] which I will give you. 22There, above the cover between the two cherubim[v] that are over the ark of the Testimony, I will meet[w] with you and give you all my commands for the Israelites.

The Table

23"Make a table[x] of acacia wood—two cubits long, a cubit wide and a cubit and a half high.[d] 24Overlay it with pure gold and make a gold molding around it. 25Also make around it a rim a handbreadth[e] wide and put a gold molding on the rim. 26Make four gold rings for the table and fasten them to the four corners, where the four legs are. 27The rings are to be close to the rim to hold the poles used in carrying the table. 28Make the poles of acacia wood, overlay them with gold and carry the table with them. 29And make its plates and dishes of pure gold, as well as its pitchers and bowls for the pouring out of offerings.[y] 30Put the bread of the Presence[z] on this table to be before me at all times.

The Lampstand

31"Make a lampstand[a] of pure gold and hammer it out, base and shaft; its flowerlike cups, buds and blossoms shall be of one piece with it. 32Six branches are to extend from the sides of the lampstand—three on one side and three on the other. 33Three cups shaped like almond flowers with buds and blossoms are to be on one branch, three on the next branch, and the same for all six branches extending from the lampstand. 34And on the lampstand there are to be four cups shaped like almond flowers with buds and blossoms. 35One bud shall be under the first pair of branches extending from the lampstand, a second bud under the second pair, and a third bud under the third pair—six branches in all. 36The buds and branches shall all be of one piece with the lampstand, hammered out of pure gold.

37"Then make its seven lamps[b] and set them up on it so that they light the space in front of it. 38Its wick trimmers and trays are to be of pure gold. 39A talent[f] of pure gold is to be used for the lampstand and all these accessories. 40See that you make them according to the pattern[c] shown you on the mountain.

The Tabernacle

26 "Make the tabernacle with ten curtains of finely twisted linen and blue, purple and scarlet yarn, with cherubim worked into them by a skilled craftsman. 2All the curtains are to be the same size—twenty-eight cubits long and four cubits wide.[g] 3Join five of the curtains together, and do the same with the other five. 4Make loops of blue material along the edge of the end curtain in one set, and do the same with the end curtain in the other set. 5Make fifty loops on one curtain and fifty loops on the end curtain of the other set, with the loops opposite each other. 6Then make fifty gold clasps and

25:7 [j]Ex 28:4,6-14 [k]Ex 28:15-30
25:8 [l]Ex 36:1-5; Heb 9:1-2 [m]Ex 29:45; 1Ki 6:13; 2Co 6:16; Rev 21:3
25:9 [n]ver 40; Ac 7:44; Heb 8:5
25:10 [o]Dt 10:1-5; Heb 9:4
25:15 [p]1Ki 8:8
25:16 [q]Dt 31:26; Heb 9:4
25:17 [r]Ro 3:25
25:20 [s]1Ki 8:7; 1Ch 28:18; Heb 9:5
25:21 [t]Ex 26:34 [u]ver 16
25:22 [v]Nu 7:89; 1Sa 4:4; 2Sa 6:2; 2Ki 19:15; Ps 80:1; Isa 37:16 [w]Ex 29:42-43
25:23 [x]Heb 9:2
25:29 [y]Nu 4:7
25:30 [z]Lev 24:5-9
25:31 [a]1Ki 7:49; Zec 4:2; Heb 9:2; Rev 1:12
25:37 [b]Ex 27:21; Lev 24:3-4; Nu 8:2
25:40 [c]Ex 26:30; Nu 8:4; Ac 7:44; Heb 8:5*

[a] *10* That is, about 3 3/4 feet (about 1.1 meters) long and 2 1/4 feet (about 0.7 meter) wide and high [b] *17* Traditionally *a mercy seat* [c] *17* That is, about 3 3/4 feet (about 1.1 meters) long and 2 1/4 feet (about 0.7 meter) wide [d] *23* That is, about 3 feet (about 0.9 meter) long and 1 1/2 feet (about 0.5 meter) wide and 2 1/4 feet (about 0.7 meter) high [e] *25* That is, about 3 inches (about 8 centimeters) [f] *39* That is, about 75 pounds (about 34 kilograms) [g] *2* That is, about 42 feet (about 12.5 meters) long and 6 feet (about 1.8 meters) wide

use them to fasten the curtains together so that the tabernacle is a unit.

7 "Make curtains of goat hair for the tent over the tabernacle—eleven altogether. 8 All eleven curtains are to be the same size—thirty cubits long and four cubits wide.[a] 9 Join five of the curtains together into one set and the other six into another set. Fold the sixth curtain double at the front of the tent. 10 Make fifty loops along the edge of the end curtain in one set and also along the edge of the end curtain in the other set. 11 Then make fifty bronze clasps and put them in the loops to fasten the tent together as a unit. 12 As for the additional length of the tent curtains, the half curtain that is left over is to hang down at the rear of the tabernacle. 13 The tent curtains will be a cubit[b] longer on both sides; what is left will hang over the sides of the tabernacle so as to cover it. 14 Make for the tent a covering of ram skins dyed red, and over that a covering of hides of sea cows.[c][d]

15 "Make upright frames of acacia wood for the tabernacle. 16 Each frame is to be ten cubits long and a cubit and a half wide,[d] 17 with two projections set parallel to each other. Make all the frames of the tabernacle in this way. 18 Make twenty frames for the south side of the tabernacle 19 and make forty silver bases to go under them—two bases for each frame, one under each projection. 20 For the other side, the north side of the tabernacle, make twenty frames 21 and forty silver bases—two under each frame. 22 Make six frames for the far end, that is, the west end of the tabernacle, 23 and make two frames for the corners at the far end. 24 At these two corners they must be double from the bottom all the way to the top, and fitted into a single ring; both shall be like that. 25 So there will be eight frames and sixteen silver bases—two under each frame.

26 "Also make crossbars of acacia wood: five for the frames on one side of the tabernacle, 27 five for those on the other side, and five for the frames on the west, at the far end of the tabernacle. 28 The center crossbar is to extend from end to end at the middle of the frames. 29 Overlay the frames with gold and make gold rings to hold the crossbars. Also overlay the crossbars with gold.

30 "Set up the tabernacle according to the plan[e] shown you on the mountain.

31 "Make a curtain[f] of blue, purple and scarlet yarn and finely twisted linen, with cherubim[g] worked into it by a skilled craftsman. 32 Hang it with gold hooks on four posts of acacia wood overlaid with gold and standing on four silver bases. 33 Hang the curtain from the clasps and place the ark of the Testimony behind the curtain.[h] The curtain will separate the Holy Place from the Most Holy Place.[i] 34 Put the atonement cover[j] on the ark of the Testimony in the Most Holy Place. 35 Place the table[k] outside the curtain on the north side of the tabernacle and put the lampstand[l] opposite it on the south side.

36 "For the entrance to the tent make a curtain of blue, purple and scarlet yarn and finely twisted linen—the work of an embroiderer. 37 Make gold hooks for this curtain and five posts of acacia wood overlaid with gold. And cast five bronze bases for them.

The Altar of Burnt Offering

27 "Build an altar[m] of acacia wood, three cubits[e] high; it is to be square, five cubits long and five cubits wide.[f] 2 Make a horn[n] at each of the four corners, so that the horns and the altar are of one piece, and overlay the altar with bronze. 3 Make all its utensils of bronze—its pots to remove the ashes, and its shovels, sprinkling bowls, meat forks and firepans. 4 Make a grating for it, a bronze network, and make a bronze ring at each of the four corners of the network. 5 Put it under the ledge of the altar so that it is halfway up the altar. 6 Make poles of acacia wood for the altar and overlay them with bronze. 7 The poles are to be inserted into the rings so they will be on two sides of the altar when it is carried. 8 Make the altar hollow, out of boards. It is to be made just as you were shown[o] on the mountain.

The Courtyard

9 "Make a courtyard for the tabernacle. The south side shall be a hundred cubits[g] long and is to have curtains of finely twisted linen, 10 with twenty posts and twenty bronze bases and with silver hooks and bands on the posts. 11 The north side shall also be a hundred cubits long and is to have curtains, with twenty posts and twenty

26:14 [d]Ex 36:19; Nu 4:25
26:30 [e]Ex 25:9,40; Ac 7:44; Heb 8:5
26:31 [f]2Ch 3:14; Mt 27:51; Heb 9:3 [g]Ex 36:35
26:33 [h]Ex 40:3,21; Lev 16:2 [i]Heb 9:2-3
26:34 [j]Ex 25:21; 40:20; Heb 9:5
26:35 [k]Heb 9:2 [l]Ex 40:22,24
27:1 [m]Eze 43:13
27:2 [n]Ps 118:27
27:8 [o]Ex 25:9,40

[a] *8* That is, about 45 feet (about 13.5 meters) long and 6 feet (about 1.8 meters) wide
[b] *13* That is, about 1 1/2 feet (about 0.5 meter)
[c] *14* That is, dugongs
[d] *16* That is, about 15 feet (about 4.5 meters) long and 2 1/4 feet (about 0.7 meter) wide
[e] *1* That is, about 4 1/2 feet (about 1.3 meters)
[f] *1* That is, about 7 1/2 feet (about 2.3 meters) long and wide
[g] *9* That is, about 150 feet (about 46 meters); also in verse 11

bronze bases and with silver hooks and bands on the posts.

12"The west end of the courtyard shall be fifty cubits[a] wide and have curtains, with ten posts and ten bases. 13On the east end, toward the sunrise, the courtyard shall also be fifty cubits wide. 14Curtains fifteen cubits[b] long are to be on one side of the entrance, with three posts and three bases, 15and curtains fifteen cubits long are to be on the other side, with three posts and three bases.

16"For the entrance to the courtyard, provide a curtain twenty cubits[c] long, of blue, purple and scarlet yarn and finely twisted linen—the work of an embroiderer—with four posts and four bases. 17All the posts around the courtyard are to have silver bands and hooks, and bronze bases. 18The courtyard shall be a hundred cubits long and fifty cubits wide,[d] with curtains of finely twisted linen five cubits[e] high, and with bronze bases. 19All the other articles used in the service of the tabernacle, whatever their function, including all the tent pegs for it and those for the courtyard, are to be of bronze.

Oil for the Lampstand

20"Command the Israelites to bring you clear oil of pressed olives for the light so that the lamps may be kept burning. 21In the Tent of Meeting,[p] outside the curtain that is in front of the Testimony,[q] Aaron and his sons are to keep the lamps[r] burning before the LORD from evening till morning. This is to be a lasting ordinance[s] among the Israelites for the generations to come.

The Priestly Garments

28 "Have Aaron[t] your brother brought to you from among the Israelites, along with his sons Nadab and Abihu, Eleazar and Ithamar, so they may serve me as priests.[u] 2Make sacred garments[v] for your brother Aaron, to give him dignity and honor. 3Tell all the skilled men[w] to whom I have given wisdom[x] in such matters that they are to make garments for Aaron, for his consecration, so he may serve me as priest. 4These are the garments they are to make: a breastpiece,[y] an ephod, a robe,[z] a woven tunic,[a] a turban and a sash. They are to make these sacred garments for your brother Aaron and his sons, so they may serve me as priests. 5Have them use gold, and blue, purple and scarlet yarn, and fine linen.

27:21
[p]Ex 28:43
[q]Ex 26:31,33
[r]Ex 25:37; 30:8; 1Sa 3:3; 2Ch 13:11
[s]Ex 29:9; Lev 3:17; 16:34; Nu 18:23; 19:21
28:1
[t]Heb 5:4
[u]Nu 18:1-7; Heb 5:1
28:2
[v]Ex 29:5,29; 31:10; 39:1; Lev 8:7-9,30
28:3
[w]Ex 31:6; 36:1
[x]Ex 31:3
28:4
[y]ver 15-30
[z]ver 31-35
[a]ver 39

The Ephod

6"Make the ephod of gold, and of blue, purple and scarlet yarn, and of finely twisted linen—the work of a skilled craftsman. 7It is to have two shoulder pieces attached to two of its corners, so it can be fastened. 8Its skillfully woven waistband is to be like it—of one piece with the ephod and made with gold, and with blue, purple and scarlet yarn, and with finely twisted linen.

9"Take two onyx stones and engrave on them the names of the sons of Israel 10in the order of their birth—six names on one stone and the remaining six on the other. 11Engrave the names of the sons of Israel on the two stones the way a gem cutter engraves a seal. Then mount the stones in gold filigree settings 12and fasten them on the shoulder pieces of the ephod as memorial stones for the sons of Israel. Aaron is to bear the names on his shoulders as a memorial before the LORD. 13Make gold filigree settings 14and two braided chains of pure gold, like a rope, and attach the chains to the settings.

The Breastpiece

15"Fashion a breastpiece for making

[a] *12* That is, about 75 feet (about 23 meters); also in verse 13 [b] *14* That is, about 22 1/2 feet (about 6.9 meters); also in verse 15
[c] *16* That is, about 30 feet (about 9 meters)
[d] *18* That is, about 150 feet (about 46 meters) long and 75 feet (about 23 meters) wide
[e] *18* That is, about 7 1/2 feet (about 2.3 meters)

28:1–29:46

PROMISE 5

HONORING GOD'S WORKERS

The priests who followed the rules for worship in these chapters were God's servants, set apart to minister to his people. As you see how carefully God wanted to recognize and dignify the position of these workers, reflect for a moment on those who serve him in your church. They are not priests in the same way as Israel's priests were, but they are set apart—in many cases ordained—to serve God by serving his people. From the pastor to the Sunday school teacher, from the deacon to the worship leader, from the usher to the outreach committee member, many of the people who work in your church feel a special calling to prepare church members and facilities for worship each week. As you reflect on these two chapters, consider how you and your fellow church members honor those who serve in your church.

For the next Promise 5 reading go to page 136.

decisions—the work of a skilled craftsman. Make it like the ephod: of gold, and of blue, purple and scarlet yarn, and of finely twisted linen. 16It is to be square—a span[a] long and a span wide—and folded double. 17Then mount four rows of precious stones on it. In the first row there shall be a ruby, a topaz and a beryl; 18in the second row a turquoise, a sapphire[b] and an emerald; 19in the third row a jacinth, an agate and an amethyst; 20in the fourth row a chrysolite, an onyx and a jasper.[c] Mount them in gold filigree settings. 21There are to be twelve stones, one for each of the names of the sons of Israel, each engraved like a seal with the name of one of the twelve tribes.

22"For the breastpiece make braided chains of pure gold, like a rope. 23Make two gold rings for it and fasten them to two corners of the breastpiece. 24Fasten the two gold chains to the rings at the corners of the breastpiece, 25and the other ends of the chains to the two settings, attaching them to the shoulder pieces of the ephod at the front. 26Make two gold rings and attach them to the other two corners of the breastpiece on the inside edge next to the ephod. 27Make two more gold rings and attach them to the bottom of the shoulder pieces on the front of the ephod, close to the seam just above the waistband of the ephod. 28The rings of the breastpiece are to be tied to the rings of the ephod with blue cord, connecting it to the waistband, so that the breastpiece will not swing out from the ephod.

29"Whenever Aaron enters the Holy Place,[b] he will bear the names of the sons of Israel over his heart on the breastpiece of decision as a continuing memorial before the LORD. 30Also put the Urim and the Thummim[c] in the breastpiece, so they may be over Aaron's heart whenever he enters the presence of the LORD. Thus Aaron will always bear the means of making decisions for the Israelites over his heart before the LORD.

Other Priestly Garments

31"Make the robe of the ephod entirely of blue cloth, 32with an opening for the head in its center. There shall be a woven edge like a collar[d] around this opening, so that it will not tear. 33Make pomegranates of blue, purple and scarlet yarn around the hem of the robe, with gold bells between them. 34The gold bells and the pomegranates are to alternate around the hem of the robe. 35Aaron must wear it when he ministers. The sound of the bells will be heard when he enters the Holy Place before the LORD and when he comes out, so that he will not die.

36"Make a plate of pure gold and engrave on it as on a seal: HOLY TO THE LORD.[d] 37Fasten a blue cord to it to attach it to the turban; it is to be on the front of the turban. 38It will be on Aaron's forehead, and he will bear the guilt[e] involved in the sacred gifts the Israelites consecrate, whatever their gifts may be. It will be on Aaron's forehead continually so that they will be acceptable to the LORD.

39"Weave the tunic of fine linen and make the turban of fine linen. The sash is to be the work of an embroiderer. 40Make tunics, sashes and headbands for Aaron's sons,[f] to give them dignity and honor. 41After you put these clothes on your brother Aaron and his sons, anoint[g] and ordain them. Consecrate them so they may serve me as priests.[h]

42"Make linen undergarments[i] as a covering for the body, reaching from the waist to the thigh. 43Aaron and his sons must wear them whenever they enter the Tent of Meeting[j] or approach the altar to minister in the Holy Place, so that they will not incur guilt and die.[k]

"This is to be a lasting ordinance[l] for Aaron and his descendants.

Consecration of the Priests

29 "This is what you are to do to consecrate them, so they may serve me as priests: Take a young bull and two rams without defect. 2And from fine wheat flour, without yeast, make bread, and cakes mixed with oil, and wafers spread with oil.[m] 3Put them in a basket and present them in it—along with the bull and the two rams. 4Then bring Aaron and his sons to the entrance to the Tent of Meeting and wash them with water.[n] 5Take the garments[o] and dress Aaron with the tunic, the robe of the ephod, the ephod itself and the breastpiece. Fasten the ephod on him by its skillfully woven waistband.[p] 6Put the turban on his head and attach the sacred diadem[q] to the turban. 7Take the anointing oil[r] and anoint him by pouring it on his head. 8Bring his sons and dress them in tunics 9and put headbands on them. Then tie sashes on Aaron and his

28:29 [b]ver 12
28:30 [c]Lev 8:8; Nu 27:21; Dt 33:8; Ezr 2:63; Ne 7:65
28:36 [d]Zec 14:20
28:38 [e]Lev 10:17; 22:9,16; Nu 18:1; Heb 9:28; 1Pe 2:24
28:40 [f]ver 4; Ex 39:41
28:41 [g]Ex 29:7; Lev 10:7 [h]Ex 29:7-9; 30:30; 40:15; Lev 8:1-36; Heb 7:28
28:42 [i]Lev 6:10; 16:4,23; Eze 44:18
28:43 [j]Ex 27:21 [k]Ex 20:26 [l]Lev 17:7
29:2 [m]Lev 2:1,4; 6:19-23
29:4 [n]Ex 40:12; Heb 10:22
29:5 [o]Ex 28:2; Lev 8:7 [p]Ex 28:8
29:6 [q]Lev 8:9
29:7 [r]Ex 30:25,30, 31; Lev 8:12; 21:10; Nu 35:25; Ps 133:2

a *16* That is, about 9 inches (about 22 centimeters) **b** *18* Or *lapis lazuli*
c *20* The precise identification of some of these precious stones is uncertain.
d *32* The meaning of the Hebrew for this word is uncertain.

sons.[a][s] The priesthood is theirs by a lasting ordinance.[t] In this way you shall ordain Aaron and his sons.

10"Bring the bull to the front of the Tent of Meeting, and Aaron and his sons shall lay their hands on its head. 11Slaughter it in the LORD's presence at the entrance to the Tent of Meeting. 12Take some of the bull's blood and put it on the horns[u] of the altar with your finger, and pour out the rest of it at the base of the altar. 13Then take all the fat[v] around the inner parts, the covering of the liver, and both kidneys with the fat on them, and burn them on the altar. 14But burn the bull's flesh and its hide and its offal outside the camp.[w] It is a sin offering.

15"Take one of the rams, and Aaron and his sons shall lay their hands on its head. 16Slaughter it and take the blood and sprinkle it against the altar on all sides. 17Cut the ram into pieces and wash the inner parts and the legs, putting them with the head and the other pieces. 18Then burn the entire ram on the altar. It is a burnt offering to the LORD, a pleasing aroma,[x] an offering made to the LORD by fire.

19"Take the other ram,[y] and Aaron and his sons shall lay their hands on its head. 20Slaughter it, take some of its blood and put it on the lobes of the right ears of Aaron and his sons, on the thumbs of their right hands, and on the big toes of their right feet. Then sprinkle blood against the altar on all sides. 21And take some of the blood[z] on the altar and some of the anointing oil[a] and sprinkle it on Aaron and his garments and on his sons and their garments. Then he and his sons and their garments will be consecrated.[b]

22"Take from this ram the fat, the fat tail, the fat around the inner parts, the covering of the liver, both kidneys with the fat on them, and the right thigh. (This is the ram for the ordination.) 23From the basket of bread made without yeast, which is before the LORD, take a loaf, and a cake made with oil, and a wafer. 24Put all these in the hands of Aaron and his sons and wave them before the LORD as a wave offering.[c] 25Then take them from their hands and burn them on the altar along with the burnt offering for a pleasing aroma to the LORD, an offering made to the LORD by fire. 26After you take the breast of the ram for Aaron's ordination, wave it before the LORD as a wave offering, and it will be your share.[d]

27"Consecrate those parts of the ordination ram that belong to Aaron and his sons:[e] the breast that was waved and the thigh that was presented. 28This is always to be the regular share from the Israelites for Aaron and his sons. It is the contribution the Israelites are to make to the LORD from their fellowship offerings.[b][f]

29"Aaron's sacred garments will belong to his descendants so that they can be anointed and ordained in them.[g] 30The son[h] who succeeds him as priest and comes to the Tent of Meeting to minister in the Holy Place is to wear them seven days.

31"Take the ram for the ordination and cook the meat in a sacred place. 32At the entrance to the Tent of Meeting, Aaron and his sons are to eat the meat of the ram and the bread[i] that is in the basket. 33They are to eat these offerings by which atonement was made for their ordination and consecration. But no one else may eat[j] them, because they are sacred. 34And if any of the meat of the ordination ram or any bread is left over till morning,[k] burn it up. It must not be eaten, because it is sacred.

35"Do for Aaron and his sons everything I have commanded you, taking seven days to ordain them. 36Sacrifice a bull each day[l] as a sin offering to make atonement. Purify the altar by making atonement for it, and anoint it to consecrate[m] it. 37For seven days make atonement for the altar and consecrate it. Then the altar will be most holy, and whatever touches it will be holy.[n]

38"This is what you are to offer on the altar regularly each day:[o] two lambs a year old. 39Offer one in the morning and the other at twilight.[p] 40With the first lamb offer a tenth of an ephah[c] of fine flour mixed with a quarter of a hin[d] of oil from pressed olives, and a quarter of a hin of wine as a drink offering. 41Sacrifice the other lamb at twilight with the same grain offering and its drink offering as in the morning—a pleasing aroma, an offering made to the LORD by fire.

42"For the generations to come[q] this burnt offering is to be made regularly at the entrance to the Tent of Meeting before the LORD. There I will meet you and speak to you;[r] 43there also I will meet with the Israelites, and the place will be consecrated by my glory.[s]

44"So I will consecrate the Tent of Meeting and the altar and will conse-

29:9 [s]Ex 28:40 [t]Ex 40:15; Nu 3:10; 18:7; 25:13; Dt 18:5
29:12 [u]Ex 27:2
29:13 [v]Lev 3:3,5,9
29:14 [w]Lev 4:11-12, 21; Heb 13:11
29:18 [x]Ge 8:21
29:19 [y]ver 3
29:21 [z]Heb 9:22 [a]Ex 30:25,31 [b]ver 1
29:24 [c]Lev 7:30
29:26 [d]Lev 7:31-34
29:27 [e]Lev 7:31,34; Dt 18:3
29:28 [f]Lev 10:15
29:29 [g]Nu 20:26,28
29:30 [h]Nu 20:28
29:32 [i]Mt 12:4
29:33 [j]Lev 10:14; 22:10,13
29:34 [k]Ex 12:10
29:36 [l]Heb 10:11 [m]Ex 40:10
29:37 [n]Ex 30:28-29; 40:10; Mt 23:19
29:38 [o]Nu 28:3-8; 1Ch 16:40; Da 12:11
29:39 [p]Eze 46:13-15
29:42 [q]Ex 30:8 [r]Ex 25:22
29:43 [s]1Ki 8:11

a *9* Hebrew; Septuagint *on them*
b *28* Traditionally *peace offerings*
c *40* That is, probably about 2 quarts (about 2 liters)
d *40* That is, probably about 1 quart (about 1 liter)

crate Aaron and his sons to serve me as priests.[t] **45**Then I will dwell[u] among the Israelites and be their God.[v] **46**They will know that I am the LORD their God, who brought them out of Egypt so that I might dwell among them. I am the LORD their God.[w]

The Altar of Incense

30 "Make an altar[x] of acacia wood for burning incense.[y] **2**It is to be square, a cubit long and a cubit wide, and two cubits high[a]—its horns[z] of one piece with it. **3**Overlay the top and all the sides and the horns with pure gold, and make a gold molding around it. **4**Make two gold rings for the altar below the molding—two on opposite sides—to hold the poles used to carry it. **5**Make the poles of acacia wood and overlay them with gold. **6**Put the altar in front of the curtain that is before the ark of the Testimony—before the atonement cover[a] that is over the Testimony—where I will meet with you.

7"Aaron must burn fragrant incense[b] on the altar every morning when he tends the lamps. **8**He must burn incense again when he lights the lamps at twilight so incense will burn regularly before the LORD for the generations to come. **9**Do not offer on this altar any other incense[c] or any burnt offering or grain offering, and do not pour a drink offering on it. **10**Once a year Aaron shall make atonement[d] on its horns. This annual atonement must be made with the blood of the atoning sin offering for the generations to come. It is most holy to the LORD."

Atonement Money

11Then the LORD said to Moses, **12**"When you take a census[e] of the Israelites to count them, each one must pay the LORD a ransom[f] for his life at the time he is counted. Then no plague[g] will come on them when you number them. **13**Each one who crosses over to those already counted is to give a half shekel,[b] according to the sanctuary shekel,[h] which weighs twenty gerahs. This half shekel is an offering to the LORD. **14**All who cross over, those twenty years old or more, are to give an offering to the LORD. **15**The rich are not to give more than a half shekel and the poor are not to give less[i] when you make the offering to the LORD to atone for your lives. **16**Receive the atonement money from the Israelites and use it for the service of the Tent of Meeting.[j] It will be a memorial for the Israelites before the LORD, making atonement for your lives."

Basin for Washing

17Then the LORD said to Moses, **18**"Make a bronze basin,[k] with its bronze stand, for washing. Place it between the Tent of Meeting and the altar, and put water in it. **19**Aaron and his sons are to wash their hands and feet[l] with water[m] from it. **20**Whenever they enter the Tent of Meeting, they shall wash with water so that they will not die. Also, when they approach the altar to minister by presenting an offering made to the LORD by fire, **21**they shall wash their hands and feet so that they will not die. This is to be a lasting ordinance[n] for Aaron and his descendants for the generations to come."

Anointing Oil

22Then the LORD said to Moses, **23**"Take the following fine spices: 500 shekels[c] of liquid myrrh,[o] half as much (that is, 250 shekels) of fragrant cinnamon, 250 shekels of fragrant cane, **24**500 shekels of cassia[p]—all according to the sanctuary shekel—and a hin[d] of olive oil. **25**Make these into a sacred anointing oil, a fragrant blend, the work of a perfumer.[q] It will be the sacred anointing oil.[r] **26**Then use it to anoint[s] the Tent of Meeting, the ark of the Testimony, **27**the table and all its articles, the lampstand and its accessories, the altar of incense, **28**the altar of burnt offering and all its utensils, and the basin with its stand. **29**You shall consecrate them so they will be most holy, and whatever touches them will be holy.[t]

30"Anoint Aaron and his sons and consecrate[u] them so they may serve me as priests. **31**Say to the Israelites, 'This is to be my sacred anointing oil for the generations to come. **32**Do not pour it on men's bodies and do not make any oil with the same formula. It is sacred, and you are to consider it sacred.[v] **33**Whoever makes perfume like it and whoever puts it on anyone other than a priest must be cut off[w] from his people.'"

Incense

34Then the LORD said to Moses, "Take fragrant spices—gum resin, on-

29:44 [t]Lev 21:15
29:45 [u]Ex 25:8; Lev 26:12; Zec 2:10; Jn 14:17 [v]2Co 6:16; Rev 21:3
29:46 [w]Ex 20:2
30:1 [x]Ex 37:25 [y]Rev 8:3
30:2 [z]Ex 27:2
30:6 [a]Ex 25:22; 26:34
30:7 [b]ver 34-35; Ex 27:21; 1Sa 2:28
30:9 [c]Lev 10:1
30:10 [d]Lev 16:18-19, 30
30:12 [e]Ex 38:25; Nu 1:2,49; 2Sa 24:1 [f]Nu 31:50; Mt 20:28 [g]2Sa 24:13
30:13 [h]Nu 3:47; Mt 17:24
30:15 [i]Pr 22:2; Eph 6:9
30:16 [j]Ex 38:25-28
30:18 [k]Ex 38:8; 40:7, 30
30:19 [l]Ex 40:31-32; Isa 52:11 [m]Ps 26:6
30:21 [n]Ex 27:21; 28:43
30:23 [o]Ge 37:25
30:24 [p]Ps 45:8
30:25 [q]Ex 37:29 [r]Ex 40:9
30:26 [s]Ex 40:9; Lev 8:10; Nu 7:1
30:29 [t]Ex 29:37
30:30 [u]Ex 29:7; Lev 8:2,12,30
30:32 [v]ver 25,37
30:33 [w]ver 38; Ge 17:14

a *2* That is, about 1 1/2 feet (about 0.5 meter) long and wide and about 3 feet (about 0.9 meter) high **b** *13* That is, about 1/5 ounce (about 6 grams); also in verse 15 **c** *23* That is, about 12 1/2 pounds (about 6 kilograms)
d *24* That is, probably about 4 quarts (about 4 liters)

ycha and galbanum—and pure frankincense, all in equal amounts, [35]and
make a fragrant blend of incense, the
work of a perfumer.[x] It is to be salted
and pure and sacred. [36]Grind some of
it to powder and place it in front of the
Testimony in the Tent of Meeting,
where I will meet with you. It shall be
most holy[y] to you. [37]Do not make any
incense with this formula for yourselves; consider it holy[z] to the LORD.
[38]Whoever makes any like it to enjoy its
fragrance must be cut off[a] from his
people."

Bezalel and Oholiab

31 Then the LORD said to Moses, [2]"See,
I have chosen Bezalel[b] son of Uri,
the son of Hur, of the tribe of Judah,
[3]and I have filled him with the Spirit of
God, with skill, ability and knowledge
in all kinds of crafts[c]— [4]to make artistic designs for work in gold, silver and
bronze, [5]to cut and set stones, to work
in wood, and to engage in all kinds of
craftsmanship. [6]Moreover, I have appointed Oholiab son of Ahisamach, of
the tribe of Dan, to help him. Also I
have given skill to all the craftsmen to
make everything I have commanded
you: [7]the Tent of Meeting,[d] the ark of
the Testimony[e] with the atonement
cover[f] on it, and all the other furnishings of the tent— [8]the table[g] and its
articles, the pure gold lampstand[h] and
all its accessories, the altar of incense,
[9]the altar of burnt offering and all its
utensils, the basin with its stand—
[10]and also the woven garments[i], both
the sacred garments for Aaron the
priest and the garments for his sons
when they serve as priests, [11]and the
anointing oil[j] and fragrant incense for
the Holy Place. They are to make them
just as I commanded you."

The Sabbath

[12]Then the LORD said to Moses,
[13]"Say to the Israelites, 'You must observe my Sabbaths.[k] This will be a
sign[l] between me and you for the
generations to come, so you may know
that I am the LORD, who makes you
holy.[a][m]
[14]" 'Observe the Sabbath, because it
is holy to you. Anyone who desecrates
it must be put to death;[n] whoever
does any work on that day must be cut
off from his people. [15]For six days,
work[o] is to be done, but the seventh
day is a Sabbath of rest,[p] holy to the
LORD. Whoever does any work on the
Sabbath day must be put to death.
[16]The Israelites are to observe the Sabbath, celebrating it for the generations
to come as a lasting covenant. [17]It will
be a sign[q] between me and the Israelites forever, for in six days the LORD
made the heavens and the earth, and
on the seventh day he abstained from
work and rested.[r]' "
[18]When the LORD finished speaking
to Moses on Mount Sinai, he gave him
the two tablets of the Testimony, the
tablets of stone[s] inscribed by the finger of God.[t]

The Golden Calf

32 When the people saw that Moses
was so long in coming down from
the mountain,[u] they gathered around
Aaron and said, "Come, make us
gods[b] who will go before us. As for this
fellow Moses who brought us up out of
Egypt, we don't know what has happened to him."[v]
[2]Aaron answered them, "Take off
the gold earrings[w] that your wives,
your sons and your daughters are
wearing, and bring them to me." [3]So all
the people took off their earrings and
brought them to Aaron. [4]He took what
they handed him and made it into an
idol cast in the shape of a calf,[x] fashioning it with a tool. Then they said,
"These are your gods,[c] O Israel, who
brought you up out of Egypt."
[5]When Aaron saw this, he built an
altar in front of the calf and announced, "Tomorrow there will be a
festival[y] to the LORD." [6]So the next day
the people rose early and sacrificed
burnt offerings and presented fellowship offerings.[d][z] Afterward they sat
down to eat and drink and got up to
indulge in revelry.[a]
[7]Then the LORD said to Moses, "Go
down, because your people, whom you
brought up out of Egypt,[b] have become corrupt.[c] [8]They have been
quick to turn away from what I commanded them and have made themselves an idol[d] cast in the shape of a
calf. They have bowed down to it and
sacrificed[e] to it and have said, 'These
are your gods, O Israel, who brought
you up out of Egypt.'[f]
[9]"I have seen these people," the
LORD said to Moses, "and they are a
stiff-necked[g] people. [10]Now leave me
alone so that my anger may burn
against them and that I may destroy
them. Then I will make you into a great
nation."[h]
[11]But Moses sought the favor[i] of
the LORD his God. "O LORD," he said,

30:35 [x]ver 25 **30:36** [y]ver 32; Ex 29:37; Lev 2:3 **30:37** [z]ver 32 **30:38** [a]ver 33 **31:2** [b]Ex 36:1,2; 1Ch 2:20 **31:3** [c]1Ki 7:14 **31:7** [d]Ex 36:8-38 [e]Ex 37:1-5 [f]Ex 37:6 **31:8** [g]Ex 37:10-16 [h]Ex 37:17-24 **31:10** [i]Ex 28:2; 39:1, 41 **31:11** [j]Ex 30:22-32 **31:13** [k]Ex 20:8; Lev 19:3,30 [l]Eze 20:12,20 [m]Lev 11:44 **31:14** [n]Nu 15:32-36 **31:15** [o]Ex 20:8-11 [p]Ge 2:3; Ex 16:23 **31:17** [q]ver 13 [r]Ge 2:2-3 **31:18** [s]Ex 24:12 [t]Ex 32:15-16; 34:1,28; Dt 4:13; 5:22 **32:1** [u]Ex 24:18; Dt 9:9-12 [v]Ac 7:40* **32:2** [w]Ex 35:22 **32:4** [x]Dt 9:16; Ne 9:18; Ps 106:19; Ac 7:41 **32:5** [y]Lev 23:2,37; 2Ki 10:20 **32:6** [z]Nu 25:2; Ac 7:41 [a]ver 17-19; 1Co 10:7* **32:7** [b]ver 4,11 [c]Ge 6:11-12; Dt 9:12 **32:8** [d]Ex 20:4 [e]Ex 22:20 [f]1Ki 12:28 **32:9** [g]Ex 33:3,5; 34:9; Isa 48:4; Ac 7:51 **32:10** [h]Nu 14:12; Dt 9:14 **32:11** [i]Dt 9:18

a *13* Or *who sanctifies you*; or *who sets you apart as holy* **b** *1* Or *a god*; also in verses 23 and 31
c *4* Or *This is your god*; also in verse 8
d *6* Traditionally *peace offerings*

AARON

The Spokesman

At last he was the real leader. Moses left Aaron in charge when he climbed up Mount Sinai to meet with God. These brothers, Aaron and Moses, acted as partners. At times people might have thought Aaron was in charge because he was the one standing and speaking in front of everyone. But everyone knew Moses gave the orders and Aaron told the people what they were. Exodus 6:28—7:2 tells us that was God's way.

Moses always met with God and came back with the decision. Then Moses told Aaron what to do and he did it. That meant Aaron did some powerful and important and essential things, but he never made the decisions. Until now. And now things were coming unraveled.

In one way, Aaron's first major decision was a tough one. But in another way, it wasn't even a decision at all. Moses had been gone longer than the people expected. Aaron's job was only to hold things together until Moses got back. He had never intended to make any major decisions, but now he was in trouble. The people "gathered around Aaron and said, 'Make us gods who will go before us' " (32:1). Aaron knew how to do what he'd been told. He reasoned, *Maybe I can buy some time by giving the people what they want. That's harmless. No hassle. Easy solution.*

The decision Aaron made was a terrible one. "He took what they handed him and made it into an idol cast in the shape of a calf, fashioning it with a tool" (32:4). Now the people of Israel had a god they could see; one they could control and that made them happy. What irony: Moses was on the mountain top with God while Aaron was in the foothills helping the people celebrate with their golden god.

Excuses, Excuses, Excuses

How could Aaron have failed so miserably? Four of Aaron's statements in Exodus 32 give us the answer to this question and some insight into his character.

It's no big deal. Moses roared at Aaron, "What did these people do to you that you led them into such great sin?" (32:21). Aaron merely answered, "Do not be angry" (32:22). Don't be angry? Of course Moses was angry. Israel was practicing idolatry, celebrating with their new golden god! Moses was furious and God was outraged. And here was Aaron telling Moses not to be angry. Aaron's response reveals his concept of sin. In his mind, this sin of idolatry was no big deal. Don't confront people or be a pain in the neck, Moses. It's just a little sin.

It's the people's fault. Aaron then tried to place the blame on the people: "You know how prone these people are to evil" (32:22). It's their fault Moses; they're just evil people. Aaron wanted to make sure everyone understood that *he* was not responsible for their sin just because it occurred on his watch. He allowed them to get out of control because they were just evil people. After all, he was only their leader.

It's Moses' fault. Aaron continued to babble about the people and how they said, "As for this fellow Moses . . . we don't know what has happened to him" (32:23). Aaron shifted the blame to Moses and suggested that if Moses hadn't been gone so long, none of this would have happened. It's all Moses' fault.

It just happened. Aaron's last feeble excuse was that he just took their gold and "threw it into the fire, and out came this calf" (32:24). It was completely and amazingly out of his control—it just happened.

Bottom line? Aaron blew it! He loused up his first leadership assignment and Moses was furious with him.

Aaron Restored

Moses was a magnificent leader and Aaron was his able spokesman. But when Aaron was promoted to a job beyond his capabilities, he messed it up. He was not ready or able to do what Moses did. He didn't have Moses' relationship with God. He couldn't fill Moses' sandals.

But that didn't end Aaron's story. When God is involved in our lives—and he always is—failure doesn't have to be the last chapter in our stories. Because Aaron repented and settled accounts with God he is not remembered as Aaron the idolater, but rather as Aaron the high priest of Israel. He is remembered as the only man on earth during his lifetime who was allowed to enter into the holy presence of God in the tabernacle and make atonement for Israel's sin. What an amazing restoration!

You probably have—or will—or *do* blow it. We all get in over our heads. We've all sinned and wanted to blame fate, or God, or anyone else for our mistakes. We certainly don't want the blame to rest on us. Aaron was like most of us in that way. But the point of Aaron's story isn't *his failure*, but rather *God's grace*. The question each man has to ask himself is: *Where does* my *story of failure end?* It can end with excuses, or it can end as Aaron's story did. After the failure, after all the excuses and explanations and finger-pointing have reached an end, we can experience repentance and restoration and service.

Aaron's story gives each one of us hope. Since each one of us has sinned inexcusably before God, we know that we can come to him and be restored and used again for his service. This story teaches us that even the Aarons of this world can become God's holy ones, sharing his blessings with others in vibrant ministry, if only they repent and return to God.

—*Dr. Sid Buzzell*

"why should your anger burn against
your people, whom you brought out of
Egypt with great power and a mighty
hand?[j] 12Why should the Egyptians
say, 'It was with evil intent that he
brought them out, to kill them in the
mountains and to wipe them off the
face of the earth'?[k] Turn from your
fierce anger; relent and do not bring
disaster on your people. 13Remem-
ber[l] your servants Abraham, Isaac
and Israel, to whom you swore by your
own self:[m] 'I will make your descendants as numerous as the stars[n] in the
sky and I will give your descendants all
this land[o] I promised them, and it will
be their inheritance forever.' " 14Then
the LORD relented[p] and did not bring
on his people the disaster he had
threatened.

15Moses turned and went down the
mountain with the two tablets of the
Testimony[q] in his hands.[r] They were
inscribed on both sides, front and
back. 16The tablets were the work of
God; the writing was the writing of
God, engraved on the tablets.[s]

17When Joshua heard the noise of
the people shouting, he said to Moses,
"There is the sound of war in the
camp."

18Moses replied:

"It is not the sound of victory,
it is not the sound of defeat;
it is the sound of singing that I
hear."

19When Moses approached the
camp and saw the calf[t] and the dancing, his anger burned and he threw the
tablets out of his hands, breaking them
to pieces[u] at the foot of the mountain.
20And he took the calf they had made
and burned it in the fire; then he
ground it to powder, scattered it on
the water[v] and made the Israelites
drink it.

21He said to Aaron, "What did these
people do to you, that you led them
into such great sin?"

22"Do not be angry, my lord," Aaron
answered. "You know how prone these
people are to evil.[w] 23They said to me,
'Make us gods who will go before us. As
for this fellow Moses who brought us
up out of Egypt, we don't know what
has happened to him.'[x] 24So I told
them, 'Whoever has any gold jewelry,
take it off.' Then they gave me the gold,
and I threw it into the fire, and out
came this calf!"[y]

25Moses saw that the people were
running wild and that Aaron had let
them get out of control and so become
a laughingstock to their enemies. 26So
he stood at the entrance to the camp
and said, "Whoever is for the LORD,
come to me." And all the Levites rallied
to him.

27Then he said to them, "This is
what the LORD, the God of Israel, says:
'Each man strap a sword to his side. Go
back and forth through the camp from
one end to the other, each killing his
brother and friend and neighbor.' "[z]
28The Levites did as Moses commanded, and that day about three thousand
of the people died. 29Then Moses said,
"You have been set apart to the LORD
today, for you were against your own
sons and brothers, and he has blessed
you this day."

30The next day Moses said to the
people, "You have committed a great
sin.[a] But now I will go up to the LORD;
perhaps I can make atonement[b] for
your sin."

31So Moses went back to the LORD
and said, "Oh, what a great sin these
people have committed![c] They have
made themselves gods of gold.[d] 32But
now, please forgive their sin—but if
not, then blot me[e] out of the book[f]
you have written."

33The LORD replied to Moses, "Whoever has sinned against me I will blot
out[g] of my book. 34Now go, lead the
people to the place[h] I spoke of, and
my angel[i] will go before you. However, when the time comes for me to
punish,[j] I will punish them for their
sin."

35And the LORD struck the people
with a plague because of what they did
with the calf[k] Aaron had made.

32:11 [j]Dt 9:26
32:12 [k]Nu 14:13-16; Dt 9:28
32:13 [l]Ex 2:24 [m]Ge 22:16; Heb 6:13 [n]Ge 15:5; 26:4 [o]Ge 12:7
32:14 [p]2Sa 24:16; Ps 106:45
32:15 [q]Ex 31:18 [r]Dt 9:15
32:16 [s]Ex 31:18
32:19 [t]Dt 9:16 [u]Dt 9:17
32:20 [v]Dt 9:21
32:22 [w]Dt 9:24
32:23 [x]ver 1
32:24 [y]ver 4
32:27 [z]Nu 25:3,5; Dt 33:9
32:30 [a]1Sa 12:20 [b]Lev 1:4; Nu 25:13
32:31 [c]Dt 9:18 [d]Ex 20:23
32:32 [e]Ro 9:3 [f]Ps 69:28; Da 12:1; Php 4:3; Rev 3:5; 21:27
32:33 [g]Dt 29:20; Ps 9:5
32:34 [h]Ex 3:17 [i]Ex 23:20 [j]Dt 32:35; Ps 99:8; Ro 2:5-6
32:35 [k]ver 4

32:31–34

PROMISE 1

REAL MEN TAKE RESPONSIBILITY

Are godly men real men? This story should dispel any doubt.

When Israel sinned against God by manufacturing and worshiping the golden calf, Moses wasn't even present. He was up on the mountain with God. Still, as the leader of Israel, Moses took charge of the situation. Did you read what Moses said to God about his responsibility? "But now, please forgive their sin—but if not . . ." (v. 32). Moses took responsibility for the people's sin, even though he didn't participate in it. But Ezekiel 18:4 talks about individual accountability for sin, and God held Moses to the same standard. The people were the ones who had sinned; they would be accountable (vv. 33–35).

Moses was a godly man. Was he a real man? Let the record decide.

For the next Promise 1 reading go to page 105.

33 Then the LORD said to Moses, "Leave this place, you and the people you brought up out of Egypt, and go up to the land I promised on oath to Abraham, Isaac and Jacob, saying, 'I will give it to your descendants.'[l] 2I will send an angel[m] before you and drive out the Canaanites, Amorites, Hittites, Perizzites, Hivites and Jebusites.[n] 3Go up to the land flowing with milk and honey.[o] But I will not go with you, because you are a stiff-necked[p] people and I might destroy[q] you on the way."

4When the people heard these distressing words, they began to mourn[r] and no one put on any ornaments. 5For the LORD had said to Moses, "Tell the Israelites, 'You are a stiff-necked people. If I were to go with you even for a moment, I might destroy you. Now take off your ornaments and I will decide what to do with you.'" 6So the Israelites stripped off their ornaments at Mount Horeb.

The Tent of Meeting

7Now Moses used to take a tent and pitch it outside the camp some distance away, calling it the "tent of meeting."[s] Anyone inquiring of the LORD would go to the tent of meeting outside the camp. 8And whenever Moses went out to the tent, all the people rose and stood at the entrances to their tents,[t] watching Moses until he entered the tent. 9As Moses went into the tent, the pillar of cloud[u] would come down and stay at the entrance, while the LORD spoke[v] with Moses. 10Whenever the people saw the pillar of cloud standing at the entrance to the tent, they all stood and worshiped, each at the entrance to his tent. 11The LORD would speak to Moses face to face,[w] as a man speaks with his friend. Then Moses would return to the camp, but his young aide Joshua son of Nun did not leave the tent.

Moses and the Glory of the LORD

12Moses said to the LORD, "You have been telling me, 'Lead these people,'[x] but you have not let me know whom you will send with me. You have said, 'I know you by name[y] and you have found favor with me.' 13If you are pleased with me, teach me your ways[z] so I may know you and continue to find favor with you. Remember that this nation is your people."[a]

1 →PG. 110

14The LORD replied, "My Presence[b] will go with you, and I will give you rest."[c]

15Then Moses said to him, "If your Presence does not go with us, do not send us up from here. 16How will anyone know that you are pleased with me and with your people unless you go with us?[d] What else will distinguish me and your people from all the other people on the face of the earth?"[e]

17And the LORD said to Moses, "I will do the very thing you have asked, because I am pleased with you and I know you by name."

18Then Moses said, "Now show me your glory."

19And the LORD said, "I will cause all my goodness to pass in front of you, and I will proclaim my name, the LORD, in your presence. I will have mercy on whom I will have mercy, and I will have compassion on whom I will have compassion.[f] 20But," he said, "you cannot see my face, for no one may see[g] me and live."

21Then the LORD said, "There is a place near me where you may stand on a rock. 22When my glory passes by, I will put you in a cleft in the rock and cover you with my hand[h] until I have passed by. 23Then I will remove my hand and you will see my back; but my face must not be seen."

The New Stone Tablets

34 The LORD said to Moses, "Chisel out two stone tablets like the first ones, and I will write on them the words that were on the first tablets,[i] which you broke.[j] 2Be ready in the morning, and then come up on Mount Sinai.[k] Present yourself to me there on top of the mountain. 3No one is to come with you or be seen anywhere on the mountain;[l] not even the flocks and herds may graze in front of the mountain."

4So Moses chiseled out two stone

33:1 [l]Ge 12:7
33:2 [m]Ex 32:34 [n]Ex 23:27-31; Jos 24:11
33:3 [o]Ex 3:8 [p]Ex 32:9 [q]Ex 32:10
33:4 [r]Nu 14:39
33:7 [s]Ex 29:42-43
33:8 [t]Nu 16:27
33:9 [u]Ex 13:21 [v]Ex 31:18; Ps 99:7
33:11 [w]Nu 12:8; Dt 34:10
33:12 [x]Ex 3:10 [y]ver 17; Jn 10:14-15; 2Ti 2:19
33:13 [z]Ps 25:4; 86:11; 119:33 [a]Ex 34:9; Dt 9:26,29
33:14 [b]Isa 63:9 [c]Jos 21:44; 22:4
33:16 [d]Nu 14:14 [e]Ex 34:10
33:19 [f]Ro 9:15*
33:20 [g]Ge 32:30; Isa 6:5
33:22 [h]Ps 91:4
34:1 [i]Dt 10:2,4 [j]Ex 32:19
34:2 [k]Ex 19:11
34:3 [l]Ex 19:12-13, 21

33:12 – 17

PROMISE **3**

PRAYER OF INTEGRITY

What qualities do you want to be characterized by? When you talk with a group and then walk away, what do you want a friend in the group to say when someone asks: "What's he like?" These verses tell us what should characterize a Christian man: a strong reputation for seeking after God, and a Christian walk that gives evidence of God's working in his life. Moses sums up what should be the prayer of every man who commits to living a life of integrity: "If you are pleased with me, teach me your ways so I may know you and continue to find favor with you" (v. 13).

For the next Promise 3 reading go to page 122.

tablets like the first ones and went up
Mount Sinai early in the morning, as
the LORD had commanded him; and he
carried the two stone tablets in his
hands. 5Then the LORD came down in
the cloud and stood there with him
and proclaimed his name, the LORD.[m]
6And he passed in front of Moses, proclaiming, "The LORD, the LORD, the
compassionate[n] and gracious God,
slow to anger,[o] abounding in love[p]
and faithfulness,[q] 7maintaining love
to thousands,[r] and forgiving wickedness, rebellion and sin.[s] Yet he does
not leave the guilty unpunished;[t] he
punishes the children and their children for the sin of the fathers to the
third and fourth generation."
8Moses bowed to the ground at once
and worshiped. 9"O Lord, if I have
found favor in your eyes," he said,
"then let the Lord go with us.[u] Although this is a stiff-necked people,
forgive our wickedness and our sin,
and take us as your inheritance."[v]
10Then the LORD said: "I am making
a covenant[w] with you. Before all your
people I will do wonders never before
done in any nation in all the world.[x]
The people you live among will see
how awesome is the work that I, the
LORD, will do for you. 11Obey what I
command you today. I will drive out
before you the Amorites, Canaanites,
Hittites, Perizzites, Hivites and Jebusites.[y] 12Be careful not to make a treaty with those who live in the land
where you are going, or they will be
a snare[z] among you. 13Break down
their altars, smash their sacred stones
and cut down their Asherah poles.[a][a]
14Do not worship any other god,[b] for
the LORD, whose name is Jealous, is a
jealous God.[c]
15"Be careful not to make a treaty
with those who live in the land; for
when they prostitute[d] themselves to
their gods and sacrifice to them, they
will invite you and you will eat their
sacrifices.[e] 16And when you choose
some of their daughters as wives[f] for
your sons and those daughters prostitute themselves to their gods,[g] they
will lead your sons to do the same.
17"Do not make cast idols.[h]
18"Celebrate the Feast of Unleavened Bread.[i] For seven days eat bread
made without yeast,[j] as I commanded you. Do this at the appointed time
in the month of Abib,[k] for in that
month you came out of Egypt.
19"The first offspring[l] of every
womb belongs to me, including all
the firstborn males of your livestock,
whether from herd or flock. 20Redeem
the firstborn donkey with a lamb, but if
you do not redeem it, break its neck.[m]
Redeem all your firstborn sons.
"No one is to appear before me
empty-handed.[n]
21"Six days you shall labor, but on
the seventh day you shall rest;[o] even
during the plowing season and harvest
you must rest.
22"Celebrate the Feast of Weeks with
the firstfruits of the wheat harvest, and
the Feast of Ingathering[p] at the turn of
the year.[b] 23Three times[q] a year all
your men are to appear before the Sovereign LORD, the God of Israel. 24I will
drive out nations[r] before you and enlarge your territory, and no one will
covet your land when you go up three
times each year to appear before the
LORD your God.
25"Do not offer the blood of a sacrifice to me along with anything containing yeast,[s] and do not let any of the
sacrifice from the Passover Feast remain until morning.[t]
26"Bring the best of the firstfruits of
your soil to the house of the LORD your
God.
"Do not cook a young goat in its
mother's milk."[u]
27Then the LORD said to Moses,
"Write[v] down these words, for in accordance with these words I have
made a covenant with you and with
Israel." 28Moses was there with the
LORD forty days and forty nights[w]
without eating bread or drinking water.
And he wrote on the tablets[x] the
words of the covenant—the Ten Commandments.[y]

The Radiant Face of Moses

29When Moses came down from
Mount Sinai with the two tablets of the
Testimony in his hands,[z] he was not
aware that his face was radiant[a] because he had spoken with the LORD.
30When Aaron and all the Israelites saw
Moses, his face was radiant, and they
were afraid to come near him. 31But
Moses called to them; so Aaron and all
the leaders of the community came
back to him, and he spoke to them.
32Afterward all the Israelites came near
him, and he gave them all the commands[b] the LORD had given him on
Mount Sinai.
33When Moses finished speaking to
them, he put a veil[c] over his face.
34But whenever he entered the LORD's
presence to speak with him, he removed the veil until he came out. And
when he came out and told the Israelites what he had been commanded,

34:5 [m]Ex 33:19
34:6 [n]Ps 86:15 [o]Nu 14:18; Ro 2:4 [p]Ne 9:17; Ps 103:8; Joel 2:13 [q]Ps 108:4
34:7 [r]Ex 20:6 [s]Ps 103:3; 130:4,8; Da 9:9; 1Jn 1:9 [t]Job 10:14; Na 1:3
34:9 [u]Ex 33:15 [v]Ps 33:12
34:10 [w]Dt 5:2-3 [x]Ex 33:16; Dt 4:32
34:11 [y]Ex 33:2
34:12 [z]Ex 23:32-33
34:13 [a]Ex 23:24; Dt 12:3; 2Ki 18:4
34:14 [b]Ex 20:3 [c]Ex 20:5; Dt 4:24
34:15 [d]Jdg 2:17 [e]Nu 25:2; 1Co 8:4
34:16 [f]Dt 7:3 [g]1Ki 11:4
34:17 [h]Ex 32:8
34:18 [i]Ex 12:17 [j]Ex 12:15 [k]Ex 12:2
34:19 [l]Ex 13:2
34:20 [m]Ex 13:13,15 [n]Ex 23:15; Dt 16:16
34:21 [o]Ex 20:9; Lk 13:14
34:22 [p]Ex 23:16
34:23 [q]Ex 23:14
34:24 [r]Ex 23:28; 33:2; Ps 78:55
34:25 [s]Ex 23:18 [t]Ex 12:8,10
34:26 [u]Ex 23:19
34:27 [v]Ex 17:14; 24:4
34:28 [w]Ge 7:4; Ex 24:18; Mt 4:2 [x]ver 1; Ex 31:18 [y]Dt 4:13; 10:4
34:29 [z]Ex 32:15 [a]Ps 34:5; Mt 17:2; 2Co 3:7,13
34:32 [b]Ex 24:3
34:33 [c]2Co 3:13

a *13* That is, symbols of the goddess Asherah
b *22* That is, in the fall

35 they saw that his face was radiant. Then Moses would put the veil back over his face until he went in to speak with the LORD.

Sabbath Regulations

35 Moses assembled the whole Israelite community and said to them, "These are the things the LORD has commanded[d] you to do: 2 For six days, work is to be done, but the seventh day shall be your holy day, a Sabbath[e] of rest to the LORD. Whoever does any work on it must be put to death. 3 Do not light a fire in any of your dwellings on the Sabbath day.[f]"

Materials for the Tabernacle

4 Moses said to the whole Israelite community, "This is what the LORD has commanded: 5 From what you have, take an offering for the LORD. Everyone who is willing is to bring to the LORD an offering of gold, silver and bronze; 6 blue, purple and scarlet yarn and fine linen; goat hair; 7 ram skins dyed red and hides of sea cows[a]; acacia wood; 8 olive oil for the light; spices for the anointing oil and for the fragrant incense; 9 and onyx stones and other gems to be mounted on the ephod and breastpiece.

10 "All who are skilled among you are to come and make everything the LORD has commanded:[g] 11 the tabernacle[h] with its tent and its covering, clasps, frames, crossbars, posts and bases; 12 the ark[i] with its poles and the atonement cover and the curtain that shields it; 13 the table[j] with its poles and all its articles and the bread of the Presence; 14 the lampstand[k] that is for light with its accessories, lamps and oil for the light; 15 the altar[l] of incense with its poles, the anointing oil[m] and the fragrant incense;[n] the curtain for the doorway at the entrance to the tabernacle; 16 the altar[o] of burnt offering with its bronze grating, its poles and all its utensils; the bronze basin with its stand; 17 the curtains of the courtyard with its posts and bases, and the curtain for the entrance to the courtyard;[p] 18 the tent pegs for the tabernacle and for the courtyard, and their ropes; 19 the woven garments worn for ministering in the sanctuary—both the sacred garments[q] for Aaron the priest and the garments for his sons when they serve as priests."

20 Then the whole Israelite community withdrew from Moses' presence, 21 and everyone who was willing and whose heart moved him came and brought an offering to the LORD for the work on the Tent of Meeting, for all its service, and for the sacred garments. 22 All who were willing, men and women alike, came and brought gold jewelry of all kinds: brooches, earrings, rings and ornaments. They all presented their gold as a wave offering to the LORD. 23 Everyone who had blue, purple or scarlet yarn[r] or fine linen, or goat hair, ram skins dyed red or hides of sea cows brought them. 24 Those presenting an offering of silver or bronze brought it as an offering to the LORD, and everyone who had acacia wood for any part of the work brought it. 25 Every skilled woman[s] spun with her hands and brought what she had spun—blue, purple or scarlet yarn or fine linen. 26 And all the women who were willing and had the skill spun the goat hair. 27 The leaders[t] brought onyx stones and other gems to be mounted on the ephod and breastpiece. 28 They also brought spices and olive oil for the light and for the anointing oil and for the fragrant incense.[u] 29 All the Israelite men and women who were willing[v] brought to the LORD freewill offerings[w] for all the work the LORD through Moses had commanded them to do.

Bezalel and Oholiab

30 Then Moses said to the Israelites, "See, the LORD has chosen Bezalel son of Uri, the son of Hur, of the tribe of Judah, 31 and he has filled him with the Spirit of God, with skill, ability and knowledge in all kinds of crafts[x]— 32 to make artistic designs for work in gold, silver and bronze, 33 to cut and set stones, to work in wood and to engage in all kinds of artistic craftsmanship. 34 And he has given both him and Oholiab[y] son of Ahisamach, of the tribe of Dan, the ability to teach[z] others. 35 He

35:1 [d]Ex 34:32
35:2 [e]Ex 20:9-10; 34:21; Lev 23:3
35:3 [f]Ex 16:23
35:10 [g]Ex 31:6
35:11 [h]Ex 26:1-37
35:12 [i]Ex 25:10-22
35:13 [j]Ex 25:23-30; Lev 24:5-6
35:14 [k]Ex 25:31
35:15 [l]Ex 30:1-6 [m]Ex 30:25 [n]Ex 30:34-38
35:16 [o]Ex 27:1-8
35:17 [p]Ex 27:9
35:19 [q]Ex 28:2; 31:10; 39:1
35:23 [r]1Ch 29:8
35:25 [s]Ex 28:3
35:27 [t]1Ch 29:6; Ezr 2:68
35:28 [u]Ex 25:6
35:29 [v]ver 21; 1Ch 29:9 [w]ver 4-9; Ex 25:1-7; 36:3; 2Ki 12:4
35:31 [x]ver 35; 2Ch 2:7,14
35:34 [y]Ex 31:6 [z]2Ch 2:14

35:1–40:38

PROMISE 1

SERIOUS WORSHIP

God takes our worship seriously. In these closing chapters of Exodus, God goes into great detail as he instructs Israel about how to worship him. When you pause to take some quiet time alone with God or when you worship God in public, think about the sense of awe and respect these last chapters of Exodus command.

God takes our worship seriously. So should we.

For the next Promise 1 reading go to page 128.

[a] *7* That is, dugongs; also in verse 23

has filled them with skill to do all kinds of work[a] as craftsmen, designers, embroiderers in blue, purple and scarlet yarn and fine linen, and weavers—all of them master craftsmen and designers.

36 1So Bezalel, Oholiab and every skilled person[b] to whom the LORD has given skill and ability to know how to carry out all the work of constructing the sanctuary[c] are to do the work just as the LORD has commanded."

2Then Moses summoned Bezalel[d] and Oholiab[e] and every skilled person to whom the LORD had given ability and who was willing[f] to come and do the work. 3They received from Moses all the offerings[g] the Israelites had brought to carry out the work of constructing the sanctuary. And the people continued to bring freewill offerings morning after morning. 4So all the skilled craftsmen who were doing all the work on the sanctuary left their work 5and said to Moses, "The people are bringing more than enough[h] for doing the work the LORD commanded to be done."

5 →PG. 191

6Then Moses gave an order and they sent this word throughout the camp: "No man or woman is to make anything else as an offering for the sanctuary." And so the people were restrained from bringing more, 7because what they already had was more[i] than enough to do all the work.

The Tabernacle

8All the skilled men among the workmen made the tabernacle with ten curtains of finely twisted linen and blue, purple and scarlet yarn, with cherubim worked into them by a skilled craftsman. 9All the curtains were the same size—twenty-eight cubits long and four cubits wide.[a] 10They joined five of the curtains together and did the same with the other five. 11Then they made loops of blue material along the edge of the end curtain in one set, and the same was done with the end curtain in the other set. 12They also made fifty loops on one curtain and fifty loops on the end curtain of the other set, with the loops opposite each other. 13Then they made fifty gold clasps and used them to fasten the two sets of curtains together so that the tabernacle was a unit.[j]

14They made curtains of goat hair for the tent over the tabernacle—eleven altogether. 15All eleven curtains were the same size—thirty cubits long and four cubits wide.[b] 16They joined five of the curtains into one set and the other six into another set. 17Then they made fifty loops along the edge of the end curtain in one set and also along the edge of the end curtain in the other set. 18They made fifty bronze clasps to fasten the tent together as a unit.[k] 19Then they made for the tent a covering of ram skins dyed red, and over that a covering of hides of sea cows.[c]

20They made upright frames of acacia wood for the tabernacle. 21Each frame was ten cubits long and a cubit and a half wide,[d] 22with two projections set parallel to each other. They made all the frames of the tabernacle in this way. 23They made twenty frames for the south side of the tabernacle 24and made forty silver bases to go under them—two bases for each frame, one under each projection. 25For the other side, the north side of the tabernacle, they made twenty frames 26and forty silver bases—two under each frame. 27They made six frames for the far end, that is, the west end of the tabernacle, 28and two frames were made for the corners of the tabernacle at the far end. 29At these two corners the frames were double from the bottom all the way to the top and fitted into a single ring; both were made alike. 30So there were eight frames and sixteen silver bases—two under each frame.

31They also made crossbars of acacia wood: five for the frames on one side of the tabernacle, 32five for those on the other side, and five for the frames on the west, at the far end of the tabernacle. 33They made the center crossbar so that it extended from end to end at the middle of the frames. 34They overlaid the frames with gold and made gold rings to hold the crossbars. They also overlaid the crossbars with gold.

35They made the curtain[l] of blue, purple and scarlet yarn and finely twisted linen, with cherubim worked into it by a skilled craftsman. 36They made four posts of acacia wood for it and overlaid them with gold. They made gold hooks for them and cast their four silver bases. 37For the entrance to the tent they made a curtain of blue, purple and scarlet yarn and finely twisted linen—the work of an embroiderer;[m] 38and they made five posts with hooks for them. They overlaid the tops of the posts and their

35:35 [a]ver 31; Ex 31:3,6; 1Ki 7:14
36:1 [b]Ex 28:3 [c]Ex 25:8
36:2 [d]Ex 31:2 [e]Ex 31:6 [f]Ex 25:2; 35:21,26; 1Ch 29:5
36:3 [g]Ex 35:29
36:5 [h]2Ch 24:14; 31:10; 2Co 8:2-3
36:7 [i]1Ki 7:47
36:13 [j]ver 18
36:18 [k]ver 13
36:35 [l]Ex 39:38; Mt 27:51; Lk 23:45; Heb 9:3
36:37 [m]Ex 27:16

a *9* That is, about 42 feet (about 12.5 meters) long and 6 feet (about 1.8 meters) wide
b *15* That is, about 45 feet (about 13.5 meters) long and 6 feet (about 1.8 meters) wide
c *19* That is, dugongs
d *21* That is, about 15 feet (about 4.5 meters) long and 2 1/4 feet (about 0.7 meter) wide

bands with gold and made their five
bases of bronze.

The Ark

37 Bezalel[n] made the ark[o] of acacia
wood—two and a half cubits long,
a cubit and a half wide, and a cubit and
a half high.[a] 2He overlaid it with pure
gold,[p] both inside and out, and made
a gold molding around it. 3He cast four
gold rings for it and fastened them to
its four feet, with two rings on one side
and two rings on the other. 4Then he
made poles of acacia wood and overlaid them with gold. 5And he inserted
the poles into the rings on the sides of
the ark to carry it.
6He made the atonement cover[q] of
pure gold—two and a half cubits long
and a cubit and a half wide.[b] 7Then he
made two cherubim[r] out of hammered gold at the ends of the cover.
8He made one cherub on one end and
the second cherub on the other; at the
two ends he made them of one piece
with the cover. 9The cherubim had
their wings spread upward, overshadowing[s] the cover with them. The
cherubim faced each other, looking toward the cover.[t]

The Table

10They[c] made the table[u] of acacia
wood—two cubits long, a cubit wide,
and a cubit and a half high.[d] 11Then
they overlaid it with pure gold[v] and
made a gold molding around it. 12They
also made around it a rim a handbreadth[e] wide and put a gold molding
on the rim. 13They cast four gold rings
for the table and fastened them to the
four corners, where the four legs were.
14The rings[w] were put close to the rim
to hold the poles used in carrying the
table. 15The poles for carrying the table
were made of acacia wood and were
overlaid with gold. 16And they made
from pure gold the articles for the
table—its plates and dishes and bowls
and its pitchers for the pouring out of
drink offerings.

The Lampstand

17They made the lampstand[x] of
pure gold and hammered it out, base
and shaft; its flowerlike cups, buds and
blossoms were of one piece with it.
18Six branches extended from the sides
of the lampstand—three on one side
and three on the other. 19Three cups
shaped like almond flowers with buds
and blossoms were on one branch,
three on the next branch and the same
for all six branches extending from the
lampstand. 20And on the lampstand
were four cups shaped like almond
flowers with buds and blossoms. 21One
bud was under the first pair of
branches extending from the lampstand, a second bud under the second
pair, and a third bud under the third
pair—six branches in all. 22The buds
and the branches were all of one piece
with the lampstand, hammered out of
pure gold.[y]
23They made its seven lamps,[z] as
well as its wick trimmers and trays, of
pure gold. 24They made the lampstand
and all its accessories from one talent[f]
of pure gold.

The Altar of Incense

25They made the altar of incense[a]
out of acacia wood. It was square, a
cubit long and a cubit wide, and two
cubits high[g]—its horns[b] of one piece
with it. 26They overlaid the top and all
the sides and the horns with pure gold,
and made a gold molding around it.
27They made two gold rings[c] below
the molding—two on opposite sides—
to hold the poles used to carry it.
28They made the poles of acacia wood
and overlaid them with gold.[d]
29They also made the sacred anointing oil[e] and the pure, fragrant incense[f]—the work of a perfumer.

The Altar of Burnt Offering

38 They[h] built the altar of burnt offering of acacia wood, three cubits[i] high; it was square, five cubits
long and five cubits wide.[j] 2They
made a horn at each of the four corners, so that the horns and the altar
were of one piece, and they overlaid
the altar with bronze.[g] 3They made all
its utensils[h] of bronze—its pots, shovels, sprinkling bowls, meat forks and
firepans. 4They made a grating for the
altar, a bronze network, to be under its
ledge, halfway up the altar. 5They cast
bronze rings to hold the poles for the
four corners of the bronze grating.
6They made the poles of acacia wood
and overlaid them with bronze. 7They
inserted the poles into the rings so they

37:1 [n] Ex 31:2 [o] Ex 30:6; 39:35; Dt 10:3
37:2 [p] ver 11,26
37:6 [q] Ex 26:34; 31:7; Heb 9:5
37:7 [r] Eze 41:18
37:9 [s] Heb 9:5 [t] Dt 10:3
37:10 [u] Heb 9:2
37:11 [v] ver 2
37:14 [w] ver 27
37:17 [x] Heb 9:2; Rev 1:12
37:22 [y] ver 17; Nu 8:4
37:23 [z] Ex 40:4,25
37:25 [a] Ex 30:34-36; Lk 1:11; Heb 9:4; Rev 8:3 [b] Ex 27:2; Rev 9:13
37:27 [c] ver 14
37:28 [d] Ex 25:13
37:29 [e] Ex 31:11 [f] Ex 30:1,25; 39:38
38:2 [g] 2Ch 1:5
38:3 [h] Ex 31:9

a *1* That is, about 3 3/4 feet (about 1.1 meters) long and 2 1/4 feet (about 0.7 meter) wide and high **b** *6* That is, about 3 3/4 feet (about 1.1 meters) long and 2 1/4 feet (about 0.7 meter) wide **c** *10* Or *He;* also in verses 11-29
d *10* That is, about 3 feet (about 0.9 meter) long, 1 1/2 feet (about 0.5 meter) wide, and 2 1/4 feet (about 0.7 meter) high **e** *12* That is, about 3 inches (about 8 centimeters) **f** *24* That is, about 75 pounds (about 34 kilograms)
g *25* That is, about 1 1/2 feet (about 0.5 meter) long and wide, and about 3 feet (about 0.9 meter) high **h** *1* Or *He;* also in verses 2-9
i *1* That is, about 4 1/2 feet (about 1.3 meters)
j *1* That is, about 7 1/2 feet (about 2.3 meters) long and wide

would be on the sides of the altar for carrying it. They made it hollow, out of boards.

Basin for Washing

8 They made the bronze basin[i] and its bronze stand from the mirrors of the women[j] who served at the entrance to the Tent of Meeting.

The Courtyard

9 Next they made the courtyard. The south side was a hundred cubits[a] long and had curtains of finely twisted linen, 10 with twenty posts and twenty bronze bases, and with silver hooks and bands on the posts. 11 The north side was also a hundred cubits long and had twenty posts and twenty bronze bases, with silver hooks and bands on the posts.

12 The west end was fifty cubits[b] wide and had curtains, with ten posts and ten bases, with silver hooks and bands on the posts. 13 The east end, toward the sunrise, was also fifty cubits wide. 14 Curtains fifteen cubits[c] long were on one side of the entrance, with three posts and three bases, 15 and curtains fifteen cubits long were on the other side of the entrance to the courtyard, with three posts and three bases. 16 All the curtains around the courtyard were of finely twisted linen. 17 The bases for the posts were bronze. The hooks and bands on the posts were silver, and their tops were overlaid with silver; so all the posts of the courtyard had silver bands.

18 The curtain for the entrance to the courtyard was of blue, purple and scarlet yarn and finely twisted linen—the work of an embroiderer. It was twenty cubits[d] long and, like the curtains of the courtyard, five cubits[e] high, 19 with four posts and four bronze bases. Their hooks and bands were silver, and their tops were overlaid with silver. 20 All the tent pegs[k] of the tabernacle and of the surrounding courtyard were bronze.

The Materials Used

21 These are the amounts of the materials used for the tabernacle, the tabernacle of the Testimony,[l] which were recorded at Moses' command by the Levites under the direction of Ithamar[m] son of Aaron, the priest. 22 (Bezalel[n] son of Uri, the son of Hur, of the tribe of Judah, made everything the LORD commanded Moses; 23 with him was Oholiab[o] son of Ahisamach, of the tribe of Dan—a craftsman and designer, and an embroiderer in blue, purple and scarlet yarn and fine linen.) 24 The total amount of the gold from the wave offering used for all the work on the sanctuary[p] was 29 talents and 730 shekels,[f] according to the sanctuary shekel.[q]

25 The silver obtained from those of the community who were counted in the census[r] was 100 talents and 1,775 shekels,[g] according to the sanctuary shekel— 26 one beka per person,[s] that is, half a shekel,[h] according to the sanctuary shekel,[t] from everyone who had crossed over to those counted, twenty years old or more,[u] a total of 603,550 men.[v] 27 The 100 talents[i] of silver were used to cast the bases[w] for the sanctuary and for the curtain—100 bases from the 100 talents, one talent for each base. 28 They used the 1,775 shekels[j] to make the hooks for the posts, to overlay the tops of the posts, and to make their bands.

29 The bronze from the wave offering was 70 talents and 2,400 shekels.[k] 30 They used it to make the bases for the entrance to the Tent of Meeting, the bronze altar with its bronze grating and all its utensils, 31 the bases for the surrounding courtyard and those for its entrance and all the tent pegs for the tabernacle and those for the surrounding courtyard.

The Priestly Garments

39 From the blue, purple and scarlet yarn[x] they made woven garments for ministering in the sanctuary.[y] They also made sacred garments[z] for Aaron, as the LORD commanded Moses.

The Ephod

2 They[l] made the ephod of gold, and of blue, purple and scarlet yarn, and of finely twisted linen. 3 They hammered out thin sheets of gold and cut strands to be worked into the blue, purple and scarlet yarn and fine linen—the work of a skilled craftsman. 4 They made shoulder pieces for the ephod, which were attached to two of its corners, so it could be fastened. 5 Its skillfully wo-

38:8 [i] Ex 30:18; 40:7 [j] Dt 23:17; 1Sa 2:22; 1Ki 14:24
38:20 [k] Ex 35:18
38:21 [l] Nu 1:50,53; 8:24; 9:15; 10:11; 17:7; 1Ch 23:32; 2Ch 24:6; Ac 7:44; Rev 15:5 [m] Nu 4:28,33
38:22 [n] Ex 31:2
38:23 [o] Ex 31:6
38:24 [p] Ex 30:16 [q] Ex 30:13; Lev 27:25; Nu 3:47; 18:16
38:25 [r] Ex 30:12
38:26 [s] Ex 30:12 [t] Ex 30:13 [u] Ex 30:14 [v] Ex 12:37; Nu 1:46
38:27 [w] Ex 26:19
39:1 [x] Ex 35:23 [y] Ex 35:19 [z] ver 41; Ex 28:2

[a] *9* That is, about 150 feet (about 46 meters)
[b] *12* That is, about 75 feet (about 23 meters)
[c] *14* That is, about 22 1/2 feet (about 6.9 meters)
[d] *18* That is, about 30 feet (about 9 meters)
[e] *18* That is, about 7 1/2 feet (about 2.3 meters)
[f] *24* The weight of the gold was a little over one ton (about 1 metric ton).
[g] *25* The weight of the silver was a little over 3 3/4 tons (about 3.4 metric tons).
[h] *26* That is, about 1/5 ounce (about 5.5 grams)
[i] *27* That is, about 3 3/4 tons (about 3.4 metric tons)
[j] *28* That is, about 45 pounds (about 20 kilograms)
[k] *29* The weight of the bronze was about 2 1/2 tons (about 2.4 metric tons).
[l] *2* Or *He*; also in verses 7, 8 and 22

ven waistband was like it—of one piece with the ephod and made with gold, and with blue, purple and scarlet yarn, and with finely twisted linen, as the LORD commanded Moses.

6They mounted the onyx stones in gold filigree settings and engraved them like a seal with the names of the sons of Israel. 7Then they fastened them on the shoulder pieces of the ephod as memorial[a] stones for the sons of Israel, as the LORD commanded Moses.

The Breastpiece

8They fashioned the breastpiece[b]—the work of a skilled craftsman. They made it like the ephod: of gold, and of blue, purple and scarlet yarn, and of finely twisted linen. 9It was square—a span[a] long and a span wide—and folded double. 10Then they mounted four rows of precious stones on it. In the first row there was a ruby, a topaz and a beryl; 11in the second row a turquoise, a sapphire[b] and an emerald; 12in the third row a jacinth, an agate and an amethyst; 13in the fourth row a chrysolite, an onyx and a jasper.[c] They were mounted in gold filigree settings. 14There were twelve stones, one for each of the names of the sons of Israel, each engraved like a seal with the name of one of the twelve tribes.[c]

15For the breastpiece they made braided chains of pure gold, like a rope. 16They made two gold filigree settings and two gold rings, and fastened the rings to two of the corners of the breastpiece. 17They fastened the two gold chains to the rings at the corners of the breastpiece, 18and the other ends of the chains to the two settings, attaching them to the shoulder pieces of the ephod at the front. 19They made two gold rings and attached them to the other two corners of the breastpiece on the inside edge next to the ephod. 20Then they made two more gold rings and attached them to the bottom of the shoulder pieces on the front of the ephod, close to the seam just above the waistband of the ephod. 21They tied the rings of the breastpiece to the rings of the ephod with blue cord, connecting it to the waistband so that the breastpiece would not swing out from the ephod—as the LORD commanded Moses.

Other Priestly Garments

22They made the robe of the ephod entirely of blue cloth—the work of a weaver— 23with an opening in the center of the robe like the opening of a collar,[d] and a band around this opening, so that it would not tear. 24They made pomegranates of blue, purple and scarlet yarn and finely twisted linen around the hem of the robe. 25And they made bells of pure gold and attached them around the hem between the pomegranates. 26The bells and pomegranates alternated around the hem of the robe to be worn for ministering, as the LORD commanded Moses.

27For Aaron and his sons, they made tunics of fine linen[d]—the work of a weaver— 28and the turban[e] of fine linen, the linen headbands and the undergarments of finely twisted linen. 29The sash was of finely twisted linen and blue, purple and scarlet yarn—the work of an embroiderer—as the LORD commanded Moses.

30They made the plate, the sacred diadem, out of pure gold and engraved on it, like an inscription on a seal: HOLY TO THE LORD. 31Then they fastened a blue cord to it to attach it to the turban, as the LORD commanded Moses.

Moses Inspects the Tabernacle

32So all the work on the tabernacle, the Tent of Meeting, was completed. The Israelites did everything just as the LORD commanded Moses.[f] 33Then they brought the tabernacle to Moses: the tent and all its furnishings, its clasps, frames, crossbars, posts and bases; 34the covering of ram skins dyed red, the covering of hides of sea cows[e] and the shielding curtain; 35the ark of the Testimony[g] with its poles and the atonement cover; 36the table with all its articles and the bread of the Presence; 37the pure gold lampstand[h] with its row of lamps and all its accessories, and the oil for the light; 38the gold altar,[i] the anointing oil, the fragrant incense, and the curtain[j] for the entrance to the tent; 39the bronze altar with its bronze grating, its poles and all its utensils; the basin with its stand; 40the curtains of the courtyard with its posts and bases, and the curtain for the entrance to the courtyard;[k] the ropes and tent pegs for the courtyard; all the furnishings for the tabernacle, the Tent of Meeting; 41and the woven garments worn for ministering in the sanctuary, both the sacred garments for Aaron the priest and the garments for his sons when serving as priests.

42The Israelites had done all the

39:7 [a]Lev 24:7; Jos 4:7
39:8 [b]Lev 8:8
39:14 [c]Rev 21:12
39:27 [d]Lev 6:10
39:28 [e]Ex 28:4
39:32 [f]ver 42-43; Ex 25:9
39:35 [g]Ex 30:6
39:37 [h]Ex 25:31
39:38 [i]Ex 30:1-10 [j]Ex 36:35
39:40 [k]Ex 27:9-19

a 9 That is, about 9 inches (about 22 centimeters) b 11 Or *lapis lazuli*
c 13 The precise identification of some of these precious stones is uncertain.
d 23 The meaning of the Hebrew for this word is uncertain. e 34 That is, dugongs

work just as the LORD had commanded
Moses.[l] 43Moses inspected the work
and saw that they had done it just as
the LORD had commanded. So Moses
blessed[m] them.

Setting Up the Tabernacle

40 Then the LORD said to Moses: 2"Set
up the tabernacle, the Tent of
Meeting,[n] on the first day of the first
month.[o] 3Place the ark[p] of the Testimony in it and shield the ark with the
curtain. 4Bring in the table and set out
what belongs on it.[q] Then bring in the
lampstand[r] and set up its lamps.
5Place the gold altar[s] of incense in
front of the ark of the Testimony and
put the curtain at the entrance to the
tabernacle.
6"Place the altar of burnt offering in
front of the entrance to the tabernacle,
the Tent of Meeting; 7place the basin[t]
between the Tent of Meeting and the
altar and put water in it. 8Set up the
courtyard around it and put the curtain
at the entrance to the courtyard.
9"Take the anointing oil and
anoint[u] the tabernacle and everything
in it; consecrate it and all its furnishings, and it will be holy. 10Then anoint
the altar of burnt offering and all its
utensils; consecrate[v] the altar, and it
will be most holy. 11Anoint the basin
and its stand and consecrate them.
12"Bring Aaron and his sons to the
entrance to the Tent of Meeting and
wash them with water.[w] 13Then dress
Aaron in the sacred garments,[x] anoint
him and consecrate[y] him so he may
serve me as priest. 14Bring his sons and
dress them in tunics. 15Anoint them
just as you anointed their father, so
they may serve me as priests. Their
anointing will be to a priesthood that
will continue for all generations to
come.[z]" 16Moses did everything just
as the LORD commanded him.
17So the tabernacle[a] was set up on
the first day of the first month[b] in the
second year. 18When Moses set up the
tabernacle, he put the bases in place,
erected the frames, inserted the crossbars and set up the posts. 19Then he
spread the tent over the tabernacle and
put the covering over the tent, as the
LORD commanded him.
20He took the Testimony[c] and
placed it in the ark, attached the poles
to the ark and put the atonement cover
over it. 21Then he brought the ark into
the tabernacle and hung the shielding
curtain[d] and shielded the ark of the
Testimony, as the LORD commanded
him.
22Moses placed the table[e] in the
Tent of Meeting on the north side of
the tabernacle outside the curtain
23and set out the bread[f] on it before
the LORD, as the LORD commanded
him.
24He placed the lampstand[g] in the
Tent of Meeting opposite the table on
the south side of the tabernacle 25and
set up the lamps[h] before the LORD, as
the LORD commanded him.
26Moses placed the gold altar[i] in
the Tent of Meeting in front of the curtain 27and burned fragrant incense on
it, as the LORD commanded[j] him.
28Then he put up the curtain[k] at the
entrance to the tabernacle.
29He set the altar of burnt offering
near the entrance to the tabernacle,
the Tent of Meeting, and offered on it
burnt offerings and grain offerings,[l]
as the LORD commanded him.
30He placed the basin[m] between the
Tent of Meeting and the altar and put
water in it for washing, 31and Moses
and Aaron and his sons used it to wash
their hands and feet. 32They washed
whenever they entered the Tent of
Meeting or approached the altar,[n] as
the LORD commanded Moses.
33Then Moses set up the courtyard[o]
around the tabernacle and altar and
put up the curtain[p] at the entrance to
the courtyard. And so Moses finished
the work.

The Glory of the LORD

34Then the cloud[q] covered the Tent
of Meeting, and the glory of the LORD
filled the tabernacle. 35Moses could not
enter the Tent of Meeting because the
cloud had settled upon it, and the glory
of the LORD filled the tabernacle.[r]
36In all the travels of the Israelites,
whenever the cloud lifted from above
the tabernacle, they would set out;[s]
37but if the cloud did not lift, they did
not set out—until the day it lifted. 38So
the cloud[t] of the LORD was over the
tabernacle by day, and fire was in the
cloud by night, in the sight of all
the house of Israel during all their travels.

1 →PG. 131

39:42 [l]Ex 25:9
39:43 [m]Lev 9:22,23; Nu 6:23-27; 2Sa 6:18; 1Ki 8:14,55; 2Ch 30:27
40:2 [n]Nu 1:1 [o]ver 17; Ex 12:2
40:3 [p]ver 21; Nu 4:5; Ex 26:33
40:4 [q]Ex 25:30 [r]ver 22-25; Ex 26:35
40:5 [s]ver 26; Ex 30:1
40:7 [t]ver 30; Ex 30:18
40:9 [u]Ex 30:26; Lev 8:10
40:10 [v]Ex 29:36
40:12 [w]Lev 8:1-13
40:13 [x]Ex 28:41 [y]Lev 8:12
40:15 [z]Ex 29:9; Nu 25:13
40:17 [a]Nu 7:1 [b]ver 2
40:20 [c]Ex 16:34; 25:16; Dt 10:5; 1Ki 8:9; Heb 9:4
40:21 [d]Ex 26:33
40:22 [e]Ex 26:35
40:23 [f]ver 4
40:24 [g]Ex 26:35
40:25 [h]ver 4; Ex 25:37
40:26 [i]ver 5; Ex 30:6
40:27 [j]Ex 30:7
40:28 [k]Ex 26:36
40:29 [l]ver 6; Ex 29:38-42
40:30 [m]ver 7
40:32 [n]Ex 30:20
40:33 [o]Ex 27:9 [p]ver 8
40:34 [q]Nu 9:15-23; 1Ki 8:12
40:35 [r]1Ki 8:11; 2Ch 5:13-14
40:36 [s]Nu 9:17-23; 10:13; Ne 9:19
40:38 [t]Ex 13:21; Nu 9:15; 1Co 10:1

LEVITICUS

AT A GLANCE

Key Principle: God is holy, and if we want to know and walk with him we must ask for his Spirit to work in us so that we can also be holy and set apart for his service.
Author: Moses
Time and Place: 1440 B.C. / Mount Sinai
Key Verses: 11:45; 17:11; 20:7–8

BENEFIT

Leviticus teaches us that God expects more than mere lip service from those who follow him—our lives in Christ should reflect a new quality of living. It also provides us with a mirror of our own depravity and need for cleansing in Christ's blood.

SETTING

Unlike Genesis and Exodus, there is no geographical movement in Leviticus; all the material in this book was revealed in the course of one month at the foot of Mount Sinai. Leviticus picks up where Exodus left off, with the construction and consecration of the tabernacle in the wilderness.

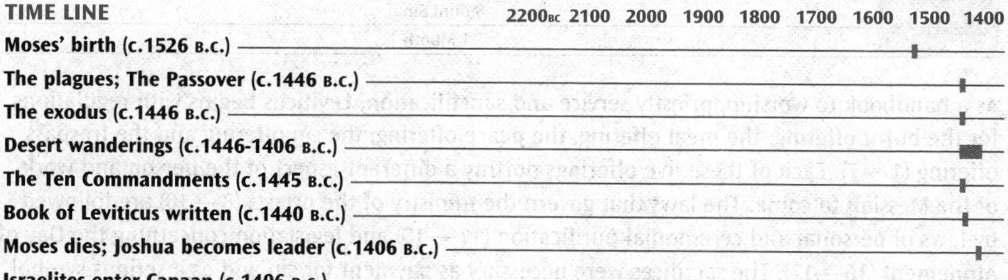

THEME AND PURPOSE

The focal point of Leviticus is the need for a redeemed people to walk in a manner consistent with their holy calling. Since God is holy, his people must also manifest holiness as a moral, civil and ceremonial community. Ancient Israel's sanctification before God required both the sacrificial system and the priestly function of mediation between God and the people. This book was written to instruct the Israelites so that their worship would be acceptable to God, and that their lives would be set apart for God's service.

UNIQUE CONTRIBUTION

Genesis records humanity's fall into sin and God's choice of Abraham as the godly seed through whom he would redeem his people. Exodus records the growth of that seed into a nation and traces God's redemption and deliverance of Israel. Leviticus continues the redemption story by developing the theme of Israel's cleansing and sanctification. While Exodus describes God's approach to man, Leviticus outlines man's approach to God. It abounds in redemptive illustrations (e.g., the five offerings, the high priest, the seven feasts), many of which are fully developed in the book of Hebrews.

LINKS TO THE NEW TESTAMENT

Each of the five offerings (1—7) anticipates an aspect of Christ's sacrificial work on the cross: He totally submitted to the will of his Father (burnt offering); his sacrifice was sinless (meal offering); his redemptive work makes it possible for us to have peace with God (peace offering); he bore our guilt (sin offering); he paid the price for the consequences of our sin (trespass offering). The seven feasts of Leviticus (23) also symbolize Christ's redemption, resurrection and return.

The Day of Atonement prefigures Christ's atoning work on the cross: "For the life of a creature is in the blood, and I have given it to you to make atonement for yourselves on the altar; it is the blood that makes atonement for one's life" (17:11). Compare Hebrews 9:22: "The law requires that nearly everything . . . be cleansed with blood, and without the shedding of blood there is no forgiveness."

OVERVIEW

FOCUS	Sacrifice	Sanctification
REFERENCE	1 — 10	11 — 27
TOPICS	How to Approach a Holy God	How to Walk with a Holy God
	Worship	Practice
	Access to God by Sacrifice	Fellowship with God by Obedience
	"I the Lord your God am holy"	"You shall be holy"
LOCATION	Mount Sinai	
TIME	1 Month	

As a handbook to worship, priestly service and sanctification, Leviticus begins with regulations for the burnt offering, the meal offering, the peace offering, the sin offering and the trespass offering (1—7). Each of these five offerings portray a different aspect of the person and work of the Messiah to come. The laws that govern the ministry of the priests (8—10) are followed by laws of personal and ceremonial purification (11—15) and legislation concerning the Day of Atonement (16—17). The sacrifices were necessary as payment for sin and as a serious symbol of repentance (17:11); Hebrews 9:22 tells us that there is no forgiveness without the shedding of blood. The rest of the book consists of laws of sanctification that extend to the people's lives (18—20), the priesthood (21—22), the seven feasts of worship (23—24), preparation for obedient living in Canaan (25—26) and consecrating vows (27).

LEVITICUS

The Burnt Offering

1 The LORD called to Moses[a] and spoke to him from the Tent of Meeting.[b] He said, 2"Speak to the Israelites and say to them: 'When any of you brings an offering to the LORD, bring as your offering an animal from either the herd or the flock.[c]

3" 'If the offering is a burnt offering from the herd, he is to offer a male without defect.[d] He must present it at the entrance to the Tent[e] of Meeting so that it[a] will be acceptable to the LORD. 4He is to lay his hand on the head[f] of the burnt offering, and it will be accepted on his behalf to make atonement[g] for him. 5He is to slaughter[h] the young bull before the LORD, and then Aaron's sons the priests shall bring the blood and sprinkle it against the altar on all sides[i] at the entrance to the Tent of Meeting. 6He is to skin[j] the burnt offering and cut it into pieces. 7The sons of Aaron the priest are to put fire on the altar and arrange wood[k] on the fire. 8Then Aaron's sons the priests shall arrange the pieces, including the head and the fat,[l] on the burning wood that is on the altar. 9He is to wash the inner parts and the legs with water, and the priest is to burn all of it on the altar.[m] It is a burnt offering, an offering made by fire, an aroma pleasing to the LORD.[n]

10" 'If the offering is a burnt offering from the flock, from either the sheep or the goats,[o] he is to offer a male without defect. 11He is to slaughter it at the north side of the altar before the LORD, and Aaron's sons the priests shall sprinkle its blood against the altar on all sides.[p] 12He is to cut it into pieces, and the priest shall arrange them, including the head and the fat, on the burning wood that is on the altar. 13He is to wash the inner parts and the legs with water, and the priest is to bring all of it and burn it on the altar. It is a burnt offering, an offering made by fire, an aroma pleasing to the LORD.

14" 'If the offering to the LORD is a burnt offering of birds, he is to offer a dove or a young pigeon.[q] 15The priest shall bring it to the altar, wring off the head and burn it on the altar; its blood shall be drained out on the side of the altar.[r] 16He is to remove the crop with its contents[b] and throw it to the east side of the altar, where the ashes[s] are. 17He shall tear it open by the wings, not severing it completely,[t] and then the priest shall burn it on the wood[u] that is on the fire on the altar. It is a burnt offering, an offering made by fire, an aroma pleasing to the LORD.

The Grain Offering

2 " 'When someone brings a grain offering[v] to the LORD, his offering is to be of fine flour. He is to pour oil[w] on it, put incense on it 2and take it to Aaron's sons the priests. The priest shall take a handful of the fine flour[x] and oil, together with all the incense,[y] and burn this as a memorial portion[z] on the altar, an offering made by fire, an aroma pleasing to the LORD. 3The rest of the grain offering belongs to Aaron and his sons;[a] it is a most holy part of the offerings made to the LORD by fire.

4" 'If you bring a grain offering baked in an oven, it is to consist of fine flour: cakes made without yeast and mixed with oil, or[c] wafers made without yeast and spread with oil.[b] 5If your grain offering is prepared on a griddle, it is to be made of fine flour mixed with oil, and without yeast. 6Crumble it and pour oil on it; it is a grain offering. 7If your grain offering is cooked in a pan,[c] it is to be made of fine flour and oil. 8Bring the grain offering made of these things to the LORD; present it to the priest, who shall take it to the altar. 9He shall take out the memorial portion[d] from the grain offering and burn it on the altar as an offering made by fire, an aroma pleasing to the LORD.[e] 10The rest of the grain offering belongs to Aaron and his sons;[f] it is a most holy part of the offerings made to the LORD by fire.

11" 'Every grain offering you bring to the LORD must be made without yeast,[g] for you are not to burn any yeast or honey in an offering made to the LORD by fire. 12You may bring them to the LORD as an offering of the firstfruits,[h] but they are not to be offered on the altar as a pleasing aroma. 13Season all your grain offerings with salt. Do not leave the salt of the covenant[i] of your God out of your grain offerings; add salt to all your offerings.

14" 'If you bring a grain offering of firstfruits[j] to the LORD, offer crushed

1:1 [a]Ex 19:3; 25:22 [b]Nu 7:89
1:2 [c]Lev 22:18-19
1:3 [d]Ex 12:5; Dt 15:21; Heb 9:14; 1Pe 1:19 [e]Lev 17:9
1:4 [f]Ex 29:10,15; Lev 3:2 [g]2Ch 29:23-24
1:5 [h]Lev 3:2,8 [i]Heb 12:24; 1Pe 1:2
1:6 [j]Lev 7:8
1:7 [k]Lev 6:12
1:8 [l]ver 12
1:9 [m]Ex 29:18 [n]ver 13; Ge 8:21; Nu 15:8-10; Eph 5:2
1:10 [o]ver 3; Ex 12:5
1:11 [p]ver 5
1:14 [q]Ge 15:9; Lev 5:7; Lk 2:24
1:15 [r]Lev 5:9
1:16 [s]Lev 6:10
1:17 [t]Ge 15:10 [u]Lev 5:8
2:1 [v]Lev 6:14-18 [w]Nu 15:4
2:2 [x]Lev 5:11 [y]Lev 6:15; Isa 66:3 [z]ver 9,16; Lev 5:12; 6:15; 24:7; Ac 10:4
2:3 [a]ver 10; Lev 6:16; 10:12,13
2:4 [b]Ex 29:2
2:7 [c]Lev 7:9
2:9 [d]ver 2 [e]Ex 29:18; Lev 6:15
2:10 [f]ver 3
2:11 [g]Ex 23:18; 34:25; Lev 6:16
2:12 [h]Lev 7:13; 23:10
2:13 [i]Nu 18:19; Eze 43:24
2:14 [j]Lev 23:10

[a] 3 Or *he* [b] 16 Or *crop and the feathers*; the meaning of the Hebrew for this word is uncertain. [c] 4 Or *and*

heads of new grain roasted in the fire. 15Put oil and incense on it; it is a grain offering. 16The priest shall burn the memorial portion[k] of the crushed grain and the oil, together with all the incense, as an offering made to the LORD by fire.

The Fellowship Offering

3 " 'If someone's offering is a fellowship offering,[a][l] and he offers an animal from the herd, whether male or female, he is to present before the LORD an animal without defect.[m] 2He is to lay his hand on the head[n] of his offering and slaughter it[o] at the entrance to the Tent of Meeting. Then Aaron's sons the priests shall sprinkle the blood against the altar on all sides. 3From the fellowship offering he is to bring a sacrifice made to the LORD by fire: all the fat[p] that covers the inner parts or is connected to them, 4both kidneys with the fat on them near the loins, and the covering of the liver, which he will remove with the kidneys. 5Then Aaron's sons[q] are to burn it on the altar on top of the burnt offering[r] that is on the burning wood, as an offering made by fire, an aroma pleasing to the LORD.

6" 'If he offers an animal from the flock as a fellowship offering[s] to the LORD, he is to offer a male or female without defect. 7If he offers a lamb, he is to present it before the LORD.[t] 8He is to lay his hand on the head of his offering and slaughter it[u] in front of the Tent of Meeting. Then Aaron's sons shall sprinkle its blood against the altar on all sides. 9From the fellowship offering he is to bring a sacrifice made to the LORD by fire: its fat, the entire fat tail cut off close to the backbone, all the fat that covers the inner parts or is connected to them, 10both kidneys with the fat on them near the loins, and the covering of the liver, which he will remove with the kidneys. 11The priest shall burn them on the altar[v] as food,[w] an offering made to the LORD by fire.

12" 'If his offering is a goat, he is to present it before the LORD. 13He is to lay his hand on its head and slaughter it in front of the Tent of Meeting. Then Aaron's sons shall sprinkle[x] its blood against the altar on all sides. 14From what he offers he is to make this offering to the LORD by fire: all the fat that covers the inner parts or is connected to them, 15both kidneys with the fat on them near the loins, and the covering of the liver, which he will remove with the kidneys. 16The priest shall burn them on the altar as food, an offering made by fire, a pleasing aroma. All the fat is the LORD's.[y]

17" 'This is a lasting ordinance for the generations to come,[z] wherever you live: You must not eat any fat or any blood.[a]' "

The Sin Offering

4 The LORD said to Moses, 2"Say to the Israelites: 'When anyone sins unintentionally[b] and does what is forbidden in any of the LORD's commands—

3" 'If the anointed priest sins, bringing guilt on the people, he must bring to the LORD a young bull[c] without defect as a sin offering[d] for the sin he has committed. 4He is to present the bull at the entrance to the Tent of Meeting before the LORD.[e] He is to lay his hand on its head and slaughter it before the LORD. 5Then the anointed priest shall take some of the bull's blood[f] and carry it into the Tent of Meeting. 6He is to dip his finger into the blood and sprinkle some of it seven times before the LORD, in front of the curtain of the sanctuary. 7The priest shall then put some of the blood on the horns of the altar of fragrant incense that is before the LORD in the Tent of Meeting. The rest of the bull's blood he shall pour out at the base of the altar[g] of burnt offering[h] at the entrance to the Tent of Meeting. 8He shall remove all the fat[i] from the bull of the sin offering—the fat that covers the inner parts or is connected to them, 9both kidneys with the fat on them near the loins, and the covering of the liver, which he will remove with the kidneys[j]— 10just as the fat is removed from the ox[b] sacrificed as a fellowship offering.[c] Then the priest shall burn them on the altar of burnt offering. 11But the hide of the bull and all its flesh, as well as the head and legs, the inner parts and offal[k]— 12that is, all the rest of the bull—he must take outside the camp[l] to a place ceremonially clean,[m] where the ashes are thrown, and burn it in a wood fire on the ash heap.

13" 'If the whole Israelite community sins unintentionally[n] and does what is forbidden in any of the LORD's commands, even though the community is unaware of the matter, they are guilty. 14When they become aware of the sin they committed, the assembly must bring a young bull[o] as a sin offering[p] and present it before the Tent of Meet-

2:16 [k]ver 2
3:1 [l]Lev 7:11-34 [m]Lev 1:3; 22:21
3:2 [n]Ex 29:10,15 [o]Lev 1:5
3:3 [p]Ex 29:13
3:5 [q]Lev 7:29-34 [r]Ex 29:13, 38-42
3:6 [s]ver 1
3:7 [t]Lev 17:8-9
3:8 [u]ver 2; Lev 1:5
3:11 [v]ver 5 [w]ver 16; Lev 21:6,17
3:13 [x]Ex 24:6
3:16 [y]1Sa 2:16
3:17 [z]Lev 6:18; 17:7 [a]Ge 9:4; Lev 7:25-26; 17:10-16; Dt 12:16; Ac 15:20
4:2 [b]Lev 5:15-18; Ps 19:12; Heb 9:7
4:3 [c]ver 14; Ps 66:15 [d]Lev 9:2-22; Heb 9:13-14
4:4 [e]Lev 1:3
4:5 [f]Lev 16:14
4:7 [g]ver 34; Lev 8:15 [h]ver 18,30; Lev 5:9; 9:9; 16:18
4:8 [i]Lev 3:3-5
4:9 [j]Lev 3:4
4:11 [k]Ex 29:14; Lev 9:11; Nu 19:5
4:12 [l]Heb 13:11 [m]Lev 6:11
4:13 [n]ver 2; Lev 5:2-4,17; Nu 15:24-26
4:14 [o]ver 3 [p]ver 23,28

[a] *1* Traditionally *peace offering*; also in verses 3, 6 and 9 [b] *10* The Hebrew word can include both male and female. [c] *10* Traditionally *peace offering*; also in verses 26, 31 and 35

ing. **15**The elders of the community are to lay their hands on the bull's head[q] before the LORD, and the bull shall be slaughtered before the LORD. **16**Then the anointed priest is to take some of the bull's blood[r] into the Tent of Meeting. **17**He shall dip his finger into the blood and sprinkle it before the LORD[s] seven times in front of the curtain. **18**He is to put some of the blood on the horns of the altar that is before the LORD[t] in the Tent of Meeting. The rest of the blood he shall pour out at the base of the altar of burnt offering at the entrance to the Tent of Meeting. **19**He shall remove all the fat[u] from it and burn it on the altar, **20**and do with this bull just as he did with the bull for the sin offering. In this way the priest will make atonement[v] for them, and they will be forgiven.[w] **21**Then he shall take the bull outside the camp and burn it as he burned the first bull. This is the sin offering for the community.[x]

22" 'When a leader[y] sins unintentionally[z] and does what is forbidden in any of the commands of the LORD his God, he is guilty. **23**When he is made aware of the sin he committed, he must bring as his offering a male goat without defect. **24**He is to lay his hand on the goat's head and slaughter it at the place where the burnt offering is slaughtered before the LORD. It is a sin offering. **25**Then the priest shall take some of the blood of the sin offering with his finger and put it on the horns of the altar of burnt offering and pour out the rest of the blood at the base of the altar.[a] **26**He shall burn all the fat on the altar as he burned the fat of the fellowship offering. In this way the priest will make atonement for the man's sin, and he will be forgiven.[b]

27" 'If a member of the community sins unintentionally[c] and does what is forbidden in any of the LORD's commands, he is guilty. **28**When he is made aware of the sin he committed, he must bring as his offering[d] for the sin he committed a female goat[e] without defect. **29**He is to lay his hand on the head[f] of the sin offering[g] and slaughter it at the place of the burnt offering. **30**Then the priest is to take some of the blood with his finger and put it on the horns of the altar of burnt offering[h] and pour out the rest of the blood at the base of the altar. **31**He shall remove all the fat, just as the fat is removed from the fellowship offering, and the priest shall burn it on the altar as an aroma pleasing to the LORD.[i] In this way the priest will make atonement for him, and he will be forgiven.

32" 'If he brings a lamb as his sin offering, he is to bring a female without defect.[j] **33**He is to lay his hand on its head and slaughter it for a sin offering at the place where the burnt offering is slaughtered.[k] **34**Then the priest shall take some of the blood of the sin offering with his finger and put it on the horns of the altar of burnt offering and pour out the rest of the blood at the base of the altar.[l] **35**He shall remove all the fat, just as the fat is removed from the lamb of the fellowship offering, and the priest shall burn it on the altar[m] on top of the offerings made to the LORD by fire. In this way the priest will make atonement for him for the sin he has committed, and he will be forgiven.

5 " 'If a person sins because he does not speak up when he hears a public charge to testify[n] regarding something he has seen or learned about, he will be held responsible.[o]

2" 'Or if a person touches anything ceremonially unclean—whether the carcasses of unclean wild animals or of unclean livestock or of unclean creatures that move along the ground[p]—even though he is unaware of it, he has become unclean and is guilty.

3" 'Or if he touches human uncleanness[q]—anything that would make him unclean—even though he is unaware of it, when he learns of it he will be guilty.

4" 'Or if a person thoughtlessly takes an oath[r] to do anything, whether good or evil—in any matter one might carelessly swear about—even though he is unaware of it, in any case when he learns of it he will be guilty.

5" 'When anyone is guilty in any of these ways, he must confess[s] in what way he has sinned **6**and, as a penalty for the sin he has committed, he must bring to the LORD a female lamb or goat from the flock as a sin offering;[t] and the priest shall make atonement for him for his sin.

7" 'If he cannot afford[u] a lamb, he is to bring two doves or two young pigeons to the LORD as a penalty for his sin—one for a sin offering and the other for a burnt offering. **8**He is to bring them to the priest, who shall first offer the one for the sin offering. He is to wring its head from its neck,[v] not severing it completely,[w] **9**and is to sprinkle some of the blood of the sin offering against the side of the altar; the rest of the blood must be drained out at the base of the altar.[x] It is a sin offering. **10**The priest shall then offer the other

4:15 [q] Lev 1:4; 8:14, 22; Nu 8:10
4:16 [r] ver 5
4:17 [s] ver 6
4:18 [t] ver 7
4:19 [u] ver 8
4:20 [v] Heb 10:10-12 [w] Nu 15:25
4:21 [x] Lev 16:5,15
4:22 [y] Nu 31:13 [z] ver 2
4:25 [a] ver 7,18,30, 34; Lev 9:9
4:26 [b] Lev 5:10
4:27 [c] ver 2; Nu 15:27
4:28 [d] ver 23 [e] ver 3
4:29 [f] ver 4,24 [g] Lev 1:4
4:30 [h] ver 7
4:31 [i] Ge 8:21
4:32 [j] ver 28
4:33 [k] ver 29
4:34 [l] ver 7
4:35 [m] ver 26,31
5:1 [n] Pr 29:24 [o] ver 17
5:2 [p] Lev 11:11, 24-40; Dt 14:8
5:3 [q] Nu 19:11-16
5:4 [r] Nu 30:6,8
5:5 [s] Lev 16:21; 26:40; Nu 5:7; Pr 28:13
5:6 [t] Lev 4:28
5:7 [u] Lev 12:8; 14:21
5:8 [v] Lev 1:15 [w] Lev 1:17
5:9 [x] Lev 4:7,18

as a burnt offering in the prescribed
way[y] and make atonement for him for
the sin he has committed, and he will
be forgiven.[z]
11" 'If, however, he cannot afford
two doves or two young pigeons, he
is to bring as an offering for his sin a
tenth of an ephah[a] of fine flour[a] for a
sin offering. He must not put oil or incense on it, because it is a sin offering.
12He is to bring it to the priest, who
shall take a handful of it as a memorial
portion and burn it on the altar on top
of the offerings made to the LORD by
fire. It is a sin offering. 13In this way the
priest will make atonement[b] for him
for any of these sins he has committed,
and he will be forgiven. The rest of the
offering will belong to the priest,[c] as
in the case of the grain offering.' "

The Guilt Offering

14The LORD said to Moses: 15"When a
person commits a violation and sins
unintentionally in regard to any of the
LORD's holy things, he is to bring to
the LORD as a penalty[d] a ram[e] from
the flock, one without defect and of the
proper value in silver, according to the
sanctuary shekel.[b][f] It is a guilt offering. 16He must make restitution[g] for
what he has failed to do in regard to the
holy things, add a fifth of the value[h] to
that and give it all to the priest, who
will make atonement for him with the
ram as a guilt offering, and he will be
forgiven.
17"If a person sins and does what is
forbidden in any of the LORD's commands, even though he does not know
it,[i] he is guilty and will be held responsible. 18He is to bring to the priest
as a guilt offering a ram from the flock,
one without defect and of the proper
value. In this way the priest will make
atonement for him for the wrong he
has committed unintentionally, and he
will be forgiven.[j] 19It is a guilt offering; he has been guilty of[c] wrongdoing
against the LORD."
6 The LORD said to Moses: 2"If anyone
sins and is unfaithful to the LORD[k]
by deceiving his neighbor[l] about
something entrusted to him or left in
his care[m] or stolen, or if he cheats him,
3or if he finds lost property and lies
about it,[n] or if he swears falsely, or if
he commits any such sin that people
may do— 4when he thus sins and becomes guilty, he must return[o] what he
has stolen or taken by extortion, or
what was entrusted to him, or the lost
property he found, 5or whatever it was
he swore falsely about. He must make
restitution[p] in full, add a fifth of the
value to it and give it all to the owner
on the day he presents his guilt offering.[q] 6And as a penalty he must bring
to the priest, that is, to the LORD, his
guilt offering,[r] a ram from the flock,
one without defect and of the proper
value. 7In this way the priest will make
atonement[s] for him before the LORD,
and he will be forgiven for any of these
things he did that made him guilty."

The Burnt Offering

8The LORD said to Moses: 9"Give Aaron and his sons this command: 'These
are the regulations for the burnt offering: The burnt offering is to remain on
the altar hearth throughout the night,
till morning, and the fire must be kept
burning on the altar. 10The priest shall
then put on his linen clothes, with lin-
en undergarments next to his body,[t]
and shall remove the ashes of the burnt
offering that the fire has consumed on
the altar and place them beside the altar. 11Then he is to take off these
clothes and put on others, and carry
the ashes outside the camp to a place
that is ceremonially clean.[u] 12The fire
on the altar must be kept burning; it
must not go out. Every morning the
priest is to add firewood and arrange
the burnt offering on the fire and burn
the fat of the fellowship offerings[d] on
it. 13The fire must be kept burning on
the altar continuously; it must not go
out.

The Grain Offering

14" 'These are the regulations for the
grain offering:[v] Aaron's sons are to
bring it before the LORD, in front of the
altar. 15The priest is to take a handful of
fine flour and oil, together with all the
incense on the grain offering,[w] and
burn the memorial portion[x] on the altar as an aroma pleasing to the LORD.
16Aaron and his sons[y] shall eat the
rest[z] of it, but it is to be eaten without
yeast[a] in a holy place;[b] they are to eat
it in the courtyard of the Tent of Meeting. 17It must not be baked with yeast;
I have given it as their share of the offerings made to me by fire. Like the sin
offering and the guilt offering, it is
most holy.[c] 18Any male descendant of
Aaron may eat it.[d] It is his regular
share of the offerings made to the LORD
by fire for the generations to come.

5:10 [y]Lev 1:14-17 [z]Lev 4:26 **5:11** [a]Lev 2:1 **5:13** [b]Lev 4:26 [c]Lev 2:3 **5:15** [d]Lev 22:14 [e]Nu 5:8 [f]Ex 30:13 **5:16** [g]Lev 6:4 [h]Lev 22:14; Nu 5:7 **5:17** [i]ver 15; Lev 4:2 **5:18** [j]ver 15 **6:2** [k]Nu 5:6; Ac 5:4; Col 3:9 [l]Pr 24:28 [m]Ex 22:7 **6:3** [n]Dt 22:1-3 **6:4** [o]Lk 19:8 **6:5** [p]Nu 5:7

[q]Lev 5:15 **6:6** [r]Lev 5:15 **6:7** [s]Lev 4:26 **6:10** [t]Ex 28:39-42, 43; 39:28 **6:11** [u]Lev 4:12 **6:14** [v]Lev 2:1; 15:4 **6:15** [w]Lev 2:9 [x]Lev 2:2 **6:16** [y]Lev 2:3 [z]Eze 44:29 [a]Lev 2:11 [b]Lev 10:13 **6:17** [c]ver 29; Ex 40:10; Nu 18:9,10 **6:18** [d]ver 29; Nu 18:9-10

a *11* That is, probably about 2 quarts (about 2 liters) **b** *15* That is, about 2/5 ounce (about 11.5 grams) **c** *19* Or *has made full expiation for his* **d** *12* Traditionally *peace offerings*

Whatever touches them will become holy.[a][e]' "

19The LORD also said to Moses, 20"This is the offering Aaron and his sons are to bring to the LORD on the day he[b] is anointed: a tenth of an ephah[c][f] of fine flour as a regular grain offering,[g] half of it in the morning and half in the evening. 21Prepare it with oil on a griddle;[h] bring it well-mixed and present the grain offering broken[d] in pieces as an aroma pleasing to the LORD. 22The son who is to succeed him as anointed priest shall prepare it. It is the LORD's regular share and is to be burned completely. 23Every grain offering of a priest shall be burned completely; it must not be eaten."

The Sin Offering

24The LORD said to Moses, 25"Say to Aaron and his sons: 'These are the regulations for the sin offering: The sin offering is to be slaughtered before the LORD[i] in the place[j] the burnt offering is slaughtered; it is most holy. 26The priest who offers it shall eat it; it is to be eaten in a holy place,[k] in the courtyard[l] of the Tent of Meeting. 27Whatever touches any of the flesh will become holy,[m] and if any of the blood is spattered on a garment, you must wash it in a holy place. 28The clay pot[n] the meat is cooked in must be broken; but if it is cooked in a bronze pot, the pot is to be scoured and rinsed with water. 29Any male in a priest's family may eat it;[o] it is most holy.[p] 30But any sin offering whose blood is brought into the Tent of Meeting to make atonement in the Holy Place[q] must not be eaten; it must be burned.[r]

The Guilt Offering

7 " 'These are the regulations for the guilt offering,[s] which is most holy: 2The guilt offering is to be slaughtered in the place where the burnt offering is slaughtered, and its blood is to be sprinkled against the altar on all sides. 3All its fat[t] shall be offered: the fat tail and the fat that covers the inner parts, 4both kidneys with the fat on them near the loins, and the covering of the liver, which is to be removed with the kidneys. 5The priest shall burn them on the altar as an offering made to the LORD by fire. It is a guilt offering. 6Any male in a priest's family may eat it,[u] but it must be eaten in a holy place; it is most holy.[v]

7" 'The same law applies to both the sin offering and the guilt offering: They belong to the priest[w] who makes atonement with them. 8The priest who offers a burnt offering for anyone may keep its hide for himself. 9Every grain offering baked in an oven or cooked in a pan or on a griddle[x] belongs to the priest who offers it, 10and every grain offering, whether mixed with oil or dry, belongs equally to all the sons of Aaron.

The Fellowship Offering

11" 'These are the regulations for the fellowship offering[e] a person may present to the LORD:

12" 'If he offers it as an expression of thankfulness, then along with this thank offering[y] he is to offer cakes of bread made without yeast and mixed with oil, wafers[z] made without yeast and spread with oil, and cakes of fine flour well-kneaded and mixed with oil. 13Along with his fellowship offering of thanksgiving he is to present an offering with cakes of bread made with yeast.[a] 14He is to bring one of each kind as an offering, a contribution to the LORD; it belongs to the priest who sprinkles the blood of the fellowship offerings. 15The meat of his fellowship offering of thanksgiving must be eaten on the day it is offered; he must leave none of it till morning.[b]

16" 'If, however, his offering is the result of a vow or is a freewill offering, the sacrifice shall be eaten on the day he offers it, but anything left over may be eaten on the next day.[c] 17Any meat of the sacrifice left over till the third day must be burned up. 18If any meat of the fellowship offering is eaten on the third day, it will not be accepted.[d] It will not be credited[e] to the one who offered it, for it is impure; the person who eats any of it will be held responsible.

19" 'Meat that touches anything ceremonially unclean must not be eaten; it must be burned up. As for other meat, anyone ceremonially clean may eat it. 20But if anyone who is unclean eats any meat of the fellowship offering belonging to the LORD, that person must be cut off from his people.[f] 21If anyone touches something unclean[g]—whether human uncleanness or an unclean animal or any unclean, detestable thing—and then eats any of the meat of the fellowship offering belonging to the LORD, that person must be cut off from his people.' "

6:18 *e*ver 27
6:20 *f*Ex 16:36 *g*Ex 29:2
6:21 *h*Lev 2:5
6:25 *i*Lev 1:3 *j*Lev 1:5,11
6:26 *k*ver 16 *l*Lev 10:17-18
6:27 *m*Ex 29:37
6:28 *n*Lev 11:33; 15:12
6:29 *o*ver 18 *p*ver 17
6:30 *q*Lev 4:18 *r*Lev 4:12
7:1 *s*Lev 5:14-6:7
7:3 *t*Ex 29:13; Lev 3:4,9
7:6 *u*Lev 6:18; Nu 18:9-10 *v*Lev 2:3
7:7 *w*Lev 6:17,26; 1Co 9:13
7:9 *x*Lev 2:5
7:12 *y*ver 13,15 *z*Lev 2:4; Nu 6:15
7:13 *a*Lev 23:17; Am 4:5
7:15 *b*Lev 22:30
7:16 *c*Lev 19:5-8
7:18 *d*Lev 19:7 *e*Nu 18:27
7:20 *f*Lev 22:3-7
7:21 *g*Lev 5:2; 11:24,28

a *18* Or *Whoever touches them must be holy*; similarly in verse 27 **b** *20* Or *each* **c** *20* That is, probably about 2 quarts (about 2 liters) **d** *21* The meaning of the Hebrew for this word is uncertain. **e** *11* Traditionally *peace offering*; also in verses 13-37

Eating Fat and Blood Forbidden

22The LORD said to Moses, 23"Say to
the Israelites: 'Do not eat any of the fat
of cattle, sheep or goats.[h] 24The fat of
an animal found dead or torn by wild
animals[i] may be used for any other
purpose, but you must not eat it.
25Anyone who eats the fat of an animal
from which an offering by fire may be[a]
made to the LORD must be cut off from
his people. 26And wherever you live,
you must not eat the blood[j] of any
bird or animal. 27If anyone eats
blood,[k] that person must be cut off
from his people.' "

The Priests' Share

28The LORD said to Moses, 29"Say to
the Israelites: 'Anyone who brings a fellowship offering to the LORD is to bring
part of it as his sacrifice to the LORD.
30With his own hands he is to bring the
offering made to the LORD by fire; he
is to bring the fat, together with the
breast, and wave the breast before the
LORD as a wave offering.[l] 31The priest
shall burn the fat on the altar, but the
breast belongs to Aaron and his sons.[m]
32You are to give the right thigh of your
fellowship offerings to the priest as a
contribution.[n] 33The son of Aaron
who offers the blood and the fat of the
fellowship offering shall have the right
thigh as his share. 34From the fellowship offerings of the Israelites, I have
taken the breast that is waved and the
thigh[o] that is presented and have giv-
en them to Aaron the priest and his
sons[p] as their regular share from the
Israelites.' "
35This is the portion of the offerings
made to the LORD by fire that were allotted to Aaron and his sons on the day
they were presented to serve the LORD
as priests. 36On the day they were
anointed,[q] the LORD commanded that
the Israelites give this to them as their
regular share for the generations to
come.

37These, then, are the regulations for
the burnt offering,[r] the grain offering,[s] the sin offering, the guilt offering, the ordination offering[t] and the
fellowship offering, 38which the LORD
gave Moses on Mount Sinai on the day
he commanded the Israelites to bring
their offerings to the LORD,[u] in the
Desert of Sinai.

The Ordination of Aaron and His Sons

8 The LORD said to Moses, 2"Bring Aaron and his sons, their garments, the
anointing oil,[v] the bull for the sin
offering, the two rams and the basket containing bread made without
yeast,[w] 3and gather the entire assembly[x] at the entrance to the Tent of
Meeting." 4Moses did as the LORD commanded him, and the assembly gathered at the entrance to the Tent of
Meeting.
5Moses said to the assembly, "This is
what the LORD has commanded to be
done." 6Then Moses brought Aaron
and his sons forward and washed them
with water.[y] 7He put the tunic on Aaron, tied the sash around him, clothed
him with the robe and put the ephod
on him. He also tied the ephod to him
by its skillfully woven waistband; so it
was fastened on him.[z] 8He placed the
breastpiece on him and put the Urim
and Thummim[a] in the breastpiece.
9Then he placed the turban on Aaron's
head and set the gold plate, the sacred
diadem,[b] on the front of it, as the
LORD commanded Moses.
10Then Moses took the anointing
oil[c] and anointed[d] the tabernacle
and everything in it, and so consecrated them. 11He sprinkled some of the oil
on the altar seven times, anointing the
altar and all its utensils and the basin
with its stand, to consecrate them.[e]
12He poured some of the anointing oil
on Aaron's head and anointed[f] him to
consecrate him.[g] 13Then he brought
Aaron's sons forward, put tunics on
them, tied sashes around them and put

7:23 [h]Lev 3:17; 17:13-14 **7:24** [i]Ex 22:31 **7:26** [j]Ge 9:4 **7:27** [k]Lev 17:10-24; Ac 15:20,29 **7:30** [l]Ex 29:24; Nu 6:20 **7:31** [m]ver 34 **7:32** [n]ver 34; Lev 9:21; Nu 6:20 **7:34** [o]Lev 10:15 [p]Ex 29:27; Nu 18:18-19 **7:36** [q]Ex 40:13,15; Lev 8:12,30 **7:37** [r]Lev 6:9 [s]Lev 6:14 [t]ver 1,11 **7:38** [u]Lev 1:2 **8:2** [v]Ex 30:23-25, 30 [w]Ex 29:2-3 **8:3** [x]Nu 8:9 **8:6** [y]Ex 29:4; 30:19; Ps 26:6; Ac 22:16; 1Co 6:11; Eph 5:26 **8:7** [z]Ex 28:4 **8:8** [a]Ex 28:30 **8:9** [b]Ex 28:36 **8:10** [c]ver 2 [d]Ex 30:26 **8:11** [e]Ex 30:29 **8:12** [f]Lev 21:10,12 [g]Ex 30:30

[a]25 Or *fire is*

8:1 – 9:24

PROMISE 7

OUR HIGH CALLING

The elaborate ceremony used to ordain Israel's priests demonstrated the dignity of their office. Each priest acted as a liaison between God and the people; his task was to represent God to the people and to approach God with the people's concerns.

When Peter wrote, "But you are a chosen people, a royal priesthood, a holy nation, a people belonging to God" (1 Peter 2:9), he declared each Christian a priest and put both privilege and responsibility on each of us. Even though we don't participate in a ceremony as did Israel's priests, we still have a high and holy calling to act as God's representatives to lost people and to our brothers and sisters in Christ. Read these chapters and take a moment, privately, to acknowledge your role as God's priest. Thank him for this privilege, and recommit your life to fulfilling this function in the most effective way possible.

For the next Promise 7 reading go to page 180.

headbands on them, as the LORD commanded Moses.

14He then presented the bull[h] for the sin offering,[i] and Aaron and his sons laid their hands on its head. **15**Moses slaughtered the bull and took some of the blood, and with his finger he put it on all the horns of the altar[j] to purify the altar.[k] He poured out the rest of the blood at the base of the altar. So he consecrated it to make atonement for it.[l] **16**Moses also took all the fat around the inner parts, the covering of the liver, and both kidneys and their fat, and burned it on the altar. **17**But the bull with its hide and its flesh and its offal[m] he burned up outside the camp,[n] as the LORD commanded Moses.

18He then presented the ram[o] for the burnt offering, and Aaron and his sons laid their hands on its head. **19**Then Moses slaughtered the ram and sprinkled the blood against the altar on all sides. **20**He cut the ram into pieces and burned the head, the pieces and the fat. **21**He washed the inner parts and the legs with water and burned the whole ram on the altar as a burnt offering, a pleasing aroma, an offering made to the LORD by fire, as the LORD commanded Moses.

22He then presented the other ram, the ram for the ordination,[p] and Aaron and his sons laid their hands on its head. **23**Moses slaughtered the ram and took some of its blood and put it on the lobe of Aaron's right ear, on the thumb of his right hand and on the big toe of his right foot. **24**Moses also brought Aaron's sons forward and put some of the blood on the lobes of their right ears, on the thumbs of their right hands and on the big toes of their right feet. Then he sprinkled blood against the altar on all sides.[q] **25**He took the fat, the fat tail, all the fat around the inner parts, the covering of the liver, both kidneys and their fat and the right thigh. **26**Then from the basket of bread made without yeast, which was before the LORD, he took a cake of bread, and one made with oil, and a wafer; he put these on the fat portions and on the right thigh. **27**He put all these in the hands of Aaron and his sons and waved them before the LORD as a wave offering. **28**Then Moses took them from their hands and burned them on the altar on top of the burnt offering as an ordination offering, a pleasing aroma, an offering made to the LORD by fire. **29**He also took the breast—Moses' share of the ordination ram[r]—and waved it before the LORD as a wave offering, as the LORD commanded Moses.

30Then Moses took some of the anointing oil and some of the blood from the altar and sprinkled them on Aaron and his garments[s] and on his sons and their garments. So he consecrated[t] Aaron and his garments and his sons and their garments.

31Moses then said to Aaron and his sons, "Cook the meat at the entrance to the Tent of Meeting and eat it there with the bread from the basket of ordination offerings, as I commanded, saying,[a] 'Aaron and his sons are to eat it.' **32**Then burn up the rest of the meat and the bread. **33**Do not leave the entrance to the Tent of Meeting for seven days, until the days of your ordination are completed, for your ordination will last seven days. **34**What has been done today was commanded by the LORD[u] to make atonement for you. **35**You must stay at the entrance to the Tent of Meeting day and night for seven days and do what the LORD requires,[v] so you will not die; for that is what I have been commanded." **36**So Aaron and his sons did everything the LORD commanded through Moses.

The Priests Begin Their Ministry

9 On the eighth day[w] Moses summoned Aaron and his sons and the elders of Israel. **2**He said to Aaron, "Take a bull calf for your sin offering and a ram for your burnt offering, both without defect, and present them before the LORD. **3**Then say to the Israelites: 'Take a male goat for a sin offering, a calf and a lamb—both a year old and without defect—for a burnt offering, **4**and an ox[b] and a ram for a fellowship offering[c] to sacrifice before the LORD, together with a grain offering mixed with oil. For today the LORD will appear to you.[x]' "

5They took the things Moses commanded to the front of the Tent of Meeting, and the entire assembly came near and stood before the LORD. **6**Then Moses said, "This is what the LORD has commanded you to do, so that the glory of the LORD[y] may appear to you."

7Moses said to Aaron, "Come to the altar and sacrifice your sin offering and your burnt offering and make atonement for yourself and the people; sacrifice the offering that is for the people and make atonement for them, as the LORD has commanded.[z]"

8:14 [h]Lev 4:3 [i]Ps 66:15; Eze 43:19
8:15 [j]Lev 4:7 [k]Heb 9:22 [l]Eze 43:20
8:17 [m]Lev 4:11 [n]Lev 4:12
8:18 [o]ver 2
8:22 [p]ver 2
8:24 [q]Heb 9:18-22
8:29 [r]Lev 7:31-34
8:30 [s]Ex 28:2 [t]Nu 3:3
8:34 [u]Heb 7:16
8:35 [v]Nu 3:7; 9:19; Dt 11:1; 1Ki 2:3; Eze 48:11
9:1 [w]Eze 43:27
9:4 [x]Ex 29:43
9:6 [y]ver 23; Ex 24:16
9:7 [z]Heb 5:1,3; 7:27

[a] *31* Or *I was commanded:* [b] *4* The Hebrew word can include both male and female; also in verses 18 and 19. [c] *4* Traditionally *peace offering*; also in verses 18 and 22

8 So Aaron came to the altar and
slaughtered the calf as a sin offering[a]
for himself. 9 His sons brought the
blood to him,[b] and he dipped his finger into the blood and put it on the
horns of the altar; the rest of the blood
he poured out at the base of the altar.[c]
10 On the altar he burned the fat, the
kidneys and the covering of the liver
from the sin offering, as the LORD commanded Moses; 11 the flesh and the
hide[d] he burned up outside the
camp.[e]

12 Then he slaughtered the burnt offering. His sons handed him the blood,
and he sprinkled it against the altar on
all sides. 13 They handed him the burnt
offering piece by piece, including the
head, and he burned them on the altar.[f] 14 He washed the inner parts and
the legs and burned them on top of the
burnt offering on the altar.

15 Aaron then brought the offering
that was for the people.[g] He took the
goat for the people's sin offering and
slaughtered it and offered it for a sin
offering as he did with the first one.

16 He brought the burnt offering and
offered it in the prescribed way.[h] 17 He
also brought the grain offering, took a
handful of it and burned it on the altar
in addition to the morning's burnt offering.[i]

18 He slaughtered the ox and the ram
as the fellowship offering for the people.[j] His sons handed him the blood,
and he sprinkled it against the altar on
all sides. 19 But the fat portions of the ox
and the ram—the fat tail, the layer of
fat, the kidneys and the covering of the
liver— 20 these they laid on the breasts,
and then Aaron burned the fat on the
altar. 21 Aaron waved the breasts and
the right thigh before the LORD as
a wave offering,[k] as Moses commanded.

22 Then Aaron lifted his hands toward the people and blessed them.[l]
And having sacrificed the sin offering,
the burnt offering and the fellowship
offering, he stepped down.

23 Moses and Aaron then went into
the Tent of Meeting. When they came
out, they blessed the people; and the
glory of the LORD[m] appeared to all the
people. 24 Fire[n] came out from
the presence of the LORD and consumed the burnt offering and the fat
portions on the altar. And when all the
people saw it, they shouted for joy and
fell facedown.[o]

The Death of Nadab and Abihu

10 Aaron's sons Nadab and Abihu[p]
took their censers, put fire in
them[q] and added incense; and they
offered unauthorized fire before the
LORD, contrary to his command.[r] 2 So
fire came out from the presence of the
LORD and consumed them,[s] and they
died before the LORD. 3 Moses then said
to Aaron, "This is what the LORD spoke
of when he said:

" 'Among those who approach
me[t]
I will show myself holy;[u]
in the sight of all the people
I will be honored.[v]' "

Aaron remained silent.

4 Moses summoned Mishael and Elzaphan,[w] sons of Aaron's uncle Uzziel,[x] and said to them, "Come here;
carry your cousins outside the camp,[y]
away from the front of the sanctuary."
5 So they came and carried them, still in
their tunics,[z] outside the camp, as
Moses ordered.

6 Then Moses said to Aaron and his
sons Eleazar and Ithamar, "Do not let
your hair become unkempt,[a][a] and do
not tear your clothes, or you will die
and the LORD will be angry with the
whole community.[b] But your relatives, all the house of Israel, may
mourn for those the LORD has destroyed by fire. 7 Do not leave the entrance to the Tent of Meeting or you
will die, because the LORD's anointing
oil[c] is on you." So they did as Moses
said.

8 Then the LORD said to Aaron, 9 "You
and your sons are not to drink wine[d]
or other fermented drink[e] whenever
you go into the Tent of Meeting, or you
will die. This is a lasting ordinance for
the generations to come. 10 You must
distinguish between the holy and the
common, between the unclean and the
clean,[f] 11 and you must teach[g] the Israelites all the decrees the LORD has
given them through Moses.[h]"

3 →PG. 122

12 Moses said to Aaron and his remaining sons, Eleazar and Ithamar,
"Take the grain offering left over from
the offerings made to the LORD by fire
and eat it prepared without yeast beside the altar,[i] for it is most holy. 13 Eat
it in a holy place, because it is your
share and your sons' share of the offerings made to the LORD by fire; for so I
have been commanded. 14 But you and
your sons and your daughters may eat
the breast that was waved and the
thigh that was presented. Eat them in a
ceremonially clean place;[j] they have
been given to you and your children as
your share of the Israelites' fellowship

9:8 *a* Lev 4:1-12
9:9 *b* ver 12,18 *c* Lev 4:7
9:11 *d* Lev 4:11 *e* Lev 4:12; 8:17
9:13 *f* Lev 1:8
9:15 *g* Lev 4:27-31
9:16 *h* Lev 1:1-13
9:17 *i* Lev 2:1-2; 3:5
9:18 *j* Lev 3:1-11
9:21 *k* Ex 29:24,26; Lev 7:30-34
9:22 *l* Nu 6:23; Dt 21:5; Lk 24:50
9:23 *m* ver 6
9:24 *n* Jdg 6:21; 2Ch 7:1 *o* 1Ki 18:39
10:1 *p* Ex 24:1; Nu 3:2-4; 26:61 *q* Lev 16:12 *r* Ex 30:9
10:2 *s* Nu 3:4; 16:35; 26:61
10:3 *t* Ex 19:22 *u* Ex 30:29; Lev 21:6; Eze 28:22 *v* Ex Isa 49:3
10:4 *w* Ex 6:22 *x* Ex 6:18 *y* Ac 5:6,9,10
10:5 *z* Lev 8:13
10:6 *a* Lev 21:10 *b* Nu 1:53; 16:22; Jos 7:1; 22:18; 2Sa 24:1
10:7 *c* Ex 28:41; Lev 21:12
10:9 *d* Hos 4:11 *e* Pr 20:1; Isa 28:7; Eze 44:21; Lk 1:15; Eph 5:18; 1Ti 3:3; Tit 1:7
10:10 *f* Lev 11:47; 20:25; Eze 22:26
10:11 *g* Mal 2:7 *h* Dt 24:8
10:12 *i* Lev 6:14-18; 21:22
10:14 *j* Ex 29:24, 26-27; Lev 7:31,34; Nu 18:11

a 6 Or *Do not uncover your heads*

offerings.[a] 15The thigh[k] that was presented and the breast that was waved must be brought with the fat portions of the offerings made by fire, to be waved before the LORD as a wave offering. This will be the regular share for you and your children, as the LORD has commanded."

16When Moses inquired about the goat of the sin offering[l] and found that it had been burned up, he was angry with Eleazar and Ithamar, Aaron's remaining sons, and asked, 17"Why didn't you eat the sin offering[m] in the sanctuary area? It is most holy; it was given to you to take away the guilt of the community by making atonement for them before the LORD. 18Since its blood was not taken into the Holy Place,[n] you should have eaten the goat in the sanctuary area, as I commanded."

19Aaron replied to Moses, "Today they sacrificed their sin offering and their burnt offering[o] before the LORD, but such things as this have happened to me. Would the LORD have been pleased if I had eaten the sin offering today?" 20When Moses heard this, he was satisfied.

Clean and Unclean Food

11 The LORD said to Moses and Aaron, 2"Say to the Israelites: 'Of all the animals that live on land, these are the ones you may eat:[p] 3You may eat any animal that has a split hoof completely divided and that chews the cud.

4" 'There are some that only chew the cud or only have a split hoof, but you must not eat them. The camel, though it chews the cud, does not have a split hoof; it is ceremonially unclean for you. 5The coney,[b] though it chews the cud, does not have a split hoof; it is unclean for you. 6The rabbit, though it chews the cud, does not have a split hoof; it is unclean for you. 7And the pig,[q] though it has a split hoof completely divided, does not chew the cud; it is unclean for you. 8You must not eat their meat or touch their carcasses; they are unclean for you.[r]

9" 'Of all the creatures living in the water of the seas and the streams, you may eat any that have fins and scales. 10But all creatures in the seas or streams that do not have fins and scales—whether among all the swarming things or among all the other living creatures in the water—you are to detest.[s] 11And since you are to detest them, you must not eat their meat and you must detest their carcasses. 12Anything living in the water that does not have fins and scales is to be detestable to you.

13" 'These are the birds you are to detest and not eat because they are detestable: the eagle, the vulture, the black vulture, 14the red kite, any kind of black kite, 15any kind of raven, 16the horned owl, the screech owl, the gull, any kind of hawk, 17the little owl, the cormorant, the great owl, 18the white owl, the desert owl, the osprey, 19the stork, any kind of heron, the hoopoe and the bat.[c]

20" 'All flying insects that walk on all fours are to be detestable to you.[t] 21There are, however, some winged creatures that walk on all fours that you may eat: those that have jointed legs for hopping on the ground. 22Of these you may eat any kind of locust,[u] katydid, cricket or grasshopper. 23But all other winged creatures that have four legs you are to detest.

24" 'You will make yourselves unclean by these; whoever touches their carcasses will be unclean till evening. 25Whoever picks up one of their carcasses must wash his clothes,[v] and he will be unclean till evening.[w]

26" 'Every animal that has a split hoof not completely divided or that does not chew the cud is unclean for you; whoever touches ⌞the carcass of⌟ any of them will be unclean. 27Of all the animals that walk on all fours, those that walk on their paws are unclean for you; whoever touches their carcasses will be unclean till evening. 28Anyone who picks up their carcasses must wash his clothes, and he will be unclean till evening. They are unclean for you.

29" 'Of the animals that move about on the ground, these are unclean for you: the weasel, the rat,[x] any kind of great lizard, 30the gecko, the monitor lizard, the wall lizard, the skink and the chameleon. 31Of all those that move along the ground, these are unclean for you. Whoever touches them when they are dead will be unclean till evening. 32When one of them dies and falls on something, that article, whatever its use, will be unclean, whether it is made of wood, cloth, hide or sackcloth.[y] Put it in water; it will be unclean till evening, and then it will be clean. 33If one of them falls into a clay pot, everything in it will be unclean, and you must break the pot.[z] 34Any food that could be eaten but has water on it from such

10:15 [k]Lev 7:34
10:16 [l]Lev 9:3
10:17 [m]Lev 6:24-30
10:18 [n]Lev 6:26,30
10:19 [o]Lev 9:12
11:2 [p]Ac 10:12-14
11:7 [q]Isa 65:4; 66:3, 17
11:8 [r]Isa 52:11; Heb 9:10
11:10 [s]Lev 7:18
11:20 [t]Ac 10:14
11:22 [u]Mt 3:4; Mk 1:6
11:25 [v]Lev 14:8,47; 15:5 [w]ver 40; Nu 31:24
11:29 [x]Isa 66:17
11:32 [y]Lev 15:12
11:33 [z]Lev 6:28; 15:12

[a] *14* Traditionally *peace offerings* [b] *5* That is, the hyrax or rock badger [c] *19* The precise identification of some of the birds, insects and animals in this chapter is uncertain.

a pot is unclean, and any liquid that could be drunk from it is unclean. 35 Anything that one of their carcasses falls on becomes unclean; an oven or cooking pot must be broken up. They are unclean, and you are to regard them as unclean. 36 A spring, however, or a cistern for collecting water remains clean, but anyone who touches one of these carcasses is unclean. 37 If a carcass falls on any seeds that are to be planted, they remain clean. 38 But if water has been put on the seed and a carcass falls on it, it is unclean for you.

39 " 'If an animal that you are allowed to eat dies, anyone who touches the carcass will be unclean till evening. 40 Anyone who eats some of the carcass must wash his clothes, and he will be unclean till evening.[a] Anyone who picks up the carcass must wash his clothes, and he will be unclean till evening.

41 " 'Every creature that moves about on the ground is detestable; it is not to be eaten. 42 You are not to eat any creature that moves about on the ground, whether it moves on its belly or walks on all fours or on many feet; it is detestable. 43 Do not defile yourselves by any of these creatures.[b] Do not make yourselves unclean by means of them or be made unclean by them. 44 I am the LORD your God;[c] consecrate yourselves[d] and be holy,[e] because I am holy.[f] Do not make yourselves unclean by any creature that moves about on the ground. 45 I am the LORD who brought you up out of Egypt[g] to be your God;[h] therefore be holy, because I am holy.[i]

3 →PG. 131

46 " 'These are the regulations concerning animals, birds, every living thing that moves in the water and every creature that moves about on the ground. 47 You must distinguish between the unclean and the clean, between living creatures that may be eaten and those that may not be eaten.[j] ' "

Purification After Childbirth

12 The LORD said to Moses, 2 "Say to the Israelites: 'A woman who becomes pregnant and gives birth to a son will be ceremonially unclean for seven days, just as she is unclean during her monthly period.[k] 3 On the eighth day the boy is to be circumcised.[l] 4 Then the woman must wait thirty-three days to be purified from her bleeding. She must not touch anything sacred or go to the sanctuary until the days of her purification are over. 5 If she gives birth to a daughter, for two weeks the woman will be unclean, as during her period. Then she must wait sixty-six days to be purified from her bleeding.

6 " 'When the days of her purification for a son or daughter are over,[m] she is to bring to the priest at the entrance to the Tent of Meeting a year-old lamb[n] for a burnt offering and a young pigeon or a dove for a sin offering.[o] 7 He shall offer them before the LORD to make atonement for her, and then she will be ceremonially clean from her flow of blood.

" 'These are the regulations for the woman who gives birth to a boy or a girl. 8 If she cannot afford a lamb, she is to bring two doves or two young pigeons,[p] one for a burnt offering and the other for a sin offering.[q] In this way the priest will make atonement for her, and she will be clean.[r] ' "

Regulations About Infectious Skin Diseases

13 The LORD said to Moses and Aaron, 2 "When anyone has a swelling[s] or a rash or a bright spot[t] on his skin that may become an infectious skin

---

11:43–45 PROMISE 3

CHOW LINE REGULATIONS

Who could possibly remember all these dietary regulations? While the list may seem confusing to people like us who live with such modern conveniences as supermarkets, food expiration dates and refrigerators, God gave Israel these laws to protect his people from illness, pain and premature death. God knew what was healthy and what could potentially injure his people, and directed the Israelites to avoid the latter.

But verses 43–45 introduce a bigger issue. Here God reminds us that we are created for him, and gives us the incentive for obedience—the possibility for purity and the potential to have a relationship with him. Jesus (Matthew 15:11) and Paul (Galatians 3) taught us that we are not under these dietary laws today, but we still live under the timeless law of obedience to God.

Don't miss the crucial principle buried in these laws. Holiness is *always* a matter of obedience to God's Word. Pray that the Spirit will empower you so that your obedience will be evident to others.

For the next Promise 3 reading go to page 130.

11:40 [a] Lev 17:15; 22:8; Eze 44:31
11:43 [b] Lev 20:25
11:44 [c] Ex 6:2,7; Isa 43:3; 51:15 [d] Lev 20:7 [e] Ex 19:6 [f] Lev 19:2; Ps 99:3; Eph 1:4; 1Th 4:7; 1Pe 1:15,16*
11:45 [g] Lev 25:38,55; Ex 6:7; 20:2 [h] Ge 17:7 [i] Ex 19:6; 1Pe 1:16*
11:47 [j] Lev 10:10
12:2 [k] Lev 15:19; 18:19
12:3 [l] Ge 17:12; Lk 1:59; 2:21
12:6 [m] Lk 2:22 [n] Ex 29:38; Lev 23:12; Nu 6:12,14; 7:15 [o] Lev 5:7
12:8 [p] Ge 15:9; Lev 14:22 [q] Lev 5:7; Lk 2:22-24* [r] Lev 4:26
13:2 [s] ver 10,19,28, 43 [t] ver 4,38,39; Lev 14:56

disease,[a][u] he must be brought to Aaron the priest[v] or to one of his sons[b] who is a priest. 3The priest is to examine the sore on his skin, and if the hair in the sore has turned white and the sore appears to be more than skin deep,[c] it is an infectious skin disease. When the priest examines him, he shall pronounce him ceremonially unclean.[w] 4If the spot[x] on his skin is white but does not appear to be more than skin deep and the hair in it has not turned white, the priest is to put the infected person in isolation for seven days.[y] 5On the seventh day[z] the priest is to examine him,[a] and if he sees that the sore is unchanged and has not spread in the skin, he is to keep him in isolation another seven days. 6On the seventh day the priest is to examine him again, and if the sore has faded and has not spread in the skin, the priest shall pronounce him clean;[b] it is only a rash. The man must wash his clothes,[c] and he will be clean.[d] 7But if the rash does spread in his skin after he has shown himself to the priest to be pronounced clean, he must appear before the priest again.[e] 8The priest is to examine him, and if the rash has spread in the skin, he shall pronounce him unclean; it is an infectious disease.

9"When anyone has an infectious skin disease, he must be brought to the priest. 10The priest is to examine him, and if there is a white swelling in the skin that has turned the hair white and if there is raw flesh in the swelling, 11it is a chronic skin disease[f] and the priest shall pronounce him unclean. He is not to put him in isolation, because he is already unclean.

12"If the disease breaks out all over his skin and, so far as the priest can see, it covers all the skin of the infected person from head to foot, 13the priest is to examine him, and if the disease has covered his whole body, he shall pronounce that person clean. Since it has all turned white, he is clean. 14But whenever raw flesh appears on him, he will be unclean. 15When the priest sees the raw flesh, he shall pronounce him unclean. The raw flesh is unclean; he has an infectious disease.[g] 16Should the raw flesh change and turn white, he must go to the priest. 17The priest is to examine him, and if the sores have turned white, the priest shall pronounce the infected person clean;[h] then he will be clean.

18"When someone has a boil[i] on his skin and it heals, 19and in the place where the boil was, a white swelling or reddish-white[j] spot[k] appears, he must present himself to the priest. 20The priest is to examine it, and if it appears to be more than skin deep and the hair in it has turned white, the priest shall pronounce him unclean. It is an infectious skin disease[l] that has broken out where the boil was. 21But if, when the priest examines it, there is no white hair in it and it is not more than skin deep and has faded, then the priest is to put him in isolation for seven days. 22If it is spreading in the skin, the priest shall pronounce him unclean; it is infectious. 23But if the spot is unchanged and has not spread, it is only a scar from the boil, and the priest shall pronounce him clean.[m]

24"When someone has a burn on his skin and a reddish-white or white spot appears in the raw flesh of the burn, 25the priest is to examine the spot, and if the hair in it has turned white, and it appears to be more than skin deep, it is an infectious disease that has broken out in the burn. The priest shall pronounce him unclean; it is an infectious skin disease.[n] 26But if the priest examines it and there is no white hair in the spot and if it is not more than skin deep and has faded, then the priest is to put him in isolation for seven days.[o] 27On the seventh day the priest is to examine him,[p] and if it is spreading in the skin, the priest shall pronounce him unclean; it is an infectious skin disease. 28If, however, the spot is unchanged and has not spread in the skin but has faded, it is a swelling from the burn, and the priest shall pronounce him clean; it is only a scar from the burn.[q]

29"If a man or woman has a sore on the head[r] or on the chin, 30the priest is to examine the sore, and if it appears to be more than skin deep and the hair in it is yellow and thin, the priest shall pronounce that person unclean; it is an itch, an infectious disease of the head or chin. 31But if, when the priest examines this kind of sore, it does not seem to be more than skin deep and there is no black hair in it, then the priest is to put the infected person in isolation for seven days.[s] 32On the seventh day the priest is to examine the sore,[t] and if the itch has not spread and there is no yellow hair in it and it does not appear to be more than skin deep, 33he must be shaved except for the diseased area, and the priest is to keep him in isolation another seven days. 34On the sev-

13:2 [u]ver 3,9,15; Ex 4:6; Lev 14:3,32; Nu 5:2; Dt 24:8 [v]Dt 24:8 **13:3** [w]ver 8,11,20, 30; Lev 21:1; Nu 9:6 **13:4** [x]ver 2 [y]ver 5,21,26, 33,46; Lev 14:38; Nu 12:14,15; Dt 24:9 **13:5** [z]Lev 14:9 [a]ver 27,32,34, 51 **13:6** [b]ver 13,17,23, 28,34; Mt 8:3; Lk 5:12-14 [c]Lev 11:25 [d]Lev 11:25; 14:8,9,20,48; 15:8; Nu 8:7 **13:7** [e]Lk 5:14 **13:11** [f]Ex 4:6; Lev 14:8; Nu 12:10; Mt 8:2 **13:15** [g]ver 2 **13:17** [h]ver 6 **13:18** [i]Ex 9:9 **13:19** [j]ver 24,42; Lev 14:37 [k]ver 2 **13:20** [l]ver 2 **13:23** [m]ver 6 **13:25** [n]ver 11 **13:26** [o]ver 4 **13:27** [p]ver 5 **13:28** [q]ver 2 **13:29** [r]ver 43,44 **13:31** [s]ver 4 **13:32** [t]ver 5

[a]2 Traditionally *leprosy*; the Hebrew word was used for various diseases affecting the skin—not necessarily leprosy; also elsewhere in this chapter. [b]2 Or *descendants* [c]3 Or *be lower than the rest of the skin*; also elsewhere in this chapter

enth day the priest is to examine the
itch,[u] and if it has not spread in the
skin and appears to be no more than
skin deep, the priest shall pronounce
him clean. He must wash his clothes,
and he will be clean.[v] 35But if the itch
does spread in the skin after he is pronounced clean, 36the priest is to examine him, and if the itch has spread in
the skin, the priest does not need to
look for yellow hair; the person is unclean.[w] 37If, however, in his judgment
it is unchanged and black hair has
grown in it, the itch is healed. He is
clean, and the priest shall pronounce
him clean.

38"When a man or woman has white
spots on the skin, 39the priest is to examine them, and if the spots are dull
white, it is a harmless rash that has
broken out on the skin; that person is
clean.

40"When a man has lost his hair and
is bald,[x] he is clean. 41If he has lost his
hair from the front of his scalp and has
a bald forehead, he is clean. 42But if he
has a reddish-white sore on his bald
head or forehead, it is an infectious
disease breaking out on his head or
forehead. 43The priest is to examine
him, and if the swollen sore on his
head or forehead is reddish-white like
an infectious skin disease, 44the man
is diseased and is unclean. The priest
shall pronounce him unclean because
of the sore on his head.

45"The person with such an infectious disease must wear torn clothes,[y]
let his hair be unkempt,[a] cover the
lower part of his face[z] and cry out,
'Unclean! Unclean!'[a] 46As long as he
has the infection he remains unclean.
He must live alone; he must live outside the camp.[b]

Regulations About Mildew

47"If any clothing is contaminated
with mildew—any woolen or linen
clothing, 48any woven or knitted material of linen or wool, any leather or
anything made of leather— 49and if the
contamination in the clothing, or
leather, or woven or knitted material,
or any leather article, is greenish or
reddish, it is a spreading mildew and
must be shown to the priest.[c] 50The
priest is to examine the mildew[d] and
isolate the affected article for seven
days. 51On the seventh day he is to examine it,[e] and if the mildew has
spread in the clothing, or the woven or
knitted material, or the leather, whatever its use, it is a destructive mildew;
the article is unclean.[f] 52He must
burn up the clothing, or the woven or
knitted material of wool or linen, or
any leather article that has the contamination in it, because the mildew
is destructive; the article must be
burned up.[g]

53"But if, when the priest examines
it, the mildew has not spread in the
clothing, or the woven or knitted material, or the leather article, 54he shall
order that the contaminated article be
washed. Then he is to isolate it for another seven days. 55After the affected
article has been washed, the priest is to
examine it, and if the mildew has not
changed its appearance, even though it
has not spread, it is unclean. Burn it
with fire, whether the mildew has affected one side or the other. 56If, when
the priest examines it, the mildew has
faded after the article has been
washed, he is to tear the contaminated
part out of the clothing, or the leather,
or the woven or knitted material. 57But
if it reappears in the clothing, or in the
woven or knitted material, or in the
leather article, it is spreading, and
whatever has the mildew must be
burned with fire. 58The clothing, or the
woven or knitted material, or any
leather article that has been washed
and is rid of the mildew, must be
washed again, and it will be clean."

59These are the regulations concerning contamination by mildew in wool-
en or linen clothing, woven or knitted
material, or any leather article, for pro-
nouncing them clean or unclean.

Cleansing From Infectious Skin Diseases

14 The LORD said to Moses, 2"These
are the regulations for the diseased
person at the time of his ceremonial
cleansing, when he is brought to the
priest:[h] 3The priest is to go outside the
camp and examine him.[i] If the person has been healed of his infectious
skin disease,[b] 4the priest shall order
that two live clean birds and some cedar wood, scarlet yarn and hyssop be
brought for the one to be cleansed.[j]
5Then the priest shall order that one of
the birds be killed over fresh water in a
clay pot. 6He is then to take the live
bird and dip it, together with the cedar
wood, the scarlet yarn and the hyssop,
into the blood of the bird that was
killed over the fresh water.[k] 7Seven
times he shall sprinkle[l] the one to be
cleansed of the infectious disease and
pronounce him clean. Then he is to

13:34 [u]ver 5 [v]Lev 11:25 **13:36** [w]ver 30 **13:40** [x]Lev 21:5; 2Ki 2:23; Isa 3:24; 15:2; 22:12; Eze 27:31; 29:18; Am 8:10; Mic 1:16 **13:45** [y]Lev 10:6 [z]Eze 24:17,22; Mic 3:7 [a]Lev 5:2; La 4:15; Lk 17:12 **13:46** [b]Nu 5:1-4; 12:14; 2Ki 7:3; 15:5; Lk 17:12 **13:49** [c]Mk 1:44 **13:50** [d]Eze 44:23 **13:51** [e]ver 5 [f]Lev 14:44

13:52 [g]ver 55,57 **14:2** [h]Mt 8:2-4; Mk 1:40-44; Lk 5:12-14; 17:14 **14:3** [i]Lev 13:46 **14:4** [j]ver 6,49,51, 52; Nu 19:6; Ps 51:7 **14:6** [k]ver 4 **14:7** [l]2Ki 5:10,14; Isa 52:15; Eze 36:25

[a] *45* Or *clothes, uncover his head*
[b] *3* Traditionally *leprosy;* the Hebrew word was used for various diseases affecting the skin—not necessarily leprosy; also elsewhere in this chapter.

release the live bird in the open fields.
8"The person to be cleansed must
wash his clothes,[m] shave off all his hair
and bathe with water;[n] then he will be
ceremonially clean.[o] After this he may
come into the camp,[p] but he must
stay outside his tent for seven days.
9On the seventh day he must shave off
all his hair; he must shave his head, his
beard, his eyebrows and the rest of his
hair. He must wash his clothes and
bathe himself with water, and he will
be clean.

10"On the eighth day[q] he must
bring two male lambs and one ewe
lamb a year old, each without defect,
along with three-tenths of an ephah[a]
of fine flour mixed with oil for a grain
offering,[r] and one log[b] of oil.[s] 11The
priest who pronounces him clean shall
present both the one to be cleansed
and his offerings before the LORD at the
entrance to the Tent of Meeting.

12"Then the priest is to take one of
the male lambs and offer it as a guilt
offering,[t] along with the log of oil; he
shall wave them before the LORD as a
wave offering.[u] 13He is to slaughter
the lamb in the holy place[v] where the
sin offering and the burnt offering are
slaughtered. Like the sin offering, the
guilt offering belongs to the priest;[w]
it is most holy. 14The priest is to take
some of the blood of the guilt offering
and put it on the lobe of the right ear
of the one to be cleansed, on the
thumb of his right hand and on the big
toe of his right foot.[x] 15The priest shall
then take some of the log of oil, pour it
in the palm of his own left hand, 16dip
his right forefinger into the oil in his
palm, and with his finger sprinkle
some of it before the LORD seven times.
17The priest is to put some of the oil
remaining in his palm on the lobe of
the right ear of the one to be cleansed,
on the thumb of his right hand and on
the big toe of his right foot, on top of
the blood of the guilt offering. 18The
rest of the oil in his palm the priest
shall put on the head of the one to be
cleansed and make atonement for him
before the LORD.

19"Then the priest is to sacrifice the
sin offering and make atonement for
the one to be cleansed from his uncleanness. After that, the priest shall
slaughter the burnt offering 20and offer
it on the altar, together with the grain
offering, and make atonement for him,
and he will be clean.[y]

21"If, however, he is poor[z] and cannot afford these,[a] he must take one
male lamb as a guilt offering to be
waved to make atonement for him, together with a tenth of an ephah[c] of
fine flour mixed with oil for a grain offering, a log of oil, 22and two doves or
two young pigeons,[b] which he can afford, one for a sin offering and the other for a burnt offering.

23"On the eighth day he must bring
them for his cleansing to the priest at
the entrance to the Tent of Meeting,
before the LORD.[c] 24The priest is to
take the lamb for the guilt offering,[d]
together with the log of oil,[e] and wave
them before the LORD as a wave offering.[f] 25He shall slaughter the lamb for
the guilt offering and take some of its
blood and put it on the lobe of the right
ear of the one to be cleansed, on the
thumb of his right hand and on the big
toe of his right foot.[g] 26The priest is to
pour some of the oil into the palm of
his own left hand,[h] 27and with his
right forefinger sprinkle some of the oil
from his palm seven times before the
LORD. 28Some of the oil in his palm he
is to put on the same places he put the
blood of the guilt offering—on the lobe
of the right ear of the one to be
cleansed, on the thumb of his right
hand and on the big toe of his right
foot. 29The rest of the oil in his palm
the priest shall put on the head of the
one to be cleansed, to make atonement
for him before the LORD.[i] 30Then he
shall sacrifice the doves or the young
pigeons, which the person can afford,[j] 31one[d] as a sin offering and the
other as a burnt offering,[k] together
with the grain offering. In this way the
priest will make atonement before the
LORD on behalf of the one to be
cleansed.[l]"

32These are the regulations for anyone who has an infectious skin disease[m] and who cannot afford the regular offerings[n] for his cleansing.

Cleansing From Mildew

33The LORD said to Moses and Aaron,
34"When you enter the land of Canaan,[o] which I am giving you as your
possession,[p] and I put a spreading
mildew in a house in that land, 35the
owner of the house must go and tell the
priest, 'I have seen something that
looks like mildew in my house.' 36The
priest is to order the house to be emptied before he goes in to examine the
mildew, so that nothing in the house
will be pronounced unclean. After this
the priest is to go in and inspect the
house. 37He is to examine the mildew

14:8 [m]Lev 11:25; 13:6 [n]ver 9 [o]ver 20 [p]Nu 5:2,3; 12:14,15; 2Ch 26:21
14:10 [q]Mt 8:4; Mk 1:44; Lk 5:14 [r]Lev 2:1 [s]ver 12,15,21, 24
14:12 [t]Lev 5:18; 6:6-7 [u]Ex 29:24
14:13 [v]Ex 29:11 [w]Lev 6:24-30; 7:7
14:14 [x]Ex 29:20; Lev 8:23
14:20 [y]ver 8
14:21 [z]Lev 5:7; 12:8 [a]ver 22,32
14:22 [b]Lev 5:7
14:23 [c]ver 10,11
14:24 [d]Nu 6:14 [e]ver 10 [f]ver 12
14:25 [g]ver 14; Ex 29:20
14:26 [h]ver 15
14:29 [i]ver 18
14:30 [j]Lev 5:7
14:31 [k]ver 22; Lev 5:7; 15:15, 30 [l]ver 18,19
14:32 [m]Lev 13:2 [n]ver 21
14:34 [o]Ge 12:5; Ex 6:4; Nu 13:2 [p]Ge 17:8; 48:4; Nu 27:12; 32:22; Dt 3:27; 7:1; 32:49

a *10* That is, probably about 6 quarts (about 6.5 liters) b *10* That is, probably about 2/3 pint (about 0.3 liter); also in verses 12, 15, 21 and 24 c *21* That is, probably about 2 quarts (about 2 liters) d *31* Septuagint and Syriac; Hebrew *31such as the person can afford, one*

on the walls, and if it has greenish or reddish[q] depressions that appear to be deeper than the surface of the wall, 38the priest shall go out the doorway of the house and close it up for seven days.[r] 39On the seventh day[s] the priest shall return to inspect the house. If the mildew has spread on the walls, 40he is to order that the contaminated stones be torn out and thrown into an unclean place outside the town.[t] 41He must have all the inside walls of the house scraped and the material that is scraped off dumped into an unclean place outside the town. 42Then they are to take other stones to replace these and take new clay and plaster the house.

43"If the mildew reappears in the house after the stones have been torn out and the house scraped and plastered, 44the priest is to go and examine it and, if the mildew has spread in the house, it is a destructive mildew; the house is unclean.[u] 45It must be torn down—its stones, timbers and all the plaster—and taken out of the town to an unclean place.

46"Anyone who goes into the house while it is closed up will be unclean till evening.[v] 47Anyone who sleeps or eats in the house must wash his clothes.[w]

48"But if the priest comes to examine it and the mildew has not spread after the house has been plastered, he shall pronounce the house clean,[x] because the mildew is gone. 49To purify the house he is to take two birds and some cedar wood, scarlet yarn and hyssop.[y] 50He shall kill one of the birds over fresh water in a clay pot.[z] 51Then he is to take the cedar wood, the hyssop,[a] the scarlet yarn and the live bird, dip them into the blood of the dead bird and the fresh water, and sprinkle the house seven times.[b] 52He shall purify the house with the bird's blood, the fresh water, the live bird, the cedar wood, the hyssop and the scarlet yarn. 53Then he is to release the live bird in the open fields[c] outside the town. In this way he will make atonement for the house, and it will be clean.[d]"

54These are the regulations for any infectious skin disease,[e] for an itch, 55for mildew[f] in clothing or in a house, 56and for a swelling, a rash or a bright spot,[g] 57to determine when something is clean or unclean.

These are the regulations for infectious skin diseases and mildew.[h]

Discharges Causing Uncleanness

15 The LORD said to Moses and Aaron, 2"Speak to the Israelites and say to them: 'When any man has a bodily discharge,[i] the discharge is unclean. 3Whether it continues flowing from his body or is blocked, it will make him unclean. This is how his discharge will bring about uncleanness:

4" 'Any bed the man with a discharge lies on will be unclean, and anything he sits on will be unclean. 5Anyone who touches his bed must wash his clothes[j] and bathe with water,[k] and he will be unclean till evening.[l] 6Whoever sits on anything that the man with a discharge sat on must wash his clothes and bathe with water, and he will be unclean till evening.

7" 'Whoever touches the man[m] who has a discharge[n] must wash his clothes and bathe with water, and he will be unclean till evening.

8" 'If the man with the discharge spits[o] on someone who is clean, that person must wash his clothes and bathe with water, and he will be unclean till evening.

9" 'Everything the man sits on when riding will be unclean, 10and whoever touches any of the things that were under him will be unclean till evening; whoever picks up those things[p] must wash his clothes and bathe with water, and he will be unclean till evening.

11" 'Anyone the man with a discharge touches without rinsing his hands with water must wash his clothes and bathe with water, and he will be unclean till evening.

12" 'A clay pot[q] that the man touches must be broken, and any wooden article[r] is to be rinsed with water.

13" 'When a man is cleansed from his discharge, he is to count off seven days[s] for his ceremonial cleansing; he must wash his clothes and bathe himself with fresh water, and he will be clean.[t] 14On the eighth day he must take two doves or two young pigeons[u] and come before the LORD to the entrance to the Tent of Meeting and give them to the priest. 15The priest is to sacrifice them, the one for a sin offering[v] and the other for a burnt offering.[w] In this way he will make atonement before the LORD for the man because of his discharge.[x]

16" 'When a man has an emission of semen,[y] he must bathe his whole body with water, and he will be unclean till evening.[z] 17Any clothing or leather that has semen on it must be washed with water, and it will be unclean till evening. 18When a man lies

14:37 [q]Lev 13:19
14:38 [r]Lev 13:4
14:39 [s]Lev 13:5
14:40 [t]ver 45
14:44 [u]Lev 13:51
14:46 [v]Lev 11:24
14:47 [w]Lev 11:25
14:48 [x]Lev 13:6
14:49 [y]ver 4; 1Ki 4:33; ver 4
14:50 [z]ver 5
14:51 [a]ver 6; Ps 51:7 [b]ver 4,7
14:53 [c]ver 7 [d]ver 20
14:54 [e]Lev 13:2,30
14:55 [f]Lev 13:47-52
14:56 [g]Lev 13:2
14:57 [h]Lev 10:10
15:2 [i]ver 16,32; Lev 22:4; Nu 5:2; 2Sa 3:29; Mt 9:20
15:5 [j]Lev 11:25 [k]Lev 14:8 [l]Lev 11:24
15:7 [m]ver 19; Lev 22:5 [n]ver 16; Lev 22:4
15:8 [o]Nu 12:14
15:10 [p]Nu 19:10
15:12 [q]Lev 6:28 [r]Lev 11:32
15:13 [s]Lev 8:33 [t]ver 5
15:14 [u]Lev 14:22
15:15 [v]Lev 5:7 [w]Lev 14:31 [x]Lev 14:18,19
15:16 [y]ver 2; Lev 22:4; Dt 23:10 [z]ver 5; Dt 23:11

with a woman and there is an emission
of semen,[a] both must bathe with water, and they will be unclean till evening.
19" 'When a woman has her regular
flow of blood, the impurity of her
monthly period[b] will last seven days,
and anyone who touches her will be
unclean till evening.
20" 'Anything she lies on during her
period will be unclean, and anything
she sits on will be unclean. 21Whoever
touches her bed must wash his clothes
and bathe with water, and he will
be unclean till evening.[c] 22Whoever
touches anything she sits on must
wash his clothes and bathe with water,
and he will be unclean till evening.
23Whether it is the bed or anything she
was sitting on, when anyone touches it,
he will be unclean till evening.
24" 'If a man lies with her and her
monthly flow[d] touches him, he will be
unclean for seven days; any bed he lies
on will be unclean.
25" 'When a woman has a discharge
of blood for many days at a time other
than her monthly period[e] or has a discharge that continues beyond her period, she will be unclean as long as she
has the discharge, just as in the days of
her period. 26Any bed she lies on while
her discharge continues will be unclean, as is her bed during her monthly
period, and anything she sits on will be
unclean, as during her period. 27Who-
ever touches them will be unclean; he
must wash his clothes and bathe with
water, and he will be unclean till evening.
28" 'When she is cleansed from her
discharge, she must count off seven
days, and after that she will be ceremonially clean. 29On the eighth day she
must take two doves or two young pigeons[f] and bring them to the priest at
the entrance to the Tent of Meeting.
30The priest is to sacrifice one for a sin
offering and the other for a burnt offering. In this way he will make atonement for her before the LORD for the
uncleanness of her discharge.[g]
31" 'You must keep the Israelites
separate from things that make them
unclean, so they will not die in their
uncleanness for defiling my dwelling
place,[a][h] which is among them.' "
32These are the regulations for a
man with a discharge, for anyone
made unclean by an emission of semen,[i] 33for a woman in her monthly
period, for a man or a woman with a
discharge, and for a man who lies with
a woman who is ceremonially unclean.[j]

15:18 [a]1Sa 21:4
15:19 [b]ver 24; Lev 12:2
15:21 [c]ver 27
15:24 [d]ver 19; Lev 12:2; 18:19; 20:18; Eze 18:6
15:25 [e]Mt 9:20; Mk 5:25; Lk 8:43
15:29 [f]Lev 14:22
15:30 [g]Lev 5:10; 14:20,31; 18:19; 2Sa 11:4; Mk 5:25; Lk 8:43
15:31 [h]Lev 20:3; Nu 5:3; 19:13, 20; 2Sa 15:25; 2Ki 21:7; Ps 33:14; 74:7; 76:2; Eze 5:11; 23:38
15:32 [i]ver 2
15:33 [j]ver 19,24,25

16:1 [k]Lev 10:1
16:2 [l]Ex 30:10; Heb 9:7 [m]Heb 9:25; 10:19 [n]Ex 25:22 [o]Ex 40:34
16:3 [p]Heb 9:24,25
16:4 [q]Ex 28:39 [r]Ex 28:42 [s]ver 24; Heb 10:22
16:5 [t]Lev 4:13-21 [u]2Ch 29:23
16:6 [v]Lev 9:7; Heb 5:3; 7:27; 9:7,12
16:10 [w]Isa 53:4-10; Ro 3:25; 1Jn 2:2
16:11 [x]Heb 7:27; 9:7
16:12 [y]Lev 10:1 [z]Ex 30:34-38
16:13 [a]Ex 28:43; Lev 22:9
16:14 [b]Lev 4:5; Heb 9:7,13,25 [c]Lev 4:6
16:15 [d]Heb 9:7,12 [e]Heb 9:3

The Day of Atonement

16 The LORD spoke to Moses after the
death of the two sons of Aaron who
died when they approached the
LORD.[k] 2The LORD said to Moses: "Tell
your brother Aaron not to come whenever he chooses[l] into the Most Holy
Place[m] behind the curtain in front of
the atonement cover on the ark, or else
he will die, because I appear[n] in the
cloud[o] over the atonement cover.
3"This is how Aaron is to enter the
sanctuary area:[p] with a young bull for
a sin offering and a ram for a burnt
offering. 4He is to put on the sacred
linen tunic, with linen undergarments
next to his body; he is to tie the linen
sash around him and put on the linen
turban.[q] These are sacred garments;[r]
so he must bathe himself with water[s]
before he puts them on. 5From the Israelite community[t] he is to take two
male goats[u] for a sin offering and a
ram for a burnt offering.
6"Aaron is to offer the bull for his
own sin offering to make atonement
for himself and his household.[v] 7Then
he is to take the two goats and present
them before the LORD at the entrance
to the Tent of Meeting. 8He is to cast
lots for the two goats—one lot for the
LORD and the other for the scapegoat.[b]
9Aaron shall bring the goat whose lot
falls to the LORD and sacrifice it for a sin
offering. 10But the goat chosen by lot as
the scapegoat shall be presented alive
before the LORD to be used for making
atonement[w] by sending it into the
desert as a scapegoat.
11"Aaron shall bring the bull for his
own sin offering to make atonement
for himself and his household,[x] and
he is to slaughter the bull for his own
sin offering. 12He is to take a censer full
of burning coals[y] from the altar before the LORD and two handfuls of finely ground fragrant incense[z] and take
them behind the curtain. 13He is to put
the incense on the fire before the LORD,
and the smoke of the incense will conceal the atonement cover above the
Testimony, so that he will not die.[a]
14He is to take some of the bull's
blood[b] and with his finger sprinkle it
on the front of the atonement cover;
then he shall sprinkle some of it with
his finger seven times before the atonement cover.[c]
15"He shall then slaughter the goat
for the sin offering for the people[d] and
take its blood behind the curtain[e] and
do with it as he did with the bull's

[a]31 Or *my tabernacle* [b]8 That is, the goat of removal; Hebrew *azazel*; also in verses 10 and 26

16:1–34

PROMISE 1

THE DAY OF ATONEMENT

All Christians are under the Great Commission. It is our responsibility and privilege to be Jesus' witnesses to all the world (Acts 1:8); to make disciples of all nations (Matthew 28:19). Our message is that God offers salvation to all people as a gift. To us it is free—but it cost God his only Son, Jesus.

Leviticus 16 is an important part of the salvation story. When we hear or tell others about the gospel, it sounds so simple and easy. And, for us, it is simple and easy. But its roots, found here in the description of the Jewish Day of Atonement, add a richness that leads the thinking Christian to a deeper love for and worship of God for offering us such a magnificent gift.

In ancient Israel, sin was not removed by accepting Jesus as Savior. But it was removed once each year, on the Day of Atonement. Leviticus 16 describes the process Israel followed to deal with their sin. It began with the high priest's preparation to offer a sacrifice for the sin. He had to take several animals—a bull and a ram for himself and two goats and a ram for the people—into the Most Holy Place, the room where God said he appeared (v. 2). Before offering these animals to God, the high priest had to bathe himself and put on a special linen outfit (3–5). With his personal preparations completed, the priest then began the Day of Atonement ritual. As you read verses 6 through 28, use this simple outline to help you sort through the activities involved in the ritual required to take away Israel's sin and purify the Most Holy Place.

1. The high priest offered a bull to make atonement for himself and his family (vv. 6, 11).
2. He took coals from the altar, which stood outside in the tabernacle court, behind the curtain into the Most Holy Place. He put incense on the coals to produce a fragrant smoke in the presence of God (vv. 12–13).
3. He took some of the sacrificed bull's blood and put it on and in front of the atonement cover (v. 14).
4. He slaughtered the goat selected as the sacrifice for the people's sin and sprinkled some of its blood on and in front of the atonement cover (v. 15).
5. He took some of the bull's blood and some of the goat's blood and wiped it on the horns of the altar (vv. 18–19).
6. He placed his hands on the live goat's head and confessed Israel's sin. Then a specifically appointed man took the live goat (called a "scapegoat") into the wilderness and set it free (20–22).
7. The high priest went into the Tent of Meeting, bathed and changed his clothes (vv. 23–24).
8. After changing his clothes, he slaughtered the two rams, combined them with the fat from the sacrificial bull and goat and made a burnt offering to God (vv. 24–25).
9. The carcasses and all that remained of the bull and goat whose blood was used in the cleansing part of the atonement ritual were taken outside the camp and completely burned (v. 27).
10. Both the man who took the goat into the wilderness and the man who burned the remains of the sacrificial animals bathed, washed their clothes and returned to the congregation of Israel (v. 28).

What was the outcome of this elaborate ritual?

1. Atonement was made for the Most Holy Place and the Tent of Meeting (v. 16).
2. Atonement was made for the high priest, his family and the whole community of Israel (v. 17).
3. Atonement was made for "the altar that is before the LORD" (vv. 18, 19).
4. The scapegoat carried the sins of all the people into the wilderness (v. 22).
5. In summary, "On this day atonement will be made for you, to cleanse you. Then, before the LORD you will be clean from all your sins" (vv. 30–33).

Acts 16 records a man asking Paul, "What must I do to be saved?" (v. 30). Imagine what would have happened if Paul had answered, "Well, first the high priest has to get a bull, then put on sacred linens to go into the Most Holy Place. Then . . ." Instead Paul answered, "Believe on the Lord Jesus, and you will be saved" (Acts 16:31). In Hebrews chapters 4, 9 and 10, Jesus is presented as God's fulfillment of all the ritual described in Leviticus 16.

The careful process that the ancient Israelites followed on the Day of Atonement shows us that God takes sin—and its removal—very seriously. Next time you think about the free gift of salvation, reflect on what Jesus accomplished by shedding his blood as a sacrifice for your sin. Stop and take a moment to express your gratitude to Jesus and worship him, for Jesus "did not enter [into God's presence] by means of the blood of goats and calves; but he entered the Most Holy Place once for all by his own blood, having obtained eternal redemption. The blood of goats and bulls and the ashes of a heifer sprinkled on those who are ceremonially unclean sanctify them so that they are outwardly clean. How much more, then, will the blood of Christ, who through the eternal Spirit offered himself unblemished to God, cleanse our consciences from acts that lead to death, so that we may serve the living God!" (Hebrews 9:12–14).

For the next Promise 1 reading go to page 139.

blood: He shall sprinkle it on the
atonement cover and in front of it. 16 In
this way he will make atonement[f] for
the Most Holy Place because of the uncleanness and rebellion of the Israelites, whatever their sins have been. He
is to do the same for the Tent of Meeting, which is among them in the midst
of their uncleanness. 17 No one is to be
in the Tent of Meeting from the time
Aaron goes in to make atonement in
the Most Holy Place until he comes
out, having made atonement for himself, his household and the whole community of Israel.
18 "Then he shall come out to the altar[g] that is before the LORD and make
atonement for it. He shall take some of
the bull's blood and some of the goat's
blood and put it on all the horns of the
altar.[h] 19 He shall sprinkle some of the
blood on it with his finger seven times
to cleanse it and to consecrate it from
the uncleanness of the Israelites.[i]
20 "When Aaron has finished making
atonement for the Most Holy Place, the
Tent of Meeting and the altar, he shall
bring forward the live goat. 21 He is to
lay both hands on the head of the live
goat and confess[j] over it all the wickedness and rebellion of the Israelites—
all their sins—and put them on the
goat's head. He shall send the goat
away into the desert in the care of a
man appointed for the task. 22 The goat
will carry on itself all their sins[k] to a
solitary place; and the man shall release it in the desert.
23 "Then Aaron is to go into the Tent
of Meeting and take off the linen garments he put on before he entered the
Most Holy Place, and he is to leave
them there.[l] 24 He shall bathe himself
with water in a holy place and put on
his regular garments.[m] Then he shall
come out and sacrifice the burnt offering for himself and the burnt offering
for the people, to make atonement for
himself and for the people. 25 He shall
also burn the fat of the sin offering on
the altar.
26 "The man who releases the goat as
a scapegoat must wash his clothes[n]
and bathe himself with water; afterward he may come into the camp.
27 The bull and the goat for the sin offerings, whose blood was brought into
the Most Holy Place to make atonement, must be taken outside the
camp;[o] their hides, flesh and offal are
to be burned up. 28 The man who burns
them must wash his clothes and bathe
himself with water; afterward he may
come into the camp.
29 "This is to be a lasting ordinance
for you: On the tenth day of the seventh month you must deny yourselves[a][p] and not do any work—
whether native-born or an alien living
among you— 30 because on this day
atonement will be made for you, to
cleanse you. Then, before the LORD,
you will be clean from all your sins.[q]
31 It is a sabbath of rest, and you must
deny yourselves;[r] it is a lasting ordinance. 32 The priest who is anointed
and ordained to succeed his father as
high priest is to make atonement. He is
to put on the sacred linen garments[s]
33 and make atonement for the Most
Holy Place, for the Tent of Meeting and
the altar, and for the priests and all the
people of the community.[t]
34 "This is to be a lasting ordinance
for you: Atonement is to be made once
a year[u] for all the sins of the Israelites."
And it was done, as the LORD commanded Moses.

Eating Blood Forbidden

17 The LORD said to Moses, 2 "Speak to
Aaron and his sons and to all the
Israelites and say to them: 'This is what
the LORD has commanded: 3 Any Israelite who sacrifices an ox,[b] a lamb or a
goat in the camp or outside of it 4 instead of bringing it to the entrance to
the Tent of Meeting to present it as an
offering to the LORD in front of the tabernacle of the LORD[v]—that man shall
be considered guilty of bloodshed; he
has shed blood and must be cut off
from his people.[w] 5 This is so the Israelites will bring to the LORD the sacrifices they are now making in the open
fields. They must bring them to the
priest, that is, to the LORD, at the entrance to the Tent of Meeting and sacrifice them as fellowship offerings.[c]
6 The priest is to sprinkle the blood
against the altar of the LORD[x] at the
entrance to the Tent of Meeting and
burn the fat as an aroma pleasing to
the LORD.[y] 7 They must no longer offer
any of their sacrifices to the goat
idols[d][z] to whom they prostitute
themselves.[a] This is to be a lasting ordinance for them and for the generations to come.'
8 "Say to them: 'Any Israelite or any
alien living among them who offers a
burnt offering or sacrifice 9 and does
not bring it to the entrance to the Tent
of Meeting[b] to sacrifice it to the
LORD—that man must be cut off from
his people.

16:16 [f]Ex 29:36 **16:18** [g]Lev 4:7 [h]Lev 4:25 **16:19** [i]Eze 43:20 **16:21** [j]Lev 5:5 **16:22** [k]Isa 53:12 **16:23** [l]Eze 42:14; 44:19 **16:24** [m]ver 3-5 **16:26** [n]Lev 11:25 **16:27** [o]Lev 4:12,21; Heb 13:11

16:29 [p]Lev 23:27,32; Nu 29:7; Isa 58:3 **16:30** [q]Jer 33:8; Eph 5:26 **16:31** [r]Isa 58:3,5 **16:32** [s]ver 4; Nu 20:26,28 **16:33** [t]ver 11,16-18 **16:34** [u]Heb 9:7,25 **17:4** [v]Dt 12:5-21 [w]Ge 17:14 **17:6** [x]Lev 3:2 [y]Nu 18:17 **17:7** [z]Ex 22:20; 2Ch 11:15 [a]Ex 32:8; 34:15; Dt 32:17; 1Co 10:20 **17:9** [b]ver 4

[a] *29* Or *must fast*; also in verse 31 [b] *3* The Hebrew word can include both male and female. [c] *5* Traditionally *peace offerings* [d] *7* Or *demons*

10" 'Any Israelite or any alien living among them who eats any blood—I will set my face against that person who eats blood[c] and will cut him off from his people. 11For the life of a creature is in the blood,[d] and I have given it to you to make atonement for yourselves on the altar; it is the blood that makes atonement for one's life.[e] 12Therefore I say to the Israelites, "None of you may eat blood, nor may an alien living among you eat blood."

13" 'Any Israelite or any alien living among you who hunts any animal or bird that may be eaten must drain out the blood and cover it with earth,[f] 14because the life of every creature is its blood. That is why I have said to the Israelites, "You must not eat the blood of any creature, because the life of every creature is its blood; anyone who eats it must be cut off."[g]

15" 'Anyone, whether native-born or alien, who eats anything found dead or torn by wild animals[h] must wash his clothes and bathe with water, and he will be ceremonially unclean till evening; then he will be clean. 16But if he does not wash his clothes and bathe himself, he will be held responsible.' "

Unlawful Sexual Relations

18 The LORD said to Moses, 2"Speak to the Israelites and say to them: 'I am the LORD your God.[i] 3You must not do as they do in Egypt, where you used to live, and you must not do as they do in the land of Canaan, where I am bringing you. Do not follow their practices.[j] 4You must obey my laws and be careful to follow my decrees. I am the LORD your God.[k] 5Keep my decrees and laws, for the man who obeys them will live by them.[l] I am the LORD.

6" 'No one is to approach any close relative to have sexual relations. I am the LORD.

7" 'Do not dishonor your father[m] by having sexual relations with your mother.[n] She is your mother; do not have relations with her.

8" 'Do not have sexual relations with your father's wife;[o] that would dishonor your father.[p]

9" 'Do not have sexual relations with your sister,[q] either your father's daughter or your mother's daughter, whether she was born in the same home or elsewhere.

10" 'Do not have sexual relations with your son's daughter or your daughter's daughter; that would dishonor you.

11" 'Do not have sexual relations with the daughter of your father's wife, born to your father; she is your sister.

12" 'Do not have sexual relations with your father's sister;[r] she is your father's close relative.

13" 'Do not have sexual relations with your mother's sister, because she is your mother's close relative.

14" 'Do not dishonor your father's brother by approaching his wife to have sexual relations; she is your aunt.[s]

15" 'Do not have sexual relations with your daughter-in-law.[t] She is your son's wife; do not have relations with her.

16" 'Do not have sexual relations with your brother's wife;[u] that would dishonor your brother.

17" 'Do not have sexual relations with both a woman and her daughter.[v] Do not have sexual relations with either her son's daughter or her daughter's daughter; they are her close relatives. That is wickedness.

18" 'Do not take your wife's sister as a rival wife and have sexual relations with her while your wife is living.

19" 'Do not approach a woman to have sexual relations during the uncleanness of her monthly period.[w]

20" 'Do not have sexual relations with your neighbor's wife[x] and defile yourself with her.

21" 'Do not give any of your children[y] to be sacrificed[a] to Molech,[z] for you must not profane the name of your God.[a] I am the LORD.

22" 'Do not lie with a man as one lies with a woman;[b] that is detestable.

a21 Or *to be passed through ⌊the fire⌋*

17:10 [c]Ge 9:4; Lev 3:17; Dt 12:16,23; 1Sa 14:33
17:11 [d]ver 14; Ge 9:4 [e]Heb 9:22
17:13 [f]Lev 7:26; Dt 12:16
17:14 [g]ver 11; Ge 9:4
17:15 [h]Ex 22:31; Dt 14:21
18:2 [i]Ex 6:7; Lev 11:44; Eze 20:5
18:3 [j]ver 24-30; Ex 23:24; Lev 20:23
18:4 [k]ver 2
18:5 [l]Eze 20:11; Ro 10:5*; Gal 3:12*
18:7 [m]Lev 20:11 [n]Eze 22:10
18:8 [o]1Co 5:1 [p]Lev 20:11
18:9 [q]Lev 20:17
18:12 [r]Lev 20:19
18:14 [s]Lev 20:20
18:15 [t]Lev 20:12
18:16 [u]Lev 20:21
18:17 [v]Lev 20:14
18:19 [w]Lev 15:24; 20:18
18:20 [x]Ex 20:14; Lev 20:10; Mt 5:27,28; 1Co 6:9; Heb 13:4
18:21 [y]Dt 12:31 [z]Lev 20:2-5 [a]Lev 19:12; 21:6; Eze 36:20
18:22 [b]Lev 20:13; Dt 23:18; Ro 1:27

18:1–5

PROMISE **3**

CULTURAL COUNSEL

In this book, God lists the laws that will protect his people and help them live effective, productive lives. And he keeps dropping these reminders in the long lists of laws to give his readers a proper perspective. God's people live in a world that doesn't obey him. Verse 3 warns that the cultural pull of both the Egyptians (in the past) and the Canaanites (in the future) will draw Israel away from God's lifestyle.

As Christians, we're always living in an environment that is hostile to God's standards. Read this warning carefully, and ask yourself, "What old habits (Egypt) do I need to be wary of, and what new fascinations and fads (Canaan) do I need to deal with?"

For the next Promise 3 reading go to page 167.

23" 'Do not have sexual relations
with an animal and defile yourself with
it. A woman must not present herself
to an animal to have sexual relations
with it; that is a perversion.[c]
24" 'Do not defile yourselves in any
of these ways, because this is how the
nations that I am going to drive out
before you[d] became defiled.[e] 25Even
the land was defiled; so I punished it
for its sin,[f] and the land vomited out
its inhabitants.[g] 26But you must keep
my decrees and my laws. The native-
born and the aliens living among you
must not do any of these detestable
things, 27for all these things were done
by the people who lived in the land
before you, and the land became defiled. 28And if you defile the land, it will
vomit you out as it vomited out the
nations that were before you.
29" 'Everyone who does any of these
detestable things—such persons must
be cut off from their people. 30Keep my
requirements[h] and do not follow any
of the detestable customs that were
practiced before you came and do not
defile yourselves with them. I am the
LORD your God.[i]' "

Various Laws

1 →PG. 156

19 The LORD said to Moses, 2"Speak to
the entire assembly of Israel and
say to them: 'Be holy because I, the
LORD your God, am holy.[j]
3" 'Each of you must respect his
mother and father,[k] and you must observe my Sabbaths. I am the LORD your
God.[l]
4" 'Do not turn to idols or make gods
of cast metal for yourselves.[m] I am the
LORD your God.
5" 'When you sacrifice a fellowship
offering[a] to the LORD, sacrifice it in
such a way that it will be accepted on
your behalf. 6It shall be eaten on the
day you sacrifice it or on the next day;
anything left over until the third day
must be burned up. 7If any of it is eaten
on the third day, it is impure and will
not be accepted. 8Whoever eats it will
be held responsible because he has
desecrated what is holy to the LORD;
that person must be cut off from his
people.
9" 'When you reap the harvest of
your land, do not reap to the very edges
of your field or gather the gleanings of
your harvest.[n] 10Do not go over your
vineyard a second time or pick up the
grapes that have fallen. Leave them for
the poor and the alien. I am the LORD
your God.
11" 'Do not steal.[o]
" 'Do not lie.[p]
" 'Do not deceive one another.
12" 'Do not swear falsely by my
name[q] and so profane the name of
your God. I am the LORD.
13" 'Do not defraud your neighbor or
rob him.[r]
" 'Do not hold back the wages of a
hired man overnight.[s]
14" 'Do not curse the deaf or put a
stumbling block in front of the blind,[t]
but fear your God. I am the LORD.
15" 'Do not pervert justice;[u] do not
show partiality[v] to the poor or favoritism to the great, but judge your neighbor fairly.

3 →PG. 132

16" 'Do not go about spreading slander[w] among your people.
" 'Do not do anything that endan-
gers your neighbor's life.[x] I am the
LORD.
17" 'Do not hate your brother in your
heart.[y] Rebuke your neighbor frank-
ly[z] so you will not share in his guilt.
18" 'Do not seek revenge[a] or bear a
grudge[b] against one of your people,
but love your neighbor as yourself.[c] I
am the LORD.

7 →PG. 136

19" 'Keep my decrees.
" 'Do not mate different kinds of animals.
" 'Do not plant your field with two
kinds of seed.[d]
" 'Do not wear clothing woven of
two kinds of material.[e]
20" 'If a man sleeps with a woman
who is a slave girl promised to another
man but who has not been ransomed
or given her freedom, there must be
due punishment. Yet they are not to be
put to death, because she had not been
freed. 21The man, however, must bring
a ram to the entrance to the Tent of
Meeting for a guilt offering to the
LORD.[f] 22With the ram of the guilt offering the priest is to make atonement
for him before the LORD for the sin he
has committed, and his sin will be forgiven.
23" 'When you enter the land and
plant any kind of fruit tree, regard its
fruit as forbidden.[b] For three years
you are to consider it forbidden[b]; it
must not be eaten. 24In the fourth year
all its fruit will be holy,[g] an offering of
praise to the LORD. 25But in the fifth
year you may eat its fruit. In this way
your harvest will be increased. I am the
LORD your God.
26" 'Do not eat any meat with the
blood still in it.[h]
" 'Do not practice divination or sorcery.[i]
27" 'Do not cut the hair at the sides

18:23 [c]Ex 22:19; Lev 20:15; Dt 27:21
18:24 [d]ver 3,27,30 [e]Dt 18:12
18:25 [f]Lev 20:23; Dt 9:5; 18:12 [g]ver 28; Lev 20:22
18:30 [h]Dt 11:1 [i]ver 2
19:2 [j]1Pe 1:16*; Lev 11:44
19:3 [k]Ex 20:12 [l]Lev 11:44
19:4 [m]Ex 20:4,23; 34:17; Lev 26:1; Ps 96:5; 115:4-7
19:9 [n]Lev 23:10,22; Dt 24:19-22
19:11 [o]Ex 20:15 [p]Eph 4:25
19:12 [q]Ex 20:7; Mt 5:33
19:13 [r]Ex 22:15, 25-27 [s]Dt 24:15; Jas 5:4
19:14 [t]Dt 27:18
19:15 [u]Ex 23:2,6 [v]Dt 1:17
19:16 [w]Ps 15:3; Eze 22:9 [x]Ex 23:7
19:17 [y]1Jn 2:9; 3:15 [z]Mt 18:15; Lk 17:3
19:18 [a]Ro 12:19 [b]Ps 103:9 [c]Mt 5:43*; 19:16*; 22:39*; Mk 12:31*; Lk 10:27*; Jn 13:34; Ro 13:9*; Gal 5:14*; Jas 2:8*
19:19 [d]Dt 22:9 [e]Dt 22:11
19:21 [f]Lev 5:15
19:24 [g]Pr 3:9
19:26 [h]Lev 17:10 [i]Dt 18:10

[a]5 Traditionally *peace offering* [b]23 Hebrew *uncircumcised*

of your head or clip off the edges of your beard.[j]

28 " 'Do not cut your bodies for the dead or put tattoo marks on yourselves. I am the LORD.

29 " 'Do not degrade your daughter by making her a prostitute,[k] or the land will turn to prostitution and be filled with wickedness.

30 " 'Observe my Sabbaths and have reverence for my sanctuary. I am the LORD.[l]

31 " 'Do not turn to mediums or seek out spiritists,[m] for you will be defiled by them. I am the LORD your God.

6 →PG. 199

32 " 'Rise in the presence of the aged, show respect for the elderly[n] and revere your God. I am the LORD.

33 " 'When an alien lives with you in your land, do not mistreat him. **34** The alien living with you must be treated as one of your native-born.[o] Love him as yourself, for you were aliens in Egypt.[p] I am the LORD your God.

35 " 'Do not use dishonest standards when measuring length, weight or quantity. **36** Use honest scales and honest weights, an honest ephah[a] and an honest hin.[b][q] I am the LORD your God, who brought you out of Egypt.

37 " 'Keep all my decrees and all my laws and follow them. I am the LORD.' "

Punishments for Sin

20 The LORD said to Moses, **2** "Say to the Israelites: 'Any Israelite or any alien living in Israel who gives[c] any of his children to Molech must be put to death. The people of the community are to stone him. **3** I will set my face against that man and I will cut him off from his people; for by giving his children to Molech, he has defiled my sanctuary[r] and profaned my holy name.[s] **4** If the people of the community close their eyes when that man gives one of his children to Molech and they fail to put him to death,[t] **5** I will set my face against that man and his family and will cut off from their people both him and all who follow him in prostituting themselves to Molech.

6 " 'I will set my face against the person who turns to mediums and spiritists to prostitute himself by following them, and I will cut him off from his people.[u]

3 →PG. 189

7 " 'Consecrate yourselves and be holy,[v] because I am the LORD your God. **8** Keep my decrees and follow them. I am the LORD, who makes you holy.[d][w]

9 " 'If anyone curses his father or mother,[x] he must be put to death.[y] He has cursed his father or his mother, and his blood will be on his own head.[z]

10 " 'If a man commits adultery with another man's wife[a]—with the wife of his neighbor—both the adulterer and the adulteress must be put to death.

11 " 'If a man sleeps with his father's wife, he has dishonored his father.[b] Both the man and the woman must be put to death; their blood will be on their own heads.

12 " 'If a man sleeps with his daughter-in-law,[c] both of them must be put to death. What they have done is a perversion; their blood will be on their own heads.

13 " 'If a man lies with a man as one lies with a woman, both of them have done what is detestable.[d] They must be put to death; their blood will be on their own heads.

14 " 'If a man marries both a woman and her mother,[e] it is wicked. Both he and they must be burned in the fire, so that no wickedness will be among you.[f]

15 " 'If a man has sexual relations with an animal,[g] he must be put to death, and you must kill the animal.

16 " 'If a woman approaches an animal to have sexual relations with it, kill both the woman and the animal. They must be put to death; their blood will be on their own heads.

17 " 'If a man marries his sister[h], the daughter of either his father or his mother, and they have sexual relations, it is a disgrace. They must be cut off before the eyes of their people. He has dishonored his sister and will be held responsible.

18 " 'If a man lies with a woman during her monthly period[i] and has sexual relations with her, he has exposed the source of her flow, and she has also uncovered it. Both of them must be cut off from their people.

19 " 'Do not have sexual relations with the sister of either your mother or your father,[j] for that would dishonor a close relative; both of you would be held responsible.

20 " 'If a man sleeps with his aunt,[k] he has dishonored his uncle. They will be held responsible; they will die childless.

21 " 'If a man marries his brother's wife,[l] it is an act of impurity; he has dishonored his brother. They will be childless.

22 " 'Keep all my decrees and laws

19:27 *j* Lev 21:5
19:29 *k* Dt 23:18
19:30 *l* Lev 26:2
19:31 *m* Lev 20:6; Isa 8:19
19:32 *n* 1Ti 5:1
19:34 *o* Ex 12:48 *p* Dt 10:19
19:36 *q* Dt 25:13-15
20:3 *r* Lev 15:31 *s* Lev 18:21
20:4 *t* Dt 17:2-5
20:6 *u* Lev 19:31
20:7 *v* Eph 1:4; 1Pe 1:16*
20:8 *w* Ex 31:13
20:9 *x* Dt 27:16 *y* Ex 21:17; Mt 15:4*; Mk 7:10* *z* ver 11; 2Sa 1:16
20:10 *a* Ex 20:14; Dt 5:18; 22:22
20:11 *b* Lev 18:7; Dt 27:23
20:12 *c* Lev 18:15
20:13 *d* Lev 18:22
20:14 *e* Lev 18:17 *f* Dt 27:23
20:15 *g* Lev 18:23
20:17 *h* Lev 18:9
20:18 *i* Lev 15:24; 18:19
20:19 *j* Lev 18:12-13
20:20 *k* Lev 18:14
20:21 *l* Lev 18:16

a *36* An ephah was a dry measure. **b** *36* A hin was a liquid measure. **c** *2* Or *sacrifices*; also in verses 3 and 4 **d** *8* Or *who sanctifies you*; or *who sets you apart as holy*

and follow them, so that the land[m] where I am bringing you to live may not vomit you out. 23You must not live according to the customs of the nations[n] I am going to drive out before you.[o] Because they did all these things, I abhorred them. 24But I said to you, "You will possess their land; I will give it to you as an inheritance, a land flowing with milk and honey."[p] I am the LORD your God, who has set you apart from the nations.[q]

25" 'You must therefore make a distinction between clean and unclean animals and between unclean and clean birds.[r] Do not defile yourselves by any animal or bird or anything that moves along the ground—those which I have set apart as unclean for you. 26You are to be holy to me[a] because I, the LORD, am holy,[s] and I have set you apart from the nations to be my own.

27" 'A man or woman who is a medium or spiritist among you must be put to death.[t] You are to stone them; their blood will be on their own heads.' "

Rules for Priests

21 The LORD said to Moses, "Speak to the priests, the sons of Aaron, and say to them: 'A priest must not make himself ceremonially unclean for any of his people who die,[u] 2except for a close relative, such as his mother or father, his son or daughter, his brother, 3or an unmarried sister who is dependent on him since she has no husband—for her he may make himself unclean. 4He must not make himself unclean for people related to him by marriage,[b] and so defile himself.

5" 'Priests must not shave their heads or shave off the edges of their beards[v] or cut their bodies.[w] 6They must be holy to their God and must not profane the name of their God.[x] Because they present the offerings made to the LORD by fire,[y] the food of their God, they are to be holy.

7" 'They must not marry women defiled by prostitution or divorced from their husbands,[z] because priests are holy to their God.[a] 8Regard them as holy,[b] because they offer up the food of your God. Consider them holy, because I the LORD am holy—I who make you holy.[c]

9" 'If a priest's daughter defiles herself by becoming a prostitute, she disgraces her father; she must be burned in the fire.[c]

10" 'The high priest, the one among his brothers who has had the anointing oil poured on his head and who has been ordained to wear the priestly garments,[d] must not let his hair become unkempt[d] or tear his clothes.[e] 11He must not enter a place where there is a dead body.[f] He must not make himself unclean,[g] even for his father or mother, 12nor leave the sanctuary of his God or desecrate it, because he has been dedicated by the anointing oil[h] of his God. I am the LORD.

13" 'The woman he marries must be a virgin.[i] 14He must not marry a widow, a divorced woman, or a woman defiled by prostitution, but only a virgin from his own people, 15so he will not defile his offspring among his people. I am the LORD, who makes him holy.[e] ' "

16The LORD said to Moses, 17"Say to Aaron: 'For the generations to come none of your descendants who has a defect may come near to offer the food of his God.[j] 18No man who has any defect[k] may come near: no man who is blind or lame, disfigured or deformed; 19no man with a crippled foot or hand, 20or who is hunchbacked or dwarfed, or who has any eye defect, or who has festering or running sores or damaged testicles.[l] 21No descendant of Aaron the priest who has any defect is to come near to present the offerings made to the LORD by fire. He has a defect; he must not come near to offer the food of his God. 22He may eat the most holy food of his God,[m] as well as the holy food; 23yet because of his defect, he must not go near the curtain or approach the altar, and so desecrate my sanctuary. I am the LORD, who makes them holy.[f] ' "

24So Moses told this to Aaron and his sons and to all the Israelites.

22 The LORD said to Moses, 2"Tell Aaron and his sons to treat with respect the sacred offerings the Israelites consecrate to me, so they will not profane my holy name. I am the LORD.

3"Say to them: 'For the generations to come, if any of your descendants is ceremonially unclean and yet comes near the sacred offerings that the Israelites consecrate to the LORD, that person must be cut off from my presence.[n] I am the LORD.

4" 'If a descendant of Aaron has an infectious skin disease[g] or a bodily discharge,[o] he may not eat the sacred offerings until he is cleansed. He will

20:22 [m]Lev 18:25-28 **20:23** [n]Lev 18:3 [o]Lev 18:24,27, 30 **20:24** [p]Ex 3:8; 13:5; 33:3 [q]Ex 33:16 **20:25** [r]Lev 11:1-47; Dt 14:3-21 **20:26** [s]Lev 19:2 **20:27** [t]Lev 19:31 **21:1** [u]Eze 44:25 **21:5** [v]Eze 44:20 [w]Lev 19:28; Dt 14:1 **21:6** [x]Lev 18:21 [y]Lev 3:11 **21:7** [z]ver 13,14 [a]Eze 44:22 **21:8** [b]ver 6 **21:9** [c]Ge 38:24; Lev 19:29

21:10 [d]Lev 16:32 [e]Lev 10:6 **21:11** [f]Nu 19:11,13, 14 [g]Lev 19:28 **21:12** [h]Ex 29:6-7; Lev 10:7 **21:13** [i]Eze 44:22 **21:17** [j]ver 6 **21:18** [k]Lev 22:19-25 **21:20** [l]Dt 23:1; Isa 56:3 **21:22** [m]1Co 9:13 **22:3** [n]Lev 7:20,21; Nu 19:13 **22:4** [o]Lev 14:1-32; 15:2-15

[a]26 Or *be my holy ones* [b]4 Or *unclean as a leader among his people* [c]8 Or *who sanctify you*; or *who set you apart as holy* [d]10 Or *not uncover his head* [e]15 Or *who sanctifies him*; or *who sets him apart as holy* [f]23 Or *who sanctifies them*; or *who sets them apart as holy*
[g]4 Traditionally *leprosy*; the Hebrew word was used for various diseases affecting the skin—not necessarily leprosy.

also be unclean if he touches something defiled by a corpse[p] or by anyone who has an emission of semen, 5or if he touches any crawling thing[q] that makes him unclean, or any person[r] who makes him unclean, whatever the uncleanness may be. 6The one who touches any such thing will be unclean till evening. He must not eat any of the sacred offerings unless he has bathed himself with water. 7When the sun goes down, he will be clean, and after that he may eat the sacred offerings, for they are his food.[s] 8He must not eat anything found dead[t] or torn by wild animals,[u] and so become unclean[v] through it. I am the LORD.

9" 'The priests are to keep my requirements so that they do not become guilty and die[w] for treating them with contempt. I am the LORD, who makes them holy.[a]

10" 'No one outside a priest's family may eat the sacred offering, nor may the guest of a priest or his hired worker eat it. 11But if a priest buys a slave with money, or if a slave is born in his household, that slave may eat his food.[x] 12If a priest's daughter marries anyone other than a priest, she may not eat any of the sacred contributions. 13But if a priest's daughter becomes a widow or is divorced, yet has no children, and she returns to live in her father's house as in her youth, she may eat of her father's food. No unauthorized person, however, may eat any of it.

14" 'If anyone eats a sacred offering by mistake, he must make restitution to the priest for the offering and add a fifth of the value[y] to it. 15The priests must not desecrate the sacred offerings the Israelites present to the LORD[z] 16by allowing them to eat the sacred offerings and so bring upon them guilt requiring payment.[a] I am the LORD, who makes them holy.' "

Unacceptable Sacrifices

17The LORD said to Moses, 18"Speak to Aaron and his sons and to all the Israelites and say to them: 'If any of you—either an Israelite or an alien living in Israel—presents a gift[b] for a burnt offering to the LORD, either to fulfill a vow or as a freewill offering, 19you must present a male without defect[c] from the cattle, sheep or goats in order that it may be accepted on your behalf. 20Do not bring anything with a defect,[d] because it will not be accepted on your behalf. 21When anyone brings from the herd or flock a fellowship offering[b][e] to the LORD to fulfill a special vow or as a freewill offering, it must be without defect or blemish to be acceptable. 22Do not offer to the LORD the blind, the injured or the maimed, or anything with warts or festering or running sores. Do not place any of these on the altar as an offering made to the LORD by fire. 23You may, however, present as a freewill offering an ox[c] or a sheep that is deformed or stunted, but it will not be accepted in fulfillment of a vow. 24You must not offer to the LORD an animal whose testicles are bruised, crushed, torn or cut.[f] You must not do this in your own land, 25and you must not accept such animals from the hand of a foreigner and offer them as the food of your God.[g] They will not be accepted on your behalf, because they are deformed and have defects.' "

26The LORD said to Moses, 27"When a calf, a lamb or a goat is born, it is to remain with its mother for seven days.[h] From the eighth day on, it will be acceptable as an offering made to the LORD by fire. 28Do not slaughter a cow or a sheep and its young on the same day.[i]

29"When you sacrifice a thank offering[j] to the LORD, sacrifice it in such a way that it will be accepted on your behalf. 30It must be eaten that same day; leave none of it till morning.[k] I am the LORD.

31"Keep[l] my commands and follow them. I am the LORD. 32Do not profane my holy name.[m] I must be acknowledged as holy by the Israelites.[n] I am the LORD, who makes[d] you holy[e] 33and who brought you out of Egypt to be your God.[o] I am the LORD."

23 The LORD said to Moses, 2"Speak to the Israelites and say to them: 'These are my appointed feasts,[p] the appointed feasts of the LORD, which you are to proclaim as sacred assemblies.[q]

The Sabbath

3" 'There are six days when you may work,[r] but the seventh day is a Sabbath of rest,[s] a day of sacred assembly. You are not to do any work; wherever you live, it is a Sabbath to the LORD.

22:4 [p]Lev 11:24-28, 39
22:5 [q]Lev 11:24-28, 43 [r]Lev 15:7
22:7 [s]Nu 18:11
22:8 [t]Lev 11:39 [u]Ex 22:31; Lev 17:15 [v]Lev 11:40
22:9 [w]ver 16; Ex 28:43
22:11 [x]Ge 17:13; Ex 12:44
22:14 [y]Lev 5:15
22:15 [z]Nu 18:32
22:16 [a]ver 9
22:18 [b]Lev 1:2
22:19 [c]Lev 1:3
22:20 [d]Dt 15:21; 17:1; Mal 1:8, 14; Heb 9:14; 1Pe 1:19
22:21 [e]Lev 3:6; Nu 15:3,8
22:24 [f]Lev 21:20
22:25 [g]Lev 21:6
22:27 [h]Ex 22:30
22:28 [i]Dt 22:6,7
22:29 [j]Lev 7:12; Ps 107:22
22:30 [k]Lev 7:15
22:31 [l]Dt 4:2,40; Ps 105:45
22:32 [m]Lev 18:21 [n]Lev 10:3
22:33 [o]Lev 11:45
23:2 [p]ver 4,37,44; Nu 29:39 [q]ver 21,27
23:3 [r]Ex 20:9 [s]Ex 20:10; 31:13-17; Lev 19:3; Dt 5:13; Heb 4:9,10

a *9* Or *who sanctifies them*; or *who sets them apart as holy*; also in verse 16
b *21* Traditionally *peace offering*
c *23* The Hebrew word can include both male and female.
d *32* Or *made*
e *32* Or *who sanctifies you*; or *who sets you apart as holy*

OLD TESTAMENT FEASTS				
Name	**OT References**	**Time**	**Description**	**NT References**
SABBATH	*Exodus 20:8-11; 31:12-17; Leviticus 23:3; Deuteronomy 5:12-15*	7th day	Day of rest; no work	*Matthew 12:1-14; Mark 2:23–3:5; Luke 4:16-30; 6:1-10; 13:10-16; 14:1-5; John 5:1-15; 9:1-34; Acts 13:14-48; 17:2; 18:4; Hebrews 4:1-11*
SABBATH YEAR	*Exodus 23:10-11; Leviticus 25:1-7*	7th year	Year of rest; fallow fields	
YEAR OF JUBILEE	*Leviticus 25:8-55; 27:17-24; Numbers 36:4*	50th year	Canceled debts; liberation of slaves and indentured servants; land returned to original family owners	
PASSOVER	*Exodus 12:1-14; Leviticus 23:5; Numbers 9:1-14; 28:16; Deuteronomy 16:1-7*	1st month (Abib) 14	Slaying and eating a lamb, together with bitter herbs and bread made without yeast in every household	*Matthew 26:1-2,17-29; Mark 14:12-26; Luke 22:7-38; John 2:13-25; 11:55-56; 13:1-30; 1 Corinthians 5:7*
UNLEAVENED BREAD	*Exodus 12:15-20; 13:3-10; 23:15; Leviticus 23:6-8; Numbers 28:17-25; Deuteronomy 16:3-4,8*	1st month (Abib) 15-21	Eating bread made without yeast; holding several assemblies; making designated offerings	*Matthew 26:17; Mark 14:1,12; Luke 22:1,7; Acts 12:3; 20:6; 1 Corinthians 5:6-8*
FIRSTFRUITS	*Leviticus 23:9-14*	1st month (Abib) 16	Presenting a sheaf of the first of the barley harvest as a wave offering; making a burnt offering and a grain offering	*Romans 8:23; 1 Corinthians 15:20-23*
WEEKS (Pentecost) (Harvest)	*Exodus 23:16a; 34:22a; Leviticus 23:15-21; Numbers 28:26-31; Deuteronomy 16:9-12*	3rd month (Sivan) 6	A festival of joy; mandatory and voluntary offerings, including the firstfruits of the wheat harvest	*Acts 2:1-41; 20:16; 1 Corinthians 16:8*
TRUMPETS (Later: Rosh Hashanah—New Year's Day)	*Leviticus 23:23-25; Numbers 29:1-6*	7th month (Tishri) 1	An assembly on a day of rest commemorated with trumpet blasts and sacrifices	
DAY OF ATONEMENT (Yom Kippur)	*Leviticus 16; 23:26-32; Numbers 29:7-11*	7th month (Tishri) 10	A day of rest, fasting and and sacrifices of atonement for priests and people and atonement for the tabernacle and altar	*Acts 27:9; Romans 3:24-26; Hebrews 9:1-14,23-26; 10:19-22*
TABERNACLES (Booths) (Ingathering)	*Exodus 23:16b; 34:22b; Leviticus 23:33-36,39-43; Numbers 29:12-34; Deuteronomy 16:13-15*	7th month (Tishri) 15-21	A week of celebration for the harvest; living in booths and offering sacrifices	*John 7:2-37*
SACRED ASSEMBLY	*Leviticus 23:36; Numbers 29:35-38*	7th month (Tishri) 22	A day of convocation, rest and offering sacrifices	*John 7:37-44*
DEDICATION		9th month	A commemoration of the purification of the temple in the Maccabean era (166-160 B.C.)	*John 10:22-39*
PURIM	*Esther 9:18-32*	12th month (Adar) 14,15	A day of joy and feasting and giving presents	

The Passover and Unleavened Bread

4 " 'These are the LORD's appointed feasts, the sacred assemblies you are to proclaim at their appointed times: 5 The LORD's Passover begins at twilight on the fourteenth day of the first month.[t] 6 On the fifteenth day of that month the LORD's Feast of Unleavened Bread begins; for seven days you must eat bread made without yeast. 7 On the first day hold a sacred assembly[u] and do no regular work. 8 For seven days present an offering made to the LORD by fire. And on the seventh day hold a sacred assembly and do no regular work.' "

Firstfruits

9 The LORD said to Moses, 10 "Speak to the Israelites and say to them: 'When you enter the land I am going to give you and you reap its harvest, bring to the priest a sheaf[v] of the first grain you harvest. 11 He is to wave the sheaf before the LORD[w] so it will be accepted on your behalf; the priest is to wave it on the day after the Sabbath. 12 On the day you wave the sheaf, you must sacrifice as a burnt offering to the LORD a lamb a year old without defect, 13 together with its grain offering[x] of two-tenths of an ephah[a] of fine flour mixed with oil—an offering made to the LORD by fire, a pleasing aroma—and its drink offering of a quarter of a hin[b] of wine. 14 You must not eat any bread, or roasted or new grain, until the very day you bring this offering to your God.[y] This is to be a lasting ordinance for the generations to come,[z] wherever you live.

Feast of Weeks

15 " 'From the day after the Sabbath, the day you brought the sheaf of the wave offering, count off seven full weeks. 16 Count off fifty days up to the day after the seventh Sabbath,[a] and then present an offering of new grain to the LORD. 17 From wherever you live, bring two loaves made of two-tenths of an ephah of fine flour, baked with yeast, as a wave offering of firstfruits[b] to the LORD. 18 Present with this bread seven male lambs, each a year old and without defect, one young bull and two rams. They will be a burnt offering to the LORD, together with their grain offerings and drink offerings—an offering made by fire, an aroma pleasing to the LORD. 19 Then sacrifice one male goat for a sin offering and two lambs, each a year old, for a fellowship offering.[c] 20 The priest is to wave the two lambs before the LORD as a wave offering, together with the bread of the firstfruits. They are a sacred offering to the LORD for the priest. 21 On that same day you are to proclaim a sacred assembly[c] and do no regular work.[d] This is to be a lasting ordinance for the generations to come, wherever you live.

22 " 'When you reap the harvest[e] of your land, do not reap to the very edges of your field or gather the gleanings of your harvest.[f] Leave them for the poor and the alien. I am the LORD your God.' "

7 →PG. 139

Feast of Trumpets

23 The LORD said to Moses, 24 "Say to the Israelites: 'On the first day of the seventh month you are to have a day of rest, a sacred assembly commemorated with trumpet blasts.[g] 25 Do no regular work,[h] but present an offering made to the LORD by fire.' "

Day of Atonement

26 The LORD said to Moses, 27 "The tenth day of this seventh month[i] is the Day of Atonement.[j] Hold a sacred assembly[k] and deny yourselves,[d] and present an offering made to the LORD by fire. 28 Do no work on that day, because it is the Day of Atonement, when

23:5 [t] Ex 12:18-19; Nu 28:16-17; Dt 16:1-8
23:7 [u] ver 3,8
23:10 [v] Ex 23:16,19; 34:26
23:11 [w] Ex 29:24
23:13 [x] Lev 2:14-16; 6:20
23:14 [y] Ex 34:26 [z] Nu 15:21
23:16 [a] Nu 28:26; Ac 2:1
23:17 [b] Ex 34:22; Lev 2:12
23:21 [c] ver 2 [d] ver 3
23:22 [e] Lev 19:9 [f] Lev 19:10; Dt 24:19-21; Ru 2:15
23:24 [g] Lev 25:9; Nu 10:9,10; 29:1
23:25 [h] ver 21
23:27 [i] Lev 16:29 [j] Ex 30:10 [k] Nu 29:7

[a] *13* That is, probably about 4 quarts (about 4.5 liters); also in verse 17 [b] *13* That is, probably about 1 quart (about 1 liter) [c] *19* Traditionally *peace offering* [d] *27* Or *and fast*; also in verses 29 and 32

23:9-14

PROMISE 5

WORKING GRATEFULLY

God's intent in this passage was for the Israelites (and us) to maintain a proper perspective on work. After they arrived in Canaan, the land God had promised them, each Israelite farmer was to set aside the first-ripened grain—the very best (or "firstfruits") of his crops—as an offering to God. After laboring in the field through the planting and growing season—tilling, weeding, praying for rain—the farmers were excited that they had fresh, newly harvested crops to eat. "But first," God says in this passage, "remember my gifts to you, and remember that all your work, by itself, won't bring home the barley."

Today we cultivate deals, we write, we teach, we manufacture, we do an endless variety of jobs. Whatever activity you perform to put groceries on your table, take time regularly to offer some firstfruits to the One who provides it all.

For the next Promise 5 reading go to page 204.

atonement is made for you before the LORD your God. 29Anyone who does not deny himself on that day must be cut off from his people.[l] 30I will destroy from among his people[m] anyone who does any work on that day. 31You shall do no work at all. This is to be a lasting ordinance for the generations to come, wherever you live. 32It is a sabbath of rest for you, and you must deny yourselves. From the evening of the ninth day of the month until the following evening you are to observe your sabbath."

Feast of Tabernacles

33The LORD said to Moses, 34"Say to the Israelites: 'On the fifteenth day of the seventh month the LORD's Feast of Tabernacles[n] begins, and it lasts for seven days. 35The first day is a sacred assembly; do no regular work. 36For seven days present offerings made to the LORD by fire, and on the eighth day hold a sacred assembly[o] and present an offering made to the LORD by fire. It is the closing assembly; do no regular work.

37(" 'These are the LORD's appointed feasts, which you are to proclaim as sacred assemblies for bringing offerings made to the LORD by fire—the burnt offerings and grain offerings, sacrifices and drink offerings[p] required for each day. 38These offerings are in addition to those for the LORD's Sabbaths[q] and[a] in addition to your gifts and whatever you have vowed and all the freewill offerings you give to the LORD.)

39" 'So beginning with the fifteenth day of the seventh month, after you have gathered the crops of the land, celebrate the festival to the LORD for seven days;[r] the first day is a day of rest, and the eighth day also is a day of rest. 40On the first day you are to take choice fruit from the trees, and palm fronds, leafy branches and poplars,[s] and rejoice before the LORD your God for seven days. 41Celebrate this as a festival to the LORD for seven days each year. This is to be a lasting ordinance for the generations to come; celebrate it in the seventh month. 42Live in booths[t] for seven days: All native-born Israelites are to live in booths 43so your descendants will know[u] that I had the Israelites live in booths when I brought them out of Egypt. I am the LORD your God.' "

44So Moses announced to the Israelites the appointed feasts of the LORD.

23:29 [l]Ge 17:14; Nu 5:2
23:30 [m]Lev 20:3
23:34 [n]Ex 23:16; Dt 16:13; Ezr 3:4; Ne 8:14; Zec 14:16; Jn 7:2
23:36 [o]2Ch 7:9; Ne 8:18; Jn 7:37
23:37 [p]ver 2,4
23:38 [q]Eze 45:17
23:39 [r]Ex 23:16; Dt 16:13
23:40 [s]Ne 8:14-17
23:42 [t]Ne 8:14-16
23:43 [u]Dt 31:13; Ps 78:5

24:4 [v]Ex 25:31; 31:8
24:5 [w]Ex 25:30
24:6 [x]Ex 25:23-30; 1Ki 7:48
24:7 [y]Lev 2:2
24:8 [z]Nu 4:7; 1Ch 9:32; 2Ch 2:4 [a]Mt 12:5
24:9 [b]Lev 8:31; Mt 12:4; Mk 2:26; Lk 6:4
24:11 [c]Ex 3:15
24:12 [d]Ex 18:16; Nu 15:34
24:14 [e]Lev 20:27; Dt 13:9; 17:5, 7; 21:21
24:15 [f]Ex 22:28
24:16 [g]1Ki 21:10,13; Mt 26:66
24:17 [h]Ge 9:6; Ex 21:12; Nu 35:30-31; Dt 27:24
24:18 [i]ver 21

Oil and Bread Set Before the LORD

24 The LORD said to Moses, 2"Command the Israelites to bring you clear oil of pressed olives for the light so that the lamps may be kept burning continually. 3Outside the curtain of the Testimony in the Tent of Meeting, Aaron is to tend the lamps before the LORD from evening till morning, continually. This is to be a lasting ordinance for the generations to come. 4The lamps on the pure gold lampstand[v] before the LORD must be tended continually.

5"Take fine flour and bake twelve loaves of bread,[w] using two-tenths of an ephah[b] for each loaf. 6Set them in two rows, six in each row, on the table of pure gold[x] before the LORD. 7Along each row put some pure incense as a memorial portion[y] to represent the bread and to be an offering made to the LORD by fire. 8This bread is to be set out before the LORD regularly,[z] Sabbath after Sabbath,[a] on behalf of the Israelites, as a lasting covenant. 9It belongs to Aaron and his sons,[b] who are to eat it in a holy place, because it is a most holy part of their regular share of the offerings made to the LORD by fire."

A Blasphemer Stoned

10Now the son of an Israelite mother and an Egyptian father went out among the Israelites, and a fight broke out in the camp between him and an Israelite. 11The son of the Israelite woman blasphemed the Name[c] with a curse; so they brought him to Moses. (His mother's name was Shelomith, the daughter of Dibri the Danite.) 12They put him in custody until the will of the LORD should be made clear to them.[d]

13Then the LORD said to Moses: 14"Take the blasphemer outside the camp. All those who heard him are to lay their hands on his head, and the entire assembly is to stone him.[e] 15Say to the Israelites: 'If anyone curses his God,[f] he will be held responsible; 16anyone who blasphemes the name of the LORD must be put to death.[g] The entire assembly must stone him. Whether an alien or native-born, when he blasphemes the Name, he must be put to death.

17" 'If anyone takes the life of a human being, he must be put to death.[h] 18Anyone who takes the life of someone's animal must make restitution[i]—life for life. 19If anyone

[a] *38* Or *These feasts are in addition to the LORD's Sabbaths, and these offerings are* [b] *5* That is, probably about 4 quarts (about 4.5 liters)

injures his neighbor, whatever he has
done must be done to him: 20fracture
for fracture, eye for eye, tooth for
tooth.[j] As he has injured the other, so
he is to be injured. 21Whoever kills an
animal must make restitution, but
whoever kills a man must be put to
death.[k] 22You are to have the same
law for the alien[l] and the native-
born.[m] I am the LORD your God.' "
23Then Moses spoke to the Israelites,
and they took the blasphemer outside
the camp and stoned him. The Israelites did as the LORD commanded Moses.

The Sabbath Year

25 The LORD said to Moses on Mount
Sinai, 2"Speak to the Israelites and
say to them: 'When you enter the land
I am going to give you, the land itself
must observe a sabbath to the LORD.
3For six years sow your fields, and for
six years prune your vineyards and
gather their crops.[n] 4But in the seventh year the land is to have a sabbath
of rest, a sabbath to the LORD. Do not
sow your fields or prune your vineyards. 5Do not reap what grows of itself
or harvest the grapes of your untended
vines. The land is to have a year of rest.
6Whatever the land yields during the
sabbath year[o] will be food for you—
for yourself, your manservant and
maidservant, and the hired worker and
temporary resident who live among
you, 7as well as for your livestock and
the wild animals in your land. Whatever the land produces may be eaten.

The Year of Jubilee

8" 'Count off seven sabbaths of
years—seven times seven years—so
that the seven sabbaths of years
amount to a period of forty-nine years.
9Then have the trumpet[p] sounded everywhere on the tenth day of the seventh month; on the Day of Atonement
sound the trumpet throughout your
land. 10Consecrate the fiftieth year and
proclaim liberty[q] throughout the land
to all its inhabitants. It shall be a jubilee[r] for you; each one of you is to return to his family property and each to
his own clan. 11The fiftieth year shall be
a jubilee for you; do not sow and do not
reap what grows of itself or harvest the
untended vines. 12For it is a jubilee and
is to be holy for you; eat only what is
taken directly from the fields.
13" 'In this Year of Jubilee[s] everyone is to return to his own property.
14" 'If you sell land to one of your
countrymen or buy any from him, do
not take advantage of each other.[t]
15You are to buy from your countryman on the basis of the number of
years[u] since the Jubilee. And he is to
sell to you on the basis of the number
of years left for harvesting crops.
16When the years are many, you are to
increase the price, and when the years
are few, you are to decrease the
price,[v] because what he is really selling you is the number of crops. 17Do
not take advantage of each other,[w] but
fear your God.[x] I am the LORD your
God.[y]
18" 'Follow my decrees and be careful to obey my laws, and you will live
safely in the land.[z] 19Then the land
will yield its fruit,[a] and you will eat
your fill and live there in safety. 20You
may ask, "What will we eat in the seventh year[b] if we do not plant or harvest our crops?" 21I will send you such
a blessing[c] in the sixth year that the
land will yield enough for three years.
22While you plant during the eighth
year, you will eat from the old crop and
will continue to eat from it until the
harvest of the ninth year comes in.[d]
23" 'The land must not be sold permanently, because the land is mine[e]
and you are but aliens[f] and my tenants. 24Throughout the country that
you hold as a possession, you must
provide for the redemption of the land.
25" 'If one of your countrymen becomes poor and sells some of his property, his nearest relative[g] is to come
and redeem[h] what his countryman
has sold. 26If, however, a man has no
one to redeem it for him but he himself
prospers and acquires sufficient means
to redeem it, 27he is to determine the
value for the years since he sold it and
refund the balance to the man to
whom he sold it; he can then go back
to his own property. 28But if he does
not acquire the means to repay him,
what he sold will remain in the possession of the buyer until the Year of Jubilee. It will be returned in the Jubilee,
and he can then go back to his property.[i]
29" 'If a man sells a house in a walled
city, he retains the right of redemption
a full year after its sale. During that
time he may redeem it. 30If it is not
redeemed before a full year has passed,
the house in the walled city shall belong permanently to the buyer and his
descendants. It is not to be returned in
the Jubilee. 31But houses in villages
without walls around them are to be
considered as open country. They can
be redeemed, and they are to be returned in the Jubilee.
32" 'The Levites always have the
right to redeem their houses in the Le-

24:20 [j]Ex 21:24; Mt 5:38*
24:21 [k]ver 17
24:22 [l]Ex 12:49 [m]Nu 9:14; 15:16
25:3 [n]Ex 23:10
25:6 [o]ver 20
25:9 [p]Lev 23:24
25:10 [q]Isa 61:1; Jer 34:8,15,17; Lk 4:19 [r]Nu 36:4
25:13 [s]ver 10
25:14 [t]Lev 19:13; 1Sa 12:3,4
25:15 [u]Lev 27:18,23
25:16 [v]ver 27,51,52
25:17 [w]Pr 22:22; Jer 7:5,6; 1Th 4:6 [x]Lev 19:14 [y]Lev 19:32
25:18 [z]Lev 26:4,5; Dt 12:10; Ps 4:8; Jer 23:6
25:19 [a]Lev 26:4
25:20 [b]ver 4
25:21 [c]Dt 28:8,12; Hag 2:19; Mal 3:10
25:22 [d]Lev 26:10
25:23 [e]Ex 19:5 [f]Ge 23:4; 1Ch 29:15; Ps 39:12; Heb 11:13; 1Pe 2:11
25:25 [g]Ru 2:20; Jer 32:7 [h]Lev 27:13,19, 31; Ru 4:4
25:28 [i]ver 10

vitical towns,[j] which they possess. 33So the property of the Levites is redeemable—that is, a house sold in any town they hold—and is to be returned in the Jubilee, because the houses in the towns of the Levites are their property among the Israelites. 34But the pastureland belonging to their towns must not be sold; it is their permanent possession.[k]

7 →PG. 199

35" 'If one of your countrymen becomes poor[l] and is unable to support himself among you, help him[m] as you would an alien or a temporary resident, so he can continue to live among you. 36Do not take interest[n] of any kind[a] from him, but fear your God, so that your countryman may continue to live among you. 37You must not lend him money at interest or sell him food at a profit. 38I am the LORD your God, who brought you out of Egypt to give you the land of Canaan and to be your God.[o]

39" 'If one of your countrymen becomes poor among you and sells himself to you, do not make him work as a slave.[p] 40He is to be treated as a hired worker or a temporary resident among you; he is to work for you until the Year of Jubilee. 41Then he and his children are to be released, and he will go back to his own clan and to the property[q] of his forefathers. 42Because the Israelites are my servants, whom I brought out of Egypt, they must not be sold as slaves. 43Do not rule over them ruthlessly,[r] but fear your God.

44" 'Your male and female slaves are to come from the nations around you; from them you may buy slaves. 45You may also buy some of the temporary residents living among you and members of their clans born in your country, and they will become your property. 46You can will them to your children as inherited property and can make them slaves for life, but you must not rule over your fellow Israelites ruthlessly.

47" 'If an alien or a temporary resident among you becomes rich and one of your countrymen becomes poor and sells himself to the alien living among you or to a member of the alien's clan, 48he retains the right of redemption after he has sold himself. One of his relatives[s] may redeem him: 49An uncle or a cousin or any blood relative in his clan may redeem him. Or if he prospers,[t] he may redeem himself. 50He and his buyer are to count the time from the year he sold himself up to the Year of Jubilee. The price for his release is to be based on the rate paid to a hired man[u] for that number of years.

25:32 [j]Nu 35:1-8; Jos 21:2
25:34 [k]Nu 35:2-5
25:35 [l]Dt 24:14,15 [m]Dt 15:8; Ps 37:21,26; Lk 6:35
25:36 [n]Ex 22:25; Dt 23:19-20
25:38 [o]Ge 17:7; Lev 11:45
25:39 [p]Ex 21:2; Dt 15:12; 1Ki 9:22
25:41 [q]ver 28
25:43 [r]Ex 1:13; Eze 34:4; Col 4:1
25:48 [s]Ne 5:5
25:49 [t]ver 26
25:50 [u]Job 7:1; Isa 16:14; 21:16

26:1 [v]Ex 20:4; Lev 19:4; Dt 5:8 [w]Ex 23:24 [x]Nu 33:52
26:2 [y]Lev 19:30

51If many years remain, he must pay for his redemption a larger share of the price paid for him. 52If only a few years remain until the Year of Jubilee, he is to compute that and pay for his redemption accordingly. 53He is to be treated as a man hired from year to year; you must see to it that his owner does not rule over him ruthlessly.

54" 'Even if he is not redeemed in any of these ways, he and his children are to be released in the Year of Jubilee, 55for the Israelites belong to me as servants. They are my servants, whom I brought out of Egypt. I am the LORD your God.

Reward for Obedience

26 " 'Do not make idols[v] or set up an image or a sacred stone[w] for yourselves, and do not place a carved stone[x] in your land to bow down before it. I am the LORD your God.

2" 'Observe my Sabbaths and have reverence for my sanctuary.[y] I am the LORD.

3" 'If you follow my decrees and are

[a]36 Or *take excessive interest*; similarly in verse 37

26:1–46

PROMISE 1

FOLLOWING INSTRUCTIONS

Ever try to put something together without reading the instructions? Sure you have. C'mon, admit it. The man-hours guys waste in putting together toys and bicycles without instructions could probably bolster the economy of a small country.

In this chapter, God made things pretty simple for the Israelites by giving them an instruction manual for living life. He told Israel, in essence, "I invented life. I created and manufactured you guys. Here's your instruction manual, written by the inventor / manufacturer. If you want life to work, follow these instructions (vv. 1–13). You don't follow the instructions, you'll mess it up" (vv. 14–46). Make no mistake about it, this is a sobering chapter.

But God's instructions are simple. He demands obedience to his Word because he knows how life should be lived. This chapter's principles are still operative—God blesses obedience and disciplines disobedience. Take a few minutes and reflect on your life as you read Leviticus 26 very carefully. Then choose daily what you will do with your life: either follow God's instructions, or try to put it together on your own.

For the next Promise 1 reading go to page 163.

careful to obey[z] my commands, **4**I will
send you rain[a] in its season, and the
ground will yield its crops and the trees
of the field their fruit.[b] **5**Your threshing will continue until grape harvest
and the grape harvest will continue until planting, and you will eat all the
food you want[c] and live in safety in
your land.[d]

6" 'I will grant peace in the land,[e]
and you will lie down[f] and no one will
make you afraid.[g] I will remove savage beasts[h] from the land, and the
sword will not pass through your country. **7**You will pursue your enemies, and
they will fall by the sword before you.
8Five of you will chase a hundred, and
a hundred of you will chase ten thousand, and your enemies will fall by the
sword before you.[i]

9" 'I will look on you with favor and
make you fruitful and increase your
numbers,[j] and I will keep my covenant[k] with you. **10**You will still be
eating last year's harvest when you will
have to move it out to make room for
the new.[l] **11**I will put my dwelling
place[a][m] among you, and I will not abhor you. **12**I will walk[n] among you and
be your God, and you will be my people.[o] **13**I am the LORD your God, who
brought you out of Egypt so that you
would no longer be slaves to the Egyptians; I broke the bars of your yoke[p]
and enabled you to walk with heads
held high.

Punishment for Disobedience

14" 'But if you will not listen to me
and carry out all these commands,[q]
15and if you reject my decrees and abhor my laws and fail to carry out all my
commands and so violate my cov-
enant, **16**then I will do this to you: I will
bring upon you sudden terror, wasting
diseases and fever[r] that will destroy
your sight and drain away your life.[s]
You will plant seed in vain, because
your enemies will eat it.[t] **17**I will set
my face[u] against you so that you will
be defeated by your enemies; those
who hate you will rule over you,[v] and
you will flee even when no one is pursuing you.[w]

18" 'If after all this you will not listen
to me, I will punish you for your sins
seven times over.[x] **19**I will break down
your stubborn pride[y] and make the
sky above you like iron and the ground
beneath you like bronze.[z] **20**Your
strength will be spent in vain,[a] because your soil will not yield its crops,
nor will the trees of the land yield their
fruit.[b]

21" 'If you remain hostile toward me
and refuse to listen to me, I will multiply your afflictions seven times over,[c]
as your sins deserve. **22**I will send wild
animals[d] against you, and they will
rob you of your children, destroy your
cattle and make you so few in number
that your roads will be deserted.

23" 'If in spite of these things you do
not accept my correction[e] but continue to be hostile toward me, **24**I myself
will be hostile toward you and will afflict you for your sins seven times over.
25And I will bring the sword upon you
to avenge the breaking of the covenant.
When you withdraw into your cities, I
will send a plague[f] among you, and
you will be given into enemy hands.
26When I cut off your supply of
bread,[g] ten women will be able to
bake your bread in one oven, and they
will dole out the bread by weight. You
will eat, but you will not be satisfied.

27" 'If in spite of this you still do not
listen to me but continue to be hostile
toward me, **28**then in my anger I will be
hostile toward you, and I myself will
punish you for your sins seven times
over. **29**You will eat the flesh of your
sons and the flesh of your daughters.[h]
30I will destroy your high places,[i] cut
down your incense altars[j] and pile
your dead bodies on the lifeless forms
of your idols,[k] and I will abhor you. **31**I
will turn your cities into ruins and lay
waste your sanctuaries,[l] and I will
take no delight in the pleasing aroma
of your offerings. **32**I will lay waste the
land,[m] so that your enemies who live
there will be appalled. **33**I will scatter
you among the nations[n] and will draw
out my sword and pursue you. Your
land will be laid waste, and your cities
will lie in ruins. **34**Then the land will
enjoy its sabbath years all the time that
it lies desolate and you are in the country of your enemies;[o] then the land
will rest and enjoy its sabbaths. **35**All
the time that it lies desolate, the land
will have the rest it did not have during
the sabbaths you lived in it.

36" 'As for those of you who are left,
I will make their hearts so fearful in the
lands of their enemies that the sound
of a windblown leaf will put them to
flight.[p] They will run as though fleeing
from the sword, and they will fall, even
though no one is pursuing them.
37They will stumble over one another
as though fleeing from the sword, even
though no one is pursuing them. So
you will not be able to stand before
your enemies.[q] **38**You will perish
among the nations; the land of your

26:3 [z]Dt 7:12; 11:13,22; 28:1,9
26:4 [a]Dt 11:14 [b]Ps 67:6
26:5 [c]Dt 11:15; Joel 2:19,26; Am 9_:13 [d]Lev 25:18
26:6 [e]Ps 29:11; 85:8; 147:14 [f]Ps 4:8 [g]Zep 3:13 [h]ver 22
26:8 [i]Dt 32:30; Jos 23:10
26:9 [j]Ge 17:6; Ne 9:23 [k]Ge 17:7
26:10 [l]Lev 25:22
26:11 [m]Ex 25:8; Ps 76:2; Eze 37:27
26:12 [n]Ge 3:8 [o]2Co 6:16*
26:13 [p]Eze 34:27
26:14 [q]Dt 28:15-68; Mal 2:2
26:16 [r]Dt 28:22,35 [s]1Sa 2:33 [t]Job 31:8
26:17 [u]Lev 17:10 [v]Ps 106:41 [w]ver 36,37; Dt 28:7,25; Ps 53:5
26:18 [x]ver 21
26:19 [y]Isa 25:11 [z]Dt 28:23
26:20 [a]Ps 127:1; Isa 17:11 [b]Dt 11:17
26:21 [c]ver 18
26:22 [d]Dt 32:24
26:23 [e]Jer 2:30; 5:3
26:25 [f]Nu 14:12; Eze 5:17
26:26 [g]Ps 105:16; Isa 3:1; Mic 6:14
26:29 [h]Dt 28:53
26:30 [i]2Ch 34:3; Eze 6:3 [j]Eze 6:6 [k]Eze 6:13
26:31 [l]Ps 74:3-7
26:32 [m]Jer 9:11
26:33 [n]Dt 4:27; Eze 12:15; 20:23; Zec 7:14
26:34 [o]ver 43; 2Ch 36:21
26:36 [p]Eze 21:7
26:37 [q]Jos 7:12

[a] *11* Or *my tabernacle*

enemies will devour you.[r] 39Those of you who are left will waste away in the lands of their enemies because of their sins; also because of their fathers' sins they will waste away.[s]

40" 'But if they will confess their sins and the sins of their fathers[t]—their treachery against me and their hostility toward me, 41which made me hostile toward them so that I sent them into the land of their enemies—then when their uncircumcised hearts[u] are humbled and they pay for their sin, 42I will remember my covenant with Jacob[v] and my covenant with Isaac[w] and my covenant with Abraham, and I will remember the land. 43For the land will be deserted by them and will enjoy its sabbaths while it lies desolate without them. They will pay for their sins because they rejected my laws and abhorred my decrees. 44Yet in spite of this, when they are in the land of their enemies, I will not reject them or abhor[x] them so as to destroy them completely,[y] breaking my covenant[z] with them. I am the LORD their God. 45But for their sake I will remember[a] the covenant with their ancestors whom I brought out of Egypt[b] in the sight of the nations to be their God. I am the LORD.' "

46These are the decrees, the laws and the regulations that the LORD established on Mount Sinai between himself and the Israelites through Moses.[c]

Redeeming What Is the LORD's

27 The LORD said to Moses, 2"Speak to the Israelites and say to them: 'If anyone makes a special vow[d] to dedicate persons to the LORD by giving equivalent values, 3set the value of a male between the ages of twenty and sixty at fifty shekels[a] of silver, according to the sanctuary shekel[b];[e] 4and if it is a female, set her value at thirty shekels.[c] 5If it is a person between the ages of five and twenty, set the value of a male at twenty shekels[d] and of a female at ten shekels.[e] 6If it is a person between one month and five years, set the value of a male at five shekels[f][f] of silver and that of a female at three shekels[g] of silver. 7If it is a person sixty years old or more, set the value of a male at fifteen shekels[h] and of a female at ten shekels. 8If anyone making the vow is too poor to pay[g] the specified amount, he is to present the person to the priest, who will set the value[h] for him according to what the man making the vow can afford.

9" 'If what he vowed is an animal that is acceptable as an offering to the LORD, such an animal given to the LORD becomes holy. 10He must not exchange it or substitute a good one for a bad one, or a bad one for a good one;[i] if he should substitute one animal for another, both it and the substitute become holy. 11If what he vowed is a ceremonially unclean animal—one that is not acceptable as an offering to the LORD—the animal must be presented to the priest, 12who will judge its quality as good or bad. Whatever value the priest then sets, that is what it will be. 13If the owner wishes to redeem[j] the animal, he must add a fifth to its value.

14" 'If a man dedicates his house as something holy to the LORD, the priest will judge its quality as good or bad. Whatever value the priest then sets, so it will remain. 15If the man who dedicates his house redeems it,[k] he must add a fifth to its value, and the house will again become his.

16" 'If a man dedicates to the LORD part of his family land, its value is to be set according to the amount of seed required for it—fifty shekels of silver to a homer[i] of barley seed. 17If he dedicates his field during the Year of Jubilee, the value that has been set remains. 18But if he dedicates his field after the Jubilee, the priest will determine the value according to the number of years that remain[l] until the next Year of Jubilee, and its set value will be reduced. 19If the man who dedicates the field wishes to redeem it, he must add a fifth to its value, and the field will again become his. 20If, however, he does not redeem the field, or if he has sold it to someone else, it can never be redeemed. 21When the field is released in the Jubilee,[m] it will become holy, like a field devoted to the LORD;[n] it will become the property of the priests.[j]

22" 'If a man dedicates to the LORD a field he has bought, which is not part of his family land, 23the priest will determine its value up to the Year of Jubilee, and the man must pay its value on that day as something holy to the LORD. 24In the Year of Jubilee the field will revert to the person from whom he bought

26:38 [r]Dt 4:26
26:39 [s]Eze 4:17
26:40 [t]Jer 3:12-15; Lk 15:18; 1Jn 1:9
26:41 [u]Eze 44:7,9; Ac 7:51
26:42 [v]Ge 22:15-18; 28:15 [w]Ge 26:5
26:44 [x]Ro 11:2 [y]Dt 4:31; Jer 30:11 [z]Jer 33:26
26:45 [a]Ge 17:7 [b]Ex 6:8; Lev 25:38
26:46 [c]Lev 7:38; 27:34
27:2 [d]Nu 6:2
27:3 [e]Ex 30:13; Nu 3:47; 18:16
27:6 [f]Nu 18:16
27:8 [g]Lev 5:11 [h]ver 12,14
27:10 [i]ver 33
27:13 [j]ver 15,19; Lev 25:25
27:15 [k]ver 13,20
27:18 [l]Lev 25:15
27:21 [m]Lev 25:10 [n]ver 28; Nu 18:14; Eze 44:29

a *3* That is, about 1 1/4 pounds (about 0.6 kilogram); also in verse 16
b *3* That is, about 2/5 ounce (about 11.5 grams); also in verse 25
c *4* That is, about 12 ounces (about 0.3 kilogram)
d *5* That is, about 8 ounces (about 0.2 kilogram)
e *5* That is, about 4 ounces (about 110 grams); also in verse 7
f *6* That is, about 2 ounces (about 55 grams)
g *6* That is, about 1 1/4 ounces (about 35 grams)
h *7* That is, about 6 ounces (about 170 grams)
i *16* That is, probably about 6 bushels (about 220 liters)
j *21* Or *priest*

it,[o] the one whose land it was. 25Every
value is to be set according to the sanctuary shekel,[p] twenty gerahs[q] to the
shekel.
26" 'No one, however, may dedicate
the firstborn of an animal, since the
firstborn already belongs to the
LORD;[r] whether an ox[a] or a sheep, it
is the LORD's. 27If it is one of the unclean animals,[s] he may buy it back at
its set value, adding a fifth of the value
to it. If he does not redeem it, it is to be
sold at its set value.
28" 'But nothing that a man owns
and devotes[b][t] to the LORD—whether
man or animal or family land—may be
sold or redeemed; everything so devoted is most holy to the LORD.
29" 'No person devoted to destruction[c] may be ransomed; he must be
put to death.
30" 'A tithe[u] of everything from the
land, whether grain from the soil or
fruit from the trees, belongs to the
LORD; it is holy to the LORD. 31If a man
redeems any of his tithe, he must add
a fifth of the value to it. 32The entire
tithe of the herd and flock—every
tenth animal that passes under the
shepherd's rod[v]—will be holy to the
LORD. 33He must not pick out the good
from the bad or make any substitution.[w] If he does make a substitution,
both the animal and its substitute become holy and cannot be redeemed.' "

34These are the commands the LORD
gave Moses on Mount Sinai for the Israelites.[x]

27:24 [o]Lev 25:28
27:25 [p]Ex 30:13; Nu 18:16 [q]Nu 3:47; Eze 45:12
27:26 [r]Ex 13:2,12
27:27 [s]ver 11
27:28 [t]Nu 18:14; Jos 6:17-19
27:30 [u]Ge 28:22; 2Ch 31:6; Mal 3:8
27:32 [v]Jer 33:13; Eze 20:37
27:33 [w]ver 10
27:34 [x]Lev 26:46; Dt 4:5

[a] *26* The Hebrew word can include both male and female. [b] *28* The Hebrew term refers to the irrevocable giving over of things or persons to the LORD. [c] *29* The Hebrew term refers to the irrevocable giving over of things or persons to the LORD, often by totally destroying them.

NUMBERS

AT A GLANCE

Key Principle: God tests us after he teaches us. If we repeatedly fail to obey him, he will eventually discipline us and we could miss significant opportunities.
Author: Moses
Time and Place: 1446 B.C. to 1406 B.C. / From Mount Sinai to the plains of Moab
Key Verses: 14:22–23; 20:12

BENEFIT

Numbers reminds us of God's holiness and outlines the danger of dishonoring him by the sin of unbelief. It teaches us that without an eternal perspective, we will live by sight rather than faith and we will be unwilling to take the risks of obedience.

SETTING

Numbers traces Israel's wilderness experiences. It begins at the foot of Mount Sinai right after the month of revelation recorded in Leviticus. After receiving additional revelation through Moses, the people depart from Mount Sinai and journey to Kadesh where they send out the twelve spies. Because of their unbelief, they are consigned to wander for 38 years in the wilderness. God then prepares a new generation for his service and for life in the plains of Moab—the promised land.

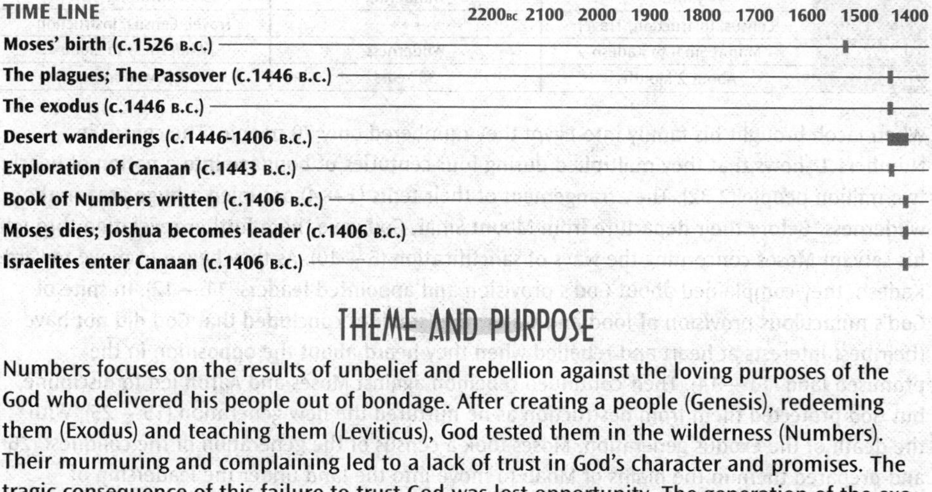

THEME AND PURPOSE

Numbers focuses on the results of unbelief and rebellion against the loving purposes of the God who delivered his people out of bondage. After creating a people (Genesis), redeeming them (Exodus) and teaching them (Leviticus), God tested them in the wilderness (Numbers). Their murmuring and complaining led to a lack of trust in God's character and promises. The tragic consequence of this failure to trust God was lost opportunity. The generation of the exodus would not be the generation of the conquest; instead, they were consigned to literally kill time for an extra 38 years until those who were twenty years and older died in the wilderness. (Some scholars estimate that an average of almost ninety people perished per day during this 38-year period.) Numbers was written to record this sad transition from one generation to the next.

UNIQUE CONTRIBUTION

Numbers illustrates God's pattern of teaching and testing more clearly than any other portion of Scripture. It develops the truth that perspective is critical to obedience: When Moses sent the twelve spies to check out the promised land, ten viewed the situation from a human perspective; their testimony filled the people with fear and doubt. But Joshua and Caleb saw the same situation through the lens of God's provision and promises. When the people drew back into disbelief they missed their moment, and God began to prepare a new generation to be taught and tested.

LINKS TO THE NEW TESTAMENT

"Just as Moses lifted up the snake in the desert, so the Son of Man must be lifted up, that everyone who believes in him may have eternal life" (John 3:14–15). The bronze snake that Moses put on a pole (21:6–9) was a portrait of Jesus' crucifixion.

"They all ate the same spiritual food and drank the same spiritual drink; for they drank from the spiritual rock that accompanied them, and that rock was Christ" (1 Corinthians 10:3 – 4). The daily manna that sustained the children of Israel prefigured the Bread of Life that came down from heaven (John 6:31–35), and the rock that satisfied their thirst was also an illustration of Christ.

OVERVIEW

FOCUS	The First Generation	The Lost Opportunity	The Second Generation
REFERENCE	1 — 14	15 — 20	21 — 36
TOPICS	Preparation	Postponement	Promise
	Waiting	Wandering	Waiting
	Census, Instruction, Travel	♦♦♦	Travel, Census, Instruction
LOCATION	Mount Sinai to Kadesh	Wilderness	Wilderness to Moab
TIME	About 2 Months	38 Years	A Few Months

When Jacob brought his family into Egypt they numbered only 70 people. The census in Numbers 1 shows that they multiplied during four centuries of bondage into a nation of nearly two million people (2:32). The arrangement of their tents (1—4) occupied a huge area in the wilderness. Before their departure from Mount Sinai, God gave them further revelation through his servant Moses concerning the ways of sanctification (5—10). As they began to move toward Kadesh, they complained about God's provision and appointed leaders (11—12). In spite of God's miraculous provision of food and water, the Israelites concluded that God did not have their best interests at heart and rebelled when they heard about the opposition in the promised land (13—14). Their continued rebellion against Moses and Aaron led to discipline, but God protected them from destruction as he nurtured the new generation (15—25). With the death of the exodus generation, Moses took a census of the generation of the conquest (26) and prepared them in the plains of Moab to move into the land under the leadership of Joshua, his successor (27—36).

NUMBERS

The Census

1 The LORD spoke to Moses in the Tent
of Meeting[a] in the Desert of Sinai[b]
on the first day of the second month[c]
of the second year after the Israelites
came out of Egypt. He said: 2"Take a
census[d] of the whole Israelite community by their clans and families, listing every man by name, one by one.
3You and Aaron are to number by their
divisions all the men in Israel twenty
years old or more[e] who are able to
serve in the army. 4One man from each
tribe, each the head of his family,[f] is
to help you.[g] 5These are the names of
the men who are to assist you:

from Reuben,[h] Elizur son of
Shedeur;
6from Simeon, Shelumiel son of
Zurishaddai;
7from Judah,[i] Nahshon son of
Amminadab;[j]
8from Issachar,[k] Nethanel son of
Zuar;
9from Zebulun,[l] Eliab son of Helon;
10from the sons of Joseph:
from Ephraim,[m] Elishama son
of Ammihud;
from Manasseh, Gamaliel son
of Pedahzur;
11from Benjamin, Abidan son of
Gideoni;
12from Dan,[n] Ahiezer son of Ammishaddai;
13from Asher,[o] Pagiel son of Ocran;
14from Gad, Eliasaph son of
Deuel;[p]
15from Naphtali,[q] Ahira son of
Enan."

16These were the men appointed
from the community, the leaders[r] of
their ancestral tribes. They were the
heads of the clans of Israel.[s]

17Moses and Aaron took these men
whose names had been given, 18and
they called the whole community together on the first day of the second
month.[t] The people indicated their
ancestry[u] by their clans and families,
and the men twenty years old or more
were listed by name, one by one, 19as
the LORD commanded Moses. And so
he counted them in the Desert of Sinai:

20From the descendants of Reuben[v]
the firstborn son of Israel:
All the men twenty years old or
more who were able to serve in
the army were listed by name,
one by one, according to the
records of their clans and families. 21The number from the
tribe of Reuben was 46,500.

22From the descendants of Simeon:[w]
All the men twenty years old or
more who were able to serve in
the army were counted and
listed by name, one by one, according to the records of their
clans and families. 23The number from the tribe of Simeon
was 59,300.

24From the descendants of Gad:[x]
All the men twenty years old or
more who were able to serve in
the army were listed by name,
according to the records of
their clans and families. 25The
number from the tribe of Gad
was 45,650.

26From the descendants of Judah:[y]
All the men twenty years old or
more who were able to serve in
the army were listed by name,
according to the records of
their clans and families. 27The
number from the tribe of Judah was 74,600.

28From the descendants of Issachar:[z]
All the men twenty years old or
more who were able to serve in
the army were listed by name,
according to the records of
their clans and families. 29The
number from the tribe of Issachar was 54,400.

30From the descendants of Zebulun:[a]
All the men twenty years old or
more who were able to serve in
the army were listed by name,
according to the records of
their clans and families. 31The
number from the tribe of Zebulun was 57,400.

32From the sons of Joseph:
From the descendants of Ephraim:[b]
All the men twenty years old or
more who were able to serve in
the army were listed by name,
according to the records of
their clans and families. 33The
number from the tribe of
Ephraim was 40,500.

1:1 [a]Ex 40:2 [b]Ex 19:1 [c]Ex 40:17
1:2 [d]Ex 30:11-16; Nu 26:2
1:3 [e]Ex 30:14
1:4 [f]ver 16 [g]Ex 18:21; Dt 1:15
1:5 [h]Ge 29:32; Dt 33:6; Rev 7:5
1:7 [i]Ge 29:35; Ps 78:68 [j]Ru 4:20; 1Ch 2:10; Lk 3:32
1:8 [k]Ge 30:18
1:9 [l]ver 30
1:10 [m]ver 32
1:12 [n]ver 38
1:13 [o]ver 40
1:14 [p]Nu 2:14
1:15 [q]ver 42
1:16 [r]Ex 18:25 [s]ver 4; Ex 18:21; Nu 7:2
1:18 [t]ver 1 [u]Ezr 2:59; Heb 7:3
1:20 [v]Nu 26:5-11; Rev 7:5
1:22 [w]Nu 26:12-14; Rev 7:7
1:24 [x]Ge 30:11; Nu 26:15-18; Rev 7:5
1:26 [y]Ge 29:35; Nu 26:19-22; Mt 1:2; Rev 7:5
1:28 [z]Nu 26:23-25; Rev 7:7
1:30 [a]Nu 26:26-27; Rev 7:8
1:32 [b]Nu 26:35-37

34From the descendants of Manasseh:[c]

All the men twenty years old or
more who were able to serve in
the army were listed by name,
according to the records of
their clans and families. 35The
number from the tribe of Manasseh was 32,200.

36From the descendants of Benjamin:[d]

All the men twenty years old or
more who were able to serve in
the army were listed by name,
according to the records of
their clans and families. 37The
number from the tribe of Benjamin was 35,400.

38From the descendants of Dan:[e]

All the men twenty years old or
more who were able to serve in
the army were listed by name,
according to the records of
their clans and families. 39The
number from the tribe of Dan
was 62,700.

40From the descendants of Asher:[f]

All the men twenty years old or
more who were able to serve in
the army were listed by name,
according to the records of
their clans and families. 41The
number from the tribe of Asher was 41,500.

42From the descendants of Naphtali:[g]

All the men twenty years old or
more who were able to serve in
the army were listed by name,
according to the records of
their clans and families. 43The
number from the tribe of
Naphtali was 53,400.

44These were the men counted by
Moses and Aaron[h] and the twelve
leaders of Israel, each one representing
his family. 45All the Israelites twenty
years old or more who were able to
serve in Israel's army were counted according to their families. 46The total
number was 603,550.[i]
47The families of the tribe of Levi,[j]
however, were not counted[k] along
with the others. 48The LORD had said to
Moses: 49"You must not count the tribe
of Levi or include them in the census of
the other Israelites. 50Instead, appoint
the Levites to be in charge of the tabernacle of the Testimony[l]—over all its
furnishings and everything belonging
to it. They are to carry the tabernacle
and all its furnishings; they are to take
care of it and encamp around it.
51Whenever the tabernacle is to move,
the Levites are to take it down, and
whenever the tabernacle is to be set up,
the Levites shall do it.[m] Anyone else
who goes near it shall be put to death.
52The Israelites are to set up their tents
by divisions, each man in his own
camp under his own standard.[n] 53The
Levites, however, are to set up their
tents around the tabernacle of the Testimony so that wrath will not fall[o] on
the Israelite community. The Levites
are to be responsible for the care of the
tabernacle of the Testimony.[p]"
54The Israelites did all this just as the
LORD commanded Moses.

1:34 [c]Nu 26:28-34; Rev 7:6
1:36 [d]Nu 26:38-41; 2Ch 17:17; Rev 7:8
1:38 [e]Ge 30:6; Nu 26:42-43
1:40 [f]Nu 26:44-47; Rev 7:6
1:42 [g]Nu 26:48-50; Rev 7:6
1:44 [h]Nu 26:64
1:46 [i]Ex 12:37; 38:26; Nu 2:32; 26:51
1:47 [j]Nu 2:33; 26:57 [k]Nu 4:3,49
1:50 [l]Ex 38:21; Ac 7:44
1:51 [m]Nu 3:38; 4:1-33
1:52 [n]Nu 2:2; Ps 20:5
1:53 [o]Lev 10:6; Nu 16:46; 18:5 [p]Nu 18:2-4
2:2 [q]Nu 1:52; Ps 74:4; Isa 31:9
2:3 [r]Nu 10:14; Ru 4:20; 1Ch 2:10
2:5 [s]Nu 1:8
2:7 [t]Nu 1:9
2:9 [u]Nu 10:14
2:10 [v]Nu 1:5
2:12 [w]Nu 1:6
2:14 [x]Nu 1:14

The Arrangement of the Tribal Camps

2 The LORD said to Moses and Aaron:
2"The Israelites are to camp around
the Tent of Meeting some distance
from it, each man under his standard[q]
with the banners of his family."

3On the east, toward the sunrise, the divisions of the camp of
Judah are to encamp under their
standard. The leader of the people
of Judah is Nahshon son of Amminadab.[r] 4His division numbers 74,600.
5The tribe of Issachar will camp
next to them. The leader of the
people of Issachar is Nethanel son
of Zuar.[s] 6His division numbers
54,400.
7The tribe of Zebulun will be
next. The leader of the people of
Zebulun is Eliab son of Helon.[t]
8His division numbers 57,400.
9All the men assigned to the
camp of Judah, according to their
divisions, number 186,400. They
will set out first.[u]

10On the south will be the divisions of the camp of Reuben under their standard. The leader of
the people of Reuben is Elizur son
of Shedeur.[v] 11His division numbers 46,500.
12The tribe of Simeon will camp
next to them. The leader of the
people of Simeon is Shelumiel son
of Zurishaddai.[w] 13His division
numbers 59,300.
14The tribe of Gad will be next.
The leader of the people of Gad is
Eliasaph son of Deuel.[a][x] 15His
division numbers 45,650.

a *14* Many manuscripts of the Masoretic Text, Samaritan Pentateuch and Vulgate (see also Num. 1:14); most manuscripts of the Masoretic Text *Reuel*

16All the men assigned to the camp of Reuben,[y] according to their divisions, number 151,450. They will set out second.

17Then the Tent of Meeting and the camp of the Levites[z] will set out in the middle of the camps. They will set out in the same order as they encamp, each in his own place under his standard.

18On the west will be the divisions of the camp of Ephraim[a] under their standard. The leader of the people of Ephraim is Elishama son of Ammihud.[b] 19His division numbers 40,500.

20The tribe of Manasseh will be next to them. The leader of the people of Manasseh is Gamaliel son of Pedahzur.[c] 21His division numbers 32,200.

22The tribe of Benjamin will be next. The leader of the people of Benjamin is Abidan son of Gideoni.[d] 23His division numbers 35,400.

24All the men assigned to the camp of Ephraim,[e] according to their divisions, number 108,100. They will set out third.[f]

25On the north will be the divisions of the camp of Dan, under their standard. The leader of the people of Dan is Ahiezer son of Ammishaddai.[g] 26His division numbers 62,700.

27The tribe of Asher will camp next to them. The leader of the people of Asher is Pagiel son of Ocran.[h] 28His division numbers 41,500.

29The tribe of Naphtali will be next. The leader of the people of Naphtali is Ahira son of Enan.[i] 30His division numbers 53,400.

31All the men assigned to the camp of Dan number 157,600. They will set out last,[j] under their standards.

32These are the Israelites, counted according to their families. All those in the camps, by their divisions, number 603,550.[k] 33The Levites, however, were not counted[l] along with the other Israelites, as the LORD commanded Moses.

34So the Israelites did everything the LORD commanded Moses; that is the way they encamped under their standards, and that is the way they set out, each with his clan and family.

The Levites

3 This is the account of the family of Aaron and Moses[m] at the time the LORD talked with Moses on Mount Sinai.

2The names of the sons of Aaron were Nadab the firstborn and Abihu, Eleazar and Ithamar.[n] 3Those were the names of Aaron's sons, the anointed priests,[o] who were ordained to serve as priests. 4Nadab and Abihu, however, fell dead before the LORD[p] when they made an offering with unauthorized fire before him in the Desert of Sinai.[q] They had no sons; so only Eleazar and Ithamar served as priests during the lifetime of their father Aaron.[r]

5The LORD said to Moses, 6"Bring the tribe of Levi[s] and present them to Aaron the priest to assist him.[t] 7They are to perform duties for him and for the whole community at the Tent of Meeting by doing the work[u] of the tabernacle. 8They are to take care of all the furnishings of the Tent of Meeting, fulfilling the obligations of the Israelites by doing the work of the tabernacle. 9Give the Levites to Aaron and his sons;[v] they are the Israelites who are to be given wholly to him.[a] 10Appoint Aaron and his sons to serve as priests;[w] anyone else who approaches the sanctuary must be put to death."[x]

11The LORD also said to Moses, 12"I have taken the Levites[y] from among the Israelites in place of the first male offspring[z] of every Israelite woman. The Levites are mine,[a] 13for all the firstborn are mine.[b] When I struck down all the firstborn in Egypt, I set apart for myself every firstborn in Israel, whether man or animal. They are to be mine. I am the LORD."

14The LORD said to Moses in the Desert of Sinai, 15"Count[c] the Levites by their families and clans. Count every male a month old or more."[d] 16So Moses counted them, as he was commanded by the word of the LORD.

17These were the names of the sons of Levi:[e]
Gershon, Kohath and Merari.[f]
18These were the names of the Gershonite clans:
Libni and Shimei.[g]
19The Kohathite clans:
Amram, Izhar, Hebron and Uzziel.[h]
20The Merarite clans:[i]
Mahli and Mushi.[j]

2:16 [y]Nu 10:18
2:17 [z]Nu 1:53; 10:21
2:18 [a]Ge 48:20; Jer 31:18-20 [b]Nu 1:10
2:20 [c]Nu 1:10
2:22 [d]Nu 1:11; Ps 68:27
2:24 [e]Nu 10:22 [f]Ps 80:2
2:25 [g]Nu 1:12
2:27 [h]Nu 1:13
2:29 [i]Nu 1:15
2:31 [j]Nu 10:25
2:32 [k]Ex 38:26; Nu 1:46
2:33 [l]Nu 1:47; 26:57-62
3:1 [m]Ex 6:27
3:2 [n]Ex 6:23; Nu 26:60
3:3 [o]Ex 28:41
3:4 [p]Lev 10:2 [q]Lev 10:1 [r]1Ch 24:1
3:6 [s]Dt 10:8; 31:9; 1Ch 15:2 [t]Nu 8:6-22; 18:1-7; 2Ch 29:11
3:7 [u]Lev 8:35; Nu 1:50
3:9 [v]Nu 8:19; 18:6
3:10 [w]Ex 29:9 [x]Nu 1:51
3:12 [y]Mal 2:4 [z]ver 41; Nu 8:16,18 [a]Ex 13:2
3:13 [b]Ex 13:12
3:15 [c]ver 39 [d]Nu 26:62
3:17 [e]Ge 46:11 [f]Ex 6:16
3:18 [g]Ex 6:17
3:19 [h]Ex 6:18
3:20 [i]Ge 46:11 [j]Ex 6:19

[a]9 Most manuscripts of the Masoretic Text; some manuscripts of the Masoretic Text, Samaritan Pentateuch and Septuagint (see also Num. 8:16) *to me*

These were the Levite clans, according to their families.

21 To Gershon belonged the clans of the Libnites and Shimeites;[k] these were the Gershonite clans. 22 The number of all the males a month old or more who were counted was 7,500. 23 The Gershonite clans were to camp on the west, behind the tabernacle. 24 The leader of the families of the Gershonites was Eliasaph son of Lael. 25 At the Tent of Meeting the Gershonites were responsible for the care of the tabernacle[l] and tent, its coverings,[m] the curtain at the entrance[n] to the Tent of Meeting, 26 the curtains of the courtyard[o], the curtain at the entrance to the courtyard surrounding the tabernacle and altar, and the ropes[p]—and everything related to their use.

27 To Kohath belonged the clans of the Amramites, Izharites, Hebronites and Uzzielites;[q] these were the Kohathite clans. 28 The number of all the males a month old or more was 8,600.[a] The Kohathites were responsible for the care of the sanctuary. 29 The Kohathite clans were to camp on the south side[r] of the tabernacle. 30 The leader of the families of the Kohathite clans was Elizaphan son of Uzziel. 31 They were responsible for the care of the ark,[s] the table,[t] the lampstand,[u] the altars,[v] the articles of the sanctuary used in ministering, the curtain,[w] and everything related to their use.[x] 32 The chief leader of the Levites was Eleazar son of Aaron, the priest. He was appointed over those who were responsible for the care of the sanctuary.

33 To Merari belonged the clans of the Mahlites and the Mushites;[y] these were the Merarite clans. 34 The number of all the males a month old or more who were counted was 6,200. 35 The leader of the families of the Merarite clans was Zuriel son of Abihail; they were to camp on the north side of the tabernacle.[z] 36 The Merarites were appointed[a] to take care of the frames of the tabernacle, its crossbars, posts, bases, all its equipment, and everything related to their use, 37 as well as the posts of the surrounding courtyard with their bases, tent pegs and ropes.

38 Moses and Aaron and his sons were to camp to the east[b] of the tabernacle, toward the sunrise, in front of the Tent of Meeting.[c] They were responsible for the care of the sanctuary[d] on behalf of the Israelites. Anyone else who approached the sanctuary was to be put to death.[e]

39 The total number of Levites counted at the LORD's command by Moses and Aaron according to their clans, including every male a month old or more, was 22,000.[f]

40 The LORD said to Moses, "Count all the firstborn Israelite males who are a month old or more[g] and make a list of their names. 41 Take the Levites for me in place of all the firstborn of the Israelites,[h] and the livestock of the Levites in place of all the firstborn of the livestock of the Israelites. I am the LORD."

42 So Moses counted all the firstborn of the Israelites, as the LORD commanded him. 43 The total number of firstborn males a month old or more, listed by name, was 22,273.[i]

44 The LORD also said to Moses, 45 "Take the Levites in place of all the firstborn of Israel, and the livestock of the Levites in place of their livestock. The Levites are to be mine. I am the LORD. 46 To redeem[j] the 273 firstborn Israelites who exceed the number of the Levites, 47 collect five shekels[b][k] for each one, according to the sanctuary shekel,[l] which weighs twenty gerahs.[m] 48 Give the money for the redemption of the additional Israelites to Aaron and his sons."

49 So Moses collected the redemption money from those who exceeded the number redeemed by the Levites. 50 From the firstborn of the Israelites he collected silver weighing 1,365 shekels,[c][n] according to the sanctuary shekel. 51 Moses gave the redemption money to Aaron and his sons, as he was commanded by the word of the LORD.

The Kohathites

4 The LORD said to Moses and Aaron: 2 "Take a census[o] of the Kohathite branch of the Levites by their clans and families. 3 Count all the men from thirty to fifty years of age[p] who come to serve in the work in the Tent of Meeting.

4 "This is the work of the Kohathites in the Tent of Meeting: the care of the most holy things.[q] 5 When the camp is to move, Aaron and his sons are to go in and take down the shielding curtain[r] and cover the ark of the Testimony with it.[s] 6 Then they are to cover

3:21 [k]Ex 6:17
3:25 [l]Ex 25:9 [m]Ex 26:14 [n]Ex 26:36; Nu 4:25
3:26 [o]Ex 27:9 [p]Ex 35:18
3:27 [q]1Ch 26:23
3:29 [r]Nu 1:53
3:31 [s]Ex 25:10-22 [t]Ex 25:23 [u]Ex 25:31 [v]Ex 27:1; 30:1 [w]Ex 26:33 [x]Nu 4:15
3:33 [y]Ex 6:19
3:35 [z]Nu 1:53; 2:25
3:36 [a]Nu 4:32
3:38 [b]Nu 2:3 [c]Nu 1:53
[d]ver 7; Nu 18:5 [e]ver 10; Nu 1:51
3:39 [f]Nu 26:62
3:40 [g]ver 15
3:41 [h]ver 12
3:43 [i]ver 39
3:46 [j]Ex 13:13; Nu 18:15
3:47 [k]Lev 27:6 [l]Ex 30:13 [m]Lev 27:25
3:50 [n]ver 46-48
4:2 [o]Ex 30:12
4:3 [p]ver 23; Nu 8:25; 1Ch 23:3,24,27; Ezr 3:8
4:4 [q]ver 19
4:5 [r]Ex 26:31,33 [s]Ex 25:10,16

[a] *28* Hebrew; some Septuagint manuscripts *8,300*
[b] *47* That is, about 2 ounces (about 55 grams)
[c] *50* That is, about 35 pounds (about 15.5 kilograms)

this with hides of sea cows,[a] spread a cloth of solid blue over that and put the poles[t] in place.

7"Over the table of the Presence[u] they are to spread a blue cloth and put on it the plates, dishes and bowls, and the jars for drink offerings; the bread that is continually there[v] is to remain on it. 8Over these they are to spread a scarlet cloth, cover that with hides of sea cows and put its poles in place.

9"They are to take a blue cloth and cover the lampstand that is for light, together with its lamps, its wick trimmers and trays,[w] and all its jars for the oil used to supply it. 10Then they are to wrap it and all its accessories in a covering of hides of sea cows and put it on a carrying frame.

11"Over the gold altar[x] they are to spread a blue cloth and cover that with hides of sea cows and put its poles in place.

12"They are to take all the articles used for ministering in the sanctuary, wrap them in a blue cloth, cover that with hides of sea cows and put them on a carrying frame.

13"They are to remove the ashes from the bronze altar[y] and spread a purple cloth over it. 14Then they are to place on it all the utensils used for ministering at the altar, including the firepans, meat forks,[z] shovels and sprinkling bowls.[a] Over it they are to spread a covering of hides of sea cows and put its poles[b] in place.

15"After Aaron and his sons have finished covering the holy furnishings and all the holy articles, and when the camp is ready to move, the Kohathites are to come to do the carrying.[c] But they must not touch the holy things or they will die.[d] The Kohathites are to carry those things that are in the Tent of Meeting.

16"Eleazar[e] son of Aaron, the priest, is to have charge of the oil for the light,[f] the fragrant incense, the regular grain offering[g] and the anointing oil. He is to be in charge of the entire tabernacle and everything in it, including its holy furnishings and articles."

17The LORD said to Moses and Aaron, 18"See that the Kohathite tribal clans are not cut off from the Levites. 19So that they may live and not die when they come near the most holy things,[h] do this for them: Aaron and his sons are to go into the sanctuary and assign to each man his work and what he is to carry. 20But the Kohathites must not go in to look[i] at the holy things, even for a moment, or they will die."

4:6 [t]Ex 25:13-15; 1Ki 8:7; 2Ch 5:8 **4:7** [u]Ex 25:23,29; Lev 24:6 [v]Ex 25:30 **4:9** [w]Ex 25:31,37,38 **4:11** [x]Ex 30:1 **4:13** [y]Ex 27:1-8 **4:14** [z]2Ch 4:16 [a]Jer 52:18 [b]Ex 27:6 **4:15** [c]Nu 7:9 [d]Nu 1:51; 2Sa 6:6,7 **4:16** [e]Lev 10:6 [f]Ex 25:6 [g]Ex 29:41; Lev 6:14-23 **4:19** [h]ver 15 **4:20** [i]Ex 19:21; 1Sa 6:19

The Gershonites

21The LORD said to Moses, 22"Take a census also of the Gershonites by their families and clans. 23Count all the men from thirty to fifty years of age[j] who come to serve in the work at the Tent of Meeting.

24"This is the service of the Gershonite clans as they work and carry burdens: 25They are to carry the curtains of the tabernacle,[k] the Tent of Meeting,[l] its covering[m] and the outer covering of hides of sea cows, the curtains for the entrance to the Tent of Meeting, 26the curtains of the courtyard surrounding the tabernacle and altar, the curtain for the entrance, the ropes and all the equipment used in its service. The Gershonites are to do all that needs to be done with these things. 27All their service, whether carrying or doing other work, is to be done under the direction of Aaron and his sons. You shall assign to them as their responsibility all they are to carry. 28This is the service of the Gershonite clans[n] at the Tent of Meeting. Their duties are to be under the direction of Ithamar son of Aaron, the priest.

The Merarites

29"Count the Merarites by their clans and families.[o] 30Count all the men from thirty to fifty years of age who come to serve in the work at the Tent of Meeting. 31This is their duty as they perform service at the Tent of Meeting: to carry the frames of the tabernacle, its crossbars, posts and bases,[p] 32as well as the posts of the surrounding courtyard with their bases, tent pegs, ropes, all their equipment and everything related to their use. Assign to each man the specific things he is to carry. 33This is the service of the Merarite clans as they work at the Tent of Meeting under the direction of Ithamar son of Aaron, the priest."

The Numbering of the Levite Clans

34Moses, Aaron and the leaders of the community counted the Kohathites[q] by their clans and families. 35All the men from thirty to fifty years of age who came to serve in the work in the Tent of Meeting, 36counted by clans, were 2,750. 37This was the total of all those in the Kohathite clans[r] who served in the Tent of Meeting. Moses and Aaron counted them according to the LORD's command through Moses.

38The Gershonites[s] were counted

4:23 [j]ver 3; 1Ch 23:3,24,27 **4:25** [k]Ex 27:10-18; Nu 3:26 [l]Nu 3:25 [m]Ex 26:14 **4:28** [n]Nu 7:7 **4:29** [o]Ge 46:11 **4:31** [p]Nu 3:36 **4:34** [q]ver 2 **4:37** [r]Nu 3:27 **4:38** [s]Ge 46:11

[a]6 That is, dugongs; also in verses 8, 10, 11, 12, 14 and 25

by their clans and families. 39All the men from thirty to fifty years of age who came to serve in the work at the Tent of Meeting, 40counted by their clans and families, were 2,630. 41This was the total of those in the Gershonite clans who served at the Tent of Meeting. Moses and Aaron counted them according to the LORD's command.

42The Merarites were counted by their clans and families. 43All the men from thirty to fifty years of age who came to serve in the work at the Tent of Meeting, 44counted by their clans, were 3,200. 45This was the total of those in the Merarite clans.[t] Moses and Aaron counted them according to the LORD's command through Moses.

46So Moses, Aaron and the leaders of Israel counted all the Levites by their clans and families. 47All the men from thirty to fifty years of age[u] who came to do the work of serving and carrying the Tent of Meeting 48numbered 8,580.[v] 49At the LORD's command through Moses, each was assigned his work and told what to carry.

Thus they were counted,[w] as the LORD commanded Moses.

The Purity of the Camp

5 The LORD said to Moses, 2"Command the Israelites to send away from the camp anyone who has an infectious skin disease[a][x] or a discharge[y] of any kind, or who is ceremonially unclean[z] because of a dead body. 3Send away male and female alike; send them outside the camp so they will not defile their camp, where I dwell among them.[a]" 4The Israelites did this; they sent them outside the camp. They did just as the LORD had instructed Moses.

Restitution for Wrongs

5The LORD said to Moses, 6"Say to the Israelites: 'When a man or woman wrongs another in any way[b] and so is unfaithful[b] to the LORD, that person is guilty[c] 7and must confess[d] the sin he has committed. He must make full restitution[e] for his wrong, add one fifth to it and give it all to the person he has wronged. 8But if that person has no close relative to whom restitution can be made for the wrong, the restitution belongs to the LORD and must be given to the priest, along with the ram with which atonement is made for him.[f] 9All the sacred contributions the Israelites bring to a priest will belong to him.[g] 10Each man's sacred gifts are his own, but what he gives to the priest will belong to the priest.[h]' "

The Test for an Unfaithful Wife

11Then the LORD said to Moses, 12"Speak to the Israelites and say to them: 'If a man's wife goes astray[i] and is unfaithful to him 13by sleeping with another man,[j] and this is hidden from her husband and her impurity is undetected (since there is no witness against her and she has not been caught in the act), 14and if feelings of jealousy[k] come over her husband and he suspects his wife and she is impure—or if he is jealous and suspects her even though she is not impure— 15then he is to take his wife to the priest. He must also take an offering of a tenth of an ephah[c][l] of barley flour[m] on her behalf. He must not pour oil on it or put incense on it, because it is a grain offering for jealousy, a reminder[n] offering to draw attention to guilt.

16" 'The priest shall bring her and have her stand before the LORD. 17Then he shall take some holy water in a clay jar and put some dust from the taber-

[a] *2* Traditionally *leprosy*; the Hebrew word was used for various diseases affecting the skin—not necessarily leprosy. [b] *6* Or *woman commits any wrong common to mankind* [c] *15* That is, probably about 2 quarts (about 2 liters)

4:45 [t]ver 29 **4:47** [u]ver 3 **4:48** [v]Nu 3:39 **4:49** [w]Nu 1:47 **5:2** [x]Lev 13:46 [y]Lev 15:2; Mt 9:20 [z]Lev 13:3; Nu 9:6-10 **5:3** [a]Lev 26:12; Nu 35:34; 2Co 6:16 **5:6** [b]Lev 6:2 [c]Lev 5:14-6:7 **5:7** [d]Lev 5:5; 26:40; Jos 7:19; Lk 19:8 [e]Lev 6:5 **5:8** [f]Lev 6:6,7; 7:7 **5:9** [g]Lev 6:17; 7:6-14 **5:10** [h]Lev 10:13 **5:12** [i]Ex 20:14 **5:13** [j]Lev 18:20; 20:10 **5:14** [k]Pr 6:34; SS 8:6 **5:15** [l]Ex 16:36 [m]Lev 6:20 [n]Eze 29:16

5:5-7

PROMISE 6

ANY AND EVERY LITTLE SIN

God put a critical emphasis on relationships here. "When a man or woman wrongs another in any way . . ." Okay, God, now, do you mean any way? Little insults or discriminations or injustices or unresolved anger or . . . ANY way? ANYBODY? Yep. That's what God is saying here. So it's real easy to sin against someone isn't it?

Look at verse 5 again: "and so is unfaithful to the LORD . . ." See it? That statement ups the ante. Any sin against any other human being (who, by the way, is created in God's image and purchased with the blood of his Son, Jesus Christ) is not primarily a personal, gender, race, age or any other issue. Regardless of the person's status, the stakes are the same because the issue is between you and God.

Remember this the next time someone cuts you off in traffic, or makes you wait in a long line at the store, or yells at your kid on the playing field. In those irritating moments, act with great caution toward anyone who ruffles your feathers; remember, you're not dealing with just Anyone.

For the next Promise 6 reading go to page 158.

nacle floor into the water. **18**After the
priest has had the woman stand before
the LORD, he shall loosen her hair[o]
and place in her hands the reminder
offering, the grain offering for jealousy,
while he himself holds the bitter water
that brings a curse. **19**Then the priest
shall put the woman under oath and
say to her, "If no other man has slept
with you and you have not gone
astray[p] and become impure while
married to your husband, may this bitter water that brings a curse not harm
you. **20**But if you have gone astray[q]
while married to your husband and
you have defiled yourself by sleeping with a man other than your
husband"— **21**here the priest is to put
the woman under this curse of the
oath[r]—"may the LORD cause your
people to curse and denounce you
when he causes your thigh to waste
away and your abdomen to swell.[a]
22May this water[s] that brings a
curse[t] enter your body so that your
abdomen swells and your thigh wastes
away.[b]"

" 'Then the woman is to say, "Amen.
So be it.[u]"

23" 'The priest is to write these
curses on a scroll[v] and then wash
them off into the bitter water. **24**He
shall have the woman drink the bitter
water that brings a curse, and this water will enter her and cause bitter suffering. **25**The priest is to take from her
hands the grain offering for jealousy,
wave it before the LORD[w] and bring it
to the altar. **26**The priest is then to take
a handful of the grain offering as a memorial offering and burn it on the altar;
after that, he is to have the woman
drink the water. **27**If she has defiled
herself and been unfaithful to her husband, then when she is made to drink
the water that brings a curse, it will go
into her and cause bitter suffering; her
abdomen will swell and her thigh
waste away,[c] and she will become accursed[x] among her people. **28**If, however, the woman has not defiled herself
and is free from impurity, she will be
cleared of guilt and will be able to have
children.

29" 'This, then, is the law of jealousy
when a woman goes astray[y] and defiles herself while married to her husband, **30**or when feelings of jealousy
come over a man because he suspects
his wife. The priest is to have her stand
before the LORD and is to apply this
entire law to her. **31**The husband will be
innocent of any wrongdoing, but the
woman will bear the consequences[z]
of her sin.' "

The Nazirite

6 The LORD said to Moses, **2**"Speak to
the Israelites and say to them: 'If a
man or woman wants to make a special
vow[a], a vow of separation to the LORD
as a Nazirite,[b] **3**he must abstain from
wine[c] and other fermented drink and
must not drink vinegar[d] made from
wine or from other fermented drink.
He must not drink grape juice or eat
grapes or raisins. **4**As long as he is a
Nazirite, he must not eat anything that
comes from the grapevine, not even
the seeds or skins.

5" 'During the entire period of his
vow of separation no razor[e] may be
used on his head.[f] He must be holy
until the period of his separation to the
LORD is over; he must let the hair of his
head grow long. **6**Throughout the period of his separation to the LORD he
must not go near a dead body.[g] **7**Even
if his own father or mother or brother
or sister dies, he must not make himself ceremonially unclean[h] on account of them, because the symbol of
his separation to God is on his head.
8Throughout the period of his separation he is consecrated to the LORD.

9" 'If someone dies suddenly in his
presence, thus defiling the hair he has
dedicated,[i] he must shave his head
on the day of his cleansing[j]—the seventh day. **10**Then on the eighth day he
must bring two doves or two young pigeons[k] to the priest at the entrance to
the Tent of Meeting. **11**The priest is to
offer one as a sin offering and the other
as a burnt offering[l] to make atonement[m] for him because he sinned by
being in the presence of the dead body.
That same day he is to consecrate his
head. **12**He must dedicate himself to
the LORD for the period of his separation and must bring a year-old male
lamb as a guilt offering. The previous
days do not count, because he became
defiled during his separation.

13" 'Now this is the law for the Nazirite when the period of his separation
is over.[n] He is to be brought to the
entrance to the Tent of Meeting.
14There he is to present his offerings to
the LORD: a year-old male lamb without defect for a burnt offering, a year-
old ewe lamb without defect for a sin
offering,[o] a ram without defect for a
fellowship offering,[d] **15**together with
their grain offerings and drink offer-

5:18 [o]Lev 10:6; 1Co 11:6
5:19 [p]ver 12,29
5:20 [q]ver 12
5:21 [r]Jos 6:26; 1Sa 14:24; Ne 10:29
5:22 [s]Ps 109:18 [t]ver 18 [u]Dt 27:15
5:23 [v]Jer 45:1
5:25 [w]Lev 8:27
5:27 [x]Isa 43:28; 65:15; Jer 26:6; 29:18; 42:18; 44:12,22; Zec 8:13
5:29 [y]ver 19
5:31 [z]Lev 5:1; 20:17
6:2 [a]Ge 28:20; Ac 21:23 [b]Jdg 13:5; 16:17; Am 2:11,12
6:3 [c]Lk 1:15 [d]Ru 2:14; Ps 69:21; Pr 10:26
6:5 [e]Ps 52:2; 57:4; 59:7; Isa 7:20; Eze 5:1 [f]1Sa 1:11
6:6 [g]Lev 21:1-3; Nu 19:11-22
6:7 [h]Nu 9:6
6:9 [i]ver 18 [j]Lev 14:9
6:10 [k]Lev 5:7; 14:22
6:11 [l]Ge 8:20 [m]Ex 29:36
6:13 [n]Ac 21:26
6:14 [o]Lev 14:10; Nu 15:27

[a] *21* Or *causes you to have a miscarrying womb and barrenness* [b] *22* Or *body and cause you to be barren and have a miscarrying womb* [c] *27* Or *suffering; she will have barrenness and a miscarrying womb* [d] *14* Traditionally *peace offering*; also in verses 17 and 18

ings,[p] and a basket of bread made without yeast—cakes made of fine flour mixed with oil, and wafers spread with oil.[q]

16" 'The priest is to present them before the LORD and make the sin offering and the burnt offering. 17He is to present the basket of unleavened bread and is to sacrifice the ram as a fellowship offering to the LORD, together with its grain offering and drink offering.

18" 'Then at the entrance to the Tent of Meeting, the Nazirite must shave off the hair that he dedicated.[r] He is to take the hair and put it in the fire that is under the sacrifice of the fellowship offering.

19" 'After the Nazirite has shaved off the hair of his dedication, the priest is to place in his hands a boiled shoulder of the ram, and a cake and a wafer from the basket, both made without yeast. 20The priest shall then wave them before the LORD as a wave offering; they are holy and belong to the priest, together with the breast that was waved and the thigh that was presented. After that, the Nazirite may drink wine.[s]

21" 'This is the law of the Nazirite who vows his offering to the LORD in accordance with his separation, in addition to whatever else he can afford. He must fulfill the vow he has made, according to the law of the Nazirite.' "

The Priestly Blessing

22The LORD said to Moses, 23"Tell Aaron and his sons, 'This is how you are to bless[t] the Israelites. Say to them:

24" ' "The LORD bless you[u]
and keep you;[v]
25the LORD make his face shine upon you[w]
and be gracious to you;[x]
26the LORD turn his face[y] toward you
and give you peace."[z] '

27"So they will put my name[a] on the Israelites, and I will bless them."

Offerings at the Dedication of the Tabernacle

7 When Moses finished setting up the tabernacle,[b] he anointed it and consecrated it and all its furnishings.[c] He also anointed and consecrated the altar and all its utensils.[d] 2Then the leaders of Israel,[e] the heads of families who were the tribal leaders in charge of those who were counted, made offerings. 3They brought as their gifts before the LORD six covered carts and twelve oxen—an ox from each leader and a cart from every two. These they presented before the tabernacle.

4The LORD said to Moses, 5"Accept these from them, that they may be used in the work at the Tent of Meeting. Give them to the Levites as each man's work requires."

6So Moses took the carts and oxen and gave them to the Levites. 7He gave two carts and four oxen to the Gershonites,[f] as their work required, 8and he gave four carts and eight oxen to the Merarites,[g] as their work required. They were all under the direction of Ithamar son of Aaron, the priest. 9But Moses did not give any to the Kohathites, because they were to carry on their shoulders[h] the holy things, for which they were responsible.

10When the altar was anointed,[i] the leaders brought their offerings for its dedication[j] and presented them before the altar. 11For the LORD had said to Moses, "Each day one leader is to bring his offering for the dedication of the altar."

12The one who brought his offering on the first day was Nahshon son of Amminadab of the tribe of Judah.

13His offering was one silver plate weighing a hundred and thirty shekels,**a** and one silver sprinkling bowl weighing seventy shekels,**b** both according to the sanctuary shekel,[k] each filled with fine flour mixed with oil as a grain offering;[l] 14one gold dish weighing ten shekels,**c** filled with incense;[m] 15one young bull,[n] one ram and one male lamb a year old, for a burnt offering;[o] 16one male goat for a sin offering;[p] 17and two oxen, five rams, five male goats and five male lambs a year old, to be sacrificed as a fellowship offering.**d**[q] This was the offering of Nahshon son of Amminadab.[r]

18On the second day Nethanel son of Zuar,[s] the leader of Issachar, brought his offering.

19The offering he brought was one silver plate weighing a hundred and thirty shekels, and one silver sprinkling bowl weighing seventy

6:15 [p]Nu 15:1-7 [q]Ex 29:2; Lev 2:4 **6:18** [r]ver 9; Ac 21:24 **6:20** [s]Ecc 9:7 **6:23** [t]Dt 21:5; 1Ch 23:13 **6:24** [u]Dt 28:3-6; Ps 28:9 [v]1Sa 2:9; Ps 17:8 **6:25** [w]Job 29:24; Ps 31:16; 80:3; 119:135 [x]Ge 43:29; Ps 25:16; 86:16 **6:26** [y]Ps 4:6; 44:3 [z]Ps 29:11; 37:11,37; Jn 14:27 **6:27** [a]Dt 28:10; 2Sa 7:23; 2Ch 7:14; Ne 9:10; Jer 25:29 **7:1** [b]Ex 40:17 [c]Ex 40:9 [d]ver 84,88; Ex 40:10 **7:2** [e]Nu 1:5-16 **7:7** [f]Nu 4:24-26,28 **7:8** [g]Nu 4:31-33 **7:9** [h]Nu 4:15 **7:10** [i]ver 1 [j]2Ch 7:9 **7:13** [k]Ex 30:13; Nu 3:47 [l]Lev 2:1 **7:14** [m]Ex 30:34 **7:15** [n]Ex 24:5; 29:3; Nu 28:11 [o]Lev 1:3 **7:16** [p]Lev 4:3,23 **7:17** [q]Lev 3:1 [r]Nu 1:7 **7:18** [s]Nu 1:8

a *13* That is, about 3 1/4 pounds (about 1.5 kilograms); also elsewhere in this chapter
b *13* That is, about 1 3/4 pounds (about 0.8 kilogram); also elsewhere in this chapter
c *14* That is, about 4 ounces (about 110 grams); also elsewhere in this chapter
d *17* Traditionally *peace offering*; also elsewhere in this chapter

shekels, both according to the sanctuary shekel, each filled with fine flour mixed with oil as a grain offering; **20**one gold dish[t] weighing ten shekels, filled with incense; **21**one young bull, one ram and one male lamb a year old, for a burnt offering; **22**one male goat for a sin offering; **23**and two oxen, five rams, five male goats and five male lambs a year old, to be sacrificed as a fellowship offering. This was the offering of Nethanel son of Zuar.

24On the third day, Eliab son of Helon,[u] the leader of the people of Zebulun, brought his offering.

25His offering was one silver plate weighing a hundred and thirty shekels, and one silver sprinkling bowl weighing seventy shekels, both according to the sanctuary shekel, each filled with fine flour mixed with oil as a grain offering; **26**one gold dish weighing ten shekels, filled with incense; **27**one young bull, one ram and one male lamb a year old, for a burnt offering; **28**one male goat for a sin offering; **29**and two oxen, five rams, five male goats and five male lambs a year old, to be sacrificed as a fellowship offering. This was the offering of Eliab son of Helon.

30On the fourth day Elizur son of Shedeur,[v] the leader of the people of Reuben, brought his offering.

31His offering was one silver plate weighing a hundred and thirty shekels, and one silver sprinkling bowl weighing seventy shekels, both according to the sanctuary shekel, each filled with fine flour mixed with oil as a grain offering; **32**one gold dish weighing ten shekels, filled with incense; **33**one young bull, one ram and one male lamb a year old, for a burnt offering; **34**one male goat for a sin offering; **35**and two oxen, five rams, five male goats and five male lambs a year old, to be sacrificed as a fellowship offering. This was the offering of Elizur son of Shedeur.

36On the fifth day Shelumiel son of Zurishaddai,[w] the leader of the people of Simeon, brought his offering.

37His offering was one silver plate weighing a hundred and thirty shekels, and one silver sprinkling bowl weighing seventy shekels, both according to the sanctuary shekel, each filled with fine flour mixed with oil as a grain offering; **38**one gold dish weighing ten shekels, filled with incense; **39**one young bull, one ram and one male lamb a year old, for a burnt offering; **40**one male goat for a sin offering; **41**and two oxen, five rams, five male goats and five male lambs a year old, to be sacrificed as a fellowship offering. This was the offering of Shelumiel son of Zurishaddai.

42On the sixth day Eliasaph son of Deuel,[x] the leader of the people of Gad, brought his offering.

43His offering was one silver plate weighing a hundred and thirty shekels, and one silver sprinkling bowl weighing seventy shekels, both according to the sanctuary shekel, each filled with fine flour mixed with oil as a grain offering; **44**one gold dish weighing ten shekels, filled with incense; **45**one young bull, one ram and one male lamb a year old, for a burnt offering; **46**one male goat for a sin offering; **47**and two oxen, five rams, five male goats and five male lambs a year old, to be sacrificed as a fellowship offering. This was the offering of Eliasaph son of Deuel.

48On the seventh day Elishama son of Ammihud,[y] the leader of the people of Ephraim, brought his offering.

49His offering was one silver plate weighing a hundred and thirty shekels, and one silver sprinkling bowl weighing seventy shekels, both according to the sanctuary shekel, each filled with fine flour mixed with oil as a grain offering; **50**one gold dish weighing ten shekels, filled with incense; **51**one young bull, one ram and one male lamb a year old, for a burnt offering; **52**one male goat for a sin offering; **53**and two oxen, five rams, five male goats and five male lambs a year old, to be sacrificed as a fellowship offering. This was the offering of Elishama son of Ammihud.[z]

54On the eighth day Gamaliel son of Pedahzur,[a] the leader of the people of Manasseh, brought his offering.

55His offering was one silver plate weighing a hundred and thirty shekels, and one silver sprinkling bowl weighing seventy shekels, both according to the sanctuary shekel, each filled with fine flour mixed with oil as a grain offering;

7:20 [t] ver 14
7:24 [u] Nu 1:9
7:30 [v] Nu 1:5
7:36 [w] Nu 1:6
7:42 [x] Nu 1:14
7:48 [y] Nu 1:10
7:53 [z] Nu 1:10
7:54 [a] Nu 1:10; 2:20

56 one gold dish weighing ten shekels, filled with incense; 57 one young bull, one ram and one male lamb a year old, for a burnt offering; 58 one male goat for a sin offering; 59 and two oxen, five rams, five male goats and five male lambs a year old, to be sacrificed as a fellowship offering. This was the offering of Gamaliel son of Pedahzur.

60 On the ninth day Abidan son of Gideoni,[b] the leader of the people of Benjamin, brought his offering.

61 His offering was one silver plate weighing a hundred and thirty shekels, and one silver sprinkling bowl weighing seventy shekels, both according to the sanctuary shekel, each filled with fine flour mixed with oil as a grain offering; 62 one gold dish weighing ten shekels, filled with incense; 63 one young bull, one ram and one male lamb a year old, for a burnt offering; 64 one male goat for a sin offering; 65 and two oxen, five rams, five male goats and five male lambs a year old, to be sacrificed as a fellowship offering. This was the offering of Abidan son of Gideoni.

66 On the tenth day Ahiezer son of Ammishaddai,[c] the leader of the people of Dan, brought his offering.

67 His offering was one silver plate weighing a hundred and thirty shekels, and one silver sprinkling bowl weighing seventy shekels, both according to the sanctuary shekel, each filled with fine flour mixed with oil as a grain offering; 68 one gold dish weighing ten shekels, filled with incense; 69 one young bull, one ram and one male lamb a year old, for a burnt offering; 70 one male goat for a sin offering; 71 and two oxen, five rams, five male goats and five male lambs a year old, to be sacrificed as a fellowship offering. This was the offering of Ahiezer son of Ammishaddai.

72 On the eleventh day Pagiel son of Ocran,[d] the leader of the people of Asher, brought his offering.

73 His offering was one silver plate weighing a hundred and thirty shekels, and one silver sprinkling bowl weighing seventy shekels, both according to the sanctuary shekel, each filled with fine flour mixed with oil as a grain offering; 74 one gold dish weighing ten shekels, filled with incense; 75 one young bull, one ram and one male lamb a year old, for a burnt offering; 76 one male goat for a sin offering; 77 and two oxen, five rams, five male goats and five male lambs a year old, to be sacrificed as a fellowship offering. This was the offering of Pagiel son of Ocran.

78 On the twelfth day Ahira son of Enan,[e] the leader of the people of Naphtali, brought his offering.

79 His offering was one silver plate weighing a hundred and thirty shekels, and one silver sprinkling bowl weighing seventy shekels, both according to the sanctuary shekel, each filled with fine flour mixed with oil as a grain offering; 80 one gold dish weighing ten shekels, filled with incense; 81 one young bull, one ram and one male lamb a year old, for a burnt offering; 82 one male goat for a sin offering; 83 and two oxen, five rams, five male goats and five male lambs a year old, to be sacrificed as a fellowship offering. This was the offering of Ahira son of Enan.

84 These were the offerings of the Israelite leaders for the dedication of the altar when it was anointed:[f] twelve silver plates, twelve silver sprinkling bowls[g] and twelve gold dishes.[h] 85 Each silver plate weighed a hundred and thirty shekels, and each sprinkling bowl seventy shekels. Altogether, the silver dishes weighed two thousand four hundred shekels,[a] according to the sanctuary shekel. 86 The twelve gold dishes filled with incense weighed ten shekels each, according to the sanctuary shekel. Altogether, the gold dishes weighed a hundred and twenty shekels.[b] 87 The total number of animals for the burnt offering came to twelve young bulls, twelve rams and twelve male lambs a year old, together with their grain offering. Twelve male goats were used for the sin offering. 88 The total number of animals for the sacrifice of the fellowship offering came to twenty-four oxen, sixty rams, sixty male goats and sixty male lambs a year old. These were the offerings for the dedication of the altar after it was anointed.[i]

89 When Moses entered the Tent of Meeting to speak with the LORD,[j] he heard the voice speaking to him from

7:60 [b] Nu 1:11
7:66 [c] Nu 1:12; 2:25
7:72 [d] Nu 1:13
7:78 [e] Nu 1:15; 2:29
7:84 [f] ver 1,10 [g] Nu 4:14 [h] ver 14
7:88 [i] ver 1,10
7:89 [j] Ex 25:21,22; 33:9,11

[a] *85* That is, about 60 pounds (about 28 kilograms) [b] *86* That is, about 3 pounds (about 1.4 kilograms)

between the two cherubim above the atonement cover[k] on the ark of the Testimony. And he spoke with him.

Setting Up the Lamps

8 The LORD said to Moses, 2"Speak to Aaron and say to him, 'When you set up the seven lamps, they are to light the area in front of the lampstand.[l]' "

3Aaron did so; he set up the lamps so that they faced forward on the lampstand, just as the LORD commanded Moses. 4This is how the lampstand was made: It was made of hammered gold[m]—from its base to its blossoms. The lampstand was made exactly like the pattern[n] the LORD had shown Moses.

The Setting Apart of the Levites

5The LORD said to Moses: 6"Take the Levites from among the other Israelites and make them ceremonially clean.[o] 7To purify them, do this: Sprinkle the water of cleansing[p] on them; then have them shave their whole bodies[q] and wash their clothes,[r] and so purify themselves. 8Have them take a young bull with its grain offering of fine flour mixed with oil;[s] then you are to take a second young bull for a sin offering. 9Bring the Levites to the front of the Tent of Meeting[t] and assemble the whole Israelite community.[u] 10You are to bring the Levites before the LORD, and the Israelites are to lay their hands on them.[v] 11Aaron is to present the Levites before the LORD as a wave offering[w] from the Israelites, so that they may be ready to do the work of the LORD.

12"After the Levites lay their hands on the heads of the bulls,[x] use the one for a sin offering to the LORD and the other for a burnt offering, to make atonement[y] for the Levites. 13Have the Levites stand in front of Aaron and his sons and then present them as a wave offering to the LORD. 14In this way you are to set the Levites apart from the other Israelites, and the Levites will be mine.[z]

15"After you have purified the Levites and presented them as a wave offering,[a] they are to come to do their work at the Tent of Meeting. 16They are the Israelites who are to be given wholly to me. I have taken them as my own in place of the firstborn, the first male offspring[b] from every Israelite woman. 17Every firstborn male in Israel, whether man or animal,[c] is mine. When I struck down all the firstborn in Egypt, I set them apart for myself.[d] 18And I have taken the Levites in place of all the firstborn sons in Israel.[e] 19Of all the Israelites, I have given the Levites as gifts to Aaron and his sons[f] to do the work at the Tent of Meeting on behalf of the Israelites[g] and to make atonement for them[h] so that no plague will strike the Israelites when they go near the sanctuary."

20Moses, Aaron and the whole Israelite community did with the Levites just as the LORD commanded Moses. 21The Levites purified themselves and washed their clothes.[i] Then Aaron presented them as a wave offering before the LORD and made atonement for them to purify them.[j] 22After that, the Levites came to do their work at the Tent of Meeting under the supervision of Aaron and his sons. They did with the Levites just as the LORD commanded Moses.

23The LORD said to Moses, 24"This applies to the Levites: Men twenty-five years old or more[k] shall come to take part in the work at the Tent of Meeting,[l] 25but at the age of fifty, they must retire from their regular service and work no longer. 26They may assist their brothers in performing their duties at the Tent of Meeting, but they themselves must not do the work. This, then, is how you are to assign the responsibilities of the Levites."

The Passover

9 The LORD spoke to Moses in the Desert of Sinai in the first month[m] of the second year after they came out of Egypt.[n] He said, 2"Have the Israelites celebrate the Passover at the appointed time. 3Celebrate it at the appointed time, at twilight on the fourteenth day of this month, in accordance with all its rules and regulations.[o]"

4So Moses told the Israelites to celebrate the Passover, 5and they did so in the Desert of Sinai at twilight on the fourteenth day of the first month.[p] The Israelites did everything just as the LORD commanded Moses.

6But some of them could not celebrate the Passover on that day because they were ceremonially unclean[q] on account of a dead body. So they came to Moses and Aaron[r] that same day 7and said to Moses, "We have become unclean because of a dead body, but why should we be kept from presenting the LORD's offering with the other Israelites at the appointed time?"

8Moses answered them, "Wait until I find out what the LORD commands concerning you."[s]

9Then the LORD said to Moses,

7:89 [k]Ps 80:1; 99:1
8:2 [l]Ex 25:37; Lev 24:2,4
8:4 [m]Ex 25:18,36; 25:18 [n]Ex 25:9
8:6 [o]Lev 22:2; Isa 1:16; 52:11
8:7 [p]Nu 19:9,17 [q]Lev 14:9; Dt 21:12 [r]Lev 14:8
8:8 [s]Lev 2:1; Nu 15:8-10
8:9 [t]Ex 40:12 [u]Lev 8:3
8:10 [v]Ac 6:6
8:11 [w]Lev 7:30
8:12 [x]Ex 29:10 [y]Ex 29:36
8:14 [z]Nu 3:12
8:15 [a]Ex 29:24
8:16 [b]Nu 3:12
8:17 [c]Ex 4:23 [d]Ex 13:2; Lk 2:23
8:18 [e]Nu 3:12
8:19 [f]Nu 3:9 [g]Nu 1:53 [h]Nu 16:46
8:21 [i]ver 7 [j]ver 12
8:24 [k]1Ch 23:3 [l]Ex 38:21; Nu 4:3
9:1 [m]Ex 40:2 [n]Nu 1:1
9:3 [o]Ex 12:2-11, 43-49; Lev 23:5-8; Dt 16:1-8
9:5 [p]Ex 12:1-13; Jos 5:10
9:6 [q]Lev 5:3 [r]Ex 18:15; Nu 27:2
9:8 [s]Ex 18:15; Nu 27:5,21; Ps 85:8

10“Tell the Israelites: ‘When any of you or your descendants are unclean because of a dead body or are away on a journey, they may still celebrate[t] the LORD’s Passover. 11They are to celebrate it on the fourteenth day of the second month at twilight. They are to eat the lamb, together with unleavened bread and bitter herbs.[u] 12They must not leave any of it till morning[v] or break any of its bones.[w] When they celebrate the Passover, they must follow all the regulations. 13But if a man who is ceremonially clean and not on a journey fails to celebrate the Passover, that person must be cut off from his people[x] because he did not present the LORD’s offering at the appointed time. That man will bear the consequences of his sin.

14“ ‘An alien[y] living among you who wants to celebrate the LORD’s Passover must do so in accordance with its rules and regulations. You must have the same regulations for the alien and the native-born.’ ”

The Cloud Above the Tabernacle

1 →PG. 160

15On the day the tabernacle, the Tent of the Testimony, was set up, the cloud[z] covered it. From evening till morning the cloud above the tabernacle looked like fire.[a] 16That is how it continued to be; the cloud covered it, and at night it looked like fire. 17Whenever the cloud lifted from above the Tent, the Israelites set out; wherever the cloud settled, the Israelites encamped.[b] 18At the LORD’s command the Israelites set out, and at his command they encamped. As long as the cloud stayed over the tabernacle, they remained in camp. 19When the cloud remained over the tabernacle a long time, the Israelites obeyed the LORD’s order and did not set out. 20Sometimes the cloud was over the tabernacle only a few days; at the LORD’s command they would encamp, and then at his command they would set out. 21Sometimes the cloud stayed only from evening till morning, and when it lifted in the morning, they set out. Whether by day or by night, whenever the cloud lifted, they set out. 22Whether the cloud stayed over the tabernacle for two days or a month or a year, the Israelites would remain in camp and not set out; but when it lifted, they would set out. 23At the LORD’s command they encamped, and at the LORD’s command they set out. They obeyed the LORD’s order, in accordance with his command through Moses.

The Silver Trumpets

10 The LORD said to Moses: 2“Make two trumpets[c] of hammered silver, and use them for calling the community[d] together and for having the camps set out. 3When both are sounded, the whole community is to assemble before you at the entrance to the Tent of Meeting. 4If only one is sounded, the leaders[e]—the heads of the clans of Israel—are to assemble before you. 5When a trumpet blast is sounded, the tribes camping on the east are to set out.[f] 6At the sounding of a second blast, the camps on the south are to set out.[g] The blast will be the signal for setting out. 7To gather the assembly, blow the trumpets,[h] but not with the same signal.[i]

8“The sons of Aaron, the priests, are to blow the trumpets. This is to be a lasting ordinance for you and the generations to come.[j] 9When you go into battle in your own land against an enemy who is oppressing you,[k] sound a blast on the trumpets. Then you will be remembered[l] by the LORD your God and rescued from your enemies.[m] 10Also at your times of rejoicing—your appointed feasts and New Moon festivals[n]—you are to sound the trumpets[o] over your burnt offerings and fellowship offerings,[a] and they will be a memorial for you before your God. I am the LORD your God.”

The Israelites Leave Sinai

11On the twentieth day of the second month of the second year,[p] the cloud lifted[q] from above the tabernacle of the Testimony. 12Then the Israelites set out from the Desert of Sinai and traveled from place to place until the cloud came to rest in the Desert of Paran. 13They set out, this first time, at the LORD’s command through Moses.[r]

14The divisions of the camp of Judah went first, under their standard.[s] Nahshon son of Amminadab[t] was in command. 15Nethanel son of Zuar was over the division of the tribe of Issachar, 16and Eliab son of Helon was over the division of the tribe of Zebulun. 17Then the tabernacle was taken down, and the Gershonites and Merarites, who carried it, set out.[u]

18The divisions of the camp of Reuben went next, under their standard.[v] Elizur son of Shedeur was in command. 19Shelumiel son of Zurishaddai was over the division of the tribe of Simeon, 20and Eliasaph son of Deuel was over the division of the tribe of

9:10 t2Ch 30:2
9:11 uEx 12:8
9:12 vEx 12:10,43 wEx 12:46; Jn 19:36*
9:13 xGe 17:14; Ex 12:15
9:14 yEx 12:48,49
9:15 zEx 40:34 aEx 13:21
9:17 bEx 40:36-38; Nu 10:11,12; 1Co 10:1
10:2 cNe 12:35; Ps 47:5 dJer 4:5,19; 6:1; Hos 5:8; Joel 2:1,15; Am 3:6
10:4 eEx 18:21; Nu 1:16; 7:2
10:5 fver 14
10:6 gver 18
10:7 hEze 33:3; Joel 2:1 i1Co 14:8
10:8 jNu 31:6
10:9 kJdg 2:18; 6:9; 1Sa 10:18; Ps 106:42 lGe 8:1 mPs 106:4
10:10 nPs 81:3 oLev 23:24
10:11 pEx 40:17 qNu 9:17
10:13 rDt 1:6
10:14 sNu 2:3-9 tNu 1:7
10:17 uNu 4:21-32
10:18 vNu 2:10-16

a *10* Traditionally *peace offerings*

Gad. 21Then the Kohathites set out, carrying the holy things.[w] The tabernacle was to be set up before they arrived.[x]

22The divisions of the camp of Ephraim[y] went next, under their standard. Elishama son of Ammihud was in command. 23Gamaliel son of Pedahzur was over the division of the tribe of Manasseh, 24and Abidan son of Gideoni was over the division of the tribe of Benjamin.

25Finally, as the rear guard[z] for all the units, the divisions of the camp of Dan set out, under their standard. Ahiezer son of Ammishaddai was in command. 26Pagiel son of Ocran was over the division of the tribe of Asher, 27and Ahira son of Enan was over the division of the tribe of Naphtali. 28This was the order of march for the Israelite divisions as they set out.

29Now Moses said to Hobab[a] son of Reuel[b] the Midianite, Moses' father-in-law,[c] "We are setting out for the place about which the LORD said, 'I will give it to you.'[d] Come with us and we will treat you well, for the LORD has promised good things to Israel."

30He answered, "No, I will not go;[e] I am going back to my own land and my own people."

31But Moses said, "Please do not leave us. You know where we should camp in the desert, and you can be our eyes.[f] 32If you come with us, we will share with you[g] whatever good things the LORD gives us.[h]"

33So they set out[i] from the mountain of the LORD and traveled for three days. The ark of the covenant of the LORD[j] went before them during those three days to find them a place to rest. 34The cloud of the LORD was over them by day when they set out from the camp.[k]

35Whenever the ark set out, Moses said,

"Rise up, O LORD!
May your enemies be
scattered;[l]
may your foes flee before you.[m]"

36Whenever it came to rest, he said,

"Return,[n] O LORD,
to the countless thousands of
Israel.[o]"

Fire From the LORD

11 Now the people complained about their hardships in the hearing of the LORD, and when he heard them his anger was aroused. Then fire from the LORD burned among them[p] and consumed some of the outskirts of the camp. 2When the people cried out to Moses, he prayed to the LORD[q] and the fire died down. 3So that place was called Taberah,[a][r] because fire from the LORD had burned among them.

Quail From the LORD

4The rabble with them began to crave other food,[s] and again the Israelites started wailing[t] and said, "If only we had meat to eat! 5We remember the fish we ate in Egypt at no cost—also the cucumbers, melons, leeks, onions and garlic.[u] 6But now we have lost our appetite; we never see anything but this manna!"

7The manna was like coriander seed[v] and looked like resin.[w] 8The people went around gathering it, and then ground it in a handmill or crushed it in a mortar. They cooked it in a pot or made it into cakes. And it tasted like something made with olive oil. 9When the dew[x] settled on the camp at night, the manna also came down.

10Moses heard the people of every family wailing, each at the entrance to his tent. The LORD became exceedingly angry, and Moses was troubled. 11He asked the LORD, "Why have you brought this trouble on your servant? What have I done to displease you that you put the burden of all these people on me?[y] 12Did I conceive all these people? Did I give them birth? Why do you tell me to carry them in my arms, as a nurse carries an infant,[z] to the land you promised on oath to their forefathers?[a] 13Where can I get meat for all these people?[b] They keep wailing to me, 'Give us meat to eat!' 14I cannot carry all these people by myself; the burden is too heavy for me.[c] 15If this is how you are going to treat me, put me to death[d] right now[e]—if I have found favor in your eyes—and do not let me face my own ruin."

16The LORD said to Moses: "Bring me seventy of Israel's elders who are known to you as leaders and officials among the people. Have them come to the Tent of Meeting, that they may stand there with you. 17I will come down and speak with you there, and I will take of the Spirit that is on you and put the Spirit on them.[f] They will help you carry the burden of the people so that you will not have to carry it alone.[g]

18"Tell the people: 'Consecrate yourselves[h] in preparation for tomorrow, when you will eat meat. The LORD heard you when you wailed,[i] "If only

10:21 [w]Nu 4:20 [x]ver 17
10:22 [y]Nu 2:24
10:25 [z]Nu 2:31; Jos 6:9
10:29 [a]Jdg 4:11 [b]Ex 2:18 [c]Ex 3:1 [d]Ge 12:7
10:30 [e]Mt 21:29
10:31 [f]Job 29:15
10:32 [g]Dt 10:18 [h]Ps 22:27-31; 67:5-7
10:33 [i]ver 12; Dt 1:33 [j]Jos 3:3
10:34 [k]Nu 9:15-23
10:35 [l]Ps 68:1 [m]Dt 7:10; 32:41; Ps 68:2; Isa 17:12-14
10:36 [n]Isa 63:17 [o]Dt 1:10
11:1 [p]Lev 10:2
11:2 [q]Nu 21:7
11:3 [r]Dt 9:22
11:4 [s]Ex 12:38 [t]Ps 78:18; 1Co 10:6
11:5 [u]Ex 16:3
11:7 [v]Ex 16:31 [w]Ge 2:12
11:9 [x]Ex 16:13
11:11 [y]Ex 5:22
11:12 [z]Isa 40:11; 49:23 [a]Ex 13:5
11:13 [b]Jn 6:5-9
11:14 [c]Ex 18:18
11:15 [d]Ex 32:32 [e]1Ki 19:4; Jnh 4:3
11:17 [f]ver 25,29; 1Sa 10:6; 2Ki 2:9,15; Joel 2:28 [g]Ex 18:18
11:18 [h]Ex 19:10 [i]Ex 16:7

[a]3 *Taberah* means *burning.*

we had meat to eat! We were better off
in Egypt!"[j] Now the LORD will give you
meat, and you will eat it. 19You will not
eat it for just one day, or two days, or
five, ten or twenty days, 20but for a
whole month—until it comes out of
your nostrils and you loathe it[k]—
because you have rejected the LORD,[l]
who is among you, and have wailed
before him, saying, "Why did we ever
leave Egypt?" ' "

21But Moses said, "Here I am among
six hundred thousand men[m] on foot,
and you say, 'I will give them meat to
eat for a whole month!' 22Would they
have enough if flocks and herds were
slaughtered for them? Would they have
enough if all the fish in the sea were
caught for them?"[n]

23The LORD answered Moses, "Is the
LORD's arm too short?[o] You will now
see whether or not what I say will come
true for you.[p]"

24So Moses went out and told the
people what the LORD had said. He
brought together seventy of their elders and had them stand around the
Tent. 25Then the LORD came down in
the cloud[q] and spoke with him,[r] and
he took of the Spirit[s] that was on him
and put the Spirit on the seventy elders.[t] When the Spirit rested on them,
they prophesied,[u] but they did not do
so again.[a]

26However, two men, whose names
were Eldad and Medad, had remained
in the camp. They were listed among
the elders, but did not go out to the
Tent. Yet the Spirit also rested on them,
and they prophesied in the camp. 27A
young man ran and told Moses, "Eldad
and Medad are prophesying in the
camp."

28Joshua son of Nun, who had been
Moses' aide[v] since youth, spoke up
and said, "Moses, my lord, stop
them!"[w]

29But Moses replied, "Are you jealous for my sake? I wish that all the
LORD's people were prophets[x] and
that the LORD would put his Spirit on
them!" 30Then Moses and the elders of
Israel returned to the camp.

31Now a wind went out from the
LORD and drove quail[y] in from the sea.
It brought them[b] down all around the
camp to about three feet[c] above the
ground, as far as a day's walk in any
direction. 32All that day and night and
all the next day the people went out
and gathered quail. No one gathered
less than ten homers.[d] Then they
spread them out all around the camp.
33But while the meat was still between
their teeth[z] and before it could be
consumed, the anger of the LORD
burned against the people, and he
struck them with a severe plague.[a]
34Therefore the place was named Kibroth Hattaavah,[e][b] because there they
buried the people who had craved other food.

35From Kibroth Hattaavah the people traveled to Hazeroth[c] and stayed
there.

Miriam and Aaron Oppose Moses

12 Miriam and Aaron began to talk
against Moses because of his Cushite wife,[d] for he had married a Cushite. 2"Has the LORD spoken only
through Moses?" they asked. "Hasn't
he also spoken through us?"[e] And the
LORD heard this.[f]

3(Now Moses was a very humble
man,[g] more humble than anyone else
on the face of the earth.)

4At once the LORD said to Moses,
Aaron and Miriam, "Come out to the
Tent of Meeting, all three of you." So
the three of them came out. 5Then the
LORD came down in a pillar of cloud;[h]
he stood at the entrance to the Tent
and summoned Aaron and Miriam.

11:18 [j]ver 5; Ac 7:39
11:20 [k]Ps 78:29; 106:14,15 [l]Jos 24:27; 1Sa 10:19
11:21 [m]Ex 12:37
11:22 [n]Mt 15:33
11:23 [o]Isa 50:2; 59:1 [p]Nu 23:19; Eze 12:25; 24:14
11:25 [q]Nu 12:5 [r]ver 17 [s]1Sa 10:6 [t]Ac 2:17 [u]1Sa 10:10
11:28 [v]Ex 33:11; Jos 1:1 [w]Mk 9:38-40
11:29 [x]1Co 14:5
11:31 [y]Ex 16:13; Ps 78:26-28
11:33 [z]Ps 78:30
[a]Ps 106:15
11:34 [b]Dt 9:22
11:35 [c]Nu 33:17
12:1 [d]Ex 2:21
12:2 [e]Nu 16:3 [f]Nu 11:1
12:3 [g]Mt 11:29
12:5 [h]Nu 11:25

a *25* Or *prophesied and continued to do so*
b *31* Or *They flew* **c** *31* Hebrew *two cubits* (about 1 meter) **d** *32* That is, probably about 60 bushels (about 2.2 kiloliters) **e** *34 Kibroth Hattaavah* means *graves of craving.*

12:1–13

PROMISE 6

HEARD ANY GOOD CRITICISM LATELY?

How could Moses so consistently please God (vv. 6–8) and at the same time so consistently aggravate people (vv. 1–2)? It's hard enough to be criticized, but to be criticized by your own family members when you know you're right? That's the worst. When we read what God did to those who wronged Moses (vv. 4–12), a voice inside says, "Yeah! Way to go! I wish God would do that for me!"

So what does a man who walks with God do when he has been criticized unfairly? Read verse 13.

Who among us hasn't been wronged? Some terribly, some for centuries? Reconciliation—between people and peoples—must and can happen as we draw closer to our common Savior. As you consider Moses' actions in this passage, try to imitate his pattern for dealing with someone who has wronged you. Write down the names of people you are alienated from and pray Moses' prayer for them every day for a week. Then act on your own prayers.

For the next Promise 6 reading go to page 173.

When both of them stepped forward,
6he said, "Listen to my words:

"When a prophet of the LORD is
among you,
I reveal myself to him in
visions,[i]
I speak to him in dreams.[j]
7But this is not true of my servant
Moses;[k]
he is faithful in all my house.[l]
8With him I speak face to face,
clearly and not in riddles;[m]
he sees the form of the LORD.[n]
Why then were you not afraid
to speak against my servant
Moses?"

9The anger of the LORD burned
against them, and he left them.[o]
10When the cloud lifted from above
the Tent, there stood Miriam—
leprous,[a] like snow.[p] Aaron turned
toward her and saw that she had leprosy;[q] 11and he said to Moses, "Please,
my lord, do not hold against us the sin
we have so foolishly committed.[r]
12Do not let her be like a stillborn infant coming from its mother's womb
with its flesh half eaten away."
13So Moses cried out to the LORD,
"O God, please heal her![s]"
14The LORD replied to Moses, "If her
father had spit in her face,[t] would she
not have been in disgrace for seven
days? Confine her outside the camp[u]
for seven days; after that she can be
brought back." 15So Miriam was confined outside the camp for seven days,
and the people did not move on till she
was brought back.
16After that, the people left Hazeroth[v] and encamped in the Desert of
Paran.

Exploring Canaan

13 The LORD said to Moses, 2"Send
some men to explore[w] the land of
Canaan, which I am giving to the Israelites. From each ancestral tribe send
one of its leaders."
3So at the LORD's command Moses
sent them out from the Desert of Paran. All of them were leaders of the Israelites. 4These are their names:

from the tribe of Reuben, Shammua son of Zaccur;
5from the tribe of Simeon, Shaphat son of Hori;
6from the tribe of Judah, Caleb
son of Jephunneh;[x]
7from the tribe of Issachar, Igal
son of Joseph;
8from the tribe of Ephraim, Hoshea son of Nun;
9from the tribe of Benjamin, Palti
son of Raphu;
10from the tribe of Zebulun, Gaddi-
el son of Sodi;
11from the tribe of Manasseh (a
tribe of Joseph), Gaddi son of
Susi;
12from the tribe of Dan, Ammiel
son of Gemalli;
13from the tribe of Asher, Sethur
son of Michael;
14from the tribe of Naphtali, Nahbi
son of Vophsi;
15from the tribe of Gad, Geuel son
of Maki.

16These are the names of the men Moses sent to explore the land. (Moses
gave Hoshea son of Nun[y] the name
Joshua.)[z]
17When Moses sent them to explore
Canaan, he said, "Go up through the
Negev[a] and on into the hill country.[b]
18See what the land is like and whether
the people who live there are strong or
weak, few or many. 19What kind of land
do they live in? Is it good or bad? What
kind of towns do they live in? Are they
unwalled or fortified? 20How is the soil?
Is it fertile or poor? Are there trees on
it or not? Do your best to bring back
some of the fruit of the land.[c]" (It was
the season for the first ripe grapes.)
21So they went up and explored the
land from the Desert of Zin[d] as far
as Rehob,[e] toward Lebo[b] Hamath.[f]
22They went up through the Negev and
came to Hebron, where Ahiman, Sheshai and Talmai,[g] the descendants of
Anak,[h] lived. (Hebron had been built
seven years before Zoan in Egypt.)[i]
23When they reached the Valley of Eshcol,[c] they cut off a branch bearing a
single cluster of grapes. Two of them
carried it on a pole between them,
along with some pomegranates and
figs. 24That place was called the Valley
of Eshcol because of the cluster of
grapes the Israelites cut off there. 25At
the end of forty days they returned
from exploring the land.

Report on the Exploration

26They came back to Moses and Aaron and the whole Israelite community
at Kadesh in the Desert of Paran. There
they reported to them[j] and to the
whole assembly and showed them the
fruit of the land. 27They gave Moses
this account: "We went into the land to
which you sent us, and it does flow
with milk and honey![k] Here is its

12:6 [i]Ge 15:1; 46:2 [j]Ge 31:10; 1Ki 3:5; Heb 1:1
12:7 [k]Jos 1:1-2; Ps 105:26 [l]Heb 3:2,5
12:8 [m]Dt 34:10 [n]Ex 20:4; Ps 17:15
12:9 [o]Ge 17:22
12:10 [p]Ex 4:6; Dt 24:9 [q]2Ki 5:1,27
12:11 [r]2Sa 19:19; 24:10
12:13 [s]Isa 30:26; Jer 17:14
12:14 [t]Dt 25:9; Job 17:6; 30:9-10; Isa 50:6 [u]Lev 13:46; Nu 5:2-3
12:16 [v]Nu 11:35
13:2 [w]Dt 1:22
13:6 [x]ver 30; Nu 14:6,24; 34:19; Jdg 1:12-15
13:16 [y]ver 8 [z]Dt 32:44
13:17 [a]Ge 12:9 [b]Jdg 1:9
13:20 [c]Dt 1:25
13:21 [d]Nu 20:1; 27:14; 33:36; Jos 15:1 [e]Jos 19:28 [f]Jos 13:5
13:22 [g]Jos 15:14 [h]Jos 15:13 [i]Ps 78:12,43; Isa 19:11,13
13:26 [j]Nu 32:8
13:27 [k]Ex 3:8

a *10* The Hebrew word was used for various diseases affecting the skin—not necessarily leprosy. b *21* Or *toward the entrance to*
c *23* *Eshcol* means *cluster*; also in verse 24.

fruit.[l] 28 But the people who live there are powerful, and the cities are fortified and very large.[m] We even saw descendants of Anak there. 29 The Amalekites live in the Negev; the Hittites, Jebusites and Amorites live in the hill country; and the Canaanites live near the sea and along the Jordan."

30 Then Caleb silenced the people before Moses and said, "We should go up and take possession of the land, for we can certainly do it."

31 But the men who had gone up with him said, "We can't attack those people; they are stronger than we are."[n] 32 And they spread among the Israelites a bad report[o] about the land they had explored. They said, "The land we explored devours[p] those living in it. All the people we saw there are of great size.[q] 33 We saw the Nephilim[r] there (the descendants of Anak[s] come from the Nephilim). We seemed like grasshoppers in our own eyes, and we looked the same to them."

The People Rebel

14 That night all the people of the community raised their voices and wept aloud. 2 All the Israelites grumbled against Moses and Aaron, and the whole assembly said to them, "If only we had died in Egypt! Or in this desert![t] 3 Why is the LORD bringing us to this land only to let us fall by the sword? Our wives and children will be taken as plunder. Wouldn't it be better for us to go back to Egypt?" 4 And they said to each other, "We should choose a leader and go back to Egypt.[u]"

5 Then Moses and Aaron fell facedown[v] in front of the whole Israelite assembly gathered there. 6 Joshua son of Nun and Caleb son of Jephunneh, who were among those who had explored the land, tore their clothes 7 and said to the entire Israelite assembly, "The land we passed through and explored is exceedingly good.[w] 8 If the LORD is pleased with us,[x] he will lead us into that land, a land flowing with milk and honey,[y] and will give it to us. 9 Only do not rebel[z] against the LORD. And do not be afraid of the people of the land,[a] because we will swallow them up. Their protection is gone, but the LORD is with us. Do not be afraid of them."

10 But the whole assembly talked about stoning[b] them. Then the glory of the LORD[c] appeared at the Tent of Meeting to all the Israelites. 11 The LORD said to Moses, "How long will these people treat me with contempt? How long will they refuse to believe in me,[d] in spite of all the miraculous signs I have performed among them? 12 I will strike them down with a plague and destroy them, but I will make you into a nation[e] greater and stronger than they."

13 Moses said to the LORD, "Then the Egyptians will hear about it! By your power you brought these people up from among them.[f] 14 And they will tell the inhabitants of this land about it. They have already heard[g] that you, O LORD, are with these people and that you, O LORD, have been seen face to face, that your cloud stays over them, and that you go before them in a pillar of cloud by day and a pillar of fire by night.[h] 15 If you put these people to death all at one time, the nations who have heard this report about you will say, 16 'The LORD was not able to bring these people into the land he promised them on oath; so he slaughtered them in the desert.'[i]

17 "Now may the Lord's strength be displayed, just as you have declared: 18 'The LORD is slow to anger, abounding in love and forgiving sin and rebellion.[j] Yet he does not leave the guilty unpunished; he punishes the children for the sin of the fathers to the third and fourth generation.'[k] 19 In accordance with your great love, forgive[l] the sin of these people,[m] just as you have pardoned them from the time they left Egypt until now."[n]

20 The LORD replied, "I have forgiven them,[o] as you asked. 21 Nevertheless, as surely as I live[p] and as surely as the glory of the LORD fills the whole earth,[q] 22 not one of the men who saw my glory and the miraculous signs I performed in Egypt and in the desert but who disobeyed me and tested me ten times[r]— 23 not one of them will ever see the land I promised on oath[s] to their forefathers. No one who has treated me with contempt will ever see it.[t] 24 But because my servant Caleb has a different spirit and follows me wholeheartedly,[u] I will bring him into the land he went to, and his descendants will inherit it.[v] 25 Since the Amalekites and Canaanites are living in the valleys, turn[w] back tomorrow and set out toward the desert along the route to the Red Sea.[a]"

1 →PG. 194

26 The LORD said to Moses and Aaron: 27 "How long will this wicked community grumble against me? I have heard the complaints of these grumbling Israelites.[x] 28 So tell them, 'As surely as I live,[y] declares the LORD, I will do to you the very things I heard you say:

a 25 Hebrew *Yam Suph;* that is, Sea of Reeds

13:27 [l]Dt 1:25
13:28 [m]Dt 1:28; 9:1,2
13:31 [n]Dt 1:28; 9:1; Jos 14:8
13:32 [o]Nu 14:36,37 [p]Eze 36:13,14 [q]Am 2:9
13:33 [r]Ge 6:4 [s]Dt 1:28
14:2 [t]Nu 11:1
14:4 [u]Ne 9:17
14:5 [v]Nu 16:4,22,45
14:7 [w]Nu 13:27; Dt 1:25
14:8 [x]Dt 10:15 [y]Nu 13:27
14:9 [z]Dt 1:26; 9:7, 23,24 [a]Dt 1:21; 7:18; 20:1
14:10 [b]Ex 17:4 [c]Lev 9:23
14:11 [d]Ps 78:22; 106:24
14:12 [e]Ex 32:10
14:13 [f]Ex 32:11-14; Ps 106:23
14:14 [g]Ex 15:14 [h]Ex 13:21
14:16 [i]Jos 7:7
14:18 [j]Ex 34:6; Ps 145:8; Jnh 4:2 [k]Ex 20:5
14:19 [l]Ex 34:9 [m]Ps 106:45 [n]Ps 78:38
14:20 [o]Ps 106:23; Mic 7:18-20
14:21 [p]Dt 32:40; Isa 49:18 [q]Ps 72:19; Isa 6:3; Hab 2:14
14:22 [r]Ex 14:11; 32:1; 1Co 10:5
14:23 [s]Nu 32:11 [t]Heb 3:18
14:24 [u]ver 6-9; Jos 14:8,14 [v]Nu 32:12
14:25 [w]Dt 1:40
14:27 [x]Ex 16:12
14:28 [y]ver 21

29In this desert your bodies will fall[z]—
every one of you twenty years old or
more[a] who was counted in the census
and who has grumbled against me.
30Not one of you will enter the land I
swore with uplifted hand to make your
home, except Caleb son of Jephunneh
and Joshua son of Nun. 31As for your
children that you said would be taken
as plunder, I will bring them in to enjoy
the land you have rejected.[b] 32But
you—your bodies will fall[c] in this
desert. 33Your children will be shepherds here for forty years, suffering for
your unfaithfulness, until the last of
your bodies lies in the desert. 34For forty years—one year for each of the forty
days you explored the land[d]—you will
suffer for your sins and know what it is
like to have me against you.' 35I, the
LORD, have spoken, and I will surely do
these things[e] to this whole wicked
community, which has banded together against me. They will meet their end
in this desert; here they will die."

36So the men Moses had sent[f] to
explore the land, who returned and
made the whole community grumble
against him by spreading a bad report[g] about it— 37these men responsible for spreading the bad report[h]
about the land were struck down and
died of a plague[i] before the LORD. 38Of
the men who went to explore the land,
only Joshua son of Nun and Caleb son
of Jephunneh survived.[j]

39When Moses reported this to all
the Israelites, they mourned[k] bitterly.
40Early the next morning they went up
toward the high hill country. "We have
sinned[l]," they said. "We will go up to
the place the LORD promised."

41But Moses said, "Why are you disobeying the LORD's command? This
will not succeed![m] 42Do not go up, because the LORD is not with you. You will
be defeated by your enemies,[n] 43for
the Amalekites and Canaanites will
face you there. Because you have
turned away from the LORD, he will not
be with you and you will fall by the
sword."

44Nevertheless, in their presumption
they went up[o] toward the high hill
country, though neither Moses nor the
ark of the LORD's covenant moved from
the camp.[p] 45Then the Amalekites and
Canaanites who lived in that hill country came down and attacked them and
beat them down all the way to Hormah.[q]

Supplementary Offerings

15 The LORD said to Moses, 2"Speak to
the Israelites and say to them: 'After you enter the land I am giving you[r]
as a home 3and you present to the LORD
offerings made by fire, from the herd or
the flock,[s] as an aroma pleasing to the
LORD[t]—whether burnt offerings[u] or
sacrifices, for special vows or freewill
offerings[v] or festival offerings[w]—
4then the one who brings his offering
shall present to the LORD a grain offering[x] of a tenth of an ephah[a] of fine
flour mixed with a quarter of a hin[b] of
oil. 5With each lamb for the burnt offering or the sacrifice, prepare a quarter of a hin of wine[y] as a drink offering.

6" 'With a ram[z] prepare a grain offering[a] of two-tenths of an ephah[c] of
fine flour mixed with a third of a hin[d]
of oil,[b] 7and a third of a hin of wine as
a drink offering. Offer it as an aroma
pleasing to the LORD.

8" 'When you prepare a young bull
as a burnt offering or sacrifice, for
a special vow or a fellowship offering[e][c] to the LORD, 9bring with the bull
a grain offering of three-tenths of an
ephah[f][d] of fine flour mixed with half
a hin[g] of oil. 10Also bring half a hin of
wine as a drink offering. It will be an
offering made by fire, an aroma pleasing to the LORD. 11Each bull or ram,
each lamb or young goat, is to be prepared in this manner. 12Do this for
each one, for as many as you prepare.

13" 'Everyone who is native-born[e]
must do these things in this way when
he brings an offering made by fire as an
aroma pleasing to the LORD. 14For the
generations to come, whenever an
alien or anyone else living among you
presents an offering made by fire as an
aroma pleasing to the LORD, he must
do exactly as you do. 15The community
is to have the same rules for you and
for the alien living among you; this is a
lasting ordinance for the generations
to come.[f] You and the alien shall be
the same before the LORD: 16The same
laws and regulations will apply both to
you and to the alien living among
you.[g]' "

17The LORD said to Moses, 18"Speak
to the Israelites and say to them:
'When you enter the land to which I
am taking you 19and you eat the food of
the land,[h] present a portion as an offering to the LORD. 20Present a cake

14:29 [z]Nu 26:65 [a]Nu 1:45 **14:31** [b]Ps 106:24 **14:32** [c]1Co 10:5 **14:34** [d]Nu 13:25 **14:35** [e]Nu 23:19 **14:36** [f]Nu 13:4-16 [g]Nu 13:32 **14:37** [h]1Co 10:10 [i]Nu 16:49 **14:38** [j]Jos 14:6 **14:39** [k]Ex 33:4 **14:40** [l]Dt 1:41 **14:41** [m]2Ch 24:20 **14:42** [n]Dt 1:42 **14:44** [o]Dt 1:43 [p]Nu 31:6 **14:45** [q]Nu 21:3; Dt 1:44; Jdg 1:17

15:2 [r]Lev 23:10 **15:3** [s]Lev 1:2 [t]ver 24; Ge 8:21; Ex 29:18 [u]Nu 28:19,27 [v]Lev 22:18,21; Ezr 1:4 [w]Lev 23:1-44 **15:4** [x]Lev 2:1; 6:14 **15:5** [y]Nu 28:7,14 **15:6** [z]Lev 5:15 [a]Nu 28:12 [b]Eze 46:14 **15:8** [c]Lev 1:3; 3:1 **15:9** [d]Lev 14:10 **15:13** [e]Lev 16:29 **15:15** [f]ver 29; Nu 9:14 **15:16** [g]Nu 9:14 **15:19** [h]Jos 5:11,12

[a]*4* That is, probably about 2 quarts (about 2 liters) [b]*4* That is, probably about 1 quart (about 1 liter); also in verse 5 [c]*6* That is, probably about 4 quarts (about 4.5 liters) [d]*6* That is, probably about 1 1/4 quarts (about 1.2 liters); also in verse 7 [e]*8* Traditionally *peace offering* [f]*9* That is, probably about 6 quarts (about 6.5 liters) [g]*9* That is, probably about 2 quarts (about 2 liters); also in verse 10

from the first of your ground meal[i] and present it as an offering from the threshing floor.[j] 21Throughout the generations to come you are to give this offering to the LORD from the first of your ground meal.[k]

Offerings for Unintentional Sins

22" 'Now if you unintentionally fail to keep any of these commands the LORD gave Moses[l]— 23any of the LORD's commands to you through him, from the day the LORD gave them and continuing through the generations to come— 24and if this is done unintentionally without the community being aware of it,[m] then the whole community is to offer a young bull for a burnt offering[n] as an aroma pleasing to the LORD, along with its prescribed grain offering and drink offering, and a male goat for a sin offering.[o] 25The priest is to make atonement for the whole Israelite community, and they will be forgiven,[p] for it was not intentional and they have brought to the LORD for their wrong an offering made by fire and a sin offering. 26The whole Israelite community and the aliens living among them will be forgiven, because all the people were involved in the unintentional wrong.[q]

27" 'But if just one person sins unintentionally,[r] he must bring a year-old female goat for a sin offering. 28The priest is to make atonement before the LORD for the one who erred by sinning unintentionally, and when atonement has been made for him, he will be forgiven.[s] 29One and the same law applies to everyone who sins unintentionally, whether he is a native-born Israelite or an alien.

30" 'But anyone who sins defiantly,[t] whether native-born or alien,[u] blasphemes the LORD, and that person must be cut off from his people. 31Because he has despised the LORD's word and broken his commands,[v] that person must surely be cut off; his guilt remains on him.[w]' "

The Sabbath-Breaker Put to Death

32While the Israelites were in the desert, a man was found gathering wood on the Sabbath day.[x] 33Those who found him gathering wood brought him to Moses and Aaron and the whole assembly, 34and they kept him in custody, because it was not clear what should be done to him.[y] 35Then the LORD said to Moses, "The man must die.[z] The whole assembly must stone him outside the camp.[a]" 36So the assembly took him outside the camp and stoned him to death, as the LORD commanded Moses.

Tassels on Garments

37The LORD said to Moses, 38"Speak to the Israelites and say to them: 'Throughout the generations to come you are to make tassels on the corners of your garments,[b] with a blue cord on each tassel. 39You will have these tassels to look at and so you will remember[c] all the commands of the LORD, that you may obey them and not prostitute yourselves by going after the lusts of your own hearts and eyes. 40Then you will remember to obey all my commands and will be consecrated to your God.[d] 41I am the LORD your God, who brought you out of Egypt to be your God. I am the LORD your God.' "

Korah, Dathan and Abiram

16 Korah[e] son of Izhar, the son of Kohath, the son of Levi, and certain Reubenites—Dathan and Abiram, sons of Eliab,[f] and On son of Peleth—became insolent[a] 2and rose up against Moses. With them were 250 Israelite men, well-known community leaders who had been appointed members of the council.[g] 3They came as a group to oppose Moses and Aaron[h] and said to them, "You have gone too far! The whole community is holy,[i] every one of them, and the LORD is with them.[j] Why then do you set yourselves above the LORD's assembly?"[k]

4When Moses heard this, he fell facedown.[l] 5Then he said to Korah and all his followers: "In the morning the LORD will show who belongs to him and who is holy,[m] and he will have that person come near him. The man he chooses[n] he will cause to come near him. 6You, Korah, and all your followers are to do this: Take censers 7and tomorrow put fire and incense in them before the LORD. The man the LORD chooses will be the one who is holy. You Levites have gone too far!"

8Moses also said to Korah, "Now listen, you Levites! 9Isn't it enough for you that the God of Israel has separated you from the rest of the Israelite community and brought you near himself to do the work at the LORD's tabernacle and to stand before the community and minister to them?[o] 10He has brought you and all your fellow Levites near himself, but now you are trying to get the priesthood too.[p] 11It is against the LORD that you and all your follow-

15:20 [i]Ex 34:26; Lev 23:14; Dt 26:2,10 [j]Lev 2:14
15:21 [k]Ro 11:16
15:22 [l]Lev 4:2
15:24 [m]Lev 5:15 [n]Lev 4:14 [o]Lev 4:3
15:25 [p]Lev 4:20; Ro 3:25; Heb 2:17
15:26 [q]ver 24
15:27 [r]Lev 4:27
15:28 [s]Lev 4:35
15:30 [t]Nu 14:40-44; Dt 1:43; 17:13; Ps 19:13 [u]ver 14
15:31 [v]2Sa 12:9; Ps 119:126; Pr 13:13 [w]Lev 5:1; Eze 18:20
15:32 [x]Ex 31:14,15; 35:2,3
15:34 [y]Nu 9:8
15:35 [z]Ex 31:14,15; Dt 21:21 [a]Lev 20:2; 24:14; Ac 7:58
15:38 [b]Dt 22:12; Mt 23:5
15:39 [c]Dt 4:23; 6:12; Ps 73:27
15:40 [d]Lev 11:44; Ro 12:1; Col 1:22; 1Pe 1:15
16:1 [e]Jude 1:11 [f]Nu 26:8; Dt 11:6
16:2 [g]Nu 1:16; 26:9
16:3 [h]ver 7; Ps 106:16 [i]Ex 19:6 [j]Nu 14:14 [k]Nu 12:2
16:4 [l]Nu 14:5
16:5 [m]Lev 10:3; 2Ti 2:19* [n]Nu 17:5; Ps 65:4
16:9 [o]Nu 3:6; Dt 10:8
16:10 [p]Nu 3:10; 18:7

a 1 Or *Peleth—took ⌞men⌟*

16:1–11

PROMISE 1

COMPLAINING AND CONFLICT MANAGEMENT

Leaders spend plenty of time dealing with griping, so an overview of Israel's grumbling and Moses' response is instructive for any leader. Read through the following passages and list the principles that you learn about how to handle grumblers. Also consider how paralyzing it is to God's work when people attack each other instead of the work at hand.

THE OPPOSITION	MOSES' RESPONSE
Exodus	
Blamed Moses because they were trapped at the Red Sea (14:10-12).	Moses assured the people of God's help (13-26). God gave Moses a plan (15-18).
At Marah—complained about bitter water (15:22-24).	Moses prayed and God solved the problem (25,26).
At the Wilderness of Sin—grumbled because they were hungry (16:2,3).	God gave manna from heaven (4-12).
At Rephidim—no water (17:1-3).	Moses prayed and God solved the problem (4-7).
At Sinai—complained because Moses was gone too long. Made the golden calf (32:1-6).	Moses prayed for the people (7-14). Moses confronted the people and stopped the idol worship by force (15-30). Moses asked God to forgive the people (31-34).
Numbers	
People complained in the ear of God (11:1a).	God sent fire to judge the people (1b). Moses prayed and the fire stopped (2).
People wailed about manna: Who will give us meat? (11:49).	Moses heard and prayed (10-15). God raised up additional leaders to help Moses (16-17). God provided meat (18-23; 31-35). Excellent insight into Moses' character (24-30).
Aaron and Miriam rebelled against Moses' leadership (12:1-3).	God judged Miriam with leprosy (4-12). Moses prayed for Miriam's restoration (13-15).
At the border of the land, the people grumbled because there were giants in the land and wanted to appoint new leaders who would lead them back to Egypt (14:1-4).	Moses, Aaron, Joshua and Caleb tried to persuade the people to trust God (5-10). God decided to wipe Israel out and start over with Moses' descendants (11,12). Moses prayed and God changed His mind (13-19).
Korah's rebellion: 250 of Israel's leaders confront Moses (16:1-3).	Moses tried to reason with Korah and suggested a test to allow God to decide who the people should follow (4-14). Moses continued to reason (15-27). God supernaturally took Korah and the 250 (28-40).
The people blamed Moses for Korah's death (16:41).	God sent a plague that killed 14,700 people. Moses prayed and Aaron offered atonement for the people to stop the plague (42-50).
At the Wilderness of Zin—complained that there was no water (20:1-5).	Moses and Aaron came to God and God gave instructions. Moses disobeyed God and was refused entrance into the land (6-13).
At Mt. Hor—complained about the route they were taking and about the food and the water—a general gripe session (21:4,5).	God sent fiery serpents (6-7). Moses prayed for the people and God told him to make a bronze snake and put it on a pole to save the people from dying (7-9).

Notice that no matter what the gripe, no matter what the Israelites did to him, Moses prayed for, and confronted, and provided for the people. This mighty man of God fully understood servant leadership. With God's help, he navigated a rebellious people through the desert and up to the land God had promised them. The Israelites griped; Moses listened, prayed and led.

For the next Promise 1 reading go to page 189.

ers have banded together. Who is Aaron that you should grumble[q] against him?[r]"

12 Then Moses summoned Dathan and Abiram, the sons of Eliab. But they said, "We will not come! 13 Isn't it enough that you have brought us up out of a land flowing with milk and honey to kill us in the desert?[s] And now you also want to lord it over us?[t] 14 Moreover, you haven't brought us into a land flowing with milk and honey[u] or given us an inheritance of fields and vineyards.[v] Will you gouge out the eyes of[a] these men?[w] No, we will not come!"

15 Then Moses became very angry and said to the LORD, "Do not accept their offering. I have not taken so much as a donkey[x] from them, nor have I wronged any of them."

16 Moses said to Korah, "You and all your followers are to appear before the LORD tomorrow—you and they and Aaron.[y] 17 Each man is to take his censer and put incense in it—250 censers in all—and present it before the LORD. You and Aaron are to present your censers also." 18 So each man took his censer, put fire and incense in it, and stood with Moses and Aaron at the entrance to the Tent of Meeting. 19 When Korah had gathered all his followers in opposition to them[z] at the entrance to the Tent of Meeting, the glory of the LORD[a] appeared to the entire assembly. 20 The LORD said to Moses and Aaron, 21 "Separate yourselves from this assembly so I can put an end to them at once."[b]

22 But Moses and Aaron fell facedown[c] and cried out, "O God, God of the spirits of all mankind,[d] will you be angry with the entire assembly when only one man sins?"[e]

23 Then the LORD said to Moses, 24 "Say to the assembly, 'Move away from the tents of Korah, Dathan and Abiram.' "

25 Moses got up and went to Dathan and Abiram, and the elders of Israel followed him. 26 He warned the assembly, "Move back from the tents of these wicked men![f] Do not touch anything belonging to them, or you will be swept away[g] because of all their sins." 27 So they moved away from the tents of Korah, Dathan and Abiram. Dathan and Abiram had come out and were standing with their wives, children and little ones at the entrances to their tents.

28 Then Moses said, "This is how you will know that the LORD has sent me[h] to do all these things and that it was not my idea: 29 If these men die a natural death and experience only what usually happens to men, then the LORD has not sent me.[i] 30 But if the LORD brings about something totally new, and the earth opens its mouth and swallows them, with everything that belongs to them, and they go down alive into the grave,[b][j] then you will know that these men have treated the LORD with contempt."

31 As soon as he finished saying all this, the ground under them split apart[k] 32 and the earth opened its mouth and swallowed them,[l] with their households and all Korah's men and all their possessions. 33 They went down alive into the grave, with everything they owned; the earth closed over them, and they perished and were gone from the community. 34 At their cries, all the Israelites around them fled, shouting, "The earth is going to swallow us too!"

35 And fire came out from the LORD[m] and consumed[n] the 250 men who were offering the incense.

36 The LORD said to Moses, 37 "Tell Eleazar son of Aaron, the priest, to take the censers out of the smoldering remains and scatter the coals some distance away, for the censers are holy— 38 the censers of the men who sinned at the cost of their lives.[o] Hammer the censers into sheets to overlay the altar, for they were presented before the LORD and have become holy. Let them be a sign[p] to the Israelites."

39 So Eleazar the priest collected the bronze censers brought by those who had been burned up, and he had them hammered out to overlay the altar, 40 as the LORD directed him through Moses. This was to remind the Israelites that no one except a descendant of Aaron should come to burn incense[q] before the LORD,[r] or he would become like Korah and his followers.[s]

41 The next day the whole Israelite community grumbled against Moses and Aaron. "You have killed the LORD's people," they said.

42 But when the assembly gathered in opposition[t] to Moses and Aaron and turned toward the Tent of Meeting, suddenly the cloud covered it and the glory of the LORD appeared. 43 Then Moses and Aaron went to the front of the Tent of Meeting, 44 and the LORD said to Moses, 45 "Get away from this assembly so I can put an end to them at once." And they fell facedown.

46 Then Moses said to Aaron, "Take your censer and put incense in it, along with fire from the altar, and hurry to

16:11 [q]1Co 10:10 [r]Ex 16:7
16:13 [s]Nu 14:2 [t]Ac 7:27,35
16:14 [u]Lev 20:24 [v]Ex 22:5; 23:11; Nu 20:5 [w]Jdg 16:21; 1Sa 11:2
16:15 [x]1Sa 12:3
16:16 [y]ver 6
16:19 [z]ver 42 [a]Ex 16:7; Nu 14:10; 20:6
16:21 [b]Ex 32:10
16:22 [c]Nu 14:5 [d]Nu 27:16; Job 12:10; Heb 12:9 [e]Ge 18:23
16:26 [f]Isa 52:11 [g]Ge 19:15
16:28 [h]Ex 3:12; Jn 5:36; 6:38
16:29 [i]Ecc 3:19
16:30 [j]ver 33; Ps 55:15
16:31 [k]Mic 1:3-4
16:32 [l]Nu 26:11; Dt 11:6; Ps 106:17
16:35 [m]Nu 11:1-3; 26:10 [n]Lev 10:2
16:38 [o]Pr 20:2 [p]Nu 26:10; Eze 14:8; 2Pe 2:6
16:40 [q]Ex 30:7-10; Nu 1:51 [r]2Ch 26:18 [s]Nu 3:10
16:42 [t]ver 19; Nu 20:6

a *14* Or *you make slaves of*; or *you deceive*
b *30* Hebrew *Sheol*; also in verse 33

the assembly[u] to make atonement[v] for them. Wrath has come out from the LORD; the plague[w] has started." 47So Aaron did as Moses said, and ran into the midst of the assembly. The plague had already started among the people,[x] but Aaron offered the incense and made atonement for them. 48He stood between the living and the dead, and the plague stopped.[y] 49But 14,700 people died from the plague, in addition to those who had died because of Korah.[z] 50Then Aaron returned to Moses at the entrance to the Tent of Meeting, for the plague had stopped.

The Budding of Aaron's Staff

17 The LORD said to Moses, 2"Speak to the Israelites and get twelve staffs from them, one from the leader of each of their ancestral tribes. Write the name of each man on his staff. 3On the staff of Levi write Aaron's name,[a] for there must be one staff for the head of each ancestral tribe. 4Place them in the Tent of Meeting in front of the Testimony,[b] where I meet with you.[c] 5The staff belonging to the man I choose[d] will sprout, and I will rid myself of this constant grumbling against you by the Israelites."

6So Moses spoke to the Israelites, and their leaders gave him twelve staffs, one for the leader of each of their ancestral tribes, and Aaron's staff was among them. 7Moses placed the staffs before the LORD in the Tent of the Testimony.[e]

8The next day Moses entered the Tent of the Testimony and saw that Aaron's staff, which represented the house of Levi, had not only sprouted but had budded, blossomed and produced almonds.[f] 9Then Moses brought out all the staffs from the LORD's presence to all the Israelites. They looked at them, and each man took his own staff.

10The LORD said to Moses, "Put back Aaron's staff in front of the Testimony, to be kept as a sign to the rebellious.[g] This will put an end to their grumbling against me, so that they will not die." 11Moses did just as the LORD commanded him.

12The Israelites said to Moses, "We will die! We are lost, we are all lost![h] 13Anyone who even comes near the tabernacle of the LORD will die.[i] Are we all going to die?"

Duties of Priests and Levites

18 The LORD said to Aaron, "You, your sons and your father's family are to bear the responsibility for offenses against the sanctuary,[j] and you and your sons alone are to bear the responsibility for offenses against the priesthood. 2Bring your fellow Levites from your ancestral tribe to join you and assist you when you and your sons minister[k] before the Tent of the Testimony. 3They are to be responsible to you and are to perform all the duties of the Tent,[l] but they must not go near the furnishings of the sanctuary or the altar, or both they and you will die.[m] 4They are to join you and be responsible for the care of the Tent of Meeting—all the work at the Tent—and no one else may come near where you are.

5"You are to be responsible for the care of the sanctuary and the altar,[n] so that wrath will not fall on the Israelites again. 6I myself have selected your fellow Levites from among the Israelites as a gift to you,[o] dedicated to the LORD to do the work at the Tent of Meeting. 7But only you and your sons may serve as priests in connection with everything at the altar and inside the curtain.[p] I am giving you the service of the priesthood as a gift.[q] Anyone else who comes near the sanctuary must be put to death.[r]"

Offerings for Priests and Levites

8Then the LORD said to Aaron, "I myself have put you in charge of the offerings presented to me; all the holy offerings the Israelites give me I give to you and your sons as your portion and regular share.[s] 9You are to have the part of the most holy offerings that is kept from the fire. From all the gifts they bring me as most holy offerings, whether grain[t] or sin[u] or guilt offerings,[v] that part belongs to you and your sons. 10Eat it as something most holy; every male shall eat it.[w] You must regard it as holy.

11"This also is yours: whatever is set aside from the gifts of all the wave offerings[x] of the Israelites. I give this to you and your sons and daughters as your regular share. Everyone in your household who is ceremonially clean[y] may eat it.

12"I give you all the finest olive oil and all the finest new wine and grain they give the LORD as the firstfruits of their harvest.[z] 13All the land's firstfruits that they bring to the LORD will be yours.[a] Everyone in your household who is ceremonially clean may eat it.

14"Everything in Israel that is devoted[a] to the LORD[b] is yours. 15The first

16:46 [u]Lev 10:6 [v]Nu 18:5; 25:13; Dt 9:22 [w]Nu 8:19; Ps 106:29
16:47 [x]Nu 25:6-8
16:48 [y]Nu 25:8; Ps 106:30
16:49 [z]ver 32
17:3 [a]Nu 1:3
17:4 [b]ver 7 [c]Ex 25:22
17:5 [d]Nu 16:5
17:7 [e]Ex 38:21; Ac 7:44
17:8 [f]Eze 17:24; Heb 9:4
17:10 [g]Dt 9:24
17:12 [h]Isa 6:5
17:13 [i]Nu 1:51
18:1 [j]Ex 28:38
18:2 [k]Nu 3:10
18:3 [l]Nu 1:51 [m]ver 7; Nu 4:15
18:5 [n]Nu 16:46
18:6 [o]Nu 3:9
18:7 [p]Heb 9:3,6 [q]ver 20; Ex 29:9 [r]Nu 3:10
18:8 [s]Lev 6:16; 7:6, 31-34,36
18:9 [t]Lev 2:1 [u]Lev 6:25 [v]Lev 5:15; 7:7
18:10 [w]Lev 6:16
18:11 [x]Ex 29:26 [y]Lev 22:1-16
18:12 [z]Ex 23:19; Ne 10:35
18:13 [a]Ex 22:29; 23:19
18:14 [b]Lev 27:28

[a] *14* The Hebrew term refers to the irrevocable giving over of things or persons to the LORD.

offspring of every womb, both man and animal, that is offered to the LORD is yours.[c] But you must redeem[d] every firstborn son and every firstborn male of unclean animals.[e] 16When they are a month old, you must redeem them at the redemption price set at five shekels[a][f] of silver, according to the sanctuary shekel,[g] which weighs twenty gerahs.

17"But you must not redeem the firstborn of an ox, a sheep or a goat; they are holy.[h] Sprinkle their blood[i] on the altar and burn their fat as an offering made by fire, an aroma pleasing to the LORD. 18Their meat is to be yours, just as the breast of the wave offering[j] and the right thigh are yours. 19Whatever is set aside from the holy offerings the Israelites present to the LORD I give to you and your sons and daughters as your regular share. It is an everlasting covenant of salt[k] before the LORD for both you and your offspring."

20The LORD said to Aaron, "You will have no inheritance in their land, nor will you have any share among them;[l] I am your share and your inheritance[m] among the Israelites.

21"I give to the Levites all the tithes[n] in Israel as their inheritance[o] in return for the work they do while serving at the Tent of Meeting. 22From now on the Israelites must not go near the Tent of Meeting, or they will bear the consequences of their sin and will die.[p] 23It is the Levites who are to do the work at the Tent of Meeting and bear the responsibility for offenses against it. This is a lasting ordinance for the generations to come. They will receive no inheritance[q] among the Israelites. 24Instead, I give to the Levites as their inheritance the tithes that the Israelites present as an offering to the LORD. That is why I said concerning them: 'They will have no inheritance among the Israelites.' "

25The LORD said to Moses, 26"Speak to the Levites and say to them: 'When you receive from the Israelites the tithe I give you[r] as your inheritance, you must present a tenth of that tithe as the LORD's offering.[s] 27Your offering will be reckoned to you as grain from the threshing floor or juice from the winepress. 28In this way you also will present an offering to the LORD from all the tithes[t] you receive from the Israelites. From these tithes you must give the LORD's portion to Aaron the priest. 29You must present as the LORD's portion the best and holiest part of everything given to you.'

30"Say to the Levites: 'When you present the best part, it will be reckoned to you as the product of the threshing floor or the winepress.[u] 31You and your households may eat the rest of it anywhere, for it is your wages for your work at the Tent of Meeting. 32By presenting the best part[v] of it you will not be guilty in this matter; then you will not defile the holy offerings[w] of the Israelites, and you will not die.' "

The Water of Cleansing

19 The LORD said to Moses and Aaron: 2"This is a requirement of the law that the LORD has commanded: Tell the Israelites to bring you a red heifer[x] without defect or blemish[y] and that has never been under a yoke.[z] 3Give it to Eleazar[a] the priest; it is to be taken outside the camp[b] and slaughtered in his presence. 4Then Eleazar the priest is to take some of its blood on his finger and sprinkle[c] it seven times toward the front of the Tent of Meeting. 5While he watches, the heifer is to be burned—its hide, flesh, blood and offal.[d] 6The priest is to take some cedar wood, hyssop[e] and scarlet wool[f] and throw them onto the burning heifer. 7After that, the priest must wash his clothes and bathe himself with water.[g] He may then come into the camp, but he will be ceremonially unclean till evening. 8The man who burns it must also wash his clothes and bathe with water, and he too will be unclean till evening.

9"A man who is clean shall gather up the ashes of the heifer[h] and put them in a ceremonially clean place outside the camp. They shall be kept by the Israelite community for use in the water of cleansing;[i] it is for purification from sin. 10The man who gathers up the ashes of the heifer must also wash his clothes, and he too will be unclean till evening. This will be a lasting ordinance both for the Israelites and for the aliens living among them.

11"Whoever touches the dead body[j] of anyone will be unclean for seven days.[k] 12He must purify himself with the water on the third day and on the seventh day;[l] then he will be clean. But if he does not purify himself on the third and seventh days, he will not be clean. 13Whoever touches the dead body[m] of anyone and fails to purify himself defiles the LORD's tabernacle.[n] That person must be cut off from Israel.[o] Because the water of cleansing has not been sprinkled on him, he is

18:15 [c]Ex 13:2 [d]Nu 3:46 [e]Ex 13:13
18:16 [f]Lev 27:6 [g]Ex 30:13
18:17 [h]Dt 15:19 [i]Lev 3:2
18:18 [j]Lev 7:30
18:19 [k]Lev 2:13; 2Ch 13:5
18:20 [l]Dt 12:12 [m]Dt 10:9; 14:27; 18:1-2; Jos 13:33; Eze 44:28
18:21 [n]Dt 14:22; Mal 3:8 [o]Lev 27:30-33; Heb 7:5
18:22 [p]Lev 22:9; Nu 1:51
18:23 [q]ver 20
18:26 [r]ver 21 [s]Ne 10:38
18:28 [t]Mal 3:8
18:30 [u]ver 27
18:32 [v]Lev 22:15 [w]Lev 19:8
19:2 [x]Ge 15:9; Heb 9:13 [y]Lev 22:19-25 [z]Dt 21:3; 1Sa 6:7
19:3 [a]Nu 3:4 [b]Lev 4:12,21; Heb 13:11
19:4 [c]Lev 4:17
19:5 [d]Ex 29:14
19:6 [e]ver 18; Ps 51:7 [f]Lev 14:4
19:7 [g]Lev 11:25; 16:26,28; 22:6
19:9 [h]Heb 9:13 [i]ver 13; Nu 8:7
19:11 [j]Lev 21:1; Nu 5:2 [k]Nu 31:19
19:12 [l]ver 19; Nu 31:19
19:13 [m]Lev 20:3 [n]Lev 15:31; 2Ch 36:14 [o]Lev 7:20; 22:3

[a] *16* That is, about 2 ounces (about 55 grams)

unclean;[p] his uncleanness remains on him.

14“This is the law that applies when a person dies in a tent: Anyone who enters the tent and anyone who is in it will be unclean for seven days, 15and every open container without a lid fastened on it will be unclean.

16“Anyone out in the open who touches someone who has been killed with a sword or someone who has died a natural death,[q] or anyone who touches a human bone or a grave,[r] will be unclean for seven days.

17“For the unclean person, put some ashes[s] from the burned purification offering into a jar and pour fresh water over them. 18Then a man who is ceremonially clean is to take some hyssop,[t] dip it in the water and sprinkle the tent and all the furnishings and the people who were there. He must also sprinkle anyone who has touched a human bone or a grave or someone who has been killed or someone who has died a natural death. 19The man who is clean is to sprinkle the unclean person on the third and seventh days, and on the seventh day he is to purify him.[u] The person being cleansed must wash his clothes and bathe with water, and that evening he will be clean. 20But if a person who is unclean does not purify himself, he must be cut off from the community, because he has defiled the sanctuary of the LORD. The water of cleansing has not been sprinkled on him, and he is unclean. 21This is a lasting ordinance for them.

“The man who sprinkles the water of cleansing must also wash his clothes, and anyone who touches the water of cleansing will be unclean till evening. 22Anything that an unclean[v] person touches becomes unclean, and anyone who touches it becomes unclean till evening.”

Water From the Rock

20 In the first month the whole Israelite community arrived at the Desert of Zin,[w] and they stayed at Kadesh.[x] There Miriam[y] died and was buried.

2Now there was no water for the community,[z] and the people gathered in opposition[a] to Moses and Aaron. 3They quarreled[b] with Moses and said, “If only we had died when our brothers fell dead before the LORD![c] 4Why did you bring the LORD’s community into this desert, that we and our livestock should die here?[d] 5Why did you bring us up out of Egypt to this terrible place? It has no grain or figs, grapevines or pomegranates.[e] And there is no water to drink!”

6Moses and Aaron went from the assembly to the entrance to the Tent of Meeting and fell facedown,[f] and the glory of the LORD[g] appeared to them. 7The LORD said to Moses, 8“Take the staff,[h] and you and your brother Aaron gather the assembly together. Speak to that rock before their eyes and it will pour out its water.[i] You will bring water out of the rock for the community so they and their livestock can drink.”

9So Moses took the staff from the LORD’s presence,[j] just as he commanded him. 10He and Aaron gathered the assembly together in front of the rock and Moses said to them, “Listen, you rebels, must we bring you water out of this rock?”[k] 11Then Moses raised his arm and struck the rock twice with his staff. Water[l] gushed out, and the community and their livestock drank.

12But the LORD said to Moses and Aaron, “Because you did not trust in me enough to honor me as holy[m] in the sight of the Israelites, you will not bring this community into the land I give them.”[n]

13These were the waters of Meribah,[a][o] where the Israelites quarreled[p] with the LORD and where he showed himself holy among them.

[a] *13 Meribah* means *quarreling.*

19:13 [p]Hag 2:13 **19:16** [q]Nu 31:19 [r]Mt 23:27 **19:17** [s]ver 9 **19:18** [t]ver 6 **19:19** [u]Eze 36:25; Heb 10:22 **19:22** [v]Lev 5:2; Hag 2:13,14 **20:1** [w]Nu 13:21 [x]Nu 33:36 [y]Ex 15:20 **20:2** [z]Ex 17:1 [a]Nu 16:19 **20:3** [b]Ex 17:2 [c]Nu 14:2; 16:31-35 **20:4** [d]Ex 14:11; 17:3; Nu 14:3; 16:13

20:5 [e]Nu 16:14 **20:6** [f]Nu 14:5 [g]Nu 16:19 **20:8** [h]Ex 4:17,20 [i]Ex 17:6; Isa 43:20 **20:9** [j]Nu 17:10 **20:10** [k]Ps 106:32,33 **20:11** [l]Ex 17:6; Dt 8:15; Ps 78:16; Isa 48:2; 1Co 10:4 **20:12** [m]Nu 27:14 [n]ver 24; Dt 1:37; 3:27 **20:13** [o]Ex 17:7 [p]Dt 33:8; Ps 95:8; 106:32

20:1–29

PROMISE 3

HARSH SENTENCE?

Like water flowed from the rock, the life-lessons flow from this story. Read it meditatively and ask God to satiate your soul with it.

Here’s one subtle lesson to prime your pump. Verse 12 describes a harsh sentence for a seemingly light offense. Instead of speaking to the rock as God commanded (v. 8), Moses hit it with his staff. But read the verse again. The indictment on Moses (and Aaron, who didn’t hit the rock) says nothing about hitting the rock. Notice the offense in verse 12; Moses’ actions dishonored God and showed a lack of trust in him.

We do many things (some good, some bad) for many reasons (some good, some bad). As you do good things and not so good things, remember why Moses was forbidden to lead the people into the land, and examine your motives and your actions.

For the next Promise 3 reading go to page 183.

Edom Denies Israel Passage

14 Moses sent messengers from Kadesh[q] to the king of Edom,[r] saying:

"This is what your brother Israel says: You know[s] about all the hardships that have come upon us. 15 Our forefathers went down into Egypt,[t] and we lived there many years.[u] The Egyptians mistreated[v] us and our fathers, 16 but when we cried out to the LORD, he heard our cry[w] and sent an angel[x] and brought us out of Egypt.

"Now we are here at Kadesh, a town on the edge of your territory. 17 Please let us pass through your country. We will not go through any field or vineyard, or drink water from any well. We will travel along the king's highway and not turn to the right or to the left until we have passed through your territory.[y]"

18 But Edom answered:

"You may not pass through here; if you try, we will march out and attack you with the sword."

19 The Israelites replied:

"We will go along the main road, and if we or our livestock[z] drink any of your water, we will pay for it.[a] We only want to pass through on foot—nothing else."

20 Again they answered:

"You may not pass through."

Then Edom came out against them with a large and powerful army. 21 Since Edom refused to let them go through their territory, Israel turned away from them.[b]

The Death of Aaron

22 The whole Israelite community set out from Kadesh and came to Mount Hor.[c] 23 At Mount Hor, near the border of Edom,[d] the LORD said to Moses and Aaron, 24 "Aaron will be gathered to his people.[e] He will not enter the land I give the Israelites, because both of you rebelled against my command[f] at the waters of Meribah. 25 Get Aaron and his son Eleazar and take them up Mount Hor.[g] 26 Remove Aaron's garments and put them on his son Eleazar, for Aaron will be gathered to his people;[h] he will die there."

27 Moses did as the LORD commanded: They went up Mount Hor in the sight of the whole community. 28 Moses removed Aaron's garments and put them on his son Eleazar.[i] And Aaron died there[j] on top of the mountain. Then Moses and Eleazar came down from the mountain, 29 and when the whole community learned that Aaron had died, the entire house of Israel mourned for him[k] thirty days.

Arad Destroyed

21 When the Canaanite king of Arad,[l] who lived in the Negev,[m] heard that Israel was coming along the road to Atharim, he attacked the Israelites and captured some of them. 2 Then Israel made this vow to the LORD: "If you will deliver these people into our hands, we will totally destroy[a] their cities." 3 The LORD listened to Israel's plea and gave the Canaanites over to them. They completely destroyed them and their towns; so the place was named Hormah.[b]

The Bronze Snake

4 They traveled from Mount Hor[n] along the route to the Red Sea,[c] to go around Edom. But the people grew impatient on the way;[o] 5 they spoke against God[p] and against Moses, and said, "Why have you brought us up out of Egypt to die in the desert?[q] There is no bread! There is no water! And we detest this miserable food!"[r]

6 Then the LORD sent venomous snakes[s] among them; they bit the people and many Israelites died.[t] 7 The people came to Moses[u] and said, "We sinned when we spoke against the LORD and against you. Pray that the LORD[v] will take the snakes away from us." So Moses prayed[w] for the people.

8 The LORD said to Moses, "Make a snake and put it up on a pole;[x] anyone who is bitten can look at it and live." 9 So Moses made a bronze snake[y] and put it up on a pole. Then when anyone was bitten by a snake and looked at the bronze snake, he lived.[z]

The Journey to Moab

10 The Israelites moved on and camped at Oboth.[a] 11 Then they set out from Oboth and camped in Iye Abarim, in the desert that faces Moab[b] toward the sunrise. 12 From there they moved on and camped in the Zered Valley.[c] 13 They set out from there and camped alongside the Arnon[d], which is in the desert extending into Amorite territory. The Arnon is the border of

20:14 [q] Jdg 11:16-17 [r] Dt 2:4 [s] Jos 2:11; 9:9
20:15 [t] Ge 46:6 [u] Ge 15:13; Ex 12:40 [v] Ex 1:11; Dt 26:6
20:16 [w] Ex 2:23; 3:7 [x] Ex 14:19
20:17 [y] Nu 21:22
20:19 [z] Ex 12:38 [a] Dt 2:6,28
20:21 [b] Dt 2:8; Jdg 11:18
20:22 [c] Nu 33:37
20:23 [d] Nu 33:37
20:24 [e] Ge 25:8 [f] ver 10
20:25 [g] Nu 33:38
20:26 [h] ver 24
20:28 [i] Ex 29:29 [j] Nu 33:38; Dt 10:6; 32:50
20:29 [k] Dt 34:8
21:1 [l] Nu 33:40; Jos 12:14 [m] Jdg 1:9,16
21:4 [n] Nu 20:22 [o] Dt 2:8; Jdg 11:18
21:5 [p] Ps 78:19 [q] Nu 14:2,3 [r] Nu 11:6
21:6 [s] Dt 8:15; Jer 8:17 [t] 1Co 10:9
21:7 [u] Ps 78:34; Hos 5:15 [v] Ex 8:8; Ac 8:24 [w] Nu 11:2
21:8 [x] Jn 3:14
21:9 [y] 2Ki 18:4 [z] Jn 3:14-15
21:10 [a] Nu 33:43
21:11 [b] Nu 33:44
21:12 [c] Dt 2:13,14
21:13 [d] Nu 22:36; Jdg 11:13,18

[a] 2 The Hebrew term refers to the irrevocable giving over of things or persons to the LORD, often by totally destroying them; also in verse 3.
[b] 3 *Hormah* means *destruction.*
[c] 4 Hebrew *Yam Suph;* that is, Sea of Reeds

Moab, between Moab and the Amorites. **14**That is why the Book of the Wars of the LORD says:

"... Waheb in Suphah[a] and the ravines,
the Arnon **15**and[b] the slopes of the ravines
that lead to the site of Ar[e]
and lie along the border of Moab."

16From there they continued on to Beer,[f] the well where the LORD said to Moses, "Gather the people together and I will give them water."

17Then Israel sang this song:[g]

"Spring up, O well!
Sing about it,
18about the well that the princes dug,
that the nobles of the people sank—
the nobles with scepters and staffs."

Then they went from the desert to Mattanah, **19**from Mattanah to Nahaliel, from Nahaliel to Bamoth, **20**and from Bamoth to the valley in Moab where the top of Pisgah overlooks the wasteland.

Defeat of Sihon and Og

21Israel sent messengers to say to Sihon[h] king of the Amorites:

22"Let us pass through your country. We will not turn aside into any field or vineyard, or drink water from any well. We will travel along the king's highway until we have passed through your territory.[i]"

23But Sihon would not let Israel pass through his territory.[j] He mustered his entire army and marched out into the desert against Israel. When he reached Jahaz,[k] he fought with Israel. **24**Israel, however, put him to the sword[l] and took over his land from the Arnon to the Jabbok, but only as far as the Ammonites,[m] because their border was fortified. **25**Israel captured all the cities of the Amorites[n] and occupied them, including Heshbon and all its surrounding settlements. **26**Heshbon was the city of Sihon[o] king of the Amorites, who had fought against the former king of Moab and had taken from him all his land as far as the Arnon.

27That is why the poets say:

"Come to Heshbon and let it be rebuilt;
let Sihon's city be restored.
28"Fire went out from Heshbon,
a blaze from the city of Sihon.[p]
It consumed Ar[q] of Moab,
the citizens of Arnon's heights.[r]
29Woe to you, O Moab![s]
You are destroyed, O people of Chemosh![t]
He has given up his sons as fugitives[u]
and his daughters as captives[v]
to Sihon king of the Amorites.

30"But we have overthrown them;
Heshbon is destroyed all the way to Dibon.[w]
We have demolished them as far as Nophah,
which extends to Medeba."

31So Israel settled in the land of the Amorites.

32After Moses had sent spies to Jazer,[x] the Israelites captured its surrounding settlements and drove out the Amorites who were there. **33**Then they turned and went up along the road toward Bashan[y,z] and Og king of Bashan and his whole army marched out to meet them in battle at Edrei.[a]

34The LORD said to Moses, "Do not be afraid of him, for I have handed him over to you, with his whole army and his land. Do to him what you did to Sihon king of the Amorites, who reigned in Heshbon.[b]"

35So they struck him down, together with his sons and his whole army, leaving them no survivors. And they took possession of his land.

Balak Summons Balaam

22 Then the Israelites traveled to the plains of Moab and camped along the Jordan across from Jericho.[c][c]

2Now Balak son of Zippor[d] saw all that Israel had done to the Amorites, **3**and Moab was terrified because there were so many people. Indeed, Moab was filled with dread[e] because of the Israelites.

4The Moabites said to the elders of Midian, "This horde is going to lick up everything around us, as an ox licks up the grass of the field."

So Balak son of Zippor, who was king of Moab at that time, **5**sent messengers to summon Balaam son of Beor,[f] who was at Pethor, near the River,[d] in his native land. Balak said:

21:15 [e]ver 28; Dt 2:9,18
21:16 [f]Jdg 9:21
21:17 [g]Ex 15:1
21:21 [h]Dt 1:4; 2:26-27; Jdg 11:19-21
21:22 [i]Nu 20:17
21:23 [j]Nu 20:21 [k]Dt 2:32; Jdg 11:20
21:24 [l]Dt 2:33; Ps 135:10-11; Am 2:9 [m]Dt 2:37
21:25 [n]Nu 13:29; Jdg 10:11; Am 2:10
21:26 [o]Dt 29:7; Ps 135:11
21:28 [p]Jer 48:45 [q]ver 15 [r]Nu 22:41; Isa 15:2
21:29 [s]Isa 25:10; Jer 48:46 [t]Jdg 11:24; 1Ki 11:7,33; 2Ki 23:13; Jer 48:7,46 [u]Isa 15:5 [v]Isa 16:2
21:30 [w]Nu 32:3; Isa 15:2; Jer 48:18,22
21:32 [x]Nu 32:1,3,35; Jer 48:32
21:33 [y]Dt 3:3 [z]Dt 3:4 [a]Dt 1:4; 3:1,10; Jos 13:12,31
21:34 [b]Dt 3:2
22:1 [c]Nu 33:48
22:2 [d]Jdg 11:25
22:3 [e]Ex 15:15
22:5 [f]Dt 23:4; Jos 13:22; 24:9; Ne 13:2; Mic 6:5; 2Pe 2:15

[a] *14* The meaning of the Hebrew for this phrase is uncertain. [b] *14,15* Or *"I have been given from Suphah and the ravines / of the Arnon* [15]*to*
[c] *1* Hebrew *Jordan of Jericho*; possibly an ancient name for the Jordan River [d] *5* That is, the Euphrates

“A people has come out of
Egypt; they cover the face of the
land and have settled next to me.
6Now come and put a curse[g] on
these people, because they are too
powerful for me. Perhaps then I
will be able to defeat them and
drive them out of the country. For
I know that those you bless are
blessed, and those you curse are
cursed.”

7The elders of Moab and Midian left,
taking with them the fee for divination.[h] When they came to Balaam,
they told him what Balak had said.
8“Spend the night here,” Balaam
said to them, “and I will bring you
back the answer the LORD gives me.[i]”
So the Moabite princes stayed with
him.
9God came to Balaam[j] and asked,[k]
“Who are these men with you?”
10Balaam said to God, “Balak son of
Zippor, king of Moab, sent me this
message: 11‘A people that has come out
of Egypt covers the face of the land.
Now come and put a curse on them for
me. Perhaps then I will be able to fight
them and drive them away.’ ”
12But God said to Balaam, “Do not
go with them. You must not put a curse
on those people, because they are
blessed.[l]”
13The next morning Balaam got up
and said to Balak’s princes, “Go back to
your own country, for the LORD has refused to let me go with you.”
14So the Moabite princes returned to
Balak and said, “Balaam refused to
come with us.”
15Then Balak sent other princes,
more numerous and more distinguished than the first. 16They came to
Balaam and said:

“This is what Balak son of Zippor says: Do not let anything keep
you from coming to me, 17be-
cause I will reward you hand-
somely[m] and do whatever you
say. Come and put a curse[n] on
these people for me.”

18But Balaam answered them, “Even
if Balak gave me his palace filled with
silver and gold, I could not do anything
great or small to go beyond the command of the LORD my God.[o] 19Now
stay here tonight as the others did, and
I will find out what else the LORD will
tell me.[p]”
20That night God came to Balaam[q]
and said, “Since these men have come
to summon you, go with them, but do
only what I tell you.”[r]

22:6 [g]ver 12,17; Nu 23:7,11,13 **22:7** [h]Nu 23:23; 24:1 **22:8** [i]ver 19 **22:9** [j]Ge 20:3 [k]ver 20 **22:12** [l]Ge 12:2; 22:17; Nu 23:20 **22:17** [m]ver 37; Nu 24:11 [n]ver 6 **22:18** [o]ver 38; Nu 23:12,26; 24:13; 1Ki 22:14; 2Ch 18:13; Jer 42:4 **22:19** [p]ver 8 **22:20** [q]Ge 20:3 [r]ver 35,38; Nu 23:5,12,16, 26; 24:13; 2Ch 18:13

22:22 [s]Ex 4:14 [t]Ge 16:7; Ex 23:20; Jdg 13:3,6,13 **22:23** [u]Jos 5:13 [v]ver 25,27 **22:27** [w]Nu 11:1; Jas 1:19 **22:28** [x]2Pe 2:16 [y]ver 32 **22:29** [z]Dt 25:4; Pr 12:10; 27:23-27; Mt 15:19 **22:31** [a]Ge 21:19 **22:33** [b]ver 29 **22:34** [c]Ge 39:9; Nu 14:40; 1Sa 15:24,30; 2Sa 12:13; 24:10; Job 33:27; Ps 51:4

Balaam’s Donkey

21Balaam got up in the morning,
saddled his donkey and went with the
princes of Moab. 22But God was very
angry[s] when he went, and the angel of
the LORD[t] stood in the road to oppose
him. Balaam was riding on his donkey,
and his two servants were with him.
23When the donkey saw the angel of
the LORD standing in the road with a
drawn sword[u] in his hand, she turned
off the road into a field. Balaam beat
her[v] to get her back on the road.
24Then the angel of the LORD stood
in a narrow path between two vineyards, with walls on both sides. 25When
the donkey saw the angel of the LORD,
she pressed close to the wall, crushing
Balaam’s foot against it. So he beat her
again.
26Then the angel of the LORD moved
on ahead and stood in a narrow place
where there was no room to turn, either to the right or to the left. 27When
the donkey saw the angel of the LORD,
she lay down under Balaam, and he
was angry[w] and beat her with his staff.
28Then the LORD opened the donkey’s
mouth,[x] and she said to Balaam,
“What have I done to you to make you
beat me these three times?[y]”
29Balaam answered the donkey,
“You have made a fool of me! If I had
a sword in my hand, I would kill you
right now.[z]”
30The donkey said to Balaam, “Am I
not your own donkey, which you have
always ridden, to this day? Have I been
in the habit of doing this to you?”
“No,” he said.
31Then the LORD opened Balaam’s
eyes,[a] and he saw the angel of the
LORD standing in the road with his
sword drawn. So he bowed low and fell
facedown.
32The angel of the LORD asked him,
“Why have you beaten your donkey
these three times? I have come here
to oppose you because your path is a
reckless one before me.[a] 33The donkey
saw me and turned away from me
these three times. If she had not turned
away, I would certainly have killed you
by now,[b] but I would have spared
her.”
34Balaam said to the angel of the
LORD, “I have sinned.[c] I did not realize
you were standing in the road to oppose me. Now if you are displeased, I
will go back.”
35The angel of the LORD said to Balaam, “Go with the men, but speak only

[a] *32* The meaning of the Hebrew for this clause is uncertain.

what I tell you." So Balaam went with the princes of Balak.

36When Balak heard that Balaam was coming, he went out to meet him at the Moabite town on the Arnon[d] border, at the edge of his territory. 37Balak said to Balaam, "Did I not send you an urgent summons? Why didn't you come to me? Am I really not able to reward you?"

38"Well, I have come to you now," Balaam replied. "But can I say just anything? I must speak only what God puts in my mouth."[e]

39Then Balaam went with Balak to Kiriath Huzoth. 40Balak sacrificed cattle and sheep,[f] and gave some to Balaam and the princes who were with him. 41The next morning Balak took Balaam up to Bamoth Baal,[g] and from there he saw part of the people.[h]

Balaam's First Oracle

23 Balaam said, "Build me seven altars here, and prepare seven bulls and seven rams[i] for me." 2Balak did as Balaam said, and the two of them offered a bull and a ram on each altar.[j]

3Then Balaam said to Balak, "Stay here beside your offering while I go aside. Perhaps the LORD will come to meet with me.[k] Whatever he reveals to me I will tell you." Then he went off to a barren height.

4God met with him,[l] and Balaam said, "I have prepared seven altars, and on each altar I have offered a bull and a ram."

5The LORD put a message in Balaam's mouth[m] and said, "Go back to Balak and give him this message."[n]

6So he went back to him and found him standing beside his offering, with all the princes of Moab.[o] 7Then Balaam[p] uttered his oracle:[q]

"Balak brought me from Aram,
the king of Moab from the
eastern mountains.
'Come,' he said, 'curse Jacob for
me;
come, denounce Israel.'[r]
8How can I curse
those whom God has not
cursed?[s]
How can I denounce
those whom the LORD has not
denounced?
9From the rocky peaks I see them,
from the heights I view them.
I see a people who live apart
and do not consider themselves
one of the nations.[t]
10Who can count the dust of Jacob[u]
or number the fourth part of
Israel?
Let me die the death of the
righteous,[v]
and may my end be like
theirs![w]"

11Balak said to Balaam, "What have you done to me? I brought you to curse my enemies, but you have done nothing but bless them!"[x]

12He answered, "Must I not speak what the LORD puts in my mouth?"[y]

Balaam's Second Oracle

13Then Balak said to him, "Come with me to another place where you can see them; you will see only a part but not all of them. And from there, curse them for me." 14So he took him to the field of Zophim on the top of Pisgah, and there he built seven altars and offered a bull and a ram on each altar.[z]

15Balaam said to Balak, "Stay here beside your offering while I meet with him over there."

16The LORD met with Balaam and put a message in his mouth[a] and said, "Go back to Balak and give him this message."

17So he went to him and found him standing beside his offering, with the princes of Moab. Balak asked him, "What did the LORD say?"

18Then he uttered his oracle:

"Arise, Balak, and listen;
hear me, son of Zippor.
19God is not a man,[b] that he should
lie,
nor a son of man, that he should
change his mind.[c]
Does he speak and then not act?
Does he promise and not fulfill?
20I have received a command to
bless;
he has blessed,[d] and I cannot
change it.[e]
21"No misfortune is seen in Jacob,[f]
no misery observed in Israel.[a][g]
The LORD their God is with them;[h]
the shout of the King[i] is among
them.
22God brought them out of Egypt;[j]
they have the strength of a wild
ox.[k]
23There is no sorcery against Jacob,
no divination[l] against Israel.
It will now be said of Jacob
and of Israel, 'See what God has
done!'
24The people rise like a lioness;[m]

22:36 [d]Nu 21:13 **22:38** [e]Nu 23:5,16,26 **22:40** [f]Nu 23:1,14, 29; Eze 45:23 **22:41** [g]Nu 21:28 [h]Nu 23:13 **23:1** [i]Nu 22:40 **23:2** [j]ver 14,30 **23:3** [k]ver 15 **23:4** [l]ver 16 **23:5** [m]Dt 18:18; Jer 1:9 [n]Nu 22:20 **23:6** [o]ver 17 **23:7** [p]Nu 22:5 [q]ver 18; Nu 24:3,21 [r]Nu 22:6; Dt 23:4 **23:8** [s]Nu 22:12 **23:9** [t]Ex 33:16; Dt 32:8; 33:28 **23:10** [u]Ge 13:16 [v]Ps 116:15; Isa 57:1 [w]Ps 37:37 **23:11** [x]Nu 24:10; Ne 13:2 **23:12** [y]Nu 22:20,38 **23:14** [z]ver 2 **23:16** [a]Nu 22:38 **23:19** [b]Isa 55:9; Hos 11:9 [c]1Sa 15:29; Mal 3:6; Tit 1:2; Jas 1:17 **23:20** [d]Ge 22:17; Nu 22:12 [e]Isa 43:13 **23:21** [f]Ps 32:2,5; Ro 4:7-8 [g]Isa 40:2; Jer 50:20 [h]Ex 29:45,46; Ps 145:18 [i]Dt 33:5; Ps 89:15-18 **23:22** [j]Nu 24:8 [k]Dt 33:17; Job 39:9 **23:23** [l]Nu 24:1; Jos 13:22 **23:24** [m]Na 2:11

[a] *21* Or *He has not looked on Jacob's offenses / or on the wrongs found in Israel.*

they rouse themselves like a
lion[n]
that does not rest till he devours
his prey
and drinks the blood of his
victims."

25Then Balak said to Balaam, "Neither curse them at all nor bless them at
all!"
26Balaam answered, "Did I not tell
you I must do whatever the LORD says?"

Balaam's Third Oracle

27Then Balak said to Balaam,
"Come, let me take you to another
place.[o] Perhaps it will please God to
let you curse them for me from there."
28And Balak took Balaam to the top of
Peor,[p] overlooking the wasteland.
29Balaam said, "Build me seven altars here, and prepare seven bulls and
seven rams for me." 30Balak did as Balaam had said, and offered a bull and a
ram on each altar.

24 Now when Balaam saw that it
pleased the LORD to bless Israel, he
did not resort to sorcery[q] as at other
times, but turned his face toward the
desert.[r] 2When Balaam looked out
and saw Israel encamped tribe by tribe,
the Spirit of God came upon him[s]
3and he uttered his oracle:

"The oracle of Balaam son of Beor,
the oracle of one whose eye sees
clearly,
4the oracle of one who hears the
words of God,[t]
who sees a vision from the
Almighty,[a][u]
who falls prostrate, and whose
eyes are opened:

5"How beautiful are your tents,
O Jacob,
your dwelling places, O Israel!

6"Like valleys they spread out,
like gardens beside a river,
like aloes[v] planted by the LORD,
like cedars beside the waters.[w]
7Water will flow from their buckets;
their seed will have abundant
water.

"Their king will be greater than
Agag;[x]
their kingdom will be exalted.[y]

8"God brought them out of Egypt;
they have the strength of a wild
ox.
They devour hostile nations
and break their bones in
pieces;[z]
with their arrows they pierce
them.[a]

23:24 [n]Ge 49:9
23:27 [o]ver 13
23:28 [p]Ps 106:28
24:1 [q]Nu 23:23 [r]Nu 23:28
24:2 [s]Nu 11:25,26; 1Sa 10:10; 19:20; 2Ch 15:1
24:4 [t]Nu 22:20 [u]Ge 15:1
24:6 [v]Ps 45:8 [w]Ps 1:3; 104:16
24:7 [x]2Sa 15:8 [y]2Sa 5:12; 1Ch 14:2; Ps 145:11-13
24:8 [z]Ps 2:9; Jer 50:17 [a]Ps 45:5
24:9 [b]Ge 49:9; Nu 23:24 [c]Ge 12:3
24:10 [d]Eze 21:14 [e]Nu 23:11 [f]Ne 13:2
24:11 [g]Nu 22:17
24:12 [h]Nu 22:18
24:13 [i]Nu 22:18 [j]Nu 22:20
24:14 [k]Ge 49:1; Nu 31:8,16; Da 2:28; Mic 6:5
24:17 [l]Rev 1:7 [m]Mt 2:2 [n]Ge 49:10 [o]Nu 21:29; Isa 15:1-16:14
24:18 [p]Am 9:12
24:19 [q]Ge 49:10; Mic 5:2

9Like a lion they crouch and lie
down,
like a lioness[b]—who dares to
rouse them?

"May those who bless you be
blessed
and those who curse you be
cursed!"[c]

10Then Balak's anger burned against
Balaam. He struck his hands together[d] and said to him, "I summoned you
to curse my enemies, but you have
blessed them[e] these three times.[f]
11Now leave at once and go home! I
said I would reward you handsome-
ly,[g] but the LORD has kept you from
being rewarded."
12Balaam answered Balak, "Did I not
tell the messengers you sent me,[h]
13'Even if Balak gave me his palace
filled with silver and gold, I could not
do anything of my own accord, good or
bad, to go beyond the command of the
LORD[i]—and I must say only what the
LORD says'?[j] 14Now I am going back to
my people, but come, let me warn you
of what this people will do to your people in days to come."[k]

Balaam's Fourth Oracle

15Then he uttered his oracle:
"The oracle of Balaam son of Beor,
the oracle of one whose eye sees
clearly,
16the oracle of one who hears the
words of God,
who has knowledge from the
Most High,
who sees a vision from the
Almighty,
who falls prostrate, and whose
eyes are opened:

17"I see him, but not now;
I behold him, but not near.[l]
A star will come out of Jacob;[m]
a scepter will rise out of Israel.[n]
He will crush the foreheads of
Moab,[o]
the skulls[b] of[c] all the sons of
Sheth.[d]
18Edom[p] will be conquered;
Seir, his enemy, will be
conquered,
but Israel will grow strong.
19A ruler will come out of Jacob[q]
and destroy the survivors of the
city."

[a]4 Hebrew *Shaddai*; also in verse 16
[b]17 Samaritan Pentateuch (see also Jer. 48:45); the meaning of the word in the Masoretic Text is uncertain.
[c]17 Or possibly *Moab, / batter*
[d]17 Or *all the noisy boasters*

Balaam's Final Oracles

[20]Then Balaam saw Amalek[r] and
uttered his oracle:

"Amalek was first among the
nations,
but he will come to ruin at last."

[21]Then he saw the Kenites[s] and uttered his oracle:

"Your dwelling place is secure,
your nest is set in a rock;
[22]yet you Kenites will be destroyed
when Asshur[t] takes you
captive."

[23]Then he uttered his oracle:

"Ah, who can live when God does
this?[a]
[24] Ships will come from the shores
of Kittim;[u]
they will subdue Asshur and
Eber,[v]
but they too will come to
ruin.[w]"

[25]Then Balaam[x] got up and returned home and Balak went his own
way.

Moab Seduces Israel

25 While Israel was staying in
Shittim,[y] the men began to indulge in sexual immorality[z] with Moabite women,[a] [2]who invited them to
the sacrifices[b] to their gods.[c] The
people ate and bowed down before
these gods. [3]So Israel joined in worshiping the Baal of Peor.[d] And the
LORD's anger burned against them.
[4]The LORD said to Moses, "Take all
the leaders of these people, kill them
and expose them in broad daylight before the LORD,[e] so that the LORD's
fierce anger[f] may turn away from Israel."
[5]So Moses said to Israel's judges,
"Each of you must put to death[g] those
of your men who have joined in worshiping the Baal of Peor."
[6]Then an Israelite man brought to
his family a Midianite woman right before the eyes of Moses and the whole
assembly of Israel while they were
weeping at the entrance to the Tent of
Meeting. [7]When Phinehas son of Eleazar, the son of Aaron, the priest, saw
this, he left the assembly, took a spear
in his hand [8]and followed the Israelite
into the tent. He drove the spear
through both of them—through the Israelite and into the woman's body.
Then the plague against the Israelites
was stopped;[h] [9]but those who died in
the plague[i] numbered 24,000.[j]
[10]The LORD said to Moses, [11]"Phinehas son of Eleazar, the son of Aaron,
the priest, has turned my anger away
from the Israelites;[k] for he was as
zealous as I am for my honor[l] among
them, so that in my zeal I did not put
an end to them. [12]Therefore tell him
I am making my covenant of peace[m]
with him. [13]He and his descendants
will have a covenant of a lasting priesthood,[n] because he was zealous for the
honor of his God and made atonement[o] for the Israelites."
[14]The name of the Israelite who was
killed with the Midianite woman was
Zimri son of Salu, the leader of a Sime-
onite family. [15]And the name of the
Midianite woman who was put to
death was Cozbi[p] daughter of Zur, a
tribal chief of a Midianite family.[q]
[16]The LORD said to Moses, [17]"Treat
the Midianites[r] as enemies and kill
them, [18]because they treated you as
enemies when they deceived you in the
affair of Peor[s] and their sister Cozbi,
the daughter of a Midianite leader, the

24:20 [r]Ex 17:14 **24:21** [s]Ge 15:19 **24:22** [t]Ge 10:22 **24:24** [u]Ge 10:4 [v]Ge 10:21 [w]ver 20 **24:25** [x]Nu 31:8 **25:1** [y]Jos 2:1; Mic 6:5 [z]1Co 10:8; Rev 2:14 [a]Nu 31:16 **25:2** [b]Ex 34:15 [c]Ex 20:5; Dt 32:38; 1Co 10:20 **25:3** [d]Ps 106:28; Hos 9:10 **25:4** [e]Dt 4:3 [f]Dt 13:17 **25:5** [g]Ex 32:27 **25:8** [h]Nu 16:46-48; Ps 106:30 **25:9** [i]Nu 14:37; 1Co 10:8 [j]Nu 31:16 **25:11** [k]Ps 106:30 [l]Ex 20:5; Dt 32:16,21; Ps 78:58 **25:12** [m]Isa 54:10; Eze 34:25; Mal 2:4,5 **25:13** [n]Ex 29:9 [o]Nu 16:46 **25:15** [p]ver 18 [q]Nu 31:8; Jos 13:21 **25:17** [r]Nu 31:1-3 **25:18** [s]Nu 31:16

[a]*23* Masoretic Text; with a different word division of the Hebrew *A people will gather from the north.*

25:1–18

PROMISE 6

BIBLICAL SEGREGATION?

Was God acting the racist in this story? Was the plague on Israel a result of their associating with the Moabites? Was the Israelite in verses 6–8 killed because he befriended a Moabite woman?

Read the chapter carefully and you'll see that Israel's practice of pagan religion incited God's wrath, not their association with people of a different culture group. In fact, God recorded the Moabite woman's name in Scripture (v. 15). Although known to us only for her disobedience and judgment, God recognized her in this way.

As God's holy people, the ancient Israelites were required to worship YHWH alone. God's command that the Israelites separate themselves from participating in pagan religion was not divinely inspired racism; nor is it a defense for isolationism in our day. Learn to live as a holy man among people who desperately need to see what God does in a person's life. God wants us to bring people to him through our contact with them, not become like those who do not know him. As the apostle Paul said, "Do not conform any longer to the pattern of this world, but be transformed by the renewing of your mind. Then you will be able to test and approve what God's will is—his good, pleasing and perfect will" (Romans 12:2).

For the next Promise 6 reading go to page 209.

woman who was killed when the
plague came as a result of Peor.”

The Second Census

26 After the plague the LORD said
to Moses and Eleazar son of Aaron, the priest, 2“Take a census[t] of
the whole Israelite community by
families—all those twenty years old or
more who are able to serve in the
army[u] of Israel.” 3So on the plains of
Moab[v] by the Jordan across from Jericho,[a][w] Moses and Eleazar the priest
spoke with them and said, 4“Take a
census of the men twenty years old or
more, as the LORD commanded Moses.”

These were the Israelites who came
out of Egypt:

5The descendants of Reuben, the firstborn son of Israel, were:
through Hanoch,[x] the Hanoch-
ite clan;
through Pallu,[y] the Palluite
clan;
6through Hezron, the Hezronite
clan;
through Carmi, the Carmite clan.
7These were the clans of Reuben; those
numbered were 43,730.
8The son of Pallu was Eliab, 9and the
sons of Eliab[z] were Nemuel, Dathan
and Abiram. The same Dathan and
Abiram were the community[a] officials
who rebelled against Moses and Aaron
and were among Korah’s followers
when they rebelled against the LORD.[b]
10The earth opened its mouth and
swallowed them along with Korah,
whose followers died when the fire devoured the 250 men. And they served
as a warning sign.[c] 11The line of Korah,[d] however, did not die out.[e]

12The descendants of Simeon by their
clans were:
through Nemuel, the Nemuelite
clan;
through Jamin,[f] the Jaminite
clan;
through Jakin, the Jakinite clan;
13through Zerah,[g] the Zerahite
clan;
through Shaul, the Shaulite clan.
14These were the clans of Simeon;
there were 22,200 men.[h]

15The descendants of Gad by their
clans were:
through Zephon,[i] the Zephon-
ite clan;
through Haggi, the Haggite clan;
through Shuni, the Shunite clan;
16through Ozni, the Oznite clan;
through Eri, the Erite clan;
17through Arodi,[b] the Arodite clan;
through Areli, the Arelite clan.
18These were the clans of Gad;[j] those
numbered were 40,500.

19Er and Onan were sons of Judah, but
they died[k] in Canaan.
20The descendants of Judah by their
clans were:
through Shelah,[l] the Shelanite
clan;
through Perez, the Perezite clan;
through Zerah, the Zerahite
clan.[m]
21The descendants of Perez were:
through Hezron,[n] the Hezronite clan;
through Hamul, the Hamulite
clan.
22These were the clans of Judah;[o]
those numbered were 76,500.

23The descendants of Issachar by their
clans were:
through Tola,[p] the Tolaite clan;
through Puah, the Puite[c] clan;
24through Jashub,[q] the Jashubite
clan;
through Shimron, the Shimronite
clan.
25These were the clans of Issachar;[r]
those numbered were 64,300.

26The descendants of Zebulun by their
clans were:
through Sered, the Seredite clan;
through Elon, the Elonite clan;
through Jahleel, the Jahleelite
clan.
27These were the clans of Zebulun;[s]
those numbered were 60,500.

28The descendants of Joseph by their
clans through Manasseh and Ephraim
were:

29The descendants of Manasseh:
through Makir,[t] the Makirite
clan (Makir was the father of
Gilead[u]);
through Gilead, the Gileadite
clan.
30These were the descendants of
Gilead:
through Iezer,[v] the Iezerite
clan;
through Helek, the Helekite
clan;
31through Asriel, the Asrielite
clan;
through Shechem, the She-
chemite clan;

26:2 [t]Ex 30:11-16; 38:25-26; Nu 1:2 [u]Nu 1:3
26:3 [v]Nu 33:48 [w]Nu 22:1
26:5 [x]Ge 46:9 [y]1Ch 5:3
26:9 [z]Nu 16:1 [a]Nu 1:16 [b]Nu 16:2
26:10 [c]Nu 16:35,38
26:11 [d]Ex 6:24 [e]Nu 16:33; Dt 24:16
26:12 [f]1Ch 4:24
26:13 [g]Ge 46:10
26:14 [h]Nu 1:23
26:15 [i]Ge 46:16
26:18 [j]Nu 1:25; Jos 13:24-28
26:19 [k]Ge 38:2-10; 46:12
26:20 [l]1Ch 2:3 [m]Jos 7:17
26:21 [n]Ru 4:19; 1Ch 2:9
26:22 [o]Nu 1:27
26:23 [p]Ge 46:13; 1Ch 7:1
26:24 [q]Ge 46:13
26:25 [r]Nu 1:29
26:27 [s]Nu 1:31
26:29 [t]Jos 17:1 [u]Jdg 11:1
26:30 [v]Jos 17:2; Jdg 6:11

a *3* Hebrew *Jordan of Jericho*; possibly an ancient name for the Jordan River; also in verse 63 b *17* Samaritan Pentateuch and Syriac (see also Gen. 46:16); Masoretic Text *Arod* c *23* Samaritan Pentateuch, Septuagint, Vulgate and Syriac (see also 1 Chron. 7:1); Masoretic Text *through Puvah, the Punite*

32 through Shemida, the Shemidaite clan;
through Hepher, the Hepherite clan.
33 (Zelophehad[w] son of Hepher had no sons; he had only daughters, whose names were Mahlah, Noah, Hoglah, Milcah and Tirzah.)[x]

34 These were the clans of Manasseh; those numbered were 52,700.[y]

35 These were the descendants of Ephraim by their clans:
through Shuthelah, the Shuthelahite clan;
through Beker, the Bekerite clan;
through Tahan, the Tahanite clan.
36 These were the descendants of Shuthelah:
through Eran, the Eranite clan.

37 These were the clans of Ephraim;[z] those numbered were 32,500.

These were the descendants of Joseph by their clans.

38 The descendants of Benjamin[a] by their clans were:
through Bela, the Belaite clan;
through Ashbel, the Ashbelite clan;
through Ahiram, the Ahiramite clan;
39 through Shupham,**a** the Shuphamite clan;
through Hupham, the Huphamite clan.
40 The descendants of Bela through Ard[b] and Naaman were:
through Ard,**b** the Ardite clan;
through Naaman, the Naamite clan.

41 These were the clans of Benjamin;[c] those numbered were 45,600.

42 These were the descendants of Dan by their clans:
through Shuham,[d] the Shuhamite clan.
These were the clans of Dan: 43 All of them were Shuhamite clans; and those numbered were 64,400.

44 The descendants of Asher by their clans were:
through Imnah, the Imnite clan;
through Ishvi, the Ishvite clan;
through Beriah, the Beriite clan;
45 and through the descendants of Beriah:
through Heber, the Heberite clan;
through Malkiel, the Malkielite clan.
46 (Asher had a daughter named Serah.)

26:33 [w]Nu 27:1 [x]Nu 36:11
26:34 [y]Nu 1:35
26:37 [z]Nu 1:33
26:38 [a]Ge 46:21; 1Ch 7:6
26:40 [b]Ge 46:21; 1Ch 8:3
26:41 [c]Nu 1:37
26:42 [d]Ge 46:23
26:47 [e]Nu 1:41
26:48 [f]Ge 46:24; 1Ch 7:13
26:50 [g]Nu 1:43
26:51 [h]Ex 12:37; 38:26; Nu 1:46; 11:21
26:53 [i]Jos 11:23; 14:1; Eze 45:8
26:54 [j]Nu 33:54
26:55 [k]Nu 34:14
26:57 [l]Ge 46:11; Ex 6:16-19
26:58 [m]Ex 6:20
26:59 [n]Ex 2:1 [o]Ex 6:20
26:60 [p]Nu 3:2
26:61 [q]Lev 10:1-2 [r]Nu 3:4
26:62 [s]Nu 3:39

47 These were the clans of Asher;[e] those numbered were 53,400.

48 The descendants of Naphtali[f] by their clans were:
through Jahzeel, the Jahzeelite clan;
through Guni, the Gunite clan;
49 through Jezer, the Jezerite clan;
through Shillem, the Shillemite clan.

50 These were the clans of Naphtali;[g] those numbered were 45,400.

51 The total number of the men of Israel was 601,730.[h]

52 The LORD said to Moses, 53 "The land is to be allotted to them as an inheritance based on the number of names.[i] 54 To a larger group give a larger inheritance, and to a smaller group a smaller one; each is to receive its inheritance according to the number[j] of those listed. 55 Be sure that the land is distributed by lot.[k] What each group inherits will be according to the names for its ancestral tribe. 56 Each inheritance is to be distributed by lot among the larger and smaller groups."

57 These were the Levites[l] who were counted by their clans:
through Gershon, the Gershonite clan;
through Kohath, the Kohathite clan;
through Merari, the Merarite clan.
58 These also were Levite clans:
the Libnite clan,
the Hebronite clan,
the Mahlite clan,
the Mushite clan,
the Korahite clan.
(Kohath was the forefather of Amram;[m] 59 the name of Amram's wife was Jochebed,[n] a descendant of Levi, who was born to the Levites**c** in Egypt. To Amram she bore Aaron, Moses[o] and their sister Miriam. 60 Aaron was the father of Nadab and Abihu, Eleazar and Ithamar.[p] 61 But Nadab and Abihu[q] died when they made an offering before the LORD with unauthorized fire.)[r]

62 All the male Levites a month old or more numbered 23,000.[s] They were

a *39* A few manuscripts of the Masoretic Text, Samaritan Pentateuch, Vulgate and Syriac (see also Septuagint); most manuscripts of the Masoretic Text *Shephupham* **b** *40* Samaritan Pentateuch and Vulgate (see also Septuagint); Masoretic Text does not have *through Ard.*
c *59* Or *Jochebed, a daughter of Levi, who was born to Levi*

not counted[t] along with the other Israelites because they received no inheritance[u] among them.[v]

63These are the ones counted by Moses and Eleazar the priest when they counted the Israelites on the plains of Moab[w] by the Jordan across from Jericho. 64Not one of them was among those counted[x] by Moses and Aaron the priest when they counted the Israelites in the Desert of Sinai. 65For the LORD had told those Israelites they would surely die in the desert,[y] and not one of them was left except Caleb son of Jephunneh and Joshua son of Nun.[z]

Zelophehad's Daughters

27 The daughters of Zelophehad[a] son of Hepher,[b] the son of Gilead, the son of Makir,[c] the son of Manasseh, belonged to the clans of Manasseh son of Joseph. The names of the daughters were Mahlah, Noah, Hoglah, Milcah and Tirzah. They approached 2the entrance to the Tent of Meeting and stood before Moses, Eleazar the priest, the leaders and the whole assembly, and said, 3"Our father died in the desert.[d] He was not among Korah's followers, who banded together against the LORD,[e] but he died for his own sin and left no sons.[f] 4Why should our father's name disappear from his clan because he had no son? Give us property among our father's relatives."

5So Moses brought their case[g] before the LORD[h] 6and the LORD said to him, 7"What Zelophehad's daughters are saying is right. You must certainly give them property as an inheritance[i] among their father's relatives and turn their father's inheritance over to them.[j]

8"Say to the Israelites, 'If a man dies and leaves no son, turn his inheritance over to his daughter. 9If he has no daughter, give his inheritance to his brothers. 10If he has no brothers, give his inheritance to his father's brothers. 11If his father had no brothers, give his inheritance to the nearest relative in his clan, that he may possess it. This is to be a legal requirement[k] for the Israelites, as the LORD commanded Moses.' "

Joshua to Succeed Moses

12Then the LORD said to Moses, "Go up this mountain in the Abarim range[l] and see the land[m] I have given the Israelites. 13After you have seen it, you too will be gathered to your people,[n] as your brother Aaron[o] was, 14for when the community rebelled at the waters in the Desert of Zin, both of you disobeyed my command to honor me as holy[p] before their eyes." (These were the waters of Meribah[q] Kadesh, in the Desert of Zin.)

15Moses said to the LORD, 16"May the LORD, the God of the spirits of all mankind,[r] appoint a man over this community 17to go out and come in before them, one who will lead them out and bring them in, so the LORD's people will not be like sheep without a shepherd."[s]

18So the LORD said to Moses, "Take Joshua son of Nun, a man in whom is the spirit,[a][t] and lay your hand on him.[u] 19Have him stand before Eleazar the priest and the entire assembly and commission him[v] in their presence.[w] 20Give him some of your authority so the whole Israelite community will obey him.[x] 21He is to stand before Eleazar the priest, who will obtain decisions for him by inquiring[y] of the Urim[z] before the LORD. At his command he and the entire community of the Israelites will go out, and at his command they will come in."

22Moses did as the LORD commanded him. He took Joshua and had him stand before Eleazar the priest and the whole assembly. 23Then he laid his hands on him and commissioned him, as the LORD instructed through Moses.

2 →PG. 191

Daily Offerings

28 The LORD said to Moses, 2"Give this command to the Israelites and say to them: 'See that you present to me at the appointed time the food[a] for my offerings made by fire, as an aroma pleasing to me.' 3Say to them: 'This is the offering made by fire that you are to present to the LORD: two lambs a year old without defect, as a regular burnt offering each day.[b] 4Prepare one lamb in the morning and the other at twilight, 5together with a grain offering of a tenth of an ephah[b] of fine flour mixed with a quarter of a hin[c] of oil[c] from pressed olives. 6This is the regular burnt offering instituted at Mount Sinai[d] as a pleasing aroma, an offering made to the LORD by fire. 7The accompanying drink offering[e] is to be a quarter of a hin of fermented drink with each lamb. Pour out the drink offering to the LORD at the sanctuary.[f] 8Prepare the second lamb at twilight, along with the same kind of grain offer-

26:62 [t]Nu 1:47 [u]Nu 18:23 [v]Nu 2:33; Dt 10:9
26:63 [w]ver 3
26:64 [x]Nu 14:29; Dt 2:14-15; Heb 3:17
26:65 [y]Nu 14:28; 1Co 10:5 [z]Jos 14:6-10
27:1 [a]Nu 26:33 [b]Jos 17:2,3 [c]Nu 36:1
27:3 [d]Nu 26:65 [e]Nu 16:2 [f]Nu 26:33
27:5 [g]Ex 18:19 [h]Nu 9:8
27:7 [i]Job 42:15 [j]Jos 17:4
27:11 [k]Nu 35:29
27:12 [l]Nu 33:47; Jer 22:20 [m]Dt 3:23-27; 32:48-52
27:13 [n]Nu 31:2 [o]Nu 20:28
27:14 [p]Nu 20:12 [q]Ex 17:7; Dt 32:51; Ps 106:32
27:16 [r]Nu 16:22
27:17 [s]Dt 31:2; 1Ki 22:17; Eze 34:5; Zec 10:2; Mt 9:36; Mk 6:34
27:18 [t]Ge 41:38; Nu 11:25-29 [u]ver 23; Dt 34:9
27:19 [v]Dt 3:28; 31:14,23 [w]Dt 31:7
27:20 [x]Jos 1:16,17
27:21 [y]Jos 9:14 [z]Ex 28:30
28:2 [a]Lev 3:11
28:3 [b]Ex 29:38
28:5 [c]Lev 2:1; Nu 15:4
28:6 [d]Ex 19:3
28:7 [e]Ex 29:41 [f]Lev 3:7

a *18* Or *Spirit* **b** *5* That is, probably about 2 quarts (about 2 liters); also in verses 13, 21 and 29 **c** *5* That is, probably about 1 quart (about 1 liter); also in verses 7 and 14

ing and drink offering that you prepare
in the morning. This is an offering
made by fire, an aroma pleasing to the
LORD.[g]

Sabbath Offerings

9“ ‘On the Sabbath[h] day, make an
offering of two lambs a year old without defect, together with its drink offering and a grain offering of two-tenths
of an ephah[a][i] of fine flour mixed
with oil. 10This is the burnt offering for
every Sabbath, in addition to the regular burnt offering[j] and its drink offering.

Monthly Offerings

11“ ‘On the first of every month,[k]
present to the LORD a burnt offering of
two young bulls, one ram and seven
male lambs a year old, all without defect.[l] 12With each bull there is to be a
grain offering[m] of three-tenths of an
ephah[b][n] of fine flour mixed with oil;
with the ram, a grain offering of two-
tenths of an ephah of fine flour mixed
with oil; 13and with each lamb, a grain
offering[o] of a tenth of an ephah of fine
flour mixed with oil. This is for a burnt
offering, a pleasing aroma, an offering
made to the LORD by fire. 14With each
bull there is to be a drink offering[p] of
half a hin[c] of wine; with the ram, a
third of a hin[d]; and with each lamb, a
quarter of a hin. This is the monthly
burnt offering to be made at each new
moon[q] during the year. 15Besides the
regular burnt offering[r] with its drink
offering, one male goat is to be presented to the LORD as a sin offering.[s]

The Passover

16“ ‘On the fourteenth day of the first
month the LORD’s Passover[t] is to be
held. 17On the fifteenth day of this
month there is to be a festival; for sev-
en days[u] eat bread made without
yeast.[v] 18On the first day hold a sacred
assembly and do no regular work.[w]
19Present to the LORD an offering made
by fire, a burnt offering of two young
bulls, one ram and seven male lambs
a year old, all without defect. 20With
each bull prepare a grain offering of
three-tenths of an ephah[x] of fine flour
mixed with oil; with the ram, two-
tenths; 21and with each of the seven
lambs, one-tenth. 22Include one male
goat as a sin offering[y] to make atonement for you.[z] 23Prepare these in addition to the regular morning burnt offering. 24In this way prepare the food
for the offering made by fire every day
for seven days as an aroma pleasing to
the LORD; it is to be prepared in addition to the regular burnt offering and
its drink offering. 25On the seventh day
hold a sacred assembly and do no regular work.

Feast of Weeks

26“ ‘On the day of firstfruits,[a] when
you present to the LORD an offering of
new grain during the Feast of Weeks,[b]
hold a sacred assembly and do no regular work.[c] 27Present a burnt offering
of two young bulls, one ram and seven
male lambs a year old as an aroma
pleasing to the LORD. 28With each bull
there is to be a grain offering of three-
tenths of an ephah of fine flour mixed
with oil; with the ram, two-tenths;
29and with each of the seven lambs,
one-tenth.[d] 30Include one male goat
to make atonement for you. 31Prepare
these together with their drink offerings, in addition to the regular burnt
offering[e] and its grain offering. Be
sure the animals are without defect.

Feast of Trumpets

29 “ ‘On the first day of the seventh
month hold a sacred assembly and
do no regular work.[f] It is a day for you
to sound the trumpets. 2As an aroma
pleasing to the LORD,[g] prepare a burnt
offering of one young bull, one ram
and seven male lambs a year old, all
without defect.[h] 3With the bull prepare a grain offering of three-tenths of
an ephah[e] of fine flour mixed with oil;
with the ram, two-tenths[f]; 4and with
each of the seven lambs, one-tenth.[g]
5Include one male goat[i] as a sin offering to make atonement for you. 6These
are in addition to the monthly[j] and
daily burnt offerings[k] with their grain
offerings and drink offerings as specified. They are offerings made to the
LORD by fire—a pleasing aroma.

Day of Atonement

7“ ‘On the tenth day of this seventh
month hold a sacred assembly. You
must deny yourselves[h][l] and do no
work.[m] 8Present as an aroma pleasing
to the LORD a burnt offering of one
young bull, one ram and seven male
lambs a year old, all without defect.

28:8 [g]Lev 1:9
28:9 [h]Ex 20:10 [i]Lev 23:13
28:10 [j]ver 3
28:11 [k]Nu 10:10 [l]Lev 1:3
28:12 [m]Nu 15:6 [n]Nu 15:9
28:13 [o]Lev 6:14
28:14 [p]Nu 15:7 [q]Ezr 3:5
28:15 [r]ver 3,23,24 [s]Lev 4:3
28:16 [t]Ex 12:6,18; Lev 23:5; Dt 16:1
28:17 [u]Ex 12:19 [v]Ex 23:15; 34:18; Lev 23:6; Dt 16:3-8
28:18 [w]Ex 12:16; Lev 23:7
28:20 [x]Lev 14:10
28:22 [y]Ro 8:3 [z]Nu 15:28
28:26 [a]Ex 34:22 [b]Ex 23:16 [c]ver 18; Dt 16:10
28:29 [d]ver 13
28:31 [e]ver 3,19
29:1 [f]Lev 23:24
29:2 [g]Nu 28:2 [h]Nu 28:3
29:5 [i]Nu 28:15
29:6 [j]Nu 28:11 [k]Nu 28:3
29:7 [l]Ac 27:9 [m]Ex 31:15; Lev 16:29; 23:26-32

[a] *9* That is, probably about 4 quarts (about 4.5 liters); also in verses 12, 20 and 28
[b] *12* That is, probably about 6 quarts (about 6.5 liters); also in verses 20 and 28
[c] *14* That is, probably about 2 quarts (about 2 liters)
[d] *14* That is, probably about 1 1/4 quarts (about 1.2 liters)
[e] *3* That is, probably about 6 quarts (about 6.5 liters); also in verses 9 and 14
[f] *3* That is, probably about 4 quarts (about 4.5 liters); also in verses 9 and 14
[g] *4* That is, probably about 2 quarts (about 2 liters); also in verses 10 and 15
[h] *7* Or *must fast*

9With the bull prepare a grain offering[n] of three-tenths of an ephah of
fine flour mixed with oil; with the ram,
two-tenths; **10**and with each of the sev-
en lambs, one-tenth.[o] **11**Include one
male goat as a sin offering, in addition
to the sin offering for atonement and
the regular burnt offering[p] with its
grain offering, and their drink offerings.

Feast of Tabernacles

12" 'On the fifteenth day of the seventh[q] month,[r] hold a sacred assembly and do no regular work. Celebrate
a festival to the LORD for seven days.
13Present an offering made by fire as an
aroma pleasing to the LORD, a burnt
offering of thirteen young bulls, two
rams and fourteen male lambs a year
old, all without defect. **14**With each of
the thirteen bulls prepare a grain offering[s] of three-tenths of an ephah of
fine flour mixed with oil; with each of
the two rams, two-tenths; **15**and with
each of the fourteen lambs, one-tenth.
16Include one male goat as a sin offering, in addition to the regular burnt offering with its grain offering and drink
offering.[t]

17" 'On the second day[u] prepare
twelve young bulls, two rams and fourteen male lambs a year old, all without
defect.[v] **18**With the bulls, rams and
lambs, prepare their grain offerings[w]
and drink offerings[x] according to the
number specified.[y] **19**Include one
male goat as a sin offering,[z] in addition to the regular burnt offering with
its grain offering, and their drink offerings.

20" 'On the third day prepare eleven
bulls, two rams and fourteen male
lambs a year old, all without defect.[a]
21With the bulls, rams and lambs, prepare their grain offerings and drink offerings according to the number specified.[b] **22**Include one male goat as a sin
offering, in addition to the regular
burnt offering with its grain offering
and drink offering.

23" 'On the fourth day prepare ten
bulls, two rams and fourteen male
lambs a year old, all without defect.
24With the bulls, rams and lambs, prepare their grain offerings and drink offerings according to the number specified. **25**Include one male goat as a sin
offering, in addition to the regular
burnt offering with its grain offering
and drink offering.

26" 'On the fifth day prepare nine
bulls, two rams and fourteen male
lambs a year old, all without defect.
27With the bulls, rams and lambs, prepare their grain offerings and drink offerings according to the number specified. **28**Include one male goat as a sin
offering, in addition to the regular
burnt offering with its grain offering
and drink offering.

29" 'On the sixth day prepare eight
bulls, two rams and fourteen male
lambs a year old, all without defect.
30With the bulls, rams and lambs, prepare their grain offerings and drink offerings according to the number specified. **31**Include one male goat as a sin
offering, in addition to the regular
burnt offering with its grain offering
and drink offering.

32" 'On the seventh day prepare sev-
en bulls, two rams and fourteen male
lambs a year old, all without defect.
33With the bulls, rams and lambs, prepare their grain offerings and drink offerings according to the number specified. **34**Include one male goat as a sin
offering, in addition to the regular
burnt offering with its grain offering
and drink offering.

35" 'On the eighth day hold an assembly[c] and do no regular work.
36Present an offering made by fire as an
aroma pleasing to the LORD,[d] a burnt
offering of one bull, one ram and seven
male lambs a year old,[e] all without
defect. **37**With the bull, the ram and the
lambs, prepare their grain offerings
and drink offerings according to the
number specified. **38**Include one male
goat as a sin offering, in addition to the
regular burnt offering with its grain offering and drink offering.

39" 'In addition to what you vow[f]
and your freewill offerings, prepare
these for the LORD at your appointed
feasts:[g] your burnt offerings,[h] grain
offerings, drink offerings and fellowship offerings.[a]' "

40Moses told the Israelites all that
the LORD commanded him.

Vows

30 Moses said to the heads of the
tribes of Israel:[i] "This is what the
LORD commands: **2**When a man makes
a vow to the LORD or takes an oath to
obligate himself by a pledge, he must
not break his word but must do everything he said.[j]

3"When a young woman still living
in her father's house makes a vow to
the LORD or obligates herself by a
pledge **4**and her father hears about her
vow or pledge but says nothing to her,
then all her vows and every pledge
by which she obligated herself will

29:9 [n]ver 3,18
29:10 [o]Nu 28:13
29:11 [p]Lev 16:3; Nu 28:3
29:12 [q]1Ki 8:2 [r]Lev 23:24
29:14 [s]ver 3
29:16 [t]ver 6
29:17 [u]Lev 23:36 [v]Nu 28:3
29:18 [w]ver 9 [x]Nu 28:7 [y]Nu 15:4-12
29:19 [z]Nu 28:15
29:20 [a]ver 17
29:21 [b]ver 18
29:35 [c]Lev 23:36
29:36 [d]Lev 1:9 [e]ver 2
29:39 [f]Nu 6:2 [g]Lev 23:2 [h]Lev 1:3; 1Ch 23:31; 2Ch 31:3
30:1 [i]Nu 1:4
30:2 [j]Dt 23:21-23; Jdg 11:35; Job 22:27; Ps 22:25; 50:14; 116:14; Pr 20:25; Ecc 5:4,5; Jnh 1:16

a *39* Traditionally *peace offerings*

stand.[k] 5But if her father forbids her
when he hears about it, none of her
vows or the pledges by which she obligated herself will stand; the LORD will
release her because her father has forbidden her.

6"If she marries after she makes a
vow[l] or after her lips utter a rash
promise by which she obligates herself
7and her husband hears about it but
says nothing to her, then her vows or
the pledges by which she obligated
herself will stand. 8But if her husband[m] forbids her when he hears
about it, he nullifies the vow that obligates her or the rash promise by which
she obligates herself, and the LORD will
release her.

9"Any vow or obligation taken by a
widow or divorced woman will be
binding on her.

10"If a woman living with her husband makes a vow or obligates herself
by a pledge under oath 11and her husband hears about it but says nothing to
her and does not forbid her, then all
her vows or the pledges by which she
obligated herself will stand. 12But if her
husband nullifies them when he hears
about them, then none of the vows or
pledges that came from her lips will
stand.[n] Her husband has nullified
them, and the LORD will release her.
13Her husband may confirm or nullify
any vow she makes or any sworn
pledge to deny herself. 14But if her husband says nothing to her about it from
day to day, then he confirms all her
vows or the pledges binding on her. He
confirms them by saying nothing to
her when he hears about them. 15If,
however, he nullifies them some time
after he hears about them, then he is
responsible for her guilt."

16These are the regulations the LORD
gave Moses concerning relationships
between a man and his wife, and between a father and his young daughter
still living in his house.

Vengeance on the Midianites

31 The LORD said to Moses, 2"Take
vengeance on the Midianites[o] for
the Israelites. After that, you will be
gathered to your people.[p]"

3So Moses said to the people, "Arm
some of your men to go to war against
the Midianites and to carry out the
LORD's vengeance[q] on them. 4Send
into battle a thousand men from each
of the tribes of Israel." 5So twelve thousand men armed for battle, a thousand
from each tribe, were supplied from
the clans of Israel. 6Moses sent them
into battle, a thousand from each tribe,
along with Phinehas son of Eleazar, the
priest, who took with him articles from
the sanctuary[r] and the trumpets[s] for
signaling.

7They fought against Midian, as the
LORD commanded Moses, and killed
every man.[t] 8Among their victims
were Evi, Rekem, Zur, Hur and
Reba[u]—the five kings of Midian.[v]
They also killed Balaam son of Beor
with the sword.[w] 9The Israelites captured the Midianite women and children and took all the Midianite herds,
flocks and goods as plunder. 10They
burned all the towns where the Midianites had settled, as well as all their
camps.[x] 11They took all the plunder
and spoils, including the people and
animals,[y] 12and brought the captives,
spoils and plunder to Moses and Eleazar the priest and the Israelite assembly[z] at their camp on the plains of
Moab, by the Jordan across from Jericho.[a]

13Moses, Eleazar the priest and all
the leaders of the community went to
meet them outside the camp. 14Moses
was angry with the officers of the
army[a]—the commanders of thousands and commanders of hundreds—
who returned from the battle.

15"Have you allowed all the women
to live?" he asked them. 16"They were
the ones who followed Balaam's advice[b] and were the means of turning
the Israelites away from the LORD in
what happened at Peor,[c] so that a
plague struck the LORD's people. 17Now
kill all the boys. And kill every woman
who has slept with a man,[d] 18but save
for yourselves every girl who has never
slept with a man.

19"All of you who have killed anyone
or touched anyone who was killed[e]
must stay outside the camp seven days.
On the third and seventh days you
must purify yourselves[f] and your captives. 20Purify every garment[g] as well
as everything made of leather, goat
hair or wood."

21Then Eleazar the priest said to the
soldiers who had gone into battle,
"This is the requirement of the law that
the LORD gave Moses: 22Gold, silver,
bronze, iron,[h] tin, lead 23and anything
else that can withstand fire must be put
through the fire,[i] and then it will be
clean. But it must also be purified with
the water of cleansing.[j] And whatever
cannot withstand fire must be put
through that water. 24On the seventh
day wash your clothes and you will be

30:4 [k]ver 7
30:6 [l]Lev 5:4
30:8 [m]Ge 3:16
30:12 [n]Eph 5:22; Col 3:18
31:2 [o]Ge 25:2 [p]Nu 20:26; 27:13
31:3 [q]Jdg 11:36; 1Sa 24:12; 2Sa 4:8; 22:48; Ps 94:1; 149:7
31:6 [r]Nu 14:44 [s]Nu 10:9
31:7 [t]Dt 20:13; Jdg 21:11; 1Ki 11:15,16
31:8 [u]Jos 13:21 [v]Nu 25:15 [w]Jos 13:22
31:10 [x]Ge 25:16; 1Ch 6:54; Ps 69:25; Eze 25:4
31:11 [y]Dt 20:14
31:12 [z]Nu 27:2
31:14 [a]ver 48; Ex 18:21; Dt 1:15
31:16 [b]2Pe 2:15; Rev 2:14 [c]Nu 25:1-9
31:17 [d]Dt 7:2; 20:16-18; Jdg 21:11
31:19 [e]Nu 19:16 [f]Nu 19:12
31:20 [g]Nu 19:19
31:22 [h]Jos 6:19; 22:8
31:23 [i]1Co 3:13 [j]Nu 19:9,17

a *12* Hebrew *Jordan of Jericho*; possibly an ancient name for the Jordan River

clean.[k] Then you may come into the camp."

Dividing the Spoils

25The LORD said to Moses, 26"You and Eleazar the priest and the family heads of the community are to count all the people[l] and animals that were captured. 27Divide[m] the spoils between the soldiers who took part in the battle and the rest of the community. 28From the soldiers who fought in the battle, set apart as tribute for the LORD[n] one out of every five hundred, whether persons, cattle, donkeys, sheep or goats. 29Take this tribute from their half share and give it to Eleazar the priest as the LORD's part. 30From the Israelites' half, select one out of every fifty, whether persons, cattle, donkeys, sheep, goats or other animals. Give them to the Levites, who are responsible for the care of the LORD's tabernacle.[o]" 31So Moses and Eleazar the priest did as the LORD commanded Moses.

32The plunder remaining from the spoils that the soldiers took was 675,000 sheep, 3372,000 cattle, 3461,000 donkeys 35and 32,000 women who had never slept with a man.

36The half share of those who fought in the battle was:

> 337,500 sheep, 37of which the tribute for the LORD[p] was 675;
> 3836,000 cattle, of which the tribute for the LORD was 72;
> 3930,500 donkeys, of which the tribute for the LORD was 61;
> 4016,000 people, of which the tribute for the LORD was 32.

41Moses gave the tribute to Eleazar the priest as the LORD's part,[q] as the LORD commanded Moses.

42The half belonging to the Israelites, which Moses set apart from that of the fighting men— 43the community's half—was 337,500 sheep, 4436,000 cattle, 4530,500 donkeys 46and 16,000 people. 47From the Israelites' half, Moses selected one out of every fifty persons and animals, as the LORD commanded him, and gave them to the Levites, who were responsible for the care of the LORD's tabernacle.

48Then the officers who were over the units of the army—the commanders of thousands and commanders of hundreds—went to Moses 49and said to him, "Your servants have counted the soldiers under our command, and not one is missing.[r] 50So we have brought as an offering to the LORD the gold articles each of us acquired—armlets, bracelets, signet rings, earrings and necklaces—to make atonement for ourselves[s] before the LORD."

51Moses and Eleazar the priest accepted from them the gold—all the crafted articles. 52All the gold from the commanders of thousands and commanders of hundreds that Moses and Eleazar presented as a gift to the LORD weighed 16,750 shekels.[a] 53Each soldier had taken plunder[t] for himself. 54Moses and Eleazar the priest accepted the gold from the commanders of thousands and commanders of hundreds and brought it into the Tent of Meeting as a memorial[u] for the Israelites before the LORD.

The Transjordan Tribes

32 The Reubenites and Gadites, who had very large herds and flocks, saw that the lands of Jazer[v] and Gilead were suitable for livestock.[w] 2So they came to Moses and Eleazar the priest and to the leaders of the community, and said, 3"Ataroth,[x] Dibon, Jazer, Nimrah,[y] Heshbon, Elealeh,[z] Sebam, Nebo and Beon[a]— 4the land the LORD subdued[b] before the people of Israel—are suitable for livestock,[c] and your servants have livestock. 5If we have found favor in your eyes," they said, "let this land be given to your servants as our possession. Do not make us cross the Jordan."

6Moses said to the Gadites and Reubenites, "Shall your countrymen go to war while you sit here? 7Why do you discourage the Israelites from going over into the land the LORD has given them?[d] 8This is what your fathers did

31:24 [k]Lev 11:25 **31:26** [l]Nu 1:19 **31:27** [m]Jos 22:8; 1Sa 30:24 **31:28** [n]Nu 18:21 **31:30** [o]Nu 3:7; 18:3 **31:37** [p]ver 38-41 **31:41** [q]Nu 5:9; 18:8 **31:49** [r]Jer 23:4 **31:50** [s]Ex 30:16 **31:53** [t]Dt 20:14 **31:54** [u]Ex 28:12 **32:1** [v]Nu 21:32 [w]Ex 12:38 **32:3** [x]ver 34 [y]ver 36 [z]ver 37; Isa 15:4; 16:9; Jer 48:34 [a]ver 38; Jos 13:17; Eze 25:9 **32:4** [b]Nu 21:34 [c]Ex 12:38 **32:7** [d]Nu 13:27-14:4

[a] *52* That is, about 420 pounds (about 190 kilograms)

32:6

PROMISE 7

DIFFERENT BRANCHES OF SERVICE

This is a timeless question for God's people. He sends some of his saints to labor in hard places while some are able to stay in softer assignments. Moses allowed those who wanted to stay east of the Jordan to do so, but commanded them to participate in the battles required of their countrymen.

When you consider those who accept hardship and sacrifice to serve God, ask yourself the question in verse 6 and say to yourself, "What can I do for my brothers and sisters who have gone to war?"

For the next Promise 7 reading go to page 208.

when I sent them from Kadesh Barnea
to look over the land.[e] 9After they
went up to the Valley of Eshcol[f] and
viewed the land, they discouraged the
Israelites from entering the land the
LORD had given them. 10The LORD's anger was aroused[g] that day and he
swore this oath: 11'Because they have
not followed me wholeheartedly, not
one of the men twenty years old or
more[h] who came up out of Egypt will
see the land I promised on oath[i] to
Abraham, Isaac and Jacob[j]— 12not
one except Caleb son of Jephunneh the
Kenizzite and Joshua son of Nun, for
they followed the LORD wholeheartedly.'[k] 13The LORD's anger burned
against Israel[l] and he made them
wander in the desert forty years, until
the whole generation of those who had
done evil in his sight was gone.[m]

14"And here you are, a brood of sinners, standing in the place of your fathers and making the LORD even more
angry with Israel.[n] 15If you turn away
from following him, he will again leave
all this people in the desert, and you
will be the cause of their destruction.[o]"

16Then they came up to him and
said, "We would like to build pens here
for our livestock[p] and cities for our
women and children. 17But we are
ready to arm ourselves and go ahead of
the Israelites[q] until we have brought
them to their place.[r] Meanwhile our
women and children will live in fortified cities, for protection from the inhabitants of the land. 18We will not return to our homes until every Israelite
has received his inheritance.[s] 19We
will not receive any inheritance with
them on the other side of the Jordan,
because our inheritance has come to
us on the east side of the Jordan."[t]

20Then Moses said to them, "If you
will do this—if you will arm yourselves
before the LORD for battle,[u] 21and if all
of you will go armed over the Jordan
before the LORD until he has driven his
enemies out before him— 22then when
the land is subdued before the LORD,
you may return[v] and be free from
your obligation to the LORD and to Israel. And this land will be your possession before the LORD.[w]

23"But if you fail to do this, you will
be sinning against the LORD; and you
may be sure that your sin will find you
out.[x] 24Build cities for your women
and children, and pens for your
flocks,[y] but do what you have promised.[z]"

25The Gadites and Reubenites said
to Moses, "We your servants will do as
our lord commands. 26Our children
and wives, our flocks and herds will remain here in the cities of Gilead.[a]
27But your servants, every man armed
for battle, will cross over to fight before
the LORD, just as our lord says."

28Then Moses gave orders about
them[b] to Eleazar the priest and Joshua son of Nun and to the family heads
of the Israelite tribes. 29He said to
them, "If the Gadites and Reubenites,
every man armed for battle, cross over
the Jordan with you before the LORD,
then when the land is subdued before
you, give them the land of Gilead as
their possession. 30But if they do not
cross over with you armed, they must
accept their possession with you in Canaan."

31The Gadites and Reubenites answered, "Your servants will do what the
LORD has said.[c] 32We will cross over
before the LORD into Canaan armed,
but the property we inherit will be on
this side of the Jordan."

33Then Moses gave to the Gadites,[d]
the Reubenites and the half-tribe of
Manasseh son of Joseph the kingdom
of Sihon king of the Amorites[e] and the
kingdom of Og king of Bashan—the
whole land with its cities and the territory around them.[f]

34The Gadites built up Dibon, Ataroth, Aroer,[g] 35Atroth Shophan, Jazer,[h] Jogbehah, 36Beth Nimrah[i] and
Beth Haran as fortified cities, and built
pens for their flocks. 37And the Reubenites rebuilt Heshbon, Elealeh and
Kiriathaim, 38as well as Nebo[j] and
Baal Meon (these names were
changed) and Sibmah. They gave
names to the cities they rebuilt.

39The descendants of Makir[k] son of
Manasseh went to Gilead, captured it
and drove out the Amorites who were
there. 40So Moses gave Gilead to the
Makirites,[l] the descendants of Manasseh, and they settled there. 41Jair,
a descendant of Manasseh, captured
their settlements and called them Havvoth Jair.[a][m] 42And Nobah captured
Kenath and its surrounding settlements and called it Nobah after himself.[n]

Stages in Israel's Journey

33 Here are the stages in the journey
of the Israelites when they came
out of Egypt[o] by divisions under the
leadership of Moses and Aaron.[p] 2At
the LORD's command Moses recorded
the stages in their journey. This is their
journey by stages:

3The Israelites set out from

32:8 [e]Nu 13:3,26; Dt 1:19-25
32:9 [f]Nu 13:23; Dt 1:24
32:10 [g]Nu 11:1
32:11 [h]Ex 30:14 [i]Nu 14:23 [j]Nu 14:28-30
32:12 [k]Nu 14:24,30; Dt 1:36; Ps 63:8
32:13 [l]Ex 4:14 [m]Nu 14:28-35; 26:64,65
32:14 [n]ver 10; Dt 1:34; Ps 78:59
32:15 [o]Dt 30:17-18; 2Ch 7:20
32:16 [p]Ex 12:38; Dt 3:19
32:17 [q]Jos 4:12,13 [r]Nu 22:4; Dt 3:20
32:18 [s]Jos 22:1-4
32:19 [t]Jos 12:1
32:20 [u]Dt 3:18
32:22 [v]Jos 22:4 [w]Dt 3:18-20
32:23 [x]Ge 4:7; 44:16; Isa 59:12
32:24 [y]ver 1,16 [z]Nu 30:2
32:26 [a]Jos 1:14
32:28 [b]Dt 3:18-20; Jos 1:13
32:31 [c]ver 29
32:33 [d]Jos 13:24-28; 1Sa 13:7 [e]Dt 2:26 [f]Nu 21:24; Jos 12:6
32:34 [g]Dt 2:36; Jdg 11:26
32:35 [h]ver 3
32:36 [i]ver 3
32:38 [j]ver 3; Isa 15:2; Jer 48:1,22
32:39 [k]Ge 50:23
32:40 [l]Dt 3:15; Jos 17:1
32:41 [m]Dt 3:14; Jos 13:30; Jdg 10:4; 1Ch 2:23
32:42 [n]2Sa 18:18; Ps 49:11
33:1 [o]Mic 6:4 [p]Ps 77:20

a *41* Or *them the settlements of Jair*

Rameses on the fifteenth day of
the first month, the day after the
Passover.[q] They marched out
boldly[r] in full view of all the
Egyptians, 4who were burying all
their firstborn, whom the LORD
had struck down among them; for
the LORD had brought judgment
on their gods.[s]
5The Israelites left Rameses and
camped at Succoth.[t]
6They left Succoth and camped
at Etham, on the edge of the
desert.[u]
7They left Etham, turned back
to Pi Hahiroth, to the east of Baal
Zephon,[v] and camped near Migdol.[w]
8They left Pi Hahiroth[a] and
passed through the sea[x] into the
desert, and when they had traveled for three days in the Desert of
Etham, they camped at Marah.[y]
9They left Marah and went to
Elim, where there were twelve
springs and seventy palm trees,
and they camped[z] there.
10They left Elim and camped by
the Red Sea.[b]
11They left the Red Sea and
camped in the Desert of Sin.[a]
12They left the Desert of Sin and
camped at Dophkah.
13They left Dophkah and
camped at Alush.
14They left Alush and camped
at Rephidim, where there was no
water for the people to drink.
15They left Rephidim[b] and
camped in the Desert of Sinai.[c]
16They left the Desert of Sinai
and camped at Kibroth Hattaavah.[d]
17They left Kibroth Hattaavah
and camped at Hazeroth.[e]
18They left Hazeroth and
camped at Rithmah.
19They left Rithmah and
camped at Rimmon Perez.
20They left Rimmon Perez and
camped at Libnah.[f]
21They left Libnah and camped
at Rissah.
22They left Rissah and camped
at Kehelathah.
23They left Kehelathah and
camped at Mount Shepher.
24They left Mount Shepher and
camped at Haradah.
25They left Haradah and
camped at Makheloth.
26They left Makheloth and
camped at Tahath.
27They left Tahath and camped
at Terah.
28They left Terah and camped
at Mithcah.
29They left Mithcah and
camped at Hashmonah.
30They left Hashmonah and
camped at Moseroth.[g]
31They left Moseroth and
camped at Bene Jaakan.
32They left Bene Jaakan and
camped at Hor Haggidgad.
33They left Hor Haggidgad
and camped at Jotbathah.[h]
34They left Jotbathah and
camped at Abronah.
35They left Abronah and
camped at Ezion Geber.[i]
36They left Ezion Geber and
camped at Kadesh, in the Desert
of Zin.[j]
37They left Kadesh and camped
at Mount Hor,[k] on the border of
Edom.[l] 38At the LORD's command Aaron the priest went up
Mount Hor, where he died[m] on
the first day of the fifth month of
the fortieth year after the Israelites came out of Egypt.[n] 39Aaron
was a hundred and twenty-three
years old when he died on Mount
Hor.
40The Canaanite king of Arad,[o]
who lived in the Negev of Canaan,
heard that the Israelites were
coming.
41They left Mount Hor and
camped at Zalmonah.
42They left Zalmonah and
camped at Punon.
43They left Punon and camped
at Oboth.[p]
44They left Oboth and camped
at Iye Abarim, on the border of
Moab.[q]
45They left Iyim[c] and camped
at Dibon Gad.
46They left Dibon Gad and
camped at Almon Diblathaim.
47They left Almon Diblathaim
and camped in the mountains of
Abarim,[r] near Nebo.
48They left the mountains of
Abarim and camped on the plains
of Moab by the Jordan across
from Jericho.[d][s] 49There on the
plains of Moab they camped
along the Jordan from Beth Jeshimoth to Abel Shittim.[t]
50On the plains of Moab by the Jor-

33:3 [q]Ex 13:4 [r]Ex 14:8
33:4 [s]Ex 12:12
33:5 [t]Ex 12:37
33:6 [u]Ex 13:20
33:7 [v]Ex 14:9 [w]Ex 14:2
33:8 [x]Ex 14:22 [y]Ex 15:23
33:9 [z]Ex 15:27
33:11 [a]Ex 16:1
33:15 [b]Ex 17:1 [c]Ex 19:1
33:16 [d]Nu 11:34
33:17 [e]Nu 11:35
33:20 [f]Jos 10:29
33:30 [g]Dt 10:6
33:33 [h]Dt 10:7
33:35 [i]Dt 2:8; 1Ki 9:26; 22:48
33:36 [j]Nu 20:1
33:37 [k]Nu 20:22 [l]Nu 20:16; 21:4
33:38 [m]Dt 10:6 [n]Nu 20:25-28
33:40 [o]Nu 21:1
33:43 [p]Nu 21:10
33:44 [q]Nu 21:11
33:47 [r]Nu 27:12
33:48 [s]Nu 22:1
33:49 [t]Nu 25:1

[a] *8* Many manuscripts of the Masoretic Text, Samaritan Pentateuch and Vulgate; most manuscripts of the Masoretic Text *left from before Hahiroth* [b] *10* Hebrew *Yam Suph*; that is, Sea of Reeds; also in verse 11 [c] *45* That is, Iye Abarim [d] *48* Hebrew *Jordan of Jericho*; possibly an ancient name for the Jordan River; also in verse 50

dan across from Jericho the LORD said
to Moses, **51**“Speak to the Israelites and
say to them: ‘When you cross the Jordan into Canaan,[u] **52**drive out all the
inhabitants of the land before you. Destroy all their carved images and their
cast idols, and demolish all their high
places.[v] **53**Take possession of the land
and settle in it, for I have given you the
land to possess.[w] **54**Distribute the land
by lot, according to your clans.[x] To a
larger group give a larger inheritance,
and to a smaller group a smaller one.
Whatever falls to them by lot will be
theirs. Distribute it according to your
ancestral tribes.

55“ ‘But if you do not drive out the
inhabitants of the land, those you allow to remain will become barbs in
your eyes and thorns[y] in your sides.
They will give you trouble in the land
where you will live. **56**And then I will do
to you what I plan to do to them.’ ”

Boundaries of Canaan

34 The LORD said to Moses, **2**“Command the Israelites and say to
them: ‘When you enter Canaan, the
land that will be allotted to you as an
inheritance[z] will have these boundaries:[a]

3“ ‘Your southern side will include
some of the Desert of Zin[b] along the
border of Edom. On the east, your
southern boundary will start from the
end of the Salt Sea,[a][c] **4**cross south of
Scorpion[b] Pass,[d] continue on to Zin
and go south of Kadesh Barnea.[e] Then
it will go to Hazar Addar and over to
Azmon, **5**where it will turn, join the
Wadi of Egypt[f] and end at the Sea.[c]

6“ ‘Your western boundary will be
the coast of the Great Sea. This will be
your boundary on the west.

7“ ‘For your northern boundary,[g]
run a line from the Great Sea to Mount
Hor **8**and from Mount Hor to Lebo[d]
Hamath.[h] Then the boundary will go
to Zedad, **9**continue to Ziphron and
end at Hazar Enan. This will be your
boundary on the north.

10“ ‘For your eastern boundary, run
a line from Hazar Enan to Shepham.
11The boundary will go down from
Shepham to Riblah[i] on the east side
of Ain and continue along the slopes
east of the Sea of Kinnereth.[e][j] **12**Then
the boundary will go down along the
Jordan and end at the Salt Sea.

“ ‘This will be your land, with its
boundaries on every side.’ ”

13Moses commanded the Israelites:
“Assign this land by lot as an inheritance.[k] The LORD has ordered that it
be given to the nine and a half tribes,
14because the families of the tribe of
Reuben, the tribe of Gad and the half-
tribe of Manasseh have received their
inheritance.[l] **15**These two and a half
tribes have received their inheritance
on the east side of the Jordan of Jericho,[f] toward the sunrise.”

16The LORD said to Moses, **17**“These
are the names of the men who are to
assign the land for you as an inheritance: Eleazar the priest and Joshua[m]
son of Nun. **18**And appoint one leader
from each tribe to help[n] assign the
land. **19**These are their names:

Caleb[o] son of Jephunneh,
from the tribe of Judah;[p]
20Shemuel son of Ammihud,
from the tribe of Simeon;[q]
21Elidad son of Kislon,
from the tribe of Benjamin;[r]
22Bukki son of Jogli,
the leader from the tribe of Dan;
23Hanniel son of Ephod,
the leader from the tribe of Manasseh son of Joseph;
24Kemuel son of Shiphtan,
the leader from the tribe of Ephraim son of Joseph;
25Elizaphan son of Parnach,
the leader from the tribe of Zebulun;
26Paltiel son of Azzan,
the leader from the tribe of Issachar;
27Ahihud son of Shelomi,
the leader from the tribe of Asher;[s]
28Pedahel son of Ammihud,

> **33:52–53**
>
> **PROMISE 3**
>
> ### TEAMWORK
>
> God and the Israelites—what a team! God said in verse 52, “You drive out the people and clean up the land.” But in verse 53 God said, “for I have given the land to you.” God assured the victory in this chapter, but Israel had to step up and do the work.
>
> God gives many of his blessings to those who obey him. And usually obedience demands disciplined, consistent effort on our part. Don’t sit and wait to become spiritually mature. God includes you in the process of your own growth.
>
> *For the next Promise 3 reading go to page 205.*

33:51 [u]Jos 3:17
33:52 [v]Ex 23:24; 34:13; Lev 26:1; Dt 7:2,5; 12:3; Jos 11:12; Ps 106:34-36
33:53 [w]Dt 11:31; Jos 21:43
33:54 [x]Nu 26:54
33:55 [y]Jos 23:13; Jdg 2:3; Ps 106:36
34:2 [z]Ge 17:8; Dt 1:7-8; Ps 78:54-55 [a]Eze 47:15
34:3 [b]Jos 15:1-3 [c]Ge 14:3
34:4 [d]Jos 15:3 [e]Nu 32:8
34:5 [f]Ge 15:18; Jos 15:4
34:7 [g]Eze 47:15-17
34:8 [h]Nu 13:21; Jos 13:5
34:11 [i]2Ki 23:33; Jer 39:5 [j]Dt 3:17; Jos 11:2; 13:27
34:13 [k]Jos 14:1-5
34:14 [l]Nu 32:33; Jos 14:3
34:17 [m]Jos 14:1
34:18 [n]Nu 1:4,16
34:19 [o]Nu 26:65 [p]Ge 29:35; Dt 33:7
34:20 [q]Ge 49:5
34:21 [r]Ge 49:27; Ps 68:27
34:27 [s]Nu 1:40

a *3* That is, the Dead Sea; also in verse 12
b *4* Hebrew *Akrabbim*
c *5* That is, the Mediterranean; also in verses 6 and 7
d *8* Or *to the entrance to*
e *11* That is, Galilee
f *15 Jordan of Jericho* was possibly an ancient name for the Jordan River.

the leader from the tribe of Naphtali."

29 These are the men the LORD commanded to assign the inheritance to the Israelites in the land of Canaan.

Towns for the Levites

35 On the plains of Moab by the Jordan across from Jericho,[a] the LORD said to Moses, 2 "Command the Israelites to give the Levites towns to live in[t] from the inheritance the Israelites will possess. And give them pasturelands around the towns. 3 Then they will have towns to live in and pasturelands for their cattle, flocks and all their other livestock.

4 "The pasturelands around the towns that you give the Levites will extend out fifteen hundred feet[b] from the town wall. 5 Outside the town, measure three thousand feet[c] on the east side, three thousand on the south side, three thousand on the west and three thousand on the north, with the town in the center. They will have this area as pastureland for the towns.

Cities of Refuge

6 "Six of the towns you give the Levites will be cities of refuge, to which a person who has killed someone may flee.[u] In addition, give them forty-two other towns. 7 In all you must give the Levites forty-eight towns, together with their pasturelands. 8 The towns you give the Levites from the land the Israelites possess are to be given in proportion to the inheritance of each tribe: Take many towns from a tribe that has many, but few from one that has few."[v]

9 Then the LORD said to Moses: 10 "Speak to the Israelites and say to them: 'When you cross the Jordan into Canaan,[w] 11 select some towns to be your cities of refuge, to which a person who has killed someone[x] accidentally[y] may flee. 12 They will be places of refuge from the avenger,[z] so that a person accused of murder may not die before he stands trial before the assembly. 13 These six towns you give will be your cities of refuge. 14 Give three on this side of the Jordan and three in Canaan as cities of refuge. 15 These six towns will be a place of refuge for Israelites, aliens and any other people living among them, so that anyone who has killed another accidentally can flee there.

16 " 'If a man strikes someone with an iron object so that he dies, he is a murderer; the murderer shall be put to death.[a] 17 Or if anyone has a stone in his hand that could kill, and he strikes someone so that he dies, he is a murderer; the murderer shall be put to death. 18 Or if anyone has a wooden object in his hand that could kill, and he hits someone so that he dies, he is a murderer; the murderer shall be put to death. 19 The avenger of blood shall put the murderer to death; when he meets him, he shall put him to death.[b] 20 If anyone with malice aforethought shoves another or throws something at him intentionally[c] so that he dies 21 or if in hostility he hits him with his fist so that he dies, that person shall be put to death; he is a murderer. The avenger of blood shall put the murderer to death when he meets him.

22 " 'But if without hostility someone suddenly shoves another or throws something at him unintentionally[d] 23 or, without seeing him, drops a stone on him that could kill him, and he dies, then since he was not his enemy and he did not intend to harm him, 24 the assembly[e] must judge between him and the avenger of blood according to these regulations. 25 The assembly must protect the one accused of murder from the avenger of blood and send him back to the city of refuge to which he fled. He must stay there until the death of the high priest, who was anointed with the holy oil.[f]

26 " 'But if the accused ever goes outside the limits of the city of refuge to which he has fled 27 and the avenger of blood finds him outside the city, the avenger of blood may kill the accused without being guilty of murder. 28 The accused must stay in his city of refuge until the death of the high priest; only after the death of the high priest may he return to his own property.

29 " 'These are to be legal requirements[g] for you throughout the generations to come, wherever you live.

30 " 'Anyone who kills a person is to be put to death as a murderer only on the testimony of witnesses. But no one is to be put to death on the testimony of only one witness.[h]

31 " 'Do not accept a ransom for the life of a murderer, who deserves to die. He must surely be put to death.

32 " 'Do not accept a ransom for anyone who has fled to a city of refuge and so allow him to go back and live on his own land before the death of the high priest.

33 " 'Do not pollute the land where

35:2 [t]Lev 25:32-34; Jos 14:3,4
35:6 [u]Jos 20:7-9; 21:3,13
35:8 [v]Nu 26:54; 33:54; Jos 21:1-42
35:10 [w]Jos 20:2
35:11 [x]ver 22-25 [y]Ex 21:13; Dt 19:1-13
35:12 [z]Dt 19:6; Jos 20:3
35:16 [a]Ex 21:12; Lev 24:17
35:19 [b]ver 21
35:20 [c]Ge 4:8; Ex 21:14; Dt 19:11; 2Sa 3:27; 20:10
35:22 [d]ver 11; Ex 21:13
35:24 [e]ver 12; Jos 20:6
35:25 [f]Ex 29:7
35:29 [g]Nu 27:11
35:30 [h]ver 16; Dt 17:6; 19:15; Mt 18:16; Jn 7:51; 2Co 13:1; Heb 10:28

[a] *1* Hebrew *Jordan of Jericho;* possibly an ancient name for the Jordan River
[b] *4* Hebrew *a thousand cubits* (about 450 meters) [c] *5* Hebrew *two thousand cubits* (about 900 meters)

you are. Bloodshed pollutes the land,[i] and atonement cannot be made for the land on which blood has been shed, except by the blood of the one who shed it. 34Do not defile the land[j] where you live and where I dwell,[k] for I, the LORD, dwell among the Israelites.' "

Inheritance of Zelophehad's Daughters

36 The family heads of the clan of Gilead[l] son of Makir, the son of Manasseh, who were from the clans of the descendants of Joseph, came and spoke before Moses and the leaders,[m] the heads of the Israelite families. 2They said, "When the LORD commanded my lord to give the land as an inheritance to the Israelites by lot, he ordered you to give the inheritance of our brother Zelophehad[n] to his daughters. 3Now suppose they marry men from other Israelite tribes; then their inheritance will be taken from our ancestral inheritance and added to that of the tribe they marry into. And so part of the inheritance allotted to us will be taken away. 4When the Year of Jubilee[o] for the Israelites comes, their inheritance will be added to that of the tribe into which they marry, and their property will be taken from the tribal inheritance of our forefathers."

5Then at the LORD's command Moses gave this order to the Israelites: "What the tribe of the descendants of Joseph is saying is right. 6This is what the LORD commands for Zelophehad's daughters: They may marry anyone they please as long as they marry within the tribal clan of their father. 7No inheritance[p] in Israel is to pass from tribe to tribe, for every Israelite shall keep the tribal land inherited from his forefathers. 8Every daughter who inherits land in any Israelite tribe must marry someone in her father's tribal clan,[q] so that every Israelite will possess the inheritance of his fathers. 9No inheritance may pass from tribe to tribe, for each Israelite tribe is to keep the land it inherits."

10So Zelophehad's daughters did as the LORD commanded Moses. 11Zelophehad's daughters—Mahlah, Tirzah, Hoglah, Milcah and Noah[r]—married their cousins on their father's side. 12They married within the clans of the descendants of Manasseh son of Joseph, and their inheritance remained in their father's clan and tribe.

13These are the commands and regulations the LORD gave through Moses[s] to the Israelites on the plains of Moab by the Jordan across from Jericho.[a] [t]

35:33 [i]Ge 9:6; Ps 106:38; Mic 4:11
35:34 [j]Lev 18:24,25 [k]Ex 29:45
36:1 [l]Nu 26:29 [m]Nu 27:2
36:2 [n]Nu 26:33; 27:1,7
36:4 [o]Lev 25:10
36:7 [p]1Ki 21:3
36:8 [q]1Ch 23:22
36:11 [r]Nu 26:33; 27:1
36:13 [s]Lev 26:46; 27:34 [t]Nu 22:1

[a] *13* Hebrew *Jordan of Jericho*; possibly an ancient name for the Jordan River

DEUTERONOMY

AT A GLANCE

Key Principle: It is always wise to obey God because obedience leads to blessing; it is always foolish to disobey God because disobedience leads to discipline.

Author: Moses (34:1–12 possibly written by Joshua)

Time and Place: 1406 B.C. / The plains of Moab

Key Verses: 4:1; 5:29; 6:4–5; 10:12–13; 30:19–20

BENEFIT

Deuteronomy completes the Pentateuch by offering a theological perspective on the historical events developed in Genesis through Numbers. It summarizes the lessons gained in Israel's Exodus and wilderness experiences. It also encourages us to pursue the sanity of holiness—the truth that, in the long run, disobedience to God's Word is always more painful than obedience.

SETTING

Deuteronomy is similar to Leviticus in that it records no geographical progression; it focuses on God's revelation and how he prepared the new generation that would conquer the land under Joshua. Like Leviticus, it covers only about one month's time. The setting is in the plains of Moab east of the Jordan river, at the end of Israel's 40-year sojourn in the wilderness, in Moses' 120th year.

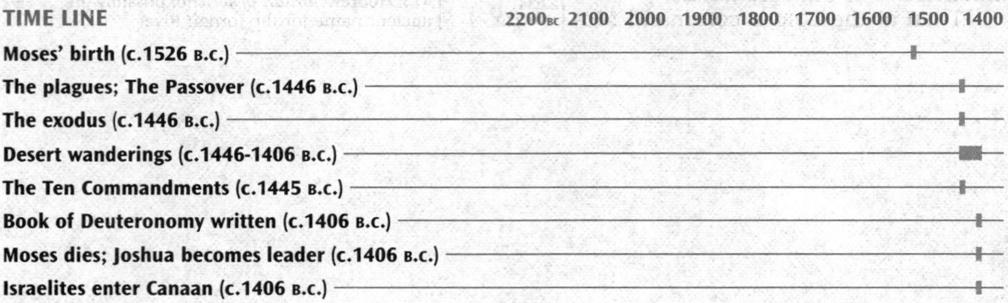

THEME AND PURPOSE

Deuteronomy focuses on the need to develop a divine perspective on human circumstances. It is a collection of three sermons delivered by Moses to the generation that would possess the promised land. These sermons were designed to prepare the people spiritually for what they were about to face in Canaan. In this book of remembrance, Moses warns the people of the dangers of forgetting that their blessings come from the hand of God. He invites the people of Israel to love the Lord their God, to embrace God's commands and to order their lives in conformity with God's will. Moses also warns them of the consequences of disobedience, and uses the experience of the generation that perished in the wilderness to illustrate the dangers of disbelief.

UNIQUE CONTRIBUTION

Deuteronomy is to the first four books of the Pentateuch what the Gospel of John is to the synoptic gospels; it supplements the historical narrative by reviewing it from the standpoint of God's purposes for his people. It also focuses on God's love (4:37; 7:7–9; 10:12–15; 23:5) for his people and calls them to reciprocate this love by walking in obedience to him.

Deuteronomy is a covenant renewal document that follows the form used in the Hittite culture and other ancient Near East cultures in Moses' time.

LINKS TO THE NEW TESTAMENT

The clearest portrait of Christ in Deuteronomy is the prophet who will come: "The LORD your God will raise up for you a prophet like me from among your own brothers. You must listen to him" (18:15; compare Acts 7:37). "Since then no prophet has risen in Israel like Moses, whom the LORD knew face to face, who did all those miraculous signs and wonders the LORD sent him to do in Egypt" (34:10–11). Like Christ, Moses was a prophet, a priest and a king (he served as Israel's ruler); like Christ, he was endangered in his childhood, he was rejected by his people, he performed miraculous works, he delivered and interceded for his people and he was a man of extraordinary humility (Numbers 12:3).

OVERVIEW

FOCUS	Remembering the Past	Reviewing the Present	Revealing the Future	Retirement of a Leader
REFERENCE	1 — 4	5 — 26	27 — 30	31 — 34
TOPICS	Moses' First Sermon	Moses' Second Sermon	Moses' Third Sermon	Moses' Parting Words
	Historical	Legal	Prophetic	Historical
	Retrospective	Introspective	Prospective	
LOCATION	The Plains of Moab			
TIME	1 Month			

Deuteronomy outlines how Moses prepared the new generation to take possession of the promised land. It also covers God's renewal of the covenant he made with their fathers at Mount Sinai. In his first sermon (1—4), Moses reminds the people of lessons to be gained from the past, particularly concerning the consequences of disbelief and the blessings of belief as expressed through obedience. His second sermon (5—26) comprises the bulk of the book as it reviews their present walk with God. This section outlines the three components of the law: the testimonies or moral duties (5—11), the statutes or ceremonial duties (12—16), and the ordinances or civil and social duties (17—26). Moses' third sermon (27—30) anticipates future blessings and curses and the later dispersion of Israel among the nations due to their rebellion against God. As Deuteronomy concludes, Moses appoints Joshua as his successor and gives his parting words to the people.

DEUTERONOMY

The Command to Leave Horeb

1 These are the words Moses spoke to all Israel in the desert east of the Jordan—that is, in the Arabah—opposite Suph, between Paran and Tophel, Laban, Hazeroth and Dizahab. **2**(It takes eleven days to go from Horeb[a] to Kadesh Barnea[b] by the Mount Seir road.)

3In the fortieth year,[c] on the first day of the eleventh month, Moses proclaimed[d] to the Israelites all that the LORD had commanded him concerning them. **4**This was after he had defeated Sihon[e] king of the Amorites, who reigned in Heshbon,[f] and at Edrei had defeated Og[g] king of Bashan, who reigned in Ashtaroth.

5East of the Jordan in the territory of Moab, Moses began to expound this law, saying:

6The LORD our God said to us[h] at Horeb,[i] "You have stayed long enough at this mountain. **7**Break camp and advance into the hill country of the Amorites; go to all the neighboring peoples in the Arabah, in the mountains, in the western foothills, in the Negev[j] and along the coast, to the land of the Canaanites and to Lebanon,[k] as far as the great river, the Euphrates. **8**See, I have given you this land. Go in and take possession of the land that the LORD swore[l] he would give to your fathers—to Abraham, Isaac and Jacob—and to their descendants after them."

The Appointment of Leaders

9At that time I said to you, "You are too heavy a burden for me to carry alone.[m] **10**The LORD your God has increased your numbers so that today you are as many[n] as the stars in the sky.[o] **11**May the LORD, the God of your fathers, increase you a thousand times and bless you as he has promised![p] **12**But how can I bear your problems and your burdens and your disputes all by myself? **13**Choose some wise, understanding and respected men[q] from each of your tribes, and I will set them over you."

14You answered me, "What you propose to do is good."

15So I took[r] the leading men of your tribes, wise and respected men, and appointed them to have authority over you—as commanders of thousands, of hundreds, of fifties and of tens and as tribal officials. **16**And I charged your judges at that time: Hear the disputes between your brothers and judge fairly,[s] whether the case is between brother Israelites or between one of them and an alien.[t] **17**Do not show partiality[u] in judging; hear both small and great alike. Do not be afraid of any man,[v] for judgment belongs to God. Bring me any case too hard for you, and I will hear it.[w] **18**And at that time I told you everything you were to do.

Spies Sent Out

19Then, as the LORD our God commanded us, we set out from Horeb and went toward the hill country of the Amorites through all that vast and dreadful desert[x] that you have seen, and so we reached Kadesh Barnea.[y] **20**Then I said to you, "You have reached the hill country of the Amorites, which the LORD our God is giving us. **21**See, the LORD your God has given you the land. Go up and take possession of it as the LORD, the God of your fathers, told you. Do not be afraid;[z] do not be discouraged."

22Then all of you came to me and said, "Let us send men ahead to spy out the land for us and bring back a report about the route we are to take and the towns we will come to."

23The idea seemed good to me; so I selected[a] twelve of you, one man from each tribe. **24**They left and went up into the hill country, and came to the Valley of Eshcol[b] and explored it. **25**Taking with them some of the fruit of the land, they brought it down to us and reported,[c] "It is a good land that the LORD our God is giving us."

Rebellion Against the LORD

26But you were unwilling to go up;[d] you rebelled against the command of the LORD your God. **27**You grumbled[e] in your tents and said, "The LORD hates us; so he brought us out of Egypt to deliver us into the hands of the Amorites to destroy us. **28**Where can we go? Our brothers have made us lose heart. They say, 'The people are stronger and taller[f] than we are; the cities are large, with walls up to the sky. We even saw the Anakites[g] there.' "

29Then I said to you, "Do not be terrified; do not be afraid of them. **30**The LORD your God, who is going before

1:2 [a]Ex 3:1 [b]Nu 13:26; Dt 9:23
1:3 [c]Nu 33:38 [d]Dt 4:1-2
1:4 [e]Nu 21:21-26 [f]Nu 21:25 [g]Nu 21:33-35; Jos 13:12
1:6 [h]Nu 10:13 [i]Ex 3:1
1:7 [j]Jos 10:40 [k]Dt 11:24
1:8 [l]Ge 12:7; 15:18; 17:7-8; 26:4; 28:13
1:9 [m]Ex 18:18
1:10 [n]Ge 15:5 [o]Dt 10:22; 28:62
1:11 [p]Ge 22:17; Ex 32:13
1:13 [q]Ex 18:21
1:15 [r]Ex 18:25
1:16 [s]Dt 16:18; Jn 7:24 [t]Lev 24:22
1:17 [u]Lev 19:15; Dt 16:19; Pr 24:23; Jas 2:1 [v]2Ch 19:6 [w]Ex 18:26
1:19 [x]Dt 8:15; Jer 2:2,6 [y]ver 2; Nu 13:26
1:21 [z]Jos 1:6,9,18
1:23 [a]Nu 13:1-3
1:24 [b]Nu 13:21-25
1:25 [c]Nu 13:27
1:26 [d]Nu 14:1-4
1:27 [e]Dt 9:28; Ps 106:25
1:28 [f]Nu 13:32 [g]Nu 13:33; Dt 9:1-3

you, will fight[h] for you, as he did for you in Egypt, before your very eyes, 31 and in the desert. There you saw how the LORD your God carried[i] you, as a father carries his son, all the way you went until you reached this place."

32 In spite of this, you did not trust[j] in the LORD your God, 33 who went ahead of you on your journey, in fire by night and in a cloud by day,[k] to search[l] out places for you to camp and to show you the way you should go.

34 When the LORD heard what you said, he was angry and solemnly swore:[m] 35 "Not a man of this evil generation shall see the good land[n] I swore to give your forefathers, 36 except Caleb son of Jephunneh. He will see it, and I will give him and his descendants the land he set his feet on, because he followed the LORD wholeheartedly.[o]"

3 →PG. 193
5 →PG. 191

37 Because of you the LORD became angry[p] with me also and said, "You shall not enter[q] it, either. 38 But your assistant, Joshua[r] son of Nun, will enter it. Encourage[s] him, because he will lead[t] Israel to inherit it. 39 And the little ones that you said would be taken captive,[u] your children who do not yet know[v] good from bad—they will enter the land. I will give it to them and they will take possession of it. 40 But as for you, turn around and set out toward the desert along the route to the Red Sea.[a][w]"

41 Then you replied, "We have sinned against the LORD. We will go up and fight, as the LORD our God commanded us." So every one of you put on his weapons, thinking it easy to go up into the hill country.

42 But the LORD said to me, "Tell them, 'Do not go up and fight, because I will not be with you. You will be defeated by your enemies.' "[x]

43 So I told you, but you would not listen. You rebelled against the LORD's command and in your arrogance you marched up into the hill country. 44 The Amorites who lived in those hills came out against you; they chased you like a swarm of bees[y] and beat you down from Seir all the way to Hormah. 45 You came back and wept before the LORD, but he paid no attention to your weeping and turned a deaf ear to you. 46 And so you stayed in Kadesh[z] many days—all the time you spent there.

Wanderings in the Desert

2 Then we turned back and set out toward the desert along the route to the Red Sea,[a][a] as the LORD had directed me. For a long time we made our way around the hill country of Seir.

2 Then the LORD said to me, 3 "You have made your way around this hill country long enough; now turn north. 4 Give the people these orders:[b] 'You are about to pass through the territory of your brothers the descendants of Esau, who live in Seir. They will be afraid of you, but be very careful. 5 Do not provoke them to war, for I will not give you any of their land, not even enough to put your foot on. I have given Esau the hill country of Seir as his own.[c] 6 You are to pay them in silver for the food you eat and the water you drink.' "

7 The LORD your God has blessed you in all the work of your hands. He has watched[d] over your journey through this vast desert. These forty years the LORD your God has been with you, and you have not lacked anything.

8 So we went on past our brothers the descendants of Esau, who live in Seir. We turned from the Arabah road, which comes up from Elath and Ezion Geber,[e] and traveled along the desert road of Moab.[f]

9 Then the LORD said to me, "Do not harass the Moabites or provoke them to war, for I will not give you any part of their land. I have given Ar[g] to the descendants of Lot[h] as a possession."

10 (The Emites[i] used to live there—a people strong and numerous, and as tall as the Anakites.[j] 11 Like the Anakites, they too were considered Rephaites, but the Moabites called them Emites. 12 Horites used to live in Seir, but the descendants of Esau drove them out. They destroyed the Horites from before them and settled in their place, just as Israel did[k] in the land the LORD gave them as their possession.)

[a] 40,1 Hebrew *Yam Suph*; that is, Sea of Reeds

1:30 [h]Ex 14:14; Dt 3:22; Ne 4:20
1:31 [i]Dt 32:10-12; Isa 46:3-4; 63:9; Hos 11:3; Ac 13:18
1:32 [j]Ps 106:24; Jude 1:5
1:33 [k]Ex 13:21; Ps 78:14 [l]Nu 10:33
1:34 [m]Nu 14:23, 28-30
1:35 [n]Ps 95:11
1:36 [o]Nu 14:24; Jos 14:9
1:37 [p]Dt 3:26; 4:21 [q]Nu 20:12
1:38 [r]Nu 14:30 [s]Dt 31:7 [t]Dt 3:28
1:39 [u]Nu 14:3 [v]Isa 7:15-16
1:40 [w]Nu 14:25
1:42 [x]Nu 14:41-43
1:44 [y]Ps 118:12
1:46 [z]Nu 20:1; Jdg 11:17
2:1 [a]Nu 21:4
2:4 [b]Nu 20:14-21
2:5 [c]Ge 36:8; Jos 24:4
2:7 [d]Dt 8:2-4
2:8 [e]1Ki 9:26 [f]Jdg 11:18
2:9 [g]Nu 21:15 [h]Ge 19:36-38
2:10 [i]Ge 14:5 [j]Nu 13:22,33
2:12 [k]ver 22

2:1 PROMISE 1

CLOSE ENOUGH TO TASTE IT

What a horrible moment! The Israelites could look across the Jordan and see the land God promised them, but they couldn't enter because they had flagrantly and belligerently disobeyed God (see 1:26–36). The decision to obey must have been difficult, but the people turned back instead of moving ahead. They set out toward the desert instead of entering the land flowing with milk and honey. Think this story through when choosing whether to obey God's Word or ignore it.

For the next Promise 1 reading go to page 192.

13And the LORD said, "Now get up and cross the Zered Valley." So we crossed the valley.

14Thirty-eight years passed from the time we left Kadesh Barnea[l] until we crossed the Zered Valley. By then, that entire generation[m] of fighting men had perished from the camp, as the LORD had sworn to them.[n] 15The LORD's hand was against them until he had completely eliminated[o] them from the camp.

16Now when the last of these fighting men among the people had died, 17the LORD said to me, 18"Today you are to pass by the region of Moab at Ar. 19When you come to the Ammonites,[p] do not harass them or provoke them to war, for I will not give you possession of any land belonging to the Ammonites. I have given it as a possession to the descendants of Lot.[q]"

20(That too was considered a land of the Rephaites, who used to live there; but the Ammonites called them Zamzummites. 21They were a people strong and numerous, and as tall as the Anakites.[r] The LORD destroyed them from before the Ammonites, who drove them out and settled in their place. 22The LORD had done the same for the descendants of Esau, who lived in Seir,[s] when he destroyed the Horites from before them. They drove them out and have lived in their place to this day. 23And as for the Avvites[t] who lived in villages as far as Gaza, the Caphtorites[u] coming out from Caphtor[a][v] destroyed them and settled in their place.)

Defeat of Sihon King of Heshbon

24"Set out now and cross the Arnon Gorge.[w] See, I have given into your hand Sihon the Amorite, king of Heshbon, and his country. Begin to take possession of it and engage him in battle. 25This very day I will begin to put the terror[x] and fear[y] of you on all the nations under heaven. They will hear reports of you and will tremble[z] and be in anguish because of you."

26From the desert of Kedemoth I sent messengers to Sihon king of Heshbon offering peace and saying, 27"Let us pass through your country. We will stay on the main road; we will not turn aside to the right or to the left.[a] 28Sell us food to eat and water to drink for their price in silver. Only let us pass through on foot[b]— 29as the descendants of Esau, who live in Seir, and the Moabites, who live in Ar, did for us—until we cross the Jordan into the land the LORD our God is giving us." 30But Sihon king of Heshbon refused to let us pass through. For the LORD[c] your God had made his spirit stubborn[d] and his heart obstinate in order to give him into your hands, as he has now done.

31The LORD said to me, "See, I have begun to deliver Sihon and his country over to you. Now begin to conquer and possess his land."[e]

32When Sihon and all his army came out to meet us in battle[f] at Jahaz, 33the LORD our God delivered him over to us and we struck him down,[g] together with his sons and his whole army. 34At that time we took all his towns and completely destroyed[b][h] them—men, women and children. We left no survivors. 35But the livestock and the plunder from the towns we had captured we carried off for ourselves. 36From Aroer[i] on the rim of the Arnon Gorge, and from the town in the gorge, even as far as Gilead, not one town was too strong for us. The LORD our God gave[j] us all of them. 37But in accordance with the command of the LORD our God,[k] you did not encroach on any of the land of the Ammonites,[l] neither the land along the course of the Jabbok[m] nor that around the towns in the hills.

Defeat of Og King of Bashan

3 Next we turned and went up along the road toward Bashan, and Og king of Bashan with his whole army marched out to meet us in battle at Edrei.[n] 2The LORD said to me, "Do not be afraid[o] of him, for I have handed him over to you with his whole army and his land. Do to him what you did to Sihon king of the Amorites, who reigned in Heshbon."

3So the LORD our God also gave into our hands Og king of Bashan and all his army. We struck them down, leaving no survivors.[p] 4At that time we took all his cities. There was not one of the sixty cities that we did not take from them—the whole region of Argob, Og's kingdom in Bashan.[q] 5All these cities were fortified with high walls and with gates and bars, and there were also a great many unwalled villages. 6We completely destroyed[b] them, as we had done with Sihon king of Heshbon, destroying[b][r] every city—men, women and children. 7But all the livestock and the plunder from their cities we carried off for ourselves.

8So at that time we took from these

2:14 [l]Nu 13:26 [m]Nu 14:29-35 [n]Dt 1:34-35
2:15 [o]Ps 106:26
2:19 [p]Ge 19:38 [q]ver 9
2:21 [r]ver 10
2:22 [s]Ge 36:8
2:23 [t]Jos 13:3 [u]Ge 10:14 [v]Am 9:7
2:24 [w]Nu 21:13-14; Jdg 11:13,18
2:25 [x]Dt 11:25 [y]Jos 2:9,11 [z]Ex 15:14-16
2:27 [a]Nu 21:21-22
2:28 [b]Nu 20:19
2:30 [c]Jos 11:20 [d]Ex 4:21; Nu 21:23; Ro 9:18
2:31 [e]Dt 1:8
2:32 [f]Nu 21:23
2:33 [g]Dt 29:7
2:34 [h]Dt 3:6; 7:2
2:36 [i]Dt 3:12; 4:48; Jos 13:9 [j]Ps 44:3
2:37 [k]ver 18-19 [l]Nu 21:24 [m]Ge 32:22; Dt 3:16
3:1 [n]Nu 21:33
3:2 [o]Nu 21:34
3:3 [p]Nu 21:35
3:4 [q]1Ki 4:13
3:6 [r]Dt 2:24,34

a *23* That is, Crete b *34,6* The Hebrew term refers to the irrevocable giving over of things or persons to the LORD, often by totally destroying them.

two kings of the Amorites the territory east of the Jordan, from the Arnon Gorge as far as Mount Hermon. 9(Hermon is called Sirion[s] by the Sidonians; the Amorites call it Senir.)[t] 10We took all the towns on the plateau, and all Gilead, and all Bashan as far as Salecah[u] and Edrei, towns of Og's kingdom in Bashan. 11(Only Og king of Bashan was left of the remnant of the Rephaites.[v] His bed**[a]** was made of iron and was more than thirteen feet long and six feet wide.**[b]** It is still in Rabbah[w] of the Ammonites.)

Division of the Land

12Of the land that we took over at that time, I gave the Reubenites and the Gadites the territory north of Aroer[x] by the Arnon Gorge, including half the hill country of Gilead, together with its towns. 13The rest of Gilead and also all of Bashan, the kingdom of Og, I gave to the half tribe of Manasseh. (The whole region of Argob in Bashan used to be known as a land of the Rephaites. 14Jair,[y] a descendant of Manasseh, took the whole region of Argob as far as the border of the Geshurites and the Maacathites; it was named after him, so that to this day Bashan is called Havvoth Jair.**[c]**) 15And I gave Gilead to Makir.[z] 16But to the Reubenites and the Gadites I gave the territory extending from Gilead down to the Arnon Gorge (the middle of the gorge being the border) and out to the Jabbok River,[a] which is the border of the Ammonites. 17Its western border was the Jordan in the Arabah, from Kinnereth[b] to the Sea of the Arabah (the Salt Sea**[d]**[c]), below the slopes of Pisgah.

2 →PG. 203

18I commanded you at that time: "The LORD your God has given you this land to take possession of it. But all your able-bodied men, armed for battle, must cross over ahead of your brother Israelites.[d] 19However, your wives, your children and your livestock (I know you have much livestock) may stay in the towns I have given you, 20until the LORD gives rest to your brothers as he has to you, and they too have taken over the land that the LORD your God is giving them, across the Jordan. After that, each of you may go back to the possession I have given you."

Moses Forbidden to Cross the Jordan

21At that time I commanded Joshua: "You have seen with your own eyes all that the LORD your God has done to these two kings. The LORD will do the same to all the kingdoms over there where you are going. 22Do not be afraid[e] of them; the LORD your God himself will fight[f] for you."

23At that time I pleaded with the LORD: 24"O Sovereign LORD, you have begun to show to your servant your greatness[g] and your strong hand. For what god[h] is there in heaven or on earth who can do the deeds and mighty works[i] you do?[j] 25Let me go over and see the good land[k] beyond the Jordan—that fine hill country and Lebanon."

26But because of you the LORD was angry[l] with me and would not listen to me. "That is enough," the LORD said. "Do not speak to me anymore about this matter. 27Go up to the top of Pisgah and look west and north and south and east. Look at the land with your own eyes, since you are not going to cross this Jordan.[m] 28But commission[n] Joshua, and encourage and strengthen him, for he will lead this people across[o] and will cause them to inherit the land that you will see." 29So we stayed in the valley near Beth Peor.[p]

5 →PG. 201

Obedience Commanded

4 Hear now, O Israel, the decrees and laws I am about to teach you. Follow them so that you may live[q] and may go in and take possession of the land that the LORD, the God of your fathers, is giving you. 2Do not add[r] to what I command you and do not subtract from it, but keep the commands of the LORD your God that I give you.

3You saw with your own eyes what the LORD did at Baal Peor.[s] The LORD your God destroyed from among you everyone who followed the Baal of Peor, 4but all of you who held fast to the LORD your God are still alive today.

5See, I have taught you decrees and laws as the LORD my God commanded me, so that you may follow them in the land you are entering to take possession of it. 6Observe them carefully, for this will show your wisdom[t] and understanding to the nations, who will hear about all these decrees and say, "Surely this great nation is a wise and understanding people."[u] 7What other nation is so great[v] as to have their gods near[w] them the way the LORD our God is near us whenever we pray to him? 8And what other nation is so great as to have such righteous decrees and

3:9 [s]Dt 4:48; Ps 29:6 [t]1Ch 5:23
3:10 [u]Jos 13:11
3:11 [v]Ge 14:5 [w]2Sa 12:26; Jer 49:2
3:12 [x]Nu 32:32-38; Dt 2:36; Jos 13:8-13
3:14 [y]Nu 32:41; 1Ch 2:22
3:15 [z]Nu 32:39-40
3:16 [a]Nu 21:24
3:17 [b]Nu 34:11; Jos 13:27 [c]Ge 14:3; Jos 12:3
3:18 [d]Nu 32:17
3:22 [e]Dt 1:29 [f]Ex 14:14; Dt 20:4
3:24 [g]Dt 11:2 [h]Ex 15:11; Ps 86:8 [i]Ps 71:16,19 [j]2Sa 7:22
3:25 [k]Dt 4:22
3:26 [l]Dt 1:37; 31:2
3:27 [m]Nu 27:12
3:28 [n]Nu 27:18-23 [o]Dt 31:3,23
3:29 [p]Dt 4:46; 34:6
4:1 [q]Dt 5:33; 8:1; 16:20; 30:15-20; Eze 20:11; Ro 10:5
4:2 [r]Dt 12:32; Jos 1:7; Rev 22:18-19
4:3 [s]Nu 25:1-9; Ps 106:28
4:6 [t]Dt 30:19-20; Ps 19:7; Pr 1:7 [u]Job 28:28
4:7 [v]2Sa 7:23 [w]Ps 46:1; Isa 55:6

a *11* Or *sarcophagus* **b** *11* Hebrew *nine cubits long and four cubits wide* (about 4 meters long and 1.8 meters wide) **c** *14* Or *called the settlements of Jair* **d** *17* That is, the Dead Sea

laws as this body of laws I am setting before you today?

4 →PG. 194

[9]Only be careful,[x] and watch yourselves closely so that you do not forget the things your eyes have seen or let them slip from your heart as long as you live. Teach[y] them to your children[z] and to their children after them. [10]Remember the day you stood before the LORD your God at Horeb,[a] when he said to me, "Assemble the people before me to hear my words so that they may learn to revere me as long as they live in the land and may teach them to their children." [11]You came near and stood at the foot of the mountain while it blazed with fire[b] to the very heavens, with black clouds and deep darkness. [12]Then the LORD spoke[c] to you out of the fire. You heard the sound of words but saw no form; there was only a voice. [13]He declared to you his covenant,[d] the Ten Commandments,[e] which he commanded you to follow and then wrote them on two stone tablets. [14]And the LORD directed me at that time to teach you the decrees and laws you are to follow in the land that you are crossing the Jordan to possess.

Idolatry Forbidden

[15]You saw no form[f] of any kind the day the LORD spoke to you at Horeb out of the fire. Therefore watch yourselves very carefully,[g] [16]so that you do not become corrupt and make for yourselves an idol,[h] an image of any shape, whether formed like a man or a woman, [17]or like any animal on earth or any bird that flies in the air, [18]or like any creature that moves along the ground or any fish in the waters below. [19]And when you look up to the sky and see the sun,[i] the moon and the stars—all the heavenly array[j]—do not be enticed into bowing down to them and worshiping things the LORD your God has apportioned to all the nations under heaven. [20]But as for you, the LORD took you and brought you out of the iron-smelting furnace,[k] out of Egypt, to be the people of his inheritance,[l] as you now are.

[21]The LORD was angry with me[m] because of you, and he solemnly swore that I would not cross the Jordan and enter the good land the LORD your God is giving you as your inheritance. [22]I will die in this land; I will not cross the Jordan; but you are about to cross over and take possession of that good land.[n] [23]Be careful not to forget the covenant[o] of the LORD your God that he made with you; do not make for yourselves an idol[p] in the form of anything the LORD your God has forbidden. [24]For the LORD your God is a consuming fire,[q] a jealous God.

[25]After you have had children and grandchildren and have lived in the land a long time—if you then become corrupt and make any kind of idol, doing evil[r] in the eyes of the LORD your God and provoking him to anger, [26]I call heaven and earth as witnesses against you[s] this day that you will quickly perish from the land that you are crossing the Jordan to possess. You will not live there long but will certainly be destroyed. [27]The LORD will scatter[t] you among the peoples, and only a few of you will survive among the nations to which the LORD will drive you. [28]There you will worship man-made gods[u] of wood and stone, which cannot see or hear or eat or smell.[v] [29]But if from there you seek[w] the LORD your God, you will find him if you look for him with all your heart[x] and with all your soul.[y] [30]When you are in distress and all these things have happened to you, then in later days[z] you will return to the LORD your God and obey him. [31]For the LORD your God is a merciful[a] God; he will not abandon or destroy you or forget the covenant with your forefathers, which he confirmed to them by oath.

The LORD Is God

[32]Ask[b] now about the former days, long before your time, from the day God created man on the earth;[c] ask from one end of the heavens to the other.[d] Has anything so great as this ever happened, or has anything like it ever been heard of? [33]Has any other people heard the voice of God[a] speaking out of fire, as you have, and lived?[e]

[a]33 Or *of a god*

4:5-14

PROMISE 1

FOLLOWING GOD'S WAY

If you're discouraged about being a godly man, read this paragraph carefully. Write it out and tape it to your mirror so you can read it every day. Memorize it. Moses here encourages the people to follow the Lord and so be an example to the surrounding nations (v. 6) and to their own children (v. 9). This call to "conspicuous holiness" applies to us today as well.

God's people, in any generation, are a noble people with a high calling. This passage is a strong reminder of that fact.

For the next Promise 1 reading go to page 200.

4:9 [x]Pr 4:23 [y]Ge 18:19; Eph 6:4 [z]Ps 78:5-6
4:10 [a]Ex 19:9,16
4:11 [b]Ex 19:18; Heb 12:18-19
4:12 [c]Ex 20:22; Dt 5:4,22
4:13 [d]Dt 9:9,11 [e]Ex 24:12; 31:18; 34:28
4:15 [f]Isa 40:18 [g]Jos 23:11
4:16 [h]Ex 20:4-5; 32:7; Dt 5:8; Ro 1:23
4:19 [i]Dt 17:3; Job 31:26 [j]2Ki 17:16; 21:3; Ro 1:25
4:20 [k]1Ki 8:51; Jer 11:4 [l]Ex 19:5; Dt 9:29
4:21 [m]Nu 20:12; Dt 1:37
4:22 [n]Dt 3:25
4:23 [o]ver 9,16 [p]Ex 20:4
4:24 [q]Ex 24:17; Dt 9:3; Heb 12:29
4:25 [r]2Ki 17:2,17
4:26 [s]Dt 30:18-19; Isa 1:2; Mic 6:2
4:27 [t]Lev 26:33; Dt 28:36,64; Ne 1:8
4:28 [u]Dt 28:36,64; 1Sa 26:19; Jer 16:13 [v]Ps 115:4-8; 135:15-18
4:29 [w]2Ch 15:4; Isa 55:6 [x]Jer 29:13 [y]Dt 30:1-3,10
4:30 [z]Dt 31:29; Jer 23:20; Hos 3:5
4:31 [a]2Ch 30:9; Ne 9:31; Ps 116:5; Jnh 4:2
4:32 [b]Dt 32:7; Job 8:8 [c]Ge 1:27 [d]Mt 24:31
4:33 [e]Ex 20:22; Dt 5:24-26

34 Has any god ever tried to take for himself one nation out of another nation,[f] by testings, by miraculous signs[g] and wonders,[h] by war, by a mighty hand and an outstretched arm,[i] or by great and awesome deeds,[j] like all the things the LORD your God did for you in Egypt before your very eyes?

35 You were shown these things so that you might know that the LORD is God; besides him there is no other.[k] 36 From heaven he made you hear his voice[l] to discipline you. On earth he showed you his great fire, and you heard his words from out of the fire. 37 Because he loved[m] your forefathers and chose their descendants after them, he brought you out of Egypt by his Presence and his great strength,[n] 38 to drive out before you nations greater and stronger than you and to bring you into their land to give it to you for your inheritance,[o] as it is today.

39 Acknowledge and take to heart this day that the LORD is God in heaven above and on the earth below. There is no other.[p] 40 Keep[q] his decrees and commands, which I am giving you today, so that it may go well[r] with you and your children after you and that you may live long[s] in the land the LORD your God gives you for all time.

Cities of Refuge

41 Then Moses set aside three cities east of the Jordan, 42 to which anyone who had killed a person could flee if he had unintentionally killed his neighbor without malice aforethought. He could flee into one of these cities and save his life. 43 The cities were these: Bezer in the desert plateau, for the Reubenites; Ramoth in Gilead, for the Gadites; and Golan in Bashan, for the Manassites.

Introduction to the Law

44 This is the law Moses set before the Israelites. 45 These are the stipulations, decrees and laws Moses gave them when they came out of Egypt 46 and were in the valley near Beth Peor east of the Jordan, in the land of Sihon[t] king of the Amorites, who reigned in Heshbon and was defeated by Moses and the Israelites as they came out of Egypt. 47 They took possession of his land and the land of Og king of Bashan, the two Amorite kings east of the Jordan. 48 This land extended from Aroer[u] on the rim of the Arnon Gorge to Mount Siyon[a][v] (that is, Hermon), 49 and included all the Arabah east of the Jordan, as far as the Sea of the Arabah,[b] below the slopes of Pisgah.

4:34 [f]Ex 6:6 [g]Ex 7:3 [h]Dt 7:19; 26:8 [i]Ex 13:3 [j]Dt 34:12
4:35 [k]Dt 32:39; 1Sa 2:2; Isa 45:5,18
4:36 [l]Ex 19:9,19
4:37 [m]Dt 10:15 [n]Ex 13:3,9,14
4:38 [o]Dt 7:1; 9:5
4:39 [p]ver 35; Jos 2:11
4:40 [q]Lev 22:31; Dt 5:33 [r]Dt 5:16 [s]Dt 6:3,18; Eph 6:2-3
4:46 [t]Nu 21:26; Dt 3:29
4:48 [u]Dt 2:36 [v]Dt 3:9

The Ten Commandments

5 Moses summoned all Israel and said:

Hear, O Israel, the decrees and laws I declare in your hearing today. Learn them and be sure to follow them. 2 The LORD our God made a covenant[w] with us at Horeb. 3 It was not with our fathers that the LORD made this covenant, but with us, with all of us who are alive here today.[x] 4 The LORD spoke[y] to you face to face out of the fire on the mountain. 5 (At that time I stood between[z] the LORD and you to declare to you the word of the LORD, because you were afraid[a] of the fire and did not go up the mountain.) And he said:

3 →PG. 202

6 "I am the LORD your God, who brought you out of Egypt, out of the land of slavery.

7 "You shall have no other gods before[c] me.

8 "You shall not make for yourself an idol in the form of anything in heaven above or on the earth beneath or in the waters below. 9 You shall not bow down to them or worship them; for I, the LORD your God, am a jealous God, punishing the children for the sin of the fathers to the third and fourth generation of those who hate me,[b] 10 but showing love to a thousand ⌊generations⌋ of those who love me and keep my commandments.[c]

11 "You shall not misuse the name of the LORD your God, for the LORD will not hold anyone guiltless who misuses his name.[d]

12 "Observe the Sabbath day by keeping it holy,[e] as the LORD your God has commanded you. 13 Six days you shall labor and do all your work, 14 but the seventh day[f] is a Sabbath to the LORD your God. On it you shall not do any work, neither you, nor your son or daughter, nor your manservant or maidservant, nor your ox, your donkey or any of your animals, nor the alien within your gates, so that your manservant and maidservant may rest, as

5:2 [w]Ex 19:5
5:3 [x]Heb 8:9
5:4 [y]Dt 4:12,33,36
5:5 [z]Gal 3:19 [a]Ex 20:18,21
5:9 [b]Ex 34:7
5:10 [c]Jer 32:18
5:11 [d]Lev 19:12; Mt 5:33-37
5:12 [e]Ex 20:8
5:14 [f]Ge 2:2; Heb 4:4

a 48 Hebrew; Syriac (see also Deut. 3:9) *Sirion*
b 49 That is, the Dead Sea
c 7 Or *besides*

you do. 15Remember that you were slaves in Egypt and that the LORD your God brought you out of there with a mighty hand and an outstretched arm.[g] Therefore the LORD your God has commanded you to observe the Sabbath day.

16"Honor your father and your mother,[h] as the LORD your God has commanded you, so that you may live long[i] and that it may go well with you in the land the LORD your God is giving you.

17"You shall not murder.[j]

18"You shall not commit adultery.[k]

19"You shall not steal.

20"You shall not give false testimony against your neighbor.

21"You shall not covet your neighbor's wife. You shall not set your desire on your neighbor's house or land, his manservant or maidservant, his ox or donkey, or anything that belongs to your neighbor."[l]

22These are the commandments the LORD proclaimed in a loud voice to your whole assembly there on the mountain from out of the fire, the cloud and the deep darkness; and he added nothing more. Then he wrote them on two stone tablets[m] and gave them to me.

23When you heard the voice out of the darkness, while the mountain was ablaze with fire, all the leading men of your tribes and your elders came to me. 24And you said, "The LORD our God has shown us his glory and his majesty, and we have heard his voice from the fire. Today we have seen that a man can live even if God speaks with him.[n] 25But now, why should we die? This great fire will consume us, and we will die if we hear the voice of the LORD our God any longer.[o] 26For what mortal man has ever heard the voice of the living God speaking out of fire, as we have, and survived?[p] 27Go near and listen to all that the LORD our God says. Then tell us whatever the LORD our God tells you. We will listen and obey."

28The LORD heard you when you spoke to me and the LORD said to me, "I have heard what this people said to you. Everything they said was good.[q]

4 →PG. 194

29Oh, that their hearts would be inclined to fear me[r] and keep all my commands[s] always, so that it might go well with them and their children forever![t]

30"Go, tell them to return to their tents. 31But you stay here[u] with me so that I may give you all the commands, decrees and laws you are to teach them to follow in the land I am giving them to possess."

32So be careful to do what the LORD your God has commanded you; do not turn aside to the right or to the left.[v] 33Walk in all the way that the LORD your God has commanded you,[w] so that you may live and prosper and prolong your days[x] in the land that you will possess.

Love the LORD Your God

6 These are the commands, decrees and laws the LORD your God directed me to teach you to observe in the land that you are crossing the Jordan to possess, 2so that you, your children and their children after them may fear[y] the LORD your God as long as you live by keeping all his decrees and commands that I give you, and so that you may enjoy long life. 3Hear, O Israel, and be careful to obey so that it may go well with you and that you may increase greatly[z] in a land flowing with milk and honey,[a] just as the LORD, the God of your fathers, promised you.

1 →PG. 199

4Hear, O Israel: The LORD our God, the LORD is one.[a][b] 5Love[c] the LORD your God with all your heart and with all your soul and with all your strength.[d] 6These commandments that I give you today are to be upon your hearts.[e] 7Impress them on your children. Talk about them when you sit at home and when you walk along the road, when you lie down and when you

4 →PG. 199

5:15 gDt 4:34
5:16 hEx 20:12; Lev 19:3; Dt 27:16; Eph 6:2-3*; Col 3:20 iDt 4:40
5:17 jMt 5:21-22*
5:18 kMt 5:27-30; Lk 18:20*; Jas 2:11*
5:21 lRo 7:7*; 13:9*
5:22 mEx 24:12; 31:18; Dt 4:13
5:24 nEx 19:19
5:25 oDt 18:16
5:26 pDt 4:33
5:28 qDt 18:17
5:29 rPs 81:8,13 sDt 11:1; Isa 48:18 tDt 4:1,40
5:31 uEx 24:12
5:32 vDt 17:11,20; 28:14; Jos 1:7; 23:6; Pr 4:27
5:33 wJer 7:23 xDt 4:40
6:2 yEx 20:20; Dt 10:12-13
6:3 zDt 5:33 aEx 3:8
6:4 bMk 12:29*; 1Co 8:4
6:5 cMt 22:37*; Mk 12:30*; Lk 10:27* dDt 10:12
6:6 eDt 11:18

a4 Or *The LORD our God is one LORD;* or *The LORD is our God, the LORD is one;* or *The LORD is our God, the LORD alone*

6:6

PROMISE 4

TOTAL INTEGRATION

Jesus quoted this statement when the Pharisees asked him to name the greatest commandment (Matthew 22:37–38). Carefully read your way through Deuteronomy 6:1–9. Moses said, "these commandments . . . are to be upon your hearts." This passage contains some *essential* requirements for your role as a godly man and a godly father. Read it. Meditate on it. Memorize it. Integrate it into every area of your life. In short, place it "upon your heart."

For the next Promise 4 reading go to page 195.

get up.[f] **8**Tie them as symbols on your
hands and bind them on your foreheads.[g] **9**Write them on the doorframes of your houses and on your
gates.[h]
10When the LORD your God brings
you into the land he swore to your fathers, to Abraham, Isaac and Jacob, to
give you—a land with large, flourishing
cities you did not build,[i] **11**houses
filled with all kinds of good things you
did not provide, wells you did not dig,
and vineyards and olive groves you did
not plant—then when you eat and are
satisfied,[j] **12**be careful that you do not
forget the LORD, who brought you out
of Egypt, out of the land of slavery.
13Fear the LORD[k] your God, serve
him only[l] and take your oaths in his
name. **14**Do not follow other gods, the
gods of the peoples around you; **15**for
the LORD your God[m], who is among
you, is a jealous God and his anger will
burn against you, and he will destroy
you from the face of the land. **16**Do not
test the LORD your God[n] as you did at
Massah. **17**Be sure to keep the commands of the LORD your God and the
stipulations and decrees he has given
you.[o] **18**Do what is right and good in
the LORD's sight, so that it may go
well[p] with you and you may go in and
take over the good land that the LORD
promised on oath to your forefathers,
19thrusting out all your enemies before
you, as the LORD said.
20In the future, when your son asks
you,[q] "What is the meaning of the
stipulations, decrees and laws the LORD
our God has commanded you?" **21**tell
him: "We were slaves of Pharaoh in
Egypt, but the LORD brought us out of
Egypt with a mighty hand. **22**Before our
eyes the LORD sent miraculous signs
and wonders—great and terrible—
upon Egypt and Pharaoh and his whole
household. **23**But he brought us out
from there to bring us in and give us
the land that he promised on oath to
our forefathers. **24**The LORD commanded us to obey all these decrees and to
fear the LORD our God,[r] so that we
might always prosper and be kept
alive, as is the case today.[s] **25**And if we

6:7 [f]Dt 4:9; 11:19; Eph 6:4 **6:8** [g]Ex 13:9,16; Dt 11:18 **6:9** [h]Dt 11:20 **6:10** [i]Jos 24:13 **6:11** [j]Dt 8:10 **6:13** [k]Dt 10:20 [l]Mt 4:10*; Lk 4:8* **6:15** [m]Dt 4:24 **6:16** [n]Ex 17:7; Mt 4:7*; Lk 4:12* **6:17** [o]Dt 11:22; Ps 119:4 **6:18** [p]Dt 4:40 **6:20** [q]Ex 13:14 **6:24** [r]Dt 10:12; Jer 32:39 [s]Ps 41:2

6:1–9

PROMISE 4

PASSING FAITH ON TO THE CHILDREN

The disobedient generation had died in the wilderness (Book of Numbers) and their children, now adults, were about to enter the land God had promised to Israel when they left Egypt. But before they did, God again gave the law to them (5:6–21).

The name *Deuteronomy* is made up of two Greek words, *deutero* meaning "second" and *nomos* meaning "law." This "second law" was a personalized rendition for this generation. Read 6:1 again; God wanted this generation to see the law as their own possession, not as something they had seen violated and abused by their parents. This is important because in these two paragraphs, God instructed this generation how *they* were to pass his law on to the next generation and the next (2, 3).

Moses offered six important principles to help the people keep and teach God's law.

1. Know who your God is: "The LORD our God, the LORD is one" (v. 4). In other words, never be confused about who your God is or what he is like. This message was especially important as the Israelites were about to enter a pagan land where the locals worshiped many false gods.

2. "Love the LORD your God with all your heart and with all your soul and with all your strength" (v. 5). God must be a proper theological reality, but at the same time he must be much more than that.

3. "These commandments that I give you today are to be upon your hearts" (v. 6). What is in your heart is what will be in your home. Out of the abundance of the heart the mouth speaks. God's commands must live in the core of your being.

4. "Impress them on your children" (v. 7). Here Moses spoke of a formal, planned, prepared strategy for teaching God's Word to the next generation. This kind of education was too important to leave to chance.

5. "Talk about them when . . ." (v. 7). The figure of speech Moses used here named the extremes to include the whole. The Israelites needed to remember God's law not *just* when they sat and walked, laid down and rose up, but at all times and in all places. In other words, Moses instructed them to use and discuss God's law in more casual conversations around the home to add to the formal teaching times.

6. Verses 8 and 9 state that God's Word should direct what we do with our hands, where we point our faces (give attention to), and what characterizes the activities in our homes and business (business was conducted at the city gates).

If we want to pass God's Word on to the next generation with enough conviction that they pass it on to the next, we must understand it correctly. It must be the most important thing in our lives and we must teach it, live it, model it. All of the principles outlined above are still operational today. Any godly man will want to master this passage of Scripture; for his own kids and for those he ministers to as God's messenger to the next generation.

For the next Promise 4 reading go to page 227.

are careful to obey all this law before the LORD our God, as he has commanded us, that will be our righteousness.[t]"

Driving Out the Nations

7 When the LORD your God brings you into the land you are entering to possess and drives out before you many nations[u]—the Hittites, Girgashites, Amorites, Canaanites, Perizzites, Hivites and Jebusites, seven nations larger and stronger than you— 2and when the LORD your God has delivered them over to you and you have defeated them, then you must destroy them totally.[a] Make no treaty[v] with them, and show them no mercy.[w] 3Do not intermarry with them.[x] Do not give your daughters to their sons or take their daughters for your sons, 4for they will turn your sons away from following me to serve other gods, and the LORD's anger will burn against you and will quickly destroy[y] you. 5This is what you are to do to them: Break down their altars, smash their sacred stones, cut down their Asherah poles[b] and burn their idols in the fire.[z] 6For you are a people holy[a] to the LORD your God.[b] The LORD your God has chosen[c] you out of all the peoples on the face of the earth to be his people, his treasured possession.

7The LORD did not set his affection on you and choose you because you were more numerous than other peoples, for you were the fewest of all peoples.[d] 8But it was because the LORD loved[e] you and kept the oath he swore[f] to your forefathers that he brought you out with a mighty hand and redeemed you from the land of slavery,[g] from the power of Pharaoh king of Egypt. 9Know therefore that the LORD your God is God;[h] he is the faithful God,[i] keeping his covenant of love[j] to a thousand generations of those who love him and keep his commands. 10But

those who hate him he will repay
to their face by destruction;
he will not be slow to repay to
their face those who hate
him.

11Therefore, take care to follow the commands, decrees and laws I give you today.

12If you pay attention to these laws and are careful to follow them, then the LORD your God will keep his covenant of love with you, as he swore to your forefathers.[k] 13He will love you and bless you[l] and increase your numbers. He will bless the fruit of your womb, the crops of your land—your grain, new wine and oil—the calves of your herds and the lambs of your flocks in the land that he swore to your forefathers to give you.[m] 14You will be blessed more than any other people; none of your men or women will be childless, nor any of your livestock without young.[n] 15The LORD will keep you free from every disease.[o] He will not inflict on you the horrible diseases you knew in Egypt, but he will inflict them on all who hate you. 16You must destroy all the peoples the LORD your God gives over to you. Do not look on them with pity[p] and do not serve their gods, for that will be a snare[q] to you.

17You may say to yourselves, "These nations are stronger than we are. How can we drive them out?[r]" 18But do not be afraid[s] of them; remember well what the LORD your God did to Pharaoh and to all Egypt.[t] 19You saw with your own eyes the great trials, the miraculous signs and wonders, the mighty hand and outstretched arm, with which the LORD your God brought you out. The LORD your God will do the same to all the peoples you now fear.[u] 20Moreover, the LORD your God will send the hornet[v] among them until even the survivors who hide from you have perished. 21Do not be terrified by them, for the LORD your God, who is among you,[w] is a great and awesome God.[x] 22The LORD your God will drive out those nations before you, little by little.[y] You will not be allowed to eliminate them all at once, or the wild animals will multiply around you. 23But the LORD your God will deliver them over to you, throwing them into great confusion until they are destroyed. 24He will give their kings into your hand, and you will wipe out their names from under heaven. No one will be able to stand up against you;[z] you will destroy them. 25The images of their gods you are to burn[a] in the fire. Do not covet[b] the silver and gold on them, and do not take it for yourselves, or you will be ensnared[c] by it, for it is detestable[d] to the LORD your God. 26Do not bring a detestable thing into your house or you, like it, will be set apart for destruction.[e] Utterly abhor and detest it, for it is set apart for destruction.

6:25 [t]Dt 24:13; Ro 10:3,5
7:1 [u]Dt 31:3; Ac 13:19
7:2 [v]Ex 23:32 [w]Dt 13:8
7:3 [x]Ex 34:15-16; Ezr 9:2
7:4 [y]Dt 6:15
7:5 [z]Ex 23:24; Dt 12:2-3
7:6 [a]Ex 19:5-6; 1Pe 2:9 [b]Ps 50:5; Jer 2:3 [c]Dt 14:2
7:7 [d]Dt 10:22
7:8 [e]Dt 10:15 [f]Ex 32:13 [g]Ex 13:14
7:9 [h]Dt 4:35 [i]1Co 1:9; 2Ti 2:13 [j]Ne 1:5; Da 9:4
7:12 [k]Lev 26:3-13; Dt 28:1-14; Ps 105:8-9
7:13 [l]Jn 14:21 [m]Dt 28:4
7:14 [n]Ex 23:26
7:15 [o]Ex 15:26
7:16 [p]ver 2; Ex 23:33 [q]Jdg 8:27
7:17 [r]Nu 33:53
7:18 [s]Dt 31:6 [t]Ps 105:5
7:19 [u]Dt 4:34
7:20 [v]Ex 23:28; Jos 24:12
7:21 [w]Jos 3:10 [x]Dt 10:17; Ne 9:32
7:22 [y]Ex 23:28-30
7:24 [z]Jos 23:9
7:25 [a]Ex 32:20; 1Ch 14:12 [b]Jos 7:21 [c]Jdg 8:27 [d]Dt 17:1
7:26 [e]Lev 27:28-29

[a]*2* The Hebrew term refers to the irrevocable giving over of things or persons to the LORD, often by totally destroying them; also in verse 26. [b]*5* That is, symbols of the goddess Asherah; here and elsewhere in Deuteronomy

Do Not Forget the LORD

8 Be careful to follow every command I am giving you today, so that you may live[f] and increase and may enter and possess the land that the LORD promised on oath to your forefathers. 2 Remember how the LORD your God led[g] you all the way in the desert these forty years, to humble you and to test you in order to know what was in your heart, whether or not you would keep his commands. 3 He humbled you, causing you to hunger and then feeding you with manna,[h] which neither you nor your fathers had known, to teach you that man does not live on bread alone but on every word that comes from the mouth of the LORD.[i] 4 Your clothes did not wear out and your feet did not swell during these forty years.[j] 5 Know then in your heart that as a man disciplines his son, so the LORD your God disciplines you.[k]

6 Observe the commands of the LORD your God, walking in his ways and revering him.[l] 7 For the LORD your God is bringing you into a good land—a land with streams and pools of water, with springs flowing in the valleys and hills;[m] 8 a land with wheat and barley, vines and fig trees, pomegranates, olive oil and honey; 9 a land where bread will not be scarce and you will lack nothing; a land where the rocks are iron and you can dig copper out of the hills.

10 When you have eaten and are satisfied,[n] praise the LORD your God for the good land he has given you. 11 Be careful that you do not forget the LORD your God, failing to observe his commands, his laws and his decrees that I am giving you this day. 12 Otherwise, when you eat and are satisfied, when you build fine houses and settle down,[o] 13 and when your herds and flocks grow large and your silver and gold increase and all you have is multiplied, 14 then your heart will become proud and you will forget[p] the LORD your God, who brought you out of Egypt, out of the land of slavery. 15 He led you through the vast and dreadful desert,[q] that thirsty and waterless land, with its venomous snakes[r] and scorpions. He brought you water out of hard rock.[s] 16 He gave you manna to eat in the desert, something your fathers had never known,[t] to humble and to test you so that in the end it might go well with you. 17 You may say to yourself,[u] "My power and the strength of my hands have produced this wealth for me." 18 But remember the LORD your God, for it is he who gives you the ability to produce wealth,[v] and so confirms his covenant, which he swore to your forefathers, as it is today.

19 If you ever forget the LORD your God and follow other gods and worship and bow down to them, I testify against you today that you will surely be destroyed.[w] 20 Like the nations the LORD destroyed before you, so you will be destroyed for not obeying the LORD your God.

Not Because of Israel's Righteousness

9 Hear, O Israel. You are now about to cross the Jordan to go in and dispossess nations greater and stronger than you,[x] with large cities that have walls up to the sky.[y] 2 The people are strong and tall—Anakites! You know about them and have heard it said: "Who can stand up against the Anakites?"[z] 3 But be assured today that the LORD your God is the one who goes across ahead of you[a] like a devouring fire.[b] He will destroy them; he will subdue them before you. And you will drive them out and annihilate them quickly,[c] as the LORD has promised you.

4 After the LORD your God has driven them out before you, do not say to yourself,[d] "The LORD has brought me here to take possession of this land because of my righteousness." No, it is on account of the wickedness of these nations[e] that the LORD is going to drive them out before you. 5 It is not because of your righteousness or your integrity[f] that you are going in to take possession of their land; but on account of the wickedness of these nations, the LORD your God will drive them out before you, to accomplish what he swore[g] to your fathers, to Abraham, Isaac and Jacob. 6 Understand, then, that it is not because of your righteousness that the LORD your God is giving you this good land to possess, for you are a stiff-necked people.[h]

The Golden Calf

7 Remember this and never forget how you provoked the LORD your God to anger in the desert. From the day you left Egypt until you arrived here, you have been rebellious against the LORD. 8 At Horeb you aroused the LORD's wrath so that he was angry enough to destroy you.[i] 9 When I went up on the mountain to receive the tablets of stone, the tablets of the covenant that the LORD had made with you, I stayed on the mountain forty days and forty nights; I ate no bread and drank no water.[j] 10 The LORD gave me two stone tablets inscribed by the

8:1 [f] Dt 4:1
8:2 [g] Am 2:10
8:3 [h] Ex 16:12,14,35 [i] Ex 16:2-3; Mt 4:4*; Lk 4:4*
8:4 [j] Dt 29:5; Ne 9:21
8:5 [k] 2Sa 7:14; Pr 3:11-12; Heb 12:5-11; Rev 3:19
8:6 [l] Dt 5:33
8:7 [m] Dt 11:9-12
8:10 [n] Dt 6:10-12
8:12 [o] Hos 13:6
8:14 [p] Ps 106:21
8:15 [q] Jer 2:6 [r] Nu 21:6 [s] Nu 20:11; Ps 78:15; 114:8
8:16 [t] Ex 16:15
8:17 [u] Dt 9:4,7,24
8:18 [v] Pr 10:22; Hos 2:8
8:19 [w] Dt 4:26; 30:18
9:1 [x] Dt 4:38; 11:23,31 [y] Dt 1:28
9:2 [z] Nu 13:22,28,32-33
9:3 [a] Dt 31:3; Jos 3:11 [b] Dt 4:24; Heb 12:29 [c] Ex 23:31; Dt 7:23-24
9:4 [d] Dt 8:17 [e] Lev 18:21,24-30; Dt 18:9-14
9:5 [f] Tit 3:5 [g] Ge 12:7; 13:15; 15:7; 17:8; 26:4
9:6 [h] ver 13; Ex 32:9; Dt 31:27
9:8 [i] Ex 32:7-10; Ps 106:19
9:9 [j] Ex 24:12,15,18; 34:28

finger of God.[k] On them were all the commandments the LORD proclaimed to you on the mountain out of the fire, on the day of the assembly.

11At the end of the forty days and forty nights, the LORD gave me the two stone tablets, the tablets of the covenant. 12Then the LORD told me, "Go down from here at once, because your people whom you brought out of Egypt have become corrupt.[l] They have turned away quickly[m] from what I commanded them and have made a cast idol for themselves."

13And the LORD said to me, "I have seen this people[n], and they are a stiff-necked people indeed! 14Let me alone,[o] so that I may destroy them and blot out[p] their name from under heaven. And I will make you into a nation stronger and more numerous than they."

15So I turned and went down from the mountain while it was ablaze with fire. And the two tablets of the covenant were in my hands.[a][q] 16When I looked, I saw that you had sinned against the LORD your God; you had made for yourselves an idol cast in the shape of a calf.[r] You had turned aside quickly from the way that the LORD had commanded you. 17So I took the two tablets and threw them out of my hands, breaking them to pieces before your eyes.

18Then once again I fell[s] prostrate before the LORD for forty days and forty nights; I ate no bread and drank no water, because of all the sin you had committed, doing what was evil in the LORD's sight and so provoking him to anger. 19I feared the anger and wrath of the LORD, for he was angry enough with you to destroy you.[t] But again the LORD listened to me.[u] 20And the LORD was angry enough with Aaron to destroy him, but at that time I prayed for Aaron too. 21Also I took that sinful thing of yours, the calf you had made, and burned it in the fire. Then I crushed it and ground it to powder as fine as dust and threw the dust into a stream that flowed down the mountain.[v]

22You also made the LORD angry at Taberah,[w] at Massah[x] and at Kibroth Hattaavah.[y]

23And when the LORD sent you out from Kadesh Barnea, he said, "Go up and take possession of the land I have given you." But you rebelled against the command of the LORD your God. You did not trust[z] him or obey him. 24You have been rebellious against the LORD ever since I have known you.[a]

25I lay prostrate before the LORD those forty days and forty nights because the LORD had said he would destroy you.[b] 26I prayed to the LORD and said, "O Sovereign LORD, do not destroy your people, your own inheritance that you redeemed by your great power and brought out of Egypt with a mighty hand.[c] 27Remember your servants Abraham, Isaac and Jacob. Overlook the stubbornness of this people, their wickedness and their sin. 28Otherwise, the country from which you brought us will say, 'Because the LORD was not able to take them into the land he had promised them, and because he hated them, he brought them out to put them to death in the desert.'[d] 29But they are your people, your inheritance[e] that you brought out by your great power and your outstretched arm.[f]"

Tablets Like the First Ones

10 At that time the LORD said to me, "Chisel out two stone tablets[g] like the first ones and come up to me on the mountain. Also make a wooden chest.[b] 2I will write on the tablets the words that were on the first tablets, which you broke. Then you are to put them in the chest."[h]

3So I made the ark out of acacia wood[i] and chiseled[j] out two stone tablets like the first ones, and I went up on the mountain with the two tablets in my hands. 4The LORD wrote on these tablets what he had written before, the Ten Commandments he had proclaimed[k] to you on the mountain, out of the fire, on the day of the assembly. And the LORD gave them to me. 5Then I came back down the mountain[l] and put the tablets in the ark[m] I had made, as the LORD commanded me, and they are there now.[n]

6(The Israelites traveled from the wells of the Jaakanites to Moserah.[o] There Aaron died and was buried, and Eleazar his son succeeded him as priest.[p] 7From there they traveled to Gudgodah and on to Jotbathah, a land with streams of water.[q] 8At that time the LORD set apart the tribe of Levi[r] to carry the ark of the covenant of the LORD, to stand before the LORD to minister[s] and to pronounce blessings[t] in his name, as they still do today. 9That is why the Levites have no share or inheritance among their brothers; the LORD is their inheritance,[u] as the LORD your God told them.)

10Now I had stayed on the mountain forty days and nights, as I did the first time, and the LORD listened to me at

9:10 [k]Ex 31:18; Dt 4:13
9:12 [l]Ex 32:7-8; Dt 31:29 [m]Jdg 2:17
9:13 [n]ver 6; Ex 32:9; Dt 10:16
9:14 [o]Ex 32:10 [p]Nu 14:12; Dt 29:20
9:15 [q]Ex 19:18; 32:15
9:16 [r]Ex 32:19
9:18 [s]Ex 34:28
9:19 [t]Ex 32:10-11, 14 [u]Dt 10:10
9:21 [v]Ex 32:20
9:22 [w]Nu 11:3 [x]Ex 17:7 [y]Nu 11:34
9:23 [z]Ps 106:24
9:24 [a]ver 7; Dt 31:27
9:25 [b]ver 18
9:26 [c]Ex 32:11
9:28 [d]Ex 32:12; Nu 14:16
9:29 [e]Dt 4:20; 1Ki 8:51 [f]Dt 4:34; Ne 1:10
10:1 [g]Ex 25:10; 34:1-2
10:2 [h]Ex 25:16,21; Dt 4:13
10:3 [i]Ex 25:5,10; 37:1-9 [j]Ex 34:4
10:4 [k]Ex 20:1
10:5 [l]Ex 34:29 [m]Ex 40:20 [n]1Ki 8:9
10:6 [o]Nu 33:30-31, 38 [p]Nu 20:25-28
10:7 [q]Nu 33:32-34
10:8 [r]Nu 3:6 [s]Dt 18:5 [t]Dt 21:5
10:9 [u]Nu 18:20; Dt 18:1-2; Eze 44:28

a *15* Or *And I had the two tablets of the covenant with me, one in each hand* **b** *1* That is, an ark

this time also. It was not his will to destroy you.[v] 11“Go,” the LORD said to me, “and lead the people on their way, so that they may enter and possess the land that I swore to their fathers to give them.”

Fear the LORD

12And now, O Israel, what does the LORD your God ask of you[w] but to fear the LORD your God, to walk in all his ways, to love him,[x] to serve the LORD your God with all your heart[y] and with all your soul, 13and to observe the LORD’s commands and decrees that I am giving you today for your own good?

1 →PG. 212
6 →PG. 277
7 →PG. 203

14To the LORD your God belong the heavens, even the highest heavens,[z] the earth and everything in it.[a] 15Yet the LORD set his affection on your forefathers and loved[b] them, and he chose you, their descendants, above all the nations, as it is today. 16Circumcise[c] your hearts, therefore, and do not be stiff-necked[d] any longer. 17For the LORD your God is God of gods[e] and Lord of lords, the great God, mighty and awesome, who shows no partiality[f] and accepts no bribes. 18He defends the cause of the fatherless and the widow,[g] and loves the alien, giving him food and clothing. 19And you are to love those who are aliens, for you yourselves were aliens in Egypt.[h] 20Fear the LORD your God and serve him.[i] Hold fast[j] to him and take your oaths in his name.[k] 21He is your praise;[l] he is your God, who performed for you those great and awesome wonders[m] you saw with your own eyes. 22Your forefathers who went down into Egypt were seventy in all,[n] and now the LORD your God has made you as numerous as the stars in the sky.[o]

Love and Obey the LORD

11 Love[p] the LORD your God and keep his requirements, his decrees, his laws and his commands always.[q] 2Remember today that your children were not the ones who saw and experienced the discipline of the LORD your God:[r] his majesty, his mighty hand, his outstretched arm; 3the signs he performed and the things he did in the heart of Egypt, both to Pharaoh king of Egypt and to his whole country; 4what he did to the Egyptian army, to its horses and chariots, how he overwhelmed them with the waters of the Red Sea[a][s] as they were pursuing you, and how the LORD brought lasting ruin on them. 5It was not your children who saw what he did for you in the desert until you arrived at this place, 6and what he did[t] to Dathan and Abiram, sons of Eliab the Reubenite, when the earth opened its mouth right in the middle of all Israel and swallowed them up with their households, their tents and every living thing that belonged to them. 7But it was your own eyes that saw all these great things the LORD has done.

8Observe therefore all the commands I am giving you today, so that you may have the strength to go in and take over the land that you are crossing the Jordan to possess,[u] 9and so that you may live long[v] in the land that the LORD swore[w] to your forefathers to give to them and their descendants, a land flowing with milk and honey.[x] 10The land you are entering to take over is not like the land of Egypt, from which you have come, where you planted your seed and irrigated it by foot as in a vegetable garden. 11But the land you are crossing the Jordan to take possession of is a land of mountains and valleys that drinks rain from heaven.[y] 12It is a land the LORD your God cares for; the eyes[z] of the LORD your God are continually on it from the beginning of the year to its end.

13So if you faithfully obey[a] the commands I am giving you today—to love[b] the LORD your God and to serve him with all your heart and with all your soul— 14then I will send rain[c] on your land in its season, both autumn and spring rains,[d] so that you may gather in your grain, new wine and oil. 15I will provide grass[e] in the fields for your cattle, and you will eat and be satisfied.[f]

16Be careful, or you will be enticed to turn away and worship other gods and bow down to them.[g] 17Then the LORD’s anger[h] will burn against you, and he will shut[i] the heavens so that it will not rain and the ground will yield no produce, and you will soon perish[j] from the good land the LORD is giving you. 18Fix these words of mine in your hearts and minds; tie them as symbols on your hands and bind them on your foreheads.[k] 19Teach them to your children,[l] talking about them when you sit at home and when you walk along the road, when you lie down and when you get up.[m] 20Write them on the doorframes of your houses and on your gates,[n] 21so that your days and the days of your children may be many[o] in the land that the LORD swore to give your forefathers, as many as the

4 →PG. 220

10:10 [v]Ex 33:17; 34:28; Dt 9:18-19,25
10:12 [w]Mic 6:8 [x]Dt 5:33; 6:13; Mt 22:37 [y]Dt 6:5
10:14 [z]1Ki 8:27 [a]Ex 19:5
10:15 [b]Dt 4:37
10:16 [c]Jer 4:4 [d]Dt 9:6
10:17 [e]Jos 22:22; Da 2:47 [f]Ac 10:34; Ro 2:11; Eph 6:9
10:18 [g]Ps 68:5
10:19 [h]Lev 19:34
10:20 [i]Mt 4:10 [j]Dt 11:22 [k]Ps 63:11
10:21 [l]Ex 15:2; Jer 17:14 [m]Ps 106:21-22
10:22 [n]Ge 46:26-27 [o]Ge 15:5; Dt 1:10
11:1 [p]Dt 10:12 [q]Zec 3:7
11:2 [r]Dt 5:24; 8:5
11:4 [s]Ex 14:27
11:6 [t]Nu 16:1-35
11:8 [u]Jos 1:7
11:9 [v]Dt 4:40; Pr 10:27 [w]Dt 9:5 [x]Ex 3:8
11:11 [y]Dt 8:7
11:12 [z]1Ki 9:3
11:13 [a]Dt 6:17 [b]Dt 10:12
11:14 [c]Lev 26:4; Dt 28:12 [d]Joel 2:23; Jas 5:7
11:15 [e]Ps 104:14 [f]Dt 6:11
11:16 [g]Dt 8:19; 29:18; Job 31:9,27
11:17 [h]Dt 6:15 [i]1Ki 8:35; 2Ch 6:26 [j]Dt 4:26
11:18 [k]Dt 6:6-8
11:19 [l]Dt 6:7 [m]Dt 4:9-10
11:20 [n]Dt 6:9
11:21 [o]Pr 3:2; 4:10

[a]4 Hebrew *Yam Suph*; that is, Sea of Reeds

days that the heavens are above the earth.[p]

22If you carefully observe[q] all these commands I am giving you to follow—to love the LORD your God, to walk in all his ways and to hold fast[r] to him—23then the LORD will drive out all these nations before you, and you will dispossess nations larger and stronger than you.[s] 24Every place where you set your foot will be yours:[t] Your territory will extend from the desert to Lebanon, and from the Euphrates River to the western sea.[a] 25No man will be able to stand against you. The LORD your God, as he promised you, will put the terror and fear of you on the whole land, wherever you go.[u]

26See, I am setting before you today a blessing and a curse[v]— 27the blessing[w] if you obey the commands of the LORD your God that I am giving you today; 28the curse if you disobey[x] the commands of the LORD your God and turn from the way that I command you today by following other gods, which you have not known. 29When the LORD your God has brought you into the land you are entering to possess, you are to proclaim on Mount Gerizim the blessings, and on Mount Ebal the curses.[y] 30As you know, these mountains are across the Jordan, west of the road,[b] toward the setting sun, near the great trees of Moreh,[z] in the territory of those Canaanites living in the Arabah in the vicinity of Gilgal.[a] 31You are about to cross the Jordan to enter and take possession[b] of the land the LORD your God is giving you. When you have taken it over and are living there, 32be sure that you obey all the decrees and laws I am setting before you today.

The One Place of Worship

12 These are the decrees and laws you must be careful to follow in the land that the LORD, the God of your fathers, has given you to possess—as long as you live in the land.[c] 2Destroy completely all the places on the high mountains and on the hills and under every spreading tree[d] where the nations you are dispossessing worship their gods. 3Break down their altars, smash[e] their sacred stones and burn their Asherah poles in the fire; cut down the idols of their gods and wipe out their names from those places.

4You must not worship the LORD your God in their way. 5But you are to seek the place the LORD your God will choose from among all your tribes to put his Name there for his dwelling.[f] To that place you must go; 6there bring your burnt offerings and sacrifices, your tithes[g] and special gifts, what you have vowed to give and your freewill offerings, and the firstborn of your herds and flocks. 7There, in the presence of the LORD your God, you and your families shall eat and shall rejoice[h] in everything you have put your hand to, because the LORD your God has blessed you.

8You are not to do as we do here today, everyone as he sees fit, 9since you have not yet reached the resting place and the inheritance the LORD your God is giving you. 10But you will cross the Jordan and settle in the land the LORD your God is giving[i] you as an inheritance, and he will give you rest from all your enemies around you so that you will live in safety. 11Then to the place the LORD your God will choose as a dwelling for his Name[j]—there you are to bring everything I command you: your burnt offerings and sacrifices, your tithes and special gifts, and all the choice possessions you have vowed to the LORD. 12And there rejoice[k] before the LORD your God, you, your sons and daughters, your menservants and maidservants, and the Levites from your towns, who have no allotment or inheritance[l] of their own. 13Be careful not to sacrifice your burnt offerings anywhere you please. 14Offer them only at the place the LORD will choose[m] in one of your tribes, and there observe everything I command you.

15Nevertheless, you may slaughter your animals in any of your towns and eat as much of the meat as you want, as if it were gazelle or deer,[n] according to the blessing the LORD your God gives

11:21 [p]Ps 72:5
11:22 [q]Dt 6:17 [r]Dt 10:20
11:23 [s]Dt 4:38; 9:1
11:24 [t]Ge 15:18; Ex 23:31; Jos 1:3; 14:9
11:25 [u]Ex 23:27; Dt 7:24
11:26 [v]Dt 30:1,15,19
11:27 [w]Dt 28:1-14
11:28 [x]Dt 28:15
11:29 [y]Dt 27:12-13; Jos 8:33
11:30 [z]Ge 12:6 [a]Jos 4:19
11:31 [b]Dt 9:1; Jos 1:11
12:1 [c]Dt 4:9-10; 1Ki 8:40
12:2 [d]2Ki 16:4; 17:10
12:3 [e]Nu 33:52; Dt 7:5; Jdg 2:2
12:5 [f]ver 11,13; 2Ch 7:12,16
12:6 [g]Dt 14:22-23
12:7 [h]ver 12,18; Lev 23:40; Dt 14:26
12:10 [i]Dt 11:31
12:11 [j]ver 5; Dt 15:20; 16:2
12:12 [k]ver 7 [l]Dt 10:9; 14:29
12:14 [m]ver 11
12:15 [n]ver 20-23; Dt 14:5; 15:22

[a]*24* That is, the Mediterranean [b]*30* Or *Jordan, westward*

12:1–3

PROMISE 1

RULE #1: WORSHIP GOD

All the laws and commandments are based on this one: The key to following God is in worshiping him correctly. The Ten Commandments themselves start with the same emphasis (Exodus 20, Deuteronomy 5).

Life isn't about keeping commandments; it's about loving (Deuteronomy 6:5) and worshiping God (Proverbs 1:7). Don't fall into a trap of reducing your Christian life to following a set of rules; if you do, you'll miss out on having a relationship with the living God.

For the next Promise 1 reading go to page 216.

you. Both the ceremonially unclean and the clean may eat it. 16But you must not eat the blood;[o] pour it out on the ground like water.[p] 17You must not eat in your own towns the tithe of your grain and new wine and oil, or the firstborn of your herds and flocks, or whatever you have vowed to give, or your freewill offerings or special gifts. 18Instead, you are to eat[q] them in the presence of the LORD your God at the place the LORD your God will choose[r]—you, your sons and daughters, your menservants and maidservants, and the Levites from your towns—and you are to rejoice[s] before the LORD your God in everything you put your hand to. 19Be careful not to neglect the Levites[t] as long as you live in your land.

5 →PG. 202

20When the LORD your God has enlarged your territory[u] as he promised[v] you, and you crave meat and say, "I would like some meat," then you may eat as much of it as you want. 21If the place where the LORD your God chooses to put his Name is too far away from you, you may slaughter animals from the herds and flocks the LORD has given you, as I have commanded you, and in your own towns you may eat as much of them as you want. 22Eat them as you would gazelle or deer.[w] Both the ceremonially unclean and the clean may eat. 23But be sure you do not eat the blood,[x] because the blood is the life, and you must not eat the life with the meat. 24You must not eat the blood; pour it out on the ground like water. 25Do not eat it, so that it may go well[y] with you and your children after you, because you will be doing what is right[z] in the eyes of the LORD.

26But take your consecrated things and whatever you have vowed to give,[a] and go to the place the LORD will choose. 27Present your burnt offerings[b] on the altar of the LORD your God, both the meat and the blood. The blood of your sacrifices must be poured beside the altar of the LORD your God, but you may eat the meat. 28Be careful to obey all these regulations I am giving you, so that it may always go well[c] with you and your children after you, because you will be doing what is good and right in the eyes of the LORD your God.

29The LORD your God will cut off[d] before you the nations you are about to invade and dispossess. But when you have driven them out and settled in their land, 30and after they have been destroyed before you, be careful not to be ensnared by inquiring about their gods, saying, "How do these nations serve their gods? We will do the same." 31You must not worship the LORD your God in their way, because in worshiping their gods, they do all kinds of detestable things the LORD hates.[e] They even burn their sons[f] and daughters in the fire as sacrifices to their gods.

32See that you do all I command you; do not add[g] to it or take away from it.

Worshiping Other Gods

13 If a prophet,[h] or one who foretells by dreams, appears among you and announces to you a miraculous sign or wonder, 2and if the sign or wonder of which he has spoken takes place, and he says, "Let us follow other gods"[i] (gods you have not known) "and let us worship them," 3you must not listen to the words of that prophet or dreamer. The LORD your God is testing[j] you to find out whether you love him with all your heart and with all your soul. 4It is the LORD your God you must follow,[k] and him you must revere. Keep his commands and obey him; serve him and hold fast[l] to him. 5That prophet or dreamer must be put to death, because he preached rebellion against the LORD your God, who brought you out of Egypt and redeemed you from the land of slavery; he has tried to turn you from the way the LORD your God commanded you to follow. You must purge the evil[m] from among you.

6If your very own brother, or your son or daughter, or the wife you love, or your closest friend secretly entices[n] you, saying, "Let us go and worship other gods" (gods that neither you nor your fathers have known, 7gods of the peoples around you, whether near or far, from one end of the land to the other), 8do not yield[o] to him or listen to him. Show him no pity. Do not spare him or shield him. 9You must certainly put him to death.[p] Your hand must be the first in putting him to death, and then the hands of all the people. 10Stone him to death, because he tried to turn you away from the LORD your God, who brought you out of Egypt, out of the land of slavery. 11Then all Israel will hear and be afraid,[q] and no one among you will do such an evil thing again.

12If you hear it said about one of the towns the LORD your God is giving you to live in 13that wicked men[r] have arisen among you and have led the people of their town astray, saying, "Let us go and worship other gods" (gods you have not known), 14then you must inquire, probe and investigate it thoroughly. And if it is true and it has

12:16 [o]Ge 9:4; Lev 7:26; 17:10-12 [p]Dt 15:23
12:18 [q]Dt 14:23 [r]ver 5 [s]ver 7,12
12:19 [t]Dt 14:27
12:20 [u]Dt 19:8 [v]Ge 15:18; Dt 11:24
12:22 [w]ver 15
12:23 [x]ver 16; Ge 9:4; Lev 17:11,14
12:25 [y]Dt 4:40; Isa 3:10 [z]Ex 15:26; Dt 13:18; 1Ki 11:38
12:26 [a]ver 17; Nu 5:9-10
12:27 [b]Lev 1:5,9,13
12:28 [c]ver 25; Dt 4:40
12:29 [d]Jos 23:4
12:31 [e]Dt 9:5 [f]Dt 18:10; Jer 32:35
12:32 [g]Dt 4:2; Jos 1:7; Rev 22:18-19
13:1 [h]Mt 24:24; Mk 13:22; 2Th 2:9
13:2 [i]ver 6,13
13:3 [j]Dt 8:2,16
13:4 [k]2Ki 23:3; 2Ch 34:31 [l]Dt 10:20
13:5 [m]Dt 17:7,12; 1Co 5:13
13:6 [n]Dt 17:2-7; 29:18
13:8 [o]Pr 1:10
13:9 [p]Dt 17:5,7
13:11 [q]Dt 19:20
13:13 [r]ver 2,6; 1Jn 2:19

been proved that this detestable thing has been done among you, **15**you must certainly put to the sword all who live in that town. Destroy it completely,[a] both its people and its livestock. **16**Gather all the plunder of the town into the middle of the public square and completely burn the town and all its plunder as a whole burnt offering to the LORD your God.[s] It is to remain a ruin[t] forever, never to be rebuilt. **17**None of those condemned things[a] shall be found in your hands, so that the LORD will turn from his fierce anger;[u] he will show you mercy, have compassion[v] on you, and increase your numbers,[w] as he promised[x] on oath to your forefathers, **18**because you obey the LORD your God, keeping all his commands that I am giving you today and doing what is right[y] in his eyes.

Clean and Unclean Food

14 You are the children[z] of the LORD your God. Do not cut yourselves or shave the front of your heads for the dead, **2**for you are a people holy to the LORD your God.[a] Out of all the peoples on the face of the earth, the LORD has chosen you to be his treasured possession.[b]

3 →PG. 204

3Do not eat any detestable thing.[c] **4**These are the animals you may eat:[d] the ox, the sheep, the goat, **5**the deer, the gazelle, the roe deer, the wild goat, the ibex, the antelope and the mountain sheep.[b] **6**You may eat any animal that has a split hoof divided in two and that chews the cud. **7**However, of those that chew the cud or that have a split hoof completely divided you may not eat the camel, the rabbit or the coney.[c] Although they chew the cud, they do not have a split hoof; they are ceremonially unclean for you. **8**The pig is also unclean; although it has a split hoof, it does not chew the cud. You are not to eat their meat or touch their carcasses.[e]

9Of all the creatures living in the water, you may eat any that has fins and scales. **10**But anything that does not have fins and scales you may not eat; for you it is unclean.

11You may eat any clean bird. **12**But these you may not eat: the eagle, the vulture, the black vulture, **13**the red kite, the black kite, any kind of falcon, **14**any kind of raven, **15**the horned owl, the screech owl, the gull, any kind of hawk, **16**the little owl, the great owl, the white owl, **17**the desert owl, the osprey, the cormorant, **18**the stork, any kind of heron, the hoopoe and the bat.

19All flying insects that swarm are unclean to you; do not eat them. **20**But any winged creature that is clean you may eat.

21Do not eat anything you find already dead.[f] You may give it to an alien living in any of your towns, and he may eat it, or you may sell it to a foreigner. But you are a people holy to the LORD your God.[g]

Do not cook a young goat in its mother's milk.[h]

Tithes

22Be sure to set aside a tenth[i] of all that your fields produce each year. **23**Eat the tithe of your grain, new wine and oil, and the firstborn of your herds and flocks in the presence of the LORD your God at the place he will choose as a dwelling for his Name,[j] so that you may learn[k] to revere the LORD your God always. **24**But if that place is too distant and you have been blessed by the LORD your God and cannot carry your tithe (because the place where the LORD will choose to put his Name is so far away), **25**then exchange your tithe for silver, and take the silver with you and go to the place the LORD your God will choose. **26**Use the silver to buy whatever you like: cattle, sheep, wine or other fermented drink, or anything you wish. Then you and your household shall eat there in the presence of the LORD your God and rejoice.[l] **27**And do not neglect the Levites[m] living in your towns, for they have no allotment or inheritance of their own.[n]

5 →PG. 387

28At the end of every three years, bring all the tithes of that year's produce and store it in your towns,[o] **29**so that the Levites (who have no allotment[p] or inheritance of their own) and the aliens,[q] the fatherless and the widows who live in your towns may come and eat and be satisfied, and so that the LORD your God may bless[r] you in all the work of your hands.

The Year for Canceling Debts

15 At the end of every seven years you must cancel debts.[s] **2**This is how it is to be done: Every creditor shall cancel the loan he has made to his fellow Israelite. He shall not require payment from his fellow Israelite or brother, because the LORD's time for canceling debts has been proclaimed. **3**You may require payment from a foreigner,[t]

13:16 [s]Jos 6:24 [t]Jos 8:28; Jer 49:2
13:17 [u]Nu 25:4 [v]Dt 30:3 [w]Dt 7:13 [x]Ge 22:17; 26:4,24; 28:14
13:18 [y]Dt 12:25,28
14:1 [z]Lev 19:28; 21:5; Jer 16:6; 41:5; Ro 8:14; 9:8; Gal 3:26
14:2 [a]Lev 20:26 [b]Dt 7:6; 26:18-19
14:3 [c]Eze 4:14
14:4 [d]Lev 11:2-45; Ac 10:14
14:8 [e]Lev 11:26-27
14:21 [f]Lev 17:15; 22:8 [g]ver 2 [h]Ex 23:19; 34:26
14:22 [i]Lev 27:30; Dt 12:6,17; Ne 10:37
14:23 [j]Dt 12:5 [k]Dt 4:10
14:26 [l]Dt 12:7-8
14:27 [m]Dt 12:19 [n]Nu 18:20
14:28 [o]Dt 26:12
14:29 [p]ver 27 [q]Dt 26:12 [r]Dt 15:10; Mal 3:10
15:1 [s]Dt 31:10
15:3 [t]Dt 23:20

[a] *15,17* The Hebrew term refers to the irrevocable giving over of things or persons to the LORD, often by totally destroying them.
[b] *5* The precise identification of some of the birds and animals in this chapter is uncertain.
[c] *7* That is, the hyrax or rock badger

but you must cancel any debt your brother owes you. 4However, there should be no poor among you, for in the land the LORD your God is giving you to possess as your inheritance, he will richly bless[u] you, 5if only you fully obey the LORD your God and are careful to follow[v] all these commands I am giving you today. 6For the LORD your God will bless you as he has promised, and you will lend to many nations but will borrow from none. You will rule over many nations but none will rule over you.[w]

2 →PG. 208

7If there is a poor man among your brothers in any of the towns of the land that the LORD your God is giving you, do not be hardhearted or tightfisted[x] toward your poor brother. 8Rather be openhanded[y] and freely lend him whatever he needs. 9Be careful not to harbor this wicked thought: "The seventh year, the year for canceling debts,[z] is near," so that you do not show ill will[a] toward your needy brother and give him nothing. He may then appeal to the LORD against you, and you will be found guilty of sin.[b] 10Give generously to him and do so without a grudging heart;[c] then because of this the LORD your God will bless[d] you in all your work and in everything you put your hand to. 11There will always be poor people in the land. Therefore I command you to be openhanded toward your brothers and toward the poor and needy in your land.[e]

7 →PG. 210

Freeing Servants

12If a fellow Hebrew, a man or a woman, sells himself to you and serves you six years, in the seventh year you must let him go free.[f] 13And when you release him, do not send him away empty-handed. 14Supply him liberally from your flock, your threshing floor and your winepress. Give to him as the LORD your God has blessed you. 15Remember that you were slaves[g] in Egypt and the LORD your God redeemed you.[h] That is why I give you this command today.

16But if your servant says to you, "I do not want to leave you," because he loves you and your family and is well off with you, 17then take an awl and push it through his ear lobe into the door, and he will become your servant for life. Do the same for your maidservant.

18Do not consider it a hardship to set your servant free, because his service to you these six years has been worth twice as much as that of a hired hand.

15:4 [u]Dt 28:8
15:5 [v]Dt 28:1
15:6 [w]Dt 28:12-13, 44
15:7 [x]1Jn 3:17
15:8 [y]Mt 5:42; Lk 6:34
15:9 [z]ver 1 [a]Mt 20:15 [b]Dt 24:15
15:10 [c]2Co 9:5 [d]Dt 14:29; 24:19
15:11 [e]Mt 26:11; Mk 14:7; Jn 12:8
15:12 [f]Ex 21:2; Lev 25:39; Jer 34:14
15:15 [g]Dt 5:15 [h]Dt 16:12
15:19 [i]Ex 13:2
15:20 [j]Dt 12:5-7,17, 18; 14:23
15:21 [k]Lev 22:19-25
15:22 [l]Dt 12:15,22
15:23 [m]Dt 12:16
16:1 [n]Ex 12:2; 13:4
16:2 [o]Dt 12:5,26
16:3 [p]Ex 12:8,39; 34:18 [q]Ex 12:11,15, 19 [r]Ex 13:3,6-7
16:4 [s]Ex 12:10; 34:25
16:6 [t]Ex 12:6; Dt 12:5
16:7 [u]Ex 12:8; 2Ch 35:13
16:8 [v]Ex 12:16; 13:6; Lev 23:8
16:9 [w]Ex 34:22; Lev 23:15 [x]Ex 23:16; Nu 28:26

And the LORD your God will bless you in everything you do.

The Firstborn Animals

19Set apart for the LORD your God every firstborn male[i] of your herds and flocks. Do not put the firstborn of your oxen to work, and do not shear the firstborn of your sheep. 20Each year you and your family are to eat them in the presence of the LORD your God at the place he will choose.[j] 21If an animal has a defect, is lame or blind, or has any serious flaw, you must not sacrifice it to the LORD your God.[k] 22You are to eat it in your own towns. Both the ceremonially unclean and the clean may eat it, as if it were gazelle or deer.[l] 23But you must not eat the blood; pour it out on the ground like water.[m]

Passover

16 Observe the month of Abib[n] and celebrate the Passover of the LORD your God, because in the month of Abib he brought you out of Egypt by night. 2Sacrifice as the Passover to the LORD your God an animal from your flock or herd at the place the LORD will choose as a dwelling for his Name.[o] 3Do not eat it with bread made with yeast, but for seven days eat unleavened bread, the bread of affliction,[p] because you left Egypt in haste[q]—so that all the days of your life you may remember the time of your departure from Egypt.[r] 4Let no yeast be found in your possession in all your land for seven days. Do not let any of the meat you sacrifice on the evening of the first day remain until morning.[s]

5You must not sacrifice the Passover in any town the LORD your God gives you 6except in the place he will choose as a dwelling for his Name. There you must sacrifice the Passover in the evening, when the sun goes down, on the anniversary[a][t] of your departure from Egypt. 7Roast[u] it and eat it at the place the LORD your God will choose. Then in the morning return to your tents. 8For six days eat unleavened bread and on the seventh day hold an assembly[v] to the LORD your God and do no work.

Feast of Weeks

9Count off seven weeks[w] from the time you begin to put the sickle to the standing grain.[x] 10Then celebrate the Feast of Weeks to the LORD your God by giving a freewill offering in proportion to the blessings the LORD your God has

[a]6 Or *down, at the time of day*

given you. 11 And rejoice[y] before the LORD your God at the place he will choose as a dwelling for his Name—you, your sons and daughters, your menservants and maidservants, the Levites[z] in your towns, and the aliens, the fatherless and the widows living among you. 12 Remember that you were slaves in Egypt,[a] and follow carefully these decrees.

Feast of Tabernacles

13 Celebrate the Feast of Tabernacles for seven days after you have gathered the produce of your threshing floor[b] and your winepress.[c] 14 Be joyful[d] at your Feast—you, your sons and daughters, your menservants and maidservants, and the Levites, the aliens, the fatherless and the widows who live in your towns. 15 For seven days celebrate the Feast to the LORD your God at the place the LORD will choose. For the LORD your God will bless you in all your harvest and in all the work of your hands, and your joy[e] will be complete.

16 Three times a year all your men must appear before the LORD your God at the place he will choose: at the Feast of Unleavened Bread, the Feast of Weeks and the Feast of Tabernacles.[f] No man should appear before the LORD empty-handed:[g] 17 Each of you must bring a gift in proportion to the way the LORD your God has blessed you.

Judges

18 Appoint judges[h] and officials for each of your tribes in every town the LORD your God is giving you, and they shall judge the people fairly. 19 Do not pervert justice[i] or show partiality.[j] Do not accept a bribe,[k] for a bribe blinds the eyes of the wise and twists the words of the righteous. 20 Follow justice and justice alone, so that you may live and possess the land the LORD your God is giving you.

3 →PG. 211

Worshiping Other Gods

21 Do not set up any wooden Asherah pole[a][l] beside the altar you build to the LORD your God,[m] 22 and do not erect a sacred stone,[n] for these the LORD your God hates.

17 Do not sacrifice to the LORD your God an ox or a sheep that has any defect[o] or flaw in it, for that would be detestable to him.[p]

2 If a man or woman living among you in one of the towns the LORD gives you is found doing evil in the eyes of the LORD your God in violation of his covenant,[q] 3 and contrary to my command[r] has worshiped other gods, bowing down to them or to the sun[s] or the moon or the stars of the sky, 4 and this has been brought to your attention, then you must investigate it thoroughly. If it is true and it has been proved that this detestable thing has been done in Israel,[t] 5 take the man or woman who has done this evil deed to your city gate and stone that person to death.[u] 6 On the testimony of two or three witnesses a man shall be put to death, but no one shall be put to death on the testimony of only one witness.[v] 7 The hands of the witnesses must be the first in putting him to death, and then the hands of all the people. You must purge the evil[w] from among you.

Law Courts

8 If cases come before your courts that are too difficult for you to judge—whether bloodshed, lawsuits or assaults[x]—take them to the place the LORD your God will choose.[y] 9 Go to the priests, who are Levites, and to the judge who is in office at that time. Inquire of them and they will give you the verdict.[z] 10 You must act according to the decisions they give you at the place the LORD will choose. Be careful to do everything they direct you to do. 11 Act according to the law they teach you and the decisions they give you. Do not turn aside from what they tell you, to the right or to the left.[a] 12 The man who shows contempt[b] for the judge or for the priest who stands ministering there to the LORD your God must be put to death. You must purge the evil from Israel. 13 All the people will hear and be afraid, and will not be contemptuous again.[c]

[a]21 Or *Do not plant any tree dedicated to Asherah*

16:11 [y]Dt 12:7 [z]Dt 12:12
16:12 [a]Dt 15:15
16:13 [b]Lev 23:34 [c]Ex 23:16
16:14 [d]ver 11
16:15 [e]Lev 23:39
16:16 [f]Ex 23:14,16 [g]Ex 34:20
16:18 [h]Dt 1:16
16:19 [i]Ex 23:2,8 [j]Lev 19:15; Dt 1:17 [k]Ecc 7:7
16:21 [l]Dt 7:5 [m]Ex 34:13; 2Ki 17:16; 21:3; 2Ch 33:3
16:22 [n]Lev 26:1
17:1 [o]Mal 1:8,13 [p]Dt 15:21
17:2 [q]Dt 13:6-11
17:3 [r]Jer 7:22-23 [s]Job 31:26
17:4 [t]Dt 13:12-14
17:5 [u]Lev 24:14
17:6 [v]Nu 35:30; Dt 19:15; Jos 7:25; Mt 18:16; Jn 8:17; 2Co 13:1; 1Ti 5:19; Heb 10:28
17:7 [w]Dt 13:5,9
17:8 [x]2Ch 19:10 [y]Dt 12:5; Hag 2:11
17:9 [z]Dt 19:17; Eze 44:24
17:11 [a]Dt 25:1
17:12 [b]Nu 15:30
17:13 [c]Dt 13:11; 19:20

16:16–17

PROMISE 5

PROPORTIONAL GIVING

Notice the basis of giving as outlined in this verse. God didn't ask for a percentage of the people's wealth when they came to worship him, but for a proportion. He asked them to consider what the Lord had done for them and give out of gratitude for those gifts.

Consider the generosity of God's grace in your own life. Consider the sacrifice that he gave you in Jesus, his only Son. Then offer him your gifts in proportion.

For the next Promise 5 reading go to page 238.

The King

14When you enter the land the LORD your God is giving you and have taken possession of it and settled in it, and you say, "Let us set a king over us like all the nations around us,"[d] **15**be sure to appoint over you the king the LORD your God chooses. He must be from among your own brothers.[e] Do not place a foreigner over you, one who is not a brother Israelite. **16**The king, moreover, must not acquire great numbers of horses for himself[f] or make the people return to Egypt[g] to get more of them,[h] for the LORD has told you, "You are not to go back that way again."[i] **17**He must not take many wives,[j] or his heart will be led astray. He must not accumulate large amounts of silver and gold.

18When he takes the throne of his kingdom, he is to write[k] for himself on a scroll a copy of this law, taken from that of the priests, who are Levites. **19**It is to be with him, and he is to read it all the days of his life[l] so that he may learn to revere the LORD his God and follow carefully all the words of this law and these decrees **20**and not consider himself better than his brothers and turn from the law[m] to the right or to the left.[n] Then he and his descendants will reign a long time over his kingdom in Israel.

Offerings for Priests and Levites

18 The priests, who are Levites—indeed the whole tribe of Levi—are to have no allotment or inheritance with Israel. They shall live on the offerings made to the LORD by fire, for that is their inheritance.[o] **2**They shall have no inheritance among their brothers; the LORD is their inheritance, as he promised them.

3This is the share due the priests from the people who sacrifice a bull or a sheep: the shoulder, the jowls and the inner parts.[p] **4**You are to give them the firstfruits of your grain, new wine and oil, and the first wool from the shearing of your sheep,[q] **5**for the LORD your God has chosen them[r] and their descendants out of all your tribes to stand and minister[s] in the LORD's name always.

6If a Levite moves from one of your towns anywhere in Israel where he is living, and comes in all earnestness to the place the LORD will choose,[t] **7**he may minister in the name of the LORD his God like all his fellow Levites who serve there in the presence of the LORD. **8**He is to share equally in their benefits, even though he has received money from the sale of family possessions.[u]

Detestable Practices

9When you enter the land the LORD your God is giving you, do not learn to imitate[v] the detestable ways of the nations there. **10**Let no one be found among you who sacrifices his son or daughter in[a] the fire, who practices divination[w] or sorcery, interprets omens, engages in witchcraft,[x] **11**or casts spells, or who is a medium or spiritist or who consults the dead. **12**Anyone who does these things is detestable to the LORD, and because of these detestable practices the LORD your God will drive out those nations before you.[y] **13**You must be blameless before the LORD your God.

The Prophet

14The nations you will dispossess listen to those who practice sorcery or divination. But as for you, the LORD your God has not permitted you to do so. **15**The LORD your God will raise up for you a prophet like me from among your own brothers.[z] You must listen to him. **16**For this is what you asked of the LORD your God at Horeb on the day of the assembly when you said, "Let us not hear the voice of the LORD our God nor see this great fire anymore, or we will die."[a]

17The LORD said to me: "What they say is good. **18**I will raise up for them

[a] 10 Or *who makes his son or daughter pass through*

17:14 [d]Dt 11:31; 1Sa 8:5,19-20
17:15 [e]Jer 30:21
17:16 [f]1Ki 4:26; 10:26 [g]Isa 31:1; Hos 11:5 [h]1Ki 10:28; Eze 17:15 [i]Ex 13:17
17:17 [j]1Ki 11:3
17:18 [k]Dt 31:22,24
17:19 [l]Jos 1:8
17:20 [m]1Ki 15:5 [n]Dt 5:32
18:1 [o]Dt 10:9; 1Co 9:13
18:3 [p]Lev 7:28-34
18:4 [q]Ex 22:29; Nu 18:12
18:5 [r]Ex 28:1 [s]Dt 10:8
18:6 [t]Nu 35:2-3
18:8 [u]2Ch 31:4; Ne 12:44,47
18:9 [v]Dt 12:29-31
18:10 [w]Dt 12:31 [x]Lev 19:31
18:12 [y]Lev 18:24; Dt 9:4
18:15 [z]Jn 1:21; Ac 3:22*; 7:37*
18:16 [a]Ex 20:19; Dt 5:23-27

18:10–13

PROMISE 3

HARMLESS PRACTICES?

Israel must have thought it was harmless to indulge in the practices mentioned in this passage. And we have our own forms of these today. After all, what's wrong with having a little fun with a horoscope? What's the big deal about using a Ouija board or visiting a medium? If you don't believe in these things, it's just a little harmless fun, isn't it?

God didn't think so, and neither should we as his people. The Bible takes these activities seriously. In consulting these other sources for information, guidance or revelation, the ancient Israelites—and we today—trust in something other than God to direct our lives. One who is blameless before God does not play around with things that are tied to God's sworn enemy.

For the next Promise 3 reading go to page 230.

a prophet like you from among their brothers; I will put my words[b] in his mouth, and he will tell them everything I command him.[c] 19If anyone does not listen to my words that the prophet speaks in my name, I myself will call him to account.[d] 20But a prophet who presumes to speak in my name anything I have not commanded him to say, or a prophet who speaks in the name of other gods,[e] must be put to death."[f]

21You may say to yourselves, "How can we know when a message has not been spoken by the LORD?" 22If what a prophet proclaims in the name of the LORD does not take place or come true, that is a message the LORD has not spoken.[g] That prophet has spoken presumptuously.[h] Do not be afraid of him.

Cities of Refuge

19 When the LORD your God has destroyed the nations whose land he is giving you, and when you have driven them out and settled in their towns and houses,[i] 2then set aside for yourselves three cities centrally located in the land the LORD your God is giving you to possess. 3Build roads to them and divide into three parts the land the LORD your God is giving you as an inheritance, so that anyone who kills a man may flee there.

4This is the rule concerning the man who kills another and flees there to save his life—one who kills his neighbor unintentionally, without malice aforethought. 5For instance, a man may go into the forest with his neighbor to cut wood, and as he swings his ax to fell a tree, the head may fly off and hit his neighbor and kill him. That man may flee to one of these cities and save his life. 6Otherwise, the avenger of blood[j] might pursue him in a rage, overtake him if the distance is too great, and kill him even though he is not deserving of death, since he did it to his neighbor without malice aforethought. 7This is why I command you to set aside for yourselves three cities.

8If the LORD your God enlarges your territory, as he promised on oath to your forefathers, and gives you the whole land he promised them, 9because you carefully follow all these laws I command you today—to love the LORD your God and to walk always in his ways[k]—then you are to set aside three more cities. 10Do this so that innocent blood will not be shed in your land, which the LORD your God is giving you as your inheritance, and so that you will not be guilty of bloodshed.[l]

11But if a man hates his neighbor and lies in wait for him, assaults and kills him,[m] and then flees to one of these cities, 12the elders of his town shall send for him, bring him back from the city, and hand him over to the avenger of blood to die. 13Show him no pity.[n] You must purge from Israel the guilt of shedding innocent blood,[o] so that it may go well with you.

14Do not move your neighbor's boundary stone set up by your predecessors in the inheritance you receive in the land the LORD your God is giving you to possess.[p]

Witnesses

15One witness is not enough to convict a man accused of any crime or offense he may have committed. A matter must be established by the testimony of two or three witnesses.[q]

16If a malicious witness[r] takes the stand to accuse a man of a crime, 17the two men involved in the dispute must stand in the presence of the LORD before the priests and the judges[s] who are in office at the time. 18The judges must make a thorough investigation, and if the witness proves to be a liar, giving false testimony against his brother, 19then do to him as he intended to do to his brother.[t] You must purge the evil from among you. 20The rest of the people will hear of this and be afraid,[u] and never again will such an evil thing be done among you. 21Show no pity:[v] life for life, eye for eye, tooth for tooth, hand for hand, foot for foot.[w]

Going to War

20 When you go to war against your enemies and see horses and chariots and an army greater than yours,[x] do not be afraid[y] of them,[z] because the LORD your God, who brought you up out of Egypt, will be with you. 2When you are about to go into battle, the priest shall come forward and address the army. 3He shall say: "Hear, O Israel, today you are going into battle against your enemies. Do not be fainthearted[a] or afraid; do not be terrified or give way to panic before them. 4For the LORD your God is the one who goes with you to fight[b] for you against your enemies to give you victory."

5The officers shall say to the army: "Has anyone built a new house and not dedicated[c] it? Let him go home, or he may die in battle and someone else may dedicate it. 6Has anyone planted a

18:18 [b]Isa 51:16; Jn 17:8 [c]Jn 4:25-26; 8:28; 12:49-50
18:19 [d]Ac 3:23*
18:20 [e]Jer 14:14 [f]Dt 13:1-5
18:22 [g]Jer 28:9 [h]ver 20
19:1 [i]Dt 12:29
19:6 [j]Nu 35:12
19:9 [k]Jos 20:7-8
19:10 [l]Nu 35:33; Dt 21:1-9
19:11 [m]Nu 35:16
19:13 [n]Dt 7:2 [o]1Ki 2:31
19:14 [p]Dt 27:17; Pr 22:28; Hos 5:10
19:15 [q]Nu 35:30; Dt 17:6; Mt 18:16*; Jn 8:17; 2Co 13:1*; 1Ti 5:19; Heb 10:28
19:16 [r]Ex 23:1; Ps 27:12
19:17 [s]Dt 17:9
19:19 [t]Pr 19:5,9
19:20 [u]Dt 17:13; 21:21
19:21 [v]ver 13 [w]Ex 21:24; Lev 24:20; Mt 5:38*
20:1 [x]Ps 20:7; Isa 31:1 [y]Dt 31:6,8 [z]2Ch 32:7-8
20:3 [a]Jos 23:10
20:4 [b]Dt 1:30; 3:22; Jos 23:10
20:5 [c]Ne 12:27

vineyard and not begun to enjoy it? Let
him go home, or he may die in battle
and someone else enjoy it. [7]Has anyone become pledged to a woman and
not married her? Let him go home, or
he may die in battle and someone else
marry her.[d]" [8]Then the officers shall
add, "Is any man afraid or fainthearted? Let him go home so that his brothers will not become disheartened
too."[e] [9]When the officers have finished speaking to the army, they shall
appoint commanders over it.

[10]When you march up to attack a
city, make its people an offer of
peace.[f] [11]If they accept and open
their gates, all the people in it shall be
subject to forced labor[g] and shall
work for you. [12]If they refuse to make
peace and they engage you in battle,
lay siege to that city. [13]When the LORD
your God delivers it into your hand, put
to the sword all the men in it.[h] [14]As
for the women, the children, the livestock[i] and everything else in the city,
you may take these as plunder for
yourselves. And you may use the plunder the LORD your God gives you from
your enemies. [15]This is how you are to
treat all the cities that are at a distance
from you and do not belong to the nations nearby.

[16]However, in the cities of the nations the LORD your God is giving you
as an inheritance, do not leave alive
anything that breathes.[j] [17]Completely
destroy[a] them—the Hittites, Amorites, Canaanites, Perizzites, Hivites
and Jebusites—as the LORD your God
has commanded you. [18]Otherwise,
they will teach you to follow all the detestable things they do in worshiping
their gods,[k] and you will sin[l] against
the LORD your God.

[19]When you lay siege to a city for a
long time, fighting against it to capture
it, do not destroy its trees by putting an
ax to them, because you can eat their
fruit. Do not cut them down. Are the
trees of the field people, that you
should besiege them?[b] [20]However,
you may cut down trees that you know
are not fruit trees and use them to
build siege works until the city at war
with you falls.

Atonement for an Unsolved Murder

21 If a man is found slain, lying in a
field in the land the LORD your God
is giving you to possess, and it is not
known who killed him, [2]your elders
and judges shall go out and measure
the distance from the body to the
neighboring towns. [3]Then the elders of
the town nearest the body shall take a
heifer that has never been worked and
has never worn a yoke [4]and lead her
down to a valley that has not been
plowed or planted and where there is a
flowing stream. There in the valley they
are to break the heifer's neck. [5]The
priests, the sons of Levi, shall step forward, for the LORD your God has chosen them to minister and to pronounce
blessings[m] in the name of the LORD
and to decide all cases of dispute and
assault.[n] [6]Then all the elders of the
town nearest the body shall wash their
hands[o] over the heifer whose neck
was broken in the valley, [7]and they
shall declare: "Our hands did not shed
this blood, nor did our eyes see it done.
[8]Accept this atonement for your people
Israel, whom you have redeemed,
O LORD, and do not hold your people
guilty of the blood of an innocent
man." And the bloodshed will be
atoned for.[p] [9]So you will purge[q] from
yourselves the guilt of shedding innocent blood, since you have done what
is right in the eyes of the LORD.

Marrying a Captive Woman

[10]When you go to war against your
enemies and the LORD your God delivers them into your hands[r] and you
take captives, [11]if you notice among
the captives a beautiful woman and are
attracted to her, you may take her as
your wife. [12]Bring her into your home
and have her shave her head,[s] trim
her nails [13]and put aside the clothes
she was wearing when captured. After
she has lived in your house and
mourned her father and mother for a
full month,[t] then you may go to her
and be her husband and she shall be
your wife. [14]If you are not pleased with
her, let her go wherever she wishes.
You must not sell her or treat her as
a slave, since you have dishonored
her.[u]

The Right of the Firstborn

[15]If a man has two wives, and he
loves one but not the other, and both
bear him sons but the firstborn is the
son of the wife he does not love,[v]
[16]when he wills his property to his
sons, he must not give the rights of the
firstborn to the son of the wife he loves
in preference to his actual firstborn,
the son of the wife he does not love.[w]
[17]He must acknowledge the son of his
unloved wife as the firstborn by giving

20:7 [d]Dt 24:5
20:8 [e]Jdg 7:3
20:10 [f]Lk 14:31-32
20:11 [g]1Ki 9:21
20:13 [h]Nu 31:7
20:14 [i]Jos 8:2; 22:8
20:16 [j]Ex 23:31-33; Nu 21:2-3; Dt 7:2; Jos 11:14
20:18 [k]Ex 34:16; Dt 7:4; 12:30-31 [l]Ex 23:33
21:5 [m]1Ch 23:13 [n]Dt 17:8-11
21:6 [o]Mt 27:24
21:8 [p]Nu 35:33-34
21:9 [q]Dt 19:13
21:10 [r]Jos 21:44
21:12 [s]Lev 14:9; Nu 6:9
21:13 [t]Ps 45:10
21:14 [u]Ge 34:2
21:15 [v]Ge 29:33
21:16 [w]1Ch 26:10

a *17* The Hebrew term refers to the irrevocable giving over of things or persons to the LORD, often by totally destroying them. b *19* Or *down to use in the siege, for the fruit trees are for the benefit of man.*

him a double share of all he has. That son is the first sign of his father's strength.[x] The right of the firstborn belongs to him.[y]

A Rebellious Son

18If a man has a stubborn and rebellious son who does not obey his father and mother[z] and will not listen to them when they discipline him, 19his father and mother shall take hold of him and bring him to the elders at the gate of his town. 20They shall say to the elders, "This son of ours is stubborn and rebellious. He will not obey us. He is a profligate and a drunkard." 21Then all the men of his town shall stone him to death. You must purge the evil[a] from among you. All Israel will hear of it and be afraid.[b]

Various Laws

22If a man guilty of a capital offense[c] is put to death and his body is hung on a tree, 23you must not leave his body on the tree overnight.[d] Be sure to bury him that same day, because anyone who is hung on a tree is under God's curse.[e] You must not desecrate[f] the land the LORD your God is giving you as an inheritance.

2 →PG. 225

22 If you see your brother's ox or sheep straying, do not ignore it but be sure to take it back to him.[g] 2If the brother does not live near you or if you do not know who he is, take it home with you and keep it until he comes looking for it. Then give it back to him. 3Do the same if you find your brother's donkey or his cloak or anything he loses. Do not ignore it.

4If you see your brother's donkey[h] or his ox fallen on the road, do not ignore it. Help him get it to its feet.

5A woman must not wear men's clothing, nor a man wear women's clothing, for the LORD your God detests anyone who does this.

6If you come across a bird's nest beside the road, either in a tree or on the ground, and the mother is sitting on the young or on the eggs, do not take the mother with the young.[i] 7You may take the young, but be sure to let the mother go, so that it may go well with you and you may have a long life.[j]

8When you build a new house, make a parapet around your roof so that you may not bring the guilt of bloodshed on your house if someone falls from the roof.

9Do not plant two kinds of seed in your vineyard;[k] if you do, not only the crops you plant but also the fruit of the vineyard will be defiled.[a]

10Do not plow with an ox and a donkey yoked together.[l]

11Do not wear clothes of wool and linen woven together.[m]

12Make tassels on the four corners of the cloak you wear.[n]

Marriage Violations

13If a man takes a wife and, after lying with her[o], dislikes her 14and slanders her and gives her a bad name, saying, "I married this woman, but when I approached her, I did not find proof of her virginity," 15then the girl's father and mother shall bring proof that she was a virgin to the town elders at the gate. 16The girl's father will say to the elders, "I gave my daughter in marriage to this man, but he dislikes her. 17Now he has slandered her and said, 'I did not find your daughter to be a virgin.' But here is the proof of my daughter's virginity." Then her parents shall display the cloth before the elders of the town, 18and the elders[p] shall take the man and punish him. 19They shall fine him a hundred shekels of silver[b] and give them to the girl's father, because this man has given an Israelite virgin a bad name. She shall continue to be his wife; he must not divorce her as long as he lives.

20If, however, the charge is true and no proof of the girl's virginity can be found, 21she shall be brought to the door of her father's house and there the men of her town shall stone her to death. She has done a disgraceful thing[q] in Israel by being promiscuous while still in her father's house. You must purge the evil from among you.

22If a man is found sleeping with another man's wife, both the man who

---

22:1–4

PROMISE 7

A TRUE NEIGHBOR

Man, could our generation ever use a dose of this old-fashioned neighborliness! Jesus repeated this theme in the parable of the good Samaritan (Luke 10:25–37). True, we need to exercise caution in our modern society. But we need to be careful not to be so cautious as to avoid or ignore people in real need. Read the spirit of this law, and whenever the opportunity to be of service to another person presents itself, ask "What would God have me do here?"

For the next Promise 7 reading go to page 233.

21:17 [x]Ge 49:3 [y]Ge 25:31 **21:18** [z]Pr 1:8; Isa 30:1; Eph 6:1-3 **21:21** [a]Dt 19:19; 1Co 5:13* [b]Dt 13:11 **21:22** [c]Dt 22:26; Mk 14:64; Ac 23:29 **21:23** [d]Jos 8:29; 10:27; Jn 19:31 [e]Gal 3:13* [f]Lev 18:25; Nu 35:34 **22:1** [g]Ex 23:4-5 **22:4** [h]Ex 23:5 **22:6** [i]Lev 22:28 **22:7** [j]Dt 4:40 **22:9** [k]Lev 19:19 **22:10** [l]2Co 6:14 **22:11** [m]Lev 19:19 **22:12** [n]Nu 15:37-41; Mt 23:5 **22:13** [o]Dt 24:1 **22:18** [p]Ex 18:21 **22:21** [q]Ge 34:7; Dt 13:5; 23:17-18; Jdg 20:6; 2Sa 13:12

[a]9 Or *be forfeited to the sanctuary* [b]19 That is, about 2 1/2 pounds (about 1 kilogram)

slept with her and the woman must
die.[r] You must purge the evil from Israel.
23If a man happens to meet in a
town a virgin pledged to be married
and he sleeps with her, 24you shall take
both of them to the gate of that town
and stone them to death—the girl because she was in a town and did not
scream for help, and the man because
he violated another man's wife. You
must purge the evil from among you.[s]
25But if out in the country a man
happens to meet a girl pledged to be
married and rapes her, only the man
who has done this shall die. 26Do nothing to the girl; she has committed no
sin deserving death. This case is like
that of someone who attacks and murders his neighbor, 27for the man found
the girl out in the country, and though
the betrothed girl screamed, there was
no one to rescue her.
28If a man happens to meet a virgin
who is not pledged to be married and
rapes her and they are discovered,[t]
29he shall pay the girl's father fifty
shekels of silver.[a] He must marry the
girl, for he has violated her. He can
never divorce her as long as he lives.
30A man is not to marry his father's
wife; he must not dishonor his father's
bed.[u]

Exclusion From the Assembly

23 No one who has been emasculated
by crushing or cutting may enter
the assembly of the LORD.
2No one born of a forbidden marriage[b] nor any of his descendants may
enter the assembly of the LORD, even
down to the tenth generation.
3No Ammonite or Moabite or any of
his descendants may enter the assembly of the LORD, even down to the tenth
generation.[v] 4For they did not come
to meet you with bread and water on
your way when you came out of Egypt,
and they hired Balaam[w] son of Beor
from Pethor in Aram Naharaim[c] to
pronounce a curse on you. 5However,
the LORD your God would not listen to
Balaam but turned the curse[x] into a
blessing for you, because the LORD your
God loves you. 6Do not seek a treaty of
friendship with them as long as you
live.[y]
7Do not abhor an Edomite, for he is
your brother.[z] Do not abhor an Egyptian, because you lived as an alien in
his country.[a] 8The third generation of
children born to them may enter the
assembly of the LORD.

Uncleanness in the Camp

9When you are encamped against
your enemies, keep away from everything impure. 10If one of your men is
unclean because of a nocturnal emission, he is to go outside the camp and
stay there.[b] 11But as evening approaches he is to wash himself, and at
sunset he may return to the camp.
12Designate a place outside the
camp where you can go to relieve yourself. 13As part of your equipment have
something to dig with, and when you
relieve yourself, dig a hole and cover
up your excrement. 14For the LORD
your God moves[c] about in your camp
to protect you and to deliver your enemies to you. Your camp must be
holy,[d] so that he will not see among
you anything indecent and turn away
from you.

Miscellaneous Laws

15If a slave has taken refuge with
you, do not hand him over to his master.[e] 16Let him live among you wherever he likes and in whatever town he
chooses. Do not oppress[f] him.
17No Israelite man[g] or woman is to
become a shrine prostitute.[h] 18You
must not bring the earnings of a female
prostitute or of a male prostitute[d] into
the house of the LORD your God to pay
any vow, because the LORD your God
detests them both.
19Do not charge your brother inter-

23:1–7

PROMISE 6

GOD'S STANDARD OF ACCEPTANCE

This is a hard passage. Some people were to be included in and some excluded from Israel's assembly. Notice that no one was excluded by race or nationality; rather, individuals were excluded based on behavior. God doesn't include or exclude anyone from fellowship because of *anything* except disobedience. Observe, in fact, that although the Moabites are excluded (v. 3), the Book of Ruth (p. 282) tells the story of a Moabitess who was accepted into the community, married a prominent Israelite citizen and is listed in Jesus' genealogy (see Matthew 1:5).

God does not accept or reject individuals because of their ethnic heritage. He accepts individuals on one basis—their acceptance or rejection of his beloved Son, Jesus Christ (Ephesians 2:8–10).

For the next Promise 6 reading go to page 256.

22:22 [r]Lev 20:10; Jn 8:5
22:24 [s]ver 21-22; 1Co 5:13*
22:28 [t]Ex 22:16
22:30 [u]Lev 18:8; 20:11; 18:8; Dt 27:20; 1Co 5:1
23:3 [v]Ne 13:2
23:4 [w]Nu 22:5-6; 23:7; 2Pe 2:15
23:5 [x]Pr 26:2
23:6 [y]Ezr 9:12
23:7 [z]Ge 25:26; Ob 1:10,12 [a]Ex 22:21; 23:9; Lev 19:34; Dt 10:19
23:10 [b]Lev 15:16
23:14 [c]Lev 26:12 [d]Ex 3:5
23:15 [e]1Sa 30:15
23:16 [f]Ex 22:21
23:17 [g]Ge 19:25; 2Ki 23:7 [h]Lev 19:29; Dt 22:21

[a] *29* That is, about 1 1/4 pounds (about 0.6 kilogram) [b] *2* Or *one of illegitimate birth*
[c] *4* That is, Northwest Mesopotamia
[d] *18* Hebrew *of a dog*

est, whether on money or food or anything else that may earn interest.[i]
20You may charge a foreigner interest,
but not a brother Israelite, so that the
LORD your God may bless[j] you in everything you put your hand to in the
land you are entering to possess.
21If you make a vow to the LORD your
God, do not be slow to pay it, for the
LORD your God will certainly demand it
of you and you will be guilty of sin.[k]
22But if you refrain from making a vow,
you will not be guilty. 23Whatever your
lips utter you must be sure to do, because you made your vow freely to the
LORD your God with your own mouth.
24If you enter your neighbor's vineyard, you may eat all the grapes you
want, but do not put any in your basket. 25If you enter your neighbor's
grainfield, you may pick kernels with
your hands, but you must not put a
sickle to his standing grain.[l]
24 If a man marries a woman who becomes displeasing to him[m] because he finds something indecent
about her, and he writes her a certificate of divorce,[n] gives it to her and
sends her from his house, 2and if after
she leaves his house she becomes the
wife of another man, 3and her second
husband dislikes her and writes her a
certificate of divorce, gives it to her and
sends her from his house, or if he dies,
4then her first husband, who divorced
her, is not allowed to marry her again
after she has been defiled. That would
be detestable in the eyes of the LORD.
Do not bring sin upon the land the
LORD[o] your God is giving you as an
inheritance.
5If a man has recently married, he
must not be sent to war or have any
other duty laid on him. For one year he
is to be free to stay at home and bring
happiness to the wife he has married.[p]
6Do not take a pair of millstones—
not even the upper one—as security
for a debt, because that would be taking a man's livelihood as security.
7If a man is caught kidnapping one
of his brother Israelites and treats him
as a slave or sells him, the kidnapper
must die.[q] You must purge the evil
from among you.
8In cases of leprous[a] diseases be
very careful to do exactly as the priests,
who are Levites, instruct you. You must
follow carefully what I have commanded them.[r] 9Remember what the LORD
your God did to Miriam along the way
after you came out of Egypt.[s]
10When you make a loan of any kind
to your neighbor, do not go into his
house to get what he is offering as a
pledge. 11Stay outside and let the man
to whom you are making the loan bring
the pledge out to you. 12If the man is
poor, do not go to sleep with his pledge
in your possession. 13Return his cloak
to him by sunset[t] so that he may sleep
in it. Then he will thank you, and it will
be regarded as a righteous act in the
sight of the LORD your God.[u]
14Do not take advantage of a hired
man who is poor and needy, whether
he is a brother Israelite or an alien living in one of your towns.[v] 15Pay him
his wages each day before sunset, because he is poor[w] and is counting on
it.[x] Otherwise he may cry to the LORD
against you, and you will be guilty of
sin.[y]
16Fathers shall not be put to death
for their children, nor children put to
death for their fathers; each is to die for
his own sin.[z]
17Do not deprive the alien or the fatherless of justice,[a] or take the cloak of
the widow as a pledge. 18Remember
that you were slaves in Egypt and the
LORD your God redeemed you from
there. That is why I command you to
do this.
19When you are harvesting in your
field and you overlook a sheaf, do not
go back to get it.[b] Leave it for the
alien, the fatherless and the widow, so
that the LORD your God may bless[c]
you in all the work of your hands.
20When you beat the olives from your
trees, do not go over the branches a
second time.[d] Leave what remains for
the alien, the fatherless and the widow.
21When you harvest the grapes in your
vineyard, do not go over the vines
again. Leave what remains for the
alien, the fatherless and the widow.
22Remember that you were slaves in
Egypt. That is why I command you to
do this.[e]
25 When men have a dispute, they are
to take it to court and the judges
will decide the case,[f] acquitting the
innocent and condemning the guilty.[g]
2If the guilty man deserves to be beat-
en,[h] the judge shall make him lie
down and have him flogged in his presence with the number of lashes his
crime deserves, 3but he must not give
him more than forty lashes.[i] If he is
flogged more than that, your brother
will be degraded in your eyes.[j]
4Do not muzzle an ox while it is
treading out the grain.[k]
5If brothers are living together and
one of them dies without a son, his

7 →PG. 450

23:19 [i]Ex 22:25; Lev 25:35-37
23:20 [j]Dt 15:10; 28:12
23:21 [k]Nu 30:1-2; Ecc 5:4-5; Mt 5:33
23:25 [l]Mt 12:1; Mk 2:23; Lk 6:1
24:1 [m]Dt 22:13 [n]Mt 5:31*; 19:7-9; Mk 10:4-5
24:4 [o]Jer 3:1
24:5 [p]Dt 20:7
24:7 [q]Ex 21:16
24:8 [r]Lev 13:1-46; 14:2
24:9 [s]Nu 12:10
24:13 [t]Ex 22:26 [u]Dt 6:25; Da 4:27
24:14 [v]Lev 25:35-43; Dt 15:12-18
24:15 [w]Jer 22:13 [x]Lev 19:13 [y]Dt 15:9; Jas 5:4
24:16 [z]2Ki 14:6; 2Ch 25:4; Jer 31:29-30; Eze 18:20
24:17 [a]Dt 1:17; 10:17-18; 16:19
24:19 [b]Lev 19:9; 23:22 [c]Pr 19:17
24:20 [d]Lev 19:10
24:22 [e]ver 18
25:1 [f]Dt 19:17 [g]Dt 1:16-17
25:2 [h]Lk 12:47-48
25:3 [i]2Co 11:24 [j]Job 18:3
25:4 [k]Pr 12:10; 1Co 9:9*; 1Ti 5:18*

[a]8 The Hebrew word was used for various diseases affecting the skin—not necessarily leprosy.

widow must not marry outside the family. Her husband's brother shall take her and marry her and fulfill the duty of a brother-in-law to her.[l] 6The first son she bears shall carry on the name of the dead brother so that his name will not be blotted out from Israel.[m]

7However, if a man does not want to marry his brother's wife, she shall go to the elders at the town gate and say, "My husband's brother refuses to carry on his brother's name in Israel. He will not fulfill the duty of a brother-in-law to me."[n] 8Then the elders of his town shall summon him and talk to him. If he persists in saying, "I do not want to marry her," 9his brother's widow shall go up to him in the presence of the elders, take off one of his sandals,[o] spit in his face and say, "This is what is done to the man who will not build up his brother's family line." 10That man's line shall be known in Israel as The Family of the Unsandaled.

11If two men are fighting and the wife of one of them comes to rescue her husband from his assailant, and she reaches out and seizes him by his private parts, 12you shall cut off her hand. Show her no pity.[p]

13Do not have two differing weights in your bag—one heavy, one light.[q]

3 →PG. 356

14Do not have two differing measures in your house—one large, one small. 15You must have accurate and honest weights and measures, so that you may live long[r] in the land the LORD your God is giving you. 16For the LORD your God detests anyone who does these things, anyone who deals dishonestly.[s]

17Remember what the Amalekites[t] did to you along the way when you came out of Egypt. 18When you were weary and worn out, they met you on your journey and cut off all who were lagging behind; they had no fear of God.[u] 19When the LORD your God gives you rest from all the enemies around you in the land he is giving you to possess as an inheritance, you shall blot out the memory of Amalek[v] from under heaven. Do not forget!

Firstfruits and Tithes

26 When you have entered the land the LORD your God is giving you as an inheritance and have taken possession of it and settled in it, 2take some of the firstfruits[w] of all that you produce from the soil of the land the LORD your God is giving you and put them in a basket. Then go to the place the LORD your God will choose as a dwelling for his Name[x] 3and say to the priest in office at the time, "I declare today to the LORD your God that I have come to the land the LORD swore to our forefathers to give us." 4The priest shall take the basket from your hands and set it down in front of the altar of the LORD your God. 5Then you shall declare before the LORD your God: "My father was a wandering Aramean,[y] and he went down into Egypt with a few people[z] and lived there and became a great nation, powerful and numerous. 6But the Egyptians mistreated us and made us suffer,[a] putting us to hard labor. 7Then we cried out to the LORD, the God of our fathers, and the LORD heard our voice[b] and saw[c] our misery, toil and oppression. 8So the LORD brought us out of Egypt with a mighty hand and an outstretched arm, with great terror and with miraculous signs and wonders.[d] 9He brought us to this place and gave us this land, a land flowing with milk and honey;[e] 10and now I bring the firstfruits of the soil that you, O LORD, have given me." Place the basket before the LORD your God and bow down before him. 11And you and the Levites[f] and the aliens among you shall rejoice[g] in all the good things the LORD your God has given to you and your household.

12When you have finished setting aside a tenth[h] of all your produce in the third year, the year of the tithe,[i] you shall give it to the Levite, the alien, the fatherless and the widow, so that they may eat in your towns and be satisfied. 13Then say to the LORD your God: "I have removed from my house the sacred portion and have given it to the Levite, the alien, the fatherless and the widow, according to all you commanded. I have not turned aside from your commands nor have I forgotten any of them.[j] 14I have not eaten any of the sacred portion while I was in mourning, nor have I removed any of it while I was unclean,[k] nor have I offered any of it to the dead. I have obeyed the LORD my God; I have done everything you commanded me. 15Look down from heaven,[l] your holy dwelling place, and bless your people Israel and the land you have given us as you promised on oath to our forefathers, a land flowing with milk and honey."

Follow the LORD's Commands

16The LORD your God commands you this day to follow these decrees and laws; carefully observe them with all your heart and with all your soul.[m]

25:5 [l] Mt 22:24; Mk 12:19; Lk 20:28
25:6 [m] Ge 38:9; Ru 4:5,10
25:7 [n] Ru 4:1-2,5-6
25:9 [o] Ru 4:7-8,11
25:12 [p] Dt 19:13
25:13 [q] Lev 19:35-37; Pr 11:1; Eze 45:10; Mic 6:11
25:15 [r] Ex 20:12
25:16 [s] Pr 11:1
25:17 [t] Ex 17:8
25:18 [u] Ps 36:1; Ro 3:18
25:19 [v] 1Sa 15:2-3
26:2 [w] Ex 22:29; 23:16,19; Nu 18:13; Pr 3:9
[x] Dt 12:5
26:5 [y] Hos 12:12 [z] Ge 43:1-2; 45:7,11; 46:27; Dt 10:22
26:6 [a] Ex 1:11,14
26:7 [b] Ex 2:23-25 [c] Ex 3:9
26:8 [d] Dt 4:34
26:9 [e] Ex 3:8
26:11 [f] Dt 12:7 [g] Dt 16:11
26:12 [h] Lev 27:30 [i] Nu 18:24; Dt 14:28-29; Heb 7:5,9
26:13 [j] Ps 119:141,153,176
26:14 [k] Lev 7:20; Hos 9:4
26:15 [l] Isa 63:15; Zec 2:13
26:16 [m] Dt 4:29

17You have declared this day that the LORD is your God and that you will walk in his ways, that you will keep his decrees, commands and laws, and that you will obey him. 18And the LORD has declared this day that you are his people, his treasured possession[n] as he promised, and that you are to keep all his commands. 19He has declared that he will set you in praise, fame and honor high above all the nations[o] he has made and that you will be a people holy[p] to the LORD your God, as he promised.

1 →PG. 217

The Altar on Mount Ebal

27 Moses and the elders of Israel commanded the people: "Keep all these commands that I give you today. 2When you have crossed the Jordan into the land the LORD your God is giving you, set up some large stones and coat them with plaster.[q] 3Write on them all the words of this law when you have crossed over to enter the land the LORD your God is giving you, a land flowing with milk and honey,[r] just as the LORD, the God of your fathers, promised you. 4And when you have crossed the Jordan, set up these stones on Mount Ebal,[s] as I command you today, and coat them with plaster. 5Build there an altar[t] to the LORD your God, an altar of stones. Do not use any iron tool[u] upon them. 6Build the altar of the LORD your God with fieldstones and offer burnt offerings on it to the LORD your God. 7Sacrifice fellowship offerings[a] there, eating them and rejoicing in the presence of the LORD your God. 8And you shall write very clearly all the words of this law on these stones you have set up."

Curses From Mount Ebal

9Then Moses and the priests, who are Levites, said to all Israel, "Be silent, O Israel, and listen! You have now become the people of the LORD your God.[v] 10Obey the LORD your God and follow his commands and decrees that I give you today."

11On the same day Moses commanded the people:

12When you have crossed the Jordan, these tribes shall stand on Mount Gerizim[w] to bless the people: Simeon, Levi, Judah, Issachar, Joseph and Benjamin.[x] 13And these tribes shall stand on Mount Ebal to pronounce curses: Reuben, Gad, Asher, Zebulun, Dan and Naphtali.

14The Levites shall recite to all the people of Israel in a loud voice:

15"Cursed is the man who carves an image or casts an idol[y]—a thing detestable to the LORD, the work of the craftsman's hands—and sets it up in secret."

Then all the people shall say, "Amen!"

16"Cursed is the man who dishonors his father or his mother."[z]

Then all the people shall say, "Amen!"

17"Cursed is the man who moves his neighbor's boundary stone."[a]

Then all the people shall say, "Amen!"

18"Cursed is the man who leads the blind astray on the road."[b]

Then all the people shall say, "Amen!"

19"Cursed is the man who withholds justice from the alien,[c] the fatherless or the widow."[d]

Then all the people shall say, "Amen!"

20"Cursed is the man who sleeps with his father's wife, for he dishonors his father's bed."[e]

Then all the people shall say, "Amen!"

21"Cursed is the man who has sexual relations with any animal."[f]

Then all the people shall say, "Amen!"

22"Cursed is the man who sleeps with his sister, the daughter of his father or the daughter of his mother."[g]

Then all the people shall say, "Amen!"

23"Cursed is the man who sleeps with his mother-in-law."[h]

Then all the people shall say, "Amen!"

24"Cursed is the man who kills[i] his neighbor secretly."

Then all the people shall say, "Amen!"

25"Cursed is the man who accepts a bribe to kill an innocent person."[j]

Then all the people shall say, "Amen!"

26"Cursed is the man who does not uphold the words of this law by carrying them out."[k]

Then all the people shall say, "Amen!"

Blessings for Obedience

28 If you fully obey the LORD your God and carefully follow all his com-

26:18 [n]Ex 6:7; 19:5; Dt 7:6; 14:2; 28:9
26:19 [o]Dt 4:7-8; 28:1,13,44 [p]Ex 19:6; Dt 7:6; 1Pe 2:9
27:2 [q]Jos 8:31
27:3 [r]Dt 26:9
27:4 [s]Dt 11:29
27:5 [t]Jos 8:31 [u]Ex 20:25
27:9 [v]Dt 26:18
27:12 [w]Dt 11:29 [x]Jos 8:35
27:15 [y]Ex 20:4; 34:17; Lev 19:4; 26:1; Dt 4:16,23; 5:8; Isa 44:9
27:16 [z]Ex 20:12; 21:17; Lev 19:3; 20:9
27:17 [a]Dt 19:14; Pr 22:28
27:18 [b]Lev 19:14
27:19 [c]Ex 22:21; Dt 24:19 [d]Dt 10:18
27:20 [e]Lev 18:7; Dt 22:30
27:21 [f]Lev 18:23
27:22 [g]Lev 18:9; 20:17
27:23 [h]Lev 20:14
27:24 [i]Lev 24:17; Nu 35:31
27:25 [j]Ex 23:7-8; Dt 10:17; Eze 22:12
27:26 [k]Jer 11:3; Gal 3:10*

[a]7 Traditionally *peace offerings*

mands[l] I give you today, the LORD
your God will set you high above all the
nations on earth.[m] 2All these blessings
will come upon you[n] and accompany
you if you obey the LORD your God:

3You will be blessed[o] in the
city and blessed in the country.[p]
4The fruit of your womb will
be blessed, and the crops of
your land and the young of your
livestock—the calves of your
herds and the lambs of your
flocks.[q]
5Your basket and your kneading trough will be blessed.
6You will be blessed when you
come in and blessed when you go
out.[r]

7The LORD will grant that the enemies who rise up against you will be
defeated before you. They will come at
you from one direction but flee from
you in seven.[s]
8The LORD will send a blessing on
your barns and on everything you put
your hand to. The LORD your God will
bless you in the land he is giving you.
9The LORD will establish you as his
holy people,[t] as he promised you on
oath, if you keep the commands of the
LORD your God and walk in his ways.
10Then all the peoples on earth will
see that you are called by the name[u]
of the LORD, and they will fear you.
11The LORD will grant you abundant
prosperity—in the fruit of your womb,
the young of your livestock and the
crops of your ground—in the land he
swore to your forefathers to give you.[v]
12The LORD will open the heavens,
the storehouse of his bounty, to send
rain[w] on your land in season and to
bless all the work of your hands. You
will lend to many nations but will borrow from none.[x] 13The LORD will make
you the head, not the tail. If you pay
attention to the commands of the LORD
your God that I give you this day and
carefully follow them, you will always
be at the top, never at the bottom. 14Do
not turn aside from any of the commands I give you today, to the right or
to the left,[y] following other gods and
serving them.

Curses for Disobedience

15However, if you do not obey[z] the
LORD your God and do not carefully follow all his commands and decrees I am
giving you today, all these curses will
come upon you and overtake you:[a]

16You will be cursed in the city
and cursed in the country.
17Your basket and your kneading trough will be cursed.
18The fruit of your womb will
be cursed, and the crops of your
land, and the calves of your herds
and the lambs of your flocks.
19You will be cursed when you
come in and cursed when you go
out.

20The LORD will send on you
curses,[b] confusion and rebuke[c] in
everything you put your hand to, until
you are destroyed and come to sudden
ruin[d] because of the evil you have
done in forsaking him.[a] 21The LORD
will plague you with diseases until he
has destroyed you from the land you
are entering to possess.[e] 22The LORD
will strike you with wasting disease,
with fever and inflammation, with
scorching heat and drought,[f] with
blight and mildew, which will plague
you until you perish.[g] 23The sky over
your head will be bronze, the ground
beneath you iron.[h] 24The LORD will
turn the rain of your country into dust
and powder; it will come down from
the skies until you are destroyed.
25The LORD will cause you to be defeated before your enemies. You will
come at them from one direction but
flee from them in seven,[i] and you will
become a thing of horror to all the
kingdoms on earth.[j] 26Your carcasses
will be food for all the birds of the air
and the beasts of the earth, and there
will be no one to frighten them away.[k]
27The LORD will afflict you with the
boils of Egypt[l] and with tumors, festering sores and the itch, from which
you cannot be cured. 28The LORD will
afflict you with madness, blindness
and confusion of mind. 29At midday
you will grope[m] about like a blind man
in the dark. You will be unsuccessful in
everything you do; day after day you
will be oppressed and robbed, with no
one to rescue you.
30You will be pledged to be married
to a woman, but another will take her
and ravish her.[n] You will build a
house, but you will not live in it.[o] You
will plant a vineyard, but you will not
even begin to enjoy its fruit.[p] 31Your
ox will be slaughtered before your eyes,
but you will eat none of it. Your donkey
will be forcibly taken from you and will
not be returned. Your sheep will be giv-
en to your enemies, and no one will
rescue them. 32Your sons and daughters will be given to another nation,[q]
and you will wear out your eyes watching for them day after day, powerless to

[a] 20 Hebrew *me*

28:1 [l]Ex 15:26; Lev 26:3; Dt 7:12-26 [m]Dt 26:19
28:2 [n]Zec 1:6
28:3 [o]Ps 128:1,4 [p]Ge 39:5
28:4 [q]Ge 49:25; Pr 10:22
28:6 [r]Ps 121:8
28:7 [s]Lev 26:8,17
28:9 [t]Ex 19:6; Dt 7:6
28:10 [u]2Ch 7:14
28:11 [v]Dt 30:9; Pr 10:22
28:12 [w]Lev 26:4 [x]Dt 15:3,6
28:14 [y]Dt 5:32
28:15 [z]Lev 26:14 [a]Jos 23:15; Da 9:11; Mal 2:2
28:20 [b]Mal 2:2 [c]Isa 51:20; 66:15 [d]Dt 4:26
28:21 [e]Lev 26:25; Jer 24:10
28:22 [f]Lev 26:16 [g]Am 4:9
28:23 [h]Lev 26:19
28:24 [i]Isa 30:17 [j]Jer 15:4; 24:9; Eze 23:46
28:26 [k]Jer 7:33; 16:4; 34:20
28:27 [l]ver 60-61; 1Sa 5:6
28:29 [m]Job 5:14; Isa 59:10
28:30 [n]Job 31:10; Jer 8:10 [o]Am 5:11 [p]Jer 12:13
28:32 [q]ver 41

lift a hand. 33A people that you do not
know will eat what your land and labor
produce, and you will have nothing but
cruel oppression all your days.[r] 34The
sights you see will drive you mad.
35The LORD will afflict your knees and
legs with painful boils[s] that cannot be
cured, spreading from the soles of your
feet to the top of your head.

36The LORD will drive you and the
king[t] you set over you to a nation unknown to you or your fathers.[u] There
you will worship other gods, gods of
wood and stone.[v] 37You will become a
thing of horror and an object of scorn
and ridicule to all the nations where
the LORD will drive you.[w]

38You will sow much seed in the field
but you will harvest little,[x] because locusts will devour[y] it. 39You will plant
vineyards and cultivate them but you
will not drink the wine or gather the
grapes, because worms will eat them.[z]
40You will have olive trees throughout
your country but you will not use the
oil, because the olives will drop off.[a]
41You will have sons and daughters but
you will not keep them, because they
will go into captivity.[b] 42Swarms of locusts will take over all your trees and
the crops of your land.

43The alien who lives among you will
rise above you higher and higher, but
you will sink lower and lower.[c] 44He
will lend to you, but you will not lend
to him.[d] He will be the head, but you
will be the tail.[e]

45All these curses will come upon
you. They will pursue you and overtake
you until you are destroyed,[f] because
you did not obey the LORD your God
and observe the commands and decrees he gave you. 46They will be a sign
and a wonder to you and your descendants forever.[g] 47Because you did not
serve[h] the LORD your God joyfully and
gladly[i] in the time of prosperity,
48therefore in hunger and thirst, in nakedness and dire poverty, you will
serve the enemies the LORD sends
against you. He will put an iron yoke[j]
on your neck until he has destroyed
you.

49The LORD will bring a nation
against you from far away, from the
ends of the earth,[k] like an eagle[l]
swooping down, a nation whose language you will not understand, 50a
fierce-looking nation without respect
for the old[m] or pity for the young.
51They will devour the young of your
livestock and the crops of your land
until you are destroyed. They will leave
you no grain, new wine or oil, nor any
calves of your herds or lambs of your
flocks until you are ruined.[n] 52They
will lay siege to all the cities throughout
your land until the high fortified walls
in which you trust fall down. They will
besiege all the cities throughout the
land the LORD your God is giving you.[o]

53Because of the suffering that your
enemy will inflict on you during the
siege, you will eat the fruit of the
womb, the flesh of the sons and daughters the LORD your God has given
you.[p] 54Even the most gentle and sensitive man among you will have no
compassion on his own brother or the
wife he loves or his surviving children,
55and he will not give to one of them
any of the flesh of his children that he
is eating. It will be all he has left because of the suffering your enemy will
inflict on you during the siege of all
your cities. 56The most gentle and sensitive[q] woman among you—so sensitive and gentle that she would not venture to touch the ground with the sole
of her foot—will begrudge the husband she loves and her own son or
daughter 57the afterbirth from her
womb and the children she bears. For
she intends to eat them secretly during
the siege and in the distress that your
enemy will inflict on you in your cities.

58If you do not carefully follow all
the words of this law, which are written
in this book, and do not revere[r] this
glorious and awesome name[s]—the
LORD your God— 59the LORD will send
fearful plagues on you and your
descendants, harsh and prolonged disasters, and severe and lingering illnesses. 60He will bring upon you all the
diseases of Egypt[t] that you dreaded,
and they will cling to you. 61The LORD
will also bring on you every kind of
sickness and disaster not recorded in
this Book of the Law, until you are destroyed.[u] 62You who were as numerous as the stars in the sky[v] will be left
but few in number, because you did
not obey the LORD your God. 63Just as
it pleased[w] the LORD to make you
prosper and increase in number, so it
will please[x] him to ruin and destroy
you. You will be uprooted[y] from the
land you are entering to possess.

64Then the LORD will scatter[z] you
among all nations,[a] from one end of
the earth to the other. There you will
worship other gods—gods of wood
and stone, which neither you nor your
fathers have known. 65Among those
nations you will find no repose, no
resting place for the sole of your foot.
There the LORD will give you an anxious
mind, eyes weary with longing, and a
despairing heart.[b] 66You will live in
constant suspense, filled with dread
both night and day, never sure of your

28:33 [r]Jer 5:15-17
28:35 [s]ver 27
28:36 [t]2Ki 17:4,6; 24:12,14; 25:7,11 [u]Jer 16:13 [v]Dt 4:28
28:37 [w]Jer 24:9
28:38 [x]Mic 6:15; Hag 1:6,9 [y]Joel 1:4
28:39 [z]Isa 5:10; 17:10-11
28:40 [a]Mic 6:15
28:41 [b]ver 32
28:43 [c]ver 13
28:44 [d]ver 12 [e]ver 13
28:45 [f]ver 15
28:46 [g]Isa 8:18; Eze 14:8
28:47 [h]Dt 32:15 [i]Ne 9:35
28:48 [j]Jer 28:13-14
28:49 [k]Jer 5:15; 6:22 [l]La 4:19; Hos 8:1
28:50 [m]Isa 47:6
28:51 [n]ver 33
28:52 [o]Jer 10:18; Zep 1:14-16,17
28:53 [p]Lev 26:29; 2Ki 6:28-29; Jer 19:9; La 2:20; 4:10
28:56 [q]ver 54
28:58 [r]Mal 1:14 [s]Ex 6:3
28:60 [t]ver 27
28:61 [u]Dt 4:25-26
28:62 [v]Dt 4:27; 10:22; Ne 9:23
28:63 [w]Jer 32:41 [x]Pr 1:26 [y]Jer 12:14; 45:4
28:64 [z]Lev 26:33; Dt 4:27 [a]Ne 1:8
28:65 [b]Lev 26:16,36

life. 67 In the morning you will say, "If only it were evening!" and in the evening, "If only it were morning!"—because of the terror that will fill your hearts and the sights that your eyes will see.[c] 68 The LORD will send you back in ships to Egypt on a journey I said you should never make again. There you will offer yourselves for sale to your enemies as male and female slaves, but no one will buy you.

Renewal of the Covenant

29 These are the terms of the covenant the LORD commanded Moses to make with the Israelites in Moab, in addition to the covenant he had made with them at Horeb.[d]

2 Moses summoned all the Israelites and said to them:

Your eyes have seen all that the LORD did in Egypt to Pharaoh, to all his officials and to all his land.[e] 3 With your own eyes you saw those great trials, those miraculous signs and great wonders.[f] 4 But to this day the LORD has not given you a mind that understands or eyes that see or ears that hear.[g] 5 During the forty years that I led you through the desert, your clothes did not wear out, nor did the sandals on your feet.[h] 6 You ate no bread and drank no wine or other fermented drink. I did this so that you might know that I am the LORD your God.[i]

7 When you reached this place, Sihon[j] king of Heshbon and Og king of Bashan came out to fight against us, but we defeated them.[k] 8 We took their land and gave it as an inheritance to the Reubenites, the Gadites and the half-tribe of Manasseh.[l]

9 Carefully follow[m] the terms of this covenant, so that you may prosper in everything you do.[n] 10 All of you are standing today in the presence of the LORD your God—your leaders and chief men, your elders and officials, and all the other men of Israel, 11 together with your children and your wives, and the aliens living in your camps who chop your wood and carry your water.[o] 12 You are standing here in order to enter into a covenant with the LORD your God, a covenant the LORD is making with you this day and sealing with an oath, 13 to confirm you this day as his people,[p] that he may be your God[q] as he promised you and as he swore to your fathers, Abraham, Isaac and Jacob. 14 I am making this covenant,[r] with its oath, not only with you 15 who are standing here with us today in the presence of the LORD our God but also with those who are not here today.[s]

16 You yourselves know how we lived in Egypt and how we passed through the countries on the way here. 17 You saw among them their detestable images and idols of wood and stone, of silver and gold.[t] 18 Make sure there is no man or woman, clan or tribe among you today whose heart turns away from the LORD our God to go and worship the gods of those nations; make sure there is no root among you that produces such bitter poison.[u]

19 When such a person hears the words of this oath, he invokes a blessing on himself and therefore thinks, "I will be safe, even though I persist in going my own way." This will bring disaster on the watered land as well as the dry.[a] 20 The LORD will never be willing to forgive him; his wrath and zeal[v] will burn[w] against that man. All the curses written in this book will fall upon him, and the LORD will blot[x] out his name from under heaven. 21 The LORD will single him out from all the tribes of Israel for disaster, according to all the curses of the covenant written in this Book of the Law.

22 Your children who follow you in later generations and foreigners who come from distant lands will see the calamities that have fallen on the land and the diseases with which the LORD has afflicted it.[y] 23 The whole land will be a burning waste[z] of salt[a] and sulfur—nothing planted, nothing sprouting, no vegetation growing on it. It will be like the destruction of Sodom and Gomorrah,[b] Admah and Zeboiim, which the LORD overthrew in fierce anger. 24 All the nations will ask: "Why has the LORD done this to this land?[c] Why this fierce, burning anger?"

25 And the answer will be: "It is because this people abandoned the covenant of the LORD, the God of their fathers, the covenant he made with them when he brought them out of Egypt. 26 They went off and worshiped other gods and bowed down to them, gods they did not know, gods he had not given them. 27 Therefore the LORD's anger burned against this land, so that he brought on it all the curses written in this book.[d] 28 In furious anger and in great wrath the LORD uprooted[e] them from their land and thrust them into another land, as it is now."

29 The secret things belong to the LORD our God, but the things revealed belong to us and to our children forev-

28:67 [c]ver 34; Job 7:4
29:1 [d]Dt 5:2-3
29:2 [e]Ex 19:4
29:3 [f]Dt 4:34; 7:19
29:4 [g]Isa 6:10; Ac 28:26-27; Ro 11:8*; Eph 4:18
29:5 [h]Dt 8:4
29:6 [i]Dt 8:3
29:7 [j]Dt 2:32; 3:1 [k]Nu 21:21-24, 33-35
29:8 [l]Nu 32:33; Dt 3:12-13
29:9 [m]Dt 4:6; Jos 1:7 [n]1Ki 2:3
29:11 [o]Jos 9:21,23,27
29:13 [p]Dt 28:9 [q]Ge 17:7; Ex 6:7
29:14 [r]Jer 31:31
29:15 [s]Ac 2:39
29:17 [t]Dt 28:36
29:18 [u]Dt 11:16; Heb 12:15
29:20 [v]Eze 23:25 [w]Ps 74:1; 79:5 [x]Ex 32:33; Dt 9:14
29:22 [y]Jer 19:8
29:23 [z]Isa 34:9 [a]Jer 17:6 [b]Ge 19:24,25; Zep 2:9
29:24 [c]1Ki 9:8; Jer 22:8-9
29:27 [d]Da 9:11,13,14
29:28 [e]1Ki 14:15; 2Ch 7:20; Ps 52:5; Pr 2:22

[a] *19* Or *way, in order to add drunkenness to thirst."*

er, that we may follow all the words of
this law.

Prosperity After Turning to the LORD

30 When all these blessings and
curses[f] I have set before you
come upon you and you take them to
heart wherever the LORD your God disperses you among the nations,[g] 2and
when you and your children return[h]
to the LORD your God and obey him
with all your heart and with all your
soul according to everything I command you today, 3then the LORD your
God will restore your fortunes[a][i] and
have compassion on you and gather[j]
you again from all the nations where
he scattered you.[k] 4Even if you have
been banished to the most distant land
under the heavens, from there the
LORD your God will gather you and
bring you back.[l] 5He will bring[m] you
to the land that belonged to your fathers, and you will take possession of
it. He will make you more prosperous
and numerous than your fathers. 6The
LORD your God will circumcise your
hearts and the hearts of your descendants,[n] so that you may love him with
all your heart and with all your soul,
and live. 7The LORD your God will put
all these curses on your enemies who
hate and persecute you.[o] 8You will
again obey the LORD and follow all his
commands I am giving you today.
9Then the LORD your God will make
you most prosperous in all the work
of your hands and in the fruit of your
womb, the young of your livestock and
the crops of your land.[p] The LORD will
again delight in you and make you
prosperous, just as he delighted in your
fathers, 10if you obey the LORD your
God and keep his commands and decrees that are written in this Book of
the Law and turn to the LORD your God

a 3 Or *will bring you back from captivity*

30:1 f ver 15,19; Dt 11:26 g Lev 26:40-45; Dt 28:64; 29:28; 1Ki 8:47 **30:2** h Dt 4:30; Ne 1:9 **30:3** i Ps 126:4 j Ps 147:2; Jer 32:37; Eze 34:13 k Jer 29:14 **30:4** l Ne 1:8-9; Isa 43:6 **30:5** m Jer 29:14 **30:6** n Dt 10:16; Jer 32:39 **30:7** o Dt 7:15 **30:9** p Dt 28:11; Jer 31:28; 32:41

29:29

PROMISE 1

GOD'S SECRETS

In the Book of Deuteronomy, Moses described how God wanted his people to live. He told them what they should do and warned them against things they should not do. God, through Moses, was thorough and specific.

In the midst of all this instruction comes a brief statement about the nature of truth. It teaches a simple but amazingly profound fact. It says that all knowledge, all truth exists in only two realms: the secret things and the revealed things. All the truth that exists in the universe resides in what God has revealed and what he has not.

Notice first that "The secret things belong to the LORD our God." In this chapter, Moses had just given the people a load of information about how to live. Beyond that information, Moses said, is another world of information. It is a reality, but it belongs to the Lord our God—it doesn't belong to us. It is valid and true and affects us, but it is secret.

Just because we can't understand something, doesn't mean it doesn't belong or isn't true or doesn't exist. Just because God's actions defy our logic, our sense of justice or goodness, that doesn't mean they shouldn't be happening. Suffering and pain often seem wrong; they sometimes confuse us or make us angry. We wonder, "Why is this happening to me?" or "Why did God allow this?" When we come to the end of our understanding, we are at the beginning of understanding God. Until what we know is exhausted, we have not entered the realm of faith.

The other realm of truth is "The things revealed." All through Scripture, God is portrayed as One who is generous about teaching us his nature and will. Genesis 1:26–28 and 2:4–24 teach us that of all God's creation, only humans are created in God's image. Of all the earth's creatures, only we can understand and respond to what God has revealed. In Deuteronomy 3:24 and 4:5–6, Joshua spoke of how God had literally revealed himself to the people of Israel to guide their way. God reveals himself to us today, but not as physically and literally as he did for the ancient Israelites. Psalm 19 tells us God is revealed in creation and in his Word, and Psalm 119 is an intricately constructed poem about the value of God's revealed Word. Finally, John 1:1–4 and Hebrews 1:1–4 present Jesus Christ as God's ultimate self-revelation.

"The secret things belong to the LORD our God, but the things revealed belong to us and to our children." Why? "That we may follow all the words of this law." God has revealed his will to protect us from destruction and to guide us in growth.

Many great mysteries confuse and befuddle us. Some annoy and some enrage us. Moses assured us that the secret things, all the things that we don't understand, belong; but not to us. Some people focus on the secret things. They doubt or deny God because they can't accept a God who is bigger than their intellect. Moses urged us to accept the secret things but to focus on the revealed things—God's Word, his creation, and his Son, Jesus Christ. These revelations belong to us and to our children, and are intended to guide us to God. As you read God's Word, own it because it's yours. Follow it because it's his.

For the next Promise 1 reading go to page 217.

with all your heart and with all your soul.[q]

The Offer of Life or Death

11Now what I am commanding you today is not too difficult for you or beyond your reach.[r] 12It is not up in heaven, so that you have to ask, "Who will ascend into heaven to get it and proclaim it to us so we may obey it?"[s] 13Nor is it beyond the sea, so that you have to ask, "Who will cross the sea to get it and proclaim it to us so we may obey it?" 14No, the word is very near you; it is in your mouth and in your heart so you may obey it.

1 →PG. 225

15See, I set before you today life and prosperity, death and destruction.[t] 16For I command you today to love the LORD your God, to walk in his ways, and to keep his commands, decrees and laws; then you will live and increase, and the LORD your God will bless you in the land you are entering to possess.

17But if your heart turns away and you are not obedient, and if you are drawn away to bow down to other gods and worship them, 18I declare to you this day that you will certainly be destroyed.[u] You will not live long in the land you are crossing the Jordan to enter and possess.

19This day I call heaven and earth as witnesses against you[v] that I have set before you life and death, blessings and curses.[w] Now choose life, so that you and your children may live 20and that you may love[x] the LORD your God, listen to his voice, and hold fast to him. For the LORD is your life,[y] and he will give you many years in the land he swore to give to your fathers, Abraham, Isaac and Jacob.

Joshua to Succeed Moses

31 Then Moses went out and spoke these words to all Israel: 2"I am now a hundred and twenty years old[z] and I am no longer able to lead you.[a] The LORD has said to me, 'You shall not cross the Jordan.'[b] 3The LORD your God himself will cross[c] over ahead of you.[d] He will destroy these nations before you, and you will take possession of their land. Joshua also will cross[e] over ahead of you, as the LORD said. 4And the LORD will do to them what he did to Sihon and Og, the kings of the Amorites, whom he destroyed along with their land. 5The LORD will deliver[f] them to you, and you must do to them all that I have commanded you. 6Be strong and courageous.[g] Do not be afraid or terrified[h] because of them, for the LORD your God goes with you;[i] he will never leave you[j] nor forsake[k] you."

7Then Moses summoned Joshua and said[l] to him in the presence of all Israel, "Be strong and courageous, for you must go with this people into the land that the LORD swore to their forefathers to give them, and you must divide it among them as their inheritance. 8The LORD himself goes before you and will be with you;[m] he will never leave you nor forsake you. Do not be afraid; do not be discouraged."

The Reading of the Law

9So Moses wrote down this law and gave it to the priests, the sons of Levi, who carried[n] the ark of the covenant of the LORD, and to all the elders of Israel. 10Then Moses commanded them: "At the end of every seven years, in the year for canceling debts,[o] during the Feast of Tabernacles,[p] 11when all Israel comes to appear[q] before the LORD your God at the place he will choose, you shall read this law[r] before them in their hearing. 12Assemble the people—men, women and children, and the aliens living in your towns—so they can listen and learn[s] to fear the LORD your God and follow carefully all the words of this law. 13Their children,[t] who do not know this law, must hear it and learn to fear the LORD your God as long as you live in the land you are crossing the Jordan to possess."

Israel's Rebellion Predicted

14The LORD said to Moses, "Now the

30:10 [q]Dt 4:29
30:11 [r]Isa 45:19,23
30:12 [s]Ro 10:6*
30:15 [t]Dt 11:26
30:18 [u]Dt 8:19
30:19 [v]Dt 4:26 [w]ver 1
30:20 [x]Dt 6:5; 10:20 [y]Ps 27:1; Jn 11:25
31:2 [z]Dt 34:7 [a]Nu 27:17; 1Ki 3:7 [b]Dt 3:23,26
31:3 [c]Nu 27:18 [d]Dt 9:3 [e]Dt 3:28
31:5 [f]Dt 7:2
31:6 [g]Jos 10:25; 1Ch 22:13 [h]Dt 7:18 [i]Dt 1:29; 20:4 [j]Jos 1:5 [k]Heb 13:5*
31:7 [l]Dt 1:38; 3:28
31:8 [m]Ex 13:21; 33:14
31:9 [n]ver 25; Nu 4:15; Jos 3:3
31:10 [o]Dt 15:1 [p]Lev 23:34
31:11 [q]Dt 16:16 [r]Jos 8:34-35; 2Ki 23:2
31:12 [s]Dt 4:10
31:13 [t]Dt 11:2; Ps 78:6-7

31:7-8

PROMISE 1

GOD'S PROVISION

Think about this: The measure of a man's need is the measure of God's response.

Joshua was the man chosen to follow Moses as Israel's leader (how would you like to follow *that* act?). In his new position, he faced two daunting tasks: First, he had to conquer Canaan; second, he had to divide the land up among God's people. Who can tell which of those jobs was tougher? Even though he had some real needs in the face of these two tasks, God responded with the promise to be with him.

God gave Joshua what he needed by specifically addressing Joshua's fear and discouragement. You serve the same God, and he still promises to fill your needs. Call out to him in your need and trust in his presence to encourage and calm you.

For the next Promise 1 reading go to page 225.

day of your death[u] is near. Call Joshua
and present yourselves at the Tent of
Meeting, where I will commission
him." So Moses and Joshua came and
presented themselves at the Tent of
Meeting.
15Then the LORD appeared at the
Tent in a pillar of cloud, and the cloud
stood over the entrance to the Tent.[v]
16And the LORD said to Moses: "You are
going to rest with your fathers, and
these people will soon prostitute[w]
themselves to the foreign gods of the
land they are entering. They will forsake[x] me and break the covenant I
made with them. **17**On that day I will
become angry[y] with them and forsake[z] them; I will hide[a] my face from
them, and they will be destroyed. Many
disasters and difficulties will come
upon them, and on that day they will
ask, 'Have not these disasters come
upon us because our God is not with
us?'[b] **18**And I will certainly hide my
face on that day because of all their
wickedness in turning to other gods.
19"Now write down for yourselves
this song and teach it to the Israelites
and have them sing it, so that it may be
a witness for me against them. **20**When
I have brought them into the land flowing with milk and honey, the land I
promised on oath to their forefathers,[c] and when they eat their fill and
thrive, they will turn to other gods[d]
and worship them, rejecting me and
breaking my covenant.[e] **21**And when
many disasters and difficulties come
upon them,[f] this song will testify
against them, because it will not be forgotten by their descendants. I know
what they are disposed to do,[g] even
before I bring them into the land I
promised them on oath." **22**So Moses
wrote[h] down this song that day and
taught it to the Israelites.
23The LORD gave this command[i] to
Joshua son of Nun: "Be strong and
courageous,[j] for you will bring the Israelites into the land I promised them
on oath, and I myself will be with you."
24After Moses finished writing in a
book the words of this law from beginning to end, **25**he gave this command to
the Levites who carried the ark of the
covenant of the LORD: **26**"Take this
Book of the Law and place it beside the
ark of the covenant of the LORD your
God. There it will remain as a witness
against you.[k] **27**For I know how rebellious and stiff-necked[l] you are. If you
have been rebellious against the LORD
while I am still alive and with you, how
much more will you rebel after I die!
28Assemble before me all the elders of
your tribes and all your officials, so that
I can speak these words in their hearing and call heaven and earth to testify
against them.[m] **29**For I know that after
my death you are sure to become utterly corrupt[n] and to turn from the way
I have commanded you. In days to
come, disaster[o] will fall upon you because you will do evil in the sight of the
LORD and provoke him to anger by
what your hands have made."

The Song of Moses

30And Moses recited the words of
this song from beginning to end in the
hearing of the whole assembly of Israel:

32 Listen, O heavens,[p] and I will speak;
hear, O earth, the words of my mouth.
2Let my teaching fall like rain
and my words descend like dew,[q]
like showers[r] on new grass,
like abundant rain on tender plants.
3I will proclaim the name of the LORD.[s]
Oh, praise the greatness[t] of our God!
4He is the Rock,[u] his works are perfect,[v]
and all his ways are just.
A faithful God[w] who does no wrong,
upright and just is he.
5They have acted corruptly toward him;
to their shame they are no longer his children,
but a warped and crooked generation.[a][x]
6Is this the way you repay[y] the LORD,
O foolish and unwise people?[z]
Is he not your Father,[a] your Creator,[b]
who made you and formed you?[b]
7Remember the days of old;
consider the generations long past.
Ask your father and he will tell you,
your elders, and they will explain to you.[c]
8When the Most High gave the nations their inheritance,
when he divided all mankind,[d]
he set up boundaries for the peoples

31:14 [u]Nu 27:13; Dt 32:49-50 **31:15** [v]Ex 33:9 **31:16** [w]Jdg 2:12 [x]Jdg 10:6,13 **31:17** [y]Jdg 2:14,20 [z]Jdg 6:13; 2Ch 15:2 [a]Dt 32:20; Isa 1:15; 8:17 [b]Nu 14:42 **31:20** [c]Dt 6:10-12 [d]Dt 32:15-17 [e]ver 16 **31:21** [f]ver 17 [g]Hos 5:3 **31:22** [h]ver 19 **31:23** [i]ver 7 [j]Jos 1:6 **31:26** [k]ver 19 **31:27** [l]Ex 32:9; Dt 9:6,24 **31:28** [m]Dt 4:26; 30:19; 32:1 **31:29** [n]Dt 32:5; Jdg 2:19 [o]Dt 28:15 **32:1** [p]Isa 1:2 **32:2** [q]Isa 55:11 [r]Ps 72:6 **32:3** [s]Ex 33:19 [t]Dt 3:24 **32:4** [u]ver 15,18,30 [v]2Sa 22:31 [w]Dt 7:9 **32:5** [x]Dt 31:29 **32:6** [y]Ps 116:12 [z]Ps 74:2 [a]Dt 1:31; Isa 63:16 [b]ver 15 **32:7** [c]Ex 13:14 **32:8** [d]Ge 11:8; Ac 17:26

[a] 5 Or *Corrupt are they and not his children, / a generation warped and twisted to their shame*
[b] 6 Or *Father, who bought you*

according to the number of the sons of Israel.[a]
9For the LORD's portion[e] is his people,
Jacob his allotted inheritance.[f]
10In a desert[g] land he found him,
in a barren and howling waste.
He shielded him and cared for him;
he guarded him as the apple of his eye,[h]
11like an eagle that stirs up its nest
and hovers over its young,[i]
that spreads its wings to catch them
and carries them on its pinions.
12The LORD alone led him;
no foreign god was with him.[j]
13He made him ride on the heights[k] of the land
and fed him with the fruit of the fields.
He nourished him with honey from the rock,
and with oil[l] from the flinty crag,
14with curds and milk from herd and flock
and with fattened lambs and goats,
with choice rams of Bashan
and the finest kernels of wheat.[m]
You drank the foaming blood of the grape.[n]

15Jeshurun[b] grew fat[o] and kicked;
filled with food, he became heavy and sleek.
He abandoned[p] the God who made him
and rejected the Rock[q] his Savior.
16They made him jealous[r] with their foreign gods
and angered[s] him with their detestable idols.
17They sacrificed to demons, which are not God—
gods they had not known,[t]
gods that recently appeared,[u]
gods your fathers did not fear.
18You deserted the Rock, who fathered you;
you forgot[v] the God who gave you birth.

19The LORD saw this and rejected them[w]
because he was angered by his sons and daughters.[x]
20"I will hide my face[y] from them," he said,
"and see what their end will be;
for they are a perverse generation,[z]
children who are unfaithful.
21They made me jealous[a] by what is no god
and angered me with their worthless idols.[b]
I will make them envious by those who are not a people;
I will make them angry by a nation that has no understanding.[c]
22For a fire has been kindled by my wrath,
one that burns to the realm of death[c] below.[d]
It will devour the earth and its harvests
and set afire the foundations of the mountains.

23"I will heap calamities[e] upon them
and spend my arrows[f] against them.
24I will send wasting famine against them,
consuming pestilence[g] and deadly plague;[h]
I will send against them the fangs of wild beasts,[i]
the venom of vipers[j] that glide in the dust.
25In the street the sword will make them childless;
in their homes terror will reign.[k]
Young men and young women will perish,
infants and gray-haired men.[l]
26I said I would scatter[m] them
and blot out their memory from mankind,[n]
27but I dreaded the taunt of the enemy,
lest the adversary misunderstand
and say, 'Our hand has triumphed;
the LORD has not done all this.'"[o]

28They are a nation without sense,
there is no discernment in them.
29If only they were wise and would understand this[p]
and discern what their end will be!
30How could one man chase a thousand,
or two put ten thousand to flight,[q]
unless their Rock had sold them,
unless the LORD had given them up?[r]
31For their rock is not like our Rock,
as even our enemies concede.

[a] *8* Masoretic Text; Dead Sea Scrolls (see also Septuagint) *sons of God* [b] *15 Jeshurun* means *the upright one,* that is, Israel. [c] *22* Hebrew *to Sheol*

32:9 [e]Jer 10:16 [f]1Ki 8:51,53 **32:10** [g]Jer 2:6 [h]Ps 17:8; Zec 2:8 **32:11** [i]Ex 19:4 **32:12** [j]ver 39 **32:13** [k]Isa 58:14 [l]Job 29:6 **32:14** [m]Ps 81:16; 147:14 [n]Ge 49:11 **32:15** [o]Dt 31:20 [p]ver 6; Isa 1:4,28 [q]ver 4 **32:16** [r]1Co 10:22 [s]Ps 78:58 **32:17** [t]Dt 28:64 [u]Jdg 5:8 **32:18** [v]Isa 17:10 **32:19** [w]Jer 44:21-23 [x]Ps 106:40 **32:20** [y]Dt 31:17,29 [z]ver 5

32:21 [a]1Co 10:22 [b]1Ki 16:13,26 [c]Ro 10:19* **32:22** [d]Ps 18:7-8; Jer 15:14; La 4:11 **32:23** [e]Dt 29:21 [f]Ps 7:13; Eze 5:16 **32:24** [g]Dt 28:22 [h]Ps 91:6 [i]Lev 26:22 [j]Am 5:18-19 **32:25** [k]Eze 7:15 [l]2Ch 36:17; La 2:21 **32:26** [m]Dt 4:27 [n]Ps 34:16 **32:27** [o]Isa 10:13 **32:29** [p]Dt 5:29; Ps 81:13 **32:30** [q]Lev 26:8 [r]Ps 44:12

32Their vine comes from the vine of
Sodom
and from the fields of Gomorrah.
Their grapes are filled with poison,
and their clusters with bitterness.
33Their wine is the venom of
serpents,
the deadly poison of cobras.[s]

34"Have I not kept this in reserve
and sealed it in my vaults?[t]
35It is mine to avenge; I will repay.[u]
In due time their foot will slip;[v]
their day of disaster is near
and their doom rushes upon
them."[w]
36The LORD will judge his people
and have compassion on his
servants[x]
when he sees their strength is gone
and no one is left, slave or free.
37He will say: "Now where are their
gods,
the rock they took refuge in,[y]
38the gods who ate the fat of their
sacrifices
and drank the wine of their drink
offerings?
Let them rise up to help you!
Let them give you shelter!

39"See now that I myself am He![z]
There is no god besides me.[a]
I put to death and I bring to life,[b]
I have wounded and I will
heal,[c]
and no one can deliver out of
my hand.[d]
40I lift my hand to heaven and
declare:
As surely as I live forever,
41when I sharpen my flashing
sword[e]
and my hand grasps it in
judgment,
I will take vengeance on my
adversaries
and repay those who hate me.[f]
42I will make my arrows drunk with
blood,[g]
while my sword devours flesh:[h]
the blood of the slain and the
captives,
the heads of the enemy leaders."

43Rejoice,[i] O nations, with his
people,[a,b]
for he will avenge the blood of
his servants;[j]
he will take vengeance on his
enemies
and make atonement for his land
and people.[k]

44Moses came with Joshua[c][l] son
of Nun and spoke all the words of this
song in the hearing of the people.
45When Moses finished reciting all
these words to all Israel, 46he said to
them, "Take to heart all the words I
have solemnly declared to you this
day,[m] so that you may command your
children to obey carefully all the words
of this law. 47They are not just idle
words for you—they are your life.[n] By
them you will live long in the land you
are crossing the Jordan to possess."

4 →PG. 249

Moses to Die on Mount Nebo

48On that same day the LORD told
Moses, 49"Go up into the Abarim[o]
Range to Mount Nebo in Moab, across
from Jericho, and view Canaan, the
land I am giving the Israelites as their
own possession. 50There on the mountain that you have climbed you will
die[p] and be gathered to your people,
just as your brother Aaron died on
Mount Hor and was gathered to his
people. 51This is because both of you
broke faith with me in the presence of
the Israelites at the waters of Meribah
Kadesh in the Desert of Zin[q] and because you did not uphold my holiness
among the Israelites.[r] 52Therefore,
you will see the land only from a distance;[s] you will not enter[t] the land I
am giving to the people of Israel."

Moses Blesses the Tribes

33 This is the blessing that Moses the
man of God[u] pronounced on the
Israelites before his death. 2He said:

"The LORD came from Sinai[v]
and dawned over them from
Seir;[w]
he shone forth from Mount
Paran.[x]
He came with[d] myriads of holy
ones[y]
from the south, from his
mountain slopes.[e]
3Surely it is you who love[z] the
people;
all the holy ones are in your
hand.[a]
At your feet they all bow down,[b]
and from you receive instruction,
4the law that Moses gave us,[c]
the possession of the assembly of
Jacob.[d]
5He was king over Jeshurun[f]

32:33 [s]Ps 58:4
32:34 [t]Jer 2:22; Hos 13:12
32:35 [u]Ro 12:19*; Heb 10:30* [v]Jer 23:12 [w]Eze 7:8-9
32:36 [x]Dt 30:1-3; Ps 135:14; Joel 2:14
32:37 [y]Jdg 10:14; Jer 2:28
32:39 [z]Isa 41:4 [a]Isa 45:5 [b]1Sa 2:6; Ps 68:20 [c]Hos 6:1 [d]Ps 50:22
32:41 [e]Isa 34:6; 66:16; Eze 21:9-10 [f]Jer 50:29
32:42 [g]ver 23 [h]Jer 46:10,14
32:43 [i]Ro 15:10* [j]2Ki 9:7 [k]Ps 65:3; 85:1; Rev 19:2
32:44 [l]Nu 13:8,16
32:46 [m]Eze 40:4
32:47 [n]Dt 30:20
32:49 [o]Nu 27:12
32:50 [p]Ge 25:8
32:51 [q]Nu 20:11-13 [r]Nu 27:14
32:52 [s]Dt 34:1-3 [t]Dt 1:37
33:1 [u]Jos 14:6
33:2 [v]Ex 19:18; Ps 68:8 [w]Jdg 5:4 [x]Hab 3:3 [y]Da 7:10; Ac 7:53; Rev 5:11
33:3 [z]Hos 11:1 [a]Dt 14:2 [b]Lk 10:39
33:4 [c]Jn 1:17 [d]Ps 119:111

a 43 Or *Make his people rejoice, O nations*
b 43 Masoretic Text; Dead Sea Scrolls (see also Septuagint) *people, / and let all the angels worship him /*
c 44 Hebrew *Hoshea,* a variant of *Joshua*
d 2 Or *from*
e 2 The meaning of the Hebrew for this phrase is uncertain.
f 5 *Jeshurun* means *the upright one,* that is, Israel; also in verse 26.

when the leaders of the people
assembled,
along with the tribes of Israel.

6"Let Reuben live and not die,
nor[a] his men be few."

7And this he said about Judah:[e]

"Hear, O LORD, the cry of Judah;
bring him to his people.
With his own hands he defends his
cause.
Oh, be his help against his foes!"

8About Levi he said:

"Your Thummim and Urim[f]
belong
to the man you favored.
You tested him at Massah;
you contended with him at the
waters of Meribah.[g]
9He said of his father and mother,[h]
'I have no regard for them.'
He did not recognize his brothers
or acknowledge his own
children,
but he watched over your word
and guarded your covenant.[i]
10He teaches your precepts to Jacob
and your law to Israel.[j]
He offers incense before you
and whole burnt offerings on
your altar.[k]
11Bless all his skills, O LORD,
and be pleased with the work of
his hands.[l]
Smite the loins of those who rise
up against him;
strike his foes till they rise no
more."

12About Benjamin he said:

"Let the beloved of the LORD rest
secure in him,[m]
for he shields him all day long,
and the one the LORD loves rests
between his shoulders.[n]"

13About Joseph[o] he said:

"May the LORD bless his land
with the precious dew from
heaven above
and with the deep waters that lie
below;[p]
14with the best the sun brings forth
and the finest the moon can
yield;
15with the choicest gifts of the
ancient mountains[q]
and the fruitfulness of the
everlasting hills;
16with the best gifts of the earth and
its fullness
and the favor of him who dwelt
in the burning bush.[r]
Let all these rest on the head of
Joseph,
on the brow of the prince
among[b] his brothers.
17In majesty he is like a firstborn
bull;
his horns are the horns of a wild
ox.[s]
With them he will gore[t] the
nations,
even those at the ends of the
earth.
Such are the ten thousands of
Ephraim;
such are the thousands of
Manasseh."

18About Zebulun[u] he said:

"Rejoice, Zebulun, in your going
out,
and you, Issachar, in your tents.
19They will summon peoples to the
mountain[v]
and there offer sacrifices of
righteousness;[w]
they will feast on the abundance of
the seas,[x]
on the treasures hidden in the
sand."

20About Gad[y] he said:

"Blessed is he who enlarges Gad's
domain!
Gad lives there like a lion,
tearing at arm or head.
21He chose the best land for
himself;[z]
the leader's portion was kept for
him.
When the heads of the people
assembled,
he carried out the LORD's
righteous will,[a]
and his judgments concerning
Israel."

22About Dan[b] he said:

"Dan is a lion's cub,
springing out of Bashan."

23About Naphtali he said:

"Naphtali is abounding with the
favor of the LORD
and is full of his blessing;
he will inherit southward to the
lake."

24About Asher[c] he said:

"Most blessed of sons is Asher;
let him be favored by his
brothers,
and let him bathe his feet in
oil.[d]

33:7 [e]Ge 49:10 **33:8** [f]Ex 28:30 [g]Ex 17:7 **33:9** [h]Ex 32:26-29 [i]Mal 2:5 **33:10** [j]Lev 10:11; Dt 31:9-13 [k]Ps 51:19 **33:11** [l]2Sa 24:23 **33:12** [m]Dt 12:10 [n]Ex 28:12 **33:13** [o]Ge 49:25 [p]Ge 27:28 **33:15** [q]Hab 3:6 **33:16** [r]Ex 3:2

33:17 [s]Nu 23:22 [t]1Ki 22:11; Ps 44:5 **33:18** [u]Ge 49:13-15 **33:19** [v]Ex 15:17; Isa 2:3 [w]Ps 4:5 [x]Isa 60:5,11 **33:20** [y]Ge 49:19 **33:21** [z]Nu 32:1-5, 31-32 [a]Jos 4:12; 22:1-3 **33:22** [b]Ge 49:16 **33:24** [c]Ge 49:21 [d]Ge 49:20; Job 29:6

[a]6 Or *but let* [b]16 Or *of the one separated from*

25The bolts of your gates will be iron
and bronze,
and your strength will equal your
days.[e]

26"There is no one like the God of
Jeshurun,[f]
who rides on the heavens to help
you[g]
and on the clouds in his majesty.
27The eternal God is your refuge,[h]
and underneath are the
everlasting arms.
He will drive out your enemy
before you,[i]
saying, 'Destroy him!'[j]
28So Israel will live in safety alone;[k]
Jacob's spring is secure
in a land of grain and new wine,
where the heavens drop dew.[l]
29Blessed are you, O Israel![m]
Who is like you,[n]
a people saved by the LORD?[o]
He is your shield and helper[p]
and your glorious sword.
Your enemies will cower before
you,
and you will trample down their
high places.[a][q]"

The Death of Moses

34 Then Moses climbed Mount Nebo
from the plains of Moab to the top
of Pisgah, across from Jericho.[r] There
the LORD showed[s] him the whole
land—from Gilead to Dan, 2all of
Naphtali, the territory of Ephraim and
Manasseh, all the land of Judah as far
as the western sea,[b][t] 3the Negev and
the whole region from the Valley of Jericho, the City of Palms,[u] as far as Zoar.
4Then the LORD said to him, "This is the
land I promised on oath[v] to Abraham,
Isaac and Jacob when I said, 'I will give
it[w] to your descendants.' I have let you
see it with your eyes, but you will not
cross[x] over into it."
5And Moses the servant of the
LORD[y] died[z] there in Moab, as the
LORD had said. 6He buried him[c] in
Moab, in the valley opposite Beth
Peor,[a] but to this day no one knows
where his grave is.[b] 7Moses was a
hundred and twenty years old[c] when
he died, yet his eyes were not weak[d]
nor his strength gone. 8The Israelites
grieved for Moses in the plains of Moab
thirty days, until the time of weeping
and mourning[e] was over.
9Now Joshua son of Nun was filled
with the spirit[d] of wisdom[f] because
Moses had laid his hands on him.[g] So
the Israelites listened to him and did
what the LORD had commanded Moses.
10Since then, no prophet has risen in
Israel like Moses,[h] whom the LORD
knew face to face,[i] 11who did all those
miraculous signs and wonders[j] the
LORD sent him to do in Egypt—to Pharaoh and to all his officials[k] and to his
whole land. 12For no one has ever
shown the mighty power or performed
the awesome deeds that Moses did in
the sight of all Israel.

33:25 [e]Dt 4:40; 32:47
33:26 [f]Ex 15:11 [g]Ps 104:3
33:27 [h]Ps 90:1 [i]Jos 24:18 [j]Dt 7:2
33:28 [k]Nu 23:9; Jer 23:6 [l]Ge 27:28
33:29 [m]Ps 144:15 [n]Ps 18:44 [o]2Sa 7:23 [p]Ps 115:9-11 [q]Dt 32:13
34:1 [r]Dt 32:49 [s]Dt 32:52
34:2 [t]Dt 11:24
34:3 [u]Jdg 1:16; 3:13; 2Ch 28:15
34:4 [v]Ge 28:13 [w]Ge 12:7 [x]Dt 3:27
34:5 [y]Nu 12:7 [z]Dt 32:50; Jos 1:1-2
34:6 [a]Dt 3:29 [b]Jude 1:9
34:7 [c]Dt 31:2 [d]Ge 27:1
34:8 [e]Ge 50:3,10; 2Sa 11:27
34:9 [f]Ge 41:38; Isa 11:2; Da 6:3 [g]Nu 27:18,23
34:10 [h]Dt 18:15,18 [i]Ex 33:11; Nu 12:6,8; Dt 5:4
34:11 [j]Dt 4:34 [k]Dt 7:19

[a]29 Or *will tread upon their bodies* [b]2 That is, the Mediterranean [c]6 Or *He was buried* [d]9 Or *Spirit*

JOSHUA

AT A GLANCE

Key Principle: God demonstrates his power and blessings to us when we are willing to trust him enough to take the risks of obedience.
Author: Joshua (24:29–33 unknown)
Time and Place: 1406 B.C. to 1390 B.C. / From Moab to Canaan
Key Verses: 1:8; 11:23; 21:45; 24:15

BENEFIT

Joshua encourages us to lay hold of God's promises and walk in his victory through trust and obedience. It continues the story of Israel after the death of Moses, and does so through the eyes of his faithful successor. Finally, this book demonstrates the blessings of courageous service to God in a context of adversity.

SETTING

This book begins with Joshua's commissioning following Moses' death in Moab. After a month of preparation, Joshua led the people across the Jordan into Canaan and launched a military campaign that required about seven years to complete. The bulk of Joshua concerns Israelite settlements in the land—2 1/2 tribes on the east of the Jordan River, the remaining 9 1/2 tribes west of the Jordan in Canaan, and the Levites in the cities of refuge. The Canaanites at that time were morally and spiritually corrupt and politically weak. Tablets from Ras Shamra reveal their practices of brutality, corruption, infant sacrifice, serpent worship and male and female prostitution. God used Israel as his instrument of judgment against the Canaanites, because their iniquity had reached its full measure (Genesis 15:16).

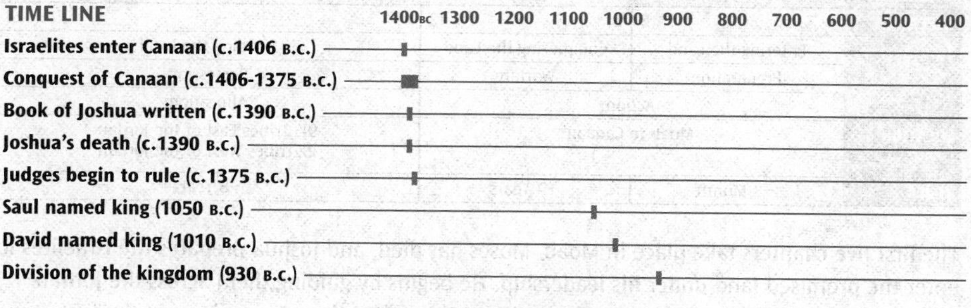

THEME AND PURPOSE

The theme of Joshua centers around Israel's conquest and settlement of the promised land. God had pledged to provide this land for his people as the reward for their obedience to his holy commands. This book was written to chronicle Israel's three-part conquest of Canaan and the division of the land among the twelve tribes. It teaches by example that true success is a byproduct of obedient faith and commitment to the God of Abraham, Isaac and Jacob. The generation of the exodus lost their opportunity to be the generation of the conquest; they had failed to trust in God's character and the promises he gave to them at Mount Sinai. After the death of the old generation, Moses taught the new generation the ways and will of God (Deuteronomy). God tested this generation under Joshua's leadership, especially as they prepared to conquer the first city, Jericho. The people trusted and obeyed the Lord at Jericho, and this became the pattern for the rest of the conquest.

UNIQUE CONTRIBUTION

Joshua continues the geographical and chronological narrative of Israel and links the Pentateuch with the following historical books. It offers a theological perspective on history, and shows how a nomadic, desert-dwelling people conquered a land of walled cities and opposing armies and became a new nation. Joshua is also a study in courageous heroism and settled confidence in God's divine guidance and purposes. The battles in this book are models of martial strategies, but the militarily unorthodox conquest of Jericho demonstrated that all subsequent victories would be accomplished by God, not by Israel's cunning or military prowess.

LINKS TO THE NEW TESTAMENT

In a number of ways, Joshua is a picture of Christ. His Hebrew name, Yeshua, is the Hebrew equivalent of the name "Jesus," which means "Yahweh is salvation." Just as Joshua succeeded Moses and won the victory that Moses did not attain, so Christ succeeded the Mosaic law and won the victory that the Mosaic law could not attain. "For the law was given through Moses; grace and truth came through Jesus Christ" (John 1:17).

The preincarnate Christ evidently appeared to Joshua in the form of "the commander of the army of the LORD" (5:13–15) and told Joshua how the Israelites were to conquer Jericho. In a scene reminiscent of Moses before the burning bush, he commanded Joshua to take off his sandals, "for the place where you are standing is holy" (5:15).

The scarlet cord Rahab tied in her window (2:21) is often seen as a picture of safety through Christ's blood (Hebrews 9:19–22).

OVERVIEW

FOCUS	Conquest		Settlement
REFERENCE	1 ... 5	6 ... 12	13 ... 24
TOPICS	Entering the Land	Conquering the Land	Dividing the Land
	Preparation	Warfare	Possession
	Action		Allocation
LOCATION	Moab to Canaan		9½ Tribes East of the Jordan 2½Tribes West of the Jordan
TIME	~1 Month	~7 Years	~8 Years

The first five chapters take place in Moab. Moses has died, and Joshua prepares the Israelites to enter the promised land under his leadership. He begins by guiding them across the Jordan River on dry land. The seven-year conquest (6—12) involves three campaigns; in the first campaign (6—8), Joshua takes the central Canaanite cities in order to drive a wedge between the northern and southern cities. In the second campaign (9—10), Joshua conquers cities in southern Canaan. In the third campaign (11—12), Joshua conquers the cities of northern Canaan.

Following the conquest, Joshua allocates the land to the twelve tribes (13—24). The settlement east of the Jordan (13) involves the boundaries of Reuben, Gad, and the half tribe of Manasseh; the settlement west of the Jordan (14—19) involves the boundaries of the remaining 9 1/2 tribes. The Levites are assigned to cities of refuge (20—21). The remainder of the book outlines the conditions under which God will continue his blessings as they settle in the land (22—24). Finally, Joshua challenges the people of Israel to keep God's law, and to serve the Lord rather than idols.

JOSHUA

The LORD Commands Joshua

1 After the death of Moses the servant of the LORD,[a] the LORD said to Joshua[b] son of Nun, Moses' aide: 2"Moses my servant is dead. Now then, you and all these people, get ready to cross the Jordan River[c] into the land I am about to give to them—to the Israelites. 3I will give you every place where you set your foot,[d] as I promised Moses. 4Your territory will extend from the desert to Lebanon, and from the great river, the Euphrates[e]—all the Hittite country—to the Great Sea**a** on the west.[f] 5No one will be able to stand up against you[g] all the days of your life. As I was with[h] Moses, so I will be with you; I will never leave you nor forsake[i] you.

6"Be strong and courageous, because you will lead these people to inherit the land I swore to their forefathers[j] to give them. 7Be strong and very courageous. Be careful to obey all the law my servant Moses gave you; do not turn from it to the right or to the left,[k] that you may be successful wherever you go.[l] 8Do not let this Book of the Law depart from your mouth; meditate on it day and night, so that you may be careful to do everything written in it. Then you will be prosperous and successful.[m] 9Have I not commanded you? Be strong and courageous. Do not be terrified;[n] do not be discouraged, for the LORD your God will be with you wherever you go."[o]

1 →PG. 225

10So Joshua ordered the officers of the people: 11"Go through the camp and tell the people, 'Get your supplies ready. Three days from now you will cross the Jordan here to go in and take possession[p] of the land the LORD your God is giving you for your own.'"

12But to the Reubenites, the Gadites and the half-tribe of Manasseh,[q] Joshua said, 13"Remember the command that Moses the servant of the LORD gave you: 'The LORD your God is giving you rest[r] and has granted you this land.' 14Your wives, your children and your livestock may stay in the land that Moses gave you east of the Jordan, but all your fighting men, fully armed, must cross over ahead of your brothers. You are to help your brothers 15until the LORD gives them rest, as he has done for you, and until they too have taken possession of the land that the LORD your God is giving them. After that, you may go back and occupy your own land, which Moses the servant of the LORD gave you east of the Jordan toward the sunrise."[s]

1 →PG. 232
2 →PG. 293

16Then they answered Joshua, "Whatever you have commanded us we will do, and wherever you send us we will go. 17Just as we fully obeyed Moses, so we will obey you.[t] Only may the LORD your God be with you as he was with Moses. 18Whoever rebels against your word and does not obey your words, whatever you may command them, will be put to death. Only be strong and courageous!"

Rahab and the Spies

2 Then Joshua son of Nun secretly sent two spies[u] from Shittim.[v] "Go, look over the land," he said, "especially Jericho." So they went and entered the house of a prostitute**b** named Rahab[w] and stayed there.

a *4* That is, the Mediterranean **b** *1* Or possibly *an innkeeper*

1:1 [a]Nu 12:7; Dt 34:5 [b]Ex 24:13; Dt 1:38
1:2 [c]ver 11
1:3 [d]Dt 11:24
1:4 [e]Ge 15:18 [f]Nu 34:2-12
1:5 [g]Dt 7:24 [h]Jos 3:7; 6:27 [i]Dt 31:6-8
1:6 [j]Dt 31:23
1:7 [k]Dt 5:32; 28:14 [l]Jos 11:15
1:8 [m]Dt 29:9; Ps 1:1-3
1:9 [n]Ps 27:1 [o]ver 7; Dt 31:7-8; Jer 1:8
1:11 [p]Joel 3:2
1:12 [q]Nu 32:20-22
1:13 [r]Dt 3:18-20
1:15 [s]Jos 22:1-4
1:17 [t]ver 5,9
2:1 [u]Jas 2:25 [v]Nu 25:1; Jos 3:1 [w]Heb 11:31

1:6–9 PROMISE **1**

THE KEY TO COURAGE

What does it take to succeed in an impossible job? Take a look at Joshua's situation. Joshua became Israel's leader when success seemed humanly impossible. But this paragraph summarizes God's instructions to the new leader of Israel.

The phrase "Be strong and courageous" (vv. 6, 7, 9) provides the key to Joshua's success as a leader. How could Joshua be inwardly strong and courageous? First, by relating properly to God's Word. Notice the number of different ways God told Joshua to use Biblical teaching (vv. 7–8). Second, by trusting in God's continual presence and guidance.

Life's pace and complexity often seem overwhelming. Whatever your role as a Christian man—husband, father, son, employee, employer, church member, teacher—God offers you the same instruction and gives you the same promises. Inner strength and courage grow out of a knowledge of God's Word and assurance of his presence. Read and meditate on God's Word daily. And pray regularly that he will remind you of his presence in your life.

For the next Promise 1 reading go to page 226.

2The king of Jericho was told, "Look! Some of the Israelites have come here tonight to spy out the land." 3So the king of Jericho sent this message to Rahab: "Bring out the men who came to you and entered your house, because they have come to spy out the whole land."

4But the woman had taken the two men and hidden them.[x] She said, "Yes, the men came to me, but I did not know where they had come from. 5At dusk, when it was time to close the city gate, the men left. I don't know which way they went. Go after them quickly. You may catch up with them." 6(But she had taken them up to the roof and hidden them under the stalks of flax[y] she had laid out on the roof.)[z] 7So the men set out in pursuit of the spies on the road that leads to the fords of the Jordan, and as soon as the pursuers had gone out, the gate was shut.

8Before the spies lay down for the night, she went up on the roof 9and said to them, "I know that the LORD has given this land to you and that a great fear[a] of you has fallen on us, so that all who live in this country are melting in fear because of you. 10We have heard how the LORD dried up[b] the water of the Red Sea[a] for you when you came out of Egypt,[c] and what you did to Sihon and Og,[d] the two kings of the Amorites east of the Jordan, whom you completely destroyed.[b] 11When we heard of it, our hearts melted and everyone's courage failed because of you,[e] for the LORD your God is God in heaven above and on the earth[f] below. 12Now then, please swear to me by the LORD that you will show kindness to my family, because I have shown kindness to you. Give me a sure sign[g] 13that you will spare the lives of my father and mother, my brothers and sisters, and all who belong to them, and that you will save us from death."

14"Our lives for your lives!" the men assured her. "If you don't tell what we are doing, we will treat you kindly and faithfully[h] when the LORD gives us the land."

15So she let them down by a rope through the window,[i] for the house she lived in was part of the city wall. 16Now she had said to them, "Go to the hills so the pursuers will not find you. Hide yourselves there three days[j] until they return, and then go on your way."[k]

17The men said to her, "This oath[l] you made us swear will not be binding on us 18unless, when we enter the land, you have tied this scarlet cord in the window through which you let us down, and unless you have brought your father and mother, your brothers and all your family[m] into your house. 19If anyone goes outside your house into the street, his blood will be on his own head;[n] we will not be responsible. As for anyone who is in the house with you, his blood will be on our head[o] if a hand is laid on him. 20But if you tell what we are doing, we will be released from the oath you made us swear."

21"Agreed," she replied. "Let it be as you say." So she sent them away and they departed. And she tied the scarlet cord in the window.

22When they left, they went into the hills and stayed there three days, until the pursuers had searched all along the road and returned without finding them. 23Then the two men started back. They went down out of the hills, forded the river and came to Joshua son of Nun and told him everything that had happened to them. 24They said to Joshua, "The LORD has surely given the whole land into our hands;[p] all the people are melting in fear because of us."

Crossing the Jordan

3 Early in the morning Joshua and all the Israelites set out from Shittim[q] and went to the Jordan, where they camped before crossing over. 2After

2:4 [x]2Sa 17:19-20 **2:6** [y]Jas 2:25 [z]Ex 1:17,19; 2Sa 17:19 **2:9** [a]Ge 35:5; Ex 23:27; Dt 2:25 **2:10** [b]Ex 14:21 [c]Nu 23:22 [d]Nu 21:21,24, 34-35 **2:11** [e]Ex 15:14; Jos 5:1; 7:5; Ps 22:14; Isa 13:7 [f]Dt 4:39

2:12 [g]ver 18 **2:14** [h]Jdg 1:24; Mt 5:7 **2:15** [i]Ac 9:25 **2:16** [j]Jas 2:25 [k]Heb 11:31 **2:17** [l]Ge 24:8 **2:18** [m]ver 12; Jos 6:23 **2:19** [n]Eze 33:4 [o]Mt 27:25 **2:24** [p]ver 9; Jos 6:2 **3:1** [q]Jos 2:1

a *10* Hebrew *Yam Suph*; that is, Sea of Reeds
b *10* The Hebrew term refers to the irrevocable giving over of things or persons to the LORD, often by totally destroying them.

2:8–13 PROMISE 1

A MODEL OF OBEDIENCE

Amazing things happen when we perceive that God is at work. Rahab, a Gentile prostitute, was as far from God's covenant community as we can imagine. But she believed in and obeyed God, and the Bible remembers her for her faith.

Aside from being the main character in this story, Rahab is mentioned three times in the New Testament. She is in Jesus' genealogy (Matthew 1:5), she is listed among the heroes of the faith (Hebrews 11:31) and James uses her as an example of faith in action (James 2:25). Rahab wasn't a great preacher or theologian, but she believed God and did what he said. That's all God asks of us.

Guess what? If she can believe in and obey God, you can too. Read, believe and act on God's revealed truth in the Bible.

For the next Promise 1 reading go to page 243.

three days the officers went throughout the camp,[r] 3giving orders to the
people: "When you see the ark of the
covenant[s] of the LORD your God, and
the priests,[t] who are Levites, carrying
it, you are to move out from your positions and follow it. 4Then you will
know which way to go, since you have
never been this way before. But keep a
distance of about a thousand yards[a]
between you and the ark; do not go
near it."

5Joshua told the people, "Consecrate
yourselves,[u] for tomorrow the LORD
will do amazing things among you."

6Joshua said to the priests, "Take up
the ark of the covenant and pass on
ahead of the people." So they took it up
and went ahead of them.

7And the LORD said to Joshua, "Today I will begin to exalt you[v] in the
eyes of all Israel, so they may know that
I am with you as I was with Moses.[w]
8Tell the priests[x] who carry the ark
of the covenant: 'When you reach the
edge of the Jordan's waters, go and
stand in the river.' "

9Joshua said to the Israelites, "Come
here and listen to the words of the
LORD your God. 10This is how you will
know that the living God[y] is among
you and that he will certainly drive out
before you the Canaanites, Hittites, Hivites, Perizzites, Girgashites, Amorites
and Jebusites.[z] 11See, the ark of the
covenant of the Lord of all the earth[a]
will go into the Jordan ahead of you.
12Now then, choose twelve men[b] from
the tribes of Israel, one from each tribe.
13And as soon as the priests who carry
the ark of the LORD—the Lord of all the
earth[c]—set foot in the Jordan, its waters flowing downstream[d] will be cut
off and stand up in a heap.[e]"

14So when the people broke camp to
cross the Jordan, the priests carrying
the ark of the covenant[f] went ahead[g]
of them. 15Now the Jordan is at flood
stage[h] all during harvest. Yet as soon
as the priests who carried the ark
reached the Jordan and their feet
touched the water's edge, 16the water
from upstream stopped flowing.[i] It
piled up in a heap a great distance
away, at a town called Adam in the vicinity of Zarethan,[j] while the water
flowing down[k] to the Sea of the Arabah[l] (the Salt Sea[b][m]) was completely cut off. So the people crossed over
opposite Jericho. 17The priests who
carried the ark of the covenant of the
LORD stood firm on dry ground in the
middle of the Jordan, while all Israel
passed by until the whole nation had
completed the crossing on dry
ground.[n]

3:2 [r]Jos 1:11
3:3 [s]Nu 10:33 [t]Dt 31:9
3:5 [u]Ex 19:10,14; Lev 20:7; Jos 7:13; 1Sa 16:5; Joel 2:16
3:7 [v]Jos 4:14; 1Ch 29:25 [w]Jos 1:5
3:8 [x]ver 3
3:10 [y]Dt 5:26; 1Sa 17:26,36; 2Ki 19:4,16; Hos 1:10; Mt 16:16; 1Th 1:9 [z]Ex 33:2; Dt 7:1
3:11 [a]ver 13; Job 41:11; Zec 6:5
3:12 [b]Jos 4:2,4
3:13 [c]ver 11 [d]ver 16 [e]Ex 15:8; Ps 78:13
3:14 [f]Ps 132:8 [g]Ac 7:44-45
3:15 [h]Jos 4:18; 1Ch 12:15
3:16 [i]Ps 66:6; 74:15 [j]1Ki 4:12; 7:46 [k]ver 13 [l]Dt 1:1 [m]Ge 14:3
3:17 [n]Ex 14:22,29

4 When the whole nation had finished
crossing the Jordan,[o] the LORD said
to Joshua, 2"Choose twelve men[p]
from among the people, one from each
tribe, 3and tell them to take up twelve
stones[q] from the middle of the Jordan
from right where the priests stood and
to carry them over with you and put
them down at the place where you stay
tonight.[r]"

4So Joshua called together the
twelve men he had appointed from the
Israelites, one from each tribe, 5and
said to them, "Go over before the ark of
the LORD your God into the middle of
the Jordan. Each of you is to take up a
stone on his shoulder, according to the
number of the tribes of the Israelites,
6to serve as a sign among you. In the
future, when your children ask you,
'What do these stones mean?'[s] 7tell
them that the flow of the Jordan was
cut off[t] before the ark of the covenant
of the LORD. When it crossed the Jordan, the waters of the Jordan were cut
off. These stones are to be a memorial[u] to the people of Israel forever."

8So the Israelites did as Joshua commanded them. They took twelve stones
from the middle of the Jordan, according to the number of the tribes of the
Israelites, as the LORD had told Joshua;[v] and they carried them over with
them to their camp, where they put
them down. 9Joshua set up the twelve

4:1 [o]Dt 27:2
4:2 [p]Jos 3:12
4:3 [q]ver 20 [r]ver 19
4:6 [s]ver 21; Ex 12:26; 13:14
4:7 [t]Jos 3:13 [u]Ex 12:14
4:8 [v]ver 20

a 4 Hebrew *about two thousand cubits* (about 900 meters) b 16 That is, the Dead Sea

4:1–6, 21–24

PROMISE 4

MONUMENTS TO GOD'S POWER

As Israel crossed the Jordan in fulfillment of God's promise of a new homeland, God commanded that his people remember his faithfulness. He told them to build a memorial to remind them of this day, and gave three reasons why. First, so that the people's children would learn from the things God did in their lives (vv. 6, 21). Second, so that other people who didn't know God would see his power at work in the life of Israel (v. 24). Third, as a personal and abiding reminder to fear God above all (v. 24).

As you reflect on the way God's sovereign hand has led you through your life, don't miss the marker events. Use them as testimonies to God's power and grace at work in you. Allow them to stand as reminders to you and your children, and as solid examples of God's power to those who do not know him yet.

For the next Promise 4 reading go to page 250.

stones[w] that had been[a] in the middle
of the Jordan at the spot where the
priests who carried the ark of the covenant had stood. And they are there to
this day.
10 Now the priests who carried the
ark remained standing in the middle of
the Jordan until everything the LORD
had commanded Joshua was done by
the people, just as Moses had directed
Joshua. The people hurried over, 11 and
as soon as all of them had crossed, the
ark of the LORD and the priests came
to the other side while the people
watched. 12 The men of Reuben, Gad
and the half-tribe of Manasseh crossed
over, armed, in front of the Israelites,[x]
as Moses had directed them. 13 About
forty thousand armed for battle
crossed over before the LORD to the
plains of Jericho for war.
14 That day the LORD exalted[y] Joshua in the sight of all Israel; and they
revered him all the days of his life, just
as they had revered Moses.
15 Then the LORD said to Joshua,
16 "Command the priests carrying the
ark of the Testimony[z] to come up out
of the Jordan."
17 So Joshua commanded the priests,
"Come up out of the Jordan."
18 And the priests came up out of the
river carrying the ark of the covenant of
the LORD. No sooner had they set their
feet on the dry ground than the waters
of the Jordan returned to their place
and ran at flood stage[a] as before.
19 On the tenth day of the first month
the people went up from the Jordan
and camped at Gilgal[b] on the eastern
border of Jericho. 20 And Joshua set up
at Gilgal the twelve stones[c] they had
taken out of the Jordan. 21 He said to
the Israelites, "In the future when your
descendants ask their fathers, 'What
do these stones mean?'[d] 22 tell them,
'Israel crossed the Jordan on dry
ground.'[e] 23 For the LORD your God
dried up the Jordan before you until
you had crossed over. The LORD your
God did to the Jordan just what he had
done to the Red Sea[b] when he dried
it up before us until we had crossed
over.[f] 24 He did this so that all the peoples of the earth might know[g] that the
hand of the LORD is powerful[h] and so
that you might always fear the LORD
your God.[i]"

Circumcision at Gilgal

5 Now when all the Amorite kings
west of the Jordan and all the Canaanite kings along the coast[j] heard
how the LORD had dried up the Jordan
before the Israelites until we had
crossed over, their hearts melted[k] and
they no longer had the courage to face
the Israelites.
2 At that time the LORD said to Joshua, "Make flint knives[l] and circumcise the Israelites again." 3 So Joshua
made flint knives and circumcised the
Israelites at Gibeath Haaraloth.[c]
4 Now this is why he did so: All those
who came out of Egypt—all the men of
military age—died in the desert on the
way after leaving Egypt.[m] 5 All the people that came out had been circumcised, but all the people born in the
desert during the journey from Egypt
had not. 6 The Israelites had moved
about in the desert forty years[n] until
all the men who were of military age
when they left Egypt had died, since
they had not obeyed the LORD. For the
LORD had sworn to them that they
would not see the land that he had solemnly promised their fathers to give
us,[o] a land flowing with milk and honey.[p] 7 So he raised up their sons in
their place, and these were the ones
Joshua circumcised. They were still uncircumcised because they had not
been circumcised on the way. 8 And after the whole nation had been circumcised, they remained where they were
in camp until they were healed.[q]
9 Then the LORD said to Joshua, "Today I have rolled away the reproach of
Egypt from you." So the place has been
called Gilgal[d] to this day.
10 On the evening of the fourteenth
day of the month,[r] while camped at
Gilgal on the plains of Jericho, the Israelites celebrated the Passover. 11 The
day after the Passover, that very day,
they ate some of the produce of the
land:[s] unleavened bread and roasted
grain.[t] 12 The manna stopped the day
after[e] they ate this food from the land;
there was no longer any manna for the
Israelites, but that year they ate of the
produce of Canaan.[u]

The Fall of Jericho

13 Now when Joshua was near Jericho, he looked up and saw a man[v]
standing in front of him with a drawn
sword[w] in his hand. Joshua went up to
him and asked, "Are you for us or for
our enemies?"
14 "Neither," he replied, "but as commander of the army of the LORD I have
now come." Then Joshua fell facedown[x] to the ground in reverence,

4:9 [w] Ge 28:18; Jos 24:26; 1Sa 7:12
4:12 [x] Nu 32:27
4:14 [y] Jos 3:7
4:16 [z] Ex 25:22
4:18 [a] Jos 3:15
4:19 [b] Jos 5:9
4:20 [c] ver 3,8
4:21 [d] ver 6
4:22 [e] Jos 3:17
4:23 [f] Ex 14:21
4:24 [g] 1Ki 8:42-43; 2Ki 19:19; Ps 106:8; Jer 10:7 [h] Ex 15:16; 1Ch 29:12; Ps 89:13 [i] Ex 14:31
5:1 [j] Nu 13:29 [k] Jos 2:9-11
5:2 [l] Ex 4:25
5:4 [m] Dt 2:14
5:6 [n] Dt 2:7 [o] Nu 14:23, 29-35; Dt 2:14 [p] Ex 3:8
5:8 [q] Ge 34:25
5:10 [r] Ex 12:6
5:11 [s] Nu 15:19 [t] Lev 23:14
5:12 [u] Ex 16:35
5:13 [v] Ge 18:2; 32:24 [w] Nu 22:23
5:14 [x] Ge 17:3

a *9* Or *Joshua also set up twelve stones*
b *23* Hebrew *Yam Suph*; that is, Sea of Reeds
c *3* *Gibeath Haaraloth* means *hill of foreskins.*
d *9* *Gilgal* sounds like the Hebrew for *roll.*
e *12* Or *the day*

and asked him, "What message does
my Lord[a] have for his servant?"
15The commander of the LORD's
army replied, "Take off your sandals,
for the place where you are standing is
holy."[y] And Joshua did so.

6 Now Jericho[z] was tightly shut up
because of the Israelites. No one
went out and no one came in.
2Then the LORD said to Joshua, "See,
I have delivered[a] Jericho into your
hands, along with its king and its fighting men. 3March around the city once
with all the armed men. Do this for six
days. 4Have seven priests carry trumpets of rams' horns in front of the ark.
On the seventh day, march around the
city seven times, with the priests blowing the trumpets.[b] 5When you hear
them sound a long blast[c] on the trumpets, have all the people give a loud
shout;[d] then the wall of the city will
collapse and the people will go up, every man straight in."
6So Joshua son of Nun called the
priests and said to them, "Take up the
ark of the covenant of the LORD and
have seven priests carry trumpets in
front of it." 7And he ordered the people, "Advance[e]! March around the
city, with the armed guard going ahead
of the ark of the LORD."
8When Joshua had spoken to the
people, the seven priests carrying the
seven trumpets before the LORD went
forward, blowing their trumpets, and
the ark of the LORD's covenant followed
them. 9The armed guard marched
ahead of the priests who blew the
trumpets, and the rear guard[f] followed the ark. All this time the trumpets were sounding. 10But Joshua had
commanded the people, "Do not give a
war cry, do not raise your voices, do
not say a word until the day I tell you
to shout. Then shout![g]" 11So he had
the ark of the LORD carried around the
city, circling it once. Then the people
returned to camp and spent the night
there.
12Joshua got up early the next morning and the priests took up the ark of
the LORD. 13The seven priests carrying
the seven trumpets went forward,
marching before the ark of the LORD
and blowing the trumpets. The armed
men went ahead of them and the rear
guard followed the ark of the LORD,
while the trumpets kept sounding. 14So
on the second day they marched
around the city once and returned to
the camp. They did this for six days.
15On the seventh day, they got up at
daybreak and marched around the city
seven times in the same manner, except that on that day they circled the
city seven times.[h] 16The seventh time
around, when the priests sounded the
trumpet blast, Joshua commanded the
people, "Shout! For the LORD has given
you the city! 17The city and all that is in
it are to be devoted[b][i] to the LORD.
Only Rahab the prostitute[c] and all
who are with her in her house shall be
spared, because she hid[j] the spies we
sent. 18But keep away from the devoted
things,[k] so that you will not bring
about your own destruction by taking
any of them. Otherwise you will make
the camp of Israel liable to destruction[l] and bring trouble[m] on it. 19All
the silver and gold and the articles of
bronze and iron[n] are sacred to the
LORD and must go into his treasury."
20When the trumpets sounded,[o]
the people shouted, and at the sound
of the trumpet, when the people gave a
loud shout,[p] the wall collapsed; so every man charged straight in, and they
took the city.[q] 21They devoted the city
to the LORD and destroyed[r] with the
sword every living thing in it—men
and women, young and old, cattle,
sheep and donkeys.
22Joshua said to the two men who
had spied out the land, "Go into the
prostitute's house and bring her out
and all who belong to her, in accordance with your oath to her.[s]" 23So
the young men who had done the spying went in and brought out Rahab, her
father and mother and brothers and all
who belonged to her.[t] They brought
out her entire family and put them in a
place outside the camp of Israel.
24Then they burned the whole city
and everything in it, but they put the
silver and gold and the articles of
bronze and iron[u] into the treasury of
the LORD's house. 25But Joshua spared
Rahab the prostitute,[v] with her family
and all who belonged to her, because
she hid the men Joshua had sent as
spies to Jericho[w]—and she lives
among the Israelites to this day.
26At that time Joshua pronounced
this solemn oath: "Cursed before the
LORD is the man who undertakes to rebuild this city, Jericho:

"At the cost of his firstborn son
  will he lay its foundations;
at the cost of his youngest
  will he set up its gates."[x]

27So the LORD was with Joshua,[y]
and his fame spread[z] throughout the
land.

5:15 [y]Ex 3:5; Ac 7:33
6:1 [z]Jos 24:11
6:2 [a]Dt 7:24; Jos 2:9,24; 8:1
6:4 [b]Lev 25:9; Nu 10:8
6:5 [c]Ex 19:13 [d]ver 20; 1Sa 4:5; Ps 42:4; Isa 42:13
6:7 [e]Ex 14:15
6:9 [f]ver 13; Isa 52:12
6:10 [g]ver 20
6:15 [h]1Ki 18:44
6:17 [i]Lev 27:28; Dt 20:17 [j]Jos 2:4
6:18 [k]Jos 7:1 [l]Jos 7:12 [m]Jos 7:25,26
6:19 [n]ver 24; Nu 31:22
6:20 [o]Jdg 6:34; Jer 4:21; Am 2:2 [p]ver 5 [q]Heb 11:30
6:21 [r]Dt 20:16
6:22 [s]Jos 2:14; Heb 11:31
6:23 [t]Jos 2:13
6:24 [u]ver 19
6:25 [v]Heb 11:31 [w]Jos 2:6
6:26 [x]1Ki 16:34
6:27 [y]Ge 39:2; Jos 1:5 [z]Jos 9:1

a *14* Or *lord* b *17* The Hebrew term refers to the irrevocable giving over of things or persons to the LORD, often by totally destroying them; also in verses 18 and 21. c *17* Or possibly *innkeeper*; also in verses 22 and 25

Achan's Sin

7 But the Israelites acted unfaithfully
in regard to the devoted things[a];[a]
Achan son of Carmi, the son of Zimri,[b]
the son of Zerah,[b] of the tribe of Judah, took some of them. So the LORD's
anger burned against Israel.
2 Now Joshua sent men from Jericho
to Ai, which is near Beth Aven[c] to the
east of Bethel, and told them, "Go up
and spy out the region." So the men
went up and spied out Ai.
3 When they returned to Joshua, they
said, "Not all the people will have to go
up against Ai. Send two or three thousand men to take it and do not weary
all the people, for only a few men are
there." 4 So about three thousand men
went up; but they were routed by the
men of Ai,[d] 5 who killed about thirty-
six of them. They chased the Israelites
from the city gate as far as the stone
quarries[c] and struck them down on
the slopes. At this the hearts of the people melted[e] and became like water.
6 Then Joshua tore his clothes[f] and
fell facedown to the ground before the
ark of the LORD, remaining there till
evening. The elders of Israel did the
same, and sprinkled dust[g] on their
heads. 7 And Joshua said, "Ah, Sovereign LORD, why did you ever bring this
people across the Jordan to deliver us
into the hands of the Amorites to destroy us?[h] If only we had been content
to stay on the other side of the Jordan!
8 O Lord, what can I say, now that Israel
has been routed by its enemies? 9 The
Canaanites and the other people of the
country will hear about this and they
will surround us and wipe out our
name from the earth.[i] What then will
you do for your own great name?"
10 The LORD said to Joshua, "Stand
up! What are you doing down on your
face? 11 Israel has sinned; they have violated my covenant,[j] which I commanded them to keep. They have taken
some of the devoted things; they have
stolen, they have lied,[k] they have put
them with their own possessions.
12 That is why the Israelites cannot
stand against their enemies;[l] they
turn their backs and run because they
have been made liable to destruction.[m] I will not be with you anymore
unless you destroy whatever among
you is devoted to destruction.
13 "Go, consecrate the people. Tell
them, 'Consecrate yourselves[n] in
preparation for tomorrow; for this is
what the LORD, the God of Israel, says:
That which is devoted is among you,
O Israel. You cannot stand against
your enemies until you remove it.
14 " 'In the morning, present yourselves tribe by tribe. The tribe that the
LORD takes[o] shall come forward clan
by clan; the clan that the LORD takes
shall come forward family by family;
and the family that the LORD takes shall
come forward man by man. 15 He who
is caught with the devoted things shall
be destroyed by fire, along with all that
belongs to him.[p] He has violated the
covenant[q] of the LORD and has done a
disgraceful thing in Israel!' "[r]
16 Early the next morning Joshua had
Israel come forward by tribes, and Judah was taken. 17 The clans of Judah
came forward, and he took the Zerahites.[s] He had the clan of the Zerahites come forward by families, and
Zimri was taken. 18 Joshua had his family come forward man by man, and
Achan son of Carmi, the son of Zimri,
the son of Zerah, of the tribe of Judah,
was taken.
19 Then Joshua said to Achan, "My

7:1 *a* Jos 6:18 *b* Jos 22:20 **7:2** *c* Jos 18:12; 1Sa 13:5; 14:23 **7:4** *d* Lev 26:17; Dt 28:25 **7:5** *e* Lev 26:36; Jos 2:9,11; Eze 21:7; Na 2:10 **7:6** *f* Ge 37:29 *g* 1Sa 4:12; 2Sa 13:19; Ne 9:1; Job 2:12; La 2:10; Rev 18:19 **7:7** *h* Ex 5:22 **7:9** *i* Ex 32:12; Dt 9:28 **7:11** *j* Jos 6:17-19 *k* Ac 5:1-2 **7:12** *l* Nu 14:45; Jdg 2:14 *m* Jos 6:18 **7:13** *n* Jos 3:5; 6:18 **7:14** *o* Pr 16:33 **7:15** *p* 1Sa 14:39 *q* ver 11 *r* Ge 34:7 **7:17** *s* Nu 26:20

a *1* The Hebrew term refers to the irrevocable giving over of things or persons to the LORD, often by totally destroying them; also in verses 11, 12, 13 and 15. **b** *1* See Septuagint and 1 Chron. 2:6; Hebrew *Zabdi*; also in verses 17 and 18. **c** *5* Or *as far as Shebarim*

7:6–12 — PROMISE 3

DEALING WITH SIN

In their divinely mandated conquest of Canaan, Israel sent spies to check out the city of Ai. The spies reported that this tiny, vulnerable city wasn't even worth Israel's full attention, "for only a few men are there" (v. 3). What happened? The army of Israel, fresh from defeating Jericho, one of the area's heavyweight champs, was routed by Ai, a 90-pound weakling by comparison.

Such a great defeat after such a great victory! Joshua fell on his face before God in confusion and anguish. "Why did you ever bring this people across the Jordan . . . ?" (v. 7). In answer, God said, "It's very simple Joshua, it's sin. You want my presence and power? Deal with the sin in your community."

Sometimes we question why God is so far away, why he doesn't come to help us in our circumstances. The answer, based on this passage, is that sometimes God uses difficult circumstances to show us the sin in our lives. But God has given us a simple, uncomplicated way for us to deal with our sin. We must acknowledge it, confess it and repent of it (1 John 1:9).

Sin will destroy us as it would destroy Israel. Joshua cleaned it out—rather brutally (vv. 19–26). So must we.

For the next Promise 3 reading go to page 255.

son, give glory[t] to the LORD,[a] the God
of Israel, and give him the praise.[b]
Tell[u] me what you have done; do not
hide it from me."
20 Achan replied, "It is true! I have
sinned against the LORD, the God of Israel. This is what I have done: 21 When
I saw in the plunder a beautiful robe
from Babylonia,[c] two hundred shekels[d] of silver and a wedge of gold
weighing fifty shekels,[e] I coveted[v]
them and took them. They are hidden
in the ground inside my tent, with the
silver underneath."
22 So Joshua sent messengers, and
they ran to the tent, and there it was,
hidden in his tent, with the silver underneath. 23 They took the things from
the tent, brought them to Joshua and
all the Israelites and spread them out
before the LORD.
24 Then Joshua, together with all Israel, took Achan son of Zerah, the silver, the robe, the gold wedge, his sons
and daughters, his cattle, donkeys and
sheep, his tent and all that he had, to
the Valley of Achor.[w] 25 Joshua said,
"Why have you brought this trouble[x]
on us? The LORD will bring trouble on
you today."
Then all Israel stoned him,[y] and after they had stoned the rest, they
burned them. 26 Over Achan they
heaped up a large pile of rocks, which
remains to this day. Then the LORD
turned from his fierce anger.[z] Therefore that place has been called the Valley of Achor[f][a] ever since.

Ai Destroyed

8 Then the LORD said to Joshua, "Do
not be afraid;[b] do not be discouraged.[c] Take the whole army[d]
with you, and go up and attack Ai. For
I have delivered[e] into your hands the
king of Ai, his people, his city and his
land. 2 You shall do to Ai and its king as
you did to Jericho and its king, except
that you may carry off their plunder
and livestock for yourselves.[f] Set an
ambush behind the city."
3 So Joshua and the whole army
moved out to attack Ai. He chose thirty
thousand of his best fighting men and
sent them out at night 4 with these orders: "Listen carefully. You are to set an
ambush behind the city. Don't go very
far from it. All of you be on the alert. 5 I
and all those with me will advance on
the city, and when the men come out
against us, as they did before, we will
flee from them. 6 They will pursue us
until we have lured them away from
the city, for they will say, 'They are running away from us as they did before.'
So when we flee from them, 7 you are to
rise up from ambush and take the city.
The LORD your God will give it into your
hand.[g] 8 When you have taken the city,
set it on fire.[h] Do what the LORD has
commanded.[i] See to it; you have my
orders."
9 Then Joshua sent them off, and
they went to the place of ambush[j]
and lay in wait between Bethel and Ai,
to the west of Ai—but Joshua spent
that night with the people.
10 Early the next morning[k] Joshua
mustered his men, and he and the
leaders of Israel[l] marched before
them to Ai. 11 The entire force that was
with him marched up and approached
the city and arrived in front of it. They
set up camp north of Ai, with the valley between them and the city. 12 Joshua had taken about five thousand
men and set them in ambush between
Bethel and Ai, to the west of the city.
13 They had the soldiers take up their
positions—all those in the camp to the
north of the city and the ambush to the
west of it. That night Joshua went into
the valley.
14 When the king of Ai saw this, he
and all the men of the city hurried out
early in the morning to meet Israel in
battle at a certain place overlooking the
Arabah.[m] But he did not know[n] that
an ambush had been set against him
behind the city. 15 Joshua and all Israel
let themselves be driven back[o] before
them, and they fled toward the
desert.[p] 16 All the men of Ai were called
to pursue them, and they pursued
Joshua and were lured away[q] from the
city. 17 Not a man remained in Ai or
Bethel who did not go after Israel. They
left the city open and went in pursuit of
Israel.
18 Then the LORD said to Joshua,
"Hold out toward Ai the javelin[r] that
is in your hand,[s] for into your hand I
will deliver the city." So Joshua held
out his javelin[t] toward Ai. 19 As soon
as he did this, the men in the ambush
rose quickly[u] from their position and
rushed forward. They entered the city
and captured it and quickly set it on
fire.[v]
20 The men of Ai looked back and saw
the smoke of the city rising against the
sky,[w] but they had no chance to escape in any direction, for the Israelites
who had been fleeing toward the
desert had turned back against their

7:19 [t] 1Sa 6:5; Jer 13:16; Jn 9:24* [u] 1Sa 14:43 **7:21** [v] Dt 7:25; Eph 5:5; 1Ti 6:10 **7:24** [w] ver 26; Jos 15:7 **7:25** [x] Jos 6:18 [y] Dt 17:5 **7:26** [z] Nu 25:4; Dt 13:17 [a] ver 24; Isa 65:10; Hos 2:15 **8:1** [b] Dt 31:6 [c] Dt 1:21; 7:18; Jos 1:9 [d] Jos 10:7 [e] Jos 6:2 **8:2** [f] ver 27; Dt 20:14

8:7 [g] Jdg 7:7; 1Sa 23:4 **8:8** [h] Jdg 20:29-38 [i] ver 19 **8:9** [j] 2Ch 13:13 **8:10** [k] Ge 22:3 [l] Jos 7:6 **8:14** [m] Dt 1:1 [n] Jdg 20:34 **8:15** [o] Jdg 20:36 [p] Jos 15:61; 16:1; 18:12 **8:16** [q] Jdg 20:31 **8:18** [r] Job 41:26; Ps 35:3 [s] Ex 4:2; 14:16; 17:9-12 [t] ver 26 **8:19** [u] Jdg 20:33 [v] ver 8 **8:20** [w] Jdg 20:40

a *19* A solemn charge to tell the truth b *19* Or *and confess to him* c *21* Hebrew *Shinar* d *21* That is, about 5 pounds (about 2.3 kilograms) e *21* That is, about 1 1/4 pounds (about 0.6 kilogram) f *26* *Achor* means *trouble.*

pursuers. 21For when Joshua and all Israel saw that the ambush had taken the city and that smoke was going up from the city, they turned around and attacked the men of Ai. 22The men of the ambush also came out of the city against them, so that they were caught in the middle, with Israelites on both sides. Israel cut them down, leaving them neither survivors nor fugitives.[x] 23But they took the king of Ai alive[y] and brought him to Joshua.

24When Israel had finished killing all the men of Ai in the fields and in the desert where they had chased them, and when every one of them had been put to the sword, all the Israelites returned to Ai and killed those who were in it. 25Twelve thousand men and women fell that day—all the people of Ai.[z] 26For Joshua did not draw back the hand that held out his javelin until he had destroyed[a][a] all who lived in Ai.[b] 27But Israel did carry off for themselves the livestock and plunder of this city, as the LORD had instructed Joshua.[c]

28So Joshua burned[d] Ai[e] and made it a permanent heap of ruins,[f] a desolate place to this day.[g] 29He hung the king of Ai on a tree and left him there until evening. At sunset,[h] Joshua ordered them to take his body from the tree and throw it down at the entrance of the city gate. And they raised a large pile of rocks[i] over it, which remains to this day.

The Covenant Renewed at Mount Ebal

1 →PG. 247

30Then Joshua built on Mount Ebal[j] an altar[k] to the LORD, the God of Israel, 31as Moses the servant of the LORD had commanded the Israelites. He built it according to what is written in the Book of the Law of Moses—an altar of uncut stones, on which no iron tool[l] had been used. On it they offered to the LORD burnt offerings and sacrificed fellowship offerings.[b][m] 32There, in the presence of the Israelites, Joshua copied on stones the law of Moses, which he had written.[n] 33All Israel, aliens and citizens[o] alike, with their elders, officials and judges, were standing on both sides of the ark of the covenant of the LORD, facing those who carried it—the priests, who were Levites.[p] Half of the people stood in front of Mount Gerizim and half of them in front of Mount Ebal,[q] as Moses the servant of the LORD had formerly commanded when he gave instructions to bless the people of Israel.

34Afterward, Joshua read all the words of the law—the blessings and the curses—just as it is written in the Book of the Law.[r] 35There was not a word of all that Moses had commanded that Joshua did not read to the whole assembly of Israel, including the women and children, and the aliens who lived among them.[s]

The Gibeonite Deception

9 Now when all the kings west of the Jordan heard about these things—those in the hill country, in the western foothills, and along the entire coast of the Great Sea[c][t] as far as Lebanon (the kings of the Hittites, Amorites, Canaanites, Perizzites, Hivites and Jebusites)[u]— 2they came together to make war against Joshua and Israel.

3However, when the people of Gibeon[v] heard what Joshua had done to Jericho and Ai, 4they resorted to a ruse: They went as a delegation whose donkeys were loaded[d] with worn-out sacks and old wineskins, cracked and mended. 5The men put worn and patched sandals on their feet and wore old clothes. All the bread of their food supply was dry and moldy. 6Then they went to Joshua in the camp at Gilgal[w] and said to him and the men of Israel, "We have come from a distant country; make a treaty with us."

7The men of Israel said to the Hivites,[x] "But perhaps you live near us. How then can we make a treaty[y] with you?"

8"We are your servants,[z]" they said to Joshua.

But Joshua asked, "Who are you and where do you come from?"

9They answered: "Your servants have come from a very distant country[a] because of the fame of the LORD your God. For we have heard reports[b] of him: all that he did in Egypt, 10and all that he did to the two kings of the Amorites east of the Jordan—Sihon king of Heshbon, and Og king of Bashan,[c] who reigned in Ashtaroth.[d] 11And our elders and all those living in our country said to us, 'Take provisions for your journey; go and meet them and say to them, "We are your servants; make a treaty with us."' 12This bread of ours was warm when we packed it at home on the day we left to come to you. But now see how dry and moldy it is. 13And these wineskins

8:22 [x]Dt 7:2; Jos 10:1 **8:23** [y]1Sa 15:8 **8:25** [z]Dt 20:16-18 **8:26** [a]Nu 21:2 [b]Ex 17:12 **8:27** [c]ver 2 **8:28** [d]Nu 31:10 [e]Jos 7:2; Jer 49:3 [f]Dt 13:16; Jos 10:1 [g]Ge 35:20 **8:29** [h]Dt 21:23; Jn 19:31 [i]2Sa 18:17 **8:30** [j]Dt 11:29 [k]Ex 20:24 **8:31** [l]Ex 20:25 [m]Dt 27:6-7 **8:32** [n]Dt 27:8 **8:33** [o]Lev 16:29 [p]Dt 31:12 [q]Dt 11:29; 27:11-14

8:34 [r]Dt 28:61; 31:11; Jos 1:8 **8:35** [s]Ex 12:38; Dt 31:12 **9:1** [t]Nu 34:6 [u]Ex 3:17; Jos 3:10 **9:3** [v]ver 17; Jos 10:2; 2Sa 2:12; 2Ch 1:3; Isa 28:21 **9:6** [w]Jos 5:10 **9:7** [x]ver 1; Jos 11:19 [y]Ex 23:32; Dt 7:2 **9:8** [z]Dt 20:11; 2Ki 10:5 **9:9** [a]Dt 20:15 [b]ver 24; Jos 2:9 **9:10** [c]Nu 21:33 [d]Nu 21:24,35

[a] *26* The Hebrew term refers to the irrevocable giving over of things or persons to the LORD, often by totally destroying them.
[b] *31* Traditionally *peace offerings*
[c] *1* That is, the Mediterranean
[d] *4* Most Hebrew manuscripts; some Hebrew manuscripts, Vulgate and Syriac (see also Septuagint) *They prepared provisions and loaded their donkeys*

that we filled were new, but see how
cracked they are. And our clothes and
sandals are worn out by the very long
journey."
14The men of Israel sampled their
provisions but did not inquire[e] of the
LORD. 15Then Joshua made a treaty of
peace[f] with them to let them live, and
the leaders of the assembly ratified it
by oath.
16Three days after they made the
treaty with the Gibeonites, the Israelites heard that they were neighbors,
living near them. 17So the Israelites set
out and on the third day came to their
cities: Gibeon, Kephirah, Beeroth[g]
and Kiriath Jearim.[h] 18But the Israelites did not attack them, because the
leaders of the assembly had sworn an
oath[i] to them by the LORD, the God of
Israel.
The whole assembly grumbled[j]
against the leaders, 19but all the leaders
answered, "We have given them our
oath by the LORD, the God of Israel, and
we cannot touch them now. 20This is
what we will do to them: We will let
them live, so that wrath will not fall on
us for breaking the oath we swore to
them." 21They continued, "Let them
live,[k] but let them be woodcutters and
water carriers[l] for the entire community." So the leaders' promise to them
was kept.
22Then Joshua summoned the Gibeonites and said, "Why did you deceive
us by saying, 'We live a long way[m]
from you,' while actually you live
near[n] us? 23You are now under a
curse:[o] You will never cease to serve
as woodcutters and water carriers for
the house of my God."
24They answered Joshua, "Your servants were clearly told[p] how the LORD
your God had commanded his servant
Moses to give you the whole land and
to wipe out all its inhabitants from before you. So we feared for our lives because of you, and that is why we did
this. 25We are now in your hands.[q] Do
to us whatever seems good and right to
you."
26So Joshua saved them from the Israelites, and they did not kill them.
27That day he made the Gibeonites
woodcutters and water carriers for the
community and for the altar of the
LORD at the place the LORD would
choose.[r] And that is what they are to
this day.

The Sun Stands Still

10 Now Adoni-Zedek king of Jerusalem[s] heard that Joshua had taken
Ai[t] and totally destroyed[a][u] it, doing
to Ai and its king as he had done to
Jericho and its king, and that the people of Gibeon had made a treaty of
peace[v] with Israel and were living
near them. 2He and his people were
very much alarmed at this, because
Gibeon was an important city, like one
of the royal cities; it was larger than Ai,
and all its men were good fighters. 3So
Adoni-Zedek king of Jerusalem appealed to Hoham king of Hebron,[w]
Piram king of Jarmuth, Japhia king of
Lachish[x] and Debir king of Eglon.
4"Come up and help me attack Gibeon," he said, "because it has made
peace[y] with Joshua and the Israelites."
5Then the five kings of the Amorites[z]—the kings of Jerusalem, Hebron, Jarmuth, Lachish and Eglon—
joined forces. They moved up with all
their troops and took up positions
against Gibeon and attacked it.
6The Gibeonites then sent word to
Joshua in the camp at Gilgal: "Do not
abandon your servants. Come up to us

9:14 [e]Nu 27:21 **9:15** [f]Ex 23:32; Jos 11:19; 2Sa 21:2 **9:17** [g]Jos 18:25 [h]1Sa 7:1-2 **9:18** [i]Ps 15:4 [j]Ex 15:24 **9:21** [k]ver 15 [l]Dt 29:11 **9:22** [m]ver 6 [n]ver 16 **9:23** [o]Ge 9:25 **9:24** [p]ver 9 **9:25** [q]Ge 16:6 **9:27** [r]Dt 12:5 **10:1** [s]Jdg 1:7 [t]Jos 8:1 [u]Dt 20:16; Jos 8:22

[v]Jos 9:15 **10:3** [w]Ge 13:18 [x]2Ch 11:9; 25:27; Ne 11:30; Isa 36:2; 37:8; Jer 34:7; Mic 1:13 **10:4** [y]Jos 9:15 **10:5** [z]Nu 13:29

a *1* The Hebrew term refers to the irrevocable giving over of things or persons to the LORD, often by totally destroying them; also in verses 28, 35, 37, 39 and 40.

9:24

PROMISE 7

LIVING BY A NEW COMMAND

To protect the purity of his covenant people, God commanded Israel to remove all other nations from Canaan. The book of Joshua tells how God's Old Testament people obeyed this command.

We live in a different era today. Since God came in Jesus Christ and made salvation available to all people, we live by a new command. Our commission is to make disciples of all the nations (Matthew 28:19–20). Instead of driving people away, we are to draw them in and lead them to a saving knowledge of Jesus Christ.

What a wonderful privilege it is to be an evangelist instead of a warrior; a discipler instead of a soldier! While we are called to put on the "full armor of God" (Ephesians 6:10–17), we aren't called to the same kind of warlike activity as was ancient Israel. These chapters in Joshua are hard, and sometimes confusing. But the Great Commission to disciple all nations is clear and simple truth. Explore what you don't understand. Never stop praying and meditating on the mysteries of God. But never let what's confusing keep you from acting on what's clear. Go and make disciples of all races, nationalities and peoples.

For the next Promise 7 reading go to page 282.

quickly and save us! Help us, because all the Amorite kings from the hill country have joined forces against us."

7So Joshua marched up from Gilgal with his entire army,[a] including all the best fighting men. 8The LORD said to Joshua, "Do not be afraid[b] of them; I have given them into your hand. Not one of them will be able to withstand you."

9After an all-night march from Gilgal, Joshua took them by surprise. 10The LORD threw them into confusion before Israel,[c] who defeated them in a great victory at Gibeon. Israel pursued them along the road going up to Beth Horon[d] and cut them down all the way to Azekah[e] and Makkedah. 11As they fled before Israel on the road down from Beth Horon to Azekah, the LORD hurled large hailstones[f] down on them from the sky, and more of them died from the hailstones than were killed by the swords of the Israelites.

12On the day the LORD gave the Amorites[g] over to Israel, Joshua said to the LORD in the presence of Israel:

"O sun, stand still over Gibeon,
O moon, over the Valley of
Aijalon.[h]"
13So the sun stood still,[i]
and the moon stopped,
till the nation avenged itself on[a]
its enemies,

as it is written in the Book of Jashar.[j]

The sun stopped[k] in the middle of the sky and delayed going down about a full day. 14There has never been a day like it before or since, a day when the LORD listened to a man. Surely the LORD was fighting[l] for Israel!

15Then Joshua returned with all Israel to the camp at Gilgal.[m]

Five Amorite Kings Killed

16Now the five kings had fled and hidden in the cave at Makkedah. 17When Joshua was told that the five kings had been found hiding in the cave at Makkedah, 18he said, "Roll large rocks up to the mouth of the cave, and post some men there to guard it. 19But don't stop! Pursue your enemies, attack them from the rear and don't let them reach their cities, for the LORD your God has given them into your hand."

20So Joshua and the Israelites destroyed them completely[n]—almost to a man—but the few who were left reached their fortified cities. 21The whole army then returned safely to Joshua in the camp at Makkedah, and no one uttered a word against the Israelites.

22Joshua said, "Open the mouth of the cave and bring those five kings out to me." 23So they brought the five kings out of the cave—the kings of Jerusalem, Hebron, Jarmuth, Lachish and Eglon. 24When they had brought these kings to Joshua, he summoned all the men of Israel and said to the army commanders who had come with him, "Come here and put your feet[o] on the necks of these kings." So they came forward and placed their feet[p] on their necks.

25Joshua said to them, "Do not be afraid; do not be discouraged. Be strong and courageous.[q] This is what the LORD will do to all the enemies you are going to fight." 26Then Joshua struck and killed the kings and hung them on five trees, and they were left hanging on the trees until evening.

27At sunset[r] Joshua gave the order and they took them down from the trees and threw them into the cave where they had been hiding. At the mouth of the cave they placed large rocks, which are there to this day.

28That day Joshua took Makkedah. He put the city and its king to the sword and totally destroyed everyone in it. He left no survivors.[s] And he did to the king of Makkedah as he had done to the king of Jericho.[t]

Southern Cities Conquered

29Then Joshua and all Israel with him moved on from Makkedah to Libnah and attacked it. 30The LORD also gave that city and its king into Israel's hand. The city and everyone in it Joshua put to the sword. He left no survivors there. And he did to its king as he had done to the king of Jericho.

31Then Joshua and all Israel with him moved on from Libnah to Lachish; he took up positions against it and attacked it. 32The LORD handed Lachish over to Israel, and Joshua took it on the second day. The city and everyone in it he put to the sword, just as he had done to Libnah. 33Meanwhile, Horam king of Gezer[u] had come up to help Lachish, but Joshua defeated him and his army—until no survivors were left.

34Then Joshua and all Israel with him moved on from Lachish to Eglon; they took up positions against it and attacked it. 35They captured it that same day and put it to the sword and totally destroyed everyone in it, just as they had done to Lachish.

10:7 [a]Jos 8:1
10:8 [b]Dt 3:2; Jos 1:9
10:10 [c]Dt 7:23 [d]Jos 16:3,5 [e]Jos 15:35
10:11 [f]Ps 18:12; Isa 28:2,17
10:12 [g]Am 2:9 [h]Jdg 1:35; 12:12
10:13 [i]Hab 3:11 [j]2Sa 1:18 [k]Isa 38:8
10:14 [l]ver 42; Ex 14:14; Dt 1:30; Ps 106:43; 136:24
10:15 [m]ver 43
10:20 [n]Dt 20:16
10:24 [o]Mal 4:3 [p]Ps 110:1
10:25 [q]Dt 31:6
10:27 [r]Dt 21:23; Jos 8:9,29
10:28 [s]Dt 20:16 [t]Jos 6:21
10:33 [u]Jos 16:3,10; Jdg 1:29; 1Ki 9:15

a *13* Or *nation triumphed over*

36 Then Joshua and all Israel with him went up from Eglon to Hebron[v] and attacked it. 37 They took the city and put it to the sword, together with its king, its villages and everyone in it. They left no survivors. Just as at Eglon, they totally destroyed it and everyone in it.

38 Then Joshua and all Israel with him turned around and attacked Debir.[w] 39 They took the city, its king and its villages, and put them to the sword. Everyone in it they totally destroyed. They left no survivors. They did to Debir and its king as they had done to Libnah and its king and to Hebron.

40 So Joshua subdued the whole region, including the hill country, the Negev,[x] the western foothills and the mountain slopes,[y] together with all their kings.[z] He left no survivors. He totally destroyed all who breathed, just as the LORD, the God of Israel, had commanded.[a] 41 Joshua subdued them from Kadesh Barnea[b] to Gaza[c] and from the whole region of Goshen[d] to Gibeon. 42 All these kings and their lands Joshua conquered in one campaign, because the LORD, the God of Israel, fought[e] for Israel.

43 Then Joshua returned with all Israel to the camp at Gilgal.[f]

Northern Kings Defeated

11 When Jabin[g] king of Hazor[h] heard of this, he sent word to Jobab king of Madon, to the kings of Shimron[i] and Acshaph, 2 and to the northern kings who were in the mountains, in the Arabah[j] south of Kinnereth,[k] in the western foothills and in Naphoth Dor[a][l] on the west; 3 to the Canaanites in the east and west; to the Amorites, Hittites, Perizzites and Jebusites in the hill country; and to the Hivites[m] below Hermon in the region of Mizpah.[n] 4 They came out with all their troops and a large number of horses and chariots—a huge army, as numerous as the sand on the seashore.[o] 5 All these kings joined forces[p] and made camp together at the Waters of Merom, to fight against Israel.

6 The LORD said to Joshua, "Do not be afraid of them, because by this time tomorrow I will hand all of them over[q] to Israel, slain. You are to hamstring[r] their horses and burn their chariots."

7 So Joshua and his whole army came against them suddenly at the Waters of Merom and attacked them, 8 and the LORD gave them into the hand of Israel. They defeated them and pursued them all the way to Greater Sidon, to Misrephoth Maim,[s] and to the Valley of Mizpah on the east, until no survivors were left. 9 Joshua did to them as the LORD had directed: He hamstrung their horses and burned their chariots.

10 At that time Joshua turned back and captured Hazor and put its king to the sword. (Hazor had been the head of all these kingdoms.) 11 Everyone in it they put to the sword. They totally destroyed[b] them, not sparing anything that breathed,[t] and he burned up Hazor itself.

12 Joshua took all these royal cities and their kings and put them to the sword. He totally destroyed them, as Moses the servant of the LORD had commanded.[u] 13 Yet Israel did not burn any of the cities built on their mounds—except Hazor, which Joshua burned. 14 The Israelites carried off for themselves all the plunder and livestock of these cities, but all the people they put to the sword until they completely destroyed them, not sparing anyone that breathed.[v] 15 As the LORD commanded his servant Moses, so Moses commanded Joshua, and Joshua did it; he left nothing undone of all that the LORD commanded Moses.[w]

16 So Joshua took this entire land: the hill country, all the Negev, the whole region of Goshen, the western foothills,[x] the Arabah and the mountains of Israel with their foothills, 17 from Mount Halak, which rises toward Seir, to Baal Gad in the Valley of Lebanon[y] below Mount Hermon. He captured all their kings and struck them down, putting them to death.[z] 18 Joshua waged war against all these kings for a long time. 19 Except for the Hivites living in Gibeon,[a] not one city made a treaty of peace with the Israelites, who took them all in battle. 20 For it was the LORD himself who hardened their hearts[b] to wage war against Israel, so that he might destroy them totally, exterminating them without mercy, as the LORD had commanded Moses.[c]

21 At that time Joshua went and destroyed the Anakites[d] from the hill country: from Hebron, Debir and Anab, from all the hill country of Judah, and from all the hill country of Israel. Joshua totally destroyed them and their towns. 22 No Anakites were left in Israelite territory; only in Gaza, Gath[e] and Ashdod[f] did any survive. 23 So Joshua took the entire land,[g] just as the LORD had directed Moses, and he

10:36 [v] Jos 14:13; 15:13; Jdg 1:10
10:38 [w] Jos 15:15; Jdg 1:11
10:40 [x] Ge 12:9; Jos 12:8 [y] Dt 1:7 [z] Dt 7:24 [a] Dt 20:16-17
10:41 [b] Ge 14:7 [c] Ge 10:19 [d] Jos 11:16; 15:51
10:42 [e] ver 14
10:43 [f] ver 15; Jos 5:9
11:1 [g] Jdg 4:2,7,23 [h] ver 10; 1Sa 12:9 [i] Jos 19:15
11:2 [j] Jos 12:3 [k] Nu 34:11 [l] Jos 17:11; Jdg 1:27; 1Ki 4:11
11:3 [m] Dt 7:1; Jdg 3:3,5; 1Ki 9:20 [n] Ge 31:49; Jos 15:38; 18:26
11:4 [o] Jdg 7:12; 1Sa 13:5
11:5 [p] Jdg 5:19
11:6 [q] Jos 10:8 [r] 2Sa 8:4
11:8 [s] Jos 13:6
11:11 [t] Dt 20:16-17
11:12 [u] Nu 33:50-52; Dt 7:2
11:14 [v] Nu 31:11-12
11:15 [w] Ex 34:11; Jos 1:7
11:16 [x] Jos 10:41
11:17 [y] Jos 12:7 [z] Dt 7:24
11:19 [a] Jos 9:3
11:20 [b] Ex 14:17; Ro 9:18 [c] Dt 7:16; Jdg 14:4
11:21 [d] Nu 13:22,33; Dt 9:2
11:22 [e] 1Sa 17:4; 1Ki 2:39; 1Ch 8:13 [f] 1Sa 5:1; Isa 20:1
11:23 [g] Jos 21:43-45

[a] *2* Or *in the heights of Dor* [b] *11* The Hebrew term refers to the irrevocable giving over of things or persons to the LORD, often by totally destroying them; also in verses 12, 20 and 21.

gave it as an inheritance[h] to Israel according to their tribal divisions.[i]

Then the land had rest from war.[j]

List of Defeated Kings

12 These are the kings of the land whom the Israelites had defeated and whose territory they took over east of the Jordan, from the Arnon Gorge to Mount Hermon,[k] including all the eastern side of the Arabah:

2Sihon king of the Amorites,
who reigned in Heshbon. He ruled from Aroer on the rim of the Arnon Gorge—from the middle of the gorge—to the Jabbok River, which is the border of the Ammonites. This included half of Gilead.[l] 3He also ruled over the eastern Arabah from the Sea of Kinnereth[a][m] to the Sea of the Arabah (the Salt Sea[b]), to Beth Jeshimoth,[n] and then southward below the slopes of Pisgah.

4And the territory of Og king of Bashan,[o]
one of the last of the Rephaites, who reigned in Ashtaroth[p] and Edrei. 5He ruled over Mount Hermon, Salecah,[q] all of Bashan to the border of the people of Geshur[r] and Maacah,[s] and half of Gilead to the border of Sihon king of Heshbon.

6Moses, the servant of the LORD, and the Israelites conquered them. And Moses the servant of the LORD gave their land to the Reubenites, the Gadites and the half-tribe of Manasseh to be their possession.[t]

7These are the kings of the land that Joshua and the Israelites conquered on the west side of the Jordan, from Baal Gad in the Valley of Lebanon[u] to Mount Halak, which rises toward Seir (their lands Joshua gave as an inheritance to the tribes of Israel according to their tribal divisions— 8the hill country, the western foothills, the Arabah, the mountain slopes, the desert and the Negev[v]—the lands of the Hittites, Amorites, Canaanites, Perizzites, Hivites and Jebusites):

9the king of Jericho[w] one
the king of Ai[x] (near Bethel) one
10the king of Jerusalem[y] one
the king of Hebron one
11the king of Jarmuth one
the king of Lachish one
12the king of Eglon one
the king of Gezer[z] one
13the king of Debir one
the king of Geder one
14the king of Hormah one
the king of Arad[a] one
15the king of Libnah one
the king of Adullam one
16the king of Makkedah one
the king of Bethel[b] one
17the king of Tappuah one
the king of Hepher[c] one
18the king of Aphek[d] one
the king of Lasharon one
19the king of Madon one
the king of Hazor one
20the king of Shimron Meron one
the king of Acshaph[e] one
21the king of Taanach one
the king of Megiddo one
22the king of Kedesh[f] one
the king of Jokneam in Carmel[g] one
23the king of Dor (in Naphoth Dor[c][h]) one
the king of Goyim in Gilgal one
24the king of Tirzah one
thirty-one kings in all.[i]

Land Still to Be Taken

13 When Joshua was old and well advanced in years,[j] the LORD said to him, "You are very old, and there are still very large areas of land to be taken over.

2"This is the land that remains: all the regions of the Philistines and Geshurites: 3from the Shihor River[k] on the east of Egypt to the territory of Ekron[l] on the north, all of it counted as Canaanite (the territory of the five Philistine rulers[m] in Gaza, Ashdod, Ashkelon, Gath and Ekron—that of the Avvites);[n] 4from the south, all the land of the Canaanites, from Arah of the Sidonians as far as Aphek,[o] the region of the Amorites,[p] 5the area of the Gebalites[d];[q] and all Lebanon[r] to the east, from Baal Gad below Mount Hermon to Lebo[e] Hamath.

6"As for all the inhabitants of the mountain regions from Lebanon to Misrephoth Maim,[s] that is, all the Sidonians, I myself will drive them out before the Israelites. Be sure to allocate this land to Israel for an inheritance, as I have instructed you,[t] 7and divide it as an inheritance[u] among the nine tribes and half of the tribe of Manasseh."

11:23 [h]Dt 1:38; 12:9-10; 25:19 [i]Nu 26:53 [j]Jos 14:15
12:1 [k]Dt 3:8
12:2 [l]Dt 2:36
12:3 [m]Jos 11:2 [n]Jos 13:20
12:4 [o]Nu 21:21,33; Dt 3:11 [p]Dt 1:4
12:5 [q]Dt 3:10 [r]1Sa 27:8 [s]Dt 3:14
12:6 [t]Nu 32:29,33; Jos 13:8
12:7 [u]Jos 11:17
12:8 [v]Jos 11:16
12:9 [w]Jos 6:2 [x]Jos 8:29
12:10 [y]Jos 10:23
12:12 [z]Jos 10:33
12:14 [a]Nu 21:1
12:16 [b]Jos 7:2
12:17 [c]1Ki 4:10
12:18 [d]Jos 13:4
12:20 [e]Jos 11:1
12:22 [f]Jos 19:37; 20:7; 21:32 [g]1Sa 15:12
12:23 [h]Jos 11:2
12:24 [i]Ps 135:11; Dt 7:24
13:1 [j]Ge 24:1; Jos 14:10
13:3 [k]Jer 2:18 [l]Jdg 1:18 [m]Jdg 3:3 [n]Dt 2:23
13:4 [o]Jos 12:18; 19:30 [p]Am 2:10
13:5 [q]1Ki 5:18; Ps 83:7; Eze 27:9 [r]Jos 12:7
13:6 [s]Jos 11:8 [t]Nu 33:54
13:7 [u]Jos 11:23; Ps 78:55

[a]3 That is, Galilee [b]3 That is, the Dead Sea [c]23 Or *in the heights of Dor* [d]5 That is, the area of Byblos [e]5 Or *to the entrance to*

Division of the Land East of the Jordan

8The other half of Manasseh,[a] the
Reubenites and the Gadites had received the inheritance that Moses had
given them east of the Jordan, as he,
the servant of the LORD, had assigned[v]
it to them.

9It extended from Aroer[w] on the
rim of the Arnon Gorge, and from
the town in the middle of the
gorge, and included the whole
plateau[x] of Medeba as far as Dibon,[y] 10and all the towns of Sihon king of the Amorites, who
ruled in Heshbon, out to the border of the Ammonites.[z] 11It also
included Gilead, the territory of
the people of Geshur and Maacah,
all of Mount Hermon and all Bashan as far as Salecah[a]— 12that
is, the whole kingdom of Og in Bashan,[b] who had reigned in Ashtaroth[c] and Edrei and had survived
as one of the last of the Rephaites.[d] Moses had defeated them
and taken over their land. 13But
the Israelites did not drive out the
people of Geshur[e] and Maacah,[f] so they continue to live
among the Israelites to this day.

14But to the tribe of Levi he gave no
inheritance, since the offerings made
by fire to the LORD, the God of Israel,
are their inheritance, as he promised
them.[g]

15This is what Moses had given to the
tribe of Reuben, clan by clan:

16The territory from Aroer[h] on
the rim of the Arnon Gorge, and
from the town in the middle of the
gorge, and the whole plateau past
Medeba[i] 17to Heshbon and all
its towns on the plateau, including Dibon,[j] Bamoth Baal, Beth
Baal Meon,[k] 18Jahaz,[l] Kedemoth,
Mephaath,[m] 19Kiriathaim,[n] Sibmah, Zereth Shahar on the hill
in the valley, 20Beth Peor,[o] the
slopes of Pisgah, and Beth Jeshimoth 21—all the towns on the
plateau and the entire realm of
Sihon king of the Amorites, who
ruled at Heshbon. Moses had defeated him and the Midianite
chiefs,[p] Evi, Rekem, Zur, Hur
and Reba[q]—princes allied with
Sihon—who lived in that country.
22In addition to those slain in
battle, the Israelites had put to
the sword Balaam son of Beor,[r]
who practiced divination. 23The
boundary of the Reubenites was
the bank of the Jordan. These
towns and their villages were
the inheritance of the Reubenites,
clan by clan.

24This is what Moses had given to the
tribe of Gad, clan by clan:

25The territory of Jazer,[s] all the
towns of Gilead and half the Ammonite country as far as Aroer,
near Rabbah; 26and from Heshbon[t] to Ramath Mizpah and Bet-
onim, and from Mahanaim to the
territory of Debir;[u] 27and in the
valley, Beth Haram, Beth Nimrah,
Succoth[v] and Zaphon with the
rest of the realm of Sihon king of
Heshbon (the east side of the Jordan, the territory up to the end of
the Sea of Kinnereth[b][w]). 28These
towns and their villages were the
inheritance of the Gadites,[x] clan
by clan.

29This is what Moses had given to the
half-tribe of Manasseh, that is, to half
the family of the descendants of Manasseh, clan by clan:

30The territory extending from
Mahanaim[y] and including all of
Bashan, the entire realm of Og
king of Bashan—all the settlements of Jair[z] in Bashan, sixty
towns, 31half of Gilead, and Ashtaroth and Edrei (the royal cities of
Og in Bashan). This was for the
descendants of Makir[a] son of
Manasseh—for half of the sons of
Makir, clan by clan.

32This is the inheritance Moses had
given when he was in the plains of
Moab across the Jordan east of Jericho.
33But to the tribe of Levi, Moses had
given no inheritance; the LORD, the
God of Israel, is their inheritance,[b] as
he promised them.[c]

Division of the Land West of the Jordan

14 Now these are the areas the Israelites received as an inheritance in
the land of Canaan, which Eleazar the
priest, Joshua son of Nun and the
heads of the tribal clans of Israel allotted to them.[d] 2Their inheritances
were assigned by lot[e] to the nine-
and-a-half tribes, as the LORD had
commanded through Moses. 3Moses
had granted the two-and-a-half tribes
their inheritance east of the Jordan[f]
but had not granted the Levites an inheritance among the rest,[g] 4for the
sons of Joseph had become two
tribes—Manasseh and Ephraim.[h] The

13:8 [v]Jos 12:6
13:9 [w]ver 16; Jdg 11:26 [x]Jer 48:8,21 [y]Nu 21:30
13:10 [z]Nu 21:24
13:11 [a]Jos 12:5
13:12 [b]Dt 3:11 [c]Jos 12:4 [d]Ge 14:5
13:13 [e]Jos 12:5 [f]Dt 3:14
13:14 [g]ver 33; Dt 18:1-2
13:16 [h]ver 9; Jos 12:2 [i]Nu 21:30
13:17 [j]Nu 32:3 [k]1Ch 5:8
13:18 [l]Nu 21:23 [m]Jer 48:21
13:19 [n]Nu 32:37
13:20 [o]Dt 3:29
13:21 [p]Nu 25:15 [q]Nu 31:8
13:22 [r]Nu 22:5; 31:8
13:25 [s]Nu 21:32; Jos 21:39
13:26 [t]Nu 21:25; Jer 49:3 [u]Jos 10:3
13:27 [v]Ge 33:17 [w]Nu 34:11
13:28 [x]Nu 32:33
13:30 [y]Ge 32:2 [z]Nu 32:41
13:31 [a]Ge 50:23
13:33 [b]Nu 18:20 [c]ver 14; Jos 18:7
14:1 [d]Nu 34:17-18
14:2 [e]Nu 26:55
14:3 [f]Nu 32:33 [g]Jos 13:14
14:4 [h]Ge 41:52; 48:5

[a]8 Hebrew *With it* (that is, with the other half of Manasseh) [b]27 That is, Galilee

Levites received no share of the land
but only towns to live in, with pasturelands for their flocks and herds. 5So the
Israelites divided the land, just as the
LORD had commanded Moses.[i]

Hebron Given to Caleb

6Now the men of Judah approached
Joshua at Gilgal, and Caleb son of Jephunneh[j] the Kenizzite said to him,
"You know what the LORD said to Moses the man of God at Kadesh Barnea[k]
about you and me. 7I was forty years
old when Moses the servant of the
LORD sent me from Kadesh Barnea to
explore the land.[l] And I brought him
back a report according to my convictions,[m] 8but my brothers who went up
with me made the hearts of the people
melt with fear.[n] I, however, followed
the LORD my God wholeheartedly.[o]
9So on that day Moses swore to me,
'The land on which your feet have
walked will be your inheritance and
that of your children[p] forever, because you have followed the LORD my
God wholeheartedly.'[a]

10"Now then, just as the LORD promised,[q] he has kept me alive for forty-
five years since the time he said this to
Moses, while Israel moved about in the
desert. So here I am today, eighty-five
years old! 11I am still as strong[r] today
as the day Moses sent me out; I'm just
as vigorous to go out to battle now as
I was then. 12Now give me this hill
country that the LORD promised me
that day. You yourself heard then that
the Anakites[s] were there and their cities were large and fortified,[t] but, the
LORD helping me, I will drive them out
just as he said."

13Then Joshua blessed[u] Caleb son
of Jephunneh and gave him Hebron[v]
as his inheritance.[w] 14So Hebron has
belonged to Caleb son of Jephunneh
the Kenizzite ever since, because he
followed the LORD, the God of Israel,
wholeheartedly. 15(Hebron used to be
called Kiriath Arba[x] after Arba,[y] who
was the greatest man among the Anakites.)

Then the land had rest[z] from war.

Allotment for Judah

15 The allotment for the tribe of Judah, clan by clan, extended down
to the territory of Edom,[a] to the
Desert of Zin[b] in the extreme south.

2Their southern boundary
started from the bay at the southern end of the Salt Sea,[b] 3crossed
south of Scorpion[c] Pass,[c] continued on to Zin and went over to
the south of Kadesh Barnea. Then
it ran past Hezron up to Addar
and curved around to Karka. 4It
then passed along to Azmon[d]
and joined the Wadi of Egypt,[e]
ending at the sea. This is their[d]
southern boundary.

5The eastern boundary[f] is the
Salt Sea as far as the mouth of the
Jordan.

The northern boundary[g] started from the bay of the sea at the
mouth of the Jordan, 6went up to
Beth Hoglah[h] and continued
north of Beth Arabah to the Stone
of Bohan[i] son of Reuben. 7The
boundary then went up to Debir
from the Valley of Achor[j] and
turned north to Gilgal, which
faces the Pass of Adummim south
of the gorge. It continued along to
the waters of En Shemesh and
came out at En Rogel.[k] 8Then it
ran up the Valley of Ben Hinnom
along the southern slope of the
Jebusite[l] city (that is, Jerusalem).
From there it climbed to the top of
the hill west of the Hinnom Valley
at the northern end of the Valley
of Rephaim. 9From the hilltop the
boundary headed toward the
spring of the waters of Nephtoah,[m] came out at the towns of
Mount Ephron and went down toward Baalah[n] (that is, Kiriath Jearim). 10Then it curved westward

[a]9 Deut. 1:36 [b]2 That is, the Dead Sea; also in verse 5 [c]3 Hebrew *Akrabbim* [d]4 Hebrew *your*

14:5 [i]Nu 34:13; 35:2; Jos 21:2
14:6 [j]Nu 13:6; 14:30 [k]Nu 13:26
14:7 [l]Nu 13:17 [m]Nu 13:30; 14:6-9
14:8 [n]Nu 13:31 [o]Nu 14:24
14:9 [p]Nu 14:24; Dt 1:36
14:10 [q]Nu 14:30
14:11 [r]Dt 34:7
14:12 [s]Nu 13:33 [t]Nu 13:28
14:13 [u]Jos 22:6,7 [v]Jos 10:36 [w]Jdg 1:20; 1Ch 6:56
14:15 [x]Ge 23:2 [y]Jos 15:13 [z]Jos 11:23
15:1 [a]Nu 34:3 [b]Nu 33:36
15:3 [c]Nu 34:4
15:4 [d]Nu 34:5 [e]Ge 15:18
15:5 [f]Nu 34:10 [g]Jos 18:15-19
15:6 [h]Jos 18:19,21 [i]Jos 18:17
15:7 [j]Jos 7:24 [k]2Sa 17:17; 1Ki 1:9
15:8 [l]ver 63; Jos 18:16,28; Jdg 1:21; 19:10
15:9 [m]Jos 18:15 [n]1Ch 13:6

14:6–15

PROMISE 5

RETIREMENT? HAH!

You gotta love Caleb. Because he followed God with his whole heart (vv. 8–9; Numbers 14:24), God gave him first choice of a place to settle down. Of all the land in Canaan, Caleb could pick any spot.

At the time, Caleb was 85 years old. Many of the most fertile plains had been conquered, and he could have settled into an easy life in a place where the enemy had been driven out. "Well, Caleb, where do you want to retire?" Joshua asks. "Give me that hill country. I hear there are giants living there, and I'm ready for 'em. Is there work to do for God? Let me at it!"

What a spirit! And man do we need it today. The church is desperate for Calebs—men of any age who are vigorous to do God's work where others are intimidated. Ask your pastor where the hill country is, where the giants are. Be your pastor's Caleb.

For the next Promise 5 reading go to page 254.

CALEB

A Wholehearted Man

He had been a nomad in the desert for forty-five years; before that, a slave in Egypt, working another man's soil. Now he was eighty-five years old, and Caleb had a great reward coming from God: first choice of all the real estate in the land of Canaan. All the land he wanted, anywhere he wanted it. All that fertile soil along the Jordan River. Flat, green, plenty of water. A peaceful place to live. So Caleb, where's your spread going to be?

Caleb's answer is shocking only to those who don't know Caleb. "Now give me this hill country that the LORD promised me . . . You yourself heard then that the Anakites (giants) were there and their cities were large and fortified, but, the LORD helping me, I will drive them out" (Joshua 14:12). Wow! This old guy says, "Where are the *giants*? Give me that mountain and I'll chase 'em outta there!" And folks probably responded, "But, Caleb, you're eighty-five years old! You've fought your battles. You've got your medals. Go buy a rocking chair and relax!"

Not Caleb. In Joshua 15 we read that Caleb drove out the Anakites (giants), then marched against the people living in Debir. Why fight giants when there are places with no enemy at all? Why live in the mountains when there are plains available? Because you're Caleb, that's why!

Trusting in God's Faithfulness

We first meet Caleb as a young spy in Numbers 13. Israel had come out of Egypt and stopped at Sinai to receive God's law. Now they were ready to march into their new land, drive out the natives and settle down. Before the entire population moved in, Moses sent twelve spies into Canaan to check it out. The spies came back with a strong word of assurance for Israel—but not a positive assurance. They assured God's people that there was no way God would keep his promise to give them that land because of the fierce armies and walled cities they found there. Ten of the twelve spies concluded that the Israelites would be like grasshoppers before the giants in the land.

That's when we meet Caleb for the first time. Caleb stood in front of Moses and the people and called for silence. His words rang out, "We should go up and take possession of the land, for we can certainly do it" (Numbers 13:30). Ten spies told the people to dump the sand out of their sandals, water their camels and head back into the desert. Only Joshua and Caleb offered dissenting opinions. Caleb was one gutsy character!

But where did Caleb's courage come from? Caleb never denied the greatness of the cities or the fierceness of the warriors. Those facts were readily observable. But Caleb looked at things differently. He didn't measure reality by the size of the problem, but rather measured his problem by the size of his God. Caleb told the Israelites, "The LORD is with us. Do not be afraid of them" (Numbers 14:9). Caleb was courageous because he wholeheartedly trusted in God's faithfulness.

No doubt Caleb and Joshua could have beaten those giants. Giants are no match for men who trust in God's strength instead of their own. But Caleb and Joshua, men who could whip giants, were hamstrung by a people with puny faith who ended up wandering for forty years and dying in the desert. Tragic? Sad? Yes. But a good reminder that even giant killers can be stifled if God's people lack faith.

So now, forty years later, the people are ready to enter the land. And because of Caleb's faithful report and his courageous stand for God's truth forty years ago, Caleb points to the giant-filled mountains as his choice for a new home. Was he crazy? No way! For forty years Caleb had waited to prove God was right, that he would be able to drive out the giants. The obstacle that scared the people the most was the very thing that challenged Caleb. The giants who had made their parents turn and run were no match for God. Caleb wanted to prove that, with a little faith, Israel could have settled into Canaan long ago.

Caleb's Giant-Fighting Secret

What made a guy like Caleb tick? Six times throughout Numbers, Deuteronomy and Joshua the Bible described Caleb as one who "followed the LORD, the God of Israel, wholeheartedly" (Joshua 14:14). Six times we read that truth about him. If giants and great cities and fierce mountain fighting was what the people thought were too much for God, then giants and great cities and fierce mountain fighting were what Caleb would face in God's name. Caleb had to prove to everyone that these obstacles weren't barriers to God's will. That attitude of wholehearted trust is what drove Caleb!

What About You?

Do you have any giants in your life? Giants are scary things. When they live in walled cities in the mountains they seem unconquerable. The Israelites were even afraid to try. But wholehearted men of God try anyway. While others are whimpering and scurrying for the safe places, the few, the brave, the Calebs are saying: "Where are the giants? Give me that mountain!"

Caleb's attitude of wholehearted trust demonstrates what any wholehearted man of God can do with the giants in his own life.

—Dr. Sid Buzzell

from Baalah to Mount Seir, ran
along the northern slope of
Mount Jearim (that is, Kesalon),
continued down to Beth Shemesh
and crossed to Timnah.[o] 11It
went to the northern slope of Ekron, turned toward Shikkeron,
passed along to Mount Baalah
and reached Jabneel.[p] The
boundary ended at the sea.
12The western boundary is the
coastline of the Great Sea.**a**[q]
These are the boundaries around the
people of Judah by their clans.

13In accordance with the LORD's
command to him, Joshua gave to Caleb
son of Jephunneh a portion in Judah—
Kiriath Arba, that is, Hebron. (Arba
was the forefather of Anak.)[r] 14From
Hebron Caleb drove out the
three Anakites[s]—Sheshai, Ahiman
and Talmai[t]—descendants of Anak.[u]
15From there he marched against the
people living in Debir (formerly called
Kiriath Sepher). 16And Caleb said, "I
will give my daughter Acsah[v] in marriage to the man who attacks and captures Kiriath Sepher." 17Othniel[w] son
of Kenaz, Caleb's brother, took it; so
Caleb gave his daughter Acsah to him
in marriage.
18One day when she came to Othni-
el, she urged him**b** to ask her father for
a field. When she got off her donkey,
Caleb asked her, "What can I do for
you?"
19She replied, "Do me a special favor. Since you have given me land in
the Negev, give me also springs of water." So Caleb gave her the upper and
lower springs.

20This is the inheritance of the tribe
of Judah, clan by clan:

21The southernmost towns of the tribe
of Judah in the Negev toward the
boundary of Edom were:
Kabzeel, Eder,[x] Jagur, 22Kinah,
Dimonah, Adadah, 23Kedesh, Hazor, Ithnan, 24Ziph,[y] Telem, Bea-
loth, 25Hazor Hadattah, Kerioth
Hezron (that is, Hazor), 26Amam,
Shema, Moladah,[z] 27Hazar Gad-
dah, Heshmon, Beth Pelet, 28Ha-
zar Shual, Beersheba,[a] Biziothi-
ah, 29Baalah,[b] Iim, Ezem,
30Eltolad,[c] Kesil, Hormah, 31Zik-
lag,[d] Madmannah, Sansannah,
32Lebaoth, Shilhim, Ain and
Rimmon[e]—a total of twenty-
nine towns and their villages.

33In the western foothills:
Eshtaol,[f] Zorah, Ashnah, 34Za-
noah,[g] En Gannim, Tappuah,
Enam, 35Jarmuth,[h] Adullam,[i]
Socoh, Azekah, 36Shaaraim, Adi-
thaim and Gederah[j] (or Gederothaim)**c**—fourteen towns and
their villages.
37Zenan, Hadashah, Migdal
Gad, 38Dilean, Mizpah, Joktheel,[k] 39Lachish,[l] Bozkath,[m] Eglon, 40Cabbon, Lahmas, Kitlish,
41Gederoth, Beth Dagon, Naamah
and Makkedah[n]—sixteen towns
and their villages.
42Libnah, Ether, Ashan,[o]
43Iphtah, Ashnah, Nezib, 44Keilah,
Aczib[p] and Mareshah[q]—nine
towns and their villages.
45Ekron, with its surrounding
settlements and villages; 46west of
Ekron, all that were in the vicinity
of Ashdod, together with their villages; 47Ashdod,[r] its surrounding
settlements and villages; and
Gaza, its settlements and villages,
as far as the Wadi of Egypt[s] and
the coastline of the Great Sea.[t]

48In the hill country:
Shamir, Jattir,[u] Socoh, 49Dan-
nah, Kiriath Sannah (that is,
Debir[v]), 50Anab, Eshtemoh,[w]
Anim, 51Goshen,[x] Holon and
Giloh—eleven towns and their
villages.
52Arab, Dumah,[y] Eshan, 53Ja-
nim, Beth Tappuah, Aphekah,
54Humtah, Kiriath Arba (that is,
Hebron) and Zior—nine towns
and their villages.
55Maon, Carmel,[z] Ziph, Juttah,
56Jezreel,[a] Jokdeam, Zanoah,
57Kain, Gibeah[b] and Timnah—
ten towns and their villages.
58Halhul, Beth Zur,[c] Gedor,
59Maarath, Beth Anoth and
Eltekon—six towns and their villages.
60Kiriath Baal (that is, Kiriath
Jearim[d]) and Rabbah[e]—two
towns and their villages.

61In the desert:
Beth Arabah, Middin, Secacah,
62Nibshan, the City of Salt and En
Gedi[f]—six towns and their villages.
63Judah could not[g] dislodge the
Jebusites[h], who were living in Jerusalem; to this day the Jebusites live there
with the people of Judah.

15:10 [o]Ge 38:12; Jdg 14:1
15:11 [p]Jos 19:33
15:12 [q]Nu 34:6
15:13 [r]Jos 14:13-15
15:14 [s]Nu 13:33 [t]Nu 13:22 [u]Jdg 1:10,20
15:16 [v]Jdg 1:12
15:17 [w]Jdg 3:9,11
15:21 [x]Ge 35:21
15:24 [y]1Sa 23:14
15:26 [z]1Ch 4:28
15:28 [a]Ge 21:31
15:29 [b]ver 9
15:30 [c]Jos 19:4
15:31 [d]1Sa 27:6
15:32 [e]Jdg 20:45
15:33 [f]Jdg 13:25; 16:31
15:34 [g]1Ch 4:18; Ne 3:13
15:35 [h]Jos 10:3 [i]1Sa 22:1
15:36 [j]1Ch 12:4
15:38 [k]2Ki 14:7
15:39 [l]Jos 10:3; 2Ki 14:19 [m]2Ki 22:1
15:41 [n]Jos 10:10
15:42 [o]1Sa 30:30
15:44 [p]Jdg 1:31 [q]Mic 1:15
15:47 [r]Jos 11:22 [s]ver 4 [t]Nu 34:6
15:48 [u]1Sa 30:27
15:49 [v]Jos 10:3
15:50 [w]Jos 21:14
15:51 [x]Jos 10:41; 11:16
15:52 [y]Ge 25:14
15:55 [z]Jos 12:22
15:56 [a]Jos 17:16
15:57 [b]Jos 18:28; Jdg 19:12
15:58 [c]1Ch 2:45
15:60 [d]Jos 18:14 [e]Dt 3:11
15:62 [f]1Sa 23:29
15:63 [g]Jdg 1:21 [h]2Sa 5:6

a *12* That is, the Mediterranean; also in verse 47
b *18* Hebrew and some Septuagint manuscripts; other Septuagint manuscripts (see also note at Judges 1:14) *Othniel, he urged her*
c *36* Or *Gederah and Gederothaim*

Allotment for Ephraim and Manasseh

16 The allotment for Joseph began at the Jordan of Jericho,[a] east of the waters of Jericho, and went up from there through the desert[i] into the hill country of Bethel. 2 It went on from Bethel (that is, Luz[j]),[b] crossed over to the territory of the Arkites in Ataroth, 3 descended westward to the territory of the Japhletites as far as the region of Lower Beth Horon[k] and on to Gezer,[l] ending at the sea.

4 So Manasseh and Ephraim, the descendants of Joseph, received their inheritance.[m]

5 This was the territory of Ephraim, clan by clan:

The boundary of their inheritance went from Ataroth Addar[n] in the east to Upper Beth Horon 6 and continued to the sea. From Micmethath[o] on the north it curved eastward to Taanath Shiloh, passing by it to Janoah on the east. 7 Then it went down from Janoah to Ataroth[p] and Naarah, touched Jericho and came out at the Jordan. 8 From Tappuah the border went west to the Kanah Ravine[q] and ended at the sea. This was the inheritance of the tribe of the Ephraimites, clan by clan. 9 It also included all the towns and their villages that were set aside for the Ephraimites within the inheritance of the Manassites.

10 They did not dislodge the Canaanites living in Gezer; to this day the Canaanites live among the people of Ephraim but are required to do forced labor.[r]

17 This was the allotment for the tribe of Manasseh as Joseph's firstborn,[s] that is, for Makir,[t] Manasseh's firstborn. Makir was the ancestor of the Gileadites, who had received Gilead and Bashan because the Makirites were great soldiers. 2 So this allotment was for the rest of the people of Manasseh—the clans of Abiezer,[u] Helek, Asriel, Shechem, Hepher and Shemida. These are the other male descendants of Manasseh son of Joseph by their clans.

3 Now Zelophehad son of Hepher,[v] the son of Gilead, the son of Makir, the son of Manasseh, had no sons but only daughters,[w] whose names were Mahlah, Noah, Hoglah, Milcah and Tirzah. 4 They went to Eleazar the priest, Joshua son of Nun, and the leaders and said, "The LORD commanded Moses to give us an inheritance among our brothers." So Joshua gave them an inheritance along with the brothers of their father, according to the LORD's command.[x] 5 Manasseh's share consisted of ten tracts of land besides Gilead and Bashan east of the Jordan, 6 because the daughters of the tribe of Manasseh received an inheritance among the sons. The land of Gilead belonged to the rest of the descendants of Manasseh.

7 The territory of Manasseh extended from Asher to Micmethath[y] east of Shechem.[z] The boundary ran southward from there to include the people living at En Tappuah. 8 (Manasseh had the land of Tappuah, but Tappuah[a] itself, on the boundary of Manasseh, belonged to the Ephraimites.) 9 Then the boundary continued south to the Kanah Ravine.[b] There were towns belonging to Ephraim lying among the towns of Manasseh, but the boundary of Manasseh was the northern side of the ravine and ended at the sea. 10 On the south the land belonged to Ephraim, on the north to Manasseh. The territory of Manasseh reached the sea and bordered Asher on the north and Issachar[c] on the east.

11 Within Issachar and Asher, Manasseh also had Beth Shan,[d] Ibleam and the people of Dor,[e] Endor,[f] Taanach and Megiddo,[g] together with their surrounding settlements (the third in the list is Naphoth[c]).

12 Yet the Manassites were not able[h] to occupy these towns, for the Canaanites were determined to live in that region. 13 However, when the Israelites grew stronger, they subjected the Canaanites to forced labor but did not drive them out completely.[i]

14 The people of Joseph said to Joshua, "Why have you given us only one allotment and one portion for an inheritance? We are a numerous people and the LORD has blessed us abundantly."[j]

15 "If you are so numerous," Joshua answered, "and if the hill country of Ephraim is too small for you, go up into the forest and clear land for yourselves there in the land of the Perizzites and Rephaites.[k]"

16:1 [i] Jos 8:15; 18:12
16:2 [j] Jos 18:13
16:3 [k] 2Ch 8:5 [l] Jos 10:33; 1Ki 9:15
16:4 [m] Jos 17:14
16:5 [n] Jos 18:13
16:6 [o] Jos 17:7
16:7 [p] 1Ch 7:28
16:8 [q] Jos 17:9
16:10 [r] Jos 17:13; Jdg 1:28-29; 1Ki 9:16
17:1 [s] Ge 41:51 [t] Ge 50:23
17:2 [u] Nu 26:30; 1Ch 7:18
17:3 [v] Nu 27:1 [w] Nu 26:33
17:4 [x] Nu 27:5-7
17:7 [y] Jos 16:6 [z] Ge 12:6; Jos 21:21
17:8 [a] Jos 16:8
17:9 [b] Jos 16:8
17:10 [c] Ge 30:18
17:11 [d] 1Sa 31:10; 1Ki 4:12; 1Ch 7:29 [e] Jos 11:2 [f] 1Sa 28:7; Ps 83:10 [g] 1Ki 9:15
17:12 [h] Jdg 1:27
17:13 [i] Jos 16:10
17:14 [j] Nu 26:28-37
17:15 [k] Ge 14:5

[a] *1 Jordan of Jericho* was possibly an ancient name for the Jordan River. [b] *2* Septuagint; Hebrew *Bethel to Luz* [c] *11* That is, Naphoth Dor

16The people of Joseph replied, "The
hill country is not enough for us, and
all the Canaanites who live in the plain
have iron chariots,[l] both those in
Beth Shan and its settlements and
those in the Valley of Jezreel."
17But Joshua said to the house of
Joseph—to Ephraim and Manasseh—
"You are numerous and very powerful.
You will have not only one allotment
18but the forested hill country as well.
Clear it, and its farthest limits will be
yours; though the Canaanites have iron
chariots[m] and though they are strong,
you can drive them out."

Division of the Rest of the Land

18 The whole assembly of the Israelites gathered at Shiloh[n] and set up
the Tent of Meeting[o] there. The country was brought under their control,
2but there were still seven Israelite
tribes who had not yet received their
inheritance.
3So Joshua said to the Israelites:
"How long will you wait before you begin to take possession of the land that
the LORD, the God of your fathers, has
given you? 4Appoint three men from
each tribe. I will send them out to make
a survey of the land and to write a description of it, according to the inheritance of each.[p] Then they will return
to me. 5You are to divide the land into
seven parts. Judah is to remain in its
territory on the south[q] and the house
of Joseph in its territory on the north.[r]
6After you have written descriptions of
the seven parts of the land, bring them
here to me and I will cast lots[s] for you
in the presence of the LORD our God.
7The Levites, however, do not get a
portion among you, because the
priestly service of the LORD is their inheritance.[t] And Gad, Reuben and the
half-tribe of Manasseh have already
received their inheritance on the east
side of the Jordan. Moses the servant of
the LORD gave it to them.[u]"
8As the men started on their way to
map out the land, Joshua instructed
them, "Go and make a survey of the
land and write a description of it. Then
return to me, and I will cast lots for you
here at Shiloh[v] in the presence of the
LORD." 9So the men left and went
through the land. They wrote its description on a scroll, town by town, in
seven parts, and returned to Joshua in
the camp at Shiloh. 10Joshua then cast
lots[w] for them in Shiloh in the presence[x] of the LORD, and there he distributed the land to the Israelites according to their tribal divisions.[y]

Allotment for Benjamin

11The lot came up for the tribe of Benjamin, clan by clan. Their allotted territory lay between the tribes of Judah
and Joseph:
12On the north side their
boundary began at the Jordan,
passed the northern slope of Jericho and headed west into the hill
country, coming out at the
desert[z] of Beth Aven.[a] 13From
there it crossed to the south slope
of Luz[b] (that is, Bethel[c]) and
went down to Ataroth Addar[d] on
the hill south of Lower Beth Horon.
14From the hill facing Beth Horon[e] on the south the boundary
turned south along the western
side and came out at Kiriath Baal
(that is, Kiriath Jearim), a town of
the people of Judah. This was the
western side.
15The southern side began at
the outskirts of Kiriath Jearim on
the west, and the boundary came
out at the spring of the waters
of Nephtoah.[f] 16The boundary
went down to the foot of the hill
facing the Valley of Ben Hinnom,
north of the Valley of Rephaim. It
continued down the Hinnom Valley[g] along the southern slope of
the Jebusite city and so to En Rogel.[h] 17It then curved north, went
to En Shemesh, continued to Geliloth, which faces the Pass of
Adummim, and ran down to the
Stone of Bohan[i] son of Reuben.
18It continued to the northern
slope of Beth Arabah[a][j] and on
down into the Arabah. 19It then

17:16 [l]Jdg 1:19; 4:3, 13
17:18 [m]ver 16
18:1 [n]Jos 19:51; 21:2; Jdg 18:31; 21:12,19; 1Sa 1:3; 4:3; Jer 7:12; 26:6 [o]Ex 27:21
18:4 [p]Mic 2:5
18:5 [q]Jos 15:1 [r]Jos 16:1-4
18:6 [s]Jos 14:2
18:7 [t]Jos 13:33 [u]Jos 13:8
18:8 [v]ver 1
18:10 [w]Nu 34:13 [x]ver 1; Jer 7:12 [y]Nu 33:54; Jos 19:51
18:12 [z]Jos 16:1 [a]Jos 7:2
18:13 [b]Ge 28:19 [c]Jdg 1:23 [d]Jos 16:5
18:14 [e]Jos 10:10
18:15 [f]Jos 15:9
18:16 [g]Jos 15:8; 2Ki 23:10 [h]Jos 15:7
18:17 [i]Jos 15:6
18:18 [j]Jos 15:6

18:3 — PROMISE 1

WAIT FOR WHAT?

"How long will you wait before you begin to take possession of the land that the LORD, the God of your fathers, has given you?" What a haunting question. Many men have become Christians. They, like these seven tribes, have crossed the river. They've made their commitments, and live on the banks of God's promises. Now they sit and wait—but for what?

The Seven Promises of a Promise Keeper provide a starting point. Read them over again and envision what your life will be like when you begin integrating their Biblical principles and living as God intends. How long will *you* wait?

For the next Promise 1 reading go to page 249.

a *18* Septuagint; Hebrew *slope facing the Arabah*

went to the northern slope of Beth Hoglah and came out at the northern bay of the Salt Sea,[a][k] at the mouth of the Jordan in the south. This was the southern boundary.

20The Jordan formed the boundary on the eastern side.

These were the boundaries that marked out the inheritance of the clans of Benjamin on all sides.[l]

21The tribe of Benjamin, clan by clan, had the following cities:

Jericho, Beth Hoglah, Emek Keziz, 22Beth Arabah, Zemaraim, Bethel,[m] 23Avvim, Parah, Ophrah, 24Kephar Ammoni, Ophni and Geba[n]—twelve towns and their villages.

25Gibeon,[o] Ramah,[p] Beeroth,[q] 26Mizpah,[r] Kephirah, Mozah, 27Rekem, Irpeel, Taralah, 28Zelah,[s] Haeleph, the Jebusite city[t] (that is, Jerusalem[u]), Gibeah[v] and Kiriath—fourteen towns and their villages.

This was the inheritance of Benjamin for its clans.

Allotment for Simeon

19 The second lot came out for the tribe of Simeon, clan by clan. Their inheritance lay within the territory of Judah.[w] 2It included:

Beersheba[x] (or Sheba),[b] Moladah, 3Hazar Shual, Balah, Ezem, 4Eltolad, Bethul, Hormah, 5Ziklag, Beth Marcaboth, Hazar Susah, 6Beth Lebaoth and Sharuhen—thirteen towns and their villages;

7Ain, Rimmon, Ether and Ashan[y]—four towns and their villages— 8and all the villages around these towns as far as Baalath Beer (Ramah in the Negev).[z]

This was the inheritance of the tribe of the Simeonites, clan by clan. 9The inheritance of the Simeonites was taken from the share of Judah,[a] because Judah's portion was more than they needed. So the Simeonites received their inheritance within the territory of Judah.[b]

Allotment for Zebulun

10The third lot came up for Zebulun,[c] clan by clan:

The boundary of their inheritance went as far as Sarid. 11Going west it ran to Maralah, touched Dabbesheth, and extended to the ravine near Jokneam.[d] 12It turned east from Sarid toward the sunrise to the territory of Kisloth Tabor and went on to Daberath and up to Japhia. 13Then it continued eastward to Gath Hepher and Eth Kazin; it came out at Rimmon[e] and turned toward Neah. 14There the boundary went around on the north to Hannathon and ended at the Valley of Iphtah El. 15Included were Kattath, Nahalal, Shimron, Idalah and Bethlehem.[f] There were twelve towns and their villages.

16These towns and their villages were the inheritance of Zebulun,[g] clan by clan.[h]

Allotment for Issachar

17The fourth lot came out for Issachar,[i] clan by clan. 18Their territory included:

Jezreel,[j] Kesulloth, Shunem,[k] 19Hapharaim, Shion, Anaharath, 20Rabbith, Kishion, Ebez, 21Remeth, En Gannim, En Haddah and Beth Pazzez. 22The boundary touched Tabor,[l] Shahazumah and Beth Shemesh,[m] and ended at the Jordan. There were sixteen towns and their villages.

23These towns and their villages were the inheritance of the tribe of Issachar,[n] clan by clan.[o]

Allotment for Asher

24The fifth lot came out for the tribe of Asher,[p] clan by clan. 25Their territory included:

Helkath, Hali, Beten, Acshaph, 26Allammelech, Amad and Mishal. On the west the boundary touched Carmel[q] and Shihor Libnath. 27It then turned east toward Beth Dagon, touched Zebulun[r] and the Valley of Iphtah El, and went north to Beth Emek and Neiel, passing Cabul[s] on the left. 28It went to Abdon,[c] Rehob,[t] Hammon[u] and Kanah, as far as Greater Sidon.[v] 29The boundary then turned back toward Ramah[w] and went to the fortified city of Tyre,[x] turned toward Hosah and came out at the sea in the region of Aczib,[y] 30Ummah, Aphek and Rehob. There were twenty-two towns and their villages.

31These towns and their villages were the inheritance of the tribe of Asher,[z] clan by clan.

18:19 [k]Ge 14:3
18:20 [l]Jos 21:4,17; 1Sa 9:1
18:22 [m]Jos 16:1
18:24 [n]Isa 10:29
18:25 [o]Jos 9:3 [p]Jdg 4:5 [q]Jos 9:17
18:26 [r]Jos 11:3
18:28 [s]2Sa 21:14 [t]Jos 15:8 [u]Jos 10:1 [v]Jos 15:57
19:1 [w]ver 9; Ge 49:7
19:2 [x]Ge 21:14; 1Ki 19:3
19:7 [y]Jos 15:42
19:8 [z]Jos 10:40
19:9 [a]Ge 49:7 [b]Eze 48:24
19:10 [c]Jos 21:7,34
19:11 [d]Jos 12:22
19:13 [e]Jos 15:32
19:15 [f]Ge 35:19
19:16 [g]ver 10; Jos 21:7 [h]Eze 48:26
19:17 [i]Ge 30:18
19:18 [j]Jos 15:56 [k]1Sa 28:4; 2Ki 4:8
19:22 [l]Jdg 4:6,12; Ps 89:12 [m]Jos 15:10
19:23 [n]Jos 17:10 [o]Ge 49:15; Eze 48:25
19:24 [p]Jos 17:7
19:26 [q]Jos 12:22
19:27 [r]ver 10 [s]1Ki 9:13
19:28 [t]Jdg 1:31 [u]1Ch 6:76 [v]Ge 10:19; Jos 11:8
19:29 [w]Jos 18:25 [x]2Sa 5:11; 24:7; Isa 23:1; Jer 25:22; Eze 26:2 [y]Jdg 1:31
19:31 [z]Ge 30:13; Eze 48:2

a *19* That is, the Dead Sea **b** *2* Or *Beersheba, Sheba*; 1 Chron. 4:28 does not have *Sheba*. **c** *28* Some Hebrew manuscripts (see also Joshua 21:30); most Hebrew manuscripts *Ebron*

Allotment for Naphtali

32The sixth lot came out for Naphtali,
clan by clan:

33Their boundary went from
Heleph and the large tree in Zaanannim, passing Adami Nekeb
and Jabneel to Lakkum and ending at the Jordan. 34The boundary
ran west through Aznoth Tabor
and came out at Hukkok. It
touched Zebulun on the south,
Asher on the west and the Jordan[a] on the east. 35The fortified cities were Ziddim, Zer,
Hammath, Rakkath, Kinnereth,[a]
36Adamah, Ramah,[b] Hazor,[c] 37Ked-
esh, Edrei,[d] En Hazor, 38Iron,
Migdal El, Horem, Beth Anath
and Beth Shemesh. There were
nineteen towns and their villages.

39These towns and their villages were
the inheritance of the tribe of Naphtali,
clan by clan.[e]

Allotment for Dan

40The seventh lot came out for the tribe
of Dan, clan by clan. 41The territory of
their inheritance included:

Zorah, Eshtaol, Ir Shemesh,
42Shaalabbin, Aijalon,[f] Ithlah,
43Elon, Timnah,[g] Ekron, 44Elte-
keh, Gibbethon, Baalath, 45Jehud,
Bene Berak, Gath Rimmon,[h]
46Me Jarkon and Rakkon, with the
area facing Joppa.[i]

47(But the Danites had difficulty taking possession of their territory,[j] so
they went up and attacked Leshem[k],
took it, put it to the sword and occupied it. They settled in Leshem and
named it Dan after their forefather.)[l]
48These towns and their villages were
the inheritance of the tribe of Dan,[m]
clan by clan.

Allotment for Joshua

49When they had finished dividing
the land into its allotted portions, the
Israelites gave Joshua son of Nun an
inheritance among them, 50as the LORD
had commanded. They gave him the
town he asked for—Timnath Serah[b][n]
in the hill country of Ephraim. And he
built up the town and settled there.

51These are the territories that Eleazar the priest, Joshua son of Nun and
the heads of the tribal clans of Israel
assigned by lot at Shiloh in the presence of the LORD at the entrance to the
Tent of Meeting. And so they finished
dividing the land.[o]

19:35 [a]Jos 11:2
19:36 [b]Jos 18:25 [c]Jos 11:1
19:37 [d]Nu 21:33
19:39 [e]Dt 33:23; Eze 48:3
19:42 [f]Jdg 1:35
19:43 [g]Ge 38:12
19:45 [h]Jos 21:24; 1Ch 6:69
19:46 [i]2Ch 2:16; Jnh 1:3
19:47 [j]Jdg 18:1 [k]Jdg 18:7,14 [l]Jdg 18:27,29
19:48 [m]Ge 30:6
19:50 [n]Jos 24:30
19:51 [o]Jos 14:1; 18:10; Ac 13:19

Cities of Refuge

20 Then the LORD said to Joshua:
2"Tell the Israelites to designate
the cities of refuge, as I instructed
you through Moses, 3so that anyone
who kills a person accidentally and
unintentionally[p] may flee there and
find protection from the avenger of
blood.[q]

4"When he flees to one of these cities, he is to stand in the entrance of the
city gate[r] and state his case before the
elders[s] of that city. Then they are to
admit him into their city and give him
a place to live with them. 5If the avenger of blood pursues him, they must not
surrender the one accused, because he
killed his neighbor unintentionally and
without malice aforethought. 6He is to
stay in that city until he has stood trial
before the assembly[t] and until the
death of the high priest who is serving
at that time. Then he may go back to
his own home in the town from which
he fled."

7So they set apart Kedesh[u] in Galilee in the hill country of Naphtali, Shechem[v] in the hill country of Ephraim,
and Kiriath Arba (that is, Hebron[w]) in
the hill country of Judah.[x] 8On the
east side of the Jordan of Jericho[c] they
designated Bezer[y] in the desert on the
plateau in the tribe of Reuben, Ramoth
in Gilead[z] in the tribe of Gad, and Golan in Bashan in the tribe of Manasseh.
9Any of the Israelites or any alien living
among them who killed someone accidentally could flee to these designated
cities and not be killed by the avenger
of blood prior to standing trial before
the assembly.[a]

Towns for the Levites

21 Now the family heads of the Levites
approached Eleazar the priest,
Joshua son of Nun, and the heads of
the other tribal families of Israel[b] 2at
Shiloh[c] in Canaan and said to them,
"The LORD commanded through Moses that you give us towns to live in,
with pasturelands for our livestock."[d]
3So, as the LORD had commanded, the
Israelites gave the Levites the following
towns and pasturelands out of their
own inheritance:

4The first lot came out for the Kohathites, clan by clan. The Levites who
were descendants of Aaron the priest
were allotted thirteen towns from the
tribes of Judah, Simeon and Benja-

20:3 [p]Lev 4:2 [q]Nu 35:12
20:4 [r]Ru 4:1; Jer 38:7 [s]Jos 7:6
20:6 [t]Nu 35:12
20:7 [u]Jos 21:32; 1Ch 6:76 [v]Ge 12:6 [w]Jos 10:36; 21:11 [x]Lk 1:39
20:8 [y]Jos 21:36; 1Ch 6:78 [z]Jos 12:2
20:9 [a]Ex 21:13; Nu 35:15
21:1 [b]Jos 14:1
21:2 [c]Jos 18:1 [d]Nu 35:2-3

a 34 Septuagint; Hebrew *west, and Judah, the Jordan,* b 50 Also known as *Timnath Heres* (see Judges 2:9) c 8 *Jordan of Jericho* was possibly an ancient name for the Jordan River.

min.[e] 5The rest of Kohath's descendants were allotted ten towns from the
clans of the tribes of Ephraim, Dan and
half of Manasseh.[f]
6The descendants of Gershon were
allotted thirteen towns from the clans
of the tribes of Issachar,[g] Asher,
Naphtali and the half-tribe of Manasseh in Bashan.
7The descendants of Merari,[h] clan
by clan, received twelve towns from
the tribes of Reuben, Gad and Zebulun.[i]
8So the Israelites allotted to the Levites these towns and their pasturelands, as the LORD had commanded
through Moses.

9From the tribes of Judah and Simeon
they allotted the following towns by
name 10(these towns were assigned to
the descendants of Aaron who were
from the Kohathite clans of the Levites,
because the first lot fell to them):

11They gave them Kiriath Arba
(that is, Hebron[j]), with its surrounding pastureland, in the hill
country of Judah. (Arba was the
forefather of Anak.) 12But the
fields and villages around the city
they had given to Caleb son of Jephunneh as his possession.
13So to the descendants of Aaron the priest they gave Hebron (a
city of refuge for one accused of
murder), Libnah,[k] 14Jattir,[l] Eshtemoa,[m] 15Holon,[n] Debir, 16Ain,
Juttah[o] and Beth Shemesh,[p] together with their pasturelands—
nine towns from these two tribes.
17And from the tribe of Benjamin they gave them Gibeon,
Geba,[q] 18Anathoth and Almon,
together with their pasturelands—four towns.

19All the towns for the priests, the
descendants of Aaron, were thirteen,
together with their pasturelands.

20The rest of the Kohathite clans of the
Levites were allotted towns from the
tribe of Ephraim:

21In the hill country of Ephraim
they were given Shechem[r] (a city
of refuge for one accused of murder) and Gezer, 22Kibzaim and
Beth Horon,[s] together with their
pasturelands—four towns.[t]
23Also from the tribe of Dan
they received Eltekeh, Gibbethon,
24Aijalon and Gath Rimmon,[u] together with their pasturelands—
four towns.
25From half the tribe of Manasseh they received Taanach and
Gath Rimmon, together with their
pasturelands—two towns.

26All these ten towns and their pasturelands were given to the rest of the Kohathite clans.

27The Levite clans of the Gershonites
were given:

from the half-tribe of Manasseh,
Golan in Bashan[v] (a city of refuge for one accused of murder[w])
and Be Eshtarah, together with
their pasturelands—two towns;
28from the tribe of Issachar,[x]
Kishion, Daberath, 29Jarmuth and
En Gannim, together with their
pasturelands—four towns;
30from the tribe of Asher,[y]
Mishal, Abdon, 31Helkath and Rehob, together with their pasturelands—four towns;
32from the tribe of Naphtali,
Kedesh[z] in Galilee (a city of refuge for one accused of murder[a]),
Hammoth Dor and Kartan, together with their pasturelands—
three towns.

33All the towns of the Gershonite[b]
clans were thirteen, together with their
pasturelands.

34The Merarite clans (the rest of the
Levites) were given:

from the tribe of Zebulun,[c]
Jokneam, Kartah, 35Dimnah and
Nahalal, together with their
pasturelands—four towns;
36from the tribe of Reuben,
Bezer,[d] Jahaz, 37Kedemoth and
Mephaath, together with their
pasturelands—four towns;
38from the tribe of Gad,
Ramoth[e] in Gilead (a city of refuge for one accused of murder),
Mahanaim,[f] 39Heshbon and Jazer, together with their pasturelands—four towns in all.

40All the towns allotted to the Merarite
clans, who were the rest of the Levites,
were twelve.

41The towns of the Levites in the territory held by the Israelites were forty-
eight in all, together with their pasturelands.[g] 42Each of these towns had
pasturelands surrounding it; this was
true for all these towns.

43So the LORD gave Israel all the land
he had sworn to give their forefathers,[h] and they took possession[i] of
it and settled there.[j] 44The LORD gave
them rest[k] on every side, just as he
had sworn to their forefathers. Not one
of their enemies[l] withstood them; the
LORD handed all their enemies[m] over
to them.[n] 45Not one of all the LORD's
good promises[o] to the house of Israel
failed; every one was fulfilled.

21:4 [e] ver 19
21:5 [f] ver 26
21:6 [g] Ge 30:18
21:7 [h] Ex 6:16 [i] Jos 19:10
21:11 [j] Jos 15:13; 1Ch 6:55
21:13 [k] Jos 15:42; 1Ch 6:57
21:14 [l] Jos 15:48 [m] Jos 15:50
21:15 [n] Jos 15:51
21:16 [o] Jos 15:55 [p] Jos 15:10
21:17 [q] Jos 18:24
21:21 [r] Jos 17:7; 20:7
21:22 [s] Jos 10:10 [t] 1Sa 1:1
21:24 [u] Jos 19:45
21:27 [v] Jos 12:5 [w] Nu 35:6
21:28 [x] Ge 30:18
21:30 [y] Jos 17:7
21:32 [z] Jos 12:22 [a] Nu 35:6; Jos 20:7
21:33 [b] ver 6
21:34 [c] Jos 19:10; 1Ch 6:77
21:36 [d] Jos 20:8
21:38 [e] Dt 4:43 [f] Ge 32:2
21:41 [g] Nu 35:7
21:43 [h] Dt 34:4 [i] Dt 11:31 [j] Dt 17:14
21:44 [k] Ex 33:14; Jos 1:13 [l] Dt 6:19 [m] Ex 23:31 [n] Dt 7:24; 21:10
21:45 [o] Jos 23:14; Ne 9:8

Eastern Tribes Return Home

22 Then Joshua summoned the Reubenites, the Gadites and the half-tribe of Manasseh 2 and said to them, "You have done all that Moses the servant of the LORD commanded,[p] and you have obeyed me in everything I commanded. 3 For a long time now—to this very day—you have not deserted your brothers but have carried out the mission the LORD your God gave you. 4 Now that the LORD your God has given your brothers rest as he promised, return to your homes[q] in the land that Moses the servant of the LORD gave you on the other side of the Jordan.[r] 5 But be very careful to keep the commandment[s] and the law that Moses the servant of the LORD gave you: to love the LORD your God, to walk in all his ways, to obey his commands,[t] to hold fast to him and to serve him with all your heart and all your soul.[u]"

1 →PG. 249

6 Then Joshua blessed[v] them and sent them away, and they went to their homes. 7 (To the half-tribe of Manasseh Moses had given land in Bashan,[w] and to the other half of the tribe Joshua gave land on the west side[x] of the Jordan with their brothers.) When Joshua sent them home, he blessed them, 8 saying, "Return to your homes with your great wealth—with large herds of livestock,[y] with silver, gold, bronze and iron, and a great quantity of clothing—and divide[z] with your brothers the plunder[a] from your enemies."

9 So the Reubenites, the Gadites and the half-tribe of Manasseh left the Israelites at Shiloh in Canaan to return to Gilead,[b] their own land, which they had acquired in accordance with the command of the LORD through Moses.

10 When they came to Geliloth near the Jordan in the land of Canaan, the Reubenites, the Gadites and the half-tribe of Manasseh built an imposing altar there by the Jordan. 11 And when the Israelites heard that they had built the altar on the border of Canaan at Geliloth near the Jordan on the Israelite side, 12 the whole assembly of Israel gathered at Shiloh[c] to go to war against them.

13 So the Israelites sent Phinehas[d] son of Eleazar,[e] the priest, to the land of Gilead—to Reuben, Gad and the half-tribe of Manasseh. 14 With him they sent ten of the chief men, one for each of the tribes of Israel, each the head of a family division among the Israelite clans.[f]

15 When they went to Gilead—to Reuben, Gad and the half-tribe of Manasseh—they said to them: 16 "The whole assembly of the LORD says: 'How could you break faith[g] with the God of Israel like this? How could you turn away from the LORD and build yourselves an altar in rebellion[h] against him now? 17 Was not the sin of Peor[i] enough for us? Up to this very day we have not cleansed ourselves from that sin, even though a plague fell on the community of the LORD! 18 And are you now turning away from the LORD?

" 'If you rebel against the LORD today, tomorrow he will be angry with the whole community[j] of Israel. 19 If the land you possess is defiled, come over to the LORD's land, where the LORD's tabernacle stands, and share the land with us. But do not rebel against the LORD or against us by building an altar for yourselves, other than the altar of the LORD our God. 20 When Achan son of Zerah acted unfaithfully regarding the devoted things,[a][k] did not wrath[l] come upon the whole community of Israel? He was not the only one who died for his sin.' "[m]

21 Then Reuben, Gad and the half-tribe of Manasseh replied to the heads of the clans of Israel: 22 "The Mighty One, God, the LORD! The Mighty One, God,[n] the LORD![o] He knows![p] And let Israel know! If this has been in rebellion or disobedience to the LORD, do not spare us this day. 23 If we have built our own altar to turn away from the LORD and to offer burnt offerings and grain offerings,[q] or to sacrifice fellowship offerings[b] on it, may the LORD himself call us to account.[r]

24 "No! We did it for fear that some day your descendants might say to ours, 'What do you have to do with the LORD, the God of Israel? 25 The LORD has made the Jordan a boundary between us and you—you Reubenites and Gadites! You have no share in the LORD.' So your descendants might cause ours to stop fearing the LORD.

26 "That is why we said, 'Let us get ready and build an altar—but not for burnt offerings or sacrifices.' 27 On the contrary, it is to be a witness[s] between us and you and the generations that follow, that we will worship the LORD at his sanctuary with our burnt offerings, sacrifices and fellowship offerings.[t] Then in the future your descendants will not be able to say to ours, 'You have no share in the LORD.'

28 "And we said, 'If they ever say this

22:2 [p]Nu 32:25
22:4 [q]Nu 32:22; Dt 3:20 [r]Nu 32:18; Jos 1:13-15
22:5 [s]Isa 43:22 [t]Dt 5:29 [u]Dt 6:6,17
22:6 [v]Ex 39:43
22:7 [w]Nu 32:33; Jos 12:5 [x]Jos 17:2,5
22:8 [y]Dt 20:14 [z]Nu 31:27 [a]Ge 49:27; 1Sa 30:16; Isa 9:3
22:9 [b]Nu 32:26,29
22:12 [c]Jos 18:1
22:13 [d]Nu 25:7 [e]Nu 3:32; Jos 24:33
22:14 [f]Nu 1:4
22:16 [g]Dt 13:14 [h]Dt 12:13-14
22:17 [i]Nu 25:1-9
22:18 [j]Lev 10:6; Nu 16:22
22:20 [k]Jos 7:1 [l]Ps 7:11 [m]Jos 7:5
22:22 [n]Dt 10:17 [o]Ps 50:1 [p]1Ki 8:39; Job 10:7; Ps 44:21; Jer 17:10
22:23 [q]Jer 41:5 [r]Dt 12:11; 18:19; 1Sa 20:16
22:27 [s]Ge 21:30; Jos 24:27 [t]Dt 12:6

a *20* The Hebrew term refers to the irrevocable giving over of things or persons to the LORD, often by totally destroying them.
b *23* Traditionally *peace offerings*; also in verse 27

to us, or to our descendants, we will answer: Look at the replica of the LORD's altar, which our fathers built, not for burnt offerings and sacrifices, but as a witness between us and you.'

29"Far be it from us to rebel[u] against the LORD and turn away from him today by building an altar for burnt offerings, grain offerings and sacrifices, other than the altar of the LORD our God that stands before his tabernacle.[v]"

30When Phinehas the priest and the leaders of the community—the heads of the clans of the Israelites—heard what Reuben, Gad and Manasseh had to say, they were pleased. 31And Phinehas son of Eleazar, the priest, said to Reuben, Gad and Manasseh, "Today we know that the LORD is with us,[w] because you have not acted unfaithfully toward the LORD in this matter. Now you have rescued the Israelites from the LORD's hand."

32Then Phinehas son of Eleazar, the priest, and the leaders returned to Canaan from their meeting with the Reubenites and Gadites in Gilead and reported to the Israelites. 33They were glad to hear the report and praised God.[x] And they talked no more about going to war against them to devastate the country where the Reubenites and the Gadites lived.

34And the Reubenites and the Gadites gave the altar this name: A Witness[y] Between Us that the LORD is God.

Joshua's Farewell to the Leaders

23 After a long time had passed and the LORD had given Israel rest[z] from all their enemies around them, Joshua, by then old and well advanced in years,[a] 2summoned all Israel—their elders,[b] leaders, judges and officials[c]—and said to them: "I am old and well advanced in years. 3You yourselves have seen everything the LORD your God has done to all these nations for your sake; it was the LORD your God who fought for you.[d] 4Remember how I have allotted[e] as an inheritance for your tribes all the land of the nations that remain—the nations I conquered—between the Jordan and the Great Sea[a][f] in the west. 5The LORD your God himself will drive them out of your way. He will push them out before you, and you will take possession of their land, as the LORD your God promised you.[g]

6"Be very strong; be careful to obey all that is written in the Book of the Law of Moses, without turning aside to the right or to the left.[h] 7Do not associate with these nations that remain among you; do not invoke the names of their gods or swear[i] by them. You must not serve them or bow down[j] to them. 8But you are to hold fast to the LORD[k] your God, as you have until now.

9"The LORD has driven out before you great and powerful nations;[l] to this day no one has been able to withstand you.[m] 10One of you routs a thousand,[n] because the LORD your God fights for you,[o] just as he promised. 11So be very careful to love the LORD[p] your God.

12"But if you turn away and ally yourselves with the survivors of these nations that remain among you and if you intermarry with them[q] and associate with them,[r] 13then you may be sure that the LORD your God will no longer drive out these nations before you. Instead, they will become snares[s] and traps for you, whips on your backs and thorns in your eyes,[t] until you perish from this good land, which the LORD your God has given you.

14"Now I am about to go the way of all the earth.[u] You know with all your heart and soul that not one of all the good promises the LORD your God gave you has failed. Every promise has been fulfilled; not one has failed.[v] 15But just as every good promise of the LORD your God has come true, so the LORD will bring on you all the evil he has threatened, until he has destroyed you from this good land he has given you.[w] 16If you violate the covenant of the LORD your God, which he commanded you, and go and serve other gods and bow down to them, the LORD's anger will burn against you, and you will quickly perish from the good land he has given you.[x]"

The Covenant Renewed at Shechem

24 Then Joshua assembled all the tribes of Israel at Shechem. He summoned the elders, leaders, judges and officials of Israel,[y] and they presented themselves before God.

2Joshua said to all the people, "This is what the LORD, the God of Israel, says: 'Long ago your forefathers, including Terah the father of Abraham and Nahor, lived beyond the River[b] and worshiped other gods.[z] 3But I took your father Abraham from the land beyond the River and led him throughout Canaan[a] and gave him many descendants.[b] I gave

22:29 [u]Jos 24:16 [v]Dt 12:13-14
22:31 [w]Lev 26:11-12; 2Ch 15:2
22:33 [x]1Ch 29:20; Da 2:19; Lk 2:28
22:34 [y]Ge 21:30
23:1 [z]Dt 12:9; Jos 21:44 [a]Jos 13:1
23:2 [b]Jos 7:6 [c]Jos 24:1
23:3 [d]Ex 14:14
23:4 [e]Jos 19:51 [f]Nu 34:6
23:5 [g]Ex 23:30; Nu 33:53
23:6 [h]Dt 5:32; Jos 1:7
23:7 [i]Ex 23:13; Ps 16:4; Jer 5:7 [j]Ex 20:5
23:8 [k]Dt 10:20
23:9 [l]Dt 11:23 [m]Dt 7:24
23:10 [n]Lev 26:8 [o]Ex 14:14; Dt 3:22
23:11 [p]Jos 22:5
23:12 [q]Dt 7:3 [r]Ex 34:16; Ps 106:34-35
23:13 [s]Ex 23:33 [t]Nu 33:55
23:14 [u]1Ki 2:2 [v]Jos 21:45
23:15 [w]Lev 26:17; Dt 28:15
23:16 [x]Dt 4:25-26
24:1 [y]Jos 23:2
24:2 [z]Ge 11:32
24:3 [a]Ge 12:1 [b]Ge 15:5

a *4* That is, the Mediterranean **b** *2* That is, the Euphrates; also in verses 3, 14 and 15

him Isaac,[c] 4and to Isaac I gave Jacob and Esau.[d] I assigned the hill country of Seir[e] to Esau, but Jacob and his sons went down to Egypt.[f]

5" 'Then I sent Moses and Aaron,[g] and I afflicted the Egyptians by what I did there, and I brought you out. 6When I brought your fathers out of Egypt, you came to the sea, and the Egyptians pursued them with chariots and horsemen[a][h] as far as the Red Sea.[b] 7But they cried to the LORD for help, and he put darkness[i] between you and the Egyptians; he brought the sea over them and covered them.[j] You saw with your own eyes what I did to the Egyptians. Then you lived in the desert for a long time.[k]

8" 'I brought you to the land of the Amorites who lived east of the Jordan. They fought against you, but I gave them into your hands. I destroyed them from before you, and you took possession of their land.[l] 9When Balak son of Zippor,[m] the king of Moab, prepared to fight against Israel, he sent for Balaam son of Beor to put a curse on you.[n] 10But I would not listen to Balaam, so he blessed you[o] again and again, and I delivered you out of his hand.

11" 'Then you crossed the Jordan[p] and came to Jericho.[q] The citizens of Jericho fought against you, as did also the Amorites, Perizzites, Canaanites, Hittites, Girgashites, Hivites and Jebusites, but I gave them into your hands.[r] 12I sent the hornet[s] ahead of you, which drove them out before you—also the two Amorite kings. You did not do it with your own sword and bow. 13So I gave you a land on which you did not toil and cities you did not build; and you live in them and eat from vineyards and olive groves that you did not plant.'[t]

14"Now fear the LORD and serve him with all faithfulness.[u] Throw away the gods[v] your forefathers worshiped beyond the River and in Egypt,[w] and serve the LORD. 15But if serving the LORD seems undesirable to you, then choose for yourselves this day whom you will serve, whether the gods your forefathers served beyond the River, or the gods of the Amorites,[x] in whose land you are living. But as for me and my household, we will serve the LORD."[y]

1 →PG. 297
4 →PG. 290

16Then the people answered, "Far be it from us to forsake the LORD to serve other gods! 17It was the LORD our God himself who brought us and our fathers up out of Egypt, from that land of slavery, and performed those great signs before our eyes. He protected us on our entire journey and among all the nations through which we traveled. 18And the LORD drove out before us all the nations, including the Amorites, who lived in the land. We too will serve the LORD, because he is our God."

19Joshua said to the people, "You are not able to serve the LORD. He is a holy God;[z] he is a jealous God.[a] He will not forgive your rebellion[b] and your sins. 20If you forsake the LORD[c] and serve foreign gods, he will turn[d] and bring disaster on you and make an end of you,[e] after he has been good to you."

21But the people said to Joshua, "No! We will serve the LORD."

22Then Joshua said, "You are witnesses against yourselves that you have chosen[f] to serve the LORD."

"Yes, we are witnesses," they replied.

23"Now then," said Joshua, "throw away the foreign gods[g] that are among you and yield your hearts[h] to the LORD, the God of Israel."

24And the people said to Joshua, "We will serve the LORD our God and obey him."[i]

25On that day Joshua made a covenant[j] for the people, and there at Shechem he drew up for them decrees and laws.[k] 26And Joshua recorded these things in the Book of the Law of God.[l] Then he took a large stone[m] and set it up there under the oak near the holy place of the LORD.

27"See!" he said to all the people.

24:3 [c]Ge 21:3
24:4 [d]Ge 25:26 [e]Dt 2:5 [f]Ge 46:5-6
24:5 [g]Ex 3:10
24:6 [h]Ex 14:9
24:7 [i]Ex 14:20 [j]Ex 14:28 [k]Dt 1:46
24:8 [l]Nu 21:31
24:9 [m]Nu 22:2 [n]Nu 22:6
24:10 [o]Nu 23:11; Dt 23:5
24:11 [p]Jos 3:16-17 [q]Jos 6:1 [r]Ex 23:23; Dt 7:1
24:12 [s]Ex 23:28; Dt 7:20; Ps 44:3,6-7
24:13 [t]Dt 6:10-11
24:14 [u]Dt 10:12; 18:13; 1Sa 12:24; 2Co 1:12 [v]ver 23 [w]Eze 23:3
24:15 [x]Jdg 6:10; Ru 1:15 [y]Ru 1:16; 1Ki 18:21
24:19 [z]Lev 19:2; 20:26 [a]Ex 20:5 [b]Ex 23:21
24:20 [c]1Ch 28:9,20 [d]Ac 7:42 [e]Jos 23:15
24:22 [f]Ps 119:30,173
24:23 [g]ver 14 [h]1Ki 8:58; Ps 119:36; 141:4
24:24 [i]Ex 19:8; 24:3,7; Dt 5:27
24:25 [j]Ex 24:8 [k]Ex 15:25
24:26 [l]Dt 31:24 [m]Ge 28:18

23:14–16 PROMISE 1

BLESSING AND DISCIPLINE

Joshua understood life well. He knew the road to victory was not a one-way street. God had blessed Israel's obedience and kept every promise he had made. God does that. That's why verse 15 is so sobering: As surely as God blessed obedience, he would also discipline disobedience.

Israel's history, as recorded for our learning in the Old Testament, is God's great gift to us. We learn from their success and from their failure. Prayerfully read through Joshua 23 and 24. If you have never done so before, set today as a memorial day. Write it down as the day you decided to serve God completely. Then renew that commitment to serve him every day.

For the next Promise 1 reading go to page 266.

[a]6 Or *charioteers* [b]6 Hebrew *Yam Suph;* that is, Sea of Reeds

"This stone will be a witness[n] against
us. It has heard all the words the LORD
has said to us. It will be a witness
against you if you are untrue to your
God."

Buried in the Promised Land

28 Then Joshua sent the people away,
each to his own inheritance.

24:31

PROMISE 4

GENERATIONAL GODLINESS

This verse contains both encouragement and warning. A godly man can make a difference. Joshua and his team of elders had a positive influence on Israel. But the implied warning comes in the thoughtful reader's question, "What happened after Joshua and the elders?" Flip over a few pages to Judges 2:6–15 for the answer.

It is important to model godliness and encourage others to live for him. But it is equally important to teach the values and behaviors of godliness to those who will be left after you've passed on. Live, model, encourage and cultivate godliness in the next generation.

For the next Promise 4 reading go to page 291.

29 After these things, Joshua son of
Nun, the servant of the LORD, died at
the age of a hundred and ten.[o] 30 And
they buried him in the land of his
inheritance, at Timnath Serah[a][p] in
the hill country of Ephraim, north of
Mount Gaash.

31 Israel served the LORD throughout
the lifetime of Joshua and of the elders[q] who outlived him and who had
experienced everything the LORD had
done for Israel.

32 And Joseph's bones, which the Israelites had brought up from Egypt,[r]
were buried at Shechem in the tract of
land[s] that Jacob bought for a hundred
pieces of silver[b] from the sons of
Hamor, the father of Shechem. This
became the inheritance of Joseph's
descendants.

33 And Eleazar son of Aaron[t] died
and was buried at Gibeah, which had
been allotted to his son Phinehas[u] in
the hill country of Ephraim.

24:27 [n]Jos 22:27
24:29 [o]Jdg 2:8
24:30 [p]Jos 19:50
24:31 [q]Jdg 2:7
24:32 [r]Ge 50:25; Ex 13:19 [s]Ge 33:19; Jn 4:5; Ac 7:16
24:33 [t]Jos 22:13 [u]Ex 6:25

[a] *30* Also known as *Timnath Heres* (see Judges 2:9)
[b] *32* Hebrew *hundred kesitahs*; a kesitah was a unit of money of unknown weight and value.

JUDGES

AT A GLANCE

Key Principle: Sin leads to a monotonous trap, but God responds to repentance with creative acts of deliverance.
Author: Possibly Samuel
Time and Place: 1390 B.C. to 1045 B.C. / Canaan and Transjordan
Key Verses: 2:12; 21:25

BENEFIT

Judges delivers a startling warning about the consequences of sliding from serving God to serving ourselves. It reminds us of the folly of disobedience and our need to turn back to God rather than wallow in defeat.

SETTING

Judges was compiled between 1050 B.C. (the beginning of Saul's reign) and 1004 B.C. (when David removed the Jebusites from Jerusalem). The events described in this book cover about 1390 B.C. to 1045 B.C., but the period of the judges extends an additional thirty years into the life of Samuel, the last of the judges (1 Samuel 1—25). Not all of the judges ruled over the entire land, and some of them reigned concurrently. The book opens with the continued conquest of Canaan, since the conquest under Joshua was general and not complete. It records the pattern of idolatry, oppression, and deliverance in the south (3), the north (4—5), the central region (6—9), the east (10—12) and the west (13—16).

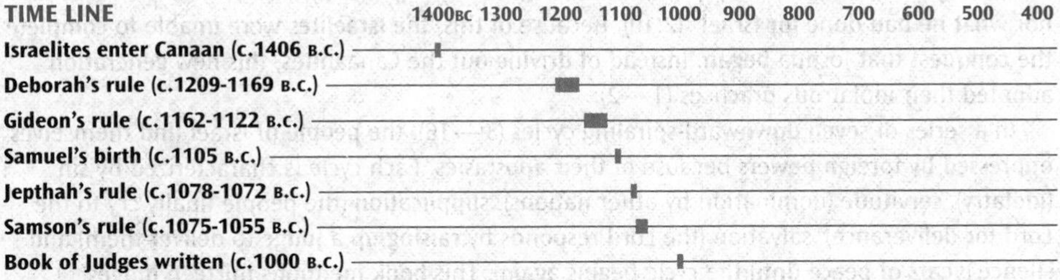

THEME AND PURPOSE

The theme of Judges is the stark contrast of Israel's apostasy and immorality with the grace, faithfulness and righteousness of God. Sin leads to sorrow and affliction, but repentance leads to deliverance. The Israelites experienced oppression and hardship because of their idolatry and disobedience to the covenant they had made with God. But each time the people turned in repentance to him, God raised up a deliverer to save them.

Judges continues the historical narrative of Israel from the time of Joshua's death to the time of Samuel, the last of the judges. After Samuel, Israel would no longer be a theocracy (directly ruled by God) but a monarchy (ruled by earthly kings).

UNIQUE CONTRIBUTION

The seven cycles in the book of Judges offer a unique view of a process that begins with sin and ends with deliverance. In each of these cycles, Judges contrasts the freedom and progress brought about by obedience with the bondage and regression brought about by disobedience. Israel's conquests were the result of their belief and service to God, but her defeats were the result of disbelief and selfishness. More than any other book of the Bible, Judges sets forth the outcome of an objective morality based on God's law versus the outcome of a subjective morality based on human opinions ("Everyone did as he saw fit"—21:25).

LINKS TO THE NEW TESTAMENT

God sent the judges not only to save the people from the consequences of their sins, but also to rule over them in righteousness. In this way, these deliverers anticipated Christ's work as the Savior and King of his people. Two of the 17 judges mentioned in Judges and 1 Samuel functioned not only as rulers, but also in the offices of prophet (Samuel) and priest (Eli). Thus, taken as a whole, the judges filled the three offices of prophet, priest and king that were perfectly fulfilled in the person of Christ.

OVERVIEW

FOCUS	Decline	Deliverances	Degradation
REFERENCE	1 — 2	3 — 16	17 — 21
TOPICS	Reasons for the Cycles	The Seven Cycles	Depravity During the Cycles
	Prologue	Narrative	Epilogue
	Explanation	Manifestation	Illustration
LOCATION	Canaan and Transjordan		
TIME	~345 Years		

After the generation of the conquest, "Another generation grew up, who knew neither the LORD nor what he had done for Israel" (2:10). Because of this, the Israelites were unable to complete the conquest that Joshua began. Instead of driving out the Canaanites, this new generation adopted their idolatrous practices (1—2).

In a series of seven downward-spiraling cycles (3—16), the people of Israel find themselves oppressed by foreign powers because of their apostasies. Each cycle is characterized by sin (idolatry), servitude (domination by other nations), supplication (the people finally cry to the Lord for deliverance), salvation (the Lord responds by raising up a judge to deliver them) and silence (years of peace until the cycle begins again). This book mentions thirteen judges; 1 Samuel mentions four more. Several incidents in the last section of the book illustrate the people's religious and moral degradation during this centuries-long time of spiritual degeneration (17—21).

JUDGES

Israel Fights the Remaining Canaanites

1 After the death[a] of Joshua, the Israelites asked the LORD, "Who will be the first[b] to go up and fight for us against the Canaanites?[c]"

2 The LORD answered, "Judah[d] is to go; I have given the land into their hands.[e]"

3 Then the men of Judah said to the Simeonites their brothers, "Come up with us into the territory allotted to us, to fight against the Canaanites. We in turn will go with you into yours." So the Simeonites[f] went with them.

4 When Judah attacked, the LORD gave the Canaanites and Perizzites[g] into their hands and they struck down ten thousand men at Bezek.[h] 5 It was there that they found Adoni-Bezek and fought against him, putting to rout the Canaanites and Perizzites. 6 Adoni-Bezek fled, but they chased him and caught him, and cut off his thumbs and big toes.

7 Then Adoni-Bezek said, "Seventy kings with their thumbs and big toes cut off have picked up scraps under my table. Now God has paid me back[i] for what I did to them." They brought him to Jerusalem, and he died there.

8 The men of Judah attacked Jerusalem[j] also and took it. They put the city to the sword and set it on fire.

9 After that, the men of Judah went down to fight against the Canaanites living in the hill country,[k] the Negev[l] and the western foothills. 10 They advanced against the Canaanites living in Hebron[m] (formerly called Kiriath Arba[n]) and defeated Sheshai, Ahiman and Talmai.[o]

11 From there they advanced against the people living in Debir[p] (formerly called Kiriath Sepher). 12 And Caleb said, "I will give my daughter Acsah in marriage to the man who attacks and captures Kiriath Sepher." 13 Othniel son of Kenaz, Caleb's younger brother, took it; so Caleb gave his daughter Acsah to him in marriage.

14 One day when she came to Othniel, she urged him**a** to ask her father for a field. When she got off her donkey, Caleb asked her, "What can I do for you?"

15 She replied, "Do me a special favor. Since you have given me land in the Negev, give me also springs of water." Then Caleb gave her the upper and lower springs.

16 The descendants of Moses' father-in-law,[q] the Kenite,[r] went up from the City of Palms**b**[s] with the men of Judah to live among the people of the Desert of Judah in the Negev near Arad.[t]

17 Then the men of Judah went with the Simeonites[u] their brothers and attacked the Canaanites living in Zephath, and they totally destroyed**c** the city. Therefore it was called Hormah.**d**[v] 18 The men of Judah also took**e** Gaza,[w] Ashkelon and Ekron—each city with its territory.

19 The LORD was with[x] the men of Judah. They took possession of the hill country, but they were unable to drive the people from the plains, because they had iron chariots.[y] 20 As Moses had promised, Hebron[z] was given to Caleb, who drove from it the three sons of Anak.[a] 21 The Benjamites, however, failed[b] to dislodge the Jebusites, who were living in Jerusalem;[c] to this day the Jebusites live there with the Benjamites.

22 Now the house of Joseph attacked Bethel, and the LORD was with them. 23 When they sent men to spy out Bethel (formerly called Luz),[d] 24 the spies saw a man coming out of the city and they said to him, "Show us how to get into the city and we will see that you are treated well.[e]" 25 So he showed them, and they put the city to the sword but spared[f] the man and his whole family. 26 He then went to the land of the Hittites, where he built a city and called it Luz, which is its name to this day.

27 But Manasseh did not drive out the people of Beth Shan or Taanach or Dor or Ibleam[g] or Megiddo and their surrounding settlements, for the Canaanites[h] were determined to live in that land. 28 When Israel became strong, they pressed the Canaanites into forced labor but never drove them out completely. 29 Nor did Ephraim drive out the Canaanites living in Gezer,[i] but the Canaanites continued to live there among them.[j] 30 Neither did

1:1 [a]Jos 24:29 [b]Nu 27:21 [c]ver 27; Jdg 3:1-6
1:2 [d]Ge 49:8 [e]ver 4; Jdg 3:28
1:3 [f]ver 17
1:4 [g]Ge 13:7; Jos 3:10 [h]1Sa 11:8
1:7 [i]Lev 24:19
1:8 [j]ver 21; Jos 15:63
1:9 [k]Nu 13:17 [l]Nu 21:1
1:10 [m]Ge 13:18 [n]Ge 35:27 [o]Jos 15:14
1:11 [p]Jos 15:15
1:16 [q]Nu 10:29 [r]Ge 15:19; Jdg 4:11 [s]Dt 34:3; Jdg 3:13 [t]Nu 21:1
1:17 [u]ver 3 [v]Nu 21:3
1:18 [w]Jos 11:22
1:19 [x]ver 2 [y]Jos 17:16
1:20 [z]Jos 14:9; 15:13-14 [a]ver 10; Jos 14:13
1:21 [b]Jos 15:63 [c]ver 8
1:23 [d]Ge 28:19
1:24 [e]Jos 2:12,14
1:25 [f]Jos 6:25
1:27 [g]Jos 17:11 [h]ver 1
1:29 [i]1Ki 9:16 [j]Jos 16:10

a *14* Hebrew; Septuagint and Vulgate *Othniel, he urged her* **b** *16* That is, Jericho **c** *17* The Hebrew term refers to the irrevocable giving over of things or persons to the LORD, often by totally destroying them. **d** *17* *Hormah* means *destruction.* **e** *18* Hebrew; Septuagint *Judah did not take*

Zebulun drive out the Canaanites living in Kitron or Nahalol, who remained
among them; but they did subject
them to forced labor. 31Nor did Asher
drive out those living in Acco or Sidon
or Ahlab or Aczib[k] or Helbah or Aphek
or Rehob, 32and because of this the
people of Asher lived among the Canaanite inhabitants of the land. 33Nei-
ther did Naphtali drive out those living
in Beth Shemesh or Beth Anath[l]; but
the Naphtalites too lived among the
Canaanite inhabitants of the land, and
those living in Beth Shemesh and Beth
Anath became forced laborers for
them. 34The Amorites[m] confined the
Danites to the hill country, not allowing them to come down into the plain.
35And the Amorites were determined
also to hold out in Mount Heres, Aijalon[n] and Shaalbim, but when the
power of the house of Joseph increased, they too were pressed into
forced labor. 36The boundary of the
Amorites was from Scorpion[a] Pass[o]
to Sela and beyond.

The Angel of the LORD at Bokim

2 The angel of the LORD[p] went up
from Gilgal to Bokim[q] and said, "I
brought you up out of Egypt[r] and led
you into the land that I swore to give to
your forefathers.[s] I said, 'I will never
break my covenant with you,[t] 2and
you shall not make a covenant with the
people of this land,[u] but you shall
break down their altars.[v]' Yet you
have disobeyed me. Why have you
done this? 3Now therefore I tell
you that I will not drive them out before you;[w] they will be ⌊thorns⌋[x] in
your sides and their gods will be a
snare[y] to you."
4When the angel of the LORD had
spoken these things to all the Israelites,
the people wept aloud, 5and they
called that place Bokim.[b] There they
offered sacrifices to the LORD.

Disobedience and Defeat

6After Joshua had dismissed the Israelites, they went to take possession of
the land, each to his own inheritance.
7The people served the LORD throughout the lifetime of Joshua and of the
elders who outlived him and who had
seen all the great things the LORD had
done for Israel.
8Joshua son of Nun, the servant of
the LORD, died at the age of a hundred
and ten. 9And they buried him in the
land of his inheritance, at Timnath Heres[c][z] in the hill country of Ephraim,
north of Mount Gaash.
10After that whole generation had
been gathered to their fathers, another
generation grew up, who knew neither
the LORD nor what he had done for Israel.[a] 11Then the Israelites did evil in
the eyes of the LORD[b] and served the
Baals.[c] 12They forsook the LORD, the
God of their fathers, who had brought
them out of Egypt. They followed and
worshiped various gods[d] of the peoples around them.[e] They provoked
the LORD to anger 13because they forsook him and served Baal and the Ashtoreths.[f] 14In his anger[g] against Israel the LORD handed them over[h] to
raiders who plundered them. He sold
them[i] to their enemies all around,
whom they were no longer able to resist.[j] 15Whenever Israel went out to
fight, the hand of the LORD was against
them to defeat them, just as he had
sworn to them. They were in great distress.
16Then the LORD raised up
judges,[d][k] who saved[l] them out of
the hands of these raiders. 17Yet they
would not listen to their judges but
prostituted[m] themselves to other gods
and worshiped them. Unlike their fathers, they quickly turned from the way
in which their fathers had walked, the
way of obedience to the LORD's commands.[n] 18Whenever the LORD raised
up a judge for them, he was with the

[a]*36* Hebrew *Akrabbim* [b]*5* *Bokim* means *weepers.* [c]*9* Also known as *Timnath Serah* (see Joshua 19:50 and 24:30) [d]*16* Or *leaders;* similarly in verses 17-19

1:31 [k]Jdg 10:6 **1:33** [l]Jos 19:38 **1:34** [m]Ex 3:17 **1:35** [n]Jos 19:42 **1:36** [o]Jos 15:3 **2:1** [p]Jdg 6:11 [q]ver 5 [r]Ex 20:2 [s]Ge 17:8 [t]Lev 26:42-44; Dt 7:9 **2:2** [u]Ex 23:32; 34:12; Dt 7:2 [v]Ex 34:13 **2:3** [w]Jos 23:13 [x]Nu 33:55 [y]Dt 7:16; Jdg 3:6; Ps 106:36 **2:9** [z]Jos 19:50 **2:10** [a]Ex 5:2; 1Sa 2:12; 1Ch 28:9; Gal 4:8 **2:11** [b]Jdg 3:12; 4:1; 6:1; 10:6 [c]Jdg 3:7; 8:33 **2:12** [d]Ps 106:36 [e]Dt 31:16; Jdg 10:6 **2:13** [f]Jdg 10:6 **2:14** [g]Dt 31:17 [h]Ps 106:41 [i]Dt 32:30; Jdg 3:8 [j]Dt 28:25 **2:16** [k]Ac 13:20 [l]Ps 106:43 **2:17** [m]Ex 34:15 [n]ver 7

2:10 PROMISE **5**

PASS IT ON

An interesting contrast jumps out of this text. Notice what characterized this generation of Israelites, then look back at Joshua 24:31 and see what characterized Joshua's generation. While the older generation had experienced God in their lives, this new generation had neither knowledge of nor experience with God.

Each generation of children needs to be involved in worship, ministry, and other faith experiences where they can see God at work. The cliché, "God has no grandchildren" is well illustrated in this passage. Each person must be confronted with the reality of God's work and decide for him or herself whether or not to become God's child. Consider your role in presenting God to others, especially the younger generation. Make a conscious effort to help your church and family experience God at work in their lives in concrete ways.

For the next Promise 5 reading go to page 264.

judge and saved them out of the hands
of their enemies as long as the judge
lived; for the LORD had compassion[o]
on them as they groaned[p] under those
who oppressed and afflicted them.
19 But when the judge died, the people
returned to ways even more corrupt[q]
than those of their fathers, following
other gods and serving and worshiping
them.[r] They refused to give up their
evil practices and stubborn ways.

20 Therefore the LORD was very angry[s] with Israel and said, "Because
this nation has violated the covenant
that I laid down for their forefathers
and has not listened to me, 21 I will no
longer drive out[t] before them any of
the nations Joshua left when he died.
22 I will use them to test[u] Israel and see
whether they will keep the way of the
LORD and walk in it as their forefathers
did." 23 The LORD had allowed those nations to remain; he did not drive them
out at once by giving them into the
hands of Joshua.

3 These are the nations the LORD left
to test[v] all those Israelites who had
not experienced any of the wars in Canaan 2 (he did this only to teach warfare
to the descendants of the Israelites
who had not had previous battle experience): 3 the five[w] rulers of the Philistines, all the Canaanites, the Sidonians,
and the Hivites living in the Lebanon
mountains from Mount Baal Hermon
to Lebo[a] Hamath. 4 They were left to
test[x] the Israelites to see whether they
would obey the LORD's commands,
which he had given their forefathers
through Moses.

5 The Israelites lived[y] among the
Canaanites, Hittites, Amorites, Perizzites, Hivites and Jebusites. 6 They took
their daughters in marriage and gave
their own daughters to their sons, and
served their gods.[z]

Othniel

7 The Israelites did evil in the eyes of
the LORD; they forgot the LORD[a] their
God and served the Baals and the
Asherahs.[b] 8 The anger of the LORD
burned against Israel so that he sold[c]
them into the hands of Cushan-
Rishathaim king of Aram Naharaim,[b]
to whom the Israelites were subject for
eight years. 9 But when they cried out[d]
to the LORD, he raised up for them a
deliverer, Othniel[e] son of Kenaz, Caleb's younger brother, who saved
them. 10 The Spirit of the LORD came
upon him,[f] so that he became Israel's
judge[c] and went to war. The LORD

2:18 [o] Dt 32:36; Jos 1:5 [p] Ps 106:44
2:19 [q] Jdg 3:12 [r] Jdg 4:1; 8:33
2:20 [s] ver 14; Jos 23:16
2:21 [t] Jos 23:13
2:22 [u] Dt 8:2,16; Jdg 3:1,14
3:1 [v] Jdg 2:21-22
3:3 [w] Jos 13:3
3:4 [x] Dt 8:2; Jdg 2:22
3:5 [y] Ps 106:35
3:6 [z] Ex 34:16; Dt 7:3-4
3:7 [a] Dt 4:9 [b] Ex 34:13; Jdg 2:11,13
3:8 [c] Jdg 2:14
3:9 [d] ver 15; Jdg 6:6,7; 10:10; Ps 106:44 [e] Jdg 1:13
3:10 [f] Nu 11:25,29; 24:2; Jdg 6:34; 11:29; 13:25; 14:6,19; 1Sa 11:6

[a] *3* Or *to the entrance to* [b] *8* That is, Northwest Mesopotamia [c] *10* Or *leader*

2:18–23

PROMISE 3

SMALL COMPROMISES—DIRE CONSEQUENCES

This is the story of a man who seemed destined for greatness. At age 14 he ran away from home to fight in the French and Indian War. When the American Revolution broke out, he joined the American army as a colonel. Later he shared a command with Ethan Allen in the capture of Ticonderoga. In 1775, he led 1,000 men into Canada to fight the British. In recognition of his courage, Congress promoted him to major general.

But somewhere, somehow, something went wrong. Compromise slowly ate away at his patriotic zeal. Finally, the unthinkable happened. In 1780 the Colonial army discovered his plot to hand over West Point to the British. Later, he led the British in the burning of Richmond, Virginia. Today, instead of being recognized as a hero, Benedict Arnold remains the most infamous traitor in American history.

Compromise made the life of Benedict Arnold a story of what could have been. How tragic. More tragic is the man who has so much to live for and gives it away through a series of small compromises. That's what happened to the ancient Israelites.

In the period of the judges, Israel had the ideal king—God himself. No enemy could stand before them if they looked to God and obeyed his commands. And, under the leadership of the judges, they did just that. The Israelites rallied behind the judges and experienced both military victories and God's blessing. But when the dust settled and the conflict was over, Israel allowed compromise to eat away at their spiritual zeal. Before long, they quit worshiping the God who had so often delivered them from their enemies. Instead, they bowed down before foreign gods. They trusted in empty images to meet their deepest needs. And, tragically, each generation was worse than the one before it.

What a profound thought! Our sins are passed on to our children where they are magnified in their lives—along with the consequences.

The story of these ancient men should cause us all to step back and take inventory of our own lives. Compromise is always a series of small steps in the wrong direction. Since that's the case, it's imperative that we take a few minutes every day to make sure we're not allowing something, besides God, to take over our lives. If you spot something that's leading you down the wrong path, remember this: Right choices today will make your life a story that honors God, rather than a story of what could have been.

For the next Promise 3 reading go to page 263.

gave Cushan-Rishathaim king of Aram into the hands of Othniel, who overpowered him. 11So the land had peace for forty years, until Othniel son of Kenaz died.

Ehud

12Once again the Israelites did evil in the eyes of the LORD,[g] and because they did this evil the LORD gave Eglon king of Moab[h] power over Israel. 13Getting the Ammonites and Amalekites to join him, Eglon came and attacked Israel, and they took possession of the City of Palms.[a][i] 14The Israelites were subject to Eglon king of Moab for eighteen years.

15Again the Israelites cried out to the LORD, and he gave them a deliverer[j]—Ehud, a left-handed man, the son of Gera the Benjamite. The Israelites sent him with tribute to Eglon king of Moab. 16Now Ehud had made a double-edged sword about a foot and a half[b] long, which he strapped to his right thigh under his clothing. 17He presented the tribute to Eglon king of Moab, who was a very fat man.[k] 18After Ehud had presented the tribute, he sent on their way the men who had carried it. 19At the idols[c] near Gilgal he himself turned back and said, "I have a secret message for you, O king."

The king said, "Quiet!" And all his attendants left him.

20Ehud then approached him while he was sitting alone in the upper room of his summer palace[d] and said, "I have a message from God for you." As the king rose from his seat, 21Ehud reached with his left hand, drew the sword from his right thigh and plunged it into the king's belly. 22Even the handle sank in after the blade, which came out his back. Ehud did not pull the sword out, and the fat closed in over it. 23Then Ehud went out to the porch[e]; he shut the doors of the upper room behind him and locked them.

24After he had gone, the servants came and found the doors of the upper room locked. They said, "He must be relieving himself[l] in the inner room of the house." 25They waited to the point of embarrassment,[m] but when he did not open the doors of the room, they took a key and unlocked them. There they saw their lord fallen to the floor, dead.

26While they waited, Ehud got away. He passed by the idols and escaped to Seirah. 27When he arrived there, he blew a trumpet[n] in the hill country of Ephraim, and the Israelites went down with him from the hills, with him leading them.

28"Follow me," he ordered, "for the LORD has given Moab, your enemy, into your hands.[o]" So they followed him down and, taking possession of the fords of the Jordan[p] that led to Moab, they allowed no one to cross over. 29At that time they struck down about ten thousand Moabites, all vigorous and strong; not a man escaped. 30That day Moab was made subject to Israel, and the land had peace[q] for eighty years.

Shamgar

31After Ehud came Shamgar son of Anath,[r] who struck down six hundred[s] Philistines with an oxgoad. He too saved Israel.

Deborah

4 After Ehud died, the Israelites once again did evil[t] in the eyes of the LORD. 2So the LORD sold them into the

3:12 [g]Jdg 2:11,14 [h]1Sa 12:9
3:13 [i]Jdg 1:16
3:15 [j]ver 9; Ps 78:34; 107:13
3:17 [k]ver 12
3:24 [l]1Sa 24:3
3:25 [m]2Ki 2:17; 8:11
3:27 [n]Jdg 6:34; 1Sa 13:3
3:28 [o]Jdg 7:9,15 [p]Jos 2:7; Jdg 7:24; 12:5
3:30 [q]ver 11
3:31 [r]Jdg 5:6 [s]Jos 23:10
4:1 [t]Jdg 2:19

[a]13 That is, Jericho [b]16 Hebrew *a cubit* (about 0.5 meter) [c]19 Or *the stone quarries*; also in verse 26 [d]20 The meaning of the Hebrew for this phrase is uncertain. [e]23 The meaning of the Hebrew for this word is uncertain.

4:1–16

PROMISE 6

DEBORAH: BREAKING NEW GROUND

This chapter contains the story of Deborah, a woman who was way ahead of her time. In an era when women had no voice in the community and very few rights, Deborah served as judge over the nation of Israel. She settled disputes and gave direction to the people.

The fact that Deborah was a woman in no way diminished her effectiveness as a leader. In fact, she demonstrated several leadership practices that are very valuable for our study today. First, she listened to God (4:1–5) while the rest of the nation had turned a deaf ear. Second, she declared God's Word to others (4:6–9). Third, she led with tenderness and compassion, calling herself "a mother in Israel" (5:7). Fourth, Deborah encouraged others to serve God (4:7–23).

In our day it's very common for women to hold positions of authority and leadership in business, government, education and all other sectors of society. Deborah is an excellent example of how God uses people with different talents and abilities to accomplish his purposes regardless of gender considerations.

For the next Promise 6 reading go to page 275.

hands of Jabin, a king of Canaan, who reigned in Hazor.[u] The commander of his army was Sisera,[v] who lived in Harosheth Haggoyim. 3 Because he had nine hundred iron chariots[w] and had cruelly oppressed[x] the Israelites for twenty years, they cried to the LORD for help.

4 Deborah, a prophetess, the wife of Lappidoth, was leading[a] Israel at that time. 5 She held court under the Palm of Deborah between Ramah and Bethel[y] in the hill country of Ephraim, and the Israelites came to her to have their disputes decided. 6 She sent for Barak son of Abinoam[z] from Kedesh in Naphtali and said to him, "The LORD, the God of Israel, commands you: 'Go, take with you ten thousand men of Naphtali and Zebulun and lead the way to Mount Tabor. 7 I will lure Sisera, the commander of Jabin's army, with his chariots and his troops to the Kishon River[a] and give him into your hands.' "

8 Barak said to her, "If you go with me, I will go; but if you don't go with me, I won't go."

9 "Very well," Deborah said, "I will go with you. But because of the way you are going about this,[b] the honor will not be yours, for the LORD will hand Sisera over to a woman." So Deborah went with Barak to Kedesh,[b] 10 where he summoned[c] Zebulun and Naphtali. Ten thousand men followed him, and Deborah also went with him.

11 Now Heber the Kenite had left the other Kenites,[d] the descendants of Hobab,[e] Moses' brother-in-law,[c] and pitched his tent by the great tree in Zaanannim[f] near Kedesh.

12 When they told Sisera that Barak son of Abinoam had gone up to Mount Tabor, 13 Sisera gathered together his nine hundred iron chariots[g] and all the men with him, from Harosheth Haggoyim to the Kishon River.

14 Then Deborah said to Barak, "Go! This is the day the LORD has given Sisera into your hands. Has not the LORD gone ahead[h] of you?" So Barak went down Mount Tabor, followed by ten thousand men. 15 At Barak's advance, the LORD routed[i] Sisera and all his chariots and army by the sword, and Sisera abandoned his chariot and fled on foot. 16 But Barak pursued the chariots and army as far as Harosheth Haggoyim. All the troops of Sisera fell by the sword; not a man was left.[j]

17 Sisera, however, fled on foot to the tent of Jael, the wife of Heber the Kenite, because there were friendly relations between Jabin king of Hazor and the clan of Heber the Kenite.

18 Jael went out to meet Sisera and said to him, "Come, my lord, come right in. Don't be afraid." So he entered her tent, and she put a covering over him.

19 "I'm thirsty," he said. "Please give me some water." She opened a skin of milk,[k] gave him a drink, and covered him up.

20 "Stand in the doorway of the tent," he told her. "If someone comes by and asks you, 'Is anyone here?' say 'No.' "

21 But Jael, Heber's wife, picked up a tent peg and a hammer and went quietly to him while he lay fast asleep, exhausted. She drove the peg through his temple into the ground, and he died.[l]

22 Barak came by in pursuit of Sisera, and Jael went out to meet him. "Come," she said, "I will show you the man you're looking for." So he went in with her, and there lay Sisera with the tent peg through his temple—dead.

23 On that day God subdued[m] Jabin, the Canaanite king, before the Israelites. 24 And the hand of the Israelites grew stronger and stronger against Jabin, the Canaanite king, until they destroyed him.

The Song of Deborah

5 On that day Deborah and Barak son of Abinoam sang this song:[n]

2 "When the princes in Israel take
the lead,
when the people willingly offer[o]
themselves—
praise the LORD![p]

3 "Hear this, you kings! Listen, you
rulers!
I will sing to[d] the LORD, I will
sing;
I will make music to[e] the LORD,
the God of Israel.[q]

4 "O LORD, when you went out from
Seir,[r]
when you marched from the
land of Edom,
the earth shook, the heavens
poured,
the clouds poured down water.[s]
5 The mountains quaked[t] before
the LORD, the One of Sinai,
before the LORD, the God of
Israel.

6 "In the days of Shamgar son of
Anath,[u]
in the days of Jael,[v] the roads[w]
were abandoned;

4:2 [u] Jos 11:1 [v] ver 13,16; 1Sa 12:9; Ps 83:9 **4:3** [w] Jdg 1:19 [x] Ps 106:42 **4:5** [y] Ge 35:8 **4:6** [z] Heb 11:32 **4:7** [a] Ps 83:9 **4:9** [b] ver 21; Jdg 2:14 **4:10** [c] ver 14; Jdg 5:15,18 **4:11** [d] Jdg 1:16 [e] Nu 10:29 [f] Jos 19:33 **4:13** [g] ver 3 **4:14** [h] Dt 9:3; 2Sa 5:24; Ps 68:7 **4:15** [i] Ps 83:9-10 **4:16** [j] Ps 83:9

4:19 [k] Jdg 5:25 **4:21** [l] Jdg 5:26 **4:23** [m] Ne 9:24; Ps 18:47 **5:1** [n] Ex 15:1 **5:2** [o] 2Ch 17:16; Ps 110:3 [p] ver 9 **5:3** [q] Ps 27:6 **5:4** [r] Dt 33:2 [s] Ps 68:8 **5:5** [t] Ex 19:18; Ps 68:8; 97:5; Isa 64:3 **5:6** [u] Jdg 3:31 [v] Jdg 4:17 [w] Isa 33:8

a 4 Traditionally *judging* b 9 Or *But on the expedition you are undertaking* c 11 Or *father-in-law* d 3 Or *of* e 3 Or / *with song I will praise*

travelers took to winding paths.
7 Village life[a] in Israel ceased,
ceased until I,[b] Deborah, arose,
arose a mother in Israel.
8 When they chose new gods,[x]
war came to the city gates,
and not a shield or spear was seen
among forty thousand in Israel.
9 My heart is with Israel's princes,
with the willing volunteers[y]
among the people.
Praise the LORD!

10 "You who ride on white donkeys,[z]
sitting on your saddle blankets,
and you who walk along the
road,
consider 11 the voice of the singers[c]
at the watering places.
They recite the righteous acts[a]
of the LORD,
the righteous acts of his
warriors[d] in Israel.

"Then the people of the LORD
went down to the city gates.[b]
12 'Wake up,[c] wake up, Deborah!
Wake up, wake up, break out in
song!
Arise, O Barak!
Take captive your captives,[d]
O son of Abinoam.'

13 "Then the men who were left
came down to the nobles;
the people of the LORD
came to me with the mighty.
14 Some came from Ephraim, whose
roots were in Amalek;[e]
Benjamin was with the people
who followed you.
From Makir captains came down,
from Zebulun those who bear a
commander's staff.
15 The princes of Issachar were with
Deborah;[f]
yes, Issachar was with Barak,
rushing after him into the valley.
In the districts of Reuben
there was much searching of
heart.
16 Why did you stay among the
campfires[e]
to hear the whistling for the
flocks?[g]
In the districts of Reuben
there was much searching of
heart.
17 Gilead stayed beyond the Jordan.
And Dan, why did he linger by
the ships?
Asher remained on the coast[h]
and stayed in his coves.
18 The people of Zebulun risked their
very lives;
so did Naphtali on the heights of
the field.[i]

5:8 *x*Dt 32:17
5:9 *y*ver 2
5:10 *z*Jdg 10:4; 12:14
5:11 *a*1Sa 12:7; Mic 6:5 *b*ver 8
5:12 *c*Ps 57:8 *d*Ps 68:18; Eph 4:8
5:14 *e*Jdg 3:13
5:15 *f*Jdg 4:10
5:16 *g*Nu 32:1
5:17 *h*Jos 19:29
5:18 *i*Jdg 4:6,10

19 "Kings came[j], they fought;
the kings of Canaan fought
at Taanach by the waters of
Megiddo,[k]
but they carried off no silver, no
plunder.[l]
20 From the heavens[m] the stars
fought,
from their courses they fought
against Sisera.
21 The river Kishon[n] swept them
away,
the age-old river, the river
Kishon.
March on, my soul; be strong!
22 Then thundered the horses'
hoofs—
galloping, galloping go his
mighty steeds.
23 'Curse Meroz,' said the angel of the
LORD.
'Curse its people bitterly,
because they did not come to help
the LORD,
to help the LORD against the
mighty.'

24 "Most blessed of women be Jael,[o]
the wife of Heber the Kenite,
most blessed of tent-dwelling
women.
25 He asked for water, and she gave
him milk;[p]
in a bowl fit for nobles she
brought him curdled milk.
26 Her hand reached for the tent peg,
her right hand for the workman's
hammer.
She struck Sisera, she crushed his
head,
she shattered and pierced his
temple.[q]
27 At her feet he sank,
he fell; there he lay.
At her feet he sank, he fell;
where he sank, there he fell—
dead.

28 "Through the window peered
Sisera's mother;
behind the lattice she cried
out,[r]
'Why is his chariot so long in
coming?
Why is the clatter of his chariots
delayed?'
29 The wisest of her ladies answer her;
indeed, she keeps saying to
herself,
30 'Are they not finding and dividing
the spoils:[s]
a girl or two for each man,

5:19 *j*Jos 11:5; Jdg 4:13 *k*Jdg 1:27 *l*ver 30
5:20 *m*Jos 10:11
5:21 *n*Jdg 4:7
5:24 *o*Jdg 4:17
5:25 *p*Jdg 4:19
5:26 *q*Jdg 4:21
5:28 *r*Pr 7:6
5:30 *s*Ex 15:9; 1Sa 30:24

a *7* Or *Warriors* **b** *7* Or *you* **c** *11* Or *archers;* the meaning of the Hebrew for this word is uncertain. **d** *11* Or *villagers* **e** *16* Or *saddlebags*

colorful garments as plunder for
Sisera,
colorful garments embroidered,
highly embroidered garments for
my neck—
all this as plunder?'

31"So may all your enemies perish,
O LORD!
But may they who love you be
like the sun[t]
when it rises in its strength."

Then the land had peace[u] forty
years.

Gideon

6 Again the Israelites did evil in the
eyes of the LORD,[v] and for seven
years he gave them into the hands of
the Midianites.[w] **2**Because the power
of Midian was so oppressive,[x] the Israelites prepared shelters for themselves in mountain clefts, caves and
strongholds.[y] **3**Whenever the Israelites planted their crops, the Midianites,
Amalekites[z] and other eastern peoples invaded the country. **4**They
camped on the land and ruined the
crops[a] all the way to Gaza and did not
spare a living thing for Israel, neither
sheep nor cattle nor donkeys. **5**They
came up with their livestock and their
tents like swarms of locusts.[b] It was
impossible to count the men and their
camels;[c] they invaded the land to ravage it. **6**Midian so impoverished the Israelites that they cried out[d] to the
LORD for help.

7When the Israelites cried to the
LORD because of Midian, **8**he sent them
a prophet, who said, "This is what the
LORD, the God of Israel, says: I brought
you up out of Egypt,[e] out of the land
of slavery. **9**I snatched you from the
power of Egypt and from the hand of
all your oppressors. I drove them from
before you and gave you their land.[f]
10I said to you, 'I am the LORD your
God; do not worship[g] the gods of the
Amorites,[h] in whose land you live.'
But you have not listened to me."

11The angel of the LORD[i] came and
sat down under the oak in Ophrah that
belonged to Joash the Abiezrite,[j]
where his son Gideon[k] was threshing
wheat in a winepress to keep it from
the Midianites. **12**When the angel of the
LORD appeared to Gideon, he said,
"The LORD is with you,[l] mighty warrior."

13"But sir," Gideon replied, "if the
LORD is with us, why has all this happened to us? Where are all his wonders
that our fathers told[m] us about when
they said, 'Did not the LORD bring us up
out of Egypt?' But now the LORD has
abandoned[n] us and put us into the
hand of Midian."

14The LORD turned to him and said,
"Go in the strength you have[o] and
save Israel out of Midian's hand. Am I
not sending you?"

15"But Lord,[a]" Gideon asked, "how
can I save Israel? My clan is the weakest in Manasseh, and I am the least in
my family.[p]"

16The LORD answered, "I will be with
you[q], and you will strike down all the
Midianites together."

17Gideon replied, "If now I have
found favor in your eyes, give me a
sign[r] that it is really you talking to me.
18Please do not go away until I come
back and bring my offering and set it
before you."

And the LORD said, "I will wait until
you return."

19Gideon went in, prepared a young
goat, and from an ephah[b] of flour he
made bread without yeast. Putting the
meat in a basket and its broth in a pot,
he brought them out and offered them
to him under the oak.[s]

20The angel of God said to him,
"Take the meat and the unleavened
bread, place them on this rock,[t] and
pour out the broth." And Gideon did
so. **21**With the tip of the staff that was
in his hand, the angel of the LORD
touched the meat and the unleavened
bread.[u] Fire flared from the rock, consuming the meat and the bread. And
the angel of the LORD disappeared.
22When Gideon realized[v] that it was
the angel of the LORD, he exclaimed,
"Ah, Sovereign LORD! I have seen the
angel of the LORD face to face!"[w]

23But the LORD said to him, "Peace!
Do not be afraid.[x] You are not going
to die."

24So Gideon built an altar to the
LORD there and called[y] it The LORD is
Peace. To this day it stands in Oph-
rah[z] of the Abiezrites.

25That same night the LORD said to
him, "Take the second bull from your
father's herd, the one seven years
old.[c] Tear down your father's altar to
Baal and cut down the Asherah
pole[d][a] beside it. **26**Then build a proper kind of[e] altar to the LORD your God
on the top of this height. Using the
wood of the Asherah pole that you cut

5:31 [t]2Sa 23:4; Ps 19:4; 89:36 [u]Jdg 3:11
6:1 [v]Jdg 2:11 [w]Nu 25:15-18; 31:1-3
6:2 [x]1Sa 13:6; Isa 8:21 [y]Heb 11:38
6:3 [z]Jdg 3:13
6:4 [a]Lev 26:16; Dt 28:30,51
6:5 [b]Jdg 7:12 [c]Jdg 8:10
6:6 [d]Jdg 3:9
6:8 [e]Jdg 2:1
6:9 [f]Ps 44:2
6:10 [g]2Ki 17:35 [h]Jer 10:2
6:11 [i]Ge 16:7 [j]Jos 17:2 [k]Heb 11:32
6:12 [l]Jos 1:5; Jdg 13:3; Lk 1:11,28
6:13 [m]Ps 44:1 [n]2Ch 15:2
6:14 [o]Heb 11:34
6:15 [p]Ex 3:11; 1Sa 9:21
6:16 [q]Ex 3:12; Jos 1:5
6:17 [r]ver 36-37; Ge 24:14; Isa 38:7-8
6:19 [s]Ge 18:7-8
6:20 [t]Jdg 13:19
6:21 [u]Lev 9:24
6:22 [v]Jdg 13:16,21 [w]Ge 32:30; Ex 33:20; Jdg 13:22
6:23 [x]Da 10:19
6:24 [y]Ge 22:14 [z]Jdg 8:32
6:25 [a]Ex 34:13; Dt 7:5

a *15* Or *sir* **b** *19* That is, probably about 3/5 bushel (about 22 liters) **c** *25* Or *Take a full-grown, mature bull from your father's herd* **d** *25* That is, a symbol of the goddess Asherah; here and elsewhere in Judges **e** *26* Or *build with layers of stone an*

GIDEON

A Man Convinced

Gideon was a regular guy who blended into any crowd with the best of the blenders. Life was not easy in Gideon's day: "The Israelites did evil in the eyes of the LORD, and for seven years he gave them into the hands of the Midianites" (6:1). Because the Midianites were so powerful, the Israelites moved to caves in the mountains whenever the Midianites showed up. Judges 6:2–6 indicates these neighborly visits turned out to be a seasonal event, always at harvest time. But there was more bad news coming. The Midianites joined with the Amalekites and some smaller countries and "settled in the valley, thick as locusts. Their camels could no more be counted than the sand on the seashore" (7:12).

Israel was no match for such a formidable enemy. These gathered peoples were starving them off their land and out of existence. The Israelites were farmers and shepherds. They had no government, no army, no weapons. Worst of all, they worshiped the Canaanite gods and had more reverence for them than for the Lord (6:25–31). So while Israel was under siege by their enemies, they were also under God's judgment for disobedience. Not a good place to be.

An Unlikely Choice

But the situation was not hopeless to God. All he needed was one man who would trust him. And God chose Gideon.

Such an unlikely hero. No one knew this guy. He wasn't a big shot. Even Gideon couldn't believe God wanted him. He asked God, "how can I save Israel? My clan is the weakest in Manasseh, and I am least in my family" (6:15). Now *there* are some credentials for a superhero.

If we follow Gideon's dialogue with God through Judges 6—8, it's almost laughable. God's angel came and said, "The LORD is with you, mighty warrior" (6:12). Gideon replied that it sure didn't look like it. But the Lord said, "I'm sending you." Gideon's reply of "I can't do that" was answered with the Lord's assurance "I'll be with you." "Prove it," Gideon said. So God gave him a miraculous sign (6:21). Gideon then realized he had been speaking to God's angel and that God really meant what he said. Gideon swallowed hard and said, "Okay, I'll try," and "the Spirit of the LORD came upon Gideon" (6:34).

Though Gideon was now headed in the right direction, he was still unsure about God's sincerity. Twice Gideon asked God for miracles with a woolen fleece as proof that God wanted to use him to attack the Midianites. And twice God obliged him. But Gideon needed something more. Finally, after three miracles and six statements directly affirming God's commission, presence and power, God told Gideon to eavesdrop on a Midianite soldier's recitation of a recent dream (7:10–14).

The overheard dream was the final turning point for Gideon, for "when Gideon heard the dream and its interpretation, he worshiped God. He returned to the camp of Israel and called out, 'Get up! The LORD has given the Midianite camp into your hands' " (7:15). God whittled Gideon's army down to 300 farmer-soldiers. This rag-tag army, each armed with a trumpet, a jug and a lamp, approached on foot to go up against 135,000 trained, mobile, and heavily armed soldiers. The odds were only 450 to 1. Poor Midianites. But God won the victory for Gideon and Israel—just as he said he would.

Facing Our Fears

God commissioned Gideon much like he commissions us. In Matthew 28:18–20 Jesus tells us to make disciples of all nations, beginning with our own sphere of influence. Very few men are actively involved in that commission. We doubt the validity of God's call, just like Gideon. We doubt the sincerity of God's promised help, just like Gideon. We struggle against the odds, just like Gideon. But in the end, Gideon went! Gideon won! Gideon succeeded! Why? Because Gideon was honest about his doubts. He wrestled with his torments. Ultimately Gideon succeeded because he was a man convinced by God. And a man convinced by God is a man possessed by God and used by God.

If you struggle with your response to God's commission for your life, face your doubts. Read books such as *Mere Christianity* by C. S. Lewis or *Disappointment with God* by Philip Yancey. Talk to your pastor. Read and meditate on God's Word. Pray for faith that God is real and that his call to service is genuine. Get involved with—or form—a Bible study / support group where you can ask questions and deal with your misgivings. You, too, can be a man like Gideon—a man convinced.

Remember, a man convinced by God is a man possessed by God. And a man possessed by God is a man used by God.

—*Dr. Sid Buzzell*

down, offer the second[a] bull as a burnt offering."

[27]So Gideon took ten of his servants and did as the LORD told him. But because he was afraid of his family and the men of the town, he did it at night rather than in the daytime.

[28]In the morning when the men of the town got up, there was Baal's altar,[b] demolished, with the Asherah pole beside it cut down and the second bull sacrificed on the newly built altar! [29]They asked each other, "Who did this?"

When they carefully investigated, they were told, "Gideon son of Joash did it."

[30]The men of the town demanded of Joash, "Bring out your son. He must die, because he has broken down Baal's altar and cut down the Asherah pole beside it."

[31]But Joash replied to the hostile crowd around him, "Are you going to plead Baal's cause? Are you trying to save him? Whoever fights for him shall be put to death by morning! If Baal really is a god, he can defend himself when someone breaks down his altar." [32]So that day they called Gideon "Jerub-Baal,[b][c]" saying, "Let Baal contend with him," because he broke down Baal's altar.

[33]Now all the Midianites, Amalekites and other eastern peoples[d] joined forces and crossed over the Jordan and camped in the Valley of Jezreel.[e] [34]Then the Spirit of the LORD came upon[f] Gideon, and he blew a trumpet,[g] summoning the Abiezrites to follow him. [35]He sent messengers throughout Manasseh, calling them to arms, and also into Asher, Zebulun and Naphtali,[h] so that they too went up to meet them.

[36]Gideon said to God, "If you will save[i] Israel by my hand as you have promised— [37]look, I will place a wool fleece on the threshing floor.[j] If there is dew only on the fleece and all the ground is dry, then I will know[k] that you will save Israel by my hand, as you said." [38]And that is what happened. Gideon rose early the next day; he squeezed the fleece and wrung out the dew—a bowlful of water.

[39]Then Gideon said to God, "Do not be angry with me. Let me make just one more request.[l] Allow me one more test with the fleece. This time make the fleece dry and the ground covered with dew." [40]That night God did so. Only the fleece was dry; all the ground was covered with dew.

Gideon Defeats the Midianites

7 Early in the morning, Jerub-Baal[m] (that is, Gideon) and all his men camped at the spring of Harod. The camp of Midian was north of them in the valley near the hill of Moreh.[n] [2]The LORD said to Gideon, "You have too many men for me to deliver Midian into their hands. In order that Israel may not boast against me that her own strength[o] has saved her, [3]announce now to the people, 'Anyone who trembles with fear may turn back and leave Mount Gilead.[p]' " So twenty-two thousand men left, while ten thousand remained.

[4]But the LORD said to Gideon, "There are still too many[q] men. Take them down to the water, and I will sift them for you there. If I say, 'This one shall go with you,' he shall go; but if I say, 'This one shall not go with you,' he shall not go."

[5]So Gideon took the men down to the water. There the LORD told him, "Separate those who lap the water with their tongues like a dog from those who kneel down to drink." [6]Three hundred men lapped with their hands to their mouths. All the rest got down on their knees to drink.

[7]The LORD said to Gideon, "With the three hundred men that lapped I will save you and give the Midianites into your hands. Let all the other men go, each to his own place."[r] [8]So Gideon sent the rest of the Israelites to their tents but kept the three hundred, who took over the provisions and trumpets of the others.

Now the camp of Midian lay below him in the valley. [9]During that night the LORD said to Gideon, "Get up, go down against the camp, because I am going to give it into your hands.[s] [10]If you are afraid to attack, go down to the camp with your servant Purah [11]and listen to what they are saying. Afterward, you will be encouraged to attack the camp." So he and Purah his servant went down to the outposts of the camp. [12]The Midianites, the Amalekites[t] and all the other eastern peoples had settled in the valley, thick as locusts.[u] Their camels[v] could no more be counted than the sand on the seashore.[w]

[13]Gideon arrived just as a man was telling a friend his dream. "I had a dream," he was saying. "A round loaf of barley bread came tumbling into the Midianite camp. It struck the tent with

6:28 [b]1Ki 16:32
6:32 [c]Jdg 7:1; 8:29, 35; 1Sa 12:11
6:33 [d]ver 3 [e]Jos 17:16
6:34 [f]Jdg 3:10; 1Ch 12:18; 2Ch 24:20 [g]Jdg 3:27
6:35 [h]Jdg 4:6
6:36 [i]ver 14
6:37 [j]Ex 4:3-7 [k]Ge 24:14
6:39 [l]Ge 18:32

7:1 [m]Jdg 6:32 [n]Ge 12:6
7:2 [o]Dt 8:17; 2Co 4:7
7:3 [p]Dt 20:8
7:4 [q]1Sa 14:6
7:7 [r]1Sa 14:6
7:9 [s]Jos 2:24; 10:8; 11:6
7:12 [t]Jdg 8:10 [u]Jdg 6:5 [v]Jer 49:29 [w]Jos 11:4

[a] *26* Or *full-grown;* also in verse 28
[b] *32* *Jerub-Baal* means *let Baal contend.*

such force that the tent overturned and
collapsed."
14 His friend responded, "This can be
nothing other than the sword of Gideon son of Joash, the Israelite. God has
given the Midianites and the whole
camp into his hands."
15 When Gideon heard the dream
and its interpretation, he worshiped
God.[x] He returned to the camp of Israel and called out, "Get up! The LORD
has given the Midianite camp into your
hands." 16 Dividing the three hundred
men[y] into three companies,[z] he
placed trumpets and empty jars in the
hands of all of them, with torches inside.
17 "Watch me," he told them. "Follow
my lead. When I get to the edge of the
camp, do exactly as I do. 18 When I and
all who are with me blow our trumpets,[a] then from all around the camp
blow yours and shout, 'For the LORD
and for Gideon.' "
19 Gideon and the hundred men with
him reached the edge of the camp at
the beginning of the middle watch, just
after they had changed the guard. They
blew their trumpets and broke the jars
that were in their hands. 20 The three
companies blew the trumpets and
smashed the jars. Grasping the torches
in their left hands and holding in their
right hands the trumpets they were to
blow, they shouted, "A sword[b] for the
LORD and for Gideon!" 21 While each
man held his position around the
camp, all the Midianites ran, crying out
as they fled.[c]
22 When the three hundred trumpets
sounded,[d] the LORD caused the men
throughout the camp to turn on each
other[e] with their swords. The army
fled to Beth Shittah toward Zererah as
far as the border of Abel Meholah[f]
near Tabbath. 23 Israelites from Naphtali, Asher and all Manasseh were
called out,[g] and they pursued the
Midianites. 24 Gideon sent messengers
throughout the hill country of Ephraim, saying, "Come down against the
Midianites and seize the waters of the
Jordan[h] ahead of them as far as Beth
Barah."
So all the men of Ephraim were
called out and they took the waters of
the Jordan as far as Beth Barah. 25 They
also captured two of the Midianite
leaders, Oreb and Zeeb[i]. They killed
Oreb at the rock of Oreb,[j] and Zeeb at
the winepress of Zeeb. They pursued
the Midianites and brought the heads
of Oreb and Zeeb to Gideon, who was
by the Jordan.[k]

7:15 [x] 1Sa 15:31
7:16 [y] Ge 14:15 [z] 2Sa 18:2
7:18 [a] Jdg 3:27
7:20 [b] ver 14
7:21 [c] 2Ki 7:7
7:22 [d] Jos 6:20 [e] 1Sa 14:20; 2Ch 20:23 [f] 1Ki 4:12; 19:16
7:23 [g] Jdg 6:35
7:24 [h] Jdg 3:28
7:25 [i] Jdg 8:3; Ps 83:11 [j] Isa 10:26 [k] Jdg 8:4

8:1 [l] Jdg 12:1 [m] 2Sa 19:41
8:3 [n] Jdg 7:25; Pr 15:1
8:4 [o] Jdg 7:25
8:5 [p] Ge 33:17 [q] Ps 83:11
8:6 [r] 1Sa 25:11 [s] ver 15
8:7 [t] Jdg 7:15
8:8 [u] Ge 32:30; 1Ki 12:25
8:9 [v] ver 17
8:10 [w] Jdg 6:5; 7:12; Isa 9:4
8:11 [x] Nu 32:42 [y] Nu 32:35

Zebah and Zalmunna

8 Now the Ephraimites asked Gideon,
"Why have you treated us like this?
Why didn't you call us when you went
to fight Midian?"[l] And they criticized
him sharply.[m]
2 But he answered them, "What have
I accomplished compared to you?
Aren't the gleanings of Ephraim's
grapes better than the full grape harvest of Abiezer? 3 God gave Oreb and
Zeeb,[n] the Midianite leaders, into
your hands. What was I able to do compared to you?" At this, their resentment
against him subsided.
4 Gideon and his three hundred men,
exhausted yet keeping up the pursuit,
came to the Jordan[o] and crossed it.
5 He said to the men of Succoth,[p]
"Give my troops some bread; they are
worn out, and I am still pursuing Zebah and Zalmunna,[q] the kings of Midian."
6 But the officials of Succoth said,
"Do you already have the hands of Zebah and Zalmunna in your possession?
Why should we give bread[r] to your
troops?"[s]
7 Then Gideon replied, "Just for that,
when the LORD has given Zebah and
Zalmunna[t] into my hand, I will tear
your flesh with desert thorns and briers."
8 From there he went up to Peniel[a][u] and made the same request of
them, but they answered as the men of
Succoth had. 9 So he said to the men
of Peniel, "When I return in triumph, I
will tear down this tower."[v]
10 Now Zebah and Zalmunna were in
Karkor with a force of about fifteen
thousand men, all that were left of the
armies of the eastern peoples; a hundred and twenty thousand swordsmen
had fallen.[w] 11 Gideon went up by the
route of the nomads east of Nobah[x]
and Jogbehah[y] and fell upon the unsuspecting army. 12 Zebah and Zalmunna, the two kings of Midian, fled, but
he pursued them and captured them,
routing their entire army.
13 Gideon son of Joash then returned
from the battle by the Pass of Heres.
14 He caught a young man of Succoth
and questioned him, and the young
man wrote down for him the names of
the seventy-seven officials of Succoth,
the elders of the town. 15 Then Gideon
came and said to the men of Succoth,
"Here are Zebah and Zalmunna, about
whom you taunted me by saying, 'Do
you already have the hands of Zebah

[a] *8* Hebrew *Penuel,* a variant of *Peniel;* also in verses 9 and 17

and Zalmunna in your possession?
Why should we give bread to your exhausted men?[z]' " 16He took the elders
of the town and taught the men of Succoth a lesson[a] by punishing them
with desert thorns and briers. 17He also
pulled down the tower of Peniel and
killed the men of the town.[b]
18Then he asked Zebah and Zalmunna, "What kind of men did you kill at
Tabor?[c]"

"Men like you," they answered,
"each one with the bearing of a
prince."

19Gideon replied, "Those were my
brothers, the sons of my own mother.
As surely as the LORD lives, if you had
spared their lives, I would not kill you."
20Turning to Jether, his oldest son, he
said, "Kill them!" But Jether did not
draw his sword, because he was only a
boy and was afraid.

21Zebah and Zalmunna said, "Come,
do it yourself. 'As is the man, so is his
strength.' " So Gideon stepped forward
and killed them, and took the ornaments[d] off their camels' necks.

Gideon's Ephod

22The Israelites said to Gideon,
"Rule over us—you, your son and your
grandson—because you have saved us
out of the hand of Midian."

23But Gideon told them, "I will not
rule over you, nor will my son rule over
you. The LORD will rule[e] over you."
24And he said, "I do have one request,
that each of you give me an earring
from your share of the plunder." (It was
the custom of the Ishmaelites[f] to
wear gold earrings.)

25They answered, "We'll be glad to
give them." So they spread out a garment, and each man threw a ring from
his plunder onto it. 26The weight of the
gold rings he asked for came to seventeen hundred shekels,[a] not counting
the ornaments, the pendants and the
purple garments worn by the kings of
Midian or the chains that were on their
camels' necks. 27Gideon made the gold
into an ephod,[g] which he placed in
Ophrah, his town. All Israel prostituted
themselves by worshiping it there, and
it became a snare[h] to Gideon and his
family.

Gideon's Death

28Thus Midian was subdued before
the Israelites and did not raise its head
again. During Gideon's lifetime, the
land enjoyed peace[i] forty years.

29Jerub-Baal[j] son of Joash went
back home to live. 30He had seventy
sons[k] of his own, for he had many
wives. 31His concubine, who lived in
Shechem, also bore him a son, whom
he named Abimelech.[l] 32Gideon son
of Joash died at a good old age[m] and
was buried in the tomb of his father
Joash in Ophrah of the Abiezrites.

33No sooner had Gideon died than
the Israelites again prostituted themselves to the Baals.[n] They set up Baal-
Berith[o] as their god[p] and 34did not
remember[q] the LORD their God, who
had rescued them from the hands of all
their enemies on every side. 35They
also failed to show kindness to the

8:15 [z]ver 6 **8:16** [a]ver 7 **8:17** [b]ver 9 **8:18** [c]Jos 19:22; Jdg 4:6 **8:21** [d]ver 26; Ps 83:11 **8:23** [e]Ex 16:8; 1Sa 8:7; 10:19; 12:12 **8:24** [f]Ge 25:13

8:27 [g]Jdg 17:5; 18:14 [h]Dt 7:16; Ps 106:39 **8:28** [i]Jdg 5:31 **8:29** [j]Jdg 7:1 **8:30** [k]Jdg 9:2,5,18, 24 **8:31** [l]Jdg 9:1 **8:32** [m]Ge 25:8 **8:33** [n]Jdg 2:11,13, 19 [o]Jdg 9:4 [p]Jdg 9:27,46 **8:34** [q]Jdg 3:7; Dt 4:9; Ps 78:11,42

[a] *26* That is, about 43 pounds (about 19.5 kilograms)

8:22–35

PROMISE 3

GIDEON'S BIG MISTAKE

Judges 7:1–25 tells the well-known story of how, with God's help, Gideon and his army routed the Midianites. What's not so well known is the rest of the story. Following the great victory, the Israelites asked Gideon to be their king. Realizing the danger of accepting their offer, Gideon refused. So far so good.

Gideon then made a serious mistake. He created an ephod—a divinely prescribed apron worn by a priest over his robe (Exodus 28:6–14). That ephod "became a snare to Gideon and his family" (v. 27). It also became an idol that all Israel worshiped. Instead of worshiping the God who gave them victory, the nation bowed down to a symbol of that victory. The Israelites' involvement with pagan gods after Gideon's death can also be traced back to this misstep.

Gideon did a great job leading the nation into battle. But he failed to work as diligently at preserving the purity of his faith after the victory. What can we learn from his example? First, the next time you experience a great victory, be on the alert. If you let your guard down, you'll be vulnerable to temptation. Second, don't act without seeking God's direction. Gideon should have consulted with God and some other godly men before having the ephod made. Third, keep your faith, and that of your family, focused on God, not on the symbols of God's greatness.

To help you do this, take a few minutes and reread the story of Gideon. Ask God to show you if you have any "ephods" in your house. If you do, get rid of them at once. Finally, focus your faith on God and ask for the grace you need to keep it there.

For the next Promise 3 reading go to page 274.

family of Jerub-Baal (that is, Gideon)
for all the good things he had done for
them.[r]

Abimelech

9 Abimelech[s] son of Jerub-Baal went
to his mother's brothers in Shechem
and said to them and to all his mother's clan, 2"Ask all the citizens of Shechem, 'Which is better for you: to have
all seventy of Jerub-Baal's sons rule
over you, or just one man?' Remember,
I am your flesh and blood.[t]"
3When the brothers repeated all this
to the citizens of Shechem, they were
inclined to follow Abimelech, for they
said, "He is our brother." 4They gave
him seventy shekels[a] of silver from the
temple of Baal-Berith,[u] and Abimelech used it to hire reckless adventurers,[v] who became his followers. 5He
went to his father's home in Ophrah
and on one stone murdered his seventy brothers,[w] the sons of Jerub-Baal.
But Jotham, the youngest son of Jerub-
Baal, escaped by hiding.[x] 6Then all
the citizens of Shechem and Beth Millo
gathered beside the great tree at the
pillar in Shechem to crown Abimelech
king.
7When Jotham was told about this,
he climbed up on the top of Mount
Gerizim[y] and shouted to them, "Listen to me, citizens of Shechem, so that
God may listen to you. 8One day the
trees went out to anoint a king for
themselves. They said to the olive tree,
'Be our king.'
9"But the olive tree answered,
'Should I give up my oil, by which both
gods and men are honored, to hold
sway over the trees?'
10"Next, the trees said to the fig tree,
'Come and be our king.'
11"But the fig tree replied, 'Should I
give up my fruit, so good and sweet, to
hold sway over the trees?'

9:8-15

PROMISE **5**

THE TREE KING

When the able are unwilling to lead, they will be led by the willing but unable. This story of the trees demonstrates a sad fact. Then as now, God's gifted men are often so busy in their own pursuits they will not use their expertise to help lead God's people. If you genuinely love God and have leadership gifts and abilities, you may be asked to invest your time in serving on a board or in some other leadership role. Carefully consider this story as you weigh your decision.

For the next Promise 5 reading go to page 360.

8:35 [r]Jdg 9:16
9:1 [s]Jdg 8:31
9:2 [t]Ge 29:14; Jdg 8:30
9:4 [u]Jdg 8:33 [v]Jdg 11:3; 2Ch 13:7
9:5 [w]ver 2; Jdg 8:30 [x]2Ki 11:2
9:7 [y]Dt 11:29; 27:12; Jn 4:20
9:13 [z]Ecc 2:3
9:15 [a]Isa 30:2 [b]ver 20 [c]Isa 2:13
9:18 [d]ver 5-6; Jdg 8:30
9:20 [e]ver 15
9:23 [f]1Sa 16:14,23; 18:10; 1Ki 22:22; Isa 19:14; 33:1
9:24 [g]Nu 35:33; 1Ki 2:32 [h]ver 56-57 [i]Dt 27:25
9:27 [j]Am 9:13 [k]Jdg 8:33

12"Then the trees said to the vine,
'Come and be our king.'
13"But the vine answered, 'Should I
give up my wine,[z] which cheers both
gods and men, to hold sway over the
trees?'
14"Finally all the trees said to the
thornbush, 'Come and be our king.'
15"The thornbush said to the trees,
'If you really want to anoint me king
over you, come and take refuge in my
shade;[a] but if not, then let fire come
out[b] of the thornbush and consume
the cedars of Lebanon!'[c]
16"Now if you have acted honorably
and in good faith when you made
Abimelech king, and if you have been
fair to Jerub-Baal and his family, and if
you have treated him as he deserves—
17and to think that my father fought for
you, risked his life to rescue you from
the hand of Midian 18(but today you
have revolted against my father's family, murdered his seventy sons[d] on a
single stone, and made Abimelech, the
son of his slave girl, king over the citizens of Shechem because he is your
brother)— 19if then you have acted
honorably and in good faith toward
Jerub-Baal and his family today, may
Abimelech be your joy, and may you be
his, too! 20But if you have not, let fire
come out[e] from Abimelech and consume you, citizens of Shechem and
Beth Millo, and let fire come out from
you, citizens of Shechem and Beth Millo, and consume Abimelech!"
21Then Jotham fled, escaping to
Beer, and he lived there because he
was afraid of his brother Abimelech.
22After Abimelech had governed
Israel three years, 23God sent an evil
spirit[f] between Abimelech and the
citizens of Shechem, who acted treacherously against Abimelech. 24God
did this in order that the crime
against Jerub-Baal's seventy sons, the
shedding[g] of their blood, might be
avenged[h] on their brother Abimelech
and on the citizens of Shechem, who
had helped him[i] murder his brothers.
25In opposition to him these citizens of
Shechem set men on the hilltops to
ambush and rob everyone who passed
by, and this was reported to Abimelech.
26Now Gaal son of Ebed moved with
his brothers into Shechem, and its citizens put their confidence in him. 27Af-
ter they had gone out into the fields
and gathered the grapes and trodden[j]
them, they held a festival in the temple
of their god.[k] While they were eating

a *4* That is, about 1 3/4 pounds (about 0.8 kilogram)

and drinking, they cursed Abimelech. 28Then Gaal son of Ebed said, "Who[l] is Abimelech, and who is Shechem, that we should be subject to him? Isn't he Jerub-Baal's son, and isn't Zebul his deputy? Serve the men of Hamor,[m] Shechem's father! Why should we serve Abimelech? 29If only this people were under my command![n] Then I would get rid of him. I would say to Abimelech, 'Call out your whole army!' "[a]

30When Zebul the governor of the city heard what Gaal son of Ebed said, he was very angry. 31Under cover he sent messengers to Abimelech, saying, "Gaal son of Ebed and his brothers have come to Shechem and are stirring up the city against you. 32Now then, during the night you and your men should come and lie in wait[o] in the fields. 33In the morning at sunrise, advance against the city. When Gaal and his men come out against you, do whatever your hand finds to do.[p]"

34So Abimelech and all his troops set out by night and took up concealed positions near Shechem in four companies. 35Now Gaal son of Ebed had gone out and was standing at the entrance to the city gate just as Abimelech and his soldiers came out from their hiding place.[q]

36When Gaal saw them, he said to Zebul, "Look, people are coming down from the tops of the mountains!"

Zebul replied, "You mistake the shadows of the mountains for men."

37But Gaal spoke up again: "Look, people are coming down from the center of the land, and a company is coming from the direction of the soothsayers' tree."

38Then Zebul said to him, "Where is your big talk now, you who said, 'Who is Abimelech that we should be subject to him?' Aren't these the men you ridiculed?[r] Go out and fight them!"

39So Gaal led out[b] the citizens of Shechem and fought Abimelech. 40Abimelech chased him, and many fell wounded in the flight—all the way to the entrance to the gate. 41Abimelech stayed in Arumah, and Zebul drove Gaal and his brothers out of Shechem.

42The next day the people of Shechem went out to the fields, and this was reported to Abimelech. 43So he took his men, divided them into three companies[s] and set an ambush in the fields. When he saw the people coming out of the city, he rose to attack them. 44Abimelech and the companies with him rushed forward to a position at the entrance to the city gate. Then two companies rushed upon those in the fields and struck them down. 45All that day Abimelech pressed his attack against the city until he had captured it and killed its people. Then he destroyed the city[t] and scattered salt[u] over it.

46On hearing this, the citizens in the tower of Shechem went into the stronghold of the temple[v] of El-Berith. 47When Abimelech heard that they had assembled there, 48he and all his men went up Mount Zalmon.[w] He took an ax and cut off some branches, which he lifted to his shoulders. He ordered the men with him, "Quick! Do what you have seen me do!" 49So all the men cut branches and followed Abimelech. They piled them against the stronghold and set it on fire over the people inside. So all the people in the tower of Shechem, about a thousand men and women, also died.

50Next Abimelech went to Thebez[x] and besieged it and captured it. 51Inside the city, however, was a strong tower, to which all the men and women—all the people of the city—fled. They locked themselves in and climbed up on the tower roof. 52Abimelech went to the tower and stormed it. But as he approached the entrance to the tower to set it on fire, 53a woman dropped an upper millstone on his head and cracked his skull.[y]

54Hurriedly he called to his armor-bearer, "Draw your sword and kill me,[z] so that they can't say, 'A woman killed him.' " So his servant ran him through, and he died. 55When the Israelites saw that Abimelech was dead, they went home.

56Thus God repaid the wickedness that Abimelech had done to his father by murdering his seventy brothers. 57God also made the men of Shechem pay for all their wickedness.[a] The curse of Jotham son of Jerub-Baal came on them.

Tola

10 After the time of Abimelech a man of Issachar,[b] Tola son of Puah,[c] the son of Dodo, rose to save[d] Israel. He lived in Shamir, in the hill country of Ephraim. 2He led[c] Israel twenty-three years; then he died, and was buried in Shamir.

Jair

3He was followed by Jair of Gilead, who led Israel twenty-two years. 4He

9:28 [l]1Sa 25:10; 1Ki 12:16 [m]Ge 34:2,6
9:29 [n]2Sa 15:4
9:32 [o]Jos 8:2
9:33 [p]1Sa 10:7
9:35 [q]Ps 32:7; Jer 49:10
9:38 [r]ver 28-29
9:43 [s]Jdg 7:16
9:45 [t]ver 20; 2Ki 3:25 [u]Dt 29:23
9:46 [v]Jdg 8:33
9:48 [w]Ps 68:14
9:50 [x]2Sa 11:21
9:53 [y]2Sa 11:21
9:54 [z]1Sa 31:4; 2Sa 1:9
9:57 [a]ver 20
10:1 [b]Ge 30:18 [c]Ge 46:13 [d]Jdg 2:16; 6:14

[a] 29 Septuagint; Hebrew *him." Then he said to Abimelech, "Call out your whole army!"*
[b] 39 Or *Gaal went out in the sight of*
[c] 2 Traditionally *judged*; also in verse 3

had thirty sons, who rode thirty donkeys. They controlled thirty towns in Gilead, which to this day are called Havvoth Jair.[a][e] **5**When Jair died, he was buried in Kamon.

Jephthah

6Again the Israelites did evil in the eyes of the LORD.[f] They served the Baals and the Ashtoreths,[g] and the gods of Aram, the gods of Sidon, the gods of Moab, the gods of the Ammonites and the gods of the Philistines.[h] And because the Israelites forsook the LORD[i] and no longer served him, **7**he became angry[j] with them. He sold them[k] into the hands of the Philistines and the Ammonites, **8**who that year shattered and crushed them. For eighteen years they oppressed all the Israelites on the east side of the Jordan in Gilead, the land of the Amorites. **9**The Ammonites also crossed the Jordan to fight against Judah, Benjamin and the house of Ephraim; and Israel was in great distress. **10**Then the Israelites cried out to the LORD, "We have sinned against you, forsaking our God and serving the Baals."[l]

11The LORD replied, "When the Egyptians,[m] the Amorites, the Ammonites,[n] the Philistines,[o] **12**the Sidonians, the Amalekites and the Maonites[b] oppressed you[p] and you cried to me for help, did I not save you from their hands? **13**But you have forsaken me and served other gods, so I will no longer save you. **14**Go and cry out to the gods you have chosen. Let them save you when you are in trouble![q]"

15But the Israelites said to the LORD, "We have sinned. Do with us whatever you think best,[r] but please rescue us now." **16**Then they got rid of the foreign gods among them and served the LORD.[s] And he could bear Israel's misery[t] no longer.[u]

17When the Ammonites were called to arms and camped in Gilead, the Israelites assembled and camped at Mizpah.[v] **18**The leaders of the people of Gilead said to each other, "Whoever will launch the attack against the Ammonites will be the head[w] of all those living in Gilead."

11 Jephthah[x] the Gileadite was a mighty warrior.[y] His father was Gilead; his mother was a prostitute. **2**Gilead's wife also bore him sons, and when they were grown up, they drove Jephthah away. "You are not going to get any inheritance in our family," they said, "because you are the son of another woman." **3**So Jephthah fled from his brothers and settled in the land of Tob,[z] where a group of adventurers[a] gathered around him and followed him.

4Some time later, when the Ammonites[b] made war on Israel, **5**the elders of Gilead went to get Jephthah from the land of Tob. **6**"Come," they said, "be our commander, so we can fight the Ammonites."

7Jephthah said to them, "Didn't you hate me and drive me from my father's house?[c] Why do you come to me now, when you're in trouble?"

8The elders of Gilead said to him, "Nevertheless, we are turning to you now; come with us to fight the Ammonites, and you will be our head[d] over all who live in Gilead."

9Jephthah answered, "Suppose you take me back to fight the Ammonites and the LORD gives them to me—will I really be your head?"

10The elders of Gilead replied, "The LORD is our witness;[e] we will certainly

10:4 [e]Nu 32:41
10:6 [f]Jdg 2:11; [g]Jdg 2:13; [h]Jdg 2:12; [i]Dt 32:15
10:7 [j]Dt 31:17; [k]Dt 32:30; Jdg 2:14; 1Sa 12:9
10:10 [l]1Sa 12:10
10:11 [m]Ex 14:30; [n]Nu 21:21; Jdg 3:13; [o]Jdg 3:31
10:12 [p]Ps 106:42
10:14 [q]Dt 32:37
10:15 [r]1Sa 3:18; 2Sa 15:26
10:16 [s]Jos 24:23; Jer 18:8; [t]Isa 63:9; [u]Dt 32:36; Ps 106:44-45
10:17 [v]Ge 31:49; Jdg 11:29
10:18 [w]Jdg 11:8,9
11:1 [x]Heb 11:32; [y]Jdg 6:12
11:3 [z]2Sa 10:6,8; [a]Jdg 9:4
11:4 [b]Jdg 10:9
11:7 [c]Ge 26:27
11:8 [d]Jdg 10:18
11:10 [e]Ge 31:50; Jer 42:5

[a] *4* Or *called the settlements of Jair*
[b] *12* Hebrew; some Septuagint manuscripts *Midianites*

11:1 – 12:15

PROMISE 1

FOXHOLE PROMISES

Most of us can remember a time when, out of anxiety or out of sheer desperation, we made a promise to God in an attempt to bargain for his favor. Such "foxhole promises" are usually feeble attempts to bribe God, as if changing our behavior or making some kind of pledge to serve him will influence God favorably toward us. How many people haven't made foxhole promises they either forgot or couldn't keep? Foxholes take many forms: the hospital, classroom during final exams, the business office; wherever we feel God's intervention will pull us out of a tough situation.

In these chapters, Jephthah teaches us the danger of trying to bribe God. Finding himself in a desperate situation, Jephthah tried to win God's favor by making a pledge to him. The disastrous results of his rash oath to God (vv. 30–31) makes for one of the most tragic stories in the Bible.

God's help and blessing don't go to the highest bidder. He is the sovereign God and isn't involved in trading his blessing for our panicked promises. When you need God's help, don't reduce him to a huckster who will help you if the price is right. Pray to him as your loving Father, trusting his sovereign wisdom to know what you need and his gracious love to provide it.

For the next Promise 1 reading go to page 286.

do as you say." **11**So Jephthah went with the elders of Gilead, and the people made him head and commander over them. And he repeated all his words before the LORD in Mizpah.[f]

12Then Jephthah sent messengers to the Ammonite king with the question: "What do you have against us that you have attacked our country?"

13The king of the Ammonites answered Jephthah's messengers, "When Israel came up out of Egypt, they took away my land from the Arnon to the Jabbok,[g] all the way to the Jordan. Now give it back peaceably."

14Jephthah sent back messengers to the Ammonite king, **15**saying:

"This is what Jephthah says: Israel did not take the land of Moab[h] or the land of the Ammonites.[i] **16**But when they came up out of Egypt, Israel went through the desert to the Red Sea[a][j] and on to Kadesh.[k] **17**Then Israel sent messengers[l] to the king of Edom, saying, 'Give us permission to go through your country,'[m] but the king of Edom would not listen. They sent also to the king of Moab, and he refused.[n] So Israel stayed at Kadesh.

18"Next they traveled through the desert, skirted the lands of Edom[o] and Moab, passed along the eastern side[p] of the country of Moab, and camped on the other side of the Arnon.[q] They did not enter the territory of Moab, for the Arnon was its border.

19"Then Israel sent messengers to Sihon king of the Amorites, who ruled in Heshbon, and said to him, 'Let us pass through your country to our own place.'[r] **20**Sihon, however, did not trust Israel[b] to pass through his territory. He mustered all his men and encamped at Jahaz and fought with Israel.[s]

21"Then the LORD, the God of Israel, gave Sihon and all his men into Israel's hands, and they defeated them. Israel took over all the land of the Amorites who lived in that country, **22**capturing all of it from the Arnon to the Jabbok and from the desert to the Jordan.[t]

23"Now since the LORD, the God of Israel, has driven the Amorites out before his people Israel, what right have you to take it over? **24**Will you not take what your god Chemosh[u] gives you? Likewise, whatever the LORD our God has given us, we will possess. **25**Are you better than Balak son of Zippor,[v] king of Moab? Did he ever quarrel with Israel or fight with them?[w] **26**For three hundred years Israel occupied[x] Heshbon, Aroer, the surrounding settlements and all the towns along the Arnon. Why didn't you retake them during that time? **27**I have not wronged you, but you are doing me wrong by waging war against me. Let the LORD, the Judge,[c][y] decide[z] the dispute this day between the Israelites and the Ammonites."

11:11 [f]Jos 11:3; Jdg 10:17; 20:1; 1Sa 10:17
11:13 [g]Ge 32:22; Nu 21:24
11:15 [h]Dt 2:9 [i]Dt 2:19
11:16 [j]Nu 14:25; Dt 1:40 [k]Nu 20:1
11:17 [l]Nu 20:14 [m]Nu 20:18,21 [n]Jos 24:9
11:18 [o]Nu 21:4 [p]Dt 2:8 [q]Nu 21:13
11:19 [r]Nu 21:21-22; Dt 2:26-27
11:20 [s]Nu 21:23; Dt 2:32
11:22 [t]Dt 2:36
11:24 [u]Nu 21:29; Jos 3:10; 1Ki 11:7
11:25 [v]Nu 22:2 [w]Jos 24:9
11:26 [x]Nu 21:25
11:27 [y]Ge 18:25 [z]Ge 16:5; 31:53; 1Sa 24:12,15
11:29 [a]Nu 11:25; Jdg 3:10; 6:34; 14:6,19; 15:14; 1Sa 11:6; 16:13; Isa 11:2
11:30 [b]Ge 28:20
11:33 [c]Eze 27:17
11:34 [d]Ex 15:20; Jer 31:4
11:35 [e]Nu 30:2; Ecc 5:2,4,5
11:36 [f]Lk 1:38 [g]2Sa 18:19

28The king of Ammon, however, paid no attention to the message Jephthah sent him.

29Then the Spirit[a] of the LORD came upon Jephthah. He crossed Gilead and Manasseh, passed through Mizpah of Gilead, and from there he advanced against the Ammonites. **30**And Jephthah made a vow[b] to the LORD: "If you give the Ammonites into my hands, **31**whatever comes out of the door of my house to meet me when I return in triumph from the Ammonites will be the LORD's, and I will sacrifice it as a burnt offering."

32Then Jephthah went over to fight the Ammonites, and the LORD gave them into his hands. **33**He devastated twenty towns from Aroer to the vicinity of Minnith,[c] as far as Abel Keramim. Thus Israel subdued Ammon.

34When Jephthah returned to his home in Mizpah, who should come out to meet him but his daughter, dancing to the sound of tambourines![d] She was an only child. Except for her he had neither son nor daughter. **35**When he saw her, he tore his clothes and cried, "Oh! My daughter! You have made me miserable and wretched, because I have made a vow to the LORD that I cannot break.[e]"

36"My father," she replied, "you have given your word to the LORD. Do to me just as you promised,[f] now that the LORD has avenged you of your enemies,[g] the Ammonites. **37**But grant me this one request," she said. "Give me two months to roam the hills and weep with my friends, because I will never marry."

38"You may go," he said. And he let her go for two months. She and the girls went into the hills and wept because she would never marry. **39**After the two months, she returned to her

a *16* Hebrew *Yam Suph*; that is, Sea of Reeds
b *20* Or *however, would not make an agreement for Israel* **c** *27* Or *Ruler*

father and he did to her as he had vowed. And she was a virgin.

From this comes the Israelite custom 40that each year the young women of Israel go out for four days to commemorate the daughter of Jephthah the Gileadite.

Jephthah and Ephraim

12 The men of Ephraim called out their forces, crossed over to Zaphon and said to Jephthah, "Why did you go to fight the Ammonites without calling us to go with you?[h] We're going to burn down your house over your head."

2Jephthah answered, "I and my people were engaged in a great struggle with the Ammonites, and although I called, you didn't save me out of their hands. 3When I saw that you wouldn't help, I took my life in my hands[i] and crossed over to fight the Ammonites, and the LORD gave me the victory over them. Now why have you come up today to fight me?"

4Jephthah then called together the men of Gilead and fought against Ephraim. The Gileadites struck them down because the Ephraimites had said, "You Gileadites are renegades from Ephraim and Manasseh." 5The Gileadites captured the fords of the Jordan[j] leading to Ephraim, and whenever a survivor of Ephraim said, "Let me cross over," the men of Gilead asked him, "Are you an Ephraimite?" If he replied, "No," 6they said, "All right, say 'Shibboleth.' " If he said, "Sibboleth," because he could not pronounce the word correctly, they seized him and killed him at the fords of the Jordan. Forty-two thousand Ephraimites were killed at that time.

7Jephthah led[a] Israel six years. Then Jephthah the Gileadite died, and was buried in a town in Gilead.

Ibzan, Elon and Abdon

8After him, Ibzan of Bethlehem led Israel. 9He had thirty sons and thirty daughters. He gave his daughters away in marriage to those outside his clan, and for his sons he brought in thirty young women as wives from outside his clan. Ibzan led Israel seven years. 10Then Ibzan died, and was buried in Bethlehem.

11After him, Elon the Zebulunite led Israel ten years. 12Then Elon died, and was buried in Aijalon in the land of Zebulun.

13After him, Abdon son of Hillel, from Pirathon, led Israel. 14He had forty sons and thirty grandsons,[k] who rode on seventy donkeys.[l] He led Israel eight years. 15Then Abdon son of Hillel died, and was buried at Pirathon in Ephraim, in the hill country of the Amalekites.[m]

The Birth of Samson

13 Again the Israelites did evil in the eyes of the LORD, so the LORD delivered them into the hands of the Philistines[n] for forty years.

2A certain man of Zorah,[o] named Manoah, from the clan of the Danites, had a wife who was sterile and remained childless. 3The angel of the LORD[p] appeared to her[q] and said, "You are sterile and childless, but you are going to conceive and have a son.[r] 4Now see to it that you drink no wine or other fermented drink and that you do not eat anything unclean,[s] 5because you will conceive and give birth to a son. No razor[t] may be used on his head, because the boy is to be a Nazirite,[u] set apart to God from birth, and he will begin[v] the deliverance of Israel from the hands of the Philistines."

6Then the woman went to her husband and told him, "A man of God[w] came to me. He looked like an angel of God,[x] very awesome. I didn't ask him where he came from, and he didn't tell me his name. 7But he said to me, 'You will conceive and give birth to a son. Now then, drink no wine or other fermented drink and do not eat anything unclean, because the boy will be a Nazirite of God from birth until the day of his death.' "

8Then Manoah prayed to the LORD: "O Lord, I beg you, let the man of God you sent to us come again to teach us how to bring up the boy who is to be born."

9God heard Manoah, and the angel of God came again to the woman while she was out in the field; but her husband Manoah was not with her. 10The woman hurried to tell her husband, "He's here! The man who appeared to me the other day!"

11Manoah got up and followed his wife. When he came to the man, he said, "Are you the one who talked to my wife?"

"I am," he said.

12So Manoah asked him, "When your words are fulfilled, what is to be the rule for the boy's life and work?"

13The angel of the LORD answered, "Your wife must do all that I have told her. 14She must not eat anything that comes from the grapevine, nor drink

12:1 [h]Jdg 8:1
12:3 [i]1Sa 19:5; 28:21; Job 13:14
12:5 [j]Jos 22:11; Jdg 3:28
12:14 [k]Jdg 10:4
[l]Jdg 5:10
12:15 [m]Jdg 5:14
13:1 [n]Jdg 2:11; 1Sa 12:9
13:2 [o]Jos 15:33; 19:41
13:3 [p]ver 6,8; Jdg 6:12 [q]ver 10 [r]Lk 1:13
13:4 [s]ver 14; Nu 6:2-4; Lk 1:15
13:5 [t]Nu 6:5; 1Sa 1:11 [u]Nu 6:2,13 [v]1Sa 7:13
13:6 [w]ver 8; 1Sa 2:27; 9:6 [x]ver 17-18; Mt 28:3

[a] 7 Traditionally *judged*; also in verses 8-14

any wine or other fermented drink[y]
nor eat anything unclean.[z] She must
do everything I have commanded her."
15Manoah said to the angel of the
LORD, "We would like you to stay until
we prepare a young goat[a] for you."
16The angel of the LORD replied,
"Even though you detain me, I will not
eat any of your food. But if you prepare
a burnt offering,[b] offer it to the LORD."
(Manoah did not realize that it was the
angel of the LORD.)
17Then Manoah inquired of the angel of the LORD, "What is your name,[c]
so that we may honor you when your
word comes true?"
18He replied, "Why do you ask my
name?[d] It is beyond understanding.[a]" 19Then Manoah took a young
goat, together with the grain offering,
and sacrificed it on a rock[e] to the
LORD. And the LORD did an amazing
thing while Manoah and his wife
watched: 20As the flame[f] blazed up
from the altar toward heaven, the angel
of the LORD ascended in the flame. Seeing this, Manoah and his wife fell with
their faces to the ground.[g] 21When the
angel of the LORD did not show himself
again to Manoah and his wife, Manoah
realized[h] that it was the angel of the
LORD.
22"We are doomed[i] to die!" he said
to his wife. "We have seen[j] God!"
23But his wife answered, "If the LORD
had meant to kill us, he would not have
accepted a burnt offering and grain offering from our hands, nor shown us all
these things or now told us this."[k]
24The woman gave birth to a boy and
named him Samson.[l] He grew[m] and
the LORD blessed him,[n] 25and the Spirit of the LORD began to stir[o] him while
he was in Mahaneh Dan,[p] between
Zorah and Eshtaol.

Samson's Marriage

14 Samson went down to Timnah[q]
and saw there a young Philistine
woman. 2When he returned, he said to
his father and mother, "I have seen a
Philistine woman in Timnah; now get
her for me as my wife."[r]
3His father and mother replied,
"Isn't there an acceptable woman
among your relatives or among all our
people?[s] Must you go to the uncircumcised[t] Philistines to get a wife?[u]"
But Samson said to his father, "Get
her for me. She's the right one for me."
4(His parents did not know that this
was from the LORD, who was seeking an
occasion to confront the Philistines;[v]
for at that time they were ruling over
Israel.)[w] 5Samson went down to Timnah together with his father and mother. As they approached the vineyards of
Timnah, suddenly a young lion came
roaring toward him. 6The Spirit of the
LORD came upon him in power[x] so
that he tore the lion apart with his bare
hands as he might have torn a young
goat. But he told neither his father nor
his mother what he had done. 7Then
he went down and talked with the
woman, and he liked her.
8Some time later, when he went
back to marry her, he turned aside to
look at the lion's carcass. In it was a
swarm of bees and some honey,
9which he scooped out with his hands
and ate as he went along. When he re-
joined his parents, he gave them some,
and they too ate it. But he did not tell
them that he had taken the honey from
the lion's carcass.
10Now his father went down to see
the woman. And Samson made a feast
there, as was customary for bride-
grooms. 11When he appeared, he was
given thirty companions.
12"Let me tell you a riddle,[y]" Samson said to them. "If you can give me
the answer within the seven days of the
feast,[z] I will give you thirty linen garments and thirty sets of clothes.[a] 13If
you can't tell me the answer, you must
give me thirty linen garments and thirty sets of clothes."
"Tell us your riddle," they said.
"Let's hear it."
14He replied,

"Out of the eater, something to eat;
out of the strong, something
sweet."

For three days they could not give the
answer.
15On the fourth[b] day, they said to
Samson's wife, "Coax[b] your husband
into explaining the riddle for us, or we
will burn you and your father's household to death.[c] Did you invite us here
to rob us?"
16Then Samson's wife threw herself
on him, sobbing, "You hate me! You
don't really love me.[d] You've given my
people a riddle, but you haven't told
me the answer."
"I haven't even explained it to my
father or mother," he replied, "so why
should I explain it to you?" 17She cried
the whole seven days[e] of the feast. So
on the seventh day he finally told her,
because she continued to press him.
She in turn explained the riddle to her
people.

13:14 [y]Nu 6:4 [z]ver 4
13:15 [a]ver 3; Jdg 6:19
13:16 [b]Jdg 6:20
13:17 [c]Ge 32:29
13:18 [d]Isa 9:6
13:19 [e]Jdg 6:20
13:20 [f]Lev 9:24 [g]1Ch 21:16; Eze 1:28; Mt 17:6
13:21 [h]ver 16; Jdg 6:22
13:22 [i]Dt 5:26 [j]Ge 32:30; Jdg 6:22
13:23 [k]Ps 25:14
13:24 [l]Heb 11:32 [m]1Sa 3:19 [n]Lk 1:80
13:25 [o]Jdg 3:10 [p]Jdg 18:12
14:1 [q]Ge 38:12
14:2 [r]Ge 21:21; 34:4
14:3 [s]Ge 24:4 [t]Dt 7:3 [u]Ex 34:16
14:4 [v]Jos 11:20 [w]Jdg 13:1
14:6 [x]Jdg 3:10; 13:25
14:12 [y]1Ki 10:1; Eze 17:2 [z]Ge 29:27 [a]Ge 45:22; 2Ki 5:5
14:15 [b]Jdg 16:5; Ecc 7:26 [c]Jdg 15:6
14:16 [d]Jdg 16:15
14:17 [e]Est 1:5

[a] *18* Or *is wonderful* [b] *15* Some Septuagint manuscripts and Syriac; Hebrew *seventh*

SAMSON

A Man Out of Control

Superheroes from the comic strips never tell a lie, always do what is moral, and fight for truth and justice. But what would happen if a comic strip superhero decided to put aside his values and pursue anything and anyone his little heart desired? No one would be able to stop him. Scary thought. Samson was a real, flesh-and-blood superman who pursued his appetites without restraint until one day he was consumed by them. But let's not get ahead of the story.

Abuse of Power

An Israelite named Manoah and his wife had been unable to have children. This was probably a good thing, since God's people had once again done "evil in the eyes of the LORD," and were subject to the Philistines for forty years (Judges 13:1). Life was hard under Philistine rule, but God heard the prayers of his people. He appeared to Manoah's wife and informed her that she would have a son who would grow up and "begin the deliverance of Israel from the hands of the Philistines" (13:5). The boy was to be "set apart to God from birth" as a Nazarite (13:5). That meant he could not drink wine or "other fermented drink" and "no razor" was to be used on his head (13:4–5). When this boy was born, his parents named him Samson (13:24).

Samson grew up to be the strongest man around. He could tear apart a lion with his bare hands (14:6). Samson knew God's hand was upon him, but he ignored the fact that with great privilege comes great responsibility. Samson thought he was invincible because of his special gift and used his supernatural strength to fulfill his own lusts.

This *he*-man had a definite *she*-problem. His greatest mistake was to marry a Philistine woman named Delilah. Delilah talked Samson into revealing the secret to his strength—his uncut hair. So one night while he slept, Delilah pulled out her scissors and gave Samson a crew cut.

No Strength Left

Samson's way of living had tried God's patience. But this was the "final straw." Over and over God had given Samson opportunities to walk in *God's* will and *God's* ways. But Samson had refused to respond to God's grace. The Lord then gave Samson over to the consequences of his sinful actions to draw Samson back to himself. When Samson's Nazirite vow was broken, the Lord withdrew his presence and strength from Samson. For the first time, the Philistines were able to capture and control him. They were cruel and heartless in their victory. They "gouged out his eyes and took him down to Gaza" where they put him in prison (16:21).

During his imprisonment, Samson's hair began to grow again. On one occasion, three thousand Philistines assembled to offer a great sacrifice to their god, Dagon, to celebrate their victory over Samson. Samson, the Philistines' most hated enemy and best-known prisoner, was taken out of prison to the temple of Dagon to entertain the Philistines.

Blind Samson asked the servant attending him to lead him to the two huge pillars that supported the temple. His excuse was that he needed a place to lean, a place to rest. But when placed between the pillars, Samson asked God to give him strength one more time. The Lord heard and answered Samson's final prayer. With supernatural strength, Samson pushed the pillars outward and the structure collapsed, destroying the temple and killing everyone in it, including himself (16:26–30). In the end, the Lord used Samson to achieve his purposes. In fact, the Bible says Samson accomplished more in his death than he did in his life.

The Lessons of Samson

Samson's wild lifestyle reminds us to practice restraint. Removing the brakes from your car may make for a thrilling ride for a while, but a wreck is inevitable! Take away the brakes of restraint in your life, and you are destined for disaster. There is a better way: God's way. Learn to say "No!" to sin.

Samson's life also demonstrates God's desire to bring us back to himself, no matter what the cost. God may permit good things to happen to us when we walk outside his divine will. But there will come a time when he will say, "Enough is enough!" He will discipline us for our own good and we will reap the consequences of our sins. Before that happens, we should remember Samson's example and correct our sinful behavior rather than wait until the Lord forces us to deal with our sin.

Samson's story ultimately shows us there is no wasted experience for a believer. God uses all of our experiences—the good and not so good—to shape his character within us and accomplish his purpose through us. It wasn't until Samson was in prison that he finally learned to depend upon God for his ultimate deliverance.

Samson's story tells us that, while it is never too late to make an impact for God, the sooner we cooperate with him, the greater that impact will be.

—Dr. Gene Getz

18 Before sunset on the seventh day the men of the town said to him,

"What is sweeter than honey?
What is stronger than a lion?"[f]

Samson said to them,

"If you had not plowed with my heifer,
you would not have solved my riddle."

19 Then the Spirit of the LORD came upon him in power.[g] He went down to Ashkelon, struck down thirty of their men, stripped them of their belongings and gave their clothes to those who had explained the riddle. Burning with anger,[h] he went up to his father's house. 20 And Samson's wife was given to the friend[i] who had attended him at his wedding.

Samson's Vengeance on the Philistines

15 Later on, at the time of wheat harvest, Samson took a young goat[j] and went to visit his wife. He said, "I'm going to my wife's room." But her father would not let him go in.

2 "I was so sure you thoroughly hated her," he said, "that I gave her to your friend.[k] Isn't her younger sister more attractive? Take her instead."

3 Samson said to them, "This time I have a right to get even with the Philistines; I will really harm them." 4 So he went out and caught three hundred foxes and tied them tail to tail in pairs. He then fastened a torch to every pair of tails, 5 lit the torches and let the foxes loose in the standing grain of the Philistines. He burned up the shocks and standing grain, together with the vineyards and olive groves.

6 When the Philistines asked, "Who did this?" they were told, "Samson, the Timnite's son-in-law, because his wife was given to his friend."

So the Philistines went up and burned her and her father to death.[l] 7 Samson said to them, "Since you've acted like this, I won't stop until I get my revenge on you." 8 He attacked them viciously and slaughtered many of them. Then he went down and stayed in a cave in the rock of Etam.

9 The Philistines went up and camped in Judah, spreading out near Lehi.[m] 10 The men of Judah asked, "Why have you come to fight us?"

"We have come to take Samson prisoner," they answered, "to do to him as he did to us."

11 Then three thousand men from Judah went down to the cave in the rock of Etam and said to Samson, "Don't you realize that the Philistines are rulers over us?[n] What have you done to us?"

He answered, "I merely did to them what they did to me."

12 They said to him, "We've come to tie you up and hand you over to the Philistines."

Samson said, "Swear to me that you won't kill me yourselves."

13 "Agreed," they answered. "We will only tie you up and hand you over to them. We will not kill you." So they bound him with two new ropes and led him up from the rock. 14 As he approached Lehi, the Philistines came toward him shouting. The Spirit of the LORD came upon him in power.[o] The ropes on his arms became like charred flax, and the bindings dropped from his hands. 15 Finding a fresh jawbone of a donkey, he grabbed it and struck down a thousand men.[p]

16 Then Samson said,

"With a donkey's jawbone
I have made donkeys of them.[a]
With a donkey's jawbone
I have killed a thousand men."

17 When he finished speaking, he threw away the jawbone; and the place was called Ramath Lehi.[b]

18 Because he was very thirsty, he cried out to the LORD,[q] "You have given your servant this great victory. Must I now die of thirst and fall into the hands of the uncircumcised?" 19 Then God opened up the hollow place in Lehi, and water came out of it. When Samson drank, his strength returned and he revived.[r] So the spring was called En Hakkore,[c] and it is still there in Lehi.

20 Samson led[d] Israel for twenty years[s] in the days of the Philistines.

Samson and Delilah

16 One day Samson went to Gaza, where he saw a prostitute. He went in to spend the night with her. 2 The people of Gaza were told, "Samson is here!" So they surrounded the place and lay in wait for him all night at the city gate.[t] They made no move during the night, saying, "At dawn we'll kill him."

3 But Samson lay there only until the middle of the night. Then he got up and took hold of the doors of the city gate, together with the two posts, and

14:18 [f] ver 14
14:19 [g] Nu 11:25; Jdg 3:10; 6:34; 11:29; 13:25; 15:14; 1Sa 11:6; 16:13; 1Ki 18:46; 2Ch 24:20; Isa 11:2 [h] 1Sa 11:6
14:20 [i] Jdg 15:2,6; Jn 3:29
15:1 [j] Ge 38:17
15:2 [k] Jdg 14:20
15:6 [l] Jdg 14:15
15:9 [m] ver 14,17,19
15:11 [n] Jdg 13:1; 14:4; Ps 106:40-42
15:14 [o] Jdg 3:10; 14:19; 1Sa 11:6
15:15 [p] Lev 26:8; Jos 23:10; Jdg 3:31
15:18 [q] Jdg 16:28
15:19 [r] Ge 45:27; Isa 40:29
15:20 [s] Jdg 13:1; 16:31; Heb 11:32
16:2 [t] 1Sa 23:26; Ps 118:10-12; Ac 9:24

a *16* Or *made a heap or two*; the Hebrew for *donkey* sounds like the Hebrew for *heap.*
b *17* *Ramath Lehi* means *jawbone hill.*
c *19* *En Hakkore* means *caller's spring.*
d *20* Traditionally *judged*

tore them loose, bar and all. He lifted
them to his shoulders and carried them
to the top of the hill that faces Hebron.[u]
4Some time later, he fell in love[v]
with a woman in the Valley of Sorek
whose name was Delilah. **5**The rulers of
the Philistines[w] went to her and said,
"See if you can lure[x] him into showing
you the secret of his great strength and
how we can overpower him so we may
tie him up and subdue him. Each one
of us will give you eleven hundred
shekels[a] of silver."[y]
6So Delilah said to Samson, "Tell me
the secret of your great strength and
how you can be tied up and subdued."
7Samson answered her, "If anyone
ties me with seven fresh thongs[b] that
have not been dried, I'll become as
weak as any other man."
8Then the rulers of the Philistines
brought her seven fresh thongs that
had not been dried, and she tied him
with them. **9**With men hidden in the
room,[z] she called to him, "Samson,
the Philistines are upon you!" But he
snapped the thongs as easily as a piece
of string snaps when it comes close to
a flame. So the secret of his strength
was not discovered.
10Then Delilah said to Samson, "You
have made a fool of me;[a] you lied to
me. Come now, tell me how you can be
tied."
11He said, "If anyone ties me securely with new ropes[b] that have never
been used, I'll become as weak as any
other man."
12So Delilah took new ropes and tied
him with them. Then, with men hidden
in the room, she called to him, "Samson, the Philistines are upon you!" But
he snapped the ropes off his arms as if
they were threads.
13Delilah then said to Samson, "Until now, you have been making a fool of
me and lying to me. Tell me how you
can be tied."
He replied, "If you weave the seven
braids of my head into the fabric ⌞on
the loom⌟ and tighten it with the pin,
I'll become as weak as any other man."
So while he was sleeping, Delilah took
the seven braids of his head, wove
them into the fabric **14**and[c] tightened
it with the pin.
Again she called to him, "Samson,
the Philistines are upon you!"[c] He
awoke from his sleep and pulled up the
pin and the loom, with the fabric.
15Then she said to him, "How can
you say, 'I love you,'[d] when you won't
confide in me? This is the third time[e]
you have made a fool of me and
haven't told me the secret of your great
strength.[f]" **16**With such nagging she
prodded him day after day until he was
tired to death.
17So he told her everything.[g] "No
razor has ever been used on my head,"
he said, "because I have been a Nazirite[h] set apart to God since birth. If
my head were shaved, my strength
would leave me, and I would become
as weak as any other man."
18When Delilah saw that he had told
her everything, she sent word to the
rulers of the Philistines[i], "Come back
once more; he has told me everything."
So the rulers of the Philistines returned
with the silver in their hands. **19**Having
put him to sleep on her lap, she called
a man to shave off the seven braids of
his hair, and so began to subdue him.[d]
And his strength left him.[j]
20Then she called, "Samson, the Philistines are upon you!"
He awoke from his sleep and
thought, "I'll go out as before and
shake myself free." But he did not
know that the LORD had left him.[k]
21Then the Philistines[l] seized him,
gouged out his eyes[m] and took him
down to Gaza. Binding him with
bronze shackles, they set him to grinding[n] in the prison. **22**But the hair on
his head began to grow again after it
had been shaved.

The Death of Samson

23Now the rulers of the Philistines
assembled to offer a great sacrifice to
Dagon[o] their god and to celebrate,
saying, "Our god has delivered Samson, our enemy, into our hands."
24When the people saw him, they
praised their god,[p] saying,

"Our god has delivered our enemy
into our hands,[q]
the one who laid waste our land
and multiplied our slain."

25While they were in high spirits,[r]
they shouted, "Bring out Samson to
entertain us." So they called Samson
out of the prison, and he performed for
them.
When they stood him among the pillars, **26**Samson said to the servant who
held his hand, "Put me where I can feel
the pillars that support the temple, so
that I may lean against them." **27**Now
the temple was crowded with men and
women; all the rulers of the Philis-

16:3 [u]Jos 10:36
16:4 [v]Ge 24:67
16:5 [w]Jos 13:3 [x]Ex 10:7; Jdg 14:15 [y]ver 18
16:9 [z]ver 12
16:10 [a]ver 13
16:11 [b]Jdg 15:13
16:14 [c]ver 9,20
16:15 [d]Jdg 14:16 [e]Nu 24:10 [f]ver 5
16:17 [g]Mic 7:5 [h]Nu 6:2,5; Jdg 13:5
16:18 [i]Jos 13:3; 1Sa 5:8
16:19 [j]Pr 7:26-27
16:20 [k]Nu 14:42; Jos 7:12; 1Sa 16:14; 18:12; 28:15
16:21 [l]Jer 47:1 [m]Nu 16:14 [n]Job 31:10; Isa 47:2
16:23 [o]1Sa 5:2; 1Ch 10:10
16:24 [p]Da 5:4 [q]1Sa 31:9; 1Ch 10:9
16:25 [r]Jdg 9:27; Ru 3:7; Est 1:10

[a] *5* That is, about 28 pounds (about 13 kilograms) [b] *7* Or *bowstrings*; also in verses 8 and 9 [c] *13,14* Some Septuagint manuscripts; Hebrew "⌞*I can*⌟ *if you weave the seven braids of my head into the fabric* ⌞*on the loom*⌟." [14]*So she* [d] *19* Hebrew; some Septuagint manuscripts *and he began to weaken*

tines were there, and on the roof[s]
were about three thousand men and
women watching Samson perform.
28Then Samson prayed to the LORD,[t]
"O Sovereign LORD, remember me.
O God, please strengthen me just once
more, and let me with one blow get
revenge[u] on the Philistines for my two
eyes." 29Then Samson reached toward
the two central pillars on which the
temple stood. Bracing himself against
them, his right hand on the one and his
left hand on the other, 30Samson said,
"Let me die with the Philistines!" Then
he pushed with all his might, and down
came the temple on the rulers and all
the people in it. Thus he killed many
more when he died than while he lived.
31Then his brothers and his father's
whole family went down to get him.
They brought him back and buried him
between Zorah and Eshtaol in the
tomb of Manoah[v] his father. He had
led[a][w] Israel twenty years.[x]

Micah's Idols

17 Now a man named Micah[y] from
the hill country of Ephraim 2said to
his mother, "The eleven hundred shekels[b] of silver that were taken from you
and about which I heard you utter a
curse—I have that silver with me; I
took it."

16:23–25

PROMISE 3

THE SAMSON SYNDROME

Samson, a man who had been greatly blessed by God, here became entertainment for God's enemies. While this passage shows the outcome of Samson's failures, chapters 13–16 relate the whole story of his life. Over the centuries, Samson has been portrayed as both a hero and a tragic figure. His own failures and weaknesses made him prey to the people he had, in the past, so creatively defeated.

The lesson of Samson is also a lesson for our times. When we identify ourselves with Christ yet consistently fail to exhibit ethical and moral purity, the scoffers have a field day. They are convinced that their gods (the things they value most) are more valid than the God of heaven. Without knowing it, many Christian men provide office entertainment for their unbelieving coworkers.

We are all tempted, as Samson was, to compromise our Christian standards. For God's sake and your own, ask God every day to keep you from the Samson syndrome.

For the next Promise 3 reading go to page 276.

Then his mother said, "The LORD
bless you,[z] my son!"
3When he returned the eleven hundred shekels of silver to his mother, she
said, "I solemnly consecrate my silver
to the LORD for my son to make a
carved image and a cast idol.[a] I will
give it back to you."
4So he returned the silver to his
mother, and she took two hundred
shekels[c] of silver and gave them to a
silversmith, who made them into the
image and the idol.[b] And they were
put in Micah's house.
5Now this man Micah had a
shrine,[c] and he made an ephod[d] and
some idols[e] and installed[f] one of his
sons as his priest.[g] 6In those days Israel had no king;[h] everyone did as he
saw fit.[i]
7A young Levite from Bethlehem in
Judah,[j] who had been living within
the clan of Judah, 8left that town in
search of some other place to stay. On
his way[d] he came to Micah's house in
the hill country of Ephraim.
9Micah asked him, "Where are you
from?"
"I'm a Levite from Bethlehem in Judah," he said, "and I'm looking for a
place to stay."
10Then Micah said to him, "Live with
me and be my father and priest,[k] and
I'll give you ten shekels[e] of silver a
year, your clothes and your food." 11So
the Levite agreed to live with him, and
the young man was to him like one of
his sons. 12Then Micah installed[l] the
Levite, and the young man became his
priest and lived in his house. 13And Micah said, "Now I know that the LORD
will be good to me, since this Levite has
become my priest."

Danites Settle in Laish

18 In those days Israel had no king.[m]
And in those days the tribe of the
Danites was seeking a place of their
own where they might settle, because
they had not yet come into an inheritance among the tribes of Israel.[n] 2So
the Danites[o] sent five warriors from
Zorah and Eshtaol to spy out the land
and explore it. These men represented
all their clans. They told them, "Go, explore the land."[p]
The men entered the hill country of
Ephraim and came to the house of Micah,[q] where they spent the night.
3When they were near Micah's house,

16:27 [s]Dt 22:8; Jos 2:8
16:28 [t]Jdg 15:18 [u]Jer 15:15
16:31 [v]Jdg 13:2 [w]Ru 1:1; 1Sa 4:18 [x]Jdg 15:20
17:1 [y]Jdg 18:2,13
17:2 [z]Ru 2:20; 1Sa 15:13; 2Sa 2:5
17:3 [a]Ex 20:4,23; 34:17; Lev 19:4
17:4 [b]Ex 32:4; Isa 17:8
17:5 [c]Isa 44:13; Eze 8:10 [d]Jdg 8:27 [e]Ge 31:19; Jdg 18:14 [f]Nu 16:10 [g]Ex 29:9; Jdg 18:24
17:6 [h]Jdg 18:1; 19:1; 21:25 [i]Dt 12:8
17:7 [j]Jdg 19:1; Ru 1:1-2; Mic 5:2; Mt 2:1
17:10 [k]Jdg 18:19
17:12 [l]Nu 16:10
18:1 [m]Jdg 17:6; 19:1 [n]Jos 19:47
18:2 [o]Jdg 13:25 [p]Jos 2:1 [q]Jdg 17:1

[a]*31* Traditionally *judged* [b]*2* That is, about 28 pounds (about 13 kilograms) [c]*4* That is, about 5 pounds (about 2.3 kilograms) [d]*8* Or *To carry on his profession* [e]*10* That is, about 4 ounces (about 110 grams)

they recognized the voice of the young
Levite; so they turned in there and
asked him, "Who brought you here?
What are you doing in this place? Why
are you here?"
4He told them what Micah had done
for him, and said, "He has hired me
and I am his priest.[r]"
5Then they said to him, "Please inquire of God[s] to learn whether our
journey will be successful."
6The priest answered them, "Go in
peace[t]. Your journey has the LORD's
approval."
7So the five men left and came to
Laish,[u] where they saw that the people were living in safety, like the Sidonians, unsuspecting and secure. And
since their land lacked nothing, they
were prosperous.[a] Also, they lived a
long way from the Sidonians[v] and had
no relationship with anyone else.[b]
8When they returned to Zorah and
Eshtaol, their brothers asked them,
"How did you find things?"
9They answered, "Come on, let's attack them! We have seen that the land
is very good. Aren't you going to do
something? Don't hesitate to go there
and take it over.[w] **10**When you get
there, you will find an unsuspecting
people and a spacious land that God
has put into your hands, a land that
lacks nothing[x] whatever.[y]"
11Then six hundred men[z] from the
clan of the Danites,[a] armed for battle,
set out from Zorah and Eshtaol. **12**On
their way they set up camp near Kiriath
Jearim in Judah. This is why the place
west of Kiriath Jearim is called Mahaneh Dan[c][b] to this day. **13**From there
they went on to the hill country of
Ephraim and came to Micah's house.
14Then the five men who had spied
out the land of Laish said to their
brothers, "Do you know that one of
these houses has an ephod, other
household gods, a carved image and
a cast idol?[c] Now you know what to
do." **15**So they turned in there and went
to the house of the young Levite at Micah's place and greeted him. **16**The six
hundred Danites,[d] armed for battle,
stood at the entrance to the gate. **17**The
five men who had spied out the land
went inside and took the carved image,
the ephod, the other household gods[e]
and the cast idol while the priest and
the six hundred armed men stood at
the entrance to the gate.
18When these men went into Micah's house and took[f] the carved image, the ephod, the other household
gods and the cast idol, the priest said to
them, "What are you doing?"
19They answered him, "Be quiet![g]
Don't say a word. Come with us, and
be our father and priest.[h] Isn't it better that you serve a tribe and clan in
Israel as priest rather than just one
man's household?" **20**Then the priest
was glad. He took the ephod, the other
household gods and the carved image
and went along with the people. **21**Putting their little children, their livestock
and their possessions in front of them,
they turned away and left.
22When they had gone some distance from Micah's house, the men
who lived near Micah were called together and overtook the Danites. **23**As
they shouted after them, the Danites
turned and said to Micah, "What's the
matter with you that you called out
your men to fight?"
24He replied, "You took the gods I
made, and my priest, and went away.
What else do I have? How can you ask,
'What's the matter with you?' "
25The Danites answered, "Don't argue with us, or some hot-tempered
men will attack you, and you and your
family will lose your lives." **26**So the
Danites went their way, and Micah,
seeing that they were too strong for
him,[i] turned around and went back
home.
27Then they took what Micah had
made, and his priest, and went on to
Laish, against a peaceful and unsuspecting people.[j] They attacked them
with the sword and burned down their
city.[k] **28**There was no one to rescue
them because they lived a long way
from Sidon[l] and had no relationship

18:4 [r]Jdg 17:12 **18:5** [s]1Ki 22:5 **18:6** [t]1Ki 22:6 **18:7** [u]Jos 19:47 [v]ver 28 **18:9** [w]Nu 13:30; 1Ki 22:3 **18:10** [x]ver 7,27; Dt 8:9 [y]1Ch 4:40 **18:11** [z]ver 16,17 [a]Jdg 13:2 **18:12** [b]Jdg 13:25

18:14 [c]Ge 31:19; Jdg 17:5 **18:16** [d]ver 11 **18:17** [e]Ge 31:19; Mic 5:13 **18:18** [f]Isa 46:2; Jer 43:11; Hos 10:5 **18:19** [g]Job 21:5; 29:9; 40:4; Mic 7:16 [h]Jdg 17:10 **18:26** [i]Ps 18:17; 35:10 **18:27** [j]ver 7,10 [k]Ge 49:17; Jos 19:47 **18:28** [l]ver 7

18:1–20:48

PROMISE 6

DEFLECTING DIVISION

The series of stories in these three chapters clearly illustrates how selfishness, greed and lust lead to division among individuals and peoples. Reconciliation will never be realized until we heed Paul's teaching to "Do nothing out of selfish ambition or vain conceit, but in humility consider others better than yourselves" (Philippians 2:3). As you read this tragic series of events among God's people, commit to doing whatever you can to build a spirit of reconciliation and unity among God's people. Reconciliation begins when you take the first step.

For the next Promise 6 reading go to page 283.

[a] *7* The meaning of the Hebrew for this clause is uncertain. [b] *7* Hebrew; some Septuagint manuscripts *with the Arameans*
[c] *12* *Mahaneh Dan* means *Dan's camp.*

with anyone else. The city was in a valley near Beth Rehob.[m]
The Danites rebuilt the city and settled there. 29They named it Dan[n] after
their forefather Dan, who was born to
Israel—though the city used to be
called Laish.[o] 30There the Danites set
up for themselves the idols, and Jonathan son of Gershom,[p] the son of Moses,[a] and his sons were priests for the
tribe of Dan until the time of the captivity of the land. 31They continued to
use the idols Micah had made, all the
time the house of God[q] was in Shiloh.[r]

A Levite and His Concubine

19 In those days Israel had no king.
Now a Levite who lived in a remote
area in the hill country of Ephraim[s]
took a concubine from Bethlehem in
Judah.[t] 2But she was unfaithful to
him. She left him and went back to her
father's house in Bethlehem, Judah. After she had been there four months,
3her husband went to her to persuade
her to return. He had with him his servant and two donkeys. She took him
into her father's house, and when her
father saw him, he gladly welcomed
him. 4His father-in-law, the girl's father, prevailed upon him to stay; so he
remained with him three days, eating
and drinking,[u] and sleeping there.
5On the fourth day they got up early
and he prepared to leave, but the girl's
father said to his son-in-law, "Refresh
yourself[v] with something to eat; then
you can go." 6So the two of them sat
down to eat and drink together. Afterward the girl's father said, "Please stay
tonight and enjoy yourself."[w] 7And
when the man got up to go, his father-
in-law persuaded him, so he stayed
there that night. 8On the morning of
the fifth day, when he rose to go, the
girl's father said, "Refresh yourself.
Wait till afternoon!" So the two of them
ate together.
9Then when the man, with his concubine and his servant, got up to leave,
his father-in-law, the girl's father, said,
"Now look, it's almost evening. Spend
the night here; the day is nearly over.
Stay and enjoy yourself. Early tomorrow morning you can get up and be on
your way home." 10But, unwilling to
stay another night, the man left and
went toward Jebus[x] (that is, Jerusalem), with his two saddled donkeys and
his concubine.
11When they were near Jebus and
the day was almost gone, the servant
said to his master, "Come, let's stop at
this city of the Jebusites[y] and spend
the night."
12His master replied, "No. We won't
go into an alien city, whose people are
not Israelites. We will go on to Gibeah."
13He added, "Come, let's try to reach
Gibeah or Ramah[z] and spend the
night in one of those places." 14So they
went on, and the sun set as they neared
Gibeah in Benjamin.[a] 15There they
stopped to spend the night. They went
and sat in the city square,[b] but no one
took them into his home for the night.
16That evening[c] an old man from
the hill country of Ephraim,[d] who was
living in Gibeah (the men of the place
were Benjamites), came in from his
work in the fields. 17When he looked
and saw the traveler in the city square,
the old man asked, "Where are you going? Where did you come from?"[e]
18He answered, "We are on our way
from Bethlehem in Judah to a remote
area in the hill country of Ephraim
where I live. I have been to Bethlehem
in Judah and now I am going to the
house of the LORD.[f] No one has taken
me into his house. 19We have both
straw and fodder[g] for our donkeys
and bread and wine[h] for ourselves
your servants—me, your maidservant,
and the young man with us. We don't
need anything."
20"You are welcome at my house,"
the old man said. "Let me supply whatever you need. Only don't spend the
night in the square." 21So he took him
into his house and fed his donkeys. Af-

[a]30 An ancient Hebrew scribal tradition, some Septuagint manuscripts and Vulgate; Masoretic Text *Manasseh*

19:1–20:48

PROMISE 3

GUARDING EVIL

Few Biblical stories better illustrate the danger of guarding evil than the one found in Judges 19–21. Not only did the men of Gibeah commit a terrible sin against the man's concubine, but the citizens of the city also committed an equally serious sin by protecting the guilty men. If they had handed the perpetrators over, a terrible war could have been avoided.

In light of this story, take a minute for some introspection. Are there any sins you're tolerating in yourself? How about your accountability group? Are you, and the men you meet with, openly dealing with sin or brushing it under the rug? The prospect of dealing with sin in your life can be threatening. But the danger of tolerating sin is a greater threat.

For the next Promise 3 reading go to page 303.

18:28 [m]Nu 13:21; 2Sa 10:6
18:29 [n]Ge 14:14 [o]Jos 19:47; 1Ki 15:20
18:30 [p]Ex 2:22; Jdg 17:3,5
18:31 [q]Jdg 19:18 [r]Jos 18:1; Jer 7:14
19:1 [s]Jdg 18:1 [t]Ru 1:1
19:4 [u]Ex 32:6
19:5 [v]ver 8; Ge 18:5
19:6 [w]ver 9,22; Jdg 16:25
19:10 [x]Ge 10:16; Jos 15:8; 1Ch 11:4-5
19:11 [y]Jos 3:10
19:13 [z]Jos 18:25
19:14 [a]1Sa 10:26; Isa 10:29
19:15 [b]Ge 19:2
19:16 [c]Ps 104:23 [d]ver 1
19:17 [e]Ge 29:4
19:18 [f]Jdg 18:31
19:19 [g]Ge 24:25 [h]Ge 14:18

ter they had washed their feet, they had something to eat and drink.[i]

22While they were enjoying themselves,[j] some of the wicked men[k] of the city surrounded the house. Pounding on the door, they shouted to the old man who owned the house, "Bring out the man who came to your house so we can have sex with him.[l]"

23The owner of the house went outside[m] and said to them, "No, my friends, don't be so vile. Since this man is my guest, don't do this disgraceful thing.[n] 24Look, here is my virgin daughter,[o] and his concubine. I will bring them out to you now, and you can use them and do to them whatever you wish. But to this man, don't do such a disgraceful thing."

25But the men would not listen to him. So the man took his concubine and sent her outside to them, and they raped her and abused her[p] throughout the night, and at dawn they let her go. 26At daybreak the woman went back to the house where her master was staying, fell down at the door and lay there until daylight.

27When her master got up in the morning and opened the door of the house and stepped out to continue on his way, there lay his concubine, fallen in the doorway of the house, with her hands on the threshold. 28He said to her, "Get up; let's go." But there was no answer. Then the man put her on his donkey and set out for home.

29When he reached home, he took a knife[q] and cut up his concubine, limb by limb, into twelve parts and sent them into all the areas of Israel.[r] 30Everyone who saw it said, "Such a thing has never been seen or done, not since the day the Israelites came up out of Egypt.[s] Think about it! Consider it! Tell us what to do![t]"

Israelites Fight the Benjamites

20 Then all the Israelites[u] from Dan to Beersheba[v] and from the land of Gilead came out as one man[w] and assembled[x] before the LORD in Mizpah. 2The leaders of all the people of the tribes of Israel took their places in the assembly of the people of God, four hundred thousand soldiers[y] armed with swords. 3(The Benjamites heard that the Israelites had gone up to Mizpah.) Then the Israelites said, "Tell us how this awful thing happened."

4So the Levite, the husband of the murdered woman, said, "I and my concubine came to Gibeah[z] in Benjamin to spend the night.[a] 5During the night the men of Gibeah came after me and surrounded the house, intending to kill me.[b] They raped my concubine, and she died.[c] 6I took my concubine, cut her into pieces and sent one piece to each region of Israel's inheritance,[d] because they committed this lewd and disgraceful act[e] in Israel. 7Now, all you Israelites, speak up and give your verdict.[f]"

8All the people rose as one man, saying, "None of us will go home. No, not one of us will return to his house. 9But now this is what we'll do to Gibeah: We'll go up against it as the lot directs.[g] 10We'll take ten men out of every hundred from all the tribes of Israel, and a hundred from a thousand, and a thousand from ten thousand, to get provisions for the army. Then, when the army arrives at Gibeah[a] in Benjamin, it can give them what they deserve for all this vileness done in Israel." 11So all the men of Israel got together and united as one man[h] against the city.

6 →PG. 282

12The tribes of Israel sent men throughout the tribe of Benjamin, saying, "What about this awful crime that was committed among you? 13Now surrender those wicked men[i] of Gibeah so that we may put them to death and purge the evil from Israel.[j]"

But the Benjamites would not listen to their fellow Israelites. 14From their towns they came together at Gibeah to fight against the Israelites. 15At once the Benjamites mobilized twenty-six thousand swordsmen from their towns, in addition to seven hundred chosen men from those living in Gibeah. 16Among all these soldiers there were seven hundred chosen men who were left-handed,[k] each of whom could sling a stone at a hair and not miss.

17Israel, apart from Benjamin, mustered four hundred thousand swordsmen, all of them fighting men.

18The Israelites went up to Bethel[b] and inquired of God.[l] They said, "Who of us shall go first to fight[m] against the Benjamites?"

The LORD replied, "Judah shall go first."

19The next morning the Israelites got up and pitched camp near Gibeah. 20The men of Israel went out to fight the Benjamites and took up battle positions against them at Gibeah. 21The Benjamites came out of Gibeah and cut down twenty-two thousand Israelites[n] on the battlefield that day. 22But

19:21 [i]Ge 24:32-33; Lk 7:44
19:22 [j]Jdg 16:25 [k]Dt 13:13 [l]Ge 19:4-5; Jdg 20:5; Ro 1:26-27
19:23 [m]Ge 19:6 [n]Ge 34:7; Lev 19:29; Dt 22:21; Jdg 20:6; 2Sa 13:12; Ro 1:27
19:24 [o]Ge 19:8; Dt 21:14
19:25 [p]1Sa 31:4
19:29 [q]Ge 22:6 [r]Jdg 20:6; 1Sa 11:7
19:30 [s]Hos 9:9 [t]Jdg 20:7; Pr 13:10
20:1 [u]Jdg 21:5 [v]1Sa 3:20; 2Sa 3:10; 1Ki 4:25 [w]1Sa 11:7 [x]1Sa 7:5
20:2 [y]Jdg 8:10
20:4 [z]Jos 15:57 [a]Jdg 19:15
20:5 [b]Jdg 19:22 [c]Jdg 19:25-26
20:6 [d]Jdg 19:29 [e]Jos 7:15; Jdg 19:23
20:7 [f]Jdg 19:30
20:9 [g]Lev 16:8
20:11 [h]ver 1
20:13 [i]Dt 13:13; Jdg 19:22 [j]Dt 17:12
20:16 [k]Jdg 3:15; 1Ch 12:2
20:18 [l]ver 26-27; Nu 27:21 [m]ver 23,28
20:21 [n]ver 25

[a] *10* One Hebrew manuscript; most Hebrew manuscripts *Geba,* a variant of *Gibeah*
[b] *18* Or *to the house of God*; also in verse 26

the men of Israel encouraged one another and again took up their positions where they had stationed themselves the first day. 23The Israelites went up and wept before the LORD until evening,[o] and they inquired of the LORD. They said, "Shall we go up again to battle[p] against the Benjamites, our brothers?"

The LORD answered, "Go up against them."

24Then the Israelites drew near to Benjamin the second day. 25This time, when the Benjamites came out from Gibeah to oppose them, they cut down another eighteen thousand Israelites,[q] all of them armed with swords.

26Then the Israelites, all the people, went up to Bethel, and there they sat weeping before the LORD.[r] They fasted that day until evening and presented burnt offerings and fellowship offerings[a] to the LORD.[s] 27And the Israelites inquired of the LORD. (In those days the ark of the covenant of God[t] was there, 28with Phinehas son of Eleazar,[u] the son of Aaron, ministering before it.)[v] They asked, "Shall we go up again to battle with Benjamin our brother, or not?"

The LORD responded, "Go, for tomorrow I will give them into your hands.[w]"

29Then Israel set an ambush[x] around Gibeah. 30They went up against the Benjamites on the third day and took up positions against Gibeah as they had done before. 31The Benjamites came out to meet them and were drawn away[y] from the city. They began to inflict casualties on the Israelites as before, so that about thirty men fell in the open field and on the roads—the one leading to Bethel and the other to Gibeah.

32While the Benjamites were saying, "We are defeating them as before,"[z] the Israelites were saying, "Let's retreat and draw them away from the city to the roads."

33All the men of Israel moved from their places and took up positions at Baal Tamar, and the Israelite ambush charged out of its place[a] on the west[b] of Gibeah.[c] 34Then ten thousand of Israel's finest men made a frontal attack on Gibeah. The fighting was so heavy that the Benjamites did not realize[b] how near disaster was.[c] 35The LORD defeated Benjamin[d] before Israel, and on that day the Israelites struck down 25,100 Benjamites, all armed with swords. 36Then the Benjamites saw that they were beaten.

Now the men of Israel had given way[e] before Benjamin, because they relied on the ambush they had set near Gibeah. 37The men who had been in ambush made a sudden dash into Gibeah, spread out and put the whole city to the sword.[f] 38The men of Israel had arranged with the ambush that they should send up a great cloud of smoke[g] from the city, 39and then the men of Israel would turn in the battle.

The Benjamites had begun to inflict casualties on the men of Israel (about thirty), and they said, "We are defeating them as in the first battle."[h] 40But when the column of smoke began to rise from the city, the Benjamites turned and saw the smoke of the whole city going up into the sky.[i] 41Then the men of Israel turned on them, and the men of Benjamin were terrified, because they realized that disaster had come upon them. 42So they fled before the Israelites in the direction of the desert, but they could not escape the battle. And the men of Israel who came out of the towns cut them down there. 43They surrounded the Benjamites, chased them and easily[d] overran them in the vicinity of Gibeah on the east. 44Eighteen thousand Benjamites fell, all of them valiant fighters.[j] 45As they turned and fled toward the desert to the rock of Rimmon,[k] the Israelites cut down five thousand men along the roads. They kept pressing after the Benjamites as far as Gidom and struck down two thousand more.

46On that day twenty-five thousand Benjamite swordsmen fell, all of them valiant fighters. 47But six hundred men turned and fled into the desert to the rock of Rimmon, where they stayed four months. 48The men of Israel went back to Benjamin and put all the towns to the sword, including the animals and everything else they found. All the towns they came across they set on fire.[l]

Wives for the Benjamites

21 The men of Israel had taken an oath[m] at Mizpah:[n] "Not one of us will give[o] his daughter in marriage to a Benjamite."

2The people went to Bethel,[e] where they sat before God until evening, raising their voices and weeping bitterly. 3"O LORD, the God of Israel," they cried, "why has this happened to Isra-

20:23 [o]Jos 7:6 [p]ver 18 **20:25** [q]ver 21 **20:26** [r]ver 23 [s]Jdg 21:4 **20:27** [t]Jos 18:1 **20:28** [u]Jos 24:33 [v]Dt 18:5 [w]Jdg 7:9 **20:29** [x]Jos 8:2,4 **20:31** [y]Jos 8:16 **20:32** [z]ver 39 **20:33** [a]Jos 8:19 **20:34** [b]Jos 8:14 [c]Isa 47:11 **20:35** [d]1Sa 9:21 **20:36** [e]Jos 8:15 **20:37** [f]Jos 8:19 **20:38** [g]Jos 8:20 **20:39** [h]ver 32 **20:40** [i]Jos 8:20 **20:44** [j]Ps 76:5 **20:45** [k]Jos 15:32; Jdg 21:13 **20:48** [l]Jdg 21:23 **21:1** [m]Jos 9:18 [n]Jdg 20:1 [o]ver 7,18

[a]26 Traditionally *peace offerings* [b]33 Some Septuagint manuscripts and Vulgate; the meaning of the Hebrew for this word is uncertain. [c]33 Hebrew *Geba,* a variant of *Gibeah* [d]43 The meaning of the Hebrew for this word is uncertain. [e]2 Or *to the house of God*

el? Why should one tribe be missing from Israel today?"

4 Early the next day the people built an altar and presented burnt offerings and fellowship offerings.[a][p]

5 Then the Israelites asked, "Who from all the tribes of Israel[q] has failed to assemble before the LORD?" For they had taken a solemn oath that anyone who failed to assemble before the LORD at Mizpah should certainly be put to death.

6 Now the Israelites grieved for their brothers, the Benjamites. "Today one tribe is cut off from Israel," they said. 7 "How can we provide wives for those who are left, since we have taken an oath[r] by the LORD not to give them any of our daughters in marriage?" 8 Then they asked, "Which one of the tribes of Israel failed to assemble before the LORD at Mizpah?" They discovered that no one from Jabesh Gilead[s] had come to the camp for the assembly. 9 For when they counted the people, they found that none of the people of Jabesh Gilead were there.

10 So the assembly sent twelve thousand fighting men with instructions to go to Jabesh Gilead and put to the sword those living there, including the women and children. 11 "This is what you are to do," they said. "Kill every male and every woman who is not a virgin.[t]" 12 They found among the people living in Jabesh Gilead four hundred young women who had never slept with a man, and they took them to the camp at Shiloh[u] in Canaan.

13 Then the whole assembly sent an offer of peace[v] to the Benjamites at the rock of Rimmon.[w] 14 So the Benjamites returned at that time and were given the women of Jabesh Gilead who had been spared. But there were not enough for all of them.

21:4 [p]Jdg 20:26; 2Sa 24:25
21:5 [q]Jdg 5:23; 20:1
21:7 [r]ver 1
21:8 [s]1Sa 11:1; 31:11
21:11 [t]Nu 31:17-18
21:12 [u]Jos 18:1
21:13 [v]Dt 20:10 [w]Jdg 20:47
21:15 [x]ver 6
21:18 [y]ver 1
21:19 [z]Jos 18:1; Jdg 18:31; 1Sa 1:3
21:21 [a]Ex 15:20; Jdg 11:34
21:22 [b]ver 1,18
21:23 [c]Jdg 20:48
21:25 [d]Dt 12:8; Jdg 17:6; 18:1; 19:1

15 The people grieved for Benjamin,[x] because the LORD had made a gap in the tribes of Israel. 16 And the elders of the assembly said, "With the women of Benjamin destroyed, how shall we provide wives for the men who are left? 17 The Benjamite survivors must have heirs," they said, "so that a tribe of Israel will not be wiped out. 18 We can't give them our daughters as wives, since we Israelites have taken this oath: 'Cursed be anyone who gives[y] a wife to a Benjamite.' 19 But look, there is the annual festival of the LORD in Shiloh,[z] to the north of Bethel, and east of the road that goes from Bethel to Shechem, and to the south of Lebonah."

20 So they instructed the Benjamites, saying, "Go and hide in the vineyards 21 and watch. When the girls of Shiloh come out to join in the dancing,[a] then rush from the vineyards and each of you seize a wife from the girls of Shiloh and go to the land of Benjamin. 22 When their fathers or brothers complain to us, we will say to them, 'Do us a kindness by helping them, because we did not get wives for them during the war, and you are innocent, since you did not give[b] your daughters to them.' "

23 So that is what the Benjamites did. While the girls were dancing, each man caught one and carried her off to be his wife. Then they returned to their inheritance and rebuilt the towns and settled in them.[c]

24 At that time the Israelites left that place and went home to their tribes and clans, each to his own inheritance.

25 In those days Israel had no king; everyone did as he saw fit.[d]

[a] *4* Traditionally *peace offerings*

RUTH

AT A GLANCE

Key Principle: God honors and provides for people who commit their ways to him.

Author: Unknown; probably written during David's reign.

Time and Place: ~1150 B.C. to ~1120 B.C. / Moab and Bethlehem

Key Verses: 1:16–17; 3:11

BENEFIT

The book of Ruth is a beautiful cameo of devotion, allegiance and romance that illustrates God's loving concern for people who cling to his character and promises in the midst of adverse circumstances. It is a heartwarming story of God's tender concern and involvement in the lives of unassuming people.

SETTING

The account of Ruth takes place during the time of the judges—a time of moral corruption, idolatry, warfare, and anarchy. It begins in the land of Moab and traces the life of a Moabite woman who embraces the God of Israel and moves with her mother-in-law, Naomi, to Bethlehem after the death of their husbands.

Moab was a region northeast of the Dead Sea whose inhabitants were descendants of Lot. The Moabites worshiped Chemosh and other gods and had a generally hostile relationship to Israel (Judges 3:12–30; 1 Samuel 14:47).

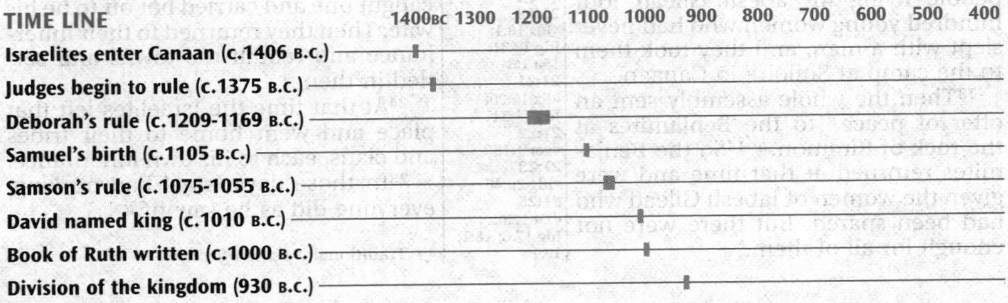

THEME AND PURPOSE

Ruth centers around the theme of redemption as it portrays Boaz as Ruth's kinsman-redeemer. Acting as Ruth's kinsman through Naomi, Boaz redeems her from widowhood and poverty to marriage and wealth. This beautiful story was written to illustrate the godly remnant who held fast to the God of Abraham, Isaac and Jacob in spite of the immorality and apostasy that ran rampant during this time in Israel's history. It also tells of God's divine preparation for the Davidic dynasty; Ruth, a Gentile, was one of David's direct ancestors (4:18–22).

UNIQUE CONTRIBUTION

This simple but profound book portrays faithfulness, love and obedience in a time of faithlessness, hatred and disobedience. It shows that, even in the worst of times, God always has a remnant who will honor and trust him. Since it anticipates the reign of King David, the book of Ruth serves as a historical link between the time of the judges and the time of the kings.

Ruth and Esther, the only two Biblical books named after women, are both stories of faith and blessing. Ruth was a Gentile woman who lived among the Jews; Esther was a Jewish woman who lived among the Gentiles. Ruth married a Jewish man who was in the royal ancestry of David; Esther married a Gentile who ruled the Persian Empire.

LINKS TO THE NEW TESTAMENT

Boaz, as Ruth's kinsman-redeemer, is an illustration of Christ. The Hebrew word *goel* (close relative or kinsman-redeemer) appears 13 times in Ruth and anticipates Christ's work as our mediator and advocate. The *goel* had to be a blood relative of the person(s) he redeemed, he had to be able and willing to pay the price of redemption, and he had to be free himself. This beautifully typifies Christ, who became our blood relative through his incarnation, who was able to redeem us because he is the God-Man, who was willing to redeem us because he loves us and who was free from the curse of sin.

OVERVIEW

FOCUS	Ruth's Devotion		Ruth's Reward	
REFERENCE	1	2	3	4
TOPICS	Ruth and Naomi		Ruth and Boaz	
	Discouragement	Discovery	Decision	Development
LOCATION	Moab	Bethlehem in Judah		
TIME	~30 Years			

Ruth was an extraordinary woman whose commitment to Naomi and devotion to Naomi's God (1:16–17) was rewarded by "the LORD, the God of Israel, under whose wings you have come to take refuge" (2:12). The story opens with a famine in Israel and records Elimelech's decision to move his family from Bethlehem to Moab because of the hardship. When Elimelech and his two sons die, his widow Naomi tells her Moabite daughters-in-law to seek new husbands. Ruth refuses to leave Naomi, and accompanies her on her return to Bethlehem (1:1–22).

At first Naomi saw God as her enemy, but later realized that God had plans for her that she could not have foreseen. In his providential care, the Lord guided Ruth to glean in the field of Boaz, Naomi's kinsman. Boaz immediately began to protect and provide for Ruth (2:1–23). When Naomi instructed Ruth to ask Boaz to exercise his right as her kinsman-redeemer, Boaz expressed his willingness to do so (3:1–18). Ruth's faithfulness and devotion was rewarded when Boaz married her. Finally, Naomi rejoiced in her grandson, Obed, who was to become King David's grandfather (4:1–22).

RUTH

Naomi and Ruth

1 In the days when the judges
ruled,[a][a] there was a famine in the
land,[b] and a man from Bethlehem in
Judah, together with his wife and two
sons, went to live for a while in the
country of Moab.[c] **2**The man's name
was Elimelech, his wife's name Naomi,
and the names of his two sons were
Mahlon and Kilion. They were Eph-
rathites from Bethlehem,[d] Judah. And
they went to Moab and lived there.
3Now Elimelech, Naomi's husband,
died, and she was left with her two
sons. **4**They married Moabite women,
one named Orpah and the other
Ruth.[e] After they had lived there
about ten years, **5**both Mahlon and Kilion also died, and Naomi was left without her two sons and her husband.
6When she heard in Moab that the
LORD had come to the aid of his people[f] by providing food[g] for them,
Naomi and her daughters-in-law prepared to return home from there.
7With her two daughters-in-law she
left the place where she had been living
and set out on the road that would take
them back to the land of Judah.
8Then Naomi said to her two
daughters-in-law, "Go back, each of
you, to your mother's home. May the
LORD show kindness[h] to you, as you
have shown to your dead[i] and to me.
9May the LORD grant that each of you
will find rest[j] in the home of another
husband."
Then she kissed them and they wept
aloud **10**and said to her, "We will go
back with you to your people."
11But Naomi said, "Return home,
my daughters. Why would you come
with me? Am I going to have any more
sons, who could become your husbands?[k] **12**Return home, my daughters; I am too old to have another husband. Even if I thought there was still
hope for me—even if I had a husband
tonight and then gave birth to sons—
13would you wait until they grew up?
Would you remain unmarried for
them? No, my daughters. It is more
bitter for me than for you, because
the LORD's hand has gone out
against me![l]"
14At this they wept again. Then Orpah kissed her mother-in-law[m] good-
by, but Ruth clung to her.[n]
15"Look," said Naomi, "your sister-
in-law is going back to her people and
her gods.[o] Go back with her."
16But Ruth replied, "Don't urge me
to leave you[p] or to turn back from
you. Where you go I will go, and where
you stay I will stay. Your people will be
my people and your God my God.[q]
17Where you die I will die, and there I
will be buried. May the LORD deal with
me, be it ever so severely,[r] if anything
but death separates you and me."
18When Naomi realized that Ruth was
determined to go with her, she stopped
urging her.[s]
19So the two women went on until
they came to Bethlehem. When they
arrived in Bethlehem, the whole town
was stirred[t] because of them, and the
women exclaimed, "Can this be Naomi?"
20"Don't call me Naomi,[b]" she told
them. "Call me Mara,[c] because the Almighty[d][u] has made my life very bitter.[v] **21**I went away full, but the LORD
has brought me back empty.[w] Why
call me Naomi? The LORD has afflicted[e] me; the Almighty has brought
misfortune upon me."
22So Naomi returned from Moab accompanied by Ruth the Moabitess, her
daughter-in-law, arriving in Bethlehem as the barley harvest[x] was beginning.[y]

6 →PG. 338

1:1 *a* Jdg 2:16-18 *b* Ge 12:10; Ps 105:16 *c* Jdg 3:30 **1:2** *d* Ge 35:19 **1:4** *e* Mt 1:5 **1:6** *f* Ex 4:31; Jer 29:10; Zep 2:7 *g* Ps 132:15; Mt 6:11 **1:8** *h* Ru 2:20; 2Ti 1:16 *i* ver 5 **1:9** *j* Ru 3:1 **1:11** *k* Ge 38:11; Dt 25:5 **1:13** *l* Jdg 2:15; Job 4:5; 19:21; Ps 32:4 **1:14** *m* Ru 2:11 *n* Pr 17:17; 18:24 **1:15** *o* Jos 24:14; Jdg 11:24 **1:16** *p* 2Ki 2:2 *q* Ru 2:11,12 **1:17** *r* 1Sa 3:17; 25:22; 2Sa 19:13; 2Ki 6:31 **1:18** *s* Ac 21:14 **1:19** *t* Mt 21:10 **1:20** *u* Ex 6:3 *v* ver 13; Job 6:4 **1:21** *w* Job 1:21 **1:22** *x* Ex 9:31; Ru 2:23 *y* 2Sa 21:9

a *1* Traditionally *judged* **b** *20* *Naomi* means *pleasant*; also in verse 21. **c** *20* *Mara* means *bitter.* **d** *20* Hebrew *Shaddai*; also in verse 21 **e** *21* Or *has testified against*

1:16 PROMISE **7**

FOLLOWING NAOMI

"Your God will be my God." Ruth was a gentile who knew nothing about God except through Naomi's example. Something about the way Naomi dealt with the bitter loss (1:20) of her husband and sons made Ruth want to follow Naomi's God. Life had dealt bitterly with Naomi, but apparently Naomi wasn't bitter toward God. Ruth, her closest relative, was devoted to Naomi and wanted to stay with her.

Consider your life with God and ask if people around you find him attractive enough to say, "I can see by the way you live and the hope you have that God is working in your life. I want that for myself, too. Your God will be my God."

For the next Promise 7 reading go to page 310.

Ruth Meets Boaz

2 Now Naomi had a relative[z] on her husband's side, from the clan of Elimelech,[a] a man of standing, whose name was Boaz.[b]

2 And Ruth the Moabitess said to Naomi, "Let me go to the fields and pick up the leftover grain[c] behind anyone in whose eyes I find favor."

Naomi said to her, "Go ahead, my daughter." 3 So she went out and began to glean in the fields behind the harvesters. As it turned out, she found herself working in a field belonging to Boaz, who was from the clan of Elimelech.

4 Just then Boaz arrived from Bethlehem and greeted the harvesters, "The LORD be with you![d]"

"The LORD bless you![e]" they called back.

5 Boaz asked the foreman of his harvesters, "Whose young woman is that?"

6 The foreman replied, "She is the Moabitess[f] who came back from Moab with Naomi. 7 She said, 'Please let me glean and gather among the sheaves behind the harvesters.' She went into the field and has worked steadily from morning till now, except for a short rest in the shelter."

8 So Boaz said to Ruth, "My daughter, listen to me. Don't go and glean in another field and don't go away from here. Stay here with my servant girls. 9 Watch the field where the men are harvesting, and follow along after the girls. I have told the men not to touch you. And whenever you are thirsty, go and get a drink from the water jars the men have filled."

10 At this, she bowed down with her face to the ground.[g] She exclaimed, "Why have I found such favor in your eyes that you notice me[h]—a foreigner?[i]"

11 Boaz replied, "I've been told all about what you have done for your mother-in-law[j] since the death of your husband—how you left your father and mother and your homeland and came to live with a people you did not know before.[k] 12 May the LORD repay you for what you have done. May you be richly rewarded by the LORD,[l] the God of Israel, under whose wings[m] you have come to take refuge.[n]"

13 "May I continue to find favor in your eyes, my lord," she said. "You have given me comfort and have spoken kindly to your servant—though I do not have the standing of one of your servant girls."

14 At mealtime Boaz said to her, "Come over here. Have some bread and dip it in the wine vinegar."

When she sat down with the harvesters, he offered her some roasted grain. She ate all she wanted and had some left over.[o] 15 As she got up to glean, Boaz gave orders to his men, "Even if she gathers among the sheaves, don't embarrass her. 16 Rather, pull out some stalks for her from the bundles and leave them for her to pick up, and don't rebuke her."

17 So Ruth gleaned in the field until evening. Then she threshed the barley she had gathered, and it amounted to about an ephah.[a] 18 She carried it back to town, and her mother-in-law saw how much she had gathered. Ruth also brought out and gave her what she had left over[p] after she had eaten enough.

19 Her mother-in-law asked her, "Where did you glean today? Where did you work? Blessed be the man who took notice of you![q]"

Then Ruth told her mother-in-law about the one at whose place she had been working. "The name of the man I worked with today is Boaz," she said.

20 "The LORD bless him!" Naomi said to her daughter-in-law. "He has not stopped showing his kindness[r] to the living and the dead." She added, "That man is our close relative; he is one of our kinsman-redeemers.[s]"

21 Then Ruth the Moabitess said, "He even said to me, 'Stay with my workers until they finish harvesting all my grain.' "

22 Naomi said to Ruth her daughter-in-law, "It will be good for you, my daughter, to go with his girls, because

2:1 [z]Ru 3:2,12 [a]Ru 1:2 [b]Ru 4:21 **2:2** [c]ver 7; Lev 19:9; 23:22; Dt 24:19 **2:4** [d]Jdg 6:12; Lk 1:28; 2Th 3:16 [e]Ps 129:7-8 **2:6** [f]Ru 1:22 **2:10** [g]1Sa 25:23 [h]Ps 41:1 [i]Dt 15:3 **2:11** [j]Ru 1:14 [k]Ru 1:16-17 **2:12** [l]1Sa 24:19 [m]Ps 17:8; 36:7; 57:1; 61:4; 63:7; 91:4 [n]Ru 1:16 **2:14** [o]ver 18 **2:18** [p]ver 14 **2:19** [q]ver 10; Ps 41:1 **2:20** [r]Ru 3:10; 2Sa 2:5; Pr 17:17 [s]Ru 3:9,12; 4:1,14

[a] *17* That is, probably about 3/5 bushel (about 22 liters)

2:6,8

PROMISE 6

BOAZ'S VISION

Ruth was a Moabitess. She was a stranger in a strange land; a foreigner from a country that had been hostile with Israel for years. Yet Boaz, a godly man, overlooked racial and ethnic prejudice and saw a woman of integrity who was also in need. He made sure she had what she needed to survive, and followed God's law for caring for the poor and widowed (see Leviticus 19:9–10; 23:22).

A powerful theme running through the Book of Ruth is Boaz's commitment to doing what God's spirit led him to do. As you read this book, take special note of Boaz's gentle, accepting behavior and his spirit of reconciliation.

For the next Promise 6 reading go to page 319.

NAOMI

God's Bitter Hand

She went out with dreams and returned with nightmares. She left with a husband and two sons and returned a childless widow. She left with hope and returned in despair. She was Naomi.

Naomi had moved to Moab ten years earlier with her husband and two sons to escape a famine in Judah. They bought a piece of land and started a life in their new country. Then, "Elimelech, Naomi's husband, died, and she was left with her two sons" (Ruth 1:3). A widow she was, but she still had two sons to protect and provide for her.

When the boys married Moabite girls, Naomi could dream of grandchildren and better days. She got along well with her sons' wives. They worked the land and experienced God's blessing in their lives. No grandchildren yet, but life was still good.

In a short time, however, Naomi had another funeral. One of her sons died. Then came the knockout punch. The other son died too. Naomi was now a widow indeed. Not only did she mourn for her husband and sons, she mourned for herself and her daughters-in-law.

What Do We Do Now?

These three women, all widows, were in a bad situation. Widows generally had a tough life, but these widows had an extra burden. Ruth and Orpah, the daughters-in-law, were Moabite women and Naomi was from Judah. Naomi was living in a foreign country away from her extended family. As miserable as it would be for Naomi to live as a widow in Judah, it would be better than staying in Moab. The choice was clear for Naomi. Go home.

Ruth and Orpah had two options: stay in Moab or go to Israel. They decided to go with Naomi. Naomi knew the consequences of both options. She knew that her foreign, widowed daughters-in-law would be despised in Judah. As they walked along the road, Naomi urged the girls to stay in Moab and find other husbands, have children, be happy. Naomi was so certain that this was the right decision she even kissed the girls good-bye. What a painful choice this must have been! But, in Naomi's mind, it was a good one.

Orpah had enough sense to leave. But Ruth clung to Naomi and begged to stay with her (1:14–16). So the two women came trudging into Bethlehem—a tired, defeated old woman and her young, foreign daughter-in-law. The women of the town saw them and exclaimed, "Can this be Naomi?" (1:19). Naomi's response was straight from the shoulder, no nonsense. "'Don't call me Naomi,' she told them. 'Call me Mara, because the Almighty has made my life very bitter. I went away full, but the LORD has brought me back empty'" (1:20–21). With these words the women understood her situation: she had left Judah as Naomi (which is translated "pleasant") and had come back as Mara (which means "bitter"). And who could disagree?

No Reproach

But notice carefully what Naomi actually said. She claimed the name Mara because "the Almighty has made my life very bitter" (1:20). Naomi had good theology. She believed the circumstances and events in her life were connected to her sovereign God. We don't know why God allowed things to happen as they did. Yet, bad things happened. That reality is not unique to Naomi's story or time. Bitter realities have always brought pain and misery. But don't miss Naomi's response to it.

Naomi was in a tough spot. She had trusted God for better things. But did her bitter circumstances turn her into a bitter person? Did she blame others and take it out on them? Did she drive everyone away with her whining? No. Naomi took inventory of her life and faced into her storm with clear reality. She was honest about her difficulty without making life difficult for those around her. No vindictiveness. No reproachfulness.

It was this response to the bitterness of life that generated Ruth's loyalty to Naomi. This Moabite woman's only information about the God of Israel came through Naomi and her family. Ruth was present when the awful truth of complete widowhood exploded in Naomi's life. What she learned about God from Naomi in those bitter times led her to say, "your God will be my God" (1:16). With every reason in the world for a perfect opportunity to escape, Ruth said, "I'm staying with you."

Wow! Ruth would rather face the dangers of going to a foreign culture than leave this woman who trusted in the Almighty God.

Doubtless in your life there have been, or will be, circumstances and events beyond your control—a disabled child, a slow death from cancer, a stalled career, the list goes on. Remember Naomi. Her bitter realities did not make her bitter. Though we do not have any of Naomi's speeches beyond the words she spoke to the women of her hometown, Naomi would certainly have said with Habakkuk: "Though the fig tree does not bud and there are no grapes on the vines, though the olive crop fails and the fields produce no food, though there are no sheep in the pen and no cattle in the stalls, yet I will rejoice in the LORD, I will be joyful in God my Savior" (Habakkuk 3:17–18).

Can you say the same?

—Dr. Sid Buzzell

in someone else's field you might be
harmed."
23 So Ruth stayed close to the servant
girls of Boaz to glean until the barley
and wheat harvests[t] were finished.
And she lived with her mother-in-law.

Ruth and Boaz at the Threshing Floor

3 One day Naomi her mother-in-law
said to her, "My daughter, should I
not try to find a home[a][u] for you,
where you will be well provided for? 2 Is
not Boaz, with whose servant girls you
have been, a kinsman[v] of ours? Tonight he will be winnowing barley on
the threshing floor. 3 Wash and perfume yourself,[w] and put on your best
clothes. Then go down to the threshing
floor, but don't let him know you are
there until he has finished eating and
drinking. 4 When he lies down, note the
place where he is lying. Then go and
uncover his feet and lie down. He will
tell you what to do."
5 "I will do whatever you say,"[x] Ruth
answered. 6 So she went down to the
threshing floor and did everything her
mother-in-law told her to do.
7 When Boaz had finished eating and
drinking and was in good spirits,[y] he
went over to lie down at the far end of
the grain pile. Ruth approached quietly, uncovered his feet and lay down. 8 In
the middle of the night something startled the man, and he turned and discovered a woman lying at his feet.
9 "Who are you?" he asked.
"I am your servant Ruth," she said.
"Spread the corner of your garment[z]
over me, since you are a kinsman-
redeemer.[a]"
10 "The LORD bless you, my daughter," he replied. "This kindness is
greater than that which you showed
earlier: You have not run after the
younger men, whether rich or poor.
11 And now, my daughter, don't be
afraid. I will do for you all you ask. All
my fellow townsmen know that you are
a woman of noble character.[b] 12 Although it is true that I am near of kin,
there is a kinsman-redeemer[c] nearer
than[d] I. 13 Stay here for the night, and
in the morning if he wants to redeem,[e] good; let him redeem. But if
he is not willing, as surely as the LORD
lives[f] I will do it. Lie here until morning."
14 So she lay at his feet until morning,
but got up before anyone could be recognized; and he said, "Don't let it be
known that a woman came to the
threshing floor."[g]
15 He also said, "Bring me the shawl
you are wearing and hold it out." When
she did so, he poured into it six measures of barley and put it on her. Then
he[b] went back to town.
16 When Ruth came to her mother-
in-law, Naomi asked, "How did it go,
my daughter?"
Then she told her everything Boaz
had done for her 17 and added, "He
gave me these six measures of barley,
saying, 'Don't go back to your mother-
in-law empty-handed.' "
18 Then Naomi said, "Wait, my
daughter, until you find out what happens. For the man will not rest until the
matter is settled today."[h]

Boaz Marries Ruth

4 Meanwhile Boaz went up to the
town gate and sat there. When the
kinsman-redeemer he had mentioned[i] came along, Boaz said, "Come
over here, my friend, and sit down." So
he went over and sat down.
2 Boaz took ten of the elders[j] of the
town and said, "Sit here," and they did
so. 3 Then he said to the kinsman-
redeemer, "Naomi, who has come
back from Moab, is selling the piece
of land that belonged to our brother
Elimelech. 4 I thought I should bring
the matter to your attention and suggest that you buy it in the presence of
these seated here and in the presence
of the elders of my people. If you will

2:23 [t]Dt 16:9
3:1 [u]Ru 1:9
3:2 [v]Dt 25:5-10; Ru 2:1
3:3 [w]2Sa 14:2
3:5 [x]Eph 6:1; Col 3:20
3:7 [y]Jdg 19:6,9,22; 2Sa 13:28; 1Ki 21:7; Est 1:10
3:9 [z]Eze 16:8 [a]ver 12; Ru 2:20
3:11 [b]Pr 12:4; 31:10
3:12 [c]ver 9 [d]Ru 4:1
3:13 [e]Dt 25:5; Ru 4:5; Mt 22:24 [f]Jdg 8:19; Jer 4:2
3:14 [g]Ro 14:16; 2Co 8:21
3:18 [h]Ps 37:3-5
4:1 [i]Ru 3:12
4:2 [j]1Ki 21:8; Pr 31:23

[a] *1* Hebrew *find rest* (see Ruth 1:9) [b] *15* Most Hebrew manuscripts; many Hebrew manuscripts, Vulgate and Syriac *she*

4:1–22

PROMISE 1

NO MATTER WHAT THE COST

Many of us are good men until it costs us. For a clearer picture, contrast the kinsman-redeemer and Boaz in this chapter. When presented with a chance for personal gain from fulfilling God's law of the kinsman-redeemer, the kinsman was willing to help Naomi (v. 4). When he found it would also cost him to help, he backed out (v. 6). Boaz followed through. He bought the land, married Ruth and fulfilled his legal obligation. Doing what God has commanded sometimes costs us in the short run. Boaz paid the short-term price and reaped the long-term blessing.

God gives us many opportunities in this lifetime to demonstrate our obedience to him. Some of the decisions to obey are small, others are life-changing. Counting the cost of obedience is the wrong place to start. Look what disobedience has cost you in the past, and then make the right decision.

For the next Promise 1 reading go to page 331.

redeem it, do so. But if you[a] will not,
tell me, so I will know. For no one has
the right to do it except you,[k] and I am
next in line."
"I will redeem it," he said.
5Then Boaz said, "On the day you
buy the land from Naomi and from
Ruth the Moabitess, you acquire[b] the
dead man's widow, in order to maintain the name of the dead with his
property."[l]
6At this, the kinsman-redeemer said,
"Then I cannot redeem[m] it because I
might endanger my own estate. You redeem it yourself. I cannot do it."
7(Now in earlier times in Israel, for
the redemption and transfer of property to become final, one party took off
his sandal and gave it to the other. This
was the method of legalizing transactions in Israel.)[n]
8So the kinsman-redeemer said to
Boaz, "Buy it yourself." And he removed his sandal.
9Then Boaz announced to the elders
and all the people, "Today you are witnesses that I have bought from Naomi
all the property of Elimelech, Kilion
and Mahlon. 10I have also acquired
Ruth the Moabitess, Mahlon's widow,
as my wife, in order to maintain the
name of the dead with his property, so
that his name will not disappear from
among his family or from the town
records.[o] Today you are witnesses!"
11Then the elders and all those at the
gate said, "We are witnesses.[p] May the
LORD make the woman who is coming
into your home like Rachel and Leah,[q]
who together built up the house of Israel. May you have standing in Ephrathah[r] and be famous in Bethlehem.
12Through the offspring the LORD gives
you by this young woman, may your
family be like that of Perez,[s] whom
Tamar bore to Judah."

The Genealogy of David

13So Boaz took Ruth and she became
his wife. Then he went to her, and the
LORD enabled her to conceive,[t] and
she gave birth to a son. 14The women[u]
said to Naomi: "Praise be to the LORD,
who this day has not left you without a
kinsman-redeemer. May he become
famous throughout Israel! 15He will renew your life and sustain you in your
old age. For your daughter-in-law,
who loves you and who is better to you
than seven sons,[v] has given him
birth."
16Then Naomi took the child, laid
him in her lap and cared for him. 17The
women living there said, "Naomi has a
son." And they named him Obed. He
was the father of Jesse,[w] the father of
David.
18This, then, is the family line of Perez[x]:

Perez was the father of Hezron,
19Hezron the father of Ram,
Ram the father of Amminadab,[y]
20Amminadab the father of Nahshon,
Nahshon the father of Salmon,[c]
21Salmon the father of Boaz,[z]
Boaz the father of Obed,
22Obed the father of Jesse,
and Jesse the father of David.

4:4 [k]Lev 25:25; Jer 32:7-8 **4:5** [l]Ge 38:8; Dt 25:5-6; Ru 3:13; Mt 22:24 **4:6** [m]Lev 25:25; Ru 3:13 **4:7** [n]Dt 25:7-9 **4:10** [o]Dt 25:6 **4:11** [p]Dt 25:9 [q]Ps 127:3; 128:3 [r]Ge 35:16 **4:12** [s]ver 18; Ge 38:29 **4:13** [t]Ge 29:31; 33:5; Ru 3:11 **4:14** [u]Lk 1:58 **4:15** [v]Ru 1:16-17; 2:11-12; 1Sa 1:8 **4:17** [w]ver 22; 1Sa 16:1,18; 1Ch 2:12,13 **4:18** [x]Mt 1:3-6 **4:19** [y]Ex 6:23 **4:21** [z]Ru 2:1

[a] *4* Many Hebrew manuscripts, Septuagint, Vulgate and Syriac; most Hebrew manuscripts *he* [b] *5* Hebrew; Vulgate and Syriac *Naomi, you acquire Ruth the Moabitess,* [c] *20* A few Hebrew manuscripts, some Septuagint manuscripts and Vulgate (see also verse 21 and Septuagint of 1 Chron. 2:11); most Hebrew manuscripts *Salma*

1 SAMUEL

AT A GLANCE

Key Principle: The Lord looks at our hearts and not on our outward appearances and circumstances, and he establishes people whose hearts are given fully to him.
Author: Unknown; Samuel may have written the first portion of the book.
Time and Place: ~1105 B.C. to 1011 B.C. / Canaan
Key Verses: 2:30; 8:5–9, 12–22; 13:14; 15:22–23

BENEFIT

The tragedy of Saul and the rise of David in this book teach us about the kind of person God wants to use. Jesus warned that God knows the hearts of those who justify themselves in the eyes of other people. "What is highly valued among men is detestable in God's sight" (Luke 16:15). First Samuel graphically portrays the difference between playing to people and following hard after God, and the consequences that follow each activity.

SETTING

First and 2 Samuel were originally one book in the Hebrew Bible, and they trace the stories of Samuel, the last of the judges and Saul and David, the first two kings of Israel. Samuel was born around 1105 B.C. and served as a judge and prophet for almost 50 years until his death in 1015 B.C. During this time, Israel was oppressed by the Philistines who lived on the coastal plains; the Israelites would have been totally overcome were it not for the fact that they lived in the hill country. Under Samuel's leadership Israel defeated the Philistines (7:7–14), but they rose up again in the time of Saul.

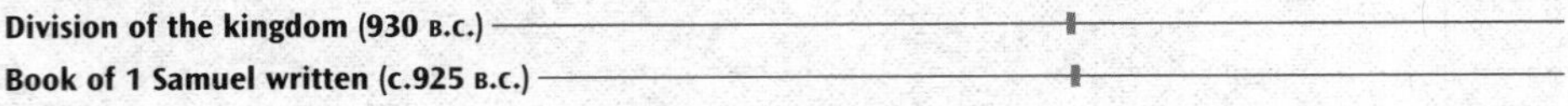

THEME AND PURPOSE

First Samuel begins late in the time of the judges and continues the historical narrative after Samson's death in Judges 16:31. The theme of this book is Israel's transition from a theocracy (God's rulership through appointed judges) to a monarchy. The people rejected the Lord as their king (8:7) and clamored for a visible earthly king. God had actually intended to give Israel a king (Deuteronomy 17:14–20), but the people refused to depend upon God and his timing. The Lord responded by instructing Samuel to anoint Saul as king, but 1 Samuel makes clear that God, not any earthly king, maintained sovereign rule in Israel's history. Because of Saul's disobedience, God deposes him. God then instructs Samuel to anoint David as Israel's future king.

UNIQUE CONTRIBUTION

This fast-paced historical narrative explains the transition in Israel's history from the period of the judges to the period of the monarchy, and reveals God's sovereign purpose behind these events. It offers a detailed spiritual portrait of Samuel, Saul and David, and shows how their interwoven lives contributed to the Lord's plan to further establish his people Israel.

The famous words Ichabod ("no glory" in 4:21) and Ebenezer ("stone of help" in 7:12) come from 1 Samuel.

LINKS TO THE NEW TESTAMENT

Samuel, like Christ, filled the three offices of prophet, priest and judge. The multitudes revered Samuel, and he heralded a new era in Israel's history. But the clearest picture of Christ in 1 Samuel is David. As Israel's anointed king (the word *Messiah,* or "anointed," appears in the Bible for the first time in 2:10), he anticipated the ultimate King who would rule on the throne of David (Luke 1:32–33). This greatest of Israel's kings was born in Bethlehem, became a shepherd, and cultivated a heart that was wholly devoted to God (13:14). Christ is a direct descendant of David (Matthew 1:1; Romans 1:3), and called himself "the Root and the Offspring of David" in Revelation 22:16.

OVERVIEW

FOCUS	Samuel	Saul	Saul and David
REFERENCE	1 — 8	9 — 15	16 — 31
TOPICS	The Last Judge	The First King	The King-Elect
	Transition from Judges to Kings	The Rise of Saul	The Decline of Saul and the Rise of David
LOCATION	Israel in Canaan		
TIME	~94 Years		

When Hannah is given a child in answer to her prayers, she dedicates her son Samuel to the Lord. This young boy is raised in the presence of Eli, Israel's judge and priest (1—2). The word of the Lord comes to Samuel, and he is confirmed as a prophet (3). The Philistines defeat Israel and Eli dies, but under Samuel's leadership, Israel experiences revival and victory (4—7). Nevertheless, the people reject God as their king and ask Samuel for an earthly king so they can be like all the other nations (8).

Samuel anoints Saul as king and though Saul begins well, he soon rebels against God's commands. Samuel announces to Saul that God has rejected him as king (9—15). God instructs Samuel to anoint David as king, and removes his Spirit from Saul (16). After David defeats Goliath (17), Saul degenerates into a selfish and jealous tyrant and continually seeks to kill David (18—20). In exile, David builds an army in the wilderness, and God protects him from Saul's attempts to hunt him down (21—27). After Saul foolishly consults a medium, his decline culminates when he and his sons are killed in a battle with the Philistines (28—31).

1 SAMUEL

The Birth of Samuel

1 There was a certain man from Ramathaim, a Zuphite[a] from the hill country[a] of Ephraim, whose name was Elkanah[b] son of Jeroham, the son of Elihu, the son of Tohu, the son of Zuph, an Ephraimite. 2He had two wives;[c] one was called Hannah and the other Peninnah. Peninnah had children, but Hannah had none.

3Year after year[d] this man went up from his town to worship[e] and sacrifice to the LORD Almighty at Shiloh,[f] where Hophni and Phinehas, the two sons of Eli, were priests of the LORD. 4Whenever the day came for Elkanah to sacrifice,[g] he would give portions of the meat to his wife Peninnah and to all her sons and daughters. 5But to Hannah he gave a double portion because he loved her, and the LORD had closed her womb.[h] 6And because the LORD had closed her womb, her rival kept provoking her in order to irritate her.[i] 7This went on year after year. Whenever Hannah went up to the house of the LORD, her rival provoked her till she wept and would not eat. 8Elkanah her husband would say to her, "Hannah, why are you weeping? Why don't you eat? Why are you downhearted? Don't I mean more to you than ten sons?[j]"

9Once when they had finished eating and drinking in Shiloh, Hannah stood up. Now Eli the priest was sitting on a chair by the doorpost of the LORD's temple.[b][k] 10In bitterness of soul[l] Hannah wept much and prayed to the LORD. 11And she made a vow, saying, "O LORD Almighty, if you will only look upon your servant's misery and remember[m] me, and not forget your servant but give her a son, then I will give him to the LORD for all the days of his life, and no razor[n] will ever be used on his head."

12As she kept on praying to the LORD, Eli observed her mouth. 13Hannah was praying in her heart, and her lips were moving but her voice was not heard. Eli thought she was drunk 14and said to her, "How long will you keep on getting drunk? Get rid of your wine."

15"Not so, my lord," Hannah replied, "I am a woman who is deeply troubled. I have not been drinking wine or beer; I was pouring[o] out my soul to the LORD. 16Do not take your servant for a wicked woman; I have been praying here out of my great anguish and grief."

17Eli answered, "Go in peace,[p] and may the God of Israel grant you what you have asked of him.[q]"

18She said, "May your servant find favor in your eyes.[r]" Then she went her way and ate something, and her face was no longer downcast.[s]

19Early the next morning they arose and worshiped before the LORD and then went back to their home at Ramah. Elkanah lay with Hannah his wife, and the LORD remembered[t] her. 20So in the course of time Hannah conceived and gave birth to a son. She named[u] him Samuel,[c] saying, "Because I asked the LORD for him."

Hannah Dedicates Samuel

4 →PG. 364

21When the man Elkanah went up with all his family to offer the annual[v] sacrifice to the LORD and to fulfill his vow,[w] 22Hannah did not go. She said to her husband, "After the boy is weaned, I will take him and present[x] him before the LORD, and he will live there always."

23"Do what seems best to you," Elkanah her husband told her. "Stay here until you have weaned him; only may the LORD make good[y] his[d] word." So the woman stayed at home and nursed her son until she had weaned him.

24After he was weaned, she took the boy with her, young as he was, along with a three-year-old bull,[e][z] an ephah[f] of flour and a skin of wine, and brought him to the house of the LORD at Shiloh. 25When they had slaughtered the bull, they brought the boy to Eli, 26and she said to him, "As surely as you live, my lord, I am the woman who stood here beside you praying to the LORD. 27I prayed[a] for this child, and the LORD has granted me what I asked of him. 28So now I give him to the LORD. For his whole life[b] he will be given over to the LORD." And he worshiped the LORD there.

1:1 [a] Jos 17:17-18 [b] 1Ch 6:27,34
1:2 [c] Dt 21:15-17; Lk 2:36
1:3 [d] ver 21; Ex 23:14; 34:23; Lk 2:41 [e] Dt 12:5-7 [f] Jos 18:1
1:4 [g] Dt 12:17-18
1:5 [h] Ge 16:1; 30:2
1:6 [i] Job 24:21
1:8 [j] Ru 4:15
1:9 [k] 1Sa 3:3
1:10 [l] Job 7:11
1:11 [m] Ge 8:1; 28:20; 29:32 [n] Nu 6:1-21; Jdg 13:5
1:15 [o] Ps 42:4; 62:8; La 2:19
1:17 [p] Jdg 18:6; 1Sa 25:35; 2Ki 5:19; Mk 5:34 [q] Ps 20:3-5
1:18 [r] Ru 2:13 [s] Ecc 9:7; Ro 15:13
1:19 [t] Ge 4:1; 30:22
1:20 [u] Ge 41:51-52; Ex 2:10,22; Mt 1:21
1:21 [v] ver 3 [w] Dt 12:11
1:22 [x] ver 11,28; Lk 2:22
1:23 [y] ver 17; Nu 30:7
1:24 [z] Nu 15:8-10; Dt 12:5; Jos 18:1
1:27 [a] ver 11-13; Ps 66:19-20
1:28 [b] ver 11,22; Ge 24:26,52

[a] *1* Or *from Ramathaim Zuphim* [b] *9* That is, tabernacle [c] *20* *Samuel* sounds like the Hebrew for *heard of God.* [d] *23* Masoretic Text; Dead Sea Scrolls, Septuagint and Syriac *your* [e] *24* Dead Sea Scrolls, Septuagint and Syriac; Masoretic Text *with three bulls* [f] *24* That is, probably about 3/5 bushel (about 22 liters)

Hannah's Prayer

2 Then Hannah prayed and said:[c]

"My heart rejoices[d] in the LORD;
in the LORD my horn[a][e] is lifted high.
My mouth boasts over my enemies,
for I delight in your deliverance.

2"There is no one holy[b][f] like the LORD;
there is no one besides you;
there is no Rock[g] like our God.

3"Do not keep talking so proudly
or let your mouth speak such arrogance,[h]
for the LORD is a God who knows,
and by him deeds[i] are weighed.[j]

4"The bows of the warriors are broken,[k]
but those who stumbled are armed with strength.
5Those who were full hire themselves out for food,
but those who were hungry hunger no more.
She who was barren[l] has borne seven children,
but she who has had many sons pines away.

6"The LORD brings death and makes alive;[m]
he brings down to the grave[c] and raises up.[n]
7The LORD sends poverty and wealth;[o]
he humbles and he exalts.[p]
8He raises[q] the poor from the dust
and lifts the needy from the ash heap;
he seats them with princes
and has them inherit a throne of honor.[r]

"For the foundations[s] of the earth are the LORD's;
upon them he has set the world.
9He will guard the feet[t] of his saints,
but the wicked will be silenced in darkness.[u]

"It is not by strength[v] that one prevails;
10 those who oppose the LORD will be shattered.[w]
He will thunder[x] against them from heaven;
the LORD will judge[y] the ends of the earth.

"He will give strength[z] to his king
and exalt the horn[a] of his anointed."

11Then Elkanah went home to Ramah, but the boy ministered[b] before the LORD under Eli the priest.

Eli's Wicked Sons

12Eli's sons were wicked men; they had no regard[c] for the LORD. 13Now it was the practice of the priests with the people that whenever anyone offered a sacrifice and while the meat[d] was being boiled, the servant of the priest would come with a three-pronged fork in his hand. 14He would plunge it into the pan or kettle or caldron or pot, and the priest would take for himself whatever the fork brought up. This is how they treated all the Israelites who came to Shiloh. 15But even before the fat was

[a] *1* Horn here symbolizes strength; also in verse 10. [b] *2* Or *no Holy One* [c] *6* Hebrew *Sheol*

2:1 [c]Lk 1:46-55 [d]Ps 9:14; 13:5 [e]Ps 89:17,24; 92:10; Isa 12:2-3
2:2 [f]Ex 15:11; Lev 19:2 [g]Dt 32:30-31; 2Sa 22:2,32
2:3 [h]Pr 8:13 [i]1Sa 16:7; 1Ki 8:39 [j]Pr 16:2; 24:11-12
2:4 [k]Ps 37:15
2:5 [l]Ps 113:9; Jer 15:9
2:6 [m]Dt 32:39 [n]Isa 26:19
2:7 [o]Dt 8:18 [p]Job 5:11; Ps 75:7
2:8 [q]Ps 113:7-8 [r]Job 36:7 [s]Job 38:4
2:9 [t]Ps 91:12 [u]Mt 8:12 [v]Ps 33:16-17
2:10 [w]Ps 2:9 [x]Ps 18:13 [y]Ps 96:13 [z]Ps 21:1 [a]Ps 89:24
2:11 [b]ver 18; 1Sa 3:1
2:12 [c]Jer 2:8; 9:6
2:13 [d]Lev 7:29-34

1:27–28

PROMISE 4

GOD'S CHILDREN

Hannah knew her son was a gift from God, and she gave him back to God. Hannah couldn't guarantee how Samuel would turn out. But Hannah trusted God with her son's life, saying, "For his whole life he will be given over to the LORD."

If you have a child, think of what it would mean to give that child to God and to see yourself as a teacher and shaper of a human soul who belongs to God. When you talk to him, when you reach out to correct some behavior, when you decide to take him to church, when he asks you a question, you are responding to God's property.

The thousands upon thousands of decisions you make in regard to your child through his or her lifetime shape a living soul whom God has entrusted to your care. You may not have given your child back to God like Hannah did in these verses, but that doesn't change the fact that he or she is God's gift to you (Psalm 127). Why not stop right now and pray verse 28, inserting your child's (or children's) name(s) in the first sentence: "So now I give ________ to the LORD. For his or her whole life he or she will be given over to the LORD."

If you have no children, think of the young people and others whom you come into contact with. All people, no matter what their age, have been created in God's image and deserve the dignity of that position. Keep in mind that when you respond to another person, you're responding to God's child.

For the next Promise 4 reading go to page 294.

ELI

A Father's Contribution

Eli was Israel's high priest, an honored position that only the descendants of Aaron could occupy. The book of Hebrews informs us that "every high priest is selected from among men and is appointed to represent them in matters related to God, to offer gifts and sacrifices for sins . . . No one takes this honor upon himself; he must be called by God, just as Aaron was" (Hebrews 5:1, 4).

Eli was not only the high priest of Israel, but he was also a father and a discipler for his sons Hophni and Phinehas. Yet Eli was not faithful to this high calling of fatherhood. He gave his sons privilege and responsibility, but provided them with little direction and discipline.

Spiritual Poverty

When Hophni and Phinehas were young men, they began serving as priests in the tabernacle. Yet these two men "had no regard for the LORD" (2:12). They stole what people were offering to God by taking the best of the sacrifice for themselves. They threatened the worshipers with physical violence and said, "Hand it over now; if you don't, I'll take it by force" (1 Samuel 2:16). That's serious business. In addition, Hophni and Phinehas used their influence to have illicit sex with women who served in the tabernacle (2:22). Eli's sons were priests, but they were bums.

Eli was displeased with his sons and told them they were in danger, but that was as far as his involvement went (2:25). He talked to his sons, but he did not act. After all, they were big boys now, and he was an old man. Yet Eli still had responsibility for directing and influencing his sons, as does any father at any age. Moreover, Eli was still the high priest, Israel's moral leader.

So God spoke to Eli: "Why do you honor your sons more than me by fattening yourselves on the choice parts of every offering . . . Those who honor me I will honor, but those who despise me will be disdained . . . in your family line there will never be an old man" (2:29, 30, 32). God confirmed these words of judgment on Eli when he spoke to young Samuel: "I told [Eli] that I would judge his family forever because of the sin he knew about; his sons made themselves contemptible, and he failed to restrain them" (3:13).

Though Eli and his sons were descendants of Aaron, Israel's high priestly family, Eli was a passive father. He employed his sons, but he never discipled them. He ignored their waywardness. And God's judgment fell on the whole family.

Spiritual Wealth

Yet Eli wasn't a complete failure. The Bible says Eli raised *three* boys. Two were his sons and one was not. That other boy was Samuel. To the extent we blame Eli for his sons' sinfulness, we also have to give him credit for Samuel's successes.

Eli was entrusted with Samuel from the time the boy was weaned (1:24). "The boy ministered before the LORD under Eli the priest" and "continued to grow in stature and in favor with the LORD and with men" (2:11, 26). These brief glimpses don't give us a full picture of Eli's style of discipling the lad, but it is instructive to note that when Samuel heard the voice in the night, Eli recognized that it was God (3:8). Eli also held Samuel accountable with a stern warning to obey him by telling him everything God had said. That stern insistence on obedience was something Eli had failed to do with his own sons. Ultimately, because of Eli's influence, Samuel grew up to become one of Israel's most godly leaders.

What made the difference? What did Eli do with Samuel that he didn't do with his own sons? How could Eli blow it so badly with his sons and succeed so well with Samuel?

First, Eli actively discipled Samuel (2:11), but failed to disciple Hophni and Phinehas. It's a subtle mistake many men make. Many men invest more quality time with a scout troop or Little League baseball team than with their own kids. They are kinder and gentler with kids who live in their neighborhood than with the kids who live in their house.

Second, Eli recognized Samuel as a gift from God. We don't know what Eli thought when his sons were born, but Samuel's mother reminded Eli of a fact that is true of every child: He was a gift from God (1:27–28). In fact, Psalm 127:3 tells us that all children are a reward from the Lord. Could it be that Eli treated Samuel as God's gift and failed to see his sons in that same light?

We may commend Eli for what he contributed to his disciple Samuel, but God condemned him for what he *didn't* contribute to his sons. The bottom line for Eli becomes a stern warning for any father: Having a disciple who is not a son never compensates for having sons who are not disciples.

—Dr. Sid Buzzell

burned, the servant of the priest would
come and say to the man who was sacrificing, "Give the priest some meat to
roast; he won't accept boiled meat
from you, but only raw."
16If the man said to him, "Let the fat
be burned up first, and then take whatever you want," the servant would then
answer, "No, hand it over now; if you
don't, I'll take it by force."
17This sin of the young men was very
great in the LORD's sight, for they[a]
were treating the LORD's offering with
contempt.[e]
18But Samuel was ministering[f] before the LORD—a boy wearing a linen
ephod.[g] 19Each year his mother made
him a little robe and took it to him
when she went up with her husband to
offer the annual[h] sacrifice. 20Eli would
bless Elkanah and his wife, saying,
"May the LORD give you children by
this woman to take the place of the one
she prayed[i] for and gave to the LORD."
Then they would go home. 21And the
LORD was gracious to Hannah;[j] she
conceived and gave birth to three sons
and two daughters. Meanwhile, the
boy Samuel grew[k] up in the presence
of the LORD.
22Now Eli, who was very old, heard
about everything his sons were doing
to all Israel and how they slept with the
women[l] who served at the entrance
to the Tent of Meeting. 23So he said to
them, "Why do you do such things? I
hear from all the people about these
wicked deeds of yours. 24No, my sons;
it is not a good report that I hear
spreading among the LORD's people.
25If a man sins against another man,
God[b] may mediate for him; but if a
man sins against the LORD, who will[m]
intercede[n] for him?" His sons, however, did not listen to their father's rebuke, for it was the LORD's will to put
them to death.
26And the boy Samuel continued to
grow[o] in stature and in favor with the
LORD and with men.

Prophecy Against the House of Eli

27Now a man of God[p] came to Eli
and said to him, "This is what the LORD
says: 'Did I not clearly reveal myself to
your father's house when they were in
Egypt under Pharaoh? 28I chose[q] your
father out of all the tribes of Israel to be
my priest, to go up to my altar, to burn
incense, and to wear an ephod[r] in my
presence. I also gave your father's
house all the offerings made with fire
by the Israelites. 29Why do you[c] scorn
my sacrifice and offering[s] that I prescribed for my dwelling?[t] Why do you
honor your sons more than me by fattening yourselves on the choice parts
of every offering made by my people
Israel?'
30"Therefore the LORD, the God of Israel, declares: 'I promised that your
house and your father's house would
minister before me forever.[u]' But now
the LORD declares: 'Far be it from me!
Those who honor me I will honor,[v]
but those who despise[w] me will be disdained. 31The time is coming when I
will cut short your strength and the
strength of your father's house, so that
there will not be an old man in your
family line[x] 32and you will see distress
in my dwelling. Although good will be
done to Israel, in your family line there
will never be an old man.[y] 33Every one
of you that I do not cut off from my
altar will be spared only to blind your
eyes with tears and to grieve your
heart, and all your descendants will die
in the prime of life.
34" 'And what happens to your two
sons, Hophni and Phinehas, will be a
sign to you—they will both die[z] on
the same day.[a] 35I will raise up for myself a faithful priest,[b] who will do according to what is in my heart and
mind. I will firmly establish his house,
and he will minister before my anointed[c] one always. 36Then everyone left
in your family line will come and bow
down before him for a piece of silver
and a crust of bread and plead, "Appoint me to some priestly office so I
can have food to eat.[d]" ' "

The LORD Calls Samuel

3 The boy Samuel ministered[e] before
the LORD under Eli. In those days the
word of the LORD was rare;[f] there
were not many visions.[g]
2One night Eli, whose eyes[h] were
becoming so weak that he could barely
see, was lying down in his usual place.
3The lamp[i] of God had not yet gone
out, and Samuel was lying down in the
temple[d] of the LORD, where the ark of
God was. 4Then the LORD called Samuel.
Samuel answered, "Here I am.[j]"
5And he ran to Eli and said, "Here I am;
you called me."
But Eli said, "I did not call; go back
and lie down." So he went and lay
down.
6Again the LORD called, "Samuel!"
And Samuel got up and went to Eli and
said, "Here I am; you called me."

2 →PG. 312

2:17 [e]Mal 2:7-9
2:18 [f]ver 11; 1Sa 3:1 [g]ver 28
2:19 [h]1Sa 1:3
2:20 [i]1Sa 1:11, 27-28; Lk 2:34
2:21 [j]Ge 21:1 [k]ver 26; Jdg 13:24; 1Sa 3:19; Lk 2:40
2:22 [l]Ex 38:8
2:25 [m]Nu 15:30; Jos 11:20 [n]Dt 1:17; 1Sa 3:14; Heb 10:26
2:26 [o]ver 21; Lk 2:52
2:27 [p]Ex 4:14-16; 1Ki 13:1
2:28 [q]Ex 28:1 [r]Lev 8:7-8
2:29 [s]ver 12-17 [t]Dt 12:5; Mt 10:37
2:30 [u]Ex 29:9 [v]Ps 50:23; 91:15 [w]Mal 2:9
2:31 [x]1Sa 4:11-18; 22:16-20
2:32 [y]1Ki 2:26-27; Zec 8:4
2:34 [z]1Sa 4:11 [a]1Ki 13:3
2:35 [b]1Sa 12:3; 1Ki 2:35 [c]1Sa 16:13; 2Sa 7:11,27; 1Ki 11:38
2:36 [d]1Ki 2:27
3:1 [e]1Sa 2:11 [f]Ps 74:9 [g]Am 8:11
3:2 [h]1Sa 4:15
3:3 [i]Lev 24:1-4
3:4 [j]Isa 6:8

[a]17 Or *men* [b]25 Or *the judges* [c]29 The Hebrew is plural. [d]3 That is, tabernacle

"My son," Eli said, "I did not call; go back and lie down."

7 Now Samuel did not yet know the LORD: The word of the LORD had not yet been revealed[k] to him.

8 The LORD called Samuel a third time, and Samuel got up and went to Eli and said, "Here I am; you called me."

Then Eli realized that the LORD was calling the boy. 9 So Eli told Samuel, "Go and lie down, and if he calls you, say, 'Speak, LORD, for your servant is listening.' " So Samuel went and lay down in his place.

10 The LORD came and stood there, calling as at the other times, "Samuel! Samuel!"

Then Samuel said, "Speak, for your servant is listening."

11 And the LORD said to Samuel: "See, I am about to do something in Israel that will make the ears of everyone who hears of it tingle.[l] 12 At that time I will carry out against Eli everything[m] I spoke against his family—from beginning to end. 13 For I told him that I would judge his family forever because of the sin he knew about; his sons made themselves contemptible,[a] and he failed to restrain[n] them. 14 Therefore, I swore to the house of Eli, 'The guilt of Eli's house will never be atoned[o] for by sacrifice or offering.' "

15 Samuel lay down until morning and then opened the doors of the house of the LORD. He was afraid to tell Eli the vision, 16 but Eli called him and said, "Samuel, my son."

Samuel answered, "Here I am."

17 "What was it he said to you?" Eli asked. "Do not hide it from me. May God deal with you, be it ever so severely,[p] if you hide from me anything he told you." 18 So Samuel told him everything, hiding nothing from him. Then Eli said, "He is the LORD; let him do what is good in his eyes."[q]

19 The LORD was with[r] Samuel as he grew[s] up, and he let none[t] of his words fall to the ground. 20 And all Israel from Dan to Beersheba[u] recognized that Samuel was attested as a prophet of the LORD. 21 The LORD continued to appear at Shiloh, and there he revealed[v] himself to Samuel through his word.

4 And Samuel's word came to all Israel.

The Philistines Capture the Ark

Now the Israelites went out to fight against the Philistines. The Israelites camped at Ebenezer,[w] and the Philistines at Aphek.[x] 2 The Philistines deployed their forces to meet Israel, and as the battle spread, Israel was defeated by the Philistines, who killed about four thousand of them on the battlefield. 3 When the soldiers returned to camp, the elders of Israel asked, "Why[y] did the LORD bring defeat upon us today before the Philistines? Let us bring the ark[z] of the LORD's covenant from Shiloh, so that it[b] may go with us and save us from the hand of our enemies."

4 So the people sent men to Shiloh, and they brought back the ark of the covenant of the LORD Almighty, who is enthroned between the cherubim.[a] And Eli's two sons, Hophni and Phine-

3:7 [k]Ac 19:12
3:11 [l]2Ki 21:12; Jer 19:3
3:12 [m]1Sa 2:27-36
3:13 [n]1Sa 2:12,17, 22,29-31
3:14 [o]Lev 15:30-31; 1Sa 2:25; Isa 22:14
3:17 [p]Ru 1:17; 2Sa 3:35
3:18 [q]Job 2:10; Isa 39:8
3:19 [r]Ge 21:22; 39:2 [s]1Sa 2:21 [t]1Sa 9:6
3:20 [u]Jdg 20:1
3:21 [v]ver 10
4:1 [w]1Sa 7:12 [x]Jos 12:18; 1Sa 29:1
4:3 [y]Jos 7:7 [z]Nu 10:35; Jos 6:7
4:4 [a]Ex 25:22; 2Sa 6:2

a *13* Masoretic Text; an ancient Hebrew scribal tradition and Septuagint *sons blasphemed God*
b *3* Or *he*

3:13

PROMISE 4

HONORING YOUR CHILDREN MORE THAN GOD

Eli's sons abused their position as his helpers in the temple, and he did nothing to restrain or correct their sin. In so doing Eli allowed them to dishonor the sanctity of the temple and corrupt Israelite worship. Even though the sons were the offenders, this passage makes clear that Eli shared in the responsibility for the state of worship at this time (see 2:12–17, 22–25).

In reference to this activity, God made two telling statements about fathering that we do well to examine. First, "Why do you honor your sons more than me?" (2:29). Eli failed to honor God because he placed his sons' desire to sin above his desire to obey God's command. He failed to address his sons' behavior forcefully enough to stop their corrupt activity. God's second statement is this: "Those who honor me I will honor, but those who despise me I will disdain" (2:30). These statements add a sobering element to fathering, especially in an age where choices are based less on the existence of a higher power than they are on individual ideas of right and wrong. In this passage, God revealed his view of our responsibility to address our children's moral choices. At its heart this is an issue of how highly we honor God.

Discuss with your wife, a friend, or write out on a sheet of paper your plan to model and teach moral responsibility to your children. Include some ideas about how you will correct your children when they disobey and affirm them when they keep God's commands.

For the next Promise 4 reading go to page 348.

has, were there with the ark of the covenant of God.

5When the ark of the LORD's covenant came into the camp, all Israel raised such a great shout[b] that the ground shook. 6Hearing the uproar, the Philistines asked, "What's all this shouting in the Hebrew camp?"

When they learned that the ark of the LORD had come into the camp, 7the Philistines were afraid.[c] "A god has come into the camp," they said. "We're in trouble! Nothing like this has happened before. 8Woe to us! Who will deliver us from the hand of these mighty gods? They are the gods who struck the Egyptians with all kinds of plagues in the desert. 9Be strong, Philistines! Be men, or you will be subject to the Hebrews, as they[d] have been to you. Be men, and fight!"

10So the Philistines fought, and the Israelites were defeated[e] and every man fled to his tent. The slaughter was very great; Israel lost thirty thousand foot soldiers. 11The ark of God was captured, and Eli's two sons, Hophni and Phinehas, died.[f]

Death of Eli

12That same day a Benjamite ran from the battle line and went to Shiloh, his clothes torn and dust[g] on his head. 13When he arrived, there was Eli[h] sitting on his chair by the side of the road, watching, because his heart feared for the ark of God. When the man entered the town and told what had happened, the whole town sent up a cry.

14Eli heard the outcry and asked, "What is the meaning of this uproar?"

The man hurried over to Eli, 15who was ninety-eight years old and whose eyes[i] were set so that he could not see. 16He told Eli, "I have just come from the battle line; I fled from it this very day."

Eli asked, "What happened, my son?"

17The man who brought the news replied, "Israel fled before the Philistines, and the army has suffered heavy losses. Also your two sons, Hophni and Phinehas, are dead, and the ark of God has been captured."

18When he mentioned the ark of God, Eli fell backward off his chair by the side of the gate. His neck was broken and he died, for he was an old man and heavy. He had led[a][j] Israel forty years.

19His daughter-in-law, the wife of Phinehas, was pregnant and near the time of delivery. When she heard the news that the ark of God had been captured and that her father-in-law and her husband were dead, she went into labor and gave birth, but was overcome by her labor pains. 20As she was dying, the women attending her said, "Don't despair; you have given birth to a son." But she did not respond or pay any attention.

21She named the boy Ichabod,[b][k] saying, "The glory[l] has departed from Israel"—because of the capture of the ark of God and the deaths of her father-in-law and her husband. 22She said, "The glory has departed from Israel, for the ark of God has been captured."

The Ark in Ashdod and Ekron

5 After the Philistines had captured the ark of God, they took it from Ebenezer[m] to Ashdod.[n] 2Then they carried the ark into Dagon's temple and set it beside Dagon.[o] 3When the people of Ashdod rose early the next day, there was Dagon, fallen[p] on his face on the ground before the ark of the LORD! They took Dagon and put him back in his place. 4But the following morning when they rose, there was Dagon, fallen on his face on the ground before the ark of the LORD! His head and hands had been broken[q] off and were lying on the threshold; only his body remained. 5That is why to this day neither the priests of Dagon nor any others who enter Dagon's temple at Ashdod step on the threshold.[r]

6The LORD's hand[s] was heavy upon the people of Ashdod and its vicinity; he brought devastation[t] upon them and afflicted them with tumors.[c][u] 7When the men of Ashdod saw what was happening, they said, "The ark of the god of Israel must not stay here with us, because his hand is heavy upon us and upon Dagon our god." 8So they called together all the rulers of the Philistines and asked them, "What shall we do with the ark of the god of Israel?"

They answered, "Have the ark of the god of Israel moved to Gath.[v]" So they moved the ark of the God of Israel.

9But after they had moved it, the LORD's hand was against that city, throwing it into a great panic.[w] He afflicted the people of the city, both young and old, with an outbreak of tumors.[d] 10So they sent the ark of God to Ekron.

As the ark of God was entering Ek-

4:5 [b]Jos 6:5,10
4:7 [c]Ex 15:14
4:9 [d]Jdg 13:1; 1Co 16:13
4:10 [e]ver 2; Dt 28:25; 2Sa 18:17; 2Ki 14:12
4:11 [f]1Sa 2:34; Ps 78:61,64
4:12 [g]Jos 7:6; 2Sa 1:2; 15:32; Ne 9:1; Job 2:12
4:13 [h]ver 18; 1Sa 1:9
4:15 [i]1Sa 3:2
4:18 [j]ver 13
4:21 [k]Ge 35:18 [l]Ps 26:8; Jer 2:11
5:1 [m]1Sa 4:1; 7:12 [n]Jos 13:3
5:2 [o]Jdg 16:23
5:3 [p]Isa 19:1; 46:7
5:4 [q]Eze 6:6; Mic 1:7
5:5 [r]Zep 1:9
5:6 [s]ver 7; Ex 9:3; Ps 32:4; Ac 13:11 [t]ver 11; Ps 78:66 [u]Dt 28:27; 1Sa 6:5
5:8 [v]ver 11
5:9 [w]ver 6,11; Dt 2:15; 1Sa 7:13; Ps 78:66

[a] *18* Traditionally *judged* [b] *21 Ichabod* means *no glory.* [c] *6* Hebrew; Septuagint and Vulgate *tumors. And rats appeared in their land, and death and destruction were throughout the city* [d] *9* Or *with tumors in the groin* (see Septuagint)

ron, the people of Ekron cried out, "They have brought the ark of the god of Israel around to us to kill us and our people." 11So they called together all the rulers[x] of the Philistines and said, "Send the ark of the god of Israel away; let it go back to its own place, or it[a] will kill us and our people." For death had filled the city with panic; God's hand was very heavy upon it. 12Those who did not die were afflicted with tumors, and the outcry of the city went up to heaven.

The Ark Returned to Israel

6 When the ark of the LORD had been in Philistine territory seven months, 2the Philistines called for the priests and the diviners[y] and said, "What shall we do with the ark of the LORD? Tell us how we should send it back to its place."

3They answered, "If you return the ark of the god of Israel, do not send it away empty,[z] but by all means send a guilt offering[a] to him. Then you will be healed, and you will know why his hand[b] has not been lifted from you."

4The Philistines asked, "What guilt offering should we send to him?"

They replied, "Five gold tumors and five gold rats, according to the number[c] of the Philistine rulers, because the same plague has struck both you and your rulers. 5Make models of the tumors[d] and of the rats that are destroying the country, and pay honor[e] to Israel's god. Perhaps he will lift his hand from you and your gods and your land. 6Why do you harden[f] your hearts as the Egyptians and Pharaoh did? When he[b] treated them harshly, did they[g] not send the Israelites out so they could go on their way?

7"Now then, get a new cart[h] ready, with two cows that have calved and have never been yoked.[i] Hitch the cows to the cart, but take their calves away and pen them up. 8Take the ark of the LORD and put it on the cart, and in a chest beside it put the gold objects you are sending back to him as a guilt offering. Send it on its way, 9but keep watching it. If it goes up to its own territory, toward Beth Shemesh,[j] then the LORD has brought this great disaster on us. But if it does not, then we will know that it was not his hand that struck us and that it happened to us by chance."

10So they did this. They took two such cows and hitched them to the cart and penned up their calves. 11They placed the ark of the LORD on the cart and along with it the chest containing the gold rats and the models of the tumors. 12Then the cows went straight up toward Beth Shemesh, keeping on the road and lowing all the way; they did not turn to the right or to the left. The rulers of the Philistines followed them as far as the border of Beth Shemesh.

13Now the people of Beth Shemesh were harvesting their wheat in the valley, and when they looked up and saw the ark, they rejoiced at the sight. 14The cart came to the field of Joshua of Beth Shemesh, and there it stopped beside a large rock. The people chopped up the wood of the cart and sacrificed the cows as a burnt offering[k] to the LORD. 15The Levites[l] took down the ark of the LORD, together with the chest containing the gold objects, and placed them on the large rock. On that day the people of Beth Shemesh offered burnt offerings and made sacrifices to the LORD. 16The five rulers of the Philistines saw all this and then returned that same day to Ekron.

17These are the gold tumors the Philistines sent as a guilt offering to the LORD—one each[m] for Ashdod, Gaza, Ashkelon, Gath and Ekron. 18And the number of the gold rats was according to the number of Philistine towns belonging to the five rulers—the fortified towns with their country villages. The large rock, on which[c] they set the ark of the LORD, is a witness to this day in the field of Joshua of Beth Shemesh.

19But God struck down[n] some of the men of Beth Shemesh, putting seventy[d] of them to death because they had looked[o] into the ark of the LORD. The people mourned because of the heavy blow the LORD had dealt them, 20and the men of Beth Shemesh asked, "Who can stand[p] in the presence of the LORD, this holy[q] God? To whom will the ark go up from here?"

21Then they sent messengers to the people of Kiriath Jearim,[r] saying, "The Philistines have returned the ark of the LORD. Come down and take it up

7 to your place." 1So the men of Kiriath Jearim came and took up the ark of the LORD. They took it to Abinadab's[s] house on the hill and consecrated Eleazar his son to guard the ark of the LORD.

Samuel Subdues the Philistines at Mizpah

2It was a long time, twenty years in all, that the ark remained at Kiriath Jea-

5:11 [x] ver 6,8-9
6:2 [y] Ge 41:8; Ex 7:11; Isa 2:6
6:3 [z] Ex 23:15; Dt 16:16 [a] Lev 5:15 [b] ver 9
6:4 [c] ver 17-18; Jos 13:3; Jdg 3:3
6:5 [d] 1Sa 5:6-11 [e] Jos 7:19; Isa 42:12; Jn 9:24; Rev 14:7
6:6 [f] Ex 7:13; 8:15; 9:34; 14:17 [g] Ex 12:31,33
6:7 [h] 2Sa 6:3 [i] Nu 19:2
6:9 [j] ver 3; Jos 15:10; 21:16
6:14 [k] 2Sa 24:22; 1Ki 19:21
6:15 [l] Jos 3:3
6:17 [m] ver 4
6:19 [n] 2Sa 6:7 [o] Ex 19:21; Nu 4:5,15,20
6:20 [p] 2Sa 6:9; Mal 3:2; Rev 6:17 [q] Lev 11:45
6:21 [r] Jos 9:17; 15:9, 60; 1Ch 13:5-6
7:1 [s] 2Sa 6:3

[a] *11* Or *he* [b] *6* That is, God [c] *18* A few Hebrew manuscripts (see also Septuagint); most Hebrew manuscripts *villages as far as Greater Abel, where* [d] *19* A few Hebrew manuscripts; most Hebrew manuscripts and Septuagint *50,070*

rim, and all the people of Israel mourned and sought after the LORD. 3And Samuel said to the whole house of Israel, "If you are returning[t] to the LORD with all your hearts, then rid[u] yourselves of the foreign gods and the Ashtoreths[v] and commit[w] yourselves to the LORD and serve him only,[x] and he will deliver you out of the hand of the Philistines." 4So the Israelites put away their Baals and Ashtoreths, and served the LORD only.

5Then Samuel said, "Assemble all Israel at Mizpah[y] and I will intercede with the LORD for you." 6When they had assembled at Mizpah, they drew water and poured[z] it out before the LORD. On that day they fasted and there they confessed, "We have sinned against the LORD." And Samuel was leader[a][a] of Israel at Mizpah.

7When the Philistines heard that Israel had assembled at Mizpah, the rulers of the Philistines came up to attack them. And when the Israelites heard of it, they were afraid[b] because of the Philistines. 8They said to Samuel, "Do not stop crying[c] out to the LORD our God for us, that he may rescue us from the hand of the Philistines." 9Then Samuel[d] took a suckling lamb and offered it up as a whole burnt offering to the LORD. He cried out to the LORD on Israel's behalf, and the LORD answered him.[e]

1 →PG. 303

10While Samuel was sacrificing the burnt offering, the Philistines drew near to engage Israel in battle. But that day the LORD thundered[f] with loud thunder against the Philistines and threw them into such a panic[g] that they were routed before the Israelites. 11The men of Israel rushed out of Mizpah and pursued the Philistines, slaughtering them along the way to a point below Beth Car.

12Then Samuel took a stone[h] and set it up between Mizpah and Shen. He named it Ebenezer,[b] saying, "Thus far has the LORD helped us." 13So the Philistines were subdued[i] and did not invade Israelite territory again.

Throughout Samuel's lifetime, the hand of the LORD was against the Philistines. 14The towns from Ekron to Gath that the Philistines had captured from Israel were restored to her, and Israel delivered the neighboring territory from the power of the Philistines. And there was peace between Israel and the Amorites.

15Samuel[j] continued as judge over Israel all the days of his life. 16From year to year he went on a circuit from Bethel to Gilgal to Mizpah, judging Israel in all those places. 17But he always went back to Ramah,[k] where his home was, and there he also judged Israel. And he built an altar[l] there to the LORD.

Israel Asks for a King

8 When Samuel grew old, he appointed[m] his sons as judges for Israel. 2The name of his firstborn was Joel and the name of his second was Abijah, and they served at Beersheba.[n] 3But his sons did not walk in his ways. They turned aside after dishonest gain and accepted bribes[o] and perverted justice.

4So all the elders of Israel gathered together and came to Samuel at Ramah.[p] 5They said to him, "You are old, and your sons do not walk in your ways; now appoint a king[q] to lead[c] us, such as all the other nations have."

6But when they said, "Give us a king to lead us," this displeased[r] Samuel; so he prayed to the LORD. 7And the LORD told him: "Listen to all that the people are saying to you; it is not you they have rejected, but they have rejected me as their king.[s] 8As they have done from the day I brought them up out of Egypt until this day, forsaking me and serving other gods, so they are doing to you. 9Now listen to them; but warn them solemnly and let them know[t] what the king who will reign over them will do."

10Samuel told all the words of the LORD to the people who were asking him for a king. 11He said, "This is what the king who will reign over you will do: He will take[u] your sons and make them serve with his chariots and horses, and they will run in front of his chariots.[v] 12Some he will assign to be commanders[w] of thousands and commanders of fifties, and others to plow his ground and reap his harvest, and still others to make weapons of war and equipment for his chariots. 13He will take your daughters to be perfumers and cooks and bakers. 14He will take the best of your[x] fields and vineyards[y] and olive groves and give them to his attendants. 15He will take a tenth of your grain and of your vintage and give it to his officials and attendants. 16Your menservants and maidservants and the best of your cattle[d] and donkeys he will take for his own use. 17He will take a tenth of your flocks, and you yourselves will become his slaves. 18When that day comes, you will cry

7:3 [t]Dt 30:10; Isa 55:7; Hos 6:1 [u]Ge 35:2; Jos 24:14 [v]Jdg 2:12-13; 1Sa 31:10 [w]Joel 2:12 [x]Dt 6:13; Mt 4:10; Lk 4:8
7:5 [y]Jdg 20:1
7:6 [z]Ps 62:8; La 2:19 [a]Jdg 10:10; Ne 9:1; Ps 106:6
7:7 [b]1Sa 17:11
7:8 [c]1Sa 12:19,23; Isa 37:4; Jer 15:1
7:9 [d]Ps 99:6 [e]Jer 15:1
7:10 [f]1Sa 2:10; 2Sa 22:14-15 [g]Jos 10:10
7:12 [h]Ge 35:14; Jos 4:9
7:13 [i]Jdg 13:1,5; 1Sa 13:5
7:15 [j]ver 6; 1Sa 12:11
7:17 [k]1Sa 1:19; 8:4 [l]Jdg 21:4
8:1 [m]Dt 16:18-19
8:2 [n]Ge 22:19; 1Ki 19:3; Am 5:4-5
8:3 [o]Ex 23:8; Dt 16:19; Ps 15:5
8:4 [p]1Sa 7:17
8:5 [q]Dt 17:14-20
8:6 [r]1Sa 15:11
8:7 [s]Ex 16:8; 1Sa 10:19
8:9 [t]ver 11-18; 1Sa 10:25
8:11 [u]1Sa 10:25; 14:52 [v]Dt 17:16; 2Sa 15:1
8:12 [w]1Sa 22:7
8:14 [x]Eze 46:18 [y]1Ki 21:7,15

[a]*6* Traditionally *judge* [b]*12* *Ebenezer* means *stone of help.* [c]*5* Traditionally *judge;* also in verses 6 and 20 [d]*16* Septuagint; Hebrew *young men*

out for relief from the king you have chosen, and the LORD will not answer[z] you in that day."

19 But the people refused[a] to listen to Samuel. "No!" they said. "We want a king over us. 20 Then we will be like all the other nations,[b] with a king to lead us and to go out before us and fight our battles."

21 When Samuel heard all that the people said, he repeated[c] it before the LORD. 22 The LORD answered, "Listen[d] to them and give them a king."

Then Samuel said to the men of Israel, "Everyone go back to his town."

Samuel Anoints Saul

9 There was a Benjamite, a man of standing, whose name was Kish[e] son of Abiel, the son of Zeror, the son of Becorath, the son of Aphiah of Benjamin. 2 He had a son named Saul, an impressive young man without equal[f] among the Israelites—a head taller[g] than any of the others.

3 Now the donkeys belonging to Saul's father Kish were lost, and Kish said to his son Saul, "Take one of the servants with you and go and look for the donkeys." 4 So he passed through the hill[h] country of Ephraim and through the area around Shalisha,[i] but they did not find them. They went on into the district of Shaalim, but the donkeys were not there. Then he passed through the territory of Benjamin, but they did not find them.

5 When they reached the district of Zuph,[j] Saul said to the servant who was with him, "Come, let's go back, or my father will stop thinking about the donkeys and start worrying[k] about us."

6 But the servant replied, "Look, in this town there is a man of God;[l] he is highly respected, and everything[m] he says comes true. Let's go there now. Perhaps he will tell us what way to take."

7 Saul said to his servant, "If we go, what can we give the man? The food in our sacks is gone. We have no gift[n] to take to the man of God. What do we have?"

8 The servant answered him again. "Look," he said, "I have a quarter of a shekel[a] of silver. I will give it to the man of God so that he will tell us what way to take." 9 (Formerly in Israel, if a man went to inquire of God, he would say, "Come, let us go to the seer," because the prophet of today used to be called a seer.)[o]

10 "Good," Saul said to his servant. "Come, let's go." So they set out for the town where the man of God was.

11 As they were going up the hill to the town, they met some girls coming out to draw[p] water, and they asked them, "Is the seer here?"

12 "He is," they answered. "He's ahead of you. Hurry now; he has just come to our town today, for the people have a sacrifice[q] at the high place.[r] 13 As soon as you enter the town, you will find him before he goes up to the high place to eat. The people will not begin eating until he comes, because he must bless the sacrifice; afterward, those who are invited will eat. Go up now; you should find him about this time."

14 They went up to the town, and as they were entering it, there was Samuel, coming toward them on his way up to the high place.

15 Now the day before Saul came, the LORD had revealed this to Samuel: 16 "About this time tomorrow I will send you a man from the land of Benjamin. Anoint[s] him leader over my people Israel; he will deliver[t] my people from the hand of the Philistines. I have looked upon my people, for their cry has reached me."

17 When Samuel caught sight of Saul, the LORD said to him, "This[u] is the man I spoke to you about; he will govern my people."

18 Saul approached Samuel in the gateway and asked, "Would you please tell me where the seer's house is?"

19 "I am the seer," Samuel replied. "Go up ahead of me to the high place, for today you are to eat with me, and in the morning I will let you go and will tell you all that is in your heart. 20 As for the donkeys[v] you lost three days ago, do not worry about them; they have been found. And to whom is all the desire[w] of Israel turned, if not to you and all your father's family?"

21 Saul answered, "But am I not a Benjamite, from the smallest tribe[x] of Israel, and is not my clan the least of all the clans of the tribe of Benjamin?[y] Why do you say such a thing to me?"

22 Then Samuel brought Saul and his servant into the hall and seated them at the head of those who were invited—about thirty in number. 23 Samuel said to the cook, "Bring the piece of meat I gave you, the one I told you to lay aside."

24 So the cook took up the leg[z] with what was on it and set it in front of Saul. Samuel said, "Here is what has been kept for you. Eat, because it was

8:18 [z]Pr 1:28; Isa 1:15; Mic 3:4 **8:19** [a]Isa 66:4; Jer 44:16 **8:20** [b]ver 5 **8:21** [c]Jdg 11:11 **8:22** [d]ver 7 **9:1** [e]1Sa 14:51; 1Ch 8:33; 9:39 **9:2** [f]1Sa 10:24 [g]1Sa 10:23 **9:4** [h]Jos 24:33 [i]2Ki 4:42 **9:5** [j]1Sa 1:1 [k]1Sa 10:2 **9:6** [l]Dt 33:1; 1Ki 13:1 [m]1Sa 3:19 **9:7** [n]1Ki 14:3; 2Ki 5:5,15; 8:8 **9:9** [o]2Sa 24:11; 2Ki 17:13; 1Ch 9:22; 26:28; 29:29; Isa 30:10; Am 7:12

9:11 [p]Ge 24:11,13 **9:12** [q]Nu 28:11-15; 1Sa 7:17 [r]Ge 31:54; 1Sa 10:5; 1Ki 3:2 **9:16** [s]1Sa 10:1 [t]Ex 3:7-9 **9:17** [u]1Sa 16:12 **9:20** [v]ver 3 [w]1Sa 8:5; 12:13 **9:21** [x]1Sa 15:17 [y]Jdg 20:35,46 **9:24** [z]Lev 7:32-34; Nu 18:18

[a] *8* That is, about 1/10 ounce (about 3 grams)

set aside for you for this occasion, from
the time I said, 'I have invited guests.' "
And Saul dined with Samuel that day.
25After they came down from the
high place to the town, Samuel talked
with Saul on the roof[a] of his house.
26They rose about daybreak and Samuel called to Saul on the roof, "Get
ready, and I will send you on your
way." When Saul got ready, he and
Samuel went outside together. 27As
they were going down to the edge of
the town, Samuel said to Saul, "Tell the
servant to go on ahead of us"—and the
servant did so—"but you stay here
awhile, so that I may give you a message from God."

10 Then Samuel took a flask[b] of oil
and poured it on Saul's head and
kissed him, saying, "Has not the LORD
anointed[c] you leader over his inheritance?[a][d] 2When you leave me today,
you will meet two men near Rachel's
tomb,[e] at Zelzah on the border of
Benjamin. They will say to you, 'The
donkeys[f] you set out to look for have
been found. And now your father has
stopped thinking about them and is
worried[g] about you. He is asking,
"What shall I do about my son?" '
3"Then you will go on from there until you reach the great tree of Tabor.
Three men going up to God at Bethel[h]
will meet you there. One will be carrying three young goats, another three
loaves of bread, and another a skin of
wine. 4They will greet you and offer
you two loaves of bread, which you will
accept from them.
5"After that you will go to Gibeah of
God, where there is a Philistine outpost.[i] As you approach the town, you
will meet a procession of prophets
coming down from the high place[j]
with lyres, tambourines, flutes and
harps[k] being played before them, and
they will be prophesying.[l] 6The Spirit[m] of the LORD will come upon you
in power, and you will prophesy with
them; and you will be changed into a
different person. 7Once these signs are
fulfilled, do whatever[n] your hand
finds to do, for God is with[o] you.
8"Go down ahead of me to Gilgal.[p]
I will surely come down to you to sacrifice burnt offerings and fellowship offerings,[b] but you must wait seven days
until I come to you and tell you what
you are to do."

Saul Made King

9As Saul turned to leave Samuel,
God changed[q] Saul's heart, and all
these signs were fulfilled that day.
10When they arrived at Gibeah, a procession of prophets met him; the Spirit
of God came upon him in power, and
he joined in their prophesying.[r]
11When all those who had formerly
known him saw him prophesying with
the prophets, they asked each other,
"What is this[s] that has happened to
the son of Kish? Is Saul also among the
prophets?"[t]
12A man who lived there answered,
"And who is their father?" So it became
a saying: "Is Saul also among the
prophets?" 13After Saul stopped prophesying, he went to the high place.
14Now Saul's uncle[u] asked him and
his servant, "Where have you been?"
"Looking for the donkeys," he said.
"But when we saw they were not to be
found, we went to Samuel."
15Saul's uncle said, "Tell me what
Samuel said to you."
16Saul replied, "He assured us that
the donkeys[v] had been found." But he
did not tell his uncle what Samuel had
said about the kingship.
17Samuel summoned the people of
Israel to the LORD at Mizpah[w] 18and
said to them, "This is what the LORD,
the God of Israel, says: 'I brought Israel
up out of Egypt, and I delivered you
from the power of Egypt and all the
kingdoms that oppressed[x] you.' 19But
you have now rejected your God, who
saves you out of all your calamities and
distresses. And you have said, 'No, set
a king[y] over us.' So now present[z]
yourselves before the LORD by your
tribes and clans."
20When Samuel brought all the
tribes of Israel near, the tribe of Benjamin was chosen. 21Then he brought
forward the tribe of Benjamin, clan by
clan, and Matri's clan was chosen. Finally Saul son of Kish was chosen. But
when they looked for him, he was not
to be found. 22So they inquired[a] further of the LORD, "Has the man come
here yet?"
And the LORD said, "Yes, he has hidden himself among the baggage."
23They ran and brought him out,
and as he stood among the people he
was a head taller[b] than any of the others. 24Samuel said to all the people,
"Do you see the man the LORD has chosen?[c] There is no one like him among
all the people."
Then the people shouted, "Long
live[d] the king!"

9:25 [a]Dt 22:8; Ac 10:9
10:1 [b]1Sa 16:13; 2Ki 9:1,3,6 [c]Ps 2:12 [d]Dt 32:9; Ps 78:62,71
10:2 [e]Ge 35:20 [f]1Sa 9:4 [g]1Sa 9:5
10:3 [h]Ge 28:22; 35:7-8
10:5 [i]1Sa 13:3 [j]1Sa 9:12 [k]2Ki 3:15 [l]1Sa 19:20; 1Co 14:1
10:6 [m]ver 10; Nu 11:25; 1Sa 19:23-24
10:7 [n]Ecc 9:10 [o]Jos 1:5; Jdg 6:12; Heb 13:5
10:8 [p]1Sa 11:14-15
10:9 [q]ver 6
10:10 [r]ver 5-6; 1Sa 19:20
10:11 [s]Mt 13:54; Jn 7:15 [t]1Sa 19:24
10:14 [u]1Sa 14:50
10:16 [v]1Sa 9:20
10:17 [w]Jdg 20:1; 1Sa 7:5
10:18 [x]Jdg 6:8-9
10:19 [y]1Sa 8:5-7; 12:12 [z]Jos 7:14; 24:1
10:22 [a]1Sa 23:2,4, 9-11
10:23 [b]1Sa 9:2
10:24 [c]Dt 17:15; 2Sa 21:6 [d]1Ki 1:25,34, 39

a *1* Hebrew; Septuagint and Vulgate *over his people Israel? You will reign over the LORD's people and save them from the power of their enemies round about. And this will be a sign to you that the LORD has anointed you leader over his inheritance:* **b** *8* Traditionally *peace offerings*

25 Samuel explained to the people
the regulations[e] of the kingship. He
wrote them down on a scroll and deposited it before the LORD. Then Samuel dismissed the people, each to his
own home.
26 Saul also went to his home in Gibeah,[f] accompanied by valiant men
whose hearts God had touched. 27 But
some troublemakers[g] said, "How can
this fellow save us?" They despised him
and brought him no gifts.[h] But Saul
kept silent.

Saul Rescues the City of Jabesh

11 Nahash[i] the Ammonite went up
and besieged Jabesh Gilead.[j] And
all the men of Jabesh said to him,
"Make a treaty[k] with us, and we will
be subject to you."
2 But Nahash the Ammonite replied,
"I will make a treaty with you only on
the condition that I gouge[l] out the
right eye of every one of you and so
bring disgrace[m] on all Israel."
3 The elders of Jabesh said to him,
"Give us seven days so we can send
messengers throughout Israel; if no
one comes to rescue us, we will surrender to you."
4 When the messengers came to Gibeah[n] of Saul and reported these terms
to the people, they all wept[o] aloud.
5 Just then Saul was returning from the
fields, behind his oxen, and he asked,
"What is wrong with the people? Why
are they weeping?" Then they repeated
to him what the men of Jabesh had
said.
6 When Saul heard their words, the
Spirit[p] of God came upon him in power, and he burned with anger. 7 He took
a pair of oxen, cut them into pieces,
and sent the pieces by messengers
throughout Israel,[q] proclaiming, "This
is what will be done to the oxen of
anyone[r] who does not follow Saul
and Samuel." Then the terror of the
LORD fell on the people, and they
turned out as one man. 8 When Saul
mustered[s] them at Bezek,[t] the men
of Israel numbered three hundred
thousand and the men of Judah thirty
thousand.
9 They told the messengers who had
come, "Say to the men of Jabesh Gilead, 'By the time the sun is hot tomorrow, you will be delivered.' " When the
messengers went and reported this to
the men of Jabesh, they were elated.
10 They said to the Ammonites, "Tomorrow we will surrender[u] to you,
and you can do to us whatever seems
good to you."
11 The next day Saul separated his
men into three divisions;[v] during the
last watch of the night they broke into
the camp of the Ammonites and
slaughtered them until the heat of the
day. Those who survived were scattered, so that no two of them were left
together.

Saul Confirmed as King

12 The people then said to Samuel,
"Who[w] was it that asked, 'Shall Saul
reign over us?' Bring these men to us
and we will put them to death."
13 But Saul said, "No one shall be put
to death today,[x] for this day the LORD
has rescued[y] Israel."
14 Then Samuel said to the people,
"Come, let us go to Gilgal[z] and there
reaffirm the kingship.[a]" 15 So all the
people went to Gilgal[b] and confirmed
Saul as king in the presence of the
LORD. There they sacrificed fellowship
offerings[a] before the LORD, and Saul
and all the Israelites held a great celebration.

Samuel's Farewell Speech

12 Samuel said to all Israel, "I have listened[c] to everything you said to
me and have set a king[d] over you.
2 Now you have a king as your leader.[e]
As for me, I am old and gray, and my
sons are here with you. I have been
your leader from my youth until this
day. 3 Here I stand. Testify against me
in the presence of the LORD and his
anointed.[f] Whose ox have I taken?
Whose donkey[g] have I taken? Whom
have I cheated? Whom have I oppressed? From whose hand have I accepted a bribe[h] to make me shut my
eyes? If I have done[i] any of these, I
will make it right."
4 "You have not cheated or oppressed us," they replied. "You have
not taken anything from anyone's
hand."
5 Samuel said to them, "The LORD is
witness against you, and also his
anointed is witness this day, that you
have not found anything[j] in my
hand.[k]"
"He is witness," they said.
6 Then Samuel said to the people, "It
is the LORD who appointed Moses and
Aaron and brought[l] your forefathers
up out of Egypt. 7 Now then, stand here,
because I am going to confront[m] you
with evidence before the LORD as to all
the righteous acts performed by the
LORD for you and your fathers.
8 "After Jacob entered Egypt, they
cried[n] to the LORD for help, and the

10:25 [e] Dt 17:14-20; 1Sa 8:11-18
10:26 [f] 1Sa 11:4
10:27 [g] Dt 13:13 [h] 1Ki 10:25; 2Ch 17:5
11:1 [i] 1Sa 12:12 [j] Jdg 21:8 [k] 1Ki 20:34; Eze 17:13
11:2 [l] Nu 16:14 [m] 1Sa 17:26
11:4 [n] 1Sa 10:5,26; 15:34 [o] Jdg 2:4; 1Sa 30:4
11:6 [p] Jdg 3:10; 6:34; 13:25; 14:6; 1Sa 10:10; 16:13
11:7 [q] Jdg 19:29 [r] Jdg 21:5
11:8 [s] Jdg 20:2 [t] Jdg 1:4
11:10 [u] ver 3
11:11 [v] Jdg 7:16
11:12 [w] 1Sa 10:27; Lk 19:27
11:13 [x] 2Sa 19:22 [y] Ex 14:13; 1Sa 19:5
11:14 [z] 1Sa 10:8 [a] 1Sa 10:25
11:15 [b] 1Sa 10:8,17
12:1 [c] 1Sa 8:7 [d] 1Sa 10:24; 11:15
12:2 [e] 1Sa 8:5
12:3 [f] 1Sa 10:1; 24:6; 2Sa 1:14 [g] Nu 16:15 [h] Dt 16:19 [i] Ac 20:33
12:5 [j] Ac 23:9; 24:20 [k] Ex 22:4
12:6 [l] Ex 6:26; Mic 6:4
12:7 [m] Isa 1:18; Mic 6:1-5
12:8 [n] Ex 2:23

a 15 Traditionally *peace offerings*

SAMUEL

A Man Uncondemned

Samuel had been Israel's leader for decades. He served as a prophet (1 Samuel 3:19), priest, political leader and judge (7:6–15). Each of these positions offered opportunities to help shape society. But these powerful positions also offered many temptations. Power can be used to help others to a better life, but it can also be manipulated to serve the one wielding it. Because of the powerful influence inherent in each of Samuel's offices, Samuel had choices to make.

Leading God's Way

The Bible tells us God spoke to Samuel, and Samuel, in turn, spoke to God's people. Whether the message was a blessing or a judgment, Samuel delivered the goods. True prophets like Samuel often made their listeners angry because they faithfully recited what God thought about sinful people. Because of Samuel's truthful words, it is reasonable to believe that Samuel had enemies in Israel—evil people who didn't like what God had to say.

Fulfilling the office of a priest was a bit more safe. Folks didn't get mad at priests for doing their duty. But being a priest presented a different power problem. Priests were often tempted to use their office for personal gain. In fact, during much of Israel's history, the priesthood became synonymous with corruption (see 1 Samuel 1—4). Samuel, by reason of his role as a priest in Israel, was subject to those powerful temptations toward personal gain.

As Israel's political leader, Samuel was responsible for many unpopular decisions. He fought against Israel's request for a king. He proclaimed what God wanted for the people, even when the entire population believed they knew what was right. As Israel's judge, Samuel traveled throughout the land for many years, making judgments among the citizens. In most disputes, a judge is deemed wise and noble by the party who wins the decision. But in doing so, he judges against another person who believes the judge must be a moron. Or corrupt. Or both! With honest leaders or honest judges the same axiom applies: Corrupt leaders often make enemies of good people; honest leaders make enemies of evil people. And the latter can be far more dangerous.

In all of his offices and positions Samuel had proved to be an honest leader, favored by God. Good people supported him because he was just. He had confronted individuals as well as the nation. He had pointed out sin and stupidity, and he had called for restitution and repentance.

Yes, after all those years of leading Israel, Samuel probably had enemies—not because Samuel was evil, but because he was good. Doubtless there were those in Israel who wanted to see Samuel discredited in order to justify themselves. They would jump at any opportunity to see this righteous old man go up in smoke. And now here was their chance.

Judging the Judge

Samuel stood before the people. He admitted he was getting old. And he invited them to speak up if they had any grievance against him: "Here I stand. Testify against me in the presence of the LORD and his anointed. Whose ox have I taken? Whose donkey have I taken? Whom have I cheated? Whom have I oppressed? From whose hand have I accepted a bribe to make me shut my eyes? If I have done any of these, I will make it right" (12:3).

How do you suppose Samuel delivered those words? Was it a challenge to his enemies? It may well have been. But considering Samuel's character, a challenging tone hardly seems appropriate for this moment in his life. He was an old man, asking his people to help him settle accounts with them. His words were simple and sincere. If, in the performance of his duties, he had offended anyone, Samuel asked the people of Israel to make him aware of it so he could repay, restore and set the problem right.

Note how the people responded. " 'You have not cheated or oppressed us,' they replied. 'You have not taken anything from anyone's hand' " (12:4). After all the years of public service, no one could condemn or challenge Samuel. What enormous satisfaction must have welled up in Samuel during those moments. No one stood to condemn, challenge or even question him. Samuel gave them another shot at it. "Samuel said to them, 'The LORD is witness against you, and also his anointed is witness this day, that you have not found anything in my hand' " (12:5). And the people agreed with Samuel's words.

Following Samuel's Lead

Who among us would issue such an invitation? Not many! But most people don't wait for an invitation to express their opinions. We can't control how often others talk about us. But when people offer their unsolicited opinions, what do they say? When we do have occasion to extend the invitation ourselves by asking for feedback, what do we hear?

People will talk. But, like Samuel, we can make choices that honor God so that when anyone opens the door of scrutiny on our lives, no one can condemn or challenge us. Then we can hear the same sounds that Samuel heard on the day he issued his challenge—only the peaceful sounds of the birds and bugs under the silent skies of the uncondemned.

—Dr. Sid Buzzell

LORD sent[o] Moses and Aaron, who
brought your forefathers out of Egypt
and settled them in this place.
9"But they forgot[p] the LORD their
God; so he sold them into the hand of
Sisera,[q] the commander of the army
of Hazor, and into the hands of the Philistines[r] and the king of Moab,[s] who
fought against them. 10They cried out
to the LORD and said, 'We have sinned;
we have forsaken[t] the LORD and
served the Baals and the Ashtoreths.[u]
But now deliver us from the hands of
our enemies, and we will serve you.'
11Then the LORD sent Jerub-Baal,[a][v]
Barak,[b][w] Jephthah[x] and Samuel,[c]
and he delivered you from the hands of
your enemies on every side, so that you
lived securely.
12"But when you saw that Nahash[y]
king[z] of the Ammonites was moving
against you, you said to me, 'No, we
want a king to rule[a] over us'—even
though the LORD your God was your
king. 13Now here is the king[b] you have
chosen, the one you asked[c] for; see,
the LORD has set a king over you. 14If
you fear[d] the LORD and serve and obey
him and do not rebel against his commands, and if both you and the king
who reigns over you follow the LORD
your God—good! 15But if you do not
obey the LORD, and if you rebel
against[e] his commands, his hand will
be against you, as it was against your
fathers.
16"Now then, stand still and see[f]
this great thing the LORD is about to do
before your eyes! 17Is it not wheat harvest[g] now? I will call[h] upon the LORD
to send thunder and rain.[i] And you
will realize what an evil[j] thing you did
in the eyes of the LORD when you asked
for a king."
18Then Samuel called upon the
LORD, and that same day the LORD sent
thunder and rain. So all the people
stood in awe[k] of the LORD and of Samuel.
19The people all said to Samuel,
"Pray[l] to the LORD your God for your
servants so that we will not die, for we
have added to all our other sins the evil
of asking for a king."
20"Do not be afraid," Samuel replied.
"You have done all this evil; yet do not
turn away from the LORD, but serve the
LORD with all your heart. 21Do not turn
away after useless[m] idols.[n] They can
do you no good, nor can they rescue
you, because they are useless. 22For the
sake[o] of his great name[p] the LORD
will not reject[q] his people, because
the LORD was pleased to make[r] you
his own. 23As for me, far be it from me
that I should sin against the LORD by
failing to pray[s] for you. And I will
teach[t] you the way that is good and
right. 24But be sure to fear[u] the LORD
and serve him faithfully with all your
heart; consider[v] what great[w] things
he has done for you. 25Yet if you persist[x] in doing evil, both you and your
king will be swept[y] away."

1 →PG. 357

Samuel Rebukes Saul

13 Saul was ⌊thirty⌋[d] years old when
he became king, and he reigned
over Israel ⌊forty-⌋[e] two years.
2Saul[f] chose three thousand men
from Israel; two thousand were with
him at Micmash and in the hill country
of Bethel, and a thousand were with
Jonathan at Gibeah[z] in Benjamin. The
rest of the men he sent back to their
homes.
3Jonathan attacked the Philistine
outpost[a] at Geba, and the Philistines
heard about it. Then Saul had the
trumpet blown throughout the land
and said, "Let the Hebrews hear!" 4So
all Israel heard the news: "Saul has attacked the Philistine outpost, and now
Israel has become a stench[b] to the
Philistines." And the people were summoned to join Saul at Gilgal.

[a] *11* Also called *Gideon* [b] *11* Some Septuagint manuscripts and Syriac; Hebrew *Bedan* [c] *11* Hebrew; some Septuagint manuscripts and Syriac *Samson* [d] *1* A few late manuscripts of the Septuagint; Hebrew does not have *thirty.* [e] *1* See the round number in Acts 13:21; Hebrew does not have *forty-*. [f] *1,2* Or *and when he had reigned over Israel two years, 2he*

12:8 [o]Ex 3:10; 4:16
12:9 [p]Jdg 3:7 [q]Jdg 4:2 [r]Jdg 10:7; 13:1 [s]Jdg 3:12
12:10 [t]Jdg 10:10,15 [u]Jdg 2:13
12:11 [v]Jdg 6:14,32 [w]Jdg 4:6 [x]Jdg 11:1
12:12 [y]1Sa 11:1 [z]1Sa 8:5 [a]Jdg 8:23; 1Sa 8:6,19
12:13 [b]1Sa 8:5; Hos 13:11 [c]1Sa 10:24
12:14 [d]Jos 24:14
12:15 [e]ver 9; Jos 24:20; Isa 1:20
12:16 [f]Ex 14:13
12:17 [g]1Sa 7:9-10 [h]Jas 5:18 [i]Pr 26:1 [j]1Sa 8:6-7
12:18 [k]Ex 14:31
12:19 [l]ver 23; Ex 9:28; Jas 5:18; 1Jn 5:16
12:21 [m]Isa 41:24,29; Jer 16:19; Hab 2:18 [n]Dt 11:16
12:22 [o]Ps 106:8 [p]Jos 7:9 [q]1Ki 6:13 [r]Dt 7:7; 1Pe 2:9
12:23 [s]Ro 1:9-10; Col 1:9; 2Ti 1:3 [t]1Ki 8:36; Ps 34:11; Pr 4:11
12:24 [u]Ecc 12:13 [v]Isa 5:12 [w]Dt 10:21
12:25 [x]1Sa 31:1-5 [y]Jos 24:20
13:2 [z]1Sa 10:26
13:3 [a]1Sa 10:5
13:4 [b]Ge 34:30

12:1-5

PROMISE 3

MASS ACCOUNTABILITY

What a legacy! Samuel's challenge to Israel after being their leader for many years was this: "If anyone knows of any corruption in my life, let that person step forward and I will make it right." Can you imagine an American president making this statement, or a corporate CEO, or even the head of a family?

Most leaders would hesitate to be this vulnerable in front of such a crowd of people. Not Samuel. He was a man of integrity who led the nation with the same integrity. His character was evident to the people he led. In essence they replied, "As the Lord is our witness, you have done nothing corrupt."

Every day we live on this earth we write another page in the book of our legacy. At the end of our days, whether we are as bold as Samuel or not, people will remember our deeds. Begin today living with your final legacy in view.

For the next Promise 3 reading go to page 309.

5 The Philistines assembled to fight Israel, with three thousand[a] chariots, six thousand charioteers, and soldiers as numerous as the sand[c] on the seashore. They went up and camped at Micmash, east of Beth Aven. 6 When the men of Israel saw that their situation was critical and that their army was hard pressed, they hid in caves and thickets, among the rocks, and in pits and cisterns.[d] 7 Some Hebrews even crossed the Jordan to the land of Gad[e] and Gilead.

Saul remained at Gilgal, and all the troops with him were quaking with fear. 8 He waited seven[f] days, the time set by Samuel; but Samuel did not come to Gilgal, and Saul's men began to scatter. 9 So he said, "Bring me the burnt offering and the fellowship offerings.[b]" And Saul offered[g] up the burnt offering. 10 Just as he finished making the offering, Samuel[h] arrived, and Saul went out to greet him.

11 "What have you done?" asked Samuel.

Saul replied, "When I saw that the men were scattering, and that you did not come at the set time, and that the Philistines were assembling at Micmash,[i] 12 I thought, 'Now the Philistines will come down against me at Gilgal, and I have not sought the LORD's favor.[j]' So I felt compelled to offer the burnt offering."

13 "You acted foolishly,[k]" Samuel said. "You have not kept[l] the command the LORD your God gave you; if you had, he would have established your kingdom over Israel for all time. 14 But now your kingdom[m] will not endure; the LORD has sought out a man after his own heart[n] and appointed[o] him leader of his people, because you have not kept the LORD's command."

15 Then Samuel left Gilgal[c] and went up to Gibeah[p] in Benjamin, and Saul counted the men who were with him. They numbered about six hundred.

Israel Without Weapons

16 Saul and his son Jonathan and the men with them were staying in Gibeah[d] in Benjamin, while the Philistines camped at Micmash. 17 Raiding[q] parties went out from the Philistine camp in three detachments. One turned toward Ophrah[r] in the vicinity of Shual, 18 another toward Beth Horon,[s] and the third toward the borderland overlooking the Valley of Zeboim[t] facing the desert.

19 Not a blacksmith[u] could be found in the whole land of Israel, because the Philistines had said, "Otherwise the Hebrews will make swords or spears!" 20 So all Israel went down to the Philistines to have their plowshares, mattocks, axes and sickles[e] sharpened. 21 The price was two thirds of a shekel[f] for sharpening plowshares and mattocks, and a third of a shekel[g] for sharpening forks and axes and for repointing goads.

22 So on the day of the battle not a soldier with Saul and Jonathan[v] had a sword or spear[w] in his hand; only Saul and his son Jonathan had them.

Jonathan Attacks the Philistines

23 Now a detachment of Philistines had gone out to the pass[x] at Micmash.

14 1 One day Jonathan son of Saul said to the young man bearing his armor, "Come, let's go over to the Philistine outpost on the other side." But he did not tell his father.

2 Saul was staying on the outskirts of Gibeah[y] under a pomegranate tree in Migron.[z] With him were about six hundred men, 3 among whom was Ahijah, who was wearing an ephod. He was a son of Ichabod's[a] brother Ahitub[b] son of Phinehas, the son of Eli,[c] the LORD's priest in Shiloh. No one was aware that Jonathan had left.

4 On each side of the pass[d] that Jonathan intended to cross to reach the Philistine outpost was a cliff; one was called Bozez, and the other Seneh. 5 One cliff stood to the north toward Micmash, the other to the south toward Geba.

6 Jonathan said to his young armor-bearer, "Come, let's go over to the outpost of those uncircumcised[e] fellows. Perhaps the LORD will act in our behalf. Nothing[f] can hinder the LORD from saving, whether by many[g] or by few.[h]"

7 "Do all that you have in mind," his armor-bearer said. "Go ahead; I am with you heart and soul."

8 Jonathan said, "Come, then; we will cross over toward the men and let them see us. 9 If they say to us, 'Wait there until we come to you,' we will stay where we are and not go up to them. 10 But if they say, 'Come up to us,' we will climb up, because that will

13:5 *c* Jos 11:4
13:6 *d* Jdg 6:2
13:7 *e* Nu 32:33
13:8 *f* 1Sa 10:8
13:9 *g* 2Sa 24:25; 1Ki 3:4
13:10 *h* 1Sa 15:13
13:11 *i* ver 2,5,16,23
13:12 *j* Jer 26:19
13:13 *k* 2Ch 16:9 *l* 1Sa 15:23,24
13:14 *m* 1Sa 15:28 *n* Ac 7:46; 13:22 *o* 2Sa 6:21
13:15 *p* 1Sa 14:2
13:17 *q* 1Sa 14:15 *r* Jos 18:23
13:18 *s* Jos 18:13-14 *t* Ne 11:34
13:19 *u* 2Ki 24:14; Jer 24:1
13:22 *v* 1Ch 9:39 *w* Jdg 5:8
13:23 *x* 1Sa 14:4
14:2 *y* 1Sa 13:15 *z* Isa 10:28
14:3 *a* 1Sa 4:21 *b* 1Sa 22:11,20 *c* 1Sa 2:28
14:4 *d* 1Sa 13:23
14:6 *e* 1Sa 17:26,36; Jer 9:26 *f* Heb 11:34 *g* Jdg 7:4 *h* 1Sa 17:46-47

a *5* Some Septuagint manuscripts and Syriac; Hebrew *thirty thousand* b *9* Traditionally *peace offerings* c *15* Hebrew; Septuagint *Gilgal and went his way; the rest of the people went after Saul to meet the army, and they went out of Gilgal* d *16* Two Hebrew manuscripts; most Hebrew manuscripts *Geba,* a variant of *Gibeah* e *20* Septuagint; Hebrew *plowshares* f *21* Hebrew *pim;* that is, about 1/4 ounce (about 8 grams) g *21* That is, about 1/8 ounce (about 4 grams)

be our sign[i] that the LORD has given them into our hands."

11So both of them showed themselves to the Philistine outpost. "Look!" said the Philistines. "The Hebrews are crawling out of the holes they were hiding[j] in." 12The men of the outpost shouted to Jonathan and his armor-bearer, "Come up to us and we'll teach you a lesson.[k]"

So Jonathan said to his armor-bearer, "Climb up after me; the LORD has given them into the hand[l] of Israel."

13Jonathan climbed up, using his hands and feet, with his armor-bearer right behind him. The Philistines fell before Jonathan, and his armor-bearer followed and killed behind him. 14In that first attack Jonathan and his armor-bearer killed some twenty men in an area of about half an acre.[a]

Israel Routs the Philistines

15Then panic[m] struck the whole army—those in the camp and field, and those in the outposts and raiding[n] parties—and the ground shook. It was a panic sent by God.[b]

16Saul's lookouts[o] at Gibeah in Benjamin saw the army melting away in all directions. 17Then Saul said to the men who were with him, "Muster the forces and see who has left us." When they did, it was Jonathan and his armor-bearer who were not there.

18Saul said to Ahijah, "Bring[p] the ark of God." (At that time it was with the Israelites.)[c] 19While Saul was talking to the priest, the tumult in the Philistine camp increased more and more. So Saul said to the priest,[q] "Withdraw your hand."

20Then Saul and all his men assembled and went to the battle. They found the Philistines in total confusion, striking[r] each other with their swords. 21Those Hebrews who had previously been with the Philistines and had gone up with them to their camp went[s] over to the Israelites who were with Saul and Jonathan. 22When all the Israelites who had hidden[t] in the hill country of Ephraim heard that the Philistines were on the run, they joined the battle in hot pursuit. 23So the LORD rescued[u] Israel that day, and the battle moved on beyond Beth Aven.[v]

Jonathan Eats Honey

24Now the men of Israel were in distress that day, because Saul had bound the people under an oath,[w] saying, "Cursed be any man who eats food before evening comes, before I have avenged myself on my enemies!" So none of the troops tasted food.

25The entire army[d] entered the woods, and there was honey on the ground. 26When they went into the woods, they saw the honey oozing out, yet no one put his hand to his mouth, because they feared the oath. 27But Jonathan had not heard that his father had bound the people with the oath, so he reached out the end of the staff that was in his hand and dipped it into the honeycomb.[x] He raised his hand to his mouth, and his eyes brightened.[e] 28Then one of the soldiers told him, "Your father bound the army under a strict oath, saying, 'Cursed be any man who eats food today!' That is why the men are faint."

29Jonathan said, "My father has made trouble[y] for the country. See how my eyes brightened[f] when I tasted a little of this honey. 30How much better it would have been if the men had eaten today some of the plunder they took from their enemies. Would not the slaughter of the Philistines have been even greater?"

31That day, after the Israelites had struck down the Philistines from Micmash to Aijalon,[z] they were exhausted. 32They pounced on the plunder[a] and, taking sheep, cattle and calves, they butchered them on the ground and ate them, together with the blood.[b] 33Then someone said to Saul, "Look, the men are sinning against the LORD by eating meat that has blood in it."

"You have broken faith," he said. "Roll a large stone over here at once." 34Then he said, "Go out among the men and tell them, 'Each of you bring me your cattle and sheep, and slaughter them here and eat them. Do not sin against the LORD by eating meat with blood still in it.' "

So everyone brought his ox that night and slaughtered it there. 35Then Saul built an altar[c] to the LORD; it was the first time he had done this.

36Saul said, "Let us go down after the Philistines by night and plunder them till dawn, and let us not leave one of them alive."

"Do whatever seems best to you," they replied.

But the priest said, "Let us inquire of God here."

14:10 [i]Ge 24:14; Jdg 6:36-37
14:11 [j]1Sa 13:6
14:12 [k]1Sa 17:43-44 [l]2Sa 5:24
14:15 [m]Ge 35:5; 2Ki 7:5-7 [n]1Sa 13:17
14:16 [o]2Sa 18:24
14:18 [p]1Sa 30:7
14:19 [q]Nu 27:21
14:20 [r]Jdg 7:22; 2Ch 20:23
14:21 [s]1Sa 29:4
14:22 [t]1Sa 13:6
14:23 [u]Ex 14:30; Ps 44:6-7 [v]1Sa 13:5
14:24 [w]Jos 6:26
14:27 [x]ver 43; 1Sa 30:12
14:29 [y]Jos 7:25; 1Ki 18:18
14:31 [z]Jos 10:12
14:32 [a]1Sa 15:19 [b]Ge 9:4; Lev 3:17; 7:26; 17:10-14; 19:26; Dt 12:16,23-24
14:35 [c]1Sa 7:17

[a] *14* Hebrew *half a yoke*; a "yoke" was the land plowed by a yoke of oxen in one day. [b] *15* Or *a terrible panic* [c] *18* Hebrew; Septuagint *"Bring the ephod." (At that time he wore the ephod before the Israelites.)* [d] *25* Or *Now all the people of the land* [e] *27* Or *his strength was renewed* [f] *29* Or *my strength was renewed*

[37]So Saul asked God, "Shall I go down after the Philistines? Will you give them into Israel's hand?" But God did not answer[d] him that day.

[38]Saul therefore said, "Come here, all you who are leaders of the army, and let us find out what sin has been committed[e] today. [39]As surely as the LORD who rescues Israel lives,[f] even if it lies with my son Jonathan, he must die." But not one of the men said a word.

[40]Saul then said to all the Israelites, "You stand over there; I and Jonathan my son will stand over here."

"Do what seems best to you," the men replied.

[41]Then Saul prayed to the LORD, the God of Israel, "Give[g] me the right[h] answer."[a] And Jonathan and Saul were taken by lot, and the men were cleared. [42]Saul said, "Cast the lot between me and Jonathan my son." And Jonathan was taken.

[43]Then Saul said to Jonathan, "Tell me what you have done."[i]

So Jonathan told him, "I merely tasted a little honey[j] with the end of my staff. And now must I die?"

[44]Saul said, "May God deal with me, be it ever so severely,[k] if you do not die, Jonathan.[l]"

[45]But the men said to Saul, "Should Jonathan die—he who has brought about this great deliverance in Israel? Never! As surely as the LORD lives, not a hair[m] of his head will fall to the ground, for he did this today with God's help." So the men rescued[n] Jonathan, and he was not put to death.

[46]Then Saul stopped pursuing the Philistines, and they withdrew to their own land.

[47]After Saul had assumed rule over Israel, he fought against their enemies on every side: Moab, the Ammonites,[o] Edom, the kings[b] of Zobah,[p] and the Philistines. Wherever he turned, he inflicted punishment on them.[c] [48]He fought valiantly and defeated the Amalekites,[q] delivering Israel from the hands of those who had plundered them.

Saul's Family

[49]Saul's sons were Jonathan, Ishvi and Malki-Shua.[r] The name of his older daughter was Merab, and that of the younger was Michal.[s] [50]His wife's name was Ahinoam daughter of Ahimaaz. The name of the commander of Saul's army was Abner son of Ner, and Ner was Saul's uncle. [51]Saul's father Kish[t] and Abner's father Ner were sons of Abiel.

[52]All the days of Saul there was bitter war with the Philistines, and whenever Saul saw a mighty or brave man, he took[u] him into his service.

The LORD Rejects Saul as King

15 Samuel said to Saul, "I am the one the LORD sent to anoint[v] you king over his people Israel; so listen now to the message from the LORD. [2]This is what the LORD Almighty says: 'I will punish the Amalekites[w] for what they did to Israel when they waylaid them as they came up from Egypt. [3]Now go, attack the Amalekites and totally[x] destroy[d] everything that belongs to them. Do not spare them; put to death men and women, children and infants, cattle and sheep, camels and donkeys.' "

[4]So Saul summoned the men and mustered them at Telaim—two hundred thousand foot soldiers and ten thousand men from Judah. [5]Saul went to the city of Amalek and set an ambush in the ravine. [6]Then he said to the Kenites,[y] "Go away, leave the Amalekites so that I do not destroy you along with them; for you showed kindness to all the Israelites when they came up out of Egypt." So the Kenites moved away from the Amalekites.

[7]Then Saul attacked the Amalekites[z] all the way from Havilah to Shur,[a] to the east of Egypt. [8]He took Agag king of the Amalekites alive,[b] and all his people he totally destroyed with the sword. [9]But Saul and the army spared[c] Agag and the best of the sheep and cattle, the fat calves[e] and lambs—everything that was good. These they were unwilling to destroy completely, but everything that was despised and weak they totally destroyed.

[10]Then the word of the LORD came to Samuel: [11]"I am grieved[d] that I have made Saul king, because he has turned[e] away from me and has not carried out my instructions."[f] Samuel was troubled,[g] and he cried out to the LORD all that night.

[12]Early in the morning Samuel got up and went to meet Saul, but he was told, "Saul has gone to Carmel.[h] There

14:37 *d* 1Sa 10:22; 28:6,15
14:38 *e* Jos 7:11; 1Sa 10:19
14:39 *f* 2Sa 12:5
14:41 *g* Ac 1:24 *h* Pr 16:33
14:43 *i* Jos 7:19 *j* ver 27
14:44 *k* Ru 1:17 *l* ver 39
14:45 *m* 1Ki 1:52; Lk 21:18; Ac 27:34 *n* 2Sa 14:11
14:47 *o* 1Sa 11:1-13 *p* ver 52; 2Sa 10:6
14:48 *q* 1Sa 15:2,7
14:49 *r* 1Sa 31:2; 1Ch 8:33 *s* 1Sa 18:17-20
14:51 *t* 1Sa 9:1
14:52 *u* 1Sa 8:11
15:1 *v* 1Sa 9:16
15:2 *w* Ex 17:8-14; Nu 24:20; Dt 25:17-19
15:3 *x* Nu 24:20; Dt 20:16-18; Jos 6:17; 1Sa 22:19
15:6 *y* Ex 18:10,19; Nu 10:29-32; 24:22; Jdg 1:16; 4:1
15:7 *z* 1Sa 14:48 *a* Ge 16:7; 25:17-18; Ex 15:22
15:8 *b* 1Sa 30:1
15:9 *c* ver 3,15
15:11 *d* Ge 6:6; 2Sa 24:16 *e* Jos 22:16 *f* 1Sa 13:13; 1Ki 9:6-7 *g* ver 35
15:12 *h* Jos 15:55

a *41* Hebrew; Septuagint *"Why have you not answered your servant today? If the fault is in me or my son Jonathan, respond with Urim, but if the men of Israel are at fault, respond with Thummim."* **b** *47* Masoretic Text; Dead Sea Scrolls and Septuagint *king* **c** *47* Hebrew; Septuagint *he was victorious* **d** *3* The Hebrew term refers to the irrevocable giving over of things or persons to the LORD, often by totally destroying them; also in verses 8, 9, 15, 18, 20 and 21. **e** *9* Or *the grown bulls*; the meaning of the Hebrew for this phrase is uncertain.

SAUL

The Peril of a Proud Man

Aesop tells the story of a proud tortoise who wanted to be more than he was. He wanted to fly like the great eagles. One day, the tortoise came up with an idea and convinced two eagles to help him. Each bird took one end of a piece of rope. The tortoise clamped his vice-like jaws in the center, and the birds took flight.

The tortoise had his wish. He was flying! He was so proud of his achievement! Then someone on the ground looked up in admiration and remarked, "Look at the tortoise. He is flying with the eagles. I wonder who thought of that?"

Unable to resist the chance to take credit for his brilliant idea, the tortoise opened his mouth to shout, "I did" and promptly fell to earth. The moral of Aesop's story? Pride can lead to a great fall.

King Saul and the tortoise both had a problem with pride. It's ironic but true that men who appear to be the most humble on the outside are often the most vulnerable to pride. Rather than reflecting true humility, they're often reflecting insecurity and a low self-image which often form the basis of *false* humility. King Saul illustrates this more than any other Old Testament personality. Saul had a great start—and a great opportunity—but a terrible finish that eventually ended in suicide.

Looks Can Be Deceiving

Though there was not a more "impressive young man" among the men of Israel, Saul became weak through jealousy (1 Samuel 9:2). Though he was "a head taller than any of the others," he eventually reflected a shocking smallness of character (9:2).

When the prophet Samuel first approached Saul about assuming the post as the first king of Israel, Saul's response appeared to be unusually humble and sincere. He asked, "Am I not a Benjamite, from the smallest tribe of Israel, and is not my clan the least of all the clans of the tribe of Benjamin?" (9:21). And when the time came for Saul to take office, he literally hid from the leaders of Israel. They eventually found him "among the baggage" and had to persuade him to accept the position as their new ruler (10:22). That doesn't sound like a man struggling with pride.

Once Saul became king, however, he grew proud, arrogant and presumptuous. Often he took matters into his own hands. He provoked the Philistines into skirmishes when the country was not even at war by attacking those he perceived to be his enemies (13:2–4). He impulsively usurped the office of priest by not waiting for Samuel to arrive to offer a sacrifice to God (13:12). And 1 Samuel 15 records a list of Saul's errors in judgment, including flagrant disobedience of God's instructions, lies to cover up his sin, and blaming others to rationalize his own behavior (15:9–21).

Samuel heatedly chastised Saul and pointed out his failures. If only Saul had obeyed the Lord, he would have been blessed forever (13:13). But because of Saul's sinful pride, Samuel told him, "You have rejected the word of the LORD, and the LORD has rejected you as king!" (15:26). From that moment forward, Saul became even more fearful, jealous and angry. Dominated by his passions, Saul's thoughts became more bizarre, paranoid and confused, and his actions more immature and unwise.

Stay Alert

Saul's slide from humility to conceit shows how subtle pride can be. It can sneak up on our blind side and cause us to do what we never thought we would. That's why the apostle Paul wrote these sobering words: "If you think you are standing firm, be careful that you don't fall!" (1 Corinthians 10:12).

True humility, on the other hand, is based more on our view of God than on our view of ourselves. Feelings of weakness, inferiority and intimidation are not signs of humility. True humility involves an acknowledgment of our strengths and our weaknesses. We all are fallen men who have been made in the image of God, and are being "conformed to the likeness of his Son" (Romans 8:29). True humility does not cause us to run and hide but to move forward with faith, believing that God can use us even with our weaknesses and failings.

We must all guard our hearts and remember the example of Saul's perilous path of pride. God understands our struggles, mistakes and failures. He is patient with us. He wants to give us a sense of true confidence paired with true humility. He wants to live his life through us, using our talents and the spiritual gifts he has given us. Living a life so filled with God, we will humbly be able to say with Nehemiah, "this work [has] been done with the help of our God" (Nehemiah 6:16).

—*Dr. Gene Getz*

he has set up a monument in his own
honor and has turned and gone on
down to Gilgal."
13When Samuel reached him, Saul
said, "The LORD bless you! I have carried out the LORD's instructions."
14But Samuel said, "What then is this
bleating of sheep in my ears? What is
this lowing of cattle that I hear?"
15Saul answered, "The soldiers
brought them from the Amalekites;
they spared the best of the sheep and
cattle to sacrifice to the LORD your God,
but we totally destroyed the rest."
16"Stop!" Samuel said to Saul. "Let
me tell you what the LORD said to me
last night."
"Tell me," Saul replied.
17Samuel said, "Although you were
once small[i] in your own eyes, did you
not become the head of the tribes of
Israel? The LORD anointed you king
over Israel. 18And he sent you on a mission, saying, 'Go and completely destroy those wicked people, the Amalekites; make war on them until you have
wiped them out.' 19Why did you not
obey the LORD? Why did you pounce on
the plunder[j] and do evil in the eyes of
the LORD?"
20"But I did obey[k] the LORD," Saul
said. "I went on the mission the LORD
assigned me. I completely destroyed
the Amalekites and brought back Agag
their king. 21The soldiers took sheep
and cattle from the plunder, the best of
what was devoted to God, in order to
sacrifice them to the LORD your God at
Gilgal."
22But Samuel replied:

"Does the LORD delight in burnt
offerings and sacrifices
as much as in obeying the voice
of the LORD?
To obey is better than sacrifice,[l]
and to heed is better than the fat
of rams.
23For rebellion is like the sin of
divination,[m]
and arrogance like the evil of
idolatry.
Because you have rejected[n] the
word of the LORD,
he has rejected you as king."

24Then Saul said to Samuel, "I have
sinned.[o] I violated the LORD's command and your instructions. I was
afraid[p] of the people and so I gave in
to them. 25Now I beg you, forgive[q] my
sin and come back with me, so that I
may worship the LORD."
26But Samuel said to him, "I will not
go back with you. You have rejected[r]
the word of the LORD, and the LORD has
rejected you as king over Israel!"

27As Samuel turned to leave, Saul
caught hold of the hem of his robe, and
it tore.[s] 28Samuel said to him, "The
LORD has torn[t] the kingdom of Israel
from you today and has given it to one
of your neighbors—to one better than
you. 29He who is the Glory of Israel
does not lie[u] or change[v] his mind; for
he is not a man, that he should change
his mind."
30Saul replied, "I have sinned. But
please honor[w] me before the elders of
my people and before Israel; come
back with me, so that I may worship
the LORD your God." 31So Samuel went
back with Saul, and Saul worshiped the
LORD.
32Then Samuel said, "Bring me Agag
king of the Amalekites."
Agag came to him confidently,[a]
thinking, "Surely the bitterness of
death is past."
33But Samuel said,

"As your sword has made women
childless,
so will your mother be childless
among women."[x]

And Samuel put Agag to death before
the LORD at Gilgal.
34Then Samuel left for Ramah,[y] but
Saul went up to his home in Gibeah[z]
of Saul. 35Until the day Samuel[a] died,
he did not go to see Saul again, though
Samuel mourned[b] for him. And the
LORD was grieved that he had made
Saul king over Israel.

Samuel Anoints David

16 The LORD said to Samuel, "How
long will you mourn[c] for Saul,
since I have rejected[d] him as king over
Israel? Fill your horn with oil[e] and be
on your way; I am sending you to Jesse[f] of Bethlehem. I have chosen[g] one
of his sons to be king."
2But Samuel said, "How can I go?
Saul will hear about it and kill me."
The LORD said, "Take a heifer with
you and say, 'I have come to sacrifice
to the LORD.' 3Invite Jesse to the sacrifice, and I will show[h] you what to do.
You are to anoint[i] for me the one I
indicate."
4Samuel did what the LORD said.
When he arrived at Bethlehem,[j] the
elders of the town trembled when they
met him. They asked, "Do you come in
peace?[k]"
5Samuel replied, "Yes, in peace; I
have come to sacrifice to the LORD.
Consecrate[l] yourselves and come to
the sacrifice with me." Then he conse-

15:17 [i]1Sa 9:21
15:19 [j]1Sa 14:32
15:20 [k]ver 13
15:22 [l]Ps 40:6-8; 51:16; Isa 1:11-15; Jer 7:22; Hos 6:6; Mic 6:6-8; Mt 12:7; Mk 12:33; Heb 10:6-9
15:23 [m]Dt 18:10 [n]1Sa 13:13
15:24 [o]2Sa 12:13 [p]Pr 29:25; Isa 51:12-13
15:25 [q]Ex 10:17
15:26 [r]1Sa 13:14
15:27 [s]1Ki 11:11,31
15:28 [t]1Sa 28:17; 1Ki 11:31
15:29 [u]1Ch 29:11; Tit 1:2 [v]Nu 23:19; Eze 24:14
15:30 [w]Isa 29:13; Jn 5:44; 12:43
15:33 [x]Ge 9:6; Jdg 1:7
15:34 [y]1Sa 7:17 [z]1Sa 11:4
15:35 [a]1Sa 19:24 [b]1Sa 16:1
16:1 [c]1Sa 15:35 [d]1Sa 15:23 [e]2Ki 9:1 [f]Ru 4:17; 1Sa 9:16 [g]Ps 78:70; Ac 13:22
16:3 [h]Ex 4:15 [i]Dt 17:15; 1Sa 9:16
16:4 [j]Ge 48:7; Lk 2:4 [k]1Ki 2:13; 2Ki 9:17
16:5 [l]Ex 19:10,22

[a] 32 Or *him trembling, yet*

crated Jesse and his sons and invited
them to the sacrifice.
6When they arrived, Samuel saw Eliab[m] and thought, "Surely the LORD's
anointed stands here before the LORD."
7But the LORD said to Samuel, "Do
not consider his appearance or his
height, for I have rejected him. The
LORD does not look at the things man
looks at. Man looks at the outward appearance,[n] but the LORD looks at the
heart."[o]
8Then Jesse called Abinadab[p] and
had him pass in front of Samuel. But
Samuel said, "The LORD has not chosen
this one either." **9**Jesse then had Shammah pass by, but Samuel said, "Nor
has the LORD chosen this one." **10**Jesse
had seven of his sons pass before Samuel, but Samuel said to him, "The LORD
has not chosen these." **11**So he asked
Jesse, "Are these all[q] the sons you
have?"
"There is still the youngest," Jesse
answered, "but he is tending the
sheep."
Samuel said, "Send for him; we will
not sit down[a] until he arrives."
12So he[r] sent and had him brought
in. He was ruddy, with a fine appearance and handsome[s] features.
Then the LORD said, "Rise and anoint
him; he is the one."
13So Samuel took the horn of oil and

16:7

PROMISE 3

SPIRITUAL RESUMÉ

In this story, even Samuel the prophet needed to be reminded that God's eyes see much deeper than our own. Even the most thorough resumé has no place to write "My heart belongs to God." When we, in whatever arena we work and live, are desperate for leaders, we may commit the same error Samuel did.

Since only God can examine the heart, and since God *can* examine the heart, we too must examine it. That's why selecting leaders should be a process of self-education mixed with the prayer that God will lead us in the right direction.

Whether choosing leaders or seeking to be one, our focus can easily be limited to what we and others see. It's easy to ignore what God sees. But God has different resumé requirements that have nothing to do with years of employment experience or the right kind of education. Were that the case, Samuel would have chosen another brother to be king. No, God's requirements start on the inside.

What does your spiritual resumé look like?

For the next Promise 3 reading go to page 340.

16:6 [m]1Sa 17:13
16:7 [n]Ps 147:10 [o]1Ki 8:39; 1Ch 28:9; Isa 55:8
16:8 [p]1Sa 17:13
16:11 [q]1Sa 17:12
16:12 [r]1Sa 9:17 [s]Ge 39:6; 1Sa 17:42
16:13 [t]Nu 27:18; Jdg 11:29 [u]1Sa 10:1,6, 9-10; 11:6
16:14 [v]Jdg 16:20 [w]Jdg 9:23; 1Sa 18:10
16:16 [x]ver 23; 1Sa 18:10; 19:9; 2Ki 3:15
16:18 [y]1Sa 3:19; 17:32-37
16:20 [z]1Sa 10:27; Pr 18:16
16:21 [a]Ge 41:46; Pr 22:29
16:23 [b]ver 14-16
17:1 [c]1Sa 13:5 [d]Jos 15:35; 2Ch 28:18
17:2 [e]1Sa 21:9
17:4 [f]Jos 11:21-22; 2Sa 21:19

anointed him in the presence of his
brothers, and from that day on the
Spirit of the LORD[t] came upon David
in power.[u] Samuel then went to Ramah.

David in Saul's Service

14Now the Spirit of the LORD had departed[v] from Saul, and an evil[b] spirit[w] from the LORD tormented him.
15Saul's attendants said to him, "See,
an evil spirit from God is tormenting
you. **16**Let our lord command his servants here to search for someone who
can play the harp.[x] He will play when
the evil spirit from God comes upon
you, and you will feel better."
17So Saul said to his attendants,
"Find someone who plays well and
bring him to me."
18One of the servants answered, "I
have seen a son of Jesse of Bethlehem
who knows how to play the harp. He is
a brave man and a warrior. He speaks
well and is a fine-looking man. And the
LORD is with[y] him."
19Then Saul sent messengers to Jesse
and said, "Send me your son David,
who is with the sheep." **20**So Jesse took
a donkey loaded with bread,[z] a skin of
wine and a young goat and sent them
with his son David to Saul.
21David came to Saul and entered
his service.[a] Saul liked him very
much, and David became one of his
armor-bearers. **22**Then Saul sent word
to Jesse, saying, "Allow David to remain in my service, for I am pleased
with him."
23Whenever the spirit from God
came upon Saul, David would take his
harp and play. Then relief would come
to Saul; he would feel better, and the
evil spirit[b] would leave him.

David and Goliath

17 Now the Philistines gathered their
forces for war and assembled[c] at
Socoh in Judah. They pitched camp at
Ephes Dammim, between Socoh[d] and
Azekah. **2**Saul and the Israelites assembled and camped in the Valley of
Elah[e] and drew up their battle line to
meet the Philistines. **3**The Philistines
occupied one hill and the Israelites another, with the valley between them.
4A champion named Goliath,[f] who
was from Gath, came out of the Philistine camp. He was over nine feet[c] tall.
5He had a bronze helmet on his head
and wore a coat of scale armor of

[a] *11* Some Septuagint manuscripts; Hebrew *not gather around* [b] *14* Or *injurious*; also in verses 15, 16 and 23 [c] *4* Hebrew *was six cubits and a span* (about 3 meters)

bronze weighing five thousand shekels[a]; 6on his legs he wore bronze
greaves, and a bronze javelin[g] was
slung on his back. 7His spear shaft was
like a weaver's rod,[h] and its iron point
weighed six hundred shekels.[b] His
shield bearer[i] went ahead of him.
8Goliath stood and shouted to the
ranks of Israel, "Why do you come out
and line up for battle? Am I not a Philistine, and are you not the servants of
Saul? Choose[j] a man and have him
come down to me. 9If he is able to fight
and kill me, we will become your subjects; but if I overcome him and kill
him, you will become our subjects and
serve us." 10Then the Philistine said,
"This day I defy[k] the ranks of Israel!
Give me a man and let us fight each
other." 11On hearing the Philistine's
words, Saul and all the Israelites were
dismayed and terrified.
12Now David was the son of an Eph-
rathite named Jesse,[l] who was from
Bethlehem[m] in Judah. Jesse had
eight[n] sons, and in Saul's time he was
old and well advanced in years. 13Jes-
se's three oldest sons had followed
Saul to the war: The firstborn was Eliab;[o] the second, Abinadab; and the
third, Shammah.[p] 14David was the
youngest. The three oldest followed
Saul, 15but David went back and forth
from Saul to tend his father's sheep[q]
at Bethlehem.
16For forty days the Philistine came
forward every morning and evening
and took his stand.
17Now Jesse said to his son David,
"Take this ephah[c] of roasted grain[r]
and these ten loaves of bread for your
brothers and hurry to their camp.
18Take along these ten cheeses to the
commander of their unit.[d] See how
your brothers[s] are and bring back
some assurance[e] from them. 19They
are with Saul and all the men of Israel
in the Valley of Elah, fighting against
the Philistines."
20Early in the morning David left the
flock with a shepherd, loaded up and
set out, as Jesse had directed. He
reached the camp as the army was going out to its battle positions, shouting
the war cry. 21Israel and the Philistines
were drawing up their lines facing each
other. 22David left his things with the
keeper of supplies, ran to the battle
lines and greeted his brothers. 23As
he was talking with them, Goliath,
the Philistine champion from Gath,
stepped out from his lines and shouted
his usual[t] defiance, and David heard
it. 24When the Israelites saw the man,
they all ran from him in great fear.
25Now the Israelites had been saying, "Do you see how this man keeps
coming out? He comes out to defy Israel. The king will give great wealth to the
man who kills him. He will also give
him his daughter[u] in marriage and
will exempt his father's family from
taxes in Israel."
26David asked the men standing
near him, "What will be done for the
man who kills this Philistine and removes this disgrace[v] from Israel? Who
is this uncircumcised[w] Philistine that
he should defy[x] the armies of the living[y] God?"
27They repeated to him what they
had been saying and told him, "This is
what will be done for the man who kills
him."
28When Eliab, David's oldest brother, heard him speaking with the men,

17:6 [g]ver 45
17:7 [h]2Sa 21:19 [i]ver 41
17:8 [j]1Sa 8:17
17:10 [k]ver 26,45; 2Sa 21:21
17:12 [l]Ru 4:17; 1Ch 2:13-15 [m]Ge 35:19 [n]1Sa 16:11
17:13 [o]1Sa 16:6 [p]1Sa 16:9
17:15 [q]1Sa 16:19
17:17 [r]1Sa 25:18
17:18 [s]Ge 37:14
17:23 [t]ver 8-10
17:25 [u]Jos 15:16; 1Sa 18:17
17:26 [v]1Sa 11:2 [w]1Sa 14:6 [x]ver 10 [y]Dt 5:26

[a]*5* That is, about 125 pounds (about 57 kilograms) [b]*7* That is, about 15 pounds (about 7 kilograms) [c]*17* That is, probably about 3/5 bushel (about 22 liters) [d]*18* Hebrew *thousand* [e]*18* Or *some token*; or *some pledge of spoils*

17:1–58 PROMISE 7

SHOWDOWN IN THE VALLEY OF ELAH

This story, one of the most well-known of all the Bible's stories, proves conclusively that one man *can* make a difference.

Goliath had been terrorizing the Israelites and insulting their God for forty long days and nights. He defied the entire Israelite army, and his continuing verbal onslaught was demoralizing. The turning point in the story hinges on one person. One day, "Goliath . . . stepped out from his lines and shouted his usual defiance, and David heard it" (v. 23). That was the beginning of the end for Goliath.

Wouldn't it be wonderful if in a desperate situation you could walk in and become a hero? Imagine some ancient text reading, ". . . and (your name) heard it." What was it about David that made the difference? Read verse 26, where David summed up the whole situation in a single statement. You could say, "Enter David, enter God." The fact is, this is the first time in this whole Goliath incident that God's name is mentioned. David saw things differently than the troops who stood shaking in their sandals. The army saw a huge giant with great power and a nasty reputation; David saw a mere man with no power challenging *God's* reputation.

Only when we define life as David did will we begin to live life as David did.

For the next Promise 7 reading go to page 507.

he burned with anger[z] at him and
asked, "Why have you come down
here? And with whom did you leave
those few sheep in the desert? I know
how conceited you are and how wicked
your heart is; you came down only to
watch the battle."
29"Now what have I done?" said David. "Can't I even speak?" 30He then
turned away to someone else and
brought up the same matter, and the
men answered him as before. 31What
David said was overheard and reported
to Saul, and Saul sent for him.
32David said to Saul, "Let no one
lose heart[a] on account of this Philistine; your servant will go and fight
him."
33Saul replied,[b] "You are not able to
go out against this Philistine and fight
him; you are only a boy, and he has
been a fighting man from his youth."
34But David said to Saul, "Your servant has been keeping his father's
sheep. When a lion[c] or a bear came
and carried off a sheep from the flock,
35I went after it, struck it and rescued
the sheep from its mouth. When it
turned on me, I seized it by its hair,
struck it and killed it. 36Your servant
has killed both the lion and the bear;
this uncircumcised Philistine will be
like one of them, because he has defied
the armies of the living God. 37The
LORD who delivered[d] me from the paw
of the lion[e] and the paw of the bear
will deliver me from the hand of this
Philistine."
Saul said to David, "Go, and the
LORD be with[f] you."
38Then Saul dressed David in his
own tunic. He put a coat of armor on
him and a bronze helmet on his head.
39David fastened on his sword over the
tunic and tried walking around, because he was not used to them.
"I cannot go in these," he said to
Saul, "because I am not used to them."
So he took them off. 40Then he took his
staff in his hand, chose five smooth
stones from the stream, put them in
the pouch of his shepherd's bag and,
with his sling in his hand, approached
the Philistine.
41Meanwhile, the Philistine, with his
shield bearer in front of him, kept coming closer to David. 42He looked David
over and saw that he was only a boy,
ruddy and handsome,[g] and he despised[h] him. 43He said to David,
"Am I a dog,[i] that you come at me
with sticks?" And the Philistine cursed
David by his gods. 44"Come here," he
said, "and I'll give your flesh to the
birds of the air and the beasts of the
field![j]"

17:28 [z]Ge 37:4,8,11; Pr 18:19; Mt 10:36
17:32 [a]Dt 20:3; 1Sa 16:18
17:33 [b]Nu 13:31
17:34 [c]Jer 49:19; Am 3:12
17:37 [d]2Co 1:10 [e]2Ti 4:17 [f]1Sa 20:13; 1Ch 22:11,16
17:42 [g]1Sa 16:12 [h]Ps 123:3-4; Pr 16:18
17:43 [i]1Sa 24:14; 2Sa 3:8; 9:8; 2Ki 8:13
17:44 [j]1Ki 20:10-11
17:45 [k]2Sa 22:33,35; 2Ch 32:8; Ps 124:8; Heb 11:32-34 [l]ver 10
17:46 [m]Dt 28:26 [n]Jos 4:24; 1Ki 8:43; Isa 52:10 [o]1Ki 18:36; 2Ki 19:19; Isa 37:20
17:47 [p]Hos 1:7; Zec 4:6 [q]1Sa 14:6; 2Ch 14:11 [r]2Ch 20:15; Ps 44:6-7
17:50 [s]2Sa 23:21
17:51 [t]Heb 11:34 [u]1Sa 21:9
17:52 [v]Jos 15:11 [w]Jos 15:36
17:55 [x]1Sa 16:21

45David said to the Philistine, "You
come against me with sword and spear
and javelin, but I come against you in
the name[k] of the LORD Almighty, the
God of the armies of Israel, whom you
have defied.[l] 46This day the LORD will
hand you over to me, and I'll strike you
down and cut off your head. Today I
will give the carcasses[m] of the Philistine army to the birds of the air and the
beasts of the earth, and the whole
world[n] will know that there is a God in
Israel.[o] 47All those gathered here will
know that it is not by sword[p] or spear
that the LORD saves;[q] for the battle[r] is
the LORD's, and he will give all of you
into our hands."
48As the Philistine moved closer to
attack him, David ran quickly toward
the battle line to meet him. 49Reaching
into his bag and taking out a stone, he
slung it and struck the Philistine on the
forehead. The stone sank into his forehead, and he fell facedown on the
ground.
50So David triumphed over the Philistine with a sling[s] and a stone; without a sword in his hand he struck down
the Philistine and killed him.
51David ran and stood over him. He
took hold of the Philistine's sword and
drew it from the scabbard. After he
killed him, he cut[t] off his head with
the sword.[u]
When the Philistines saw that their
hero was dead, they turned and ran.
52Then the men of Israel and Judah
surged forward with a shout and pursued the Philistines to the entrance of
Gath[a] and to the gates of Ekron.[v]
Their dead were strewn along the
Shaaraim[w] road to Gath and Ekron.
53When the Israelites returned from
chasing the Philistines, they plundered
their camp. 54David took the Philistine's head and brought it to Jerusalem, and he put the Philistine's weapons in his own tent.
55As Saul watched David[x] going out
to meet the Philistine, he said to Abner,
commander of the army, "Abner,
whose son is that young man?"
Abner replied, "As surely as you live,
O king, I don't know."
56The king said, "Find out whose son
this young man is."
57As soon as David returned from
killing the Philistine, Abner took him
and brought him before Saul, with David still holding the Philistine's head.
58"Whose son are you, young man?"
Saul asked him.

[a] 52 Some Septuagint manuscripts; Hebrew *a valley*

David said, "I am the son of your servant Jesse[y] of Bethlehem."

Saul's Jealousy of David

2 →PG. 318

18 After David had finished talking with Saul, Jonathan became one in spirit with David, and he loved[z] him as himself.[a] 2From that day Saul kept David with him and did not let him return to his father's house. 3And Jonathan made a covenant[b] with David because he loved him as himself. 4Jonathan took off the robe[c] he was wearing and gave it to David, along with his tunic, and even his sword, his bow and his belt.

5Whatever Saul sent him to do, David did it so successfully[a] that Saul gave him a high rank in the army. This pleased all the people, and Saul's officers as well.

6When the men were returning home after David had killed the Philistine, the women came out from all the towns of Israel to meet King Saul with singing and dancing,[d] with joyful songs and with tambourines[e] and lutes. 7As they danced, they sang:[f]

"Saul has slain his thousands,
and David his tens[g] of thousands."

8Saul was very angry; this refrain galled him. "They have credited David with tens of thousands," he thought, "but me with only thousands. What more can he get but the kingdom?[h]" 9And from that time on Saul kept a jealous eye on David.

10The next day an evil[b] spirit[i] from God came forcefully upon Saul. He was prophesying in his house, while David was playing the harp, as he usually[j] did. Saul had a spear in his hand 11and he hurled it, saying to himself,[k] "I'll pin David to the wall." But David eluded[l] him twice.

12Saul was afraid[m] of David, because the LORD[n] was with[o] David but had left Saul. 13So he sent David away from him and gave him command over a thousand men, and David led[p] the troops in their campaigns.[q] 14In everything he did he had great success,[c][r] because the LORD was with[s] him. 15When Saul saw how successful[d] he was, he was afraid of him. 16But all Israel and Judah loved David, because he led them in their campaigns.[t]

17Saul said to David, "Here is my older daughter[u] Merab. I will give her to you in marriage; only serve me bravely and fight the battles[v] of the LORD." For Saul said to himself,[w] "I will not raise a hand against him. Let the Philistines do that!"

18But David said to Saul, "Who am I,[x] and what is my family or my father's clan in Israel, that I should become the king's son-in-law?[y]" 19So[e] when the time came for Merab,[z] Saul's daughter, to be given to David, she was given in marriage to Adriel of Meholah.[a]

20Now Saul's daughter Michal[b] was in love with David, and when they told Saul about it, he was pleased. 21"I will give her to him," he thought, "so that she may be a snare[c] to him and so that the hand of the Philistines may be against him." So Saul said to David, "Now you have a second opportunity to become my son-in-law."

22Then Saul ordered his attendants: "Speak to David privately and say, 'Look, the king is pleased with you, and his attendants all like you; now become his son-in-law.' "

23They repeated these words to David. But David said, "Do you think it is a small matter to become the king's son-in-law? I'm only a poor man and little known."

24When Saul's servants told him what David had said, 25Saul replied, "Say to David, 'The king wants no other price[d] for the bride than a hundred Philistine foreskins, to take revenge on his enemies.' " Saul's plan[e] was to have David fall by the hands of the Philistines.

26When the attendants told David these things, he was pleased to become the king's son-in-law. So before the allotted time elapsed, 27David and his men went out and killed two hundred Philistines. He brought their foreskins and presented the full number to the king so that he might become the king's son-in-law. Then Saul gave him his daughter Michal[f] in marriage.

28When Saul realized that the LORD was with David and that his daughter Michal loved David, 29Saul became still more afraid of him, and he remained his enemy the rest of his days.

30The Philistine commanders continued to go out to battle, and as often as they did, David met with more success[f][g] than the rest of Saul's officers, and his name became well known.

Saul Tries to Kill David

19 Saul told his son Jonathan[h] and all the attendants to kill[i] David. But Jonathan was very fond of David 2and

17:58 [y]ver 12
18:1 [z]2Sa 1:26 [a]Ge 44:30
18:3 [b]1Sa 20:8,16, 17,42
18:4 [c]Ge 41:42
18:6 [d]Ex 15:20 [e]Jdg 11:34; Ps 68:25
18:7 [f]Ex 15:21 [g]1Sa 21:11; 29:5
18:8 [h]1Sa 15:8
18:10 [i]1Sa 16:14 [j]1Sa 19:7
18:11 [k]1Sa 20:7,33 [l]1Sa 19:10
18:12 [m]ver 15,29 [n]1Sa 16:13 [o]1Sa 28:15
18:13 [p]ver 16; Nu 27:17 [q]2Sa 5:2
18:14 [r]Ge 39:3 [s]Ge 39:2,23; Jos 6:27; 1Sa 16:18
18:16 [t]ver 5
18:17 [u]1Sa 17:25 [v]Nu 21:14; 1Sa 25:28 [w]ver 25
18:18 [x]1Sa 9:21; 2Sa 7:18 [y]ver 23
18:19 [z]2Sa 21:8 [a]Jdg 7:22
18:20 [b]ver 28
18:21 [c]ver 17,26
18:25 [d]Ge 34:12; Ex 22:17; 1Sa 14:24 [e]ver 17
18:27 [f]ver 13; 2Sa 3:14
18:30 [g]ver 5; 2Sa 11:1
19:1 [h]1Sa 18:1 [i]1Sa 18:9

[a]5 Or *wisely* [b]10 Or *injurious* [c]14 Or *he was very wise* [d]15 Or *wise* [e]19 Or *However,* [f]30 Or *David acted more wisely*

warned him, "My father Saul is looking
for a chance to kill you. Be on your
guard tomorrow morning; go into hiding and stay there. 3I will go out and
stand with my father in the field where
you are. I'll speak[j] to him about you
and will tell you what I find out."
4Jonathan spoke[k] well of David to
Saul his father and said to him, "Let
not the king do wrong[l] to his servant
David; he has not wronged you, and
what he has done has benefited you
greatly. 5He took his life in his hands
when he killed the Philistine. The LORD
won a great victory[m] for all Israel, and
you saw it and were glad. Why then
would you do wrong to an innocent[n]
man like David by killing him for no
reason?"
6Saul listened to Jonathan and took
this oath: "As surely as the LORD lives,
David will not be put to death."
7So Jonathan called David and told
him the whole conversation. He
brought him to Saul, and David was
with Saul as before.[o]
8Once more war broke out, and David went out and fought the Philistines.
He struck them with such force that
they fled before him.
9But an evil[a] spirit[p] from the LORD
came upon Saul as he was sitting in his
house with his spear in his hand. While
David was playing the harp, 10Saul
tried to pin him to the wall with his
spear, but David eluded[q] him as Saul
drove the spear into the wall. That
night David made good his escape.
11Saul sent men to David's house to
watch[r] it and to kill him in the morning. But Michal, David's wife, warned
him, "If you don't run for your life
tonight, tomorrow you'll be killed."
12So Michal let David down through a
window,[s] and he fled and escaped.
13Then Michal took an idol[b] and laid it
on the bed, covering it with a garment
and putting some goats' hair at the
head.
14When Saul sent the men to capture
David, Michal said,[t] "He is ill."
15Then Saul sent the men back to see
David and told them, "Bring him up to
me in his bed so that I may kill him."
16But when the men entered, there was
the idol in the bed, and at the head was
some goats' hair.
17Saul said to Michal, "Why did you
deceive me like this and send my enemy away so that he escaped?"
Michal told him, "He said to me, 'Let
me get away. Why should I kill you?' "
18When David had fled and made his
escape, he went to Samuel at Ramah[u]
and told him all that Saul had done to
him. Then he and Samuel went to Naioth and stayed there. 19Word came to
Saul: "David is in Naioth at Ramah";
20so he sent men to capture him. But
when they saw a group of prophets[v]
prophesying, with Samuel standing
there as their leader, the Spirit of God
came upon[w] Saul's men and they also
prophesied.[x] 21Saul was told about it,
and he sent more men, and they
prophesied too. Saul sent men a third
time, and they also prophesied. 22Fi-
nally, he himself left for Ramah and
went to the great cistern at Secu. And
he asked, "Where are Samuel and David?"
"Over in Naioth at Ramah," they
said.
23So Saul went to Naioth at Ramah.
But the Spirit of God came even upon
him, and he walked along prophesying[y] until he came to Naioth. 24He
stripped[z] off his robes and also
prophesied in Samuel's presence. He
lay that way all that day and night. This
is why people say, "Is Saul also among
the prophets?"[a]

David and Jonathan

20 Then David fled from Naioth at Ramah and went to Jonathan and
asked, "What have I done? What is my
crime? How have I wronged[b] your father, that he is trying to take my life?"
2"Never!" Jonathan replied. "You are
not going to die! Look, my father
doesn't do anything, great or small,
without confiding in me. Why would
he hide this from me? It's not so!"
3But David took an oath[c] and said,
"Your father knows very well that I
have found favor in your eyes, and he
has said to himself, 'Jonathan must not
know this or he will be grieved.' Yet as
surely as the LORD lives and as you live,
there is only a step between me and
death."
4Jonathan said to David, "Whatever
you want me to do, I'll do for you."
5So David said, "Look, tomorrow is
the New Moon festival,[d] and I am
supposed to dine with the king; but let
me go and hide[e] in the field until the
evening of the day after tomorrow. 6If
your father misses me at all, tell him,
'David earnestly asked my permission
to hurry to Bethlehem,[f] his hometown, because an annual[g] sacrifice is
being made there for his whole clan.'
7If he says, 'Very well,' then your servant is safe. But if he loses his temper,[h] you can be sure that he is determined to harm me. 8As for you, show
kindness to your servant, for you have

19:3 [j] 1Sa 20:12
19:4 [k] 1Sa 20:32; Pr 31:8,9; Jer 18:20 [l] Ge 42:22; Pr 17:13
19:5 [m] 1Sa 11:13; 17:49-50; 1Ch 11:14 [n] Dt 19:10-13; 1Sa 20:32; Mt 27:4
19:7 [o] 1Sa 16:21; 18:2,13
19:9 [p] 1Sa 16:14; 18:10-11
19:10 [q] 1Sa 18:11
19:11 [r] Ps 59 Title
19:12 [s] Jos 2:15; Ac 9:25
19:14 [t] Jos 2:4
19:18 [u] 1Sa 7:17
19:20 [v] ver 11,14; Jn 7:32,45 [w] Nu 11:25 [x] 1Sa 10:5; Joel 2:28
19:23 [y] 1Sa 10:13
19:24 [z] 2Sa 6:20; Isa 20:2; Mic 1:8 [a] 1Sa 10:11
20:1 [b] 1Sa 24:9
20:3 [c] Dt 6:13
20:5 [d] Nu 10:10; 28:11 [e] 1Sa 19:2
20:6 [f] 1Sa 17:58 [g] Dt 12:5
20:7 [h] 1Sa 25:17

[a] *9* Or *injurious* [b] *13* Hebrew *teraphim*; also in verse 16

JONATHAN

The Picture of a Man's Loyalty

In an age when "winning at all costs" and "looking out for number one" are exalted as virtues, we have almost forgotten what *loyalty* looks like. Proverbs 20:6 sounds like a description of our times: "Many a man claims to have unfailing love, but a faithful [loyal] man who can find?"

Friendship Built on a Common Faith

Jonathan, the oldest son of Israel's King Saul and heir to the throne, illustrates what loyalty is meant to be. Jonathan is introduced to us as one of his father's military commanders (1 Samuel 13:2). In that role, Jonathan demonstrated great faith and trust in God. On one occasion, he decided to take on the whole Philistine army single-handedly, believing that the Lord would give him victory (14:1, 6). And, through supernatural intervention, God did. A "panic struck the whole army . . . It was a panic sent by God" (14:15).

Jonathan and David probably met soon after David entered Saul's service as a musician and armor bearer (16:21). David was a young man of faith, and perhaps he and Jonathan had begun to develop a friendship early on. But then came an event that likely sealed their relationship.

The Philistine giant, Goliath, challenged the Israelite army to send someone to fight him, one-on-one. No one was willing to accept his challenge—apparently not even Jonathan, one who had shown such faith and bravery earlier. Then along came David, a fiery young shepherd boy who was ready to fight anyone who dared to mock God.

That day, as Jonathan watched David take on Goliath and slay him all by himself, Jonathan felt his soul drawn toward David. He recognized that David understood and trusted God's greatness. So, "Jonathan became one in spirit with David, and he loved him as himself" (18:1). To signal his devotion to his new friend, "Jonathan took off the robe he was wearing and gave it to David, along with his tunic, and even his sword, his bow and his belt" (18:4). In their minds and hearts, Jonathan and David were bound to each other in an inseparable, loyal friendship.

Loyalty Put to the Test

As David and Jonathan became closer friends, David also became one of Saul's military commanders. God gave David great success in that role—so much success that Saul grew jealous of David and began scheming to kill him. This put a strain on Jonathan's loyalty to David. Jonathan loved his father, yet he knew David had done nothing wrong. He warned David about Saul's murderous intent and interceded with his father on David's behalf, persuading Saul to allow David to serve the king once more (19:1–7).

Unfortunately, Jonathan's success in building a bridge between his father and David was short-lived. One day while David was playing his harp, Saul flew into a horrible rage and "tried to pin him to the wall with a spear" (19:10). David deftly sidestepped and escaped.

Later, David sought out Jonathan and the two friends decided to test Saul's motives. David would be absent from his scheduled meal with the king. If Saul reacted with anger, the friends would know Saul was still determined to kill David.

When Saul noticed that "David's place was empty . . . Saul's anger flared up at Jonathan" and he accused Jonathan of treachery (20:27, 30). Saul also tried to convince Jonathan to help him find and kill David, insisting that otherwise Jonathan would lose his right to the throne (20:31).

Jonathan stood his ground. His loyalty to his godly friend compelled him to protect David. Once more he pleaded for David's life. But that only infuriated Saul even more. When "Saul hurled his spear at him," trying to kill his own son, Jonathan knew without a doubt "that his father intended to kill David" (20:33). Jonathan went to David and told him what had happened. "They kissed each other and wept together" for they knew they would have to part and David would have to flee for his life (20:41).

As David hid from murderous King Saul, Jonathan went to see him. Jonathan knew God wanted David to be the next king, and he was at peace with that fact. Jonathan encouraged David, "You will be king over Israel, and I will be second to you" (23:17). That's true loyalty to a friend!

Loyalty Today

Jonathan gives us a shining example of what it means to be loyal to a friend, even under extreme pressure. Yet loyal friends can be tough to find. At one men's retreat, two men who had developed this kind of loyal friendship described their relationship to others in the group. They told how they had shared their deepest joys and their most difficult struggles. Clearly, both men were better husbands, fathers and churchmen because of their faithful support for each other. Now one of them was moving to a different city. With tears and voices that broke periodically, the friends agreed that the separation would be tough on both of them.

As men of God, we want to be known for our loyalty to our Christian brothers, our churches and our families. Jonathan offers us a model to follow. For whom can you be a better Jonathan? How about starting today?

—Dr. Gene Getz

brought him into a covenant[i] with
you before the LORD. If I am guilty, then
kill[j] me yourself! Why hand me over
to your father?"
9"Never!" Jonathan said. "If I had the
least inkling that my father was determined to harm you, wouldn't I tell
you?"
10David asked, "Who will tell me if
your father answers you harshly?"
11"Come," Jonathan said, "let's go
out into the field." So they went there
together.
12Then Jonathan said to David: "By
the LORD, the God of Israel, I will surely
sound out my father by this time the
day after tomorrow! If he is favorably
disposed toward you, will I not send
you word and let you know? 13But if my
father is inclined to harm you, may the
LORD deal with me, be it ever so severely,[k] if I do not let you know and send
you away safely. May the LORD be
with[l] you as he has been with my father. 14But show me unfailing kindness
like that of the LORD as long as I live, so
that I may not be killed, 15and do not
ever cut off your kindness from my
family[m]—not even when the LORD has
cut off every one of David's enemies
from the face of the earth."
16So Jonathan made a covenant[n]
with the house of David, saying, "May
the LORD call David's enemies to account." 17And Jonathan had David reaffirm his oath[o] out of love for him,
because he loved him as he loved himself.
18Then Jonathan said to David: "Tomorrow is the New Moon festival. You
will be missed, because your seat will
be empty.[p] 19The day after tomorrow,
toward evening, go to the place where
you hid[q] when this trouble began, and
wait by the stone Ezel. 20I will shoot
three arrows to the side of it, as though
I were shooting at a target. 21Then I will
send a boy and say, 'Go, find the arrows.' If I say to him, 'Look, the arrows
are on this side of you; bring them
here,' then come, because, as surely as
the LORD lives, you are safe; there is no
danger. 22But if I say to the boy, 'Look,
the arrows are beyond[r] you,' then you
must go, because the LORD has sent
you away. 23And about the matter you
and I discussed—remember, the LORD
is witness[s] between you and me forever."
24So David hid in the field, and when
the New Moon festival came, the king
sat down to eat. 25He sat in his customary place by the wall, opposite Jonathan,[a] and Abner sat next to Saul, but
David's place was empty.[t] 26Saul said
nothing that day, for he thought,
"Something must have happened to
David to make him ceremonially
unclean—surely he is unclean.[u]"
27But the next day, the second day of
the month, David's place was empty
again. Then Saul said to his son Jonathan, "Why hasn't the son of Jesse
come to the meal, either yesterday or
today?"
28Jonathan answered, "David earnestly asked me for permission[v] to go
to Bethlehem. 29He said, 'Let me go,
because our family is observing a sacrifice in the town and my brother has
ordered me to be there. If I have found
favor in your eyes, let me get away to
see my brothers.' That is why he has
not come to the king's table."
30Saul's anger flared up at Jonathan
and he said to him, "You son of a perverse and rebellious woman! Don't I
know that you have sided with the son
of Jesse to your own shame and to the
shame of the mother who bore you?
31As long as the son of Jesse lives on
this earth, neither you nor your kingdom will be established. Now send and
bring him to me, for he must die!"
32"Why[w] should he be put to death?
What[x] has he done?" Jonathan asked
his father. 33But Saul hurled his spear
at him to kill him. Then Jonathan knew
that his father intended[y] to kill David.
34Jonathan got up from the table in
fierce anger; on that second day of the
month he did not eat, because he was
grieved at his father's shameful treatment of David.
35In the morning Jonathan went out
to the field for his meeting with David.
He had a small boy with him, 36and he
said to the boy, "Run and find the arrows I shoot." As the boy ran, he shot
an arrow beyond him. 37When the boy
came to the place where Jonathan's arrow had fallen, Jonathan called out after him, "Isn't the arrow beyond[z]
you?" 38Then he shouted, "Hurry! Go
quickly! Don't stop!" The boy picked
up the arrow and returned to his master. 39(The boy knew nothing of all this;
only Jonathan and David knew.)
40Then Jonathan gave his weapons to
the boy and said, "Go, carry them back
to town."
41After the boy had gone, David got
up from the south side ⌊of the stone⌋
and bowed down before Jonathan
three times, with his face to the
ground. Then they kissed each other
and wept together—but David wept
the most.
42Jonathan said to David, "Go in
peace,[a] for we have sworn friend-

20:8 [i] 1Sa 18:3; 23:18 [j] 2Sa 14:32
20:13 [k] Ru 1:17; 1Sa 3:17 [l] Jos 1:5; 1Sa 17:37; 18:12; 1Ch 22:11,16
20:15 [m] 2Sa 9:7
20:16 [n] 1Sa 25:22
20:17 [o] 1Sa 18:3
20:18 [p] ver 5,25
20:19 [q] 1Sa 19:2
20:22 [r] ver 37
20:23 [s] ver 14-15; Ge 31:50
20:25 [t] ver 18
20:26 [u] Lev 7:20-21; 15:5; 1Sa 16:5
20:28 [v] ver 6
20:32 [w] 1Sa 19:4; Mt 27:23 [x] Ge 31:36; Lk 23:22
20:33 [y] ver 7; 1Sa 18:11,17
20:37 [z] ver 22
20:42 [a] ver 22; 1Sa 1:17

[a] 25 Septuagint; Hebrew *wall. Jonathan arose*

ship[b] with each other in the name of
the LORD, saying, 'The LORD is witness
between you and me, and between
your descendants and my descendants
forever.' " Then David left, and Jonathan went back to the town.

David at Nob

21 David went to Nob,[c] to Ahimelech
the priest. Ahimelech trembled[d]
when he met him, and asked, "Why are
you alone? Why is no one with you?"
2David answered Ahimelech the
priest, "The king charged me with a
certain matter and said to me, 'No one
is to know anything about your mission and your instructions.' As for my
men, I have told them to meet me at a
certain place. 3Now then, what do you
have on hand? Give me five loaves of
bread, or whatever you can find."
4But the priest answered David, "I
don't have any ordinary bread[e] on
hand; however, there is some consecrated[f] bread here—provided the
men have kept[g] themselves from
women."
5David replied, "Indeed women
have been kept from us, as usual whenever[a] I set out. The men's things[b] are
holy[h] even on missions that are not
holy. How much more so today!" 6So
the priest gave him the consecrated
bread,[i] since there was no bread
there except the bread of the Presence
that had been removed from before the
LORD and replaced by hot bread on the
day it was taken away.
7Now one of Saul's servants was
there that day, detained before the
LORD; he was Doeg[j] the Edomite,[k]
Saul's head shepherd.
8David asked Ahimelech, "Don't you
have a spear or a sword here? I haven't
brought my sword or any other weapon, because the king's business was urgent."
9The priest replied, "The sword[l] of
Goliath the Philistine, whom you killed
in the Valley of Elah,[m] is here; it is
wrapped in a cloth behind the ephod.
If you want it, take it; there is no sword
here but that one."
David said, "There is none like it;
give it to me."

David at Gath

10That day David fled from Saul and
went[n] to Achish king of Gath. 11But
the servants of Achish said to him,
"Isn't this David, the king of the land?
Isn't he the one they sing about in their
dances:

" 'Saul has slain his thousands,
and David his tens of
thousands'?"[o]

12David took these words to heart
and was very much afraid of Achish
king of Gath. 13So he pretended to be
insane[p] in their presence; and while
he was in their hands he acted like a
madman, making marks on the doors
of the gate and letting saliva run down
his beard.
14Achish said to his servants, "Look
at the man! He is insane! Why bring
him to me? 15Am I so short of madmen
that you have to bring this fellow here
to carry on like this in front of me?
Must this man come into my house?"

David at Adullam and Mizpah

22 David left Gath and escaped to the
cave[q] of Adullam. When his
brothers and his father's household
heard about it, they went down to him
there. 2All those who were in distress
or in debt or discontented gathered[r]
around him, and he became their leader. About four hundred men were with
him.
3From there David went to Mizpah
in Moab and said to the king of Moab,
"Would you let my father and mother
come and stay with you until I learn
what God will do for me?" 4So he left
them with the king of Moab, and they
stayed with him as long as David was in
the stronghold.
5But the prophet Gad[s] said to David, "Do not stay in the stronghold. Go
into the land of Judah." So David left
and went to the forest of Hereth.

Saul Kills the Priests of Nob

6Now Saul heard that David and his
men had been discovered. And Saul,
spear in hand, was seated[t] under the
tamarisk[u] tree on the hill at Gibeah,
with all his officials standing around
him. 7Saul said to them, "Listen, men
of Benjamin! Will the son of Jesse give
all of you fields and vineyards? Will he
make all of you commanders[v] of
thousands and commanders of hundreds? 8Is that why you have all conspired against me? No one tells me
when my son makes a covenant[w] with
the son of Jesse. None of you is concerned[x] about me or tells me that my
son has incited my servant to lie in wait
for me, as he does today."
9But Doeg[y] the Edomite, who was
standing with Saul's officials, said, "I
saw the son of Jesse come to Ahimelech son of Ahitub at Nob.[z] 10Ahime-

20:42 [b] 2Sa 1:26; Pr 18:24
21:1 [c] 1Sa 14:3; 22:9,19; Ne 11:32; Isa 10:32 [d] 1Sa 16:4
21:4 [e] Lev 24:8-9 [f] Ex 25:30; Mt 12:4 [g] Ex 19:15
21:5 [h] 1Th 4:4
21:6 [i] Lev 24:8-9; Mt 12:3-4; Mk 2:25-28; Lk 6:1-5
21:7 [j] 1Sa 22:9,22 [k] 1Sa 14:47; Ps 52 Title
21:9 [l] 1Sa 17:51 [m] 1Sa 17:2
21:10 [n] 1Sa 27:2
21:11 [o] 1Sa 18:7; 29:5; Ps 56 Title
21:13 [p] Ps 34 Title
22:1 [q] 2Sa 23:13; Ps 57 Title; 142 Title
22:2 [r] 1Sa 23:13; 25:13; 2Sa 15:20
22:5 [s] 2Sa 24:11; 1Ch 21:9; 29:29; 2Ch 29:25
22:6 [t] Jdg 4:5 [u] Ge 21:33
22:7 [v] 1Sa 8:14
22:8 [w] 1Sa 18:3; 20:16 [x] 1Sa 23:21
22:9 [y] 1Sa 21:7; Ps 52 Title [z] 1Sa 21:1

[a] 5 Or *from us in the past few days since*
[b] 5 Or *bodies*

lech inquired[a] of the LORD for him; he also gave him provisions[b] and the sword of Goliath the Philistine."

11Then the king sent for the priest Ahimelech son of Ahitub and his father's whole family, who were the priests at Nob, and they all came to the king. 12Saul said, "Listen now, son of Ahitub."

"Yes, my lord," he answered.

13Saul said to him, "Why have you conspired[c] against me, you and the son of Jesse, giving him bread and a sword and inquiring of God for him, so that he has rebelled against me and lies in wait for me, as he does today?"

14Ahimelech answered the king, "Who[d] of all your servants is as loyal as David, the king's son-in-law, captain of your bodyguard and highly respected in your household? 15Was that day the first time I inquired of God for him? Of course not! Let not the king accuse your servant or any of his father's family, for your servant knows nothing at all about this whole affair."

16But the king said, "You will surely die, Ahimelech, you and your father's whole family."

17Then the king ordered the guards at his side: "Turn and kill the priests of the LORD, because they too have sided with David. They knew he was fleeing, yet they did not tell me."

But the king's officials were not willing[e] to raise a hand to strike the priests of the LORD.

18The king then ordered Doeg, "You turn and strike down the priests." So Doeg the Edomite turned and struck them down. That day he killed eighty-five men who wore the linen ephod.[f] 19He also put to the sword[g] Nob, the town of the priests, with its men and women, its children and infants, and its cattle, donkeys and sheep.

20But Abiathar,[h] a son of Ahimelech son of Ahitub, escaped and fled to join David.[i] 21He told David that Saul had killed the priests of the LORD. 22Then David said to Abiathar: "That day, when Doeg[j] the Edomite was there, I knew he would be sure to tell Saul. I am responsible for the death of your father's whole family. 23Stay with me; don't be afraid; the man who is seeking your life[k] is seeking mine also. You will be safe with me."

David Saves Keilah

23 When David was told, "Look, the Philistines are fighting against Keilah[l] and are looting the threshing floors," 2he inquired[m] of the LORD, saying, "Shall I go and attack these Philistines?"

The LORD answered him, "Go, attack the Philistines and save Keilah."

3But David's men said to him, "Here in Judah we are afraid. How much more, then, if we go to Keilah against the Philistine forces!"

4Once again David inquired of the LORD, and the LORD answered him, "Go down to Keilah, for I am going to give the Philistines into your hand."[n] 5So David and his men went to Keilah, fought the Philistines and carried off their livestock. He inflicted heavy losses on the Philistines and saved the people of Keilah. 6(Now Abiathar[o] son of Ahimelech had brought the ephod down with him when he fled to David at Keilah.)

Saul Pursues David

7Saul was told that David had gone to Keilah, and he said, "God has handed him over to me, for David has imprisoned himself by entering a town with gates and bars." 8And Saul called up all his forces for battle, to go down to Keilah to besiege David and his men.

9When David learned that Saul was plotting against him, he said to Abiathar[p] the priest, "Bring the ephod." 10David said, "O LORD, God of Israel, your servant has heard definitely that Saul plans to come to Keilah and destroy the town on account of me. 11Will the citizens of Keilah surrender me to him? Will Saul come down, as your servant has heard? O LORD, God of Israel, tell your servant."

And the LORD said, "He will."

12Again David asked, "Will the citizens of Keilah surrender[q] me and my men to Saul?"

And the LORD said, "They will."

13So David and his men,[r] about six hundred in number, left Keilah and kept moving from place to place. When Saul was told that David had escaped from Keilah, he did not go there.

14David stayed in the desert strongholds and in the hills of the Desert of Ziph.[s] Day after day Saul searched[t] for him, but God did not[u] give David into his hands.

15While David was at Horesh in the Desert of Ziph, he learned that Saul had come out to take his life. 16And Saul's son Jonathan went to David at Horesh and helped him find strength[v] in God. 17"Don't be afraid," he said. "My father Saul will not lay a hand on you. You will be king[w] over Israel, and I will be second to you. Even my father Saul knows this." 18The two of them

2 →PG. 358

22:10 [a]Nu 27:21; 1Sa 10:22 [b]1Sa 21:6
22:13 [c]ver 8
22:14 [d]1Sa 19:4
22:17 [e]Ex 1:17
22:18 [f]1Sa 2:18,31
22:19 [g]1Sa 15:3
22:20 [h]1Sa 23:6,9; 30:7; 1Ki 2:22,26,27 [i]1Sa 2:32
22:22 [j]1Sa 21:7
22:23 [k]1Ki 2:26
23:1 [l]Jos 15:44
23:2 [m]ver 4,12; 1Sa 30:8; 2Sa 5:19,23
23:4 [n]Jos 8:7; Jdg 7:7
23:6 [o]1Sa 22:20
23:9 [p]ver 6; 1Sa 22:20; 30:7
23:12 [q]ver 20
23:13 [r]1Sa 22:2; 25:13
23:14 [s]Jos 15:24,55 [t]Ps 54:3-4 [u]Ps 32:7
23:16 [v]1Sa 30:6
23:17 [w]1Sa 20:31; 24:20

made a covenant[x] before the LORD.
Then Jonathan went home, but David
remained at Horesh.
19 The Ziphites[y] went up to Saul at
Gibeah and said, "Is not David hiding
among us[z] in the strongholds at Horesh, on the hill of Hakilah,[a] south of
Jeshimon? 20 Now, O king, come down
whenever it pleases you to do so, and
we will be responsible for handing[b]
him over to the king."
21 Saul replied, "The LORD bless you
for your concern[c] for me. 22 Go and
make further preparation. Find out
where David usually goes and who has
seen him there. They tell me he is very
crafty. 23 Find out about all the hiding
places he uses and come back to me
with definite information.**[a]** Then I will
go with you; if he is in the area, I will
track him down among all the clans of
Judah."
24 So they set out and went to Ziph
ahead of Saul. Now David and his men
were in the Desert of Maon,[d] in the
Arabah south of Jeshimon. 25 Saul and
his men began the search, and when
David was told about it, he went down
to the rock and stayed in the Desert of
Maon. When Saul heard this, he went
into the Desert of Maon in pursuit of
David.
26 Saul[e] was going along one side of
the mountain, and David and his men
were on the other side, hurrying to get
away from Saul. As Saul and his forces
were closing in on David and his men
to capture them, 27 a messenger came
to Saul, saying, "Come quickly! The
Philistines are raiding the land."
28 Then Saul broke off his pursuit of David and went to meet the Philistines.
That is why they call this place Sela
Hammahlekoth.**[b]** 29 And David went
up from there and lived in the strongholds of En Gedi.[f]

David Spares Saul's Life

24 After Saul returned from pursuing
the Philistines, he was told, "David
is in the Desert of En Gedi.[g]" 2 So Saul
took three thousand chosen men from
all Israel and set out to look[h] for David
and his men near the Crags of the Wild
Goats.
3 He came to the sheep pens along
the way; a cave[i] was there, and Saul
went in to relieve[j] himself. David and
his men were far back in the cave. 4 The
men said, "This is the day the LORD
spoke[k] of when he said**[c]** to you, 'I will
give your enemy into your hands for
you to deal with as you wish.' "[l] Then
David crept up unnoticed and cut off a
corner of Saul's robe.

23:18 [x] 1Sa 18:3; 20:16,42; 2Sa 9:1; 21:7
23:19 [y] 1Sa 26:1 [z] Ps 54 Title [a] 1Sa 26:3
23:20 [b] ver 12
23:21 [c] 1Sa 22:8
23:24 [d] Jos 15:55; 1Sa 25:2
23:26 [e] Ps 17:9
23:29 [f] 2Ch 20:2
24:1 [g] 1Sa 23:28-29
24:2 [h] 1Sa 26:2
24:3 [i] Ps 57 Title; 142 Title [j] Jdg 3:24
24:4 [k] 1Sa 25:28-30 [l] 1Sa 23:17; 26:8
24:5 [m] 2Sa 24:10
24:6 [n] 1Sa 26:11
24:8 [o] 1Sa 25:23-24
24:11 [p] Ps 7:3 [q] 1Sa 23:14,23; 1Sa 26:20
24:12 [r] Ge 16:5; 31:53; Job 5:8 [s] Jdg 11:27; 1Sa 26:10

5 Afterward, David was conscience-
stricken[m] for having cut off a corner of
his robe. 6 He said to his men, "The
LORD forbid that I should do such a
thing to my master, the LORD's anointed,[n] or lift my hand against him; for
he is the anointed of the LORD." 7 With
these words David rebuked his men
and did not allow them to attack Saul.
And Saul left the cave and went his
way.
8 Then David went out of the cave
and called out to Saul, "My lord the
king!" When Saul looked behind him,
David bowed down and prostrated
himself with his face to the ground.[o]
9 He said to Saul, "Why do you listen
when men say, 'David is bent on harming you'? 10 This day you have seen with
your own eyes how the LORD delivered
you into my hands in the cave. Some
urged me to kill you, but I spared you;
I said, 'I will not lift my hand against
my master, because he is the LORD's
anointed.' 11 See, my father, look at this
piece of your robe in my hand! I cut off
the corner of your robe but did not kill
you. Now understand and recognize
that I am not guilty[p] of wrongdoing or
rebellion. I have not wronged you, but
you are hunting[q] me down to take my
life. 12 May the LORD judge[r] between
you and me. And may the LORD
avenge[s] the wrongs you have done to
me, but my hand will not touch you.

[a] *23* Or *me at Nacon* **[b]** *28 Sela Hammahlekoth* means *rock of parting.* **[c]** *4* Or *"Today the LORD is saying*

24:10–21

RESPECT FOR GOD'S ANOINTED
PROMISE 6

This is one of two opportunities David had to free himself from Saul's pursuit (see ch. 26 for the other story). In his jealous rage, Saul had tried to kill David many times. David had every right to fight back and to protect his own life, but refused to do it.

David gave two reasons for not retaliating. First, Saul was God's anointed—David would not harm Saul because God had made him king (vv. 8–11). Second, judgment belongs to God, and David trusted him to deal with Saul (vv. 12–15).

What a model David provides for us to follow when people wrong us! The David who killed Goliath, God's enemy, refused to harm Saul, God's anointed. After reading these accounts, read David's response to Saul's death in 2 Samuel 1. Then ask God to help you frame a proper response to the next person who treads on your "rights."

For the next Promise 6 reading go to page 381.

13 As the old saying goes, 'From evildoers come evil deeds,[t]' so my hand
will not touch you.
14 "Against whom has the king of Israel come out? Whom are you pursuing? A dead dog?[u] A flea?[v] 15 May the
LORD be our judge[w] and decide between us. May he consider my cause
and uphold[x] it; may he vindicate[y]
me by delivering[z] me from your
hand."
16 When David finished saying this,
Saul asked, "Is that your voice,[a] David
my son?" And he wept aloud. 17 "You
are more righteous than I,"[b] he said.
"You have treated me well,[c] but I have
treated you badly. 18 You have just now
told me of the good you did to me; the
LORD delivered[d] me into your hands,
but you did not kill me. 19 When a man
finds his enemy, does he let him get
away unharmed? May the LORD reward
you well for the way you treated me
today. 20 I know that you will surely be
king[e] and that the kingdom[f] of Israel
will be established in your hands.
21 Now swear[g] to me by the LORD that
you will not cut off my descendants or
wipe out my name from my father's
family.[h]"
22 So David gave his oath to Saul.
Then Saul returned home, but David
and his men went up to the stronghold.[i]

David, Nabal and Abigail

25 Now Samuel died,[j] and all Israel
assembled and mourned[k] for
him; and they buried him at his home
in Ramah.[l]
Then David moved down into the
Desert of Maon.[a] 2 A certain man in
Maon,[m] who had property there at
Carmel, was very wealthy. He had a
thousand goats and three thousand
sheep, which he was shearing in Carmel. 3 His name was Nabal and his
wife's name was Abigail.[n] She was an
intelligent and beautiful woman, but
her husband, a Calebite,[o] was surly
and mean in his dealings.
4 While David was in the desert, he
heard that Nabal was shearing sheep.
5 So he sent ten young men and said to
them, "Go up to Nabal at Carmel and
greet him in my name. 6 Say to him:
'Long life to you! Good health[p] to you
and your household! And good health
to all that is yours![q]
7 " 'Now I hear that it is sheep-
shearing time. When your shepherds
were with us, we did not mistreat[r]
them, and the whole time they were at
Carmel nothing of theirs was missing.
8 Ask your own servants and they will
tell you. Therefore be favorable toward
my young men, since we come at a festive time. Please give your servants and
your son David whatever[s] you can
find for them.' "
9 When David's men arrived, they
gave Nabal this message in David's
name. Then they waited.
10 Nabal answered David's servants,
"Who[t] is this David? Who is this son
of Jesse? Many servants are breaking
away from their masters these days.
11 Why should I take my bread[u] and
water, and the meat I have slaughtered
for my shearers, and give it to men
coming from who knows where?"
12 David's men turned around and
went back. When they arrived, they reported every word. 13 David said to his
men, "Put on your swords!" So they put
on their swords, and David put on his.
About four hundred men went[v] up
with David, while two hundred stayed
with the supplies.[w]
14 One of the servants told Nabal's
wife Abigail: "David sent messengers
from the desert to give our master his
greetings,[x] but he hurled insults at
them. 15 Yet these men were very good
to us. They did not mistreat[y] us, and
the whole time we were out in the
fields near them nothing was missing.[z] 16 Night and day they were a
wall[a] around us all the time we were
herding our sheep near them. 17 Now
think it over and see what you can do,
because disaster is hanging over our
master and his whole household. He is
such a wicked[b] man that no one can
talk to him."
18 Abigail lost no time. She took two
hundred loaves of bread, two skins of
wine, five dressed sheep, five seahs[b]
of roasted grain, a hundred cakes of
raisins[c] and two hundred cakes of
pressed figs, and loaded them on donkeys.[d] 19 Then she told her servants,
"Go on ahead;[e] I'll follow you." But
she did not tell her husband Nabal.
20 As she came riding her donkey into
a mountain ravine, there were David
and his men descending toward her,
and she met them. 21 David had just
said, "It's been useless—all my watching over this fellow's property in the
desert so that nothing of his was missing. He has paid[f] me back evil for
good. 22 May God deal with David,[c] be
it ever so severely,[g] if by morning I
leave alive one male[h] of all who belong to him!"

24:13 [t]Mt 7:20
24:14 [u]1Sa 17:43; 2Sa 9:8 [v]1Sa 26:20
24:15 [w]ver 12 [x]Ps 35:1,23; Mic 7:9 [y]Ps 43:1 [z]Ps 119:134, 154
24:16 [a]1Sa 26:17
24:17 [b]Ge 38:26; 1Sa 26:21 [c]Mt 5:44
24:18 [d]1Sa 26:23
24:20 [e]1Sa 23:17 [f]1Sa 13:14
24:21 [g]Ge 21:23; 2Sa 21:1-9 [h]1Sa 20:14-15
24:22 [i]1Sa 23:29
25:1 [j]1Sa 28:3 [k]Nu 20:29; Dt 34:8 [l]Ge 21:21; 2Ch 33:20
25:2 [m]Jos 15:55; 1Sa 23:24
25:3 [n]Pr 31:10 [o]Jos 15:13
25:6 [p]Ps 122:7; Lk 10:5 [q]1Ch 12:18
25:7 [r]ver 15
25:8 [s]Ne 8:10
25:10 [t]Jdg 9:28
25:11 [u]Jdg 8:6
25:13 [v]1Sa 23:13 [w]1Sa 30:24
25:14 [x]1Sa 13:10
25:15 [y]ver 7 [z]ver 21
25:16 [a]Ex 14:22; Job 1:10
25:17 [b]1Sa 20:7
25:18 [c]1Ch 12:40 [d]2Sa 16:1
25:19 [e]Ge 32:20
25:21 [f]Ps 109:5
25:22 [g]1Sa 3:17; 20:13 [h]1Ki 14:10; 21:21; 2Ki 9:8

[a] *1* Some Septuagint manuscripts; Hebrew *Paran*
[b] *18* That is, probably about a bushel (about 37 liters)
[c] *22* Some Septuagint manuscripts; Hebrew *with David's enemies*

ABIGAIL

Beauty, Intelligence, Sensitivity, Reward

Some men are married to women they don't deserve. Nabal, a "very wealthy" livestock owner, was one of these men (1 Samuel 25:2). His wife's name was Abigail, and the Scriptures mince no words in contrasting her personality and character with her husband's (25:3). Abigail's worth to her husband was amply displayed in an incident that brought her face to face with young David.

Before he became King of Israel and while he was still being chased by Saul, David and his 600 men set up headquarters in the same desert area where Nabal grazed his sheep. David demonstrated unusual kindness to Nabal's shepherds—he never harassed them, and even protected them from other intruders (25:15–16).

David's motives, however, were not completely magnanimous. Having been a shepherd himself, he knew that "sheep shearing" was a time of feasting. David knew this was his prime opportunity to approach Nabal and ask for payment for David's protective services. Consequently, he sent two young men to ask for help. They were to greet Nabal graciously and in David's name, sensitively reminding him of the way they had protected Nabal's shepherds.

Nabal's response was a brash and unexpected snub. He hurled at David the greatest insult any man could ever give another. "Who is this David?" he asked. He then went on to brand him nothing more than a renegade and a runaway (25:10). Everyone in Israel knew who David was, ever since his victory over Goliath. Nabal's insult was deliberately offensive.

Naturally, David was infuriated. It was as if all his pent-up anger and frustration over the years of mistreatment by Saul became focused on this stupid landowner. Overcome with emotion, he grabbed his sword and ordered 400 men to do the same. Right there and then he vowed he would kill every man associated with Nabal—which no doubt included Nabal himself (25:13).

Nabal's Opposite

Fortunately for all, Abigail was Nabal's opposite—wise, discerning and generous. Perhaps there had been other times when she had been called on to correct her husband's blunders. In any case, Nabal's servants obviously trusted her. One quickly ran to tell her the whole story of Nabal's churlish response and David's impending wrath. He was desperate—his own life was on the line because of Nabal's foolishness.

Abigail was no fool. She quickly grasped the danger of such a volatile situation, but her courageous response to the crisis never exceeded her role as a woman of her times. Without consulting her husband, who may have ordered her to do otherwise, she immediately prepared a "truckload of food" and went out to meet David as the mistress of the home. She approached him and humbly fell at his feet, taking the blame for her husband's irresponsible actions. Begging for mercy, she accurately described her husband's lack of judgment. At the same time, she appealed to David's better nature and reminded him of God's call on his life.

Just as quickly as David had lost control of his emotions, he regained perspective. He saw that what he was about to do was wrong and something he would regret for the rest of his life. He was touched and humbled by Abigail's openness, honesty and courage. More importantly, he recognized God's hand in what was happening (25:32–33).

God's Hand

After David received Abigail's gift of food, he sent her on her way in peace. When she returned home, she discovered that Nabal had "over celebrated." He became so drunk that he was incapable of carrying on an intelligent conversation. But, in the morning when he was sober, Abigail was just as honest with her husband as she had been with David. She told him exactly what had happened (25:37).

We're not told exactly what Nabal's reactions were to her report. He was either so filled with anger or fear—or both—that "his heart failed him and he became like a stone" (25:37). He never recovered. In ten days, he was dead. The Scriptures make it very clear that God's hand of judgment fell on this wicked and selfish man (25:38).

The final scene in this dramatic story is even more ironic. When David heard about Nabal's death, he sent a proposal to Abigail and asked her to become his wife. David undoubtedly could have had any woman he chose. He was, after all, a hero who was soon to be king in Israel. Why did he choose Abigail as the one to be at his side?

In their brief encounter, David had grasped Abigail's value in a way her own husband had not: He saw her as a gift from God. She had given him God's perspective when his own emotions got out of control, a fact that Nabal had not appreciated until it was too late!

Clear Take-away

What major lesson can we learn from this story? There is one that speaks loud and clear. As Christian men we need to listen to our wives—particularly when we become carnal, selfish and insensitive and they are spiritual, wise and prudent! Unfortunately, many men lord it over their mates and ignore their God-created talents and abilities.

Follow David's example: Appreciate the "Abigail" in your life. Learn to recognize all the ways God may want to use your wife to bring balance and perspective to your life. It will save you and your family needless trials and stress. Who knows? It may even save your life.

—Dr. Gene Getz

23When Abigail saw David, she quickly got off her donkey and bowed down before David with her face to the ground.[i] 24She fell at his feet and said: "My lord, let the blame be on me alone. Please let your servant speak to you; hear what your servant has to say. 25May my lord pay no attention to that wicked man Nabal. He is just like his name—his name is Fool,[j] and folly goes with him. But as for me, your servant, I did not see the men my master sent.

26"Now since the LORD has kept you, my master, from bloodshed[k] and from avenging[l] yourself with your own hands, as surely as the LORD lives and as you live, may your enemies and all who intend to harm my master be like Nabal.[m] 27And let this gift,[n] which your servant has brought to my master, be given to the men who follow you. 28Please forgive[o] your servant's offense, for the LORD will certainly make a lasting[p] dynasty for my master, because he fights the LORD's battles.[q] Let no wrongdoing[r] be found in you as long as you live. 29Even though someone is pursuing you to take your life, the life of my master will be bound securely in the bundle of the living by the LORD your God. But the lives of your enemies he will hurl[s] away as from the pocket of a sling. 30When the LORD has done for my master every good thing he promised concerning him and has appointed him leader[t] over Israel, 31my master will not have on his conscience the staggering burden of needless bloodshed or of having avenged himself. And when the LORD has brought my master success, remember[u] your servant."

32David said to Abigail, "Praise[v] be to the LORD, the God of Israel, who has sent you today to meet me. 33May you be blessed for your good judgment and for keeping me from bloodshed[w] this day and from avenging myself with my own hands. 34Otherwise, as surely as the LORD, the God of Israel, lives, who has kept me from harming you, if you had not come quickly to meet me, not one male belonging to Nabal would have been left alive by daybreak."

35Then David accepted from her hand what she had brought him and said, "Go home in peace. I have heard your words and granted[x] your request."

36When Abigail went to Nabal, he was in the house holding a banquet like that of a king. He was in high[y] spirits and very drunk.[z] So she told[a] him nothing until daybreak. 37Then in the morning, when Nabal was sober, his wife told him all these things, and his heart failed him and he became like a stone. 38About ten days later, the LORD struck[b] Nabal and he died.

39When David heard that Nabal was dead, he said, "Praise be to the LORD, who has upheld my cause against Nabal for treating me with contempt. He has kept his servant from doing wrong and has brought Nabal's wrongdoing down on his own head."

Then David sent word to Abigail, asking her to become his wife. 40His servants went to Carmel and said to Abigail, "David has sent us to you to take you to become his wife."

41She bowed down with her face to the ground and said, "Here is your maidservant, ready to serve you and wash the feet of my master's servants." 42Abigail[c] quickly got on a donkey and, attended by her five maids, went with David's messengers and became his wife. 43David had also married Ahinoam[d] of Jezreel, and they both were his wives.[e] 44But Saul had given his daughter Michal, David's wife, to Paltiel[a][f] son of Laish, who was from Gallim.[g]

David Again Spares Saul's Life

26 The Ziphites[h] went to Saul at Gibeah and said, "Is not David hiding[i] on the hill of Hakilah, which faces Jeshimon?"

2So Saul went down to the Desert of Ziph, with his three thousand chosen men of Israel, to search[j] there for David. 3Saul made his camp beside the road on the hill of Hakilah facing Jeshimon, but David stayed in the desert. When he saw that Saul had followed him there, 4he sent out scouts and learned that Saul had definitely arrived.[b]

5Then David set out and went to the place where Saul had camped. He saw where Saul and Abner[k] son of Ner, the commander of the army, had lain down. Saul was lying inside the camp, with the army encamped around him.

6David then asked Ahimelech the Hittite and Abishai son of Zeruiah,[l] Joab's brother, "Who will go down into the camp with me to Saul?"

"I'll go with you," said Abishai.

7So David and Abishai went to the army by night, and there was Saul, lying asleep inside the camp with his spear stuck in the ground near his head. Abner and the soldiers were lying around him.

8Abishai said to David, "Today God

25:23 [i]1Sa 20:41
25:25 [j]Pr 14:16
25:26 [k]ver 33 [l]Heb 10:30 [m]2Sa 18:32
25:27 [n]Ge 33:11; 1Sa 30:26
25:28 [o]ver 24 [p]2Sa 7:11,26 [q]1Sa 18:17 [r]1Sa 24:11
25:29 [s]Jer 10:18
25:30 [t]1Sa 13:14
25:31 [u]Ge 40:14
25:32 [v]Ge 24:27; Ex 18:10; Lk 1:68
25:33 [w]ver 26
25:35 [x]Ge 19:21; 1Sa 20:42; 2Ki 5:19
25:36 [y]2Sa 13:23 [z]Pr 20:1; Isa 5:11,22; Hos 4:11 [a]ver 19
25:38 [b]1Sa 26:10; 2Sa 6:7
25:42 [c]Ge 24:61-67
25:43 [d]Jos 15:56 [e]1Sa 27:3; 30:5
25:44 [f]2Sa 3:15 [g]Isa 10:30
26:1 [h]1Sa 23:19 [i]Ps 54 Title
26:2 [j]1Sa 13:2; 24:2
26:5 [k]1Sa 14:50; 17:55
26:6 [l]Jdg 7:10-11; 1Ch 2:16

a *44* Hebrew *Palti,* a variant of *Paltiel* **b** *4* Or *had come to Nacon*

has delivered your enemy into your
hands. Now let me pin him to the
ground with one thrust of my spear; I
won't strike him twice."
9But David said to Abishai, "Don't
destroy him! Who can lay a hand on
the LORD's anointed[m] and be guiltless?[n] **10**As surely as the LORD lives," he
said, "the LORD himself will strike[o]
him; either his time[p] will come and he
will die,[q] or he will go into battle and
perish. **11**But the LORD forbid that I
should lay a hand on the LORD's
anointed. Now get the spear and water
jug that are near his head, and
let's go."
12So David took the spear and water
jug near Saul's head, and they left. No
one saw or knew about it, nor did anyone wake up. They were all sleeping,
because the LORD had put them into a
deep sleep.[r]
13Then David crossed over to the
other side and stood on top of the hill
some distance away; there was a wide
space between them. **14**He called out
to the army and to Abner son of Ner,
"Aren't you going to answer me, Abner?"
Abner replied, "Who are you who
calls to the king?"
15David said, "You're a man, aren't
you? And who is like you in Israel? Why
didn't you guard your lord the king?
Someone came to destroy your lord the
king. **16**What you have done is not
good. As surely as the LORD lives, you
and your men deserve to die, because
you did not guard your master, the
LORD's anointed. Look around you.
Where are the king's spear and water
jug that were near his head?"
17Saul recognized David's voice and
said, "Is that your voice,[s] David my
son?"
David replied, "Yes it is, my lord the
king." **18**And he added, "Why is my lord
pursuing his servant? What have I
done, and what wrong[t] am I guilty of?
19Now let my lord the king listen to his
servant's words. If the LORD has incited
you against me, then may he accept an
offering.[u] If, however, men have done
it, may they be cursed before the LORD!
They have now driven me from my
share in the LORD's inheritance[v] and
have said, 'Go, serve other gods.'
20Now do not let my blood fall to the
ground far from the presence of the
LORD. The king of Israel has come out
to look for a flea[w]—as one hunts a
partridge in the mountains."
21Then Saul said, "I have sinned.[x]
Come back, David my son. Because
you considered my life precious[y] today, I will not try to harm you again.

26:9 [m]2Sa 1:14 [n]1Sa 24:5
26:10 [o]1Sa 25:38; Ro 12:19 [p]Ge 47:29; Dt 31:14; Ps 37:13 [q]1Sa 31:6; 2Sa 1:1
26:12 [r]Ge 2:21; 15:12
26:17 [s]1Sa 24:16
26:18 [t]1Sa 24:9, 11-14
26:19 [u]2Sa 16:11 [v]2Sa 14:16
26:20 [w]1Sa 24:14
26:21 [x]Ex 9:27; 1Sa 15:24 [y]1Sa 24:17
26:23 [z]Ps 62:12 [a]Ps 7:8; 18:20, 24
26:24 [b]Ps 54:7
27:2 [c]1Sa 25:13 [d]1Sa 21:10 [e]1Ki 2:39
27:3 [f]1Sa 25:43; 30:3
27:6 [g]Jos 15:31; 19:5; Ne 11:28
27:7 [h]1Sa 29:3
27:8 [i]Jos 13:2,13 [j]Ex 17:8; 1Sa 15:7-8 [k]Ex 15:22
27:9 [l]1Sa 15:3
27:10 [m]1Sa 30:29; 1Ch 2:9,25 [n]Jdg 1:16

Surely I have acted like a fool and have
erred greatly."
22"Here is the king's spear," David
answered. "Let one of your young men
come over and get it. **23**The LORD rewards[z] every man for his righteousness[a] and faithfulness. The LORD delivered you into my hands today, but I
would not lay a hand on the LORD's
anointed. **24**As surely as I valued your
life today, so may the LORD value my
life and deliver[b] me from all trouble."
25Then Saul said to David, "May you
be blessed, my son David; you will do
great things and surely triumph."
So David went on his way, and Saul
returned home.

David Among the Philistines

27 But David thought to himself, "One
of these days I will be destroyed by
the hand of Saul. The best thing I can
do is to escape to the land of the Philistines. Then Saul will give up searching
for me anywhere in Israel, and I will
slip out of his hand."
2So David and the six hundred
men[c] with him left and went[d] over to
Achish[e] son of Maoch king of Gath.
3David and his men settled in Gath
with Achish. Each man had his family
with him, and David had his two
wives:[f] Ahinoam of Jezreel and Abigail of Carmel, the widow of Nabal.
4When Saul was told that David had
fled to Gath, he no longer searched for
him.
5Then David said to Achish, "If I
have found favor in your eyes, let a
place be assigned to me in one of the
country towns, that I may live there.
Why should your servant live in the
royal city with you?"
6So on that day Achish gave him Ziklag,[g] and it has belonged to the kings
of Judah ever since. **7**David lived[h] in
Philistine territory a year and four
months.
8Now David and his men went up
and raided the Geshurites,[i] the Gir-
zites and the Amalekites.[j] (From ancient times these peoples had lived in
the land extending to Shur[k] and
Egypt.) **9**Whenever David attacked an
area, he did not leave a man or woman
alive,[l] but took sheep and cattle, donkeys and camels, and clothes. Then he
returned to Achish.
10When Achish asked, "Where did
you go raiding today?" David would
say, "Against the Negev of Judah" or
"Against the Negev of Jerahmeel[m]" or
"Against the Negev of the Kenites.[n]"
11He did not leave a man or woman
alive to be brought to Gath, for he

thought, "They might inform on us and say, 'This is what David did.'" And such was his practice as long as he lived in Philistine territory. 12Achish trusted David and said to himself, "He has become so odious to his people, the Israelites, that he will be my servant forever."

Saul and the Witch of Endor

28 In those days the Philistines gathered[o] their forces to fight against Israel. Achish said to David, "You must understand that you and your men will accompany me in the army."

2David said, "Then you will see for yourself what your servant can do."

Achish replied, "Very well, I will make you my bodyguard for life."

3Now Samuel was dead,[p] and all Israel had mourned for him and buried him in his own town of Ramah.[q] Saul had expelled the mediums and spiritists[r] from the land.

4The Philistines assembled and came and set up camp at Shunem,[s] while Saul gathered all the Israelites and set up camp at Gilboa.[t] 5When Saul saw the Philistine army, he was afraid; terror filled his heart. 6He inquired[u] of the LORD, but the LORD did not answer him by dreams[v] or Urim[w] or prophets. 7Saul then said to his attendants, "Find me a woman who is a medium,[x] so I may go and inquire of her."

"There is one in Endor,[y]" they said.

8So Saul disguised[z] himself, putting on other clothes, and at night he and two men went to the woman. "Consult[a] a spirit for me," he said, "and bring up for me the one I name."

9But the woman said to him, "Surely you know what Saul has done. He has cut off[b] the mediums and spiritists from the land. Why have you set a trap for my life to bring about my death?"

10Saul swore to her by the LORD, "As surely as the LORD lives, you will not be punished for this."

11Then the woman asked, "Whom shall I bring up for you?"

"Bring up Samuel," he said.

12When the woman saw Samuel, she cried out at the top of her voice and said to Saul, "Why have you deceived me? You are Saul!"

13The king said to her, "Don't be afraid. What do you see?"

The woman said, "I see a spirit[a] coming up out of the ground."

14"What does he look like?" he asked.

"An old man wearing a robe[c] is coming up," she said.

Then Saul knew it was Samuel, and he bowed down and prostrated himself with his face to the ground.

15Samuel said to Saul, "Why have you disturbed me by bringing me up?"

"I am in great distress," Saul said. "The Philistines are fighting against me, and God has turned[d] away from me. He no longer answers me, either by prophets or by dreams. So I have called on you to tell me what to do."

16Samuel said, "Why do you consult me, now that the LORD has turned away from you and become your enemy? 17The LORD has done what he predicted through me. The LORD has torn[e] the kingdom out of your hands and given it to one of your neighbors—to David. 18Because you did not obey[f] the LORD or carry out his fierce wrath[g] against the Amalekites, the LORD has done this to you today. 19The LORD will hand over both Israel and you to the Philistines, and tomorrow you and your sons[h] will be with me. The LORD will also hand over the army of Israel to the Philistines."

20Immediately Saul fell full length on the ground, filled with fear because of Samuel's words. His strength was gone, for he had eaten nothing all that day and night.

21When the woman came to Saul and saw that he was greatly shaken, she said, "Look, your maidservant has obeyed you. I took my life[i] in my hands and did what you told me to do. 22Now please listen to your servant and let me give you some food so you may eat and have the strength to go on your way."

23He refused[j] and said, "I will not eat."

But his men joined the woman in urging him, and he listened to them. He got up from the ground and sat on the couch.

24The woman had a fattened calf at the house, which she butchered at once. She took some flour, kneaded it and baked bread without yeast. 25Then she set it before Saul and his men, and they ate. That same night they got up and left.

Achish Sends David Back to Ziklag

29 The Philistines gathered[k] all their forces at Aphek,[l] and Israel camped by the spring in Jezreel.[m] 2As the Philistine rulers marched with their units of hundreds and thousands, David and his men were marching at the rear[n] with Achish. 3The commanders

28:1 [o]1Sa 29:1
28:3 [p]1Sa 25:1 [q]1Sa 7:17 [r]Ex 22:18; Lev 19:31; 20:27; Dt 18:10-11; 1Sa 15:23
28:4 [s]Jos 19:18; 2Ki 4:8 [t]1Sa 31:1,3
28:6 [u]1Sa 14:37; 1Ch 10:13-14; Pr 1:28 [v]Nu 12:6 [w]Ex 28:30; Nu 27:21
28:7 [x]Ac 16:16 [y]Jos 17:11
28:8 [z]2Ch 18:29; 35:22 [a]Dt 18:10-11; 1Ch 10:13; Isa 8:19
28:9 [b]ver 3
28:14 [c]1Sa 15:27; 24:8
28:15 [d]ver 6; 1Sa 18:12
28:17 [e]1Sa 15:28
28:18 [f]1Sa 15:20 [g]1Ki 20:42
28:19 [h]1Sa 31:2
28:21 [i]Jdg 12:3; 1Sa 19:5; Job 13:14
28:23 [j]2Ki 5:13
29:1 [k]1Sa 28:1 [l]Jos 12:18; 1Sa 4:1 [m]2Ki 9:30
29:2 [n]1Sa 28:2

a *13* Or *see spirits*; or *see gods*

of the Philistines asked, "What about
these Hebrews?"

Achish replied, "Is this not David,
who was an officer of Saul king of Israel? He has already been with me for
over a year,[o] and from the day he left
Saul until now, I have found no fault in
him."

4But the Philistine commanders
were angry with him and said, "Send[p]
the man back, that he may return to
the place you assigned him. He must
not go with us into battle, or he will
turn[q] against us during the fighting.
How better could he regain his master's favor than by taking the heads of
our own men? **5**Isn't this the David
they sang about in their dances:

" 'Saul has slain his thousands,
and David his tens of
thousands'?"[r]

6So Achish called David and said to
him, "As surely as the LORD lives, you
have been reliable, and I would be
pleased to have you serve with me in
the army. From the day[s] you came to
me until now, I have found no fault in
you, but the rulers[t] don't approve of
you. **7**Turn back and go in peace; do
nothing to displease the Philistine rulers."

8"But what have I done?" asked David. "What have you found against
your servant from the day I came to
you until now? Why can't I go and fight
against the enemies of my lord the
king?"

9Achish answered, "I know that you
have been as pleasing in my eyes as an
angel[u] of God; nevertheless, the Philistine commanders[v] have said, 'He
must not go up with us into battle.'
10Now get up early, along with your
master's servants who have come with
you, and leave[w] in the morning as
soon as it is light."

11So David and his men got up early
in the morning to go back to the land
of the Philistines, and the Philistines
went up to Jezreel.

David Destroys the Amalekites

30 David and his men reached Ziklag[x] on the third day. Now the
Amalekites[y] had raided the Negev and
Ziklag. They had attacked Ziklag and
burned it, **2**and had taken captive the
women and all who were in it, both
young and old. They killed none of
them, but carried them off as they went
on their way.

3When David and his men came to
Ziklag, they found it destroyed by fire
and their wives and sons and daughters taken captive. **4**So David and his
men wept aloud until they had no
strength left to weep. **5**David's two
wives[z] had been captured—Ahinoam
of Jezreel and Abigail, the widow of Nabal of Carmel. **6**David was greatly distressed because the men were talking
of stoning[a] him; each one was bitter
in spirit because of his sons and
daughters. But David found strength[b]
in the LORD his God.

7Then David said to Abiathar[c] the
priest, the son of Ahimelech, "Bring me
the ephod.[d]" Abiathar brought it to
him, **8**and David inquired[e] of the
LORD, "Shall I pursue this raiding party?
Will I overtake them?"

"Pursue them," he answered. "You
will certainly overtake them and succeed[f] in the rescue."

9David and the six hundred men[g]
with him came to the Besor Ravine,
where some stayed behind, **10**for two
hundred men were too exhausted[h] to
cross the ravine. But David and four
hundred men continued the pursuit.

11They found an Egyptian in a field
and brought him to David. They gave
him water to drink and food to eat—
12part of a cake of pressed figs and two
cakes of raisins. He ate and was revived,[i] for he had not eaten any food
or drunk any water for three days and
three nights.

13David asked him, "To whom do
you belong, and where do you come
from?"

He said, "I am an Egyptian, the slave
of an Amalekite. My master abandoned
me when I became ill three days ago.
14We raided the Negev of the Kerethites[j] and the territory belonging to Judah and the Negev of Caleb.[k] And we
burned[l] Ziklag."

15David asked him, "Can you lead
me down to this raiding party?"

He answered, "Swear to me before
God that you will not kill me or hand
me over to my master, and I will take
you down to them."

16He led David down, and there they
were, scattered over the countryside,
eating, drinking and reveling[m] because of the great amount of plunder[n]
they had taken from the land of the
Philistines and from Judah. **17**David
fought[o] them from dusk until the evening of the next day, and none of them
got away, except four hundred young
men who rode off on camels and
fled.[p] **18**David recovered[q] everything
the Amalekites had taken, including his
two wives. **19**Nothing was missing:
young or old, boy or girl, plunder or
anything else they had taken. David
brought everything back. **20**He took all

29:3 [o] 1Sa 27:7; Da 6:5
29:4 [p] 1Ch 12:19 [q] 1Sa 14:21
29:5 [r] 1Sa 18:7; 21:11
29:6 [s] 1Sa 27:8-12 [t] ver 3
29:9 [u] 2Sa 14:17,20; 19:27 [v] ver 4
29:10 [w] 1Ch 12:19
30:1 [x] 1Sa 29:4,11 [y] 1Sa 15:7; 27:8
30:5 [z] 1Sa 25:43; 2Sa 2:2
30:6 [a] Ex 17:4; Jn 8:59 [b] Ps 27:14; 56:3-4,11; Ro 4:20
30:7 [c] 1Sa 22:20 [d] 1Sa 23:9
30:8 [e] 1Sa 23:2 [f] ver 18
30:9 [g] 1Sa 27:2
30:10 [h] ver 9,21
30:12 [i] Jdg 15:19
30:14 [j] 2Sa 8:18; 1Ki 1:38,44; Eze 25:16; Zep 2:5 [k] ver 16; Jos 14:13; 15:13 [l] ver 1
30:16 [m] Lk 12:19 [n] ver 14
30:17 [o] 1Sa 11:11 [p] 1Sa 15:3
30:18 [q] Ge 14:16

the flocks and herds, and his men drove them ahead of the other livestock, saying, "This is David's plunder."

21Then David came to the two hundred men who had been too exhausted[r] to follow him and who were left behind at the Besor Ravine. They came out to meet David and the people with him. As David and his men approached, he greeted them. 22But all the evil men and troublemakers among David's followers said, "Because they did not go out with us, we will not share with them the plunder we recovered. However, each man may take his wife and children and go."

23David replied, "No, my brothers, you must not do that with what the LORD has given us. He has protected us and handed over to us the forces that came against us. 24Who will listen to what you say? The share of the man who stayed with the supplies is to be the same as that of him who went down to the battle. All will share alike.[s]" 25David made this a statute and ordinance for Israel from that day to this.

26When David arrived in Ziklag, he sent some of the plunder to the elders of Judah, who were his friends, saying, "Here is a present for you from the plunder of the LORD's enemies."

27He sent it to those who were in Bethel,[t] Ramoth[u] Negev and Jattir;[v] 28to those in Aroer,[w] Siphmoth, Eshtemoa[x] 29and Racal; to those in the towns of the Jerahmeelites[y] and the Kenites;[z] 30to those in Hormah,[a] Bor Ashan,[b] Athach 31and Hebron;[c] and to those in all the other places where David and his men had roamed.

Saul Takes His Life

31 Now the Philistines fought against Israel; the Israelites fled before them, and many fell slain on Mount Gilboa.[d] 2The Philistines pressed hard after Saul and his sons, and they killed his sons Jonathan, Abinadab and Malki-Shua. 3The fighting grew fierce around Saul, and when the archers overtook him, they wounded[e] him critically.

4Saul said to his armor-bearer, "Draw your sword and run me through,[f] or these uncircumcised[g] fellows will come and run me through and abuse me."

But his armor-bearer was terrified and would not do it; so Saul took his own sword and fell on it. 5When the armor-bearer saw that Saul was dead, he too fell on his sword and died with him. 6So Saul and his three sons and his armor-bearer and all his men died together that same day.

7When the Israelites along the valley and those across the Jordan saw that the Israelite army had fled and that Saul and his sons had died, they abandoned their towns and fled. And the Philistines came and occupied them.

8The next day, when the Philistines came to strip the dead, they found Saul and his three sons fallen on Mount Gilboa. 9They cut off his head and stripped off his armor, and they sent messengers throughout the land of the Philistines to proclaim the news[h] in the temple of their idols and among their people.[i] 10They put his armor in the temple of the Ashtoreths[j] and fastened his body to the wall of Beth Shan.[k]

11When the people of Jabesh Gilead[l] heard of what the Philistines had done to Saul, 12all their valiant men journeyed through the night to Beth Shan. They took down the bodies of Saul and his sons from the wall of Beth Shan and went to Jabesh, where they burned[m] them. 13Then they took their bones[n] and buried them under a tamarisk[o] tree at Jabesh, and they fasted[p] seven days.[q]

30:21 [r] ver 10
30:24 [s] Nu 31:27; Jos 22:8
30:27 [t] Jos 7:2 [u] Jos 19:8 [v] Jos 15:48
30:28 [w] Jos 13:16 [x] Jos 15:50
30:29 [y] 1Sa 27:10 [z] Jdg 1:16; 1Sa 15:6
30:30 [a] Nu 14:45; Jdg 1:17 [b] Jos 15:42
30:31 [c] Jos 14:13; 2Sa 2:1,4
31:1 [d] 1Sa 28:4; 1Ch 10:1-12
31:3 [e] 2Sa 1:6
31:4 [f] Jdg 9:54; 2Sa 1:6,10 [g] 1Sa 14:6
31:9 [h] 2Sa 1:20 [i] Jdg 16:24
31:10 [j] Jdg 2:12-13; 1Sa 7:3 [k] Jos 17:11; 2Sa 21:12
31:11 [l] 1Sa 11:1
31:12 [m] 2Sa 2:4-7; 2Ch 16:14; Am 6:10
31:13 [n] 2Sa 21:12-14 [o] 1Sa 22:6 [p] 2Sa 1:12 [q] Ge 50:10

2 SAMUEL

AT A GLANCE

Key Principle: Obedience to God's commands (1—7) leads to his blessings (8—10), and disobedience to God's commands (11) leads to his discipline (12—24).
Author: Unknown; probably compiled before the Assyrian captivity of Israel (722 B.C.).
Time and Place: 1010 B.C. to 970 B.C. / David's reign in Hebron and Jerusalem
Key Verses: 5:12; 7:12–13, 25–26; 22:21

BENEFIT

Second Samuel centers on the life and character of David, who stands in the middle of the family line between Abraham and Christ. While we have much to learn from his faithfulness and responsiveness to God, we can also learn from how he repented after committing adultery and murder and was restored to favor with God. David's passion for God is a model for us, and though he strayed from the path at times, he always returned to the Lord his God.

SETTING

In the Hebrew Bible, 1 and 2 Samuel were a single book that developed the historical transition from the theocracy under the judges to the institution of the monarchy. Second Samuel picks up the story of Saul's death at the end of 1 Samuel. It then records David's 7-year reign over Judah from Hebron (1010 B.C. to 1003 B.C.) and his 33-year reign over the united kingdom of Israel and Judah from Jerusalem (1003 B.C. to 970 B.C.).

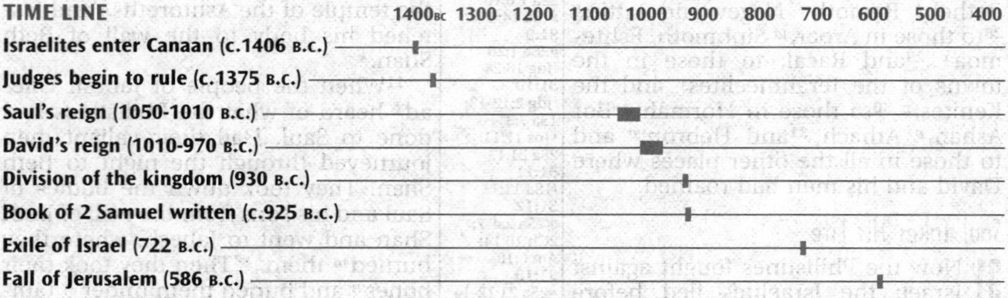

THEME AND PURPOSE

The books of Samuel offer a prophetic perspective on the status of the united kingdom of Israel and Judah. They stress that the political and military conditions of the kingdom are directly related to the spiritual condition of the king—as the king goes, so goes the nation. Second Samuel also depicts the ongoing hostility between the ten northern tribes of Israel and the two southern tribes of Judah and Benjamin. It comes as no surprise, then, that the northern and southern kingdoms that were united under Saul, David and Solomon finally split after Solomon's death in 930 B.C. Nevertheless, God's covenant with David in chapter 7 assures that David's dynasty will be established forever (in contrast to the nine dynasties of the northern kingdom).

UNIQUE CONTRIBUTION

While 1 Samuel details the establishment of the kingdom in Israel, 2 Samuel tells how David, its greatest king, solidified and expanded that kingdom. David consolidated the kingdom, captured Jerusalem, and set that city up as the royal capital. We know more about David than about any other Old Testament character; 2 Samuel portrays his military and economic accomplishments as well as his spiritual and relational successes and failures.

LINKS TO THE NEW TESTAMENT

As the parallel note in the introduction to 1 Samuel shows, David is one of the clearest Old Testament pictures of the Messiah to come. This is especially true of the first ten chapters in 2 Samuel, before David's sin against Bathsheba and Uriah in chapter 11. The Davidic covenant in chapter 7, with its promise of an eternal kingdom and lineage, relates directly to the promises Mary received concerning her son Jesus (Luke 1:32–33). Christ is the "son of David" (Matthew 21:9; 22:45), and he will reign on David's throne (Isaiah 9:6–7).

OVERVIEW

FOCUS	David's Success		David's Sin	David's Setbacks
REFERENCE	1	10	11	12 — 24
TOPICS	Obedience leads to 1 — 7	blessing; 8 — 10	disobedience	leads to discipline
	Civil War, Coronation, Conquests		Crimes	Conflicts and Consequences
	Political, Spiritual and Military Attainments		Adultery, Murder	Threats to David's House and Kingdom
LOCATION	David in Hebron	David in Jerusalem		
TIME	~7½ Years	~33 Years		

After Saul's death, David is anointed king over Judah and reigns for 7 1/2 years from Hebron. During this time, Saul's son Ish-Bosheth is king over Israel. Abner, Israel's army commander, defects and plans to join forces with David. Before he can do so, however, Abner is murdered by Joab, David's military commander (1—4). Ish-Bosheth is assassinated by his men, and David is anointed king over Israel and Judah. He conquers Jerusalem and makes it the royal capital from which he reigns for the next 33 years (5).

After David brings the ark of the covenant to Jerusalem, God makes a covenant with him (6—7) and David's righteous rule is established and blessed (8—10). His crimes of adultery and murder (11) change the course of his life. Although he repents and returns to the Lord, the consequences become evident first in his household (death, incest, and murder; 12—13) and then in his kingdom (Absalom's rebellion and David's flight from Jerusalem; 14—18). Although David returns to the throne after Absalom is overthrown, the glory and blessing that characterized the first part of his reign are never fully restored (19—24).

2 SAMUEL

David Hears of Saul's Death

1 After the death[a] of Saul, David returned from defeating[b] the Amalekites and stayed in Ziklag two days. 2On the third day a man[c] arrived from Saul's camp, with his clothes torn and with dust on his head.[d] When he came to David, he fell to the ground to pay him honor.

3"Where have you come from?" David asked him.

He answered, "I have escaped from the Israelite camp."

4"What happened?" David asked. "Tell me."

He said, "The men fled from the battle. Many of them fell and died. And Saul and his son Jonathan are dead."

5Then David said to the young man who brought him the report, "How do you know that Saul and his son Jonathan are dead?"

6"I happened to be on Mount Gilboa,[e]" the young man said, "and there was Saul, leaning on his spear, with the chariots and riders almost upon him. 7When he turned around and saw me, he called out to me, and I said, 'What can I do?'

8"He asked me, 'Who are you?'

" 'An Amalekite,[f]' I answered.

9"Then he said to me, 'Stand over me and kill me! I am in the throes of death, but I'm still alive.'

10"So I stood over him and killed him, because I knew that after he had fallen he could not survive. And I took the crown[g] that was on his head and the band on his arm and have brought them here to my lord."

11Then David and all the men with him took hold of their clothes and tore[h] them. 12They mourned and wept and fasted till evening for Saul and his son Jonathan, and for the army of the LORD and the house of Israel, because they had fallen by the sword.

13David said to the young man who brought him the report, "Where are you from?"

"I am the son of an alien, an Amalekite,[i]" he answered.

14David asked him, "Why were you not afraid to lift your hand to destroy the LORD's anointed?[j]"

15Then David called one of his men and said, "Go, strike him down!"[k] So he struck him down, and he died.[l] 16For David had said to him, "Your blood be on your own head.[m] Your own mouth testified against you when you said, 'I killed the LORD's anointed.' "

1:1 [a]1Sa 31:6 [b]1Sa 30:17 **1:2** [c]2Sa 4:10 [d]1Sa 4:12 **1:6** [e]1Sa 28:4; 31:2-4 **1:8** [f]1Sa 15:2; 30:13,17 **1:10** [g]Jdg 9:54; 2Ki 11:12 **1:11** [h]Ge 37:29; 2Sa 3:31; 13:31 **1:13** [i]ver 8 **1:14** [j]1Sa 24:6; 26:9 **1:15** [k]2Sa 4:12 [l]2Sa 4:10 **1:16** [m]Lev 20:9; 2Sa 3:28-29; 1Ki 2:32; Mt 27:24-25; Ac 18:6 **1:17** [n]2Ch 35:25 **1:18** [o]Jos 10:13; 1Sa 31:3 **1:19** [p]ver 27 **1:20** [q]Mic 1:10 [r]1Sa 31:8 [s]Ex 15:20; 1Sa 18:6 **1:21** [t]ver 6; 1Sa 31:1 [u]Eze 31:15 [v]Isa 21:5 **1:22** [w]Isa 34:3,7 [x]Dt 32:42; 1Sa 18:4 **1:23** [y]Dt 28:49; Jer 4:13 [z]Jdg 14:18 **1:26** [a]1Sa 20:42 [b]1Sa 18:1

David's Lament for Saul and Jonathan

17David took up this lament[n] concerning Saul and his son Jonathan, 18and ordered that the men of Judah be taught this lament of the bow (it is written in the Book of Jashar):[o]

19"Your glory, O Israel, lies slain on your heights.
How the mighty have fallen![p]

20"Tell it not in Gath,[q]
proclaim it not in the streets of Ashkelon,
lest the daughters of the Philistines[r] be glad,
lest the daughters of the uncircumcised rejoice.[s]

21"O mountains of Gilboa,[t]
may you have neither dew nor rain,
nor fields that yield offerings[u] ⌞of grain⌟.
For there the shield of the mighty was defiled,
the shield of Saul—no longer rubbed with oil.[v]
22From the blood[w] of the slain,
from the flesh of the mighty,
the bow[x] of Jonathan did not turn back,
the sword of Saul did not return unsatisfied.

23"Saul and Jonathan—
in life they were loved and gracious,
and in death they were not parted.
They were swifter than eagles,[y]
they were stronger than lions.[z]

24"O daughters of Israel,
weep for Saul,
who clothed you in scarlet and finery,
who adorned your garments with ornaments of gold.

25"How the mighty have fallen in battle!
Jonathan lies slain on your heights.
26I grieve for you, Jonathan my brother;[a]
you were very dear to me.
Your love for me was wonderful,[b]

more wonderful than that of
women.

27 "How the mighty have fallen!
The weapons of war have
perished!" [c]

David Anointed King Over Judah

2 In the course of time, David inquired[d] of the LORD. "Shall I go up to one of the towns of Judah?" he asked.

The LORD said, "Go up."

David asked, "Where shall I go?"

"To Hebron,"[e] the LORD answered.

2 So David went up there with his two wives,[f] Ahinoam of Jezreel and Abigail,[g] the widow of Nabal of Carmel.
3 David also took the men who were with him,[h] each with his family, and they settled in Hebron and its towns.
4 Then the men of Judah came to Hebron[i] and there they anointed[j] David king over the house of Judah.

When David was told that it was the men of Jabesh Gilead[k] who had buried Saul,
5 he sent messengers to the men of Jabesh Gilead to say to them, "The LORD bless[l] you for showing this kindness to Saul your master by burying him.
6 May the LORD now show you kindness and faithfulness,[m] and I too will show you the same favor because you have done this.
7 Now then, be strong and brave, for Saul your master is dead, and the house of Judah has anointed me king over them."

War Between the Houses of David and Saul

8 Meanwhile, Abner[n] son of Ner, the commander of Saul's army, had taken Ish-Bosheth son of Saul and brought him over to Mahanaim.[o]
9 He made him king over Gilead,[p] Ashuri[a][q] and Jezreel, and also over Ephraim, Benjamin and all Israel.[r]

10 Ish-Bosheth son of Saul was forty years old when he became king over Israel, and he reigned two years. The house of Judah, however, followed David.
11 The length of time David was king in Hebron over the house of Judah was seven years and six months.[s]

12 Abner son of Ner, together with the men of Ish-Bosheth son of Saul, left Mahanaim and went to Gibeon.[t]
13 Joab[u] son of Zeruiah and David's men went out and met them at the pool of Gibeon. One group sat down on one side of the pool and one group on the other side.

14 Then Abner said to Joab, "Let's have some of the young men get up and fight hand to hand in front of us."

"All right, let them do it," Joab said.

15 So they stood up and were counted off—twelve men for Benjamin and Ish-Bosheth son of Saul, and twelve for David.
16 Then each man grabbed his opponent by the head and thrust his dagger into his opponent's side, and they fell down together. So that place in Gibeon was called Helkath Hazzurim.[b]

17 The battle that day was very fierce, and Abner and the men of Israel were defeated[v] by David's men.

18 The three sons of Zeruiah[w] were there: Joab,[x] Abishai[y] and Asahel.[z] Now Asahel was as fleet-footed as a wild gazelle.[a]
19 He chased Abner, turning neither to the right nor to the left as he pursued him.
20 Abner looked behind him and asked, "Is that you, Asahel?"

"It is," he answered.

21 Then Abner said to him, "Turn aside to the right or to the left; take on one of the young men and strip him of his weapons." But Asahel would not stop chasing him.

22 Again Abner warned Asahel, "Stop chasing me! Why should I strike you down? How could I look your brother Joab in the face?"[b]

23 But Asahel refused to give up the pursuit; so Abner thrust the butt of his spear into Asahel's stomach,[c] and the spear came out through his back. He fell there and died on the spot. And every man stopped when he came to the place where Asahel had fallen and died.[d]

1:27 [c] ver 19,25; 1Sa 2:4
2:1 [d] 1Sa 23:2, 11-12 [e] Ge 13:18; 1Sa 30:31
2:2 [f] 1Sa 25:43; 30:5 [g] 1Sa 25:42
2:3 [h] 1Sa 27:2; 30:9
2:4 [i] 1Sa 30:31 [j] 1Sa 2:35; 2Sa 5:3-5 [k] 1Sa 31:11-13
2:5 [l] 1Sa 23:21
2:6 [m] Ex 34:6; 1Ti 1:16
2:8 [n] 1Sa 14:50 [o] Ge 32:2
2:9 [p] Nu 32:26 [q] Jdg 1:32 [r] 1Ch 12:29
2:11 [s] 2Sa 5:5
2:12 [t] Jos 18:25
2:13 [u] 2Sa 8:16; 1Ch 2:16; 11:6
2:17 [v] 2Sa 3:1
2:18 [w] 2Sa 3:39 [x] 2Sa 3:30 [y] 1Sa 26:6 [z] 1Ch 2:16 [a] 1Ch 12:8
2:22 [b] 2Sa 3:27
2:23 [c] 2Sa 3:27; 4:6 [d] 2Sa 20:12

[a] 9 Or *Asher* [b] 16 *Helkath Hazzurim* means *field of daggers* or *field of hostilities.*

2:5–6 PROMISE 1

HONORING GOD'S ANOINTED

How many of us, having been pursued by someone whose sole obsession in life had been to kill us, would shed a tear at his death?

David did exactly that. In the previous chapter, David lamented the deaths of Saul and Jonathan, and made sure that the nation joined him in grieving for the fallen king (1:17–18). Even after Saul's death, David honored God's appointment of this man to the monarchy in Israel. He also blessed the people of Jabesh Gilead who had been careful to honor Saul's position by giving him a proper burial. As is so evident in the first book of Samuel, David consistently demonstrated a heart for and sensitivity to the things of the Lord.

For the next Promise 1 reading go to page 337.

24But Joab and Abishai pursued Abner, and as the sun was setting, they
came to the hill of Ammah, near Giah
on the way to the wasteland of Gibeon.
25Then the men of Benjamin rallied behind Abner. They formed themselves
into a group and took their stand on
top of a hill.

26Abner called out to Joab, "Must the
sword devour[e] forever? Don't you realize that this will end in bitterness?
How long before you order your men
to stop pursuing their brothers?"

27Joab answered, "As surely as God
lives, if you had not spoken, the men
would have continued the pursuit of
their brothers until morning.[a]"

28So Joab[f] blew the trumpet,[g] and
all the men came to a halt; they no
longer pursued Israel, nor did they
fight anymore.

29All that night Abner and his men
marched through the Arabah. They
crossed the Jordan, continued through
the whole Bithron[b] and came to Mahanaim.[h]

30Then Joab returned from pursuing
Abner and assembled all his men. Besides Asahel, nineteen of David's men
were found missing.
31But David's men
had killed three hundred and sixty
Benjamites who were with Abner.
32They took Asahel and buried him in
his father's tomb[i] at Bethlehem. Then
Joab and his men marched all night
and arrived at Hebron by daybreak.

3 The war between the house of Saul
and the house of David lasted a long
time.[j] David grew stronger and stronger,[k] while the house of Saul grew
weaker and weaker.[l]

2Sons were born to David in Hebron:
His firstborn was Amnon the
son of Ahinoam[m] of Jezreel;
3his second, Kileab the son of
Abigail[n] the widow of Nabal
of Carmel;
the third, Absalom[o] the son of
Maacah daughter of Talmai
king of Geshur;[p]
4the fourth, Adonijah[q] the son
of Haggith;
the fifth, Shephatiah the son of
Abital;
5and the sixth, Ithream the son
of David's wife Eglah.
These were born to David in
Hebron.

Abner Goes Over to David

6During the war between the house
of Saul and the house of David, Abner
had been strengthening his own position in the house of Saul.
7Now Saul
had had a concubine[r] named Rizpah[s] daughter of Aiah. And Ish-
Bosheth said to Abner, "Why did you
sleep with my father's concubine?"

8Abner was very angry because of
what Ish-Bosheth said and he answered, "Am I a dog's head[t]—on Judah's side? This very day I am loyal to
the house of your father Saul and to his
family and friends. I haven't handed
you over to David. Yet now you accuse
me of an offense involving this woman!
9May God deal with Abner, be it ever so
severely, if I do not do for David what
the LORD promised[u] him on oath
10and transfer the kingdom from the
house of Saul and establish David's
throne over Israel and Judah from Dan
to Beersheba."[v]
11Ish-Bosheth did not
dare to say another word to Abner, because he was afraid of him.

12Then Abner sent messengers on
his behalf to say to David, "Whose land
is it? Make an agreement with me, and
I will help you bring all Israel over to
you."

13"Good," said David. "I will make
an agreement with you. But I demand
one thing of you: Do not come into
my presence unless you bring Michal
daughter of Saul when you come to see
me."[w]
14Then David sent messengers
to Ish-Bosheth son of Saul, demanding, "Give me my wife Michal,[x] whom
I betrothed to myself for the price of a
hundred Philistine foreskins."

15So Ish-Bosheth gave orders and
had her taken away from her husband[y] Paltiel[z] son of Laish.
16Her
husband, however, went with her,
weeping behind her all the way to Bahurim.[a] Then Abner said to him, "Go
back home!" So he went back.

17Abner conferred with the elders[b]
of Israel and said, "For some time you
have wanted to make David your king.
18Now do it! For the LORD promised
David, 'By my servant David I will rescue my people Israel from the hand of
the Philistines[c] and from the hand of
all their enemies.[d]'"

19Abner also spoke to the Benjamites
in person. Then he went to Hebron to
tell David everything that Israel and
the whole house of Benjamin[e] wanted
to do.
20When Abner, who had twenty
men with him, came to David at Hebron, David prepared a feast for him
and his men.
21Then Abner said to Da-
vid, "Let me go at once and assemble

2:26 [e]Dt 32:42; Jer 46:10,14
2:28 [f]2Sa 18:16 [g]Jdg 3:27
2:29 [h]ver 8
2:32 [i]Ge 49:29
3:1 [j]1Ki 14:30 [k]2Sa 5:10 [l]2Sa 2:17
3:2 [m]1Sa 25:43; 1Ch 3:1-3
3:3 [n]1Sa 25:42 [o]2Sa 13:1,28 [p]1Sa 27:8; 2Sa 13:37; 14:32; 15:8
3:4 [q]1Ki 1:5,11
3:7 [r]2Sa 16:21-22 [s]2Sa 21:8-11
3:8 [t]1Sa 24:14; 2Sa 9:8; 16:9
3:9 [u]1Sa 15:28; 1Ki 19:2
3:10 [v]Jdg 20:1; 1Sa 3:20
3:13 [w]Ge 43:5; 1Sa 18:20
3:14 [x]1Sa 18:27
3:15 [y]Dt 24:1-4 [z]1Sa 25:44
3:16 [a]2Sa 16:5; 19:16
3:17 [b]Jdg 11:11
3:18 [c]1Sa 9:16 [d]1Sa 15:28; 2Sa 8:6
3:19 [e]1Sa 10:20-21; 1Ch 12:2,16,29

[a]*27* Or *spoken this morning, the men would not have taken up the pursuit of their brothers;* or *spoken, the men would have given up the pursuit of their brothers by morning* [b]*29* Or *morning;* or *ravine;* the meaning of the Hebrew for this word is uncertain.

all Israel for my lord the king, so that they may make a compact[f] with you, and that you may rule over all that your heart desires."[g] So David sent Abner away, and he went in peace.

Joab Murders Abner

22 Just then David's men and Joab returned from a raid and brought with them a great deal of plunder. But Abner was no longer with David in Hebron, because David had sent him away, and he had gone in peace. 23 When Joab and all the soldiers with him arrived, he was told that Abner son of Ner had come to the king and that the king had sent him away and that he had gone in peace.

24 So Joab went to the king and said, "What have you done? Look, Abner came to you. Why did you let him go? Now he is gone! 25 You know Abner son of Ner; he came to deceive you and observe your movements and find out everything you are doing."

26 Joab then left David and sent messengers after Abner, and they brought him back from the well of Sirah. But David did not know it. 27 Now when Abner[h] returned to Hebron, Joab took him aside into the gateway, as though to speak with him privately. And there, to avenge the blood of his brother Asahel, Joab stabbed him in the stomach, and he died.[i]

28 Later, when David heard about this, he said, "I and my kingdom are forever innocent[j] before the LORD concerning the blood of Abner son of Ner. 29 May his blood[k] fall upon the head of Joab and upon all his father's house![l] May Joab's house never be without someone who has a running sore[m] or leprosy[a] or who leans on a crutch or who falls by the sword or who lacks food."

30 (Joab and his brother Abishai murdered Abner because he had killed their brother Asahel in the battle at Gibeon.)

31 Then David said to Joab and all the people with him, "Tear your clothes and put on sackcloth[n] and walk in mourning[o] in front of Abner." King David himself walked behind the bier. 32 They buried Abner in Hebron, and the king wept[p] aloud at Abner's tomb. All the people wept also.

33 The king sang this lament[q] for Abner:

"Should Abner have died as the
lawless die?
34 Your hands were not bound,
your feet were not fettered.
You fell as one falls before wicked
men."

And all the people wept over him again.

35 Then they all came and urged David to eat something while it was still day; but David took an oath, saying, "May God deal with me, be it ever so severely,[r] if I taste bread[s] or anything else before the sun sets!"

36 All the people took note and were pleased; indeed, everything the king did pleased them. 37 So on that day all the people and all Israel knew that the king had no part[t] in the murder of Abner son of Ner.

38 Then the king said to his men, "Do you not realize that a prince and a great man has fallen[u] in Israel this day? 39 And today, though I am the anointed king, I am weak, and these sons of Zeruiah[v] are too strong for me.[w] May the LORD repay[x] the evildoer according to his evil deeds!"

Ish-Bosheth Murdered

4 When Ish-Bosheth son of Saul heard that Abner[y] had died in Hebron, he lost courage, and all Israel became alarmed. 2 Now Saul's son had two men who were leaders of raiding bands. One was named Baanah and the other Recab; they were sons of Rimmon the Beerothite from the tribe of Benjamin—Beeroth[z] is considered part of Benjamin, 3 because the people of Beeroth fled to Gittaim[a] and have lived there as aliens to this day.

4 (Jonathan[b] son of Saul had a son who was lame in both feet. He was five years old when the news[c] about Saul and Jonathan came from Jezreel. His nurse picked him up and fled, but as she hurried to leave, he fell and became crippled.[d] His name was Mephibosheth.)[e]

5 Now Recab and Baanah, the sons of Rimmon the Beerothite, set out for the house of Ish-Bosheth,[f] and they arrived there in the heat of the day while he was taking his noonday rest. 6 They went into the inner part of the house as if to get some wheat, and they stabbed[g] him in the stomach. Then Recab and his brother Baanah slipped away.

7 They had gone into the house while he was lying on the bed in his bedroom. After they stabbed and killed him, they cut off his head. Taking it with them, they traveled all night by

3:21 [f] ver 10,12 [g] 1Ki 11:37
3:27 [h] 2Sa 2:8 [i] 2Sa 2:22; 20:9-10; 1Ki 2:5
3:28 [j] ver 37; Dt 21:9
3:29 [k] Lev 20:9 [l] 1Ki 2:31-33 [m] Lev 15:2
3:31 [n] 2Sa 1:2,11; Ps 30:11; Isa 20:2 [o] Ge 37:34
3:32 [p] Nu 14:1; Pr 24:17
3:33 [q] 2Sa 1:17
3:35 [r] Ru 1:17; 1Sa 3:17 [s] 1Sa 31:13; 2Sa 1:12; 12:17; Jer 16:7
3:37 [t] ver 28
3:38 [u] 2Sa 1:19
3:39 [v] 2Sa 2:18 [w] 2Sa 19:5-7 [x] 1Ki 2:5-6, 33-34; Ps 41:10; 101:8
4:1 [y] 2Sa 3:27; Ezr 4:4
4:2 [z] Jos 9:17; 18:25
4:3 [a] Ne 11:33
4:4 [b] 1Sa 18:1 [c] 1Sa 31:1-4 [d] Lev 21:18 [e] 2Sa 9:3,6; 1Ch 8:34; 9:40
4:5 [f] 2Sa 2:8
4:6 [g] 2Sa 2:23

[a] *29* The Hebrew word was used for various diseases affecting the skin—not necessarily leprosy.

way of the Arabah. 8They brought the head of Ish-Bosheth to David at Hebron and said to the king, "Here is the head of Ish-Bosheth son of Saul,[h] your enemy, who tried to take your life. This day the LORD has avenged my lord the king against Saul and his offspring."

9David answered Recab and his brother Baanah, the sons of Rimmon the Beerothite, "As surely as the LORD lives, who has delivered[i] me out of all trouble, 10when a man told me, 'Saul is dead,' and thought he was bringing good news, I seized him and put him to death in Ziklag.[j] That was the reward I gave him for his news! 11How much more—when wicked men have killed an innocent man in his own house and on his own bed—should I not now demand his blood[k] from your hand and rid the earth of you!"

12So David gave an order to his men, and they killed them.[l] They cut off their hands and feet and hung the bodies by the pool in Hebron. But they took the head of Ish-Bosheth and buried it in Abner's tomb at Hebron.

David Becomes King Over Israel

5 All the tribes of Israel[m] came to David at Hebron and said, "We are your own flesh and blood.[n] 2In the past, while Saul was king over us, you were the one who led Israel on their military campaigns.[o] And the LORD said to you, 'You will shepherd[p] my people Israel, and you will become their ruler.[q]' "

3When all the elders of Israel had come to King David at Hebron, the king made a compact[r] with them at Hebron before the LORD, and they anointed[s] David king over Israel.

4David was thirty years old[t] when he became king, and he reigned[u] forty[v] years. 5In Hebron he reigned over Judah seven years and six months,[w] and in Jerusalem he reigned over all Israel and Judah thirty-three years.

David Conquers Jerusalem

6The king and his men marched to Jerusalem[x] to attack the Jebusites,[y] who lived there. The Jebusites said to David, "You will not get in here; even the blind and the lame can ward you off." They thought, "David cannot get in here." 7Nevertheless, David captured the fortress of Zion, the City of David.[z]

8On that day, David said, "Anyone who conquers the Jebusites will have to use the water shaft[a] to reach those 'lame and blind' who are David's enemies.[b]" That is why they say, "The 'blind and lame' will not enter the palace."

9David then took up residence in the fortress and called it the City of David. He built up the area around it, from the supporting terraces[c][a] inward. 10And he became more and more powerful,[b] because the LORD God Almighty was with him.

11Now Hiram[c] king of Tyre sent messengers to David, along with cedar logs and carpenters and stonemasons, and they built a palace for David. 12And David knew that the LORD had established him as king over Israel and had exalted his kingdom for the sake of his people Israel.

13After he left Hebron, David took more concubines and wives[d] in Jerusalem, and more sons and daughters were born to him. 14These are the names of the children born to him there:[e] Shammua, Shobab, Nathan, Solomon, 15Ibhar, Elishua, Nepheg, Japhia, 16Elishama, Eliada and Eliphelet.

David Defeats the Philistines

17When the Philistines heard that David had been anointed king over Israel, they went up in full force to search for him, but David heard about it and went down to the stronghold.[f] 18Now the Philistines had come and spread out in the Valley of Rephaim;[g] 19so David inquired[h] of the LORD, "Shall I go and attack the Philistines? Will you hand them over to me?"

The LORD answered him, "Go, for I will surely hand the Philistines over to you."

20So David went to Baal Perazim, and there he defeated them. He said, "As waters break out, the LORD has broken out against my enemies before me." So that place was called Baal Perazim.[d][i] 21The Philistines abandoned their idols there, and David and his men carried them off.[j]

22Once more the Philistines came up and spread out in the Valley of Rephaim; 23so David inquired of the LORD, and he answered, "Do not go straight up, but circle around behind them and attack them in front of the balsam trees. 24As soon as you hear the sound[k] of marching in the tops of the balsam trees, move quickly, because that will mean the LORD has gone out in front[l] of you to strike the Philistine army." 25So David did as the LORD commanded him, and he struck down

4:8 [h] 1Sa 24:4; 25:29
4:9 [i] Ge 48:16; 1Ki 1:29
4:10 [j] 2Sa 1:2-16
4:11 [k] Ge 9:5; Ps 9:12
4:12 [l] 2Sa 1:15
5:1 [m] 2Sa 19:43 [n] 1Ch 11:1
5:2 [o] 1Sa 18:5,13, 16 [p] 1Sa 16:1; 2Sa 7:7 [q] 1Sa 25:30
5:3 [r] 2Sa 3:21 [s] 2Sa 2:4
5:4 [t] Lk 3:23 [u] 1Ki 2:11; 1Ch 3:4 [v] 1Ch 26:31; 29:27
5:5 [w] 2Sa 2:11; 1Ch 3:4
5:6 [x] Jdg 1:8 [y] Jos 15:8
5:7 [z] 2Sa 6:12,16; 1Ki 2:10
5:9 [a] ver 7; 1Ki 9:15,24
5:10 [b] 2Sa 3:1
5:11 [c] 1Ki 5:1,18; 1Ch 14:1
5:13 [d] Dt 17:17; 1Ch 3:9
5:14 [e] 1Ch 3:5
5:17 [f] 2Sa 23:14; 1Ch 11:16
5:18 [g] Jos 15:8; 17:15; 18:16
5:19 [h] 1Sa 23:2; 2Sa 2:1
5:20 [i] Isa 28:21
5:21 [j] Dt 7:5; 1Ch 14:12; Isa 46:2
5:24 [k] 2Ki 7:6 [l] Jdg 4:14

[a] 8 Or *use scaling hooks* [b] 8 Or *are hated by David* [c] 9 Or *the Millo* [d] 20 *Baal Perazim* means *the lord who breaks out.*

the Philistines all the way from Gibeon[a][m] to Gezer.[n]

The Ark Brought to Jerusalem

6 David again brought together out of Israel chosen men, thirty thousand in all. 2He and all his men set out from Baalah[o] of Judah[b] to bring up from there the ark[p] of God, which is called by the Name,[c][q] the name of the LORD Almighty, who is enthroned[r] between the cherubim[s] that are on the ark. 3They set the ark of God on a new cart[t] and brought it from the house of Abinadab, which was on the hill. Uzzah and Ahio, sons of Abinadab, were guiding the new cart 4with the ark of God on it,[d] and Ahio was walking in front of it. 5David and the whole house of Israel were celebrating with all their might before the LORD, with songs[e] and with harps, lyres, tambourines, sistrums and cymbals.[u]

6When they came to the threshing floor of Nacon, Uzzah reached out and took hold of[v] the ark of God, because the oxen stumbled. 7The LORD's anger burned against Uzzah because of his irreverent act;[w] therefore God struck him down[x] and he died there beside the ark of God.

8Then David was angry because the LORD's wrath[y] had broken out against Uzzah, and to this day that place is called Perez Uzzah.[f][z]

9David was afraid of the LORD that day and said, "How[a] can the ark of the LORD ever come to me?" 10He was not willing to take the ark of the LORD to be with him in the City of David. Instead, he took it aside to the house of Obed-Edom[b] the Gittite. 11The ark of the LORD remained in the house of Obed-Edom the Gittite for three months, and the LORD blessed him and his entire household.[c]

12Now King David[d] was told, "The LORD has blessed the household of Obed-Edom and everything he has, because of the ark of God." So David went down and brought up the ark of God from the house of Obed-Edom to the City of David with rejoicing. 13When those who were carrying the ark of the LORD had taken six steps, he sacrificed[e] a bull and a fattened calf. 14David, wearing a linen ephod,[f] danced[g] before the LORD with all his might, 15while he and the entire house of Israel brought up the ark of the LORD with shouts and the sound of trumpets.[h]

16As the ark of the LORD was entering the City of David,[i] Michal daughter of Saul watched from a window. And when she saw King David leaping and dancing before the LORD, she despised him in her heart.

17They brought the ark of the LORD and set it in its place inside the tent that David had pitched for it,[j] and David sacrificed burnt offerings[k] and fellowship offerings[g] before the LORD. 18After he had finished sacrificing[l] the burnt offerings and fellowship offerings, he blessed the people in the name of the LORD Almighty. 19Then he gave a loaf of bread, a cake of dates and a cake of raisins[m] to each person in the whole crowd of Israelites, both men and women.[n] And all the people went to their homes.

20When David returned home to bless his household, Michal daughter of Saul came out to meet him and said, "How the king of Israel has distinguished himself today, disrobing[o] in the sight of the slave girls of his servants as any vulgar fellow would!"

21David said to Michal, "It was before the LORD, who chose me rather than your father or anyone from his house when he appointed[p] me ruler over the LORD's people Israel—I will celebrate before the LORD. 22I will become even more undignified than this, and I will be humiliated in my own eyes. But by these slave girls you spoke of, I will be held in honor."

23And Michal daughter of Saul had no children to the day of her death.

God's Promise to David

7 After the king was settled in his palace[q] and the LORD had given him rest from all his enemies around him, 2he said to Nathan the prophet, "Here I am, living in a palace[r] of cedar, while the ark of God remains in a tent."[s]

3Nathan replied to the king, "Whatever you have in mind, go ahead and do it, for the LORD is with you."

4That night the word of the LORD came to Nathan, saying:

5"Go and tell my servant David, 'This is what the LORD says: Are you[t] the one to build me a house to dwell in?[u] 6I have not dwelt in

5:25 [m]Isa 28:21 [n]1Ch 14:16
6:2 [o]Jos 15:9 [p]1Sa 4:4; 7:1 [q]Lev 24:16; Isa 63:14 [r]Ps 99:1 [s]Ex 25:22; 1Ch 13:5-6
6:3 [t]Nu 7:4-9; 1Sa 6:7
6:5 [u]1Sa 18:6-7; Ezr 3:10; Ps 150:5
6:6 [v]Nu 4:15, 19-20; 1Ch 13:9
6:7 [w]1Ch 15:13-15 [x]Ex 19:22; 1Sa 6:19
6:8 [y]Ps 7:11 [z]Ge 38:29
6:9 [a]Ps 119:120
6:10 [b]1Ch 13:13; 26:4-5
6:11 [c]Ge 30:27; 39:5
6:12 [d]1Ki 8:1; 1Ch 15:25
6:13 [e]1Ki 8:5,62
6:14 [f]Ex 19:6; 1Sa 2:18 [g]Ex 15:20
6:15 [h]Ps 47:5; 98:6
6:16 [i]2Sa 5:7
6:17 [j]1Ch 15:1; 2Ch 1:4 [k]Lev 1:1-17; 1Ki 8:62-64
6:18 [l]1Ki 8:22
6:19 [m]Hos 3:1 [n]Ne 8:10
6:20 [o]ver 14,16
6:21 [p]1Sa 13:14; 15:28
7:1 [q]1Ch 17:1
7:2 [r]2Sa 5:11 [s]Ex 26:1; Ac 7:45-46
7:5 [t]1Ki 8:19; 1Ch 22:8 [u]1Ki 5:3-5

[a] *25* Septuagint (see also 1 Chron. 14:16); Hebrew *Geba* [b] *2* That is, Kiriath Jearim; Hebrew *Baale Judah*, a variant of *Baalah of Judah* [c] *2* Hebrew; Septuagint and Vulgate do not have *the Name.* [d] *3,4* Dead Sea Scrolls and some Septuagint manuscripts; Masoretic Text *cart* [4]*and they brought it with the ark of God from the house of Abinadab, which was on the hill* [e] *5* See Dead Sea Scrolls, Septuagint and 1 Chronicles 13:8; Masoretic Text *celebrating before the LORD with all kinds of instruments made of pine.* [f] *8* *Perez Uzzah* means *outbreak against Uzzah.* [g] *17* Traditionally *peace offerings*; also in verse 18

NATHAN

Surgeon of the Soul

It was a rotten job, and only Nathan could do it. He and David had been friends for a long time, and he owed David the truth. But Nathan was also God's prophet, and just as surely as he owed David the truth, he owed God his obedience. No matter how you cut it, this job was Nathan's.

Confronting a Killer

David had committed adultery with Bathsheba and had orchestrated her husband Uriah's murder to cover it up. He had managed to keep it quiet for about a year. Only Nathan knew David's dark, tragic secret. Others may have suspected, but Nathan, David's friend and God's prophet, knew it was true. As David's friend he may have wrestled with what to do, but as God's prophet there was only his duty to perform. He had to act now.

But how? How does one confront a dear friend with something like this? How, especially when one's friend is also the king who can, and has, taken a person's life to keep his secret buried? David had killed many people in his years as a soldier. He had arranged for Uriah's death and could just as quickly kill Nathan if he needed to. Nathan knew all this. Yet as hard and dangerous as it was, Nathan had to confront David with this awful sin.

As one of David's key advisors, Nathan often spoke to David about important, even personal things (2 Samuel 7:1–3). But this was different. Nathan needed to confront David with his sin, because David needed to repent. But while Nathan needed to confront David, that wasn't his goal. Confrontation was the means to the higher end of repentance and restoration. God, David's heavenly Father, and Nathan, David's earthly friend, weren't interested in seeing David grovel. They wanted to see him restored. Leading a person to repentance and restoration was—and still is—a delicate task.

Nathan went to David. He knew that in spite of everything David was a man with a just and sensitive heart. Can you picture the setting? The prophet and the king are managing the affairs of the kingdom. They are discussing land disputes, unpaid debts, a lawsuit over selling a sick donkey—those sorts of things. And, yes, there is this matter about a cruel man who stole his neighbor's only sheep—a family pet—and slaughtered it so he could feed it to his party guests. Nathan's heart must have been racing. So much was at stake. His own life was on the line. But so was David's eternal soul. When David heard the story about the stolen sheep, he was outraged. His eyes blazed and he pronounced, "As surely as the LORD lives, the man who did this deserves to die!" (12:5).

After a pregnant pause, Nathan declared to David, "You are the man" (12:7). Nathan was deadly serious. He was direct. He told David how God had seen his sin and would discipline him for it. He pulled no punches. But something about Nathan's presentation led David exactly where God and Nathan wanted him to go. David's confession was powerful in its simplicity, "I have sinned against the LORD" (12:13).

No longer prophet and king, Nathan and David were now just men—old friends whose hearts were breaking. Murder and adultery both carried the death penalty in Israel, and David was guilty of both. David knew this, and his creative genius could find no way out. It was all over for him. Then Nathan, David's friend and God's prophet, spoke again. He didn't judge or condemn or moralize. David already knew anything Nathan could tell him. Nathan's words were clear: "The LORD has taken away your sin. You are not going to die" (12:13).

Sign On the Dotted Line

Nathan is a man every generation desperately needs. Nathan called sin sin and made David understand its consequences, but he did it all in a way that led to David's forgiveness. He was tough enough to lead David to repentance, yet tender enough to celebrate his restoration.

We need more men and women with the spiritual strength and maturity to be today's Nathans. Preachers and teachers and counselors abound, but Nathans are rare. Consider this niche if you wish to find a significant ministry in the church. But before signing on as a Nathan, remember the qualifications that Paul says you must have: "If someone is caught in a sin, *you who are spiritual* should restore him gently" (Galatians 6:1; italics added).

A Nathan is not haughty or angry or vengeful. A Nathan's place of service is a place for one who has a passion to serve God by restoring shredded souls to their loving Father. Confrontation is never the goal. God has more in mind for his wayward children than that. Nathan's example shows us how to go about this delicate work.

—Dr. Sid Buzzell

a house from the day I brought
the Israelites up out of Egypt to
this day. I have been moving from
place to place with a tent[v] as my
dwelling.[w] **7**Wherever I have
moved with all the Israelites,[x]
did I ever say to any of their rulers
whom I commanded to shep-
herd[y] my people Israel, "Why
have you not built me a house of
cedar?[z]" '
8"Now then, tell my servant David, 'This is what the LORD Almighty says: I took you from the
pasture and from following the
flock[a] to be ruler[b] over my people Israel.[c] **9**I have been with you
wherever you have gone,[d] and I
have cut off all your enemies from
before you.[e] Now I will make
your name great, like the names
of the greatest men of the earth.
10And I will provide a place for my
people Israel and will plant[f]
them so that they can have a
home of their own and no longer
be disturbed. Wicked[g] people
will not oppress them anymore,[h]
as they did at the beginning **11**and
have done ever since the time I
appointed leaders[a][i] over my
people Israel. I will also give you
rest from all your enemies.[j]
" 'The LORD declares to you that
the LORD himself will establish[k]
a house[l] for you: **12**When your
days are over and you rest[m] with
your fathers, I will raise up your
offspring to succeed you, who will
come from your own body,[n] and
I will establish his kingdom. **13**He
is the one who will build a house
for my Name,[o] and I will establish the throne of his kingdom forever.[p] **14**I will be his father, and
he will be my son.[q] When he
does wrong, I will punish him
with the rod[r] of men, with flog-
gings inflicted by men. **15**But my
love will never be taken away
from him, as I took it away from
Saul,[s] whom I removed from before you. **16**Your house and your
kingdom will endure forever before me[b]; your throne[t] will be
established forever.[u]' "
17Nathan reported to David all the
words of this entire revelation.

David's Prayer

18Then King David went in and sat
before the LORD, and he said:
"Who am I,[v] O Sovereign
LORD, and what is my family, that
you have brought me this far?
19And as if this were not enough in
your sight, O Sovereign LORD, you
have also spoken about the future
of the house of your servant. Is
this your usual way of dealing
with man,[w] O Sovereign LORD?
20"What more can David say to
you? For you know[x] your servant,[y] O Sovereign LORD. **21**For
the sake of your word and according to your will, you have done
this great thing and made it
known to your servant.
22"How great[z] you are,[a]
O Sovereign LORD! There is no one
like you, and there is no God[b]
but you, as we have heard with
our own ears.[c] **23**And who is like
your people Israel[d]—the one nation on earth that God went out to
redeem as a people for himself,
and to make a name for himself,
and to perform great and awesome wonders[e] by driving out
nations and their gods from before your people, whom you redeemed[f] from Egypt?[c] **24**You
have established your people Israel as your very own[g] forever, and
you, O LORD, have become their
God.[h]
25"And now, LORD God, keep
forever the promise you have
made concerning your servant
and his house. Do as you promised, **26**so that your name will be
great forever. Then men will say,
'The LORD Almighty is God over

7:6 [v]Ex 40:18,34 [w]1Ki 8:16
7:7 [x]Dt 23:14 [y]2Sa 5:2 [z]Lev 26:11-12
7:8 [a]1Sa 16:11 [b]2Sa 6:21 [c]Ps 78:70-72; 2Co 6:18*
7:9 [d]2Sa 5:10 [e]Ps 18:37-42
7:10 [f]Ex 15:17; Isa 5:1-7 [g]Ps 89:22-23 [h]Isa 60:18
7:11 [i]Jdg 2:16; 1Sa 12:9-11 [j]ver 1 [k]1Sa 25:28 [l]ver 27
7:12 [m]1Ki 2:1 [n]Ps 132:11-12
7:13 [o]1Ki 5:5; 8:19, 29 [p]Isa 9:7
7:14 [q]Ps 89:26; Heb 1:5* [r]Ps 89:30-33
7:15 [s]1Sa 15:23,28
7:16 [t]Ps 89:36-37 [u]ver 13
7:18 [v]Ex 3:11; 1Sa 18:18
7:19 [w]Isa 55:8-9
7:20 [x]Jn 21:17 [y]1Sa 16:7
7:22 [z]Ps 48:1; 86:10; Jer 10:6 [a]Dt 3:24 [b]Ex 15:11 [c]Ex 10:2; Ps 44:1
7:23 [d]Dt 4:32-38 [e]Dt 10:21 [f]Dt 9:26; 15:15
7:24 [g]Dt 26:18 [h]Ex 6:6-7; Ps 48:14

[a]*11* Traditionally *judges* [b]*16* Some Hebrew manuscripts and Septuagint; most Hebrew manuscripts *you* [c]*23* See Septuagint and 1 Chron. 17:21; Hebrew *wonders for your land and before your people, whom you redeemed from Egypt, from the nations and their gods.*

7:18–29 PROMISE 1

THANK YOU, LORD!

How good it is to give thanks to God! Through the prophet Nathan, David had just received God's promise of great blessings upon him and his entire family. The prayer in this passage reflects David's sincere gratitude in the face of God's goodness.

Read this prayer and meditate on God's gifts to you: family, Christian brothers and sisters, new life in Christ, God's Word to guide you, and the ultimate hope of eternal life in his presence. Expand and personalize this list while you give thanks to God for his goodness.

For the next Promise 1 reading go to page 366.

Israel!’ And the house of your servant David will be established before you.
27“O LORD Almighty, God of Israel, you have revealed this to
your servant, saying, ‘I will build
a house for you.’ So your servant
has found courage to offer you
this prayer. 28O Sovereign LORD,
you are God! Your words are trustworthy,[i] and you have promised
these good things to your servant.
29Now be pleased to bless the
house of your servant, that it may
continue forever in your sight; for
you, O Sovereign LORD, have spoken, and with your blessing[j] the
house of your servant will be
blessed forever.”

David's Victories

8 In the course of time, David defeated the Philistines and subdued
them, and he took Metheg Ammah
from the control of the Philistines.
2David also defeated the Moabites.[k] He made them lie down on the
ground and measured them off with
a length of cord. Every two lengths of
them were put to death, and the third
length was allowed to live. So the Moabites became subject to David and
brought tribute.
3Moreover, David fought Hadadezer[l] son of Rehob, king of Zobah,[m]
when he went to restore his control
along the Euphrates River. 4David captured a thousand of his chariots, seven
thousand charioteers[a] and twenty
thousand foot soldiers. He hamstrung[n] all but a hundred of the chariot horses.
5When the Arameans of Damascus[o]
came to help Hadadezer king of Zobah,
David struck down twenty-two thousand of them. 6He put garrisons in the
Aramean kingdom of Damascus, and
the Arameans became subject to him
and brought tribute. The LORD gave
David victory wherever he went.[p]
7David took the gold shields[q] that
belonged to the officers of Hadadezer
and brought them to Jerusalem. 8From
Tebah[b] and Berothai,[r] towns that belonged to Hadadezer, King David took
a great quantity of bronze.
9When Tou[c] king of Hamath[s]
heard that David had defeated the entire army of Hadadezer, 10he sent his
son Joram[d] to King David to greet him
and congratulate him on his victory in
battle over Hadadezer, who had been
at war with Tou. Joram brought with
him articles of silver and gold and
bronze.
11King David dedicated[t] these articles to the LORD, as he had done with
the silver and gold from all the nations
he had subdued: 12Edom[e] and
Moab,[u] the Ammonites[v] and the Philistines,[w] and Amalek.[x] He also dedicated the plunder taken from Hadadezer son of Rehob, king of Zobah.
13And David became famous[y] after
he returned from striking down eighteen thousand Edomites[f] in the Valley
of Salt.[z]
14He put garrisons throughout
Edom, and all the Edomites[a] became
subject to David.[b] The LORD gave David victory wherever he went.[c]

David's Officials

15David reigned over all Israel, doing
what was just and right for all his people. 16Joab[d] son of Zeruiah was over
the army; Jehoshaphat[e] son of Ahilud
was recorder; 17Zadok[f] son of Ahitub
and Ahimelech son of Abiathar were
priests; Seraiah was secretary;[g] 18Be-
naiah[h] son of Jehoiada was over the
Kerethites[i] and Pelethites; and David's sons were royal advisers.[g]

David and Mephibosheth

9 David asked, “Is there anyone still
left of the house of Saul to whom I
can show kindness for Jonathan's
sake?”[j]
2Now there was a servant of Saul's
household named Ziba.[k] They called
him to appear before David, and the
king said to him, “Are you Ziba?”
“Your servant,” he replied.
3The king asked, “Is there no one
still left of the house of Saul to whom I
can show God's kindness?”
Ziba answered the king, “There is
still a son of Jonathan;[l] he is crippled[m] in both feet.”
4“Where is he?” the king asked.
Ziba answered, “He is at the house
of Makir[n] son of Ammiel in Lo Debar.”
5So King David had him brought
from Lo Debar, from the house of Makir son of Ammiel.
6When Mephibosheth son of Jonathan, the son of Saul, came to David, he
bowed down to pay him honor.[o]

6 →PG. 665

7:28 *i* Ex 34:6; Jn 17:17
7:29 *j* Nu 6:23-27
8:2 *k* Ge 19:37; Nu 24:17
8:3 *l* 2Sa 10:16,19 *m* 1Sa 14:47
8:4 *n* Jos 11:9
8:5 *o* 1Ki 11:24
8:6 *p* ver 14; 2Sa 3:18; 7:9
8:7 *q* 1Ki 10:16
8:8 *r* Eze 47:16
8:9 *s* 1Ki 8:65; 2Ch 8:4
8:11 *t* 1Ki 7:51; 1Ch 26:26
8:12 *u* ver 2 *v* 2Sa 10:14 *w* 2Sa 5:25 *x* 1Sa 27:8
8:13 *y* 2Sa 7:9 *z* 2Ki 14:7; 1Ch 18:12
8:14 *a* Nu 24:17-18 *b* Ge 27:29, 37-40 *c* ver 6
8:16 *d* 2Sa 19:13; 1Ch 11:6 *e* 2Sa 20:24; 1Ki 4:3
8:17 *f* 2Sa 15:24,29; 1Ch 16:39; 24:3 *g* 1Ki 4:3; 2Ki 12:10
8:18 *h* 2Sa 20:23; 1Ki 1:8,38; 1Ch 18:17 *i* 1Sa 30:14
9:1 *j* 1Sa 20:14-17, 42
9:2 *k* 2Sa 16:1-4; 19:17,26,29
9:3 *l* 1Sa 20:14 *m* 2Sa 4:4
9:4 *n* 2Sa 17:27-29
9:6 *o* 2Sa 16:4; 19:24-30

a *4* Septuagint (see also Dead Sea Scrolls and 1 Chron. 18:4); Masoretic Text *captured seventeen hundred of his charioteers*
b *8* See some Septuagint manuscripts (see also 1 Chron. 18:8); Hebrew *Betah.* **c** *9* Hebrew *Toi,* a variant of *Tou;* also in verse 10
d *10* A variant of *Hadoram* **e** *12* Some Hebrew manuscripts, Septuagint and Syriac (see also 1 Chron. 18:11); most Hebrew manuscripts *Aram*
f *13* A few Hebrew manuscripts, Septuagint and Syriac (see also 1 Chron. 18:12); most Hebrew manuscripts *Aram* (that is, Arameans) **g** *18* Or *were priests*

David said, “Mephibosheth!”

“Your servant,” he replied.

7“Don’t be afraid,” David said to him, “for I will surely show you kindness for the sake of your father Jonathan. I will restore to you all the land that belonged to your grandfather Saul, and you will always eat at my table.[p]”

8Mephibosheth bowed down and said, “What is your servant, that you should notice a dead dog[q] like me?”

9Then the king summoned Ziba, Saul’s servant, and said to him, “I have given your master’s grandson everything that belonged to Saul and his family. 10You and your sons and your servants are to farm the land for him and bring in the crops, so that your master’s grandson[r] may be provided for. And Mephibosheth, grandson of your master, will always eat at my table.” (Now Ziba had fifteen sons and twenty servants.)

11Then Ziba said to the king, “Your servant will do whatever my lord the king commands his servant to do.” So Mephibosheth ate at David’s[a] table like one of the king’s sons.[s]

12Mephibosheth had a young son named Mica, and all the members of Ziba’s household were servants of Mephibosheth.[t] 13And Mephibosheth lived in Jerusalem, because he always ate at the king’s table, and he was crippled in both feet.

David Defeats the Ammonites

10 In the course of time, the king of the Ammonites died, and his son Hanun succeeded him as king. 2David thought, “I will show kindness to Hanun son of Nahash,[u] just as his father showed kindness to me.” So David sent a delegation to express his sympathy to Hanun concerning his father.

When David’s men came to the land of the Ammonites, 3the Ammonite nobles said to Hanun their lord, “Do you think David is honoring your father by sending men to you to express sympathy? Hasn’t David sent them to you to explore the city and spy it out and overthrow it?” 4So Hanun seized David’s men, shaved off half of each man’s beard,[v] cut off their garments in the middle at the buttocks,[w] and sent them away.

5When David was told about this, he sent messengers to meet the men, for they were greatly humiliated. The king said, “Stay at Jericho till your beards have grown, and then come back.”

6When the Ammonites realized that they had become a stench[x] in David’s nostrils, they hired twenty thousand Aramean[y] foot soldiers from Beth Rehob[z] and Zobah, as well as the king of Maacah[a] with a thousand men, and also twelve thousand men from Tob.

7On hearing this, David sent Joab out with the entire army of fighting men. 8The Ammonites came out and drew up in battle formation at the entrance to their city gate, while the Arameans of Zobah and Rehob and the men of Tob and Maacah were by themselves in the open country.

9Joab saw that there were battle lines in front of him and behind him; so he selected some of the best troops in Israel and deployed them against the Arameans. 10He put the rest of the men under the command of Abishai his brother and deployed them against the Ammonites. 11Joab said, “If the Arameans are too strong for me, then you are to come to my rescue; but if the Ammonites are too strong for you, then I will come to rescue you. 12Be strong[b] and let us fight bravely for our people and the cities of our God. The LORD will do what is good in his sight.”[c]

13Then Joab and the troops with him advanced to fight the Arameans, and they fled before him. 14When the Ammonites saw that the Arameans were fleeing, they fled before Abishai and went inside the city. So Joab returned from fighting the Ammonites and came to Jerusalem.

15After the Arameans saw that they had been routed by Israel, they regrouped. 16Hadadezer had Arameans brought from beyond the River[b]; they went to Helam, with Shobach the commander of Hadadezer’s army leading them.

17When David was told of this, he gathered all Israel, crossed the Jordan and went to Helam. The Arameans formed their battle lines to meet David and fought against him. 18But they fled before Israel, and David killed seven hundred of their charioteers and forty thousand of their foot soldiers.[c] He also struck down Shobach the commander of their army, and he died there. 19When all the kings who were vassals of Hadadezer saw that they had been defeated by Israel, they made peace with the Israelites and became subject[d] to them.

So the Arameans[e] were afraid to help the Ammonites anymore.

9:7 [p] ver 1,3; 2Sa 12:8; 19:28; 1Ki 2:7; 2Ki 25:29
9:8 [q] 2Sa 16:9
9:10 [r] ver 7,11,13; 2Sa 19:28
9:11 [s] Job 36:7; Ps 113:8
9:12 [t] 1Ch 8:34
10:2 [u] 1Sa 11:1
10:4 [v] Lev 19:27; Isa 15:2; Jer 48:37 [w] Isa 20:4
10:6 [x] Ge 34:30 [y] 2Sa 8:5 [z] Jdg 18:28 [a] Dt 3:14
10:12 [b] Dt 31:6; 1Co 16:13; Eph 6:10 [c] Jdg 10:15; 1Sa 3:18; Ne 4:14
10:19 [d] 2Sa 8:6 [e] 1Ki 11:25; 2Ki 5:1

[a] *11* Septuagint; Hebrew *my* [b] *16* That is, the Euphrates [c] *18* Some Septuagint manuscripts (see also 1 Chron. 19:18); Hebrew *horsemen*

David and Bathsheba

11 In the spring,[f] at the time when
kings go off to war, David sent
Joab[g] out with the king's men and the
whole Israelite army.[h] They destroyed
the Ammonites and besieged Rabbah.[i] But David remained in Jerusalem.
2 One evening David got up from his
bed and walked around on the roof[j]
of the palace. From the roof he saw[k] a
woman bathing. The woman was very
beautiful, 3 and David sent someone to
find out about her. The man said, "Isn't
this Bathsheba,[l] the daughter of Eliam[m] and the wife of Uriah[n] the Hittite?" 4 Then David sent messengers to
get her.[o] She came to him, and he
slept[p] with her. (She had purified herself from her uncleanness.)[q] Then[a]
she went back home. 5 The woman

11:1 [f] 1Ki 20:22,26 [g] 2Sa 2:18 [h] 1Ch 20:1 [i] 2Sa 12:26-28
11:2 [j] Dt 22:8; Jos 2:8 [k] Mt 5:28
11:3 [l] 1Ch 3:5 [m] 2Sa 23:34 [n] 2Sa 23:39
11:4 [o] Lev 20:10; Ps 51 Title; Jas 1:14-15 [p] Dt 22:22 [q] Lev 15:25-30; 18:19

[a] 4 Or *with her. When she purified herself from her uncleanness,*

11:1-27

PROMISE 3

SIN'S DESTRUCTIVE POWER

David defeated Goliath and became a hero. He escaped Saul's attempts to kill him. He led a band of mighty men who followed him into battle no matter how overwhelming the odds. He united Israel's tribes for the first time in their history, and organized them into one of the great military and commercial powers in the ancient world. It seemed there was nothing this man couldn't do. But whatever else David was known for, he was most known for his godliness.

Oh, how David loved God! Even after David's death, God recognized his faithfulness when speaking to Solomon, David's son: "As for you, if you walk before me in integrity of heart and uprightness, as David your father did . . ." (1 Kings 9:4). But, as chapter 11 reveals, even David was defeated by the destructive power of sin.

What happened? The story starts with a clue: "In the spring, at the time when kings go off to war, David sent Joab out with the king's army . . . but David remained in Jerusalem" (v. 1). The text doesn't condemn David for not leading the army, but it does tell us that he wasn't out there—and that he ended up in trouble. Men who aren't busy doing what they should be doing are more vulnerable to doing what they shouldn't.

The next paragraph (vv. 2–5) tells the story that changed many lives, including David's, forever. Notice the brevity and simplicity of it. Sin often sounds like that. One hitch changed what David thought would be a moment of sinful passion into a complicated problem (v. 5). But David was a genius. Not one to be beaten by a technicality, he quickly devised a plan. He had to sin again to cover up the first one. At that moment, he was caught in the trap that leads so many people into a downward spiral.

Read David's plan (vv. 6–8). Here he added lying and manipulation to his adultery, calling Uriah home in the hope that he would sleep with his wife Bathsheba. If Uriah would do so, David wouldn't have a messy pregnancy to explain. But Uriah, a soldier who held to a military code of honor, refused to go home to his wife while his fellow soldiers were camped in the fields. "I will not do such a thing!" Uriah protested (v. 11).

Ouch! The irony of this soldier's act is almost painful. Uriah, one of David's mighty men, wouldn't sleep with his wife while his fellow soldiers were in the field. But David *had* slept with Uriah's wife while Uriah and his comrades were in the field. Normally, David would be the first to sense such irony, but he was too dulled by his sin to see anything. That night David got Uriah drunk (v. 13), believing that in his drunken state he would go home to his wife. But even when drunk, honorable Uriah had more integrity than David. David had become intoxicated with sin—it made him crazy.

His plans for a cover-up thwarted, David took the next step and spiraled deeper into sin. Verse 14 states very simply that in the morning David wrote a letter. That letter involved Joab, another of David's intimate friends, in a plot to murder Uriah. For David, his sin had to be protected no matter what the cost. Covering his deed was more important than the integrity of his general or the life of a man who had risked his life and fought side-by-side with David in some of his toughest battles. In short, David's sin with Bathsheba completely took over his life. The rest of the story goes on agonizingly. When David heard news of Uriah's death (v. 25), he sent a message to Joab: "Don't let this upset you . . ." David pulled Bathsheba, Uriah, and Joab into this horrible swamp of sin and deception.

Did God rehash this story in the Bible to defame David? Not at all. God revealed it in his Word to teach us that even the best of men become crazed when sin takes over. David was a man after God's own heart, but sin turned him into a wretch. It started when David failed to be involved with what God had given him to do. It ended with a woman pregnant, a husband murdered, a general's integrity compromised and the king of Israel—God's chosen servant—acting like a reprobate.

As Christian men, we cannot afford one minute outside God's will. "Love the LORD your God with all your heart and with all your soul and with all your strength" (Deuteronomy 6:5). What's the other option? Ask David. Or Bathsheba. Or Uriah. Or Joab.

For the next Promise 3 reading go to page 379.

conceived and sent word to David, saying, "I am pregnant."
6So David sent this word to Joab:
"Send me Uriah[r] the Hittite." And
Joab sent him to David. 7When Uriah
came to him, David asked him how
Joab was, how the soldiers were and
how the war was going. 8Then David
said to Uriah, "Go down to your house
and wash your feet."[s] So Uriah left the
palace, and a gift from the king was
sent after him. 9But Uriah slept at the
entrance to the palace with all his master's servants and did not go down to
his house.
10When David was told, "Uriah did
not go home," he asked him, "Haven't
you just come from a distance? Why
didn't you go home?"
11Uriah said to David, "The ark[t]
and Israel and Judah are staying in
tents, and my master Joab and my
lord's men are camped in the open
fields. How could I go to my house to
eat and drink and lie with my wife? As
surely as you live, I will not do such a
thing!"
12Then David said to him, "Stay here
one more day, and tomorrow I will
send you back." So Uriah remained in
Jerusalem that day and the next. 13At
David's invitation, he ate and drank
with him, and David made him drunk.
But in the evening Uriah went out to
sleep on his mat among his master's
servants; he did not go home.
14In the morning David wrote a letter[u] to Joab and sent it with Uriah.
15In it he wrote, "Put Uriah in the front
line where the fighting is fiercest. Then
withdraw from him so he will be struck
down[v] and die.[w]"
16So while Joab had the city under
siege, he put Uriah at a place where he
knew the strongest defenders were.
17When the men of the city came out
and fought against Joab, some of the
men in David's army fell; moreover,
Uriah the Hittite died.
18Joab sent David a full account of
the battle. 19He instructed the messenger: "When you have finished giving
the king this account of the battle,
20the king's anger may flare up, and
he may ask you, 'Why did you get so
close to the city to fight? Didn't you
know they would shoot arrows from
the wall? 21Who killed Abimelech[x] son
of Jerub-Besheth[a]? Didn't a woman
throw an upper millstone on him from
the wall,[y] so that he died in Thebez?
Why did you get so close to the wall?' If
he asks you this, then say to him, 'Also,
your servant Uriah the Hittite is
dead.' "
22The messenger set out, and when
he arrived he told David everything
Joab had sent him to say. 23The messenger said to David, "The men overpowered us and came out against us in
the open, but we drove them back to
the entrance to the city gate. 24Then
the archers shot arrows at your servants from the wall, and some of the
king's men died. Moreover, your servant Uriah the Hittite is dead."
25David told the messenger, "Say
this to Joab: 'Don't let this upset you;
the sword devours one as well as another. Press the attack against the city
and destroy it.' Say this to encourage
Joab."
26When Uriah's wife heard that her
husband was dead, she mourned for
him. 27After the time of mourning was
over, David had her brought to his
house, and she became his wife and
bore him a son. But the thing David
had done displeased[z] the LORD.

Nathan Rebukes David

12 The LORD sent Nathan[a] to David.[b] When he came to him,[c] he
said, "There were two men in a certain
town, one rich and the other poor.
2The rich man had a very large number
of sheep and cattle, 3but the poor man
had nothing except one little ewe lamb
he had bought. He raised it, and it grew
up with him and his children. It shared
his food, drank from his cup and even
slept in his arms. It was like a daughter
to him.
4"Now a traveler came to the rich
man, but the rich man refrained from
taking one of his own sheep or cattle to
prepare a meal for the traveler who had
come to him. Instead, he took the ewe
lamb that belonged to the poor man
and prepared it for the one who had
come to him."
5David[d] burned with anger against
the man and said to Nathan, "As surely
as the LORD lives, the man who did this
deserves to die! 6He must pay for that
lamb four times over,[e] because he did
such a thing and had no pity."
7Then Nathan said to David, "You
are the man! This is what the LORD, the
God of Israel, says: 'I anointed[f] you[g]
king over Israel, and I delivered you
from the hand of Saul. 8I gave your
master's house to you,[h] and your
master's wives into your arms. I gave
you the house of Israel and Judah. And
if all this had been too little, I would
have given you even more. 9Why did
you despise[i] the word of the LORD by
doing what is evil in his eyes? You

11:6 [r]1Ch 11:41
11:8 [s]Ge 18:4; 43:24; Lk 7:44
11:11 [t]2Sa 7:2
11:14 [u]1Ki 21:8
11:15 [v]2Sa 12:9 [w]2Sa 12:12
11:21 [x]Jdg 8:31 [y]Jdg 9:50-54
11:27 [z]2Sa 12:9; Ps 51:4-5
12:1 [a]2Sa 7:2; 1Ki 20:35-41 [b]Ps 51 Title [c]2Sa 14:4
12:5 [d]1Ki 20:40
12:6 [e]Ex 22:1; Lk 19:8
12:7 [f]1Sa 16:13 [g]1Ki 20:42
12:8 [h]2Sa 9:7
12:9 [i]Nu 15:31; 1Sa 15:19

[a]21 Also known as *Jerub-Baal* (that is, Gideon)

struck down[j] Uriah the Hittite with
the sword and took his wife to be your
own. You killed him with the sword of
the Ammonites. 10Now, therefore, the
sword[k] will never depart from your
house, because you despised me and
took the wife of Uriah the Hittite to be
your own.'
11"This is what the LORD says: 'Out
of your own household I am going to
bring calamity upon you.[l] Before
your very eyes I will take your wives
and give them to one who is close to
you, and he will lie with your wives in
broad daylight. 12You did it in secret,[m]
but I will do this thing in broad daylight[n] before all Israel.' "
13Then David said to Nathan, "I have
sinned[o] against the LORD."
Nathan replied, "The LORD has taken
away[p] your sin.[q] You are not going to
die.[r] 14But because by doing this you
have made the enemies of the LORD
show utter contempt,[a][s] the son born
to you will die."
15After Nathan had gone home, the
LORD struck[t] the child that Uriah's
wife had borne to David, and he became ill. 16David pleaded with God for
the child. He fasted and went into his
house and spent the nights lying[u] on
the ground. 17The elders of his household stood beside him to get him up
from the ground, but he refused, and
he would not eat any food with them.[v]
18On the seventh day the child died.
David's servants were afraid to tell him
that the child was dead, for they
thought, "While the child was still living, we spoke to David but he would
not listen to us. How can we tell him
the child is dead? He may do something desperate."
19David noticed that his servants
were whispering among themselves
and he realized the child was dead. "Is
the child dead?" he asked.
"Yes," they replied, "he is dead."
20Then David got up from the
ground. After he had washed,[w] put on
lotions and changed his clothes,[x] he
went into the house of the LORD and
worshiped. Then he went to his own
house, and at his request they served
him food, and he ate.
21His servants asked him, "Why are
you acting this way? While the child
was alive, you fasted and wept,[y] but
now that the child is dead, you get up
and eat!"
22He answered, "While the child was
still alive, I fasted and wept. I thought,
'Who knows?[z] The LORD may be gracious to me and let the child live.'[a]
23But now that he is dead, why should
I fast? Can I bring him back again? I will
go to him,[b] but he will not return
to me."[c]
24Then David comforted his wife
Bathsheba,[d] and he went to her and
lay with her. She gave birth to a son,
and they named him Solomon.[e] The
LORD loved him; 25and because the
LORD loved him, he sent word through
Nathan the prophet to name him Jedidiah.[b][f]
26Meanwhile Joab fought against
Rabbah[g] of the Ammonites and captured the royal citadel. 27Joab then sent
messengers to David, saying, "I have
fought against Rabbah and taken its
water supply. 28Now muster the rest of
the troops and besiege the city and
capture it. Otherwise I will take the
city, and it will be named after me."
29So David mustered the entire army
and went to Rabbah, and attacked and
captured it. 30He took the crown[h]
from the head of their king[c]—its
weight was a talent[d] of gold, and it was
set with precious stones—and it was
placed on David's head. He took a
great quantity of plunder from the city

12:9 [j]2Sa 11:15 **12:10** [k]2Sa 13:28; 18:14-15; 1Ki 2:25 **12:11** [l]Dt 28:30; 2Sa 16:21-22 **12:12** [m]2Sa 11:4-15 [n]2Sa 16:22 **12:13** [o]Ge 13:13; Nu 22:34; 1Sa 15:24; 2Sa 24:10 [p]Ps 32:1-5; 51:1,9; 103:12; Zec 3:4,9 [q]Pr 28:13; Mic 7:18-19 [r]Lev 20:10; 24:17 **12:14** [s]Isa 52:5; Ro 2:24 **12:15** [t]1Sa 25:38 **12:16** [u]2Sa 13:31; Ps 5:7

12:17 [v]2Sa 3:35 **12:20** [w]Mt 6:17 [x]Job 1:20 **12:21** [y]Jdg 20:26 **12:22** [z]Jnh 3:9 [a]Isa 38:1-5 **12:23** [b]Ge 37:35 [c]1Sa 31:13; 2Sa 13:39; Job 7:10; 10:21 **12:24** [d]1Ki 1:11 [e]1Ki 1:10; 1Ch 22:9; 28:5; Mt 1:6 **12:25** [f]Ne 13:26 **12:26** [g]Dt 3:11; 1Ch 20:1-3 **12:30** [h]1Ch 20:2; Est 8:15; Ps 21:3; 132:18

[a] *14* Masoretic Text; an ancient Hebrew scribal tradition *this you have shown utter contempt for the LORD* [b] *25* *Jedidiah* means *loved by the LORD.* [c] *30* Or *of Milcom* (that is, Molech) [d] *30* That is, about 75 pounds (about 34 kilograms)

12:1–13

PROMISE 2

CONFRONTING SIN GRACIOUSLY

David had sinned. For a while after the fiasco of chapter 11, it seemed that no one knew about the sin; no one, that is, except God and Nathan, God's prophet. As a prophet and as David's friend, Nathan had an obligation to confront the sin in David's life. But notice Nathan's approach to David. He had an awful job to do, but he didn't approach the king in anger or with pious superiority. He devised a careful and wise plan to confront David in a way that would lead to repentance and restoration.

Convincing the sinner that he or she has sinned is not always the most important part of this process. He or she is usually well aware of the reality of the sin. The goal of the confrontation process is restoration. Paul's advice in the New Testament is this, "Brothers, if someone is caught in a sin, you who are spiritual should restore him gently" (see Galatians 6:1–5). Examine Nathan's strategy here. And when you confront a non-Christian or a fallen saint, first ask yourself, "What can I do to help lead this person to repentance and restoration?"

For the next Promise 2 reading go to page 358.

31 and brought out the people who were there, consigning them to labor with saws and with iron picks and axes, and he made them work at brickmaking.[a] He did this to all the Ammonite[i] towns. Then David and his entire army returned to Jerusalem.

Amnon and Tamar

13 In the course of time, Amnon[j] son of David fell in love with Tamar,[k] the beautiful sister of Absalom[l] son of David.

2 Amnon became frustrated to the point of illness on account of his sister Tamar, for she was a virgin, and it seemed impossible for him to do anything to her.

3 Now Amnon had a friend named Jonadab son of Shimeah,[m] David's brother. Jonadab was a very shrewd man. 4 He asked Amnon, "Why do you, the king's son, look so haggard morning after morning? Won't you tell me?"

Amnon said to him, "I'm in love with Tamar, my brother Absalom's sister."

5 "Go to bed and pretend to be ill," Jonadab said. "When your father comes to see you, say to him, 'I would like my sister Tamar to come and give me something to eat. Let her prepare the food in my sight so I may watch her and then eat it from her hand.' "

6 So Amnon lay down and pretended to be ill. When the king came to see him, Amnon said to him, "I would like my sister Tamar to come and make some special bread in my sight, so I may eat from her hand."

7 David sent word to Tamar at the palace: "Go to the house of your brother Amnon and prepare some food for him." 8 So Tamar went to the house of her brother Amnon, who was lying down. She took some dough, kneaded it, made the bread in his sight and baked it. 9 Then she took the pan and served him the bread, but he refused to eat.

"Send everyone out of here,"[n] Amnon said. So everyone left him. 10 Then Amnon said to Tamar, "Bring the food here into my bedroom so I may eat from your hand." And Tamar took the bread she had prepared and brought it to her brother Amnon in his bedroom. 11 But when she took it to him to eat, he grabbed[o] her and said, "Come to bed with me, my sister."[p]

12 "Don't, my brother!" she said to him. "Don't force me. Such a thing should not be done in Israel![q] Don't do this wicked thing.[r] 13 What about me?[s] Where could I get rid of my disgrace? And what about you? You would be like one of the wicked fools in Israel. Please speak to the king; he will not keep me from being married to you." 14 But he refused to listen to her, and since he was stronger than she, he raped her.[t]

15 Then Amnon hated her with intense hatred. In fact, he hated her more than he had loved her. Amnon said to her, "Get up and get out!"

16 "No!" she said to him. "Sending me away would be a greater wrong than what you have already done to me."

But he refused to listen to her. 17 He called his personal servant and said, "Get this woman out of here and bolt the door after her." 18 So his servant put her out and bolted the door after her. She was wearing a richly ornamented[b] robe,[u] for this was the kind of garment the virgin daughters of the king wore. 19 Tamar put ashes[v] on her head and tore the ornamented[c] robe she was wearing. She put her hand on her head and went away, weeping aloud as she went.

20 Her brother Absalom said to her, "Has that Amnon, your brother, been with you? Be quiet now, my sister; he is your brother. Don't take this thing to heart." And Tamar lived in her brother Absalom's house, a desolate woman.

21 When King David heard all this, he was furious.[w] 22 Absalom never said a word to Amnon, either good or bad;[x] he hated[y] Amnon because he had disgraced his sister Tamar.

Absalom Kills Amnon

23 Two years later, when Absalom's sheepshearers[z] were at Baal Hazor near the border of Ephraim, he invited all the king's sons to come there. 24 Absalom went to the king and said, "Your servant has had shearers come. Will the king and his officials please join me?"

25 "No, my son," the king replied. "All of us should not go; we would only be a burden to you." Although Absalom urged him, he still refused to go, but gave him his blessing.

26 Then Absalom said, "If not, please let my brother Amnon come with us."

The king asked him, "Why should he go with you?" 27 But Absalom urged him, so he sent with him Amnon and the rest of the king's sons.

28 Absalom[a] ordered his men, "Listen! When Amnon is in high[b] spirits

12:31 [i] 1Sa 14:47
13:1 [j] 2Sa 3:2 [k] 2Sa 14:27; 1Ch 3:9 [l] 2Sa 3:3
13:3 [m] 1Sa 16:9
13:9 [n] Ge 45:1
13:11 [o] Ge 39:12 [p] Ge 38:16
13:12 [q] Lev 20:17; Jdg 20:6 [r] Ge 34:7; Jdg 19:23
13:13 [s] Ge 20:12; Lev 18:9; Dt 22:21,23-24
13:14 [t] Ge 34:2; Dt 22:25; Eze 22:11
13:18 [u] Ge 37:23; Jdg 5:30
13:19 [v] Jos 7:6; 1Sa 4:12; 2Sa 1:2; Est 4:1; Da 9:3
13:21 [w] Ge 34:7
13:22 [x] Ge 31:24 [y] Lev 19:17-18; 1Jn 2:9-11
13:23 [z] 1Sa 25:7
13:28 [a] 2Sa 3:3 [b] Jdg 19:6,9,22; Ru 3:7; 1Sa 25:36

[a] *31* The meaning of the Hebrew for this clause is uncertain. [b] *18* The meaning of the Hebrew for this phrase is uncertain. [c] *19* The meaning of the Hebrew for this word is uncertain.

from drinking wine and I say to you,
'Strike Amnon down,' then kill him.
Don't be afraid. Have not I given you
this order? Be strong and brave.[c]"
29 So Absalom's men did to Amnon
what Absalom had ordered. Then all
the king's sons got up, mounted their
mules and fled.
30 While they were on their way, the
report came to David: "Absalom has
struck down all the king's sons; not one
of them is left." 31 The king stood up,
tore[d] his clothes and lay down on the
ground; and all his servants stood by
with their clothes torn.
32 But Jonadab son of Shimeah, David's brother, said, "My lord should not
think that they killed all the princes;
only Amnon is dead. This has been Absalom's expressed intention ever since
the day Amnon raped his sister Tamar.
33 My lord the king should not be concerned about the report that all the
king's sons are dead. Only Amnon is
dead."
34 Meanwhile, Absalom had fled.
Now the man standing watch looked
up and saw many people on the road
west of him, coming down the side of
the hill. The watchman went and told
the king, "I see men in the direction of
Horonaim, on the side of the hill."[a]
35 Jonadab said to the king, "See, the
king's sons are here; it has happened
just as your servant said."
36 As he finished speaking, the king's
sons came in, wailing loudly. The king,
too, and all his servants wept very bitterly.
37 Absalom fled and went to Talmai[e]
son of Ammihud, the king of Geshur.
But King David mourned for his son
every day.
38 After Absalom fled and went to Geshur, he stayed there three years. 39 And
the spirit of the king[b] longed to go to
Absalom,[f] for he was consoled[g] concerning Amnon's death.

Absalom Returns to Jerusalem

14 Joab[h] son of Zeruiah knew that the
king's heart longed for Absalom.
2 So Joab sent someone to Tekoa[i] and
had a wise woman[j] brought from
there. He said to her, "Pretend you are
in mourning. Dress in mourning
clothes, and don't use any cosmetic lotions.[k] Act like a woman who has
spent many days grieving for the dead.
3 Then go to the king and speak these
words to him." And Joab[l] put the
words in her mouth.
4 When the woman from Tekoa
went[c] to the king, she fell with her face
to the ground to pay him honor, and
she said, "Help me, O king!"
5 The king asked her, "What is troubling you?"
She said, "I am indeed a widow; my
husband is dead. 6 I your servant had
two sons. They got into a fight with
each other in the field, and no one was
there to separate them. One struck the
other and killed him. 7 Now the whole
clan has risen up against your servant;
they say, 'Hand over the one who
struck his brother down, so that we
may put him to death[m] for the life of
his brother whom he killed; then we
will get rid of the heir[n] as well.' They
would put out the only burning coal I
have left,[o] leaving my husband neither name nor descendant on the face
of the earth."
8 The king said to the woman, "Go
home,[p] and I will issue an order in
your behalf."
9 But the woman from Tekoa said to
him, "My lord the king, let the blame[q]
rest on me and on my father's family,[r]
and let the king and his throne be without guilt.[s]"
10 The king replied, "If anyone says
anything to you, bring him to me, and
he will not bother you again."
11 She said, "Then let the king invoke
the LORD his God to prevent the avenger[t] of blood from adding to the destruction, so that my son will not be
destroyed."
"As surely as the LORD lives," he said,
"not one hair[u] of your son's head will
fall to the ground.[v]"
12 Then the woman said, "Let your
servant speak a word to my lord the
king."
"Speak," he replied.
13 The woman said, "Why then have
you devised a thing like this against the
people of God? When the king says
this, does he not convict himself,[w] for
the king has not brought back his banished son?[x] 14 Like water[y] spilled on
the ground, which cannot be recovered, so we must die.[z] But God does
not take away life; instead, he devises
ways so that a banished person[a] may
not remain estranged from him.
15 "And now I have come to say this
to my lord the king because the people
have made me afraid. Your servant
thought, 'I will speak to the king; perhaps he will do what his servant asks.
16 Perhaps the king will agree to deliver

13:28 [c]2Sa 12:10
13:31 [d]Nu 14:6; 2Sa 1:11; 12:16
13:37 [e]ver 34; 2Sa 3:3; 14:23, 32
13:39 [f]2Sa 14:13 [g]2Sa 12:19-23
14:1 [h]2Sa 2:18
14:2 [i]2Ch 11:6; Ne 3:5; Jer 6:1; Am 1:1 [j]2Sa 20:16 [k]Ru 3:3; 2Sa 12:20; Isa 1:6
14:3 [l]ver 19
14:7 [m]Nu 35:19 [n]Mt 21:38 [o]Dt 19:10-13
14:8 [p]1Sa 25:35
14:9 [q]1Sa 25:24 [r]Mt 27:25 [s]1Sa 25:28; 1Ki 2:33
14:11 [t]Nu 35:12,21 [u]Mt 10:30 [v]1Sa 14:45
14:13 [w]2Sa 12:7; 1Ki 20:40 [x]2Sa 13:38-39
14:14 [y]Job 14:11; Ps 58:7; Isa 19:5 [z]Job 10:8; 17:13; 30:23; Ps 22:15; Heb 9:27 [a]Nu 35:15, 25-28; Job 34:15

a *34* Septuagint; Hebrew does not have this sentence. b *39* Dead Sea Scrolls and some Septuagint manuscripts; Masoretic Text *But the spirit of David the king* c *4* Many Hebrew manuscripts, Septuagint, Vulgate and Syriac; most Hebrew manuscripts *spoke*

his servant from the hand of the man who is trying to cut off both me and my son from the inheritance[b] God gave us.’

17“And now your servant says, ‘May the word of my lord the king bring me rest, for my lord the king is like an angel[c] of God in discerning[d] good and evil. May the LORD your God be with you.’ ”

18Then the king said to the woman, “Do not keep from me the answer to what I am going to ask you.”

“Let my lord the king speak,” the woman said.

19The king asked, “Isn’t the hand of Joab[e] with you in all this?”

The woman answered, “As surely as you live, my lord the king, no one can turn to the right or to the left from anything my lord the king says. Yes, it was your servant Joab who instructed me to do this and who put all these words into the mouth of your servant. 20Your servant Joab did this to change the present situation. My lord has wisdom[f] like that of an angel of God—he knows everything that happens in the land.[g]”

21The king said to Joab, “Very well, I will do it. Go, bring back the young man Absalom.”

22Joab fell with his face to the ground to pay him honor, and he blessed the king.[h] Joab said, “Today your servant knows that he has found favor in your eyes, my lord the king, because the king has granted his servant’s request.”

23Then Joab went to Geshur and brought Absalom back to Jerusalem. 24But the king said, “He must go to his own house; he must not see my face.” So Absalom went to his own house and did not see the face of the king.

25In all Israel there was not a man so highly praised for his handsome appearance as Absalom. From the top of his head to the sole of his foot there was no blemish in him. 26Whenever he cut the hair of his head[i]—he used to cut his hair from time to time when it became too heavy for him—he would weigh it, and its weight was two hundred shekels[a] by the royal standard.

27Three sons[j] and a daughter were born to Absalom. The daughter’s name was Tamar,[k] and she became a beautiful woman.

28Absalom lived two years in Jerusalem without seeing the king’s face. 29Then Absalom sent for Joab in order to send him to the king, but Joab refused to come to him. So he sent a second time, but he refused to come. 30Then he said to his servants, “Look, Joab’s field is next to mine, and he has barley[l] there. Go and set it on fire.” So Absalom’s servants set the field on fire.

31Then Joab did go to Absalom’s house and he said to him, “Why have your servants set my field on fire?[m]”

32Absalom said to Joab, “Look, I sent word to you and said, ‘Come here so I can send you to the king to ask, “Why have I come from Geshur?[n] It would be better for me if I were still there!” ’ Now then, I want to see the king’s face, and if I am guilty of anything, let him put me to death.”[o]

33So Joab went to the king and told him this. Then the king summoned Absalom, and he came in and bowed down with his face to the ground before the king. And the king kissed[p] Absalom.

14:16 [b]Ex 34:9; 1Sa 26:19
14:17 [c]ver 20; 1Sa 29:9; 2Sa 19:27 [d]1Ki 3:9; Da 2:21
14:19 [e]ver 3
14:20 [f]1Ki 3:12,28; Isa 28:6 [g]ver 17; 2Sa 18:13; 19:27
14:22 [h]Ge 47:7
14:26 [i]2Sa 18:9; Eze 44:20
14:27 [j]2Sa 18:18 [k]2Sa 13:1
14:30 [l]Ex 9:31
14:31 [m]Jdg 15:5
14:32 [n]2Sa 3:3 [o]1Sa 20:8
14:33 [p]Ge 33:4; Lk 15:20
15:1 [q]2Sa 12:11 [r]1Sa 8:11; 1Ki 1:5
15:2 [s]Ge 23:10; 2Sa 19:8
15:3 [t]Pr 12:2
15:4 [u]Jdg 9:29
15:6 [v]Ro 16:18
15:8 [w]2Sa 3:3; 13:37-38 [x]Ge 28:20

Absalom’s Conspiracy

15 In the course of time,[q] Absalom provided himself with a chariot[r] and horses and with fifty men to run ahead of him. 2He would get up early and stand by the side of the road leading to the city gate.[s] Whenever anyone came with a complaint to be placed before the king for a decision, Absalom would call out to him, “What town are you from?” He would answer, “Your servant is from one of the tribes of Israel.” 3Then Absalom would say to him, “Look, your claims are valid and proper, but there is no representative of the king to hear you.”[t] 4And Absalom would add, “If only I were appointed judge in the land![u] Then everyone who has a complaint or case could come to me and I would see that he gets justice.”

5Also, whenever anyone approached him to bow down before him, Absalom would reach out his hand, take hold of him and kiss him. 6Absalom behaved in this way toward all the Israelites who came to the king asking for justice, and so he stole the hearts[v] of the men of Israel.

7At the end of four[b] years, Absalom said to the king, “Let me go to Hebron and fulfill a vow I made to the LORD. 8While your servant was living at Geshur[w] in Aram, I made this vow:[x] ‘If the LORD takes me back to Jerusalem, I will worship the LORD in Hebron.[c]’ ”

9The king said to him, “Go in peace.” So he went to Hebron.

10Then Absalom sent secret messen-

[a]*26* That is, about 5 pounds (about 2.3 kilograms) [b]*7* Some Septuagint manuscripts, Syriac and Josephus; Hebrew *forty* [c]*8* Some Septuagint manuscripts; Hebrew does not have *in Hebron.*

ABSALOM

A Son Who Betrayed His Father

Have you ever trusted someone implicitly—a marriage partner, a brother or sister in Christ, a friend, a fellow employee—and been betrayed by that person? Betrayal can be the most devastating emotional wound any person can inflict on another. Can you imagine what it would feel like to be betrayed by your own son?

When Absalom betrayed his father, King David, the pain was almost more than his dad could bear. Even worse for David, he knew it was part of God's judgment on him because of his sins of adultery and murder. Though the Lord forgave David, he made it clear that the "sword" would "never depart" from his house (2 Samuel 12:10). And indeed, that's what happened.

The Beginning of Betrayal

Absalom had already proven a violent man. He killed his brother Amnon after Amnon had raped their sister Tamar. Following that, Absalom fled into exile for a time to wait for David's anger to cool. When David allowed him to return to Jerusalem, Absalom set about undermining his father's kingship.

He began by ingratiating himself with the people. He stood at the city gate, "shaking hands" with the people of Israel as they would come and go. With subtle innuendoes, he built himself up as a more caring person and a better leader than his father. Absalom's charms were effective; eventually, he "stole the hearts of the men of Israel" (15:6).

David was unaware of Absalom's conspiracy. He had no clue that his son had "sent secret messengers" throughout the land to plan a takeover (15:7–12). He loved and trusted Absalom too much to believe his son would do such a terrible thing.

David discovered the plot too late. The people had thrown their support behind Absalom, and King David had to flee Jerusalem and run for his life. Eventually, however, David confronted Absalom and his army of men. Though Absalom was shrewd, he could not outwit or outfight his father, an experienced warrior. In the carnage, Israel's army suffered 20,000 casualties (18:6–8).

The Price of Betrayal

On that same day, Absalom paid the ultimate price of betrayal. As he was trying to escape the battlefield, he rode under a tree. Absalom's long, beautiful hair evidently caught on the branches. His mule kept on going, leaving Absalom hanging in mid-air (18:10).

When Joab, one of David's generals, arrived on the scene, he and his armor bearer ignored David's direct orders and killed Absalom. Even after Absalom's flagrant betrayal, his father wanted to save his life. David remembered that he should have been stoned for his own sins, so how could he not have mercy on his son—especially since David knew that he was at least in part responsible for Absalom's rebellious behavior?

Of course, David's poor parenting doesn't justify Absalom's sinful choices. We're all responsible for our own actions, no matter what our parents have done. In turn, Absalom paid a terrible price for breaking God's commandment to "honor your father" (Exodus 20:12).

Now David faced almost unbelievable pain, not only because of Absalom's betrayal, but also because of his son's death. David's words of mourning reveal both the intensity of his love and the depth of his pain: "O my son Absalom! My son, my son Absalom! If only I had died instead of you—O Absalom, my son, my son! (18:33).

The Pain of Betrayal

Every time we choose to disobey the Lord, we betray our heavenly Father. The pain David felt over Absalom only hints at what God feels when his sons betray him. But how does God respond when we turn away from our sin and back to him? Here is the good news! "He does not treat us as our sins deserve or repay us according to our iniquities. For as high as the heavens are above the earth, so great is his love for those who fear him; as far as the east is from the west, so far has he removed our transgressions from us" (Psalm 103:10–12).

In light of God's mercy toward us, how should we respond when we're betrayed? We must not allow our hurt to turn into bitterness. Forgiving as we have been forgiven is the standard God has set for us. This doesn't mean we can't pray and hope for justice; however, ultimately, justice is God's to dispense. Our responsibility, with an act of the will and in the power of the Holy Spirit, is to choose to forgive our betrayer (Matthew 6:14).

The memories and the pain of betrayal may last a long time. But the "God of all comfort" (2 Corinthians 1:3), the God who can "sympathize with our weaknesses" (Hebrews 4:15), *will* sustain us.

—Dr. Gene Getz

gers throughout the tribes of Israel to
say, "As soon as you hear the sound of
the trumpets,[y] then say, 'Absalom is
king in Hebron.'" 11 Two hundred men
from Jerusalem had accompanied Absalom. They had been invited as guests
and went quite innocently, knowing
nothing about the matter. 12 While Absalom was offering sacrifices, he also
sent for Ahithophel[z] the Gilonite, David's counselor,[a] to come from Giloh,[b] his hometown. And so the conspiracy gained strength, and Absalom's
following kept on increasing.[c]

David Flees

13 A messenger came and told David,
"The hearts of the men of Israel are
with Absalom."
14 Then David said to all his officials
who were with him in Jerusalem,
"Come! We must flee,[d] or none of us
will escape from Absalom.[e] We must
leave immediately, or he will move
quickly to overtake us and bring ruin
upon us and put the city to the sword."
15 The king's officials answered him,
"Your servants are ready to do whatever our lord the king chooses."

> **15:14**
>
> **PROMISE 4**
>
> ### A PROPHECY FULFILLED
>
> Chapters 15–18 of 2 Samuel outline the results of David's sin with Bathsheba, prophesied by Nathan in 12:11: "Out of your own household I am going to bring calamity upon you." Absalom's rebellion was one of many outgrowths of David's moral failure, touched off by his adultery with Bathsheba.
>
> As a father, David had not set a good example for his sons to follow. He had not disciplined his sons after Amnon's violent sexual offense or Absalom's murderous act (ch. 13). Could it be that guilt over his sin with Bathsheba undermined his own sense of moral authority? We'll never know. We do know, however, that in this verse David found himself running for his life from his own son, in fulfillment of Nathan's prophecy.
>
> Sin has a way of surprising the sinner. Like an oil slick being pushed and stretched by the tide, time and circumstance can magnify sin's effects and push its influence into different areas of life. Is there some sin in your own life that you know is spreading its influence over your family, your career, your spiritual walk? Take a lesson from David's situation and prayerfully consider which steps you can take today to stop the slick from spreading any further.
>
> *For the next Promise 4 reading go to page 364.*

16 The king set out, with his entire
household following him; but he left
ten concubines[f] to take care of the
palace. 17 So the king set out, with all
the people following him, and they
halted at a place some distance away.
18 All his men marched past him, along
with all the Kerethites[g] and Pelethites;
and all the six hundred Gittites who
had accompanied him from Gath
marched before the king.
19 The king said to Ittai[h] the Gittite,
"Why should you come along with us?
Go back and stay with King Absalom.
You are a foreigner,[i] an exile from
your homeland. 20 You came only yesterday. And today shall I make you
wander[j] about with us, when I do not
know where I am going? Go back, and
take your countrymen. May kindness
and faithfulness[k] be with you."
21 But Ittai replied to the king, "As
surely as the LORD lives, and as my lord
the king lives, wherever my lord the
king may be, whether it means life or
death, there will your servant be."[l]
22 David said to Ittai, "Go ahead,
march on." So Ittai the Gittite marched
on with all his men and the families
that were with him.
23 The whole countryside wept aloud
as all the people passed by. The king
also crossed the Kidron Valley,[m] and
all the people moved on toward the
desert.
24 Zadok[n] was there, too, and all the
Levites who were with him were carrying the ark[o] of the covenant of God.
They set down the ark of God, and Abiathar[p] offered sacrifices[a] until all the
people had finished leaving the city.
25 Then the king said to Zadok, "Take
the ark of God back into the city. If I
find favor in the LORD's eyes, he will
bring me back and let me see it and his
dwelling place[q] again. 26 But if he says,
'I am not pleased with you,' then I am
ready; let him do to me whatever
seems good to him.[r]"
27 The king also said to Zadok the
priest, "Aren't you a seer?[s] Go back to
the city in peace, with your son Ahimaaz and Jonathan[t] son of Abiathar. You
and Abiathar take your two sons with
you. 28 I will wait at the fords[u] in the
desert until word comes from you to
inform me." 29 So Zadok and Abiathar
took the ark of God back to Jerusalem
and stayed there.
30 But David continued up the
Mount of Olives, weeping[v] as he went;
his head[w] was covered and he was
barefoot. All the people with him covered their heads too and were weeping

15:10 [y] 1Ki 1:34,39; 2Ki 9:13
15:12 [z] ver 31,34; 2Sa 16:15,23; 1Ch 27:33 [a] Job 19:14; Ps 41:9; 55:13; Jer 9:4 [b] Jos 15:51 [c] Ps 3:1
15:14 [d] 2Sa 12:11; 1Ki 2:26; Ps 132:1; Ps 3 Title [e] 2Sa 19:9
15:16 [f] 2Sa 16:21-22; 20:3
15:18 [g] 1Sa 30:14; 2Sa 8:18; 20:7, 23; 1Ki 1:38, 44; 1Ch 18:17
15:19 [h] 2Sa 18:2 [i] Ge 31:15
15:20 [j] 1Sa 23:13 [k] 2Sa 2:6
15:21 [l] Ru 1:16-17; Pr 17:17
15:23 [m] 2Ch 29:16
15:24 [n] 2Sa 8:17 [o] Nu 4:15 [p] 1Sa 22:20
15:25 [q] Ex 15:13; Ps 43:3; Jer 25:30
15:26 [r] 1Sa 3:18; 2Sa 22:20; 1Ki 10:9
15:27 [s] 1Sa 9:9 [t] 2Sa 17:17
15:28 [u] 2Sa 17:16
15:30 [v] 2Sa 19:4; Ps 126:6 [w] Est 6:12; Isa 20:2-4

[a] 24 Or *Abiathar went up*

as they went up. 31Now David had been told, "Ahithophel[x] is among the conspirators with Absalom." So David prayed, "O LORD, turn Ahithophel's counsel into foolishness."

32When David arrived at the summit, where people used to worship God, Hushai the Arkite[y] was there to meet him, his robe torn and dust[z] on his head. 33David said to him, "If you go with me, you will be a burden[a] to me. 34But if you return to the city and say to Absalom, 'I will be your servant, O king; I was your father's servant in the past, but now I will be your servant,'[b] then you can help me by frustrating Ahithophel's advice. 35Won't the priests Zadok and Abiathar be there with you? Tell them anything you hear in the king's palace.[c] 36Their two sons, Ahimaaz son of Zadok and Jonathan[d] son of Abiathar, are there with them. Send them to me with anything you hear."

37So David's friend Hushai[e] arrived at Jerusalem as Absalom[f] was entering the city.

David and Ziba

16 When David had gone a short distance beyond the summit, there was Ziba,[g] the steward of Mephibosheth, waiting to meet him. He had a string of donkeys saddled and loaded with two hundred loaves of bread, a hundred cakes of raisins, a hundred cakes of figs and a skin of wine.[h]

2The king asked Ziba, "Why have you brought these?"

Ziba answered, "The donkeys are for the king's household to ride on, the bread and fruit are for the men to eat, and the wine is to refresh[i] those who become exhausted in the desert."

3The king then asked, "Where is your master's grandson?"[j]

Ziba said to him, "He is staying in Jerusalem, because he thinks, 'Today the house of Israel will give me back my grandfather's kingdom.' "

4Then the king said to Ziba, "All that belonged to Mephibosheth is now yours."

"I humbly bow," Ziba said. "May I find favor in your eyes, my lord the king."

Shimei Curses David

5As King David approached Bahurim,[k] a man from the same clan as Saul's family came out from there. His name was Shimei[l] son of Gera, and he cursed[m] as he came out. 6He pelted David and all the king's officials with stones, though all the troops and the special guard were on David's right and left. 7As he cursed, Shimei said, "Get out, get out, you man of blood, you scoundrel! 8The LORD has repaid you for all the blood you shed in the household of Saul, in whose place you have reigned.[n] The LORD has handed the kingdom over to your son Absalom. You have come to ruin because you are a man of blood!"

9Then Abishai[o] son of Zeruiah said to the king, "Why should this dead dog curse my lord the king? Let me go over and cut off his head."[p]

10But the king said, "What do you and I have in common, you sons of Zeruiah?[q] If he is cursing because the LORD said to him, 'Curse David,' who can ask, 'Why do you do this?' "[r]

11David then said to Abishai and all his officials, "My son,[s] who is of my own flesh, is trying to take my life. How much more, then, this Benjamite! Leave him alone; let him curse, for the LORD has told him to.[t] 12It may be that the LORD will see my distress[u] and repay me with good[v] for the cursing I am receiving today.[w]"

13So David and his men continued along the road while Shimei was going along the hillside opposite him, cursing as he went and throwing stones at him and showering him with dirt. 14The king and all the people with him arrived at their destination exhausted.[x] And there he refreshed himself.

The Advice of Hushai and Ahithophel

15Meanwhile, Absalom[y] and all the men of Israel came to Jerusalem, and Ahithophel[z] was with him. 16Then Hushai[a] the Arkite, David's friend, went to Absalom and said to him, "Long live the king! Long live the king!"

17Absalom asked Hushai, "Is this the love you show your friend? Why didn't you go with your friend?"[b]

18Hushai said to Absalom, "No, the one chosen by the LORD, by these people, and by all the men of Israel—his I will be, and I will remain with him. 19Furthermore, whom should I serve? Should I not serve the son? Just as I served your father, so I will serve you."[c]

20Absalom said to Ahithophel, "Give us your advice. What should we do?"

21Ahithophel answered, "Lie with your father's concubines whom he left to take care of the palace. Then all Israel will hear that you have made yourself a stench in your father's nostrils, and the hands of everyone with you will be strengthened." 22So they pitched a tent for Absalom on the roof,

15:31 [x] ver 12; 2Sa 16:23; 17:14,23
15:32 [y] Jos 16:2 [z] 2Sa 1:2
15:33 [a] 2Sa 19:35
15:34 [b] 2Sa 16:19
15:35 [c] 2Sa 17:15-16
15:36 [d] ver 27; 2Sa 17:17
15:37 [e] 2Sa 16:16-17; 1Ch 27:33 [f] 2Sa 16:15
16:1 [g] 2Sa 9:1-13 [h] 1Sa 25:18
16:2 [i] 2Sa 17:27-29
16:3 [j] 2Sa 9:9-10; 19:26-27
16:5 [k] 2Sa 3:16 [l] 2Sa 19:16-23; 1Ki 2:8-9,36,44 [m] Ex 22:28
16:8 [n] 2Sa 21:9
16:9 [o] 2Sa 9:8 [p] Ex 22:28; Lk 9:54
16:10 [q] 2Sa 19:22 [r] Ro 9:20
16:11 [s] 2Sa 12:11 [t] Ge 45:5
16:12 [u] Ps 4:1; 25:18 [v] Dt 23:5; Ro 8:28 [w] Ps 109:28
16:14 [x] 2Sa 17:2
16:15 [y] 2Sa 15:37 [z] 2Sa 15:12
16:16 [a] 2Sa 15:37
16:17 [b] 2Sa 19:25
16:19 [c] 2Sa 15:34

and he lay with his father's concubines
in the sight of all Israel.[d]
23 Now in those days the advice[e]
Ahithophel gave was like that of one
who inquires of God. That was how
both David[f] and Absalom regarded all
of Ahithophel's advice.

17 Ahithophel said to Absalom, "I
would[a] choose twelve thousand
men and set out tonight in pursuit of
David. 2 I would[b] attack him while he
is weary and weak.[g] I would[b] strike
him with terror, and then all the people
with him will flee. I would[b] strike
down only the king[h] 3 and bring all the
people back to you. The death of the
man you seek will mean the return of
all; all the people will be unharmed."
4 This plan seemed good to Absalom
and to all the elders of Israel.
5 But Absalom said, "Summon also
Hushai[i] the Arkite, so we can hear
what he has to say." 6 When Hushai
came to him, Absalom said, "Ahithophel has given this advice. Should we
do what he says? If not, give us your
opinion."
7 Hushai replied to Absalom, "The
advice Ahithophel has given is not
good this time. 8 You know your father
and his men; they are fighters, and as
fierce as a wild bear robbed of her
cubs.[j] Besides, your father is an experienced fighter;[k] he will not spend the
night with the troops. 9 Even now, he is
hidden in a cave or some other place.[l]
If he should attack your troops first,[c]
whoever hears about it will say, 'There
has been a slaughter among the troops
who follow Absalom.' 10 Then even the
bravest soldier, whose heart is like the
heart of a lion,[m] will melt[n] with fear,
for all Israel knows that your father is
a fighter and that those with him are
brave.[o]
11 "So I advise you: Let all Israel, from
Dan to Beersheba[p]—as numerous as
the sand[q] on the seashore—be gathered to you, with you yourself leading
them into battle. 12 Then we will attack
him wherever he may be found, and we
will fall on him as dew settles on the
ground. Neither he nor any of his men
will be left alive. 13 If he withdraws into
a city, then all Israel will bring ropes to
that city, and we will drag it down to
the valley[r] until not even a piece of it
can be found."
14 Absalom and all the men of Israel
said, "The advice[s] of Hushai the Arkite is better than that of Ahithophel."[t] For the LORD had determined
to frustrate[u] the good advice of Ahithophel in order to bring disaster[v] on
Absalom.[w]
15 Hushai told Zadok and Abiathar,
the priests, "Ahithophel has advised
Absalom and the elders of Israel to do
such and such, but I have advised them
to do so and so. 16 Now send a message
immediately and tell David, 'Do not
spend the night at the fords in the
desert;[x] cross over without fail, or the
king and all the people with him will be
swallowed up.[y]' "
17 Jonathan[z] and Ahimaaz were
staying at En Rogel.[a] A servant girl
was to go and inform them, and they
were to go and tell King David, for they
could not risk being seen entering the
city. 18 But a young man saw them and
told Absalom. So the two of them left
quickly and went to the house of a man
in Bahurim.[b] He had a well in his
courtyard, and they climbed down into
it. 19 His wife took a covering and
spread it out over the opening of the
well and scattered grain over it. No one
knew anything about it.[c]
20 When Absalom's men came to the
woman[d] at the house, they asked,
"Where are Ahimaaz and Jonathan?"
The woman answered them, "They
crossed over the brook."[d] The men
searched but found no one, so they returned to Jerusalem.
21 After the men had gone, the two
climbed out of the well and went to
inform King David. They said to him,
"Set out and cross the river at once;
Ahithophel has advised such and such
against you." 22 So David and all the
people with him set out and crossed
the Jordan. By daybreak, no one was
left who had not crossed the Jordan.
23 When Ahithophel saw that his advice[e] had not been followed, he saddled his donkey and set out for his
house in his hometown. He put his
house in order[f] and then hanged
himself. So he died and was buried in
his father's tomb.
24 David went to Mahanaim,[g] and
Absalom crossed the Jordan with all
the men of Israel. 25 Absalom had appointed Amasa[h] over the army in
place of Joab. Amasa was the son of a
man named Jether,[e][i] an Israelite[f]
who had married Abigail,[g] the daughter of Nahash and sister of Zeruiah the
mother of Joab. 26 The Israelites and
Absalom camped in the land of Gilead.
27 When David came to Mahanaim,
Shobi son of Nahash[j] from Rabbah[k]

16:22 [d] 2Sa 12:11-12; 15:16
16:23 [e] 2Sa 17:14,23 [f] 2Sa 15:12
17:2 [g] 2Sa 16:14 [h] 1Ki 22:31; Zec 13:7
17:5 [i] 2Sa 15:32
17:8 [j] Hos 13:8 [k] 1Sa 16:18
17:9 [l] Jer 41:9
17:10 [m] 1Ch 12:8 [n] Jos 2:9,11; Eze 21:15 [o] 2Sa 23:8; 1Ch 11:11
17:11 [p] Jdg 20:1 [q] Ge 12:2; 22:17; Jos 11:4
17:13 [r] Mic 1:6
17:14 [s] 2Sa 16:23 [t] 2Sa 15:12 [u] 2Sa 15:34; Ne 4:15 [v] Ps 9:16 [w] 2Ch 10:8
17:16 [x] 2Sa 15:28 [y] 2Sa 15:35
17:17 [z] 2Sa 15:27,36 [a] Jos 15:7; 18:16
17:18 [b] 2Sa 3:16; 16:5
17:19 [c] Jos 2:6
17:20 [d] Ex 1:19; Jos 2:3-5; 1Sa 19:12-17
17:23 [e] 2Sa 15:12; 16:23 [f] 2Ki 20:1; Mt 27:5
17:24 [g] Ge 32:2; 2Sa 2:8
17:25 [h] 2Sa 19:13; 20:4,9-12; 1Ki 2:5,32; 1Ch 12:18 [i] 1Ch 2:13-17
17:27 [j] 1Sa 11:1 [k] Dt 3:11; 2Sa 10:1-2; 12:26,29

[a] *1* Or *Let me* [b] *2* Or *will* [c] *9* Or *When some of the men fall at the first attack*
[d] *20* Or *"They passed by the sheep pen toward the water."* [e] *25* Hebrew *Ithra,* a variant of *Jether* [f] *25* Hebrew and some Septuagint manuscripts; other Septuagint manuscripts (see also 1 Chron. 2:17) *Ishmaelite* or *Jezreelite*
[g] *25* Hebrew *Abigal,* a variant of *Abigail*

of the Ammonites, and Makir[l] son of Ammiel from Lo Debar, and Barzillai[m] the Gileadite[n] from Rogelim 28 brought bedding and bowls and articles of pottery. They also brought wheat and barley, flour and roasted grain, beans and lentils,[a] 29 honey and curds, sheep, and cheese from cows' milk for David and his people to eat.[o] For they said, "The people have become hungry and tired and thirsty in the desert.[p]"

Absalom's Death

18 David mustered the men who were with him and appointed over them commanders of thousands and commanders of hundreds. 2 David sent the troops out[q]—a third under the command of Joab, a third under Joab's brother Abishai[r] son of Zeruiah, and a third under Ittai[s] the Gittite. The king told the troops, "I myself will surely march out with you."

3 But the men said, "You must not go out; if we are forced to flee, they won't care about us. Even if half of us die, they won't care; but you are worth ten[t] thousand of us.[b] It would be better now for you to give us support from the city."[u]

4 The king answered, "I will do whatever seems best to you."

So the king stood beside the gate while all the men marched out in units of hundreds and of thousands. 5 The king commanded Joab, Abishai and Ittai, "Be gentle with the young man Absalom for my sake." And all the troops heard the king giving orders concerning Absalom to each of the commanders.

6 The army marched into the field to fight Israel, and the battle took place in the forest[v] of Ephraim. 7 There the army of Israel was defeated by David's men, and the casualties that day were great—twenty thousand men. 8 The battle spread out over the whole countryside, and the forest claimed more lives that day than the sword.

9 Now Absalom happened to meet David's men. He was riding his mule, and as the mule went under the thick branches of a large oak, Absalom's head[w] got caught in the tree. He was left hanging in midair, while the mule he was riding kept on going.

10 When one of the men saw this, he told Joab, "I just saw Absalom hanging in an oak tree."

11 Joab said to the man who had told him this, "What! You saw him? Why didn't you strike[x] him to the ground right there? Then I would have had to give you ten shekels[c] of silver and a warrior's belt.[y]"

12 But the man replied, "Even if a thousand shekels[d] were weighed out into my hands, I would not lift my hand against the king's son. In our hearing the king commanded you and Abishai and Ittai, 'Protect the young man Absalom for my sake.[e]' 13 And if I had put my life in jeopardy[f]—and nothing is hidden from the king[z]—you would have kept your distance from me."

14 Joab[a] said, "I'm not going to wait like this for you." So he took three javelins in his hand and plunged them into Absalom's heart while Absalom was still alive in the oak tree. 15 And ten of Joab's armor-bearers surrounded Absalom, struck him and killed him.[b]

16 Then Joab[c] sounded the trumpet, and the troops stopped pursuing Israel, for Joab halted them. 17 They took Absalom, threw him into a big pit in the forest and piled up[d] a large heap of rocks[e] over him. Meanwhile, all the Israelites fled to their homes.

18 During his lifetime Absalom had taken a pillar and erected it in the King's Valley[f] as a monument[g] to himself, for he thought, "I have no son[h] to carry on the memory of my name." He named the pillar after himself, and it is called Absalom's Monument to this day.

David Mourns

19 Now Ahimaaz[i] son of Zadok said, "Let me run and take the news to the king that the LORD has delivered him from the hand of his enemies.[j]"

20 "You are not the one to take the news today," Joab told him. "You may take the news another time, but you must not do so today, because the king's son is dead."

21 Then Joab said to a Cushite, "Go, tell the king what you have seen." The Cushite bowed down before Joab and ran off.

22 Ahimaaz son of Zadok again said to Joab, "Come what may, please let me run behind the Cushite."

But Joab replied, "My son, why do

17:27 [l]2Sa 9:4 [m]2Sa 19:31-39; 1Ki 2:7 [n]2Sa 19:31; Ezr 2:61
17:29 [o]1Ch 12:40 [p]2Sa 16:2; Ro 12:13
18:2 [q]Jdg 7:16; 1Sa 11:11 [r]1Sa 26:6 [s]2Sa 15:19
18:3 [t]1Sa 18:7 [u]2Sa 21:17
18:6 [v]Jos 17:18
18:9 [w]2Sa 14:26
18:11 [x]2Sa 3:39 [y]1Sa 18:4
18:13 [z]2Sa 14:19-20
18:14 [a]2Sa 2:18; 14:30
18:15 [b]2Sa 12:10
18:16 [c]2Sa 2:28; 20:22
18:17 [d]Jos 7:26 [e]Jos 8:29
18:18 [f]Ge 14:17 [g]Ge 50:5; Nu 32:42; 1Sa 15:12 [h]2Sa 14:27
18:19 [i]2Sa 15:36 [j]ver 31; Jdg 11:36

[a] *28* Most Septuagint manuscripts and Syriac; Hebrew *lentils, and roasted grain*
[b] *3* Two Hebrew manuscripts, some Septuagint manuscripts and Vulgate; most Hebrew manuscripts *care; for now there are ten thousand like us*
[c] *11* That is, about 4 ounces (about 115 grams)
[d] *12* That is, about 25 pounds (about 11 kilograms)
[e] *12* A few Hebrew manuscripts, Septuagint, Vulgate and Syriac; most Hebrew manuscripts may be translated *Absalom, whoever you may be.*
[f] *13* Or *Otherwise, if I had acted treacherously toward him*

you want to go? You don't have any news that will bring you a reward."

23He said, "Come what may, I want to run."

So Joab said, "Run!" Then Ahimaaz ran by way of the plain[a] and outran the Cushite.

24While David was sitting between the inner and outer gates, the watchman[k] went up to the roof of the gateway by the wall. As he looked out, he saw a man running alone. 25The watchman called out to the king and reported it.

The king said, "If he is alone, he must have good news." And the man came closer and closer.

26Then the watchman saw another man running, and he called down to the gatekeeper, "Look, another man running alone!"

The king said, "He must be bringing good news,[l] too."

27The watchman said, "It seems to me that the first one runs like[m] Ahimaaz son of Zadok."

"He's a good man," the king said. "He comes with good news."

28Then Ahimaaz called out to the king, "All is well!" He bowed down before the king with his face to the ground and said, "Praise be to the LORD your God! He has delivered up the men who lifted their hands against my lord the king."

29The king asked, "Is the young man Absalom safe?"

Ahimaaz answered, "I saw great confusion just as Joab was about to send the king's servant and me, your servant, but I don't know what it was."

30The king said, "Stand aside and wait here." So he stepped aside and stood there.

31Then the Cushite arrived and said, "My lord the king, hear the good news! The LORD has delivered you today from all who rose up against you."

32The king asked the Cushite, "Is the young man Absalom safe?"

The Cushite replied, "May the enemies of my lord the king and all who rise up to harm you be like that young man."[n]

33The king was shaken. He went up to the room over the gateway and wept. As he went, he said: "O my son Absalom! My son, my son Absalom! If only I had died[o] instead of you—O Absalom, my son, my son!"[p]

19 Joab was told, "The king is weeping and mourning for Absalom." 2And for the whole army the victory that day was turned into mourning, because on that day the troops heard it said, "The king is grieving for his son." 3The men stole into the city that day as men steal in who are ashamed when they flee from battle. 4The king covered his face and cried aloud, "O my son Absalom! O Absalom, my son, my son!"

5Then Joab went into the house to the king and said, "Today you have humiliated all your men, who have just saved your life and the lives of your sons and daughters and the lives of your wives and concubines. 6You love those who hate you and hate those who love you. You have made it clear today that the commanders and their men mean nothing to you. I see that you would be pleased if Absalom were alive today and all of us were dead. 7Now go out and encourage your men. I swear by the LORD that if you don't go out, not a man will be left with you by nightfall. This will be worse for you than all the calamities that have come upon you from your youth till now."[q]

8So the king got up and took his seat in the gateway. When the men were told, "The king is sitting in the gateway,[r]" they all came before him.

David Returns to Jerusalem

Meanwhile, the Israelites had fled to their homes. 9Throughout the tribes of Israel, the people were all arguing with each other, saying, "The king delivered us from the hand of our enemies; he is the one who rescued us from the hand of the Philistines.[s] But now he has fled the country because of Absalom;[t] 10and Absalom, whom we anointed to rule over us, has died in battle. So why do you say nothing about bringing the king back?"

11King David sent this message to Zadok[u] and Abiathar, the priests: "Ask the elders of Judah, 'Why should you be the last to bring the king back to his palace, since what is being said throughout Israel has reached the king at his quarters? 12You are my brothers, my own flesh and blood. So why should you be the last to bring back the king?' 13And say to Amasa,[v] 'Are you not my own flesh and blood?[w] May God deal with me, be it ever so severely,[x] if from now on you are not the commander of my army in place of Joab.[y]'"

14He won over the hearts of all the men of Judah as though they were one man. They sent word to the king, "Return, you and all your men." 15Then the king returned and went as far as the Jordan.

Now the men of Judah had come to

18:24 [k]1Sa 14:16; 2Sa 19:8; 2Ki 9:17; Jer 51:12
18:26 [l]1Ki 1:42; Isa 52:7; 61:1
18:27 [m]2Ki 9:20
18:32 [n]Jdg 5:31; 1Sa 25:26
18:33 [o]Ex 32:32 [p]Ge 43:14; 2Sa 19:4; Ro 9:3
19:7 [q]Pr 14:28
19:8 [r]2Sa 15:2
19:9 [s]2Sa 8:1-14 [t]2Sa 15:14
19:11 [u]2Sa 15:24
19:13 [v]2Sa 17:25 [w]Ge 29:14 [x]Ru 1:17; 1Ki 19:2; 8:16 [y]2Sa 2:13

[a] *23* That is, the plain of the Jordan

Gilgal[z] to go out and meet the king
and bring him across the Jordan.
16Shimei[a] son of Gera, the Benjamite
from Bahurim, hurried down with the
men of Judah to meet King David.
17With him were a thousand Benjamites, along with Ziba,[b] the steward
of Saul's household,[c] and his fifteen
sons and twenty servants. They rushed
to the Jordan, where the king was.
18They crossed at the ford to take the
king's household over and to do whatever he wished.

When Shimei son of Gera crossed
the Jordan, he fell prostrate before the
king 19and said to him, "May my lord
not hold me guilty. Do not remember
how your servant did wrong on the day
my lord the king left Jerusalem.[d] May
the king put it out of his mind. 20For I
your servant know that I have sinned,
but today I have come here as the first
of the whole house of Joseph to come
down and meet my lord the king."

21Then Abishai[e] son of Zeruiah
said, "Shouldn't Shimei be put to death
for this? He cursed[f] the LORD's
anointed."[g]

22David replied, "What do you and I
have in common, you sons of Zeruiah?[h] This day you have become my
adversaries! Should anyone be put to
death in Israel today?[i] Do I not know
that today I am king over Israel?" 23So
the king said to Shimei, "You shall not
die." And the king promised him on
oath.[j]

24Mephibosheth,[k] Saul's grandson,
also went down to meet the king. He
had not taken care of his feet or
trimmed his mustache or washed his
clothes from the day the king left until
the day he returned safely. 25When he
came from Jerusalem to meet the king,
the king asked him, "Why didn't you go
with me,[l] Mephibosheth?"

26He said, "My lord the king, since I
your servant am lame,[m] I said, 'I will
have my donkey saddled and will ride
on it, so I can go with the king.' But
Ziba[n] my servant betrayed me. 27And
he has slandered your servant to my
lord the king. My lord the king is like an
angel[o] of God; so do whatever pleases
you. 28All my grandfather's descendants deserved nothing but death[p]
from my lord the king, but you gave
your servant a place among those who
eat at your table.[q] So what right do I
have to make any more appeals to the
king?"

29The king said to him, "Why say
more? I order you and Ziba to divide
the fields."

30Mephibosheth said to the king,
"Let him take everything, now that my
lord the king has arrived home safely."

31Barzillai[r] the Gileadite also came
down from Rogelim to cross the Jordan
with the king and to send him on his
way from there. 32Now Barzillai was a
very old man, eighty years of age. He
had provided for the king during his
stay in Mahanaim, for he was a very
wealthy[s] man. 33The king said to Barzillai, "Cross over with me and stay
with me in Jerusalem, and I will provide for you."

34But Barzillai answered the king,
"How many more years will I live, that
I should go up to Jerusalem with the
king? 35I am now eighty[t] years old.
Can I tell the difference between what
is good and what is not? Can your servant taste what he eats and drinks? Can
I still hear the voices of men and wom-
en singers?[u] Why should your servant
be an added[v] burden to my lord the
king? 36Your servant will cross over the
Jordan with the king for a short distance, but why should the king reward
me in this way? 37Let your servant return, that I may die in my own town
near the tomb of my father[w] and
mother. But here is your servant Kimham.[x] Let him cross over with my lord
the king. Do for him whatever pleases
you."

38The king said, "Kimham shall cross
over with me, and I will do for him
whatever pleases you. And anything
you desire from me I will do for you."

39So all the people crossed the Jordan, and then the king crossed over.
The king kissed Barzillai and gave him
his blessing,[y] and Barzillai returned to
his home.

40When the king crossed over to Gilgal, Kimham crossed with him. All the
troops of Judah and half the troops of
Israel had taken the king over.

41Soon all the men of Israel were
coming to the king and saying to him,
"Why did our brothers, the men of Judah, steal the king away and bring him
and his household across the Jordan,
together with all his men?"[z]

42All the men of Judah answered the
men of Israel, "We did this because the
king is closely related to us. Why are
you angry about it? Have we eaten any
of the king's provisions? Have we taken
anything for ourselves?"

43Then the men of Israel[a] answered
the men of Judah, "We have ten shares
in the king; and besides, we have a
greater claim on David than you have.
So why do you treat us with contempt?
Were we not the first to speak of bringing back our king?"

But the men of Judah responded

19:15 [z]Jos 5:9; 1Sa 11:15
19:16 [a]2Sa 16:5-13; 1Ki 2:8
19:17 [b]2Sa 9:2; 16:1-2 [c]Ge 43:16
19:19 [d]1Sa 22:15; 2Sa 16:6-8
19:21 [e]1Sa 26:6 [f]Ex 22:28 [g]1Sa 12:3; 26:9; 2Sa 16:7-8
19:22 [h]2Sa 2:18; 16:10 [i]1Sa 11:13
19:23 [j]1Ki 2:8,42
19:24 [k]2Sa 4:4; 9:6-10
19:25 [l]2Sa 16:17
19:26 [m]Lev 21:18 [n]2Sa 9:2
19:27 [o]1Sa 29:9; 2Sa 14:17,20
19:28 [p]2Sa 16:8; 21:6-9 [q]2Sa 9:7,13
19:31 [r]2Sa 17:27-29, 27; 1Ki 2:7
19:32 [s]1Sa 25:2; 2Sa 17:27
19:35 [t]Ps 90:10 [u]2Ch 35:25; Ezr 2:65; Ecc 2:8; 12:1; Isa 5:11-12 [v]2Sa 15:33
19:37 [w]Ge 49:29; 1Ki 2:7 [x]ver 40; Jer 41:17
19:39 [y]Ge 31:55; Ge 47:7
19:41 [z]Jdg 8:1; 12:1
19:43 [a]2Sa 5:1

even more harshly than the men of Israel.

Sheba Rebels Against David

20 Now a troublemaker named Sheba son of Bicri, a Benjamite, happened to be there. He sounded the trumpet and shouted,

"We have no share[b] in David,[c]
  no part in Jesse's son![d]
Every man to his tent, O Israel!"

2So all the men of Israel deserted David to follow Sheba son of Bicri. But the men of Judah stayed by their king all the way from the Jordan to Jerusalem.

3When David returned to his palace in Jerusalem, he took the ten concubines[e] he had left to take care of the palace and put them in a house under guard. He provided for them, but did not lie with them. They were kept in confinement till the day of their death, living as widows.

4Then the king said to Amasa,[f] "Summon the men of Judah to come to me within three days, and be here yourself." 5But when Amasa went to summon Judah, he took longer than the time the king had set for him.

6David said to Abishai,[g] "Now Sheba son of Bicri will do us more harm than Absalom did. Take your master's men and pursue him, or he will find fortified cities and escape from us." 7So Joab's men and the Kerethites[h] and Pelethites and all the mighty warriors went out under the command of Abishai. They marched out from Jerusalem to pursue Sheba son of Bicri.

8While they were at the great rock in Gibeon,[i] Amasa came to meet them. Joab[j] was wearing his military tunic, and strapped over it at his waist was a belt with a dagger in its sheath. As he stepped forward, it dropped out of its sheath.

9Joab said to Amasa, "How are you, my brother?" Then Joab took Amasa by the beard with his right hand to kiss him. 10Amasa was not on his guard against the dagger[k] in Joab's[l] hand, and Joab plunged it into his belly, and his intestines spilled out on the ground. Without being stabbed again, Amasa died. Then Joab and his brother Abishai pursued Sheba son of Bicri.

11One of Joab's men stood beside Amasa and said, "Whoever favors Joab, and whoever is for David, let him follow Joab!" 12Amasa lay wallowing in his blood in the middle of the road, and the man saw that all the troops came to a halt[m] there. When he realized that everyone who came up to Amasa stopped, he dragged him from the road into a field and threw a garment over him. 13After Amasa had been removed from the road, all the men went on with Joab to pursue Sheba son of Bicri.

14Sheba passed through all the tribes of Israel to Abel Beth Maacah[a] and through the entire region of the Berites,[n] who gathered together and followed him. 15All the troops with Joab came and besieged Sheba in Abel Beth Maacah.[o] They built a siege ramp[p] up to the city, and it stood against the outer fortifications. While they were battering the wall to bring it down, 16a wise woman[q] called from the city, "Listen! Listen! Tell Joab to come here so I can speak to him." 17He went toward her, and she asked, "Are you Joab?"

"I am," he answered.

She said, "Listen to what your servant has to say."

"I'm listening," he said.

18She continued, "Long ago they used to say, 'Get your answer at Abel,' and that settled it. 19We are the peaceful[r] and faithful in Israel. You are trying to destroy a city that is a mother in Israel. Why do you want to swallow up the LORD's inheritance?"[s]

20"Far be it from me!" Joab replied, "Far be it from me to swallow up or destroy! 21That is not the case. A man named Sheba son of Bicri, from the hill country of Ephraim, has lifted up his hand against the king, against David. Hand over this one man, and I'll withdraw from the city."

The woman said to Joab, "His head[t] will be thrown to you from the wall."

22Then the woman went to all the people with her wise advice,[u] and they cut off the head of Sheba son of Bicri and threw it to Joab. So he sounded the trumpet, and his men dispersed from the city, each returning to his home. And Joab went back to the king in Jerusalem.

23Joab[v] was over Israel's entire army; Benaiah son of Jehoiada was over the Kerethites and Pelethites; 24Adoniram[b][w] was in charge of forced labor; Jehoshaphat[x] son of Ahilud was recorder; 25Sheva was secretary; Zadok[y] and Abiathar were priests; 26and Ira the Jairite was David's priest.

20:1 [b]Ge 31:14 [c]Ge 29:14; 1Ki 12:16 [d]1Sa 22:7-8; 2Ch 10:16 **20:3** [e]2Sa 15:16; 16:21-22 **20:4** [f]2Sa 17:25; 19:13 **20:6** [g]2Sa 21:17 **20:7** [h]1Sa 30:14; 2Sa 8:18; 15:18; 1Ki 1:38 **20:8** [i]Jos 9:3 [j]2Sa 2:18 **20:10** [k]Jdg 3:21; 2Sa 2:23; 3:27 [l]1Ki 2:5 **20:12** [m]2Sa 2:23

20:14 [n]Nu 21:16 **20:15** [o]1Ki 15:20; 2Ki 15:29 [p]2Ki 19:32; Isa 37:33; Jer 6:6; 32:24 **20:16** [q]2Sa 14:2 **20:19** [r]Dt 2:26 [s]1Sa 26:19; 2Sa 21:3 **20:21** [t]2Sa 4:8 **20:22** [u]Ecc 9:13 **20:23** [v]2Sa 2:28; 8:16-18; 24:2 **20:24** [w]1Ki 4:6; 5:14; 12:18; 2Ch 10:18 [x]2Sa 8:16; 1Ki 4:3 **20:25** [y]1Sa 2:35; 2Sa 8:17

a *14* Or *Abel, even Beth Maacah*; also in verse 15
b *24* Some Septuagint manuscripts (see also 1 Kings 4:6 and 5:14); Hebrew *Adoram*

The Gibeonites Avenged

21 During the reign of David, there
was a famine[z] for three successive
years; so David sought[a] the face of the
LORD. The LORD said, "It is on account
of Saul and his blood-stained house;
it is because he put the Gibeonites to
death."
2The king summoned the Gibeonites[b] and spoke to them. (Now the
Gibeonites were not a part of Israel but
were survivors of the Amorites; the Israelites had sworn to ⌞spare⌟ them, but
Saul in his zeal for Israel and Judah had
tried to annihilate them.) 3David asked
the Gibeonites, "What shall I do for
you? How shall I make amends so that
you will bless the LORD's inheritance?"[c]
4The Gibeonites answered him, "We
have no right to demand silver or gold
from Saul or his family, nor do we have
the right to put anyone in Israel to
death."[d]
"What do you want me to do for
you?" David asked.
5They answered the king, "As for the
man who destroyed us and plotted
against us so that we have been deci-
mated and have no place anywhere in
Israel, 6let seven of his male descendants be given to us to be killed and
exposed[e] before the LORD at Gibeah of
Saul—the LORD's chosen[f] one."
So the king said, "I will give them to
you."
7The king spared Mephibosheth[g]
son of Jonathan, the son of Saul, because of the oath[h] before the LORD between David and Jonathan son of Saul.
8But the king took Armoni and Mephibosheth, the two sons of Aiah's
daughter Rizpah,[i] whom she had
borne to Saul, together with the five
sons of Saul's daughter Merab,[a]
whom she had borne to Adriel son of
Barzillai the Meholathite.[j] 9He handed them over to the Gibeonites, who
killed and exposed them on a hill before the LORD. All seven of them fell
together; they were put to death[k] during the first days of the harvest, just as
the barley harvest was beginning.[l]
10Rizpah daughter of Aiah took sackcloth and spread it out for herself on a
rock. From the beginning of the harvest till the rain poured down from the
heavens on the bodies, she did not let
the birds of the air touch them by day
or the wild animals by night.[m] 11When
David was told what Aiah's daughter
Rizpah, Saul's concubine, had done,
12he went and took the bones of Saul[n]
and his son Jonathan from the citizens
of Jabesh Gilead. (They had taken them
secretly from the public square at Beth
Shan,[o] where the Philistines had
hung[p] them after they struck Saul
down on Gilboa.) 13David brought the
bones of Saul and his son Jonathan
from there, and the bones of those who
had been killed and exposed were
gathered up.
14They buried the bones of Saul and
his son Jonathan in the tomb of Saul's
father Kish, at Zela[q] in Benjamin, and
did everything the king commanded.
After that,[r] God answered prayer[s] in
behalf of the land.

Wars Against the Philistines

15Once again there was a battle between the Philistines[t] and Israel. David went down with his men to fight
against the Philistines, and he became
exhausted. 16And Ishbi-Benob, one of
the descendants of Rapha, whose
bronze spearhead weighed three hundred shekels[b] and who was armed
with a new ⌞sword⌟, said he would kill
David. 17But Abishai[u] son of Zeruiah
came to David's rescue; he struck the
Philistine down and killed him. Then
David's men swore to him, saying,
"Never again will you go out with us to
battle, so that the lamp[v] of Israel will
not be extinguished.[w]"
18In the course of time, there was
another battle with the Philistines, at
Gob. At that time Sibbecai[x] the Hushathite killed Saph, one of the descendants of Rapha.
19In another battle with the Philistines at Gob, Elhanan son of Jaare-
Oregim[c] the Bethlehemite killed Goliath[d] the Gittite, who had a spear with
a shaft like a weaver's rod.[y]
20In still another battle, which took
place at Gath, there was a huge man
with six fingers on each hand and six
toes on each foot—twenty-four in all.
He also was descended from Rapha.
21When he taunted Israel, Jonathan
son of Shimeah,[z] David's brother,
killed him.
22These four were descendants of
Rapha in Gath, and they fell at the
hands of David and his men.

David's Song of Praise

22 David sang[a] to the LORD the
words of this song when the LORD
delivered him from the hand of all his

21:1 [z]Ge 12:10; Dt 32:24 [a]Ex 32:11 **21:2** [b]Jos 9:15 **21:3** [c]1Sa 26:19; 2Sa 20:19 **21:4** [d]Nu 35:33-34 **21:6** [e]Nu 25:4 [f]1Sa 10:24 **21:7** [g]2Sa 4:4 [h]1Sa 18:3; 20:8,15; 2Sa 9:7 **21:8** [i]2Sa 3:7 [j]1Sa 18:19 **21:9** [k]2Sa 16:8 [l]Ru 1:22 **21:10** [m]ver 8; Dt 21:23; 1Sa 17:44 **21:12** [n]1Sa 31:11-13 [o]Jos 17:11 [p]1Sa 31:10 **21:14** [q]Jos 18:28 [r]Jos 7:26 [s]2Sa 24:25 **21:15** [t]2Sa 5:25 **21:17** [u]2Sa 20:6 [v]1Ki 11:36 [w]2Sa 18:3 **21:18** [x]1Ch 11:29; 20:4; 27:11 **21:19** [y]1Sa 17:7 **21:21** [z]1Sa 16:9 **22:1** [a]Ex 15:1; Jdg 5:1; Ps 18:2-50

[a] *8* Two Hebrew manuscripts, some Septuagint manuscripts and Syriac (see also 1 Samuel 18:19); most Hebrew and Septuagint manuscripts *Michal* [b] *16* That is, about 7 1/2 pounds (about 3.5 kilograms) [c] *19* Or *son of Jair the weaver* [d] *19* Hebrew and Septuagint; 1 Chron. 20:5 *son of Jair killed Lahmi the brother of Goliath*

enemies and from the hand of Saul.
2 He said:

"The LORD is my rock,[b] my
fortress[c] and my
deliverer;[d]
3 my God is my rock, in whom I
take refuge,[e]
my shield[f] and the horn[a][g] of
my salvation.
He is my stronghold,[h] my refuge
and my savior—
from violent men you save me.
4 I call to the LORD, who is worthy[i]
of praise,
and I am saved from my
enemies.

5 "The waves[j] of death swirled
about me;
the torrents of destruction
overwhelmed me.
6 The cords of the grave[b][k] coiled
around me;
the snares of death confronted
me.
7 In my distress[l] I called[m] to the
LORD;
I called out to my God.
From his temple he heard my
voice;
my cry came to his ears.

8 "The earth[n] trembled and
quaked,[o]
the foundations[p] of the
heavens[c] shook;
they trembled because he was
angry.
9 Smoke rose from his nostrils;
consuming fire[q] came from his
mouth,
burning coals blazed out of it.
10 He parted the heavens and came
down;
dark clouds[r] were under his
feet.
11 He mounted the cherubim and
flew;
he soared[d] on the wings of the
wind.[s]
12 He made darkness his canopy
around him—
the dark[e] rain clouds of the sky.
13 Out of the brightness of his
presence
bolts of lightning[t] blazed forth.
14 The LORD thundered[u] from
heaven;
the voice of the Most High
resounded.
15 He shot arrows[v] and scattered ⌊the
enemies⌋,
bolts of lightning and routed
them.
16 The valleys of the sea were exposed
and the foundations of the earth
laid bare
at the rebuke[w] of the LORD,
at the blast of breath from his
nostrils.

17 "He reached down from on high[x]
and took hold of me;
he drew[y] me out of deep
waters.
18 He rescued me from my powerful
enemy,
from my foes, who were too
strong for me.
19 They confronted me in the day of
my disaster,
but the LORD was my support.[z]
20 He brought me out into a
spacious[a] place;
he rescued[b] me because he
delighted[c] in me.[d]

3 →PG. 421

21 "The LORD has dealt with me
according to my
righteousness;[e]
according to the cleanness of my
hands[f] he has rewarded
me.
22 For I have kept[g] the ways of the
LORD;
I have not done evil by turning
from my God.
23 All his laws are before me;[h]
I have not turned[i] away from
his decrees.
24 I have been blameless[j] before him
and have kept myself from sin.
25 The LORD has rewarded me
according to my
righteousness,[k]
according to my cleanness[f] in
his sight.

26 "To the faithful you show yourself
faithful,
to the blameless you show
yourself blameless,
27 to the pure[l] you show yourself
pure,
but to the crooked you show
yourself shrewd.[m]
28 You save the humble,[n]
but your eyes are on the haughty
to bring them low.[o]
29 You are my lamp,[p] O LORD;
the LORD turns my darkness into
light.

22:2 [b]Dt 32:4; Ps 71:3 [c]Ps 31:3; 91:2 [d]Ps 144:2 **22:3** [e]Dt 32:37; Jer 16:19 [f]Ge 15:1 [g]Lk 1:69 [h]Ps 9:9 **22:4** [i]Ps 48:1; 96:4 **22:5** [j]Ps 69:14-15; 93:4; Jnh 2:3 **22:6** [k]Ps 116:3 **22:7** [l]Ps 120:1 [m]Ps 34:6,15; 116:4 **22:8** [n]Jdg 5:4; Ps 97:4 [o]Ps 77:18 [p]Job 26:11 **22:9** [q]Ps 97:3; Heb 12:29 **22:10** [r]1Ki 8:12; Na 1:3 **22:11** [s]Ps 104:3 **22:13** [t]ver 9 **22:14** [u]1Sa 2:10 **22:15** [v]Dt 32:23 **22:16** [w]Na 1:4 **22:17** [x]Ps 144:7 [y]Ex 2:10 **22:19** [z]Ps 23:4 **22:20** [a]Ps 31:8 [b]Ps 118:5 [c]Ps 22:8 [d]2Sa 15:26 **22:21** [e]1Sa 26:23 [f]Ps 24:4 **22:22** [g]Ge 18:19; Ps 128:1; Pr 8:32 **22:23** [h]Dt 6:4-9; Ps 119:30-32 [i]Ps 119:102 **22:24** [j]Ge 6:9; Eph 1:4 **22:25** [k]ver 21 **22:27** [l]Mt 5:8 [m]Lev 26:23-24 **22:28** [n]Ex 3:8; Ps 72:12-13 [o]Isa 2:12,17; 5:15 **22:29** [p]Ps 27:1

[a] *3* *Horn* here symbolizes strength.
[b] *6* Hebrew *Sheol*
[c] *8* Hebrew; Vulgate and Syriac (see also Psalm 18:7) *mountains*
[d] *11* Many Hebrew manuscripts (see also Psalm 18:10); most Hebrew manuscripts *appeared*
[e] *12* Septuagint and Vulgate (see also Psalm 18:11); Hebrew *massed*
[f] *25* Hebrew; Septuagint and Vulgate (see also Psalm 18:24) *to the cleanness of my hands*

30With your help I can advance against a troop[a];
with my God I can scale a wall.

1 →PG. 376

31"As for God, his way is perfect;[q]
the word of the LORD is flawless.[r]
He is a shield
for all who take refuge in him.
32For who is God besides the LORD?
And who is the Rock[s] except our God?
33It is God who arms me with strength[b]
and makes my way perfect.
34He makes my feet like the feet of a deer;[t]
he enables me to stand on the heights.[u]
35He trains my hands[v] for battle;
my arms can bend a bow of bronze.
36You give me your shield[w] of victory;
you stoop down to make me great.
37You broaden the path[x] beneath me,
so that my ankles do not turn.

38"I pursued my enemies and crushed them;
I did not turn back till they were destroyed.
39I crushed[y] them completely, and they could not rise;
they fell beneath my feet.
40You armed me with strength for battle;
you made my adversaries bow at my feet.[z]
41You made my enemies turn their backs[a] in flight,
and I destroyed my foes.
42They cried for help,[b] but there was no one to save them—[c]
to the LORD, but he did not answer.
43I beat them as fine as the dust of the earth;
I pounded and trampled[d] them like mud[e] in the streets.

44"You have delivered[f] me from the attacks of my people;
you have preserved[g] me as the head of nations.
People[h] I did not know are subject to me,
45 and foreigners come cringing[i] to me;
as soon as they hear me, they obey me.
46They all lose heart;
they come trembling[c][j] from their strongholds.

47"The LORD lives! Praise be to my Rock!
Exalted be God, the Rock, my Savior![k]
48He is the God who avenges me,[l]
who puts the nations under me,
49 who sets me free from my enemies.[m]
You exalted me above my foes;
from violent men you rescued me.
50Therefore I will praise you, O LORD, among the nations;
I will sing praises to your name.[n]
51He gives his king great victories;[o]
he shows unfailing kindness to his anointed,[p]
to David[q] and his descendants forever."[r]

The Last Words of David

23 These are the last words of David:

"The oracle of David son of Jesse,
the oracle of the man exalted[s] by the Most High,
the man anointed[t] by the God of Jacob,
Israel's singer of songs[d]:

2"The Spirit[u] of the LORD spoke through me;
his word was on my tongue.
3The God of Israel spoke,
the Rock[v] of Israel said to me:
'When one rules over men in righteousness,[w]
when he rules in the fear of God,[x]
4he is like the light of morning at sunrise[y]
on a cloudless morning,
like the brightness after rain
that brings the grass from the earth.'

5"Is not my house right with God?
Has he not made with me an everlasting covenant,[z]
arranged and secured in every part?
Will he not bring to fruition my salvation
and grant me my every desire?
6But evil men are all to be cast aside like thorns,[a]
which are not gathered with the hand.
7Whoever touches thorns

22:31 [q]Dt 32:4; Mt 5:48 [r]Ps 12:6; 119:140; Pr 30:5-6 **22:32** [s]1Sa 2:2 **22:34** [t]Hab 3:19 [u]Dt 32:13 **22:35** [v]Ps 144:1 **22:36** [w]Eph 6:16 **22:37** [x]Pr 4:11 **22:39** [y]Mal 4:3 **22:40** [z]Ps 44:5 **22:41** [a]Ex 23:27 **22:42** [b]Isa 1:15 [c]Ps 50:22 **22:43** [d]Mic 7:10 [e]Isa 10:6; Mic 7:10 **22:44** [f]2Sa 3:1 [g]Dt 28:13 [h]2Sa 8:1-14; Isa 55:3-5 **22:45** [i]Ps 66:3; 81:15 **22:46** [j]Mic 7:17 **22:47** [k]Ps 89:26 **22:48** [l]Ps 94:1; 144:2; 1Sa 25:39 **22:49** [m]Ps 140:1,4 **22:50** [n]Ro 15:9* **22:51** [o]Ps 144:9-10 [p]Ps 89:20 [q]2Sa 7:13 [r]Ps 89:24,29 **23:1** [s]2Sa 7:8-9; Ps 78:70-71; 89:27 [t]1Sa 16:12-13; Ps 89:20 **23:2** [u]Mt 22:43; 2Pe 1:21 **23:3** [v]Dt 32:4; 2Sa 22:2,32 [w]Ps 72:2 [x]2Ch 19:7,9; Isa 11:1-5 **23:4** [y]Jdg 5:31; Ps 89:36 **23:5** [z]Ps 89:29; Isa 55:3 **23:6** [a]Mt 13:40-41

[a]*30* Or *can run through a barricade*
[b]*33* Dead Sea Scrolls, some Septuagint manuscripts, Vulgate and Syriac (see also Psalm 18:32); Masoretic Text *who is my strong refuge*
[c]*46* Some Septuagint manuscripts and Vulgate (see also Psalm 18:45); Masoretic Text *they arm themselves.*
[d]*1* Or *Israel's beloved singer*

uses a tool of iron or the shaft of
a spear;
they are burned up where they
lie."

David's Mighty Men

2 →PG. 364

8These are the names of David's
mighty men:
Josheb-Basshebeth,[a] a Tahkemo-
nite,[b] was chief of the Three; he raised
his spear against eight hundred men,
whom he killed[c] in one encounter.
9Next to him was Eleazar son of Dodai[b] the Ahohite.[c] As one of the three
mighty men, he was with David when
they taunted the Philistines gathered
⌞at Pas Dammim⌟[d] for battle. Then the
men of Israel retreated, 10but he stood
his ground and struck down the Philistines till his hand grew tired and froze
to the sword. The LORD brought about
a great victory that day. The troops returned to Eleazar, but only to strip the
dead.
11Next to him was Shammah son of
Agee the Hararite. When the Philistines
banded together at a place where there
was a field full of lentils, Israel's troops
fled from them. 12But Shammah took
his stand in the middle of the field. He
defended it and struck the Philistines
down, and the LORD brought about a
great victory.
13During harvest time, three of the
thirty chief men came down to David
at the cave of Adullam,[d] while a band
of Philistines was encamped in the
Valley of Rephaim.[e] 14At that time David was in the stronghold,[f] and the Philistine garrison was at Bethlehem.[g]
15David longed for water and said, "Oh,
that someone would get me a drink of
water from the well near the gate of
Bethlehem!" 16So the three mighty
men broke through the Philistine lines,
drew water from the well near the gate
of Bethlehem and carried it back to David. But he refused to drink it; instead,
he poured[h] it out before the LORD.
17"Far be it from me, O LORD, to do
this!" he said. "Is it not the blood[i] of
men who went at the risk of their
lives?" And David would not drink it.
Such were the exploits of the three
mighty men.
18Abishai[j] the brother of Joab son
of Zeruiah was chief of the Three.[e] He
raised his spear against three hundred
men, whom he killed, and so he became as famous as the Three. 19Was
he not held in greater honor than the
Three? He became their commander,
even though he was not included
among them.
20Benaiah[k] son of Jehoiada was a
valiant fighter from Kabzeel,[l] who
performed great exploits. He struck
down two of Moab's best men. He also
went down into a pit on a snowy day
and killed a lion. 21And he struck down
a huge Egyptian. Although the Egyptian had a spear in his hand, Benaiah
went against him with a club. He
snatched the spear from the Egyptian's
hand and killed him with his own
spear. 22Such were the exploits of Benaiah son of Jehoiada; he too was as
famous as the three mighty men. 23He
was held in greater honor than any of
the Thirty, but he was not included
among the Three. And David put him
in charge of his bodyguard.

24Among the Thirty were:
Asahel[m] the brother of Joab,
Elhanan son of Dodo from
Bethlehem,
25Shammah the Harodite,[n]
Elika the Harodite,
26Helez[o] the Paltite,

23:9 [b] 1Ch 27:4 [c] 1Ch 8:4
23:13 [d] 1Sa 22:1 [e] 2Sa 5:18
23:14 [f] 1Sa 22:4-5 [g] Ru 1:19
23:16 [h] Ge 35:14
23:17 [i] Lev 17:10-12
23:18 [j] 2Sa 10:10,14; 1Ch 11:20
23:20 [k] 2Sa 8:18; 20:23 [l] Jos 15:21
23:24 [m] 2Sa 2:18
23:25 [n] Jdg 7:1; 1Ch 11:27
23:26 [o] 1Ch 27:10

a *8* Hebrew; some Septuagint manuscripts suggest *Ish-Bosheth,* that is, *Esh-Baal* (see also 1 Chron. 11:11 *Jashobeam*). **b** *8* Probably a variant of *Hacmonite* (see 1 Chron. 11:11) **c** *8* Some Septuagint manuscripts (see also 1 Chron. 11:11); Hebrew and other Septuagint manuscripts *Three; it was Adino the Eznite who killed eight hundred men* **d** *9* See 1 Chron. 11:13; Hebrew *gathered there.* **e** *18* Most Hebrew manuscripts (see also 1 Chron. 11:20); two Hebrew manuscripts and Syriac *Thirty*

23:8–39

PROMISE 2

LOYAL TO THE DEATH

How would you like to lead this group? We know little about these mighty men (cf. 21:15–22 and 1 Chronicles 11:10–47) except that they were exceptional warriors who were totally devoted to David. The stories contained in this and other passages give fascinating evidence to the power of God in the lives of these, David's closest companions.

Want to know the measure of a leader? Look at who's following. David accomplished great things partly because he could rally great people to his cause. Notice that there were no giant-killers in Saul's army, but there are several among David's men. Saul hid from the giants; David tackled them head on with God's help and inspired others to do the same.

As you read about David's life in Samuel and Chronicles, highlight passages that give clues as to why these mighty men followed David. Study your list and ask what you could do to increase your ability to influence others to do greater things for God.

For the next Promise 2 reading go to page 390.

Ira son of Ikkesh from Tekoa,
27 Abiezer from Anathoth,[p]
Mebunnai[a] the Hushathite,
28 Zalmon the Ahohite,
Maharai[q] the Netophathite,[r]
29 Heled[b] son of Baanah the Netophathite,
Ithai son of Ribai from Gibeah[s] in Benjamin,
30 Benaiah the Pirathonite,[t]
Hiddai[c] from the ravines of Gaash,[u]
31 Abi-Albon the Arbathite,
Azmaveth the Barhumite,[v]
32 Eliahba the Shaalbonite,
the sons of Jashen,
Jonathan 33 son of[d] Shammah the Hararite,
Ahiam son of Sharar[e] the Hararite,
34 Eliphelet son of Ahasbai the Maacathite,
Eliam[w] son of Ahithophel[x] the Gilonite,
35 Hezro the Carmelite,[y]
Paarai the Arbite,
36 Igal son of Nathan from Zobah,[z]
the son of Hagri,[f]
37 Zelek the Ammonite,
Naharai the Beerothite, the armor-bearer of Joab son of Zeruiah,
38 Ira the Ithrite,[a]
Gareb the Ithrite
39 and Uriah[b] the Hittite.
There were thirty-seven in all.

David Counts the Fighting Men

24 Again[c] the anger of the LORD
burned against Israel, and he incited David against them, saying, "Go and
take a census of[d] Israel and Judah."
2 So the king said to Joab[e] and the
army commanders[g] with him, "Go
throughout the tribes of Israel from
Dan to Beersheba[f] and enroll the
fighting men, so that I may know how
many there are."
3 But Joab replied to the king, "May
the LORD your God multiply the troops
a hundred times over,[g] and may the
eyes of my lord the king see it. But why
does my lord the king want to do such
a thing?"
4 The king's word, however, overruled Joab and the army commanders;
so they left the presence of the king to
enroll the fighting men of Israel.
5 After crossing the Jordan, they
camped near Aroer,[h] south of the
town in the gorge, and then went
through Gad and on to Jazer.[i] 6 They
went to Gilead and the region of Tah-
tim Hodshi, and on to Dan Jaan and
around toward Sidon.[j] 7 Then they
went toward the fortress of Tyre[k] and
all the towns of the Hivites and Canaanites. Finally, they went on to Beersheba[l] in the Negev[m] of Judah.
8 After they had gone through the entire land, they came back to Jerusalem
at the end of nine months and twenty
days.
9 Joab reported the number of
the fighting men to the king: In Israel
there were eight hundred thousand
able-bodied men who could handle
a sword, and in Judah five hundred
thousand.[n]
10 David was conscience-stricken[o]
after he had counted the fighting men,
and he said to the LORD, "I have
sinned[p] greatly in what I have done.
Now, O LORD, I beg you, take away the
guilt of your servant. I have done a very
foolish thing.[q]"
11 Before David got up the next
morning, the word of the LORD had
come to Gad[r] the prophet, David's
seer:[s] 12 "Go and tell David, 'This is
what the LORD says: I am giving you
three options. Choose one of them for
me to carry out against you.' "
13 So Gad went to David and said to
him, "Shall there come upon you
three[h] years of famine[t] in your land?
Or three months of fleeing from your
enemies while they pursue you? Or
three days of plague[u] in your land?
Now then, think it over and decide how
I should answer the one who sent me."
14 David said to Gad, "I am in deep
distress. Let us fall into the hands of the
LORD, for his mercy[v] is great; but do
not let me fall into the hands of men."
15 So the LORD sent a plague on Israel
from that morning until the end of the
time designated, and seventy thousand
of the people from Dan to Beersheba
died.[w] 16 When the angel stretched out
his hand to destroy Jerusalem, the
LORD was grieved[x] because of the calamity and said to the angel who was
afflicting the people, "Enough! Withdraw your hand." The angel of the
LORD[y] was then at the threshing floor
of Araunah the Jebusite.

23:27 [p] Jos 21:18
23:28 [q] 1Ch 27:13 [r] 2Ki 25:23; Ne 7:26
23:29 [s] Jos 15:57
23:30 [t] Jdg 12:13 [u] Jos 24:30
23:31 [v] 2Sa 3:16
23:34 [w] 2Sa 11:3 [x] 2Sa 15:12
23:35 [y] Jos 12:22
23:36 [z] 1Sa 14:47
23:38 [a] 2Sa 20:26; 1Ch 2:53
23:39 [b] 2Sa 11:3
24:1 [c] Jos 9:15 [d] 1Ch 27:23
24:2 [e] 2Sa 20:23 [f] Jdg 20:1; 2Sa 3:10
24:3 [g] Dt 1:11
24:5 [h] Dt 2:36; Jos 13:9 [i] Nu 21:32
24:6 [j] Ge 10:19; Jos 19:28; Jdg 1:31
24:7 [k] Jos 19:29 [l] Ge 21:22-33 [m] Dt 1:7; Jos 11:3
24:9 [n] Nu 1:44-46; 1Ch 21:5
24:10 [o] 1Sa 24:5 [p] 2Sa 12:13 [q] Nu 12:11; 1Sa 13:13
24:11 [r] 1Sa 22:5 [s] 1Sa 9:9; 1Ch 29:29
24:13 [t] Dt 28:38-42, 48; Eze 14:21 [u] Lev 26:25
24:14 [v] Ne 9:28; Ps 51:1; 103:8, 13; 130:4
24:15 [w] 1Ch 27:24
24:16 [x] Ge 6:6; 1Sa 15:11 [y] Ex 12:23; Ac 12:23

[a] *27* Hebrew; some Septuagint manuscripts (see also 1 Chron. 11:29) *Sibbecai* [b] *29* Some Hebrew manuscripts and Vulgate (see also 1 Chron. 11:30); most Hebrew manuscripts *Heleb* [c] *30* Hebrew; some Septuagint manuscripts (see also 1 Chron. 11:32) *Hurai* [d] *33* Some Septuagint manuscripts (see also 1 Chron. 11:34); Hebrew does not have *son of.* [e] *33* Hebrew; some Septuagint manuscripts (see also 1 Chron. 11:35) *Sacar* [f] *36* Some Septuagint manuscripts (see also 1 Chron. 11:38); Hebrew *Haggadi* [g] *2* Septuagint (see also verse 4 and 1 Chron. 21:2); Hebrew *Joab the army commander* [h] *13* Septuagint (see also 1 Chron. 21:12); Hebrew *seven*

17When David saw the angel who
was striking down the people, he said
to the LORD, "I am the one who has
sinned and done wrong. These are but
sheep.[z] What have they done? Let
your hand fall upon me and my family."[a]

David Builds an Altar

18On that day Gad went to David and
said to him, "Go up and build an altar
to the LORD on the threshing floor of

24:18–24

PROMISE 5

THE PRICE OF WORSHIP

David didn't give cheap gifts to his God. Arunah made a noble gesture (v. 22); he wanted to honor his king by giving him the land and the sacrifices. But David's response revealed his heart: "I will not sacrifice to the LORD my God burnt offerings that cost me nothing." Here David exemplified Jesus' teaching in Luke 6:45: "Out of the overflow of [a man's] heart his mouth speaks."

Take a moment to formulate the message David's heart sent to his mouth as he processed this decision to accept Arunah's gift or to pay him for the offering. David undoubtedly made the decision in a moment, but he had to go through a valuing process that led him to his decision. What was it? What can we learn from it?

For the next Promise 5 reading go to page 414.

Araunah the Jebusite." 19So David went
up, as the LORD had commanded
through Gad. 20When Araunah looked
and saw the king and his men coming
toward him, he went out and bowed
down before the king with his face to
the ground.
21Araunah said, "Why has my lord
the king come to his servant?"
"To buy your threshing floor," David
answered, "so I can build an altar to
the LORD, that the plague on the people
may be stopped."[b]
22Araunah said to David, "Let my
lord the king take whatever pleases
him and offer it up. Here are oxen[c] for
the burnt offering, and here are threshing sledges and ox yokes for the wood.
23O king, Araunah gives[d] all this to the
king." Araunah also said to him, "May
the LORD your God accept you."
24But the king replied to Araunah,
"No, I insist on paying you for it. I will
not sacrifice to the LORD my God burnt
offerings that cost me nothing."[e]
So David bought the threshing floor
and the oxen and paid fifty shekels[a] of
silver for them. 25David built an altar[f]
to the LORD there and sacrificed burnt
offerings and fellowship offerings.[b]
Then the LORD answered prayer[g] in
behalf of the land, and the plague on
Israel was stopped.

24:17 [z]Ps 74:1 [a]Jnh 1:12
24:21 [b]Nu 16:44-50
24:22 [c]1Sa 6:14; 1Ki 19:21
24:23 [d]Eze 20:40-41
24:24 [e]Mal 1:13-14
24:25 [f]1Sa 7:17 [g]2Sa 21:14

[a]*24* That is, about 1 1/4 pounds (about 0.6 kilogram) [b]*25* Traditionally *peace offerings*

1 KINGS

AT A GLANCE

Key Principle: Unless we deliberately depend on God's grace for help, we cannot properly govern ourselves.
Author: Unknown; possibly Jeremiah
Time and Place: 970 B.C. to 852 B.C. / Israel and Judah
Key Verses: 9:4–5; 11:11

BENEFIT

This book tells the story of one of the most fascinating of all Biblical characters, King Solomon. This extraordinary man had more intellectual and material resources at his disposal than any other in history, and yet none of it was enough. When he turned away from God, he discovered that he could never find satisfaction. First Kings also gives us a portrait of Elijah, a remarkable prophet who stood firm against idolatry in Israel.

SETTING

Like Samuel, 1 and 2 Kings were originally one book in the Hebrew Bible. Together they chronicle the end of the united kingdom under Solomon, the Assyrian capture of Israel in 722 B.C., and the Babylonian capture of Judah in 586 B.C. The books of 1 and 2 Kings give God's reasons for these captivities—ungodliness, idolatry, disobedience and immorality. First Kings records the highlights of Solomon's 40-year reign (970 B.C. to 930 B.C.) and traces the first 80 years of the divided kingdoms of Israel and Judah until the end of Ahaziah's reign in 852 B.C.

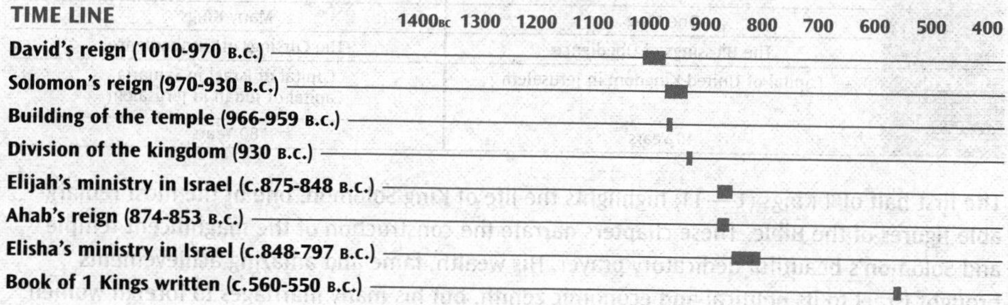

THEME AND PURPOSE

First Kings directly relates the spiritual and moral condition of the kings with the welfare of the nations under their rule. The examples in this book teach that covenant faithfulness and obedience to God's law leads to great blessing, while the inevitable consequence of apostasy and disobedience is divine judgment. While the accounts of the different kings are highly selective in nature, 1 Kings repeatedly illustrates that without humility and ongoing dependence on God's help, a king cannot properly rule himself or his people. God's grace in sending prophets to warn the king and the people contrasts with the faithless way his people responded to his initiatives.

UNIQUE CONTRIBUTION

First Kings picks up the story of Israel's history where Samuel left off. First Samuel describes the transition from the last of the judges (Samuel) to the first of the kings (Saul); 2 Samuel continues the narrative from the time the kingdom is established to the time it is consolidated under David. First Kings portrays the glory and spiritual decline of Solomon, the last ruler of the united kingdom, and alternates between the reigns of the first kings of the northern kingdom of Israel and the southern kingdom of Judah. In each case, an introductory and concluding formula assess each king. David, a man who had a whole heart for God, is the spiritual standard by which the kings of Judah are judged. This book also describes how God raised up and used a school of prophets to warn the people about the consequences of abandoning their devotion to God.

LINKS TO THE NEW TESTAMENT

During the early years of his reign, God granted Solomon unparalleled wisdom, glory, wealth and honor; this foreshadows the coming glory of Messiah's kingdom. Apart from "Christ Jesus, who has become for us wisdom from God" (1 Corinthians 1:30), Solomon was the wisest man the world had ever seen, and the source of his wisdom, glory and power was his faithfulness to God. It was his very greatness that made his spiritual downfall so tragic. By contrast, the prophet Elijah remained faithful to the end, and his ascension to heaven prefigured Christ's glorious ascension. His prophetic and miraculous ministry also anticipated the miraculous works of Christ.

OVERVIEW

FOCUS	The United Kingdom		The Divided Kingdom	
REFERENCE	1	11	12	22
TOPICS	Expansion and Glorification		Division and Decline	
	One King		Many Kings	
	The Blessings of Obedience		The Cursings of Disobedience	
LOCATION	Capital of United Kingdom in Jerusalem		Capital of Israel in Samaria Capital of Judah in Jerusalem	
TIME	40 Years		80 Years	

The first half of 1 Kings (1—11) highlights the life of King Solomon, one of the most remarkable figures of the Bible. These chapters narrate the construction of the magnificent temple and Solomon's beautiful dedicatory prayer. His wealth, fame and amazing achievements brought Israel to its political and economic zenith, but his many marriages to foreign women eventually turned his heart away from the Lord. Ironically, this wisest of men succumbed to the folly of idolatry.

The kingdom is divided in the second half of this book (12—22), a period marked by spiritual apostasy and frequent struggles between Israel and Judah. The northern kingdom of Israel never departs from the idolatrous system set up by its first king, Jeroboam. And apart from Asa and Jehoshaphat, the rulers of the southern kingdom are ungodly and unscrupulous men. The concluding chapters of this book contrast the lives of Elijah the prophet and Ahab, the wicked king who introduced Jezebel's Baal worship to Israel.

1 KINGS

Adonijah Sets Himself Up as King

1 When King David was old and well advanced in years, he could not keep warm even when they put covers over him. 2So his servants said to him, "Let us look for a young virgin to attend the king and take care of him. She can lie beside him so that our lord the king may keep warm."

3Then they searched throughout Israel for a beautiful girl and found Abishag, a Shunammite,[a] and brought her to the king. 4The girl was very beautiful; she took care of the king and waited on him, but the king had no intimate relations with her.

5Now Adonijah,[b] whose mother was Haggith, put himself forward and said, "I will be king." So he got chariots[c] and horses**a** ready, with fifty men to run ahead of him. 6(His father had never interfered[d] with him by asking, "Why do you behave as you do?" He was also very handsome and was born next after Absalom.)

7Adonijah conferred with Joab[e] son of Zeruiah and with Abiathar[f] the priest, and they gave him their support. 8But Zadok[g] the priest, Benaiah[h] son of Jehoiada, Nathan[i] the prophet, Shimei[j] and Rei**b** and David's special guard[k] did not join Adonijah.

9Adonijah then sacrificed sheep, cattle and fattened calves at the Stone of Zoheleth near En Rogel.[l] He invited all his brothers, the king's sons, and all the men of Judah who were royal officials, 10but he did not invite Nathan the prophet or Benaiah or the special guard or his brother Solomon.[m]

11Then Nathan asked Bathsheba,[n] Solomon's mother, "Have you not heard that Adonijah,[o] the son of Haggith, has become king without our lord David's knowing it? 12Now then, let me advise[p] you how you can save your own life and the life of your son Solomon. 13Go in to King David and say to him, 'My lord the king, did you not swear[q] to me your servant: "Surely Solomon your son shall be king after me, and he will sit on my throne"? Why then has Adonijah become king?' 14While you are still there talking to the king, I will come in and confirm what you have said."

15So Bathsheba went to see the aged king in his room, where Abishag[r] the Shunammite was attending him. 16Bathsheba bowed low and knelt before the king.

"What is it you want?" the king asked.

17She said to him, "My lord, you yourself swore[s] to me your servant by the LORD your God: 'Solomon your son shall be king after me, and he will sit on my throne.' 18But now Adonijah has become king, and you, my lord the king, do not know about it. 19He has sacrificed[t] great numbers of cattle, fattened calves, and sheep, and has invited all the king's sons, Abiathar the priest and Joab the commander of the army, but he has not invited Solomon your servant. 20My lord the king, the eyes of all Israel are on you, to learn from you who will sit on the throne of my lord the king after him. 21Otherwise, as soon as my lord the king is laid to rest[u] with his fathers, I and my son Solomon will be treated as criminals."

22While she was still speaking with the king, Nathan the prophet arrived. 23And they told the king, "Nathan the prophet is here." So he went before the king and bowed with his face to the ground.

24Nathan said, "Have you, my lord the king, declared that Adonijah shall be king after you, and that he will sit on your throne? 25Today he has gone down and sacrificed great numbers of cattle, fattened calves, and sheep. He has invited all the king's sons, the commanders of the army and Abiathar the priest. Right now they are eating and drinking with him and saying, 'Long live King Adonijah!' 26But me your servant, and Zadok the priest, and Benaiah son of Jehoiada, and your servant Solomon he did not invite.[v] 27Is this something my lord the king has done without letting his servants know who should sit on the throne of my lord the king after him?"

David Makes Solomon King

28Then King David said, "Call in Bathsheba." So she came into the king's presence and stood before him.

29The king then took an oath: "As surely as the LORD lives, who has delivered me out of every trouble,[w] 30I will surely carry out today what I swore[x] to you by the LORD, the God of Israel: Solomon your son shall be king after

1:3 [a]Jos 19:18
1:5 [b]2Sa 3:4 [c]2Sa 15:1
1:6 [d]2Sa 3:3-4
1:7 [e]1Ki 2:22,28; 1Ch 11:6 [f]1Sa 22:20; 2Sa 20:25
1:8 [g]2Sa 20:25 [h]2Sa 8:18 [i]2Sa 12:1 [j]1Ki 4:18 [k]2Sa 23:8
1:9 [l]2Sa 17:17
1:10 [m]2Sa 12:24
1:11 [n]2Sa 12:24 [o]2Sa 3:4
1:12 [p]Pr 15:22
1:13 [q]ver 30; 1Ch 22:9-13
1:15 [r]ver 1
1:17 [s]ver 13,30
1:19 [t]ver 9
1:21 [u]Dt 31:16; 1Ki 2:10
1:26 [v]ver 8,10
1:29 [w]2Sa 4:9
1:30 [x]ver 13,17

a5 Or *charioteers* **b**8 Or *and his friends*

me, and he will sit on my throne in my place."

31Then Bathsheba bowed low with her face to the ground and, kneeling before the king, said, "May my lord King David live forever!"

32King David said, "Call in Zadok the priest, Nathan the prophet and Benaiah son of Jehoiada." When they came before the king, 33he said to them: "Take your lord's servants with you and set Solomon my son on my own mule[y] and take him down to Gihon.[z] 34There have Zadok the priest and Nathan the prophet anoint[a] him king over Israel. Blow the trumpet[b] and shout, 'Long live King Solomon!' 35Then you are to go up with him, and he is to come and sit on my throne and reign in my place. I have appointed him ruler over Israel and Judah."

36Benaiah son of Jehoiada answered the king, "Amen! May the LORD, the God of my lord the king, so declare it. 37As the LORD was with my lord the king, so may he be with[c] Solomon to make his throne even greater[d] than the throne of my lord King David!"

38So Zadok[e] the priest, Nathan the prophet, Benaiah son of Jehoiada, the Kerethites[f] and the Pelethites went down and put Solomon on King David's mule and escorted him to Gihon.[g] 39Zadok the priest took the horn of oil[h] from the sacred tent and anointed Solomon. Then they sounded the trumpet and all the people shouted,[i] "Long live King Solomon!" 40And all the people went up after him, playing flutes and rejoicing greatly, so that the ground shook with the sound.

41Adonijah and all the guests who were with him heard it as they were finishing their feast. On hearing the sound of the trumpet, Joab asked, "What's the meaning of all the noise in the city?"

42Even as he was speaking, Jonathan[j] son of Abiathar the priest arrived. Adonijah said, "Come in. A worthy man like you must be bringing good news."[k]

43"Not at all!" Jonathan answered. "Our lord King David has made Solomon king. 44The king has sent with him Zadok the priest, Nathan the prophet, Benaiah son of Jehoiada, the Kerethites and the Pelethites, and they have put him on the king's mule, 45and Zadok the priest and Nathan the prophet have anointed him king at Gihon. From there they have gone up cheering, and the city resounds[l] with it. That's the noise you hear. 46Moreover, Solomon has taken his seat on the royal throne. 47Also, the royal officials have come to congratulate our lord King David, saying, 'May your God make Solomon's name more famous than yours and his throne greater[m] than yours!' And the king bowed in worship on his bed 48and said, 'Praise be to the LORD, the God of Israel, who has allowed my eyes to see a successor[n] on my throne today.' "

49At this, all Adonijah's guests rose in alarm and dispersed. 50But Adonijah, in fear of Solomon, went and took hold of the horns[o] of the altar. 51Then Solomon was told, "Adonijah is afraid of King Solomon and is clinging to the horns of the altar. He says, 'Let King Solomon swear to me today that he will not put his servant to death with the sword.' "

52Solomon replied, "If he shows himself to be a worthy man, not a hair[p] of his head will fall to the ground; but if evil is found in him, he will die." 53Then King Solomon sent men, and they brought him down from the altar. And Adonijah came and bowed down to King Solomon, and Solomon said, "Go to your home."

David's Charge to Solomon

2 When the time drew near for David to die,[q] he gave a charge to Solomon his son.

2"I am about to go the way of all the earth,"[r] he said. "So be strong,[s] show yourself a man, 3and observe[t] what the LORD your God requires: Walk in his ways, and keep his decrees and commands, his laws and requirements, as written in the Law of Moses, so that

2 →PG. 391
4 →PG. 463

1:33 [y]2Sa 20:6-7 [z]2Ch 32:30; 33:14
1:34 [a]1Sa 10:1; 16:3,12; 1Ki 19:16; 2Ki 9:3,13 [b]ver 25; 2Sa 5:3; 15:10
1:37 [c]Jos 1:5,17; 1Sa 20:13 [d]ver 47
1:38 [e]ver 8 [f]2Sa 8:18 [g]ver 33
1:39 [h]Ex 30:23-32; Ps 89:20 [i]ver 34; 1Sa 10:24
1:42 [j]2Sa 15:27,36 [k]2Sa 18:26
1:45 [l]ver 40
1:47 [m]ver 37; Ge 47:31
1:48 [n]2Sa 7:12; 1Ki 3:6
1:50 [o]1Ki 2:28
1:52 [p]1Sa 14:45; 2Sa 14:11
2:1 [q]Ge 47:29; Dt 31:14
2:2 [r]Jos 23:14 [s]Dt 31:7,23; Jos 1:6
2:3 [t]Dt 17:14-20; Jos 1:7

2:1–4

PROMISE 4

FATHERLY ADVICE

This fatherly advice from David to Solomon contains five elements. The verbs in verses 2 and 3 tell the story: *be* addresses character; *show*—reputation; *observe*—respectfully notice; *walk*—daily conduct; *keep*—a will to obey. David promises two outcomes to Solomon if these five verbs guide his relation to God and his Word. One promise is broad enough to apply to us (v. 3; see Joshua 1:8, Psalm 1:1–3); the other is specific to the situation (v. 4).

What a creed for life: to *be* a man of integrity; to *demonstrate* that character; to *live out a respectful obedience* to God's Word and model it to your children. Then you can confidently say, as David did, "Follow me as I have followed God" (cf. 3:6).

For the next Promise 4 reading go to page 641.

you may prosper[u] in all you do and wherever you go, 4and that the LORD may keep his promise[v] to me: 'If your descendants watch how they live, and if they walk faithfully[w] before me with all their heart and soul, you will never fail to have a man on the throne of Israel.'

5"Now you yourself know what Joab[x] son of Zeruiah did to me—what he did to the two commanders of Israel's armies, Abner[y] son of Ner and Amasa[z] son of Jether. He killed them, shedding their blood in peacetime as if in battle, and with that blood stained the belt around his waist and the sandals on his feet. 6Deal with him according to your wisdom,[a] but do not let his gray head go down to the grave[a] in peace.

7"But show kindness to the sons of Barzillai[b] of Gilead and let them be among those who eat at your table.[c] They stood by me when I fled from your brother Absalom.

8"And remember, you have with you Shimei[d] son of Gera, the Benjamite from Bahurim, who called down bitter curses on me the day I went to Mahanaim. When he came down to meet me at the Jordan, I swore[e] to him by the LORD: 'I will not put you to death by the sword.' 9But now, do not consider him innocent. You are a man of wisdom;[f] you will know what to do to him. Bring his gray head down to the grave in blood."

10Then David rested with his fathers and was buried[g] in the City of David.[h] 11He had reigned[i] forty years over Israel—seven years in Hebron and thirty-three in Jerusalem. 12So Solomon sat on the throne[j] of his father David, and his rule was firmly established.[k]

Solomon's Throne Established

13Now Adonijah, the son of Haggith, went to Bathsheba, Solomon's mother. Bathsheba asked him, "Do you come peacefully?"[l]

He answered, "Yes, peacefully." 14Then he added, "I have something to say to you."

"You may say it," she replied.

15"As you know," he said, "the kingdom was mine. All Israel looked to me as their king. But things changed, and the kingdom has gone to my brother; for it has come to him from the LORD. 16Now I have one request to make of you. Do not refuse me."

"You may make it," she said.

17So he continued, "Please ask King Solomon—he will not refuse you—to give me Abishag[m] the Shunammite as my wife."

18"Very well," Bathsheba replied, "I will speak to the king for you."

19When Bathsheba went to King Solomon to speak to him for Adonijah, the king stood up to meet her, bowed down to her and sat down on his throne. He had a throne brought for the king's mother,[n] and she sat down at his right hand.[o]

20"I have one small request to make of you," she said. "Do not refuse me."

The king replied, "Make it, my mother; I will not refuse you."

21So she said, "Let Abishag[p] the Shunammite be given in marriage to your brother Adonijah."

22King Solomon answered his mother, "Why do you request Abishag[q] the Shunammite for Adonijah? You might as well request the kingdom for him—after all, he is my older brother[r]—yes, for him and for Abiathar the priest and Joab son of Zeruiah!"

23Then King Solomon swore by the LORD: "May God deal with me, be it ever so severely,[s] if Adonijah does not pay with his life for this request! 24And now, as surely as the LORD lives—he who has established me securely on the throne of my father David and has founded a dynasty for me as he promised[t]—Adonijah shall be put to death today!" 25So King Solomon gave orders to Benaiah[u] son of Jehoiada, and he struck down Adonijah and he died.

26To Abiathar[v] the priest the king said, "Go back to your fields in Anathoth.[w] You deserve to die, but I will not put you to death now, because you carried the ark[x] of the Sovereign LORD before my father David and shared all my father's hardships."[y] 27So Solomon removed Abiathar from the priesthood of the LORD, fulfilling[z] the word the LORD had spoken at Shiloh about the house of Eli.

28When the news reached Joab, who had conspired with Adonijah though not with Absalom, he fled to the tent of the LORD and took hold of the horns[a] of the altar. 29King Solomon was told that Joab had fled to the tent of the LORD and was beside the altar. Then Solomon ordered Benaiah[b] son of Jehoiada, "Go, strike him down!"

30So Benaiah entered the tent of the LORD and said to Joab, "The king says, 'Come out![c]' "

But he answered, "No, I will die here."

[a]6 Hebrew *Sheol*; also in verse 9

2:3 [u]1Ch 22:13
2:4 [v]2Sa 7:13,25; 1Ki 8:25 [w]2Ki 20:3; Ps 132:12
2:5 [x]2Sa 2:18; 18:5,12,14 [y]2Sa 3:27 [z]2Sa 20:10
2:6 [a]ver 9
2:7 [b]2Sa 17:27; 19:31-39 [c]2Sa 9:7
2:8 [d]2Sa 16:5-13 [e]2Sa 19:18-23
2:9 [f]ver 6
2:10 [g]Ac 2:29; 13:36 [h]2Sa 5:7
2:11 [i]2Sa 5:4,5
2:12 [j]1Ch 29:23 [k]2Ch 1:1
2:13 [l]1Sa 16:4
2:17 [m]1Ki 1:3
2:19 [n]1Ki 15:13 [o]Ps 45:9
2:21 [p]1Ki 1:3
2:22 [q]2Sa 12:8; 1Ki 1:3 [r]1Ch 3:2
2:23 [s]Ru 1:17
2:24 [t]2Sa 7:11; 1Ch 22:10
2:25 [u]2Sa 8:18
2:26 [v]1Sa 22:20 [w]Jos 21:18 [x]2Sa 15:24 [y]1Sa 23:6
2:27 [z]1Sa 2:27-36
2:28 [a]1Ki 1:7,50
2:29 [b]ver 25
2:30 [c]Ex 21:14

Benaiah reported to the king, "This
is how Joab answered me."
31Then the king commanded Benaiah, "Do as he says. Strike him down
and bury him, and so clear me and my
father's house of the guilt of the innocent blood[d] that Joab shed. 32The
LORD will repay[e] him for the blood he
shed,[f] because without the knowledge of my father David he attacked
two men and killed them with the
sword. Both of them—Abner son of
Ner, commander of Israel's army, and
Amasa[g] son of Jether, commander of
Judah's army—were better[h] men and
more upright than he. 33May the guilt
of their blood rest on the head of Joab
and his descendants forever. But on
David and his descendants, his house
and his throne, may there be the
LORD's peace forever."
34So Benaiah son of Jehoiada went
up and struck down Joab and killed
him, and he was buried on his own
land**a** in the desert. 35The king put Benaiah[i] son of Jehoiada over the army
in Joab's position and replaced Abiathar with Zadok[j] the priest.
36Then the king sent for Shimei[k]
and said to him, "Build yourself a
house in Jerusalem and live there, but
do not go anywhere else. 37The day you
leave and cross the Kidron Valley,[l]
you can be sure you will die; your
blood will be on your own head."[m]
38Shimei answered the king, "What
you say is good. Your servant will do as
my lord the king has said." And Shimei
stayed in Jerusalem for a long time.
39But three years later, two of Shimei's slaves ran off to Achish[n] son of
Maacah, king of Gath, and Shimei was
told, "Your slaves are in Gath." 40At
this, he saddled his donkey and went to
Achish at Gath in search of his slaves.
So Shimei went away and brought the
slaves back from Gath.
41When Solomon was told that
Shimei had gone from Jerusalem to
Gath and had returned, 42the king
summoned Shimei and said to him,
"Did I not make you swear by the LORD
and warn you, 'On the day you leave to
go anywhere else, you can be sure you
will die'? At that time you said to me,
'What you say is good. I will obey.'
43Why then did you not keep your oath
to the LORD and obey the command I
gave you?"
44The king also said to Shimei, "You
know in your heart all the wrong[o] you
did to my father David. Now the LORD
will repay you for your wrongdoing.
45But King Solomon will be blessed,
and David's throne will remain secure[p] before the LORD forever."

2:31 [d]Nu 35:33; Dt 19:13; 21:8-9
2:32 [e]Jdg 9:57; Ps 7:16 [f]Jdg 9:24 [g]2Sa 3:27; 20:10 [h]2Ch 21:13
2:35 [i]1Ki 4:4 [j]ver 27; 1Ch 29:22
2:36 [k]ver 8; 2Sa 16:5
2:37 [l]2Sa 15:23 [m]Lev 20:9; Jos 2:19; 2Sa 1:16
2:39 [n]1Sa 27:2
2:44 [o]1Sa 25:39; 2Sa 16:5-13; Eze 17:19
2:45 [p]2Sa 7:13; Pr 25:5
2:46 [q]ver 12; 2Ch 1:1
3:1 [r]1Ki 7:8 [s]1Ki 9:24 [t]2Sa 5:7 [u]1Ki 7:1; 9:15, 19
3:2 [v]Lev 17:3-5; Dt 12:2,4-5; 1Ki 22:43
3:3 [w]Dt 6:5; Ps 31:23; 1Co 8:3 [x]1Ki 2:3; 9:4; 11:4,6,38
3:4 [y]1Ch 16:39
3:5 [z]1Ki 9:2 [a]Nu 12:6; Mt 1:20
3:6 [b]1Ki 2:4; 9:4

46Then the king gave the order to Benaiah son of Jehoiada, and he went out
and struck Shimei down and killed
him.
The kingdom was now firmly established[q] in Solomon's hands.

Solomon Asks for Wisdom

3 Solomon made an alliance with
Pharaoh king of Egypt and married[r] his daughter.[s] He brought her
to the City of David[t] until he finished
building his palace[u] and the temple of
the LORD, and the wall around Jerusalem. 2The people, however, were still
sacrificing at the high places,[v] because a temple had not yet been built
for the Name of the LORD. 3Solomon
showed his love[w] for the LORD by
walking according to the statutes[x] of
his father David, except that he offered
sacrifices and burned incense on the
high places.
4The king went to Gibeon[y] to offer
sacrifices, for that was the most important high place, and Solomon offered a
thousand burnt offerings on that altar.
5At Gibeon the LORD appeared[z] to Solomon during the night in a dream,[a]
and God said, "Ask for whatever you
want me to give you."
6Solomon answered, "You have
shown great kindness to your servant,
my father David, because he was faithful[b] to you and righteous and upright
in heart. You have continued this great

a *34* Or *buried in his tomb*

3:4–14

PROMISE **1**

ASKING FOR THE RIGHT TOOLS

Read verse 5 again! Imagine receiving this offer in a dream. What would you ask God for? Solomon asked for a full tool box. As leader and shepherd of God's people, Solomon made many decisions that affected their lives. He knew he'd need the tools of wisdom and discernment to effectively lead these many people and carry out God's will for the nation.

We aren't kings, but we are leaders in many different ways. As friends, workers, husbands and dads, we need wisdom. We must ask God for wisdom as Solomon did, because God is the one who gives it (see Proverbs 2:6; James 1:5).

Did God answer Solomon's request? Read 4:29–34, which describes this king's legendary wisdom. God invites us to pray to him about many things. The next time you pray, ask that God give you the tools for building a life that pleases him.

For the next Promise 1 reading go to page 402.

SOLOMON

A Man of Wisdom?

There is only one thing worse than not having wisdom, and that's having wisdom and not using it. Just ask Solomon.

An Amazing Dream

When Solomon became king, he realized the enormity of his task. The Lord appeared to Solomon one night in a dream, and promised to give him anything he asked for. Imagine receiving that promise from God! But Solomon had a proper perspective on his task as ruler over Israel. Rather than asking God for tangible blessings like health, wealth or victory over his enemies, Solomon asked God for "a discerning heart to govern [the] people and to distinguish between right and wrong" (1 Kings 3:9).

God was pleased to grant Solomon's unselfish request and told him, "I will give you a wise and discerning heart, so that there will never have been anyone like you, nor will there ever be. Moreover, I will give you what you have not asked for—both riches and honor—so that in your lifetime you will have no equal among kings" (3:12–13). God further told Solomon that if he walked in God's ways and obeyed his laws, God would grant him a long life (3:14).

This was no ordinary dream. It was God speaking to Solomon. And the Lord did as promised. Solomon became the wisest man that ever lived. People came from all over the world to visit him and to listen to "the wisdom God had put in his heart" (10:24).

A Downward Slide

But as the years went on, Solomon's kingdom and his personal life began to unravel. The Bible clearly tells us the reason for this downward slide: Solomon "loved many foreign women" (11:1). Solomon chose the daughter of Pharaoh as his first wife, but he didn't stop there. By the time Solomon finished marrying all his Moabite, Ammonite, Edomite, Sidonian and Hittite wives, "he had seven hundred wives of royal birth and three hundred concubines" (11:3). Talk about a flagrant disregard of God's commands! In this regard, Solomon was a serious repeat offender.

The Lord had warned the people of Israel specifically not to intermarry with people of these nations, "because they will surely turn your hearts after their gods" (11:2). But Solomon did not listen to God's warning. After all, he was wiser than most people. He figured he could handle a few foreigners. But in the end, to please his wives, Solomon began to worship their false gods. His wives led him astray, and "Solomon did evil in the eyes of the Lord; he did not follow the Lord completely, as David his father had done" (11:6).

What a tragedy! This great man of wisdom allowed wealth, sex and power to take over his life and destroy him. God "became angry with Solomon because his heart had turned away from the Lord, the God of Israel" (11:9). Then God pronounced judgment upon Solomon and promised to "tear the kingdom away" from him and give it to one of his subordinates (11:11).

Just as God had kept his earlier promise to grant Solomon wisdom and discernment, so God kept this promise too. Because of Solomon's sins, the kingdom of Israel eventually split into two parts. Both kingdoms were characterized by idolatry and immorality. The northern part of the country was ruled initially by Jeroboam, but was eventually taken into captivity by the Assyrians. The southern part of the country was ruled at first by Solomon's son Rehoboam, but ultimately was conquered by the Babylonians. As God had forewarned, judgment came on all the people because of Solomon's unwise choices. What a terrible testimony Solomon's life became to all those who had looked to him for wisdom and guidance! Solomon began his reign with a wonderful relationship to God but ended up spiritually destitute.

Could It Happen to Me?

Solomon's life speaks loudly to all of us as men. Though none of us will ever receive the degree of wisdom Solomon received from God, and most of us will never have the power and possessions he did, we must remember that Solomon's tumble was a "long way down" because he was a "long way up." In other words, the greater *our* position, the greater our fall if we violate God's will.

Most of us will face Solomon's temptations—to sell our souls for sex, power or possessions. Even one of these temptations alone is powerful enough to destroy us. But it need not happen. We have been warned! And we have the advantage of being able to look back at Solomon's life to see the whole picture and the results of his unwise living.

We also know what it means to know Jesus Christ as the true Messiah, our Savior. And we have the indwelling presence of the Holy Spirit to empower us and help us be victorious over Solomon's temptations. As men of God, we must keep our hearts fixed on the One who can keep us from falling into sin and ultimately bring us "before his glorious presence without fault and with great joy—to the only God our Savior be glory, majesty, power and authority, through Jesus Christ our Lord, before all ages, now and forevermore! Amen" (Jude 24–25).

—Dr. Gene Getz

kindness to him and have given him a
son[c] to sit on his throne this very day.
7“Now, O LORD my God, you have
made your servant king in place of my
father David. But I am only a little
child[d] and do not know how to carry
out my duties. 8Your servant is here
among the people you have chosen,[e]
a great people, too numerous to count
or number.[f] 9So give your servant a
discerning[g] heart to govern your people and to distinguish[h] between right
and wrong. For who is able[i] to govern
this great people of yours?”
10The Lord was pleased that Solomon had asked for this. 11So God said
to him, “Since you have asked[j] for
this and not for long life or wealth for
yourself, nor have asked for the death
of your enemies but for discernment
in administering justice, 12I will do
what you have asked.[k] I will give you
a wise[l] and discerning heart, so that
there will never have been anyone like
you, nor will there ever be. 13Moreover,
I will give you what you have not[m]
asked for—both riches and honor[n]—
so that in your lifetime you will have
no equal[o] among kings. 14And if you
walk[p] in my ways and obey my statutes and commands as David your father did, I will give you a long life.”[q]
15Then Solomon awoke[r]—and he realized it had been a dream.

He returned to Jerusalem, stood
before the ark of the Lord’s covenant
and sacrificed burnt offerings[s] and fellowship offerings.[a][t] Then he gave a
feast[u] for all his court.

A Wise Ruling

16Now two prostitutes came to the
king and stood before him. 17One of
them said, “My lord, this woman and I
live in the same house. I had a baby
while she was there with me. 18The
third day after my child was born, this
woman also had a baby. We were
alone; there was no one in the house
but the two of us.
19“During the night this woman’s
son died because she lay on him. 20So
she got up in the middle of the night
and took my son from my side while I
your servant was asleep. She put him
by her breast and put her dead son by
my breast. 21The next morning, I got up
to nurse my son—and he was dead!
But when I looked at him closely in the
morning light, I saw that it wasn’t the
son I had borne.”
22The other woman said, “No! The
living one is my son; the dead one is
yours.”

But the first one insisted, “No! The
dead one is yours; the living one is
mine.” And so they argued before the
king.
23The king said, “This one says, ‘My
son is alive and your son is dead,’ while
that one says, ‘No! Your son is dead
and mine is alive.’ ”
24Then the king said, “Bring me a
sword.” So they brought a sword for
the king. 25He then gave an order: “Cut
the living child in two and give half to
one and half to the other.”
26The woman whose son was alive
was filled with compassion[v] for her
son and said to the king, “Please, my
lord, give her the living baby! Don’t kill
him!”

But the other said, “Neither I nor
you shall have him. Cut him in two!”
27Then the king gave his ruling:
“Give the living baby to the first woman. Do not kill him; she is his mother.”
28When all Israel heard the verdict
the king had given, they held the king
in awe, because they saw that he had
wisdom[w] from God to administer justice.

Solomon’s Officials and Governors

4 So King Solomon ruled over all Israel. 2And these were his chief officials:

Azariah[x] son of Zadok—the
priest;
3Elihoreph and Ahijah, sons of
Shisha—secretaries;
Jehoshaphat[y] son of Ahilud—
recorder;
4Benaiah[z] son of Jehoiada—
commander in chief;
Zadok[a] and Abiathar—priests;
5Azariah son of Nathan—in
charge of the district officers;
Zabud son of Nathan—a priest
and personal adviser to the
king;
6Ahishar—in charge of the palace;
Adoniram son of Abda—in
charge of forced labor.

7Solomon also had twelve district
governors over all Israel, who supplied
provisions for the king and the royal
household. Each one had to provide
supplies for one month in the year.
8These are their names:

Ben-Hur—in the hill country[b]
of Ephraim;
9Ben-Deker—in Makaz, Shaalbim,[c] Beth Shemesh[d] and
Elon Bethhanan;
10Ben-Hesed—in Arubboth (Socoh[e] and all the land of Hepher[f] were his);

3:6 [c]1Ki 1:48 **3:7** [d]Nu 27:17; 1Ch 29:1 **3:8** [e]Dt 7:6 [f]Ge 15:5 **3:9** [g]2Sa 14:17; Jas 1:5 [h]Pr 2:3-9; Heb 5:14 [i]Ps 72:1-2 **3:11** [j]Jas 4:3 **3:12** [k]1Jn 5:14-15 [l]1Ki 4:29,30, 31; 5:12; 10:23; Ecc 1:16 **3:13** [m]Mt 6:33; Eph 3:20 [n]1Ki 4:21-24; Pr 3:1-2,16 [o]1Ki 10:23 **3:14** [p]ver 6; Pr 3:1-2,16 [q]Ps 61:6; 91:16 **3:15** [r]Ge 41:7 [s]1Ki 8:65 [t]Mk 6:21 [u]Est 1:3,9; Da 5:1

3:26 [v]Ge 43:30; Isa 49:15; Jer 31:20; Hos 11:8 **3:28** [w]ver 9,11-12; Col 2:3 **4:2** [x]1Ch 6:10 **4:3** [y]2Sa 8:16 **4:4** [z]1Ki 2:35 [a]1Ki 2:27 **4:8** [b]Jos 24:33 **4:9** [c]Jdg 1:35 [d]Jos 21:16 **4:10** [e]Jos 15:35 [f]Jos 12:17

[a] *15* Traditionally *peace offerings*

11 Ben-Abinadab—in Naphoth Dor[a][g] (he was married to Taphath daughter of Solomon);

12 Baana son of Ahilud—in Taanach and Megiddo, and in all of Beth Shan[h] next to Zarethan[i] below Jezreel, from Beth Shan to Abel Meholah[j] across to Jokmeam;[k]

13 Ben-Geber—in Ramoth Gilead (the settlements of Jair[l] son of Manasseh in Gilead were his, as well as the district of Argob in Bashan and its sixty large walled cities[m] with bronze gate bars);

14 Ahinadab son of Iddo—in Mahanaim;[n]

15 Ahimaaz[o]—in Naphtali (he had married Basemath daughter of Solomon);

16 Baana son of Hushai[p]—in Asher and in Aloth;

17 Jehoshaphat son of Paruah—in Issachar;

18 Shimei[q] son of Ela—in Benjamin;

19 Geber son of Uri—in Gilead (the country of Sihon king of the Amorites and the country of Og[r] king of Bashan). He was the only governor over the district.

Solomon's Daily Provisions

20 The people of Judah and Israel were as numerous as the sand[s] on the seashore; they ate, they drank and they were happy. 21 And Solomon ruled[t] over all the kingdoms from the River[b][u] to the land of the Philistines, as far as the border of Egypt.[v] These countries brought tribute[w] and were Solomon's subjects all his life.

22 Solomon's daily provisions were thirty cors[c] of fine flour and sixty cors[d] of meal, 23 ten head of stall-fed cattle, twenty of pasture-fed cattle and a hundred sheep and goats, as well as deer, gazelles, roebucks and choice fowl. 24 For he ruled over all the kingdoms west of the River, from Tiphsah[x] to Gaza, and had peace[y] on all sides. 25 During Solomon's lifetime Judah and Israel, from Dan to Beersheba,[z] lived in safety,[a] each man under his own vine and fig tree.[b]

26 Solomon had four[e] thousand stalls for chariot horses,[c] and twelve thousand horses.[f]

27 The district officers,[d] each in his month, supplied provisions for King Solomon and all who came to the king's table. They saw to it that nothing was lacking. 28 They also brought to the proper place their quotas of barley and straw for the chariot horses and the other horses.

Solomon's Wisdom

29 God gave Solomon wisdom[e] and very great insight, and a breadth of understanding as measureless as the sand on the seashore. 30 Solomon's wisdom was greater than the wisdom of all the men of the East,[f] and greater than all the wisdom of Egypt.[g] 31 He was wiser[h] than any other man, including Ethan the Ezrahite—wiser than Heman, Calcol and Darda, the sons of Mahol. And his fame spread to all the surrounding nations. 32 He spoke three thousand proverbs[i] and his songs[j] numbered a thousand and five. 33 He described plant life, from the cedar of Lebanon to the hyssop that grows out of walls. He also taught about animals and birds, reptiles and fish. 34 Men of all nations came to listen to Solomon's wisdom, sent by all the kings[k] of the world, who had heard of his wisdom.

Preparations for Building the Temple

5 When Hiram[l] king of Tyre heard that Solomon had been anointed king to succeed his father David, he sent his envoys to Solomon, because he had always been on friendly terms with David. 2 Solomon sent back this message to Hiram:

3 "You know that because of the wars[m] waged against my father David from all sides, he could not build a temple for the Name of the LORD his God until the LORD put his enemies under his feet. 4 But now the LORD my God has given me rest[n] on every side, and there is no adversary or disaster. 5 I intend, therefore, to build a temple[o] for the Name of the LORD my God, as the LORD told my father David, when he said, 'Your son whom I will put on the throne in your place will build the temple for my Name.'[p]

6 "So give orders that cedars of Lebanon be cut for me. My men will work with yours, and I will pay you for your men whatever wages you set. You know that we have no one so skilled in felling timber as the Sidonians."

4:11 [g] Jos 11:2
4:12 [h] Jos 17:11; Jdg 5:19 [i] Jos 3:16 [j] 1Ki 19:16 [k] 1Ch 6:68
4:13 [l] Nu 32:41 [m] Dt 3:4
4:14 [n] Jos 13:26
4:15 [o] 2Sa 15:27
4:16 [p] 2Sa 15:32
4:18 [q] 1Ki 1:8
4:19 [r] Dt 3:8-10
4:20 [s] Ge 22:17; 32:12; 1Ki 3:8
4:21 [t] 2Ch 9:26; Ps 72:11 [u] Jos 1:4; Ps 72:8 [v] Ge 15:18 [w] Ps 68:29
4:24 [x] Ps 72:11 [y] 1Ch 22:9
4:25 [z] Jdg 20:1 [a] Jer 23:6 [b] Mic 4:4; Zec 3:10
4:26 [c] 1Ki 10:26; 2Ch 1:14
4:27 [d] ver 7
4:29 [e] 1Ki 3:12
4:30 [f] Ge 25:6 [g] Ac 7:22
4:31 [h] 1Ki 3:12; 1Ch 2:6; 6:33; 15:19; Ps 89 Title
4:32 [i] Pr 1:1; Ecc 12:9 [j] SS 1:1
4:34 [k] 1Ki 10:1; 2Ch 9:23
5:1 [l] ver 10,18; 2Sa 5:11; 1Ch 14:1
5:3 [m] 1Ch 22:8; 28:3
5:4 [n] 1Ki 4:24; 1Ch 22:9
5:5 [o] 1Ch 17:12 [p] 2Sa 7:13; 1Ch 22:10

[a] *11* Or *in the heights of Dor* [b] *21* That is, the Euphrates; also in verse 24 [c] *22* That is, probably about 185 bushels (about 6.6 kiloliters) [d] *22* That is, probably about 375 bushels (about 13.2 kiloliters) [e] *26* Some Septuagint manuscripts (see also 2 Chron. 9:25); Hebrew *forty* [f] *26* Or *charioteers*

7When Hiram heard Solomon's message, he was greatly pleased and said, "Praise be to the LORD today, for he has given David a wise son to rule over this great nation."

8So Hiram sent word to Solomon:

"I have received the message you sent me and will do all you want in providing the cedar and pine logs. 9My men will haul them down from Lebanon to the sea[q], and I will float them in rafts by sea to the place you specify. There I will separate them and you can take them away. And you are to grant my wish by providing food[r] for my royal household."

10In this way Hiram kept Solomon supplied with all the cedar and pine logs he wanted, 11and Solomon gave Hiram twenty thousand cors[a] of wheat as food for his household, in addition to twenty thousand baths[b,c] of pressed olive oil. Solomon continued to do this for Hiram year after year. 12The LORD gave Solomon wisdom,[s] just as he had promised him. There were peaceful relations between Hiram and Solomon, and the two of them made a treaty.[t]

13King Solomon conscripted laborers[u] from all Israel—thirty thousand men. 14He sent them off to Lebanon in shifts of ten thousand a month, so that they spent one month in Lebanon and two months at home. Adoniram[v] was in charge of the forced labor. 15Solomon had seventy thousand carriers and eighty thousand stonecutters in the hills, 16as well as thirty-three hundred[d] foremen[w] who supervised the project and directed the workmen. 17At the king's command they removed from the quarry[x] large blocks of quality stone[y] to provide a foundation of dressed stone for the temple. 18The craftsmen of Solomon and Hiram and the men of Gebal[e][z] cut and prepared the timber and stone for the building of the temple.

Solomon Builds the Temple

6 In the four hundred and eightieth[f] year after the Israelites had come out of Egypt, in the fourth year of Solomon's reign over Israel, in the month of Ziv, the second month, he began to build the temple of the LORD.[a]

2The temple[b] that King Solomon built for the LORD was sixty cubits long, twenty wide and thirty high.[g] 3The portico at the front of the main hall of the temple extended the width of the temple, that is twenty cubits,[h] and projected ten cubits[i] from the front of the temple. 4He made narrow clerestory windows[c] in the temple. 5Against the walls of the main hall and inner sanctuary he built a structure around the building, in which there were side rooms.[d] 6The lowest floor was five cubits[j] wide, the middle floor six cubits[k] and the third floor seven.[l] He made offset ledges around the outside of the temple so that nothing would be inserted into the temple walls.

7In building the temple, only blocks dressed[e] at the quarry were used, and no hammer, chisel or any other iron tool[f] was heard at the temple site while it was being built.

8The entrance to the lowest[m] floor was on the south side of the temple; a stairway led up to the middle level and from there to the third. 9So he built the temple and completed it, roofing it with beams and cedar[g] planks. 10And he built the side rooms all along the temple. The height of each was five cubits, and they were attached to the temple by beams of cedar.

11The word of the LORD came to Solomon: 12"As for this temple you are building, if you follow my decrees, carry out my regulations and keep all my commands and obey them, I will fulfill through you the promise[h] I gave to David your father. 13And I will live among the Israelites and will not abandon[i] my people Israel."

14So Solomon built the temple and completed[j] it. 15He lined its interior walls with cedar boards, paneling them from the floor of the temple to the ceiling,[k] and covered the floor of the temple with planks of pine. 16He partitioned off twenty cubits[h] at the rear of the temple with cedar boards from floor to ceiling to form within the temple an inner sanctuary, the Most Holy Place.[l] 17The main hall in front of this room was forty cubits[n] long. 18The inside of the temple was cedar,[m] carved with gourds and open flowers. Every-

5:9 [q]Ezr 3:7 [r]Eze 27:17; Ac 12:20
5:12 [s]1Ki 3:12 [t]Am 1:9
5:13 [u]1Ki 9:15
5:14 [v]1Ki 4:6; 2Ch 10:18
5:16 [w]1Ki 9:23
5:17 [x]1Ki 6:7 [y]1Ch 22:2
5:18 [z]Jos 13:5
6:1 [a]Ac 7:47
6:2 [b]Eze 41:1
6:4 [c]Eze 40:16; 41:16
6:5 [d]ver 16,19-21; Eze 41:5-6
6:7 [e]Ex 20:25 [f]Dt 27:5
6:9 [g]ver 14,38
6:12 [h]2Sa 7:12-16; 1Ki 2:4; 9:5
6:13 [i]Ex 25:8; Lev 26:11; Dt 31:6; Heb 13:5
6:14 [j]ver 9,38
6:15 [k]1Ki 7:7
6:16 [l]Ex 26:33; Lev 16:2; 1Ki 8:6
6:18 [m]1Ki 7:24; Ps 74:6

a *11* That is, probably about 125,000 bushels (about 4,400 kiloliters) **b** *11* Septuagint (see also 2 Chron. 2:10); Hebrew *twenty cors* **c** *11* That is, about 115,000 gallons (about 440 kiloliters) **d** *16* Hebrew; some Septuagint manuscripts (see also 2 Chron. 2:2, 18) *thirty-six hundred* **e** *18* That is, Byblos **f** *1* Hebrew; Septuagint *four hundred and fortieth* **g** *2* That is, about 90 feet (about 27 meters) long and 30 feet (about 9 meters) wide and 45 feet (about 13.5 meters) high **h** *3,16* That is, about 30 feet (about 9 meters) **i** *3* That is, about 15 feet (about 4.5 meters) **j** *6* That is, about 7 1/2 feet (about 2.3 meters); also in verses 10 and 24 **k** *6* That is, about 9 feet (about 2.7 meters) **l** *6* That is, about 10 1/2 feet (about 3.1 meters) **m** *8* Septuagint; Hebrew *middle* **n** *17* That is, about 60 feet (about 18 meters)

thing was cedar; no stone was to be seen.

19 He prepared the inner sanctuary[n] within the temple to set the ark of the covenant[o] of the LORD there. 20 The inner sanctuary[p] was twenty cubits long, twenty wide and twenty high.[a] He overlaid the inside with pure gold, and he also overlaid the altar of cedar. 21 Solomon covered the inside of the temple with pure gold, and he extended gold chains across the front of the inner sanctuary, which was overlaid with gold. 22 So he overlaid the whole interior with gold. He also overlaid with gold the altar that belonged to the inner sanctuary.

23 In the inner sanctuary he made a pair of cherubim[q] of olive wood, each ten cubits[b] high. 24 One wing of the first cherub was five cubits long, and the other wing five cubits—ten cubits from wing tip to wing tip. 25 The second cherub also measured ten cubits, for the two cherubim were identical in size and shape. 26 The height of each cherub was ten cubits. 27 He placed the cherubim[r] inside the innermost room of the temple, with their wings spread out. The wing of one cherub touched one wall, while the wing of the other touched the other wall, and their wings touched each other in the middle of the room. 28 He overlaid the cherubim with gold.

29 On the walls all around the temple, in both the inner and outer rooms, he carved cherubim,[s] palm trees and open flowers. 30 He also covered the floors of both the inner and outer rooms of the temple with gold.

31 For the entrance of the inner sanctuary he made doors of olive wood with five-sided jambs. 32 And on the two olive wood doors he carved cherubim, palm trees and open flowers, and overlaid the cherubim and palm trees with beaten gold. 33 In the same way he made four-sided jambs of olive wood for the entrance to the main hall. 34 He also made two pine doors, each having two leaves that turned in sockets. 35 He carved cherubim, palm trees and open flowers on them and overlaid them with gold hammered evenly over the carvings.

36 And he built the inner courtyard of three courses[t] of dressed stone and one course of trimmed cedar beams.

37 The foundation of the temple of the LORD was laid in the fourth year, in the month of Ziv. 38 In the eleventh year in the month of Bul, the eighth month, the temple was finished in all its details according to its specifications.[u] He had spent seven years building it.

6:19 [n] 1Ki 8:6 [o] 1Sa 3:3 **6:20** [p] Eze 41:3-4 **6:23** [q] Ex 37:1-9 **6:27** [r] Ex 25:20; 37:9; 1Ki 8:7; 2Ch 5:8 **6:29** [s] ver 32,35 **6:36** [t] 1Ki 7:12; Ezr 6:4 **6:38** [u] Heb 8:5

Solomon Builds His Palace

7 It took Solomon thirteen years, however, to complete the construction of his palace.[v] 2 He built the Palace[w] of the Forest of Lebanon[x] a hundred cubits long, fifty wide and thirty high,[c] with four rows of cedar columns supporting trimmed cedar beams. 3 It was roofed with cedar above the beams that rested on the columns—forty-five beams, fifteen to a row. 4 Its windows were placed high in sets of three, facing each other. 5 All the doorways had rectangular frames; they were in the front part in sets of three, facing each other.[d]

6 He made a colonnade fifty cubits long and thirty wide.[e] In front of it was a portico, and in front of that were pillars and an overhanging roof.

7 He built the throne hall, the Hall of Justice, where he was to judge,[y] and he covered it with cedar from floor to ceiling.[f][z] 8 And the palace in which he was to live, set farther back, was similar in design. Solomon also made a palace like this hall for Pharaoh's daughter, whom he had married.[a]

9 All these structures, from the outside to the great courtyard and from foundation to eaves, were made of blocks of high-grade stone cut to size and trimmed with a saw on their inner and outer faces. 10 The foundations were laid with large stones of good quality, some measuring ten cubits[b] and some eight.[g] 11 Above were high-grade stones, cut to size, and cedar beams. 12 The great courtyard was surrounded by a wall of three courses[b] of dressed stone and one course of trimmed cedar beams, as was the inner courtyard of the temple of the LORD with its portico.

The Temple's Furnishings

13 King Solomon sent to Tyre and brought Huram,[h][c] 14 whose mother was a widow from the tribe of Naphtali and whose father was a man of Tyre and a craftsman in bronze. Huram was highly skilled[d] and experienced in all kinds of bronze work. He came to King

7:1 [v] 1Ki 9:10; 2Ch 8:1 **7:2** [w] 2Sa 7:2 [x] 1Ki 10:17; 2Ch 9:16 **7:7** [y] Ps 122:5; Pr 20:8 [z] 1Ki 6:15 **7:8** [a] 1Ki 3:1; 2Ch 8:11 **7:12** [b] 1Ki 6:36 **7:13** [c] 2Ch 2:13 **7:14** [d] Ex 31:2-5; 35:31; 36:1; 2Ch 2:14

[a] *20* That is, about 30 feet (about 9 meters) long, wide and high [b] *23,10* That is, about 15 feet (about 4.5 meters) [c] *2* That is, about 150 feet (about 46 meters) long, 75 feet (about 23 meters) wide and 45 feet (about 13.5 meters) high [d] *5* The meaning of the Hebrew for this verse is uncertain. [e] *6* That is, about 75 feet (about 23 meters) long and 45 feet (about 13.5 meters) wide [f] *7* Vulgate and Syriac; Hebrew *floor* [g] *10* That is, about 12 feet (about 3.6 meters) [h] *13* Hebrew *Hiram,* a variant of *Huram;* also in verses 40 and 45

Solomon and did all[e] the work assigned to him.
15He cast two bronze pillars,[f] each
eighteen cubits high and twelve cubits
around,[a] by line. 16He also made two
capitals[g] of cast bronze to set on the
tops of the pillars; each capital was five
cubits[b] high. 17A network of interwoven chains festooned the capitals on
top of the pillars, seven for each capital. 18He made pomegranates in two
rows[c] encircling each network to decorate the capitals on top of the pillars.[d] He did the same for each capital.
19The capitals on top of the pillars in
the portico were in the shape of lilies,
four cubits[e] high. 20On the capitals of
both pillars, above the bowl-shaped
part next to the network, were the two
hundred pomegranates[h] in rows all
around. 21He erected the pillars at the
portico of the temple. The pillar to the
south he named Jakin[f] and the one to
the north Boaz.[g][i] 22The capitals on
top were in the shape of lilies. And so
the work on the pillars was completed.
23He made the Sea[j] of cast metal,
circular in shape, measuring ten cubits[h] from rim to rim and five cubits
high. It took a line of thirty cubits[i] to
measure around it. 24Below the rim,
gourds encircled it—ten to a cubit. The
gourds were cast in two rows in one
piece with the Sea.
25The Sea stood on twelve bulls,[k]
three facing north, three facing west,
three facing south and three facing
east. The Sea rested on top of them,
and their hindquarters were toward
the center. 26It was a handbreadth[j] in
thickness, and its rim was like the rim
of a cup, like a lily blossom. It held two
thousand baths.[k]
27He also made ten movable
stands[l] of bronze; each was four cubits long, four wide and three high.[l]
28This is how the stands were made:
They had side panels attached to uprights. 29On the panels between the
uprights were lions, bulls and
cherubim—and on the uprights as
well. Above and below the lions and
bulls were wreaths of hammered work.
30Each stand[m] had four bronze wheels
with bronze axles, and each had a basin resting on four supports, cast with
wreaths on each side. 31On the inside
of the stand there was an opening that
had a circular frame one cubit[m] deep.
This opening was round, and with its
basework it measured a cubit and a
half.[n] Around its opening there was
engraving. The panels of the stands
were square, not round. 32The four
wheels were under the panels, and the
axles of the wheels were attached to
the stand. The diameter of each wheel
was a cubit and a half. 33The wheels
were made like chariot wheels; the axles, rims, spokes and hubs were all of
cast metal.
34Each stand had four handles, one
on each corner, projecting from the
stand. 35At the top of the stand there
was a circular band half a cubit[o] deep.
The supports and panels were attached
to the top of the stand. 36He engraved
cherubim, lions and palm trees on the
surfaces of the supports and on the
panels, in every available space, with
wreaths all around. 37This is the way he
made the ten stands. They were all cast
in the same molds and were identical
in size and shape.
38He then made ten bronze basins,[n] each holding forty baths[p] and
measuring four cubits across, one basin to go on each of the ten stands.
39He placed five of the stands on the
south side of the temple and five on the
north. He placed the Sea on the south
side, at the southeast corner of the
temple. 40He also made the basins and
shovels and sprinkling bowls.
So Huram finished all the work he
had undertaken for King Solomon in
the temple of the LORD:

41the two pillars;
the two bowl-shaped capitals on
top of the pillars;
the two sets of network decorating the two bowl-shaped capitals on top of the pillars;
42the four hundred pomegranates
for the two sets of network
(two rows of pomegranates for
each network, decorating the
bowl-shaped capitals[o] on top
of the pillars);
43the ten stands with their ten basins;

7:14 [e]2Ch 4:11,16
7:15 [f]2Ki 25:17; 2Ch 3:15; 4:12; 52:17,21
7:16 [g]2Ki 25:17
7:20 [h]2Ch 3:16; 4:13; Jer 52:23
7:21 [i]1Ki 6:3; 2Ch 3:17
7:23 [j]2Ki 25:13; 1Ch 18:8; Jer 52:17
7:25 [k]2Ch 4:4-5; Jer 52:20
7:27 [l]ver 38; 2Ch 4:14
7:30 [m]2Ki 16:17
7:38 [n]Ex 30:18; 2Ch 4:6
7:42 [o]ver 20

[a] *15* That is, about 27 feet (about 8.1 meters) high and 18 feet (about 5.4 meters) around
[b] *16* That is, about 7 1/2 feet (about 2.3 meters); also in verse 23
[c] *18* Two Hebrew manuscripts and Septuagint; most Hebrew manuscripts *made the pillars, and there were two rows*
[d] *18* Many Hebrew manuscripts and Syriac; most Hebrew manuscripts *pomegranates*
[e] *19* That is, about 6 feet (about 1.8 meters); also in verse 38
[f] *21* *Jakin* probably means *he establishes.*
[g] *21* *Boaz* probably means *in him is strength.*
[h] *23* That is, about 15 feet (about 4.5 meters)
[i] *23* That is, about 45 feet (about 13.5 meters)
[j] *26* That is, about 3 inches (about 8 centimeters)
[k] *26* That is, probably about 11,500 gallons (about 44 kiloliters); the Septuagint does not have this sentence.
[l] *27* That is, about 6 feet (about 1.8 meters) long and wide and about 4 1/2 feet (about 1.3 meters) high
[m] *31* That is, about 1 1/2 feet (about 0.5 meter)
[n] *31* That is, about 2 1/4 feet (about 0.7 meter); also in verse 32
[o] *35* That is, about 3/4 foot (about 0.2 meter)
[p] *38* That is, about 230 gallons (about 880 liters)

44 the Sea and the twelve bulls under it;
45 the pots, shovels and sprinkling
bowls.[p]

All these objects that Huram made
for King Solomon for the temple of the
LORD were of burnished bronze. 46 The
king had them cast in clay molds in the
plain[q] of the Jordan between Succoth[r] and Zarethan.[s] 47 Solomon left
all these things unweighed,[t] because
there were so many; the weight of the
bronze was not determined.
48 Solomon also made all the furnishings that were in the LORD's temple:

the golden altar;
the golden table[u] on which was
the bread of the Presence;[v]
49 the lampstands[w] of pure gold
(five on the right and five on
the left, in front of the inner
sanctuary);
the gold floral work and lamps
and tongs;
50 the pure gold basins, wick trimmers, sprinkling bowls, dishes
and censers;[x]
and the gold sockets for the
doors of the innermost room,
the Most Holy Place, and also
for the doors of the main hall
of the temple.

51 When all the work King Solomon
had done for the temple of the LORD
was finished, he brought in the things
his father David had dedicated[y]—the
silver and gold and the furnishings—
and he placed them in the treasuries of
the LORD's temple.

The Ark Brought to the Temple

8 Then King Solomon summoned into
his presence at Jerusalem the elders
of Israel, all the heads of the tribes and
the chiefs[z] of the Israelite families, to
bring up the ark[a] of the LORD's covenant from Zion, the City of David.[b]
2 All the men of Israel came together to
King Solomon at the time of the festival[c] in the month of Ethanim, the seventh month.[d]
3 When all the elders of Israel had arrived, the priests[e] took up the ark,
4 and they brought up the ark of the
LORD and the Tent of Meeting[f] and all
the sacred furnishings in it. The priests
and Levites carried them up, 5 and King
Solomon and the entire assembly of Israel that had gathered about him were
before the ark, sacrificing[g] so many
sheep and cattle that they could not be
recorded or counted.
6 The priests then brought the ark of
the LORD's covenant[h] to its place in
the inner sanctuary of the temple, the
Most Holy Place, and put it beneath
the wings of the cherubim.[i] 7 The
cherubim spread their wings over the
place of the ark and overshadowed the
ark and its carrying poles. 8 These poles
were so long that their ends could be
seen from the Holy Place in front of the
inner sanctuary, but not from outside
the Holy Place; and they are still there
today.[j] 9 There was nothing in the ark
except the two stone tablets[k] that Moses had placed in it at Horeb, where the
LORD made a covenant with the Israelites after they came out of Egypt.
10 When the priests withdrew from
the Holy Place, the cloud[l] filled the
temple of the LORD. 11 And the priests
could not perform their service because of the cloud, for the glory of the
LORD filled his temple.
12 Then Solomon said, "The LORD has
said that he would dwell in a dark
cloud;[m] 13 I have indeed built a magnificent temple for you, a place for you to
dwell[n] forever."
14 While the whole assembly of Israel
was standing there, the king turned
around and blessed[o] them. 15 Then he
said:

"Praise be to the LORD,[p] the
God of Israel, who with his own
hand has fulfilled what he promised with his own mouth to my
father David. For he said, 16 'Since
the day I brought my people Israel
out of Egypt, I have not chosen a
city in any tribe of Israel to have a
temple built for my Name[q] to be
there, but I have chosen[r] David[s] to rule my people Israel.'
17 "My father David had it in his
heart to build a temple[t] for the
Name of the LORD, the God of Israel. 18 But the LORD said to my father David, 'Because it was in
your heart to build a temple for
my Name, you did well to have
this in your heart. 19 Nevertheless,
you[u] are not the one to build the
temple, but your son, who is your
own flesh and blood—he is the
one who will build the temple for
my Name.'[v]
20 "The LORD has kept the promise he made: I have succeeded David my father and now I sit on the
throne of Israel, just as the LORD
promised, and I have built[w] the
temple for the Name of the LORD,
the God of Israel. 21 I have provided a place there for the ark, in
which is the covenant of the LORD
that he made with our fathers

7:45 [p] Ex 27:3
7:46 [q] 2Ch 4:17 [r] Ge 33:17; Jos 13:27 [s] Jos 3:16
7:47 [t] 1Ch 22:3
7:48 [u] Ex 37:10 [v] Ex 25:30
7:49 [w] Ex 25:31-38
7:50 [x] 2Ki 25:13
7:51 [y] 2Sa 8:11
8:1 [z] Nu 7:2 [a] 2Sa 6:17 [b] 2Sa 5:7
8:2 [c] 2Ch 7:8 [d] Lev 23:34
8:3 [e] Nu 7:9; Jos 3:3
8:4 [f] 1Ki 3:4; 2Ch 1:3
8:5 [g] 2Sa 6:13
8:6 [h] 2Sa 6:17 [i] 1Ki 6:19,27
8:8 [j] Ex 25:13-15
8:9 [k] Ex 24:7-8; 25:21; 40:20; Dt 10:2-5; Heb 9:4
8:10 [l] Ex 40:34-35; 2Ch 7:1-2
8:12 [m] Ps 18:11; 97:2
8:13 [n] Ex 15:17; 2Sa 7:13; Ps 132:13
8:14 [o] 2Sa 6:18
8:15 [p] 2Sa 7:12-13; 1Ch 29:10,20; Ne 9:5; Lk 1:68
8:16 [q] Dt 12:5 [r] 1Sa 16:1 [s] 2Sa 7:4-6,8
8:17 [t] 2Sa 7:2; 1Ch 17:1
8:19 [u] 2Sa 7:5 [v] 2Sa 7:13; 1Ki 5:3,5
8:20 [w] 1Ch 28:6

when he brought them out of
Egypt."

Solomon's Prayer of Dedication

22 Then Solomon stood before the altar of the LORD in front of the whole
assembly of Israel, spread out his
hands[x] toward heaven 23 and said:

"O LORD, God of Israel, there is
no God like[y] you in heaven
above or on earth below—you
who keep your covenant of love[z]
with your servants who continue
wholeheartedly in your way.
24 You have kept your promise to
your servant David my father;
with your mouth you have promised and with your hand you have
fulfilled it—as it is today.
25 "Now LORD, God of Israel,
keep for your servant David my
father the promises[a] you made
to him when you said, 'You shall
never fail to have a man to sit before me on the throne of Israel, if
only your sons are careful in all
they do to walk before me as you
have done.' 26 And now, O God of
Israel, let your word that you
promised[b] your servant David
my father come true.
27 "But will God really dwell[c]
on earth? The heavens, even the
highest heaven, cannot contain[d]
you. How much less this temple I
have built! 28 Yet give attention to
your servant's prayer and his plea
for mercy, O LORD my God. Hear
the cry and the prayer that your
servant is praying in your presence this day. 29 May your eyes
be open[e] toward[f] this temple
night and day, this place of which
you said, 'My Name[g] shall be
there,' so that you will hear the
prayer your servant prays toward
this place. 30 Hear the supplication
of your servant and of your people
Israel when they pray toward this
place. Hear from heaven, your
dwelling place, and when you
hear, forgive.[h]
31 "When a man wrongs his
neighbor and is required to take
an oath and he comes and swears
the oath[i] before your altar in this
temple, 32 then hear from heaven
and act. Judge between your servants, condemning the guilty and
bringing down on his own head
what he has done. Declare the innocent not guilty, and so establish
his innocence.[j]
33 "When your people Israel
have been defeated[k] by an enemy because they have sinned[l]
against you, and when they turn
back to you and confess your
name, praying and making supplication to you in this temple,
34 then hear from heaven and forgive the sin of your people Israel
and bring them back to the land
you gave to their fathers.
35 "When the heavens are shut
up and there is no rain[m] because
your people have sinned against
you, and when they pray toward
this place and confess your name
and turn from their sin because
you have afflicted them, 36 then
hear from heaven and forgive the
sin of your servants, your people
Israel. Teach[n] them the right
way[o] to live, and send rain on the
land you gave your people for an
inheritance.
37 "When famine[p] or plague
comes to the land, or blight[q] or
mildew, locusts or grasshoppers,
or when an enemy besieges them
in any of their cities, whatever disaster or disease may come, 38 and
when a prayer or plea is made by
any of your people Israel—each
one aware of the afflictions of
his own heart, and spreading out
his hands toward this temple—
39 then hear from heaven, your
dwelling place. Forgive and act;
deal with each man according to
all he does, since you know[r] his
heart (for you alone know the
hearts of all men), 40 so that they
will fear[s] you all the time they
live in the land you gave our fathers.
41 "As for the foreigner who
does not belong to your people Israel but has come from a distant
land because of your name—
42 for men will hear of your great
name and your mighty hand[t]
and your outstretched arm—
when he comes and prays toward
this temple, 43 then hear from
heaven, your dwelling place, and
do whatever the foreigner asks of
you, so that all the peoples of the
earth may know[u] your name and
fear[v] you, as do your own people
Israel, and may know that this
house I have built bears your
Name.
44 "When your people go to war
against their enemies, wherever
you send them, and when they
pray to the LORD toward the city
you have chosen and the temple I
have built for your Name, 45 then
hear from heaven their prayer and

8:22 [x] Ex 9:29; Ezr 9:5
8:23 [y] 1Sa 2:2; 2Sa 7:22 [z] Dt 7:9,12; Ne 1:5; 9:32; Da 9:4
8:25 [a] 1Ki 2:4
8:26 [b] 2Sa 7:25
8:27 [c] Ac 7:48 [d] 2Ch 2:6; Ps 139:7-16; Isa 66:1; Jer 23:24
8:29 [e] 2Ch 7:15; Ne 1:6 [f] Da 6:10 [g] Dt 12:11
8:30 [h] Ps 85:2
8:31 [i] Ex 22:11
8:32 [j] Dt 25:1
8:33 [k] Lev 26:17; Dt 28:25 [l] Lev 26:39
8:35 [m] Lev 26:19; Dt 28:24
8:36 [n] 1Sa 12:23; Ps 25:4; 94:12 [o] Ps 5:8; 27:11; Jer 6:16
8:37 [p] Lev 26:26 [q] Dt 28:22
8:39 [r] 1Sa 16:7; 1Ch 28:9; Ps 11:4; Jer 17:10; Jn 2:24; Ac 1:24
8:40 [s] Ps 130:4
8:42 [t] Dt 3:24
8:43 [u] 1Sa 17:46; 2Ki 19:19 [v] Ps 102:15

their plea, and uphold their cause.

46"When they sin against you—for there is no one who does not sin[w]—and you become angry with them and give them over to the enemy, who takes them captive[x] to his own land, far away or near; **47**and if they have a change of heart in the land where they are held captive, and repent and plead[y] with you in the land of their conquerors and say, 'We have sinned, we have done wrong, we have acted wickedly';[z] **48**and if they turn back to you with all their heart[a] and soul in the land of their enemies who took them captive, and pray[b] to you toward the land you gave their fathers, toward the city you have chosen and the temple[c] I have built for your Name; **49**then from heaven, your dwelling place, hear their prayer and their plea, and uphold their cause. **50**And forgive your people, who have sinned against you; forgive all the offenses they have committed against you, and cause their conquerors to show them mercy;[d] **51**for they are your people and your inheritance,[e] whom you brought out of Egypt, out of that iron-smelting furnace.[f]

52"May your eyes be open to your servant's plea and to the plea of your people Israel, and may you listen to them whenever they cry out to you. **53**For you singled them out from all the nations of the world to be your own inheritance,[g] just as you declared through your servant Moses when you, O Sovereign LORD, brought our fathers out of Egypt."

54When Solomon had finished all these prayers and supplications to the LORD, he rose from before the altar of the LORD, where he had been kneeling with his hands spread out toward heaven. **55**He stood and blessed[h] the whole assembly of Israel in a loud voice, saying:

1 →PG. 420

56"Praise be to the LORD, who has given rest[i] to his people Israel just as he promised. Not one word has failed of all the good promises[j] he gave through his servant Moses. **57**May the LORD our God be with us as he was with our fathers; may he never leave us nor forsake[k] us. **58**May he turn our hearts[l] to him, to walk in all his ways and to keep the commands, decrees and regulations he gave our fathers. **59**And may these words of mine, which I have prayed before the LORD, be near to the LORD our God day and night, that he may uphold the cause of his servant and the cause of his people Israel according to each day's need, **60**so that all the peoples[m] of the earth may know that the LORD is God and that there is no other.[n] **61**But your hearts must be fully committed[o] to the LORD our God, to live by his decrees and obey his commands, as at this time."

The Dedication of the Temple

62Then the king and all Israel with him offered sacrifices before the LORD. **63**Solomon offered a sacrifice of fellowship offerings[a] to the LORD: twenty-two thousand cattle and a hundred and twenty thousand sheep and goats. So the king and all the Israelites dedicated the temple of the LORD.

64On that same day the king consecrated the middle part of the courtyard in front of the temple of the LORD, and there he offered burnt offerings, grain offerings and the fat of the fellowship offerings, because the bronze altar[p] before the LORD was too small to hold the burnt offerings, the grain offerings and the fat of the fellowship offerings.

65So Solomon observed the festival[q] at that time, and all Israel with him—a vast assembly, people from Lebo[b] Hamath[r] to the Wadi of Egypt.[s] They celebrated it before the LORD our God for seven days and seven days more, fourteen days in all. **66**On the following day he sent the people away. They blessed the king and then went home, joyful and glad in heart for all the good things the LORD had done for his servant David and his people Israel.

The LORD Appears to Solomon

9 When Solomon had finished[t] building the temple of the LORD and the royal palace, and had achieved all he had desired to do, **2**the LORD appeared[u] to him a second time, as he had appeared to him at Gibeon. **3**The LORD said to him:

"I have heard[v] the prayer and plea you have made before me; I have consecrated this temple, which you have built, by putting my Name there forever. My eyes[w] and my heart will always be there.

8:46 [w]Pr 20:9; Ecc 7:20; Ro 3:9; 1Jn 1:8-10 [x]Lev 26:33-39; Dt 28:64
8:47 [y]Lev 26:40; Ne 1:6 [z]Ps 106:6; Da 9:5
8:48 [a]Dt 4:29; Jer 29:12-14 [b]Da 6:10 [c]Jnh 2:4
8:50 [d]2Ch 30:9; Ps 106:46
8:51 [e]Dt 4:20; 9:29; Ne 1:10 [f]Jer 11:4
8:53 [g]Ex 19:5; Dt 9:26-29
8:55 [h]ver 14; 2Sa 6:18
8:56 [i]Dt 12:10 [j]Jos 21:45; 23:15
8:57 [k]Dt 31:6; Jos 1:5; Heb 13:5
8:58 [l]Ps 119:36
8:60 [m]Jos 4:24; 1Sa 17:46 [n]Dt 4:35; 1Ki 18:39; Jer 10:10-12
8:61 [o]1Ki 11:4; 15:3,14; 2Ki 20:3
8:64 [p]2Ch 4:1
8:65 [q]ver 2; Lev 23:34 [r]Nu 34:8; Jos 13:5; Jdg 3:3; 2Ki 14:25 [s]Ge 15:18
9:1 [t]1Ki 7:1; 2Ch 8:6
9:2 [u]1Ki 3:5
9:3 [v]2Ki 20:5; Ps 10:17 [w]Dt 11:12; 1Ki 8:29

[a] 63 Traditionally *peace offerings*; also in verse 64
[b] 65 Or *from the entrance to*

4“As for you, if you walk before
me in integrity of heart[x] and uprightness, as David[y] your father
did, and do all I command and
observe my decrees and laws, 5I
will establish[z] your royal throne
over Israel forever, as I promised
David your father when I said,
‘You shall never fail[a] to have a
man on the throne of Israel.’
6“But if you[a] or your sons turn
away[b] from me and do not observe the commands and decrees
I have given you[a] and go off to
serve other gods and worship
them, 7then I will cut off Israel
from the land[c] I have given them
and will reject this temple I have
consecrated for my Name.[d] Israel will then become a byword[e]
and an object of ridicule[f] among
all peoples. 8And though this temple is now imposing, all who pass
by will be appalled and will scoff
and say, ‘Why has the LORD done
such a thing to this land and to
this temple?’[g] 9People will answer, ‘Because they have forsaken
the LORD their God, who brought
their fathers out of Egypt, and
have embraced other gods, worshiping and serving them—that is
why the LORD brought all this disaster on them.’ ”

Solomon's Other Activities

10At the end of twenty years, during which Solomon built these two
buildings—the temple of the LORD and
the royal palace— 11King Solomon
gave twenty towns in Galilee to Hiram
king of Tyre, because Hiram had supplied him with all the cedar and pine
and gold[h] he wanted. 12But when Hiram went from Tyre to see the towns
that Solomon had given him, he was
not pleased with them. 13“What kind of
towns are these you have given me, my
brother?” he asked. And he called them
the Land of Cabul,[b][i] a name they
have to this day. 14Now Hiram had sent
to the king 120 talents[c] of gold.
15Here is the account of the forced
labor King Solomon conscripted[j] to
build the LORD’s temple, his own palace, the supporting terraces,[d][k] the
wall of Jerusalem, and Hazor,[l] Megiddo and Gezer.[m] 16(Pharaoh king of
Egypt had attacked and captured Gezer. He had set it on fire. He killed its
Canaanite inhabitants and then gave
it as a wedding gift to his daughter, Solomon’s wife. 17And Solomon rebuilt
Gezer.) He built up Lower Beth Horon,[n] 18Baalath,[o] and Tadmor[e] in the
desert, within his land, 19as well as
all his store cities[p] and the towns for
his chariots[q] and for his horses[f]—
whatever he desired to build in Jerusalem, in Lebanon and throughout all the
territory he ruled.
20All the people left from the Amorites, Hittites, Perizzites, Hivites and
Jebusites (these peoples were not Israelites), 21that is, their descendants[r]
remaining in the land, whom the
Israelites could not exterminate[g][s]—
these Solomon conscripted for his
slave labor force,[t] as it is to this day.
22But Solomon did not make slaves[u]
of any of the Israelites; they were his
fighting men, his government officials, his officers, his captains, and the
commanders of his chariots and
charioteers. 23They were also the chief
officials[v] in charge of Solomon’s
projects—550 officials supervising the
men who did the work.
24After Pharaoh’s daughter[w] had
come up from the City of David to the
palace Solomon had built for her, he
constructed the supporting terraces.[x]
25Three[y] times a year Solomon sacrificed burnt offerings and fellowship
offerings[h] on the altar he had built for
the LORD, burning incense before the
LORD along with them, and so fulfilled
the temple obligations.
26King Solomon also built ships[z] at
Ezion Geber,[a] which is near Elath in
Edom, on the shore of the Red Sea.[i]
27And Hiram sent his men—sailors[b]
who knew the sea—to serve in the fleet
with Solomon’s men. 28They sailed to
Ophir[c] and brought back 420 talents[j]
of gold, which they delivered to King
Solomon.

The Queen of Sheba Visits Solomon

10 When the queen of Sheba[d] heard
about the fame of Solomon and his
relation to the name of the LORD, she
came to test him with hard questions.[e] 2Arriving at Jerusalem with a
very great caravan—with camels carrying spices, large quantities of gold, and
precious stones—she came to Solomon and talked with him about all that
she had on her mind. 3Solomon answered all her questions; nothing was

9:4 [x]Ge 17:1 [y]1Ki 15:5 **9:5** [z]1Ch 22:10 [a]2Sa 7:15; 1Ki 2:4 **9:6** [b]2Sa 7:14 **9:7** [c]2Ki 17:23; 25:21 [d]Jer 7:14 [e]Ps 44:14 [f]Dt 28:37 **9:8** [g]Dt 29:24; Jer 22:8-9 **9:11** [h]2Ch 8:2 **9:13** [i]Jos 19:27 **9:15** [j]Jos 16:10; 1Ki 5:13 [k]ver 24; 2Sa 5:9 [l]Jos 19:36 [m]Jos 17:11 **9:17** [n]Jos 16:3; 2Ch 8:5 **9:18** [o]Jos 19:44 **9:19** [p]ver 1 [q]1Ki 4:26 **9:21** [r]Ge 9:25-26 [s]Jos 15:63; 17:12; Jdg 1:21,27,29 [t]Ezr 2:55,58 **9:22** [u]Lev 25:39 **9:23** [v]1Ki 5:16 **9:24** [w]1Ki 3:1; 7:8 [x]2Sa 5:9; 1Ki 11:27; 2Ch 32:5 **9:25** [y]Ex 23:14; 2Ch 8:12-13,16 **9:26** [z]1Ki 22:48 [a]Nu 33:35; Dt 2:8 **9:27** [b]1Ki 10:11; Eze 27:8 **9:28** [c]1Ch 29:4 **10:1** [d]Ge 10:7,28; Mt 12:42; Lk 11:31 [e]Jdg 14:12

[a]*6* The Hebrew is plural. [b]*13* *Cabul* sounds like the Hebrew for *good-for-nothing.*
[c]*14* That is, about 4 1/2 tons (about 4 metric tons) [d]*15* Or *the Millo*; also in verse 24
[e]*18* The Hebrew may also be read *Tamar.*
[f]*19* Or *charioteers* [g]*21* The Hebrew term refers to the irrevocable giving over of things or persons to the LORD, often by totally destroying them. [h]*25* Traditionally *peace offerings*
[i]*26* Hebrew *Yam Suph*; that is, Sea of Reeds
[j]*28* That is, about 16 tons (about 14.5 metric tons)

too hard for the king to explain to her.
4 When the queen of Sheba saw all the
wisdom of Solomon and the palace he
had built, 5 the food on his table,[f] the
seating of his officials, the attending
servants in their robes, his cupbearers,
and the burnt offerings he made at[a]
the temple of the LORD, she was overwhelmed.
6 She said to the king, "The report I
heard in my own country about your
achievements and your wisdom is true.
7 But I did not believe these things until
I came and saw with my own eyes. Indeed, not even half was told me; in wisdom and wealth[g] you have far exceeded the report I heard. 8 How happy your
men must be! How happy your officials, who continually stand before you
and hear[h] your wisdom! 9 Praise[i] be
to the LORD your God, who has delighted in you and placed you on the throne
of Israel. Because of the LORD's eternal
love for Israel, he has made you king, to
maintain justice[j] and righteousness."
10 And she gave the king 120 talents[b]
of gold,[k] large quantities of spices,
and precious stones. Never again were
so many spices brought in as those the
queen of Sheba gave to King Solomon.
11 (Hiram's ships brought gold from
Ophir;[l] and from there they brought
great cargoes of almugwood[c] and precious stones. 12 The king used the almugwood to make supports for the
temple of the LORD and for the royal
palace, and to make harps and lyres for
the musicians. So much almugwood
has never been imported or seen since
that day.)
13 King Solomon gave the queen of
Sheba all she desired and asked for, besides what he had given her out of his
royal bounty. Then she left and returned with her retinue to her own
country.

Solomon's Splendor

14 The weight of the gold[m] that Solomon received yearly was 666 talents,[d]
15 not including the revenues from
merchants and traders and from all the
Arabian kings and the governors of the
land.
16 King Solomon made two hundred
large shields[n] of hammered gold; six
hundred bekas[e] of gold went into
each shield. 17 He also made three hundred small shields of hammered gold,
with three minas[f] of gold in each
shield. The king put them in the Palace
of the Forest of Lebanon.[o]
18 Then the king made a great throne
inlaid with ivory and overlaid with fine
gold. 19 The throne had six steps, and its
back had a rounded top. On both sides
of the seat were armrests, with a lion
standing beside each of them. 20 Twelve
lions stood on the six steps, one at either end of each step. Nothing like it
had ever been made for any other kingdom. 21 All King Solomon's goblets
were gold, and all the household articles in the Palace of the Forest of Lebanon were pure gold. Nothing was made
of silver, because silver was considered
of little value in Solomon's days. 22 The
king had a fleet of trading ships[g][p] at
sea along with the ships of Hiram.
Once every three years it returned, carrying gold, silver and ivory, and apes
and baboons.
23 King Solomon was greater in
riches[q] and wisdom[r] than all the
other kings of the earth. 24 The whole
world sought audience with Solomon
to hear the wisdom[s] God had put in
his heart. 25 Year after year, everyone
who came brought a gift—articles of
silver and gold, robes, weapons and
spices, and horses and mules.
26 Solomon accumulated chariots
and horses;[t] he had fourteen hundred
chariots and twelve thousand horses,[h]
which he kept in the chariot cities and
also with him in Jerusalem. 27 The king
made silver as common[u] in Jerusalem
as stones, and cedar as plentiful as
sycamore-fig trees in the foothills.
28 Solomon's horses were imported
from Egypt[i] and from Kue[j]—the royal merchants purchased them from
Kue. 29 They imported a chariot from
Egypt for six hundred shekels[k] of silver, and a horse for a hundred and fifty.[f] They also exported them to all the
kings of the Hittites[v] and of the Arameans.

Solomon's Wives

11 King Solomon, however, loved
many foreign women[w] besides
Pharaoh's daughter—Moabites, Ammonites, Edomites, Sidonians and Hittites. 2 They were from nations about
which the LORD had told the Israelites,
"You must not intermarry[x] with them,
because they will surely turn your
hearts after their gods." Nevertheless,
Solomon held fast to them in love. 3 He

10:5 [f] 1Ch 26:16
10:7 [g] 1Ch 29:25
10:8 [h] Pr 8:34
10:9 [i] 1Ki 5:7 [j] 2Sa 8:15; Ps 33:5; 72:2
10:10 [k] ver 2
10:11 [l] Ge 10:29; 1Ki 9:27-28
10:14 [m] 1Ki 9:28
10:16 [n] 1Ki 14:26-28
10:17 [o] 1Ki 7:2
10:22 [p] 1Ki 9:26
10:23 [q] 1Ki 3:13 [r] 1Ki 4:30
10:24 [s] 1Ki 3:9,12,28
10:26 [t] Dt 17:16; 1Ki 4:26; 9:19; 2Ch 1:14; 9:25
10:27 [u] Dt 17:17
10:29 [v] 2Ki 7:6-7
11:1 [w] Dt 17:17; Ne 13:26
11:2 [x] Ex 34:16; Dt 7:3-4

[a] *5* Or *the ascent by which he went up to*
[b] *10* That is, about 4 1/2 tons (about 4 metric tons)
[c] *11* Probably a variant of *algumwood*; also in verse 12
[d] *14* That is, about 25 tons (about 23 metric tons)
[e] *16* That is, about 7 1/2 pounds (about 3.5 kilograms)
[f] *17,29* That is, about 3 3/4 pounds (about 1.7 kilograms)
[g] *22* Hebrew *of ships of Tarshish*
[h] *26* Or *charioteers*
[i] *28* Or possibly *Muzur*, a region in Cilicia; also in verse 29
[j] *28* Probably *Cilicia*
[k] *29* That is, about 15 pounds (about 7 kilograms)

had seven hundred wives of royal birth
and three hundred concubines, and his
wives led him astray. **4**As Solomon
grew old, his wives turned his heart after other gods, and his heart was not
fully devoted[y] to the LORD his God, as
the heart of David his father had been.
5He followed Ashtoreth[z] the goddess
of the Sidonians, and Molech[a][a] the
detestable god of the Ammonites. **6**So
Solomon did evil in the eyes of the
LORD; he did not follow the LORD completely, as David his father had done.
7On a hill east[b] of Jerusalem, Solomon built a high place for Chemosh[c]
the detestable god of Moab, and for
Molech[d] the detestable god of the
Ammonites. **8**He did the same for all
his foreign wives, who burned incense
and offered sacrifices to their gods.
9The LORD became angry with Solomon because his heart had turned
away from the LORD, the God of Israel,
who had appeared[e] to him twice. **10**Although he had forbidden Solomon to
follow other gods,[f] Solomon did not
keep the LORD's command.[g] **11**So the
LORD said to Solomon, "Since this is
your attitude and you have not kept my
covenant and my decrees, which I
commanded you, I will most certainly
tear[h] the kingdom away from you and
give it to one of your subordinates.
12Nevertheless, for the sake of David
your father, I will not do it during your
lifetime. I will tear it out of the hand of
your son. **13**Yet I will not tear the whole
kingdom from him, but will give him
one tribe[i] for the sake[j] of David my
servant and for the sake of Jerusalem,
which I have chosen."[k]

Solomon's Adversaries

14Then the LORD raised up against
Solomon an adversary, Hadad the
Edomite, from the royal line of Edom.
15Earlier when David was fighting with
Edom, Joab the commander of the
army, who had gone up to bury the
dead, had struck down all the men in
Edom.[l] **16**Joab and all the Israelites
stayed there for six months, until they
had destroyed all the men in Edom.
17But Hadad, still only a boy, fled to
Egypt with some Edomite officials who
had served his father. **18**They set out
from Midian and went to Paran.[m]
Then taking men from Paran with
them, they went to Egypt, to Pharaoh
king of Egypt, who gave Hadad a house
and land and provided him with food.
19Pharaoh was so pleased with Ha-

11:4 [y]1Ki 8:61; 9:4
11:5 [z]ver 33; Jdg 2:13; 2Ki 23:13 [a]ver 7
11:7 [b]2Ki 23:13 [c]Nu 21:29; Jdg 11:24 [d]Lev 20:2-5; Ac 7:43
11:9 [e]ver 2-3; 1Ki 3:5; 9:2
11:10 [f]1Ki 9:6 [g]1Ki 6:12
11:11 [h]ver 31; 1Ki 12:15-16; 2Ki 17:21
11:13 [i]1Ki 12:20 [j]2Sa 7:15 [k]Dt 12:11
11:15 [l]Dt 20:13; 2Sa 8:14; 1Ch 18:12
11:18 [m]Nu 10:12

[a]5 Hebrew *Milcom;* also in verse 33

11:1–12

PROMISE 3

FINISHING WELL

Many promising leaders have not led as promised; they start well but end badly. As you consider the leadership issues present in this passage, remember that races aren't won in the first lap; they are won at the finish line.

This passage contrasts David and Solomon. David had a rough start, Solomon a quick start (1 Kings 3:7–14). David's finish set up Solomon's start; Solomon's finish jeopardized his whole lineage (11:11, 12). This passage presents some of the critical contrasts between David who finished and Solomon who fell. But before looking at differences, we look at a similarity.

Both men sinned. David and Solomon were human; men of flesh with human hearts (Jeremiah 17:9). We all have that in common. To think that David or Joseph or Daniel or any other Biblical "hero" was non-human, that their tasks were somehow easier for them, is an injustice to their relationship with God. Each person whose story is told in the Bible was subject to the same passions, emotions, and temptations as we are.

Two facts in this passage help clarify the difference between David and Solomon. First, Solomon "turned his heart after other gods, and his heart was not fully devoted to the LORD his God," and here's the contrast, "as the heart of David his father had been" (v. 4). This first contrast is at the core. David's heart, Solomon's heart. The second contrast is a consequence of the first: "Solomon did evil in the eyes of the LORD; he did not follow the LORD completely as David his father had done" (v. 6). Both in character and conduct David followed God totally and Solomon did not. David sinned—and repented (Psalms 32, 51). Solomon sinned—and sinned some more. His was a gradual slide away from God. For David, sin was a horrible detour. He immediately got back on the track to God through confession, repentance and prayer for restoration. For Solomon, sin became a road to destruction.

Wherever we are, whether close to God or in a pit, we know sin is waiting to destroy us. To Solomon, sin became a way of life; his legacy is described in 1 Kings 11. To David, sin became an awful distortion of his soul; he repented and his legacy is also described in 1 Kings 11. Think of the number 11. Two '1's'—two individuals: one remembered by God as a winner, a finisher (vv. 4, 6); the other one—well, read verses 4 and 6 again.

A heart wholly devoted to God leads to a life lived for him. A heart turned away from God leads to disaster. One finished; one fell. It's your choice: Which one will you choose to become?

For the next Promise 3 reading go to page 393.

dad that he gave him a sister of his own
wife, Queen Tahpenes, in marriage.
20The sister of Tahpenes bore him a
son named Genubath, whom Tahpenes brought up in the royal palace.
There Genubath lived with Pharaoh's
own children.
21While he was in Egypt, Hadad
heard that David rested with his fathers
and that Joab the commander of the
army was also dead. Then Hadad said
to Pharaoh, "Let me go, that I may return to my own country."
22"What have you lacked here that
you want to go back to your own country?" Pharaoh asked.
"Nothing," Hadad replied, "but do
let me go!"
23And God raised up against Solomon another adversary,[n] Rezon son
of Eliada, who had fled from his master, Hadadezer[o] king of Zobah. 24He
gathered men around him and became
the leader of a band of rebels when
David destroyed the forces[a] ⌞of Zo-
bah⌟; the rebels went to Damascus,[p]
where they settled and took control.
25Rezon was Israel's adversary as long
as Solomon lived, adding to the trouble
caused by Hadad. So Rezon ruled in
Aram[q] and was hostile toward Israel.

Jeroboam Rebels Against Solomon

26Also, Jeroboam son of Nebat rebelled[r] against the king. He was one
of Solomon's officials, an Ephraimite
from Zeredah, and his mother was a
widow named Zeruah.
27Here is the account of how he rebelled against the king: Solomon had
built the supporting terraces[b][s] and
had filled in the gap in the wall of the
city of David his father. 28Now Jeroboam was a man of standing,[t] and when
Solomon saw how well[u] the young
man did his work, he put him in charge
of the whole labor force of the house of
Joseph.
29About that time Jeroboam was going out of Jerusalem, and Ahijah[v] the
prophet of Shiloh met him on the way,
wearing a new cloak. The two of them
were alone out in the country, 30and
Ahijah took hold of the new cloak he
was wearing and tore[w] it into twelve
pieces. 31Then he said to Jeroboam,
"Take ten pieces for yourself, for this is
what the LORD, the God of Israel, says:
'See, I am going to tear[x] the kingdom
out of Solomon's hand and give you
ten tribes. 32But for the sake of my servant David and the city of Jerusalem,
which I have chosen out of all the
tribes of Israel, he will have one tribe.
33I will do this because they have[c] forsaken me and worshiped[y] Ashtoreth
the goddess of the Sidonians, Chemosh
the god of the Moabites, and Molech
the god of the Ammonites, and have
not walked in my ways, nor done what
is right in my eyes, nor kept my statutes[z] and laws as David, Solomon's
father, did.
34" 'But I will not take the whole
kingdom out of Solomon's hand; I have
made him ruler all the days of his life
for the sake of David my servant,
whom I chose and who observed my
commands and statutes. 35I will take
the kingdom from his son's hands and
give you ten tribes. 36I will give one
tribe[a] to his son so that David my servant may always have a lamp[b] before
me in Jerusalem, the city where I chose
to put my Name. 37However, as for
you, I will take you, and you will rule
over all that your heart desires;[c] you
will be king over Israel. 38If you do
whatever I command you and walk in
my ways and do what is right in my
eyes by keeping my statutes[d] and
commands, as David my servant did, I
will be with you. I will build you a dynasty[e] as enduring as the one I built
for David and will give Israel to you. 39I
will humble David's descendants because of this, but not forever.' "
40Solomon tried to kill Jeroboam,
but Jeroboam fled to Egypt, to Shishak[f] the king, and stayed there until
Solomon's death.

Solomon's Death

41As for the other events of Solomon's reign—all he did and the wisdom he displayed—are they not written in the book of the annals of
Solomon? 42Solomon reigned in Jerusalem over all Israel forty years. 43Then
he rested with his fathers and was buried in the city of David his father. And
Rehoboam[g] his son succeeded him as
king.

Israel Rebels Against Rehoboam

12 Rehoboam went to Shechem, for all
the Israelites had gone there to
make him king. 2When Jeroboam son
of Nebat heard this (he was still in
Egypt, where he had fled[h] from King
Solomon), he returned from[d] Egypt.
3So they sent for Jeroboam, and he and
the whole assembly of Israel went to
Rehoboam and said to him: 4"Your father put a heavy yoke[i] on us, but now
lighten the harsh labor and the heavy

11:23 [n]ver 14 [o]2Sa 8:3
11:24 [p]2Sa 8:5; 10:8, 18
11:25 [q]2Sa 10:19
11:26 [r]2Sa 20:21; 1Ki 12:2; 2Ch 13:6
11:27 [s]1Ki 9:24
11:28 [t]Ru 2:1 [u]Pr 22:29
11:29 [v]1Ki 12:15; 14:2; 2Ch 9:29
11:30 [w]1Sa 15:27
11:31 [x]ver 11
11:33 [y]ver 5-7 [z]1Ki 3:3
11:36 [a]ver 13; 1Ki 12:17 [b]1Ki 15:4; 2Ki 8:19
11:37 [c]2Sa 3:21
11:38 [d]Dt 17:19 [e]Jos 1:5; 2Sa 7:11,27
11:40 [f]2Ch 12:2
11:43 [g]1Ki 14:21; Mt 1:7
12:2 [h]1Ki 11:40
12:4 [i]1Sa 8:11-18; 1Ki 4:20-28

[a]24 Hebrew *destroyed them* [b]27 Or *the Millo*
[c]33 Hebrew; Septuagint, Vulgate and Syriac *because he has* [d]2 Or *he remained in*

yoke he put on us, and we will serve
you."
5Rehoboam answered, "Go away for
three days and then come back to me."
So the people went away.
6Then King Rehoboam consulted
the elders[j] who had served his father
Solomon during his lifetime. "How
would you advise me to answer these
people?" he asked.
7They replied, "If today you will be a
servant to these people and serve them
and give them a favorable answer,[k]
they will always be your servants."
8But Rehoboam rejected the advice
the elders gave him and consulted the
young men who had grown up with
him and were serving him. 9He asked
them, "What is your advice? How
should we answer these people who
say to me, 'Lighten the yoke your father
put on us'?"
10The young men who had grown up
with him replied, "Tell these people
who have said to you, 'Your father put
a heavy yoke on us, but make our yoke
lighter'—tell them, 'My little finger is
thicker than my father's waist. 11My father laid on you a heavy yoke; I will
make it even heavier. My father
scourged you with whips; I will scourge
you with scorpions.' "
12Three days later Jeroboam and all
the people returned to Rehoboam, as
the king had said, "Come back to me in
three days." 13The king answered the
people harshly. Rejecting the advice
given him by the elders, 14he followed
the advice of the young men and said,
"My father made your yoke heavy; I
will make it even heavier. My father
scourged[l] you with whips; I will
scourge you with scorpions." 15So the
king did not listen to the people, for
this turn of events was from the
LORD,[m] to fulfill the word the LORD had
spoken to Jeroboam son of Nebat
through Ahijah[n] the Shilonite.
16When all Israel saw that the king
refused to listen to them, they answered the king:

"What share do we have in David,
what part in Jesse's son?
To your tents, O Israel![o]
Look after your own house,
O David!"

So the Israelites went home. 17But as
for the Israelites who were living in the
towns of Judah,[p] Rehoboam still ruled
over them.
18King Rehoboam sent out Adoniram,[a][q] who was in charge of forced
labor, but all Israel stoned him to
death. King Rehoboam, however, managed to get into his chariot and escape
to Jerusalem. 19So Israel has been in
rebellion against the house of David[r]
to this day.
20When all the Israelites heard that
Jeroboam had returned, they sent and
called him to the assembly and made
him king over all Israel. Only the tribe
of Judah remained loyal to the house of
David.[s]
21When Rehoboam arrived in Jerusalem, he mustered the whole house of
Judah and the tribe of Benjamin—
a hundred and eighty thousand fighting men—to make war[t] against the
house of Israel and to regain the kingdom for Rehoboam son of Solomon.
22But this word of God came to Shemaiah[u] the man of God: 23"Say to Rehoboam son of Solomon king of Judah,
to the whole house of Judah and Benjamin, and to the rest of the people,
24'This is what the LORD says: Do not go
up to fight against your brothers, the
Israelites. Go home, every one of you,
for this is my doing.' " So they obeyed
the word of the LORD and went home
again, as the LORD had ordered.

Golden Calves at Bethel and Dan

25Then Jeroboam fortified Shechem[v] in the hill country of Ephraim
and lived there. From there he went
out and built up Peniel.[b][w]
26Jeroboam thought to himself, "The
kingdom will now likely revert to the
house of David. 27If these people go up
to offer sacrifices at the temple of the

12:6 [j]1Ki 4:2 **12:7** [k]Pr 15:1 **12:14** [l]Ex 1:14; 5:5-9, 16-18 **12:15** [m]ver 24; Dt 2:30; Jdg 14:4; 2Ch 22:7; 25:20 [n]1Ki 11:29 **12:16** [o]2Sa 20:1 **12:17** [p]1Ki 11:13,36 **12:18** [q]2Sa 20:24; 1Ki 4:6; 5:14 **12:19** [r]2Ki 17:21 **12:20** [s]1Ki 11:13,32 **12:21** [t]2Ch 11:1 **12:22** [u]2Ch 12:5-7 **12:25** [v]Jdg 9:45 [w]Jdg 8:8,17

[a] *18* Some Septuagint manuscripts and Syriac (see also 1 Kings 4:6 and 5:14); Hebrew *Adoram*
[b] *25* Hebrew *Penuel,* a variant of *Peniel*

12:1–33

PROMISE 6

UNITY

This tragic chapter describes Rehoboam's folly, which ultimately led to Israel's division into the two nations of Judah and Israel. Only under David and Solomon were Israel's twelve tribes united; those were her glory days. From this point in the Biblical narrative to the end of both nations, the story is one of decline and destruction.

Psalm 133 and Ephesians 4:1–3 tell of God's desire for his people to dwell in unity. Israel's history is a graphic illustration of the alternative. Reaching beyond racial, cultural, gender or denominational barriers to demonstrate the power of Biblical unity is more than a nice idea. It is God's revealed will, and we violate it to our own destruction.

For the next Promise 6 reading go to page 453.

LORD in Jerusalem,[x] they will again
give their allegiance to their lord, Rehoboam king of Judah. They will kill
me and return to King Rehoboam."
28After seeking advice, the king
made two golden calves.[y] He said to
the people, "It is too much for you to
go up to Jerusalem. Here are your gods,
O Israel, who brought you up out of
Egypt."[z] 29One he set up in Bethel,[a]
and the other in Dan.[b] 30And this
thing became a sin;[c] the people went
even as far as Dan to worship the one
there.
31Jeroboam built shrines[d] on high
places and appointed priests[e] from all
sorts of people, even though they were
not Levites. 32He instituted a festival
on the fifteenth day of the eighth[f]
month, like the festival held in Judah,
and offered sacrifices on the altar. This
he did in Bethel, sacrificing to the
calves he had made. And at Bethel he
also installed priests at the high places
he had made. 33On the fifteenth day of
the eighth month, a month of his own
choosing, he offered sacrifices on the
altar he had built at Bethel.[g] So he
instituted the festival for the Israelites
and went up to the altar to make offerings.

The Man of God From Judah

13 By the word of the LORD a man of
God[h] came from Judah to Bethel,[i] as Jeroboam was standing by the
altar to make an offering. 2He cried out
against the altar by the word of the
LORD: "O altar, altar! This is what the
LORD says: 'A son named Josiah[j] will
be born to the house of David. On you
he will sacrifice the priests of the high
places who now make offerings here,
and human bones will be burned on
you.' " 3That same day the man of God
gave a sign:[k] "This is the sign the LORD
has declared: The altar will be split
apart and the ashes on it will be poured
out."
4When King Jeroboam heard what
the man of God cried out against the
altar at Bethel, he stretched out his
hand from the altar and said, "Seize
him!" But the hand he stretched out
toward the man shriveled up, so that
he could not pull it back. 5Also, the altar was split apart and its ashes poured
out according to the sign given by the
man of God by the word of the LORD.
6Then the king said to the man of
God, "Intercede[l] with the LORD your
God and pray for me that my hand may
be restored." So the man of God interceded with the LORD, and the king's
hand was restored and became as it
was before.
7The king said to the man of God,
"Come home with me and have something to eat, and I will give you a
gift."[m]
8But the man of God answered the
king, "Even if you were to give me half
your possessions,[n] I would not go
with you, nor would I eat bread[o] or
drink water here. 9For I was commanded by the word of the LORD: 'You must
not eat bread or drink water or return
by the way you came.' " 10So he took
another road and did not return by the
way he had come to Bethel.
11Now there was a certain old
prophet living in Bethel, whose sons
came and told him all that the man of
God had done there that day. They also
told their father what he had said to
the king. 12Their father asked them,
"Which way did he go?" And his sons
showed him which road the man of
God from Judah had taken. 13So he said
to his sons, "Saddle the donkey for
me." And when they had saddled the
donkey for him, he mounted it 14and
rode after the man of God. He found
him sitting under an oak tree and
asked, "Are you the man of God who
came from Judah?"
"I am," he replied.
15So the prophet said to him, "Come
home with me and eat."
16The man of God said, "I cannot
turn back and go with you, nor can I
eat bread[p] or drink water with you in
this place. 17I have been told by the
word of the LORD: 'You must not eat
bread or drink water there or return by
the way you came.' "
18The old prophet answered, "I too
am a prophet, as you are. And an angel
said to me by the word of the LORD:
'Bring him back with you to your house
so that he may eat bread and drink water.' " (But he was lying[q] to him.) 19So
the man of God returned with him and
ate and drank in his house.
20While they were sitting at the table,
the word of the LORD came to the old
prophet who had brought him back.
21He cried out to the man of God who
had come from Judah, "This is what
the LORD says: 'You have defied[r] the
word of the LORD and have not kept the
command the LORD your God gave you.
22You came back and ate bread and
drank water in the place where he told
you not to eat or drink. Therefore your
body will not be buried in the tomb of
your fathers.' "
23When the man of God had finished
eating and drinking, the prophet who
had brought him back saddled his don-

12:27 [x]Dt 12:5-6
12:28 [y]Ex 32:4; 2Ki 10:29; 17:16 [z]Ex 32:8
12:29 [a]Ge 28:19 [b]Jdg 18:27-31
12:30 [c]1Ki 13:34; 2Ki 17:21
12:31 [d]1Ki 13:32 [e]Nu 3:10; 1Ki 13:33; 2Ki 17:32; 2Ch 11:14-15; 13:9
12:32 [f]Lev 23:33-34; Nu 29:12
12:33 [g]Nu 15:39; 1Ki 13:1; Am 7:13
13:1 [h]2Ki 23:17 [i]1Ki 12:32-33
13:2 [j]2Ki 23:15-16, 20
13:3 [k]Jdg 6:17; Isa 7:14; Jn 2:11; 1Co 1:22
13:6 [l]Ex 8:8; 9:28; 10:17; Lk 6:27-28; Ac 8:24; Jas 5:16
13:7 [m]1Sa 9:7; 2Ki 5:15
13:8 [n]Nu 22:18; 24:13 [o]ver 16
13:16 [p]ver 8
13:18 [q]Dt 13:3
13:21 [r]ver 26

key for him. 24As he went on his way, a
lion[s] met him on the road and killed
him, and his body was thrown down
on the road, with both the donkey and
the lion standing beside it. 25Some
people who passed by saw the body
thrown down there, with the lion
standing beside the body, and they
went and reported it in the city where
the old prophet lived.
26When the prophet who had
brought him back from his journey
heard of it, he said, "It is the man of
God who defied the word of the LORD.
The LORD has given him over to the
lion, which has mauled him and killed
him, as the word of the LORD had
warned him."
27The prophet said to his sons, "Saddle the donkey for me," and they did
so. 28Then he went out and found the
body thrown down on the road, with
the donkey and the lion standing beside it. The lion had neither eaten the
body nor mauled the donkey. 29So the
prophet picked up the body of the man
of God, laid it on the donkey, and
brought it back to his own city to
mourn for him and bury him. 30Then
he laid the body in his own tomb, and
they mourned over him and said, "Oh,
my brother!"[t]
31After burying him, he said to his
sons, "When I die, bury me in the grave
where the man of God is buried; lay my
bones[u] beside his bones. 32For the
message he declared by the word of the
LORD against the altar in Bethel and
against all the shrines on the high
places[v] in the towns of Samaria[w] will
certainly come true."[x]
33Even after this, Jeroboam did not
change his evil ways, but once more
appointed priests for the high places
from all sorts[y] of people. Anyone who
wanted to become a priest he consecrated for the high places. 34This was
the sin[z] of the house of Jeroboam that
led to its downfall and to its destruction[a] from the face of the earth.

Ahijah's Prophecy Against Jeroboam

14 At that time Abijah son of Jeroboam
became ill, 2and Jeroboam said to
his wife, "Go, disguise yourself, so you
won't be recognized as the wife of Jeroboam. Then go to Shiloh. Ahijah[b] the
prophet is there—the one who told me
I would be king over this people. 3Take
ten loaves of bread[c] with you, some
cakes and a jar of honey, and go to him.
He will tell you what will happen to the
boy." 4So Jeroboam's wife did what he
said and went to Ahijah's house in Shiloh.
Now Ahijah could not see; his sight
was gone because of his age. 5But the
LORD had told Ahijah, "Jeroboam's wife
is coming to ask you about her son, for
he is ill, and you are to give her such
and such an answer. When she arrives,
she will pretend to be someone else."
6So when Ahijah heard the sound of
her footsteps at the door, he said,
"Come in, wife of Jeroboam. Why this
pretense? I have been sent to you with
bad news. 7Go, tell Jeroboam that this
is what the LORD, the God of Israel,
says: 'I raised you up from among the
people and made you a leader[d] over
my people Israel. 8I tore[e] the kingdom
away from the house of David and gave
it to you, but you have not been like
my servant David, who kept my commands and followed me with all his
heart, doing only what was right[f] in
my eyes. 9You have done more evil
than all who lived before you. You have
made for yourself other gods, idols[g]
made of metal; you have provoked me
to anger and thrust me behind your
back.[h]
10" 'Because of this, I am going to
bring disaster on the house of Jeroboam. I will cut off from Jeroboam every
last male in Israel—slave or free.[i] I
will burn up the house of Jeroboam as
one burns dung, until it is all gone.[j]
11Dogs[k] will eat those belonging to
Jeroboam who die in the city, and the
birds of the air will feed on those who
die in the country. The LORD has spoken!'
12"As for you, go back home. When
you set foot in your city, the boy will
die. 13All Israel will mourn for him and
bury him. He is the only one belonging
to Jeroboam who will be buried, because he is the only one in the house of
Jeroboam in whom the LORD, the God
of Israel, has found anything good.[l]
14"The LORD will raise up for himself
a king over Israel who will cut off the
family of Jeroboam. This is the day!
What? Yes, even now.[a] 15And the LORD
will strike Israel, so that it will be like a
reed swaying in the water. He will uproot[m] Israel from this good land that
he gave to their forefathers and scatter
them beyond the River,[b] because they
provoked[n] the LORD to anger by making Asherah[o] poles.[c] 16And he will
give Israel up because of the sins[p] Jeroboam has committed and has caused
Israel to commit."
17Then Jeroboam's wife got up and

13:24 [s]1Ki 20:36 **13:30** [t]Jer 22:18 **13:31** [u]2Ki 23:18 **13:32** [v]ver 2; Lev 26:30 [w]1Ki 16:24,28 [x]2Ki 23:16 **13:33** [y]1Ki 12:31; 2Ch 11:15; 13:9 **13:34** [z]1Ki 12:30 [a]1Ki 14:10 **14:2** [b]1Sa 28:8; 2Sa 14:2; 1Ki 11:29 **14:3** [c]1Sa 9:7
14:7 [d]2Sa 12:7-8; 1Ki 16:2 **14:8** [e]1Ki 11:31,33, 38 [f]1Ki 15:5 **14:9** [g]Ex 34:17; 1Ki 12:28; 2Ch 11:15 [h]Ne 9:26; Ps 50:17; Eze 23:35 **14:10** [i]Dt 32:36; 1Ki 21:21; 2Ki 9:8-9; 14:26 [j]1Ki 15:29 **14:11** [k]1Ki 16:4; 21:24 **14:13** [l]2Ch 12:12; 19:3 **14:15** [m]Dt 29:28; 2Ki 15:29; 17:6; Ps 52:5 [n]Jos 23:15-16 [o]Ex 34:13; Dt 12:3 **14:16** [p]1Ki 12:30; 13:34; 15:30, 34; 16:2

a *14* The meaning of the Hebrew for this sentence is uncertain. **b** *15* That is, the Euphrates **c** *15* That is, symbols of the goddess Asherah; here and elsewhere in 1 Kings

left and went to Tirzah.[q] As soon as she stepped over the threshold of the house, the boy died. 18They buried him, and all Israel mourned for him, as the LORD had said through his servant the prophet Ahijah.

19The other events of Jeroboam's reign, his wars and how he ruled, are written in the book of the annals of the kings of Israel. 20He reigned for twenty-two years and then rested with his fathers. And Nadab his son succeeded him as king.

Rehoboam King of Judah

21Rehoboam son of Solomon was king in Judah. He was forty-one years old when he became king, and he reigned seventeen years in Jerusalem, the city the LORD had chosen out of all the tribes of Israel in which to put his Name. His mother's name was Naamah; she was an Ammonite.[r]

22Judah[s] did evil in the eyes of the LORD. By the sins they committed they stirred up his jealous anger[t] more than their fathers had done. 23They also set up for themselves high places, sacred stones[u] and Asherah poles on every high hill and under every spreading tree.[v] 24There were even male shrine prostitutes[w] in the land; the people engaged in all the detestable practices of the nations the LORD had driven out before the Israelites.

25In the fifth year of King Rehoboam, Shishak king of Egypt attacked[x] Jerusalem. 26He carried off the treasures of the temple[y] of the LORD and the treasures of the royal palace. He took everything, including all the gold shields[z] Solomon had made. 27So King Rehoboam made bronze shields to replace them and assigned these to the commanders of the guard on duty at the entrance to the royal palace. 28Whenever the king went to the LORD's temple, the guards bore the shields, and afterward they returned them to the guardroom.

29As for the other events of Rehoboam's reign, and all he did, are they not written in the book of the annals of the kings of Judah? 30There was continual warfare[a] between Rehoboam and Jeroboam. 31And Rehoboam rested with his fathers and was buried with them in the City of David. His mother's name was Naamah; she was an Ammonite.[b] And Abijah[a] his son succeeded him as king.

Abijah King of Judah

15 In the eighteenth year of the reign of Jeroboam son of Nebat, Abijah[b] became king of Judah, 2and he reigned in Jerusalem three years. His mother's name was Maacah[c] daughter of Abishalom.[c]

3He committed all the sins his father had done before him; his heart was not fully devoted[d] to the LORD his God, as the heart of David his forefather had been. 4Nevertheless, for David's sake the LORD his God gave him a lamp[e] in Jerusalem by raising up a son to succeed him and by making Jerusalem strong. 5For David had done what was right in the eyes of the LORD and had not failed to keep[f] any of the LORD's commands all the days of his life—except in the case of Uriah[g] the Hittite.

6There was war[h] between Rehoboam[d] and Jeroboam throughout ⌞Abijah's⌟ lifetime. 7As for the other events of Abijah's reign, and all he did, are they not written in the book of the annals of the kings of Judah? There was war between Abijah and Jeroboam. 8And Abijah rested with his fathers and was buried in the City of David. And Asa his son succeeded him as king.

Asa King of Judah

9In the twentieth year of Jeroboam king of Israel, Asa became king of Judah, 10and he reigned in Jerusalem forty-one years. His grandmother's name was Maacah[i] daughter of Abishalom.

11Asa did what was right in the eyes of the LORD, as his father David had done. 12He expelled the male shrine prostitutes[j] from the land and got rid of all the idols his fathers had made. 13He even deposed his grandmother Maacah from her position as queen mother, because she had made a repulsive Asherah pole. Asa cut the pole down[k] and burned it in the Kidron Valley. 14Although he did not remove the high places, Asa's heart was fully committed[l] to the LORD all his life. 15He brought into the temple of the LORD the silver and gold and the articles that he and his father had dedicated.[m]

16There was war[n] between Asa and Baasha king of Israel throughout their reigns. 17Baasha king of Israel went up against Judah and fortified Ramah[o] to

14:17 [q]ver 12; 1Ki 15:33; 16:6-9
14:21 [r]ver 31; 1Ki 11:1; 2Ch 12:13
14:22 [s]2Ch 12:1 [t]Dt 32:21; Ps 78:58; 1Co 10:22
14:23 [u]Dt 16:22; 2Ki 17:9-10; Eze 16:24-25 [v]Dt 12:2; Isa 57:5
14:24 [w]Dt 23:17; 1Ki 15:12; 2Ki 23:7
14:25 [x]1Ki 11:40; 2Ch 12:2
14:26 [y]1Ki 15:15,18 [z]1Ki 10:17
14:30 [a]1Ki 12:21; 15:6
14:31 [b]ver 21; 2Ch 12:16
15:2 [c]2Ch 11:20; 13:2
15:3 [d]1Ki 11:4; Ps 119:80
15:4 [e]2Sa 21:17; 1Ki 11:36; 2Ch 21:7
15:5 [f]1Ki 9:4; 14:8 [g]2Sa 11:2-27; 12:9
15:6 [h]1Ki 14:30
15:10 [i]ver 2
15:12 [j]1Ki 14:24; 22:46
15:13 [k]Ex 32:20
15:14 [l]ver 3; 1Ki 8:61; 22:43
15:15 [m]1Ki 7:51
15:16 [n]ver 32
15:17 [o]Jos 18:25; 1Ki 12:27

[a] *31* Some Hebrew manuscripts and Septuagint (see also 2 Chron. 12:16); most Hebrew manuscripts *Abijam* [b] *1* Some Hebrew manuscripts and Septuagint (see also 2 Chron. 12:16); most Hebrew manuscripts *Abijam*; also in verses 7 and 8 [c] *2* A variant of *Absalom*; also in verse 10 [d] *6* Most Hebrew manuscripts; some Hebrew manuscripts and Syriac *Abijam* (that is, Abijah)

prevent anyone from leaving or entering the territory of Asa king of Judah.
18 Asa then took all the silver and
gold that was left in the treasuries of
the LORD's temple[p] and of his own
palace. He entrusted it to his officials
and sent[q] them to Ben-Hadad[r] son
of Tabrimmon, the son of Hezion, the
king of Aram, who was ruling in Damascus. 19 "Let there be a treaty between me and you," he said, "as there
was between my father and your father. See, I am sending you a gift of
silver and gold. Now break your treaty
with Baasha king of Israel so he will
withdraw from me."
20 Ben-Hadad agreed with King Asa
and sent the commanders of his forces
against the towns of Israel. He conquered[s] Ijon, Dan, Abel Beth Maacah
and all Kinnereth in addition to Naphtali. 21 When Baasha heard this, he
stopped building Ramah and withdrew to Tirzah. 22 Then King Asa issued
an order to all Judah—no one was
exempt—and they carried away from
Ramah the stones and timber Baasha
had been using there. With them King
Asa built up Geba[t] in Benjamin, and
also Mizpah.
23 As for all the other events of Asa's
reign, all his achievements, all he did
and the cities he built, are they not
written in the book of the annals of the
kings of Judah? In his old age, however,
his feet became diseased. 24 Then Asa
rested with his fathers and was buried
with them in the city of his father David. And Jehoshaphat[u] his son succeeded him as king.

Nadab King of Israel

25 Nadab son of Jeroboam became
king of Israel in the second year of Asa
king of Judah, and he reigned over Israel two years. 26 He did evil in the eyes of
the LORD, walking in the ways of his
father[v] and in his sin, which he had
caused Israel to commit.
27 Baasha son of Ahijah of the house
of Issachar plotted against him, and he
struck him down[w] at Gibbethon,[x] a
Philistine town, while Nadab and all Israel were besieging it. 28 Baasha killed
Nadab in the third year of Asa king of
Judah and succeeded him as king.
29 As soon as he began to reign, he
killed Jeroboam's whole family.[y] He
did not leave Jeroboam anyone that
breathed, but destroyed them all, according to the word of the LORD given
through his servant Ahijah the
Shilonite— 30 because of the sins[z] Jeroboam had committed and had caused
Israel to commit, and because he pro-

15:18 [p] ver 15; 1Ki 14:26 [q] 2Ki 12:18 [r] 1Ki 11:23-24
15:20 [s] Jdg 18:29; 2Sa 20:14; 2Ki 15:29
15:22 [t] Jos 18:24; 21:17
15:24 [u] Mt 1:8
15:26 [v] 1Ki 12:30; 14:16
15:27 [w] 1Ki 14:14 [x] Jos 19:44; 21:23
15:29 [y] 1Ki 14:10,14
15:30 [z] 1Ki 14:9,16
15:32 [a] ver 16
15:34 [b] ver 26; 1Ki 12:28-29; 13:33; 14:16
16:1 [c] ver 7; 2Ch 19:2; 20:34 [d] 2Ch 16:7
16:2 [e] 1Sa 2:8 [f] 1Ki 14:7-9 [g] 1Ki 15:34
16:3 [h] ver 11; 1Ki 14:10; 15:29; 21:22
16:4 [i] 1Ki 14:11
16:5 [j] 1Ki 14:19; 15:31
16:6 [k] 1Ki 14:17; 15:33
16:7 [l] 1Ki 15:27,29 [m] ver 1
16:9 [n] 2Ki 9:30-33 [o] 1Ki 18:3
16:11 [p] ver 3

voked the LORD, the God of Israel, to
anger.
31 As for the other events of Nadab's
reign, and all he did, are they not written in the book of the annals of the
kings of Israel? 32 There was war[a] between Asa and Baasha king of Israel
throughout their reigns.

Baasha King of Israel

33 In the third year of Asa king of Judah, Baasha son of Ahijah became king
of all Israel in Tirzah, and he reigned
twenty-four years. 34 He did evil[b] in
the eyes of the LORD, walking in the
ways of Jeroboam and in his sin, which
he had caused Israel to commit.
16 Then the word of the LORD came to
Jehu[c] son of Hanani[d] against Baasha: 2 "I lifted you up from the dust[e]
and made you leader[f] of my people
Israel, but you walked in the ways of
Jeroboam and caused[g] my people Israel to sin and to provoke me to anger
by their sins. 3 So I am about to consume Baasha and his house,[h] and I
will make your house like that of Jeroboam son of Nebat. 4 Dogs[i] will eat
those belonging to Baasha who die in
the city, and the birds of the air will
feed on those who die in the country."
5 As for the other events of Baasha's
reign, what he did and his achievements, are they not written in the book
of the annals[j] of the kings of Israel?
6 Baasha rested with his fathers and was
buried in Tirzah.[k] And Elah his son
succeeded him as king.
7 Moreover, the word of the LORD
came[l] through the prophet Jehu[m]
son of Hanani to Baasha and his house,
because of all the evil he had done in
the eyes of the LORD, provoking him to
anger by the things he did, and becoming like the house of Jeroboam—and
also because he destroyed it.

Elah King of Israel

8 In the twenty-sixth year of Asa king
of Judah, Elah son of Baasha became
king of Israel, and he reigned in Tirzah
two years.
9 Zimri, one of his officials, who had
command of half his chariots, plotted
against him. Elah was in Tirzah at the
time, getting drunk[n] in the home of
Arza, the man in charge[o] of the palace
at Tirzah. 10 Zimri came in, struck him
down and killed him in the twenty-
seventh year of Asa king of Judah. Then
he succeeded him as king.
11 As soon as he began to reign and
was seated on the throne, he killed off
Baasha's whole family.[p] He did not
spare a single male, whether relative or

friend. 12So Zimri destroyed the whole
family of Baasha, in accordance with
the word of the LORD spoken against
Baasha through the prophet Jehu—
13because of all the sins Baasha and
his son Elah had committed and had
caused Israel to commit, so that they
provoked the LORD, the God of Israel,
to anger by their worthless idols.[q]
14As for the other events of Elah's
reign, and all he did, are they not written in the book of the annals of the
kings of Israel?

Zimri King of Israel

15In the twenty-seventh year of Asa
king of Judah, Zimri reigned in Tirzah
seven days. The army was encamped
near Gibbethon,[r] a Philistine town.
16When the Israelites in the camp
heard that Zimri had plotted against
the king and murdered him, they proclaimed Omri, the commander of the
army, king over Israel that very day
there in the camp. 17Then Omri and all
the Israelites with him withdrew from
Gibbethon and laid siege to Tirzah.
18When Zimri saw that the city was tak-
en, he went into the citadel of the royal
palace and set the palace on fire
around him. So he died, 19because of
the sins he had committed, doing evil
in the eyes of the LORD and walking in
the ways of Jeroboam and in the sin he
had committed and had caused Israel
to commit.
20As for the other events of Zimri's
reign, and the rebellion he carried out,
are they not written in the book of the
annals of the kings of Israel?

Omri King of Israel

21Then the people of Israel were split
into two factions; half supported Tibni
son of Ginath for king, and the other
half supported Omri. 22But Omri's followers proved stronger than those of
Tibni son of Ginath. So Tibni died and
Omri became king.
23In the thirty-first year of Asa king
of Judah, Omri became king of Israel,
and he reigned twelve years, six of
them in Tirzah.[s] 24He bought the hill
of Samaria from Shemer for two talents[a] of silver and built a city on the
hill, calling it Samaria,[t] after Shemer,
the name of the former owner of the
hill.
25But Omri did evil[u] in the eyes of
the LORD and sinned more than all
those before him. 26He walked in all
the ways of Jeroboam son of Nebat and
in his sin, which he had caused[v] Israel
to commit, so that they provoked the
LORD, the God of Israel, to anger by
their worthless idols.[w]
27As for the other events of Omri's
reign, what he did and the things he
achieved, are they not written in the
book of the annals of the kings of Israel? 28Omri rested with his fathers and
was buried in Samaria. And Ahab his
son succeeded him as king.

Ahab Becomes King of Israel

29In the thirty-eighth year of Asa
king of Judah, Ahab son of Omri became king of Israel, and he reigned in
Samaria over Israel twenty-two years.
30Ahab son of Omri did more[x] evil in
the eyes of the LORD than any of those
before him. 31He not only considered it
trivial to commit the sins of Jeroboam
son of Nebat, but he also married[y]
Jezebel daughter[z] of Ethbaal king of
the Sidonians, and began to serve
Baal[a] and worship him. 32He set up an
altar for Baal in the temple[b] of Baal
that he built in Samaria. 33Ahab also
made an Asherah pole[c] and did
more[d] to provoke the LORD, the God of
Israel, to anger than did all the kings of
Israel before him.
34In Ahab's time, Hiel of Bethel rebuilt Jericho. He laid its foundations at
the cost of his firstborn son Abiram,
and he set up its gates at the cost of his
youngest son Segub, in accordance
with the word of the LORD spoken by
Joshua son of Nun.[e]

Elijah Fed by Ravens

17 Now Elijah[f] the Tishbite, from
Tishbe[b] in Gilead,[g] said to Ahab,
"As the LORD, the God of Israel, lives,
whom I serve, there will be neither dew
nor rain[h] in the next few years except
at my word."
2Then the word of the LORD came to
Elijah: 3"Leave here, turn eastward and
hide in the Kerith Ravine, east of the
Jordan. 4You will drink from the brook,
and I have ordered the ravens[i] to feed
you there."
5So he did what the LORD had told
him. He went to the Kerith Ravine, east
of the Jordan, and stayed there. 6The
ravens brought him bread and meat in
the morning[j] and bread and meat in
the evening, and he drank from the
brook.

The Widow at Zarephath

7Some time later the brook dried up
because there had been no rain in the
land. 8Then the word of the LORD came

16:13 [q]Dt 32:21; 1Sa 12:21; Isa 41:29
16:15 [r]Jos 19:44; 1Ki 15:27
16:23 [s]1Ki 15:21
16:24 [t]1Ki 13:32; Jn 4:4
16:25 [u]Dt 4:25; Mic 6:16
16:26 [v]ver 19 [w]Dt 32:21
16:30 [x]ver 25; 1Ki 14:9
16:31 [y]Dt 7:3; 1Ki 11:2 [z]Jdg 18:7; 2Ki 9:34 [a]2Ki 10:18; 17:16
16:32 [b]2Ki 10:21,27; 11:18
16:33 [c]2Ki 13:6 [d]ver 29,30; 1Ki 14:9; 21:25
16:34 [e]Jos 6:26
17:1 [f]Mal 4:5; Jas 5:17 [g]Jdg 12:4 [h]Dt 10:8; 1Ki 18:1; 2Ki 3:14; Lk 4:25
17:4 [i]Ge 8:7
17:6 [j]Ex 16:8

[a]*24* That is, about 150 pounds (about 70 kilograms) [b]*1* Or *Tishbite, of the settlers*

to him: 9"Go at once to Zarephath[k] of Sidon and stay there. I have commanded a widow[l] in that place to supply you with food." 10So he went to Zarephath. When he came to the town gate, a widow was there gathering sticks. He called to her and asked, "Would you bring me a little water in a jar so I may have a drink?"[m] 11As she was going to get it, he called, "And bring me, please, a piece of bread."

5 →PG. 404

12"As surely as the LORD your God lives," she replied, "I don't have any bread—only a handful of flour in a jar and a little oil[n] in a jug. I am gathering a few sticks to take home and make a meal for myself and my son, that we may eat it—and die."

13Elijah said to her, "Don't be afraid. Go home and do as you have said. But first make a small cake of bread for me from what you have and bring it to me, and then make something for yourself and your son. 14For this is what the LORD, the God of Israel, says: 'The jar of flour will not be used up and the jug of oil will not run dry until the day the LORD gives rain on the land.' "

15She went away and did as Elijah had told her. So there was food every day for Elijah and for the woman and her family. 16For the jar of flour was not used up and the jug of oil did not run dry, in keeping with the word of the LORD spoken by Elijah.

17Some time later the son of the woman who owned the house became ill. He grew worse and worse, and finally stopped breathing. 18She said to Elijah, "What do you have against me, man of God? Did you come to remind me of my sin[o] and kill my son?"

19"Give me your son," Elijah replied. He took him from her arms, carried him to the upper room where he was staying, and laid him on his bed. 20Then he cried out to the LORD, "O LORD my God, have you brought tragedy also upon this widow I am staying with, by causing her son to die?" 21Then he stretched[p] himself out on the boy three times and cried to the LORD, "O LORD my God, let this boy's life return to him!"

22The LORD heard Elijah's cry, and the boy's life returned to him, and he lived. 23Elijah picked up the child and carried him down from the room into the house. He gave him to his mother and said, "Look, your son is alive!"

24Then the woman said to Elijah, "Now I know[q] that you are a man of God and that the word of the LORD from your mouth is the truth."[r]

Elijah and Obadiah

18 After a long time, in the third[s] year, the word of the LORD came to Elijah: "Go and present yourself to Ahab, and I will send rain[t] on the land." 2So Elijah went to present himself to Ahab.

Now the famine was severe in Samaria, 3and Ahab had summoned Obadiah, who was in charge[u] of his palace. (Obadiah was a devout believer[v] in the LORD. 4While Jezebel[w] was killing off the LORD's prophets, Obadiah had taken a hundred prophets and hidden[x] them in two caves, fifty in each, and had supplied them with food and water.) 5Ahab had said to Obadiah, "Go through the land to all the springs and valleys. Maybe we can find some grass to keep the horses and mules alive so we will not have to kill any of our animals." 6So they divided the land they were to cover, Ahab going in one direction and Obadiah in another.

7As Obadiah was walking along, Elijah met him. Obadiah recognized[y] him, bowed down to the ground, and said, "Is it really you, my lord Elijah?"

8"Yes," he replied. "Go tell your master, 'Elijah is here.' "

9"What have I done wrong," asked Obadiah, "that you are handing your servant over to Ahab to be put to death? 10As surely as the LORD your God lives, there is not a nation or kingdom where my master has not sent someone to look[z] for you. And whenever a nation or kingdom claimed you were not there, he made them swear they could not find you. 11But now you tell me to go to my master and say, 'Elijah is here.' 12I don't know where the Spirit[a] of the LORD may carry you when I leave you. If I go and tell Ahab and he doesn't find you, he will kill me. Yet I your servant have worshiped the LORD since my youth. 13Haven't you heard, my lord, what I did while Jezebel was killing the prophets of the LORD? I hid a hundred of the LORD's prophets in two caves, fifty in each, and supplied them with food and water. 14And now you tell me to go to my master and say, 'Elijah is here.' He will kill me!"

15Elijah said, "As the LORD Almighty lives, whom I serve, I will surely present[b] myself to Ahab today."

Elijah on Mount Carmel

16So Obadiah went to meet Ahab and told him, and Ahab went to meet Elijah. 17When he saw Elijah, he said to him, "Is that you, you troubler[c] of Israel?"

18"I have not made trouble for Isra-

17:9 [k]Ob 1:20 [l]Lk 4:26
17:10 [m]Ge 24:17; Jn 4:7
17:12 [n]ver 1; 2Ki 4:2
17:18 [o]2Ki 3:13; Lk 5:8
17:21 [p]2Ki 4:34; Ac 20:10
17:24 [q]Jn 3:2; 16:30 [r]Ps 119:43; Jn 17:17

18:1 [s]1Ki 17:1; Lk 4:25; Jas 5:17 [t]Dt 28:12
18:3 [u]1Ki 16:9 [v]Ne 7:2
18:4 [w]2Ki 9:7 [x]ver 13; Isa 16:3
18:7 [y]2Ki 1:8
18:10 [z]1Ki 17:3
18:12 [a]2Ki 2:16; Eze 3:14; Ac 8:39
18:15 [b]1Ki 17:1
18:17 [c]Jos 7:25; 1Ki 21:20; Ac 16:20

OBADIAH

A Man of Integrity

When the Port Authority of New York ran a help-wanted ad throughout the New York and New Jersey areas for electricians with expertise at using Sontag connectors, it received 170 responses. This wouldn't be all that unusual, were it not for the fact that there is no such thing as a Sontag connector! The Port Authority merely ran the ad to determine how many applicants would deliberately falsify their resumes.

All too often our society overlooks dishonesty when it will guarantee success. It can be difficult, in today's culture, to be a godly man and a successful businessman. God's ethics conflict with the world's lack of morals, creating tension that's hard to handle in a Biblical fashion.

Obadiah's life illustrates, however, that it *is* possible to be a godly man, a man of integrity, in the midst of the worst kind of environment. As an assistant to an evil king, Obadiah maintained his integrity not only through personal wisdom, but also through God's guidance and protection.

Godly Living in a Pagan World

After several years of drought in Israel, God sent the prophet Elijah to meet King Ahab. While Elijah was on the way there, he met Obadiah, who was on an errand for the king, searching for water. Obadiah was in charge of King Ahab's palace. He was a highly trusted official. But more importantly, the Bible tells us, Obadiah was "a devout believer in the LORD" (1 Kings 18:3).

How could devout Obadiah be in such a strategic position, faithfully serving a king who was promoting the worst kind of pagan idolatry? How was it possible for this man to maintain Ahab's trust and yet not violate his love for God?

Secret Agent

God had a purpose for keeping Obadiah in such a position—Obadiah was an "undercover agent" for God. While Ahab's queen, Jezebel, "was killing the prophets of the LORD," Obadiah was busy protecting the ones he could (18:13). He had taken a hundred prophets, hidden them in two caves, and kept them supplied with food and water all during the famine and drought (18:13). This was no small task. Obadiah's life hung in the balance every second of every day. If someone in Ahab's court had discovered the hidden prophets and turned Obadiah in for treason, this godly man would have certainly and instantly been put to death.

This was no game; this was a pitched battle against evil. And certainly, no one knew the danger more personally than Obadiah. He made his choice deliberately, with full knowledge of the risk he was taking. Obeying the Lord was more important to him than anything else—including life itself.

Godly Men in a Secular World

Obadiah's life demonstrates that God uses godly men who are in key positions in a secular society to accomplish his purposes. This is why we are here to begin with. God wants to communicate to a sinful world his message of redemption, and we are the means he uses to share that message.

But we don't have to be in upper-level corporate management, or the top echelons of the government as was Obadiah, to do God's work in the world. Every godly man who rubs shoulders with a non-Christian man is in a crucial strategic position. Our greatest influence may not be through speeches about ethics and morality, but rather through personal contact with people. Through interpersonal relationships we can reflect our beliefs, our eternal hope for the future, and our love for God and one another. We can demonstrate our morality and integrity by the way we live our lives, leaving a lasting impression that can be more powerful than anything words could say.

This isn't always easy. We may face difficult decisions that place us in danger of losing favor with our superiors. We may encounter enemies to our value system, just as Obadiah did. There will be a price to pay to stand for integrity in a hostile environment. But if that happens, we can trust God to honor our faith.

So, where are you? In what strategic position has God placed you? What does he want you to accomplish there? Will you make a new commitment to be God's man wherever he has placed you, whatever the cost? Obadiah made that choice. He was determined to serve God while working in Ahab's palace. If you make the same commitment, God will begin to unfold a personal strategy for you. And you never know what great things he's waiting to do through a man of integrity—a modern day Obadiah—like you.

—Dr. Gene Getz

el," Elijah replied. "But you[d] and your
father's family have. You have abandoned[e] the LORD's commands and
have followed the Baals. 19Now summon the people from all over Israel to
meet me on Mount Carmel.[f] And
bring the four hundred and fifty prophets of Baal and the four hundred
prophets of Asherah, who eat at Jezebel's table."
20So Ahab sent word throughout all
Israel and assembled the prophets on
Mount Carmel. 21Elijah went before
the people and said, "How long will
you waver[g] between two opinions? If
the LORD is God, follow him; but if Baal
is God, follow him."
But the people said nothing.
22Then Elijah said to them, "I am the
only one of the LORD's prophets left,[h]
but Baal has four hundred and fifty
prophets.[i] 23Get two bulls for us. Let
them choose one for themselves, and
let them cut it into pieces and put it on
the wood but not set fire to it. I will
prepare the other bull and put it on the
wood but not set fire to it. 24Then you
call on the name of your god, and I will
call on the name of the LORD. The god
who answers by fire[j]—he is God."
Then all the people said, "What you
say is good."
25Elijah said to the prophets of Baal,
"Choose one of the bulls and prepare it
first, since there are so many of you.
Call on the name of your god, but do
not light the fire." 26So they took the
bull given them and prepared it.
Then they called on the name of
Baal from morning till noon. "O Baal,
answer us!" they shouted. But there
was no response;[k] no one answered.
And they danced around the altar they
had made.
27At noon Elijah began to taunt
them. "Shout louder!" he said. "Surely
he is a god! Perhaps he is deep in
thought, or busy, or traveling. Maybe
he is sleeping and must be awakened."[l] 28So they shouted louder and
slashed[m] themselves with swords and
spears, as was their custom, until their
blood flowed. 29Midday passed, and
they continued their frantic prophesying until the time for the evening sacrifice.[n] But there was no response, no
one answered, no one paid attention.[o]
30Then Elijah said to all the people,
"Come here to me." They came to him,
and he repaired the altar[p] of the LORD,
which was in ruins. 31Elijah took twelve
stones, one for each of the tribes descended from Jacob, to whom the word
of the LORD had come, saying, "Your
name shall be Israel."[q] 32With the
stones he built an altar in the name[r]
of the LORD, and he dug a trench
around it large enough to hold two
seahs[a] of seed. 33He arranged[s] the
wood, cut the bull into pieces and laid
it on the wood. Then he said to them,
"Fill four large jars with water and pour
it on the offering and on the wood."
34"Do it again," he said, and they did
it again.
"Do it a third time," he ordered, and
they did it the third time. 35The water
ran down around the altar and even
filled the trench.
36At the time of sacrifice, the prophet Elijah stepped forward and prayed:
"O LORD, God of Abraham,[t] Isaac and
Israel, let it be known[u] today that you
are God in Israel and that I am your
servant and have done all these things
at your command.[v] 37Answer me,
O LORD, answer me, so these people
will know that you, O LORD, are God,
and that you are turning their hearts
back again."
38Then the fire[w] of the LORD fell and
burned up the sacrifice, the wood, the
stones and the soil, and also licked up
the water in the trench.
39When all the people saw this, they
fell prostrate and cried, "The LORD—he
is God! The LORD—he is God!"[x]
40Then Elijah commanded them,
"Seize the prophets of Baal. Don't let
anyone get away!" They seized them,
and Elijah had them brought down to
the Kishon Valley[y] and slaughtered[z]
there.
41And Elijah said to Ahab, "Go, eat
and drink, for there is the sound of a
heavy rain." 42So Ahab went off to eat
and drink, but Elijah climbed to the top
of Carmel, bent down to the ground
and put his face between his knees.[a]
43"Go and look toward the sea," he
told his servant. And he went up and
looked.
"There is nothing there," he said.
Seven times Elijah said, "Go back."
44The seventh time the servant reported, "A cloud[b] as small as a man's
hand is rising from the sea."
So Elijah said, "Go and tell Ahab,
'Hitch up your chariot and go down
before the rain stops you.' "
45Meanwhile, the sky grew black
with clouds, the wind rose, a heavy rain
came on and Ahab rode off to Jezreel.
46The power[c] of the LORD came upon
Elijah and, tucking his cloak into his
belt,[d] he ran ahead of Ahab all the way
to Jezreel.

18:18 [d]1Ki 16:31,33; 21:25 [e]2Ch 15:2
18:19 [f]Jos 19:26
18:21 [g]Jos 24:15; 2Ki 17:41; Mt 6:24
18:22 [h]1Ki 19:10 [i]ver 19
18:24 [j]ver 38; 1Ch 21:26
18:26 [k]Ps 115:4-5; Jer 10:5; 1Co 8:4; 12:2
18:27 [l]Hab 2:19
18:28 [m]Lev 19:28; Dt 14:1
18:29 [n]Ex 29:41 [o]ver 26
18:30 [p]1Ki 19:10
18:31 [q]Ge 32:28; 35:10; 2Ki 17:34
18:32 [r]Col 3:17
18:33 [s]Ge 22:9; Lev 1:6-8
18:36 [t]Ex 3:6; Mt 22:32 [u]1Ki 8:43; 2Ki 19:19 [v]Nu 16:28
18:38 [w]Lev 9:24; Jdg 6:21; 1Ch 21:26; 2Ch 7:1; Job 1:16
18:39 [x]ver 24
18:40 [y]Jdg 4:7 [z]Dt 13:5; 18:20; 2Ki 10:24-25
18:42 [a]ver 19-20; Jas 5:18
18:44 [b]Lk 12:54
18:46 [c]2Ki 3:15 [d]2Ki 4:29; 9:1

[a]32 That is, probably about 13 quarts (about 15 liters)

Elijah Flees to Horeb

19 Now Ahab told Jezebel everything Elijah had done and how he had killed[e] all the prophets with the sword. 2So Jezebel sent a messenger to Elijah to say, "May the gods deal with me, be it ever so severely,[f] if by this time tomorrow I do not make your life like that of one of them."

3Elijah was afraid[a] and ran[g] for his life. When he came to Beersheba in Judah, he left his servant there, 4while he himself went a day's journey into the desert. He came to a broom tree, sat down under it and prayed that he might die. "I have had enough, LORD," he said. "Take my life;[h] I am no better than my ancestors." 5Then he lay down under the tree and fell asleep.[i]

All at once an angel touched him and said, "Get up and eat." 6He looked around, and there by his head was a cake of bread baked over hot coals, and a jar of water. He ate and drank and then lay down again.

7The angel of the LORD came back a second time and touched him and said, "Get up and eat, for the journey is too much for you." 8So he got up and ate and drank. Strengthened by that food, he traveled forty[j] days and forty nights until he reached Horeb,[k] the mountain of God. 9There he went into a cave[l] and spent the night.

The LORD Appears to Elijah

And the word of the LORD came to him: "What are you doing here, Elijah?"

10He replied, "I have been very zealous[m] for the LORD God Almighty. The Israelites have rejected your covenant, broken down your altars, and put your prophets to death with the sword. I am the only one left,[n] and now they are trying to kill me too."

11The LORD said, "Go out and stand on the mountain[o] in the presence of the LORD, for the LORD is about to pass by."

Then a great and powerful wind[p] tore the mountains apart and shattered the rocks before the LORD, but the LORD was not in the wind. After the wind there was an earthquake, but the LORD

19:1 [e]1Ki 18:40
19:2 [f]1Ki 20:10; 2Ki 6:31; Ru 1:17
19:3 [g]Ge 31:21
19:4 [h]Nu 11:15; Jer 20:18; Jnh 4:8
19:5 [i]Ge 28:11
19:8 [j]Ex 24:18; 34:28; Dt 9:9-11,18; Mt 4:2 [k]Ex 3:1
19:9 [l]Ex 33:22
19:10 [m]Nu 25:13 [n]1Ki 18:4,22; Ro 11:3*
19:11 [o]Ex 24:12 [p]Eze 1:4; 37:7

[a]3 Or *Elijah saw*

19:1–18

PROMISE 2

GOD ENCOURAGES A DISCOURAGED SERVANT

God worked miracles through Elijah to defeat the false prophets of Baal and embarrass their sponsor, Jezebel (18:16–45). In 19:1–10, the other side of Elijah emerged. He went from being a man who performed a great public miracle to one who ran from godless Queen Jezebel. He went from the man who took the lives of the prophets of Baal to one who asked God to take his own life (19:3–5). He went from faith to fear, from courage to cowardice, from energy to exhaustion. The great prophet was, after all, human.

How did God react to his servant? God fed him (vv. 5–8) and listened to Elijah as he poured out his frustration and anxiety (vv. 9–10). God ministered to him; notice how. Elijah's response to fear and exhaustion was isolation. He ran to Beersheba, left his servant there, and then went into the desert. After God fed him and gave him a chance to rest, Elijah went even further away, found a cave, went in, and fell asleep. God then spoke to Elijah. Notice God's use of questions in verse 9 and again in verse 13. God didn't ask Elijah these questions because he didn't have the answers. He asked them because Elijah didn't have the answers, and he needed to find them.

Elijah felt afraid because he felt alone. He had seen God's power demonstrated in the battle with the priests of Baal. He had experienced God's provision of food and rest and shelter. But at this point in his life, the prophet needed God's presence more than his power. He needed to feel God working in a deeply personal way. How did God address Elijah's need for comfort? He didn't show himself in the powerful wind, or the great earthquake, or the roaring fire. God ministered to his prophet in the whispered voice, "What are you doing here, Elijah?" Again the prophet poured out his fear and frustration, but this time God's response assured Elijah that he was not alone, as he had feared. God said that there were 7000 people in Israel who still served and feared him.

God knew that Elijah needed a friend. He needed a compatriot to share his load, listen to him and encourage him. Notice how simply the text states that Elisha followed Elijah and became his attendant in ministry (vv. 19–21). These men were a team until Elijah was taken into heaven. At that time Elisha, under Elijah's mentoring ministry, was preparing to become the next great prophet. But, really, who ministered to whom?

Remember why God instructed Elijah to anoint Elisha. It's a dangerous thing to find yourself alone. Elijah, the great prophet, the man who worked miracles and who saw God's power firsthand, needed to hear God in a whispered voice. He needed another godly man to encourage and support him. Elisha was God's answer to the great prophet's need. It's part of God's answer to any Christian man. If the great Elijah needed a friend in his life, that's a pretty good indication that we do too.

For the next Promise 2 reading go to page 479.

was not in the earthquake. 12After the earthquake came a fire, but the LORD was not in the fire. And after the fire came a gentle whisper.[q] 13When Elijah heard it, he pulled his cloak over his face[r] and went out and stood at the mouth of the cave.

Then a voice said to him, "What are you doing here, Elijah?"

14He replied, "I have been very zealous for the LORD God Almighty. The Israelites have rejected your covenant, broken down your altars, and put your prophets to death with the sword. I am the only one left,[s] and now they are trying to kill me too."

15The LORD said to him, "Go back the way you came, and go to the Desert of Damascus. When you get there, anoint Hazael[t] king over Aram. 16Also, anoint[u] Jehu son of Nimshi king over Israel, and anoint Elisha[v] son of Shaphat from Abel Meholah to succeed you as prophet. 17Jehu will put to death any who escape the sword of Hazael,[w] and Elisha will put to death any who escape the sword of Jehu. 18Yet I reserve[x] seven thousand in Israel—all whose knees have not bowed down to Baal and all whose mouths have not kissed[y] him."

The Call of Elisha

2 →PG. 399

19So Elijah went from there and found Elisha son of Shaphat. He was plowing with twelve yoke of oxen, and he himself was driving the twelfth pair. Elijah went up to him and threw his cloak[z] around him. 20Elisha then left his oxen and ran after Elijah. "Let me kiss my father and mother good-by,"[a] he said, "and then I will come with you."

"Go back," Elijah replied. "What have I done to you?"

21So Elisha left him and went back. He took his yoke of oxen[b] and slaughtered them. He burned the plowing equipment to cook the meat and gave it to the people, and they ate. Then he set out to follow Elijah and became his attendant.[c]

Ben-Hadad Attacks Samaria

20 Now Ben-Hadad[d] king of Aram mustered his entire army. Accompanied by thirty-two kings with their horses and chariots, he went up and besieged Samaria and attacked it. 2He sent messengers into the city to Ahab king of Israel, saying, "This is what Ben-Hadad says: 3'Your silver and gold are mine, and the best of your wives and children are mine.' "

4The king of Israel answered, "Just as you say, my lord the king. I and all I have are yours."

5The messengers came again and said, "This is what Ben-Hadad says: 'I sent to demand your silver and gold, your wives and your children. 6But about this time tomorrow I am going to send my officials to search your palace and the houses of your officials. They will seize everything you value and carry it away.' "

7The king of Israel summoned all the elders of the land and said to them, "See how this man is looking for trouble![e] When he sent for my wives and my children, my silver and my gold, I did not refuse him."

8The elders and the people all answered, "Don't listen to him or agree to his demands."

9So he replied to Ben-Hadad's messengers, "Tell my lord the king, 'Your servant will do all you demanded the first time, but this demand I cannot meet.' " They left and took the answer back to Ben-Hadad.

10Then Ben-Hadad sent another message to Ahab: "May the gods deal with me, be it ever so severely, if enough dust[f] remains in Samaria to give each of my men a handful."

11The king of Israel answered, "Tell him: 'One who puts on his armor should not boast[g] like one who takes it off.' "

12Ben-Hadad heard this message while he and the kings were drinking[h] in their tents,[a] and he ordered his men: "Prepare to attack." So they prepared to attack the city.

Ahab Defeats Ben-Hadad

13Meanwhile a prophet came to Ahab king of Israel and announced, "This is what the LORD says: 'Do you see this vast army? I will give it into your hand today, and then you will know[i] that I am the LORD.' "

14"But who will do this?" asked Ahab.

The prophet replied, "This is what the LORD says: 'The young officers of the provincial commanders will do it.' "

"And who will start[j] the battle?" he asked.

The prophet answered, "You will."

15So Ahab summoned the young officers of the provincial commanders, 232 men. Then he assembled the rest of the Israelites, 7,000 in all. 16They set out at noon while Ben-Hadad and the 32 kings allied with him were in their

19:12 [q] Job 4:16; Zec 4:6
19:13 [r] ver 9; Ex 3:6
19:14 [s] ver 10
19:15 [t] 2Ki 8:7-15
19:16 [u] 2Ki 9:1-3,6 [v] ver 21; 2Ki 2:9,15
19:17 [w] 2Ki 8:12,29; 9:14; 13:3,7,22
19:18 [x] Ro 11:4* [y] Hos 13:2
19:19 [z] 2Ki 2:8,14
19:20 [a] Mt 8:21-22; Lk 9:61
19:21 [b] 2Sa 24:22 [c] ver 16
20:1 [d] 1Ki 15:18; 22:31; 2Ki 6:24
20:7 [e] 2Ki 5:7
20:10 [f] 2Sa 22:43; 1Ki 19:2
20:11 [g] Pr 27:1; Jer 9:23
20:12 [h] ver 16; 1Ki 16:9
20:13 [i] ver 28; Ex 6:7
20:14 [j] Jdg 1:1

[a] 12 Or *in Succoth*; also in verse 16

tents getting drunk.[k] 17The young officers of the provincial commanders
went out first.
Now Ben-Hadad had dispatched
scouts, who reported, "Men are advancing from Samaria."
18He said, "If they have come out for
peace, take them alive; if they have
come out for war, take them alive."
19The young officers of the provincial commanders marched out of the
city with the army behind them 20and
each one struck down his opponent. At
that, the Arameans fled, with the Israelites in pursuit. But Ben-Hadad king
of Aram escaped on horseback with
some of his horsemen. 21The king of
Israel advanced and overpowered the
horses and chariots and inflicted heavy
losses on the Arameans.
22Afterward, the prophet[l] came to
the king of Israel and said, "Strengthen
your position and see what must be
done, because next spring[m] the king of
Aram will attack you again."
23Meanwhile, the officials of the king
of Aram advised him, "Their gods are
gods[n] of the hills. That is why they
were too strong for us. But if we fight
them on the plains, surely we will be
stronger than they. 24Do this: Remove
all the kings from their commands and
replace them with other officers. 25You
must also raise an army like the one
you lost—horse for horse and chariot
for chariot—so we can fight Israel on
the plains. Then surely we will be
stronger than they." He agreed with
them and acted accordingly.
26The next spring[o] Ben-Hadad
mustered the Arameans and went
up to Aphek[p] to fight against Israel. 27When the Israelites were also
mustered and given provisions, they
marched out to meet them. The Israelites camped opposite them like two
small flocks of goats, while the Arameans covered the countryside.[q]
28The man of God came up and told
the king of Israel, "This is what the
LORD says: 'Because the Arameans
think the LORD is a god of the hills and
not a god[r] of the valleys, I will deliver
this vast army into your hands, and you
will know[s] that I am the LORD.' "
29For seven days they camped opposite each other, and on the seventh day
the battle was joined. The Israelites inflicted a hundred thousand casualties
on the Aramean foot soldiers in one
day. 30The rest of them escaped to the
city of Aphek,[t] where the wall collapsed on twenty-seven thousand of
them. And Ben-Hadad fled to the city
and hid[u] in an inner room.
31His officials said to him, "Look, we
have heard that the kings of the house
of Israel are merciful. Let us go to the
king of Israel with sackcloth[v] around
our waists and ropes around our
heads. Perhaps he will spare your life."
32Wearing sackcloth around their
waists and ropes around their heads,
they went to the king of Israel and said,
"Your servant Ben-Hadad says: 'Please
let me live.' "
The king answered, "Is he still alive?
He is my brother."
33The men took this as a good sign
and were quick to pick up his word.
"Yes, your brother Ben-Hadad!" they
said.
"Go and get him," the king said.
When Ben-Hadad came out, Ahab had
him come up into his chariot.
34"I will return the cities[w] my father
took from your father," Ben-Hadad offered. "You may set up your own market areas in Damascus,[x] as my father
did in Samaria."
⌊Ahab said,⌋ "On the basis of a treaty[y] I will set you free." So he made a
treaty with him, and let him go.

A Prophet Condemns Ahab

35By the word of the LORD one of the
sons of the prophets said to his companion, "Strike me with your weapon,"
but the man refused.[z]
36So the prophet said, "Because you
have not obeyed the LORD, as soon as
you leave me a lion[a] will kill you." And
after the man went away, a lion found
him and killed him.
37The prophet found another man
and said, "Strike me, please." So the
man struck him and wounded him.
38Then the prophet went and stood by
the road waiting for the king. He disguised himself with his headband
down over his eyes. 39As the king
passed by, the prophet called out to
him, "Your servant went into the thick
of the battle, and someone came to me
with a captive and said, 'Guard this
man. If he is missing, it will be your life
for his life,[b] or you must pay a talent[a]
of silver.' 40While your servant was
busy here and there, the man disappeared."
"That is your sentence," the king of
Israel said. "You have pronounced it
yourself."
41Then the prophet quickly removed
the headband from his eyes, and the
king of Israel recognized him as one of
the prophets. 42He said to the king,
"This is what the LORD says: 'You have
set free a man I had determined should

20:16 [k]ver 12; 1Ki 16:9
20:22 [l]ver 13 [m]ver 26; 2Sa 11:1
20:23 [n]1Ki 14:23; Ro 1:21-23
20:26 [o]ver 22 [p]2Ki 13:17
20:27 [q]Jdg 6:6; 1Sa 13:6
20:28 [r]ver 23 [s]ver 13
20:30 [t]ver 26 [u]1Ki 22:25; 2Ch 18:24
20:31 [v]Ge 37:34
20:34 [w]1Ki 15:20 [x]Jer 49:23-27 [y]Ex 23:32
20:35 [z]1Ki 13:21; 2Ki 2:3-7
20:36 [a]1Ki 13:24
20:39 [b]2Ki 10:24

[a] *39* That is, about 75 pounds (about 34 kilograms)

die.[a][c] Therefore it is your life for his
life,[d] your people for his people.' "
43 Sullen and angry,[e] the king of Israel
went to his palace in Samaria.

Naboth's Vineyard

21 Some time later there was an incident involving a vineyard belonging to Naboth[f] the Jezreelite. The
vineyard was in Jezreel,[g] close to the
palace of Ahab king of Samaria. 2 Ahab
said to Naboth, "Let me have your
vineyard to use for a vegetable garden,
since it is close to my palace. In exchange I will give you a better vineyard
or, if you prefer, I will pay you whatever
it is worth."
3 But Naboth replied, "The LORD forbid that I should give you the inheritance[h] of my fathers."
4 So Ahab went home, sullen and angry[i] because Naboth the Jezreelite
had said, "I will not give you the inheritance of my fathers." He lay on his bed
sulking and refused to eat.
5 His wife Jezebel came in and asked
him, "Why are you so sullen? Why
won't you eat?"
6 He answered her, "Because I said to
Naboth the Jezreelite, 'Sell me your
vineyard; or if you prefer, I will give you
another vineyard in its place.' But he
said, 'I will not give you my vineyard.' "
7 Jezebel his wife said, "Is this how
you act as king over Israel? Get up and
eat! Cheer up. I'll get you the vineyard[j] of Naboth the Jezreelite."
8 So she wrote letters in Ahab's
name, placed his seal[k] on them, and
sent them to the elders and nobles who

21:1–19 PROMISE 3

POWER PLAY

Power and greed, when unleashed, produce ugly results. If you doubt that, read this story. In varying degrees, many of us can identify these feelings in ourselves. Whether it's a vineyard, the corner office or a parking spot, we've all felt the urge to eliminate those who get what we want. Is it ever true that the difference between you and Ahab is not the desire to eliminate the other but the power to carry it out?

Examine how you deal with children, employees or anyone under your authority. Do you use your position to get what you want, or to help others get what they need? Jesus' teaching about servant leadership in Matthew 20:20–28 takes on powerful dimensions in light of this awful contrast.

For the next Promise 3 reading go to page 427.

20:42 [c]Jer 48:10 [d]ver 39; Jos 2:14; 1Ki 22:31-37
20:43 [e]1Ki 21:4
21:1 [f]2Ki 9:21 [g]1Ki 18:45-46
21:3 [h]Lev 25:23; Nu 36:7; Eze 46:18
21:4 [i]1Ki 20:43
21:7 [j]1Sa 8:14
21:8 [k]Ge 38:18; Est 3:12; 8:8, 10

lived in Naboth's city with him. 9 In
those letters she wrote:

"Proclaim a day of fasting and
seat Naboth in a prominent place
among the people. 10 But seat two
scoundrels[l] opposite him and
have them testify that he has
cursed[m] both God and the king.
Then take him out and stone him
to death."

11 So the elders and nobles who lived
in Naboth's city did as Jezebel directed
in the letters she had written to them.
12 They proclaimed a fast[n] and seated
Naboth in a prominent place among
the people. 13 Then two scoundrels
came and sat opposite him and
brought charges against Naboth before
the people, saying, "Naboth has cursed
both God and the king." So they took
him outside the city and stoned him to
death.[o] 14 Then they sent word to Jezebel: "Naboth has been stoned and is
dead."
15 As soon as Jezebel heard that Naboth had been stoned to death, she
said to Ahab, "Get up and take possession of the vineyard[p] of Naboth the
Jezreelite that he refused to sell you. He
is no longer alive, but dead." 16 When
Ahab heard that Naboth was dead, he
got up and went down to take possession of Naboth's vineyard.
17 Then the word of the LORD came to
Elijah the Tishbite: 18 "Go down to meet
Ahab king of Israel, who rules in Samaria. He is now in Naboth's vineyard,
where he has gone to take possession
of it. 19 Say to him, 'This is what the
LORD says: Have you not murdered a
man and seized his property?' Then say
to him, 'This is what the LORD says: In
the place where dogs licked up Naboth's blood,[q] dogs[r] will lick up your
blood—yes, yours!' "
20 Ahab said to Elijah, "So you have
found me, my enemy!"[s]
"I have found you," he answered,
"because you have sold[t] yourself to
do evil in the eyes of the LORD. 21 'I am
going to bring disaster on you. I will
consume your descendants and cut off
from Ahab every last male[u] in Israel—
slave or free. 22 I will make your
house[v] like that of Jeroboam son of
Nebat and that of Baasha son of Ahijah,
because you have provoked me to anger and have caused Israel to sin.'[w]
23 "And also concerning Jezebel the

21:10 [l]Ac 6:11 [m]Ex 22:28; Lev 24:15-16
21:12 [n]Isa 58:4
21:13 [o]2Ki 9:26
21:15 [p]1Sa 8:14
21:19 [q]2Ki 9:26; Ps 9:12; Isa 14:20 [r]1Ki 22:38
21:20 [s]1Ki 18:17 [t]ver 25; 2Ki 17:17; Ro 7:14
21:21 [u]1Ki 14:10; 2Ki 9:8
21:22 [v]1Ki 15:29; 16:3 [w]1Ki 12:30

[a] *42* The Hebrew term refers to the irrevocable giving over of things or persons to the LORD, often by totally destroying them.

LORD says: 'Dogs[x] will devour Jezebel
by the wall of[a] Jezreel.'
24"Dogs[y] will eat those belonging to
Ahab who die in the city, and the birds
of the air will feed on those who die in
the country."
25(There was never[z] a man like
Ahab, who sold himself to do evil in the
eyes of the LORD, urged on by Jezebel
his wife. 26He behaved in the vilest
manner by going after idols, like the
Amorites[a] the LORD drove out before
Israel.)
27When Ahab heard these words, he
tore his clothes, put on sackcloth[b] and
fasted. He lay in sackcloth and went
around meekly.
28Then the word of the LORD came to
Elijah the Tishbite: 29"Have you noticed how Ahab has humbled himself
before me? Because he has humbled
himself, I will not bring this disaster in
his day, but I will bring it on his house
in the days of his son."[c]

Micaiah Prophesies Against Ahab

22 For three years there was no war
between Aram and Israel. 2But in
the third year Jehoshaphat king of Judah went down to see the king of Israel.
3The king of Israel had said to his officials, "Don't you know that Ramoth
Gilead[d] belongs to us and yet we are
doing nothing to retake it from the king
of Aram?"
4So he asked Jehoshaphat, "Will you
go with me to fight[e] against Ramoth
Gilead?"
Jehoshaphat replied to the king of
Israel, "I am as you are, my people as
your people, my horses as your
horses." 5But Jehoshaphat also said to
the king of Israel, "First seek the counsel[f] of the LORD."
6So the king of Israel brought together the prophets—about four hundred
men—and asked them, "Shall I go to
war against Ramoth Gilead, or shall I
refrain?"
"Go,"[g] they answered, "for the Lord
will give it into the king's hand."
7But Jehoshaphat asked, "Is there
not a prophet[h] of the LORD here whom
we can inquire of?"
8The king of Israel answered Jehoshaphat, "There is still one man through
whom we can inquire of the LORD, but
I hate[i] him because he never prophesies anything good[j] about me, but always bad. He is Micaiah son of Imlah."
"The king should not say that," Jehoshaphat replied.
9So the king of Israel called one of
his officials and said, "Bring Micaiah
son of Imlah at once."
10Dressed in their royal robes, the
king of Israel and Jehoshaphat king of
Judah were sitting on their thrones at
the threshing floor[k] by the entrance of
the gate of Samaria, with all the prophets prophesying before them. 11Now
Zedekiah son of Kenaanah had made
iron horns[l] and he declared, "This is
what the LORD says: 'With these you
will gore the Arameans until they are
destroyed.' "
12All the other prophets were prophesying the same thing. "Attack Ramoth
Gilead and be victorious," they said,
"for the LORD will give it into the king's
hand."
13The messenger who had gone to
summon Micaiah said to him, "Look,
as one man the other prophets are predicting success for the king. Let your
word agree with theirs, and speak favorably."
14But Micaiah said, "As surely as the
LORD lives, I can tell him only what the
LORD tells me."[m]
15When he arrived, the king asked
him, "Micaiah, shall we go to war
against Ramoth Gilead, or shall I refrain?"
"Attack and be victorious," he answered, "for the LORD will give it into
the king's hand."
16The king said to him, "How many
times must I make you swear to tell me
nothing but the truth in the name of
the LORD?"
17Then Micaiah answered, "I saw all
Israel scattered on the hills like sheep
without a shepherd,[n] and the LORD
said, 'These people have no master. Let
each one go home in peace.' "
18The king of Israel said to Jehoshaphat, "Didn't I tell you that he never
prophesies anything good about me,
but only bad?"
19Micaiah continued, "Therefore
hear the word of the LORD: I saw the
LORD sitting on his throne[o] with all the
host[p] of heaven standing around him
on his right and on his left. 20And the
LORD said, 'Who will entice Ahab into
attacking Ramoth Gilead and going to
his death there?'
"One suggested this, and another
that. 21Finally, a spirit came forward,
stood before the LORD and said, 'I will
entice him.'
22" 'By what means?' the LORD asked.
" 'I will go out and be a lying[q] spirit
in the mouths of all his prophets,' he
said.

21:23 [x]2Ki 9:10, 34-36
21:24 [y]1Ki 14:11; 16:4
21:25 [z]ver 20; 1Ki 16:33
21:26 [a]Ge 15:16; Lev 18:25-30; 2Ki 21:11
21:27 [b]Ge 37:34; 2Sa 3:31; 2Ki 6:30
21:29 [c]2Ki 9:26
22:3 [d]Dt 4:43; Jos 21:38
22:4 [e]2Ki 3:7
22:5 [f]Ex 33:7; 2Ki 3:11
22:6 [g]1Ki 18:19
22:7 [h]2Ki 3:11
22:8 [i]Am 5:10 [j]Isa 5:20
22:10 [k]ver 6
22:11 [l]Dt 33:17; Zec 1:18-21
22:14 [m]Nu 22:18; 24:13; 1Ki 18:10,15
22:17 [n]ver 34-36; Nu 27:17; Mt 9:36
22:19 [o]Isa 6:1; Eze 1:26; Da 7:9 [p]Job 1:6; 2:1; Ps 103:20-21; Mt 18:10; Heb 1:7,14
22:22 [q]Jdg 9:23; 1Sa 16:14; 18:10; 19:9; Eze 14:9; 2Th 2:11

[a]*23* Most Hebrew manuscripts; a few Hebrew manuscripts, Vulgate and Syriac (see also 2 Kings 9:26) *the plot of ground at*

“ ‘You will succeed in enticing him,’
said the LORD. ‘Go and do it.’
23 “So now the LORD has put a lying
spirit in the mouths of all these prophets[r] of yours. The LORD has decreed
disaster for you.”
24 Then Zedekiah[s] son of Kenaanah
went up and slapped[t] Micaiah in the
face. “Which way did the spirit from[a]
the LORD go when he went from me to
speak to you?” he asked.
25 Micaiah replied, “You will find out
on the day you go to hide[u] in an inner
room.”
26 The king of Israel then ordered,
“Take Micaiah and send him back to
Amon the ruler of the city and to Joash
the king’s son 27 and say, ‘This is what
the king says: Put this fellow in prison[v] and give him nothing but bread
and water until I return safely.’ ”
28 Micaiah declared, “If you ever return safely, the LORD has not spoken[w]
through me.” Then he added, “Mark
my words, all you people!”

Ahab Killed at Ramoth Gilead

29 So the king of Israel and Jehoshaphat king of Judah went up to Ramoth
Gilead. 30 The king of Israel said to Jehoshaphat, “I will enter the battle in
disguise,[x] but you wear your royal
robes.” So the king of Israel disguised
himself and went into battle.
31 Now the king of Aram had ordered
his thirty-two chariot commanders,
“Do not fight with anyone, small or
great, except the king[y] of Israel.”
32 When the chariot commanders saw
Jehoshaphat, they thought, “Surely this
is the king of Israel.” So they turned
to attack him, but when Jehoshaphat
cried out, 33 the chariot commanders
saw that he was not the king of Israel
and stopped pursuing him.
34 But someone drew his bow[z] at
random and hit the king of Israel between the sections of his armor. The
king told his chariot driver, “Wheel
around and get me out of the fighting.
I’ve been wounded.” 35 All day long the
battle raged, and the king was propped
up in his chariot facing the Arameans.
The blood from his wound ran onto the
floor of the chariot, and that evening
he died. 36 As the sun was setting, a cry
spread through the army: “Every man
to his town; everyone to his land!”[a]
37 So the king died and was brought
to Samaria, and they buried him there.
38 They washed the chariot at a pool
in Samaria (where the prostitutes
bathed),[b] and the dogs[b] licked up his
blood, as the word of the LORD had declared.

39 As for the other events of Ahab’s
reign, including all he did, the palace
he built and inlaid with ivory,[c] and
the cities he fortified, are they not written in the book of the annals of the
kings of Israel? 40 Ahab rested with his
fathers. And Ahaziah his son succeeded him as king.

Jehoshaphat King of Judah

41 Jehoshaphat son of Asa became
king of Judah in the fourth year of Ahab
king of Israel. 42 Jehoshaphat was
thirty-five years old when he became
king, and he reigned in Jerusalem
twenty-five years. His mother’s name
was Azubah daughter of Shilhi. 43 In everything he walked in the ways of his
father Asa[d] and did not stray from
them; he did what was right in the eyes
of the LORD. The high places,[e] however, were not removed, and the people
continued to offer sacrifices and burn
incense there. 44 Jehoshaphat was also
at peace with the king of Israel.
45 As for the other events of Jehoshaphat’s reign, the things he achieved
and his military exploits, are they not
written in the book of the annals of the
kings of Judah? 46 He rid the land of the
rest of the male shrine prostitutes[f]
who remained there even after the
reign of his father Asa. 47 There was
then no king[g] in Edom; a deputy
ruled.
48 Now Jehoshaphat built a fleet of
trading ships[c][h] to go to Ophir for
gold, but they never set sail—they were
wrecked at Ezion Geber. 49 At that time
Ahaziah son of Ahab said to Jehoshaphat, “Let my men sail with your men,”
but Jehoshaphat refused.
50 Then Jehoshaphat rested with his
fathers and was buried with them in
the city of David his father. And Jehoram his son succeeded him.

Ahaziah King of Israel

51 Ahaziah son of Ahab became king
of Israel in Samaria in the seventeenth
year of Jehoshaphat king of Judah, and
he reigned over Israel two years. 52 He
did evil[i] in the eyes of the LORD, because he walked in the ways of his father and mother and in the ways of
Jeroboam son of Nebat, who caused Israel to sin. 53 He served and worshiped
Baal[j] and provoked the LORD, the God
of Israel, to anger, just as his father[k]
had done.

22:23 [r]Eze 14:9
22:24 [s]ver 11 [t]Ac 23:2
22:25 [u]1Ki 20:30
22:27 [v]2Ch 16:10
22:28 [w]Dt 18:22
22:30 [x]2Ch 35:32
22:31 [y]2Sa 17:2
22:34 [z]2Ch 35:23
22:36 [a]2Ki 14:12
22:38 [b]1Ki 21:19
22:39 [c]2Ch 9:17; Am 3:15
22:43 [d]2Ch 17:3 [e]1Ki 3:2; 15:14; 2Ki 12:3
22:46 [f]Dt 23:17; 1Ki 14:24; 15:12
22:47 [g]2Sa 8:14; 2Ki 3:9; 8:20
22:48 [h]1Ki 9:26; 10:22
22:52 [i]1Ki 15:26; 21:25
22:53 [j]Jdg 2:11 [k]1Ki 16:30-32

[a] *24* Or *Spirit of the weapons*
[b] *38* Or *Samaria and cleaned*
[c] *48* Hebrew *of ships of Tarshish*

KINGS AND PROPHETS OF THE DIVIDED NATION: ISRAEL AND JUDAH (930–415 B.C.)

Northern Kings	Dates	Years	Prophets	Dates	Southern Kings	Dates	Years
Jereboam	930–909	22			Rehoboam	930–913	17
Nadab	909–908	2			Abijah	913–910	3
Baasha	908–886	24			**Asa***	**910–869**	**41**
Elah	886–885	2					
Zimri	885	7 days					
Omri	885–874	12					
Ahab	874–853	22			**Jehoshophat**	**872–848**	**25**
Ahaziah	853–852	2					
Joram	852–841	12			Jehoram	848–841	8
Jehu	841–814	28	Obadiah: to Gentiles	853–841	Ahaziah	841	1
Jehoahaz	814–798	17	Joel: to Judah	835–796	Athaliah	841–835	7
Jehoash	798–782	16			**Joash**	**835–796**	**40**
Jereboam II	793–753	41	Jonah: to Gentiles	785–775	**Amaziah**	**796–767**	**29**
Zachariah	753–752	1/2	Amos: to Israel	760–750	**Azariah**	**792–740**	**52**
Shallum	752	30 days	Hosea: to Israel	753–715	**Jotham**	**750–732**	**19**
Menahem	752–742	10					
Pekahiah	742–740	2	Isaiah: to Israel & Judah	740–681			
Pekah	752–732	20	Micah: to Israel & Judah	742–687	Ahaz	735–715	20
Hoshea	732–722	9					
					Hezekiah	**715–686**	**29**
Destruction of Israel by Assyria	722		Nahum: to Gentiles	663–612	Manasseh	697–642	55
					Amon	642–640	2
			Zephaniah: to Judah	640–621	**Josiah**	**640–609**	**31**
			Habakkuk: to Judah	612–588	Jehoahaz	609	90 days
			Jeremiah: to Judah	626–585	Jehoiakim	609–598	9
					Jehoiachin	598–597	90 days
					Zedekiah	597–586	11
			Daniel: to Judah in Exile	605–536	*Destruction of Judah by Babylon*	586	
			Ezekiel: to Judah in Exile	593–571			
			Haggai: to reconstruction	520-480	*Reconstruction of Jerusalem under the Persians*	536–415	
			Zechariah: to reconstruction	520-480			
			Malachi: to reconstruction	440-430			

***Bold** type indicates godly kings*

2 KINGS

AT A GLANCE

Key Principle: Disobedience and rebellion against God results in slavery to sin and the loss of God's blessing.
Author: Possibly Jeremiah
Time and Place: 852 B.C. to 560 B.C. / Israel and Judah
Key Verses: 17:22–23; 23:27

BENEFIT

Second Kings tells the sad story of Israel and Judah's decline and fall. It contains far more negative than positive examples for our instruction. Of the 19 kings in the northern kingdom of Israel, none followed in God's way; of the 20 rulers in the southern kingdom of Judah, only eight pursued God. Of those eight, few remained faithful to the end. This book illustrates again and again that people never find what they're looking for when they abandon God in favor of their own interests. To reject God is to destroy oneself.

SETTING

The first 17 chapters of 2 Kings continue the story of the divided kingdom of Israel and Judah from the end of 1 Kings. These chapters begin with the death of Israel's King Ahaziah in 852 B.C. and conclude with Assyria's capture of Israel in 722 B.C. The remaining eight chapters chronicle Judah's downfall from the beginning of King Hezekiah's reign in 715 B.C. to Babylon's destruction of Jerusalem in 586 B.C. The last event recorded in this book is Jehoiachin's release from prison in Babylon in 561 B.C.

The kingdom period in Israel lasted 464 years: The united kingdom under Saul, David, and Solomon existed from 1050 B.C. to 930 B.C. (120 years), the divided kingdom of Israel and Judah went from 930 B.C. to Assyria's capture of Israel in 722 B.C. (208 years), and Judah continued on until the Babylonian invasion in 586 B.C. (136 years).

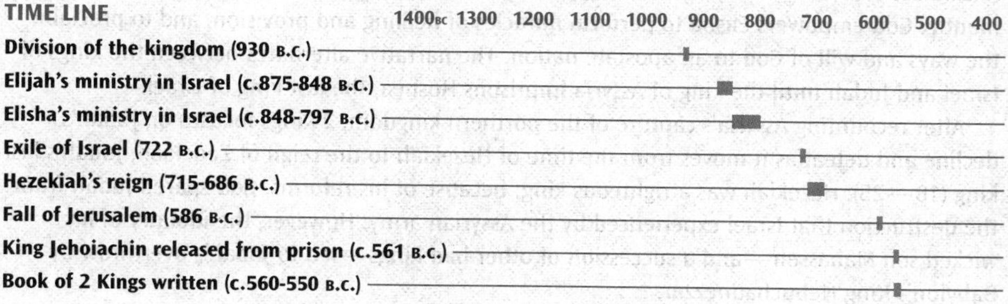

THEME AND PURPOSE

Since 1 and 2 Kings were originally one book in the Hebrew Bible, they share the same theme and purpose—namely, that there is a direct relationship between the spiritual and moral condition of the kings and the welfare of the nations under their rule. The northern kingdom of Israel didn't last as long as the southern kingdom of Judah because none of its kings did what was right in the sight of the Lord. Even Jehu's reform was half-hearted; he removed Baal worship but continued Jeroboam's apostate system of calf worship. Judah lasted an additional 136 years because of the relative righteousness of kings such as Joash, Hezekiah, and Josiah, but it too came to an end because most of its kings were immoral and disobedient. The Lord graciously sent many prophets to warn the kings of Israel and Judah about the consequences of their faithlessness, but most of the kings rejected God's messengers and paved the way for divine judgment.

UNIQUE CONTRIBUTION

Second Kings is a highly selective and thematic book that was written not to provide biographies of the kings of Israel and Judah, but to prophetically assess their lives and reigns. This book offers God's perspective on why he had to judge his people by raising up foreign powers to bring them into captivity. The kings' pride and spiritual disobedience, coupled with their refusal to heed the prophets' words, led to their shame, deterioration, and destruction.

LINKS TO THE NEW TESTAMENT

David's dynasty in Judah has a clear bearing on the coming Messiah; God promised that Christ would be a direct descendant of David. Israel saw nine short-lived dynasties, but only one dynasty could remain in Judah if the messianic prophecies were to be fulfilled. Queen Athaliah attempted to eliminate David's dynasty, but in spite of her attempt, Joash survived and continued the unbroken line.

OVERVIEW

FOCUS	The Divided Kingdom		The Kingdom of Judah
REFERENCE	1	17	18 25
TOPICS	Israel's Corruption and Captivity		Judah's Corruption and Captivity
	Elisha	Kings of Israel and Judah	Kings of Judah
	Ahaziah to Hoshea		Hezekiah to Zedekiah
LOCATION	Israel Deported to Assyria		Judah Deported to Babylonia
TIME	130 Years		154 Years

This book continues where 1 Kings left off. It traces the succession of bad kings in Israel from Ahaziah to Hoshea (1—17). After God takes Elijah into heaven, Elisha assumes his prophetic mantle. God empowers Elisha to perform miracles of healing and provision, and to proclaim the ways and will of God to an apostate nation. The narrative alternates between the kings of Israel and Judah until the king of Assyria imprisons Hoshea, the last king of Israel.

After recounting Assyria's capture of the northern kingdom, 2 Kings focuses on Judah's decline and defeat as it moves from the time of Hezekiah to the reign of Zedekiah, Judah's last king (18—25). Hezekiah was a righteous king; because of his reforms, God spared Judah from the destruction that Israel experienced by the Assyrian army. However, the idolatry of his wicked son Manasseh—and a succession of other bad kings—led to Judah's overthrow by Babylon's King Nebuchadnezzar.

2 KINGS

The LORD's Judgment on Ahaziah

1 After Ahab's death, Moab[a] rebelled against Israel. 2Now Ahaziah had fallen through the lattice of his upper room in Samaria and injured himself. So he sent messengers,[b] saying to them, "Go and consult Baal-Zebub,[c] the god of Ekron,[d] to see if I will recover[e] from this injury."

3But the angel[f] of the LORD said to Elijah[g] the Tishbite, "Go up and meet the messengers of the king of Samaria and ask them, 'Is it because there is no God in Israel[h] that you are going off to consult Baal-Zebub, the god of Ekron?' 4Therefore this is what the LORD says: 'You will not leave[i] the bed you are lying on. You will certainly die!' " So Elijah went.

5When the messengers returned to the king, he asked them, "Why have you come back?"

6"A man came to meet us," they replied. "And he said to us, 'Go back to the king who sent you and tell him, "This is what the LORD says: Is it because there is no God in Israel that you are sending men to consult Baal-Zebub, the god of Ekron? Therefore you will not leave the bed you are lying on. You will certainly die!" ' "

7The king asked them, "What kind of man was it who came to meet you and told you this?"

8They replied, "He was a man with a garment of hair[j] and with a leather belt around his waist."

The king said, "That was Elijah the Tishbite."

9Then he sent[k] to Elijah a captain[l] with his company of fifty men. The captain went up to Elijah, who was sitting on the top of a hill, and said to him, "Man of God, the king says, 'Come down!' "

10Elijah answered the captain, "If I am a man of God, may fire come down from heaven and consume you and your fifty men!" Then fire[m] fell from heaven and consumed the captain and his men.

11At this the king sent to Elijah another captain with his fifty men. The captain said to him, "Man of God, this is what the king says, 'Come down at once!' "

12"If I am a man of God," Elijah replied, "may fire come down from heaven and consume you and your fifty men!" Then the fire of God fell from heaven and consumed him and his fifty men.

13So the king sent a third captain with his fifty men. This third captain went up and fell on his knees before Elijah. "Man of God," he begged, "please have respect for my life[n] and the lives of these fifty men, your servants! 14See, fire has fallen from heaven and consumed the first two captains and all their men. But now have respect for my life!"

15The angel[o] of the LORD said to Elijah, "Go down with him; do not be afraid[p] of him." So Elijah got up and went down with him to the king.

16He told the king, "This is what the LORD says: Is it because there is no God in Israel for you to consult that you have sent messengers[q] to consult Baal-Zebub, the god of Ekron? Because you have done this, you will never leave[r] the bed you are lying on. You will certainly die!" 17So he died,[s] according to the word of the LORD that Elijah had spoken.

Because Ahaziah had no son, Joram[a][t] succeeded him as king in the second year of Jehoram son of Jehoshaphat king of Judah. 18As for all the other events of Ahaziah's reign, and what he did, are they not written in the book of the annals of the kings of Israel?

Elijah Taken Up to Heaven

2 When the LORD was about to take[u] Elijah up to heaven in a whirlwind,[v] Elijah and Elisha[w] were on their way from Gilgal.[x] 2Elijah said to Elisha, "Stay here;[y] the LORD has sent me to Bethel."

2 →PG. 487

But Elisha said, "As surely as the LORD lives and as you live, I will not leave you."[z] So they went down to Bethel.

3The company[a] of the prophets at Bethel came out to Elisha and asked, "Do you know that the LORD is going to take your master from you today?"

"Yes, I know," Elisha replied, "but do not speak of it."

4Then Elijah said to him, "Stay here, Elisha; the LORD has sent me to Jericho.[b]"

And he replied, "As surely as the

1:1 [a]Ge 19:37; 2Sa 8:2; 2Ki 3:5 **1:2** [b]ver 16 [c]Mk 3:22 [d]1Sa 6:2; Isa 2:6; 14:29; Mt 10:25 [e]Jdg 18:5; 2Ki 8:7-10 **1:3** [f]ver 15; Ge 16:7 [g]1Ki 17:1 [h]1Sa 28:8 **1:4** [i]ver 6,16; Ps 41:8 **1:8** [j]1Ki 18:7; Zec 13:4; Mt 3:4; Mk 1:6 **1:9** [k]2Ki 6:14 [l]Ex 18:25; Isa 3:3 **1:10** [m]1Ki 18:38; Lk 9:54; Rev 11:5; 13:13 **1:13** [n]1Sa 26:21; Ps 72:14 **1:15** [o]ver 3 [p]Isa 51:12; 57:11; Jer 1:17; Eze 2:6 **1:16** [q]ver 2 [r]ver 4 **1:17** [s]2Ki 8:15; Jer 20:6; 28:17 [t]2Ki 3:1; 8:16 **2:1** [u]Ge 5:24; Heb 11:5 [v]ver 11; 1Ki 19:11; Isa 5:28; 66:15; Jer 4:13; Na 1:3 [w]1Ki 19:16,21 [x]Dt 11:30; 2Ki 4:38 **2:2** [y]ver 6 [z]Ru 1:16; 1Sa 1:26; 2Ki 4:30 **2:3** [a]1Sa 10:5; 2Ki 4:1,38 **2:4** [b]Jos 3:16; 6:26

[a]17 Hebrew *Jehoram,* a variant of *Joram*

ELISHA

A Friend and a Disciple

An English publication once offered a prize for the best definition of a friend. Thousands of definitions were submitted. Of all of those, a few in particular stand out:

A friend is one who multiplies joys and divides grief.

A friend is one who understands our silence.

A friend is a watch that beats true for all time and never runs down.

Here's the definition that won first prize: "A friend is one who comes in when the whole world has gone out."

If the prophet Elijah suddenly stepped into our world and described what happened following his experience on Mount Carmel, he would agree with this prize-winning definition. He might even add, "When my whole world turned black as midnight, God brought Elisha into my life to be my friend."

Friends Are Good Medicine

God sent his prophet Elijah to the Jordan valley and a place called Abel Meholah. That's where Elisha lived (1 Kings 19:16). Elisha didn't seem surprised to see Elijah come walking into the field he was plowing. Along with most everyone in Israel, Elisha had heard about this feisty old prophet who had confronted Ahab and the prophets of Baal on Mount Carmel. Elijah wasn't surprised to see Elisha either, because the Lord had told Elijah where to find Elisha and made it clear that Elisha would eventually succeed him as God's prophet.

Elijah approached Elisha and "threw his cloak around him" (19:19). With this symbolic gesture, Elisha knew that God was calling him to be a special assistant to this great prophet. Kissing his parents goodbye, Elisha left his duties and his family and "set out to follow Elijah and [become] his attendant" (19:21).

Something important happened to Elijah when Elisha joined forces with him. Elijah could now share the deepest and most intimate details of his life with Elisha without fear of rejection, misinterpretation or betrayal. This openness led to renewed strength for Elijah. His bouts with severe depression subsided. He once again responded positively to God's commands. Without hesitation, Elijah fiercely confronted the rulers of Israel and rebuked them for their sins of idolatry. Elisha's friendship with the older prophet came at a time when Elijah needed him most.

I Will Not Leave You

On three different occasions, and in three different locations, Elijah planned to visit a group of prophets. Every time, Elijah asked Elisha to stay behind. We're not told what Elijah's motivation was in issuing these commands to his friend. However, Elisha would not hear of it. Each time Elijah commanded him to stay, Elisha responded deliberately and adamantly, "As surely as the LORD lives and as you live, I will not leave you" (2 Kings 2:2, 4, 6).

Evidently, Elisha sensed that Elijah would soon leave him. He was determined to stay by Elijah's side until that moment. "So the two of them walked on" together (2:6). That's the way it is with friends. They're loyal to each other. They "walk on" together no matter what the difficulties and problems in life.

Friends Can Be Disciples

Elisha was eager to learn everything he could from his friend and mentor. He wanted to be prepared to carry on Elijah's prophetic ministry. This added dimension of disciple and teacher must have greatly encouraged Elijah and broadened the friendship between the two men.

Elisha recognized, however, that he could never take over Elijah's powerful position in Israel without God's anointing. One day when Elijah asked Elisha what he could do for him before he was taken away, Elisha responded without hesitation: "Let me inherit a double portion of your spirit" (2:9).

Don't misunderstand this request. Elisha was not selfishly asking that he be twice as successful as Elijah. Elisha felt he needed twice the motivation and strength that Elijah had just to keep up with his mentor, so he asked for the double blessing of his spirit. Because Elisha's motives were pure, God granted his request.

In God's sight, Elijah and Elisha were brothers—spiritually equal. But from Elisha's point of view, they were separated by age and experience. Elisha was like a son who looked to Elijah as his father for guidance and help (2:11–12). He was a true disciple, a faithful friend, and eventually became one of the greatest prophets in Israel.

Do You Have Such a Friend?

All of us need a close friend, especially with the stress levels and all the passions and concerns of modern life. If you don't have that kind of friend, have you asked God for one? "My wife is my best friend," you say? Great! You are fortunate indeed! But as a man, you also need a male companion—as Elijah needed Elisha. And someone needs you. Are you available?

—Dr. Gene Getz

LORD lives and as you live, I will not
leave you." So they went to Jericho.
5 The company[c] of the prophets at
Jericho went up to Elisha and asked
him, "Do you know that the LORD is
going to take your master from you today?"
"Yes, I know," he replied, "but do
not speak of it."
6 Then Elijah said to him, "Stay
here;[d] the LORD has sent me to the
Jordan."[e]
And he replied, "As surely as the
LORD lives and as you live, I will not
leave you."[f] So the two of them
walked on.
7 Fifty men of the company of the
prophets went and stood at a distance,
facing the place where Elijah and Elisha had stopped at the Jordan. 8 Elijah
took his cloak,[g] rolled it up and
struck[h] the water with it. The water
divided[i] to the right and to the left,
and the two of them crossed over on
dry[j] ground.
9 When they had crossed, Elijah said
to Elisha, "Tell me, what can I do for
you before I am taken from you?"
"Let me inherit a double[k] portion
of your spirit,"[l] Elisha replied.
10 "You have asked a difficult thing,"
Elijah said, "yet if you see me when I
am taken from you, it will be yours—
otherwise not."
11 As they were walking along and
talking together, suddenly a chariot of
fire[m] and horses of fire appeared and
separated the two of them, and Elijah
went up to heaven[n] in a whirlwind.[o]
12 Elisha saw this and cried out, "My
father! My father! The chariots[p] and
horsemen of Israel!" And Elisha saw
him no more. Then he took hold of his
own clothes and tore[q] them apart.
13 He picked up the cloak that had
fallen from Elijah and went back and
stood on the bank of the Jordan.
14 Then he took the cloak[r] that had
fallen from him and struck[s] the water
with it. "Where now is the LORD, the
God of Elijah?" he asked. When he
struck the water, it divided to the right
and to the left, and he crossed over.
15 The company[t] of the prophets
from Jericho, who were watching, said,
"The spirit[u] of Elijah is resting on Elisha." And they went to meet him and
bowed to the ground before him.
16 "Look," they said, "we your servants
have fifty able men. Let them go and
look for your master. Perhaps the Spirit[v] of the LORD has picked him up[w]
and set him down on some mountain
or in some valley."
"No," Elisha replied, "do not send
them."
17 But they persisted until he was too
ashamed[x] to refuse. So he said, "Send
them." And they sent fifty men, who
searched for three days but did not find
him. 18 When they returned to Elisha,
who was staying in Jericho, he said to
them, "Didn't I tell you not to go?"

Healing of the Water

19 The men of the city said to Elisha,
"Look, our lord, this town is well situated, as you can see, but the water is bad
and the land is unproductive."
20 "Bring me a new bowl," he said,
"and put salt in it." So they brought it
to him.
21 Then he went out to the spring and
threw[y] the salt into it, saying, "This is
what the LORD says: 'I have healed this
water. Never again will it cause death
or make the land unproductive.' "
22 And the water has remained wholesome[z] to this day, according to the
word Elisha had spoken.

Elisha Is Jeered

23 From there Elisha went up to Bethel. As he was walking along the road,
some youths came out of the town and
jeered[a] at him. "Go on up, you bald-
head!" they said. "Go on up, you bald-
head!" 24 He turned around, looked at
them and called down a curse[b] on
them in the name[c] of the LORD. Then
two bears came out of the woods and
mauled forty-two of the youths. 25 And
he went on to Mount Carmel[d] and
from there returned to Samaria.

2:5 c ver 3 **2:6** d ver 2 e Jos 3:15 f Ru 1:16 **2:8** g 1Ki 19:19 h ver 14 i Ex 14:21 j Ex 14:22,29 **2:9** k Dt 21:17 l Nu 11:17 **2:11** m 2Ki 6:17; Ps 68:17; 104:3,4; Isa 66:15; Hab 3:8; Zec 6:1 n Ge 5:24 o ver 1 **2:12** p 2Ki 6:17; 13:14 q Ge 37:29 **2:14** r 1Ki 19:19 s ver 8 **2:15** t ver 7; 1Sa 10:5 u Nu 11:17 **2:16** v 1Ki 18:12 w Ac 8:39 **2:17** x 2Ki 8:11 **2:21** y Ex 15:25; 2Ki 4:41; 6:6 **2:22** z Ex 15:25 **2:23** a Ex 22:28; 2Ch 36:16; Job 19:18; Ps 31:18 **2:24** b Ge 4:11; Ne 13:25-27 c Dt 18:19 **2:25** d 1Ki 18:20; 2Ki 4:25

2:9–15

PROMISE 1

ELIJAH TIMES TWO, PLEASE

"What do you want from me?" Elijah asked his disciple. Elisha's answer is a powerful commentary on the character of both men.

Elisha wanted the spirit this godly older prophet exhibited. Not his estate, or his reputation, or his contacts—no, his spirit. And what a compliment to Elijah. Elisha said, in effect, "Whatever it is that drives you—I want it doubled!" Read Elijah's story (1 Kings 17–22 and 2 Kings 1–2, about 10 pages) and discover what Elisha wanted. Look for answers to the question, "What was Elijah's spirit?" As you discover facts about Elijah that bear modeling, ask God for a double portion of his spirit in your life.

For the next Promise 1 reading go to page 407.

Moab Revolts

3 Joram[a][e] son of Ahab became king
of Israel in Samaria in the eighteenth
year of Jehoshaphat king of Judah, and
he reigned twelve years. 2He did evil[f]
in the eyes of the LORD, but not as his
father[g] and mother had done. He got
rid of the sacred stone[h] of Baal that
his father had made. 3Nevertheless he
clung to the sins[i] of Jeroboam son of
Nebat, which he had caused Israel to
commit; he did not turn away from
them.
4Now Mesha king of Moab[j] raised
sheep, and he had to supply the king
of Israel with a hundred thousand
lambs[k] and with the wool of a hundred thousand rams. 5But after Ahab
died, the king of Moab rebelled[l]
against the king of Israel. 6So at that
time King Joram set out from Samaria
and mobilized all Israel. 7He also sent
this message to Jehoshaphat king of Judah: "The king of Moab has rebelled
against me. Will you go with me to
fight[m] against Moab?"
"I will go with you," he replied. "I am
as you are, my people as your people,
my horses as your horses."
8"By what route shall we attack?" he
asked.
"Through the Desert of Edom," he
answered.
9So the king of Israel set out with the
king of Judah and the king of Edom.[n]
After a roundabout march of seven
days, the army had no more water for
themselves or for the animals with
them.
10"What!" exclaimed the king of Israel. "Has the LORD called us three kings
together only to hand us over to
Moab?"
11But Jehoshaphat asked, "Is there
no prophet of the LORD here, that we
may inquire[o] of the LORD through
him?"
An officer of the king of Israel answered, "Elisha[p] son of Shaphat is
here. He used to pour water on the
hands of Elijah.[b][q]"
12Jehoshaphat said, "The word[r] of
the LORD is with him." So the king of
Israel and Jehoshaphat and the king of
Edom went down to him.
13Elisha said to the king of Israel,
"What do we have to do with each other? Go to the prophets of your father
and the prophets of your mother."
"No," the king of Israel answered,
"because it was the LORD who called us
three kings together to hand us over to
Moab."
14Elisha said, "As surely as the LORD
Almighty lives, whom I serve, if I did
not have respect for the presence of
Jehoshaphat king of Judah, I would not
look at you or even notice you. 15But
now bring me a harpist."[s]
While the harpist was playing, the
hand[t] of the LORD came upon Elisha
16and he said, "This is what the LORD
says: Make this valley full of ditches.
17For this is what the LORD says: You
will see neither wind nor rain, yet this
valley will be filled with water,[u] and
you, your cattle and your other animals
will drink. 18This is an easy[v] thing in
the eyes of the LORD; he will also hand
Moab over to you. 19You will overthrow
every fortified city and every major
town. You will cut down every good
tree, stop up all the springs, and ruin
every good field with stones."
20The next morning, about the
time[w] for offering the sacrifice, there it
was—water flowing from the direction
of Edom! And the land was filled with
water.[x]
21Now all the Moabites had heard
that the kings had come to fight against
them; so every man, young and old,
who could bear arms was called up and
stationed on the border. 22When they
got up early in the morning, the sun
was shining on the water. To the Moabites across the way, the water looked
red—like blood. 23"That's blood!" they
said. "Those kings must have fought
and slaughtered each other. Now to the
plunder, Moab!"
24But when the Moabites came to
the camp of Israel, the Israelites rose
up and fought them until they fled.
And the Israelites invaded the land and
slaughtered the Moabites. 25They destroyed the towns, and each man threw
a stone on every good field until it was
covered. They stopped up all the
springs and cut down every good tree.
Only Kir Hareseth[y] was left with its
stones in place, but men armed with
slings surrounded it and attacked it as
well.
26When the king of Moab saw that
the battle had gone against him, he
took with him seven hundred swordsmen to break through to the king of
Edom, but they failed. 27Then he took
his firstborn[z] son, who was to succeed
him as king, and offered him as a sacrifice on the city wall. The fury against
Israel was great; they withdrew and returned to their own land.

3:1 [e]2Ki 1:17 **3:2** [f]1Ki 15:26 [g]1Ki 16:30-32 [h]Ex 23:24; 2Ki 10:18, 26-28 **3:3** [i]1Ki 12:28-32; 14:9,16 **3:4** [j]Ge 19:37; 2Ki 1:1 [k]Ezr 7:17; Isa 16:1 **3:5** [l]2Ki 1:1 **3:7** [m]1Ki 22:4 **3:9** [n]1Ki 22:47 **3:11** [o]Ge 25:22; 1Ki 22:7 [p]Ge 20:7 [q]1Ki 19:16 **3:12** [r]Nu 11:17 **3:15** [s]1Sa 16:23 [t]Jer 15:17; Eze 1:3 **3:17** [u]Ps 107:35; Isa 32:2; 35:6; 41:18 **3:18** [v]Ge 18:14; 2Ki 20:10; Isa 49:6; Jer 32:17,27; Mk 10:27 **3:20** [w]Ex 29:39-40 [x]Ex 17:6 **3:25** [y]ver 19; Isa 15:1; 16:7; Jer 48:31,36 **3:27** [z]Dt 12:31; 2Ki 16:3; 21:6; 2Ch 28:3; Ps 106:38; Jer 19:4-5; Am 2:1; Mic 6:7

[a] *1* Hebrew *Jehoram*, a variant of *Joram*; also in verse 6 [b] *11* That is, he was Elijah's personal servant.

The Widow's Oil

4 The wife of a man from the company[a] of the prophets cried out to Elisha, "Your servant my husband is
dead, and you know that he revered
the LORD. But now his creditor[b] is
coming to take my two boys as his
slaves."
2Elisha replied to her, "How can I
help you? Tell me, what do you have in
your house?"
"Your servant has nothing there at
all," she said, "except a little oil."[c]
3Elisha said, "Go around and ask all
your neighbors for empty jars. Don't
ask for just a few. 4Then go inside and
shut the door behind you and your
sons. Pour oil into all the jars, and as
each is filled, put it to one side."
5She left him and afterward shut the
door behind her and her sons. They
brought the jars to her and she kept
pouring. 6When all the jars were full,
she said to her son, "Bring me another
one."
But he replied, "There is not a jar
left." Then the oil stopped flowing.
7She went and told the man of
God,[d] and he said, "Go, sell the oil and
pay your debts. You and your sons can
live on what is left."

The Shunammite's Son Restored to Life

8One day Elisha went to Shunem.[e] 5 →PG. 462
And a well-to-do woman was there,
who urged him to stay for a meal. So
whenever he came by, he stopped
there to eat. 9She said to her husband,
"I know that this man who often comes
our way is a holy man of God. 10Let's
make a small room on the roof and put
in it a bed and a table, a chair and a
lamp for him. Then he can stay[f] there
whenever he comes to us."
11One day when Elisha came, he
went up to his room and lay down
there. 12He said to his servant Gehazi,
"Call the Shunammite."[g] So he called
her, and she stood before him. 13Elisha
said to him, "Tell her, 'You have gone
to all this trouble for us. Now what can
be done for you? Can we speak on your
behalf to the king or the commander of
the army?' "
She replied, "I have a home among
my own people."
14"What can be done for her?" Elisha
asked.

4:1 [a] 1Sa 10:5; 2Ki 2:3 [b] Ex 22:26; Lev 25:39-43; Ne 5:3-5; Job 22:6; 24:9
4:2 [c] 1Ki 17:12
4:7 [d] 1Ki 12:22
4:8 [e] Jos 19:18
4:10 [f] Mt 10:41; Ro 12:13
4:12 [g] 2Ki 8:1

4:1-7

PE

A TALE OF TWO PROPHETS

Two of Israel's greatest prophets have no recorded writings. There is no book of Elijah or Elisha that contains their personal memoirs. There is, however, an enormous amount to be learned from these two prophets. Elijah's story begins in 1 Kings 17:1 and goes to 2 Kings 2:11. Elisha's story begins in 1 Kings 19:16 and ends in 2 Kings 13:21. These two prophets served God and his people during some difficult days, and their stories provide some of the most exciting reading in the Old Testament. The chart below lists the miracles God performed through these two men to demonstrate his power and to validate their ministries.

MIRACLES OF TWO AMAZING PROPHETS

Elijah	Elisha
Elijah was fed by ravens (1 Kings 17:1-6).	Elisha parted the Jordan River (2 Kings 2:13-14).
The widow's grain and oil were replenished (1 Kings 17:7-16).	Poisoned water made pure (2 Kings 2:19-22).
The widow's son was raised from death (1 Kings 17:17-24).	The widow's oil sustained (2 Kings 4:1-7).
Elijah defeated the prophets of Baal (1 Kings 18:16-42).	The Shunamite's son raised from the dead (2 Kings 4:8-37).
Ahaziah's soldiers consumed by fire (2 Kings 1:1-18).	The poison stew purified (2 Kings 4:38-41).
Elijah parted the Jordan river (2 Kings 2:1-9).	The multiplication of the prophet's bread (2 Kings 4:42-44).
Elijah was supernaturally transported to heaven (2 Kings 2:11-12).	Healing of General Naaman's leprosy (2 Kings 5:1-19).
	Elisha's servant Gehazi's leprosy (2 Kings 5:19-27).
	Recovery of the axehead from the river (2 Kings 6:1-7).
	Elisha's servant enabled to see host of God (2 Kings 6:8-17).
	The Aramean soldiers blinded and delivered (2 Kings 6:18-23).

These events are filled with demonstrations of God's power and man's faithfulness. Think your way through them as you read and allow God's Spirit to encourage you as he did these godly prophets.

Gehazi said, "Well, she has no son
and her husband is old."
15Then Elisha said, "Call her." So he
called her, and she stood in the doorway. **16**"About this time[h] next year,"
Elisha said, "you will hold a son in your
arms."
"No, my lord," she objected. "Don't
mislead your servant, O man of God!"
17But the woman became pregnant,
and the next year about that same time
she gave birth to a son, just as Elisha
had told her.
18The child grew, and one day he
went out to his father, who was with
the reapers.[i] **19**"My head! My head!"
he said to his father.
His father told a servant, "Carry him
to his mother." **20**After the servant had
lifted him up and carried him to his
mother, the boy sat on her lap until
noon, and then he died. **21**She went up
and laid him on the bed[j] of the man
of God, then shut the door and went
out.
22She called her husband and said,
"Please send me one of the servants
and a donkey so I can go to the man of
God quickly and return."
23"Why go to him today?" he asked.
"It's not the New Moon[k] or the Sabbath."
"It's all right," she said.
24She saddled the donkey and said
to her servant, "Lead on; don't slow
down for me unless I tell you." **25**So she
set out and came to the man of God at
Mount Carmel.[l]
When he saw her in the distance, the
man of God said to his servant Gehazi,
"Look! There's the Shunammite! **26**Run
to meet her and ask her, 'Are you all
right? Is your husband all right? Is your
child all right?' "
"Everything is all right," she said.
27When she reached the man of God
at the mountain, she took hold of his
feet. Gehazi came over to push her
away, but the man of God said, "Leave
her alone! She is in bitter distress,[m]
but the LORD has hidden it from me
and has not told me why."
28"Did I ask you for a son, my lord?"
she said. "Didn't I tell you, 'Don't raise
my hopes'?"
29Elisha said to Gehazi, "Tuck your
cloak into your belt,[n] take my staff[o]
in your hand and run. If you meet anyone, do not greet him, and if anyone
greets you, do not answer. Lay my staff
on the boy's face."
30But the child's mother said, "As
surely as the LORD lives and as you live,
I will not leave you." So he got up and
followed her.
31Gehazi went on ahead and laid the
staff on the boy's face, but there was no
sound or response. So Gehazi went
back to meet Elisha and told him, "The
boy has not awakened."
32When Elisha reached the house,
there was the boy lying dead on his
couch.[p] **33**He went in, shut the door
on the two of them and prayed[q] to the
LORD. **34**Then he got on the bed and lay
upon the boy, mouth to mouth, eyes to
eyes, hands to hands. As he stretched[r]
himself out upon him, the boy's body
grew warm. **35**Elisha turned away and
walked back and forth in the room and
then got on the bed and stretched out
upon him once more. The boy sneezed
seven times[s] and opened his eyes.[t]
36Elisha summoned Gehazi and
said, "Call the Shunammite." And he
did. When she came, he said, "Take
your son."[u] **37**She came in, fell at his
feet and bowed to the ground. Then
she took her son and went out.

Death in the Pot

38Elisha returned to Gilgal[v] and
there was a famine[w] in that region.
While the company of the prophets
was meeting with him, he said to his
servant, "Put on the large pot and cook
some stew for these men."
39One of them went out into the
fields to gather herbs and found a wild
vine. He gathered some of its gourds
and filled the fold of his cloak. When he
returned, he cut them up into the pot
of stew, though no one knew what they
were. **40**The stew was poured out for
the men, but as they began to eat it,
they cried out, "O man of God, there is
death in the pot!" And they could not
eat it.
41Elisha said, "Get some flour." He
put it into the pot and said, "Serve it to
the people to eat." And there was nothing harmful in the pot.[x]

Feeding of a Hundred

42A man came from Baal Shali-
shah,[y] bringing the man of God twenty loaves[z] of barley bread[a] baked
from the first ripe grain, along with
some heads of new grain. "Give it to
the people to eat," Elisha said.
43"How can I set this before a hundred men?" his servant asked.
But Elisha answered, "Give it to the
people to eat.[b] For this is what the
LORD says: 'They will eat and have
some left over.[c]' " **44**Then he set it before them, and they ate and had some
left over, according to the word of the
LORD.

4:16 [h] Ge 18:10
4:18 [i] Ru 2:3
4:21 [j] ver 32
4:23 [k] Nu 10:10; 1Ch 23:31; Ps 81:3
4:25 [l] 1Ki 18:20; 2Ki 2:25
4:27 [m] 1Sa 1:15
4:29 [n] 1Ki 18:46; 2Ki 2:8,14; 9:1 [o] Ex 4:2; 7:19; 14:16
4:32 [p] ver 21
4:33 [q] 1Ki 17:20; Mt 6:6
4:34 [r] 1Ki 17:21; Ac 20:10
4:35 [s] Jos 6:15 [t] 2Ki 8:5
4:36 [u] Heb 11:35
4:38 [v] 2Ki 2:1 [w] Lev 26:26; 2Ki 8:1
4:41 [x] Ex 15:25; 2Ki 2:21
4:42 [y] 1Sa 9:4 [z] Mt 14:17; 15:36 [a] 1Sa 9:7
4:43 [b] Lk 9:13 [c] Mt 14:20; Jn 6:12

Naaman Healed of Leprosy

5 Now Naaman was commander of
the army of the king of Aram.[d] He
was a great man in the sight of his master and highly regarded, because
through him the LORD had given victory to Aram. He was a valiant soldier,
but he had leprosy.[a][e]
2 Now bands[f] from Aram had gone
out and had taken captive a young girl
from Israel, and she served Naaman's
wife. 3 She said to her mistress, "If only
my master would see the prophet[g]
who is in Samaria! He would cure him
of his leprosy."
4 Naaman went to his master and
told him what the girl from Israel had
said. 5 "By all means, go," the king of
Aram replied. "I will send a letter to the
king of Israel." So Naaman left, taking
with him ten talents[b] of silver, six
thousand shekels[c] of gold and ten sets
of clothing.[h] 6 The letter that he took
to the king of Israel read: "With this
letter I am sending my servant Naaman
to you so that you may cure him of his
leprosy."
7 As soon as the king of Israel read
the letter,[i] he tore his robes and said,
"Am I God?[j] Can I kill and bring back
to life?[k] Why does this fellow send
someone to me to be cured of his leprosy? See how he is trying to pick a
quarrel[l] with me!"
8 When Elisha the man of God heard
that the king of Israel had torn his
robes, he sent him this message: "Why
have you torn your robes? Have the
man come to me and he will know that
there is a prophet[m] in Israel." 9 So Naaman went with his horses and chariots
and stopped at the door of Elisha's
house. 10 Elisha sent a messenger to say
to him, "Go, wash[n] yourself seven
times[o] in the Jordan, and your flesh
will be restored and you will be
cleansed."
11 But Naaman went away angry and
said, "I thought that he would surely
come out to me and stand and call on
the name of the LORD his God, wave his
hand[p] over the spot and cure me of
my leprosy. 12 Are not Abana and Phar-
par, the rivers of Damascus, better
than any of the waters[q] of Israel?
Couldn't I wash in them and be
cleansed?" So he turned and went off
in a rage.[r]
13 Naaman's servants went to him
and said, "My father,[s] if the prophet
had told you to do some great thing,
would you not have done it? How
much more, then, when he tells you,
'Wash and be cleansed'!" 14 So he went
down and dipped himself in the Jordan
seven times,[t] as the man of God had
told him, and his flesh was restored[u]
and became clean like that of a young
boy.[v]
15 Then Naaman and all his attendants went back to the man of God[w].
He stood before him and said, "Now I
know[x] that there is no God in all the
world except in Israel. Please accept
now a gift[y] from your servant."
16 The prophet answered, "As surely
as the LORD lives, whom I serve, I will
not accept a thing." And even though
Naaman urged him, he refused.[z]
17 "If you will not," said Naaman,
"please let me, your servant, be given
as much earth[a] as a pair of mules can
carry, for your servant will never again
make burnt offerings and sacrifices to
any other god but the LORD. 18 But may
the LORD forgive your servant for this
one thing: When my master enters the
temple of Rimmon to bow down and
he is leaning[b] on my arm and I bow
there also—when I bow down in the
temple of Rimmon, may the LORD forgive your servant for this."
19 "Go in peace,"[c] Elisha said.
After Naaman had traveled some
distance, 20 Gehazi, the servant of Elisha the man of God, said to himself,
"My master was too easy on Naaman,
this Aramean, by not accepting from
him what he brought. As surely as the
LORD[d] lives, I will run after him and
get something from him."
21 So Gehazi hurried after Naaman.
When Naaman saw him running toward him, he got down from the chariot to meet him. "Is everything all
right?" he asked.
22 "Everything is all right," Gehazi
answered. "My master sent me to say,
'Two young men from the company of
the prophets have just come to me
from the hill country of Ephraim.
Please give them a talent[d] of silver and
two sets of clothing.' "[e]
23 "By all means, take two talents,"
said Naaman. He urged Gehazi to accept them, and then tied up the two
talents of silver in two bags, with two
sets of clothing. He gave them to two of
his servants, and they carried them
ahead of Gehazi. 24 When Gehazi came
to the hill, he took the things from the
servants and put them away in the
house. He sent the men away and they

5:1 [d]Ge 10:22; 2Sa 10:19 [e]Ex 4:6; Nu 12:10; Lk 4:27
5:2 [f]2Ki 6:23; 13:20; 24:2
5:3 [g]Ge 20:7
5:5 [h]ver 22; Ge 24:53; Jdg 14:12; 1Sa 9:7
5:7 [i]2Ki 19:14 [j]Ge 30:2 [k]Dt 32:39; 1Sa 2:6 [l]1Ki 20:7
5:8 [m]1Ki 22:7
5:10 [n]Jn 9:7 [o]Ge 33:3; Lev 14:7
5:11 [p]Ex 7:19
5:12 [q]Isa 8:6 [r]Pr 14:17,29; 19:11; 29:11
5:13 [s]2Ki 6:21; 13:14
5:14 [t]Ge 33:3; Lev 14:7; Jos 6:15 [u]Ex 4:7 [v]Job 33:25; Lk 4:27
5:15 [w]Jos 2:11 [x]Jos 4:24; 1Sa 17:46; Da 2:47 [y]1Sa 9:7; 25:27
5:16 [z]ver 20,26; Ge 14:23; Da 5:17
5:17 [a]Ex 20:24
5:18 [b]2Ki 7:2
5:19 [c]1Sa 1:17; Ac 15:33
5:20 [d]Ex 20:7
5:22 [e]ver 5; Ge 45:22

[a] *1* The Hebrew word was used for various diseases affecting the skin—not necessarily leprosy; also in verses 3, 6, 7, 11 and 27.
[b] *5* That is, about 750 pounds (about 340 kilograms) [c] *5* That is, about 150 pounds (about 70 kilograms) [d] *22* That is, about 75 pounds (about 34 kilograms)

left. 25 Then he went in and stood before his master Elisha.

"Where have you been, Gehazi?" Elisha asked.

"Your servant didn't go anywhere," Gehazi answered.

26 But Elisha said to him, "Was not my spirit with you when the man got down from his chariot to meet you? Is this the time[f] to take money, or to accept clothes, olive groves, vineyards, flocks, herds, or menservants and maidservants?[g] 27 Naaman's leprosy[h] will cling to you and to your descendants forever." Then Gehazi[i] went from Elisha's presence and he was leprous, as white as snow.[j]

An Axhead Floats

6 The company[k] of the prophets said to Elisha, "Look, the place where we meet with you is too small for us. 2 Let us go to the Jordan, where each of us can get a pole; and let us build a place there for us to live."

And he said, "Go."

3 Then one of them said, "Won't you please come with your servants?"

"I will," Elisha replied. 4 And he went with them.

They went to the Jordan and began to cut down trees. 5 As one of them was cutting down a tree, the iron axhead fell into the water. "Oh, my lord," he cried out, "it was borrowed!"

6 The man of God asked, "Where did it fall?" When he showed him the place, Elisha cut a stick and threw[l] it there, and made the iron float. 7 "Lift it out," he said. Then the man reached out his hand and took it.

Elisha Traps Blinded Arameans

8 Now the king of Aram was at war with Israel. After conferring with his officers, he said, "I will set up my camp in such and such a place."

9 The man of God sent word to the king[m] of Israel: "Beware of passing that place, because the Arameans are going down there." 10 So the king of Israel checked on the place indicated by the man of God. Time and again Elisha warned[n] the king, so that he was on his guard in such places.

11 This enraged the king of Aram. He summoned his officers and demanded of them, "Will you not tell me which of us is on the side of the king of Israel?"

12 "None of us, my lord the king[o]," said one of his officers, "but Elisha, the prophet who is in Israel, tells the king of Israel the very words you speak in your bedroom."

13 "Go, find out where he is," the king ordered, "so I can send men and capture him." The report came back: "He is in Dothan."[p] 14 Then he sent[q] horses and chariots and a strong force there. They went by night and surrounded the city.

15 When the servant of the man of God got up and went out early the next morning, an army with horses and chariots had surrounded the city. "Oh, my lord, what shall we do?" the servant asked.

16 "Don't be afraid,"[r] the prophet answered. "Those who are with us are more[s] than those who are with them."

17 And Elisha prayed, "O LORD, open his eyes so he may see." Then the LORD opened the servant's eyes, and he looked and saw the hills full of horses and chariots[t] of fire all around Elisha.

18 As the enemy came down toward him, Elisha prayed to the LORD, "Strike these people with blindness."[u] So he struck them with blindness, as Elisha had asked.

19 Elisha told them, "This is not the road and this is not the city. Follow me, and I will lead you to the man you are looking for." And he led them to Samaria.

20 After they entered the city, Elisha said, "LORD, open the eyes of these men so they can see." Then the LORD opened their eyes and they looked, and there they were, inside Samaria.

21 When the king of Israel saw them, he asked Elisha, "Shall I kill them, my father?[v] Shall I kill them?"

22 "Do not kill them," he answered. "Would you kill men you have captured[w] with your own sword or bow? Set food and water before them so that they may eat and drink and then go back to their master." 23 So he prepared a great feast for them, and after they had finished eating and drinking, he sent them away, and they returned to their master. So the bands[x] from Aram stopped raiding Israel's territory.

5:26 [f] ver 16 [g] Jer 45:5
5:27 [h] Nu 12:10; 2Ki 15:5 [i] Col 3:5 [j] Ex 4:6
6:1 [k] 1Sa 10:5; 2Ki 4:38
6:6 [l] Ex 15:25; 2Ki 2:21
6:9 [m] ver 12
6:10 [n] Jer 11:18
6:12 [o] ver 9
6:13 [p] Ge 37:17
6:14 [q] 2Ki 1:9
6:16 [r] Ge 15:1 [s] 2Ch 32:7; Ps 55:18; Ro 8:31; 1Jn 4:4
6:17 [t] 2Ki 2:11,12; Ps 68:17; Zec 6:1-7
6:18 [u] Ge 19:11; Ac 13:11
6:21 [v] 2Ki 5:13
6:22 [w] Dt 20:11; 2Ch 28:8-15; Ro 12:20
6:23 [x] 2Ki 5:2

6:8–23

PROMISE 1

SPECIAL VISION

The difference between Elisha and his servant was their focus. A man who believes in God sees a reality behind the reality. He is not limited to what meets the eye. The God whose army stood between Elisha and his enemies is the same God you serve. List the things in your life that are beyond your power, then read verses 16 and 17 as your prayer to God about them.

For the next Promise 1 reading go to page 419.

Famine in Besieged Samaria

[24]Some time later, Ben-Hadad[y] king of Aram mobilized his entire army and marched up and laid siege[z] to Samaria. [25]There was a great famine[a] in the city; the siege lasted so long that a donkey's head sold for eighty shekels[a] of silver, and a quarter of a cab[b] of seed pods[c][b] for five shekels.[d]

[26]As the king of Israel was passing by on the wall, a woman cried to him, "Help me, my lord the king!"

[27]The king replied, "If the LORD does not help you, where can I get help for you? From the threshing floor? From the winepress?" [28]Then he asked her, "What's the matter?"

She answered, "This woman said to me, 'Give up your son so we may eat him today, and tomorrow we'll eat my son.' [29]So we cooked my son and ate[c] him. The next day I said to her, 'Give up your son so we may eat him,' but she had hidden him."

[30]When the king heard the woman's words, he tore[d] his robes. As he went along the wall, the people looked, and there, underneath, he had sackcloth[e] on his body. [31]He said, "May God deal with me, be it ever so severely, if the head of Elisha son of Shaphat remains on his shoulders today!"

[32]Now Elisha was sitting in his house, and the elders[f] were sitting with him. The king sent a messenger ahead, but before he arrived, Elisha said to the elders, "Don't you see how this murderer[g] is sending someone to cut off my head?[h] Look, when the messenger comes, shut the door and hold it shut against him. Is not the sound of his master's footsteps behind him?"

[33]While he was still talking to them, the messenger came down to him. And ⌊the king⌋ said, "This disaster is from the LORD. Why should I wait[i] for the LORD any longer?"

7 Elisha said, "Hear the word of the LORD. This is what the LORD says: About this time tomorrow, a seah[e] of flour will sell for a shekel[f] and two seahs[g] of barley for a shekel[j] at the gate of Samaria."

[2]The officer on whose arm the king was leaning[k] said to the man of God, "Look, even if the LORD should open the floodgates[l] of the heavens, could this happen?"

"You will see it with your own eyes," answered Elisha, "but you will not eat[m] any of it!"

The Siege Lifted

[3]Now there were four men with leprosy[h][n] at the entrance of the city gate. They said to each other, "Why stay here until we die? [4]If we say, 'We'll go into the city'—the famine is there, and we will die. And if we stay here, we will die. So let's go over to the camp of the Arameans and surrender. If they spare us, we live; if they kill us, then we die."

[5]At dusk they got up and went to the camp of the Arameans. When they reached the edge of the camp, not a man was there, [6]for the Lord had caused the Arameans to hear the sound[o] of chariots and horses and a great army, so that they said to one another, "Look, the king of Israel has hired[p] the Hittite[q] and Egyptian kings to attack us!" [7]So they got up and fled[r] in the dusk and abandoned their tents and their horses and donkeys. They left the camp as it was and ran for their lives.

[8]The men who had leprosy[s] reached the edge of the camp and entered one of the tents. They ate and drank, and carried away silver, gold and clothes, and went off and hid them. They returned and entered another tent and took some things from it and hid them also.

[9]Then they said to each other, "We're not doing right. This is a day of good news and we are keeping it to ourselves. If we wait until daylight, punishment will overtake us. Let's go at once and report this to the royal palace."

[10]So they went and called out to the city gatekeepers and told them, "We went into the Aramean camp and not a man was there—not a sound of anyone—only tethered horses and donkeys, and the tents left just as they were." [11]The gatekeepers shouted the news, and it was reported within the palace.

[12]The king got up in the night and said to his officers, "I will tell you what the Arameans have done to us. They know we are starving; so they have left the camp to hide[t] in the countryside, thinking, 'They will surely come out, and then we will take them alive and get into the city.' "

[13]One of his officers answered,

6:24 [y]1Ki 15:18; 20:1; 2Ki 8:7 [z]Dt 28:52
6:25 [a]Lev 26:26; Ru 1:1 [b]Isa 36:12
6:29 [c]Lev 26:29; Dt 28:53-55
6:30 [d]2Ki 18:37; Isa 22:15 [e]Ge 37:34; 1Ki 21:27
6:32 [f]Eze 8:1; 14:1; 20:1 [g]1Ki 18:4 [h]ver 31
6:33 [i]Lev 24:11; Job 2:9; 14:14; Isa 40:31
7:1 [j]ver 16
7:2 [k]2Ki 5:18 [l]ver 19; Ge 7:11; Ps 78:23; Mal 3:10 [m]ver 17
7:3 [n]Lev 13:45-46; Nu 5:1-4
7:6 [o]Ex 14:24; 2Sa 5:24; Eze 1:24 [p]2Sa 10:6; Jer 46:21 [q]Nu 13:29
7:7 [r]Jdg 7:21; Ps 48:4-6; Pr 28:1; Isa 30:17
7:8 [s]Isa 33:23; 35:6
7:12 [t]Jos 8:4; 2Ki 6:25-29

[a] *25* That is, about 2 pounds (about 1 kilogram) [b] *25* That is, probably about 1/2 pint (about 0.3 liter) [c] *25* Or *of dove's dung* [d] *25* That is, about 2 ounces (about 55 grams) [e] *1* That is, probably about 7 quarts (about 7.3 liters); also in verses 16 and 18 [f] *1* That is, about 2/5 ounce (about 11 grams); also in verses 16 and 18 [g] *1* That is, probably about 13 quarts (about 15 liters); also in verses 16 and 18 [h] *3* The Hebrew word is used for various diseases affecting the skin—not necessarily leprosy; also in verse 8.

"Have some men take five of the horses
that are left in the city. Their plight will
be like that of all the Israelites left
here—yes, they will only be like all
these Israelites who are doomed. So let
us send them to find out what happened."
14So they selected two chariots with
their horses, and the king sent them
after the Aramean army. He commanded the drivers, "Go and find out
what has happened." 15They followed
them as far as the Jordan, and they
found the whole road strewn with the
clothing and equipment the Arameans
had thrown away in their headlong
flight. So the messengers returned and
reported to the king. 16Then the people
went out and plundered[u] the camp of
the Arameans. So a seah of flour sold
for a shekel, and two seahs of barley
sold for a shekel,[v] as the LORD had
said.
17Now the king had put the officer
on whose arm he leaned in charge of
the gate, and the people trampled him
in the gateway, and he died,[w] just as
the man of God had foretold when the
king came down to his house. 18It happened as the man of God had said to
the king: "About this time tomorrow, a
seah of flour will sell for a shekel and
two seahs of barley for a shekel at the
gate of Samaria."
19The officer had said to the man of
God, "Look, even if the LORD should
open the floodgates[x] of the heavens,
could this happen?" The man of God
had replied, "You will see it with your
own eyes, but you will not eat any of
it!" 20And that is exactly what happened to him, for the people trampled
him in the gateway, and he died.

The Shunammite's Land Restored

8 Now Elisha had said to the woman[y]
whose son he had restored to life,
"Go away with your family and stay for
a while wherever you can, because the
LORD has decreed a famine[z] in the
land that will last seven years."[a] 2The
woman proceeded to do as the man
of God said. She and her family went
away and stayed in the land of the Philistines seven years.
3At the end of the seven years she
came back from the land of the Philistines and went to the king to beg for
her house and land. 4The king was talking to Gehazi, the servant of the man of
God, and had said, "Tell me about all
the great things Elisha has done." 5Just
as Gehazi was telling the king how Elisha had restored[b] the dead to life, the
woman whose son Elisha had brought
back to life came to beg the king for her
house and land.
Gehazi said, "This is the woman, my
lord the king, and this is her son whom
Elisha restored to life." 6The king asked
the woman about it, and she told him.
Then he assigned an official to her
case and said to him, "Give back everything that belonged to her, including
all the income from her land from the
day she left the country until now."

Hazael Murders Ben-Hadad

7Elisha went to Damascus,[c] and
Ben-Hadad[d] king of Aram was ill.
When the king was told, "The man of
God has come all the way up here," 8he
said to Hazael,[e] "Take a gift[f] with
you and go to meet the man of God.
Consult[g] the LORD through him; ask
him, 'Will I recover from this illness?' "
9Hazael went to meet Elisha, taking
with him as a gift forty camel-loads of
all the finest wares of Damascus. He
went in and stood before him, and
said, "Your son Ben-Hadad king of
Aram has sent me to ask, 'Will I recover
from this illness?' "
10Elisha answered, "Go and say to
him, 'You will certainly recover';[h]
but[a] the LORD has revealed to me that
he will in fact die." 11He stared at him
with a fixed gaze until Hazael felt
ashamed.[i] Then the man of God began to weep.[j]
12"Why is my lord weeping?" asked
Hazael.
"Because I know the harm[k] you will
do to the Israelites," he answered. "You
will set fire to their fortified places, kill
their young men with the sword,
dash[l] their little children[m] to the
ground, and rip open[n] their pregnant
women."
13Hazael said, "How could your servant, a mere dog,[o] accomplish such a
feat?"
"The LORD has shown me that you
will become king[p] of Aram," answered
Elisha.
14Then Hazael left Elisha and returned to his master. When Ben-
Hadad asked, "What did Elisha say to
you?" Hazael replied, "He told me that
you would certainly recover." 15But the
next day he took a thick cloth, soaked
it in water and spread it over the king's
face, so that he died.[q] Then Hazael
succeeded him as king.

Jehoram King of Judah

16In the fifth year of Joram[r] son of

7:16 [u]Isa 33:4,23 [v]ver 1
7:17 [w]ver 2; 2Ki 6:32
7:19 [x]ver 2
8:1 [y]2Ki 4:8-37 [z]Lev 26:26; Dt 28:22; Ru 1:1 [a]Ge 12:10; Ps 105:16; Hag 1:11
8:5 [b]2Ki 4:35
8:7 [c]2Sa 8:5; 1Ki 11:24 [d]2Ki 6:24
8:8 [e]1Ki 19:15 [f]Ge 32:20; 1Sa 9:7; 2Ki 1:2 [g]Jdg 18:5
8:10 [h]Isa 38:1
8:11 [i]Jdg 3:25 [j]Lk 19:41
8:12 [k]1Ki 19:17; 2Ki 10:32; 12:17; 13:3,7 [l]Ps 137:9; Isa 13:16; Hos 13:16; Na 3:10; Lk 19:44 [m]Ge 34:29 [n]2Ki 15:16; Am 1:13
8:13 [o]1Sa 17:43; 2Sa 3:8 [p]1Ki 19:15
8:15 [q]2Ki 1:17
8:16 [r]2Ki 1:17; 3:1

a *10* The Hebrew may also be read *Go and say, 'You will certainly not recover,' for.*

Ahab king of Israel, when Jehoshaphat was king of Judah, Jehoram[s] son of Jehoshaphat began his reign as king of Judah. 17He was thirty-two years old when he became king, and he reigned in Jerusalem eight years. 18He walked in the ways of the kings of Israel, as the house of Ahab had done, for he married a daughter[t] of Ahab. He did evil in the eyes of the LORD. 19Nevertheless, for the sake of his servant David, the LORD was not willing to destroy[u] Judah. He had promised to maintain a lamp[v] for David and his descendants forever.

20In the time of Jehoram, Edom rebelled against Judah and set up its own king.[w] 21So Jehoram[a] went to Zair with all his chariots. The Edomites surrounded him and his chariot commanders, but he rose up and broke through by night; his army, however, fled back home. 22To this day Edom has been in rebellion[x] against Judah. Libnah[y] revolted at the same time.

23As for the other events of Jehoram's reign, and all he did, are they not written in the book of the annals of the kings of Judah? 24Jehoram rested with his fathers and was buried with them in the City of David. And Ahaziah his son succeeded him as king.

Ahaziah King of Judah

25In the twelfth[z] year of Joram son of Ahab king of Israel, Ahaziah son of Jehoram king of Judah began to reign. 26Ahaziah was twenty-two years old when he became king, and he reigned in Jerusalem one year. His mother's name was Athaliah,[a] a granddaughter of Omri[b] king of Israel. 27He walked in the ways of the house of Ahab[c] and did evil[d] in the eyes of the LORD, as the house of Ahab had done, for he was related by marriage to Ahab's family.

28Ahaziah went with Joram son of Ahab to war against Hazael king of Aram at Ramoth Gilead.[e] The Arameans wounded Joram; 29so King Joram returned to Jezreel[f] to recover from the wounds the Arameans had inflicted on him at Ramoth[b] in his battle with Hazael[g] king of Aram.

Then Ahaziah son of Jehoram king of Judah went down to Jezreel to see Joram son of Ahab, because he had been wounded.

Jehu Anointed King of Israel

9 The prophet Elisha summoned a man from the company[h] of the prophets and said to him, "Tuck your cloak into your belt,[i] take this flask of oil[j] with you and go to Ramoth Gilead.[k] 2When you get there, look for Jehu son of Jehoshaphat, the son of Nimshi. Go to him, get him away from his companions and take him into an inner room. 3Then take the flask and pour the oil[l] on his head and declare, 'This is what the LORD says: I anoint you king over Israel.' Then open the door and run; don't delay!"

4So the young man, the prophet, went to Ramoth Gilead. 5When he arrived, he found the army officers sitting together. "I have a message for you, commander," he said.

"For which of us?" asked Jehu.

"For you, commander," he replied.

6Jehu got up and went into the house. Then the prophet poured the oil[m] on Jehu's head and declared, "This is what the LORD, the God of Israel, says: 'I anoint you king over the LORD's people Israel. 7You are to destroy the house of Ahab your master, and I will avenge[n] the blood of my servants[o] the prophets and the blood of all the LORD's servants shed by Jezebel.[p] 8The whole house[q] of Ahab will perish. I will cut off from Ahab every last male[r] in Israel—slave or free. 9I will make the house of Ahab like the house of Jeroboam[s] son of Nebat and like the house of Baasha[t] son of Ahijah. 10As for Jezebel, dogs[u] will devour her on the plot of ground at Jezreel, and no one will bury her.' " Then he opened the door and ran.

11When Jehu went out to his fellow officers, one of them asked him, "Is everything all right? Why did this madman[v] come to you?"

"You know the man and the sort of things he says," Jehu replied.

12"That's not true!" they said. "Tell us."

Jehu said, "Here is what he told me: 'This is what the LORD says: I anoint you king over Israel.' "

13They hurried and took their cloaks and spread[w] them under him on the bare steps. Then they blew the trumpet[x] and shouted, "Jehu is king!"

Jehu Kills Joram and Ahaziah

14So Jehu son of Jehoshaphat, the son of Nimshi, conspired against Joram. (Now Joram and all Israel had been defending Ramoth Gilead[y] against Hazael king of Aram, 15but King Joram[c] had returned to Jezreel to recover[z] from the wounds the Arameans had inflicted on him in the battle

8:16 [s] 2Ch 21:1-4
8:18 [t] ver 26; 2Ki 11:1
8:19 [u] Ge 6:13 [v] 2Sa 21:17; 7:13; 1Ki 11:36; Rev 21:23
8:20 [w] 1Ki 22:47
8:22 [x] Ge 27:40 [y] Nu 33:20; Jos 21:13; 2Ki 19:8
8:25 [z] 2Ki 9:29
8:26 [a] ver 18 [b] 1Ki 16:23
8:27 [c] 1Ki 16:30 [d] 1Ki 15:26
8:28 [e] Dt 4:43; 1Ki 22:3,29
8:29 [f] 2Ki 9:15 [g] 1Ki 19:15,17
9:1 [h] 1Sa 10:5 [i] 2Ki 4:29 [j] 1Sa 10:1
[k] 2Ki 8:28
9:3 [l] 1Ki 19:16
9:6 [m] 1Ki 19:16; 2Ch 22:7
9:7 [n] Ge 4:24; Rev 6:10 [o] Dt 32:43 [p] 1Ki 18:4; 21:15
9:8 [q] 2Ki 10:17 [r] Dt 32:36; 1Sa 25:22; 1Ki 21:21; 2Ki 14:26
9:9 [s] 1Ki 14:10; 15:29; 16:3,11 [t] 1Ki 16:3
9:10 [u] ver 35-36; 1Ki 21:23
9:11 [v] Jer 29:26; Jn 10:20; Ac 26:24
9:13 [w] Mt 21:8; Lk 19:36 [x] 2Sa 15:10; 1Ki 1:34,39
9:14 [y] Dt 4:43; 2Ki 8:28
9:15 [z] 2Ki 8:29

[a] *21* Hebrew *Joram,* a variant of *Jehoram;* also in verses 23 and 24 [b] *29* Hebrew *Ramah,* a variant of *Ramoth* [c] *15* Hebrew *Jehoram,* a variant of *Joram;* also in verses 17 and 21-24

with Hazael king of Aram.) Jehu said,
"If this is the way you feel, don't let
anyone slip out of the city to go and tell
the news in Jezreel." 16Then he got into
his chariot and rode to Jezreel, because
Joram was resting there and Ahaziah[a]
king of Judah had gone down to see
him.
17When the lookout[b] standing on
the tower in Jezreel saw Jehu's troops
approaching, he called out, "I see some
troops coming."
"Get a horseman," Joram ordered.
"Send him to meet them and ask, 'Do
you come in peace?[c]' "
18The horseman rode off to meet
Jehu and said, "This is what the king
says: 'Do you come in peace?' "
"What do you have to do with
peace?" Jehu replied. "Fall in behind me."
The lookout reported, "The messenger has reached them, but he isn't
coming back."
19So the king sent out a second
horseman. When he came to them he
said, "This is what the king says: 'Do
you come in peace?' "
Jehu replied, "What do you have to
do with peace? Fall in behind me."
20The lookout reported, "He has
reached them, but he isn't coming
back either. The driving is like[d] that of
Jehu son of Nimshi—he drives like a
madman."
21"Hitch up my chariot," Joram ordered. And when it was hitched up, Joram king of Israel and Ahaziah king of
Judah rode out, each in his own chariot, to meet Jehu. They met him at the
plot of ground that had belonged to
Naboth[e] the Jezreelite. 22When Joram
saw Jehu he asked, "Have you come in
peace, Jehu?"
"How can there be peace," Jehu replied, "as long as all the idolatry and
witchcraft of your mother Jezebel[f]
abound?"
23Joram turned about and fled, calling out to Ahaziah, "Treachery,[g] Ahaziah!"
24Then Jehu drew his bow[h] and
shot Joram between the shoulders. The
arrow pierced his heart and he
slumped down in his chariot. 25Jehu
said to Bidkar, his chariot officer, "Pick
him up and throw him on the field that
belonged to Naboth the Jezreelite. Remember how you and I were riding
together in chariots behind Ahab his
father when the LORD made this
prophecy[i] about him: 26'Yesterday I
saw the blood of Naboth[j] and the
blood of his sons, declares the LORD,
and I will surely make you pay for it
on this plot of ground, declares the
LORD.'[a] Now then, pick him up and
throw him on that plot, in accordance
with the word of the LORD."[k]
27When Ahaziah king of Judah saw
what had happened, he fled up the
road to Beth Haggan.[b] Jehu chased
him, shouting, "Kill him too!" They
wounded him in his chariot on the way
up to Gur near Ibleam,[l] but he escaped to Megiddo[m] and died there.
28His servants took him by chariot[n] to
Jerusalem and buried him with his fathers in his tomb in the City of David.
29(In the eleventh[o] year of Joram son
of Ahab, Ahaziah had become king of
Judah.)

Jezebel Killed

30Then Jehu went to Jezreel. When
Jezebel heard about it, she painted[p]
her eyes, arranged her hair and looked
out of a window. 31As Jehu entered the
gate, she asked, "Have you come in
peace, Zimri,[q] you murderer of your
master?"[c]
32He looked up at the window and
called out, "Who is on my side? Who?"
Two or three eunuchs looked down at
him. 33"Throw her down!" Jehu said.
So they threw her down, and some of
her blood spattered the wall and the
horses as they trampled her underfoot.[r]
34Jehu went in and ate and drank.
"Take care of that cursed woman," he
said, "and bury her, for she was a king's
daughter."[s] 35But when they went out
to bury her, they found nothing except
her skull, her feet and her hands.
36They went back and told Jehu, who
said, "This is the word of the LORD that
he spoke through his servant Elijah
the Tishbite: On the plot of ground
at Jezreel dogs[t] will devour Jezebel's
flesh.[d][u] 37Jezebel's body will be like
refuse[v] on the ground in the plot at
Jezreel, so that no one will be able to
say, 'This is Jezebel.' "

Ahab's Family Killed

10 Now there were in Samaria[w] seventy sons[x] of the house of Ahab.
So Jehu wrote letters and sent them to
Samaria: to the officials of Jezreel,[e][y]
to the elders and to the guardians[z] of
Ahab's children. He said, 2"As soon as
this letter reaches you, since your master's sons are with you and you have
chariots and horses, a fortified city and
weapons, 3choose the best and most

9:16 [a]2Ch 22:7
9:17 [b]Isa 21:6 [c]1Sa 16:4
9:20 [d]2Sa 18:27
9:21 [e]ver 26; 1Ki 21:1-7, 15-19
9:22 [f]1Ki 16:30-33; 18:19; 2Ch 21:13; Rev 2:20
9:23 [g]2Ki 11:14
9:24 [h]1Ki 22:34
9:25 [i]1Ki 21:19-22, 24-29
9:26 [j]1Ki 21:19 [k]1Ki 21:29
9:27 [l]Jdg 1:27 [m]2Ki 23:29
9:28 [n]2Ki 14:20; 23:30
9:29 [o]2Ki 8:25
9:30 [p]Jer 4:30; Eze 23:40
9:31 [q]1Ki 16:9-10
9:33 [r]Ps 7:5
9:34 [s]1Ki 16:31; 21:25
9:36 [t]Ps 68:23; Jer 15:3 [u]1Ki 21:23
9:37 [v]Ps 83:10; Isa 5:25; Jer 8:2; 9:22; 16:4; 25:33; Zep 1:17
10:1 [w]1Ki 13:32 [x]Jdg 8:30 [y]1Ki 21:1 [z]ver 5

[a]26 See 1 Kings 21:19. [b]27 Or *fled by way of the garden house* [c]31 Or *"Did Zimri have peace, who murdered his master?"*
[d]36 See 1 Kings 21:23. [e]1 Hebrew; some Septuagint manuscripts and Vulgate *of the city*

worthy of your master's sons and set
him on his father's throne. Then fight
for your master's house."
4 But they were terrified and said, "If
two kings could not resist him, how
can we?"
5 So the palace administrator, the
city governor, the elders and the guardians sent this message to Jehu: "We are
your servants[a] and we will do anything you say. We will not appoint anyone as king; you do whatever you think
best."
6 Then Jehu wrote them a second letter, saying, "If you are on my side and
will obey me, take the heads of your
master's sons and come to me in Jezreel by this time tomorrow."
Now the royal princes, seventy of
them, were with the leading men of the
city, who were rearing them. 7 When
the letter arrived, these men took the
princes and slaughtered all seventy[b]
of them. They put their heads[c] in baskets and sent them to Jehu in Jezreel.
8 When the messenger arrived, he told
Jehu, "They have brought the heads of
the princes."
Then Jehu ordered, "Put them in
two piles at the entrance of the city
gate until morning."
9 The next morning Jehu went out.
He stood before all the people and
said, "You are innocent. It was I who
conspired against my master and killed
him, but who killed all these? 10 Know
then, that not a word the LORD has spoken against the house of Ahab will fail.
The LORD has done what he promised[d] through his servant Elijah."[e]
11 So Jehu[f] killed everyone in Jezreel
who remained of the house of Ahab,
as well as all his chief men, his close
friends and his priests, leaving him no
survivor.[g]
12 Jehu then set out and went toward
Samaria. At Beth Eked of the Shepherds, 13 he met some relatives of Ahaziah king of Judah and asked, "Who are
you?"
They said, "We are relatives of Ahaziah,[h] and we have come down to
greet the families of the king and of the
queen mother.[i]"
14 "Take them alive!" he ordered. So
they took them alive and slaughtered
them by the well of Beth Eked—forty-
two men. He left no survivor.
15 After he left there, he came upon
Jehonadab[j] son of Recab,[k] who was
on his way to meet him. Jehu greeted
him and said, "Are you in accord with
me, as I am with you?"
"I am," Jehonadab answered.
"If so," said Jehu, "give me your
hand."[l] So he did, and Jehu helped
him up into the chariot. 16 Jehu said,
"Come with me and see my zeal[m] for
the LORD." Then he had him ride along
in his chariot.
17 When Jehu came to Samaria, he
killed all who were left there of Ahab's
family;[n] he destroyed them, according
to the word of the LORD spoken to Elijah.

Ministers of Baal Killed

18 Then Jehu brought all the people
together and said to them, "Ahab
served[o] Baal a little; Jehu will serve
him much. 19 Now summon[p] all the
prophets of Baal, all his ministers and
all his priests. See that no one is missing, because I am going to hold a great
sacrifice for Baal. Anyone who fails to
come will no longer live." But Jehu was
acting deceptively in order to destroy
the ministers of Baal.
20 Jehu said, "Call an assembly[q] in
honor of Baal." So they proclaimed it.
21 Then he sent word throughout Israel,
and all the ministers of Baal came; not
one stayed away. They crowded into
the temple of Baal until it was full from
one end to the other. 22 And Jehu said
to the keeper of the wardrobe, "Bring
robes for all the ministers of Baal." So
he brought out robes for them.
23 Then Jehu and Jehonadab son of
Recab went into the temple of Baal.
Jehu said to the ministers of Baal,
"Look around and see that no servants
of the LORD are here with you—only
ministers of Baal." 24 So they went in to
make sacrifices and burnt offerings.
Now Jehu had posted eighty men outside with this warning: "If one of you
lets any of the men I am placing in your
hands escape, it will be your life for his
life."[r]
25 As soon as Jehu had finished making the burnt offering, he ordered the
guards and officers: "Go in and kill[s]
them; let no one escape."[t] So they cut
them down with the sword. The guards
and officers threw the bodies out and
then entered the inner shrine of the
temple of Baal. 26 They brought the sacred stone[u] out of the temple of Baal
and burned it. 27 They demolished the
sacred stone of Baal and tore down the
temple[v] of Baal, and people have used
it for a latrine to this day.
28 So Jehu[w] destroyed Baal worship
in Israel. 29 However, he did not turn
away from the sins[x] of Jeroboam son
of Nebat, which he had caused Israel to
commit—the worship of the golden
calves[y] at Bethel[z] and Dan.
30 The LORD said to Jehu, "Because
you have done well in accomplishing

10:5 [a] Jos 9:8; 1Ki 20:4,32
10:7 [b] 1Ki 21:21 [c] 2Sa 4:8
10:10 [d] 2Ki 9:7-10 [e] 1Ki 21:29
10:11 [f] Hos 1:4 [g] ver 14; Job 18:19
10:13 [h] 2Ki 8:24,29; 2Ch 22:8 [i] 1Ki 2:19
10:15 [j] Jer 35:6,14-19 [k] 1Ch 2:55; Jer 35:2 [l] Ezr 10:19; Eze 17:18
10:16 [m] Nu 25:13; 1Ki 19:10
10:17 [n] 2Ki 9:8
10:18 [o] Jdg 2:11; 1Ki 16:31-32
10:19 [p] 1Ki 18:19; 22:6
10:20 [q] Ex 32:5; Joel 1:14
10:24 [r] 1Ki 20:39
10:25 [s] Ex 22:20; 2Ki 11:18 [t] 1Ki 18:40
10:26 [u] 1Ki 14:23
10:27 [v] 1Ki 16:32
10:28 [w] 1Ki 19:17
10:29 [x] 1Ki 12:30 [y] 1Ki 12:28-29 [z] 1Ki 12:32

what is right in my eyes and have done
to the house of Ahab all I had in mind
to do, your descendants will sit on the
throne of Israel to the fourth generation."[a] **31**Yet Jehu was not careful[b] to
keep the law of the LORD, the God of
Israel, with all his heart. He did not
turn away from the sins[c] of Jeroboam,
which he had caused Israel to commit.
32In those days the LORD began to
reduce[d] the size of Israel. Hazael[e]
overpowered the Israelites throughout
their territory **33**east of the Jordan in all
the land of Gilead (the region of Gad,
Reuben and Manasseh), from Aroer[f]
by the Arnon Gorge through Gilead to
Bashan.
34As for the other events of Jehu's
reign, all he did, and all his achievements, are they not written in the book
of the annals[g] of the kings of Israel?
35Jehu rested with his fathers and
was buried in Samaria. And Jehoahaz
his son succeeded him as king. **36**The
time that Jehu reigned over Israel in
Samaria was twenty-eight years.

Athaliah and Joash

11 When Athaliah[h] the mother of
Ahaziah saw that her son was dead,
she proceeded to destroy the whole
royal family. **2**But Jehosheba, the
daughter of King Jehoram[a] and sister
of Ahaziah, took Joash[i] son of Ahaziah and stole him away from among the
royal princes, who were about to be
murdered. She put him and his nurse
in a bedroom to hide him from Athaliah; so he was not killed.[j] **3**He remained hidden with his nurse at the
temple of the LORD for six years while
Athaliah ruled the land.
4In the seventh year Jehoiada sent
for the commanders of units of a hundred, the Carites[k] and the guards and
had them brought to him at the temple
of the LORD. He made a covenant with
them and put them under oath at the
temple of the LORD. Then he showed
them the king's son. **5**He commanded
them, saying, "This is what you are to
do: You who are in the three companies that are going on duty on the
Sabbath[l]—a third of you guarding
the royal palace,[m] **6**a third at the Sur
Gate, and a third at the gate behind the
guard, who take turns guarding the
temple— **7**and you who are in the other two companies that normally go off
Sabbath duty are all to guard the temple for the king. **8**Station yourselves
around the king, each man with his
weapon in his hand. Anyone who approaches your ranks[b] must be put to
death. Stay close to the king wherever
he goes."
9The commanders of units of a hundred did just as Jehoiada the priest ordered. Each one took his men—those
who were going on duty on the Sabbath and those who were going off
duty—and came to Jehoiada the priest.
10Then he gave the commanders the
spears and shields[n] that had belonged
to King David and that were in the temple of the LORD. **11**The guards, each
with his weapon in his hand, stationed
themselves around the king—near the
altar and the temple, from the south
side to the north side of the temple.
12Jehoiada brought out the king's
son and put the crown on him; he presented him with a copy of the covenant[o] and proclaimed him king.
They anointed[p] him, and the people
clapped their hands[q] and shouted,
"Long live the king!"[r]
13When Athaliah heard the noise
made by the guards and the people,
she went to the people at the temple of
the LORD. **14**She looked and there was
the king, standing by the pillar,[s] as the
custom was. The officers and the trumpeters were beside the king, and all
the people of the land were rejoicing
and blowing trumpets.[t] Then Athaliah
tore[u] her robes and called out, "Treason! Treason!"[v]
15Jehoiada the priest ordered the
commanders of units of a hundred,
who were in charge of the troops:
"Bring her out between the ranks[c] and
put to the sword anyone who follows
her." For the priest had said, "She must
not be put to death in the temple[w] of
the LORD." **16**So they seized her as she
reached the place where the horses enter[x] the palace grounds, and there she
was put to death.[y]
17Jehoiada then made a covenant[z]
between the LORD and the king and
people that they would be the LORD's
people. He also made a covenant between the king and the people.[a] **18**All
the people of the land went to the temple[b] of Baal and tore it down. They
smashed[c] the altars and idols to
pieces and killed Mattan the priest[d] of
Baal in front of the altars.
Then Jehoiada the priest posted
guards at the temple of the LORD. **19**He
took with him the commanders of
hundreds, the Carites,[e] the guards
and all the people of the land, and together they brought the king down
from the temple of the LORD and went

10:30 [a]ver 35; 2Ki 15:12
10:31 [b]Pr 4:23 [c]1Ki 12:30
10:32 [d]2Ki 13:25 [e]1Ki 19:17; 2Ki 8:12
10:33 [f]Nu 32:34; Dt 2:36; Jdg 11:26; Isa 17:2
10:34 [g]1Ki 15:31
11:1 [h]2Ki 8:18
11:2 [i]ver 21; 2Ki 12:1 [j]Jdg 9:5
11:4 [k]ver 19
11:5 [l]1Ch 9:25 [m]1Ki 14:27
11:10 [n]2Sa 8:7; 1Ch 18:7
11:12 [o]Ex 25:16; 2Ki 23:3 [p]1Sa 9:16; 1Ki 1:39 [q]Ps 47:1; 98:8; Isa 55:12 [r]1Sa 10:24
11:14 [s]1Ki 7:15; 2Ki 23:3; 2Ch 34:31 [t]1Ki 1:39 [u]Ge 37:29 [v]2Ki 9:23
11:15 [w]1Ki 2:30
11:16 [x]Ne 3:28; Jer 31:40 [y]Ge 4:14
11:17 [z]Ex 24:8; 2Sa 5:3; 2Ch 15:12; 23:3; 29:10; 34:31; Ezr 10:3 [a]2Ki 23:3; Jer 34:8
11:18 [b]1Ki 16:32 [c]Dt 12:3 [d]1Ki 18:40; 2Ki 10:25; 23:20
11:19 [e]ver 4

a *2* Hebrew *Joram*, a variant of *Jehoram*
b *8* Or *approaches the precincts*
c *15* Or *out from the precincts*

into the palace, entering by way of the gate of the guards. The king then took his place on the royal throne, 20and all the people of the land rejoiced.[f] And the city was quiet, because Athaliah had been slain with the sword at the palace.

21Joash[a] was seven years old when he began to reign.

Joash Repairs the Temple

12 In the seventh year of Jehu, Joash[b][g] became king, and he reigned in Jerusalem forty years. His mother's name was Zibiah; she was from Beersheba. 2Joash did what was right in the eyes of the LORD all the years Jehoiada the priest instructed him. 3The high places,[h] however, were not removed; the people continued to offer sacrifices and burn incense there.

4Joash said to the priests, "Collect[i] all the money that is brought as sacred offerings[j] to the temple of the LORD—the money collected in the census,[k] the money received from personal vows and the money brought voluntarily[l] to the temple. 5Let every priest receive the money from one of the treasurers, and let it be used to repair whatever damage is found in the temple."

6But by the twenty-third year of King Joash the priests still had not repaired the temple. 7Therefore King Joash summoned Jehoiada the priest and the other priests and asked them, "Why aren't you repairing the damage done to the temple? Take no more money from your treasurers, but hand it over for repairing the temple." 8The priests agreed that they would not collect any more money from the people and that they would not repair the temple themselves.

9Jehoiada the priest took a chest and bored a hole in its lid. He placed it beside the altar, on the right side as one enters the temple of the LORD. The priests who guarded the entrance[m] put into the chest all the money[n] that was brought to the temple of the LORD. 10Whenever they saw that there was a large amount of money in the chest, the royal secretary[o] and the high priest came, counted the money that had been brought into the temple of the LORD and put it into bags. 11When the amount had been determined, they gave the money to the men appointed to supervise the work on the temple. With it they paid those who worked on the temple of the LORD—the carpenters and builders, 12the masons and stonecutters.[p] They purchased timber and dressed stone for the repair of the temple of the LORD, and met all the other expenses of restoring the temple.

13The money brought into the temple was not spent for making silver basins, wick trimmers, sprinkling bowls, trumpets or any other articles of gold[q] or silver for the temple of the LORD; 14it was paid to the workmen, who used it to repair the temple. 15They did not require an accounting from those to whom they gave the money to pay the workers, because they acted with com-

11:20 [f]Pr 11:10; 28:12; 29:2
12:1 [g]2Ki 11:2
12:3 [h]1Ki 3:3; 2Ki 14:4; 15:35; 18:4
12:4 [i]2Ki 22:4 [j]Ex 35:5 [k]Ex 30:12 [l]Ex 35:29; 1Ch 29:3-9
12:9 [m]Jer 35:4 [n]2Ch 24:8; Mk 12:41; Lk 21:1
12:10 [o]2Sa 8:17
12:12 [p]2Ki 22:5-6
12:13 [q]1Ki 7:48-51; 2Ch 24:14

[a] *21* Hebrew *Jehoash,* a variant of *Joash*
[b] *1* Hebrew *Jehoash,* a variant of *Joash*; also in verses 2, 4, 6, 7 and 18

12:1–16

PROMISE **5**

BUILDING THE KINGDOM—LITERALLY

Sometimes building God's kingdom requires putting saw to wood and hammer to nail. That's what Joash intended at the beginning of his reign—that the temple be restored to its former glory. But in the 23rd year of his 40-year rule, the work still had not been done. He'd asked the wrong people to complete the repairs. After questioning the priests, Joash cranked up the building committee and devoted all temple funds to repair work.

Jehoiada the priest collected the funds and gave them to sub-contracters who hired "the carpenters and builders, the masons and stonecutters" (vv. 11–12). Finally, the right men were on the job. One can almost hear the sounds around the construction site when reading these verses.

One verse stands out in this passage: "They [the priests] did not require an accounting from those to whom they gave the money to pay the workers [the sub-contractors], because they acted with complete honesty" (v. 15). That's saying a lot about the integrity of the men who supervised the work on the temple. They had respect for God's house and carried out their task with complete financial responsibility.

All of us as members of a congregation have responsibility for the building in which we worship. When the call comes, either for funds or for hands to do the work, are you willing to give of your time and money? If you have responsibility for church finances, do you act with the same unquestionable integrity as the men in verse 15? Your challenge today is to follow the example of the men in this story; men who responsibly gave of their time and money and got dirty for God.

For the next Promise 5 reading go to page 511.

plete honesty.[r] 16The money from the guilt offerings[s] and sin offerings[t] was not brought into the temple of the LORD; it belonged[u] to the priests.

17About this time Hazael[v] king of Aram went up and attacked Gath and captured it. Then he turned to attack Jerusalem. 18But Joash king of Judah took all the sacred objects dedicated by his fathers—Jehoshaphat, Jehoram and Ahaziah, the kings of Judah—and the gifts he himself had dedicated and all the gold found in the treasuries of the temple of the LORD and of the royal palace, and he sent[w] them to Hazael king of Aram, who then withdrew[x] from Jerusalem.

19As for the other events of the reign of Joash, and all he did, are they not written in the book of the annals of the kings of Judah? 20His officials[y] conspired against him and assassinated[z] him at Beth Millo,[a] on the road down to Silla. 21The officials who murdered him were Jozabad son of Shimeath and Jehozabad son of Shomer. He died and was buried with his fathers in the City of David. And Amaziah his son succeeded him as king.

Jehoahaz King of Israel

13 In the twenty-third year of Joash son of Ahaziah king of Judah, Jehoahaz son of Jehu became king of Israel in Samaria, and he reigned seventeen years. 2He did evil[b] in the eyes of the LORD by following the sins of Jeroboam son of Nebat, which he had caused Israel to commit, and he did not turn away from them. 3So the LORD's anger[c] burned against Israel, and for a long time he kept them under the power[d] of Hazael king of Aram and Ben-Hadad[e] his son.

4Then Jehoahaz sought[f] the LORD's favor, and the LORD listened to him, for he saw[g] how severely the king of Aram was oppressing[h] Israel. 5The LORD provided a deliverer[i] for Israel, and they escaped from the power of Aram. So the Israelites lived in their own homes as they had before. 6But they did not turn away from the sins[j] of the house of Jeroboam, which he had caused Israel to commit; they continued in them. Also, the Asherah pole[a][k] remained standing in Samaria.

7Nothing had been left[l] of the army of Jehoahaz except fifty horsemen, ten chariots and ten thousand foot soldiers, for the king of Aram had destroyed the rest and made them like the dust[m] at threshing time.

8As for the other events of the reign of Jehoahaz, all he did and his achievements, are they not written in the book of the annals of the kings of Israel? 9Jehoahaz rested with his fathers and was buried in Samaria. And Jehoash[b] his son succeeded him as king.

Jehoash King of Israel

10In the thirty-seventh year of Joash king of Judah, Jehoash son of Jehoahaz became king of Israel in Samaria, and he reigned sixteen years. 11He did evil in the eyes of the LORD and did not turn away from any of the sins of Jeroboam son of Nebat, which he had caused Israel to commit; he continued in them.

12As for the other events of the reign of Jehoash, all he did and his achievements, including his war against Amaziah[n] king of Judah, are they not written in the book of the annals[o] of the kings of Israel? 13Jehoash rested with his fathers, and Jeroboam[p] succeeded him on the throne. Jehoash was buried in Samaria with the kings of Israel.

14Now Elisha was suffering from the illness from which he died. Jehoash king of Israel went down to see him and wept over him. "My father! My father!" he cried. "The chariots[q] and horsemen of Israel!"

15Elisha said, "Get a bow and some arrows,"[r] and he did so. 16"Take the bow in your hands," he said to the king of Israel. When he had taken it, Elisha put his hands on the king's hands.

17"Open the east window," he said, and he opened it. "Shoot!"[s] Elisha said, and he shot. "The LORD's arrow of victory, the arrow of victory over Aram!" Elisha declared. "You will completely destroy the Arameans at Aphek."[t]

18Then he said, "Take the arrows," and the king took them. Elisha told him, "Strike the ground." He struck it three times and stopped. 19The man of God was angry with him and said, "You should have struck the ground five or six times; then you would have defeated Aram and completely destroyed it. But now you will defeat it only three times."[u]

20Elisha died and was buried.

Now Moabite raiders[v] used to enter the country every spring. 21Once while some Israelites were burying a man, suddenly they saw a band of raiders; so they threw the man's body into Elisha's tomb. When the body touched Elisha's bones, the man came to life[w] and stood up on his feet.

12:15 [r]2Ki 22:7; 1Co 4:2
12:16 [s]Lev 5:14-19; Nu 18:9 [t]Lev 4:1-35 [u]Lev 7:7
12:17 [v]2Ki 8:12
12:18 [w]1Ki 15:18; 2Ch 21:16-17 [x]1Ki 15:21
12:20 [y]2Ki 14:5 [z]2Ch 24:25 [a]Jdg 9:6
13:2 [b]1Ki 12:26-33
13:3 [c]Dt 31:17; Jdg 2:14 [d]1Ki 8:12; 12:17; 19:17 [e]ver 24
13:4 [f]Dt 4:29; Ps 78:34 [g]Ex 3:7; Dt 26:7 [h]2Ki 14:26
13:5 [i]ver 25; 2Ki 14:25,27
13:6 [j]1Ki 12:30 [k]1Ki 16:33
13:7 [l]2Ki 10:32-33 [m]2Sa 22:43
13:12 [n]2Ki 14:15 [o]1Ki 15:31
13:13 [p]2Ki 14:23; Hos 1:1
13:14 [q]2Ki 2:12
13:15 [r]1Sa 20:20
13:17 [s]Jos 8:18 [t]1Ki 20:26
13:19 [u]ver 25
13:20 [v]2Ki 3:7; 24:2
13:21 [w]Mt 27:52

[a]6 That is, a symbol of the goddess Asherah; here and elsewhere in 2 Kings [b]9 Hebrew *Joash,* a variant of *Jehoash;* also in verses 12-14 and 25

22 Hazael king of Aram oppressed[x]
Israel throughout the reign of Jehoahaz. 23 But the LORD was gracious to
them and had compassion and showed
concern for them because of his covenant[y] with Abraham, Isaac and Jacob. To this day he has been unwilling
to destroy[z] them or banish them from
his presence.[a]

24 Hazael king of Aram died, and
Ben-Hadad[b] his son succeeded him
as king. 25 Then Jehoash son of Jehoahaz recaptured from Ben-Hadad son
of Hazael the towns he had taken in
battle from his father Jehoahaz. Three
times[c] Jehoash defeated him, and so
he recovered[d] the Israelite towns.

Amaziah King of Judah

14 In the second year of Jehoash[a] son
of Jehoahaz king of Israel, Amaziah
son of Joash king of Judah began to
reign. 2 He was twenty-five years old
when he became king, and he reigned
in Jerusalem twenty-nine years. His
mother's name was Jehoaddin; she was
from Jerusalem. 3 He did what was right
in the eyes of the LORD, but not as his
father David had done. In everything
he followed the example of his father
Joash. 4 The high places,[e] however,
were not removed; the people continued to offer sacrifices and burn incense
there.

5 After the kingdom was firmly in his
grasp, he executed[f] the officials[g]
who had murdered his father the king.
6 Yet he did not put the sons of the as-
sassins to death, in accordance with
what is written in the Book of the
Law[h] of Moses where the LORD commanded: "Fathers shall not be put to
death for their children, nor children
put to death for their fathers; each is to
die for his own sins."[b][i]

7 He was the one who defeated ten
thousand Edomites in the Valley of
Salt[j] and captured Sela[k] in battle,
calling it Joktheel, the name it has to
this day.

8 Then Amaziah sent messengers to
Jehoash son of Jehoahaz, the son of
Jehu, king of Israel, with the challenge:
"Come, meet me face to face."

9 But Jehoash king of Israel replied to
Amaziah king of Judah: "A thistle[l] in
Lebanon sent a message to a cedar in
Lebanon, 'Give your daughter to my
son in marriage.' Then a wild beast in
Lebanon came along and trampled the
thistle underfoot. 10 You have indeed
defeated Edom and now you are arrogant.[m] Glory in your victory, but stay
at home! Why ask for trouble and cause
your own downfall and that of Judah
also?"

11 Amaziah, however, would not listen, so Jehoash king of Israel attacked.
He and Amaziah king of Judah faced
each other at Beth Shemesh[n] in Judah. 12 Judah was routed by Israel, and
every man fled to his home.[o] 13 Jehoash king of Israel captured Amaziah
king of Judah, the son of Joash, the son
of Ahaziah, at Beth Shemesh. Then Jehoash went to Jerusalem and broke
down the wall[p] of Jerusalem from
the Ephraim Gate[q] to the Corner
Gate[r]—a section about six hundred
feet long.[c] 14 He took all the gold and
silver and all the articles found in the
temple of the LORD and in the treasuries of the royal palace. He also took
hostages and returned to Samaria.

15 As for the other events of the reign
of Jehoash, what he did and his
achievements, including his war[s]
against Amaziah king of Judah, are
they not written in the book of the annals of the kings of Israel? 16 Jehoash
rested with his fathers and was buried
in Samaria with the kings of Israel. And
Jeroboam his son succeeded him as
king.

17 Amaziah son of Joash king of Judah lived for fifteen years after the
death of Jehoash son of Jehoahaz king
of Israel. 18 As for the other events of
Amaziah's reign, are they not written in
the book of the annals of the kings of
Judah?

19 They conspired[t] against him in
Jerusalem, and he fled to Lachish,[u]
but they sent men after him to Lachish
and killed him there. 20 He was brought
back by horse[v] and was buried in Jerusalem with his fathers, in the City of
David.

21 Then all the people of Judah took
Azariah,[d][w] who was sixteen years old,
and made him king in place of his father Amaziah. 22 He was the one who
rebuilt Elath[x] and restored it to Judah
after Amaziah rested with his fathers.

Jeroboam II King of Israel

23 In the fifteenth year of Amaziah
son of Joash king of Judah, Jeroboam[y]
son of Jehoash king of Israel became
king in Samaria, and he reigned forty-
one years. 24 He did evil in the eyes of
the LORD and did not turn away from
any of the sins of Jeroboam son of Nebat, which he had caused Israel to
commit.[z] 25 He was the one who re-

13:22 [x] 1Ki 19:17; 2Ki 8:12
13:23 [y] Ge 13:16-17; Ex 2:24 [z] Dt 29:20 [a] Ex 33:15; 2Ki 14:27; 17:18; 24:3,20
13:24 [b] ver 3
13:25 [c] ver 18,19 [d] 2Ki 10:32
14:4 [e] 2Ki 12:3; 16:4
14:5 [f] 2Ki 21:24 [g] 2Ki 12:20
14:6 [h] Dt 28:61 [i] Nu 26:11; Job 21:20; Jer 31:30; 44:3; Eze 18:4,20
14:7 [j] 2Sa 8:13; 2Ch 25:11 [k] Jdg 1:36
14:9 [l] Jdg 9:8-15
14:10 [m] Dt 8:14; 2Ch 26:16; 32:25
14:11 [n] Jos 15:10
14:12 [o] 2Sa 18:17
14:13 [p] 1Ki 3:1; 2Ch 33:14; 36:19; Jer 39:2 [q] Ne 8:16; 12:39 [r] 2Ch 25:23; Jer 31:38; Zec 14:10
14:15 [s] 2Ki 13:12
14:19 [t] 2Ki 12:20 [u] Jos 10:3; 2Ki 18:14,17
14:20 [v] 2Ki 9:28
14:21 [w] 2Ki 15:1; 2Ch 26:23
14:22 [x] 1Ki 9:26; 2Ki 16:6
14:23 [y] 2Ki 13:13
14:24 [z] 1Ki 15:30

[a] *1* Hebrew *Joash,* a variant of *Jehoash;* also in verses 13, 23 and 27 [b] *6* Deut. 24:16
[c] *13* Hebrew *four hundred cubits* (about 180 meters) [d] *21* Also called *Uzziah*

stored the boundaries of Israel from Lebo[a] Hamath[a] to the Sea of the Arabah,[b][b] in accordance with the word of the LORD, the God of Israel, spoken through his servant Jonah[c] son of Amittai, the prophet from Gath Hepher.

26 The LORD had seen how bitterly everyone in Israel, whether slave or free,[d] was suffering;[e] there was no one to help them.[f] 27 And since the LORD had not said he would blot out[g] the name of Israel from under heaven, he saved[h] them by the hand of Jeroboam son of Jehoash.

28 As for the other events of Jeroboam's reign, all he did, and his military achievements, including how he recovered for Israel both Damascus[i] and Hamath,[j] which had belonged to Yaudi,[c] are they not written in the book of the annals[k] of the kings of Israel? 29 Jeroboam rested with his fathers, the kings of Israel. And Zechariah his son succeeded him as king.

Azariah King of Judah

15 In the twenty-seventh year of Jeroboam king of Israel, Azariah[l] son of Amaziah king of Judah began to reign. 2 He was sixteen years old when he became king, and he reigned in Jerusalem fifty-two years. His mother's name was Jecoliah; she was from Jerusalem. 3 He did what was right in the eyes of the LORD, just as his father Amaziah had done. 4 The high places, however, were not removed; the people continued to offer sacrifices and burn incense there.

5 The LORD afflicted[m] the king with leprosy[d] until the day he died, and he lived in a separate house.[e][n] Jotham[o] the king's son had charge of the palace[p] and governed the people of the land.

6 As for the other events of Azariah's reign, and all he did, are they not written in the book of the annals of the kings of Judah? 7 Azariah rested[q] with his fathers and was buried near them in the City of David. And Jotham[r] his son succeeded him as king.

Zechariah King of Israel

8 In the thirty-eighth year of Azariah king of Judah, Zechariah son of Jeroboam became king of Israel in Samaria, and he reigned six months. 9 He did evil[s] in the eyes of the LORD, as his fathers had done. He did not turn away from the sins of Jeroboam son of Nebat, which he had caused Israel to commit.

10 Shallum son of Jabesh conspired against Zechariah. He attacked him in front of the people,[f] assassinated[t] him and succeeded him as king. 11 The other events of Zechariah's reign are written in the book of the annals[u] of the kings of Israel. 12 So the word of the LORD spoken to Jehu was fulfilled:[v] "Your descendants will sit on the throne of Israel to the fourth generation."[g]

Shallum King of Israel

13 Shallum son of Jabesh became king in the thirty-ninth year of Uzziah king of Judah, and he reigned in Samaria[w] one month. 14 Then Menahem son of Gadi went from Tirzah[x] up to Samaria. He attacked Shallum son of Jabesh in Samaria, assassinated[y] him and succeeded him as king.

15 The other events of Shallum's reign, and the conspiracy he led, are written in the book of the annals[z] of the kings of Israel.

16 At that time Menahem, starting out from Tirzah, attacked Tiphsah[a] and everyone in the city and its vicinity, because they refused to open[b] their gates. He sacked Tiphsah and ripped open all the pregnant women.

Menahem King of Israel

17 In the thirty-ninth year of Azariah king of Judah, Menahem son of Gadi became king of Israel, and he reigned in Samaria ten years. 18 He did evil in the eyes of the LORD. During his entire reign he did not turn away from the sins of Jeroboam son of Nebat, which he had caused Israel to commit.

19 Then Pul[h][c] king of Assyria invaded the land, and Menahem gave him a thousand talents[i] of silver to gain his support and strengthen his own hold on the kingdom. 20 Menahem exacted this money from Israel. Every wealthy man had to contribute fifty shekels[j] of silver to be given to the king of Assyria. So the king of Assyria withdrew[d] and stayed in the land no longer.

21 As for the other events of Menahem's reign, and all he did, are they not written in the book of the annals of the kings of Israel? 22 Menahem rested with his fathers. And Pekahiah his son succeeded him as king.

14:25 [a]Nu 13:21; 1Ki 8:65 [b]Dt 3:17 [c]Jnh 1:1; Mt 12:39
14:26 [d]Dt 32:36 [e]2Ki 13:4 [f]Ps 18:41; 22:11; 72:12; 107:12; Isa 63:5; La 1:7
14:27 [g]2Ki 13:23 [h]Jdg 6:14
14:28 [i]2Sa 8:5; 1Ki 11:24 [j]2Ch 8:3 [k]1Ki 15:31
15:1 [l]ver 32; 2Ki 14:21
15:5 [m]Ge 12:17 [n]Lev 13:46 [o]2Ch 27:1 [p]Ge 41:40
15:7 [q]Isa 6:1; 14:28 [r]ver 5
15:9 [s]1Ki 15:26
15:10 [t]2Ki 12:20
15:11 [u]1Ki 15:31
15:12 [v]2Ki 10:30
15:13 [w]ver 1,8
15:14 [x]1Ki 14:17 [y]2Ki 12:20
15:15 [z]1Ki 15:31
15:16 [a]1Ki 4:24 [b]2Ki 8:12; Hos 13:16
15:19 [c]1Ch 5:6,26
15:20 [d]2Ki 12:18

[a] *25* Or *from the entrance to* [b] *25* That is, the Dead Sea [c] *28* Or *Judah* [d] *5* The Hebrew word was used for various diseases affecting the skin—not necessarily leprosy. [e] *5* Or *in a house where he was relieved of responsibility* [f] *10* Hebrew; some Septuagint manuscripts *in Ibleam* [g] *12* 2 Kings 10:30 [h] *19* Also called *Tiglath-Pileser* [i] *19* That is, about 37 tons (about 34 metric tons) [j] *20* That is, about 1 1/4 pounds (about 0.6 kilogram)

Pekahiah King of Israel

23 In the fiftieth year of Azariah king of Judah, Pekahiah son of Menahem became king of Israel in Samaria, and he reigned two years. 24 Pekahiah did evil in the eyes of the LORD. He did not turn away from the sins of Jeroboam son of Nebat, which he had caused Israel to commit. 25 One of his chief officers, Pekah[e] son of Remaliah, conspired against him. Taking fifty men of Gilead with him, he assassinated[f] Pekahiah, along with Argob and Arieh, in the citadel of the royal palace at Samaria. So Pekah killed Pekahiah and succeeded him as king.

26 The other events of Pekahiah's reign, and all he did, are written in the book of the annals of the kings of Israel.

Pekah King of Israel

27 In the fifty-second year of Azariah king of Judah, Pekah[g] son of Remaliah[h] became king of Israel in Samaria, and he reigned twenty years. 28 He did evil in the eyes of the LORD. He did not turn away from the sins of Jeroboam son of Nebat, which he had caused Israel to commit.

29 In the time of Pekah king of Israel, Tiglath-Pileser[i] king of Assyria came and took Ijon,[j] Abel Beth Maacah, Janoah, Kedesh and Hazor. He took Gilead and Galilee, including all the land of Naphtali,[k] and deported[l] the people to Assyria. 30 Then Hoshea[m] son of Elah conspired against Pekah son of Remaliah. He attacked and assassinated[n] him, and then succeeded him as king in the twentieth year of Jotham son of Uzziah.

31 As for the other events of Pekah's reign, and all he did, are they not written in the book of the annals of the kings of Israel?

Jotham King of Judah

32 In the second year of Pekah son of Remaliah king of Israel, Jotham[o] son of Uzziah king of Judah began to reign. 33 He was twenty-five years old when he became king, and he reigned in Jerusalem sixteen years. His mother's name was Jerusha daughter of Zadok. 34 He did what was right[p] in the eyes of the LORD, just as his father Uzziah had done. 35 The high places,[q] however, were not removed; the people continued to offer sacrifices and burn incense there. Jotham rebuilt the Upper Gate[r] of the temple of the LORD.

36 As for the other events of Jotham's reign, and what he did, are they not written in the book of the annals of the kings of Judah? 37 (In those days the LORD began to send Rezin[s] king of Aram and Pekah son of Remaliah against Judah.) 38 Jotham rested with his fathers and was buried with them in the City of David, the city of his father. And Ahaz his son succeeded him as king.

Ahaz King of Judah

16 In the seventeenth year of Pekah son of Remaliah, Ahaz[t] son of Jotham king of Judah began to reign. 2 Ahaz was twenty years old when he became king, and he reigned in Jerusalem sixteen years. Unlike David his father, he did not do what was right[u] in the eyes of the LORD his God. 3 He walked in the ways of the kings of Israel and even sacrificed his son[v] in[a] the fire, following the detestable[w] ways of the nations the LORD had driven out before the Israelites. 4 He offered sacrifices and burned incense at the high places, on the hilltops and under every spreading tree.[x]

5 Then Rezin[y] king of Aram and Pekah son of Remaliah king of Israel marched up to fight against Jerusalem and besieged Ahaz, but they could not overpower him. 6 At that time, Rezin[z] king of Aram recovered Elath[a] for Aram by driving out the men of Judah. Edomites then moved into Elath and have lived there to this day.

7 Ahaz sent messengers to say to Tiglath-Pileser[b] king of Assyria, "I am your servant and vassal. Come up and save[c] me out of the hand of the king of Aram and of the king of Israel, who are attacking me." 8 And Ahaz took the silver and gold found in the temple of the LORD and in the treasuries of the royal palace and sent it as a gift[d] to the king of Assyria. 9 The king of Assyria complied by attacking Damascus[e] and capturing it. He deported its inhabitants to Kir[f] and put Rezin to death.

10 Then King Ahaz went to Damascus to meet Tiglath-Pileser king of Assyria. He saw an altar in Damascus and sent to Uriah[g] the priest a sketch of the altar, with detailed plans for its construction. 11 So Uriah the priest built an altar in accordance with all the plans that King Ahaz had sent from Damascus and finished it before King Ahaz returned. 12 When the king came back from Damascus and saw the altar, he approached it and presented offerings[b][h] on it. 13 He offered up his burnt

[a] *3* Or *even made his son pass through*
[b] *12* Or *and went up*

15:25 [e] 2Ch 28:6; Isa 7:1 [f] 2Ki 12:20
15:27 [g] 2Ch 28:6; Isa 7:1 [h] Isa 7:4
15:29 [i] 2Ki 16:7; 17:6; 1Ch 5:26; 2Ch 28:20; Jer 50:17 [j] 1Ki 15:20 [k] 2Ki 16:9; 17:24; 2Ch 16:4; Isa 9:1 [l] 2Ki 24:14-16; 1Ch 5:22; Isa 14:6,17; 36:17; 45:13
15:30 [m] 2Ki 17:1 [n] 2Ki 12:20
15:32 [o] 1Ch 5:17
15:34 [p] ver 3; 1Ki 14:8; 2Ch 26:4-5
15:35 [q] 2Ki 12:3 [r] 2Ch 23:20
15:37 [s] 2Ki 16:5; Isa 7:1
16:1 [t] Isa 1:1; 14:28
16:2 [u] 1Ki 14:8
16:3 [v] Lev 18:21; 2Ki 21:6 [w] Lev 18:3; Dt 9:4; 12:31
16:4 [x] Dt 12:2; Eze 6:13
16:5 [y] 2Ki 15:37; Isa 7:1,4
16:6 [z] Isa 9:12 [a] 2Ki 14:22; 2Ch 26:2
16:7 [b] 2Ki 15:29 [c] Isa 2:6; Jer 2:18; Eze 16:28; Hos 10:6
16:8 [d] 2Ki 12:18
16:9 [e] 2Ki 15:29 [f] Isa 22:6; Am 1:5; 9:7
16:10 [g] Isa 8:2
16:12 [h] 2Ch 26:16

offering[i] and grain offering, poured
out his drink offering, and sprinkled
the blood of his fellowship offerings[a][j] on the altar. 14The bronze altar[k] that stood before the LORD he
brought from the front of the temple—
from between the new altar and the
temple of the LORD—and put it on the
north side of the new altar.
15King Ahaz then gave these orders
to Uriah the priest: "On the large new
altar, offer the morning[l] burnt offering and the evening grain offering, the
king's burnt offering and his grain offering, and the burnt offering of all the
people of the land, and their grain offering and their drink offering. Sprinkle
on the altar all the blood of the burnt
offerings and sacrifices. But I will use
the bronze altar for seeking guidance."[m] 16And Uriah the priest did just
as King Ahaz had ordered.
17King Ahaz took away the side panels and removed the basins from the
movable stands. He removed the Sea
from the bronze bulls that supported it
and set it on a stone base.[n] 18He took
away the Sabbath canopy[b] that had
been built at the temple and removed
the royal entryway outside the temple
of the LORD, in deference to the king of
Assyria.[o]
19As for the other events of the reign
of Ahaz, and what he did, are they not
written in the book of the annals of the
kings of Judah? 20Ahaz rested with his
fathers and was buried with them in
the City of David. And Hezekiah his son
succeeded him as king.

Hoshea Last King of Israel

17 In the twelfth year of Ahaz king of
Judah, Hoshea[p] son of Elah became king of Israel in Samaria, and he
reigned nine years. 2He did evil in the
eyes of the LORD, but not like the kings
of Israel who preceded him.
3Shalmaneser[q] king of Assyria
came up to attack Hoshea, who had
been Shalmaneser's vassal and had
paid him tribute. 4But the king of Assyria discovered that Hoshea was a
traitor, for he had sent envoys to So[c]
king of Egypt, and he no longer paid
tribute to the king of Assyria, as he had
done year by year. Therefore Shalmaneser seized him and put him in prison.
5The king of Assyria invaded the entire
land, marched against Samaria and
laid siege[r] to it for three years. 6In the
ninth year of Hoshea, the king of Assyria captured Samaria[s] and deported[t]
the Israelites to Assyria. He settled
them in Halah, in Gozan[u] on the Habor River and in the towns of the
Medes.

Israel Exiled Because of Sin

7All this took place because the Israelites had sinned[v] against the LORD
their God, who had brought them up
out of Egypt[w] from under the power of
Pharaoh king of Egypt. They worshiped
other gods 8and followed the practices
of the nations[x] the LORD had driven
out before them, as well as the practices that the kings of Israel had introduced. 9The Israelites secretly did
things against the LORD their God that
were not right. From watchtower to
fortified city[y] they built themselves
high places in all their towns. 10They
set up sacred stones and Asherah
poles[z] on every high hill and under
every spreading tree.[a] 11At every high
place they burned incense, as the nations whom the LORD had driven out
before them had done. They did wicked things that provoked the LORD to
anger. 12They worshiped idols,[b]
though the LORD had said, "You shall
not do this."[d] 13The LORD warned Israel and Judah through all his prophets
and seers:[c] "Turn from your evil

16:13 [i]Lev 6:8-13 [j]Lev 7:11-21 **16:14** [k]2Ch 4:1 **16:15** [l]Ex 29:38-41 [m]1Sa 9:9 **16:17** [n]1Ki 7:27 **16:18** [o]Eze 16:28 **17:1** [p]2Ki 15:30 **17:3** [q]2Ki 18:9-12; Hos 10:14 **17:5** [r]Hos 13:16 **17:6** [s]Hos 13:16 [t]Dt 28:36,64; 2Ki 18:10-11 [u]1Ch 5:26

17:7 [v]Jos 23:16; Jdg 6:10 [w]Ex 14:15-31 **17:8** [x]Lev 18:3; Dt 18:9; 2Ki 16:3 **17:9** [y]2Ki 18:8 **17:10** [z]Ex 34:13; Mic 5:14 [a]1Ki 14:23 **17:12** [b]Ex 20:4 **17:13** [c]1Sa 9:9

[a] *13* Traditionally *peace offerings* [b] *18* Or *the dais of his throne* (see Septuagint) [c] *4* Or *to Sais, to the; So* is possibly an abbreviation for *Osorkon.* [d] *12* Exodus 20:4, 5

17:7–23

PROMISE 1

THE MOST IMPORTANT RELATIONSHIP

Can we single out one sin as the most damaging? Read this explanation of why God allowed Israel's destruction and notice the number of times idolatry (including the sin of Jeroboam) is mentioned!

Israel committed every sin imaginable. All sin grieves God, but his focus is on our worship of and obedience to him. No single factor is more important than your relationship to God, because that determines everything else. The phrase "Love the Lord your God with all your heart, mind, soul and strength" (Deuteronomy 6; Matthew 22) is not called the Great Commandment for no reason.

Consistently check the quality and amount of time you spend cultivating and enjoying your relationship with God. Ask yourself regularly (maybe every Sunday morning) how the past week reflected what you love and worship most. If "God" isn't the answer to that reflection, it's time for an adjustment.

For the next Promise 1 reading go to page 445.

ways.[d] Observe my commands and
decrees, in accordance with the entire
Law that I commanded your fathers to
obey and that I delivered to you
through my servants the prophets."
14But they would not listen and were
as stiff-necked[e] as their fathers, who
did not trust in the LORD their God.
15They rejected his decrees and the
covenant[f] he had made with their fathers and the warnings he had given
them. They followed worthless idols[g]
and themselves became worthless.
They imitated the nations[h] around
them although the LORD had ordered
them, "Do not do as they do," and they
did the things the LORD had forbidden
them to do.
16They forsook all the commands of
the LORD their God and made for themselves two idols cast in the shape of
calves,[i] and an Asherah[j] pole. They
bowed down to all the starry hosts,[k]
and they worshiped Baal.[l] 17They sacrificed[m] their sons and daughters in[a]
the fire. They practiced divination and
sorcery[n] and sold[o] themselves to do
evil in the eyes of the LORD, provoking
him to anger.
18So the LORD was very angry with
Israel and removed them from his
presence. Only the tribe of Judah was
left, 19and even Judah did not keep the
commands of the LORD their God. They
followed the practices Israel had introduced.[p] 20Therefore the LORD rejected
all the people of Israel; he afflicted
them and gave them into the hands
of plunderers,[q] until he thrust them
from his presence.
21When he tore[r] Israel away from
the house of David, they made Jeroboam son of Nebat their king.[s] Jeroboam enticed Israel away from following
the LORD and caused them to commit a
great sin. 22The Israelites persisted in
all the sins of Jeroboam and did not
turn away from them 23until the LORD
removed them from his presence, as he
had warned through all his servants
the prophets. So the people of Israel
were taken from their homeland into
exile in Assyria, and they are still there.

Samaria Resettled

24The king of Assyria[t] brought people from Babylon, Cuthah, Avva, Hamath and Sepharvaim[u] and settled
them in the towns of Samaria to replace the Israelites. They took over Samaria and lived in its towns. 25When
they first lived there, they did not worship the LORD; so he sent lions[v]
among them and they killed some of
the people. 26It was reported to the
king of Assyria: "The people you deported and resettled in the towns of
Samaria do not know what the god of
that country requires. He has sent lions
among them, which are killing them
off, because the people do not know
what he requires."
27Then the king of Assyria gave this
order: "Have one of the priests you
took captive from Samaria go back to
live there and teach the people what
the god of the land requires." 28So one
of the priests who had been exiled from
Samaria came to live in Bethel and
taught them how to worship the LORD.
29Nevertheless, each national group
made its own gods in the several
towns[w] where they settled, and set
them up in the shrines[x] the people of
Samaria had made at the high places.[y]
30The men from Babylon made Succoth Benoth, the men from Cuthah
made Nergal, and the men from Hamath made Ashima; 31the Avvites
made Nibhaz and Tartak, and the Se-
pharvites burned their children in the
fire as sacrifices to Adrammelech[z]
and Anammelech, the gods of Sepharvaim.[a] 32They worshiped the LORD,
but they also appointed all sorts[b] of
their own people to officiate for them
as priests in the shrines at the high
places. 33They worshiped the LORD, but
they also served their own gods in accordance with the customs of the nations from which they had been
brought.
34To this day they persist in their former practices. They neither worship
the LORD nor adhere to the decrees and
ordinances, the laws and commands
that the LORD gave the descendants of
Jacob, whom he named Israel.[c]
35When the LORD made a covenant
with the Israelites, he commanded
them: "Do not worship[d] any other
gods or bow down to them, serve them
or sacrifice to them. 36But the LORD,
who brought you up out of Egypt with
mighty power and outstretched arm,[e]
is the one you must worship. To him
you shall bow down and to him offer
sacrifices. 37You must always be careful[f] to keep the decrees and ordinances, the laws and commands he
wrote for you. Do not worship other
gods. 38Do not forget[g] the covenant I
have made with you, and do not worship other gods. 39Rather, worship the
LORD your God; it is he who will deliver
you from the hand of all your enemies."
40They would not listen, however,

1 →PG. 450

[a] 17 Or *They made their sons and daughters pass through*

17:13 [d] Jer 18:11; 25:5; 35:15
17:14 [e] Ex 32:9; Dt 31:27; Ac 7:51
17:15 [f] Dt 29:25 [g] Dt 32:21; Ro 1:21-23 [h] Dt 12:30-31
17:16 [i] 1Ki 12:28 [j] 1Ki 14:15,23 [k] 2Ki 21:3 [l] 1Ki 16:31
17:17 [m] Dt 18:10-12; 2Ki 16:3 [n] Lev 19:26 [o] 1Ki 21:20
17:19 [p] 1Ki 14:22-23; 2Ki 16:3
17:20 [q] 2Ki 15:29
17:21 [r] 1Ki 11:11 [s] 1Ki 12:20
17:24 [t] Ezr 4:2,10 [u] 2Ki 18:34
17:25 [v] Ge 37:20
17:29 [w] Jer 2:28 [x] 1Ki 12:31 [y] Mic 4:5
17:31 [z] 2Ki 19:37 [a] ver 24
17:32 [b] 1Ki 12:31
17:34 [c] Ge 32:28; 35:10; 1Ki 18:31
17:35 [d] Ex 20:5; Jdg 6:10
17:36 [e] Ex 3:20; 6:6; Ps 136:12
17:37 [f] Dt 5:32
17:38 [g] Dt 4:23; 6:12

but persisted in their former practices. [41]Even while these people were worshiping the LORD,[h] they were serving their idols. To this day their children and grandchildren continue to do as their fathers did.

Hezekiah King of Judah

18 In the third year of Hoshea son of Elah king of Israel, Hezekiah[i] son of Ahaz king of Judah began to reign. [2]He was twenty-five years old when he became king, and he reigned in Jerusalem twenty-nine years.[j] His mother's name was Abijah[a] daughter of Zechariah. [3]He did what was right in the eyes of the LORD, just as his father David[k] had done. [4]He removed[l] the high places, smashed the sacred stones[m] and cut down the Asherah poles. He broke into pieces the bronze snake[n] Moses had made, for up to that time the Israelites had been burning incense to it. (It was called[b] Nehushtan.[c])

3 →PG. 424

[5]Hezekiah trusted[o] in the LORD, the God of Israel. There was no one like him among all the kings of Judah, either before him or after him. [6]He held fast[p] to the LORD and did not cease to follow him; he kept the commands the LORD had given Moses. [7]And the LORD was with him; he was successful[q] in whatever he undertook. He rebelled[r] against the king of Assyria and did not serve him. [8]From watchtower to fortified city,[s] he defeated the Philistines, as far as Gaza and its territory.

[9]In King Hezekiah's fourth year,[t] which was the seventh year of Hoshea son of Elah king of Israel, Shalmaneser king of Assyria marched against Samaria and laid siege to it. [10]At the end of three years the Assyrians took it. So Samaria was captured in Hezekiah's sixth year, which was the ninth year of Hoshea king of Israel. [11]The king[u] of Assyria deported Israel to Assyria and settled them in Halah, in Gozan on the Habor River and in towns of the Medes. [12]This happened because they had not obeyed the LORD their God, but had violated his covenant[v]—all that Moses the servant of the LORD commanded.[w] They neither listened to the commands[x] nor carried them out.

[13]In the fourteenth year of King Hezekiah's reign, Sennacherib king of Assyria attacked all the fortified cities of Judah[y] and captured them. [14]So Hezekiah king of Judah sent this message to the king of Assyria at Lachish: "I have done wrong.[z] Withdraw from me, and I will pay whatever you demand of me." The king of Assyria exacted from Hezekiah king of Judah three hundred talents[d] of silver and thirty talents[e] of gold. [15]So Hezekiah gave[a] him all the silver that was found in the temple of the LORD and in the treasuries of the royal palace.

[16]At this time Hezekiah king of Judah stripped off the gold with which he had covered the doors and doorposts of the temple of the LORD, and gave it to the king of Assyria.

Sennacherib Threatens Jerusalem

[17]The king of Assyria sent his supreme commander,[b] his chief officer and his field commander with a large army, from Lachish to King Hezekiah at Jerusalem. They came up to Jerusalem and stopped at the aqueduct of the Upper Pool,[c] on the road to the Washerman's Field. [18]They called for the king; and Eliakim[d] son of Hilkiah the palace administrator, Shebna[e] the secretary, and Joah son of Asaph the recorder went out to them.

[19]The field commander said to them, "Tell Hezekiah:

" 'This is what the great king, the king of Assyria, says: On what are you basing this confidence of yours? [20]You say you have strategy and military strength—but you speak only empty words. On whom are you depending, that you rebel against me? [21]Look now, you are depending on Egypt,[f] that splintered reed of a staff,[g] which pierces a man's hand and wounds him if he leans on it! Such is Pharaoh king of Egypt to all who depend on him. [22]And if you say to me, "We are depending on the LORD our God"—isn't he the one whose high places and altars Hezekiah removed, saying to Judah and Jerusalem, "You must worship before this altar in Jerusalem"?

[23]" 'Come now, make a bargain with my master, the king of Assyria: I will give you two thousand horses—if you can put riders on them! [24]How can you repulse one officer[h] of the least of my master's officials, even though you are depending on Egypt for chariots and horsemen[f]? [25]Furthermore, have I come to attack and destroy this place without word from the

17:41 [h]ver 32-33; 1Ki 18:21; Mt 6:24
18:1 [i]Isa 1:1; 2Ch 28:27
18:2 [j]Isa 38:5
18:3 [k]Isa 38:5
18:4 [l]2Ch 31:1 [m]Ex 23:24 [n]Nu 21:9
18:5 [o]2Ki 19:10; 23:25
18:6 [p]Dt 10:20; Jos 23:8
18:7 [q]Ge 39:3; 1Sa 18:14 [r]2Ki 16:7
18:8 [s]2Ki 17:9; Isa 14:29
18:9 [t]Isa 1:1
18:11 [u]Isa 37:12
18:12 [v]2Ki 17:15 [w]Da 9:6,10 [x]1Ki 9:6
18:13 [y]2Ch 32:1; Isa 1:7; Mic 1:9
18:14 [z]Isa 24:5
18:15 [a]1Ki 15:18; 2Ki 16:8
18:17 [b]Isa 20:1 [c]2Ki 20:20; 2Ch 32:4,30; Isa 7:3
18:18 [d]2Ki 19:2; Isa 22:20 [e]Isa 22:15
18:21 [f]Isa 20:5; Eze 29:6 [g]Isa 30:5,7
18:24 [h]Isa 10:8

[a]*2* Hebrew *Abi,* a variant of *Abijah* [b]*4* Or *He called it* [c]*4* *Nehushtan* sounds like the Hebrew for *bronze* and *snake* and *unclean thing.* [d]*14* That is, about 11 tons (about 10 metric tons) [e]*14* That is, about 1 ton (about 1 metric ton) [f]*24* Or *charioteers*

LORD?[i] The LORD himself told me to march against this country and destroy it.' "

26 Then Eliakim son of Hilkiah, and Shebna and Joah said to the field commander, "Please speak to your servants in Aramaic,[j] since we understand it. Don't speak to us in Hebrew in the hearing of the people on the wall."

27 But the commander replied, "Was it only to your master and you that my master sent me to say these things, and not to the men sitting on the wall—who, like you, will have to eat their own filth and drink their own urine?"

28 Then the commander stood and called out in Hebrew: "Hear the word of the great king, the king of Assyria! 29 This is what the king says: Do not let Hezekiah deceive[k] you. He cannot deliver you from my hand. 30 Do not let Hezekiah persuade you to trust in the LORD when he says, 'The LORD will surely deliver us; this city will not be given into the hand of the king of Assyria.'

31 "Do not listen to Hezekiah. This is what the king of Assyria says: Make peace with me and come out to me. Then every one of you will eat from his own vine and fig tree[l] and drink water from his own cistern,[m] 32 until I come and take you to a land like your own, a land of grain and new wine, a land of bread and vineyards, a land of olive trees and honey. Choose life[n] and not death!

"Do not listen to Hezekiah, for he is misleading you when he says, 'The LORD will deliver us.' 33 Has the god[o] of any nation ever delivered his land from the hand of the king of Assyria? 34 Where are the gods of Hamath[p] and Arpad?[q] Where are the gods of Sepharvaim, Hena and Ivvah? Have they rescued Samaria from my hand? 35 Who of all the gods of these countries has been able to save his land from me? How then can the LORD deliver Jerusalem from my hand?"[r]

36 But the people remained silent and said nothing in reply, because the king had commanded, "Do not answer him."

37 Then Eliakim son of Hilkiah the palace administrator, Shebna the secretary and Joah son of Asaph the recorder went to Hezekiah, with their clothes torn,[s] and told him what the field commander had said.

Jerusalem's Deliverance Foretold

19 When King Hezekiah heard this, he tore[t] his clothes and put on sackcloth and went into the temple of the LORD. 2 He sent Eliakim the palace administrator, Shebna the secretary and the leading priests, all wearing sackcloth, to the prophet Isaiah[u] son of Amoz. 3 They told him, "This is what Hezekiah says: This day is a day of distress and rebuke and disgrace, as when children come to the point of birth and there is no strength to deliver them. 4 It may be that the LORD your God will hear all the words of the field commander, whom his master, the king of Assyria, has sent to ridicule[v] the living God, and that he will rebuke[w] him for the words the LORD your God has heard. Therefore pray for the remnant that still survives."

5 When King Hezekiah's officials came to Isaiah, 6 Isaiah said to them, "Tell your master, 'This is what the LORD says: Do not be afraid of what you have heard—those words with which the underlings of the king of Assyria have blasphemed[x] me. 7 Listen! I am going to put such a spirit in him that when he hears a certain report, he will return to his own country, and there I will have him cut down with the sword.[y] ' "

8 When the field commander heard that the king of Assyria had left Lachish,[z] he withdrew and found the king fighting against Libnah.

9 Now Sennacherib received a report that Tirhakah, the Cushite[a] king ⌞of Egypt⌟, was marching out to fight against him. So he again sent messengers to Hezekiah with this word: 10 "Say to Hezekiah king of Judah: Do not let the god you depend[a] on deceive[b] you when he says, 'Jerusalem will not be handed over to the king of Assyria.' 11 Surely you have heard what the kings of Assyria have done to all the countries, destroying them completely. And will you be delivered? 12 Did the gods of the nations that were destroyed by my forefathers deliver[c] them: the gods of Gozan,[d] Haran,[e] Rezeph and the people of Eden who were in Tel Assar? 13 Where is the king of Hamath, the king of Arpad, the king of the city of Sepharvaim, or of Hena or Ivvah?"[f]

Hezekiah's Prayer

14 Hezekiah received the letter from the messengers and read it. Then he went up to the temple of the LORD and spread it out before the LORD. 15 And Hezekiah prayed to the LORD: "O LORD, God of Israel, enthroned between the cherubim,[g] you alone are God over all the kingdoms of the earth. You have

18:25 [i] 2Ki 19:6,22
18:26 [j] Ezr 4:7
18:29 [k] 2Ki 19:10
18:31 [l] Nu 13:23; 1Ki 4:25 [m] Jer 14:3; La 4:4
18:32 [n] Dt 8:7-9; 30:19
18:33 [o] 2Ki 19:12; Isa 10:10-11
18:34 [p] 2Ki 17:24; 19:13 [q] Isa 10:9
18:35 [r] Ps 2:1-2
18:37 [s] 2Ki 6:30
19:1 [t] Ge 37:34; 1Ki 21:27; 2Ch 32:20-22
19:2 [u] Isa 1:1
19:4 [v] 2Ki 18:35 [w] 2Sa 16:12
19:6 [x] 2Ki 18:25
19:7 [y] ver 37
19:8 [z] 2Ki 18:14
19:10 [a] 2Ki 18:5 [b] 2Ki 18:29
19:12 [c] 2Ki 18:33 [d] 2Ki 17:6 [e] Ge 11:31
19:13 [f] 2Ki 18:34
19:15 [g] Ex 25:22

a 9 That is, from the upper Nile region

made heaven and earth. 16Give ear,[h]
O LORD, and hear;[i] open your eyes,[j]
O LORD, and see; listen to the words
Sennacherib has sent to insult the living God.
17"It is true, O LORD, that the Assyrian kings have laid waste these nations
and their lands. 18They have thrown
their gods into the fire and destroyed
them, for they were not gods[k] but
only wood and stone, fashioned by
men's hands.[l] 19Now, O LORD our
God, deliver us from his hand, so that
all kingdoms[m] on earth may know[n]
that you alone, O LORD, are God."

Isaiah Prophesies Sennacherib's Fall

20Then Isaiah son of Amoz sent a
message to Hezekiah: "This is what the
LORD, the God of Israel, says: I have
heard[o] your prayer concerning Sennacherib king of Assyria. 21This is the
word that the LORD has spoken against
him:

" 'The Virgin Daughter[p] of Zion
despises you and mocks[q] you.
The Daughter of Jerusalem
tosses her head[r] as you flee.
22Who is it you have insulted and
blasphemed?
Against whom have you raised
your voice
and lifted your eyes in pride?
Against the Holy One[s] of Israel!
23By your messengers
you have heaped insults on the
Lord.
And you have said,[t]
"With my many chariots[u]
I have ascended the heights of the
mountains,
the utmost heights of Lebanon.
I have cut down its tallest cedars,
the choicest of its pines.
I have reached its remotest parts,
the finest of its forests.
24I have dug wells in foreign lands
and drunk the water there.
With the soles of my feet
I have dried up all the streams of
Egypt."
25" 'Have you not heard?[v]
Long ago I ordained it.
In days of old I planned[w] it;
now I have brought it to pass,
that you have turned fortified cities
into piles of stone.[x]
26Their people, drained of power,
are dismayed[y] and put to
shame.
They are like plants in the field,
like tender green shoots,[z]
like grass sprouting on the roof,
scorched[a] before it grows up.

27" 'But I know[b] where you stay
and when you come and go
and how you rage against
me.
28Because you rage against me
and your insolence has reached
my ears,
I will put my hook[c] in your nose
and my bit[d] in your mouth,
and I will make you return[e]
by the way you came.'

29"This will be the sign[f] for you,
O Hezekiah:

"This year you will eat what grows
by itself,[g]
and the second year what
springs from that.
But in the third year sow and reap,
plant vineyards[h] and eat their
fruit.
30Once more a remnant of the house
of Judah
will take root[i] below and bear
fruit above.
31For out of Jerusalem will come a
remnant,
and out of Mount Zion a band of
survivors.

The zeal[j] of the LORD Almighty will
accomplish this.

32"Therefore this is what the LORD
says concerning the king of Assyria:
"He will not enter this city
or shoot an arrow here.
He will not come before it with
shield
or build a siege ramp against it.
33By the way that he came he will
return;[k]
he will not enter this city,
declares the LORD.
34I will defend[l] this city and save it,
for my sake and for the sake of
David[m] my servant."

35That night the angel of the LORD[n]
went out and put to death a hundred
and eighty-five thousand men in the
Assyrian camp. When the people got
up the next morning—there were all
the dead bodies![o] 36So Sennacherib
king of Assyria broke camp and withdrew. He returned to Nineveh[p] and
stayed there.
37One day, while he was worshiping
in the temple of his god Nisroch, his
sons Adrammelech and Sharezer cut
him down with the sword,[q] and they
escaped to the land of Ararat.[r] And
Esarhaddon[s] his son succeeded him
as king.

19:16 [h]Ps 31:2 [i]1Ki 8:29 [j]ver 4; 2Ch 6:40
19:18 [k]Isa 44:9-11; Jer 10:3-10 [l]Ps 115:4; Ac 17:29
19:19 [m]1Ki 8:43 [n]Ps 83:18
19:20 [o]2Ki 20:5
19:21 [p]Jer 14:17; La 2:13 [q]Ps 22:7-8 [r]Job 16:4; Ps 109:25
19:22 [s]Ps 71:22; Isa 5:24
19:23 [t]Isa 10:18 [u]Ps 20:7
19:25 [v]Isa 40:21,28 [w]Isa 10:5; 45:7 [x]Mic 1:6
19:26 [y]Ps 6:10 [z]Isa 4:2 [a]Ps 129:6
19:27 [b]Ps 139:1-4
19:28 [c]Eze 19:9; 29:4 [d]Isa 30:28 [e]ver 33
19:29 [f]2Ki 20:8-9; Lk 2:12 [g]Lev 25:5 [h]Ps 107:37
19:30 [i]2Ch 32:22-23
19:31 [j]Isa 9:7
19:33 [k]ver 28
19:34 [l]2Ki 20:6 [m]1Ki 11:12-13
19:35 [n]Ex 12:23 [o]Job 24:24
19:36 [p]Ge 10:11; Jnh 1:2
19:37 [q]ver 7 [r]Ge 8:4 [s]Ezr 4:2

Hezekiah's Illness

3 →PG. 463

20 In those days Hezekiah became ill
and was at the point of death. The
prophet Isaiah son of Amoz went to
him and said, "This is what the LORD
says: Put your house in order, because
you are going to die; you will not recover."
2Hezekiah turned his face to the wall
and prayed to the LORD, 3"Remember,[t] O LORD, how I have walked before you faithfully[u] and with wholehearted devotion and have done what
is good in your eyes." And Hezekiah
wept bitterly.
4Before Isaiah had left the middle
court, the word of the LORD came to
him: 5"Go back and tell Hezekiah, the
leader of my people, 'This is what the
LORD, the God of your father David,
says: I have heard[v] your prayer and
seen your tears;[w] I will heal you. On
the third day from now you will go up
to the temple of the LORD. 6I will add
fifteen years to your life. And I will deliver you and this city from the hand of
the king of Assyria. I will defend[x] this
city for my sake and for the sake of my
servant David.' "
7Then Isaiah said, "Prepare a poultice of figs." They did so and applied it
to the boil,[y] and he recovered.
8Hezekiah had asked Isaiah, "What
will be the sign that the LORD will heal
me and that I will go up to the temple
of the LORD on the third day from
now?"
9Isaiah answered, "This is the LORD's
sign[z] to you that the LORD will do what
he has promised: Shall the shadow go
forward ten steps, or shall it go back
ten steps?"
10"It is a simple matter for the shadow to go forward ten steps," said Hezekiah. "Rather, have it go back ten
steps."
11Then the prophet Isaiah called
upon the LORD, and the LORD made the
shadow go back[a] the ten steps it had
gone down on the stairway of Ahaz.

Envoys From Babylon

12At that time Merodach-Baladan
son of Baladan king of Babylon sent
Hezekiah letters and a gift, because he
had heard of Hezekiah's illness. 13Hez-
ekiah received the messengers and
showed them all that was in his
storehouses—the silver, the gold, the
spices and the fine oil—his armory and
everything found among his treasures.
There was nothing in his palace or in
all his kingdom that Hezekiah did not
show them.
14Then Isaiah the prophet went to
King Hezekiah and asked, "What did
those men say, and where did they
come from?"
"From a distant land," Hezekiah replied. "They came from Babylon."
15The prophet asked, "What did they
see in your palace?"
"They saw everything in my palace,"
Hezekiah said. "There is nothing
among my treasures that I did not
show them."
16Then Isaiah said to Hezekiah,
"Hear the word of the LORD: 17The time
will surely come when everything in
your palace, and all that your fathers
have stored up until this day, will be
carried off to Babylon.[b] Nothing will
be left, says the LORD. 18And some of
your descendants,[c] your own flesh
and blood, that will be born to you, will
be taken away, and they will become
eunuchs in the palace of the king of
Babylon."
19"The word of the LORD you have
spoken is good," Hezekiah replied. For
he thought, "Will there not be peace
and security in my lifetime?"
20As for the other events of Hezekiah's reign, all his achievements and
how he made the pool[d] and the tun-
nel by which he brought water into the
city, are they not written in the book of
the annals of the kings of Judah? 21Hez-
ekiah rested with his fathers. And Manasseh his son succeeded him as king.

Manasseh King of Judah

21 Manasseh was twelve years old
when he became king, and he
reigned in Jerusalem fifty-five years.
His mother's name was Hephzibah.[e]
2He did evil[f] in the eyes of the LORD,
following the detestable practices[g] of
the nations the LORD had driven out
before the Israelites. 3He rebuilt the
high places[h] his father Hezekiah had
destroyed; he also erected altars to
Baal[i] and made an Asherah pole, as
Ahab king of Israel had done. He
bowed down to all the starry hosts[j]
and worshiped them. 4He built altars[k]
in the temple of the LORD, of which the
LORD had said, "In Jerusalem I will put
my Name."[l] 5In both courts[m] of the
temple of the LORD, he built altars to all
the starry hosts. 6He sacrificed his own
son[n] in[a] the fire, practiced sorcery
and divination, and consulted mediums and spiritists.[o] He did much evil
in the eyes of the LORD, provoking him
to anger.
7He took the carved Asherah pole[p]
he had made and put it in the temple,

20:3 [t]Ne 13:22 [u]2Ki 18:3-6 **20:5** [v]1Sa 9:16; 1Ki 9:3; 2Ki 19:20 [w]Ps 39:12; 56:8 **20:6** [x]2Ki 19:34 **20:7** [y]Isa 38:21 **20:9** [z]Dt 13:2; Jer 44:29 **20:11** [a]Jos 10:13

20:17 [b]2Ki 24:13; 25:13; 2Ch 36:10; Jer 27:22; 52:17-23 **20:18** [c]2Ki 24:15; 2Ch 33:11; Da 1:3 **20:20** [d]Ne 3:16 **21:1** [e]Isa 62:4 **21:2** [f]Jer 15:4 [g]2Ki 16:3 **21:3** [h]2Ki 18:4 [i]Jdg 6:28; 1Ki 16:32 [j]Dt 17:3; 2Ki 17:16 **21:4** [k]Jer 32:34 [l]2Sa 7:13; 1Ki 8:29 **21:5** [m]1Ki 7:12; 2Ki 23:12 **21:6** [n]Lev 18:21; Dt 18:10; 2Ki 16:3; 17:17 [o]Lev 19:31 **21:7** [p]Dt 16:21; 2Ki 23:4

[a]6 Or *He made his own son pass through*

of which the LORD had said to David
and to his son Solomon, "In this temple and in Jerusalem, which I have chosen out of all the tribes of Israel, I will
put my Name[q] forever. 8 I will not
again[r] make the feet of the Israelites
wander from the land I gave their forefathers, if only they will be careful to do
everything I commanded them and
will keep the whole Law that my servant Moses[s] gave them." 9 But the
people did not listen. Manasseh led
them astray, so that they did more
evil[t] than the nations[u] the LORD had
destroyed before the Israelites.

10 The LORD said through his servants
the prophets: 11 "Manasseh king of Judah has committed these detestable
sins. He has done more evil[v] than the
Amorites[w] who preceded him and has
led Judah into sin with his idols.
12 Therefore this is what the LORD, the
God of Israel, says: I am going to bring
such disaster[x] on Jerusalem and Judah that the ears of everyone who
hears of it will tingle.[y] 13 I will stretch
out over Jerusalem the measuring line
used against Samaria and the plumb
line[z] used against the house of Ahab.
I will wipe[a] out Jerusalem as one
wipes a dish, wiping it and turning it
upside down. 14 I will forsake[b] the
remnant[c] of my inheritance and hand
them over to their enemies. They will
be looted and plundered by all their
foes, 15 because they have done evil[d]
in my eyes and have provoked[e] me to
anger from the day their forefathers
came out of Egypt until this day."

16 Moreover, Manasseh also shed so
much innocent blood[f] that he filled
Jerusalem from end to end—besides
the sin that he had caused Judah to
commit, so that they did evil in the
eyes of the LORD.

17 As for the other events of Manasseh's reign, and all he did, including
the sin he committed, are they not
written in the book of the annals of the
kings of Judah? 18 Manasseh rested with
his fathers and was buried in his palace
garden,[g] the garden of Uzza. And
Amon his son succeeded him as king.

Amon King of Judah

19 Amon was twenty-two years old
when he became king, and he reigned
in Jerusalem two years. His mother's
name was Meshullemeth daughter of
Haruz; she was from Jotbah. 20 He did
evil[h] in the eyes of the LORD, as his
father Manasseh had done. 21 He
walked in all the ways of his father; he
worshiped the idols his father had worshiped, and bowed down to them. 22 He
forsook the LORD, the God of his fathers, and did not walk[i] in the way of
the LORD.

23 Amon's officials conspired against
him and assassinated[j] the king in his
palace. 24 Then the people of the land
killed[k] all who had plotted against
King Amon, and they made Josiah his
son king in his place.

25 As for the other events of Amon's
reign, and what he did, are they not
written in the book of the annals of the
kings of Judah? 26 He was buried in his
grave in the garden[l] of Uzza. And Josiah his son succeeded him as king.

The Book of the Law Found

22 Josiah was eight years old when he
became king, and he reigned in Jerusalem thirty-one years. His mother's
name was Jedidah daughter of Adaiah;
she was from Bozkath.[m] 2 He did what
was right[n] in the eyes of the LORD and
walked in all the ways of his father David, not turning aside to the right[o] or
to the left.

3 In the eighteenth year of his reign,
King Josiah sent the secretary, Shaphan[p] son of Azaliah, the son of Meshullam, to the temple of the LORD. He
said: 4 "Go up to Hilkiah the high priest
and have him get ready the money that
has been brought into the temple of
the LORD, which the doorkeepers have
collected[q] from the people. 5 Have
them entrust it to the men appointed
to supervise the work on the temple.
And have these men pay the workers
who repair[r] the temple of the LORD—
6 the carpenters, the builders and the
masons. Also have them purchase timber and dressed stone to repair the
temple.[s] 7 But they need not account
for the money entrusted to them, because they are acting faithfully."[t]

8 Hilkiah the high priest said to Shaphan the secretary, "I have found the
Book of the Law[u] in the temple of the
LORD." He gave it to Shaphan, who read
it. 9 Then Shaphan the secretary went
to the king and reported to him: "Your
officials have paid out the money that
was in the temple of the LORD and have
entrusted it to the workers and supervisors at the temple." 10 Then Shaphan
the secretary informed the king, "Hilkiah the priest has given me a book." And
Shaphan read from it in the presence
of the king.[v]

11 When the king heard the words of
the Book of the Law, he tore his robes.
12 He gave these orders to Hilkiah the
priest, Ahikam[w] son of Shaphan, Acbor son of Micaiah, Shaphan the secretary and Asaiah the king's attendant:

21:7 [q] 2Sa 7:13; 1Ki 8:29; 9:3; 2Ki 23:27; Jer 32:34
21:8 [r] 2Sa 7:10 [s] 2Ki 18:12
21:9 [t] Pr 29:12 [u] Dt 9:4
21:11 [v] 2Ki 24:3-4 [w] Ge 15:16; 1Ki 21:26
21:12 [x] 2Ki 23:26; 24:3; Jer 15:4 [y] 1Sa 3:11; Jer 19:3
21:13 [z] Isa 34:11; La 2:8; Am 7:7-9 [a] 2Ki 23:27
21:14 [b] Ps 78:58-60 [c] 2Ki 19:4; Mic 2:12
21:15 [d] Ex 32:22 [e] Jer 25:7
21:16 [f] 2Ki 24:4
21:18 [g] ver 26
21:20 [h] ver 2-6
21:22 [i] 1Ki 11:33
21:23 [j] 2Ki 12:20; 2Ch 33:24-25
21:24 [k] 2Ki 14:5
21:26 [l] ver 18
22:1 [m] Jos 15:39
22:2 [n] Dt 17:19 [o] Dt 5:32
22:3 [p] 2Ch 34:20; Jer 39:14
22:4 [q] 2Ki 12:4-5
22:5 [r] 2Ki 12:5, 11-14
22:6 [s] 2Ki 12:11-12
22:7 [t] 2Ki 12:15
22:8 [u] Dt 31:24
22:10 [v] Jer 36:21
22:12 [w] 2Ki 25:22; Jer 26:24

13 "Go and inquire of the LORD for me
and for the people and for all Judah
about what is written in this book that
has been found. Great is the LORD's anger[x] that burns against us because our
fathers have not obeyed the words of
this book; they have not acted in accordance with all that is written there concerning us."

14 Hilkiah the priest, Ahikam, Acbor,
Shaphan and Asaiah went to speak to
the prophetess Huldah, who was the
wife of Shallum son of Tikvah, the son
of Harhas, keeper of the wardrobe. She
lived in Jerusalem, in the Second District.

15 She said to them, "This is what the
LORD, the God of Israel, says: Tell the
man who sent you to me, 16 'This is
what the LORD says: I am going to bring
disaster[y] on this place and its people,
according to everything written in the
book[z] the king of Judah has read.
17 Because they have forsaken[a] me
and burned incense to other gods and
provoked me to anger by all the idols
their hands have made,[a] my anger will
burn against this place and will not be
quenched.' 18 Tell the king of Judah,
who sent you to inquire[b] of the LORD,
'This is what the LORD, the God of Israel, says concerning the words you
heard: 19 Because your heart was responsive and you humbled[c] yourself
before the LORD when you heard what
I have spoken against this place and its
people, that they would become accursed[d] and laid waste,[e] and because
you tore your robes and wept in my
presence, I have heard you, declares
the LORD. 20 Therefore I will gather you
to your fathers, and you will be buried
in peace.[f] Your eyes will not see all
the disaster I am going to bring on this
place.' "

So they took her answer back to the
king.

Josiah Renews the Covenant

23 Then the king called together all
the elders of Judah and Jerusalem.
2 He went up to the temple of the LORD
with the men of Judah, the people
of Jerusalem, the priests and the
prophets—all the people from the least
to the greatest. He read[g] in their hearing all the words of the Book of the
Covenant, which had been found in
the temple of the LORD. 3 The king stood
by the pillar and renewed the covenant[h] in the presence of the LORD—
to follow[i] the LORD and keep his commands, regulations and decrees with
all his heart and all his soul, thus confirming the words of the covenant written in this book. Then all the people
pledged themselves to the covenant.

4 The king ordered Hilkiah the high
priest, the priests next in rank and the
doorkeepers[j] to remove[k] from the
temple of the LORD all the articles made
for Baal and Asherah and all the starry
hosts. He burned them outside Jerusalem in the fields of the Kidron Valley
and took the ashes to Bethel. 5 He did
away with the pagan priests appointed
by the kings of Judah to burn incense
on the high places of the towns of Judah and on those around Jerusalem—
those who burned incense to Baal, to
the sun and moon, to the constellations and to all the starry hosts.[l] 6 He
took the Asherah pole from the temple
of the LORD to the Kidron Valley outside Jerusalem and burned it there. He
ground it to powder and scattered the
dust over the graves of the common
people.[m] 7 He also tore down the quarters of the male shrine prostitutes,[n]
which were in the temple of the LORD
and where women did weaving for
Asherah.

8 Josiah brought all the priests from
the towns of Judah and desecrated the
high places, from Geba[o] to Beersheba,
where the priests had burned incense.
He broke down the shrines[b] at the
gates—at the entrance to the Gate of
Joshua, the city governor, which is on
the left of the city gate. 9 Although the
priests of the high places did not
serve[p] at the altar of the LORD in Jerusalem, they ate unleavened bread with
their fellow priests.

10 He desecrated Topheth,[q] which
was in the Valley of Ben Hinnom,[r] so
no one could use it to sacrifice his
son[s] or daughter in[c] the fire to Molech. 11 He removed from the entrance
to the temple of the LORD the horses
that the kings of Judah had dedicated
to the sun. They were in the court near
the room of an official named Nathan-
Melech. Josiah then burned the chariots dedicated to the sun.[t]

12 He pulled down the altars the
kings of Judah had erected on the
roof[u] near the upper room of Ahaz,
and the altars Manasseh had built in
the two courts[v] of the temple of the
LORD. He removed them from there,
smashed them to pieces and threw the
rubble into the Kidron Valley. 13 The
king also desecrated the high places
that were east of Jerusalem on the
south of the Hill of Corruption—the
ones Solomon[w] king of Israel had built

22:13 [x] Dt 29:24-28; 31:17
22:16 [y] Dt 31:29; Jos 23:15 [z] Dt 29:27; Da 9:11
22:17 [a] Dt 29:25-27
22:18 [b] 2Ch 34:26; Jer 21:2
22:19 [c] Ex 10:3; 1Ki 21:29; Ps 51:17; Isa 57:15; Mic 6:8 [d] Jer 26:6 [e] Lev 26:31
22:20 [f] Isa 57:1
23:2 [g] Dt 31:11; 2Ki 22:8
23:3 [h] 2Ki 11:14,17 [i] Dt 13:4
23:4 [j] 2Ki 25:18 [k] 2Ki 21:7
23:5 [l] 2Ki 21:3; Jer 8:2
23:6 [m] Jer 26:23
23:7 [n] 1Ki 14:24; 15:12; Eze 16:16
23:8 [o] 1Ki 15:22
23:9 [p] Eze 44:10-14
23:10 [q] Isa 30:33; Jer 7:31,32; 19:6 [r] Jos 15:8 [s] Lev 18:21; Dt 18:10
23:11 [t] Dt 4:19
23:12 [u] Jer 19:13; Zep 1:5 [v] 2Ki 21:5
23:13 [w] 1Ki 11:7

a 17 Or *by everything they have done* b 8 Or *high places* c 10 Or *to make his son or daughter pass through*

for Ashtoreth the vile goddess of the
Sidonians, for Chemosh the vile god of
Moab, and for Molech[a] the detestable
god of the people of Ammon. 14 Josiah
smashed[x] the sacred stones and cut
down the Asherah poles and covered
the sites with human bones.
15 Even the altar[y] at Bethel, the high
place made by Jeroboam[z] son of Nebat, who had caused Israel to sin—
even that altar and high place he demolished. He burned the high place
and ground it to powder, and burned
the Asherah pole also. 16 Then Josiah[a]
looked around, and when he saw the
tombs that were there on the hillside,
he had the bones removed from them
and burned on the altar to defile it, in
accordance with the word of the LORD
proclaimed by the man of God who
foretold these things.
17 The king asked, "What is that
tombstone I see?"
The men of the city said, "It marks
the tomb of the man of God who came
from Judah and pronounced against
the altar of Bethel the very things you
have done to it."
18 "Leave it alone," he said. "Don't let
anyone disturb his bones[b]." So they
spared his bones and those of the
prophet who had come from Samaria.
19 Just as he had done at Bethel, Josiah removed and defiled all the shrines
at the high places that the kings of Israel had built in the towns of Samaria
that had provoked the LORD to anger.
20 Josiah slaughtered[c] all the priests of
those high places on the altars and
burned human bones[d] on them. Then
he went back to Jerusalem.
21 The king gave this order to all the
people: "Celebrate the Passover[e] to
the LORD your God, as it is written in
this Book of the Covenant." 22 Not since
the days of the judges who led Israel,
nor throughout the days of the kings of
Israel and the kings of Judah, had any
such Passover been observed. 23 But in
the eighteenth year of King Josiah, this
Passover was celebrated to the LORD in
Jerusalem.
24 Furthermore, Josiah got rid of the
mediums and spiritists,[f] the household gods,[g] the idols and all the other
detestable things seen in Judah and Jerusalem. This he did to fulfill the requirements of the law written in the
book that Hilkiah the priest had discovered in the temple of the LORD.
25 Neither before nor after Josiah was
there a king like him who turned[h] to
the LORD as he did—with all his heart
and with all his soul and with all his
strength, in accordance with all the
Law of Moses.
26 Nevertheless, the LORD did not
turn away from the heat of his fierce
anger, which burned against Judah because of all that Manasseh[i] had done
to provoke him to anger. 27 So the LORD
said, "I will remove[j] Judah also from
my presence[k] as I removed Israel, and
I will reject Jerusalem, the city I chose,
and this temple, about which I said,
'There shall my Name be.'[b]"
28 As for the other events of Josiah's
reign, and all he did, are they not written in the book of the annals of the
kings of Judah?
29 While Josiah was king, Pharaoh
Neco[l] king of Egypt went up to the
Euphrates River to help the king of Assyria. King Josiah marched out to meet
him in battle, but Neco faced him and
killed him at Megiddo.[m] 30 Josiah's servants brought his body in a chariot[n]
from Megiddo to Jerusalem and buried
him in his own tomb. And the people
of the land took Jehoahaz son of Josiah
and anointed him and made him king
in place of his father.

Jehoahaz King of Judah

31 Jehoahaz[o] was twenty-three years
old when he became king, and he
reigned in Jerusalem three months. His
mother's name was Hamutal[p] daughter of Jeremiah; she was from Libnah.
32 He did evil in the eyes of the LORD,
just as his fathers had done. 33 Pharaoh
Neco put him in chains at Riblah[q] in
the land of Hamath[c][r] so that he
might not reign in Jerusalem, and he
imposed on Judah a levy of a hundred
talents[d] of silver and a talent[e] of gold.

23:14 [x]Ex 23:24; Dt 7:5,25
23:15 [y]1Ki 13:1-3 [z]1Ki 12:33
23:16 [a]1Ki 13:2
23:18 [b]1Ki 13:31
23:20 [c]Ex 22:20; 2Ki 10:25; 11:18 [d]1Ki 13:2
23:21 [e]Ex 12:11; Nu 9:2; Dt 16:1-8
23:24 [f]Lev 19:31; Dt 18:11; 2Ki 21:6 [g]Ge 31:19
23:25 [h]2Ki 18:5
23:26 [i]2Ki 21:12; Jer 15:4
23:27 [j]2Ki 21:13 [k]2Ki 18:11
23:29 [l]Jer 46:2 [m]Zec 12:11
23:30 [n]2Ki 9:28
23:31 [o]1Ch 3:15; Jer 22:11 [p]2Ki 24:18
23:33 [q]2Ki 25:6 [r]1Ki 8:65

23:17–18 PROMISE 3

MAN OF GOD REMEMBERED

Over 300 years after the event described in this passage, God still remembered and honored this unnamed man of God. Thoughtfully read his story in 1 Kings 13.

This man of God refused the king's invitation because it violated God's command. He was then deceived into disobedience by an old prophet whose turf he had invaded. That story, plus this memorial passage to this faithful but naive man of God, is *full* of rich instruction for the thoughtful reader. Read, meditate on, learn and grow from this loaded passage.

For the next Promise 3 reading go to page 510.

[a] *13* Hebrew *Milcom* [b] *27* 1 Kings 8:29
[c] *33* Hebrew; Septuagint (see also 2 Chron. 36:3) *Neco at Riblah in Hamath removed him*
[d] *33* That is, about 3 3/4 tons (about 3.4 metric tons) [e] *33* That is, about 75 pounds (about 34 kilograms)

34 Pharaoh Neco made Eliakim[s] son of Josiah king in place of his father Josiah and changed Eliakim's name to Jehoiakim. But he took Jehoahaz and carried him off to Egypt, and there he died.[t] 35 Jehoiakim paid Pharaoh Neco the silver and gold he demanded. In order to do so, he taxed the land and exacted the silver and gold from the people of the land according to their assessments.[u]

Jehoiakim King of Judah

36 Jehoiakim[v] was twenty-five years old when he became king, and he reigned in Jerusalem eleven years. His mother's name was Zebidah daughter of Pedaiah; she was from Rumah. 37 And he did evil in the eyes of the LORD, just as his fathers had done.

24 During Jehoiakim's reign, Nebuchadnezzar[w] king of Babylon invaded the land, and Jehoiakim became his vassal for three years. But then he changed his mind and rebelled against Nebuchadnezzar. 2 The LORD sent Babylonian,[a] Aramean,[x] Moabite and Ammonite raiders against him. He sent them to destroy[y] Judah, in accordance with the word of the LORD proclaimed by his servants the prophets. 3 Surely these things happened to Judah according to the LORD's command,[z] in order to remove them from his presence because of the sins of Manasseh[a] and all he had done, 4 including the shedding of innocent blood.[b] For he had filled Jerusalem with innocent blood, and the LORD was not willing to forgive.

5 As for the other events of Jehoiakim's reign, and all he did, are they not written in the book of the annals of the kings of Judah? 6 Jehoiakim rested[c] with his fathers. And Jehoiachin his son succeeded him as king.

7 The king of Egypt[d] did not march out from his own country again, because the king of Babylon[e] had taken all his territory, from the Wadi of Egypt to the Euphrates River.

Jehoiachin King of Judah

8 Jehoiachin[f] was eighteen years old when he became king, and he reigned in Jerusalem three months. His mother's name was Nehushta daughter of Elnathan; she was from Jerusalem. 9 He did evil in the eyes of the LORD, just as his father had done.

10 At that time the officers of Nebuchadnezzar[g] king of Babylon advanced on Jerusalem and laid siege to it, 11 and Nebuchadnezzar himself came up to the city while his officers were besieging it. 12 Jehoiachin king of Judah, his mother, his attendants, his nobles and his officials all surrendered[h] to him.

In the eighth year of the reign of the king of Babylon, he took Jehoiachin prisoner. 13 As the LORD had declared,[i] Nebuchadnezzar removed all the treasures[j] from the temple of the LORD and from the royal palace, and took away all the gold articles[k] that Solomon[l] king of Israel had made for the temple of the LORD. 14 He carried into exile[m] all Jerusalem: all the officers and fighting men, and all the craftsmen and artisans—a total of ten thousand. Only the poorest[n] people of the land were left.

15 Nebuchadnezzar took Jehoiachin captive to Babylon. He also took from Jerusalem to Babylon the king's mother,[o] his wives, his officials and the leading men[p] of the land. 16 The king of Babylon also deported to Babylon the entire force of seven thousand fighting men, strong and fit for war, and a thousand craftsmen and artisans.[q] 17 He made Mattaniah, Jehoiachin's uncle, king in his place and changed his name to Zedekiah.[r]

Zedekiah King of Judah

18 Zedekiah[s] was twenty-one years old when he became king, and he reigned in Jerusalem eleven years. His mother's name was Hamutal[t] daughter of Jeremiah; she was from Libnah. 19 He did evil in the eyes of the LORD, just as Jehoiakim had done. 20 It was because of the LORD's anger that all this happened to Jerusalem and Judah, and in the end he thrust[u] them from his presence.

The Fall of Jerusalem

Now Zedekiah rebelled against the king of Babylon.

25 So in the ninth year of Zedekiah's reign, on the tenth day of the tenth month, Nebuchadnezzar[v] king of Babylon marched against Jerusalem with his whole army. He encamped outside the city and built siege works[w] all around it. 2 The city was kept under siege until the eleventh year of King Zedekiah. 3 By the ninth day of the ⌊fourth⌋[b] month the famine[x] in the city had become so severe that there was no food for the people to eat. 4 Then the city wall was broken through,[y] and the whole army fled at night through the gate between the two walls near the king's garden, though

23:34 [s] 1Ch 3:15; 2Ch 36:5-8 [t] Jer 22:12; Eze 19:3-4
23:35 [u] ver 33
23:36 [v] Jer 26:1
24:1 [w] Jer 25:1,9; Da 1:1
24:2 [x] Jer 35:11 [y] Jer 25:9
24:3 [z] 2Ki 18:25 [a] 2Ki 21:12; 23:26
24:4 [b] 2Ki 21:16
24:6 [c] Jer 22:19
24:7 [d] Ge 15:18 [e] Jer 37:5-7; 46:2
24:8 [f] 1Ch 3:16
24:10 [g] Da 1:1
24:12 [h] 2Ki 25:27; Jer 22:24-30; 24:1; 25:1; 29:2; 52:28
24:13 [i] 2Ki 20:17 [j] 2Ki 25:15; Isa 39:6 [k] 2Ki 25:14; Jer 20:5 [l] 1Ki 7:51
24:14 [m] Jer 24:1; 52:28 [n] 2Ki 25:12; Jer 40:7; 52:16
24:15 [o] Jer 22:24-28 [p] Est 2:6; Eze 17:12-14
24:16 [q] Jer 52:28
24:17 [r] 1Ch 3:15; 2Ch 36:11; Jer 37:1
24:18 [s] Jer 52:1 [t] 2Ki 23:31
24:20 [u] Dt 4:26; 29:27
25:1 [v] Jer 34:1-7 [w] Eze 24:2
25:3 [x] Jer 14:18; La 4:9
25:4 [y] Eze 33:21

a 2 Or *Chaldean*   b 3 See Jer. 52:6.

the Babylonians[a] were surrounding[z] the city. They fled toward the Arabah,[b] [5]but the Babylonian[c] army pursued the king and overtook him in the plains of Jericho. All his soldiers were separated from him and scattered,[a] [6]and he was captured.[b] He was taken to the king of Babylon at Riblah,[c] where sentence was pronounced on him. [7]They killed the sons of Zedekiah before his eyes. Then they put out his eyes, bound him with bronze shackles and took him to Babylon.[d]

[8]On the seventh day of the fifth month, in the nineteenth year of Nebuchadnezzar king of Babylon, Nebuzaradan commander of the imperial guard, an official of the king of Babylon, came to Jerusalem. [9]He set fire[e] to the temple of the LORD, the royal palace and all the houses of Jerusalem. Every important building he burned down.[f] [10]The whole Babylonian army, under the commander of the imperial guard, broke down the walls[g] around Jerusalem. [11]Nebuzaradan the commander of the guard carried into exile[h] the people who remained in the city, along with the rest of the populace and those who had gone over to the king of Babylon.[i] [12]But the commander left behind some of the poorest people[j] of the land to work the vineyards and fields.

[13]The Babylonians broke up the bronze pillars, the movable stands and the bronze Sea that were at the temple of the LORD and they carried the bronze to Babylon. [14]They also took away the pots, shovels, wick trimmers, dishes and all the bronze articles[k] used in the temple service. [15]The commander of the imperial guard took away the censers and sprinkling bowls—all that were made of pure gold or silver.

[16]The bronze from the two pillars, the Sea and the movable stands, which Solomon had made for the temple of the LORD, was more than could be weighed. [17]Each pillar[l] was twenty-seven feet[d] high. The bronze capital on top of one pillar was four and a half feet[e] high and was decorated with a network and pomegranates of bronze all around. The other pillar, with its network, was similar.

[18]The commander of the guard took as prisoners Seraiah[m] the chief priest, Zephaniah[n] the priest next in rank and the three doorkeepers. [19]Of those still in the city, he took the officer in charge of the fighting men and five royal advisers. He also took the secretary who was chief officer in charge of conscripting the people of the land and sixty of his men who were found in the city. [20]Nebuzaradan the commander took them all and brought them to the king of Babylon at Riblah. [21]There at Riblah, in the land of Hamath, the king had them executed.

So Judah went into captivity, away from her land.[o]

[22]Nebuchadnezzar king of Babylon appointed Gedaliah[p] son of Ahikam, the son of Shaphan, to be over the people he had left behind in Judah. [23]When all the army officers and their men heard that the king of Babylon had appointed Gedaliah as governor, they came to Gedaliah at Mizpah—Ishmael son of Nethaniah, Johanan son of Kareah, Seraiah son of Tanhumeth the Netophathite, Jaazaniah the son of the Maacathite, and their men. [24]Gedaliah took an oath to reassure them and their men. "Do not be afraid of the Babylonian officials," he said. "Settle down in the land and serve the king of Babylon, and it will go well with you."

[25]In the seventh month, however, Ishmael son of Nethaniah, the son of Elishama, who was of royal blood, came with ten men and assassinated Gedaliah and also the men of Judah and the Babylonians who were with him at Mizpah. [26]At this, all the people from the least to the greatest, together with the army officers, fled to Egypt[q] for fear of the Babylonians.

Jehoiachin Released

[27]In the thirty-seventh year of the exile of Jehoiachin king of Judah, in the year Evil-Merodach[f] became king of Babylon, he released Jehoiachin[r] from prison on the twenty-seventh day of the twelfth month. [28]He spoke kindly to him and gave him a seat of honor[s] higher than those of the other kings who were with him in Babylon. [29]So Jehoiachin put aside his prison clothes and for the rest of his life ate regularly at the king's table.[t] [30]Day by day the king gave Jehoiachin a regular allowance as long as he lived.[u]

25:4 [z]Jer 4:17
25:5 [a]Eze 12:14
25:6 [b]Jer 34:21-22 [c]2Ki 23:33
25:7 [d]Jer 21:7; 32:4-5; Eze 12:11
25:9 [e]Isa 60:7 [f]Ps 74:3-8; Jer 2:15; Am 2:5; Mic 3:12
25:10 [g]Ne 1:3
25:11 [h]2Ki 24:14 [i]2Ki 24:1
25:12 [j]2Ki 24:14
25:14 [k]Ex 27:3; 1Ki 7:47-50
25:17 [l]1Ki 7:15-22
25:18 [m]1Ch 6:14; Ezr 7:1; Ne 11:11 [n]Jer 21:1; 29:25
25:21 [o]Ge 12:7; Dt 28:64; Jos 23:13; 2Ki 23:27
25:22 [p]Jer 39:14; 40:5,7
25:26 [q]Isa 30:2; Jer 43:7
25:27 [r]2Ki 24:12; Jer 52:31-34
25:28 [s]Ezr 5:5; Ne 2:1; Da 2:48
25:29 [t]2Sa 9:7
25:30 [u]Est 2:9; Jer 28:4

[a] *4* Or *Chaldeans*; also in verses 13, 25 and 26 [b] *4* Or *the Jordan Valley* [c] *5* Or *Chaldean*; also in verses 10 and 24 [d] *17* Hebrew *eighteen cubits* (about 8.1 meters) [e] *17* Hebrew *three cubits* (about 1.3 meters) [f] *27* Also called *Amel-Marduk*

1 CHRONICLES

AT A GLANCE

Key Principle: God is pleased to honor us when we make God's will and his kingdom our top priority.
Author: Possibly Ezra the priest
Time and Place: 4000 (??)+ B.C. to 971 B.C. / Israel
Key Verses: 17:11–14; 29:11–12

BENEFIT

Unlike 1 and 2 Samuel, 1 Chronicles omits key events in David's life including his victory over Goliath, his years of struggle with Saul, his early reign in Hebron, his sin with Bathsheba and Absalom's rebellion. In place of these omissions, 1 Chronicles adds details about the recovery of the ark of the covenant, the temple construction and dedication and Israel's temple worship. This book emphasizes God's grace and forgiveness as it minimizes David's shortcomings and stresses his service to God.

SETTING

First Chronicles was written around 450 B.C. to 400 B.C. Its first readers were the remnant of Jews who had returned from captivity in Babylonia / Persia. Some historical evidence supports the Jewish Talmud tradition that Ezra compiled this book after returning to Jerusalem with some of the exiles in 458 B.C. During those years, Ezra, Nehemiah and Malachi led the people in restoring Jerusalem and refining their worship in the second temple built decades earlier under Zerubbabel's leadership. During these difficult times, this account encouraged the people to remain true to God's covenant as the spiritual heirs of God's promises to Abraham and to David.

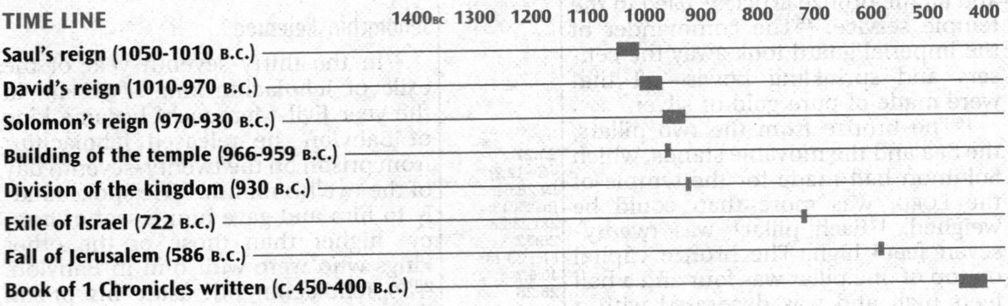

THEME AND PURPOSE

One of the evidences Ezra the priest may have written 1 Chronicles is its focus on the temple, the role of the priesthood and the royal line of David. This priestly and spiritual perspective helped the returned remnant of Jewish people understand their history and the unique purpose God still had for them. That's why the two books of Chronicles emphasize the glorious days of David and Solomon and their preparation of the temple and its system of worship. Chronicles was written from a more positive perspective than Samuel and Kings; it was meant to encourage the remnant to rebuild their heritage, and to help them see that God had a future for them even though they were still dominated by Gentile nations.

UNIQUE CONTRIBUTION

Chronicles covers much of the same material as Samuel and Kings, but it does so from an entirely different perspective. Chronicles is to Samuel and Kings what Deuteronomy is to the first four books of the Pentateuch and John is to the synoptic gospels. Chronicles, Deuteronomy and John provide a spiritual perspective on the historical events recorded in them. To be more specific, Samuel and Kings emphasize the prophetic theme that divine judgment results when people disobey and rebel against God's purposes. Chronicles emphasizes the priestly theme that God faithfully keeps his covenant promises in spite of human failures.

Unlike in the English Bible, Chronicles is the last book of the Hebrew Bible. That being the case, think of the genealogies in 1 Chronicles 1—9 as the preamble to Christ's genealogy in Matthew 1.

LINKS TO THE NEW TESTAMENT

The sections on "Links to the New Testament" in 1 and 2 Samuel discuss some of the ways in which King David is one of the clearest Old Testament illustrations of the Messiah to come. First Chronicles 17 repeats the 2 Samuel 7 account of God's covenant with David, a central part of which is the promise that David's kingly line will be eternal. This promise will ultimately be fulfilled by the coming King who will rule over the entire earth from David's throne in Jerusalem (Isaiah 9:6–7; Matthew 21:9; 22:45; Luke 1:32–33).

OVERVIEW

FOCUS	David's Ancestry	David's Activity
REFERENCE	1 — 9	10 — 29
TOPICS	Geneology	History
	From Adam to Saul	The Ark, the Temple, and the Priesthood
	A Priestly View of David's Reign	
LOCATION	Israel	
TIME	Thousands of Years	40 Years

First Chronicles begins with a set of genealogies that trace David's lineage back to Adam (1—9). Since Chronicles is concerned exclusively with the southern kingdom of Judah, these genealogies disproportionately represent the tribes of Judah and Benjamin. Because of the worship focus of this book, the geneaologies also detail the priestly line of Levi. These records extend to about 500 B.C., since they mention Zerubbabel and his grandsons (3:21), and they demonstrate that God will continue to preserve David's descendants.

The remainder of 1 Chronicles records David's reign (10—29). These chapters provide a highly selective history that illustrates David's concern for the things of the Lord. These chapters chronicle Saul's death (10), David's anointing as king, his conquest of Jerusalem, his thirty mighty men (11—12), his recovery of the ark of the covenant (13—16), God's covenant with him (17), his military victories (18—20) and his preparation for the future temple (21—27). The book concludes with David's public prayer of praise and thanksgiving, Solomon's coronation and David's death (28—29).

1 CHRONICLES

Historical Records From Adam to Abraham

To Noah's Sons

1 Adam,[a] Seth, Enosh, 2Kenan,[b] Mahalalel,[c] Jared,[d] 3Enoch,[e] Methuselah,[f] Lamech,[g] Noah.[h]

4The sons of Noah:[a][i]
Shem, Ham and Japheth.[j]

The Japhethites

5The sons[b] of Japheth:
Gomer, Magog, Madai, Javan, Tubal, Meshech and Tiras.
6The sons of Gomer:
Ashkenaz, Riphath[c] and Togarmah.
7The sons of Javan:
Elishah, Tarshish, the Kittim and the Rodanim.

The Hamites

8The sons of Ham:
Cush, Mizraim,[d] Put and Canaan.
9The sons of Cush:
Seba, Havilah, Sabta, Raamah and Sabteca.
The sons of Raamah:
Sheba and Dedan.
10Cush was the father[e] of
Nimrod, who grew to be a mighty warrior on earth.
11Mizraim was the father of
the Ludites, Anamites, Lehabites, Naphtuhites, 12Pathrusites, Casluhites (from whom the Philistines came) and Caphtorites.
13Canaan was the father of
Sidon his firstborn,[f] and of the Hittites, 14Jebusites, Amorites, Girgashites, 15Hivites, Arkites, Sinites, 16Arvadites, Zemarites and Hamathites.

The Semites

17The sons of Shem:
Elam, Asshur, Arphaxad, Lud and Aram.
The sons of Aram[g]:
Uz, Hul, Gether and Meshech.
18Arphaxad was the father of Shelah,
and Shelah the father of Eber.
19Two sons were born to Eber:
One was named Peleg,[h] because in his time the earth was divided; his brother was named Joktan.
20Joktan was the father of
Almodad, Sheleph, Hazarmaveth, Jerah, 21Hadoram, Uzal, Diklah, 22Obal,[i] Abimael, Sheba, 23Ophir, Havilah and Jobab. All these were sons of Joktan.

24Shem,[k] Arphaxad,[j] Shelah,
25Eber, Peleg, Reu,
26Serug, Nahor, Terah
27and Abram (that is, Abraham).

The Family of Abraham

28The sons of Abraham:
Isaac and Ishmael.

Descendants of Hagar

29These were their descendants:
Nebaioth the firstborn of Ishmael, Kedar, Adbeel, Mibsam, 30Mishma, Dumah, Massa, Hadad, Tema, 31Jetur, Naphish and Kedemah. These were the sons of Ishmael.

Descendants of Keturah

32The sons born to Keturah, Abraham's concubine:[l]
Zimran, Jokshan, Medan, Midian, Ishbak and Shuah.
The sons of Jokshan:
Sheba and Dedan.[m]
33The sons of Midian:
Ephah, Epher, Hanoch, Abida and Eldaah.
All these were descendants of Keturah.

Descendants of Sarah

34Abraham[n] was the father of Isaac.[o]

1:1 [a]Ge 5:1-32; Lk 3:36-38
1:2 [b]Ge 5:9 [c]Ge 5:12 [d]Ge 5:15
1:3 [e]Ge 5:18; Jude 1:14 [f]Ge 5:21 [g]Ge 5:25 [h]Ge 5:29
1:4 [i]Ge 6:10; 10:1 [j]Ge 5:32
1:24 [k]Ge 10:21-25; Lk 3:34-36
1:32 [l]Ge 22:24 [m]Ge 10:7
1:34 [n]Lk 3:34 [o]Ge 21:2-3; Mt 1:2; Ac 7:8

[a]*4* Septuagint; Hebrew does not have *The sons of Noah:* [b]*5* *Sons* may mean *descendants* or *successors* or *nations*; also in verses 6-10, 17 and 20. [c]*6* Many Hebrew manuscripts and Vulgate (see also Septuagint and Gen. 10:3); most Hebrew manuscripts *Diphath* [d]*8* That is, Egypt; also in verse 11 [e]*10* *Father* may mean *ancestor* or *predecessor* or *founder*, also in verses 11, 13, 18 and 20. [f]*13* Or *of the Sidonians, the foremost* [g]*17* One Hebrew manuscript and some Septuagint manuscripts (see also Gen. 10:23); most Hebrew manuscripts do not have this line. [h]*19* *Peleg* means *division.* [i]*22* Some Hebrew manuscripts and Syriac (see also Gen. 10:28); most Hebrew manuscripts *Ebal* [j]*24* Hebrew; some Septuagint manuscripts *Arphaxad, Cainan* (see also note at Gen. 11:10)

The sons of Isaac:
Esau and Israel.[p]

Esau's Sons

35 The sons of Esau:[q]
Eliphaz, Reuel,[r] Jeush, Jalam and Korah.
36 The sons of Eliphaz:
Teman, Omar, Zepho,[a] Gatam and Kenaz;
by Timna: Amalek.[b][s]
37 The sons of Reuel:[t]
Nahath, Zerah, Shammah and Mizzah.

The People of Seir in Edom

38 The sons of Seir:
Lotan, Shobal, Zibeon, Anah, Dishon, Ezer and Dishan.
39 The sons of Lotan:
Hori and Homam. Timna was Lotan's sister.
40 The sons of Shobal:
Alvan,[c] Manahath, Ebal, Shepho and Onam.
The sons of Zibeon:
Aiah and Anah.[u]
41 The son of Anah:
Dishon.
The sons of Dishon:
Hemdan,[d] Eshban, Ithran and Keran.
42 The sons of Ezer:
Bilhan, Zaavan and Akan.[e]
The sons of Dishan[f]:
Uz and Aran.

The Rulers of Edom

43 These were the kings who reigned in Edom before any Israelite king reigned[g]:
Bela son of Beor, whose city was named Dinhabah.
44 When Bela died, Jobab son of Zerah from Bozrah succeeded him as king.
45 When Jobab died, Husham from the land of the Temanites[v] succeeded him as king.
46 When Husham died, Hadad son of Bedad, who defeated Midian in the country of Moab, succeeded him as king. His city was named Avith.
47 When Hadad died, Samlah from Masrekah succeeded him as king.
48 When Samlah died, Shaul from Rehoboth on the river[h] succeeded him as king.
49 When Shaul died, Baal-Hanan son of Acbor succeeded him as king.
50 When Baal-Hanan died, Hadad succeeded him as king. His city was named Pau,[i] and his wife's name was Mehetabel daughter of Matred, the daughter of Me-Zahab. 51 Hadad also died.

The chiefs of Edom were:
Timna, Alvah, Jetheth, 52 Oholibamah, Elah, Pinon, 53 Kenaz, Teman, Mibzar, 54 Magdiel and Iram. These were the chiefs of Edom.

Israel's Sons

2 These were the sons of Israel:
Reuben, Simeon, Levi, Judah, Issachar, Zebulun, 2 Dan, Joseph, Benjamin, Naphtali, Gad and Asher.

Judah

To Hezron's Sons

3 The sons of Judah:[w]
Er, Onan and Shelah.[x] These three were born to him by a Canaanite woman, the daughter of Shua.[y] Er, Judah's firstborn, was wicked in the LORD's sight; so the LORD put him to death.[z] 4 Tamar,[a] Judah's daughter-in-law,[b] bore him Perez[c] and Zerah. Judah had five sons in all.

5 The sons of Perez:[d]
Hezron[e] and Hamul.
6 The sons of Zerah:
Zimri, Ethan, Heman, Calcol and Darda[j]—five in all.
7 The son of Carmi:
Achar,[k][f] who brought trouble on Israel by violating

1:34 [p]Ge 17:5; 25:25-26
1:35 [q]Ge 36:19 [r]Ge 36:4
1:36 [s]Ex 17:14
1:37 [t]Ge 36:17
1:40 [u]Ge 36:2
1:45 [v]Ge 36:11
2:3 [w]Ge 29:35; 38:2-10 [x]Ge 38:5 [y]Ge 38:2 [z]Nu 26:19
2:4 [a]Ge 38:11-30 [b]Ge 11:31 [c]Ge 38:29
2:5 [d]Ge 46:12 [e]Nu 26:21
2:7 [f]Jos 7:1

[a] *36* Many Hebrew manuscripts, some Septuagint manuscripts and Syriac (see also Gen. 36:11); most Hebrew manuscripts *Zephi*
[b] *36* Some Septuagint manuscripts (see also Gen. 36:12); Hebrew *Gatam, Kenaz, Timna and Amalek*
[c] *40* Many Hebrew manuscripts and some Septuagint manuscripts (see also Gen. 36:23); most Hebrew manuscripts *Alian*
[d] *41* Many Hebrew manuscripts and some Septuagint manuscripts (see also Gen. 36:26); most Hebrew manuscripts *Hamran*
[e] *42* Many Hebrew and Septuagint manuscripts (see also Gen. 36:27); most Hebrew manuscripts *Zaavan, Jaakan*
[f] *42* Hebrew *Dishon,* a variant of *Dishan*
[g] *43* Or *before an Israelite king reigned over them*
[h] *48* Possibly the Euphrates
[i] *50* Many Hebrew manuscripts, some Septuagint manuscripts, Vulgate and Syriac (see also Gen. 36:39); most Hebrew manuscripts *Pai*
[j] *6* Many Hebrew manuscripts, some Septuagint manuscripts and Syriac (see also 1 Kings 4:31); most Hebrew manuscripts *Dara*
[k] *7* *Achar* means *trouble*; *Achar* is called *Achan* in Joshua.

the ban on taking devoted
things.[a][g]
8 The son of Ethan:
Azariah.
9 The sons born to Hezron[h] were:
Jerahmeel, Ram and Caleb.[b]

From Ram Son of Hezron

10 Ram[i] was the father of
Amminadab[j], and Ammina-
dab the father of Nahshon,[k]
the leader of the people of Judah. 11 Nahshon was the father
of Salmon,[c] Salmon the father
of Boaz, 12 Boaz[l] the father of
Obed and Obed the father of
Jesse.[m]
13 Jesse[n] was the father of
Eliab[o] his firstborn; the second son was Abinadab, the
third Shimea, 14 the fourth Nethanel, the fifth Raddai, 15 the
sixth Ozem and the seventh
David. 16 Their sisters were
Zeruiah[p] and Abigail. Zeruiah's[q] three sons were Abishai,
Joab[r] and Asahel. 17 Abigail
was the mother of Amasa,[s]
whose father was Jether the
Ishmaelite.

Caleb Son of Hezron

18 Caleb son of Hezron had children
by his wife Azubah (and by Jer-
ioth). These were her sons:
Jesher, Shobab and Ardon.
19 When Azubah died, Caleb[t]
married Ephrath, who bore
him Hur. 20 Hur was the father
of Uri, and Uri the father of
Bezalel.[u]
21 Later, Hezron lay with the daughter of Makir the father of
Gilead[v] (he had married her
when he was sixty years old),
and she bore him Segub.
22 Segub was the father of Jair,
who controlled twenty-three
towns in Gilead. 23 (But Geshur
and Aram captured Havvoth
Jair,[d][w] as well as Kenath[x]
with its surrounding settlements—sixty towns.) All these
were descendants of Makir
the father of Gilead.

24 After Hezron died in Caleb Ephrathah, Abijah the wife of Hezron bore him Ashhur[y] the father[e] of Tekoa.

Jerahmeel Son of Hezron

25 The sons of Jerahmeel the first-
born of Hezron:
Ram his firstborn, Bunah,
Oren, Ozem and[f] Ahijah.
26 Jerahmeel had another wife,
whose name was Atarah; she
was the mother of Onam.
27 The sons of Ram the firstborn of
Jerahmeel:
Maaz, Jamin and Eker.
28 The sons of Onam:
Shammai and Jada.
The sons of Shammai:
Nadab and Abishur.
29 Abishur's wife was named Abihail, who bore him Ahban and
Molid.
30 The sons of Nadab:
Seled and Appaim. Seled died
without children.
31 The son of Appaim:
Ishi, who was the father of
Sheshan.
Sheshan was the father of Ahlai.
32 The sons of Jada, Shammai's
brother:
Jether and Jonathan. Jether
died without children.
33 The sons of Jonathan:
Peleth and Zaza.
These were the descendants of
Jerahmeel.
34 Sheshan had no sons—only
daughters.
He had an Egyptian servant
named Jarha. 35 Sheshan gave
his daughter in marriage to his
servant Jarha, and she bore
him Attai.
36 Attai was the father of Nathan,
Nathan the father of Zabad,[z]
37 Zabad the father of Ephlal,
Ephlal the father of Obed,
38 Obed the father of Jehu,
Jehu the father of Azariah,
39 Azariah the father of Helez,
Helez the father of Eleasah,
40 Eleasah the father of Sismai,
Sismai the father of Shallum,
41 Shallum the father of Jekamiah,
and Jekamiah the father of
Elishama.

The Clans of Caleb

42 The sons of Caleb[a] the brother
of Jerahmeel:
Mesha his firstborn, who was
the father of Ziph, and his son

2:7 [g] Jos 6:18
2:9 [h] Nu 26:21
2:10 [i] Lk 3:32-33 [j] Ex 6:23 [k] Nu 1:7
2:12 [l] Ru 2:1 [m] Ru 4:17
2:13 [n] Ru 4:17 [o] 1Sa 16:6
2:16 [p] 1Sa 26:6 [q] 2Sa 2:18 [r] 2Sa 2:13
2:17 [s] 2Sa 17:25
2:19 [t] ver 42,50
2:20 [u] Ex 31:2
2:21 [v] Nu 27:1
2:23 [w] Nu 32:41; Dt 3:14; Jos 13:30 [x] Nu 32:42
2:24 [y] 1Ch 4:5
2:36 [z] 1Ch 11:41
2:42 [a] ver 19

[a] *7* The Hebrew term refers to the irrevocable giving over of things or persons to the LORD, often by totally destroying them. [b] *9* Hebrew *Kelubai,* a variant of *Caleb* [c] *11* Septuagint (see also Ruth 4:21); Hebrew *Salma* [d] *23* Or *captured the settlements of Jair* [e] *24* *Father* may mean *civic leader* or *military leader*; also in verses 42, 45, 49-52 and possibly elsewhere. [f] *25* Or *Oren and Ozem, by*

Mareshah,[a] who was the father of Hebron.
43 The sons of Hebron:
Korah, Tappuah, Rekem and
Shema. 44 Shema was the father of Raham, and Raham the
father of Jorkeam. Rekem was
the father of Shammai. 45 The
son of Shammai was Maon[b],
and Maon was the father of
Beth Zur.[c]
46 Caleb's concubine Ephah was
the mother of Haran, Moza
and Gazez. Haran was the father of Gazez.
47 The sons of Jahdai:
Regem, Jotham, Geshan, Pelet,
Ephah and Shaaph.
48 Caleb's concubine Maacah was
the mother of Sheber and Tir-
hanah. 49 She also gave birth to
Shaaph the father of Madmannah[d] and to Sheva the father
of Macbenah and Gibea. Caleb's daughter was Acsah.[e]
50 These were the descendants
of Caleb.

The sons of Hur[f] the firstborn of
Ephrathah:
Shobal the father of Kiriath Jearim,[g] 51 Salma the father of
Bethlehem, and Hareph the father of Beth Gader.
52 The descendants of Shobal the
father of Kiriath Jearim were:
Haroeh, half the Manahathites, 53 and the clans of Kiriath
Jearim: the Ithrites,[h] Puthites,
Shumathites and Mishraites.
From these descended the Zorathites and Eshtaolites.
54 The descendants of Salma:
Bethlehem, the Netopha-
thites,[i] Atroth Beth Joab, half
the Manahathites, the Zorites,
55 and the clans of scribes[b]
who lived at Jabez: the Tirath-
ites, Shimeathites and Sucath-
ites. These are the Kenites[j]
who came from Hammath,[k]
the father of the house of Recab.[c][l]

The Sons of David

3 These were the sons of David[m] born
to him in Hebron:
The firstborn was Amnon the
son of Ahinoam of Jezreel;[n]
the second, Daniel the son of
Abigail[o] of Carmel;
2 the third, Absalom the son of
Maacah daughter of Talmai
king of Geshur;
the fourth, Adonijah[p] the son
of Haggith;
3 the fifth, Shephatiah the son of
Abital;
and the sixth, Ithream, by his
wife Eglah.
4 These six were born to David
in Hebron,[q] where he reigned
seven years and six months.[r]
David reigned in Jerusalem thirty-
three years, 5 and these were the children born to him there:
Shammua,[d] Shobab, Nathan
and Solomon. These four
were by Bathsheba[e][s] daughter
of Ammiel. 6 There were also
Ibhar, Elishua,[f] Eliphelet,
7 Nogah, Nepheg, Japhia,
8 Elishama, Eliada and Eliphelet—nine in all. 9 All these
were the sons of David, besides
his sons by his concubines.
And Tamar[t] was their sister.[u]

The Kings of Judah

10 Solomon's son was Rehoboam,[v]
Abijah his son,
Asa his son,
Jehoshaphat[w] his son,
11 Jehoram[g][x] his son,
Ahaziah[y] his son,
Joash[z] his son,
12 Amaziah[a] his son,
Azariah his son,
Jotham[b] his son,
13 Ahaz[c] his son,
Hezekiah[d] his son,
Manasseh[e] his son,
14 Amon[f] his son,
Josiah[g] his son.
15 The sons of Josiah:
Johanan the firstborn,
Jehoiakim[h] the second son,
Zedekiah[i] the third,
Shallum[j] the fourth.
16 The successors of Jehoiakim:
Jehoiachin[h][k] his son,
and Zedekiah.[l]

The Royal Line After the Exile

17 The descendants of Jehoiachin
the captive:
Shealtiel[m] his son, 18 Malki-
ram, Pedaiah, Shenazzar,[n]
Jekamiah, Hoshama and Ned-
abiah.[o]

2:45 [b] Jos 15:55 [c] Jos 15:58 **2:49** [d] Jos 15:31 [e] Jos 15:16 **2:50** [f] 1Ch 4:4 [g] ver 19 **2:53** [h] 2Sa 23:38 **2:54** [i] Ezr 2:22; Ne 7:26; 12:28 **2:55** [j] Ge 15:19; Jdg 1:16; Jdg 4:11 [k] Jos 19:35 [l] 2Ki 10:15,23; Jer 35:2-19 **3:1** [m] 1Ch 14:3; 28:5 [n] Jos 15:56 [o] 1Sa 25:42 **3:2** [p] 1Ki 2:22 **3:4** [q] 2Sa 5:4; 1Ch 29:27 [r] 2Sa 2:11; 5:5 **3:5** [s] 2Sa 11:3; 12:24 **3:9** [t] 2Sa 13:1 [u] 1Ch 14:4 **3:10** [v] 1Ki 11:43; 14:21-31; 2Ch 12:16 [w] 2Ch 17:1-21:3 **3:11** [x] 2Ki 8:16-24; 2Ch 21:1 [y] 2Ch 22:1-10 [z] 2Ki 11:1-12:21 **3:12** [a] 2Ki 14:1-22; 2Ch 25:1-28 [b] Isa 1:1; Hos 1:1; Mic 1:1 **3:13** [c] 2Ki 16:1-20; 2Ch 28:1; Isa 7:1 [d] 2Ki 18:1-20:21; 2Ch 29:1; Jer 26:19 [e] 2Ch 33:1 **3:14** [f] 2Ki 21:19-26; 2Ch 33:21; Zep 1:1 [g] 2Ch 34:1; Jer 1:2; 3:6; 25:3 **3:15** [h] 2Ki 23:34 [i] Jer 37:1 [j] 2Ki 23:31 **3:16** [k] 2Ki 24:6,8; Mt 1:11 [l] 2Ki 24:18 **3:17** [m] Ezr 3:2 **3:18** [n] Ezr 1:8; 5:14 [o] Jer 22:30

a *42* The meaning of the Hebrew for this phrase is uncertain. **b** *55* Or *of the Sopherites* **c** *55* Or *father of Beth Recab* **d** *5* Hebrew *Shimea,* a variant of *Shammua* **e** *5* One Hebrew manuscript and Vulgate (see also Septuagint and 2 Samuel 11:3); most Hebrew manuscripts *Bathshua* **f** *6* Two Hebrew manuscripts (see also 2 Samuel 5:15 and 1 Chron. 14:5); most Hebrew manuscripts *Elishama* **g** *11* Hebrew *Joram,* a variant of *Jehoram* **h** *16* Hebrew *Jeconiah,* a variant of *Jehoiachin*; also in verse 17

19 The sons of Pedaiah:
Zerubbabel[p] and Shimei.
The sons of Zerubbabel:
Meshullam and Hananiah.
Shelomith was their sister.
20 There were also five others:
Hashubah, Ohel, Berekiah, Hasadiah and Jushab-Hesed.
21 The descendants of Hananiah:
Pelatiah and Jeshaiah, and the sons of Rephaiah, of Arnan, of Obadiah and of Shecaniah.
22 The descendants of Shecaniah:
Shemaiah and his sons:
Hattush,[q] Igal, Bariah, Neariah and Shaphat—six in all.
23 The sons of Neariah:
Elioenai, Hizkiah and Azrikam—three in all.
24 The sons of Elioenai:
Hodaviah, Eliashib, Pelaiah, Akkub, Johanan, Delaiah and Anani—seven in all.

Other Clans of Judah

4 The descendants of Judah:[r]
Perez, Hezron,[s] Carmi, Hur and Shobal.
2 Reaiah son of Shobal was the father of Jahath, and Jahath the father of Ahumai and Lahad. These were the clans of the Zorathites.
3 These were the sons[a] of Etam:
Jezreel, Ishma and Idbash. Their sister was named Hazzelelponi. 4 Penuel was the father of Gedor, and Ezer the father of Hushah.
These were the descendants of Hur,[t] the firstborn of Ephrathah and father[b] of Bethlehem.[u]
5 Ashhur[v] the father of Tekoa had two wives, Helah and Naarah.
6 Naarah bore him Ahuzzam, Hepher, Temeni and Haahashtari. These were the descendants of Naarah.
7 The sons of Helah:
Zereth, Zohar, Ethnan, 8 and Koz, who was the father of Anub and Hazzobebah and of the clans of Aharhel son of Harum.

9 Jabez was more honorable than his
brothers. His mother had named him
Jabez,[c] saying, "I gave birth to him in
pain." 10 Jabez cried out to the God of
Israel, "Oh, that you would bless me and enlarge my territory! Let your hand be with me, and keep me from harm so that I will be free from pain." And God granted his request.

11 Kelub, Shuhah's brother, was the father of Mehir, who was the father of Eshton. 12 Eshton was the father of Beth Rapha, Paseah and Tehinnah the father of Ir Nahash.[d] These were the men of Recah.
13 The sons of Kenaz:
Othniel[w] and Seraiah.
The sons of Othniel:
Hathath and Meonothai.[e]
14 Meonothai was the father of Ophrah.
Seraiah was the father of Joab, the father of Ge Harashim.[f] It was called this because its people were craftsmen.
15 The sons of Caleb son of Jephunneh:
Iru, Elah and Naam.
The son of Elah:
Kenaz.
16 The sons of Jehallelel:
Ziph, Ziphah, Tiria and Asarel.
17 The sons of Ezrah:
Jether, Mered, Epher and Jalon. One of Mered's wives gave birth to Miriam,[x] Shammai and Ishbah the father of Eshtemoa. 18 (His Judean wife gave birth to Jered the father of Gedor, Heber the father of Soco, and Jekuthiel the father of Zanoah.[y]) These were the children of Pharaoh's daughter Bithiah, whom Mered had married.
19 The sons of Hodiah's wife, the sister of Naham:
the father of Keilah[z] the Garmite, and Eshtemoa the Maacathite.[a]
20 The sons of Shimon:
Amnon, Rinnah, Ben-Hanan and Tilon.
The descendants of Ishi:
Zoheth and Ben-Zoheth.
21 The sons of Shelah[b] son of Judah:
Er the father of Lecah, Laadah the father of Mareshah and the clans of the linen workers at Beth Ashbea, 22 Jokim, the men of Cozeba, and Joash and Saraph, who ruled in Moab and Jashubi Lehem. (These records are from ancient times.)

3:19 [p] Ezr 2:2; 3:2; 5:2; Ne 7:7; 12:1; Hag 1:1; 2:2; Zec 4:6
3:22 [q] Ezr 8:2-3
4:1 [r] Ge 29:35; 46:12; 1Ch 2:3 [s] Nu 26:21
4:4 [t] 1Ch 2:50 [u] Ru 1:19
4:5 [v] 1Ch 2:24
4:13 [w] Jos 15:17
4:17 [x] Ex 15:20
4:18 [y] Jos 15:34
4:19 [z] Jos 15:44 [a] Dt 3:14
4:21 [b] Ge 38:5

[a] *3* Some Septuagint manuscripts (see also Vulgate); Hebrew *father* [b] *4* *Father* may mean *civic leader* or *military leader*; also in verses 12, 14, 17, 18 and possibly elsewhere. [c] *9* *Jabez* sounds like the Hebrew for *pain.* [d] *12* Or *of the city of Nahash* [e] *13* Some Septuagint manuscripts and Vulgate; Hebrew does not have *and Meonothai.* [f] *14* *Ge Harashim* means *valley of craftsmen.*

23 They were the potters who
lived at Netaim and Gederah;
they stayed there and worked
for the king.

Simeon

24 The descendants of Simeon:[c]
Nemuel, Jamin, Jarib,[d] Zerah
and Shaul;
25 Shallum was Shaul's son, Mibsam his son and Mishma his
son.
26 The descendants of Mishma:
Hammuel his son, Zaccur his
son and Shimei his son.
27 Shimei had sixteen sons and six
daughters, but his brothers did not
have many children; so their entire
clan did not become as numerous
as the people of Judah. 28 They lived in
Beersheba,[e] Moladah,[f] Hazar Shual,
29 Bilhah, Ezem,[g] Tolad, 30 Bethuel,
Hormah,[h] Ziklag, 31 Beth Marcaboth,
Hazar Susim, Beth Biri and Shaaraim.[i] These were their towns until the
reign of David. 32 Their surrounding villages were Etam, Ain,[j] Rimmon, Token and Ashan[k]—five towns— 33 and
all the villages around these towns as
far as Baalath.[a] These were their settlements. And they kept a genealogical
record.

34 Meshobab, Jamlech, Joshah son
of Amaziah, 35 Joel, Jehu son of
Joshibiah, the son of Seraiah, the
son of Asiel, 36 also Elioenai, Jaa-
kobah, Jeshohaiah, Asaiah, Adiel,
Jesimiel, Benaiah, 37 and Ziza son
of Shiphi, the son of Allon, the son
of Jedaiah, the son of Shimri, the
son of Shemaiah.

38 The men listed above by name
were leaders of their clans. Their families increased greatly, 39 and they went
to the outskirts of Gedor[l] to the east
of the valley in search of pasture for
their flocks. 40 They found rich, good
pasture, and the land was spacious,
peaceful and quiet.[m] Some Hamites
had lived there formerly.
41 The men whose names were listed
came in the days of Hezekiah king of
Judah. They attacked the Hamites in
their dwellings and also the Meunites[n] who were there and completely
destroyed[b] them, as is evident to this
day. Then they settled in their place,
because there was pasture for their
flocks. 42 And five hundred of these
Simeonites, led by Pelatiah, Neariah,
Rephaiah and Uzziel, the sons of Ishi,
invaded the hill country of Seir.[o]
43 They killed the remaining Amalekites[p] who had escaped, and they have
lived there to this day.

Reuben

5 The sons of Reuben[q] the firstborn
of Israel (he was the firstborn, but
when he defiled his father's marriage
bed,[r] his rights as firstborn were given
to the sons of Joseph[s] son of Israel;[t]
so he could not be listed in the genealogical record in accordance with his
birthright,[u] 2 and though Judah[v] was
the strongest of his brothers and a
ruler[w] came from him, the rights of
the firstborn[x] belonged to Joseph)—
3 the sons of Reuben[y] the firstborn of
Israel:
Hanoch, Pallu,[z] Hezron and
Carmi.
4 The descendants of Joel:
Shemaiah his son, Gog his son,
Shimei his son, 5 Micah his son,
Reaiah his son, Baal his son,
6 and Beerah his son, whom
Tiglath-Pileser[c][a] king of Assyria took into exile. Beerah
was a leader of the Reubenites.
7 Their relatives by clans,[b] listed
according to their genealogical
records:
Jeiel the chief, Zechariah, 8 and
Bela son of Azaz, the son of
Shema, the son of Joel. They
settled in the area from Aroer[c] to Nebo and Baal Meon.
9 To the east they occupied the
land up to the edge of the
desert that extends to the Euphrates River, because their
livestock had increased in Gilead.[d]
10 During Saul's reign they
waged war against the Hagrites[e], who were defeated at
their hands; they occupied the
dwellings of the Hagrites
throughout the entire region east
of Gilead.

Gad

11 The Gadites[f] lived next to them
in Bashan, as far as Salecah:[g]
12 Joel was the chief, Shapham
the second, then Janai and
Shaphat, in Bashan.
13 Their relatives, by families, were:
Michael, Meshullam, Sheba,
Jorai, Jacan, Zia and Eber—
seven in all.

4:24 [c]Ge 29:33 [d]Nu 26:12 **4:28** [e]Ge 21:14 [f]Jos 15:26 **4:29** [g]Jos 15:29 **4:30** [h]Nu 14:45 **4:31** [i]Jos 15:36 **4:32** [j]Nu 34:11 [k]Jos 15:42 **4:39** [l]Jos 15:58 **4:40** [m]Jdg 18:7-10 **4:41** [n]2Ch 20:1; 26:7 **4:42** [o]Ge 14:6 **4:43** [p]1Sa 15:8; 30:17; 2Sa 8:12; Est 3:1; 9:16 **5:1** [q]Ge 29:32 [r]Ge 35:22; 49:4 [s]Ge 48:16,22; 49:26 [t]Ge 48:5 [u]1Ch 26:10 **5:2** [v]Ge 49:10,12 [w]1Sa 9:16; 12:12; 2Sa 6:21; 1Ch 11:2; 2Ch 7:18; Ps 60:7; Mic 5:2; Mt 2:6 [x]Ge 25:31 **5:3** [y]Ge 29:32; 46:9; Ex 6:14; Nu 26:5-11 [z]Nu 26:5 **5:6** [a]ver 26; 2Ki 15:19; 16:10; 2Ch 28:20 **5:7** [b]ver 17 **5:8** [c]Nu 32:34 **5:9** [d]Nu 32:26; Jos 22:9 **5:10** [e]ver 18-21 **5:11** [f]Jos 13:24-28 [g]Dt 3:10; Jos 13:11

[a] *33* Some Septuagint manuscripts (see also Joshua 19:8); Hebrew *Baal* [b] *41* The Hebrew term refers to the irrevocable giving over of things or persons to the LORD, often by totally destroying them. [c] *6* Hebrew *Tilgath-Pilneser,* a variant of *Tiglath-Pileser,* also in verse 26

14 These were the sons of Abihail
son of Huri, the son of Jaroah,
the son of Gilead, the son of
Michael, the son of Jeshishai,
the son of Jahdo, the son of
Buz.
15 Ahi son of Abdiel, the son of
Guni, was head of their family.
16 The Gadites lived in Gilead, in
Bashan and its outlying villages, and on all the pasturelands of Sharon as far as they
extended.
17 All these were entered in the genealogical records during the reigns of Jotham[h] king of Judah and Jeroboam[i]
king of Israel.

18 The Reubenites, the Gadites and
the half-tribe of Manasseh had 44,760
men ready for military service[j]—
able-bodied men who could handle
shield and sword, who could use a
bow, and who were trained for battle.
19 They waged war against the Hagrites,
Jetur,[k] Naphish and Nodab. 20 They
were helped[l] in fighting them, and
God handed the Hagrites and all their
allies over to them, because they
cried[m] out to him during the battle. He
answered their prayers, because they
trusted[n] in him. 21 They seized the
livestock of the Hagrites—fifty thousand camels, two hundred fifty thousand sheep and two thousand donkeys. They also took one hundred
thousand people captive, 22 and many
others fell slain, because the battle[o]
was God's. And they occupied the land
until the exile.[p]

The Half-Tribe of Manasseh

23 The people of the half-tribe of Manasseh were numerous; they settled in
the land from Bashan to Baal Hermon,
that is, to Senir (Mount Hermon).[q]
24 These were the heads of their families: Epher, Ishi, Eliel, Azriel, Jeremiah,
Hodaviah and Jahdiel. They were brave
warriors, famous men, and heads of
their families. 25 But they were unfaithful[r] to the God of their fathers and
prostituted[s] themselves to the gods of
the peoples of the land, whom God had
destroyed before them. 26 So the God of
Israel stirred up the spirit of Pul[t] king
of Assyria (that is, Tiglath-Pileser[u]
king of Assyria), who took the Reubenites, the Gadites and the half-tribe of
Manasseh into exile. He took them to
Halah,[v] Habor, Hara and the river of
Gozan, where they are to this day.

Levi

6 The sons of Levi:[w]
Gershon, Kohath and Merari.

5:17 [h] 2Ki 15:32 [i] 2Ki 14:16,28
5:18 [j] Nu 1:3
5:19 [k] ver 10; Ge 25:15; 1Ch 1:31
5:20 [l] Ps 37:40 [m] 1Ki 8:44; 2Ch 13:14; 14:11; Ps 20:7-9; 22:5 [n] Ps 26:1; Da 6:23
5:22 [o] 2Ch 32:8 [p] 2Ki 15:29; 17:6
5:23 [q] Dt 3:8,9; SS 4:8
5:25 [r] Dt 32:15-18; 2Ki 17:7; 1Ch 9:1; 2Ch 26:16 [s] Ex 34:15
5:26 [t] 2Ki 15:19 [u] 2Ki 15:29 [v] 2Ki 17:6; 18:11
6:1 [w] Ge 46:11; Ex 6:16; Nu 26:57; 1Ch 23:6
6:3 [x] Lev 10:1
6:8 [y] 2Sa 8:17; 15:27; Ezr 7:2
6:10 [z] 1Ki 4:2; 6:1; 2Ch 3:1; 26:17-18
6:13 [a] 2Ki 22:1-20; 2Ch 34:9; 35:8
6:14 [b] 2Ki 25:18; Ezr 2:2; Ne 11:11
6:15 [c] 2Ki 25:18; Ne 12:1; Hag 1:1,14; 2:2,4; Zec 6:11
6:16 [d] Ge 29:34; Ex 6:16; Nu 3:17-20 [e] Nu 26:57
6:19 [f] Ge 46:11; 1Ch 23:21; 24:26

2 The sons of Kohath:
Amram, Izhar, Hebron and
Uzziel.
3 The children of Amram:
Aaron, Moses and Miriam.
The sons of Aaron:
Nadab, Abihu,[x] Eleazar and
Ithamar.
4 Eleazar was the father of Phinehas,
Phinehas the father of
Abishua,
5 Abishua the father of Bukki,
Bukki the father of Uzzi,
6 Uzzi the father of Zerahiah,
Zerahiah the father of Meraioth,
7 Meraioth the father of Amariah,
Amariah the father of Ahitub,
8 Ahitub the father of Zadok,[y]
Zadok the father of Ahimaaz,
9 Ahimaaz the father of Azariah,
Azariah the father of Johanan,
10 Johanan the father of Azariah[z] (it was he who served as
priest in the temple Solomon
built in Jerusalem),
11 Azariah the father of Amariah,
Amariah the father of Ahitub,
12 Ahitub the father of Zadok,
Zadok the father of Shallum,
13 Shallum the father of Hilkiah,[a]
Hilkiah the father of Azariah,
14 Azariah the father of Seraiah,[b]
and Seraiah the father of Jehozadak.
15 Jehozadak[c] was deported when
the LORD sent Judah and Jerusalem into exile by the hand of
Nebuchadnezzar.

16 The sons of Levi:[d]
Gershon,[a] Kohath and Merari.[e]
17 These are the names of the sons
of Gershon:
Libni and Shimei.
18 The sons of Kohath:
Amram, Izhar, Hebron and
Uzziel.
19 The sons of Merari:[f]
Mahli and Mushi.
These are the clans of the Levites
listed according to their fathers:
20 Of Gershon:
Libni his son, Jehath his son,
Zimmah his son, 21 Joah his
son,
Iddo his son, Zerah his son
and Jeatherai his son.

[a] *16* Hebrew *Gershom,* a variant of *Gershon;* also in verses 17, 20, 43, 62 and 71

22 The descendants of Kohath:
Amminadab his son, Korah[g] his son,
Assir his son, 23 Elkanah his son,
Ebiasaph his son, Assir his son,
24 Tahath his son, Uriel[h] his son,
Uzziah his son and Shaul his son.
25 The descendants of Elkanah:
Amasai, Ahimoth,
26 Elkanah his son,[a] Zophai his son,
Nahath his son, 27 Eliab his son,
Jeroham his son, Elkanah[i] his son
and Samuel[j] his son.[b]
28 The sons of Samuel:
Joel[c][k] the firstborn
and Abijah the second son.
29 The descendants of Merari:
Mahli, Libni his son,
Shimei his son, Uzzah his son,
30 Shimea his son, Haggiah his son
and Asaiah his son.

The Temple Musicians

31 These are the men[l] David put in
charge of the music[m] in the house of
the LORD after the ark came to rest
there. 32 They ministered with music
before the tabernacle, the Tent of
Meeting, until Solomon built the temple of the LORD in Jerusalem. They performed their duties according to the
regulations laid down for them.
33 Here are the men who served, together with their sons:

From the Kohathites:
Heman,[n] the musician,
the son of Joel,[o] the son of Samuel,
34 the son of Elkanah,[p] the son of Jeroham,
the son of Eliel, the son of Toah,
35 the son of Zuph, the son of Elkanah,
the son of Mahath, the son of Amasai,
36 the son of Elkanah, the son of Joel,
the son of Azariah, the son of Zephaniah,
37 the son of Tahath, the son of Assir,
the son of Ebiasaph, the son of Korah,[q]
38 the son of Izhar,[r] the son of Kohath,
the son of Levi, the son of Israel;
39 and Heman's associate Asaph,[s]
who served at his right hand:
Asaph son of Berekiah, the son of Shimea,[t]
40 the son of Michael, the son of Baaseiah,[d]
the son of Malkijah, 41 the son of Ethni,
the son of Zerah, the son of Adaiah,
42 the son of Ethan, the son of Zimmah,
the son of Shimei, 43 the son of Jahath,
the son of Gershon, the son of Levi;
44 and from their associates, the Merarites, at his left hand:
Ethan son of Kishi, the son of Abdi,
the son of Malluch, 45 the son of Hashabiah,
the son of Amaziah, the son of Hilkiah,
46 the son of Amzi, the son of Bani,
the son of Shemer, 47 the son of Mahli,
the son of Mushi, the son of Merari,
the son of Levi.

48 Their fellow Levites[u] were assigned to all the other duties of the tabernacle, the house of God. 49 But Aaron
and his descendants were the ones
who presented offerings on the altar[v]
of burnt offering and on the altar of
incense[w] in connection with all that
was done in the Most Holy Place, making atonement for Israel, in accordance
with all that Moses the servant of God
had commanded.

50 These were the descendants of Aaron:
Eleazar his son, Phinehas his son,
Abishua his son, 51 Bukki his son,
Uzzi his son, Zerahiah his son,
52 Meraioth his son, Amariah his son,
Ahitub his son, 53 Zadok[x] his son
and Ahimaaz his son.

6:22 [g] Ex 6:24 **6:24** [h] 1Ch 15:5 **6:27** [i] 1Sa 1:1 [j] 1Sa 1:20 **6:28** [k] ver 33; 1Sa 8:2 **6:31** [l] 1Ch 25:1; 2Ch 29:25-26; Ne 12:45 [m] 1Ch 9:33; 15:19; Ezr 3:10; Ps 68:25 **6:33** [n] 1Ki 4:31; 1Ch 15:17; 25:1 [o] ver 28 **6:34** [p] 1Sa 1:1 **6:37** [q] Ex 6:24 **6:38** [r] Ex 6:21 **6:39** [s] 1Ch 25:1,9; 2Ch 29:13; Ne 11:17 [t] 1Ch 15:17 **6:48** [u] 1Ch 23:32 **6:49** [v] Ex 27:1-8 [w] Ex 30:1-7,10; 2Ch 26:18 **6:53** [x] 2Sa 8:17

[a] *26* Some Hebrew manuscripts, Septuagint and Syriac; most Hebrew manuscripts *Ahimoth 26 and Elkanah. The sons of Elkanah:*
[b] *27* Some Septuagint manuscripts (see also 1 Samuel 1:19,20 and 1 Chron. 6:33,34); Hebrew does not have *and Samuel his son.*
[c] *28* Some Septuagint manuscripts and Syriac (see also 1 Samuel 8:2 and 1 Chron. 6:33); Hebrew does not have *Joel.*
[d] *40* Most Hebrew manuscripts; some Hebrew manuscripts, one Septuagint manuscript and Syriac *Maaseiah*

54These were the locations of their settlements[y] allotted as their territory (they were assigned to the descendants of Aaron who were from the Kohathite clan, because the first lot was for them):

55They were given Hebron in Judah with its surrounding pasturelands. 56But the fields and villages around the city were given to Caleb son of Jephunneh.[z]

57So the descendants of Aaron were given Hebron (a city of refuge), and Libnah,[a][a] Jattir,[b] Eshtemoa, 58Hilen, Debir,[c] 59Ashan,[d] Juttah[b] and Beth Shemesh, together with their pasturelands. 60And from the tribe of Benjamin they were given Gibeon,[c] Geba, Alemeth and Anathoth,[e] together with their pasturelands.

These towns, which were distributed among the Kohathite clans, were thirteen in all.

61The rest of Kohath's descendants were allotted ten towns from the clans of half the tribe of Manasseh.

62The descendants of Gershon, clan by clan, were allotted thirteen towns from the tribes of Issachar, Asher and Naphtali, and from the part of the tribe of Manasseh that is in Bashan.

63The descendants of Merari, clan by clan, were allotted twelve towns from the tribes of Reuben, Gad and Zebulun.

64So the Israelites gave the Levites these towns[f] and their pasturelands. 65From the tribes of Judah, Simeon and Benjamin they allotted the previously named towns.

66Some of the Kohathite clans were given as their territory towns from the tribe of Ephraim.

67In the hill country of Ephraim they were given Shechem (a city of refuge), and Gezer,[d][g] 68Jokmeam,[h] Beth Horon,[i] 69Aijalon[j] and Gath Rimmon,[k] together with their pasturelands.

70And from half the tribe of Manasseh the Israelites gave Aner and Bileam, together with their pasturelands, to the rest of the Kohathite clans.

71The Gershonites[l] received the following:
From the clan of the half-tribe of Manasseh
they received Golan in Bashan[m] and also Ashtaroth, together with their pasturelands;
72from the tribe of Issachar
they received Kedesh, Daberath,[n] 73Ramoth and Anem, together with their pasturelands;
74from the tribe of Asher
they received Mashal, Abdon,[o] 75Hukok[p] and Rehob,[q] together with their pasturelands;
76and from the tribe of Naphtali
they received Kedesh in Galilee, Hammon[r] and Kiriathaim,[s] together with their pasturelands.

77The Merarites (the rest of the Levites) received the following:
From the tribe of Zebulun
they received Jokneam, Kartah,[e] Rimmono and Tabor, together with their pasturelands;
78from the tribe of Reuben across the Jordan east of Jericho
they received Bezer[t] in the desert, Jahzah, 79Kedemoth[u] and Mephaath, together with their pasturelands;
80and from the tribe of Gad
they received Ramoth in Gilead,[v] Mahanaim,[w] 81Heshbon and Jazer,[x] together with their pasturelands.[y]

Issachar

7 The sons of Issachar:[z]
Tola, Puah,[a] Jashub and Shimron—four in all.
2The sons of Tola:
Uzzi, Rephaiah, Jeriel, Jahmai, Ibsam and Samuel—heads of their families. During the reign of David, the descendants of Tola listed as fighting men in their genealogy numbered 22,600.
3The son of Uzzi:
Izrahiah.
The sons of Izrahiah:
Michael, Obadiah, Joel and Isshiah. All five of them were chiefs. 4According to their family genealogy, they had 36,000 men ready for battle, for they had many wives and children.
5The relatives who were fighting men belonging to all the clans of Issachar, as listed in their genealogy, were 87,000 in all.

6:54 [y]Nu 31:10 **6:56** [z]Jos 14:13; 15:13 **6:57** [a]Nu 33:20 [b]Jos 15:48 **6:58** [c]Jos 10:3 **6:59** [d]Jos 15:42 **6:60** [e]Jer 1:1 **6:64** [f]Nu 35:1-8; Jos 21:3,41-42 **6:67** [g]Jos 10:33 **6:68** [h]1Ki 4:12 [i]Jos 10:10 **6:69** [j]Jos 10:12 [k]Jos 19:45 **6:71** [l]1Ch 23:7 [m]Jos 20:8 **6:72** [n]Jos 19:12

6:74 [o]Jos 19:28 **6:75** [p]Jos 19:34 [q]Nu 13:21 **6:76** [r]Jos 19:28 [s]Nu 32:37 **6:78** [t]Jos 20:8 **6:79** [u]Dt 2:26 **6:80** [v]Jos 20:8 [w]Ge 32:2 **6:81** [x]Nu 21:32 [y]2Ch 11:14 **7:1** [z]Ge 30:18; Nu 26:23 [a]Ge 46:13

[a]57 See Joshua 21:13; Hebrew *given the cities of refuge: Hebron, Libnah.* [b]59 Syriac (see also Septuagint and Joshua 21:16); Hebrew does not have *Juttah.* [c]60 See Joshua 21:17; Hebrew does not have *Gibeon.* [d]67 See Joshua 21:21; Hebrew *given the cities of refuge: Shechem, Gezer.* [e]77 See Septuagint and Joshua 21:34; Hebrew does not have *Jokneam, Kartah.*

Benjamin

6Three sons of Benjamin:[b]
Bela, Beker and Jediael.
7The sons of Bela:
Ezbon, Uzzi, Uzziel, Jerimoth and Iri, heads of families—five in all. Their genealogical record listed 22,034 fighting men.
8The sons of Beker:
Zemirah, Joash, Eliezer, Elioenai, Omri, Jeremoth, Abijah, Anathoth and Alemeth. All these were the sons of Beker.
9Their genealogical record listed the heads of families and 20,200 fighting men.
10The son of Jediael:
Bilhan.
The sons of Bilhan:
Jeush, Benjamin, Ehud, Kenaanah, Zethan, Tarshish and
Ahishahar. 11All these sons of Jediael were heads of families. There were 17,200 fighting men ready to go out to war.
12The Shuppites and Huppites were the descendants of Ir, and the Hushites the descendants of Aher.

Naphtali

13The sons of Naphtali:[c]
Jahziel, Guni, Jezer and Shillem[a]—the descendants of Bilhah.

Manasseh

14The descendants of Manasseh:[d]
Asriel was his descendant through his Aramean concubine. She gave birth to Makir the father
of Gilead.[e] 15Makir took a wife from among the Huppites and Shuppites. His sister's name was Maacah.
Another descendant was named Zelophehad,[f] who had only daughters.
16Makir's wife Maacah gave birth to a son and named him Peresh. His brother was named Sheresh, and his sons were Ulam and Rakem.
17The son of Ulam:
Bedan.
These were the sons of Gilead[g] son of Makir, the son of Manasseh.
18His sister Hammoleketh gave birth to Ishhod, Abiezer[h] and Mahlah.
19The sons of Shemida were:
Ahian, Shechem, Likhi and Aniam.

Ephraim

20The descendants of Ephraim:[i]
Shuthelah, Bered his son,
Tahath his son, Eleadah his son,
Tahath his son, 21Zabad his son
and Shuthelah his son.
Ezer and Elead were killed by the native-born men of Gath, when they went down to seize their livestock.
22Their father Ephraim mourned for them many days, and his relatives came to comfort him.
23Then he lay with his wife again, and she became pregnant and gave birth to a son. He named him Beriah,[b] because there had been misfortune in his family.
24His daughter was Sheerah, who built Lower and Upper Beth Horon[j] as well as Uzzen Sheerah.
25Rephah was his son, Resheph his son,[c]
Telah his son, Tahan his son,
26Ladan his son, Ammihud his son,
Elishama his son, 27Nun his son
and Joshua his son.
28Their lands and settlements included Bethel and its surrounding villages, Naaran to the east, Gezer[k] and its villages to the west, and Shechem and its villages all the way to Ayyah and its villages.
29Along the borders of Manasseh were Beth Shan,[l] Taanach, Megiddo and Dor,[m] together with their villages. The descendants of Joseph son of Israel lived in these towns.

Asher

30The sons of Asher:[n]
Imnah, Ishvah, Ishvi and Beriah. Their sister was Serah.
31The sons of Beriah:
Heber and Malkiel, who was the father of Birzaith.
32Heber was the father of Japhlet, Shomer and Hotham and of their sister Shua.
33The sons of Japhlet:
Pasach, Bimhal and Ashvath.
These were Japhlet's sons.
34The sons of Shomer:
Ahi, Rohgah,[d] Hubbah and Aram.

7:6 *b* Ge 46:21; Nu 26:38; 1Ch 8:1-40
7:13 *c* Ge 30:8; 46:24
7:14 *d* Ge 41:51; Jos 17:1; 1Ch 5:23 *e* Nu 26:30
7:15 *f* Nu 26:33; 36:1-12
7:17 *g* Nu 26:30; 1Sa 12:11
7:18 *h* Jos 17:2
7:20 *i* Ge 41:52; Nu 1:33; 26:35
7:24 *j* Jos 10:10; 16:3,5
7:28 *k* Jos 10:33; 16:7
7:29 *l* Jos 17:11 *m* Jos 11:2
7:30 *n* Ge 46:17; Nu 1:40; 26:44

---

a *13* Some Hebrew and Septuagint manuscripts (see also Gen. 46:24 and Num. 26:49); most Hebrew manuscripts *Shallum* **b** *23* *Beriah* sounds like the Hebrew for *misfortune.* **c** *25* Some Septuagint manuscripts; Hebrew does not have *his son.* **d** *34* Or *of his brother Shomer: Rohgah*

35 The sons of his brother Helem:
Zophah, Imna, Shelesh and Amal.
36 The sons of Zophah:
Suah, Harnepher, Shual, Beri,
Imrah, 37 Bezer, Hod, Shamma,
Shilshah, Ithran[a] and Beera.
38 The sons of Jether:
Jephunneh, Pispah and Ara.
39 The sons of Ulla:
Arah, Hanniel and Rizia.
40 All these were descendants of Asher—heads of families, choice men, brave warriors and outstanding leaders. The number of men ready for battle, as listed in their genealogy, was 26,000.

The Genealogy of Saul the Benjamite

8 Benjamin[o] was the father of Bela
his firstborn,
Ashbel the second son, Aharah
the third,
2 Nohah the fourth and Rapha
the fifth.
3 The sons of Bela were:
Addar,[p] Gera, Abihud,[b]
4 Abishua, Naaman, Ahoah,[q]
5 Gera, Shephuphan and Huram.
6 These were the descendants of Ehud,[r] who were heads of families of those living in Geba and were deported to Manahath:
7 Naaman, Ahijah, and Gera, who deported them and who was the father of Uzza and Ahihud.
8 Sons were born to Shaharaim in
Moab after he had divorced his
wives Hushim and Baara. 9 By
his wife Hodesh he had Jobab,
Zibia, Mesha, Malcam, 10 Jeuz,
Sakia and Mirmah. These were
his sons, heads of families.
11 By Hushim he had Abitub
and Elpaal.
12 The sons of Elpaal:
Eber, Misham, Shemed (who
built Ono[s] and Lod with its
surrounding villages), 13 and
Beriah and Shema, who were
heads of families of those living in Aijalon[t] and who drove out the inhabitants of Gath.[u]
14 Ahio, Shashak, Jeremoth, 15 Zebadiah, Arad, Eder, 16 Michael,
Ishpah and Joha were the sons
of Beriah.
17 Zebadiah, Meshullam, Hizki, Heber, 18 Ishmerai, Izliah and Jobab were the sons of Elpaal.
19 Jakim, Zicri, Zabdi, 20 Elienai, Zillethai, Eliel, 21 Adaiah, Beraiah
and Shimrath were the sons of
Shimei.
22 Ishpan, Eber, Eliel, 23 Abdon, Zicri, Hanan, 24 Hananiah, Elam,
Anthothijah, 25 Iphdeiah and
Penuel were the sons of Shashak.
26 Shamsherai, Shehariah, Athaliah,
27 Jaareshiah, Elijah and Zicri
were the sons of Jeroham.
28 All these were heads of families, chiefs as listed in their genealogy, and they lived in Jerusalem.
29 Jeiel[c] the father[d] of Gibeon
lived in Gibeon.[v]
His wife's name was Maacah,
30 and his firstborn son was Abdon, followed by Zur, Kish,
Baal, Ner,[e] Nadab, 31 Gedor,
Ahio, Zeker 32 and Mikloth,
who was the father of Shimeah. They too lived near their relatives in Jerusalem.
33 Ner[w] was the father of Kish,[x]
Kish the father of Saul[y], and
Saul the father of Jonathan,
Malki-Shua, Abinadab and
Esh-Baal.[f][z]
34 The son of Jonathan:[a]
Merib-Baal,[g][b] who was the
father of Micah.
35 The sons of Micah:
Pithon, Melech, Tarea and
Ahaz.
36 Ahaz was the father of Jehoaddah, Jehoaddah was the father
of Alemeth, Azmaveth and
Zimri, and Zimri was the father
of Moza. 37 Moza was the father
of Binea; Raphah was his son,
Eleasah his son and Azel his
son.
38 Azel had six sons, and these were
their names:
Azrikam, Bokeru, Ishmael,
Sheariah, Obadiah and Hanan.
All these were the sons of Azel.
39 The sons of his brother Eshek:
Ulam his firstborn, Jeush the
second son and Eliphelet the
third. 40 The sons of Ulam were
brave warriors who could handle the bow. They had many
sons and grandsons—150 in
all.
All these were the descendants of
Benjamin.[c]

8:1 [o]Ge 46:21; 1Ch 7:6 **8:3** [p]Ge 46:21 **8:4** [q]2Sa 23:9 **8:6** [r]Jdg 3:12-30; 1Ch 2:52 **8:12** [s]Ezr 2:33; Ne 6:2; 7:37; 11:35 **8:13** [t]Jos 10:12 [u]Jos 11:22 **8:29** [v]Jos 9:3 **8:33** [w]1Sa 28:19 [x]1Sa 9:1 [y]1Sa 14:49 [z]2Sa 2:8 **8:34** [a]2Sa 9:12 [b]2Sa 4:4 **8:40** [c]Nu 26:38

[a]37 Possibly a variant of *Jether* [b]3 Or *Gera the father of Ehud* [c]29 Some Septuagint manuscripts (see also 1 Chron. 9:35); Hebrew does not have *Jeiel.* [d]29 *Father* may mean *civic leader* or *military leader.* [e]30 Some Septuagint manuscripts (see also 1 Chron. 9:36); Hebrew does not have *Ner.* [f]33 Also known as *Ish-Bosheth* [g]34 Also known as *Mephibosheth*

9 All Israel was listed in the genealogies recorded in the book of the
kings of Israel.

The People in Jerusalem

The people of Judah were taken captive to Babylon because of their unfaithfulness.[d] 2Now the first to resettle
on their own property in their own
towns[e] were some Israelites, priests,
Levites and temple servants.[f]
3Those from Judah, from Benjamin,
and from Ephraim and Manasseh who
lived in Jerusalem were:
4Uthai son of Ammihud, the son
of Omri, the son of Imri, the
son of Bani, a descendant of
Perez son of Judah.[g]
5Of the Shilonites:
Asaiah the firstborn and his
sons.
6Of the Zerahites:
Jeuel.
The people from Judah numbered 690.
7Of the Benjamites:
Sallu son of Meshullam, the
son of Hodaviah, the son of
Hassenuah;
8Ibneiah son of Jeroham; Elah
son of Uzzi, the son of Micri;
and Meshullam son of Shephatiah, the son of Reuel, the son
of Ibnijah.
9The people from Benjamin, as
listed in their genealogy, numbered 956. All these men were
heads of their families.
10Of the priests:
Jedaiah; Jehoiarib; Jakin;
11Azariah son of Hilkiah, the son
of Meshullam, the son of Zadok, the son of Meraioth, the
son of Ahitub, the official in
charge of the house of God;
12Adaiah son of Jeroham, the
son of Pashhur,[h] the son of
Malkijah; and Maasai son of
Adiel, the son of Jahzerah, the
son of Meshullam, the son of
Meshillemith, the son of Immer.
13The priests, who were heads
of families, numbered 1,760.
They were able men, responsible for ministering in the
house of God.
14Of the Levites:
Shemaiah son of Hasshub, the
son of Azrikam, the son of
Hashabiah, a Merarite; 15Bak-
bakkar, Heresh, Galal and
Mattaniah[i] son of Mica, the
son of Zicri, the son of Asaph;
16Obadiah son of Shemaiah,
the son of Galal, the son of Jeduthun; and Berekiah son of
Asa, the son of Elkanah, who
lived in the villages of the Netophathites.[j]
17The gatekeepers:[k]
Shallum, Akkub, Talmon, Ahiman and their brothers, Shallum their chief 18being stationed at the King's Gate[l] on
the east, up to the present
time. These were the gatekeepers belonging to the camp
of the Levites. 19Shallum[m] son
of Kore, the son of Ebiasaph,
the son of Korah, and his
fellow gatekeepers from his
family (the Korahites) were
responsible for guarding the
thresholds of the Tent[a] just as
their fathers had been responsible for guarding the entrance
to the dwelling of the LORD.
20In earlier times Phinehas[n]
son of Eleazar was in charge of
the gatekeepers, and the LORD
was with him. 21Zechariah[o]
son of Meshelemiah was the
gatekeeper at the entrance to
the Tent of Meeting.
22Altogether, those chosen to be
gatekeepers[p] at the thresholds numbered 212. They were registered by genealogy in their villages. The gatekeepers had been assigned to their
positions of trust by David and Samuel
the seer.[q] 23They and their descendants were in charge of guarding the
gates of the house of the LORD—the
house called the Tent. 24The gatekeepers were on the four sides: east, west,
north and south. 25Their brothers in
their villages had to come from time to
time and share their duties for seven-
day[r] periods. 26But the four principal
gatekeepers, who were Levites, were
entrusted with the responsibility for
the rooms and treasuries[s] in the
house of God. 27They would spend the
night stationed around the house of
God,[t] because they had to guard it;
and they had charge of the key[u] for
opening it each morning.
28Some of them were in charge of
the articles used in the temple service;
they counted them when they were
brought in and when they were taken
out. 29Others were assigned to take
care of the furnishings and all the other
articles of the sanctuary,[v] as well as
the flour and wine, and the oil, incense
and spices. 30But some[w] of the priests
took care of mixing the spices. 31A Levite named Mattithiah, the firstborn

9:1 [d] 1Ch 5:25 **9:2** [e] Jos 9:27; Ezr 2:70 [f] Ezr 2:43,58; 8:20; Ne 7:60 **9:4** [g] Ge 38:29; 46:12 **9:12** [h] Ezr 2:38; 10:22; Ne 10:3; Jer 21:1; 38:1 **9:15** [i] 2Ch 20:14; Ne 11:22

9:16 [j] Ne 12:28 **9:17** [k] ver 22; 1Ch 26:1; 2Ch 8:14; 31:14; Ezr 2:42; Ne 7:45 **9:18** [l] 1Ch 26:14; Eze 43:1; 46:1 **9:19** [m] Jer 35:4 **9:20** [n] Nu 25:7-13 **9:21** [o] 1Ch 26:2,14 **9:22** [p] ver 17; 1Ch 26:1-2; 2Ch 31:15,18 [q] 1Sa 9:9 **9:25** [r] 2Ki 11:5; 2Ch 23:8 **9:26** [s] 1Ch 26:22 **9:27** [t] Nu 3:38; 1Ch 23:30-32 [u] Isa 22:22 **9:29** [v] Nu 3:28; 1Ch 23:29 **9:30** [w] Ex 30:23-25

[a] *19* That is, the temple; also in verses 21 and 23

son of Shallum the Korahite, was entrusted with the responsibility for baking the offering bread. 32Some of their
Kohathite brothers were in charge of
preparing for every Sabbath the bread
set out on the table.[x]
33Those who were musicians,[y]
heads of Levite families, stayed in the
rooms of the temple and were exempt
from other duties because they were
responsible for the work day and
night.[z]
34All these were heads of Levite families, chiefs as listed in their genealogy,
and they lived in Jerusalem.

The Genealogy of Saul

35Jeiel[a] the father[a] of Gibeon
lived in Gibeon.
His wife's name was Maacah,
36and his firstborn son was Ab-
don, followed by Zur, Kish,
Baal, Ner, Nadab, 37Gedor,
Ahio, Zechariah and Mikloth.
38Mikloth was the father of
Shimeam. They too lived near
their relatives in Jerusalem.
39Ner[b] was the father of Kish,[c]
Kish the father of Saul, and
Saul the father of Jonathan,[d]
Malki-Shua, Abinadab and
Esh-Baal.[b][e]
40The son of Jonathan:
Merib-Baal,[c][f] who was the
father of Micah.
41The sons of Micah:
Pithon, Melech, Tahrea and
Ahaz.[d]
42Ahaz was the father of Jadah,
Jadah[e] was the father of Ale-
meth, Azmaveth and Zimri,
and Zimri was the father of
Moza. 43Moza was the father of
Binea; Rephaiah was his son,
Eleasah his son and Azel his
son.
44Azel had six sons, and these were
their names:
Azrikam, Bokeru, Ishmael,
Sheariah, Obadiah and Hanan.
These were the sons of Azel.

Saul Takes His Life

10 Now the Philistines fought against
Israel; the Israelites fled before
them, and many fell slain on Mount
Gilboa. 2The Philistines pressed hard
after Saul and his sons, and they killed
his sons Jonathan, Abinadab and
Malki-Shua. 3The fighting grew fierce
around Saul, and when the archers
overtook him, they wounded him.
4Saul said to his armor-bearer,
"Draw your sword and run me
through, or these uncircumcised fellows will come and abuse me."
But his armor-bearer was terrified
and would not do it; so Saul took his
own sword and fell on it. 5When the
armor-bearer saw that Saul was dead,
he too fell on his sword and died. 6So
Saul and his three sons died, and all his
house died together.
7When all the Israelites in the valley
saw that the army had fled and that
Saul and his sons had died, they abandoned their towns and fled. And the
Philistines came and occupied them.
8The next day, when the Philistines
came to strip the dead, they found Saul
and his sons fallen on Mount Gilboa.
9They stripped him and took his head
and his armor, and sent messengers
throughout the land of the Philistines
to proclaim the news among their idols
and their people. 10They put his armor
in the temple of their gods and hung
up his head in the temple of Dagon.[g]
11When all the inhabitants of Jabesh
Gilead[h] heard of everything the Philistines had done to Saul, 12all their valiant men went and took the bodies of
Saul and his sons and brought them to
Jabesh. Then they buried their bones
under the great tree in Jabesh, and they
fasted seven days.
13Saul died[i] because he was unfaithful[j] to the LORD; he did not
keep[k] the word of the LORD and even
consulted a medium[l] for guidance,
14and did not inquire of the LORD. So
the LORD put him to death and
turned[m] the kingdom[n] over to David
son of Jesse.

David Becomes King Over Israel

11 All Israel[o] came together to David
at Hebron[p] and said, "We are your
own flesh and blood. 2In the past, even
while Saul was king, you were the one
who led Israel on their military campaigns.[q] And the LORD your God said
to you, 'You will shepherd[r] my people
Israel, and you will become their
ruler.[s]' "
3When all the elders of Israel had
come to King David at Hebron, he
made a compact with them at Hebron
before the LORD, and they anointed[t]
David king over Israel, as the LORD had
promised through Samuel.

9:32 [x] Lev 24:5-8; 1Ch 23:29; 2Ch 13:11
9:33 [y] 1Ch 6:31; 25:1-31 [z] Ps 134:1
9:35 [a] 1Ch 8:29
9:39 [b] 1Ch 8:33 [c] 1Sa 9:1 [d] 1Sa 13:22 [e] 2Sa 2:8
9:40 [f] 2Sa 4:4
10:10 [g] Jdg 16:23
10:11 [h] Jdg 21:8
10:13 [i] 2Sa 1:1 [j] 1Sa 15:23; 1Ch 5:25 [k] 1Sa 13:13 [l] Lev 19:31; 20:6; Dt 18:9-14; 1Sa 28:7
10:14 [m] 1Ch 12:23 [n] 1Sa 13:14; 15:28
11:1 [o] 1Ch 9:1 [p] Ge 13:18; 23:19
11:2 [q] 1Sa 18:5,16 [r] Ps 78:71; Mt 2:6 [s] 1Ch 5:2
11:3 [t] 1Sa 16:1-13

[a] *35 Father* may mean *civic leader* or *military leader.* [b] *39* Also known as *Ish-Bosheth*
[c] *40* Also known as *Mephibosheth*
[d] *41* Vulgate and Syriac (see also Septuagint and 1 Chron. 8:35); Hebrew does not have *and Ahaz.*
[e] *42* Some Hebrew manuscripts and Septuagint (see also 1 Chron. 8:36); most Hebrew manuscripts *Jarah, Jarah*

David Conquers Jerusalem

4David and all the Israelites
marched to Jerusalem (that is, Jebus).
The Jebusites[u] who lived there 5said
to David, "You will not get in here."
Nevertheless, David captured the fortress of Zion, the City of David.

6David had said, "Whoever leads the
attack on the Jebusites will become
commander-in-chief." Joab[v] son of
Zeruiah went up first, and so he received the command.

7David then took up residence in the
fortress, and so it was called the City of

11:4 [u]Ge 10:16; 15:18-21; Jos 3:10; 15:8; Jdg 1:21; 19:10
11:6 [v]2Sa 2:13; 8:16

11:1-3

PROMISE 1

WAITING ON GOD

Are you the kind of guy who always wants it done yesterday? Have you bought into the idea that macho men are impatient, that successful men push to get it done ASAP, that efficiency must reign?

David was as successful as they come—a macho man if one ever lived. But this man of action and accomplishment knew how to wait on God. What a hard lesson for many of us to learn, but an absolutely essential one to live with. This passage illustrates David's ability to wait on God. As a boy, God anointed David as Israel's next king (v. 2, 1 Samuel 16). Now as a 30-year-old man, God placed him on Israel's throne (v. 3). What's missing from this account are the years of hiding from Saul, the anxiety, the wars, injustices, disappointments—years of turmoil and agony. But David loved, trusted and waited on God.

What an illustration of a man walking with God over the long haul. The man who loves God like David did is the man who will wait on God and, sometimes later instead of sooner, receive God's promise. But it all begins with cultivating that personal, intimate relationship with God through prayer and meditation on Scripture. The following statements, taken from some of David's psalms, provide a glimpse of the heart of a man who waits on God.

Psalm 25:1–3: "To you, O LORD, I lift up my soul; in you I trust, O my God. Do not let me be put to shame, nor let my enemies triumph over me. No one whose hope is in you will ever be put to shame, but they will be put to shame who are treacherous without excuse."

Psalm 25:16–21: "Turn to me and be gracious to me, for I am lonely and afflicted. The troubles of my heart have multiplied; free me from my anguish. Look upon my affliction and my distress and take away all my sins. See how my enemies have increased and how fiercely they hate me! Guard my life and rescue me; let me not be put to shame, for I take refuge in you. May integrity and uprightness protect me, because my hope is in you."

Psalm 27:1–3: "The LORD is my light and my salvation—whom shall I fear? The LORD is the stronghold of my life—of whom shall I be afraid? When evil men advance against me to devour my flesh, when my enemies and my foes attack me, they will stumble and fall. Though an army besiege me, my heart will not fear; though war break out against me, even then I will be confident."

Psalm 27:11–14: "Teach me your way, O LORD; lead me in a straight path because of my oppressors. Do not turn me over to the desire of my foes, for false witnesses rise up against me, breathing out violence. I am still confident of this: I will see the goodness of the LORD in the land of the living. Wait for the LORD; be strong and take heart and wait for the LORD."

Psalm 33:18–22: "But the eyes of the LORD are on those who fear him, on those whose hope is in his unfailing love, to deliver them from death and keep them alive in famine. We wait in hope for the LORD; he is our help and our shield. In him our hearts rejoice, for we trust in his holy name. May your unfailing love rest upon us, O LORD, even as we put our hope in you."

Psalm 37:7–11: "Be still before the LORD and wait patiently for him; do not fret when men succeed in their ways, when they carry out their wicked schemes. Refrain from anger and turn from wrath; do not fret—it leads only to evil. For evil men will be cut off, but those who hope in the LORD will inherit the land. A little while, and the wicked will be no more; though you look for them, they will not be found. But the meek will inherit the land and enjoy great peace."

Psalm 37:34: "Wait for the LORD and keep his way. He will exalt you to inherit the land; when the wicked are cut off, you will see it."

Psalm 40:1–5: "I waited patiently for the LORD; he turned to me and heard my cry. He lifted me out of the slimy pit, out of the mud and mire; he set my feet on a rock and gave me a firm place to stand. He put a new song in my mouth, a hymn of praise to our God. Many will see and fear and put their trust in the LORD. Blessed is the man who makes the LORD his trust, who does not look to the proud, to those who turn aside to false gods. Many, O LORD my God, are the wonders you have done. The things you planned for us no one can recount to you; were I to speak and tell of them, they would be too many to declare."

Psalm 62:5–8: "Find rest, O my soul, in God alone; my hope comes from him. He alone is my rock and my salvation; he is my fortress, I will not be shaken. My salvation and my honor depend on God; he is my mighty rock, my refuge. Trust in him at all times, O people; pour out your hearts to him, for God is our refuge."

For the next Promise 1 reading go to page 455.

David. 8 He built up the city around it,
from the supporting terraces[a][w] to the
surrounding wall, while Joab restored
the rest of the city. 9 And David became
more and more powerful,[x] because
the LORD Almighty was with him.

David's Mighty Men

10 These were the chiefs of David's
mighty men—they, together with all
Israel,[y] gave his kingship strong support to extend it over the whole land, as
the LORD had promised[z]— 11 this is
the list of David's mighty men:[a]

Jashobeam,[b] a Hacmonite, was
chief of the officers[c]; he raised his
spear against three hundred men,
whom he killed in one encounter.

12 Next to him was Eleazar son of Dodai the Ahohite, one of the three
mighty men. 13 He was with David at
Pas Dammim when the Philistines
gathered there for battle. At a place
where there was a field full of barley,
the troops fled from the Philistines.
14 But they took their stand in the middle of the field. They defended it and
struck the Philistines down, and the
LORD brought about a great victory.[b]

15 Three of the thirty chiefs came
down to David to the rock at the cave
of Adullam, while a band of Philistines
was encamped in the Valley[c] of Rephaim. 16 At that time David was in the
stronghold,[d] and the Philistine garrison was at Bethlehem. 17 David longed
for water and said, "Oh, that someone
would get me a drink of water from the
well near the gate of Bethlehem!" 18 So
the Three broke through the Philistine
lines, drew water from the well near
the gate of Bethlehem and carried it
back to David. But he refused to drink
it; instead, he poured[e] it out before
the LORD. 19 "God forbid that I should
do this!" he said. "Should I drink the
blood of these men who went at the
risk of their lives?" Because they risked
their lives to bring it back, David would
not drink it.

Such were the exploits of the three
mighty men.

20 Abishai[f] the brother of Joab was
chief of the Three. He raised his spear
against three hundred men, whom he
killed, and so he became as famous as
the Three. 21 He was doubly honored
above the Three and became their
commander, even though he was not
included among them.

22 Benaiah son of Jehoiada was a valiant fighter from Kabzeel,[g] who performed great exploits. He struck down
two of Moab's best men. He also went
down into a pit on a snowy day and
killed a lion.[h] 23 And he struck down
an Egyptian who was seven and a half
feet[d] tall. Although the Egyptian had a
spear like a weaver's rod[i] in his hand,
Benaiah went against him with a club.
He snatched the spear from the Egyptian's hand and killed him with his own
spear. 24 Such were the exploits of Benaiah son of Jehoiada; he too was as
famous as the three mighty men. 25 He
was held in greater honor than any of
the Thirty, but he was not included
among the Three. And David put him
in charge of his bodyguard.

26 The mighty men were:
Asahel[j] the brother of Joab,
Elhanan son of Dodo from
Bethlehem,
27 Shammoth[k] the Harorite,
Helez the Pelonite,
28 Ira son of Ikkesh from Tekoa,
Abiezer[l] from Anathoth,
29 Sibbecai[m] the Hushathite,
Ilai the Ahohite,
30 Maharai the Netophathite,
Heled son of Baanah the Netophathite,
31 Ithai son of Ribai from Gibeah
in Benjamin,
Benaiah[n] the Pirathonite,[o]
32 Hurai from the ravines of Gaash,
Abiel the Arbathite,
33 Azmaveth the Baharumite,
Eliahba the Shaalbonite,
34 the sons of Hashem the Gizo-
nite,
Jonathan son of Shagee the
Hararite,
35 Ahiam son of Sacar the Hararite,
Eliphal son of Ur,
36 Hepher the Mekerathite,
Ahijah the Pelonite,
37 Hezro the Carmelite,
Naarai son of Ezbai,
38 Joel the brother of Nathan,
Mibhar son of Hagri,
39 Zelek the Ammonite,
Naharai the Berothite, the
armor-bearer of Joab son of
Zeruiah,
40 Ira the Ithrite,
Gareb the Ithrite,
41 Uriah[p] the Hittite,
Zabad[q] son of Ahlai,
42 Adina son of Shiza the Reubenite, who was chief of the
Reubenites, and the thirty with
him,
43 Hanan son of Maacah,

11:8 [w] 2Sa 5:9; 2Ch 32:5
11:9 [x] 2Sa 3:1; Est 9:4
11:10 [y] ver 1 [z] ver 3; 1Ch 12:23
11:11 [a] 2Sa 17:10
11:14 [b] Ex 14:30; 1Sa 11:13
11:15 [c] 1Ch 14:9; Isa 17:5
11:16 [d] 2Sa 5:17
11:18 [e] Dt 12:16
11:20 [f] 1Sa 26:6
11:22 [g] Jos 15:21 [h] 1Sa 17:36
11:23 [i] 1Sa 17:7
11:26 [j] 2Sa 2:18
11:27 [k] 1Ch 27:8
11:28 [l] 1Ch 27:12
11:29 [m] 2Sa 21:18
11:31 [n] 1Ch 27:14 [o] Jdg 12:13
11:41 [p] 2Sa 11:6 [q] 1Ch 2:36

[a] *8* Or *the Millo* [b] *11* Possibly a variant of *Jashob-Baal* [c] *11* Or *Thirty;* some Septuagint manuscripts *Three* (see also 2 Samuel 23:8) [d] *23* Hebrew *five cubits* (about 2.3 meters)

Joshaphat the Mithnite,
44 Uzzia the Ashterathite,[r]
Shama and Jeiel the sons of
Hotham the Aroerite,
45 Jediael son of Shimri,
his brother Joha the Tizite,
46 Eliel the Mahavite,
Jeribai and Joshaviah the sons
of Elnaam,
Ithmah the Moabite,
47 Eliel, Obed and Jaasiel the Me-
zobaite.

Warriors Join David

12 These were the men who came to
David at Ziklag,[s] while he was
banished from the presence of Saul son
of Kish (they were among the warriors
who helped him in battle; 2 they were
armed with bows and were able to
shoot arrows or to sling stones right-
handed or left-handed;[t] they were
kinsmen of Saul[u] from the tribe of
Benjamin):

3 Ahiezer their chief and Joash the
sons of Shemaah the Gibeathite;
Jeziel and Pelet the sons of Azmaveth; Beracah, Jehu the Anathothite, 4 and Ishmaiah the Gibeonite,
a mighty man among the Thirty,
who was a leader of the Thirty;
Jeremiah, Jahaziel, Johanan, Jozabad the Gederathite,[v] 5 Eluzai,
Jerimoth, Bealiah, Shemariah and
Shephatiah the Haruphite; 6 Elkanah, Isshiah, Azarel, Joezer and
Jashobeam the Korahites; 7 and Jo-
elah and Zebadiah the sons of Jeroham from Gedor.[w]

8 Some Gadites[x] defected to David
at his stronghold in the desert. They
were brave warriors, ready for battle
and able to handle the shield and
spear. Their faces were the faces of lions,[y] and they were as swift as gazelles[z] in the mountains.

9 Ezer was the chief,
Obadiah the second in command, Eliab the third,
10 Mishmannah the fourth, Jeremiah the fifth,
11 Attai the sixth, Eliel the seventh,
12 Johanan the eighth, Elzabad the
ninth,
13 Jeremiah the tenth and Macban-
nai the eleventh.

14 These Gadites were army commanders; the least was a match for a
hundred,[a] and the greatest for a thousand.[b] 15 It was they who crossed the
Jordan in the first month when it was
overflowing all its banks,[c] and they
put to flight everyone living in the valleys, to the east and to the west.

11:44 [r] Dt 1:4
12:1 [s] Jos 15:31; 1Sa 27:2-6
12:2 [t] Jdg 3:15; 20:16 [u] 2Sa 3:19
12:4 [v] Jos 15:36
12:7 [w] Jos 15:58
12:8 [x] Ge 30:11 [y] 2Sa 17:10 [z] 2Sa 2:18
12:14 [a] Lev 26:8 [b] Dt 32:30
12:15 [c] Jos 3:15

12:16 [d] 2Sa 3:19
12:18 [e] Jdg 3:10; 6:34; 1Ch 28:12; 2Ch 15:1; 20:14; 24:20 [f] 2Sa 17:25 [g] 1Sa 25:5-6
12:19 [h] 1Sa 29:2-11
12:20 [i] 1Sa 27:6
12:23 [j] 2Sa 2:3-4 [k] 1Ch 10:14 [l] 1Sa 16:1; 1Ch 11:10
12:28 [m] 2Sa 8:17; 1Ch 6:8; 15:11; 16:39; 27:17
12:29 [n] 2Sa 3:19 [o] 2Sa 2:8-9

16 Other Benjamites[d] and some men
from Judah also came to David in his
stronghold. 17 David went out to meet
them and said to them, "If you have
come to me in peace, to help me, I am
ready to have you unite with me. But if
you have come to betray me to my enemies when my hands are free from violence, may the God of our fathers see it
and judge you."

18 Then the Spirit[e] came upon Amasai,[f] chief of the Thirty, and he said:

"We are yours, O David!
We are with you, O son of Jesse!
Success,[g] success to you,
and success to those who help
you,
for your God will help you."

So David received them and made
them leaders of his raiding bands.

19 Some of the men of Manasseh defected to David when he went with the
Philistines to fight against Saul. (He
and his men did not help the Philistines because, after consultation, their
rulers sent him away. They said, "It will
cost us our heads if he deserts to his
master Saul.")[h] 20 When David went to
Ziklag,[i] these were the men of Manasseh who defected to him: Adnah, Jozabad, Jediael, Michael, Jozabad, Elihu
and Zillethai, leaders of units of a thousand in Manasseh. 21 They helped David against raiding bands, for all of
them were brave warriors, and they
were commanders in his army. 22 Day
after day men came to help David, until he had a great army, like the army of
God.[a]

Others Join David at Hebron

23 These are the numbers of the men
armed for battle who came to David
at Hebron[j] to turn[k] Saul's kingdom
over to him, as the LORD had said:[l]

24 men of Judah, carrying shield
and spear—6,800 armed for
battle;
25 men of Simeon, warriors ready
for battle—7,100;
26 men of Levi—4,600, 27 including
Jehoiada, leader of the family
of Aaron, with 3,700 men,
28 and Zadok,[m] a brave young
warrior, with 22 officers from
his family;
29 men of Benjamin,[n] Saul's kinsmen—3,000, most[o] of whom
had remained loyal to Saul's
house until then;
30 men of Ephraim, brave warriors,

[a] 22 Or *a great and mighty army*

famous in their own clans—
20,800;
31 men of half the tribe of Manasseh, designated by name to
come and make David king—
18,000;
32 men of Issachar, who understood
the times and knew what Israel
should do[p]—200 chiefs, with
all their relatives under their
command;
33 men of Zebulun, experienced
soldiers prepared for battle
with every type of weapon, to
help David with undivided
loyalty—50,000;
34 men of Naphtali—1,000 officers,
together with 37,000 men carrying shields and spears;
35 men of Dan, ready for battle—
28,600;
36 men of Asher, experienced soldiers prepared for battle—
40,000;
37 and from east of the Jordan, men
of Reuben, Gad and the half-
tribe of Manasseh, armed
with every type of weapon—
120,000.

38 All these were fighting men who
volunteered to serve in the ranks. They
came to Hebron fully determined to
make David king over all Israel.[q] All
the rest of the Israelites were also of
one mind to make David king. 39 The
men spent three days there with David,
eating and drinking,[r] for their families
had supplied provisions for them.
40 Also, their neighbors from as far away
as Issachar, Zebulun and Naphtali
came bringing food on donkeys, camels, mules and oxen. There were plentiful supplies[s] of flour, fig cakes, raisin[t] cakes, wine, oil, cattle and sheep,
for there was joy[u] in Israel.

Bringing Back the Ark

13 David conferred with each of his officers, the commanders of thousands and commanders of hundreds.
2 He then said to the whole assembly of
Israel, "If it seems good to you and if it
is the will of the LORD our God, let us
send word far and wide to the rest of
our brothers throughout the territories
of Israel, and also to the priests and
Levites who are with them in their
towns and pasturelands, to come and
join us. 3 Let us bring the ark of our God
back to us,[v] for we did not inquire[w]
of[a] it[b] during the reign of Saul." 4 The
whole assembly agreed to do this, because it seemed right to all the people.
5 So David assembled all the Israelites,[x] from the Shihor River[y] in Egypt
to Lebo[c] Hamath,[z] to bring the ark
of God from Kiriath Jearim.[a] 6 David
and all the Israelites with him went to
Baalah[b] of Judah (Kiriath Jearim) to
bring up from there the ark of God the
LORD, who is enthroned between the
cherubim[c]—the ark that is called by
the Name.

7 They moved the ark of God from
Abinadab's[d] house on a new cart, with
Uzzah and Ahio guiding it. 8 David and
all the Israelites were celebrating with
all their might before God, with songs
and with harps, lyres, tambourines,
cymbals and trumpets.[e]

9 When they came to the threshing
floor of Kidon, Uzzah reached out his
hand to steady the ark, because the
oxen stumbled. 10 The LORD's anger[f]
burned against Uzzah, and he struck
him down[g] because he had put his
hand on the ark. So he died there before God.

11 Then David was angry because the
LORD's wrath had broken out against
Uzzah, and to this day that place is
called Perez Uzzah.[d][h]

12 David was afraid of God that day
and asked, "How can I ever bring the
ark of God to me?" 13 He did not take
the ark to be with him in the City
of David. Instead, he took it aside to
the house of Obed-Edom[i] the Gittite.
14 The ark of God remained with the
family of Obed-Edom in his house for
three months, and the LORD blessed his
household[j] and everything he had.

David's House and Family

14 Now Hiram king of Tyre sent messengers to David, along with cedar
logs,[k] stonemasons and carpenters to
build a palace for him. 2 And David
knew that the LORD had established
him as king over Israel and that his
kingdom had been highly exalted[l] for
the sake of his people Israel.

3 In Jerusalem David took more
wives and became the father of more
sons[m] and daughters. 4 These are the
names of the children born to him
there:[n] Shammua, Shobab, Nathan,
Solomon, 5 Ibhar, Elishua, Elpelet, 6 Nogah, Nepheg, Japhia, 7 Elishama, Beeli-
ada[e] and Eliphelet.

David Defeats the Philistines

8 When the Philistines heard that David had been anointed king over all Israel,[o] they went up in full force to
search for him, but David heard about

12:32 [p] Est 1:13
12:38 [q] 2Sa 5:1-3; 1Ch 9:1
12:39 [r] 2Sa 3:20; Isa 25:6-8
12:40 [s] 2Sa 16:1; 17:29 [t] 1Sa 25:18 [u] 1Ch 29:22
13:3 [v] 1Sa 7:1-2 [w] 2Ch 1:5
13:5 [x] 1Ch 11:1; 15:3 [y] Jos 13:3 [z] Nu 13:21 [a] 1Sa 6:21; 7:2
13:6 [b] Jos 15:9; 2Sa 6:2 [c] Ex 25:22; 2Ki 19:15
13:7 [d] Nu 4:15; 1Sa 7:1
13:8 [e] 2Sa 6:5; 1Ch 15:16,19, 24; 2Ch 5:12; Ps 92:3
13:10 [f] 1Ch 15:13,15 [g] Lev 10:2
13:11 [h] 1Ch 15:13; Ps 7:11
13:13 [i] 1Ch 15:18,24; 16:38; 26:4-5, 15
13:14 [j] 2Sa 6:11; 1Ch 26:4-5
14:1 [k] 2Ch 2:3; Ezr 3:7
14:2 [l] Nu 24:7; Dt 26:19
14:3 [m] 1Ch 3:1
14:4 [n] 1Ch 3:9
14:8 [o] 1Ch 11:1

[a] 3 Or *we neglected* [b] 3 Or *him* [c] 5 Or *to the entrance to* [d] 11 *Perez Uzzah* means *outbreak against Uzzah.* [e] 7 A variant of *Eliada*

it and went out to meet them. **9**Now the Philistines had come and raided the Valley[p] of Rephaim; **10**so David inquired of God: "Shall I go and attack the Philistines? Will you hand them over to me?"

The LORD answered him, "Go, I will hand them over to you."

11So David and his men went up to Baal Perazim,[q] and there he defeated them. He said, "As waters break out, God has broken out against my enemies by my hand." So that place was called Baal Perazim.[a] **12**The Philistines had abandoned their gods there, and David gave orders to burn[r] them in the fire.[s]

13Once more the Philistines raided the valley;[t] **14**so David inquired of God again, and God answered him, "Do not go straight up, but circle around them and attack them in front of the balsam trees. **15**As soon as you hear the sound of marching in the tops of the balsam trees, move out to battle, because that will mean God has gone out in front of you to strike the Philistine army." **16**So David did as God commanded him, and they struck down the Philistine army, all the way from Gibeon[u] to Gezer.[v]

17So David's fame[w] spread throughout every land, and the LORD made all the nations fear[x] him.

The Ark Brought to Jerusalem

15 After David had constructed buildings for himself in the City of David, he prepared[y] a place for the ark of God and pitched[z] a tent for it. **2**Then David said, "No one but the Levites[a] may carry[b] the ark of God, because the LORD chose them to carry the ark of the LORD and to minister[c] before him forever."

3David assembled all Israel[d] in Jerusalem to bring up the ark of the LORD to the place he had prepared for it. **4**He called together the descendants of Aaron and the Levites:

5From the descendants of Kohath,
Uriel the leader and 120 relatives;
6from the descendants of Merari,
Asaiah the leader and 220 relatives;
7from the descendants of Gershon,[b]
Joel the leader and 130 relatives;
8from the descendants of Elizaphan,[e]
Shemaiah the leader and 200 relatives;
9from the descendants of Hebron,[f]
Eliel the leader and 80 relatives;
10from the descendants of Uzziel,
Amminadab the leader and 112 relatives.

11Then David summoned Zadok[g] and Abiathar[h] the priests, and Uriel, Asaiah, Joel, Shemaiah, Eliel and Amminadab the Levites. **12**He said to them, "You are the heads of the Levitical families; you and your fellow Levites are to consecrate[i] yourselves and bring up the ark of the LORD, the God of Israel, to the place I have prepared for it. **13**It was because you, the Levites,[j] did not bring it up the first time that the LORD our God broke out in anger against us.[k] We did not inquire of him about how to do it in the prescribed way." **14**So the priests and Levites consecrated themselves in order to bring up the ark of the LORD, the God of Israel. **15**And the Levites carried the ark of God with the poles on their shoulders, as Moses had commanded[l] in accordance with the word of the LORD.

16David told the leaders of the Levites to appoint their brothers as singers[m] to sing joyful songs, accompanied by musical instruments: lyres, harps and cymbals.[n]

17So the Levites appointed Heman[o] son of Joel; from his brothers, Asaph[p] son of Berekiah; and from their brothers the Merarites,[q] Ethan son of Kushaiah; **18**and with them their brothers next in rank: Zechariah,[c] Jaaziel, Shemiramoth, Jehiel, Unni, Eliab, Benaiah, Maaseiah, Mattithiah, Eliphelehu, Mikneiah, Obed-Edom[r] and Jeiel,[d] the gatekeepers.

19The musicians Heman,[s] Asaph and Ethan were to sound the bronze cymbals; **20**Zechariah, Aziel, Shemiramoth, Jehiel, Unni, Eliab, Maaseiah and Benaiah were to play the lyres according to *alamoth,*[e] **21**and Mattithiah, Eliphelehu, Mikneiah, Obed-Edom, Jeiel and Azaziah were to play the harps, directing according to *sheminith.*[e] **22**Kenaniah the head Levite was in charge of the singing; that was his responsibility because he was skillful at it.

23Berekiah and Elkanah were to be

14:9 [p]ver 13; Jos 15:8; 1Ch 11:15
14:11 [q]Isa 28:21
14:12 [r]Ex 32:20 [s]Jos 7:15
14:13 [t]ver 9
14:16 [u]Jos 9:3 [v]Jos 10:33
14:17 [w]Jos 6:27; 2Ch 26:8 [x]Ex 15:14-16; Dt 2:25
15:1 [y]Ps 132:1-18 [z]1Ch 16:1; 17:1
15:2 [a]Nu 4:15; Dt 10:8; 2Ch 5:5 [b]Dt 31:9 [c]1Ch 23:13
15:3 [d]1Ki 8:1; 1Ch 13:5
15:8 [e]Ex 6:22
15:9 [f]Ex 6:18
15:11 [g]1Ch 12:28 [h]1Sa 22:20
15:12 [i]Ex 19:14-15; Lev 11:44; 2Ch 35:6
15:13 [j]1Ki 8:4 [k]2Sa 6:3; 1Ch 13:7-10
15:15 [l]Ex 25:14; Nu 4:5,15
15:16 [m]Ps 68:25 [n]1Ch 13:8; 25:1; Ne 12:27,36
15:17 [o]1Ch 6:33 [p]1Ch 6:39 [q]1Ch 6:44
15:18 [r]1Ch 26:4-5
15:19 [s]1Ch 25:6

[a] 11 *Baal Perazim* means *the lord who breaks out.* [b] 7 Hebrew *Gershom,* a variant of *Gershon* [c] 18 Three Hebrew manuscripts and most Septuagint manuscripts (see also verse 20 and 1 Chron. 16:5); most Hebrew manuscripts *Zechariah son and* or *Zechariah, Ben and* [d] 18 Hebrew; Septuagint (see also verse 21) *Jeiel and Azaziah* [e] 20,21 Probably a musical term

doorkeepers for the ark. 24 Shebaniah,
Joshaphat, Nethanel, Amasai, Zechariah, Benaiah and Eliezer the priests
were to blow trumpets[t] before the ark
of God. Obed-Edom and Jehiah were
also to be doorkeepers for the ark.
25 So David and the elders of Israel
and the commanders of units of a
thousand went to bring up the ark[u]
of the covenant of the LORD from the
house of Obed-Edom, with rejoicing.
26 Because God had helped the Levites
who were carrying the ark of the covenant of the LORD, seven bulls and sev-
en rams[v] were sacrificed. 27 Now David was clothed in a robe of fine linen,
as were all the Levites who were carrying the ark, and as were the singers,
and Kenaniah, who was in charge of
the singing of the choirs. David also
wore a linen ephod. 28 So all Israel
brought up the ark of the covenant of
the LORD with shouts, with the sounding of rams' horns[w] and trumpets, and
of cymbals, and the playing of lyres
and harps.
29 As the ark of the covenant of the
LORD was entering the City of David,
Michal daughter of Saul watched from
a window. And when she saw King David dancing and celebrating, she despised him in her heart.

16 They brought the ark of God and
set it inside the tent that David had
pitched[x] for it, and they presented
burnt offerings and fellowship offerings[a] before God. 2 After David had
finished sacrificing the burnt offerings
and fellowship offerings, he blessed[y]
the people in the name of the LORD.
3 Then he gave a loaf of bread, a cake of
dates and a cake of raisins to each Israelite man and woman.
4 He appointed some of the Levites to
minister[z] before the ark of the LORD,
to make petition, to give thanks, and
to praise the LORD, the God of Israel:
5 Asaph was the chief, Zechariah second, then Jeiel, Shemiramoth, Jehiel,
Mattithiah, Eliab, Benaiah, Obed-
Edom and Jeiel. They were to play the
lyres and harps, Asaph was to sound
the cymbals, 6 and Benaiah and Jahaziel the priests were to blow the trumpets regularly before the ark of the covenant of God.

David's Psalm of Thanks

7 That day David first committed to
Asaph and his associates this psalm[a]
of thanks to the LORD:

7 →PG. 450

8 Give thanks[b] to the LORD, call on
his name;
make known among the
nations[c] what he has done.
9 Sing to him, sing praise[d] to him;
tell of all his wonderful acts.
10 Glory in his holy name;
let the hearts of those who seek
the LORD rejoice.
11 Look to the LORD and his strength;
seek[e] his face always.
12 Remember[f] the wonders he has
done,
his miracles,[g] and the
judgments he pronounced,

1 →PG. 451

13 O descendants of Israel his servant,
O sons of Jacob, his chosen
ones.

14 He is the LORD our God;
his judgments[h] are in all the
earth.
15 He remembers[b] his covenant
forever,
the word he commanded, for a
thousand generations,
16 the covenant[i] he made with
Abraham,
the oath he swore to Isaac.
17 He confirmed it to Jacob[j] as a
decree,
to Israel as an everlasting
covenant:
18 "To you I will give the land of
Canaan[k]
as the portion you will inherit."

19 When they were but few in
number,[l]
few indeed, and strangers in it,
20 they[c] wandered from nation to
nation,
from one kingdom to another.
21 He allowed no man to oppress
them;
for their sake he rebuked
kings:[m]
22 "Do not touch my anointed ones;
do my prophets[n] no harm."

7 →PG. 518

23 Sing to the LORD, all the earth;
proclaim his salvation day after
day.
24 Declare his glory among the
nations,
his marvelous deeds among all
peoples.
25 For great is the LORD and most
worthy of praise;[o]
he is to be feared[p] above all
gods.[q]
26 For all the gods of the nations are
idols,
but the LORD made the
heavens.[r]

15:24 *t* ver 28; 1Ch 16:6; 2Ch 7:6 **15:25** *u* 1Ch 13:13; 2Ch 1:4 **15:26** *v* Nu 23:1-4,29 **15:28** *w* 1Ch 13:8 **16:1** *x* 1Ch 15:1 **16:2** *y* Ex 39:43 **16:4** *z* 1Ch 15:2 **16:7** *a* 2Sa 23:1 **16:8** *b* ver 34; Ps 136:1 *c* 2Ki 19:19

16:9 *d* Ex 15:1 **16:11** *e* 1Ch 28:9; 2Ch 7:14; Ps 24:6; 119:2, 58 **16:12** *f* Ps 77:11 *g* Ps 78:43 **16:14** *h* Isa 26:9 **16:16** *i* Ge 12:7; 15:18; 17:2; 22:16-18; 26:3; 28:13; 35:11 **16:17** *j* Ge 35:9-12 **16:18** *k* Ge 13:14-17 **16:19** *l* Ge 34:30; Dt 7:7 **16:21** *m* Ge 12:17; 20:3; Ex 7:15-18 **16:22** *n* Ge 20:7 **16:25** *o* Ps 48:1 *p* Ps 76:7; 89:7 *q* Dt 32:39 **16:26** *r* Lev 19:4; Ps 102:25

a *1* Traditionally *peace offerings*; also in verse 2 **b** *15* Some Septuagint manuscripts (see also Psalm 105:8); Hebrew *Remember* **c** *18-20* One Hebrew manuscript, Septuagint and Vulgate (see also Psalm 105:12); most Hebrew manuscripts *inherit, / 19 though you are but few in number, / few indeed, and strangers in it." / 20 They*

27Splendor and majesty are before
him;
strength and joy in his dwelling
place.
1 →PG. 472
28Ascribe to the LORD, O families of
nations,
ascribe to the LORD glory and
strength,[s]
29 ascribe to the LORD the glory due
his name.
Bring an offering and come before
him;
worship the LORD in the splendor
of his[a] holiness.[t]
30Tremble[u] before him, all the earth!
The world is firmly established; it
cannot be moved.
31Let the heavens rejoice, let the
earth be glad;[v]
let them say among the nations,
"The LORD reigns![w]"
32Let the sea resound, and all that is
in it;[x]
let the fields be jubilant, and
everything in them!
33Then the trees[y] of the forest will
sing,
they will sing for joy before the
LORD,
for he comes to judge[z] the
earth.

34Give thanks[a] to the LORD, for he is
good;[b]
his love endures forever.[c]
35Cry out, "Save us, O God our
Savior;[d]
gather us and deliver us from the
nations,
that we may give thanks to your
holy name,
that we may glory in your
praise."
36Praise be to the LORD, the God of
Israel,[e]
from everlasting to everlasting.
Then all the people said "Amen" and
"Praise the LORD."

37David left Asaph and his associates
before the ark of the covenant of the
LORD to minister there regularly, according to each day's requirements.[f]
38He also left Obed-Edom[g] and his
sixty-eight associates to minister with
them. Obed-Edom son of Jeduthun,
and also Hosah,[h] were gatekeepers.
39David left Zadok[i] the priest and
his fellow priests before the tabernacle
of the LORD at the high place in Gibeon[j] 40to present burnt offerings to the
LORD on the altar of burnt offering regularly, morning and evening, in accordance with everything written in the
Law[k] of the LORD, which he had given
Israel. 41With them were Heman[l] and
Jeduthun and the rest of those chosen
and designated by name to give thanks
to the LORD, "for his love endures forever." 42Heman and Jeduthun were responsible for the sounding of the trumpets and cymbals and for the playing
of the other instruments for sacred
song.[m] The sons of Jeduthun were stationed at the gate.
43Then all the people left, each for
his own home, and David returned
home to bless his family.

God's Promise to David

17 After David was settled in his palace, he said to Nathan the prophet,
"Here I am, living in a palace of cedar,
while the ark of the covenant of the
LORD is under a tent.[n]"
2Nathan replied to David, "Whatever
you have in mind,[o] do it, for God is
with you."
3That night the word of God came to
Nathan, saying:
4"Go and tell my servant David,
'This is what the LORD says: You[p]
are not the one to build me a
house to dwell in. 5I have not
dwelt in a house from the day I
brought Israel up out of Egypt to
this day. I have moved from one
tent site to another, from one
dwelling place to another. 6Wher-
ever I have moved with all the Israelites, did I ever say to any of
their leaders[b] whom I commanded to shepherd my people, "Why
have you not built me a house of
cedar?" '
7"Now then, tell my servant David, 'This is what the LORD Almighty says: I took you from the
pasture and from following the
flock, to be ruler[q] over my people
Israel. 8I have been with you
wherever you have gone, and I
have cut off all your enemies from
before you. Now I will make your
name like the names of the greatest men of the earth. 9And I will
provide a place for my people Israel and will plant them so that
they can have a home of their own
and no longer be disturbed. Wicked people will not oppress them
anymore, as they did at the beginning 10and have done ever since
the time I appointed leaders[r]
over my people Israel. I will also
subdue all your enemies.
" 'I declare to you that the LORD
will build a house for you: 11When

16:28 [s]Ps 29:1-2
16:29 [t]Ps 29:1-2
16:30 [u]Ps 114:7
16:31 [v]Isa 44:23; 49:13 [w]Ps 93:1
16:32 [x]Ps 98:7
16:33 [y]Isa 55:12 [z]Ps 96:10; 98:9
16:34 [a]ver 8 [b]Na 1:7 [c]2Ch 5:13; 7:3; Ezr 3:11; Ps 136:1-26; Jer 33:11
16:35 [d]Mic 7:7
16:36 [e]Dt 27:15; 1Ki 8:15; Ps 72:18-19
16:37 [f]2Ch 8:14
16:38 [g]1Ch 13:13 [h]1Ch 26:10
16:39 [i]2Sa 8:17; 1Ch 15:11 [j]1Ki 3:4; 2Ch 1:3
16:40 [k]Ex 29:38; Nu 28:1-8
16:41 [l]1Ch 6:33; 25:1-6; 2Ch 5:13
16:42 [m]2Ch 7:6
17:1 [n]1Ch 15:1
17:2 [o]2Ch 6:7
17:4 [p]1Ch 28:3
17:7 [q]2Sa 6:21
17:10 [r]Jdg 2:16

[a]29 Or *LORD with the splendor of*
[b]6 Traditionally *judges*; also in verse 10

your days are over and you go to
be with your fathers, I will raise up
your offspring to succeed you,
one of your own sons, and I will
establish his kingdom. 12He is the
one who will build[s] a house for
me, and I will establish his throne
forever.[t] 13I will be his father,[u]
and he will be my son.[v] I will
never take my love away from
him, as I took it away from your
predecessor. 14I will set him over
my house and my kingdom forever; his throne[w] will be established
forever.[x]' "

15Nathan reported to David all the
words of this entire revelation.

David's Prayer

16Then King David went in and sat
before the LORD, and he said:

"Who am I, O LORD God, and
what is my family, that you have
brought me this far? 17And as if
this were not enough in your
sight, O God, you have spoken
about the future of the house of
your servant. You have looked on
me as though I were the most exalted of men, O LORD God.

18"What more can David say to
you for honoring your servant?
For you know your servant,
19O LORD. For the sake[y] of your
servant and according to your
will, you have done this great
thing and made known all these
great promises.[z]

20"There is no one like you,
O LORD, and there is no God but
you,[a] as we have heard with our
own ears. 21And who is like your
people Israel—the one nation on
earth whose God went out to redeem[b] a people for himself, and
to make a name for yourself, and
to perform great and awesome
wonders by driving out nations
from before your people, whom
you redeemed from Egypt? 22You
made your people Israel your very
own forever,[c] and you, O LORD,
have become their God.

23"And now, LORD, let the
promise[d] you have made concerning your servant and his
house be established forever. Do
as you promised, 24so that it will
be established and that your
name will be great forever. Then
men will say, 'The LORD Almighty,
the God over Israel, is Israel's
God!' And the house of your servant David will be established before you.

25"You, my God, have revealed
to your servant that you will build
a house for him. So your servant
has found courage to pray to you.
26O LORD, you are God! You have
promised these good things to
your servant. 27Now you have
been pleased to bless the house of
your servant, that it may continue
forever in your sight;[e] for you,
O LORD, have blessed it, and it will
be blessed forever."

David's Victories

18 In the course of time, David defeated the Philistines and subdued
them, and he took Gath and its surrounding villages from the control of
the Philistines.

2David also defeated the Moabites,[f] and they became subject to him
and brought tribute.

3Moreover, David fought Hadadezer
king of Zobah,[g] as far as Hamath,
when he went to establish his control
along the Euphrates River.[h] 4David
captured a thousand of his chariots,
seven thousand charioteers and twenty
thousand foot soldiers. He hamstrung[i] all but a hundred of the chariot horses.

5When the Arameans of Damascus[j]
came to help Hadadezer king of Zobah,
David struck down twenty-two thousand of them. 6He put garrisons in the
Aramean kingdom of Damascus, and
the Arameans became subject to him
and brought tribute. The LORD gave
David victory everywhere he went.

7David took the gold shields carried
by the officers of Hadadezer and
brought them to Jerusalem. 8From Tebah[a] and Cun, towns that belonged to
Hadadezer, David took a great quantity
of bronze, which Solomon used to
make the bronze Sea,[k] the pillars and
various bronze articles.

9When Tou king of Hamath heard
that David had defeated the entire
army of Hadadezer king of Zobah, 10he
sent his son Hadoram to King David to
greet him and congratulate him on his
victory in battle over Hadadezer, who
had been at war with Tou. Hadoram
brought all kinds of articles of gold and
silver and bronze.

11King David dedicated these articles to the LORD, as he had done with
the silver and gold he had taken from
all these nations: Edom[l] and Moab,

17:12 [s]1Ki 5:5 [t]2Ch 7:18
17:13 [u]2Co 6:18 [v]Lk 1:32; Heb 1:5*
17:14 [w]1Ki 2:12; 1Ch 28:5 [x]Ps 132:11; Jer 33:17
17:19 [y]2Sa 7:16-17; 2Ki 20:6; Isa 9:7; 37:35; 55:3 [z]2Sa 7:25
17:20 [a]Ex 8:10; 9:14; 15:11; Isa 44:6; 46:9
17:21 [b]Ex 6:6
17:22 [c]Ex 19:5-6
17:23 [d]1Ki 8:25
17:27 [e]Ps 16:11; 21:6
18:2 [f]Nu 21:29
18:3 [g]1Ch 19:6 [h]Ge 2:14
18:4 [i]Ge 49:6
18:5 [j]2Ki 16:9; 1Ch 19:6
18:8 [k]1Ki 7:23; 2Ch 4:12,15-16
18:11 [l]Nu 24:18

[a] 8 Hebrew *Tibhath,* a variant of *Tebah*

the Ammonites and the Philistines, and Amalek.[m]

12 Abishai son of Zeruiah struck down eighteen thousand Edomites[n] in the Valley of Salt. 13 He put garrisons in Edom, and all the Edomites became subject to David. The LORD gave David victory everywhere he went.

David's Officials

14 David reigned[o] over all Israel,[p] doing what was just and right for all his people. 15 Joab[q] son of Zeruiah was over the army; Jehoshaphat son of Ahilud was recorder; 16 Zadok[r] son of Ahitub and Ahimelech[a][s] son of Abiathar were priests; Shavsha was secretary; 17 Benaiah son of Jehoiada was over the Kerethites and Pelethites;[t] and David's sons were chief officials at the king's side.

The Battle Against the Ammonites

19 In the course of time, Nahash king of the Ammonites[u] died, and his son succeeded him as king. 2 David thought, "I will show kindness to Hanun son of Nahash, because his father showed kindness to me." So David sent a delegation to express his sympathy to Hanun concerning his father.

When David's men came to Hanun in the land of the Ammonites to express sympathy to him, 3 the Ammonite nobles said to Hanun, "Do you think David is honoring your father by sending men to you to express sympathy? Haven't his men come to you to explore and spy out[v] the country and overthrow it?" 4 So Hanun seized David's men, shaved them, cut off their garments in the middle at the buttocks, and sent them away.

5 When someone came and told David about the men, he sent messengers to meet them, for they were greatly humiliated. The king said, "Stay at Jericho till your beards have grown, and then come back."

6 When the Ammonites realized that they had become a stench[w] in David's nostrils, Hanun and the Ammonites sent a thousand talents[b] of silver to hire chariots and charioteers from Aram Naharaim,[c] Aram Maacah and Zobah.[x] 7 They hired thirty-two thousand chariots and charioteers, as well as the king of Maacah with his troops, who came and camped near Medeba,[y] while the Ammonites were mustered from their towns and moved out for battle.

8 On hearing this, David sent Joab out with the entire army of fighting men. 9 The Ammonites came out and drew up in battle formation at the entrance to their city, while the kings who had come were by themselves in the open country.

10 Joab saw that there were battle lines in front of him and behind him; so he selected some of the best troops in Israel and deployed them against the Arameans. 11 He put the rest of the men under the command of Abishai[z] his brother, and they were deployed against the Ammonites. 12 Joab said, "If the Arameans are too strong for me, then you are to rescue me; but if the Ammonites are too strong for you, then I will rescue you. 13 Be strong and let us fight bravely for our people and the cities of our God. The LORD will do what is good in his sight."

14 Then Joab and the troops with him advanced to fight the Arameans, and they fled before him. 15 When the Ammonites saw that the Arameans were fleeing, they too fled before his brother Abishai and went inside the city. So Joab went back to Jerusalem.

16 After the Arameans saw that they had been routed by Israel, they sent messengers and had Arameans brought from beyond the River,[d] with Shophach the commander of Hadadezer's army leading them.

17 When David was told of this, he gathered all Israel[a] and crossed the Jordan; he advanced against them and formed his battle lines opposite them. David formed his lines to meet the Arameans in battle, and they fought against him. 18 But they fled before Israel, and David killed seven thousand of their charioteers and forty thousand of

19:1–19 PROMISE 6

SENSELESS VIOLENCE

Some people just seem to want enemies! This needless war that killed 47,000 men sounds a sharp warning against bickering. The circumstances and outcomes of our spats and divisions today are different, but the causes are similar: a misunderstood gesture, bad advice, hasty escalation instead of reconciliation, gathering allies to show strength instead of admitting error and asking forgiveness. Read about Hanun's actions as a case study of how *not* to act in relationships.

For the next Promise 6 reading go to page 476.

18:11 [m] Nu 24:20
18:12 [n] 1Ki 11:15
18:14 [o] 1Ch 29:26; [p] 1Ch 11:1
18:15 [q] 2Sa 5:6-8; 1Ch 11:6
18:16 [r] 2Sa 8:17; 1Ch 6:8; [s] 1Ch 24:6
18:17 [t] 1Sa 30:14; 2Sa 8:18; 15:18
19:1 [u] Ge 19:38; Jdg 10:17-11:33; 2Ch 20:1-2; Zep 2:8-11
19:3 [v] Nu 21:32
19:6 [w] Ge 34:30; [x] 1Ch 18:3,5,9
19:7 [y] Nu 21:30; Jos 13:9,16
19:11 [z] 1Sa 26:6
19:17 [a] 1Ch 9:1

[a] *16* Some Hebrew manuscripts, Vulgate and Syriac (see also 2 Samuel 8:17); most Hebrew manuscripts *Abimelech* [b] *6* That is, about 37 tons (about 34 metric tons) [c] *6* That is, Northwest Mesopotamia [d] *16* That is, the Euphrates

their foot soldiers. He also killed Shophach the commander of their army.

19When the vassals of Hadadezer saw that they had been defeated by Israel, they made peace with David and became subject to him.

So the Arameans were not willing to help the Ammonites anymore.

The Capture of Rabbah

20 In the spring, at the time when kings go off to war, Joab led out the armed forces. He laid waste the land of the Ammonites and went to Rabbah[b] and besieged it, but David remained in Jerusalem. Joab attacked Rabbah and left it in ruins.[c] 2David took the crown from the head of their king[a]—its weight was found to be a talent[b] of gold, and it was set with precious stones—and it was placed on David's head. He took a great quantity of plunder from the city 3and brought out the people who were there, consigning them to labor with saws and with iron picks and axes.[d] David did this to all the Ammonite towns. Then David and his entire army returned to Jerusalem.

War With the Philistines

4In the course of time, war broke out with the Philistines, at Gezer.[e] At that time Sibbecai the Hushathite killed Sippai, one of the descendants of the Rephaites,[f] and the Philistines were subjugated.

5In another battle with the Philistines, Elhanan son of Jair killed Lahmi the brother of Goliath the Gittite, who had a spear with a shaft like a weaver's rod.[g]

6In still another battle, which took place at Gath, there was a huge man with six fingers on each hand and six toes on each foot—twenty-four in all. He also was descended from Rapha. 7When he taunted Israel, Jonathan son of Shimea, David's brother, killed him.

8These were descendants of Rapha in Gath, and they fell at the hands of David and his men.

David Numbers the Fighting Men

21 Satan[h] rose up against Israel and incited David to take a census[i] of Israel. 2So David said to Joab and the commanders of the troops, "Go and count[j] the Israelites from Beersheba to Dan. Then report back to me so that I may know how many there are."

3But Joab replied, "May the LORD multiply his troops a hundred times over.[k] My lord the king, are they not all my lord's subjects? Why does my lord want to do this? Why should he bring guilt on Israel?"

4The king's word, however, overruled Joab; so Joab left and went throughout Israel and then came back to Jerusalem. 5Joab reported the number of the fighting men to David: In all Israel[l] there were one million one hundred thousand men who could handle a sword, including four hundred and seventy thousand in Judah.

6But Joab did not include Levi and Benjamin in the numbering, because the king's command was repulsive to him. 7This command was also evil in the sight of God; so he punished Israel.

8Then David said to God, "I have sinned greatly by doing this. Now, I beg you, take away the guilt of your servant. I have done a very foolish thing."

9The LORD said to Gad,[m] David's seer,[n] 10"Go and tell David, 'This is what the LORD says: I am giving you three options. Choose one of them for me to carry out against you.' "

11So Gad went to David and said to him, "This is what the LORD says: 'Take your choice: 12three years of famine,[o] three months of being swept away[c] before your enemies, with their swords overtaking you, or three days of the sword[p] of the LORD[q]—days of plague in the land, with the angel of the LORD ravaging every part of Israel.' Now then, decide how I should answer the one who sent me."

13David said to Gad, "I am in deep distress. Let me fall into the hands of the LORD, for his mercy[r] is very great; but do not let me fall into the hands of men."

14So the LORD sent a plague on Israel, and seventy thousand men of Israel fell dead.[s] 15And God sent an angel[t] to destroy Jerusalem.[u] But as the angel was doing so, the LORD saw it and was grieved[v] because of the calamity and said to the angel who was destroying[w] the people, "Enough! Withdraw your hand." The angel of the LORD was then standing at the threshing floor of Araunah[d] the Jebusite.

16David looked up and saw the angel of the LORD standing between heaven and earth, with a drawn sword in his hand extended over Jerusalem. Then David and the elders, clothed in sackcloth, fell facedown.[x]

17David said to God, "Was it not I who ordered the fighting men to be

20:1 [b]Dt 3:11; 2Sa 12:26 [c]Am 1:13-15 **20:3** [d]Dt 29:11 **20:4** [e]Jos 10:33 [f]Ge 14:5 **20:5** [g]1Sa 17:7 **21:1** [h]2Ch 18:21; Ps 109:6 [i]2Ch 14:8; 25:5 **21:2** [j]1Ch 27:23-24 **21:3** [k]Dt 1:11 **21:5** [l]1Ch 9:1 **21:9** [m]1Sa 22:5 [n]1Sa 9:9 **21:12** [o]Dt 32:24 [p]Eze 30:25 [q]Ge 19:13 **21:13** [r]Ps 6:4; 86:15; 130:4,7 **21:14** [s]1Ch 27:24 **21:15** [t]Ge 32:1 [u]Ps 125:2 [v]Ge 6:6; Ex 32:14 [w]Ge 19:13 **21:16** [x]Nu 14:5; Jos 7:6

[a]*2* Or *of Milcom,* that is, Molech [b]*2* That is, about 75 pounds (about 34 kilograms) [c]*12* Hebrew; Septuagint and Vulgate (see also 2 Samuel 24:13) *of fleeing* [d]*15* Hebrew *Ornan,* a variant of *Araunah*; also in verses 18-28

counted? I am the one who has sinned
and done wrong. These are but
sheep.[y] What have they done? O LORD
my God, let your hand fall upon me
and my family,[z] but do not let this
plague remain on your people."
18Then the angel of the LORD ordered
Gad to tell David to go up and build
an altar to the LORD on the threshing
floor[a] of Araunah the Jebusite. 19So
David went up in obedience to the
word that Gad had spoken in the name
of the LORD.
20While Araunah was threshing
wheat,[b] he turned and saw the angel;
his four sons who were with him hid
themselves. 21Then David approached,
and when Araunah looked and saw
him, he left the threshing floor and
bowed down before David with his face
to the ground.
22David said to him, "Let me have
the site of your threshing floor so I can
build an altar to the LORD, that the
plague on the people may be stopped.
Sell it to me at the full price."
23Araunah said to David, "Take it!
Let my lord the king do whatever
pleases him. Look, I will give the oxen
for the burnt offerings, the threshing
sledges for the wood, and the wheat for
the grain offering. I will give all this."
24But King David replied to Araunah,
"No, I insist on paying the full price. I
will not take for the LORD what is yours,
or sacrifice a burnt offering that costs
me nothing."
25So David paid Araunah six hundred shekels[a] of gold for the site. 26Da-
vid built an altar to the LORD there and
sacrificed burnt offerings and fellowship offerings.[b] He called on the LORD,
and the LORD answered him with fire[c]
from heaven on the altar of burnt offering.
27Then the LORD spoke to the angel,
and he put his sword back into its
sheath. 28At that time, when David saw
that the LORD had answered him on the
threshing floor of Araunah the Jebusite, he offered sacrifices there. 29The
tabernacle of the LORD, which Moses
had made in the desert, and the altar of
burnt offering were at that time on the
high place at Gibeon.[d] 30But David
could not go before it to inquire of
God, because he was afraid of the
sword of the angel of the LORD.
22 Then David said, "The house of the
LORD God[e] is to be here, and also
the altar of burnt offering for Israel."

Preparations for the Temple

2So David gave orders to assemble
the aliens[f] living in Israel, and from
among them he appointed stonecutters[g] to prepare dressed stone for
building the house of God. 3He provided a large amount of iron to make nails
for the doors of the gateways and for
the fittings, and more bronze than
could be weighed.[h] 4He also provided
more cedar logs[i] than could be
counted, for the Sidonians and Tyrians
had brought large numbers of them to
David.
5David said, "My son Solomon is
young[j] and inexperienced, and the
house to be built for the LORD should
be of great magnificence and fame and
splendor in the sight of all the nations.
Therefore I will make preparations for
it." So David made extensive preparations before his death.
6Then he called for his son Solomon
and charged him to build[k] a house
for the LORD, the God of Israel. 7David
said to Solomon: "My son, I had it in
my heart[l] to build[m] a house for the
Name[n] of the LORD my God. 8But this
word of the LORD came to me: 'You
have shed much blood and have fought
many wars.[o] You are not to build a
house for my Name,[p] because you
have shed much blood on the earth in
my sight. 9But you will have a son who
will be a man of peace[q] and rest, and
I will give him rest from all his enemies
on every side. His name will be Solomon,[c][r] and I will grant Israel peace

21:17 [y]2Sa 7:8; Ps 74:1 [z]Jnh 1:12 **21:18** [a]2Ch 3:1 **21:20** [b]Jdg 6:11 **21:26** [c]Lev 9:24; Jdg 6:21 **21:29** [d]1Ki 3:4; 1Ch 16:39 **22:1** [e]Ge 28:17; 1Ch 21:18-29; 2Ch 3:1 **22:2** [f]1Ki 9:21; Isa 56:6 [g]1Ki 5:17-18 **22:3** [h]ver 14; 1Ki 7:47; 1Ch 29:2-5 **22:4** [i]1Ki 5:6 **22:5** [j]1Ki 3:7; 1Ch 29:1 **22:6** [k]Ac 7:47 **22:7** [l]1Ch 17:2 [m]2Sa 7:2; 1Ki 8:17 [n]Dt 12:5,11 **22:8** [o]1Ki 5:3 [p]1Ch 28:3 **22:9** [q]1Ki 5:4 [r]2Sa 12:24

[a]*25* That is, about 15 pounds (about 7 kilograms) [b]*26* Traditionally *peace offerings* [c]*9* *Solomon* sounds like and may be derived from the Hebrew for *peace.*

22:6–14

PROMISE 1

DEALING WITH DISAPPOINTMENT

David wanted to build a temple for God (vv. 6–7) and God wouldn't let him (vv. 8–10). So David contributed to Solomon's success in building it, through prayer (vv. 11–12), encouragement (v. 13), financial and human resources (vv.14–16), and leadership support (vv.17–19). David had taken great pains to lay all the groundwork for the temple, but God put a stop to his plans. How do you think you would deal with that kind of disappointment?

Recognize that Solomon was going to accomplish what David had set his heart on doing. Then read verses 11–13 again, and ask what kind of man deals that way with disappointment and potential jealousy. This kind of man isn't built in a day; he is built over a period of loving and following God, no matter where God leads.

For the next Promise 1 reading go to page 463.

and quiet[s] during his reign. 10He is
the one who will build a house for my
Name.[t] He will be my son,[u] and I will
be his father. And I will establish the
throne of his kingdom over Israel forever.'[v]
11"Now, my son, the LORD be with[w]
you, and may you have success and
build the house of the LORD your God,
as he said you would. 12May the LORD
give you discretion and understanding[x] when he puts you in command
over Israel, so that you may keep the
law of the LORD your God. 13Then you
will have success if you are careful to
observe the decrees and laws[y] that the
LORD gave Moses for Israel. Be strong
and courageous.[z] Do not be afraid or
discouraged.
14"I have taken great pains to
provide for the temple of the LORD a
hundred thousand talents[a] of gold, a
million talents[b] of silver, quantities
of bronze and iron too great to be
weighed, and wood and stone. And you
may add to them.[a] 15You have many
workmen: stonecutters, masons and
carpenters, as well as men skilled in
every kind of work 16in gold and silver,
bronze and iron—craftsmen[b] beyond
number. Now begin the work, and the
LORD be with you."
17Then David ordered[c] all the leaders of Israel to help his son Solomon.
18He said to them, "Is not the LORD
your God with you? And has he not
granted you rest[d] on every side?[e] For
he has handed the inhabitants of the
land over to me, and the land is subject
to the LORD and to his people. 19Now
devote your heart and soul to seeking
the LORD your God.[f] Begin to build
the sanctuary of the LORD God, so that
you may bring the ark of the covenant
of the LORD and the sacred articles belonging to God into the temple that will
be built for the Name of the LORD."

The Levites

23 When David was old and full of
years, he made his son Solomon[g]
king over Israel.[h]
2He also gathered together all the
leaders of Israel, as well as the priests
and Levites. 3The Levites thirty years
old or more[i] were counted, and the
total number of men was thirty-eight
thousand.[j] 4David said, "Of these,
twenty-four thousand are to supervise[k] the work of the temple of the
LORD and six thousand are to be officials and judges.[l] 5Four thousand are
to be gatekeepers and four thousand
are to praise the LORD with the musical
instruments[m] I have provided for that
purpose."[n]
6David divided[o] the Levites into
groups corresponding to the sons of
Levi: Gershon, Kohath and Merari.

Gershonites

7Belonging to the Gershonites:
Ladan and Shimei.
8The sons of Ladan:
Jehiel the first, Zetham and
Joel—three in all.
9The sons of Shimei:
Shelomoth, Haziel and Ha-
ran—three in all.
These were the heads of the
families of Ladan.
10And the sons of Shimei:
Jahath, Ziza,[c] Jeush and Beriah.
These were the sons of Shimei—four in all.
11Jahath was the first and Ziza
the second, but Jeush and Beriah did not have many sons;
so they were counted as one
family with one assignment.

Kohathites

12The sons of Kohath:[p]
Amram, Izhar, Hebron and
Uzziel—four in all.
13The sons of Amram:[q]
Aaron and Moses.
Aaron was set apart,[r] he and
his descendants forever, to
consecrate the most holy
things, to offer sacrifices before the LORD, to minister before him and to pronounce
blessings[s] in his name forever. 14The sons of Moses the
man[t] of God were counted as
part of the tribe of Levi.
15The sons of Moses:
Gershom and Eliezer.[u]
16The descendants of Gershom:[v]
Shubael was the first.
17The descendants of Eliezer:
Rehabiah was the first.
Eliezer had no other sons, but
the sons of Rehabiah were very
numerous.
18The sons of Izhar:
Shelomith was the first.
19The sons of Hebron:[w]
Jeriah the first, Amariah the
second, Jahaziel the third and
Jekameam the fourth.
20The sons of Uzziel:

22:9 [s] 1Ki 4:20
22:10 [t] 1Ch 17:12 [u] 2Sa 7:13 [v] 2Sa 7:14; 2Ch 6:15
22:11 [w] ver 16
22:12 [x] 1Ki 3:9-12; 2Ch 1:10
22:13 [y] 1Ch 28:7 [z] Dt 31:6; Jos 1:6-9; 1Ch 28:20
22:14 [a] ver 3; 1Ch 29:2-5,19
22:16 [b] ver 11; 2Ch 2:7
22:17 [c] 1Ch 28:1-6
22:18 [d] ver 9; 1Ch 23:25 [e] 2Sa 7:1
22:19 [f] ver 7; 1Ki 8:6; 1Ch 28:9; 2Ch 5:7; 7:14
23:1 [g] 1Ki 1:33-39; 1Ch 28:5 [h] 1Ki 1:30; 1Ch 29:28
23:3 [i] ver 24; Nu 8:24 [j] Nu 4:3-49
23:4 [k] Ezr 3:8 [l] 1Ch 26:29; 2Ch 19:8
23:5 [m] 1Ch 15:16 [n] Ne 12:45
23:6 [o] 2Ch 8:14; 29:25
23:12 [p] Ex 6:18
23:13 [q] Ex 6:20; 28:1 [r] Ex 30:7-10; Dt 21:5 [s] Nu 6:23
23:14 [t] Dt 33:1
23:15 [u] Ex 18:4
23:16 [v] 1Ch 26:24-28
23:19 [w] 1Ch 24:23

a *14* That is, about 3,750 tons (about 3,450 metric tons) **b** *14* That is, about 37,500 tons (about 34,500 metric tons) **c** *10* One Hebrew manuscript, Septuagint and Vulgate (see also verse 11); most Hebrew manuscripts *Zina*

Micah the first and Isshiah the second.

Merarites

21The sons of Merari:[x]
Mahli and Mushi.
The sons of Mahli:
Eleazar and Kish.
22Eleazar died without having sons: he had only daughters. Their cousins, the sons of Kish, married them.
23The sons of Mushi:
Mahli, Eder and Jerimoth—three in all.

24These were the descendants of Levi by their families—the heads of families as they were registered under their names and counted individually, that is, the workers twenty years old or more[y] who served in the temple of the LORD. 25For David had said, "Since the LORD, the God of Israel, has granted rest[z] to his people and has come to dwell in Jerusalem forever, 26the Levites no longer need to carry the tabernacle or any of the articles used in its service."[a] 27According to the last instructions of David, the Levites were counted from those twenty years old or more.

28The duty of the Levites was to help Aaron's descendants in the service of the temple of the LORD: to be in charge of the courtyards, the side rooms, the purification[b] of all sacred things and the performance of other duties at the house of God. 29They were in charge of the bread set out on the table,[c] the flour for the grain offerings,[d] the unleavened wafers, the baking and the mixing, and all measurements of quantity and size.[e] 30They were also to stand every morning to thank and praise the LORD. They were to do the same in the evening[f] 31and whenever burnt offerings were presented to the LORD on Sabbaths and at New Moon[g] festivals and at appointed feasts.[h] They were to serve before the LORD regularly in the proper number and in the way prescribed for them.

32And so the Levites[i] carried out their responsibilities for the Tent of Meeting,[j] for the Holy Place and, under their brothers the descendants of Aaron, for the service of the temple of the LORD.[k]

The Divisions of Priests

24 These were the divisions[l] of the sons of Aaron:[m]

The sons of Aaron were Nadab, Abihu, Eleazar and Ithamar.[n] 2But Nadab and Abihu died before their father did,[o] and they had no sons; so Eleazar and Ithamar served as the priests. 3With the help of Zadok[p] a descendant of Eleazar and Ahimelech a descendant of Ithamar, David separated them into divisions for their appointed order of ministering. 4A larger number of leaders were found among Eleazar's descendants than among Ithamar's, and they were divided accordingly: sixteen heads of families from Eleazar's descendants and eight heads of families from Ithamar's descendants. 5They divided them impartially by drawing lots,[q] for there were officials of the sanctuary and officials of God among the descendants of both Eleazar and Ithamar.

6The scribe Shemaiah son of Nethanel, a Levite, recorded their names in the presence of the king and of the officials: Zadok the priest, Ahimelech[r] son of Abiathar and the heads of families of the priests and of the Levites—one family being taken from Eleazar and then one from Ithamar.

7The first lot fell to Jehoiarib,
the second to Jedaiah,[s]
8the third to Harim,[t]
the fourth to Seorim,
9the fifth to Malkijah,
the sixth to Mijamin,
10the seventh to Hakkoz,
the eighth to Abijah,[u]
11the ninth to Jeshua,
the tenth to Shecaniah,
12the eleventh to Eliashib,
the twelfth to Jakim,
13the thirteenth to Huppah,
the fourteenth to Jeshebeab,
14the fifteenth to Bilgah,
the sixteenth to Immer,[v]
15the seventeenth to Hezir,[w]
the eighteenth to Happizzez,
16the nineteenth to Pethahiah,
the twentieth to Jehezkel,
17the twenty-first to Jakin,
the twenty-second to Gamul,
18the twenty-third to Delaiah
and the twenty-fourth to Maaziah.

19This was their appointed order of ministering when they entered the temple of the LORD, according to the regulations prescribed for them by their forefather Aaron, as the LORD, the God of Israel, had commanded him.

The Rest of the Levites

20As for the rest of the descendants of Levi:[x]
from the sons of Amram: Shubael;

23:21 x 1Ch 24:26
23:24 y Nu 4:3; 10:17, 21
23:25 z 1Ch 22:9
23:26 a Nu 4:5,15; 7:9; Dt 10:8
23:28 b 2Ch 29:15; Ne 13:9; Mal 3:3
23:29 c Ex 25:30 d Lev 2:4-7; 6:20-23 e Lev 19:35-36; 1Ch 9:29,32
23:30 f 1Ch 9:33; Ps 134:1
23:31 g 2Ki 4:23 h Lev 23:4; Nu 28:9-29:39; Isa 1:13-14; Col 2:16
23:32 i Nu 1:53; 1Ch 6:48 j Nu 3:6-8,38 k 2Ch 23:18; 31:2; Eze 44:14
24:1 l 1Ch 23:6; 28:13; 2Ch 5:11; 8:14; 23:8; 31:2; 35:4,5; Ezr 6:18 m Nu 3:2-4 n Ex 6:23
24:2 o Lev 10:1-2; Nu 3:4
24:3 p 2Sa 8:17
24:5 q ver 31; 1Ch 25:8
24:6 r 1Ch 18:16
24:7 s Ezr 2:36; Ne 12:6
24:8 t Ezr 2:39; Ne 10:5
24:10 u Ne 12:4,17; Lk 1:5
24:14 v Jer 20:1
24:15 w Ne 10:20
24:20 x 1Ch 23:6

from the sons of Shubael: Jehdeiah.
21As for Rehabiah,[y] from his sons:
Isshiah was the first.
22From the Izharites: Shelomoth;
from the sons of Shelomoth: Jahath.
23The sons of Hebron:[z] Jeriah the first,[a] Amariah the second, Jahaziel the third and Jekameam the fourth.
24The son of Uzziel: Micah;
from the sons of Micah: Shamir.
25The brother of Micah: Isshiah;
from the sons of Isshiah: Zechariah.
26The sons of Merari:[a] Mahli and Mushi.
The son of Jaaziah: Beno.
27The sons of Merari:
from Jaaziah: Beno, Shoham, Zaccur and Ibri.
28From Mahli: Eleazar, who had no sons.
29From Kish: the son of Kish:
Jerahmeel.
30And the sons of Mushi: Mahli, Eder and Jerimoth.

These were the Levites, according to
their families. 31They also cast lots,[b]
just as their brothers the descendants
of Aaron did, in the presence of King
David and of Zadok, Ahimelech, and
the heads of families of the priests and
of the Levites. The families of the oldest
brother were treated the same as those
of the youngest.

The Singers

25 David, together with the commanders of the army, set apart
some of the sons of Asaph,[c] Heman[d]
and Jeduthun[e] for the ministry of
prophesying,[f] accompanied by harps,
lyres and cymbals.[g] Here is the list of
the men[h] who performed this service:[i]

2From the sons of Asaph:
Zaccur, Joseph, Nethaniah and Asarelah. The sons of Asaph were under the supervision of Asaph, who prophesied under the king's supervision.
3As for Jeduthun, from his sons:[j]
Gedaliah, Zeri, Jeshaiah, Shimei,[b] Hashabiah and Mattithiah, six in all, under the supervision of their father Jeduthun, who prophesied, using the harp[k] in thanking and praising the LORD.
4As for Heman, from his sons:
Bukkiah, Mattaniah, Uzziel, Shubael and Jerimoth; Hananiah, Hanani, Eliathah, Giddalti and Romamti-Ezer; Joshbekashah, Mallothi, Hothir and Mahazioth.
5All these were sons of Heman the king's seer. They were given him through the promises of God to exalt him.[c] God gave Heman fourteen sons and three daughters.

6All these men were under the supervision of their fathers[l] for the music of the temple of the LORD, with cymbals, lyres and harps, for the ministry
at the house of God. Asaph, Jeduthun
and Heman[m] were under the supervision of the king.[n] 7Along with
their relatives—all of them trained and
skilled in music for the LORD—they
numbered 288. 8Young and old alike,
teacher as well as student, cast lots[o]
for their duties.

9The first lot, which was for Asaph,[p] fell to Joseph, his sons and relatives,[d]	12[e]
the second to Gedaliah, he and his relatives and sons,	12
10the third to Zaccur, his sons and relatives,	12
11the fourth to Izri,[f] his sons and relatives,	12
12the fifth to Nethaniah, his sons and relatives,	12
13the sixth to Bukkiah, his sons and relatives,	12
14the seventh to Jesarelah,[g] his sons and relatives,	12
15the eighth to Jeshaiah, his sons and relatives,	12
16the ninth to Mattaniah, his sons and relatives,	12
17the tenth to Shimei, his sons and relatives,	12
18the eleventh to Azarel,[h] his sons and relatives,	12
19the twelfth to Hashabiah, his sons and relatives,	12
20the thirteenth to Shubael, his sons and relatives,	12
21the fourteenth to Mattithiah,	

24:21 [y]1Ch 23:17 **24:23** [z]1Ch 23:19 **24:26** [a]1Ch 6:19; 23:21 **24:31** [b]ver 5 **25:1** [c]1Ch 6:39 [d]1Ch 6:33 [e]1Ch 16:41,42; Ne 11:17 [f]1Sa 10:5; 2Ki 3:15 [g]1Ch 15:16 [h]1Ch 6:31 [i]2Ch 5:12; 8:14; 34:12; 35:15; Ezr 3:10 **25:3** [j]1Ch 16:41-42 [k]Ge 4:21; Ps 33:2 **25:6** [l]1Ch 15:16 [m]1Ch 15:19 [n]2Ch 23:18; 29:25 **25:8** [o]1Ch 26:13 **25:9** [p]1Ch 6:39

a *23* Two Hebrew manuscripts and some Septuagint manuscripts (see also 1 Chron. 23:19); most Hebrew manuscripts *The sons of Jeriah:* b *3* One Hebrew manuscript and some Septuagint manuscripts (see also verse 17); most Hebrew manuscripts do not have *Shimei.* c *5* Hebrew *exalt the horn* d *9* See Septuagint; Hebrew does not have *his sons and relatives.* e *9* See the total in verse 7; Hebrew does not have *twelve.* f *11* A variant of *Zeri* g *14* A variant of *Asarelah* h *18* A variant of *Uzziel*

his sons and relatives, 12
22 the fifteenth to Jerimoth,
his sons and relatives, 12
23 the sixteenth to
Hananiah,
his sons and relatives, 12
24 the seventeenth to
Joshbekashah,
his sons and relatives, 12
25 the eighteenth to Hanani,
his sons and relatives, 12
26 the nineteenth to Mallothi,
his sons and relatives, 12
27 the twentieth to Eliathah,
his sons and relatives, 12
28 the twenty-first to Hothir,
his sons and relatives, 12
29 the twenty-second to
Giddalti,
his sons and relatives, 12
30 the twenty-third to
Mahazioth,
his sons and relatives, 12
31 the twenty-fourth to
Romamti-Ezer,
his sons and relatives, 12[q]

The Gatekeepers

26 The divisions of the gatekeepers:[r]

From the Korahites: Meshelemiah son of Kore, one of the sons of Asaph.
2 Meshelemiah had sons:
Zechariah[s] the firstborn,
Jediael the second,
Zebadiah the third,
Jathniel the fourth,
3 Elam the fifth,
Jehohanan the sixth
and Eliehoenai the seventh.
4 Obed-Edom also had sons:
Shemaiah the firstborn,
Jehozabad the second,
Joah the third,
Sacar the fourth,
Nethanel the fifth,
5 Ammiel the sixth,
Issachar the seventh
and Peullethai the eighth.
(For God had blessed Obed-Edom.[t])

6 His son Shemaiah also had sons,
who were leaders in their father's family because they
were very capable men. 7 The
sons of Shemaiah: Othni, Rephael, Obed and Elzabad; his
relatives Elihu and Semakiah
were also able men. 8 All these
were descendants of Obed-Edom; they and their sons and
their relatives were capable
men with the strength to
do the work—descendants of Obed-Edom, 62 in all.
9 Meshelemiah had sons and relatives, who were able men—18 in all.

10 Hosah the Merarite had sons:
Shimri the first (although he was not the firstborn, his father had appointed him the
first),[u] 11 Hilkiah the second,
Tabaliah the third and Zechariah the fourth. The sons and relatives of Hosah were 13 in all.

12 These divisions of the gatekeepers,
through their chief men, had duties
for ministering[v] in the temple of
the LORD, just as their relatives had.
13 Lots[w] were cast for each gate, according to their families, young and old
alike.
14 The lot for the East Gate[x] fell to
Shelemiah.[a] Then lots were cast for
his son Zechariah,[y] a wise counselor,
and the lot for the North Gate fell to
him. 15 The lot for the South Gate fell
to Obed-Edom,[z] and the lot for the
storehouse fell to his sons. 16 The lots
for the West Gate and the Shalleketh
Gate on the upper road fell to Shuppim
and Hosah.
Guard was alongside of guard:
17 There were six Levites a day on the
east, four a day on the north, four a day
on the south and two at a time at the
storehouse. 18 As for the court to the
west, there were four at the road and
two at the court itself.
19 These were the divisions of the
gatekeepers who were descendants of
Korah and Merari.[a]

The Treasurers and Other Officials

20 Their fellow Levites[b] were[b] in
charge of the treasuries of the house of
God and the treasuries for the dedicated things.[c]
21 The descendants of Ladan, who
were Gershonites through Ladan and
who were heads of families belonging
to Ladan the Gershonite,[d] were Jehieli,
22 the sons of Jehieli, Zetham and his
brother Joel. They were in charge of the
treasuries[e] of the temple of the LORD.
23 From the Amramites, the Izharites,
the Hebronites and the Uzzielites:[f]
24 Shubael,[g] a descendant of Gershom son of Moses, was the officer in charge of the treasuries.
25 His relatives through Eliezer: Rehabiah his son, Jesha-

25:31 [q] 1Ch 9:33
26:1 [r] 1Ch 9:17
26:2 [s] 1Ch 9:21
26:5 [t] 2Sa 6:10; 1Ch 13:13; 16:38
26:10 [u] Dt 21:16; 1Ch 5:1
26:12 [v] 1Ch 9:22
26:13 [w] 1Ch 24:5,31; 25:8
26:14 [x] 1Ch 9:18 [y] 1Ch 9:21
26:15 [z] 1Ch 13:13; 2Ch 25:24
26:19 [a] 2Ch 35:15; Ne 7:1; Eze 44:11
26:20 [b] 2Ch 24:5 [c] 1Ch 28:12
26:21 [d] 1Ch 23:7; 29:8
26:22 [e] 1Ch 9:26
26:23 [f] Nu 3:27
26:24 [g] 1Ch 23:16

a *14* A variant of *Meshelemiah*
b *20* Septuagint; Hebrew *As for the Levites, Ahijah was*

iah his son, Joram his son,
Zicri his son and Shelomith[h]
his son. 26 Shelomith and his
relatives were in charge of all
the treasuries for the things
dedicated[i] by King David, by
the heads of families who were
the commanders of thousands
and commanders of hundreds,
and by the other army commanders. 27 Some of the plunder taken in battle they dedicated for the repair of the
temple of the LORD. 28 And everything dedicated by Samuel
the seer[j] and by Saul son of
Kish, Abner son of Ner and
Joab son of Zeruiah, and all the
other dedicated things were in
the care of Shelomith and his
relatives.
29 From the Izharites: Kenaniah and
his sons were assigned duties
away from the temple, as officials and judges[k] over Israel.
30 From the Hebronites: Hashabiah[l] and his relatives—
seventeen hundred able
men—were responsible in Israel west of the Jordan for all
the work of the LORD and for
the king's service. 31 As for the
Hebronites,[m] Jeriah was their
chief according to the genealogical records of their families. In the fortieth[n] year of
David's reign a search was
made in the records, and capable men among the Hebron-
ites were found at Jazer in Gilead. 32 Jeriah had twenty-seven
hundred relatives, who were
able men and heads of families, and King David put them
in charge of the Reubenites,
the Gadites and the half-tribe
of Manasseh for every matter
pertaining to God and for the
affairs of the king.

Army Divisions

27 This is the list of the Israelites—
heads of families, commanders of
thousands and commanders of hundreds, and their officers, who served
the king in all that concerned the army
divisions that were on duty month by
month throughout the year. Each division consisted of 24,000 men.

2 In charge of the first division, for the
first month, was Jashobeam[o] son
of Zabdiel. There were 24,000 men
in his division. 3 He was a descendant of Perez and chief of all the
army officers for the first month.
4 In charge of the division for the second month was Dodai[p] the Ahohite; Mikloth was the leader of his
division. There were 24,000 men
in his division.
5 The third army commander, for the
third month, was Benaiah[q] son of
Jehoiada the priest. He was chief
and there were 24,000 men in his
division. 6 This was the Benaiah
who was a mighty man among the
Thirty and was over the Thirty. His
son Ammizabad was in charge of
his division.
7 The fourth, for the fourth month,
was Asahel[r] the brother of Joab;
his son Zebadiah was his successor. There were 24,000 men in his
division.
8 The fifth, for the fifth month, was the
commander Shamhuth[s] the Izra-
hite. There were 24,000 men in his
division.
9 The sixth, for the sixth month, was
Ira[t] the son of Ikkesh the Tekoite.
There were 24,000 men in his division.
10 The seventh, for the seventh month,
was Helez[u] the Pelonite, an
Ephraimite. There were 24,000
men in his division.
11 The eighth, for the eighth month,
was Sibbecai[v] the Hushathite, a
Zerahite. There were 24,000 men
in his division.
12 The ninth, for the ninth month, was
Abiezer[w] the Anathothite, a Benjamite. There were 24,000 men in
his division.
13 The tenth, for the tenth month, was
Maharai[x] the Netophathite, a Zerahite. There were 24,000 men in
his division.
14 The eleventh, for the eleventh
month, was Benaiah[y] the Pirathonite, an Ephraimite. There
were 24,000 men in his division.
15 The twelfth, for the twelfth month,
was Heldai[z] the Netophathite,
from the family of Othniel.[a]
There were 24,000 men in his division.

Officers of the Tribes

16 The officers over the tribes of Israel:
over the Reubenites: Eliezer son
of Zicri;
over the Simeonites: Shephatiah
son of Maacah;
17 over Levi: Hashabiah[b] son of
Kemuel;
over Aaron: Zadok;[c]

26:25 [h] 1Ch 23:18
26:26 [i] 2Sa 8:11
26:28 [j] 1Sa 9:9
26:29 [k] Dt 17:8-13; 1Ch 23:4; Ne 11:16
26:30 [l] 1Ch 27:17
26:31 [m] 1Ch 23:19 [n] 2Sa 5:4
27:2 [o] 2Sa 23:8; 1Ch 11:11
27:4 [p] 2Sa 23:9
27:5 [q] 2Sa 23:20
27:7 [r] 2Sa 2:18; 1Ch 11:26
27:8 [s] 1Ch 11:27
27:9 [t] 2Sa 23:26; 1Ch 11:28
27:10 [u] 2Sa 23:26; 1Ch 11:27
27:11 [v] 2Sa 21:18
27:12 [w] 2Sa 23:27; 1Ch 11:28
27:13 [x] 2Sa 23:28; 1Ch 11:30
27:14 [y] 1Ch 11:31
27:15 [z] 2Sa 23:29 [a] Jos 15:17
27:17 [b] 1Ch 26:30 [c] 2Sa 8:17; 1Ch 12:28

18over Judah: Elihu, a brother of David;
over Issachar: Omri son of Michael;
19over Zebulun: Ishmaiah son of Obadiah;
over Naphtali: Jerimoth son of Azriel;
20over the Ephraimites: Hoshea son of Azaziah;
over half the tribe of Manasseh: Joel son of Pedaiah;
21over the half-tribe of Manasseh in Gilead: Iddo son of Zechariah;
over Benjamin: Jaasiel son of Abner;
22over Dan: Azarel son of Jeroham.
These were the officers over the tribes of Israel.

23David did not take the number of
the men twenty years old or less,[d] because the LORD had promised to make
Israel as numerous as the stars[e] in the
sky. 24Joab son of Zeruiah began to
count the men but did not finish.
Wrath came on Israel on account of
this numbering,[f] and the number was
not entered in the book[a] of the annals
of King David.

The King's Overseers

25Azmaveth son of Adiel was in
charge of the royal storehouses.
Jonathan son of Uzziah was in
charge of the storehouses in the outlying districts, in the towns, the villages
and the watchtowers.
26Ezri son of Kelub was in charge of
the field workers who farmed the land.
27Shimei the Ramathite was in
charge of the vineyards.
Zabdi the Shiphmite was in charge
of the produce of the vineyards for the
wine vats.
28Baal-Hanan the Gederite was in
charge of the olive and sycamore-fig[g]
trees in the western foothills.
Joash was in charge of the supplies
of olive oil.
29Shitrai the Sharonite was in charge
of the herds grazing in Sharon.
Shaphat son of Adlai was in charge
of the herds in the valleys.
30Obil the Ishmaelite was in charge
of the camels.
Jehdeiah the Meronothite was in
charge of the donkeys.
31Jaziz the Hagrite[h] was in charge of
the flocks.
All these were the officials in charge
of King David's property.

32Jonathan, David's uncle, was a
counselor, a man of insight and a
scribe. Jehiel son of Hacmoni took care
of the king's sons.
33Ahithophel[i] was the king's counselor.
Hushai[j] the Arkite was the king's
friend. 34Ahithophel was succeeded by
Jehoiada son of Benaiah and by Abiathar.[k]
Joab[l] was the commander of the
royal army.

David's Plans for the Temple

28 David summoned all the officials[m]
of Israel to assemble at Jerusalem:
the officers over the tribes, the commanders of the divisions in the service
of the king, the commanders of thousands and commanders of hundreds,
and the officials in charge of all the
property and livestock belonging to the
king and his sons, together with
the palace officials, the mighty men
and all the brave warriors.
2King David rose to his feet and said:
"Listen to me, my brothers and my
people. I had it in my heart[n] to build
a house as a place of rest for the ark of
the covenant of the LORD, for the footstool[o] of our God, and I made plans to
build it. 3But God said to me,[p] 'You
are not to build a house for my
Name,[q] because you are a warrior and
have shed blood.'[r]
4"Yet the LORD, the God of Israel,
chose me[s] from my whole family[t] to
be king over Israel forever. He chose
Judah[u] as leader, and from the house
of Judah he chose my family, and from
my father's sons he was pleased to
make me king over all Israel. 5Of all
my sons—and the LORD has given me
many[v]—he has chosen my son Solomon[w] to sit on the throne of the kingdom of the LORD over Israel. 6He said to
me: 'Solomon your son is the one who
will build my house and my courts, for
I have chosen him to be my son,[x] and
I will be his father. 7I will establish his
kingdom forever if he is unswerving in
carrying out my commands and
laws,[y] as is being done at this time.'
8"So now I charge you in the sight of
all Israel and of the assembly of the
LORD, and in the hearing of our God: Be
careful to follow all the commands[z] of
the LORD your God, that you may possess this good land and pass it on as an
inheritance to your descendants forever.[a]
9"And you, my son Solomon, acknowledge the God of your father, and
serve him with wholehearted devotion[b] and with a willing mind, for the

27:23 [d]1Ch 21:2-5 [e]Ge 15:5
27:24 [f]2Sa 24:15; 1Ch 21:7
27:28 [g]1Ki 10:27; 2Ch 1:15
27:31 [h]1Ch 5:10
27:33 [i]2Sa 15:12 [j]2Sa 15:37
27:34 [k]1Ki 1:7 [l]1Ch 11:6
28:1 [m]1Ch 11:10; 27:1-31
28:2 [n]1Ch 17:2 [o]Ps 99:5; 132:7
28:3 [p]2Sa 7:5 [q]1Ch 22:8 [r]1Ki 5:3; 1Ch 17:4
28:4 [s]1Ch 17:23,27; 2Ch 6:6 [t]1Sa 16:1-13 [u]Ge 49:10; 1Ch 5:2
28:5 [v]1Ch 3:1 [w]1Ch 22:9; 23:1
28:6 [x]2Sa 7:13; 1Ch 22:9-10
28:7 [y]1Ch 22:13
28:8 [z]Dt 6:1 [a]Dt 4:1
28:9 [b]1Ch 29:19

[a]*24* Septuagint; Hebrew *number*

LORD searches every heart[c] and understands every motive behind the thoughts. If you seek him,[d] he will be found by you; but if you forsake[e] him, he will reject[f] you forever. 10Consider now, for the LORD has chosen you to build a temple as a sanctuary. Be strong and do the work."

11Then David gave his son Solomon the plans[g] for the portico of the temple, its buildings, its storerooms, its upper parts, its inner rooms and the place of atonement. 12He gave him the plans of all that the Spirit[h] had put in his mind for the courts of the temple of the LORD and all the surrounding rooms, for the treasuries of the temple of God and for the treasuries for the dedicated things.[i] 13He gave him instructions for the divisions[j] of the priests and Levites, and for all the work of serving in the temple of the LORD, as well as for all the articles to be used in its service. 14He designated the weight of gold for all the gold articles to be used in various kinds of service, and the weight of silver for all the silver articles to be used in various kinds of service: 15the weight of gold for the gold lampstands[k] and their lamps, with the weight for each lampstand and its lamps; and the weight of silver for each silver lampstand and its lamps, according to the use of each lampstand; 16the weight of gold for each table[l] for consecrated bread; the weight of silver for the silver tables; 17the weight of pure gold for the forks, sprinkling bowls[m] and pitchers; the weight of gold for each gold dish; the weight of silver for each silver dish; 18and the weight of the refined gold for the altar of incense.[n] He also gave him the plan for the chariot,[o] that is, the cherubim of gold that spread their wings and shelter[p] the ark of the covenant of the LORD.

19"All this," David said, "I have in writing from the hand of the LORD upon me, and he gave me understanding in all the details[q] of the plan.[r]"

20David also said to Solomon his son, "Be strong and courageous,[s] and do the work. Do not be afraid or discouraged, for the LORD God, my God, is with you. He will not fail you or forsake[t] you until all the work for the service of the temple of the LORD is finished.[u] 21The divisions of the priests and Levites are ready for all the work on the temple of God, and every willing man skilled[v] in any craft will help you in all the work. The officials and all the people will obey your every command."

28:9 [c]1Sa 16:7; Ps 7:9 [d]Ps 40:16; Jer 29:13 [e]Jos 24:20; 2Ch 15:2 [f]Ps 44:23
28:11 [g]Ex 25:9
28:12 [h]1Ch 12:18 [i]1Ch 26:20
28:13 [j]1Ch 24:1
28:15 [k]Ex 25:31
28:16 [l]Ex 25:23
28:17 [m]Ex 27:3
28:18 [n]Ex 30:1-10 [o]Ex 25:18-22 [p]Ex 25:20
28:19 [q]1Ki 6:38 [r]Ex 25:9
28:20 [s]Dt 31:6; 1Ch 22:13; 2Ch 19:11; Hag 2:4 [t]Dt 4:31; Jos 24:20 [u]1Ki 6:14; 2Ch 7:11
28:21 [v]Ex 35:25-36:5

29:1 [w]1Ki 3:7; 1Ch 22:5; 2Ch 13:7
29:2 [x]ver 7,14,16; Ezr 1:4; 6:5; Hag 2:8 [y]Isa 54:11 [z]1Ch 22:2-5
29:3 [a]2Ch 24:10; 31:3; 35:8
29:4 [b]Ge 10:29 [c]1Ch 22:14
29:6 [d]1Ch 27:1; 28:1 [e]ver 9; Ex 25:1-8; 35:20-29; 36:2; 2Ch 24:10; Ezr 7:15
29:7 [f]Ex 25:2; Ne 7:70-71
29:8 [g]Ex 35:27 [h]1Ch 26:21
29:9 [i]1Ki 8:61; 2Co 9:7

Gifts for Building the Temple

29 Then King David said to the whole assembly: "My son Solomon, the one whom God has chosen, is young and inexperienced.[w] The task is great, because this palatial structure is not for man but for the LORD God. 2With all my resources I have provided for the temple of my God—gold[x] for the gold work, silver for the silver, bronze for the bronze, iron for the iron and wood for the wood, as well as onyx for the settings, turquoise,[a][y] stones of various colors, and all kinds of fine stone and marble—all of these in large quantities.[z] 3Besides, in my devotion to the temple of my God I now give my personal treasures of gold and silver for the temple of my God, over and above everything I have provided[a] for this holy temple: 4three thousand talents[b] of gold (gold of Ophir)[b] and seven thousand talents[c] of refined silver,[c] for the overlaying of the walls of the buildings, 5for the gold work and the silver work, and for all the work to be done by the craftsmen. Now, who is willing to consecrate himself today to the LORD?"

6Then the leaders of families, the officers of the tribes of Israel, the commanders of thousands and commanders of hundreds, and the officials[d] in charge of the king's work gave willingly.[e] 7They[f] gave toward the work on the temple of God five thousand talents[d] and ten thousand darics[e] of gold, ten thousand talents[f] of silver, eighteen thousand talents[g] of bronze and a hundred thousand talents[h] of iron. 8Any who had precious stones[g] gave them to the treasury of the temple of the LORD in the custody of Jehiel the Gershonite.[h] 9The people rejoiced at the willing response of their leaders, for they had given freely and wholeheartedly[i] to the LORD. David the king also rejoiced greatly.

5 →PG. 486

David's Prayer

10David praised the LORD in the presence of the whole assembly, saying,

"Praise be to you, O LORD,
  God of our father Israel,
  from everlasting to everlasting.

[a]*2* The meaning of the Hebrew for this word is uncertain. [b]*4* That is, about 110 tons (about 100 metric tons) [c]*4* That is, about 260 tons (about 240 metric tons) [d]*7* That is, about 190 tons (about 170 metric tons) [e]*7* That is, about 185 pounds (about 84 kilograms) [f]*7* That is, about 375 tons (about 345 metric tons) [g]*7* That is, about 675 tons (about 610 metric tons) [h]*7* That is, about 3,750 tons (about 3,450 metric tons)

11Yours, O LORD, is the greatness and
the power[j]
and the glory and the majesty
and the splendor,
for everything in heaven and
earth is yours.[k]
Yours, O LORD, is the kingdom;
you are exalted as head over
all.[l]
12Wealth and honor[m] come from
you;
you are the ruler[n] of all things.
In your hands are strength and
power
to exalt and give strength to all.
13Now, our God, we give you thanks,
and praise your glorious name.

14"But who am I, and who are my
people, that we should be able to give
as generously as this? Everything
comes from you, and we have given
you only what comes from your hand.
15We are aliens and strangers[o] in your
sight, as were all our forefathers. Our
days on earth are like a shadow,[p]
without hope. 16O LORD our God, as for
all this abundance that we have provided for building you a temple for
your Holy Name, it comes from your
3 →PG. 480
hand, and all of it belongs to you. 17I
know, my God, that you test the
heart[q] and are pleased with integrity.
All these things have I given willingly
and with honest intent. And now I have
seen with joy how willingly your people
who are here have given to you.[r]
18O LORD, God of our fathers Abraham,
Isaac and Israel, keep this desire in the
hearts of your people forever, and keep
their hearts loyal to you. 19And give my
son Solomon the wholehearted devotion[s] to keep your commands, requirements and decrees[t] and to do
everything to build the palatial structure for which I have provided."[u]
4 →PG. 511
20Then David said to the whole assembly, "Praise the LORD your God." So
they all praised the LORD, the God of
their fathers; they bowed low and fell
prostrate before the LORD and the king.

Solomon Acknowledged as King

21The next day they made sacrifices
to the LORD and presented burnt offerings to him:[v] a thousand bulls, a thousand rams and a thousand male lambs,
together with their drink offerings, and
other sacrifices in abundance for all Israel. 22They ate and drank with great
joy[w] in the presence of the LORD that
day.

Then they acknowledged Solomon
son of David as king a second time,
anointing him before the LORD to be
ruler and Zadok[x] to be priest. 23So
Solomon sat on the throne[y] of the
LORD as king in place of his father David. He prospered and all Israel obeyed
him. 24All the officers and mighty men,
as well as all of King David's sons,
pledged their submission to King Solomon.

25The LORD highly exalted Solomon
in the sight of all Israel and bestowed
on him royal splendor[z] such as no
king over Israel ever had before.[a]

The Death of David

26David son of Jesse was king[b] over
all Israel. 27He ruled over Israel forty
years—seven in Hebron and thirty-
three in Jerusalem.[c] 28He died[d] at a
good old age, having enjoyed long life,
wealth and honor. His son Solomon
succeeded him as king.[e]

29As for the events of King David's
reign, from beginning to end, they are
written in the records of Samuel the
seer,[f] the records of Nathan[g] the
prophet and the records of Gad[h]
the seer, 30together with the details of
his reign and power, and the circumstances that surrounded him and Israel
and the kingdoms of all the other
lands.

29:11 [j]Ps 24:8; 59:17; 62:11 [k]Ps 89:11 [l]Rev 5:12-13
29:12 [m]2Ch 1:12 [n]2Ch 20:6; Ro 11:36
29:15 [o]Ps 39:12; Heb 11:13 [p]Job 14:2
29:17 [q]Ps 139:23; Pr 15:11; 17:3; Jer 11:20; 17:10 [r]1Ch 28:9; Ps 15:1-5
29:19 [s]1Ch 28:9 [t]Ps 72:1 [u]1Ch 22:14
29:21 [v]1Ki 8:62
29:22 [w]1Ch 23:1 [x]1Ki 1:33-39
29:23 [y]1Ki 2:12
29:25 [z]2Ch 1:1,12 [a]1Ki 3:13; Ecc 2:9
29:26 [b]1Ch 18:14
29:27 [c]2Sa 5:4-5; 1Ki 2:11; 1Ch 3:4
29:28 [d]Ge 15:15; Ac 13:36 [e]1Ch 23:1
29:29 [f]1Sa 9:9 [g]2Sa 7:2 [h]1Sa 22:5

29:10–19

PROMISE 1

IN TUNE WITH GOD

This short prayer of David reveals his perspective on life and helps us understand why he experienced such intimacy with God. List or underline the things David said to God that strike you, and pray that he will deepen your awareness of these realities. To believe as David believed is to live as David lived and die as David died: to God's everlasting glory.

For the next Promise 1 reading go to page 469.

2 CHRONICLES

AT A GLANCE

Key Principle: **The real mission of God's people is to bring others to know and worship him. When we place our own agenda before God's, we miss our purpose and destiny.**

Author: Possibly Ezra the priest

Time and Place: 970 B.C. to 538 B.C. / Judah

Key Verses: 7:14; 16:9; 20:20

BENEFIT

The books we know as 1 and 2 Chronicles were originally one book that was placed at the end of the Hebrew Bible. Unlike Samuel and Kings, which reflect a prophetic perspective, Chronicles reflects a priestly perspective. It is concerned with the central sanctuary in Jerusalem as a symbol of God's covenant promises, God's presence among his people and worship as the key to Israel's very existence. This book is a solemn reminder to us that when we don't make God a priority in our lives, our worship will grow cold and we will no longer enjoy God's blessings.

SETTING

As the "Setting" section in 1 Chronicles indicates, Chronicles was probably compiled by Ezra the priest around 450 B.C. to 400 B.C. for the remnant of Jews who had returned from captivity in Babylonia / Persia. Ezra used a variety of official and prophetic records such as "the annotations on the book of the kings" (24:27) and "the records of the seers" (33:19) to compile this book. Second Chronicles devotes nine chapters to the 40-year reign of King Solomon (970 B.C. to 930 B.C.). Beginning with the division of Israel and Judah, the remainder of the book records the reigns of Judah's kings until the destruction of Jerusalem and its temple by Nebuchadnezzar in 586 B.C. The last account in 2 Chronicles is a decree by King Cyrus of Persia in 538 B.C. that the temple in Jerusalem be rebuilt.

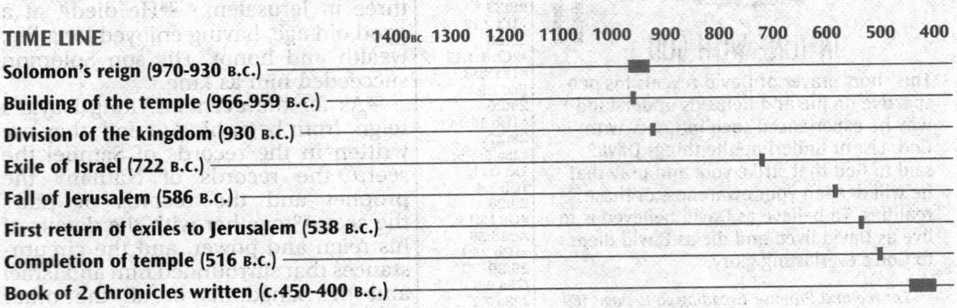

THEME AND PURPOSE

Second Chronicles offers a spiritual editorial on the history of God's covenant people from the end of the united kingdom under Solomon to the Babylonian captivity of Judah. While 1 and 2 Kings move back and forth from the kings of Judah to the kings of Israel, this book focuses exclusively on the southern kingdom of Judah. The theme of Chronicles is the preparation, consecration and worship in the temple in Jerusalem, and the temple's subsequent decline, degradation and destruction. In view of this theme, it is appropriate for this book to ignore the kings of the northern kingdom of Israel; they never acknowledged the legitimacy of the temple, and instead promoted an apostate system of calf worship.

This book encouraged the returning remnant to realize that although the glory of the past had departed, they had a new temple (built in 516 B.C.), the priesthood and Davidic line were still intact, and they still had a future hope.

UNIQUE CONTRIBUTION

Since 1 and 2 Chronicles go back to Adam and stretch to the Persian decree to rebuild the temple, they cover more time and history than any other Biblical book. These books offer a unique perspective on historical events covered in the books of Samuel and Kings. The unifying theme of the temple—its conception, consecration, corruption, destruction and its rebuilding by the remnant who returned from Persia—points to God's faithfulness to his covenant promises in the past, the present and the future. Chronicles shows that God works behind the scenes of human history, and that no one who opposes his purposes will endure.

LINKS TO THE NEW TESTAMENT

One Messianic theme in Chronicles is the royal line of David that would remain unbroken until Christ himself fulfilled it. This single dynasty was often threatened, and on a few occasions almost severed—as in the case of Joash whom God protected from the murderous intentions of Queen Athaliah (22—23).

OVERVIEW

FOCUS	Solomon's Glory	Judah's Decline and Deportation
REFERENCE	1 — 9	10 — 36
TOPICS	The Temple Constructed and Consecrated	The Temple Desecrated and Destroyed
	The Reign of Solomon	The Ruin of Judah
	Splendor	Degeneration and Disaster
	A Priestly View of Judah's History	
LOCATION	Judah	
TIME	40 Years	392 Years

Chapters 1—9 focus on King Solomon's glorious reign and the construction and consecration of the temple. This was a time of great prosperity and peace, and Israel's borders reached their greatest extent under Solomon. During this time Solomon's wealth and wisdom became legendary; people traveled from surrounding nations to pay tribute to Israel, to see Solomon's achievements and to listen to his wisdom.

Sadly, the splendor of the united kingdom was lost after Solomon's death. The nation was divided into two kingdoms that gradually declined politically, economically and morally as a result of spiritual compromise and rebellion against the Lord. Chapters 10—36 chronicle the reigns of Judah's kings (ignoring the kings of Israel) from a spiritual and priestly vantage point. Only 30 percent of this material deals with the twelve evil kings of Judah; the remaining 70 percent is devoted to the reigns of the eight kings who followed God and did his will.

2 CHRONICLES

Solomon Asks for Wisdom

1 Solomon son of David established[a] himself firmly over his kingdom, for the LORD his God was with[b] him and made him exceedingly great.[c]

2Then Solomon spoke to all Israel[d]—to the commanders of thousands and commanders of hundreds, to the judges and to all the leaders in Israel, the heads of families— 3and Solomon and the whole assembly went to the high place at Gibeon, for God's Tent of Meeting[e] was there, which Moses[f] the LORD's servant had made in the desert. 4Now David had brought up the ark[g] of God from Kiriath Jearim to the place he had prepared for it, because he had pitched a tent[h] for it in Jerusalem. 5But the bronze altar[i] that Bezalel[j] son of Uri, the son of Hur, had made was in Gibeon in front of the tabernacle of the LORD; so Solomon and the assembly inquired[k] of him there. 6Solomon went up to the bronze altar before the LORD in the Tent of Meeting and offered a thousand burnt offerings on it.

7That night God appeared[l] to Solomon and said to him, "Ask for whatever you want me to give you."

8Solomon answered God, "You have shown great kindness to David my father and have made me[m] king in his place. 9Now, LORD God, let your promise[n] to my father David be confirmed, for you have made me king over a people who are as numerous as the dust of the earth.[o] 10Give me wisdom and knowledge, that I may lead[p] this people, for who is able to govern this great people of yours?"

11God said to Solomon, "Since this is your heart's desire and you have not asked for wealth,[q] riches or honor, nor for the death of your enemies, and since you have not asked for a long life but for wisdom and knowledge to govern my people over whom I have made you king, 12therefore wisdom and knowledge will be given you. And I will also give you wealth, riches and honor,[r] such as no king who was before you ever had and none after you will have.[s]"

13Then Solomon went to Jerusalem from the high place at Gibeon, from before the Tent of Meeting. And he reigned over Israel.

14Solomon accumulated chariots[t] and horses; he had fourteen hundred chariots and twelve thousand horses,[a] which he kept in the chariot cities and also with him in Jerusalem. 15The king made silver and gold[u] as common in Jerusalem as stones, and cedar as plentiful as sycamore-fig trees in the foothills. 16Solomon's horses were imported from Egypt[b] and from Kue[c]—the royal merchants purchased them from Kue. 17They imported a chariot[v] from Egypt for six hundred shekels[d] of silver, and a horse for a hundred and fifty.[e] They also exported them to all the kings of the Hittites and of the Arameans.

Preparations for Building the Temple

2 Solomon gave orders to build a temple[w] for the Name of the LORD and a royal palace for himself.[x] 2He conscripted seventy thousand men as carriers and eighty thousand as stonecutters in the hills and thirty-six hundred as foremen over them.[y]

3Solomon sent this message to Hiram[f][z] king of Tyre:

"Send me cedar logs[a] as you did for my father David when you sent him cedar to build a palace to live in. 4Now I am about to build a temple[b] for the Name of the LORD my God and to dedicate it to him for burning fragrant incense[c] before him, for setting out the consecrated bread[d] regularly, and for making burnt offerings[e] every morning and evening and on Sabbaths[f] and New Moons and at the appointed feasts of the LORD our God. This is a lasting ordinance for Israel.

5"The temple I am going to build will be great,[g] because our God is greater than all other gods.[h] 6But who is able to build a temple for him, since the heavens, even the highest heavens, cannot contain him?[i] Who then am I[j] to build a temple for him, except as a place to burn sacrifices before him?

7"Send me, therefore, a man

1:1 [a] 1Ki 2:12,26; 2Ch 12:1 [b] Ge 21:22; 39:2; Nu 14:43 [c] 1Ch 29:25
1:2 [d] 1Ch 9:1; 28:1
1:3 [e] Ex 36:8 [f] Ex 40:18
1:4 [g] 2Sa 6:2; 1Ch 15:25 [h] 2Sa 6:17; 1Ch 15:1
1:5 [i] Ex 38:2 [j] Ex 31:2 [k] 1Ch 13:3
1:7 [l] 2Ch 7:12
1:8 [m] 1Ch 23:1; 28:5
1:9 [n] 2Sa 7:25; 1Ki 8:25 [o] Ge 12:2
1:10 [p] Nu 27:17; 2Sa 5:2; Pr 8:15-16
1:11 [q] Dt 17:17
1:12 [r] 1Ch 29:12 [s] 1Ch 29:25; 2Ch 9:22; Ne 13:26
1:14 [t] 1Sa 8:11; 1Ki 4:26; 9:19
1:15 [u] 1Ki 9:28; Isa 60:5
1:17 [v] SS 1:9
2:1 [w] Dt 12:5 [x] Ecc 2:4
2:2 [y] ver 18; 2Ch 10:4
2:3 [z] 2Sa 5:11 [a] 1Ch 14:1
2:4 [b] ver 1; Dt 12:5 [c] Ex 30:7 [d] Ex 25:30 [e] Ex 29:42; 2Ch 13:11 [f] Nu 28:9-10
2:5 [g] 1Ch 22:5; Ps 135:5 [h] 1Ch 16:25
2:6 [i] 1Ki 8:27; 2Ch 6:18; Jer 23:24 [j] Ex 3:11

[a] 14 Or *charioteers* [b] 16 Or possibly *Muzur*, a region in Cilicia; also in verse 17 [c] 16 Probably Cilicia [d] 17 That is, about 15 pounds (about 7 kilograms) [e] 17 That is, about 3 3/4 pounds (about 1.7 kilograms) [f] 3 Hebrew *Huram*, a variant of *Hiram*; also in verses 11 and 12

skilled to work in gold and silver, bronze and iron, and in purple, crimson and blue yarn, and experienced in the art of engraving, to work in Judah and Jerusalem with my skilled craftsmen,[k] whom my father David provided.

8“Send me also cedar, pine and algum[a] logs from Lebanon, for I know that your men are skilled in cutting timber there. My men will work with yours 9to provide me with plenty of lumber, because the temple I build must be large and magnificent. 10I will give your servants, the woodsmen who cut the timber, twenty thousand cors[b] of ground wheat, twenty thousand cors of barley, twenty thousand baths[c] of wine and twenty thousand baths of olive oil.[l]”

11Hiram king of Tyre replied by letter to Solomon:

“Because the LORD loves[m] his people, he has made you their king.”

12And Hiram added:

“Praise be to the LORD, the God of Israel, who made heaven and earth![n] He has given King David a wise son, endowed with intelligence and discernment, who will build a temple for the LORD and a palace for himself.

13“I am sending you Huram-Abi,[o] a man of great skill, 14whose mother was from Dan[p] and whose father was from Tyre. He is trained[q] to work in gold and silver, bronze and iron, stone and wood, and with purple and blue[r] and crimson yarn and fine linen. He is experienced in all kinds of engraving and can execute any design given to him. He will work with your craftsmen and with those of my lord, David your father.

15“Now let my lord send his servants the wheat and barley and the olive oil[s] and wine he promised, 16and we will cut all the logs from Lebanon that you need and will float them in rafts by sea down to Joppa.[t] You can then take them up to Jerusalem.”

17Solomon took a census of all the aliens[u] who were in Israel, after the census[v] his father David had taken; and they were found to be 153,600. 18He assigned[w] 70,000 of them to be carriers and 80,000 to be stonecutters in the hills, with 3,600 foremen over them to keep the people working.

Solomon Builds the Temple

3 Then Solomon began to build[x] the temple of the LORD[y] in Jerusalem on Mount Moriah, where the LORD had appeared to his father David. It was on the threshing floor of Araunah[d][z] the Jebusite, the place provided by David. 2He began building on the second day of the second month in the fourth year of his reign.[a]

3The foundation Solomon laid for building the temple of God was sixty cubits long and twenty cubits wide[e][b] (using the cubit of the old standard). 4The portico at the front of the temple was twenty cubits[f] long across the width of the building and twenty cubits[g] high.

He overlaid the inside with pure gold. 5He paneled the main hall with pine and covered it with fine gold and decorated it with palm tree[c] and chain designs. 6He adorned the temple with precious stones. And the gold he used was gold of Parvaim. 7He overlaid the ceiling beams, doorframes, walls and doors of the temple with gold, and he carved cherubim[d] on the walls.

8He built the Most Holy Place,[e] its length corresponding to the width of the temple—twenty cubits long and twenty cubits wide. He overlaid the inside with six hundred talents[h] of fine gold. 9The gold nails[f] weighed fifty shekels.[i] He also overlaid the upper parts with gold.

10In the Most Holy Place he made a pair[g] of sculptured cherubim and overlaid them with gold. 11The total wingspan of the cherubim was twenty cubits. One wing of the first cherub was five cubits[j] long and touched the temple wall, while its other wing, also five cubits long, touched the wing of the other cherub. 12Similarly one wing of the second cherub was five cubits long and touched the other temple wall, and its other wing, also five cubits long, touched the wing of the first cherub. 13The wings of these cherubim[h] ex-

2:7 [k]ver 13-14; Ex 35:31; 1Ch 22:16 **2:10** [l]Ezr 3:7 **2:11** [m]1Ki 10:9; 2Ch 9:8 **2:12** [n]Ne 9:6; Ps 8:3; 33:6; 102:25 **2:13** [o]1Ki 7:13 **2:14** [p]Ex 31:6 [q]Ex 35:31 [r]Ex 35:35 **2:15** [s]ver 10; Ezr 3:7 **2:16** [t]Jos 19:46; Jnh 1:3 **2:17** [u]1Ch 22:2 [v]2Sa 24:2 **2:18** [w]ver 2; 1Ch 22:2; 2Ch 8:8

3:1 [x]Ac 7:47 [y]Ge 28:17 [z]2Sa 24:18; 1Ch 21:18 **3:2** [a]Ezr 5:11 **3:3** [b]Eze 41:2 **3:5** [c]Eze 40:16 **3:7** [d]Ge 3:24; 1Ki 6:29-35; Eze 41:18 **3:8** [e]Ex 26:33 **3:9** [f]Ex 26:32 **3:10** [g]Ex 25:18 **3:13** [h]Ex 25:18

[a] *8* Probably a variant of *almug*; possibly juniper [b] *10* That is, probably about 125,000 bushels (about 4,400 kiloliters) [c] *10* That is, probably about 115,000 gallons (about 440 kiloliters) [d] *1* Hebrew *Ornan*, a variant of *Araunah* [e] *3* That is, about 90 feet (about 27 meters) long and 30 feet (about 9 meters) wide [f] *4* That is, about 30 feet (about 9 meters); also in verses 8, 11 and 13 [g] *4* Some Septuagint and Syriac manuscripts; Hebrew *and a hundred and twenty* [h] *8* That is, about 23 tons (about 21 metric tons) [i] *9* That is, about 1 1/4 pounds (about 0.6 kilogram) [j] *11* That is, about 7 1/2 feet (about 2.3 meters); also in verse 15

tended twenty cubits. They stood on
their feet, facing the main hall.[a]
14He made the curtain[i] of blue,
purple and crimson yarn and fine lin-
en, with cherubim[j] worked into it.
15In the front of the temple he made
two pillars,[k] which ⌞together⌟ were
thirty-five cubits[b] long, each with a
capital[l] on top measuring five cubits.
16He made interwoven chains[c][m] and
put them on top of the pillars. He also
made a hundred pomegranates[n] and
attached them to the chains. 17He
erected the pillars in the front of the
temple, one to the south and one to the
north. The one to the south he named
Jakin[d] and the one to the north
Boaz.[e]

The Temple's Furnishings

4 He made a bronze altar[o] twenty cubits long, twenty cubits wide and ten
cubits high.[f] 2He made the Sea[p] of
cast metal, circular in shape, measuring ten cubits from rim to rim and five
cubits[g] high. It took a line of thirty
cubits[h] to measure around it. 3Below
the rim, figures of bulls encircled it—
ten to a cubit.[i] The bulls were cast in
two rows in one piece with the Sea.
4The Sea stood on twelve bulls, three
facing north, three facing west, three
facing south and three facing east.[q]
The Sea rested on top of them, and
their hindquarters were toward the
center. 5It was a handbreadth[j] in
thickness, and its rim was like the rim
of a cup, like a lily blossom. It held
three thousand baths.[k]
6He then made ten basins[r] for
washing and placed five on the south
side and five on the north. In them the
things to be used for the burnt offerings[s] were rinsed, but the Sea was to
be used by the priests for washing.
7He made ten gold lampstands[t] according to the specifications[u] for
them and placed them in the temple,
five on the south side and five on the
north.
8He made ten tables[v] and placed
them in the temple, five on the south
side and five on the north. He also
made a hundred gold sprinkling
bowls.[w]
9He made the courtyard[x] of the
priests, and the large court and the
doors for the court, and overlaid the
doors with bronze. 10He placed the Sea
on the south side, at the southeast corner.
11He also made the pots and shovels
and sprinkling bowls.
So Huram finished[y] the work he
had undertaken for King Solomon in
the temple of God:

12the two pillars;
the two bowl-shaped capitals on
top of the pillars;
the two sets of network decorating the two bowl-shaped capitals on top of the pillars;
13the four hundred pomegranates
for the two sets of network
(two rows of pomegranates for
each network, decorating the
bowl-shaped capitals on top
of the pillars);
14the stands[z] with their basins;
15the Sea and the twelve bulls under it;
16the pots, shovels, meat forks and
all related articles.

All the objects that Huram-Abi[a]
made for King Solomon for the temple
of the LORD were of polished bronze.
17The king had them cast in clay molds
in the plain of the Jordan between Succoth[b] and Zarethan.[l] 18All these
things that Solomon made amounted
to so much that the weight of the
bronze[c] was not determined.
19Solomon also made all the furnishings that were in God's temple:

the golden altar;
the tables[d] on which was the
bread of the Presence;
20the lampstands[e] of pure gold
with their lamps, to burn in
front of the inner sanctuary as
prescribed;
21the gold floral work and lamps
and tongs (they were solid
gold);
22the pure gold wick trimmers,
sprinkling bowls, dishes[f] and
censers;[g] and the gold doors
of the temple: the inner doors
to the Most Holy Place and the
doors of the main hall.

5 When all the work Solomon had
done for the temple of the LORD was
finished,[h] he brought in the things his
father David had dedicated[i]—the silver and gold and all the furnishings—

3:14 [i]Ex 26:31,33; Heb 9:3 [j]Ge 3:24
3:15 [k]1Ki 7:15; Rev 3:12 [l]1Ki 7:22
3:16 [m]1Ki 7:17 [n]1Ki 7:20
4:1 [o]Ex 20:24; 27:1-2; 40:6; 1Ki 8:64; 2Ki 16:14
4:2 [p]Rev 4:6; 15:2
4:4 [q]Nu 2:3-25; Eze 48:30-34; Rev 21:13
4:6 [r]Ex 30:18 [s]Ne 13:5,9; Eze 40:38
4:7 [t]Ex 25:31 [u]Ex 25:40
4:8 [v]Ex 25:23 [w]Nu 4:14
4:9 [x]1Ki 6:36; 2Ki 21:5; 2Ch 33:5
4:11 [y]1Ki 7:14
4:14 [z]1Ki 7:27-30
4:16 [a]1Ki 7:13
4:17 [b]Ge 33:17
4:18 [c]1Ki 7:23
4:19 [d]Ex 25:23,30
4:20 [e]Ex 25:31
4:22 [f]Nu 7:14 [g]Lev 10:1
5:1 [h]1Ki 6:14 [i]2Sa 8:11

[a] *13* Or *facing inward* [b] *15* That is, about 52 feet (about 16 meters) [c] *16* Or possibly *made chains in the inner sanctuary;* the meaning of the Hebrew for this phrase is uncertain.
[d] *17* *Jakin* probably means *he establishes.*
[e] *17* *Boaz* probably means *in him is strength.*
[f] *1* That is, about 30 feet (about 9 meters) long and wide, and about 15 feet (about 4.5 meters) high [g] *2* That is, about 7 1/2 feet (about 2.3 meters) [h] *2* That is, about 45 feet (about 13.5 meters) [i] *3* That is, about 1 1/2 feet (about 0.5 meter) [j] *5* That is, about 3 inches (about 8 centimeters) [k] *5* That is, about 17,500 gallons (about 66 kiloliters) [l] *17* Hebrew *Zeredatha,* a variant of *Zarethan*

and he placed them in the treasuries of God's temple.

The Ark Brought to the Temple

[2]Then Solomon summoned to Jerusalem the elders of Israel, all the heads of the tribes and the chiefs of the Israelite families, to bring up the ark[j] of the LORD's covenant from Zion, the City of David. [3]And all the men of Israel[k] came together to the king at the time of the festival in the seventh month.

[4]When all the elders of Israel had arrived, the Levites took up the ark, [5]and they brought up the ark and the Tent of Meeting and all the sacred furnishings in it. The priests, who were Levites,[l] carried them up; [6]and King Solomon and the entire assembly of Israel that had gathered about him were before the ark, sacrificing so many sheep and cattle that they could not be recorded or counted.

[7]The priests then brought the ark[m] of the LORD's covenant to its place in the inner sanctuary of the temple, the Most Holy Place, and put it beneath the wings of the cherubim. [8]The cherubim[n] spread their wings over the place of the ark and covered the ark and its carrying poles. [9]These poles were so long that their ends, extending from the ark, could be seen from in front of the inner sanctuary, but not from outside the Holy Place; and they are still there today. [10]There was nothing in the ark except[o] the two tablets[p] that Moses had placed in it at Horeb, where the LORD made a covenant with the Israelites after they came out of Egypt.

[11]The priests then withdrew from the Holy Place. All the priests who were there had consecrated themselves, regardless of their divisions.[q] [12]All the Levites who were musicians[r]—Asaph, Heman, Jeduthun and their sons and relatives—stood on the east side of the altar, dressed in fine linen and playing cymbals, harps and lyres. They were accompanied by 120 priests sounding trumpets.[s] [13]The trumpeters and singers joined in unison, as with one voice, to give praise and thanks to the LORD. Accompanied by trumpets, cymbals and other instruments, they raised their voices in praise to the LORD and sang:

"He is good;
his love endures forever."[t]

Then the temple of the LORD was filled with a cloud, [14]and the priests could not perform[u] their service because of the cloud,[v] for the glory[w] of the LORD filled the temple of God.

6

Then Solomon said, "The LORD has said that he would dwell in a dark cloud;[x] [2]I have built a magnificent temple for you, a place for you to dwell forever.[y]"

[3]While the whole assembly of Israel was standing there, the king turned around and blessed them. [4]Then he said:

"Praise be to the LORD, the God of Israel, who with his hands has fulfilled what he promised with his mouth to my father David. For he said, [5]'Since the day I brought my people out of Egypt, I have not chosen a city in any tribe of Israel to have a temple built for my Name to be there, nor have I chosen anyone to be the leader over my people Israel. [6]But now I have chosen Jerusalem[z] for my Name[a] to be there, and I have chosen David[b] to rule my people Israel.'

[7]"My father David had it in his heart[c] to build a temple for the Name of the LORD, the God of Israel. [8]But the LORD said to my father David, 'Because it was in your heart to build a temple for my Name, you did well to have this in your heart. [9]Nevertheless, you are

5:2 [j]Nu 3:31; 2Sa 6:12; 1Ch 15:25 **5:3** [k]1Ch 9:1; 2Ch 7:8-10 **5:5** [l]Nu 3:31; 1Ch 15:2 **5:7** [m]Rev 11:19 **5:8** [n]Ge 3:24 **5:10** [o]Heb 9:4 [p]Ex 16:34; Dt 10:2 **5:11** [q]1Ch 24:1 **5:12** [r]1Ki 10:12; 1Ch 25:1; Ps 68:25 [s]1Ch 13:8; 15:24 **5:13** [t]1Ch 16:34,41; 2Ch 7:3; 20:21; Ezr 3:11; Ps 100:5; 136:1; Jer 33:11 **5:14** [u]Ex 40:35; Rev 15:8

[v]Ex 19:16 [w]Ex 29:43; 2Ch 7:2 **6:1** [x]Ex 19:9; 1Ki 8:12-50 **6:2** [y]Ezr 6:12; 7:15; Ps 135:21 **6:6** [z]Dt 12:5; Isa 14:1 [a]Ex 20:24; 2Ch 12:13 [b]1Ch 28:4 **6:7** [c]1Sa 10:7; 1Ch 17:2; 28:2; Ac 7:46

5:13–14 PROMISE 1

PREPARING FOR WORSHIP

"The glory of the LORD filled the temple." Notice the care and the cost that went into the building that God occupied. From chapter 2 through chapter 5 the chronicler impresses upon the thoughtful reader that because Israel would worship God at this temple, its construction demanded their best. A key word follows the people's expression of praise to God: "*Then* the temple of the LORD was filled." God entered when the people praised him as the culmination to all their careful work. Solomon's prayer of praise in chapter 6 reveals his attitude toward worship, one that follows along the lines of his father David.

As you enter God's presence—either in your personal worship or as you prepare for the worship service at your church—consider how Israel prepared to meet with God. Verses 1–6 of this chapter discuss how Solomon prepared for this event; learn from this story, and prepare daily to connect with God with the same kind of reverence.

For the next Promise 1 reading go to page 472.

not the one to build the temple, but your son, who is your own flesh and blood—he is the one who will build the temple for my Name.'

10"The LORD has kept the promise he made. I have succeeded David my father and now I sit on the throne of Israel, just as the LORD promised, and I have built the temple for the Name of the LORD, the God of Israel. 11There I have placed the ark, in which is the covenant[d] of the LORD that he made with the people of Israel."

Solomon's Prayer of Dedication

12Then Solomon stood before the altar of the LORD in front of the whole assembly of Israel and spread out his hands. 13Now he had made a bronze platform,[e] five cubits[a] long, five cubits wide and three cubits[b] high, and had placed it in the center of the outer court. He stood on the platform and then knelt down[f] before the whole assembly of Israel and spread out his hands toward heaven. 14He said:

"O LORD, God of Israel, there is no God like you[g] in heaven or on earth—you who keep your covenant of love[h] with your servants who continue wholeheartedly in your way. 15You have kept your promise to your servant David my father; with your mouth you have promised[i] and with your hand you have fulfilled it—as it is today.

16"Now LORD, God of Israel, keep for your servant David my father the promises you made to him when you said, 'You shall never fail[j] to have a man to sit before me on the throne of Israel, if only your sons are careful in all they do to walk before me according to my law,[k] as you have done.' 17And now, O LORD, God of Israel, let your word that you promised your servant David come true.

18"But will God really dwell[l] on earth with men? The heavens,[m] even the highest heavens, cannot contain you. How much less this temple I have built! 19Yet give attention to your servant's prayer and his plea for mercy, O LORD my God. Hear the cry and the prayer that your servant is praying in your presence. 20May your eyes[n] be open toward this temple day and night, this place of which you said you would put your Name[o] there. May you hear[p] the prayer your servant prays toward this place. 21Hear the supplications of your servant and of your people Israel when they pray toward this place. Hear from heaven, your dwelling place; and when you hear, forgive.[q]

22"When a man wrongs his neighbor and is required to take an oath[r] and he comes and swears the oath before your altar in this temple, 23then hear from heaven and act. Judge between your servants, repaying[s] the guilty by bringing down on his own head what he has done. Declare the innocent not guilty and so establish his innocence.

24"When your people Israel have been defeated[t] by an enemy because they have sinned against you and when they turn back and confess your name, praying and making supplication before you in this temple, 25then hear from heaven and forgive the sin of your people Israel and bring them back to the land you gave to them and their fathers.

26"When the heavens are shut up and there is no rain[u] because your people have sinned against you, and when they pray toward this place and confess your name and turn from their sin because you have afflicted them, 27then hear from heaven and forgive[v] the sin of your servants, your people Israel. Teach them the right way to live, and send rain on the land you gave your people for an inheritance.

28"When famine[w] or plague comes to the land, or blight or mildew, locusts or grasshoppers, or when enemies besiege them in any of their cities, whatever disaster or disease may come, 29and when a prayer or plea is made by any of your people Israel—each one aware of his afflictions and pains, and spreading out his hands toward this temple— 30then hear from heaven, your dwelling place. Forgive,[x] and deal with each man according to all he does, since you know his heart (for you alone know the hearts of men),[y] 31so that they will fear you[z] and walk in your ways all the time they live in the land you gave our fathers.

6:11 [d]Dt 10:2; 2Ch 5:10; Ps 25:10; 50:5
6:13 [e]Ne 8:4 [f]Ps 95:6
6:14 [g]Ex 8:10; 15:11 [h]Dt 7:9
6:15 [i]1Ch 22:10
6:16 [j]2Sa 7:13,15; 1Ki 2:4; 2Ch 7:18; 23:3 [k]Ps 132:12
6:18 [l]Rev 21:3 [m]2Ch 2:6; Ps 11:4; Isa 40:22; 66:1; Ac 7:49
6:20 [n]Ex 3:16; Ps 34:15 [o]Dt 12:11 [p]2Ch 7:14; 30:20
6:21 [q]Ps 51:1; Isa 33:24; 40:2; 43:25; 44:22; 55:7; Mic 7:18
6:22 [r]Ex 22:11
6:23 [s]Isa 3:11; 65:6; Mt 16:27
6:24 [t]Lev 26:17
6:26 [u]Lev 26:19; Dt 11:17; 28:24; 2Sa 1:21; 1Ki 17:1
6:27 [v]ver 30,39; 2Ch 7:14
6:28 [w]2Ch 20:9
6:30 [x]ver 27 [y]1Sa 16:7; 1Ch 28:9; Ps 7:9; 44:21; Pr 16:2; 17:3
6:31 [z]Ps 103:11,13; Pr 8:13

a *13* That is, about 7 1/2 feet (about 2.3 meters)
b *13* That is, about 4 1/2 feet (about 1.3 meters)

32 "As for the foreigner who
does not belong to your people Israel but has come[a] from a distant
land because of your great name
and your mighty hand[b] and your
outstretched arm—when he
comes and prays toward this temple, 33 then hear from heaven,
your dwelling place, and do whatever the foreigner[c] asks of you,
so that all the peoples of the earth
may know your name and fear
you, as do your own people Israel,
and may know that this house I
have built bears your Name.
34 "When your people go to war
against their enemies,[d] wherever
you send them, and when they
pray[e] to you toward this city you
have chosen and the temple I
have built for your Name, 35 then
hear from heaven their prayer and
their plea, and uphold their cause.
36 "When they sin against you—
for there is no one who does not
sin[f]—and you become angry
with them and give them over to
the enemy, who takes them captive[g] to a land far away or near;
37 and if they have a change of
heart[h] in the land where they are
held captive, and repent and
plead with you in the land of their
captivity and say, 'We have
sinned, we have done wrong and
acted wickedly'; 38 and if they turn
back to you with all their heart
and soul in the land of their captivity where they were taken, and
pray toward the land you gave
their fathers, toward the city you
have chosen and toward the temple I have built for your Name;
39 then from heaven, your dwelling
place, hear their prayer and their
pleas, and uphold their cause.
And forgive your people, who
have sinned against you.
40 "Now, my God, may your
eyes be open and your ears attentive[i] to the prayers offered in this
place.

41 "Now arise,[j] O LORD God,
and come to your
resting place,[k]
you and the ark of your
might.
May your priests,[l] O LORD
God, be clothed with
salvation,
may your saints rejoice in
your goodness.[m]
42 O LORD God, do not reject
your anointed one.
Remember the great love[n]
promised to David your
servant."

6:32 [a] 2Ch 9:6; Jn 12:20; Ac 8:27 [b] Ex 3:19,20 **6:33** [c] 2Ch 7:14 **6:34** [d] Dt 28:7 [e] 1Ch 5:20 **6:36** [f] Job 15:14; Ps 143:2; Ecc 7:20; Jer 17:9; Jas 3:1; 1Jn 1:8-10 [g] Lev 26:44 **6:37** [h] 2Ch 7:14; 33:12,19,23; Jer 29:13 **6:40** [i] 2Ch 7:15; Ne 1:6,11; Ps 17:1,6 **6:41** [j] Isa 33:10 [k] 1Ch 28:2 [l] Ps 132:16 [m] Ps 116:12 **6:42** [n] Ps 89:24,28; Isa 55:3

The Dedication of the Temple

7 When Solomon finished praying,
fire[o] came down from heaven and
consumed the burnt offering and the
sacrifices, and the glory of the LORD
filled[p] the temple.[q] 2 The priests
could not enter[r] the temple of the
LORD because the glory[s] of the LORD
filled it. 3 When all the Israelites saw the
fire coming down and the glory of the
LORD above the temple, they knelt on
the pavement with their faces to the
ground, and they worshiped and gave
thanks to the LORD, saying,

"He is good;
his love endures forever."[t]

4 Then the king and all the people offered sacrifices before the LORD. 5 And
King Solomon offered a sacrifice of
twenty-two thousand head of cattle
and a hundred and twenty thousand
sheep and goats. So the king and all the
people dedicated the temple of God.
6 The priests took their positions, as did
the Levites[u] with the LORD's musical
instruments,[v] which King David had
made for praising the LORD and which
were used when he gave thanks, saying, "His love endures forever." Opposite the Levites, the priests blew their
trumpets, and all the Israelites were
standing.
7 Solomon consecrated the middle
part of the courtyard in front of the
temple of the LORD, and there he offered burnt offerings and the fat of the
fellowship offerings,[a] because the
bronze altar he had made could not
hold the burnt offerings, the grain offerings and the fat portions.
8 So Solomon observed the festival[w]
at that time for seven days, and all Israel with him—a vast assembly, people
from Lebo[b] Hamath to the Wadi of
Egypt.[x] 9 On the eighth day they held
an assembly, for they had celebrated
the dedication of the altar for seven
days and the festival[y] for seven days
more. 10 On the twenty-third day of the
seventh month he sent the people to
their homes, joyful and glad in heart
for the good things the LORD had done
for David and Solomon and for his
people Israel.

The LORD Appears to Solomon

11 When Solomon had finished the
temple of the LORD and the royal pal-

7:1 [o] Lev 9:24; 1Ki 18:38 [p] Ex 16:10 [q] Ps 26:8 **7:2** [r] 1Ki 8:11 [s] Ex 29:43; 40:35; 2Ch 5:14 **7:3** [t] 1Ch 16:34; 2Ch 5:13; 20:21 **7:6** [u] 1Ch 15:16 [v] 2Ch 5:12 **7:8** [w] 2Ch 30:26 [x] Ge 15:18 **7:9** [y] Lev 23:36

a 7 Traditionally *peace offerings* b 8 Or *from the entrance to*

ace, and had succeeded in carrying out
all he had in mind to do in the temple
of the LORD and in his own palace,
12the LORD appeared to him at night
and said:

1 →PG. 480

"I have heard your prayer and
have chosen this place for myself[z] as a temple for sacrifices.
13"When I shut up the heavens
so that there is no rain,[a] or command locusts to devour the land
or send a plague among my people, 14if my people, who are called
by my name, will humble[b] themselves and pray and seek my
face[c] and turn[d] from their wicked ways, then will I hear from
heaven and will forgive[e] their sin
and will heal[f] their land. 15Now
my eyes will be open and my ears
attentive to the prayers offered
in this place.[g] 16I have chosen[h]
and consecrated this temple so
that my Name may be there forever. My eyes and my heart will always be there.
17"As for you, if you walk before
me[i] as David your father did,
and do all I command, and observe my decrees and laws, 18I will
establish your royal throne, as I
covenanted with David your father when I said, 'You shall never
fail to have a man[j] to rule over
Israel.'[k]

19"But if you[a] turn away[l] and
forsake[m] the decrees and commands I have given you[a] and go
off to serve other gods and worship them, 20then I will uproot[n]
Israel from my land,[o] which I
have given them, and will reject
this temple I have consecrated for
my Name. I will make it a byword
and an object of ridicule[p] among
all peoples. 21And though this
temple is now so imposing, all
who pass by will be appalled and
say,[q] 'Why has the LORD done
such a thing to this land and to
this temple?' 22People will answer,
'Because they have forsaken the
LORD, the God of their fathers,
who brought them out of Egypt,
and have embraced other gods,
worshiping and serving them—
that is why he brought all this disaster on them.' "

Solomon's Other Activities

8 At the end of twenty years, during
which Solomon built the temple of
the LORD and his own palace, 2Solo-
mon rebuilt the villages that Hiram[b]
had given him, and settled Israelites in
them. 3Solomon then went to Hamath
Zobah and captured it. 4He also built

7:12 [z]Dt 12:5
7:13 [a]2Ch 6:26-28; Am 4:7
7:14 [b]Lev 26:41; 2Ch 6:37; Jas 4:10 [c]1Ch 16:11 [d]Isa 55:7; Zec 1:4 [e]2Ch 6:27 [f]2Ch 30:20; Isa 30:26; 57:18
7:15 [g]2Ch 6:40
7:16 [h]ver 12; 2Ch 6:6
7:17 [i]1Ki 9:4
7:18 [j]2Ch 6:16 [k]2Sa 7:13; 2Ch 13:5
7:19 [l]Dt 28:15 [m]Lev 26:14,33
7:20 [n]Dt 29:28 [o]1Ki 14:15 [p]Dt 28:37
7:21 [q]Dt 29:24

a *19* The Hebrew is plural. b *2* Hebrew *Huram,* a variant of *Hiram;* also in verse 18

7:14–15

PROMISE 1

FOUR STEPS TO WHAT GOD WANTS

"Just tell me what you want!" Many men have made this frustrated exclamation to someone they are trying to please—or at least satisfy—and just can't figure out what it takes to do so. Relatives, employers, employees and friends all make demands on us that, at times, bring out this kind of a statement.

God never stutters when he tells us what he wants. This passage names four things. As you study this passage, first notice *whom* God is addressing: "*My* people who are called by my name." This is a personal matter between God and those who claim to be his followers. What does he want? Only the following: (1) "Humble [your]selves," (2) "pray," (3) "seek my face," (4) "turn from [your] wicked ways."

These four steps are very easy to understand and, if taken in sequence, to do. Thinking about the sequence, however, is important. (1) *Humble yourself.* Until we admit we can't live as God intended, we are not in a position to seek his help. Jesus told his disciples that "whoever exalts himself will be humbled, and whoever humbles himself will be exalted" (Matthew 23:12). Nothing else in the Christian's life works until we recognize our frailty and become serious about our complete need for God. (2) *Pray.* Prayer is the link between "I can't" and "God can." Only after admitting that we can't will we call out in a new attitude of urgency to the one who can. (3) *Seek his face.* This meditative, lingering search for God's face suggests more than a prayer for help; it calls for a quiet time of seeking after him. God wants a face-to-face relationship with each of his people. (4) *Turn from your wicked ways.* This fourth demand is the tough one for most of us. Priorities, habits, peer pressure and pleasure all pull at us to do what we know we shouldn't. Only with the first three steps in place can we tackle the fourth.

God makes a promise to people who seriously pursue him through humility, prayer, a personal relationship and repentance from sin: "Then will I hear from heaven and will forgive their sin and will heal their land" (v. 14). Note Solomon's prayer in 6:26–31; this passage (7:14–15) is a direct response to that prayer. God's answer is, "You do your part (humble yourself, pray, seek my face, turn from your wicked ways) and I will do mine (hear from heaven, forgive your sins and heal your land)."

Life still works that way.

For the next Promise 1 reading go to page 508.

up Tadmor in the desert and all the
store cities he had built in Hamath. 5He
rebuilt Upper Beth Horon[r] and Lower
Beth Horon as fortified cities, with
walls and with gates and bars, 6as well
as Baalath and all his store cities, and
all the cities for his chariots and for his
horses[a]—whatever he desired to build
in Jerusalem, in Lebanon and throughout all the territory he ruled.
7All the people left from the Hittites,
Amorites, Perizzites, Hivites and Jebusites[s] (these peoples were not Israelites), 8that is, their descendants remaining in the land, whom the
Israelites had not destroyed—these
Solomon conscripted[t] for his slave labor force, as it is to this day. 9But Solomon did not make slaves of the Israelites for his work; they were his fighting
men, commanders of his captains, and
commanders of his chariots and charioteers. 10They were also King Solomon's chief officials—two hundred
and fifty officials supervising the
men.
11Solomon brought Pharaoh's
daughter[u] up from the City of David
to the palace he had built for her, for he
said, "My wife must not live in the palace of David king of Israel, because the
places the ark of the LORD has entered
are holy."
12On the altar[v] of the LORD that he
had built in front of the portico, Solomon sacrificed burnt offerings to the
LORD, 13according to the daily requirement[w] for offerings commanded by
Moses for Sabbaths,[x] New Moons and
the three[y] annual feasts—the Feast
of Unleavened Bread, the Feast of
Weeks[z] and the Feast of Tabernacles.
14In keeping with the ordinance of his
father David, he appointed the divisions[a] of the priests for their duties,
and the Levites[b] to lead the praise and
to assist the priests according to each
day's requirement. He also appointed
the gatekeepers[c] by divisions for the
various gates, because this was what
David the man of God[d] had ordered.[e] 15They did not deviate from
the king's commands to the priests or
to the Levites in any matter, including
that of the treasuries.
16All Solomon's work was carried
out, from the day the foundation of the
temple of the LORD was laid until its
completion. So the temple of the LORD
was finished.
17Then Solomon went to Ezion Geber and Elath on the coast of Edom.
18And Hiram sent him ships commanded by his own officers, men who
knew the sea. These, with Solomon's
men, sailed to Ophir and brought back
four hundred and fifty talents[b] of
gold,[f] which they delivered to King
Solomon.

The Queen of Sheba Visits Solomon

9 When the queen of Sheba[g] heard of
Solomon's fame, she came to Jerusalem to test him with hard questions.
Arriving with a very great caravan—
with camels carrying spices, large
quantities of gold, and precious
stones—she came to Solomon and
talked with him about all she had on
her mind. 2Solomon answered all her
questions; nothing was too hard for
him to explain to her. 3When the queen
of Sheba saw the wisdom of Solomon,[h] as well as the palace he had
built, 4the food on his table, the seating
of his officials, the attending servants
in their robes, the cupbearers in their
robes and the burnt offerings he made
at[c] the temple of the LORD, she was
overwhelmed.
5She said to the king, "The report I
heard in my own country about your
achievements and your wisdom is true.
6But I did not believe what they said
until I came[i] and saw with my own
eyes. Indeed, not even half the greatness of your wisdom was told me; you
have far exceeded the report I heard.
7How happy your men must be! How
happy your officials, who continually
stand before you and hear your wisdom! 8Praise be to the LORD your God,
who has delighted in you and placed
you on his throne[j] as king to rule for
the LORD your God. Because of the love
of your God for Israel and his desire to
uphold them forever, he has made you
king[k] over them, to maintain justice
and righteousness."
9Then she gave the king 120 talents[d]
of gold,[l] large quantities of spices,
and precious stones. There had never
been such spices as those the queen of
Sheba gave to King Solomon.
10(The men of Hiram and the men of
Solomon brought gold from Ophir;[m]
they also brought algumwood[e] and
precious stones. 11The king used the
algumwood to make steps for the temple of the LORD and for the royal palace,
and to make harps and lyres for the
musicians. Nothing like them had ever
been seen in Judah.)
12King Solomon gave the queen of
Sheba all she desired and asked for; he
gave her more than she had brought to

8:5 [r]1Ch 7:24; 2Ch 14:7 **8:7** [s]Ge 10:16 **8:8** [t]1Ki 4:6; 9:21 **8:11** [u]1Ki 3:1; 7:8 **8:12** [v]1Ki 8:64; 2Ch 4:1; 15:8 **8:13** [w]Ex 29:38; Nu 28:3 [x]Nu 28:9 [y]Ex 23:14; Dt 16:16 [z]Ex 23:16 **8:14** [a]1Ch 24:1 [b]1Ch 25:1 [c]1Ch 9:17; 26:1 [d]Ne 12:24,36 [e]1Ch 23:6; Ne 12:45

8:18 [f]2Ch 9:9 **9:1** [g]Ge 10:7; Eze 23:42; Mt 12:42; Lk 11:31 **9:3** [h]1Ki 5:12 **9:6** [i]2Ch 6:32 **9:8** [j]1Ki 2:12; 1Ch 17:14; 28:5; 29:23; 2Ch 13:8 [k]2Ch 2:11 **9:9** [l]2Ch 8:18 **9:10** [m]2Ch 8:18

[a]*6* Or *charioteers* [b]*18* That is, about 17 tons (about 16 metric tons) [c]*4* Or *the ascent by which he went up to* [d]*9* That is, about 4 1/2 tons (about 4 metric tons) [e]*10* Probably a variant of *almugwood*

him. Then she left and returned with
her retinue to her own country.

Solomon's Splendor

13The weight of the gold that Solomon received yearly was 666 talents,[a]
14not including the revenues brought
in by merchants and traders. Also all
the kings of Arabia[n] and the governors
of the land brought gold and silver to
Solomon.
15King Solomon made two hundred
large shields of hammered gold; six
hundred bekas[b] of hammered gold
went into each shield. 16He also made
three hundred small shields[o] of hammered gold, with three hundred bekas[c] of gold in each shield. The king
put them in the Palace of the Forest of
Lebanon.[p]
17Then the king made a great throne
inlaid with ivory[q] and overlaid with
pure gold. 18The throne had six steps,
and a footstool of gold was attached to
it. On both sides of the seat were armrests, with a lion standing beside each
of them. 19Twelve lions stood on the six
steps, one at either end of each step.
Nothing like it had ever been made for
any other kingdom. 20All King Solomon's goblets were gold, and all the
household articles in the Palace of the
Forest of Lebanon were pure gold.
Nothing was made of silver, because
silver was considered of little value in
Solomon's day. 21The king had a fleet
of trading ships[d] manned by Hiram's[e] men. Once every three years it
returned, carrying gold, silver and ivory, and apes and baboons.
22King Solomon was greater in
riches and wisdom than all the other
kings of the earth.[r] 23All the kings[s] of
the earth sought audience with Solomon to hear the wisdom God had put
in his heart. 24Year after year, everyone
who came brought a gift[t]—articles of
silver and gold, and robes, weapons
and spices, and horses and mules.
25Solomon had four thousand stalls
for horses and chariots,[u] and twelve
thousand horses,[f] which he kept in
the chariot cities and also with him in
Jerusalem. 26He ruled[v] over all the
kings from the River[g][w] to the land of
the Philistines, as far as the border of
Egypt.[x] 27The king made silver as
common in Jerusalem as stones, and
cedar as plentiful as sycamore-fig trees
in the foothills. 28Solomon's horses
were imported from Egypt[h] and from
all other countries.

Solomon's Death

29As for the other events of Solomon's reign, from beginning to end,
are they not written in the records of
Nathan[y] the prophet, in the prophecy
of Ahijah[z] the Shilonite and in the visions of Iddo the seer concerning Jeroboam[a] son of Nebat? 30Solomon
reigned in Jerusalem over all Israel forty years. 31Then he rested with his fathers and was buried in the city of David[b] his father. And Rehoboam his son
succeeded him as king.

Israel Rebels Against Rehoboam

10 Rehoboam went to Shechem, for all
the Israelites had gone there to
make him king. 2When Jeroboam[c]
son of Nebat heard this (he was in
Egypt, where he had fled[d] from King
Solomon), he returned from Egypt. 3So
they sent for Jeroboam, and he and all
Israel[e] went to Rehoboam and said to
him: 4"Your father put a heavy yoke on
us,[f] but now lighten the harsh labor
and the heavy yoke he put on us, and
we will serve you."
5Rehoboam answered, "Come back
to me in three days." So the people
went away.
6Then King Rehoboam consulted
the elders[g] who had served his father
Solomon during his lifetime. "How
would you advise me to answer these
people?" he asked.
7They replied, "If you will be kind to
these people and please them and give
them a favorable answer,[h] they will
always be your servants."
8But Rehoboam rejected[i] the advice the elders[j] gave him and consulted the young men who had grown up
with him and were serving him. 9He
asked them, "What is your advice? How
should we answer these people who
say to me, 'Lighten the yoke your father
put on us'?"
10The young men who had grown up
with him replied, "Tell the people who
have said to you, 'Your father put a
heavy yoke on us, but make our yoke
lighter'—tell them, 'My little finger is
thicker than my father's waist. 11My father laid on you a heavy yoke; I will
make it even heavier. My father
scourged you with whips; I will scourge
you with scorpions.' "
12Three days later Jeroboam and all
the people returned to Rehoboam, as
the king had said, "Come back to me in

9:14 [n]2Ch 17:11; Isa 21:13; Jer 25:24; Eze 27:21; 30:5
9:16 [o]2Ch 12:9 [p]1Ki 7:2
9:17 [q]1Ki 22:39
9:22 [r]1Ki 3:13; 2Ch 1:12
9:23 [s]1Ki 4:34
9:24 [t]2Ch 32:23; Ps 45:12; 68:29; 72:10; Isa 18:7
9:25 [u]1Sa 8:11; 1Ki 4:26
9:26 [v]1Ki 4:21 [w]Ps 72:8-9 [x]Ge 15:18-21
9:29 [y]2Sa 7:2; 1Ch 29:29 [z]1Ki 11:29 [a]2Ch 10:2
9:31 [b]1Ki 2:10
10:2 [c]2Ch 9:29 [d]1Ki 11:40
10:3 [e]1Ch 9:1
10:4 [f]2Ch 2:2
10:6 [g]Job 8:8-9; 12:12; 15:10; 32:7
10:7 [h]Pr 15:1
10:8 [i]2Sa 17:14 [j]Pr 13:20

[a] *13* That is, about 25 tons (about 23 metric tons) [b] *15* That is, about 7 1/2 pounds (about 3.5 kilograms) [c] *16* That is, about 3 3/4 pounds (about 1.7 kilograms) [d] *21* Hebrew *of ships that could go to Tarshish* [e] *21* Hebrew *Huram,* a variant of *Hiram* [f] *25* Or *charioteers* [g] *26* That is, the Euphrates [h] *28* Or possibly *Muzur,* a region in Cilicia

three days." 13The king answered them harshly. Rejecting the advice of the elders, 14he followed the advice of the young men and said, "My father made your yoke heavy; I will make it even heavier. My father scourged you with whips; I will scourge you with scorpions." 15So the king did not listen to the people, for this turn of events was from God,[k] to fulfill the word the LORD had spoken to Jeroboam son of Nebat through Ahijah the Shilonite.[l]

16When all Israel[m] saw that the king refused to listen to them, they answered the king:

> "What share do we have in
> David,[n]
> what part in Jesse's son?
> To your tents, O Israel!
> Look after your own house,
> O David!"

So all the Israelites went home. 17But as for the Israelites who were living in the towns of Judah, Rehoboam still ruled over them.

18King Rehoboam sent out Adoniram,**a**[o] who was in charge of forced labor, but the Israelites stoned him to death. King Rehoboam, however, managed to get into his chariot and escape to Jerusalem. 19So Israel has been in rebellion against the house of David to this day.

11 When Rehoboam arrived in Jerusalem,[p] he mustered the house of Judah and Benjamin—a hundred and eighty thousand fighting men—to make war against Israel and to regain the kingdom for Rehoboam.

2But this word of the LORD came to Shemaiah[q] the man of God: 3"Say to Rehoboam son of Solomon king of Judah and to all the Israelites in Judah and Benjamin, 4'This is what the LORD says: Do not go up to fight against your brothers.[r] Go home, every one of you, for this is my doing.' " So they obeyed the words of the LORD and turned back from marching against Jeroboam.

Rehoboam Fortifies Judah

5Rehoboam lived in Jerusalem and built up towns for defense in Judah: 6Bethlehem, Etam, Tekoa, 7Beth Zur, Soco, Adullam, 8Gath, Mareshah, Ziph, 9Adoraim, Lachish, Azekah, 10Zorah, Aijalon and Hebron. These were fortified cities in Judah and Benjamin. 11He strengthened their defenses and put commanders in them, with supplies of food, olive oil and wine. 12He put shields and spears in all the cities, and made them very strong. So Judah and Benjamin were his.

13The priests and Levites from all their districts throughout Israel sided with him. 14The Levites[s] even abandoned their pasturelands and property,[t] and came to Judah and Jerusalem because Jeroboam and his sons had rejected them as priests of the LORD. 15And he appointed[u] his own priests[v] for the high places and for the goat[w] and calf[x] idols he had made. 16Those from every tribe of Israel[y] who set their hearts on seeking the LORD, the God of Israel, followed the Levites to Jerusalem to offer sacrifices to the LORD, the God of their fathers. 17They strengthened[z] the kingdom of Judah and supported Rehoboam son of Solomon three years, walking in the ways of David and Solomon during this time.

Rehoboam's Family

18Rehoboam married Mahalath, who was the daughter of David's son Jerimoth and of Abihail, the daughter of Jesse's son Eliab. 19She bore him sons: Jeush, Shemariah and Zaham. 20Then he married Maacah[a] daughter of Absalom, who bore him Abijah,[b] Attai, Ziza and Shelomith. 21Rehoboam loved Maacah daughter of Absalom more than any of his other wives and concubines. In all, he had eighteen wives[c] and sixty concubines, twenty-eight sons and sixty daughters.

22Rehoboam appointed Abijah[d] son of Maacah to be the chief prince among his brothers, in order to make him king. 23He acted wisely, dispersing some of his sons throughout the districts of Judah and Benjamin, and to all the fortified cities. He gave them abundant provisions and took many wives for them.

Shishak Attacks Jerusalem

12 After Rehoboam's position as king was established[e] and he had become strong,[f] he and all Israel**b** with him abandoned the law of the LORD. 2Because they had been unfaithful[g] to the LORD, Shishak[h] king of Egypt attacked Jerusalem in the fifth year of King Rehoboam. 3With twelve hundred chariots and sixty thousand horsemen and the innumerable troops of Libyans, Sukkites and Cushites**c**[i] that came with him from Egypt, 4he captured the fortified cities[j] of Judah and came as far as Jerusalem.

5Then the prophet Shemaiah[k] came to Rehoboam and to the leaders

10:15 [k]2Ch 11:4; 25:16-20 [l]1Ki 11:29
10:16 [m]1Ch 9:1 [n]ver 19; 2Sa 20:1
10:18 [o]1Ki 5:14
11:1 [p]1Ki 12:21
11:2 [q]2Ch 12:5-7, 15
11:4 [r]2Ch 28:8-11
11:14 [s]Nu 35:2-5 [t]2Ch 13:9
11:15 [u]1Ki 13:33 [v]1Ki 12:31 [w]Lev 17:7 [x]1Ki 12:28; 2Ch 13:8
11:16 [y]2Ch 15:9
11:17 [z]2Ch 12:1
11:20 [a]1Ki 15:2 [b]2Ch 13:2
11:21 [c]Dt 17:17
11:22 [d]Dt 21:15-17
12:1 [e]ver 13 [f]2Ch 11:17
12:2 [g]1Ki 14:22-24 [h]1Ki 11:40
12:3 [i]2Ch 16:8; Na 3:9
12:4 [j]2Ch 11:10
12:5 [k]2Ch 11:2

a *18* Hebrew *Hadoram,* a variant of *Adoniram*
b *1* That is, Judah, as frequently in 2 Chronicles
c *3* That is, people from the upper Nile region

of Judah who had assembled in Jerusalem for fear of Shishak, and he said to
them, "This is what the LORD says, 'You
have abandoned me; therefore, I now
abandon[l] you to Shishak.' "
6The leaders of Israel and the king
humbled themselves and said, "The
LORD is just."[m]
7When the LORD saw that they humbled themselves, this word of the LORD
came to Shemaiah: "Since they have
humbled themselves, I will not destroy
them but will soon give them deliverance.[n] My wrath will not be poured
out on Jerusalem through Shishak.
8They will, however, become subject[o]
to him, so that they may learn the difference between serving me and serving the kings of other lands."
9When Shishak king of Egypt attacked Jerusalem, he carried off the
treasures of the temple of the LORD and

12:5 [l]Dt 28:15; 2Ch 15:2
12:6 [m]Ex 9:27; Da 9:14
12:7 [n]1Ki 21:29; Ps 78:38
12:8 [o]Dt 28:48

11:4

PROMISE 6

ONE BAD APPLE?

Israel went to war with itself. The twelve tribes, united under David (2 Samuel 5:4–5) had risen to great heights under him and his son Solomon. After Solomon died, Israel ripped itself apart and became the two separate nations of Israel and Judah.

Why did they split? That's a simple question with a complex answer. As you read chapter 10 it appears that Rehoboam was the cause. He was harsh, egocentric and arrogant, and he rejected good advice for bad. The ten tribes who broke away had good cause. But read 1 Kings 12:12–33; it appears that Jeroboam has to carry some of the blame. As the ruler of the ten tribes of Israel he had his own problems. His practice of idolatry only made matters worse. So how do we distribute blame? Is it 50/50? 60/40? Assigning blame quickly becomes a fool's game, even though many have tried to play it over the years.

But wait, there's more to the story. Much of what happened to Rehoboam and Jeroboam was orchestrated by God as judgment on sin—not Rehoboam's sin or Jeroboam's sin, but Solomon's sin! The "subordinate" mentioned in 1 Kings 11:11 is Jeroboam. This tragic event in Israel's history was a result of Solomon's idolatry (11:9–13). To conclude that Solomon had it all together and that Rehoboam and Jeroboam were responsible for the split is to miss one of history's great lessons.

So was the root of the nation's division Solomon's idolatry? Not quite. We have to go back another step to see what tragically changed Israel's history for all time. The root of Solomon's problem is described in 1 Kings 11:1–7. Because Solomon ignored one of God's laws, his heart was turned away from God and toward other gods (v. 4). Slowly read verses 3 and 4 and let this truth grip your soul. It's not about women or sex as much as it is about whatever any man will substitute for God's place in his life. The summary of it all is written in 1 Kings 11:9: "His heart had turned away from the LORD his God." Stop for a moment and examine what your heart is devoted to; this story certainly tells us it makes a difference.

Brothers going to war against brothers because of sin. Jeroboam's sin? Rehoboam's sin? Yes, both are responsible for their actions, as we are for ours. But what's amazing—and terrifying—about Israel's story is Solomon's role. Sin is so subtle, so sneaky, so enormously powerful. As you follow the progression from Solomon's desire for women to his idolatry to God's judgment on this divided nation, think of the unknown consequences of your own potential disobedience.

From Solomon's idolatry on, Israel's history is a story of Abraham's divided descendants—two nations going their separate ways. Their resources are divided. Their testimony to God's glory is compromised. Frequently the two sides engage in open warfare with Jewish brother killing Jewish brother. Although the "Why?" of all this destruction and ruin is complicated in how it plays out, it goes back to the all-too-familiar root: Someone thought he was smarter than God.

The rest of Old Testament history (Kings and Chronicles), and the writings of the prophets refer frequently to Israel and Judah as the people of God. It is important to remember that the one Israel is now two nations, Israel and Judah. A few points of comparison and contrast will help as you read the rest of the Old Testament.

ISRAEL	JUDAH
Located in the North	Located in the South
Capital in various cities, eventually Samaria	Capital was always Jerusalem
Consisted of 10 tribes	Consisted of 2 tribes, Judah and Benjamin
Lasted from 930B.C. to 721B.C.	Lasted from 930B.C. to 586B.C.
Had 19 kings; none followed God	Had 20 kings; 8 followed God
Four dynasties	One dynasty: Davidic
Destroyed by the Assyrians in 721B.C.	Destroyed by the Babylonians in 586B.C.
Nation was never restored	Restored under Darius in 516B.C., reconstruction story written in Ezra and Nehemiah

For the next Promise 6 reading go to page 504.

the treasures of the royal palace. He took everything, including the gold shields[p] Solomon had made. 10So King Rehoboam made bronze shields to replace them and assigned these to the commanders of the guard on duty at the entrance to the royal palace. 11Whenever the king went to the LORD's temple, the guards went with him, bearing the shields, and afterward they returned them to the guardroom.

12Because Rehoboam humbled himself, the LORD's anger turned from him, and he was not totally destroyed. Indeed, there was some good[q] in Judah.

13King Rehoboam established himself firmly in Jerusalem and continued as king. He was forty-one years old when he became king, and he reigned seventeen years in Jerusalem, the city the LORD had chosen out of all the tribes of Israel in which to put his Name.[r] His mother's name was Naamah; she was an Ammonite. 14He did evil because he had not set his heart on seeking the LORD.

15As for the events of Rehoboam's reign, from beginning to end, are they not written in the records of Shemaiah[s] the prophet and of Iddo the seer that deal with genealogies? There was continual warfare between Rehoboam and Jeroboam. 16Rehoboam rested with his fathers and was buried in the City of David. And Abijah[t] his son succeeded him as king.

Abijah King of Judah

13 In the eighteenth year of the reign of Jeroboam, Abijah became king of Judah, 2and he reigned in Jerusalem three years. His mother's name was Maacah,[a] a daughter[b] of Uriel of Gibeah.

There was war between Abijah[u] and Jeroboam.[v] 3Abijah went into battle with a force of four hundred thousand able fighting men, and Jeroboam drew up a battle line against him with eight hundred thousand able troops.

4Abijah stood on Mount Zemaraim,[w] in the hill country of Ephraim, and said, "Jeroboam and all Israel,[x] listen to me! 5Don't you know that the LORD, the God of Israel, has given the kingship of Israel to David and his descendants forever[y] by a covenant of salt?[z] 6Yet Jeroboam son of Nebat, an official of Solomon son of David, rebelled[a] against his master. 7Some worthless scoundrels[b] gathered around him and opposed Rehoboam son of Solomon when he was young and indecisive and not strong enough to resist them.

8"And now you plan to resist the kingdom of the LORD, which is in the hands of David's descendants. You are indeed a vast army and have with you the golden calves[c] that Jeroboam made to be your gods. 9But didn't you drive out the priests of the LORD,[d] the sons of Aaron, and the Levites, and make priests of your own as the peoples of other lands do? Whoever comes to consecrate himself with a young bull[e] and seven rams may become a priest of what are not gods.[f]

10"As for us, the LORD is our God, and we have not forsaken him. The priests who serve the LORD are sons of Aaron, and the Levites assist them. 11Every morning and evening[g] they present burnt offerings and fragrant incense to the LORD. They set out the bread on the ceremonially clean table[h] and light the lamps on the gold lampstand every evening. We are observing the requirements of the LORD our God. But you have forsaken him. 12God is with us; he is our leader. His priests with their trumpets will sound the battle cry against you.[i] Men of Israel, do not fight against the LORD,[j] the God of your fathers, for you will not succeed."

13Now Jeroboam had sent troops around to the rear, so that while he was in front of Judah the ambush[k] was behind them. 14Judah turned and saw that they were being attacked at both front and rear. Then they cried out[l] to the LORD. The priests blew their trumpets 15and the men of Judah raised the battle cry. At the sound of their battle cry, God routed Jeroboam and all Israel[m] before Abijah and Judah. 16The Israelites fled before Judah, and God delivered[n] them into their hands. 17Abijah and his men inflicted heavy losses on them, so that there were five hundred thousand casualties among Israel's able men. 18The men of Israel were subdued on that occasion, and the men of Judah were victorious because they relied[o] on the LORD, the God of their fathers.

19Abijah pursued Jeroboam and took from him the towns of Bethel, Jeshanah and Ephron, with their surrounding villages. 20Jeroboam did not regain power during the time of Abijah. And the LORD struck him down and he died.

21But Abijah grew in strength. He married fourteen wives and had

12:9 [p]2Ch 9:16
12:12 [q]1Ki 14:13; 2Ch 19:3
12:13 [r]Dt 12:5; 2Ch 6:6
12:15 [s]2Ch 9:29; 11:2
12:16 [t]2Ch 11:20
13:2 [u]2Ch 11:20 [v]1Ki 15:6
13:4 [w]Jos 18:22 [x]1Ch 11:1
13:5 [y]2Sa 7:13 [z]Lev 2:13; Nu 18:19
13:6 [a]1Ki 11:26
13:7 [b]Jdg 9:4
13:8 [c]1Ki 12:28; 2Ch 11:15
13:9 [d]2Ch 11:14-15 [e]Ex 29:35-36 [f]Jer 2:11
13:11 [g]Ex 29:39; 2Ch 2:4 [h]Lev 24:5-9
13:12 [i]Nu 10:8-9 [j]Ac 5:39
13:13 [k]Jos 8:9
13:14 [l]2Ch 14:11
13:15 [m]2Ch 14:12
13:16 [n]2Ch 16:8
13:18 [o]1Ch 5:20; 2Ch 14:11; Ps 22:5

[a] *2* Most Septuagint manuscripts and Syriac (see also 2 Chron. 11:20 and 1 Kings 15:2); Hebrew *Micaiah* [b] *2* Or *granddaughter*

twenty-two sons and sixteen daughters.
22The other events of Abijah's reign,
what he did and what he said, are written in the annotations of the prophet
Iddo.
14 And Abijah rested with his fathers
and was buried in the City of David.
Asa his son succeeded him as king, and
in his days the country was at peace for
ten years.

Asa King of Judah

2Asa did what was good and right in
the eyes of the LORD his God. 3He removed the foreign altars and the high
places, smashed the sacred stones and
cut down the Asherah poles.[a][p] 4He
commanded Judah to seek the LORD,
the God of their fathers, and to obey his
laws and commands. 5He removed the
high places and incense altars[q] in every town in Judah, and the kingdom
was at peace under him. 6He built up
the fortified cities of Judah, since the
land was at peace. No one was at war
with him during those years, for the
LORD gave him rest.[r]
7"Let us build up these towns," he
said to Judah, "and put walls around
them, with towers, gates and bars. The
land is still ours, because we have
sought the LORD our God; we sought
him and he has given us rest on every
side." So they built and prospered.
8Asa had an army of three hundred
thousand men from Judah, equipped
with large shields and with spears, and
two hundred and eighty thousand
from Benjamin, armed with small
shields and with bows. All these were
brave fighting men.
9Zerah the Cushite[s] marched out
against them with a vast army[b] and
three hundred chariots, and came as
far as Mareshah.[t] 10Asa went out to
meet him, and they took up battle positions in the Valley of Zephathah near
Mareshah.
11Then Asa called[u] to the LORD his
God and said, "LORD, there is no one
like you to help the powerless against
the mighty. Help us, O LORD our God,
for we rely[v] on you, and in your
name[w] we have come against this vast
army. O LORD, you are our God; do not
let man prevail[x] against you."
12The LORD struck down[y] the Cushites before Asa and Judah. The Cushites fled, 13and Asa and his army pursued them as far as Gerar.[z] Such a
great number of Cushites fell that they
could not recover; they were crushed
before the LORD and his forces. The
men of Judah carried off a large
amount of plunder. 14They destroyed
all the villages around Gerar, for the
terror[a] of the LORD had fallen upon
them. They plundered all these villages, since there was much booty
there. 15They also attacked the camps
of the herdsmen and carried off droves
of sheep and goats and camels. Then
they returned to Jerusalem.

Asa's Reform

15 The Spirit of God came upon[b] Azariah son of Oded. 2He went out to
meet Asa and said to him, "Listen to
me, Asa and all Judah and Benjamin.
The LORD is with you[c] when you are
with him.[d] If you seek[e] him, he will
be found by you, but if you forsake
him, he will forsake you.[f] 3For a long
time Israel was without the true God,
without a priest to teach[g] and without
the law.[h] 4But in their distress they
turned to the LORD, the God of Israel,
and sought him,[i] and he was found
by them. 5In those days it was not safe
to travel about,[j] for all the inhabitants
of the lands were in great turmoil. 6One
nation was being crushed by another
and one city by another,[k] because
God was troubling them with every
kind of distress. 7But as for you, be
strong[l] and do not give up, for your
work will be rewarded."[m]
8When Asa heard these words and
the prophecy of Azariah son of[c] Oded
the prophet, he took courage. He removed the detestable idols from the
whole land of Judah and Benjamin and
from the towns he had captured[n] in
the hills of Ephraim. He repaired the
altar[o] of the LORD that was in front of
the portico of the LORD's temple.
9Then he assembled all Judah and
Benjamin and the people from Ephraim, Manasseh and Simeon who had
settled among them, for large numbers[p] had come over to him from Israel when they saw that the LORD his God
was with him.
10They assembled at Jerusalem in
the third month of the fifteenth year of
Asa's reign. 11At that time they sacrificed to the LORD seven hundred head
of cattle and seven thousand sheep
and goats from the plunder[q] they had
brought back. 12They entered into a
covenant[r] to seek the LORD,[s] the God
of their fathers, with all their heart and
soul. 13All who would not seek the

14:3 [p]Ex 34:13; Dt 7:5; 1Ki 15:12-14
14:5 [q]2Ch 34:4,7
14:6 [r]1Ch 22:9; 2Ch 15:15
14:9 [s]2Ch 12:3; 16:8 [t]2Ch 11:8
14:11 [u]2Ch 13:14 [v]2Ch 13:18 [w]1Sa 17:45 [x]1Sa 14:6; Ps 9:19
14:12 [y]2Ch 13:15
14:13 [z]Ge 10:19
14:14 [a]Ge 35:5; 2Ch 17:10
15:1 [b]Nu 11:25,26; 24:2; 2Ch 20:14; 24:20
15:2 [c]ver 4,15; 2Ch 20:17 [d]Jas 4:8 [e]Jer 29:13 [f]1Ch 28:9; 2Ch 24:20
15:3 [g]Lev 10:11 [h]2Ch 17:9; La 2:9
15:4 [i]Dt 4:29
15:5 [j]Jdg 5:6
15:6 [k]Mt 24:7
15:7 [l]Jos 1:7,9 [m]Ps 58:11
15:8 [n]2Ch 13:19 [o]2Ch 8:12
15:9 [p]2Ch 11:16-17
15:11 [q]2Ch 14:13
15:12 [r]2Ki 11:17; 2Ch 23:16; 34:31 [s]1Ch 16:11

a 3 That is, symbols of the goddess Asherah; here and elsewhere in 2 Chronicles
b 9 Hebrew *with an army of a thousand thousands* or *with an army of thousands upon thousands*
c 8 Vulgate and Syriac (see also Septuagint and verse 1); Hebrew does not have *Azariah son of.*

LORD, the God of Israel, were to be put to death,[t] whether small or great, man or woman. 14They took an oath to the LORD with loud acclamation, with shouting and with trumpets and horns. 15All Judah rejoiced about the oath because they had sworn it wholeheartedly. They sought God[u] eagerly, and he was found by them. So the LORD gave them rest[v] on every side.

16King Asa also deposed his grandmother Maacah from her position as queen mother, because she had made a repulsive Asherah pole.[w] Asa cut the pole down, broke it up and burned it in the Kidron Valley. 17Although he did not remove the high places from Israel, Asa's heart was fully committed ⌞to the LORD⌟ all his life. 18He brought into the temple of God the silver and gold and the articles that he and his father had dedicated.

19There was no more war until the thirty-fifth year of Asa's reign.

Asa's Last Years

16 In the thirty-sixth year of Asa's reign Baasha[x] king of Israel went up against Judah and fortified Ramah to prevent anyone from leaving or entering the territory of Asa king of Judah.

2Asa then took the silver and gold out of the treasuries of the LORD's temple and of his own palace and sent it to Ben-Hadad king of Aram, who was ruling in Damascus. 3"Let there be a treaty[y] between me and you," he said, "as there was between my father and your father. See, I am sending you silver and gold. Now break your treaty with Baasha king of Israel so he will withdraw from me."

4Ben-Hadad agreed with King Asa and sent the commanders of his forces against the towns of Israel. They conquered Ijon, Dan, Abel Maim[a] and all the store cities of Naphtali. 5When Baasha heard this, he stopped building Ramah and abandoned his work. 6Then King Asa brought all the men of Judah, and they carried away from Ramah the stones and timber Baasha had been using. With them he built up Geba and Mizpah.

7At that time Hanani[z] the seer came to Asa king of Judah and said to him: "Because you relied on the king of Aram and not on the LORD your God, the army of the king of Aram has escaped from your hand. 8Were not the Cushites[b][a] and Libyans a mighty army with great numbers of chariots and horsemen[c]? Yet when you relied on the LORD, he delivered[b] them into your hand. 9For the eyes[c] of the LORD range throughout the earth to strengthen those whose hearts are fully committed to him. You have done a foolish[d] thing, and from now on you will be at war."

10Asa was angry with the seer because of this; he was so enraged that he put him in prison. At the same time Asa brutally oppressed some of the people.

11The events of Asa's reign, from beginning to end, are written in the book of the kings of Judah and Israel. 12In the thirty-ninth year of his reign Asa was afflicted with a disease in his feet. Though his disease was severe, even in his illness he did not seek help from the LORD,[e] but only from the physicians. 13Then in the forty-first year of his reign Asa died and rested with his fathers. 14They buried him in the tomb that he had cut out for himself in the City of David. They laid him on a bier covered with spices and various blended perfumes,[f] and they made a huge fire[g] in his honor.

Jehoshaphat King of Judah

17 Jehoshaphat his son succeeded him as king and strengthened himself against Israel. 2He stationed troops in all the fortified cities of Judah and put garrisons in Judah and in the towns of

15:13 [t]Ex 22:20; Dt 13:9-16
15:15 [u]Dt 4:29 [v]1Ch 22:9; 2Ch 14:7
15:16 [w]Ex 34:13; 2Ch 14:2-5
16:1 [x]Jer 41:9
16:3 [y]2Ch 20:35
16:7 [z]1Ki 16:1
16:8 [a]2Ch 12:3; 14:9 [b]2Ch 13:16
16:9 [c]Pr 15:3; Jer 16:17; Zec 4:10 [d]1Sa 13:13
16:12 [e]Jer 17:5-6
16:14 [f]Ge 50:2; Jn 19:39-40 [g]2Ch 21:19; Jer 34:5

[a]4 Also known as *Abel Beth Maacah* [b]8 That is, people from the upper Nile region [c]8 Or *charioteers*

16:7–10

PROMISE 2

A BAD CALL

Even good men have chinks in their armor. Asa was a good man (15:17); his attitude reveals why God blessed him (14:11). Late in life, when he found himself under pressure, he made a mistake—a bad call. God sent a messenger to warn the king that he had stepped outside of God's will, and Asa punished the messenger. In recording this event, the writer of 2 Chronicles chastises him for this rash action.

Learn from Asa that even good men make bad decisions; that smart guys do dumb things. When someone cares enough to tell you when you've strayed from the path, swallow hard and say "Thank you, come again." Encourage your brothers and sisters in Christ to keep on helping you by telling you the truth. Solomon wrote, "Wounds from a friend can be trusted, but an enemy multiplies kisses" (Proverbs 27:6). Asa hurt himself badly by not believing that.

For the next Promise 2 reading go to page 523.

Ephraim that his father Asa had captured.[h]

1 →PG. 509
3 →PG. 549

3The LORD was with Jehoshaphat because in his early years he walked in the ways his father David[i] had followed. He did not consult the Baals 4but sought[j] the God of his father and followed his commands rather than the practices of Israel. 5The LORD established the kingdom under his control; and all Judah brought gifts[k] to Jehoshaphat, so that he had great wealth and honor.[l] 6His heart was devoted[m] to the ways of the LORD; furthermore, he removed the high places[n] and the Asherah poles[o] from Judah.[p]

7In the third year of his reign he sent his officials Ben-Hail, Obadiah, Zechariah, Nethanel and Micaiah to teach[q] in the towns of Judah. 8With them were certain Levites[r]—Shemaiah, Nethaniah, Zebadiah, Asahel, Shemiramoth, Jehonathan, Adonijah, Tobijah and Tob-Adonijah—and the priests Elishama and Jehoram. 9They taught throughout Judah, taking with them the Book of the Law[s] of the LORD; they went around to all the towns of Judah and taught the people.

10The fear[t] of the LORD fell on all the kingdoms of the lands surrounding Judah, so that they did not make war with Jehoshaphat. 11Some Philistines brought Jehoshaphat gifts and silver as tribute, and the Arabs[u] brought him flocks:[v] seven thousand seven hundred rams and seven thousand seven hundred goats.

12Jehoshaphat became more and more powerful; he built forts and store cities in Judah 13and had large supplies in the towns of Judah. He also kept experienced fighting men in Jerusalem. 14Their enrollment[w] by families was as follows:

From Judah, commanders of units of 1,000:
Adnah the commander, with 300,000 fighting men;
15next, Jehohanan the commander, with 280,000;
16next, Amasiah son of Zicri, who volunteered[x] himself for the service of the LORD, with 200,000.
17From Benjamin:[y]
Eliada, a valiant soldier, with 200,000 men armed with bows and shields;
18next, Jehozabad, with 180,000 men armed for battle.

19These were the men who served the king, besides those he stationed in the fortified cities[z] throughout Judah.[a]

17:2 [h]2Ch 15:8
17:3 [i]1Ki 22:43
17:4 [j]1Ki 12:28; 2Ch 22:9
17:5 [k]1Sa 10:27 [l]2Ch 18:1
17:6 [m]1Ki 8:61; 2Ch 15:17 [n]1Ki 15:14; 2Ch 19:3; 20:33 [o]Ex 34:13 [p]2Ch 21:12
17:7 [q]Lev 10:11; Dt 6:4-9; 2Ch 15:3; 35:3
17:8 [r]2Ch 19:8; Ne 8:7-8
17:9 [s]Dt 6:4-9; 28:61
17:10 [t]Ge 35:5; Dt 2:25; 2Ch 14:14
17:11 [u]2Ch 9:14; 26:8 [v]2Ch 21:16
17:14 [w]2Sa 24:2
17:16 [x]Jdg 5:9; 1Ch 29:9
17:17 [y]Nu 1:36
17:19 [z]2Ch 11:10 [a]2Ch 25:5

18:1 [b]2Ch 17:5 [c]2Ch 19:1-3; 22:3 [d]2Ch 21:6
18:11 [e]2Ch 22:5
18:13 [f]Nu 22:18,20, 35

Micaiah Prophesies Against Ahab

18 Now Jehoshaphat had great wealth and honor,[b] and he allied[c] himself with Ahab[d] by marriage. 2Some years later he went down to visit Ahab in Samaria. Ahab slaughtered many sheep and cattle for him and the people with him and urged him to attack Ramoth Gilead. 3Ahab king of Israel asked Jehoshaphat king of Judah, "Will you go with me against Ramoth Gilead?"

Jehoshaphat replied, "I am as you are, and my people as your people; we will join you in the war." 4But Jehoshaphat also said to the king of Israel, "First seek the counsel of the LORD."

5So the king of Israel brought together the prophets—four hundred men—and asked them, "Shall we go to war against Ramoth Gilead, or shall I refrain?"

"Go," they answered, "for God will give it into the king's hand."

6But Jehoshaphat asked, "Is there not a prophet of the LORD here whom we can inquire of?"

7The king of Israel answered Jehoshaphat, "There is still one man through whom we can inquire of the LORD, but I hate him because he never prophesies anything good about me, but always bad. He is Micaiah son of Imlah."

"The king should not say that," Jehoshaphat replied.

8So the king of Israel called one of his officials and said, "Bring Micaiah son of Imlah at once."

9Dressed in their royal robes, the king of Israel and Jehoshaphat king of Judah were sitting on their thrones at the threshing floor by the entrance to the gate of Samaria, with all the prophets prophesying before them. 10Now Zedekiah son of Kenaanah had made iron horns, and he declared, "This is what the LORD says: 'With these you will gore the Arameans until they are destroyed.' "

11All the other prophets were prophesying the same thing. "Attack Ramoth Gilead[e] and be victorious," they said, "for the LORD will give it into the king's hand."

12The messenger who had gone to summon Micaiah said to him, "Look, as one man the other prophets are predicting success for the king. Let your word agree with theirs, and speak favorably."

13But Micaiah said, "As surely as the LORD lives, I can tell him only what my God says."[f]

14When he arrived, the king asked him, "Micaiah, shall we go to war

against Ramoth Gilead, or shall I refrain?"
"Attack and be victorious," he answered, "for they will be given into
your hand."
15The king said to him, "How many
times must I make you swear to tell me
nothing but the truth in the name of
the LORD?"
16Then Micaiah answered, "I saw all
Israel[g] scattered on the hills like
sheep without a shepherd,[h] and the
LORD said, 'These people have no master. Let each one go home in peace.' "
17The king of Israel said to Jehoshaphat, "Didn't I tell you that he never
prophesies anything good about me,
but only bad?"
18Micaiah continued, "Therefore
hear the word of the LORD: I saw the
LORD sitting on his throne[i] with all the
host of heaven standing on his right
and on his left. 19And the LORD said,
'Who will entice Ahab king of Israel
into attacking Ramoth Gilead and going to his death there?'
"One suggested this, and another
that. 20Finally, a spirit came forward,
stood before the LORD and said, 'I will
entice him.'
" 'By what means?' the LORD asked.
21" 'I will go and be a lying spirit[j] in
the mouths of all his prophets,' he said.
" 'You will succeed in enticing him,'
said the LORD. 'Go and do it.'
22"So now the LORD has put a lying
spirit in the mouths of these prophets
of yours.[k] The LORD has decreed disaster for you."
23Then Zedekiah son of Kenaanah
went up and slapped[l] Micaiah in the
face. "Which way did the spirit from[a]
the LORD go when he went from me to
speak to you?" he asked.
24Micaiah replied, "You will find out
on the day you go to hide in an inner
room."
25The king of Israel then ordered,
"Take Micaiah and send him back to
Amon the ruler of the city and to Joash
the king's son, 26and say, 'This is what
the king says: Put this fellow in prison[m] and give him nothing but bread
and water until I return safely.' "
27Micaiah declared, "If you ever return safely, the LORD has not spoken
through me." Then he added, "Mark
my words, all you people!"

Ahab Killed at Ramoth Gilead

28So the king of Israel and Jehoshaphat king of Judah went up to Ramoth
Gilead. 29The king of Israel said to Jehoshaphat, "I will enter the battle in
disguise, but you wear your royal
robes." So the king of Israel disguised[n]
himself and went into battle.
30Now the king of Aram had ordered
his chariot commanders, "Do not fight
with anyone, small or great, except the
king of Israel." 31When the chariot
commanders saw Jehoshaphat, they
thought, "This is the king of Israel." So
they turned to attack him, but Jehoshaphat cried out,[o] and the LORD helped
him. God drew them away from him,
32for when the chariot commanders
saw that he was not the king of Israel,
they stopped pursuing him.
33But someone drew his bow at random and hit the king of Israel between
the sections of his armor. The king told
the chariot driver, "Wheel around and
get me out of the fighting. I've been
wounded." 34All day long the battle
raged, and the king of Israel propped
himself up in his chariot facing the Arameans until evening. Then at sunset he
died.[p]
19 When Jehoshaphat king of Judah
returned safely to his palace in Jerusalem, 2Jehu[q] the seer, the son of
Hanani, went out to meet him and said
to the king, "Should you help the wicked[r] and love[b] those who hate the
LORD?[s] Because of this, the wrath[t] of
the LORD is upon you. 3There is, however, some good[u] in you, for you have
rid the land of the Asherah poles[v] and
have set your heart on seeking God.[w]"

Jehoshaphat Appoints Judges

4Jehoshaphat lived in Jerusalem,
and he went out again among the people from Beersheba to the hill country
of Ephraim and turned them back to
the LORD, the God of their fathers. 5He
appointed judges[x] in the land, in each
of the fortified cities of Judah. 6He told
them, "Consider carefully what you
do,[y] because you are not judging for
man[z] but for the LORD, who is with
you whenever you give a verdict. 7Now
let the fear of the LORD be upon you.
Judge carefully, for with the LORD our
God there is no injustice[a] or partiality[b] or bribery."
8In Jerusalem also, Jehoshaphat appointed some of the Levites, priests
and heads of Israelite families to administer[c] the law of the LORD and to
settle disputes. And they lived in Jerusalem. 9He gave them these orders:
"You must serve faithfully and wholeheartedly in the fear of the LORD. 10In
every case that comes before you from
your fellow countrymen who live in the
cities—whether bloodshed or other

18:16 [g] 1Ch 9:1 [h] Nu 27:17; Eze 34:5-8
18:18 [i] Da 7:9
18:21 [j] 1Ch 21:1; Job 1:6; Zec 3:1; Jn 8:44
18:22 [k] Job 12:16; Isa 19:14; Eze 14:9
18:23 [l] Jer 20:2; Mk 14:65; Ac 23:2
18:26 [m] 2Ch 16:10; Heb 11:36
18:29 [n] 1Sa 28:8
18:31 [o] 2Ch 13:14
18:34 [p] 2Ch 22:5
19:2 [q] 1Ki 16:1 [r] 2Ch 16:2-9 [s] Ps 139:21-22 [t] 2Ch 24:18; 32:25; Ps 7:11
19:3 [u] 1Ki 14:13; 2Ch 12:12 [v] 2Ch 17:6 [w] 2Ch 18:1; 20:35; 25:7; Ezr 7:10
19:5 [x] Ge 47:6; Ex 18:26
19:6 [y] Lev 19:15 [z] Dt 1:17; 16:18-20; 17:8-13
19:7 [a] Ge 18:25; Dt 32:4 [b] Dt 10:17; Job 34:19; Ro 2:11; Col 3:25
19:8 [c] 2Ch 17:8-9

[a] 23 Or *Spirit of with*   [b] 2 Or *and make alliances*

concerns of the law, commands, decrees or ordinances—you are to warn
them not to sin against the LORD;[d]
otherwise his wrath will come on you
and your brothers. Do this, and you
will not sin.
11 "Amariah the chief priest will be
over you in any matter concerning the
LORD, and Zebadiah son of Ishmael, the
leader of the tribe of Judah, will be over
you in any matter concerning the king,
and the Levites will serve as officials
before you. Act with courage,[e] and
may the LORD be with those who do
well."

Jehoshaphat Defeats Moab and Ammon

20 After this, the Moabites and Ammonites with some of the Meunites[a][f] came to make war on Jehoshaphat.
2 Some men came and told Jehosha-
phat, "A vast army is coming against
you from Edom,[b] from the other side
of the Sea.[c] It is already in Hazazon
Tamar[g]" (that is, En Gedi). 3 Alarmed,
Jehoshaphat resolved to inquire of the
LORD, and he proclaimed a fast[h] for all
Judah. 4 The people of Judah came together to seek help from the LORD; indeed, they came from every town in
Judah to seek him.
5 Then Jehoshaphat stood up in the
assembly of Judah and Jerusalem at the
temple of the LORD in the front of the
new courtyard 6 and said:

"O LORD, God of our fathers,[i]
are you not the God who is in
heaven?[j] You rule over all the
kingdoms[k] of the nations. Power
and might are in your hand, and
no one can withstand you. 7 O our
God, did you not drive out the inhabitants of this land before your
people Israel and give it forever to
the descendants of Abraham your
friend?[l] 8 They have lived in it
and have built in it a sanctuary[m]
for your Name, saying, 9 'If calamity comes upon us, whether the
sword of judgment, or plague or
famine,[n] we will stand in your
presence before this temple that
bears your Name and will cry out
to you in our distress, and you will
hear us and save us.'
10 "But now here are men from
Ammon, Moab and Mount Seir,
whose territory you would not allow Israel to invade when they
came from Egypt;[o] so they
turned away from them and did
not destroy them. 11 See how they
are repaying us by coming to drive
us out of the possession[p] you
gave us as an inheritance. 12 O our
God, will you not judge them?[q]
For we have no power to face this
vast army that is attacking us. We
do not know what to do, but our
eyes are upon you.[r]"

13 All the men of Judah, with their
wives and children and little ones,
stood there before the LORD.
14 Then the Spirit[s] of the LORD came
upon Jahaziel son of Zechariah, the son
of Benaiah, the son of Jeiel, the son of
Mattaniah, a Levite and descendant of
Asaph, as he stood in the assembly.
15 He said: "Listen, King Jehoshaphat
and all who live in Judah and Jerusalem! This is what the LORD says to you:
'Do not be afraid or discouraged[t] because of this vast army. For the battle[u]
is not yours, but God's. 16 Tomorrow
march down against them. They will be
climbing up by the Pass of Ziz, and you
will find them at the end of the gorge in
the Desert of Jeruel. 17 You will not have
to fight this battle. Take up your positions; stand firm and see[v] the deliverance the LORD will give you, O Judah
and Jerusalem. Do not be afraid; do not
be discouraged. Go out to face them
tomorrow, and the LORD will be with
you.' "
18 Jehoshaphat bowed[w] with his face
to the ground, and all the people of
Judah and Jerusalem fell down in worship before the LORD. 19 Then some Levites from the Kohathites and Korahites stood up and praised the LORD, the
God of Israel, with very loud voice.
20 Early in the morning they left for
the Desert of Tekoa. As they set out,
Jehoshaphat stood and said, "Listen to
me, Judah and people of Jerusalem!
Have faith[x] in the LORD your God and
you will be upheld; have faith in his
prophets and you will be successful.[y]"
21 After consulting the people, Jehoshaphat appointed men to sing to the
LORD and to praise him for the splendor of his[d] holiness[z] as they went out
at the head of the army, saying:

"Give thanks to the LORD,
for his love endures forever."[a]

22 As they began to sing and praise,
the LORD set ambushes[b] against the
men of Ammon and Moab and Mount
Seir who were invading Judah, and
they were defeated. 23 The men of Ammon[c] and Moab rose up against the
men from Mount Seir[d] to destroy and

19:10 [d]Dt 17:8-13
19:11 [e]1Ch 28:20
20:1 [f]1Ch 4:41
20:2 [g]Ge 14:7
20:3 [h]1Sa 7:6; 2Ch 19:3; Ezr 8:21; Jer 36:9; Jnh 3:5,7
20:6 [i]Mt 6:9 [j]Dt 4:39 [k]1Ch 29:11-12
20:7 [l]Isa 41:8; Jas 2:23
20:8 [m]2Ch 6:20
20:9 [n]2Ch 6:28
20:10 [o]Nu 20:14-21; Dt 2:4-6,9, 18-19
20:11 [p]Ps 83:1-12
20:12 [q]Jdg 11:27 [r]Ps 25:15; 121:1-2
20:14 [s]2Ch 15:1
20:15 [t]2Ch 32:7 [u]Ex 14:13-14; 1Sa 17:47
20:17 [v]Ex 14:13; 2Ch 15:2
20:18 [w]Ex 4:31
20:20 [x]Isa 7:9 [y]Ge 39:3; Pr 16:3
20:21 [z]1Ch 16:29; Ps 29:2 [a]2Ch 5:13; Ps 136:1
20:22 [b]Jdg 7:22; 2Ch 13:13
20:23 [c]Ge 19:38 [d]2Ch 21:8

a *1* Some Septuagint manuscripts; Hebrew *Ammonites* **b** *2* One Hebrew manuscript; most Hebrew manuscripts, Septuagint and Vulgate *Aram* **c** *2* That is, the Dead Sea **d** *21* Or *him with the splendor of*

annihilate them. After they finished
slaughtering the men from Seir, they
helped to destroy one another.[e]
24When the men of Judah came to
the place that overlooks the desert and
looked toward the vast army, they saw
only dead bodies lying on the ground;
no one had escaped. 25So Jehoshaphat
and his men went to carry off their
plunder, and they found among them a
great amount of equipment and clothing[a] and also articles of value—more
than they could take away. There was
so much plunder that it took three days
to collect it. 26On the fourth day they
assembled in the Valley of Beracah,
where they praised the LORD. This is
why it is called the Valley of Beracah[b]
to this day.
27Then, led by Jehoshaphat, all the
men of Judah and Jerusalem returned
joyfully to Jerusalem, for the LORD had
given them cause to rejoice over their
enemies. 28They entered Jerusalem
and went to the temple of the LORD
with harps and lutes and trumpets.
29The fear[f] of God came upon all
the kingdoms of the countries when
they heard how the LORD had fought[g]
against the enemies of Israel. 30And the
kingdom of Jehoshaphat was at peace,
for his God had given him rest[h] on
every side.

The End of Jehoshaphat's Reign

31So Jehoshaphat reigned over Judah. He was thirty-five years old when
he became king of Judah, and he
reigned in Jerusalem twenty-five years.
His mother's name was Azubah daughter of Shilhi. 32He walked in the ways of
his father Asa and did not stray from
them; he did what was right in the eyes
of the LORD. 33The high places,[i] however, were not removed, and the people still had not set their hearts on the
God of their fathers.
34The other events of Jehoshaphat's
reign, from beginning to end, are written in the annals of Jehu[j] son of Hanani, which are recorded in the book of
the kings of Israel.
35Later, Jehoshaphat king of Judah
made an alliance[k] with Ahaziah king
of Israel, who was guilty of wickedness.[l] 36He agreed with him to construct a fleet of trading ships.[c] After
these were built at Ezion Geber, 37Elie-
zer son of Dodavahu of Mareshah
prophesied against Jehoshaphat, saying, "Because you have made an alliance with Ahaziah, the LORD will destroy what you have made." The
ships[m] were wrecked and were not
able to set sail to trade.[d]

21 Then Jehoshaphat rested with his
fathers and was buried with them
in the City of David. And Jehoram[n] his
son succeeded him as king. 2Jehoram's
brothers, the sons of Jehoshaphat,
were Azariah, Jehiel, Zechariah, Azaria-
hu, Michael and Shephatiah. All these
were sons of Jehoshaphat king of Israel.[e] 3Their father had given them
many gifts[o] of silver and gold and articles of value, as well as fortified cities[p]
in Judah, but he had given the kingdom
to Jehoram because he was his firstborn son.

Jehoram King of Judah

4When Jehoram established[q] himself firmly over his father's kingdom,
he put all his brothers[r] to the sword
along with some of the princes of Israel. 5Jehoram was thirty-two years old
when he became king, and he reigned
in Jerusalem eight years. 6He walked in
the ways of the kings of Israel,[s] as the
house of Ahab had done, for he married a daughter of Ahab.[t] He did evil
in the eyes of the LORD. 7Nevertheless,
because of the covenant the LORD had
made with David,[u] the LORD was not
willing to destroy the house of David.[v]
He had promised to maintain a lamp[w]
for him and his descendants forever.
8In the time of Jehoram, Edom[x] rebelled against Judah and set up its own
king. 9So Jehoram went there with his
officers and all his chariots. The Edomites surrounded him and his chariot
commanders, but he rose up and broke
through by night. 10To this day Edom
has been in rebellion against Judah.
Libnah[y] revolted at the same time,
because Jehoram had forsaken the
LORD, the God of his fathers. 11He had
also built high places on the hills of
Judah and had caused the people of
Jerusalem to prostitute themselves and
had led Judah astray.
12Jehoram received a letter from Elijah[z] the prophet, which said:
"This is what the LORD, the God of
your father[a] David, says: 'You
have not walked in the ways
of your father Jehoshaphat or
of Asa[b] king of Judah. 13But you
have walked in the ways of the
kings of Israel, and you have led
Judah and the people of Jerusalem to prostitute themselves, just
as the house of Ahab did.[c] You

20:23 [e]Jdg 7:22; 1Sa 14:20; Eze 38:21
20:29 [f]Ge 35:5; Dt 2:25; 2Ch 14:14; 17:10 [g]Ex 14:14
20:30 [h]1Ch 22:9; 2Ch 14:6-7; 15:15
20:33 [i]2Ch 17:6; 19:3
20:34 [j]1Ki 16:1
20:35 [k]2Ch 16:3 [l]2Ch 19:1-3
20:37 [m]1Ki 9:26; 2Ch 9:21
21:1 [n]1Ch 3:11
21:3 [o]2Ch 11:23 [p]2Ch 11:10
21:4 [q]1Ki 2:12 [r]Jdg 9:5
21:6 [s]1Ki 12:28-30 [t]2Ch 18:1; 22:3
21:7 [u]2Sa 7:13 [v]2Sa 7:15; 2Ch 23:3 [w]2Sa 21:17; 1Ki 11:36
21:8 [x]2Ch 20:22-23
21:10 [y]Nu 33:20
21:12 [z]2Ki 1:16-17 [a]2Ch 17:3-6 [b]2Ch 14:2
21:13 [c]ver 6,11; 1Ki 16:29-33

[a]*25* Some Hebrew manuscripts and Vulgate; most Hebrew manuscripts *corpses*
[b]*26* *Beracah* means *praise.*
[c]*36* Hebrew *of ships that could go to Tarshish*
[d]*37* Hebrew *sail for Tarshish*
[e]*2* That is, Judah, as frequently in 2 Chronicles

have also murdered your own brothers, members of your father's house, men who were better[d] than you. 14So now the LORD is about to strike your people, your sons, your wives and everything that is yours, with a heavy blow. 15You yourself will be very ill with a lingering disease[e] of the bowels, until the disease causes your bowels to come out.'"

16The LORD aroused against Jehoram the hostility of the Philistines and of the Arabs[f] who lived near the Cushites. 17They attacked Judah, invaded it and carried off all the goods found in the king's palace, together with his sons and wives. Not a son was left to him except Ahaziah,[a] the youngest.[g]

18After all this, the LORD afflicted Jehoram with an incurable disease of the bowels. 19In the course of time, at the end of the second year, his bowels came out because of the disease, and he died in great pain. His people made no fire in his honor,[h] as they had for his fathers.

20Jehoram was thirty-two years old when he became king, and he reigned in Jerusalem eight years. He passed away, to no one's regret, and was buried[i] in the City of David, but not in the tombs of the kings.

Ahaziah King of Judah

22 The people[j] of Jerusalem[k] made Ahaziah, Jehoram's youngest son, king in his place, since the raiders,[l] who came with the Arabs into the camp, had killed all the older sons. So Ahaziah son of Jehoram king of Judah began to reign.

2Ahaziah was twenty-two[b] years old when he became king, and he reigned in Jerusalem one year. His mother's name was Athaliah, a granddaughter of Omri.

3He too walked[m] in the ways of the house of Ahab,[n] for his mother encouraged him in doing wrong. 4He did evil in the eyes of the LORD, as the house of Ahab had done, for after his father's death they became his advisers, to his undoing. 5He also followed their counsel when he went with Joram[c] son of Ahab king of Israel to war against Hazael king of Aram at Ramoth Gilead.[o] The Arameans wounded Joram; 6so he returned to Jezreel to recover from the wounds they had inflicted on him at Ramoth[d] in his battle with Hazael[p] king of Aram.

Then Ahaziah[e] son of Jehoram king of Judah went down to Jezreel to see Joram son of Ahab because he had been wounded.

7Through Ahaziah's[q] visit to Joram, God brought about Ahaziah's downfall. When Ahaziah arrived, he went out with Joram to meet Jehu son of Nimshi, whom the LORD had anointed to destroy the house of Ahab. 8While Jehu was executing judgment on the house of Ahab,[r] he found the princes of Judah and the sons of Ahaziah's relatives, who had been attending Ahaziah, and he killed them. 9He then went in search of Ahaziah, and his men captured him while he was hiding[s] in Samaria. He was brought to Jehu and put to death. They buried him, for they said, "He was a son of Jehoshaphat, who sought[t] the LORD with all his heart." So there was no one in the house of Ahaziah powerful enough to retain the kingdom.

Athaliah and Joash

10When Athaliah the mother of Ahaziah saw that her son was dead, she proceeded to destroy the whole royal family of the house of Judah. 11But Jehosheba,[f] the daughter of King Jehoram, took Joash son of Ahaziah and stole him away from among the royal princes who were about to be murdered and put him and his nurse in a bedroom. Because Jehosheba,[f] the daughter of King Jehoram and wife of the priest Jehoiada, was Ahaziah's sister, she hid the child from Athaliah so she could not kill him. 12He remained hidden with them at the temple of God for six years while Athaliah ruled the land.

23 In the seventh year Jehoiada showed his strength. He made a covenant with the commanders of units of a hundred: Azariah son of Jeroham, Ishmael son of Jehohanan, Azariah son of Obed, Maaseiah son of Adaiah, and Elishaphat son of Zicri. 2They went throughout Judah and gathered the Levites[u] and the heads of Israelite families from all the towns. When they came to Jerusalem, 3the whole assembly made a covenant[v] with the king at the temple of God.

Jehoiada said to them, "The king's son shall reign, as the LORD promised concerning the descendants of Da-

21:13 [d]ver 4; 1Ki 2:32 **21:15** [e]ver 18-19; Nu 12:10 **21:16** [f]2Ch 17:10-11; 22:1; 26:7 **21:17** [g]2Ki 12:18; 2Ch 22:1; 25:23; Joel 3:5 **21:19** [h]2Ch 16:14 **21:20** [i]2Ch 24:25; 28:27; 33:20; Jer 22:18,28 **22:1** [j]2Ch 33:25; 36:1 [k]2Ch 23:20-21; 26:1 [l]2Ch 21:16-17 **22:3** [m]2Ch 18:1 [n]2Ch 21:6 **22:5** [o]2Ch 18:11,34 **22:6** [p]1Ki 19:15; 2Ki 8:13-15; 9:15 **22:7** [q]2Ki 9:16; 2Ch 10:15 **22:8** [r]2Ki 10:13 **22:9** [s]Jdg 9:5 [t]2Ch 17:4 **23:2** [u]Nu 35:2-5 **23:3** [v]2Ki 11:17

[a]17 Hebrew *Jehoahaz,* a variant of *Ahaziah*
[b]2 Some Septuagint manuscripts and Syriac (see also 2 Kings 8:26); Hebrew *forty-two*
[c]5 Hebrew *Jehoram,* a variant of *Joram;* also in verses 6 and 7
[d]6 Hebrew *Ramah,* a variant of *Ramoth*
[e]6 Some Hebrew manuscripts, Septuagint, Vulgate and Syriac (see also 2 Kings 8:29); most Hebrew manuscripts *Azariah*
[f]11 Hebrew *Jehoshabeath,* a variant of *Jehosheba*

vid.[w] 4Now this is what you are to do:
A third of you priests and Levites who
are going on duty on the Sabbath are to
keep watch at the doors, 5a third of you
at the royal palace and a third at the
Foundation Gate, and all the other
men are to be in the courtyards of the
temple of the LORD. 6No one is to enter
the temple of the LORD except the
priests and Levites on duty; they may
enter because they are consecrated,
but all the other men are to guard[x]
what the LORD has assigned to them.[a]
7The Levites are to station themselves
around the king, each man with his
weapons in his hand. Anyone who enters the temple must be put to death.
Stay close to the king wherever he
goes."
8The Levites and all the men of Judah did just as Jehoiada the priest ordered.[y] Each one took his men—
those who were going on duty on the
Sabbath and those who were going off
duty—for Jehoiada the priest had not
released any of the divisions.[z] 9Then
he gave the commanders of units of a
hundred the spears and the large and
small shields that had belonged to King
David and that were in the temple of
God. 10He stationed all the men, each
with his weapon in his hand, around
the king—near the altar and the temple, from the south side to the north
side of the temple.
11Jehoiada and his sons brought out
the king's son and put the crown on
him; they presented him with a copy[a]
of the covenant and proclaimed him
king. They anointed him and shouted,
"Long live the king!"
12When Athaliah heard the noise of
the people running and cheering the
king, she went to them at the temple of
the LORD. 13She looked, and there was
the king,[b] standing by his pillar[c] at
the entrance. The officers and the
trumpeters were beside the king, and
all the people of the land were rejoicing
and blowing trumpets, and singers
with musical instruments were leading
the praises. Then Athaliah tore her
robes and shouted, "Treason! Treason!"
14Jehoiada the priest sent out the
commanders of units of a hundred,
who were in charge of the troops, and
said to them: "Bring her out between
the ranks[b] and put to the sword anyone who follows her." For the priest
had said, "Do not put her to death at
the temple of the LORD." 15So they
seized her as she reached the entrance
of the Horse Gate[d] on the palace
grounds, and there they put her to
death.
16Jehoiada then made a covenant[e]
that he and the people and the king[c]
would be the LORD's people. 17All the
people went to the temple of Baal and
tore it down. They smashed the altars
and idols and killed[f] Mattan the
priest of Baal in front of the altars.
18Then Jehoiada placed the oversight of the temple of the LORD in the
hands of the priests, who were Levites,[g] to whom David had made assignments in the temple,[h] to present
the burnt offerings of the LORD as written in the Law of Moses, with rejoicing
and singing, as David had ordered.
19He also stationed doorkeepers[i] at
the gates of the LORD's temple so that
no one who was in any way unclean
might enter.
20He took with him the commanders
of hundreds, the nobles, the rulers of
the people and all the people of the
land and brought the king down from
the temple of the LORD. They went into
the palace through the Upper Gate[j]
and seated the king on the royal
throne, 21and all the people of the land
rejoiced. And the city was quiet, because Athaliah had been slain with the
sword.[k]

Joash Repairs the Temple

24 Joash was seven years old when he
became king, and he reigned in Jerusalem forty years. His mother's name
was Zibiah; she was from Beersheba.
2Joash did what was right in the eyes of
the LORD[l] all the years of Jehoiada the
priest. 3Jehoiada chose two wives for
him, and he had sons and daughters.
4Some time later Joash decided to
restore the temple of the LORD. 5He
called together the priests and Levites
and said to them, "Go to the towns of
Judah and collect the money[m] due annually from all Israel,[n] to repair the
temple of your God. Do it now." But
the Levites[o] did not act at once.
6Therefore the king summoned Jehoiada the chief priest and said to him,
"Why haven't you required the Levites
to bring in from Judah and Jerusalem
the tax imposed by Moses the servant
of the LORD and by the assembly of Israel for the Tent of the Testimony?"[p]
7Now the sons of that wicked woman Athaliah had broken into the temple
of God and had used even its sacred
objects for the Baals.
8At the king's command, a chest was
made and placed outside, at the gate of

23:3 [w]2Sa 7:12; 1Ki 2:4; 2Ch 6:16; 7:18; 21:7
23:6 [x]1Ch 23:28-29; Zec 3:7
23:8 [y]2Ki 11:9 [z]1Ch 24:1
23:11 [a]Ex 25:16; Dt 17:18; 1Sa 10:24
23:13 [b]1Ki 1:41 [c]1Ki 7:15
23:15 [d]Ne 3:28; Jer 31:40
23:16 [e]2Ch 29:10; 34:31; Ne 9:38
23:17 [f]Dt 13:6-9
23:18 [g]1Ch 23:28-32; 2Ch 5:5 [h]1Ch 23:6; 25:6
23:19 [i]1Ch 9:22
23:20 [j]2Ki 15:35
23:21 [k]2Ch 22:1
24:2 [l]2Ch 25:2; 26:5
24:5 [m]Ex 30:16; Ne 10:32-33; Mt 17:24 [n]1Ch 11:1 [o]1Ch 26:20
24:6 [p]Ex 30:12-16; Nu 1:50

[a]6 Or *to observe the LORD's command ⌞not to enter⌟*
[b]14 Or *out from the precincts*
[c]16 Or *covenant between ⌞the LORD⌟ and the people and the king that they* (see 2 Kings 11:17)

the temple of the LORD. [9]A proclamation was then issued in Judah and Jerusalem that they should bring to the LORD the tax that Moses the servant of God had required of Israel in the desert. 5 →PG. 679 [10]All the officials and all the people brought their contributions gladly,[q] dropping them into the chest until it was full. [11]Whenever the chest was brought in by the Levites to the king's officials and they saw that there was a large amount of money, the royal secretary and the officer of the chief priest would come and empty the chest and carry it back to its place. They did this regularly and collected a great amount of money. [12]The king and Jehoiada gave it to the men who carried out the work required for the temple of the LORD. They hired[r] masons and carpenters to restore the LORD's temple, and also workers in iron and bronze to repair the temple.

[13]The men in charge of the work were diligent, and the repairs progressed under them. They rebuilt the temple of God according to its original design and reinforced it. [14]When they had finished, they brought the rest of the money to the king and Jehoiada, and with it were made articles for the LORD's temple: articles for the service and for the burnt offerings, and also dishes and other objects of gold and silver. As long as Jehoiada lived, burnt offerings were presented continually in the temple of the LORD.

[15]Now Jehoiada was old and full of years, and he died at the age of a hundred and thirty. [16]He was buried with the kings in the City of David, because of the good he had done in Israel for God and his temple.

The Wickedness of Joash

[17]After the death of Jehoiada, the officials of Judah came and paid homage to the king, and he listened to them. [18]They abandoned[s] the temple of the LORD, the God of their fathers, and worshiped Asherah poles and idols.[t] Because of their guilt, God's anger[u] came upon Judah and Jerusalem. [19]Although the LORD sent prophets to the people to bring them back to him, and though they testified against them, they would not listen.[v]

[20]Then the Spirit[w] of God came upon Zechariah[x] son of Jehoiada the priest. He stood before the people and said, "This is what God says: 'Why do you disobey the LORD's commands? You will not prosper.[y] Because you have forsaken the LORD, he has forsaken[z] you.' "

[21]But they plotted against him, and by order of the king they stoned[a] him to death[b] in the courtyard of the LORD's temple.[c] [22]King Joash did not remember the kindness Zechariah's father Jehoiada had shown him but killed his son, who said as he lay dying, "May the LORD see this and call you to account."[d]

[23]At the turn of the year,[a] the army of Aram marched against Joash; it invaded Judah and Jerusalem and killed all the leaders of the people.[e] They sent all the plunder to their king in Damascus. [24]Although the Aramean army had come with only a few men,[f] the LORD delivered into their hands a much larger army.[g] Because Judah had forsaken the LORD, the God of their fathers, judgment was executed on Joash. [25]When the Arameans withdrew, they left Joash severely wounded. His officials conspired against him for murdering the son of Jehoiada the priest, and they killed him in his bed. So he died and was buried[h] in the City of David, but not in the tombs of the kings.

[26]Those who conspired against him were Zabad,[b] son of Shimeath an Ammonite woman, and Jehozabad, son of Shimrith[c][i] a Moabite woman.[j] [27]The account of his sons, the many prophecies about him, and the record of the restoration of the temple of God are written in the annotations on the book of the kings. And Amaziah his son succeeded him as king.

Amaziah King of Judah

25 Amaziah was twenty-five years old when he became king, and he reigned in Jerusalem twenty-nine years. His mother's name was Jehoaddin[d]; she was from Jerusalem. [2]He did what was right in the eyes of the LORD, but not wholeheartedly.[k] [3]After the kingdom was firmly in his control, he executed the officials who had murdered his father the king. [4]Yet he did not put their sons to death, but acted in accordance with what is written in the Law, in the Book of Moses,[l] where the LORD commanded: "Fathers shall not be put to death for their children, nor children put to death for their fathers; each is to die for his own sins."[e][m]

[5]Amaziah called the people of Judah together and assigned them according to their families to commanders of thousands and commanders of hun-

24:10 [q]Ex 25:2; 1Ch 29:3,6,9
24:12 [r]2Ch 34:11
24:18 [s]ver 4; Jos 24:20; 2Ch 7:19 [t]Ex 34:13; 1Ki 14:23; 2Ch 33:3; Jer 17:2 [u]Jos 22:20; 2Ch 19:2
24:19 [v]Nu 11:29; Jer 7:25; Zec 1:4
24:20 [w]Jdg 3:10; 1Ch 12:18; 2Ch 20:14 [x]Mt 23:35; Lk 11:51 [y]Nu 14:41 [z]Dt 31:17; 2Ch 15:2
24:21 [a]Jos 7:25; Ac 7:58-59 [b]Ne 9:26; Jer 26:21 [c]Jer 20:2; Mt 23:35
24:22 [d]Ge 9:5
24:23 [e]2Ki 12:17-18
24:24 [f]2Ch 14:9; 16:8; 20:2,12 [g]Lev 26:23-25; Dt 28:25
24:25 [h]2Ch 21:20
24:26 [i]2Ki 12:21 [j]Ru 1:4
25:2 [k]ver 14; 1Ki 8:61; 2Ch 24:2
25:4 [l]Dt 28:61 [m]Nu 26:11; Dt 24:16

[a]23 Probably in the spring [b]26 A variant of *Jozabad* [c]26 A variant of *Shomer*
[d]1 Hebrew *Jehoaddan,* a variant of *Jehoaddin*
[e]4 Deut. 24:16

dreds for all Judah and Benjamin. He then mustered[n] those twenty years old[o] or more and found that there were three hundred thousand men ready for military service,[p] able to handle the spear and shield. 6He also hired a hundred thousand fighting men from Israel for a hundred talents[a] of silver.

7But a man of God came to him and said, "O king, these troops from Israel[q] must not march with you, for the LORD is not with Israel—not with any of the people of Ephraim. 8Even if you go and fight courageously in battle, God will overthrow you before the enemy, for God has the power to help or to overthrow."[r]

9Amaziah asked the man of God, "But what about the hundred talents I paid for these Israelite troops?"

The man of God replied, "The LORD can give you much more than that."[s]

10So Amaziah dismissed the troops who had come to him from Ephraim and sent them home. They were furious with Judah and left for home in a great rage.[t]

11Amaziah then marshaled his strength and led his army to the Valley of Salt, where he killed ten thousand men of Seir. 12The army of Judah also captured ten thousand men alive, took them to the top of a cliff and threw them down so that all were dashed to pieces.[u]

13Meanwhile the troops that Amaziah had sent back and had not allowed to take part in the war raided Judean towns from Samaria to Beth Horon. They killed three thousand people and carried off great quantities of plunder.

14When Amaziah returned from slaughtering the Edomites, he brought back the gods of the people of Seir. He set them up as his own gods,[v] bowed down to them and burned sacrifices to them. 15The anger of the LORD burned against Amaziah, and he sent a prophet to him, who said, "Why do you consult this people's gods, which could not save[w] their own people from your hand?"

16While he was still speaking, the king said to him, "Have we appointed you an adviser to the king? Stop! Why be struck down?"

So the prophet stopped but said, "I know that God has determined to destroy you, because you have done this and have not listened to my counsel."

17After Amaziah king of Judah consulted his advisers, he sent this challenge to Jehoash[b] son of Jehoahaz, the son of Jehu, king of Israel: "Come, meet me face to face."

25:5 [n]2Sa 24:2 [o]Ex 30:14 [p]Nu 1:3; 1Ch 21:1; 2Ch 17:14-19
25:7 [q]2Ch 16:2-9; 19:1-3
25:8 [r]2Ch 14:11; 20:6
25:9 [s]Dt 8:18; Pr 10:22
25:10 [t]ver 13
25:12 [u]Ps 141:6; Ob 1:3
25:14 [v]Ex 20:3; 2Ch 28:23; Isa 44:15
25:15 [w]Ps 96:5; Isa 36:20

18But Jehoash king of Israel replied to Amaziah king of Judah: "A thistle[x] in Lebanon sent a message to a cedar in Lebanon, 'Give your daughter to my son in marriage.' Then a wild beast in Lebanon came along and trampled the thistle underfoot. 19You say to yourself that you have defeated Edom, and now you are arrogant and proud. But stay at home! Why ask for trouble and cause your own downfall and that of Judah also?"

20Amaziah, however, would not listen, for God so worked that he might hand them over to ⌞Jehoash⌟, because they sought the gods of Edom.[y] 21So Jehoash king of Israel attacked. He and Amaziah king of Judah faced each other at Beth Shemesh in Judah. 22Judah was routed by Israel, and every man fled to his home. 23Jehoash king of Israel captured Amaziah king of Judah, the son of Joash, the son of Ahaziah,[c] at Beth Shemesh. Then Jehoash brought him to Jerusalem and broke down the wall of Jerusalem from the Ephraim Gate[z] to the Corner Gate[a]—a section about six hundred feet[d] long. 24He took all the gold and silver and all the articles found in the temple of God that had been in the care of Obed-Edom,[b] together with the palace treasures and the hostages, and returned to Samaria.

25Amaziah son of Joash king of Judah lived for fifteen years after the death of Jehoash son of Jehoahaz king of Israel. 26As for the other events of Amaziah's reign, from beginning to end, are they not written in the book of the kings of Judah and Israel? 27From the time that Amaziah turned away from following the LORD, they conspired against him in Jerusalem and he fled to Lachish[c], but they sent men after him to Lachish and killed him there. 28He was brought back by horse and was buried with his fathers in the City of Judah.

Uzziah King of Judah

26 Then all the people of Judah[d] took Uzziah,[e] who was sixteen years old, and made him king in place of his father Amaziah. 2He was the one who rebuilt Elath and restored it to Judah after Amaziah rested with his fathers.

3Uzziah was sixteen years old when he became king, and he reigned in Jerusalem fifty-two years. His mother's name was Jecoliah; she was from Jeru-

2 →PG. 522

25:18 [x]Jdg 9:8-15
25:20 [y]1Ki 12:15; 2Ch 10:15; 22:7
25:23 [z]2Ki 14:13; Ne 8:16; 12:39 [a]2Ch 26:9; Jer 31:38
25:24 [b]1Ch 26:15
25:27 [c]Jos 10:3
26:1 [d]2Ch 22:1

[a]*6* That is, about 3 3/4 tons (about 3.4 metric tons); also in verse 9 [b]*17* Hebrew *Joash,* a variant of *Jehoash*; also in verses 18, 21, 23 and 25 [c]*23* Hebrew *Jehoahaz,* a variant of *Ahaziah* [d]*23* Hebrew *four hundred cubits* (about 180 meters) [e]*1* Also called *Azariah*

salem. 4He did what was right in the eyes of the LORD, just as his father Amaziah had done. 5He sought God during the days of Zechariah, who instructed him in the fear[a] of God.[e] As long as he sought the LORD, God gave him success.[f]

6He went to war against the Philistines[g] and broke down the walls of Gath, Jabneh and Ashdod.[h] He then rebuilt towns near Ashdod and elsewhere among the Philistines. 7God helped him against the Philistines and against the Arabs[i] who lived in Gur Baal and against the Meunites.[j] 8The Ammonites[k] brought tribute to Uzziah, and his fame spread as far as the border of Egypt, because he had become very powerful.

9Uzziah built towers in Jerusalem at the Corner Gate,[l] at the Valley Gate[m] and at the angle of the wall, and he fortified them. 10He also built towers in the desert and dug many cisterns, because he had much livestock in the foothills and in the plain. He had people working his fields and vineyards in the hills and in the fertile lands, for he loved the soil.

11Uzziah had a well-trained army, ready to go out by divisions according to their numbers as mustered by Jeiel the secretary and Maaseiah the officer under the direction of Hananiah, one of the royal officials. 12The total number of family leaders over the fighting men was 2,600. 13Under their command was an army of 307,500 men trained for war, a powerful force to support the king against his enemies. 14Uzziah provided shields, spears, helmets, coats of armor, bows and slingstones for the entire army.[n] 15In Jerusalem he made machines designed by skillful men for use on the towers and on the corner defenses to shoot arrows and hurl large stones. His fame spread far and wide, for he was greatly helped until he became powerful.

16But after Uzziah became powerful, his pride[o] led to his downfall.[p] He was unfaithful[q] to the LORD his God, and entered the temple of the LORD to burn incense[r] on the altar of incense. 17Azariah[s] the priest with eighty other courageous priests of the LORD followed him in. 18They confronted him and said, "It is not right for you, Uzziah, to burn incense to the LORD. That is for the priests,[t] the descendants[u] of Aaron,[v] who have been consecrated to burn incense.[w] Leave the sanctuary, for you have been unfaithful; and you will not be honored by the LORD God."

19Uzziah, who had a censer in his hand ready to burn incense, became angry. While he was raging at the priests in their presence before the incense altar in the LORD's temple, leprosy[b][x] broke out on his forehead. 20When Azariah the chief priest and all the other priests looked at him, they saw that he had leprosy on his forehead, so they hurried him out. Indeed, he himself was eager to leave, because the LORD had afflicted him.

21King Uzziah had leprosy until the day he died. He lived in a separate house[c][y]—leprous, and excluded from the temple of the LORD. Jotham his son had charge of the palace and governed the people of the land.

22The other events of Uzziah's reign, from beginning to end, are recorded by the prophet Isaiah[z] son of Amoz. 23Uzziah[a] rested with his fathers and was buried near them in a field for burial that belonged to the kings, for people said, "He had leprosy." And Jotham his son succeeded him as king.[b]

Jotham King of Judah

27 Jotham[c] was twenty-five years old when he became king, and he reigned in Jerusalem sixteen years. His mother's name was Jerusha daughter of Zadok. 2He did what was right in the eyes of the LORD, just as his father Uzziah had done, but unlike him he did not enter the temple of the LORD. The people, however, continued their corrupt practices. 3Jotham rebuilt the Upper Gate of the temple of the LORD and did extensive work on the wall at the hill of Ophel.[d] 4He built towns in the Judean hills and forts and towers in the wooded areas.

5Jotham made war on the king of the Ammonites[e] and conquered them. That year the Ammonites paid him a hundred talents[d] of silver, ten thousand cors[e] of wheat and ten thousand cors of barley. The Ammonites brought him the same amount also in the second and third years.

6Jotham grew powerful[f] because he walked steadfastly before the LORD his God.

7The other events in Jotham's reign, including all his wars and the other things he did, are written in the book of the kings of Israel and Judah. 8He was twenty-five years old when he became

26:5 [e]2Ch 15:2; 24:2; Da 1:17 [f]2Ch 27:6
26:6 [g]Isa 2:6; 11:14; 14:29; Jer 25:20 [h]Am 1:8; 3:9
26:7 [i]2Ch 21:16 [j]2Ch 20:1
26:8 [k]Ge 19:38; 2Ch 17:11
26:9 [l]2Ki 14:13; 2Ch 25:23 [m]Ne 2:13; 3:13
26:14 [n]Jer 46:4
26:16 [o]2Ki 14:10 [p]Dt 32:15; 2Ch 25:19 [q]1Ch 5:25 [r]2Ki 16:12
26:17 [s]1Ki 4:2; 1Ch 6:10
26:18 [t]Nu 16:39 [u]Nu 18:1-7 [v]Ex 30:7 [w]1Ch 6:49
26:19 [x]Nu 12:10; 2Ki 5:25-27
26:21 [y]Ex 4:6; Lev 13:46; 14:8; Nu 5:2; 19:12
26:22 [z]2Ki 15:1; Isa 1:1; 6:1
26:23 [a]Isa 1:1; 6:1 [b]2Ki 14:21; 15:7; Am 1:1
27:1 [c]2Ki 15:5,32; 1Ch 3:12
27:3 [d]2Ch 33:14; Ne 3:26
27:5 [e]Ge 19:38
27:6 [f]2Ch 26:5

[a] *5* Many Hebrew manuscripts, Septuagint and Syriac; other Hebrew manuscripts *vision*
[b] *19* The Hebrew word was used for various diseases affecting the skin—not necessarily leprosy; also in verses 20, 21 and 23.
[c] *21* Or *in a house where he was relieved of responsibilities*
[d] *5* That is, about 3 3/4 tons (about 3.4 metric tons)
[e] *5* That is, probably about 62,000 bushels (about 2,200 kiloliters)

king, and he reigned in Jerusalem sixteen years. 9 Jotham rested with his fathers and was buried in the City of David. And Ahaz his son succeeded him
as king.

Ahaz King of Judah

28 Ahaz[g] was twenty years old when
he became king, and he reigned in
Jerusalem sixteen years. Unlike David
his father, he did not do what was right
in the eyes of the LORD. 2 He walked in
the ways of the kings of Israel and also
made cast idols[h] for worshiping the
Baals. 3 He burned sacrifices in the Valley of Ben Hinnom[i] and sacrificed his
sons[j] in the fire, following the detestable[k] ways of the nations the LORD
had driven out before the Israelites.
4 He offered sacrifices and burned incense at the high places, on the hilltops
and under every spreading tree.
5 Therefore the LORD his God handed
him over to the king of Aram.[l] The
Arameans defeated him and took
many of his people as prisoners and
brought them to Damascus.

He was also given into the hands of
the king of Israel, who inflicted heavy
casualties on him. 6 In one day Pekah[m]
son of Remaliah killed a hundred and
twenty thousand soldiers in Judah[n]—
because Judah had forsaken the LORD,
the God of their fathers. 7 Zicri, an
Ephraimite warrior, killed Maaseiah
the king's son, Azrikam the officer in
charge of the palace, and Elkanah, second to the king. 8 The Israelites took
captive from their kinsmen[o] two hundred thousand wives, sons and daughters. They also took a great deal of
plunder, which they carried back to Samaria.[p]

9 But a prophet of the LORD named
Oded was there, and he went out to
meet the army when it returned to Samaria. He said to them, "Because the
LORD, the God of your fathers, was angry[q] with Judah, he gave them into
your hand. But you have slaughtered
them in a rage that reaches to heav-
en.[r] 10 And now you intend to make
the men and women of Judah and Jerusalem your slaves.[s] But aren't you
also guilty of sins against the LORD your
God? 11 Now listen to me! Send back
your fellow countrymen you have tak-
en as prisoners, for the LORD's fierce
anger rests on you.[t]"

12 Then some of the leaders in
Ephraim—Azariah son of Jehohanan,
Berekiah son of Meshillemoth, Jehizki-
ah son of Shallum, and Amasa son of
Hadlai—confronted those who were
arriving from the war. 13 "You must not
bring those prisoners here," they said,
"or we will be guilty before the LORD.
Do you intend to add to our sin and
guilt? For our guilt is already great, and
his fierce anger rests on Israel."

14 So the soldiers gave up the prisoners and plunder in the presence of the
officials and all the assembly. 15 The
men designated by name took the prisoners, and from the plunder they
clothed all who were naked. They provided them with clothes and sandals,
food and drink,[u] and healing balm. All
those who were weak they put on donkeys. So they took them back to their
fellow countrymen at Jericho, the City
of Palms,[v] and returned to Samaria.

16 At that time King Ahaz sent to
the king**a** of Assyria[w] for help. 17 The
Edomites[x] had again come and attacked Judah and carried away prisoners,[y] 18 while the Philistines[z] had
raided towns in the foothills and in the
Negev of Judah. They captured and occupied Beth Shemesh, Aijalon[a] and
Gederoth, as well as Soco, Timnah and
Gimzo, with their surrounding villages.
19 The LORD had humbled Judah because of Ahaz king of Israel,**b** for he
had promoted wickedness in Judah
and had been most unfaithful[b] to the
LORD. 20 Tiglath-Pileser**c**[c] king of Assyria came to him, but he gave him
trouble instead of help.[d] 21 Ahaz took
some of the things from the temple of
the LORD and from the royal palace and
from the princes and presented them
to the king of Assyria, but that did not
help him.

22 In his time of trouble King Ahaz
became even more unfaithful[e] to the
LORD. 23 He offered sacrifices to the
gods[f] of Damascus, who had defeated
him; for he thought, "Since the gods of
the kings of Aram have helped them, I
will sacrifice to them so they will help
me."[g] But they were his downfall and
the downfall of all Israel.

24 Ahaz gathered together the furnishings from the temple of God[h] and
took them away.**d** He shut the doors[i]
of the LORD's temple and set up altars[j]
at every street corner in Jerusalem. 25 In
every town in Judah he built high
places to burn sacrifices to other gods
and provoked the LORD, the God of his
fathers, to anger.

26 The other events of his reign and
all his ways, from beginning to end, are
written in the book of the kings of Ju-

28:1 [g]1Ch 3:13; Isa 1:1
28:2 [h]Ex 34:17; 2Ch 22:3
28:3 [i]Jos 15:8; 2Ki 23:10 [j]Lev 18:21; 2Ki 3:27; 2Ch 33:6; Eze 20:26 [k]Dt 18:9; 2Ch 33:2
28:5 [l]Isa 7:1
28:6 [m]2Ki 15:25,27 [n]ver 8; Isa 9:21; 11:13
28:8 [o]Dt 28:25-41; 2Ch 11:4 [p]2Ch 29:9
28:9 [q]2Ch 25:15; Isa 10:6; 47:6; Zec 1:15 [r]Ezr 9:6; Rev 18:5
28:10 [s]Lev 25:39-46
28:11 [t]2Ch 11:4; Jas 2:13
28:15 [u]2Ki 6:22; Pr 25:21-22 [v]Dt 34:3; Jdg 1:16
28:16 [w]2Ki 16:7
28:17 [x]Ps 137:7; Isa 34:5 [y]2Ch 29:9
28:18 [z]Eze 16:27,57 [a]Jos 10:12
28:19 [b]2Ch 21:2
28:20 [c]2Ki 15:29; 1Ch 5:6 [d]2Ki 16:7
28:22 [e]Jer 5:3
28:23 [f]2Ch 25:14 [g]Jer 44:17-18
28:24 [h]2Ki 16:18 [i]2Ch 29:7 [j]2Ch 30:14

a *16* One Hebrew manuscript, Septuagint and Vulgate (see also 2 Kings 16:7); most Hebrew manuscripts *kings* **b** *19* That is, Judah, as frequently in 2 Chronicles **c** *20* Hebrew *Tilgath-Pilneser*, a variant of *Tiglath-Pileser*
d *24* Or *and cut them up*

dah and Israel. 27Ahaz rested[k] with his fathers and was buried[l] in the city of Jerusalem, but he was not placed in the tombs of the kings of Israel. And Hezekiah his son succeeded him as king.

Hezekiah Purifies the Temple

29 Hezekiah[m] was twenty-five years old when he became king, and he reigned in Jerusalem twenty-nine years. His mother's name was Abijah daughter of Zechariah. 2He did what was right in the eyes of the LORD, just as his father David[n] had done.

3In the first month of the first year of his reign, he opened the doors of the temple of the LORD and repaired[o] them. 4He brought in the priests and the Levites, assembled them in the square on the east side 5and said: "Listen to me, Levites! Consecrate[p] yourselves now and consecrate the temple of the LORD, the God of your fathers. Remove all defilement from the sanctuary. 6Our fathers[q] were unfaithful;[r] they did evil in the eyes of the LORD our God and forsook him. They turned their faces away from the LORD's dwelling place and turned their backs on him. 7They also shut the doors of the portico and put out the lamps. They did not burn incense or present any burnt offerings at the sanctuary to the God of Israel. 8Therefore, the anger of the LORD has fallen on Judah and Jerusalem; he has made them an object of dread and horror[s] and scorn,[t] as you can see with your own eyes. 9This is why our fathers have fallen by the sword and why our sons and daughters and our wives are in captivity.[u] 10Now I intend to make a covenant[v] with the LORD, the God of Israel, so that his fierce anger will turn away from us. 11My sons, do not be negligent now, for the LORD has chosen you to stand before him and serve him,[w] to minister[x] before him and to burn incense."

12Then these Levites[y] set to work:
from the Kohathites,
Mahath son of Amasai and Joel son of Azariah;
from the Merarites,
Kish son of Abdi and Azariah son of Jehallelel;
from the Gershonites,
Joah son of Zimmah and Eden[z] son of Joah;
13from the descendants of Elizaphan,
Shimri and Jeiel;
from the descendants of Asaph,[a]
Zechariah and Mattaniah;
14from the descendants of Heman,
Jehiel and Shimei;
from the descendants of Jeduthun,
Shemaiah and Uzziel.

15When they had assembled their brothers and consecrated themselves, they went in to purify[b] the temple of the LORD, as the king had ordered, following the word of the LORD. 16The priests went into the sanctuary of the LORD to purify it. They brought out to the courtyard of the LORD's temple everything unclean that they found in the temple of the LORD. The Levites took it and carried it out to the Kidron Valley.[c] 17They began the consecration on the first day of the first month, and by the eighth day of the month they reached the portico of the LORD. For eight more days they consecrated the temple of the LORD itself, finishing on the sixteenth day of the first month.

18Then they went in to King Hezekiah and reported: "We have purified the entire temple of the LORD, the altar of burnt offering with all its utensils, and the table for setting out the consecrated bread, with all its articles. 19We have prepared and consecrated all the articles[d] that King Ahaz removed in his unfaithfulness while he was king. They are now in front of the LORD's altar."

20Early the next morning King Hezekiah gathered the city officials together and went up to the temple of the LORD. 21They brought seven bulls, seven rams, seven male lambs and seven male goats as a sin offering[e] for the kingdom, for the sanctuary and for Judah. The king commanded the priests, the descendants of Aaron, to offer these on the altar of the LORD. 22So they slaughtered the bulls, and the priests took the blood and sprinkled it on the altar; next they slaughtered the rams and sprinkled their blood on the altar; then they slaughtered the lambs and sprinkled their blood[f] on the altar. 23The goats for the sin offering were brought before the king and the assembly, and they laid their hands[g] on them. 24The priests then slaughtered the goats and presented their blood on the altar for a sin offering to atone[h] for all Israel, because the king had ordered the burnt offering and the sin offering for all Israel.

25He stationed the Levites in the temple of the LORD with cymbals, harps and lyres in the way prescribed by David[i] and Gad[j] the king's seer and Nathan the prophet; this was commanded by the LORD through his prophets. 26So the Levites stood ready with David's instruments,[k] and the priests with their trumpets.[l]

27Hezekiah gave the order to sacri-

28:27 [k]Isa 14:28-32 [l]2Ch 21:20; 24:25
29:1 [m]1Ch 3:13
29:2 [n]2Ch 28:1; 34:2
29:3 [o]2Ch 28:24
29:5 [p]2Ch 35:6
29:6 [q]Ps 106:6-47; Jer 2:27 [r]1Ch 5:25; Eze 8:16
29:8 [s]Dt 28:25; 2Ch 24:18 [t]Jer 18:16; 19:8; 25:9,18
29:9 [u]2Ch 28:5-8, 17
29:10 [v]2Ch 15:12; 23:16
29:11 [w]Nu 3:6; 8:6, 14 [x]1Ch 15:2
29:12 [y]Nu 3:17-20 [z]2Ch 31:15
29:13 [a]1Ch 6:39
29:15 [b]ver 5; 1Ch 23:28; 2Ch 30:12
29:16 [c]2Sa 15:23
29:19 [d]2Ch 28:24
29:21 [e]Lev 4:13-14
29:22 [f]Lev 4:18
29:23 [g]Lev 4:15
29:24 [h]Ex 29:36; Lev 4:26
29:25 [i]1Ch 25:6; 2Ch 8:14 [j]1Sa 22:5; 2Sa 24:11
29:26 [k]1Ch 15:16 [l]1Ch 15:24; 23:5; 2Ch 5:12

fice the burnt offering on the altar. As the offering began, singing to the LORD began also, accompanied by trumpets and the instruments[m] of David king of Israel. 28The whole assembly bowed in worship, while the singers sang and the trumpeters played. All this continued until the sacrifice of the burnt offering was completed.

29When the offerings were finished, the king and everyone present with him knelt down and worshiped.[n] 30King Hezekiah and his officials ordered the Levites to praise the LORD with the words of David and of Asaph the seer. So they sang praises with gladness and bowed their heads and worshiped.

31Then Hezekiah said, "You have now dedicated yourselves to the LORD. Come and bring sacrifices[o] and thank offerings to the temple of the LORD." So the assembly brought sacrifices and thank offerings, and all whose hearts were willing[p] brought burnt offerings.

32The number of burnt offerings the assembly brought was seventy bulls, a hundred rams and two hundred male lambs—all of them for burnt offerings to the LORD. 33The animals consecrated as sacrifices amounted to six hundred bulls and three thousand sheep and goats. 34The priests, however, were too few to skin all the burnt offerings;[q] so their kinsmen the Levites helped them until the task was finished and until other priests had been consecrated,[r] for the Levites had been more conscientious in consecrating themselves than the priests had been. 35There were burnt offerings in abundance, together with the fat[s] of the fellowship offerings[a][t] and the drink offerings[u] that accompanied the burnt offerings.

So the service of the temple of the LORD was reestablished. 36Hezekiah and all the people rejoiced at what God had brought about for his people, because it was done so quickly.

Hezekiah Celebrates the Passover

30 Hezekiah sent word to all Israel and Judah and also wrote letters to Ephraim and Manasseh,[v] inviting them to come to the temple of the LORD in Jerusalem and celebrate the Passover[w] to the LORD, the God of Israel. 2The king and his officials and the whole assembly in Jerusalem decided to celebrate[x] the Passover in the second month. 3They had not been able to celebrate it at the regular time because not enough priests had consecrated[y] themselves and the people had not assembled in Jerusalem. 4The plan seemed right both to the king and to the whole assembly. 5They decided to send a proclamation throughout Israel, from Beersheba to Dan,[z] calling the people to come to Jerusalem and celebrate the Passover to the LORD, the God of Israel. It had not been celebrated in large numbers according to what was written.

6At the king's command, couriers went throughout Israel and Judah with letters from the king and from his officials, which read:

> "People of Israel, return to the LORD, the God of Abraham, Isaac and Israel, that he may return to you who are left, who have escaped from the hand of the kings of Assyria. 7Do not be like your fathers[a] and brothers, who were unfaithful to the LORD, the God of their fathers, so that he made them an object of horror,[b] as you see. 8Do not be stiff-necked,[c] as your fathers were; submit to the LORD. Come to the sanctuary, which he has consecrated forever. Serve the LORD your God, so that his fierce anger[d] will turn away from you. 9If you return[e] to the LORD, then your brothers and your children will be shown compassion[f] by their captors and will come back to this land, for the LORD your God is gracious and compassionate.[g] He will not turn his face from you if you return to him."

10The couriers went from town to town in Ephraim and Manasseh, as far as Zebulun, but the people scorned and ridiculed[h] them. 11Nevertheless, some men of Asher, Manasseh and Zebulun humbled themselves and went to Jerusalem.[i] 12Also in Judah the hand of God was on the people to give them unity[j] of mind to carry out what the king and his officials had ordered, following the word of the LORD.

13A very large crowd of people assembled in Jerusalem to celebrate the Feast of Unleavened Bread[k] in the second month. 14They removed the altars[l] in Jerusalem and cleared away the incense altars and threw them into the Kidron Valley.[m]

15They slaughtered the Passover lamb on the fourteenth day of the second month. The priests and the Levites were ashamed and consecrated[n] themselves and brought burnt offerings to the temple of the LORD. 16Then they took up their regular positions[o]

29:27 [m]2Ch 23:18
29:29 [n]2Ch 20:18
29:31 [o]Heb 13:15-16 [p]Ex 25:2; 35:22
29:34 [q]2Ch 35:11 [r]2Ch 30:3,15
29:35 [s]Ex 29:13; Lev 3:16 [t]Lev 7:11-21 [u]Nu 15:5-10
30:1 [v]Ge 41:52 [w]Ex 12:11; Nu 28:16
30:2 [x]Nu 9:10
30:3 [y]2Ch 29:34
30:5 [z]Jdg 20:1
30:7 [a]Ps 78:8,57; 106:6; Eze 20:18 [b]2Ch 29:8
30:8 [c]Ex 32:9 [d]Nu 25:4; 2Ch 29:10
30:9 [e]Dt 30:2-5; Isa 1:16; 55:7 [f]1Ki 8:50; Ps 106:46 [g]Ex 34:6-7; Dt 4:31; Mic 7:18
30:10 [h]2Ch 36:16
30:11 [i]ver 25
30:12 [j]Jer 32:39; Eze 11:19; Php 2:13
30:13 [k]Nu 28:16
30:14 [l]2Ch 28:24 [m]2Sa 15:23
30:15 [n]2Ch 29:34
30:16 [o]2Ch 35:10

[a] 35 Traditionally *peace offerings*

as prescribed in the Law of Moses the
man of God. The priests sprinkled the
blood handed to them by the Levites.
17Since many in the crowd had not
consecrated themselves, the Levites
had to kill[p] the Passover lambs for all
those who were not ceremonially clean
and could not consecrate ⌊their lambs⌋
to the LORD. 18Although most of the
many people who came from Ephraim,
Manasseh, Issachar and Zebulun had
not purified themselves,[q] yet they ate
the Passover, contrary to what was
written. But Hezekiah prayed for them,
saying, "May the LORD, who is good,
pardon everyone 19who sets his heart
on seeking God—the LORD, the God of
his fathers—even if he is not clean according to the rules of the sanctuary."
20And the LORD heard[r] Hezekiah and
healed[s] the people.[t]

21The Israelites who were present in
Jerusalem celebrated the Feast of Unleavened Bread[u] for seven days with
great rejoicing, while the Levites and
priests sang to the LORD every day, accompanied by the LORD's instruments
of praise.[a]

22Hezekiah spoke encouragingly to
all the Levites, who showed good understanding of the service of the LORD.
For the seven days they ate their assigned portion and offered fellowship
offerings[b] and praised the LORD, the
God of their fathers.

23The whole assembly then agreed
to celebrate[v] the festival seven more
days; so for another seven days they
celebrated joyfully. 24Hezekiah king of
Judah provided[w] a thousand bulls and
seven thousand sheep and goats for
the assembly, and the officials provided them with a thousand bulls and ten
thousand sheep and goats. A great
number of priests consecrated themselves. 25The entire assembly of Judah
rejoiced, along with the priests and Levites and all who had assembled from
Israel[x], including the aliens who had
come from Israel and those who lived
in Judah. 26There was great joy in Jerusalem, for since the days of Solomon[y]
son of David king of Israel there had
been nothing like this in Jerusalem.
27The priests and the Levites stood to
bless[z] the people, and God heard
them, for their prayer reached heaven,
his holy dwelling place.

31 When all this had ended, the Israelites who were there went out to the
towns of Judah, smashed the sacred
stones and cut down[a] the Asherah
poles. They destroyed the high places
and the altars throughout Judah and
Benjamin and in Ephraim and Manasseh. After they had destroyed all of
them, the Israelites returned to their
own towns and to their own property.

Contributions for Worship

2Hezekiah[b] assigned the priests
and Levites to divisions[c]—each of
them according to their duties as
priests or Levites—to offer burnt offerings and fellowship offerings,[b] to minister,[d] to give thanks and to sing
praises[e] at the gates of the LORD's
dwelling.[f] 3The king contributed[g]
from his own possessions for the
morning and evening burnt offerings
and for the burnt offerings on the Sabbaths, New Moons and appointed
feasts as written in the Law of the
LORD.[h] 4He ordered the people living
in Jerusalem to give the portion[i] due
the priests and Levites so they could
devote themselves to the Law of the
LORD. 5As soon as the order went out,
the Israelites generously gave the firstfruits[j] of their grain, new wine,[k] oil
and honey and all that the fields produced. They brought a great amount, a
tithe of everything. 6The men of Israel
and Judah who lived in the towns of
Judah also brought a tithe[l] of their
herds and flocks and a tithe of the holy
things dedicated to the LORD their God,
and they piled them in heaps.[m] 7They
began doing this in the third month
and finished in the seventh month.[n]
8When Hezekiah and his officials came
and saw the heaps, they praised the
LORD and blessed[o] his people Israel.

9Hezekiah asked the priests and Levites about the heaps; 10and Azariah
the chief priest, from the family of Zadok,[p] answered, "Since the people began to bring their contributions to the
temple of the LORD, we have had
enough to eat and plenty to spare, because the LORD has blessed his people,
and this great amount is left over."[q]

11Hezekiah gave orders to prepare
storerooms in the temple of the LORD,
and this was done. 12Then they faithfully brought in the contributions,
tithes and dedicated gifts. Conaniah,[r]
a Levite, was in charge of these things,
and his brother Shimei was next in
rank. 13Jehiel, Azaziah, Nahath, Asahel,
Jerimoth, Jozabad,[s] Eliel, Ismakiah,
Mahath and Benaiah were supervisors
under Conaniah and Shimei his brother, by appointment of King Hezekiah
and Azariah the official in charge of the
temple of God.

14Kore son of Imnah the Levite,
keeper of the East Gate, was in charge

30:17 [p]2Ch 29:34
30:18 [q]Ex 12:43-49; Nu 9:6-10
30:20 [r]2Ch 6:20 [s]2Ch 7:14; Mal 4:2 [t]Jas 5:16
30:21 [u]Ex 12:15,17; 13:6
30:23 [v]1Ki 8:65; 2Ch 7:9
30:24 [w]1Ki 8:5; 2Ch 29:34; 35:7; Ezr 6:17; 8:35
30:25 [x]ver 11
30:26 [y]2Ch 7:8
30:27 [z]Ex 39:43; Nu 6:23; Dt 26:15; 2Ch 23:18; Ps 68:5
31:1 [a]2Ki 18:4; 2Ch 32:12; Isa 36:7
31:2 [b]2Ch 29:9 [c]1Ch 24:1 [d]1Ch 15:2 [e]Ps 7:17; 9:2; 47:6; 71:22 [f]1Ch 23:28-32
31:3 [g]1Ch 29:3; 2Ch 35:7; Eze 45:17 [h]Nu 28:1-29:40
31:4 [i]Nu 18:8; Dt 18:8; Ne 13:10; Mal 2:7
31:5 [j]Nu 18:12,24; Ne 13:12; Eze 44:30 [k]Dt 12:17
31:6 [l]Lev 27:30; Ne 13:10-12 [m]Dt 14:28; Ru 3:7
31:7 [n]Ex 23:16
31:8 [o]Ps 144:13-15
31:10 [p]2Sa 8:17 [q]Ex 36:5; Eze 44:30; Mal 3:10-12
31:12 [r]2Ch 35:9
31:13 [s]2Ch 35:9

[a] 21 Or *priests praised the LORD every day with resounding instruments belonging to the LORD*
[b] 22,2 Traditionally *peace offerings*

of the freewill offerings given to God, distributing the contributions made to the LORD and also the consecrated gifts. [15]Eden,[t] Miniamin, Jeshua, Shemaiah, Amariah and Shecaniah assisted him faithfully in the towns[u] of the priests, distributing to their fellow priests according to their divisions, old and young alike.

[16]In addition, they distributed to the males three years old or more whose names were in the genealogical records[v]—all who would enter the temple of the LORD to perform the daily duties of their various tasks, according to their responsibilities and their divisions. [17]And they distributed to the priests enrolled by their families in the genealogical records and likewise to the Levites twenty years old or more, according to their responsibilities and their divisions. [18]They included all the little ones, the wives, and the sons and daughters of the whole community listed in these genealogical records. For they were faithful in consecrating themselves.

[19]As for the priests, the descendants of Aaron, who lived on the farm lands around their towns or in any other towns,[w] men were designated by name to distribute portions to every male among them and to all who were recorded in the genealogies of the Levites.

[20]This is what Hezekiah did throughout Judah, doing what was good and right and faithful[x] before the LORD his God. [21]In everything that he undertook in the service of God's temple and in obedience to the law and the commands, he sought his God and worked wholeheartedly. And so he prospered.[y]

Sennacherib Threatens Jerusalem

32 After all that Hezekiah had so faithfully done, Sennacherib[z] king of Assyria came and invaded Judah. He laid siege to the fortified cities, thinking to conquer them for himself. [2]When Hezekiah saw that Sennacherib had come and that he intended to make war on Jerusalem,[a] [3]he consulted with his officials and military staff about blocking off the water from the springs outside the city, and they helped him. [4]A large force of men assembled, and they blocked all the springs[b] and the stream that flowed through the land. "Why should the kings[a] of Assyria come and find plenty of water?" they said. [5]Then he worked hard repairing all the broken sections of the wall[c] and building towers on it. He built another wall outside that one and reinforced the supporting terraces[b][d] of the City of David. He also made large numbers of weapons[e] and shields.

[6]He appointed military officers over the people and assembled them before him in the square at the city gate and encouraged them with these words: [7]"Be strong and courageous.[f] Do not be afraid or discouraged[g] because of the king of Assyria and the vast army with him, for there is a greater power with us than with him.[h] [8]With him is only the arm of flesh,[i] but with us[j] is the LORD our God to help us and to fight our battles."[k] And the people gained confidence from what Hezekiah the king of Judah said.

[9]Later, when Sennacherib king of Assyria and all his forces were laying siege to Lachish,[l] he sent his officers to Jerusalem with this message for Hezekiah king of Judah and for all the people of Judah who were there:

> [10]"This is what Sennacherib king of Assyria says: On what are you basing your confidence,[m] that you remain in Jerusalem under siege? [11]When Hezekiah says, 'The LORD our God will save us from the hand of the king of Assyria,' he is misleading[n] you, to let you die of hunger and thirst. [12]Did not Hezekiah himself remove this god's high places and altars, saying to Judah and Jerusalem, 'You must worship before one altar[o] and burn sacrifices on it'?
>
> [13]"Do you not know what I and my fathers have done to all the peoples of the other lands? Were the gods of those nations ever able to deliver their land from my hand?[p] [14]Who of all the gods of these nations that my fathers destroyed has been able to save his people from me? How then can your god deliver you from my hand? [15]Now do not let Hezekiah deceive[q] you and mislead you like this. Do not believe him, for no god of any nation or kingdom has been able to deliver[r] his people from my hand or the hand of my fathers.[s] How much less will your god deliver you from my hand!"

[16]Sennacherib's officers spoke further against the LORD God and against his servant Hezekiah. [17]The king also

31:15 [t]2Ch 29:12 [u]Jos 21:9-19
31:16 [v]1Ch 23:3; Ezr 3:4
31:19 [w]ver 12-15; Lev 25:34; Nu 35:2-5
31:20 [x]2Ki 20:3; 22:2
31:21 [y]Dt 29:9
32:1 [z]2Ki 18:13-19; Isa 36:1; 37:9, 17,37
32:2 [a]Isa 22:7; Jer 1:15
32:4 [b]2Ki 18:17; 20:20; Isa 22:9, 11; Na 3:14
32:5 [c]2Ch 25:23; Isa 22:10 [d]1Ki 9:24; 1Ch 11:8 [e]Isa 22:8
32:7 [f]Dt 31:6; 1Ch 22:13 [g]2Ch 20:15 [h]Nu 14:9; 2Ki 6:16
32:8 [i]Job 40:9; Isa 52:10; Jer 17:5; 32:21 [j]Dt 3:22; 1Sa 17:45; 2Ch 13:12 [k]1Ch 5:22; 2Ch 20:17; Ps 20:7; Isa 28:6
32:9 [l]Jos 10:3,31
32:10 [m]Eze 29:16
32:11 [n]Isa 37:10
32:12 [o]2Ch 31:1
32:13 [p]ver 15
32:15 [q]Isa 37:10 [r]Da 3:15 [s]Ex 5:2

[a] *4* Hebrew; Septuagint and Syriac *king*
[b] *5* Or *the Millo*

wrote letters[t] insulting[u] the LORD, the God of Israel, and saying this against him: "Just as the gods[v] of the peoples of the other lands did not rescue their people from my hand, so the god of Hezekiah will not rescue his people from my hand." **18**Then they called out in Hebrew to the people of Jerusalem who were on the wall, to terrify them and make them afraid in order to capture the city. **19**They spoke about the God of Jerusalem as they did about the gods of the other peoples of the world—the work of men's hands.[w]

20King Hezekiah and the prophet Isaiah son of Amoz cried out in prayer to heaven about this. **21**And the LORD sent an angel,[x] who annihilated all the fighting men and the leaders and officers in the camp of the Assyrian king. So he withdrew to his own land in disgrace. And when he went into the temple of his god, some of his sons cut him down with the sword.[y]

22So the LORD saved Hezekiah and the people of Jerusalem from the hand of Sennacherib king of Assyria and from the hand of all others. He took care of them[a] on every side. **23**Many brought offerings to Jerusalem for the LORD and valuable gifts[z] for Hezekiah king of Judah. From then on he was highly regarded by all the nations.

Hezekiah's Pride, Success and Death

24In those days Hezekiah became ill and was at the point of death. He prayed to the LORD, who answered him and gave him a miraculous sign. **25**But Hezekiah's heart was proud[a] and he did not respond to the kindness shown him; therefore the LORD's wrath[b] was on him and on Judah and Jerusalem. **26**Then Hezekiah repented[c] of the pride of his heart, as did the people of Jerusalem; therefore the LORD's wrath did not come upon them during the days of Hezekiah.[d]

27Hezekiah had very great riches and honor,[e] and he made treasuries for his silver and gold and for his precious stones, spices, shields and all kinds of valuables. **28**He also made buildings to store the harvest of grain, new wine and oil; and he made stalls for various kinds of cattle, and pens for the flocks. **29**He built villages and acquired great numbers of flocks and herds, for God had given him very great riches.[f]

30It was Hezekiah who blocked[g] the upper outlet of the Gihon[h] spring and channeled the water down to the west side of the City of David. He succeeded in everything he undertook. **31**But when envoys were sent by the rulers of Babylon[i] to ask him about the miraculous sign[j] that had occurred in the land, God left him to test[k] him and to know everything that was in his heart.

32The other events of Hezekiah's reign and his acts of devotion are written in the vision of the prophet Isaiah son of Amoz in the book of the kings of Judah and Israel. **33**Hezekiah rested with his fathers and was buried on the hill where the tombs of David's descendants are. All Judah and the people of Jerusalem honored him when he died. And Manasseh his son succeeded him as king.

Manasseh King of Judah

33 Manasseh[l] was twelve years old when he became king, and he reigned in Jerusalem fifty-five years. **2**He did evil in the eyes of the LORD,[m] following the detestable[n] practices of the nations the LORD had driven out before the Israelites. **3**He rebuilt the high places his father Hezekiah had demolished; he also erected altars to the Baals and made Asherah poles.[o] He bowed down[p] to all the starry hosts and worshiped them. **4**He built altars in the temple of the LORD, of which the LORD had said, "My Name[q] will remain in Jerusalem forever." **5**In both courts of the temple of the LORD,[r] he built altars to all the starry hosts. **6**He sacrificed his sons[s] in[b] the fire in the Valley of Ben Hinnom, practiced sorcery, divination and witchcraft, and consulted mediums[t] and spiritists.[u] He did much evil in the eyes of the LORD, provoking him to anger.

7He took the carved image he had made and put it in God's temple,[v] of which God had said to David and to his son Solomon, "In this temple and in Jerusalem, which I have chosen out of all the tribes of Israel, I will put my Name forever. **8**I will not again make the feet of the Israelites leave the land[w] I assigned to your forefathers, if only they will be careful to do everything I commanded them concerning all the laws, decrees and ordinances given through Moses." **9**But Manasseh led Judah and the people of Jerusalem astray, so that they did more evil than the nations the LORD had destroyed before the Israelites.[x]

10The LORD spoke to Manasseh and his people, but they paid no attention. **11**So the LORD brought against them the army commanders of the king of Assyria, who took Manasseh prisoner,[y] put

32:17 [t]Isa 37:14 [u]Ps 74:22; Isa 37:4,17 [v]2Ki 19:12
32:19 [w]2Ki 19:18; Ps 115:4,4-8; Isa 2:8; 17:8
32:21 [x]Ge 19:13 [y]2Ki 19:7
32:23 [z]2Ch 9:24; 17:5; Isa 45:14; Zec 14:16-17
32:25 [a]2Ki 14:10; 2Ch 26:16 [b]2Ch 19:2; 24:18
32:26 [c]Jer 26:18-19 [d]2Ch 34:27,28; Isa 39:8
32:27 [e]1Ch 29:12
32:29 [f]1Ch 29:12
32:30 [g]2Ki 18:17 [h]1Ki 1:33
32:31 [i]Isa 39:1 [j]ver 24; Isa 38:7 [k]Ge 22:1; Dt 8:16
33:1 [l]1Ch 3:13
33:2 [m]Jer 15:4 [n]Dt 18:9; 2Ch 28:3
33:3 [o]Dt 16:21-22 [p]Dt 17:3; 2Ch 31:1
33:4 [q]2Ch 7:16
33:5 [r]2Ch 4:9
33:6 [s]Lev 18:21; Dt 18:10; 2Ch 28:3 [t]Lev 19:31 [u]1Sa 28:13
33:7 [v]2Ch 7:16
33:8 [w]2Sa 7:10
33:9 [x]Jer 15:4
33:11 [y]Dt 28:36

[a] *22* Hebrew; Septuagint and Vulgate *He gave them rest* [b] *6* Or *He made his sons pass through*

a hook in his nose, bound him with bronze shackles[z] and took him to Babylon. 12In his distress he sought the favor of the LORD his God and humbled[a] himself greatly before the God of his fathers. 13And when he prayed to him, the LORD was moved by his entreaty and listened to his plea; so he brought him back to Jerusalem and to his kingdom. Then Manasseh knew that the LORD is God.

14Afterward he rebuilt the outer wall of the City of David, west of the Gihon[b] spring in the valley, as far as the entrance of the Fish Gate[c] and encircling the hill of Ophel;[d] he also made it much higher. He stationed military commanders in all the fortified cities in Judah.

15He got rid of the foreign gods and removed[e] the image from the temple of the LORD, as well as all the altars he had built on the temple hill and in Jerusalem; and he threw them out of the city. 16Then he restored the altar of the LORD and sacrificed fellowship offerings[a] and thank offerings[f] on it, and told Judah to serve the LORD, the God of Israel. 17The people, however, continued to sacrifice at the high places, but only to the LORD their God.

18The other events of Manasseh's reign, including his prayer to his God and the words the seers spoke to him in the name of the LORD, the God of Israel, are written in the annals of the kings of Israel.[b] 19His prayer and how God was moved by his entreaty, as well as all his sins and unfaithfulness, and the sites where he built high places and set up Asherah poles and idols before he humbled[g] himself—all are written in the records of the seers.[c][h] 20Manasseh rested with his fathers and was buried[i] in his palace. And Amon his son succeeded him as king.

Amon King of Judah

21Amon[j] was twenty-two years old when he became king, and he reigned in Jerusalem two years. 22He did evil in the eyes of the LORD, as his father Manasseh had done. Amon worshiped and offered sacrifices to all the idols Manasseh had made. 23But unlike his father Manasseh, he did not humble[k] himself before the LORD; Amon increased his guilt.

24Amon's officials conspired against him and assassinated him in his palace. 25Then the people[l] of the land killed all who had plotted against King Amon, and they made Josiah his son king in his place.

33:11 [z]Ps 149:8
33:12 [a]2Ch 6:37; 32:26; 1Pe 5:6
33:14 [b]1Ki 1:33 [c]Ne 3:3; 12:39; Zep 1:10 [d]2Ch 27:3; Ne 3:26
33:15 [e]ver 3-7; 2Ki 23:12
33:16 [f]Lev 7:11-18
33:19 [g]2Ch 6:37 [h]2Ki 21:17
33:20 [i]2Ki 21:18; 2Ch 21:20
33:21 [j]1Ch 3:14
33:23 [k]ver 12; Ex 10:3; 2Ch 7:14; Ps 18:27; 147:6; Pr 3:34
33:25 [l]2Ch 22:1

34:1 [m]1Ch 3:14 [n]Zep 1:1
34:2 [o]2Ch 29:2
34:3 [p]1Ki 13:2; 1Ch 16:11; 2Ch 15:2; 33:17,22
34:4 [q]Ex 34:13 [r]Ex 32:20; Lev 26:30; 2Ki 23:11; Mic 1:5
34:5 [s]1Ki 13:2
34:7 [t]Ex 32:20; 2Ch 31:1
34:9 [u]1Ch 6:13; 2Ch 35:8
34:11 [v]2Ch 24:12 [w]2Ch 33:4-7
34:12 [x]2Ki 12:15

Josiah's Reforms

34 Josiah[m] was eight years old when he became king,[n] and he reigned in Jerusalem thirty-one years. 2He did what was right in the eyes of the LORD and walked in the ways of his father David,[o] not turning aside to the right or to the left.

3In the eighth year of his reign, while he was still young, he began to seek the God[p] of his father David. In his twelfth year he began to purge Judah and Jerusalem of high places, Asherah poles, carved idols and cast images. 4Under his direction the altars of the Baals were torn down; he cut to pieces the incense altars that were above them, and smashed the Asherah poles,[q] the idols and the images. These he broke to pieces and scattered over the graves of those who had sacrificed to them.[r] 5He burned[s] the bones of the priests on their altars, and so he purged Judah and Jerusalem. 6In the towns of Manasseh, Ephraim and Simeon, as far as Naphtali, and in the ruins around them, 7he tore down the altars and the Asherah poles and crushed the idols to powder[t] and cut to pieces all the incense altars throughout Israel. Then he went back to Jerusalem.

8In the eighteenth year of Josiah's reign, to purify the land and the temple, he sent Shaphan son of Azaliah and Maaseiah the ruler of the city, with Joah son of Joahaz, the recorder, to repair the temple of the LORD his God.

9They went to Hilkiah[u] the high priest and gave him the money that had been brought into the temple of God, which the Levites who were the doorkeepers had collected from the people of Manasseh, Ephraim and the entire remnant of Israel and from all the people of Judah and Benjamin and the inhabitants of Jerusalem. 10Then they entrusted it to the men appointed to supervise the work on the LORD's temple. These men paid the workers who repaired and restored the temple. 11They also gave money[v] to the carpenters and builders to purchase dressed stone, and timber for joists and beams for the buildings that the kings of Judah had allowed to fall into ruin.[w]

12The men did the work faithfully.[x] Over them to direct them were Jahath and Obadiah, Levites descended from Merari, and Zechariah and Meshullam, descended from Kohath. The Levites—

[a] *16* Traditionally *peace offerings* [b] *18* That is, Judah, as frequently in 2 Chronicles [c] *19* One Hebrew manuscript and Septuagint; most Hebrew manuscripts *of Hozai*

all who were skilled in playing musical
instruments—[y] 13had charge of the
laborers[z] and supervised all the workers from job to job. Some of the Levites
were secretaries, scribes and doorkeepers.

The Book of the Law Found

14While they were bringing out the
money that had been taken into the
temple of the LORD, Hilkiah the priest
found the Book of the Law of the LORD
that had been given through Moses.
15Hilkiah said to Shaphan the secretary, "I have found the Book of the
Law[a] in the temple of the LORD." He
gave it to Shaphan.

16Then Shaphan took the book to
the king and reported to him: "Your
officials are doing everything that has
been committed to them. 17They have
paid out the money that was in the
temple of the LORD and have entrusted
it to the supervisors and workers."
18Then Shaphan the secretary informed the king, "Hilkiah the priest has
given me a book." And Shaphan read
from it in the presence of the king.

19When the king heard the words of
the Law,[b] he tore[c] his robes. 20He
gave these orders to Hilkiah, Ahikam
son of Shaphan[d], Abdon son of Micah,[a] Shaphan the secretary and Asaiah the king's attendant: 21"Go and inquire of the LORD for me and for the
remnant in Israel and Judah about
what is written in this book that has
been found. Great is the LORD's anger
that is poured out[e] on us because our
fathers have not kept the word of the
LORD; they have not acted in accordance with all that is written in this
book."

22Hilkiah and those the king had
sent with him[b] went to speak to the
prophetess[f] Huldah, who was the
wife of Shallum son of Tokhath,[c]
the son of Hasrah,[d] keeper of the
wardrobe. She lived in Jerusalem, in
the Second District.

23She said to them, "This is what the
LORD, the God of Israel, says: Tell the
man who sent you to me, 24'This is
what the LORD says: I am going to bring
disaster[g] on this place and its
people[h]—all the curses[i] written in
the book that has been read in the
presence of the king of Judah. 25Be-
cause they have forsaken me[j] and
burned incense to other gods and provoked me to anger by all that their
hands have made,[e] my anger will be
poured out on this place and will not
be quenched.' 26Tell the king of Judah,
who sent you to inquire of the LORD,
'This is what the LORD, the God of Israel, says concerning the words you
heard: 27Because your heart was responsive[k] and you humbled[l] yourself before God when you heard what
he spoke against this place and its people, and because you humbled yourself
before me and tore your robes and
wept in my presence, I have heard you,
declares the LORD. 28Now I will gather
you to your fathers,[m] and you will be
buried in peace. Your eyes will not see
all the disaster I am going to bring on
this place and on those who live
here.' "[n]

So they took her answer back to the
king.

29Then the king called together all
the elders of Judah and Jerusalem.
30He went up to the temple of the
LORD[o] with the men of Judah, the people of Jerusalem, the priests and the
Levites—all the people from the least
to the greatest. He read in their hearing
all the words of the Book of the Covenant, which had been found in the
temple of the LORD. 31The king stood
by his pillar[p] and renewed the covenant[q] in the presence of the LORD—
to follow[r] the LORD and keep his commands, regulations and decrees with
all his heart and all his soul, and to
obey the words of the covenant written
in this book.

32Then he had everyone in Jerusalem and Benjamin pledge themselves
to it; the people of Jerusalem did this in
accordance with the covenant of God,
the God of their fathers.

33Josiah removed all the detestable[s] idols from all the territory belonging to the Israelites, and he had all
who were present in Israel serve the
LORD their God. As long as he lived,
they did not fail to follow the LORD, the
God of their fathers.

Josiah Celebrates the Passover

35 Josiah celebrated the Passover[t] to
the LORD in Jerusalem, and the
Passover lamb was slaughtered on the
fourteenth day of the first month. 2He
appointed the priests to their duties
and encouraged them in the service of
the LORD's temple. 3He said to the Levites, who instructed[u] all Israel and
who had been consecrated to the LORD:
"Put the sacred ark in the temple that
Solomon son of David king of Israel
built. It is not to be carried about on

34:12 [y] 1Ch 25:1
34:13 [z] 1Ch 23:4
34:15 [a] 2Ki 22:8; Ezr 7:6; Ne 8:1
34:19 [b] Dt 28:3-68 [c] Jos 7:6; Isa 36:22; 37:1
34:20 [d] 2Ki 22:3
34:21 [e] 2Ch 29:8; La 2:4; 4:11; Eze 36:18
34:22 [f] Ex 15:20; Ne 6:14
34:24 [g] Pr 16:4; Isa 3:9; Jer 40:2; 42:10; 44:2,11 [h] 2Ch 36:14-20 [i] Dt 28:15-68
34:25 [j] 2Ch 33:3-6; Jer 22:9
34:27 [k] 2Ch 12:7; 32:26 [l] Ex 10:3; 2Ch 6:37
34:28 [m] 2Ch 35:20-25 [n] 2Ch 32:26
34:30 [o] 2Ki 23:2; Ne 8:1-3
34:31 [p] 1Ki 7:15; 2Ki 11:14 [q] 2Ki 11:17; 2Ch 23:16; 29:10 [r] Dt 13:4
34:33 [s] ver 3-7; Dt 18:9
35:1 [t] Ex 12:1-30; Nu 9:3; 28:16
35:3 [u] Dt 33:10; 1Ch 23:26; 2Ch 5:7; 17:7

[a] 20 Also called *Acbor son of Micaiah*
[b] 22 One Hebrew manuscript, Vulgate and Syriac; most Hebrew manuscripts do not have *had sent with him.*
[c] 22 Also called *Tikvah*
[d] 22 Also called *Harhas*
[e] 25 Or *by everything they have done*

your shoulders. Now serve the LORD
your God and his people Israel. 4Pre-
pare yourselves by families in your divisions,[v] according to the directions
written by David king of Israel and by
his son Solomon.
5"Stand in the holy place with a
group of Levites for each subdivision of
the families of your fellow countrymen,
the lay people. 6Slaughter the Passover
lambs, consecrate yourselves[w] and
prepare ⌞the lambs⌟ for your fellow
countrymen, doing what the LORD
commanded through Moses."
7Josiah provided for all the lay people who were there a total of thirty
thousand sheep and goats for the Passover offerings,[x] and also three thousand cattle—all from the king's own
possessions.[y]
8His officials also contributed[z] voluntarily to the people and the priests
and Levites. Hilkiah,[a] Zechariah and
Jehiel, the administrators of God's
temple, gave the priests twenty-six
hundred Passover offerings and three
hundred cattle. 9Also Conaniah[b]
along with Shemaiah and Nethanel, his
brothers, and Hashabiah, Jeiel and Jozabad,[c] the leaders of the Levites, provided five thousand Passover offerings
and five hundred head of cattle for the
Levites.
10The service was arranged and the
priests stood in their places with the
Levites in their divisions[d] as the king
had ordered.[e] 11The Passover lambs
were slaughtered,[f] and the priests
sprinkled the blood handed to them,
while the Levites skinned the animals.
12They set aside the burnt offerings to
give them to the subdivisions of the
families of the people to offer to the
LORD, as is written in the Book of Moses. They did the same with the cattle.
13They roasted the Passover animals
over the fire as prescribed,[g] and
boiled the holy offerings in pots, cal-
drons and pans and served them
quickly to all the people. 14After this,
they made preparations for themselves
and for the priests, because the priests,
the descendants of Aaron, were sacrificing the burnt offerings and the fat
portions[h] until nightfall. So the Levites made preparations for themselves
and for the Aaronic priests.
15The musicians,[i] the descendants
of Asaph, were in the places prescribed
by David, Asaph, Heman and Jeduthun
the king's seer. The gatekeepers at each
gate did not need to leave their posts,
because their fellow Levites made the
preparations for them.
16So at that time the entire service of
the LORD was carried out for the cele-

35:4 [v]ver 10; 1Ch 9:10-13; 24:1; 2Ch 8:14; Ezr 6:18
35:6 [w]Lev 11:44; 2Ch 29:5,15
35:7 [x]2Ch 30:24 [y]2Ch 31:3
35:8 [z]1Ch 29:3; 2Ch 29:31-36 [a]1Ch 6:13
35:9 [b]2Ch 31:12 [c]2Ch 31:13
35:10 [d]ver 4; Ezr 6:18 [e]2Ch 30:16
35:11 [f]2Ch 29:22,34; 30:17
35:13 [g]Ex 12:2-11; Lev 6:25; 1Sa 2:13-15
35:14 [h]Ex 29:13
35:15 [i]1Ch 25:1; 26:12-19; 2Ch 29:30; Ne 12:46; Ps 68:25
35:20 [j]Isa 10:9; Jer 46:2 [k]Ge 2:14
35:21 [l]1Ki 13:18; 2Ki 18:25
35:22 [m]Jdg 5:19; 1Sa 28:8; 2Ch 18:29
35:23 [n]1Ki 22:34
35:25 [o]Jer 22:10, 15-16

bration of the Passover and the offering of burnt offerings on the altar of
the LORD, as King Josiah had ordered.
17The Israelites who were present celebrated the Passover at that time and
observed the Feast of Unleavened
Bread for seven days. 18The Passover
had not been observed like this in Israel since the days of the prophet Samuel; and none of the kings of Israel had
ever celebrated such a Passover as did
Josiah, with the priests, the Levites and
all Judah and Israel who were there
with the people of Jerusalem. 19This
Passover was celebrated in the eighteenth year of Josiah's reign.

The Death of Josiah

20After all this, when Josiah had set
the temple in order, Neco king of Egypt
went up to fight at Carchemish[j] on
the Euphrates,[k] and Josiah marched
out to meet him in battle. 21But Neco
sent messengers to him, saying, "What
quarrel is there between you and me,
O king of Judah? It is not you I am attacking at this time, but the house with
which I am at war. God has told[l] me
to hurry; so stop opposing God, who is
with me, or he will destroy you."
22Josiah, however, would not turn
away from him, but disguised[m] himself to engage him in battle. He would
not listen to what Neco had said at
God's command but went to fight him
on the plain of Megiddo.
23Archers[n] shot King Josiah, and he
told his officers, "Take me away; I am
badly wounded." 24So they took him
out of his chariot, put him in the other
chariot he had and brought him to Jerusalem, where he died. He was buried
in the tombs of his fathers, and all Judah and Jerusalem mourned for him.
25Jeremiah composed laments for
Josiah, and to this day all the men and
women singers commemorate Josiah
in the laments.[o] These became a tradition in Israel and are written in the
Laments.
26The other events of Josiah's reign
and his acts of devotion, according to
what is written in the Law of the LORD—
27all the events, from beginning to end,
are written in the book of the kings of
36 Israel and Judah. 1And the people
of the land took Jehoahaz son of
Josiah and made him king in Jerusalem
in place of his father.

Jehoahaz King of Judah

2Jehoahaz[a] was twenty-three years

[a] *2* Hebrew *Joahaz,* a variant of *Jehoahaz;* also in verse 4

old when he became king, and he reigned in Jerusalem three months. 3The king of Egypt dethroned him in Jerusalem and imposed on Judah a levy of a hundred talents[a] of silver and a talent[b] of gold. 4The king of Egypt made Eliakim, a brother of Jehoahaz, king over Judah and Jerusalem and changed Eliakim's name to Jehoiakim. But Neco[p] took Eliakim's brother Jehoahaz and carried him off to Egypt.

Jehoiakim King of Judah

5Jehoiakim[q] was twenty-five years old when he became king, and he reigned in Jerusalem eleven years. He did evil in the eyes of the LORD his God. 6Nebuchadnezzar[r] king of Babylon attacked him and bound him with bronze shackles to take him to Babylon.[s] 7Nebuchadnezzar also took to Babylon articles from the temple of the LORD and put them in his temple[c] there.[t]

8The other events of Jehoiakim's reign, the detestable things he did and all that was found against him, are written in the book of the kings of Israel and Judah. And Jehoiachin his son succeeded him as king.

Jehoiachin King of Judah

9Jehoiachin[u] was eighteen[d] years old when he became king, and he reigned in Jerusalem three months and ten days. He did evil in the eyes of the LORD. 10In the spring, King Nebuchadnezzar sent for him and brought him to Babylon,[v] together with articles of value from the temple of the LORD, and he made Jehoiachin's uncle,[e] Zedekiah, king over Judah and Jerusalem.

Zedekiah King of Judah

11Zedekiah[w] was twenty-one years old when he became king, and he reigned in Jerusalem eleven years. 12He did evil in the eyes of the LORD[x] his God and did not humble[y] himself before Jeremiah the prophet, who spoke the word of the LORD. 13He also rebelled against King Nebuchadnezzar, who had made him take an oath[z] in God's name. He became stiff-necked[a] and hardened his heart and would not turn to the LORD, the God of Israel. 14Furthermore, all the leaders of the priests and the people became more and more unfaithful,[b] following all the detestable practices of the nations and defiling the temple of the LORD, which he had consecrated in Jerusalem.

The Fall of Jerusalem

15The LORD, the God of their fathers, sent word to them through his messengers[c] again and again,[d] because he had pity on his people and on his dwelling place. 16But they mocked God's messengers, despised his words and scoffed[e] at his prophets until the wrath[f] of the LORD was aroused against his people and there was no remedy.[g] 17He brought up against them the king of the Babylonians,[f] who killed their young men with the sword in the sanctuary, and spared neither young man[h] nor young woman, old man or aged. God handed all of them over to Nebuchadnezzar.[i] 18He carried to Babylon all the articles[j] from the temple of God, both large and small, and the treasures of the LORD's temple and the treasures of the king and his officials. 19They set fire[k] to God's temple[l] and broke down the wall[m] of Jerusalem; they burned all the palaces and destroyed[n] everything of value there.[o]

20He carried into exile[p] to Babylon the remnant, who escaped from the sword, and they became servants[q] to him and his sons until the kingdom of Persia came to power. 21The land enjoyed its sabbath rests;[r] all the time of its desolation it rested,[s] until the seventy years[t] were completed in fulfillment of the word of the LORD spoken by Jeremiah.

22In the first year of Cyrus[u] king of Persia, in order to fulfill the word of the LORD spoken by Jeremiah, the LORD moved the heart of Cyrus king of Persia to make a proclamation throughout his realm and to put it in writing:

23"This is what Cyrus king of Persia says:

" 'The LORD, the God of heaven, has given me all the kingdoms of the earth and he has appointed[v] me to build a temple for him at Jerusalem in Judah. Anyone of his people among you—may the LORD his God be with him, and let him go up.' "

36:4 p Jer 22:10-12 **36:5** q Jer 22:18; 26:1; 35:1 **36:6** r Jer 25:9; 27:6; Eze 29:18 s 2Ch 33:11; Eze 19:9; Da 1:1 **36:7** t 2Ki 24:13; Ezr 1:7; Da 1:2 **36:9** u Jer 22:24-28; 52:31 **36:10** v ver 18; 2Ki 20:17; Ezr 1:7; Jer 22:25; 24:1; 29:1; 37:1; Eze 17:12 **36:11** w 2Ki 24:17; Jer 27:1; 28:1 **36:12** x Jer 37:1-39:18 y Dt 8:3; 2Ch 7:14; 2Ch 33:23; Jer 21:3-7 **36:13** z Eze 17:13 a 2Ki 17:14; 2Ch 30:8 **36:14** b 1Ch 5:25 **36:15** c Isa 5:4; 44:26; Jer 7:25; Hag 1:13; Zec 1:4; Mal 2:7; 3:1 d Jer 7:13,25; 25:3-4; 35:14, 15; 44:4-6 **36:16** e 2Ki 2:23; Pr 1:25; Jer 5:13 f Ezr 5:12; Pr 1:30-31 g 2Ch 30:10; Pr 29:1; Zec 1:2 **36:17** h Jer 6:11 i Ezr 5:12; Jer 32:28 **36:18** j ver 7,10 **36:19** k Jer 11:16; 17:27; 21:10, 14; 22:7; 32:29; 39:8; La 4:11; Eze 20:47; Am 2:5; Zec 11:1 l 1Ki 9:8-9 m 2Ki 14:13 n La 2:6 o Ps 79:1-3 **36:20** p Lev 26:44; 2Ki 24:14; Ezr 2:1; Ne 7:6 q Jer 27:7 **36:21** r Lev 25:4; 26:34 s 1Ch 22:9 t Jer 1:1; 25:11; 27:22; 29:10; 40:1; Da 9:2; Zec 1:12; 7:5 **36:22** u Isa 44:28; 45:1,13; Jer 25:12; 29:10; Da 1:21; 6:28; 10:1 **36:23** v Jdg 4:10

a *3* That is, about 3 3/4 tons (about 3.4 metric tons) b *3* That is, about 75 pounds (about 34 kilograms) c *7* Or *palace* d *9* One Hebrew manuscript, some Septuagint manuscripts and Syriac (see also 2 Kings 24:8); most Hebrew manuscripts *eight* e *10* Hebrew *brother,* that is, relative (see 2 Kings 24:17) f *17* Or *Chaldeans*

EZRA

AT A GLANCE

Key Principle: In spite of his people's faithlessness, God always faithfully fulfills the promises he makes. There is no limit to the amazing means God uses to keep his promises.
Author: Probably Ezra the priest
Time and Place: Ezra 1—6: 539 B.C. to 516 B.C. / Persia to Jerusalem; Ezra 7—10: 458 B.C. / Persia to Jerusalem
Key Verses: 1:3; 6:14; 7:10

BENEFIT

Ezra teaches us that even when all seems lost, God is continually at work behind the scenes of history. While he may sometimes appear uninvolved, God steadily pursues his purposes for his people in the best times and ways. The prophet Jeremiah predicted that after seventy years of Babylonian captivity, God would restore the fortunes of the remaining remnant. "'For I know the plans I have for you,' declares the LORD, 'plans to prosper you and not to harm you, plans to give you hope and a future. . . . I will be found by you,' declares the LORD, 'and will bring you back from captivity'" (Jeremiah 29:11, 14). Ezra records how God fulfilled this promise.

SETTING

The books of the Kings and Chronicles detail the decline of Israel and Judah and their capture at the hands of foreign powers. Judah fell to Babylon, who eventually fell to Persia. The book of Ezra picks up the timeline, telling the first two of three stories about the Jewish remnant's return to Jerusalem from Persia.

Zerubbabel led the first return (1—6) in 538 B.C. and began construction on the second temple in 536 B.C. After a lengthy interruption, the remnant completed temple construction in 516 B.C. Ezra led the second return (7—10) 80 years after the first return (458 B.C.). Nehemiah led the third return in 445 B.C.; the book by that name contains a full account of that time period. The book of Esther fits in chronologically during the gap between Ezra 6 and 7, the first and second return to Jerusalem.

Zerubbabel	Esther	Ezra	Jeremiah
First Return		Second Return	Third Return
Ezra 1–6	Book of Esther	Ezra 7–10	Book of Nehemiah
538–515 B.C.	483–473 B.C.	458 B.C.	445– c.425 B.C.

Persian Kings During This Period

Cyrus	Cambyses	Smerdis	Darius I	Ahasuerus (Xerxes)	Artaxerxes I
559–530 B.C.	530–522 B.C.	522 B.C.	521–486 B.C.	486–464 B.C.	464–423 B.C.

TIME LINE 1400BC 1300 1200 1100 1000 900 800 700 600 500 400

Fall of Jerusalem (586 B.C.)
Persia's conquest of Babylon (539 B.C.)
First return of exiles to Jerusalem (538 B.C.)
Ministries of Haggai and Zechariah (c.520-480 B.C.)
Completion of temple (516 B.C.)
Second return to Jerusalem under Ezra (458 B.C.)
Third return to Jerusalem under Nehemiah (445 B.C.)

THEME AND PURPOSE

Ezra probably wrote this book between 457 B.C. and 440 B.C. to show his readers how the Lord returned the faithful remnant of Israel to their land and guided them as they rebuilt the temple and the city. Looking back to the time of Zerubbabel, Ezra describes the people who returned and how they rebuilt the altar, restored the religious feasts and reconstructed and dedicated the temple. Zerubbabel lead the people to rebuild the sanctuary and restore proper worship; Ezra led the people into spiritual and moral revival. Although the glorious days of David and Solomon were over, this book encouraged the remnant to see that they still had their spiritual heritage and that God would continue to use them to accomplish his purposes.

UNIQUE CONTRIBUTION

The book of Ezra continues the story left off at the end of 2 Chronicles; this is why it appears after Chronicles in the English Bible. (The Hebrew Bible combines the books of Ezra and Nehemiah into one and places it just before Chronicles, the last book in that Bible.) The final event in Chronicles is the edict of Cyrus in 538 B.C. allowing the Jews to return to Jerusalem and rebuild their temple. Ezra 1—6 tells us what happened during that return under Zerubbabel, and Ezra 7—10 gives us the history of the second return under Ezra. This book strongly emphasizes the importance of knowing and responding to God's revealed Word (1:1; 3:2; 6:14, 18; 7:6, 10; 9:4).

LINKS TO THE NEW TESTAMENT

One of the key themes in the books of Samuel through Chronicles has been the royal line of David that would ultimately usher in the coming Messiah. Ezra continues this theme, showing that even though Israel's monarchy has ended, the royal line of David's descendants has not. Zerubbabel, the key figure in chapters 1—6, is a part of this line (see Matthew 1:12–13). And the return of Jews to Jerusalem prepares the way for the Messiah to be born in the land of promise (Micah 5:2) rather than the land of captivity.

OVERVIEW

FOCUS	Rebuilding the Temple			Rebuilding the People	
REFERENCE	1 2	3 6	Book of Esther	7 8	9 10
TOPICS	The First Return under Zerubbabel			The Second Return under Ezra	
	Restoration			Reformation	
	Decree and Journey	Work		Decree and Journey	Work
LOCATION	Persia to Jerusalem			Persia to Jerusalem	
TIME	23 Years (538 B.C. to 516 B.C.)		58 Year Gap	1 Year (458 B.C.)	

In 538 B.C., a year after the Persian king Cyrus defeated Babylon, he decreed that the exiled Jews could return to their homeland and rebuild their temple (1). According to the census of the Jews who returned under Zerubbabel's leadership, only 49,897 people (including the priests and Levites) responded to this offer (2). While the vast majority of the Jewish population chose to remain in the relative comfort of Persia, this dedicated remnant endured a difficult journey and took on the challenge of rebuilding the ruined city and temple of Jerusalem. After building an altar, these dedicated Jews completed the temple foundation in 536 B.C. (3). Temple construction stalled from 534–520 B.C. due to local opposition. But when the prophets

Haggai and Zechariah inspired the people to resume the work in spite of that opposition, the faithful remnant completed the temple in 516 B.C. and dedicated it to the Lord (4—6).

In 458 B.C., Ezra led a second return of Jewish exiles from Persia to Jerusalem. This time, however, only 1,754 people returned (7—8). They carried valuable gifts for the temple, and God protected them during their journey. But when Ezra arrived he discovered that during the years since the first return, many of his countrymen had intermarried with foreign women. Ezra offered a moving intercessory prayer because of the sins of his people, and the people responded by confessing their sins and promising to put away their foreign wives and live in obedience to God's Word (9—10).

EZRA

Cyrus Helps the Exiles to Return

1 In the first year of Cyrus king of
Persia, in order to fulfill the word
of the LORD spoken by Jeremiah,[a] the
LORD moved the heart[b] of Cyrus king
of Persia to make a proclamation
throughout his realm and to put it in
writing:

2"This is what Cyrus king of Persia
says:
" 'The LORD, the God of heaven,
has given me all the kingdoms of
the earth and he has appointed[c]
me to build[d] a temple for him at
Jerusalem in Judah. 3Anyone of
his people among you—may his
God be with him, and let him go
up to Jerusalem in Judah and
build the temple of the LORD, the
God of Israel, the God who is in
Jerusalem. 4And the people of any
place where survivors[e] may now
be living are to provide him with
silver and gold, with goods and
livestock, and with freewill offerings[f] for the temple of God in
Jerusalem.' "[g]

5Then the family heads of Judah and
Benjamin,[h] and the priests and
Levites—everyone whose heart God
had moved[i]—prepared to go up and
build the house[j] of the LORD in Jerusalem. 6All their neighbors assisted
them with articles of silver and gold,
with goods and livestock, and with
valuable gifts, in addition to all the
freewill offerings. 7Moreover, King Cyrus brought out the articles belonging
to the temple of the LORD, which Nebuchadnezzar had carried away from Jerusalem and had placed in the temple
of his god.[a][k] 8Cyrus king of Persia
had them brought by Mithredath the
treasurer, who counted them out to
Sheshbazzar[l] the prince of Judah.
9This was the inventory:

gold dishes	30
silver dishes	1,000
silver pans[b]	29
10gold bowls	30
matching silver bowls	410
other articles	1,000

11In all, there were 5,400 articles of
gold and of silver. Sheshbazzar brought
all these along when the exiles came up
from Babylon to Jerusalem.

1:1 [a]Jer 25:11-12; 29:10-14 [b]2Ch 36:22,23 **1:2** [c]Isa 44:28; 45:13 [d]Ezr 5:13 **1:4** [e]Isa 10:20-22 [f]Nu 15:3; Ps 50:14; 54:6; 116:17 [g]Ezr 4:3; 5:13; 6:3,14 **1:5** [h]Ezr 4:1; Ne 11:4 [i]ver 1; Ex 35:20-22; 2Ch 36:22; Hag 1:14; Php 2:13 [j]Ps 127:1 **1:7** [k]2Ki 24:13; 2Ch 36:7,10; Ezr 5:14; 6:5 **1:8** [l]Ezr 5:14

2:1 [m]2Ch 36:20; Ne 7:6 [n]2Ki 24:16; 25:12 [o]Ne 7:73 **2:2** [p]1Ch 3:19 [q]Ezr 3:2 [r]Ne 10:2 **2:3** [s]Ezr 8:3 **2:13** [t]Ezr 8:13 **2:21** [u]Mic 5:2 **2:26** [v]Jos 18:25 **2:28** [w]Ge 12:8 **2:34** [x]1Ki 16:34; 2Ch 28:15 **2:36** [y]1Ch 24:7

The List of the Exiles Who Returned

2 Now these are the people of the
province who came up from the
captivity of the exiles,[m] whom Nebuchadnezzar king of Babylon[n] had tak-
en captive to Babylon (they returned to
Jerusalem and Judah, each to his own
town,[o] 2in company with Zerubbabel,[p] Jeshua,[q] Nehemiah, Seraiah,[r]
Reelaiah, Mordecai, Bilshan, Mispar,
Bigvai, Rehum and Baanah):

The list of the men of the people of Israel:

3the descendants of Parosh[s]	2,172
4of Shephatiah	372
5of Arah	775
6of Pahath-Moab (through the line of Jeshua and Joab)	2,812
7of Elam	1,254
8of Zattu	945
9of Zaccai	760
10of Bani	642
11of Bebai	623
12of Azgad	1,222
13of Adonikam[t]	666
14of Bigvai	2,056
15of Adin	454
16of Ater (through Hezekiah)	98
17of Bezai	323
18of Jorah	112
19of Hashum	223
20of Gibbar	95
21the men of Bethlehem[u]	123
22of Netophah	56
23of Anathoth	128
24of Azmaveth	42
25of Kiriath Jearim,[c] Kephirah and Beeroth	743
26of Ramah[v] and Geba	621
27of Micmash	122
28of Bethel and Ai[w]	223
29of Nebo	52
30of Magbish	156
31of the other Elam	1,254
32of Harim	320
33of Lod, Hadid and Ono	725
34of Jericho[x]	345
35of Senaah	3,630

36The priests:

the descendants of Jedaiah[y] (through the family of Jeshua)	973

[a] *7* Or *gods* [b] *9* The meaning of the Hebrew for this word is uncertain. [c] *25* See Septuagint (see also Neh. 7:29); Hebrew *Kiriath Arim.*

37 of Immer[z]	1,052
38 of Pashhur[a]	1,247
39 of Harim[b]	1,017

40 The Levites:[c]

the descendants of Jeshua[d] and Kadmiel (through the line of Hodaviah)	74

41 The singers:[e]

the descendants of Asaph	128

42 The gatekeepers[f] of the temple:

the descendants of Shallum, Ater, Talmon, Akkub, Hatita and Shobai	139

43 The temple servants:[g]

the descendants of
Ziha, Hasupha, Tabbaoth,
44 Keros, Siaha, Padon,
45 Lebanah, Hagabah, Akkub,
46 Hagab, Shalmai, Hanan,
47 Giddel, Gahar, Reaiah,
48 Rezin, Nekoda, Gazzam,
49 Uzza, Paseah, Besai,
50 Asnah, Meunim, Nephussim,
51 Bakbuk, Hakupha, Harhur,
52 Bazluth, Mehida, Harsha,
53 Barkos, Sisera, Temah,
54 Neziah and Hatipha

55 The descendants of the servants of Solomon:

the descendants of
Sotai, Hassophereth, Peruda,
56 Jaala, Darkon, Giddel,
57 Shephatiah, Hattil,
Pokereth-Hazzebaim and Ami

58 The temple servants[h] and the descendants of the servants of Solomon	392

59 The following came up from
the towns of Tel Melah, Tel Harsha, Kerub, Addon and Immer, but they could not show that their families were descended[i] from Israel:

60 The descendants of Delaiah, Tobiah and Nekoda	652

61 And from among the priests:

The descendants of
Hobaiah, Hakkoz and
Barzillai (a man who had married a daughter of Barzillai the Gileadite[j] and was called by that name).

62 These searched for their family records, but they could not find them and so were excluded from the priesthood[k] as unclean.
63 The governor ordered them not to eat any of the most sacred food[l] until there was a priest ministering with the Urim and Thummim.[m]

64 The whole company numbered 42,360,
65 besides their 7,337 menservants and maidservants; and they also had 200 men and women singers.[n]
66 They had 736 horses,[o] 245 mules,
67 435 camels and 6,720 donkeys.

68 When they arrived at the house of the LORD in Jerusalem, some of the heads of the families[p] gave freewill offerings toward the rebuilding of the house of God on its site.
69 According to their ability they gave to the treasury for this work 61,000 drachmas[a] of gold, 5,000 minas[b] of silver and 100 priestly garments.

70 The priests, the Levites, the singers, the gatekeepers and the temple servants settled in their own towns, along with some of the other people, and the rest of the Israelites settled in their towns.[q]

Rebuilding the Altar

3 When the seventh month came and the Israelites had settled in their towns,[r] the people assembled[s] as one man in Jerusalem.
2 Then Jeshua[t] son of Jozadak[u] and his fellow priests and Zerubbabel son of Shealtiel[v] and his associates began to build the altar of the God of Israel to sacrifice burnt offerings on it, in accordance with what is written in the Law of Moses[w] the man of God.
3 Despite their fear[x] of the peoples around them, they built the altar on its foundation and sacrificed burnt offerings on it to the LORD, both the morning and evening sacrifices.[y]
4 Then in accordance with what is written, they celebrated the Feast of Tabernacles[z] with the required number of burnt offerings prescribed for each day.
5 After that, they presented the regular burnt offerings, the New Moon[a] sacrifices and the sacrifices for all the appointed sacred feasts of the LORD,[b] as well as those brought as freewill offerings to the LORD.
6 On the first day of the seventh month they began to offer burnt offerings to the LORD, though the foundation of the LORD's temple had not yet been laid.

2:37 [z] 1Ch 24:14 **2:38** [a] 1Ch 9:12 **2:39** [b] 1Ch 24:8 **2:40** [c] Ge 29:34; Nu 3:9; Dt 18:6-7; 1Ch 16:4; Ezr 7:7; 8:15; Ne 12:24 [d] Ezr 3:9 **2:41** [e] 1Ch 15:16 **2:42** [f] 1Sa 3:15; 1Ch 9:17 **2:43** [g] 1Ch 9:2; Ne 11:21 **2:58** [h] 1Ki 9:21; 1Ch 9:2 **2:59** [i] Nu 1:18 **2:61** [j] 2Sa 17:27 **2:62** [k] Nu 3:10; 16:39-40 **2:63** [l] Lev 2:3,10 [m] Ex 28:30; Nu 27:21 **2:65** [n] 2Sa 19:35 **2:66** [o] Isa 66:20 **2:68** [p] Ex 25:2 **2:70** [q] ver 1; 1Ch 9:2; Ne 11:3-4 **3:1** [r] Ne 7:73; 8:1 [s] Lev 23:24 **3:2** [t] Ezr 2:2; Ne 12:1,8; Hag 2:2 [u] Hag 1:1; Zec 6:11 [v] 1Ch 3:17 [w] Ex 20:24; Dt 12:5-6 **3:3** [x] Ezr 4:4; Da 9:25 [y] Ex 29:39; Nu 28:1-8 **3:4** [z] Ex 23:16; Nu 29:12-38; Ne 8:14-18; Zec 14:16-19 **3:5** [a] Nu 28:3,11,14; Col 2:16 [b] Lev 23:1-44; Nu 29:39

[a] *69* That is, about 1,100 pounds (about 500 kilograms) [b] *69* That is, about 3 tons (about 2.9 metric tons)

Rebuilding the Temple

7 Then they gave money to the masons and carpenters, and gave food
and drink and oil to the people of Sidon and Tyre, so that they would bring
cedar logs[c] by sea from Lebanon[d] to
Joppa, as authorized by Cyrus[e] king of
Persia.

8 In the second month of the second
year after their arrival at the house of
God in Jerusalem, Zerubbabel[f] son of
Shealtiel, Jeshua son of Jozadak and
the rest of their brothers (the priests
and the Levites and all who had returned from the captivity to Jerusalem)
began the work, appointing Levites
twenty[g] years of age and older to supervise the building of the house of the
LORD. 9 Jeshua[h] and his sons and
brothers and Kadmiel and his sons
(descendants of Hodaviah[a]) and the
sons of Henadad and their sons and
brothers—all Levites—joined together
in supervising those working on the
house of God.

10 When the builders laid[i] the foundation of the temple of the LORD, the
priests in their vestments and with
trumpets,[j] and the Levites (the sons
of Asaph) with cymbals, took their
places to praise[k] the LORD, as prescribed by David[l] king of Israel.[m]
11 With praise and thanksgiving they
sang to the LORD:

"He is good;
his love to Israel endures
forever."[n]

And all the people gave a great shout[o]
of praise to the LORD, because the
foundation of the house of the LORD
was laid. 12 But many of the older
priests and Levites and family heads,
who had seen the former temple,[p]
wept aloud when they saw the foundation of this temple being laid, while
many others shouted for joy. 13 No one
could distinguish the sound of the
shouts of joy[q] from the sound of
weeping, because the people made so
much noise. And the sound was heard
far away.

Opposition to the Rebuilding

4 When the enemies of Judah and
Benjamin heard that the exiles were
building a temple for the LORD, the God
of Israel, 2 they came to Zerubbabel and
to the heads of the families and said,
"Let us help you build because, like
you, we seek your God and have been
sacrificing to him since the time of
Esarhaddon[r] king of Assyria, who
brought us here."[s]
3 But Zerubbabel, Jeshua and the rest
of the heads of the families of Israel
answered, "You have no part with us in
building a temple to our God. We alone
will build it for the LORD, the God of
Israel, as King Cyrus, the king of Persia,
commanded us."[t]

4 Then the peoples around them set
out to discourage the people of Judah
and make them afraid to go on building.[b][u] 5 They hired counselors to work
against them and frustrate their plans
during the entire reign of Cyrus king of
Persia and down to the reign of Darius
king of Persia.

Later Opposition Under Xerxes and Artaxerxes

6 At the beginning of the reign of
Xerxes,[c][v] they lodged an accusation
against the people of Judah and Jerusalem.[w]

7 And in the days of Artaxerxes[x] king
of Persia, Bishlam, Mithredath, Tabeel
and the rest of his associates wrote a
letter to Artaxerxes. The letter was writ-

3:7 [c]1Ch 14:1 [d]Isa 35:2 [e]Ezr 1:2-4; 6:3
3:8 [f]Zec 4:9 [g]1Ch 23:24
3:9 [h]Ezr 2:40
3:10 [i]Ezr 5:16 [j]Nu 10:2; 1Ch 16:6 [k]1Ch 25:1 [l]1Ch 6:31 [m]Zec 6:12
3:11 [n]1Ch 16:34,41; 2Ch 7:3; Ps 107:1; 118:1 [o]Ne 12:24
3:12 [p]Hag 2:3,9
3:13 [q]Job 8:21; Ps 27:6; Isa 16:9
4:2 [r]2Ki 17:24; 19:37 [s]2Ki 17:41
4:3 [t]Ezr 1:1-4; Ne 2:20
4:4 [u]Ezr 3:3
4:6 [v]Est 1:1; Da 9:1 [w]Est 3:13; 9:5
4:7 [x]Ezr 7:1; Ne 2:1

[a]9 Hebrew *Yehudah,* probably a variant of *Hodaviah* [b]4 Or *and troubled them as they built* [c]6 Hebrew *Ahasuerus,* a variant of Xerxes' Persian name

3:11–13

PROMISE 6

ONE CHEERING SECTION

Picture this: The game is on the line with only a few seconds left to play. The teams are evenly matched, and neither one has been able to gain an advantage throughout the game. As the seconds wear down, one team pulls it together and makes the final score. One side cheers and the other side moans. It's all a matter of perspective.

When workmen began to lay the foundation for a new temple in Jerusalem, a similar thing happened. Some shouted for joy that the temple was on its way to being rebuilt; others wept aloud because this construction was a poor reflection of the original temple that Solomon had built.

When God works, the results may not be what we expect. We may look at God's work in someone's life or in the life of an organization and think it could have been different, or better, or that God could have worked through another person or church or organization. But when God is at work, the sound coming from his people should never be mixed. Be one of God's cheerleaders, even if you don't completely understand what he's doing.

For the next Promise 6 reading go to page 518.

ten in Aramaic script and in the Aramaic[y] language.[a,b]

8 Rehum the commanding officer and Shimshai the secretary wrote a letter against Jerusalem to Artaxerxes the king as follows:

> 9 Rehum the commanding officer and Shimshai the secretary, together with the rest of their associates[z]—the judges and officials over the men from Tripolis, Persia,[c] Erech and Babylon, the Elamites of Susa, 10 and the other people whom the great and honorable Ashurbanipal[d] deported and settled in the city of Samaria and elsewhere in Trans-Euphrates.[a]

11 (This is a copy of the letter they sent him.)

> To King Artaxerxes,
>
> From your servants, the men of Trans-Euphrates:
>
> 12 The king should know that the Jews who came up to us from you have gone to Jerusalem and are rebuilding that rebellious and wicked city. They are restoring the walls and repairing the foundations.[b]
>
> 13 Furthermore, the king should know that if this city is built and its walls are restored, no more taxes, tribute or duty[c] will be paid, and the royal revenues will suffer. 14 Now since we are under obligation to the palace and it is not proper for us to see the king dishonored, we are sending this message to inform the king, 15 so that a search may be made in the archives[d] of your predecessors. In these records you will find that this city is a rebellious city, troublesome to kings and provinces, a place of rebellion from ancient times. That is why this city was destroyed.[e] 16 We inform the king that if this city is built and its walls are restored, you will be left with nothing in Trans-Euphrates.

17 The king sent this reply:

> To Rehum the commanding officer, Shimshai the secretary and the rest of their associates living in Samaria and elsewhere in Trans-Euphrates:[f]
>
> Greetings.
>
> 18 The letter you sent us has been read and translated in my presence. 19 I issued an order and a search was made, and it was found that this city has a long history of revolt[g] against kings and has been a place of rebellion and sedition. 20 Jerusalem has had powerful kings ruling over the whole of Trans-Euphrates,[h] and taxes, tribute and duty were paid to them. 21 Now issue an order to these men to stop work, so that this city will not be rebuilt until I so order. 22 Be careful not to neglect this matter. Why let this threat grow, to the detriment of the royal interests?[i]

23 As soon as the copy of the letter of King Artaxerxes was read to Rehum and Shimshai the secretary and their associates,[j] they went immediately to the Jews in Jerusalem and compelled them by force to stop.

24 Thus the work on the house of God in Jerusalem came to a standstill until the second year of the reign of Darius[k] king of Persia.

Tattenai's Letter to Darius

5 Now Haggai[l] the prophet and Zechariah[m] the prophet, a descendant of Iddo, prophesied[n] to the Jews in Judah and Jerusalem in the name of the God of Israel, who was over them. 2 Then Zerubbabel[o] son of Shealtiel and Jeshua[p] son of Jozadak set to work[q] to rebuild the house of God in Jerusalem. And the prophets of God were with them, helping them.

3 At that time Tattenai,[r] governor of Trans-Euphrates, and Shethar-Bozenai[s] and their associates went to them and asked, "Who authorized you to rebuild this temple and restore this structure?"[t] 4 They also asked, "What are the names of the men constructing this building?"[e] 5 But the eye of their God[u] was watching over the elders of the Jews, and they were not stopped until a report could go to Darius and his written reply be received.

6 This is a copy of the letter that Tattenai, governor of Trans-Euphrates, and Shethar-Bozenai and their associates, the officials of Trans-Euphrates, sent to King Darius. 7 The report they sent him read as follows:

4:7 [y] 2Ki 18:26; Isa 36:11; Da 2:4
4:9 [z] Ezr 5:6; 6:6, 13
4:10 [a] ver 17; Ne 4:2
4:12 [b] Ezr 5:3,9
4:13 [c] Ezr 7:24; Ne 5:4
4:15 [d] Ezr 5:17; 6:1 [e] Est 3:8
4:17 [f] ver 10
4:19 [g] 2Ki 18:7
4:20 [h] Ge 15:18-21; Ex 23:31; Jos 1:4; 1Ki 4:21; 1Ch 18:3; Ps 72:8-11
4:22 [i] Da 6:2
4:23 [j] ver 9
4:24 [k] Ne 2:1-8; Da 9:25; Hag 1:1,15; Zec 1:1
5:1 [l] Ezr 6:14; Hag 1:1,3,12; 2:1,10,20 [m] Zec 1:1; 7:1 [n] Hag 1:14-2:9; Zec 4:9-10; 8:9
5:2 [o] 1Ch 3:19; Hag 1:14; 2:21; Zec 4:6-10 [p] Ezr 2:2; 3:2 [q] ver 8; Hag 2:2-5
5:3 [r] Ezr 6:6 [s] Ezr 6:6 [t] ver 9; Ezr 1:3; 4:12
5:5 [u] 2Ki 25:28; Ezr 7:6,9,28; 8:18,22,31; Ne 2:8,18; Ps 33:18; Isa 66:14

a 7 Or *written in Aramaic and translated*
b 7 The text of Ezra 4:8—6:18 is in Aramaic.
c 9 Or *officials, magistrates and governors over the men from*
d 10 Aramaic *Osnappar,* a variant of *Ashurbanipal*
e 4 See Septuagint; Aramaic *4We told them the names of the men constructing this building.*

To King Darius:

Cordial greetings.

8The king should know that we
went to the district of Judah, to
the temple of the great God. The
people are building it with large
stones and placing the timbers in
the walls. The work[v] is being carried on with diligence and is making rapid progress under their direction.
9We questioned the elders and
asked them, "Who authorized you
to rebuild this temple and restore
this structure?"[w] 10We also asked
them their names, so that we
could write down the names of
their leaders for your information.
11This is the answer they
gave us:

"We are the servants of the God
of heaven and earth, and we are
rebuilding the temple[x] that was
built many years ago, one that a
great king of Israel built and finished. 12But because our fathers
angered[y] the God of heaven, he
handed them over to Nebuchadnezzar the Chaldean, king of Babylon, who destroyed this temple
and deported the people to Babylon.[z]
13"However, in the first year of
Cyrus king of Babylon, King Cyrus
issued a decree[a] to rebuild this
house of God. 14He even removed
from the temple[a] of Babylon the
gold and silver articles of the
house of God, which Nebuchadnezzar had taken from the temple
in Jerusalem and brought to the
temple[a] in Babylon.[b]
"Then King Cyrus gave them
to a man named Sheshbazzar,[c]
whom he had appointed governor, 15and he told him, 'Take
these articles and go and deposit
them in the temple in Jerusalem.
And rebuild the house of God on
its site.' 16So this Sheshbazzar
came and laid the foundations of
the house of God[d] in Jerusalem.
From that day to the present it has
been under construction but is
not yet finished."

17Now if it pleases the king, let
a search be made in the royal archives[e] of Babylon to see if King
Cyrus did in fact issue a decree to
rebuild this house of God in Jerusalem. Then let the king send us
his decision in this matter.

5:8 [v]ver 2
5:9 [w]Ezr 4:12
5:11 [x]1Ki 6:1; 2Ch 3:1-2
5:12 [y]2Ch 36:16 [z]Dt 21:10; 28:36; 2Ki 24:1; 25:8, 9,11; Jer 1:3
5:13 [a]Ezr 1:1
5:14 [b]Ezr 1:7; 6:5; Da 5:2 [c]1Ch 3:18
5:16 [d]Ezr 3:10; 6:15
5:17 [e]Ezr 4:15; 6:1,2

The Decree of Darius

6 King Darius then issued an order,
and they searched in the archives[f]
stored in the treasury at Babylon. 2A
scroll was found in the citadel of Ecbat-
ana in the province of Media, and this
was written on it:

Memorandum:
3In the first year of King Cyrus,
the king issued a decree concerning the temple of God in Jerusalem:

Let the temple be rebuilt as a
place to present sacrifices, and let
its foundations be laid.[g] It is to
be ninety feet[b] high and ninety
feet wide, 4with three courses[h] of
large stones and one of timbers.
The costs are to be paid by the
royal treasury.[i] 5Also, the gold[j]
and silver articles of the house of
God, which Nebuchadnezzar took
from the temple in Jerusalem and
brought to Babylon, are to be returned to their places in the temple in Jerusalem; they are to be
deposited in the house of God.[k]

6Now then, Tattenai,[l] governor of Trans-Euphrates, and
Shethar-Bozenai[m] and you, their
fellow officials of that province,
stay away from there. 7Do not interfere with the work on this temple of God. Let the governor of the
Jews and the Jewish elders rebuild
this house of God on its site.
8Moreover, I hereby decree
what you are to do for these elders
of the Jews in the construction of
this house of God:
The expenses of these men are
to be fully paid out of the royal
treasury,[n] from the revenues[o] of
Trans-Euphrates, so that the work
will not stop. 9Whatever is
needed—young bulls, rams, male
lambs for burnt offerings[p] to the
God of heaven, and wheat, salt,
wine and oil, as requested by the
priests in Jerusalem—must be
given them daily without fail, 10so
that they may offer sacrifices
pleasing to the God of heaven and
pray for the well-being of the king
and his sons.[q]
11Furthermore, I decree that if
anyone changes this edict, a beam
is to be pulled from his house and
he is to be lifted up and impaled[r]
on it. And for this crime his house

6:1 [f]Ezr 4:15; 5:17
6:3 [g]Ezr 3:10; Hag 2:3
6:4 [h]1Ki 6:36 [i]ver 8; Ezr 7:20
6:5 [j]1Ch 29:2 [k]Ezr 1:7; 5:14
6:6 [l]Ezr 5:3 [m]Ezr 5:3
6:8 [n]ver 4 [o]1Sa 9:20
6:9 [p]Lev 1:3,10
6:10 [q]Ezr 7:23; 1Ti 2:1-2
6:11 [r]Dt 21:22-23; Est 2:23; 5:14; 9:14

a *14* Or *palace* **b** *3* Aramaic *sixty cubits* (about 27 meters)

is to be made a pile of rubble.[s]
12May God, who has caused his
Name to dwell there,[t] overthrow
any king or people who lifts a
hand to change this decree or to
destroy this temple in Jerusalem.
I Darius[u] have decreed it. Let it
be carried out with diligence.

Completion and Dedication of the Temple

13Then, because of the decree King
Darius had sent, Tattenai, governor of
Trans-Euphrates, and Shethar-Bozenai and their associates[v] carried it
out with diligence. 14So the elders of
the Jews continued to build and prosper under the preaching[w] of Haggai
the prophet and Zechariah, a descendant of Iddo. They finished building
the temple according to the command
of the God of Israel and the decrees of
Cyrus,[x] Darius[y] and Artaxerxes,[z]
kings of Persia. 15The temple was completed on the third day of the month
Adar, in the sixth year of the reign of
King Darius.[a]
16Then the people of Israel—the
priests, the Levites and the rest of the
exiles—celebrated the dedication[b] of
the house of God with joy. 17For the
dedication of this house of God they
offered[c] a hundred bulls, two hundred rams, four hundred male lambs
and, as a sin offering for all Israel,
twelve male goats, one for each of the
tribes of Israel. 18And they installed the
priests in their divisions[d] and the Levites in their groups[e] for the service of
God at Jerusalem, according to what is
written in the Book of Moses.[f]

6:11 [s]Ezr 7:26; Da 2:5; 3:29
6:12 [t]Ex 20:24; Dt 12:5; 1Ki 9:3; 2Ch 6:2 [u]ver 14
6:13 [v]Ezr 4:9
6:14 [w]Ezr 5:1 [x]Ezr 1:1-4 [y]ver 12 [z]Ezr 7:1; Ne 2:1
6:15 [a]Zec 1:1; 4:9
6:16 [b]1Ki 8:63; 2Ch 7:5
6:17 [c]2Sa 6:13; 2Ch 29:21; 30:24; Ezr 8:35
6:18 [d]1Ch 23:6; 2Ch 35:4; Lk 1:5 [e]1Ch 24:1
[f]Nu 3:6-9; 8:9-11; 18:1-32
6:19 [g]Ex 12:11; Nu 28:16
6:20 [h]2Ch 30:15,17; 35:11
6:21 [i]Ezr 9:1; Ne 9:2 [j]Dt 18:9; Ezr 9:11; Eze 36:25 [k]1Ch 22:19; Ps 14:2
6:22 [l]Ex 12:17 [m]Ezr 1:1
7:1 [n]Ezr 4:7; 6:14; Ne 2:1 [o]2Ki 22:4
7:2 [p]1Ki 1:8; 1Ch 6:8 [q]Ne 11:11
7:6 [r]Ne 12:36 [s]Ezr 5:5; Isa 41:20
7:7 [t]Ezr 8:1
7:9 [u]ver 6
7:10 [v]ver 25; Dt 33:10; Ne 8:1-8

The Passover

19On the fourteenth day of the first
month, the exiles celebrated the Passover.[g] 20The priests and Levites had
purified themselves and were all ceremonially clean. The Levites slaughtered[h] the Passover lamb for all the
exiles, for their brothers the priests and
for themselves. 21So the Israelites who
had returned from the exile ate it, together with all who had separated
themselves[i] from the unclean practices[j] of their Gentile neighbors in order to seek the LORD,[k] the God of Israel. 22For seven days they celebrated
with joy the Feast of Unleavened
Bread,[l] because the LORD had filled
them with joy by changing the attitude[m] of the king of Assyria, so that he
assisted them in the work on the house
of God, the God of Israel.

Ezra Comes to Jerusalem

7 After these things, during the reign
of Artaxerxes[n] king of Persia, Ezra
son of Seraiah, the son of Azariah, the
son of Hilkiah,[o] 2the son of Shallum,
the son of Zadok,[p] the son of Ahitub,[q] 3the son of Amariah, the son of
Azariah, the son of Meraioth, 4the son
of Zerahiah, the son of Uzzi, the son of
Bukki, 5the son of Abishua, the son of
Phinehas, the son of Eleazar, the son
of Aaron the chief priest— 6this Ezra[r]
came up from Babylon. He was a
teacher well versed in the Law of Moses, which the LORD, the God of Israel,
had given. The king had granted him
everything he asked, for the hand of
the LORD his God was on him.[s] 7Some
of the Israelites, including priests, Levites, singers, gatekeepers and temple
servants, also came up to Jerusalem in
the seventh year of King Artaxerxes.[t]
8Ezra arrived in Jerusalem in the
fifth month of the seventh year of the
king. 9He had begun his journey from
Babylon on the first day of the first
month, and he arrived in Jerusalem on
the first day of the fifth month, for the
gracious hand of his God was on
him.[u] 10For Ezra had devoted himself
to the study and observance of the Law
of the LORD, and to teaching[v] its decrees and laws in Israel.

King Artaxerxes' Letter to Ezra

11This is a copy of the letter King Artaxerxes had given to Ezra the priest
and teacher, a man learned in matters
concerning the commands and decrees of the LORD for Israel:

6:13–15

PROMISE 7

TEAM EFFORT

God's work required many resources. A Persian king and Israelite elders, prophets and laborers all had to pitch in and work together. They put aside professional, ethnic and ideological differences and combined their efforts to accomplish something none of them could have done without the others.

Imagine what we can do as we focus on the Great Commission and the Great Commandment, combine our resources and get at God's work. Take a moment now to consider where there are divisions among the fellowship of which you're a part. Then pray for reconciliation and unity among God's people in your community and around the world. Together we can accomplish what none of us could do alone.

For the next Promise 7 reading go to page 509.

12[a]Artaxerxes, king of kings,[w]

To Ezra the priest, a teacher of the
Law of the God of heaven:

Greetings.

13Now I decree that any of the
Israelites in my kingdom, including priests and Levites, who wish
to go to Jerusalem with you, may
go. **14**You are sent by the king and
his seven advisers[x] to inquire
about Judah and Jerusalem with
regard to the Law of your God,
which is in your hand. **15**Moreover, you are to take with you the
silver and gold that the king and
his advisers have freely given[y] to
the God of Israel, whose dwelling[z] is in Jerusalem, **16**together
with all the silver and gold[a] you
may obtain from the province of
Babylon, as well as the freewill offerings of the people and priests
for the temple of their God in Jerusalem.[b] **17**With this money be
sure to buy bulls, rams and male
lambs,[c] together with their grain
offerings and drink offerings,[d]
and sacrifice[e] them on the altar
of the temple of your God in Jerusalem.

18You and your brother Jews
may then do whatever seems best
with the rest of the silver and gold,
in accordance with the will of
your God. **19**Deliver[f] to the God
of Jerusalem all the articles entrusted to you for worship in the
temple of your God. **20**And anything else needed for the temple
of your God that you may have
occasion to supply, you may provide from the royal treasury.[g]

7:10

PROMISE **1**

GOD'S MAN FOR WHAT'S NEXT

Now that the temple had been completed, God needed a different kind of leader for his people. He chose Ezra, because this priest was prepared in a particular way for what God was going to do next.

As in Ezra's time, God needs men who can rally the troops, men who can build things and men who know his Word and have a heart to teach. God has prepared a place for you in his work. Each man of God needs to lead in his time and let others lead in theirs. We accomplish great things for God when great men lead well and follow well—each in his own appropriate time. As Ezra did, you too can become God's man for what's next.

For the next Promise 1 reading go to page 518.

21Now I, King Artaxerxes, order
all the treasurers of Trans-
Euphrates to provide with diligence whatever Ezra the priest, a
teacher of the Law of the God of
heaven, may ask of you— **22**up to
a hundred talents[b] of silver, a
hundred cors[c] of wheat, a hundred baths[d] of wine, a hundred
baths[d] of olive oil, and salt without limit. **23**Whatever the God of
heaven has prescribed, let it be
done with diligence for the temple
of the God of heaven. Why should
there be wrath against the realm
of the king and of his sons?[h]
24You are also to know that you
have no authority to impose taxes,
tribute or duty[i] on any of the
priests, Levites, singers, gatekeepers, temple servants or other
workers at this house of God.[j]

25And you, Ezra, in accordance
with the wisdom of your God,
which you possess, appoint[k]
magistrates and judges to administer justice to all the people of
Trans-Euphrates—all who know
the laws of your God. And you are
to teach[l] any who do not know
them. **26**Whoever does not obey
the law of your God and the law of
the king must surely be punished
by death, banishment, confiscation of property, or imprisonment.[m]

27Praise be to the LORD, the God of
our fathers, who has put it into the
king's heart[n] to bring honor[o] to the
house of the LORD in Jerusalem in this
way **28**and who has extended his good
favor[p] to me before the king and his
advisers and all the king's powerful officials. Because the hand of the LORD
my God was on me,[q] I took courage
and gathered leading men from Israel
to go up with me.

List of the Family Heads Returning With Ezra

8 These are the family heads and
those registered with them who
came up with me from Babylon during
the reign of King Artaxerxes:[r]

2of the descendants of Phinehas,
Gershom;
of the descendants of Ithamar,
Daniel;
of the descendants of David, Hat-

7:12 [w]Eze 26:7; Da 2:37
7:14 [x]Est 1:14
7:15 [y]1Ch 29:6 [z]1Ch 29:6,9; 2Ch 6:2
7:16 [a]Ezr 8:25 [b]Zec 6:10
7:17 [c]2Ki 3:4 [d]Nu 15:5-12 [e]Dt 12:5-11
7:19 [f]Ezr 5:14; Jer 27:22
7:20 [g]Ezr 6:4
7:23 [h]Ezr 6:10
7:24 [i]Ezr 4:13 [j]Ezr 8:36
7:25 [k]Ex 18:21,26; Dt 16:18 [l]ver 10; Lev 10:11
7:26 [m]Ezr 6:11
7:27 [n]Ezr 1:1; 6:22 [o]1Ch 29:12
7:28 [p]2Ki 25:28 [q]Ezr 5:5; 9:9
8:1 [r]Ezr 7:7

[a] *12* The text of Ezra 7:12-26 is in Aramaic.
[b] *22* That is, about 3 3/4 tons (about 3.4 metric tons) [c] *22* That is, probably about 600 bushels (about 22 kiloliters) [d] *22* That is, probably about 600 gallons (about 2.2 kiloliters)

tush 3of the descendants of
Shecaniah;[s]

of the descendants of Parosh,[t]
Zechariah, and with him were
registered 150 men;
4of the descendants of Pahath-
Moab,[u] Eliehoenai son of Zerahiah, and with him 200 men;
5of the descendants of Zattu,[a]
Shecaniah son of Jahaziel, and
with him 300 men;
6of the descendants of Adin,[v]
Ebed son of Jonathan, and
with him 50 men;
7of the descendants of Elam, Jeshaiah son of Athaliah, and
with him 70 men;
8of the descendants of Shephatiah, Zebadiah son of Michael,
and with him 80 men;
9of the descendants of Joab, Obadiah son of Jehiel, and with
him 218 men;
10of the descendants of Bani,[b]
Shelomith son of Josiphiah,
and with him 160 men;
11of the descendants of Bebai,
Zechariah son of Bebai, and
with him 28 men;
12of the descendants of Azgad, Johanan son of Hakkatan, and
with him 110 men;
13of the descendants of Adoni-
kam,[w] the last ones, whose
names were Eliphelet, Jeuel
and Shemaiah, and with them
60 men;
14of the descendants of Bigvai,
Uthai and Zaccur, and with
them 70 men.

The Return to Jerusalem

15I assembled them at the canal that
flows toward Ahava,[x] and we camped
there three days. When I checked
among the people and the priests, I
found no Levites[y] there. 16So I summoned Eliezer, Ariel, Shemaiah, Elnathan, Jarib, Elnathan, Nathan, Zechariah and Meshullam, who were leaders,
and Joiarib and Elnathan, who were
men of learning, 17and I sent them to
Iddo, the leader in Casiphia. I told
them what to say to Iddo and his kinsmen, the temple servants[z] in Casiphia, so that they might bring attendants
to us for the house of our God. 18Be-
cause the gracious hand of our God
was on us,[a] they brought us Sherebiah, a capable man, from the descendants of Mahli son of Levi, the son of
Israel, and Sherebiah's sons and brothers, 18 men; 19and Hashabiah, together
with Jeshaiah from the descendants of
Merari, and his brothers and nephews,
20 men. 20They also brought 220 of the
temple servants[b]—a body that David
and the officials had established to assist the Levites. All were registered by
name.
21There, by the Ahava Canal,[c] I proclaimed a fast, so that we might humble ourselves before our God and ask
him for a safe journey[d] for us and our
children, with all our possessions. 22I
was ashamed to ask the king for soldiers[e] and horsemen to protect us
from enemies on the road, because we
had told the king, "The gracious hand
of our God is on everyone[f] who looks
to him, but his great anger is against all
who forsake him.[g]" 23So we fasted[h]
and petitioned our God about this, and
he answered our prayer.

1 →PG. 511

24Then I set apart twelve of the leading priests, together with Sherebiah,[i]
Hashabiah and ten of their brothers,
25and I weighed out[j] to them the offering of silver and gold and the articles
that the king, his advisers, his officials
and all Israel present there had donat-
ed for the house of our God. 26I
weighed out to them 650 talents[c] of
silver, silver articles weighing 100 talents,[d] 100 talents[d] of gold, 2720 bowls
of gold valued at 1,000 darics,[e] and
two fine articles of polished bronze, as
precious as gold.
28I said to them, "You as well as
these articles are consecrated to the
LORD.[k] The silver and gold are a freewill offering to the LORD, the God of
your fathers. 29Guard them carefully
until you weigh them out in the cham-

8:3 [s] 1Ch 3:22 [t] Ezr 2:3 **8:4** [u] Ezr 2:6 **8:6** [v] Ezr 2:15; Ne 7:20; 10:16 **8:13** [w] Ezr 2:13 **8:15** [x] ver 21,31 [y] Ezr 2:40; 7:7 **8:17** [z] Ezr 2:43 **8:18** [a] Ezr 5:5 **8:20** [b] 1Ch 9:2; Ezr 2:43 **8:21** [c] ver 15; 2Ch 20:3 [d] Ps 5:8; 107:7 **8:22** [e] Ne 2:9; Ezr 7:6,9,28 [f] Ezr 5:5 [g] Dt 31:17; 2Ch 15:2 **8:23** [h] 2Ch 20:3; 33:13 **8:24** [i] ver 18 **8:25** [j] ver 33; Ezr 7:15,16 **8:28** [k] Lev 21:6; 22:2-3

[a] *5* Some Septuagint manuscripts (also 1 Esdras 8:32); Hebrew does not have *Zattu.* [b] *10* Some Septuagint manuscripts (also 1 Esdras 8:36); Hebrew does not have *Bani.* [c] *26* That is, about 25 tons (about 22 metric tons) [d] *26* That is, about 3 3/4 tons (about 3.4 metric tons) [e] *27* That is, about 19 pounds (about 8.5 kilograms)

8:21–23

PROMISE 7

POWER SOURCE

Ezra had impressive financial and human resources (7:11–8:14) as he set out for Jerusalem. But he took time to draw on the only Resource that brings success in God's work.

Stop! Read over these verses again. Before you go out your door each morning, follow Ezra's example and, in some way, get in touch with the Master. Every Christian man is under the Great Commission and Great Commandment, and needs to draw on God's power before going into the world to represent him.

For the next Promise 7 reading go to page 517.

bers of the house of the LORD in Jerusalem before the leading priests and the
Levites and the family heads of Israel."
30Then the priests and Levites received
the silver and gold and sacred articles
that had been weighed out to be taken
to the house of our God in Jerusalem.
31On the twelfth day of the first
month we set out from the Ahava Canal[l] to go to Jerusalem. The hand of
our God was on us, and he protected us
from enemies and bandits along the
way. 32So we arrived in Jerusalem,
where we rested three days.[m]
33On the fourth day, in the house of
our God, we weighed out the silver and
gold and the sacred articles into the
hands of Meremoth[n] son of Uriah, the
priest. Eleazar son of Phinehas was
with him, and so were the Levites Jozabad son of Jeshua and Noadiah son of
Binnui.[o] 34Everything was accounted
for by number and weight, and the entire weight was recorded at that time.
35Then the exiles who had returned
from captivity sacrificed burnt offerings to the God of Israel: twelve bulls
for all Israel, ninety-six rams, seventy-
seven male lambs and, as a sin offering, twelve male goats.[p] All this was a
burnt offering to the LORD. 36They also
delivered the king's orders[q] to the royal satraps and to the governors of
Trans-Euphrates, who then gave assistance to the people and to the house of
God.[r]

Ezra's Prayer About Intermarriage

9 After these things had been done,
the leaders came to me and said,
"The people of Israel, including the
priests and the Levites, have not kept
themselves separate[s] from the neighboring peoples with their detestable
practices, like those of the Canaanites,
Hittites, Perizzites, Jebusites, Ammonites,[t] Moabites, Egyptians and Amorites.[u] 2They have taken some of their
daughters[v] as wives for themselves
and their sons, and have mingled the
holy race[w] with the peoples around
them. And the leaders and officials
have led the way in this unfaithfulness."[x]
3When I heard this, I tore my tunic
and cloak, pulled hair from my head
and beard and sat down appalled.
4Then everyone who trembled[y] at the
words of the God of Israel gathered
around me because of this unfaithfulness of the exiles. And I sat there appalled until the evening sacrifice.
5Then, at the evening sacrifice,[z] I
rose from my self-abasement, with my
tunic and cloak torn, and fell on my
knees with my hands spread out to the
LORD my God 6and prayed:

"O my God, I am too ashamed
and disgraced to lift up my face to
you, my God, because our sins are
higher than our heads and our
guilt has reached to the heavens.[a] 7From the days of our forefathers[b] until now, our guilt has
been great. Because of our sins,
we and our kings and our priests
have been subjected to the
sword[c] and captivity,[d] to pillage
and humiliation[e] at the hand of
foreign kings, as it is today.
8"But now, for a brief moment,
the LORD our God has been gracious[f] in leaving us a remnant[g]
and giving us a firm place[h] in his
sanctuary, and so our God gives
light to our eyes[i] and a little relief
in our bondage. 9Though we are
slaves,[j] our God has not deserted
us in our bondage. He has shown
us kindness[k] in the sight of the
kings of Persia: He has granted
us new life to rebuild the house
of our God and repair its ruins,[l]
and he has given us a wall of protection in Judah and Jerusalem.
10"But now, O our God, what
can we say after this? For we have

8:31 [l]ver 15 **8:32** [m]Ge 40:13; Ne 2:11 **8:33** [n]Ne 3:4,21 [o]Ne 3:24 **8:35** [p]2Ch 29:21; Ezr 6:17 **8:36** [q]Ezr 7:21-24 [r]Est 9:3 **9:1** [s]Ezr 6:21; Ne 9:2 [t]Ge 19:38 [u]Ex 13:5 **9:2** [v]Ex 34:16 [w]Ex 22:31 [x]Ezr 10:2 **9:4** [y]Ezr 10:3 **9:5** [z]Ex 29:41

9:6 [a]2Ch 28:9; Job 42:6; Ps 38:4; Rev 18:5 **9:7** [b]2Ch 29:6 [c]Eze 21:1-32 [d]Dt 28:64 [e]Dt 28:37 **9:8** [f]Ps 25:16; Isa 33:2 [g]Ge 45:7 [h]Ecc 12:11; Isa 22:23 [i]Ps 13:3 **9:9** [j]Ex 1:14; Ne 9:36 [k]Ezr 7:28 [l]Ps 69:35; Isa 43:1; Jer 32:44

9:3–4

PROMISE **3**

PASSION FOR PURITY

Ezra understood sin's destructive power. The people of Israel, against God's direct commands, had intermarried with people from surrounding nations. They had taken up the "detestable practices" of these nations, and in so doing had corrupted their worship of and commitment to God. Ezra's reaction in this passage indicates his deep shock and sorrow over the nation's sin. Only this kind of deep repentance leads to revival.

Meditate on Ezra's prayer (vv. 5–15) and pray that God will give you this kind of sensitivity to sin and passion for purity among God's people. Are there any "detestable practices" in your life that you need to do something about? The Israelites vowed to keep God's command in an extremely dramatic fashion after seeing Ezra's sorrow (see 10:1–2). They repented of their sin and kept God's commands. Perhaps you will become someone's Ezra—demonstrating a concern for a friend's sin and leading him or her to repentence. Perhaps you will be an Israel, seeing Ezra's sorrow for sin and coming to repentence before God.

For the next Promise 3 reading go to page 591.

disregarded the commands[m]
11you gave through your servants
the prophets when you said: 'The
land you are entering to possess is
a land polluted[n] by the corruption of its peoples. By their detestable practices[o] they have filled it
with their impurity from one end
4 →PG. 522
to the other. 12Therefore, do not
give your daughters in marriage to
their sons or take their daughters
for your sons. Do not seek a treaty
of friendship with them[p] at any
time, that you may be strong and
eat the good things of the land
and leave it to your children as an
everlasting inheritance.'
13"What has happened to us is
a result of our evil deeds and our
great guilt, and yet, our God, you
have punished us less than our
sins have deserved[q] and have
given us a remnant like this.
14Shall we again break your commands and intermarry[r] with the
peoples who commit such detestable practices? Would you not be
angry enough with us to destroy
us,[s] leaving us no remnant[t] or
survivor? 15O LORD, God of Israel,
you are righteous![u] We are left
this day as a remnant. Here we are
before you in our guilt, though because of it not one of us can
stand[v] in your presence.[w]"

The People's Confession of Sin

10 While Ezra was praying and confessing,[x] weeping and throwing
himself down before the house of
God, a large crowd of Israelites—
men, women and children—gathered
around him. They too wept bitterly.
2Then Shecaniah son of Jehiel, one of
the descendants of Elam, said to Ezra,
"We have been unfaithful[y] to our God
by marrying foreign women from the
peoples around us. But in spite of this,
there is still hope for Israel.[z] 3Now let
us make a covenant[a] before our God
to send away[b] all these women and
their children, in accordance with the
counsel of my lord and of those who
fear the commands of our God. Let it
be done according to the Law. 4Rise up;
this matter is in your hands. We will
support you, so take courage and
do it."
5So Ezra rose up and put the leading
priests and Levites and all Israel under
oath[c] to do what had been suggested.
1 →PG. 527
And they took the oath. 6Then Ezra
withdrew from before the house of God
and went to the room of Jehohanan
son of Eliashib. While he was there, he
ate no food and drank no water,[d] because he continued to mourn over the
unfaithfulness of the exiles.
7A proclamation was then issued
throughout Judah and Jerusalem for all
the exiles to assemble in Jerusalem.
8Anyone who failed to appear within
three days would forfeit all his property, in accordance with the decision of
the officials and elders, and would
himself be expelled from the assembly
of the exiles.

9Within the three days, all the men
of Judah and Benjamin[e] had gathered
in Jerusalem. And on the twentieth day
of the ninth month, all the people were
sitting in the square before the house
of God, greatly distressed by the occasion and because of the rain. 10Then
Ezra the priest stood up and said to
them, "You have been unfaithful; you
have married foreign women, adding
to Israel's guilt. 11Now make confession to the LORD, the God of your fathers, and do his will. Separate yourselves from the peoples around you
and from your foreign wives."[f]
12The whole assembly responded
with a loud voice:[g] "You are right! We
must do as you say. 13But there are
many people here and it is the rainy
season; so we cannot stand outside.
Besides, this matter cannot be taken
care of in a day or two, because we
have sinned greatly in this thing. 14Let
our officials act for the whole assembly. Then let everyone in our towns
who has married a foreign woman
come at a set time, along with the elders and judges[h] of each town, until
the fierce anger[i] of our God in this
matter is turned away from us." 15Only
Jonathan son of Asahel and Jahzeiah
son of Tikvah, supported by Meshullam and Shabbethai[j] the Levite, opposed this.
16So the exiles did as was proposed.

9:10 [m]Dt 11:8; Isa 1:19-20 **9:11** [n]Lev 18:25-28 [o]Dt 9:4 **9:12** [p]Ex 34:15; Dt 7:3; 23:6 **9:13** [q]Job 11:6; Ps 103:10 **9:14** [r]Ne 13:27 [s]Dt 9:8 [t]Dt 9:14 **9:15** [u]Ge 18:25; Ps 51:4; Jer 12:1; Da 9:7 [v]Ne 9:33; Ps 130:3; Mal 3:2 [w]1Ki 8:47 **10:1** [x]2Ch 20:9; Da 9:20 **10:2** [y]Ezr 9:2; Ne 13:27 [z]Dt 30:8-10 **10:3** [a]2Ch 34:31 [b]Ex 34:16; Dt 7:2-3; Ezr 9:4 **10:5** [c]Ne 5:12; 13:25

10:6 [d]Ex 34:28; Dt 9:18 **10:9** [e]Ezr 1:5 **10:11** [f]ver 3; Dt 24:1; Ne 9:2; Mal 2:10-16 **10:12** [g]Jos 6:5 **10:14** [h]Dt 16:18 [i]Nu 25:4; 2Ch 29:10; 30:8 **10:15** [j]Ne 11:16

10:1-4

PROMISE 5

MODEL BEHAVIOR

When people have a good model to follow, amazing things happen. Ezra's repentance and prayer for restoration encouraged others to join him in repentance. The priest so motivated the people that they dramatically acted to reverse the sins that they had committed.

Every church can be inspired and empowered by a man who will be known for his righteousness and humility before God. Why not you?

For the next Promise 5 reading go to page 519.

Ezra the priest selected men who were
family heads, one from each family division, and all of them designated by
name. On the first day of the tenth
month they sat down to investigate the
cases, 17 and by the first day of the first
month they finished dealing with all
the men who had married foreign
women.

Those Guilty of Intermarriage

18 Among the descendants of the
priests, the following had married foreign women:[k]

From the descendants of Jeshua[l] son of Jozadak, and his
brothers: Maaseiah, Eliezer,
Jarib and Gedaliah. 19 (They all
gave their hands[m] in pledge to
put away their wives, and for
their guilt they each presented
a ram from the flock as a guilt
offering.)[n]

20 From the descendants of Immer:[o]
Hanani and Zebadiah.

21 From the descendants of Ha-
rim:[p]
Maaseiah, Elijah, Shemaiah,
Jehiel and Uzziah.

22 From the descendants of Pash-
hur:[q]
Elioenai, Maaseiah, Ishmael,
Nethanel, Jozabad and Elasah.

23 Among the Levites:[r]

Jozabad, Shimei, Kelaiah (that
is, Kelita), Pethahiah, Judah
and Eliezer.

24 From the singers:
Eliashib.[s]

From the gatekeepers:
Shallum, Telem and Uri.

25 And among the other Israelites:

From the descendants of Parosh:[t]
Ramiah, Izziah, Malkijah, Mijamin, Eleazar, Malkijah and
Benaiah.

26 From the descendants of Elam:[u]
Mattaniah, Zechariah, Jehiel,
Abdi, Jeremoth and Elijah.

27 From the descendants of Zattu:
Elioenai, Eliashib, Mattaniah,
Jeremoth, Zabad and Aziza.

28 From the descendants of Bebai:
Jehohanan, Hananiah, Zabbai
and Athlai.

29 From the descendants of Bani:
Meshullam, Malluch, Adaiah,
Jashub, Sheal and Jeremoth.

30 From the descendants of Pahath-
Moab:
Adna, Kelal, Benaiah, Maaseiah, Mattaniah, Bezalel, Binnui
and Manasseh.

31 From the descendants of Harim:
Eliezer, Ishijah, Malkijah, She-
maiah, Shimeon, 32 Benjamin,
Malluch and Shemariah.

33 From the descendants of Hashum:
Mattenai, Mattattah, Zabad,
Eliphelet, Jeremai, Manasseh
and Shimei.

34 From the descendants of Bani:
Maadai, Amram, Uel, 35 Benaiah, Bedeiah, Keluhi, 36 Vaniah,
Meremoth, Eliashib, 37 Mattaniah, Mattenai and Jaasu.

38 From the descendants of Binnui:[a]
Shimei, 39 Shelemiah, Nathan,
Adaiah, 40 Macnadebai, Sha-
shai, Sharai, 41 Azarel, Shelemiah, Shemariah, 42 Shallum,
Amariah and Joseph.

43 From the descendants of Nebo:
Jeiel, Mattithiah, Zabad, Zebi-
na, Jaddai, Joel and Benaiah.

44 All these had married foreign
women, and some of them had children by these wives.[b]

10:18 [k] Jdg 3:6 [l] Ezr 2:2
10:19 [m] 2Ki 10:15 [n] Lev 5:15; 6:6
10:20 [o] 1Ch 24:14
10:21 [p] 1Ch 24:8
10:22 [q] 1Ch 9:12
10:23 [r] Ne 8:7; 9:4
10:24 [s] Ne 3:1; 12:10; 13:7,28
10:25 [t] Ezr 2:3
10:26 [u] ver 2

[a] *37,38* See Septuagint (also 1 Esdras 9:34); Hebrew *Jaasu* [38] *and Bani and Binnui,*
[b] *44* Or *and they sent them away with their children*

CHRONOLOGY OF THE EXILE AND RECONSTRUCTION PERIODS

	JUDAH'S CAPTIVITY		RISE OF GREEKS		DEVELOPMENT OF GREEKS		NEHEMIAH IN BABYLON (PERSIA)	
GENTILE WORLD	Babylonians 586–539 (Daniel 5) Persians 539– Buddha 557 Confucious 551 *Ezekiel* 570 *Daniel* 530	22 YRS	Defeated Persians at Marathon 490 at Salamis 480 **Persian Kings** Darius 522–486 Zerxes 486–465 **ARTAXERXES I** 465–424 *Esther* 481	2 YRS	Socrates 470–399 Herodotus 485–425	12 YRS	Plato 428–348	10 YRS
	605 530		515 458		456 445		433 425	

	DESTRUCTION		ZERUBBABEL'S RETURN		EZRA'S RETURN		NEHEMIAH'S 1ST RETURN		NEHEMIAH'S 2ND RETURN
JUDAH	Israel by Assyria 722 Judah by Babylon 586 2 Chronicles 36 facts = what? Jeremiah Interpretation = why?	75 YRS	**Temple Rebuilt** Ezra 1–6 *Haggai* 520 *Zechariah* 520	57 YRS	**People Revived** Ezra 7–10	11 YRS	**Walls Rebuilt** Nehemiah 1–6 **People Revived** Nehemiah 7–12 *Malachi* 432	8 YRS	**People Reformed** Nehemiah 13
	722 586		538 516		458 456		445 433		425

NEHEMIAH

AT A GLANCE

Key Principle: When God calls us to a great work, we can always expect opposition; during such times we must rely upon God's strength and intervention rather than our own resources.
Author: Nehemiah; possibly edited by Ezra
Time and Place: 445 B.C. to ~425 B.C. / Jerusalem
Key Verses: 2:17; 4:6; 6:15–16; 8:8

BENEFIT

Nehemiah recounts the mission of a godly man whose life is a model of servant leadership. This book not only provides us with a variety of leadership principles, but it also abounds with lessons on day-to-day reliance upon God during times of opposition and upheaval. Nehemiah also teaches that a people's spiritual condition before God is the key to the quality of their political and social condition before one another.

SETTING

Nehemiah the governor and Ezra the priest were contemporaries; their stories intertwine. This is why Ezra-Nehemiah was originally one book in the Hebrew Bible. Nehemiah led the third portion of the Jewish remnant from Persia to Jerusalem in 445 B.C. Nehemiah's return came 93 years after the first Jewish return to Jerusalem under Zerubbabel (538 B.C.) and thirteen years after the second return under Ezra (458 B.C.).

The events in this book took place during the reign of the Persian King Artaxerxes I (464–423 B.C.; Esther was his stepmother) under whom Nehemiah served as the king's cupbearer (1:11). Nehemiah led the return to Jerusalem in Artaxerxes' twentieth year; after the events recorded in chapters 1—10, he returned to Persia in the king's thirty-second year (13:6). Soon after this (~425 B.C.) Nehemiah returned to Jerusalem and instituted reforms (11—13). Malachi, the last of the Old Testament prophets and another contemporary of Nehemiah and Ezra, supplemented their ministries.

TIME LINE 1400BC 1300 1200 1100 1000 900 800 700 600 500 400

Fall of Jerusalem (586 B.C.)
Persia's conquest of Babylon (539 B.C.)
First return of exiles to Jerusalem (538 B.C.)
Ministries of Haggai and Zechariah (c.520-480 B.C.)
Temple restoration completed (516 B.C.)
Second return to Jerusalem under Ezra (458 B.C.)
Third return to Jerusalem under Nehemiah (445 B.C.)
Jerusalem's wall rebuilt (445 B.C.)
Book of Nehemiah written (c.430 B.C.)

THEME AND PURPOSE

Nehemiah demonstrates God's sovereign protection and guidance of the returning Jews who sought to rebuild their lives in the land that God had promised to the descendants of

Abraham, Isaac and Jacob. That God was at work behind the scenes is evident in the way he enabled his people to overcome their enemies' opposition and to rebuild the walls of Jerusalem in such a short time. This book begins with the people's political and geographical restoration (1—7), but it also meshes well with Ezra in its later themes of spiritual revival and moral reform (8—13).

UNIQUE CONTRIBUTION

Just as Ezra continues the historical account of the Jewish people after 2 Chronicles, so Nehemiah picks up the story from the end of Ezra. The book of Ezra details the first two returns to Jerusalem from Persia led by Zerubbabel and Ezra; Nehemiah focuses on the history of the third return. Thus the books of Ezra and Nehemiah, for centuries regarded as a unit, combine to give us the historical background for the three prophets who ministered after the Babylonian exile—Haggai, Zechariah, and Malachi:

First Return		Second Return		Third Return
Rebuilding the Temple	58 Year Gap (Esther)	Rebuilding the People	13 Year Gap	Rebuilding the Walls
Zerubbabel		Ezra		Nehemiah
Prophets: Haggai and Zechariah				Prophet: Malachi
538–516 B.C.		458 B.C.		445– C.425 B.C.
Ezra 1–6		Ezra 7–10		Nehemiah 1–13

As a leader, Nehemiah offers a perfect illustration of the Biblical balance between prayer and action. While he was a practical and resourceful man, he was also a dependent man. He knew that unless the Lord was the builder of the walls and of the people, his efforts would be in vain.

LINKS TO THE NEW TESTAMENT

Ezra and Nehemiah are books of restoration, both physical and spiritual. In these books the leaders and people rebuild the altar, the temple and Jerusalem's walls; they also restore the priesthood and the sacrificial system. In the process they experience moral and spiritual reform. But while the Messianic line still exists, they no longer have a king. The restoration under Nehemiah anticipates the ultimate restoration of all things—including the rightful kingdom when Messiah comes.

OVERVIEW

FOCUS	Rebuilding	Revival	Reform
REFERENCE	1 — 7	8 — 10	11 — 13
TOPICS	Renewed Walls	Renewed Covenant	Renewed Nation
	Civil Reform	Religious Reform	Political Reform
	Construction of the City	Instruction of the People	
	Political	Spiritual	
LOCATION	Jerusalem		
TIME	~20 Years		

While in exile, Nehemiah heard (1:3) that the walls of Jerusalem had been destroyed. The rebuilding process begun earlier had been squelched by the opposition recorded in Ezra 4:6–23. The first portion of this book (1—7) details how Nehemiah led the third return of the Jewish remnant from Persia to Jerusalem. After Nehemiah inspected the walls and gates and exhorted the people to rebuild them, they immediately began their work. The people worked on those portions closest to where they lived, and in spite of constant opposition, they completed the task in a mere 52 days.

In chapters 8—10, Ezra the priest leads a revival by convening the people and reading the law to them, translating from the Hebrew into Aramaic so they understand. After a great prayer led by the Levites and priests, the people consecrate themselves to the Lord and renew their covenant vows. Although he had to return to Persia for some time, Nehemiah returns and reforms the people once again (11—13). The book of Nehemiah completes the Old Testament's historical story line by taking us to the time of Malachi the prophet (~425 B.C.).

NEHEMIAH

Nehemiah's Prayer

1 The words of Nehemiah son of Hacaliah:

In the month of Kislev[a] in the twentieth year, while I was in the citadel of
Susa, 2Hanani,[b] one of my brothers,
came from Judah with some other
men, and I questioned them about the
Jewish remnant[c] that survived the exile, and also about Jerusalem.
3They said to me, "Those who survived the exile and are back in the
province are in great trouble and disgrace. The wall of Jerusalem is broken
down, and its gates have been burned
with fire.[d]"
4When I heard these things, I sat
down and wept.[e] For some days I
mourned and fasted[f] and prayed before the God of heaven. 5Then I said:

"O LORD, God of heaven, the
great and awesome God,[g] who
keeps his covenant of love[h] with
those who love him and obey his
commands, 6let your ear be attentive and your eyes open to hear[i]
the prayer[j] your servant is praying before you day and night for
your servants, the people of Israel.
I confess the sins we Israelites, including myself and my father's
house, have committed against
you. 7We have acted very wickedly[k] toward you. We have not
obeyed the commands, decrees
and laws you gave your servant
Moses.
8"Remember[l] the instruction
you gave your servant Moses, saying, 'If you are unfaithful, I will
scatter[m] you among the nations,
9but if you return to me and obey
my commands, then even if your
exiled people are at the farthest
horizon, I will gather[n] them from
there and bring them to the place
I have chosen as a dwelling for my
Name.'[o]
10"They are your servants and
your people, whom you redeemed
by your great strength and your
mighty hand.[p] 11O Lord, let your
ear be attentive[q] to the prayer of
this your servant and to the prayer
of your servants who delight in revering your name. Give your servant success today by granting
him favor in the presence of this
man."

I was cupbearer[r] to the king.

Artaxerxes Sends Nehemiah to Jerusalem

2 In the month of Nisan in the twentieth year of King Artaxerxes,[s] when
wine was brought for him, I took the
wine and gave it to the king. I had not
been sad in his presence before; 2so the
king asked me, "Why does your face
look so sad when you are not ill? This
can be nothing but sadness of heart."
I was very much afraid, 3but I said to
the king, "May the king live forever![t]
Why should my face not look sad when
the city[u] where my fathers are buried
lies in ruins, and its gates have been
destroyed by fire?[v]"
4The king said to me, "What is it you
want?"
Then I prayed to the God of heaven,
5and I answered the king, "If it pleases
the king and if your servant has found
favor in his sight, let him send me to
the city in Judah where my fathers are
buried so that I can rebuild it."
6Then the king[w], with the queen sitting beside him, asked me, "How long
will your journey take, and when will
you get back?" It pleased the king to
send me; so I set a time.
7I also said to him, "If it pleases the

1:1 [a]Ne 10:1; Zec 7:1 **1:2** [b]Ne 7:2 [c]Jer 52:28 **1:3** [d]2Ki 25:10; Ne 2:3,13,17 **1:4** [e]Ps 137:1 [f]Ezr 9:4 **1:5** [g]Dt 7:21; Ne 4:14 [h]Ex 20:6; Da 9:4 **1:6** [i]1Ki 8:29 [j]Da 9:17 **1:7** [k]Dt 28:14-15; Ps 106:6 **1:8** [l]2Ki 20:3 [m]Lev 26:33 **1:9** [n]Dt 30:4 [o]1Ki 8:48; Jer 29:14 **1:10** [p]Ex 32:11; Dt 9:29 **1:11** [q]ver 6 [r]Ge 40:1 **2:1** [s]Ezr 7:1 **2:3** [t]1Ki 1:31; Da 2:4; 5:10; 6:6,21 [u]Ps 137:6 [v]Ne 1:3 **2:6** [w]Ne 5:14; 13:6

1:1–4

PROMISE 7

CARING AND TRUSTING

Nehemiah had a comfortable life—a good job, a secure place to live. When he heard his people were in trouble and disgrace and that the walls of Jerusalem were not being rebuilt, he could have said, "Tough luck guys, I'll pray for you (from right here in the palace)." But verse 4 reveals two keys to Nehemiah's leadership success. First, he cared about his people; second, he trusted in his God. Nehemiah would probably not have done the heroic job this book describes if he hadn't cared so deeply and trusted so fully.

God has commissioned each one of us to be involved with hurting people. Think back to your response the last few times you heard of people in need. Then read Nehemiah 1:1–4 again. Nehemiah made a difference. So can you—if you care and if you trust God to use you.

For the next Promise 7 reading go to page 524.

king, may I have letters to the governors of Trans-Euphrates,[x] so that they will provide me safe-conduct until I arrive in Judah? 8 And may I have a letter to Asaph, keeper of the king's forest, so he will give me timber to make beams for the gates of the citadel[y] by the temple and for the city wall and for the residence I will occupy?" And because the gracious hand of my God was upon me,[z] the king granted my requests. 9 So I went to the governors of Trans-Euphrates and gave them the king's letters. The king had also sent army officers and cavalry[a] with me.

10 When Sanballat[b] the Horonite and Tobiah[c] the Ammonite official heard about this, they were very much disturbed that someone had come to promote the welfare of the Israelites.[d]

Nehemiah Inspects Jerusalem's Walls

11 I went to Jerusalem, and after staying there three days[e] 12 I set out during the night with a few men. I had not told anyone what my God had put in my heart to do for Jerusalem. There were no mounts with me except the one I was riding on.

13 By night I went out through the Valley Gate[f] toward the Jackal[a] Well and the Dung Gate,[g] examining the walls[h] of Jerusalem, which had been broken down, and its gates, which had been destroyed by fire. 14 Then I moved on toward the Fountain Gate[i] and the King's Pool,[j] but there was not enough room for my mount to get through; 15 so I went up the valley by night, examining the wall. Finally, I turned back and reentered through the Valley Gate. 16 The officials did not know where I had gone or what I was doing, because as yet I had said nothing to the Jews or the priests or nobles or officials or any others who would be doing the work.

17 Then I said to them, "You see the trouble we are in: Jerusalem lies in ruins, and its gates have been burned with fire.[k] Come, let us rebuild the wall[l] of Jerusalem, and we will no longer be in disgrace.[m]" 18 I also told them about the gracious hand of my God upon me[n] and what the king had said to me.

7 →PG. 569

They replied, "Let us start rebuilding." So they began this good work.

19 But when Sanballat the Horonite, Tobiah the Ammonite official and Geshem[o] the Arab heard about it, they mocked and ridiculed us.[p] "What is this you are doing?" they asked. "Are you rebelling against the king?"

20 I answered them by saying, "The God of heaven will give us success. We his servants will start rebuilding, but as for you, you have no share[q] in Jerusalem or any claim or historic right to it."

Builders of the Wall

3 Eliashib[r] the high priest and his fellow priests went to work and rebuilt[s] the Sheep Gate.[t] They dedicated it and set its doors in place, building as far as the Tower of the Hundred, which they dedicated, and as far as the Tower of Hananel.[u] 2 The men of Jericho[v] built the adjoining section, and Zaccur son of Imri built next to them.

3 The Fish Gate[w] was rebuilt by the sons of Hassenaah. They laid its beams

a 13 Or *Serpent* or *Fig*

2:7 [x]Ezr 8:36
2:8 [y]Ne 7:2 [z]ver 18; Ezr 5:5; 7:6
2:9 [a]Ezr 8:22
2:10 [b]ver 19; Ne 4:1,7 [c]Ne 4:3; 13:4-7 [d]Est 10:3
2:11 [e]Ge 40:13
2:13 [f]2Ch 26:9 [g]Ne 3:13 [h]Ne 1:3
2:14 [i]Ne 3:15 [j]2Ki 18:17
2:17 [k]Ne 1:3 [l]Ps 102:16; Isa 30:13; 58:12 [m]Eze 5:14
2:18 [n]2Sa 2:7
2:19 [o]Ne 6:1,2,6 [p]Ps 44:13-16
2:20 [q]Ezr 4:3
3:1 [r]Ezr 10:24 [s]Isa 58:12 [t]ver 32; Ne 12:39 [u]Ne 12:39; Jer 31:38; Zec 14:10
3:2 [v]Ne 7:36
3:3 [w]2Ch 33:14; Ne 12:39

2:6–9

PROMISE 1

MOMENT OF TRUTH

This was the moment. Nehemiah had fasted and prayed for four months. Now he stood before King Artaxerxes to ask if he could go to Jerusalem and help the Jewish people. Notice Nehemiah's response to the king's question (vv. 6–9). Nehemiah knew what time, material, personnel and documents he would need for his journey. Psalm 37:3 says, "Trust the LORD and do good." In this same vein, Nehemiah prayed and fasted, but he also planned. He'd done his homework.

When serving God we must prepare spiritually as Nehemiah did in chapter 1, but we must also use the minds God gave us. Give God your absolute best effort when you serve him. He expects and deserves no less.

For the next Promise 1 reading go to page 528.

2:19

PROMISE 6

THE THREE SCROOGES

Sanballat, Tobiah and Geshem—three natural enemies who were drawn together around a common, though evil, cause. Often the forces of evil reach beyond all barriers to unite their efforts for corrupt ends.

Can God's people expect to win the spiritual war unless we realize that God has already broken down the barriers between his people? Only by exercising the power of Biblical unity can we succeed in a battle where the enemy rallies together to defeat us. In this battle, "Lone Rangers" cannot win.

For the next Promise 6 reading go to page 539.

and put its doors and bolts and bars in
place. 4 Meremoth son of Uriah, the son
of Hakkoz, repaired the next section.
Next to him Meshullam son of Berekiah, the son of Meshezabel, made repairs, and next to him Zadok son of
Baana also made repairs. 5 The next
section was repaired by the men of Tekoa,[x] but their nobles would not put
their shoulders to the work under their
supervisors.[a]

6 The Jeshanah[b] Gate[y] was repaired
by Joiada son of Paseah and Meshullam son of Besodeiah. They laid its
beams and put its doors and bolts and
bars in place. 7 Next to them, repairs
were made by men from Gibeon[z] and
Mizpah—Melatiah of Gibeon and Ja-
don of Meronoth—places under the
authority of the governor of Trans-
Euphrates. 8 Uzziel son of Harhaiah,
one of the goldsmiths, repaired the
next section; and Hananiah, one of the
perfume-makers, made repairs next to
that. They restored[c] Jerusalem as far
as the Broad Wall.[a] 9 Rephaiah son of
Hur, ruler of a half-district of Jerusalem, repaired the next section. 10 Adjoining this, Jedaiah son of Harumaph
made repairs opposite his house, and
Hattush son of Hashabneiah made repairs next to him. 11 Malkijah son of
Harim and Hasshub son of Pahath-
Moab repaired another section and the
Tower of the Ovens.[b] 12 Shallum son of
Hallohesh, ruler of a half-district of Jerusalem, repaired the next section with
the help of his daughters.

13 The Valley Gate[c] was repaired by
Hanun and the residents of Zanoah.[d]
They rebuilt it and put its doors and
bolts and bars in place. They also repaired five hundred yards[d] of the wall
as far as the Dung Gate.[e]

14 The Dung Gate was repaired by
Malkijah son of Recab, ruler of the district of Beth Hakkerem.[f] He rebuilt it
and put its doors and bolts and bars in
place.

15 The Fountain Gate was repaired by
Shallun son of Col-Hozeh, ruler of the
district of Mizpah. He rebuilt it, roofing
it over and putting its doors and bolts
and bars in place. He also repaired
the wall of the Pool of Siloam,[e][g] by
the King's Garden, as far as the steps
going down from the City of David.
16 Beyond him, Nehemiah son of Az-
buk, ruler of a half-district of Beth Zur,[h]
made repairs up to a point opposite the

3:5 [x] 2Sa 14:2
3:6 [y] Ne 12:39
3:7 [z] Jos 9:3; Ne 2:7
3:8 [a] Ne 12:38
3:11 [b] Ne 12:38
3:13 [c] 2Ch 26:9 [d] Jos 15:34 [e] Ne 2:13
3:14 [f] Jer 6:1
3:15 [g] Isa 8:6; Jn 9:7
3:16 [h] Jos 15:58

a *5* Or *their Lord* or *the governor* **b** *6* Or *Old*
c *8* Or *They left out part of* **d** *13* Hebrew *a thousand cubits* (about 450 meters)
e *15* Hebrew *Shelah,* a variant of *Shiloah,* that is, Siloam

3:1–32

PROMISE **5**

THE CREW

What a model of teamwork! Chapter 3 describes the actual process of rebuilding Jerusalem's walls. The events of chapters 4, 5 and 6 occurred during the time period described in chapter 3. That the walls were built under such pressure and opposition is truly amazing. It happened because Nehemiah practiced brilliant leadership and management.

Chapter 3, with its lists and repetition, comes alive when we examine it a little. Five crucial principles combine in this chapter to tell a great story of dynamic leadership. They are:

Recognition: The list of names demonstrates that Nehemiah knew his people. They were important members of the team and he recognized them by name.

Mobilization: The names of the workers include nine different teams of people grouped into 42 work crews. Nehemiah got the high priest, the priests, Tekoites, officials, temple servants, goldsmiths, merchants, foreigners and children to work on the wall.

Cooperation: In the Hebrew text, the word for "next to" occurs 15 times in this chapter. These people were building a fortified wall out of stone. Each segment had to fit, almost seamlessly, with the ones on either side of it. These 42 crews worked under threat from their enemies and under tight time constraints. They needed to work together—and they did.

Coordination: The word for "after him" also occurs 15 times in the original language. Nehemiah planned the work so that when one crew was done with its work, another crew could come in and do its part.

Completion: Forty-one times the word "repaired" (or done) is used. Everyone knew what had to be done and did it until they finished.

Add the facts of direction—he knew where they were going with the work; and motivation—the fact that all this occurred when the builders' lives were constantly threatened, and we have an impressive model for getting great tasks accomplished. Men like Nehemiah make a great statement for God in a day when excuses are more evident than results. Study this book carefully and learn how one man, blessed by God, moved into an impossible situation with a demoralized people and opposition all around, and got the job done anyway!

For the next Promise 5 reading go to page 525.

NEHEMIAH

Working and Trusting God

A wise man once said, "Work as if everything depended on you. Pray as if everything depended on God." As Christian men we tend to go to extremes. We either work like crazy to achieve our goals on our own, or we sit back and wait for God to solve our problems, barely lifting a finger until he does. The fact is, we need to work hard *and* entrust our plans to God. We need to find the balance between relying on God's supernatural promises, power and provision, while at the same time using all our energy and skills to accomplish our goal—just like Nehemiah.

Success Comes from God

Nehemiah was a Jew living in exile in Babylon. He had been made the king of Babylon's personal cupbearer—the man who tasted King Artaxerxes' wine to ensure it wasn't poisoned.

One day Nehemiah's routine was interrupted by a group of men from Judah who reported, "The wall of Jerusalem is broken down, and its gates have been burned with fire" (Nehemiah 1:3). Nehemiah was so distressed about this news from Jerusalem that he wept and mourned for days. He refused to eat, and spent hours in prayer (1:4).

Not many days later, while Nehemiah was performing his usual duties, King Artaxerxes noticed Nehemiah's sad expression. Artaxerxes sensed that something was seriously wrong and asked how he could help. After hearing Nehemiah describe the sad state of affairs in Jerusalem, Artaxerxes miraculously gave permission for his cupbearer to go back to Jerusalem for a period of time to help rebuild the wall.

This was the opportunity Nehemiah had been waiting for. And Nehemiah had a "game plan." He knew he would need more than just Artaxerxes' permission to travel. In order to get the walls of Jerusalem rebuilt, Nehemiah was going to need letters of permission from the king allowing him unopposed passage through the various provinces between Babylon and Jerusalem (2:7). Nehemiah also asked for a letter to Asaph, the man in charge of the king's forest. When Artaxerxes gave Nehemiah that letter as well, Nehemiah knew he would have access to the materials needed to rebuild the wall (2:8).

Throughout this encounter, Nehemiah recognized the balance between the divine and the human. Though Nehemiah had worked and prayed hard and had planned a way to share his burden with the king, and though the king had been alert to Nehemiah's downcast spirit, Nehemiah said, "Because the gracious hand of my God was upon me, the king granted my requests" (2:8). Nehemiah's success was not due to the king's greatness or Nehemiah's hard work. His success came about because of God's help.

Doing the Work

When he arrived in Jerusalem, Nehemiah again exhibited his awareness of the need for balance between making plans and depending on God. Nehemiah noticed that the people were discouraged. Morale was low. During the night, he inspected the wall, surveyed the damage and developed a plan (2:11-13).

Then Nehemiah spoke to the people. He challenged them to rebuild the wall of Jerusalem so that they would no longer be disgraced. He gave the people a divine perspective on their labor as he told them his story of God's miraculous provision through Artaxerxes. He reminded the people that God had already answered prayer and was involved in this whole process. And the people responded, "Let us start rebuilding" (2:18).

As word of the rebuilding spread, enemies tried to undermine Nehemiah's work by ridiculing the people. Nehemiah handled this new situation just as he had every other problem—he prayed *and* he worked (4:4, 6). The Jews' enemies saw that the people kept on building, so they conspired together and threatened a larger attack from all sides. Nehemiah countered their "corporate threat" with "corporate prayer." Not only did Nehemiah pray, but the people prayed too. They had finally learned from Nehemiah's example that prayer and hard work go together.

To further repel the enemy threat, the people prayed for divine help and also "posted a guard day and night" (4:9). Against overwhelming odds, with lots of hard work, prayer and God's help, the people completed the wall of Jerusalem in only 52 days (6:15).

Finding Balance for Ourselves

Like Nehemiah, we need to rely on God's supernatural power, provision and guidance when faced with problems or goals that seem unreachable. At the same time, we need to use all our skill, energy and abilities as God directs in each situation. We need to find the balance that Nehemiah found between work and trust. While we work and trust, we must also realize that every success we achieve is because of God's hand of blessing. Let's make sure, as Nehemiah did, that we give God the glory for it all.

—Dr. Gene Getz

tombs[a][i] of David, as far as the artificial pool and the House of the Heroes.
17Next to him, the repairs were made
by the Levites under Rehum son of
Bani. Beside him, Hashabiah, ruler of
half the district of Keilah,[j] carried out
repairs for his district. 18Next to him,
the repairs were made by their countrymen under Binnui[b] son of Henadad, ruler of the other half-district of
Keilah. 19Next to him, Ezer son of Jeshua, ruler of Mizpah, repaired another
section, from a point facing the ascent
to the armory as far as the angle. 20Next
to him, Baruch son of Zabbai zealously
repaired another section, from the angle to the entrance of the house of Eliashib the high priest. 21Next to him,
Meremoth[k] son of Uriah, the son of
Hakkoz, repaired another section, from
the entrance of Eliashib's house to
the end of it.
22The repairs next to him were made
by the priests from the surrounding region. 23Beyond them, Benjamin and
Hasshub made repairs in front of their
house; and next to them, Azariah son
of Maaseiah, the son of Ananiah, made
repairs beside his house. 24Next to him,
Binnui[l] son of Henadad repaired another section, from Azariah's house to
the angle and the corner, 25and Palal
son of Uzai worked opposite the angle
and the tower projecting from the upper palace near the court of the
guard.[m] Next to him, Pedaiah son of
Parosh[n] 26and the temple servants[o]
living on the hill of Ophel[p] made repairs up to a point opposite the Water
Gate[q] toward the east and the projecting tower. 27Next to them, the men
of Tekoa[r] repaired another section,
from the great projecting tower[s] to
the wall of Ophel.

28Above the Horse Gate,[t] the
priests made repairs, each in front of
his own house. 29Next to them, Zadok
son of Immer made repairs opposite
his house. Next to him, Shemaiah son
of Shecaniah, the guard at the East
Gate, made repairs. 30Next to him,
Hananiah son of Shelemiah, and Hanun, the sixth son of Zalaph, repaired
another section. Next to them, Meshullam son of Berekiah made repairs opposite his living quarters. 31Next to
him, Malkijah, one of the goldsmiths,
made repairs as far as the house of the
temple servants and the merchants,
opposite the Inspection Gate, and as
far as the room above the corner; 32and
between the room above the corner
and the Sheep Gate[u] the goldsmiths
and merchants made repairs.

3:16 [i]Ac 2:29
3:17 [j]Jos 15:44
3:21 [k]Ezr 8:33
3:24 [l]Ezr 8:33
3:25 [m]Jer 32:2; 37:21; 39:14 [n]Ezr 2:3
3:26 [o]Ne 7:46; 11:21 [p]2Ch 33:14 [q]Ne 8:1,3,16; 12:37
3:27 [r]ver 5 [s]Ps 48:12
3:28 [t]2Ki 11:16; 2Ch 23:15; Jer 31:40
3:32 [u]ver 1; Jn 5:2

4:1 [v]Ne 2:10
4:2 [w]Ezr 4:9-10 [x]Ps 79:1; Jer 26:18
4:3 [y]Ne 2:10 [z]Job 13:12; 15:3
4:4 [a]Ps 44:13; 79:12; 123:3-4; Jer 33:24
4:5 [b]Isa 2:9; La 1:22 [c]2Ki 14:27; Ps 51:1; 69:27-28; 109:14; Jer 18:23
4:7 [d]Ne 2:10
4:8 [e]Ps 2:2; 83:1-18
4:10 [f]1Ch 23:4

Opposition to the Rebuilding

4 When Sanballat[v] heard that we
were rebuilding the wall, he became
angry and was greatly incensed. He
ridiculed the Jews, 2and in the presence of his associates[w] and the army
of Samaria, he said, "What are those
feeble Jews doing? Will they restore
their wall? Will they offer sacrifices?
Will they finish in a day? Can they bring
the stones back to life from those
heaps of rubble[x]—burned as they
are?"
3Tobiah[y] the Ammonite, who was
at his side, said, "What they are
building—if even a fox climbed up on
it, he would break down their wall of
stones!"[z]

4Hear us, O our God, for we are despised.[a] Turn their insults back on
their own heads. Give them over as
plunder in a land of captivity. 5Do not
cover up their guilt[b] or blot out their
sins from your sight,[c] for they have
thrown insults in the face of[c] the
builders.

6So we rebuilt the wall till all of it
reached half its height, for the people
worked with all their heart.
7But when Sanballat, Tobiah,[d] the
Arabs, the Ammonites and the men of
Ashdod heard that the repairs to Jerusalem's walls had gone ahead and that
the gaps were being closed, they were
very angry. 8They all plotted together[e]
to come and fight against Jerusalem
and stir up trouble against it. 9But we
prayed to our God and posted a guard
day and night to meet this threat.
10Meanwhile, the people in Judah
said, "The strength of the laborers[f] is
giving out, and there is so much rubble
that we cannot rebuild the wall."
11Also our enemies said, "Before
they know it or see us, we will be right
there among them and will kill them
and put an end to the work."
12Then the Jews who lived near them
came and told us ten times over,
"Wherever you turn, they will attack us."
13Therefore I stationed some of the
people behind the lowest points of the
wall at the exposed places, posting
them by families, with their swords,
spears and bows. 14After I looked
things over, I stood up and said to the
nobles, the officials and the rest of the

2 → PG. 523
4 → PG. 538

[a] *16* Hebrew; Septuagint, some Vulgate manuscripts and Syriac *tomb* [b] *18* Two Hebrew manuscripts and Syriac (see also Septuagint and verse 24); most Hebrew manuscripts *Bavvai* [c] *5* Or *have provoked you to anger before*

people, "Don't be afraid[g] of them. Remember[h] the Lord, who is great and
awesome,[i] and fight[j] for your brothers, your sons and your daughters,
your wives and your homes."
15When our enemies heard that we
were aware of their plot and that God
had frustrated it,[k] we all returned to
the wall, each to his own work.
16From that day on, half of my men
did the work, while the other half were
equipped with spears, shields, bows
and armor. The officers posted themselves behind all the people of Judah
17who were building the wall. Those
who carried materials did their work
with one hand and held a weapon[l] in
the other, 18and each of the builders
wore his sword at his side as he
worked. But the man who sounded the
trumpet[m] stayed with me.
2 →PG. 549
19Then I said to the nobles, the officials and the rest of the people, "The
work is extensive and spread out, and
we are widely separated from each other along the wall. 20Wherever you hear
the sound of the trumpet,[n] join us
there. Our God will fight[o] for us!"
21So we continued the work with
half the men holding spears, from the
first light of dawn till the stars came
out. 22At that time I also said to the
people, "Have every man and his helper stay inside Jerusalem at night, so
they can serve us as guards by night
and workmen by day." 23Neither I nor
my brothers nor my men nor the
guards with me took off our clothes;
each had his weapon, even when he
went for water.[a]

Nehemiah Helps the Poor

5 Now the men and their wives raised
a great outcry against their Jewish
brothers. 2Some were saying, "We and
our sons and daughters are numerous;
in order for us to eat and stay alive, we
must get grain."
3Others were saying, "We are mort-
gaging our fields,[p] our vineyards and
our homes to get grain during the famine."[q]
4Still others were saying, "We have
had to borrow money to pay the king's
tax[r] on our fields and vineyards. 5Al-
though we are of the same flesh
and blood[s] as our countrymen and
though our sons are as good as theirs,
yet we have to subject our sons and
daughters to slavery.[t] Some of our
daughters have already been enslaved,
but we are powerless, because our
fields and our vineyards belong to others."[u]
6When I heard their outcry and these
charges, I was very angry. 7I pondered
them in my mind and then accused the
nobles and officials. I told them, "You
are exacting usury[v] from your own
countrymen!" So I called together a
large meeting to deal with them 8and
said: "As far as possible, we have
bought[w] back our Jewish brothers
who were sold to the Gentiles. Now you
are selling your brothers, only for them
to be sold back to us!" They kept quiet,
because they could find nothing to
say.[x]
9So I continued, "What you are doing is not right. Shouldn't you walk in
the fear of our God to avoid the reproach[y] of our Gentile enemies? 10I
and my brothers and my men are also
lending the people money and grain.
But let the exacting of usury stop![z]
11Give back to them immediately their
fields, vineyards, olive groves and
houses, and also the usury[a] you are
charging them—the hundredth part of
the money, grain, new wine and oil."
12"We will give it back," they said.
"And we will not demand anything
more from them. We will do as you
say."
Then I summoned the priests and
made the nobles and officials take an
oath[b] to do what they had promised.

[a]23 The meaning of the Hebrew for this clause is uncertain.

4:14 [g]Ge 28:15; Nu 14:9; Dt 1:29 [h]Ne 1:8 [i]Ne 1:5 [j]2Sa 10:12
4:15 [k]2Sa 17:14; Job 5:12
4:17 [l]Ps 149:6
4:18 [m]Nu 10:2
4:20 [n]Eze 33:3 [o]Ex 14:14; Dt 1:30; 20:4; Jos 10:14
5:3 [p]Ps 109:11 [q]Ge 47:23
5:4 [r]Ezr 4:13
5:5 [s]Ge 29:14 [t]Lev 25:39-43, 47; 2Ki 4:1; Isa 50:1 [u]Dt 15:7-11; 2Ki 4:1
5:7 [v]Ex 22:25-27; Lev 25:35-37; Dt 23:19-20; 24:10-13
5:8 [w]Lev 25:47 [x]Jer 34:8
5:9 [y]Isa 52:5
5:10 [z]Ex 22:25
5:11 [a]Isa 58:6
5:12 [b]Ezr 10:5

4:19-20

PROMISE 2

STRENGTH IN NUMBERS

Nehemiah faced a tough situation from a military strategy point of view. While the workers were spread out around the wall, enemy soldiers watched from outside. In short, his military resources were spread thin over a large geographic area. Besides that, the workers were concerned with building the wall in addition to defending the city—their attention was divided. Nehemiah told his people to listen for the trumpet and come running to that spot to help if trouble arose. He assured his people that God would win any battle that broke out. But God used faithful people to do it.

During the week, the church that gathers on Sunday is scattered throughout the community doing God's work. We need the same assurance as we build God's kingdom that Nehemiah's crew had: Even though we often work alone, we are never alone in our work. Band together with a few other godly men and provide this kind of support for one another. It's easier to work alone if you aren't alone in your work.

For the next Promise 2 reading go to page 540.

13I also shook[c] out the folds of my
robe and said, "In this way may God
shake out of his house and possessions
every man who does not keep this
promise. So may such a man be shaken
out and emptied!"
At this the whole assembly said,
"Amen,"[d] and praised the LORD. And
the people did as they had promised.
14Moreover, from the twentieth year
of King Artaxerxes,[e] when I was appointed to be their governor[f] in the
land of Judah, until his thirty-second
year—twelve years—neither I nor my
brothers ate the food allotted to the
governor. 15But the earlier governors—
those preceding me—placed a heavy
burden on the people and took forty
shekels[a] of silver from them in addition to food and wine. Their assistants
also lorded it over the people. But out
of reverence for God[g] I did not act like
that. 16Instead,[h] I devoted myself to
the work on this wall. All my men were
assembled there for the work; we[b] did
not acquire any land.
17Furthermore, a hundred and fifty
Jews and officials ate at my table, as
well as those who came to us from the
surrounding nations. 18Each day one
ox, six choice sheep and some poul-
try[i] were prepared for me, and every
ten days an abundant supply of wine of
all kinds. In spite of all this, I never
demanded the food allotted to the governor, because the demands were
heavy on these people.
19Remember[j] me with favor, O my
God, for all I have done for these people.

Further Opposition to the Rebuilding

6 When word came to Sanballat, Tobiah,[k] Geshem[l] the Arab and the
rest of our enemies that I had rebuilt
the wall and not a gap was left in it—
though up to that time I had not set the
doors in the gates— 2Sanballat and Geshem sent me this message: "Come, let
us meet together in one of the villages[c] on the plain of Ono.[m]"
But they were scheming to harm me;
3so I sent messengers to them with this
reply: "I am carrying on a great project
and cannot go down. Why should the
work stop while I leave it and go down
to you?" 4Four times they sent me the
same message, and each time I gave
them the same answer.
5Then, the fifth time, Sanballat[n]
sent his aide to me with the same message, and in his hand was an unsealed
letter 6in which was written:

> "It is reported among the
> nations—and Geshem[d][o] says it
> is true—that you and the Jews are
> plotting to revolt, and therefore
> you are building the wall. More-
> over, according to these reports
> you are about to become their
> king 7and have even appointed
> prophets to make this proclama-
> tion about you in Jerusalem:
> 'There is a king in Judah!' Now
> this report will get back to the
> king; so come, let us confer to-
> gether."

8I sent him this reply: "Nothing like
what you are saying is happening; you
are just making it up out of your head."
9They were all trying to frighten us,
thinking, "Their hands will get too
weak for the work, and it will not be
completed."
⌊But I prayed,⌋ "Now strengthen my
hands."
10One day I went to the house of
Shemaiah son of Delaiah, the son of
Mehetabel, who was shut in at his
home. He said, "Let us meet in the
house of God, inside the temple[p], and
let us close the temple doors, because
men are coming to kill you—by night
they are coming to kill you."
11But I said, "Should a man like me
run away? Or should one like me go
into the temple to save his life? I will
not go!" 12I realized that God had not
sent him, but that he had prophesied
against me[q] because Tobiah and Sanballat[r] had hired him. 13He had been
hired to intimidate me so that I would
commit a sin by doing this, and then
they would give me a bad name to discredit me.[s]

5:14-18

PROMISE 7

LEADING BY EXAMPLE

Nehemiah here confronted a terrible injustice in the community. He minced no words when dealing with the guilty officials (vv. 6–11). He could speak powerfully enough to correct the situation (vv. 12–13) because of the example he had set (vv. 14–18).

Take stock of the example you set in your home, your church and your workplace. Can you confront sin, injustice and prejudice, and set things right? God, the church, and our society need men whose life allows them to faithfully fill this honorable role of leading by example.

For the next Promise 7 reading go to page 533.

5:13 [c]Mt 10:14; Ac 18:6 [d]Dt 27:15-26
5:14 [e]Ne 2:6; 13:6 [f]Ge 42:6; Ezr 6:7; Jer 40:7; Hag 1:1
5:15 [g]Ge 20:11
5:16 [h]2Th 3:7-10
5:18 [i]1Ki 4:23
5:19 [j]Ge 8:1; 2Ki 20:3; Ne 1:8; 13:14, 22,31
6:1 [k]Ne 2:10 [l]Ne 2:19
6:2 [m]1Ch 8:12
6:5 [n]Ne 2:10
6:6 [o]Ne 2:19
6:10 [p]Nu 18:7
6:12 [q]Eze 13:22-23 [r]Ne 2:10
6:13 [s]Jer 20:10

a *15* That is, about 1 pound (about 0.5 kilogram)
b *16* Most Hebrew manuscripts; some Hebrew manuscripts, Septuagint, Vulgate and Syriac *I*
c *2* Or *in Kephirim*
d *6* Hebrew *Gashmu,* a variant of *Geshem*

14Remember[t] Tobiah and Sanballat,[u] O my God, because of what they
have done; remember also the prophetess[v] Noadiah and the rest of the
prophets[w] who have been trying to intimidate me.

The Completion of the Wall

15So the wall was completed on the
twenty-fifth of Elul, in fifty-two days.
16When all our enemies heard about
this, all the surrounding nations were
afraid and lost their self-confidence,
because they realized that this work
had been done with the help of our
God.

17Also, in those days the nobles of
Judah were sending many letters to Tobiah, and replies from Tobiah kept
coming to them. 18For many in Judah
were under oath to him, since he was
son-in-law to Shecaniah son of Arah,
and his son Jehohanan had married
the daughter of Meshullam son of Berekiah. 19Moreover, they kept reporting
to me his good deeds and then telling
him what I said. And Tobiah sent letters to intimidate me.

7 After the wall had been rebuilt and I
had set the doors in place, the gatekeepers[x] and the singers[y] and the
Levites[z] were appointed. 2I put in
charge of Jerusalem my brother Hanani,[a] along with[a] Hananiah[b] the
commander of the citadel,[c] because
he was a man of integrity and feared[d]
God more than most men do. 3I said to
them, "The gates of Jerusalem are not
to be opened until the sun is hot. While
the gatekeepers are still on duty, have
them shut the doors and bar them.
Also appoint residents of Jerusalem as
guards, some at their posts and some
near their own houses."

The List of the Exiles Who Returned

4Now the city was large and spacious, but there were few people in it,[e]
and the houses had not yet been rebuilt. 5So my God put it into my heart
to assemble the nobles, the officials
and the common people for registra-
tion by families. I found the genealogical record of those who had been the
first to return. This is what I found written there:

6These are the people of the
province who came up from the
captivity of the exiles[f] whom
Nebuchadnezzar king of Babylon
had taken captive (they returned
to Jerusalem and Judah, each to
his own town, 7in company with
Zerubbabel,[g] Jeshua, Nehemiah,
Azariah, Raamiah, Nahamani, Mordecai, Bilshan, Mispereth, Bigvai, Nehum and Baanah):

The list of the men of Israel:

8the descendants of Parosh	2,172
9of Shephatiah	372
10of Arah	652
11of Pahath-Moab (through the line of Jeshua and Joab)	2,818
12of Elam	1,254
13of Zattu	845
14of Zaccai	760
15of Binnui	648
16of Bebai	628
17of Azgad	2,322
18of Adonikam	667
19of Bigvai	2,067
20of Adin[h]	655
21of Ater (through Hezekiah)	98
22of Hashum	328
23of Bezai	324
24of Hariph	112
25of Gibeon	95
26the men of Bethlehem and Netophah[i]	188
27of Anathoth[j]	128
28of Beth Azmaveth	42
29of Kiriath Jearim, Kephirah[k] and Beeroth[l]	743
30of Ramah and Geba	621
31of Micmash	122
32of Bethel and Ai[m]	123
33of the other Nebo	52
34of the other Elam	1,254
35of Harim	320
36of Jericho[n]	345
37of Lod, Hadid and Ono[o]	721
38of Senaah	3,930

39The priests:

6:15-16

PROMISE 5

ON TIME AND WITHIN BUDGET

In spite of opposition from enemies outside the city, corruption inside the city and personal attacks against Nehemiah, we read that "The wall was completed . . . in 52 days." Even God's enemies had to admit that God had helped the Jews. Pray for God to bless your church so obviously that even those opposed to God's work will have indisputable evidence that he is at work within the walls—and the hearts—of your church and its members.

For the next Promise 5 reading go to page 1037.

6:14 [t]Ne 1:8 [u]Ne 2:10 [v]Ex 15:20; Eze 13:17-23; Ac 21:9; Rev 2:20 [w]Ne 13:29; Jer 23:9-40; Zec 13:2-3
7:1 [x]1Ch 9:27; 26:12-19; Ne 6:1,15 [y]Ps 68:25 [z]Ne 8:9
7:2 [a]Ne 1:2 [b]Ne 10:23 [c]Ne 2:8 [d]1Ki 18:3
7:4 [e]Ne 11:1
7:6 [f]2Ch 36:20; Ezr 2:1-70; Ne 1:2
7:7 [g]1Ch 3:19; Ezr 2:2
7:20 [h]Ezr 8:6
7:26 [i]2Sa 23:28; 1Ch 2:54
7:27 [j]Jos 21:18
7:29 [k]Jos 18:26 [l]Jos 18:25
7:32 [m]Ge 12:8
7:36 [n]Ne 3:2
7:37 [o]1Ch 8:12

[a]2 Or *Hanani, that is,*

the descendants of Jedaiah (through the family of Jeshua) 973
40of Immer 1,052
41of Pashhur 1,247
42of Harim 1,017

43The Levites:

the descendants of Jeshua (through Kadmiel through the line of Hodaviah) 74

44The singers:[p]

the descendants of Asaph 148

45The gatekeepers:[q]

the descendants of Shallum, Ater, Talmon, Akkub, Hatita and Shobai 138

46The temple servants:[r]

the descendants of
Ziha, Hasupha, Tabbaoth,
47Keros, Sia, Padon,
48Lebana, Hagaba, Shalmai,
49Hanan, Giddel, Gahar,
50Reaiah, Rezin, Nekoda,
51Gazzam, Uzza, Paseah,
52Besai, Meunim, Nephussim,
53Bakbuk, Hakupha, Harhur,
54Bazluth, Mehida, Harsha,
55Barkos, Sisera, Temah,
56Neziah and Hatipha

57The descendants of the servants of Solomon:

the descendants of
Sotai, Sophereth, Perida,
58Jaala, Darkon, Giddel,
59Shephatiah, Hattil, Pokereth-Hazzebaim and Amon

60The temple servants and the descendants of the servants of Solomon[s] 392

61The following came up from the towns of Tel Melah, Tel Harsha, Kerub, Addon and Immer, but they could not show that their families were descended from Israel:

62the descendants of Delaiah, Tobiah and Nekoda 642

63And from among the priests:

the descendants of Hobaiah, Hakkoz and Barzillai (a man who had married a daughter of Barzillai the Gileadite and was called by that name).

64These searched for their family records, but they could not find them and so were excluded from the priesthood as unclean. 65The governor, therefore, ordered them not to eat any of the most sacred food until there should be a priest ministering with the Urim and Thummim.[t]

66The whole company numbered 42,360, 67besides their 7,337 menservants and maidservants; and they also had 245 men and women singers. 68There were 736 horses, 245 mules,[a] 69435 camels and 6,720 donkeys.

70Some of the heads of the families contributed to the work. The governor gave to the treasury 1,000 drachmas[b] of gold, 50 bowls and 530 garments for priests. 71Some of the heads of the families[u] gave to the treasury for the work 20,000 drachmas[c] of gold and 2,200 minas[d] of silver. 72The total given by the rest of the people was 20,000 drachmas of gold, 2,000 minas[e] of silver and 67 garments for priests.[v]

73The priests, the Levites, the gatekeepers, the singers and the temple servants,[w] along with certain of the people and the rest of the Israelites, settled in their own towns.[x]

Ezra Reads the Law

When the seventh month came and the Israelites had settled in their
8 towns,[y] 1all the people assembled as one man in the square before the Water Gate.[z] They told Ezra the scribe to bring out the Book of the Law of Moses,[a] which the LORD had commanded for Israel.

2So on the first day of the seventh month[b] Ezra the priest brought the Law[c] before the assembly, which was made up of men and women and all who were able to understand. 3He read it aloud from daybreak till noon as he faced the square before the Water Gate[d] in the presence of the men, women and others who could understand. And all the people listened attentively to the Book of the Law.

4Ezra the scribe stood on a high

7:44 [p]Ne 11:23
7:45 [q]1Ch 9:17
7:46 [r]Ne 3:26
7:60 [s]1Ch 9:2
7:65 [t]Ex 28:30; Ne 8:9
7:71 [u]1Ch 29:7
7:72 [v]Ex 25:2
7:73 [w]Ne 1:10; Ps 34:22; 103:21; 113:1; 135:1 [x]Ezr 3:1; Ne 11:1 [y]Ezr 3:1
8:1 [z]Ne 3:26 [a]Dt 28:61; 2Ch 34:15; Ezr 7:6
8:2 [b]Lev 23:23-25; Nu 29:1-6 [c]Dt 31:11
8:3 [d]Ne 3:26

[a] *68* Some Hebrew manuscripts (see also Ezra 2:66); most Hebrew manuscripts do not have this verse. [b] *70* That is, about 19 pounds (about 8.5 kilograms) [c] *71* That is, about 375 pounds (about 170 kilograms); also in verse 72 [d] *71* That is, about 1 1/3 tons (about 1.2 metric tons) [e] *72* That is, about 1 1/4 tons (about 1.1 metric tons)

wooden platform[e] built for the occasion. Beside him on his right stood Mattithiah, Shema, Anaiah, Uriah, Hilkiah and Maaseiah; and on his left were Pedaiah, Mishael, Malkijah, Hashum, Hashbaddanah, Zechariah and Meshullam.

5 Ezra opened the book. All the people could see him because he was standing[f] above them; and as he opened it, the people all stood up. 6 Ezra praised the LORD, the great God; and all the people lifted their hands[g] and responded, "Amen! Amen!" Then they bowed down and worshiped the LORD with their faces to the ground.

7 The Levites[h]—Jeshua, Bani, Sherebiah, Jamin, Akkub, Shabbethai, Hodiah, Maaseiah, Kelita, Azariah, Jozabad, Hanan and Pelaiah—instructed[i] the people in the Law while the people were standing there. 8 They read from the Book of the Law of God, making it clear[a] and giving the meaning so that the people could understand what was being read.

9 Then Nehemiah the governor, Ezra the priest and scribe, and the Levites[j] who were instructing the people said to them all, "This day is sacred to the LORD your God. Do not mourn or weep."[k] For all the people had been weeping as they listened to the words of the Law.

10 Nehemiah said, "Go and enjoy choice food and sweet drinks, and send some to those who have nothing[l] prepared. This day is sacred to our Lord. Do not grieve, for the joy[m] of the LORD is your strength."

11 The Levites calmed all the people, saying, "Be still, for this is a sacred day. Do not grieve."

12 Then all the people went away to eat and drink, to send portions of food and to celebrate with great joy,[n] because they now understood the words that had been made known to them.

13 On the second day of the month, the heads of all the families, along with the priests and the Levites, gathered around Ezra the scribe to give attention to the words of the Law. 14 They found written in the Law, which the LORD had commanded through Moses, that the Israelites were to live in booths during the feast of the seventh month 15 and that they should proclaim this word and spread it throughout their towns and in Jerusalem: "Go out into the hill country and bring back branches from olive and wild olive trees, and from myrtles, palms and shade trees, to make booths"—as it is written.[b]

16 So the people went out and brought back branches and built themselves booths on their own roofs, in their courtyards, in the courts of the house of God and in the square by the Water Gate and the one by the Gate of Ephraim.[o] 17 The whole company that had returned from exile built booths and lived in them. From the days of Joshua son of Nun until that day, the Israelites had not celebrated[p] it like this. And their joy was very great.

18 Day after day, from the first day to the last, Ezra read[q] from the Book of the Law of God. They celebrated the feast for seven days, and on the eighth day, in accordance with the regulation,[r] there was an assembly.

The Israelites Confess Their Sins

9 On the twenty-fourth day of the same month, the Israelites gathered together, fasting and wearing sackcloth and having dust on their heads.[s] 2 Those of Israelite descent had separated themselves from all foreigners.[t] They stood in their places and confessed their sins and the wickedness of their fathers.[u] 3 They stood where they were and read from the Book of the Law of the LORD their God for a quarter of the day, and spent another quarter in confession and in worshiping the LORD their God. 4 Standing on the stairs were the Levites[v]—Jeshua, Bani, Kadmiel, Shebaniah, Bunni, Sherebiah, Bani and Kenani—who called with loud voices to the LORD their God. 5 And the Levites—Jeshua, Kadmiel, Bani, Hashabneiah, Sherebiah, Hodiah, Shebaniah and Pethahiah—said: "Stand up and praise the LORD your God,[w] who is from everlasting to everlasting.[c]"

1 →PG. 540

"Blessed be your glorious name, and may it be exalted above all blessing and praise.
6 You alone are the LORD.[x] You made the heavens,[y] even the highest heavens, and all their starry host, the earth[z] and all that is on it, the seas[a] and all that is in them.[b] You give life to everything, and the multitudes of heaven worship you.

7 "You are the LORD God, who chose Abram and brought him out of Ur of the Chaldeans[c] and named him Abraham.[d] 8 You found his heart faithful to you, and you made a covenant with him to give to his descendants the land of the Canaanites, Hittites, Amorites, Perizzites, Jebusites

8:4 [e] 2Ch 6:13
8:5 [f] Jdg 3:20
8:6 [g] Ex 4:31; Ezr 9:5; 1Ti 2:8
8:7 [h] Ezr 10:23 [i] Lev 10:11; 2Ch 17:7
8:9 [j] Ne 7:1,65,70 [k] Dt 12:7,12; 16:14-15
8:10 [l] 1Sa 25:8; Lk 14:12-14 [m] Lev 23:40; Dt 12:18; 16:11,14-15
8:12 [n] Est 9:22
8:16 [o] 2Ki 14:13; Ne 12:39
8:17 [p] 2Ch 7:8; 8:13; 30:21
8:18 [q] Dt 31:11 [r] Lev 23:36,40; Nu 29:35
9:1 [s] Jos 7:6; 1Sa 4:12
9:2 [t] Ne 13:3,30 [u] Ezr 10:11; Ps 106:6
9:4 [v] Ezr 10:23
9:5 [w] Ps 78:4
9:6 [x] Dt 6:4 [y] 2Ki 19:15 [z] Ge 1:1; Isa 37:16 [a] Ps 95:5 [b] Dt 10:14
9:7 [c] Ge 11:31 [d] Ge 17:5

[a] 8 Or *God, translating it* [b] 15 See Lev. 23:37-40. [c] 5 Or *God for ever and ever*

and Girgashites.[e] You have kept
your promise[f] because you are
righteous.[g]
9“You saw the suffering of our
forefathers in Egypt;[h] you heard
their cry at the Red Sea.[a][i] 10You
sent miraculous signs[j] and wonders against Pharaoh, against all
his officials and all the people of
his land, for you knew how arrogantly the Egyptians treated them.
You made a name[k] for yourself,
which remains to this day. 11You
divided the sea before them,[l] so
that they passed through it on dry
ground, but you hurled their pursuers into the depths, like a stone
into mighty waters.[m] 12By day
you led[n] them with a pillar of
cloud,[o] and by night with a pillar
of fire to give them light on the
way they were to take.
13“You came down on Mount
Sinai;[p] you spoke[q] to them from
heaven. You gave them regulations and laws that are just[r] and
right, and decrees and commands
that are good.[s] 14You made
known to them your holy Sabbath[t] and gave them commands,
decrees and laws through your
servant Moses. 15In their hunger
you gave them bread from heav-
en[u] and in their thirst you
brought them water from the
rock;[v] you told them to go in and
take possession of the land you
had sworn with uplifted hand to
give them.[w]
16“But they, our forefathers, became arrogant and stiff-necked,
and did not obey your commands.[x] 17They refused to listen
and failed to remember[y] the miracles you performed among them.
They became stiff-necked and in
their rebellion appointed a leader
in order to return to their slavery.[z] But you are a forgiving God,
gracious and compassionate,
slow to anger[a] and abounding
in love.[b] Therefore you did not
desert them,[c] 18even when they
cast for themselves an image of a
calf[d] and said, ‘This is your god,
who brought you up out of Egypt,’
or when they committed awful
blasphemies.
19“Because of your great compassion you did not abandon
them in the desert. By day the pillar of cloud did not cease to guide
them on their path, nor the pillar
of fire by night to shine on the way
they were to take. 20You gave your
good Spirit[e] to instruct them.
You did not withhold your manna[f] from their mouths, and you
gave them water[g] for their thirst.
21For forty years you sustained
them in the desert; they lacked
nothing,[h] their clothes did not
wear out nor did their feet become swollen.[i]
22“You gave them kingdoms
and nations, allotting to them
even the remotest frontiers. They
took over the country of Sihon[b][j]
king of Heshbon and the country
of Og king of Bashan.[k] 23You
made their sons as numerous as
the stars in the sky, and you
brought them into the land that
you told their fathers to enter and
possess. 24Their sons went in and
took possession of the land.[l] You
subdued before them the Canaanites, who lived in the land;
you handed the Canaanites over
to them, along with their kings
and the peoples of the land, to
deal with them as they pleased.
25They captured fortified cities
and fertile land; they took possession of houses filled with all kinds
of good things, wells already
dug, vineyards, olive groves and
fruit trees in abundance. They
ate to the full and were well-
nourished;[m] they reveled in your
great goodness.[n]
26“But they were disobedient

9:8 [e]Ge 15:18-21 [f]Jos 21:45 [g]Ge 15:6; Ezr 9:15
9:9 [h]Ex 3:7 [i]Ex 14:10-30
9:10 [j]Ex 10:1 [k]Jer 32:20; Da 9:15
9:11 [l]Ex 14:21; Ps 78:13 [m]Ex 15:4-5,10; Heb 11:29
9:12 [n]Ex 15:13 [o]Ex 13:21
9:13 [p]Ex 19:11 [q]Ex 19:19 [r]Ps 119:137 [s]Ex 20:1
9:14 [t]Ge 2:3; Ex 20:8-11
9:15 [u]Ex 16:4; Jn 6:31 [v]Ex 17:6; Nu 20:7-13 [w]Dt 1:8,21
9:16 [x]Dt 1:26-33; 31:29
9:17 [y]Ps 78:42 [z]Nu 14:1-4 [a]Ex 34:6 [b]Nu 14:17-19 [c]Ps 78:11
9:18 [d]Ex 32:4
9:20 [e]Nu 11:17; Isa 63:11,14 [f]Ex 16:15 [g]Ex 17:6
9:21 [h]Dt 2:7 [i]Dt 8:4
9:22 [j]Nu 21:21 [k]Nu 21:33
9:24 [l]Jos 11:23
9:25 [m]Dt 6:10-12 [n]Nu 13:27; Dt 32:12-15

9:1–38 PROMISE 1

JUST DO IT

What contributed to the revival described in this chapter? Notice in chapter 8 that Ezra read God’s Word to the people. When the people heard Ezra read a directive from the law, they went and did it. Then they came back and said, “What else you got for us to do?” This went on for 24 days. Then God broke through to them, and they confessed their sins and repented.

Let this chapter inspire you to follow the people’s example. Take the next month—30 days—and read God’s Word every day. Whatever you find God telling you to do, do it. Commit to being responsive to him. See what happens in your soul. Give God’s truth a chance to transform your life.

For the next Promise 1 reading go to page 533.

[a] *9* Hebrew *Yam Suph*; that is, Sea of Reeds
[b] *22* One Hebrew manuscript and Septuagint; most Hebrew manuscripts *Sihon, that is, the country of the*

and rebelled against you; they put
your law behind their backs.[o]
They killed your prophets,[p] who
had admonished them in order to
turn them back to you; they committed awful blasphemies.[q] 27So
you handed them over to their
enemies,[r] who oppressed them.
But when they were oppressed
they cried out to you. From heav-
en you heard them, and in your
great compassion[s] you gave
them deliverers, who rescued
them from the hand of their enemies.

28"But as soon as they were at
rest, they again did what was evil
in your sight. Then you abandoned them to the hand of their
enemies so that they ruled over
them. And when they cried out to
you again, you heard from heav-
en, and in your compassion you
delivered them[t] time after time.

29"You warned them to return
to your law, but they became arrogant[u] and disobeyed your commands. They sinned against your
ordinances, by which a man will
live if he obeys them.[v] Stubbornly they turned their backs on you,
became stiff-necked and refused
to listen.[w] 30For many years you
were patient with them. By your
Spirit you admonished them
through your prophets.[x] Yet they
paid no attention, so you handed
them over to the neighboring peoples. 31But in your great mercy
you did not put an end[y] to them
or abandon them, for you are a
gracious and merciful God.

32"Now therefore, O our God,
the great, mighty[z] and awesome
God, who keeps his covenant of
love,[a] do not let all this hardship
seem trifling in your eyes—the
hardship that has come upon us,
upon our kings and leaders, upon
our priests and prophets, upon
our fathers and all your people,
from the days of the kings of Assyria until today. 33In all that has
happened to us, you have been
just;[b] you have acted faithfully,
while we did wrong.[c] 34Our
kings,[d] our leaders, our priests
and our fathers[e] did not follow
your law; they did not pay attention to your commands or the
warnings you gave them. 35Even
while they were in their kingdom,
enjoying your great goodness[f] to
them in the spacious and fertile
land you gave them, they did not

9:26
[o]1Ki 14:9
[p]Mt 21:35-36
[q]Jdg 2:12-13
9:27
[r]Jdg 2:14
[s]Ps 106:45
9:28
[t]Ps 106:43
9:29
[u]Ps 5:5; Isa 2:11; Jer 43:2
[v]Dt 30:16
[w]Zec 7:11-12
9:30
[x]2Ki 17:13-18; 2Ch 36:16
9:31
[y]Isa 48:9; Jer 4:27
9:32
[z]Ps 24:8
[a]Dt 7:9
9:33
[b]Ge 18:25
[c]Jer 44:3; Da 9:7-8,14
9:34
[d]2Ki 23:11
[e]Jer 44:17
9:35
[f]Isa 63:7

[g]Dt 28:45-48
9:36
[h]Dt 28:48; Ezr 9:9
9:37
[i]Dt 28:33; La 5:5
9:38
[j]2Ch 23:16
[k]Isa 44:5
10:2
[l]Ezr 2:2
10:3
[m]1Ch 9:12
10:5
[n]1Ch 24:8
10:9
[o]Ne 12:1
10:16
[p]Ezr 8:6
10:20
[q]1Ch 24:15
10:23
[r]Ne 7:2
10:28
[s]Ps 135:1

serve you[g] or turn from their evil
ways.

36"But see, we are slaves[h] today, slaves in the land you gave
our forefathers so they could eat
its fruit and the other good things
it produces. 37Because of our sins,
its abundant harvest goes to the
kings you have placed over us.
They rule over our bodies and our
cattle as they please. We are in
great distress.[i]

The Agreement of the People

38"In view of all this, we are making
a binding agreement,[j] putting it in
writing,[k] and our leaders, our Levites
and our priests are affixing their seals
to it."

10 Those who sealed it were:

Nehemiah the governor, the son of Hacaliah.

Zedekiah, 2Seraiah,[l] Azariah, Jeremiah,
3Pashhur,[m] Amariah, Malkijah,
4Hattush, Shebaniah, Malluch,
5Harim,[n] Meremoth, Obadiah,
6Daniel, Ginnethon, Baruch,
7Meshullam, Abijah, Mijamin,
8Maaziah, Bilgai and Shemaiah.
These were the priests.

9The Levites:[o]

Jeshua son of Azaniah, Binnui of the sons of Henadad, Kadmiel,
10and their associates: Shebaniah,
Hodiah, Kelita, Pelaiah, Hanan,
11Mica, Rehob, Hashabiah,
12Zaccur, Sherebiah, Shebaniah,
13Hodiah, Bani and Beninu.

14The leaders of the people:

Parosh, Pahath-Moab, Elam, Zattu, Bani,
15Bunni, Azgad, Bebai,
16Adonijah, Bigvai, Adin,[p]
17Ater, Hezekiah, Azzur,
18Hodiah, Hashum, Bezai,
19Hariph, Anathoth, Nebai,
20Magpiash, Meshullam, Hezir,[q]
21Meshezabel, Zadok, Jaddua,
22Pelatiah, Hanan, Anaiah,
23Hoshea, Hananiah,[r] Hasshub,
24Hallohesh, Pilha, Shobek,
25Rehum, Hashabnah, Maaseiah,
26Ahiah, Hanan, Anan,
27Malluch, Harim and Baanah.

28"The rest of the people—
priests, Levites, gatekeepers, singers, temple servants[s] and all who
separated themselves from the

neighboring peoples[t] for the
sake of the Law of God, together
with their wives and all their sons
and daughters who are able to
understand— 29all these now join
their brothers the nobles, and
bind themselves with a curse and
an oath[u] to follow the Law of God
given through Moses the servant
of God and to obey carefully all
the commands, regulations and
decrees of the LORD our Lord.

30"We promise not to give our
daughters in marriage to the peoples around us or take their
daughters for our sons.[v]

31"When the neighboring peoples bring merchandise or grain to
sell on the Sabbath,[w] we will not
buy from them on the Sabbath or
on any holy day. Every seventh
year we will forgo working the
land[x] and will cancel all debts.[y]

32"We assume the responsibility for carrying out the commands
to give a third of a shekel[a] each
year for the service of the house of
our God: 33for the bread set out on
the table;[z] for the regular grain
offerings and burnt offerings; for
the offerings on the Sabbaths,
New Moon[a] festivals and appointed feasts; for the holy offerings; for sin offerings to make
atonement for Israel; and for all
the duties of the house of our
God.[b]

34"We—the priests, the Levites
and the people—have cast lots[c]
to determine when each of our
families is to bring to the house of
our God at set times each year a
contribution of wood[d] to burn
on the altar of the LORD our God,
as it is written in the Law.

35"We also assume responsibility for bringing to the house of the
LORD each year the firstfruits[e] of
our crops and of every fruit tree.[f]

36"As it is also written in the
Law, we will bring the firstborn[g]
of our sons and of our cattle, of
our herds and of our flocks to the
house of our God, to the priests
ministering there.[h]

37"Moreover, we will bring to
the storerooms of the house of
our God, to the priests, the first of
our ground meal, of our ⌞grain⌟
offerings, of the fruit of all our
trees and of our new wine and
oil.[i] And we will bring a tithe[j] of
our crops to the Levites,[k] for it is
the Levites who collect the tithes
in all the towns where we work.[l]
38A priest descended from Aaron
is to accompany the Levites when
they receive the tithes, and the Levites are to bring a tenth of the
tithes[m] up to the house of our
God, to the storerooms of the
treasury. 39The people of Israel,
including the Levites, are to bring
their contributions of grain, new
wine and oil to the storerooms
where the articles for the sanctuary are kept and where the ministering priests, the gatekeepers and
the singers stay.

"We will not neglect the house
of our God."[n]

10:28 [t]2Ch 6:26; Ne 9:2
10:29 [u]Nu 5:21; Ps 119:106
10:30 [v]Ex 34:16; Dt 7:3; Ne 13:23
10:31 [w]Ne 13:16,18; Jer 17:27; Eze 23:38; Am 8:5 [x]Ex 23:11; Lev 25:1-7 [y]Dt 15:1
10:33 [z]Lev 24:6 [a]Nu 10:10; Ps 81:3; Isa 1:14 [b]2Ch 24:5
10:34 [c]Lev 16:8 [d]Ne 13:31
10:35 [e]Ex 22:29; 23:19; Nu 18:12 [f]Dt 26:1-11
10:36 [g]Ex 13:2; Nu 18:14-16 [h]Ne 13:31
10:37 [i]Lev 23:17; Nu 18:12 [j]Lev 27:30; Nu 18:21 [k]Dt 14:22-29 [l]Eze 44:30
10:38 [m]Nu 18:26
10:39 [n]Dt 12:6; Ne 13:11,12
11:1 [o]Ne 7:4 [p]ver 18; Isa 48:2; 52:1; 64:10; Zec 14:20-21 [q]Ne 7:73
11:3 [r]1Ch 9:2-3; Ezr 2:1
11:4 [s]Ezr 1:5 [t]Ezr 2:70
11:11 [u]2Ki 25:18; Ezr 2:2

The New Residents of Jerusalem

11 Now the leaders of the people settled in Jerusalem, and the rest of the
people cast lots to bring one out of every ten to live in Jerusalem,[o] the holy
city,[p] while the remaining nine were
to stay in their own towns.[q] 2The people commended all the men who volunteered to live in Jerusalem.

3These are the provincial leaders
who settled in Jerusalem (now some
Israelites, priests, Levites, temple servants and descendants of Solomon's
servants lived in the towns of Judah,
each on his own property in the various towns,[r] 4while other people from
both Judah and Benjamin[s] lived in Jerusalem):[t]

From the descendants of Judah:

Athaiah son of Uzziah, the son of
Zechariah, the son of Amariah,
the son of Shephatiah, the son of
Mahalalel, a descendant of Perez;
5and Maaseiah son of Baruch, the
son of Col-Hozeh, the son of Ha-
zaiah, the son of Adaiah, the son
of Joiarib, the son of Zechariah,
a descendant of Shelah. 6The
descendants of Perez who lived in
Jerusalem totaled 468 able men.

7From the descendants of Benjamin:

Sallu son of Meshullam, the son of
Joed, the son of Pedaiah, the son
of Kolaiah, the son of Maaseiah,
the son of Ithiel, the son of Jeshaiah, 8and his followers, Gabbai
and Sallai—928 men. 9Joel son of
Zicri was their chief officer, and
Judah son of Hassenuah was over
the Second District of the city.

10From the priests:

Jedaiah; the son of Joiarib; Jakin;
11Seraiah[u] son of Hilkiah, the son
of Meshullam, the son of Zadok,

[a] *32* That is, about 1/8 ounce (about 4 grams)

the son of Meraioth, the son of
Ahitub,[v] supervisor in the house
of God, 12and their associates,
who carried on work for the
temple—822 men; Adaiah son of
Jeroham, the son of Pelaliah, the
son of Amzi, the son of Zechariah,
the son of Pashhur, the son of
Malkijah, 13and his associates,
who were heads of families—242
men; Amashsai son of Azarel, the
son of Ahzai, the son of Meshillemoth, the son of Immer, 14and
his[a] associates, who were able
men—128. Their chief officer was
Zabdiel son of Haggedolim.

15From the Levites:

Shemaiah son of Hasshub, the
son of Azrikam, the son of Hashabiah, the son of Bunni; 16Shabbe-
thai[w] and Jozabad,[x] two of the
heads of the Levites, who had
charge of the outside work of the
house of God; 17Mattaniah[y] son
of Mica, the son of Zabdi, the son
of Asaph,[z] the director who led
in thanksgiving and prayer; Bakbukiah, second among his associates; and Abda son of Shammua,
the son of Galal, the son of Jeduthun.[a] 18The Levites in the holy
city[b] totaled 284.

19The gatekeepers:

Akkub, Talmon and their associates, who kept watch at the
gates—172 men.

20The rest of the Israelites, with the
priests and Levites, were in all the
towns of Judah, each on his ancestral
property.
21The temple servants[c] lived on the
hill of Ophel, and Ziha and Gishpa
were in charge of them.
22The chief officer of the Levites in
Jerusalem was Uzzi son of Bani, the
son of Hashabiah, the son of Mattaniah,[d] the son of Mica. Uzzi was one of
Asaph's descendants, who were the
singers responsible for the service of
the house of God. 23The singers[e] were
under the king's orders, which regulat-
ed their daily activity.
24Pethahiah son of Meshezabel, one
of the descendants of Zerah[f] son of
Judah, was the king's agent in all affairs
relating to the people.
25As for the villages with their fields,
some of the people of Judah lived in
Kiriath Arba[g] and its surrounding settlements, in Dibon[h] and its settlements, in Jekabzeel and its villages,
26in Jeshua, in Moladah, in Beth Pelet,[i] 27in Hazar Shual, in Beersheba[j]
and its settlements, 28in Ziklag,[k] in
Meconah and its settlements, 29in En
Rimmon, in Zorah,[l] in Jarmuth,[m]
30Zanoah, Adullam[n] and their villages,
in Lachish[o] and its fields, and in Azekah[p] and its settlements. So they were
living all the way from Beersheba[q] to
the Valley of Hinnom.
31The descendants of the Benjamites
from Geba[r] lived in Micmash,[s] Aija,
Bethel and its settlements, 32in Anathoth,[t] Nob[u] and Ananiah, 33in Hazor,[v] Ramah and Gittaim,[w] 34in Ha-
did, Zeboim[x] and Neballat, 35in Lod
and Ono,[y] and in the Valley of the
Craftsmen.
36Some of the divisions of the Levites
of Judah settled in Benjamin.

Priests and Levites

12 These were the priests[z] and Levites who returned with Zerubbabel[a] son of Shealtiel and with
Jeshua:[b]

Seraiah,[c] Jeremiah, Ezra,
2Amariah, Malluch, Hattush,
3Shecaniah, Rehum, Meremoth,
4Iddo,[d] Ginnethon,[b] Abijah,[e]
5Mijamin,[c] Moadiah, Bilgah,
6Shemaiah, Joiarib, Jedaiah,[f]
7Sallu, Amok, Hilkiah and Jedaiah.

These were the leaders of the priests
and their associates in the days of
Jeshua.
8The Levites were Jeshua, Binnui,
Kadmiel, Sherebiah, Judah, and also
Mattaniah,[g] who, together with his
associates, was in charge of the songs
of thanksgiving. 9Bakbukiah and Unni,
their associates, stood opposite them
in the services.
10Jeshua was the father of Joiakim,
Joiakim the father of Eliashib,[h] Eliashib the father of Joiada, 11Joiada the
father of Jonathan, and Jonathan the
father of Jaddua.
12In the days of Joiakim, these were
the heads of the priestly families:

of Seraiah's family, Meraiah;
of Jeremiah's, Hananiah;
13of Ezra's, Meshullam;
of Amariah's, Jehohanan;
14of Malluch's, Jonathan;
of Shecaniah's,[d] Joseph;
15of Harim's, Adna;
of Meremoth's,[e] Helkai;

11:11 [v]Ezr 7:2
11:16 [w]Ezr 10:15 [x]Ezr 8:33
11:17 [y]1Ch 9:15; Ne 12:8 [z]2Ch 5:12 [a]1Ch 25:1
11:18 [b]Rev 21:2
11:21 [c]Ezr 2:43; Ne 3:26
11:22 [d]1Ch 9:15
11:23 [e]Ne 7:44
11:24 [f]Ge 38:30
11:25 [g]Ge 35:27; Jos 14:15 [h]Nu 21:30
11:26 [i]Jos 15:27
11:27 [j]Ge 21:14
11:28 [k]1Sa 27:6
11:29 [l]Jos 15:33 [m]Jos 10:3
11:30 [n]Jos 15:35 [o]Jos 10:3 [p]Jos 10:10 [q]Jos 15:28
11:31 [r]Jos 21:17; Isa 10:29 [s]1Sa 13:2
11:32 [t]Jos 21:18; Isa 10:30 [u]1Sa 21:1
11:33 [v]Jos 11:1 [w]2Sa 4:3
11:34 [x]1Sa 13:18
11:35 [y]1Ch 8:12
12:1 [z]Ne 10:1-8 [a]1Ch 3:19 [b]Ezr 2:2 [c]Ezr 2:2
12:4 [d]Zec 1:1 [e]Lk 1:5
12:6 [f]1Ch 24:7
12:8 [g]Ne 11:17
12:10 [h]Ezr 10:24

a *14* Most Septuagint manuscripts; Hebrew *their*
b *4* Many Hebrew manuscripts and Vulgate (see also Neh. 12:16); most Hebrew manuscripts *Ginnethoi*
c *5* A variant of *Miniamin*
d *14* Very many Hebrew manuscripts, some Septuagint manuscripts and Syriac (see also Neh. 12:3); most Hebrew manuscripts *Shebaniah's*
e *15* Some Septuagint manuscripts (see also Neh. 12:3); Hebrew *Meraioth's*

16 of Iddo's,[i] Zechariah;
of Ginnethon's, Meshullam;
17 of Abijah's, Zicri;
of Miniamin's and of Moadiah's,
Piltai;
18 of Bilgah's, Shammua;
of Shemaiah's, Jehonathan;
19 of Joiarib's, Mattenai;
of Jedaiah's, Uzzi;
20 of Sallu's, Kallai;
of Amok's, Eber;
21 of Hilkiah's, Hashabiah;
of Jedaiah's, Nethanel.

22 The family heads of the Levites in the days of Eliashib, Joiada, Johanan and Jaddua, as well as those of the priests, were recorded in the reign of Darius the Persian. 23 The family heads among the descendants of Levi up to the time of Johanan son of Eliashib were recorded in the book of the annals. 24 And the leaders of the Levites[j] were Hashabiah, Sherebiah, Jeshua son of Kadmiel, and their associates, who stood opposite them to give praise and thanksgiving, one section responding to the other, as prescribed by David the man of God.

25 Mattaniah, Bakbukiah, Obadiah, Meshullam, Talmon and Akkub were gatekeepers who guarded the storerooms at the gates. 26 They served in the days of Joiakim son of Jeshua, the son of Jozadak, and in the days of Nehemiah the governor and of Ezra the priest and scribe.

Dedication of the Wall of Jerusalem

27 At the dedication[k] of the wall of Jerusalem, the Levites were sought out from where they lived and were brought to Jerusalem to celebrate joyfully the dedication with songs of thanksgiving and with the music of cymbals,[l] harps and lyres.[m] 28 The singers also were brought together from the region around Jerusalem—from the villages of the Netophathites,[n] 29 from Beth Gilgal, and from the area of Geba and Azmaveth, for the singers had built villages for themselves around Jerusalem. 30 When the priests and Levites had purified themselves ceremonially, they purified the people,[o] the gates and the wall.

31 I had the leaders of Judah go up on top[a] of the wall. I also assigned two large choirs to give thanks. One was to proceed on top[b] of the wall to the right, toward the Dung Gate.[p] 32 Hoshaiah and half the leaders of Judah followed them, 33 along with Azariah, Ezra, Meshullam, 34 Judah, Benjamin,[q] Shemaiah, Jeremiah, 35 as well as some priests with trumpets,[r] and also Zechariah son of Jonathan, the son of Shemaiah, the son of Mattaniah, the son of Micaiah, the son of Zaccur, the son of Asaph, 36 and his associates—Shemaiah, Azarel, Milalai, Gilalai, Maai, Nethanel, Judah and Hanani—with musical instruments[s] ⌞prescribed by⌟ David the man of God.[t] Ezra[u] the scribe led the procession. 37 At the Fountain Gate[v] they continued directly up the steps of the City of David on the ascent to the wall and passed above the house of David to the Water Gate[w] on the east.

38 The second choir proceeded in the opposite direction. I followed them on top[c] of the wall, together with half the people—past the Tower of the Ovens[x] to the Broad Wall,[y] 39 over the Gate of Ephraim,[z] the Jeshanah[d] Gate,[a] the Fish Gate,[b] the Tower of Hananel[c] and the Tower of the Hundred,[d] as far as the Sheep Gate.[e] At the Gate of the Guard they stopped.

40 The two choirs that gave thanks then took their places in the house of God; so did I, together with half the officials, 41 as well as the priests—Eliakim, Maaseiah, Miniamin, Micaiah, Elioenai, Zechariah and Hananiah with their trumpets— 42 and also Maaseiah, Shemaiah, Eleazar, Uzzi, Jehohanan, Malkijah, Elam and Ezer. The choirs sang under the direction of Jezrahiah. 43 And on that day they offered great sacrifices, rejoicing because God had given them great joy. The women and children also rejoiced. The sound of rejoicing in Jerusalem could be heard far away.

44 At that time men were appointed to be in charge of the storerooms[f] for the contributions, firstfruits and tithes.[g] From the fields around the towns they were to bring into the storerooms the portions required by the Law for the priests and the Levites, for Judah was pleased with the ministering priests and Levites.[h] 45 They performed the service of their God and the service of purification, as did also the singers and gatekeepers, according to the commands of David[i] and his son Solomon.[j] 46 For long ago, in the days of David and Asaph,[k] there had been directors for the singers and for the songs of praise[l] and thanksgiving to God. 47 So in the days of Zerubbabel and of Nehemiah, all Israel contributed the daily portions for the singers and gatekeepers. They also set aside the portion for the other Levites, and

12:16 [i] ver 4
12:24 [j] Ezr 2:40
12:27 [k] Dt 20:5 [l] 2Sa 6:5 [m] 1Ch 15:16, 28; 25:6; Ps 92:3
12:28 [n] 1Ch 2:54; 9:16
12:30 [o] Ex 19:10; Job 1:5
12:31 [p] Ne 2:13
12:34 [q] Ezr 1:5
12:35 [r] Ezr 3:10
12:36 [s] 1Ch 15:16 [t] 2Ch 8:14 [u] Ezr 7:6
12:37 [v] Ne 2:14; 3:15 [w] Ne 3:26
12:38 [x] Ne 3:11 [y] Ne 3:8
12:39 [z] 2Ki 14:13; Ne 8:16 [a] Ne 3:6 [b] 2Ch 33:14; Ne 3:3 [c] Ne 3:1 [d] Ne 3:1 [e] Ne 3:1
12:44 [f] Ne 13:4,13 [g] Lev 27:30 [h] Dt 18:8
12:45 [i] 1Ch 25:1; 2Ch 8:14 [j] 1Ch 6:31; 23:5
12:46 [k] 2Ch 35:15 [l] 2Ch 29:27; Ps 137:4

a 31 Or *go alongside* b 31 Or *proceed alongside* c 38 Or *them alongside* d 39 Or *Old*

the Levites set aside the portion for the descendants of Aaron.[m]

Nehemiah's Final Reforms

13 On that day the Book of Moses was read aloud in the hearing of the people and there it was found written that no Ammonite or Moabite should ever be admitted into the assembly of God,[n] 2because they had not met the Israelites with food and water but had hired Balaam[o] to call a curse down on them.[p] (Our God, however, turned the curse into a blessing.)[q] 3When the people heard this law, they excluded from Israel all who were of foreign descent.[r]

4Before this, Eliashib the priest had been put in charge of the storerooms[s] of the house of our God. He was closely associated with Tobiah,[t] 5and he had provided him with a large room formerly used to store the grain offerings and incense and temple articles, and also the tithes[u] of grain, new wine and oil prescribed for the Levites, singers and gatekeepers, as well as the contributions for the priests.

6But while all this was going on, I was not in Jerusalem, for in the thirty-second year of Artaxerxes[v] king of Babylon I had returned to the king. Some time later I asked his permission 7and came back to Jerusalem. Here I learned about the evil thing Eliashib[w] had done in providing Tobiah a room in the courts of the house of God. 8I was greatly displeased and threw all Tobiah's household goods out of the room.[x] 9I gave orders to purify the rooms,[y] and then I put back into them the equipment of the house of God, with the grain offerings and the incense.

10I also learned that the portions assigned to the Levites had not been given to them,[z] and that all the Levites and singers responsible for the service had gone back to their own fields. 11So I rebuked the officials and asked them, "Why is the house of God neglected?"[a] Then I called them together and stationed them at their posts.

12All Judah brought the tithes[b] of grain, new wine and oil into the storerooms.[c] 13I put Shelemiah the priest, Zadok the scribe, and a Levite named Pedaiah in charge of the storerooms and made Hanan son of Zaccur, the son of Mattaniah, their assistant, because these men were considered trustworthy. They were made responsible for distributing the supplies to their brothers.[d]

14Remember[e] me for this, O my God, and do not blot out what I have so faithfully done for the house of my God and its services.

15In those days I saw men in Judah treading winepresses on the Sabbath and bringing in grain and loading it on donkeys, together with wine, grapes, figs and all other kinds of loads. And they were bringing all this into Jerusalem on the Sabbath.[f] Therefore I warned them against selling food on that day. 16Men from Tyre who lived in Jerusalem were bringing in fish and all kinds of merchandise and selling them in Jerusalem on the Sabbath[g] to the people of Judah. 17I rebuked the nobles of Judah and said to them, "What is

12:47 [m]Nu 18:21; Dt 18:8
13:1 [n]ver 23; Dt 23:3
13:2 [o]Nu 22:3-11 [p]Nu 23:7; Dt 23:3 [q]Nu 23:11; Dt 23:4-5
13:3 [r]ver 23; Ne 9:2
13:4 [s]Ne 12:44 [t]Ne 2:10
13:5 [u]Lev 27:30; Nu 18:21
13:6 [v]Ne 2:6; 5:14
13:7 [w]Ezr 10:24
13:8 [x]Mt 21:12-13; Jn 2:13-16
13:9 [y]1Ch 23:28; 2Ch 29:5
13:10 [z]Dt 12:19
13:11 [a]Ne 10:37-39; Hag 1:1-9
13:12 [b]2Ch 31:6 [c]1Ki 7:51; Ne 10:37-39; Mal 3:10
13:13 [d]Ne 12:44; Ac 6:1-5
13:14 [e]Ge 8:1
13:15 [f]Ex 20:8-11; 34:21; Dt 5:12-15; Ne 10:31
13:16 [g]Ne 10:31

13:3

PROMISE 7

THE COURAGE OF CONVICTION

One man who is passionately sold out to God *can* make a difference. Between chapter 12 and chapter 13 there is a gap of leadership in which Nehemiah was away in Babylon (13:6). His time away could have lasted as long as 8 years. While he was gone, the people abandoned all the reforms made in the revival (ch. 8—12). From 13:7 to the end of the book, Nehemiah describes how he came back, discovered the disobedience and began whipping things (sometimes literally) back into shape.

Anyone can wring their hands and complain about evil. Nehemiah demonstrated that one man with courage fired by conviction can make a difference.

For the next Promise 7 reading go to page 588.

13:14

PROMISE 1

NEHEMIAH REMEMBERED

"Remember me for this, O my God." This clause recurs throughout the book of Nehemiah. It helps explain why Nehemiah the man made such a difference in his times. Throughout the book, Nehemiah lived to receive one vote of approval. He could stand against enemies from outside and inside the walls. He could revive the revival, even if doing so meant making more enemies. He looked only to God for a nod of approval, and his recurring prayer was answered.

Nehemiah was a man of action who consistently prayed for God's help. He was a warrior who began his battles on his knees. We do well to follow his example as we go through the struggles of our own lives.

For the next Promise 1 reading go to page 549.

this wicked thing you are doing—desecrating the Sabbath day? 18Didn't your forefathers do the same things, so that our God brought all this calamity upon us and upon this city? Now you are stirring up more wrath against Israel by desecrating the Sabbath."[h]

19When evening shadows fell on the gates of Jerusalem before the Sabbath,[i] I ordered the doors to be shut and not opened until the Sabbath was over. I stationed some of my own men at the gates so that no load could be brought in on the Sabbath day. 20Once or twice the merchants and sellers of all kinds of goods spent the night outside Jerusalem. 21But I warned them and said, "Why do you spend the night by the wall? If you do this again, I will lay hands on you." From that time on they no longer came on the Sabbath. 22Then I commanded the Levites to purify themselves and go and guard the gates in order to keep the Sabbath day holy.

Remember[j] me for this also, O my God, and show mercy to me according to your great love.

23Moreover, in those days I saw men of Judah who had married[k] women from Ashdod, Ammon and Moab.[l] 24Half of their children spoke the language of Ashdod or the language of one of the other peoples, and did not know how to speak the language of Judah. 25I rebuked them and called curses down on them. I beat some of the men and pulled out their hair. I made them take an oath[m] in God's name and said: "You are not to give your daughters in marriage to their sons, nor are you to take their daughters in marriage for your sons or for yourselves. 26Was it not because of marriages like these that Solomon king of Israel sinned? Among the many nations there was no king like him.[n] He was loved by his God,[o] and God made him king over all Israel, but even he was led into sin by foreign women.[p] 27Must we hear now that you too are doing all this terrible wickedness and are being unfaithful to our God by marrying[q] foreign women?"

28One of the sons of Joiada son of Eliashib[r] the high priest was son-in-law to Sanballat[s] the Horonite. And I drove him away from me.

29Remember[t] them, O my God, because they defiled the priestly office and the covenant of the priesthood and of the Levites.

30So I purified the priests and the Levites of everything foreign,[u] and assigned them duties, each to his own task. 31I also made provision for contributions of wood[v] at designated times, and for the firstfruits.

Remember[w] me with favor, O my God.

13:18 [h]Ne 10:31; Jer 17:21-23
13:19 [i]Lev 23:32
13:22 [j]Ge 8:1; Ne 12:30
13:23 [k]Ezr 9:1-2; Mal 2:11 [l]ver 1; Ne 10:30
13:25 [m]Ezr 10:5
13:26 [n]1Ki 3:13; 2Ch 1:12 [o]2Sa 12:25 [p]1Ki 11:3
13:27 [q]Ezr 9:14; 10:2
13:28 [r]Ezr 10:24 [s]Ne 2:10
13:29 [t]Ne 6:14
13:30 [u]Ne 10:30
13:31 [v]Ne 10:34 [w]ver 14,22; Ge 8:1

ESTHER

AT A GLANCE

Key Principle: Even though God sometimes seems removed from our experience, his providential care is always at work in our lives—often in times and ways we could never guess.
Author: A Persian Jew
Time and Place: 483 to 473 B.C. / Persia
Key Verses: 4:14; 8:17

BENEFIT

While Ezra and Nehemiah tell us about the Jews who returned from captivity to rebuild their homeland, Esther gives us insight into the lives of the vast majority of Jews who chose to remain in Persia after it defeated Babylon. Esther is a beautiful drama that is full of suspense, irony and heroic risks, and even though God's name is never mentioned in it, the whole book points to his providential hand in protecting and preserving his people in captivity.

SETTING

The story of Queen Esther takes place in the 58-year gap between Ezra 6 and 7 during the reign of the Persian king Xerxes (486 B.C. to 464 B.C.). Esther opens with a banquet that took place in 483 B.C., the third year of Xerxes' reign. According to the historian Herodotus, this banquet celebrated Xerxes' plans to conquer Greece, but in 479 B.C. he suffered defeat and returned to his palace in Susa. Most of the events in the book of Esther occurred in Xerxes' twelfth year (473 B.C.; 3:7). After Cyrus of Persia conquered Babylon in 539 B.C., three leaders took bands of Jews back to their homeland (Zerubbabel in 538 B.C., Ezra in 458 B.C., and Nehemiah in 445 B.C.). This book was addressed to the majority of the Jews who chose to remain in Persia.

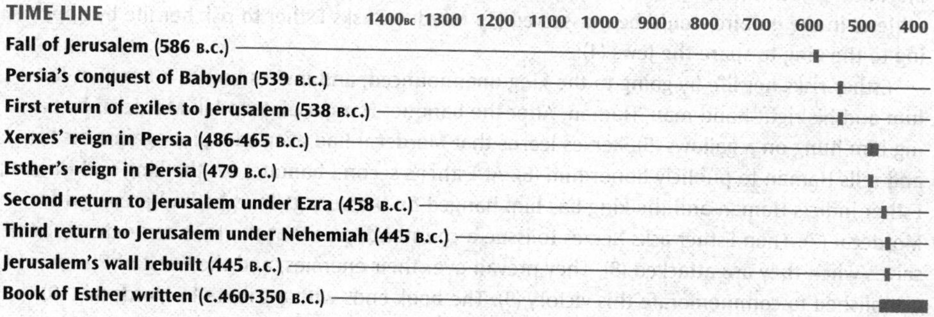

THEME AND PURPOSE

The account of Esther demonstrates God's gracious protection and preservation of the Jews who remained in voluntary exile in the Persian Empire. The story of Esther's elevation from obscurity to become the queen of Persia, of Mordecai's loyal deed and the timeliness in which the king heard of it, of Esther's two feasts and her unusual favor in the eyes of Xerxes, of Haman's ironic hanging on the gallows he constructed for Mordecai, of the Jews' victory over their enemies—all of these and other events converge to demonstrate God's continuing care for his people.

UNIQUE CONTRIBUTION

Esther is unique in that it is more like a drama than a historical narrative, with its ironic twists and suspenseful timing. Scholars questioned the inspiration of this book for a time because of the indirect way it points to God's hand behind every event and its failure to mention anything of a supernatural nature. Some scholars have speculated that God is silent in Esther due to the disobedience of many of the Jews who preferred conditions in Persia to the hardship of returning to rebuild Israel. Others believe that God's name is omitted to demonstrate his care for his people behind the scenes, even when they were among the Gentiles.

LINKS TO THE NEW TESTAMENT

This book shows how God's people, through whom would come the promised Messiah, were sovereignly preserved throughout the generations in spite of frequent attempts to destroy them.

OVERVIEW

FOCUS	Plotting Destruction		Preventing Destruction	
REFERENCE	1	4	5	10
TOPICS	Grave Danger		Great Deliverance	
	Conflict	Cunning	Courage	Conquest
	Exaltation	Persecution	Preservation	Commemoration
	Feast of Ahasuerus	Fast of Mordecai	Feasts of Esther	Feasts of Purim
LOCATION	Persia			
TIME	10 Years			

When Queen Vashti refuses to display herself before Xerxes' banquet guests, the king deposes her (1). He later selects Esther as his new queen from among many beautiful candidates, and she chooses not to reveal her Jewish identity to the king (2). Haman rises to a position of power over all the princes, but Esther's relative Mordecai refuses to bow to him. Learning that Mordecai is Jewish, Haman plots to destroy all the Jews and has Xerxes decree a day on which all Jews in the empire would be massacred (3). Mordecai asks Esther to risk her life by appealing to the king to spare the Jews (4).

Esther risks her life by going to the king unannounced, and invites him to a banquet for him and his right-hand man, Haman. After the banquet Haman plots to kill Mordecai by having him hung on a gallows (5). Xerxes learns that Mordecai had averted a plot against his life and tells Haman to publicly honor him (6). At Esther's second banquet for the king and Haman, Esther indicts Haman and the king has him hanged on the very gallows he had prepared for Mordecai (7). Then Esther asks Xerxes to issue a counter-decree that the Jews can defend themselves when they are attacked (8). They prevail over their enemies, and the Feast of Purim is established to commemorate this victory (9). The book ends with a tribute to Mordecai (10).

ESTHER

Queen Vashti Deposed

1 This is what happened during the time of Xerxes,[a][a] the Xerxes who ruled over 127 provinces[b] stretching from India to Cush[b]:[c] **2**At that time King Xerxes reigned from his royal throne in the citadel of Susa,[d] **3**and in the third year of his reign he gave a banquet[e] for all his nobles and officials. The military leaders of Persia and Media, the princes, and the nobles of the provinces were present.

4For a full 180 days he displayed the vast wealth of his kingdom and the splendor and glory of his majesty. **5**When these days were over, the king gave a banquet, lasting seven days,[f] in the enclosed garden[g] of the king's palace, for all the people from the least to the greatest, who were in the citadel of Susa. **6**The garden had hangings of white and blue linen, fastened with cords of white linen and purple material to silver rings on marble pillars. There were couches[h] of gold and silver on a mosaic pavement of porphyry, marble, mother-of-pearl and other costly stones. **7**Wine was served in goblets of gold, each one different from the other, and the royal wine was abundant, in keeping with the king's liberality.[i] **8**By the king's command each guest was allowed to drink in his own way, for the king instructed all the wine stewards to serve each man what he wished.

9Queen Vashti also gave a banquet[j] for the women in the royal palace of King Xerxes.

10On the seventh day, when King Xerxes was in high spirits[k] from wine,[l] he commanded the seven eunuchs who served him—Mehuman, Biztha, Harbona,[m] Bigtha, Abagtha, Zethar and Carcas— **11**to bring[n] before him Queen Vashti, wearing her royal crown, in order to display her beauty[o] to the people and nobles, for she was lovely to look at. **12**But when the attendants delivered the king's command, Queen Vashti refused to come. Then the king became furious and burned with anger.[p]

13Since it was customary for the king to consult experts in matters of law and justice, he spoke with the wise men who understood the times[q] **14**and were closest to the king—Carshena, Shethar, Admatha, Tarshish, Meres, Marsena and Memucan, the seven nobles[r] of Persia and Media who had special access to the king and were highest in the kingdom.

15"According to law, what must be done to Queen Vashti?" he asked. "She has not obeyed the command of King Xerxes that the eunuchs have taken to her."

16Then Memucan replied in the presence of the king and the nobles, "Queen Vashti has done wrong, not only against the king but also against all the nobles and the peoples of all the provinces of King Xerxes. **17**For the queen's conduct will become known to all the women, and so they will despise their husbands and say, 'King Xerxes commanded Queen Vashti to be brought before him, but she would not come.' **18**This very day the Persian and Median women of the nobility who have heard about the queen's conduct will respond to all the king's nobles in the same way. There will be no end of disrespect and discord.[s]

19"Therefore, if it pleases the king,[t] let him issue a royal decree and let it be written in the laws of Persia and Media, which cannot be repealed,[u] that Vashti is never again to enter the presence of King Xerxes. Also let the king give her royal position to someone else who is better than she. **20**Then when the king's edict is proclaimed throughout all his vast realm, all the women will respect their husbands, from the least to the greatest."

21The king and his nobles were pleased with this advice, so the king did as Memucan proposed. **22**He sent dispatches to all parts of the kingdom, to each province in its own script and to each people in its own language,[v] proclaiming in each people's tongue that every man should be ruler over his own household.

Esther Made Queen

2 Later when the anger of King Xerxes had subsided,[w] he remembered Vashti and what she had done and what he had decreed about her. **2**Then the king's personal attendants proposed, "Let a search be made for beautiful young virgins for the king. **3**Let the king appoint commissioners in every

1:1 [a]Ezr 4:6; Da 9:1 [b]Est 9:30; Da 3:2; 6:1 [c]Est 8:9
1:2 [d]Ezr 4:9; Ne 1:1; Est 2:8
1:3 [e]1Ki 3:15; Est 2:18
1:5 [f]Jdg 14:17 [g]2Ki 21:18; Est 7:7-8
1:6 [h]Est 7:8; Eze 23:41; Am 3:12; 6:4
1:7 [i]Est 2:18; Da 5:2
1:9 [j]1Ki 3:15
1:10 [k]Jdg 16:25; Ru 3:7 [l]Ge 14:18; Est 3:15; 5:6; 7:2; Pr 31:4-7; Da 5:1-4 [m]Est 7:9
1:11 [n]SS 2:4 [o]Ps 45:11; Eze 16:14
1:12 [p]Ge 39:19; Est 2:21; 7:7; Pr 19:12
1:13 [q]1Ch 12:32; Jer 10:7; Da 2:12
1:14 [r]2Ki 25:19; Ezr 7:14
1:18 [s]Pr 19:13; 27:15
1:19 [t]Ecc 8:4 [u]Est 8:8; Da 6:8,12
1:22 [v]Ne 13:24; Est 8:9; Eph 5:22-24; 1Ti 2:12
2:1 [w]Est 1:19-20; 7:10

a *1* Hebrew *Ahasuerus,* a variant of Xerxes' Persian name; here and throughout Esther
b *1* That is, the upper Nile region

province of his realm to bring all these beautiful girls into the harem at the citadel of Susa. Let them be placed under the care of Hegai, the king's eunuch, who is in charge of the women; and let beauty treatments be given to them. 4Then let the girl who pleases the king be queen instead of Vashti." This advice appealed to the king, and he followed it.

5Now there was in the citadel of Susa a Jew of the tribe of Benjamin, named Mordecai son of Jair, the son of Shimei, the son of Kish,[x] 6who had been carried into exile from Jerusalem by Nebuchadnezzar king of Babylon, among those taken captive with Jehoiachin[a][y] king of Judah.[z] 7Mordecai had a cousin named Hadassah, whom he had brought up because she had neither father nor mother. This girl, who was also known as Esther,[a] was lovely[b] in form and features, and Mordecai had taken her as his own daughter when her father and mother died.

8When the king's order and edict had been proclaimed, many girls were brought to the citadel of Susa[c] and put under the care of Hegai. Esther also was taken to the king's palace and entrusted to Hegai, who had charge of the harem. 9The girl pleased him and won his favor.[d] Immediately he provided her with her beauty treatments and special food.[e] He assigned to her seven maids selected from the king's palace and moved her and her maids into the best place in the harem.

4 →PG. 548

10Esther had not revealed her nationality and family background, because Mordecai had forbidden her to do so.[f] 11Every day he walked back and forth near the courtyard of the harem to find out how Esther was and what was happening to her.

12Before a girl's turn came to go in to King Xerxes, she had to complete twelve months of beauty treatments prescribed for the women, six months with oil of myrrh and six with perfumes[g] and cosmetics. 13And this is how she would go to the king: Anything she wanted was given her to take with her from the harem to the king's palace. 14In the evening she would go there and in the morning return to another part of the harem to the care of Shaashgaz, the king's eunuch who was in charge of the concubines.[h] She would not return to the king unless he was pleased with her and summoned her by name.[i]

15When the turn came for Esther (the girl Mordecai had adopted, the daughter of his uncle Abihail[j]) to go to the king,[k] she asked for nothing other than what Hegai, the king's eunuch who was in charge of the harem, suggested. And Esther won the favor[l] of everyone who saw her. 16She was taken to King Xerxes in the royal residence in the tenth month, the month of Tebeth, in the seventh year of his reign.

17Now the king was attracted to Esther more than to any of the other women, and she won his favor and approval more than any of the other virgins. So he set a royal crown on her head and made her queen[m] instead of Vashti. 18And the king gave a great banquet,[n] Esther's banquet, for all his nobles and officials.[o] He proclaimed a holiday throughout the provinces and distributed gifts with royal liberality.[p]

Mordecai Uncovers a Conspiracy

19When the virgins were assembled a second time, Mordecai was sitting at the king's gate.[q] 20But Esther had kept secret her family background and nationality just as Mordecai had told her to do, for she continued to follow Mordecai's instructions as she had done when he was bringing her up.[r]

21During the time Mordecai was sitting at the king's gate, Bigthana[b] and Teresh, two of the king's officers[s] who guarded the doorway, became angry[t] and conspired to assassinate King Xerxes. 22But Mordecai found out about the plot and told Queen Esther, who in turn reported it to the king, giving credit to Mordecai. 23And when the report was investigated and found to be true, the two officials were hanged[u] on a gallows.[c] All this was recorded in the book of the annals[v] in the presence of the king.

Haman's Plot to Destroy the Jews

3 After these events, King Xerxes honored Haman son of Hammedatha, the Agagite,[w] elevating him and giving him a seat of honor higher than that of all the other nobles. 2All the royal officials at the king's gate knelt down and paid honor to Haman, for the king had commanded this concerning him. But Mordecai would not kneel down or pay him honor.

3Then the royal officials at the king's gate asked Mordecai, "Why do you disobey the king's command?"[x] 4Day after day they spoke to him but he refused to comply.[y] Therefore they told Haman about it to see whether Morde-

2:5 [x]1Sa 9:1; Est 3:2
2:6 [y]2Ki 24:6,15; 2Ch 36:10,20 [z]Da 1:1-5; 5:13
2:7 [a]Ge 41:45 [b]Ge 39:6
2:8 [c]ver 3,15; Ne 1:1; Est 1:2; Da 8:2
2:9 [d]Ge 39:21 [e]ver 3,12; Ge 37:3; 1Sa 9:22-24; 2Ki 25:30; Eze 16:9-13; Da 1:5
2:10 [f]ver 20
2:12 [g]Pr 27:9; SS 1:3; Isa 3:24
2:14 [h]1Ki 11:3; SS 6:8; Da 5:2 [i]Est 4:11
2:15 [j]Est 9:29 [k]Ps 45:14 [l]Ge 18:3; 30:27; Est 5:8
2:17 [m]Est 1:11; Eze 16:9-13
2:18 [n]1Ki 3:15; Est 1:3 [o]Ge 40:20 [p]Est 1:7
2:19 [q]ver 21; Est 3:2; 4:2; 5:13
2:20 [r]ver 10
2:21 [s]Ge 40:2; Est 6:2 [t]Est 1:12; 3:5; 5:9; 7:7
2:23 [u]Ge 40:19; Ps 7:14-16; Pr 26:27 [v]Est 6:1; 10:2
3:1 [w]ver 10; Ex 17:8-16; Nu 24:7; Dt 25:17-19; 1Sa 14:48; Est 5:11
3:3 [x]Est 5:9; Da 3:12
3:4 [y]Ge 39:10

[a]6 Hebrew *Jeconiah*, a variant of *Jehoiachin*
[b]21 Hebrew *Bigthan*, a variant of *Bigthana*
[c]23 Or *were hung* (or *impaled*) *on poles*; similarly elsewhere in Esther

cai's behavior would be tolerated, for he had told them he was a Jew.

5 When Haman saw that Mordecai would not kneel down or pay him honor, he was enraged.[z] 6 Yet having learned who Mordecai's people were, he scorned the idea of killing only Mordecai. Instead Haman looked for a way[a] to destroy[b] all Mordecai's people, the Jews,[c] throughout the whole kingdom of Xerxes.

7 In the twelfth year of King Xerxes, in the first month, the month of Nisan, they cast the *pur*[d] (that is, the lot[e]) in the presence of Haman to select a day and month. And the lot fell on[a] the twelfth month, the month of Adar.[f]

8 Then Haman said to King Xerxes, "There is a certain people dispersed and scattered among the peoples in all the provinces of your kingdom whose customs[g] are different from those of all other people and who do not obey[h] the king's laws; it is not in the king's best interest to tolerate them.[i] 9 If it pleases the king, let a decree be issued to destroy them, and I will put ten thousand talents[b] of silver into the royal treasury for the men who carry out this business."[j]

10 So the king took his signet ring[k] from his finger and gave it to Haman son of Hammedatha, the Agagite, the enemy of the Jews. 11 "Keep the money," the king said to Haman, "and do with the people as you please."

12 Then on the thirteenth day of the first month the royal secretaries were summoned. They wrote out in the script of each province and in the language[l] of each people all Haman's orders to the king's satraps, the governors of the various provinces and the nobles of the various peoples. These were written in the name of King Xerxes himself and sealed[m] with his own ring. 13 Dispatches were sent by couriers to all the king's provinces with the order to destroy, kill and annihilate all the Jews[n]—young and old, women and little children—on a single day, the thirteenth day of the twelfth month, the month of Adar,[o] and to plunder[p] their goods. 14 A copy of the text of the edict was to be issued as law in every province and made known to the people of every nationality so they would be ready for that day.[q]

15 Spurred on by the king's command, the couriers went out, and the edict was issued in the citadel of Susa.[r] The king and Haman sat down to drink,[s] but the city of Susa was bewildered.[t]

Mordecai Persuades Esther to Help

4 When Mordecai learned of all that had been done, he tore his clothes,[u] put on sackcloth and ashes,[v] and went out into the city, wailing[w] loudly and bitterly. 2 But he went only as far as the king's gate,[x] because no one clothed in sackcloth was allowed to enter it. 3 In every province to which the edict and order of the king came, there was great mourning among the Jews, with fasting, weeping and wailing. Many lay in sackcloth and ashes.

4 When Esther's maids and eunuchs came and told her about Mordecai, she was in great distress. She sent clothes for him to put on instead of his sackcloth, but he would not accept them. 5 Then Esther summoned Hathach, one of the king's eunuchs assigned to attend her, and ordered him to find out what was troubling Mordecai and why.

6 So Hathach went out to Mordecai in the open square of the city in front of the king's gate. 7 Mordecai told him everything that had happened to him, including the exact amount of money Haman had promised to pay into the royal treasury for the destruction of the Jews.[y] 8 He also gave him a copy of the text of the edict for their annihila-

3:5 [z]Est 2:21; 5:9
3:6 [a]Pr 16:25 [b]Ps 74:8; 83:4 [c]Est 9:24
3:7 [d]Est 9:24,26 [e]Lev 16:8; 1Sa 10:21 [f]ver 13; Ezr 6:15; Est 9:19
3:8 [g]Ac 16:20-21 [h]Jer 29:7; Da 6:13 [i]Ezr 4:15
3:9 [j]Est 7:4
3:10 [k]Ge 41:42; Est 7:6; 8:2
3:12 [l]Ne 13:24 [m]Ge 38:18; 1Ki 21:8; Est 8:8-10
3:13 [n]1Sa 15:3; Ezr 4:6; Est 8:10-14 [o]ver 7 [p]Est 8:11; 9:10
3:14 [q]Est 8:8; 9:1
3:15 [r]Est 8:14 [s]Est 1:10 [t]Est 8:15
4:1 [u]Nu 14:6 [v]2Sa 13:19; Eze 27:30-31; Jnh 3:5-6 [w]Ex 11:6; Ps 30:11
4:2 [x]Est 2:19
4:7 [y]Est 3:9; 7:4

[a]7 Septuagint; Hebrew does not have *And the lot fell on.* [b]9 That is, about 375 tons (about 345 metric tons)

3:8

PROMISE 6

DIFFERENCES ENCOURAGED

Haman's accusation against the Jews has created turmoil since the days of Abraham. This royal advisor wanted to get rid of the Jews because their "customs [were] different from those of all other people." He advised that "It is not in the king's best interest to tolerate them." Throughout history, the sentence for the crime of being "different" has been humiliation, exclusion, even death. When God's people today practice Haman's sinful game against fellow Christians, the church is sentenced to hypocrisy and impotence.

The Scriptures encourage different ways of approaching God in worship. Churches have a wonderful freedom in Christ to express different customs. Suspicion, accusation, and superior or inferior attitudes based on expression of that freedom violate both the spirit and the letter of God's Word. One of the church's great strengths is that among its members "customs are different," and they enrich us all.

For the next Promise 6 reading go to page 581.

tion, which had been published in
Susa, to show to Esther and explain it
to her, and he told him to urge her to
go into the king's presence to beg for
mercy and plead with him for her people.
⁹Hathach went back and reported to
Esther what Mordecai had said. ¹⁰Then
she instructed him to say to Mordecai,
¹¹"All the king's officials and the people
of the royal provinces know that for
any man or woman who approaches
the king in the inner court without being summoned[z] the king has but one
law:[a] that he be put to death. The only
exception to this is for the king to extend the gold scepter[b] to him and
spare his life. But thirty days have
passed since I was called to go to the
king."
¹²When Esther's words were reported to Mordecai, ¹³he sent back this answer: "Do not think that because you
are in the king's house you alone of all
the Jews will escape. ¹⁴For if you remain silent[c] at this time, relief[d] and
deliverance[e] for the Jews will arise
from another place, but you and your
father's family will perish. And who
knows but that you have come to royal
position for such a time as this?"[f]
¹⁵Then Esther sent this reply to Mor-
1 →PG. 585
decai: ¹⁶"Go, gather together all the
Jews who are in Susa, and fast[g] for me.
Do not eat or drink for three days,
night or day. I and my maids will fast as
you do. When this is done, I will go to
the king, even though it is against the
law. And if I perish, I perish."[h]
¹⁷So Mordecai went away and carried out all of Esther's instructions.

Esther's Request to the King

5 On the third day Esther put on her
royal robes[i] and stood in the inner
court of the palace, in front of the
king's[j] hall. The king was sitting on
his royal throne in the hall, facing the
entrance. ²When he saw Queen Esther
standing in the court, he was pleased
with her and held out to her the gold
scepter that was in his hand. So Esther
approached and touched the tip of the
scepter.[k]
³Then the king asked, "What is it,
Queen Esther? What is your request?
Even up to half the kingdom,[l] it will
be given you."
⁴"If it pleases the king," replied Esther, "let the king, together with Haman, come today to a banquet I have
prepared for him."
⁵"Bring Haman at once," the king
said, "so that we may do what Esther
asks."
So the king and Haman went to the
banquet Esther had prepared. ⁶As they
were drinking wine,[m] the king again
asked Esther, "Now what is your petition? It will be given you. And what is
your request? Even up to half the kingdom,[n] it will be granted."[o]
⁷Esther replied, "My petition and my
request is this: ⁸If the king regards me
with favor[p] and if it pleases the king
to grant my petition and fulfill my request, let the king and Haman come
tomorrow to the banquet[q] I will prepare for them. Then I will answer the
king's question."

Haman's Rage Against Mordecai

⁹Haman went out that day happy
and in high spirits. But when he saw
Mordecai at the king's gate and observed that he neither rose nor showed
fear in his presence, he was filled
with rage[r] against Mordecai.[s] ¹⁰Never-
theless, Haman restrained himself and
went home.
Calling together his friends and Zeresh,[t] his wife, ¹¹Haman boasted[u] to
them about his vast wealth, his many
sons,[v] and all the ways the king had
honored him and how he had elevated
him above the other nobles and officials. ¹²"And that's not all," Haman
added. "I'm the only person[w] Queen
Esther invited to accompany the king
to the banquet she gave. And she has
invited me along with the king tomorrow. ¹³But all this gives me no satisfaction as long as I see that Jew Mordecai
sitting at the king's gate.[x]"
¹⁴His wife Zeresh and all his friends
said to him, "Have a gallows built,

4:12–16

PROMISE 2

LAYING IT ON THE LINE

Esther put her life on the line for her people by going before the king without being summoned. Before doing so she made one request of her people: "Fast for me. Do not eat or drink for three days . . . I and my maids will do as you do" (v. 16).

Different people prepare in different ways for great events, but no way is more important than spending time with God. Prayer, fasting and sensing his almighty presence has to be the focus for a godly man. Whatever expected or unexpected events you face today, take time to pray to God and consider his will for you. And when you're facing a big crisis, call a few godly friends and say, "Fast for me . . . I will do as you do."

For the next Promise 2 reading go to page 550.

4:11 [z]Est 2:14 [a]Da 2:9 [b]Est 5:1,2; 8:4
4:14 [c]Ecc 3:7; Isa 62:1; Am 5:13 [d]Est 9:16,22 [e]Ge 45:7; Dt 28:29 [f]Ge 50:20
4:16 [g]2Ch 20:3; Est 9:31 [h]Ge 43:14
5:1 [i]Est 4:16; Eze 16:13 [j]Est 6:4; Pr 21:1
5:2 [k]Est 4:11; 8:4; Pr 21:1
5:3 [l]Est 7:2; Da 5:16; Mk 6:23
5:6 [m]Est 1:10 [n]Mk 6:23 [o]Est 7:2; 9:12
5:8 [p]Est 2:15; 7:3; 8:5 [q]1Ki 3:15; Est 6:14
5:9 [r]Est 2:21; Pr 14:17 [s]Est 3:3,5
5:10 [t]Est 6:13
5:11 [u]Pr 13:16 [v]Est 9:7-10,13
5:12 [w]Job 22:29; Pr 16:18; 29:23
5:13 [x]Est 2:19

seventy-five feet[a] high,[y] and ask the king in the morning to have Mordecai hanged[z] on it. Then go with the king to the dinner and be happy." This suggestion delighted Haman, and he had the gallows built.

Mordecai Honored

6 That night the king could not sleep;[a] so he ordered the book of the chronicles,[b] the record of his reign, to be brought in and read to him. 2It was found recorded there that Mordecai had exposed Bigthana and Teresh, two of the king's officers who guarded the doorway, who had conspired to assassinate King Xerxes.

3"What honor and recognition has Mordecai received for this?" the king asked.

"Nothing has been done for him,"[c] his attendants answered.

4The king said, "Who is in the court?" Now Haman had just entered the outer court of the palace to speak to the king about hanging Mordecai on the gallows he had erected for him.

5His attendants answered, "Haman is standing in the court."

"Bring him in," the king ordered.

6When Haman entered, the king asked him, "What should be done for the man the king delights to honor?"

Now Haman thought to himself, "Who is there that the king would rather honor than me?" 7So he answered the king, "For the man the king delights to honor, 8have them bring a royal robe[d] the king has worn and a horse[e] the king has ridden, one with a royal crest placed on its head. 9Then let the robe and horse be entrusted to one of the king's most noble princes. Let them robe the man the king delights to honor, and lead him on the horse through the city streets, proclaiming before him, 'This is what is done for the man the king delights to honor!'[f]"

10"Go at once," the king commanded Haman. "Get the robe and the horse and do just as you have suggested for Mordecai the Jew, who sits at the king's gate. Do not neglect anything you have recommended."

11So Haman got[g] the robe and the horse. He robed Mordecai, and led him on horseback through the city streets, proclaiming before him, "This is what is done for the man the king delights to honor!"

12Afterward Mordecai returned to the king's gate. But Haman rushed home, with his head covered[h] in grief, 13and told Zeresh[i] his wife and all his friends everything that had happened to him.

His advisers and his wife Zeresh said to him, "Since Mordecai, before whom your downfall[j] has started, is of Jewish origin, you cannot stand against him—you will surely come to ruin!" 14While they were still talking with him, the king's eunuchs arrived and hurried Haman away to the banquet[k] Esther had prepared.

Haman Hanged

7 So the king and Haman went to dine[l] with Queen Esther, 2and as they were drinking wine[m] on that second day, the king again asked, "Queen Esther, what is your petition? It will be given you. What is your request? Even up to half the kingdom,[n] it will be granted.[o]"

3Then Queen Esther answered, "If I have found favor[p] with you, O king, and if it pleases your majesty, grant me my life—this is my petition. And spare my people—this is my request. 4For I and my people have been sold for destruction and slaughter and annihilation.[q] If we had merely been sold as male and female slaves, I would have kept quiet, because no such distress would justify disturbing the king.[b]"

5King Xerxes asked Queen Esther, "Who is he? Where is the man who has dared to do such a thing?"

6Esther said, "The adversary and enemy is this vile Haman."

Then Haman was terrified before the king and queen. 7The king got up in a rage,[r] left his wine and went out into the palace garden.[s] But Haman, realizing that the king had already decided his fate,[t] stayed behind to beg Queen Esther for his life.

8Just as the king returned from the palace garden to the banquet hall, Haman was falling on the couch[u] where Esther was reclining.[v]

The king exclaimed, "Will he even molest the queen while she is with me in the house?"[w]

As soon as the word left the king's mouth, they covered Haman's face.[x] 9Then Harbona,[y] one of the eunuchs attending the king, said, "A gallows seventy-five feet[a] high[z] stands by Haman's house. He had it made for

5:14 [y]Est 7:9 [z]Ezr 6:11; Est 6:4
6:1 [a]Da 2:1; 6:18 [b]Est 2:23; 10:2
6:3 [c]Ecc 9:13-16
6:8 [d]Ge 41:42; Isa 52:1 [e]1Ki 1:33
6:9 [f]Ge 41:43
6:11 [g]Ge 41:42
6:12 [h]2Sa 15:30; Jer 14:3,4; Mic 3:7
6:13 [i]Est 5:10 [j]Ps 57:6; Pr 26:27; 28:18
6:14 [k]1Ki 3:15; Est 5:8
7:1 [l]Ge 40:20-22; Mt 22:1-14
7:2 [m]Est 1:10 [n]Est 5:3 [o]Est 9:12
7:3 [p]Est 2:15
7:4 [q]Est 3:9
7:7 [r]Ge 34:7; Est 1:12; Pr 19:12; 20:1-2 [s]2Ki 21:18 [t]Est 6:13
7:8 [u]Est 1:6 [v]Ge 39:14 [w]Ge 34:7 [x]Est 6:12
7:9 [y]Est 1:10 [z]Est 5:14

a *14,9* Hebrew *fifty cubits* (about 23 meters)
b *4* Or *quiet, but the compensation our adversary offers cannot be compared with the loss the king would suffer*

Mordecai, who spoke up to help the king."

The king said, "Hang him on it!"[a] 10So they hanged Haman[b] on the gallows[c] he had prepared for Mordecai.[d] Then the king's fury subsided.[e]

The King's Edict in Behalf of the Jews

8 That same day King Xerxes gave Queen Esther the estate of Haman,[f] the enemy of the Jews. And Mordecai came into the presence of the king, for Esther had told how he was related to her. 2The king took off his signet ring,[g] which he had reclaimed from Haman, and presented it to Mordecai. And Esther appointed him over Haman's estate.[h]

3Esther again pleaded with the king, falling at his feet and weeping. She begged him to put an end to the evil plan of Haman the Agagite, which he had devised against the Jews. 4Then the king extended the gold scepter[i] to Esther and she arose and stood before him.

5"If it pleases the king," she said, "and if he regards me with favor and thinks it the right thing to do, and if he is pleased with me, let an order be written overruling the dispatches that Haman son of Hammedatha, the Agagite, devised and wrote to destroy the Jews in all the king's provinces. 6For how can I bear to see disaster fall on my people? How can I bear to see the destruction of my family?"[j]

7King Xerxes replied to Queen Esther and to Mordecai the Jew, "Because Haman attacked the Jews, I have given his estate to Esther, and they have hanged him on the gallows. 8Now write another decree[k] in the king's name in behalf of the Jews as seems best to you, and seal it with the king's signet ring[l]—for no document written in the king's name and sealed with his ring can be revoked."[m]

9At once the royal secretaries were summoned—on the twenty-third day of the third month, the month of Sivan. They wrote out all Mordecai's orders to the Jews, and to the satraps, governors and nobles of the 127 provinces stretching from India to Cush.[a][n] These orders were written in the script of each province and the language of each people and also to the Jews in their own script and language.[o] 10Mordecai wrote in the name of King Xerxes, sealed the dispatches with the king's signet ring, and sent them by mounted couriers, who rode fast horses especially bred for the king.

11The king's edict granted the Jews in every city the right to assemble and protect themselves; to destroy, kill and annihilate any armed force of any nationality or province that might attack them and their women and children; and to plunder[p] the property of their enemies. 12The day appointed for the Jews to do this in all the provinces of King Xerxes was the thirteenth day of the twelfth month, the month of Adar.[q] 13A copy of the text of the edict was to be issued as law in every province and made known to the people of every nationality so that the Jews would be ready on that day[r] to avenge themselves on their enemies.

14The couriers, riding the royal horses, raced out, spurred on by the king's command. And the edict was also issued in the citadel of Susa.

15Mordecai[s] left the king's presence wearing royal garments of blue and white, a large crown of gold and a purple robe of fine linen.[t] And the city of Susa held a joyous celebration.[u] 16For the Jews it was a time of happiness and joy,[v] gladness and honor.[w] 17In every province and in every city, wherever the edict of the king went, there was joy[x] and gladness among the Jews, with feasting and celebrating. And many people of other nationalities became Jews because fear[y] of the Jews had seized them.[z]

Triumph of the Jews

9 On the thirteenth day of the twelfth month, the month of Adar,[a] the edict commanded by the king was to be carried out. On this day the enemies of the Jews had hoped to overpower them, but now the tables were turned and the Jews got the upper hand[b] over those who hated them.[c] 2The Jews assembled in their cities[d] in all the provinces of King Xerxes to attack those seeking their destruction. No one could stand against them,[e] because the people of all the other nationalities were afraid of them. 3And all the nobles of the provinces, the satraps, the governors and the king's administrators helped the Jews,[f] because fear of Mordecai had seized them. 4Mordecai was prominent[g] in the palace; his reputation spread throughout the provinces, and he became more and more powerful.[h]

5The Jews struck down all their enemies with the sword, killing and de-

7:9 [a]Ps 7:14-16; 9:16; Pr 11:5-6; 26:27; Mt 7:2
7:10 [b]Pr 10:28 [c]Est 9:25 [d]Da 6:24 [e]Est 2:1
8:1 [f]Est 2:7; 7:6; Pr 22:22-23
8:2 [g]Ge 41:42; Est 3:10 [h]Pr 13:22; Da 2:48
8:4 [i]Est 4:11; 5:2
8:6 [j]Est 7:4; 9:1
8:8 [k]Est 3:12-14 [l]Ge 41:42 [m]Est 1:19; Da 6:15
8:9 [n]Est 1:1 [o]Est 1:22
8:11 [p]Est 9:10,15,16
8:12 [q]Est 3:13; 9:1
8:13 [r]Est 3:14
8:15 [s]Est 9:4 [t]Ge 41:42 [u]Est 3:15
8:16 [v]Ps 97:10-12 [w]Ps 112:4
8:17 [x]Est 9:19,27; Ps 35:27; Pr 11:10 [y]Ex 15:14,16; Dt 11:25 [z]Est 9:3
9:1 [a]Est 8:12 [b]Jer 29:4-7 [c]Est 3:12-14; Pr 22:22-23
9:2 [d]ver 15-18 [e]Est 8:11,17; Ps 71:13,24
9:3 [f]Ezr 8:36
9:4 [g]Ex 11:3 [h]2Sa 3:1; 1Ch 11:9

a9 That is, the upper Nile region

stroying them,[i] and they did what
they pleased to those who hated them.
6In the citadel of Susa, the Jews killed
and destroyed five hundred men.
7They also killed Parshandatha, Dal-
phon, Aspatha, **8**Poratha, Adalia, Arida-
tha, **9**Parmashta, Arisai, Aridai and Vai-
zatha, **10**the ten sons[j] of Haman son
of Hammedatha, the enemy of the
Jews. But they did not lay their hands
on the plunder.[k]
11The number of those slain in the
citadel of Susa was reported to the king
that same day. **12**The king said to
Queen Esther, "The Jews have killed
and destroyed five hundred men and
the ten sons of Haman in the citadel of
Susa. What have they done in the rest
of the king's provinces? Now what is
your petition? It will be given you.
What is your request? It will also be
granted."[l]
13"If it pleases the king," Esther answered, "give the Jews in Susa permission to carry out this day's edict tomorrow also, and let Haman's ten sons[m]
be hanged[n] on gallows."
14So the king commanded that this
be done. An edict was issued in Susa,
and they hanged[o] the ten sons of Haman. **15**The Jews in Susa came together
on the fourteenth day of the month of
Adar, and they put to death in Susa
three hundred men, but they did not
lay their hands on the plunder.[p]
16Meanwhile, the remainder of the
Jews who were in the king's provinces
also assembled to protect themselves
and get relief[q] from their enemies.[r]
They killed seventy-five thousand of
them[s] but did not lay their hands on
the plunder. **17**This happened on the
thirteenth day of the month of Adar,
and on the fourteenth they rested and
made it a day of feasting[t] and joy.

Purim Celebrated

18The Jews in Susa, however, had assembled on the thirteenth and fourteenth, and then on the fifteenth they
rested and made it a day of feasting
and joy.
19That is why rural Jews—those living in villages—observe the fourteenth
of the month of Adar[u] as a day of joy
and feasting, a day for giving presents
to each other.[v]
20Mordecai recorded these events,
and he sent letters to all the Jews
throughout the provinces of King Xerxes, near and far, **21**to have them celebrate annually the fourteenth and fifteenth days of the month of Adar **22**as
the time when the Jews got relief[w]
from their enemies, and as the month
when their sorrow was turned into joy
and their mourning into a day of celebration.[x] He wrote them to observe
the days as days of feasting and joy and
giving presents of food[y] to one another and gifts to the poor.
23So the Jews agreed to continue the
celebration they had begun, doing
what Mordecai had written to them.
24For Haman son of Hammedatha, the
Agagite,[z] the enemy of all the Jews,
had plotted against the Jews to destroy
them and had cast the *pur*[a] (that is,
the lot[b]) for their ruin and destruction. **25**But when the plot came to the
king's attention,[a] he issued written orders that the evil scheme Haman had
devised against the Jews should come
back onto his own head,[c] and that he
and his sons should be hanged[d] on
the gallows.[e] **26**(Therefore these days
were called Purim, from the word
pur.[f]) Because of everything written
in this letter and because of what they
had seen and what had happened to
them, **27**the Jews took it upon themselves to establish the custom that they
and their descendants and all who join
them should without fail observe these
two days every year, in the way prescribed and at the time appointed.
28These days should be remembered
and observed in every generation by
every family, and in every province and
in every city. And these days of Purim
should never cease to be celebrated
by the Jews, nor should the memory
of them die out among their descendants.
29So Queen Esther, daughter of Abihail,[g] along with Mordecai the Jew,
wrote with full authority to confirm
this second letter concerning Purim.
30And Mordecai sent letters to all the
Jews in the 127 provinces[h] of the kingdom of Xerxes—words of goodwill and
assurance— **31**to establish these days
of Purim at their designated times, as
Mordecai the Jew and Queen Esther
had decreed for them, and as they had
established for themselves and their
descendants in regard to their times of
fasting[i] and lamentation.[j] **32**Esther's
decree confirmed these regulations
about Purim, and it was written down
in the records.

The Greatness of Mordecai

10 King Xerxes imposed tribute
throughout the empire, to its distant shores.[k] **2**And all his acts of power

9:5 [i]Ezr 4:6
9:10 [j]Est 5:11 [k]Ge 14:23; 1Sa 14:32; Est 3:13; 8:11
9:12 [l]Est 5:6; 7:2
9:13 [m]Est 5:11 [n]Dt 21:22-23
9:14 [o]Ezr 6:11
9:15 [p]Ge 14:23; Est 8:11
9:16 [q]Est 4:14 [r]Dt 25:19 [s]1Ch 4:43
9:17 [t]1Ki 3:15
9:19 [u]Est 3:7 [v]ver 22; Dt 16:11,14; Ne 8:10,12; Est 2:9; Rev 11:10
9:22 [w]Est 4:14 [x]Ne 8:12; Ps 30:11-12 [y]2Ki 25:30
9:24 [z]Ex 17:8-16 [a]Est 3:7 [b]Lev 16:8
9:25 [c]Ps 7:16 [d]Dt 21:22-23 [e]Est 7:10
9:26 [f]ver 20; Est 3:7
9:29 [g]Est 2:15
9:30 [h]Est 1:1
9:31 [i]Est 4:16 [j]Est 4:1-3
10:1 [k]Ps 72:10; 97:1; Isa 24:15

[a] *25* Or *when Esther came before the king*

and might, together with a full account
of the greatness of Mordecai[l] to
which the king had raised him,[m] are
they not written in the book of the annals[n] of the kings of Media and Persia?
3Mordecai the Jew was second[o] in
rank[p] to King Xerxes,[q] preeminent
among the Jews, and held in high esteem by his many fellow Jews, because
he worked for the good of his people
and spoke up for the welfare of all the
Jews.[r]

10:2 [l]Est 8:15; 9:4 [m]Ge 41:44 [n]Est 2:23
10:3 [o]Da 5:7 [p]Ge 41:43 [q]Ge 41:40 [r]Ne 2:10; Jer 29:4-7; Da 6:3

JOB

AT A GLANCE

Key Principle: God is in control over all things and is worthy of our worship, even though we may not understand what he is doing in our lives.
Author: Unknown
Time and Place: Patriarchal period, perhaps ~2000 B.C. / Land of Uz (Area of Edom / Northern Arabia)
Key Verses: 13:15; 23:10; 37:23–24

BENEFIT

Suffering is part of the human experience, and Job is a valuable resource to turn to when suffering overwhelms us. This poetic book deals more thoroughly with this theme than any other book in the Bible. It offers God's perspective on the adversity and affliction we sometimes face. Job teaches us that God may allow suffering to enter our lives for a number of reasons: to test us (2:3), to discipline us (5:17), to humble us (22:29), to change our perspective (42:5–6) and to prepare us for blessings in the future (42:10).

SETTING

According to Lamentations 4:21, Uz was located in the area of Edom, which was southeast of the Dead Sea in the region of northern Arabia. Several literary clues help us to associate Job with the patriarchal period (about the time of Abraham, ~2000 B.C.). The book of Job includes no references to Israel or to the Mosaic law; it often uses the patriarchal name *Shaddai* ("the Almighty") for God; it portrays Job as the priest of his family as were the patriarchs Abraham, Isaac and Jacob; Job's longevity rivals Abraham's (42:16); Job's wealth is measured in livestock, not in silver and gold (1:3; 42:12).

No one knows when this book was written. Either Job or Elihu could have written it, Moses could have compiled this account when he was in Midian (1485–1445 B.C.) or perhaps an unknown individual edited it around Solomon's time. Job is mentioned in other places in the Bible (Ezekiel 14:14, 20; James 5:11), so we know that his story was well known through years of retelling in the oral tradition.

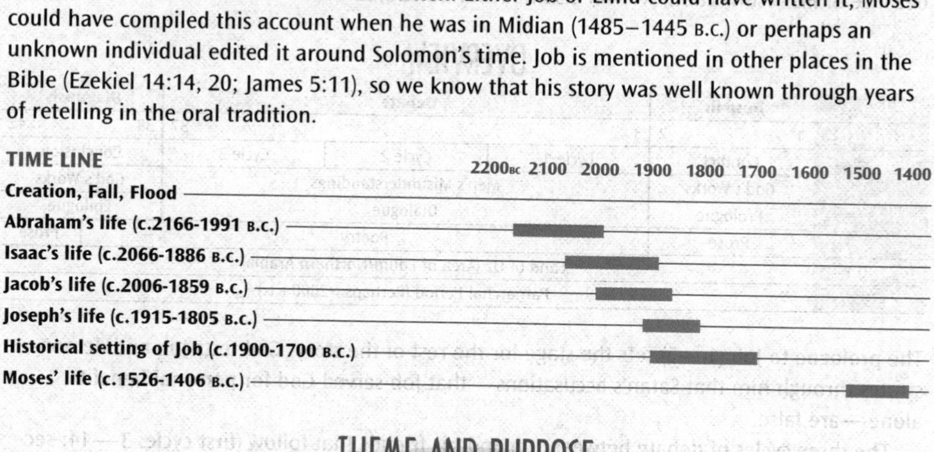

THEME AND PURPOSE

The real issue in Job is not suffering, but sovereignty. The lesson Job ultimately learned through his sufferings is that God alone is in sovereign control of all things. To think God has lost control or that he does not have our best interests at heart is to judge according to our human perspective. When we do so, we fail to take God's perfect character into account. We are often too nearsighted to see the things God has in mind.

This book poses many reasons for the existence of suffering, but the simplistic answers of Job's three friends are unworthy of the God of Scripture. The final chapters show us that God is far more concerned that we trust him than that we understand him, since his ways and his wisdom far exceed our own.

UNIQUE CONTRIBUTION

Job is the first of the five poetical books in the Bible (the others are Psalms, Proverbs, Ecclesiastes, and Song of Songs). Apart from chapters 1—2 and 42, Job is a book of dramatic poetry that is both profound and beautiful. It analyzes human suffering with extraordinary depth and subtlety, and gives us principles that are universal and timeless. God's speech to Job in chapters 38—41 is a vivid and beautiful portrait of the divine wisdom and providential care that we see in creation.

Hebrew poetry does not rhyme sounds; it relates ideas through carefully arranging parallel thoughts. The three most common forms of this literary device, called "parallelism," are synonymous (the second line reinforces the thought of the first line using similar words or concepts), synthetic (the second line adds to or completes the idea of the first line) and antithetic (the second line contrasts the thought of the first line). Hebrew poetry also makes rich use of figures of speech, including simile (using similar words that add depth of meaning), metaphor (a simple image representing a complex idea), hyperbole (exaggeration), anthropomorphism (speaking of God in human terms) and synecdoche (representing the whole by a part). Look for these literary devices as you work your way through the Old Testament books of poetry.

LINKS TO THE NEW TESTAMENT

Job anticipates the coming Messiah when he says, "I know that my Redeemer lives, and that in the end he will stand upon the earth" (19:25). Job also cries out for a mediator to stand between himself and God (9:33). Christ is our Redeemer, our Mediator, and our Advocate before God. He has identified with us in our sufferings (Hebrews 2:14–18; 4:14–16), and because of his resurrection, we will also be resurrected (Job 19:26–27).

OVERVIEW

FOCUS	Despair	Debate			Diagnosis
REFERENCE	1 — 2	3		37	38 — 42
TOPICS	Conflict	Cycle 1	Cycle 2	Cycle 3	Conclusion
	God's Works	Men's Misunderstandings			God's Works
	Prologue	Dialogue			Epilogue
	Prose	Poetry			Prose
LOCATION	Land of Uz (Area of Edom/Northern Arabia)				
TIME	Patriarchal Period (Perhaps ~2000 B.C.)				

The prologue to Job (1—2) sets the stage for the rest of the story. God tests Job and demonstrates through him that Satan's accusations—that Job served God for personal benefits alone—are false.

The three cycles of debate between Job and his friends that follow (first cycle: 3—14; second cycle: 15—21; third cycle: 22—26) increase in emotional intensity. Eliphaz, Bildad and Zophar claim that Job is suffering because of his sins, while Job defends his innocence with growing vehemence. Eliphaz is a theologian who appeals to observation and experience;

Bildad is a historian who appeals to tradition and history; and Zophar is a moralist who simply assumes that Job is sinning. Job's responses, including his closing monologue (27—31) become increasingly self-righteous as he accuses God of not listening to him and of unjustly punishing him while allowing the wicked to prosper. Elihu finally speaks and urges Job to humble himself while God purifies him through these trials (32—37).

God himself ends the debate by speaking to Job of his power and wisdom in creating and sustaining creation (38—39). When Job acknowledges his insignificance and presumption, God illustrates his power to control all things (40—41). This time Job responds in humility and repentance. Finally, God restores Job's fortunes after he prays for his three friends (42).

JOB

Prologue

4 →PG. 605

1 In the land of Uz[a] there lived a man whose name was Job.[b] This man was blameless[c] and upright; he feared God[d] and shunned evil. 2He had seven sons and three daughters,[e] 3and he owned seven thousand sheep, three thousand camels, five hundred yoke of oxen and five hundred donkeys, and had a large number of servants. He was the greatest man[f] among all the people of the East.

4His sons used to take turns holding feasts in their homes, and they would invite their three sisters to eat and drink with them. 5When a period of feasting had run its course, Job would send and have them purified. Early in the morning he would sacrifice a burnt offering[g] for each of them, thinking, "Perhaps my children have sinned[h] and cursed God[i] in their hearts." This was Job's regular custom.

Job's First Test

6One day the angels[a][j] came to present themselves before the LORD, and Satan[b] also came with them.[k] 7The LORD said to Satan, "Where have you come from?"

Satan answered the LORD, "From roaming through the earth and going back and forth in it."[l]

8Then the LORD said to Satan, "Have you considered my servant Job?[m] There is no one on earth like him; he is blameless and upright, a man who fears God and shuns evil."[n]

9"Does Job fear God for nothing?"[o] Satan replied. 10"Have you not put a hedge around him and his household and everything he has?[p] You have blessed the work of his hands, so that his flocks and herds are spread throughout the land.[q] 11But stretch out your hand and strike everything he has,[r] and he will surely curse you to your face."[s]

12The LORD said to Satan, "Very well, then, everything he has is in your hands, but on the man himself do not lay a finger."

Then Satan went out from the presence of the LORD.

13One day when Job's sons and daughters were feasting and drinking wine at the oldest brother's house, 14a messenger came to Job and said, "The oxen were plowing and the donkeys were grazing nearby, 15and the Sabeans[t] attacked and carried them off. They put the servants to the sword, and I am the only one who has escaped to tell you!"

16While he was still speaking, another messenger came and said, "The fire of God fell from the sky[u] and burned up the sheep and the servants,[v] and I am the only one who has escaped to tell you!"

17While he was still speaking, another messenger came and said, "The Chaldeans[w] formed three raiding parties and swept down on your camels and carried them off. They put the servants to the sword, and I am the only one who has escaped to tell you!"

18While he was still speaking, yet another messenger came and said, "Your sons and daughters were feasting and drinking wine at the oldest brother's house, 19when suddenly a mighty wind[x] swept in from the desert and struck the four corners of the house. It collapsed on them and they are dead, and I am the only one who has escaped to tell you!"

20At this, Job got up and tore his robe[y] and shaved his head. Then he fell to the ground in worship[z] 21and said:

"Naked I came from my mother's
    womb,
  and naked I will depart.[c][a]
The LORD gave and the LORD has
    taken away;[b]
  may the name of the LORD be
    praised."[c]

22In all this, Job did not sin by charging God with wrongdoing.[d]

Job's Second Test

2 On another day the angels[a] came to present themselves before the LORD, and Satan also came with them[e] to present himself before him. 2And the LORD said to Satan, "Where have you come from?"

Satan answered the LORD, "From roaming through the earth and going back and forth in it."

3Then the LORD said to Satan, "Have you considered my servant Job? There is no one on earth like him; he is blameless and upright, a man who

1:1 [a]Jer 25:20 [b]Eze 14:14,20; Jas 5:11 [c]Ge 6:9; 17:1 [d]Ge 22:12; Ex 18:21 **1:2** [e]Job 42:13 **1:3** [f]Job 29:25 **1:5** [g]Ge 8:20; Job 42:8 [h]Job 8:4 [i]1Ki 21:10,13 **1:6** [j]Job 38:7 [k]Job 2:1 **1:7** [l]1Pe 5:8 **1:8** [m]Jos 1:7; Job 42:7-8 [n]ver 1 **1:9** [o]1Ti 6:5 **1:10** [p]Ps 34:7 [q]ver 3; Job 29:6; 31:25; Ps 128:1-2 **1:11** [r]Job 19:21 [s]Job 2:5

1:15 [t]Ge 10:7; Job 6:19 **1:16** [u]Ge 19:24 [v]Lev 10:2; Nu 11:1-3 **1:17** [w]Ge 11:28,31 **1:19** [x]Jer 4:11; 13:24 **1:20** [y]Ge 37:29 [z]1Pe 5:6 **1:21** [a]Ecc 5:15; 1Ti 6:7 [b]1Sa 2:7 [c]Job 2:10; Eph 5:20; 1Th 5:18 **1:22** [d]Job 2:10 **2:1** [e]Job 1:6

a6,1 Hebrew *the sons of God* **b**6 *Satan* means *accuser.* **c**21 Or *will return there*

fears God and shuns evil.[f] And he still
maintains his integrity,[g] though you
incited me against him to ruin him
without any reason."[h]
3 →PG. 549
4"Skin for skin!" Satan replied. "A
man will give all he has for his own life.
5But stretch out your hand and strike
his flesh and bones,[i] and he will surely curse you to your face."[j]
6The LORD said to Satan, "Very well,
then, he is in your hands; but you must
spare his life."[k]
7So Satan went out from the presence of the LORD and afflicted Job with
painful sores from the soles of his feet
to the top of his head.[l] 8Then Job took
a piece of broken pottery and scraped

2:3 [f]Job 1:1,8 [g]Job 27:6 [h]Job 9:17
2:5 [i]Job 19:20 [j]Job 1:11
2:6 [k]Job 1:12
2:7 [l]Dt 28:35; Job 7:5
2:8 [m]Job 42:6; Jer 6:26; Eze 27:30; Mt 11:21
2:10 [n]Job 1:21 [o]Job 1:22; Ps 39:1; Jas 1:12; 5:11

himself with it as he sat among the
ashes.[m]
3 →PG. 569
9His wife said to him, "Are you still
holding on to your integrity? Curse
God and die!"
10He replied, "You are talking like a
foolish[a] woman. Shall we accept good
from God, and not trouble?"[n]
In all this, Job did not sin in what he
said.[o]

Job's Three Friends

2 →PG. 581
11When Job's three friends, Eliphaz

[a]*10* The Hebrew word rendered *foolish* denotes moral deficiency.

1:1–2:13

PROMISE 1

WHY DID JOB, A GOOD MAN, SUFFER?

Some people do evil things and suffer the consequences; their suffering, it seems, is natural. Other people live seemingly neutral lives; their suffering is problematic. But when someone suffers while actively pursuing God and trying to do good, the question "Why?" can become deeply troubling and difficult.

In this story, a good man suffers. The term "good" is carefully defined in the first few verses of chapter 1. The author of Job takes pains to let us know Job was a *good* man. Job's suffering increased because other good and well-intentioned men tried to explain his suffering to him. Their explanations turned to accusations, and only confused the issue. Their "comfort" became his torment.

Through the ages people have struggled to understand why good people suffer. We can't read the book of Job without feeling some need to grapple with that question. The issue is, at its most fundamental level, one of believing God. Passage upon passage in the Bible tell us that we will never understand all God does. Our finite intellect must bow to God's infinite understanding. Sin, at its base, involves believing and following our own understanding when it disagrees with God's truth. God encourages us to question and search his will; he created us with the ability to do so. But if, at the end of our search, our logic is not satisfied, we must bow our heads at his feet, not shake our fists in his face.

This brief note will not solve a problem with which entire volumes have struggled. There is no ultimate answer to human suffering, but there is greater understanding of it for those who read Scripture with a searching and humble mind. A quick study reviews at least five passages that address the question of why good people suffer.

1. *To develop character.* James 1 teaches that "the testing of your faith develops perseverance." If we remain true to God through the suffering process we will be "mature and complete, not lacking anything" (James 1:1–4).
2. *To demonstrate the nature of our character.* Job was God's demonstration to Satan that there was a man who truly loved him and was truly righteous (Job 1:1–6). No matter what cruelty Satan devised, *this* man, God said, would endure in his righteousness.
3. *To allow God to demonstrate the strength he makes available to us* (2 Corinthians 12:7–10). Paul was greatly blessed by God; he was a truly good man. He wrote that his suffering was God's way of keeping him dependent on God. The "thorn in his flesh" helped him understand that God was sufficient for all his needs.
4. *To test us.* Genesis 22 (see the note there) describes the process by which God perfected Abraham's faith. Both the story in Genesis and God's explanation of it in James 2:20–24 tell us that God was showing Abraham what Abraham was made of.
5. *To discipline and correct us.* All people, even the most godly among us, sin. Proverbs 3:11–12 and Hebrews 12:4–11 tell us that God uses suffering to guide us back to his way when we stray from it. Both passages show God as a loving Father who wants to correct behavior that will destroy us if we persist in it. Throughout Scripture, God deals with sin; not to vindictively punish us, but to lovingly correct us.

God's people must use their minds and attempt to understand all he has revealed. But God knows that the finite sometimes slams into the infinite; we cannot grasp all he is doing. At that point, God trusts our faith to keep us coming to back to him.

In the final analysis the question of why good people suffer has reasonable explanations but, for many, no sufficient answer. Where the intellect boggles, faith in God's sovereign love must step in. The story of Job, with all his pain, is not only a *story* of one man's faith in God's love, it is an *exercise* of man's faith in God's love. It will be so for you if you read it as it was written.

For the next Promise 1 reading go to page 562.

the Temanite,[p] Bildad the Shuhite[q]
and Zophar the Naamathite, heard
about all the troubles that had come
upon him, they set out from their
homes and met together by agreement
to go and sympathize with him and
comfort him.[r] 12When they saw him
from a distance, they could hardly recognize him; they began to weep aloud,
and they tore their robes and sprinkled
dust on their heads.[s] 13Then they sat
on the ground with him for seven days
and seven nights.[t] No one said a word
to him, because they saw how great his
suffering was.

Job Speaks

3 After this, Job opened his mouth and
cursed the day of his birth. 2He said:

3"May the day of my birth perish,
and the night it was said, 'A boy
is born!'[u]
4That day—may it turn to darkness;
may God above not care about
it;
may no light shine upon it.
5May darkness and deep shadow[a][v]
claim it once more;
may a cloud settle over it;
may blackness overwhelm its
light.
6That night—may thick darkness[w]
seize it;
may it not be included among
the days of the year
nor be entered in any of the
months.
7May that night be barren;
may no shout of joy be heard in
it.
8May those who curse days[b] curse
that day,
those who are ready to rouse
Leviathan.[x]
9May its morning stars become
dark;
may it wait for daylight in vain
and not see the first rays of
dawn,[y]
10for it did not shut the doors of the
womb on me
to hide trouble from my eyes.

11"Why did I not perish at birth,
and die as I came from the
womb?[z]
12Why were there knees to receive
me[a]
and breasts that I might be
nursed?
13For now I would be lying down[b]
in peace;
I would be asleep and at rest[c]
14with kings and counselors of the
earth,[d]
who built for themselves places
now lying in ruins,[e]
15with rulers[f] who had gold,
who filled their houses with
silver.[g]
16Or why was I not hidden in the
ground like a stillborn
child,[h]
like an infant who never saw the
light of day?
17There the wicked cease from
turmoil,
and there the weary are at rest.[i]
18Captives also enjoy their ease;
they no longer hear the slave
driver's shout.[j]
19The small and the great are there,
and the slave is freed from his
master.

20"Why is light given to those in
misery,
and life to the bitter of soul,[k]
21to those who long for death that
does not come,[l]
who search for it more than for
hidden treasure,[m]
22who are filled with gladness
and rejoice when they reach the
grave?
23Why is life given to a man
whose way is hidden,
whom God has hedged in?[n]
24For sighing comes to me instead of
food;[o]
my groans pour out like water.[p]
25What I feared has come upon me;
what I dreaded[q] has happened
to me.
26I have no peace, no quietness;

[a]5 Or *and the shadow of death* [b]8 Or *the sea*

2:11 [p]Ge 36:11; Jer 49:7 [q]Ge 25:2 [r]Job 42:11; Ro 12:15 **2:12** [s]Jos 7:6; Ne 9:1; La 2:10; Eze 27:30 **2:13** [t]Ge 50:10; Eze 3:15 **3:3** [u]Job 10:18-19; Jer 20:14-18 **3:5** [v]Job 10:21,22; Ps 23:4; Jer 2:6; 13:16 **3:6** [w]Job 23:17 **3:8** [x]Job 41:1,8,10, 25 **3:9** [y]Job 41:18 **3:11** [z]Job 10:18 **3:12** [a]Ge 30:3; Isa 66:12 **3:13** [b]Job 17:13 [c]Job 7:8-10,21; 10:22; 14:10-12; 19:27; 21:13,23 **3:14** [d]Job 12:17 [e]Job 15:28 **3:15** [f]Job 12:21 [g]Job 27:17 **3:16** [h]Ps 58:8; Ecc 6:3 **3:17** [i]Job 17:16 **3:18** [j]Job 39:7 **3:20** [k]1Sa 1:10; Jer 20:18; Eze 27:30-31 **3:21** [l]Rev 9:6 [m]Pr 2:4 **3:23** [n]Job 19:6,8,12; Ps 88:8; La 3:7 **3:24** [o]Job 6:7; 33:20 [p]Ps 42:3,4 **3:25** [q]Job 30:15

2:11–13

PROMISE 2

FAITHFUL FRIENDS

Job's cultivation of friendships like these is a mark of his greatness. Note how these men responded to news of Job's suffering. When they heard of his trouble, they traveled from their homes to be with him. They wept and mourned with him, and for seven days they just sat on the ground suffering in silence with their friend. These men spoke volumes to Job's heart without saying a word.

Think about what it takes to develop friends who will do that. Think about what it would mean for you to suffer like that with one of your friends. The investment of quality time in a few other men can pay off for all of you in the tough times.

For the next Promise 2 reading go to page 560.

I have no rest,[r] but only
turmoil."

Eliphaz

4 Then Eliphaz the Temanite replied:

2"If someone ventures a word with
you, will you be impatient?
But who can keep from
speaking?[s]
3Think how you have instructed
many,
how you have strengthened
feeble hands.[t]
4Your words have supported those
who stumbled;
you have strengthened faltering
knees.[u]
5But now trouble comes to you, and
you are discouraged;
it strikes[v] you, and you are
dismayed.[w]
6Should not your piety be your
confidence[x]
and your blameless[y] ways your
hope?

7"Consider now: Who, being
innocent, has ever
perished?[z]
Where were the upright ever
destroyed?[a]
8As I have observed, those who plow
evil[b]
and those who sow trouble reap
it.[c]
9At the breath of God[d] they are
destroyed;
at the blast of his anger they
perish.[e]
10The lions may roar and growl,
yet the teeth of the great lions
are broken.[f]
11The lion perishes for lack of prey,[g]
and the cubs of the lioness are
scattered.

12"A word was secretly brought to
me,
my ears caught a whisper[h] of
it.[i]
13Amid disquieting dreams in the
night,
when deep sleep falls on men,[j]
14fear and trembling seized me
and made all my bones shake.[k]
15A spirit glided past my face,
and the hair on my body stood
on end.
16It stopped,
but I could not tell what it was.
A form stood before my eyes,
and I heard a hushed voice:
17'Can a mortal be more righteous
than God?[l]
Can a man be more pure than
his Maker?[m]
18If God places no trust in his
servants,
if he charges his angels with
error,[n]
19how much more those who live in
houses of clay,[o]
whose foundations[p] are in the
dust,[q]
who are crushed more readily
than a moth!
20Between dawn and dusk they are
broken to pieces;
unnoticed, they perish forever.[r]
21Are not the cords of their tent
pulled up,[s]
so that they die without
wisdom?'[a][t]

5 "Call if you will, but who will
answer you?
To which of the holy ones[u] will
you turn?
2Resentment kills a fool,
and envy slays the simple.[v]
3I myself have seen a fool taking
root,[w]
but suddenly his house was
cursed.[x]
4His children are far from safety,[y]
crushed in court[z] without a
defender.
5The hungry consume his harvest,[a]
taking it even from among
thorns,
and the thirsty pant after his
wealth.
6For hardship does not spring from
the soil,
nor does trouble sprout from the
ground.
7Yet man is born to trouble[b]
as surely as sparks fly upward.

8"But if it were I, I would appeal to
God;
I would lay my cause before
him.[c]
9He performs wonders that cannot
be fathomed,[d]
miracles that cannot be counted.
10He bestows rain on the earth;
he sends water upon the
countryside.[e]
11The lowly he sets on high,[f]
and those who mourn are lifted
to safety.
12He thwarts the plans[g] of the
crafty,
so that their hands achieve no
success.
13He catches the wise in their
craftiness,[h]

[a]21 Some interpreters end the quotation after verse 17.

3:26 [r]Job 7:4,14
4:2 [s]Job 32:20
4:3 [t]Isa 35:3; Heb 12:12
4:4 [u]Isa 35:3; Heb 12:12
4:5 [v]Job 19:21 [w]Job 6:14
4:6 [x]Pr 3:26 [y]Job 1:1
4:7 [z]Job 36:7 [a]Job 8:20; Ps 37:25
4:8 [b]Job 15:35 [c]Pr 22:8; Hos 10:13; Gal 6:7-8
4:9 [d]Job 15:30; Isa 30:33; 2Th 2:8 [e]Job 40:13
4:10 [f]Job 5:15; Ps 58:6
4:11 [g]Job 27:14; Ps 34:10
4:12 [h]Job 26:14 [i]Job 33:14
4:13 [j]Job 33:15
4:14 [k]Jer 23:9; Hab 3:16
4:17 [l]Job 9:2 [m]Job 35:10
4:18 [n]Job 15:15
4:19 [o]Job 10:9 [p]Job 22:16 [q]Ge 2:7
4:20 [r]Job 14:2,20; 20:7; Ps 90:5-6
4:21 [s]Job 8:22 [t]Job 18:21; 36:12
5:1 [u]Job 15:15
5:2 [v]Pr 12:16
5:3 [w]Ps 37:35; Jer 12:2 [x]Job 24:18
5:4 [y]Job 4:11 [z]Am 5:12
5:5 [a]Job 18:8-10
5:7 [b]Job 14:1
5:8 [c]Ps 35:23; 50:15
5:9 [d]Job 42:3; Ps 40:5
5:10 [e]Job 36:28
5:11 [f]Ps 113:7-8
5:12 [g]Ne 4:15; Ps 33:10
5:13 [h]1Co 3:19*

and the schemes of the wily are
swept away.
14Darkness[i] comes upon them in
the daytime;
at noon they grope as in the
night.[j]
15He saves the needy[k] from the
sword in their mouth;
he saves them from the clutches
of the powerful.[l]
16So the poor have hope,
and injustice shuts its mouth.[m]

17"Blessed is the man whom God
corrects;[n]
so do not despise the
discipline[o] of the
Almighty.[a][p]
18For he wounds, but he also binds
up;[q]
he injures, but his hands also
heal.[r]
19From six calamities he will rescue
you;
in seven no harm will befall
you.[s]
20In famine[t] he will ransom you
from death,
and in battle from the stroke of
the sword.[u]
21You will be protected from the lash
of the tongue,[v]
and need not fear[w] when
destruction comes.
22You will laugh at destruction and
famine,
and need not fear the beasts of
the earth.[x]
23For you will have a covenant with
the stones[y] of the field,
and the wild animals will be at
peace with you.[z]
24You will know that your tent is
secure;
you will take stock of your
property and find nothing
missing.[a]
25You will know that your children
will be many,[b]
and your descendants like the
grass of the earth.[c]
26You will come to the grave in full
vigor,[d]
like sheaves gathered in season.

27"We have examined this, and it is
true.
So hear it and apply it to
yourself."

Job

6 Then Job replied:

2"If only my anguish could be
weighed
and all my misery be placed on
the scales![e]
3It would surely outweigh the
sand[f] of the seas—
no wonder my words have been
impetuous.[g]
4The arrows[h] of the Almighty are in
me,[i]
my spirit drinks[j] in their
poison;
God's terrors[k] are marshaled
against me.[l]
5Does a wild donkey bray when it
has grass,
or an ox bellow when it has
fodder?
6Is tasteless food eaten without salt,
or is there flavor in the white of
an egg[b]?
7I refuse to touch it;
such food makes me ill.[m]

8"Oh, that I might have my request,
that God would grant what I
hope for,[n]
9that God would be willing to crush
me,
to let loose his hand and cut me
off![o]
10Then I would still have this
consolation—
my joy in unrelenting pain—
that I had not denied the
words[p] of the Holy One.[q]

11"What strength do I have, that I
should still hope?
What prospects, that I should be
patient?[r]
12Do I have the strength of stone?
Is my flesh bronze?
13Do I have any power to help
myself,[s]
now that success has been
driven from me?

14"A despairing man[t] should have
the devotion[u] of his
friends,
even though he forsakes the fear
of the Almighty.
15But my brothers are as
undependable as
intermittent streams,[v]
as the streams that overflow
16when darkened by thawing ice
and swollen with melting snow,
17but that cease to flow in the dry
season,
and in the heat[w] vanish from
their channels.
18Caravans turn aside from their
routes;

5:14 [i]Job 12:25 [j]Dt 28:29 **5:15** [k]Ps 35:10 [l]Job 4:10 **5:16** [m]Ps 107:42 **5:17** [n]Jas 1:12 [o]Ps 94:12; Pr 3:11 [p]Heb 12:5-11 **5:18** [q]Isa 30:26 [r]1Sa 2:6 **5:19** [s]Ps 34:19; 91:10 **5:20** [t]Ps 33:19 [u]Ps 144:10 **5:21** [v]Ps 31:20 [w]Ps 91:5 **5:22** [x]Ps 91:13; Eze 34:25 **5:23** [y]Ps 91:12 [z]Isa 11:6-9 **5:24** [a]Job 8:6 **5:25** [b]Ps 112:2 [c]Ps 72:16; Isa 44:3-4 **5:26** [d]Ge 15:15

6:2 [e]Job 31:6 **6:3** [f]Pr 27:3 [g]Job 23:2 **6:4** [h]Ps 38:2 [i]Job 16:12,13 [j]Job 21:20 [k]Job 30:15 [l]Ps 88:15-18 **6:7** [m]Job 3:24 **6:8** [n]Job 14:13 **6:9** [o]Nu 11:15; 1Ki 19:4 **6:10** [p]Job 22:22; 23:12 [q]Lev 19:2; Isa 57:15 **6:11** [r]Job 21:4 **6:13** [s]Job 26:2 **6:14** [t]Job 4:5 [u]Job 15:4 **6:15** [v]Ps 38:11; Jer 15:18 **6:17** [w]Job 24:19

a *17* Hebrew *Shaddai*; here and throughout Job
b *6* The meaning of the Hebrew for this phrase is uncertain.

they go up into the wasteland
and perish.
19The caravans of Tema[x] look for
water,
the traveling merchants of Sheba
look in hope.
20They are distressed, because they
had been confident;
they arrive there, only to be
disappointed.[y]
21Now you too have proved to be of
no help;
you see something dreadful and
are afraid.[z]
22Have I ever said, 'Give something
on my behalf,
pay a ransom for me from your
wealth,
23deliver me from the hand of the
enemy,
ransom me from the clutches of
the ruthless'?

24"Teach me, and I will be quiet;[a]
show me where I have been
wrong.
25How painful are honest words![b]
But what do your arguments
prove?
26Do you mean to correct what I say,
and treat the words of a
despairing man as wind?[c]
27You would even cast lots[d] for the
fatherless
and barter away your friend.

28"But now be so kind as to look at
me.
Would I lie to your face?[e]
29Relent, do not be unjust;
reconsider, for my integrity is at
stake.[a][f]
30Is there any wickedness on my
lips?[g]
Can my mouth not discern[h]
malice?

7 "Does not man have hard service[i]
on earth?[j]
Are not his days like those of a
hired man?[k]
2Like a slave longing for the evening
shadows,
or a hired man waiting eagerly
for his wages,[l]
3so I have been allotted months of
futility,
and nights of misery have been
assigned to me.[m]
4When I lie down I think, 'How long
before I get up?'[n]
The night drags on, and I toss till
dawn.
5My body is clothed with worms[o]
and scabs,
my skin is broken and festering.

6"My days are swifter than a
weaver's shuttle,[p]
and they come to an end
without hope.[q]
7Remember, O God, that my life is
but a breath;[r]
my eyes will never see happiness
again.[s]
8The eye that now sees me will see
me no longer;
you will look for me, but I will
be no more.[t]
9As a cloud vanishes and is gone,
so he who goes down to the
grave[b][u] does not return.[v]
10He will never come to his house
again;
his place[w] will know him no
more.[x]

11"Therefore I will not keep silent;[y]
I will speak out in the anguish of
my spirit,
I will complain in the bitterness
of my soul.[z]
12Am I the sea, or the monster of the
deep,[a]
that you put me under guard?
13When I think my bed will comfort
me
and my couch will ease my
complaint,[b]
14even then you frighten me with
dreams
and terrify[c] me with visions,
15so that I prefer strangling and
death,[d]
rather than this body of mine.
16I despise my life;[e] I would not live
forever.
Let me alone; my days have no
meaning.

17"What is man that you make so
much of him,
that you give him so much
attention,[f]
18that you examine him every
morning
and test him every moment?[g]
19Will you never look away from me,
or let me alone even for an
instant?[h]
20If I have sinned, what have I done
to you,[i]
O watcher of men?
Why have you made me your
target?[j]
Have I become a burden to
you?[c]

6:19 [x]Ge 25:15; Isa 21:14
6:20 [y]Jer 14:3
6:21 [z]Ps 38:11
6:24 [a]Ps 39:1
6:25 [b]Ecc 12:11
6:26 [c]Job 8:2; 15:3
6:27 [d]Joel 3:3; Na 3:10; 2Pe 2:3
6:28 [e]Job 27:4; 33:1,3; 36:3,4
6:29 [f]Job 23:7,10; 34:5,36; 42:6
6:30 [g]Job 27:4 [h]Job 12:11
7:1 [i]Job 14:14; Isa 40:2 [j]Job 5:7 [k]Job 14:6
7:2 [l]Lev 19:13
7:3 [m]Job 16:7; Ps 6:6
7:4 [n]Dt 28:67
7:5 [o]Job 17:14; Isa 14:11
7:6 [p]Job 9:25 [q]Job 13:15; 17:11,15
7:7 [r]Ps 78:39; Jas 4:14 [s]Job 9:25
7:8 [t]Job 20:7,9,21
7:9 [u]Job 11:8 [v]2Sa 12:23; Job 30:15
7:10 [w]Job 27:21,23 [x]Job 8:18
7:11 [y]Ps 40:9 [z]1Sa 1:10
7:12 [a]Eze 32:2-3
7:13 [b]Job 9:27
7:14 [c]Job 9:34
7:15 [d]1Ki 19:4
7:16 [e]Job 9:21; 10:1
7:17 [f]Ps 8:4; 144:3; Heb 2:6
7:18 [g]Job 14:3
7:19 [h]Job 9:18
7:20 [i]Job 35:6 [j]Job 16:12

[a]29 Or *my righteousness still stands*
[b]9 Hebrew *Sheol* [c]20 A few manuscripts of the Masoretic Text, an ancient Hebrew scribal tradition and Septuagint; most manuscripts of the Masoretic Text *I have become a burden to myself.*

21 Why do you not pardon my
offenses
and forgive my sins?[k]
For I will soon lie down in the
dust;[l]
you will search for me, but I will
be no more."

Bildad

8 Then Bildad the Shuhite replied:

2 "How long will you say such
things?
Your words are a blustering
wind.[m]
3 Does God pervert justice?[n]
Does the Almighty pervert what
is right?[o]
4 When your children sinned against
him,
he gave them over to the penalty
of their sin.[p]
5 But if you will look to God
and plead[q] with the Almighty,
6 if you are pure and upright,
even now he will rouse himself
on your behalf[r]
and restore you to your rightful
place.[s]
7 Your beginnings will seem humble,
so prosperous[t] will your future
be.

8 "Ask the former generations[u]
and find out what their fathers
learned,
9 for we were born only yesterday
and know nothing,[v]
and our days on earth are but a
shadow.[w]
10 Will they not instruct you and tell
you?
Will they not bring forth words
from their understanding?
11 Can papyrus grow tall where there
is no marsh?
Can reeds thrive without water?
12 While still growing and uncut,
they wither more quickly than
grass.[x]
13 Such is the destiny of all who
forget God;[y]
so perishes the hope of the
godless.[z]
14 What he trusts in is fragile[a];
what he relies on is a spider's
web.[a]
15 He leans on his web,[b] but it gives
way;
he clings to it, but it does not
hold.[c]
16 He is like a well-watered plant in
the sunshine,
spreading its shoots[d] over the
garden;[e]
17 it entwines its roots around a pile
of rocks
and looks for a place among the
stones.
18 But when it is torn from its spot,
that place disowns it and says, 'I
never saw you.'[f]
19 Surely its life withers[g] away,
and[b] from the soil other plants
grow.[h]

20 "Surely God does not reject a
blameless[i] man
or strengthen the hands of
evildoers.[j]
21 He will yet fill your mouth with
laughter[k]
and your lips with shouts of
joy.[l]
22 Your enemies will be clothed in
shame,[m]
and the tents of the wicked will
be no more."[n]

Job

9 Then Job replied:

2 "Indeed, I know that this is true.
But how can a mortal be
righteous before God?[o]
3 Though one wished to dispute with
him,
he could not answer him one
time out of a thousand.[p]
4 His wisdom[q] is profound, his
power is vast.[r]
Who has resisted him and come
out unscathed?[s]
5 He moves mountains without their
knowing it
and overturns them in his
anger.[t]
6 He shakes the earth[u] from its
place
and makes its pillars tremble.[v]
7 He speaks to the sun and it does
not shine;
he seals off the light of the
stars.[w]
8 He alone stretches out the
heavens[x]
and treads on the waves of the
sea.[y]
9 He is the Maker of the Bear and
Orion,
the Pleiades and the
constellations of the
south.[z]
10 He performs wonders[a] that cannot
be fathomed,
miracles that cannot be
counted.[b]

7:21 [k]Job 10:14 [l]Job 10:9; Ps 104:29
8:2 [m]Job 6:26
8:3 [n]Dt 32:4; 2Ch 19:7; Ro 3:5 [o]Ge 18:25
8:4 [p]Job 1:19
8:5 [q]Job 11:13
8:6 [r]Ps 7:6 [s]Job 5:24
8:7 [t]Job 42:12
8:8 [u]Dt 4:32; 32:7; Job 15:18
8:9 [v]Ge 47:9 [w]1Ch 29:15; Job 7:6
8:12 [x]Ps 129:6; Jer 17:6
8:13 [y]Ps 9:17 [z]Job 11:20; 13:16; 15:34; Pr 10:28
8:14 [a]Isa 59:5
8:15 [b]Job 27:18 [c]Ps 49:11
8:16 [d]Ps 80:11 [e]Ps 37:35; Jer 11:16
8:18 [f]Job 7:8; Ps 37:36
8:19 [g]Job 20:5 [h]Ecc 1:4
8:20 [i]Job 1:1 [j]Job 21:30
8:21 [k]Job 5:22 [l]Ps 126:2; 132:16
8:22 [m]Ps 35:26; 109:29; 132:18 [n]Job 18:6,14, 21
9:2 [o]Job 4:17; Ps 143:2; Ro 3:20
9:3 [p]Job 10:2; 40:2
9:4 [q]Job 11:6 [r]Job 36:5 [s]2Ch 13:12
9:5 [t]Mic 1:4
9:6 [u]Isa 2:21; Hag 2:6; Heb 12:26 [v]Job 26:11
9:7 [w]Isa 13:10; Eze 32:8
9:8 [x]Ge 1:6; Ps 104:2-3 [y]Job 38:16; Ps 77:19
9:9 [z]Ge 1:16; Job 38:31; Am 5:8
9:10 [a]Ps 71:15 [b]Job 5:9

[a] *14* The meaning of the Hebrew for this word is uncertain. [b] *19* Or *Surely all the joy it has / is that*

11When he passes me, I cannot see him;
when he goes by, I cannot perceive him.[c]
12If he snatches away, who can stop him?[d]
Who can say to him, 'What are you doing?'[e]
13God does not restrain his anger;
even the cohorts of Rahab[f] cowered at his feet.

14"How then can I dispute with him?
How can I find words to argue with him?
15Though I were innocent, I could not answer him;[g]
I could only plead[h] with my Judge for mercy.
16Even if I summoned him and he responded,
I do not believe he would give me a hearing.
17He would crush me[i] with a storm[j]
and multiply[k] my wounds for no reason.[l]
18He would not let me regain my breath
but would overwhelm me with misery.[m]
19If it is a matter of strength, he is mighty!
And if it is a matter of justice, who will summon him[a]?
20Even if I were innocent, my mouth would condemn me;
if I were blameless, it would pronounce me guilty.

21"Although I am blameless,[n]
I have no concern for myself;
I despise my own life.[o]
22It is all the same; that is why I say,
'He destroys both the blameless and the wicked.'[p]
23When a scourge[q] brings sudden death,
he mocks the despair of the innocent.[r]
24When a land falls into the hands of the wicked,[s]
he blindfolds its judges.[t]
If it is not he, then who is it?

25"My days are swifter than a runner;[u]
they fly away without a glimpse of joy.
26They skim past like boats of papyrus,[v]
like eagles swooping down on their prey.[w]
27If I say, 'I will forget my complaint,[x]
I will change my expression, and smile,'
28I still dread[y] all my sufferings,
for I know you will not hold me innocent.[z]
29Since I am already found guilty,
why should I struggle in vain?[a]
30Even if I washed myself with soap[b]
and my hands[b] with washing soda,[c]
31you would plunge me into a slime pit
so that even my clothes would detest me.

32"He is not a man like me that I might answer him,[d]
that we might confront each other in court.[e]
33If only there were someone to arbitrate between us,[f]
to lay his hand upon us both,
34someone to remove God's rod from me,[g]
so that his terror would frighten me no more.
35Then I would speak up without fear of him,
but as it now stands with me, I cannot.[h]

10

"I loathe my very life;[i]
therefore I will give free rein to my complaint
and speak out in the bitterness of my soul.[j]
2I will say to God: Do not condemn me,
but tell me what charges[k] you have against me.
3Does it please you to oppress me,[l]
to spurn the work of your hands,[m]
while you smile on the schemes of the wicked?[n]
4Do you have eyes of flesh?
Do you see as a mortal sees?[o]
5Are your days like those of a mortal
or your years like those of a man,[p]
6that you must search out my faults
and probe after my sin[q]—
7though you know that I am not guilty
and that no one can rescue me from your hand?

8"Your hands shaped[r] me and made me.
Will you now turn and destroy me?
9Remember that you molded me like clay.[s]
Will you now turn me to dust again?[t]

9:11 [c]Job 23:8-9; 35:14
9:12 [d]Job 11:10 [e]Isa 45:9; Ro 9:20
9:13 [f]Job 26:12; Ps 89:10; Isa 30:7; 51:9
9:15 [g]Job 10:15 [h]Job 8:5
9:17 [i]Job 16:12 [j]Job 30:22 [k]Job 16:14 [l]Job 2:3
9:18 [m]Job 7:19; 27:2
9:21 [n]Job 1:1 [o]Job 7:16
9:22 [p]Job 10:8; Ecc 9:2,3; Eze 21:3
9:23 [q]Heb 11:36 [r]Job 24:1,12
9:24 [s]Job 10:3; 16:11 [t]Job 12:6
9:25 [u]Job 7:6
9:26 [v]Isa 18:2 [w]Hab 1:8
9:27 [x]Job 7:11
9:28 [y]Job 3:25; Ps 119:120 [z]Job 7:21
9:29 [a]Ps 37:33
9:30 [b]Job 31:7 [c]Jer 2:22
9:32 [d]Ro 9:20 [e]Ps 143:2; Ecc 6:10
9:33 [f]1Sa 2:25
9:34 [g]Job 13:21; Ps 39:10
9:35 [h]Job 13:21
10:1 [i]1Ki 19:4 [j]Job 7:11
10:2 [k]Job 9:29
10:3 [l]Job 9:22 [m]Job 14:15; Ps 138:8; Isa 64:8 [n]Job 21:16; 22:18
10:4 [o]1Sa 16:7
10:5 [p]Ps 90:2,4; 2Pe 3:8
10:6 [q]Job 14:16
10:8 [r]Ps 119:73
10:9 [s]Isa 64:8 [t]Ge 2:7

a *19* See Septuagint; Hebrew *me.* **b** *30* Or *snow*

10Did you not pour me out like milk
and curdle me like cheese,
11clothe me with skin and flesh
and knit me together[u] with
bones and sinews?
12You gave me life[v] and showed me
kindness,
and in your providence watched
over my spirit.

13"But this is what you concealed in
your heart,
and I know that this was in your
mind:[w]
14If I sinned, you would be watching
me
and would not let my offense go
unpunished.[x]
15If I am guilty—woe to me![y]
Even if I am innocent, I cannot
lift my head,[z]
for I am full of shame
and drowned in[a] my affliction.
16If I hold my head high, you stalk
me like a lion[a]
and again display your awesome
power against me.[b]
17You bring new witnesses against
me[c]
and increase your anger toward
me;[d]
your forces come against me
wave upon wave.

18"Why then did you bring me out of
the womb?[e]
I wish I had died before any eye
saw me.
19If only I had never come into
being,
or had been carried straight from
the womb to the grave!
20Are not my few days[f] almost
over?[g]
Turn away from me[h] so I can
have a moment's joy
21before I go to the place of no
return,[i]
to the land of gloom and deep
shadow,[b][j]
22to the land of deepest night,
of deep shadow and disorder,
where even the light is like
darkness."

Zophar

11 Then Zophar the Naamathite replied:

2"Are all these words to go
unanswered?[k]
Is this talker to be vindicated?
3Will your idle talk reduce men to
silence?
Will no one rebuke you when
you mock?[l]

10:11 [u]Ps 139:13,15
10:12 [v]Job 33:4
10:13 [w]Job 23:13
10:14 [x]Job 7:21
10:15 [y]Job 9:13; Isa 3:11 [z]Job 9:15
10:16 [a]Isa 38:13; La 3:10 [b]Job 5:9
10:17 [c]Job 16:8 [d]Ru 1:21
10:18 [e]Job 3:11
10:20 [f]Job 14:1 [g]Job 7:19 [h]Job 7:16
10:21 [i]2Sa 12:23; Job 3:13; 16:22 [j]Ps 23:4; 88:12
11:2 [k]Job 8:2
11:3 [l]Job 17:2; 21:3
11:4 [m]Job 6:10 [n]Job 10:7
11:6 [o]Job 9:4 [p]Ezr 9:13; Job 15:5
11:7 [q]Ecc 3:11; Ro 11:33
11:8 [r]Job 22:12
11:10 [s]Job 9:12; Rev 3:7
11:11 [t]Job 34:21-25; Ps 10:14
11:13 [u]1Sa 7:3; Ps 78:8 [v]Ps 88:9
11:14 [w]Ps 101:4 [x]Job 22:23
11:15 [y]Job 22:26; 1Jn 3:21
11:16 [z]Isa 65:16 [a]Job 22:11
11:17 [b]Job 22:28; Ps 37:6; Isa 58:8,10
11:18 [c]Ps 3:5 [d]Lev 26:6; Pr 3:24

4You say to God, 'My beliefs are
flawless[m]
and I am pure[n] in your sight.'
5Oh, how I wish that God would
speak,
that he would open his lips
against you
6and disclose to you the secrets of
wisdom,[o]
for true wisdom has two sides.
Know this: God has even
forgotten some of your
sin.[p]

7"Can you fathom[q] the mysteries of
God?
Can you probe the limits of the
Almighty?
8They are higher than the
heavens[r]—what can you
do?
They are deeper than the depths
of the grave[c]—what can
you know?
9Their measure is longer than the
earth
and wider than the sea.

10"If he comes along and confines
you in prison
and convenes a court, who can
oppose him?[s]
11Surely he recognizes deceitful men;
and when he sees evil, does he
not take note?[t]
12But a witless man can no more
become wise
than a wild donkey's colt can be
born a man.[d]

13"Yet if you devote your heart[u] to
him
and stretch out your hands to
him,[v]
14if you put away the sin that is in
your hand
and allow no evil[w] to dwell in
your tent,[x]
15then you will lift up your face[y]
without shame;
you will stand firm and without
fear.
16You will surely forget your
trouble,[z]
recalling it only as waters gone
by.[a]
17Life will be brighter than
noonday,[b]
and darkness will become like
morning.
18You will be secure, because there is
hope;
you will look about you and take
your rest[c] in safety.[d]

[a]*15* Or *and aware of* [b]*21* Or *and the shadow of death*; also in verse 22 [c]*8* Hebrew *than Sheol* [d]*12* Or *wild donkey can be born tame*

19You will lie down, with no one to
make you afraid,[e]
and many will court your
favor.[f]
20But the eyes of the wicked will
fail,[g]
and escape will elude them;[h]
their hope will become a dying
gasp."[i]

Job

12 Then Job replied:

2"Doubtless you are the people,
and wisdom will die with you![j]
3But I have a mind as well as you;
I am not inferior to you.
Who does not know all these
things?[k]

4"I have become a laughingstock[l]
to my friends,
though I called upon God and he
answered[m]—
a mere laughingstock, though
righteous and blameless![n]
5Men at ease have contempt for
misfortune
as the fate of those whose feet
are slipping.
6The tents of marauders are
undisturbed,[o]
and those who provoke God are
secure[p]—
those who carry their god in
their hands.[a]

7"But ask the animals, and they will
teach you,
or the birds of the air, and they
will tell you;
8or speak to the earth, and it will
teach you,
or let the fish of the sea inform
you.
9Which of all these does not know
that the hand of the LORD has
done this?[q]
10In his hand is the life of every
creature
and the breath of all mankind.[r]
11Does not the ear test words
as the tongue tastes food?[s]
12Is not wisdom found among the
aged?[t]
Does not long life bring
understanding?[u]

13"To God belong wisdom[v] and
power;[w]
counsel and understanding are
his.[x]
14What he tears down[y] cannot be
rebuilt;[z]
the man he imprisons cannot be
released.
15If he holds back the waters,[a] there
is drought;[b]
if he lets them loose, they
devastate the land.[c]
16To him belong strength and
victory;
both deceived and deceiver are
his.[d]
17He leads counselors away
stripped[e]
and makes fools of judges.[f]
18He takes off the shackles[g] put on
by kings
and ties a loincloth[b] around
their waist.
19He leads priests away stripped
and overthrows men long
established.[h]
20He silences the lips of trusted
advisers
and takes away the discernment
of elders.[i]
21He pours contempt on nobles
and disarms the mighty.
22He reveals the deep things of
darkness[j]
and brings deep shadows[k] into
the light.[l]
23He makes nations great, and
destroys them;[m]
he enlarges nations,[n] and
disperses them.
24He deprives the leaders of the earth
of their reason;
he sends them wandering
through a trackless waste.[o]
25They grope in darkness with no
light;[p]
he makes them stagger like
drunkards.[q]

13 "My eyes have seen all this,
my ears have heard and
understood it.
2What you know, I also know;
I am not inferior to you.[r]
3But I desire to speak to the
Almighty
and to argue my case with
God.[s]
4You, however, smear me with
lies;[t]
you are worthless physicians, all
of you!
5If only you would be altogether
silent!
For you, that would be
wisdom.[u]
6Hear now my argument;
listen to the plea of my lips.
7Will you speak wickedly on God's
behalf?

11:19 [e]Lev 26:6 [f]Isa 45:14
11:20 [g]Dt 28:65; Job 17:5 [h]Job 27:22; 34:22 [i]Job 8:13
12:2 [j]Job 17:10
12:3 [k]Job 13:2
12:4 [l]Job 21:3 [m]Ps 91:15 [n]Job 6:29
12:6 [o]Job 22:18 [p]Job 9:24; 21:9
12:9 [q]Isa 41:20
12:10 [r]Job 27:3; 33:4; Ac 17:28
12:11 [s]Job 34:3
12:12 [t]Job 15:10 [u]Job 32:7,9
12:13 [v]Job 11:6 [w]Job 9:4 [x]Job 32:8; 38:36
12:14 [y]Job 19:10 [z]Job 37:7; Isa 25:2
12:15 [a]1Ki 8:35 [b]1Ki 17:1 [c]Ge 7:11
12:16 [d]Job 13:7,9
12:17 [e]Job 19:9 [f]Job 3:14
12:18 [g]Ps 116:16
12:19 [h]Job 24:12,22; 34:20,28; 35:9
12:20 [i]Job 32:9
12:22 [j]1Co 4:5 [k]Job 3:5 [l]Da 2:22
12:23 [m]Jer 25:9 [n]Ps 107:38; Isa 9:3; 26:15
12:24 [o]Ps 107:40
12:25 [p]Job 5:14 [q]Ps 107:27; Isa 24:20
13:2 [r]Job 12:3
13:3 [s]Job 23:3-4
13:4 [t]Ps 119:69; Jer 23:32
13:5 [u]Pr 17:28

a6 Or *secure / in what God's hand brings them*
b18 Or *shackles of kings / and ties a belt*

Will you speak deceitfully for
him?[v]
8Will you show him partiality?[w]
Will you argue the case for God?
9Would it turn out well if he
examined you?
Could you deceive him as you
might deceive men?[x]
10He would surely rebuke you
if you secretly showed partiality.
11Would not his splendor[y] terrify
you?
Would not the dread of him fall
on you?
12Your maxims are proverbs of ashes;
your defenses are defenses of
clay.

13"Keep silent and let me speak;
then let come to me what may.
14Why do I put myself in jeopardy
and take my life in my hands?
15Though he slay me, yet will I
hope[z] in him;[a]
I will surely[a] defend my ways to
his face.[b]
16Indeed, this will turn out for my
deliverance,[c]
for no godless man would dare
come before him!
17Listen carefully to my words;[d]
let your ears take in what I say.
18Now that I have prepared my
case,[e]
I know I will be vindicated.
19Can anyone bring charges against
me?[f]
If so, I will be silent and die.[g]

20"Only grant me these two things,
O God,
and then I will not hide from
you:
21Withdraw your hand[h] far from me,
and stop frightening me with
your terrors.
22Then summon me and I will
answer,[i]
or let me speak, and you reply.[j]
23How many wrongs and sins have I
committed?[k]
Show me my offense and my sin.
24Why do you hide your face[l]
and consider me your enemy?[m]
25Will you torment a windblown
leaf?[n]
Will you chase after dry chaff?[o]
26For you write down bitter things
against me
and make me inherit the sins of
my youth.[p]
27You fasten my feet in shackles;[q]
you keep close watch on all my
paths
by putting marks on the soles of
my feet.

13:7 [v]Job 36:4
13:8 [w]Lev 19:15
13:9 [x]Job 12:16; Gal 6:7
13:11 [y]Job 31:23
13:15 [z]Job 7:6 [a]Ps 23:4; Pr 14:32 [b]Job 27:5
13:16 [c]Isa 12:1
13:17 [d]Job 21:2
13:18 [e]Job 23:4
13:19 [f]Job 40:4; Isa 50:8 [g]Job 10:8
13:21 [h]Ps 39:10
13:22 [i]Job 14:15 [j]Job 9:16
13:23 [k]1Sa 26:18
13:24 [l]Dt 32:20; Ps 13:1; Isa 8:17 [m]Job 19:11; La 2:5
13:25 [n]Lev 26:36 [o]Job 21:18; Isa 42:3
13:26 [p]Ps 25:7
13:27 [q]Job 33:11
13:28 [r]Isa 50:9; Jas 5:2
14:1 [s]Job 5:7; Ecc 2:23
14:2 [t]Jas 1:10 [u]Ps 90:5-6 [v]Job 8:9
14:3 [w]Ps 8:4; 144:3 [x]Ps 143:2
14:4 [y]Ps 51:10 [z]Eph 2:1-3 [a]Jn 3:6; Ro 5:12
14:5 [b]Job 21:21
14:6 [c]Job 7:19 [d]Job 7:1,2; Ps 39:13
14:10 [e]Job 13:19
14:11 [f]Isa 19:5
14:12 [g]Rev 20:11; 21:1 [h]Ac 3:21
14:13 [i]Isa 26:20
14:15 [j]Job 13:22

28"So man wastes away like
something rotten,
like a garment eaten by moths.[r]

14

"Man born of woman
is of few days and full of
trouble.[s]
2He springs up like a flower[t] and
withers away;[u]
like a fleeting shadow,[v] he does
not endure.
3Do you fix your eye on such a
one?[w]
Will you bring him[b] before you
for judgment?[x]
4Who can bring what is pure[y] from
the impure?[z]
No one![a]
5Man's days are determined;
you have decreed the number of
his months[b]
and have set limits he cannot
exceed.
6So look away from him and let him
alone,[c]
till he has put in his time like a
hired man.[d]

7"At least there is hope for a tree:
If it is cut down, it will sprout
again,
and its new shoots will not fail.
8Its roots may grow old in the
ground
and its stump die in the soil,
9yet at the scent of water it will bud
and put forth shoots like a plant.
10But man dies and is laid low;
he breathes his last and is no
more.[e]
11As water disappears from the sea
or a riverbed becomes parched
and dry,[f]
12so man lies down and does not
rise;
till the heavens are no more,[g]
men will not awake
or be roused from their sleep.[h]

13"If only you would hide me in the
grave[c]
and conceal me till your anger
has passed![i]
If only you would set me a time
and then remember me!
14If a man dies, will he live again?
All the days of my hard service
I will wait for my renewal[d] to
come.
15You will call and I will answer
you;[j]
you will long for the creature
your hands have made.

[a]*15* Or *He will surely slay me; I have no hope — / yet I will* [b]*3* Septuagint, Vulgate and Syriac; Hebrew *me* [c]*13* Hebrew *Sheol* [d]*14* Or *release*

16 Surely then you will count my steps[k]
but not keep track of my sin.[l]
17 My offenses will be sealed up in a bag;[m]
you will cover over my sin.[n]

18 "But as a mountain erodes and crumbles
and as a rock is moved from its place,
19 as water wears away stones
and torrents wash away the soil,
so you destroy man's hope.[o]
20 You overpower him once for all,
and he is gone;
you change his countenance and send him away.
21 If his sons are honored, he does not know it;
if they are brought low, he does not see it.[p]
22 He feels but the pain of his own body
and mourns only for himself."

Eliphaz

15 Then Eliphaz the Temanite replied:

2 "Would a wise man answer with empty notions
or fill his belly with the hot east wind?[q]
3 Would he argue with useless words,
with speeches that have no value?
4 But you even undermine piety
and hinder devotion to God.
5 Your sin prompts your mouth;
you adopt the tongue of the crafty.[r]
6 Your own mouth condemns you, not mine;
your own lips testify against you.[s]

7 "Are you the first man ever born?[t]
Were you brought forth before the hills?[u]
8 Do you listen in on God's council?[v]
Do you limit wisdom to yourself?
9 What do you know that we do not know?
What insights do you have that we do not have?[w]
10 The gray-haired and the aged[x] are on our side,
men even older than your father.
11 Are God's consolations[y] not enough for you,
words[z] spoken gently to you?[a]
12 Why has your heart[b] carried you away,
and why do your eyes flash,

14:16 [k]Ps 139:1-3; Pr 5:21; Jer 32:19 [l]Job 10:6
14:17 [m]Dt 32:34 [n]Hos 13:12
14:19 [o]Job 7:6
14:21 [p]Ecc 9:5; Isa 63:16
15:2 [q]Job 6:26
15:5 [r]Job 5:13
15:6 [s]Lk 19:22
15:7 [t]Job 38:21 [u]Ps 90:2; Pr 8:25
15:8 [v]Ro 11:34; 1Co 2:11
15:9 [w]Job 13:2
15:10 [x]Job 32:6-7
15:11 [y]2Co 1:3-4 [z]Zec 1:13 [a]Job 36:16
15:12 [b]Job 11:13
15:14 [c]Job 14:4; 25:4 [d]Pr 20:9; Ecc 7:20
15:15 [e]Job 4:18; 25:5
15:16 [f]Ps 14:1 [g]Job 34:7; Pr 19:28
15:18 [h]Job 8:8
15:20 [i]Job 24:1; 27:13-23
15:21 [j]Job 18:11; 20:25 [k]Job 27:20; 1Th 5:3
15:22 [l]Job 19:29; 27:14
15:23 [m]Ps 59:15; 109:10 [n]Job 18:12
15:25 [o]Job 36:9
15:27 [p]Ps 17:10
15:28 [q]Isa 5:9 [r]Job 3:14
15:29 [s]Job 27:16-17
15:30 [t]Job 5:14 [u]Job 22:20 [v]Job 4:9

13 so that you vent your rage against God
and pour out such words from your mouth?

14 "What is man, that he could be pure,
or one born of woman,[c] that he could be righteous?[d]
15 If God places no trust in his holy ones,
if even the heavens are not pure in his eyes,[e]
16 how much less man, who is vile and corrupt,[f]
who drinks up evil like water![g]

17 "Listen to me and I will explain to you;
let me tell you what I have seen,
18 what wise men have declared,
hiding nothing received from their fathers[h]
19 (to whom alone the land was given
when no alien passed among them):
20 All his days the wicked man suffers torment,
the ruthless through all the years stored up for him.[i]
21 Terrifying sounds fill his ears;[j]
when all seems well, marauders attack him.[k]
22 He despairs of escaping the darkness;
he is marked for the sword.[l]
23 He wanders about[m]—food for vultures[a];
he knows the day of darkness is at hand.[n]
24 Distress and anguish fill him with terror;
they overwhelm him, like a king poised to attack,
25 because he shakes his fist at God
and vaunts himself against the Almighty,[o]
26 defiantly charging against him
with a thick, strong shield.

27 "Though his face is covered with fat
and his waist bulges with flesh,[p]
28 he will inhabit ruined towns
and houses where no one lives,[q]
houses crumbling to rubble.[r]
29 He will no longer be rich and his wealth will not endure,[s]
nor will his possessions spread over the land.
30 He will not escape the darkness;[t]
a flame[u] will wither his shoots,
and the breath of God's mouth[v] will carry him away.

[a] *23* Or *about, looking for food*

31Let him not deceive himself by
trusting what is worthless,[w]
for he will get nothing in return.
32Before his time[x] he will be paid in
full,[y]
and his branches will not
flourish.[z]
33He will be like a vine stripped of its
unripe grapes,[a]
like an olive tree shedding its
blossoms.
34For the company of the godless will
be barren,
and fire will consume the tents
of those who love bribes.[b]
35They conceive trouble and give
birth to evil;[c]
their womb fashions deceit."

Job

16 Then Job replied:

2"I have heard many things like
these;
miserable comforters are you
all![d]
3Will your long-winded speeches
never end?
What ails you that you keep on
arguing?[e]
4I also could speak like you,
if you were in my place;
I could make fine speeches against
you
and shake my head[f] at you.
5But my mouth would encourage
you;
comfort from my lips would
bring you relief.

6"Yet if I speak, my pain is not
relieved;
and if I refrain, it does not go
away.
7Surely, O God, you have worn me
out;[g]
you have devastated my entire
household.

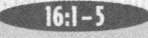

16:1–5

PROMISE 2

MISERABLE COMFORTERS

Even the strongest of friendships can be strained when people try to explain God's great mysteries. What started with seven days of quietly being there (2:11–13) broke down when Job's friends tried to encourage him and fix him with explanations and advice. This passage, and Job's reaction to his friends in it, is proof that we sometimes show the greatest command of language by not using it.

For the next Promise 2 reading go to page 569.

15:31 [w]Isa 59:4
15:32 [x]Ecc 7:17 [y]Job 22:16; Ps 55:23 [z]Job 18:16
15:33 [a]Hab 3:17
15:34 [b]Job 8:22
15:35 [c]Ps 7:14; Isa 59:4; Hos 10:13
16:2 [d]Job 13:4
16:3 [e]Job 6:26
16:4 [f]Ps 22:7; 109:25; La 2:15; Zep 2:15; Mt 27:39
16:7 [g]Job 7:3
16:8 [h]Job 19:20 [i]Job 10:17
16:9 [j]Hos 6:1 [k]Ps 35:16; La 2:16; Ac 7:54 [l]Job 13:24
16:10 [m]Ps 22:13 [n]Isa 50:6; La 3:30; Mic 5:1; Ac 23:2 [o]Ps 35:15
16:11 [p]Job 1:15,17
16:12 [q]Job 9:17 [r]La 3:12
16:13 [s]Job 20:24
16:14 [t]Job 9:17 [u]Joel 2:7
16:15 [v]Ge 37:34
16:17 [w]Isa 59:6; Jnh 3:8
16:18 [x]Isa 26:21 [y]Ps 66:18-19
16:19 [z]Ge 31:50; Ro 1:9; 1Th 2:5
16:20 [a]La 2:19
16:21 [b]Ps 9:4
16:22 [c]Ecc 12:5
17:1 [d]Ps 88:3-4
17:2 [e]1Sa 1:6-7
17:3 [f]Ps 119:122 [g]Pr 6:1 [h]Isa 38:14

8You have bound me—and it has
become a witness;
my gauntness[h] rises up and
testifies against me.[i]
9God assails me and tears[j] me in
his anger
and gnashes his teeth at me;[k]
my opponent fastens on me his
piercing eyes.[l]
10Men open their mouths[m] to jeer at
me;
they strike my cheek[n] in scorn
and unite together against me.[o]
11God has turned me over to evil
men
and thrown me into the clutches
of the wicked.[p]
12All was well with me, but he
shattered me;
he seized me by the neck and
crushed me.[q]
He has made me his target;[r]
13 his archers surround me.
Without pity, he pierces[s] my
kidneys
and spills my gall on the ground.
14Again and again[t] he bursts upon
me;
he rushes at me like a warrior.[u]

15"I have sewed sackcloth[v] over my
skin
and buried my brow in the dust.
16My face is red with weeping,
deep shadows ring my eyes;
17yet my hands have been free of
violence[w]
and my prayer is pure.

18"O earth, do not cover my blood;[x]
may my cry never be laid to
rest![y]
19Even now my witness[z] is in
heaven;
my advocate is on high.
20My intercessor is my friend[a]
as my eyes pour out[a] tears to
God;
21on behalf of a man he pleads[b]
with God
as a man pleads for his friend.

22"Only a few years will pass
before I go on the journey of no
return.[c]

17 1My spirit is broken,
my days are cut short,
the grave awaits me.[d]
2Surely mockers[e] surround me;
my eyes must dwell on their
hostility.

3"Give me, O God, the pledge you
demand.[f]
Who else will put up security[g]
for me?[h]

[a]20 Or *My friends treat me with scorn*

4You have closed their minds to
understanding;
therefore you will not let them
triumph.
5If a man denounces his friends for
reward,
the eyes of his children will
fail.[i]
6"God has made me a byword[j] to
everyone,
a man in whose face people spit.
7My eyes have grown dim with
grief;[k]
my whole frame is but a shadow.
8Upright men are appalled at this;
the innocent are aroused[l]
against the ungodly.
9Nevertheless, the righteous[m] will
hold to their ways,
and those with clean hands[n]
will grow stronger.
10"But come on, all of you, try again!
I will not find a wise man among
you.[o]
11My days have passed, my plans are
shattered,
and so are the desires of my
heart.[p]
12These men turn night into day;
in the face of darkness they say,
'Light is near.'
13If the only home I hope for is the
grave,**a**[q]
if I spread out my bed in
darkness,
14if I say to corruption,[r] 'You are
my father,'
and to the worm,[s] 'My mother'
or 'My sister,'
15where then is my hope?[t]
Who can see any hope for me?
16Will it go down to the gates of
death**a**?[u]
Will we descend together into
the dust?"

Bildad

18 Then Bildad the Shuhite replied:

2"When will you end these
speeches?
Be sensible, and then we can
talk.
3Why are we regarded as cattle
and considered stupid in your
sight?[v]
4You who tear yourself[w] to pieces
in your anger,
is the earth to be abandoned for
your sake?
Or must the rocks be moved
from their place?
5"The lamp of the wicked is snuffed
out;[x]
the flame of his fire stops
burning.
6The light in his tent becomes dark;
the lamp beside him goes out.
7The vigor of his step is
weakened;[y]
his own schemes[z] throw him
down.[a]
8His feet thrust him into a net[b]
and he wanders into its mesh.
9A trap seizes him by the heel;
a snare holds him fast.
10A noose is hidden for him on the
ground;
a trap lies in his path.
11Terrors startle him on every side[c]
and dog[d] his every step.
12Calamity is hungry[e] for him;
disaster is ready for him when
he falls.
13It eats away parts of his skin;
death's firstborn devours his
limbs.[f]
14He is torn from the security of his
tent[g]
and marched off to the king of
terrors.
15Fire resides**b** in his tent;
burning sulfur[h] is scattered over
his dwelling.
16His roots dry up below[i]
and his branches wither above.[j]
17The memory of him perishes from
the earth;
he has no name in the land.[k]
18He is driven from light into
darkness[l]
and is banished from the world.
19He has no offspring[m] or
descendants[n] among his
people,
no survivor where once he
lived.[o]
20Men of the west are appalled at his
fate;[p]
men of the east are seized with
horror.
21Surely such is the dwelling[q] of an
evil man;
such is the place of one who
knows not God."[r]

Job

19 Then Job replied:

2"How long will you torment me
and crush me with words?
3Ten times now you have
reproached me;
shamelessly you attack me.
4If it is true that I have gone astray,
my error[s] remains my concern
alone.

17:5 [i]Job 11:20
17:6 [j]Job 30:9
17:7 [k]Job 16:8
17:8 [l]Job 22:19
17:9 [m]Pr 4:18 [n]Job 22:30
17:10 [o]Job 12:2
17:11 [p]Job 7:6
17:13 [q]Job 3:13
17:14 [r]Job 13:28; 30:28,30; Ps 16:10 [s]Job 21:26
17:15 [t]Job 7:6
17:16 [u]Job 3:17-19; Jnh 2:6
18:3 [v]Ps 73:22
18:4 [w]Job 13:14
18:5 [x]Job 21:17; Pr 13:9; 20:20; 24:20
18:7 [y]Pr 4:12 [z]Job 5:13 [a]Job 15:6
18:8 [b]Job 22:10; Ps 9:15; 35:7
18:11 [c]Job 15:21; Jer 6:25; 20:3 [d]Job 20:8
18:12 [e]Isa 8:21
18:13 [f]Zec 14:12
18:14 [g]Job 8:22
18:15 [h]Ps 11:6
18:16 [i]Isa 5:24; Hos 9:1-16; Am 2:9 [j]Job 15:30; Mal 4:1
18:17 [k]Ps 34:16; Pr 2:22; 10:7
18:18 [l]Job 5:14
18:19 [m]Jer 22:30 [n]Isa 14:22 [o]Job 27:14-15
18:20 [p]Ps 37:13; Jer 50:27,31
18:21 [q]Job 21:28 [r]Jer 9:3; 1Th 4:5
19:4 [s]Job 6:24

a *13,16* Hebrew *Sheol* **b** *15* Or *Nothing he had remains*

5 If indeed you would exalt
yourselves above me[t]
and use my humiliation against
me,
6 then know that God has wronged
me[u]
and drawn his net[v] around me.

7 "Though I cry, 'I've been wronged!'
I get no response;[w]
though I call for help, there is no
justice.[x]
8 He has blocked my way so I cannot
pass;[y]
he has shrouded my paths in
darkness.[z]
9 He has stripped[a] me of my honor
and removed the crown from my
head.[b]
10 He tears me down[c] on every side
till I am gone;
he uproots my hope[d] like a
tree.[e]
11 His anger[f] burns against me;
he counts me among his
enemies.[g]
12 His troops advance in force;[h]
they build a siege ramp[i] against
me
and encamp around my tent.

13 "He has alienated my brothers[j]
from me;
my acquaintances are completely
estranged from me.[k]
14 My kinsmen have gone away;
my friends have forgotten me.
15 My guests and my maidservants
count me a stranger;
they look upon me as an alien.
16 I summon my servant, but he does
not answer,
though I beg him with my own
mouth.
17 My breath is offensive to my wife;
I am loathsome to my own
brothers.
18 Even the little boys[l] scorn me;
when I appear, they ridicule me.
19 All my intimate friends[m] detest
me;[n]
those I love have turned against
me.
20 I am nothing but skin and bones;[o]
I have escaped with only the skin
of my teeth.**[a]**

21 "Have pity on me, my friends, have
pity,
for the hand of God has struck
me.
22 Why do you pursue[p] me as God
does?
Will you never get enough of my
flesh?[q]

23 "Oh, that my words were recorded,
that they were written on a
scroll,[r]
24 that they were inscribed with an
iron tool on**[b]** lead,
or engraved in rock forever!
25 I know that my Redeemer**[c]**[s]
lives,[t]
and that in the end he will stand
upon the earth.**[d]**
26 And after my skin has been
destroyed,
yet**[e]** in**[f]** my flesh I will see
God;[u]
27 I myself will see him
with my own eyes—I, and not
another.
How my heart yearns[v] within
me!

28 "If you say, 'How we will hound
him,
since the root of the trouble lies
in him,**[g]**'
29 you should fear the sword
yourselves;
for wrath will bring punishment
by the sword,[w]
and then you will know that
there is judgment.**[h]**"[x]

19:5 [t]Ps 35:26; 38:16; 55:12 **19:6** [u]Job 27:2 [v]Job 18:8 **19:7** [w]Job 30:20 [x]Job 9:24; Hab 1:2-4 **19:8** [y]Job 3:23; La 3:7 [z]Job 30:26 **19:9** [a]Job 12:17 [b]Ps 89:39,44; La 5:16 **19:10** [c]Job 12:14 [d]Job 7:6 [e]Job 24:20 **19:11** [f]Job 16:9 [g]Job 13:24 **19:12** [h]Job 16:13 [i]Job 30:12 **19:13** [j]Ps 69:8 [k]Job 16:7; Ps 88:8 **19:18** [l]2Ki 2:23 **19:19** [m]Ps 55:12-13 [n]Ps 38:11 **19:20** [o]Job 33:21; Ps 102:5 **19:22** [p]Job 13:25; 16:11 [q]Ps 69:26 **19:23** [r]Isa 30:8 **19:25** [s]Ps 78:35; Pr 23:11; Isa 43:14; Jer 50:34 [t]Job 16:19 **19:26** [u]Ps 17:15; Mt 5:8; 1Co 13:12; 1Jn 3:2 **19:27** [v]Ps 73:26 **19:29** [w]Job 15:22 [x]Job 22:4; Ps 1:5; 9:7

Zophar

20 Then Zophar the Naamathite replied:

a *20* Or *only my gums* **b** *24* Or *and* **c** *25* Or *defender* **d** *25* Or *upon my grave* **e** *26* Or *And after I awake, / though this ⌊body⌋ has been destroyed, / then* **f** *26* Or */ apart from* **g** *28* Many Hebrew manuscripts, Septuagint and Vulgate; most Hebrew manuscripts *me* **h** *29* Or / *that you may come to know the Almighty*

19:25–27

THE TEST FOR TOUGH TIMES

PROMISE 1

One test of a man's greatness is what he grabs for on his way down. Job clung to his belief in God's deliverance. Even in the deepest pit of despair Job knew his Redeemer was alive and would not abandon him. Job believed that even though his disease would probably bring about his death, he would see God with his own eyes after death. His heart yearned to do so.

Where is your center of gravity? What (or who) do you hold on to when you feel your stability slipping? To understand Job's response in this tough time, read the comment about Job in Job 1:1. What we do about God in the normal times determines what we do about the tough times.

For the next Promise 1 reading go to page 566.

2"My troubled thoughts prompt me
to answer
because I am greatly disturbed.
3I hear a rebuke[y] that dishonors
me,
and my understanding inspires
me to reply.

4"Surely you know how it has been
from of old,
ever since man**a** was placed on
the earth,
5that the mirth of the wicked is
brief,
the joy of the godless lasts but a
moment.[z]
6Though his pride reaches to the
heavens
and his head touches the
clouds,[a]
7he will perish forever,[b] like his
own dung;
those who have seen him will
say, 'Where is he?'[c]
8Like a dream[d] he flies away,[e] no
more to be found,
banished[f] like a vision of the
night.[g]
9The eye that saw him will not see
him again;
his place will look on him no
more.[h]
10His children[i] must make amends
to the poor;
his own hands must give back
his wealth.[j]
11The youthful vigor[k] that fills his
bones
will lie with him in the dust.[l]

12"Though evil is sweet in his mouth
and he hides it under his tongue,
13though he cannot bear to let it go
and keeps it in his mouth,[m]
14yet his food will turn sour in his
stomach;
it will become the venom of
serpents within him.
15He will spit out the riches he
swallowed;
God will make his stomach
vomit them up.
16He will suck the poison[n] of
serpents;
the fangs of an adder will kill
him.[o]
17He will not enjoy the streams,
the rivers flowing with honey[p]
and cream.[q]
18What he toiled for he must give
back uneaten;
he will not enjoy the profit from
his trading.
19For he has oppressed the poor and
left them destitute;[r]
he has seized houses he did not
build.

20:3 [y]Job 19:3 **20:5** [z]Job 8:12; Ps 37:35-36; 73:19 **20:6** [a]Isa 14:13-14; Ob 1:3-4 **20:7** [b]Job 4:20 [c]Job 7:10; 8:18 **20:8** [d]Ps 73:20 [e]Job 27:21-23 [f]Job 18:18 [g]Ps 90:5 **20:9** [h]Job 7:8 **20:10** [i]Job 5:4 [j]Job 27:16-17 **20:11** [k]Job 13:26 [l]Job 21:26 **20:13** [m]Nu 11:18-20 **20:16** [n]Dt 32:32 [o]Dt 32:24 **20:17** [p]Dt 32:13 [q]Job 29:6 **20:19** [r]Job 24:4,14; 35:9

20:20 [s]Ecc 5:12-14 **20:21** [t]Job 15:29 **20:23** [u]Ps 78:30-31 **20:24** [v]Isa 24:18; Am 5:19 **20:25** [w]Job 18:11 [x]Job 16:13 **20:26** [y]Job 18:18 [z]Ps 21:9 **20:27** [a]Dt 31:28 **20:28** [b]Dt 28:31 [c]Job 21:17,20, 30 **20:29** [d]Job 27:13 **21:3** [e]Job 16:10 **21:4** [f]Job 6:11 **21:5** [g]Jdg 18:19; Job 29:9; 40:4 **21:7** [h]Job 12:6; Ps 73:3; Jer 12:1; Hab 1:13

20"Surely he will have no respite
from his craving;[s]
he cannot save himself by his
treasure.
21Nothing is left for him to devour;
his prosperity will not endure.[t]
22In the midst of his plenty, distress
will overtake him;
the full force of misery will come
upon him.
23When he has filled his belly,
God will vent his burning anger
against him
and rain down his blows upon
him.[u]
24Though he flees[v] from an iron
weapon,
a bronze-tipped arrow pierces
him.
25He pulls it out of his back,
the gleaming point out of his
liver.
Terrors[w] will come over him;[x]
26 total darkness[y] lies in wait for
his treasures.
A fire unfanned will consume
him[z]
and devour what is left in his
tent.
27The heavens will expose his guilt;
the earth will rise up against
him.[a]
28A flood will carry off his house,[b]
rushing waters**b** on the day of
God's wrath.[c]
29Such is the fate God allots the
wicked,
the heritage appointed for them
by God."[d]

Job

21 Then Job replied:

2"Listen carefully to my words;
let this be the consolation you
give me.
3Bear with me while I speak,
and after I have spoken, mock
on.[e]

4"Is my complaint directed to man?
Why should I not be
impatient?[f]
5Look at me and be astonished;
clap your hand over your
mouth.[g]
6When I think about this, I am
terrified;
trembling seizes my body.
7Why do the wicked live on,
growing old and increasing in
power?[h]

a4 Or *Adam* **b**28 Or *The possessions in his house will be carried off, / washed away*

8They see their children established
around them,
their offspring before their
eyes.[i]
9Their homes are safe and free from
fear;[j]
the rod of God is not upon them.
10Their bulls never fail to breed;
their cows calve and do not
miscarry.[k]
11They send forth their children as a
flock;
their little ones dance about.
12They sing to the music of
tambourine and harp;
they make merry to the sound of
the flute.[l]
13They spend their years in
prosperity[m]
and go down to the grave[a] in
peace.[b]
14Yet they say to God, 'Leave us
alone![n]
We have no desire to know your
ways.[o]
15Who is the Almighty, that we
should serve him?
What would we gain by praying
to him?'[p]
16But their prosperity is not in their
own hands,
so I stand aloof from the counsel
of the wicked.

17"Yet how often is the lamp of the
wicked snuffed out?[q]
How often does calamity come
upon them,
the fate God allots in his anger?
18How often are they like straw
before the wind,
like chaff[r] swept away by a
gale?
19⌊It is said,⌋ 'God stores up a man's
punishment for his sons.'[s]
Let him repay the man himself,
so that he will know it!
20Let his own eyes see his
destruction;
let him drink[t] of the wrath of
the Almighty.[c][u]
21For what does he care about the
family he leaves behind
when his allotted months[v]
come to an end?

22"Can anyone teach knowledge to
God,[w]
since he judges even the
highest?[x]
23One man dies in full vigor,
completely secure and at ease,
24his body[d] well nourished,
his bones rich with marrow.[y]
25Another man dies in bitterness of
soul,
never having enjoyed anything
good.
26Side by side they lie in the dust,
and worms cover them both.[z]

27"I know full well what you are
thinking,
the schemes by which you would
wrong me.
28You say, 'Where now is the great
man's[a] house,
the tents where wicked men
lived?'[b]
29Have you never questioned those
who travel?
Have you paid no regard to their
accounts—
30that the evil man is spared from
the day of calamity,[c]
that he is delivered from[e] the
day of wrath?[d]
31Who denounces his conduct to his
face?
Who repays him for what he has
done?
32He is carried to the grave,
and watch is kept over his tomb.
33The soil in the valley is sweet to
him;[e]
all men follow after him,
and a countless throng goes[f]
before him.[f]

34"So how can you console me[g]
with your nonsense?
Nothing is left of your answers
but falsehood!"

Eliphaz

22 Then Eliphaz the Temanite replied:

2"Can a man be of benefit to God?[h]
Can even a wise man benefit
him?
3What pleasure would it give the
Almighty if you were
righteous?
What would he gain if your ways
were blameless?

4"Is it for your piety that he rebukes
you
and brings charges against
you?[i]
5Is not your wickedness great?
Are not your sins[j] endless?
6You demanded security[k] from
your brothers for no reason;

21:8 [i]Ps 17:14 **21:9** [j]Ps 73:5 **21:10** [k]Ex 23:26 **21:12** [l]Ps 81:2 **21:13** [m]Job 36:11 **21:14** [n]Job 22:17 [o]Pr 1:29 **21:15** [p]Ex 5:2; Job 34:9; Mal 3:14 **21:17** [q]Job 18:5 **21:18** [r]Job 13:25; Ps 1:4 **21:19** [s]Ex 20:5; Jer 31:29; Eze 18:2 **21:20** [t]Ps 75:8; Isa 51:17 [u]Jer 25:15; Rev 14:10 **21:21** [v]Job 14:5 **21:22** [w]Job 35:11; 36:22; Isa 40:13-14; Ro 11:34 [x]Ps 82:1 **21:24** [y]Pr 3:8 **21:26** [z]Job 24:20; Ecc 9:2-3; Isa 14:11 **21:28** [a]Job 1:3; 12:21; 31:37 [b]Job 8:22 **21:30** [c]Pr 16:4 [d]Job 20:22,28; 2Pe 2:9 **21:33** [e]Job 3:22; 17:16; 24:24 [f]Job 3:19 **21:34** [g]Job 16:2 **22:2** [h]Lk 17:10 **22:4** [i]Job 14:3; 19:29; Ps 143:2 **22:5** [j]Job 11:6; 15:5 **22:6** [k]Ex 22:26; Dt 24:6,17; Eze 18:12,16

[a]*13* Hebrew *Sheol* [b]*13* Or *in an instant* [c]*17-20* Verses 17 and 18 may be taken as exclamations and 19 and 20 as declarations. [d]*24* The meaning of the Hebrew for this word is uncertain. [e]*30* Or *man is reserved for the day of calamity, / that he is brought forth to* [f]*33* Or / *as a countless throng went*

you stripped men of their
clothing, leaving them
naked.
7You gave no water to the weary
and you withheld food from the
hungry,[l]
8though you were a powerful man,
owning land—
an honored man,[m] living on it.
9And you sent widows away
empty-handed[n]
and broke the strength of the
fatherless.
10That is why snares are all around
you,
why sudden peril terrifies you,
11why it is so dark[o] you cannot see,
and why a flood of water covers
you.[p]

12"Is not God in the heights of
heaven?[q]
And see how lofty are the highest
stars!
13Yet you say, 'What does God
know?[r]
Does he judge through such
darkness?[s]
14Thick clouds[t] veil him, so he does
not see us
as he goes about in the vaulted
heavens.'
15Will you keep to the old path
that evil men have trod?
16They were carried off before their
time,[u]
their foundations washed away
by a flood.[v]
17They said to God, 'Leave us alone!
What can the Almighty do to
us?'[w]
18Yet it was he who filled their
houses with good things,[x]
so I stand aloof from the counsel
of the wicked.[y]

19"The righteous see their ruin and
rejoice;[z]
the innocent mock[a] them,
saying,
20'Surely our foes are destroyed,
and fire[b] devours their wealth.'

21"Submit to God and be at peace
with him;
in this way prosperity will come
to you.[c]
22Accept instruction from his mouth
and lay up his words in your
heart.
23If you return[d] to the Almighty, you
will be restored:[e]
If you remove wickedness far
from your tent[f]
24and assign your nuggets to the
dust,
your gold of Ophir to the rocks
in the ravines,[g]
25then the Almighty will be your
gold,
the choicest silver for you.[h]
26Surely then you will find delight in
the Almighty[i]
and will lift up your face to God.
27You will pray to him,[j] and he will
hear you,
and you will fulfill your vows.
28What you decide on will be done,
and light will shine on your
ways.
29When men are brought low and
you say, 'Lift them up!'
then he will save the downcast.[k]
30He will deliver even one who is not
innocent,
who will be delivered through
the cleanness of your
hands."[l]

Job

23 Then Job replied:

2"Even today my complaint[m] is
bitter;[n]
his hand[a] is heavy in spite of[b]
my groaning.
3If only I knew where to find him;
if only I could go to his dwelling!
4I would state my case[o] before him
and fill my mouth with
arguments.
5I would find out what he would
answer me,
and consider what he would say.
6Would he oppose me with great
power?[p]
No, he would not press charges
against me.
7There an upright man could
present his case before
him,[q]
and I would be delivered forever
from my judge.

8"But if I go to the east, he is not
there;
if I go to the west, I do not find
him.
9When he is at work in the north, I
do not see him;
when he turns to the south, I
catch no glimpse of him.[r]
10But he knows the way that I take;
when he has tested me,[s] I will
come forth as gold.[t]
11My feet have closely followed his
steps;[u]
I have kept to his way without
turning aside.[v]

22:7 [l]Job 31:17,21,31
22:8 [m]Isa 3:3; 9:15
22:9 [n]Job 24:3,21
22:11 [o]Job 5:14 [p]Ps 69:1-2; 124:4-5; La 3:54
22:12 [q]Job 11:8
22:13 [r]Ps 10:11; Isa 29:15 [s]Eze 8:12
22:14 [t]Job 26:9
22:16 [u]Job 15:32 [v]Job 14:19; Mt 7:26-27
22:17 [w]Job 21:15
22:18 [x]Job 12:6 [y]Job 21:16
22:19 [z]Ps 58:10; 107:42 [a]Ps 52:6
22:20 [b]Job 15:30
22:21 [c]Ps 34:8-10
22:23 [d]Job 8:5; Isa 31:6; Zec 1:3 [e]Isa 19:22; Ac 20:32 [f]Job 11:14
22:24 [g]Job 31:25
22:25 [h]Isa 33:6
22:26 [i]Job 27:10; Isa 58:14
22:27 [j]Job 33:26; 34:28; Isa 58:9
22:29 [k]Mt 23:12; 1Pe 5:5
22:30 [l]Job 42:7-8
23:2 [m]Job 7:11 [n]Job 6:3
23:4 [o]Job 13:18
23:6 [p]Job 9:4
23:7 [q]Job 13:3
23:9 [r]Job 9:11
23:10 [s]Ps 66:10; 139:1-3 [t]1Pe 1:7
23:11 [u]Ps 17:5 [v]Ps 44:18

[a]2 Septuagint and Syriac; Hebrew / *the hand on me* [b]2 Or *heavy on me in*

12I have not departed from the
commands of his lips;[w]
I have treasured the words of his
mouth more than my daily
bread.[x]
13"But he stands alone, and who can
oppose him?
He does whatever he pleases.[y]
14He carries out his decree against
me,
and many such plans he still has
in store.[z]
15That is why I am terrified before
him;
when I think of all this, I fear him.
16God has made my heart faint;[a]
the Almighty[b] has terrified me.
17Yet I am not silenced by the
darkness,[c]
by the thick darkness that covers
my face.

24 "Why does the Almighty not set
times for judgment?[d]
Why must those who know him
look in vain for such days?[e]
2Men move boundary stones;[f]
they pasture flocks they have
stolen.
3They drive away the orphan's
donkey
and take the widow's ox in
pledge.[g]
4They thrust the needy from the
path
and force all the poor[h] of the
land into hiding.[i]
5Like wild donkeys in the desert,
the poor go about their labor[j]
of foraging food;
the wasteland provides food for
their children.
6They gather fodder in the fields
and glean in the vineyards of the
wicked.
7Lacking clothes, they spend the
night naked;
they have nothing to cover
themselves in the cold.[k]
8They are drenched by mountain
rains
and hug[l] the rocks for lack of
shelter.
9The fatherless[m] child is snatched
from the breast;
the infant of the poor is seized
for a debt.
10Lacking clothes, they go about
naked;
they carry the sheaves, but still
go hungry.
11They crush olives among the
terraces[a];
they tread the winepresses, yet
suffer thirst.
12The groans of the dying rise from
the city,
and the souls of the wounded
cry out for help.[n]
But God charges no one with
wrongdoing.[o]
13"There are those who rebel against
the light,[p]
who do not know its ways
or stay in its paths.[q]
14When daylight is gone, the
murderer rises up
and kills the poor and needy;
in the night he steals forth like a
thief.[r]
15The eye of the adulterer watches
for dusk;[s]
he thinks, 'No eye will see me,'[t]
and he keeps his face concealed.
16In the dark, men break into
houses,[u]
but by day they shut themselves
in;
they want nothing to do with the
light.[v]
17For all of them, deep darkness is
their morning[b];
they make friends with the
terrors of darkness.[c]
18"Yet they are foam[w] on the surface
of the water;[x]
their portion of the land is
cursed,
so that no one goes to the
vineyards.
19As heat and drought snatch away
the melted snow,[y]

23:12 [w]Job 6:10 [x]Jn 4:32,34 **23:13** [y]Ps 115:3 **23:14** [z]1Th 3:3 **23:16** [a]Dt 20:3; Ps 22:14; Jer 51:46 [b]Job 27:2 **23:17** [c]Job 19:8 **24:1** [d]Jer 46:10 [e]Ac 1:7 **24:2** [f]Dt 19:14; 27:17; Pr 23:10 **24:3** [g]Dt 24:6,10,12,17; Job 22:6 **24:4** [h]Job 29:12; 30:25; Ps 41:1 [i]Pr 28:28 **24:5** [j]Ps 104:23 **24:7** [k]Ex 22:27; Job 22:6 **24:8** [l]La 4:5 **24:9** [m]Dt 24:17 **24:12** [n]Eze 26:15 [o]Job 9:23 **24:13** [p]Jn 3:19-20 [q]Isa 5:20 **24:14** [r]Ps 10:9 **24:15** [s]Pr 7:8-9 [t]Ps 10:11 **24:16** [u]Ex 22:2; Mt 6:19 [v]Jn 3:20 **24:18** [w]Job 9:26 [x]Job 22:16 **24:19** [y]Job 6:17

[a]11 Or *olives between the millstones*; the meaning of the Hebrew for this word is uncertain. [b]17 Or *them, their morning is like the shadow of death* [c]17 Or *of the shadow of death*

23:8-12 PROMISE 1

JOB'S BENCHMARK

Even though Job searched for God and couldn't find him, he never forgot that God had not lost him. Why was Job so confident? Read verses 10–12 carefully and notice how Job piled statement upon statement to describe how he stayed close to God.

The infinite God will never lose anyone, but we often lose sight of God. Make a list of the statements Job used to describe how he related to God, then use it as a benchmark to evaluate how you relate to him. Your focus in the good times influences your field of vision in the hard times.

For the next Promise 1 reading go to page 579.

so the grave[a][z] snatches away
those who have sinned.
20The womb forgets them,
the worm feasts on them;
evil men are no longer
remembered[a]
but are broken like a tree.[b]
21They prey on the barren and
childless woman,
and to the widow show no
kindness.[c]
22But God drags away the mighty by
his power;
though they become established,
they have no assurance of
life.[d]
23He may let them rest in a feeling of
security,[e]
but his eyes are on their ways.[f]
24For a little while they are exalted,
and then they are gone;[g]
they are brought low and
gathered up like all others;
they are cut off like heads of
grain.[h]
25"If this is not so, who can prove
me false
and reduce my words to
nothing?"[i]

Bildad

25 Then Bildad the Shuhite replied:

2"Dominion and awe belong to
God;[j]
he establishes order in the
heights of heaven.
3Can his forces be numbered?
Upon whom does his light not
rise?[k]
4How then can a man be righteous
before God?
How can one born of woman be
pure?[l]
5If even the moon[m] is not bright
and the stars are not pure in his
eyes,[n]
6how much less man, who is but a
maggot—
a son of man,[o] who is only a
worm!"[p]

Job

26 Then Job replied:

2"How you have helped the
powerless![q]
How you have saved the arm
that is feeble![r]
3What advice you have offered to
one without wisdom!
And what great insight you have
displayed!
4Who has helped you utter these
words?
And whose spirit spoke from
your mouth?

5"The dead are in deep anguish,[s]
those beneath the waters and all
that live in them.
6Death[b][t] is naked before God;
Destruction[b] lies uncovered.[u]
7He spreads out the northern
⌞skies⌟[v] over empty space;
he suspends the earth over
nothing.
8He wraps up the waters[w] in his
clouds,[x]
yet the clouds do not burst
under their weight.
9He covers the face of the full
moon,
spreading his clouds[y] over it.
10He marks out the horizon on the
face of the waters[z]
for a boundary between light
and darkness.[a]
11The pillars of the heavens quake,
aghast at his rebuke.
12By his power he churned up the
sea;[b]
by his wisdom[c] he cut Rahab to
pieces.
13By his breath the skies became fair;
his hand pierced the gliding
serpent.[d]
14And these are but the outer fringe
of his works;
how faint the whisper we hear of
him!
Who then can understand the
thunder of his power?"[e]

27 And Job continued his discourse:[f]

2"As surely as God lives, who has
denied me justice,[g]
the Almighty, who has made me
taste bitterness of soul,[h]
3as long as I have life within me,
the breath of God[i] in my
nostrils,
4my lips will not speak wickedness,
and my tongue will utter no
deceit.[j]
5I will never admit you are in the
right;
till I die, I will not deny my
integrity.[k]
6I will maintain my righteousness
and never let go of it;
my conscience will not reproach
me as long as I live.[l]

7"May my enemies be like the
wicked,
my adversaries like the unjust!
8For what hope has the godless[m]
when he is cut off,

24:19 [z]Job 21:13
24:20 [a]Job 18:17; Pr 10:7 [b]Ps 31:12; Da 4:14
24:21 [c]Job 22:9
24:22 [d]Dt 28:66
24:23 [e]Job 12:6 [f]Job 11:11
24:24 [g]Job 14:21; Ps 37:10 [h]Isa 17:5
24:25 [i]Job 6:28; 27:4
25:2 [j]Job 9:4; Rev 1:6
25:3 [k]Jas 1:17
25:4 [l]Job 4:17; 14:4
25:5 [m]Job 31:26 [n]Job 15:15
25:6 [o]Job 7:17 [p]Ps 22:6
26:2 [q]Job 6:12 [r]Ps 71:9
26:5 [s]Ps 88:10
26:6 [t]Ps 139:8 [u]Job 41:11; Pr 15:11; Heb 4:13
26:7 [v]Job 9:8
26:8 [w]Pr 30:4 [x]Job 37:11
26:9 [y]Job 22:14; Ps 97:2
26:10 [z]Pr 8:27,29 [a]Job 38:8-11
26:12 [b]Ex 14:21; Isa 51:15; Jer 31:35 [c]Job 12:13
26:13 [d]Isa 27:1
26:14 [e]Job 36:29
27:1 [f]Job 29:1
27:2 [g]Job 34:5 [h]Job 9:18
27:3 [i]Job 32:8; 33:4
27:4 [j]Job 6:28
27:5 [k]Job 2:9; 13:15
27:6 [l]Job 2:3
27:8 [m]Job 8:13

a 19,6 Hebrew *Sheol* b 6 Hebrew *Abaddon*

when God takes away his life?[n]
9Does God listen to his cry
when distress comes upon him?[o]
10Will he find delight in the Almighty?[p]
Will he call upon God at all times?

11"I will teach you about the power of God;
the ways of the Almighty I will not conceal.
12You have all seen this yourselves.
Why then this meaningless talk?

13"Here is the fate God allots to the wicked,
the heritage a ruthless man receives from the Almighty:[q]
14However many his children, their fate is the sword;[r]
his offspring will never have enough to eat.[s]
15The plague will bury those who survive him,
and their widows will not weep for them.[t]
16Though he heaps up silver like dust
and clothes like piles of clay,[u]
17what he lays up the righteous will wear,[v]
and the innocent will divide his silver.
18The house he builds is like a moth's cocoon,[w]
like a hut[x] made by a watchman.
19He lies down wealthy, but will do so no more;[y]
when he opens his eyes, all is gone.
20Terrors overtake him like a flood;[z]
a tempest snatches him away in the night.[a]
21The east wind carries him off, and he is gone;
it sweeps him out of his place.[b]
22It hurls itself against him without mercy[c]
as he flees headlong from its power.[d]
23It claps its hands in derision
and hisses him out of his place.[e]

28 "There is a mine for silver
and a place where gold is refined.
2Iron is taken from the earth,
and copper is smelted from ore.[f]
3Man puts an end to the darkness;[g]
he searches the farthest recesses
for ore in the blackest darkness.
4Far from where people dwell he cuts a shaft,
in places forgotten by the foot of man;
far from men he dangles and sways.
5The earth, from which food comes,[h]
is transformed below as by fire;
6sapphires[a] come from its rocks,
and its dust contains nuggets of gold.
7No bird of prey knows that hidden path,
no falcon's eye has seen it.
8Proud beasts do not set foot on it,
and no lion prowls there.
9Man's hand assaults the flinty rock
and lays bare the roots of the mountains.
10He tunnels through the rock;
his eyes see all its treasures.
11He searches[b] the sources of the rivers
and brings hidden things to light.

12"But where can wisdom be found?[i]
Where does understanding dwell?
13Man does not comprehend its worth;[j]
it cannot be found in the land of the living.
14The deep says, 'It is not in me';
the sea says, 'It is not with me.'
15It cannot be bought with the finest gold,
nor can its price be weighed in silver.[k]
16It cannot be bought with the gold of Ophir,
with precious onyx or sapphires.
17Neither gold nor crystal can compare with it,
nor can it be had for jewels of gold.[l]
18Coral and jasper are not worthy of mention;
the price of wisdom is beyond rubies.[m]
19The topaz of Cush cannot compare with it;
it cannot be bought with pure gold.[n]

20"Where then does wisdom come from?
Where does understanding dwell?[o]
21It is hidden from the eyes of every living thing,

27:8 [n]Job 11:20; Lk 12:20 **27:9** [o]Job 35:12; Pr 1:28; Isa 1:15; Jer 14:12; Mic 3:4 **27:10** [p]Job 22:26 **27:13** [q]Job 15:20; 20:29 **27:14** [r]Dt 28:41; Job 15:22; Hos 9:13 [s]Job 20:10 **27:15** [t]Ps 78:64 **27:16** [u]Zec 9:3 **27:17** [v]Pr 28:8; Ecc 2:26 **27:18** [w]Job 8:14 [x]Isa 1:8 **27:19** [y]Job 7:8 **27:20** [z]Job 15:21 [a]Job 20:8 **27:21** [b]Job 7:10; 21:18 **27:22** [c]Jer 13:14; Eze 5:11; 24:14 [d]Job 11:20 **27:23** [e]Job 18:18 **28:2** [f]Dt 8:9 **28:3** [g]Ecc 1:13 **28:5** [h]Ps 104:14 **28:12** [i]Ecc 7:24 **28:13** [j]Pr 3:15; Mt 13:44-46 **28:15** [k]Pr 3:13-14; 8:10-11; 16:16 **28:17** [l]Pr 16:16 **28:18** [m]Pr 3:15 **28:19** [n]Pr 8:19 **28:20** [o]ver 23,28

[a]*6* Or *lapis lazuli*; also in verse 16
[b]*11* Septuagint, Aquila and Vulgate; Hebrew *He dams up*

concealed even from the birds of the air.
22Destruction[a][p] and Death say,
'Only a rumor of it has reached our ears.'
23God understands the way to it
and he alone knows where it dwells,[q]
24for he views the ends of the earth[r]
and sees everything under the heavens.[s]
25When he established the force of the wind
and measured out the waters,[t]
26when he made a decree for the rain
and a path for the thunderstorm,[u]
27then he looked at wisdom and appraised it;
he confirmed it and tested it.

3 →PG. 571

28And he said to man,
'The fear of the Lord—that is wisdom,
and to shun evil is understanding.[v]'"

29

Job continued his discourse:[w]

2"How I long for the months gone by,
for the days when God watched over me,[x]
3when his lamp shone upon my head
and by his light I walked through darkness![y]
4Oh, for the days when I was in my prime,
when God's intimate friendship blessed my house,[z]
5when the Almighty was still with me
and my children were around me,
6when my path was drenched with cream[a]
and the rock[b] poured out for me streams of olive oil.[c]

7"When I went to the gate[d] of the city
and took my seat in the public square,
8the young men saw me and stepped aside
and the old men rose to their feet;
9the chief men refrained from speaking
and covered their mouths with their hands;[e]
10the voices of the nobles were hushed,
and their tongues stuck to the roof of their mouths.[f]

7 →PG. 569

11Whoever heard me spoke well of me,
and those who saw me commended me,
12because I rescued the poor[g] who cried for help,
and the fatherless[h] who had none to assist him.[i]
13The man who was dying blessed me;[j]
I made the widow's[k] heart sing.
14I put on righteousness[l] as my clothing;
justice was my robe and my turban.

7 →PG. 588

15I was eyes[m] to the blind
and feet to the lame.
16I was a father to the needy;[n]
I took up the case of the stranger.
17I broke the fangs of the wicked
and snatched the victims from their teeth.[o]

18"I thought, 'I will die in my own house,
my days as numerous as the grains of sand.[p]
19My roots will reach to the water,[q]
and the dew will lie all night on my branches.
20My glory will remain fresh in me,
the bow[r] ever new in my hand.'[s]

21"Men listened to me expectantly,
waiting in silence for my counsel.
22After I had spoken, they spoke no more;
my words fell gently on their ears.[t]

28:22 [p]Job 26:6 **28:23** [q]Pr 8:22-31 **28:24** [r]Ps 33:13-14 [s]Pr 15:3 **28:25** [t]Job 12:15; Ps 135:7 **28:26** [u]Job 37:3,8,11; 38:25,27 **28:28** [v]Dt 4:6; Ps 111:10; Pr 1:7; 9:10 **29:1** [w]Job 13:12; 27:1 **29:2** [x]Jer 31:28 **29:3** [y]Job 11:17 **29:4** [z]Ps 25:14; Pr 3:32

29:6 [a]Job 20:17 [b]Ps 81:16 [c]Dt 32:13 **29:7** [d]Job 31:21 **29:9** [e]Job 21:5 **29:10** [f]Ps 137:6 **29:12** [g]Job 24:4 [h]Job 31:17,21 [i]Ps 72:12; Pr 21:13 **29:13** [j]Job 31:20 [k]Job 22:9 **29:14** [l]Job 27:6; Ps 132:9; Isa 59:17; 61:10; Eph 6:14 **29:15** [m]Nu 10:31 **29:16** [n]Job 24:4; Pr 29:7 **29:17** [o]Ps 3:7 **29:18** [p]Ps 30:6 **29:19** [q]Job 18:16; Jer 17:8 **29:20** [r]Ps 18:34 [s]Ge 49:24 **29:22** [t]Dt 32:2

a22 Hebrew *Abaddon*

29:1–31:40

LIKE SALT IN AN OPEN WOUND

PROMISE 2

What a tragedy. Job's well-intentioned friends became his greatest burden. His losses and physical pains could not break him, but his friends' hollow, judgmental (though sincere and holy-sounding) advice almost did him in.

We need friends, and we need to be friends, but friends only speak the *truth* in love (Ephesians 4:15). After his experience, Job would caution us to be extremely careful about what we say to a hurting friend. God did not ignore this assault on his servant Job (see 42:7–9). Let this story serve as a reminder to avoid coming to hasty conclusions and dispensing bad advice to a hurting friend.

For the next Promise 2 reading go to page 577.

23They waited for me as for showers
and drank in my words as the
spring rain.
24When I smiled at them, they
scarcely believed it;
the light of my face was precious
to them.[a]
25I chose the way for them and sat as
their chief;
I dwelt as a king[u] among his
troops;
I was like one who comforts
mourners.[v]

30 "But now they mock me,[w]
men younger than I,
whose fathers I would have
disdained
to put with my sheep dogs.
2Of what use was the strength of
their hands to me,
since their vigor had gone from
them?
3Haggard from want and hunger,
they roamed[b] the parched land
in desolate wastelands at night.
4In the brush they gathered salt
herbs,
and their food[c] was the root of
the broom tree.
5They were banished from their
fellow men,
shouted at as if they were
thieves.
6They were forced to live in the dry
stream beds,
among the rocks and in holes in
the ground.
7They brayed among the bushes
and huddled in the undergrowth.
8A base and nameless brood,
they were driven out of the land.

9"And now their sons mock me[x] in
song;[y]
I have become a byword[z]
among them.
10They detest me and keep their
distance;
they do not hesitate to spit in
my face.[a]
11Now that God has unstrung my
bow and afflicted me,[b]
they throw off restraint[c] in my
presence.
12On my right the tribe[d] attacks;
they lay snares for my feet,[d]
they build their siege ramps
against me.[e]
13They break up my road;[f]
they succeed in destroying me—
without anyone's helping them.[e]
14They advance as through a gaping
breach;
amid the ruins they come rolling
in.
15Terrors overwhelm me;[g]
my dignity is driven away as by
the wind,
my safety vanishes like a
cloud.[h]

16"And now my life ebbs away;[i]
days of suffering grip me.
17Night pierces my bones;
my gnawing pains never rest.
18In his great power ⌞God⌟ becomes
like clothing to me[f];
he binds me like the neck of my
garment.
19He throws me into the mud,[j]
and I am reduced to dust and
ashes.

20"I cry out to you, O God, but you
do not answer;[k]
I stand up, but you merely look
at me.
21You turn on me ruthlessly;[l]
with the might of your hand[m]
you attack me.[n]
22You snatch me up and drive me
before the wind;[o]
you toss me about in the
storm.[p]
23I know you will bring me down to
death,[q]
to the place appointed for all the
living.[r]

24"Surely no one lays a hand on a
broken man
when he cries for help in his
distress.[s]
25Have I not wept for those in
trouble?
Has not my soul grieved for the
poor?[t]
26Yet when I hoped for good, evil
came;
when I looked for light, then
came darkness.[u]
27The churning inside me never
stops;[v]
days of suffering confront me.
28I go about blackened,[w] but not by
the sun;
I stand up in the assembly and
cry for help.[x]
29I have become a brother of
jackals,[y]
a companion of owls.[z]
30My skin grows black and peels;[a]
my body burns with fever.[b]
31My harp is tuned to mourning,[c]
and my flute to the sound of
wailing.

29:25 *u*Job 1:3; 31:37 *v*Job 4:4
30:1 *w*Job 12:4
30:9 *x*Ps 69:11 *y*Job 12:4; La 3:14,63 *z*Job 17:6
30:10 *a*Nu 12:14; Dt 25:9; Isa 50:6; Mt 26:67
30:11 *b*Ru 1:21 *c*Ps 32:9
30:12 *d*Ps 140:4-5 *e*Job 19:12
30:13 *f*Isa 3:12
30:15 *g*Job 31:23; Ps 55:4-5 *h*Job 3:25; Hos 13:3
30:16 *i*Job 3:24; Ps 22:14; 42:4
30:19 *j*Ps 69:2,14
30:20 *k*Job 19:7
30:21 *l*Job 19:6,22 *m*Job 16:9,14 *n*Job 10:3
30:22 *o*Job 27:21 *p*Job 9:17
30:23 *q*Job 9:22; 10:8 *r*Job 3:19
30:24 *s*Job 19:7
30:25 *t*Job 24:4; Ps 35:13-14; Ro 12:15
30:26 *u*Job 3:25-26; 19:8; Jer 8:15
30:27 *v*La 2:11
30:28 *w*Ps 38:6; 42:9; 43:2 *x*Job 19:7
30:29 *y*Ps 44:19 *z*Ps 102:6; Mic 1:8
30:30 *a*La 4:8 *b*Ps 102:3
30:31 *c*Isa 24:8

a24 The meaning of the Hebrew for this clause is uncertain. **b**3 Or *gnawed* **c**4 Or *fuel* **d**12 The meaning of the Hebrew for this word is uncertain. **e**13 Or *me. / 'No one can help him,' ⌞they say⌟.* **f**18 Hebrew; Septuagint *⌞God⌟ grasps my clothing*

3 →PG. 585

31 “I made a covenant with my eyes
not to look lustfully at a girl.[d]
2For what is man’s lot from God
above,
his heritage from the Almighty
on high?[e]
3Is it not ruin[f] for the wicked,
disaster for those who do
wrong?[g]
4Does he not see my ways[h]
and count my every step?[i]

5“If I have walked in falsehood
or my foot has hurried after
deceit[j]—
6let God weigh me in honest
scales[k]
and he will know that I am
blameless—
7if my steps have turned from the
path,[l]
if my heart has been led by my
eyes,
or if my hands[m] have been
defiled,
8then may others eat what I have
sown,[n]
and may my crops be
uprooted.[o]

9“If my heart has been enticed[p] by
a woman,
or if I have lurked at my
neighbor’s door,
10then may my wife grind another
man’s grain,
and may other men sleep with
her.[q]
11For that would have been
shameful,
a sin to be judged.[r]
12It is a fire[s] that burns to
Destruction[a];[t]
it would have uprooted my
harvest.[u]

13“If I have denied justice to my
menservants and
maidservants
when they had a grievance
against me,[v]
14what will I do when God confronts
me?
What will I answer when called
to account?
15Did not he who made me in the
womb make them?
Did not the same one form us
both within our mothers?[w]

16“If I have denied the desires of the
poor[x]
or let the eyes of the widow[y]
grow weary,
17if I have kept my bread to myself,
not sharing it with the
fatherless[z]—
18but from my youth I reared him as
would a father,
and from my birth I guided the
widow—
19if I have seen anyone perishing for
lack of clothing,[a]
or a needy[b] man without a
garment,
20and his heart did not bless me
for warming him with the fleece
from my sheep,
21if I have raised my hand against
the fatherless,[c]
knowing that I had influence in
court,
22then let my arm fall from the
shoulder,
let it be broken off at the joint.[d]
23For I dreaded destruction from
God,
and for fear of his splendor[e] I
could not do such things.

24“If I have put my trust in gold[f]
or said to pure gold, ‘You are my
security,’[g]
25if I have rejoiced over my great
wealth,[h]
the fortune my hands had
gained,
26if I have regarded the sun[i] in its
radiance
or the moon moving in splendor,
27so that my heart was secretly
enticed
and my hand offered them a kiss
of homage,
28then these also would be sins to be
judged,[j]
for I would have been unfaithful
to God on high.

29“If I have rejoiced at my enemy’s
misfortune[k]
or gloated over the trouble that
came to him[l]—
30I have not allowed my mouth to
sin
by invoking a curse against his
life—
31if the men of my household have
never said,
‘Who has not had his fill of Job’s
meat?’[m]—
32but no stranger had to spend the
night in the street,
for my door was always open to
the traveler[n]—
33if I have concealed[o] my sin as
men do,[b]
by hiding[p] my guilt in my heart
34because I so feared the crowd[q]
and so dreaded the contempt of
the clans

31:1 [d]Mt 5:28
31:2 [e]Job 20:29
31:3 [f]Job 21:30 [g]Job 34:22
31:4 [h]2Ch 16:9 [i]Pr 5:21
31:5 [j]Mic 2:11
31:6 [k]Job 6:2; 27:5-6
31:7 [l]Job 23:11 [m]Job 9:30
31:8 [n]Lev 26:16; Job 20:18 [o]Mic 6:15
31:9 [p]Job 24:15
31:10 [q]Dt 28:30; Jer 8:10
31:11 [r]Ge 38:24; Lev 20:10; Dt 22:22-24
31:12 [s]Job 15:30 [t]Job 26:6 [u]Job 20:28
31:13 [v]Dt 24:14-15
31:15 [w]Job 10:3
31:16 [x]Job 5:16; 20:19 [y]Job 22:9
31:17 [z]Job 22:7; 29:12
31:19 [a]Job 22:6 [b]Job 24:4
31:21 [c]Job 22:9
31:22 [d]Job 38:15
31:23 [e]Job 13:11
31:24 [f]Job 22:25 [g]Mt 6:24; Mk 10:24
31:25 [h]Ps 62:10
31:26 [i]Eze 8:16
31:28 [j]Dt 17:2-7
31:29 [k]Ob 1:12 [l]Pr 17:5; 24:17-18
31:31 [m]Job 22:7
31:32 [n]Ge 19:2-3; Ro 12:13
31:33 [o]Pr 28:13 [p]Ge 3:8
31:34 [q]Ex 23:2

a *12* Hebrew *Abaddon* **b** *33* Or *as Adam did*

that I kept silent and would not go outside
35 ("Oh, that I had someone to hear me![r]
I sign now my defense—let the Almighty answer me;
let my accuser[s] put his indictment in writing.
36 Surely I would wear it on my shoulder,
I would put it on like a crown.
37 I would give him an account of my every step;
like a prince[t] I would approach him.)—
38 "if my land cries out against me[u]
and all its furrows are wet with tears,
39 if I have devoured its yield without payment[v]
or broken the spirit of its tenants,[w]
40 then let briers[x] come up instead of wheat
and weeds instead of barley."

The words of Job are ended.

Elihu

32 So these three men stopped answering Job, because he was righteous in his own eyes.[y] 2 But Elihu son
of Barakel the Buzite,[z] of the family of
Ram, became very angry with Job for
justifying himself rather than God.[a]
3 He was also angry with the three
friends, because they had found no
way to refute Job, and yet had condemned him.[a] 4 Now Elihu had waited
before speaking to Job because they
were older than he. 5 But when he saw
that the three men had nothing more
to say, his anger was aroused.
6 So Elihu son of Barakel the Buzite
said:

"I am young in years,
and you are old;[b]
that is why I was fearful,
not daring to tell you what I know.
7 I thought, 'Age should speak;
advanced years should teach wisdom.'
8 But it is the spirit[b] in a man,
the breath of the Almighty,[c]
that gives him understanding.[d]
9 It is not only the old[c] who are wise,[e]
not only the aged who understand what is right.
10 "Therefore I say: Listen to me;
I too will tell you what I know.
11 I waited while you spoke,
I listened to your reasoning;
while you were searching for words,
12 I gave you my full attention.
But not one of you has proved Job wrong;
none of you has answered his arguments.
13 Do not say, 'We have found wisdom;[f]
let God refute him, not man.'
14 But Job has not marshaled his words against me,
and I will not answer him with your arguments.
15 "They are dismayed and have no more to say;
words have failed them.
16 Must I wait, now that they are silent,
now that they stand there with no reply?
17 I too will have my say;
I too will tell what I know.
18 For I am full of words,
and the spirit within me compels me;
19 inside I am like bottled-up wine,
like new wineskins ready to burst.
20 I must speak and find relief;
I must open my lips and reply.
21 I will show partiality[g] to no one,[h]
nor will I flatter any man;
22 for if I were skilled in flattery,
my Maker would soon take me away.

33 "But now, Job, listen to my words;
pay attention to everything I say.[i]
2 I am about to open my mouth;
my words are on the tip of my tongue.
3 My words come from an upright heart;
my lips sincerely speak what I know.[j]
4 The Spirit of God has made me;[k]
the breath of the Almighty[l] gives me life.
5 Answer me[m] then, if you can;
prepare[n] yourself and confront me.
6 I am just like you before God;
I too have been taken from clay.[o]
7 No fear of me should alarm you,
nor should my hand be heavy upon you.[p]

31:35 [r] Job 19:7; 30:28 [s] Job 27:7; 35:14 **31:37** [t] Job 1:3; 29:25 **31:38** [u] Ge 4:10 **31:39** [v] 1Ki 21:19 [w] Lev 19:13; Jas 5:4 **31:40** [x] Ge 3:18 **32:1** [y] Job 10:7; 33:9 **32:2** [z] Ge 22:21 [a] Job 27:5; 30:21 **32:6** [b] Job 15:10 **32:8** [c] Job 27:3; 33:4 [d] Pr 2:6 **32:9** [e] 1Co 1:26 **32:13** [f] Jer 9:23 **32:21** [g] Lev 19:15; Job 13:10 [h] Mt 22:16 **33:1** [i] Job 13:6 **33:3** [j] Job 6:28; 27:4; 36:4 **33:4** [k] Ge 2:7; Job 10:3 [l] Job 27:3 **33:5** [m] ver 32 [n] Job 13:18 **33:6** [o] Job 4:19 **33:7** [p] Job 9:34; 13:21; 2Co 2:4

[a] *3* Masoretic Text; an ancient Hebrew scribal tradition *Job, and so had condemned God* [b] *8* Or *Spirit*; also in verse 18 [c] *9* Or *many*; or *great*

8"But you have said in my
hearing—
I heard the very words—
9'I am pure[q] and without sin;[r]
I am clean and free from guilt.
10Yet God has found fault with me;
he considers me his enemy.[s]
11He fastens my feet in shackles;[t]
he keeps close watch on all my
paths.'[u]

12"But I tell you, in this you are not
right,
for God is greater than man.[v]
13Why do you complain to him[w]
that he answers none of man's
words[a]?
14For God does speak[x]—now one
way, now another—
though man may not perceive it.
15In a dream,[y] in a vision of the
night,
when deep sleep falls on men
as they slumber in their beds,
16he may speak[z] in their ears
and terrify them with warnings,
17to turn man from wrongdoing
and keep him from pride,
18to preserve his soul from the
pit,[b][a]
his life from perishing by the
sword.[c][b]
19Or a man may be chastened on a
bed of pain
with constant distress in his
bones,[c]
20so that his very being finds food[d]
repulsive
and his soul loathes the choicest
meal.[e]
21His flesh wastes away to nothing,
and his bones, once hidden, now
stick out.[f]
22His soul draws near to the pit,[d]
and his life to the messengers of
death.[e][g]
23"Yet if there is an angel on his side
as a mediator, one out of a
thousand,
to tell a man what is right for
him,[h]
24to be gracious to him and say,
'Spare him from going down to
the pit[f];[i]
I have found a ransom for
him'—
25then his flesh is renewed like a
child's;
it is restored as in the days of his
youth.[j]
26He prays to God and finds favor
with him,[k]
he sees God's face and shouts
for joy;[l]
he is restored by God to his
righteous state.[m]
27Then he comes to men and says,
'I sinned,[n] and perverted what
was right,[o]
but I did not get what I
deserved.[p]
28He redeemed my soul from going
down to the pit,[g]
and I will live to enjoy the
light.'[q]

29"God does all these things to a
man[r]—
twice, even three times—
30to turn back his soul from the pit,[h]
that the light of life[s] may shine
on him.

31"Pay attention, Job, and listen to
me;
be silent, and I will speak.
32If you have anything to say, answer
me;
speak up, for I want you to be
cleared.
33But if not, then listen to me;
be silent, and I will teach you
wisdom.[t]"

34 Then Elihu said:

2"Hear my words, you wise men;
listen to me, you men of
learning.
3For the ear tests words
as the tongue tastes food.[u]
4Let us discern for ourselves what is
right;
let us learn together what is
good.[v]

5"Job says, 'I am innocent,[w]
but God denies me justice.[x]
6Although I am right,
I am considered a liar;
although I am guiltless,
his arrow inflicts an incurable
wound.'[y]
7What man is like Job,
who drinks scorn like water?[z]
8He keeps company with evildoers;
he associates with wicked men.[a]
9For he says, 'It profits a man
nothing
when he tries to please God.'[b]

10"So listen to me, you men of
understanding.
Far be it from God to do evil,[c]
from the Almighty to do
wrong.[d]

33:9 *q*Job 10:7 *r*Job 13:23; 16:17
33:10 *s*Job 13:24
33:11 *t*Job 13:27 *u*Job 14:16
33:12 *v*Ecc 7:20
33:13 *w*Job 40:2; Isa 45:9
33:14 *x*Ps 62:11
33:15 *y*Job 4:13
33:16 *z*Job 36:10,15
33:18 *a*ver 22,24,28, 30 *b*Job 15:22
33:19 *c*Job 30:17
33:20 *d*Ps 107:18 *e*Job 3:24; 6:6
33:21 *f*Job 16:8; 19:20
33:22 *g*Ps 88:3
33:23 *h*Mic 6:8
33:24 *i*Isa 38:17
33:25 *j*2Ki 5:14
33:26 *k*Job 34:28 *l*Job 22:26 *m*Ps 50:15; 51:12
33:27 *n*2Sa 12:13 *o*Lk 15:21 *p*Ro 6:21
33:28 *q*Job 22:28
33:29 *r*1Co 12:6; Eph 1:11; Php 2:13
33:30 *s*Ps 56:13
33:33 *t*Ps 34:11
34:3 *u*Job 12:11
34:4 *v*1Th 5:21
34:5 *w*Job 33:9 *x*Job 27:2
34:6 *y*Job 6:4
34:7 *z*Job 15:16
34:8 *a*Job 22:15; Ps 50:18
34:9 *b*Job 21:15; 35:3
34:10 *c*Ge 18:25 *d*Dt 32:4; Job 8:3; Ro 9:14

[a] 13 Or *that he does not answer for any of his actions* [b] 18 Or *preserve him from the grave* [c] 18 Or *from crossing the River* [d] 22 Or *He draws near to the grave* [e] 22 Or *to the dead* [f] 24 Or *grave* [g] 28 Or *redeemed me from going down to the grave* [h] 30 Or *turn him back from the grave*

11He repays a man for what he has
done;[e]
he brings upon him what his
conduct deserves.[f]
12It is unthinkable that God would
do wrong,
that the Almighty would pervert
justice.[g]
13Who appointed him over the earth?
Who put him in charge of the
whole world?[h]
14If it were his intention
and he withdrew his spirit[a] and
breath,[i]
15all mankind would perish together
and man would return to the
dust.[j]

16"If you have understanding, hear
this;
listen to what I say.
17Can he who hates justice govern?[k]
Will you condemn the just and
mighty One?[l]
18Is he not the One who says to
kings, 'You are worthless,'
and to nobles, 'You are
wicked,'[m]
19who shows no partiality[n] to
princes
and does not favor the rich over
the poor,[o]
for they are all the work of his
hands?[p]
20They die in an instant, in the
middle of the night;[q]
the people are shaken and they
pass away;
the mighty are removed without
human hand.[r]

21"His eyes are on the ways of men;
he sees their every step.[s]
22There is no dark place,[t] no deep
shadow,[u]
where evildoers can hide.
23God has no need to examine men
further,
that they should come before
him for judgment.[v]
24Without inquiry he shatters the
mighty[w]
and sets up others in their
place.[x]
25Because he takes note of their
deeds,
he overthrows them in the night
and they are crushed.
26He punishes them for their
wickedness
where everyone can see them,
27because they turned from following
him[y]
and had no regard for any of his
ways.[z]
28They caused the cry of the poor to
come before him,
so that he heard the cry of the
needy.[a]
29But if he remains silent, who can
condemn him?
If he hides his face, who can see
him?
Yet he is over man and nation
alike,
30 to keep a godless man from
ruling,
from laying snares for the
people.[b]

31"Suppose a man says to God,
'I am guilty but will offend no
more.
32Teach me what I cannot see;[c]
if I have done wrong, I will not
do so again.'[d]
33Should God then reward you on
your terms,
when you refuse to repent?[e]
You must decide, not I;
so tell me what you know.

34"Men of understanding declare,
wise men who hear me say to
me,
35'Job speaks without knowledge;[f]
his words lack insight.'
36Oh, that Job might be tested to the
utmost
for answering like a wicked
man![g]
37To his sin he adds rebellion;
scornfully he claps his hands[h]
among us
and multiplies his words against
God."[i]

35

Then Elihu said:

2"Do you think this is just?
You say, 'I will be cleared by
God.[b]'
3Yet you ask him, 'What profit is it
to me,[c]
and what do I gain by not
sinning?'[j]

4"I would like to reply to you
and to your friends with you.
5Look up at the heavens[k] and see;
gaze at the clouds so high above
you.[l]
6If you sin, how does that affect
him?
If your sins are many, what does
that do to him?[m]
7If you are righteous, what do you
give to him,[n]
or what does he receive[o] from
your hand?[p]

34:11 [e]Ps 62:12; Mt 16:27; Ro 2:6; 2Co 5:10 [f]Jer 32:19; Eze 33:20 **34:12** [g]Job 8:3 **34:13** [h]Job 38:4,6 **34:14** [i]Ps 104:29 **34:15** [j]Ge 3:19; Job 9:22 **34:17** [k]2Sa 23:3-4 [l]Job 40:8 **34:18** [m]Ex 22:28 **34:19** [n]Dt 10:17; Ac 10:34 [o]Lev 19:15 [p]Job 10:3 **34:20** [q]Ex 12:29 [r]Job 12:19 **34:21** [s]Job 31:4; Pr 15:3 **34:22** [t]Ps 139:12 [u]Am 9:2-3 **34:23** [v]Job 11:11 **34:24** [w]Job 12:19 [x]Da 2:21 **34:27** [y]Ps 28:5; Isa 5:12 [z]1Sa 15:11

34:28 [a]Ex 22:23; Job 35:9; Jas 5:4 **34:30** [b]Pr 29:2-12 **34:32** [c]Job 35:11; Ps 25:4 [d]Job 33:27 **34:33** [e]Job 41:11 **34:35** [f]Job 35:16; 38:2 **34:36** [g]Job 22:15 **34:37** [h]Job 27:23 [i]Job 23:2 **35:3** [j]Job 9:29-31; 34:9 **35:5** [k]Ge 15:5 [l]Job 22:12 **35:6** [m]Pr 8:36 **35:7** [n]Ro 11:35 [o]Pr 9:12 [p]Job 22:2-3; Lk 17:10

a 14 Or *Spirit* **b** 2 Or *My righteousness is more than God's* **c** 3 Or *you*

8Your wickedness affects only a man
like yourself,
and your righteousness only the
sons of men.

9"Men cry out[q] under a load of
oppression;
they plead for relief from the
arm of the powerful.[r]
10But no one says, 'Where is God my
Maker,[s]
who gives songs in the night,[t]
11who teaches[u] more to us than to[a]
the beasts of the earth
and makes us wiser than[b] the
birds of the air?'
12He does not answer[v] when men
cry out
because of the arrogance of the
wicked.
13Indeed, God does not listen to their
empty plea;
the Almighty pays no attention
to it.[w]
14How much less, then, will he listen
when you say that you do not
see him,[x]
that your case[y] is before him
and you must wait for him,
15and further, that his anger never
punishes
and he does not take the least
notice of wickedness.[c]
16So Job opens his mouth with
empty talk;
without knowledge he multiplies
words."[z]

36

Elihu continued:

2"Bear with me a little longer and I
will show you
that there is more to be said in
God's behalf.
3I get my knowledge from afar;
I will ascribe justice to my
Maker.[a]
4Be assured that my words are not
false;[b]
one perfect in knowledge[c] is
with you.

5"God is mighty, but does not
despise men;[d]
he is mighty, and firm in his
purpose.[e]
6He does not keep the wicked
alive[f]
but gives the afflicted their
rights.[g]
7He does not take his eyes off the
righteous;[h]
he enthrones them with kings[i]
and exalts them forever.
8But if men are bound in chains,[j]
held fast by cords of affliction,
9he tells them what they have
done—
that they have sinned
arrogantly.[k]
10He makes them listen[l] to
correction
and commands them to repent
of their evil.[m]
11If they obey and serve him,[n]
they will spend the rest of their
days in prosperity
and their years in contentment.
12But if they do not listen,
they will perish by the sword[d][o]
and die without knowledge.[p]

13"The godless in heart[q] harbor
resentment;
even when he fetters them, they
do not cry for help.
14They die in their youth,
among male prostitutes of the
shrines.[r]
15But those who suffer he delivers in
their suffering;
he speaks to them in their
affliction.

16"He is wooing[s] you from the jaws
of distress
to a spacious place free from
restriction,
to the comfort of your table[t]
laden with choice food.
17But now you are laden with the
judgment due the wicked;
judgment and justice have taken
hold of you.[u]
18Be careful that no one entices you
by riches;
do not let a large bribe turn you
aside.[v]
19Would your wealth
or even all your mighty efforts
sustain you so you would not be
in distress?
20Do not long for the night,[w]
to drag people away from their
homes.[e]
21Beware of turning to evil,[x]
which you seem to prefer to
affliction.[y]

22"God is exalted in his power.
Who is a teacher like him?[z]
23Who has prescribed his ways for
him,[a]
or said to him, 'You have done
wrong'?[b]
24Remember to extol his work,[c]

35:9 [q]Ex 2:23 [r]Job 12:19
35:10 [s]Job 27:10; Isa 51:13 [t]Ps 42:8; 149:5; Ac 16:25
35:11 [u]Ps 94:12
35:12 [v]Pr 1:28
35:13 [w]Job 27:9; Pr 15:29; Isa 1:15; Jer 11:11
35:14 [x]Job 9:11 [y]Ps 37:6
35:16 [z]Job 34:35,37
36:3 [a]Job 8:3; 37:23
36:4 [b]Job 33:3 [c]Job 37:5,16, 23
36:5 [d]Ps 22:24 [e]Job 12:13
36:6 [f]Job 8:22 [g]Job 5:15
36:7 [h]Ps 33:18 [i]Ps 113:8
36:8 [j]Ps 107:10,14
36:9 [k]Job 15:25
36:10 [l]Job 33:16 [m]2Ki 17:13
36:11 [n]Isa 1:19
36:12 [o]Job 15:22 [p]Job 4:21
36:13 [q]Ro 2:5
36:14 [r]Dt 23:17
36:16 [s]Hos 2:14 [t]Ps 23:5
36:17 [u]Job 22:11
36:18 [v]Job 34:33
36:20 [w]Job 34:20,25
36:21 [x]Ps 66:18 [y]Heb 11:25
36:22 [z]Isa 40:13; 1Co 2:16
36:23 [a]Job 34:13 [b]Job 8:3
36:24 [c]Ps 92:5; 138:5

[a] *11* Or *teaches us by* [b] *11* Or *us wise by*
[c] *15* Symmachus, Theodotion and Vulgate; the meaning of the Hebrew for this word is uncertain. [d] *12* Or *will cross the River*
[e] *20* The meaning of the Hebrew for verses 18-20 is uncertain.

which men have praised in song.[d]
25All mankind has seen it;
men gaze on it from afar.
26How great is God—beyond our understanding![e]
The number of his years is past finding out.[f]

27"He draws up the drops of water,
which distill as rain to the streams[a];[g]
28the clouds pour down their moisture
and abundant showers fall on mankind.[h]
29Who can understand how he spreads out the clouds,
how he thunders from his pavilion?[i]
30See how he scatters his lightning about him,
bathing the depths of the sea.
31This is the way he governs[b] the nations[j]
and provides food in abundance.[k]
32He fills his hands with lightning
and commands it to strike its mark.[l]
33His thunder announces the coming storm;
even the cattle make known its approach.[c]

37 "At this my heart pounds
and leaps from its place.
2Listen! Listen to the roar of his voice,
to the rumbling that comes from his mouth.[m]
3He unleashes his lightning beneath the whole heaven
and sends it to the ends of the earth.
4After that comes the sound of his roar;
he thunders with his majestic voice.
When his voice resounds,
he holds nothing back.
5God's voice thunders in marvelous ways;
he does great things beyond our understanding.[n]
6He says to the snow,[o] 'Fall on the earth,'
and to the rain shower, 'Be a mighty downpour.'[p]
7So that all men he has made may know his work,
he stops every man from his labor.[d][q]
8The animals take cover;
they remain in their dens.[r]
9The tempest comes out from its chamber,
the cold from the driving winds.
10The breath of God produces ice,
and the broad waters become frozen.[s]
11He loads the clouds with moisture;
he scatters his lightning through them.[t]
12At his direction they swirl around
over the face of the whole earth
to do whatever he commands them.[u]
13He brings the clouds to punish men,[v]
or to water his earth[e] and show his love.[w]

14"Listen to this, Job;
stop and consider God's wonders.
15Do you know how God controls the clouds
and makes his lightning flash?
16Do you know how the clouds hang poised,
those wonders of him who is perfect in knowledge?[x]
17You who swelter in your clothes
when the land lies hushed under the south wind,
18can you join him in spreading out the skies,[y]
hard as a mirror of cast bronze?

19"Tell us what we should say to him;
we cannot draw up our case because of our darkness.
20Should he be told that I want to speak?
Would any man ask to be swallowed up?
21Now no one can look at the sun,
bright as it is in the skies
after the wind has swept them clean.
22Out of the north he comes in golden splendor;
God comes in awesome majesty.
23The Almighty is beyond our reach and exalted in power;[z]
in his justice[a] and great righteousness, he does not oppress.[b]
24Therefore, men revere him,[c]
for does he not have regard for all the wise[d] in heart?[f]"

The LORD Speaks

38 Then the LORD answered Job out of the storm.[e] He said:

36:24 [d]Ps 59:16; Rev 15:3
36:26 [e]1Co 13:12 [f]Job 10:5; Ps 90:2; 102:24; Heb 1:12
36:27 [g]Job 38:28; Ps 147:8
36:28 [h]Job 5:10
36:29 [i]Job 26:14; 37:16
36:31 [j]Job 37:13 [k]Ps 136:25; Ac 14:17
36:32 [l]Job 37:12,15
37:2 [m]Ps 29:3-9
37:5 [n]Job 5:9
37:6 [o]Job 38:22 [p]Job 36:27
37:7 [q]Job 12:14
37:8 [r]Job 38:40; Ps 104:22
37:10 [s]Job 38:29-30; Ps 147:17
37:11 [t]Job 36:27,29
37:12 [u]Ps 148:8
37:13 [v]1Sa 12:17 [w]Ex 9:18; 1Ki 18:45; Job 38:27
37:16 [x]Job 36:4
37:18 [y]Job 9:8; Ps 104:2; Isa 44:24
37:23 [z]Job 9:4; 36:4; 1Ti 6:16 [a]Job 8:3 [b]Isa 63:9; Eze 18:23,32
37:24 [c]Mt 10:28 [d]Mt 11:25
38:1 [e]Job 40:6

a27 Or *distill from the mist as rain* b31 Or *nourishes* c33 Or *announces his coming— / the One zealous against evil* d7 Or / *he fills all men with fear by his power* e13 Or *to favor them* f24 Or *for he does not have regard for any who think they are wise.*

2“Who is this that darkens my
counsel
with words without knowledge?[f]
3Brace yourself like a man;
I will question you,
and you shall answer me.[g]

4“Where were you when I laid the
earth’s foundation?[h]
Tell me, if you understand.
5Who marked off its dimensions?[i]
Surely you know!
Who stretched a measuring line
across it?
6On what were its footings set,
or who laid its cornerstone[j]—
7while the morning stars sang
together
and all the angels[a] shouted for
joy?

8“Who shut up the sea behind doors[k]
when it burst forth from the
womb,[l]
9when I made the clouds its
garment
and wrapped it in thick darkness,
10when I fixed limits for it[m]
and set its doors and bars in
place,[n]
11when I said, ‘This far you may
come and no farther;
here is where your proud waves
halt’?[o]

12“Have you ever given orders to the
morning,
or shown the dawn its place,
13that it might take the earth by the
edges
and shake the wicked[p] out of it?
14The earth takes shape like clay
under a seal;
its features stand out like those
of a garment.
15The wicked are denied their light,[q]
and their upraised arm is
broken.[r]

16“Have you journeyed to the springs
of the sea
or walked in the recesses of the
deep?[s]
17Have the gates of death[t] been
shown to you?
Have you seen the gates of the
shadow of death[b]?
18Have you comprehended the vast
expanses of the earth?[u]
Tell me, if you know all this.

19“What is the way to the abode of
light?
And where does darkness reside?
20Can you take them to their places?
Do you know the paths[v] to
their dwellings?
21Surely you know, for you were
already born![w]
You have lived so many years!

22“Have you entered the storehouses
of the snow[x]
or seen the storehouses of the
hail,
23which I reserve for times of
trouble,[y]
for days of war and battle?[z]
24What is the way to the place where
the lightning is dispersed,
or the place where the east
winds are scattered over the
earth?
25Who cuts a channel for the torrents
of rain,
and a path for the
thunderstorm,[a]
26to water[b] a land where no man
lives,
a desert with no one in it,
27to satisfy a desolate wasteland
and make it sprout with grass?[c]
28Does the rain have a father?[d]
Who fathers the drops of dew?
29From whose womb comes the ice?
Who gives birth to the frost from
the heavens[e]
30when the waters become hard as
stone,
when the surface of the deep is
frozen?[f]

31“Can you bind the beautiful[c]
Pleiades?
Can you loose the cords of
Orion?[g]
32Can you bring forth the
constellations in their
seasons[d]

38:2 [f]Job 35:16; 42:3; 1Ti 1:7 **38:3** [g]Job 40:7 **38:4** [h]Ps 104:5; Pr 8:29 **38:5** [i]Pr 8:29; Isa 40:12 **38:6** [j]Job 26:7 **38:8** [k]Jer 5:22 [l]Ge 1:9-10 **38:10** [m]Ps 33:7; 104:9 [n]Job 26:10 **38:11** [o]Ps 89:9 **38:13** [p]Ps 104:35 **38:15** [q]Job 18:5 [r]Ps 10:15 **38:16** [s]Ps 77:19 **38:17** [t]Ps 9:13 **38:18** [u]Job 28:24 **38:20** [v]Job 26:10 **38:21** [w]Job 15:7 **38:22** [x]Job 37:6 **38:23** [y]Isa 30:30; Eze 13:11 [z]Ex 9:18; Jos 10:11; Rev 16:21 **38:25** [a]Job 28:26 **38:26** [b]Job 36:27 **38:27** [c]Ps 104:14; 107:35 **38:28** [d]Ps 147:8; Jer 14:22 **38:29** [e]Ps 147:16-17 **38:30** [f]Job 37:10 **38:31** [g]Job 9:9; Am 5:8

38:2

PROMISE 2

AN INCREDIBLE CONTRAST

Notice the enormous contrast between God’s response to Job and his friends’ response. It’s laughable! For the last several chapters, these foolish men have been speaking in categorical statements to Job. They’ve frustrated, discouraged and, finally, infuriated him. But the Almighty, all-knowing God comes to Job with questions. He corrects and comforts Job.

The men who do not know—tell! The God who knows all—asks! When trying to help a family member or friend, observe how God handled the questions of his troubled servant.

For the next Promise 2 reading go to page 716.

[a]7 Hebrew *the sons of God* [b]17 Or *gates of deep shadows* [c]31 Or *the twinkling;* or *the chains of the* [d]32 Or *the morning star in its season*

or lead out the Bear[a] with its
cubs?
33Do you know the laws[h] of the
heavens?
Can you set up ⌞God's[b]⌟
dominion over the earth?

34"Can you raise your voice to the
clouds
and cover yourself with a flood
of water?[i]
35Do you send the lightning bolts on
their way?[j]
Do they report to you, 'Here we
are'?
36Who endowed the heart[c] with
wisdom[k]
or gave understanding[l] to the
mind[c]?
37Who has the wisdom to count the
clouds?
Who can tip over the water jars
of the heavens
38when the dust becomes hard
and the clods of earth stick
together?

39"Do you hunt the prey for the
lioness
and satisfy the hunger of the
lions[m]
40when they crouch in their dens[n]
or lie in wait in a thicket?
41Who provides food for the raven[o]
when its young cry out to God
and wander about for lack of
food?[p]

39 "Do you know when the
mountain goats[q] give birth?
Do you watch when the doe
bears her fawn?
2Do you count the months till they
bear?
Do you know the time they give
birth?
3They crouch down and bring forth
their young;
their labor pains are ended.
4Their young thrive and grow strong
in the wilds;
they leave and do not return.

5"Who let the wild donkey[r] go
free?
Who untied his ropes?
6I gave him the wasteland[s] as his
home,
the salt flats as his habitat.[t]
7He laughs at the commotion in the
town;
he does not hear a driver's
shout.[u]
8He ranges the hills for his pasture
and searches for any green thing.

9"Will the wild ox[v] consent to serve
you?
Will he stay by your manger at
night?
10Can you hold him to the furrow
with a harness?
Will he till the valleys behind
you?
11Will you rely on him for his great
strength?
Will you leave your heavy work
to him?
12Can you trust him to bring in your
grain
and gather it to your threshing
floor?

13"The wings of the ostrich flap
joyfully,
but they cannot compare with
the pinions and feathers of
the stork.
14She lays her eggs on the ground
and lets them warm in the sand,
15unmindful that a foot may crush
them,
that some wild animal may
trample them.
16She treats her young harshly,[w] as
if they were not hers;
she cares not that her labor was
in vain,
17for God did not endow her with
wisdom
or give her a share of good
sense.[x]
18Yet when she spreads her feathers
to run,
she laughs at horse and rider.

19"Do you give the horse his strength
or clothe his neck with a flowing
mane?
20Do you make him leap like a
locust,[y]
striking terror with his proud
snorting?[z]
21He paws fiercely, rejoicing in his
strength,
and charges into the fray.[a]
22He laughs at fear, afraid of nothing;
he does not shy away from the
sword.
23The quiver rattles against his side,
along with the flashing spear and
lance.
24In frenzied excitement he eats up
the ground;
he cannot stand still when the
trumpet sounds.[b]
25At the blast of the trumpet[c] he
snorts, 'Aha!'
He catches the scent of battle
from afar,

38:33 [h]Ps 148:6; Jer 31:36
38:34 [i]Job 22:11; 36:27-28
38:35 [j]Job 36:32; 37:3
38:36 [k]Job 9:4 [l]Job 32:8; Ps 51:6; Ecc 2:26
38:39 [m]Ps 104:21
38:40 [n]Job 37:8
38:41 [o]Lk 12:24 [p]Ps 147:9; Mt 6:26
39:1 [q]Dt 14:5
39:5 [r]Job 6:5; 11:12; 24:5
39:6 [s]Job 24:5; Ps 107:34; Jer 2:24 [t]Hos 8:9
39:7 [u]Job 3:18
39:9 [v]Nu 23:22; Dt 33:17
39:16 [w]La 4:3
39:17 [x]Job 35:11
39:20 [y]Joel 2:4-5 [z]Jer 8:16
39:21 [a]Jer 8:6
39:24 [b]Jer 4:5,19; Eze 7:14; Am 3:6
39:25 [c]Jos 6:5

[a]*32* Or *out Leo* [b]*33* Or *his*; or *their*
[c]*36* The meaning of the Hebrew for this word is uncertain.

the shout of commanders and
the battle cry.[d]
26"Does the hawk take flight by your
wisdom
and spread his wings toward the
south?
27Does the eagle soar at your
command
and build his nest on high?[e]
28He dwells on a cliff and stays there
at night;
a rocky crag is his stronghold.
29From there he seeks out his food;[f]
his eyes detect it from afar.
30His young ones feast on blood,
and where the slain are, there is
he."[g]

40 The LORD said to Job:[h]
2"Will the one who contends with
the Almighty correct him?
Let him who accuses God answer
him!"

3Then Job answered the LORD:
4"I am unworthy[i]—how can I
reply to you?
I put my hand over my mouth.[j]
5I spoke once, but I have no
answer[k]—
twice, but I will say no more."[l]

6Then the LORD spoke to Job out of
the storm:[m]

7"Brace yourself like a man;
I will question you,
and you shall answer me.[n]

8"Would you discredit my justice?[o]
Would you condemn me to
justify yourself?
9Do you have an arm like God's,[p]
and can your voice thunder like
his?[q]
10Then adorn yourself with glory and
splendor,
and clothe yourself in honor and
majesty.[r]
11Unleash the fury of your wrath,[s]
look at every proud man and
bring him low,[t]
12look at every proud man and
humble him,[u]
crush[v] the wicked where they
stand.
13Bury them all in the dust together;
shroud their faces in the grave.
14Then I myself will admit to you
that your own right hand can
save you.[w]

15"Look at the behemoth,[a]
which I made along with you
and which feeds on grass like an
ox.
16What strength he has in his loins,
what power in the muscles of his
belly!
17His tail[b] sways like a cedar;
the sinews of his thighs are
close-knit.
18His bones are tubes of bronze,
his limbs like rods of iron.
19He ranks first among the works of
God,[x]
yet his Maker can approach him
with his sword.
20The hills bring him their
produce,[y]
and all the wild animals play[z]
nearby.
21Under the lotus plants he lies,
hidden among the reeds in the
marsh.
22The lotuses conceal him in their
shadow;
the poplars by the stream[a]
surround him.
23When the river rages, he is not
alarmed;
he is secure, though the Jordan
should surge against his
mouth.
24Can anyone capture him by the
eyes,[c]
or trap him and pierce his
nose?[b]

41 "Can you pull in the leviathan[d][c]
with a fishhook

39:25 [d]Am 1:14; 2:2 **39:27** [e]Jer 49:16; Ob 1:4 **39:29** [f]Job 9:26 **39:30** [g]Mt 24:28; Lk 17:37 **40:1** [h]Job 10:2; 13:3; 23:4; 31:35; 33:13 **40:4** [i]Job 42:6 [j]Job 29:9 **40:5** [k]Job 9:3 [l]Job 9:15 **40:6** [m]Job 38:1 **40:7** [n]Job 38:3; 42:4

40:8 [o]Job 27:2; Ro 3:3 **40:9** [p]2Ch 32:8 [q]Job 37:5; Ps 29:3-4 **40:10** [r]Ps 93:1; 104:1 **40:11** [s]Isa 42:25; Na 1:6 [t]Isa 2:11,12, 17; Da 4:37 **40:12** [u]1Sa 2:7 [v]Isa 13:11; 63:2-3,6 **40:14** [w]Ps 20:6; 60:5; 108:6 **40:19** [x]Job 41:33 **40:20** [y]Ps 104:14 [z]Ps 104:26 **40:22** [a]Isa 44:4 **40:24** [b]Job 41:2,7,26 **41:1** [c]Job 3:8; Ps 104:26; Isa 27:1

40:1–2

PROMISE 1

QUESTIONING GOD

It is not unusual for men to question God. He often acts outside our realm of understanding and contrary to our sense of justice and goodness. We honestly ask, "Lord, what are you *doing* this for?" That's the same question Job asked in this book.

Read these verses carefully. Then go back to 38:4 and start answering the questions God asked Job. If you work through to the end of chapter 41 you will have an exalted (and more accurate) view of God.

Take a few questions at a time. Read them, meditate on them and savor the answers. The answers we get when we question God can lead to worship or cynicism, depending on how we view God. The answers we give to the questions God asked Job will give us better answers to the questions we ask God.

For the next Promise 1 reading go to page 581.

---

a *15* Possibly the hippopotamus or the elephant
b *17* Possibly trunk c *24* Or *by a water hole*
d *1* Possibly the crocodile

or tie down his tongue with a
rope?
2Can you put a cord through his
nose
or pierce his jaw with a hook?[d]
3Will he keep begging you for
mercy?
Will he speak to you with gentle
words?
4Will he make an agreement with
you
for you to take him as your slave
for life?[e]
5Can you make a pet of him like a
bird
or put him on a leash for your
girls?
6Will traders barter for him?
Will they divide him up among
the merchants?
7Can you fill his hide with harpoons
or his head with fishing spears?
8If you lay a hand on him,
you will remember the struggle
and never do it again!
9Any hope of subduing him is false;
the mere sight of him is
overpowering.
10No one is fierce enough to rouse
him.[f]
Who then is able to stand
against me?[g]
11Who has a claim against me that I
must pay?[h]
Everything under heaven belongs
to me.[i]
12"I will not fail to speak of his
limbs,
his strength and his graceful
form.
13Who can strip off his outer coat?
Who would approach him with a
bridle?
14Who dares open the doors of his
mouth,
ringed about with his fearsome
teeth?
15His back has[a] rows of shields
tightly sealed together;
16each is so close to the next
that no air can pass between.
17They are joined fast to one
another;
they cling together and cannot
be parted.
18His snorting throws out flashes of
light;
his eyes are like the rays of
dawn.[j]
19Firebrands stream from his mouth;
sparks of fire shoot out.
20Smoke pours from his nostrils
as from a boiling pot over a fire
of reeds.
21His breath[k] sets coals ablaze,
and flames dart from his
mouth.[l]
22Strength resides in his neck;
dismay goes before him.
23The folds of his flesh are tightly
joined;
they are firm and immovable.
24His chest is hard as rock,
hard as a lower millstone.
25When he rises up, the mighty are
terrified;
they retreat before his thrashing.
26The sword that reaches him has no
effect,
nor does the spear or the dart or
the javelin.
27Iron he treats like straw
and bronze like rotten wood.
28Arrows do not make him flee;
slingstones are like chaff to him.
29A club seems to him but a piece of
straw;
he laughs at the rattling of the
lance.
30His undersides are jagged
potsherds,
leaving a trail in the mud like a
threshing sledge.[m]
31He makes the depths churn like a
boiling caldron
and stirs up the sea like a pot of
ointment.
32Behind him he leaves a glistening
wake;
one would think the deep had
white hair.
33Nothing on earth is his equal[n]—
a creature without fear.
34He looks down on all that are
haughty;
he is king over all that are
proud.[o]"

Job

42 Then Job replied to the LORD:
2"I know that you can do all
things;[p]
no plan of yours can be
thwarted.[q]
3⌊You asked,⌋ 'Who is this that
obscures my counsel
without knowledge?'[r]
Surely I spoke of things I did not
understand,
things too wonderful for me to
know.[s]
4⌊"You said,⌋ 'Listen now, and I will
speak;
I will question you,
and you shall answer me.'[t]
5My ears had heard of you[u]

41:2 [d]Isa 37:29
41:4 [e]Ex 21:6
41:10 [f]Job 3:8 [g]Jer 50:44
41:11 [h]Ro 11:35 [i]Ex 19:5; Dt 10:14; Ps 24:1; 50:12; 1Co 10:26
41:18 [j]Job 3:9
41:21 [k]Isa 40:7 [l]Ps 18:8
41:30 [m]Isa 41:15
41:33 [n]Job 40:19
41:34 [o]Job 28:8
42:2 [p]Ge 18:14; Mt 19:26 [q]2Ch 20:6
42:3 [r]Job 38:2 [s]Ps 40:5; 131:1; 139:6
42:4 [t]Job 38:3; 40:7
42:5 [u]Job 26:14; Ro 10:17

a 15 Or *His pride is his*

but now my eyes have seen
you.[v]
6Therefore I despise myself[w]
and repent in dust and ashes."[x]

Epilogue

7After the LORD had said these things to Job, he said to Eliphaz the Temanite, "I am angry with you and your two friends,[y] because you have not spoken of me what is right, as my servant Job has. 8So now take seven bulls and seven rams[z] and go to my servant Job and sacrifice a burnt offering[a] for yourselves. My servant Job will pray for you, and I will accept his prayer[b] and not deal with you according to your folly.[c] You have not spoken of me what is right, as my servant Job has." 9So Eliphaz the Temanite, Bildad the Shuhite and Zophar the Naamathite did what the LORD told them; and the LORD accepted Job's prayer.

10After Job had prayed for his friends, the LORD made him prosperous again[d] and gave him twice as much as he had before.[e] 11All his brothers and sisters and everyone who had known him before[f] came and ate with him in his house. They comforted and consoled him over all the trouble the LORD had brought upon him, and each one gave him a piece of silver[a] and a gold ring.

2 →PG. 597

12The LORD blessed the latter part of Job's life more than the first. He had fourteen thousand sheep, six thousand camels, a thousand yoke of oxen and a thousand donkeys. 13And he also had seven sons and three daughters. 14The first daughter he named Jemimah, the second Keziah and the third Keren-Happuch. 15Nowhere in all the land were there found women as beautiful as Job's daughters, and their father granted them an inheritance along with their brothers.

16After this, Job lived a hundred and forty years; he saw his children and their children to the fourth generation. 17And so he died, old and full of years.[g]

42:5 [v]Jdg 13:22; Isa 6:5; Eph 1:17-18 **42:6** [w]Job 40:4 [x]Ezr 9:6 **42:7** [y]Job 32:3 **42:8** [z]Nu 23:1,29 [a]Job 1:5 [b]Ge 20:17; Jas 5:15-16; 1Jn 5:16 [c]Job 22:30 **42:10** [d]Dt 30:3; Ps 14:7 [e]Job 1:3; Ps 85:1-3; 126:5-6 **42:11** [f]Job 19:13 **42:17** [g]Ge 15:15; 25:8

[a] 11 Hebrew *him a kesitah*; a kesitah was a unit of money of unknown weight and value.

42:1-6

PROMISE 1

THE END OF THE ORDEAL

Job ended his ordeal a better man than he started (and he started well). God allowed his faith to be tested—severely. Job struggled—terribly. God helped him—graciously. Job came through—triumphantly.

The key? Check out verses 3 and 4. Job learned when to listen and when to talk. "Everyone should be quick to listen, slow to speak and slow to become angry" (James 1:19). That's good advice that Job learned the hard way. You don't have to.

For the next Promise 1 reading go to page 585.

42:7-10

PROMISE 6

FORGIVENESS PLUS PRAYER

God forgave Job's friends because they offered a sacrifice and because Job prayed for them. Reconciliation goes further than forgiveness; it involves prayer for those who violate you. Job's friends' well-being (v. 8) and his own (v. 10) were based on his prayer for those who made his life miserable.

Consider this view of forgiveness and reconciliation. Forgive those who have wronged you *and* pray for their restoration to God and their well-being. It takes a good and godly man to do so. Think about it.

For the next Promise 6 reading go to page 665.

PSALMS

AT A GLANCE

Key Principle: The God of Abraham, Isaac and Jacob, the Ruler of all creation, is worthy of all blessing, honor and praise because of who he is and what he has done.
Author: David (73 psalms), Asaph (12 psalms), sons of Korah (10 psalms), Solomon (2 psalms), Moses (1 psalm), Heman (1 psalm), Ethan (1 psalm), anonymous (50 psalms)
Time and Place: ~1410 B.C. to 430 B.C. / Israel
Key Verses: 19:14; 145:21

BENEFIT

The Book of Psalms, also called the "Psalter," is actually five books in one. The New Testament quotes this compilation of Hebrew songs more than any other book. Its power, beauty and depiction of the whole range of human emotions—from anger and fear to joy and delight—have made it the most comforting and relevant book of the Bible for generations of believers. Each of the psalms teaches us about God's character and his ways, and about how we should respond to the variety of circumstances we encounter. The psalms show us how to praise and worship God in good times and difficult times, and call us to put our hope in God instead of other people or our own resources.

SETTING

The five books of psalms stretch back to the time of Moses (Psalm 90, ~1410 B.C.) and forward to the time of Ezra and Nehemiah after the Babylonian exile (Psalm 126, ~430 B.C.). Many psalms were originally incorporated in Israel's temple worship as songs that were sung antiphonally. Although the psalms were composed and collected over many centuries, a number of smaller psalm anthologies gradually made their way into the final five-book Psalter. The psalm compilers included David (1 Chronicles 15:16), Hezekiah (2 Chronicles 29:30) and Ezra (Nehemiah 8). David wrote 73 psalms, several of which have superscriptions that relate them to specific events in David's life. The anonymous Psalms 2 and 95 are also Davidic, according to the New Testament.

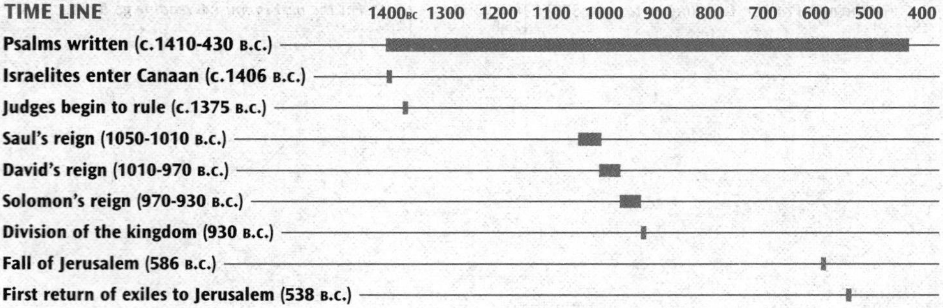

THEME AND PURPOSE

Worship is the primary theme that runs throughout the book of Psalms. The temple liturgy David instituted featured singing hymns of praise, worship and thanksgiving to the infinite and personal God who created all things and called Israel to be his people. The Psalter was designed to be a devotional guide for individuals, families and the community as a whole. It assisted God's people in responding to his truth, his character and his acts of redemption and deliverance. The psalms review God's mighty work in the past, his loving kindness in the present and the hope of his everlasting care in the future. They also encourage readers to trust in the Lord during times of adversity.

UNIQUE CONTRIBUTION

Psalms is the largest and most widely used book in Scripture. It touches hearts and emotions more than any other book in the Bible; it provides comfort, encouragement and perspective in times of sorrow, and it amplifies our adoration and thanksgiving in times of blessing. Not only was it central to Israel's communal worship, but it also played a key role in early New Testament church worship (1 Corinthians 14:26; Ephesians 5:19; Colossians 3:16). Judging by Jesus' frequent use of the psalms, it may have been his favorite portion of Scripture. He often incorporated the psalms in his teaching and in his responses to the Jewish leaders.

LINKS TO THE NEW TESTAMENT

Many psalms anticipate Christ as the coming Servant who would shepherd his people and suffer on their behalf (22, 41, 69), as well as the coming King who would establish an eternal kingdom (24, 47,110). Some scholars have linked Christ to the psalms using the following terms. *Typical Messianic* psalms portray types of Christ (34:20; 69:4,9). *Indirectly Messianic* psalms relate to the royal line of David, but are ultimately fulfilled in Christ (2, 45, 72). *Purely prophetic* psalms speak only of Christ rather than a person who typifies Christ (110). *Typical prophetic* psalms use language that points beyond the psalmist's experience and toward the Messiah to come (22). *Enthronement* psalms look ahead to the consummation of God's kingdom, which will be fulfilled in the reign of Messiah (96—99).

OVERVIEW

FIVE BOOKS	Book 1	Book 2	Book 3	Book 4	Book 5
REFERENCE	1 41	42 72	73 89	90 106	107 150
GENERAL CONTENT	Songs of Worship	Hymns Concerning Israel		Songs of Praise	
PRIMARY AUTHOR	David	David/Sons of Korah	Asaph	Anonymous	David/Anonymous
CONCLUDING DOXOLOGY	41:13	72:18-19	89:52	106:48	150:1-6
POSSIBLE EDITOR AND TIME OF COMPILATION	David ~1020–970 B.C.	Hezekiah or Josiah ~970–610 B.C.		Ezra or Nehemiah ~430 B.C.	
LOCATION	Israel				
TIME	~1000 Years				

Each of the five books of Psalms is a unit that concludes with a doxology, and the final doxology (Psalm 150) applies to the entire Psalter. While the psalms have been classified in several ways, the most basic classification is that of petition, thanksgiving and praise (1 Chronicles 16:4).

Under the category of petition, there are two types of lament psalms: individual and communal. The *individual lament* psalms (e.g., 3—7, 25—28, 38—40, 69—71, 109, 140—143) are the most common, and usually include a call to God, a lament, a confession of trust in

God, a petition and a declaration or vow of praise. The *communal lament* psalms (e.g., 44, 60, 79—80, 90, 123) follow the same pattern but apply to the nation rather than to an individual.

Psalms of thanksgiving are also categorized as individual or communal. The *individual thanksgiving* psalms (e.g., 18, 30, 34, 40—41, 106, 138) usually include a proclamation of praise, a summary statement, a report of what God has done and a renewed vow of praise. The *communal thanksgiving* psalms (e.g., 124, 129) follow the same pattern but apply to the nation as a whole.

Psalms of praise are categorized as general or descriptive. The *general praise* psalms (e.g., 8, 19, 103—104, 139, 150) glorify God by proclaiming his greatness. The *descriptive praise* psalms (e.g., 33, 36, 105, 113, 117, 136, 147) glorify God by describing his attributes and works.

The Psalter also contains *enthronement* psalms that describe God's sovereign rule (e.g., 96—99), *pilgrimage songs* that pilgrims sang as they went to Jerusalem to worship (e.g., 46, 76, 87, 120—134), *royal* psalms that focus on the reign of the earthly and heavenly king (e.g., 2, 18, 45, 72, 110, 132, 144) and *wisdom* psalms that instruct the reader in the way of righteousness (e.g., 1, 37, 119).

PSALMS

BOOK I

Psalms 1–41

Psalm 1

1 →PG. 586
3 →PG. 586

1 Blessed is the man
who does not walk[a] in the
counsel of the wicked
or stand in the way of sinners
or sit[b] in the seat of mockers.
2 But his delight[c] is in the law of
the LORD,[d]
and on his law he meditates[e]
day and night.
3 He is like a tree[f] planted by
streams of water,[g]
which yields its fruit[h] in season
and whose leaf does not wither.
Whatever he does prospers.[i]

4 Not so the wicked!
They are like chaff[j]
that the wind blows away.
5 Therefore the wicked will not
stand[k] in the judgment,[l]
nor sinners in the assembly of
the righteous.
6 For the LORD watches over[m] the
way of the righteous,
but the way of the wicked will
perish.[n]

Psalm 2

1 Why do the nations conspire[a]
and the peoples plot[o] in vain?
2 The kings[p] of the earth take their
stand
and the rulers gather together
against the LORD
and against his Anointed[q]
One.[b][r]
3 "Let us break their chains," they
say,
"and throw off their fetters."[s]

4 The One enthroned in heaven
laughs;[t]
the Lord scoffs at them.
5 Then he rebukes them in his anger
and terrifies them in his wrath,[u]
saying,
6 "I have installed my King[c]
on Zion, my holy hill."

7 I will proclaim the decree of the
LORD:

He said to me, "You are my Son[d];
today I have become your
Father.[e][v]
8 Ask of me,
and I will make the nations your
inheritance,
the ends of the earth[w] your
possession.
9 You will rule them with an iron
scepter[f];[x]
you will dash them to pieces[y]
like pottery.[z]"

10 Therefore, you kings, be wise;
be warned, you rulers of the
earth.
11 Serve the LORD with fear
and rejoice[a] with trembling.[b]
12 Kiss the Son,[c] lest he be angry
and you be destroyed in your
way,
for his wrath[d] can flare up in a
moment.
Blessed are all who take refuge[e]
in him.

[a] *1* Hebrew; Septuagint *rage* [b] *2* Or *anointed one* [c] *6* Or *king* [d] *7* Or *son*; also in verse 12 [e] *7* Or *have begotten you* [f] *9* Or *will break them with a rod of iron*

1:1 [a]Pr 4:14 [b]Ps 26:4; Jer 15:17 **1:2** [c]Ps 119:16,35 [d]Ps 119:1 [e]Jos 1:8 **1:3** [f]Ps 128:3 [g]Jer 17:8 [h]Eze 47:12 [i]Ge 39:3 **1:4** [j]Job 21:18; Isa 17:13 **1:5** [k]Ps 5:5 [l]Ps 9:7-8,16 **1:6** [m]Ps 37:18; 2Ti 2:19 [n]Ps 9:6 **2:1** [o]Ps 21:11 **2:2** [p]Ps 48:4 [q]Jn 1:41 [r]Ps 74:18,23; Ac 4:25-26* **2:3** [s]Jer 5:5 **2:4** [t]Ps 37:13; 59:8; Pr 1:26 **2:5** [u]Ps 21:9; 78:49-50 **2:7** [v]Ac 13:33*; Heb 1:5* **2:8** [w]Ps 22:27 **2:9** [x]Rev 12:5 [y]Ps 89:23 [z]Rev 2:27* **2:11** [a]Heb 12:28 [b]Ps 119:119-120 **2:12** [c]Jn 5:23 [d]Rev 6:16 [e]Ps 34:8; Ro 9:33

1:3

PROMISE 1

LIKE A TREE?

Oh boy! Bet you've always wanted to be like a tree. What in the world was the psalmist saying here?

To excite us about avoiding sin and pursuing God's Word, the writer used four images to explain what happens to the man God blesses. A tree planted by a stream is *stable*. Its roots are deeply embedded in the rich earth and irrigated by the stream. It is *productive*. Season after season it produces the fruit God intended for it to produce. It is *consistent*. When the vegetation around it withers and wilts under the heat of the summer sun, this tree is healthy. In the fourth image the psalmist switched to people instead of trees and summarized what happens when God blesses a man. Whatever he does *prospers* under God's good hand. These are outcomes in the life of a man who avoids sin (v. 1) and pursues God's Word (v. 2).

Think back over the past week and ask yourself what you did when temptation assaulted you. Look over your schedule and ask how much time you spent in the Bible. The psalmist tells us that the four important outcomes in our life, outlined above, are linked to what we discover by asking these two questions.

For the next Promise 1 reading go to page 590.

Psalm 3

A psalm of David. When he fled from his son Absalom.[f]

1 O LORD, how many are my foes!
How many rise up against me!
2 Many are saying of me,
"God will not deliver him.[g]"
Selah[a]
3 But you are a shield[h] around me,
O LORD;
you bestow glory on me and
lift[b] up my head.[i]
4 To the LORD I cry aloud,
and he answers me from his holy
hill.[j] *Selah*
5 I lie down and sleep;[k]
I wake again, because the LORD
sustains me.
6 I will not fear[l] the tens of
thousands
drawn up against me on every
side.

7 Arise,[m] O LORD!
Deliver me,[n] O my God!
Strike[o] all my enemies on the jaw;
break the teeth[p] of the wicked.

8 From the LORD comes
deliverance.[q]
May your blessing be on your
people. *Selah*

Psalm 4

For the director of music. With stringed instruments. A psalm of David.

1 Answer me when I call to you,
O my righteous God.
Give me relief from my distress;
be merciful[r] to me and hear my
prayer.[s]

2 How long, O men, will you turn my
glory into shame[c]?
How long will you love delusions
and seek false gods[d]?[t]
Selah

3 Know that the LORD has set apart
the godly[u] for himself;
the LORD will hear[v] when I call
to him.

3 →PG. 591
4 In your anger do not sin;[w]
when you are on your beds,[x]
search your hearts and be silent.
Selah
5 Offer right sacrifices
and trust in the LORD.[y]

6 Many are asking, "Who can show
us any good?"
Let the light of your face shine
upon us,[z] O LORD.
7 You have filled my heart[a] with
greater joy[b]
than when their grain and new
wine abound.
8 I will lie down and sleep[c] in
peace,
for you alone, O LORD,
make me dwell in safety.[d]
1 →PG. 586

Psalm 5

For the director of music. For flutes. A psalm of David.

1 Give ear to my words, O LORD,
consider my sighing.
2 Listen to my cry for help,[e]
my King and my God,[f]
for to you I pray.
3 In the morning,[g] O LORD, you hear
my voice;
in the morning I lay my requests
before you
and wait in expectation.

4 You are not a God who takes
pleasure in evil;
with you the wicked[h] cannot
dwell.
5 The arrogant[i] cannot stand[j] in
your presence;
you hate[k] all who do wrong.
6 You destroy those who tell lies;[l]
bloodthirsty and deceitful men
the LORD abhors.

7 But I, by your great mercy,
will come into your house;
in reverence will I bow down[m]
toward your holy temple.
1 →PG. 589
8 Lead me, O LORD, in your
righteousness[n]
because of my enemies—
make straight your way[o] before
me.

9 Not a word from their mouth can
be trusted;
their heart is filled with
destruction.
Their throat is an open grave;[p]
with their tongue they speak
deceit.[q]
10 Declare them guilty, O God!
Let their intrigues be their
downfall.
Banish them for their many sins,[r]
for they have rebelled[s] against
you.

3 Title [f]2Sa 15:14
3:2 [g]Ps 71:11
3:3 [h]Ge 15:1; Ps 28:7 [i]Ps 27:6
3:4 [j]Ps 2:6
3:5 [k]Lev 26:6; Pr 3:24
3:6 [l]Ps 27:3
3:7 [m]Ps 7:6 [n]Ps 6:4 [o]Job 16:10 [p]Ps 58:6
3:8 [q]Isa 43:3,11
4:1 [r]Ps 25:16 [s]Ps 17:6
4:2 [t]Ps 31:6
4:3 [u]Ps 31:23 [v]Ps 6:8
4:4 [w]Eph 4:26* [x]Ps 77:6
4:5 [y]Dt 33:19; Ps 37:3
4:6 [z]Nu 6:25
4:7 [a]Ac 14:17 [b]Isa 9:3
4:8 [c]Ps 3:5 [d]Lev 25:18
5:2 [e]Ps 3:4 [f]Ps 84:3
5:3 [g]Ps 88:13
5:4 [h]Ps 11:5; 92:15
5:5 [i]Ps 73:3 [j]Ps 1:5 [k]Ps 11:5
5:6 [l]Ps 55:23; Rev 21:8
5:7 [m]Ps 138:2
5:8 [n]Ps 31:1 [o]Ps 27:11
5:9 [p]Lk 11:44 [q]Ro 3:13*
5:10 [r]Ps 9:16 [s]Ps 107:11

a *2* A word of uncertain meaning, occurring frequently in the Psalms; possibly a musical term **b** *3* Or *LORD, / my Glorious One, who lifts* **c** *2* Or *you dishonor my Glorious One* **d** *2* Or *seek lies*

11But let all who take refuge in you
be glad;
let them ever sing for joy.[t]
Spread your protection over them,
that those who love your name[u]
may rejoice in you.[v]
12For surely, O LORD, you bless the
righteous;
you surround them[w] with your
favor as with a shield.

Psalm 6

For the director of music. With stringed instruments. According to *sheminith*.[a] A psalm of David.

1O LORD, do not rebuke me in your
anger[x]
or discipline me in your wrath.
2Be merciful to me, LORD, for I am
faint;
O LORD, heal me,[y] for my bones
are in agony.[z]
3My soul is in anguish.[a]
How long,[b] O LORD, how long?

4Turn, O LORD, and deliver me;
save me because of your
unfailing love.[c]
5No one remembers you when he is
dead.
Who praises you from the
grave[b]?[d]

6I am worn out[e] from groaning;
all night long I flood my bed
with weeping
and drench my couch with
tears.[f]
7My eyes grow weak[g] with sorrow;
they fail because of all my foes.

8Away from me,[h] all you who do
evil,[i]
for the LORD has heard my
weeping.
9The LORD has heard my cry for
mercy;[j]
the LORD accepts my prayer.
10All my enemies will be ashamed
and dismayed;
they will turn back in sudden
disgrace.[k]

Psalm 7

A *shiggaion*[c] of David, which he sang to the LORD concerning Cush, a Benjamite.

1O LORD my God, I take refuge in
you;
save and deliver me from all who
pursue me,[l]
2or they will tear me like a lion[m]
and rip me to pieces with no one
to rescue[n] me.

3O LORD my God, if I have done this
and there is guilt on my
hands[o]—
4if I have done evil to him who is at
peace with me
or without cause have robbed
my foe—
5then let my enemy pursue and
overtake me;
let him trample my life to the
ground
and make me sleep in the dust.
Selah

6Arise,[p] O LORD, in your anger;
rise up against the rage of my
enemies.[q]
Awake,[r] my God; decree justice.
7Let the assembled peoples gather
around you.
Rule over them from on high;
8 let the LORD judge the peoples.
Judge me, O LORD, according to my
righteousness,[s]
according to my integrity,
O Most High.
9O righteous God,[t]
who searches minds and
hearts,[u]
bring to an end the violence of the
wicked
and make the righteous secure.[v]

10My shield[d] is God Most High,
who saves the upright in heart.[w]
11God is a righteous judge,[x]
a God who expresses his wrath
every day.
12If he does not relent,
he[e] will sharpen his sword;[y]
he will bend and string his bow.
13He has prepared his deadly
weapons;
he makes ready his flaming
arrows.

14He who is pregnant with evil
and conceives trouble gives
birth[z] to disillusionment.
15He who digs a hole and scoops it
out
falls into the pit he has made.[a]
16The trouble he causes recoils on
himself;
his violence comes down on his
own head.

17I will give thanks to the LORD
because of his
righteousness[b]

5:11 [t]Ps 2:12 [u]Ps 69:36 [v]Isa 65:13 **5:12** [w]Ps 32:7 **6:1** [x]Ps 38:1 **6:2** [y]Hos 6:1 [z]Ps 22:14; 31:10 **6:3** [a]Jn 12:27 [b]Ps 90:13 **6:4** [c]Ps 17:13 **6:5** [d]Ps 30:9; 88:10-12; Ecc 9:10; Isa 38:18 **6:6** [e]Ps 69:3 [f]Ps 42:3 **6:7** [g]Ps 31:9 **6:8** [h]Ps 119:115 [i]Mt 7:23; Lk 13:27 **6:9** [j]Ps 116:1 **6:10** [k]Ps 71:24; 73:19 **7:1** [l]Ps 31:15 **7:2** [m]Isa 38:13 [n]Ps 50:22 **7:3** [o]1Sa 24:11; Isa 59:3 **7:6** [p]Ps 94:2 [q]Ps 138:7 [r]Ps 44:23 **7:8** [s]Ps 18:20; 96:13 **7:9** [t]Jer 11:20 [u]1Ch 28:9; Ps 26:2; Rev 2:23 [v]Ps 37:23 **7:10** [w]Ps 125:4 **7:11** [x]Ps 50:6 **7:12** [y]Dt 32:41 **7:14** [z]Job 15:35; Isa 59:4; Jas 1:15 **7:15** [a]Job 4:8 **7:17** [b]Ps 71:15-16

[a]Title: Probably a musical term [b]5 Hebrew *Sheol* [c]Title: Probably a literary or musical term [d]10 Or *sovereign* [e]12 Or *If a man does not repent, / God*

and will sing praise[c] to the
name of the LORD Most
High.

Psalm 8

For the director of music. According
to *gittith*.[a] A psalm of David.

1 O LORD, our Lord,
how majestic is your name in all
the earth!

You have set your glory
above the heavens.[d]
2 From the lips of children and
infants
you have ordained praise[b][e]
because of your enemies,
to silence the foe[f] and the
avenger.
3 When I consider your heavens,[g]
the work of your fingers,
the moon and the stars,[h]
which you have set in place,
4 what is man that you are mindful
of him,
the son of man that you care for
him?[i]
5 You made him a little lower than
the heavenly beings[c]
and crowned him with glory and
honor.[j]

8:3–7

PROMISE 7

CREATION'S CARETAKERS

The question in verse 4 brings us up short. We ask with the psalmist, "Yes, 'What *is* man that you are mindful of him?'" After contemplating God's majesty and his work displayed in the heavens, the psalmist exclaimed his question: "What in the world makes us so special to you, O God?" The answer lies in the first words of verses 5 and 6: "You made him . . ."

God made us only one level lower than the heavenly beings (v. 5) and made us stewards of his earthly creation (vv. 6–8). This truth demands some think time. *We* are rulers over the works of God's hands? All the creatures of the earth are under *our* care? A man can't save all the endangered species by himself, but he can be careful of any part of God's creation he does touch. The fact that men and women are caretakers of God's creation carries enormous responsibility. List some things you can do this week to act out your role as a steward of God's creation.

For the next Promise 7 reading go to page 677.

6 You made him ruler[k] over the
works of your hands;
you put everything under his
feet:[l][m]
7 all flocks and herds,
and the beasts of the field,
8 the birds of the air,
and the fish of the sea,
all that swim the paths of the
seas.

9 O LORD, our Lord,
how majestic is your name in all
the earth![n]

Psalm 9[d]

For the director of music. To ⌞the
tune of⌟ "The Death of the Son."
A psalm of David.

1 I will praise you, O LORD, with all
my heart;[o]
I will tell of all your wonders.[p]
2 I will be glad and rejoice[q] in you;
I will sing praise to your name,[r]
O Most High.

3 My enemies turn back;
they stumble and perish before
you.
4 For you have upheld my right and
my cause;[s]
you have sat on your throne,
judging righteously.[t]
5 You have rebuked the nations and
destroyed the wicked;
you have blotted out their
name[u] for ever and ever.
6 Endless ruin has overtaken the
enemy,
you have uprooted their cities;
even the memory of them[v] has
perished.

7 The LORD reigns forever;
he has established his throne[w]
for judgment.
8 He will judge the world in
righteousness;[x]
he will govern the peoples with
justice.
9 The LORD is a refuge for the
oppressed,
a stronghold in times of
trouble.[y]
10 Those who know your name[z] will
trust in you,
for you, LORD, have never
forsaken[a] those who seek
you.

7 →PG. 627

7:17 [c]Ps 9:2
8:1 [d]Ps 57:5; 113:4; 148:13
8:2 [e]Mt 21:16* [f]Ps 44:16; 1Co 1:27
8:3 [g]Ps 89:11 [h]Ps 136:9
8:4 [i]Job 7:17; Ps 144:3; Heb 2:6
8:5 [j]Ps 21:5; 103:4
8:6 [k]Ge 1:28 [l]Heb 2:6-8* [m]1Co 15:25, 27*; Eph 1:22
8:9 [n]ver 1
9:1 [o]Ps 86:12 [p]Ps 26:7
9:2 [q]Ps 5:11 [r]Ps 92:1; 83:18
9:4 [s]Ps 140:12 [t]1Pe 2:23
9:5 [u]Pr 10:7
9:6 [v]Ps 34:16
9:7 [w]Ps 89:14
9:8 [x]Ps 96:13
9:9 [y]Ps 32:7
9:10 [z]Ps 91:14 [a]Ps 37:28

[a]Title: Probably a musical term [b]2 Or *strength* [c]5 Or *than God* [d]Psalms 9 and 10 may have been originally a single acrostic poem, the stanzas of which begin with the successive letters of the Hebrew alphabet. In the Septuagint they constitute one psalm.

11 Sing praises to the LORD, enthroned
in Zion;[b]
proclaim among the nations[c]
what he has done.[d]
12 For he who avenges blood[e]
remembers;
he does not ignore the cry of the
afflicted.

13 O LORD, see how my enemies[f]
persecute me!
Have mercy and lift me up from
the gates of death,
14 that I may declare your praises[g]
in the gates of the Daughter of
Zion
and there rejoice in your
salvation.[h]
15 The nations have fallen into the pit
they have dug;[i]
their feet are caught in the net
they have hidden.[j]
16 The LORD is known by his justice;
the wicked are ensnared by the
work of their hands.
Higgaion.[a] *Selah*
17 The wicked return to the grave,[b][k]
all the nations that forget God.[l]
18 But the needy will not always be
forgotten,
nor the hope[m] of the afflicted[n]
ever perish.

19 Arise, O LORD, let not man triumph;
let the nations be judged in your
presence.
20 Strike them with terror, O LORD;
let the nations know they are but
men.[o] *Selah*

Psalm 10[c]

1 Why, O LORD, do you stand far
off?[p]
Why do you hide yourself[q] in
times of trouble?

2 In his arrogance the wicked man
hunts down the weak,
who are caught in the schemes
he devises.
3 He boasts[r] of the cravings of his
heart;
he blesses the greedy and reviles
the LORD.
4 In his pride the wicked does not
seek him;
in all his thoughts there is no
room for God.[s]
5 His ways are always prosperous;
he is haughty and your laws are
far from him;
he sneers at all his enemies.
6 He says to himself, "Nothing will
shake me;
I'll always be happy[t] and never
have trouble."
7 His mouth is full of curses[u] and
lies and threats;[v]
trouble and evil are under his
tongue.[w]
8 He lies in wait near the villages;
from ambush he murders the
innocent,[x]
watching in secret for his
victims.
9 He lies in wait like a lion in
cover;
he lies in wait to catch the
helpless;[y]
he catches the helpless and
drags them off in his net.
10 His victims are crushed, they
collapse;
they fall under his strength.
11 He says to himself, "God has
forgotten;[z]
he covers his face and never
sees."

12 Arise, LORD! Lift up your hand,[a]
O God.
Do not forget the helpless.[b]
13 Why does the wicked man revile
God?
Why does he say to himself,
"He won't call me to account"?
14 But you, O God, do see trouble[c]
and grief;
you consider it to take it in
hand.
The victim commits himself to
you;[d]
you are the helper[e] of the
fatherless.
15 Break the arm of the wicked and
evil man;[f]
call him to account for his
wickedness
that would not be found out.

16 The LORD is King for ever and
ever;[g]
the nations[h] will perish from his
land.
17 You hear, O LORD, the desire of the
afflicted;[i]
you encourage them, and you
listen to their cry,
18 defending the fatherless[j] and the
oppressed,[k]
in order that man, who is of the
earth, may terrify no more.

1 →PG. 592

9:11 [b]Ps 76:2 [c]Ps 107:22 [d]Ps 105:1 **9:12** [e]Ge 9:5 **9:13** [f]Ps 38:19 **9:14** [g]Ps 106:2 [h]Ps 13:5; 51:12 **9:15** [i]Ps 7:15-16 [j]Ps 35:8; 57:6 **9:17** [k]Ps 49:14 [l]Job 8:13; Ps 50:22 **9:18** [m]Ps 71:5; Pr 23:18 [n]Ps 12:5 **9:20** [o]Ps 62:9; Isa 31:3 **10:1** [p]Ps 22:1,11 [q]Ps 13:1 **10:3** [r]Ps 94:4 **10:4** [s]Ps 14:1; 36:1

10:6 [t]Rev 18:7 **10:7** [u]Ro 3:14* [v]Ps 73:8 [w]Ps 140:3 **10:8** [x]Ps 94:6 **10:9** [y]Ps 17:12; 59:3; 140:5 **10:11** [z]Job 22:13 **10:12** [a]Ps 17:7; Mic 5:9 [b]Ps 9:12 **10:14** [c]Ps 22:11 [d]Ps 37:5 [e]Ps 68:5 **10:15** [f]Ps 37:17 **10:16** [g]Ps 29:10 [h]Dt 8:20 **10:17** [i]1Ch 29:18; Ps 34:15 **10:18** [j]Ps 82:3 [k]Ps 9:9

a *16* Or *Meditation*; possibly a musical notation **b** *17* Hebrew *Sheol* **c** Psalms 9 and 10 may have been originally a single acrostic poem, the stanzas of which begin with the successive letters of the Hebrew alphabet. In the Septuagint they constitute one psalm.

Psalm 11

For the director of music. Of David.

1 In the LORD I take refuge.[l]
How then can you say to me:
"Flee like a bird to your mountain.
2 For look, the wicked bend their bows;
they set their arrows[m] against the strings
to shoot from the shadows
at the upright in heart.[n]
3 When the foundations[o] are being destroyed,
what can the righteous do[a]?"

4 The LORD is in his holy temple;[p]
the LORD is on his heavenly throne.[q]
He observes the sons of men;[r]
his eyes examine[s] them.
5 The LORD examines the righteous,[t]
but the wicked[b] and those who love violence
his soul hates.[u]
6 On the wicked he will rain
fiery coals and burning sulfur;[v]
a scorching wind[w] will be their lot.

7 For the LORD is righteous,[x]
he loves justice;[y]
upright men will see his face.[z]

Psalm 12

For the director of music. According to *sheminith*.[c] A psalm of David.

1 Help, LORD, for the godly are no more;[a]
the faithful have vanished from among men.
2 Everyone lies to his neighbor;
their flattering lips speak with deception.[b]

3 May the LORD cut off all flattering lips
and every boastful tongue[c]
4 that says, "We will triumph with our tongues;
we own our lips[d]—who is our master?"

5 "Because of the oppression of the weak
and the groaning of the needy,
I will now arise," says the LORD.
"I will protect them[d] from those who malign them."
6 And the words of the LORD are flawless,[e]
like silver refined in a furnace of clay,
purified seven times.

7 O LORD, you will keep us safe
and protect us from such people forever.[f]
8 The wicked freely strut[g] about
when what is vile is honored among men.

Psalm 13

For the director of music. A psalm of David.

1 How long, O LORD? Will you forget me forever?
How long will you hide your face[h] from me?
2 How long must I wrestle with my thoughts[i]
and every day have sorrow in my heart?
How long will my enemy triumph over me?[j]

3 Look on me and answer,[k] O LORD my God.
Give light to my eyes,[l] or I will sleep in death;[m]
4 my enemy will say, "I have overcome him,[n]"

11:1 [l]Ps 56:11 **11:2** [m]Ps 7:13 [n]Ps 64:3-4 **11:3** [o]Ps 82:5 **11:4** [p]Ps 18:6 [q]Ps 103:19 [r]Ps 33:13 [s]Ps 34:15-16 **11:5** [t]Ge 22:1; Jas 1:12 [u]Ps 5:5 **11:6** [v]Eze 38:22 [w]Jer 4:11-12 **11:7** [x]Ps 7:9,11; 45:7 [y]Ps 33:5 [z]Ps 17:15 **12:1** [a]Isa 57:1 **12:2** [b]Ps 10:7; 41:6; 55:21; Ro 16:18 **12:3** [c]Da 7:8; Rev 13:5 **12:5** [d]Ps 10:18; 34:6 **12:6** [e]2Sa 22:31; Ps 18:30; Pr 30:5 **12:7** [f]Ps 37:28 **12:8** [g]Ps 55:10-11 **13:1** [h]Job 13:24; Ps 44:24 **13:2** [i]Ps 42:4 [j]Ps 42:9 **13:3** [k]Ps 5:1 [l]Ezr 9:8 [m]Jer 51:39 **13:4** [n]Ps 25:2

[a]3 Or *what is the Righteous One doing* [b]5 Or *The LORD, the Righteous One, examines the wicked, /* [c]Title: Probably a musical term [d]4 Or */ our lips are our plowshares*

13:1–6

PROMISE 1

HOW LONG?

Have you ever been frustrated with God because you asked him for something and he didn't deliver? Most everyone who has asked for God's help has wondered when—or if—he was going to deliver.

Four times in the first two verses of this psalm David asked, "How long?" which basically means, "When are you going to act?" What's amazing about this psalm is not that David was impatient over God's timing but that, without getting any help, he concluded the psalm with statements of trust in God.

Read verses 5 and 6 carefully. Remember that when David prayed this prayer he had asked God for help during a time of serious trouble and God had not acted. Pray that God will develop your faith to the point where you can pray this psalm, asking God for help and then trusting him completely to act in love and care for your best interests.

For the next Promise 1 reading go to page 595.

and my foes will rejoice when I
fall.

5 But I trust in your unfailing love;[o]
my heart rejoices in your
salvation.[p]
6 I will sing[q] to the LORD,
for he has been good to me.

Psalm 14

For the director of music. Of David.

1 The fool[a] says in his heart,
"There is no God."[r]
They are corrupt, their deeds are
vile;
there is no one who does good.
2 The LORD looks down from
heaven[s]
on the sons of men
to see if there are any who
understand,[t]
any who seek God.
3 All have turned aside,
they have together become
corrupt;[u]
there is no one who does good,[v]
not even one.[w]

4 Will evildoers never learn—[x]
those who devour my people[y]
as men eat bread
and who do not call on the
LORD?[z]
5 There they are, overwhelmed with
dread,
for God is present in the
company of the righteous.
6 You evildoers frustrate the plans of
the poor,
but the LORD is their refuge.[a]
7 Oh, that salvation for Israel would
come out of Zion!
When the LORD restores the
fortunes[b] of his people,
let Jacob rejoice and Israel be
glad!

Psalm 15

A psalm of David.

3 →PG. 593

1 LORD, who may dwell in your
sanctuary?[c]
Who may live on your holy
hill?[d]
2 He whose walk is blameless
and who does what is righteous,
who speaks the truth[e] from his
heart
3 and has no slander[f] on his
tongue,
who does his neighbor no wrong

13:5 [o]Ps 52:8 [p]Ps 9:14 **13:6** [q]Ps 116:7 **14:1** [r]Ps 10:4 **14:2** [s]Ps 33:13 [t]Ps 92:6 **14:3** [u]Ps 58:3 [v]Ps 143:2 [w]Ro 3:10-12* **14:4** [x]Ps 82:5 [y]Ps 27:2 [z]Ps 79:6; Isa 64:7 **14:6** [a]Ps 9:9; 40:17 **14:7** [b]Ps 53:6 **15:1** [c]Ps 27:5-6 [d]Ps 24:3-5 **15:2** [e]Ps 24:4; Zec 8:3,16; Eph 4:25 **15:3** [f]Ex 23:1

15:4 [g]Ac 28:10 [h]Jdg 11:35 **15:5** [i]Ex 22:25 [j]Ex 23:8; Dt 16:19 [k]2Pe 1:10 **16:1** [l]Ps 17:8 [m]Ps 7:1

and casts no slur on his
fellowman,
4 who despises a vile man
but honors[g] those who fear the
LORD,
who keeps his oath[h]
even when it hurts,
5 who lends his money without
usury[i]
and does not accept a bribe[j]
against the innocent.

He who does these things
will never be shaken.[k]

Psalm 16

A *miktam*[b] of David.

1 Keep me safe,[l] O God,
for in you I take refuge.[m]

2 I said to the LORD, "You are my
Lord;

[a] *1* The Hebrew words rendered *fool* in Psalms denote one who is morally deficient. [b] Title: Probably a literary or musical term

15:1–5

PROMISE 3

FINDING PEACE AMID PANIC

David attracted pressure like a magnet. Most powerful leaders do. He regularly made life-and-death decisions that affected thousands of people. He was surrounded with temptations. Every day was like running the gauntlet. Imagine David in the rush and crush of life, asking, "How can I dwell in the serenity of your presence, O God?" Many men today know they can't escape life's pressure, but they can find a calm place in the midst of it.

"Who may dwell in your sanctuary? Who may live on your holy hill?" Verses 2–5 give ten specific conditions for living in God's presence no matter where you are. Any man would do well to memorize this psalm as a reminder of what kind of man feels welcome in God's holy presence. Note especially that this man "keeps his oath even when it hurts . . . lends his money without usury and does not accept a bribe against the innocent" (vv. 4–5). God entertains the man whose promise stands regardless of what it costs.

What does it take for a man to renege on his promises? How generous is a man when there is no pay back? How strongly will a man stand against making money off the innocence of the naive? In the pressure of life, God offers his sanctuary to those who feel at home there because their life is consistent with his holiness.

"He who does these things will never be shaken."

For the next Promise 3 reading go to page 679.

apart from you I have no good
thing."[n]
3 As for the saints who are in the
land,[o]
they are the glorious ones in
whom is all my delight.[a]
4 The sorrows[p] of those will
increase
who run after other gods.[q]
I will not pour out their libations of
blood
or take up their names[r] on my
lips.

5 LORD, you have assigned me my
portion[s] and my cup;[t]
you have made my lot secure.
6 The boundary lines have fallen for
me in pleasant places;
surely I have a delightful
inheritance.[u]

7 I will praise the LORD, who
counsels me;[v]
even at night[w] my heart
instructs me.
8 I have set the LORD always before
me.
Because he is at my right
hand,[x]
I will not be shaken.

9 Therefore my heart is glad[y] and
my tongue rejoices;
my body also will rest secure,[z]
10 because you will not abandon me
to the grave,[b]
nor will you let your Holy One[c]
see decay.[a]

11 You have made[d] known to me the
path of life;[b]
you will fill me with joy in your
presence,[c]
with eternal pleasures[d] at your
right hand.

Psalm 17

A prayer of David.

1 Hear, O LORD, my righteous plea;
listen to my cry.[e]
Give ear to my prayer—
it does not rise from deceitful
lips.[f]
2 May my vindication come from
you;
may your eyes see what is right.
3 Though you probe my heart and
examine me at night,
though you test me,[g] you will
find nothing;[h]
I have resolved that my mouth
will not sin.[i]
4 As for the deeds of men—
by the word of your lips
I have kept myself
from the ways of the violent.
5 My steps have held to your
paths;[j]
my feet have not slipped.[k]

1 →PG. 594

6 I call on you, O God, for you will
answer me;[l]
give ear to me[m] and hear my
prayer.[n]
7 Show the wonder of your great
love,[o]
you who save by your right
hand[p]
those who take refuge in you
from their foes.
8 Keep me as the apple of your
eye;[q]
hide me in the shadow of your
wings
9 from the wicked who assail me,
from my mortal enemies who
surround me.[r]

10 They close up their callous
hearts,[s]
and their mouths speak with
arrogance.[t]
11 They have tracked me down, they
now surround me,[u]
with eyes alert, to throw me to
the ground.
12 They are like a lion[v] hungry for
prey,
like a great lion crouching in
cover.

13 Rise up, O LORD, confront them,
bring them down;[w]
rescue me from the wicked by
your sword.
14 O LORD, by your hand save me
from such men,
from men of this world[x] whose
reward is in this life.

You still the hunger of those you
cherish;
their sons have plenty,
and they store up wealth[y] for
their children.
15 And I—in righteousness I will see
your face;
when I awake, I will be satisfied
with seeing your likeness.[z]

16:2 *n* Ps 73:25
16:3 *o* Ps 101:6
16:4 *p* Ps 32:10 *q* Ps 106:37-38 *r* Ex 23:13
16:5 *s* Ps 73:26 *t* Ps 23:5
16:6 *u* Ps 78:55; Jer 3:19
16:7 *v* Ps 73:24 *w* Ps 77:6
16:8 *x* Ps 73:23
16:9 *y* Ps 4:7; 30:11 *z* Ps 4:8
16:10 *a* Ac 13:35*
16:11 *b* Mt 7:14 *c* Ac 2:25-28* *d* Ps 36:7-8
17:1 *e* Ps 61:1 *f* Isa 29:13
17:3 *g* Ps 26:2; 66:10 *h* Job 23:10; Jer 50:20 *i* Ps 39:1
17:5 *j* Ps 44:18; 119:133 *k* Ps 18:36
17:6 *l* Ps 86:7 *m* Ps 116:2 *n* Ps 88:2
17:7 *o* Ps 31:21 *p* Ps 20:6
17:8 *q* Dt 32:10
17:9 *r* Ps 31:20; 109:3
17:10 *s* Ps 73:7 *t* 1Sa 2:3
17:11 *u* Ps 37:14; 88:17
17:12 *v* Ps 7:2; 10:9
17:13 *w* Ps 7:12; 22:20; 73:18
17:14 *x* Lk 16:8 *y* Ps 73:3-7
17:15 *z* Nu 12:8; Ps 4:6-7; 16:11; 1Jn 3:2

a *3* Or *As for the pagan priests who are in the land / and the nobles in whom all delight, I said:*
b *10* Hebrew *Sheol* **c** *10* Or *your faithful one*
d *11* Or *You will make*

Psalm 18

For the director of music. Of David the servant of the LORD. He sang to the LORD the words of this song when the LORD delivered him from the hand of all his enemies and from the hand of Saul. He said:

1 I love you, O LORD, my strength.

2 The LORD is my rock,[a] my fortress
and my deliverer;
my God is my rock, in whom I
take refuge.
He is my shield[b] and the horn[a]
of my salvation,[c] my
stronghold.
3 I call to the LORD, who is worthy of
praise,[d]
and I am saved from my
enemies.

4 The cords of death[e] entangled me;
the torrents[f] of destruction
overwhelmed me.
5 The cords of the grave[b] coiled
around me;
the snares of death[g] confronted
me.
6 In my distress I called to the LORD;
I cried to my God for help.
From his temple he heard my
voice;[h]
my cry came before him, into his
ears.

7 The earth trembled and quaked,[i]
and the foundations of the
mountains shook;
they trembled because he was
angry.[j]
8 Smoke rose from his nostrils;
consuming fire[k] came from his
mouth,
burning coals blazed out of it.
9 He parted the heavens and came
down;[l]
dark clouds were under his feet.
10 He mounted the cherubim[m] and
flew;
he soared on the wings of the
wind.[n]
11 He made darkness his covering,[o]
his canopy around him—
the dark rain clouds of the sky.
12 Out of the brightness of his
presence[p] clouds advanced,
with hailstones and bolts of
lightning.[q]
13 The LORD thundered[r] from
heaven;
the voice of the Most High
resounded.[c]
14 He shot his arrows and scattered
⌊the enemies⌋,
great bolts of lightning and
routed them.[s]
15 The valleys of the sea were exposed
and the foundations of the earth
laid bare
at your rebuke,[t] O LORD,
at the blast of breath from your
nostrils.

16 He reached down from on high
and took hold of me;
he drew me out of deep
waters.[u]
17 He rescued me from my powerful
enemy,
from my foes, who were too
strong for me.[v]
18 They confronted me in the day of
my disaster,
but the LORD was my support.[w]
19 He brought me out into a spacious
place;[x]
he rescued me because he
delighted in me.[y]

20 The LORD has dealt with me
according to my
righteousness;
according to the cleanness of my
hands[z] he has rewarded
me.
21 For I have kept the ways of the
LORD;[a]
I have not done evil by turning[b]
from my God.
22 All his laws are before me;[c]
I have not turned away from his
decrees.
23 I have been blameless before him
and have kept myself from sin.
24 The LORD has rewarded me
according to my
righteousness,[d]
according to the cleanness of my
hands in his sight.

25 To the faithful[e] you show yourself
faithful,
to the blameless you show
yourself blameless,
26 to the pure you show yourself pure,
but to the crooked you show
yourself shrewd.[f]
27 You save the humble
but bring low those whose eyes
are haughty.[g]
28 You, O LORD, keep my lamp
burning;
my God turns my darkness into
light.[h]

3 →PG. 598

a *2 Horn* here symbolizes strength.
b *5* Hebrew *Sheol*
c *13* Some Hebrew manuscripts and Septuagint (see also 2 Samuel 22:14); most Hebrew manuscripts *resounded, / amid hailstones and bolts of lightning*

18:2 [a]Ps 19:14 [b]Ps 59:11 [c]Ps 75:10
18:3 [d]Ps 48:1
18:4 [e]Ps 116:3 [f]Ps 124:4
18:5 [g]Ps 116:3
18:6 [h]Ps 34:15
18:7 [i]Jdg 5:4 [j]Ps 68:7-8
18:8 [k]Ps 50:3
18:9 [l]Ps 144:5
18:10 [m]Ps 80:1 [n]Ps 104:3
18:11 [o]Dt 4:11; Ps 97:2
18:12 [p]Ps 104:2 [q]Ps 97:3
18:13 [r]Ps 29:3; 104:7
18:14 [s]Ps 144:6
18:15 [t]Ps 76:6; 106:9
18:16 [u]Ps 144:7
18:17 [v]Ps 35:10
18:18 [w]Ps 59:16
18:19 [x]Ps 31:8 [y]Ps 118:5
18:20 [z]Ps 24:4
18:21 [a]2Ch 34:33 [b]Ps 119:102
18:22 [c]Ps 119:30
18:24 [d]1Sa 26:23
18:25 [e]1Ki 8:32; Ps 62:12; Mt 5:7
18:26 [f]Pr 3:34
18:27 [g]Pr 6:17
18:28 [h]Job 18:6; 29:3

29With your help[i] I can advance
against a troop[a];
with my God I can scale a wall.

1 →PG. 594

30As for God, his way is perfect;[j]
the word of the LORD is
flawless.[k]
He is a shield
for all who take refuge[l] in him.
31For who is God besides the LORD?[m]
And who is the Rock[n] except
our God?
32It is God who arms me with
strength[o]
and makes my way perfect.
33He makes my feet like the feet of a
deer;[p]
he enables me to stand on the
heights.[q]
34He trains my hands for battle;[r]
my arms can bend a bow of
bronze.
35You give me your shield of victory,
and your right hand sustains[s]
me;
you stoop down to make me
great.
36You broaden the path beneath me,
so that my ankles do not turn.

37I pursued my enemies[t] and
overtook them;
I did not turn back till they were
destroyed.
38I crushed them so that they could
not rise;[u]
they fell beneath my feet.[v]
39You armed me with strength for
battle;
you made my adversaries bow at
my feet.
40You made my enemies turn their
backs[w] in flight,
and I destroyed[x] my foes.
41They cried for help, but there was
no one to save them[y]—
to the LORD, but he did not
answer.[z]
42I beat them as fine as dust borne
on the wind;
I poured them out like mud in
the streets.
43You have delivered me from the
attacks of the people;
you have made me the head of
nations;[a]
people I did not know[b] are
subject to me.
44As soon as they hear me, they obey
me;
foreigners[c] cringe before me.
45They all lose heart;
they come trembling from their
strongholds.[d]

46The LORD lives! Praise be to my
Rock!
Exalted be God my Savior![e]
47He is the God who avenges me,
who subdues nations[f] under
me,
48 who saves[g] me from my
enemies.
You exalted me above my foes;
from violent men you rescued
me.
49Therefore I will praise you among
the nations, O LORD;
I will sing[h] praises to your
name.[i]
50He gives his king great victories;
he shows unfailing kindness to
his anointed,
to David[j] and his descendants
forever.[k]

Psalm 19

For the director of music. A psalm
of David.

1 →PG. 599

1The heavens[l] declare[m] the glory
of God;
the skies proclaim the work of
his hands.
2Day after day they pour forth
speech;
night after night they display
knowledge.[n]
3There is no speech or language
where their voice is not heard.[b]
4Their voice[c] goes out into all the
earth,
their words to the ends of the
world.[o]
In the heavens he has pitched a
tent[p] for the sun,
5 which is like a bridegroom
coming forth from his
pavilion,
like a champion rejoicing to run
his course.
6It rises at one end of the heavens
and makes its circuit to the
other;[q]
nothing is hidden from its heat.

7The law of the LORD is perfect,
reviving the soul.[r]
The statutes of the LORD are
trustworthy,[s]
making wise the simple.[t]
8The precepts of the LORD are
right,[u]
giving joy to the heart.
The commands of the LORD are
radiant,
giving light to the eyes.

18:29 [i]Heb 11:34 **18:30** [j]Dt 32:4; Rev 15:3 [k]Ps 12:6 [l]Ps 17:7 **18:31** [m]Dt 32:39; 86:8; Isa 45:5, 6,14,18,21 [n]Dt 32:31; 1Sa 2:2 **18:32** [o]Isa 45:5 **18:33** [p]Hab 3:19 [q]Dt 32:13 **18:34** [r]Ps 144:1 **18:35** [s]Ps 119:116 **18:37** [t]Ps 37:20; 44:5 **18:38** [u]Ps 36:12 [v]Ps 47:3 **18:40** [w]Ps 21:12 [x]Ps 94:23 **18:41** [y]Ps 50:22 [z]Job 27:9; Pr 1:28 **18:43** [a]2Sa 8:1-14 [b]Isa 52:15; 55:5 **18:44** [c]Ps 66:3 **18:45** [d]Mic 7:17 **18:46** [e]Ps 51:14 **18:47** [f]Ps 47:3 **18:48** [g]Ps 59:1 **18:49** [h]Ps 108:1 [i]Ro 15:9* **18:50** [j]Ps 144:10 [k]Ps 89:4 **19:1** [l]Isa 40:22 [m]Ps 50:6; Ro 1:19 **19:2** [n]Ps 74:16 **19:4** [o]Ro 10:18* [p]Ps 104:2 **19:6** [q]Ps 113:3; Ecc 1:5 **19:7** [r]Ps 23:3 [s]Ps 93:5; 111:7 [t]Ps 119:98-100 **19:8** [u]Ps 12:6; 119:128

a29 Or *can run through a barricade* **b**3 Or *They have no speech, there are no words; / no sound is heard from them* **c**4 Septuagint, Jerome and Syriac; Hebrew *line*

9The fear of the LORD is pure,
enduring forever.
The ordinances of the LORD are sure
and altogether righteous.[v]
10They are more precious than gold,[w]
than much pure gold;
they are sweeter than honey,
than honey from the comb.
11By them is your servant warned;
in keeping them there is great reward.

12Who can discern his errors?
Forgive my hidden faults.[x]
13Keep your servant also from willful sins;
may they not rule over me.
Then will I be blameless,
innocent of great transgression.

14May the words of my mouth and
the meditation of my heart
be pleasing[y] in your sight,
O LORD, my Rock[z] and my
Redeemer.[a]

19:9 [v]Ps 119:138, 142 **19:10** [w]Pr 8:10 **19:12** [x]Ps 51:2; 90:8; 139:6 **19:14** [y]Ps 104:34 [z]Ps 18:2 [a]Isa 47:4 **20:1** [b]Ps 46:7,11 [c]Ps 91:14 **20:2** [d]Ps 3:4 **20:3** [e]Ac 10:4 [f]Ps 51:19 **20:4** [g]Ps 21:2; 145:16,19

Psalm 20

For the director of music. A psalm of David.

1May the LORD answer you when
you are in distress;
may the name of the God of
Jacob[b] protect you.[c]
2May he send you help from the
sanctuary[d]
and grant you support from
Zion.
3May he remember[e] all your
sacrifices
and accept your burnt
offerings.[f] *Selah*
4May he give you the desire of your
heart[g]

19:1–14

PROMISE 1

THE GOD WHO SPEAKS

"Can man know God?" That's one of life's most fundamental questions. David's answer in this psalm is a resounding "Yes!" The inescapable evidence of God's reality is all around us. But David isn't offering a philosophical argument to answer the skeptic; he's writing a poem to encourage the saint. In Psalm 19 we discover that God wants us to know him. He reveals himself to us.

David described two sources of information that reveal God. In verses 1–6 he wrote about natural revelation (the created world), and in 7–11, special revelation (God's Word, the Bible). Then David burst forth with his own response to this overwhelming truth in verses 12–14.

Read verses 1 and 2 and notice the words David selected: "declare," "proclaim," "pour forth," "display." David the shepherd boy had spent countless hours in the open fields with his sheep. This brilliant, sensitive soul, lying under the midnight sky with no unnatural light to diminish his view, could see God's universe in all its glory. But David's vision wasn't limited to stars. When he looked up to the heavens on those occasions he saw evidence of his God. Just examine one of the images David used: "Day after day [the heavens] pour forth speech" (v. 2). God is not stingy with his revelation. Information about God *pours* out of what he created. Looking up into the sky is like sitting under Niagara Falls with a bucket. It's as if the black night sky has holes in it through which God pours knowledge about himself. David is encouraging us to use all our senses to know God—use our eyes, our ears; feel the wind, the warm sun. Smell the scents God has designed into the world for our pleasure. Rip off the blinders and bask in knowing God. It's a twenty-four-hour-a-day (v. 2), worldwide (v. 4) experience.

As important and awesome (literally) as this revelation is, God wants us to know him in more specific ways than stars and flowers can speak of him. In verses 7–11 we read of a special revelation where God has used written words to reveal truth about himself: the Bible. Notice again the words he chooses to describe what this revelation does: "renewing," "making wise," "giving joy," "giving light." This book has purpose far beyond dispensing information, even information about God. God didn't give us the Bible so it would be read or preached or taught. He gave it to us to change our lives. Reading the Bible, as important as that is, is never an end in itself. It is always a means to an end: That our life is better because we know and live by God's revealed will.

Work your way through verses 7–11 phrase by phrase, asking what each one means and how you can integrate each claim in your own life. What you'll discover is a powerful argument for meditating on the Scriptures. In fact, verses 12–14 present two advantages of knowing God's Word. First, it keeps us from sin (vv. 12–13). Note the phrases in verses 7–11 that refer to a standard of conduct and the joy related to living a righteous life. But even beyond keeping us out of trouble, God teaches us in his Word how to *please* him. It's a good thing not to offend God, but how much more wonderful that we can actually please him. Read the prayer of verse 14 as your prayer. How can you know what is pleasing to God? God has told you.

God's Word is a guidebook for how to live an aggressively holy life. Reread the statements in verses 7–11 that refer to personal growth. Can anyone expect to live a whole and good life apart from reading and following God's instructions?

For the next Promise 1 reading go to page 597.

and make all your plans succeed.
5We will shout for joy when you are victorious
and will lift up our banners[h] in the name of our God.
May the LORD grant all your requests.[i]

6Now I know that the LORD saves his anointed;[j]
he answers him from his holy heaven
with the saving power of his right hand.
7Some trust in chariots and some in horses,[k]
but we trust in the name of the LORD our God.[l]
8They are brought to their knees and fall,
but we rise up[m] and stand firm.[n]
9O LORD, save the king!
Answer[a] us[o] when we call!

Psalm 21

For the director of music. A psalm of David.

1O LORD, the king rejoices in your strength.
How great is his joy in the victories you give![p]
2You have granted him the desire of his heart[q]
and have not withheld the request of his lips. *Selah*
3You welcomed him with rich blessings
and placed a crown of pure gold[r] on his head.
4He asked you for life, and you gave it to him—
length of days, for ever and ever.[s]
5Through the victories[t] you gave, his glory is great;
you have bestowed on him splendor and majesty.
6Surely you have granted him eternal blessings
and made him glad with the joy[u] of your presence.[v]
7For the king trusts in the LORD;
through the unfailing love of the Most High
he will not be shaken.

8Your hand will lay hold[w] on all your enemies;
your right hand will seize your foes.
9At the time of your appearing
you will make them like a fiery furnace.

20:5 [h]Ps 9:14; 60:4 [i]1Sa 1:17
20:6 [j]Ps 28:8; 41:11; Isa 58:9
20:7 [k]Ps 33:17; Isa 31:1 [l]2Ch 32:8
20:8 [m]Mic 7:8 [n]Ps 37:23
20:9 [o]Ps 3:7; 17:6
21:1 [p]Ps 59:16-17
21:2 [q]Ps 37:4
21:3 [r]2Sa 12:30
21:4 [s]Ps 61:5-6; 91:16; 133:3
21:5 [t]Ps 18:50
21:6 [u]Ps 43:4 [v]1Ch 17:27
21:8 [w]Isa 10:10
21:9 [x]Ps 50:3; La 2:2; Mal 4:1
21:10 [y]Dt 28:18; Ps 37:28
21:11 [z]Ps 2:1 [a]Ps 10:2
21:12 [b]Ps 7:12-13; 18:40
22:1 [c]Mt 27:46*; Mk 15:34* [d]Ps 10:1
22:2 [e]Ps 42:3
22:3 [f]Ps 99:9 [g]Dt 10:21
22:5 [h]Isa 49:23
22:6 [i]Job 25:6; Isa 41:14 [j]Ps 31:11 [k]Isa 49:7; 53:3
22:7 [l]Mt 27:39,44 [m]Mk 15:29
22:8 [n]Ps 91:14 [o]Mt 27:43
22:9 [p]Ps 71:6
22:10 [q]Isa 46:3

In his wrath the LORD will swallow them up,
and his fire will consume them.[x]
10You will destroy their descendants from the earth,
their posterity from mankind.[y]
11Though they plot evil[z] against you
and devise wicked schemes,[a]
they cannot succeed;
12for you will make them turn their backs[b]
when you aim at them with drawn bow.

13Be exalted, O LORD, in your strength;
we will sing and praise your might.

Psalm 22

For the director of music. To ⌊the tune of⌋ "The Doe of the Morning." A psalm of David.

1My God, my God, why have you forsaken me?[c]
Why are you so far[d] from saving me,
so far from the words of my groaning?
2O my God, I cry out by day, but you do not answer,
by night,[e] and am not silent.
3Yet you are enthroned as the Holy One;[f]
you are the praise[g] of Israel.[b]
4In you our fathers put their trust;
they trusted and you delivered them.
5They cried to you and were saved;
in you they trusted and were not disappointed.[h]

6But I am a worm[i] and not a man,
scorned by men[j] and despised[k] by the people.
7All who see me mock me;
they hurl insults,[l] shaking their heads:[m]
8"He trusts in the LORD;
let the LORD rescue him.[n]
Let him deliver him,
since he delights[o] in him."

9Yet you brought me out of the womb;[p]
you made me trust in you
even at my mother's breast.
10From birth[q] I was cast upon you;
from my mother's womb you have been my God.

[a]9 Or *save! / O King, answer* [b]3 Or *Yet you are holy, / enthroned on the praises of Israel*

11Do not be far from me,
for trouble is near
and there is no one to help.[r]

12Many bulls[s] surround me;
strong bulls of Bashan[t] encircle me.
13Roaring lions[u] tearing their prey
open their mouths wide[v]
against me.
14I am poured out like water,
and all my bones are out of joint.[w]
My heart has turned to wax;
it has melted away[x] within me.
15My strength is dried up like a potsherd,
and my tongue sticks to the roof of my mouth;[y]
you lay me[a] in the dust[z] of death.
16Dogs[a] have surrounded me;
a band of evil men has encircled me,
they have pierced[b] [b] my hands and my feet.
17I can count all my bones;
people stare[c] and gloat over me.[d]

18They divide my garments among them
and cast lots[e] for my clothing.

19But you, O LORD, be not far off;
O my Strength, come quickly[f] to help me.
20Deliver my life from the sword,
my precious life[g] from the power of the dogs.
21Rescue me from the mouth of the lions;
save[c] me from the horns of the wild oxen.

22I will declare your name to my brothers;
in the congregation I will praise you.[h]
2 →PG. 665
23You who fear the LORD, praise him![i]
All you descendants of Jacob, honor him!
Revere him,[j] all you descendants of Israel!
24For he has not despised or disdained
the suffering of the afflicted one;
he has not hidden his face[k] from him
but has listened to his cry for help.[l]

25From you comes the theme of my praise in the great assembly;[m]
before those who fear you[d] will I fulfill my vows.[n]
26The poor will eat[o] and be satisfied;
they who seek the LORD will praise him—[p]
may your hearts live forever!
27All the ends of the earth[q]
will remember and turn to the LORD,
and all the families of the nations
will bow down before him,[r]
28for dominion belongs to the LORD[s]
and he rules over the nations.

29All the rich[t] of the earth will feast and worship;
all who go down to the dust[u]
will kneel before him—
those who cannot keep themselves alive.
30Posterity[v] will serve him;
future generations will be told about the Lord.

22:11 [r]Ps 72:12 **22:12** [s]Ps 68:30 [t]Dt 32:14 **22:13** [u]Ps 17:12 [v]Ps 35:21 **22:14** [w]Ps 31:10 [x]Job 30:16; Da 5:6 **22:15** [y]Ps 38:10; Jn 19:28 [z]Ps 104:29 **22:16** [a]Ps 59:6 [b]Isa 53:5; Zec 12:10; Jn 19:34 **22:17** [c]Lk 23:35 [d]Lk 23:27

22:18 [e]Mt 27:35*; Lk 23:34; Jn 19:24* **22:19** [f]Ps 70:5 **22:20** [g]Ps 35:17 **22:22** [h]Heb 2:12* **22:23** [i]Ps 86:12; 135:19 [j]Ps 33:8 **22:24** [k]Ps 69:17 [l]Heb 5:7 **22:25** [m]Ps 35:18 [n]Ecc 5:4 **22:26** [o]Ps 107:9 [p]Ps 40:16 **22:27** [q]Ps 2:8 [r]Ps 86:9 **22:28** [s]Ps 47:7-8 **22:29** [t]Ps 45:12 [u]Isa 26:19 **22:30** [v]Ps 102:28

a 15 Or / *I am laid* b 16 Some Hebrew manuscripts, Septuagint and Syriac; most Hebrew manuscripts / *like the lion,* c 21 Or / *you have heard* d 25 Hebrew *him*

22:1–31

PROMISE 1

"WHERE ARE YOU, GOD?"

"My God, where are you?" (vv. 1–2). Who hasn't felt this gut-wrenching fear? David wrote this psalm as a reflection of the weakness and discouragement he felt after being relentlessly pursued by murderers (vv. 11–21). Jesus quoted parts of this psalm from the cross in his darkest hours (Matthew 27:46). Most of us have or will feel this powerful dread of being abandoned by God. Most of us will make our own scream of despair. What separates David and Jesus from most of us is not trouble, or praying in trouble, or feeling abandoned when God's response is not as we asked. The mark of a man is what he does when he is desperate. That's when we cross the line from espoused to practiced theology.

What David expressed in verses 1–2 is not what set David apart from most men. What he felt and expressed in verses 3 through 5 revealed his true character. These beliefs continued to develop David's character throughout his life. Read these short verses again and think about how these same beliefs have, can, and will develop your own character.

In their darkest, most critical hours, both David and Jesus submitted to God the Father. Study this psalm as an instructional booklet on how a man of God responds when God seems nowhere near.

For the next Promise 1 reading go to page 598.

31 They will proclaim his
righteousness
to a people yet unborn[w]—
for he has done it.

Psalm 23

A psalm of David.

1 The LORD is my shepherd,[x] I shall
not be in want.[y]
2 He makes me lie down in green
pastures,
he leads me beside quiet waters,[z]
3 he restores my soul.[a]
He guides me in paths of
righteousness[b]
for his name's sake.
4 Even though I walk
through the valley of the shadow
of death,[a][c]
I will fear no evil,[d]
for you are with me;[e]
your rod and your staff,
they comfort me.

5 You prepare a table before me
in the presence of my enemies.
You anoint my head with oil;[f]
my cup[g] overflows.
6 Surely goodness and love will
follow me
all the days of my life,
and I will dwell in the house of the
LORD
forever.

23:1–6

PROMISE 1

OUR SHEPHERD

This may well be the best-known psalm because of its theme: "The LORD is my shepherd." Jesus, the great Shepherd himself, expanded on that thought in John 10:11–18. It is important to understand how the Shepherd views his role if we are going to appreciate what it means for us. Think of the phrase with the following emphases: The *Lord* is my shepherd; The Lord is *my* shepherd; The Lord is my *shepherd.*

David's understanding of God as his shepherd is organized around three themes. Since "the LORD is my shepherd," I will want for nothing (vv. 1–3); I will fear nothing (v. 4); I will be anxious for nothing (vv. 5–6). The closing thought, like the opening one, is a summary statement: Because the Lord is my shepherd, both time and eternity are cared for. I have goodness and mercy in this life, and after this life I will dwell in God's house forever.

For the next Promise 1 reading go to page 600.

22:31 [w]Ps 78:6
23:1 [x]Isa 40:11; Jn 10:11; 1Pe 2:25 [y]Php 4:19
23:2 [z]Eze 34:14; Rev 7:17
23:3 [a]Ps 19:7 [b]Ps 5:8; 85:13
23:4 [c]Job 10:21-22 [d]Ps 3:6; 27:1 [e]Isa 43:2
23:5 [f]Ps 92:10 [g]Ps 16:5

Psalm 24

Of David. A psalm.

1 The earth is the LORD's,[h] and
everything in it,
the world, and all who live in
it;[i]
2 for he founded it upon the seas
and established it upon the
waters.

3 Who may ascend the hill[j] of the
LORD?
Who may stand in his holy
place?[k]
4 He who has clean hands[l] and a
pure heart,[m]
who does not lift up his soul to
an idol
or swear by what is false.[b]
5 He will receive blessing from the
LORD
and vindication from God his
Savior.
6 Such is the generation of those
who seek him,
who seek your face,[n] O God of
Jacob.[c] *Selah*

3 → PG. 599

7 Lift up your heads, O you gates;[o]
be lifted up, you ancient doors,
that the King of glory[p] may
come in.
8 Who is this King of glory?
The LORD strong and mighty,
the LORD mighty in battle.[q]
9 Lift up your heads, O you gates;
lift them up, you ancient doors,
that the King of glory may come
in.
10 Who is he, this King of glory?
The LORD Almighty—
he is the King of glory. *Selah*

Psalm 25[d]

Of David.

1 To you, O LORD, I lift up my soul;[r]
2 in you I trust,[s] O my God.
Do not let me be put to shame,
nor let my enemies triumph over
me.
3 No one whose hope is in you
will ever be put to shame,[t]
but they will be put to shame
who are treacherous without
excuse.

4 Show me your ways, O LORD,

24:1 [h]Ex 9:29; Job 41:11; Ps 89:11 [i]1Co 10:26*
24:3 [j]Ps 2:6 [k]Ps 15:1; 65:4
24:4 [l]Job 17:9 [m]Mt 5:8
24:6 [n]Ps 27:8
24:7 [o]Isa 26:2 [p]Ps 97:6; 1Co 2:8
24:8 [q]Ps 76:3-6
25:1 [r]Ps 86:4
25:2 [s]Ps 41:11
25:3 [t]Isa 49:23

[a] 4 Or *through the darkest valley* [b] 4 Or *swear falsely* [c] 6 Two Hebrew manuscripts and Syriac (see also Septuagint); most Hebrew manuscripts *face, Jacob* [d] This psalm is an acrostic poem, the verses of which begin with the successive letters of the Hebrew alphabet.

teach me your paths;[u]
5guide me in your truth and teach
me,
for you are God my Savior,
and my hope is in you all day
long.
6Remember, O LORD, your great
mercy and love,[v]
for they are from of old.
7Remember not the sins of my
youth[w]
and my rebellious ways;
according to your love[x] remember
me,
for you are good, O LORD.

8Good and upright[y] is the LORD;
therefore he instructs[z] sinners
in his ways.
9He guides[a] the humble in what is
right
and teaches them[b] his way.
10All the ways of the LORD are loving
and faithful[c]
for those who keep the demands
of his covenant.[d]
11For the sake of your name,[e]
O LORD,
forgive my iniquity, though it is
great.
12Who, then, is the man that fears
the LORD?
He will instruct him in the way[f]
chosen for him.
13He will spend his days in
prosperity,[g]
and his descendants will inherit
the land.[h]
14The LORD confides[i] in those who
fear him;
he makes his covenant known[j]
to them.
15My eyes are ever on the LORD,[k]
for only he will release my feet
from the snare.
16Turn to me[l] and be gracious to
me,
for I am lonely and afflicted.
17The troubles of my heart have
multiplied;
free me from my anguish.[m]
18Look upon my affliction and my
distress[n]
and take away all my sins.
19See how my enemies[o] have
increased
and how fiercely they hate me!
20Guard my life[p] and rescue me;
let me not be put to shame,
for I take refuge in you.
21May integrity[q] and uprightness
protect me,
because my hope is in you.

22Redeem Israel,[r] O God,
from all their troubles!

Psalm 26

Of David.

3 →PG. 602

1Vindicate me, O LORD,
for I have led a blameless life;[s]
I have trusted[t] in the LORD
without wavering.[u]
2Test me,[v] O LORD, and try me,
examine my heart and my
mind;[w]
3for your love is ever before me,
and I walk continually[x] in your
truth.
4I do not sit[y] with deceitful men,
nor do I consort with hypocrites;
5I abhor[z] the assembly of evildoers
and refuse to sit with the wicked.
6I wash my hands in innocence,[a]
and go about your altar, O LORD,
7proclaiming aloud your praise
and telling of all your wonderful
deeds.[b]
8I love[c] the house where you live,
O LORD,
the place where your glory
dwells.

9Do not take away my soul along
with sinners,
my life with bloodthirsty men,[d]
10in whose hands are wicked
schemes,
whose right hands are full of
bribes.[e]
11But I lead a blameless life;
redeem me[f] and be merciful to
me.
12My feet stand on level ground;[g]
in the great assembly[h] I will
praise the LORD.

Psalm 27

Of David.

1 →PG. 600

1The LORD is my light[i] and my
salvation[j]—
whom shall I fear?
The LORD is the stronghold of my
life—
of whom shall I be afraid?[k]
2When evil men advance against me
to devour my flesh,[a]
when my enemies and my foes
attack me,
they will stumble and fall.[l]
3Though an army besiege me,
my heart will not fear;[m]
though war break out against me,
even then will I be confident.[n]

25:4 [u]Ex 33:13 **25:6** [v]Ps 103:17; Isa 63:7,15 **25:7** [w]Job 13:26; Jer 3:25 [x]Ps 51:1 **25:8** [y]Ps 92:15 [z]Ps 32:8 **25:9** [a]Ps 23:3 [b]Ps 27:11 **25:10** [c]Ps 40:11 [d]Ps 103:18 **25:11** [e]Ps 31:3; 79:9 **25:12** [f]Ps 37:23 **25:13** [g]Pr 19:23 [h]Ps 37:11 **25:14** [i]Pr 3:32 [j]Jn 7:17 **25:15** [k]Ps 141:8 **25:16** [l]Ps 69:16 **25:17** [m]Ps 107:6 **25:18** [n]2Sa 16:12 **25:19** [o]Ps 3:1 **25:20** [p]Ps 86:2 **25:21** [q]Ps 41:12 **25:22** [r]Ps 130:8

26:1 [s]Ps 7:8; Pr 20:7 [t]Ps 28:7 [u]2Ki 20:3; Heb 10:23 **26:2** [v]Ps 17:3 [w]Ps 7:9 **26:3** [x]2Ki 20:3 **26:4** [y]Ps 1:1 **26:5** [z]Ps 31:6; 139:21 **26:6** [a]Ps 73:13 **26:7** [b]Ps 9:1 **26:8** [c]Ps 27:4 **26:9** [d]Ps 28:3 **26:10** [e]1Sa 8:3 **26:11** [f]Ps 69:18 **26:12** [g]Ps 27:11; 40:2 [h]Ps 22:22 **27:1** [i]Isa 60:19 [j]Ex 15:2 [k]Ps 118:6 **27:2** [l]Ps 9:3; 14:4 **27:3** [m]Ps 3:6 [n]Job 4:6

[a]2 Or *to slander me*

4One thing[o] I ask of the LORD,
this is what I seek:
that I may dwell in the house of the LORD
all the days of my life,[p]
to gaze upon the beauty of the LORD
and to seek him in his temple.
5For in the day of trouble
he will keep me safe in his dwelling;
he will hide me[q] in the shelter of his tabernacle
and set me high upon a rock.[r]
6Then my head will be exalted[s]
above the enemies who surround me;
at his tabernacle will I sacrifice[t]
with shouts of joy;
I will sing and make music to the LORD.

7Hear my voice when I call, O LORD;
be merciful to me and answer me.[u]
8My heart says of you, "Seek his[a] face!"
Your face, LORD, I will seek.
9Do not hide your face[v] from me,
do not turn your servant away in anger;
you have been my helper.
Do not reject me or forsake me,
O God my Savior.
10Though my father and mother forsake me,
the LORD will receive me.
11Teach me your way, O LORD;
lead me in a straight path[w]
because of my oppressors.
12Do not turn me over to the desire of my foes,
for false witnesses[x] rise up against me,
breathing out violence.

13I am still confident of this:
I will see the goodness of the LORD[y]
in the land of the living.[z]
14Wait[a] for the LORD;
be strong and take heart
and wait for the LORD.

27:1–14

PROMISE 1

SPLIT PER"PSALM"ALITY

This Psalm reads like it was written either by two people or by one really confused person. Verses 1–6 comprise a powerful expression of confidence and faith in God. Read through them and identify the numerous statements of confidence. Then we stumble into the fearful and almost desperate statements of verses 7–12. If we could ask David, the author, why this psalm has two such different tones, he might well reply, "Welcome to reality." In the space of a single prayer he went from feeling great to feeling scared. How often do we swing from one end of the spectrum to the other? David, in this psalm, expressed both feelings candidly.

As surely as we praise God, we can tell him our fears. It is as important to express our anxieties to God as to express our trust in his provision and protection. Read the two movements again (vv. 1–6 and 7–12), seeing how many specific statements of confidence and fear you can relate to. Then focus for a few moments on the closing statement (vv. 13–14) and pray for the confidence (v. 13), patience and strength (v. 14) David expressed.

David had trust and he had fears. After working his way through both emotions before God, he concluded that he would "be strong and take heart and wait for the LORD."

For the next Promise 1 reading go to page 603.

Psalm 28

Of David.

1To you I call, O LORD my Rock;
do not turn a deaf ear to me.
For if you remain silent,[b]
I will be like those who have gone down to the pit.[c]
2Hear my cry for mercy[d]
as I call to you for help,
as I lift up my hands
toward your Most Holy Place.[e]

3Do not drag me away with the wicked,
with those who do evil,
who speak cordially with their neighbors
but harbor malice in their hearts.[f]
4Repay them for their deeds
and for their evil work;
repay them for what their hands have done[g]
and bring back upon them what they deserve.[h]
5Since they show no regard for the works of the LORD
and what his hands have done,[i]
he will tear them down
and never build them up again.

6Praise be to the LORD,
for he has heard my cry for mercy.

27:4 [o]Ps 90:17 [p]Ps 23:6; 26:8 **27:5** [q]Ps 17:8; 31:20 [r]Ps 40:2 **27:6** [s]Ps 3:3 [t]Ps 107:22 **27:7** [u]Ps 13:3 **27:9** [v]Ps 69:17 **27:11** [w]Ps 5:8; 25:4; 86:11 **27:12** [x]Mt 26:60; Ac 9:1 **27:13** [y]Ps 31:19 [z]Jer 11:19; Eze 26:20 **27:14** [a]Ps 40:1 **28:1** [b]Ps 83:1 [c]Ps 88:4 **28:2** [d]Ps 138:2; 140:6 [e]Ps 5:7 **28:3** [f]Ps 12:2; Ps 26:9; Jer 9:8 **28:4** [g]2Ti 4:14; Rev 22:12 [h]Rev 18:6 **28:5** [i]Isa 5:12

[a]8 Or *To you, O my heart, he has said, "Seek my*

7The LORD is my strength[j] and my
shield;
my heart trusts[k] in him, and I
am helped.
My heart leaps for joy
and I will give thanks to him in
song.[l]
8The LORD is the strength of his
people,
a fortress of salvation for his
anointed one.[m]
9Save your people and bless your
inheritance;[n]
be their shepherd[o] and carry
them[p] forever.

Psalm 29

A psalm of David.

1Ascribe to the LORD,[q] O mighty
ones,
ascribe to the LORD glory[r] and
strength.
2Ascribe to the LORD the glory due
his name;
worship the LORD in the splendor
of his[a] holiness.[s]

1 →PG. 621

3The voice[t] of the LORD is over the
waters;
the God of glory thunders,[u]
the LORD thunders over the
mighty waters.
4The voice of the LORD is
powerful;[v]
the voice of the LORD is majestic.
5The voice of the LORD breaks the
cedars;
the LORD breaks in pieces the
cedars of Lebanon.[w]
6He makes Lebanon skip[x] like a
calf,
Sirion[b][y] like a young wild ox.
7The voice of the LORD strikes
with flashes of lightning.
8The voice of the LORD shakes the
desert;
the LORD shakes the Desert of
Kadesh.[z]
9The voice of the LORD twists the
oaks[c]
and strips the forests bare.
And in his temple all cry, "Glory!"[a]

10The LORD sits[d] enthroned over the
flood;[b]
the LORD is enthroned as King
forever.[c]
11The LORD gives strength to his
people;[d]
the LORD blesses his people with
peace.[e]

28:7 [j]Ps 18:1 [k]Ps 13:5 [l]Ps 40:3; 69:30 **28:8** [m]Ps 20:6 **28:9** [n]Dt 9:29; Ezr 1:4 [o]Isa 40:11 [p]Dt 1:31; 32:11 **29:1** [q]1Ch 16:28 [r]Ps 96:7-9 **29:2** [s]2Ch 20:21 **29:3** [t]Job 37:5 [u]Ps 18:13 **29:4** [v]Ps 68:33 **29:5** [w]Jdg 9:15 **29:6** [x]Ps 114:4 [y]Dt 3:9 **29:8** [z]Nu 13:26 **29:9** [a]Ps 26:8 **29:10** [b]Ge 6:17 [c]Ps 10:16 **29:11** [d]Ps 28:8 [e]Ps 37:11

Psalm 30

A psalm. A song. For the dedication
of the temple.[e] Of David.

1I will exalt you, O LORD,
for you lifted me out of the
depths
and did not let my enemies gloat
over me.[f]
2O LORD my God, I called to you for
help[g]
and you healed me.[h]
3O LORD, you brought me up from
the grave[f];
you spared me from going down
into the pit.[i]

4Sing to the LORD, you saints[j] of
his;
praise his holy name.[k]
5For his anger[l] lasts only a
moment,
but his favor lasts a lifetime;
weeping may remain for a night,
but rejoicing comes in the
morning.[m]

6When I felt secure, I said,
"I will never be shaken."
7O LORD, when you favored me,
you made my mountain[g] stand
firm;
but when you hid your face,[n]
I was dismayed.

8To you, O LORD, I called;
to the Lord I cried for mercy:
9"What gain is there in my
destruction,[h]
in my going down into the pit?
Will the dust praise you?
Will it proclaim your
faithfulness?[o]
10Hear, O LORD, and be merciful to
me;
O LORD, be my help."

11You turned my wailing into
dancing;
you removed my sackcloth and
clothed me with joy,[p]
12that my heart may sing to you and
not be silent.
O LORD my God, I will give you
thanks[q] forever.[r]

30:1 [f]Ps 25:2; 28:9 **30:2** [g]Ps 88:13 [h]Ps 6:2 **30:3** [i]Ps 28:1; 86:13 **30:4** [j]Ps 149:1 [k]Ps 97:12 **30:5** [l]Ps 103:9 [m]2Co 4:17 **30:7** [n]Dt 31:17; Ps 104:29 **30:9** [o]Ps 6:5 **30:11** [p]Ps 4:7; Jer 31:4,13 **30:12** [q]Ps 16:9 [r]Ps 44:8

[a]2 Or *LORD with the splendor of* [b]6 That is, Mount Hermon [c]9 Or *LORD makes the deer give birth* [d]10 Or *sat* [e]Title: Or *palace* [f]3 Hebrew *Sheol* [g]7 Or *hill country* [h]9 Or *there if I am silenced*

Psalm 31

For the director of music. A psalm of David.

1In you, O LORD, I have taken
refuge;
let me never be put to shame;
deliver me in your righteousness.
2Turn your ear to me,
come quickly to my rescue;
be my rock of refuge,[s]
a strong fortress to save me.
3Since you are my rock and my
fortress,[t]
for the sake of your name[u] lead
and guide me.
4Free me from the trap that is set
for me,
for you are my refuge.[v]
5Into your hands I commit my
spirit;[w]
redeem me, O LORD, the God of
truth.

6I hate those who cling to worthless
idols;
I trust in the LORD.[x]
7I will be glad and rejoice in your
love,
for you saw my affliction[y]
and knew the anguish[z] of my
soul.
8You have not handed me over[a] to
the enemy
but have set my feet in a
spacious place.

9Be merciful to me, O LORD, for I
am in distress;
my eyes grow weak with
sorrow,[b]
my soul and my body with grief.
10My life is consumed by anguish
and my years by groaning;[c]
my strength fails because of my
affliction,[a]
and my bones grow weak.[d]
11Because of all my enemies,
I am the utter contempt of my
neighbors;[e]
I am a dread to my friends—
those who see me on the street
flee from me.
12I am forgotten by them as though I
were dead;[f]
I have become like broken
pottery.
13For I hear the slander of many;
there is terror on every side;[g]
they conspire against me
and plot to take my life.[h]

14But I trust[i] in you, O LORD;
I say, "You are my God."
15My times[j] are in your hands;
deliver me from my enemies
and from those who pursue me.
16Let your face shine[k] on your
servant;
save me in your unfailing love.
17Let me not be put to shame,[l]
O LORD,
for I have cried out to you;
but let the wicked be put to shame
and lie silent[m] in the grave.[b]
18Let their lying lips[n] be silenced,
for with pride and contempt
they speak arrogantly[o] against
the righteous.

19How great is your goodness,[p]
which you have stored up for
those who fear you,
which you bestow in the sight of
men[q]
on those who take refuge in you.
20In the shelter of your presence you
hide[r] them
from the intrigues of men;[s]
in your dwelling you keep them
safe
from accusing tongues.

21Praise be to the LORD,
for he showed his wonderful
love[t] to me
when I was in a besieged city.[u]
22In my alarm[v] I said,
"I am cut off from your sight!"
Yet you heard my cry[w] for mercy
when I called to you for help.

23Love the LORD, all his saints![x]
The LORD preserves the
faithful,[y]
but the proud he pays back[z] in
full.
24Be strong and take heart,[a]
all you who hope in the LORD.

Psalm 32

Of David. A *maskil*.[c]

3 →PG. 608

1Blessed is he
whose transgressions are
forgiven,
whose sins are covered.[b]
2Blessed is the man
whose sin the LORD does not
count against him[c]
and in whose spirit is no
deceit.[d]

3When I kept silent,
my bones wasted away[e]
through my groaning all day
long.
4For day and night
your hand was heavy[f] upon me;

31:2 [s]Ps 18:2
31:3 [t]Ps 18:2 [u]Ps 23:3
31:4 [v]Ps 25:15
31:5 [w]Lk 23:46; Ac 7:59
31:6 [x]Jnh 2:8
31:7 [y]Ps 90:14 [z]Ps 10:14; Jn 10:27
31:8 [a]Dt 32:30
31:9 [b]Ps 6:7
31:10 [c]Ps 13:2 [d]Ps 38:3; 39:11
31:11 [e]Job 19:13; Ps 38:11; 64:8; Isa 53:4
31:12 [f]Ps 88:4
31:13 [g]Jer 20:3,10; La 2:22 [h]Mt 27:1
31:14 [i]Ps 140:6
31:15 [j]Job 24:1; Ps 143:9
31:16 [k]Nu 6:25; Ps 4:6
31:17 [l]Ps 25:2-3 [m]Ps 115:17
31:18 [n]Ps 120:2 [o]Ps 94:4
31:19 [p]Ro 11:22 [q]Isa 64:4
31:20 [r]Ps 27:5 [s]Job 5:21
31:21 [t]Ps 17:7 [u]1Sa 23:7
31:22 [v]Ps 116:11 [w]La 3:54
31:23 [x]Ps 34:9 [y]Ps 145:20 [z]Ps 94:2
31:24 [a]Ps 27:14
32:1 [b]Ps 85:2
32:2 [c]Ro 4:7-8*; 2Co 5:19 [d]Jn 1:47
32:3 [e]Ps 31:10
32:4 [f]Job 33:7

[a] *10* Or *guilt* [b] *17* Hebrew *Sheol* [c] Title: Probably a literary or musical term

my strength was sapped
as in the heat of summer. *Selah*
5Then I acknowledged my sin to you
and did not cover up my
iniquity.
I said, "I will confess[g]
my transgressions[h] to the
LORD"—
and you forgave
the guilt of my sin.[i] *Selah*

6Therefore let everyone who is godly
pray to you
while you may be found;[j]
surely when the mighty waters rise,
they will not reach him.[k]
7You are my hiding place;
you will protect me from
trouble[l]
and surround me with songs of
deliverance.[m] *Selah*
8I will instruct[n] you and teach you
in the way you should go;
I will counsel you and watch
over[o] you.
9Do not be like the horse or the
mule,
which have no understanding
but must be controlled by bit and
bridle[p]
or they will not come to you.
10Many are the woes of the wicked,[q]
but the LORD's unfailing love
surrounds the man who trusts[r]
in him.

11Rejoice in the LORD[s] and be glad,
you righteous;
sing, all you who are upright in
heart!

Psalm 33

1Sing joyfully to the LORD, you
righteous;
it is fitting[t] for the upright[u] to
praise him.
2Praise the LORD with the harp;
make music to him on the
ten-stringed lyre.[v]
3Sing to him a new song;[w]
play skillfully, and shout for joy.

4For the word of the LORD is right[x]
and true;
he is faithful in all he does.

32:5 [g]Pr 28:13 [h]Ps 103:12 [i]Lev 26:40
32:6 [j]Ps 69:13; Isa 55:6 [k]Isa 43:2
32:7 [l]Ps 9:9 [m]Ex 15:1
32:8 [n]Ps 25:8 [o]Ps 33:18
32:9 [p]Pr 26:3
32:10 [q]Ro 2:9 [r]Pr 16:20
32:11 [s]Ps 64:10
33:1 [t]Ps 147:1 [u]Ps 32:11
33:2 [v]Ps 92:3
33:3 [w]Ps 96:1
33:4 [x]Ps 19:8

32, 40, 51

PROMISE 1

WHEN A MAN DOESN'T KEEP HIS PROMISES

What should a man do when he sins? David's answer to this question is one of the most important things his psalms teach us. Combining Psalms 32, 51 and parts of 40, we discover insights into a great mystery about David. After David's death, God's commentary on him was that he had followed God with his whole heart (1 Kings 3:14; 9:4; 11:4, 6, 33–36). Yet we know David broke God's law. Among other things, he committed adultery and murder (2 Samuel 11); those sins were punishable by death. How could it be said, then, that David followed God completely?

Because we all sin, it's important to think our way through David's response to his own sin. In Psalm 32:3–4 David described the agony he experienced between the time he sinned and the time he confessed and repented. Read those verses and summarize David's attitude about sin in his life. Verse 5 describes David's confession, but Psalm 51:1–17 is a more complete statement of that prayer. Read it and note that David asked for mercy and compassion (v. 1); confessed his sin and asked for cleansing and restoration (vv. 1–12); presented God with a broken spirit and contrite heart rather than sacrifice (vv. 16–17). Note also that in verses 13 and 14 he promised God he would teach transgressors God's ways so sinners could turn back to him.

What can we learn from David about how we should come back to God when we sin?

1. *David didn't admit to a problem, he confessed sin.* He didn't talk about his addictions, his failures, his dysfunctions. He confessed, "Against you I have sinned, O God" (51:3–4).
2. *David didn't explain, he repented.* He didn't say he was tired, he had a bad marriage, he had lousy parents; no, he said, "I am guilty and I am broken over it" (51:6–12). He asked for cleansing and for a pure heart (51:10).
3. *David didn't ask how he could make restitution to God, he asked for mercy* (51:1). We are completely unable to counterbalance the sin in our lives with good works. Only by God's mercy can we approach him and ask for his forgiveness.
4. *David didn't offer to do some religious exercise, even a God-ordained one; he offered God his whole life* (40:6–8). No amount of religious devotion or exercise will substitute for the need to confess our sin.
5. *David didn't ask to be excused, he asked to be forgiven* (Psalm 32:5). We never go to God and say "Excuse me for sinning." There is no excuse for our sin; there is only forgiveness.

Until a man sees sin as David did, he will never repent as David did. Only a hatred of sin that leads to genuine repentance and a personal renewal of commitment to holiness will do. Why did God say that David followed him wholeheartedly? Because David was a man who hated his sin and loved God's holiness.

For the next Promise 1 reading go to page 604.

5The LORD loves righteousness and
justice;[y]
the earth is full of his unfailing
love.[z]
6By the word[a] of the LORD were the
heavens made,
their starry host by the breath of
his mouth.
7He gathers the waters of the sea
into jars[a];
he puts the deep into
storehouses.
8Let all the earth fear the LORD;
let all the people of the world
revere him.[b]
9For he spoke, and it came to be;
he commanded,[c] and it stood
firm.
10The LORD foils the plans of the
nations;[d]
he thwarts the purposes of the
peoples.
11But the plans of the LORD stand
firm forever,
the purposes[e] of his heart
through all generations.

12Blessed is the nation whose God is
the LORD,[f]
the people he chose[g] for his
inheritance.
13From heaven the LORD looks down
and sees all mankind;[h]
14from his dwelling place[i] he
watches
all who live on earth—
15he who forms[j] the hearts of all,
who considers everything they
do.[k]
16No king is saved by the size of his
army;[l]
no warrior escapes by his great
strength.
17A horse[m] is a vain hope for
deliverance;
despite all its great strength it
cannot save.
18But the eyes[n] of the LORD are on
those who fear him,
on those whose hope is in his
unfailing love,[o]
19to deliver them from death
and keep them alive in famine.[p]
20We wait[q] in hope for the LORD;
he is our help and our shield.
21In him our hearts rejoice,[r]
for we trust in his holy name.
22May your unfailing love rest upon
us, O LORD,
even as we put our hope in you.

33:1–22

PROMISE 1

SOURCE OF SECURITY

Our God is sovereign. Verses 18–22 of this psalm tell us that our life is ultimately in God's hands. Our modern society surrounds us with cushions and protections that range from seat belts to dead bolts, from warning labels to health insurance. Wisdom tells us to use these things to protect ourselves. But ultimately and finally, the psalmist reminds us, "We wait in hope for the LORD; he is our help and our shield" (v. 20).

In verses 16 and 17 the psalmist listed some of the primary protections of his time and said they were insufficient in themselves—they could not save. Isn't it interesting that our modern era of protection devices and insurance is also an era of great fear and anxiety? Regardless of what other protections we have, our only sense of security must be in our God as he is described in verses 1–15. Read that passage and let its truths about God sink into your mind. Then read verses 16–19 and meditate on the truth of that passage. Now explain the psalmist's sense of security described in verses 20–22.

The size of our God is the size of our security and peace.

For the next Promise 1 reading go to page 607.

Psalm 34[b]

Of David. When he pretended to be insane[s] before Abimelech, who drove him away, and he left.

1I will extol the LORD at all times;[t]
his praise will always be on my
lips.
2My soul will boast[u] in the LORD;
let the afflicted hear and
rejoice.[v]
3Glorify the LORD with me;
let us exalt[w] his name together.

4I sought the LORD,[x] and he
answered me;
he delivered me from all my
fears.
5Those who look to him are
radiant;[y]
their faces are never covered
with shame.[z]
6This poor man called, and the LORD
heard him;
he saved him out of all his
troubles.
7The angel of the LORD[a] encamps
around those who fear him,
and he delivers them.
8Taste and see that the LORD is
good;[b]

33:5 [y]Ps 11:7 [z]Ps 119:64 **33:6** [a]Heb 11:3 **33:8** [b]Ps 67:7; 96:9 **33:9** [c]Ge 1:3; Ps 148:5 **33:10** [d]Isa 8:10 **33:11** [e]Job 23:13 **33:12** [f]Ps 144:15 [g]Ex 19:5; Dt 7:6 **33:13** [h]Job 28:24; Ps 11:4 **33:14** [i]1Ki 8:39 **33:15** [j]Job 10:8 [k]Jer 32:19 **33:16** [l]Ps 44:6 **33:17** [m]Ps 20:7; Pr 21:31 **33:18** [n]Job 36:7; Ps 34:15 [o]Ps 147:11 **33:19** [p]Job 5:20 **33:20** [q]Ps 130:6 **33:21** [r]Zec 10:7; Jn 16:22 **34 Title** [s]1Sa 21:13 **34:1** [t]Ps 71:6; Eph 5:20 **34:2** [u]Jer 9:24; 1Co 1:31 [v]Ps 119:74 **34:3** [w]Lk 1:46 **34:4** [x]Mt 7:7 **34:5** [y]Ps 36:9 [z]Ps 25:3 **34:7** [a]2Ki 6:17; Da 6:22 **34:8** [b]1Pe 2:3

a7 Or *sea as into a heap* **b**This psalm is an acrostic poem, the verses of which begin with the successive letters of the Hebrew alphabet.

blessed is the man who takes
refuge[c] in him.
9Fear the LORD, you his saints,
for those who fear him lack
nothing.[d]
10The lions may grow weak and
hungry,
but those who seek the LORD
lack no good thing.[e]

4 →PG. 631

11Come, my children, listen to me;
I will teach you[f] the fear of the
LORD.
12Whoever of you loves life[g]
and desires to see many good
days,
13keep your tongue from evil
and your lips from speaking
lies.[h]
14Turn from evil and do good;[i]
seek peace[j] and pursue it.
15The eyes of the LORD[k] are on the
righteous[l]
and his ears are attentive to their
cry;
16the face of the LORD is against[m]
those who do evil,[n]
to cut off the memory[o] of them
from the earth.
17The righteous cry out, and the
LORD hears[p] them;
he delivers them from all their
troubles.
18The LORD is close[q] to the
brokenhearted[r]
and saves those who are crushed
in spirit.
19A righteous man may have many
troubles,[s]
but the LORD delivers him from
them all;[t]
20he protects all his bones,
not one of them will be
broken.[u]
21Evil will slay the wicked;[v]
the foes of the righteous will be
condemned.
22The LORD redeems[w] his servants;
no one will be condemned who
takes refuge in him.

Psalm 35

Of David.

1Contend, O LORD, with those who
contend with me;
fight[x] against those who fight
against me.
2Take up shield and buckler;
arise[y] and come to my aid.
3Brandish spear and javelin[a]
against those who pursue me.
Say to my soul,
"I am your salvation."
4May those who seek my life
be disgraced[z] and put to
shame;
may those who plot my ruin
be turned back in dismay.
5May they be like chaff[a] before the
wind,
with the angel of the LORD
driving them away;
6may their path be dark and
slippery,
with the angel of the LORD
pursuing them.
7Since they hid their net for me
without cause
and without cause dug a pit for
me,
8may ruin overtake them by
surprise—[b]
may the net they hid entangle
them,
may they fall into the pit,[c] to
their ruin.
9Then my soul will rejoice[d] in the
LORD
and delight in his salvation.[e]
10My whole being will exclaim,
"Who is like you,[f] O LORD?
You rescue the poor from those too
strong[g] for them,
the poor and needy[h] from those
who rob them."
11Ruthless witnesses[i] come forward;
they question me on things I
know nothing about.
12They repay me evil for good[j]
and leave my soul forlorn.
13Yet when they were ill, I put on
sackcloth
and humbled myself with
fasting.[k]
When my prayers returned to me
unanswered,
14 I went about mourning
as though for my friend or
brother.
I bowed my head in grief
as though weeping for my
mother.
15But when I stumbled, they
gathered in glee;
attackers gathered against me
when I was unaware.
They slandered[l] me without
ceasing.
16Like the ungodly they maliciously
mocked[b];
they gnashed their teeth[m] at me.
17O Lord, how long[n] will you look
on?

34:8 [c]Ps 2:12
34:9 [d]Ps 23:1
34:10 [e]Ps 84:11
34:11 [f]Ps 32:8
34:12 [g]1Pe 3:10
34:13 [h]1Pe 2:22
34:14 [i]Ps 37:27 [j]Heb 12:14
34:15 [k]Ps 33:18 [l]Job 36:7
34:16 [m]Lev 17:10; Jer 44:11 [n]1Pe 3:10-12* [o]Pr 10:7
34:17 [p]Ps 145:19
34:18 [q]Ps 145:18 [r]Isa 57:15
34:19 [s]ver 17 [t]ver 4,6; Pr 24:16
34:20 [u]Jn 19:36*
34:21 [v]Ps 94:23
34:22 [w]1Ki 1:29; Ps 71:23
35:1 [x]Ps 43:1
35:2 [y]Ps 62:2
35:4 [z]Ps 70:2
35:5 [a]Job 21:18; Ps 1:4; Isa 29:5
35:8 [b]1Th 5:3 [c]Ps 9:15
35:9 [d]Lk 1:47 [e]Isa 61:10
35:10 [f]Ex 15:11 [g]Ps 18:17 [h]Ps 37:14
35:11 [i]Ps 27:12
35:12 [j]Jn 10:32
35:13 [k]Job 30:25; Ps 69:10
35:15 [l]Job 30:1,8
35:16 [m]Job 16:9; La 2:16
35:17 [n]Hab 1:13

a*3* Or *and block the way* b*16* Septuagint; Hebrew may mean *ungodly circle of mockers.*

Rescue my life from their
ravages,
my precious life[o] from these
lions.
18 I will give you thanks in the great
assembly;[p]
among throngs of people I will
praise you.[q]

19 Let not those gloat over me
who are my enemies without
cause;
let not those who hate me without
reason[r]
maliciously wink the eye.[s]
20 They do not speak peaceably,
but devise false accusations
against those who live quietly in
the land.
21 They gape[t] at me and say, "Aha!
Aha![u]
With our own eyes we have seen
it."

22 O LORD, you have seen[v] this; be
not silent.
Do not be far[w] from me,
O Lord.
23 Awake,[x] and rise to my defense!
Contend for me, my God and
Lord.
24 Vindicate me in your righteousness,
O LORD my God;
do not let them gloat over me.
25 Do not let them think, "Aha, just
what we wanted!"
or say, "We have swallowed him
up."[y]

26 May all who gloat over my distress
be put to shame[z] and
confusion;
may all who exalt themselves over
me[a]
be clothed with shame and
disgrace.
27 May those who delight in my
vindication[b]
shout for joy[c] and gladness;
may they always say, "The LORD be
exalted,
who delights[d] in the well-being
of his servant."
28 My tongue will speak of your
righteousness[e]
and of your praises all day long.

Psalm 36

For the director of music. Of David
the servant of the LORD.

1 An oracle is within my heart
concerning the sinfulness of the
wicked:[a]
There is no fear of God
before his eyes.[f]
2 For in his own eyes he flatters
himself
too much to detect or hate his
sin.
3 The words of his mouth[g] are
wicked and deceitful;
he has ceased to be wise[h] and
to do good.[i]
4 Even on his bed he plots evil;[j]
he commits himself to a sinful
course[k]
and does not reject what is
wrong.[l]

5 Your love, O LORD, reaches to the
heavens,
your faithfulness to the skies.
6 Your righteousness is like the
mighty mountains,
your justice like the great deep.[m]
O LORD, you preserve both man
and beast.
7 How priceless is your unfailing
love!
Both high and low among men
find[b] refuge in the shadow of
your wings.[n]
8 They feast on the abundance of
your house;[o]
you give them drink from your
river[p] of delights.
9 For with you is the fountain of
life;[q]
in your light[r] we see light.

10 Continue your love to those who
know you,
your righteousness to the upright
in heart.
11 May the foot of the proud not
come against me,
nor the hand of the wicked drive
me away.
12 See how the evildoers lie fallen—
thrown down, not able to rise![s]

Psalm 37[c]

Of David.

1 Do not fret because of evil men
or be envious[t] of those who do
wrong;[u]
2 for like the grass they will soon
wither,
like green plants they will soon
die away.[v]

3 Trust in the LORD and do good;
dwell in the land[w] and enjoy
safe pasture.[x]

35:17 [o]Ps 22:20 **35:18** [p]Ps 22:25 [q]Ps 22:22 **35:19** [r]Ps 38:19; 69:4; Jn 15:25* [s]Ps 13:4; Pr 6:13 **35:21** [t]Ps 22:13 [u]Ps 40:15 **35:22** [v]Ex 3:7 [w]Ps 10:1; 28:1 **35:23** [x]Ps 44:23 **35:25** [y]La 2:16 **35:26** [z]Ps 40:14; 109:29 [a]Ps 38:16 **35:27** [b]Ps 9:4 [c]Ps 32:11 [d]Ps 40:16; 147:11 **35:28** [e]Ps 51:14 **36:1** [f]Ro 3:18* **36:3** [g]Ps 10:7 [h]Ps 94:8 [i]Jer 4:22 **36:4** [j]Pr 4:16; Mic 2:1 [k]Isa 65:2 [l]Ps 52:3; Ro 12:9 **36:6** [m]Job 11:8; Ps 77:19; Ro 11:33 **36:7** [n]Ru 2:12; Ps 17:8 **36:8** [o]Ps 65:4 [p]Job 20:17; Rev 22:1 **36:9** [q]Jer 2:13 [r]1Pe 2:9 **36:12** [s]Ps 140:10 **37:1** [t]Pr 23:17-18 [u]Ps 73:3 **37:2** [v]Ps 90:6 **37:3** [w]Dt 30:20 [x]Isa 40:11; Jn 10:9

a *1* Or *heart: / Sin proceeds from the wicked.*
b *7* Or *love, O God! / Men find*; or *love! / Both heavenly beings and men / find*
c This psalm is an acrostic poem, the stanzas of which begin with the successive letters of the Hebrew alphabet.

4 Delight[y] yourself in the LORD
and he will give you the desires
of your heart.

5 Commit your way to the LORD;
trust in him[z] and he will do
this:
6 He will make your righteousness[a]
shine like the dawn,[b]
the justice of your cause like the
noonday sun.

7 Be still[c] before the LORD and wait
patiently[d] for him;
do not fret when men succeed in
their ways,
when they carry out their wicked
schemes.

8 Refrain from anger[e] and turn from
wrath;
do not fret—it leads only to evil.
9 For evil men will be cut off,
but those who hope in the LORD
will inherit the land.[f]

10 A little while, and the wicked will
be no more;[g]
though you look for them, they
will not be found.
11 But the meek will inherit the land[h]
and enjoy great peace.

12 The wicked plot against the
righteous
and gnash their teeth[i] at them;
13 but the Lord laughs at the wicked,
for he knows their day is
coming.[j]

14 The wicked draw the sword
and bend the bow[k]
to bring down the poor and
needy,[l]
to slay those whose ways are
upright.
15 But their swords will pierce their
own hearts,[m]
and their bows will be broken.

16 Better the little that the righteous
have
than the wealth[n] of many
wicked;
17 for the power of the wicked will be
broken,[o]
but the LORD upholds the
righteous.

18 The days of the blameless are
known to the LORD,[p]
and their inheritance will endure
forever.
19 In times of disaster they will not
wither;
in days of famine they will enjoy
plenty.

20 But the wicked will perish:
The LORD's enemies will be like
the beauty of the fields,
they will vanish—vanish like
smoke.[q]

21 The wicked borrow and do not
repay,
but the righteous give
generously;[r]
22 those the LORD blesses will inherit
the land,
but those he curses[s] will be cut
off.

23 If the LORD delights[t] in a man's
way,
he makes his steps firm;[u]
24 though he stumble, he will not
fall,[v]
for the LORD upholds[w] him with
his hand.

25 I was young and now I am old,
yet I have never seen the
righteous forsaken[x]
or their children begging bread.
26 They are always generous and lend
freely;
their children will be blessed.[y]

37:4 [y]Isa 58:14 **37:5** [z]Ps 4:5; Ps 55:22; Pr 16:3; 1Pe 5:7 **37:6** [a]Mic 7:9 [b]Job 11:17 **37:7** [c]Ps 62:5; La 3:26 [d]Ps 40:1 **37:8** [e]Eph 4:31; Col 3:8 **37:9** [f]Isa 57:13; 60:21 **37:10** [g]Job 7:10; 24:24

37:11 [h]Mt 5:5 **37:12** [i]Ps 35:16 **37:13** [j]1Sa 26:10; Ps 2:4 **37:14** [k]Ps 11:2 [l]Ps 35:10 **37:15** [m]Ps 9:16 **37:16** [n]Pr 15:16 **37:17** [o]Job 38:15; Ps 10:15 **37:18** [p]Ps 1:6 **37:20** [q]Ps 102:3 **37:21** [r]Ps 112:5 **37:22** [s]Job 5:3; Pr 3:33 **37:23** [t]Ps 147:11 [u]1Sa 2:9 **37:24** [v]Pr 24:16 [w]Ps 145:14; 147:6 **37:25** [x]Heb 13:5 **37:26** [y]Ps 147:13

37:1–40

PROMISE 1

HIGHWAY CHEATS

They're everywhere: Guys who break the rules and get ahead. Even on the road in construction zones they zoom down the shoulder, squeeze into line and are gone while we sit and wait. David, speaking with the perspective of an old and wise man (v. 25) advised: "Do not fret . . . trust in the LORD and do good" (vv. 1, 3).

Sound simplistic? We've all seen the rule breaker get ahead while the guy who does good falls further behind. This whole psalm powerfully addresses that tough issue. The summary, contained in verses 1–9, bears careful study by anyone who has been outraged by the injustice of the rule breakers winning. Note especially three particulars that occur throughout the psalm: (1) the frequent use of the word "but" as the writer contrasted the short-term gain of the wicked with the long-term gain of the righteous; (2) the references to the "land" (vv. 3, 9, 11, 22, 27, 29, 34) which represented resources, longevity and stability; (3) the value the writer put on the Lord's approval.

Ultimately, no matter who makes the gains in this life and economy, the psalmist measures value in a different currency. Read the psalm again, noting the references to "the LORD." As you face the choices of your day, how do you measure true wealth? How does this psalm teach us to gain it?

For the next Promise 1 reading go to page 611.

3 →PG. 616

27Turn from evil and do good;[z]
then you will dwell in the land
forever.
28For the LORD loves the just
and will not forsake his faithful
ones.

They will be protected forever,
but the offspring of the wicked
will be cut off;[a]
29the righteous will inherit the land[b]
and dwell in it forever.

30The mouth of the righteous man
utters wisdom,
and his tongue speaks what is
just.
31The law of his God is in his
heart;[c]
his feet do not slip.[d]
32The wicked lie in wait[e] for the
righteous,
seeking their very lives;
33but the LORD will not leave them in
their power
or let them be condemned when
brought to trial.[f]

34Wait for the LORD[g]
and keep his way.
He will exalt you to inherit the
land;
when the wicked are cut off, you
will see[h] it.

35I have seen a wicked and ruthless
man
flourishing[i] like a green tree in
its native soil,
36but he soon passed away and was
no more;
though I looked for him, he
could not be found.[j]

37Consider the blameless, observe the
upright;
there is a future**a** for the man of
peace.[k]
38But all sinners will be destroyed;
the future**b** of the wicked will be
cut off.[l]

39The salvation[m] of the righteous
comes from the LORD;
he is their stronghold in time of
trouble.[n]
40The LORD helps[o] them and
delivers[p] them;
he delivers them from the
wicked and saves them,
because they take refuge in him.

Psalm 38

A psalm of David. A petition.

1O LORD, do not rebuke me in your
anger
or discipline me in your wrath.[q]
2For your arrows[r] have pierced me,
and your hand has come down
upon me.
3Because of your wrath there is no
health in my body;
my bones[s] have no soundness
because of my sin.
4My guilt has overwhelmed me
like a burden too heavy to
bear.[t]

5My wounds fester and are
loathsome
because of my sinful folly.[u]
6I am bowed down and brought
very low;
all day long I go about
mourning.[v]
7My back is filled with searing
pain;[w]
there is no health in my body.
8I am feeble and utterly crushed;
I groan[x] in anguish of heart.

9All my longings lie open before
you, O Lord;
my sighing[y] is not hidden from
you.
10My heart pounds, my strength
fails[z] me;
even the light has gone from my
eyes.[a]
11My friends and companions avoid
me because of my
wounds;[b]
my neighbors stay far away.
12Those who seek my life set their
traps,[c]
those who would harm me talk
of my ruin;[d]
all day long they plot
deception.[e]

13I am like a deaf man, who cannot
hear,
like a mute, who cannot open
his mouth;
14I have become like a man who
does not hear,
whose mouth can offer no reply.
15I wait[f] for you, O LORD;
you will answer,[g] O Lord my
God.
16For I said, "Do not let them gloat[h]
or exalt themselves over me
when my foot slips."[i]

17For I am about to fall,
and my pain is ever with me.
18I confess my iniquity;[j]
I am troubled by my sin.
19Many are those who are my
vigorous enemies;[k]

a37 Or *there will be posterity* **b**38 Or *posterity*

37:27 [z]Ps 34:14
37:28 [a]Ps 21:10; Isa 14:20
37:29 [b]ver 9; Pr 2:21
37:31 [c]Dt 6:6; Ps 40:8; Isa 51:7 [d]ver 23
37:32 [e]Ps 10:8
37:33 [f]Ps 109:31; 2Pe 2:9
37:34 [g]Ps 27:14 [h]Ps 52:6
37:35 [i]Job 5:3
37:36 [j]Job 20:5
37:37 [k]Isa 57:1-2
37:38 [l]Ps 1:4
37:39 [m]Ps 3:8 [n]Ps 9:9
37:40 [o]1Ch 5:20 [p]Isa 31:5
38:1 [q]Ps 6:1
38:2 [r]Job 6:4; Ps 32:4
38:3 [s]Ps 6:2; Isa 1:6
38:4 [t]Ezr 9:6
38:5 [u]Ps 69:5
38:6 [v]Job 30:28; Ps 35:14; 42:9
38:7 [w]Ps 102:3
38:8 [x]Ps 22:1
38:9 [y]Job 3:24; Ps 6:6; 10:17
38:10 [z]Ps 31:10 [a]Ps 6:7
38:11 [b]Ps 31:11
38:12 [c]Ps 140:5 [d]Ps 35:4; 54:3 [e]Ps 35:20
38:15 [f]Ps 39:7 [g]Ps 17:6
38:16 [h]Ps 35:26 [i]Ps 13:4
38:18 [j]Ps 32:5
38:19 [k]Ps 18:17

those who hate me without
reason[l] are numerous.
20 Those who repay my good with
evil[m]
slander me when I pursue what
is good.

21 O LORD, do not forsake me;
be not far[n] from me, O my God.
22 Come quickly to help me,[o]
O Lord my Savior.[p]

Psalm 39

For the director of music. For Jeduthun. A psalm of David.

1 I said, "I will watch my ways[q]
and keep my tongue from sin;[r]
I will put a muzzle on my mouth
as long as the wicked are in my
presence."
2 But when I was silent[s] and still,
not even saying anything good,
my anguish increased.
3 My heart grew hot within me,
and as I meditated, the fire
burned;
then I spoke with my tongue:

4 "Show me, O LORD, my life's end
and the number of my days;[t]
let me know how fleeting is my
life.[u]
5 You have made my days[v] a mere
handbreadth;
the span of my years is as
nothing before you.
Each man's life is but a breath.[w]
Selah
6 Man is a mere phantom[x] as he
goes to and fro:
He bustles about, but only in
vain;[y]
he heaps up wealth, not knowing
who will get it.[z]

7 "But now, Lord, what do I look for?
My hope is in you.[a]
8 Save me[b] from all my
transgressions;[c]
do not make me the scorn of
fools.
9 I was silent; I would not open my
mouth,[d]
for you are the one who has
done this.
10 Remove your scourge from me;
I am overcome by the blow of
your hand.[e]
11 You rebuke[f] and discipline men
for their sin;
you consume their wealth like a
moth[g]—
each man is but a breath. *Selah*

12 "Hear my prayer, O LORD,
listen to my cry for help;
be not deaf to my weeping.
For I dwell with you as an alien,[h]
a stranger,[i] as all my fathers
were.
13 Look away from me, that I may
rejoice again
before I depart and am no
more."[j]

Psalm 40

For the director of music. Of David. A psalm.

1 I waited patiently[k] for the LORD;
he turned to me and heard my
cry.[l]
2 He lifted me out of the slimy pit,
out of the mud and mire;[m]
he set my feet on a rock[n]
and gave me a firm place to
stand.
3 He put a new song[o] in my mouth,
a hymn of praise to our God.
Many will see and fear
and put their trust in the LORD.

4 Blessed is the man[p]
who makes the LORD his trust,[q]
who does not look to the proud,
to those who turn aside to false
gods.[a]
5 Many, O LORD my God,
are the wonders[r] you have
done.
The things you planned for us
no one can recount[s] to you;
were I to speak and tell of them,
they would be too many to
declare.

6 Sacrifice and offering you did not
desire,[t]
but my ears you have
pierced[b,c];
burnt offerings[u] and sin offerings
you did not require.
7 Then I said, "Here I am, I have
come—
it is written about me in the
scroll.[d]
8 I desire to do your will,[v] O my
God;
your law is within my heart."[w]
9 I proclaim righteousness in the
great assembly;[x]
I do not seal my lips,
as you know,[y] O LORD.
10 I do not hide your righteousness in
my heart;

38:19 [l]Ps 35:19
38:20 [m]Ps 35:12; 1Jn 3:12
38:21 [n]Ps 35:22
38:22 [o]Ps 40:13 [p]Ps 27:1
39:1 [q]1Ki 2:4 [r]Job 2:10; Jas 3:2
39:2 [s]Ps 38:13
39:4 [t]Ps 90:12 [u]Ps 103:14
39:5 [v]Ps 89:45 [w]Ps 62:9
39:6 [x]1Pe 1:24 [y]Ps 127:2 [z]Lk 12:20
39:7 [a]Ps 38:15
39:8 [b]Ps 51:9 [c]Ps 44:13
39:9 [d]Job 2:10
39:10 [e]Job 9:34; Ps 32:4
39:11 [f]2Pe 2:16 [g]Job 13:28
39:12 [h]1Pe 2:11 [i]Heb 11:13
39:13 [j]Job 10:21; 14:10
40:1 [k]Ps 27:14 [l]Ps 34:15
40:2 [m]Ps 69:14 [n]Ps 27:5
40:3 [o]Ps 33:3
40:4 [p]Ps 34:8 [q]Ps 84:12
40:5 [r]Ps 136:4 [s]Ps 139:18; Isa 55:8
40:6 [t]1Sa 15:22; Am 5:22 [u]Isa 1:11
40:8 [v]Jn 4:34 [w]Ps 37:31
40:9 [x]Ps 22:25 [y]Jos 22:22; Ps 119:13

[a]4 Or *to falsehood* [b]6 Hebrew; Septuagint *but a body you have prepared for me* (see also Symmachus and Theodotion) [c]6 Or *opened* [d]7 Or *come / with the scroll written for me*

I speak of your faithfulness[z]
and salvation.
I do not conceal your love and
your truth
from the great assembly.[a]

11Do not withhold your mercy from
me, O LORD;
may your love[b] and your
truth[c] always protect me.
12For troubles[d] without number
surround me;
my sins have overtaken me, and
I cannot see.[e]
They are more than the hairs of my
head,[f]
and my heart fails[g] within me.

13Be pleased, O LORD, to save me;
O LORD, come quickly to help
me.[h]
14May all who seek to take my life
be put to shame and confusion;
may all who desire my ruin[i]
be turned back in disgrace.
15May those who say to me, "Aha!
Aha!"
be appalled at their own shame.
16But may all who seek you
rejoice and be glad in you;
may those who love your salvation
always say,
"The LORD be exalted!"[j]

17Yet I am poor and needy;
may the Lord think of me.
You are my help and my deliverer;
O my God, do not delay.[k]

Psalm 41

For the director of music. A psalm
of David.

1Blessed is he who has regard for
the weak;[l]
the LORD delivers him in times of
trouble.
2The LORD will protect him and
preserve his life;
he will bless him in the land[m]
and not surrender him to the
desire of his foes.[n]
3The LORD will sustain him on his
sickbed
and restore him from his bed of
illness.

4I said, "O LORD, have mercy[o] on
me;
heal me, for I have sinned[p]
against you."
5My enemies say of me in malice,
"When will he die and his name
perish?[q]"
6Whenever one comes to see me,
he speaks falsely,[r] while his
heart gathers slander;[s]
then he goes out and spreads it
abroad.

7All my enemies whisper together[t]
against me;
they imagine the worst for me,
saying,
8"A vile disease has beset him;
he will never get up from the
place where he lies."
9Even my close friend,[u] whom I
trusted,
he who shared my bread,
has lifted up his heel against
me.[v]

10But you, O LORD, have mercy on
me;
raise me up,[w] that I may repay
them.
11I know that you are pleased with
me,[x]
for my enemy does not triumph
over me.[y]
12In my integrity you uphold me[z]
and set me in your presence
forever.[a]

13Praise be to the LORD, the God of
Israel,[b]
from everlasting to everlasting.
Amen and Amen.[c]

BOOK II

Psalms 42–72

Psalm 42[a]

For the director of music. A *maskil*[b]
of the Sons of Korah.

1As the deer pants for streams of
water,
so my soul pants[d] for you,
O God.
2My soul thirsts[e] for God, for the
living God.[f]
When can I go[g] and meet with
God?
3My tears[h] have been my food
day and night,
while men say to me all day long,
"Where is your God?"[i]
4These things I remember
as I pour out my soul:
how I used to go with the
multitude,
leading the procession to the
house of God,[j]

40:10 [z]Ps 89:1 [a]Ac 20:20 **40:11** [b]Pr 20:28 [c]Ps 43:3 **40:12** [d]Ps 116:3 [e]Ps 38:4 [f]Ps 69:4 [g]Ps 73:26 **40:13** [h]Ps 70:1 **40:14** [i]Ps 35:4 **40:16** [j]Ps 35:27 **40:17** [k]Ps 70:5 **41:1** [l]Ps 82:3-4; Pr 14:21 **41:2** [m]Ps 37:22 [n]Ps 27:12 **41:4** [o]Ps 6:2 [p]Ps 51:4 **41:5** [q]Ps 38:12 **41:6** [r]Ps 12:2 [s]Pr 26:24 **41:7** [t]Ps 56:5; 71:10-11 **41:9** [u]2Sa 15:12; Ps 55:12 [v]Job 19:19; Ps 55:20; Mt 26:23; Jn 13:18* **41:10** [w]Ps 3:3 **41:11** [x]Ps 147:11 [y]Ps 25:2 **41:12** [z]Ps 37:17 [a]Job 36:7 **41:13** [b]Ps 72:18 [c]Ps 89:52; 106:48 **42:1** [d]Ps 119:131 **42:2** [e]Ps 63:1 [f]Jer 10:10 [g]Ps 43:4 **42:3** [h]Ps 80:5 [i]Ps 79:10 **42:4** [j]Isa 30:29

[a]In many Hebrew manuscripts Psalms 42 and 43 constitute one psalm. [b]Title: Probably a literary or musical term

with shouts of joy and
thanksgiving[k]
among the festive throng.

5Why are you downcast,[l] O my
soul?
Why so disturbed within me?
Put your hope in God,[m]
for I will yet praise him,
my Savior[n] and 6my God.

My**[a]** soul is downcast within me;
therefore I will remember you
from the land of the Jordan,
the heights of Hermon—from
Mount Mizar.
7Deep calls to deep
in the roar of your waterfalls;
all your waves and breakers
have swept over me.[o]
8By day the LORD directs his love,[p]
at night[q] his song[r] is with
me—
a prayer to the God of my life.
9I say to God my Rock,
"Why have you forgotten me?
Why must I go about mourning,[s]
oppressed by the enemy?"
10My bones suffer mortal agony
as my foes taunt me,
saying to me all day long,
"Where is your God?"

11Why are you downcast, O my soul?
Why so disturbed within me?
Put your hope in God,
for I will yet praise him,
my Savior and my God.[t]

42:1–43:5

PROMISE 1

HELP FOR HARD TIMES

"I'm depressed, so I'm going to . . ." How a man finishes that sentence says a lot about him. Psalms 42 and 43 (originally one psalm) describe the kind of hard times we all experience. Misunderstanding, feeling abandoned by God, even tears were part of the writer's struggle. When he was in the pits ("Why are you downcast O my soul?" 42:5, 11; 43:5), he told himself what to do: "Put your hope in God, for I will yet praise him."

The opening of this Psalm sounds almost like the words of an addict: "My soul *pants* for God . . . my soul *thirsts* for God . . . When can I go and meet with God?" The psalmist compared his craving for God to the way a deer on the run pants for a drink from a cold stream.

Finish the sentence posed above, "I'm depressed, so I'm going to . . . put my hope in God, for I will yet praise him" (42:5, 11; 43:5).

For the next Promise 1 reading go to page 615.

42:4 [k]Ps 100:4
42:5 [l]Ps 38:6; 77:3 [m]La 3:24 [n]Ps 44:3
42:7 [o]Ps 88:7; Jnh 2:3
42:8 [p]Ps 57:3 [q]Job 35:10 [r]Ps 63:6; 149:5
42:9 [s]Ps 38:6
42:11 [t]Ps 43:5
43:1 [u]1Sa 24:15; Ps 26:1; 35:1 [v]Ps 5:6
43:2 [w]Ps 44:9 [x]Ps 42:9
43:3 [y]Ps 36:9 [z]Ps 42:4 [a]Ps 84:1
43:4 [b]Ps 26:6 [c]Ps 33:2
43:5 [d]Ps 42:6
44:1 [e]Ex 12:26; Ps 78:3
44:2 [f]Ps 78:55 [g]Ex 15:17 [h]Ps 80:9
44:3 [i]Dt 8:17; Jos 24:12 [j]Ps 77:15 [k]Dt 4:37; 7:7-8
44:4 [l]Ps 74:12
44:5 [m]Ps 108:13
44:6 [n]Ps 33:16

Psalm 43**[b]**

1Vindicate me, O God,
and plead my cause[u] against an
ungodly nation;
rescue me from deceitful and
wicked men.[v]
2You are God my stronghold.
Why have you rejected[w] me?
Why must I go about mourning,
oppressed by the enemy?[x]
3Send forth your light[y] and your
truth,
let them guide me;
let them bring me to your holy
mountain,[z]
to the place where you dwell.[a]
4Then will I go to the altar[b] of God,
to God, my joy and my delight.
I will praise you with the harp,[c]
O God, my God.
5Why are you downcast, O my soul?
Why so disturbed within me?
Put your hope in God,
for I will yet praise him,
my Savior and my God.[d]

Psalm 44

For the director of music. Of the Sons of Korah. A *maskil*.**[c]**

1We have heard with our ears,
O God;
our fathers have told us[e]
what you did in their days,
in days long ago.
2With your hand you drove out[f]
the nations
and planted[g] our fathers;
you crushed the peoples
and made our fathers flourish.[h]
3It was not by their sword[i] that
they won the land,
nor did their arm bring them
victory;
it was your right hand, your arm,[j]
and the light of your face, for
you loved[k] them.

4You are my King[l] and my God,
who decrees**[d]** victories for Jacob.
5Through you we push back our
enemies;
through your name we trample[m]
our foes.
6I do not trust in my bow,[n]

a *5,6* A few Hebrew manuscripts, Septuagint and Syriac; most Hebrew manuscripts *praise him for his saving help. / 6O my God, my* **b** In many Hebrew manuscripts Psalms 42 and 43 constitute one psalm. **c** Title: Probably a literary or musical term **d** *4* Septuagint, Aquila and Syriac; Hebrew *King, O God; / command*

my sword does not bring me
victory;
7but you give us victory[o] over our
enemies,
you put our adversaries to
shame.[p]
8In God we make our boast[q] all
day long,
and we will praise your name
forever.[r] *Selah*

9But now you have rejected[s] and
humbled us;
you no longer go out with our
armies.[t]
10You made us retreat[u] before the
enemy,
and our adversaries have
plundered us.
11You gave us up to be devoured like
sheep[v]
and have scattered us among the
nations.[w]
12You sold your people for a
pittance,[x]
gaining nothing from their sale.

13You have made us a reproach to
our neighbors,[y]
the scorn[z] and derision of those
around us.
14You have made us a byword
among the nations;
the peoples shake their heads[a]
at us.
15My disgrace is before me all day
long,
and my face is covered with
shame
16at the taunts of those who reproach
and revile[b] me,
because of the enemy, who is
bent on revenge.

17All this happened to us,
though we had not forgotten[c]
you
or been false to your covenant.
18Our hearts had not turned[d] back;
our feet had not strayed from
your path.
19But you crushed[e] us and made us
a haunt for jackals
and covered us over with deep
darkness.[f]
20If we had forgotten[g] the name of
our God
or spread out our hands to a
foreign god,[h]
21would not God have discovered it,
since he knows the secrets of the
heart?[i]
22Yet for your sake we face death all
day long;
we are considered as sheep to be
slaughtered.[j]

44:7
[o]Ps 136:24
[p]Ps 53:5
44:8
[q]Ps 34:2
[r]Ps 30:12
44:9
[s]Ps 74:1
[t]Ps 60:1,10
44:10
[u]Lev 26:17;
Jos 7:8;
Ps 89:41
44:11
[v]Ro 8:36
[w]Dt 4:27;
28:64;
Ps 106:27
44:12
[x]Isa 52:3;
Jer 15:13; 52:3;
Jer 15:13
44:13
[y]Ps 79:4; 80:6
[z]Dt 28:37
44:14
[a]Ps 109:25;
Jer 24:9
44:16
[b]Ps 74:10
44:17
[c]Ps 78:7,57;
Da 9:13
44:18
[d]Job 23:11
44:19
[e]Ps 51:8
[f]Job 3:5
44:20
[g]Ps 78:11
[h]Dt 6:14;
Ps 81:9
44:21
[i]Ps 139:1-2;
Jer 17:10
44:22
[j]Isa 53:7;
Ro 8:36*

44:23
[k]Ps 7:6
[l]Ps 78:65
[m]Ps 77:7
44:24
[n]Job 13:24
[o]Ps 42:9
44:25
[p]Ps 119:25
44:26
[q]Ps 35:2
[r]Ps 25:22
45:2
[s]Lk 4:22
45:3
[t]Heb 4:12;
Rev 1:16
[u]Isa 9:6
45:4
[v]Rev 6:2
45:6
[w]Ps 93:2; 98:9
45:7
[x]Ps 33:5
[y]Isa 61:1
[z]Ps 21:6;
Heb 1:8-9*
45:8
[a]SS 1:3
45:9
[b]SS 6:8
[c]1Ki 2:19

23Awake,[k] O Lord! Why do you
sleep?[l]
Rouse yourself! Do not reject us
forever.[m]
24Why do you hide your face[n]
and forget our misery and
oppression?[o]

25We are brought down to the
dust;[p]
our bodies cling to the ground.
26Rise up[q] and help us;
redeem[r] us because of your
unfailing love.

Psalm 45

For the director of music. To ˻the
tune of˼ "Lilies." Of the Sons of
Korah. A *maskil*.[a] A wedding song.

1My heart is stirred by a noble
theme
as I recite my verses for the king;
my tongue is the pen of a skillful
writer.

2You are the most excellent of men
and your lips have been
anointed with grace,[s]
since God has blessed you
forever.
3Gird your sword[t] upon your side,
O mighty one;[u]
clothe yourself with splendor and
majesty.
4In your majesty ride forth
victoriously[v]
in behalf of truth, humility and
righteousness;
let your right hand display
awesome deeds.
5Let your sharp arrows pierce the
hearts of the king's enemies;
let the nations fall beneath your
feet.
6Your throne, O God, will last for
ever and ever;[w]
a scepter of justice will be the
scepter of your kingdom.
7You love righteousness[x] and hate
wickedness;
therefore God, your God, has set
you above your companions
by anointing[y] you with the oil
of joy.[z]
8All your robes are fragrant[a] with
myrrh and aloes and cassia;
from palaces adorned with ivory
the music of the strings makes
you glad.
9Daughters of kings[b] are among
your honored women;
at your right hand[c] is the royal
bride in gold of Ophir.

[a]Title: Probably a literary or musical term

10 Listen, O daughter, consider and
give ear:
Forget your people[d] and your
father's house.
11 The king is enthralled by your
beauty;
honor[e] him, for he is your
lord.[f]
12 The Daughter of Tyre will come
with a gift,[a][g]
men of wealth will seek your
favor.
13 All glorious[h] is the princess within
⌞her chamber⌟;
her gown is interwoven with
gold.
14 In embroidered garments she is led
to the king;[i]
her virgin companions follow her
and are brought to you.
15 They are led in with joy and
gladness;
they enter the palace of the king.

16 Your sons will take the place of
your fathers;
you will make them princes
throughout the land.
17 I will perpetuate your memory
through all generations;[j]
therefore the nations will praise
you[k] for ever and ever.

Psalm 46

For the director of music. Of the Sons of Korah. According to *alamoth*.[b] A song.

1 God is our refuge[l] and strength,
an ever-present[m] help in
trouble.
2 Therefore we will not fear,[n]
though the earth give way[o]
and the mountains fall[p] into the
heart of the sea,
3 though its waters roar[q] and foam
and the mountains quake with
their surging. *Selah*
4 There is a river whose streams
make glad the city of God,[r]
the holy place where the Most
High dwells.
5 God is within her,[s] she will not
fall;
God will help[t] her at break of
day.
6 Nations[u] are in uproar,
kingdoms[v] fall;
he lifts his voice, the earth
melts.[w]
7 The LORD Almighty is with us;[x]
the God of Jacob is our
fortress.[y] *Selah*

45:10 [d]Dt 21:13 **45:11** [e]Ps 95:6 [f]Isa 54:5 **45:12** [g]Ps 22:29; Isa 49:23 **45:13** [h]Isa 61:10 **45:14** [i]SS 1:4 **45:17** [j]Mal 1:11 [k]Ps 138:4 **46:1** [l]Ps 9:9; 14:6 [m]Dt 4:7 **46:2** [n]Ps 23:4 [o]Ps 82:5 [p]Ps 18:7 **46:3** [q]Ps 93:3 **46:4** [r]Ps 48:1,8; Isa 60:14 **46:5** [s]Isa 12:6; Eze 43:7 [t]Ps 37:40 **46:6** [u]Ps 2:1 [v]Ps 68:32 [w]Mic 1:4 **46:7** [x]2Ch 13:12 [y]Ps 9:9 **46:8** [z]Ps 66:5 [a]Isa 61:4 **46:9** [b]Isa 2:4 [c]Ps 76:3 [d]Eze 39:9 **46:10** [e]Ps 100:3 [f]Isa 2:11 **47:1** [g]Ps 98:8; Isa 55:12 [h]Ps 106:47 **47:2** [i]Dt 7:21 [j]Mal 1:14 **47:3** [k]Ps 18:39,47 **47:4** [l]1Pe 1:4 **47:5** [m]Ps 68:33; 98:6 **47:6** [n]Ps 68:4; 89:18 **47:7** [o]Zec 14:9 [p]Col 3:16 **47:8** [q]1Ch 16:31 **47:9** [r]Ps 72:11; 89:18 [s]Ps 97:9

8 Come and see the works of the
LORD,[z]
the desolations[a] he has brought
on the earth.
9 He makes wars[b] cease to the ends
of the earth;
he breaks the bow[c] and shatters
the spear,
he burns the shields[c] with
fire.[d]
10 "Be still, and know that I am
God;[e]
I will be exalted[f] among the
nations,
I will be exalted in the earth."
11 The LORD Almighty is with us;
the God of Jacob is our fortress.
Selah

Psalm 47

For the director of music. Of the Sons of Korah. A psalm.

1 Clap your hands,[g] all you nations;
shout to God with cries of joy.[h]
2 How awesome[i] is the LORD Most
High,
the great King[j] over all the
earth!
3 He subdued[k] nations under us,
peoples under our feet.
4 He chose our inheritance[l]
for us,
the pride of Jacob, whom
he loved. *Selah*

5 God has ascended amid shouts of
joy,
the LORD amid the sounding of
trumpets.[m]
6 Sing praises[n] to God, sing praises;
sing praises to our King, sing
praises.

7 For God is the King of all the
earth;[o]
sing to him a psalm[d][p] of
praise.
8 God reigns[q] over the nations;
God is seated on his holy throne.
9 The nobles of the nations assemble
as the people of the God of
Abraham,
for the kings[e] of the earth belong
to God;[r]
he is greatly exalted.[s]

[a] *12* Or *A Tyrian robe is among the gifts*
[b] Title: Probably a musical term [c] *9* Or *chariots* [d] *7* Or *a maskil* (probably a literary or musical term) [e] *9* Or *shields*

Psalm 48

A song. A psalm of the Sons of Korah.

1Great is the LORD,[t] and most
worthy of praise,
in the city of our God,[u] his holy
mountain.[v]
2It is beautiful[w] in its loftiness,
the joy of the whole earth.
Like the utmost heights of
Zaphon[a] is Mount Zion,
the[b] city of the Great King.[x]
3God is in her citadels;
he has shown himself to be her
fortress.[y]

4When the kings joined forces,
when they advanced together,[z]
5they saw ⌊her⌋ and were astounded;
they fled in terror.[a]
6Trembling seized them there,
pain like that of a woman in
labor.
7You destroyed them like ships of
Tarshish
shattered by an east wind.[b]
8As we have heard,
so have we seen
in the city of the LORD Almighty,
in the city of our God:
God makes her secure forever.[c]
Selah

9Within your temple, O God,
we meditate on your unfailing
love.[d]
10Like your name,[e] O God,
your praise reaches to the ends
of the earth;[f]
your right hand is filled with
righteousness.
11Mount Zion rejoices,
the villages of Judah are glad
because of your judgments.[g]

12Walk about Zion, go around her,
count her towers,
13consider well her ramparts,
view her citadels,[h]
that you may tell of them to the
next generation.[i]
14For this God is our God for ever
and ever;
he will be our guide[j] even to
the end.

Psalm 49

For the director of music. Of the Sons of Korah. A psalm.

1Hear this, all you peoples;[k]
listen, all who live in this
world,[l]
2both low and high,
rich and poor alike:
3My mouth will speak words of
wisdom;[m]
the utterance from my heart will
give understanding.[n]
4I will turn my ear to a proverb;[o]
with the harp I will expound my
riddle:[p]

5Why should I fear[q] when evil days
come,
when wicked deceivers surround
me—
6those who trust in their wealth[r]
and boast of their great riches?
7No man can redeem the life of
another
or give to God a ransom for
him—
8the ransom for a life is costly,
no payment is ever enough—[s]
9that he should live on[t] forever
and not see decay.

10For all can see that wise men die;[u]
the foolish and the senseless
alike perish
and leave their wealth to
others.[v]
11Their tombs will remain their
houses[c] forever,
their dwellings for endless
generations,
though they had[d] named[w]
lands after themselves.

12But man, despite his riches, does
not endure;
he is[e] like the beasts that
perish.

13This is the fate of those who trust
in themselves,[x]
and of their followers, who
approve their sayings. *Selah*
14Like sheep they are destined for
the grave,[f][y]
and death will feed on them.
The upright will rule[z] over them
in the morning;
their forms will decay in the
grave,[f]
far from their princely mansions.
15But God will redeem my life[g] from
the grave;[a]
he will surely take me to
himself.[b] *Selah*

48:1 [t]Ps 96:4 [u]Ps 46:4 [v]Isa 2:2-3; Mic 4:1; Zec 8:3
48:2 [w]Ps 50:2; La 2:15 [x]Mt 5:35
48:3 [y]Ps 46:7
48:4 [z]2Sa 10:1-19
48:5 [a]Ex 15:16
48:7 [b]Jer 18:17; Eze 27:26
48:8 [c]Ps 87:5
48:9 [d]Ps 26:3
48:10 [e]Dt 28:58; Jos 7:9 [f]Isa 41:10
48:11 [g]Ps 97:8
48:13 [h]ver 3; Ps 122:7 [i]Ps 78:6
48:14 [j]Ps 23:4
49:1 [k]Ps 78:1 [l]Ps 33:8
49:3 [m]Ps 37:30 [n]Ps 119:130
49:4 [o]Ps 78:2 [p]Nu 12:8
49:5 [q]Ps 23:4
49:6 [r]Job 31:24
49:8 [s]Mt 16:26
49:9 [t]Ps 22:29; 89:48
49:10 [u]Ecc 2:16 [v]Ecc 2:18,21
49:11 [w]Ge 4:17; Dt 3:14
49:13 [x]Lk 12:20
49:14 [y]Job 24:19; Ps 9:17 [z]Da 7:18; Mal 4:3; 1Co 6:2; Rev 2:26
49:15 [a]Ps 56:13; Hos 13:14 [b]Ps 73:24

[a]*2 Zaphon* can refer to a sacred mountain or the direction north. [b]*2* Or *earth, / Mount Zion, on the northern side / of the* [c]*11* Septuagint and Syriac; Hebrew *In their thoughts their houses will remain* [d]*11* Or / *for they have* [e]*12* Hebrew; Septuagint and Syriac read verse 12 the same as verse 20. [f]*14* Hebrew *Sheol*; also in verse 15 [g]*15* Or *soul*

16 Do not be overawed when a man
grows rich,
when the splendor of his house
increases;
17 for he will take nothing with him
when he dies,
his splendor will not descend
with him.[c]
18 Though while he lived he counted
himself blessed—[d]
and men praise you when you
prosper—
19 he will join the generation of his
fathers,[e]
who will never see the light[f] ⌞of
life⌟.
20 A man who has riches without
understanding
is like the beasts that perish.[g]

Psalm 50

A psalm of Asaph.

1 The Mighty One, God, the LORD,[h]
speaks and summons the earth
from the rising of the sun to the
place where it sets.[i]
2 From Zion, perfect in beauty,[j]
God shines forth.[k]
3 Our God comes[l] and will not be
silent;
a fire devours before him,[m]
and around him a tempest rages.
4 He summons the heavens above,
and the earth,[n] that he may
judge his people:
5 "Gather to me my consecrated
ones,[o]
who made a covenant[p] with me
by sacrifice."

49:20

A DOSE OF REALITY

PROMISE 1

What a contrast! Like a cold shower on a hot day, this psalm jolts anyone who has just read about God's glory in Psalms 46–48. This psalm is a stern warning about becoming overly impressed by or secure in personal wealth and power. This is not a statement against either of these gifts from God, but a warning that they can give us a false sense of reality. To know the God of Psalms 46–48 is to gain the understanding called for in Psalm 49:20.

Get a running start on Psalm 49 by reading Psalms 46–48. Then Psalm 49:20 makes a powerful statement about honoring and obeying God.

For the next Promise 1 reading go to page 623.

49:17 [c]Ps 17:14; 1Ti 6:7
49:18 [d]Dt 29:19; Lk 12:19
49:19 [e]Ge 15:15 [f]Job 33:30
49:20 [g]Ecc 3:19
50:1 [h]Jos 22:22 [i]Ps 113:3
50:2 [j]Ps 48:2 [k]Dt 33:2; Ps 80:1
50:3 [l]Ps 96:13 [m]Ps 97:3; Da 7:10
50:4 [n]Dt 4:26; Isa 1:2
50:5 [o]Ps 30:4 [p]Ex 24:7

50:6 [q]Ps 89:5 [r]Ps 75:7
50:7 [s]Ps 81:8 [t]Ex 20:2
50:8 [u]Ps 40:6; Hos 6:6
50:9 [v]Ps 69:31
50:10 [w]Ps 104:24
50:12 [x]Ex 19:5
50:14 [y]Heb 13:15 [z]Dt 23:21
50:15 [a]Ps 81:7 [b]Ps 22:23
50:16 [c]Isa 29:13
50:17 [d]Ne 9:26; Ro 2:21-22
50:18 [e]Ro 1:32; 1Ti 5:22
50:19 [f]Ps 10:7; 52:2
50:20 [g]Mt 10:21
50:21 [h]Ecc 8:11; Isa 42:14 [i]Ps 90:8
50:22 [j]Job 8:13; Ps 9:17

6 And the heavens proclaim[q] his
righteousness,
for God himself is judge.[r] *Selah*
7 "Hear, O my people, and I will
speak,
O Israel, and I will testify[s]
against you:
I am God, your God.[t]
8 I do not rebuke you for your
sacrifices
or your burnt offerings,[u] which
are ever before me.
9 I have no need of a bull[v] from
your stall
or of goats from your pens,
10 for every animal of the forest is
mine,
and the cattle on a thousand
hills.[w]
11 I know every bird in the
mountains,
and the creatures of the field are
mine.
12 If I were hungry I would not tell
you,
for the world[x] is mine, and all
that is in it.
13 Do I eat the flesh of bulls
or drink the blood of goats?
14 Sacrifice thank offerings[y] to God,
fulfill your vows[z] to the Most
High,
15 and call[a] upon me in the day of
trouble;
I will deliver you, and you will
honor[b] me."

16 But to the wicked, God says:

"What right have you to recite my
laws
or take my covenant on your
lips?[c]
17 You hate my instruction
and cast my words behind[d] you.
18 When you see a thief, you join[e]
with him;
you throw in your lot with
adulterers.
19 You use your mouth for evil
and harness your tongue to
deceit.[f]
20 You speak continually against your
brother[g]
and slander your own mother's
son.
21 These things you have done and I
kept silent;[h]
you thought I was altogether[a]
like you.
But I will rebuke you
and accuse[i] you to your face.
22 "Consider this, you who forget
God,[j]

[a]21 Or *thought the 'I AM' was*

or I will tear you to pieces, with
none to rescue:[k]
23He who sacrifices thank offerings
honors me,
and he prepares the way[l]
so that I may show him[a] the
salvation of God.[m]"

Psalm 51

For the director of music. A psalm of David. When the prophet Nathan came to him after David had committed adultery with Bathsheba.

3 →PG. 628

1Have mercy on me, O God,
according to your unfailing love;
according to your great compassion
blot out[n] my transgressions.[o]
2Wash away[p] all my iniquity
and cleanse[q] me from my sin.
3For I know my transgressions,
and my sin is always before
me.[r]
4Against you, you only, have I
sinned
and done what is evil in your
sight,[s]
so that you are proved right when
you speak
and justified when you judge.[t]
5Surely I was sinful[u] at birth,
sinful from the time my mother
conceived me.
6Surely you desire truth in the inner
parts[b];
you teach[c] me wisdom[v] in the
inmost place.[w]
7Cleanse me with hyssop,[x] and I
will be clean;
wash me, and I will be whiter
than snow.[y]
8Let me hear joy and gladness;[z]
let the bones you have crushed
rejoice.
9Hide your face from my sins[a]
and blot out all my iniquity.
10Create in me a pure heart,[b]
O God,
and renew a steadfast spirit
within me.[c]
11Do not cast me from your presence
or take your Holy Spirit[d] from
me.
12Restore to me the joy of your
salvation[e]
and grant me a willing spirit, to
sustain me.
13Then I will teach transgressors your
ways,[f]
and sinners will turn back to
you.[g]
14Save me from bloodguilt,[h] O God,
the God who saves me,[i]

50:22 [k]Ps 7:2
50:23 [l]Ps 85:13 [m]Ps 91:16
51:1 [n]Ac 3:19 [o]Isa 43:25; Col 2:14
51:2 [p]1Jn 1:9 [q]Heb 9:14
51:3 [r]Isa 59:12
51:4 [s]Ge 20:6; Lk 15:21 [t]Ro 3:4*
51:5 [u]Job 14:4
51:6 [v]Pr 2:6 [w]Ps 15:2
51:7 [x]Lev 14:4; Heb 9:19 [y]Isa 1:18
51:8 [z]Isa 35:10
51:9 [a]Jer 16:17
51:10 [b]Ps 78:37; Ac 15:9 [c]Eze 18:31
51:11 [d]Eph 4:30
51:12 [e]Ps 13:5
51:13 [f]Ac 9:21-22 [g]Ps 22:27
51:14 [h]2Sa 12:9 [i]Ps 25:5
[j]Ps 35:28
51:15 [k]Ps 9:14
51:16 [l]1Sa 15:22; Ps 40:6
51:17 [m]Ps 34:18
51:18 [n]Ps 102:16; Isa 51:3
51:19 [o]Ps 4:5 [p]Ps 66:13 [q]Ps 66:15
52 Title [r]1Sa 22:9
52:1 [s]Ps 94:4
52:2 [t]Ps 57:4 [u]Ps 50:19
52:3 [v]Jer 9:5
52:4 [w]Ps 120:2,3
52:5 [x]Isa 22:19 [y]Pr 2:22 [z]Ps 27:13
52:6 [a]Job 22:19; Ps 37:34; 40:3
52:7 [b]Ps 49:6
52:8 [c]Jer 11:16

and my tongue will sing of your
righteousness.[j]
15O Lord, open my lips,[k]
and my mouth will declare your
praise.
16You do not delight in sacrifice,[l] or
I would bring it;
you do not take pleasure in
burnt offerings.
17The sacrifices of God are[d] a
broken spirit;
a broken and contrite heart,[m]
O God, you will not despise.
18In your good pleasure make Zion[n]
prosper;
build up the walls of Jerusalem.
19Then there will be righteous
sacrifices,[o]
whole burnt offerings[p] to
delight you;
then bulls[q] will be offered on
your altar.

Psalm 52

For the director of music. A *maskil*[e] of David. When Doeg the Edomite[r] had gone to Saul and told him: "David has gone to the house of Ahimelech."

1Why do you boast of evil, you
mighty man?
Why do you boast[s] all day long,
you who are a disgrace in the
eyes of God?
2Your tongue plots destruction;
it is like a sharpened razor,[t]
you who practice deceit.[u]
3You love evil rather than good,
falsehood[v] rather than speaking
the truth. *Selah*
4You love every harmful word,
O you deceitful tongue![w]
5Surely God will bring you down to
everlasting ruin:
He will snatch you up and tear[x]
you from your tent;
he will uproot[y] you from the
land of the living.[z] *Selah*
6The righteous will see and fear;
they will laugh[a] at him, saying,
7"Here now is the man
who did not make God his
stronghold
but trusted in his great wealth[b]
and grew strong by destroying
others!"
8But I am like an olive tree[c]

a23 Or *and to him who considers his way / I will show* **b**6 The meaning of the Hebrew for this phrase is uncertain. **c**6 Or *you desired . . . ; / you taught* **d**17 Or *My sacrifice, O God, is* **e**Title: Probably a literary or musical term

flourishing in the house of God;
I trust[d] in God's unfailing love
for ever and ever.
9 I will praise you forever[e] for what
you have done;
in your name I will hope, for
your name is good.[f]
I will praise you in the presence
of your saints.

Psalm 53

For the director of music. According to *mahalath*.[a] A *maskil*[b] of David.

1 The fool[g] says in his heart,
"There is no God."[h]
They are corrupt, and their ways
are vile;
there is no one who does good.

2 God looks down from heaven[i]
on the sons of men
to see if there are any who
understand,
any who seek God.[j]
3 Everyone has turned away,
they have together become
corrupt;
there is no one who does good,
not even one.[k]

4 Will the evildoers never learn—
those who devour my people as
men eat bread
and who do not call on God?
5 There they were, overwhelmed with
dread,
where there was nothing to
dread.[l]
God scattered the bones[m] of those
who attacked you;
you put them to shame, for God
despised them.

6 Oh, that salvation for Israel would
come out of Zion!
When God restores the fortunes
of his people,
let Jacob rejoice and Israel be
glad!

Psalm 54

For the director of music. With stringed instruments. A *maskil*[b] of David. When the Ziphites had gone to Saul and said, "Is not David hiding among us?"

1 Save me, O God, by your name;[n]
vindicate me by your might.[o]
2 Hear my prayer, O God;[p]
listen to the words of my mouth.

3 Strangers are attacking me;[q]
ruthless men seek my life[r]—
men without regard for God.[s]
Selah

4 Surely God is my help;[t]
the Lord is the one who sustains
me.[u]

5 Let evil recoil[v] on those who
slander me;
in your faithfulness[w] destroy
them.

6 I will sacrifice a freewill offering[x]
to you;
I will praise your name, O LORD,
for it is good.[y]
7 For he has delivered me[z] from all
my troubles,
and my eyes have looked in
triumph on my foes.[a]

Psalm 55

For the director of music. With stringed instruments. A *maskil*[b] of David.

1 Listen to my prayer, O God,
do not ignore my plea;[b]
2 hear me and answer me.[c]
My thoughts trouble me and I am
distraught[d]
3 at the voice of the enemy,
at the stares of the wicked;
for they bring down suffering upon
me[e]
and revile me in their anger.[f]

4 My heart is in anguish within me;
the terrors[g] of death assail me.
5 Fear and trembling[h] have beset
me;
horror has overwhelmed me.
6 I said, "Oh, that I had the wings of
a dove!
I would fly away and be at rest—
7 I would flee far away
and stay in the desert; *Selah*
8 I would hurry to my place of
shelter,
far from the tempest and
storm.[i]"

9 Confuse the wicked, O Lord,
confound their speech,
for I see violence and strife[j] in
the city.
10 Day and night they prowl about on
its walls;
malice and abuse are within it.
11 Destructive forces[k] are at work in
the city;
threats and lies[l] never leave its
streets.

12 If an enemy were insulting me,

[a]Title: Probably a musical term [b]Title: Probably a literary or musical term

52:8 [d]Ps 13:5
52:9 [e]Ps 30:12 [f]Ps 54:6
53:1 [g]Ps 14:1-7; Ro 3:10 [h]Ps 10:4
53:2 [i]Ps 33:13 [j]2Ch 15:2
53:3 [k]Ro 3:10-12*
53:5 [l]Lev 26:17 [m]Eze 6:5
54:1 [n]Ps 20:1 [o]2Ch 20:6
54:2 [p]Ps 5:1; 55:1
54:3 [q]Ps 86:14 [r]Ps 40:14 [s]Ps 36:1
54:4 [t]Ps 118:7 [u]Ps 41:12
54:5 [v]Ps 94:23 [w]Ps 89:49; 143:12
54:6 [x]Ps 50:14 [y]Ps 52:9
54:7 [z]Ps 34:6 [a]Ps 59:10
55:1 [b]Ps 27:9; 61:1
55:2 [c]Ps 66:19 [d]Ps 77:3; Isa 38:14
55:3 [e]2Sa 16:6-8; Ps 17:9 [f]Ps 71:11
55:4 [g]Ps 116:3
55:5 [h]Job 21:6; Ps 119:120
55:8 [i]Isa 4:6
55:9 [j]Jer 6:7
55:11 [k]Ps 5:9 [l]Ps 10:7

I could endure it;
if a foe were raising himself against me,
I could hide from him.
13But it is you, a man like myself,
my companion, my close friend,[m]
14with whom I once enjoyed sweet fellowship
as we walked with the throng at the house of God.[n]

15Let death take my enemies by surprise;[o]
let them go down alive to the grave,[a][p]
for evil finds lodging among them.

16But I call to God,
and the LORD saves me.
17Evening,[q] morning[r] and noon
I cry out in distress,
and he hears my voice.
18He ransoms me unharmed
from the battle waged against me,
even though many oppose me.
19God, who is enthroned forever,[s]
will hear[t] them and afflict them— *Selah*
men who never change their ways
and have no fear of God.

20My companion attacks his friends;[u]
he violates his covenant.[v]
21His speech is smooth as butter,
yet war is in his heart;
his words are more soothing than oil,[w]
yet they are drawn swords.[x]

22Cast your cares on the LORD
and he will sustain you;[y]
he will never let the righteous fall.[z]
23But you, O God, will bring down the wicked
into the pit[a] of corruption;
bloodthirsty and deceitful men[b]
will not live out half their days.[c]

But as for me, I trust in you.[d]

Psalm 56

For the director of music. To ⌞the tune of⌟ "A Dove on Distant Oaks." Of David. A *miktam*.[b] When the Philistines had seized him in Gath.

1Be merciful to me, O God, for men hotly pursue me;[e]
all day long they press their attack.
2My slanderers pursue me all day long;[f]

55:13 [m]2Sa 15:12; Ps 41:9 **55:14** [n]Ps 42:4 **55:15** [o]Ps 64:7 [p]Nu 16:30,33 **55:17** [q]Ps 141:2; Ac 3:1 [r]Ps 5:3 **55:19** [s]Dt 33:27 [t]Ps 78:59 **55:20** [u]Ps 7:4 [v]Ps 89:34 **55:21** [w]Pr 5:3 [x]Ps 28:3; Ps 57:4; 59:7 **55:22** [y]Ps 37:5; Mt 6:25-34; 1Pe 5:7 [z]Ps 37:24 **55:23** [a]Ps 73:18 [b]Ps 5:6 [c]Job 15:32; Pr 10:27 [d]Ps 25:2 **56:1** [e]Ps 57:1-3 **56:2** [f]Ps 57:3

[g]Ps 35:1 **56:3** [h]Ps 55:4-5 **56:4** [i]Ps 118:6; Heb 13:6 **56:5** [j]Ps 41:7 **56:6** [k]Ps 59:3 [l]Ps 71:10 **56:7** [m]Ps 36:12; 55:23 **56:8** [n]Mal 3:16 **56:9** [o]Ps 9:3 [p]Ps 102:2 [q]Ro 8:31 **56:12** [r]Ps 50:14 **56:13** [s]Ps 116:8 [t]Job 33:30 **57:1** [u]Ps 2:12 [v]Ps 17:8 [w]Isa 26:20 **57:2** [x]Ps 138:8 **57:3** [y]Ps 18:9,16

many are attacking me in their pride.[g]
3When I am afraid,[h]
I will trust in you.
4In God, whose word I praise,
in God I trust; I will not be afraid.
What can mortal man do to me?[i]

5All day long they twist my words;[j]
they are always plotting to harm me.
6They conspire,[k] they lurk,
they watch my steps,
eager to take my life.[l]
7On no account let them escape;
in your anger, O God, bring down the nations.[m]
8Record my lament;
list my tears on your scroll[c]—
are they not in your record?[n]
9Then my enemies will turn back[o]
when I call for help.[p]
By this I will know that God is for me.[q]
10In God, whose word I praise,
in the LORD, whose word I praise—
11in God I trust; I will not be afraid.
What can man do to me?

12I am under vows[r] to you, O God;
I will present my thank offerings to you.
13For you have delivered me[d] from death[s]
and my feet from stumbling,
that I may walk before God
in the light of life.[e][t]

Psalm 57

For the director of music. ⌞To the tune of⌟ "Do Not Destroy." Of David. A *miktam*.[b] When he had fled from Saul into the cave.

1Have mercy on me, O God, have mercy on me,
for in you my soul takes refuge.[u]
I will take refuge in the shadow of your wings[v]
until the disaster has passed.[w]

2I cry out to God Most High,
to God, who fulfills ⌞his purpose⌟ for me.[x]
3He sends from heaven and saves me,[y]

[a]*15* Hebrew *Sheol* [b]Title: Probably a literary or musical term [c]*8* Or / *put my tears in your wineskin* [d]*13* Or *my soul* [e]*13* Or *the land of the living*

rebuking those who hotly pursue
me;[z] *Selah*
God sends his love and his
faithfulness.[a]

4I am in the midst of lions;[b]
I lie among ravenous beasts—
men whose teeth are spears and
arrows,
whose tongues are sharp
swords.[c]

5Be exalted, O God, above the
heavens;
let your glory be over all the
earth.[d]

6They spread a net for my feet—
I was bowed down[e] in distress.
They dug a pit[f] in my path—
but they have fallen into it
themselves.[g] *Selah*

7My heart is steadfast, O God,
my heart is steadfast;[h]
I will sing and make music.
8Awake, my soul!
Awake, harp and lyre![i]
I will awaken the dawn.

9I will praise you, O Lord, among
the nations;
I will sing of you among the
peoples.
10For great is your love, reaching to
the heavens;
your faithfulness reaches to the
skies.[j]

11Be exalted, O God, above the
heavens;
let your glory be over all the
earth.[k]

Psalm 58

For the director of music. ⌞To the tune of⌟ "Do Not Destroy." Of David. A *miktam*.[a]

1Do you rulers indeed speak
justly?[l]
Do you judge uprightly among
men?
2No, in your heart you devise
injustice,
and your hands mete out
violence on the earth.[m]
3Even from birth the wicked go
astray;
from the womb they are
wayward and speak lies.
4Their venom is like the venom of a
snake,[n]
like that of a cobra that has
stopped its ears,
5that will not heed the tune of the
charmer,

57:3 [z]Ps 56:1 [a]Ps 40:11 **57:4** [b]Ps 35:17 [c]Ps 55:21; Pr 30:14 **57:5** [d]Ps 108:5 **57:6** [e]Ps 145:14 [f]Ps 35:7 [g]Ps 7:15; Pr 28:10 **57:7** [h]Ps 108:1 **57:8** [i]Ps 16:9; 30:12; 150:3 **57:10** [j]Ps 36:5; 103:11 **57:11** [k]ver 5 **58:1** [l]Ps 82:2 **58:2** [m]Ps 94:20; Mal 3:15 **58:4** [n]Ps 140:3; Ecc 10:11

58:6 [o]Ps 3:7 [p]Job 4:10 **58:7** [q]Jos 7:5; Ps 112:10 [r]Ps 64:3 **58:8** [s]Job 3:16 **58:9** [t]Ps 118:12 [u]Pr 10:25 **58:10** [v]Ps 64:10; 91:8 [w]Ps 68:23 **58:11** [x]Ps 9:8; 18:20 **59:1** [y]Ps 143:9 **59:2** [z]Ps 139:19 **59:3** [a]Ps 56:6 **59:4** [b]Ps 35:19,23 **59:5** [c]Jer 18:23

however skillful the enchanter
may be.

6Break the teeth in their mouths,
O God;[o]
tear out, O LORD, the fangs of the
lions![p]
7Let them vanish like water that
flows away;[q]
when they draw the bow, let
their arrows be blunted.[r]
8Like a slug melting away as it
moves along,
like a stillborn child,[s] may they
not see the sun.

9Before your pots can feel ⌞the heat
of⌟ the thorns[t]—
whether they be green or dry—
the wicked will be swept
away.[b] [u]
10The righteous will be glad when
they are avenged,[v]
when they bathe their feet in the
blood of the wicked.[w]
11Then men will say,
"Surely the righteous still are
rewarded;
surely there is a God who judges
the earth."[x]

Psalm 59

For the director of music. ⌞To the tune of⌟ "Do Not Destroy." Of David. A *miktam*.[a] When Saul had sent men to watch David's house in order to kill him.

1Deliver me from my enemies,
O God;[y]
protect me from those who rise
up against me.
2Deliver me from evildoers
and save me from bloodthirsty
men.[z]
3See how they lie in wait for me!
Fierce men conspire[a] against
me
for no offense or sin of mine,
O LORD.
4I have done no wrong, yet they are
ready to attack me.[b]
Arise to help me; look on my
plight!
5O LORD God Almighty, the God of
Israel,
rouse yourself to punish all the
nations;
show no mercy to wicked
traitors.[c] *Selah*

6They return at evening,

[a]Title: Probably a literary or musical term
[b]9 The meaning of the Hebrew for this verse is uncertain.

snarling like dogs,[d]
and prowl about the city.
7 See what they spew from their mouths—
they spew out swords[e] from their lips,
and they say, "Who can hear us?"[f]
8 But you, O LORD, laugh at them;[g]
you scoff at all those nations.[h]

9 O my Strength, I watch for you;
you, O God, are my fortress,[i]
10 my loving God.

God will go before me
and will let me gloat over those who slander me.
11 But do not kill them, O Lord our shield,[a][j]
or my people will forget.[k]
In your might make them wander about,
and bring them down.[l]
12 For the sins of their mouths,[m]
for the words of their lips,[n]
let them be caught in their pride.[o]
For the curses and lies they utter,
13 consume them in wrath,
consume them till they are no more.[p]
Then it will be known to the ends of the earth
that God rules over Jacob.[q]
Selah
14 They return at evening,
snarling like dogs,
and prowl about the city.
15 They wander about for food[r]
and howl if not satisfied.
16 But I will sing of your strength,[s]
in the morning[t] I will sing of your love;[u]
for you are my fortress,
my refuge in times of trouble.[v]
17 O my Strength, I sing praise to you;
you, O God, are my fortress, my loving God.

Psalm 60

For the director of music. To ⌊the tune of⌋ "The Lily of the Covenant." A *miktam*[b] of David. For teaching. When he fought Aram Naharaim[c] and Aram Zobah,[d] and when Joab returned and struck down twelve thousand Edomites in the Valley of Salt.

1 You have rejected us,[w] O God, and burst forth upon us;
you have been angry[x]—now restore us![y]
2 You have shaken the land[z] and torn it open;
mend its fractures,[a] for it is quaking.
3 You have shown your people desperate times;[b]
you have given us wine that makes us stagger.[c]

4 But for those who fear you, you have raised a banner
to be unfurled against the bow.
Selah

5 Save us and help us with your right hand,[d]
that those you love[e] may be delivered.
6 God has spoken from his sanctuary:
"In triumph I will parcel out Shechem[f]
and measure off the Valley of Succoth.
7 Gilead[g] is mine, and Manasseh is mine;
Ephraim is my helmet,
Judah[h] my scepter.[i]
8 Moab is my washbasin,
upon Edom I toss my sandal;
over Philistia I shout in triumph.[j]"

9 Who will bring me to the fortified city?
Who will lead me to Edom?
10 Is it not you, O God, you who have rejected us
and no longer go out with our armies?[k]
11 Give us aid against the enemy,
for the help of man is worthless.[l]
12 With God we will gain the victory,
and he will trample down our enemies.[m]

Psalm 61

For the director of music. With stringed instruments. Of David.

1 Hear my cry, O God;[n]
listen to my prayer.[o]

2 From the ends of the earth I call to you,
I call as my heart grows faint;[p]
lead me to the rock[q] that is higher than I.
3 For you have been my refuge,[r]
a strong tower against the foe.[s]

59:6 [d]ver 14
59:7 [e]Ps 57:4 [f]Ps 10:11
59:8 [g]Ps 37:13; Pr 1:26 [h]Ps 2:4
59:9 [i]Ps 9:9; 62:2
59:11 [j]Ps 84:9 [k]Dt 4:9 [l]Ps 106:27
59:12 [m]Ps 10:7 [n]Pr 12:13 [o]Zep 3:11
59:13 [p]Ps 104:35 [q]Ps 83:18
59:15 [r]Job 15:23
59:16 [s]Ps 21:13 [t]Ps 88:13 [u]Ps 101:1 [v]Ps 46:1
60:1 [w]2Sa 5:20; Ps 44:9 [x]Ps 79:5 [y]Ps 80:3
60:2 [z]Ps 18:7 [a]2Ch 7:14
60:3 [b]Ps 71:20 [c]Isa 51:17; Jer 25:16
60:5 [d]Ps 17:7; 108:6 [e]Ps 127:2
60:6 [f]Ge 12:6
60:7 [g]Jos 13:31 [h]Dt 33:17 [i]Ge 49:10
60:8 [j]2Sa 8:1
60:10 [k]Jos 7:12; Ps 44:9; 108:11
60:11 [l]Ps 146:3
60:12 [m]Nu 24:18; Ps 44:5
61:1 [n]Ps 64:1 [o]Ps 86:6
61:2 [p]Ps 77:3 [q]Ps 18:2
61:3 [r]Ps 62:7 [s]Pr 18:10

[a] *11* Or *sovereign* [b] Title: Probably a literary or musical term [c] Title: That is, Arameans of Northwest Mesopotamia [d] Title: That is, Arameans of central Syria

4 I long to dwell[t] in your tent
forever
and take refuge in the shelter of
your wings.[u] *Selah*
5 For you have heard my vows,[v]
O God;
you have given me the heritage
of those who fear your
name.[w]

6 Increase the days of the king's life,
his years for many generations.[x]
7 May he be enthroned in God's
presence forever;[y]
appoint your love and
faithfulness to protect
him.[z]

8 Then will I ever sing praise to your
name[a]
and fulfill my vows day after day.

Psalm 62

For the director of music. For
Jeduthun. A psalm of David.

1 My soul finds rest[b] in God alone;
my salvation comes from him.
2 He alone is my rock[c] and my
salvation;
he is my fortress, I will never be
shaken.

3 How long will you assault a man?
Would all of you throw him
down—
this leaning wall,[d] this tottering
fence?
4 They fully intend to topple him
from his lofty place;
they take delight in lies.
With their mouths they bless,
but in their hearts they curse.[e]
Selah
5 Find rest, O my soul, in God alone;
my hope comes from him.
6 He alone is my rock and my
salvation;
he is my fortress, I will not be
shaken.
7 My salvation and my honor depend
on God**a**;
he is my mighty rock, my
refuge.[f]
8 Trust in him at all times, O people;
pour out your hearts to him,[g]
for God is our refuge. *Selah*

9 Lowborn men are but a breath,[h]
the highborn are but a lie;
if weighed on a balance,[i] they are
nothing;
together they are only a breath.
10 Do not trust in extortion
or take pride in stolen goods;[j]
though your riches increase,
do not set your heart on them.[k]

11 One thing God has spoken,
two things have I heard:
that you, O God, are strong,
12 and that you, O Lord, are loving.
Surely you will reward each person
according to what he has
done.[l]

Psalm 63

A psalm of David. When he was in
the Desert of Judah.

1 →PG. 622

1 O God, you are my God,
earnestly I seek you;
my soul thirsts for you,[m]
my body longs for you,
in a dry and weary land
where there is no water.

2 I have seen you in the sanctuary[n]
and beheld your power and your
glory.
3 Because your love is better than
life,[o]
my lips will glorify you.
4 I will praise you as long as I live,[p]
and in your name I will lift up
my hands.[q]
5 My soul will be satisfied as with the
richest of foods;[r]
with singing lips my mouth will
praise you.

6 On my bed I remember you;
I think of you through the
watches of the night.[s]
7 Because you are my help,[t]
I sing in the shadow of your
wings.
8 My soul clings to you;
your right hand upholds me.[u]

9 They who seek my life will be
destroyed;[v]
they will go down to the depths
of the earth.[w]
10 They will be given over to the
sword
and become food for jackals.

11 But the king will rejoice in God;
all who swear by God's name
will praise him,[x]
while the mouths of liars will be
silenced.

61:4 [t]Ps 23:6 [u]Ps 91:4 **61:5** [v]Ps 56:12 [w]Ps 86:11 **61:6** [x]Ps 21:4 **61:7** [y]Ps 41:12 [z]Ps 40:11 **61:8** [a]Ps 65:1; 71:22 **62:1** [b]Ps 33:20 **62:2** [c]Ps 89:26 **62:3** [d]Isa 30:13 **62:4** [e]Ps 28:3 **62:7** [f]Ps 46:1; 85:9; Jer 3:23 **62:8** [g]1Sa 1:15; Ps 42:4; La 2:19 **62:9** [h]Ps 39:5,11 [i]Isa 40:15 **62:10** [j]Isa 61:8 [k]Job 31:25; 1Ti 6:6-10 **62:12** [l]Job 34:11; Mt 16:27 **63:1** [m]Ps 42:2; 84:2 **63:2** [n]Ps 27:4 **63:3** [o]Ps 69:16 **63:4** [p]Ps 104:33 [q]Ps 28:2 **63:5** [r]Ps 36:8 **63:6** [s]Ps 42:8 **63:7** [t]Ps 27:9 **63:8** [u]Ps 18:35 **63:9** [v]Ps 40:14 [w]Ps 55:15 **63:11** [x]Dt 6:13; Ps 21:1; Isa 45:23

a 7 Or / *God Most High is my salvation and my honor*

Psalm 64

For the director of music. A psalm of David.

[1]Hear me, O God, as I voice my complaint;[y]
protect my life from the threat of the enemy.[z]
[2]Hide me from the conspiracy of the wicked,[a]
from that noisy crowd of evildoers.

[3]They sharpen their tongues like swords
and aim their words like deadly arrows.[b]
[4]They shoot from ambush at the innocent man;[c]
they shoot at him suddenly, without fear.[d]

[5]They encourage each other in evil plans,
they talk about hiding their snares;
they say, "Who will see them[a]?"[e]
[6]They plot injustice and say,
"We have devised a perfect plan!"
Surely the mind and heart of man are cunning.

[7]But God will shoot them with arrows;
suddenly they will be struck down.
[8]He will turn their own tongues against them[f]
and bring them to ruin;
all who see them will shake their heads[g] in scorn.

[9]All mankind will fear;
they will proclaim the works of God
and ponder what he has done.[h]
[10]Let the righteous rejoice in the LORD
and take refuge in him;[i]
let all the upright in heart praise him![j]

Psalm 65

For the director of music. A psalm of David. A song.

1 →PG. 623

[1]Praise awaits[b] you, O God, in Zion;
to you our vows will be fulfilled.[k]
[2]O you who hear prayer,
to you all men will come.[l]
[3]When we were overwhelmed by sins,[m]
you forgave[c] our transgressions.[n]
[4]Blessed are those you choose[o]
and bring near to live in your courts!
We are filled with the good things of your house,[p]
of your holy temple.

[5]You answer us with awesome deeds of righteousness,
O God our Savior,[q]
the hope of all the ends of the earth
and of the farthest seas,[r]
[6]who formed the mountains by your power,
having armed yourself with strength,[s]
[7]who stilled the roaring of the seas,[t]
the roaring of their waves,
and the turmoil of the nations.[u]
[8]Those living far away fear your wonders;
where morning dawns and evening fades
you call forth songs of joy.

[9]You care for the land and water it;[v]
you enrich it abundantly.
The streams of God are filled with water
to provide the people with grain,[w]
for so you have ordained it.[d]
[10]You drench its furrows
and level its ridges;
you soften it with showers
and bless its crops.
[11]You crown the year with your bounty,
and your carts overflow with abundance.
[12]The grasslands of the desert overflow;[x]
the hills are clothed with gladness.
[13]The meadows are covered with flocks[y]
and the valleys are mantled with grain;[z]
they shout for joy and sing.[a]

Psalm 66

For the director of music. A song. A psalm.

[1]Shout with joy to God, all the earth![b]

64:1 [y]Ps 55:2 [z]Ps 140:1 **64:2** [a]Ps 56:6; 59:2 **64:3** [b]Ps 58:7 **64:4** [c]Ps 11:2 [d]Ps 55:19 **64:5** [e]Ps 10:11 **64:8** [f]Ps 9:3; Pr 18:7 [g]Ps 22:7 **64:9** [h]Jer 51:10 **64:10** [i]Ps 25:20 [j]Ps 32:11 **65:1** [k]Ps 116:18 **65:2** [l]Isa 66:23 **65:3** [m]Ps 38:4 [n]Heb 9:14 **65:4** [o]Ps 4:3; 33:12 [p]Ps 36:8 **65:5** [q]Ps 85:4 [r]Ps 107:23 **65:6** [s]Ps 93:1 **65:7** [t]Mt 8:26 [u]Isa 17:12-13 **65:9** [v]Ps 68:9-10 [w]Ps 46:4; 104:14 **65:12** [x]Job 28:26 **65:13** [y]Ps 144:13 [z]Ps 72:16 [a]Ps 98:8; Isa 55:12 **66:1** [b]Ps 100:1

[a]5 Or *us* [b]1 Or *befits*; the meaning of the Hebrew for this word is uncertain. [c]3 Or *made atonement for* [d]9 Or *for that is how you prepare the land*

2 Sing the glory of his name;[c]
make his praise glorious!
3Say to God, "How awesome are
your deeds![d]
So great is your power
that your enemies cringe[e]
before you.
4All the earth bows down[f] to you;
they sing praise[g] to you,
they sing praise to your name."
Selah

5Come and see what God has
done,
how awesome his works[h] in
man's behalf!
6He turned the sea into dry land,[i]
they passed through the waters
on foot—
come, let us rejoice in him.
7He rules forever[j] by his power,
his eyes watch[k] the nations—
let not the rebellious[l] rise up
against him. *Selah*

8Praise[m] our God, O peoples,
let the sound of his praise be
heard;
9he has preserved our lives
and kept our feet from
slipping.[n]
10For you, O God, tested us;
you refined us like silver.[o]
11You brought us into prison
and laid burdens[p] on our backs.
12You let men ride over our heads;[q]
we went through fire and water,
but you brought us to a place of
abundance.[r]

13I will come to your temple with
burnt offerings
and fulfill my vows[s] to you—
14vows my lips promised and my
mouth spoke
when I was in trouble.
15I will sacrifice fat animals to you
and an offering of rams;
I will offer bulls and goats.[t]
Selah

1 →PG. 628

16Come and listen,[u] all you who fear
God;
let me tell[v] you what he has
done for me.
17I cried out to him with my mouth;
his praise was on my tongue.
18If I had cherished sin in my heart,
the Lord would not have
listened;[w]
19but God has surely listened
and heard my voice[x] in prayer.
20Praise be to God,
who has not rejected[y] my
prayer
or withheld his love from me!

66:2 [c]Ps 79:9 **66:3** [d]Ps 65:5 [e]Ps 18:44 **66:4** [f]Ps 22:27 [g]Ps 67:3 **66:5** [h]Ps 106:22 **66:6** [i]Ex 14:22 **66:7** [j]Ps 145:13 [k]Ps 11:4 [l]Ps 140:8 **66:8** [m]Ps 98:4 **66:9** [n]Ps 121:3 **66:10** [o]Ps 17:3; Isa 48:10; Zec 13:9; 1Pe 1:6-7 **66:11** [p]La 1:13 **66:12** [q]Isa 51:23 [r]Isa 43:2 **66:13** [s]Ecc 5:4 **66:15** [t]Nu 6:14; Ps 51:19 **66:16** [u]Ps 34:11 [v]Ps 71:15,24 **66:18** [w]Job 36:21; Isa 1:15; Jas 4:3 **66:19** [x]Ps 116:1-2 **66:20** [y]Ps 22:24; 68:35

Psalm 67

For the director of music. With stringed instruments. A psalm. A song.

1May God be gracious to us and
bless us
and make his face shine upon
us,[z] *Selah*
2that your ways may be known on
earth,
your salvation[a] among all
nations.[b]

3May the peoples praise you, O God;
may all the peoples praise you.
4May the nations be glad and sing
for joy,
for you rule the peoples justly[c]
and guide the nations of the
earth. *Selah*
5May the peoples praise you, O God;
may all the peoples praise you.

6Then the land will yield its
harvest,[d]
and God, our God, will bless us.
7God will bless us,
and all the ends of the earth will
fear him.[e]

67:1 [z]Nu 6:24-26; Ps 4:6 **67:2** [a]Isa 52:10 [b]Tit 2:11 **67:4** [c]Ps 96:10-13 **67:6** [d]Lev 26:4; Ps 85:12; Eze 34:27 **67:7** [e]Ps 33:8

66:18

PROMISE 1

SIN BLOCKS OUR PRAISE

Now *this* was a godly man. He was afraid God wouldn't hear his prayers, but for an unusual reason.

Early in the psalm, the writer urged his readers to get a fix on Biblical reality because the greater people's understanding, the greater their praise. To help them along, he recounted the wonder of God's power and provision for his people throughout history (vv. 5–12). And this man didn't just tell his readers to worship God, he practiced what he told others to do (vv. 13–20). He was a man of praise and worship. But reread verse 18. Does this sound familiar? Does it sound like someone saying, "I'd better not sin or God won't give me what I ask for"? Look again. This man is saying, "If I cherish sin in my heart God won't hear my *praise*."

This psalmist wasn't saying, "Gimme something, God." This whole psalm is about giving something *to* God. The writer was concerned that sin in his heart would mar his ability to praise God. Chew on *that* while you read this psalm a few times, asking how you can express your praise and worship to the great God presented in this song of praise.

For the next Promise 1 reading go to page 630.

Psalm 68

For the director of music. Of David.
A psalm. A song.

1 May God arise, may his enemies be
scattered;
may his foes flee[f] before him.
2 As smoke[g] is blown away by the
wind,
may you blow them away;
as wax melts[h] before the fire,
may the wicked perish before
God.
3 But may the righteous be glad
and rejoice[i] before God;
may they be happy and joyful.
4 Sing to God, sing praise to his
name,[j]
extol him who rides on the
clouds[a][k]—
his name is the LORD[l]—
and rejoice before him.
5 A father to the fatherless,[m] a
defender of widows,[n]
is God in his holy dwelling.[o]
6 God sets the lonely in families,[b][p]
he leads forth the prisoners[q]
with singing;
but the rebellious live in a
sun-scorched land.[r]

7 When you went out[s] before your
people, O God,
when you marched through the
wasteland, *Selah*
8 the earth shook,
the heavens poured down rain,[t]
before God, the One of Sinai,[u]
before God, the God of Israel.
9 You gave abundant showers,[v]
O God;
you refreshed your weary
inheritance.
10 Your people settled in it,
and from your bounty, O God,
you provided[w] for the poor.

11 The Lord announced the word,
and great was the company of
those who proclaimed it:
12 "Kings and armies flee[x] in haste;
in the camps men divide the
plunder.
13 Even while you sleep among the
campfires,[c][y]
the wings of ⌞my⌟ dove are
sheathed with silver,
its feathers with shining gold."
14 When the Almighty[d] scattered[z]
the kings in the land,
it was like snow fallen on
Zalmon.

15 The mountains of Bashan are
majestic mountains;
rugged are the mountains of
Bashan.
16 Why gaze in envy, O rugged
mountains,
at the mountain where God
chooses[a] to reign,
where the LORD himself will
dwell forever?
17 The chariots of God are tens of
thousands
and thousands of thousands;[b]
the Lord ⌞has come⌟ from Sinai
into his sanctuary.
18 When you ascended on high,
you led captives[c] in your train;
you received gifts from men,[d]
even from[e] the rebellious—
that you,[f] O LORD God, might
dwell there.

19 Praise be to the Lord, to God our
Savior,[e]
who daily bears our burdens.[f]
Selah
20 Our God is a God who saves;
from the Sovereign LORD comes
escape from death.[g]

21 Surely God will crush the heads[h]
of his enemies,
the hairy crowns of those who go
on in their sins.
22 The Lord says, "I will bring them
from Bashan;
I will bring them from the
depths of the sea,[i]
23 that you may plunge your feet in
the blood of your foes,[j]
while the tongues of your dogs[k]
have their share."

24 Your procession has come into
view, O God,
the procession of my God and
King into the sanctuary.[l]
25 In front are the singers, after them
the musicians;
with them are the maidens
playing tambourines.[m]
26 Praise God in the great
congregation;
praise the LORD in the assembly
of Israel.[n]
27 There is the little tribe[o] of
Benjamin, leading them,
there the great throng of Judah's
princes,
and there the princes of Zebulun
and of Naphtali.

68:1 [f]Nu 10:35; Isa 33:3 **68:2** [g]Hos 13:3 [h]Isa 9:18; Mic 1:4 **68:3** [i]Ps 32:11 **68:4** [j]Ps 66:2 [k]Dt 33:26 [l]Ex 6:3; Ps 83:18 **68:5** [m]Ps 10:14 [n]Dt 10:18 [o]Dt 26:15 **68:6** [p]Ps 113:9 [q]Ac 12:6 [r]Ps 107:34 **68:7** [s]Ex 13:21; Jdg 4:14 **68:8** [t]Jdg 5:4 [u]Ex 19:16,18 **68:9** [v]Dt 11:11 **68:10** [w]Ps 74:19 **68:12** [x]Jos 10:16 **68:13** [y]Ge 49:14 **68:14** [z]Jos 10:10

68:16 [a]Dt 12:5 **68:17** [b]Dt 33:2; Da 7:10 **68:18** [c]Jdg 5:12 [d]Eph 4:8* **68:19** [e]Ps 65:5 [f]Ps 55:22 **68:20** [g]Ps 56:13 **68:21** [h]Ps 110:5; Hab 3:13 **68:22** [i]Nu 21:33 **68:23** [j]Ps 58:10 [k]1Ki 21:19 **68:24** [l]Ps 63:2 **68:25** [m]Jdg 11:34; 1Ch 13:8 **68:26** [n]Ps 26:12; Isa 48:1 **68:27** [o]1Sa 9:21

[a] *4* Or / *prepare the way for him who rides through the deserts* [b] *6* Or *the desolate in a homeland* [c] *13* Or *saddlebags* [d] *14* Hebrew *Shaddai* [e] *18* Or *gifts for men, / even* [f] *18* Or *they*

28Summon your power, O God[a];
show us your strength, O God, as
you have done before.
29Because of your temple at
Jerusalem
kings will bring you gifts.[p]
30Rebuke the beast among the reeds,
the herd of bulls[q] among the
calves of the nations.
Humbled, may it bring bars of
silver.
Scatter the nations[r] who delight
in war.
31Envoys will come from Egypt;[s]
Cush[b] will submit herself to
God.

32Sing to God, O kingdoms of the
earth,
sing praise to the Lord, *Selah*
33to him who rides[t] the ancient
skies above,
who thunders with mighty
voice.[u]
34Proclaim the power[v] of God,
whose majesty is over Israel,
whose power is in the skies.
35You are awesome, O God, in your
sanctuary;
the God of Israel gives power
and strength to his
people.[w]

Praise be to God![x]

Psalm 69

For the director of music. To ⌊the tune of⌋ "Lilies." Of David.

1Save me, O God,
for the waters have come up to
my neck.[y]
2I sink in the miry depths,[z]
where there is no foothold.
I have come into the deep waters;
the floods engulf me.
3I am worn out calling for help;[a]
my throat is parched.
My eyes fail,[b]
looking for my God.
4Those who hate me without
reason[c]
outnumber the hairs of my head;
many are my enemies without
cause,[d]
those who seek to destroy me.
I am forced to restore
what I did not steal.
5You know my folly,[e] O God;
my guilt is not hidden from
you.[f]
6May those who hope in you
not be disgraced because of me,
O Lord, the LORD Almighty;
may those who seek you
not be put to shame because of
me,
O God of Israel.
7For I endure scorn for your sake,[g]
and shame covers my face.[h]
8I am a stranger to my brothers,
an alien to my own mother's
sons;[i]
9for zeal for your house consumes
me,[j]
and the insults of those who
insult you fall on me.[k]
10When I weep and fast,[l]
I must endure scorn;
11when I put on sackcloth,[m]
people make sport of me.
12Those who sit at the gate mock me,
and I am the song of the
drunkards.[n]

13But I pray to you, O LORD,
in the time of your favor;[o]
in your great love,[p] O God,
answer me with your sure
salvation.
14Rescue me from the mire,
do not let me sink;
deliver me from those who hate
me,
from the deep waters.[q]
15Do not let the floodwaters[r] engulf
me
or the depths swallow me up[s]
or the pit close its mouth over
me.
16Answer me, O LORD, out of the
goodness of your love;[t]
in your great mercy turn to me.
17Do not hide your face[u] from your
servant;
answer me quickly, for I am in
trouble.[v]
18Come near and rescue me;
redeem[w] me because of my
foes.

19You know how I am scorned,[x]
disgraced and shamed;
all my enemies are before you.
20Scorn has broken my heart
and has left me helpless;
I looked for sympathy, but there
was none,
for comforters,[y] but I found
none.[z]
21They put gall in my food
and gave me vinegar for my
thirst.[a]

22May the table set before them
become a snare;

68:29 [p]Ps 72:10
68:30 [q]Ps 22:12 [r]Ps 89:10
68:31 [s]Isa 19:19; 45:14
68:33 [t]Ps 18:10 [u]Ps 29:4
68:34 [v]Ps 29:1
68:35 [w]Ps 29:11 [x]Ps 66:20
69:1 [y]Jnh 2:5
69:2 [z]Ps 40:2
69:3 [a]Ps 6:6 [b]Ps 119:82; Isa 38:14
69:4 [c]Jn 15:25* [d]Ps 35:19; 38:19
69:5 [e]Ps 38:5 [f]Ps 44:21
69:7 [g]Jer 15:15 [h]Ps 44:15
69:8 [i]Ps 31:11; Isa 53:3
69:9 [j]Jn 2:17* [k]Ps 89:50-51; Ro 15:3*
69:10 [l]Ps 35:13
69:11 [m]Ps 35:13
69:12 [n]Job 30:9
69:13 [o]Isa 49:8; 2Co 6:2 [p]Ps 51:1
69:14 [q]ver 2; Ps 144:7
69:15 [r]Ps 124:4-5 [s]Nu 16:33
69:16 [t]Ps 63:3
69:17 [u]Ps 27:9 [v]Ps 66:14
69:18 [w]Ps 49:15
69:19 [x]Ps 22:6
69:20 [y]Job 16:2 [z]Isa 63:5
69:21 [a]Mt 27:34; Mk 15:23; Jn 19:28-30

a *28* Many Hebrew manuscripts, Septuagint and Syriac; most Hebrew manuscripts *Your God has summoned power for you* **b** *31* That is, the upper Nile region

may it become retribution and[a]
a trap.
23May their eyes be darkened so they
cannot see,
and their backs be bent
forever.[b]
24Pour out your wrath[c] on them;
let your fierce anger overtake
them.
25May their place be deserted;[d]
let there be no one to dwell in
their tents.[e]
26For they persecute those you
wound
and talk about the pain of those
you hurt.[f]
27Charge them with crime upon
crime;[g]
do not let them share in your
salvation.[h]
28May they be blotted out of the
book of life[i]
and not be listed with the
righteous.[j]

29I am in pain and distress;
may your salvation, O God,
protect me.[k]

30I will praise God's name in song[l]
and glorify him[m] with
thanksgiving.
31This will please the LORD more
than an ox,
more than a bull with its horns
and hoofs.[n]
32The poor will see and be glad[o]—
you who seek God, may your
hearts live![p]
33The LORD hears the needy[q]
and does not despise his captive
people.

34Let heaven and earth praise him,
the seas and all that move in
them,[r]
35for God will save Zion[s]
and rebuild the cities of Judah.[t]
Then people will settle there and
possess it;
36 the children of his servants will
inherit it,
and those who love his name
will dwell there.[u]

Psalm 70

For the director of music. Of David.
A petition.

1Hasten, O God, to save me;
O LORD, come quickly to help
me.[v]
2May those who seek my life[w]
be put to shame and confusion;
may all who desire my ruin
be turned back in disgrace.[x]
3May those who say to me, "Aha!
Aha!"
turn back because of their
shame.
4But may all who seek you
rejoice and be glad in you;
may those who love your salvation
always say,
"Let God be exalted!"

5Yet I am poor and needy;[y]
come quickly to me,[z] O God.
You are my help and my deliverer;
O LORD, do not delay.

Psalm 71

1In you, O LORD, I have taken
refuge;
let me never be put to shame.[a]
2Rescue me and deliver me in your
righteousness;
turn your ear[b] to me and save
me.
3Be my rock of refuge,
to which I can always go;
give the command to save me,
for you are my rock and my
fortress.[c]
4Deliver me, O my God, from the
hand of the wicked,[d]
from the grasp of evil and cruel
men.

5For you have been my hope,
O Sovereign LORD,
my confidence[e] since my youth.
6From birth[f] I have relied on you;
you brought me forth from my
mother's womb.[g]
I will ever praise[h] you.
7I have become like a portent[i] to
many,
but you are my strong refuge.[j]
8My mouth[k] is filled with your
praise,
declaring your splendor[l] all day
long.

9Do not cast[m] me away when I am
old;[n]
do not forsake me when my
strength is gone.
10For my enemies speak against me;
those who wait to kill[o] me
conspire[p] together.
11They say, "God has forsaken him;
pursue him and seize him,
for no one will rescue[q] him."
12Be not far[r] from me, O God;
come quickly, O my God, to
help[s] me.
13May my accusers perish in shame;
may those who want to harm me

69:23 [b]Isa 6:9-10; Ro 11:9-10*
69:24 [c]Ps 79:6
69:25 [d]Mt 23:38 [e]Ac 1:20*
69:26 [f]Isa 53:4; Zec 1:15
69:27 [g]Ne 4:5 [h]Ps 109:14; Isa 26:10
69:28 [i]Ex 32:32-33; Lk 10:20; Php 4:3 [j]Eze 13:9
69:29 [k]Ps 59:1; 70:5
69:30 [l]Ps 28:7 [m]Ps 34:3
69:31 [n]Ps 50:9-13
69:32 [o]Ps 34:2 [p]Ps 22:26
69:33 [q]Ps 12:5; 68:6
69:34 [r]Ps 96:11; 148:1; Isa 44:23; 49:13; 55:12
69:35 [s]Ob 1:17 [t]Ps 51:18; Isa 44:26
69:36 [u]Ps 37:29; 102:28
70:1 [v]Ps 40:13
70:2 [w]Ps 35:4 [x]Ps 35:26
70:5 [y]Ps 40:17 [z]Ps 141:1
71:1 [a]Ps 25:2-3; 31:1
71:2 [b]Ps 17:6
71:3 [c]Ps 18:2; 31:2-3; 44:4
71:4 [d]Ps 140:4
71:5 [e]Job 4:6; Jer 17:7
71:6 [f]Ps 22:10 [g]Ps 22:9; Isa 46:3 [h]Ps 9:1; 34:1; 52:9; 119:164; 145:2
71:7 [i]Isa 8:18; 1Co 4:9 [j]2Sa 22:3; Ps 61:3
71:8 [k]Ps 51:15; 63:5 [l]Ps 35:28; 96:6; 104:1
71:9 [m]Ps 51:11 [n]ver 18; Ps 92:14; Isa 46:4
71:10 [o]Ps 10:8; 59:3; Pr 1:18 [p]Ps 31:13; 56:6; Mt 12:14
71:11 [q]Ps 7:2
71:12 [r]Ps 35:22; 38:21 [s]Ps 38:22; 70:1

[a]22 Or *snare / and their fellowship become*

be covered with scorn and
disgrace.[t]

7 →PG. 635

14 But as for me, I will always have
hope;[u]
I will praise you more and more.
15 My mouth will tell[v] of your
righteousness,
of your salvation all day long,
though I know not its measure.
16 I will come and proclaim your
mighty acts,[w] O Sovereign
LORD;
I will proclaim your
righteousness, yours alone.
17 Since my youth, O God, you have
taught[x] me,
and to this day I declare your
marvelous deeds.[y]
18 Even when I am old and gray,[z]
do not forsake me, O God,
till I declare your power to the next
generation,
your might to all who are to
come.[a]

19 Your righteousness reaches to the
skies,[b] O God,
you who have done great
things.[c]
Who, O God, is like you?[d]
20 Though you have made me see
troubles,[e] many and bitter,
you will restore[f] my life again;
from the depths of the earth
you will again bring me up.
21 You will increase my honor[g]
and comfort[h] me once again.

22 I will praise you with the harp[i]
for your faithfulness, O my God;
I will sing praise to you with the
lyre,[j]
O Holy One of Israel.[k]
23 My lips will shout for joy
when I sing praise to you—
I, whom you have redeemed.[l]
24 My tongue will tell of your
righteous acts
all day long,[m]
for those who wanted to harm
me[n]
have been put to shame and
confusion.

Psalm 72

Of Solomon.

1 Endow the king with your justice,
O God,
the royal son with your
righteousness.
2 He will[a] judge your people in
righteousness,[o]
your afflicted ones with justice.
3 The mountains will bring
prosperity to the people,
the hills the fruit of
righteousness.
4 He will defend the afflicted among
the people
and save the children of the
needy;[p]
he will crush the oppressor.
5 He will endure[b] as long as the
sun,
as long as the moon, through all
generations.
6 He will be like rain[q] falling on a
mown field,
like showers watering the earth.
7 In his days the righteous will
flourish;[r]
prosperity will abound till the
moon is no more.

8 He will rule from sea to sea
and from the River[c][s] to the
ends of the earth.[d][t]
9 The desert tribes will bow before
him
and his enemies will lick the
dust.
10 The kings of Tarshish and of
distant shores
will bring tribute to him;
the kings of Sheba[u] and Seba
will present him gifts.[v]
11 All kings will bow down to him
and all nations will serve him.
12 For he will deliver the needy who
cry out,
the afflicted who have no one to
help.
13 He will take pity on the weak and
the needy
and save the needy from death.
14 He will rescue[w] them from
oppression and violence,
for precious[x] is their blood in
his sight.

15 Long may he live!
May gold from Sheba[y] be given
him.
May people ever pray for him
and bless him all day long.
16 Let grain abound throughout the
land;
on the tops of the hills may it
sway.
Let its fruit flourish like Lebanon;[z]
let it thrive like the grass of the
field.
17 May his name endure forever;[a]

71:13 [t]ver 24
71:14 [u]Ps 130:7
71:15 [v]Ps 35:28; 40:5
71:16 [w]Ps 106:2
71:17 [x]Dt 4:5 [y]Ps 26:7
71:18 [z]ver 9 [a]Ps 22:30,31; 78:4
71:19 [b]Ps 36:5; 57:10 [c]Ps 126:2; Lk 1:49 [d]Ps 35:10
71:20 [e]Ps 60:3 [f]Hos 6:2
71:21 [g]Ps 18:35 [h]Ps 23:4; 86:17; Isa 12:1; 49:13
71:22 [i]Ps 33:2 [j]Ps 92:3; 144:9 [k]2Ki 19:22
71:23 [l]Ps 103:4
71:24 [m]Ps 35:28 [n]ver 13
72:2 [o]Isa 9:7; 11:4-5; 32:1
72:4 [p]Isa 11:4
72:6 [q]Dt 32:2; Hos 6:3
72:7 [r]Ps 92:12; Isa 2:4
72:8 [s]Ex 23:31 [t]Zec 9:10
72:10 [u]Ge 10:7 [v]2Ch 9:24
72:14 [w]Ps 69:18 [x]1Sa 26:21; Ps 116:15
72:15 [y]Isa 60:6
72:16 [z]Ps 104:16
72:17 [a]Ex 3:15

[a]*2* Or *May he*; similarly in verses 3-11 and 17
[b]*5* Septuagint; Hebrew *You will be feared*
[c]*8* That is, the Euphrates
[d]*8* Or *the end of the land*

may it continue as long as the
sun.[b]
All nations will be blessed through
him,
and they will call him blessed.[c]

18 Praise be to the LORD God, the God
of Israel,[d]
who alone does marvelous
deeds.[e]
19 Praise be to his glorious name
forever;
may the whole earth be filled
with his glory.[f]
Amen and Amen.[g]

20 This concludes the prayers of
David son of Jesse.

BOOK III

Psalms 73–89

Psalm 73

A psalm of Asaph.

3 →PG. 642

1 Surely God is good to Israel,
to those who are pure in heart.[h]
2 But as for me, my feet had almost
slipped;
I had nearly lost my foothold.
3 For I envied[i] the arrogant
when I saw the prosperity of the
wicked.[j]

4 They have no struggles;
their bodies are healthy and
strong.[a]
5 They are free[k] from the burdens
common to man;
they are not plagued by human
ills.
6 Therefore pride is their necklace;[l]
they clothe themselves with
violence.[m]
7 From their callous hearts[n] comes
iniquity[b];
the evil conceits of their minds
know no limits.
8 They scoff, and speak with malice;
in their arrogance[o] they
threaten oppression.
9 Their mouths lay claim to heaven,
and their tongues take
possession of the earth.
10 Therefore their people turn to them
and drink up waters in
abundance.[c]
11 They say, "How can God know?
Does the Most High have
knowledge?"
12 This is what the wicked are like—
always carefree, they increase in
wealth.[p]

13 Surely in vain[q] have I kept my
heart pure;
in vain have I washed my hands
in innocence.[r]
14 All day long I have been plagued;
I have been punished every
morning.

15 If I had said, "I will speak thus,"
I would have betrayed your
children.
16 When I tried to understand[s] all
this,
it was oppressive to me
17 till I entered the sanctuary[t] of
God;
then I understood their final
destiny.[u]

18 Surely you place them on slippery
ground;[v]
you cast them down to ruin.
19 How suddenly[w] are they
destroyed,
completely swept away by
terrors!
20 As a dream[x] when one awakes,[y]
so when you arise, O Lord,
you will despise them as
fantasies.

21 When my heart was grieved
and my spirit embittered,
22 I was senseless[z] and ignorant;
I was a brute beast[a] before you.

1 →PG. 636

23 Yet I am always with you;
you hold me by my right hand.
24 You guide[b] me with your
counsel,[c]
and afterward you will take me
into glory.
25 Whom have I in heaven but you?
And earth has nothing I desire
besides you.[d]
26 My flesh and my heart[e] may
fail,[f]
but God is the strength of my
heart
and my portion forever.

27 Those who are far from you will
perish;[g]
you destroy all who are
unfaithful to you.
28 But as for me, it is good to be near
God.[h]
I have made the Sovereign LORD
my refuge;
I will tell of all your deeds.[i]

72:17 [b]Ps 89:36 [c]Ge 12:3; Lk 1:48
72:18 [d]1Ch 29:10; Ps 41:13; 106:48 [e]Job 5:9
72:19 [f]Nu 14:21; Ne 9:5 [g]Ps 41:13
73:1 [h]Mt 5:8
73:3 [i]Ps 37:1; Pr 23:17 [j]Job 21:7; Jer 12:1
73:5 [k]Job 21:9
73:6 [l]Ge 41:42 [m]Ps 109:18
73:7 [n]Ps 17:10
73:8 [o]Ps 17:10; Jude 16
73:12 [p]Ps 49:6
73:13 [q]Job 21:15; 34:9 [r]Ps 26:6
73:16 [s]Ecc 8:17
73:17 [t]Ps 77:13 [u]Ps 37:38
73:18 [v]Ps 35:6
73:19 [w]Isa 47:11
73:20 [x]Job 20:8 [y]Ps 78:65
73:22 [z]Ps 49:10; 92:6 [a]Ecc 3:18
73:24 [b]Ps 48:14 [c]Ps 32:8
73:25 [d]Php 3:8
73:26 [e]Ps 84:2 [f]Ps 40:12
73:27 [g]Ps 119:155
73:28 [h]Heb 10:22; Jas 4:8 [i]Ps 40:5

a *4* With a different word division of the Hebrew; Masoretic Text *struggles at their death; / their bodies are healthy* **b** *7* Syriac (see also Septuagint); Hebrew *Their eyes bulge with fat* **c** *10* The meaning of the Hebrew for this verse is uncertain.

Psalm 74

A *maskil*[a] of Asaph.

1Why have you rejected us
forever,[j] O God?
Why does your anger smolder
against the sheep of your
pasture?[k]
2Remember the people you
purchased[l] of old,[m]
the tribe of your inheritance,
whom you redeemed[n]—
Mount Zion, where you dwelt.[o]
3Turn your steps toward these
everlasting ruins,
all this destruction the enemy
has brought on the
sanctuary.

4Your foes roared[p] in the place
where you met with us;
they set up their standards[q] as
signs.
5They behaved like men wielding
axes
to cut through a thicket of
trees.[r]
6They smashed all the carved[s]
paneling
with their axes and hatchets.
7They burned your sanctuary to the
ground;
they defiled the dwelling place of
your Name.
8They said in their hearts, "We will
crush[t] them completely!"
They burned every place where
God was worshiped in the
land.
9We are given no miraculous signs;
no prophets[u] are left,
and none of us knows how long
this will be.

10How long will the enemy mock
you, O God?
Will the foe revile[v] your name
forever?
11Why do you hold back your hand,
your right hand?[w]
Take it from the folds of your
garment and destroy them!

12But you, O God, are my king[x]
from of old;
you bring salvation upon the
earth.
13It was you who split open the sea[y]
by your power;
you broke the heads of the
monster[z] in the waters.
14It was you who crushed the heads
of Leviathan
and gave him as food to the
creatures of the desert.

74:1 [j]Dt 29:20; Ps 44:23 [k]Ps 79:13; 95:7; 100:3
74:2 [l]Ex 15:16 [m]Dt 32:7 [n]Ex 15:13 [o]Ps 68:16
74:4 [p]La 2:7 [q]Nu 2:2
74:5 [r]Jer 46:22
74:6 [s]1Ki 6:18
74:8 [t]Ps 83:4
74:9 [u]1Sa 3:1
74:10 [v]Ps 44:16
74:11 [w]La 2:3
74:12 [x]Ps 44:4
74:13 [y]Ex 14:21 [z]Isa 51:9; Eze 29:3
74:15 [a]Ex 17:6; Nu 20:11 [b]Jos 2:10; 3:13
74:16 [c]Ge 1:16; Ps 136:7-9
74:17 [d]Dt 32:8; Ac 17:26 [e]Ge 8:22
74:18 [f]Dt 32:6; Ps 39:8
74:19 [g]Ps 9:18
74:20 [h]Ge 17:7; Ps 106:45
74:21 [i]Ps 103:6 [j]Ps 35:10
74:22 [k]Ps 53:1
74:23 [l]Ps 65:7
75:1 [m]Ps 145:18 [n]Ps 44:1; 71:16
75:3 [o]Isa 24:19 [p]1Sa 2:8
75:4 [q]Zec 1:21

15It was you who opened up
springs[a] and streams;
you dried up[b] the ever flowing
rivers.
16The day is yours, and yours also
the night;
you established the sun and
moon.[c]
17It was you who set all the
boundaries[d] of the earth;
you made both summer and
winter.[e]

18Remember how the enemy has
mocked you, O LORD,
how foolish people[f] have
reviled your name.
19Do not hand over the life of your
dove to wild beasts;
do not forget the lives of your
afflicted[g] people forever.
20Have regard for your covenant,[h]
because haunts of violence fill
the dark places of the land.
21Do not let the oppressed[i] retreat
in disgrace;
may the poor and needy[j] praise
your name.

22Rise up, O God, and defend your
cause;
remember how fools[k] mock you
all day long.
23Do not ignore the clamor of your
adversaries,[l]
the uproar of your enemies,
which rises continually.

Psalm 75

For the director of music. ⌞To the tune of,⌟ "Do Not Destroy." A psalm of Asaph. A song.

1We give thanks to you, O God,
we give thanks, for your Name is
near;[m]
men tell of your wonderful
deeds.[n]
2You say, "I choose the appointed
time;
it is I who judge uprightly.
3When the earth and all its people
quake,[o]
it is I who hold its pillars[p] firm.
Selah
4To the arrogant I say, 'Boast no
more,'
and to the wicked, 'Do not lift
up your horns.[q]
5Do not lift your horns against
heaven;
do not speak with outstretched
neck.' "

[a]Title: Probably a literary or musical term

6No one from the east or the west
or from the desert can exalt a
man.
7But it is God who judges:[r]
He brings one down, he exalts
another.[s]
8In the hand of the LORD is a cup
full of foaming wine mixed[t]
with spices;
he pours it out, and all the wicked
of the earth
drink it down to its very dregs.[u]

9As for me, I will declare[v] this
forever;
I will sing praise to the God of
Jacob.
10I will cut off the horns of all the
wicked,
but the horns of the righteous
will be lifted up.[w]

Psalm 76

For the director of music. With stringed instruments. A psalm of Asaph. A song.

1In Judah God is known;
his name is great in Israel.
2His tent is in Salem,[x]
his dwelling place in Zion.
3There he broke the flashing arrows,
the shields and the swords, the
weapons of war.[y] *Selah*
4You are resplendent with light,
more majestic than mountains
rich with game.
5Valiant men lie plundered,
they sleep their last sleep;[z]
not one of the warriors
can lift his hands.
6At your rebuke, O God of Jacob,
both horse and chariot[a] lie still.
7You alone are to be feared.[b]
Who can stand[c] before you
when you are angry?[d]
8From heaven you pronounced
judgment,
and the land feared[e] and was
quiet—
9when you, O God, rose up to
judge,[f]
to save all the afflicted of the
land. *Selah*
10Surely your wrath against men
brings you praise,[g]
and the survivors of your wrath
are restrained.[a]
11Make vows to the LORD your God
and fulfill them;[h]
let all the neighboring lands
bring gifts[i] to the One to be
feared.
12He breaks the spirit of rulers;
he is feared by the kings of the
earth.

Psalm 77

For the director of music. For Jeduthun. Of Asaph. A psalm.

1I cried out to God[j] for help;
I cried out to God to hear me.
2When I was in distress,[k] I sought
the Lord;
at night I stretched out untiring
hands[l]
and my soul refused to be
comforted.[m]

3I remembered you, O God, and I
groaned;
I mused, and my spirit grew
faint.[n] *Selah*
4You kept my eyes from closing;
I was too troubled to speak.
5I thought about the former days,[o]
the years of long ago;
6I remembered my songs in the
night.
My heart mused and my spirit
inquired:

a *10* Or *Surely the wrath of men brings you praise, / and with the remainder of wrath you arm yourself*

75:7 [r]Ps 50:6 [s]1Sa 2:7; Ps 147:6; Da 2:21 **75:8** [t]Pr 23:30 [u]Job 21:20; Jer 25:15 **75:9** [v]Ps 40:10 **75:10** [w]Ps 89:17; 92:10; 148:14 **76:2** [x]Ge 14:18 **76:3** [y]Ps 46:9 **76:5** [z]Ps 13:3 **76:6** [a]Ex 15:1 **76:7** [b]1Ch 16:25 [c]Ezr 9:15; Rev 6:17 [d]Ps 2:5; Na 1:6 **76:8** [e]1Ch 16:30; 2Ch 20:29-30 **76:9** [f]Ps 9:8 **76:10** [g]Ex 9:16; Ro 9:17 **76:11** [h]Ps 50:14; Ecc 5:4-5 [i]2Ch 32:23; Ps 68:29 **77:1** [j]Ps 3:4 **77:2** [k]Ps 50:15; Isa 26:9,16 [l]Job 11:13 [m]Ge 37:35 **77:3** [n]Ps 143:4 **77:5** [o]Dt 32:7; Ps 44:1; 143:5; Isa 51:9

75:1-10

PROMISE 1

MAKING IT TO THE TOP

Many men find that their lives are heavily influenced by recognition and promotion in the workplace. Influence, income, ego fulfillment—all of these are prizes that go with promotion and recognition. Men spend time, money, and in some cases lives and fortunes maneuvering for the few spots at the top of their world.

But the way to the *real* top is not through arrogance or assertiveness (vv. 2–6) or through impressing the right people (v. 6). Ultimately it all comes back to the same starting point: *The fear of the LORD.* All the promotion, recognition, position and power that matters is controlled by God himself.

Verses 6 and 7 are essential truths to carry into a world where position and promotion are facts of life. What are some ways you can impress the One who handles all promotion? This wonderful book you hold in your hands instructs and guides men and women into that kind of life. Read it daily with a view toward pleasing God, the Creator of the universe, by acting on what you read.

For the next Promise 1 reading go to page 640.

7"Will the Lord reject forever?
Will he never show his favor[p] again?
8Has his unfailing love vanished forever?
Has his promise[q] failed for all time?
9Has God forgotten to be merciful?[r]
Has he in anger withheld his compassion?[s]" *Selah*

10Then I thought, "To this I will appeal:
the years of the right hand[t] of the Most High."
11I will remember the deeds of the LORD;
yes, I will remember your miracles[u] of long ago.
12I will meditate on all your works
and consider all your mighty deeds.

13Your ways, O God, are holy.
What god is so great as our God?[v]
14You are the God who performs miracles;
you display your power among the peoples.
15With your mighty arm you redeemed your people,[w]
the descendants of Jacob and Joseph. *Selah*

16The waters[x] saw you, O God,
the waters saw you and writhed;[y]
the very depths were convulsed.
17The clouds poured down water,[z]
the skies resounded with thunder;
your arrows flashed back and forth.
18Your thunder was heard in the whirlwind,
your lightning lit up the world;
the earth trembled and quaked.[a]
19Your path led through the sea,[b]
your way through the mighty waters,
though your footprints were not seen.

20You led your people[c] like a flock[d]
by the hand of Moses and Aaron.

Psalm 78

A *maskil*[a] of Asaph.

1O my people, hear my teaching;[e]
listen to the words of my mouth.
2I will open my mouth in parables,[f]
I will utter hidden things, things from of old—
3what we have heard and known,
what our fathers have told us.[g]
4We will not hide them from their children;[h]
we will tell the next generation
the praiseworthy deeds[i] of the LORD,
his power, and the wonders he has done.
5He decreed statutes[j] for Jacob[k]
and established the law in Israel,
which he commanded our forefathers
to teach their children,
6so the next generation would know them,
even the children yet to be born,[l]
and they in turn would tell their children.
7Then they would put their trust in God
and would not forget[m] his deeds
but would keep his commands.[n]
8They would not be like their forefathers[o]—
a stubborn[p] and rebellious[q] generation,
whose hearts were not loyal to God,
whose spirits were not faithful to him.

4 →PG. 647

9The men of Ephraim, though armed with bows,[r]
turned back on the day of battle;[s]
10they did not keep God's covenant[t]
and refused to live by his law.
11They forgot what he had done,[u]
the wonders he had shown them.
12He did miracles[v] in the sight of their fathers
in the land of Egypt,[w] in the region of Zoan.[x]
13He divided the sea[y] and led them through;
he made the water stand firm like a wall.[z]
14He guided them with the cloud by day
and with light from the fire all night.[a]
15He split the rocks[b] in the desert
and gave them water as abundant as the seas;
16he brought streams out of a rocky crag
and made water flow down like rivers.

77:7 [p]Ps 85:1 **77:8** [q]2Pe 3:9 **77:9** [r]Ps 25:6; 40:11; 51:1 [s]Isa 49:15 **77:10** [t]Ps 31:22 **77:11** [u]Ps 143:5 **77:13** [v]Ex 15:11; Ps 71:19; 86:8 **77:15** [w]Ex 6:6; Dt 9:29 **77:16** [x]Ex 14:21,28; Hab 3:8 [y]Ps 114:4; Hab 3:10 **77:17** [z]Jdg 5:4 **77:18** [a]Jdg 5:4 **77:19** [b]Hab 3:15 **77:20** [c]Ex 13:21 [d]Ps 78:52; Isa 63:11 **78:1** [e]Isa 51:4; 55:3 **78:2** [f]Ps 49:4; Mt 13:35*

78:3 [g]Ps 44:1 **78:4** [h]Dt 11:19 [i]Ps 26:7; 71:17 **78:5** [j]Ps 19:7; 81:5 [k]Ps 147:19 **78:6** [l]Ps 22:31; 102:18 **78:7** [m]Dt 6:12 [n]Dt 5:29 **78:8** [o]2Ch 30:7 [p]Ex 32:9 [q]ver 37; Isa 30:9 **78:9** [r]ver 57; 1Ch 12:2 [s]Jdg 20:39 **78:10** [t]2Ki 17:15 **78:11** [u]Ps 106:13 **78:12** [v]Ps 106:22 [w]Ex 7-12 [x]Nu 13:22 **78:13** [y]Ex 14:21; Ps 136:13 [z]Ex 15:8 **78:14** [a]Ex 13:21; Ps 105:39 **78:15** [b]Nu 20:11; 1Co 10:4

[a]Title: Probably a literary or musical term

17 But they continued to sin[c] against
him,
rebelling in the desert against
the Most High.
18 They willfully put God to the test[d]
by demanding the food they
craved.[e]
19 They spoke against God,[f] saying,
"Can God spread a table in the
desert?
20 When he struck the rock, water
gushed out,[g]
and streams flowed abundantly.
But can he also give us food?
Can he supply meat[h] for his
people?"
21 When the LORD heard them, he was
very angry;
his fire broke out[i] against
Jacob,
and his wrath rose against Israel,
22 for they did not believe in God
or trust[j] in his deliverance.
23 Yet he gave a command to the
skies above
and opened the doors of the
heavens;[k]
24 he rained down manna[l] for the
people to eat,
he gave them the grain of
heaven.
25 Men ate the bread of angels;
he sent them all the food they
could eat.
26 He let loose the east wind[m] from
the heavens
and led forth the south wind by
his power.
27 He rained meat down on them like
dust,
flying birds like sand on the
seashore.
28 He made them come down inside
their camp,
all around their tents.
29 They ate till they had more than
enough,[n]
for he had given them what they
craved.
30 But before they turned from the
food they craved,
even while it was still in their
mouths,[o]
31 God's anger rose against them;
he put to death the sturdiest[p]
among them,
cutting down the young men of
Israel.
32 In spite of all this, they kept on
sinning;
in spite of his wonders,[q] they
did not believe.[r]
33 So he ended their days in futility[s]
and their years in terror.

78:17 [c] Dt 9:22; Isa 63:10; Heb 3:16
78:18 [d] 1Co 10:9 [e] Ex 16:2; Nu 11:4
78:19 [f] Nu 21:5
78:20 [g] Nu 20:11 [h] Nu 11:18
78:21 [i] Nu 11:1
78:22 [j] Dt 1:32; Heb 3:19
78:23 [k] Ge 7:11; Mal 3:10
78:24 [l] Ex 16:4; Jn 6:31*
78:26 [m] Nu 11:31
78:29 [n] Nu 11:20
78:30 [o] Nu 11:33
78:31 [p] Isa 10:16
78:32 [q] ver 11 [r] ver 22
78:33 [s] Nu 14:29,35

34 Whenever God slew them, they
would seek[t] him;
they eagerly turned to him again.
35 They remembered that God was
their Rock,[u]
that God Most High was their
Redeemer.[v]
36 But then they would flatter him
with their mouths,[w]
lying to him with their tongues;
37 their hearts were not loyal[x] to
him,
they were not faithful to his
covenant.
38 Yet he was merciful;[y]
he forgave[z] their iniquities[a]
and did not destroy them.
Time after time he restrained his
anger
and did not stir up his full wrath.
39 He remembered that they were but
flesh,[b]
a passing breeze[c] that does not
return.
40 How often they rebelled[d] against
him in the desert[e]
and grieved him[f] in the
wasteland!
41 Again and again they put God to
the test;[g]
they vexed the Holy One of
Israel.[h]
42 They did not remember his
power—
the day he redeemed them from
the oppressor,
43 the day he displayed his
miraculous signs in Egypt,
his wonders in the region of
Zoan.
44 He turned their rivers to blood;[i]
they could not drink from their
streams.
45 He sent swarms of flies[j] that
devoured them,
and frogs[k] that devastated
them.
46 He gave their crops to the
grasshopper,
their produce to the locust.[l]
47 He destroyed their vines with hail[m]
and their sycamore-figs with
sleet.
48 He gave over their cattle to the
hail,
their livestock[n] to bolts of
lightning.
49 He unleashed against them his hot
anger,[o]
his wrath, indignation and
hostility—
a band of destroying angels.
50 He prepared a path for his anger;
he did not spare them from
death

78:34 [t] Hos 5:15
78:35 [u] Dt 32:4 [v] Dt 9:26
78:36 [w] Eze 33:31
78:37 [x] ver 8; Ac 8:21
78:38 [y] Ex 34:6 [z] Isa 48:10 [a] Nu 14:18,20
78:39 [b] Ge 6:3; Ps 103:14 [c] Job 7:7; Jas 4:14
78:40 [d] Heb 3:16 [e] Ps 95:8; 106:14 [f] Eph 4:30
78:41 [g] Nu 14:22 [h] 2Ki 19:22; Ps 89:18
78:44 [i] Ex 7:20-21; Ps 105:29
78:45 [j] Ex 8:24; Ps 105:31 [k] Ex 8:2,6
78:46 [l] Ex 10:13
78:47 [m] Ex 9:23; Ps 105:32
78:48 [n] Ex 9:25
78:49 [o] Ex 15:7

but gave them over to the
plague.
51 He struck down all the firstborn of
Egypt,[p]
the firstfruits of manhood in the
tents of Ham.[q]
52 But he brought his people out like
a flock;[r]
he led them like sheep through
the desert.
53 He guided them safely, so they
were unafraid;
but the sea engulfed[s] their
enemies.[t]
54 Thus he brought them to the
border of his holy land,
to the hill country his right
hand[u] had taken.
55 He drove out nations[v] before
them
and allotted their lands to them
as an inheritance;[w]
he settled the tribes of Israel in
their homes.

56 But they put God to the test
and rebelled against the Most
High;
they did not keep his statutes.
57 Like their fathers[x] they were
disloyal and faithless,
as unreliable as a faulty bow.[y]
58 They angered him[z] with their high
places;[a]
they aroused his jealousy with
their idols.[b]
59 When God heard them, he was very
angry;
he rejected Israel[c] completely.
60 He abandoned the tabernacle of
Shiloh,[d]
the tent he had set up among
men.
61 He sent ⌊the ark of⌋ his might[e]
into captivity,[f]
his splendor into the hands of
the enemy.
62 He gave his people over to the
sword;
he was very angry with his
inheritance.
63 Fire consumed[g] their young men,
and their maidens had no
wedding songs;[h]
64 their priests were put to the
sword,[i]
and their widows could not
weep.

65 Then the Lord awoke as from
sleep,[j]
as a man wakes from the stupor
of wine.
66 He beat back his enemies;
he put them to everlasting
shame.[k]

78:51 [p]Ex 12:29; Ps 135:8 [q]Ps 105:23; 106:22 **78:52** [r]Ps 77:20 **78:53** [s]Ex 14:28 [t]Ps 106:10 **78:54** [u]Ex 15:17; Ps 44:3 **78:55** [v]Ps 44:2 [w]Jos 13:7 **78:57** [x]Eze 20:27 [y]Hos 7:16 **78:58** [z]Jdg 2:12 [a]Lev 26:30 [b]Ex 20:4; Dt 32:21 **78:59** [c]Dt 32:19 **78:60** [d]Jos 18:1 **78:61** [e]Ps 132:8 [f]1Sa 4:17 **78:63** [g]Nu 11:1 [h]Jer 7:34; 16:9 **78:64** [i]1Sa 4:17; 22:18 **78:65** [j]Ps 44:23 **78:66** [k]1Sa 5:6

78:68 [l]Ps 87:2 **78:70** [m]1Sa 16:1 **78:71** [n]2Sa 5:2; Ps 28:9 **78:72** [o]1Ki 9:4 **79:1** [p]Ps 74:2 [q]2Ki 25:9 **79:2** [r]Dt 28:26; Jer 7:33 **79:3** [s]Jer 16:4 **79:4** [t]Ps 44:13; 80:6 **79:5** [u]Ps 74:10 [v]Ps 74:1; 85:5 [w]Dt 29:20; Ps 89:46; Zep 3:8 **79:6** [x]Ps 69:24; Rev 16:1 [y]Jer 10:25; 2Th 1:8 [z]Ps 14:4 **79:8** [a]Isa 64:9 [b]Ps 116:6; 142:6 **79:9** [c]2Ch 14:11

67 Then he rejected the tents of
Joseph,
he did not choose the tribe of
Ephraim;
68 but he chose the tribe of Judah,
Mount Zion,[l] which he loved.
69 He built his sanctuary like the
heights,
like the earth that he established
forever.
70 He chose David[m] his servant
and took him from the sheep
pens;
71 from tending the sheep he brought
him
to be the shepherd[n] of his
people Jacob,
of Israel his inheritance.
72 And David shepherded them with
integrity of heart;[o]
with skillful hands he led them.

Psalm 79

A psalm of Asaph.

1 O God, the nations have invaded
your inheritance;[p]
they have defiled your holy
temple,
they have reduced Jerusalem to
rubble.[q]
2 They have given the dead bodies of
your servants
as food to the birds of the air,
the flesh of your saints to the
beasts of the earth.[r]
3 They have poured out blood like
water
all around Jerusalem,
and there is no one to bury the
dead.[s]
4 We are objects of reproach to our
neighbors,
of scorn and derision to those
around us.[t]

5 How long,[u] O LORD? Will you be
angry[v] forever?
How long will your jealousy burn
like fire?[w]
6 Pour out your wrath[x] on the
nations
that do not acknowledge[y] you,
on the kingdoms
that do not call on your name;[z]
7 for they have devoured Jacob
and destroyed his homeland.
8 Do not hold against us the sins of
the fathers;[a]
may your mercy come quickly to
meet us,
for we are in desperate need.[b]
9 Help us,[c] O God our Savior,
for the glory of your name;

deliver us and forgive our sins
for your name's sake.[d]
10Why should the nations say,
"Where is their God?"[e]
Before our eyes, make known
among the nations
that you avenge[f] the outpoured
blood of your servants.
11May the groans of the prisoners
come before you;
by the strength of your arm
preserve those condemned to
die.
12Pay back into the laps[g] of our
neighbors seven times[h]
the reproach they have hurled at
you, O Lord.
13Then we your people, the sheep of
your pasture,[i]
will praise you forever;[j]
from generation to generation
we will recount your praise.

Psalm 80

For the director of music. To ⌊the tune of⌋ "The Lilies of the Covenant." Of Asaph. A psalm.

1Hear us, O Shepherd of Israel,
you who lead Joseph like a
flock;[k]
you who sit enthroned between the
cherubim,[l] shine forth
2 before Ephraim, Benjamin and
Manasseh.[m]
Awaken[n] your might;
come and save us.

3Restore[o] us,[p] O God;
make your face shine upon us,
that we may be saved.

4O LORD God Almighty,
how long will your anger
smolder
against the prayers of your
people?
5You have fed them with the bread
of tears;
you have made them drink tears
by the bowlful.[q]
6You have made us a source of
contention to our neighbors,
and our enemies mock us.[r]

7Restore us, O God Almighty;
make your face shine upon us,
that we may be saved.

8You brought a vine[s] out of Egypt;
you drove out[t] the nations and
planted it.
9You cleared the ground for it,
and it took root and filled the
land.
10The mountains were covered with
its shade,
the mighty cedars with its
branches.
11It sent out its boughs to the Sea,[a]
its shoots as far as the River.[b][u]
12Why have you broken down its
walls[v]
so that all who pass by pick its
grapes?
13Boars from the forest ravage[w] it
and the creatures of the field
feed on it.
14Return to us, O God Almighty!
Look down from heaven and
see![x]
Watch over this vine,
15 the root your right hand has
planted,
the son[c] you have raised up for
yourself.
16Your vine is cut down, it is burned
with fire;
at your rebuke[y] your people
perish.
17Let your hand rest on the man at
your right hand,
the son of man you have raised
up for yourself.
18Then we will not turn away from
you;
revive us, and we will call on
your name.
19Restore us, O LORD God Almighty;
make your face shine upon us,
that we may be saved.

Psalm 81

For the director of music. According to *gittith*.[d] Of Asaph.

1Sing for joy to God our strength;
shout aloud to the God of
Jacob![z]
2Begin the music, strike the
tambourine,[a]
play the melodious harp[b] and
lyre.
3Sound the ram's horn at the New
Moon,
and when the moon is full, on
the day of our Feast;
4this is a decree for Israel,
an ordinance of the God of
Jacob.
5He established it as a statute for
Joseph
when he went out against
Egypt,[c]

79:9 [d]Ps 25:11; 31:3; Jer 14:7 **79:10** [e]Ps 42:10 [f]Ps 94:1 **79:12** [g]Isa 65:6; Jer 32:18 [h]Ge 4:15 **79:13** [i]Ps 74:1; 95:7 [j]Ps 44:8 **80:1** [k]Ps 77:20 [l]Ex 25:22 **80:2** [m]Nu 2:18-24 [n]Ps 35:23 **80:3** [o]Ps 85:4; La 5:21 [p]Nu 6:25 **80:5** [q]Ps 42:3; Isa 30:20 **80:6** [r]Ps 79:4 **80:8** [s]Isa 5:1-2; Jer 2:21 [t]Jos 13:6; Ac 7:45

80:11 [u]Ps 72:8 **80:12** [v]Ps 89:40; Isa 5:5 **80:13** [w]Jer 5:6 **80:14** [x]Isa 63:15 **80:16** [y]Ps 39:11; 76:6 **81:1** [z]Ps 66:1 **81:2** [a]Ex 15:20 [b]Ps 92:3 **81:5** [c]Ex 11:4

a *11* Probably the Mediterranean b *11* That is, the Euphrates c *15* Or *branch* d Title: Probably a musical term

where we heard a language we
did not understand.[a][d]

6He says, "I removed the burden
from their shoulders;[e]
their hands were set free from
the basket.
7In your distress you called[f] and I
rescued you,
I answered[g] you out of a
thundercloud;
I tested you at the waters of
Meribah.[h] *Selah*

8"Hear, O my people,[i] and I will
warn you—
if you would but listen to me,
O Israel!
9You shall have no foreign god[j]
among you;
you shall not bow down to an
alien god.
10I am the LORD your God,
who brought you up out of
Egypt.[k]
Open wide your mouth and I will
fill[l] it.

11"But my people would not listen to
me;
Israel would not submit to me.[m]
12So I gave them over[n] to their
stubborn hearts
to follow their own devices.

13"If my people would but listen to
me,[o]
if Israel would follow my ways,
14how quickly would I subdue[p] their
enemies
and turn my hand against[q] their
foes!
15Those who hate the LORD would
cringe before him,
and their punishment would last
forever.
16But you would be fed with the
finest of wheat;[r]
with honey from the rock I
would satisfy you."

Psalm 82

A psalm of Asaph.

1God presides in the great assembly;
he gives judgment[s] among the
"gods":

2"How long will you[b] defend the
unjust
and show partiality[t] to the
wicked?[u] *Selah*
7 →PG. 671
3Defend the cause of the weak and
fatherless;[v]
maintain the rights of the poor[w]
and oppressed.
4Rescue the weak and needy;
deliver them from the hand of
the wicked.

5"They know nothing, they
understand nothing.[x]
They walk about in darkness;[y]
all the foundations[z] of the earth
are shaken.

6"I said, 'You are "gods";[a]
you are all sons of the Most
High.'
7But you will die[b] like mere men;
you will fall like every other
ruler."

8Rise up,[c] O God, judge the earth,
for all the nations are your
inheritance.[d]

Psalm 83

A song. A psalm of Asaph.

1O God, do not keep silent;[e]
be not quiet, O God, be not still.
2See how your enemies are astir,[f]
how your foes rear their heads.[g]
3With cunning they conspire[h]
against your people;
they plot against those you
cherish.
4"Come," they say, "let us destroy[i]
them as a nation,
that the name of Israel be
remembered[j] no more."

5With one mind they plot
together;[k]
they form an alliance against
you—
6the tents of Edom[l] and the
Ishmaelites,
of Moab[m] and the Hagrites,[n]
7Gebal,[c][o] Ammon and Amalek,
Philistia, with the people of
Tyre.[p]
8Even Assyria has joined them
to lend strength to the
descendants of Lot.[q] *Selah*

9Do to them as you did to Midian,[r]
as you did to Sisera and Jabin at
the river Kishon,[s]
10who perished at Endor
and became like refuse[t] on the
ground.
11Make their nobles like Oreb and
Zeeb,[u]
all their princes like Zebah and
Zalmunna,[v]
12who said, "Let us take possession[w]
of the pasturelands of God."

81:5 [d]Ps 114:1 **81:6** [e]Isa 9:4 **81:7** [f]Ex 2:23; Ps 50:15 [g]Ex 19:19 [h]Ex 17:7 **81:8** [i]Ps 50:7 **81:9** [j]Ex 20:3; Dt 32:12; Isa 43:12 **81:10** [k]Ex 20:2 [l]Ps 107:9 **81:11** [m]Ex 32:1-6 **81:12** [n]Ac 7:42; Ro 1:24 **81:13** [o]Dt 5:29; Isa 48:18 **81:14** [p]Ps 47:3 [q]Am 1:8 **81:16** [r]Dt 32:14 **82:1** [s]Ps 58:11; Isa 3:13 **82:2** [t]Dt 1:17 [u]Ps 58:1-2; Pr 18:5 **82:3** [v]Dt 24:17 [w]Jer 22:16 **82:5** [x]Ps 14:4; Mic 3:1 [y]Isa 59:9 [z]Ps 11:3 **82:6** [a]Jn 10:34* **82:7** [b]Ps 49:12; Eze 31:14 **82:8** [c]Ps 12:5 [d]Ps 2:8; Rev 11:15 **83:1** [e]Ps 28:1; 35:22 **83:2** [f]Ps 2:1; Isa 17:12 [g]Jdg 8:28; Ps 81:15 **83:3** [h]Ps 31:13 **83:4** [i]Est 3:6 [j]Jer 11:19 **83:5** [k]Ps 2:2 **83:6** [l]Ps 137:7 [m]2Ch 20:1 [n]Ge 25:16 **83:7** [o]Jos 13:5 [p]Eze 27:3 **83:8** [q]Dt 2:9 **83:9** [r]Jdg 7:1-23 [s]Jdg 4:23-24 **83:10** [t]Zep 1:17 **83:11** [u]Jdg 7:25 [v]Jdg 8:12,21 **83:12** [w]2Ch 20:11

a5 Or / *and we heard a voice we had not known*
b2 The Hebrew is plural.
c7 That is, Byblos

13Make them like tumbleweed, O my God,
like chaff[x] before the wind.
14As fire consumes the forest
or a flame sets the mountains ablaze,[y]
15so pursue them with your tempest
and terrify them with your storm.[z]
16Cover their faces with shame[a]
so that men will seek your name, O LORD.
17May they ever be ashamed and dismayed;
may they perish in disgrace.[b]
18Let them know that you, whose name is the LORD—
that you alone are the Most High over all the earth.[c]

Psalm 84

For the director of music. According to *gittith*.[a] Of the Sons of Korah. A psalm.

1 →PG. 637

1How lovely is your dwelling place,[d]
O LORD Almighty!
2My soul yearns,[e] even faints,
for the courts of the LORD;
my heart and my flesh cry out
for the living God.

3Even the sparrow has found a home,
and the swallow a nest for herself,
where she may have her young—
a place near your altar,[f]
O LORD Almighty, my King and my God.[g]
4Blessed are those who dwell in your house;
they are ever praising you. *Selah*

5Blessed are those whose strength[h] is in you,
who have set their hearts on pilgrimage.[i]
6As they pass through the Valley of Baca,
they make it a place of springs;
the autumn[j] rains also cover it with pools.[b]
7They go from strength to strength,[k]
till each appears[l] before God in Zion.

8Hear my prayer, O LORD God Almighty;
listen to me, O God of Jacob. *Selah*
9Look upon our shield,[c][m] O God;
look with favor on your anointed one.[n]

10Better is one day in your courts
than a thousand elsewhere;
I would rather be a doorkeeper[o] in the house of my God
than dwell in the tents of the wicked.
11For the LORD God is a sun[p] and shield;[q]
the LORD bestows favor and honor;
no good thing does he withhold[r]
from those whose walk is blameless.

12O LORD Almighty,
blessed[s] is the man who trusts in you.

Psalm 85

For the director of music. Of the Sons of Korah. A psalm.

1You showed favor to your land, O LORD;
you restored the fortunes[t] of Jacob.
2You forgave[u] the iniquity[v] of your people
and covered all their sins. *Selah*
3You set aside all your wrath[w]
and turned from your fierce anger.[x]

4Restore[y] us again, O God our Savior,
and put away your displeasure toward us.
5Will you be angry with us forever?[z]
Will you prolong your anger through all generations?
6Will you not revive[a] us again,
that your people may rejoice in you?
7Show us your unfailing love, O LORD,
and grant us your salvation.

8I will listen to what God the LORD will say;
he promises peace[b] to his people, his saints—
but let them not return to folly.
9Surely his salvation[c] is near those who fear him,
that his glory[d] may dwell in our land.

83:13 [x]Ps 35:5; Isa 17:13 **83:14** [y]Dt 32:22; Isa 9:18 **83:15** [z]Job 9:17 **83:16** [a]Ps 109:29; 132:18 **83:17** [b]Ps 35:4 **83:18** [c]Ps 59:13 **84:1** [d]Ps 27:4; 43:3; 132:5 **84:2** [e]Ps 42:1-2 **84:3** [f]Ps 43:4 [g]Ps 5:2 **84:5** [h]Ps 81:1 [i]Jer 31:6 **84:6** [j]Joel 2:23 **84:7** [k]Pr 4:18 [l]Dt 16:16 **84:9** [m]Ps 59:11 [n]1Sa 16:6; Ps 2:2; 132:17 **84:10** [o]1Ch 23:5 **84:11** [p]Isa 60:19; Rev 21:23 [q]Ge 15:1 [r]Ps 34:10 **84:12** [s]Ps 2:12 **85:1** [t]Ps 14:7; Jer 30:18; Eze 39:25 **85:2** [u]Nu 14:19 [v]Ps 78:38 **85:3** [w]Ps 106:23 [x]Ex 32:12; Dt 13:17; Ps 78:38; Jnh 3:9 **85:4** [y]Ps 80:3,7 **85:5** [z]Ps 79:5 **85:6** [a]Ps 80:18; Hab 3:2 **85:8** [b]Zec 9:10 **85:9** [c]Isa 46:13 [d]Zec 2:5

[a]Title: Probably a musical term [b]6 Or *blessings* [c]9 Or *sovereign*

10Love and faithfulness[e] meet
together;
righteousness[f] and peace kiss
each other.
11Faithfulness springs forth from the
earth,
and righteousness[g] looks down
from heaven.
12The LORD will indeed give what is
good,[h]
and our land will yield[i] its
harvest.
13Righteousness goes before him
and prepares the way for his
steps.

Psalm 86

A prayer of David.

1Hear, O LORD, and answer[j] me,
for I am poor and needy.
2Guard my life, for I am devoted to
you.
You are my God; save your
servant
who trusts in you.[k]
3Have mercy[l] on me, O Lord,
for I call[m] to you all day long.
4Bring joy to your servant,
for to you, O Lord,
I lift[n] up my soul.
5You are forgiving and good,
O Lord,
abounding in love[o] to all who
call to you.
6Hear my prayer, O LORD;
listen to my cry for mercy.
7In the day of my trouble[p] I will
call to you,
for you will answer me.
8Among the gods there is none like
you,[q] O Lord;
no deeds can compare with
yours.
9All the nations you have made
will come and worship[r] before
you, O Lord;
they will bring glory[s] to your
name.
10For you are great and do marvelous
deeds;[t]
you alone[u] are God.

1 →PG. 642

11Teach me your way,[v] O LORD,
and I will walk in your truth;
give me an undivided[w] heart,
that I may fear your name.
12I will praise you, O Lord my God,
with all my heart;
I will glorify your name forever.
13For great is your love toward me;
you have delivered me from the
depths of the grave.[a]

85:10 [e]Ps 89:14; Pr 3:3 [f]Ps 72:2-3; Isa 32:17
85:11 [g]Isa 45:8
85:12 [h]Ps 84:11; Jas 1:17 [i]Lev 26:4; Ps 67:6; Zec 8:12
86:1 [j]Ps 17:6
86:2 [k]Ps 25:2; 31:14
86:3 [l]Ps 4:1; 57:1 [m]Ps 88:9
86:4 [n]Ps 25:1; 143:8
86:5 [o]Ex 34:6; Ne 9:17; Ps 103:8; 145:8; Joel 2:13; Jnh 4:2
86:7 [p]Ps 50:15
86:8 [q]Ex 15:11; Dt 3:24; Ps 89:6
86:9 [r]Ps 66:4; Rev 15:4 [s]Isa 43:7
86:10 [t]Ps 72:18 [u]Dt 6:4; Mk 12:29; 1Co 8:4
86:11 [v]Ps 25:5 [w]Jer 32:39

86:14 [x]Ps 54:3
86:15 [y]Ps 103:8 [z]Ex 34:6; Ne 9:17; Joel 2:13
86:16 [a]Ps 116:16
87:2 [b]Ps 78:68
87:3 [c]Ps 46:4; Isa 60:1
87:4 [d]Job 9:13 [e]Ps 45:12 [f]Isa 19:25
87:6 [g]Ps 69:28; Isa 4:3; Eze 13:9
87:7 [h]Ps 149:3 [i]Ps 36:9

14The arrogant are attacking me,
O God;
a band of ruthless men seeks my
life—
men without regard for you.[x]
15But you, O Lord, are a
compassionate and
gracious[y] God,
slow to anger, abounding in love
and faithfulness.[z]
16Turn to me and have mercy on
me;
grant your strength to your
servant
and save the son of your
maidservant.[b][a]
17Give me a sign of your goodness,
that my enemies may see it and
be put to shame,
for you, O LORD, have helped me
and comforted me.

Psalm 87

Of the Sons of Korah. A psalm.
A song.

1He has set his foundation on the
holy mountain;
2 the LORD loves the gates of
Zion[b]
more than all the dwellings of
Jacob.
3Glorious things are said of you,
O city of God:[c] *Selah*
4"I will record Rahab[c][d] and
Babylon
among those who acknowledge
me—
Philistia too, and Tyre[e], along with
Cush[d]—
and will say, 'This[e] one was
born in Zion.[f]' "
5Indeed, of Zion it will be said,
"This one and that one were
born in her,
and the Most High himself will
establish her."
6The LORD will write in the
register[g] of the peoples:
"This one was born in Zion."
Selah
7As they make music[h] they will
sing,
"All my fountains[i] are in you."

[a] 13 Hebrew *Sheol* [b] 16 Or *save your faithful son* [c] 4 A poetic name for Egypt [d] 4 That is, the upper Nile region [e] 4 Or *"O Rahab and Babylon, / Philistia, Tyre and Cush, / I will record concerning those who acknowledge me: / 'This*

Psalm 88

A song. A psalm of the Sons of Korah. For the director of music. According to *mahalath leannoth*.[a] A *maskil*[b] of Heman the Ezrahite.

1 O LORD, the God who saves me,[j]
day and night I cry out[k] before you.
2 May my prayer come before you;
turn your ear to my cry.
3 For my soul is full of trouble
and my life draws near the grave.[c][l]
4 I am counted among those who go down to the pit;[m]
I am like a man without strength.
5 I am set apart with the dead,
like the slain who lie in the grave,
whom you remember no more,
who are cut off[n] from your care.
6 You have put me in the lowest pit,
in the darkest depths.[o]
7 Your wrath lies heavily upon me;
you have overwhelmed me with all your waves.[p] *Selah*
8 You have taken from me my closest friends[q]
and have made me repulsive to them.
I am confined[r] and cannot escape;
9 my eyes[s] are dim with grief.
I call[t] to you, O LORD, every day;
I spread out my hands[u] to you.
10 Do you show your wonders to the dead?
Do those who are dead rise up and praise you?[v] *Selah*
11 Is your love declared in the grave,
your faithfulness[w] in Destruction[d]?
12 Are your wonders known in the place of darkness,
or your righteous deeds in the land of oblivion?
13 But I cry to you for help,[x] O LORD;
in the morning[y] my prayer comes before you.[z]
14 Why, O LORD, do you reject[a] me
and hide your face[b] from me?
15 From my youth I have been afflicted and close to death;
I have suffered your terrors[c] and am in despair.
16 Your wrath has swept over me;
your terrors have destroyed me.
17 All day long they surround me like a flood;[d]
they have completely engulfed me.
18 You have taken my companions[e]
and loved ones from me;
the darkness is my closest friend.

Psalm 89

A *maskil*[b] of Ethan the Ezrahite.

1 I will sing[f] of the LORD's great love forever;
with my mouth I will make your faithfulness known[g]
through all generations.
2 I will declare that your love stands firm forever,
that you established your faithfulness in heaven itself.[h]
3 You said, "I have made a covenant with my chosen one,
I have sworn to David my servant,
4 'I will establish your line forever
and make your throne firm through all generations.'"[i] *Selah*
5 The heavens[j] praise your wonders, O LORD,
your faithfulness too, in the assembly of the holy ones.
6 For who in the skies above can compare with the LORD?
Who is like the LORD among the heavenly beings?[k]
7 In the council of the holy ones God is greatly feared;
he is more awesome than all who surround him.[l]
8 O LORD God Almighty, who is like you?[m]
You are mighty, O LORD, and your faithfulness surrounds you.
9 You rule over the surging sea;
when its waves mount up, you still them.[n]
10 You crushed Rahab[o] like one of the slain;
with your strong arm you scattered[p] your enemies.
11 The heavens are yours, and yours also the earth;[q]
you founded the world and all that is in it.[r]
12 You created the north and the south;
Tabor[s] and Hermon[t] sing for joy[u] at your name.

88:1 [j]Ps 51:14 [k]Ps 22:2; 27:9; Lk 18:7 **88:3** [l]Ps 107:18,26 **88:4** [m]Ps 28:1 **88:5** [n]Ps 31:22; Isa 53:8 **88:6** [o]Ps 69:15; La 3:55 **88:7** [p]Ps 42:7 **88:8** [q]Job 19:13; Ps 31:11 [r]Jer 32:2 **88:9** [s]Ps 38:10 [t]Ps 86:3 [u]Job 11:13; Ps 143:6 **88:10** [v]Ps 6:5 **88:11** [w]Ps 30:9 **88:13** [x]Ps 30:2 [y]Ps 5:3 [z]Ps 119:147 **88:14** [a]Ps 43:2 [b]Job 13:24; Ps 13:1 **88:15** [c]Job 6:4 **88:17** [d]Ps 22:16; 124:4 **88:18** [e]ver 8; Job 19:13; Ps 38:11 **89:1** [f]Ps 59:16; Ps 101:1 [g]Ps 36:5; 40:10 **89:2** [h]Ps 36:5 **89:4** [i]2Sa 7:12-16; 1Ki 8:16; Ps 132:11-12; Isa 9:7; Lk 1:33 **89:5** [j]Ps 19:1 **89:6** [k]Ps 113:5 **89:7** [l]Ps 47:2 **89:8** [m]Ps 71:19 **89:9** [n]Ps 65:7 **89:10** [o]Ps 87:4 [p]Ps 68:1 **89:11** [q]1Ch 29:11; Ps 24:1 [r]Ge 1:1 **89:12** [s]Jos 19:22 [t]Dt 3:8; Jos 12:1 [u]Ps 98:8

a Title: Possibly a tune, "The Suffering of Affliction" **b** Title: Probably a literary or musical term **c** *3* Hebrew *Sheol* **d** *11* Hebrew *Abaddon*

13 Your arm is endued with power;
your hand is strong, your right hand exalted.

14 Righteousness and justice are the foundation of your throne;[v]
love and faithfulness go before you.
15 Blessed are those who have learned to acclaim you,
who walk in the light[w] of your presence, O LORD.
16 They rejoice in your name[x] all day long;
they exult in your righteousness.
17 For you are their glory and strength,
and by your favor you exalt our horn.[a][y]
18 Indeed, our shield[b] belongs to the LORD,
our king[z] to the Holy One of Israel.

19 Once you spoke in a vision,
to your faithful people you said:
"I have bestowed strength on a warrior;
I have exalted a young man from among the people.
20 I have found David[a] my servant;[b]
with my sacred oil I have anointed[c] him.
21 My hand will sustain him;
surely my arm will strengthen him.[d]
22 No enemy will subject him to tribute;
no wicked man will oppress[e] him.
23 I will crush his foes before him[f]
and strike down his adversaries.[g]
24 My faithful love will be with him,[h]
and through my name his horn[c] will be exalted.
25 I will set his hand over the sea,
his right hand over the rivers.[i]
26 He will call out to me, 'You are my Father,[j]
my God, the Rock my Savior.'[k]
27 I will also appoint him my firstborn,[l]
the most exalted[m] of the kings[n] of the earth.
28 I will maintain my love to him forever,
and my covenant with him will never fail.[o]
29 I will establish his line forever,
his throne as long as the heavens endure.[p]

30 "If his sons forsake my law
and do not follow my statutes,
31 if they violate my decrees
and fail to keep my commands,

89:14 [v]Ps 97:2
89:15 [w]Ps 44:3
89:16 [x]Ps 105:3
89:17 [y]Ps 75:10; 92:10; 148:14
89:18 [z]Ps 47:9
89:20 [a]Ac 13:22 [b]Ps 78:70 [c]1Sa 16:1,12
89:21 [d]Ps 18:35
89:22 [e]2Sa 7:10
89:23 [f]Ps 18:40 [g]2Sa 7:9
89:24 [h]2Sa 7:15
89:25 [i]Ps 72:8
89:26 [j]2Sa 7:14 [k]2Sa 22:47
89:27 [l]Col 1:18 [m]Nu 24:7 [n]Rev 1:5; 19:16
89:28 [o]ver 33-34; Isa 55:3
89:29 [p]ver 4,36; Dt 11:21; Jer 33:17
89:32 [q]2Sa 7:14
89:33 [r]2Sa 7:15
89:34 [s]Nu 23:19
89:38 [t]Dt 32:19; 1Ch 28:9; Ps 44:9
89:39 [u]La 5:16
89:40 [v]Ps 80:12 [w]La 2:2
89:41 [x]Ps 44:13
89:42 [y]Ps 13:2; 80:6
89:43 [z]Ps 44:10
89:45 [a]Ps 44:15; 109:29
89:46 [b]Ps 79:5
89:47 [c]Job 7:7; Ps 39:5

32 I will punish their sin with the rod,
their iniquity with flogging;[q]
33 but I will not take my love from him,[r]
nor will I ever betray my faithfulness.
34 I will not violate my covenant
or alter what my lips have uttered.[s]
35 Once for all, I have sworn by my holiness—
and I will not lie to David—
36 that his line will continue forever
and his throne endure before me like the sun;
37 it will be established forever like the moon,
the faithful witness in the sky."
Selah

38 But you have rejected,[t] you have spurned,
you have been very angry with your anointed one.
39 You have renounced the covenant with your servant
and have defiled his crown in the dust.[u]
40 You have broken through all his walls[v]
and reduced his strongholds[w] to ruins.
41 All who pass by have plundered him;
he has become the scorn of his neighbors.[x]
42 You have exalted the right hand of his foes;
you have made all his enemies rejoice.[y]
43 You have turned back the edge of his sword
and have not supported him in battle.[z]
44 You have put an end to his splendor
and cast his throne to the ground.
45 You have cut short the days of his youth;
you have covered him with a mantle of shame.[a] *Selah*

46 How long, O LORD? Will you hide yourself forever?
How long will your wrath burn like fire?[b]
47 Remember how fleeting is my life.[c]
For what futility you have created all men!
48 What man can live and not see death,

[a] *17 Horn* here symbolizes strong one.
[b] *18* Or *sovereign*
[c] *24 Horn* here symbolizes strength.

or save himself from the power
of the grave[a]?[d] *Selah*
49 O Lord, where is your former great
love,
which in your faithfulness you
swore to David?
50 Remember, Lord, how your servant
has[b] been mocked,[e]
how I bear in my heart the
taunts of all the nations,
51 the taunts with which your
enemies have mocked,
O LORD,
with which they have mocked
every step of your anointed
one.[f]

52 Praise be to the LORD forever!
Amen and Amen.[g]

BOOK IV

Psalms 90–106

Psalm 90

A prayer of Moses the man of God.

1 Lord, you have been our dwelling
place[h]
throughout all generations.
2 Before the mountains were born[i]
or you brought forth the earth
and the world,
from everlasting to everlasting
you are God.[j]

3 You turn men back to dust,
saying, "Return to dust, O sons
of men."[k]
4 For a thousand years in your sight
are like a day that has just gone
by,
or like a watch in the night.[l]
5 You sweep men away[m] in the
sleep of death;
they are like the new grass of the
morning—
6 though in the morning it springs
up new,
by evening it is dry and
withered.[n]

7 We are consumed by your anger
and terrified by your indignation.
8 You have set our iniquities before
you,
our secret sins[o] in the light of
your presence.
9 All our days pass away under your
wrath;
we finish our years with a
moan.[p]
10 The length of our days is seventy
years—

89:48 [d]Ps 22:29; 49:9 **89:50** [e]Ps 69:19 **89:51** [f]Ps 74:10 **89:52** [g]Ps 41:13; 72:19 **90:1** [h]Dt 33:27; Eze 11:16 **90:2** [i]Job 15:7; Pr 8:25 [j]Ps 102:24-27 **90:3** [k]Ge 3:19; Job 34:15 **90:4** [l]2Pe 3:8 **90:5** [m]Ps 73:20; Isa 40:6 **90:6** [n]Mt 6:30; Jas 1:10 **90:8** [o]Ps 19:12 **90:9** [p]Ps 78:33

90:10 [q]Job 20:8 **90:11** [r]Ps 76:7 **90:12** [s]Ps 39:4 [t]Dt 32:29 **90:13** [u]Ps 6:3 [v]Dt 32:36; Ps 135:14 **90:14** [w]Ps 103:5 [x]Ps 85:6 [y]Ps 31:7

or eighty, if we have the
strength;
yet their span[c] is but trouble and
sorrow,
for they quickly pass, and we fly
away.[q]

11 Who knows the power of your
anger?
For your wrath is as great as the
fear that is due you.[r]
12 Teach us to number our days[s]
aright,
that we may gain a heart of
wisdom.[t]

13 Relent, O LORD! How long[u] will it
be?
Have compassion on your
servants.[v]
14 Satisfy[w] us in the morning with
your unfailing love,
that we may sing for joy[x] and
be glad all our days.[y]
15 Make us glad for as many days as
you have afflicted us,

[a] *48* Hebrew *Sheol* [b] *50* Or *your servants have* [c] *10* Or *yet the best of them*

90:1–17

PROMISE 1

DOES MY WORK MATTER?

Many of us spend quiet lives in a cubicle or in front of a machine where no one notices our work unless we mess up. If we don't show up for work, someone else takes the pile off our desk or bench and life goes on. So how significant is what I do with those 40-plus hours of my week?

This psalm was written by Moses during Israel's 40 years in the wilderness (see the book of Numbers for the full story). It is a plea for God to give meaning to otherwise meaningless lives (v. 17). Think through the structure of this poem, and its impact hits like a sledge hammer. God is eternal (vv. 1–2); man is temporary (vv. 3–6). Apart from God, humans have no hope of significance (vv. 7–11). So Moses prayed for wisdom (v. 12) and for God's compassion on man's condition (vv. 13–15). The request of Moses' prayer (vv. 16–17) was that God would let man understand God's workings, and then incorporate human work into his grand, eternal plan.

Moses recognized that God's involvement in a man's life is his only hope of real significance. Meditate on verses 1–11 and then carefully read verses 12–17 as your own prayer. As you go to work, offer up your activity to God as part of his eternal work through you.

For the next Promise 1 reading go to page 646.

for as many years as we have
seen trouble.
16May your deeds be shown to your
servants,
your splendor to their children.[z]
17May the favor[a] of the Lord our
God rest upon us;
establish the work of our hands
for us—
yes, establish the work of our
hands.[a]

Psalm 91

1He who dwells in the shelter[b] of
the Most High
will rest in the shadow[c] of the
Almighty.[b]
2I will say[c] of the LORD, "He is my
refuge[d] and my fortress,
my God, in whom I trust."
3Surely he will save you from the
fowler's snare[e]
and from the deadly
pestilence.[f]
4He will cover you with his feathers,
and under his wings you will
find refuge;[g]
his faithfulness will be your
shield[h] and rampart.
5You will not fear[i] the terror of
night,
nor the arrow that flies by day,
6nor the pestilence that stalks in the
darkness,
nor the plague that destroys at
midday.
7A thousand may fall at your side,
ten thousand at your right hand,
but it will not come near you.
8You will only observe with your
eyes
and see the punishment of the
wicked.[j]
9If you make the Most High your
dwelling—
even the LORD, who is my
refuge—
10then no harm[k] will befall you,
no disaster will come near your
tent.
11For he will command his angels[l]
concerning you
to guard you in all your ways;[m]
12they will lift you up in their hands,
so that you will not strike your
foot against a stone.[n]
13You will tread upon the lion and
the cobra;
you will trample the great lion
and the serpent.[o]
14"Because he loves me," says the
LORD, "I will rescue him;
I will protect him, for he
acknowledges my name.
15He will call upon me, and I will
answer him;
I will be with him in trouble,
I will deliver him and honor
him.[p]
16With long life[q] will I satisfy him
and show him my salvation.[r]"

Psalm 92

A psalm. A song.
For the Sabbath day.

1It is good to praise the LORD
and make music to your name,[s]
O Most High,[t]
2to proclaim your love in the
morning[u]
and your faithfulness at night,
3to the music of the ten-stringed
lyre
and the melody of the harp.[v]
4For you make me glad by your
deeds, O LORD;
I sing for joy at the works of
your hands.[w]

91:1–16 PROMISE 4

RESTING IN GOD'S SHADOW

As men we want to protect ourselves and those whom God has entrusted to our care. What could you do physically to *absolutely* insure and protect yourself against anything earth or hell could throw at you? Nothing! So what is a man to do? This psalm holds the answer.

Verses 1 and 2 describe the one thing that gives confidence, and nothing you can do physically makes it work. It is not a matter of guardedness but of godliness; not of fighting but of faith. The psalm elaborates and explains, but verses 1 and 2 state it clearly: *Your only real place of security is in God.*

List three or four of your greatest fears, then ask how powerful they are in light of God's strength. Imagine yourself with God's arms around you, and then read this psalm again. If you struggle with worry, take time to memorize this psalm. Write it on a 3 x 5 card and refer to it during the day until you have it fixed in your mind. That is the first step to dwelling "in the shelter of the Most High"; the only absolutely safe place in the universe.

For the next Promise 4 reading go to page 663.

90:16 [z]Ps 44:1; Hab 3:2
90:17 [a]Isa 26:12
91:1 [b]Ps 31:20 [c]Ps 17:8
91:2 [d]Ps 142:5
91:3 [e]Ps 124:7; Pr 6:5 [f]1Ki 8:37
91:4 [g]Ps 17:8 [h]Ps 35:2
91:5 [i]Job 5:21
91:8 [j]Ps 37:34; 58:10; Mal 1:5
91:10 [k]Pr 12:21
91:11 [l]Heb 1:14 [m]Ps 34:7
91:12 [n]Mt 4:6*; Lk 4:10-11*
91:13 [o]Da 6:22; Lk 10:19
91:15 [p]1Sa 2:30; Ps 50:15; Jn 12:26
91:16 [q]Dt 6:2; Ps 21:4 [r]Ps 50:23
92:1 [s]Ps 147:1 [t]Ps 135:3
92:2 [u]Ps 89:1
92:3 [v]1Sa 10:5; Ne 12:27; Ps 33:2
92:4 [w]Ps 8:6; 143:5

a 17 Or *beauty* b 1 Hebrew *Shaddai* c 2 Or *He says*

5How great are your works,[x]
O LORD,
how profound your thoughts![y]
6The senseless man[z] does not
know,
fools do not understand,
7that though the wicked spring up
like grass
and all evildoers flourish,
they will be forever destroyed.

8But you, O LORD, are exalted
forever.

9For surely your enemies, O LORD,
surely your enemies will perish;
all evildoers will be scattered.[a]
10You have exalted my horn[a][b] like
that of a wild ox;
fine oils[c] have been poured
upon me.
11My eyes have seen the defeat of my
adversaries;
my ears have heard the rout of
my wicked foes.[d]

12The righteous will flourish like a
palm tree,
they will grow like a cedar of
Lebanon;[e]
13planted in the house of the LORD,
they will flourish in the courts of
our God.[f]
14They will still bear fruit[g] in old
age,
they will stay fresh and green,
15proclaiming, "The LORD is upright;
he is my Rock, and there is no
wickedness in him.[h]"

Psalm 93

1The LORD reigns,[i] he is robed in
majesty;[j]
the LORD is robed in majesty
and is armed with strength.[k]
The world is firmly established;
it cannot be moved.[l]
2Your throne was established long
ago;
you are from all eternity.[m]

3The seas[n] have lifted up, O LORD,
the seas have lifted up their
voice;
the seas have lifted up their
pounding waves.
4Mightier than the thunder[o] of the
great waters,
mightier than the breakers of the
sea—
the LORD on high is mighty.

5Your statutes stand firm;
holiness[p] adorns your house
for endless days, O LORD.

Psalm 94

1O LORD, the God who avenges,[q]
O God who avenges, shine
forth.[r]
2Rise up, O Judge[s] of the earth;
pay back[t] to the proud what
they deserve.
3How long will the wicked, O LORD,
how long will the wicked be
jubilant?

4They pour out arrogant[u] words;
all the evildoers are full of
boasting.[v]
5They crush your people,[w] O LORD;
they oppress your inheritance.
6They slay the widow and the alien;
they murder the fatherless.
7They say, "The LORD does not
see;[x]
the God of Jacob pays no heed."

8Take heed, you senseless ones[y]
among the people;
you fools, when will you become
wise?
9Does he who implanted the ear not
hear?
Does he who formed the eye not
see?[z]
10Does he who disciplines nations
not punish?
Does he who teaches[a] man lack
knowledge?
11The LORD knows the thoughts of
man;
he knows that they are futile.[b]

12Blessed is the man you
discipline,[c] O LORD,
the man you teach[d] from your
law;
13you grant him relief from days of
trouble,
till a pit[e] is dug for the wicked.
14For the LORD will not reject his
people;[f]
he will never forsake his
inheritance.
15Judgment will again be founded on
righteousness,[g]
and all the upright in heart will
follow it.

3 →PG. 644

16Who will rise up[h] for me against
the wicked?
Who will take a stand for me
against evildoers?[i]
17Unless the LORD had given me
help,[j]
I would soon have dwelt in the
silence of death.
18When I said, "My foot is
slipping,[k]"

1 →PG. 643

a *10 Horn* here symbolizes strength.

92:5 [x]Rev 15:3 [y]Ps 40:5; 139:17; Isa 28:29; Ro 11:33
92:6 [z]Ps 73:22
92:9 [a]Ps 68:1; 89:10
92:10 [b]Ps 89:17 [c]Ps 23:5
92:11 [d]Ps 54:7; 91:8
92:12 [e]Ps 1:3; 52:8; Jer 17:8; Hos 14:6
92:13 [f]Ps 100:4
92:14 [g]Jn 15:2
92:15 [h]Job 34:10
93:1 [i]Ps 97:1 [j]Ps 104:1 [k]Ps 65:6 [l]Ps 96:10
93:2 [m]Ps 45:6
93:3 [n]Ps 96:11
93:4 [o]Ps 65:7
93:5 [p]Ps 29:2
94:1 [q]Na 1:2; Ro 12:19 [r]Ps 80:1
94:2 [s]Ge 18:25 [t]Ps 31:23
94:4 [u]Ps 31:18 [v]Ps 52:1
94:5 [w]Isa 3:15
94:7 [x]Job 22:14; Ps 10:11
94:8 [y]Ps 92:6
94:9 [z]Ex 4:11; Pr 20:12
94:10 [a]Job 35:11; Isa 28:26
94:11 [b]1Co 3:20*
94:12 [c]Job 5:17; Heb 12:5 [d]Dt 8:3
94:13 [e]Ps 55:23
94:14 [f]1Sa 12:22; Ps 37:28; Ro 11:2
94:15 [g]Ps 97:2
94:16 [h]Nu 10:35; Ps 17:13 [i]Ps 59:2
94:17 [j]Ps 124:2
94:18 [k]Ps 38:16

your love, O LORD, supported
me.
19When anxiety was great within me,
your consolation brought joy to
my soul.
20Can a corrupt throne be allied with
you—
one that brings on misery by its
decrees?[l]
21They band together[m] against the
righteous
and condemn the innocent[n] to
death.
22But the LORD has become my
fortress,
and my God the rock in whom I
take refuge.[o]
23He will repay[p] them for their sins
and destroy them for their
wickedness;
the LORD our God will destroy
them.

Psalm 95

1 →PG. 644

1Come, let us sing for joy to the
LORD;
let us shout aloud[q] to the
Rock[r] of our salvation.
2Let us come before him[s] with
thanksgiving
and extol him with music[t] and
song.

3For the LORD is the great God,[u]
the great King above all gods.[v]
4In his hand are the depths of the
earth,
and the mountain peaks belong
to him.
5The sea is his, for he made it,
and his hands formed the dry
land.[w]

6Come, let us bow down[x] in
worship,
let us kneel[y] before the LORD
our Maker;[z]
7for he is our God
and we are the people of his
pasture,[a]
the flock under his care.

Today, if you hear his voice,
8 do not harden your hearts as you
did at Meribah,[a][b]
as you did that day at Massah[b]
in the desert,
9where your fathers tested[c] and
tried me,
though they had seen what I did.
10For forty years[d] I was angry with
that generation;
I said, "They are a people whose
hearts go astray,
and they have not known my
ways."
11So I declared on oath[e] in my
anger,
"They shall never enter my
rest."[f]

Psalm 96

1Sing to the LORD[g] a new song;
sing to the LORD, all the earth.
2Sing to the LORD, praise his name;
proclaim his salvation[h] day after
day.
3Declare his glory among the
nations,
his marvelous deeds among all
peoples.

4For great is the LORD and most
worthy of praise;[i]
he is to be feared[j] above all
gods.[k]
5For all the gods of the nations are
idols,
but the LORD made the
heavens.[l]
6Splendor and majesty are before
him;
strength and glory[m] are in his
sanctuary.

7Ascribe to the LORD,[n] O families of
nations,[o]
ascribe to the LORD glory and
strength.
8Ascribe to the LORD the glory due
his name;
bring an offering[p] and come
into his courts.
9Worship the LORD in the splendor
of his[c] holiness;[q]
tremble[r] before him, all the
earth.[s]

10Say among the nations, "The LORD
reigns.[t]"
The world is firmly established, it
cannot be moved;[u]
he will judge the peoples with
equity.[v]
11Let the heavens rejoice, let the
earth be glad;[w]
let the sea resound, and all that
is in it;
12 let the fields be jubilant, and
everything in them.
Then all the trees of the forest[x]
will sing for joy;[y]
13 they will sing before the LORD,
for he comes,
he comes to judge[z] the earth.
He will judge the world in
righteousness
and the peoples in his truth.

94:20 [l]Ps 58:2
94:21 [m]Ps 56:6 [n]Ps 106:38; Pr 17:15,26
94:22 [o]Ps 18:2; 59:9
94:23 [p]Ps 7:16
95:1 [q]Ps 81:1 [r]2Sa 22:47
95:2 [s]Mic 6:6 [t]Ps 81:2; Eph 5:19
95:3 [u]Ps 48:1; 145:3 [v]Ps 96:4; 97:9
95:5 [w]Ge 1:9; Ps 146:6
95:6 [x]Php 2:10 [y]2Ch 6:13 [z]Ps 100:3; 149:2; Isa 17:7; Da 6:10-11; Hos 8:14
95:7 [a]Ps 74:1; 79:13
95:8 [b]Ex 17:7
95:9 [c]Nu 14:22; Ps 78:18; 1Co 10:9
95:10 [d]Ac 7:36; Heb 3:17
95:11 [e]Nu 14:23 [f]Dt 1:35; Heb 4:3*
96:1 [g]1Ch 16:23
96:2 [h]Ps 71:15
96:4 [i]Ps 18:3; 145:3 [j]Ps 89:7 [k]Ps 95:3
96:5 [l]Ps 115:15
96:6 [m]Ps 29:1
96:7 [n]Ps 29:1 [o]Ps 22:27
96:8 [p]Ps 45:12; 72:10
96:9 [q]Ps 29:2 [r]Ps 114:7 [s]Ps 33:8
96:10 [t]Ps 97:1 [u]Ps 93:1 [v]Ps 67:4
96:11 [w]Ps 97:1; 98:7; Isa 49:13
96:12 [x]Isa 44:23 [y]Ps 65:13
96:13 [z]Rev 19:11

[a]8 *Meribah* means *quarreling.* [b]8 *Massah* means *testing.* [c]9 Or *LORD with the splendor of*

Psalm 97

1The LORD reigns,[a] let the earth be
glad;[b]
let the distant shores rejoice.

2Clouds and thick darkness[c]
surround him;
righteousness and justice are the
foundation of his throne.[d]
3Fire[e] goes before[f] him
and consumes[g] his foes on
every side.
4His lightning lights up the world;
the earth sees and trembles.[h]
5The mountains melt[i] like wax
before the LORD,
before the Lord of all the
earth.[j]
6The heavens proclaim his
righteousness,[k]
and all the peoples see his
glory.[l]

7All who worship images[m] are put
to shame,[n]
those who boast in idols—
worship him,[o] all you gods!
8Zion hears and rejoices
and the villages of Judah are glad
because of your judgments,[p]
O LORD.
9For you, O LORD, are the Most High
over all the earth;[q]
you are exalted[r] far above all
gods.

3 →PG. 645
10Let those who love the LORD hate
evil,[s]
for he guards the lives of his
faithful ones[t]
and delivers[u] them from the
hand of the wicked.[v]
11Light is shed[w] upon the righteous
and joy on the upright in heart.
12Rejoice in the LORD, you who are
righteous,
and praise his holy name.[x]

Psalm 98

A psalm.

1Sing to the LORD a new song,[y]
for he has done marvelous
things;[z]
his right hand[a] and his holy arm[b]
have worked salvation for him.
1 →PG. 645
2The LORD has made his salvation
known[c]
and revealed his righteousness to
the nations.
3He has remembered[d] his love
and his faithfulness to the house
of Israel;
all the ends of the earth have seen
the salvation of our God.

4Shout for joy[e] to the LORD, all the
earth,
burst into jubilant song with
music;
5make music to the LORD with the
harp,[f]
with the harp and the sound of
singing,[g]
6with trumpets[h] and the blast of
the ram's horn—
shout for joy before the LORD,
the King.[i]

7Let the sea resound, and everything
in it,
the world, and all who live in it.[j]
8Let the rivers clap their hands,
let the mountains[k] sing together
for joy;
9let them sing before the LORD,
for he comes to judge the earth.
He will judge the world in
righteousness
and the peoples with equity.[l]

Psalm 99

1The LORD reigns,[m]
let the nations tremble;
he sits enthroned between the
cherubim,[n]
let the earth shake.
2Great is the LORD[o] in Zion;
he is exalted[p] over all the
nations.
3Let them praise your great and
awesome name[q]—
he is holy.
4The King is mighty, he loves
justice[r]—
you have established equity;[s]
in Jacob you have done
what is just and right.
5Exalt[t] the LORD our God
and worship at his footstool;
he is holy.

6Moses[u] and Aaron were among
his priests,
Samuel[v] was among those who
called on his name;
they called on the LORD
and he answered[w] them.
7He spoke to them from the pillar of
cloud;[x]
they kept his statutes and the
decrees he gave them.

8O LORD our God,
you answered them;
you were to Israel[a] a forgiving
God,[y]

[a] *8* Hebrew *them*

97:1 [a]Ps 96:10 [b]Ps 96:11 **97:2** [c]Ex 19:9; Ps 18:11 [d]Ps 89:14 **97:3** [e]Da 7:10 [f]Hab 3:5 [g]Ps 18:8 **97:4** [h]Ps 104:32 **97:5** [i]Ps 46:2,6; Mic 1:4 [j]Jos 3:11 **97:6** [k]Ps 50:6 [l]Ps 19:1 **97:7** [m]Lev 26:1 [n]Jer 10:14 [o]Heb 1:6 **97:8** [p]Ps 48:11 **97:9** [q]Ps 83:18; 95:3 [r]Ex 18:11 **97:10** [s]Ps 34:14; Am 5:15; Ro 12:9 [t]Pr 2:8 [u]Da 3:28 [v]Ps 37:40; Jer 15:21 **97:11** [w]Job 22:28 **97:12** [x]Ps 30:4 **98:1** [y]Ps 96:1 [z]Ps 96:3 [a]Ex 15:6 [b]Isa 52:10 **98:2** [c]Isa 52:10 **98:3** [d]Lk 1:54 **98:4** [e]Isa 44:23 **98:5** [f]Ps 92:3 [g]Isa 51:3 **98:6** [h]Nu 10:10 [i]Ps 47:7 **98:7** [j]Ps 24:1 **98:8** [k]Isa 55:12 **98:9** [l]Ps 96:10 **99:1** [m]Ps 97:1 [n]Ex 25:22 **99:2** [o]Ps 48:1 [p]Ps 97:9; 113:4 **99:3** [q]Ps 76:1 **99:4** [r]Ps 11:7 [s]Ps 98:9 **99:5** [t]Ps 132:7 **99:6** [u]Ex 24:6 [v]Jer 15:1 [w]1Sa 7:9 **99:7** [x]Ex 33:9 **99:8** [y]Nu 14:20

though you punished their
misdeeds.[a]
9 Exalt the LORD our God
and worship at his holy
mountain,
for the LORD our God is holy.

Psalm 100

A psalm. For giving thanks.

1 →PG. 646

1 Shout for joy[z] to the LORD, all the
earth.
2 Worship the LORD with gladness;
come before him[a] with joyful
songs.
3 Know that the LORD is God.[b]
It is he who made us,[c] and we
are his[b];
we are his people, the sheep of
his pasture.[d]
4 Enter his gates with thanksgiving
and his courts with praise;
give thanks to him and praise his
name.[e]
5 For the LORD is good[f] and his love
endures forever;[g]
his faithfulness[h] continues
through all generations.

Psalm 101

Of David. A psalm.

1 I will sing of your love[i] and
justice;
to you, O LORD, I will sing praise.

3 →PG. 677

2 I will be careful to lead a blameless
life—
when will you come to me?

I will walk in my house
with blameless heart.
3 I will set before my eyes
no vile thing.[j]

The deeds of faithless men I
hate;[k]
they will not cling to me.
4 Men of perverse heart[l] shall be far
from me;
I will have nothing to do with
evil.

5 Whoever slanders his neighbor[m] in
secret,
him will I put to silence;
whoever has haughty eyes[n] and a
proud heart,
him will I not endure.

6 My eyes will be on the faithful in
the land,
that they may dwell with me;
he whose walk is blameless[o]
will minister to me.

7 No one who practices deceit
will dwell in my house;
no one who speaks falsely
will stand in my presence.

8 Every morning[p] I will put to
silence
all the wicked[q] in the land;
I will cut off every evildoer[r]
from the city of the LORD.[s]

Psalm 102

A prayer of an afflicted man. When
he is faint and pours out his lament
before the LORD.

1 Hear my prayer, O LORD;
let my cry for help[t] come to
you.
2 Do not hide your face[u] from me
when I am in distress.
Turn your ear to me;
when I call, answer me quickly.

3 For my days vanish like smoke;[v]
my bones burn like glowing
embers.
4 My heart is blighted and withered
like grass;[w]
I forget to eat my food.
5 Because of my loud groaning
I am reduced to skin and bones.
6 I am like a desert owl,[x]
like an owl among the ruins.
7 I lie awake;[y] I have become
like a bird alone[z] on a roof.
8 All day long my enemies taunt me;
those who rail against me use
my name as a curse.
9 For I eat ashes as my food
and mingle my drink with
tears[a]
10 because of your great wrath,[b]
for you have taken me up and
thrown me aside.
11 My days are like the evening
shadow;[c]
I wither away like grass.

12 But you, O LORD, sit enthroned
forever;[d]
your renown endures[e] through
all generations.
13 You will arise and have
compassion[f] on Zion,
for it is time to show favor to
her;
the appointed time has come.
14 For her stones are dear to your
servants;
her very dust moves them to
pity.

100:1 [z]Ps 98:4 **100:2** [a]Ps 95:2 **100:3** [b]Ps 46:10 [c]Job 10:3 [d]Ps 74:1; Eze 34:31 **100:4** [e]Ps 116:17 **100:5** [f]1Ch 16:34; Ps 25:8 [g]Ezr 3:11; Ps 106:1 [h]Ps 119:90 **101:1** [i]Ps 51:14; 89:1; 145:7 **101:3** [j]Dt 15:9 [k]Ps 40:4 **101:4** [l]Pr 11:20 **101:5** [m]Ps 50:20 [n]Ps 10:5; Pr 6:17 **101:6** [o]Ps 119:1

101:8 [p]Jer 21:12 [q]Ps 75:10 [r]Ps 118:10-12 [s]Ps 46:4 **102:1** [t]Ex 2:23 **102:2** [u]Ps 69:17 **102:3** [v]Jas 4:14 **102:4** [w]Ps 37:2 **102:6** [x]Job 30:29; Isa 34:11 **102:7** [y]Ps 77:4 [z]Ps 38:11 **102:9** [a]Ps 42:3 **102:10** [b]Ps 38:3 **102:11** [c]Job 14:2 **102:12** [d]Ps 9:7 [e]Ps 135:13 **102:13** [f]Isa 60:10

a 8 Or / *an avenger of the wrongs done to them*
b 3 Or *and not we ourselves*

15The nations will fear[g] the name of
the LORD,
all the kings[h] of the earth will
revere your glory.
16For the LORD will rebuild Zion
and appear in his glory.[i]
17He will respond to the prayer[j] of
the destitute;
he will not despise their plea.

18Let this be written[k] for a future
generation,
that a people not yet created[l]
may praise the LORD:
19"The LORD looked down[m] from his
sanctuary on high,
from heaven he viewed the
earth,
20to hear the groans of the
prisoners[n]
and release those condemned to
death."
21So the name of the LORD will be
declared[o] in Zion
and his praise in Jerusalem
22when the peoples and the
kingdoms
assemble to worship the LORD.

23In the course of my life[a] he broke
my strength;
he cut short my days.
24So I said:
"Do not take me away, O my
God, in the midst of my
days;
your years go on[p] through all
generations.
25In the beginning[q] you laid the
foundations of the earth,
and the heavens are the work of
your hands.
26They will perish,[r] but you remain;
they will all wear out like a
garment.
Like clothing you will change them
and they will be discarded.
27But you remain the same,[s]
and your years will never end.
28The children of your servants[t] will
live in your presence;
their descendants[u] will be
established before you."

Psalm 103

Of David.

1 →PG. 655

1Praise the LORD, O my soul;[v]
all my inmost being, praise his
holy name.
2Praise the LORD, O my soul,
and forget not all his benefits—
3who forgives all your sins[w]
and heals[x] all your diseases,
4who redeems your life from the pit
and crowns you with love and
compassion,
5who satisfies your desires with
good things
so that your youth is renewed
like the eagle's.[y]

6The LORD works righteousness
and justice for all the oppressed.

7He made known[z] his ways[a] to
Moses,
his deeds[b] to the people of
Israel:
8The LORD is compassionate and
gracious,[c]
slow to anger, abounding in love.
9He will not always accuse,
nor will he harbor his anger
forever;[d]
10he does not treat us as our sins
deserve[e]
or repay us according to our
iniquities.
11For as high as the heavens are
above the earth,
so great is his love[f] for those
who fear him;
12as far as the east is from the west,
so far has he removed our
transgressions[g] from us.
13As a father has compassion[h] on
his children,
so the LORD has compassion on
those who fear him;
14for he knows how we are formed,[i]
he remembers that we are dust.
15As for man, his days are like
grass,[j]
he flourishes like a flower[k] of
the field;
16the wind blows[l] over it and it is
gone,

102:15 [g]1Ki 8:43 [h]Ps 138:4
102:16 [i]Isa 60:1-2
102:17 [j]Ne 1:6
102:18 [k]Ro 15:4 [l]Ps 22:31
102:19 [m]Dt 26:15
102:20 [n]Ps 79:11
102:21 [o]Ps 22:22
102:24 [p]Ps 90:2; Isa 38:10
102:25 [q]Ge 1:1; Heb 1:10-12*
102:26 [r]Isa 34:4; Mt 24:35; 2Pe 3:7-10; Rev 20:11
102:27 [s]Mal 3:6; Heb 13:8; Jas 1:17
102:28 [t]Ps 69:36 [u]Ps 89:4
103:1 [v]Ps 104:1
103:3 [w]Ps 130:8 [x]Ex 15:26
103:5 [y]Isa 40:31
103:7 [z]Ps 99:7; 147:19 [a]Ex 33:13 [b]Ps 106:22
103:8 [c]Ex 34:6; Ps 86:15; Jas 5:11
103:9 [d]Ps 30:5; Isa 57:16; Jer 3:5,12; Mic 7:18
103:10 [e]Ezr 9:13
103:11 [f]Ps 57:10
103:12 [g]2Sa 12:13
103:13 [h]Mal 3:17
103:14 [i]Isa 29:16
103:15 [j]Ps 90:5 [k]Job 14:2; Jas 1:10; 1Pe 1:24
103:16 [l]Isa 40:7

[a]23 Or *By his power*

103:1–22

PROMISE 1

THE BEST ADVICE

This psalm opens and closes with the greatest advice anyone can give: A simple six-word line where the psalmist tells the core of his being to think properly about God. What we do with God is the most important thing in this life, and this psalm explains why we should praise God. Read it with a mind to respond to what it teaches.

What a way to start and end your day! Take a week—seven consecutive days—and read this psalm at different times throughout each day. When you do, write down one new reason given in the psalm to "Praise the LORD." Then do it!

For the next Promise 1 reading go to page 668.

and its place[m] remembers it no
more.
17But from everlasting to everlasting
the LORD's love is with those who
fear him,
and his righteousness with their
children's children—
18with those who keep his covenant
and remember to obey his
precepts.[n]

4 →PG. 663

19The LORD has established his
throne in heaven,
and his kingdom rules[o] over all.

20Praise the LORD, you his angels,[p]
you mighty ones[q] who do his
bidding,
who obey his word.
21Praise the LORD, all his heavenly
hosts,[r]
you his servants who do his will.
22Praise the LORD, all his works[s]
everywhere in his dominion.

Praise the LORD, O my soul.

Psalm 104

1Praise the LORD, O my soul.[t]

O LORD my God, you are very great;
you are clothed with splendor
and majesty.
2He wraps[u] himself in light as with
a garment;
he stretches out the heavens[v]
like a tent
3 and lays the beams[w] of his
upper chambers on their
waters.
He makes the clouds[x] his chariot
and rides on the wings of the
wind.[y]
4He makes winds his
messengers,[a][z]
flames of fire[a] his servants.

5He set the earth[b] on its
foundations;
it can never be moved.
6You covered it[c] with the deep[d] as
with a garment;
the waters stood above the
mountains.
7But at your rebuke[e] the waters
fled,
at the sound of your thunder
they took to flight;
8they flowed over the mountains,
they went down into the valleys,
to the place you assigned[f] for
them.
9You set a boundary they cannot
cross;
never again will they cover the
earth.

10He makes springs[g] pour water
into the ravines;
it flows between the mountains.
11They give water to all the beasts of
the field;
the wild donkeys quench their
thirst.
12The birds of the air[h] nest by the
waters;
they sing among the branches.
13He waters the mountains[i] from
his upper chambers;
the earth is satisfied by the fruit
of his work.
14He makes grass grow[j] for the
cattle,
and plants for man to cultivate—
bringing forth food[k] from the
earth:
15wine[l] that gladdens the heart of
man,
oil[m] to make his face shine,
and bread that sustains his heart.
16The trees of the LORD are well
watered,
the cedars of Lebanon that he
planted.
17There the birds[n] make their nests;
the stork has its home in the
pine trees.
18The high mountains belong to the
wild goats;
the crags are a refuge for the
coneys.[b][o]

19The moon marks off the seasons,[p]
and the sun[q] knows when to go
down.
20You bring darkness,[r] it becomes
night,[s]
and all the beasts of the forest[t]
prowl.
21The lions roar for their prey
and seek their food from God.[u]
22The sun rises, and they steal away;
they return and lie down in their
dens.[v]
23Then man goes out to his work,[w]
to his labor until evening.

24How many are your works,[x]
O LORD!
In wisdom you made[y] them all;
the earth is full of your creatures.
25There is the sea,[z] vast and
spacious,
teeming with creatures beyond
number—
living things both large and
small.
26There the ships[a] go to and fro,
and the leviathan,[b] which you
formed to frolic there.

a 4 Or *angels* b 18 That is, the hyrax or rock badger

103:16 [m]Job 7:10 **103:18** [n]Dt 7:9 **103:19** [o]Ps 47:2 **103:20** [p]Ps 148:2; Heb 1:14 [q]Ps 29:1 **103:21** [r]1Ki 22:19 **103:22** [s]Ps 145:10 **104:1** [t]Ps 103:22 **104:2** [u]Da 7:9 [v]Isa 40:22 **104:3** [w]Am 9:6 [x]Isa 19:1 [y]Ps 18:10 **104:4** [z]Ps 148:8; Heb 1:7* [a]2Ki 2:11 **104:5** [b]Job 26:7; Ps 24:1-2 **104:6** [c]Ge 7:19 [d]Ge 1:2 **104:7** [e]Ps 18:15 **104:8** [f]Ps 33:7

104:10 [g]Ps 107:33; Isa 41:18 **104:12** [h]Mt 8:20 **104:13** [i]Ps 147:8; Jer 10:13 **104:14** [j]Job 38:27; Ps 147:8 [k]Ge 1:30; Job 28:5 **104:15** [l]Jdg 9:13 [m]Ps 23:5; 92:10; Lk 7:46 **104:17** [n]ver 12 **104:18** [o]Pr 30:26 **104:19** [p]Ge 1:14 [q]Ps 19:6 **104:20** [r]Isa 45:7 [s]Ps 74:16 [t]Ps 50:10 **104:21** [u]Job 38:39; Ps 145:15; Joel 1:20 **104:22** [v]Job 37:8 **104:23** [w]Ge 3:19 **104:24** [x]Ps 40:5 [y]Pr 3:19 **104:25** [z]Ps 69:34 **104:26** [a]Ps 107:23; Eze 27:9 [b]Job 41:1

27These all look to you
to give them their food[c] at the proper time.
28When you give it to them,
they gather it up;
when you open your hand,
they are satisfied[d] with good things.
29When you hide your face,[e]
they are terrified;
when you take away their breath,
they die and return to the dust.[f]
30When you send your Spirit,
they are created,
and you renew the face of the earth.

31May the glory of the LORD endure forever;
may the LORD rejoice in his works[g]—
32he who looks at the earth, and it trembles,[h]
who touches the mountains,[i] and they smoke.[j]

33I will sing[k] to the LORD all my life;
I will sing praise to my God as long as I live.
34May my meditation be pleasing to him,
as I rejoice[l] in the LORD.
35But may sinners vanish[m] from the earth
and the wicked be no more.

Praise the LORD, O my soul.

Praise the LORD.[a][n]

Psalm 105

1Give thanks to the LORD,[o] call on his name;[p]
make known among the nations what he has done.
2Sing to him,[q] sing praise to him;
tell of all his wonderful acts.
3Glory in his holy name;
let the hearts of those who seek the LORD rejoice.
4Look to the LORD and his strength;
seek his face[r] always.

5Remember the wonders[s] he has done,
his miracles, and the judgments he pronounced,[t]
6O descendants of Abraham his servant,[u]
O sons of Jacob, his chosen[v] ones.
7He is the LORD our God;
his judgments are in all the earth.

8He remembers his covenant[w] forever,
the word he commanded, for a thousand generations,
9the covenant he made with Abraham,[x]
the oath he swore to Isaac.
10He confirmed it[y] to Jacob as a decree,
to Israel as an everlasting covenant:
11"To you I will give the land of Canaan[z]
as the portion you will inherit."

12When they were but few in number,[a]
few indeed, and strangers in it,[b]
13they wandered from nation to nation,
from one kingdom to another.
14He allowed no one to oppress[c] them;
for their sake he rebuked kings:[d]
15"Do not touch[e] my anointed ones;
do my prophets no harm."

16He called down famine[f] on the land
and destroyed all their supplies of food;
17and he sent a man before them—
Joseph, sold as a slave.[g]
18They bruised his feet with shackles,[h]
his neck was put in irons,
19till what he foretold[i] came to pass,
till the word of the LORD proved him true.
20The king sent and released him,
the ruler of peoples set him free.[j]
21He made him master of his household,
ruler over all he possessed,
22to instruct his princes[k] as he pleased
and teach his elders wisdom.

23Then Israel entered Egypt;[l]
Jacob lived as an alien in the land of Ham.
24The LORD made his people very fruitful;
he made them too numerous[m] for their foes,
25whose hearts he turned[n] to hate his people,
to conspire[o] against his servants.
26He sent Moses[p] his servant,
and Aaron, whom he had chosen.[q]

104:27 [c]Job 36:31; Ps 136:25; 145:15; 147:9 **104:28** [d]Ps 145:16 **104:29** [e]Dt 31:17 [f]Job 34:14; Ecc 12:7 **104:31** [g]Ge 1:31 **104:32** [h]Ps 97:4 [i]Ex 19:18 [j]Ps 144:5 **104:33** [k]Ps 63:4 **104:34** [l]Ps 9:2 **104:35** [m]Ps 37:38 [n]Ps 105:45; 106:48 **105:1** [o]1Ch 16:34 [p]Ps 99:6 **105:2** [q]Ps 96:1 **105:4** [r]Ps 27:8 **105:5** [s]Ps 40:5 [t]Ps 77:11 **105:6** [u]ver 42 [v]Ps 106:5 **105:8** [w]Ps 106:45; Lk 1:72 **105:9** [x]Ge 12:7; 17:2; 22:16-18; Gal 3:15-18 **105:10** [y]Ge 28:13-15 **105:11** [z]Ge 13:15; 15:18 **105:12** [a]Ge 34:30; Dt 7:7 [b]Ge 23:4; Heb 11:9 **105:14** [c]Ge 35:5 [d]Ge 12:17-20 **105:15** [e]Ge 26:11 **105:16** [f]Ge 41:54; Lev 26:26; Isa 3:1; Eze 4:16 **105:17** [g]Ge 37:28; 45:5; Ac 7:9 **105:18** [h]Ge 40:15 **105:19** [i]Ge 40:20-22 **105:20** [j]Ge 41:14 **105:22** [k]Ge 41:43-44 **105:23** [l]Ge 46:6; Ac 13:17 **105:24** [m]Ex 1:7,9 **105:25** [n]Ex 4:21 [o]Ex 1:6-10; Ac 7:19 **105:26** [p]Ex 3:10 [q]Nu 16:5; 17:5-8

a *35* Hebrew *Hallelu Yah*; in the Septuagint this line stands at the beginning of Psalm 105.

27They performed[r] his miraculous
signs among them,
his wonders in the land of Ham.
28He sent darkness[s] and made the
land dark—
for had they not rebelled against
his words?
29He turned their waters into
blood,[t]
causing their fish to die.[u]
30Their land teemed with frogs,[v]
which went up into the
bedrooms of their rulers.
31He spoke, and there came swarms
of flies,[w]
and gnats[x] throughout their
country.
32He turned their rain into hail,[y]
with lightning throughout their
land;
33he struck down their vines[z] and
fig trees
and shattered the trees of their
country.
34He spoke, and the locusts came,[a]
grasshoppers without number;
35they ate up every green thing in
their land,
ate up the produce of their
soil.
36Then he struck down all the
firstborn[b] in their land,
the firstfruits of all their
manhood.

37He brought out Israel, laden with
silver and gold,[c]
and from among their tribes no
one faltered.
38Egypt was glad when they left,
because dread of Israel[d] had
fallen on them.
39He spread out a cloud[e] as a
covering,
and a fire to give light at night.[f]
40They asked,[g] and he brought them
quail[h]
and satisfied them with the
bread of heaven.[i]
41He opened the rock,[j] and water
gushed out;
like a river it flowed in the
desert.

42For he remembered his holy
promise[k]
given to his servant Abraham.
43He brought out his people with
rejoicing,[l]
his chosen ones with shouts of
joy;
44he gave them the lands of the
nations,[m]
and they fell heir to what others
had toiled for—

105:27 [r]Ex 7:8-12:51
105:28 [s]Ex 10:22
105:29 [t]Ps 78:44 [u]Ex 7:21
105:30 [v]Ex 8:2,6
105:31 [w]Ex 8:21-24 [x]Ex 8:16-18
105:32 [y]Ex 9:22-25
105:33 [z]Ps 78:47
105:34 [a]Ex 10:4,12-15
105:36 [b]Ex 12:29
105:37 [c]Ex 12:35
105:38 [d]Ex 12:33; 15:16
105:39 [e]Ex 13:21 [f]Ne 9:12; Ps 78:14
105:40 [g]Ps 78:18,24 [h]Ex 16:13 [i]Jn 6:31
105:41 [j]Ex 17:6; Nu 20:11; Ps 78:15-16; 1Co 10:4
105:42 [k]Ge 15:13-16
105:43 [l]Ex 15:1-18; Ps 106:12
105:44 [m]Jos 13:6-7
105:45 [n]Dt 4:40; 6:21-24
106:1 [o]Ps 100:5; 105:1
106:2 [p]Ps 145:4,12
106:3 [q]Ps 15:2
106:4 [r]Ps 119:132
106:5 [s]Ps 1:3 [t]Ps 118:15
106:6 [u]Da 9:5
106:7 [v]Ps 78:11,42 [w]Ex 14:11-12
106:8 [x]Ex 9:16
106:9 [y]Ps 18:15 [z]Ex 14:21; Na 1:4 [a]Isa 63:11-14
106:10 [b]Ex 14:30 [c]Ps 107:2
106:11 [d]Ex 14:28; 15:5
106:12 [e]Ex 15:1-21
106:13 [f]Ex 15:24

45that they might keep his precepts
and observe his laws.[n]

Praise the LORD.[a]

Psalm 106

1Praise the LORD.[b]

Give thanks to the LORD, for he is
good;[o]
his love endures forever.
2Who can proclaim the mighty
acts[p] of the LORD
or fully declare his praise?
3Blessed are they who maintain
justice,
who constantly do what is
right.[q]
4Remember me,[r] O LORD, when
you show favor to your
people,
come to my aid when you save
them,
5that I may enjoy the prosperity[s] of
your chosen ones,
that I may share in the joy[t] of
your nation
and join your inheritance in
giving praise.

6We have sinned,[u] even as our
fathers did;
we have done wrong and acted
wickedly.
7When our fathers were in Egypt,
they gave no thought to your
miracles;
they did not remember[v] your
many kindnesses,
and they rebelled by the sea,[w]
the Red Sea.[c]
8Yet he saved them for his name's
sake,[x]
to make his mighty power known.
9He rebuked[y] the Red Sea, and it
dried up;[z]
he led them through[a] the
depths as through a desert.
10He saved them[b] from the hand of
the foe;
from the hand of the enemy he
redeemed them.[c]
11The waters covered[d] their
adversaries;
not one of them survived.
12Then they believed his promises
and sang his praise.[e]
13But they soon forgot[f] what he had
done
and did not wait for his counsel.
14In the desert they gave in to their
craving;

[a]*45* Hebrew *Hallelu Yah* [b]*1* Hebrew *Hallelu Yah*; also in verse 48 [c]*7* Hebrew *Yam Suph*; that is, Sea of Reeds; also in verses 9 and 22

in the wasteland they put God to
the test.[g]
15So he gave them[h] what they asked
for,
but sent a wasting disease[i]
upon them.

16In the camp they grew envious[j] of
Moses
and of Aaron, who was
consecrated to the LORD.
17The earth opened[k] up and
swallowed Dathan;
it buried the company of Abiram.
18Fire blazed[l] among their
followers;
a flame consumed the wicked.

19At Horeb they made a calf[m]
and worshiped an idol cast from
metal.
20They exchanged their Glory[n]
for an image of a bull, which
eats grass.
21They forgot the God[o] who saved
them,
who had done great things[p] in
Egypt,
22miracles in the land of Ham[q]
and awesome deeds by the Red
Sea.
23So he said he would destroy[r]
them—
had not Moses, his chosen one,
stood in the breach[s] before him
to keep his wrath from
destroying them.

24Then they despised the pleasant
land;[t]
they did not believe[u] his
promise.
25They grumbled[v] in their tents
and did not obey the LORD.
26So he swore[w] to them with
uplifted hand
that he would make them fall in
the desert,[x]
27make their descendants fall among
the nations
and scatter[y] them throughout
the lands.

28They yoked themselves to the Baal
of Peor[z]
and ate sacrifices offered to
lifeless gods;
29they provoked the LORD to anger by
their wicked deeds,
and a plague broke out among
them.
30But Phinehas stood up and
intervened,
and the plague was checked.[a]
31This was credited to him[b] as
righteousness
for endless generations to come.
32By the waters of Meribah[c] they
angered the LORD,
and trouble came to Moses
because of them;
33for they rebelled against the Spirit
of God,
and rash words came from
Moses' lips.[a][d]

34They did not destroy[e] the peoples
as the LORD had commanded[f]
them,
35but they mingled[g] with the
nations
and adopted their customs.
36They worshiped their idols,[h]
which became a snare to them.
37They sacrificed their sons[i]
and their daughters to demons.
38They shed innocent blood,
the blood of their sons[j] and
daughters,
whom they sacrificed to the idols
of Canaan,
and the land was desecrated by
their blood.
39They defiled themselves[k] by what
they did;
by their deeds they prostituted[l]
themselves.

40Therefore the LORD was angry[m]
with his people
and abhorred his inheritance.[n]
41He handed them over[o] to the
nations,
and their foes ruled over them.
42Their enemies oppressed them
and subjected them to their
power.
43Many times he delivered them,
but they were bent on
rebellion[p]
and they wasted away in their
sin.

44But he took note of their distress
when he heard their cry;[q]
45for their sake he remembered his
covenant[r]
and out of his great love[s] he
relented.
46He caused them to be pitied[t]
by all who held them captive.

47Save us, O LORD our God,
and gather us[u] from the
nations,
that we may give thanks to your
holy name
and glory in your praise.

106:14 [g]1Co 10:9
106:15 [h]Nu 11:31 [i]Isa 10:16
106:16 [j]Nu 16:1-3
106:17 [k]Dt 11:6
106:18 [l]Nu 16:35
106:19 [m]Ex 32:4
106:20 [n]Jer 2:11; Ro 1:23
106:21 [o]Ps 78:11 [p]Dt 10:21
106:22 [q]Ps 105:27
106:23 [r]Ex 32:10 [s]Ex 32:11-14
106:24 [t]Dt 8:7; Eze 20:6 [u]Heb 3:18-19
106:25 [v]Nu 14:2
106:26 [w]Eze 20:15; Heb 3:11 [x]Nu 14:28-35
106:27 [y]Lev 26:33; Ps 44:11
106:28 [z]Nu 25:2-3; Hos 9:10
106:30 [a]Nu 25:8
106:31 [b]Nu 25:11-13
106:32 [c]Nu 20:2-13; Ps 81:7
106:33 [d]Nu 20:8-12
106:34 [e]Jdg 1:21 [f]Dt 7:16
106:35 [g]Jdg 3:5-6
106:36 [h]Jdg 2:12
106:37 [i]2Ki 16:3; 17:17
106:38 [j]Nu 35:33
106:39 [k]Eze 20:18 [l]Lev 17:7; Nu 15:39
106:40 [m]Jdg 2:14; Ps 78:59 [n]Dt 9:29
106:41 [o]Jdg 2:14; Ne 9:27
106:43 [p]Jdg 2:16-19
106:44 [q]Jdg 3:9; 10:10
106:45 [r]Lev 26:42; Ps 105:8 [s]Jdg 2:18
106:46 [t]Ezr 9:9; Jer 42:12
106:47 [u]Ps 147:2

[a]*33* Or *against his spirit, / and rash words came from his lips*

48Praise be to the LORD, the God of
Israel,
from everlasting to everlasting.
Let all the people say, "Amen!"[v]

Praise the LORD.

BOOK V

Psalms 107–150

Psalm 107

1Give thanks to the LORD,[w] for he is
good;
his love endures forever.
2Let the redeemed[x] of the LORD say
this—
those he redeemed from the
hand of the foe,
3those he gathered[y] from the lands,
from east and west, from north
and south.[a]

4Some wandered in desert[z]
wastelands,
finding no way to a city where
they could settle.
5They were hungry and thirsty,
and their lives ebbed away.
6Then they cried out[a] to the LORD
in their trouble,
and he delivered them from their
distress.
7He led them by a straight way[b]
to a city where they could settle.
8Let them give thanks to the LORD
for his unfailing love
and his wonderful deeds for
men,
9for he satisfies[c] the thirsty
and fills the hungry with good
things.[d]

10Some sat in darkness[e] and the
deepest gloom,
prisoners suffering in iron
chains,[f]
11for they had rebelled[g] against the
words of God
and despised the counsel[h] of
the Most High.
12So he subjected them to bitter
labor;
they stumbled, and there was no
one to help.[i]
13Then they cried to the LORD in
their trouble,
and he saved them from their
distress.
14He brought them out of darkness
and the deepest gloom
and broke away their chains.[j]
15Let them give thanks to the LORD
for his unfailing love
and his wonderful deeds for
men,
16for he breaks down gates of bronze
and cuts through bars of iron.
17Some became fools through their
rebellious ways
and suffered affliction[k] because
of their iniquities.
18They loathed all food[l]
and drew near the gates of
death.[m]
19Then they cried to the LORD in
their trouble,
and he saved them from their
distress.
20He sent forth his word[n] and
healed them;[o]
he rescued[p] them from the
grave.[q]
21Let them give thanks to the LORD
for his unfailing love
and his wonderful deeds for
men.
22Let them sacrifice thank offerings[r]
and tell of his works[s] with
songs of joy.

23Others went out on the sea in
ships;
they were merchants on the
mighty waters.
24They saw the works of the LORD,
his wonderful deeds in the deep.
25For he spoke[t] and stirred up a
tempest[u]
that lifted high the waves.[v]
26They mounted up to the heavens
and went down to the
depths;
in their peril their courage
melted[w] away.
27They reeled and staggered like
drunken men;
they were at their wits' end.
28Then they cried out to the LORD in
their trouble,
and he brought them out of their
distress.
29He stilled the storm[x] to a whisper;
the waves[y] of the sea were
hushed.
30They were glad when it grew calm,
and he guided them to their
desired haven.
31Let them give thanks to the LORD
for his unfailing love
and his wonderful deeds for men.
32Let them exalt him in the
assembly[z] of the people
and praise him in the council of
the elders.

33He turned rivers into a desert,[a]
flowing springs into thirsty
ground,

106:48 [v]Ps 41:13
107:1 [w]Ps 106:1
107:2 [x]Ps 106:10
107:3 [y]Ps 106:47; Isa 43:5-6
107:4 [z]Nu 14:33; 32:13
107:6 [a]Ps 50:15
107:7 [b]Ezr 8:21
107:9 [c]Ps 22:26; Lk 1:53 [d]Ps 34:10
107:10 [e]Lk 1:79 [f]Job 36:8
107:11 [g]Ps 106:7; La 3:42 [h]2Ch 36:16
107:12 [i]Ps 22:11
107:14 [j]Ps 116:16; Lk 13:16; Ac 12:7
107:17 [k]Isa 65:6-7; La 3:39
107:18 [l]Job 33:20 [m]Job 33:22; Ps 9:13; 88:3
107:20 [n]Mt 8:8 [o]Ps 103:3 [p]Job 33:28 [q]Ps 30:3; 49:15
107:22 [r]Lev 7:12; Ps 50:14; 116:17 [s]Ps 9:11; 73:28; 118:17
107:25 [t]Ps 105:31 [u]Jnh 1:4 [v]Ps 93:3
107:26 [w]Ps 22:14
107:29 [x]Mt 8:26 [y]Ps 89:9
107:32 [z]Ps 22:22,25; 35:18
107:33 [a]1Ki 17:1; Ps 74:15

[a]3 Hebrew *north and the sea*

34and fruitful land into a salt
waste,[b]
because of the wickedness of
those who lived there.
35He turned the desert into pools of
water[c]
and the parched ground into
flowing springs;
36there he brought the hungry to live,
and they founded a city where
they could settle.
37They sowed fields and planted
vineyards[d]
that yielded a fruitful harvest;
38he blessed them, and their
numbers greatly
increased,[e]
and he did not let their herds
diminish.

39Then their numbers decreased,[f]
and they were humbled
by oppression, calamity and
sorrow;
40he who pours contempt on
nobles[g]
made them wander in a trackless
waste.[h]
41But he lifted the needy[i] out of
their affliction
and increased their families like
flocks.
42The upright see and rejoice,[j]
but all the wicked shut their
mouths.[k]

43Whoever is wise,[l] let him heed
these things
and consider the great love[m] of
the LORD.

Psalm 108

A song. A psalm of David.

1My heart is steadfast, O God;
I will sing and make music with
all my soul.
2Awake, harp and lyre!
I will awaken the dawn.
3I will praise you, O LORD, among
the nations;
I will sing of you among the
peoples.
4For great is your love, higher than
the heavens;
your faithfulness reaches to the
skies.
5Be exalted, O God, above the
heavens,
and let your glory be over all the
earth.[n]

6Save us and help us with your right
hand,
that those you love may be
delivered.
7God has spoken from his
sanctuary:
"In triumph I will parcel out
Shechem
and measure off the Valley of
Succoth.
8Gilead is mine, Manasseh is mine;
Ephraim is my helmet,
Judah[o] my scepter.
9Moab is my washbasin,
upon Edom I toss my sandal;
over Philistia I shout in
triumph."

10Who will bring me to the fortified
city?
Who will lead me to Edom?
11Is it not you, O God, you who have
rejected us
and no longer go out with our
armies?[p]
12Give us aid against the enemy,
for the help of man is worthless.
13With God we will gain the victory,
and he will trample down our
enemies.

Psalm 109

For the director of music. Of David.
A psalm.

1O God, whom I praise,
do not remain silent,[q]
2for wicked and deceitful men
have opened their mouths
against me;
they have spoken against me
with lying tongues.[r]
3With words of hatred[s] they
surround me;
they attack me without cause.[t]
4In return for my friendship they
accuse me,
but I am a man of prayer.[u]
5They repay me evil for good,[v]
and hatred for my friendship.

6Appoint[a] an evil man[b] to oppose
him;
let an accuser[c][w] stand at his
right hand.
7When he is tried, let him be found
guilty,
and may his prayers condemn[x]
him.
8May his days be few;
may another take his place[y] of
leadership.
9May his children be fatherless
and his wife a widow.[z]

107:34 [b]Ge 13:10; 14:3; 19:25
107:35 [c]Ps 114:8; Isa 41:18
107:37 [d]Isa 65:21
107:38 [e]Ge 12:2; 17:16,20; Ex 1:7
107:39 [f]2Ki 10:32; Eze 5:12
107:40 [g]Job 12:21 [h]Job 12:24
107:41 [i]1Sa 2:8; Ps 113:7-9
107:42 [j]Job 22:19 [k]Job 5:16; Ps 63:11; Ro 3:19
107:43 [l]Jer 9:12; Hos 14:9 [m]Ps 64:9
108:5 [n]Ps 57:5
108:8 [o]Ge 49:10
108:11 [p]Ps 44:9
109:1 [q]Ps 83:1
109:2 [r]Ps 52:4; 120:2
109:3 [s]Ps 69:4 [t]Ps 35:7; Jn 15:25
109:4 [u]Ps 69:13
109:5 [v]Ps 35:12; 38:20
109:6 [w]Zec 3:1
109:7 [x]Pr 28:9
109:8 [y]Ac 1:20*
109:9 [z]Ex 22:24

[a]6 Or *They say:* "*Appoint* (with quotation marks at the end of verse 19) [b]6 Or *the Evil One* [c]6 Or *let Satan*

10 May his children be wandering beggars;
may they be driven[a] from their ruined homes.
11 May a creditor seize all he has;
may strangers plunder the fruits of his labor.[a]
12 May no one extend kindness to him
or take pity[b] on his fatherless children.
13 May his descendants be cut off,[c]
their names blotted out[d] from the next generation.
14 May the iniquity of his fathers[e] be remembered before the LORD;
may the sin of his mother never be blotted out.
15 May their sins always remain before the LORD,
that he may cut off the memory[f] of them from the earth.

16 For he never thought of doing a kindness,
but hounded to death the poor
and the needy[g] and the brokenhearted.[h]
17 He loved to pronounce a curse—
may it[b] come on him;[i]
he found no pleasure in blessing—
may it be[c] far from him.
18 He wore cursing[j] as his garment;
it entered into his body like water,[k]
into his bones like oil.
19 May it be like a cloak wrapped about him,
like a belt tied forever around him.
20 May this be the LORD's payment[l] to my accusers,
to those who speak evil[m] of me.

21 But you, O Sovereign LORD,
deal well with me for your name's sake;[n]
out of the goodness of your love,[o] deliver me.
22 For I am poor and needy,
and my heart is wounded within me.
23 I fade away like an evening shadow;[p]
I am shaken off like a locust.
24 My knees give[q] way from fasting;
my body is thin and gaunt.
25 I am an object of scorn[r] to my accusers;
when they see me, they shake their heads.[s]

109:11 [a]Job 5:5 **109:12** [b]Isa 9:17 **109:13** [c]Job 18:19; Ps 37:28 [d]Pr 10:7 **109:14** [e]Ex 20:5; Ne 4:5; Jer 18:23 **109:15** [f]Job 18:17; Ps 34:16 **109:16** [g]Ps 37:14,32 [h]Ps 34:18 **109:17** [i]Pr 14:14; Eze 35:6 **109:18** [j]Ps 73:6 [k]Nu 5:22 **109:20** [l]Ps 94:23; 2Ti 4:14 [m]Ps 71:10 **109:21** [n]Ps 79:9 [o]Ps 69:16 **109:23** [p]Ps 102:11 **109:24** [q]Heb 12:12 **109:25** [r]Ps 22:6 [s]Mt 27:39; Mk 15:29

109:26 [t]Ps 119:86 **109:27** [u]Job 37:7 **109:28** [v]2Sa 16:12 [w]Isa 65:14 **109:29** [x]Ps 35:26; 132:18 **109:30** [y]Ps 35:18; 111:1 **109:31** [z]Ps 16:8; 73:23; 121:5 **110:1** [a]Mt 22:44*; Mk 12:36*; Lk 20:42*; Ac 2:34* [b]1Co 15:25 **110:2** [c]Ps 45:6 **110:3** [d]Jdg 5:2; Ps 96:9 **110:4** [e]Nu 23:19 [f]Heb 5:6*; 7:21* [g]Heb 7:15-17* **110:5** [h]Ps 16:8 [i]Ps 2:12 [j]Ps 2:5; Ro 2:5 **110:6** [k]Isa 2:4 [l]Isa 66:24 [m]Ps 68:21 **110:7** [n]Ps 27:6

26 Help me,[t] O LORD my God;
save me in accordance with your love.
27 Let them know[u] that it is your hand,
that you, O LORD, have done it.
28 They may curse,[v] but you will bless;
when they attack they will be put to shame,
but your servant will rejoice.[w]
29 My accusers will be clothed with disgrace
and wrapped in shame[x] as in a cloak.

30 With my mouth I will greatly extol the LORD;
in the great throng[y] I will praise him.
31 For he stands at the right hand[z] of the needy one,
to save his life from those who condemn him.

Psalm 110

Of David. A psalm.

1 The LORD says[a] to my Lord:
"Sit at my right hand
until I make your enemies
a footstool for your feet."[b]

2 The LORD will extend your mighty scepter[c] from Zion;
you will rule in the midst of your enemies.
3 Your troops will be willing
on your day of battle.
Arrayed in holy majesty,[d]
from the womb of the dawn
you will receive the dew of your youth.[d]

4 The LORD has sworn
and will not change his mind:[e]
"You are a priest forever,[f]
in the order of Melchizedek.[g]"

5 The Lord is at your right hand;[h]
he will crush kings[i] on the day of his wrath.[j]
6 He will judge the nations,[k]
heaping up the dead[l]
and crushing the rulers[m] of the whole earth.
7 He will drink from a brook beside the way[e];
therefore he will lift up his head.[n]

[a] 10 Septuagint; Hebrew *sought* [b] 17 Or *curse, / and it has* [c] 17 Or *blessing, / and it is* [d] 3 Or / *your young men will come to you like the dew* [e] 7 Or / *The One who grants succession will set him in authority*

Psalm 111[a]

1Praise the LORD.[b]

I will extol the LORD with all my heart
in the council of the upright and in the assembly.

2Great are the works[o] of the LORD;
they are pondered by all who delight in them.
3Glorious and majestic are his deeds,
and his righteousness endures forever.
4He has caused his wonders to be remembered;
the LORD is gracious and compassionate.[p]
5He provides food[q] for those who fear him;
he remembers his covenant forever.
6He has shown his people the power of his works,
giving them the lands of other nations.
7The works of his hands are faithful and just;
all his precepts are trustworthy.[r]
8They are steadfast for ever[s] and ever,
done in faithfulness and uprightness.
9He provided redemption[t] for his people;
he ordained his covenant forever—
holy and awesome[u] is his name.
10The fear of the LORD is the beginning of wisdom;[v]
all who follow his precepts have good understanding.[w]
To him belongs eternal praise.[x]

Psalm 112[a]

1Praise the LORD.[b]

Blessed is the man who fears the LORD,[y]
who finds great delight[z] in his commands.

2His children will be mighty in the land;
the generation of the upright will be blessed.
3Wealth and riches are in his house,
and his righteousness endures forever.
4Even in darkness light dawns[a] for the upright,
for the gracious and compassionate and righteous[b] man.[c]
5Good will come to him who is generous and lends freely,[c]
who conducts his affairs with justice.
6Surely he will never be shaken;
a righteous man will be remembered[d] forever.
7He will have no fear of bad news;
his heart is steadfast,[e] trusting in the LORD.
8His heart is secure, he will have no fear;
in the end he will look in triumph on his foes.[f]
9He has scattered abroad his gifts to the poor,[g]
his righteousness endures forever;
his horn[d] will be lifted[h] high in honor.
10The wicked man will see[i] and be vexed,
he will gnash his teeth[j] and waste away;[k]
the longings of the wicked will come to nothing.[l]

Psalm 113

1Praise the LORD.[e]

Praise, O servants of the LORD,[m]
praise the name of the LORD.
2Let the name of the LORD be praised,
both now and forevermore.[n]
3From the rising of the sun[o] to the place where it sets,
the name of the LORD is to be praised.

4The LORD is exalted[p] over all the nations,
his glory above the heavens.[q]
5Who is like the LORD our God,[r]
the One who sits enthroned[s] on high,
6who stoops down to look[t]
on the heavens and the earth?

7He raises the poor[u] from the dust
and lifts the needy[v] from the ash heap;
8he seats them[w] with princes,
with the princes of their people.

111:2 [o]Ps 92:5; 143:5 **111:4** [p]Ps 103:8 **111:5** [q]Mt 6:26, 31-33 **111:7** [r]Ps 19:7; Rev 15:3 **111:8** [s]Isa 40:8; Mt 5:18 **111:9** [t]Lk 1:68 [u]Ps 99:3; Lk 1:49 **111:10** [v]Pr 9:10 [w]Ecc 12:13 [x]Ps 145:2 **112:1** [y]Ps 128:1 [z]Ps 119:14,16, 47,92 **112:4** [a]Job 11:17 [b]Ps 97:11 **112:5** [c]Ps 37:21,26 **112:6** [d]Pr 10:7 **112:7** [e]Ps 57:7; Pr 1:33 **112:8** [f]Ps 59:10 **112:9** [g]2Co 9:9* [h]Ps 75:10 **112:10** [i]Ps 86:17 [j]Ps 37:12 [k]Ps 58:7-8 [l]Pr 11:7 **113:1** [m]Ps 135:1 **113:2** [n]Da 2:20 **113:3** [o]Isa 59:19; Mal 1:11 **113:4** [p]Ps 99:2 [q]Ps 8:1; 97:9 **113:5** [r]Ps 89:6 [s]Ps 103:19 **113:6** [t]Ps 11:4; 138:6; Isa 57:15 **113:7** [u]1Sa 2:8 [v]Ps 107:41 **113:8** [w]Job 36:7

[a]This psalm is an acrostic poem, the lines of which begin with the successive letters of the Hebrew alphabet. [b]*1* Hebrew *Hallelu Yah* [c]*4* Or / *for* ⌞*the LORD*⌟ *is gracious and compassionate and righteous* [d]*9* *Horn* here symbolizes dignity. [e]*1* Hebrew *Hallelu Yah;* also in verse 9

9He settles the barren[x] woman in
her home
as a happy mother of children.

Praise the LORD.

Psalm 114

1When Israel came out of Egypt,[y]
the house of Jacob from a people
of foreign tongue,
2Judah became God's sanctuary,
Israel his dominion.

3The sea looked and fled,[z]
the Jordan turned back;[a]
4the mountains skipped like rams,
the hills like lambs.

5Why was it, O sea, that you fled,
O Jordan, that you turned back,
6you mountains, that you skipped
like rams,
you hills, like lambs?

7Tremble, O earth,[b] at the presence
of the Lord,
at the presence of the God of
Jacob,
8who turned the rock into a pool,
the hard rock into springs of
water.[c]

Psalm 115

1Not to us, O LORD, not to us
but to your name be the glory,[d]
because of your love and
faithfulness.

2Why do the nations say,
"Where is their God?"[e]
3Our God is in heaven;[f]
he does whatever pleases him.[g]
4But their idols are silver and gold,
made by the hands of men.[h]
5They have mouths, but cannot
speak,[i]
eyes, but they cannot see;
6they have ears, but cannot hear,
noses, but they cannot smell;
7they have hands, but cannot feel,
feet, but they cannot walk;
nor can they utter a sound with
their throats.
8Those who make them will be like
them,
and so will all who trust in them.

9O house of Israel, trust in the
LORD—
he is their help and shield.
10O house of Aaron,[j] trust in the
LORD—
he is their help and shield.
11You who fear him, trust in the
LORD—
he is their help and shield.

12The LORD remembers us and will
bless us:
He will bless the house of Israel,
he will bless the house of Aaron,
13he will bless those who fear[k] the
LORD—
small and great alike.

14May the LORD make you increase,[l]
both you and your children.
15May you be blessed by the LORD,
the Maker of heaven[m] and earth.

16The highest heavens belong to the
LORD,[n]
but the earth he has given[o] to
man.
17It is not the dead[p] who praise the
LORD,
those who go down to silence;
18it is we who extol the LORD,
both now and forevermore.[q]

Praise the LORD.[a]

Psalm 116

1I love the LORD,[r] for he heard my
voice;
he heard my cry[s] for mercy.
2Because he turned his ear[t] to me,
I will call on him as long as I
live.

3The cords of death[u] entangled me,
the anguish of the grave[b] came
upon me;
I was overcome by trouble and
sorrow.
4Then I called on the name[v] of the
LORD:
"O LORD, save me![w]"

5The LORD is gracious and
righteous;[x]
our God is full of compassion.
6The LORD protects the
simplehearted;
when I was in great need,[y] he
saved me.

7Be at rest[z] once more, O my soul,
for the LORD has been good[a] to
you.

8For you, O LORD, have delivered my
soul[b] from death,
my eyes from tears,
my feet from stumbling,
9that I may walk before the LORD
in the land of the living.[c]
10I believed;[d] therefore[c] I said,
"I am greatly afflicted."
11And in my dismay I said,
"All men are liars."[e]

12How can I repay the LORD

113:9 [x]1Sa 2:5; Ps 68:6; Isa 54:1
114:1 [y]Ex 13:3
114:3 [z]Ex 14:21; Ps 77:16 [a]Jos 3:16
114:7 [b]Ps 96:9
114:8 [c]Ex 17:6; Nu 20:11; Ps 107:35
115:1 [d]Ps 96:8; Isa 48:11; Eze 36:32
115:2 [e]Ps 42:3; 79:10
115:3 [f]Ps 103:19 [g]Ps 135:6; Da 4:35
115:4 [h]Dt 4:28; Jer 10:3-5
115:5 [i]Jer 10:5
115:10 [j]Ps 118:3
115:13 [k]Ps 128:1,4
115:14 [l]Dt 1:11
115:15 [m]Ge 1:1; 14:19; Ps 96:5
115:16 [n]Ps 89:11 [o]Ps 8:6-8
115:17 [p]Ps 6:5; 88:10-12; Isa 38:18
115:18 [q]Ps 113:2; Da 2:20
116:1 [r]Ps 18:1 [s]Ps 66:19
116:2 [t]Ps 40:1
116:3 [u]Ps 18:4-5
116:4 [v]Ps 118:5 [w]Ps 22:20
116:5 [x]Ezr 9:15; Ne 9:8; Ps 103:8; 145:17
116:6 [y]Ps 19:7; 79:8
116:7 [z]Jer 6:16; Mt 11:29 [a]Ps 13:6
116:8 [b]Ps 56:13
116:9 [c]Ps 27:13
116:10 [d]2Co 4:13*
116:11 [e]Ro 3:4

a 18 Hebrew *Hallelu Yah* b 3 Hebrew *Sheol*
c 10 Or *believed even when*

1 → PG. 657

for all his goodness to me?
13 I will lift up the cup of salvation
and call on the name[f] of the LORD.
14 I will fulfill my vows[g] to the LORD
in the presence of all his people.

15 Precious in the sight[h] of the LORD
is the death of his saints.
16 O LORD, truly I am your servant;[i]
I am your servant, the son of your maidservant[a];[j]
you have freed me from my chains.

17 I will sacrifice a thank offering[k] to you
and call on the name of the LORD.
18 I will fulfill my vows to the LORD
in the presence of all his people,
19 in the courts[l] of the house of the LORD—
in your midst, O Jerusalem.

Praise the LORD.[b]

Psalm 117

1 Praise the LORD, all you nations;[m]
extol him, all you peoples.
2 For great is his love toward us,
and the faithfulness of the LORD[n] endures forever.

Praise the LORD.[b]

Psalm 118

1 Give thanks to the LORD,[o] for he is good;
his love endures forever.[p]

2 Let Israel say:[q]
"His love endures forever."
3 Let the house of Aaron say:
"His love endures forever."
4 Let those who fear the LORD say:
"His love endures forever."

5 In my anguish[r] I cried to the LORD,
and he answered[s] by setting me free.
6 The LORD is with me;[t] I will not be afraid.
What can man do to me?[u]
7 The LORD is with me; he is my helper.[v]
I will look in triumph on my enemies.[w]

8 It is better to take refuge in the LORD[x]
than to trust in man.[y]
9 It is better to take refuge in the LORD
than to trust in princes.[z]
10 All the nations surrounded me,
but in the name of the LORD I cut them off.[a]
11 They surrounded me[b] on every side,[c]
but in the name of the LORD I cut them off.
12 They swarmed around me like bees,[d]
but they died out as quickly as burning thorns;[e]
in the name of the LORD I cut them off.
13 I was pushed back and about to fall,
but the LORD helped me.[f]
14 The LORD is my strength[g] and my song;
he has become my salvation.[h]

15 Shouts of joy[i] and victory
resound in the tents of the righteous:
"The LORD's right hand[j] has done mighty things!
16 The LORD's right hand is lifted high;
the LORD's right hand has done mighty things!"
17 I will not die[k] but live,
and will proclaim[l] what the LORD has done.
18 The LORD has chastened me severely,
but he has not given me over to death.[m]

19 Open for me the gates[n] of righteousness;
I will enter and give thanks to the LORD.
20 This is the gate of the LORD
through which the righteous may enter.[o]
21 I will give you thanks, for you answered me;[p]
you have become my salvation.

22 The stone the builders rejected
has become the capstone;[q]
23 the LORD has done this,
and it is marvelous in our eyes.
24 This is the day the LORD has made;
let us rejoice and be glad in it.

25 O LORD, save us;
O LORD, grant us success.
26 Blessed is he who comes[r] in the name of the LORD.
From the house of the LORD we bless you.[c]
27 The LORD is God,
and he has made his light shine[s] upon us.

a *16* Or *servant, your faithful son*
b *19,2* Hebrew *Hallelu Yah*
c *26* The Hebrew is plural.

116:13 fPs 16:5; 80:18 **116:14** gPs 22:25; Jnh 2:9 **116:15** hPs 72:14 **116:16** iPs 119:125; 143:12 jPs 86:16 **116:17** kLev 7:12; Ps 50:14 **116:19** lPs 96:8; 135:2 **117:1** mRo 15:11* **117:2** nPs 100:5 **118:1** o1Ch 16:8 pPs 106:1; 136:1 **118:2** qPs 115:9 **118:5** rPs 120:1 sPs 18:19 **118:6** tHeb 13:6* uPs 27:1; 56:4 **118:7** vPs 54:4 wPs 59:10 **118:8** xPs 40:4 yJer 17:5 **118:9** zPs 146:3

118:10 aPs 18:40 **118:11** bPs 88:17 cPs 3:6 **118:12** dDt 1:44 ePs 58:9 **118:13** fPs 86:17; 140:4 **118:14** gEx 15:2 hIsa 12:2 **118:15** iPs 68:3 jPs 89:13 **118:17** kPs 6:5; Hab 1:12 lEx 15:6; Ps 73:28 **118:18** m2Co 6:9 **118:19** nIsa 26:2 **118:20** oPs 24:7; Isa 35:8; Rev 22:14 **118:21** pPs 116:1 **118:22** qMt 21:42; Mk 12:10; Lk 20:17*; Ac 4:11*; 1Pe 2:7* **118:26** rMt 21:9*; Mk 11:9*; Lk 13:35*; 19:38*; Jn 12:13* **118:27** s1Pe 2:9

With boughs in hand, join in the festal procession
up[a] to the horns of the altar.
28You are my God, and I will give you thanks;
you are my God,[t] and I will exalt[u] you.
29Give thanks to the LORD, for he is good;
his love endures forever.

Psalm 119[b]

א Aleph

1 →PG. 657

1Blessed are they whose ways are blameless,
who walk[v] according to the law of the LORD.
2Blessed are they who keep his statutes
and seek him with all their heart.[w]
3They do nothing wrong;[x]
they walk in his ways.
4You have laid down precepts
that are to be fully obeyed.
5Oh, that my ways were steadfast
in obeying your decrees!
6Then I would not be put to shame
when I consider all your commands.
7I will praise you with an upright heart
as I learn your righteous laws.[y]
8I will obey your decrees;
do not utterly forsake me.

ב Beth

9How can a young man keep his way pure?
By living according to your word.[z]
10I seek you with all my heart;[a]
do not let me stray from your commands.[b]
11I have hidden your word in my heart[c]
that I might not sin against you.
12Praise be to you, O LORD;
teach me your decrees.[d]
13With my lips I recount
all the laws that come from your mouth.[e]
14I rejoice in following your statutes
as one rejoices in great riches.
15I meditate on your precepts[f]
and consider your ways.
16I delight[g] in your decrees;
I will not neglect your word.

ג Gimel

17Do good to your servant,[h] and I will live;
I will obey your word.
18Open my eyes that I may see
wonderful things in your law.
19I am a stranger on earth;[i]
do not hide your commands from me.
20My soul is consumed[j] with longing
for your laws[k] at all times.
21You rebuke the arrogant, who are cursed
and who stray[l] from your commands.
22Remove from me scorn[m] and contempt,
for I keep your statutes.
23Though rulers sit together and slander me,
your servant will meditate on your decrees.
24Your statutes are my delight;
they are my counselors.

ד Daleth

25I am laid low in the dust;[n]
preserve my life[o] according to your word.
26I recounted my ways and you answered me;
teach me your decrees.[p]
27Let me understand the teaching of your precepts;
then I will meditate on your wonders.[q]
28My soul is weary with sorrow;[r]
strengthen me[s] according to your word.
29Keep me from deceitful ways;
be gracious to me through your law.
30I have chosen the way of truth;
I have set my heart on your laws.
31I hold fast[t] to your statutes, O LORD;
do not let me be put to shame.
32I run in the path of your commands,
for you have set my heart free.

ה He

1 →PG. 658

33Teach me,[u] O LORD, to follow your decrees;
then I will keep them to the end.
34Give me understanding, and I will keep your law
and obey it with all my heart.
35Direct me in the path of your commands,
for there I find delight.
36Turn my heart[v] toward your statutes
and not toward selfish gain.[w]

[a]27 Or *Bind the festal sacrifice with ropes / and take it* [b]This psalm is an acrostic poem; the verses of each stanza begin with the same letter of the Hebrew alphabet.

118:28 [t]Isa 25:1 [u]Ex 15:2
119:1 [v]Ps 128:1
119:2 [w]Dt 6:5
119:3 [x]1Jn 3:9; 5:18
119:7 [y]S Dt 4:8
119:9 [z]2Ch 6:16
119:10 [a]2Ch 15:15 [b]ver 21,118
119:11 [c]Ps 37:31; Lk 2:19,51
119:12 [d]ver 26
119:13 [e]Ps 40:9
119:15 [f]Ps 1:2
119:16 [g]Ps 1:2
119:17 [h]Ps 13:6; 116:7
119:19 [i]1Ch 29:15; Ps 39:12; 2Co 5:6; Heb 11:13
119:20 [j]Ps 42:2; 84:2 [k]Ps 63:1
119:21 [l]ver 10
119:22 [m]Ps 39:8
119:25 [n]Ps 44:25 [o]Ps 143:11
119:26 [p]Ps 25:4; 27:11; 86:11
119:27 [q]Ps 145:5
119:28 [r]Ps 107:26 [s]Ps 20:2; 1Pe 5:10
119:31 [t]Dt 11:22
119:33 [u]ver 12
119:36 [v]1Ki 8:58 [w]Eze 33:31; Mk 7:21-22; Lk 12:15; Heb 13:5

37Turn my eyes away from worthless things;
preserve my life[x] according to your word.[a]
38Fulfill your promise[y] to your servant,
so that you may be feared.
39Take away the disgrace I dread,
for your laws are good.
40How I long[z] for your precepts!
Preserve my life in your righteousness.

ו Waw

41May your unfailing love come to me, O LORD,
your salvation according to your promise;
42then I will answer[a] the one who taunts me,
for I trust in your word.
43Do not snatch the word of truth from my mouth,
for I have put my hope in your laws.
44I will always obey your law,
for ever and ever.
45I will walk about in freedom,
for I have sought out your precepts.
46I will speak of your statutes before kings[b]
and will not be put to shame,
47for I delight in your commands
because I love them.
48I lift up my hands to[b] your commands, which I love,
and I meditate on your decrees.

ז Zayin

49Remember your word to your servant,
for you have given me hope.
50My comfort in my suffering is this:
Your promise preserves my life.[c]
51The arrogant mock me[d] without restraint,
but I do not turn[e] from your law.
52I remember[f] your ancient laws, O LORD,
and I find comfort in them.
53Indignation grips me[g] because of the wicked,
who have forsaken your law.[h]
54Your decrees are the theme of my song
wherever I lodge.
55In the night I remember[i] your name, O LORD,
and I will keep your law.
56This has been my practice:
I obey your precepts.

119:37 [x]Ps 71:20; Isa 33:15 **119:38** [y]2Sa 7:25 **119:40** [z]ver 20 **119:42** [a]Pr 27:11 **119:46** [b]Mt 10:18; Ac 26:1-2 **119:50** [c]Ro 15:4 **119:51** [d]Jer 20:7 [e]ver 157; Job 23:11; Ps 44:18 **119:52** [f]Ps 103:18 **119:53** [g]Ezr 9:3 [h]Ps 89:30 **119:55** [i]Ps 63:6

119:57 [j]Ps 16:5; La 3:24 **119:58** [k]1Ki 13:6 [l]ver 41 **119:59** [m]Lk 15:17-18 **119:61** [n]Ps 140:5 **119:62** [o]Ac 16:25 **119:63** [p]Ps 101:6-7 **119:64** [q]Ps 33:5 **119:67** [r]Jer 31:18-19; Heb 12:11 **119:68** [s]Ps 106:1; 107:1; Mt 19:17 [t]ver 12 **119:69** [u]Job 13:4; Ps 109:2 **119:70** [v]Ps 17:10; Isa 6:10; Ac 28:27 **119:72** [w]Ps 19:10; Pr 8:10-11,19 **119:73** [x]Job 10:8; Ps 100:3; 138:8; 139:13-16 **119:74** [y]Ps 34:2

ח Heth

57You are my portion,[j] O LORD;
I have promised to obey your words.
58I have sought your face with all my heart;
be gracious to me[k] according to your promise.[l]
59I have considered my ways[m]
and have turned my steps to your statutes.
60I will hasten and not delay
to obey your commands.
61Though the wicked bind me with ropes,
I will not forget[n] your law.
62At midnight[o] I rise to give you thanks
for your righteous laws.
63I am a friend to all who fear you,[p]
to all who follow your precepts.
64The earth is filled with your love,[q] O LORD;
teach me your decrees.

1 →PG. 659

ט Teth

65Do good to your servant
according to your word, O LORD.
66Teach me knowledge and good judgment,
for I believe in your commands.
67Before I was afflicted I went astray,[r]
but now I obey your word.
68You are good,[s] and what you do is good;
teach me your decrees.[t]
69Though the arrogant have smeared me with lies,[u]
I keep your precepts with all my heart.
70Their hearts are callous[v] and unfeeling,
but I delight in your law.
71It was good for me to be afflicted
so that I might learn your decrees.
72The law from your mouth is more precious to me
than thousands of pieces of silver and gold.[w]

י Yodh

73Your hands made me[x] and formed me;
give me understanding to learn your commands.
74May those who fear you rejoice[y] when they see me,
for I have put my hope in your word.

[a] *37* Two manuscripts of the Masoretic Text and Dead Sea Scrolls; most manuscripts of the Masoretic Text *life in your way* [b] *48* Or *for*

75I know, O LORD, that your laws are
righteous,
and in faithfulness[z] you have
afflicted me.
76May your unfailing love be my
comfort,
according to your promise to
your servant.
77Let your compassion[a] come to me
that I may live,
for your law is my delight.
78May the arrogant[b] be put to
shame for wronging me
without cause;[c]
but I will meditate on your
precepts.
79May those who fear you turn to
me,
those who understand your
statutes.
80May my heart be blameless toward
your decrees,
that I may not be put to shame.

כ Kaph

81My soul faints[d] with longing for
your salvation,
but I have put my hope in your
word.
82My eyes fail,[e] looking for your
promise;
I say, "When will you comfort
me?"
83Though I am like a wineskin in the
smoke,
I do not forget your decrees.
84How long[f] must your servant
wait?
When will you punish my
persecutors?
85The arrogant dig pitfalls[g] for me,
contrary to your law.
86All your commands are
trustworthy;[h]
help me,[i] for men persecute me
without cause.[j]
87They almost wiped me from the
earth,
but I have not forsaken[k] your
precepts.
88Preserve my life according to your
love,
and I will obey the statutes of
your mouth.

ל Lamedh

1 →PG. 661
89Your word, O LORD, is eternal;[l]
it stands firm in the heavens.
90Your faithfulness[m] continues
through all generations;
you established the earth, and it
endures.[n]
91Your laws endure[o] to this day,
for all things serve you.
92If your law had not been my
delight,
I would have perished in my
affliction.
93I will never forget your precepts,
for by them you have preserved
my life.
94Save me, for I am yours;
I have sought out your precepts.
95The wicked are waiting to destroy
me,
but I will ponder your statutes.
96To all perfection I see a limit;
but your commands are
boundless.

מ Mem

97Oh, how I love your law!
I meditate[p] on it all day long.
98Your commands make me wiser[q]
than my enemies,
for they are ever with me.
99I have more insight than all my
teachers,
for I meditate on your statutes.
100I have more understanding than
the elders,
for I obey your precepts.[r]
101I have kept my feet[s] from every
evil path
so that I might obey your word.
102I have not departed from your
laws,
for you yourself have taught me.
103How sweet are your words to my
taste,
sweeter than honey[t] to my
mouth![u]
104I gain understanding from your
precepts;
therefore I hate every wrong
path.[v]

נ Nun

105Your word is a lamp to my feet
and a light[w] for my path.
106I have taken an oath[x] and
confirmed it,
that I will follow your righteous
laws.
107I have suffered much;
preserve my life, O LORD,
according to your word.
108Accept, O LORD, the willing praise
of my mouth,[y]
and teach me your laws.
109Though I constantly take my life
in my hands,[z]
I will not forget your law.
110The wicked have set a snare[a]
for me,
but I have not strayed[b] from
your precepts.
111Your statutes are my heritage
forever;
they are the joy of my heart.

119:75 [z]Heb 12:5-11
119:77 [a]ver 41
119:78 [b]Jer 50:32 [c]ver 86,161
119:81 [d]Ps 84:2
119:82 [e]Ps 69:3; La 2:11
119:84 [f]Ps 39:4; Rev 6:10
119:85 [g]Ps 35:7; Jer 18:20,22
119:86 [h]Ps 35:19 [i]Ps 109:26 [j]ver 78
119:87 [k]Isa 58:2
119:89 [l]Mt 24:34-35; 1Pe 1:25
119:90 [m]Ps 36:5 [n]Ps 148:6; Ecc 1:4
119:91 [o]Jer 33:25
119:97 [p]Ps 1:2
119:98 [q]Dt 4:6
119:100 [r]Job 32:7-9
119:101 [s]Pr 1:15
119:103 [t]Ps 19:10; Pr 8:11 [u]Pr 24:13-14
119:104 [v]ver 128
119:105 [w]Pr 6:23
119:106 [x]Ne 10:29
119:108 [y]Hos 14:2; Heb 13:15
119:109 [z]Jdg 12:3; Job 13:14
119:110 [a]Ps 140:5; 141:9 [b]ver 10

112My heart is set on keeping your decrees
to the very end.[c]

ס Samekh

113I hate double-minded men,[d]
but I love your law.
114You are my refuge and my shield;[e]
I have put my hope[f] in your word.
115Away from me,[g] you evildoers,
that I may keep the commands of my God!
116Sustain me[h] according to your promise, and I will live;
do not let my hopes be dashed.[i]
117Uphold me, and I will be delivered;
I will always have regard for your decrees.
118You reject all who stray from your decrees,
for their deceitfulness is in vain.
119All the wicked of the earth you discard like dross;[j]
therefore I love your statutes.
120My flesh trembles[k] in fear of you;
I stand in awe of your laws.

ע Ayin

121I have done what is righteous and just;
do not leave me to my oppressors.
122Ensure your servant's well-being;[l]
let not the arrogant oppress me.
123My eyes fail, looking for your salvation,
looking for your righteous promise.[m]
124Deal with your servant according to your love
and teach me your decrees.[n]
125I am your servant;[o] give me discernment
that I may understand your statutes.
126It is time for you to act, O LORD;
your law is being broken.
127Because I love your commands
more than gold,[p] more than pure gold,
128and because I consider all your precepts right,
I hate every wrong path.[q]

פ Pe

129Your statutes are wonderful;
therefore I obey them.
130The unfolding of your words gives light;[r]
it gives understanding to the simple.[s]
131I open my mouth and pant,[t]
longing for your commands.[u]
132Turn to me and have mercy[v] on me,
as you always do to those who love your name.
133Direct my footsteps according to your word;[w]
let no sin rule[x] over me.
134Redeem me from the oppression of men,[y]
that I may obey your precepts.
135Make your face shine[z] upon your servant
and teach me your decrees.
136Streams of tears[a] flow from my eyes,
for your law is not obeyed.[b]

צ Tsadhe

137Righteous are you,[c] O LORD,
and your laws are right.[d]
138The statutes you have laid down are righteous;[e]
they are fully trustworthy.
139My zeal wears me out,[f]
for my enemies ignore your words.
140Your promises have been thoroughly tested,[g]
and your servant loves them.
141Though I am lowly and despised,[h]
I do not forget your precepts.
142Your righteousness is everlasting
and your law is true.[i]
143Trouble and distress have come upon me,
but your commands are my delight.
144Your statutes are forever right;
give me understanding[j] that I may live.

ק Qoph

145I call with all my heart; answer me, O LORD,
and I will obey your decrees.
146I call out to you; save me
and I will keep your statutes.
147I rise before dawn[k] and cry for help;
I have put my hope in your word.
148My eyes stay open through the watches of the night,[l]
that I may meditate on your promises.
149Hear my voice in accordance with your love;
preserve my life, O LORD,
according to your laws.
150Those who devise wicked schemes are near,
but they are far from your law.
151Yet you are near,[m] O LORD,

119:112 [c]ver 33 **119:113** [d]Jas 1:8 **119:114** [e]Ps 32:7; 91:1 [f]ver 74 **119:115** [g]Ps 6:8; 139:19; Mt 7:23 **119:116** [h]Ps 54:4 [i]Ps 25:2; Ro 5:5; 9:33 **119:119** [j]Eze 22:18,19 **119:120** [k]Hab 3:16 **119:122** [l]Job 17:3 **119:123** [m]ver 82 **119:124** [n]ver 12 **119:125** [o]Ps 116:16 **119:127** [p]Ps 19:10 **119:128** [q]ver 104,163 **119:130** [r]Pr 6:23 [s]Ps 19:7

119:131 [t]Ps 42:1 [u]ver 20 **119:132** [v]Ps 25:16; 106:4 **119:133** [w]Ps 17:5 [x]Ps 19:13; Ro 6:12 **119:134** [y]Ps 142:6; Lk 1:74 **119:135** [z]Nu 6:25; Ps 4:6 **119:136** [a]Jer 9:1,18 [b]Eze 9:4 **119:137** [c]Ezr 9:15; Jer 12:1 [d]Ne 9:13 **119:138** [e]Ps 19:7 **119:139** [f]Ps 69:9; Jn 2:17 **119:140** [g]Ps 12:6 **119:141** [h]Ps 22:6 **119:142** [i]Ps 19:7 **119:144** [j]Ps 19:9 **119:147** [k]Ps 5:3; 57:8; 108:2 **119:148** [l]Ps 63:6 **119:151** [m]Ps 34:18; 145:18

and all your commands are
true.[n]
152 Long ago I learned from your
statutes
that you established them to last
forever.[o]

ר Resh

153 Look upon my suffering[p] and
deliver me,
for I have not forgotten[q] your
law.
154 Defend my cause[r] and
redeem me;[s]
preserve my life according to
your promise.
155 Salvation is far from the wicked,
for they do not seek out[t] your
decrees.
156 Your compassion is great, O LORD;
preserve my life[u] according to
your laws.
157 Many are the foes who
persecute me,[v]
but I have not turned from your
statutes.
158 I look on the faithless with
loathing,[w]
for they do not obey your word.
159 See how I love your precepts;
preserve my life, O LORD,
according to your love.
160 All your words are true;
all your righteous laws are
eternal.

ש Sin and Shin

161 Rulers persecute me[x] without
cause,
but my heart trembles at your
word.
162 I rejoice in your promise
like one who finds great spoil.[y]
163 I hate and abhor falsehood
but I love your law.
164 Seven times a day I praise you
for your righteous laws.
165 Great peace[z] have they who love
your law,
and nothing can make them
stumble.
166 I wait for your salvation,[a]
O LORD,
and I follow your commands.
167 I obey your statutes,
for I love them greatly.
168 I obey your precepts and your
statutes,
for all my ways are known[b] to
you.

ת Taw

1 →PG. 662
169 May my cry come[c] before you,
O LORD;
give me understanding according
to your word.
170 May my supplication come[d]
before you;
deliver me[e] according to your
promise.
171 May my lips overflow with
praise,[f]
for you teach me[g] your decrees.
172 May my tongue sing of your word,
for all your commands are
righteous.
173 May your hand be ready to
help[h] me,
for I have chosen[i] your
precepts.
174 I long for your salvation,[j]
O LORD,
and your law is my delight.
175 Let me live[k] that I may praise
you,
and may your laws sustain me.
176 I have strayed like a lost sheep.[l]
Seek your servant,
for I have not forgotten your
commands.

Psalm 120

A song of ascents.

1 I call on the LORD in my distress,[m]
and he answers me.
2 Save me, O LORD, from lying lips[n]
and from deceitful tongues.[o]

3 What will he do to you,
and what more besides,
O deceitful tongue?
4 He will punish you with a warrior's
sharp arrows,[p]
with burning coals of the broom
tree.

5 Woe to me that I dwell in
Meshech,
that I live among the tents of
Kedar![q]
6 Too long have I lived
among those who hate peace.
7 I am a man of peace;
but when I speak, they are for
war.

Psalm 121

A song of ascents.

1 I lift up my eyes to the hills—
where does my help come from?
2 My help comes from the LORD,
the Maker of heaven and earth.[r]
3 He will not let your foot slip—
he who watches over you will
not slumber;
4 indeed, he who watches over Israel
will neither slumber nor sleep.

119:151 [n] ver 142
119:152 [o] Lk 21:33
119:153 [p] La 5:1 [q] Pr 3:1
119:154 [r] Mic 7:9 [s] 1Sa 24:15
119:155 [t] Job 5:4
119:156 [u] 2Sa 24:14
119:157 [v] Ps 7:1
119:158 [w] Ps 139:21
119:161 [x] 1Sa 24:11
119:162 [y] 1Sa 30:16
119:165 [z] Pr 3:2; Isa 26:3,12; 32:17
119:166 [a] Ge 49:18
119:168 [b] Pr 5:21
119:169 [c] Ps 18:6
119:170 [d] Ps 28:2 [e] Ps 31:2
119:171 [f] Ps 51:15 [g] Ps 94:12
119:173 [h] Ps 37:24 [i] Jos 24:22
119:174 [j] ver 166
119:175 [k] Isa 55:3
119:176 [l] Isa 53:6
120:1 [m] Ps 102:2; Jnh 2:2
120:2 [n] Pr 12:22 [o] Ps 52:4
120:4 [p] Ps 45:5
120:5 [q] Ge 25:13; Jer 49:28
121:2 [r] Ps 115:15; 124:8

5 The LORD watches over[s] you—
the LORD is your shade at your right hand;
6 the sun[t] will not harm you by day,
nor the moon by night.
7 The LORD will keep you from all harm[u]—
he will watch over your life;
8 the LORD will watch over your coming and going
both now and forevermore.[v]

Psalm 122

A song of ascents. Of David.

1 I rejoiced with those who said to me,
"Let us go to the house of the LORD."
2 Our feet are standing
in your gates, O Jerusalem.

3 Jerusalem is built like a city
that is closely compacted together.
4 That is where the tribes go up,
the tribes of the LORD,
to praise the name of the LORD
according to the statute given to Israel.
5 There the thrones for judgment stand,
the thrones of the house of David.

6 Pray for the peace of Jerusalem:
"May those who love[w] you be secure.
7 May there be peace within your walls
and security within your citadels."
8 For the sake of my brothers and friends,
I will say, "Peace be within you."
9 For the sake of the house of the LORD our God,
I will seek your prosperity.[x]

Psalm 123

A song of ascents.

1 →PG. 667
1 I lift up my eyes to you,
to you whose throne[y] is in heaven.
2 As the eyes of slaves look to the hand of their master,
as the eyes of a maid look to the hand of her mistress,
so our eyes look to the LORD[z] our God,
till he shows us his mercy.

3 Have mercy on us, O LORD, have mercy on us,
for we have endured much contempt.
4 We have endured much ridicule from the proud,
much contempt from the arrogant.

Psalm 124

A song of ascents. Of David.

1 If the LORD had not been on our side—
let Israel say[a]—
2 if the LORD had not been on our side
when men attacked us,
3 when their anger flared against us,
they would have swallowed us alive;
4 the flood would have engulfed us,
the torrent would have swept over us,
5 the raging waters
would have swept us away.

6 Praise be to the LORD,
who has not let us be torn by their teeth.
7 We have escaped like a bird
out of the fowler's snare;[b]
the snare has been broken,
and we have escaped.
8 Our help is in the name of the LORD,
the Maker of heaven[c] and earth.

Psalm 125

A song of ascents.

1 Those who trust in the LORD are like Mount Zion,
which cannot be shaken[d] but endures forever.
2 As the mountains surround Jerusalem,
so the LORD surrounds[e] his people
both now and forevermore.

3 The scepter of the wicked will not remain[f]
over the land allotted to the righteous,
for then the righteous might use their hands to do evil.[g]

121:5 [s]Isa 25:4
121:6 [t]Ps 91:5; Isa 49:10; Rev 7:16
121:7 [u]Ps 41:2; 91:10-12
121:8 [v]Dt 28:6
122:6 [w]Ps 51:18
122:9 [x]Ne 2:10
123:1 [y]Ps 11:4; 121:1; 141:8
123:2 [z]Ps 25:15
124:1 [a]Ps 129:1
124:7 [b]Ps 91:3; Pr 6:5
124:8 [c]Ge 1:1; Ps 121:2; 134:3
125:1 [d]Ps 46:5
125:2 [e]Ps 121:8; Zec 2:4-5
125:3 [f]Ps 89:22; Pr 22:8; Isa 14:5 [g]1Sa 24:10; Ps 55:20

4 Do good, O LORD,[h] to those who
are good,
to those who are upright in
heart.[i]
5 But those who turn[j] to crooked
ways[k]
the LORD will banish with the
evildoers.

Peace be upon Israel.[l]

Psalm 126

A song of ascents.

1 When the LORD brought back[m] the
captives to[a] Zion,
we were like men who
dreamed.[b]
2 Our mouths were filled with
laughter,
our tongues with songs of joy.[n]
Then it was said among the
nations,
"The LORD has done great
things[o] for them."
3 The LORD has done great things for
us,
and we are filled with joy.[p]

4 Restore our fortunes,[c] O LORD,
like streams in the Negev.[q]
5 Those who sow in tears
will reap with songs of joy.[r]
6 He who goes out weeping,
carrying seed to sow,
will return with songs of joy,
carrying sheaves with him.

Psalm 127

A song of ascents. Of Solomon.

4 →PG. 663

1 Unless the LORD builds[s] the
house,
its builders labor in vain.
Unless the LORD watches[t] over the
city,
the watchmen stand guard in
vain.
2 In vain you rise early
and stay up late,
toiling for food[u] to eat—
for he grants sleep[v] to[d] those
he loves.

3 Sons are a heritage from the LORD,
children a reward[w] from him.
4 Like arrows in the hands of a
warrior
are sons born in one's youth.
5 Blessed is the man
whose quiver is full of them.
They will not be put to shame
when they contend with their
enemies[x] in the gate.

125:4 [h]Ps 119:68 [i]Ps 7:10; 36:10; 94:15
125:5 [j]Job 23:11 [k]Pr 2:15; Isa 59:8
125:5 [l]Ps 128:6
126:1 [m]Ps 85:1; Hos 6:11
126:2 [n]Job 8:21; Ps 51:14 [o]Ps 71:19
126:3 [p]Isa 25:9
126:4 [q]Isa 35:6; 43:19
126:5 [r]Isa 35:10
127:1 [s]Ps 78:69 [t]Ps 121:4
127:2 [u]Ge 3:17 [v]Job 11:18
127:3 [w]Ge 33:5
127:5 [x]Pr 27:11
128:1 [y]Ps 112:1 [z]Ps 119:1-3
128:2 [a]Isa 3:10 [b]Ecc 8:12
128:3 [c]Eze 19:10 [d]Ps 52:8; 144:12
128:5 [e]Ps 20:2; 134:3
128:6 [f]Ge 50:23; Job 42:16 [g]Ps 125:5

Psalm 128

A song of ascents.

4 →PG. 682

1 Blessed are all who fear the LORD,[y]
who walk in his ways.[z]
2 You will eat the fruit of your
labor;[a]
blessings and prosperity[b] will be
yours.
3 Your wife will be like a fruitful
vine[c]
within your house;
your sons will be like olive shoots[d]
around your table.
4 Thus is the man blessed
who fears the LORD.

5 May the LORD bless you from
Zion[e]
all the days of your life;
may you see the prosperity of
Jerusalem,
6 and may you live to see your
children's children.[f]

Peace be upon Israel.[g]

[a] *1* Or *LORD restored the fortunes of* [b] *1* Or *men restored to health* [c] *4* Or *Bring back our captives* [d] *2* Or *eat— / for while they sleep he provides for*

127:1–5

PROMISE 4

THE SOURCE OF SUCCESS

Success comes from God. The Scriptures encourage hard work, but work alone won't ultimately bring success. Verses 1 and 2 present an important general principle: Unless God is involved in whatever you're trying to achieve, you may as well forget it. Based on that principle, the focus of the psalm turns to sons—to children (vv. 3–5). Food, houses and cities are important, but a man's responsibilities increase dramatically when children come along. If we need God to build, protect and sustain our material goods, how much more do we need his help in our responsibility to raise the lives he has entrusted to our care?

Take a moment right now and ask God to guide you and place his good hand on you for guidance and provision. If you are a dad, pray the same prayer for your wife and your children. It's tough for some of us to admit we need help, but we need to listen to Solomon when he says, "God's help is your only hope!"

For the next Promise 4 reading go to page 726.

Psalm 129

A song of ascents.

1 They have greatly oppressed me
from my youth[h]—
let Israel say[i]—
2 they have greatly oppressed me
from my youth,
but they have not gained the
victory[j] over me.
3 Plowmen have plowed my back
and made their furrows long.
4 But the LORD is righteous;[k]
he has cut me free from the
cords of the wicked.

5 May all who hate Zion[l]
be turned back in shame.[m]
6 May they be like grass on the roof,
which withers[n] before it can
grow;
7 with it the reaper cannot fill his
hands,
nor the one who gathers fill his
arms.
8 May those who pass by not say,
"The blessing of the LORD be
upon you;
we bless you[o] in the name of
the LORD."

Psalm 130

A song of ascents.

1 Out of the depths[p] I cry to you,
O LORD;
2 O Lord, hear my voice.[q]
Let your ears be attentive[r]
to my cry for mercy.

3 If you, O LORD, kept a record of
sins,
O Lord, who could stand?[s]
4 But with you there is forgiveness;[t]
therefore you are feared.[u]

5 I wait for the LORD,[v] my soul
waits,
and in his word[w] I put my
hope.
6 My soul waits for the Lord
more than watchmen[x] wait for
the morning,
more than watchmen wait for
the morning.[y]

7 O Israel, put your hope[z] in the
LORD,
for with the LORD is unfailing
love
and with him is full redemption.
8 He himself will redeem[a] Israel
from all their sins.

129:1 [h]Ps 88:15; Hos 2:15 [i]Ps 124:1 **129:2** [j]Mt 16:18 **129:4** [k]Ps 119:137 **129:5** [l]Mic 4:11 [m]Ps 71:13 **129:6** [n]Ps 37:2 **129:8** [o]Ru 2:4; Ps 118:26 **130:1** [p]Ps 42:7; 69:2; La 3:55 **130:2** [q]Ps 28:2 [r]2Ch 6:40; Ps 64:1 **130:3** [s]Ps 76:7; 143:2 **130:4** [t]Ex 34:7; Isa 55:7; Jer 33:8 [u]1Ki 8:40 **130:5** [v]Ps 27:14; 33:20; Isa 8:17 [w]Ps 119:81 **130:6** [x]Ps 63:6 [y]Ps 119:147 **130:7** [z]Ps 131:3 **130:8** [a]Lk 1:68

131:1 [b]Ps 101:5; Ro 12:16 **131:2** [c]Mt 18:3; 1Co 14:20 **131:3** [d]Ps 130:7 **132:2** [e]Ge 49:24 **132:5** [f]Ac 7:46 **132:6** [g]1Sa 17:12 [h]1Sa 7:2 **132:7** [i]Ps 5:7 [j]Ps 99:5 **132:8** [k]Nu 10:35; Ps 78:61 **132:9** [l]Job 29:14; Isa 61:3,10 **132:11** [m]Ps 89:3-4,35 [n]2Sa 7:12

Psalm 131

A song of ascents. Of David.

1 My heart is not proud,[b] O LORD,
my eyes are not haughty;
I do not concern myself with great
matters
or things too wonderful for me.
2 But I have stilled and quieted my
soul;
like a weaned child with its
mother,
like a weaned child is my soul[c]
within me.

3 O Israel, put your hope[d] in the
LORD
both now and forevermore.

Psalm 132

A song of ascents.

1 O LORD, remember David
and all the hardships he
endured.

2 He swore an oath to the LORD
and made a vow to the Mighty
One of Jacob:[e]
3 "I will not enter my house
or go to my bed—
4 I will allow no sleep to my eyes,
no slumber to my eyelids,
5 till I find a place[f] for the LORD,
a dwelling for the Mighty One of
Jacob."
6 We heard it in Ephrathah,[g]
we came upon it in the fields of
Jaar[a]:[b][h]
7 "Let us go to his dwelling place;[i]
let us worship at his
footstool[j]—
8 arise, O LORD,[k] and come to your
resting place,
you and the ark of your might.
9 May your priests be clothed with
righteousness;[l]
may your saints sing for joy."

10 For the sake of David your servant,
do not reject your anointed one.

11 The LORD swore an oath to
David,[m]
a sure oath that he will not
revoke:
"One of your own descendants[n]
I will place on your throne—
12 if your sons keep my covenant
and the statutes I teach them,
then their sons will sit

[a]6 That is, Kiriath Jearim [b]6 Or *heard of it in Ephrathah, / we found it in the fields of Jaar.* (And no quotes around verses 7-9)

on your throne[o] for ever and
ever."

13 For the LORD has chosen Zion,[p]
he has desired it for his dwelling:
14 "This is my resting place for ever
and ever;[q]
here I will sit enthroned, for I
have desired it—
15 I will bless her with abundant
provisions;
her poor will I satisfy with
food.[r]
16 I will clothe her priests[s] with
salvation,
and her saints will ever sing for
joy.

17 "Here I will make a horn[a] grow[t]
for David
and set up a lamp[u] for my
anointed one.
18 I will clothe his enemies with
shame,[v]
but the crown on his head will
be resplendent."

Psalm 133

A song of ascents. Of David.

2 →PG. 692
6 →PG. 699

1 How good and pleasant it is
when brothers live together[w] in
unity!
2 It is like precious oil poured on the
head,[x]
running down on the beard,
running down on Aaron's beard,
down upon the collar of his
robes.
3 It is as if the dew of Hermon[y]
were falling on Mount Zion.
For there the LORD bestows his
blessing,[z]
even life forevermore.[a]

Psalm 134

A song of ascents.

1 Praise the LORD, all you servants[b]
of the LORD
who minister by night[c] in the
house of the LORD.
2 Lift up your hands[d] in the
sanctuary
and praise the LORD.
3 May the LORD, the Maker of
heaven[e] and earth,
bless you from Zion.[f]

Psalm 135

1 Praise the LORD.[b]

Praise the name of the LORD;
praise him, you servants[g] of the
LORD,
2 you who minister in the house[h] of
the LORD,
in the courts[i] of the house of
our God.

3 Praise the LORD, for the LORD is
good;[j]
sing praise to his name, for that
is pleasant.[k]
4 For the LORD has chosen Jacob[l] to
be his own,
Israel to be his treasured
possession.[m]

132:12 [o]Lk 1:32; Ac 2:30
132:13 [p]Ps 48:1-2
132:14 [q]Ps 68:16
132:15 [r]Ps 107:9; 147:14
132:16 [s]2Ch 6:41
132:17 [t]Eze 29:21; Lk 1:69 [u]1Ki 11:36; 2Ch 21:7
132:18 [v]Ps 35:26; 109:29
133:1 [w]Ge 13:8; Heb 13:1
133:2 [x]Ex 30:25
133:3 [y]Dt 4:48 [z]Lev 25:21; Dt 28:8 [a]Ps 42:8
134:1 [b]Ps 135:1-2 [c]1Ch 9:33
134:2 [d]Ps 28:2; 1Ti 2:8
134:3 [e]Ps 124:8 [f]Ps 128:5
135:1 [g]Ps 113:1; 134:1
135:2 [h]Lk 2:37 [i]Ps 116:19
135:3 [j]Ps 119:68 [k]Ps 147:1
135:4 [l]Dt 10:15; 1Pe 2:9 [m]Ex 19:5; Dt 7:6

[a] *17 Horn* here symbolizes strong one, that is, king. [b] *1* Hebrew *Hallelu Yah*; also in verses 3 and 21

133:1-3

PROMISE 6

DAVID'S VIEWS ON UNITY

David knew both teamwork and hostility. In his life he made both friends who would have died for him and enemies who would have loved to kill him. As he considered these two extremes, he wrote in this psalm, "Unity is good and pleasant."

The imagery of this poem made a powerful statement to David's countrymen. Only under David and Solomon did the twelve tribes of Israel dwell in unity. For the rest of their history they bickered and fought as two separate nations. There's a lesson in the fact that Israel reached her political and religious pinnacle when David and Solomon were her kings. United, the twelve tribes did what they could never have done divided. During those glory years they set the standard for worship and left a legacy that has inspired Jewish people throughout history.

God's Word states here and in many other places: "It is good and it is pleasant when God's people dwell together in unity." Anyone who isolates himself from other believers, regardless of the reason, is disobedient to God's Word and is crippling his Christian witness. David and other Biblical writers teach that reconciliation is not just a good idea, it is God's will and command.

Join those who work for unity among God's people. Make one phone call or initiate one conversation today that will build a bridge to someone you might not normally contact. Find out for yourself how "good and pleasant" it is when God's people dwell together in unity.

For the next Promise 6 reading go to page 682.

5I know that the LORD is great,[n]
that our Lord is greater than all
gods.[o]
6The LORD does whatever pleases
him,[p]
in the heavens and on the earth,
in the seas and all their depths.
7He makes clouds rise from the
ends of the earth;
he sends lightning with the
rain[q]
and brings out the wind[r] from
his storehouses.[s]

8He struck down the firstborn[t] of
Egypt,
the firstborn of men and
animals.
9He sent his signs[u] and wonders
into your midst, O Egypt,
against Pharaoh and all his
servants.[v]
10He struck down many[w] nations
and killed mighty kings—
11Sihon[x] king of the Amorites,
Og king of Bashan
and all the kings of Canaan[y]—
12and he gave their land as an
inheritance,[z]
an inheritance to his people
Israel.

13Your name, O LORD, endures
forever,[a]
your renown,[b] O LORD, through
all generations.
14For the LORD will vindicate his
people
and have compassion on his
servants.[c]

15The idols of the nations are silver
and gold,
made by the hands of men.
16They have mouths, but cannot
speak,
eyes, but they cannot see;
17they have ears, but cannot hear,
nor is there breath in their
mouths.
18Those who make them will be like
them,
and so will all who trust in
them.

19O house of Israel, praise the
LORD;
O house of Aaron, praise the
LORD;
20O house of Levi, praise the LORD;
you who fear him, praise the
LORD.
21Praise be to the LORD from Zion,[d]
to him who dwells in Jerusalem.

Praise the LORD.

135:5
[n]Ps 48:1
[o]Ps 97:9
135:6
[p]Ps 115:3
135:7
[q]Jer 10:13; Zec 10:1
[r]Job 28:25
[s]Job 38:22
135:8
[t]Ex 12:12; Ps 78:51
135:9
[u]Dt 6:22
[v]Ps 136:10-15
135:10
[w]Nu 21:21-25; Ps 136:17-21
135:11
[x]Nu 21:21
[y]Jos 12:7-24
135:12
[z]Ps 78:55
135:13
[a]Ex 3:15
[b]Ps 102:12
135:14
[c]Dt 32:36
135:21
[d]Ps 134:3

136:1
[e]Ps 106:1
[f]1Ch 16:34; 2Ch 20:21
136:2
[g]Dt 10:17
136:4
[h]Ps 72:18
136:5
[i]Pr 3:19; Jer 51:15
[j]Ge 1:1
136:6
[k]Ge 1:9; Jer 10:12
[l]Ps 24:2
136:7
[m]Ge 1:14,16
136:8
[n]Ge 1:16
136:10
[o]Ex 12:29; Ps 135:8
136:11
[p]Ex 6:6; 12:51
136:12
[q]Dt 4:34; Ps 44:3
136:13
[r]Ex 14:21; Ps 78:13
136:14
[s]Ex 14:22
136:15
[t]Ex 14:27; Ps 135:9
136:16
[u]Ex 13:18
136:17
[v]Ps 135:9-12
136:18
[w]Dt 29:7
136:19
[x]Nu 21:21-25
136:21
[y]Jos 12:1

Psalm 136

1Give thanks to the LORD, for he is
good.[e]
His love endures forever.[f]
2Give thanks to the God of gods.[g]
His love endures forever.
3Give thanks to the Lord of lords:
His love endures forever.

4to him who alone does great
wonders,[h]
His love endures forever.
5who by his understanding[i] made
the heavens,[j]
His love endures forever.
6who spread out the earth[k] upon
the waters,[l]
His love endures forever.
7who made the great lights[m]—
His love endures forever.
8the sun to govern[n] the day,
His love endures forever.
9the moon and stars to govern the
night;
His love endures forever.

10to him who struck down the
firstborn[o] of Egypt
His love endures forever.
11and brought Israel out[p] from
among them
His love endures forever.
12with a mighty hand and
outstretched arm;[q]
His love endures forever.

13to him who divided the Red
Sea[a][r] asunder
His love endures forever.
14and brought Israel through[s] the
midst of it,
His love endures forever.
15but swept Pharaoh and his army
into the Red Sea;[t]
His love endures forever.

16to him who led his people through
the desert,[u]
His love endures forever.
17who struck down great kings,[v]
His love endures forever.
18and killed mighty kings[w]—
His love endures forever.
19Sihon king of the Amorites[x]
His love endures forever.
20and Og king of Bashan—
His love endures forever.
21and gave their land[y] as an
inheritance,
His love endures forever.
22an inheritance to his servant Israel;
His love endures forever.

a *13* Hebrew *Yam Suph*; that is, Sea of Reeds; also in verse 15

23to the One who remembered us[z]
in our low estate
His love endures forever.
24and freed us from our enemies,[a]
His love endures forever.
25and who gives food[b] to every
creature.
His love endures forever.
26Give thanks to the God of heaven.
His love endures forever.

Psalm 137

1By the rivers of Babylon[c] we sat
and wept[d]
when we remembered Zion.
2There on the poplars
we hung our harps,
3for there our captors asked us for
songs,
our tormentors demanded[e]
songs of joy;
they said, "Sing us one of the
songs of Zion!"

4How can we sing the songs of the
LORD
while in a foreign land?
5If I forget you, O Jerusalem,
may my right hand forget ⌞its
skill⌟.
6May my tongue cling to the roof[f]
of my mouth
if I do not remember you,
if I do not consider Jerusalem
my highest joy.

7Remember, O LORD, what the
Edomites[g] did
on the day Jerusalem fell.[h]
"Tear it down," they cried,
"tear it down to its foundations!"
8O Daughter of Babylon, doomed to
destruction,[i]
happy is he who repays you
for what you have done to us—
9he who seizes your infants
and dashes them[j] against the
rocks.

Psalm 138

Of David.

1I will praise you, O LORD, with all
my heart;
before the "gods"[k] I will sing
your praise.
1 →PG. 667
2I will bow down toward your holy
temple[l]
and will praise your name
for your love and your
faithfulness,
for you have exalted above all
things

136:23 [z]Ps 113:7
136:24 [a]Ps 107:2
136:25 [b]Ps 104:27; 145:15
137:1 [c]Eze 1:1,3 [d]Ne 1:4
137:3 [e]Ps 80:6
137:6 [f]Eze 3:26
137:7 [g]Jer 49:7; La 4:21-22; Eze 25:12 [h]Ob 1:11
137:8 [i]Isa 13:1,19; Jer 25:12,26; Jer 50:15; Rev 18:6
137:9 [j]2Ki 8:12; Isa 13:16
138:1 [k]Ps 95:3; 96:4
138:2 [l]1Ki 8:29; Ps 5:7; 28:2

[m]Isa 42:21
138:3 [n]Ps 28:7
138:4 [o]Ps 102:15
138:6 [p]Ps 113:6; Isa 57:15 [q]Pr 3:34; Jas 4:6
138:7 [r]Ps 23:4 [s]Jer 51:25 [t]Ps 20:6 [u]Ps 71:20
138:8 [v]Ps 57:2; Php 1:6 [w]Job 10:3,8; 14:15
139:1 [x]Ps 17:3 [y]Jer 12:3
139:2 [z]2Ki 19:27 [a]Mt 9:4; Jn 2:24
139:3 [b]Job 31:4
139:4 [c]Heb 4:13
139:5 [d]Ps 34:7
139:6 [e]Job 42:3; Ro 11:33
139:7 [f]Jer 23:24; Jnh 1:3
139:8 [g]Am 9:2-3 [h]Pr 15:11

your name and your word.[m]
3When I called, you answered me;
you made me bold and
stouthearted.[n]

4May all the kings of the earth[o]
praise you, O LORD,
when they hear the words of
your mouth.
5May they sing of the ways of the
LORD,
for the glory of the LORD is great.

6Though the LORD is on high, he
looks upon the lowly,[p]
but the proud[q] he knows from
afar.
7Though I walk[r] in the midst of
trouble,
you preserve my life;
you stretch out your hand against
the anger of my foes,[s]
with your right hand[t] you save
me.[u]
8The LORD will fulfill ⌞his purpose⌟[v]
for me;
your love, O LORD, endures
forever—
do not abandon the works of
your hands.[w]

Psalm 139

For the director of music. Of David.
A psalm.

1 →PG. 669
1O LORD, you have searched me[x]
and you know[y] me.
2You know when I sit and when I
rise;[z]
you perceive my thoughts[a] from
afar.
3You discern my going out and my
lying down;
you are familiar with all my
ways.[b]
4Before a word is on my tongue
you know it completely,[c]
O LORD.
5You hem me in[d]—behind and
before;
you have laid your hand upon
me.
6Such knowledge is too wonderful
for me,
too lofty[e] for me to attain.

7Where can I go from your Spirit?
Where can I flee[f] from your
presence?
8If I go up to the heavens,[g] you are
there;
if I make my bed[h] in the
depths,**a** you are there.
9If I rise on the wings of the dawn,

a *8* Hebrew *Sheol*

if I settle on the far side of the sea,
10even there your hand will guide me,[i]
your right hand will hold me fast.
11If I say, "Surely the darkness will hide me
and the light become night around me,"
12even the darkness will not be dark[j] to you;
the night will shine like the day,
for darkness is as light to you.

13For you created my inmost being;[k]
you knit me together[l] in my mother's womb.
14I praise you because I am fearfully and wonderfully made;
your works are wonderful,[m]
I know that full well.
15My frame was not hidden from you
when I was made in the secret place.
When I was woven together[n] in the depths of the earth,[o]
16 your eyes saw my unformed body.
All the days ordained for me
were written in your book
before one of them came to be.

17How precious to[a] me are your thoughts, O God![p]
How vast is the sum of them!
18Were I to count them,
they would outnumber the grains of sand.
When I awake,
I am still with you.

19If only you would slay the wicked,[q] O God!
Away from me,[r] you bloodthirsty men!
20They speak of you with evil intent;
your adversaries misuse your name.[s]
21Do I not hate those[t] who hate you, O LORD,
and abhor those who rise up against you?
22I have nothing but hatred for them;
I count them my enemies.

23Search me,[u] O God, and know my heart;[v]
test me and know my anxious thoughts.
24See if there is any offensive way in me,
and lead me[w] in the way everlasting.

Psalm 140

For the director of music. A psalm of David.

1Rescue me,[x] O LORD, from evil men;
protect me from men of violence,[y]
2who devise evil plans[z] in their hearts
and stir up war every day.
3They make their tongues as sharp as[a] a serpent's;
the poison of vipers[b] is on their lips. *Selah*
4Keep me,[c] O LORD, from the hands of the wicked;[d]
protect me from men of violence
who plan to trip my feet.
5Proud men have hidden a snare for me;
they have spread out the cords of their net
and have set traps[e] for me along my path. *Selah*

6O LORD, I say to you, "You are my God."[f]
Hear, O LORD, my cry for mercy.[g]
7O Sovereign LORD,[h] my strong deliverer,
who shields my head in the day of battle—
8do not grant the wicked[i] their desires, O LORD;

139:10 [i]Ps 23:3
139:12 [j]Job 34:22; Da 2:22
139:13 [k]Ps 119:73 [l]Job 10:11
139:14 [m]Ps 40:5
139:15 [n]Job 10:11 [o]Ps 63:9
139:17 [p]Ps 40:5
139:19 [q]Isa 11:4 [r]Ps 119:115
139:20 [s]Jude 15
139:21 [t]2Ch 19:2; Ps 31:6; 119:113; 119:158
139:23 [u]Job 31:6; Ps 26:2 [v]Jer 11:20
139:24 [w]Ps 5:8; 143:10; Pr 15:9
140:1 [x]Ps 17:13 [y]Ps 18:48
140:2 [z]Ps 36:4; 56:6
140:3 [a]Ps 57:4 [b]Ps 58:4; Jas 3:8
140:4 [c]Ps 141:9 [d]Ps 71:4
140:5 [e]Ps 31:4; 35:7
140:6 [f]Ps 16:2 [g]Ps 116:1; 143:1
140:7 [h]Ps 28:8
140:8 [i]Ps 10:2-3

[a]17 Or *concerning*

139:1–24

PROMISE 1

GOD'S CONTINUAL PRESENCE

The truth of this psalm is both comforting and scary at the same time. David said, "I am never alone, never away from God's awareness. No matter where I go, God is there; no danger, no act, no thought escapes his guiding hand" (vv. 5–10). Many read this psalm as a threat. God not only guides with his hand, but he also observes with his eye (vv. 1–4, 7–12).

Knowing we cannot escape God's observation and intervention can be comforting or discomforting (or even downright terrifying). The difference lies in what God sees in the darkest corners of our minds. Think back over yesterday. Consider your schedule for today and tomorrow. Is God's all-seeing, all-knowing presence a source of comfort or terror for you? What, specifically, makes the difference? Read this psalm through a couple of times and, thinking through your schedule and lifestyle, ask, "What can I do to conform both to God's will?"

For the next Promise 1 reading go to page 671.

do not let their plans succeed,
or they will become proud. *Selah*
9 Let the heads of those who
surround me
be covered with the trouble their
lips have caused.[j]
10 Let burning coals fall upon them;
may they be thrown into the
fire,[k]
into miry pits, never to rise.
11 Let slanderers not be established in
the land;
may disaster hunt down men of
violence.[l]

12 I know that the LORD secures
justice for the poor
and upholds the cause[m] of the
needy.[n]
13 Surely the righteous will praise
your name[o]
and the upright will live[p] before
you.

Psalm 141

A psalm of David.

1 →PG. 670

1 O LORD, I call to you; come
quickly[q] to me.
Hear my voice[r] when I call to
you.
2 May my prayer be set before you
like incense;[s]
may the lifting up of my hands[t]
be like the evening
sacrifice.[u]

3 Set a guard over my mouth,
O LORD;
keep watch over the door of my
lips.
4 Let not my heart be drawn to what
is evil,
to take part in wicked deeds
with men who are evildoers;
let me not eat of their
delicacies.[v]

5 Let a righteous man[a] strike me—it
is a kindness;
let him rebuke me[w]—it is oil on
my head.[x]
My head will not refuse it.

Yet my prayer is ever against the
deeds of evildoers;
6 their rulers will be thrown down
from the cliffs,
and the wicked will learn that
my words were well spoken.
7 They will say, "As one plows and
breaks up the earth,
so our bones have been
scattered at the mouth[y] of
the grave.[b]"

8 But my eyes are fixed[z] on you,
O Sovereign LORD;
in you I take refuge[a]—do not
give me over to death.
9 Keep me[b] from the snares they
have laid for me,
from the traps set[c] by evildoers.
10 Let the wicked fall[d] into their own
nets,
while I pass by in safety.

Psalm 142

A *maskil*[c] of David. When he was in
the cave. A prayer.

1 I cry aloud to the LORD;
I lift up my voice to the LORD for
mercy.[e]
2 I pour out my complaint[f] before
him;
before him I tell my trouble.

3 When my spirit grows faint[g]
within me,
it is you who know my way.
In the path where I walk
men have hidden a snare for me.
4 Look to my right and see;
no one is concerned for me.
I have no refuge;
no one cares[h] for my life.

5 I cry to you, O LORD;
I say, "You are my refuge,[i]
my portion[j] in the land of the
living."[k]
6 Listen to my cry,[l]
for I am in desperate need;[m]
rescue me from those who pursue
me,
for they are too strong for me.
7 Set me free from my prison,[n]
that I may praise your name.

Then the righteous will gather
about me
because of your goodness to
me.[o]

Psalm 143

A psalm of David.

1 O LORD, hear my prayer,
listen to my cry for mercy;[p]
in your faithfulness[q] and
righteousness[r]
come to my relief.
2 Do not bring your servant into
judgment,
for no one living is righteous[s]
before you.

140:9 [j]Ps 7:16
140:10 [k]Ps 11:6; 21:9
140:11 [l]Ps 34:21
140:12 [m]Ps 9:4 [n]Ps 35:10
140:13 [o]Ps 97:12 [p]Ps 11:7
141:1 [q]Ps 22:19; 70:5 [r]Ps 143:1
141:2 [s]Rev 5:8; 8:3 [t]1Ti 2:8 [u]Ex 29:39,41
141:4 [v]Pr 23:6
141:5 [w]Pr 9:8 [x]Ps 23:5
141:7 [y]Ps 53:5
141:8 [z]Ps 25:15 [a]Ps 2:12
141:9 [b]Ps 140:4 [c]Ps 38:12
141:10 [d]Ps 35:8
142:1 [e]Ps 30:8
142:2 [f]Isa 26:16
142:3 [g]Ps 140:5; 143:4,7
142:4 [h]Ps 31:11; Jer 30:17
142:5 [i]Ps 46:1 [j]Ps 16:5 [k]Ps 27:13
142:6 [l]Ps 17:1 [m]Ps 79:8; 116:6
142:7 [n]Ps 146:7 [o]Ps 13:6
143:1 [p]Ps 140:6 [q]Ps 89:1-2 [r]Ps 71:2
143:2 [s]Ps 14:3; Ecc 7:20; Ro 3:20

[a] 5 Or *Let the Righteous One* [b] 7 Hebrew *Sheol* [c] Title: Probably a literary or musical term

3The enemy pursues me,
he crushes me to the ground;
he makes me dwell in darkness
like those long dead.
4So my spirit grows faint within me;
my heart within me is
dismayed.[t]

5I remember[u] the days of long ago;
I meditate on all your works
and consider what your hands
have done.

6I spread out my hands[v] to you;
my soul thirsts for you like a
parched land. *Selah*

7Answer me quickly,[w] O LORD;
my spirit fails.
Do not hide your face[x] from me
or I will be like those who go
down to the pit.
8Let the morning bring me word of
your unfailing love,[y]
for I have put my trust in you.
Show me the way[z] I should go,
for to you I lift up my soul.[a]
9Rescue me from my enemies,[b]
O LORD,
for I hide myself in you.
10Teach me to do your will,
for you are my God;
may your good Spirit
lead[c] me on level ground.

11For your name's sake, O LORD,
preserve my life;[d]
in your righteousness,[e] bring
me out of trouble.
12In your unfailing love, silence my
enemies;
destroy all my foes,[f]
for I am your servant.[g]

Psalm 144

Of David.

1Praise be to the LORD my Rock,[h]
who trains my hands for war,
my fingers for battle.
2He is my loving God and my
fortress,[i]
my stronghold and my deliverer,
my shield,[j] in whom I take refuge,
who subdues peoples**[a]** under
me.

3O LORD, what is man[k] that you
care for him,
the son of man that you think of
him?
4Man is like a breath;
his days are like a fleeting
shadow.[l]

5Part your heavens,[m] O LORD, and
come down;
touch the mountains, so that
they smoke.[n]
6Send forth lightning and scatter
⌞the enemies⌟;
shoot your arrows[o] and rout
them.
7Reach down your hand from on
high;
deliver me and rescue me
from the mighty waters,[p]
from the hands of foreigners[q]
8whose mouths are full of lies,[r]
whose right hands are deceitful.

9I will sing a new song to you,
O God;
on the ten-stringed lyre[s] I will
make music to you,
10to the One who gives victory to
kings,
who delivers his servant David[t]
from the deadly sword.

11Deliver me and rescue me
from the hands of foreigners
whose mouths are full of lies,
whose right hands are
deceitful.[u]

12Then our sons in their youth
will be like well-nurtured
plants,[v]
and our daughters will be like
pillars
carved to adorn a palace.
13Our barns will be filled
with every kind of provision.
Our sheep will increase by
thousands,
by tens of thousands in our
fields;
14 our oxen will draw heavy loads.**[b]**
There will be no breaching of walls,
no going into captivity,
no cry of distress in our streets.

15Blessed are the people[w] of whom
this is true;
blessed are the people whose
God is the LORD.

Psalm 145**[c]**

A psalm of praise. Of David.

1I will exalt you,[x] my God the
King;[y]
I will praise your name for ever
and ever.
2Every day I will praise[z] you

1 →PG. 679

143:4 [t]Ps 142:3 **143:5** [u]Ps 77:6 **143:6** [v]Ps 63:1; 88:9 **143:7** [w]Ps 69:17 [x]Ps 27:9; 28:1 **143:8** [y]Ps 46:5; 90:14 [z]Ps 27:11 [a]Ps 25:1-2 **143:9** [b]Ps 31:15 **143:10** [c]Ne 9:20; Ps 23:3; 25:4-5 **143:11** [d]Ps 119:25 [e]Ps 31:1 **143:12** [f]Ps 52:5; 54:5 [g]Ps 116:16 **144:1** [h]Ps 18:2,34 **144:2** [i]Ps 59:9; 91:2 [j]Ps 84:9 **144:3** [k]Ps 8:4; Heb 2:6 **144:4** [l]Ps 39:11; 102:11 **144:5** [m]Ps 18:9; Isa 64:1

[n]Ps 104:32 **144:6** [o]Ps 7:12-13; 18:14 **144:7** [p]Ps 69:2 [q]Ps 18:44 **144:8** [r]Ps 12:2 **144:9** [s]Ps 33:2-3 **144:10** [t]Ps 18:50 **144:11** [u]Ps 12:2; Isa 44:20 **144:12** [v]Ps 128:3 **144:15** [w]Ps 33:12 **145:1** [x]Ps 30:1; 34:1 [y]Ps 5:2 **145:2** [z]Ps 71:6

a *2* Many manuscripts of the Masoretic Text, Dead Sea Scrolls, Aquila, Jerome and Syriac; most manuscripts of the Masoretic Text *subdues my people* **b** *14* Or *our chieftains will be firmly established* **c** This psalm is an acrostic poem, the verses of which (including verse 13b) begin with the successive letters of the Hebrew alphabet.

and extol your name for ever
and ever.

7 →PG. 691

3Great is the LORD and most worthy
of praise;
his greatness no one can
fathom.[a]
4One generation[b] will commend
your works to another;
they will tell of your mighty acts.
5They will speak of the glorious
splendor of your majesty,
and I will meditate on your
wonderful works.[a][c]
6They will tell of the power of your
awesome works,[d]
and I will proclaim[e] your great
deeds.
7They will celebrate your abundant
goodness[f]
and joyfully sing of your
righteousness.[g]
8The LORD is gracious and
compassionate,[h]
slow to anger and rich in love.[i]
9The LORD is good[j] to all;
he has compassion on all he has
made.
10All you have made will praise
you,[k] O LORD;
your saints will extol you.[l]
11They will tell of the glory of your
kingdom
and speak of your might,
12so that all men may know of your
mighty acts[m]
and the glorious splendor of
your kingdom.
13Your kingdom is an everlasting
kingdom,[n]
and your dominion endures
through all generations.
The LORD is faithful to all his
promises
and loving toward all he has
made.[b]
14The LORD upholds[o] all those who
fall
and lifts up all[p] who are bowed
down.
15The eyes of all look to you,
and you give them their food[q]
at the proper time.
16You open your hand
and satisfy the desires[r] of every
living thing.
17The LORD is righteous in all his
ways
and loving toward all he has
made.
18The LORD is near[s] to all who call
on him,[t]
to all who call on him in truth.
19He fulfills the desires[u] of those
who fear him;
he hears their cry[v] and saves
them.
20The LORD watches over all who love
him,[w]
but all the wicked he will
destroy.[x]
21My mouth will speak[y] in praise of
the LORD.
Let every creature[z] praise his
holy name
for ever and ever.

Psalm 146

1Praise the LORD.[c]

Praise the LORD,[a] O my soul.
2 I will praise the LORD all my
life;[b]
I will sing praise to my God as
long as I live.

145:3 [a]Job 5:9; Ps 147:5; Ro 11:33
145:4 [b]Isa 38:19
145:5 [c]Ps 119:27
145:6 [d]Ps 66:3 [e]Dt 32:3
145:7 [f]Isa 63:7 [g]Ps 51:14
145:8 [h]Ps 86:15 [i]Ex 34:6; Nu 14:18
145:9 [j]Ps 100:5
145:10 [k]Ps 19:1 [l]Ps 68:26
145:12 [m]Ps 105:1
145:13 [n]1Ti 1:17; 2Pe 1:11
145:14 [o]Ps 37:24 [p]Ps 146:8
145:15 [q]Ps 104:27; 136:25
145:16 [r]Ps 104:28
145:18 [s]Dt 4:7 [t]Jn 4:24
145:19 [u]Ps 37:4 [v]Pr 15:29
145:20 [w]Ps 31:23; 97:10 [x]Ps 9:5
145:21 [y]Ps 71:8 [z]Ps 65:2
146:1 [a]Ps 103:1
146:2 [b]Ps 104:33

[a]*5* Dead Sea Scrolls and Syriac (see also Septuagint); Masoretic Text *On the glorious splendor of your majesty / and on your wonderful works I will meditate* [b]*13* One manuscript of the Masoretic Text, Dead Sea Scrolls and Syriac (see also Septuagint); most manuscripts of the Masoretic Text do not have the last two lines of verse 13. [c]*1* Hebrew *Hallelu Yah*; also in verse 10

145:1–21

PROMISE 1

A LIFE OF PRAISE

What wonderful praise! Wouldn't it be great to experience such love and praise for God? This psalm not only expresses enviable feelings for God, but also gives a clue about where such feelings come from. David could praise God as he did (vv. 1–7, 21) because he experienced God as he did (vv. 8–20).

How deep and rich and genuine is your love for and praise of God? Likely it is as deep and rich and genuine as your life with God. A distant relationship will breed shallow trust and praise; a life lived up to its ears in God will more likely develop the kind of relationship and praise this psalm expresses.

Reflect on your experience of God. Do you read his Word with a mind to act on what it says? Do you talk of him with your family and friends? Are you involved with a group of guys who study the Bible and pray together? Are you involved in your church in any meaningful way?

Until we experience life as God instructs, we cannot expect to experience God as we desire. Take a lesson from David, the great saint of God: Live a godly life to the hilt and experience a relationship with God that makes you want to shout his praise.

For the next Promise 1 reading go to page 673.

3Do not put your trust in princes,[c]
in mortal men,[d] who cannot
save.
4When their spirit departs, they
return to the ground;[e]
on that very day their plans
come to nothing.[f]

5Blessed is he[g] whose help[h] is the
God of Jacob,
whose hope is in the LORD his
God,
6the Maker of heaven[i] and earth,
the sea, and everything in
them—
the LORD, who remains faithful[j]
forever.
7He upholds the cause of the
oppressed[k]
and gives food to the hungry.[l]
The LORD sets prisoners free,[m]
8 the LORD gives sight to the
blind,[n]
the LORD lifts up those who are
bowed down,
the LORD loves the righteous.
9The LORD watches over the alien
and sustains the fatherless and
the widow,[o]
but he frustrates the ways of the
wicked.

10The LORD reigns[p] forever,
your God, O Zion, for all
generations.

Praise the LORD.

Psalm 147

1Praise the LORD.[a]

How good it is to sing praises to
our God,
how pleasant[q] and fitting to
praise him![r]

2The LORD builds up Jerusalem;[s]
he gathers the exiles[t] of Israel.
3He heals the brokenhearted
and binds up their wounds.

4He determines the number of the
stars[u]
and calls them each by name.
5Great is our Lord[v] and mighty in
power;
his understanding has no limit.[w]
6The LORD sustains the humble[x]
but casts the wicked to the
ground.

7Sing to the LORD[y] with
thanksgiving;
make music to our God on the
harp.
8He covers the sky with clouds;
he supplies the earth with rain[z]
and makes grass grow[a] on the
hills.
9He provides food[b] for the cattle
and for the young ravens[c] when
they call.

10His pleasure is not in the
strength[d] of the horse,[e]
nor his delight in the legs of a
man;
11the LORD delights in those who fear
him,
who put their hope in his
unfailing love.

12Extol the LORD, O Jerusalem;
praise your God, O Zion,
13for he strengthens the bars of your
gates
and blesses your people within
you.
14He grants peace[f] to your borders
and satisfies you[g] with the
finest of wheat.

15He sends his command[h] to the
earth;
his word runs swiftly.
16He spreads the snow[i] like wool
and scatters the frost[j] like
ashes.
17He hurls down his hail like
pebbles.
Who can withstand his icy blast?
18He sends his word[k] and melts
them;
he stirs up his breezes, and the
waters flow.

19He has revealed his word to Jacob,
his laws and decrees[l] to Israel.
20He has done this for no other
nation;[m]
they do not know his laws.

Praise the LORD.

Psalm 148

1Praise the LORD.[b]

Praise the LORD from the heavens,
praise him in the heights above.
2Praise him, all his angels,[n]
praise him, all his heavenly
hosts.
3Praise him, sun and moon,
praise him, all you shining stars.
4Praise him, you highest heavens
and you waters above the
skies.[o]
5Let them praise the name of the
LORD,
for he commanded[p] and they
were created.

146:3 [c]Ps 118:9 [d]Isa 2:22 **146:4** [e]Ps 104:29; Ecc 12:7 [f]Ps 33:10; 1Co 2:6 **146:5** [g]Ps 144:15; Jer 17:7 [h]Ps 71:5 **146:6** [i]Ps 115:15; Ac 14:15; Rev 14:7 [j]Ps 117:2 **146:7** [k]Ps 103:6 [l]Ps 107:9 [m]Ps 68:6 **146:8** [n]Mt 9:30 **146:9** [o]Ex 22:22; Dt 10:18; Ps 68:5 **146:10** [p]Ex 15:18; Ps 10:16 **147:1** [q]Ps 135:3 [r]Ps 33:1 **147:2** [s]Ps 102:16 [t]Dt 30:3 **147:4** [u]Isa 40:26 **147:5** [v]Ps 48:1 [w]Isa 40:28 **147:6** [x]Ps 146:8-9 **147:7** [y]Ps 33:3 **147:8** [z]Job 38:26 [a]Ps 104:14 **147:9** [b]Ps 104:27-28; Mt 6:26 [c]Job 38:41 **147:10** [d]1Sa 16:7 [e]Ps 33:16-17 **147:14** [f]Isa 60:17-18 [g]Ps 132:15 **147:15** [h]Job 37:12 **147:16** [i]Job 37:6 [j]Job 38:29 **147:18** [k]Ps 33:9 **147:19** [l]Dt 33:4; Mal 4:4 **147:20** [m]Dt 4:7-8, 32-34 **148:2** [n]Ps 103:20 **148:4** [o]Ge 1:7; 1Ki 8:27 **148:5** [p]Ge 1:1,6; Ps 33:6,9

a *1* Hebrew *Hallelu Yah*; also in verse 20
b *1* Hebrew *Hallelu Yah*; also in verse 14

6He set them in place for ever and
ever;
he gave a decree[q] that will
never pass away.

7Praise the LORD from the earth,
you great sea creatures[r] and all
ocean depths,
8lightning and hail, snow and
clouds,
stormy winds that do his
bidding,[s]
9you mountains and all hills,[t]
fruit trees and all cedars,
10wild animals and all cattle,
small creatures and flying birds,
11kings of the earth and all nations,
you princes and all rulers on
earth,
12young men and maidens,
old men and children.
13Let them praise the name of the
LORD,[u]
for his name alone is exalted;
his splendor is above the earth
and the heavens.[v]
14He has raised up for his people a
horn,**[a]**[w]
the praise of all his saints,
of Israel, the people close to his
heart.

Praise the LORD.

Psalm 149

1Praise the LORD.**[b]**[x]

Sing to the LORD a new song,
his praise in the assembly[y] of
the saints.
2Let Israel rejoice in their Maker;[z]
let the people of Zion be glad in
their King.[a]
3Let them praise his name with
dancing
and make music to him with
tambourine and harp.[b]
4For the LORD takes delight[c] in his
people;
he crowns the humble with
salvation.[d]
5Let the saints rejoice[e] in this
honor
and sing for joy on their beds.[f]

6May the praise of God be in their
mouths[g]
and a double-edged[h] sword in
their hands,
7to inflict vengeance on the nations
and punishment on the peoples,
8to bind their kings with fetters,
their nobles with shackles of
iron,
9to carry out the sentence written
against them.[i]
This is the glory of all his
saints.[j]

Praise the LORD.

Psalm 150

1Praise the LORD.**[c]**

Praise God in his sanctuary;[k]
praise him in his mighty
heavens.[l]
2Praise him for his acts of power;[m]
praise him for his surpassing
greatness.[n]
3Praise him with the sounding of
the trumpet,
praise him with the harp and
lyre,[o]
4praise him with tambourine and
dancing,[p]
praise him with the strings[q] and
flute,
5praise him with the clash of
cymbals,[r]
praise him with resounding
cymbals.

6Let everything[s] that has breath
praise the LORD.

Praise the LORD.

148:6 [q]Job 38:33; Ps 89:37; Jer 33:25
148:7 [r]Ps 74:13-14
148:8 [s]Ps 147:15-18
148:9 [t]Isa 44:23; 49:13; 55:12
148:13 [u]Isa 12:4 [v]Ps 8:1; 113:4
148:14 [w]Ps 75:10
149:1 [x]Ps 33:2 [y]Ps 35:18
149:2 [z]Ps 95:6 [a]Ps 47:6; Zec 9:9
149:3 [b]Ps 81:2; 150:4
149:4 [c]Ps 35:27 [d]Ps 132:16
149:5 [e]Ps 132:16 [f]Job 35:10
149:6 [g]Ps 66:17 [h]Heb 4:12; Rev 1:16
149:9 [i]Dt 7:1; Eze 28:26 [j]Ps 148:14
150:1 [k]Ps 102:19 [l]Ps 19:1
150:2 [m]Dt 3:24 [n]Ps 145:5-6
150:3 [o]Ps 149:3
150:4 [p]Ex 15:20 [q]Isa 38:20
150:5 [r]1Ch 13:8; 15:16
150:6 [s]Ps 145:21

a *14 Horn* here symbolizes strong one, that is, king. **b** *1* Hebrew *Hallelu Yah*; also in verse 9
c *1* Hebrew *Hallelu Yah*; also in verse 6

150:1–6

PROMISE **1**

CATCH THE FEVER

This last psalm ends this book in an appropriate way. A person can't fake what this psalm demonstrates—a raucous love for and praise of God for all he's done. This psalmist demonstrates a fever for praising God that is extremely contagious.

As we read the psalms, we find a lot of language that sounds quite pious and godly. It's easy to fake being a spiritual leader if one knows the lingo. But this psalm isn't about lingo. In fact, the language is downright repetitive. It is the well out of which this song bursts forth that makes this psalm great.

This book is a masterpiece of praise. It not only gives us the language of praise, it gives us reasons for praise that are as contemporary as the daily newspaper. As you read through these psalms, look for God in a personal way. Catch the fever this psalmist exhibits and sing your own songs of praise to our awesome God!

For the next Promise 1 reading go to page 678.

PROVERBS

AT A GLANCE

Key Principle: Skill in the art of living God's way is built on the foundation of an attitude of radical dependence on God.
Author: Solomon, anonymous wise men, Agur and Lemuel
Time and Place: ~970 B.C. to ~686 B.C. / Judah
Key Verses: 1:5–7; 3:5–6; 6:23; 9:10; 15:33

BENEFIT

Proverbs is an extremely practical and specific book that challenges us to pursue wisdom in each area of everyday life. It counsels us to depend upon God in our relationships with our wives, children, work, friends and neighbors. It also encourages us to develop a godly character that is evident in our speech, our use of money and time and our decision-making process. These maxims are concise and practical; read them slowly and carefully with an eye toward bringing your behavior in line with God's common-sense directives and divine will.

SETTING

The wisdom school of Israel consisted of sages or elders who instructed the people in how to apply God's teachings to specific areas of daily life. The book of Proverbs is an assortment of the kind of perceptive sayings and insights studied in such schools. This book was finally collected into a single volume of practical wisdom by the men of Hezekiah (25:1) around 700 B.C. The principal contributor to this book of wisdom literature is Solomon (d. 930 B.C.) who spoke 3,000 proverbs (1 Kings 4:32), of which about 800 are included in the two Solomonic collections in 10:1—22:16 and chapters 25—29. As the uniquely gifted Teacher of Israel, he "pondered and searched out and set in order many proverbs" (Ecclesiastes 12:9). It is possible that he collected and edited the section called "the sayings of the wise" (22:17—24:34). The origin of the sayings of Agur (30) and of King Lemuel (31) is unknown, since this is the only appearance of these names in the Bible.

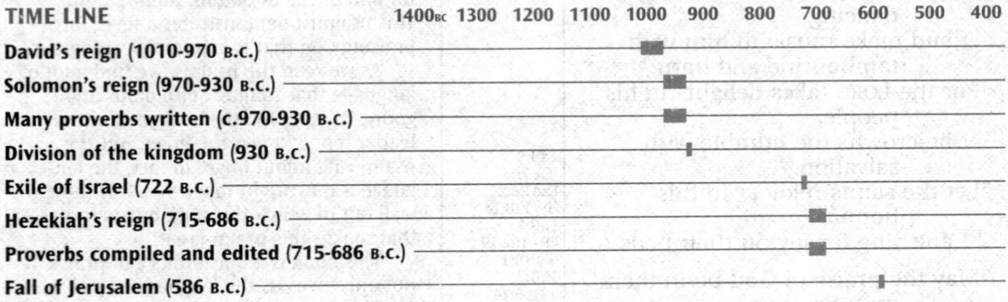

THEME AND PURPOSE

The purpose of Proverbs is stated clearly in 1:2–6. This book was collected first to teach moral insight and astuteness (1:2a, 3–5), and second to help the reader develop mental ability and understanding (1:2b, 6). The theme of this book is captured in 1:7—"The fear of the LORD is the beginning of knowledge, but fools despise wisdom and discipline" (compare 9:10). The word translated "wisdom" (*hokhmah*) relates to the idea of skill; this book stresses that it is through instruction, discipline and practice that we learn the skill of living our lives in such a way that they amount to something excellent and worthwhile. When we fear the Lord by developing a sense of awe, humility and dependence upon him, God refines us and shapes us into the people he wants us to become, much as a skilled artist takes raw materials and transforms them into a beautiful work.

UNIQUE CONTRIBUTION

Job, Proverbs and Ecclesiastes are the three wisdom books of the Old Testament (James is the wisdom book of the New Testament). Evidently, ancient Israel had schools of wise men who were prudent and discerning observers of life (1 Kings 4:29–34). There is evidence that such wise men traveled even to other countries to learn from one another. Some of the examples of wisdom writings from the ancient Near East date back to 2700 B.C. The sayings of the wise (22:17—24:34) in Proverbs are similar to *The Wisdom of Amenemope,* written by an Egyptian who lived sometime after 1000 B.C.

The Hebrew word for "proverb" (*mashal*) means a comparison or a likeness, and the proverbs use figures of speech to make comparisons and penetrating insights. The proverbs were designed for ease of memorization, and are simple illustrations that expose fundamental realities about life. These illustrations are moral, practical and pithy. They're based on the central truth that the fear of the Lord is the basic starting point for living a life that reflects a balanced application of God's Word in our everyday lives.

LINKS TO THE NEW TESTAMENT

Proverbs stresses that wisdom is not limited to an elite class of people, but is accessible to all who are willing to seek it. As the New Testament teaches, Christ Jesus the incarnation of wisdom: He has "become for us wisdom from God—that is, our righteousness, holiness and redemption" (1 Corinthians 1:30). In Christ "are hidden all the treasures of wisdom and knowledge" (Colossians 2:3).

OVERVIEW

FOCUS	Preparation for Wisdom		Proverbs on Wisdom		Precepts
REFERENCE	1 9	10		29	30 31
TOPICS	Prologue	Maxims			Epilogue
	Personification of Wisdom	Principles of Wisdom			Practice of Wisdom
	Commendation of Wisdom	Counsel of Wisdom			Comparisons
AUTHORS	Solomon (1-22a)		Wise Men (22b-24)	Solomon (25-29)	Agur and Lemuel
LOCATION	Judah				
TIME	~250 Years				

The book of Proverbs begins by preparing the reader to receive instruction (1—9). A clear statement of the book's purpose (1:1–7) is followed by a series of ten exhortations as from a father to a son. These are designed to encourage the student to treasure and pursue the priceless gem of wisdom. The benefits of wisdom are many, since they lead to true success and character in life as opposed to the pain and destruction that results from a life of folly. The discipline of wisdom leads to freedom and skillful living, but the path of foolishness and rebellion makes a person vulnerable to the deadly lusts and seductions of this world.

The proverbs themselves do not begin until chapter 10. These pithy sayings of Solomon cover a wide variety of issues, and for the most part are not arranged in any topical manner (10—24). They deal with instruction concerning the use of the tongue, poverty and wealth, relationships between husbands and wives and parents and children, relationships with one's neighbors, industry versus slothfulness, self-control versus anger, humility versus pride, justice versus vengeance and character versus wickedness. The second set of Solomon's proverbs, copied by King Hezekiah's men, develop the same themes as the first collection (25—29).

Proverbs concludes with a number of precepts and comparisons by Agur (30) and Lemuel (31), ending with an acrostic (the first letter of each verse consecutively moves through the alphabet of 22 Hebrew letters) that depicts a wife of noble character.

PROVERBS

Prologue: Purpose and Theme

1 The proverbs of Solomon[a] son of David, king of Israel:[b]

3 →PG. 679

2for attaining wisdom and
discipline;
for understanding words of
insight;
3for acquiring a disciplined and
prudent life,
doing what is right and just and
fair;
4for giving prudence to the
simple,[c]
knowledge and discretion[d] to
the young—
5let the wise listen and add to their
learning,[e]
and let the discerning get
guidance—
6for understanding proverbs and
parables,[f]
the sayings and riddles[g] of the
wise.

7The fear of the LORD[h] is the
beginning of knowledge,
but fools**a** despise wisdom and
discipline.

Exhortations to Embrace Wisdom

Warning Against Enticement

8Listen, my son,[i] to your father's
instruction
and do not forsake your
mother's teaching.[j]
9They will be a garland to grace
your head
and a chain to adorn your
neck.[k]

10My son, if sinners entice[l] you,
do not give in[m] to them.[n]
11If they say, "Come along with us;
let's lie in wait[o] for someone's
blood,
let's waylay some harmless soul;
12let's swallow them alive, like the
grave,**b**
and whole, like those who go
down to the pit;[p]
13we will get all sorts of valuable
things
and fill our houses with plunder;
14throw in your lot with us,
and we will share a common
purse"—
15my son, do not go along with
them,
do not set foot[q] on their
paths;[r]
16for their feet rush into sin,
they are swift to shed blood.[s]
17How useless to spread a net
in full view of all the birds!
18These men lie in wait for their own
blood;
they waylay only themselves!
19Such is the end of all who go after
ill-gotten gain;
it takes away the lives of those
who get it.[t]

Warning Against Rejecting Wisdom

20Wisdom calls aloud[u] in the street,
she raises her voice in the public
squares;
21at the head of the noisy streets**c**
she cries out,
in the gateways of the city she
makes her speech:

22"How long will you simple ones**d**[v]
love your simple ways?
How long will mockers delight in
mockery
and fools hate knowledge?
23If you had responded to my
rebuke,
I would have poured out my
heart to you

1:1–6

PROMISE 7

WANTED: WISE MEN

Our world is desperate for wise men. This passage tells us that the proverbs were written to develop wisdom and insight in people who study them. Look at the statements in verses 2–6 that begin with the word "for" and you'll discover the writer's intent. Meditate on each statement. Ask yourself what you would be like if you developed each of the characteristics listed. Then as you read Proverbs, ask God to help you grow in each dimension. Imagine how you can contribute to your sphere of influence as you grow.

For the next Promise 7 reading go to page 743.

1:1 [a]1Ki 4:29-34 [b]Pr 10:1; 25:1; Ecc 1:1
1:4 [c]Pr 8:5 [d]Pr 2:10-11; 8:12
1:5 [e]Pr 9:9
1:6 [f]Ps 49:4; 78:2 [g]Nu 12:8
1:7 [h]Job 28:28; Ps 111:10; Pr 9:10; 15:33; Ecc 12:13
1:8 [i]Pr 4:1 [j]Pr 6:20
1:9 [k]Pr 4:1-9
1:10 [l]Ge 39:7 [m]Dt 13:8 [n]Pr 16:29; Eph 5:11
1:11 [o]Ps 10:8
1:12 [p]Ps 28:1
1:15 [q]Ps 119:101 [r]Ps 1:1; Pr 4:14
1:16 [s]Pr 6:18; Isa 59:7
1:19 [t]Pr 15:27
1:20 [u]Pr 8:1; 9:1-3, 13-15
1:22 [v]Pr 8:5; 9:4,16

---

a *7* The Hebrew words rendered *fool* in Proverbs, and often elsewhere in the Old Testament, denote one who is morally deficient.
b *12* Hebrew *Sheol*
c *21* Hebrew; Septuagint / *on the tops of the walls*
d *22* The Hebrew word rendered *simple* in Proverbs generally denotes one without moral direction and inclined to evil.

and made my thoughts known to
you.
24But since you rejected me when I
called[w]
and no one gave heed when I
stretched out my hand,
25since you ignored all my advice
and would not accept my
rebuke,
26I in turn will laugh[x] at your
disaster;
I will mock when calamity
overtakes you[y]—
27when calamity overtakes you like a
storm,
when disaster sweeps over you
like a whirlwind,
when distress and trouble
overwhelm you.

28"Then they will call to me but I will
not answer;[z]
they will look for me but will not
find me.[a]
29Since they hated knowledge
and did not choose to fear the
LORD,[b]
30since they would not accept my
advice
and spurned my rebuke,[c]
31they will eat the fruit of their ways
and be filled with the fruit of
their schemes.[d]
32For the waywardness of the simple
will kill them,
and the complacency of fools
will destroy them;[e]
33but whoever listens to me will live
in safety[f]
and be at ease, without fear of
harm."[g]

Moral Benefits of Wisdom

2 My son, if you accept my words
and store up my commands
within you,
2turning your ear to wisdom
and applying your heart to
understanding,[h]
3and if you call out for insight
and cry aloud for understanding,
4and if you look for it as for silver
and search for it as for hidden
treasure,[i]
5then you will understand the fear
of the LORD
and find the knowledge of
God.[j]

1:24 [w]Isa 65:12; 66:4; Jer 7:13; Zec 7:11
1:26 [x]Ps 2:4 [y]Pr 6:15; 10:24
1:28 [z]1Sa 8:18; Isa 1:15; Jer 11:11; Mic 3:4 [a]Job 27:9; Pr 8:17; Eze 8:18; Zec 7:13
1:29 [b]Job 21:14
1:30 [c]ver 25; Ps 81:11
1:31 [d]Job 4:8; Pr 14:14; Isa 3:11; Jer 6:19
1:32 [e]Jer 2:19
1:33 [f]Ps 25:12; Pr 3:23 [g]Ps 112:8
2:2 [h]Pr 22:17
2:4 [i]Job 3:21; Pr 3:14; Mt 13:44
2:5 [j]Pr 1:7

1:7

PROMISE 1

ONE SOURCE OF WISDOM

In this opening chapter, Solomon laid a foundation for those who read the proverbs found in this book. He presented and developed his purpose in verses 1–6. In verse 7 he informed the reader that this purpose cannot possibly be attained apart from a correct understanding of and response to God.

Defining three key terms in verse 7 will help in understanding this passage. *Fear* does not mean "to be afraid of"; rather, it means that we must be in awe of, have ultimate respect for and be realistic about the power of God. *Beginning* refers to the first step or starting point on the path we take as we attempt to reach a destination. *Knowledge* refers to our attempts to understand and make sense of what is around us. Decisions ranging from simple to complex, from harmless to disastrous are made on the basis of what we believe to be accurate knowledge. Our approach to knowledge is essential to discovering truth.

Solomon combined these terms to inform us that our idea of God functions like a lens for our minds to see through. If that lens is missing or flawed, the data that confronts our minds is distorted and the raw material out of which we attempt to construct our view of reality is skewed. If that lens is in place and is clear and accurate, we have taken the primary step toward correct definitions, on-target values and right understanding. What we think of God is the first and foundational decision. It shapes how we view every other critical bit of knowledge we process.

Two decisions affect the way we understand concepts and ideas, construct our ethical and moral code and handle our responsibilities, freedoms and obligations. First, do we believe God exists or not? If we say there is a God, our second decision determines how we choose to relate to him. If God is who the Bible teaches, he must not be taken lightly. In fact, he is to be feared. If we view the world and our role and responsibility in it without serious regard for God's all-powerful, trustworthy, and moral will, we misunderstand everything else.

The first step in accurately defining and understanding everything else is defining and understanding our position before God and bowing before him. If his explanation of reality disagrees with ours, we must accept his or we will not have true knowledge.

Take a moment and reflect on how you view God. If he is all-powerful, then all that he has communicated in his Word is absolute and undeniable. We do not debate or disagree with God, we obey. If we take any other view of the knowledge we discover in this book, we distort that knowledge. Remember, "The fear of the LORD is the beginning of knowledge." No matter what sphere of knowledge you pursue—whether you're in college, starting a family, or learning a new way of doing business—make sure your first step is in the right direction.

For the next Promise 1 reading go to page 680.

6 For the LORD gives wisdom,[k]
and from his mouth come
knowledge and
understanding.
7 He holds victory in store for the
upright,
he is a shield[l] to those whose
walk is blameless,[m]
8 for he guards the course of the just
and protects the way of his
faithful ones.[n]

9 Then you will understand what is
right and just
and fair—every good path.
10 For wisdom will enter your heart,[o]
and knowledge will be pleasant
to your soul.
11 Discretion will protect you,
and understanding will guard
you.[p]

12 Wisdom will save you from the
ways of wicked men,
from men whose words are
perverse,
13 who leave the straight paths
to walk in dark ways,[q]
14 who delight in doing wrong
and rejoice in the perverseness
of evil,[r]
15 whose paths are crooked[s]
and who are devious in their
ways.[t]

16 It will save you also from the
adulteress,[u]
from the wayward wife with her
seductive words,
17 who has left the partner of her
youth
and ignored the covenant she
made before God.[a][v]
18 For her house leads down to death
and her paths to the spirits of
the dead.[w]
19 None who go to her return
or attain the paths of life.[x]

20 Thus you will walk in the ways of
good men
and keep to the paths of the
righteous.
21 For the upright will live in the
land,[y]
and the blameless will remain in
it;
22 but the wicked will be cut off from
the land,[z]
and the unfaithful will be torn
from it.[a]

3 →PG. 679

Further Benefits of Wisdom

3 My son, do not forget my
teaching,[b]
but keep my commands in your
heart,
2 for they will prolong your life many
years[c]
and bring you prosperity.

3 Let love and faithfulness never
leave you;
bind them around your neck,
write them on the tablet of your
heart.[d]
4 Then you will win favor and a good
name
in the sight of God and man.[e]

3 →PG. 681

5 Trust in the LORD[f] with all your
heart
and lean not on your own
understanding;
6 in all your ways acknowledge him,
and he will make your paths[g]
straight.[b][h]

1 →PG. 681

7 Do not be wise in your own eyes;[i]
fear the LORD and shun evil.[j]
8 This will bring health to your
body[k]
and nourishment to your
bones.[l]

9 Honor the LORD with your wealth,
with the firstfruits[m] of all your
crops;
10 then your barns will be filled[n] to
overflowing,
and your vats will brim over with
new wine.[o]

5 →PG. 797

2:6 [k] 1Ki 3:9,12; Jas 1:5
2:7 [l] Pr 30:5-6 [m] Ps 84:11
2:8 [n] 1Sa 2:9; Ps 66:9
2:10 [o] Pr 14:33
2:11 [p] Pr 4:6; 6:22
2:13 [q] Pr 4:19; Jn 3:19
2:14 [r] Pr 10:23; Jer 11:15
2:15 [s] Ps 125:5 [t] Pr 21:8
2:16 [u] Pr 5:1-6; 6:20-29; 7:5-27
2:17 [v] Mal 2:14
2:18 [w] Pr 7:27
2:19 [x] Ecc 7:26
2:21 [y] Ps 37:29
2:22 [z] Job 18:17; Ps 37:38 [a] Dt 28:63; Pr 10:30
3:1 [b] Pr 4:5
3:2 [c] Pr 4:10
3:3 [d] Ex 13:9; Pr 6:21; 7:3; 2Co 3:3
3:4 [e] 1Sa 2:26; Lk 2:52
3:5 [f] Ps 37:3,5
3:6 [g] 1Ch 28:9 [h] Pr 16:3; Isa 45:13
3:7 [i] Ro 12:16 [j] Job 1:1; Pr 16:6
3:8 [k] Pr 4:22 [l] Job 21:24
3:9 [m] Ex 22:29; 23:19; Dt 26:1-15
3:10 [n] Dt 28:8 [o] Joel 2:24

2:1–22

PROMISE 3

CALL TO ACTION

This chapter answers two questions: "How do I gain wisdom?" (vv. 1–8) and "Is it worth the effort?" (vv. 9–22). We gain wisdom by the focused effort described in verses 1–4. Eight verbs call us to action and tell us what is involved in gaining wisdom: "accept," "store up," "turning your ear," "applying," "call out," "cry aloud," "look" and "search." Think for a minute about what you would actually do in response to each action. Verses 5–6 tell us what we should be accepting, searching and listening to: God and his Word. The Bible is the focus of the activity described in verses 1–4.

Is wisdom worth all that effort? Verses 7–22 say, "Yes!" These verses tell us of growth opportunities related to wisdom and warn us of disasters awaiting those who choose not to pursue wisdom. Read this chapter very carefully; it could strongly influence whether you pursue the way of the wise or the way of the fool.

For the next Promise 3 reading go to page 681.

[a] 17 Or *covenant of her God* [b] 6 Or *will direct your paths*

11My son, do not despise the LORD's discipline[p]
and do not resent his rebuke,
12because the LORD disciplines those he loves,[q]
as a father[a] the son he delights in.[r]

13Blessed is the man who finds wisdom,
the man who gains understanding,
14for she is more profitable than silver
and yields better returns than gold.[s]
15She is more precious than rubies;[t]
nothing you desire can compare with her.[u]
16Long life is in her right hand;
in her left hand are riches and honor.[v]
17Her ways are pleasant ways,
and all her paths are peace.[w]
18She is a tree of life[x] to those who embrace her;
those who lay hold of her will be blessed.

19By wisdom the LORD laid the earth's foundations,[y]
by understanding he set the heavens[z] in place;
20by his knowledge the deeps were divided,
and the clouds let drop the dew.

21My son, preserve sound judgment and discernment,
do not let them out of your sight;[a]
22they will be life for you,
an ornament to grace your neck.[b]
23Then you will go on your way in safety,
and your foot will not stumble;[c]
24when you lie down,[d] you will not be afraid;
when you lie down, your sleep[e] will be sweet.
25Have no fear of sudden disaster
or of the ruin that overtakes the wicked,
26for the LORD will be your confidence
and will keep your foot[f] from being snared.

27Do not withhold good from those who deserve it,
when it is in your power to act.
28Do not say to your neighbor,
"Come back later; I'll give it tomorrow"—
when you now have it with you.[g]

29Do not plot harm against your neighbor,
who lives trustfully near you.
30Do not accuse a man for no reason—
when he has done you no harm.

31Do not envy[h] a violent man
or choose any of his ways,
32for the LORD detests a perverse man[i]
but takes the upright into his confidence.[j]
33The LORD's curse[k] is on the house of the wicked,[l]
but he blesses the home of the righteous.[m]
34He mocks proud mockers
but gives grace to the humble.[n]
35The wise inherit honor,
but fools he holds up to shame.

Wisdom Is Supreme

4 Listen, my sons,[o] to a father's instruction;
pay attention and gain understanding.
2I give you sound learning,
so do not forsake my teaching.

3:11 [p]Job 5:17
3:12 [q]Pr 13:24; Rev 3:19 [r]Dt 8:5; Heb 12:5-6*
3:14 [s]Job 28:15; Pr 8:19; 16:16
3:15 [t]Job 28:18 [u]Pr 8:11
3:16 [v]Pr 8:18
3:17 [w]Pr 16:7; Mt 11:28-30
3:18 [x]Ge 2:9; Pr 11:30; Rev 2:7
3:19 [y]Ps 104:24 [z]Pr 8:27-29
3:21 [a]Pr 4:20-22
3:22 [b]Pr 1:8-9
3:23 [c]Ps 37:24; Pr 4:12
3:24 [d]Lev 26:6; Ps 3:5 [e]Job 11:18
3:26 [f]1Sa 2:9
3:28 [g]Lev 19:13; Dt 24:15
3:31 [h]Ps 37:1; Pr 24:1-2
3:32 [i]Pr 11:20 [j]Job 29:4; Ps 25:14
3:33 [k]Dt 11:28; Mal 2:2 [l]Zec 5:4 [m]Ps 1:3
3:34 [n]Jas 4:6*; 1Pe 5:5*
4:1 [o]Pr 1:8

a 12 Hebrew; Septuagint / *and he punishes*

3:5–6

PROMISE 1

TRUST, FEAR, HONOR THE LORD

Verses 5–10 present three exhortations about living life as a godly man: Trust in the Lord (vv. 5–6), fear the Lord (vv. 7–8) and honor the Lord (vv. 9–10). Any man would do well to examine this trio carefully because it covers most of life.

The first of the three is all-encompassing. In a book that promotes the pursuit of wisdom, Solomon told us that ultimately we are to trust in the Lord with all our hearts. Second, in every way or path we are to acknowledge God, which means living in the knowledge that God exists and is the source of all wisdom. A danger of gaining wisdom and insight is that we can forget that wisdom comes from God and begin believing we are its source. Finally, our intellectual (vv. 5–6), moral (vv. 7–8) and stewardship (vv. 9–10) activities must acknowledge and honor God.

These verses are a practical outworking of this book's theme (presented in 1:7). Think about and write down some specific ways you can apply this trilogy of wisdom to your life this week.

For the next Promise 1 reading go to page 713.

3When I was a boy in my father's
house,
still tender, and an only child of
my mother,
4he taught me and said,
"Lay hold of my words with all
your heart;
keep my commands and you will
live.[p]
5Get wisdom,[q] get understanding;
do not forget my words or
swerve from them.
6Do not forsake wisdom, and she
will protect you;[r]
love her, and she will watch over
you.
7Wisdom is supreme; therefore get
wisdom.
Though it cost all[s] you have,[a]
get understanding.[t]
8Esteem her, and she will exalt you;
embrace her, and she will honor
you.[u]
9She will set a garland of grace on
your head
and present you with a crown of
splendor.[v]"
10Listen, my son, accept what I say,
and the years of your life will be
many.[w]
11I guide[x] you in the way of wisdom
and lead you along straight
paths.
12When you walk, your steps will not
be hampered;
when you run, you will not
stumble.[y]
13Hold on to instruction, do not let it
go;
guard it well, for it is your life.[z]
14Do not set foot on the path of the
wicked
or walk in the way of evil men.[a]
15Avoid it, do not travel on it;
turn from it and go on your way.
16For they cannot sleep till they do
evil;[b]
they are robbed of slumber till
they make someone fall.
17They eat the bread of wickedness
and drink the wine of violence.
18The path of the righteous[c] is like
the first gleam of dawn,
shining ever brighter till the full
light of day.[d]
19But the way of the wicked is like
deep darkness;[e]
they do not know what makes
them stumble.

1 →PG. 706

20My son, pay attention to what I
say;
listen closely to my words.[f]
21Do not let them out of your
sight,[g]
keep them within your heart;
22for they are life to those who find
them
and health to a man's whole
body.[h]

3 →PG. 687

23Above all else, guard your heart,
for it is the wellspring of life.[i]
24Put away perversity from your
mouth;
keep corrupt talk far from your
lips.
25Let your eyes look straight ahead,
fix your gaze directly before you.
26Make level[b] paths for your feet[j]
and take only ways that are firm.
27Do not swerve to the right or the
left;[k]
keep your foot from evil.

Warning Against Adultery

5 My son, pay attention to my
wisdom,
listen well to my words[l] of
insight,
2that you may maintain discretion
and your lips may preserve
knowledge.
3For the lips of an adulteress drip
honey,
and her speech is smoother than
oil;[m]

4:4 [p]Pr 7:2
4:5 [q]Pr 16:16
4:6 [r]2Th 2:10
4:7 [s]Mt 13:44-46 [t]Pr 23:23
4:8 [u]1Sa 2:30; Pr 3:18
4:9 [v]Pr 1:8-9
4:10 [w]Pr 3:2
4:11 [x]1Sa 12:23
4:12 [y]Job 18:7; Pr 3:23
4:13 [z]Pr 3:22
4:14 [a]Ps 1:1; Pr 1:15
4:16 [b]Ps 36:4; Mic 2:1
4:18 [c]Isa 26:7 [d]2Sa 23:4; Da 12:3; Mt 5:14; Php 2:15
4:19 [e]Job 18:5; Pr 2:13; Isa 59:9-10; Jn 12:35
4:20 [f]Pr 5:1
4:21 [g]Pr 3:21; 7:1-2
4:22 [h]Pr 3:8; 12:18
4:23 [i]Mt 12:34; Lk 6:45
4:26 [j]Heb 12:13*
4:27 [k]Dt 5:32; 28:14
5:1 [l]Pr 4:20; 22:17
5:3 [m]Ps 55:21; Pr 2:16; 7:5

[a]7 Or *Whatever else you get the* [b]26 Or *Consider*

5:1–23

PROMISE 3

A TIMELY WARNING

We must read this chapter, along with 2:16–22 and 7:5–27, as a literal warning against sexual immorality, a danger that exists in epidemic proportions today as it did in Solomon's time. We are surrounded by a culture preoccupied with illicit sex. In addition to this literal warning, we must not miss the fact that the immoral woman in Proverbs is presented in contrast to the woman called "Wisdom" (1:20–33; 3:13–18; 8:1–36; 9:1–6; 31:10–31). Folly, personified as a seductress, will destroy just as surely as will involvement with an immoral woman. Wisdom, personified as a noble and pure woman, will build and benefit as a good mother and/or wife does.

Folly is as seductive as a tempting woman, and just as destructive. As a good wife is far more valuable than a self-seeking mistress, so is wisdom far more desirable than the temptations of folly. In language most men will readily understand, Solomon issued this dual warning and exhortation.

For the next Promise 3 reading go to page 684.

4but in the end she is bitter as
gall,[n]
sharp as a double-edged sword.
5Her feet go down to death;
her steps lead straight to the
grave.[a][o]
6She gives no thought to the way of
life;
her paths are crooked, but she
knows it not.[p]

7Now then, my sons, listen[q] to me;
do not turn aside from what I
say.
8Keep to a path far from her,[r]
do not go near the door of her
house,
9lest you give your best strength to
others
and your years to one who is
cruel,
10lest strangers feast on your wealth
and your toil enrich another
man's house.
11At the end of your life you will
groan,
when your flesh and body are
spent.
12You will say, "How I hated
discipline!
How my heart spurned
correction![s]
13I would not obey my teachers
or listen to my instructors.
14I have come to the brink of utter
ruin
in the midst of the whole
assembly."

15Drink water from your own cistern,
running water from your own
well.
16Should your springs overflow in the
streets,
your streams of water in the
public squares?
17Let them be yours alone,
never to be shared with
strangers.
4 →PG. 690
18May your fountain[t] be blessed,
and may you rejoice in the wife
of your youth.[u]
19A loving doe, a graceful deer[v]—
may her breasts satisfy you
always,
may you ever be captivated by
her love.
20Why be captivated, my son, by an
adulteress?
Why embrace the bosom of
another man's wife?

21For a man's ways are in full view[w]
of the LORD,
and he examines all his paths.[x]
22The evil deeds of a wicked man
ensnare him;[y]
the cords of his sin hold him
fast.[z]
23He will die for lack of discipline,[a]
led astray by his own great folly.

Warnings Against Folly

6 My son, if you have put up
security for your neighbor,[b]
if you have struck hands in
pledge[c] for another,
2if you have been trapped by what
you said,
ensnared by the words of your
mouth,
3then do this, my son, to free
yourself,
since you have fallen into your
neighbor's hands:
Go and humble yourself;
press your plea with your
neighbor!
4Allow no sleep to your eyes,
no slumber to your eyelids.[d]
5Free yourself, like a gazelle from
the hand of the hunter,
like a bird from the snare of the
fowler.[e]

6Go to the ant, you sluggard;[f]

5:4 [n]Ecc 7:26
5:5 [o]Pr 7:26-27
5:6 [p]Pr 30:20
5:7 [q]Pr 7:24
5:8 [r]Pr 7:1-27
5:12 [s]Pr 1:29; 12:1
5:18 [t]SS 4:12-15 [u]Ecc 9:9; Mal 2:14
5:19 [v]SS 2:9; 4:5
5:21 [w]Ps 119:168; Hos 7:2 [x]Job 14:16; Job 31:4; 34:21; Pr 15:3; Jer 16:17; 32:19; Heb 4:13
5:22 [y]Ps 9:16 [z]Nu 32:23; Ps 7:15-16; Pr 1:31-32
5:23 [a]Job 4:21; 36:12
6:1 [b]Pr 17:18 [c]Pr 11:15; 22:26-27
6:4 [d]Ps 132:4
6:5 [e]Ps 91:3
6:6 [f]Pr 20:4

[a]5 Hebrew *Sheol*

6:1–35

PROMISE 6

WHAT GOD HATES

This chapter lists six "things" God hates, seven that he detests (vv. 16–19). The writer used this startling language to grab his readers' attention. We should take notice of things God hates and finds detestable. Some are obvious: shedding innocent blood, a heart that devises wicked schemes, lying (named twice) and quickly rushing into evil. Other sins seem less severe than those mentioned in the list: haughty eyes and stirring up dissension. We might think of many sins omitted from this list that seem far worse than these last two.

The last in the list, "stirring up dissension," is singled out by the literary device of "six things . . . seven" in verse 16. This sin is also addressed in verses 12–15: "A scoundrel and villain . . . always stirs up dissension." Hardly the harmless habit some might think, God singled out dissension as something he hates and detests.

We do well to read this list carefully and avoid these "things." While we must guard ourselves against sin of any kind, these sins are specially named as things God hates and detests. We may have our own list of detestable sins, but what God hates we too must hate.

For the next Promise 6 reading go to page 752.

consider its ways and be wise!
7 It has no commander,
no overseer or ruler,
8 yet it stores its provisions in summer
and gathers its food at harvest.[g]

9 How long will you lie there, you sluggard?[h]
When will you get up from your sleep?
10 A little sleep, a little slumber,
a little folding of the hands to rest[i]—
11 and poverty[j] will come on you like a bandit
and scarcity like an armed man.[a]

12 A scoundrel and villain,
who goes about with a corrupt mouth,
13 who winks with his eye,[k]
signals with his feet
and motions with his fingers,
14 who plots evil[l] with deceit in his heart—
he always stirs up dissension.[m]
15 Therefore disaster will overtake him in an instant;
he will suddenly be destroyed—without remedy.[n]

16 There are six things the LORD hates,
seven that are detestable to him:
17 haughty eyes,
a lying tongue,[o]
hands that shed innocent blood,[p]
18 a heart that devises wicked schemes,
feet that are quick to rush into evil,[q]
19 a false witness[r] who pours out lies
and a man who stirs up dissension among brothers.[s]

Warning Against Adultery

20 My son, keep your father's commands
and do not forsake your mother's teaching.[t]
21 Bind them upon your heart forever;
fasten them around your neck.[u]
22 When you walk, they will guide you;
when you sleep, they will watch over you;
when you awake, they will speak to you.
23 For these commands are a lamp,
this teaching is a light,[v]
and the corrections of discipline
are the way to life,
24 keeping you from the immoral woman,
from the smooth tongue of the wayward wife.[w]
25 Do not lust in your heart after her beauty
or let her captivate you with her eyes,
26 for the prostitute reduces you to a loaf of bread,
and the adulteress preys upon your very life.[x]
27 Can a man scoop fire into his lap
without his clothes being burned?
28 Can a man walk on hot coals
without his feet being scorched?
29 So is he who sleeps[y] with another man's wife;[z]
no one who touches her will go unpunished.

30 Men do not despise a thief if he steals
to satisfy his hunger when he is starving.
31 Yet if he is caught, he must pay sevenfold,[a]
though it costs him all the wealth of his house.
32 But a man who commits adultery[b] lacks judgment;[c]
whoever does so destroys himself.
33 Blows and disgrace are his lot,
and his shame will never[d] be wiped away;
34 for jealousy[e] arouses a husband's fury,[f]
and he will show no mercy when he takes revenge.
35 He will not accept any compensation;
he will refuse the bribe, however great it is.[g]

Warning Against the Adulteress

7 My son,[h] keep my words
and store up my commands within you.
2 Keep my commands and you will live;[i]
guard my teachings as the apple of your eye.
3 Bind them on your fingers;
write them on the tablet of your heart.[j]
4 Say to wisdom, "You are my sister,"
and call understanding your kinsman;
5 they will keep you from the adulteress,
from the wayward wife with her seductive words.[k]

6:8 [g]Pr 10:4
6:9 [h]Pr 24:30-34
6:10 [i]Pr 24:33
6:11 [j]Pr 24:30-34
6:13 [k]Ps 35:19
6:14 [l]Mic 2:1 [m]ver 16-19
6:15 [n]2Ch 36:16
6:17 [o]Ps 120:2; Pr 12:22 [p]Dt 19:10; Isa 1:15; 59:7
6:18 [q]Ge 6:5
6:19 [r]Ps 27:12 [s]ver 12-15
6:20 [t]Pr 1:8
6:21 [u]Pr 3:3; 7:1-3
6:23 [v]Ps 19:8; 119:105
6:24 [w]Pr 2:16; 7:5
6:26 [x]Pr 7:22-23; 29:3
6:29 [y]Ex 20:14 [z]Pr 2:16-19; 5:8
6:31 [a]Ex 22:1-14
6:32 [b]Ex 20:14 [c]Pr 7:7; 9:4,16
6:33 [d]Pr 5:9-14
6:34 [e]Nu 5:14 [f]Ge 34:7
6:35 [g]Job 31:9-11; SS 8:7
7:1 [h]Pr 1:8; 2:1
7:2 [i]Pr 4:4
7:3 [j]Dt 6:8; Pr 3:3
7:5 [k]ver 21; Job 31:9; Pr 2:16; 6:24

[a] 11 Or *like a vagrant / and scarcity like a beggar*

[6]At the window of my house
I looked out through the lattice.
[7]I saw among the simple,
I noticed among the young men,
a youth who lacked judgment.[l]
[8]He was going down the street near her corner,
walking along in the direction of her house
[9]at twilight,[m] as the day was fading,
as the dark of night set in.

[10]Then out came a woman to meet him,
dressed like a prostitute and with crafty intent.
[11](She is loud[n] and defiant,
her feet never stay at home;
[12]now in the street, now in the squares,
at every corner she lurks.)[o]
[13]She took hold of him[p] and kissed him
and with a brazen face she said:[q]

[14]"I have fellowship offerings[a][r] at home;
today I fulfilled my vows.
[15]So I came out to meet you;
I looked for you and have found you!
[16]I have covered my bed
with colored linens from Egypt.
[17]I have perfumed my bed[s]
with myrrh,[t] aloes and cinnamon.
[18]Come, let's drink deep of love till morning;
let's enjoy ourselves with love![u]
[19]My husband is not at home;
he has gone on a long journey.
[20]He took his purse filled with money
and will not be home till full moon."

[21]With persuasive words she led him astray;
she seduced him with her smooth talk.[v]
[22]All at once he followed her
like an ox going to the slaughter,
like a deer[b] stepping into a noose[c][w]
[23] till an arrow pierces[x] his liver,
like a bird darting into a snare,
little knowing it will cost him his life.[y]

[24]Now then, my sons, listen[z] to me;
pay attention to what I say.
[25]Do not let your heart turn to her ways
or stray into her paths.[a]
[26]Many are the victims she has brought down;
her slain are a mighty throng.
[27]Her house is a highway to the grave,[d]
leading down to the chambers of death.[b]

Wisdom's Call

8 Does not wisdom call out?[c]
Does not understanding raise her voice?
[2]On the heights along the way, where the paths meet, she takes her stand;
[3]beside the gates leading into the city,
at the entrances, she cries aloud:[d]
[4]"To you, O men, I call out;
I raise my voice to all mankind.
[5]You who are simple,[e] gain prudence;[f]
you who are foolish, gain understanding.

7:1–27

PROMISE 3

SEVENTH COMMANDMENT REVISITED

This chapter presents the last in a series of four warnings against adultery (2:16–19; 5:3–20; 6:20–35; 7:1–27). In the space of seven chapters, Solomon issued four warnings about this destructive sin. The fact that he warned so frequently, and that each warning is so long and so intense, should get our attention.

Each of the warnings moves the focus from the short-term pleasure of sexual sin to its long-range destruction. The warning against adultery, as with other warnings in Proverbs, distinguishes between the fool and the wise man. The wise one in this situation takes the long-range view; the fool lives for the moment. A second common theme in this directive is that succumbing to the wayward woman is always presented as being in direct opposition to wisdom.

Solomon was frantically warning his reader about a terrible danger (perhaps because of his own failures in this regard). He offered three preventative measures that will keep us from this sin: Love your own wife (5:15–20); recognize sin as an issue with the God who observes all (5:21); and think the act through to its ultimate end (2:18–19; 5:7–14; 6:26–35; 7:24–27). Let these passages sink deeply into your soul.

For the next Promise 3 reading go to page 685.

7:7 [l]Pr 1:22; 6:32
7:9 [m]Job 24:15
7:11 [n]Pr 9:13; 1Ti 5:13
7:12 [o]Pr 8:1-36; 23:26-28
7:13 [p]Ge 39:12 [q]Pr 1:20
7:14 [r]Lev 7:11-18
7:17 [s]Est 1:6; Isa 57:7; Eze 23:41; Am 6:4 [t]Ge 37:25
7:18 [u]Ge 39:7
7:21 [v]Pr 5:3
7:22 [w]Job 18:10
7:23 [x]Job 15:22; 16:13 [y]Pr 6:26; Ecc 7:26; 9:12
7:24 [z]Pr 1:8-9; 5:7; 8:32
7:25 [a]Pr 5:7-8
7:27 [b]Pr 2:18; 5:5; 9:18; Rev 22:15
8:1 [c]Pr 1:20; 9:3
8:3 [d]Job 29:7
8:5 [e]Pr 1:22 [f]Pr 1:4

---

a *14* Traditionally *peace offerings* **b** *22* Syriac (see also Septuagint); Hebrew *fool* **c** *22* The meaning of the Hebrew for this line is uncertain. **d** *27* Hebrew *Sheol*

[6]Listen, for I have worthy things to say;
I open my lips to speak what is right.
[7]My mouth speaks what is true,[g]
for my lips detest wickedness.
[8]All the words of my mouth are just;
none of them is crooked or perverse.
[9]To the discerning all of them are right;
they are faultless to those who have knowledge.
[10]Choose my instruction instead of silver,
knowledge rather than choice gold,[h]
[11]for wisdom is more precious[i] than rubies,
and nothing you desire can compare with her.[j]

[12]"I, wisdom, dwell together with prudence;
I possess knowledge and discretion.[k]
[13]To fear the LORD is to hate evil;[l]
I hate[m] pride and arrogance,
evil behavior and perverse speech.
[14]Counsel and sound judgment are mine;
I have understanding and power.[n]
[15]By me kings reign
and rulers[o] make laws that are just;
[16]by me princes govern,
and all nobles who rule on earth.[a]
[17]I love those who love me,[p]
and those who seek me find me.[q]
[18]With me are riches and honor,[r]
enduring wealth and prosperity.[s]
[19]My fruit is better than fine gold;
what I yield surpasses choice silver.[t]
[20]I walk in the way of righteousness,
along the paths of justice,
[21]bestowing wealth on those who love me
and making their treasuries full.[u]

[22]"The LORD brought me forth as the first of his works,[b,c]
before his deeds of old;
[23]I was appointed[d] from eternity,
from the beginning, before the world began.
[24]When there were no oceans, I was given birth,
when there were no springs abounding with water;[v]
[25]before the mountains were settled in place,
before the hills, I was given birth,[w]
[26]before he made the earth or its fields
or any of the dust of the world.[x]
[27]I was there when he set the heavens in place,[y]
when he marked out the horizon on the face of the deep,
[28]when he established the clouds above
and fixed securely the fountains of the deep,
[29]when he gave the sea its boundary[z]
so the waters would not overstep his command,[a]
and when he marked out the foundations of the earth.[b]
[30] Then I was the craftsman at his side.[c]
I was filled with delight day after day,
rejoicing always in his presence,

8:7 [g]Ps 37:30; Jn 8:14
8:10 [h]Pr 3:14-15
8:11 [i]Job 28:17-19 [j]Pr 3:13-15
8:12 [k]Pr 1:4
8:13 [l]Pr 16:6 [m]Jer 44:4
8:14 [n]Pr 21:22; Ecc 7:19
8:15 [o]Da 2:21; Ro 13:1
8:17 [p]1Sa 2:30; Ps 91:14; Jn 14:21-24 [q]Pr 1:28; Jas 1:5
8:18 [r]Pr 3:16 [s]Dt 8:18; Mt 6:33
8:19 [t]Pr 3:13-14; 10:20
8:21 [u]Pr 24:4
8:24 [v]Ge 7:11
8:25 [w]Job 15:7
8:26 [x]Ps 90:2
8:27 [y]Pr 3:19
8:29 [z]Ge 1:9; Job 38:10; Ps 16:6 [a]Ps 104:9 [b]Job 38:5
8:30 [c]Jn 1:1-3

8:1–9:18

PROMISE 3

PLAY IT AGAIN, SOL

Before launching into the actual proverbs, Solomon here made one more attempt to convince the reader to choose wisdom instead of folly. His tactic was to let Lady Wisdom make an extended statement (8:1 to 9:12).

Wisdom urges her listeners to hear her credentials and consider the rewards of following her. Note the contrasts between her promises and the claims of folly as presented in the passages about the wayward woman. While folly can offer immediate and short-lived pleasures, these experiences destroy in the long run. The rewards of wisdom, however, are rich and everlasting.

Solomon said the Proverbs were designed to develop wisdom, discipline and insight (1:1–6). He urged the reader to fear the Lord because that is the first step in knowing (1:7). Then for nine chapters he painted portraits of folly and wisdom so we could graphically see the difference. Most of the rest of this book contains his actual proverbial statements. Read them and meditate on them as a way to avoid folly and pursue wisdom.

For the next Promise 3 reading go to page 687.

[a]*16* Many Hebrew manuscripts and Septuagint; most Hebrew manuscripts *and nobles—all righteous rulers* [b]*22* Or *way,* or *dominion* [c]*22* Or *The LORD possessed me at the beginning of his work;* or *The LORD brought me forth at the beginning of his work* [d]*23* Or *fashioned*

31 rejoicing in his whole world
and delighting in mankind.[d]

32 "Now then, my sons, listen to me;
blessed are[e] those who keep my ways.[f]
33 Listen to my instruction and be wise;
do not ignore it.
34 Blessed is the man who listens[g] to me,
watching daily at my doors,
waiting at my doorway.
35 For whoever finds me[h] finds life
and receives favor from the LORD.[i]
36 But whoever fails to find me harms himself;[j]
all who hate me love death."

Invitations of Wisdom and of Folly

9 Wisdom has built[k] her house;
she has hewn out its seven pillars.
2 She has prepared her meat and mixed her wine;
she has also set her table.[l]
3 She has sent out her maids, and she calls[m]
from the highest point of the city.[n]
4 "Let all who are simple come in here!"
she says to those who lack judgment.[o]
5 "Come, eat my food
and drink the wine I have mixed.[p]
6 Leave your simple ways and you will live;[q]
walk in the way of understanding.

7 "Whoever corrects a mocker invites insult;
whoever rebukes a wicked man incurs abuse.[r]
8 Do not rebuke a mocker[s] or he will hate you;
rebuke a wise man and he will love you.[t]
9 Instruct a wise man and he will be wiser still;
teach a righteous man and he will add to his learning.[u]

10 "The fear of the LORD[v] is the beginning of wisdom,
and knowledge of the Holy One is understanding.
11 For through me your days will be many,
and years will be added to your life.[w]
12 If you are wise, your wisdom will reward you;
if you are a mocker, you alone will suffer."

13 The woman Folly is loud;[x]
she is undisciplined and without knowledge.[y]
14 She sits at the door of her house,
on a seat at the highest point of the city,[z]
15 calling out to those who pass by,
who go straight on their way.
16 "Let all who are simple come in here!"
she says to those who lack judgment.
17 "Stolen water is sweet;
food eaten in secret is delicious![a]"
18 But little do they know that the dead are there,
that her guests are in the depths of the grave.[a][b]

Proverbs of Solomon

10 The proverbs of Solomon:[c]

A wise son brings joy to his father,[d]
but a foolish son grief to his mother.

2 Ill-gotten treasures are of no value,[e]
but righteousness delivers from death.[f]

3 The LORD does not let the righteous go hungry[g]
but he thwarts the craving of the wicked.

4 Lazy hands make a man poor,[h]
but diligent hands bring wealth.[i]

5 He who gathers crops in summer is a wise son,
but he who sleeps during harvest is a disgraceful son.

6 Blessings crown the head of the righteous,
but violence overwhelms the mouth of the wicked.[b][j]

7 The memory of the righteous[k] will be a blessing,
but the name of the wicked[l] will rot.[m]

8 The wise in heart accept commands,
but a chattering fool comes to ruin.[n]

8:31 [d]Ps 16:3; 104:1-30
8:32 [e]Lk 11:28 [f]Ps 119:1-2
8:34 [g]Pr 3:13,18
8:35 [h]Pr 3:13-18 [i]Pr 12:2
8:36 [j]Pr 15:32
9:1 [k]Eph 2:20-22; 1Pe 2:5
9:2 [l]Lk 14:16-23
9:3 [m]Pr 8:1-3 [n]ver 14
9:4 [o]Pr 6:32
9:5 [p]Isa 55:1
9:6 [q]Pr 8:35
9:7 [r]Pr 23:9
9:8 [s]Pr 15:12 [t]Ps 141:5
9:9 [u]Pr 1:5,7
9:10 [v]Job 28:28; Pr 1:7
9:11 [w]Pr 3:16; 10:27
9:13 [x]Pr 7:11 [y]Pr 5:6
9:14 [z]ver 3
9:17 [a]Pr 20:17
9:18 [b]Pr 2:18; 7:26-27
10:1 [c]Pr 1:1 [d]Pr 15:20; 29:3
10:2 [e]Pr 21:6 [f]Pr 11:4,19
10:3 [g]Mt 6:25-34
10:4 [h]Pr 19:15 [i]Pr 12:24; 13:4; 21:5
10:6 [j]ver 8,11,14
10:7 [k]Ps 112:6 [l]Ps 109:13 [m]Ps 9:6
10:8 [n]Mt 7:24-27

[a] *18* Hebrew *Sheol* [b] *6* Or *but the mouth of the wicked conceals violence*; also in verse 11

3 →PG. 688

9The man of integrity[o] walks
securely,[p]
but he who takes crooked paths
will be found out.[q]

10He who winks maliciously[r] causes
grief,
and a chattering fool comes to
ruin.

11The mouth of the righteous is a
fountain of life,[s]
but violence overwhelms the
mouth of the wicked.[t]

12Hatred stirs up dissension,
but love covers over all
wrongs.[u]

13Wisdom is found on the lips of the
discerning,[v]
but a rod is for the back of him
who lacks judgment.[w]

14Wise men store up knowledge,
but the mouth of a fool invites
ruin.[x]

15The wealth of the rich is their
fortified city,[y]
but poverty is the ruin of the
poor.[z]

16The wages of the righteous bring
them life,
but the income of the wicked
brings them punishment.[a]

10:9 [o]Isa 33:15 [p]Ps 23:4 [q]Pr 28:18 **10:10** [r]Ps 35:19 **10:11** [s]Ps 37:30; Pr 13:12,14,19 [t]ver 6 **10:12** [u]Pr 17:9; 1Co 13:4-7; 1Pe 4:8 **10:13** [v]ver 31 [w]Pr 26:3 **10:14** [x]Pr 18:6,7 **10:15** [y]Pr 18:11 [z]Pr 19:7 **10:16** [a]Pr 11:18-19

10:17 [b]Pr 6:23 **10:19** [c]Pr 17:28; Ecc 5:3; Jas 1:19; 3:2-12 **10:21** [d]Pr 5:22-23; Hos 4:1,6,14 **10:22** [e]Ge 24:35; Ps 37:22 **10:23** [f]Pr 2:14; 15:21 **10:24** [g]Isa 66:4 [h]Ps 145:17-19; Mt 5:6; 1Jn 5:14-15

17He who heeds discipline shows the
way to life,[b]
but whoever ignores correction
leads others astray.

18He who conceals his hatred has
lying lips,
and whoever spreads slander is a
fool.

19When words are many, sin is not
absent,
but he who holds his tongue is
wise.[c]

20The tongue of the righteous is
choice silver,
but the heart of the wicked is of
little value.

21The lips of the righteous nourish
many,
but fools die for lack of
judgment.[d]

22The blessing of the LORD brings
wealth,[e]
and he adds no trouble to it.

23A fool finds pleasure in evil
conduct,[f]
but a man of understanding
delights in wisdom.

24What the wicked dreads[g] will
overtake him;
what the righteous desire will be
granted.[h]

10:8

PROMISE 3

SPEAKING IN PROVERBS

The Book of Proverbs is known for its practical application of God's truth to life's issues. Communication is one of those issues. In the home, the workplace, the community or wherever we may find ourselves, we communicate. In fact, we don't ever *not* communicate. Even our silence makes a statement.

Communication involves both understanding and being understood. This brief summary will focus on the speaking half of the equation. James wrote, "If anyone is never at fault in what he says, he is a perfect man . . ." (James 3:2). As you think about your speaking, ask if what you say helps or hurts, develops or deteriorates those with whom you communicate.

Proverbs addresses both helpful and hurtful speaking. By their very nature, the proverbs compare and contrast these two kinds of statements in the same verse. As you read these wise sayings, notice these two categories, but don't fail to see the power of understanding one in relation to the other.

THE WAY WORDS ARE USED	REFERENCES IN PROVERBS
Tell the Truth / Deceive	6:16-17; 7:19-20; 10:18; 12:2,17,19,22; 14:5, 25; 15:4; 17:4,7; 19:5,9,22; 21:6; 25:23; 26:28
Build Up / Tear Down Others	10:11, 20-21; 12:14,18; 15:4; 18:4,20-21; 26:23, 28; 28:23; 29:5
Kind and Affirming / Mocking and Quarreling	10:32; 12:25; 13:1, 10; 14:6; 15:1,4,12,18,23; 16:24; 17:5,14,19; 19:13,29; 20:3; 21:9,11,19; 22:10; 24:9; 25:11,15,24; 26:17, 20-21; 30:17
Wise / Foolish	10:13, 31; 14:3,7; 15:2, 7-14; 16:10,21,23; 18:6,7; 20:15
Careful / Careless	10:31-32; 12:18; 13:3; 14:3; 15:1,28; 16:3; 19:1,28; 21:23
Few / Many	10:8, 10, 18-19; 13:3; 17:27-28; 18:2; 20:19
Gossip / Slander	10:18; 11:13; 16:28; 17:9; 18:8; 20:19; 26:20, 22; 30:10
Boasting	17:17; 20:14; 25:14; 27:1-2

For the next Promise 3 reading go to page 726.

25 When the storm has swept by, the
wicked are gone,
but the righteous stand firm[i]
forever.[j]

26 As vinegar to the teeth and smoke
to the eyes,
so is a sluggard to those who
send him.[k]

27 The fear of the LORD adds length to
life,[l]
but the years of the wicked are
cut short.[m]

28 The prospect of the righteous is
joy,
but the hopes of the wicked
come to nothing.[n]

29 The way of the LORD is a refuge for
the righteous,
but it is the ruin of those who do
evil.[o]

30 The righteous will never be
uprooted,
but the wicked will not remain
in the land.[p]

31 The mouth of the righteous brings
forth wisdom,[q]
but a perverse tongue will be cut
out.

32 The lips of the righteous know
what is fitting,[r]
but the mouth of the wicked
only what is perverse.

11 The LORD abhors dishonest
scales,[s]
but accurate weights are his
delight.[t]

2 When pride comes, then comes
disgrace,[u]
but with humility comes
wisdom.[v]

3 The integrity of the upright guides
them,
but the unfaithful are destroyed
by their duplicity.[w]

4 Wealth is worthless in the day of
wrath,[x]
but righteousness delivers from
death.[y]

3 →PG. 692

5 The righteousness of the blameless
makes a straight way for
them,
but the wicked are brought down
by their own wickedness.[z]

6 The righteousness of the upright
delivers them,
but the unfaithful are trapped by
evil desires.

7 When a wicked man dies, his hope
perishes;
all he expected from his power
comes to nothing.[a]

8 The righteous man is rescued from
trouble,
and it comes on the wicked
instead.[b]

9 With his mouth the godless
destroys his neighbor,
but through knowledge the
righteous escape.

10 When the righteous prosper, the
city rejoices;[c]
when the wicked perish, there
are shouts of joy.

11 Through the blessing of the upright
a city is exalted,
but by the mouth of the wicked
it is destroyed.[d]

12 A man who lacks judgment derides
his neighbor,[e]
but a man of understanding
holds his tongue.

13 A gossip betrays a confidence,[f]
but a trustworthy man keeps a
secret.

14 For lack of guidance a nation
falls,[g]
but many advisers make victory
sure.[h]

15 He who puts up security[i] for
another will surely suffer,
but whoever refuses to strike
hands in pledge is safe.

16 A kindhearted woman gains
respect,[j]
but ruthless men gain only
wealth.

17 A kind man benefits himself,
but a cruel man brings trouble
on himself.

18 The wicked man earns deceptive
wages,
but he who sows righteousness
reaps a sure reward.[k]

19 The truly righteous man attains life,
but he who pursues evil goes to
his death.

20 The LORD detests men of perverse
heart
but he delights in those whose
ways are blameless.[l]

21 Be sure of this: The wicked will not
go unpunished,
but those who are righteous will
go free.[m]

22 Like a gold ring in a pig's snout
is a beautiful woman who shows
no discretion.

10:25 [i]Ps 15:5 [j]Pr 12:3,7; Mt 7:24-27
10:26 [k]Pr 26:6
10:27 [l]Pr 9:10-11 [m]Job 15:32
10:28 [n]Job 8:13; Pr 11:7
10:29 [o]Pr 21:15
10:30 [p]Ps 37:9, 28-29; Pr 2:20-22
10:31 [q]Ps 37:30
10:32 [r]Ecc 10:12
11:1 [s]Lev 19:36; Dt 25:13-16; Pr 20:10,23 [t]Pr 16:11
11:2 [u]Pr 16:18 [v]Pr 18:12; 29:23
11:3 [w]Pr 13:6
11:4 [x]Eze 7:19; Zep 1:18 [y]Ge 7:1; Pr 10:2
11:5 [z]Pr 5:21-23
11:7 [a]Pr 10:28
11:8 [b]Pr 21:18
11:10 [c]Pr 28:12
11:11 [d]Pr 29:8
11:12 [e]Pr 14:21
11:13 [f]Lev 19:16; Pr 20:19; 1Ti 5:13
11:14 [g]Pr 20:18 [h]Pr 15:22; 24:6
11:15 [i]Pr 6:1
11:16 [j]Pr 31:31
11:18 [k]Hos 10:12-13
11:20 [l]1Ch 29:17; Ps 119:1; Pr 12:2,22
11:21 [m]Pr 16:5

23 The desire of the righteous ends
only in good,
but the hope of the wicked only
in wrath.

24 One man gives freely, yet gains
even more;
another withholds unduly, but
comes to poverty.

25 A generous man will prosper;
he who refreshes others will
himself be refreshed.[n]

26 People curse the man who hoards
grain,
but blessing crowns him who is
willing to sell.

27 He who seeks good finds goodwill,
but evil comes to him who
searches for it.[o]

28 Whoever trusts in his riches will
fall,[p]
but the righteous will thrive like
a green leaf.[q]

29 He who brings trouble on his
family will inherit only
wind,
and the fool will be servant to
the wise.[r]

30 The fruit of the righteous is a tree
of life,[s]
and he who wins souls is wise.

31 If the righteous receive their due[t]
on earth,
how much more the ungodly
and the sinner!

12 Whoever loves discipline loves
knowledge,
but he who hates correction is
stupid.[u]

2 A good man obtains favor from the
LORD,
but the LORD condemns a crafty
man.

3 A man cannot be established
through wickedness,
but the righteous cannot be
uprooted.[v]

4 A wife of noble character is her
husband's crown,
but a disgraceful wife is like
decay in his bones.[w]

5 The plans of the righteous are just,
but the advice of the wicked is
deceitful.

6 The words of the wicked lie in wait
for blood,
but the speech of the upright
rescues them.[x]

11:25 [n]Mt 5:7; 2Co 9:6-9 **11:27** [o]Est 7:10; Ps 7:15-16 **11:28** [p]Job 31:24-28; Ps 49:6; 52:7; Mk 10:25; 1Ti 6:17 [q]Ps 1:3; 92:12-14; Jer 17:8 **11:29** [r]Pr 14:19 **11:30** [s]Jas 5:20 **11:31** [t]Pr 13:21; Jer 25:29; 1Pe 4:18 **12:1** [u]Pr 9:7-9; 15:5,10,12,32 **12:3** [v]Pr 10:25 **12:4** [w]Pr 14:30 **12:6** [x]Pr 14:3

7 Wicked men are overthrown and
are no more,[y]
but the house of the righteous
stands firm.[z]

8 A man is praised according to his
wisdom,
but men with warped minds are
despised.

9 Better to be a nobody and yet have
a servant
than pretend to be somebody
and have no food.

10 A righteous man cares for the
needs of his animal,
but the kindest acts of the
wicked are cruel.

11 He who works his land will have
abundant food,
but he who chases fantasies
lacks judgment.[a]

12 The wicked desire the plunder of
evil men,
but the root of the righteous
flourishes.

13 An evil man is trapped by his sinful
talk,[b]
but a righteous man escapes
trouble.[c]

14 From the fruit of his lips a man is
filled with good things[d]
as surely as the work of his
hands rewards him.[e]

15 The way of a fool seems right to
him,[f]
but a wise man listens to advice.

16 A fool shows his annoyance at
once,
but a prudent man overlooks an
insult.[g]

17 A truthful witness gives honest
testimony,
but a false witness tells lies.[h]

18 Reckless words pierce like a
sword,[i]
but the tongue of the wise brings
healing.[j]

19 Truthful lips endure forever,
but a lying tongue lasts only a
moment.

20 There is deceit in the hearts of
those who plot evil,
but joy for those who promote
peace.

21 No harm befalls the righteous,[k]
but the wicked have their fill of
trouble.

22 The LORD detests lying lips,[l]

12:7 [y]Ps 37:36 [z]Pr 10:25 **12:11** [a]Pr 28:19 **12:13** [b]Pr 18:7 [c]Pr 21:23; 2Pe 2:9 **12:14** [d]Pr 13:2; 15:23; 18:20 [e]Isa 3:10-11 **12:15** [f]Pr 14:12; 16:2,25; Lk 18:11 **12:16** [g]Pr 29:11 **12:17** [h]Pr 14:5,25 **12:18** [i]Ps 57:4 [j]Pr 15:4 **12:21** [k]Ps 91:10 **12:22** [l]Pr 6:17; Rev 22:15

but he delights in men who are
truthful.[m]

23A prudent man keeps his
knowledge to himself,[n]
but the heart of fools blurts out
folly.

24Diligent hands will rule,
but laziness ends in slave
labor.[o]

25An anxious heart weighs a man
down,[p]
but a kind word cheers him up.

26A righteous man is cautious in
friendship,[a]
but the way of the wicked leads
them astray.

27The lazy man does not roast[b] his
game,
but the diligent man prizes his
possessions.

28In the way of righteousness there is
life;[q]
along that path is immortality.

4 →PG. 690

13

1A wise son heeds his father's
instruction,
but a mocker does not listen to
rebuke.[r]

2From the fruit of his lips a man
enjoys good things,[s]
but the unfaithful have a craving
for violence.

3He who guards his lips[t] guards his
life,[u]
but he who speaks rashly will
come to ruin.[v]

4The sluggard craves and gets
nothing,
but the desires of the diligent are
fully satisfied.

5The righteous hate what is false,
but the wicked bring shame and
disgrace.

6Righteousness guards the man of
integrity,
but wickedness overthrows the
sinner.[w]

7One man pretends to be rich, yet
has nothing;
another pretends to be poor, yet
has great wealth.[x]

8A man's riches may ransom his life,
but a poor man hears no threat.

9The light of the righteous shines
brightly,
but the lamp of the wicked is
snuffed out.[y]

10Pride only breeds quarrels,
but wisdom is found in those
who take advice.

11Dishonest money dwindles away,[z]
but he who gathers money little
by little makes it grow.

12Hope deferred makes the heart
sick,
but a longing fulfilled is a tree of
life.

13He who scorns instruction will pay
for it,[a]
but he who respects a command
is rewarded.

14The teaching of the wise is a
fountain of life,[b]
turning a man from the snares of
death.[c]

15Good understanding wins favor,
but the way of the unfaithful is
hard.[c]

16Every prudent man acts out of
knowledge,
but a fool exposes his folly.[d]

17A wicked messenger falls into
trouble,
but a trustworthy envoy brings
healing.[e]

18He who ignores discipline comes to
poverty and shame,
but whoever heeds correction is
honored.[f]

19A longing fulfilled is sweet to the
soul,
but fools detest turning from
evil.

20He who walks with the wise grows
wise,
but a companion of fools suffers
harm.[g]

21Misfortune pursues the sinner,
but prosperity is the reward of
the righteous.[h]

22A good man leaves an inheritance
for his children's children,
but a sinner's wealth is stored up
for the righteous.[i]

4 →PG. 690

23A poor man's field may produce
abundant food,
but injustice sweeps it away.

24He who spares the rod hates his
son,
but he who loves him is careful
to discipline him.[j]

4 →PG. 694

25The righteous eat to their hearts'
content,

[a]26 Or *man is a guide to his neighbor*
[b]27 The meaning of the Hebrew for this word is uncertain.
[c]15 Or *unfaithful does not endure*

12:22 [m]Pr 11:20
12:23 [n]Pr 10:14; 13:16
12:24 [o]Pr 10:4
12:25 [p]Pr 15:13; Isa 50:4
12:28 [q]Dt 30:15
13:1 [r]Pr 10:1
13:2 [s]Pr 12:14
13:3 [t]Jas 3:2 [u]Pr 21:23 [v]Pr 18:7,20-21
13:6 [w]Pr 11:3,5
13:7 [x]2Co 6:10
13:9 [y]Job 18:5; Pr 4:18-19; 24:20
13:11 [z]Pr 10:2
13:13 [a]Nu 15:31; 2Ch 36:16
13:14 [b]Pr 10:11 [c]Pr 14:27
13:16 [d]Pr 12:23
13:17 [e]Pr 25:13
13:18 [f]Pr 15:5,31-32
13:20 [g]Pr 15:31
13:21 [h]Ps 32:10
13:22 [i]Job 27:17; Ecc 2:26
13:24 [j]Pr 19:18; 22:15; 23:13-14; 29:15,17; Heb 12:7

but the stomach of the wicked
goes hungry.[k]

14 The wise woman builds her
house,[l]
but with her own hands the
foolish one tears hers down.

2He whose walk is upright fears the
LORD,
but he whose ways are devious
despises him.

3A fool's talk brings a rod to his
back,
but the lips of the wise protect
them.[m]

4Where there are no oxen, the
manger is empty,
but from the strength of an ox
comes an abundant harvest.

5A truthful witness does not deceive,
but a false witness pours out
lies.[n]

6The mocker seeks wisdom and
finds none,
but knowledge comes easily to
the discerning.

7Stay away from a foolish man,
for you will not find knowledge
on his lips.

8The wisdom of the prudent is to
give thought to their ways,
but the folly of fools is
deception.[o]

9Fools mock at making amends for
sin,
but goodwill is found among the
upright.

10Each heart knows its own
bitterness,
and no one else can share its
joy.

11The house of the wicked will be
destroyed,
but the tent of the upright will
flourish.[p]

12There is a way that seems right to a
man,[q]
but in the end it leads to
death.[r]

13Even in laughter[s] the heart may
ache,
and joy may end in grief.

14The faithless will be fully repaid for
their ways,[t]
and the good man rewarded for
his.[u]

15A simple man believes anything,
but a prudent man gives thought
to his steps.

16A wise man fears the LORD and
shuns evil,[v]
but a fool is hotheaded and
reckless.

17A quick-tempered man does foolish
things,[w]
and a crafty man is hated.

18The simple inherit folly,
but the prudent are crowned
with knowledge.

19Evil men will bow down in the
presence of the good,
and the wicked at the gates of
the righteous.[x]

7 →PG. 697

20The poor are shunned even by
their neighbors,
but the rich have many
friends.[y]

21He who despises his neighbor
sins,[z]
but blessed is he who is kind to
the needy.[a]

22Do not those who plot evil go
astray?
But those who plan what is good
find[a] love and faithfulness.

23All hard work brings a profit,
but mere talk leads only to
poverty.

24The wealth of the wise is their
crown,
but the folly of fools yields folly.

25A truthful witness saves lives,
but a false witness is deceitful.[b]

26He who fears the LORD has a secure
fortress,[c]
and for his children it will be a
refuge.

27The fear of the LORD is a fountain
of life,
turning a man from the snares of
death.[d]

28A large population is a king's glory,
but without subjects a prince is
ruined.

29A patient man has great
understanding,
but a quick-tempered man
displays folly.[e]

30A heart at peace gives life to the
body,
but envy rots the bones.[f]

31He who oppresses the poor shows
contempt for their Maker,[g]
but whoever is kind to the needy
honors God.

13:25 [k]Ps 34:10; Pr 10:3
14:1 [l]Pr 24:3
14:3 [m]Pr 12:6
14:5 [n]Pr 6:19; 12:17
14:8 [o]ver 24
14:11 [p]Pr 3:33; 12:7
14:12 [q]Pr 12:15 [r]Pr 16:25
14:13 [s]Ecc 2:2
14:14 [t]Pr 1:31 [u]Pr 12:14
14:16 [v]Pr 22:3
14:17 [w]ver 29
14:19 [x]Pr 11:29
14:20 [y]Pr 19:4,7
14:21 [z]Pr 11:12 [a]Ps 41:1; Pr 19:17
14:25 [b]ver 5
14:26 [c]Pr 18:10; 19:23; Isa 33:6
14:27 [d]Pr 13:14
14:29 [e]Ecc 7:8-9; Jas 1:19
14:30 [f]Pr 12:4
14:31 [g]Pr 17:5

[a]22 Or *show*

32When calamity comes, the wicked
are brought down,[h]
but even in death the righteous
have a refuge.[i]

33Wisdom reposes in the heart of the
discerning[j]
and even among fools she lets
herself be known.[a]

34Righteousness exalts a nation,[k]
but sin is a disgrace to any
people.

35A king delights in a wise servant,
but a shameful servant incurs his
wrath.[l]

3 →PG. 699

15 A gentle answer turns away
wrath,[m]
but a harsh word stirs up anger.

2The tongue of the wise commends
knowledge,
but the mouth of the fool gushes
folly.[n]

3The eyes[o] of the LORD are
everywhere,[p]
keeping watch on the wicked
and the good.[q]

4The tongue that brings healing is a
tree of life,
but a deceitful tongue crushes
the spirit.

5A fool spurns his father's discipline,
but whoever heeds correction
shows prudence.[r]

6The house of the righteous
contains great treasure,[s]
but the income of the wicked
brings them trouble.

7The lips of the wise spread
knowledge;
not so the hearts of fools.

8The LORD detests the sacrifice of
the wicked,[t]
but the prayer of the upright
pleases him.[u]

9The LORD detests the way of the
wicked
but he loves those who pursue
righteousness.[v]

10Stern discipline awaits him who
leaves the path;
he who hates correction will
die.[w]

11Death and Destruction[b] lie open
before the LORD[x]—
how much more the hearts of
men![y]

12A mocker resents correction;[z]
he will not consult the wise.

14:32 [h]Pr 6:15 [i]Job 13:15; 2Ti 4:18
14:33 [j]Pr 2:6-10
14:34 [k]Pr 11:11
14:35 [l]Mt 24:45-51; 25:14-30
15:1 [m]Pr 25:15
15:2 [n]Pr 12:23
15:3 [o]2Ch 16:9 [p]Job 31:4; Heb 4:13 [q]Job 34:21; Jer 16:17
15:5 [r]Pr 13:1
15:6 [s]Pr 8:21
15:8 [t]Pr 21:27; Isa 1:11; Jer 6:20 [u]ver 29
15:9 [v]Pr 21:21; 1Ti 6:11
15:10 [w]Pr 1:31-32; 5:12
15:11 [x]Job 26:6; Ps 139:8 [y]2Ch 6:30; Ps 44:21
15:12 [z]Am 5:10
15:13 [a]Pr 12:25; 17:22; 18:14
15:14 [b]Pr 18:15
15:15 [c]ver 13
15:16 [d]Ps 37:16-17; Pr 16:8; 1Ti 6:6
15:17 [e]Pr 17:1
15:18 [f]Pr 26:21 [g]Ge 13:8
15:19 [h]Pr 22:5
15:20 [i]Pr 10:1
15:21 [j]Pr 10:23
15:22 [k]Pr 11:14
15:23 [l]Pr 12:14 [m]Pr 25:11
15:25 [n]Pr 12:7 [o]Dt 19:14; Ps 68:5-6; Pr 23:10-11
15:26 [p]Pr 6:16

13A happy heart makes the face
cheerful,
but heartache crushes the
spirit.[a]

14The discerning heart seeks
knowledge,[b]
but the mouth of a fool feeds on
folly.

15All the days of the oppressed are
wretched,
but the cheerful heart has a
continual feast.[c]

16Better a little with the fear of the
LORD
than great wealth with turmoil.[d]

17Better a meal of vegetables where
there is love
than a fattened calf with
hatred.[e]

18A hot-tempered man stirs up
dissension,[f]
but a patient man calms a
quarrel.[g]

19The way of the sluggard is blocked
with thorns,[h]
but the path of the upright is a
highway.

20A wise son brings joy to his
father,[i]
but a foolish man despises his
mother.

21Folly delights a man who lacks
judgment,[j]
but a man of understanding
keeps a straight course.

2 →PG. 695

22Plans fail for lack of counsel,
but with many advisers they
succeed.[k]

23A man finds joy in giving an apt
reply[l]—
and how good is a timely
word![m]

24The path of life leads upward for
the wise
to keep him from going down to
the grave.[c]

25The LORD tears down the proud
man's house[n]
but he keeps the widow's
boundaries intact.[o]

26The LORD detests the thoughts of
the wicked,[p]
but those of the pure are
pleasing to him.

[a] 33 Hebrew; Septuagint and Syriac / *but in the heart of fools she is not known* [b] 11 Hebrew *Sheol and Abaddon* [c] 24 Hebrew *Sheol*

27 A greedy man brings trouble to his family,
but he who hates bribes will live.[q]

28 The heart of the righteous weighs its answers,[r]
but the mouth of the wicked gushes evil.

29 The LORD is far from the wicked
but he hears the prayer of the righteous.[s]

30 A cheerful look brings joy to the heart,
and good news gives health to the bones.

31 He who listens to a life-giving rebuke
will be at home among the wise.[t]

32 He who ignores discipline despises himself,[u]
but whoever heeds correction gains understanding.

33 The fear of the LORD[v] teaches a man wisdom,[a]
and humility comes before honor.[w]

16 To man belong the plans of the heart,
but from the LORD comes the reply of the tongue.[x]

2 All a man's ways seem innocent to him,
but motives are weighed by the LORD.[y]

3 Commit to the LORD whatever you do,
and your plans will succeed.[z]

4 The LORD works out everything for his own ends[a]—
even the wicked for a day of disaster.[b]

5 The LORD detests all the proud of heart.[c]
Be sure of this: They will not go unpunished.[d]

6 Through love and faithfulness sin is atoned for;
through the fear of the LORD a man avoids evil.[e]

7 When a man's ways are pleasing to the LORD,
he makes even his enemies live at peace with him.

8 Better a little with righteousness
than much gain[f] with injustice.

9 In his heart a man plans his course,
but the LORD determines his steps.[g]

10 The lips of a king speak as an oracle,
and his mouth should not betray justice.

11 Honest scales and balances are from the LORD;
all the weights in the bag are of his making.[h]

12 Kings detest wrongdoing,
for a throne is established through righteousness.[i]

13 Kings take pleasure in honest lips;
they value a man who speaks the truth.[j]

14 A king's wrath is a messenger of death,[k]
but a wise man will appease it.

15 When a king's face brightens, it means life;[l]
his favor is like a rain cloud in spring.

16 How much better to get wisdom than gold,
to choose understanding rather than silver![m]

17 The highway of the upright avoids evil;
he who guards his way guards his life.

18 Pride goes before destruction,
a haughty spirit before a fall.[n]

19 Better to be lowly in spirit and among the oppressed
than to share plunder with the proud.

20 Whoever gives heed to instruction prospers,
and blessed is he who trusts in the LORD.[o]

21 The wise in heart are called discerning,
and pleasant words promote instruction.[b][p]

22 Understanding is a fountain of life to those who have it,[q]
but folly brings punishment to fools.

23 A wise man's heart guides his mouth,
and his lips promote instruction.[c]

24 Pleasant words are a honeycomb,

15:27 [q]Ex 23:8; Isa 33:15 **15:28** [r]1Pe 3:15 **15:29** [s]Ps 145:18-19 **15:31** [t]ver 5 **15:32** [u]Pr 1:7 **15:33** [v]Pr 1:7 [w]Pr 18:12 **16:1** [x]Pr 19:21 **16:2** [y]Pr 21:2 **16:3** [z]Ps 37:5-6; Pr 3:5-6 **16:4** [a]Isa 43:7 [b]Ro 9:22 **16:5** [c]Pr 6:16 [d]Pr 11:20-21 **16:6** [e]Pr 14:16 **16:8** [f]Ps 37:16

16:9 [g]Jer 10:23 **16:11** [h]Pr 11:1 **16:12** [i]Pr 25:5 **16:13** [j]Pr 14:35 **16:14** [k]Pr 19:12 **16:15** [l]Job 29:24 **16:16** [m]Pr 8:10,19 **16:18** [n]Pr 11:2; 18:12 **16:20** [o]Ps 2:12; 34:8; Pr 19:8; Jer 17:7 **16:21** [p]ver 23 **16:22** [q]Pr 13:14

[a]33 Or *Wisdom teaches the fear of the LORD*
[b]21 Or *words make a man persuasive*
[c]23 Or *mouth / and makes his lips persuasive*

sweet to the soul and healing to
the bones.[r]

25 There is a way that seems right to a
man,[s]
but in the end it leads to
death.[t]

26 The laborer's appetite works for
him;
his hunger drives him on.

27 A scoundrel plots evil,
and his speech is like a
scorching fire.[u]

28 A perverse man stirs up
dissension,[v]
and a gossip separates close
friends.[w]

29 A violent man entices his neighbor
and leads him down a path that
is not good.[x]

30 He who winks with his eye is
plotting perversity;
he who purses his lips is bent on
evil.

31 Gray hair is a crown of splendor;[y]
it is attained by a righteous life.

32 Better a patient man than a
warrior,
a man who controls his temper
than one who takes a city.

33 The lot is cast into the lap,
but its every decision is from the
LORD.[z]

17 Better a dry crust with peace and
quiet
than a house full of feasting,[a]
with strife.[a]

2 A wise servant will rule over a
disgraceful son,
and will share the inheritance as
one of the brothers.

3 The crucible for silver and the
furnace for gold,[b]
but the LORD tests the heart.[c]

4 A wicked man listens to evil lips;
a liar pays attention to a
malicious tongue.

5 He who mocks the poor shows
contempt for their Maker;[d]
whoever gloats over disaster[e]
will not go unpunished.[f]

4 →PG. 695

6 Children's children[g] are a crown
to the aged,
and parents are the pride of their
children.

7 Arrogant[b] lips are unsuited to a
fool—
how much worse lying lips to a
ruler!

8 A bribe is a charm to the one who
gives it;
wherever he turns, he succeeds.

9 He who covers over an offense
promotes love,[h]
but whoever repeats the matter
separates close friends.[i]

10 A rebuke impresses a man of
discernment
more than a hundred lashes a
fool.

11 An evil man is bent only on
rebellion;
a merciless official will be sent
against him.

12 Better to meet a bear robbed of her
cubs
than a fool in his folly.

13 If a man pays back evil[j] for good,
evil will never leave his house.

14 Starting a quarrel is like breaching
a dam;
so drop the matter before a
dispute breaks out.[k]

15 Acquitting the guilty and
condemning the
innocent[l]—
the LORD detests them both.[m]

16 Of what use is money in the hand
of a fool,
since he has no desire to get
wisdom?[n]

17 A friend loves at all times,
and a brother is born for
adversity.

18 A man lacking in judgment strikes
hands in pledge
and puts up security for his
neighbor.[o]

19 He who loves a quarrel loves sin;
he who builds a high gate invites
destruction.

20 A man of perverse heart does not
prosper;
he whose tongue is deceitful falls
into trouble.

21 To have a fool for a son brings
grief;
there is no joy for the father of a
fool.[p]

22 A cheerful heart is good medicine,
but a crushed spirit dries up the
bones.[q]

23 A wicked man accepts a bribe[r] in
secret
to pervert the course of justice.

16:24 [r] Pr 24:13-14
16:25 [s] Pr 12:15 [t] Pr 14:12
16:27 [u] Jas 3:6
16:28 [v] Pr 15:18 [w] Pr 17:9
16:29 [x] Pr 1:10; 12:26
16:31 [y] Pr 20:29
16:33 [z] Pr 18:18; 29:26
17:1 [a] Pr 15:16,17
17:3 [b] Pr 27:21 [c] 1Ch 29:17; Ps 26:2; Jer 17:10
17:5 [d] Pr 14:31 [e] Job 31:29 [f] Ob 1:12
17:6 [g] Pr 13:22
17:9 [h] Pr 10:12 [i] Pr 16:28
17:13 [j] Ps 109:4-5; Jer 18:20
17:14 [k] Pr 20:3
17:15 [l] Pr 18:5 [m] Ex 23:6-7; Isa 5:23
17:16 [n] Pr 23:23
17:18 [o] Pr 6:1-5; 11:15; 22:26-27
17:21 [p] Pr 10:1
17:22 [q] Ps 22:15; Pr 15:13
17:23 [r] Ex 23:8

[a] *1* Hebrew *sacrifices* [b] *7* Or *Eloquent*

24 A discerning man keeps wisdom in view,
but a fool's eyes[s] wander to the ends of the earth.

25 A foolish son brings grief to his father
and bitterness to the one who bore him.[t]

26 It is not good to punish an innocent man,[u]
or to flog officials for their integrity.

27 A man of knowledge uses words with restraint,
and a man of understanding is even-tempered.[v]

28 Even a fool is thought wise if he keeps silent,
and discerning if he holds his tongue.[w]

18 An unfriendly man pursues selfish ends;
he defies all sound judgment.

2 A fool finds no pleasure in understanding
but delights in airing his own opinions.[x]

3 When wickedness comes, so does contempt,
and with shame comes disgrace.

4 The words of a man's mouth are deep waters,
but the fountain of wisdom is a bubbling brook.

5 It is not good to be partial to the wicked[y]
or to deprive the innocent of justice.[z]

6 A fool's lips bring him strife,
and his mouth invites a beating.

7 A fool's mouth is his undoing,
and his lips are a snare[a] to his soul.[b]

8 The words of a gossip are like choice morsels;
they go down to a man's inmost parts.[c]

9 One who is slack in his work
is brother to one who destroys.[d]

10 The name of the LORD is a strong tower;[e]
the righteous run to it and are safe.

11 The wealth of the rich is their fortified city;[f]
they imagine it an unscalable wall.

12 Before his downfall a man's heart is proud,
but humility comes before honor.[g]

13 He who answers before listening—
that is his folly and his shame.[h]

14 A man's spirit sustains him in sickness,
but a crushed spirit who can bear?[i]

15 The heart of the discerning acquires knowledge;[j]
the ears of the wise seek it out.

16 A gift[k] opens the way for the giver
and ushers him into the presence of the great.

17 The first to present his case seems right,
till another comes forward and questions him.

18 Casting the lot settles disputes[l]
and keeps strong opponents apart.

19 An offended brother is more unyielding than a fortified city,
and disputes are like the barred gates of a citadel.

20 From the fruit of his mouth a man's stomach is filled;
with the harvest from his lips he is satisfied.[m]

21 The tongue has the power of life and death,
and those who love it will eat its fruit.[n]

22 He who finds a wife finds what is good[o]
and receives favor from the LORD.[p]

4 →PG. 697

23 A poor man pleads for mercy,
but a rich man answers harshly.

24 A man of many companions may come to ruin,
but there is a friend who sticks closer than a brother.[q]

2 →PG. 701

19 Better a poor man whose walk is blameless
than a fool whose lips are perverse.[r]

2 It is not good to have zeal without knowledge,
nor to be hasty and miss the way.[s]

3 A man's own folly ruins his life,
yet his heart rages against the LORD.

4 Wealth brings many friends,

17:24 [s]Ecc 2:14 **17:25** [t]Pr 10:1 **17:26** [u]Pr 18:5 **17:27** [v]Pr 14:29; Jas 1:19 **17:28** [w]Job 13:5 **18:2** [x]Pr 12:23 **18:5** [y]Lev 19:15; Pr 24:23-25; 28:21 [z]Ps 82:2; Pr 17:15 **18:7** [a]Ps 140:9 [b]Ps 64:8; Pr 10:14; 12:13; 13:3; Ecc 10:12 **18:8** [c]Pr 26:22 **18:9** [d]Pr 28:24 **18:10** [e]2Sa 22:3; Ps 61:3 **18:11** [f]Pr 10:15 **18:12** [g]Pr 11:2; 15:33; 16:18 **18:13** [h]Pr 20:25; Jn 7:51 **18:14** [i]Pr 15:13; 17:22 **18:15** [j]Pr 15:14 **18:16** [k]Ge 32:20 **18:18** [l]Pr 16:33 **18:20** [m]Pr 12:14 **18:21** [n]Pr 13:2-3; Mt 12:37 **18:22** [o]Pr 12:4 [p]Pr 19:14; 31:10 **18:24** [q]Pr 17:17; Jn 15:13-15 **19:1** [r]Pr 28:6 **19:2** [s]Pr 29:20

but a poor man's friend deserts
him.[t]

5A false witness[u] will not go
unpunished,
and he who pours out lies will
not go free.[v]

6Many curry favor with a ruler,[w]
and everyone is the friend of a
man who gives gifts.[x]

7A poor man is shunned by all his
relatives—
how much more do his friends
avoid him!
Though he pursues them with
pleading,
they are nowhere to be
found.[a][y]

8He who gets wisdom loves his own
soul;
he who cherishes understanding
prospers.[z]

19:4 [t]Pr 14:20
19:5 [u]Ex 23:1 [v]Dt 19:19; Pr 21:28
19:6 [w]Pr 29:26 [x]Pr 17:8; 18:16
19:7 [y]ver 4; Ps 38:11
19:8 [z]Pr 16:20

[a]7 The meaning of the Hebrew for this sentence is uncertain.

19:1

PE

PROVERBS' MAIN PLAYERS

The Book of Proverbs contains an enormous amount of teaching and advice: statements about money, marriage, sex, work, relationships, communication, education, discipline, godliness . . . and the list goes on. The teaching can be organized around four main characters who keep surfacing throughout the book.

Two characters, the Wise and the Godly, are presented as models for those who follow the teaching of Proverbs. Their counterparts, the Fool and the Wicked, are presented as warnings against ignoring what Proverbs teaches. Carefully study these four characters as models and as warnings.

The references to each of these characters are too numerous to include, so as you read this chart understand that the passages included are extremely limited. You might want to do a more thorough study on your own.

WHAT CHARACTERIZES	
The Wise	**The Fool**
In Proverbs the wise person is seen as one who develops four skills and uses them well. 1. The ability to gather information, to learn facts, to seek and find knowledge (2:1-5; 8:10-11; 10:14; 15:14). 2. The ability to develop insight, sharpness of understanding and discernment. A wise person works to understand the information he gathers (1:5; 10:13; 14:6; 16:21; 17:28; 19:11). 3. The ability to comprehend issues, develop mental sophistication and expand breadth of experience (1:3; 10:15; 16:20; 19; 19:11, 20; 21:11). 4. To combine the three functions in a way that results in skilled use of the mind. The word translated "wisdom" in Proverbs is translated "skill" in many other Old Testament passages. It is used 312 times in Proverbs (1:2,7; 2:2; 4:5,11).	Three words are translated "fool" in Proverbs. 1. The first kind of fool has no desire to learn (1:22; 18:2) and is interested only in foolishness (15:2,14). He is characterized by insufficient mental ability. 2. The second kind, a bit more intense in his foolishness, is morally perverse and insolent. He is more sinful than stupid (1:7; 14:9) and he is a trouble maker (12:16; 20:3). 3. The third kind of fool is ignoble. He has no sense of ethics or religion and is shameless and uncaring (17:7,21; 30:32).

WHAT HAPPENS TO	
The Wise	**The Fool**
He is equipped for a life of growth (9:8, 9; 10:8). He is protected from problems and tragedy (4:6; 29:8,11). His mouth is guided (10:19; 16:23). He has power over the powerful (21:22). He is equipped to help others (10:1; 12:18; 13:14,20).	He rejects learning and growth (18:2; 17:10; 26:11) He creates problems for himself (14:3; 29:11) and for others (13:20; 17:12). He is unrepentant (14:9). He becomes known for his folly (12:33).

HOW DOES ONE BECOME	
The Wise	**The Fool**
Through diligent application of the mind (4:5; 6:6; 8:33; 23:19; 27:11) Through reading and applying Proverbs 1:1-6. Through listening to instruction (9:9; 13:20; 19:20). Through asking the Lord (2:6; 9:10; 29:15).	Do nothing. Better question: How does one avoid becoming a fool? Study and apply God's Word to life (1:1-7). Practice the process of becoming wise.

9 A false witness will not go
unpunished,
and he who pours out lies will
perish.[a]

10 It is not fitting for a fool[b] to live
in luxury—
how much worse for a slave to
rule over princes![c]

11 A man's wisdom gives him
patience;[d]
it is to his glory to overlook an
offense.

12 A king's rage is like the roar of a
lion,
but his favor is like dew[e] on the
grass.[f]

13 A foolish son is his father's ruin,[g]
and a quarrelsome wife is like a
constant dripping.[h]

4 →PG. 697
14 Houses and wealth are inherited
from parents,[i]
but a prudent wife is from the
LORD.[j]

15 Laziness brings on deep sleep,
and the shiftless man goes
hungry.[k]

16 He who obeys instructions guards
his life,
but he who is contemptuous of
his ways will die.[l]

7 →PG. 706
17 He who is kind to the poor lends to
the LORD,
and he will reward him for what
he has done.[m]

4 →PG. 697
18 Discipline your son, for in that
there is hope;
do not be a willing party to his
death.[n]

19 A hot-tempered man must pay the
penalty;
if you rescue him, you will have
to do it again.

20 Listen to advice and accept
instruction,[o]
and in the end you will be
wise.[p]

21 Many are the plans in a man's
heart,
but it is the LORD's purpose that
prevails.[q]

22 What a man desires is unfailing
love[a];
better to be poor than a liar.

23 The fear of the LORD leads to life:
Then one rests content,
untouched by trouble.[r]

24 The sluggard buries his hand in the
dish;
he will not even bring it back to
his mouth![s]

25 Flog a mocker, and the simple will
learn prudence;
rebuke a discerning man, and he
will gain knowledge.[t]

26 He who robs his father and drives
out his mother[u]
is a son who brings shame and
disgrace.

27 Stop listening to instruction, my
son,
and you will stray from the
words of knowledge.

28 A corrupt witness mocks at justice,
and the mouth of the wicked
gulps down evil.[v]

29 Penalties are prepared for mockers,
and beatings for the backs of
fools.[w]

20

1 Wine is a mocker and beer a
brawler;
whoever is led astray by them is
not wise.[x]

2 A king's wrath is like the roar of a
lion;[y]
he who angers him forfeits his
life.[z]

3 It is to a man's honor to avoid
strife,
but every fool is quick to
quarrel.[a]

4 A sluggard does not plow in
season;
so at harvest time he looks but
finds nothing.

5 The purposes of a man's heart are
deep waters,
but a man of understanding
draws them out.

6 Many a man claims to have
unfailing love,
but a faithful man who can
find?[b] 4 →PG. 699

7 The righteous man leads a
blameless life;
blessed are his children after
him.[c]

8 When a king sits on his throne to
judge,
he winnows out all evil with his
eyes.[d]

9 Who can say, "I have kept my heart
pure;
I am clean and without sin"?[e]

19:9 [a]ver 5
19:10 [b]Pr 26:1 [c]Pr 30:21-23; Ecc 10:5-7
19:11 [d]Pr 16:32
19:12 [e]Ps 133:3 [f]Pr 16:14-15
19:13 [g]Pr 10:1 [h]Pr 21:9
19:14 [i]2Co 12:14 [j]Pr 18:22
19:15 [k]Pr 6:9; 10:4
19:16 [l]Pr 16:17; Lk 10:28
19:17 [m]Mt 10:42; 2Co 9:6-8
19:18 [n]Pr 13:24; 23:13-14
19:20 [o]Pr 4:1 [p]Pr 12:15
19:21 [q]Ps 33:11; Pr 16:9; Isa 14:24,27
19:23 [r]Ps 25:13; Pr 12:21; 1Ti 4:8
19:24 [s]Pr 26:15
19:25 [t]Pr 9:9; 21:11
19:26 [u]Pr 28:24
19:28 [v]Job 15:16
19:29 [w]Pr 26:3
20:1 [x]Pr 31:4
20:2 [y]Pr 19:12 [z]Pr 8:36
20:3 [a]Pr 17:14
20:6 [b]Ps 12:1
20:7 [c]Ps 37:25-26; 112:2
20:8 [d]ver 26; Pr 25:4-5
20:9 [e]1Ki 8:46; Ecc 7:20; 1Jn 1:8

[a] 22 Or *A man's greed is his shame*

10 Differing weights and differing
measures—
the LORD detests them both.[f]

11 Even a child is known by his
actions,
by whether his conduct is pure[g]
and right.

12 Ears that hear and eyes that see—
the LORD has made them both.[h]

13 Do not love sleep or you will grow
poor;[i]
stay awake and you will have
food to spare.

14 "It's no good, it's no good!" says
the buyer;
then off he goes and boasts
about his purchase.

15 Gold there is, and rubies in
abundance,
but lips that speak knowledge
are a rare jewel.

16 Take the garment of one who puts
up security for a stranger;
hold it in pledge[j] if he does it
for a wayward woman.[k]

17 Food gained by fraud tastes sweet
to a man,[l]
but he ends up with a mouth full
of gravel.

18 Make plans by seeking advice;
if you wage war, obtain
guidance.[m]

19 A gossip betrays a confidence;[n]
so avoid a man who talks too
much.

20 If a man curses his father or
mother,[o]
his lamp will be snuffed out in
pitch darkness.[p]

21 An inheritance quickly gained at
the beginning
will not be blessed at the end.

22 Do not say, "I'll pay you back for
this wrong!"[q]
Wait for the LORD, and he will
deliver you.[r]

23 The LORD detests differing weights,
and dishonest scales do not
please him.[s]

24 A man's steps are directed by the
LORD.
How then can anyone
understand his own way?[t]

25 It is a trap for a man to dedicate
something rashly
and only later to consider his
vows.[u]

26 A wise king winnows out the
wicked;
he drives the threshing wheel
over them.[v]

27 The lamp of the LORD searches the
spirit of a man[a];
it searches out his inmost being.

28 Love and faithfulness keep a king
safe;
through love his throne is made
secure.[w]

29 The glory of young men is their
strength,
gray hair the splendor of the
old.[x]

30 Blows and wounds cleanse[y] away
evil,
and beatings purge the inmost
being.

21

1 The king's heart is in the hand of
the LORD;
he directs it like a watercourse
wherever he pleases.

2 All a man's ways seem right to him,
but the LORD weighs the heart.[z]

3 To do what is right and just
is more acceptable to the LORD
than sacrifice.[a]

4 Haughty eyes[b] and a proud heart,
the lamp of the wicked, are sin!

5 The plans of the diligent lead to
profit[c]
as surely as haste leads to
poverty.

6 A fortune made by a lying tongue
is a fleeting vapor and a deadly
snare.[b][d]

7 The violence of the wicked will
drag them away,
for they refuse to do what is
right.

8 The way of the guilty is devious,[e]
but the conduct of the innocent
is upright.

9 Better to live on a corner of the
roof
than share a house with a
quarrelsome wife.[f]

10 The wicked man craves evil;
his neighbor gets no mercy from
him.

11 When a mocker is punished, the
simple gain wisdom;

20:10 *f* ver 23; Pr 11:1
20:11 *g* Mt 7:16
20:12 *h* Ps 94:9
20:13 *i* Pr 6:11; 19:15
20:16 *j* Ex 22:26 *k* Pr 27:13
20:17 *l* Pr 9:17
20:18 *m* Pr 11:14; 24:6
20:19 *n* Pr 11:13
20:20 *o* Pr 30:11 *p* Ex 21:17; Job 18:5
20:22 *q* Pr 24:29 *r* Ro 12:19
20:23 *s* ver 10
20:24 *t* Jer 10:23
20:25 *u* Ecc 5:2,4-5
20:26 *v* ver 8
20:28 *w* Pr 29:14
20:29 *x* Pr 16:31
20:30 *y* Pr 22:15
21:2 *z* Pr 16:2; 24:12; Lk 16:15
21:3 *a* 1Sa 15:22; Pr 15:8; Isa 1:11; Hos 6:6; Mic 6:6-8
21:4 *b* Pr 6:17
21:5 *c* Pr 10:4; 28:22
21:6 *d* 2Pe 2:3
21:8 *e* Pr 2:15
21:9 *f* Pr 25:24

[a] *27* Or *The spirit of man is the LORD's lamp*
[b] *6* Some Hebrew manuscripts, Septuagint and Vulgate; most Hebrew manuscripts *vapor for those who seek death*

when a wise man is instructed,
he gets knowledge.[g]

12 The Righteous One[a] takes note of
the house of the wicked
and brings the wicked to ruin.[h]

13 If a man shuts his ears to the cry of
the poor,
he too will cry out and not be
answered.[i]

14 A gift given in secret soothes anger,
and a bribe concealed in the
cloak pacifies great wrath.[j]

15 When justice is done, it brings joy
to the righteous
but terror to evildoers.[k]

16 A man who strays from the path of
understanding
comes to rest in the company of
the dead.[l]

17 He who loves pleasure will become
poor;
whoever loves wine and oil will
never be rich.[m]

18 The wicked become a ransom[n] for
the righteous,
and the unfaithful for the
upright.

19 Better to live in a desert
than with a quarrelsome and
ill-tempered wife.[o]

20 In the house of the wise are stores
of choice food and oil,
but a foolish man devours all he
has.

3 →PG. 699

21 He who pursues righteousness and
love
finds life, prosperity[b] and
honor.[p]

22 A wise man attacks the city of the
mighty[q]
and pulls down the stronghold in
which they trust.

23 He who guards his mouth[r] and
his tongue
keeps himself from calamity.[s]

24 The proud and arrogant[t] man—
"Mocker" is his name;
he behaves with overweening
pride.

25 The sluggard's craving will be the
death of him,[u]
because his hands refuse to
work.

26 All day long he craves for more,
but the righteous give without
sparing.[v]

27 The sacrifice of the wicked is
detestable[w]—
how much more so when
brought with evil intent![x]

28 A false witness will perish,[y]
and whoever listens to him will
be destroyed forever.[c]

29 A wicked man puts up a bold front,
but an upright man gives
thought to his ways.

30 There is no wisdom,[z] no insight,
no plan
that can succeed against the
LORD.[a]

31 The horse is made ready for the
day of battle,
but victory rests with the LORD.[b]

22 A good name is more desirable
than great riches;
to be esteemed is better than
silver or gold.[c]

3 →PG. 705
6 →PG. 1038

2 Rich and poor have this in
common:
The LORD is the Maker of them
all.[d]

3 A prudent man sees danger and
takes refuge,[e]
but the simple keep going and
suffer for it.[f]

4 Humility and the fear of the LORD
bring wealth and honor and life.

5 In the paths of the wicked lie
thorns and snares,[g]
but he who guards his soul stays
far from them.

6 Train[d] a child in the way he
should go,[h]
and when he is old he will not
turn from it.

4 →PG. 700

7 The rich rule over the poor,
and the borrower is servant to
the lender.

8 He who sows wickedness reaps
trouble,[i]
and the rod of his fury will be
destroyed.[j]

9 A generous man will himself be
blessed,[k]
for he shares his food with the
poor.[l]

10 Drive out the mocker, and out goes
strife;
quarrels and insults are ended.[m]

11 He who loves a pure heart and
whose speech is gracious
will have the king for his
friend.[n]

21:11 [g]Pr 19:25 **21:12** [h]Pr 14:11 **21:13** [i]Mt 18:30-34; Jas 2:13 **21:14** [j]Pr 18:16; 19:6 **21:15** [k]Pr 10:29 **21:16** [l]Ps 49:14 **21:17** [m]Pr 23:20-21, 29-35 **21:18** [n]Pr 11:8; Isa 43:3 **21:19** [o]ver 9 **21:21** [p]Mt 5:6 **21:22** [q]Ecc 9:15-16 **21:23** [r]Jas 3:2 [s]Pr 12:13; 13:3 **21:24** [t]Ps 1:1; Pr 1:22; Isa 16:6; Jer 48:29 **21:25** [u]Pr 13:4 **21:26** [v]Ps 37:26; Mt 5:42; Eph 4:28 **21:27** [w]Isa 66:3; Jer 6:20; Am 5:22 [x]Pr 15:8 **21:28** [y]Pr 19:5 **21:30** [z]Jer 9:23 [a]Isa 8:10; Ac 5:39 **21:31** [b]Ps 3:8; 33:12-19; Isa 31:1 **22:1** [c]Ecc 7:1 **22:2** [d]Job 31:15 **22:3** [e]Pr 14:16 [f]Pr 27:12 **22:5** [g]Pr 15:19 **22:6** [h]Eph 6:4 **22:8** [i]Job 4:8 [j]Ps 125:3 **22:9** [k]2Co 9:6 [l]Pr 19:17 **22:10** [m]Pr 18:6; 26:20 **22:11** [n]Pr 16:13; Mt 5:8

[a] 12 Or *The righteous man* [b] 21 Or *righteousness* [c] 28 Or */ but the words of an obedient man will live on* [d] 6 Or *Start*

12 The eyes of the LORD keep watch
over knowledge,
but he frustrates the words of
the unfaithful.

13 The sluggard says, "There is a lion
outside!"[o]
or, "I will be murdered in the
streets!"

14 The mouth of an adulteress is a
deep pit;[p]
he who is under the LORD's
wrath will fall into it.[q]

4 →PG. 701

15 Folly is bound up in the heart of a
child,
but the rod of discipline will
drive it far from him.[r]

16 He who oppresses the poor to
increase his wealth
and he who gives gifts to the
rich—both come to poverty.

Sayings of the Wise

17 Pay attention and listen to the
sayings of the wise;[s]
apply your heart to what I teach,
18 for it is pleasing when you keep
them in your heart
and have all of them ready on
your lips.
19 So that your trust may be in the
LORD,
I teach you today, even you.
20 Have I not written thirty[a] sayings
for you,
sayings of counsel and
knowledge,
21 teaching you true and reliable
words,[t]
so that you can give sound
answers
to him who sent you?

22 Do not exploit the poor[u] because
they are poor
and do not crush the needy in
court,[v]
23 for the LORD will take up their
case[w]
and will plunder those who
plunder them.[x]

24 Do not make friends with a
hot-tempered man,
do not associate with one easily
angered,
25 or you may learn his ways
and get yourself ensnared.[y]

26 Do not be a man who strikes hands
in pledge[z]
or puts up security for debts;
27 if you lack the means to pay,
your very bed will be snatched
from under you.[a]

28 Do not move an ancient boundary
stone[b]
set up by your forefathers.

29 Do you see a man skilled in his
work?
He will serve[c] before kings;
he will not serve before obscure
men.

23

1 When you sit to dine with a
ruler,
note well what[b] is before you,
2 and put a knife to your throat
if you are given to gluttony.
3 Do not crave his delicacies,[d]
for that food is deceptive.

4 Do not wear yourself out to get
rich;
have the wisdom to show
restraint.
5 Cast but a glance at riches, and
they are gone,
for they will surely sprout wings
and fly off to the sky like an
eagle.[e]

6 Do not eat the food of a stingy
man,
do not crave his delicacies;[f]
7 for he is the kind of man
who is always thinking about the
cost.[c]
"Eat and drink," he says to you,
but his heart is not with you.
8 You will vomit up the little you
have eaten
and will have wasted your
compliments.

9 Do not speak to a fool,
for he will scorn the wisdom of
your words.[g]

10 Do not move an ancient boundary
stone[h]
or encroach on the fields of the
fatherless,
11 for their Defender[i] is strong;
he will take up their case against
you.[j]

12 Apply your heart to instruction
and your ears to words of
knowledge.

13 Do not withhold discipline from a
child;
if you punish him with the rod,
he will not die.
14 Punish him with the rod
and save his soul from death.[d]

15 My son, if your heart is wise,
then my heart will be glad;

22:13 [o]Pr 26:13 **22:14** [p]Pr 2:16; 5:3-5; 7:5; 23:27 [q]Ecc 7:26 **22:15** [r]Pr 13:24; 23:14 **22:17** [s]Pr 5:1 **22:21** [t]Lk 1:3-4; 1Pe 3:15 **22:22** [u]Zec 7:10 [v]Ex 23:6; Mal 3:5 **22:23** [w]Ps 12:5 [x]1Sa 25:39; Pr 23:10-11 **22:25** [y]1Co 15:33 **22:26** [z]Pr 11:15 **22:27** [a]Pr 17:18

22:28 [b]Dt 19:14; Pr 23:10 **22:29** [c]Ge 41:46 **23:3** [d]ver 6-8 **23:5** [e]Pr 27:24 **23:6** [f]Ps 141:4 **23:9** [g]Pr 1:7; 9:7; Mt 7:6 **23:10** [h]Dt 19:14; Pr 22:28 **23:11** [i]Job 19:25 [j]Pr 22:22-23

[a] *20* Or *not formerly written*; or *not written excellent* [b] *1* Or *who* [c] *7* Or *for as he thinks within himself, / so he is*; or *for as he puts on a feast, / so he is* [d] *14* Hebrew *Sheol*

16my inmost being will rejoice
when your lips speak what is
right.[k]
17Do not let your heart envy[l]
sinners,
but always be zealous for the
fear of the LORD.
18There is surely a future hope for
you,
and your hope will not be cut
off.[m]
19Listen, my son, and be wise,
and keep your heart on the right
path.
20Do not join those who drink too
much wine[n]
or gorge themselves on meat,
21for drunkards and gluttons become
poor,[o]
and drowsiness clothes them in
rags.

4 →PG. 701

22Listen to your father, who gave you
life,
and do not despise your mother
when she is old.[p]
23Buy the truth and do not sell it;
get wisdom, discipline and
understanding.[q]
24The father of a righteous man has
great joy;
he who has a wise son delights
in him.[r]
25May your father and mother be
glad;
may she who gave you birth
rejoice!

26My son,[s] give me your heart
and let your eyes keep to my
ways,[t]
27for a prostitute is a deep pit[u]
and a wayward wife is a narrow
well.
28Like a bandit she lies in wait,[v]
and multiplies the unfaithful
among men.
29Who has woe? Who has sorrow?
Who has strife? Who has
complaints?
Who has needless bruises? Who
has bloodshot eyes?
30Those who linger over wine,[w]
who go to sample bowls of
mixed wine.
31Do not gaze at wine when it is red,
when it sparkles in the cup,
when it goes down smoothly!
32In the end it bites like a snake
and poisons like a viper.
33Your eyes will see strange sights
and your mind imagine
confusing things.
34You will be like one sleeping on the
high seas,
lying on top of the rigging.
35"They hit me," you will say, "but
I'm not hurt!
They beat me, but I don't feel it!
When will I wake up
so I can find another drink?"

24 Do not envy[x] wicked men,
do not desire their company;
2for their hearts plot violence,
and their lips talk about making
trouble.[y]

2 →PG. 704
4 →PG. 708

3By wisdom a house is built,[z]
and through understanding it is
established;
4through knowledge its rooms are
filled
with rare and beautiful
treasures.[a]
5A wise man has great power,
and a man of knowledge
increases strength;
6for waging war you need guidance,
and for victory many advisers.[b]

7Wisdom is too high for a fool;
in the assembly at the gate he
has nothing to say.

8He who plots evil
will be known as a schemer.
9The schemes of folly are sin,
and men detest a mocker.

10If you falter in times of trouble,
how small is your strength![c]
11Rescue those being led away to
death;
hold back those staggering
toward slaughter.[d]
12If you say, "But we knew nothing
about this,"
does not he who weighs[e] the
heart perceive it?
Does not he who guards your life
know it?
Will he not repay each person
according to what he has
done?[f]

13Eat honey, my son, for it is good;
honey from the comb is sweet to
your taste.
14Know also that wisdom is sweet to
your soul;
if you find it, there is a future
hope for you,
and your hope will not be cut
off.[g h]

15Do not lie in wait like an outlaw
against a righteous man's
house,
do not raid his dwelling place;
16for though a righteous man falls
seven times, he rises again,

23:16 [k]ver 24; Pr 27:11
23:17 [l]Ps 37:1; Pr 28:14
23:18 [m]Ps 9:18; Pr 24:14,19-20
23:20 [n]Isa 5:11,22; Ro 13:13; Eph 5:18
23:21 [o]Pr 21:17
23:22 [p]Lev 19:32; Pr 1:8; 30:17; Eph 6:1-2
23:23 [q]Pr 4:7
23:24 [r]ver 15-16; Pr 10:1; 15:20
23:26 [s]Pr 3:1; 5:1-6 [t]Ps 18:21; Pr 4:4
23:27 [u]Pr 22:14
23:28 [v]Pr 7:11-12; Ecc 7:26
23:30 [w]Ps 75:8; Isa 5:11; Eph 5:18
24:1 [x]Ps 37:1; 73:3; Pr 3:31-32; 23:17-18
24:2 [y]Ps 10:7
24:3 [z]Pr 14:1
24:4 [a]Pr 8:21
24:6 [b]Pr 11:14; 20:18; Lk 14:31
24:10 [c]Job 4:5; Jer 51:46; Heb 12:3
24:11 [d]Ps 82:4; Isa 58:6-7
24:12 [e]Pr 21:2 [f]Job 34:11; Ps 62:12; Ro 2:6*
24:14 [g]Ps 119:103; Pr 16:24 [h]Pr 23:18

but the wicked are brought down
by calamity.[i]

17 Do not gloat[j] when your enemy
falls;
when he stumbles, do not let
your heart rejoice,[k]
18 or the LORD will see and disapprove
and turn his wrath away from
him.

19 Do not fret[l] because of evil men
or be envious of the wicked,
20 for the evil man has no future
hope,
and the lamp of the wicked will
be snuffed out.[m]

21 Fear the LORD and the king,[n] my
son,
and do not join with the
rebellious,
22 for those two will send sudden
destruction upon them,
and who knows what calamities
they can bring?

Further Sayings of the Wise

23 These also are sayings of the wise:[o]

To show partiality[p] in judging is
not good:[q]
24 Whoever says to the guilty, "You
are innocent"[r]—
peoples will curse him and
nations denounce him.
25 But it will go well with those who
convict the guilty,
and rich blessing will come upon
them.

26 An honest answer
is like a kiss on the lips.

27 Finish your outdoor work
and get your fields ready;
after that, build your house.

28 Do not testify against your
neighbor without cause,[s]
or use your lips to deceive.
29 Do not say, "I'll do to him as he
has done to me;
I'll pay that man back for what
he did."[t]

30 I went past the field of the
sluggard,[u]
past the vineyard of the man
who lacks judgment;
31 thorns had come up everywhere,
the ground was covered with
weeds,
and the stone wall was in ruins.
32 I applied my heart to what I
observed
and learned a lesson from what I
saw:
33 A little sleep, a little slumber,
a little folding of the hands to
rest[v]—
34 and poverty will come on you like
a bandit
and scarcity like an armed
man.[a][w]

More Proverbs of Solomon

25 These are more proverbs[x] of Solomon, copied by the men of Hezekiah king of Judah:[y]

2 It is the glory of God to conceal a
matter;
to search out a matter is the
glory of kings.[z]
3 As the heavens are high and the
earth is deep,
so the hearts of kings are
unsearchable.

4 Remove the dross from the silver,
and out comes material for[b] the
silversmith;
5 remove the wicked from the king's
presence,[a]
and his throne will be
established[b] through
righteousness.[c]

6 Do not exalt yourself in the king's
presence,
and do not claim a place among
great men;
7 it is better for him to say to you,
"Come up here,"[d]
than for him to humiliate you
before a nobleman.

What you have seen with your eyes
8 do not bring[c] hastily to court,
for what will you do in the end
if your neighbor puts you to
shame?[e]

9 If you argue your case with a
neighbor,
do not betray another man's
confidence,
10 or he who hears it may shame you
and you will never lose your bad
reputation.

11 A word aptly spoken
is like apples of gold in settings
of silver.[f]

12 Like an earring of gold or an
ornament of fine gold
is a wise man's rebuke to a
listening ear.[g]

13 Like the coolness of snow at
harvest time

24:16 [i]Job 5:19; Ps 34:19; Mic 7:8 **24:17** [j]Ob 1:12 [k]Job 31:29 **24:19** [l]Ps 37:1 **24:20** [m]Job 18:5; Pr 13:9; 23:17-18 **24:21** [n]Ro 13:1-5; 1Pe 2:17 **24:23** [o]Pr 1:6 [p]Lev 19:15 [q]Pr 28:21 **24:24** [r]Pr 17:15 **24:28** [s]Ps 7:4; Pr 25:18; Eph 4:25 **24:29** [t]Pr 20:22; Mt 5:38-41; Ro 12:17 **24:30** [u]Pr 6:6-11; 26:13-16

24:33 [v]Pr 6:10 **24:34** [w]Pr 10:4; Ecc 10:18 **25:1** [x]1Ki 4:32 [y]Pr 1:1 **25:2** [z]Pr 16:10-15 **25:5** [a]Pr 20:8 [b]2Sa 7:13 [c]Pr 16:12; 29:14 **25:7** [d]Lk 14:7-10 **25:8** [e]Mt 5:25-26 **25:11** [f]ver 12; Pr 15:23 **25:12** [g]ver 11; Ps 141:5; Pr 13:18; 15:31

[a] 34 Or *like a vagrant / and scarcity like a beggar*
[b] 4 Or *comes a vessel from*
[c] 7,8 Or *nobleman / on whom you had set your eyes. / 8Do not go*

is a trustworthy messenger to
those who send him;
he refreshes the spirit of his
masters.[h]

14Like clouds and wind without rain
is a man who boasts of gifts he
does not give.

15Through patience a ruler can be
persuaded,[i]
and a gentle tongue can break a
bone.[j]

16If you find honey, eat just
enough—
too much of it, and you will
vomit.[k]

17Seldom set foot in your neighbor's
house—
too much of you, and he will
hate you.

18Like a club or a sword or a sharp
arrow
is the man who gives false
testimony against his
neighbor.[l]

19Like a bad tooth or a lame foot
is reliance on the unfaithful in
times of trouble.

20Like one who takes away a garment
on a cold day,
or like vinegar poured on soda,
is one who sings songs to a
heavy heart.

21If your enemy is hungry, give him
food to eat;
if he is thirsty, give him water to
drink.
22In doing this, you will heap
burning coals[m] on his head,
and the LORD will reward you.[n]

23As a north wind brings rain,
so a sly tongue brings angry
looks.

24Better to live on a corner of the
roof
than share a house with a
quarrelsome wife.[o]

25Like cold water to a weary soul
is good news from a distant
land.[p]

26Like a muddied spring or a
polluted well
is a righteous man who gives
way to the wicked.

27It is not good to eat too much
honey,[q]
nor is it honorable to seek one's
own honor.[r]

28Like a city whose walls are broken
down
is a man who lacks self-control.

25:13 [h]Pr 10:26; 13:17 **25:15** [i]Ecc 10:4 [j]Pr 15:1 **25:16** [k]ver 27 **25:18** [l]Ps 57:4; Pr 12:18 **25:22** [m]Ps 18:8 [n]2Sa 16:12; 2Ch 28:15; Mt 5:44; Ro 12:20* **25:24** [o]Pr 21:9 **25:25** [p]Pr 15:30 **25:27** [q]ver 16 [r]Pr 27:2; Mt 23:12

26

Like snow in summer or rain[s] in
harvest,
honor is not fitting for a fool.[t]

2Like a fluttering sparrow or a
darting swallow,
an undeserved curse does not
come to rest.[u]

3A whip for the horse, a halter for
the donkey,[v]
and a rod for the backs of
fools![w]

4Do not answer a fool according to
his folly,
or you will be like him
yourself.[x]

5Answer a fool according to his folly,
or he will be wise in his own
eyes.[y]

6Like cutting off one's feet or
drinking violence
is the sending of a message by
the hand of a fool.[z]

7Like a lame man's legs that hang
limp
is a proverb in the mouth of a
fool.[a]

8Like tying a stone in a sling
is the giving of honor to a fool.[b]

9Like a thornbush in a drunkard's
hand
is a proverb in the mouth of a
fool.[c]

10Like an archer who wounds at
random
is he who hires a fool or any
passer-by.

11As a dog returns to its vomit,[d]
so a fool repeats his folly.[e]

12Do you see a man wise in his own
eyes?[f]
There is more hope for a fool
than for him.[g]

13The sluggard says,[h] "There is a
lion in the road,
a fierce lion roaming the
streets!"[i]

14As a door turns on its hinges,
so a sluggard turns on his bed.[j]

15The sluggard buries his hand in the
dish;
he is too lazy to bring it back to
his mouth.[k]

16The sluggard is wiser in his own
eyes
than seven men who answer
discreetly.

26:1 [s]1Sa 12:17 [t]ver 8; Pr 19:10 **26:2** [u]Nu 23:8; Dt 23:5 **26:3** [v]Ps 32:9 [w]Pr 10:13 **26:4** [x]ver 5; Isa 36:21 **26:5** [y]ver 4; Pr 3:7 **26:6** [z]Pr 10:26 **26:7** [a]ver 9 **26:8** [b]ver 1 **26:9** [c]ver 7 **26:11** [d]2Pe 2:22* [e]Ex 8:15; Ps 85:8 **26:12** [f]Pr 3:7 [g]Pr 29:20 **26:13** [h]Pr 6:6-11; 24:30-34 [i]Pr 22:13 **26:14** [j]Pr 6:9 **26:15** [k]Pr 19:24

17 Like one who seizes a dog by the
ears
is a passer-by who meddles in a
quarrel not his own.

18 Like a madman shooting
firebrands or deadly arrows
19 is a man who deceives his neighbor
and says, "I was only joking!"

20 Without wood a fire goes out;
without gossip a quarrel dies
down.[l]

21 As charcoal to embers and as wood
to fire,
so is a quarrelsome man for
kindling strife.[m]

22 The words of a gossip are like
choice morsels;
they go down to a man's inmost
parts.[n]

23 Like a coating of glaze[a] over
earthenware
are fervent lips with an evil
heart.

24 A malicious man disguises himself
with his lips,[o]
but in his heart he harbors
deceit.[p]
25 Though his speech is charming,[q]
do not believe him,
for seven abominations fill his
heart.[r]
26 His malice may be concealed by
deception,
but his wickedness will be
exposed in the assembly.

27 If a man digs a pit,[s] he will fall
into it;[t]
if a man rolls a stone, it will roll
back on him.[u]

28 A lying tongue hates those it hurts,
and a flattering mouth[v] works
ruin.

27

Do not boast[w] about tomorrow,
for you do not know what a day
may bring forth.[x]

2 Let another praise you, and not
your own mouth;
someone else, and not your own
lips.[y]

3 Stone is heavy and sand[z] a
burden,
but provocation by a fool is
heavier than both.

4 Anger is cruel and fury
overwhelming,
but who can stand before
jealousy?[a]

5 Better is open rebuke
than hidden love.

6 Wounds from a friend can be
trusted,
but an enemy multiplies kisses.[b]

7 He who is full loathes honey,
but to the hungry even what is
bitter tastes sweet.

8 Like a bird that strays from its
nest[c]
is a man who strays from his
home.

9 Perfume[d] and incense bring joy to
the heart,
and the pleasantness of one's
friend springs from his
earnest counsel.

10 Do not forsake your friend and the
friend of your father,
and do not go to your brother's
house when disaster[e]
strikes you—
better a neighbor nearby than a
brother far away.

11 Be wise, my son, and bring joy to
my heart;[f]
then I can answer anyone who
treats me with contempt.[g]

12 The prudent see danger and take
refuge,
but the simple keep going and
suffer for it.[h]

13 Take the garment of one who puts
up security for a stranger;
hold it in pledge if he does it for
a wayward woman.[i]

14 If a man loudly blesses his
neighbor early in the
morning,
it will be taken as a curse.

15 A quarrelsome wife is like
a constant dripping[j] on a rainy
day;
16 restraining her is like restraining
the wind
or grasping oil with the hand.

17 As iron sharpens iron,
so one man sharpens another. 2 →PG. 716

18 He who tends a fig tree will eat its
fruit,[k]
and he who looks after his
master will be honored.[l]

19 As water reflects a face,
so a man's heart reflects the
man.

20 Death and Destruction[b] are never
satisfied,[m]

[a] *23* With a different word division of the Hebrew; Masoretic Text *of silver dross*
[b] *20* Hebrew *Sheol and Abaddon*

26:20 [l] Pr 22:10
26:21 [m] Pr 14:17; 15:18
26:22 [n] Pr 18:8
26:24 [o] Ps 31:18 [p] Ps 41:6; Pr 10:18; 12:20
26:25 [q] Ps 28:3 [r] Jer 9:4-8
26:27 [s] Ps 7:15 [t] Est 6:13 [u] Est 2:23; 7:9; Ps 35:8; 141:10; Pr 28:10; 29:6; Isa 50:11
26:28 [v] Ps 12:3; Pr 29:5
27:1 [w] 1Ki 20:11 [x] Mt 6:34; Lk 12:19-20; Jas 4:13-16
27:2 [y] Pr 25:27
27:3 [z] Job 6:3
27:4 [a] Nu 5:14
27:6 [b] Ps 141:5; Pr 28:23
27:8 [c] Isa 16:2
27:9 [d] Est 2:12; Ps 45:8
27:10 [e] Pr 17:17; 18:24
27:11 [f] Pr 10:1; 23:15-16 [g] Ge 24:60
27:12 [h] Pr 22:3
27:13 [i] Pr 20:16
27:15 [j] Est 1:18; Pr 19:13
27:18 [k] 1Co 9:7 [l] Lk 19:12-27
27:20 [m] Pr 30:15-16; Hab 2:5

and neither are the eyes of
man.[n]

3 →PG. 706

21The crucible for silver and the
furnace for gold,[o]
but man is tested by the praise
he receives.

22Though you grind a fool in a
mortar,
grinding him like grain with a
pestle,
you will not remove his folly
from him.

23Be sure you know the condition of
your flocks,[p]
give careful attention to your
herds;
24for riches do not endure forever,[q]
and a crown is not secure for all
generations.
25When the hay is removed and new
growth appears
and the grass from the hills is
gathered in,
26the lambs will provide you with
clothing,
and the goats with the price of a
field.
27You will have plenty of goats' milk
to feed you and your family
and to nourish your servant girls.

28 The wicked man flees[r] though
no one pursues,[s]
but the righteous are as bold as
a lion.[t]

2When a country is rebellious, it has
many rulers,
but a man of understanding and
knowledge maintains order.

3A ruler[a] who oppresses the poor
is like a driving rain that leaves
no crops.

4Those who forsake the law praise
the wicked,
but those who keep the law
resist them.

5Evil men do not understand justice,
but those who seek the LORD
understand it fully.

6Better a poor man whose walk is
blameless
than a rich man whose ways are
perverse.[u]

7He who keeps the law is a
discerning son,
but a companion of gluttons
disgraces his father.[v]

8He who increases his wealth by
exorbitant interest[w]
amasses it for another,[x] who
will be kind to the poor.[y]

9If anyone turns a deaf ear to the
law,
even his prayers are detestable.[z]

10He who leads the upright along an
evil path
will fall into his own trap,[a]
but the blameless will receive a
good inheritance.

11A rich man may be wise in his own
eyes,
but a poor man who has
discernment sees through
him.

12When the righteous triumph, there
is great elation;[b]
but when the wicked rise to
power, men go into
hiding.[c]

13He who conceals his sins[d] does
not prosper,
but whoever confesses and
renounces them finds
mercy.[e]

14Blessed is the man who always
fears the LORD,
but he who hardens his heart
falls into trouble.

15Like a roaring lion or a charging
bear
is a wicked man ruling over a
helpless people.

16A tyrannical ruler lacks judgment,
but he who hates ill-gotten gain
will enjoy a long life.

17A man tormented by the guilt of
murder
will be a fugitive[f] till death;
let no one support him.

18He whose walk is blameless is kept
safe,
but he whose ways are perverse
will suddenly fall.[g]

19He who works his land will have
abundant food,
but the one who chases fantasies
will have his fill of
poverty.[h]

20A faithful man will be richly
blessed,
but one eager to get rich will not
go unpunished.[i]

21To show partiality is not good[j] —
yet a man will do wrong for a
piece of bread.[k]

22A stingy man is eager to get rich
and is unaware that poverty
awaits him.[l]

27:20 [n]Ecc 1:8; 6:7 **27:21** [o]Pr 17:3 **27:23** [p]Pr 12:10 **27:24** [q]Pr 23:5 **28:1** [r]2Ki 7:7 [s]Lev 26:17; Ps 53:5 [t]Ps 138:3 **28:6** [u]Pr 19:1 **28:7** [v]Pr 23:19-21 **28:8** [w]Ex 18:21 [x]Job 27:17; Pr 13:22 [y]Ps 112:9; Pr 14:31; Lk 14:12-14

28:9 [z]Ps 66:18; 109:7; Pr 15:8; Isa 1:13 **28:10** [a]Pr 26:27 **28:12** [b]2Ki 11:20 [c]Pr 11:10; 29:2 **28:13** [d]Job 31:33 [e]Ps 32:1-5; 1Jn 1:9 **28:17** [f]Ge 9:6 **28:18** [g]Pr 10:9 **28:19** [h]Pr 12:11 **28:20** [i]ver 22; Pr 10:6; 1Ti 6:9 **28:21** [j]Pr 18:5 [k]Eze 13:19 **28:22** [l]ver 20; Pr 23:6

[a]3 Or *A poor man*

23 He who rebukes a man will in the
end gain more favor
than he who has a flattering
tongue.[m]

24 He who robs his father or mother[n]
and says, "It's not wrong"—
he is partner to him who
destroys.[o]

25 A greedy man stirs up dissension,
but he who trusts in the LORD[p]
will prosper.

26 He who trusts in himself is a
fool,[q]
but he who walks in wisdom is
kept safe.

7 →PG. 737
27 He who gives to the poor will lack
nothing,[r]
but he who closes his eyes to
them receives many curses.

28 When the wicked rise to power,
people go into hiding;[s]
but when the wicked perish, the
righteous thrive.

29

1 A man who remains stiff-necked
after many rebukes
will suddenly be destroyed—
without remedy.[t]

2 When the righteous thrive, the
people rejoice;[u]
when the wicked rule, the people
groan.[v]

3 A man who loves wisdom brings
joy to his father,[w]
but a companion of prostitutes
squanders his wealth.[x]

4 By justice a king gives a country
stability,[y]
but one who is greedy for bribes
tears it down.

5 Whoever flatters his neighbor
is spreading a net for his feet.

6 An evil man is snared by his own
sin,[z]
but a righteous one can sing and
be glad.

7 The righteous care about justice for
the poor,[a]
but the wicked have no such
concern.

8 Mockers stir up a city,
but wise men turn away anger.[b]

9 If a wise man goes to court with a
fool,
the fool rages and scoffs, and
there is no peace.

3 →PG. 708
10 Bloodthirsty men hate a man of
integrity
and seek to kill the upright.[c]

11 A fool gives full vent to his anger,
but a wise man keeps himself
under control.[d]

12 If a ruler listens to lies,
all his officials become wicked.

13 The poor man and the oppressor
have this in common:
The LORD gives sight to the eyes
of both.[e]

14 If a king judges the poor with
fairness,
his throne will always be
secure.[f]

15 The rod of correction imparts
wisdom,
but a child left to himself
disgraces his mother.[g]

16 When the wicked thrive, so does
sin,
but the righteous will see their
downfall.[h]

17 Discipline your son, and he will
give you peace;
he will bring delight to your
soul.[i]

18 Where there is no revelation, the
people cast off restraint;
but blessed is he who keeps the
law.[j]
1 →PG. 707

19 A servant cannot be corrected by
mere words;
though he understands, he will
not respond.

20 Do you see a man who speaks in
haste?
There is more hope for a fool
than for him.[k]

21 If a man pampers his servant from
youth,
he will bring grief[a] in the end.

22 An angry man stirs up dissension,
and a hot-tempered one
commits many sins.[l]

23 A man's pride brings him low,
but a man of lowly spirit gains
honor.[m]

24 The accomplice of a thief is his
own enemy;
he is put under oath and dare
not testify.[n]

25 Fear of man will prove to be a
snare,
but whoever trusts in the LORD[o]
is kept safe.

28:23 [m] Pr 27:5-6
28:24 [n] Pr 19:26 [o] Pr 18:9
28:25 [p] Pr 29:25
28:26 [q] Ps 4:5; Pr 3:5
28:27 [r] Dt 15:7; 24:19; Pr 19:17; 22:9
28:28 [s] ver 12
29:1 [t] 2Ch 36:16; Pr 6:15
29:2 [u] Est 8:15 [v] Pr 28:12
29:3 [w] Pr 10:1 [x] Pr 5:8-10; Lk 15:11-32
29:4 [y] Pr 8:15-16
29:6 [z] Ecc 9:12
29:7 [a] Job 29:16; Ps 41:1; Pr 31:8-9
29:8 [b] Pr 11:11; 16:14
29:10 [c] 1Jn 3:12
29:11 [d] Pr 12:16; 19:11
29:13 [e] Pr 22:2; Mt 5:45
29:14 [f] Ps 72:1-5; Pr 16:12
29:15 [g] Pr 10:1; 13:24; 17:21,25
29:16 [h] Ps 37:35-36; 58:10; 91:8; 92:11
29:17 [i] ver 15; Pr 10:1
29:18 [j] Ps 1:1-2; 119:1-2; Jn 13:17
29:20 [k] Pr 26:12; Jas 1:19
29:22 [l] Pr 14:17; 15:18; 26:21
29:23 [m] Pr 11:2; 15:33; 16:18; Isa 66:2; Mt 23:12
29:24 [n] Lev 5:1
29:25 [o] Pr 28:25

a *21* The meaning of the Hebrew for this word is uncertain.

[26]Many seek an audience with a
ruler,[p]
but it is from the LORD that man
gets justice.
[27]The righteous detest the dishonest;
the wicked detest the upright.[q]

Sayings of Agur

30 The sayings of Agur son of Jakeh—
an oracle[a]:

This man declared to Ithiel,
to Ithiel and to Ucal:[b]

[2]"I am the most ignorant of men;
I do not have a man's
understanding.
[3]I have not learned wisdom,
nor have I knowledge of the Holy
One.[r]
[4]Who has gone up[s] to heaven and
come down?
Who has gathered up the wind
in the hollow[t] of his
hands?
Who has wrapped up the waters[u]
in his cloak?[v]
Who has established all the ends
of the earth?
What is his name,[w] and the name
of his son?
Tell me if you know!

1 →PG. 738

[5]"Every word of God is flawless;[x]
he is a shield[y] to those who
take refuge in him.
[6]Do not add[z] to his words,
or he will rebuke you and prove
you a liar.

[7]"Two things I ask of you, O LORD;
do not refuse me before I die:
[8]Keep falsehood and lies far from
me;
give me neither poverty nor
riches,
but give me only my daily
bread.[a]
[9]Otherwise, I may have too much
and disown[b] you
and say, 'Who is the LORD?'[c]
Or I may become poor and steal,
and so dishonor the name of my
God.[d]

[10]"Do not slander a servant to his
master,
or he will curse you, and you will
pay for it.

[11]"There are those who curse their
fathers
and do not bless their mothers;[e]
[12]those who are pure in their own
eyes[f]
and yet are not cleansed of their
filth;[g]
[13]those whose eyes are ever so
haughty,[h]
whose glances are so disdainful;
[14]those whose teeth[i] are swords
and whose jaws are set with
knives[j]
to devour[k] the poor[l] from the
earth,
the needy from among
mankind.[m]

[15]"The leech has two daughters.
'Give! Give!' they cry.

"There are three things that are
never satisfied,[n]
four that never say, 'Enough!':
[16]the grave,[c][o] the barren womb,
land, which is never satisfied
with water,
and fire, which never says,
'Enough!'

[17]"The eye that mocks[p] a father,
that scorns obedience to a
mother,
will be pecked out by the ravens of
the valley,
will be eaten by the vultures.[q]

[18]"There are three things that are too
amazing for me,
four that I do not understand:
[19]the way of an eagle in the sky,
the way of a snake on a rock,
the way of a ship on the high seas,
and the way of a man with a
maiden.

[20]"This is the way of an adulteress:
She eats and wipes her mouth
and says, 'I've done nothing
wrong.'[r]

[21]"Under three things the earth
trembles,
under four it cannot bear up:
[22]a servant who becomes king,[s]
a fool who is full of food,
[23]an unloved woman who is married,
and a maidservant who displaces
her mistress.

[24]"Four things on earth are small,
yet they are extremely wise:
[25]Ants are creatures of little strength,
yet they store up their food in
the summer;[t]
[26]coneys[d][u] are creatures of little
power,
yet they make their home in the
crags;

29:26 [p]Pr 19:6
29:27 [q]ver 10
30:3 [r]Pr 9:10
30:4 [s]Ps 24:1-2; Jn 3:13; Eph 4:7-10 [t]Ps 104:3; Isa 40:12 [u]Job 26:8; 38:8-9 [v]Ge 1:2 [w]Rev 19:12
30:5 [x]Ps 12:6; 18:30 [y]Ge 15:1; Ps 84:11
30:6 [z]Dt 4:2; 12:32; Rev 22:18
30:8 [a]Mt 6:11
30:9 [b]Jos 24:27; Isa 1:4; 59:13 [c]Dt 6:12; 8:10-14; Hos 13:6 [d]Dt 8:12
30:11 [e]Pr 20:20
30:12 [f]Pr 16:2; Lk 18:11 [g]Jer 2:23,35
30:13 [h]2Sa 22:28; Job 41:34; Ps 131:1; Pr 6:17
30:14 [i]Job 4:11; 29:17; Ps 3:7 [j]Ps 57:4 [k]Job 24:9; Ps 14:4 [l]Am 8:4; Mic 2:2 [m]Job 19:22
30:15 [n]Pr 27:20
30:16 [o]Pr 27:20; Isa 5:14; 14:9, 11; Hab 2:5
30:17 [p]Dt 21:18-21; Pr 23:22 [q]Job 15:23
30:20 [r]Pr 5:6
30:22 [s]Pr 19:10; 29:2
30:25 [t]Pr 6:6-8
30:26 [u]Ps 104:18

[a] *1* Or *Jakeh of Massa* [b] *1* Masoretic Text; with a different word division of the Hebrew *declared, "I am weary, O God; / I am weary, O God, and faint.* [c] *16* Hebrew *Sheol*
[d] *26* That is, the hyrax or rock badger

[27]locusts[v] have no king,
yet they advance together in ranks;
[28]a lizard can be caught with the hand,
yet it is found in kings' palaces.

[29]"There are three things that are stately in their stride,
four that move with stately bearing:
[30]a lion, mighty among beasts,
who retreats before nothing;
[31]a strutting rooster, a he-goat,
and a king with his army around him.[a]

3 →PG. 717

[32]"If you have played the fool and exalted yourself,
or if you have planned evil,
clap your hand over your mouth![w]
[33]For as churning the milk produces butter,
and as twisting the nose produces blood,
so stirring up anger produces strife."

Sayings of King Lemuel

31 The sayings[x] of King Lemuel—an oracle[b] his mother taught him:

[2]"O my son, O son of my womb,
O son of my vows,[c][y]
[3]do not spend your strength on women,
your vigor on those who ruin kings.[z]

[4]"It is not for kings, O Lemuel—
not for kings to drink wine,[a]
not for rulers to crave beer,
[5]lest they drink[b] and forget what the law decrees,[c]
and deprive all the oppressed of their rights.
[6]Give beer to those who are perishing,
wine[d] to those who are in anguish;
[7]let them drink[e] and forget their poverty
and remember their misery no more.

[8]"Speak[f] up for those who cannot speak for themselves,
for the rights of all who are destitute.
[9]Speak up and judge fairly;
defend the rights of the poor and needy."[g]

Epilogue: The Wife of Noble Character

[10][d]A wife of noble character[h] who can find?[i]
She is worth far more than rubies.
[11]Her husband[j] has full confidence in her
and lacks nothing of value.[k]
[12]She brings him good, not harm,
all the days of her life.
[13]She selects wool and flax
and works with eager hands.[l]
[14]She is like the merchant ships,
bringing her food from afar.
[15]She gets up while it is still dark;
she provides food for her family
and portions for her servant girls.
[16]She considers a field and buys it;
out of her earnings she plants a vineyard.
[17]She sets about her work vigorously;
her arms are strong for her tasks.
[18]She sees that her trading is profitable,
and her lamp does not go out at night.
[19]In her hand she holds the distaff
and grasps the spindle with her fingers.
[20]She opens her arms to the poor
and extends her hands to the needy.[m]
[21]When it snows, she has no fear for her household;
for all of them are clothed in scarlet.
[22]She makes coverings for her bed;
she is clothed in fine linen and purple.
[23]Her husband is respected at the city gate,
where he takes his seat among the elders[n] of the land.
[24]She makes linen garments and sells them,
and supplies the merchants with sashes.
[25]She is clothed with strength and dignity;
she can laugh at the days to come.
[26]She speaks with wisdom,
and faithful instruction is on her tongue.[o]
[27]She watches over the affairs of her household

4 →PG. 720

30:27 [v]Ex 10:4 **30:32** [w]Job 21:5; 29:9 **31:1** [x]Pr 22:17 **31:2** [y]Jdg 11:30; Isa 49:15 **31:3** [z]Dt 17:17; 1Ki 11:3; Ne 13:26; Pr 5:1-14 **31:4** [a]Pr 20:1; Ecc 10:16-17; Isa 5:22 **31:5** [b]1Ki 16:9 [c]Pr 16:12; Hos 4:11 **31:6** [d]Ge 14:18 **31:7** [e]Est 1:10 **31:8** [f]1Sa 19:4; Job 29:12-17 **31:9** [g]Lev 19:15; Dt 1:16; Pr 24:23; 29:7; Isa 1:17; Jer 22:16 **31:10** [h]Ru 3:11; Pr 12:4; 18:22 [i]Pr 8:35; 19:14 **31:11** [j]Ge 2:18 [k]Pr 12:4 **31:13** [l]1Ti 2:9-10 **31:20** [m]Dt 15:11; Eph 4:28; Heb 13:16 **31:23** [n]Ex 3:16; Ru 4:1,11; Pr 12:4 **31:26** [o]Pr 10:31

[a]*31* Or *king secure against revolt* [b]*1* Or *of Lemuel king of Massa, which* [c]*2* Or */ the answer to my prayers* [d]*10* Verses 10-31 are an acrostic, each verse beginning with a successive letter of the Hebrew alphabet.

and does not eat the bread of
idleness.
28 Her children arise and call her
blessed;
her husband also, and he praises
her:
29 "Many women do noble things,
but you surpass them all."
30 Charm is deceptive, and beauty is
fleeting;
but a woman who fears the LORD
is to be praised.
31 Give her the reward she has
earned,
and let her works bring her
praise[p] at the city gate.

31:31 [p] Pr 11:16

ECCLESIASTES

AT A GLANCE

Key Principle: The human quest for meaning and purpose can never be satisfied through earthly pursuits ("under the sun"), but only by embracing an eternal perspective (looking "beyond the sun").
Author: Probably Solomon
Time and Place: ~970 – ~930 B.C. / Written in Israel from a universal perspective
Key Verses: 2:24; 3:14; 8:17; 12:13–14

BENEFIT

The need for satisfaction and significance in life drives most people to pursue these things in the wrong places. They look for meaning in the created order, rather than in the Creator of order. Ecclesiastes, written by a man whose abilities, assets and attainments are far beyond our own, is a road map that shows us where the human quest apart from God ends. This man, who quite literally had it all, warns us that the world will never satisfy our deepest longings. Since we have been created in God's image and he has "set eternity in [our] hearts" (3:11), our deepest longings can only be satisfied in relationship with him.

SETTING

The Jewish Talmud identifies "the Teacher, son of David, king in Jerusalem" (1:1) who wrote Ecclesiastes with Solomon, but suggests the book was later edited by scribes in the days of Hezekiah. Some scholars argue that this book may have been written after the exile around the time of Ezra, but there are good reasons to accept the traditional Jewish and Christian views that Qoheleth ("the preacher") was Solomon himself. He was the only son of David who ruled over Israel from Jerusalem (1:12), and the extraordinary resources and projects listed in chapters 1—2 fit him better than any other man.

Solomon possessed the greatest combination of intellectual, economic and political resources that the world has ever known, and he based his profound observations on his experiences with these tremendous resources. Jewish tradition says that Solomon wrote Song of Songs in his youth, Proverbs in his middle years, and Ecclesiastes near the end of his life (~935 B.C.). In his final years, Solomon had good reason to regret the foolish path of idolatry and carnality he had followed and promoted; it was leading to the decline and division of his kingdom (1 Kings 11).

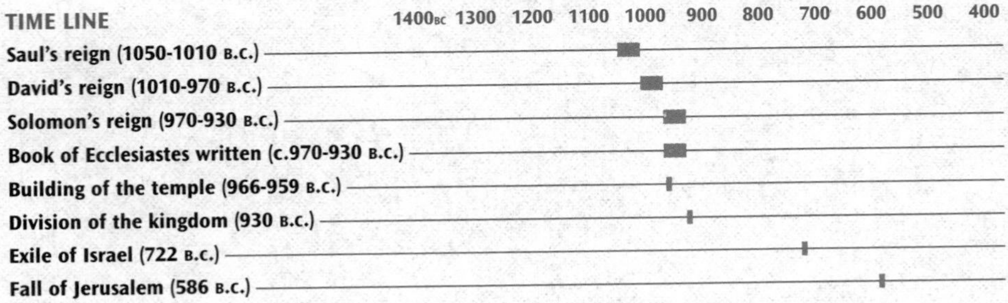

THEME AND PURPOSE

Ecclesiastes was written at the end of a life characterized by an unprecedented pursuit of wisdom, power, pleasure, possessions and accomplishments. It uses these experiences to demonstrate that none of these things can fill the empty void in the human heart. Augustine said that God created us for himself, and our hearts are restless until they find their rest in him; Ecclesiastes is an earlier commentary on this truth.

This book develops the theme that our search for the highest good must not be limited to life lived "under the sun" (this expression appears 29 times), but must end in fearing and obeying God (12:13). Without God life is empty, meaningless and futile, and is characterized by inequity, injustice and uncertainty. With God our lives have hope, meaning and joy. While life is full of difficulties and unexpected turns, hope in God keeps our lives from degenerating into a cycle of cynicism and despair.

UNIQUE CONTRIBUTION

Ecclesiastes is the most "modern" of all Biblical books; it speaks directly to the spirit of our age. It explores what life has to offer from a vantage point of unaided human wisdom. This "under the sun" perspective made Ecclesiastes a controversial book over the centuries. Jewish scholars questioned its inclusion in the canon (recognized list) of Scriptural books until the matter was finally settled in A.D. 90 at the Council of Jamnia. Even now, some scholars believe that Ecclesiastes is an uninspired, naturalistic work marked by materialism and pessimism; others say it is partially inspired as an example of the farthest human reason can reach apart from God. While Ecclesiastes has a number of difficult passages that can easily be misconstrued if one overlooks the purpose and perspective of the book, it rightly belongs to the canon of inspired books when taken as a whole.

LINKS TO THE NEW TESTAMENT

In many ways, Ecclesiastes is a timeless work that points to the emptiness and despair that follows a life lived apart from Christ. Most unbelievers don't recognize the implications of this book on their own. They avoid thinking about the brevity and apparent absurdity of life through escapism, workaholism, medication, entertainment and other activities. Try as people might, however, they cannot eliminate eternity from their hearts (3:11). This book, and the entire Biblical narrative, tells us there is only "one Shepherd" (12:11) who imparts true wisdom and who can satisfy the deepest longings of the human heart.

OVERVIEW

FOCUS	Exclamation	Experience and Exploration	Exhortation and Explanation	Epilogue
REFERENCE	1:1-11	1:12 — 6:12	7:1 — 12:8	12:9-14
TOPICS	Declaration	Demonstration and Development	Deductions	Denouement
	Thesis	Proof		Conclusion
	Subject	Sermons		Summary
	Vanity Under the Sun Versus Fear of the Lord			
LOCATION	Written in Israel from a Universal ("Under the Sun") Perspective			
TIME	Decades of Searching			

Ecclesiastes begins with a statement that everything under the sun appears to be a meaningless series of endless cycles (1:1–11). Following this exclamation is a profile of the Teacher's quest for meaning through pursuing wisdom, wine, great projects, women and wealth (1:12—2:26).

In spite of his vast resources, none of these delivered the satisfaction they promised. Taking a more philosophical bent, the Teacher explores the changeless order of events, the brevity of life, the absurdity of death and the futility of social and religious relationships. He then questions whether wisdom and righteousness are better in the long run than folly and wickedness, and whether there is any hope for true satisfaction in this life (3—6).

The Teacher then offers a series of lessons on practical wisdom (7:1—9:12) and presents a number of general observations on wisdom and folly (9:13—11:6). He then exhorts his readers to live fully and well, and to acknowledge God early in life (11:7—12:8). This section closes with a picturesque allegory of old age (12:1–8). The concluding epilogue (12:9–14) is the climax of the book because it calls us to find meaning by ordering our lives before God.

ECCLESIASTES

Everything Is Meaningless

1 The words of the Teacher,[a][a] son of David, king in Jerusalem:[b]

2"Meaningless! Meaningless!"
says the Teacher.
"Utterly meaningless!
Everything is meaningless."[c]

3What does man gain from all his labor
at which he toils under the sun?[d]
4Generations come and generations go,
but the earth remains forever.[e]
5The sun rises and the sun sets,
and hurries back to where it rises.[f]
6The wind blows to the south
and turns to the north;
round and round it goes,
ever returning on its course.
7All streams flow into the sea,
yet the sea is never full.
To the place the streams come from,
there they return again.[g]
8All things are wearisome,
more than one can say.
The eye never has enough of seeing,[h]
nor the ear its fill of hearing.
9What has been will be again,
what has been done will be done again;[i]
there is nothing new under the sun.
10Is there anything of which one can say,
"Look! This is something new"?
It was here already, long ago;
it was here before our time.
11There is no remembrance of men of old,
and even those who are yet to come
will not be remembered
by those who follow.[j]

Wisdom Is Meaningless

12I, the Teacher,[k] was king over Israel in Jerusalem. 13I devoted myself to
study and to explore by wisdom all that
is done under heaven. What a heavy
burden God has laid on men![l] 14I have
seen all the things that are done under
the sun; all of them are meaningless, a
chasing after the wind.[m]

15What is twisted cannot be straightened;[n]
what is lacking cannot be counted.

16I thought to myself, "Look, I have
grown and increased in wisdom more
than anyone who has ruled over Jerusalem before me;[o] I have experienced
much of wisdom and knowledge."
17Then I applied myself to the understanding of wisdom,[p] and also of

1:1 [a]ver 12; Ecc 7:27; 12:10 [b]Pr 1:1
1:2 [c]Ps 39:5-6; 62:9; 144:4; Ecc 12:8; Ro 8:20-21
1:3 [d]Ecc 2:11,22; 3:9; 5:15-16
1:4 [e]Ps 104:5; 119:90
1:5 [f]Ps 19:5-6
1:7 [g]Job 36:28
1:8 [h]Pr 27:20
1:9 [i]Ecc 2:12; 3:15
1:11 [j]Ecc 2:16
1:12 [k]ver 1
1:13 [l]Ge 3:17; Ecc 3:10
1:14 [m]Ecc 2:11,17
1:15 [n]Ecc 7:13
1:16 [o]1Ki 3:12; 4:30; Ecc 2:9
1:17 [p]Ecc 7:23

[a] *1* Or *leader of the assembly*; also in verses 2 and 12

1:1–11

PROMISE 1

MEANINGLESS?

There's nothing a man wants more than to believe his life matters. We want to be a part of something important, something that lasts. Yet at times our lives seem to consist of nothing more than making a living, perhaps raising a family, paying our taxes and dying.

It may impress you to learn that Solomon came to the same conclusion. He noted that all of life "under the sun"—that is, in our earthly existence and apart from God—is meaningless. Like sand castles on the beach that are swept away by the high tide, so everything we do is washed away and eventually amounts to nothing.

To prove his point, Solomon gave a few illustrations. The results of a man's labor won't remain; after a few generations the man himself is forgotten. In the natural world, the sun circles overhead every day only to make the same journey the next day. Water follows an endless cycle from a river to the sea, from the sea to the sky, and from the sky back to the ground where it runs into a river. All of these cycles continue regardless of any significance we try to build into our lives.

It would be easy to throw up our hands in despair after reading Solomon's words. But remember, he was talking about life "under the sun"—life without God. Solomon's words make sense, don't they? Just ask yourself, "What have I done that has eternal value if I take God out of the equation?" The answer should reveal two things. First, life without God is, as Solomon said, "meaningless." Second, the opposite is equally true: The presence of God adds meaning to everything you do.

For the next Promise 1 reading go to page 715.

madness and folly,[q] but I learned that
this, too, is a chasing after the wind.

18For with much wisdom comes
much sorrow;
the more knowledge, the more
grief.[r]

Pleasures Are Meaningless

2 I thought in my heart, "Come now, I
will test you with pleasure[s] to find
out what is good." But that also proved
to be meaningless. 2"Laughter,"[t] I
said, "is foolish. And what does pleasure accomplish?" 3I tried cheering
myself with wine,[u] and embracing
folly[v]—my mind still guiding me with
wisdom. I wanted to see what was
worthwhile for men to do under heav-
en during the few days of their
lives.
4I undertook great projects: I built
houses for myself[w] and planted vineyards.[x] 5I made gardens and parks
and planted all kinds of fruit trees in
them. 6I made reservoirs to water
groves of flourishing trees. 7I bought
male and female slaves and had other
slaves who were born in my house. I
also owned more herds and flocks than
anyone in Jerusalem before me. 8I
amassed silver and gold[y] for myself,
and the treasure of kings and provinces. I acquired men and women
singers,[z] and a harem[a] as well—the
delights of the heart of man. 9I became
greater by far than anyone in Jerusalem
before me.[a] In all this my wisdom
stayed with me.

10I denied myself nothing my eyes
desired;
I refused my heart no pleasure.
My heart took delight in all my
work,
and this was the reward for all
my labor.
11Yet when I surveyed all that my
hands had done
and what I had toiled to achieve,
everything was meaningless, a
chasing after the wind;[b]
nothing was gained under the
sun.[c]

Wisdom and Folly Are Meaningless

12Then I turned my thoughts to
consider wisdom,
and also madness and folly.[d]
What more can the king's successor
do
than what has already been
done?[e]
13I saw that wisdom[f] is better than
folly,[g]
just as light is better than
darkness.
14The wise man has eyes in his head,
while the fool walks in the
darkness;
but I came to realize
that the same fate overtakes
them both.[h]

15Then I thought in my heart,

"The fate of the fool will overtake
me also.
What then do I gain by being
wise?"[i]
I said in my heart,
"This too is meaningless."
16For the wise man, like the fool, will
not be long remembered;
in days to come both will be
forgotten.[j]
Like the fool, the wise man too
must die!

Toil Is Meaningless

17So I hated life, because the work
that is done under the sun was grievous to me. All of it is meaningless, a
chasing after the wind.[k] 18I hated all
the things I had toiled for under the
sun, because I must leave them to the
one who comes after me.[l] 19And who
knows whether he will be a wise man
or a fool? Yet he will have control over
all the work into which I have poured
my effort and skill under the sun. This
too is meaningless. 20So my heart began to despair over all my toilsome labor under the sun. 21For a man may do
his work with wisdom, knowledge and
skill, and then he must leave all he
owns to someone who has not worked
for it. This too is meaningless and a
great misfortune. 22What does a man
get for all the toil and anxious striving
with which he labors under the sun?[m]
23All his days his work is pain and
grief;[n] even at night his mind does not
rest. This too is meaningless.
24A man can do nothing better than
to eat and drink[o] and find satisfaction
in his work.[p] This too, I see, is from
the hand of God,[q] 25for without him,
who can eat or find enjoyment? 26To
the man who pleases him, God gives
wisdom, knowledge and happiness,
but to the sinner he gives the task of
gathering and storing up wealth[r] to
hand it over to the one who pleases
God.[s] This too is meaningless, a chasing after the wind.

1:17 [q]Ecc 2:3,12; 7:25
1:18 [r]Ecc 2:23; 12:12
2:1 [s]Ecc 7:4; 8:15; Lk 12:19
2:2 [t]Pr 14:13; Ecc 7:6
2:3 [u]ver 24-25; Ecc 3:12-13 [v]Ecc 1:17
2:4 [w]1Ki 7:1-12 [x]SS 8:11
2:8 [y]1Ki 9:28; 10:10,14,21 [z]2Sa 19:35
2:9 [a]1Ch 29:25; Ecc 1:16
2:11 [b]Ecc 1:14 [c]Ecc 1:3
2:12 [d]Ecc 1:17 [e]Ecc 1:9; 7:25
2:13 [f]Ecc 7:19; 9:18 [g]Ecc 7:11-12
2:14 [h]Ps 49:10; Pr 17:24; Ecc 3:19; 6:6; 7:2; 9:3,11-12
2:15 [i]Ecc 6:8
2:16 [j]Ecc 1:11; 9:5
2:17 [k]Ecc 4:2
2:18 [l]Ps 39:6; 49:10
2:22 [m]Ecc 1:3; 3:9
2:23 [n]Job 5:7; 14:1; Ecc 1:18
2:24 [o]Ecc 8:15; 1Co 15:32 [p]Ecc 3:22 [q]Ecc 3:12-13; 5:17-19; 9:7-10
2:26 [r]Job 27:17 [s]Pr 13:22

[a]8 The meaning of the Hebrew for this phrase is uncertain.

A Time for Everything

3 There is a time[t] for everything,
and a season for every activity
under heaven:

2 a time to be born and a time to
die,
a time to plant and a time to
uproot,
3 a time to kill and a time to heal,
a time to tear down and a time
to build,
4 a time to weep and a time to
laugh,
a time to mourn and a time to
dance,
5 a time to scatter stones and a
time to gather them,
a time to embrace and a time to
refrain,
6 a time to search and a time to
give up,
a time to keep and a time to
throw away,
7 a time to tear and a time to
mend,
a time to be silent[u] and a time
to speak,
8 a time to love and a time to
hate,
a time for war and a time for
peace.

9 What does the worker gain from his
toil?[v] 10 I have seen the burden God
has laid on men.[w] 11 He has made everything beautiful in its time.[x] He has
also set eternity in the hearts of men;
yet they cannot fathom[y] what God
has done from beginning to end.[z] 12 I
know that there is nothing better for
men than to be happy and do good
while they live. 13 That everyone may
eat and drink,[a] and find satisfaction[b]
in all his toil—this is the gift of God.[c]
14 I know that everything God does will
endure forever; nothing can be added
to it and nothing taken from it. God
does it so that men will revere him.[d]

15 Whatever is has already been,[e]
and what will be has been
before;[f]
and God will call the past to
account.[a]

16 And I saw something else under
the sun:

In the place of judgment—
wickedness was there,
in the place of justice—
wickedness was there.

17 I thought in my heart,

"God will bring to judgment[g]
both the righteous and the
wicked,

3:1 [t]ver 11,17; Ecc 8:6 **3:7** [u]Am 5:13 **3:9** [v]Ecc 1:3 **3:10** [w]Ecc 1:13 **3:11** [x]ver 1 [y]Job 11:7; Ecc 8:17 [z]Job 28:23; Ro 11:33 **3:13** [a]Ecc 2:3 [b]Ps 34:12 [c]Dt 12:7,18; Ecc 2:24; 5:19 **3:14** [d]Job 23:15; Ecc 5:7; 7:18; 8:12-13; Jas 1:17 **3:15** [e]Ecc 6:10 [f]Ecc 1:9 **3:17** [g]Job 19:29; Ecc 11:9; Mt 16:27; Ro 2:6-8; 2Th 1:6-7

[a] 15 Or *God calls back the past*

3:1–11

CHANGE: THE ONLY SURE THING

PROMISE 1

As we live through the different seasons of life, sometimes we are faced with unexpected change. Accidents, natural disasters, job transfers and the like take us by surprise and change our perspective—for better or for worse. Perhaps you've been fortunate enough to have seen a difficult situation turn around for the better. Or maybe you've gone through a sudden change in your life, a time when things went from good to bad or from bad to worse.

It's easy and natural at times to wonder why God allows certain events to happen. In what has become the best-known portion of Ecclesiastes, Solomon lets us know that, this side of heaven, we'll never fully understand why such things occur. But Solomon's perspective is that all changes in life are arranged by God. In that context Solomon said, "there is a time for everything" and followed that statement with a balanced list of fourteen negative and positive life experiences (vv. 2–8). Read through the list and try to think of a situation in which each of these "times" has been or will be true in your life.

Understanding every part of life can be as perplexing as figuring out the placement of each piece of a large puzzle without looking at the top of the box. We know each piece contributes to the beauty of the picture, but we don't know how. Similarly, Solomon said God has made everything beautiful "in its time." That's a promise that overflows with optimism. *Everything* will eventually fit together to form a beautiful picture.

Wouldn't it be nice to see the box top? But God doesn't always give it to us. Instead, he gives us something better: He offers us hope. We can know that God has drawn a bigger picture for our lives, a picture that will make sense of all the unexpected changes that happen in life.

As you look back on your life, can you see any events or experiences that at the time seemed useless—or worse, even harmful? Over time, what good has resulted from those experiences? Have you found it possible to thank God for these changes? Perhaps you've had experiences for which you can see no positive benefit whatsoever. That's when faith enters the picture. Because we read that "in all things God works for the good of those who love him, who have been called according to his purpose" (Romans 8:28), we can believe and rely on God to keep his promise to us.

For the next Promise 1 reading go to page 717.

for there will be a time for every
activity,
a time for every deed."[h]

18I also thought, "As for men, God
tests them so that they may see that
they are like the animals.[i] **19**Man's
fate[j] is like that of the animals; the
same fate awaits them both: As one
dies, so dies the other. All have the
same breath[a]; man has no advantage
over the animal. Everything is meaningless. **20**All go to the same place; all
come from dust, and to dust all return.[k] **21**Who knows if the spirit of
man rises upward[l] and if the spirit
of the animal[b] goes down into the
earth?"

22So I saw that there is nothing better for a man than to enjoy his work,[m]
because that is his lot.[n] For who can
bring him to see what will happen after
him?

Oppression, Toil, Friendlessness

4 Again I looked and saw all the oppression[o] that was taking place under the sun:

I saw the tears of the oppressed—
and they have no comforter;
power was on the side of their
oppressors—
and they have no comforter.[p]
2And I declared that the dead,[q]
who had already died,
are happier than the living,
who are still alive.[r]
3But better than both
is he who has not yet been,[s]
who has not seen the evil
that is done under the sun.[t]

4And I saw that all labor and all
achievement spring from man's envy
of his neighbor. This too is meaningless, a chasing after the wind.[u]

5The fool folds his hands[v]
and ruins himself.
6Better one handful with tranquillity
than two handfuls with toil[w]
and chasing after the wind.

7Again I saw something meaningless
under the sun:

8There was a man all alone;
he had neither son nor brother.
There was no end to his toil,
yet his eyes were not content[x]
with his wealth.
"For whom am I toiling," he asked,
"and why am I depriving myself
of enjoyment?"
This too is meaningless—
a miserable business!

2 →PG. 932
9Two are better than one,
because they have a good return
for their work:
10If one falls down,
his friend can help him up.
But pity the man who falls
and has no one to help him up!
11Also, if two lie down together, they
will keep warm.
But how can one keep warm
alone?
12Though one may be overpowered,
two can defend themselves.
A cord of three strands is not
quickly broken.

Advancement Is Meaningless

13Better a poor but wise youth than
an old but foolish king who no longer
knows how to take warning. **14**The
youth may have come from prison to
the kingship, or he may have been

3:17 [h]ver 1
3:18 [i]Ps 73:22
3:19 [j]Ecc 2:14
3:20 [k]Ge 2:7; 3:19; Job 34:15
3:21 [l]Ecc 12:7
3:22 [m]Ecc 2:24; 5:18 [n]Job 31:2
4:1 [o]Ps 12:5; Ecc 3:16 [p]La 1:16
4:2 [q]Jer 20:17-18; 22:10 [r]Job 3:17; 10:18
4:3 [s]Job 3:16; Ecc 6:3 [t]Job 3:22
4:4 [u]Ecc 1:14
4:5 [v]Pr 6:10
4:6 [w]Pr 15:16-17; 16:8
4:8 [x]Pr 27:20

[a]*19* Or *spirit* [b]*21* Or *Who knows the spirit of man, which rises upward, or the spirit of the animal, which*

4:9–12

PROMISE 2

WANTED: GOOD FRIENDS

Good friends seem in short supply today. We're living in a time when men find it hard to develop close relationships with other men. We might have achieved that as boys, but as adults we tend to see other men as competitors. And we're reluctant to get close to the competition—doing so might give them an edge.

The Bible doesn't portray friends as competitors. Instead, they're seen as companions. Solomon points out several reasons why having a friend is better than going it alone. First, two can reap a bigger profit than one. Any job—chopping wood, building a deck or painting a house—can be done more quickly and better with two men working side by side. It's also more fun! Second, friends can support one another. While most men like to think they can make it alone, we all need someone to lighten our load and help us get back up when we stumble. Third, friends offer warmth. Solomon meant for this to have a wider application than to a marriage. Friends offer warmth when we face threatening situations, and they are there to encourage us when we feel vulnerable. Fourth, friends increase our strength. And if two men are strong, how much stronger are they if the Lord locks arms with them?

Considering the above points, do you have any close friends? Remember, finding a friend is only half the job. The other half is being one.

For the next Promise 2 reading go to page 881.

born in poverty within his kingdom. 15I
saw that all who lived and walked under the sun followed the youth, the
king's successor. 16There was no end to
all the people who were before them.
But those who came later were not
pleased with the successor. This too is
meaningless, a chasing after the wind.

Stand in Awe of God

5 Guard your steps when you go to the
house of God. Go near to listen rather than to offer the sacrifice of fools,
who do not know that they do wrong.

2Do not be quick with your mouth,
do not be hasty in your heart
to utter anything before God.[y]
God is in heaven
and you are on earth,
so let your words be few.[z]
3As a dream[a] comes when there
are many cares,
so the speech of a fool when
there are many words.[b]

4When you make a vow to God, do
not delay in fulfilling it.[c] He has no
pleasure in fools; fulfill your vow.[d] 5It
is better not to vow than to make a vow
and not fulfill it.[e] 6Do not let your
mouth lead you into sin. And do not
protest to the ⌊temple⌋ messenger, "My
vow was a mistake." Why should God
be angry at what you say and destroy
the work of your hands? 7Much dream-
ing and many words are meaningless.
Therefore stand in awe of God.[f]

5:1–5

PROMISE 1

AWESTRUCK

If you've ever stood on the edge of an oceanside cliff and watched huge waves crash against the rocks below, you know what it's like to stand in awe. The power and beauty of such a sight are enough to take the breath from the most passive spectator.

As believers, we're to enter God's presence with an even greater sense of awe. That means we'll enter his presence with reverence, listen to what he has to say to us, and take care in what we promise to God (vv. 4–5).

Solomon's words are easy to understand. The bigger challenge involves applying them to our lives. How exactly will you listen for what God has to say to you? And how will you be sure you'll only promise God those things that, by his grace and by his power, you can do?

For the next Promise 1 reading go to page 722.

5:2 [y]Jdg 11:35 [z]Job 6:24; Pr 10:19; 20:25
5:3 [a]Job 20:8 [b]Ecc 10:14
5:4 [c]Dt 23:21; Jdg 11:35; Ps 119:60 [d]Nu 30:2; Ps 66:13-14; 76:11
5:5 [e]Nu 30:2-4; Pr 20:25; Jnh 2:9; Ac 5:4
5:7 [f]Ecc 3:14; 12:13

Riches Are Meaningless

8If you see the poor oppressed[g] in a
district, and justice and rights denied,
do not be surprised at such things; for
one official is eyed by a higher one, and
over them both are others higher still.
9The increase from the land is taken by 3 →PG. 718
all; the king himself profits from the
fields.

10Whoever loves money never has
money enough;
whoever loves wealth is never
satisfied with his income.
This too is meaningless.

11As goods increase,
so do those who consume them.
And what benefit are they to the
owner
except to feast his eyes on them?

12The sleep of a laborer is sweet,
whether he eats little or much,
but the abundance of a rich man
permits him no sleep.[h]

13I have seen a grievous evil under
the sun:[i]

wealth hoarded to the harm of its
owner,
14 or wealth lost through some
misfortune,
so that when he has a son
there is nothing left for him.
15Naked a man comes from his
mother's womb,
and as he comes, so he
departs.[j]
He takes nothing from his labor[k]
that he can carry in his hand.[l]

16This too is a grievous evil:

As a man comes, so he departs,
and what does he gain,
since he toils for the wind?[m]
17All his days he eats in darkness,
with great frustration, affliction
and anger.

18Then I realized that it is good and
proper for a man to eat and drink,[n]
and to find satisfaction in his toilsome
labor[o] under the sun during the few
days of life God has given him—for this
is his lot. 19Moreover, when God gives
any man wealth and possessions,[p]
and enables him to enjoy them,[q] to
accept his lot[r] and be happy in his
work—this is a gift of God.[s] 20He seldom reflects on the days of his life, because God keeps him occupied with
gladness of heart.[t]

6 I have seen another evil under the
sun, and it weighs heavily on men:
2God gives a man wealth, possessions
and honor, so that he lacks nothing his

5:8 [g]Ps 12:5; Ecc 4:1
5:12 [h]Job 20:20
5:13 [i]Ecc 6:1-2
5:15 [j]Job 1:21 [k]Ps 49:17; 1Ti 6:7 [l]Ecc 1:3
5:16 [m]Pr 11:29; Ecc 1:3
5:18 [n]Ecc 2:3 [o]Ecc 2:10,24
5:19 [p]1Ch 29:12; 2Ch 1:12 [q]Ecc 6:2 [r]Job 31:2 [s]Ecc 2:24; 3:13
5:20 [t]Dt 12:7,18

heart desires, but God does not enable
him to enjoy them,[u] and a stranger
enjoys them instead. This is meaningless, a grievous evil.[v]
3A man may have a hundred children and live many years; yet no matter how long he lives, if he cannot enjoy
his prosperity and does not receive
proper burial, I say that a stillborn[w]
child is better off than he.[x] 4It comes
without meaning, it departs in darkness, and in darkness its name is
shrouded. 5Though it never saw the
sun or knew anything, it has more rest
than does that man— 6even if he lives
a thousand years twice over but fails to
enjoy his prosperity. Do not all go to
the same place?

7All man's efforts are for his mouth,
yet his appetite is never
satisfied.[y]
8What advantage has a wise man
over a fool?[z]
What does a poor man gain
by knowing how to conduct
himself before others?
9Better what the eye sees
than the roving of the appetite.
This too is meaningless,
a chasing after the wind.[a]

10Whatever exists has already been
named,
and what man is has been
known;
no man can contend
with one who is stronger than
he.
11The more the words,
the less the meaning,
and how does that profit
anyone?

12For who knows what is good for a
man in life, during the few and meaningless days[b] he passes through like a
shadow?[c] Who can tell him what will
happen under the sun after he is gone?

Wisdom

7 A good name is better than fine
perfume,[d]
and the day of death better than
the day of birth.
2It is better to go to a house of
mourning
than to go to a house of feasting,
for death[e] is the destiny[f] of every
man;
the living should take this to
heart.
3Sorrow is better than laughter,[g]
because a sad face is good for
the heart.
4The heart of the wise is in the
house of mourning,
but the heart of fools is in the
house of pleasure.[h]
5It is better to heed a wise man's
rebuke[i]
than to listen to the song of
fools.
6Like the crackling of thorns[j]
under the pot,
so is the laughter[k] of fools.
This too is meaningless.

7Extortion turns a wise man into a
fool,
and a bribe[l] corrupts the heart.

8The end of a matter is better than
its beginning,
and patience[m] is better than
pride.
9Do not be quickly provoked[n] in
your spirit,
for anger resides in the lap of
fools.

10Do not say, "Why were the old
days better than these?"
For it is not wise to ask such
questions.

11Wisdom, like an inheritance, is a
good thing[o]
and benefits those who see the
sun.[p]
12Wisdom is a shelter
as money is a shelter,
but the advantage of knowledge is
this:
that wisdom preserves the life of
its possessor.

3 →PG. 720

13Consider what God has done:[q]

Who can straighten
what he has made crooked?[r]
14When times are good, be happy;
but when times are bad,
consider:
God has made the one
as well as the other.
Therefore, a man cannot discover
anything about his future.

15In this meaningless life[s] of mine I
have seen both of these:

a righteous man perishing in his
righteousness,
and a wicked man living long in
his wickedness.[t]
16Do not be overrighteous,
neither be overwise—
why destroy yourself?
17Do not be overwicked,
and do not be a fool—
why die before your time?[u]
18It is good to grasp the one
and not let go of the other.

6:2 [u]Ps 17:14; Ecc 5:19 [v]Ecc 5:13
6:3 [w]Job 3:16; Ecc 4:3 [x]Job 3:3
6:7 [y]Pr 16:26; 27:20
6:8 [z]Ecc 2:15
6:9 [a]Ecc 1:14
6:12 [b]Job 10:20 [c]Job 14:2; Ps 39:6; Jas 4:14
7:1 [d]Pr 22:1; SS 1:3
7:2 [e]Pr 11:19 [f]Ps 90:12
7:3 [g]Pr 14:13
7:4 [h]Ecc 2:1; Jer 16:8
7:5 [i]Ps 141:5; Pr 13:18; 15:31-32
7:6 [j]Ps 58:9; 118:12 [k]Ecc 2:2
7:7 [l]Ex 18:21; 23:8; Dt 16:19
7:8 [m]Pr 14:29; Gal 5:22; Eph 4:2
7:9 [n]Mt 5:22; Pr 14:17; Jas 1:19
7:11 [o]Pr 8:10-11; Ecc 2:13 [p]Ecc 11:7
7:13 [q]Ecc 2:24 [r]Ecc 1:15
7:15 [s]Job 7:7 [t]Ecc 8:12-14; Jer 12:1
7:17 [u]Job 15:32; Ps 55:23

The man who fears God[v] will
avoid all ⌞extremes⌟.[a]

19Wisdom[w] makes one wise man
more powerful[x]
than ten rulers in a city.

20There is not a righteous man[y] on
earth
who does what is right and never
sins.[z]

21Do not pay attention to every word
people say,
or you[a] may hear your servant
cursing you—
22for you know in your heart
that many times you yourself
have cursed others.

23All this I tested by wisdom and I
said,

"I am determined to be wise"[b]—
but this was beyond me.
24Whatever wisdom may be,
it is far off and most profound—
who can discover it?[c]
25So I turned my mind to
understand,
to investigate and to search out
wisdom and the scheme of
things[d]
and to understand the stupidity of
wickedness
and the madness of folly.[e]

26I find more bitter than death
the woman who is a snare,[f]
whose heart is a trap
and whose hands are chains.
The man who pleases God will
escape her,
but the sinner she will
ensnare.[g]

27"Look," says the Teacher,[b][h] "this
is what I have discovered:

"Adding one thing to another to
discover the scheme of
things—
28 while I was still searching
but not finding—
I found one ⌞upright⌟ man among a
thousand,
but not one ⌞upright⌟ woman[i]
among them all.
29This only have I found:
God made mankind upright,
but men have gone in search of
many schemes."

7:18 [v]Ecc 3:14
7:19 [w]Ecc 2:13 [x]Ecc 9:13-18
7:20 [y]Ps 14:3 [z]1Ki 8:46; 2Ch 6:36; Pr 20:9; Ro 3:23
7:21 [a]Pr 30:10
7:23 [b]Ecc 1:17; Ro 1:22
7:24 [c]Job 28:12
7:25 [d]Job 28:3 [e]Ecc 1:17
7:26 [f]Ex 10:7; Jdg 14:15 [g]Pr 2:16-19; 5:3-5; 7:23; 22:14
7:27 [h]Ecc 1:1
7:28 [i]1Ki 11:3

8 Who is like the wise man?
Who knows the explanation of
things?
Wisdom brightens a man's face
and changes its hard
appearance.

Obey the King

2Obey the king's command, I say,
because you took an oath before
God. 3Do not be in a hurry to leave the
king's presence.[j] Do not stand up for
a bad cause, for he will do whatever
he pleases. 4Since a king's word is supreme, who can say to him, "What are
you doing?[k]"

5Whoever obeys his command will
come to no harm,
and the wise heart will know the
proper time and procedure.
6For there is a proper time and
procedure for every
matter,[l]
though a man's misery weighs
heavily upon him.

7Since no man knows the future,
who can tell him what is to
come?
8No man has power over the wind
to contain it[c];
so no one has power over the
day of his death.
As no one is discharged in time of
war,
so wickedness will not release
those who practice it.

9All this I saw, as I applied my mind
to everything done under the sun.
There is a time when a man lords it
over others to his own[d] hurt. 10Then
too, I saw the wicked buried[m]—those
who used to come and go from the holy
place and receive praise[e] in the city
where they did this. This too is meaningless.
11When the sentence for a crime is
not quickly carried out, the hearts of
the people are filled with schemes to
do wrong. 12Although a wicked man
commits a hundred crimes and still
lives a long time, I know that it will go
better[n] with God-fearing men,[o] who
are reverent before God.[p] 13Yet because the wicked do not fear God,[q] it
will not go well with them, and their
days[r] will not lengthen like a shadow.
14There is something else meaningless that occurs on earth: righteous
men who get what the wicked deserve,
and wicked men who get what the righteous deserve.[s] This too, I say, is
meaningless.[t] 15So I commend the
enjoyment of life[u], because nothing is
better for a man under the sun than to
eat and drink[v] and be glad.[w] Then joy

8:3 [j]Ecc 10:4
8:4 [k]Job 9:12; Est 1:19; Da 4:35
8:6 [l]Ecc 3:1
8:10 [m]Ecc 1:11
8:12 [n]Dt 12:28; Ps 37:11, 18-19; Pr 1:32-33; Isa 3:10-11 [o]Ex 1:20 [p]Ecc 3:14
8:13 [q]Ecc 3:14; Isa 3:11 [r]Dt 4:40; Job 5:26; Ps 34:12; Isa 65:20
8:14 [s]Job 21:7; Ps 73:14; Mal 3:15 [t]Ecc 7:15
8:15 [u]Ps 42:8 [v]Ex 32:6; Ecc 2:3 [w]Ecc 2:24; 3:12-13; 5:18; 9:7

[a]18 Or *will follow them both* [b]27 Or *leader of the assembly* [c]8 Or *over his spirit to retain it* [d]9 Or *to their* [e]10 Some Hebrew manuscripts and Septuagint (Aquila); most Hebrew manuscripts *and are forgotten*

will accompany him in his work all the
days of the life God has given him under the sun.
16 When I applied my mind to know
wisdom[x] and to observe man's labor
on earth[y]—his eyes not seeing sleep
day or night— 17 then I saw all that God
has done.[z] No one can comprehend
what goes on under the sun. Despite all
his efforts to search it out, man cannot
discover its meaning. Even if a wise
man claims he knows, he cannot really
comprehend it.[a]

A Common Destiny for All

9 So I reflected on all this and concluded that the righteous and the
wise and what they do are in God's
hands, but no man knows whether love
or hate awaits him.[b] 2 All share a common destiny—the righteous and the
wicked, the good and the bad,[a] the
clean and the unclean, those who offer
sacrifices and those who do not.

As it is with the good man,
so with the sinner;
as it is with those who take oaths,
so with those who are afraid to
take them.[c]

3 This is the evil in everything that
happens under the sun: The same destiny overtakes all.[d] The hearts of men,
moreover, are full of evil and there is
madness in their hearts while they
live,[e] and afterward they join the
dead.[f] 4 Anyone who is among the living has hope[b]—even a live dog is better off than a dead lion!

5 For the living know that they will
die,
but the dead know nothing;[g]
they have no further reward,
and even the memory of them[h]
is forgotten.[i]
6 Their love, their hate
and their jealousy have long
since vanished;
never again will they have a part
in anything that happens under
the sun.[j]

7 Go, eat your food with gladness,
and drink your wine[k] with a joyful
heart,[l] for it is now that God favors
what you do. 8 Always be clothed in
white,[m] and always anoint your head
with oil. 9 Enjoy life with your wife,[n]
whom you love, all the days of this
meaningless life that God has given
you under the sun— all your meaningless days. For this is your lot[o] in life
and in your toilsome labor under the
sun. 10 Whatever[p] your hand finds to
do, do it with all your might,[q] for in

4 →PG. 727
3 →PG. 722

8:16 xEcc 1:17 yEcc 1:13
8:17 zJob 28:3 aJob 5:9; 28:23; Ecc 3:11; Ro 11:33
9:1 bDt 33:3; Job 12:10; Ecc 10:14
9:2 cJob 9:22; Ecc 2:14; 6:6; 7:2
9:3 dJob 9:22; Ecc 2:14 eJer 11:8; 13:10; 16:12; 17:9 fJob 21:26
9:5 gJob 14:21 hPs 9:6 iEcc 1:11; 2:16; Isa 26:14
9:6 jJob 21:21
9:7 kNu 6:20 lEcc 2:24; 8:15
9:8 mPs 23:5; Rev 3:4
9:9 nPr 5:18 oJob 31:2
9:10 p1Sa 10:7 qEcc 11:6; Ro 12:11; Col 3:23
rNu 16:33 sEcc 2:24
9:11 tAm 2:14-15 uJob 32:13; Isa 47:10; Jer 9:23 vEcc 2:14 wDt 8:18
9:12 xPr 29:6 yPs 73:22; Ecc 2:14; 8:7
9:13 z2Sa 20:22
9:15 aGe 40:14; Ecc 1:11; 2:16; 4:13
9:16 bPr 21:22; Ecc 7:19
9:18 cver 16
10:1 dPr 13:16; 18:2
10:3 ePr 13:16; 18:2
10:4 fEcc 8:3 gPr 16:14; 25:15

the grave,[c][r] where you are going,
there is neither working nor planning
nor knowledge nor wisdom.[s]

11 I have seen something else under
the sun:

The race is not to the swift
or the battle to the strong,[t]
nor does food come to the wise[u]
or wealth to the brilliant
or favor to the learned;
but time and chance[v] happen to
them all.[w]

12 Moreover, no man knows when his
hour will come:

As fish are caught in a cruel net,
or birds are taken in a snare,
so men are trapped by evil times[x]
that fall unexpectedly upon
them.[y]

Wisdom Better Than Folly

13 I also saw under the sun this example of wisdom[z] that greatly impressed
me: 14 There was once a small city with
only a few people in it. And a powerful
king came against it, surrounded it and
built huge siegeworks against it. 15 Now
there lived in that city a man poor but
wise, and he saved the city by his wisdom. But nobody remembered that
poor man.[a] 16 So I said, "Wisdom is
better than strength." But the poor
man's wisdom is despised, and his
words are no longer heeded.[b]

17 The quiet words of the wise are
more to be heeded
than the shouts of a ruler of
fools.
18 Wisdom[c] is better than weapons
of war,
but one sinner destroys much
good.

10 As dead flies give perfume a bad
smell,
so a little folly[d] outweighs
wisdom and honor.
2 The heart of the wise inclines to
the right,
but the heart of the fool to the
left.
3 Even as he walks along the road,
the fool lacks sense
and shows everyone[e] how
stupid he is.
4 If a ruler's anger rises against you,
do not leave your post;[f]
calmness can lay great errors to
rest.[g]

a 2 Septuagint (Aquila), Vulgate and Syriac; Hebrew does not have *and the bad.* b 4 Or *What then is to be chosen? With all who live, there is hope* c 10 Hebrew *Sheol*

5There is an evil I have seen under
the sun,
the sort of error that arises from
a ruler:
6Fools are put in many high
positions,[h]
while the rich occupy the low
ones.
7I have seen slaves on horseback,
while princes go on foot like
slaves.[i]

8Whoever digs a pit may fall into
it;[j]
whoever breaks through a wall
may be bitten by a snake.[k]
9Whoever quarries stones may be
injured by them;
whoever splits logs may be
endangered by them.[l]

10If the ax is dull
and its edge unsharpened,
more strength is needed
but skill will bring success.

11If a snake bites before it is
charmed,
there is no profit for the
charmer.[m]

12Words from a wise man's mouth
are gracious,[n]
but a fool is consumed by his
own lips.[o]
13At the beginning his words are
folly;
at the end they are wicked
madness—
14 and the fool multiplies words.[p]

No one knows what is coming—
who can tell him what will
happen after him?[q]

15A fool's work wearies him;
he does not know the way to
town.

16Woe to you, O land whose king was
a servant[a][r]
and whose princes feast in the
morning.
17Blessed are you, O land whose king
is of noble birth
and whose princes eat at a
proper time—
for strength and not for
drunkenness.[s]

18If a man is lazy, the rafters sag;
if his hands are idle, the house
leaks.[t]

19A feast is made for laughter,
and wine[u] makes life merry,
but money is the answer for
everything.

20Do not revile the king[v] even in
your thoughts,
or curse the rich in your
bedroom,
because a bird of the air may carry
your words,
and a bird on the wing may
report what you say.

Bread Upon the Waters

11 Cast[w] your bread upon the
waters,
for after many days you will find
it again.[x]
2Give portions to seven, yes to eight,
for you do not know what
disaster may come upon the
land.

3If clouds are full of water,
they pour rain upon the earth.
Whether a tree falls to the south or
to the north,
in the place where it falls, there
will it lie.
4Whoever watches the wind will not
plant;
whoever looks at the clouds will
not reap.

5As you do not know the path of the
wind,[y]
or how the body is formed[b] in a
mother's womb,[z]
so you cannot understand the work
of God,
the Maker of all things.

6Sow your seed in the morning,
and at evening let not your
hands be idle,[a]
for you do not know which will
succeed,
whether this or that,
or whether both will do equally
well.

Remember Your Creator While Young

7Light is sweet,
and it pleases the eyes to see the
sun.[b]
8However many years a man may
live,
let him enjoy them all.
But let him remember[c] the days
of darkness,
for they will be many.
Everything to come is
meaningless.

9Be happy, young man, while you
are young,
and let your heart give you joy in
the days of your youth.
Follow the ways of your heart
and whatever your eyes see,

10:6 [h]Pr 29:2
10:7 [i]Pr 19:10
10:8 [j]Ps 7:15; 57:6; Pr 26:27 [k]Est 2:23; Ps 9:16; Am 5:19
10:9 [l]Pr 26:27
10:11 [m]Ps 58:5; Isa 3:3
10:12 [n]Pr 10:32 [o]Pr 10:14; 14:3; 15:2; 18:7
10:14 [p]Pr 15:2; Ecc 5:3; 6:12; 8:7 [q]Ecc 9:1
10:16 [r]Isa 3:4-5,12
10:17 [s]Dt 14:26; 1Sa 25:36; Pr 31:4
10:18 [t]Pr 20:4; 24:30-34
10:19 [u]Ge 14:18; Jdg 9:13
10:20 [v]Ex 22:28
11:1 [w]ver 6; Isa 32:20; Hos 10:12 [x]Dt 24:19; Pr 19:17; Mt 10:42
11:5 [y]Jn 3:8-10 [z]Ps 139:14-16
11:6 [a]Ecc 9:10
11:7 [b]Ecc 7:11
11:8 [c]Ecc 12:1

[a] *16* Or *king is a child* [b] *5* Or *know how life* (or *the spirit*) / *enters the body being formed*

but know that for all these things
God will bring you to
judgment.[d]
10So then, banish anxiety[e] from
your heart
and cast off the troubles of your
body,
for youth and vigor are
meaningless.[f]

12 Remember[g] your Creator
in the days of your youth,
before the days of trouble[h] come
and the years approach when
you will say,
"I find no pleasure in them"—
2before the sun and the light
and the moon and the stars grow
dark,
and the clouds return after the
rain;
3when the keepers of the house
tremble,
and the strong men stoop,
when the grinders cease because
they are few,
and those looking through the
windows grow dim;
4when the doors to the street are
closed
and the sound of grinding fades;
when men rise up at the sound of
birds,
but all their songs grow faint;[i]
5when men are afraid of heights
and of dangers in the streets;
when the almond tree blossoms
and the grasshopper drags
himself along
and desire no longer is stirred.
Then man goes to his eternal
home[j]
and mourners[k] go about the
streets.

6Remember him—before the silver
cord is severed,
or the golden bowl is broken;
before the pitcher is shattered at
the spring,
or the wheel broken at the well,
7and the dust returns[l] to the
ground it came from,
and the spirit returns to God[m]
who gave it.[n]

8"Meaningless! Meaningless!" says
the Teacher.[a]
"Everything is meaningless![o]"

The Conclusion of the Matter

9Not only was the Teacher wise, but
also he imparted knowledge to the
people. He pondered and searched out
and set in order many proverbs.[p]
10The Teacher searched to find just the
right words, and what he wrote was upright and true.[q]
11The words of the wise are like
goads, their collected sayings like firmly embedded nails[r]—given by one
Shepherd. 12Be warned, my son, of
anything in addition to them.
Of making many books there is no
end, and much study wearies the
body.[s]

13Now all has been heard;
here is the conclusion of the
matter:
Fear God and keep his
commandments,[t]
for this is the whole ⌊duty⌋ of
man.[u]
14For God will bring every deed into
judgment,[v]
including every hidden thing,[w]
whether it is good or evil.

3 →PG. 742

a *8* Or *the leader of the assembly;* also in verses 9 and 10

11:9 [d]Job 19:29; Ecc 2:24; 3:17; 12:14; Ro 14:10
11:10 [e]Ps 94:19 [f]Ecc 2:24
12:1 [g]Ecc 11:8 [h]2Sa 19:35
12:4 [i]Jer 25:10
12:5 [j]Job 17:13; 10:21 [k]Jer 9:17; Am 5:16
12:7 [l]Ge 3:19; Job 34:15; Ps 146:4 [m]Ecc 3:21 [n]Job 20:8; Zec 12:1
12:8 [o]Ecc 1:2
12:9 [p]1Ki 4:32
12:10 [q]Pr 22:20-21
12:11 [r]Ezr 9:8
12:12 [s]Ecc 1:18
12:13 [t]Dt 4:2; 10:12 [u]Mic 6:8
12:14 [v]Ecc 3:17 [w]Mt 10:26; 1Co 4:5

12:9–14

PROMISE 1

OUR SOLITARY PURPOSE

Throughout the book of Ecclesiastes, Solomon points out the futility of "life under the sun." And his words are trustworthy—he'd seen and tried much of what this life has to offer. Solomon had the resources to search far and wide for any earthly thing that could give life meaning. He tried pleasure, wealth, wisdom and work. None of those things, Solomon concluded, gave life lasting significance.

None of us will ever have the time or money to experiment as Solomon did. And that's good; we don't have to walk down the dead-end paths he explored. Instead, we can learn from his experiences. The bottom line is that no matter how hard we try to find meaning in life, if we look anywhere "under the sun" we won't find it. We'll live our lives and then we'll die.

That's why this short epilogue urges us to look to God. While we'll never receive a key that magically unlocks the mysteries of life, we can have something better—we can know the Locksmith. Loving God and living in obedience to him in all aspects of our life is the "whole duty of man." After all is said and done, that's our whole purpose on earth.

In light of the message of Ecclesiastes, what should be the primary pursuit of your life? What possessions or tasks or relationships interfere with that pursuit? What will you do to make sure that nothing gets in the way of making that pursuit the primary focus of your life?

For the next Promise 1 reading go to page 733.

SONG OF SONGS

AT A GLANCE

Key Principle: The physical and emotional aspects of marital love are a gift from God, and are designed to be enjoyed in an other-centered way.
Author: Probably Solomon
Time and Place: ~965 B.C. / Israel: the palace in Jerusalem and the country in the north
Key Verses: 2:16; 7:10; 8:7

BENEFIT

Among the 1,005 songs Solomon wrote (1 Kings 4:32), this beautiful tribute to the love that germinates and blossoms between a man and a woman stood out as "the Song of Songs." It is a literary masterpiece of oriental symbolism, layered metaphors and rich imagery that declares the wonder and glory of romantic love. This song is intimate, but never sinks to vulgarity as it portrays attraction, desire, pleasure, consummation, separation, companionship and growth in the relationship between a man and a woman.

SETTING

While a number of scholars claim that this book is a collection of songs written after the time of Solomon, a good deal of evidence within the book supports the traditional position that Solomon, whose name appears seven times (1:1, 5; 3:7, 9, 11; 8:11–12) wrote it. The Song was probably written early in his reign (~970 B.C.), and it mentions the size of his harem as 60 queens and 80 concubines (6:8; according to 1 Kings 11:3, it would later grow to 700 wives and 300 concubines). It seems difficult to reconcile this harem with the spirit of singular devotion that marks this book, but Solomon's relationship with the Shulammite (6:13) may have been the only genuine romantic love he ever knew. It appears that this book was also written before Solomon slid into the flagrant idolatry and sensual indulgence that characterized his latter years.

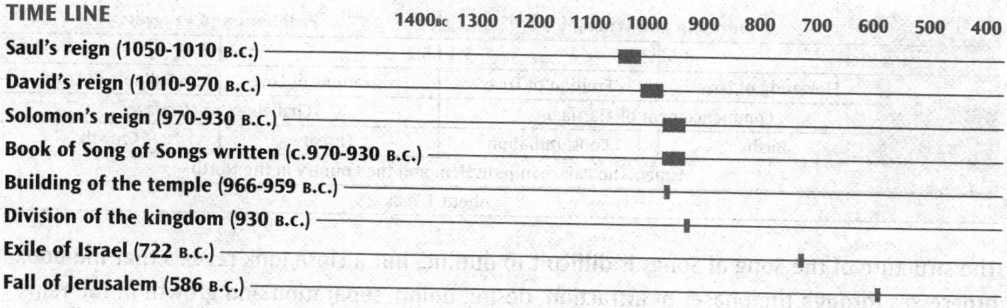

THEME AND PURPOSE

Until recently, scholars almost universally interpreted this book as an allegory of Yahweh and his bride, Israel (Hosea 2:19–20) or of Christ and his bride, the church (Ephesians 5:25–32). While these scholars differed on whether the events in the Song were historical or fictional, they agreed that the book typified the reality of God's love for his covenant people Israel and/or Christ's love for his church.

In the last century or so, commentators began to read the Song as a poetic, historical record of Solomon's actual courtship and marriage to a woman he met tending one of his vineyards in the north. This interpretation resulted from an improved view of human sexuality as a gift from God that should not be disdained as coarse or unspiritual, but should be celebrated as an integral part of the marital relationship between a man and a woman. Seen this way, the Song is an inspired guidebook to the joys of the physical and emotional relationship that God designed at creation. While this book should be interpreted historically, it can still be applied to spiritual truth; a God-honoring human relationship points to the profound oneness of the Godhead (Genesis 1:27; 2:24; 1 Corinthians 6:16–20).

UNIQUE CONTRIBUTION

Song of Songs is a rich dramatic poem complete with a chorus in the background (the daughters of Jerusalem). It consists of several scenes that depict the growing romantic relationship between two characters, a king and his beloved. The content, language, imagery and emphasis on emotions are unique in Scripture. Because of this, scholars over the centuries have challenged the Song's inclusion in the Biblical canon.

This book can be discouraging to single men and to married men for different reasons. Single men have enough trouble struggling with their sexuality without reading a poem that extols the beauty of sexual love. And married men may find the relationship between the king and his bride so ideal that their marriages simply can't compare. Single men must cultivate an understanding that Christ will meet their needs if they look first to him. Married men must realize that the Lord can use trials in their marriage relationships to make them more like Christ, if they are committed to serving him through serving their wives.

LINKS TO THE NEW TESTAMENT

Many students of this book have tied it to the New Testament imagery of Christ's marriage to his bride, the church (2 Corinthians 11:2; Ephesians 5:25–32; Revelation 19:7–9; 21:9). It depicts the covenental relationship—earthly and otherwise—as one marked by radical commitment.

OVERVIEW

FOCUS	Courtship and Wedding		Problems and Progress	
REFERENCE	1:1 3:5	3:6 5:1	5:2 7:10	7:11 8:14
TOPICS	Flowering of Love	Fruition of Love	Frustrations of Love	Fullness of Love
	Commencement of Marriage		Challenges to Marriage	
	Birth	Consummation	Threat	Growth
LOCATION	Israel: The Palace in Jerusalem and the Country in the North			
TIME	About 1 Year			

The structure of the Song of Songs is difficult to outline, but a close look reveals that the book progresses through the phases of attraction, desire, union, separation and growth in the relationship between two lovers. The poem begins with scenes from the courtship (1:1—3:5) followed by the wedding procession from the bride's home to Jerusalem (3:6–11) and the wedding night (4:1—5:1). Months later, the Shulammite responds too late to her husband's approach, and he departs. She searches in vain for him, but when he returns he reassures her of his love (5:2—7:10). The poem concludes with a journey to the Shulammite's home in the north, the deepening of their relationship, a recollection of her brothers' care for her as she was growing up and an invitation between the two lovers (7:11—8:14).

SONG OF SONGS

1 Solomon's Song of Songs.[a]

Beloved[a]

2Let him kiss me with the kisses of
his mouth—
for your love[b] is more delightful
than wine.
3Pleasing is the fragrance of your
perfumes;[c]
your name[d] is like perfume
poured out.
No wonder the maidens[e] love
you!
4Take me away with you—let us
hurry!
Let the king bring me into his
chambers.[f]

Friends

We rejoice and delight in you[b];
we will praise your love more
than wine.

Beloved

How right they are to adore you!

5Dark am I, yet lovely,[g]
O daughters of Jerusalem,[h]
dark like the tents of Kedar,
like the tent curtains of
Solomon.[c]
6Do not stare at me because I am
dark,
because I am darkened by the
sun.
My mother's sons were angry with
me
and made me take care of the
vineyards;[i]
my own vineyard I have
neglected.
7Tell me, you whom I love, where
you graze your flock
and where you rest your sheep[j]
at midday.
Why should I be like a veiled
woman
beside the flocks of your friends?

Friends

8If you do not know, most beautiful
of women,[k]
follow the tracks of the sheep
and graze your young goats
by the tents of the shepherds.

Lover

9I liken you, my darling, to a mare
harnessed to one of the
chariots[l] of Pharaoh.
10Your cheeks[m] are beautiful with
earrings,
your neck with strings of
jewels.[n]
11We will make you earrings of gold,
studded with silver.

Beloved

12While the king was at his table,
my perfume spread its
fragrance.[o]
13My lover is to me a sachet of
myrrh
resting between my breasts.
14My lover is to me a cluster of
henna[p] blossoms
from the vineyards of En Gedi.[q]

Lover

15How beautiful[r] you are, my
darling!
Oh, how beautiful!
Your eyes are doves.[s]

Beloved

16How handsome you are, my lover!
Oh, how charming!
And our bed is verdant.

Lover

17The beams of our house are
cedars;[t]
our rafters are firs.

Beloved[d]

2 I am a rose[e][u] of Sharon,[v]
a lily[w] of the valleys.

Lover

2Like a lily among thorns
is my darling among the
maidens.

Beloved

3Like an apple tree among the trees
of the forest
is my lover[x] among the young
men.

1:1 [a]1Ki 4:32 **1:2** [b]SS 4:10 **1:3** [c]SS 4:10 [d]Ecc 7:1 [e]Ps 45:14 **1:4** [f]Ps 45:15 **1:5** [g]SS 2:14; 4:3 [h]SS 2:7; 5:8; 5:16 **1:6** [i]Ps 69:8; SS 8:12 **1:7** [j]SS 3:1-4; Isa 13:20 **1:8** [k]SS 5:9; 6:1

1:9 [l]2Ch 1:17 **1:10** [m]SS 5:13 [n]Isa 61:10 **1:12** [o]SS 4:11-14 **1:14** [p]SS 4:13 [q]1Sa 23:29 **1:15** [r]SS 4:7 [s]SS 2:14; 4:1; 5:2,12; 6:9 **1:17** [t]1Ki 6:9 **2:1** [u]Isa 35:1 [v]1Ch 27:29 [w]SS 5:13; Hos 14:5 **2:3** [x]SS 1:14

[a]Primarily on the basis of the gender of the Hebrew pronouns used, male and female speakers are indicated in the margins by the captions *Lover* and *Beloved* respectively. The words of others are marked *Friends.* In some instances the divisions and their captions are debatable. [b]*4* The Hebrew is masculine singular. [c]*5* Or *Salma* [d]*1* Or *Lover* [e]*1* Possibly a member of the crocus family

I delight[y] to sit in his shade,
and his fruit is sweet to my taste.[z]
4He has taken me to the banquet hall,[a]
and his banner[b] over me is love.
5Strengthen me with raisins,
refresh me with apples,[c]
for I am faint with love.[d]
6His left arm is under my head,
and his right arm embraces me.[e]
7Daughters of Jerusalem, I charge you[f]
by the gazelles and by the does of the field:
Do not arouse or awaken love
until it so desires.[g]

8Listen! My lover!
Look! Here he comes,
leaping across the mountains,
bounding over the hills.[h]
9My lover is like a gazelle[i] or a young stag.[j]
Look! There he stands behind our wall,
gazing through the windows,
peering through the lattice.
10My lover spoke and said to me,
"Arise, my darling,
my beautiful one, and come with me.
11See! The winter is past;
the rains are over and gone.
12Flowers appear on the earth;
the season of singing has come,
the cooing of doves
is heard in our land.
13The fig tree forms its early fruit;[k]
the blossoming[l] vines spread their fragrance.
Arise, come, my darling;
my beautiful one, come with me."

Lover

14My dove[m] in the clefts of the rock,
in the hiding places on the mountainside,
show me your face,
let me hear your voice;
for your voice is sweet,
and your face is lovely.[n]
15Catch for us the foxes,[o]
the little foxes
that ruin the vineyards,[p]
our vineyards that are in bloom.[q]

Beloved

16My lover is mine and I am his;[r]
he browses among the lilies.[s]
17Until the day breaks
and the shadows flee,[t]
turn, my lover,[u]
and be like a gazelle
or like a young stag[v]
on the rugged hills.[a][w]

3 All night long on my bed
I looked[x] for the one my heart loves;
I looked for him but did not find him.

2:3 [y]SS 1:4 [z]SS 4:16
2:4 [a]Est 1:11 [b]Nu 1:52
2:5 [c]SS 7:8 [d]SS 5:8
2:6 [e]SS 8:3
2:7 [f]SS 5:8 [g]SS 3:5; 8:4
2:8 [h]ver 17; SS 8:14
2:9 [i]2Sa 2:18 [j]ver 17; SS 8:14
2:13 [k]Isa 28:4; Jer 24:2; Hos 9:10; Mic 7:1; Na 3:12 [l]SS 7:12
2:14 [m]Ge 8:8; SS 1:15 [n]SS 1:5; 8:13
2:15 [o]Jdg 15:4 [p]SS 1:6 [q]SS 7:12
2:16 [r]SS 7:10 [s]SS 4:5; 6:3
2:17 [t]SS 4:6 [u]SS 1:14 [v]ver 9 [w]ver 8
3:1 [x]SS 5:6; Isa 26:9

[a]17 Or *the hills of Bether*

2:1

PROMISE 4

TELL HER THIS

A man's love has the power to transform the way a woman views herself. That's what happened during the courtship of Solomon and his bride-to-be. During her first days in the palace, she urged him not to look at her because she felt her skin was unattractive (1:6). Yet here she describes herself as "a rose" and "a lily" (2:1).

Why the change? If you'll read carefully what Solomon said to her in the previous chapter, you'll discover the answer—he showered her with affirmation and praise. Now that's one example we should all follow!

For the next Promise 4 reading go to page 728.

2:4–7

PROMISE 3

THE WAITING

How should a single man express love to the woman he intends to wed? Two important ways emerge from these verses. To begin with, his love should be apparent to all (v. 4). It should be like a banner waving over her head. Those who hear him speak to her or about her should sense his devotion. Next, the desire to express physical love should be restrained until after marriage (v. 7). His desire for sexual contact will be held in check by his commitment to her well-being. In public and in private, he will express his love in a way that honors her.

Romance is a delicate part of a relationship that requires tenderness and strength if it's going to prosper. If you're single, reflect on the two guidelines found in this passage. Do an honest inventory and try to discover how well you fulfill these two categories. Next, identify some specific ways you can express love as Solomon did. If you can follow in his steps, not only will you benefit, so will the woman you love.

For the next Promise 3 reading go to page 730.

2 I will get up now and go about the city,
through its streets and squares;
I will search for the one my heart loves.
So I looked for him but did not find him.
3 The watchmen found me
as they made their rounds in the city.[y]
"Have you seen the one my heart loves?"
4 Scarcely had I passed them
when I found the one my heart loves.
I held him and would not let him go
till I had brought him to my mother's house,[z]
to the room of the one who conceived me.[a]
5 Daughters of Jerusalem, I charge you[b]
by the gazelles and by the does of the field:
Do not arouse or awaken love
until it so desires.[c]

6 Who is this coming up from the desert[d]
like a column of smoke,
perfumed with myrrh[e] and incense
made from all the spices[f] of the merchant?
7 Look! It is Solomon's carriage,
escorted by sixty warriors,[g]
the noblest of Israel,
8 all of them wearing the sword,
all experienced in battle,
each with his sword at his side,
prepared for the terrors of the night.[h]
9 King Solomon made for himself the carriage;
he made it of wood from Lebanon.
10 Its posts he made of silver,
its base of gold.
Its seat was upholstered with purple,
its interior lovingly inlaid
by[a] the daughters of Jerusalem.
11 Come out, you daughters of Zion,[i]
and look at King Solomon
wearing the crown,
the crown with which his mother crowned him
on the day of his wedding,
the day his heart rejoiced.[j]

Lover

4 →PG. 731

4

How beautiful you are, my darling!
Oh, how beautiful!
Your eyes behind your veil are doves.[k]
Your hair is like a flock of goats
descending from Mount Gilead.[l]
2 Your teeth are like a flock of sheep just shorn,
coming up from the washing.
Each has its twin;
not one of them is alone.[m]
3 Your lips are like a scarlet ribbon;
your mouth[n] is lovely.
Your temples behind your veil
are like the halves of a pomegranate.[o]
4 Your neck is like the tower[p] of David,
built with elegance[b];
on it hang a thousand shields,[q]
all of them shields of warriors.
5 Your two breasts[r] are like two fawns,
like twin fawns of a gazelle[s]
that browse among the lilies.[t]
6 Until the day breaks
and the shadows flee,[u]
I will go to the mountain of myrrh[v]
and to the hill of incense.
7 All beautiful[w] you are, my darling;
there is no flaw in you.

8 Come with me from Lebanon, my bride,[x]
come with me from Lebanon.
Descend from the crest of Amana,
from the top of Senir,[y] the summit of Hermon,[z]
from the lions' dens
and the mountain haunts of the leopards.
9 You have stolen my heart, my sister, my bride;
you have stolen my heart
with one glance of your eyes,
with one jewel of your necklace.[a]
10 How delightful[b] is your love[c], my sister, my bride!
How much more pleasing is your love than wine,
and the fragrance of your perfume than any spice!
11 Your lips drop sweetness as the honeycomb, my bride;
milk and honey are under your tongue.[d]
The fragrance of your garments
is like that of Lebanon.[e]
12 You are a garden locked up, my sister, my bride;
you are a spring enclosed, a sealed fountain.[f]
13 Your plants are an orchard of pomegranates[g]

3:3 [y]SS 5:7 **3:4** [z]SS 8:2 [a]SS 6:9 **3:5** [b]SS 2:7 [c]SS 8:4 **3:6** [d]SS 8:5 [e]SS 1:13; 4:6, 14 [f]Ex 30:34 **3:7** [g]1Sa 8:11 **3:8** [h]Job 15:22; Ps 91:5 **3:11** [i]Isa 4:4 [j]Isa 62:5 **4:1** [k]SS 1:15; 5:12 [l]SS 6:5; Mic 7:14 **4:2** [m]SS 6:6 **4:3** [n]SS 5:16 [o]SS 6:7 **4:4** [p]SS 7:4 [q]Eze 27:10 **4:5** [r]SS 7:3 [s]Pr 5:19 [t]SS 2:16; 6:2-3 **4:6** [u]SS 2:17 [v]ver 14 **4:7** [w]SS 1:15 **4:8** [x]SS 5:1 [y]Dt 3:9 [z]1Ch 5:23 **4:9** [a]Ge 41:42 **4:10** [b]SS 7:6 [c]SS 1:2 **4:11** [d]Ps 19:10; SS 5:1 [e]Hos 14:6 **4:12** [f]Pr 5:15-18 **4:13** [g]SS 6:11; 7:12

a *10* Or *its inlaid interior a gift of love / from*
b *4* The meaning of the Hebrew for this word is uncertain.

with choice fruits,
with henna[h] and nard,
14 nard and saffron,
calamus and cinnamon,[i]
with every kind of incense tree,
with myrrh[j] and aloes
and all the finest spices.[k]
15 You are[a] a garden fountain,
a well of flowing water
streaming down from Lebanon.

Beloved

16 Awake, north wind,
and come, south wind!
Blow on my garden,
that its fragrance may spread abroad.
Let my lover come into his garden
and taste its choice fruits.[l]

Lover

5 I have come into my garden, my sister, my bride;[m]
I have gathered my myrrh with my spice.
I have eaten my honeycomb and my honey;
I have drunk my wine and my milk.[n]

Friends

Eat, O friends, and drink;
drink your fill, O lovers.

Beloved

2 I slept but my heart was awake.
Listen! My lover is knocking:
"Open to me, my sister, my darling,
my dove, my flawless[o] one.[p]
My head is drenched with dew,
my hair with the dampness of the night."
3 I have taken off my robe—
must I put it on again?
I have washed my feet—
must I soil them again?
4 My lover thrust his hand through the latch-opening;
my heart began to pound for him.
5 I arose to open for my lover,
and my hands dripped with myrrh,[q]
my fingers with flowing myrrh,
on the handles of the lock.
6 I opened for my lover,[r]
but my lover had left; he was gone.[s]
My heart sank at his departure.[b]
I looked[t] for him but did not find him.
I called him but he did not answer.
7 The watchmen found me
as they made their rounds in the city.[u]
They beat me, they bruised me;
they took away my cloak,
those watchmen of the walls!
8 O daughters of Jerusalem, I charge you[v]—
if you find my lover,
what will you tell him?
Tell him I am faint with love.[w]

4:13 [h]SS 1:14
4:14 [i]Ex 30:23 [j]SS 3:6 [k]SS 1:12
4:16 [l]SS 2:3; 5:1
5:1 [m]SS 4:8 [n]SS 4:11; Isa 55:1
5:2 [o]SS 4:7 [p]SS 6:9
5:5 [q]ver 13
5:6 [r]SS 6:1 [s]SS 6:2 [t]SS 3:1
5:7 [u]SS 3:3
5:8 [v]SS 2:7; 3:5 [w]SS 2:5

[a] *15* Or *I am* (spoken by the *Beloved*) [b] *6* Or *heart had gone out to him when he spoke*

5:1

PROMISE 4

GOD'S VIEW OF SEX

If you've ever wondered how God feels about sexual intimacy, no verse in the Bible declares God's attitude toward it more clearly than this one.

Understanding the passage requires reflecting on what has led up it. During their wedding night Solomon tenderly praised his bride (4:1–7). Then he calmed her fearful thoughts (4:8) and they began to make love (4:9–11). Finally, through tender imagery provided by the garden metaphor, we read that they consummated their marriage (4:12–5:1). The friends respond in celebration of this relationship—this is sexuality as it is meant to be expressed. The fact that this passage appears in God's Word is a sign of divine approval for the sexual pleasure Solomon and his bride gave and received.

Today this beautiful, God-ordained activity has been distorted. Many men feel a sense of guilt about their sexual urges because what they see and hear and read about is so far removed from God's original design. Since that kind of sexual activity draws God's disapproval, it can be easy for us to think that God disapproves of all sexual activity. Nothing could be further from the truth—the same God who designed humans as sexual creatures endorses sex within the confines of marriage.

If we want to please God, we must live within the sexual boundaries he has drawn in his Word. Doing so means we must trust that he knows what's best for us. It also demands that single men believe God will provide grace and direction for them. Use this passage as a springboard for your own thoughts, or for discussion within a small group. Try to identify some specific action steps you could take to help you maintain sexual purity. Remember, romantic love wants *a* person, true love wants what's best for *the* person.

For the next Promise 4 reading go to page 729.

Friends

9How is your beloved better than
others,
most beautiful of women?[x]
How is your beloved better than
others,
that you charge us so?

Beloved

10My lover is radiant and ruddy,
outstanding among ten
thousand.[y]
11His head is purest gold;
his hair is wavy
and black as a raven.
12His eyes are like doves[z]
by the water streams,
washed in milk,[a]
mounted like jewels.
13His cheeks[b] are like beds of
spice[c]
yielding perfume.
His lips are like lilies[d]
dripping with myrrh.
14His arms are rods of gold
set with chrysolite.
His body is like polished ivory
decorated with sapphires.[a][e]
15His legs are pillars of marble
set on bases of pure gold.
His appearance is like Lebanon,[f]
choice as its cedars.
16His mouth[g] is sweetness itself;
he is altogether lovely.
This is my lover,[h] this my friend,
O daughters of Jerusalem.[i]

Friends

6 Where has your lover[j] gone,
most beautiful of women?[k]
Which way did your lover turn,
that we may look for him with
you?

Beloved

2My lover has gone[l] down to his
garden,[m]
to the beds of spices,[n]
to browse in the gardens
and to gather lilies.
3I am my lover's and my lover is
mine;[o]
he browses among the lilies.[p]

Lover

4You are beautiful, my darling, as
Tirzah,[q]
lovely as Jerusalem,[r]
majestic as troops with
banners.[s]
5Turn your eyes from me;
they overwhelm me.
Your hair is like a flock of goats
descending from Gilead.[t]
6Your teeth are like a flock of sheep
coming up from the washing.
Each has its twin,
not one of them is alone.[u]
7Your temples behind your veil[v]
are like the halves of a
pomegranate.[w]
8Sixty queens[x] there may be,
and eighty concubines,[y]
and virgins beyond number;
9but my dove,[z] my perfect one,[a] is
unique,
the only daughter of her mother,
the favorite of the one who bore
her.[b]
The maidens saw her and called
her blessed;
the queens and concubines
praised her.

Friends

10Who is this that appears like the
dawn,
fair as the moon, bright as the
sun,
majestic as the stars in
procession?

Lover

11I went down to the grove of nut
trees
to look at the new growth in the
valley,
to see if the vines had budded
or the pomegranates were in
bloom.[c]
12Before I realized it,

a 14 Or *lapis lazuli*

5:9 [x]SS 1:8; 6:1 **5:10** [y]Ps 45:2 **5:12** [z]SS 1:15; 4:1 [a]Ge 49:12 **5:13** [b]SS 1:10 [c]SS 6:2 [d]SS 2:1 **5:14** [e]Job 28:6 **5:15** [f]1Ki 4:33; SS 7:4 **5:16** [g]SS 4:3 [h]SS 7:9 [i]SS 1:5 **6:1** [j]SS 5:6 [k]SS 1:8
6:2 [l]SS 5:6 [m]SS 4:12 [n]SS 5:13 **6:3** [o]SS 7:10 [p]SS 2:16 **6:4** [q]Jos 12:24 [r]Ps 48:2; 50:2 [s]ver 10 **6:5** [t]SS 4:1 **6:6** [u]SS 4:2 **6:7** [v]Ge 24:65 [w]SS 4:3 **6:8** [x]Ps 45:9 [y]Ge 22:24 **6:9** [z]SS 1:15 [a]SS 5:2 [b]SS 3:4 **6:11** [c]SS 7:12

5:16

PROMISE 4

LOVERS AND FRIENDS

Scores of books have been written telling men and women how they can be better lovers. But no one has ever summed it up better than Solomon's bride. She described him as her lover *and* friend. Her words make sense, don't they? If you want romance and sexual excitement to flourish, then marry someone you like—someone whose company you enjoy.

To put it another way, if you want to strengthen the romance in your marriage, be a friend to your wife. In fact, why not take a few moments now and consider some ways you can express both love and friendship to her? If you're single and pursuing God's call to marriage, consider how important friendship is to romance.

For the next Promise 4 reading go to page 731.

my desire set me among the
royal chariots of my
people.[a]

Friends

13Come back, come back,
O Shulammite;
come back, come back, that we
may gaze on you!

Lover

Why would you gaze on the
Shulammite
as on the dance[d] of Mahanaim?

6:13 [d]Ex 15:20
7:1 [e]Ps 45:13
7:3 [f]SS 4:5
7:4 [g]Ps 144:12; SS 4:4

7 How beautiful your sandaled feet,
O prince's[e] daughter!
Your graceful legs are like jewels,
the work of a craftsman's hands.
2Your navel is a rounded goblet
that never lacks blended wine.
Your waist is a mound of wheat
encircled by lilies.
3Your breasts[f] are like two fawns,
twins of a gazelle.
4Your neck is like an ivory tower.[g]

a *12* Or *among the chariots of Amminadab*; or *among the chariots of the people of the prince*

7:1–13

PROMISE 3

GOD ISN'T EMBARRASSED BY SEX

This passage pictures the groom in the story describing the physical beauty of his wife and his arousal by what he sees. It is an unabashed, unapologetic, open expression of sexual enjoyment. This fact surprises many Bible readers because of an inaccurate belief that God and the Bible are against sex or are at least embarrassed by it. The best way to address error is to examine truth. So what does the Bible say about sex?

Sex is God's idea. After God created man and woman, his first recorded words to them were, "Be fruitful and increase in number" (Genesis 1:28). We don't know what Adam and Eve said next, but if they asked, "How?" we all know the answer. God created us as sexual beings ("male and female he created them" [Genesis 1:27]) and his first command requires the exercise of our sexuality. So one Biblical purpose for sex is to multiply and populate the earth with other humans.

God designed sex to be pleasurable. God didn't have to include pleasure in sex. He didn't have to place nerve endings and sensitivity in any part of the human body. But he did. God designed sex as an experience that affects our feelings and emotions and encompasses all of our senses. The Song of Songs describes the beauty of sexual pleasure between a bride and groom. The human inability to manage the use of that pleasure—both in practice and in fantasy—has contributed to an overabundance of sinful behavior.

Because God understands the power and potential danger of sex, he has given us ample warning about its abuse. Those warnings have led some to conclude that God, in the Bible, is against sex. On the contrary; God has created us so we can gain great pleasure in the marital relationship from the healthy exercise of our sexuality. In fact, it is the very pleasurable aspect of sex that leads to the third Biblical purpose for sexual expression.

Sexual expression within marriage is a preventative to sexual infidelity outside of marriage. Because sex is so pleasurable, we are tempted to use it outside the boundaries God has placed around it for our protection. In 1 Corinthians 7:1–7 Paul taught that, for married people, the best preventative against sex outside of marriage is an active, healthy sex life inside of marriage. Commitment to spouse and to God, along with a good measure of self-control, also factor into this equation. Solomon presented an even more definitive statement of this same advice in Proverbs 5:11–23.

While the last of these three points applies only to married men, the Bible also helps single men as they consider God's gift of sexuality. (See Paul's instruction on that subject in 1 Corinthians 6:18–20; 7:8–9, 32–35 and Ephesians 5:3–7. See also Psalm 73:23–28 for words about our ultimate allegiance to God and not to people.) For the single man, healthy sexuality must be balanced by a strong belief in God's directives about self-control.

Some men find complete fulfillment in remaining single; others hope to share God's gift of sexuality within marriage. Both of these are completely healthy, and come to different individuals as gifts from God. But the desire for sexual intimacy in marriage needs to be put in its proper perspective. If you're not married, finding God's will for your life in your singleness, and defining yourself along those lines, is the best way to find personal fulfillment.

God is not embarrassed or put off by sex. He created us as sexual and sensual beings. He designed both male and female bodies—sensitive organs and all. He commanded men and women to use their sexuality for procreation, for pleasure and for prevention of sexual sin. He also called us to express masculinity and femininity in other ways, such as through fostering healthy relationships with people of the other gender.

God's people should never apologize for holding a Biblical view of sex. They should never feel embarrassed about their sexuality or fail to educate their children about God's view of sexuality.

For the next Promise 3 reading go to page 758.

Your eyes are the pools of
Heshbon[h]
by the gate of Bath Rabbim.
Your nose is like the tower of
Lebanon[i]
looking toward Damascus.
5 Your head crowns you like Mount
Carmel.[j]
Your hair is like royal tapestry;
the king is held captive by its
tresses.
6 How beautiful[k] you are and how
pleasing,
O love, with your delights![l]
7 Your stature is like that of the
palm,
and your breasts[m] like clusters
of fruit.
8 I said, "I will climb the palm tree;
I will take hold of its fruit."
May your breasts be like the
clusters of the vine,
the fragrance of your breath like
apples,[n]
9 and your mouth like the best
wine.

Beloved

May the wine go straight to my
lover,[o]
flowing gently over lips and
teeth.[a]
10 I belong to my lover,
and his desire[p] is for me.[q]
11 Come, my lover, let us go to the
countryside,
let us spend the night in the
villages.[b]
12 Let us go early to the vineyards[r]
to see if the vines have
budded,[s]
if their blossoms[t] have opened,
and if the pomegranates[u] are in
bloom[v]—
there I will give you my love.
13 The mandrakes[w] send out their
fragrance,
and at our door is every delicacy,
both new and old,
that I have stored up for you, my
lover.[x]

8 If only you were to me like a
brother,
who was nursed at my mother's
breasts!
Then, if I found you outside,
I would kiss you,
and no one would despise me.
2 I would lead you
and bring you to my mother's
house[y]—
she who has taught me.
I would give you spiced wine to
drink,
the nectar of my pomegranates.

7:4 [h]Nu 21:26 [i]SS 5:15 **7:5** [j]Isa 35:2 **7:6** [k]SS 1:15 [l]SS 4:10 **7:7** [m]SS 4:5 **7:8** [n]SS 2:5 **7:9** [o]SS 5:16 **7:10** [p]Ps 45:11 [q]SS 2:16; 6:3 **7:12** [r]SS 1:6 [s]SS 2:15 [t]SS 2:13 [u]SS 4:13 [v]SS 6:11 **7:13** [w]Ge 30:14 [x]SS 4:16 **8:2** [y]SS 3:4

8:3 [z]SS 2:6 **8:4** [a]SS 2:7; 3:5 **8:5** [b]SS 3:6 [c]SS 3:4 **8:6** [d]SS 1:2 [e]Nu 5:14

3 His left arm is under my head
and his right arm embraces
me.[z]
4 Daughters of Jerusalem, I charge
you:
Do not arouse or awaken love
until it so desires.[a]

Friends

5 Who is this coming up from the
desert[b]
leaning on her lover?

Beloved

Under the apple tree I roused you;
there your mother conceived[c]
you,
there she who was in labor gave
you birth.
6 Place me like a seal over your
heart,
like a seal on your arm;
for love[d] is as strong as death,
its jealousy[c][e] unyielding as the
grave.[d]
It burns like blazing fire,
like a mighty flame.[e]
7 Many waters cannot quench love;
rivers cannot wash it away.
If one were to give

4 →PG. 773

[a]9 Septuagint, Aquila, Vulgate and Syriac; Hebrew *lips of sleepers* [b]11 Or *henna bushes* [c]6 Or *ardor* [d]6 Hebrew *Sheol* [e]6 Or / *like the very flame of the* LORD

8:13–14

PROMISE 4

BETTER WITH AGE

Do love and romance have to fade with time? Must a man tire of the woman he has taken to be his wife? Not if Solomon has anything to say about it. His final words to his wife (v. 13) are similar to those he whispered to her at the height of their courtship (2:14). Then he wished to hear her voice and learn of the person hidden within her heart. Now, at the end of the song, he still longs to hear her voice.

The thrill of romance can stay with a couple, but it requires dedication, hard work, commitment, and devotion to each other above all others (Proverbs 5:18–23). If you're married, recommit yourself to your wife. Express your affection with both words and actions. Let her know how deeply you love her and thank God for her friendship. As with a rare, mint-condition automobile, your love can increase in value, getting better and better as the years roll on.

For the next Promise 4 reading go to page 749.

all the wealth of his house for
love,
it[a] would be utterly scorned.[f]

Friends

8We have a young sister,
and her breasts are not yet
grown.
What shall we do for our sister
for the day she is spoken for?
9If she is a wall,
we will build towers of silver on
her.
If she is a door,
we will enclose her with panels
of cedar.

Beloved

10I am a wall,
and my breasts are like towers.
Thus I have become in his eyes
like one bringing contentment.
11Solomon had a vineyard[g] in Baal
Hamon;
he let out his vineyard to
tenants.
Each was to bring for its fruit
a thousand shekels[b][h] of silver.
12But my own vineyard[i] is mine to
give;
the thousand shekels are for you,
O Solomon,
and two hundred[c] are for those
who tend its fruit.

Lover

13You who dwell in the gardens
with friends in attendance,
let me hear your voice!

Beloved

14Come away, my lover,
and be like a gazelle[j]
or like a young stag[k]
on the spice-laden mountains.[l]

8:7 [f]Pr 6:35 **8:11** [g]Ecc 2:4 [h]Isa 7:23 **8:12** [i]SS 1:6 **8:14** [j]Pr 5:19 [k]SS 2:9 [l]SS 2:8,17

[a]*7* Or *he* [b]*11* That is, about 25 pounds (about 11.5 kilograms); also in verse 12
[c]*12* That is, about 5 pounds (about 2.3 kilograms)

PROMISE 1

PORTRAIT OF A PROPHET

We often see prophets depicted in film as gaunt individuals with flowing beards and heavy scowls. While the prophets' concern for their people often contained a message of rebuke and repentance, we must see the bigger picture of their character. As you read the writings of these men, see them as real men, normal men, men just like us. The prophets were like any of us, except that they were deeply aware of God's call on their life.

Have you ever wondered what a man today would be like if he took the Great Commandment (Mark 12:30–31) and the Great Commission (Matthew 28:18–20) seriously? Essentially, these prophets help us discover what this man would be like. This brief study, taken from selected passages in the prophets, gives some insight into the character of these mighty men of God. It also provides some insight into how we can be more like them.

God's prophets were:

1. *Men of uncompromising conviction.* Jeremiah struggled deeply with the persecution he endured. His suffering was so intense and frequent, he has been nicknamed "the weeping prophet." But, in spite of persecution, Jeremiah hung in there. Carefully read Jeremiah 20:7–13, a passage that provides great insight into why Jeremiah was so faithful. Notice how the statement begins and ends. It begins with, "O LORD, you deceived me" (v. 7) and ends with, "Sing to the LORD! Give praise to the LORD!" (v. 13). Kind of makes a person curious to know what's in the middle. Daniel and Hosea and Habakkuk were other prophets who were faithful when it seemed their world was coming apart.
2. *Men with a divine call.* Some had dramatic calls like Isaiah (ch. 6) and Ezekiel (ch. 1–3), but most prophets began their prophetic message with the statement, "The word of the LORD that came to . . ." What made their ministry significant was not the size of the call but the size of the God who called them. As you read these prophets, you will discover an exalted view of God that is found nowhere else in the Bible. We need to read these books to give substance to what it means that God has saved us, that God is our Father, that God has commissioned us to serve him, that God invites us to read his Word and pray to him. The prophets were tuned in to the Lord of the universe.
3. *Men who were conscious of God's authority.* The divine call means little without divine authority. Amos 3:7–8 is an excellent illustration of what it meant for a prophet to represent God. He wrote: "Surely the Sovereign LORD does nothing without revealing his plan to his servants the prophets. The lion has roared; who will not fear? The Sovereign LORD has spoken; who can but prophesy?"
4. *Men of courage.* Amos was a farmer, called by God to proclaim his word (Amos 7:14–15). When he was threatened by Amaziah the priest for preaching an upsetting message, Amos's response was honest, direct and extremely unpopular. Amos had no opportunity to soft-pedal his message. He spoke what God told him to speak regardless of the circumstances.
5. *Men of prayer and communion.* Habakkuk had prayed for insight and when he got it, he didn't like it. He objected to what God was going to do. In his prophecy, he wrote: "I will stand at my watch and station myself on the ramparts; I will look to see what [God] will say to me, and what answer I am to give to this complaint" (Habakkuk 2:1). Habakkuk's dialogue with God, which occupies much of his book, reveals an intimate and familiar relationship between the servant (Habakkuk) and his Master (the living Lord). Men who know God as Habakkuk did, serve him as Habakkuk did.
6. *Men of compassion, hope and love.* Hear Ezekiel's heart-wrenching cry. This compassionate man was obligated to proclaim Israel's destruction for their sin, but he also cried out, "As surely as I live, declares the Sovereign LORD, I take no pleasure in the death of the wicked, but rather that they turn from their ways and live. Turn! Turn from your evil ways! Why will you die, O house of Israel?" (Ezekiel 33:11). Do not see the prophets as people who knew they were on God's side and who angrily shouted out a "turn or burn" message at people they didn't care about. Ezekiel and his fellow prophets demonstrated over and over that they cared deeply about the welfare of the people to whom they spoke.
7. *Men of encouragement and optimism.* Micah spoke to the people during Israel's dark days. Sin was rampant, and God threatened destruction. Kings and false prophets preyed on the people. Then God raised up Micah as one of his prophets and gave him a message that went back and forth between one of destruction and one of hope. In the dark night of sin and judgment flashed the bright light of eternal promise. Read Micah 5:2–15 to see what the prophets longed for.

As you read what these men wrote, see them as men. Normal men. Real men. But men with something added: a burning passion for God, his truth and his will among his people. God has invited you into their ranks. Look over the qualifications listed above and pray that he will give you the right stuff to take God's Word to people who need to hear.

For the next Promise 1 reading go to page 737.

ISAIAH

AT A GLANCE

Key Principle: God is the sovereign Ruler of all things; salvation comes from him alone.
Author: Isaiah
Time and Place: ~740–681 B.C. / Jerusalem
Key Verses: 1:18–20; 6:3; 9:6–7; 41:10; 53:6; 57:15

BENEFIT

Isaiah has been called "the Shakespeare of the prophets" and "the Mount Everest of Hebrew prophecy" for good reasons. This comprehensive and superbly written book is the high-water mark of Messianic prophecy, and can be regarded as the Bible in miniature. The first 39 chapters loosely correspond to the 39 books of the Old Testament as they condemn sin and emphasize judgment, while the last 27 chapters loosely correspond to the 27 books of the New Testament as they proclaim a message of consolation and hope.

SETTING

Isaiah's extensive vocabulary and sophisticated style mark him as an intelligent and well-educated man who frequented the royal court in Jerusalem. He ministered for about 60 years (~740–681 B.C.) during the reigns of Uzziah, Jotham, Ahaz and Hezekiah (1:1). As he stood before these kings, he eloquently warned them of the foolishness of making alliances with foreign powers rather than trusting in God to protect and deliver them. Tradition says that because of his message, Isaiah was cut in two early in the reign of the ungodly King Manasseh.

Many critics argue that an unknown author wrote chapters 40—66 after the Babylonian captivity. Chapters 1—39, these critics claim, were concerned with the Assyrian threat, while the second half focuses on Babylon. They also point out differences of style and theme between the two parts of the book. However, the similarities greatly outnumber the differences, and the latter can be accounted for by the different purposes of the two parts (condemnation versus consolation). In addition, the first part of Isaiah actually deals more extensively with Babylon than the second part. Such criticism comes from the assumption that specific prophecy about future events is impossible, but this view is based on an antisupernatural bias and directly contradicts the internal claims of the book (e.g., 42:9). The New Testament often attributes both parts of this book to the prophet Isaiah (Matthew 3:3; 12:17–21; Luke 3:4–6; John 12:37–41; Acts 8:28; Romans 9—10).

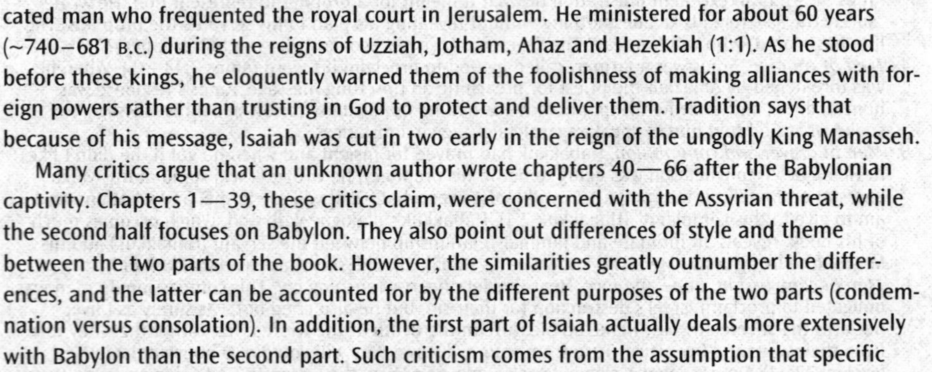

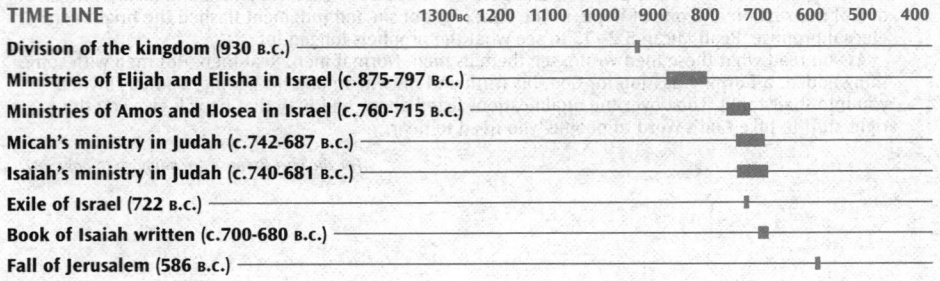

THEME AND PURPOSE

More than any other prophet, Isaiah develops the theme contained in the meaning of his own name: "Yahweh is salvation." The term "salvation" appears in Isaiah 26 times, in contrast to a total of only seven times in all the other prophets combined. The first part of Isaiah develops our profound need for salvation in light of our sinful human condition and the certainty of judgment. Here Isaiah presents the reality of God's coming judgment against the sin of his people, the surrounding nations and eventually the whole world. The second part of Isaiah points ahead to God's comfort and salvation in the person and work of his coming Servant.

UNIQUE CONTRIBUTION

Isaiah is the most comprehensive of the Old Testament prophets and offers the clearest portrait of the coming Messiah. Isaiah has rightly been called the "Saint Paul of the Old Testament" because of the systematic commentary, clarity and power, sweeping scope and striking imagery contained in his book. He is quoted in the New Testament more than any other prophet, with about 85 allusions to chapter 53 alone.

LINKS TO THE NEW TESTAMENT

Isaiah contains the most explicit and detailed Old Testament prophecies of Christ. It portrays Christ in his dual role as the suffering Servant and the coming King. A significant number of the over 300 Old Testament prophecies come from Isaiah, and the same is true of the over 400 Old Testament prophecies that await fulfillment in Christ's second coming. Some of the key Messianic prophecies in Isaiah include 7:14; 9:6–7; 11:1–6; 28:16; 40:3–5; 42:1–4; 50:6; 59:20–21; 60:1–3; and 61:1–3.

Isaiah 52:13—53:12 has been called the "gospel according to Isaiah" because it sounds like the work of a New Testament writer, even though it was penned some 700 years before Jesus Christ was born on earth.

OVERVIEW

FOCUS	Prophetic Condemnation			Historical Transition	Prophetic Consolation
REFERENCE	1 12	13 23	24 35	36 39	40 66
TOPICS	Judgment			Parenthesis	Future Hope
	God's Nation				The Nation's God
	Corruption (1:4)				Comfort (40:1)
	Need for Salvation: Israel the Sinful Servant				Provision of Salvation: Messiah the Suffering Servant
LOCATION	Judah	Surrounding Nations	All Nations	Jerusalem	Israel and All Nations
TIME	About 60 Years of Prophetic Ministry				

Isaiah moves from the specific to the general in chapters 1—35. After summarizing the whole book in chapter 1, he begins a prophetic condemnation of sin by focusing on his own people in Judah (1—12). In spite of their moral and spiritual corruption, God graciously invites his people to return to him before it is too late. Next, the prophet pronounces the coming judgment upon eleven surrounding nations, including Egypt and Assyria (13—23). He then broadens his scope to include future judgment upon all nations in the little apocalypse (24—27). Then follows a series of woes on Israel and Judah (28—33) and a description of global devastation followed by universal blessing (34—35). The next four chapters (36—39) provide a historical transition between the two major sections of condemnation and of consolation. This parenthetical interlude depicts the Assyrian siege on Jerusalem in 701 B.C. in the time of Hezekiah. God delivers Judah from Assyria because of Hezekiah's prayers, but it later falls to the Babylonians.

The prophetic condemnation (1—39) is followed by a prophetic consolation (40—66) in which the Lord comforts his people with a message of hope and restoration. God's sovereignty and majesty is the foundation for Israel's hope (40—48). He alone rules the realms of nature and of nations; Isaiah contrasts God's power and greatness with the impotence of idols made by men. God's salvation centers on the redemptive work of the coming Servant, who will save God's people from their sins (49—57). God will restore all who come to him in humility and trust, and Messiah himself will reign over the earth in his glorious kingdom (58—66).

ISAIAH

1 The vision[a] concerning Judah and Jerusalem[b] that Isaiah son of Amoz saw[c] during the reigns of Uzziah,[d] Jotham, Ahaz[e] and Hezekiah, kings of Judah.

A Rebellious Nation

2Hear, O heavens! Listen, O earth!
For the LORD has spoken:[f]
"I reared children and brought them up,
but they have rebelled[g] against me.
3The ox knows his master,
the donkey his owner's manger,
but Israel does not know,[h]
my people do not understand."

4Ah, sinful nation,
a people loaded with guilt,
a brood of evildoers,[i]
children given to corruption!
They have forsaken the LORD;
they have spurned the Holy One[j] of Israel
and turned their backs on him.

5Why should you be beaten anymore?
Why do you persist in rebellion?[k]
Your whole head is injured,
your whole heart afflicted.[l]
6From the sole of your foot to the top of your head
there is no soundness[m]—
only wounds and welts
and open sores,
not cleansed or bandaged[n]
or soothed with oil.[o]

7Your country is desolate,[p]
your cities burned with fire;
your fields are being stripped by foreigners
right before you,
laid waste as when overthrown by strangers.
8The Daughter of Zion is left
like a shelter in a vineyard,
like a hut[q] in a field of melons,
like a city under siege.
9Unless the LORD Almighty
had left us some survivors,[r]
we would have become like Sodom,
we would have been like Gomorrah.[s]

10Hear the word of the LORD,[t]
you rulers of Sodom;[u]
listen to the law[v] of our God,
you people of Gomorrah!

1:1 [a]Nu 12:6 [b]Isa 40:9 [c]Isa 2:1 [d]2Ch 26:22 [e]2Ki 16:1 **1:2** [f]Mic 1:2 [g]Isa 30:1,9; 65:2 **1:3** [h]Jer 8:7; 9:3,6 **1:4** [i]Isa 14:20 [j]Isa 5:19,24 **1:5** [k]Isa 31:6 [l]Isa 33:6,24 **1:6** [m]Ps 38:3 [n]Isa 30:26; Jer 8:22 [o]Lk 10:34 **1:7** [p]Lev 26:34 **1:8** [q]Job 27:18 **1:9** [r]Isa 10:20-22; 37:4,31-32 [s]Ge 19:24; Ro 9:29* **1:10** [t]Isa 28:14 [u]Isa 3:9; Eze 16:49; Ro 9:29; Rev 11:8 [v]Isa 8:20

1:11 [w]Ps 50:8 [x]Jer 6:20 [y]1Sa 15:22; Mal 1:10 **1:12** [z]Ex 23:17 **1:13** [a]Isa 66:3 [b]Jer 7:9 [c]1Ch 23:31 **1:14** [d]Lev 23:1-44; Nu 28:11-29:39; 29:1 [e]Isa 7:13; 43:22,24 **1:15** [f]Isa 8:17; 59:2; Mic 3:4 [g]Isa 59:3 **1:16** [h]Isa 52:11 [i]Isa 55:7; Jer 25:5

11"The multitude of your sacrifices—
what are they to me?" says the LORD.
"I have more than enough of burnt offerings,
of rams and the fat of fattened animals;[w]
I have no pleasure
in the blood of bulls[x] and lambs and goats.[y]
12When you come to appear before me,
who has asked this of you,[z]
this trampling of my courts?
13Stop bringing meaningless offerings![a]
Your incense[b] is detestable to me.
New Moons, Sabbaths and convocations[c]—
I cannot bear your evil assemblies.
14Your New Moon festivals and your appointed feasts[d]
my soul hates.
They have become a burden to me;
I am weary[e] of bearing them.
15When you spread out your hands in prayer,
I will hide[f] my eyes from you;
even if you offer many prayers,
I will not listen.
Your hands are full of blood;[g]
16 wash and make yourselves clean.
Take your evil deeds
out of my sight![h]
Stop doing wrong,[i]
17 learn to do right!

7 →PG. 749

1:10–17

PROMISE 1

CONTAMINATED WORSHIP

God here referred to his people as Sodom and Gomorrah, those sinful cities he had destroyed over a thousand years earlier (Genesis 19:1–29). God told the people of Israel to stop bringing sacrifices (v. 11), to stop their worship activities (vv. 13–14) and to quit praying (v. 15). God wanted obedience, not religious activity. Because the people chose to live sinful lives, God detested Israel's practice of his sacred rituals.

Anyone who goes through the motions of worship and service but has no heart for God should read this passage with great care. God wants our hearts before he wants our religious activity.

For the next Promise 1 reading go to page 745.

Seek justice,[j]
encourage the oppressed.[a]
Defend the cause of the
fatherless,[k]
plead the case of the widow.

18"Come now, let us reason
together,"[l]
says the LORD.
"Though your sins are like scarlet,
they shall be as white as snow;[m]
though they are red as crimson,
they shall be like wool.
19If you are willing and obedient,
you will eat the best from the
land;[n]
20but if you resist and rebel,
you will be devoured by the
sword."[o]
For the mouth of the LORD
has spoken.[p]

21See how the faithful city
has become a harlot![q]
She once was full of justice;
righteousness used to dwell in
her—
but now murderers!
22Your silver has become dross,
your choice wine is diluted with
water.
23Your rulers are rebels,
companions of thieves;
they all love bribes[r]
and chase after gifts.
They do not defend the cause of
the fatherless;
the widow's case does not come
before them.[s]
24Therefore the Lord, the LORD
Almighty,
the Mighty One of Israel,
declares:
"Ah, I will get relief from my foes
and avenge[t] myself on my
enemies.
25I will turn my hand against you;
I will thoroughly purge away
your dross
and remove all your impurities.[u]
26I will restore your judges as in days
of old,[v]
your counselors as at the
beginning.
Afterward you will be called
the City of Righteousness,[w]
the Faithful City.[x]"

27Zion will be redeemed with justice,
her penitent ones with
righteousness.[y]
28But rebels and sinners will both be
broken,
and those who forsake the LORD
will perish.[z]

29"You will be ashamed because of
the sacred oaks[a]
in which you have delighted;
you will be disgraced because of
the gardens[b]
that you have chosen.
30You will be like an oak with fading
leaves,
like a garden without water.
31The mighty man will become
tinder
and his work a spark;
both will burn together,
with no one to quench the
fire.[c]"

The Mountain of the LORD

2 This is what Isaiah son of Amoz saw
concerning Judah and Jerusalem:[d]
2In the last days

the mountain[e] of the LORD's
temple will be established
as chief among the mountains;
it will be raised above the hills,
and all nations will stream to it.

3Many peoples will come and say,

"Come, let us go up to the
mountain of the LORD,
to the house of the God of Jacob.
He will teach us his ways,
so that we may walk in his
paths."
The law[f] will go out from Zion,
the word of the LORD from
Jerusalem.[g]
4He will judge between the nations
and will settle disputes for many
peoples.
They will beat their swords into
plowshares
and their spears into pruning
hooks.[h]
Nation will not take up sword
against nation,[i]
nor will they train for war
anymore.

1 →PG. 742

5Come, O house of Jacob,[j]
let us walk in the light[k] of the
LORD.

The Day of the LORD

6You have abandoned[l] your
people,
the house of Jacob.
They are full of superstitions from
the East;
they practice divination like the
Philistines[m]
and clasp hands[n] with
pagans.[o]
7Their land is full of silver and gold;
there is no end to their treasures.
Their land is full of horses;[p]

1:17 [j]Zep 2:3 [k]Ps 82:3 **1:18** [l]Isa 41:1; 43:9, 26 [m]Ps 51:7; Rev 7:14 **1:19** [n]Dt 30:15-16; Isa 55:2 **1:20** [o]Isa 3:25; 65:12 [p]Isa 34:16; 40:5; 58:14; Mic 4:4 **1:21** [q]Isa 57:3-9; Jer 2:20 **1:23** [r]Ex 23:8 [s]Isa 10:2; Jer 5:28; Eze 22:6-7; Zec 7:10 **1:24** [t]Isa 35:4; 59:17; 61:2; 63:4 **1:25** [u]Eze 22:22; Mal 3:3 **1:26** [v]Jer 33:7,11 [w]Isa 33:5; 62:1; Zec 8:3 [x]Isa 60:14; 62:2 **1:27** [y]Isa 35:10; 62:12; 63:4 **1:28** [z]Ps 9:5; Isa 24:20; 66:24; 2Th 1:8-9 **1:29** [a]Isa 57:5 [b]Isa 65:3; 66:17 **1:31** [c]Isa 5:24; 9:18-19; 26:11; 33:14; 66:15-16,24 **2:1** [d]Isa 1:1 **2:2** [e]Isa 27:13; 56:7; 66:20; Mic 4:7 **2:3** [f]Isa 51:4,7 [g]Lk 24:47 **2:4** [h]Joel 3:10 [i]Ps 46:9; Isa 9:5; 11:6-9; 32:18; Hos 2:18; Zec 9:10 **2:5** [j]Isa 58:1 [k]Isa 60:1, 19-20; 1Jn 1:5,7 **2:6** [l]Dt 31:17 [m]2Ki 1:2 [n]Pr 6:1 [o]2Ki 16:7 **2:7** [p]Dt 17:16

[a]*17* Or / *rebuke the oppressor*

there is no end to their
chariots.[q]
8Their land is full of idols;[r]
they bow down to the work of
their hands,
to what their fingers[s] have
made.
9So man will be brought low[t]
and mankind humbled[u]—
do not forgive them.[a][v]
10Go into the rocks,
hide in the ground
from dread of the LORD
and the splendor of his
majesty![w]
11The eyes of the arrogant man will
be humbled
and the pride[x] of men brought
low;
the LORD alone will be exalted in
that day.

12The LORD Almighty has a day in
store
for all the proud and lofty,
for all that is exalted[y]
(and they will be humbled),[z]
13for all the cedars of Lebanon, tall
and lofty,
and all the oaks of Bashan,[a]
14for all the towering mountains
and all the high hills,[b]
15for every lofty tower
and every fortified wall,[c]
16for every trading ship[b][d]
and every stately vessel.
17The arrogance of man will be
brought low
and the pride of men humbled;
the LORD alone will be exalted in
that day,[e]
18 and the idols will totally
disappear.[f]

19Men will flee to caves in the rocks
and to holes in the ground
from dread of the LORD
and the splendor of his majesty,
when he rises to shake the
earth.[g]
20In that day men will throw away
to the rodents and bats[h]
their idols of silver and idols of
gold,
which they made to worship.
21They will flee to caverns in the
rocks
and to the overhanging crags
from dread of the LORD
and the splendor of his majesty,
when he rises to shake the
earth.[i]

22Stop trusting in man,[j]
who has but a breath in his
nostrils.
Of what account is he?[k]

2:7 [q]Isa 31:1; Mic 5:10
2:8 [r]Isa 10:9-11 [s]Isa 17:8
2:9 [t]Ps 62:9 [u]Isa 5:15 [v]Ne 4:5
2:10 [w]2Th 1:9; Rev 6:15-16
2:11 [x]Isa 5:15; 37:23
2:12 [y]Isa 24:4,21; Mal 4:1 [z]Job 40:11
2:13 [a]Zec 11:2
2:14 [b]Isa 30:25; 40:4
2:15 [c]Isa 25:2,12
2:16 [d]1Ki 10:22
2:17 [e]ver 11
2:18 [f]Isa 21:9
2:19 [g]Heb 12:26
2:20 [h]Lev 11:19
2:21 [i]ver 19
2:22 [j]Ps 146:3; Jer 17:5 [k]Ps 8:4; 144:3; Isa 40:15; Jas 4:14

3:1 [l]Lev 26:26 [m]Isa 5:13; Eze 4:16
3:2 [n]Eze 17:13 [o]2Ki 24:14; Isa 9:14-15
3:4 [p]Ecc 10:16 *fn*
3:5 [q]Isa 9:19; Jer 9:8; Mic 7:2,6
3:7 [r]Eze 34:4; Hos 5:13
3:8 [s]Isa 1:7 [t]Isa 9:15,17 [u]Ps 73:9,11
3:9 [v]Ge 13:13 [w]Pr 8:36; Ro 6:23
3:10 [x]Dt 28:1-14 [y]Ps 128:2
3:11 [z]Dt 28:15-68
3:12 [a]ver 4

Judgment on Jerusalem and Judah

3 See now, the Lord,
the LORD Almighty,
is about to take from Jerusalem
and Judah
both supply and support:
all supplies of food[l] and all
supplies of water,[m]
2 the hero and warrior,[n]
the judge and prophet,
the soothsayer and elder,[o]
3the captain of fifty and man of
rank,
the counselor, skilled craftsman
and clever enchanter.

4I will make boys their officials;
mere children will govern
them.[p]
5People will oppress each other—
man against man, neighbor
against neighbor.[q]
The young will rise up against the
old,
the base against the honorable.

6A man will seize one of his
brothers
at his father's home, and say,
"You have a cloak, you be our
leader;
take charge of this heap of
ruins!"
7But in that day he will cry out,
"I have no remedy.[r]
I have no food or clothing in my
house;
do not make me the leader of
the people."

8Jerusalem staggers,
Judah is falling;[s]
their words[t] and deeds are against
the LORD,
defying[u] his glorious presence.
9The look on their faces testifies
against them;
they parade their sin like
Sodom;[v]
they do not hide it.
Woe to them!
They have brought disaster[w]
upon themselves.

10Tell the righteous it will be well[x]
with them,
for they will enjoy the fruit of
their deeds.[y]
11Woe to the wicked! Disaster[z] is
upon them!
They will be paid back for what
their hands have done.

12Youths[a] oppress my people,
women rule over them.

[a]9 Or *not raise them up* [b]16 Hebrew *every ship of Tarshish*

O my people, your guides lead you
astray;[b]
they turn you from the path.
13 The LORD takes his place in court;
he rises to judge[c] the people.
14 The LORD enters into judgment[d]
against the elders and leaders of
his people:
"It is you who have ruined my
vineyard;
the plunder[e] from the poor is in
your houses.
15 What do you mean by crushing my
people[f]
and grinding the faces of the
poor?"
declares the Lord,
the LORD Almighty.

16 The LORD says,
"The women of Zion[g] are
haughty,
walking along with outstretched
necks,
flirting with their eyes,
tripping along with mincing steps,
with ornaments jingling on their
ankles.
17 Therefore the Lord will bring sores
on the heads of the women
of Zion;
the LORD will make their scalps
bald."

18 In that day the Lord will snatch
away their finery: the bangles and
headbands and crescent necklaces,[h]
19 the earrings and bracelets and veils,
20 the headdresses[i] and ankle chains
and sashes, the perfume bottles and
charms, 21 the signet rings and nose
rings, 22 the fine robes and the capes
and cloaks, the purses 23 and mirrors,
and the linen garments and tiaras and
shawls.

24 Instead of fragrance[j] there will be
a stench;
instead of a sash,[k] a rope;
instead of well-dressed hair,
baldness;[l]
instead of fine clothing,
sackcloth;[m]
instead of beauty,[n] branding.
25 Your men will fall by the sword,[o]
your warriors in battle.
26 The gates of Zion will lament and
mourn;[p]
destitute, she will sit on the
ground.[q]

4 In that day seven women
will take hold of one man[r]
and say, "We will eat our own
food[s]
and provide our own clothes;
only let us be called by your name.
Take away our disgrace!"[t]

The Branch of the LORD

2 In that day the Branch of the
LORD[u] will be beautiful and glorious,
and the fruit[v] of the land will be the
pride and glory of the survivors in Israel. 3 Those who are left in Zion, who
remain[w] in Jerusalem, will be called
holy,[x] all who are recorded[y] among
the living in Jerusalem. 4 The Lord will
wash away the filth[z] of the women of
Zion; he will cleanse the bloodstains[a]
from Jerusalem by a spirit[a] of judgment[b] and a spirit[a] of fire.[c] 5 Then
the LORD will create over all of Mount
Zion and over those who assemble
there a cloud of smoke by day and a
glow of flaming fire by night;[d] over all
the glory[e] will be a canopy. 6 It will be
a shelter[f] and shade from the heat of
the day, and a refuge[g] and hiding
place from the storm and rain.

The Song of the Vineyard

5 I will sing for the one I love
a song about his vineyard:[h]
My loved one had a vineyard
on a fertile hillside.
2 He dug it up and cleared it of
stones
and planted it with the choicest
vines.[i]
He built a watchtower in it
and cut out a winepress as well.
Then he looked for a crop of good
grapes,
but it yielded only bad fruit.[j]

3 "Now you dwellers in Jerusalem
and men of Judah,
judge between me and my
vineyard.[k]
4 What more could have been done
for my vineyard
than I have done for it?[l]
When I looked for good grapes,
why did it yield only bad?
5 Now I will tell you
what I am going to do to my
vineyard:
I will take away its hedge,
and it will be destroyed;
I will break down its wall,[m]
and it will be trampled.[n]
6 I will make it a wasteland,
neither pruned nor cultivated,
and briers and thorns[o] will
grow there.
I will command the clouds
not to rain on it."

7 The vineyard[p] of the LORD
Almighty
is the house of Israel,
and the men of Judah

3:12 [b] Isa 9:16
3:13 [c] Mic 6:2
3:14 [d] Job 22:4 [e] Job 24:9; Jas 2:6
3:15 [f] Ps 94:5
3:16 [g] SS 3:11
3:18 [h] Jdg 8:21
3:20 [i] Ex 39:28
3:24 [j] Est 2:12 [k] Pr 31:24 [l] Isa 22:12 [m] La 2:10; Eze 27:30-31 [n] 1Pe 3:3
3:25 [o] Isa 1:20
3:26 [p] Jer 14:2 [q] La 2:10
4:1 [r] Isa 13:12 [s] 2Th 3:12 [t] Ge 30:23
4:2 [u] Isa 11:1-5; 53:2; Jer 23:5-6; Zec 3:8; 6:12 [v] Ps 72:16
4:3 [w] Ro 11:5 [x] Isa 52:1; 60:21 [y] Lk 10:20
4:4 [z] Isa 3:24 [a] Isa 1:15 [b] Isa 28:6 [c] Isa 1:31; Mt 3:11
4:5 [d] Ex 13:21 [e] Isa 60:1
4:6 [f] Ps 27:5 [g] Isa 25:4
5:1 [h] Ps 80:8-9
5:2 [i] Jer 2:21 [j] Mt 21:19; Mk 11:13; Lk 13:6
5:3 [k] Mt 21:40
5:4 [l] 2Ch 36:15; Jer 2:5-7; Mic 6:3-4; Mt 23:37
5:5 [m] Ps 80:12 [n] Isa 28:3,18; La 1:15; Lk 21:24
5:6 [o] Isa 7:23,24; Heb 6:8
5:7 [p] Ps 80:8

[a] 4 Or *the Spirit*

are the garden of his delight.
And he looked for justice,[q] but
saw bloodshed;
for righteousness, but heard cries
of distress.

Woes and Judgments

8Woe[r] to you who add house to
house
and join field to field[s]
till no space is left
and you live alone in the land.

9The LORD Almighty has declared in my hearing:[t]

"Surely the great houses will
become desolate,[u]
the fine mansions left without
occupants.
10A ten-acre[a] vineyard will produce
only a bath[b] of wine,
a homer[c] of seed only an
ephah[d] of grain."[v]

11Woe to those who rise early in the
morning
to run after their drinks,
who stay up late at night
till they are inflamed with
wine.[w]
12They have harps and lyres at their
banquets,
tambourines and flutes and
wine,
but they have no regard[x] for the
deeds of the LORD,
no respect for the work of his
hands.[y]
13Therefore my people will go into
exile[z]
for lack of understanding;[a]
their men of rank will die of
hunger
and their masses will be parched
with thirst.
14Therefore the grave[e][b] enlarges its
appetite
and opens its mouth[c] without
limit;
into it will descend their nobles
and masses
with all their brawlers and
revelers.
15So man will be brought low[d]
and mankind humbled,[e]
the eyes of the arrogant[f]
humbled.
16But the LORD Almighty will be
exalted by his justice,[g]
and the holy God will show
himself holy[h] by his
righteousness.
17Then sheep will graze as in their
own pasture;[i]
lambs will feed[f] among the
ruins of the rich.

18Woe to those who draw sin along
with cords of deceit,
and wickedness[j] as with cart
ropes,
19to those who say, "Let God hurry,
let him hasten his work
so we may see it.
Let it approach,
let the plan of the Holy One of
Israel come,
so we may know it."[k]

20Woe to those who call evil good
and good evil,
who put darkness for light
and light for darkness,[l]
who put bitter for sweet
and sweet for bitter.[m]

21Woe to those who are wise in their
own eyes[n]
and clever in their own sight.

22Woe to those who are heroes at
drinking wine[o]
and champions at mixing drinks,
23who acquit the guilty for a bribe,[p]
but deny justice[q] to the
innocent.[r]
24Therefore, as tongues of fire lick up
straw
and as dry grass sinks down in
the flames,
so their roots will decay[s]
and their flowers blow away like
dust;
for they have rejected the law of
the LORD Almighty
and spurned the word[t] of the
Holy One of Israel.
25Therefore the LORD's anger[u] burns
against his people;
his hand is raised and he strikes
them down.
The mountains shake,
and the dead bodies are like
refuse[v] in the streets.

Yet for all this, his anger is not
turned away,[w]
his hand is still upraised.[x]

26He lifts up a banner for the distant
nations,
he whistles[y] for those at the
ends of the earth.[z]
Here they come,
swiftly and speedily!
27Not one of them grows tired or
stumbles,
not one slumbers or sleeps;

5:7 [q]Isa 59:15
5:8 [r]Jer 22:13 [s]Mic 2:2; Hab 2:9-12
5:9 [t]Isa 22:14 [u]Isa 6:11-12; Mt 23:38
5:10 [v]Lev 26:26
5:11 [w]Pr 23:29-30
5:12 [x]Job 34:27 [y]Ps 28:5; Am 6:5-6
5:13 [z]Hos 4:6 [a]Isa 1:3; Hos 4:6
5:14 [b]Pr 30:16 [c]Nu 16:30
5:15 [d]Isa 10:33 [e]Isa 2:9 [f]Isa 2:11
5:16 [g]Isa 28:17; 30:18; 33:5; 61:8 [h]Isa 29:23
5:17 [i]Isa 7:25; Zep 2:6,14
5:18 [j]Isa 59:4-8; Jer 23:14
5:19 [k]Jer 17:15; Eze 12:22; 2Pe 3:4
5:20 [l]Mt 6:22-23; Lk 11:34-35 [m]Am 5:7
5:21 [n]Pr 3:7; Ro 12:16; 1Co 3:18-20
5:22 [o]Pr 23:20
5:23 [p]Ex 23:8 [q]Isa 10:2 [r]Ps 94:21; Jas 5:6
5:24 [s]Job 18:16 [t]Isa 8:6; 30:9, 12
5:25 [u]2Ki 22:13 [v]2Ki 9:37 [w]Jer 4:8; Da 9:16 [x]Isa 9:12,17, 21; 10:4
5:26 [y]Isa 7:18; Zec 10:8 [z]Dt 28:49; Isa 13:5; 18:3

[a] *10* Hebrew *ten-yoke,* that is, the land plowed by 10 yoke of oxen in one day [b] *10* That is, probably about 6 gallons (about 22 liters) [c] *10* That is, probably about 6 bushels (about 220 liters) [d] *10* That is, probably about 3/5 bushel (about 22 liters) [e] *14* Hebrew *Sheol* [f] *17* Septuagint; Hebrew / *strangers will eat*

not a belt is loosened at the
waist,[a]
not a sandal thong is broken.[b]
28 Their arrows are sharp,[c]
all their bows[d] are strung;
their horses' hoofs seem like flint,
their chariot wheels like a
whirlwind.
29 Their roar is like that of the lion,[e]
they roar like young lions;
they growl as they seize[f] their
prey
and carry it off with no one to
rescue.[g]
30 In that day they will roar over it
like the roaring of the sea.[h]
And if one looks at the land,
he will see darkness and
distress;[i]
even the light will be darkened[j]
by the clouds.

Isaiah's Commission

1 →PG. 749

6 In the year that King Uzziah[k]
died,[l] I saw the Lord[m] seated on
a throne,[n] high and exalted, and the
train of his robe filled the temple.
2 Above him were seraphs,[o] each with
six wings: With two wings they covered
their faces, with two they covered their
feet,[p] and with two they were flying.
3 And they were calling to one another:

"Holy, holy, holy is the LORD
Almighty;
the whole earth is full of his
glory."[q]

4 At the sound of their voices the doorposts and thresholds shook and the
temple was filled with smoke.

3 →PG. 792

5 "Woe to me!" I cried. "I am ruined!
For I am a man of unclean lips, and I
live among a people of unclean lips,[r]
and my eyes have seen the King,[s] the
LORD Almighty."
6 Then one of the seraphs flew to me
with a live coal in his hand, which he
had taken with tongs from the altar.
7 With it he touched my mouth and
said, "See, this has touched your lips;[t]
your guilt is taken away and your sin
atoned for.[u]"
8 Then I heard the voice[v] of the Lord
saying, "Whom shall I send? And who
will go for us?"
And I said, "Here am I. Send me!"
9 He said, "Go[w] and tell this people:

" 'Be ever hearing, but never
understanding;
be ever seeing, but never
perceiving.'[x]
10 Make the heart of this people
calloused;[y]
make their ears dull
and close their eyes.[a]
Otherwise they might see with their
eyes,
hear with their ears,[z]
understand with their hearts,
and turn and be healed."[a]

11 Then I said, "For how long,
O Lord?"[b]
And he answered:

"Until the cities lie ruined[c]
and without inhabitant,
until the houses are left deserted
and the fields ruined and
ravaged,
12 until the LORD has sent everyone
far away[d]
and the land is utterly
forsaken.[e]
13 And though a tenth remains[f] in
the land,
it will again be laid waste.
But as the terebinth and oak
leave stumps when they are cut
down,
so the holy seed will be the
stump in the land."[g]

The Sign of Immanuel

7 When Ahaz son of Jotham, the son of
Uzziah, was king of Judah, King Rezin[h] of Aram[i] and Pekah[j] son of
Remaliah king of Israel marched up to
fight against Jerusalem, but they could
not overpower it.
2 Now the house of David[k] was told,
"Aram has allied itself with[b] Ephraim[l]"; so the hearts of Ahaz and his
people were shaken, as the trees of the
forest are shaken by the wind.
3 Then the LORD said to Isaiah, "Go
out, you and your son Shear-Jashub,[c]
to meet Ahaz at the end of the aqueduct of the Upper Pool, on the road to
the Washerman's Field.[m] 4 Say to him,
'Be careful, keep calm[n] and don't be
afraid.[o] Do not lose heart[p] because
of these two smoldering stubs[q] of
firewood—because of the fierce anger[r] of Rezin and Aram and of the son
of Remaliah. 5 Aram, Ephraim and
Remaliah's son have plotted your ruin,
saying, 6 "Let us invade Judah; let us
tear it apart and divide it among ourselves, and make the son of Tabeel king
over it." 7 Yet this is what the Sovereign
LORD says:

" 'It will not take place,
it will not happen,[s]

5:27 [a]Job 12:18 [b]Joel 2:7-8
5:28 [c]Ps 45:5 [d]Ps 7:12
5:29 [e]Jer 51:38; Zep 3:3; Zec 11:3 [f]Isa 10:6; 49:24-25 [g]Isa 42:22; Mic 5:8
5:30 [h]Lk 21:25 [i]Isa 8:22; Jer 4:23-28 [j]Joel 2:10
6:1 [k]2Ch 26:22,23 [l]2Ki 15:7 [m]Jn 12:41 [n]Rev 4:2
6:2 [o]Rev 4:8 [p]Eze 1:11
6:3 [q]Ps 72:19; Rev 4:8
6:5 [r]Jer 9:3-8 [s]Jer 51:57
6:7 [t]Jer 1:9 [u]1Jn 1:7
6:8 [v]Ac 9:4
6:9 [w]Eze 3:11 [x]Mt 13:15*; Lk 8:10*
6:10 [y]Dt 32:15; Ps 119:70 [z]Jer 5:21 [a]Mt 13:13-15; Mk 4:12*; Ac 28:26-27*
6:11 [b]Ps 79:5 [c]Lev 26:31
6:12 [d]Dt 28:64 [e]Jer 4:29
6:13 [f]Isa 1:9 [g]Job 14:7
7:1 [h]2Ki 15:37 [i]2Ch 28:5 [j]2Ki 15:25
7:2 [k]ver 13; Isa 22:22 [l]Isa 9:9
7:3 [m]2Ki 18:17; Isa 36:2
7:4 [n]Isa 30:15 [o]Isa 35:4 [p]Dt 20:3 [q]Zec 3:2 [r]Isa 10:24
7:7 [s]Isa 8:10; Ac 4:25

[a] *9,10* Hebrew; Septuagint *'You will be ever hearing, but never understanding; / you will be ever seeing, but never perceiving.' / 10This people's heart has become calloused; / they hardly hear with their ears, / and they have closed their eyes*
[b] *2* Or *has set up camp in*
[c] *3 Shear-Jashub* means *a remnant will return.*

6:1–13

PROMISE 7

GREAT COMMISSION AND GREAT COMMANDMENT

Every Christian is called to ministry. The Great Commission in Matthew 28:18–20 belongs to every one of us. Romans 12, 1 Corinthians 12 and Ephesians 4 leave no doubt that every Christian is called by God to minister to others. Mark 12:30–31 also calls Christians to lives of love and service to others. Our call to ministry may not be as dramatic as Isaiah's experience recorded in this chapter, but it is no less certain or important. In fact, Isaiah's call reveals several essential truths for every Christian man.

Every informed man of God eventually comes to the realization that God wants to use him. When Isaiah got the call he said, "Here am I, send me!" Isaiah, like any of us, must have had a sense of anticipation when reflecting on this call: "I wonder how God will use me?" Now read Isaiah's assignment in verses 9 and 10. What God said to Isaiah can be summarized as, "From all outward appearances, I am calling you to be a flop; a wipe-out; a failure." No wonder Isaiah asked the question in verse 11, "How long?" And God's answer in verses 11–13 was no encouragement to this young prophet.

The question before us is a simple one: Why would Isaiah respond to such a call? What was his motivation for engaging in a ministry that had little ministry potential? This question begs yet another: What keeps a man today committed to fulfill the Great Commission and Great Commandment when it seems more men reject than accept the gospel? What we learn from Isaiah's manual on motivation may be among the most important lessons of our life.

A careful reading of this passage reveals Isaiah's motive to continue in ministry even when he knew ministry would be tough. He followed a logical progression of critical experiences that explain his faithfulness to God's call. First, Isaiah saw God (vv. 1–4). Notice what he said God looked like: "seated on a throne, high and exalted." Isaiah saw a majestic and powerful God, not some second-rate monarch—or even a first-rate one. He saw God as high and exalted, and "the train of his robe filled the temple." Actually, this is an absurd picture unless the one wearing the robe is so exalted that this opulent display is appropriate, and it certainly is here. Never has there been an earthly ruler with this kind of glory.

Verse 2 shifts the focus from the throne to the angels hovering around it, further amplifying God's majesty and glory. These seraphs had six wings but used only two of them to fly. The other four wings shielded their faces and feet from the glory of the One on the throne. Notice in verse 3 what these mighty angels did: They hovered about the throne praising God's holiness and glory. Verse 4 gives an idea of their power—the voices that rattled the room came not from God, but from those who praised him. These exciting images give us just a taste of the wonder that Isaiah witnessed.

Second, Isaiah responded appropriately to this vision of God. Verse 5 records Isaiah's response to this vision: "I am ruined!" He was immediately struck with his sinfulness and with the sin of his people. A proper understanding of God gave Isaiah a new view of himself and the needs of his people. Compared to this glorious God, Isaiah was a ruined, unworthy sinner. But observe what happened next. After seeing God and realizing his desperate need, Isaiah was in a position for God to help him. He mentioned a specific problem with his lips in verse 5; in verse 6, God cleansed him.

Third, Isaiah heard and responded to God's call without hesitation. Without knowing where or to what God would send him, Isaiah responded quickly and enthusiastically: "Here am I, send me!" (v. 8). Isaiah saw God as he is, which allowed Isaiah to see himself as he was. Only then could he clearly understand his need and ask God for specific help. This was a worship-oriented, spiritually prepared man who heard God's call. When *this* God calls and *this* kind of man hears, there is only one response: "Send me!"

Take a moment to reflect on five truths from Isaiah's call:

1. *Our God is the all-powerful ruler of everything.* The bigger our view of God, the more confidently we will minister for him. We will probably never have the same experience of God as Isaiah did, but we have the Bible (including Isaiah's description) which, from cover to cover, presents a holy and exalted God.
2. *A proper view of God gives a man a proper view of himself.* Isaiah understood the depth of his need when he saw God. God warns us about comparing ourselves with other people. Our only standard is his holiness.
3. *Isaiah didn't remain in his sin.* Because he saw God and saw himself, Isaiah was able to call for and receive help from God. That is what God does.
4. *Only then did Isaiah understand a higher call on his life.* No matter what our role, we are God's ambassadors, commissioned by God to represent him on earth. He has called us to serve him and will prepare and support us. No matter what we may have done in the past, God still calls and uses us to complete his purposes on earth. He is in the reconstruction business.
5. *The task is tough.* Isaiah's call was much like ours: Take God's Word and God's love to people who, in many cases, will reject it. Satanic and human opposition can be scary and discouraging. But the God Isaiah saw—and introduced us to—is the undisputed ruler of the universe. He is on the throne, lofty and exalted; he is magnificent in his glory, and his power far outshines opposition from any other source.

Isaiah teaches us that it is not the size of the job that determines our success or failure in life, but the size of our view of God. He is the One who helps us as we seek to minister to others in his name and in obedience to the Great Commission and the Great Commandment. In private devotions and public worship, focus on God in all his glory. That, ultimately and finally, will make the difference.

For the next Promise 7 reading go to page 764.

8for the head of Aram is
Damascus,[t]
and the head of Damascus is
only Rezin.
Within sixty-five years
Ephraim will be too shattered[u]
to be a people.
9The head of Ephraim is Samaria,
and the head of Samaria is only
Remaliah's son.
If you do not stand firm in your
faith,[v]
you will not stand at all.' "[w]

10Again the LORD spoke to Ahaz, 11"Ask the LORD your God for a sign, whether in the deepest depths or in the highest heights."

12But Ahaz said, "I will not ask; I will not put the LORD to the test."

13Then Isaiah said, "Hear now, you house of David! Is it not enough to try the patience of men? Will you try the patience of my God[x] also? 14Therefore the Lord himself will give you[a] a sign: The virgin will be with child and will give birth to a son,[y] and[b] will call him Immanuel.[c][z] 15He will eat curds and honey[a] when he knows enough to reject the wrong and choose the right. 16But before the boy knows[b] enough to reject the wrong and choose the right, the land of the two kings you dread will be laid waste.[c] 17The LORD will bring on you and on your people and on the house of your father a time unlike any since Ephraim broke away[d] from Judah—he will bring the king of Assyria.[e]"

18In that day the LORD will whistle[f] for flies from the distant streams of Egypt and for bees from the land of Assyria.[g] 19They will all come and settle in the steep ravines and in the crevices[h] in the rocks, on all the thornbushes and at all the water holes. 20In that day the Lord will use[i] a razor hired from beyond the River[d]—the king of Assyria[j]—to shave your head and the hair of your legs, and to take off your beards also. 21In that day, a man will keep alive a young cow and two goats. 22And because of the abundance of the milk they give, he will have curds to eat. All who remain in the land will eat curds and honey. 23In that day, in every place where there were a thousand vines worth a thousand silver shekels,[e] there will be only briers and thorns.[k] 24Men will go there with bow and arrow, for the land will be covered with briers and thorns. 25As for all the hills once cultivated by the hoe, you will no longer go there for fear of the briers and thorns; they will become places where cattle are turned loose and where sheep run.[l]

Assyria, the LORD's Instrument

8 The LORD said to me, "Take a large scroll[m] and write on it with an ordinary pen: Maher-Shalal-Hash-Baz.[f][n] 2And I will call in Uriah[o] the priest and Zechariah son of Jeberekiah as reliable witnesses for me."

3Then I went to the prophetess, and she conceived and gave birth to a son. And the LORD said to me, "Name him Maher-Shalal-Hash-Baz. 4Before the boy knows[p] how to say 'My father' or 'My mother,' the wealth of Damascus and the plunder of Samaria will be carried off by the king of Assyria.[q]"

5The LORD spoke to me again:

6"Because this people has rejected[r]
the gently flowing waters of
Shiloah[s]
and rejoices over Rezin
and the son of Remaliah,[t]
7therefore the Lord is about to bring
against them
the mighty floodwaters[u] of the
River[d]—
the king of Assyria[v] with all his
pomp.
It will overflow all its channels,
run over all its banks
8and sweep on into Judah, swirling
over it,
passing through it and reaching
up to the neck.
Its outspread wings will cover the
breadth of your land,
O Immanuel[c]!"[w]

9Raise the war cry,[g][x] you nations,
and be shattered!
Listen, all you distant lands.
Prepare[y] for battle, and be
shattered!
Prepare for battle, and be
shattered!
10Devise your strategy, but it will be
thwarted;[z]
propose your plan, but it will not
stand,[a]
for God is with us.[h][b]

Fear God

11The LORD spoke to me with his strong hand upon me,[c] warning me not to follow[d] the way of this people. He said:

7:8 [t]Ge 14:15 [u]Isa 17:1-3
7:9 [v]2Ch 20:20 [w]Isa 8:6-8; 30:12-14
7:13 [x]Isa 25:1
7:14 [y]Lk 1:31 [z]Isa 8:8,10; Mt 1:23*
7:15 [a]ver 22
7:16 [b]Isa 8:4 [c]Isa 17:3; Hos 5:9,13; Am 1:3-5
7:17 [d]1Ki 12:16 [e]2Ch 28:20
7:18 [f]Isa 5:26 [g]Isa 13:5
7:19 [h]Isa 2:19
7:20 [i]Isa 10:15 [j]Isa 8:7; 10:5
7:23 [k]Isa 5:6
7:25 [l]Isa 5:17
8:1 [m]Isa 30:8; Hab 2:2 [n]ver 3; Hab 2:2
8:2 [o]2Ki 16:10
8:4 [p]Isa 7:16 [q]Isa 7:8
8:6 [r]Isa 5:24 [s]Jn 9:7 [t]Isa 7:1
8:7 [u]Isa 17:12-13 [v]Isa 7:20
8:8 [w]Isa 7:14
8:9 [x]Isa 17:12-13 [y]Joel 3:9
8:10 [z]Job 5:12 [a]Isa 7:7 [b]Isa 7:14; Ro 8:31
8:11 [c]Eze 3:14 [d]Eze 2:8

a 14 The Hebrew is plural. b 14 Masoretic Text; Dead Sea Scrolls *and he* or *and they* c 14,8 *Immanuel* means *God with us.* d 20,7 That is, the Euphrates e 23 That is, about 25 pounds (about 11.5 kilograms) f 1 *Maher-Shalal-Hash-Baz* means *quick to the plunder, swift to the spoil*; also in verse 3. g 9 Or *Do your worst* h 10 Hebrew *Immanuel*

12"Do not call conspiracy[e]
everything that these people call
conspiracy[a];
do not fear what they fear,
and do not dread it.[f]
13The LORD Almighty is the one you
are to regard as holy,[g]
he is the one you are to fear,
he is the one you are to dread,[h]
14and he will be a sanctuary;[i]
but for both houses of Israel he
will be
a stone that causes men to stumble
and a rock that makes them
fall.[j]
And for the people of Jerusalem he
will be
a trap and a snare.[k]
15Many of them will stumble;[l]
they will fall and be broken,
they will be snared and
captured."

16Bind up the testimony
and seal[m] up the law among my
disciples.
17I will wait[n] for the LORD,
who is hiding[o] his face from the
house of Jacob.
I will put my trust in him.

18Here am I, and the children the
LORD has given me.[p] We are signs[q]
and symbols in Israel from the LORD
Almighty, who dwells on Mount
Zion.[r]
19When men tell you to consult[s]
mediums and spiritists, who whisper
and mutter,[t] should not a people inquire of their God? Why consult the
dead on behalf of the living? 20To the
law[u] and to the testimony! If they do
not speak according to this word, they
have no light[v] of dawn. 21Distressed
and hungry, they will roam through the
land; when they are famished, they will
become enraged and, looking upward,
will curse[w] their king and their God.
22Then they will look toward the earth
and see only distress and darkness and
fearful gloom, and they will be thrust
into utter darkness.[x]

To Us a Child Is Born

9 Nevertheless, there will be no more
gloom for those who were in distress. In the past he humbled the land
of Zebulun and the land of Naphtali,[y]
but in the future he will honor Galilee
of the Gentiles, by the way of the sea,
along the Jordan—

2The people walking in darkness
have seen a great light;[z]
on those living in the land of the
shadow of death[b][a]
a light has dawned.[b]
3You have enlarged the nation
and increased their joy;
they rejoice before you
as people rejoice at the harvest,
as men rejoice
when dividing the plunder.
4For as in the day of Midian's
defeat,[c]
you have shattered
the yoke[d] that burdens them,
the bar across their shoulders,[e]
the rod of their oppressor.[f]
5Every warrior's boot used in battle
and every garment rolled in
blood
will be destined for burning,[g]
will be fuel for the fire.
6For to us a child is born,[h]
to us a son is given,[i]
and the government[j] will be on
his shoulders.
And he will be called
Wonderful Counselor,[c][k] Mighty
God,[l]
Everlasting Father, Prince of
Peace.[m]
7Of the increase of his government
and peace
there will be no end.[n]
He will reign on David's throne
and over his kingdom,
establishing and upholding it
with justice[o] and righteousness
from that time on and forever.
The zeal[p] of the LORD Almighty
will accomplish this.

8:12 [e]Isa 7:2; 30:1 [f]1Pe 3:14* **8:13** [g]Nu 20:12 [h]Isa 29:23 **8:14** [i]Isa 4:6; Eze 11:16 [j]Lk 2:34; Ro 9:33*; 1Pe 2:8* [k]Isa 24:17-18 **8:15** [l]Isa 28:13; 59:10; Lk 20:18; Ro 9:32 **8:16** [m]Isa 29:11-12 **8:17** [n]Hab 2:3 [o]Dt 31:17; Isa 54:8 **8:18** [p]Heb 2:13* [q]Lk 2:34 [r]Ps 9:11 **8:19** [s]1Sa 28:8 [t]Isa 29:4 **8:20** [u]Isa 1:10; Lk 16:29

[v]Mic 3:6 **8:21** [w]Rev 16:11 **8:22** [x]ver 20; Isa 5:30 **9:1** [y]2Ki 15:29 **9:2** [z]Eph 5:8 [a]Lk 1:79 [b]Mt 4:15-16* **9:4** [c]Jdg 7:25 [d]Isa 14:25 [e]Isa 10:27 [f]Isa 14:4; 49:26; 51:13; 54:14 **9:5** [g]Isa 2:4 **9:6** [h]Isa 53:2; Lk 2:11 [i]Jn 3:16 [j]Mt 28:18 [k]Isa 28:29 [l]Isa 10:21; 11:2 [m]Isa 26:3,12; 66:12 **9:7** [n]Da 2:44; Lk 1:33 [o]Isa 11:4; 16:5; 32:1,16 [p]Isa 37:32; 59:17

8:13-14

PROMISE 1

ONLY ONE OPTION

God had promised to protect Israel from its enemies if the nation turned to him (v. 10). Still, many in Israel preferred to make alliances with other nations for protection.

God's word to Isaiah in this passage stands today as both a caution and a promise for us. To those who trust him, God is a refuge. To those who ignore him, he is a source of trouble. God never goes away and is never neutral about sin and obedience. He either forgives sin or disciplines the sinner until he or she repents. Isaiah made the only logical choice for a man who knows God. Read it in verse 17, then ponder it and follow it.

For the next Promise 1 reading go to page 749.

[a]12 Or *Do not call for a treaty / every time these people call for a treaty* [b]2 Or *land of darkness* [c]6 Or *Wonderful, Counselor*

The LORD's Anger Against Israel

8The Lord has sent a message
against Jacob;
it will fall on Israel.
9All the people will know it—
Ephraim and the inhabitants of
Samaria[q]—
who say with pride
and arrogance[r] of heart,
10"The bricks have fallen down,
but we will rebuild with dressed
stone;
the fig trees have been felled,
but we will replace them with
cedars."
11But the LORD has strengthened
Rezin's[s] foes against them
and has spurred their enemies
on.
12Arameans[t] from the east and
Philistines[u] from the west
have devoured[v] Israel with open
mouth.

Yet for all this, his anger is not
turned away,
his hand is still upraised.[w]

13But the people have not returned
to him who struck[x] them,
nor have they sought[y] the LORD
Almighty.
14So the LORD will cut off from Israel
both head and tail,
both palm branch and reed[z] in
a single day;[a]
15the elders[b] and prominent men
are the head,
the prophets who teach lies are
the tail.
16Those who guide[c] this people
mislead them,
and those who are guided are
led astray.[d]
17Therefore the Lord will take no
pleasure in the young
men,[e]
nor will he pity[f] the fatherless
and widows,
for everyone is ungodly[g] and
wicked,[h]
every mouth speaks vileness.[i]

Yet for all this, his anger is not
turned away,
his hand is still upraised.[j]

18Surely wickedness burns like a
fire;[k]
it consumes briers and thorns,
it sets the forest thickets ablaze,[l]
so that it rolls upward in a
column of smoke.
19By the wrath[m] of the LORD
Almighty
the land will be scorched
and the people will be fuel for the
fire;[n]
no one will spare his brother.[o]
20On the right they will devour,
but still be hungry;[p]
on the left they will eat,[q]
but not be satisfied.
Each will feed on the flesh of his
own offspring[a]:
21 Manasseh will feed on Ephraim,
and Ephraim on Manasseh;
together they will turn against
Judah.[r]

Yet for all this, his anger is not
turned away,
his hand is still upraised.[s]

10 Woe to those who make unjust
laws,
to those who issue oppressive
decrees,[t]
2to deprive[u] the poor of their rights
and withhold justice from the
oppressed of my people,[v]
making widows their prey
and robbing the fatherless.
3What will you do on the day of
reckoning,[w]
when disaster[x] comes from
afar?
To whom will you run for help?[y]
Where will you leave your riches?
4Nothing will remain but to cringe
among the captives[z]
or fall among the slain.[a]

Yet for all this, his anger is not
turned away,[b]
his hand is still upraised.

God's Judgment on Assyria

5"Woe to the Assyrian,[c] the rod of
my anger,
in whose hand is the club[d] of
my wrath![e]
6I send him against a godless[f]
nation,
I dispatch him against a people
who anger me,[g]
to seize loot and snatch plunder,[h]
and to trample them down like
mud in the streets.
7But this is not what he intends,[i]
this is not what he has in mind;
his purpose is to destroy,
to put an end to many nations.
8'Are not my commanders[j] all
kings?' he says.
9 'Has not Calno[k] fared like
Carchemish?[l]
Is not Hamath like Arpad,
and Samaria[m] like Damascus?[n]

[a]20 Or *arm*

9:9 [q]Isa 7:9 [r]Isa 46:12 **9:11** [s]Isa 7:8 **9:12** [t]2Ki 16:6 [u]2Ch 28:18 [v]Ps 79:7 [w]Isa 5:25 **9:13** [x]Jer 5:3 [y]Isa 31:1; Hos 7:7,10 **9:14** [z]Isa 19:15 [a]Rev 18:8 **9:15** [b]Isa 3:2-3 **9:16** [c]Mt 15:14; 23:16,24 [d]Isa 3:12 **9:17** [e]Jer 18:21 [f]Isa 27:11 [g]Isa 10:6 [h]Isa 1:4 [i]Mt 12:34 [j]Isa 5:25 **9:18** [k]Mal 4:1 [l]Ps 83:14 **9:19** [m]Isa 13:9,13
[n]Isa 1:31 [o]Mic 7:2,6 **9:20** [p]Lev 26:26 [q]Isa 49:26 **9:21** [r]2Ch 28:6 [s]Isa 5:25 **10:1** [t]Ps 58:2 **10:2** [u]Isa 3:14 [v]Isa 5:23 **10:3** [w]Job 31:14; Hos 9:7 [x]Lk 19:44 [y]Isa 20:6 **10:4** [z]Isa 24:22 [a]Isa 22:2; 34:3; 66:16 [b]Isa 5:25 **10:5** [c]Isa 14:25; Zep 2:13 [d]Jer 51:20 [e]Isa 13:3,5,13; 30:30; 66:14 **10:6** [f]Isa 9:17 [g]Isa 9:19 [h]Isa 5:29 **10:7** [i]Ge 50:20; Ac 4:23-28 **10:8** [j]2Ki 18:24 **10:9** [k]Ge 10:10 [l]2Ch 35:20 [m]2Ki 17:6 [n]2Ki 16:9

10As my hand seized the kingdoms of
the idols,[o]
kingdoms whose images excelled
those of Jerusalem and
Samaria—
11shall I not deal with Jerusalem and
her images
as I dealt with Samaria and her
idols?' "

12When the Lord has finished all his
work[p] against Mount Zion[q] and Jerusalem, he will say, "I will punish the
king of Assyria[r] for the willful pride of
his heart and the haughty look in his
eyes. 13For he says:

" 'By the strength of my hand I
have done this,[s]
and by my wisdom, because I
have understanding.
I removed the boundaries of
nations,
I plundered their treasures;[t]
like a mighty one I subdued[a]
their kings.
14As one reaches into a nest,[u]
so my hand reached for the
wealth[v] of the nations;
as men gather abandoned eggs,
so I gathered all the countries;
not one flapped a wing,
or opened its mouth to chirp.' "
15Does the ax raise itself above him
who swings it,
or the saw boast against him
who uses it?[w]
As if a rod were to wield him who
lifts it up,
or a club[x] brandish him who is
not wood!
16Therefore, the Lord, the LORD
Almighty,
will send a wasting disease[y]
upon his sturdy warriors;
under his pomp[z] a fire will be
kindled
like a blazing flame.
17The Light of Israel will become a
fire,[a]
their Holy One[b] a flame;
in a single day it will burn and
consume
his thorns[c] and his briers.[d]
18The splendor of his forests[e] and
fertile fields
it will completely destroy,
as when a sick man wastes away.
19And the remaining trees of his
forests will be so few[f]
that a child could write them
down.

The Remnant of Israel

20In that day[g] the remnant of Israel,
the survivors of the house of
Jacob,
will no longer rely[h] on him
who struck them down[i]
but will truly rely[j] on the LORD,
the Holy One of Israel.
21A remnant[k] will return,[b] a
remnant of Jacob
will return to the Mighty God.[l]
22Though your people, O Israel, be
like the sand by the sea,
only a remnant will return.[m]
Destruction has been decreed,[n]
overwhelming and righteous.
23The Lord, the LORD Almighty, will
carry out
the destruction decreed upon the
whole land.[o]

24Therefore, this is what the Lord,
the LORD Almighty, says:

"O my people who live in Zion,[p]
do not be afraid of the Assyrians,
who beat[q] you with a rod
and lift up a club against you, as
Egypt did.
25Very soon[r] my anger against you
will end
and my wrath[s] will be directed
to their destruction."

26The LORD Almighty will lash[t] them
with a whip,
as when he struck down
Midian[u] at the rock of
Oreb;
and he will raise his staff over the
waters,[v]
as he did in Egypt.
27In that day their burden will be
lifted from your shoulders,
their yoke[w] from your neck;[x]
the yoke will be broken
because you have grown so fat.[c]
28They enter Aiath;
they pass through Migron;[y]
they store supplies at
Micmash.[z]
29They go over the pass, and say,
"We will camp overnight at
Geba."
Ramah[a] trembles;
Gibeah of Saul flees.
30Cry out, O Daughter of Gallim![b]
Listen, O Laishah!
Poor Anathoth![c]
31Madmenah is in flight;
the people of Gebim take cover.
32This day they will halt at Nob;[d]
they will shake their fist

10:10 [o] 2Ki 19:18 **10:12** [p] Isa 28:21-22; 65:7 [q] 2Ki 19:31 [r] Jer 50:18 **10:13** [s] Isa 37:24; Da 4:30 [t] Eze 28:4 **10:14** [u] Jer 49:16; Ob 1:4 [v] Job 31:25 **10:15** [w] Isa 45:9; Ro 9:20-21 [x] ver 5 **10:16** [y] ver 18; Isa 17:4 [z] Isa 8:7 **10:17** [a] Isa 31:9 [b] Isa 37:23 [c] Nu 11:1-3 [d] Isa 9:18 **10:18** [e] 2Ki 19:23 **10:19** [f] Isa 21:17 **10:20** [g] Isa 11:10,11

[h] 2Ki 16:7 [i] 2Ch 28:20 [j] Isa 17:7 **10:21** [k] Isa 6:13 [l] Isa 9:6 **10:22** [m] Ro 9:27-28 [n] Isa 28:22; Da 9:27 **10:23** [o] Isa 28:22; Ro 9:27-28* **10:24** [p] Ps 87:5-6 [q] Ex 5:14 **10:25** [r] Isa 17:14 [s] ver 5; Da 11:36 **10:26** [t] Isa 37:36-38 [u] Isa 9:4 [v] Ex 14:16 **10:27** [w] Isa 9:4 [x] Isa 14:25 **10:28** [y] 1Sa 14:2 [z] 1Sa 13:2 **10:29** [a] Jos 18:25 **10:30** [b] 1Sa 25:44 [c] Ne 11:32 **10:32** [d] 1Sa 21:1

[a] 13 Or / *I subdued the mighty,* [b] *21* Hebrew *shear-jashub;* also in verse 22 [c] *27* Hebrew; Septuagint *broken / from your shoulders*

at the mount of the Daughter of
Zion,[e]
at the hill of Jerusalem.

33See, the Lord, the LORD Almighty,
will lop off the boughs with great
power.
The lofty trees will be felled,
the tall[f] ones will be brought
low.
34He will cut down the forest thickets
with an ax;
Lebanon will fall before the
Mighty One.

The Branch From Jesse

11 A shoot will come up from the
stump of Jesse;[g]
from his roots a Branch[h] will
bear fruit.
2The Spirit[i] of the LORD will rest on
him—
the Spirit of wisdom[j] and of
understanding,
the Spirit of counsel and of
power,[k]
the Spirit of knowledge and of
the fear of the LORD—
3and he will delight in the fear of
the LORD.

He will not judge by what he sees
with his eyes,[l]
or decide by what he hears with
his ears;[m]
4but with righteousness[n] he will
judge the needy,
with justice[o] he will give
decisions for the poor[p] of
the earth.
He will strike[q] the earth with the
rod of his mouth;
with the breath[r] of his lips he
will slay the wicked.
5Righteousness will be his belt
and faithfulness[s] the sash
around his waist.[t]

6The wolf will live with the lamb,[u]
the leopard will lie down with
the goat,
the calf and the lion and the
yearling[a] together;
and a little child will lead them.
7The cow will feed with the bear,
their young will lie down
together,
and the lion will eat straw like
the ox.
8The infant will play near the hole
of the cobra,
and the young child put his
hand into the viper's nest.
9They will neither harm nor
destroy[v]
on all my holy mountain,
for the earth[w] will be full of the
knowledge[x] of the LORD
as the waters cover the sea.

10In that day the Root of Jesse will
stand as a banner[y] for the peoples;
the nations[z] will rally to him,[a] and
his place of rest[b] will be glorious. 11In
that day[c] the Lord will reach out his
hand a second time to reclaim the remnant that is left of his people from Assyria,[d] from Lower Egypt, from Upper Egypt,[b] from Cush,[c] from Elam,[e]
from Babylonia,[d] from Hamath and
from the islands[f] of the sea.

12He will raise a banner for the
nations
and gather the exiles of Israel;
he will assemble the scattered
people[g] of Judah
from the four quarters of the
earth.
13Ephraim's jealousy will vanish,
and Judah's enemies[e] will be
cut off;
Ephraim will not be jealous of
Judah,
nor Judah hostile toward
Ephraim.[h]
14They will swoop down on the
slopes of Philistia to the
west;
together they will plunder the
people to the east.
They will lay hands on Edom[i] and
Moab,[j]
and the Ammonites will be
subject to them.
15The LORD will dry up
the gulf of the Egyptian sea;
with a scorching wind he will
sweep his hand[k]
over the Euphrates River.[f][l]
He will break it up into seven
streams
so that men can cross over in
sandals.
16There will be a highway[m] for the
remnant of his people
that is left from Assyria,
as there was for Israel
when they came up from
Egypt.[n]

Songs of Praise

12 In that day you will say:

"I will praise[o] you, O LORD.
Although you were angry with
me,
your anger has turned away

10:32 [e]Jer 6:23
10:33 [f]Am 2:9
11:1 [g]ver 10; Isa 9:7; Rev 5:5 [h]Isa 4:2
11:2 [i]Isa 42:1; 48:16; 61:1; Mt 3:16; Jn 1:32-33 [j]Eph 1:17 [k]2Ti 1:7
11:3 [l]Jn 7:24 [m]Jn 2:25
11:4 [n]Ps 72:2 [o]Isa 9:7 [p]Isa 3:14 [q]Mal 4:6 [r]Job 4:9; 2Th 2:8
11:5 [s]Isa 25:1 [t]Eph 6:14
11:6 [u]Isa 65:25
11:9 [v]Job 5:23 [w]Ps 98:2-3; Isa 52:10 [x]Isa 45:6,14; Hab 2:14
11:10 [y]Jn 12:32 [z]Isa 49:23; Lk 2:32 [a]Ro 15:12* [b]Isa 14:3; 28:12; 32:17-18
11:11 [c]Isa 10:20 [d]Isa 19:24; Hos 11:11; Mic 7:12; Zec 10:10 [e]Ge 10:22 [f]Isa 42:4,10,12; 66:19
11:12 [g]Zep 3:10
11:13 [h]Jer 3:18; Eze 37:16-17, 22; Hos 1:11
11:14 [i]Da 11:41; Joel 3:19 [j]Isa 16:14; 25:10
11:15 [k]Isa 19:16 [l]Isa 7:20
11:16 [m]Isa 19:23; 62:10 [n]Ex 14:26-31
12:1 [o]Isa 25:1

[a]6 Hebrew; Septuagint *lion will feed*
[b]11 Hebrew *from Pathros*
[c]11 That is, the upper Nile region
[d]11 Hebrew *Shinar*
[e]13 Or *hostility*
[f]15 Hebrew *the River*

and you have comforted me.
1 →PG. 759
2 Surely God is my salvation;
I will trust[p] and not be afraid.
The LORD, the LORD, is my strength
and my song;
he has become my salvation.[q]"
3 With joy you will draw water[r]
from the wells of salvation.

7 →PG. 778
4 In that day you will say:

"Give thanks to the LORD, call on
his name;[s]
make known among the nations
what he has done,
and proclaim that his name is
exalted.
5 Sing[t] to the LORD, for he has done
glorious things;[u]
let this be known to all the
world.
6 Shout aloud and sing for joy,
people of Zion,
for great is the Holy One of
Israel[v] among you.[w]"

A Prophecy Against Babylon

13 An oracle concerning Babylon that Isaiah son of Amoz saw:

2 Raise a banner[x] on a bare hilltop,
shout to them;
beckon to them
to enter the gates of the nobles.
3 I have commanded my holy ones;
I have summoned my warriors[y]
to carry out my wrath—
those who rejoice[z] in my
triumph.

4 Listen, a noise on the mountains,
like that of a great multitude![a]
Listen, an uproar among the
kingdoms,
like nations massing together!
The LORD Almighty is mustering
an army for war.
5 They come from faraway lands,
from the ends of the
heavens[b]—
the LORD and the weapons of his
wrath—
to destroy[c] the whole country.

6 Wail,[d] for the day[e] of the LORD is
near;
it will come like destruction from
the Almighty.a
7 Because of this, all hands will go
limp,
every man's heart will melt.[f]
8 Terror[g] will seize them,
pain and anguish will grip them;
they will writhe like a woman in
labor.
They will look aghast at each other,
their faces aflame.[h]

9 See, the day of the LORD is coming
—a cruel day, with wrath and
fierce anger—
to make the land desolate
and destroy the sinners within it.
10 The stars of heaven and their
constellations
will not show their light.
The rising sun[i] will be darkened[j]
and the moon will not give its
light.[k]
11 I will punish[l] the world for its
evil,
the wicked for their sins.
I will put an end to the arrogance
of the haughty
and will humble the pride of the
ruthless.
12 I will make man[m] scarcer than
pure gold,
more rare than the gold of
Ophir.
13 Therefore I will make the heavens
tremble;[n]
and the earth will shake from its
place
at the wrath of the LORD Almighty,
in the day of his burning anger.

14 Like a hunted gazelle,
like sheep without a shepherd,[o]
each will return to his own people,
each will flee to his native
land.[p]
15 Whoever is captured will be thrust
through;
all who are caught will fall[q] by
the sword.[r]
16 Their infants[s] will be dashed to
pieces before their eyes;
their houses will be looted and
their wives ravished.

17 See, I will stir up[t] against them
the Medes,
who do not care for silver
and have no delight in gold.[u]

12:2 [p]Isa 26:3 [q]Ex 15:2; Ps 118:14
12:3 [r]Jn 4:10,14
12:4 [s]Ps 105:1; Isa 24:15
12:5 [t]Ex 15:1 [u]Ps 98:1
12:6 [v]Isa 49:26 [w]Zep 3:14-17
13:2 [x]Jer 50:2; 51:27
13:3 [y]Joel 3:11 [z]Ps 149:2
13:4 [a]Joel 3:14
13:5 [b]Isa 5:26 [c]Isa 24:1
13:6 [d]Eze 30:2 [e]Isa 2:12; Joel 1:15
13:7 [f]Eze 21:7
13:8 [g]Isa 21:4 [h]Na 2:10
13:10 [i]Isa 24:23 [j]Isa 5:30; Rev 8:12 [k]Eze 32:7; Mt 24:29*; Mk 13:24*
13:11 [l]Isa 3:11; 11:4; 26:21
13:12 [m]Isa 4:1
13:13 [n]Isa 34:4; 51:6; Hag 2:6
13:14 [o]1Ki 22:17 [p]Jer 50:16
13:15 [q]Jer 51:4 [r]Isa 14:19; Jer 50:25
13:16 [s]Ps 137:9
13:17 [t]Jer 51:1 [u]Pr 6:34-35

a6 Hebrew *Shaddai*

12:1–6

PROMISE 1

OASIS

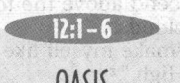

This song of the redeemed strikes deep into the heart. After plowing through eleven chapters that describe Israel's struggle against God's invitation to repent and return to him, this chapter is like an oasis. It is the song of one who lives in God's presence.

When you're worn down by life's struggles, know that God invites you to rest in him. It can—it *must*—be the song of a godly man's life.

For the next Promise 1 reading go to page 773.

18 Their bows will strike down the young men;
they will have no mercy on infants
nor will they look with compassion on children.
19 Babylon, the jewel of kingdoms,
the glory[v] of the Babylonians'[a] pride,
will be overthrown[w] by God
like Sodom and Gomorrah.[x]
20 She will never be inhabited[y]
or lived in through all generations;
no Arab[z] will pitch his tent there,
no shepherd will rest his flocks there.
21 But desert creatures[a] will lie there,
jackals will fill her houses;
there the owls will dwell,
and there the wild goats will leap about.
22 Hyenas will howl in her strongholds,[b]
jackals[c] in her luxurious palaces.
Her time is at hand,[d]
and her days will not be prolonged.

14 The LORD will have compassion[e] on Jacob;
once again he will choose[f] Israel
and will settle them in their own land.
Aliens[g] will join them
and unite with the house of Jacob.
2 Nations will take them
and bring[h] them to their own place.
And the house of Israel will possess the nations[i]
as menservants and maidservants in the LORD's land.
They will make captives of their captors
and rule over their oppressors.[j]

3 On the day the LORD gives you relief[k] from suffering and turmoil and
cruel bondage, 4 you will take up this
taunt[l] against the king of Babylon:

How the oppressor[m] has come to an end!
How his fury[b] has ended!
5 The LORD has broken the rod of the wicked,[n]
the scepter of the rulers,
6 which in anger struck down peoples[o]
with unceasing blows,
and in fury subdued nations
with relentless aggression.[p]
7 All the lands are at rest and at peace;
they break into singing.[q]
8 Even the pine trees[r] and the cedars of Lebanon
exult over you and say,
"Now that you have been laid low,
no woodsman comes to cut us down."
9 The grave[c][s] below is all astir
to meet you at your coming;
it rouses the spirits of the departed to greet you—
all those who were leaders in the world;
it makes them rise from their thrones—
all those who were kings over the nations.
10 They will all respond,
they will say to you,
"You also have become weak, as we are;
you have become like us."[t]
11 All your pomp has been brought down to the grave,
along with the noise of your harps;
maggots are spread out beneath you
and worms[u] cover you.
12 How you have fallen[v] from heaven,
O morning star,[w] son of the dawn!
You have been cast down to the earth,
you who once laid low the nations!
13 You said in your heart,
"I will ascend[x] to heaven;
I will raise my throne[y]
above the stars of God;
I will sit enthroned on the mount of assembly,
on the utmost heights of the sacred mountain.[d]
14 I will ascend above the tops of the clouds;
I will make myself like the Most High."[z]
15 But you are brought down to the grave,
to the depths[a] of the pit.
16 Those who see you stare at you,
they ponder your fate:[b]
"Is this the man who shook the earth
and made kingdoms tremble,

13:19 [v]Da 4:30 [w]Rev 14:8 [x]Ge 19:24 **13:20** [y]Isa 14:23; 34:10-15 [z]2Ch 17:11 **13:21** [a]Rev 18:2 **13:22** [b]Isa 25:2 [c]Isa 34:13 [d]Jer 51:33 **14:1** [e]Ps 102:13; Isa 49:10,13; 54:7-8,10 [f]Isa 41:8; 44:1; 49:7; Zec 1:17; 2:12 [g]Eph 2:12-19 **14:2** [h]Isa 60:9 [i]Isa 49:7,23 [j]Isa 60:14; 61:5 **14:3** [k]Isa 11:10 **14:4** [l]Hab 2:6 [m]Isa 9:4 **14:5** [n]Ps 125:3 **14:6** [o]Isa 10:14 [p]Isa 47:6 **14:7** [q]Ps 98:1; 126:1-3 **14:8** [r]Eze 31:16 **14:9** [s]Eze 32:21 **14:10** [t]Eze 32:21 **14:11** [u]Isa 51:8 **14:12** [v]Isa 34:4; Lk 10:18 [w]2Pe 1:19; Rev 2:28; 8:10; 9:1 **14:13** [x]Da 5:23; 8:10; Mt 11:23 [y]Eze 28:2; 2Th 2:4 **14:14** [z]Isa 47:8; 2Th 2:4 **14:15** [a]Mt 11:23; Lk 10:15 **14:16** [b]Jer 50:23

[a] 19 Or *Chaldeans'* [b] 4 Dead Sea Scrolls, Septuagint and Syriac; the meaning of the word in the Masoretic Text is uncertain.
[c] 9 Hebrew *Sheol*; also in verses 11 and 15
[d] 13 Or *the north*; Hebrew *Zaphon*

17the man who made the world a
desert,[c]
who overthrew its cities
and would not let his captives go
home?"

18All the kings of the nations lie in
state,
each in his own tomb.
19But you are cast out[d] of your
tomb
like a rejected branch;
you are covered with the slain,
with those pierced by the sword,
those who descend to the stones
of the pit.[e]
Like a corpse trampled underfoot,
20 you will not join them in burial,
for you have destroyed your land
and killed your people.

The offspring[f] of the wicked[g]
will never be mentioned[h] again.
21Prepare a place to slaughter his
sons
for the sins of their forefathers;[i]
they are not to rise to inherit the
land
and cover the earth with their
cities.
22"I will rise up against them,"
declares the LORD Almighty.
"I will cut off from Babylon her
name and survivors,
her offspring and
descendants,[j]"
declares the LORD.
23"I will turn her into a place for
owls[k]
and into swampland;
I will sweep her with the broom of
destruction,"
declares the LORD Almighty.

A Prophecy Against Assyria

24The LORD Almighty has sworn,[l]

"Surely, as I have planned, so it
will be,
and as I have purposed, so it will
stand.[m]
25I will crush the Assyrian[n] in my
land;
on my mountains I will trample
him down.
His yoke[o] will be taken from my
people,
and his burden removed from
their shoulders.[p]"

26This is the plan[q] determined for
the whole world;
this is the hand[r] stretched out
over all nations.
27For the LORD Almighty has
purposed, and who can
thwart him?
His hand is stretched out, and
who can turn it back?[s]

A Prophecy Against the Philistines

28This oracle[t] came in the year
King Ahaz[u] died:

29Do not rejoice, all you Philistines,[v]
that the rod that struck you is
broken;
from the root of that snake will
spring up a viper,[w]
its fruit will be a darting,
venomous serpent.
30The poorest of the poor will find
pasture,
and the needy[x] will lie down in
safety.[y]
But your root I will destroy by
famine;[z]
it will slay[a] your survivors.

31Wail, O gate![b] Howl, O city!
Melt away, all you Philistines!
A cloud of smoke comes from the
north,[c]
and there is not a straggler in its
ranks.
32What answer shall be given
to the envoys[d] of that nation?
"The LORD has established Zion,[e]
and in her his afflicted people
will find refuge.[f]"

A Prophecy Against Moab

15 An oracle concerning Moab:[g]

Ar in Moab is ruined,[h]
destroyed in a night!
Kir in Moab is ruined,
destroyed in a night!
2Dibon goes up to its temple,
to its high places[i] to weep;
Moab wails over Nebo and
Medeba.
Every head is shaved[j]
and every beard cut off.
3In the streets they wear sackcloth;
on the roofs and in the public
squares[k]
they all wail,
prostrate with weeping.[l]
4Heshbon and Elealeh[m] cry out,
their voices are heard all the way
to Jahaz.
Therefore the armed men of Moab
cry out,
and their hearts are faint.

5My heart cries out over Moab;[n]
her fugitives flee as far as Zoar,
as far as Eglath Shelishiyah.
They go up the way to Luhith,
weeping as they go;

14:17 [c]Joel 2:3
14:19 [d]Isa 22:16-18 [e]Jer 41:7-9
14:20 [f]Job 18:19 [g]Isa 1:4 [h]Ps 21:10
14:21 [i]Ex 20:5; Lev 26:39
14:22 [j]1Ki 14:10; Job 18:19
14:23 [k]Isa 34:11-15; Zep 2:14
14:24 [l]Isa 45:23 [m]Ac 4:28
14:25 [n]Isa 10:5,12 [o]Isa 9:4 [p]Isa 10:27
14:26 [q]Isa 23:9 [r]Ex 15:12
14:27 [s]2Ch 20:6; Isa 43:13; Da 4:35
14:28 [t]Isa 13:1 [u]2Ki 16:20
14:29 [v]2Ch 26:6 [w]Isa 11:8
14:30 [x]Isa 3:15 [y]Isa 7:21-22 [z]Isa 8:21; 9:20; 51:19 [a]Jer 25:16
14:31 [b]Isa 3:26 [c]Jer 1:14
14:32 [d]Isa 37:9 [e]Ps 87:2,5; Isa 44:28; 54:11 [f]Isa 4:6; Jas 2:5
15:1 [g]Isa 11:14 [h]Jer 48:24,41
15:2 [i]Jer 48:35 [j]Lev 21:5
15:3 [k]Jer 48:38 [l]Isa 22:4
15:4 [m]Nu 32:3
15:5 [n]Jer 48:31

on the road to Horonaim[o]
they lament their destruction.[p]
6 The waters of Nimrim are dried
up[q]
and the grass is withered;[r]
the vegetation is gone
and nothing green is left.
7 So the wealth they have acquired[s]
and stored up
they carry away over the Ravine
of the Poplars.
8 Their outcry echoes along the
border of Moab;
their wailing reaches as far as
Eglaim,
their lamentation as far as Beer
Elim.
9 Dimon's[a] waters are full of blood,
but I will bring still more upon
Dimon[a]—
a lion[t] upon the fugitives of Moab
and upon those who remain in
the land.

16 Send lambs[u] as tribute
to the ruler of the land,
from Sela,[v] across the desert,
to the mount of the Daughter of
Zion.[w]
2 Like fluttering birds
pushed from the nest,[x]
so are the women of Moab
at the fords of the Arnon.[y]
3 "Give us counsel,
render a decision.
Make your shadow like night—
at high noon.
Hide the fugitives,[z]
do not betray the refugees.
4 Let the Moabite fugitives stay with
you;
be their shelter from the
destroyer."

The oppressor[a] will come to an
end,
and destruction will cease;
the aggressor will vanish from
the land.
5 In love a throne[b] will be
established;
in faithfulness a man will sit on
it—
one from the house[b] of
David[c]—
one who in judging seeks justice[d]
and speeds the cause of
righteousness.

6 We have heard of Moab's[e]
pride[f]—
her overweening pride and
conceit,
her pride and her insolence—
but her boasts are empty.
7 Therefore the Moabites wail,[g]
they wail together for Moab.
Lament and grieve
for the men[c][h] of Kir
Hareseth.[i]
8 The fields of Heshbon wither,
the vines of Sibmah also.
The rulers of the nations
have trampled down the choicest
vines,
which once reached Jazer
and spread toward the desert.
Their shoots spread out
and went as far as the sea.
9 So I weep,[j] as Jazer weeps,
for the vines of Sibmah.
O Heshbon, O Elealeh,
I drench you with tears!
The shouts of joy over your ripened
fruit
and over your harvests[k] have
been stilled.
10 Joy and gladness are taken away
from the orchards;[l]
no one sings or shouts in the
vineyards;
no one treads[m] out wine at the
presses,[n]
for I have put an end to the
shouting.
11 My heart laments for Moab[o] like a
harp,

16:1–5 — PROMISE 6

LOVE YOUR ENEMIES

Moab, Israel's avowed enemy, was about to be destroyed by the Assyrians. God offered them mercy and safety through his people Israel. Mercy came in the offer of eternal peace if they would accept his Messiah (v. 5). God also offered Moab a haven from the Assyrian threat. Isaiah's reference to "fluttering birds pushed from the nest" (v. 2) is a graphic picture of Moab's panic in this situation. See verses 3 and 4 for Isaiah's incredible instructions to Israel regarding their enemies: "Let the Moabite fugitives stay with you; be their shelter from the destroyer."

What an illustration of reconciliation! Enemy or not, these desperate people needed shelter, hope and mercy. Our ministry, like Israel's, can have no ethnic, national, racial or ideological boundaries. As God's earthly instruments of peace, shelter and good news, God commands Christians to play the same role today as did ancient Israel in this passage.

For the next Promise 6 reading go to page 789.

15:5 [o]Jer 48:3,34 [p]Jer 4:20; 48:5 **15:6** [q]Isa 19:5-7; Jer 48:34 [r]Joel 1:12 **15:7** [s]Isa 30:6; Jer 48:36 **15:9** [t]2Ki 17:25 **16:1** [u]2Ki 3:4 [v]2Ki 14:7 [w]Isa 10:32 **16:2** [x]Pr 27:8 [y]Nu 21:13-14; Jer 48:20

16:3 [z]1Ki 18:4 **16:4** [a]Isa 9:4 **16:5** [b]Da 7:14; Mic 4:7 [c]Lk 1:32 [d]Isa 9:7 **16:6** [e]Am 2:1; Zep 2:8 [f]Ob 1:3; Zep 2:10 **16:7** [g]Jer 48:20 [h]1Ch 16:3 [i]2Ki 3:25 **16:9** [j]Isa 15:3 [k]Jer 40:12 **16:10** [l]Isa 24:7-8 [m]Jdg 9:27 [n]Job 24:11 **16:11** [o]Isa 15:5

a 9 Masoretic Text; Dead Sea Scrolls, some Septuagint manuscripts and Vulgate *Dibon*
b 5 Hebrew *tent*
c 7 Or *"raisin cakes,"* a wordplay

my inmost being[p] for Kir
Hareseth.
12When Moab appears at her high
place,
she only wears herself out;
when she goes to her shrine[q] to
pray,
it is to no avail.[r]

13This is the word the LORD has already spoken concerning Moab. 14But
now the LORD says: "Within three
years, as a servant bound by contract
would count them, Moab's splendor
and all her many people will be despised,[s] and her survivors will be very
few and feeble."[t]

An Oracle Against Damascus

17 An oracle concerning Damascus:[u]

"See, Damascus will no longer be a
city
but will become a heap of
ruins.[v]
2The cities of Aroer will be deserted
and left to flocks,[w] which will lie
down,
with no one to make them
afraid.[x]
3The fortified city will disappear
from Ephraim,
and royal power from Damascus;
the remnant of Aram will be
like the glory[y] of the
Israelites,"[z]
declares the LORD Almighty.

4"In that day the glory of Jacob will
fade;
the fat of his body will waste[a]
away.
5It will be as when a reaper gathers
the standing grain
and harvests[b] the grain with his
arm—
as when a man gleans heads of
grain
in the Valley of Rephaim.
6Yet some gleanings will remain,[c]
as when an olive tree is
beaten,[d]
leaving two or three olives on the
topmost branches,
four or five on the fruitful
boughs,"
declares the LORD, the God
of Israel.

7In that day men will look[e] to their
Maker
and turn their eyes to the Holy
One[f] of Israel.
8They will not look to the altars,
the work of their hands,[g]
and they will have no regard for
the Asherah poles[a]
and the incense altars their
fingers have made.

9In that day their strong cities, which
they left because of the Israelites, will
be like places abandoned to thickets
and undergrowth. And all will be desolation.

10You have forgotten[h] God your
Savior;[i]
you have not remembered the
Rock, your fortress.
Therefore, though you set out the
finest plants
and plant imported vines,
11though on the day you set them
out, you make them grow,
and on the morning[j] when you
plant them, you bring them
to bud,
yet the harvest will be as nothing[k]
in the day of disease and
incurable pain.[l]

12Oh, the raging of many nations—
they rage like the raging sea![m]
Oh, the uproar of the peoples—
they roar like the roaring of great
waters!
13Although the peoples roar like the
roar of surging waters,
when he rebukes[n] them they
flee[o] far away,
driven before the wind like chaff[p]
on the hills,
like tumbleweed before a gale.[q]
14In the evening, sudden terror!
Before the morning, they are
gone![r]
This is the portion of those who
loot us,
the lot of those who plunder us.

A Prophecy Against Cush

18 Woe to the land of whirring
wings[b]
along the rivers of Cush,[c] [s]
2which sends envoys by sea
in papyrus[t] boats over the
water.

Go, swift messengers,
to a people tall and
smooth-skinned,
to a people feared far and wide,
an aggressive[u] nation of strange
speech,
whose land is divided by
rivers.[v]

3All you people of the world,
you who live on the earth,

16:11 [p]Isa 63:15; Hos 11:8; Php 2:1 **16:12** [q]Isa 15:2 [r]1Ki 18:29 **16:14** [s]Isa 25:10; Jer 48:42 [t]Isa 21:17 **17:1** [u]Ge 14:15; Jer 49:23; Ac 9:2 [v]Isa 25:2; Am 1:3; Zec 9:1 **17:2** [w]Isa 7:21; Eze 25:5 [x]Jer 7:33; Mic 4:4 **17:3** [y]ver 4; Hos 9:11 [z]Isa 7:8,16; 8:4 **17:4** [a]Isa 10:16 **17:5** [b]ver 11; Jer 51:33; Joel 3:13; Mt 13:30 **17:6** [c]Dt 4:27; Isa 24:13 [d]Isa 27:12 **17:7** [e]Isa 10:20 [f]Mic 7:7 **17:8** [g]Isa 2:18,20; 30:22

17:10 [h]Isa 51:13 [i]Ps 68:19; Isa 12:2 **17:11** [j]Ps 90:6 [k]Hos 8:7 [l]Job 4:8 **17:12** [m]Ps 18:4; Jer 6:23; Lk 21:25 **17:13** [n]Ps 9:5 [o]Isa 13:14 [p]Isa 41:2, 15-16 [q]Job 21:18 **17:14** [r]2Ki 19:35 **18:1** [s]Isa 20:3-5; Eze 30:4-5,9; Zep 2:12; 3:10 **18:2** [t]Ex 2:3 [u]Ge 10:8-9; 2Ch 12:3 [v]ver 7

a *8* That is, symbols of the goddess Asherah
b *1* Or *of locusts* c *1* That is, the upper Nile region

when a banner[w] is raised on the mountains,
you will see it,
and when a trumpet sounds,
you will hear it.
4This is what the LORD says to me:
"I will remain quiet and will look on from my dwelling place,[x]
like shimmering heat in the sunshine,
like a cloud of dew[y] in the heat of harvest."
5For, before the harvest, when the blossom is gone
and the flower becomes a ripening grape,
he will cut off the shoots with pruning knives,
and cut down and take away the spreading branches.[z]
6They will all be left to the mountain birds of prey
and to the wild animals;[a]
the birds will feed on them all summer,
the wild animals all winter.

7At that time gifts will be brought to the LORD Almighty

from a people tall and smooth-skinned,
from a people feared far and wide,
an aggressive nation of strange speech,
whose land is divided by rivers—

the gifts will be brought to Mount Zion, the place of the Name of the LORD Almighty.[b]

A Prophecy About Egypt

19 An oracle[c] concerning Egypt:[d e]

See, the LORD rides on a swift cloud[f]
and is coming to Egypt.
The idols of Egypt tremble before him,
and the hearts of the Egyptians melt[g] within them.

2"I will stir up Egyptian against Egyptian—
brother will fight against brother,[h]
neighbor against neighbor,
city against city,
kingdom against kingdom.[i]
3The Egyptians will lose heart,
and I will bring their plans to nothing;
they will consult the idols and the spirits of the dead,
the mediums and the spiritists.[j]
4I will hand the Egyptians over
to the power of a cruel master,
and a fierce king[k] will rule over them,"
declares the Lord, the LORD Almighty.

5The waters of the river will dry up,[l]
and the riverbed will be parched and dry.
6The canals will stink;[m]
the streams of Egypt will dwindle and dry up.[n]
The reeds and rushes will wither,[o]
7 also the plants along the Nile,
at the mouth of the river.
Every sown field[p] along the Nile
will become parched, will blow away and be no more.
8The fishermen[q] will groan and lament,
all who cast hooks[r] into the Nile;
those who throw nets on the water
will pine away.
9Those who work with combed flax will despair,
the weavers of fine linen[s] will lose hope.
10The workers in cloth will be dejected,
and all the wage earners will be sick at heart.

11The officials of Zoan[t] are nothing but fools;
the wise counselors of Pharaoh give senseless advice.
How can you say to Pharaoh,
"I am one of the wise men,[u]
a disciple of the ancient kings"?
12Where are your wise men[v] now?
Let them show you and make known
what the LORD Almighty
has planned[w] against Egypt.
13The officials of Zoan have become fools,
the leaders of Memphis[a][x] are deceived;
the cornerstones of her peoples
have led Egypt astray.
14The LORD has poured into them
a spirit of dizziness;[y]
they make Egypt stagger in all that she does,
as a drunkard staggers around in his vomit.
15There is nothing Egypt can do—
head or tail, palm branch or reed.[z]

16In that day the Egyptians will be like women.[a] They will shudder with

[a] 13 Hebrew *Noph*

18:3 [w]Isa 5:26
18:4 [x]Isa 26:21; Hos 5:15 [y]Isa 26:19; Hos 14:5
18:5 [z]Isa 17:10-11; Eze 17:6
18:6 [a]Isa 56:9; Jer 7:33; Eze 32:4; 39:17
18:7 [b]Ps 68:31
19:1 [c]Isa 13:1; Jer 43:12 [d]Joel 3:19 [e]Ex 12:12 [f]Ps 18:10; 104:3; Rev 1:7 [g]Jos 2:11
19:2 [h]Jdg 7:22; Mt 10:21,36 [i]2Ch 20:23
19:3 [j]Isa 8:19; 47:13; Da 2:2, 10
19:4 [k]Isa 20:4; Jer 46:26; Eze 29:19
19:5 [l]Jer 51:36
19:6 [m]Ex 7:18 [n]Isa 37:25; Eze 30:12 [o]Isa 15:6
19:7 [p]Isa 23:3
19:8 [q]Eze 47:10 [r]Hab 1:15
19:9 [s]Pr 7:16; Eze 27:7
19:11 [t]Nu 13:22 [u]1Ki 4:30; Ac 7:22
19:12 [v]1Co 1:20 [w]Isa 14:24; Ro 9:17
19:13 [x]Jer 2:16; Eze 30:13,16
19:14 [y]Mt 17:17
19:15 [z]Isa 9:14
19:16 [a]51:30; Na 3:13

fear[b] at the uplifted hand[c] that the
LORD Almighty raises against them.
17 And the land of Judah will bring terror to the Egyptians; everyone to whom
Judah is mentioned will be terrified,
because of what the LORD Almighty is
planning[d] against them.
18 In that day five cities in Egypt will
speak the language of Canaan and
swear allegiance[e] to the LORD Almighty. One of them will be called the
City of Destruction.[a]
19 In that day there will be an altar[f]
to the LORD in the heart of Egypt, and
a monument[g] to the LORD at its border. 20 It will be a sign and witness to
the LORD Almighty in the land of Egypt.
When they cry out to the LORD because
of their oppressors, he will send them
a savior and defender, and he will rescue[h] them. 21 So the LORD will make
himself known to the Egyptians, and in
that day they will acknowledge[i] the
LORD. They will worship[j] with sacrifices and grain offerings; they will
make vows to the LORD and keep them.
22 The LORD will strike[k] Egypt with a
plague; he will strike them and heal
them. They will turn[l] to the LORD, and
he will respond to their pleas and
heal[m] them.
23 In that day there will be a highway[n] from Egypt to Assyria. The Assyrians will go to Egypt and the Egyptians to Assyria. The Egyptians and
Assyrians will worship[o] together. 24 In
that day Israel will be the third, along
with Egypt and Assyria, a blessing on
the earth. 25 The LORD Almighty will
bless them, saying, "Blessed be Egypt
my people,[p] Assyria my handiwork,[q]
and Israel my inheritance.[r]"

A Prophecy Against Egypt and Cush

20 In the year that the supreme commander,[s] sent by Sargon king of
Assyria, came to Ashdod and attacked
and captured it— 2 at that time the
LORD spoke through Isaiah son of
Amoz.[t] He said to him, "Take off the
sackcloth[u] from your body and the
sandals[v] from your feet." And he did
so, going around stripped[w] and barefoot.[x]
3 Then the LORD said, "Just as my servant Isaiah has gone stripped and
barefoot for three years, as a sign[y] and
portent against Egypt and Cush,[b][z]
4 so the king[a] of Assyria will lead away
stripped and barefoot the Egyptian
captives and Cushite exiles, young and
old, with buttocks bared—to Egypt's
shame.[b] 5 Those who trusted in Cush
and boasted in Egypt[c] will be afraid
and put to shame. 6 In that day the people who live on this coast will say, 'See
what has happened to those we relied
on, those we fled to for help[d] and deliverance from the king of Assyria! How
then can we escape?[e]' "

A Prophecy Against Babylon

21 An oracle concerning the Desert[f]
by the Sea:

Like whirlwinds sweeping through
the southland,[g]
an invader comes from the
desert,
from a land of terror.

2 A dire[h] vision has been shown to
me:
The traitor betrays,[i] the looter
takes loot.
Elam,[j] attack! Media, lay siege!
I will bring to an end all the
groaning she caused.

3 At this my body is racked with
pain,
pangs seize me, like those of a
woman in labor;[k]
I am staggered by what I hear,
I am bewildered by what I see.
4 My heart falters,
fear makes me tremble;
the twilight I longed for
has become a horror to me.

5 They set the tables,
they spread the rugs,
they eat, they drink![l]
Get up, you officers,
oil the shields!

6 This is what the Lord says to me:

"Go, post a lookout
and have him report what he
sees.
7 When he sees chariots[m]
with teams of horses,
riders on donkeys
or riders on camels,
let him be alert,
fully alert."

8 And the lookout[c][n] shouted,

"Day after day, my lord, I stand on
the watchtower;
every night I stay at my post.
9 Look, here comes a man in a
chariot
with a team of horses.
And he gives back the answer:
'Babylon[o] has fallen,[p] has
fallen!

19:16 [b]Heb 10:31 [c]Isa 11:15
19:17 [d]Isa 14:24
19:18 [e]Zep 3:9
19:19 [f]Jos 22:10 [g]Ge 28:18
19:20 [h]Isa 49:24-26
19:21 [i]Isa 11:9 [j]Isa 56:7; Mal 1:11
19:22 [k]Heb 12:11 [l]Isa 45:14; Hos 14:1 [m]Dt 32:39
19:23 [n]Isa 11:16 [o]Isa 27:13
19:25 [p]Ps 100:3 [q]Isa 29:23; 45:11; 60:21; 64:8; Eph 2:10 [r]Hos 2:23
20:1 [s]2Ki 18:17
20:2 [t]Isa 13:1 [u]Zec 13:4; Mt 3:4 [v]Eze 24:17,23 [w]1Sa 19:24 [x]Mic 1:8
20:3 [y]Isa 8:18 [z]Isa 37:9; 43:3
20:4 [a]Isa 19:4 [b]Isa 47:3; Jer 13:22,26
20:5 [c]2Ki 18:21; Isa 30:5
20:6 [d]Isa 10:3 [e]Jer 30:15-17; Mt 23:33; 1Th 5:3; Heb 2:3
21:1 [f]Isa 13:21; Jer 51:43 [g]Zec 9:14
21:2 [h]Ps 60:3 [i]Isa 33:1 [j]Isa 22:6; Jer 49:34
21:3 [k]Ps 48:6; Isa 26:17
21:5 [l]Jer 51:39,57; Da 5:2
21:7 [m]ver 9
21:8 [n]Hab 2:1
21:9 [o]Rev 14:8 [p]Jer 51:8; Rev 18:2

a *18* Most manuscripts of the Masoretic Text; some manuscripts of the Masoretic Text, Dead Sea Scrolls and Vulgate *City of the Sun* (that is, Heliopolis) **b** *3* That is, the upper Nile region; also in verse 5 **c** *8* Dead Sea Scrolls and Syriac; Masoretic Text *A lion*

All the images of its gods[q]
lie shattered on the ground!' "
10O my people, crushed on the
threshing floor,[r]
I tell you what I have heard
from the LORD Almighty,
from the God of Israel.

A Prophecy Against Edom

11An oracle concerning Dumah[a]:[s]

Someone calls to me from Seir,[t]
"Watchman, what is left of the
night?
Watchman, what is left of the
night?"
12The watchman replies,
"Morning is coming, but also the
night.
If you would ask, then ask;
and come back yet again."

A Prophecy Against Arabia

13An oracle[u] concerning Arabia:

You caravans of Dedanites,
who camp in the thickets of
Arabia,
14 bring water for the thirsty;
you who live in Tema,[v]
bring food for the fugitives.
15They flee[w] from the sword,
from the drawn sword,
from the bent bow
and from the heat of battle.

16This is what the Lord says to me:
"Within one year, as a servant bound
by contract[x] would count it, all the
pomp[y] of Kedar[z] will come to an
end. 17The survivors of the bowmen,
the warriors of Kedar, will be few.[a]"
The LORD, the God of Israel, has spoken.

A Prophecy About Jerusalem

22 An oracle[b] concerning the Valley[c] of Vision:

What troubles you now,
that you have all gone up on the
roofs,
2O town full of commotion,
O city of tumult and revelry?[d]
Your slain were not killed by the
sword,
nor did they die in battle.
3All your leaders have fled together;
they have been captured without
using the bow.
All you who were caught were
taken prisoner together,
having fled while the enemy was
still far away.
4Therefore I said, "Turn away from
me;
let me weep[e] bitterly.
Do not try to console me
over the destruction of my
people."[f]

5The Lord, the LORD Almighty, has a
day
of tumult and trampling and
terror[g]
in the Valley of Vision,
a day of battering down walls
and of crying out to the
mountains.
6Elam[h] takes up the quiver,[i]
with her charioteers and horses;
Kir[j] uncovers the shield.
7Your choicest valleys are full of
chariots,
and horsemen are posted at the
city gates;[k]
8 the defenses of Judah are
stripped away.

And you looked in that day
to the weapons[l] in the Palace
of the Forest;[m]
9you saw that the City of David
had many breaches in its
defenses;
you stored up water
in the Lower Pool.[n]
10You counted the buildings in
Jerusalem
and tore down houses to
strengthen the wall.
11You built a reservoir between the
two walls[o]
for the water of the Old Pool,[p]
but you did not look to the One
who made it,
or have regard for the One who
planned it long ago.

12The Lord, the LORD Almighty,
called you on that day
to weep[q] and to wail,
to tear out your hair[r] and put
on sackcloth.[s]
13But see, there is joy and revelry,
slaughtering of cattle and killing
of sheep,
eating of meat and drinking of
wine![t]
"Let us eat and drink," you say,
"for tomorrow we die!"[u]

14The LORD Almighty has revealed
this in my hearing:[v] "Till your dying
day this sin will not be atoned[w] for,"
says the Lord, the LORD Almighty.

15This is what the Lord, the LORD Almighty, says:

"Go, say to this steward,

21:9 [q]Isa 46:1; Jer 50:2; 51:44 **21:10** [r]Jer 51:33 **21:11** [s]Ge 25:14 [t]Ge 32:3 **21:13** [u]Isa 13:1 **21:14** [v]Ge 25:15 **21:15** [w]Isa 13:14 **21:16** [x]Isa 16:14 [y]Isa 17:3 [z]Ps 120:5; Isa 60:7 **21:17** [a]Isa 10:19 **22:1** [b]Isa 13:1 [c]Ps 125:2; Jer 21:13; Joel 3:2,12,14 **22:2** [d]Isa 32:13 **22:4** [e]Isa 15:3; Lk 19:41 [f]Jer 9:1 **22:5** [g]La 1:5 **22:6** [h]Isa 21:2 [i]Jer 49:35 [j]2Ki 16:9 **22:7** [k]2Ch 32:1-2 **22:8** [l]2Ch 32:5 [m]1Ki 7:2 **22:9** [n]2Ch 32:4 **22:11** [o]2Ki 25:4; Jer 39:4 [p]2Ch 32:4 **22:12** [q]Joel 2:17 [r]Mic 1:16 [s]Joel 1:13 **22:13** [t]Isa 5:22; 28:7-8; 56:12; Lk 17:26-29 [u]1Co 15:32* **22:14** [v]Isa 5:9 [w]Isa 13:11; 26:21; 30:13-14; Eze 24:13

a 11 *Dumah* means *silence* or *stillness,* a wordplay on *Edom.*

to Shebna,[x] who is in charge of
the palace:
16What are you doing here and who
gave you permission
to cut out a grave[y] for yourself
here,
hewing your grave on the height
and chiseling your resting place
in the rock?

17"Beware, the LORD is about to take
firm hold of you
and hurl you away, O you
mighty man.
18He will roll you up tightly like a
ball
and throw[z] you into a large
country.
There you will die
and there your splendid chariots
will remain—
you disgrace to your master's
house!
19I will depose you from your office,
and you will be ousted from
your position.

20"In that day I will summon my servant, Eliakim[a] son of Hilkiah. 21I will
clothe him with your robe and fasten
your sash around him and hand your
authority over to him. He will be a father to those who live in Jerusalem and
to the house of Judah. 22I will place on
his shoulder the key[b] to the house of
David;[c] what he opens no one can
shut, and what he shuts no one can
open.[d] 23I will drive him like a peg[e]
into a firm place;[f] he will be a seat[a]
of honor[g] for the house of his father.
24All the glory of his family will hang on
him: its offspring and offshoots—all its
lesser vessels, from the bowls to all the
jars.

25"In that day," declares the LORD Almighty, "the peg[h] driven into the firm
place will give way; it will be sheared
off and will fall, and the load hanging
on it will be cut down." The LORD has
spoken.[i]

A Prophecy About Tyre

23 An oracle concerning Tyre:[j]

Wail, O ships[k] of Tarshish![l]
For Tyre is destroyed
and left without house or harbor.
From the land of Cyprus[b]
word has come to them.

2Be silent, you people of the island
and you merchants of Sidon,
whom the seafarers have
enriched.
3On the great waters
came the grain of the Shihor;
the harvest of the Nile[c][m] was the
revenue of Tyre,[n]
and she became the marketplace
of the nations.

4Be ashamed, O Sidon,[o] and you,
O fortress of the sea,
for the sea has spoken:
"I have neither been in labor nor
given birth;
I have neither reared sons nor
brought up daughters."
5When word comes to Egypt,
they will be in anguish at the
report from Tyre.

6Cross over to Tarshish;
wail, you people of the island.
7Is this your city of revelry,[p]
the old, old city,
whose feet have taken her
to settle in far-off lands?
8Who planned this against Tyre,
the bestower of crowns,
whose merchants are princes,
whose traders are renowned in
the earth?
9The LORD Almighty planned it,
to bring low[q] the pride of all
glory
and to humble[r] all who are
renowned[s] on the earth.

10Till[d] your land as along the Nile,
O Daughter of Tarshish,
for you no longer have a harbor.
11The LORD has stretched out his
hand[t] over the sea
and made its kingdoms tremble.
He has given an order concerning
Phoenicia[e]
that her fortresses be
destroyed.[u]
12He said, "No more of your
reveling,[v]
O Virgin Daughter[w] of Sidon,
now crushed!

"Up, cross over to Cyprus[b];
even there you will find no rest."
13Look at the land of the
Babylonians,[f]
this people that is now of no
account!
The Assyrians[x] have made it
a place for desert creatures;
they raised up their siege towers,
they stripped its fortresses bare
and turned it into a ruin.[y]
14Wail, you ships of Tarshish;[z]

22:15 [x]2Ki 18:18; Isa 36:3 **22:16** [y]Mt 27:60 **22:18** [z]Isa 17:13 **22:20** [a]2Ki 18:18; Isa 36:3 **22:22** [b]Rev 3:7 [c]Isa 7:2 [d]Job 12:14 **22:23** [e]Zec 10:4 [f]Ezr 9:8 [g]1Sa 2:7-8; Job 36:7 **22:25** [h]ver 23 [i]Isa 46:11; Mic 4:4 **23:1** [j]Jos 19:29; 1Ki 5:1; Jer 47:4; Eze 26,27,28; Joel 3:4-8; Am 1:9-10; Zec 9:2-4 [k]1Ki 10:22 [l]Ge 10:4; Isa 2:16 *fn*

23:3 [m]Isa 19:7 [n]Eze 27:3 **23:4** [o]Ge 10:15,19 **23:7** [p]Isa 22:2; 32:13 **23:9** [q]Job 40:11 [r]Isa 13:11 [s]Isa 5:13; 9:15 **23:11** [t]Ex 14:21 [u]Isa 25:2; Zec 9:3-4 **23:12** [v]Rev 18:22 [w]Isa 47:1 **23:13** [x]Isa 10:5 [y]Isa 10:7 **23:14** [z]Isa 2:16 *fn*

[a]*23* Or *throne* [b]*1,12* Hebrew *Kittim* [c]*2,3* Masoretic Text; one Dead Sea Scroll *Sidon, / who cross over the sea; / your envoys* [3]*are on the great waters. / The grain of the Shihor, / the harvest of the Nile,* [d]*10* Dead Sea Scrolls and some Septuagint manuscripts; Masoretic Text *Go through* [e]*11* Hebrew *Canaan* [f]*13* Or *Chaldeans*

your fortress is destroyed!

15 At that time Tyre[a] will be forgotten for seventy years, the span of a
king's life. But at the end of these seventy years, it will happen to Tyre as in
the song of the prostitute:

16 "Take up a harp, walk through the city,
O prostitute forgotten;
play the harp well, sing many a song,
so that you will be remembered."

17 At the end of seventy years, the
LORD will deal with Tyre. She will return to her hire as a prostitute[b] and
will ply her trade with all the kingdoms
on the face of the earth. 18 Yet her profit
and her earnings will be set apart for
the LORD;[c] they will not be stored up
or hoarded. Her profits will go to those
who live before the LORD,[d] for abundant food and fine clothes.

The LORD's Devastation of the Earth

24 See, the LORD is going to lay waste the earth[e]
and devastate it;
he will ruin its face
and scatter its inhabitants—
2 it will be the same
for priest as for people,[f]
for master as for servant,
for mistress as for maid,
for seller as for buyer,[g]
for borrower as for lender,
for debtor as for creditor.[h]
3 The earth will be completely laid waste
and totally plundered.[i]
The LORD has spoken this word.

4 The earth dries up and withers,
the world languishes and withers,
the exalted[j] of the earth languish.
5 The earth is defiled[k] by its people;
they have disobeyed[l] the laws,
violated the statutes
and broken the everlasting covenant.
6 Therefore a curse consumes the earth;
its people must bear their guilt.
Therefore earth's inhabitants are burned up,[m]
and very few are left.
7 The new wine dries up and the vine withers;[n]
all the merrymakers groan.[o]
8 The gaiety of the tambourines[p] is stilled,
the noise[q] of the revelers has stopped,
the joyful harp[r] is silent.[s]
9 No longer do they drink wine[t] with a song;
the beer is bitter[u] to its drinkers.
10 The ruined city lies desolate;
the entrance to every house is barred.
11 In the streets they cry out for wine;
all joy turns to gloom,[v]
all gaiety is banished from the earth.
12 The city is left in ruins,
its gate is battered to pieces.
13 So will it be on the earth
and among the nations,
as when an olive tree is beaten,[w]
or as when gleanings are left
after the grape harvest.

14 They raise their voices, they shout for joy;[x]
from the west they acclaim the LORD's majesty.
15 Therefore in the east give glory[y] to the LORD;
exalt[z] the name of the LORD, the God of Israel,
in the islands of the sea.
16 From the ends of the earth we hear singing:
"Glory[a] to the Righteous One."

But I said, "I waste away, I waste away!
Woe to me!
The treacherous betray!

23:15 [a]Jer 25:22 **23:17** [b]Eze 16:26; Na 3:4; Rev 17:1 **23:18** [c]Ex 28:36; Ps 72:10 [d]Isa 60:5-9; Mic 4:13 **24:1** [e]ver 20; Isa 2:19-21; 33:9 **24:2** [f]Hos 4:9 [g]Eze 7:12 [h]Lev 25:35-37; Dt 23:19-20 **24:3** [i]Isa 6:11-12 **24:4** [j]Isa 2:12 **24:5** [k]Ge 3:17; Nu 35:33 [l]Isa 10:6; 59:12 **24:6** [m]Isa 1:31 **24:7** [n]Joel 1:10-12 [o]Isa 16:8-10 **24:8** [p]Isa 5:12 [q]Jer 7:34; 16:9; 25:10; Hos 2:11 [r]Rev 18:22 [s]Eze 26:13 **24:9** [t]Isa 5:11,22 [u]Isa 5:20 **24:11** [v]Isa 16:10; 32:13; Jer 14:3 **24:13** [w]Isa 17:6 **24:14** [x]Isa 12:6 **24:15** [y]Isa 66:19 [z]Isa 25:3; Mal 1:11 **24:16** [a]Isa 28:5

24:4-6

PROMISE 3

SIN'S EFFECTS

These chapters present an important reminder. Even a quick reading through Isaiah's prophecies against the nations leaves us stunned at the awful war and destruction and ruin that were to come upon nation after nation. The spirit of a godly man cries out, "Why all this pain and anguish?" The answer is stated in 24:5—very plainly, the problem is sin. People who disobey God's way of life ruin their lives.

Don't read about others' destruction without carefully evaluating where your actions are leading you. Obedience leads to blessing and disobedience to destruction. Isaiah reported this truth about nation after nation. God offers a wonderful alternative to destruction—it's called obedience and blessing. Pretty easy choice, isn't it?

For the next Promise 3 reading go to page 784.

With treachery the treacherous
betray![b]"
17 Terror and pit and snare[c] await
you,
O people of the earth.
18 Whoever flees at the sound of
terror
will fall into a pit;
whoever climbs out of the pit
will be caught in a snare.

The floodgates of the heavens[d] are
opened,
the foundations of the earth
shake.[e]
19 The earth is broken up,
the earth is split asunder,[f]
the earth is thoroughly shaken.
20 The earth reels like a drunkard,[g]
it sways like a hut in the wind;
so heavy upon it is the guilt of its
rebellion[h]
that it falls—never to rise again.

21 In that day the LORD will punish[i]
the powers in the heavens above
and the kings on the earth
below.
22 They will be herded together
like prisoners[j] bound in a
dungeon;[k]
they will be shut up in prison
and be punished**a** after many
days.[l]
23 The moon will be abashed, the
sun[m] ashamed;
for the LORD Almighty will
reign[n]
on Mount Zion[o] and in Jerusalem,
and before its elders,
gloriously.[p]

Praise to the LORD

25 O LORD, you are my God;
I will exalt you and praise your
name,
for in perfect faithfulness
you have done marvelous
things,[q]
things planned[r] long ago.
2 You have made the city a heap of
rubble,[s]
the fortified[t] town a ruin,
the foreigners' stronghold[u] a city
no more;
it will never be rebuilt.
3 Therefore strong peoples will honor
you;
cities of ruthless[v] nations will
revere you.
4 You have been a refuge[w] for the
poor,
a refuge for the needy in his
distress,
a shelter from the storm
and a shade from the heat.

24:16 [b]Isa 21:2; Jer 5:11
24:17 [c]Jer 48:43
24:18 [d]Ge 7:11 [e]Ps 18:7
24:19 [f]Dt 11:6
24:20 [g]Isa 19:14 [h]Isa 1:2,28; 43:27
24:21 [i]Isa 10:12
24:22 [j]Isa 10:4 [k]Isa 42:7,22 [l]Eze 38:8
24:23 [m]Isa 13:10 [n]Rev 22:5 [o]Heb 12:22 [p]Isa 60:19
25:1 [q]Ps 98:1 [r]Nu 23:19
25:2 [s]Isa 17:1 [t]Isa 17:3 [u]Isa 13:22
25:3 [v]Isa 13:11
25:4 [w]Isa 4:6; 17:10; 27:5; 33:16 [x]Isa 29:5; 49:25
25:5 [y]Jer 51:55
25:6 [z]Isa 2:2 [a]Isa 1:19; Mt 8:11; 22:4 [b]Pr 9:2
25:7 [c]2Co 3:15-16; Eph 4:18
25:8 [d]Hos 13:14; 1Co 15:54-55* [e]Isa 30:19; 35:10; 51:11; 65:19; Rev 7:17; 21:4 [f]Mt 5:11; 1Pe 4:14
25:9 [g]Isa 40:9 [h]Ps 20:5; Isa 33:22; 35:4; 49:25-26; 60:16 [i]Isa 35:2,10
25:10 [j]Am 2:1-3
25:11 [k]Isa 5:25; 14:26; 16:14 [l]Job 40:12
25:12 [m]Isa 15:1

For the breath of the ruthless[x]
is like a storm driving against a
wall
5 and like the heat of the desert.
You silence[y] the uproar of
foreigners;
as heat is reduced by the shadow
of a cloud,
so the song of the ruthless is
stilled.

6 On this mountain[z] the LORD
Almighty will prepare
a feast[a] of rich food for all
peoples,
a banquet of aged wine—
the best of meats and the finest
of wines.[b]
7 On this mountain he will destroy
the shroud[c] that enfolds all
peoples,
the sheet that covers all nations;
8 he will swallow up death[d]
forever.
The Sovereign LORD will wipe away
the tears[e]
from all faces;
he will remove the disgrace[f] of his
people
from all the earth.
The LORD has spoken.

9 In that day they will say,

1 →PG. 760

"Surely this is our God;[g]
we trusted in him, and he
saved[h] us.
This is the LORD, we trusted in him;
let us rejoice[i] and be glad in
his salvation."

10 The hand of the LORD will rest on
this mountain;
but Moab[j] will be trampled
under him
as straw is trampled down in the
manure.
11 They will spread out their hands in
it,
as a swimmer spreads out his
hands to swim.
God will bring down[k] their pride[l]
despite the cleverness**b** of their
hands.
12 He will bring down your high
fortified walls
and lay them low;[m]
he will bring them down to the
ground,
to the very dust.

A Song of Praise

26 In that day this song will be sung in
the land of Judah:

a *22* Or *released* **b** *11* The meaning of the Hebrew for this word is uncertain.

We have a strong city;[n]
God makes salvation
its walls[o] and ramparts.
2Open the gates
that the righteous[p] nation may
enter,
the nation that keeps faith.
3You will keep in perfect peace
him whose mind is steadfast,
because he trusts in you.
4Trust[q] in the LORD forever,
for the LORD, the LORD, is the
Rock eternal.

1 →PG. 760

5He humbles those who dwell on
high,
he lays the lofty city low;
he levels it to the ground[r]
and casts it down to the dust.
6Feet trample it down—
the feet of the oppressed,
the footsteps of the poor.[s]

7The path of the righteous is level;
O upright One, you make the
way of the righteous
smooth.[t]
8Yes, LORD, walking in the way of
your laws,[a][u]
we wait for you;
your name[v] and renown
are the desire of our hearts.
9My soul yearns for you in the
night;
in the morning my spirit longs[w]
for you.
When your judgments come upon
the earth,
the people of the world learn
righteousness.[x]

1 →PG. 775

10Though grace is shown to the
wicked,
they do not learn righteousness;
even in a land of uprightness they
go on doing evil[y]
and regard[z] not the majesty of
the LORD.
11O LORD, your hand is lifted high,
but they do not see[a] it.
Let them see your zeal for your
people and be put to
shame;
let the fire[b] reserved for your
enemies consume them.

12LORD, you establish peace for us;
all that we have accomplished
you have done for us.
13O LORD, our God, other lords[c]
besides you have ruled over
us,
but your name alone do we
honor.[d]
14They are now dead,[e] they live no
more;
those departed spirits do not
rise.
You punished them and brought
them to ruin;[f]
you wiped out all memory of
them.
15You have enlarged the nation,
O LORD;
you have enlarged the nation.
You have gained glory for yourself;
you have extended all the
borders[g] of the land.

16LORD, they came to you in their
distress;[h]
when you disciplined them,
they could barely whisper a
prayer.[b]
17As a woman with child and about
to give birth[i]
writhes and cries out in her pain,
so were we in your presence,
O LORD.
18We were with child, we writhed in
pain,
but we gave birth[j] to wind.
We have not brought salvation[k] to
the earth;
we have not given birth to
people of the world.
19But your dead[l] will live;
their bodies will rise.
You who dwell in the dust,
wake up and shout for joy.
Your dew is like the dew of the
morning;
the earth will give birth to her
dead.[m]

20Go, my people, enter your rooms
and shut the doors[n] behind
you;
hide[o] yourselves for a little while
until his wrath has passed by.[p]
21See, the LORD is coming[q] out of
his dwelling[r]
to punish[s] the people of the
earth for their sins.
The earth will disclose the blood[t]
shed upon her;
she will conceal her slain no
longer.

Deliverance of Israel

27 In that day,
the LORD will punish with his
sword,[u]
his fierce, great and powerful
sword,
Leviathan[v] the gliding serpent,
Leviathan the coiling serpent;
he will slay the monster[w] of the
sea.

2In that day—

26:1 [n]Isa 14:32 [o]Isa 60:18
26:2 [p]Isa 54:14; 58:8; 62:2
26:4 [q]Isa 12:2; 50:10
26:5 [r]Isa 25:12
26:6 [s]Isa 3:15
26:7 [t]Isa 42:16
26:8 [u]Isa 56:1 [v]Isa 12:4
26:9 [w]Ps 63:1; 78:34; Isa 55:6 [x]Mt 6:33
26:10 [y]Isa 32:6 [z]Isa 22:12-13; Hos 11:7; Jn 5:37-38; Ro 2:4
26:11 [a]Isa 44:9,18 [b]Heb 10:27
26:13 [c]Isa 2:8; 10:5, 11 [d]Isa 63:7
26:14 [e]Dt 4:28 [f]Isa 10:3
26:15 [g]Isa 33:17
26:16 [h]Hos 5:15
26:17 [i]Jn 16:21
26:18 [j]Isa 33:11; 59:4 [k]Ps 17:14
26:19 [l]Isa 25:8; Eph 5:14 [m]Eze 37:1-14; Da 12:2
26:20 [n]Ex 12:23 [o]Ps 91:1,4 [p]Ps 30:5; Isa 54:7-8
26:21 [q]Jude 1:14 [r]Mic 1:3 [s]Isa 13:9,11; 30:12-14 [t]Job 16:18; Lk 11:50-51
27:1 [u]Isa 34:6; 66:16 [v]Job 3:8 [w]Ps 74:13

a *8* Or *judgments* b *16* The meaning of the Hebrew for this clause is uncertain.

"Sing about a fruitful vineyard:[x]
3 I, the LORD, watch over it;
I water[y] it continually.
I guard it day and night
so that no one may harm it.
4 I am not angry.
If only there were briers and thorns confronting me!
I would march against them in battle;
I would set them all on fire.[z]
5 Or else let them come to me for refuge;[a]
let them make peace[b] with me,
yes, let them make peace with me."

6 In days to come Jacob will take root,
Israel will bud and blossom[c]
and fill all the world with fruit.[d]

7 Has ⌊the LORD⌋ struck her
as he struck[e] down those who struck her?
Has she been killed
as those were killed who killed her?
8 By warfare[a] and exile[f] you contend with her—
with his fierce blast he drives her out,
as on a day the east wind blows.
9 By this, then, will Jacob's guilt be atoned for,
and this will be the full fruitage of the removal of his sin:[g]
When he makes all the altar stones
to be like chalk stones crushed to pieces,
no Asherah poles[b][h] or incense altars
will be left standing.
10 The fortified city stands desolate,[i]
an abandoned settlement,
forsaken like the desert;
there the calves graze,
there they lie down;[j]
they strip its branches bare.
11 When its twigs are dry, they are broken off
and women come and make fires with them.
For this is a people without understanding;[k]
so their Maker has no compassion on them,
and their Creator[l] shows them no favor.[m]

12 In that day the LORD will thresh
from the flowing Euphrates[c] to the
Wadi of Egypt,[n] and you, O Israelites,
will be gathered[o] up one by one.
13 And in that day a great trumpet[p] will
sound. Those who were perishing in
Assyria and those who were exiled in
Egypt[q] will come and worship the
LORD on the holy mountain in Jerusalem.

Woe to Ephraim

28 Woe to that wreath, the pride of Ephraim's[r] drunkards,
to the fading flower, his glorious beauty,
set on the head of a fertile valley[s]—
to that city, the pride of those laid low by wine![t]
2 See, the Lord has one who is powerful[u] and strong.
Like a hailstorm[v] and a destructive wind,[w]
like a driving rain and a flooding[x] downpour,
he will throw it forcefully to the ground.
3 That wreath, the pride of Ephraim's[y] drunkards,
will be trampled underfoot.
4 That fading flower, his glorious beauty,
set on the head of a fertile valley,[z]
will be like a fig[a] ripe before harvest—
as soon as someone sees it and takes it in his hand,
he swallows it.

5 In that day the LORD Almighty
will be a glorious crown,[b]
a beautiful wreath
for the remnant of his people.
6 He will be a spirit of justice[c]
to him who sits in judgment,[d]
a source of strength
to those who turn back the battle[e] at the gate.

7 And these also stagger from wine[f]
and reel[g] from beer:
Priests[h] and prophets[i] stagger from beer
and are befuddled with wine;
they reel from beer,
they stagger when seeing visions,[j]
they stumble when rendering decisions.
8 All the tables are covered with vomit[k]
and there is not a spot without filth.

9 "Who is it he is trying to teach?[l]
To whom is he explaining his message?

27:2 [x]Jer 2:21 **27:3** [y]Isa 58:11 **27:4** [z]Isa 10:17; Mt 3:12; Heb 6:8 **27:5** [a]Isa 25:4 [b]Job 22:21; Ro 5:1; 2Co 5:20 **27:6** [c]Hos 14:5-6 [d]Isa 37:31 **27:7** [e]Isa 37:36-38 **27:8** [f]Isa 50:1; 54:7 **27:9** [g]Ro 11:27* [h]Ex 34:13 **27:10** [i]Isa 32:14; Jer 26:6 [j]Isa 17:2 **27:11** [k]Dt 32:28; Isa 1:3; Jer 8:7 [l]Dt 32:18; Isa 43:1,7,15; 44:1-2,21,24 [m]Isa 9:17 **27:12** [n]Ge 15:18 [o]Dt 30:4; Isa 11:12; 17:6 **27:13** [p]Lev 25:9; Mt 24:31

[q]Isa 19:21,25 **28:1** [r]ver 3; Isa 9:9 [s]ver 4 [t]Hos 7:5 **28:2** [u]Isa 40:10 [v]Isa 30:30; Eze 13:11 [w]Isa 29:6 [x]Isa 8:7 **28:3** [y]ver 1 **28:4** [z]ver 1 [a]Hos 9:10; Na 3:12 **28:5** [b]Isa 62:3 **28:6** [c]Isa 11:2-4; 32:1,16 [d]Jn 5:30 [e]2Ch 32:8 **28:7** [f]Isa 22:13 [g]Isa 56:10-12 [h]Isa 24:2 [i]Isa 9:15 [j]Isa 29:11; Hos 4:11 **28:8** [k]Jer 48:26 **28:9** [l]ver 26; Isa 30:20; 48:17; 50:4; 54:13

[a] *8* See Septuagint; the meaning of the Hebrew for this word is uncertain. [b] *9* That is, symbols of the goddess Asherah [c] *12* Hebrew *River*

To children weaned[m] from their
milk,[n]
to those just taken from the
breast?
10For it is:
Do and do, do and do,
rule on rule, rule on rule[a];
a little here, a little there."
11Very well then, with foreign lips
and strange tongues[o]
God will speak to this people,[p]
12to whom he said,
"This is the resting place, let the
weary rest";[q]
and, "This is the place of repose"—
but they would not listen.
13So then, the word of the LORD to
them will become:
Do and do, do and do,
rule on rule, rule on rule;
a little here, a little there—
so that they will go and fall
backward,
be injured[r] and snared and
captured.[s]
14Therefore hear the word of the
LORD,[t] you scoffers
who rule this people in
Jerusalem.
15You boast, "We have entered into a
covenant with death,
with the grave[b] we have made
an agreement.
When an overwhelming scourge
sweeps by,[u]
it cannot touch us,
for we have made a lie[v] our refuge
and falsehood[c] our hiding
place.[w]"
16So this is what the Sovereign LORD
says:
"See, I lay a stone in Zion,
a tested stone,[x]
a precious cornerstone for a sure
foundation;
the one who trusts will never be
dismayed.[y]
17I will make justice[z] the measuring
line
and righteousness the plumb
line;[a]
hail will sweep away your refuge,
the lie,
and water will overflow your
hiding place.
18Your covenant with death will be
annulled;
your agreement with the grave
will not stand.[b]
When the overwhelming scourge
sweeps by,[c]
you will be beaten down[d] by it.
19As often as it comes it will carry
you away;[e]
morning after morning, by day
and by night,
it will sweep through."
The understanding of this message
will bring sheer terror.[f]
20The bed is too short to stretch out
on,
the blanket too narrow to wrap
around you.[g]
21The LORD will rise up as he did at
Mount Perazim,[h]
he will rouse himself as in the
Valley of Gibeon[i]—
to do his work,[j] his strange work,
and perform his task, his alien
task.
22Now stop your mocking,
or your chains will become
heavier;
the Lord, the LORD Almighty, has
told me
of the destruction decreed[k]
against the whole land.[l]
23Listen and hear my voice;
pay attention and hear what I
say.
24When a farmer plows for planting,
does he plow continually?
Does he keep on breaking up
and harrowing the soil?
25When he has leveled the surface,
does he not sow caraway and
scatter cummin?[m]
Does he not plant wheat in its
place,[d]
barley in its plot,[d]
and spelt[n] in its field?
26His God instructs him
and teaches him the right way.
27Caraway is not threshed with a
sledge,
nor is a cartwheel rolled over
cummin;
caraway is beaten out with a rod,
and cummin with a stick.
28Grain must be ground to make
bread;
so one does not go on threshing
it forever.
Though he drives the wheels of his
threshing cart over it,
his horses do not grind it.
29All this also comes from the LORD
Almighty,
wonderful in counsel[o] and
magnificent in wisdom.[p]

28:9 [m]Ps 131:2 [n]Heb 5:12-13 **28:11** [o]Isa 33:19 [p]1Co 14:21* **28:12** [q]Isa 11:10; Mt 11:28-29 **28:13** [r]Mt 21:44 [s]Isa 8:15 **28:14** [t]Isa 1:10 **28:15** [u]ver 2,18; Isa 8:7-8; 30:28; Da 11:22 [v]Isa 9:15 [w]Isa 29:15 **28:16** [x]Ps 118:22; Isa 8:14-15; Mt 21:42; Ac 4:11; Eph 2:20 [y]Ro 9:33*; 10:11*; 1Pe 2:6* **28:17** [z]Isa 5:16 [a]2Ki 21:13 **28:18** [b]Isa 7:7 [c]ver 15 [d]Da 8:13 **28:19** [e]2Ki 24:2 [f]Job 18:11 **28:20** [g]Isa 59:6 **28:21** [h]1Ch 14:11 [i]Jos 10:10,12; 1Ch 14:16 [j]Isa 10:12; Lk 19:41-44 **28:22** [k]Isa 10:22 [l]Isa 10:23 **28:25** [m]Mt 23:23 [n]Ex 9:32 **28:29** [o]Isa 9:6 [p]Ro 11:33

a *10* Hebrew / *sav lasav sav lasav / kav lakav kav lakav* (possibly meaningless sounds; perhaps a mimicking of the prophet's words); also in verse 13 **b** *15* Hebrew *Sheol*; also in verse 18 **c** *15* Or *false gods* **d** *25* The meaning of the Hebrew for this word is uncertain.

Woe to David's City

29 Woe[q] to you, Ariel, Ariel,[r]
the city where David settled!
Add year to year
and let your cycle of festivals[s]
go on.
2 Yet I will besiege Ariel;
she will mourn and lament,[t]
she will be to me like an altar
hearth.[a]
3 I will encamp against you all
around;
I will encircle[u] you with towers
and set up my siege works
against you.
4 Brought low, you will speak from
the ground;
your speech will mumble[v] out
of the dust.
Your voice will come ghostlike from
the earth;
out of the dust your speech will
whisper.

5 But your many enemies will
become like fine dust,
the ruthless hordes like blown
chaff.[w]
Suddenly,[x] in an instant,
6 the LORD Almighty will come
with thunder and earthquake[y] and
great noise,
with windstorm and tempest and
flames of a devouring fire.
7 Then the hordes of all the
nations[z] that fight against
Ariel,
that attack her and her fortress
and besiege her,
will be as it is with a dream,[a]
with a vision in the night—
8 as when a hungry man dreams that
he is eating,
but he awakens,[b] and his
hunger remains;
as when a thirsty man dreams that
he is drinking,
but he awakens faint, with his
thirst unquenched.
So will it be with the hordes of all
the nations
that fight against Mount Zion.

9 Be stunned and amazed,
blind yourselves and be sightless;
be drunk,[c] but not from wine,[d]
stagger, but not from beer.
10 The LORD has brought over you a
deep sleep:
He has sealed your eyes[e] (the
prophets);[f]
he has covered your heads (the
seers).[g]

11 For you this whole vision is nothing but words sealed[h] in a scroll. And

29:1 [q]Isa 22:12-13 [r]2Sa 5:9 [s]Isa 1:14
29:2 [t]Isa 3:26; La 2:5
29:3 [u]Lk 19:43-44
29:4 [v]Isa 8:19
29:5 [w]Isa 17:13 [x]Isa 17:14; 1Th 5:3
29:6 [y]Mt 24:7; Mk 13:8; Lk 21:11; Rev 11:19
29:7 [z]Mic 4:11-12; Zec 12:9 [a]Job 20:8
29:8 [b]Ps 73:20
29:9 [c]Isa 51:17 [d]Isa 51:21-22
29:10 [e]Ps 69:23; Isa 6:9-10; Ro 11:8* [f]Mic 3:6 [g]1Sa 9:9
29:11 [h]Isa 8:16; Mt 13:11; Rev 5:1-2
29:13 [i]Eze 33:31 [j]Mt 15:8-9*; Mk 7:6-7*; Col 2:22
29:14 [k]Hab 1:5 [l]Jer 8:9; 49:7 [m]Isa 6:9-10; 1Co 1:19*
29:15 [n]Ps 10:11-13; 94:7; Isa 57:12 [o]Job 22:13
29:16 [p]Isa 45:9; 64:8; Ro 9:20-21*
29:17 [q]Ps 84:6 [r]Isa 32:15
29:18 [s]Mk 7:37 [t]Isa 32:3; 35:5; Mt 11:5
29:19 [u]Isa 61:1; Mt 5:5; 11:29 [v]Isa 14:30; Mt 11:5; Jas 1:9; 2:5
29:20 [w]Isa 28:22 [x]Isa 59:4; Mic 2:1
29:21 [y]Am 5:10,15

if you give the scroll to someone who
can read, and say to him, "Read this,
please," he will answer, "I can't; it is
sealed."
12 Or if you give the scroll to
someone who cannot read, and say,
"Read this, please," he will answer, "I
don't know how to read."

13 The Lord says:
"These people come near to me
with their mouth
and honor me with their lips,
but their hearts are far from
me.[i]
Their worship of me
is made up only of rules taught
by men.[b][j]
14 Therefore once more I will astound
these people
with wonder upon wonder;[k]
the wisdom of the wise[l] will
perish,
the intelligence of the intelligent
will vanish.[m]"
15 Woe to those who go to great
depths
to hide their plans from the
LORD,
who do their work in darkness and
think,
"Who sees us?[n] Who will
know?"[o]
16 You turn things upside down,
as if the potter were thought to
be like the clay!
Shall what is formed say to him
who formed it,
"He did not make me"?
Can the pot say of the potter,[p]
"He knows nothing"?

17 In a very short time, will not
Lebanon be turned into a
fertile field[q]
and the fertile field seem like a
forest?[r]
18 In that day the deaf[s] will hear the
words of the scroll,
and out of gloom and darkness
the eyes of the blind will see.[t]
19 Once more the humble[u] will
rejoice in the LORD;
the needy[v] will rejoice in the
Holy One of Israel.
20 The ruthless will vanish,
the mockers[w] will disappear,
and all who have an eye for
evil[x] will be cut down—
21 those who with a word make a
man out to be guilty,
who ensnare the defender in
court[y]

[a] *2* The Hebrew for *altar hearth* sounds like the Hebrew for *Ariel.* [b] *13* Hebrew; Septuagint *They worship me in vain; / their teachings are but rules taught by men*

and with false testimony deprive
the innocent of justice.[z]

22Therefore this is what the LORD,
who redeemed Abraham,[a] says to the
house of Jacob:

"No longer will Jacob be
ashamed;[b]
no longer will their faces grow
pale.
23When they see among them their
children,[c]
the work of my hands,[d]
they will keep my name holy;
they will acknowledge the
holiness of the Holy One of
Jacob,
and will stand in awe of the God
of Israel.
24Those who are wayward[e] in spirit
will gain understanding;[f]
those who complain will accept
instruction."[g]

Woe to the Obstinate Nation

30 "Woe[h] to the obstinate
children,"[i]
declares the LORD,
"to those who carry out plans that
are not mine,
forming an alliance,[j] but not by
my Spirit,
heaping sin upon sin;
2who go down to Egypt[k]
without consulting[l] me;
who look for help to Pharaoh's
protection,[m]
to Egypt's shade for refuge.
3But Pharaoh's protection will be to
your shame,
Egypt's shade will bring you
disgrace.[n]
4Though they have officials in
Zoan[o]
and their envoys have arrived in
Hanes,
5everyone will be put to shame
because of a people[p] useless to
them,
who bring neither help nor
advantage,
but only shame and disgrace."

6An oracle concerning the animals
of the Negev:

Through a land of hardship and
distress,[q]
of lions and lionesses,
of adders and darting snakes,[r]
the envoys carry their riches on
donkeys' backs,
their treasures[s] on the humps
of camels,
to that unprofitable nation,

29:21 [z]Isa
29:22 [a]Isa 41:8; 63:16 [b]Isa 49:23
29:23 [c]Isa 49:20-26 [d]Isa 19:25
29:24 [e]Isa 28:7; Heb 5:2 [f]Isa 41:20; 60:16 [g]Isa 30:21
30:1 [h]Isa 29:15 [i]Isa 1:2 [j]Isa 8:12
30:2 [k]Isa 31:1 [l]Nu 27:21 [m]Isa 36:9
30:3 [n]Isa 20:4-5; 36:6
30:4 [o]Isa 19:11
30:5 [p]ver 7
30:6 [q]Ex 5:10,21; Isa 8:22; Jer 11:4 [r]Dt 8:15 [s]Isa 15:7

7 to Egypt, whose help is utterly
useless.
Therefore I call her
Rahab the Do-Nothing.

8Go now, write it on a tablet for
them,
inscribe it on a scroll,[t]
that for the days to come
it may be an everlasting witness.
9These are rebellious people,
deceitful[u] children,
children unwilling to listen to the
LORD's instruction.[v]
10They say to the seers,
"See no more visions[w]!"
and to the prophets,
"Give us no more visions of what
is right!
Tell us pleasant things,[x]
prophesy illusions.[y]
11Leave this way,
get off this path,
and stop confronting[z] us
with the Holy One of Israel!"

30:8 [t]Isa 8:1; Hab 2:2
30:9 [u]Isa 28:15; 59:3-4 [v]Isa 1:10
30:10 [w]Jer 11:21; Am 7:13 [x]1Ki 22:8 [y]Eze 13:7; Ro 16:18
30:11 [z]Job 21:14

30:9 – 15

PROMISE 7

ISAIAH IN TODAY'S HEADLINES

Read Isaiah's commentary on his people in this passage. This description could have been written at any time in history—including today. Proud and rebellious people don't want to hear God's word of instruction and warning; God asks proud people to trust in him instead of in their own ability. So in verse 15, God invites people to find "salvation" through "repentance and rest." He offers "strength" through "quietness and trust." Men who find themselves in trouble, who need salvation and strength, want to *act*; they want to *do* something to save themselves.

God takes that human urge and turns it on its ear. He says there comes a time to rest, to be quiet, to trust him. He says we must repent of our proud self-sufficiency and let him help us. This is a tough assignment for a proud man, but it's God's only offer.

The godly man's message as he pursues the Great Commission and Great Commandment is this: God will save me because I cannot save myself. "God so loved the world that he gave his one and only Son, that whoever believes in him shall not perish but have eternal life" (John 3:16). Only in repentance from sin and rest in Christ's death on the cross will a man be saved. Only in quiet trust in Jesus' offer of forgiveness will a man find the strength to live his life.

For the next Promise 7 reading go to page 791.

12Therefore, this is what the Holy One of Israel says:

"Because you have rejected this
message,[a]
relied on oppression[b]
and depended on deceit,
13this sin will become for you
like a high wall,[c] cracked and
bulging,
that collapses[d] suddenly,[e] in
an instant.
14It will break in pieces like
pottery,[f]
shattered so mercilessly
that among its pieces not a
fragment will be found
for taking coals from a hearth
or scooping water out of a
cistern."

15This is what the Sovereign LORD, the Holy One of Israel, says:

"In repentance and rest is your
salvation,
in quietness and trust[g] is your
strength,
but you would have none of it.
16You said, 'No, we will flee on
horses.'[h]
Therefore you will flee!
You said, 'We will ride off on swift
horses.'
Therefore your pursuers will be
swift!
17A thousand will flee
at the threat of one;
at the threat of five[i]
you will all flee[j] away,
till you are left
like a flagstaff on a mountaintop,
like a banner on a hill."

18Yet the LORD longs[k] to be gracious
to you;
he rises to show you
compassion.
For the LORD is a God of justice.[l]
Blessed are all who wait for
him![m]

19O people of Zion, who live in Jerusalem, you will weep no more.[n] How
gracious he will be when you cry for
help! As soon as he hears, he will answer[o] you. 20Although the Lord gives
you the bread[p] of adversity and the
water of affliction, your teachers will be
hidden[q] no more; with your own eyes
you will see them. 21Whether you turn
to the right or to the left, your ears will
hear a voice[r] behind you, saying,
"This is the way; walk in it." 22Then you
will defile your idols[s] overlaid with silver and your images covered with gold;
you will throw them away like a men-
strual cloth and say to them, "Away
with you!"

23He will also send you rain[t] for the
seed you sow in the ground, and the
food that comes from the land will be
rich and plentiful. In that day your cattle will graze in broad meadows.[u]
24The oxen and donkeys that work the
soil will eat fodder and mash, spread
out with fork[v] and shovel. 25In the day
of great slaughter, when the towers[w]
fall, streams of water will flow[x] on every high mountain and every lofty hill.
26The moon will shine like the sun,[y]
and the sunlight will be seven times
brighter, like the light of seven full
days, when the LORD binds up the
bruises of his people and heals[z] the
wounds he inflicted.

27See, the Name[a] of the LORD comes
from afar,
with burning anger[b] and dense
clouds of smoke;
his lips are full of wrath,[c]
and his tongue is a consuming
fire.
28His breath[d] is like a rushing
torrent,
rising up to the neck.[e]
He shakes the nations in the
sieve[f] of destruction;
he places in the jaws of the
peoples
a bit[g] that leads them astray.
29And you will sing
as on the night you celebrate a
holy festival;
your hearts will rejoice
as when people go up with flutes
to the mountain[h] of the LORD,
to the Rock of Israel.
30The LORD will cause men to hear
his majestic voice
and will make them see his arm
coming down
with raging anger and consuming
fire,
with cloudburst, thunderstorm
and hail.
31The voice of the LORD will shatter
Assyria;[i]
with his scepter he will strike[j]
them down.
32Every stroke the LORD lays on them
with his punishing rod
will be to the music of tambourines
and harps,
as he fights them in battle with
the blows of his arm.[k]
33Topheth[l] has long been prepared;
it has been made ready for the
king.
Its fire pit has been made deep and
wide,

30:12 [a]Isa 5:24 [b]Isa 5:7
30:13 [c]Ps 62:3 [d]1Ki 20:30 [e]Isa 29:5
30:14 [f]Ps 2:9; Jer 19:10-11
30:15 [g]Isa 32:17
30:16 [h]Isa 31:1,3
30:17 [i]Lev 26:8; Jos 23:10 [j]Lev 26:36; Dt 28:25
30:18 [k]Isa 42:14; 2Pe 3:9,15 [l]Isa 5:16 [m]Isa 25:9
30:19 [n]Isa 60:20; 61:3 [o]Ps 50:15; Isa 58:9; 65:24; Mt 7:7-11
30:20 [p]1Ki 22:27 [q]Ps 74:9; Am 8:11
30:21 [r]Isa 29:24
30:22 [s]Ex 32:4
30:23 [t]Isa 65:21-22 [u]Ps 65:13
30:24 [v]Mt 3:12; Lk 3:17
30:25 [w]Isa 2:15 [x]Isa 41:18
30:26 [y]Isa 24:23; 60:19-20; Rev 21:23; 22:5 [z]Dt 32:39; Isa 1:5
30:27 [a]Isa 59:19 [b]Isa 66:14 [c]Isa 10:5
30:28 [d]Isa 11:4 [e]Isa 8:8 [f]Am 9:9 [g]2Ki 19:28; Isa 37:29
30:29 [h]Ps 42:4
30:31 [i]Isa 10:5,12 [j]Isa 11:4
30:32 [k]Isa 11:15; Eze 32:10
30:33 [l]2Ki 23:10

with an abundance of fire and
wood;
the breath of the LORD,
like a stream of burning sulfur,[m]
sets it ablaze.

Woe to Those Who Rely on Egypt

31 Woe to those who go down to
Egypt[n] for help,
who rely on horses,
who trust in the multitude of their
chariots[o]
and in the great strength of their
horsemen,
but do not look to the Holy One of
Israel,
or seek help from the LORD.[p]
2 Yet he too is wise[q] and can bring
disaster;[r]
he does not take back his
words.[s]
He will rise up against the house of
the wicked,[t]
against those who help evildoers.
3 But the Egyptians[u] are men and
not God;[v]
their horses are flesh and not
spirit.
When the LORD stretches out his
hand,[w]
he who helps will stumble,
he who is helped[x] will fall;
both will perish together.

4 This is what the LORD says to me:

"As a lion[y] growls,
a great lion over his prey—
and though a whole band of
shepherds
is called together against him,
he is not frightened by their shouts
or disturbed by their clamor—
so the LORD Almighty will come
down[z]
to do battle on Mount Zion and
on its heights.
5 Like birds hovering overhead,
the LORD Almighty will shield[a]
Jerusalem;
he will shield it and deliver[b] it,
he will 'pass over' it and will
rescue it."

6 Return to him you have so greatly
revolted against, O Israelites. 7 For in
that day every one of you will reject the
idols of silver and gold[c] your sinful
hands have made.

8 "Assyria[d] will fall by a sword that
is not of man;
a sword, not of mortals, will
devour[e] them.
They will flee before the sword
and their young men will be put
to forced labor.[f]
9 Their stronghold[g] will fall because
of terror;
at sight of the battle standard
their commanders will
panic,"
declares the LORD,
whose fire[h] is in Zion,
whose furnace is in Jerusalem.

The Kingdom of Righteousness

32 See, a king[i] will reign in
righteousness
and rulers will rule with
justice.[j]
2 Each man will be like a shelter[k]
from the wind
and a refuge from the storm,
like streams of water in the desert
and the shadow of a great rock
in a thirsty land.

3 Then the eyes of those who see will
no longer be closed,[l]
and the ears of those who hear
will listen.
4 The mind of the rash will know
and understand,[m]
and the stammering tongue will
be fluent and clear.
5 No longer will the fool[n] be called
noble
nor the scoundrel be highly
respected.
6 For the fool speaks folly,[o]
his mind is busy with evil:
He practices ungodliness[p]
and spreads error[q] concerning
the LORD;
the hungry he leaves empty[r]
and from the thirsty he
withholds water.
7 The scoundrel's methods are
wicked,[s]
he makes up evil schemes[t]
to destroy the poor with lies,
even when the plea of the
needy[u] is just.
8 But the noble man makes noble
plans,
and by noble deeds[v] he stands.

The Women of Jerusalem

9 You women who are so
complacent,
rise up and listen[w] to me;
you daughters who feel secure,[x]
hear what I have to say!
10 In little more than a year
you who feel secure will tremble;
the grape harvest will fail,[y]
and the harvest of fruit will not
come.
11 Tremble, you complacent women;
shudder, you daughters who feel
secure!
Strip off your clothes,[z]

30:33 [m]Ge 19:24
31:1 [n]Dt 17:16; Isa 30:2,5 [o]Isa 2:7 [p]Ps 20:7; Da 9:13
31:2 [q]Ro 16:27 [r]Isa 45:7 [s]Nu 23:19 [t]Isa 32:6
31:3 [u]Isa 36:9 [v]Eze 28:9; 2Th 2:4 [w]Isa 9:17,21 [x]Isa 30:5-7
31:4 [y]Nu 24:9; Hos 11:10; Am 3:8 [z]Isa 42:13
31:5 [a]Ps 91:4 [b]Isa 37:35; 38:6
31:7 [c]Isa 2:20; 30:22
31:8 [d]Isa 10:12 [e]Isa 14:25; 37:7 [f]Ge 49:15
31:9 [g]Dt 32:31,37 [h]Isa 10:17
32:1 [i]Eze 37:24 [j]Ps 72:1-4; Isa 9:7
32:2 [k]Isa 4:6
32:3 [l]Isa 29:18
32:4 [m]Isa 29:24
32:5 [n]1Sa 25:25
32:6 [o]Pr 19:3 [p]Isa 9:17 [q]Isa 9:16 [r]Isa 3:15
32:7 [s]Jer 5:26-28 [t]Mic 7:3 [u]Isa 61:1
32:8 [v]Pr 11:25
32:9 [w]Isa 28:23 [x]Isa 47:8; Am 6:1; Zep 2:15
32:10 [y]Isa 5:5-6; 24:7
32:11 [z]Isa 47:2

put sackcloth around your
waists.
12 Beat your breasts[a] for the pleasant
fields,
for the fruitful vines
13 and for the land of my people,
a land overgrown with thorns
and briers[b]—
yes, mourn for all houses of
merriment
and for this city of revelry.[c]
14 The fortress[d] will be abandoned,
the noisy city deserted;[e]
citadel and watchtower[f] will
become a wasteland forever,
the delight of donkeys,[g] a
pasture for flocks,
15 till the Spirit[h] is poured upon us
from on high,
and the desert becomes a fertile
field,[i]
and the fertile field seems like a
forest.[j]
16 Justice will dwell in the desert
and righteousness live in the
fertile field.
17 The fruit of righteousness will be
peace;[k]
the effect of righteousness will
be quietness and
confidence[l] forever.
18 My people will live in peaceful
dwelling places,
in secure homes,
in undisturbed places of rest.[m]
19 Though hail[n] flattens the forest[o]
and the city is leveled[p]
completely,
20 how blessed you will be,
sowing[q] your seed by every
stream,
and letting your cattle and
donkeys range free.[r]

Distress and Help

33 Woe to you, O destroyer,
you who have not been
destroyed!
Woe to you, O traitor,
you who have not been betrayed!
When you stop destroying,
you will be destroyed;[s]
when you stop betraying,
you will be betrayed.[t]

2 O LORD, be gracious to us;
we long for you.
Be our strength[u] every morning,
our salvation[v] in time of
distress.
3 At the thunder of your voice, the
peoples flee;
when you rise up,[w] the nations
scatter.
4 Your plunder, O nations, is
harvested as by young
locusts;
like a swarm of locusts men
pounce on it.
5 The LORD is exalted,[x] for he dwells
on high;
he will fill Zion with justice[y]
and righteousness.[z]
6 He will be the sure foundation for
your times,
a rich store of salvation[a] and
wisdom and knowledge;
the fear[b] of the LORD is the key
to this treasure.[a]
7 Look, their brave men cry aloud in
the streets;
the envoys[c] of peace weep
bitterly.
8 The highways are deserted,
no travelers are on the roads.[d]
The treaty is broken,
its witnesses[b] are despised,
no one is respected.
9 The land mourns[c][e] and wastes
away,
Lebanon[f] is ashamed and
withers;[g]
Sharon is like the Arabah,
and Bashan and Carmel drop
their leaves.
10 "Now will I arise,[h]" says the LORD.
"Now will I be exalted;
now will I be lifted up.
11 You conceive[i] chaff,
you give birth[j] to straw;
your breath is a fire[k] that
consumes you.
12 The peoples will be burned as if to
lime;
like cut thornbushes they will be
set ablaze.[l]"
13 You who are far away,[m] hear[n]
what I have done;
you who are near, acknowledge
my power!
14 The sinners in Zion are terrified;
trembling[o] grips the godless:
"Who of us can dwell with the
consuming fire?[p]
Who of us can dwell with
everlasting burning?"
15 He who walks righteously[q]
and speaks what is right,[r]
who rejects gain from extortion
and keeps his hand from
accepting bribes,
who stops his ears against plots of
murder

32:12 [a]Na 2:7
32:13 [b]Isa 5:6 [c]Isa 22:2
32:14 [d]Isa 13:22 [e]Isa 6:11; 27:10 [f]Isa 34:13 [g]Ps 104:11
32:15 [h]Isa 11:2; Joel 2:28 [i]Ps 107:35; Isa 35:1-2 [j]Isa 29:17
32:17 [k]Ps 119:165; Ro 14:17; Jas 3:18 [l]Isa 30:15
32:18 [m]Hos 2:18-23
32:19 [n]Isa 28:17; 30:30 [o]Isa 10:19; Zec 11:2 [p]Isa 24:10; 27:10
32:20 [q]Ecc 11:1 [r]Isa 30:24
33:1 [s]Hab 2:8; Mt 7:2 [t]Isa 21:2
33:2 [u]Isa 40:10; 51:9; 59:16 [v]Isa 25:9
33:3 [w]Isa 59:16-18
33:5 [x]Ps 97:9 [y]Isa 28:6 [z]Isa 1:26
33:6 [a]Isa 51:6 [b]Isa 11:2-3; Mt 6:33
33:7 [c]2Ki 18:37
33:8 [d]Jdg 5:6; Isa 35:8
33:9 [e]Isa 3:26 [f]Isa 2:13; 35:2 [g]Isa 24:4
33:10 [h]Ps 12:5; Isa 2:21
33:11 [i]Ps 7:14; Isa 59:4; Jas 1:15 [j]Isa 26:18 [k]Isa 1:31
33:12 [l]Isa 10:17
33:13 [m]Ps 48:10; 49:1 [n]Isa 49:1
33:14 [o]Isa 32:11 [p]Isa 30:30; Heb 12:29
33:15 [q]Isa 58:8 [r]Ps 15:2; 24:4

[a] 6 Or *is a treasure from him* [b] 8 Dead Sea Scrolls; Masoretic Text / *the cities* [c] 9 Or *dries up*

and shuts his eyes[s] against
contemplating evil—
16this is the man who will dwell on
the heights,
whose refuge[t] will be the
mountain fortress.[u]
His bread will be supplied,
and water will not fail[v] him.
17Your eyes will see the king[w] in his
beauty
and view a land that stretches
afar.[x]
18In your thoughts you will ponder
the former terror:[y]
"Where is that chief officer?
Where is the one who took the
revenue?
Where is the officer in charge of
the towers?"
19You will see those arrogant people
no more,
those people of an obscure
speech,
with their strange,
incomprehensible tongue.[z]
20Look upon Zion, the city of our
festivals;
your eyes will see Jerusalem,
a peaceful abode,[a] a tent that
will not be moved;[b]
its stakes will never be pulled up,
nor any of its ropes broken.
21There the LORD will be our Mighty
One.
It will be like a place of broad
rivers and streams.[c]
No galley with oars will ride them,
no mighty ship will sail them.
22For the LORD is our judge,[d]
the LORD is our lawgiver,[e]
the LORD is our king;[f]
it is he who will save[g] us.
23Your rigging hangs loose:
The mast is not held secure,
the sail is not spread.
Then an abundance of spoils will
be divided
and even the lame[h] will carry
off plunder.[i]
24No one living in Zion will say, "I
am ill";[j]
and the sins of those who dwell
there will be forgiven.[k]

Judgment Against the Nations

34 Come near, you nations, and
listen;
pay attention, you peoples![l]
Let the earth[m] hear, and all that is
in it,
the world, and all that comes out
of it![n]
2The LORD is angry with all nations;
his wrath is upon all their
armies.
He will totally destroy[a][o] them,
he will give them over to
slaughter.[p]
3Their slain will be thrown out,
their dead bodies will send up a
stench;[q]
the mountains will be soaked
with their blood.[r]
4All the stars of the heavens will be
dissolved[s]
and the sky rolled up[t] like a
scroll;
all the starry host will fall[u]
like withered leaves from the
vine,
like shriveled figs from the fig
tree.
5My sword[v] has drunk its fill in the
heavens;
see, it descends in judgment on
Edom,[w]
the people I have totally
destroyed.[x]
6The sword of the LORD is bathed in
blood,
it is covered with fat—
the blood of lambs and goats,
fat from the kidneys of rams.
For the LORD has a sacrifice in
Bozrah
and a great slaughter in Edom.
7And the wild oxen will fall with
them,
the bull calves and the great
bulls.[y]
Their land will be drenched with
blood,
and the dust will be soaked with
fat.
8For the LORD has a day of
vengeance,[z]
a year of retribution, to uphold
Zion's cause.
9Edom's streams will be turned into
pitch,
her dust into burning sulfur;
her land will become blazing
pitch!
10It will not be quenched night and
day;
its smoke will rise forever.[a]
From generation to generation it
will lie desolate;[b]
no one will ever pass through it
again.
11The desert owl[b][c] and screech
owl[b] will possess it;

33:15 [s]Ps 119:37 **33:16** [t]Isa 25:4 [u]Isa 26:1 [v]Isa 49:10 **33:17** [w]Isa 6:5 [x]Isa 26:15 **33:18** [y]Isa 17:14 **33:19** [z]Isa 28:11; Jer 5:15 **33:20** [a]Isa 32:18 [b]Ps 46:5; 125:1-2 **33:21** [c]Isa 41:18; 48:18; 66:12 **33:22** [d]Isa 11:4 [e]Isa 2:3; Jas 4:12 [f]Ps 89:18 [g]Isa 25:9 **33:23** [h]2Ki 7:8 [i]2Ki 7:16 **33:24** [j]Isa 30:26 [k]Jer 50:20; 1Jn 1:7-9 **34:1** [l]Isa 41:1; 43:9 [m]Ps 49:1 [n]Dt 32:1

34:2 [o]Isa 13:5 [p]Isa 30:25 **34:3** [q]Joel 2:20; Am 4:10 [r]ver 7; Eze 14:19; 35:6; 38:22 **34:4** [s]Isa 13:13; 2Pe 3:10 [t]Eze 32:7-8 [u]Joel 2:31; Mt 24:29*; Rev 6:13 **34:5** [v]Dt 32:41-42; Jer 46:10; Eze 21:5 [w]Am 1:11-12 [x]Isa 24:6; Mal 1:4 **34:7** [y]Ps 68:30 **34:8** [z]Isa 63:4 **34:10** [a]Rev 14:10-11; 19:3 [b]Isa 13:20; 24:1; Eze 29:12; Mal 1:3 **34:11** [c]Zep 2:14; Rev 18:2

[a] *2* The Hebrew term refers to the irrevocable giving over of things or persons to the LORD, often by totally destroying them; also in verse 5.
[b] *11* The precise identification of these birds is uncertain.

the great owl[a] and the raven
will nest there.
God will stretch out over Edom
the measuring line of chaos
and the plumb line[d] of
desolation.
12Her nobles will have nothing there
to be called a kingdom,
all her princes[e] will vanish[f]
away.
13Thorns will overrun her citadels,
nettles and brambles her
strongholds.[g]
She will become a haunt for
jackals,[h]
a home for owls.
14Desert creatures will meet with
hyenas,[i]
and wild goats will bleat to each
other;
there the night creatures will also
repose
and find for themselves places of
rest.
15The owl will nest there and lay
eggs,
she will hatch them, and care for
her young under the
shadow of her wings;
there also the falcons[j] will gather,
each with its mate.

16Look in the scroll[k] of the LORD
and read:
None of these will be missing,
not one will lack her mate.
For it is his mouth[l] that has given
the order,
and his Spirit will gather them
together.
17He allots their portions;[m]
his hand distributes them by
measure.
They will possess it forever
and dwell there from generation
to generation.[n]

Joy of the Redeemed

35 The desert[o] and the parched
land will be glad;
the wilderness will rejoice and
blossom.[p]
Like the crocus, 2it will burst into
bloom;
it will rejoice greatly and shout
for joy.[q]
The glory of Lebanon[r] will be
given to it,
the splendor of Carmel[s] and
Sharon;
they will see the glory of the LORD,
the splendor of our God.[t]

3Strengthen the feeble hands,
steady the knees[u] that give way;
4say to those with fearful hearts,
"Be strong, do not fear;
your God will come,
he will come with vengeance;[v]
with divine retribution
he will come to save you."

5Then will the eyes of the blind be
opened[w]
and the ears of the deaf[x]
unstopped.
6Then will the lame[y] leap like a
deer,
and the mute tongue[z] shout for
joy.
Water will gush forth in the
wilderness
and streams[a] in the desert.
7The burning sand will become a
pool,
the thirsty ground bubbling
springs.[b]
In the haunts where jackals[c] once
lay,
grass and reeds and papyrus will
grow.
8And a highway[d] will be there;
it will be called the Way of
Holiness.[e]
The unclean[f] will not journey on
it;
it will be for those who walk in
that Way;
wicked fools will not go about on
it.[b]
9No lion[g] will be there,
nor will any ferocious beast[h] get
up on it;
they will not be found there.
But only the redeemed[i] will walk
there,
10 and the ransomed of the LORD
will return.
They will enter Zion with singing;
everlasting joy[j] will crown their
heads.
Gladness and joy will overtake
them,
and sorrow and sighing will flee
away.[k]

Sennacherib Threatens Jerusalem

36 In the fourteenth year of King Hezekiah's reign, Sennacherib[l] king
of Assyria attacked all the fortified cities of Judah and captured them. 2Then
the king of Assyria sent his field commander with a large army from Lachish
to King Hezekiah at Jerusalem. When
the commander stopped at the aqueduct of the Upper Pool, on the road to
the Washerman's Field,[m] 3Eliakim[n]
son of Hilkiah the palace administra-

34:11 [d]2Ki 21:13; La 2:8
34:12 [e]Jer 27:20; 39:6 [f]Isa 41:11-12
34:13 [g]Isa 13:22; 32:13 [h]Ps 44:19; Jer 9:11; 10:22
34:14 [i]Isa 13:22
34:15 [j]Dt 14:13
34:16 [k]Isa 30:8 [l]Isa 1:20; 58:14
34:17 [m]Isa 17:14; Jer 13:25 [n]ver 10
35:1 [o]Isa 27:10; 41:18-19 [p]Isa 51:3
35:2 [q]Isa 25:9; 55:12 [r]Isa 32:15 [s]SS 7:5 [t]Isa 25:9
35:3 [u]Job 4:4; Heb 12:12
35:4 [v]Isa 1:24; 34:8
35:5 [w]Mt 11:5; Jn 9:6-7 [x]Isa 29:18; 50:4
35:6 [y]Mt 15:30; Jn 5:8-9; Ac 3:8 [z]Isa 32:4; Mt 9:32-33; 12:22; Lk 11:14 [a]Isa 41:18; Jn 7:38
35:7 [b]Isa 49:10 [c]Isa 13:22
35:8 [d]Isa 11:16; 33:8; Mt 7:13-14 [e]Isa 4:3; 1Pe 1:15 [f]Isa 52:1
35:9 [g]Isa 30:6 [h]Isa 34:14 [i]Isa 51:11; 62:12; 63:4
35:10 [j]Isa 25:9 [k]Isa 30:19; 51:11; Rev 7:17; 21:4
36:1 [l]2Ch 32:1
36:2 [m]Isa 7:3
36:3 [n]Isa 22:20-21

[a] *11* The precise identification of these birds is uncertain. [b] *8* Or / *the simple will not stray from it*

tor, Shebna[o] the secretary, and Joah son of Asaph the recorder went out to him.

4The field commander said to them, "Tell Hezekiah,

" 'This is what the great king, the king of Assyria, says: On what are you basing this confidence of yours? 5You say you have strategy and military strength—but you speak only empty words. On whom are you depending, that you rebel[p] against me? 6Look now, you are depending on Egypt,[q] that splintered reed[r] of a staff, which pierces a man's hand and wounds him if he leans on it! Such is Pharaoh king of Egypt to all who depend on him. 7And if you say to me, "We are depending on the LORD our God"—isn't he the one whose high places and altars Hezekiah removed,[s] saying to Judah and Jerusalem, "You must worship before this altar"?[t]

8" 'Come now, make a bargain with my master, the king of Assyria: I will give you two thousand horses—if you can put riders on them! 9How then can you repulse one officer of the least of my master's officials, even though you are depending on Egypt[u] for chariots and horsemen?[v] 10Furthermore, have I come to attack and destroy this land without the LORD? The LORD himself told[w] me to march against this country and destroy it.' "

11Then Eliakim, Shebna and Joah said to the field commander, "Please speak to your servants in Aramaic,[x] since we understand it. Don't speak to us in Hebrew in the hearing of the people on the wall."

12But the commander replied, "Was it only to your master and you that my master sent me to say these things, and not to the men sitting on the wall—who, like you, will have to eat their own filth and drink their own urine?"

13Then the commander stood and called out in Hebrew,[y] "Hear the words of the great king, the king of Assyria! 14This is what the king says: Do not let Hezekiah deceive you. He cannot deliver you! 15Do not let Hezekiah persuade you to trust in the LORD when he says, 'The LORD will surely deliver us; this city will not be given into the hand of the king of Assyria.'[z]

16"Do not listen to Hezekiah. This is what the king of Assyria says: Make peace with me and come out to me. Then every one of you will eat from his own vine and fig tree[a] and drink water from his own cistern,[b] 17until I come and take you to a land like your own—a land of grain and new wine, a land of bread and vineyards.

18"Do not let Hezekiah mislead you when he says, 'The LORD will deliver us.' Has the god of any nation ever delivered his land from the hand of the king of Assyria? 19Where are the gods of Hamath and Arpad? Where are the gods of Sepharvaim? Have they rescued Samaria from my hand? 20Who of all the gods[c] of these countries has been able to save his land from me? How then can the LORD deliver Jerusalem from my hand?"

21But the people remained silent and said nothing in reply, because the king had commanded, "Do not answer him."[d]

22Then Eliakim son of Hilkiah the palace administrator, Shebna the secretary, and Joah son of Asaph the recorder went to Hezekiah, with their clothes torn, and told him what the field commander had said.

Jerusalem's Deliverance Foretold

37 When King Hezekiah heard this, he tore his clothes and put on sackcloth and went into the temple of the LORD. 2He sent Eliakim the palace administrator, Shebna the secretary, and the leading priests, all wearing sackcloth, to the prophet Isaiah son of Amoz.[e] 3They told him, "This is what Hezekiah says: This day is a day of distress and rebuke and disgrace, as when children come to the point of birth[f] and there is no strength to deliver them. 4It may be that the LORD your God will hear the words of the field commander, whom his master, the king of Assyria, has sent to ridicule the living God, and that he will rebuke him for the words the LORD your God has heard.[g] Therefore pray for the remnant[h] that still survives."

5When King Hezekiah's officials came to Isaiah, 6Isaiah said to them, "Tell your master, 'This is what the LORD says: Do not be afraid[i] of what you have heard—those words with which the underlings of the king of Assyria have blasphemed me. 7Listen! I am going to put a spirit in him so that when he hears a certain report,[j] he will return to his own country, and there I will have him cut down with the sword.' "

8When the field commander heard that the king of Assyria had left La-

36:3 [o]2Ki 18:18
36:5 [p]2Ki 18:7
36:6 [q]Isa 30:2,5 [r]Eze 29:6-7
36:7 [s]2Ki 18:4 [t]Dt 12:2-5
36:9 [u]Isa 31:3 [v]Isa 30:2-5
36:10 [w]1Ki 13:18
36:11 [x]Ezr 4:7
36:13 [y]2Ch 32:18
36:15 [z]Isa 37:10
36:16 [a]1Ki 4:25; Zec 3:10 [b]Pr 5:15
36:20 [c]1Ki 20:23
36:21 [d]Pr 9:7-8; 26:4
37:2 [e]Isa 1:1
37:3 [f]Isa 26:18; 66:9; Hos 13:13
37:4 [g]Isa 36:13, 18-20 [h]Isa 1:9
37:6 [i]Isa 7:4
37:7 [j]ver 9

chish, he withdrew and found the king fighting against Libnah.[k]

9 Now Sennacherib received a report[l] that Tirhakah, the Cushite[a] king ⌞of Egypt⌟, was marching out to fight against him. When he heard it, he sent messengers to Hezekiah with this word: 10 "Say to Hezekiah king of Judah: Do not let the god you depend on deceive you when he says, 'Jerusalem will not be handed over to the king of Assyria.'[m] 11 Surely you have heard what the kings of Assyria have done to all the countries, destroying them completely. And will you be delivered?[n] 12 Did the gods of the nations that were destroyed by my forefathers[o] deliver them—the gods of Gozan, Haran,[p] Rezeph and the people of Eden who were in Tel Assar? 13 Where is the king of Hamath, the king of Arpad, the king of the city of Sepharvaim, or of Hena or Ivvah?"

Hezekiah's Prayer

14 Hezekiah received the letter from the messengers and read it. Then he went up to the temple of the LORD and spread it out before the LORD. 15 And Hezekiah prayed to the LORD: 16 "O LORD Almighty, God of Israel, enthroned between the cherubim, you alone are God[q] over all the kingdoms of the earth. You have made heaven and earth. 17 Give ear, O LORD, and hear;[r] open your eyes, O LORD, and see;[s] listen to all the words Sennacherib has sent to insult the living God.

18 "It is true, O LORD, that the Assyrian kings have laid waste all these peoples and their lands.[t] 19 They have thrown their gods into the fire and destroyed them,[u] for they were not gods[v] but only wood and stone, fashioned by human hands. 20 Now, O LORD our God, deliver us from his hand, so that all kingdoms on earth may know that you alone, O LORD, are God.[b][w]"

Sennacherib's Fall

21 Then Isaiah son of Amoz[x] sent a message to Hezekiah: "This is what the LORD, the God of Israel, says: Because you have prayed to me concerning Sennacherib king of Assyria, 22 this is the word the LORD has spoken against him:

"The Virgin Daughter of Zion
despises and mocks you.
The Daughter of Jerusalem
tosses her head[y] as you flee.
23 Who is it you have insulted and
blasphemed?[z]
Against whom have you raised
your voice
and lifted your eyes in pride?[a]
Against the Holy One of Israel!
24 By your messengers
you have heaped insults on the
Lord.
And you have said,
'With my many chariots
I have ascended the heights of the
mountains,
the utmost heights of Lebanon.[b]
I have cut down its tallest cedars,
the choicest of its pines.
I have reached its remotest heights,
the finest of its forests.
25 I have dug wells in foreign lands[c]
and drunk the water there.
With the soles of my feet
I have dried up all the streams of
Egypt.[c]'

26 "Have you not heard?
Long ago I ordained[d] it.
In days of old I planned[e] it;
now I have brought it to pass,
that you have turned fortified cities
into piles of stone.[f]
27 Their people, drained of power,
are dismayed and put to shame.
They are like plants in the field,
like tender green shoots,
like grass sprouting on the roof,[g]
scorched[d] before it grows up.

28 "But I know where you stay
and when you come and go[h]
and how you rage[i] against me.
29 Because you rage against me
and because your insolence[j]
has reached my ears,
I will put my hook in your nose[k]
and my bit in your mouth,
and I will make you return
by the way you came.[l]

30 "This will be the sign for you, O Hezekiah:

"This year you will eat what grows
by itself,
and the second year what
springs from that.
But in the third year sow and reap,
plant vineyards and eat their
fruit.
31 Once more a remnant of the house
of Judah
will take root below and bear
fruit[m] above.
32 For out of Jerusalem will come a
remnant,

37:8 [k]Nu 33:20
37:9 [l]ver 7
37:10 [m]Isa 36:15
37:11 [n]Isa 36:18-20
37:12 [o]2Ki 18:11 [p]Ge 11:31; 12:1-4; Ac 7:2
37:16 [q]Dt 10:17; Ps 86:10; 136:2-3
37:17 [r]2Ch 6:40 [s]Da 9:18
37:18 [t]2Ki 15:29; Na 2:11-12
37:19 [u]Isa 26:14 [v]Isa 41:24,29
37:20 [w]Ps 46:10
37:21 [x]ver 2
37:22 [y]Job 16:4
37:23 [z]ver 4 [a]Isa 2:11
37:24 [b]Isa 14:8
37:25 [c]Dt 11:10
37:26 [d]Ac 2:23; 4:27-28; 1Pe 2:8 [e]Isa 10:6; 25:1 [f]Isa 25:2
37:27 [g]Ps 129:6
37:28 [h]Ps 139:1-3 [i]Ps 2:1
37:29 [j]Isa 10:12 [k]Isa 30:28; Eze 38:4 [l]ver 34
37:31 [m]Isa 27:6

a *9* That is, from the upper Nile region
b *20* Dead Sea Scrolls (see also 2 Kings 19:19); Masoretic Text *alone are the LORD*
c *25* Dead Sea Scrolls (see also 2 Kings 19:24); Masoretic Text does not have *in foreign lands.*
d *27* Some manuscripts of the Masoretic Text, Dead Sea Scrolls and some Septuagint manuscripts (see also 2 Kings 19:26); most manuscripts of the Masoretic Text *roof / and terraced fields*

and out of Mount Zion a band of
survivors.
The zeal[n] of the LORD Almighty
will accomplish this.

33"Therefore this is what the LORD
says concerning the king of Assyria:

"He will not enter this city
or shoot an arrow here.
He will not come before it with
shield
or build a siege ramp against it.
34By the way that he came he will
return;[o]
he will not enter this city,"
declares the LORD.
35"I will defend[p] this city and save
it,
for my sake[q] and for the sake of
David[r] my servant!"

36Then the angel of the LORD went
out and put to death a hundred and
eighty-five thousand men in the Assyrian[s] camp. When the people got up
the next morning—there were all the
dead bodies! 37So Sennacherib king of
Assyria broke camp and withdrew.
He returned to Nineveh[t] and stayed
there.
38One day, while he was worshiping
in the temple of his god Nisroch, his
sons Adrammelech and Sharezer cut
him down with the sword, and they escaped to the land of Ararat.[u] And
Esarhaddon his son succeeded him as
king.

Hezekiah's Illness

38 In those days Hezekiah became ill
and was at the point of death. The
prophet Isaiah son of Amoz[v] went to
him and said, "This is what the LORD
says: Put your house in order,[w] because you are going to die; you will not
recover."
2Hezekiah turned his face to the wall
and prayed to the LORD, 3"Remember,
O LORD, how I have walked[x] before
you faithfully and with wholehearted
devotion[y] and have done what is good
in your eyes.[z]" And Hezekiah wept[a]
bitterly.
4Then the word of the LORD came to
Isaiah: 5"Go and tell Hezekiah, 'This is
what the LORD, the God of your father
David, says: I have heard your prayer
and seen your tears; I will add fifteen
years[b] to your life. 6And I will deliver
you and this city from the hand of the
king of Assyria. I will defend[c] this city.
7" 'This is the LORD's sign[d] to you
that the LORD will do what he has
promised: 8I will make the shadow cast
by the sun go back the ten steps it has
gone down on the stairway of Ahaz.' "
So the sunlight went back the ten steps
it had gone down.[e]

9A writing of Hezekiah king of Judah
after his illness and recovery:

10I said, "In the prime of my life[f]
must I go through the gates of
death[a][g]
and be robbed of the rest of my
years?[h]"
11I said, "I will not again see the
LORD,
the LORD, in the land of the
living;[i]
no longer will I look on mankind,
or be with those who now dwell
in this world.[b]
12Like a shepherd's tent[j] my house
has been pulled down[k] and
taken from me.
Like a weaver I have rolled[l] up
my life,
and he has cut me off from the
loom;[m]
day and night[n] you made an
end of me.
13I waited patiently till dawn,
but like a lion he broke[o] all my
bones;[p]
day and night you made an end
of me.
14I cried like a swift or thrush,
I moaned like a mourning
dove.[q]
My eyes grew weak as I looked to
the heavens.
I am troubled; O Lord, come to
my aid!"[r]
15But what can I say?
He has spoken to me, and he
himself has done this.[s]
I will walk humbly[t] all my years
because of this anguish of my
soul.[u]
16Lord, by such things men live;
and my spirit finds life in them
too.
You restored me to health
and let me live.[v]
17Surely it was for my benefit
that I suffered such anguish.
In your love you kept me
from the pit[w] of destruction;
you have put all my sins[x]
behind your back.[y]
18For the grave[a][z] cannot praise
you,
death cannot sing your praise;[a]
those who go down to the pit[b]
cannot hope for your
faithfulness.

[a] *10,18* Hebrew *Sheol* [b] *11* A few Hebrew manuscripts; most Hebrew manuscripts *in the place of cessation*

37:32 [n] Isa 9:7
37:34 [o] ver 29
37:35 [p] Isa 31:5; 38:6 [q] Isa 43:25; 48:9,11 [r] 2Ki 20:6
37:36 [s] Isa 10:12
37:37 [t] Ge 10:11
37:38 [u] Ge 8:4; Jer 51:27
38:1 [v] Isa 37:2 [w] 2Sa 17:23
38:3 [x] Ne 13:14; Ps 26:3 [y] 1Ch 29:19 [z] Dt 6:18 [a] Ps 6:8
38:5 [b] 2Ki 18:2
38:6 [c] Isa 31:5; 37:35
38:7 [d] Isa 7:11,14
38:8 [e] Jos 10:13
38:10 [f] Ps 102:24 [g] Ps 107:18; 2Co 1:9 [h] Job 17:11
38:11 [i] Ps 27:13; 116:9
38:12 [j] 2Co 5:1,4; 2Pe 1:13-14 [k] Job 4:21 [l] Heb 1:12 [m] Job 7:6 [n] Ps 73:14
38:13 [o] Ps 51:8 [p] Job 10:16; Da 6:24
38:14 [q] Isa 59:11 [r] Job 17:3
38:15 [s] Ps 39:9 [t] 1Ki 21:27 [u] Job 7:11
38:16 [v] Ps 119:25
38:17 [w] Ps 30:3 [x] Jer 31:34 [y] Isa 43:25; Mic 7:19
38:18 [z] Ecc 9:10 [a] Ps 6:5; 88:10-11; 115:17 [b] Ps 30:9

4 →PG. 961

19The living, the living—they praise[c]
you,
as I am doing today;
fathers tell their children[d]
about your faithfulness.

20The LORD will save me,
and we will sing[e] with stringed
instruments[f]
all the days of our lives[g]
in the temple[h] of the LORD.

21Isaiah had said, "Prepare a poultice of figs and apply it to the boil, and he will recover."

22Hezekiah had asked, "What will be the sign that I will go up to the temple of the LORD?"

Envoys From Babylon

39 At that time Merodach-Baladan son of Baladan king of Babylon[i]
sent Hezekiah letters and a gift, be-
cause he had heard of his illness and
recovery. 2Hezekiah received the en-
voys[j] gladly and showed them what was in his storehouses—the silver, the gold,[k] the spices, the fine oil, his entire armory and everything found among his treasures. There was nothing in his palace or in all his kingdom that Hezekiah did not show them.
3Then Isaiah the prophet went to King Hezekiah and asked, "What did those men say, and where did they come from?"

"From a distant land,[l]" Hezekiah replied. "They came to me from Babylon."

4The prophet asked, "What did they see in your palace?"

"They saw everything in my palace," Hezekiah said. "There is nothing among my treasures that I did not show them."

5Then Isaiah said to Hezekiah, "Hear
the word of the LORD Almighty: 6The
time will surely come when everything in your palace, and all that your fathers have stored up until this day, will be carried off to Babylon.[m] Nothing will
be left, says the LORD. 7And some of
your descendants, your own flesh and blood who will be born to you, will be taken away, and they will become eunuchs in the palace of the king of Babylon.[n]"

8"The word of the LORD you have spoken is good," Hezekiah replied. For he thought, "There will be peace and security in my lifetime.[o]"

Comfort for God's People

40 Comfort, comfort[p] my people,
says your God.
2Speak tenderly[q] to Jerusalem,
and proclaim to her
that her hard service has been
completed,[r]
that her sin has been paid for,
that she has received from the
LORD's hand
double[s] for all her sins.

3A voice of one calling:
"In the desert prepare
the way[t] for the LORD[a];
make straight in the wilderness
a highway for our God.[b][u]
4Every valley shall be raised up,
every mountain and hill made
low;
the rough ground shall become
level,[v]
the rugged places a plain.
5And the glory of the LORD will be
revealed,
and all mankind together will see
it.[w]
For the mouth of the LORD
has spoken."[x]

6A voice says, "Cry out."
And I said, "What shall I cry?"

"All men are like grass,[y]
and all their glory is like the
flowers of the field.
7The grass withers and the flowers
fall,
because the breath[z] of the LORD
blows on them.
Surely the people are grass.

38:19 [c]Dt 6:7; Ps 118:17; 119:175 [d]Dt 11:19 **38:20** [e]Ps 68:25 [f]Ps 33:2 [g]Ps 116:2 [h]Ps 116:17-19 **39:1** [i]2Ch 32:31 **39:2** [j]2Ch 32:31 [k]2Ki 18:15 **39:3** [l]Dt 28:49 **39:6** [m]2Ki 24:13; Jer 20:5 **39:7** [n]2Ki 24:15; Da 1:1-7 **39:8** [o]2Ch 32:26 **40:1** [p]Isa 12:1; 49:13; 51:3,12; 52:9; 61:2; 66:13; Jer 31:13; Zep 3:14-17; 2Co 1:3 **40:2** [q]Isa 35:4 [r]Isa 41:11-13; 49:25 [s]Isa 61:7; Jer 16:18; Zec 9:12; Rev 18:6 **40:3** [t]Mal 3:1 [u]Mt 3:3*; Mk 1:3*; Jn 1:23* **40:4** [v]Isa 45:2,13 **40:5** [w]Isa 52:10; Lk 3:4-6* [x]Isa 1:20; 58:14 **40:6** [y]Job 14:2 **40:7** [z]Job 41:21

[a]3 Or *A voice of one calling in the desert: / "Prepare the way for the LORD* [b]3 Hebrew; Septuagint *make straight the paths of our God*

38:15–19

PROMISE 1

A 15-YEAR EXTENSION

What can a man say when God spares his life? King Hezekiah knew he was going to die. In quiet desperation, he wept as he prayed for healing. In answer to this king's sincere prayer, God gave him 15 more years—*and* protection from the Assyrians, to boot!

When God gives a gift, he includes the batteries. This passage records Hezekiah's response to God's gift of extended life. First, he expressed humility (v. 15). Second, he recognized that the illness he suffered was for his benefit because it made him deal with his sin (v. 17). Finally, he saw that the purpose of his life was to praise God and to teach the next generation about his faithfulness (v. 19). Reflect on God's gift of *eternally extended* life to you through his Son. Then read Hezekiah's response to God as your own.

For the next Promise 1 reading go to page 777.

8The grass withers and the flowers
fall,
but the word[a] of our God
stands forever.[b]"

9You who bring good tidings[c] to
Zion,
go up on a high mountain.
You who bring good tidings to
Jerusalem,**a**
lift up your voice with a shout,
lift it up, do not be afraid;
say to the towns of Judah,
"Here is your God!"[d]
10See, the Sovereign LORD comes[e]
with power,
and his arm[f] rules[g] for him.
See, his reward[h] is with him,
and his recompense
accompanies him.
11He tends his flock like a
shepherd:[i]
He gathers the lambs in his arms
and carries them close to his heart;
he gently leads those that have
young.

12Who has measured the waters[j] in
the hollow of his hand,[k]
or with the breadth of his hand
marked off the heavens?[l]
Who has held the dust of the earth
in a basket,
or weighed the mountains on the
scales
and the hills in a balance?
13Who has understood the mind**b** of
the LORD,
or instructed him as his
counselor?[m]
14Whom did the LORD consult to
enlighten him,
and who taught him the right
way?
Who was it that taught him
knowledge[n]
or showed him the path of
understanding?

15Surely the nations are like a drop
in a bucket;
they are regarded as dust on the
scales;
he weighs the islands as though
they were fine dust.
16Lebanon is not sufficient for altar
fires,
nor its animals[o] enough for
burnt offerings.
17Before him all the nations[p] are as
nothing;[q]
they are regarded by him as
worthless
and less than nothing.[r]

18To whom, then, will you compare
God?[s]
What image[t] will you compare
him to?
19As for an idol,[u] a craftsman casts
it,
and a goldsmith[v] overlays it
with gold[w]
and fashions silver chains for it.
20A man too poor to present such an
offering
selects wood that will not rot.
He looks for a skilled craftsman
to set up an idol that will not
topple.[x]

21Do you not know?
Have you not heard?
Has it not been told[y] you from the
beginning?
Have you not understood[z] since
the earth was founded?[a]
22He sits enthroned above the circle
of the earth,
and its people are like
grasshoppers.[b]
He stretches out the heavens like a
canopy,[c]
and spreads them out like a
tent[d] to live in.
23He brings princes[e] to naught
and reduces the rulers of this
world to nothing.[f]
24No sooner are they planted,
no sooner are they sown,
no sooner do they take root in
the ground,
than he blows[g] on them and they
wither,
and a whirlwind sweeps them
away like chaff.

25"To whom will you compare me?[h]
Or who is my equal?" says the
Holy One.
26Lift your eyes and look to the
heavens:[i]
Who created[j] all these?
He who brings out the starry host[k]
one by one,
and calls them each by name.
Because of his great power and
mighty strength,
not one of them is missing.[l]

27Why do you say, O Jacob,
and complain, O Israel,
"My way is hidden from the LORD;
my cause is disregarded by my
God"?[m]
28Do you not know?
Have you not heard?[n]
The LORD is the everlasting[o] God,
the Creator of the ends of the
earth.
He will not grow tired or weary,

a9 Or *O Zion, bringer of good tidings, / go up on a high mountain. / O Jerusalem, bringer of good tidings* **b**13 Or *Spirit*; or *spirit*

40:8 [a]Isa 55:11; 59:21 [b]Mt 5:18; 1Pe 1:24-25* **40:9** [c]Isa 52:7-10; 61:1; Ro 10:15 [d]Isa 25:9 **40:10** [e]Rev 22:7 [f]Isa 59:16 [g]Isa 9:6-7 [h]Isa 62:11; Rev 22:12 **40:11** [i]Eze 34:23; Mic 5:4; Jn 10:11 **40:12** [j]Job 38:10 [k]Pr 30:4 [l]Heb 1:10-12 **40:13** [m]Ro 11:34*; 1Co 2:16* **40:14** [n]Job 21:22; Col 2:3 **40:16** [o]Ps 50:9-11; Mic 6:7; Heb 10:5-9 **40:17** [p]Isa 30:28 [q]Isa 29:7 [r]Da 4:35 **40:18** [s]Ex 8:10; 1Sa 2:2; Isa 46:5 [t]Ac 17:29 **40:19** [u]Ps 115:4 [v]Isa 41:7; Jer 10:3 [w]Isa 2:20 **40:20** [x]1Sa 5:3 **40:21** [y]Ps 19:1; 50:6; Ac 14:17 [z]Ro 1:19 [a]Isa 48:13; 51:13 **40:22** [b]Nu 13:33; Ps 104:2; Isa 42:5 [c]Job 22:14 [d]Job 36:29 **40:23** [e]Isa 34:12 [f]Job 12:21; Ps 107:40 **40:24** [g]Isa 41:16 **40:25** [h]ver 18 **40:26** [i]Isa 51:6 [j]Ps 89:11-13; Isa 42:5 [k]Ps 147:4 [l]Isa 34:16 **40:27** [m]Job 27:2; Lk 18:7-8 **40:28** [n]ver 21 [o]Ps 90:2

and his understanding no one
can fathom.[p]
29He gives strength to the weary[q]
and increases the power of the
weak.
30Even youths grow tired and weary,
and young men[r] stumble and
fall;
31but those who hope[s] in the LORD
will renew their strength.[t]
They will soar on wings like
eagles;[u]
they will run and not grow
weary,
they will walk and not be faint.[v]

1 →PG. 785

The Helper of Israel

41 "Be silent[w] before me, you
islands![x]
Let the nations renew their
strength!
Let them come forward[y] and
speak;
let us meet together[z] at the
place of judgment.

2"Who has stirred[a] up one from
the east,[b]
calling him in righteousness to
his service[a]?
He hands nations over to him
and subdues kings before him.
He turns them to dust[c] with his
sword,
to windblown chaff[d] with his
bow.
3He pursues them and moves on
unscathed,
by a path his feet have not
traveled before.
4Who has done this and carried it
through,
calling forth the generations
from the beginning?[e]
I, the LORD—with the first of them
and with the last[f]—I am he."

5The islands[g] have seen it and fear;
the ends of the earth tremble.
They approach and come forward;
6 each helps the other
and says to his brother, "Be
strong!"
7The craftsman encourages the
goldsmith,[h]
and he who smooths with the
hammer
spurs on him who strikes the
anvil.
He says of the welding, "It is
good."
He nails down the idol so it will
not topple.

8"But you, O Israel, my servant,
Jacob, whom I have chosen,
you descendants of Abraham[i]
my friend,[j]
9I took you from the ends of the
earth,[k]
from its farthest corners I called
you.
I said, 'You are my servant';
I have chosen[l] you and have
not rejected you.
10So do not fear, for I am with you;[m]
do not be dismayed, for I am
your God.
I will strengthen you and help[n]
you;
I will uphold you with my
righteous right hand.

11"All who rage[o] against you
will surely be ashamed and
disgraced;[p]
those who oppose[q] you
will be as nothing and perish.[r]
12Though you search for your
enemies,
you will not find them.[s]
Those who wage war against you
will be as nothing[t] at all.
13For I am the LORD, your God,
who takes hold of your right
hand[u]
and says to you, Do not fear;
I will help[v] you.
14Do not be afraid, O worm Jacob,
O little Israel,
for I myself will help you," declares
the LORD,
your Redeemer, the Holy One of
Israel.
15"See, I will make you into a
threshing sledge,[w]
new and sharp, with many teeth.
You will thresh the mountains and
crush them,
and reduce the hills to chaff.
16You will winnow[x] them, the wind
will pick them up,
and a gale will blow them away.
But you will rejoice in the LORD
and glory[y] in the Holy One of
Israel.

17"The poor and needy search for
water,[z]
but there is none;
their tongues are parched with
thirst.
But I the LORD will answer[a] them;
I, the God of Israel, will not
forsake them.
18I will make rivers flow[b] on barren
heights,
and springs within the valleys.
I will turn the desert[c] into pools
of water,

40:28 [p]Ps 147:5; Ro 11:33
40:29 [q]Isa 50:4; Jer 31:25
40:30 [r]Isa 9:17; Jer 6:11; 9:21
40:31 [s]Lk 18:1 [t]2Co 4:16 [u]Ex 19:4; Ps 103:5 [v]2Co 4:1; Heb 12:1-3
41:1 [w]Hab 2:20; Zec 2:13 [x]Isa 11:11 [y]Isa 48:16 [z]Isa 1:18; 34:1; 50:8
41:2 [a]Ezr 1:2 [b]ver 25; Isa 45:1,13 [c]2Sa 22:43 [d]Isa 40:24
41:4 [e]ver 26; Isa 46:10 [f]Isa 44:6; 48:12; Rev 1:8, 17; 22:13
41:5 [g]Eze 26:17-18
41:7 [h]Isa 40:19
41:8 [i]Isa 29:22; 51:2; 63:16 [j]2Ch 20:7; Jas 2:23
41:9 [k]Isa 11:12 [l]Dt 7:6
41:10 [m]Jos 1:9; Isa 43:2,5; Ro 8:31 [n]ver 13-14; Isa 44:2; 49:8
41:11 [o]Isa 17:12 [p]Isa 45:24 [q]Ex 23:22 [r]Isa 29:8
41:12 [s]Ps 37:35-36 [t]Isa 17:14
41:13 [u]Isa 42:6; 45:1 [v]ver 10
41:15 [w]Mic 4:13
41:16 [x]Jer 51:2 [y]Isa 45:25
41:17 [z]Isa 43:20 [a]Isa 30:19
41:18 [b]Isa 30:25 [c]Isa 43:19

[a]2 Or / *whom victory meets at every step*

and the parched ground into
springs.[d]
19I will put in the desert
the cedar and the acacia, the
myrtle and the olive.
I will set pines in the wasteland,
the fir and the cypress
together,[e]
20so that people may see and know,
may consider and understand,
that the hand of the LORD has done
this,
that the Holy One of Israel has
created[f] it.

21"Present your case," says the LORD.
"Set forth your arguments," says
Jacob's King.[g]
22"Bring in ⌞your idols⌟ to tell us
what is going to happen.[h]
Tell us what the former things
were,
so that we may consider them
and know their final outcome.
Or declare to us the things to
come,[i]
23 tell us what the future holds,
so we may know[j] that you are
gods.
Do something, whether good or
bad,[k]
so that we will be dismayed and
filled with fear.
24But you are less than nothing[l]
and your works are utterly
worthless;
he who chooses you is
detestable.[m]

25"I have stirred up one from the
north,[n] and he comes—
one from the rising sun who
calls on my name.
He treads[o] on rulers as if they
were mortar,
as if he were a potter treading
the clay.
26Who told of this from the
beginning, so we could
know,
or beforehand, so we could say,
'He was right'?
No one told of this,
no one foretold it,
no one heard any words[p] from
you.
27I was the first to tell[q] Zion, 'Look,
here they are!'
I gave to Jerusalem a messenger
of good tidings.[r]
28I look but there is no one[s]—
no one among them to give
counsel,[t]
no one to give answer when I
ask them.
29See, they are all false!
Their deeds amount to
nothing;[u]
their images are but wind[v] and
confusion.

The Servant of the LORD

42 "Here is my servant, whom I
uphold,
my chosen one[w] in whom I
delight;
I will put my Spirit[x] on him
and he will bring justice to the
nations.
2He will not shout or cry out,
or raise his voice in the streets.
3A bruised reed he will not break,
and a smoldering wick he will
not snuff out.
In faithfulness he will bring forth
justice;[y]
4 he will not falter or be
discouraged
till he establishes justice on earth.
In his law the islands will put
their hope."[z]

5This is what God the LORD says—
he who created the heavens and
stretched them out,
who spread out the earth and all
that comes out of it,[a]
who gives breath[b] to its people,
and life to those who walk on it:
6"I, the LORD, have called[c] you in
righteousness;[d]
I will take hold of your hand.
I will keep[e] you and will make
you
to be a covenant[f] for the
people
and a light for the Gentiles,[g]
7to open eyes that are blind,[h]
to free[i] captives from prison[j]
and to release from the dungeon
those who sit in darkness.
8"I am the LORD; that is my name![k]
I will not give my glory to
another[l]
or my praise to idols.
9See, the former things have taken
place,
and new things I declare;
before they spring into being
I announce them to you."

Song of Praise to the LORD

10Sing to the LORD a new song,[m]
his praise from the ends of the
earth,[n]
you who go down to the sea, and
all that is in it,[o]
you islands, and all who live in
them.
11Let the desert[p] and its towns raise
their voices;

41:18 [d]Isa 35:7
41:19 [e]Isa 60:13
41:20 [f]Job 12:9
41:21 [g]Isa 43:15
41:22 [h]Isa 43:9; 45:21 [i]Isa 46:10
41:23 [j]Isa 42:9; 44:7-8; 45:3 [k]Jer 10:5
41:24 [l]Isa 37:19; 44:9; 1Co 8:4 [m]Ps 115:8
41:25 [n]ver 2 [o]2Sa 22:43
41:26 [p]Hab 2:18-19
41:27 [q]Isa 48:3,16 [r]Isa 40:9
41:28 [s]Isa 50:2; 59:16; 63:5 [t]Isa 40:13-14
41:29 [u]ver 24 [v]Jer 5:13
42:1 [w]Isa 43:10; Lk 9:35; 1Pe 2:4,6 [x]Isa 11:2; Mt 3:16-17; Jn 3:34
42:3 [y]Ps 72:2
42:4 [z]Ge 49:10; Mt 12:18-21*
42:5 [a]Ps 24:2 [b]Ac 17:25
42:6 [c]Isa 43:1 [d]Jer 23:6 [e]Isa 26:3 [f]Isa 49:8 [g]Lk 2:32; Ac 13:47
42:7 [h]Isa 35:5 [i]Isa 49:9; 61:1 [j]Lk 4:19; 2Ti 2:26; Heb 2:14-15
42:8 [k]Ex 3:15 [l]Isa 48:11
42:10 [m]Ps 33:3; 40:3; 98:1 [n]Isa 49:6 [o]1Ch 16:32; Ps 96:11
42:11 [p]Isa 32:16

let the settlements where
Kedar[q] lives rejoice.
Let the people of Sela sing for joy;
let them shout from the
mountaintops.[r]
12Let them give glory[s] to the LORD
and proclaim his praise in the
islands.
13The LORD will march out like a
mighty[t] man,
like a warrior he will stir up his
zeal;[u]
with a shout[v] he will raise the
battle cry
and will triumph over his
enemies.[w]

14"For a long time I have kept silent,
I have been quiet and held
myself back.
But now, like a woman in
childbirth,
I cry out, I gasp and pant.
15I will lay waste[x] the mountains
and hills
and dry up all their vegetation;
I will turn rivers into islands
and dry up[y] the pools.
16I will lead[z] the blind[a] by ways
they have not known,
along unfamiliar paths I will
guide them;
I will turn the darkness into light
before them
and make the rough places
smooth.[b]
These are the things I will do;
I will not forsake[c] them.
17But those who trust in idols,
who say to images, 'You are our
gods,'
will be turned back in utter
shame.[d]

Israel Blind and Deaf

18"Hear, you deaf;[e]
look, you blind, and see!
19Who is blind[f] but my servant,[g]
and deaf like the messenger[h] I
send?
Who is blind like the one
committed[i] to me,
blind like the servant of the
LORD?
20You have seen many things, but
have paid no attention;
your ears are open, but you hear
nothing."[j]
21It pleased the LORD
for the sake of his righteousness
to make his law[k] great and
glorious.
22But this is a people plundered and
looted,
all of them trapped in pits[l]
or hidden away in prisons.[m]

42:11 [q]Isa 60:7 [r]Isa 52:7; Na 1:15 **42:12** [s]Isa 24:15 **42:13** [t]Isa 9:6 [u]Isa 26:11 [v]Hos 11:10 [w]Isa 66:14 **42:15** [x]Eze 38:20 [y]Isa 50:2; Na 1:4-6 **42:16** [z]Lk 1:78-79 [a]Isa 32:3 [b]Lk 3:5 [c]Heb 13:5 **42:17** [d]Ps 97:7; Isa 1:29; 44:11; 45:16 **42:18** [e]Isa 35:5 **42:19** [f]Isa 43:8; Eze 12:2 [g]Isa 41:8-9 [h]Isa 44:26 [i]Isa 26:3 **42:20** [j]Jer 6:10 **42:21** [k]ver 4 **42:22** [l]Isa 24:18 [m]Isa 24:22

42:23 [n]Isa 48:18 **42:24** [o]Isa 30:15 **42:25** [p]2Ki 25:9 [q]Isa 29:13; 47:7; 57:1,11; Hos 7:9 **43:1** [r]ver 7 [s]Ge 32:28; Isa 44:21 [t]Isa 44:2,6 [u]Isa 42:6; 45:3-4 **43:2** [v]Isa 8:7

They have become plunder,
with no one to rescue them;
they have been made loot,
with no one to say, "Send them
back."
23Which of you will listen to this
or pay close attention[n] in time
to come?
24Who handed Jacob over to become
loot,
and Israel to the plunderers?
Was it not the LORD,
against whom we have sinned?
For they would not follow[o] his
ways;
they did not obey his law.
25So he poured out on them his
burning anger,
the violence of war.
It enveloped them in flames,[p] yet
they did not understand;
it consumed them, but they did
not take it to heart.[q]

Israel's Only Savior

43 But now, this is what the LORD
says—
he who created you, O Jacob,
he who formed[r] you, O Israel:[s]
"Fear not, for I have redeemed[t]
you;
I have summoned you by
name;[u] you are mine.
2When you pass through the
waters,[v]

43:1–3

PROMISE 1

GOD IN THE PRESSURE COOKER

Boy, can life get tough! Sometimes the pressures seem to come from every direction. You dread the ring of the phone; a knock on the door makes you cringe. God's ancient people felt pressures as well. But in the pit of pressure, Judah's people could hear God's voice calling out comfort.

Because God knows the potential value of pressure in life (see James 1), he doesn't promise to get us out of our trouble. But he does say, "I will be with you," and that the pressure or trial "will not sweep over you." He doesn't promise deliverance, but he does promise presence. In fact, one of the values of experiencing pressure is that it increases our awareness of God's presence. Write these few verses on a 3 x 5 card and keep them close by. Memorize them. Their message from God will comfort and encourage you when life's pressures mount.

For the next Promise 1 reading go to page 802.

I will be with you;[w]
and when you pass through the rivers,
they will not sweep over you.
When you walk through the fire,[x]
you will not be burned;
the flames will not set you ablaze.[y]
3 For I am the LORD, your God,[z]
the Holy One of Israel, your Savior;
I give Egypt for your ransom,
Cush[a][a] and Seba in your stead.[b]
4 Since you are precious and honored in my sight,
and because I love[c] you,
I will give men in exchange for you,
and people in exchange for your life.
5 Do not be afraid,[d] for I am with you;[e]
I will bring your children[f] from the east
and gather you from the west.

7 →PG. 778

6 I will say to the north, 'Give them up!'
and to the south,[g] 'Do not hold them back.'
Bring my sons from afar
and my daughters[h] from the ends of the earth—
7 everyone who is called by my name,[i]
whom I created for my glory,
whom I formed and made.[j]"

8 Lead out those who have eyes but are blind,[k]
who have ears but are deaf.[l]
9 All the nations gather together[m]
and the peoples assemble.
Which of them foretold[n] this
and proclaimed to us the former things?
Let them bring in their witnesses to prove they were right,
so that others may hear and say,
"It is true."

7 →PG. 785

10 "You are my witnesses," declares the LORD,
"and my servant[o] whom I have chosen,
so that you may know and believe me
and understand that I am he.
Before me no god[p] was formed,
nor will there be one after me.
11 I, even I, am the LORD,
and apart from me there is no savior.[q]
12 I have revealed and saved and proclaimed—
I, and not some foreign god[r] among you.
You are my witnesses,[s]" declares the LORD, "that I am God.
13 Yes, and from ancient days[t] I am he.
No one can deliver out of my hand.
When I act, who can reverse it?"[u]

God's Mercy and Israel's Unfaithfulness

14 This is what the LORD says—
your Redeemer, the Holy One of Israel:
"For your sake I will send to Babylon
and bring down as fugitives[v] all the Babylonians,[b][w]
in the ships in which they took pride.
15 I am the LORD, your Holy One,
Israel's Creator, your King."

16 This is what the LORD says—
he who made a way through the sea,
a path through the mighty waters,[x]
17 who drew out[y] the chariots and horses,
the army and reinforcements together,[z]
and they lay there, never to rise again,
extinguished, snuffed out like a wick:
18 "Forget the former things;
do not dwell on the past.
19 See, I am doing a new thing![a]
Now it springs up; do you not perceive it?
I am making a way in the desert[b]
and streams in the wasteland.
20 The wild animals honor me,
the jackals[c] and the owls,
because I provide water[d] in the desert
and streams in the wasteland,
to give drink to my people, my chosen,
21 the people I formed for myself
that they may proclaim my praise.[e]

22 "Yet you have not called upon me, O Jacob,
you have not wearied yourselves for me, O Israel.[f]
23 You have not brought me sheep for burnt offerings,
nor honored[g] me with your sacrifices.[h]
I have not burdened you with grain offerings
nor wearied you with demands[i] for incense.[j]

43:2 [w] Dt 31:6,8 [x] Isa 29:6; 30:27 [y] Ps 66:12; Da 3:25-27
43:3 [z] Ex 20:2 [a] Isa 20:3 [b] Pr 21:18
43:4 [c] Isa 63:9
43:5 [d] Isa 44:2 [e] Jer 30:10-11 [f] Isa 41:8
43:6 [g] Ps 107:3 [h] 2Co 6:18
43:7 [i] Isa 56:5; 63:19; Jas 2:7 [j] ver 1,21; Ps 100:3; Eph 2:10
43:8 [k] Isa 6:9-10 [l] Isa 42:20; Eze 12:2
43:9 [m] Isa 41:1 [n] Isa 41:26
43:10 [o] Isa 41:8-9 [p] Isa 44:6,8
43:11 [q] Isa 45:21
43:12 [r] Dt 32:12; Ps 81:9 [s] Isa 44:8
43:13 [t] Ps 90:2 [u] Job 9:12; Isa 14:27
43:14 [v] Isa 13:14-15 [w] Isa 23:13
43:16 [x] Ps 77:19; Isa 11:15; 51:10
43:17 [y] Ps 118:12; Isa 1:31 [z] Ex 14:9
43:19 [a] 2Co 5:17; Rev 21:5 [b] Ex 17:6; Nu 20:11
43:20 [c] Isa 13:22 [d] Isa 48:21
43:21 [e] Ps 102:18; 1Pe 2:9
43:22 [f] Isa 30:11
43:23 [g] Zec 7:5-6; Mal 1:6-8 [h] Am 5:25 [i] Jer 7:22 [j] Ex 30:35; Lev 2:1

a *3* That is, the upper Nile region b *14* Or *Chaldeans*

24 You have not bought any fragrant
calamus[k] for me,
or lavished on me the fat of your
sacrifices.
But you have burdened me with
your sins
and wearied[l] me with your
offenses.[m]
25 "I, even I, am he who blots out
your transgressions,[n] for my
own sake,[o]
and remembers your sins no
more.[p]
26 Review the past for me,
let us argue the matter
together;[q]
state the case[r] for your
innocence.
27 Your first father sinned;
your spokesmen[s] rebelled
against me.
28 So I will disgrace the dignitaries of
your temple,
and I will consign Jacob to
destruction[a]
and Israel to scorn.[t]

Israel the Chosen

44 "But now listen, O Jacob, my
servant,[u]
Israel, whom I have chosen.
2 This is what the LORD says—
he who made you, who formed
you in the womb,
and who will help[v] you:
Do not be afraid, O Jacob, my
servant,
Jeshurun,[w] whom I have chosen.
3 For I will pour water[x] on the
thirsty land,
and streams on the dry ground;
I will pour out my Spirit[y] on your
offspring,
and my blessing on your
descendants.[z]
4 They will spring up like grass in a
meadow,
like poplar trees[a] by flowing
streams.[b]
5 One will say, 'I belong to the LORD';
another will call himself by the
name of Jacob;
still another will write on his
hand,[c] 'The LORD's,'[d]
and will take the name Israel.

The LORD, Not Idols

6 "This is what the LORD says—
Israel's King[e] and Redeemer,[f]
the LORD Almighty:
I am the first and I am the last;[g]
apart from me there is no God.
7 Who then is like me? Let him
proclaim it.
Let him declare and lay out
before me
what has happened since I
established my ancient
people,
and what is yet to come—
yes, let him foretell[h] what will
come.
8 Do not tremble, do not be afraid.
Did I not proclaim this and
foretell it long ago?
You are my witnesses. Is there any
God[i] besides me?
No, there is no other Rock;[j] I
know not one."
9 All who make idols are nothing,
and the things they treasure are
worthless.[k]
Those who would speak up for
them are blind;
they are ignorant, to their own
shame.
10 Who shapes a god and casts an
idol,
which can profit him nothing?[l]
11 He and his kind will be put to
shame;[m]
craftsmen are nothing but men.
Let them all come together and
take their stand;
they will be brought down to
terror and infamy.[n]
12 The blacksmith[o] takes a tool
and works with it in the coals;
he shapes an idol with hammers,
he forges it with the might of his
arm.[p]
He gets hungry and loses his
strength;
he drinks no water and grows
faint.
13 The carpenter[q] measures with a
line
and makes an outline with a
marker;
he roughs it out with chisels
and marks it with compasses.
He shapes it in the form of man,[r]
of man in all his glory,
that it may dwell in a shrine.[s]
14 He cut down cedars,
or perhaps took a cypress or oak.
He let it grow among the trees of
the forest,
or planted a pine, and the rain
made it grow.
15 It is man's fuel[t] for burning;
some of it he takes and warms
himself,
he kindles a fire and bakes
bread.

43:24 [k]Ex 30:23 [l]Isa 1:14; 7:13 [m]Mal 2:17
43:25 [n]Ac 3:19 [o]Isa 37:35; Eze 36:22 [p]Isa 38:17; Jer 31:34
43:26 [q]Isa 1:18 [r]Isa 41:1; 50:8
43:27 [s]Isa 9:15; 28:7; Jer 5:31
43:28 [t]Jer 24:9; Eze 5:15
44:1 [u]ver 21; Jer 30:10; 46:27-28
44:2 [v]Isa 41:10 [w]Dt 32:15
44:3 [x]Joel 3:18 [y]Joel 2:28; Ac 2:17 [z]Isa 61:9; 65:23
44:4 [a]Lev 23:40 [b]Job 40:22
44:5 [c]Ex 13:9 [d]Zec 8:20-22
44:6 [e]Isa 41:21 [f]Isa 43:1 [g]Isa 41:4; Rev 1:8,17; 22:13
44:7 [h]Isa 41:22,26
44:8 [i]Isa 43:10 [j]Dt 4:35; 1Sa 2:2
44:9 [k]Isa 41:24
44:10 [l]Isa 41:29; Jer 10:5; Ac 19:26
44:11 [m]Isa 1:29 [n]Isa 42:17
44:12 [o]Isa 40:19; 41:6-7 [p]Jer 10:3-5; Ac 17:29
44:13 [q]Isa 41:7 [r]Ps 115:4-7 [s]Jdg 17:4-5
44:15 [t]ver 19

[a] *28* The Hebrew term refers to the irrevocable giving over of things or persons to the LORD, often by totally destroying them.

But he also fashions a god and
worships it;
he makes an idol and bows[u]
down to it.
16Half of the wood he burns in the
fire;
over it he prepares his meal,
he roasts his meat and eats his
fill.
He also warms himself and says,
"Ah! I am warm; I see the fire."
17From the rest he makes a god, his
idol;
he bows down to it and
worships.
He prays[v] to it and says,
"Save[w] me; you are my god."
18They know nothing, they
understand[x] nothing;
their eyes[y] are plastered over so
they cannot see,
and their minds closed so they
cannot understand.
19No one stops to think,
no one has the knowledge or
understanding[z] to say,
"Half of it I used for fuel;
I even baked bread over its coals,
I roasted meat and I ate.
Shall I make a detestable[a] thing
from what is left?
Shall I bow down to a block of
wood?"
20He feeds on ashes,[b] a deluded[c]
heart misleads him;
he cannot save himself, or say,
"Is not this thing in my right
hand a lie?[d]"

21"Remember[e] these things,
O Jacob,
for you are my servant, O Israel.
I have made you, you are my
servant;[f]
O Israel, I will not forget you.[g]
22I have swept away[h] your offenses
like a cloud,
your sins like the morning mist.
Return[i] to me,
for I have redeemed[j] you."

23Sing for joy,[k] O heavens, for the
LORD has done this;
shout aloud, O earth[l] beneath.
Burst into song, you mountains,[m]
you forests and all your trees,
for the LORD has redeemed Jacob,
he displays his glory[n] in Israel.

Jerusalem to Be Inhabited

24"This is what the LORD says—
your Redeemer,[o] who formed
you in the womb:

I am the LORD,
who has made all things,
who alone stretched out the
heavens,[p]
who spread out the earth by
myself,
25who foils[q] the signs of false
prophets
and makes fools of diviners,[r]
who overthrows the learning of the
wise[s]
and turns it into nonsense,[t]
26who carries out the words[u] of his
servants
and fulfills[v] the predictions of
his messengers,

who says of Jerusalem, 'It shall be
inhabited,'
of the towns of Judah, 'They
shall be built,'
and of their ruins, 'I will restore
them,'[w]
27who says to the watery deep, 'Be
dry,
and I will dry up your streams,'
28who says of Cyrus,[x] 'He is my
shepherd
and will accomplish all that I
please;
he will say of Jerusalem,[y] "Let it
be rebuilt,"
and of the temple,[z] "Let its
foundations be laid." '

45 "This is what the LORD says to his
anointed,
to Cyrus, whose right hand I take
hold[a] of
to subdue nations[b] before him
and to strip kings of their armor,
to open doors before him
so that gates will not be shut:
2I will go before you
and will level[c] the mountains[a];
I will break down gates of bronze
and cut through bars of iron.[d]
3I will give you the treasures[e] of
darkness,
riches stored in secret places,[f]
so that you may know[g] that I am
the LORD,
the God of Israel, who summons
you by name.[h]
4For the sake of Jacob my servant,[i]
of Israel my chosen,
I summon you by name
and bestow on you a title of
honor,
though you do not
acknowledge[j] me.
5I am the LORD, and there is no
other;[k]
apart from me there is no God.[l]

44:15 [u]2Ch 25:14 **44:17** [v]1Ki 18:26 [w]Isa 45:20 **44:18** [x]Isa 1:3 [y]Isa 6:9-10 **44:19** [z]Isa 5:13; 27:11; 45:20 [a]Dt 27:15 **44:20** [b]Ps 102:9 [c]Job 15:31; Ro 1:21-23,28; 2Th 2:11; 2Ti 3:13 [d]Isa 59:3,4,13; Ro 1:25 **44:21** [e]Isa 46:8; Zec 10:9 [f]ver 1-2 [g]Isa 49:15 **44:22** [h]Isa 43:25; Ac 3:19 [i]Isa 55:7 [j]1Co 6:20 **44:23** [k]Isa 42:10 [l]Ps 148:7 [m]Ps 98:8 [n]Isa 61:3 **44:24** [o]Isa 43:14 [p]Isa 42:5 **44:25** [q]Ps 33:10 [r]Isa 47:13 [s]1Co 1:27 [t]2Sa 15:31; 1Co 1:19-20 **44:26** [u]Zec 1:6 [v]Isa 55:11; Mt 5:18 [w]Isa 49:8-21 **44:28** [x]2Ch 36:22 [y]Isa 14:32 [z]Ezr 1:2-4 **45:1** [a]Ps 73:23; Isa 41:13; 42:6 [b]Jer 50:35 **45:2** [c]Isa 40:4 [d]Ps 107:16; Jer 51:30 **45:3** [e]Jer 50:37 [f]Jer 41:8 [g]Isa 41:23 [h]Ex 33:12; Isa 43:1 **45:4** [i]Isa 41:8-9 [j]Ac 17:23 **45:5** [k]Isa 44:8 [l]Ps 18:31

a2 Dead Sea Scrolls and Septuagint; the meaning of the word in the Masoretic Text is uncertain.

I will strengthen you,[m]
though you have not
acknowledged me,
6so that from the rising of the sun
to the place of its setting[n]
men may know there is none
besides me.[o]
I am the LORD, and there is no
other.
7I form the light and create
darkness,
I bring prosperity and create
disaster;[p]
I, the LORD, do all these things.

8"You heavens above, rain[q] down
righteousness;[r]
let the clouds shower it down.
Let the earth open wide,
let salvation[s] spring up,
let righteousness grow with it;
I, the LORD, have created it.

9"Woe to him who quarrels[t] with
his Maker,
to him who is but a potsherd
among the potsherds on the
ground.
Does the clay say to the potter,[u]
'What are you making?'
Does your work say,
'He has no hands'?
10Woe to him who says to his father,
'What have you begotten?'
or to his mother,
'What have you brought to
birth?'

11"This is what the LORD says—
the Holy One of Israel, and its
Maker:
Concerning things to come,
do you question me about my
children,
or give me orders about the work
of my hands?[v]
12It is I who made the earth
and created mankind upon it.
My own hands stretched out the
heavens;[w]
I marshaled their starry hosts.[x]
13I will raise up Cyrus[a][y] in my
righteousness:
I will make all his ways straight.
He will rebuild my city
and set my exiles free,
but not for a price or reward,[z]
says the LORD Almighty."

14This is what the LORD says:

"The products of Egypt and the
merchandise of Cush,[b]
and those tall Sabeans—
they will come over to you
and will be yours;
they will trudge behind you,
coming over to you in chains.[a]
They will bow down before you
and plead[b] with you, saying,
'Surely God is with you,[c] and
there is no other;
there is no other god.' "

15Truly you are a God who hides[d]
himself,
O God and Savior of Israel.
16All the makers of idols will be put
to shame and disgraced;[e]
they will go off into disgrace
together.
17But Israel will be saved[f] by the
LORD
with an everlasting salvation;[g]
you will never be put to shame or
disgraced,
to ages everlasting.

18For this is what the LORD says—
he who created the heavens,
he is God;
he who fashioned and made the
earth,
he founded it;
he did not create it to be empty,[h]
but formed it to be
inhabited[i]—
he says:
"I am the LORD,
and there is no other.[j]
19I have not spoken in secret,[k]
from somewhere in a land of
darkness;
I have not said to Jacob's
descendants,[l]
'Seek me in vain.'
I, the LORD, speak the truth;
I declare what is right.[m]

20"Gather together[n] and come;
assemble, you fugitives from the
nations.
Ignorant[o] are those who carry[p]
about idols of wood,
who pray to gods that cannot
save.[q]
21Declare what is to be, present it—
let them take counsel together.
Who foretold[r] this long ago,
who declared it from the distant
past?
Was it not I, the LORD?
And there is no God apart from
me,[s]
a righteous God and a Savior;
there is none but me.

22"Turn[t] to me and be saved,[u]
all you ends of the earth;[v]
for I am God, and there is no
other.
23By myself I have sworn,[w]

45:5
[m]Ps 18:39
45:6
[n]Isa 43:5;
Mal 1:11
[o]ver 5,18
45:7
[p]Isa 31:2;
Am 3:6
45:8
[q]Ps 72:6;
Joel 3:18
[r]Ps 85:11;
Isa 60:21;
61:10,11;
Hos 10:12
[s]Isa 12:3
45:9
[t]Job 15:25
[u]Isa 29:16;
Ro 9:20-21*
45:11
[v]Isa 19:25
45:12
[w]Ge 2:1;
Isa 42:5
[x]Ne 9:6
45:13
[y]2Ch 36:22;
Isa 41:2
[z]Isa 52:3
45:14
[a]Isa 14:1-2
[b]Jer 16:19;
Zec 8:20-23
[c]1Co 14:25
45:15
[d]Ps 44:24
45:16
[e]Isa 44:9,11
45:17
[f]Ro 11:26
[g]Isa 26:4
45:18
[h]Ge 1:2
[i]Ge 1:26;
Isa 42:5
[j]ver 5
45:19
[k]Isa 48:16
[l]Isa 41:8
[m]Dt 30:11
45:20
[n]Isa 43:9
[o]Isa 44:19
[p]Isa 46:1;
Jer 10:5
[q]Isa 44:17;
46:6-7
45:21
[r]Isa 41:22
[s]ver 5
45:22
[t]Zec 12:10
[u]Nu 21:8-9;
2Ch 20:12
[v]Isa 49:6,12
45:23
[w]Ge 22:16

a *13* Hebrew *him* **b** *14* That is, the upper Nile region

my mouth has uttered in all
integrity[x]
a word that will not be
revoked:[y]
Before me every knee will bow;
by me every tongue will swear.[z]
24They will say of me, 'In the LORD
alone
are righteousness[a] and
strength.' "
All who have raged against him
will come to him and be put to
shame.[b]
25But in the LORD all the descendants
of Israel
will be found righteous and will
exult.[c]

Gods of Babylon

46 Bel[d] bows down, Nebo stoops
low;
their idols are borne by beasts of
burden.[a]
The images that are carried[e] about
are burdensome,
a burden for the weary.
2They stoop and bow down
together;
unable to rescue the burden,
they themselves go off into
captivity.[f]

3"Listen[g] to me, O house of Jacob,
all you who remain of the house
of Israel,
you whom I have upheld since you
were conceived,
and have carried since your
birth.
4Even to your old age and gray
hairs[h]
I am he,[i] I am he who will
sustain you.
I have made you and I will carry
you;
I will sustain you and I will
rescue you.

5"To whom will you compare me or
count me equal?
To whom will you liken me that
we may be compared?[j]
6Some pour out gold from their
bags
and weigh out silver on the
scales;
they hire a goldsmith[k] to make it
into a god,
and they bow down and worship
it.[l]
7They lift it to their shoulders and
carry[m] it;
they set it up in its place, and
there it stands.
From that spot it cannot move.

45:23 [x]Heb 6:13 [y]Isa 55:11 [z]Ps 63:11; Isa 19:18; Ro 14:11*; Php 2:10-11 **45:24** [a]Jer 33:16 [b]Isa 41:11 **45:25** [c]Isa 41:16 **46:1** [d]Isa 21:9; Jer 50:2; 51:44 [e]Isa 45:20 **46:2** [f]Jdg 18:17-18; 2Sa 5:21 **46:3** [g]ver 12 **46:4** [h]Ps 71:18 [i]Isa 43:13 **46:5** [j]Isa 40:18,25 **46:6** [k]Isa 40:19 [l]Isa 44:17 **46:7** [m]ver 1

Though one cries out to it, it does
not answer;
it cannot save[n] him from his
troubles.

8"Remember[o] this, fix it in mind,
take it to heart, you rebels.
9Remember the former things, those
of long ago;[p]
I am God, and there is no other;
I am God, and there is none like
me.[q]
10I make known the end from the
beginning,
from ancient times,[r] what is
still to come.
I say: My purpose will stand,[s]
and I will do all that I please.
11From the east I summon a bird of
prey;
from a far-off land, a man to
fulfill my purpose.
What I have said, that will I bring
about;
what I have planned, that will I
do.
12Listen[t] to me, you
stubborn-hearted,
you who are far from
righteousness.[u]
13I am bringing my righteousness
near,
it is not far away;
and my salvation will not be
delayed.
I will grant salvation to Zion,
my splendor[v] to Israel.

The Fall of Babylon

47 "Go down, sit in the dust,
Virgin Daughter[w] of Babylon;
sit on the ground without a throne,
Daughter of the Babylonians.[b][x]
No more will you be called
tender or delicate.[y]
2Take millstones[z] and grind[a]
flour;
take off your veil.[b]
Lift up your skirts,[c] bare your legs,
and wade through the streams.
3Your nakedness[d] will be exposed
and your shame[e] uncovered.
I will take vengeance;[f]
I will spare no one."

4Our Redeemer—the LORD Almighty
is his name[g]—
is the Holy One of Israel.

5"Sit in silence, go into darkness,[h]
Daughter of the Babylonians;
no more will you be called
queen of kingdoms.[i]
6I was angry[j] with my people

[n]Isa 44:17; Isa 45:20 **46:8** [o]Isa 44:21 **46:9** [p]Dt 32:7 [q]Isa 45:5,21 **46:10** [r]Isa 45:21 [s]Pr 19:21; Ac 5:39 **46:12** [t]ver 3 [u]Ps 119:150; Isa 48:1; Jer 2:5 **46:13** [v]Isa 44:23 **47:1** [w]Isa 23:12 [x]Ps 137:8; Jer 50:42; 51:33; Zec 2:7 [y]Dt 28:56 **47:2** [z]Ex 11:5; Mt 24:41 [a]Jdg 16:21 [b]Ge 24:65 [c]Isa 32:11 **47:3** [d]Eze 16:37; Na 3:5 [e]Isa 20:4 [f]Isa 34:8 **47:4** [g]Jer 50:34 **47:5** [h]Isa 13:10 [i]Isa 13:19 **47:6** [j]2Ch 28:9

a *1* Or *are but beasts and cattle* **b** *1* Or *Chaldeans;* also in verse 5

and desecrated my inheritance;
I gave them into your hand,[k]
and you showed them no mercy.
Even on the aged
you laid a very heavy yoke.
7You said, 'I will continue forever—
the eternal queen!'[l]
But you did not consider these
things
or reflect[m] on what might
happen.[n]

8"Now then, listen, you wanton
creature,
lounging in your security[o]
and saying to yourself,
'I am, and there is none besides
me.[p]
I will never be a widow[q]
or suffer the loss of children.'
9Both of these will overtake you
in a moment,[r] on a single day:
loss of children[s] and
widowhood.
They will come upon you in full
measure,
in spite of your many sorceries[t]
and all your potent spells.[u]
10You have trusted[v] in your
wickedness
and have said, 'No one sees
me.'[w]
Your wisdom[x] and knowledge
mislead[y] you
when you say to yourself,
'I am, and there is none besides
me.'
11Disaster will come upon you,
and you will not know how to
conjure it away.
A calamity will fall upon you
that you cannot ward off with a
ransom;
a catastrophe you cannot foresee
will suddenly[z] come upon you.

12"Keep on, then, with your magic
spells
and with your many sorceries,[a]
which you have labored at since
childhood.
Perhaps you will succeed,
perhaps you will cause terror.
13All the counsel you have received
has only worn you out![b]
Let your astrologers[c] come
forward,
those stargazers who make
predictions month by
month,
let them save[d] you from what is
coming upon you.
14Surely they are like stubble;[e]
the fire will burn them up.
They cannot even save themselves
from the power of the flame.[f]
Here are no coals to warm anyone;
here is no fire to sit by.
15That is all they can do for you—
these you have labored with
and trafficked[g] with since
childhood.
Each of them goes on in his error;
there is not one that can save
you.

Stubborn Israel

48 "Listen to this, O house of Jacob,
you who are called by the name
of Israel
and come from the line of Judah,
you who take oaths in the name of
the LORD
and invoke[h] the God of Israel—
but not in truth[i] or
righteousness—
2you who call yourselves citizens of
the holy city[j]
and rely[k] on the God of Israel—
the LORD Almighty is his name:
3I foretold the former things[l] long
ago,
my mouth announced[m] them
and I made them known;
then suddenly I acted, and they
came to pass.
4For I knew how stubborn[n] you
were;
the sinews of your neck[o] were
iron,
your forehead[p] was bronze.
5Therefore I told you these things
long ago;
before they happened I
announced them to you
so that you could not say,
'My idols did them;[q]
my wooden image and metal
god ordained them.'
6You have heard these things; look
at them all.
Will you not admit them?

"From now on I will tell you of
new things,
of hidden things unknown to
you.
7They are created now, and not long
ago;
you have not heard of them
before today.
So you cannot say,
'Yes, I knew of them.'
8You have neither heard nor
understood;
from of old your ear has not
been open.
Well do I know how treacherous
you are;
you were called a rebel[r] from
birth.
9For my own name's sake I delay
my wrath;[s]

47:6 [k]Isa 10:13
47:7 [l]ver 5; Rev 18:7 [m]Isa 42:23,25 [n]Dt 32:29
47:8 [o]Isa 32:9 [p]Isa 45:6; Zep 2:15 [q]Rev 18:7
47:9 [r]Ps 73:19; 1Th 5:3; Rev 18:8-10 [s]Isa 13:18 [t]Na 3:4 [u]Rev 18:23
47:10 [v]Ps 52:7; 62:10 [w]Isa 29:15 [x]Isa 5:21 [y]Isa 44:20
47:11 [z]1Th 5:3
47:12 [a]ver 9
47:13 [b]Isa 57:10; Jer 51:58 [c]Isa 44:25 [d]ver 15
47:14 [e]Isa 5:24; Na 1:10 [f]Isa 10:17; Jer 51:30,32,58
47:15 [g]Rev 18:11
48:1 [h]Isa 58:2 [i]Jer 4:2
48:2 [j]Isa 52:1 [k]Isa 10:20; Mic 3:11; Ro 2:17
48:3 [l]Isa 41:22 [m]Isa 45:21
48:4 [n]Dt 31:27 [o]Ex 32:9; Ac 7:51 [p]Eze 3:9
48:5 [q]Jer 44:15-18
48:8 [r]Dt 9:7,24; Ps 58:3
48:9 [s]Ps 78:38; Isa 30:18

for the sake of my praise I hold
it back from you,
so as not to cut you off.[t]
10See, I have refined you, though not
as silver;
I have tested you in the
furnace[u] of affliction.
11For my own sake,[v] for my own
sake, I do this.
How can I let myself be
defamed?[w]
I will not yield my glory to
another.[x]

Israel Freed

12"Listen[y] to me, O Jacob,
Israel, whom I have called:
I am he;
I am the first and I am the
last.[z]
13My own hand laid the foundations
of the earth,[a]
and my right hand spread out
the heavens;[b]
when I summon them,
they all stand up together.[c]
14"Come together,[d] all of you, and
listen:
Which of ⌊the idols⌋ has foretold
these things?
The LORD's chosen ally
will carry out his purpose[e]
against Babylon;
his arm will be against the
Babylonians.[a]
15I, even I, have spoken;
yes, I have called[f] him.
I will bring him,
and he will succeed in his
mission.
16"Come near[g] me and listen to
this:

48:14–22 PROMISE 3

ABANDONING BABYLON

Israel's people seemed to abandon any attempt to preserve their spiritual, moral, or ethical integrity. Through Isaiah, God pointed to the wreckage of their lives and offered a better alternative (vv. 17–19). What did Israel need to do? Abandon "Babylon." The word "Babylon" often represented sin, and in this case is used that way. Notice the process. First, "Leave Babylon"—flee the influence that is dragging you to destruction (v. 20). Second, celebrate your salvation and enjoy God's blessing (vv. 20–21). Finally, observe what happens to the wicked.

God's closing word in verse 22 is a grabber. Think about it.

For the next Promise 3 reading go to page 795.

48:9 [t]Ne 9:31
48:10 [u]1Ki 8:51
48:11 [v]1Sa 12:22; Isa 37:35 [w]Dt 32:27; Jer 14:7,21; Eze 20:9,14,22, 44 [x]Isa 42:8
48:12 [y]Isa 46:3 [z]Isa 41:4; Rev 1:17; 22:13
48:13 [a]Heb 1:10-12 [b]Ex 20:11 [c]Isa 40:26
48:14 [d]Isa 43:9 [e]Isa 46:10-11
48:15 [f]Isa 45:1
48:16 [g]Isa 41:1 [h]Isa 45:19 [i]Zec 2:9,11
48:17 [j]Isa 49:7 [k]Isa 43:14 [l]Isa 49:10 [m]Ps 32:8
48:18 [n]Dt 32:29 [o]Ps 119:165; Isa 66:12 [p]Isa 45:8
48:19 [q]Ge 22:17 [r]Isa 56:5; 66:22
48:20 [s]Jer 50:8; 51:6, 45; Zec 2:6-7; Rev 18:4 [t]Isa 49:13 [u]Isa 52:9; 63:9
48:21 [v]Isa 41:17 [w]Isa 30:25 [x]Ex 17:6; Nu 20:11; Ps 105:41; Isa 35:6
48:22 [y]Isa 57:21
49:1 [z]Isa 44:24; 46:3; Mt 1:20 [a]Isa 7:14; 9:6; 44:2; Jer 1:5; Gal 1:15
49:2 [b]Isa 11:4; Rev 1:16
49:3 [c]Zec 3:8

"From the first announcement I
have not spoken in secret;[h]
at the time it happens, I am
there."
And now the Sovereign LORD has
sent[i] me,
with his Spirit.
17This is what the LORD says—
your Redeemer,[j] the Holy
One[k] of Israel:
"I am the LORD your God,
who teaches you what is best for
you,
who directs[l] you in the way[m]
you should go.
18If only you had paid attention[n] to
my commands,
your peace[o] would have been
like a river,
your righteousness[p] like the
waves of the sea.
19Your descendants would have been
like the sand,
your children like its numberless
grains;[q]
their name would never be cut
off[r]
nor destroyed from before me."
20Leave Babylon,
flee[s] from the Babylonians!
Announce this with shouts of joy[t]
and proclaim it.
Send it out to the ends of the
earth;
say, "The LORD has redeemed[u]
his servant Jacob."
21They did not thirst[v] when he led
them through the deserts;
he made water flow[w] for them
from the rock;
he split the rock
and water gushed out.[x]
22"There is no peace," says the LORD,
"for the wicked."[y]

The Servant of the LORD

49 Listen to me, you islands;
hear this, you distant nations:
Before I was born[z] the LORD
called[a] me;
from my birth he has made
mention of my name.
2He made my mouth like a
sharpened sword,[b]
in the shadow of his hand he hid
me;
he made me into a polished arrow
and concealed me in his quiver.
3He said to me, "You are my
servant,[c]

a *14* Or *Chaldeans;* also in verse 20

Israel, in whom I will display my
splendor.[d]"
4But I said, "I have labored to no
purpose;
I have spent my strength in
vain[e] and for nothing.
Yet what is due me is in the LORD's
hand,
and my reward[f] is with my
God."

7 →PG. 788

5And now the LORD says—
he who formed me in the womb
to be his servant
to bring Jacob back to him
and gather Israel[g] to himself,
for I am honored[h] in the eyes of
the LORD
and my God has been my
strength—
6he says:
"It is too small a thing for you to
be my servant
to restore the tribes of Jacob
and bring back those of Israel I
have kept.
I will also make you a light for the
Gentiles,[i]
that you may bring my salvation
to the ends of the earth."[j]

7This is what the LORD says—
the Redeemer and Holy One of
Israel[k]—
to him who was despised[l] and
abhorred by the nation,
to the servant of rulers:
"Kings[m] will see you and rise up,
princes will see and bow down,
because of the LORD, who is
faithful,
the Holy One of Israel, who has
chosen you."

Restoration of Israel

8This is what the LORD says:

"In the time of my favor[n] I will
answer you,
and in the day of salvation I will
help you;[o]
I will keep[p] you and will make
you
to be a covenant for the
people,[q]
to restore the land[r]
and to reassign its desolate
inheritances,
9to say to the captives,[s] 'Come
out,'
and to those in darkness, 'Be
free!'

"They will feed beside the roads
and find pasture on every barren
hill.[t]
10They will neither hunger nor
thirst,[u]
nor will the desert heat or the
sun beat upon them.[v]
He who has compassion[w] on them
will guide them
and lead them beside springs[x]
of water.
11I will turn all my mountains into
roads,
and my highways[y] will be raised
up.[z]
12See, they will come from afar[a]—
some from the north, some from
the west,
some from the region of
Aswan.[a]"

1 →PG. 791

13Shout for joy, O heavens;
rejoice, O earth;
burst into song, O mountains![b]
For the LORD comforts[c] his people
and will have compassion on his
afflicted ones.

14But Zion said, "The LORD has
forsaken me,
the Lord has forgotten me."

15"Can a mother forget the baby at
her breast
and have no compassion on the
child she has borne?
Though she may forget,
I will not forget you![d]
16See, I have engraved[e] you on the
palms of my hands;
your walls[f] are ever before me.
17Your sons hasten back,
and those who laid you waste[g]
depart from you.
18Lift up your eyes and look around;
all your sons gather[h] and come
to you.
As surely as I live,[i]" declares the
LORD,
"you will wear[j] them all as
ornaments;
you will put them on, like a
bride.

19"Though you were ruined and
made desolate[k]
and your land laid waste,[l]
now you will be too small for your
people,[m]
and those who devoured you will
be far away.
20The children born during your
bereavement
will yet say in your hearing,
'This place is too small for us;
give us more space to live in.'[n]
21Then you will say in your heart,
'Who bore me these?

a *12* Dead Sea Scrolls; Masoretic Text *Sinim*

49:3 [d]Isa 44:23
49:4 [e]Isa 65:23 [f]Isa 35:4
49:5 [g]Isa 11:12 [h]Isa 43:4
49:6 [i]Lk 2:32 [j]Ac 13:47*
49:7 [k]Isa 48:17 [l]Ps 22:6; 69:7-9 [m]Isa 52:15
49:8 [n]Ps 69:13 [o]2Co 6:2* [p]Isa 26:3 [q]Isa 42:6 [r]Isa 44:26
49:9 [s]Isa 42:7; 61:1; Lk 4:19 [t]Isa 41:18
49:10 [u]Isa 33:16 [v]Ps 121:6; Rev 7:16 [w]Isa 14:1 [x]Isa 35:7
49:11 [y]Isa 11:16 [z]Isa 40:4
49:12 [a]Isa 43:5-6
49:13 [b]Isa 44:23 [c]Isa 40:1
49:15 [d]Isa 44:21
49:16 [e]SS 8:6 [f]Ps 48:12-13; Isa 62:6
49:17 [g]Isa 10:6
49:18 [h]Isa 43:5; 54:7; Isa 60:4 [i]Isa 45:23 [j]Isa 52:1
49:19 [k]Isa 54:1,3 [l]Isa 5:6 [m]Zec 10:10
49:20 [n]Isa 54:1-3

I was bereaved and barren;
I was exiled and rejected.[o]
Who brought these up?
I was left[p] all alone,
but these—where have they come from?' "

22This is what the Sovereign LORD says:

"See, I will beckon to the Gentiles,
I will lift up my banner[q] to the peoples;
they will bring your sons in their arms
and carry your daughters on their shoulders.[r]
23Kings[s] will be your foster fathers,
and their queens your nursing mothers.[t]
They will bow down before you with their faces to the ground;
they will lick the dust[u] at your feet.
Then you will know that I am the LORD;[v]
those who hope in me will not be disappointed."

24Can plunder be taken from warriors,[w]
or captives rescued from the fierce[a]?

25But this is what the LORD says:

"Yes, captives[x] will be taken from warriors,[y]
and plunder retrieved from the fierce;
I will contend with those who contend with you,
and your children I will save.[z]
26I will make your oppressors[a] eat[b] their own flesh;
they will be drunk on their own blood,[c] as with wine.
Then all mankind will know[d]
that I, the LORD, am your Savior,
your Redeemer, the Mighty One of Jacob."

Israel's Sin and the Servant's Obedience

50 This is what the LORD says:

"Where is your mother's certificate of divorce[e]
with which I sent her away?
Or to which of my creditors did I sell[f] you?
Because of your sins you were sold;[g]
because of your transgressions your mother was sent away.
2When I came, why was there no one?
When I called, why was there no one to answer?[h]
Was my arm too short[i] to ransom you?
Do I lack the strength[j] to rescue you?
By a mere rebuke I dry up the sea,[k]
I turn rivers into a desert;
their fish rot for lack of water
and die of thirst.
3I clothe the sky with darkness
and make sackcloth[l] its covering."

4The Sovereign LORD has given me an instructed tongue,[m]
to know the word that sustains the weary.[n]
He wakens me morning by morning,[o]
wakens my ear to listen like one being taught.
5The Sovereign LORD has opened my ears,[p]
and I have not been rebellious;[q]
I have not drawn back.
6I offered my back to those who beat[r] me,
my cheeks to those who pulled out my beard;
I did not hide my face
from mocking and spitting.[s]
7Because the Sovereign LORD helps[t] me,
I will not be disgraced.
Therefore have I set my face like flint,[u]
and I know I will not be put to shame.
8He who vindicates me is near.
Who then will bring charges against me?[v]
Let us face each other![w]
Who is my accuser?
Let him confront me!
9It is the Sovereign LORD who helps[x] me.
Who is he that will condemn me?
They will all wear out like a garment;
the moths[y] will eat them up.

10Who among you fears the LORD
and obeys the word of his servant?[z]
Let him who walks in the dark,
who has no light,
trust[a] in the name of the LORD
and rely on his God.
11But now, all you who light fires

49:21 [o]Isa 5:13 [p]Isa 1:8 **49:22** [q]Isa 11:10 [r]Isa 60:4 **49:23** [s]Isa 60:3,10-11 [t]Isa 60:16 [u]Ps 72:9 [v]Mic 7:17 **49:24** [w]Mt 12:29; Lk 11:21 **49:25** [x]Isa 14:2 [y]Jer 50:33-34 [z]Isa 25:9; 35:4 **49:26** [a]Isa 9:4 [b]Isa 9:20 [c]Rev 16:6 [d]Eze 39:7 **50:1** [e]Dt 24:1; Jer 3:8; Hos 2:2 [f]Ne 5:5; Mt 18:25 [g]Dt 32:30; Isa 52:3 **50:2** [h]Isa 41:28 [i]Nu 11:23; Isa 59:1 [j]Ge 18:14 [k]Ex 14:22; Jos 3:16 **50:3** [l]Rev 6:12 **50:4** [m]Ex 4:12 [n]Mt 11:28 [o]Ps 5:3; 119:147; 143:8 **50:5** [p]Isa 35:5 [q]Mt 26:39; Jn 8:29; 14:31; 15:10; Ac 26:19; Heb 5:8 **50:6** [r]Isa 53:5; Mt 27:30; Mk 14:65; 15:19; Lk 22:63 [s]La 3:30; Mt 26:67 **50:7** [t]Isa 42:1 [u]Eze 3:8-9 **50:8** [v]Isa 43:26; Ro 8:32-34 [w]Isa 41:1 **50:9** [x]Isa 41:10 [y]Job 13:28; Isa 51:8 **50:10** [z]Isa 49:3 [a]Isa 26:4

[a]24 Dead Sea Scrolls, Vulgate and Syriac (see also Septuagint and verse 25); Masoretic Text *righteous*

and provide yourselves with
flaming torches,[b]
go, walk in the light of your fires[c]
and of the torches you have set
ablaze.
This is what you shall receive from
my hand:
You will lie down in torment.[d]

Everlasting Salvation for Zion

51 "Listen[e] to me, you who pursue
righteousness[f]
and who seek the LORD:
Look to the rock from which you
were cut
and to the quarry from which
you were hewn;
2look to Abraham,[g] your father,
and to Sarah, who gave you
birth.
When I called him he was but one,
and I blessed him and made him
many.[h]
3The LORD will surely comfort[i]
Zion
and will look with compassion
on all her ruins;[j]
he will make her deserts like
Eden,[k]
her wastelands like the garden of
the LORD.
Joy and gladness[l] will be found in
her,
thanksgiving and the sound of
singing.

4"Listen to me, my people;[m]
hear me, my nation:
The law will go out from me;
my justice[n] will become a light
to the nations.[o]
5My righteousness draws near
speedily,
my salvation is on the way,[p]
and my arm[q] will bring justice
to the nations.
The islands will look to me
and wait in hope for my arm.
6Lift up your eyes to the heavens,
look at the earth beneath;
the heavens will vanish like
smoke,[r]
the earth will wear out like a
garment[s]
and its inhabitants die like flies.
But my salvation will last forever,
my righteousness will never fail.

7"Hear me, you who know what is
right,[t]
you people who have my law in
your hearts:[u]
Do not fear the reproach of men
or be terrified by their insults.[v]
8For the moth will eat them up like
a garment;[w]
the worm will devour them like
wool.
But my righteousness will last
forever,[x]
my salvation through all
generations."

9Awake, awake! Clothe yourself with
strength,[y]
O arm of the LORD;
awake, as in days gone by,
as in generations of old.[z]
Was it not you who cut Rahab to
pieces,
who pierced that monster[a]
through?
10Was it not you who dried up the
sea,[b]
the waters of the great deep,
who made a road in the depths of
the sea
so that the redeemed might
cross over?
11The ransomed[c] of the LORD will
return.
They will enter Zion with
singing;
everlasting joy will crown their
heads.
Gladness and joy[d] will overtake
them,
and sorrow and sighing will flee
away.[e]

12"I, even I, am he who comforts[f]
you.
Who are you that you fear
mortal men,[g]
the sons of men, who are but
grass,[h]
13that you forget[i] the LORD your
Maker,[j]
who stretched out the heavens[k]
and laid the foundations of the
earth,
that you live in constant terror[l]
every day
because of the wrath of the
oppressor,
who is bent on destruction?
For where is the wrath of the
oppressor?
14 The cowering prisoners will soon
be set free;
they will not die in their dungeon,
nor will they lack bread.[m]
15For I am the LORD your God,
who churns up the sea[n] so that
its waves roar—
the LORD Almighty is his name.
16I have put my words in your
mouth[o]
and covered you with the
shadow of my hand[p]—
I who set the heavens in place,
who laid the foundations of the
earth,

50:11 [b]Pr 26:18 [c]Jas 3:6 [d]Isa 65:13-15
51:1 [e]Isa 46:3 [f]ver 7; Ps 94:15; Ro 9:30-31
51:2 [g]Isa 29:22; Ro 4:16; Heb 11:11 [h]Ge 12:2
51:3 [i]Isa 40:1 [j]Isa 52:9 [k]Ge 2:8 [l]Isa 25:9; 66:10
51:4 [m]Ps 50:7 [n]Isa 2:4 [o]Isa 42:4,6
51:5 [p]Isa 46:13 [q]Isa 40:10; 63:1,5
51:6 [r]Mt 24:35; 2Pe 3:10 [s]Ps 102:25-26
51:7 [t]ver 1 [u]Ps 37:31 [v]Mt 5:11; Ac 5:41
51:8 [w]Isa 50:9 [x]ver 6
51:9 [y]Isa 52:1 [z]Dt 4:34 [a]Ps 74:13
51:10 [b]Ex 14:22
51:11 [c]Isa 35:9 [d]Jer 33:11 [e]Rev 7:17
51:12 [f]2Co 1:4 [g]Ps 118:6; Isa 2:22 [h]Isa 40:6-7; 1Pe 1:24
51:13 [i]Isa 17:10 [j]Isa 45:11 [k]Ps 104:2; Isa 48:13 [l]Isa 7:4
51:14 [m]Isa 49:10
51:15 [n]Jer 31:35
51:16 [o]Dt 18:18; Isa 59:21 [p]Ex 33:22

and who say to Zion, 'You are
my people.' "

The Cup of the LORD's Wrath

17Awake, awake![q]
Rise up, O Jerusalem,
you who have drunk from the hand
of the LORD
the cup of his wrath,[r]
you who have drained to its dregs
the goblet that makes men
stagger.[s]
18Of all the sons[t] she bore
there was none to guide her;[u]
of all the sons she reared
there was none to take her by
the hand.
19These double calamities[v] have
come upon you—
who can comfort you?—
ruin and destruction, famine[w] and
sword—
who can[a] console you?
20Your sons have fainted;
they lie at the head of every
street,[x]
like antelope caught in a net.
They are filled with the wrath of
the LORD
and the rebuke of your God.
21Therefore hear this, you afflicted
one,
made drunk,[y] but not with
wine.
22This is what your Sovereign LORD
says,
your God, who defends[z] his
people:
"See, I have taken out of your hand
the cup[a] that made you stagger;
from that cup, the goblet of my
wrath,
you will never drink again.
23I will put it into the hands of your
tormentors,[b]
who said to you,
'Fall prostrate[c] that we may
walk[d] over you.'
And you made your back like the
ground,
like a street to be walked over."

52 Awake, awake,[e] O Zion,
clothe yourself with strength.[f]
Put on your garments of
splendor,[g]
O Jerusalem, the holy city.[h]
The uncircumcised and defiled
will not enter you again.[i]
2Shake off your dust;[j]
rise up, sit enthroned,
O Jerusalem.
Free yourself from the chains on
your neck,
O captive Daughter of Zion.

3For this is what the LORD says:

"You were sold for nothing,[k]
and without money[l] you will be
redeemed."

4For this is what the Sovereign LORD
says:

"At first my people went down to
Egypt[m] to live;
lately, Assyria has oppressed
them.

5"And now what do I have here?" declares the LORD.

"For my people have been taken
away for nothing,
and those who rule them
mock,[b]"
declares the LORD.
"And all day long
my name is constantly
blasphemed.[n]
6Therefore my people will know[o]
my name;
therefore in that day they will
know
that it is I who foretold it.
Yes, it is I."

7How beautiful on the mountains
are the feet of those who bring
good news,[p]
who proclaim peace,[q]
who bring good tidings,
who proclaim salvation,
who say to Zion,
"Your God reigns!"[r]
8Listen! Your watchmen[s] lift up
their voices;
together they shout for joy.
When the LORD returns to Zion,
they will see it with their own
eyes.
9Burst into songs of joy[t] together,
you ruins[u] of Jerusalem,
for the LORD has comforted his
people,
he has redeemed Jerusalem.[v]
10The LORD will lay bare his holy arm
in the sight of all the nations,[w]
and all the ends of the earth will
see
the salvation[x] of our God.

7 →PG. 794

11Depart,[y] depart, go out from
there!
Touch no unclean thing![z]
Come out from it and be pure,[a]
you who carry the vessels of the
LORD.
12But you will not leave in haste[b]
or go in flight;
for the LORD will go before you,[c]

51:17 [q]Isa 52:1 [r]Job 21:20; Rev 14:10; 16:19 [s]Ps 60:3 **51:18** [t]Ps 88:18 [u]Isa 49:21 **51:19** [v]Isa 47:9 [w]Isa 14:30 **51:20** [x]Isa 5:25; Jer 14:16 **51:21** [y]ver 17; Isa 29:9 **51:22** [z]Isa 49:25 [a]ver 17 **51:23** [b]Isa 49:26; Jer 25:15-17, 26,28; 49:12 [c]Zec 12:2 [d]Jos 10:24 **52:1** [e]Isa 51:17 [f]Isa 51:9 [g]Ex 28:2,40; Ps 110:3; Zec 3:4 [h]Ne 11:1; Mt 4:5; Rev 21:2 [i]Na 1:15; Rev 21:27 **52:2** [j]Isa 29:4

52:3 [k]Ps 44:12 [l]Isa 45:13 **52:4** [m]Ge 46:6 **52:5** [n]Eze 36:20; Ro 2:24* **52:6** [o]Isa 49:23 **52:7** [p]Isa 40:9; Ro 10:15* [q]Na 1:15; Eph 6:15 [r]Ps 93:1 **52:8** [s]Isa 62:6 **52:9** [t]Ps 98:4 [u]Isa 51:3 [v]Isa 48:20 **52:10** [w]Isa 66:18 [x]Ps 98:2-3; Lk 3:6 **52:11** [y]Isa 48:20 [z]Isa 1:16; 2Co 6:17* [a]2Ti 2:19 **52:12** [b]Ex 12:11 [c]Mic 2:13

[a]19 Dead Sea Scrolls, Septuagint, Vulgate and Syriac; Masoretic Text / *how can I* [b]5 Dead Sea Scrolls and Vulgate; Masoretic Text *wail*

the God of Israel will be your
rear guard.[d]

The Suffering and Glory of the Servant

13See, my servant[e] will act wisely[a];
he will be raised and lifted up
and highly exalted.[f]
14Just as there were many who were
appalled at him[b]—
his appearance was so disfigured
beyond that of any man
and his form marred beyond
human likeness—
15so will he sprinkle many nations,[c]
and kings will shut their mouths
because of him.
For what they were not told, they
will see,
and what they have not heard,
they will understand.[g]

52:12 [d]Ex 14:19 **52:13** [e]Isa 42:1 [f]Isa 57:15; Php 2:9 **52:15** [g]Ro 15:21*; Eph 3:4-5 **53:1** [h]Ro 10:16* [i]Jn 12:38* **53:2** [j]Isa 52:14 **53:3** [k]ver 4,10; Lk 18:31-33

53 Who has believed our message[h]
and to whom has the arm of the
LORD been revealed?[i]
2He grew up before him like a
tender shoot,
and like a root out of dry
ground.
He had no beauty or majesty to
attract us to him,
nothing in his appearance[j] that
we should desire him.
3He was despised and rejected by
men,
a man of sorrows, and familiar
with suffering.[k]
Like one from whom men hide
their faces

[a]13 Or *will prosper* [b]14 Hebrew *you* [c]15 Hebrew; Septuagint *so will many nations marvel at him*

53:1–12

PROMISE 6

THE SUFFERING SERVANT

How does a godly man respond when he's treated unfairly? The answer to that question can be found as we look at the way the Son of God himself responded. Isaiah 53 tells us what we need to know.

Many battles are fought over "my rights" or "what's fair" or "what I've got coming to me." In families, in churches and in the workplace, many issues that could be dropped instead become sources of pain, anguish and division. Why? Because people say, "No one is going to mess with *me* and get away with it!"

Jesus presented a different approach. Without ever diminishing his strength, his authority or his intelligence, Jesus offered an alternative to negative self-assertiveness. Look at his example as Isaiah prophesied it would happen:

1. *Jesus* did *suffer* (vv. 4–9). In this passage Isaiah used the words, "stricken," "smitten," "afflicted" "pierced," "crushed," "punishment," "wounds," "oppressed," "judgment" and "cut off" to describe what would happen to God's Son. In fact, the preceding passage tells us that "his appearance was . . . disfigured beyond that of any man and his form marred beyond human likeness" (52:14). The suffering that Jesus Christ experienced in his trials and crucifixion would be considered cruel and unusual punishment by any reasonable court today. No criminal, no matter what his crime, would be allowed to go through what Jesus suffered. Why did Jesus suffer like that?
2. *Jesus did* not *suffer because he deserved it* (vv. 4–6). Isaiah clearly taught that God's suffering Servant would take our infirmities and carry our sorrows; would be pierced for our transgressions and crushed for our iniquities; that his punishment would bring us peace; that his wounds would heal us; that our iniquity would be laid on him. Jesus suffered to pay the price for *our* sin. Hebrews 4:15 teaches that Jesus "[had] been tempted in every way, just as we are—yet was without sin." Make no mistake. Isaiah is telling us that Jesus' death was not caused by his sin, but by ours.
3. *Jesus suffered for us because we deserve it.* Isaiah left no doubt about the human condition. In fact, he accused us of the most fundamental of all sins. "We all, like sheep, have gone astray, each of us has turned to his own way" (v. 6). All sins branch from this foundational sin. From the fall of humanity (described in Genesis 3) to the last judgment (described in Matthew 25), the standard decision is the same: Will we follow God's way or our own way? Jesus never went astray, never turned to his own way; he suffered because each one of us has strayed from God's path.

   Isaiah 53:4–6 tells us Jesus' suffering was unjust, unfair and cruel. He didn't deserve it. In fact, those who inflicted his wounds were the ones who deserved it, and Jesus took the punishment to pay the price for what they were doing to him. They too are included in the list of ones for whom Christ died, as are we today.
4. *Jesus' response to those who punished him was consistent with his sinless life.* That's the kicker. Notice how Jesus responded when those who deserved the punishment inflicted it on the one person in history who didn't deserve it (v. 7).

Carefully and meditatively read Isaiah 53:7. Then read 1 Peter 2:21–25. The next time you are slighted, abused or ripped off, remember Jesus' example before deciding how to respond. As a Christian man, ask why you're responding this way and what you want your response to accomplish. Ask if the "how" corresponds to the "why" of your response. Then ask how Jesus would respond in the same situation.

For the next Promise 6 reading go to page 842.

he was despised,[l] and we
esteemed him not.

4Surely he took up our infirmities
and carried our sorrows,[m]
yet we considered him stricken by
God,[n]
smitten by him, and afflicted.
5But he was pierced for our
transgressions,[o]
he was crushed for our
iniquities;
the punishment that brought us
peace was upon him,
and by his wounds we are
healed.[p]
6We all, like sheep, have gone
astray,
each of us has turned to his own
way;
and the LORD has laid on him
the iniquity of us all.

7He was oppressed and afflicted,
yet he did not open his mouth;[q]
he was led like a lamb to the
slaughter,
and as a sheep before her
shearers is silent,
so he did not open his mouth.
8By oppression[a] and judgment he
was taken away.
And who can speak of his
descendants?
For he was cut off from the land of
the living;[r]
for the transgression[s] of my
people he was stricken.[b]
9He was assigned a grave with the
wicked,
and with the rich[t] in his death,
though he had done no violence,[u]
nor was any deceit in his
mouth.[v]

10Yet it was the LORD's will[w] to
crush[x] him and cause him
to suffer,[y]
and though the LORD makes[c] his
life a guilt offering,
he will see his offspring[z] and
prolong his days,
and the will of the LORD will
prosper in his hand.
11After the suffering[a] of his soul,
he will see the light ⌞of life⌟[d]
and be satisfied[e];
by his knowledge[f] my righteous
servant will justify[b] many,
and he will bear their iniquities.
12Therefore I will give him a portion
among the great,[g][c]
and he will divide the spoils with
the strong,[h]
because he poured out his life unto
death,[d]
and was numbered with the
transgressors.[e]
For he bore the sin of many,
and made intercession for the
transgressors.

The Future Glory of Zion

54 "Sing, O barren woman,
you who never bore a child;
burst into song, shout for joy,
you who were never in labor;
because more are the children[f] of
the desolate woman
than of her who has a
husband,[g]"
says the LORD.
2"Enlarge the place of your tent,[h]
stretch your tent curtains wide,
do not hold back;
lengthen your cords,
strengthen your stakes.[i]
3For you will spread out to the right
and to the left;
your descendants will dispossess
nations
and settle in their desolate[j]
cities.

4"Do not be afraid; you will not
suffer shame.
Do not fear disgrace; you will
not be humiliated.
You will forget the shame of your
youth
and remember no more the
reproach[k] of your
widowhood.
5For your Maker is your
husband[l]—
the LORD Almighty is his name—
the Holy One of Israel is your
Redeemer;[m]
he is called the God of all the
earth.[n]
6The LORD will call you back[o]
as if you were a wife deserted[p]
and distressed in spirit—
a wife who married young,
only to be rejected," says your
God.
7"For a brief moment[q] I
abandoned you,
but with deep compassion I will
bring you back.[r]
8In a surge of anger[s]

53:3 [l]Ps 22:6; Jn 1:10-11
53:4 [m]Mt 8:17*; [n]Jn 19:7
53:5 [o]Ro 4:25; 1Co 15:3; Heb 9:28; [p]1Pe 2:24-25
53:7 [q]Mk 14:61
53:8 [r]Da 9:26; Ac 8:32-33*; [s]ver 12
53:9 [t]Mt 27:57-60; [u]Isa 42:1-3; [v]1Pe 2:22*
53:10 [w]Isa 46:10; [x]ver 5; [y]ver 3; [z]Ps 22:30
53:11 [a]Jn 10:14-18; [b]Ro 5:18-19
53:12 [c]Php 2:9; [d]Mt 26:28,38,39,42; [e]Mk 15:27*; Lk 22:37*; 23:32
54:1 [f]Isa 49:20; [g]1Sa 2:5; Gal 4:27*
54:2 [h]Isa 49:19-20; [i]Ex 35:18; 39:40
54:3 [j]Isa 49:19
54:4 [k]Isa 51:7
54:5 [l]Jer 3:14; [m]Isa 48:17; [n]Isa 6:3
54:6 [o]Isa 49:14-21; [p]Isa 50:1-2; 62:4,12
54:7 [q]Isa 26:20; [r]Isa 49:18
54:8 [s]Isa 60:10

[a]8 Or *From arrest* [b]8 Or *away. / Yet who of his generation considered / that he was cut off from the land of the living / for the transgression of my people, / to whom the blow was due?* [c]10 Hebrew *though you make* [d]11 Dead Sea Scrolls (see also Septuagint); Masoretic Text does not have *the light ⌞of life⌟*. [e]11 Or (with Masoretic Text) *11He will see the result of the suffering of his soul / and be satisfied* [f]11 Or *by knowledge of him* [g]12 Or *many* [h]12 Or *numerous*

I hid my face from you for a
moment,
but with everlasting kindness[t]
I will have compassion on you,"
says the LORD your Redeemer.

9"To me this is like the days of
Noah,
when I swore that the waters of
Noah would never again
cover the earth.[u]
So now I have sworn not to be
angry[v] with you,
never to rebuke you again.
10Though the mountains be shaken[w]
and the hills be removed,
yet my unfailing love for you will
not be shaken[x]
nor my covenant[y] of peace be
removed,"
says the LORD, who has
compassion[z] on you.

11"O afflicted[a] city, lashed by
storms[b] and not
comforted,[c]
I will build you with stones of
turquoise,[a][d]
your foundations[e] with
sapphires.[b]
12I will make your battlements of
rubies,
your gates of sparkling jewels,
and all your walls of precious
stones.
13All your sons will be taught by the
LORD,[f]
and great will be your children's
peace.[g]
14In righteousness you will be
established:
Tyranny[h] will be far from you;
you will have nothing to fear.
Terror will be far removed;
it will not come near you.
15If anyone does attack you, it will
not be my doing;
whoever attacks you will
surrender[i] to you.

16"See, it is I who created the
blacksmith
who fans the coals into flame
and forges a weapon fit for its
work.
And it is I who have created the
destroyer to work havoc;
17 no weapon forged against you
will prevail,[j]
and you will refute[k] every
tongue that accuses you.
This is the heritage of the servants
of the LORD,
and this is their vindication from
me,"
declares the LORD.

54:8 [t]ver 10
54:9 [u]Ge 8:21 [v]Isa 12:1
54:10 [w]Ps 46:2 [x]Isa 51:6 [y]Ps 89:34 [z]ver 8
54:11 [a]Isa 14:32 [b]Isa 28:2; 29:6 [c]Isa 51:19 [d]1Ch 29:2; Rev 21:18 [e]Isa 28:16; Rev 21:19-20
54:13 [f]Jn 6:45* [g]Isa 48:18
54:14 [h]Isa 9:4
54:15 [i]Isa 41:11-16
54:17 [j]Isa 29:8 [k]Isa 45:24-25

Invitation to the Thirsty

55 "Come, all you who are thirsty,[l]
come to the waters;
and you who have no money,
come, buy[m] and eat!
Come, buy wine and milk[n]
without money and without cost.[o]
2Why spend money on what is not
bread,
and your labor on what does not
satisfy?[p]
Listen, listen to me, and eat what is
good,[q]
and your soul will delight in the
richest of fare.
3Give ear and come to me;
hear me, that your soul may
live.[r]
I will make an everlasting
covenant[s] with you,
my faithful love[t] promised to
David.[u]
4See, I have made him a witness to
the peoples,
a leader and commander[v] of
the peoples.
5Surely you will summon nations[w]
you know not,
and nations that do not know
you will hasten to you,
because of the LORD your God,
the Holy One of Israel,
for he has endowed you with
splendor."[x]

6Seek the LORD while he may be
found;[y]
call[z] on him while he is near.
7Let the wicked forsake his way
and the evil man his thoughts.[a]

1 →PG. 793

55:1 [l]Jn 4:14; 7:37 [m]La 5:4; Mt 13:44; Rev 3:18 [n]SS 5:1 [o]Hos 14:4; Mt 10:8; Rev 21:6
55:2 [p]Ps 22:26; Ecc 6:2; Hos 8:7 [q]Isa 1:19
55:3 [r]Lev 18:5; Ro 10:5 [s]Isa 61:8 [t]Isa 54:8 [u]Ac 13:34*
55:4 [v]Jer 30:9; Eze 34:23-24
55:5 [w]Isa 49:6 [x]Isa 60:9
55:6 [y]Ps 32:6; Isa 49:8; 2Co 6:1-2 [z]Isa 65:24
55:7 [a]Isa 32:7; 59:7

[a]*11* The meaning of the Hebrew for this word is uncertain. [b]*11* Or *lapis lazuli*

55:5-11

PROMISE 7

ATTRACTING OTHERS TO GOD

How can a man make a difference? How can he "make disciples of all nations" in response to the Great Commission (Matthew 28:19–20)? In verse 5, God told Israel he would make them attractive so they could bring all peoples to him. How would God do that? He would forgive their sin (vv. 6–7), change their lives so they conformed to his will (vv. 8–9), and give them his life-changing Word as a guide for their lives and as a message for others (vv. 10–11).

God has given us a Great Commission along with the resources to carry it out. Use this passage as a guide to attracting others to God.

For the next Promise 7 reading go to page 797.

Let him turn[b] to the LORD, and he
will have mercy[c] on him,
and to our God, for he will freely
pardon.[d]

8"For my thoughts are not your
thoughts,
neither are your ways my
ways,"[e]
declares the LORD.
9"As the heavens are higher than the
earth,[f]
so are my ways higher than your
ways
and my thoughts than your
thoughts.
10As the rain[g] and the snow
come down from heaven,
and do not return to it
without watering the earth
and making it bud and flourish,
so that it yields seed for the
sower and bread for the
eater,[h]
11so is my word that goes out from
my mouth:
It will not return to me empty,[i]
but will accomplish what I desire
and achieve the purpose[j] for
which I sent it.
12You will go out in joy
and be led forth in peace;[k]
the mountains and hills
will burst into song before you,
and all the trees[l] of the field
will clap their hands.[m]
13Instead of the thornbush will grow
the pine tree,
and instead of briers[n] the
myrtle[o] will grow.
This will be for the LORD's
renown,[p]
for an everlasting sign,
which will not be destroyed."

Salvation for Others

3 →PG. 814

56 This is what the LORD says:

"Maintain justice[q]
and do what is right,
for my salvation[r] is close at hand
and my righteousness will soon
be revealed.
2Blessed[s] is the man who does
this,
the man who holds it fast,
who keeps the Sabbath[t] without
desecrating it,
and keeps his hand from doing
any evil."

3Let no foreigner who has bound
himself to the LORD say,
"The LORD will surely exclude me
from his people."
And let not any eunuch[u]
complain,
"I am only a dry tree."

4For this is what the LORD says:

"To the eunuchs who keep my
Sabbaths,
who choose what pleases me
and hold fast to my covenant—
5to them I will give within my
temple and its walls[v]
a memorial and a name
better than sons and daughters;
I will give them an everlasting
name
that will not be cut off.[w]
6And foreigners who bind
themselves to the LORD
to serve[x] him,
to love the name of the LORD,
and to worship him,
all who keep the Sabbath[y] without
desecrating it
and who hold fast to my
covenant—
7these I will bring to my holy
mountain[z]
and give them joy in my house
of prayer.
Their burnt offerings and
sacrifices[a]
will be accepted on my altar;
for my house will be called
a house of prayer for all
nations."[b][c]
8The Sovereign LORD declares—
he who gathers the exiles of
Israel:
"I will gather[d] still others to them
besides those already gathered."

God's Accusation Against the Wicked

9Come, all you beasts of the field,[e]
come and devour, all you beasts
of the forest!
10Israel's watchmen[f] are blind,
they all lack knowledge;
they are all mute dogs,
they cannot bark;
they lie around and dream,
they love to sleep.[g]
11They are dogs with mighty
appetites;
they never have enough.
They are shepherds[h] who lack
understanding;[i]
they all turn to their own way,
each seeks his own gain.[j]
12"Come," each one cries, "let me get
wine!
Let us drink our fill of beer!
And tomorrow will be like today,
or even far better."[k]

55:7 [b]Isa 44:22 [c]Isa 54:10 [d]Isa 1:18; 40:2 **55:8** [e]Isa 53:6 **55:9** [f]Ps 103:11 **55:10** [g]Isa 30:23 [h]2Co 9:10 **55:11** [i]Isa 45:23 [j]Isa 44:26 **55:12** [k]Isa 54:10,13 [l]1Ch 16:33 [m]Ps 98:8 **55:13** [n]Isa 5:6 [o]Isa 41:19 [p]Isa 63:12 **56:1** [q]Isa 1:17 [r]Ps 85:9 **56:2** [s]Ps 119:2 [t]Ex 20:8,10; Isa 58:13

56:3 [u]Jer 38:7 *fn*; Ac 8:27 **56:5** [v]Isa 26:1; 60:18 [w]Isa 48:19; 55:13 **56:6** [x]Isa 60:7,10; 61:5 [y]ver 2,4 **56:7** [z]Isa 2:2 [a]Ro 12:1; Heb 13:15 [b]Mt 21:13*; Lk 19:46* [c]Mk 11:17* **56:8** [d]Isa 11:12; 60:3-11; Jn 10:16 **56:9** [e]Isa 18:6; Jer 12:9 **56:10** [f]Eze 3:17 [g]Na 3:18 **56:11** [h]Eze 34:2 [i]Isa 1:3 [j]Isa 57:17; Eze 13:19; Mic 3:11 **56:12** [k]Ps 10:6; Lk 12:18-19

57 The righteous perish,[l]
and no one ponders it in his heart;[m]
devout men are taken away,
and no one understands
that the righteous are taken away
to be spared from evil.[n]
2Those who walk uprightly[o]
enter into peace;
they find rest as they lie in death.
3"But you—come here, you sons of a sorceress,
you offspring of adulterers[p] and prostitutes![q]
4Whom are you mocking?
At whom do you sneer
and stick out your tongue?
Are you not a brood of rebels,
the offspring of liars?
5You burn with lust among the oaks
and under every spreading tree;[r]
you sacrifice your children[s] in the ravines
and under the overhanging crags.
6⌞The idols⌟[t] among the smooth stones of the ravines are your portion;
they, they are your lot.
Yes, to them you have poured out drink offerings[u]
and offered grain offerings.
In the light of these things, should I relent?[v]
7You have made your bed on a high and lofty hill;[w]
there you went up to offer your sacrifices.
8Behind your doors and your doorposts
you have put your pagan symbols.
Forsaking me, you uncovered your bed,
you climbed into it and opened it wide;
you made a pact with those whose beds you love,[x]
and you looked on their nakedness.[y]
9You went to Molech[a] with olive oil
and increased your perfumes.
You sent your ambassadors[b][z] far away;
you descended to the grave[c] itself!
10You were wearied by all your ways,
but you would not say, 'It is hopeless.'[a]
You found renewal of your strength,
and so you did not faint.

11"Whom have you so dreaded and feared[b]
that you have been false to me,
and have neither remembered[c] me
nor pondered this in your hearts?
Is it not because I have long been silent[d]
that you do not fear me?
12I will expose your righteousness and your works,[e]
and they will not benefit you.
13When you cry out[f] for help,
let your collection ⌞of idols⌟ save you!
The wind will carry all of them off,
a mere breath will blow them away.
But the man who makes me his refuge
will inherit the land[g]
and possess my holy mountain."[h]

Comfort for the Contrite

14And it will be said:

"Build up, build up, prepare the road!
Remove the obstacles out of the way of my people."[i]
15For this is what the high and lofty[j] One says—
he who lives forever,[k] whose name is holy:
"I live in a high and holy place,
but also with him who is contrite[l] and lowly in spirit,[m]
to revive the spirit of the lowly
and to revive the heart of the contrite.[n]
16I will not accuse forever,
nor will I always be angry,[o]
for then the spirit of man would grow faint before me—
the breath of man that I have created.
17I was enraged by his sinful greed;[p]
I punished him, and hid my face in anger,
yet he kept on in his willful ways.[q]
18I have seen his ways, but I will heal[r] him;
I will guide him and restore comfort[s] to him,
19 creating praise on the lips[t] of the mourners in Israel.
Peace, peace,[u] to those far and near,"[v]

1 →PG. 798

57:1 [l]Ps 12:1 [m]Isa 42:25 [n]2Ki 22:20
57:2 [o]Isa 26:7
57:3 [p]Mt 16:4 [q]Isa 1:21
57:5 [r]2Ki 16:4 [s]Lev 18:21; Ps 106:37-38; Eze 16:20
57:6 [t]Jer 3:9 [u]Jer 7:18 [v]Jer 5:9,29; 9:9
57:7 [w]Jer 3:6; Eze 16:16
57:8 [x]Eze 16:26; 23:7 [y]Eze 23:18
57:9 [z]Eze 23:16,40
57:10 [a]Jer 2:25; 18:12
57:11 [b]Pr 29:25 [c]Jer 2:32; 3:21 [d]Ps 50:21
57:12 [e]Isa 29:15; Mic 3:2-4,8
57:13 [f]Jer 22:20; 30:15 [g]Ps 37:9 [h]Isa 65:9-11
57:14 [i]Isa 62:10; Jer 18:15
57:15 [j]Isa 52:13 [k]Dt 33:27 [l]Ps 147:3 [m]Ps 34:18; 51:17; Isa 66:2 [n]Isa 61:1
57:16 [o]Ps 85:5; 103:9; Mic 7:18
57:17 [p]Isa 56:11 [q]Isa 1:4
57:18 [r]Isa 30:26 [s]Isa 61:1-3
57:19 [t]Isa 6:7; Heb 13:15 [u]Eph 2:17 [v]Ac 2:39

a9 Or *to the king* b9 Or *idols* c9 Hebrew *Sheol*

says the LORD. "And I will heal
them."
20But the wicked[w] are like the
tossing sea,
which cannot rest,
whose waves cast up mire and
mud.
21"There is no peace,"[x] says my
God, "for the wicked."[y]

True Fasting

58 "Shout it aloud,[z] do not hold
back.
Raise your voice like a trumpet.
Declare to my people their
rebellion[a]
and to the house of Jacob their
sins.
2For day after day they seek[b] me
out;
they seem eager to know my
ways,
as if they were a nation that does
what is right
and has not forsaken the
commands of its God.
They ask me for just decisions
and seem eager for God to come
near[c] them.
3'Why have we fasted,'[d] they say,
'and you have not seen it?
Why have we humbled ourselves,
and you have not noticed?'[e]

"Yet on the day of your fasting, you
do as you please[f]
and exploit all your workers.
4Your fasting ends in quarreling and
strife,[g]
and in striking each other with
wicked fists.
You cannot fast as you do today
and expect your voice to be
heard[h] on high.
5Is this the kind of fast[i] I have
chosen,
only a day for a man to
humble[j] himself?
Is it only for bowing one's head
like a reed
and for lying on sackcloth and
ashes?[k]
Is that what you call a fast,
a day acceptable to the LORD?

7 →PG. 797

6"Is not this the kind of fasting I
have chosen:
to loose the chains of injustice[l]
and untie the cords of the yoke,
to set the oppressed[m] free
and break every yoke?
7Is it not to share your food with
the hungry[n]
and to provide the poor
wanderer with shelter[o]—
when you see the naked, to
clothe[p] him,
and not to turn away from your
own flesh and blood?[q]
8Then your light will break forth like
the dawn,[r]
and your healing[s] will quickly
appear;
then your righteousness[a] will go
before you,
and the glory of the LORD will be
your rear guard.[t]
9Then you will call,[u] and the LORD
will answer;
you will cry for help, and he will
say: Here am I.

"If you do away with the yoke of
oppression,
with the pointing finger[v] and
malicious talk,[w]
10and if you spend yourselves in
behalf of the hungry
and satisfy the needs of the
oppressed,[x]
then your light[y] will rise in the
darkness,
and your night will become like
the noonday.[z]
11The LORD will guide you always;
he will satisfy your needs[a] in a
sun-scorched land
and will strengthen your frame.
You will be like a well-watered
garden,[b]
like a spring[c] whose waters
never fail.
12Your people will rebuild the
ancient ruins[d]
and will raise up the age-old
foundations;[e]
you will be called Repairer of
Broken Walls,
Restorer of Streets with
Dwellings.

13"If you keep your feet from
breaking the Sabbath[f]
and from doing as you please on
my holy day,
if you call the Sabbath a delight[g]
and the LORD's holy day
honorable,
and if you honor it by not going
your own way
and not doing as you please or
speaking idle words,
14then you will find your joy[h] in the
LORD,
and I will cause you to ride on
the heights[i] of the land
and to feast on the inheritance
of your father Jacob."
The mouth of the LORD
has spoken.[j]

57:20 [w]Job 18:5-21
57:21 [x]Isa 59:8 [y]Isa 48:22
58:1 [z]Isa 40:6 [a]Isa 48:8
58:2 [b]Isa 48:1; Tit 1:16; Jas 4:8 [c]Isa 29:13
58:3 [d]Lev 16:29 [e]Mal 3:14 [f]Isa 22:13; Zec 7:5-6
58:4 [g]1Ki 21:9-13; Isa 59:6 [h]Isa 59:2
58:5 [i]Zec 7:5 [j]1Ki 21:27 [k]Job 2:8
58:6 [l]Ne 5:10-11 [m]Jer 34:9
58:7 [n]Eze 18:16; Lk 3:11 [o]Isa 16:4; Heb 13:2 [p]Job 31:19-20; Mt 25:36 [q]Ge 29:14; Lk 10:31-32
58:8 [r]Job 11:17 [s]Isa 30:26 [t]Ex 14:19
58:9 [u]Ps 50:15 [v]Pr 6:13 [w]Ps 12:2; Isa 59:13
58:10 [x]Dt 15:7-8 [y]Isa 42:16 [z]Job 11:17
58:11 [a]Ps 107:9 [b]SS 4:15 [c]Jn 4:14
58:12 [d]Isa 49:8 [e]Isa 44:28
58:13 [f]Isa 56:2 [g]Ps 84:2,10
58:14 [h]Job 22:26 [i]Dt 32:13 [j]Isa 1:20

a8 Or *your righteous One*

Sin, Confession and Redemption

59 Surely the arm of the LORD is not
too short[k] to save,
nor his ear too dull to hear.[l]
2But your iniquities have separated
you from your God;
your sins have hidden his face from
you,
so that he will not hear.[m]
3For your hands are stained with
blood,[n]
your fingers with guilt.
Your lips have spoken lies,
and your tongue mutters wicked
things.
4No one calls for justice;
no one pleads his case with
integrity.
They rely on empty arguments and
speak lies;
they conceive trouble and give
birth to evil.[o]
5They hatch the eggs of vipers
and spin a spider's web.[p]
Whoever eats their eggs will die,
and when one is broken, an
adder is hatched.
6Their cobwebs are useless for
clothing;
they cannot cover themselves
with what they make.[q]
Their deeds are evil deeds,
and acts of violence[r] are in
their hands.
7Their feet rush into sin;
they are swift to shed innocent
blood.[s]
Their thoughts are evil thoughts;[t]
ruin and destruction mark their
ways.[u]
8The way of peace they do not
know;
there is no justice in their paths.
They have turned them into
crooked roads;
no one who walks in them will
know peace.[v]

9So justice is far from us,
and righteousness does not
reach us.
We look for light, but all is
darkness;[w]
for brightness, but we walk in
deep shadows.
10Like the blind[x] we grope along the
wall,
feeling our way like men without
eyes.
At midday we stumble[y] as if it
were twilight;
among the strong, we are like
the dead.[z]
11We all growl like bears;
we moan mournfully like
doves.[a]
We look for justice, but find none;
for deliverance, but it is far away.

12For our offenses[b] are many in
your sight,
and our sins testify[c] against us.
Our offenses are ever with us,
and we acknowledge our
iniquities:
13rebellion and treachery against the
LORD,
turning our backs[d] on our God,
fomenting oppression[e] and revolt,
uttering lies[f] our hearts have
conceived.
14So justice is driven back,
and righteousness[g] stands at a
distance;
truth[h] has stumbled in the streets,
honesty cannot enter.
15Truth is nowhere to be found,
and whoever shuns evil becomes
a prey.

The LORD looked and was
displeased
that there was no justice.
16He saw that there was no one,[i]
he was appalled that there was
no one to intervene;
so his own arm worked salvation[j]
for him,
and his own righteousness
sustained him.
17He put on righteousness as his
breastplate,[k]

59:1 [k]Nu 11:23; Isa 50:2 [l]Isa 58:9; 65:24
59:2 [m]Isa 1:15; 58:4
59:3 [n]Isa 1:15
59:4 [o]Job 15:35; Ps 7:14
59:5 [p]Job 8:14
59:6 [q]Isa 28:20 [r]Isa 58:4
59:7 [s]Pr 6:17 [t]Mk 7:21-22 [u]Ro 3:15-17*
59:8 [v]Isa 57:21; Lk 1:79
59:9 [w]Isa 5:30; 8:20
59:10 [x]Dt 28:29 [y]Isa 8:15 [z]La 3:6
59:11 [a]Isa 38:14; Eze 7:16
59:12 [b]Ezr 9:6 [c]Isa 3:9
59:13 [d]Pr 30:9; Mt 10:33; Tit 1:16 [e]Isa 5:7 [f]Mk 7:21-22
59:14 [g]Isa 1:21 [h]Isa 48:1
59:16 [i]Isa 41:28 [j]Ps 98:1; Isa 63:5
59:17 [k]Eph 6:14

59:1–2

PROMISE 3

WHEN GOD TURNS HIS FACE

Isn't it strange to know God is present everywhere but not be able to find him? Often men feel like they are talking to themselves when they pray; it's as if God isn't anywhere around. Without suggesting it is the *only* reason, Isaiah taught us that sin is one *definite* reason why a man can feel cut off from God. He assured us that God is never too far away to hear us or touch us. Distance is not the issue (v. 1); sin is (v. 2).

We all sin; God has made provision for us when we do. 1 John 1:9 says that when we confess our sins to God, he is quick to forgive us. When you feel God is nowhere near, consider Isaiah's teaching in this passage. Avoid sin. When you don't avoid it, repent and confess, and live in the power and hope of God's forgiveness.

Capitalize these awful words in your thinking: "Separated" and "Hidden." There is no lonelier spot in all God's universe than the dark pocket of sin.

For the next Promise 3 reading go to page 807.

and the helmet[l] of salvation on
his head;
he put on the garments[m] of
vengeance
and wrapped himself in zeal[n] as
in a cloak.
18 According to what they have done,
so will he repay
wrath to his enemies
and retribution to his foes;
he will repay the islands their
due.
19 From the west,[o] men will fear the
name of the LORD,
and from the rising of the sun,[p]
they will revere his glory.
For he will come like a pent-up
flood
that the breath of the LORD
drives along.[a]
20 "The Redeemer will come to Zion,
to those in Jacob who repent of
their sins,"[q]
declares the LORD.

21 "As for me, this is my covenant with them," says the LORD. "My Spirit,[r] who is on you, and my words that I have put in your mouth will not depart from your mouth, or from the mouths of your children, or from the mouths of their descendants from this time on and forever," says the LORD.

The Glory of Zion

60 "Arise,[s] shine, for your light[t]
has come,
and the glory of the LORD rises
upon you.
2 See, darkness covers the earth
and thick darkness[u] is over the
peoples,
but the LORD rises upon you
and his glory appears over you.
3 Nations[v] will come to your light,
and kings[w] to the brightness of
your dawn.

4 "Lift up your eyes and look about
you:
All assemble[x] and come to you;
your sons come from afar,
and your daughters[y] are carried
on the arm.[z]
5 Then you will look and be radiant,
your heart will throb and swell
with joy;
the wealth on the seas will be
brought to you,
to you the riches of the nations
will come.
6 Herds of camels will cover your
land,
young camels of Midian[a] and
Ephah.[b]
And all from Sheba[c] will come,
bearing gold and incense[d]
and proclaiming the praise[e] of
the LORD.
7 All Kedar's[f] flocks will be gathered
to you,
the rams of Nebaioth will serve
you;
they will be accepted as offerings
on my altar,
and I will adorn my glorious
temple.[g]

8 "Who are these[h] that fly along like
clouds,
like doves to their nests?
9 Surely the islands[i] look to me;
in the lead are the ships of
Tarshish,[b][j]
bringing[k] your sons from afar,
with their silver and gold,
to the honor of the LORD your God,
the Holy One of Israel,
for he has endowed you with
splendor.[l]

10 "Foreigners[m] will rebuild your
walls,
and their kings[n] will serve you.
Though in anger I struck you,
in favor I will show you
compassion.[o]
11 Your gates[p] will always stand
open,
they will never be shut, day or
night,
so that men may bring you the
wealth of the nations[q]—
their kings[r] led in triumphal
procession.
12 For the nation or kingdom that will
not serve[s] you will perish;
it will be utterly ruined.

13 "The glory of Lebanon[t] will come
to you,
the pine, the fir and the cypress
together,[u]
to adorn the place of my sanctuary;
and I will glorify the place of my
feet.[v]
14 The sons of your oppressors[w] will
come bowing before you;
all who despise you will bow
down[x] at your feet
and will call you the City of the
LORD,
Zion[y] of the Holy One of Israel.

15 "Although you have been
forsaken[z] and hated,
with no one traveling[a] through,
I will make you the everlasting
pride[b]
and the joy[c] of all generations.

59:17 [l]Eph 6:17; 1Th 5:8 [m]Isa 63:3 [n]Isa 9:7
59:19 [o]Isa 49:12 [p]Ps 113:3
59:20 [q]Ac 2:38-39; Ro 11:26-27*
59:21 [r]Isa 11:2; 44:3
60:1 [s]Isa 52:2 [t]Eph 5:14
60:2 [u]Jer 13:16; Col 1:13
60:3 [v]Isa 45:14; Rev 21:24 [w]Isa 49:23
60:4 [x]Isa 11:12 [y]Isa 43:6 [z]Isa 49:20-22
60:6 [a]Ge 25:2 [b]Ge 25:4 [c]Ps 72:10 [d]Isa 43:23; Mt 2:11 [e]Isa 42:10
60:7 [f]Ge 25:13 [g]ver 13; Hag 2:3,7,9
60:8 [h]Isa 49:21
60:9 [i]Isa 11:11 [j]Isa 2:16 *fn* [k]Isa 14:2; 43:6 [l]Isa 55:5
60:10 [m]Isa 14:1-2 [n]Isa 49:23; Rev 21:24 [o]Isa 54:8
60:11 [p]ver 18; Isa 62:10; Rev 21:25 [q]ver 5; Rev 21:26 [r]Ps 149:8
60:12 [s]Isa 14:2
60:13 [t]Isa 35:2 [u]Isa 41:19 [v]1Ch 28:2; Ps 132:7
60:14 [w]Isa 14:2 [x]Isa 49:23; Rev 3:9 [y]Heb 12:22
60:15 [z]Isa 1:7-9; 6:12 [a]Isa 33:8 [b]Isa 4:2 [c]Isa 65:18

a 19 Or *When the enemy comes in like a flood, / the Spirit of the LORD will put him to flight*
b 9 Or *the trading ships*

16You will drink the milk of nations
and be nursed[d] at royal breasts.
Then you will know that I, the
LORD, am your Savior,
your Redeemer,[e] the Mighty
One of Jacob.
17Instead of bronze I will bring you
gold,
and silver in place of iron.
Instead of wood I will bring you
bronze,
and iron in place of stones.
I will make peace your governor
and righteousness your ruler.
18No longer will violence be heard in
your land,
nor ruin or destruction within
your borders,
but you will call your walls
Salvation[f]
and your gates Praise.
19The sun will no more be your light
by day,
nor will the brightness of the
moon shine on you,
for the LORD will be your
everlasting light,[g]
and your God will be your
glory.[h]
20Your sun[i] will never set again,
and your moon will wane no
more;
the LORD will be your everlasting
light,
and your days of sorrow[j] will
end.
21Then will all your people be
righteous[k]
and they will possess[l] the land
forever.
They are the shoot I have
planted,[m]
the work of my hands,[n]
for the display of my splendor.[o]
22The least of you will become a
thousand,
the smallest a mighty nation.
I am the LORD;
in its time I will do this swiftly."

The Year of the LORD's Favor

5 →PG. 1038
7 →PG. 798

61 The Spirit[p] of the Sovereign LORD
is on me,
because the LORD has anointed[q]
me
to preach good news to the
poor.[r]
He has sent me to bind up[s] the
brokenhearted,
to proclaim freedom for the
captives[t]
and release from darkness for
the prisoners,[a]
2to proclaim the year of the LORD's
favor[u]
and the day of vengeance[v] of
our God,
to comfort[w] all who mourn,
3 and provide for those who grieve
in Zion—
to bestow on them a crown of
beauty
instead of ashes,
the oil of gladness
instead of mourning,
and a garment of praise
instead of a spirit of despair.
They will be called oaks of
righteousness,
a planting of the LORD
for the display of his splendor.[x]

4They will rebuild the ancient
ruins[y]
and restore the places long
devastated;
they will renew the ruined cities
that have been devastated for
generations.
5Aliens[z] will shepherd your flocks;
foreigners will work your fields
and vineyards.
6And you will be called priests[a] of
the LORD,
you will be named ministers of
our God.
You will feed on the wealth[b] of
nations,
and in their riches you will
boast.

7Instead of their shame
my people will receive a
double[c] portion,
and instead of disgrace
they will rejoice in their
inheritance;

60:16 [d]Isa 49:23; 66:11,12 [e]Isa 59:20 **60:18** [f]Isa 26:1 **60:19** [g]Rev 22:5 [h]Zec 2:5; Rev 21:23 **60:20** [i]Isa 30:26 [j]Isa 35:10 **60:21** [k]Rev 21:27 [l]Ps 37:11,22; Isa 57:13; 61:7 [m]Mt 15:13 [n]Isa 19:25; 29:23; Eph 2:10 [o]Isa 52:1 **61:1** [p]Isa 11:2 [q]Ps 45:7 [r]Mt 11:5; Lk 7:22 [s]Isa 57:15 [t]Isa 42:7; 49:9 **61:2** [u]Isa 49:8; Lk 4:18-19* [v]Isa 34:8 [w]Isa 57:18; Mt 5:4 **61:3** [x]Isa 60:20-21 **61:4** [y]Isa 49:8; Eze 36:33; Am 9:14 **61:5** [z]Isa 14:1-2 **61:6** [a]Ex 19:6; 1Pe 2:5 [b]Isa 60:11 **61:7** [c]Isa 40:2; Zec 9:12

[a]*1* Hebrew; Septuagint *the blind*

61:1–2

PROMISE 7

SENT BY GOD

Isaiah knew he was God's messenger (v. 1). He also knew what that meant (v. 2). Isaiah's powerful messages and faithful ministry have taught and guided millions over the centuries. It's great for a man to know that God guides his life. It gives a man a sense of meaning and destiny.

Read Acts 1:8 and Matthew 28:18–20 as your personal commission to God's ministry of discipleship. If you are a Christian, you are commissioned. The great God of the universe has personally called you into his service. Read Isaiah 61:1–2 and emphasize the word "me" as you read. Then go and do it!

For the next Promise 7 reading go to page 806.

and so they will inherit a double
portion in their land,
and everlasting joy will be theirs.

8"For I, the LORD, love justice;[d]
I hate robbery and iniquity.
In my faithfulness I will reward
them
and make an everlasting
covenant[e] with them.
9Their descendants will be known
among the nations
and their offspring among the
peoples.
All who see them will acknowledge
that they are a people the LORD
has blessed."

10I delight greatly in the LORD;
my soul rejoices[f] in my God.
For he has clothed me with
garments of salvation
and arrayed me in a robe of
righteousness,[g]
as a bridegroom adorns his head
like a priest,
and as a bride[h] adorns herself
with her jewels.
11For as the soil makes the sprout
come up
and a garden causes seeds to
grow,
so the Sovereign LORD will make
righteousness[i] and praise
spring up before all nations.

Zion's New Name

62 For Zion's sake I will not keep
silent,
for Jerusalem's sake I will not
remain quiet,
till her righteousness[j] shines out
like the dawn,
her salvation like a blazing torch.
2The nations[k] will see your
righteousness,
and all kings your glory;
you will be called by a new name[l]
that the mouth of the LORD will
bestow.
3You will be a crown[m] of splendor
in the LORD's hand,
a royal diadem in the hand of
your God.
4No longer will they call you
Deserted,[n]
or name your land Desolate.
But you will be called Hephzibah,[a]
and your land Beulah[b];
for the LORD will take delight[o] in
you,
and your land will be married.[p]
5As a young man marries a maiden,
so will your sons[c] marry you;
as a bridegroom rejoices over his
bride,

61:8 [d]Ps 11:7; Isa 5:16 [e]Isa 55:3 **61:10** [f]Isa 25:9; Hab 3:18 [g]Ps 132:9; Isa 52:1 [h]Isa 49:18; Rev 21:2 **61:11** [i]Ps 85:11 **62:1** [j]Isa 1:26 **62:2** [k]Isa 52:10; 60:3 [l]ver 4,12 **62:3** [m]Isa 28:5; Zec 9:16; 1Th 2:19 **62:4** [n]Isa 54:6 [o]Jer 32:41; Zep 3:17 [p]Jer 3:14; Hos 2:19

62:5 [q]Isa 65:19 **62:6** [r]Isa 52:8; Eze 3:17 **62:7** [s]Mt 15:21-28; Lk 18:1-8 **62:8** [t]Dt 28:30-33; Isa 1:7; Jer 5:17 **62:10** [u]Isa 60:11 [v]Isa 57:14 [w]Isa 11:16 [x]Isa 11:10 **62:11** [y]Zec 9:9; Mt 21:5 [z]Rev 22:12 [a]Isa 40:10 **62:12** [b]ver 4 [c]1Pe 2:9 [d]Isa 35:9 [e]Isa 42:16 **63:1** [f]Am 1:12 [g]Zep 3:17 **63:3** [h]Rev 14:20; 19:15

so will your God rejoice[q] over
you.

6I have posted watchmen[r] on your
walls, O Jerusalem;
they will never be silent day or
night.
You who call on the LORD,
give yourselves no rest,
7and give him no rest[s] till he
establishes Jerusalem
and makes her the praise of the
earth.

1 →PG. 800
7 →PG. 830

8The LORD has sworn by his right
hand
and by his mighty arm:
"Never again will I give your
grain[t]
as food for your enemies,
and never again will foreigners
drink the new wine
for which you have toiled;
9but those who harvest it will eat it
and praise the LORD,
and those who gather the grapes
will drink it
in the courts of my sanctuary."

10Pass through, pass through the
gates![u]
Prepare the way for the people.
Build up, build up the highway![v][w]
Remove the stones.
Raise a banner[x] for the nations.

11The LORD has made proclamation
to the ends of the earth:
"Say to the Daughter of Zion,[y]
'See, your Savior comes![z]
See, his reward is with him,
and his recompense
accompanies him.' "[a]
12They will be called[b] the Holy
People,[c]
the Redeemed[d] of the LORD;
and you will be called Sought After,
the City No Longer Deserted.[e]

God's Day of Vengeance and Redemption

63 Who is this coming from Edom,
from Bozrah,[f] with his
garments stained crimson?
Who is this, robed in splendor,
striding forward in the greatness
of his strength?

"It is I, speaking in righteousness,
mighty to save."[g]

2Why are your garments red,
like those of one treading the
winepress?

3"I have trodden the winepress[h]
alone;

[a]4 *Hephzibah* means *my delight is in her.*
[b]4 *Beulah* means *married.* [c]5 Or *Builder*

from the nations no one was
with me.
I trampled them in my anger
and trod them down in my
wrath;[i]
their blood spattered my
garments,[j]
and I stained all my clothing.
4 For the day of vengeance was in
my heart,
and the year of my redemption
has come.
5 I looked, but there was no one[k] to
help,
I was appalled that no one gave
support;
so my own arm[l] worked salvation
for me,
and my own wrath sustained
me.[m]
6 I trampled the nations in my anger;
in my wrath I made them
drunk[n]
and poured their blood[o] on the
ground."

Praise and Prayer

7 I will tell of the kindnesses[p] of the
LORD,
the deeds for which he is to be
praised,
according to all the LORD has
done for us—
yes, the many good things he has
done
for the house of Israel,
according to his compassion[q]
and many kindnesses.
8 He said, "Surely they are my
people,[r]
sons who will not be false to
me";
and so he became their Savior.
9 In all their distress he too was
distressed,
and the angel of his presence[s]
saved them.
In his love and mercy he
redeemed[t] them;
he lifted them up and carried[u]
them
all the days of old.
10 Yet they rebelled[v]
and grieved his Holy Spirit.[w]
So he turned and became their
enemy[x]
and he himself fought against
them.
11 Then his people recalled[a] the days
of old,
the days of Moses and his
people—
where is he who brought them
through the sea,[y]
with the shepherd of his flock?

63:3 [i]Isa 22:5 [j]Rev 19:13 **63:5** [k]Isa 41:28 [l]Ps 44:3; 98:1 [m]Isa 59:16 **63:6** [n]Isa 29:9 [o]Isa 34:3 **63:7** [p]Isa 54:8 [q]Ps 51:1; Eph 2:4 **63:8** [r]Isa 51:4 **63:9** [s]Ex 33:14 [t]Dt 7:7-8 [u]Dt 1:31 **63:10** [v]Ps 78:40 [w]Ps 51:11; Ac 7:51; Eph 4:30 [x]Ps 106:40 **63:11** [y]Ex 14:22,30 [z]Nu 11:17 **63:12** [a]Ex 14:21-22; Isa 11:15 **63:13** [b]Dt 32:12 [c]Jer 31:9 **63:15** [d]Dt 26:15; Ps 80:14 [e]Ps 123:1 [f]Isa 9:7; 26:11 [g]Jer 31:20; Hos 11:8 **63:16** [h]Job 14:21 [i]Isa 41:14; 44:6 **63:17** [j]Isa 29:13 [k]Nu 10:36 **63:18** [l]Ps 74:3-8 **64:1** [m]Ps 18:9; 144:5 [n]Mic 1:3 [o]Ex 19:18

Where is he who set
his Holy Spirit[z] among them,
12 who sent his glorious arm of power
to be at Moses' right hand,
who divided the waters[a] before
them,
to gain for himself everlasting
renown,
13 who led[b] them through the
depths?
Like a horse in open country,
they did not stumble;[c]
14 like cattle that go down to the
plain,
they were given rest by the Spirit
of the LORD.
This is how you guided your people
to make for yourself a glorious
name.

15 Look down from heaven[d] and see
from your lofty throne,[e] holy
and glorious.
Where are your zeal[f] and your
might?
Your tenderness and
compassion[g] are withheld
from us.
16 But you are our Father,
though Abraham does not know
us
or Israel acknowledge[h] us;
you, O LORD, are our Father,
our Redeemer[i] from of old is
your name.
17 Why, O LORD, do you make us
wander from your ways
and harden our hearts so we do
not revere[j] you?
Return[k] for the sake of your
servants,
the tribes that are your
inheritance.
18 For a little while your people
possessed your holy place,
but now our enemies have
trampled down your
sanctuary.[l]
19 We are yours from of old;
but you have not ruled over
them,
they have not been called by
your name.[b]

64 Oh, that you would rend the
heavens[m] and come
down,[n]
that the mountains[o] would
tremble before you!
2 As when fire sets twigs ablaze
and causes water to boil,
come down to make your name
known to your enemies

[a] *11* Or *But may he recall* [b] *19* Or *We are like those you have never ruled, / like those never called by your name*

and cause the nations to quake[p] before you!
3For when you did awesome[q] things that we did not expect,
you came down, and the mountains trembled before you.
4Since ancient times no one has heard,
no ear has perceived,
no eye has seen any God besides you,
who acts on behalf of those who wait for him.[r]
5You come to the help of those who gladly do right,[s]
who remember your ways.
But when we continued to sin against them,
you were angry.
How then can we be saved?
6All of us have become like one who is unclean,
and all our righteous[t] acts are like filthy rags;
we all shrivel up like a leaf,[u]
and like the wind our sins sweep us away.
7No one[v] calls on your name
or strives to lay hold of you;
for you have hidden[w] your face from us
and made us waste away[x]
because of our sins.

1 →PG. 801
8Yet, O LORD, you are our Father.[y]
We are the clay, you are the potter;[z]
we are all the work of your hand.
9Do not be angry[a] beyond measure, O LORD;
do not remember our sins[b] forever.
Oh, look upon us, we pray,
for we are all your people.
10Your sacred cities have become a desert;
even Zion is a desert, Jerusalem a desolation.
11Our holy and glorious temple,[c]
where our fathers praised you,
has been burned with fire,
and all that we treasured[d] lies in ruins.
12After all this, O LORD, will you hold yourself back?[e]
Will you keep silent[f] and punish us beyond measure?

Judgment and Salvation

65 "I revealed myself to those who did not ask for me;
I was found by those who did not seek me.[g]
To a nation[h] that did not call on my name,
I said, 'Here am I, here am I.'
2All day long I have held out my hands
to an obstinate people,[i]
who walk in ways not good,
pursuing their own imaginations[j]—
3a people who continually provoke me
to my very face,[k]
offering sacrifices in gardens[l]
and burning incense on altars of brick;
4who sit among the graves
and spend their nights keeping secret vigil;
who eat the flesh of pigs,[m]
and whose pots hold broth of unclean meat;
5who say, 'Keep away; don't come near me,
for I am too sacred[n] for you!'
Such people are smoke in my nostrils,
a fire that keeps burning all day.

6"See, it stands written before me:
I will not keep silent[o] but will pay back[p] in full;
I will pay it back into their laps[q]—
7both your sins[r] and the sins of your fathers,"[s]
says the LORD.
"Because they burned sacrifices on the mountains
and defied me on the hills,[t]
I will measure into their laps
the full payment for their former deeds."

8This is what the LORD says:
"As when juice is still found in a cluster of grapes
and men say, 'Don't destroy it,
there is yet some good in it,'
so will I do in behalf of my servants;
I will not destroy them all.
9I will bring forth descendants[u] from Jacob,
and from Judah those who will possess[v] my mountains;
my chosen people will inherit them,
and there will my servants live.[w]
10Sharon[x] will become a pasture for flocks,
and the Valley of Achor[y] a resting place for herds,
for my people who seek[z] me.
11"But as for you who forsake[a] the LORD
and forget my holy mountain,

64:2 [p]Ps 99:1; Jer 5:22; 33:9 **64:3** [q]Ps 65:5 **64:4** [r]Isa 30:18; 1Co 2:9* **64:5** [s]Isa 26:8 **64:6** [t]Isa 46:12; 48:1 [u]Ps 90:5-6 **64:7** [v]Isa 59:4 [w]Dt 31:18; Isa 1:15; 54:8 [x]Isa 9:18 **64:8** [y]Isa 63:16 [z]Isa 29:16 **64:9** [a]Isa 57:17; 60:10 [b]Isa 43:25 **64:11** [c]Ps 74:3-7 [d]La 1:7,10 **64:12** [e]Ps 74:10-11; Isa 42:14 [f]Ps 83:1 **65:1** [g]Hos 1:10; Ro 9:24-26; 10:20*

[h]Eph 2:12 **65:2** [i]Isa 1:2,23; Ro 10:21* [j]Ps 81:11-12; Isa 66:18 **65:3** [k]Job 1:11 [l]Isa 1:29 **65:4** [m]Lev 11:7 **65:5** [n]Mt 9:11; Lk 7:39; 18:9-12 **65:6** [o]Ps 50:3 [p]Jer 16:18 [q]Ps 79:12 **65:7** [r]Isa 22:14 [s]Ex 20:5 [t]Isa 57:7 **65:9** [u]Isa 45:19 [v]Am 9:11-15 [w]Isa 32:18 **65:10** [x]Isa 35:2 [y]Jos 7:26 [z]Isa 51:1 **65:11** [a]Dt 29:24-25; Isa 1:28

who spread a table for Fortune
and fill bowls of mixed wine for
Destiny,
12I will destine you for the sword,[b]
and you will all bend down for
the slaughter;
for I called but you did not
answer,[c]
I spoke but you did not listen.[d]
You did evil in my sight
and chose what displeases me."

13Therefore this is what the Sovereign LORD says:

"My servants will eat,[e]
but you will go hungry;
my servants will drink,
but you will go thirsty;[f]
my servants will rejoice,
but you will be put to shame.[g]
14My servants will sing
out of the joy of their hearts,
but you will cry out[h]
from anguish of heart
and wail in brokenness of spirit.
15You will leave your name
to my chosen ones as a curse;[i]
the Sovereign LORD will put you to
death,
but to his servants he will give
another name.
16Whoever invokes a blessing in the
land
will do so by the God of truth;[j]
he who takes an oath in the land
will swear[k] by the God of truth.
For the past troubles will be
forgotten
and hidden from my eyes.

New Heavens and a New Earth

17"Behold, I will create
new heavens and a new earth.[l]
The former things will not be
remembered,[m]
nor will they come to mind.
18But be glad and rejoice[n] forever
in what I will create,
for I will create Jerusalem to be a
delight
and its people a joy.
19I will rejoice[o] over Jerusalem
and take delight in my people;
the sound of weeping and of
crying[p]
will be heard in it no more.

20"Never again will there be in it
an infant who lives but a few
days,
or an old man who does not live
out his years;[q]
he who dies at a hundred
will be thought a mere youth;
he who fails to reach[a] a hundred
will be considered accursed.
21They will build houses[r] and dwell
in them;
they will plant vineyards and eat
their fruit.[s]
22No longer will they build houses
and others live in them,
or plant and others eat.
For as the days of a tree,[t]
so will be the days[u] of my
people;
my chosen ones will long enjoy
the works of their hands.
23They will not toil in vain
or bear children doomed to
misfortune;
for they will be a people blessed[v]
by the LORD,
they and their descendants[w]
with them.
24Before they call[x] I will answer;
while they are still speaking[y] I
will hear.
25The wolf and the lamb[z] will feed
together,
and the lion will eat straw like
the ox,
but dust will be the serpent's[a]
food.
They will neither harm nor destroy
on all my holy mountain,"
says the LORD.

Judgment and Hope

66 This is what the LORD says:

1 →PG. 825

"Heaven is my throne,[b]
and the earth is my footstool.[c]
Where is the house[d] you will build
for me?
Where will my resting place be?
2Has not my hand made all these
things,[e]
and so they came into being?"
declares the LORD.

"This is the one I esteem:
he who is humble and contrite
in spirit,[f]
and trembles at my word.[g]
3But whoever sacrifices a bull[h]
is like one who kills a man,
and whoever offers a lamb,
like one who breaks a dog's
neck;
whoever makes a grain offering
is like one who presents pig's
blood,
and whoever burns memorial
incense,[i]
like one who worships an idol.
They have chosen their own
ways,[j]
and their souls delight in their
abominations;

65:12 [b]Isa 27:1 [c]Pr 1:24-25; Isa 41:28; 66:4 [d]2Ch 36:15-16; Jer 7:13 **65:13** [e]Isa 1:19 [f]Isa 41:17 [g]Isa 44:9 **65:14** [h]Mt 8:12; Lk 13:28 **65:15** [i]Zec 8:13 **65:16** [j]Ps 31:5 [k]Isa 19:18 **65:17** [l]Isa 66:22; 2Pe 3:13 [m]Isa 43:18; Jer 3:16 **65:18** [n]Ps 98:1-9; Isa 25:9 **65:19** [o]Isa 35:10; 62:5 [p]Isa 25:8; Rev 7:17 **65:20** [q]Ecc 8:13 **65:21** [r]Isa 32:18 [s]Isa 37:30; Am 9:14 **65:22** [t]Ps 92:12-14 [u]Ps 21:4; 91:16 **65:23** [v]Dt 28:3-12; Isa 61:9 [w]Ac 2:39 **65:24** [x]Isa 55:6 [y]Da 9:20-23; 10:12 **65:25** [z]Isa 11:6 [a]Ge 3:14; Mic 7:17 **66:1** [b]Mt 23:22 [c]1Ki 8:27; Mt 5:34-35 [d]2Sa 7:7; Jn 4:20-21; Ac 7:49*; 17:24 **66:2** [e]Isa 40:26; Ac 7:50* [f]Isa 57:15; Mt 5:3-4; Lk 18:13-14 [g]Ezr 9:4 **66:3** [h]Isa 1:11 [i]Lev 2:2 [j]Isa 57:17

[a]20 Or / *the sinner who reaches*

4so I also will choose harsh
treatment for them
and will bring upon them what
they dread.[k]
For when I called, no one
answered,[l]
when I spoke, no one listened.
They did evil[m] in my sight
and chose what displeases
me."[n]

5Hear the word of the LORD,
you who tremble at his word:
"Your brothers who hate[o] you,
and exclude you because of my
name, have said,
'Let the LORD be glorified,
that we may see your joy!'
Yet they will be put to shame.[p]
6Hear that uproar from the city,
hear that noise from the temple!
It is the sound of the LORD
repaying[q] his enemies all they
deserve.

7"Before she goes into labor,[r]
she gives birth;
before the pains come upon her,
she delivers a son.[s]
8Who has ever heard of such a
thing?
Who has ever seen[t] such
things?
Can a country be born in a day
or a nation be brought forth in a
moment?
Yet no sooner is Zion in labor
than she gives birth to her
children.
9Do I bring to the moment of
birth[u]
and not give delivery?" says the
LORD.
"Do I close up the womb
when I bring to delivery?" says
your God.
10"Rejoice[v] with Jerusalem and be
glad for her,
all you who love[w] her;
rejoice greatly with her,
all you who mourn over her.
11For you will nurse[x] and be
satisfied
at her comforting breasts;
you will drink deeply
and delight in her overflowing
abundance."

12For this is what the LORD says:

"I will extend peace to her like a
river,[y]
and the wealth[z] of nations like
a flooding stream;
you will nurse and be carried[a] on
her arm
and dandled on her knees.
13As a mother comforts her child,
so will I comfort[b] you;
and you will be comforted over
Jerusalem."

14When you see this, your heart will
rejoice
and you will flourish like grass;
the hand of the LORD will be made
known to his servants,
but his fury[c] will be shown to
his foes.
15See, the LORD is coming with fire,
and his chariots[d] are like a
whirlwind;
he will bring down his anger with
fury,
and his rebuke[e] with flames of
fire.
16For with fire[f] and with his
sword[g]
the LORD will execute judgment
upon all men,
and many will be those slain by
the LORD.
17"Those who consecrate and purify
themselves to go into the gardens,[h]

66:1–3

PROMISE 1

ESTEEM

"This is the one I esteem . . ." When God says this, we should take note.

The first part of this passage gives us a glimpse of who is speaking: "Heaven is my throne" (v. 1); "Has not my hand made all these things?" (v. 2). The more esteemed the one who esteems, the more esteemed is the esteem. Want to try that again? Look at it this way: No one's esteem means as much as God's.

Who *does* God esteem? "He who is humble and contrite in spirit, and trembles at my word." Simple statement, profound reality. How can we develop a humble and contrite spirit? First, read how Isaiah did it in chapter 6. Next read Isaiah 40:12–31, where you'll find some amazing descriptions of God. Anyone who understands God's majesty will be "humble and contrite before" him. Then read Isaiah 55:8–11 to see how God's Word addresses man's most basic needs.

A man who sees God as he is will be humble and contrite. That man is esteemed by God. A man who sees God as he is trembles at God's Word. That man is esteemed by God. The more exalted your view of God, the easier it is to be humble and contrite before him and tremble at his Word.

Could it be that the more we exalt God the more he esteems us?

For the next Promise 1 reading go to page 809.

66:4 [k]Pr 10:24 [l]Pr 1:24; Jer 7:13 [m]2Ki 21:2,4,6 [n]Isa 65:12
66:5 [o]Ps 38:20; Isa 60:15 [p]Lk 13:17
66:6 [q]Isa 65:6; Joel 3:7
66:7 [r]Isa 54:1 [s]Rev 12:5
66:8 [t]Isa 64:4
66:9 [u]Isa 37:3
66:10 [v]Dt 32:43; Ro 15:10 [w]Ps 26:8
66:11 [x]Isa 60:16
66:12 [y]Isa 48:18 [z]Ps 72:3; Isa 60:5; 61:6 [a]Isa 60:4
66:13 [b]Isa 40:1; 2Co 1:4
66:14 [c]Isa 10:5
66:15 [d]Ps 68:17 [e]Ps 9:5
66:16 [f]Isa 30:30 [g]Isa 27:1
66:17 [h]Isa 1:29

following the one in the midst of[a]
those who eat the flesh of pigs[i] and
rats and other abominable things—
they will meet their end[j] together,"
declares the LORD.
18"And I, because of their actions
and their imaginations, am about to
come[b] and gather all nations and
tongues, and they will come and see
my glory.
19"I will set a sign[k] among them,
and I will send some of those who survive to the nations—to Tarshish,[l] to
the Libyans[c] and Lydians[m] (famous
as archers), to Tubal[n] and Greece, and
to the distant islands[o] that have not
heard of my fame or seen my glory.[p]
They will proclaim my glory among the
nations. 20And they will bring all your
brothers, from all the nations, to my
holy mountain in Jerusalem as an offering to the LORD—on horses, in chariots and wagons, and on mules and
camels," says the LORD. "They will

66:17 [i]Lev 11:7 [j]Ps 37:20; Isa 1:28
66:19 [k]Isa 11:10; 49:22 [l]Isa 2:16 [m]Eze 27:10 [n]Ge 10:2 [o]Isa 11:11 [p]1Ch 16:24; Isa 24:15
66:20 [q]Isa 52:11
66:21 [r]Ex 19:6; Isa 61:6; 1Pe 2:5,9
66:22 [s]Isa 65:17; Heb 12:26-27; 2Pe 3:13; Rev 21:1 [t]Jn 10:27-29; 1Pe 1:4-5
66:23 [u]Eze 46:1-3 [v]Isa 19:21
66:24 [w]Isa 14:11 [x]Isa 1:31; Mk 9:48*

bring them, as the Israelites bring their
grain offerings, to the temple of the
LORD in ceremonially clean vessels.[q]
21And I will select some of them also
to be priests[r] and Levites," says the
LORD.
22"As the new heavens and the new
earth[s] that I make will endure before
me," declares the LORD, "so will your
name and descendants endure.[t]
23From one New Moon to another and
from one Sabbath[u] to another, all
mankind will come and bow down[v]
before me," says the LORD. 24"And they
will go out and look upon the dead
bodies of those who rebelled against
me; their worm[w] will not die, nor will
their fire be quenched,[x] and they will
be loathsome to all mankind."

a *17* Or *gardens behind one of your temples, and*
b *18* The meaning of the Hebrew for this clause is uncertain.
c *19* Some Septuagint manuscripts *Put* (Libyans); Hebrew *Pul*

JEREMIAH

AT A GLANCE

Key Principle: When we rebel against God, he graciously offers us an opportunity to repent and return to him. We would be wise to do so before he disciplines us.
Author: Jeremiah
Time and Place: ~626–585 B.C. / Judah, the surrounding nations, and Babylon
Key Verses: 1:10; 3:14; 7:23–24; 8:11–12; 9:23–24; 17:5–10; 18:11–12

BENEFIT

In response to God's commission, Jeremiah spent nearly five decades calling a rebellious people to repent of their sins. During that time, however, he worked without any significant positive response. Instead, he experienced extreme public humiliation, was put in stocks, forced to flee for his life, thrown into a cistern and was misunderstood by virtually all who encountered him. In spite of his frequent discouragement and pain, Jeremiah remained faithful to his calling and endured to the end. He is a striking model of faithfulness and steadfast endurance in the face of heated and extended opposition.

SETTING

Jeremiah prophesied during and after the reigns of Judah's last kings and was a contemporary of the prophets Zephaniah, Habakkuk, Ezekiel and Daniel. He began his ministry in the days of Josiah, Judah's last good king, and endured a series of ungodly kings from Jehoahaz to Zedekiah until Nebuchadnezzar finally conquered Jerusalem in 586 B.C. Jeremiah's prophetic ministry went through three phases: (1) the years when Assyria and Egypt threatened Judah (627–605 B.C.), (2) the years when Babylonia threatened and besieged Judah (605–586 B.C.) and (3) a few years after Jerusalem fell (586 B.C. to ~580 B.C.).

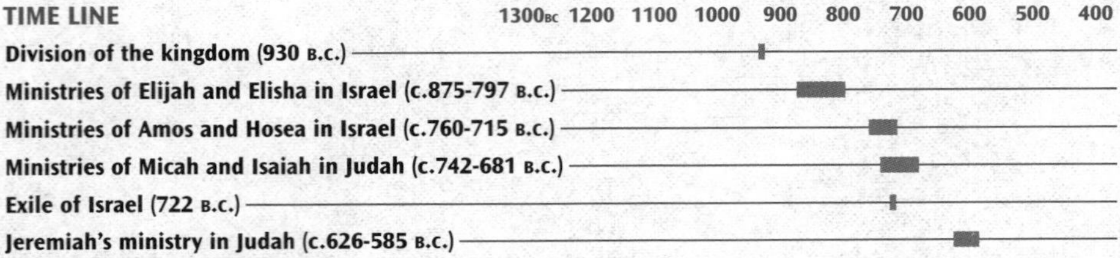

THEME AND PURPOSE

Jeremiah's recurring theme is the inevitability of divine judgment because of Judah's sin. God's purpose in commissioning Jeremiah was to call his people to repentance before it was too late, but the people met the Lord's gracious eleventh-hour appeals with a stiff-necked and rebellious response. While the clay is still wet, it is possible for the potter to repair a pot, but when it hardens, it can only be destroyed (18:1–12; 19:10–11). Judah's problem was that in spite of God's loving warnings for them to reform their ways and actions, they replied, "It's no use. We will continue with our own plans; each of us will follow the stubbornness of his evil heart"

(18:12). Yet God promised that after judgment he would preserve a remnant, and that he would establish a new covenant with them in which his law would be in their hearts.

UNIQUE CONTRIBUTION

Jeremiah more clearly demonstrates the burden of God's prophetic commission than any other book of the Bible. Jeremiah suffered profound pain and brokenness from his stubborn countrymen, and for decades he continued to love them even though they spurned his appeals and warnings.

The prophecies of Jeremiah stress God's holiness, sovereignty and compassion as well as his hatred of the corruption and immorality that follows in the wake of idolatry. These prophecies are difficult to arrange topically or chronologically, but using the order of the last kings of Judah, here is an approximate sequence:

Josiah	**Jehoahaz**	**Jehoiakim**	**Jehoiachin**	**Zedekiah**	**The Remnant in Judah and Egypt**
1–6	22:10-12	7–20; 25–26; 35–36; 45–46:12; 47–49	22–23	21; 24; 27–34; 37–39	40–44
627–609 B.C.	609 B.C.	609–598 B.C.	598–597B.C.	597–586 B.C.	586 to ~580 B.C.

LINKS TO THE NEW TESTAMENT

Jeremiah's prophecy about the coming new covenant anticipates the new covenant that Christ inaugurated through his blood (31:31–34; Matthew 26:26–29). Christ is also the righteous Branch and the coming King who will reign wisely and be called "The LORD Our Righteousness" (23:1–6).

OVERVIEW

FOCUS	Call of Jeremiah	Concerning Judah	Concerning the Nations	Consummation
REFERENCE	1	2 — 45	46 — 51	52
TOPICS	Prologue	Prophetic Declarations (Sermons and Signs)		Postlude
	Minister	Message		Fulfillment
	Designation of the Prophet	Declarations Against Judah	Declarations Against the Nations	Destruction of Jerusalem
LOCATION	Judah		Surrounding Nations	Babylon
TIME	About 47 Years of Prophetic Ministry			

God called Jeremiah to be a prophet before his birth, and this book opens with his divine commission (1). The bulk of the book contains Jeremiah's prophetic declarations—through sermons, signs and parables—against the people of Judah for their apostasy, idolatry and immorality (2—45). In these chapters, God instructs Jeremiah to use a number of object lessons so that his life and actions become a series of illustrations to Judah. In spite of God's covenant love for his people, however, they have corrupted themselves through spiritual harlotry and are beyond the point of repentance.

Chapters 46—51 contain a series of prophecies against the surrounding nations, including Egypt, Moab, Ammon and Babylon. The book concludes with an account of the fall of Jerusalem (52) in which the city is destroyed and plundered, its leaders are killed and many of the people are deported to Babylon (this event is also recorded in 2 Kings 25, 2 Chronicles 36 and Jeremiah 39).

JEREMIAH

1 The words of Jeremiah son of Hilkiah, one of the priests at Anathoth[a]
in the territory of Benjamin. 2 The word
of the LORD came to him in the thirteenth year of the reign of Josiah son of
Amon king of Judah, 3 and through the
reign of Jehoiakim[b] son of Josiah king
of Judah, down to the fifth month of
the eleventh year of Zedekiah[c] son of
Josiah king of Judah, when the people
of Jerusalem went into exile.[d]

The Call of Jeremiah

4 The word of the LORD came to me,
saying,

5 "Before I formed you in the womb
I knew[a][e] you,
before you were born[f] I set you
apart;
I appointed you as a prophet to
the nations.[g]"

6 "Ah, Sovereign LORD," I said, "I do
not know how to speak;[h] I am only a
child."[i]
7 But the LORD said to me, "Do not
say, 'I am only a child.' You must go
to everyone I send you to and say
whatever I command you. 8 Do not
be afraid[j] of them, for I am with you[k]
and will rescue you," declares the
LORD.
9 Then the LORD reached out his
hand and touched[l] my mouth and
said to me, "Now, I have put my words
in your mouth.[m] 10 See, today I appoint
you over nations and kingdoms to uproot and tear down, to destroy and
overthrow, to build and to plant."[n]
11 The word of the LORD came to me:
"What do you see, Jeremiah?"[o]
"I see the branch of an almond tree,"
I replied.
12 The LORD said to me, "You have
seen correctly, for I am watching[b] to
see that my word is fulfilled."
13 The word of the LORD came to me
again: "What do you see?"[p]
"I see a boiling pot, tilting away from
the north," I answered.
14 The LORD said to me, "From the
north disaster will be poured out on all
who live in the land. 15 I am about to
summon all the peoples of the northern kingdoms," declares the LORD.

"Their kings will come and set up
their thrones
in the entrance of the gates of
Jerusalem;
they will come against all her
surrounding walls
and against all the towns of
Judah.[q]
16 I will pronounce my judgments on
my people
because of their wickedness[r] in
forsaking me,[s]
in burning incense to other gods[t]
and in worshiping what their
hands have made.

17 "Get yourself ready! Stand up and
say to them whatever I command you.
Do not be terrified[u] by them, or I will
terrify you before them. 18 Today I have
made you[v] a fortified city, an iron pillar and a bronze wall to stand against
the whole land—against the kings of
Judah, its officials, its priests and the
people of the land. 19 They will fight
against you but will not overcome you,
for I am with you[w] and will rescue[x]
you," declares the LORD.

Israel Forsakes God

2 The word of the LORD came to me:
2 "Go and proclaim in the hearing of
Jerusalem:

" 'I remember the devotion of your
youth,[y]

1:1 [a]Jos 21:18; 1Ch 6:60; Jer 32:7-9 **1:3** [b]2Ki 23:34 [c]2Ki 24:17; Jer 39:2 [d]Jer 52:15 **1:5** [e]Ps 139:16 [f]Isa 49:1 [g]ver 10; Jer 25:15-26 **1:6** [h]Ex 4:10; 6:12 [i]1Ki 3:7 **1:8** [j]Eze 2:6 [k]Jos 1:5; Jer 15:20 **1:9** [l]Isa 6:7 [m]Ex 4:12 **1:10** [n]Jer 18:7-10; 24:6; 31:4,28 **1:11** [o]Jer 24:3; Am 7:8 **1:13** [p]Zec 4:2 **1:15** [q]Jer 4:16; 9:11 **1:16** [r]Dt 28:20 [s]Jer 17:13 [t]Jer 7:9; 19:4 **1:17** [u]Eze 2:6 **1:18** [v]Isa 50:7 **1:19** [w]Jer 20:11 [x]ver 8 **2:2** [y]Eze 16:8-14, 60; Hos 2:15

1:5–10, 17–19

PROMISE 7

GOD'S RESOURCES

God never assigns a job without supplying the resources to get it done. Faced with the call to prophecy, Jeremiah needed two things; God supplied both. First, Jeremiah was timid about being God's spokesman (v. 6), so God supplied perspective (v. 5) and courage (vv. 7–8, 17–19). Second, he needed a message, and God put his own words in Jeremiah's mouth (v. 9–11).

As you consider how fortunate Jeremiah was, read Matthew 28:18–20 and Acts 1:8. These two reports of your Great Commission to be God's witness address these same issues and supply the same resources. As you read Jeremiah's story in this book, learn how a man of courage and conviction used God's resources to do God's work.

For the next Promise 7 reading go to page 854.

[a] 5 Or *chose* [b] 12 The Hebrew for *watching* sounds like the Hebrew for *almond tree.*

how as a bride you loved me
and followed me through the
desert,[z]
through a land not sown.
3Israel was holy[a] to the LORD,[b]
the firstfruits[c] of his harvest;
all who devoured[d] her were held
guilty,[e]
and disaster overtook them,' "
declares the LORD.

4Hear the word of the LORD,
O house of Jacob,
all you clans of the house of
Israel.

5This is what the LORD says:

"What fault did your fathers find in
me,
that they strayed so far from me?
They followed worthless idols
and became worthless[f]
themselves.
6They did not ask, 'Where is the
LORD,
who brought us up out of
Egypt[g]
and led us through the barren
wilderness,
through a land of deserts[h] and
rifts,[i]
a land of drought and darkness,[a]
a land where no one travels and
no one lives?'
7I brought you into a fertile land
to eat its fruit and rich
produce.[j]
But you came and defiled my land
and made my inheritance
detestable.[k]
8The priests did not ask,
'Where is the LORD?'
Those who deal with the law did
not know me;[l]
the leaders rebelled against me.
The prophets prophesied by Baal,[m]
following worthless idols.[n]

9"Therefore I bring charges[o]
against you again,"
declares the LORD.
"And I will bring charges against
your children's children.
10Cross over to the coasts of Kittim[b]
and look,
send to Kedar[c] and observe
closely;
see if there has ever been
anything like this:
11Has a nation ever changed its gods?
(Yet they are not gods[p] at all.)
But my people have exchanged
their[d] Glory[q]
for worthless idols.
12Be appalled at this, O heavens,
and shudder with great horror,"
declares the LORD.

13"My people have committed two
sins:
They have forsaken me,
the spring of living water,[r]
and have dug their own cisterns,
broken cisterns that cannot hold
water.
14Is Israel a servant, a slave[s] by
birth?
Why then has he become
plunder?
15Lions[t] have roared;
they have growled at him.
They have laid waste[u] his land;
his towns are burned and
deserted.
16Also, the men of Memphis[e][v] and
Tahpanhes[w]
have shaved the crown of your
head.[f]
17Have you not brought this on
yourselves[x]
by forsaking the LORD your God
when he led you in the way?
18Now why go to Egypt[y]
to drink water from the
Shihor[g]?[z]

2:2 [z]Dt 2:7
2:3 [a]Dt 7:6 [b]Ex 19:6 [c]Jas 1:18; Rev 14:4 [d]Isa 41:11; Jer 30:16 [e]Jer 50:7
2:5 [f]2Ki 17:15
2:6 [g]Hos 13:4 [h]Dt 8:15 [i]Dt 32:10
2:7 [j]Nu 13:27; Dt 8:7-9; 11:10-12 [k]Ps 106:34-39; Jer 16:18
2:8 [l]Jer 4:22 [m]Jer 23:13 [n]Jer 16:19
2:9 [o]Eze 20:35-36; Mic 6:2
2:11 [p]Isa 37:19; Jer 16:20 [q]Ps 106:20; Ro 1:23
2:13 [r]Ps 36:9; Jn 4:14
2:14 [s]Ex 4:22
2:15 [t]Jer 4:7; 50:17 [u]Isa 1:7
2:16 [v]Isa 19:13 [w]Jer 43:7-9
2:17 [x]Jer 4:18
2:18 [y]Isa 30:2 [z]Jos 13:3

[a]6 Or *and the shadow of death* [b]10 That is, Cyprus and western coastlands [c]10 The home of Bedouin tribes in the Syro-Arabian desert [d]11 Masoretic Text; an ancient Hebrew scribal tradition *my* [e]16 Hebrew *Noph* [f]16 Or *have cracked your skull* [g]18 That is, a branch of the Nile

2:13

PROMISE 3

DOUBLE TROUBLE

Sin is always double trouble, and Jeremiah used a powerful image to address both of those troubles. First, when God's people forsake him, they lose great opportunity for spiritual, moral, and ethical maturity. They miss pursuing a growth strategy for their lives. Second, what they substitute for God's way of life isn't just neutral; it's negative. As Jeremiah put it, their own cisterns cannot hold water. Their search for fulfillment without God is futile.

When we substitute our own wisdom for God's wisdom, we don't just lose growth opportunities, we develop *counter*-productive lifestyles. Instead of our lives taking on quality, our lives without God seem to leak! Over time we lose quality. Think of your life as being dynamic, as Jeremiah described here. Our lives are in a constant state of change, whether that change be positive or negative, toward God or away from God. God offers growth; disobedience results in atrophy. That presents a pretty clear choice, doesn't it?

For the next Promise 3 reading go to page 850.

And why go to Assyria
to drink water from the River[a]?
19Your wickedness will punish you;
your backsliding[a] will rebuke[b] you.
Consider then and realize
how evil and bitter[c] it is for you
when you forsake the LORD your God
and have no awe[d] of me,"
declares the Lord,
the LORD Almighty.

20"Long ago you broke off your yoke[e]
and tore off your bonds;
you said, 'I will not serve you!'
Indeed, on every high hill[f]
and under every spreading tree[g]
you lay down as a prostitute.
21I had planted[h] you like a choice vine[i]
of sound and reliable stock.
How then did you turn against me
into a corrupt,[j] wild vine?
22Although you wash yourself with soda
and use an abundance of soap,
the stain of your guilt is still before me,"
declares the Sovereign LORD.
23"How can you say, 'I am not defiled;[k]
I have not run after the Baals'?[l]
See how you behaved in the valley;[m]
consider what you have done.
You are a swift she-camel
running[n] here and there,
24a wild donkey[o] accustomed to the desert,
sniffing the wind in her craving—
in her heat who can restrain her?
Any males that pursue her need not tire themselves;
at mating time they will find her.
25Do not run until your feet are bare
and your throat is dry.
But you said, 'It's no use!
I love foreign gods,[p]
and I must go after them.'

26"As a thief is disgraced[q] when he is caught,
so the house of Israel is disgraced—
they, their kings and their officials,
their priests and their prophets.
27They say to wood, 'You are my father,'
and to stone,[r] 'You gave me birth.'
They have turned their backs to me
and not their faces;[s]
yet when they are in trouble,[t]
they say,
'Come and save us!'
28Where then are the gods[u] you made for yourselves?
Let them come if they can save you
when you are in trouble![v]
For you have as many gods
as you have towns,[w] O Judah.

29"Why do you bring charges against me?
You have all[x] rebelled against me,"
declares the LORD.
30"In vain I punished your people;
they did not respond to correction.
Your sword has devoured your prophets[y]
like a ravening lion.

31"You of this generation, consider
the word of the LORD:

"Have I been a desert to Israel
or a land of great darkness?[z]
Why do my people say, 'We are free to roam;
we will come to you no more'?
32Does a maiden forget her jewelry,
a bride her wedding ornaments?
Yet my people have forgotten me,
days without number.
33How skilled you are at pursuing love!
Even the worst of women can learn from your ways.
34On your clothes men find
the lifeblood[a] of the innocent poor,
though you did not catch them breaking in.[b]
Yet in spite of all this
35 you say, 'I am innocent;
he is not angry with me.'
But I will pass judgment[c] on you
because you say, 'I have not sinned.'[d]
36Why do you go about so much,
changing[e] your ways?
You will be disappointed by Egypt[f]
as you were by Assyria.
37You will also leave that place
with your hands on your head,[g]
for the LORD has rejected those you trust;
you will not be helped[h] by them.

3 "If a man divorces[i] his wife
and she leaves him and marries another man,

2:19 [a]Jer 3:11,22 [b]Isa 3:9; Hos 5:5 [c]Job 20:14; Am 8:10 [d]Ps 36:1
2:20 [e]Lev 26:13 [f]Isa 57:7; Jer 17:2 [g]Dt 12:2
2:21 [h]Ex 15:17 [i]Ps 80:8 [j]Isa 5:4
2:23 [k]Pr 30:12 [l]Jer 9:14 [m]Jer 7:31 [n]ver 33; Jer 31:22
2:24 [o]Jer 14:6
2:25 [p]Dt 32:16; Jer 3:13; 14:10
2:26 [q]Jer 48:27
2:27 [r]Jer 3:9 [s]Jer 18:17; 32:33 [t]Jdg 10:10; Isa 26:16
2:28 [u]Isa 45:20 [v]Dt 32:37 [w]2Ki 17:29; Jer 11:13
2:29 [x]Jer 5:1; 6:13; Da 9:11
2:30 [y]Ne 9:26; Ac 7:52; 1Th 2:15
2:31 [z]Isa 45:19
2:34 [a]2Ki 21:16 [b]Ex 22:2
2:35 [c]Jer 25:31 [d]1Jn 1:8,10
2:36 [e]Jer 31:22 [f]Isa 30:2,3,7
2:37 [g]2Sa 13:19 [h]Jer 37:7
3:1 [i]Dt 24:1-4

a *18* That is, the Euphrates

should he return to her again?
Would not the land be
completely defiled?
But you have lived as a prostitute
with many lovers[j]—
would you now return to me?"
declares the LORD.
2"Look up to the barren heights and
see.
Is there any place where you
have not been ravished?
By the roadside[k] you sat waiting
for lovers,
sat like a nomad[a] in the desert.
You have defiled the land[l]
with your prostitution and
wickedness.
3Therefore the showers have been
withheld,[m]
and no spring rains[n] have
fallen.
Yet you have the brazen look of a
prostitute;
you refuse to blush with
shame.[o]
4Have you not just called to me:
'My Father,[p] my friend from my
youth,[q]
5will you always be angry?[r]
Will your wrath continue
forever?'
This is how you talk,
but you do all the evil you can."

Unfaithful Israel

6During the reign of King Josiah, the
LORD said to me, "Have you seen what
faithless Israel has done? She has gone
up on every high hill and under every
spreading tree[s] and has committed
adultery[t] there. 7I thought that after
she had done all this she would return
to me but she did not, and her unfaithful sister[u] Judah saw it. 8I gave faithless Israel her certificate of divorce and
sent her away because of all her adulteries. Yet I saw that her unfaithful sister Judah had no fear;[v] she also went
out and committed adultery. 9Because
Israel's immorality mattered so little
to her, she defiled the land[w] and
committed adultery with stone[x] and
wood.[y] 10In spite of all this, her unfaithful sister Judah did not return to
me with all her heart, but only in pretense,[z]" declares the LORD.
11The LORD said to me, "Faithless Israel is more righteous[a] than unfaithful[b] Judah. 12Go, proclaim this message toward the north:[c]

" 'Return,[d] faithless Israel,'
declares the LORD,
'I will frown on you no longer,
for I am merciful,' declares the
LORD,
'I will not be angry[e] forever.
13Only acknowledge[f] your guilt—
you have rebelled against the
LORD your God,
you have scattered your favors to
foreign gods[g]
under every spreading tree,[h]
and have not obeyed[i] me,' "
declares the LORD.

14"Return,[j] faithless people," declares the LORD, "for I am your husband. I will choose you—one from a
town and two from a clan—and bring
you to Zion. 15Then I will give you
shepherds[k] after my own heart, who
will lead you with knowledge and understanding. 16In those days, when
your numbers have increased greatly
in the land," declares the LORD, "men
will no longer say, 'The ark of the covenant of the LORD.' It will never enter
their minds or be remembered;[l] it will
not be missed, nor will another one be
made. 17At that time they will call Jerusalem The Throne[m] of the LORD, and
all nations will gather in Jerusalem to
honor[n] the name of the LORD. No
longer will they follow the stubbornness of their evil hearts.[o] 18In those
days the house of Judah will join the
house of Israel,[p] and together[q] they

3:1 [j]Jer 2:20,25; Eze 16:26,29
3:2 [k]Ge 38:14; Eze 16:25 [l]Jer 2:7
3:3 [m]Lev 26:19 [n]Jer 14:4 [o]Jer 6:15; 8:12; Zep 3:5
3:4 [p]ver 19 [q]Jer 2:2
3:5 [r]Ps 103:9; Isa 57:16
3:6 [s]Jer 17:2 [t]Jer 2:20
3:7 [u]Eze 16:46
3:8 [v]Eze 16:47; 23:11
3:9 [w]ver 2 [x]Isa 57:6 [y]Jer 2:27
3:10 [z]Jer 12:2
3:11 [a]Eze 16:52; 23:11 [b]ver 7
3:12 [c]2Ki 17:3-6 [d]ver 14; Jer 31:21,22; Eze 33:11 [e]Ps 86:15
3:13 [f]Dt 30:1-3; Jer 14:20; 1Jn 1:9 [g]Jer 2:25 [h]Dt 12:2 [i]ver 25
3:14 [j]Hos 2:19
3:15 [k]Ac 20:28
3:16 [l]Isa 65:17
3:17 [m]Jer 17:12; Eze 43:7 [n]Isa 60:9 [o]Jer 11:8
3:18 [p]Hos 1:11 [q]Isa 11:13; Jer 50:4

3:3–13

PROMISE 1

OUR DEFIANCE, GOD'S GRACE

Israel had defied God over and over again. As they interacted with their pagan neighbors, the Israelites were drawn into worshiping other gods instead of or in addition to the true God. In case anyone thought sinning against God was no big deal, God described Israel's idolatry as adultery. He pictured himself as a husband reasoning with Israel, his adulterous wife. These verses capture the spirit of God's message to his people: Although God hates sin, he will always forgive the repentant sinner.

We should never confuse God's willingness to forgive with a light view of sin. This passage bears out the extent of God's disgust with sin. His attitude toward it is uncompromising and clear. That's what makes God's gracious offer of forgiveness so astounding.

If you have never become a Christian, or if you are a Christian who is living in disobedience to God, read the prophet's message clearly and carefully. Acknowledge your guilt, confess it, and return to him. God is waiting with open arms to receive you.

For the next Promise 1 reading go to page 814.

a 2 Or *an Arab*

will come from a northern[r] land to the land[s] I gave your forefathers as an inheritance.

19"I myself said,

" 'How gladly would I treat you like sons
and give you a desirable land,
the most beautiful inheritance of any nation.'
I thought you would call me 'Father'[t]
and not turn away from following me.
20But like a woman unfaithful to her husband,
so you have been unfaithful to me, O house of Israel,"
declares the LORD.

21A cry is heard on the barren heights,[u]
the weeping and pleading of the people of Israel,
because they have perverted their ways
and have forgotten the LORD their God.

22"Return,[v] faithless people;
I will cure[w] you of backsliding."

"Yes, we will come to you,
for you are the LORD our God.
23Surely the ⌊idolatrous⌋ commotion on the hills
and mountains is a deception;
surely in the LORD our God
is the salvation[x] of Israel.
24From our youth shameful[y] gods have consumed
the fruits of our fathers' labor—
their flocks and herds,
their sons and daughters.
25Let us lie down in our shame,[z]
and let our disgrace cover us.
We have sinned against the LORD our God,
both we and our fathers;
from our youth[a] till this day
we have not obeyed the LORD our God."

4 "If you will return[b], O Israel,
return to me,"
declares the LORD.
"If you put your detestable idols[c] out of my sight
and no longer go astray,
2and if in a truthful, just and righteous way
you swear,[d] 'As surely as the LORD lives,'[e]
then the nations will be blessed[f] by him
and in him they will glory."

3This is what the LORD says to the men of Judah and to Jerusalem:

"Break up your unplowed ground[g]
and do not sow among thorns.[h]
4Circumcise yourselves to the LORD,
circumcise your hearts,[i]
you men of Judah and people of Jerusalem,
or my wrath[j] will break out and burn like fire
because of the evil you have done—
burn with no one to quench[k] it.

Disaster From the North

5"Announce in Judah and proclaim in Jerusalem and say:
'Sound the trumpet throughout the land!'
Cry aloud and say:
'Gather together!
Let us flee to the fortified cities!'[l]
6Raise the signal to go to Zion!
Flee for safety without delay!
For I am bringing disaster from the north,[m]
even terrible destruction."

7A lion[n] has come out of his lair;
a destroyer of nations has set out.
He has left his place
to lay waste[o] your land.
Your towns will lie in ruins[p]
without inhabitant.
8So put on sackcloth,[q]
lament and wail,
for the fierce anger[r] of the LORD
has not turned away from us.

9"In that day," declares the LORD,
"the king and the officials will lose heart,
the priests will be horrified,
and the prophets will be appalled."[s]

10Then I said, "Ah, Sovereign LORD, how completely you have deceived[t] this people and Jerusalem by saying, 'You will have peace,'[u] when the sword is at our throats."

11At that time this people and Jerusalem will be told, "A scorching wind[v] from the barren heights in the desert blows toward my people, but not to winnow or cleanse; 12a wind too strong for that comes from me.[a] Now I pronounce my judgments[w] against them."

13Look! He advances like the clouds,[x]

3:18 [r]Jer 16:15; 31:8 [s]Am 9:15
3:19 [t]ver 4; Isa 63:16
3:21 [u]ver 2
3:22 [v]Hos 14:4 [w]Jer 33:6; Hos 6:1
3:23 [x]Ps 3:8; Jer 17:14
3:24 [y]Hos 9:10
3:25 [z]Ezr 9:6 [a]Jer 22:21
4:1 [b]Jer 3:1,22; Joel 2:12 [c]Jer 35:15
4:2 [d]Dt 10:20; Isa 65:16 [e]Jer 12:16 [f]Ge 22:18; Gal 3:8
4:3 [g]Hos 10:12 [h]Mk 4:18
4:4 [i]Dt 10:16; Jer 9:26; Ro 2:28-29 [j]Zep 2:2 [k]Am 5:6
4:5 [l]Jos 10:20; Jer 8:14
4:6 [m]Jer 1:13-15; 50:3
4:7 [n]2Ki 24:1; Jer 2:15 [o]Isa 1:7 [p]Jer 25:9
4:8 [q]Isa 22:12; Jer 6:26 [r]Jer 30:24
4:9 [s]Isa 29:9
4:10 [t]2Th 2:11 [u]Jer 14:13
4:11 [v]Eze 17:10; Hos 13:15
4:12 [w]Jer 1:16
4:13 [x]Isa 19:1

[a]12 Or *comes at my command*

his chariots[y] come like a
whirlwind,[z]
his horses are swifter than eagles.[a]
Woe to us! We are ruined!
14O Jerusalem, wash[b] the evil from
your heart and be saved.
How long will you harbor wicked
thoughts?
15A voice is announcing from Dan,[c]
proclaiming disaster from the
hills of Ephraim.
16"Tell this to the nations,
proclaim it to Jerusalem:
'A besieging army is coming from a
distant land,
raising a war cry[d] against the
cities of Judah.
17They surround[e] her like men
guarding a field,
because she has rebelled[f]
against me,' "
declares the LORD.
18"Your own conduct and actions[g]
have brought this upon you.[h]
This is your punishment.
How bitter[i] it is!
How it pierces to the heart!"

19Oh, my anguish, my anguish![j]
I writhe in pain.
Oh, the agony of my heart!
My heart pounds within me,
I cannot keep silent.[k]
For I have heard the sound of the
trumpet;
I have heard the battle cry.[l]
20Disaster follows disaster;[m]
the whole land lies in ruins.
In an instant my tents[n] are
destroyed,
my shelter in a moment.
21How long must I see the battle
standard
and hear the sound of the
trumpet?
22"My people are fools;[o]
they do not know me.[p]
They are senseless children;
they have no understanding.
They are skilled in doing evil;[q]
they know not how to do
good."[r]
23I looked at the earth,
and it was formless and empty;[s]
and at the heavens,
and their light was gone.
24I looked at the mountains,
and they were quaking;[t]
all the hills were swaying.
25I looked, and there were no people;
every bird in the sky had flown
away.[u]
26I looked, and the fruitful land was
a desert;
all its towns lay in ruins
before the LORD, before his fierce
anger.

27This is what the LORD says:
"The whole land will be ruined,
though I will not destroy[v] it
completely.
28Therefore the earth will mourn[w]
and the heavens above grow
dark,[x]
because I have spoken and will not
relent,[y]
I have decided and will not turn
back.[z]"

29At the sound of horsemen and
archers[a]
every town takes to flight.[b]
Some go into the thickets;
some climb up among the rocks.
All the towns are deserted;[c]
no one lives in them.

30What are you doing,[d]
O devastated one?
Why dress yourself in scarlet
and put on jewels[e] of gold?
Why shade your eyes with paint?[f]
You adorn yourself in vain.
Your lovers[g] despise you;
they seek your life.

31I hear a cry as of a woman in
labor,[h]
a groan as of one bearing her
first child—
the cry of the Daughter of Zion
gasping for breath,[i]
stretching out her hands[j] and
saying,
"Alas! I am fainting;
my life is given over to
murderers."

Not One Is Upright

5 "Go up and down[k] the streets of
Jerusalem,
look around and consider,
search through her squares.
If you can find but one person[l]
who deals honestly and seeks the
truth,
I will forgive[m] this city.
2Although they say, 'As surely as the
LORD lives,'[n]
still they are swearing falsely."
3O LORD, do not your eyes[o] look for
truth?
You struck[p] them, but they felt
no pain;
you crushed them, but they
refused correction.[q]
They made their faces harder than
stone[r]
and refused to repent.

4:13 [y]Isa 66:15 [z]Isa 5:28 [a]Dt 28:49; Hab 1:8
4:14 [b]Jas 4:8
4:15 [c]Jer 8:16
4:16 [d]Eze 21:22
4:17 [e]2Ki 25:1,4 [f]Jer 5:23
4:18 [g]Ps 107:17; Isa 50:1 [h]Jer 2:17 [i]Jer 2:19
4:19 [j]Isa 16:11; 22:4; Jer 9:10 [k]Jer 20:9 [l]Nu 10:9
4:20 [m]Ps 42:7; Eze 7:26 [n]Jer 10:20
4:22 [o]Jer 10:8 [p]Jer 2:8 [q]Jer 13:23; 1Co 14:20 [r]Ro 16:19
4:23 [s]Ge 1:2
4:24 [t]Isa 5:25; Eze 38:20
4:25 [u]Jer 9:10; 12:4; Zep 1:3
4:27 [v]Jer 5:10,18; 12:12; 30:11; 46:28
4:28 [w]Jer 12:4,11; 14:2; Hos 4:3 [x]Isa 5:30; 50:3 [y]Nu 23:19 [z]Jer 23:20; 30:24
4:29 [a]Jer 6:23 [b]2Ki 25:4 [c]ver 7
4:30 [d]Isa 10:3-4 [e]Eze 23:40 [f]2Ki 9:30 [g]La 1:2; Eze 23:9,22
4:31 [h]Jer 13:21 [i]Isa 42:14 [j]Isa 1:15; La 1:17
5:1 [k]2Ch 16:9; Eze 22:30 [l]Ge 18:32 [m]Ge 18:24
5:2 [n]Jer 4:2
5:3 [o]2Ch 16:9 [p]Isa 9:13 [q]Jer 2:30; Zep 3:2 [r]Jer 7:26; 19:15; Eze 3:8-9

4I thought, "These are only the
poor;
they are foolish,
for they do not know[s] the way of
the LORD,
the requirements of their God.
5So I will go to the leaders[t]
and speak to them;
surely they know the way of the
LORD,
the requirements of their God."
But with one accord they too had
broken off the yoke
and torn off the bonds.[u]
6Therefore a lion from the forest will
attack them,
a wolf from the desert will
ravage them,
a leopard[v] will lie in wait near
their towns
to tear to pieces any who
venture out,
for their rebellion is great
and their backslidings many.[w]

7"Why should I forgive you?
Your children have forsaken me
and sworn[x] by gods that are not
gods.[y]
I supplied all their needs,
yet they committed adultery[z]
and thronged to the houses of
prostitutes.
8They are well-fed, lusty stallions,
each neighing for another man's
wife.[a]
9Should I not punish them for
this?"[b]
declares the LORD.
"Should I not avenge myself
on such a nation as this?

10"Go through her vineyards and
ravage them,
but do not destroy them
completely.[c]
Strip off her branches,
for these people do not belong
to the LORD.
11The house of Israel and the house
of Judah
have been utterly unfaithful[d] to
me,"
declares the LORD.
12They have lied about the LORD;
they said, "He will do nothing!
No harm will come to us;[e]
we will never see sword or
famine.[f]
13The prophets[g] are but wind
and the word is not in them;
so let what they say be done to
them."

14Therefore this is what the LORD
God Almighty says:

"Because the people have spoken
these words,
I will make my words in your
mouth[h] a fire[i]
and these people the wood it
consumes.
15O house of Israel," declares the
LORD,
"I am bringing a distant nation[j]
against you—
an ancient and enduring nation,
a people whose language[k] you
do not know,
whose speech you do not
understand.
16Their quivers are like an open
grave;
all of them are mighty warriors.
17They will devour[l m] your harvests
and food,
devour[n o] your sons and
daughters;
they will devour[p] your flocks and
herds,
devour your vines and fig trees.
With the sword they will destroy
the fortified cities in which you
trust.[q]

18"Yet even in those days," declares
the LORD, "I will not destroy[r] you
completely. 19And when the people
ask,[s] 'Why has the LORD our God done
all this to us?' you will tell them, 'As you
have forsaken me and served foreign
gods[t] in your own land, so now you
will serve foreigners[u] in a land not
your own.'

20"Announce this to the house of
Jacob
and proclaim it in Judah:
21Hear this, you foolish and senseless
people,
who have eyes[v] but do not see,
who have ears but do not hear:[w]
22Should you not fear[x] me?"
declares the LORD.
"Should you not tremble in my
presence?
I made the sand a boundary for the
sea,
an everlasting barrier it cannot
cross.
The waves may roll, but they
cannot prevail;
they may roar, but they cannot
cross it.
23But these people have stubborn
and rebellious[y] hearts;
they have turned aside and gone
away.
24They do not say to themselves,
'Let us fear the LORD our God,
who gives autumn and spring
rains[z] in season,

5:4 [s]Jer 8:7
5:5 [t]Mic 3:1,9 [u]Ps 2:3; Jer 2:20
5:6 [v]Hos 13:7 [w]Jer 30:14
5:7 [x]Jos 23:7; Zep 1:5 [y]Dt 32:21; Jer 2:11; Gal 4:8 [z]Nu 25:1
5:8 [a]Jer 29:23; Eze 22:11
5:9 [b]ver 29; Jer 9:9
5:10 [c]Jer 4:27
5:11 [d]Jer 3:20
5:12 [e]Jer 23:17 [f]2Ch 36:16; Jer 14:13
5:13 [g]Jer 14:15
5:14 [h]Jer 1:9; Hos 6:5 [i]Jer 23:29
5:15 [j]Dt 28:49; Isa 5:26; Jer 4:16 [k]Isa 28:11
5:17 [l]Jer 8:16 [m]Lev 26:16 [n]Jer 50:7,17 [o]Dt 28:32 [p]Dt 28:31 [q]Dt 28:33
5:18 [r]Jer 4:27
5:19 [s]Dt 29:24-26; 1Ki 9:9 [t]Jer 16:13 [u]Dt 28:48
5:21 [v]Isa 6:10; Eze 12:2 [w]Mt 13:15; Mk 8:18
5:22 [x]Dt 28:58
5:23 [y]Dt 21:18
5:24 [z]Ps 147:8; Joel 2:23

who assures us of the regular weeks of harvest.'[a]
25Your wrongdoings have kept these away;
your sins have deprived you of good.

26"Among my people are wicked men
who lie in wait[b] like men who snare birds
and like those who set traps to catch men.
27Like cages full of birds,
their houses are full of deceit;[c]
they have become rich[d] and powerful
28 and have grown fat[e] and sleek.
Their evil deeds have no limit;
they do not plead the case of the fatherless[f] to win it,
they do not defend the rights of the poor.[g]
29Should I not punish them for this?"
declares the LORD.
"Should I not avenge myself
on such a nation as this?

30"A horrible[h] and shocking thing
has happened in the land:
31The prophets prophesy lies,[i]
the priests rule by their own authority,
and my people love it this way.
But what will you do in the end?

Jerusalem Under Siege

6 "Flee for safety, people of Benjamin!
Flee from Jerusalem!
Sound the trumpet in Tekoa![j]
Raise the signal over Beth Hakkerem![k]
For disaster looms out of the north,[l]
even terrible destruction.
2I will destroy the Daughter of Zion,
so beautiful and delicate.
3Shepherds[m] with their flocks will come against her;
they will pitch their tents around[n] her,
each tending his own portion."

4"Prepare for battle against her!
Arise, let us attack at noon![o]
But, alas, the daylight is fading,
and the shadows of evening grow long.
5So arise, let us attack at night
and destroy her fortresses!"

6This is what the LORD Almighty says:

"Cut down the trees[p]
and build siege ramps[q] against Jerusalem.
This city must be punished;
it is filled with oppression.
7As a well pours out its water,
so she pours out her wickedness.
Violence[r] and destruction[s] resound in her;
her sickness and wounds are ever before me.
8Take warning, O Jerusalem,
or I will turn away[t] from you
and make your land desolate
so no one can live in it."

9This is what the LORD Almighty says:

"Let them glean the remnant of Israel
as thoroughly as a vine;
pass your hand over the branches again,
like one gathering grapes."
10To whom can I speak and give warning?
Who will listen to me?
Their ears are closed[a][u]
so they cannot hear.
The word[v] of the LORD is offensive to them;
they find no pleasure in it.
11But I am full of the wrath[w] of the LORD,
and I cannot hold it in.[x]

"Pour it out on the children in the street
and on the young men[y] gathered together;
both husband and wife will be caught in it,
and the old, those weighed down with years.
12Their houses will be turned over to others,[z]
together with their fields and their wives,[a]
when I stretch out my hand[b]
against those who live in the land,"
declares the LORD.
13"From the least to the greatest,
all are greedy for gain;[c]
prophets and priests alike,
all practice deceit.[d]
14They dress the wound of my people
as though it were not serious.
'Peace, peace,' they say,
when there is no peace.[e]
15Are they ashamed of their loathsome conduct?
No, they have no shame at all;
they do not even know how to blush.[f]
So they will fall among the fallen;

5:24 [a]Ge 8:22; Ac 14:17
5:26 [b]Ps 10:8; Pr 1:11
5:27 [c]Jer 9:6 [d]Jer 12:1
5:28 [e]Dt 32:15 [f]Zec 7:10 [g]Isa 1:23; Jer 7:6
5:30 [h]Jer 23:14; Hos 6:10
5:31 [i]Eze 13:6; Mic 2:11
6:1 [j]2Ch 11:6 [k]Ne 3:14 [l]Jer 4:6
6:3 [m]Jer 12:10 [n]2Ki 25:4; Lk 19:43
6:4 [o]Jer 15:8
6:6 [p]Dt 20:19-20 [q]Jer 32:24
6:7 [r]Ps 55:9; Eze 7:11,23 [s]Jer 20:8
6:8 [t]Eze 23:18; Hos 9:12
6:10 [u]Ac 7:51 [v]Jer 20:8
6:11 [w]Jer 7:20 [x]Job 32:20; Jer 20:9 [y]Jer 9:21
6:12 [z]Dt 28:30 [a]Jer 8:10; 38:22 [b]Isa 5:25
6:13 [c]Isa 56:11 [d]Jer 8:10
6:14 [e]Jer 4:10; 8:11; Eze 13:10
6:15 [f]Jer 3:3; 8:10-12

[a]10 Hebrew *uncircumcised*

they will be brought down when
I punish them,"
says the LORD.

3 →PG. 892

16 This is what the LORD says:

"Stand at the crossroads and look;
ask for the ancient paths,[g]
ask where the good way[h] is, and
walk in it,
and you will find rest[i] for your
souls.
But you said, 'We will not walk
in it.'
17 I appointed watchmen[j] over you
and said,
'Listen to the sound of the
trumpet!'
But you said, 'We will not
listen.'[k]
18 Therefore hear, O nations;
observe, O witnesses,
what will happen to them.
19 Hear, O earth:[l]
I am bringing disaster on this
people,
the fruit of their schemes,[m]
because they have not listened to
my words
and have rejected my law.[n]
20 What do I care about incense from
Sheba
or sweet calamus[o] from a
distant land?
Your burnt offerings are not
acceptable;[p]
your sacrifices[q] do not please
me."[r]

21 Therefore this is what the LORD
says:

"I will put obstacles before this
people.
Fathers and sons alike will
stumble[s] over them;
neighbors and friends will
perish."

22 This is what the LORD says:

"Look, an army is coming
from the land of the north;[t]
a great nation is being stirred up
from the ends of the earth.
23 They are armed with bow and
spear;
they are cruel and show no
mercy.[u]
They sound like the roaring sea
as they ride on their horses;[v]
they come like men in battle
formation
to attack you, O Daughter of
Zion."

24 We have heard reports about them,
and our hands hang limp.
Anguish[w] has gripped us,
pain like that of a woman in
labor.[x]
25 Do not go out to the fields
or walk on the roads,
for the enemy has a sword,
and there is terror on every
side.[y]
26 O my people, put on sackcloth[z]
and roll in ashes;[a]
mourn with bitter wailing
as for an only son,[b]
for suddenly the destroyer
will come upon us.

27 "I have made you a tester[c] of
metals
and my people the ore,
that you may observe
and test their ways.
28 They are all hardened rebels,[d]
going about to slander.[e]
They are bronze and iron;[f]
they all act corruptly.
29 The bellows blow fiercely
to burn away the lead with fire,
but the refining goes on in vain;
the wicked are not purged out.
30 They are called rejected silver,
because the LORD has rejected
them."[g]

False Religion Worthless

7 This is the word that came to Jeremiah from the LORD: 2 "Stand[h] at the
gate of the LORD's house and there
proclaim this message:

" 'Hear the word of the LORD, all you
people of Judah who come through
these gates to worship the LORD. 3 This
is what the LORD Almighty, the God of
Israel, says: Reform your ways[i] and
your actions, and I will let you live in
this place. 4 Do not trust in deceptive[j]
words and say, "This is the temple of
the LORD, the temple of the LORD, the
temple of the LORD!" 5 If you really
change your ways and your actions
and deal with each other justly,[k] 6 if
you do not oppress the alien, the fa-

6:16 [g] Jer 18:15 [h] Ps 119:3 [i] Mt 11:29 **6:17** [j] Eze 3:17 [k] Jer 11:7-8; 25:4 **6:19** [l] Isa 1:2; Jer 22:29 [m] Pr 1:31 [n] Jer 8:9 **6:20** [o] Ex 30:23 [p] Am 5:22 [q] Ps 50:8-10; Jer 7:21; Mic 6:7-8 [r] Isa 1:11 **6:21** [s] Isa 8:14 **6:22** [t] Jer 1:15; 10:22 **6:23** [u] Isa 13:18 [v] Jer 4:29 **6:24** [w] Jer 4:19 [x] Jer 4:31; 50:41-43 **6:25** [y] Jer 49:29 **6:26** [z] Jer 4:8 [a] Jer 25:34; Mic 1:10 [b] Zec 12:10 **6:27** [c] Jer 9:7 **6:28** [d] Jer 5:23 [e] Jer 9:4 [f] Eze 22:18 **6:30** [g] Ps 119:119; Jer 7:29; Hos 9:17 **7:2** [h] Jer 17:19 **7:3** [i] Jer 18:11; 26:13 **7:4** [j] Mic 3:11 **7:5** [k] Jer 22:3

7:3–11

PROMISE 1

AN UNCHANGING ELEMENT

Some things never change; this passage looks at one of those things. Jeremiah addressed it here. Jesus addressed it in his day (Matthew 23; Mark 11:17). Today, people use it as an excuse to reject Christianity. It's called *hypocrisy.* Jeremiah warned people who lived a double life with these simple but sobering words in verse 11: "I have been watching! declares the LORD."

For the next Promise 1 reading go to page 826.

therless or the widow and do not shed innocent blood[l] in this place, and if you do not follow other gods[m] to your own harm, 7then I will let you live in this place, in the land[n] I gave your forefathers for ever and ever. 8But look, you are trusting in deceptive words that are worthless.

9" 'Will you steal and murder, commit adultery and perjury,[a] burn incense to Baal[o] and follow other gods[p] you have not known, 10and then come and stand before me in this house,[q] which bears my Name, and say, "We are safe"—safe to do all these detestable things? 11Has this house,[r] which bears my Name, become a den of robbers[s] to you? But I have been watching![t] declares the LORD.

12" 'Go now to the place in Shiloh[u] where I first made a dwelling for my Name, and see what I did[v] to it because of the wickedness of my people Israel. 13While you were doing all these things, declares the LORD, I spoke to you again and again,[w] but you did not listen;[x] I called you, but you did not answer.[y] 14Therefore, what I did to Shiloh I will now do to the house that bears my Name,[z] the temple you trust in, the place I gave to you and your fathers. 15I will thrust you from my presence, just as I did all your brothers, the people of Ephraim.'[a]

16"So do not pray for this people nor offer any plea[b] or petition for them; do not plead with me, for I will not listen to you. 17Do you not see what they are doing in the towns of Judah and in the streets of Jerusalem? 18The children gather wood, the fathers light the fire, and the women knead the dough and make cakes of bread for the Queen of Heaven.[c] They pour out drink offerings[d] to other gods to provoke[e] me to anger. 19But am I the one they are provoking? declares the LORD. Are they not rather harming themselves, to their own shame?[f]

20" 'Therefore this is what the Sovereign LORD says: My anger[g] and my wrath will be poured out on this place, on man and beast, on the trees of the field and on the fruit of the ground, and it will burn and not be quenched.

21" 'This is what the LORD Almighty, the God of Israel, says: Go ahead, add your burnt offerings to your other sacrifices[h] and eat[i] the meat yourselves! 22For when I brought your forefathers out of Egypt and spoke to them, I did not just give them commands about burnt offerings and sacrifices,[j] 23but I gave them this command: Obey[k] me, and I will be your God and you will be my people.[l] Walk in all the ways I command you, that it may go well[m] with you. 24But they did not listen or pay attention;[n] instead, they followed the stubborn inclinations of their evil hearts. They went backward and not forward. 25From the time your forefathers left Egypt until now, day after day, again and again I sent you my servants the prophets.[o] 26But they did not listen to me or pay attention. They were stiff-necked and did more evil than their forefathers.'[p]

27"When you tell[q] them all this, they will not listen[r] to you; when you call to them, they will not answer. 28Therefore say to them, 'This is the nation that has not obeyed the LORD its God or responded to correction. Truth has perished; it has vanished from their lips. 29Cut off[s] your hair and throw it away; take up a lament on the barren heights, for the LORD has rejected and abandoned[t] this generation that is under his wrath.

The Valley of Slaughter

30" 'The people of Judah have done evil in my eyes, declares the LORD. They have set up their detestable idols[u] in the house that bears my Name and have defiled[v] it. 31They have built the high places of Topheth[w] in the Valley of Ben Hinnom to burn their sons and daughters[x] in the fire—something I did not command, nor did it enter my mind.[y] 32So beware, the days are coming, declares the LORD, when people will no longer call it Topheth or the Valley of Ben Hinnom, but the Valley of Slaughter,[z] for they will bury[a] the dead in Topheth until there is no more room. 33Then the carcasses of this people will become food[b] for the birds of the air and the beasts of the earth, and there will be no one to frighten them away. 34I will bring an end to the sounds[c] of joy and gladness and to the voices of bride and bridegroom[d] in the towns of Judah and the streets of Jerusalem, for the land will become desolate.[e]

8 " 'At that time, declares the LORD, the bones of the kings and officials of Judah, the bones of the priests and prophets, and the bones of the people of Jerusalem will be removed from their graves. 2They will be exposed to the sun and the moon and all the stars of the heavens, which they have loved and served[f] and which they have followed and consulted and worshiped. They will not be gathered up or buried, but will be like refuse lying on the

7:6 [l]Jer 2:34; 19:4 [m]Dt 8:19
7:7 [n]Dt 4:40
7:9 [o]Jer 11:13,17 [p]Ex 20:3
7:10 [q]Jer 32:34; Eze 23:38-39
7:11 [r]Isa 56:7 [s]Mt 21:13*; Mk 11:17*; Lk 19:46* [t]Jer 29:23
7:12 [u]Jos 18:1 [v]1Sa 4:10-11, 22; Ps 78:60-64
7:13 [w]2Ch 36:15 [x]Isa 65:12 [y]Jer 35:17
7:14 [z]1Ki 9:7
7:15 [a]Ps 78:67
7:16 [b]Ex 32:10; Dt 9:14; Jer 15:1
7:18 [c]Jer 44:17-19 [d]Jer 19:13 [e]1Ki 14:9
7:19 [f]Jer 9:19
7:20 [g]Jer 42:18; La 2:3-5
7:21 [h]Isa 1:11; Am 5:21-22 [i]Hos 8:13
7:22 [j]1Sa 15:22; Ps 51:16; Hos 6:6
7:23 [k]Ex 19:5 [l]Lev 26:12 [m]Ex 15:26
7:24 [n]Ps 81:11-12; Jer 11:8
7:25 [o]Jer 25:4
7:26 [p]Jer 16:12
7:27 [q]Eze 2:7 [r]Eze 3:7
7:29 [s]Job 1:20; Isa 15:2; Mic 1:16 [t]Jer 6:30
7:30 [u]Eze 7:20-22 [v]Jer 32:34
7:31 [w]2Ki 23:10 [x]Ps 106:38 [y]Jer 19:5
7:32 [z]Jer 19:6 [a]Jer 19:11
7:33 [b]Dt 28:26
7:34 [c]Isa 24:8; Eze 26:13 [d]Rev 18:23 [e]Lev 26:34
8:2 [f]2Ki 23:5; Ac 7:42

[a] 9 Or *and swear by false gods*

ground. 3Wherever I banish them, all the survivors of this evil nation will prefer death to life,[g] declares the LORD Almighty.'

Sin and Punishment

4"Say to them, 'This is what the LORD says:

" 'When men fall down, do they
not get up?[h]
When a man turns away, does he
not return?
5Why then have these people turned
away?
Why does Jerusalem always turn
away?
They cling to deceit;[i]
they refuse to return.[j]
6I have listened attentively,
but they do not say what is right.
No one repents[k] of his
wickedness,
saying, "What have I done?"
Each pursues his own course[l]
like a horse charging into battle.
7Even the stork in the sky
knows her appointed seasons,
and the dove, the swift and the
thrush
observe the time of their
migration.
But my people do not know[m]
the requirements of the LORD.
8" 'How can you say, "We are wise,
for we have the law[n] of the
LORD,"
when actually the lying pen of the
scribes
has handled it falsely?
9The wise[o] will be put to shame;
they will be dismayed and
trapped.
Since they have rejected the word[p]
of the LORD,
what kind of wisdom do they
have?
10Therefore I will give their wives to
other men
and their fields to new owners.[q]
From the least to the greatest,
all are greedy for gain;[r]
prophets and priests alike,
all practice deceit.
11They dress the wound of my
people
as though it were not serious.
"Peace, peace," they say,
when there is no peace.[s]
12Are they ashamed of their
loathsome conduct?
No, they have no shame[t] at all;
they do not even know how to
blush.
So they will fall among the fallen;
they will be brought down when
they are punished,[u]
says the LORD.[v]
13" 'I will take away their harvest,
declares the LORD.
There will be no grapes on the
vine.[w]
There will be no figs[x] on the tree,
and their leaves will wither.[y]
What I have given them
will be taken[z] from them.[a]' "

14"Why are we sitting here?
Gather together!
Let us flee to the fortified cities[a]
and perish there!
For the LORD our God has doomed
us to perish
and given us poisoned water[b] to
drink,
because we have sinned[c]
against him.
15We hoped for peace[d]
but no good has come,
for a time of healing
but there was only terror.[e]
16The snorting of the enemy's horses
is heard from Dan;[f]
at the neighing of their stallions
the whole land trembles.
They have come to devour
the land and everything in it,
the city and all who live there."

17"See, I will send venomous
snakes[g] among you,
vipers that cannot be charmed,[h]
and they will bite you,"
declares the LORD.

18O my Comforter[b] in sorrow,
my heart is faint[i] within me.
19Listen to the cry of my people
from a land far away:[j]
"Is the LORD not in Zion?
Is her King no longer there?"

"Why have they provoked me to
anger with their images,
with their worthless foreign
idols?"[k]

20"The harvest is past,
the summer has ended,
and we are not saved."
21Since my people are crushed, I am
crushed;
I mourn,[l] and horror grips me.
22Is there no balm in Gilead?[m]
Is there no physician there?
Why then is there no healing[n]
for the wound of my people?

9 1Oh, that my head were a spring of
water

8:3 [g]Job 3:22; Rev 9:6 **8:4** [h]Pr 24:16 **8:5** [i]Jer 5:27 [j]Jer 7:24; 9:6 **8:6** [k]Rev 9:20 [l]Ps 14:1-3 **8:7** [m]Isa 1:3; Jer 5:4-5 **8:8** [n]Ro 2:17 **8:9** [o]Jer 6:15 [p]Jer 6:19 **8:10** [q]Jer 6:12 [r]Isa 56:11 **8:11** [s]Jer 6:14 **8:12** [t]Jer 3:3 [u]Ps 52:5-7; Isa 3:9 [v]Jer 6:15 **8:13** [w]Joel 1:7 [x]Lk 13:6 [y]Mt 21:19 [z]Jer 5:17 **8:14** [a]Jer 4:5; Jer 35:11 [b]Dt 29:18; Jer 9:15; 23:15 [c]Jer 14:7,20 **8:15** [d]ver 11 [e]Jer 14:19 **8:16** [f]Jer 4:15 **8:17** [g]Nu 21:6; Dt 32:24 [h]Ps 58:5 **8:18** [i]La 5:17 **8:19** [j]Jer 9:16 [k]Dt 32:21 **8:21** [l]Jer 14:17 **8:22** [m]Ge 37:25 [n]Jer 30:12

a *13* The meaning of the Hebrew for this sentence is uncertain. b *18* The meaning of the Hebrew for this word is uncertain.

and my eyes a fountain of tears!
I would weep[o] day and night
for the slain of my people.[p]
2Oh, that I had in the desert
a lodging place for travelers,
so that I might leave my people
and go away from them;
for they are all adulterers,[q]
a crowd of unfaithful people.

3"They make ready their tongue
like a bow, to shoot lies;[r]
it is not by truth
that they triumph[a] in the land.
They go from one sin to another;
they do not acknowledge me,"
declares the LORD.
4"Beware of your friends;
do not trust your brothers.[s]
For every brother is a deceiver,[b][t]
and every friend a slanderer.
5Friend deceives friend,
and no one speaks the truth.
They have taught their tongues to
lie;
they weary themselves with
sinning.
6You[c] live in the midst of
deception;[u]
in their deceit they refuse to
acknowledge me,"
declares the LORD.

7Therefore this is what the LORD Almighty says:

"See, I will refine[v] and test[w]
them,
for what else can I do
because of the sin of my people?
8Their tongue[x] is a deadly arrow;
it speaks with deceit.
With his mouth each speaks
cordially to his neighbor,
but in his heart he sets a trap[y]
for him.
9Should I not punish them for this?"
declares the LORD.
"Should I not avenge[z] myself
on such a nation as this?"
10I will weep and wail for the
mountains
and take up a lament concerning
the desert pastures.
They are desolate and untraveled,
and the lowing of cattle is not
heard.
The birds of the air[a] have fled
and the animals are gone.
11"I will make Jerusalem a heap of
ruins,
a haunt of jackals;[b]
and I will lay waste the towns of
Judah
so no one can live there."[c]

12What man is wise[d] enough to understand this? Who has been instructed by the LORD and can explain it? Why has the land been ruined and laid waste like a desert that no one can cross?

13The LORD said, "It is because they have forsaken my law, which I set before them; they have not obeyed me or followed my law.[e] 14Instead, they have followed[f] the stubbornness of their hearts;[g] they have followed the Baals, as their fathers taught them."
15Therefore, this is what the LORD Almighty, the God of Israel, says: "See, I will make this people eat bitter food[h] and drink poisoned water.[i] 16I will scatter them among nations[j] that neither they nor their fathers have known,[k] and I will pursue them with the sword[l] until I have destroyed them."[m]

17This is what the LORD Almighty says:

"Consider now! Call for the wailing
women[n] to come;
send for the most skillful of
them.
18Let them come quickly
and wail over us
till our eyes overflow with tears
and water streams from our
eyelids.[o]
19The sound of wailing is heard from
Zion:
'How ruined[p] we are!
How great is our shame!
We must leave our land
because our houses are in
ruins.' "
20Now, O women, hear the word of
the LORD;
open your ears to the words of
his mouth.
Teach your daughters how to wail;
teach one another a lament.[q]
21Death has climbed in through our
windows
and has entered our fortresses;
it has cut off the children from the
streets
and the young men[r] from the
public squares.

22Say, "This is what the LORD declares:

" 'The dead bodies of men will lie
like refuse[s] on the open field,
like cut grain behind the reaper,
with no one to gather them.' "

23This is what the LORD says:

9:1 [o]Jer 13:17; La 2:11,18 [p]Isa 22:4
9:2 [q]Jer 5:7-8; 23:10; Hos 4:2
9:3 [r]Ps 64:3
9:4 [s]Mic 7:5-6 [t]Ge 27:35
9:6 [u]Jer 5:27
9:7 [v]Isa 1:25 [w]Jer 6:27
9:8 [x]ver 3 [y]Jer 5:26
9:9 [z]Jer 5:9,29
9:10 [a]Jer 4:25; 12:4; Hos 4:3
9:11 [b]Isa 34:13 [c]Isa 25:2; Jer 26:9
9:12 [d]Ps 107:43; Hos 14:9
9:13 [e]2Ch 7:19; Ps 89:30-32
9:14 [f]Jer 2:8,23 [g]Jer 7:24
9:15 [h]La 3:15 [i]Jer 8:14
9:16 [j]Lev 26:33 [k]Dt 28:64 [l]Eze 5:2 [m]Jer 44:27; Eze 5:12
9:17 [n]2Ch 35:25; Ecc 12:5; Am 5:16
9:18 [o]Jer 14:17
9:19 [p]Jer 4:13
9:20 [q]Isa 32:9-13
9:21 [r]2Ch 36:17
9:22 [s]Jer 8:2

a3 Or *lies; / they are not valiant for truth*
b4 Or *a deceiving Jacob*
c6 That is, Jeremiah (the Hebrew is singular)

"Let not the wise man boast of his
wisdom[t]
or the strong man boast of his
strength[u]
or the rich man boast of his
riches,[v]
24 but let him who boasts boast[w]
about this:
that he understands and knows
me,
that I am the LORD,[x] who exercises
kindness,[y]
justice and righteousness[z] on
earth,
for in these I delight,"
declares the LORD.

25 "The days are coming," declares
the LORD, "when I will punish all who
are circumcised only in the flesh[a]—
26 Egypt, Judah, Edom, Ammon, Moab
and all who live in the desert in distant
places.[a][b] For all these nations are
really uncircumcised, and even the
whole house of Israel is uncircumcised
in heart.[c]"

God and Idols

10 Hear what the LORD says to you,
O house of Israel. 2 This is what the
LORD says:

"Do not learn the ways of the
nations[d]
or be terrified by signs in the
sky,
though the nations are terrified
by them.
3 For the customs of the peoples are
worthless;
they cut a tree out of the forest,
and a craftsman[e] shapes it with
his chisel.
4 They adorn it with silver and gold;
they fasten it with hammer and
nails
so it will not totter.[f]
5 Like a scarecrow in a melon patch,
their idols cannot speak;[g]
they must be carried
because they cannot walk.[h]
Do not fear them;
they can do no harm
nor can they do any good."[i]

6 No one is like you, O LORD;
you are great,[j]
and your name is mighty in
power.
7 Who should not revere you,
O King of the nations?[k]
This is your due.
Among all the wise men of the
nations
and in all their kingdoms,
there is no one like you.
8 They are all senseless and foolish;[l]
they are taught by worthless
wooden idols.
9 Hammered silver is brought from
Tarshish
and gold from Uphaz.
What the craftsman and goldsmith
have made[m]
is then dressed in blue and
purple—
all made by skilled workers.
10 But the LORD is the true God;
he is the living God, the eternal
King.
When he is angry, the earth
trembles;
the nations cannot endure his
wrath.[n]

11 "Tell them this: 'These gods, who
did not make the heavens and the
earth, will perish[o] from the earth and
from under the heavens.' "[b]

12 But God made the earth by his
power;
he founded the world by his
wisdom
and stretched out the heavens[p]
by his understanding.
13 When he thunders,[q] the waters in
the heavens roar;
he makes clouds rise from the
ends of the earth.

[a] 26 Or *desert and who clip the hair by their foreheads* [b] 11 The text of this verse is in Aramaic.

9:23 [t] Ecc 9:11 [u] 1Ki 20:11 [v] Eze 28:4-5 **9:24** [w] 1Co 1:31*; Gal 6:14 [x] 2Co 10:17* [y] Ps 51:1; Mic 7:18 [z] Ps 36:6 **9:25** [a] Ro 2:8-9 **9:26** [b] Jer 25:23 [c] Lev 26:41; Ac 7:51; Ro 2:28 **10:2** [d] Lev 20:23 **10:3** [e] Isa 40:19 **10:4** [f] Isa 41:7 **10:5** [g] 1Co 12:2 [h] Ps 115:5,7 [i] Isa 41:24; 46:7 **10:6** [j] Ps 48:1 **10:7** [k] Ps 22:28; Rev 15:4 **10:8** [l] Isa 40:19; Jer 4:22 **10:9** [m] Ps 115:4; Isa 40:19 **10:10** [n] Ps 76:7 **10:11** [o] Ps 96:5; Isa 2:18 **10:12** [p] Ge 1:1,8; Job 9:8; Isa 40:22 **10:13** [q] Job 36:29

9:23–24 PE

WORTH BRAGGING ABOUT

What a man brags about provides strong commentary on his values. Some brag with certificates on their walls, some with athletic trophies on their shelves, some with the cost of their cars or the size of their houses. Most people who have used the abilities God has given to make significant achievements struggle at times with how much to hide or display their accomplishments.

God gives us something to brag about without worry. God said, "with all your working to achieve something worth bragging about, work to know me and how I work my will in the world." The Bible, the book you're holding right now, will lay the foundation for a working knowledge of God and the blueprint for entering into a relationship with him.

Think carefully about what gives you a sense of pride and significance. Whatever that is, add to it your love for and understanding of your God and his Word.

He sends lightning with the rain[r]
and brings out the wind from his storehouses.

14Everyone is senseless and without knowledge;
every goldsmith is shamed by his idols.
His images are a fraud;
they have no breath in them.
15They are worthless,[s] the objects of mockery;
when their judgment comes,
they will perish.
16He who is the Portion[t] of Jacob is not like these,
for he is the Maker of all things,[u]
including Israel, the tribe of his inheritance[v]—
the LORD Almighty is his name.[w]

Coming Destruction

17Gather up your belongings[x] to leave the land,
you who live under siege.
18For this is what the LORD says:
"At this time I will hurl[y] out
those who live in this land;
I will bring distress on them
so that they may be captured."

19Woe to me because of my injury!
My wound[z] is incurable!
Yet I said to myself,
"This is my sickness, and I must endure[a] it."
20My tent[b] is destroyed;
all its ropes are snapped.
My sons are gone from me and are no more;[c]
no one is left now to pitch my tent
or to set up my shelter.
21The shepherds are senseless
and do not inquire of the LORD;
so they do not prosper
and all their flock is scattered.[d]
22Listen! The report is coming—
a great commotion from the land of the north!
It will make the towns of Judah desolate,
a haunt of jackals.[e]

Jeremiah's Prayer

23I know, O LORD, that a man's life is not his own;
it is not for man to direct his steps.[f]
24Correct me, LORD, but only with justice—
not in your anger,[g]
lest you reduce me to nothing.[h]
25Pour out your wrath on the nations[i]
that do not acknowledge you,
on the peoples who do not call on your name.[j]
For they have devoured[k] Jacob;
they have devoured him completely
and destroyed his homeland.[l]

The Covenant Is Broken

11 This is the word that came to Jeremiah from the LORD: 2"Listen to the
terms of this covenant and tell them to
the people of Judah and to those who
live in Jerusalem. 3Tell them that this is
what the LORD, the God of Israel, says:
'Cursed[m] is the man who does not
obey the terms of this covenant— 4the
terms I commanded your forefathers
when I brought them out of Egypt, out
of the iron-smelting furnace.[n]' I said,
'Obey[o] me and do everything I command you, and you will be my people,[p] and I will be your God. 5Then I
will fulfill the oath I swore[q] to your
forefathers, to give them a land flowing
with milk and honey'—the land you
possess today."

I answered, "Amen, LORD."

6The LORD said to me, "Proclaim all
these words in the towns of Judah and
in the streets of Jerusalem: 'Listen to
the terms of this covenant and follow[r]
them. 7From the time I brought your
forefathers up from Egypt until today, I
warned them again and again,[s] saying, "Obey me." 8But they did not listen
or pay attention;[t] instead, they followed the stubbornness of their evil
hearts. So I brought on them all the
curses[u] of the covenant I had commanded them to follow but that they
did not keep.' "

9Then the LORD said to me, "There is
a conspiracy[v] among the people of Judah and those who live in Jerusalem.
10They have returned to the sins of
their forefathers,[w] who refused to listen to my words. They have followed
other gods[x] to serve them. Both the
house of Israel and the house of Judah
have broken the covenant I made with
their forefathers. 11Therefore this is
what the LORD says: 'I will bring on
them a disaster[y] they cannot escape.
Although they cry[z] out to me, I will
not listen[a] to them. 12The towns of
Judah and the people of Jerusalem will
go and cry out to the gods to whom
they burn incense,[b] but they will not
help them at all when disaster[c]
strikes. 13You have as many gods as
you have towns, O Judah; and the altars you have set up to burn incense[d]

10:13 [r]Ps 135:7
10:15 [s]Isa 41:24; Jer 14:22
10:16 [t]Dt 32:9; Ps 119:57 [u]ver 12 [v]Ps 74:2 [w]Jer 31:35; 32:18
10:17 [x]Eze 12:3-12
10:18 [y]1Sa 25:29
10:19 [z]Jer 14:17 [a]Mic 7:9
10:20 [b]Jer 4:20 [c]Jer 31:15; La 1:5
10:21 [d]Jer 23:2
10:22 [e]Jer 9:11
10:23 [f]Pr 20:24
10:24 [g]Ps 6:1; 38:1 [h]Jer 30:11
10:25 [i]Zep 3:8 [j]Job 18:21; Ps 14:4 [k]Ps 79:7; Jer 8:16 [l]Ps 79:6-7
11:3 [m]Dt 27:26; Gal 3:10
11:4 [n]Dt 4:20; 1Ki 8:51 [o]Ex 24:8 [p]Jer 7:23; 31:33
11:5 [q]Ex 13:5; Dt 7:12; Ps 105:8-11
11:6 [r]Dt 15:5; Ro 2:13; Jas 1:22
11:7 [s]2Ch 36:15
11:8 [t]Jer 7:26 [u]Lev 26:14-43
11:9 [v]Eze 22:25
11:10 [w]Dt 9:7 [x]Jdg 2:12-13
11:11 [y]2Ki 22:16 [z]Jer 14:12; Eze 8:18 [a]ver 14; Pr 1:28; Isa 1:15; Zec 7:13
11:12 [b]Jer 44:17 [c]Dt 32:37
11:13 [d]Jer 7:9

to that shameful[e] god Baal are as
many as the streets of Jerusalem.'
14"Do not pray[f] for this people nor
offer any plea or petition for them, because I will not listen[g] when they call
to me in the time of their distress.

15"What is my beloved doing in my
temple
as she works out her evil
schemes with many?
Can consecrated meat avert
⌊your punishment⌋?
When you engage in your
wickedness,
then you rejoice.[a]"

16The LORD called you a thriving
olive tree
with fruit beautiful in form.
But with the roar of a mighty storm
he will set it on fire,[h]
and its branches will be
broken.[i]

17The LORD Almighty, who planted[j]
you, has decreed disaster for you, because the house of Israel and the house
of Judah have done evil and provoked
me to anger by burning incense to
Baal.[k]

Plot Against Jeremiah

18Because the LORD revealed their
plot to me, I knew it, for at that time he
showed me what they were doing.
19I
had been like a gentle lamb led to the
slaughter; I did not realize that they
had plotted[l] against me, saying,

"Let us destroy the tree and its
fruit;
let us cut him off from the land
of the living,[m]
that his name be remembered[n]
no more."
20But, O LORD Almighty, you who
judge righteously
and test the heart and mind,[o]
let me see your vengeance upon
them,
for to you I have committed my
cause.

21"Therefore this is what the LORD
says about the men of Anathoth who
are seeking your life[p] and saying, 'Do
not prophesy in the name of the LORD
or you will die[q] by our hands'—
22therefore this is what the LORD Almighty says: 'I will punish them. Their
young men[r] will die by the sword,
their sons and daughters by famine.
23Not even a remnant[s] will be left to
them, because I will bring disaster on
the men of Anathoth in the year of their
punishment.[t]'"

11:13 [e]Jer 3:24 **11:14** [f]Ex 32:10 [g]ver 11 **11:16** [h]Jer 21:14 [i]Isa 27:11; Ro 11:17-24 **11:17** [j]Isa 5:2; Jer 12:2 [k]Jer 7:9 **11:19** [l]Jer 18:18; 20:10 [m]Job 28:13; Isa 53:8 [n]Ps 83:4 **11:20** [o]Ps 7:9 **11:21** [p]Jer 12:6 [q]Jer 26:8,11; 38:4 **11:22** [r]Jer 18:21 **11:23** [s]Jer 6:9 [t]Jer 23:12

12:1 [u]Ezr 9:15 [v]Jer 5:27-28 **12:2** [w]Jer 11:17 [x]Isa 29:13; Jer 3:10; Mt 15:8; Tit 1:16 **12:3** [y]Ps 7:9; 11:5; 139:1-4; Jer 11:20 [z]Jer 17:18 **12:4** [a]Jer 4:28 [b]Joel 1:10-12 [c]Jer 4:25; 9:10 **12:5** [d]Jer 49:19; 50:44 **12:6** [e]Pr 26:24-25; Jer 9:4 [f]Ps 12:2 **12:7** [g]Jer 7:29 **12:8** [h]Hos 9:15; Am 6:8

Jeremiah's Complaint

12 You are always righteous,[u]
O LORD,
when I bring a case before you.
Yet I would speak with you about
your justice:
Why does the way of the wicked
prosper?[v]
Why do all the faithless live at
ease?
2You have planted[w] them, and they
have taken root;
they grow and bear fruit.
You are always on their lips
but far from their hearts.[x]
3Yet you know me, O LORD;
you see me and test[y] my
thoughts about you.
Drag them off like sheep to be
butchered!
Set them apart for the day of
slaughter![z]
4How long will the land lie
parched[b][a]
and the grass in every field be
withered?[b]
Because those who live in it are
wicked,
the animals and birds have
perished.[c]
Moreover, the people are saying,
"He will not see what happens to
us."

God's Answer

5"If you have raced with men on
foot
and they have worn you out,
how can you compete with
horses?
If you stumble in safe country,[c]
how will you manage in the
thickets[d] by[d] the Jordan?
6Your brothers, your own family—
even they have betrayed you;
they have raised a loud cry
against you.[e]
Do not trust them,
though they speak well of you.[f]

7"I will forsake my house,
abandon[g] my inheritance;
I will give the one I love
into the hands of her enemies.
8My inheritance has become to me
like a lion in the forest.
She roars at me;
therefore I hate her.[h]
9Has not my inheritance become to
me
like a speckled bird of prey

[a] 15 Or *Could consecrated meat avert your punishment? / Then you would rejoice* [b] 4 Or *land mourn* [c] 5 Or *If you put your trust in a land of safety* [d] 5 Or *the flooding of*

that other birds of prey surround
and attack?
Go and gather all the wild beasts;
bring them to devour.[i]
10Many shepherds[j] will ruin my
vineyard
and trample down my field;
they will turn my pleasant field
into a desolate wasteland.[k]
11It will be made a wasteland,
parched and desolate before
me;[l]
the whole land will be laid waste
because there is no one who
cares.
12Over all the barren heights in the
desert
destroyers will swarm,
for the sword of the LORD[m] will
devour
from one end of the land to the
other;[n]
no one will be safe.
13They will sow wheat but reap
thorns;
they will wear themselves out
but gain nothing.[o]
So bear the shame of your harvest
because of the LORD's fierce
anger."[p]

14This is what the LORD says: "As for
all my wicked neighbors who seize the
inheritance I gave my people Israel, I
will uproot[q] them from their lands
and I will uproot the house of Judah
from among them. 15But after I uproot
them, I will again have compassion
and will bring[r] each of them back to
his own inheritance and his own country. 16And if they learn well the ways of
my people and swear by my name, saying, 'As surely as the LORD lives'[s]—
even as they once taught my people to
swear by Baal[t]—then they will be established among my people.[u] 17But if
any nation does not listen, I will completely uproot and destroy[v] it," declares the LORD.

A Linen Belt

13 This is what the LORD said to me:
"Go and buy a linen belt and put
it around your waist, but do not let it
touch water." 2So I bought a belt, as the
LORD directed, and put it around my
waist.

3Then the word of the LORD came to
me a second time: 4"Take the belt you
bought and are wearing around your
waist, and go now to Perath[a] and hide
it there in a crevice in the rocks." 5So I
went and hid it at Perath, as the LORD
told me.[w]

6Many days later the LORD said to
me, "Go now to Perath and get the belt
I told you to hide there." 7So I went to
Perath and dug up the belt and took it
from the place where I had hidden it,
but now it was ruined and completely
useless.

8Then the word of the LORD came to
me: 9"This is what the LORD says: 'In
the same way I will ruin the pride of
Judah and the great pride[x] of Jerusalem. 10These wicked people, who refuse to listen to my words, who follow
the stubbornness of their hearts[y] and
go after other gods[z] to serve and worship them, will be like this belt—
completely useless! 11For as a belt is
bound around a man's waist, so I
bound the whole house of Israel and
the whole house of Judah to me,' declares the LORD, 'to be my people for
my renown[a] and praise and honor.[b]
But they have not listened.'[c]

Wineskins

12"Say to them: 'This is what the
LORD, the God of Israel, says: Every
wineskin should be filled with wine.'
And if they say to you, 'Don't we know
that every wineskin should be filled
with wine?' 13then tell them, 'This is
what the LORD says: I am going to fill
with drunkenness[d] all who live in this
land, including the kings who sit on
David's throne, the priests, the prophets and all those living in Jerusalem. 14I
will smash them one against the other,
fathers and sons alike, declares the
LORD. I will allow no pity or mercy or
compassion[e] to keep me from destroying[f] them.' "

Threat of Captivity

15Hear and pay attention,
do not be arrogant,
for the LORD has spoken.
16Give glory[g] to the LORD your God
before he brings the darkness,
before your feet stumble[h]
on the darkening hills.
You hope for light,
but he will turn it to thick
darkness
and change it to deep gloom.[i]
17But if you do not listen,[j]
I will weep in secret
because of your pride;
my eyes will weep bitterly,
overflowing with tears,[k]
because the LORD's flock[l] will
be taken captive.[m]

18Say to the king and to the queen
mother,
"Come down from your thrones,
for your glorious crowns

12:9 [i]Isa 56:9; Jer 15:3; Eze 23:25 **12:10** [j]Jer 23:1 [k]Isa 5:1-7 **12:11** [l]ver 4; Isa 42:25; Jer 23:10 **12:12** [m]Jer 47:6 [n]Jer 3:2 **12:13** [o]Lev 26:20; Dt 28:38; Mic 6:15; Hag 1:6 [p]Jer 4:26 **12:14** [q]Zec 2:7-9 **12:15** [r]Am 9:14-15 **12:16** [s]Jer 4:2 [t]Jos 23:7 [u]Isa 49:6; Jer 3:17 **12:17** [v]Isa 60:12 **13:5** [w]Ex 40:16

13:9 [x]Lev 26:19 **13:10** [y]Jer 11:8; 16:12 [z]Jer 9:14 **13:11** [a]Jer 32:20; 33:9 [b]Ex 19:5-6 [c]Jer 7:26 **13:13** [d]Ps 60:3; 75:8; Isa 51:17; 63:6; Jer 51:57 **13:14** [e]Jer 16:5 [f]Dt 29:20; Eze 5:10 **13:16** [g]Jos 7:19 [h]Jer 23:12 [i]Isa 59:9 **13:17** [j]Mal 2:2 [k]Jer 9:1 [l]Ps 80:1; Jer 23:1 [m]Jer 14:18

[a] 4 Or possibly *the Euphrates*; also in verses 5-7

will fall from your heads."
19 The cities in the Negev will be shut up,
and there will be no one to open them.
All Judah[n] will be carried into exile,
carried completely away.
20 Lift up your eyes and see
those who are coming from the north.[o]
Where is the flock[p] that was entrusted to you,
the sheep of which you boasted?
21 What will you say when ⌞the LORD⌟ sets over you
those you cultivated as your special allies?[q]
Will not pain grip you
like that of a woman in labor?[r]
22 And if you ask yourself,
"Why has this happened to me?"—
it is because of your many sins[s]
that your skirts have been torn off
and your body mistreated.[t]
23 Can the Ethiopian[a] change his skin
or the leopard its spots?
Neither can you do good
who are accustomed to doing evil.
24 "I will scatter you like chaff[u]
driven by the desert wind.[v]
25 This is your lot,
the portion[w] I have decreed for you,"
declares the LORD,
"because you have forgotten me
and trusted in false gods.
26 I will pull up your skirts over your face
that your shame may be seen[x]—
27 your adulteries and lustful neighings,
your shameless prostitution![y]
I have seen your detestable acts
on the hills and in the fields.[z]
Woe to you, O Jerusalem!
How long will you be unclean?"[a]

Drought, Famine, Sword

14 This is the word of the LORD to Jeremiah concerning the drought:

2 "Judah mourns,[b]
her cities languish;
they wail for the land,
and a cry goes up from Jerusalem.
3 The nobles send their servants for water;
they go to the cisterns
but find no water.[c]
They return with their jars unfilled;
dismayed and despairing,
they cover their heads.[d]
4 The ground is cracked
because there is no rain in the land;[e]
the farmers are dismayed
and cover their heads.
5 Even the doe in the field
deserts her newborn fawn
because there is no grass.[f]
6 Wild donkeys stand on the barren heights[g]
and pant like jackals;
their eyesight fails
for lack of pasture."
7 Although our sins testify[h] against us,
O LORD, do something for the sake of your name.
For our backsliding[i] is great;
we have sinned[j] against you.
8 O Hope[k] of Israel,
its Savior in times of distress,
why are you like a stranger in the land,
like a traveler who stays only a night?
9 Why are you like a man taken by surprise,
like a warrior powerless to save?[l]
You are among[m] us, O LORD,
and we bear your name;[n]
do not forsake us!

10 This is what the LORD says about this people:

"They greatly love to wander;
they do not restrain their feet.[o]
So the LORD does not accept[p] them;
he will now remember[q] their wickedness
and punish them for their sins."[r]

11 Then the LORD said to me, "Do not pray[s] for the well-being of this people. 12 Although they fast, I will not listen to their cry;[t] though they offer burnt offerings[u] and grain offerings, I will not accept[v] them. Instead, I will destroy them with the sword, famine and plague."

13 But I said, "Ah, Sovereign LORD, the prophets keep telling them, 'You will not see the sword or suffer famine.[w] Indeed, I will give you lasting peace in this place.' "

14 Then the LORD said to me, "The

13:19 [n] Jer 20:4; 52:30 **13:20** [o] Jer 6:22; Hab 1:6 [p] Jer 23:2 **13:21** [q] Jer 38:22 [r] Jer 4:31 **13:22** [s] Jer 9:2-6; 16:10-12 [t] Eze 16:37; Na 3:5-6 **13:24** [u] Ps 1:4 [v] Lev 26:33 **13:25** [w] Job 20:29; Mt 24:51 **13:26** [x] La 1:8; Eze 16:37; Hos 2:10 **13:27** [y] Jer 2:20 [z] Eze 6:13 [a] Hos 8:5 **14:2** [b] Isa 3:26; Jer 8:21 **14:3** [c] 2Ki 18:31; Job 6:19-20 [d] 2Sa 15:30 **14:4** [e] Jer 3:3 **14:5** [f] Isa 15:6 **14:6** [g] Job 39:5-6; Jer 2:24 **14:7** [h] Hos 5:5 [i] Jer 5:6 [j] Jer 8:14 **14:8** [k] Jer 17:13 **14:9** [l] Isa 50:2 [m] Jer 8:19 [n] Isa 63:19; Jer 15:16 **14:10** [o] Ps 119:101; Jer 2:25 [p] Jer 6:20; Am 5:22 [q] Hos 9:9 [r] Jer 44:21-23; Hos 8:13 **14:11** [s] Ex 32:10 **14:12** [t] Isa 1:15; Jer 11:11 [u] Jer 7:21 [v] Jer 6:20 **14:13** [w] Jer 5:12

[a] *23* Hebrew *Cushite* (probably a person from the upper Nile region)

prophets are prophesying lies[x] in my
name. I have not sent[y] them or appointed them or spoken to them. They
are prophesying to you false visions,[z]
divinations,[a] idolatries[a] and the delusions of their own minds. 15 Therefore, this is what the LORD says about
the prophets who are prophesying in
my name: I did not send them, yet they
are saying, 'No sword or famine will
touch this land.' Those same prophets
will perish[b] by sword and famine.[c]
16 And the people they are prophesying
to will be thrown out into the streets of
Jerusalem because of the famine and
sword. There will be no one to bury[d]
them or their wives, their sons or their
daughters.[e] I will pour out on them
the calamity they deserve.[f]

17 "Speak this word to them:

" 'Let my eyes overflow with tears[g]
night and day without ceasing;
for my virgin daughter—my people—
has suffered a grievous wound,
a crushing blow.[h]
18 If I go into the country,
I see those slain by the sword;
if I go into the city,
I see the ravages of famine.[i]
Both prophet and priest
have gone to a land they know not.' "
19 Have you rejected Judah completely?[j]
Do you despise Zion?
Why have you afflicted us
so that we cannot be healed?[k]
We hoped for peace
but no good has come,
for a time of healing
but there is only terror.[l]
20 O LORD, we acknowledge our wickedness
and the guilt of our fathers;
we have indeed sinned[m] against you.
21 For the sake of your name[n] do not despise us;
do not dishonor your glorious throne.[o]
Remember your covenant with us
and do not break it.
22 Do any of the worthless idols of the nations bring rain?[p]
Do the skies themselves send down showers?
No, it is you, O LORD our God.
Therefore our hope is in you,
for you are the one who does all this.

15 Then the LORD said to me: "Even
if Moses[q] and Samuel[r] were to
stand before me, my heart would not
go out to this people.[s] Send them
away from my presence![t] Let them go!
2 And if they ask you, 'Where shall we
go?' tell them, 'This is what the LORD
says:

" 'Those destined for death, to death;
those for the sword, to the sword;[u]
those for starvation, to starvation;[v]
those for captivity, to captivity.'[w]

3 "I will send four kinds of destroyers[x] against them," declares the LORD,
"the sword to kill and the dogs to drag
away and the birds[y] of the air and the
beasts of the earth to devour and destroy.[z] 4 I will make them abhorrent[a]
to all the kingdoms of the earth[b] because of what Manasseh[c] son of Hezekiah king of Judah did in Jerusalem.

5 "Who will have pity[d] on you,
O Jerusalem?
Who will mourn for you?
Who will stop to ask how you are?
6 You have rejected[e] me," declares the LORD.
"You keep on backsliding.
So I will lay hands[f] on you and destroy you;
I can no longer show compassion.
7 I will winnow them with a winnowing fork
at the city gates of the land.
I will bring bereavement and destruction on my people,[g]
for they have not changed their ways.
8 I will make their widows more numerous
than the sand of the sea.
At midday I will bring a destroyer[h]
against the mothers of their young men;
suddenly I will bring down on them
anguish and terror.
9 The mother of seven will grow faint[i]
and breathe her last.
Her sun will set while it is still day;
she will be disgraced and humiliated.
I will put the survivors to the sword[j]
before their enemies,"
declares the LORD.

10 Alas, my mother, that you gave me birth,[k]
a man with whom the whole
land strives and contends![l]

14:14 [x] Jer 27:14 [y] Jer 23:21,32 [z] Jer 23:16 [a] Eze 12:24
14:15 [b] Eze 14:9 [c] Jer 5:12-13
14:16 [d] Ps 79:3 [e] Jer 7:33 [f] Pr 1:31
14:17 [g] Jer 9:1 [h] Jer 8:21
14:18 [i] Eze 7:15
14:19 [j] Jer 7:29 [k] Jer 30:12-13 [l] Jer 8:15
14:20 [m] Da 9:7-8
14:21 [n] ver 7 [o] Jer 3:17
14:22 [p] Ps 135:7
15:1 [q] Ex 32:11; Nu 14:13-20 [r] 1Sa 7:9 [s] Jer 7:16; Eze 14:14,20 [t] 2Ki 17:20
15:2 [u] Jer 43:11 [v] Jer 14:12 [w] Rev 13:10
15:3 [x] Lev 26:16 [y] Dt 28:26 [z] Lev 26:22; Eze 14:21
15:4 [a] Jer 24:9; 29:18 [b] Dt 28:25 [c] 2Ki 21:2; 23:26-27
15:5 [d] Isa 51:19; Jer 13:14; 21:7; Na 3:7
15:6 [e] Jer 6:19; 7:24 [f] Zep 1:4
15:7 [g] Jer 18:21
15:8 [h] Jer 6:4
15:9 [i] 1Sa 2:5 [j] Jer 21:7
15:10 [k] Job 3:1 [l] Jer 1:19

[a] 14 Or *visions, worthless divinations*

I have neither lent[m] nor borrowed,
yet everyone curses me.

11The LORD said,

"Surely I will deliver you[n] for a
good purpose;
surely I will make your enemies
plead[o] with you
in times of disaster and times of
distress.

12"Can a man break iron—
iron from the north[p]—or
bronze?
13Your wealth and your treasures
I will give as plunder, without
charge,[q]
because of all your sins
throughout your country.[r]
14I will enslave you to your enemies
in[a] a land you do not know,[s]
for my anger will kindle a fire[t]
that will burn against you."

15You understand, O LORD;
remember me and care for me.
Avenge me on my persecutors.[u]
You are long-suffering—do not
take me away;
think of how I suffer reproach
for your sake.[v]
16When your words came, I ate[w]
them;
they were my joy and my heart's
delight,[x]
for I bear your name,[y]
O LORD God Almighty.
17I never sat[z] in the company of
revelers,
never made merry with them;
I sat alone because your hand was
on me
and you had filled me with
indignation.
18Why is my pain unending
and my wound grievous and
incurable?[a]
Will you be to me like a deceptive
brook,
like a spring that fails?[b]

19Therefore this is what the LORD
says:

"If you repent, I will restore you
that you may serve[c] me;
if you utter worthy, not worthless,
words,
you will be my spokesman.
Let this people turn to you,
but you must not turn to them.
20I will make you a wall to this
people,
a fortified wall of bronze;
they will fight against you
but will not overcome you,
for I am with you
to rescue and save you,"[d]
declares the LORD.
21"I will save you from the hands of
the wicked
and redeem[e] you from the
grasp of the cruel."[f]

Day of Disaster

16 Then the word of the LORD came to
me: 2"You must not marry[g] and
have sons or daughters in this place."
3For this is what the LORD says about
the sons and daughters born in this
land and about the women who are
their mothers and the men who are
their fathers:[h] 4"They will die of deadly diseases. They will not be mourned
or buried[i] but will be like refuse lying
on the ground.[j] They will perish by
sword and famine, and their dead bodies will become food for the birds of the
air and the beasts of the earth."[k]
5For this is what the LORD says: "Do
not enter a house where there is a funeral meal; do not go to mourn or
show sympathy, because I have withdrawn my blessing, my love and my
pity from this people," declares the
LORD. 6"Both high and low will die in
this land.[l] They will not be buried or
mourned, and no one will cut[m] himself or shave[n] his head for them. 7No
one will offer food to comfort those
who mourn[o] for the dead—not even
for a father or a mother—nor will anyone give them a drink to console them.
8"And do not enter a house where
there is feasting and sit down to eat
and drink.[p] 9For this is what the LORD
Almighty, the God of Israel, says: Before your eyes and in your days I will
bring an end to the sounds[q] of joy and
gladness and to the voices of bride and
bridegroom in this place.[r]
10"When you tell these people all
this and they ask you, 'Why has the
LORD decreed such a great disaster
against us? What wrong have we done?
What sin have we committed against
the LORD our God?'[s] 11then say to
them, 'It is because your fathers forsook me,' declares the LORD, 'and followed other gods and served and worshiped them. They forsook me and did
not keep my law.[t] 12But you have behaved more wickedly than your fathers.[u] See how each of you is following the stubbornness of his evil heart[v]
instead of obeying me. 13So I will throw
you out of this land into a land neither

15:10 [m]Lev 25:36
15:11 [n]Jer 40:4 [o]Jer 21:1-2; 37:3; 42:1-3
15:12 [p]Jer 28:14
15:13 [q]Ps 44:12 [r]Jer 17:3
15:14 [s]Dt 28:36; Jer 16:13 [t]Dt 32:22; Ps 21:9
15:15 [u]Jer 12:3 [v]Ps 69:7-9
15:16 [w]Eze 3:3; Rev 10:10 [x]Ps 119:72,103 [y]Jer 14:9
15:17 [z]Ps 1:1; 26:4-5; Jer 16:8
15:18 [a]Jer 30:15; Mic 1:9 [b]Job 6:15
15:19 [c]Zec 3:7
15:20 [d]Jer 20:11; Eze 3:8
15:21 [e]Jer 50:34 [f]Ge 48:16
16:2 [g]1Co 7:26-27
16:3 [h]Jer 6:21
16:4 [i]Jer 25:33 [j]Ps 83:10; Jer 9:22 [k]Ps 79:1-3; Jer 15:3; 34:20
16:6 [l]Eze 9:5-6 [m]Lev 19:28 [n]Jer 41:5; 47:5
16:7 [o]Eze 24:17; Hos 9:4
16:8 [p]Ecc 7:2-4; Jer 15:17
16:9 [q]Isa 24:8; Eze 26:13; Hos 2:11 [r]Rev 18:23
16:10 [s]Dt 29:24; Jer 5:19
16:11 [t]Dt 29:25-26; 1Ki 9:9; Ps 106:35-43; Jer 22:9
16:12 [u]Jer 7:26 [v]Ecc 9:3; Jer 13:10

[a] 14 Some Hebrew manuscripts, Septuagint and Syriac (see also Jer. 17:4); most Hebrew manuscripts *I will cause your enemies to bring you / into*

you nor your fathers have known,[w]
and there you will serve other gods[x]
day and night, for I will show you no
favor.'[y]
14"However, the days are coming,"
declares the LORD, "when men will no
longer say, 'As surely as the LORD lives,
who brought the Israelites up out of
Egypt,'[z] 15but they will say, 'As surely
as the LORD lives, who brought the Israelites up out of the land of the north
and out of all the countries where he
had banished them.'[a] For I will restore[b] them to the land I gave their
forefathers.

16"But now I will send for many
fishermen," declares the LORD, "and
they will catch them.[c] After that I will
send for many hunters, and they will
hunt[d] them down on every mountain
and hill and from the crevices of the
rocks.[e] 17My eyes are on all their ways;
they are not hidden[f] from me, nor is
their sin concealed from my eyes.[g] 18I
will repay them double[h] for their
wickedness and their sin, because they
have defiled my land[i] with the lifeless
forms of their vile images and have
filled my inheritance with their detestable idols."

19O LORD, my strength and my
fortress,
my refuge in time of distress,
to you the nations will come[j]
from the ends of the earth and
say,
"Our fathers possessed nothing but
false gods,[k]
worthless idols that did them no
good.
20Do men make their own gods?
Yes, but they are not gods!"[l]

21"Therefore I will teach them—
this time I will teach them
my power and might.
Then they will know
that my name is the LORD.

17 "Judah's sin is engraved with an
iron tool,[m]
inscribed with a flint point,
on the tablets of their hearts[n]
and on the horns of their altars.
2Even their children remember
their altars and Asherah
poles[a][o]
beside the spreading trees
and on the high hills.[p]
3My mountain in the land
and your[b] wealth and all your
treasures
I will give away as plunder,[q]
together with your high places,[r]
because of sin throughout your
country.[s]
4Through your own fault you will
lose
the inheritance[t] I gave you.
I will enslave you to your
enemies[u]
in a land[v] you do not know,
for you have kindled my anger,
and it will burn[w] forever."

5This is what the LORD says:
"Cursed is the one who trusts in
man,[x]
who depends on flesh for his
strength
and whose heart turns away
from the LORD.
6He will be like a bush in the
wastelands;
he will not see prosperity when
it comes.
He will dwell in the parched places
of the desert,
in a salt[y] land where no one
lives.
7"But blessed is the man who
trusts[z] in the LORD,
whose confidence is in him.
8He will be like a tree planted by
the water
that sends out its roots by the
stream.
It does not fear when heat comes;
its leaves are always green.

1 →PG. 934

[a]2 That is, symbols of the goddess Asherah
[b]2,3 Or *hills / 3and the mountains of the land. / Your*

16:13 [w]Dt 28:36; Jer 5:19 [x]Dt 4:28 [y]Jer 15:5 **16:14** [z]Dt 15:15; Jer 23:7-8 **16:15** [a]Isa 11:11; Jer 23:8 [b]Jer 24:6 **16:16** [c]Am 4:2; Hab 1:14-15 [d]Am 9:3; Mic 7:2 [e]1Sa 26:20 **16:17** [f]1Co 4:5; Heb 4:13 [g]Pr 15:3 **16:18** [h]Isa 40:2; Rev 18:6 [i]Nu 35:34; Jer 2:7 **16:19** [j]Isa 2:2; Jer 3:17

[k]Ps 4:2 **16:20** [l]Ps 115:4-7; Isa 37:19; Jer 2:11 **17:1** [m]Job 19:24 [n]Pr 3:3; 2Co 3:3 **17:2** [o]2Ch 24:18 [p]Jer 2:20 **17:3** [q]2Ki 24:13 [r]Jer 26:18; Mic 3:12 [s]Jer 15:13 **17:4** [t]La 5:2 [u]Dt 28:48; Jer 12:7 [v]Jer 16:13 [w]Jer 7:20; 15:14 **17:5** [x]Isa 2:22; 30:1-3 **17:6** [y]Dt 29:23; Job 39:6 **17:7** [z]Ps 34:8; 40:4; Pr 16:20

16:10–12

PROMISE 4

"GUILTY? WHO, ME?"

Innocence is a common theme in prison. Few prisoners will actually admit to having committed a crime. Verse 10 tells us that kind of false perception isn't limited to prison, or to modern history. The people of Jeremiah's time also seemed baffled at God's judgment on their sin: "What sin have we committed? Why would God judge us?" God's answer carries greater momentum as history rolls on. Not only did Jeremiah's generation disobey God (v. 12), but they failed to learn from the failure of their fathers (vv. 10–12).

Notice a double message here. First, we must learn from history—including Israel's story, recorded in the Bible. Second, we can provide a history that instead of merely warning others from our failure, models through our goodness. Jeremiah's double rebuke—on the fathers and the sons—can also be a double challenge. We need to learn from our fathers and teach our children to follow God's way.

For the next Promise 4 reading go to page 846.

It has no worries in a year of drought[a]
and never fails to bear fruit."[b]

9The heart[c] is deceitful above all things
and beyond cure.
Who can understand it?

10"I the LORD search the heart[d]
and examine the mind,[e]
to reward[f] a man according to his conduct,
according to what his deeds deserve."[g]

11Like a partridge that hatches eggs it did not lay
is the man who gains riches by unjust means.
When his life is half gone, they will desert him,
and in the end he will prove to be a fool.[h]

12A glorious throne,[i] exalted from the beginning,
is the place of our sanctuary.
13O LORD, the hope[j] of Israel,
all who forsake[k] you will be put to shame.
Those who turn away from you will be written in the dust
because they have forsaken the LORD,
the spring of living water.

14Heal me, O LORD, and I will be healed;
save me and I will be saved,
for you are the one I praise.[l]
15They keep saying to me,
"Where is the word of the LORD?

17:8 [a]Jer 14:1-6 [b]Ps 1:3; 92:12-14
17:9 [c]Ecc 9:3; Mt 13:15; Mk 7:21-22
17:10 [d]1Sa 16:7; Rev 2:23 [e]Ps 17:3; 139:23; Jer 11:20; 20:12; Ro 8:27 [f]Ps 62:12; Jer 32:19 [g]Ro 2:6
17:11 [h]Lk 12:20
17:12 [i]Jer 3:17
17:13 [j]Jer 14:8 [k]Isa 1:28; Jer 2:17
17:14 [l]Ps 109:1

17:5–10

PROMISE 1

WHAT IS THE HEART?

Here Jeremiah makes a strong case against trusting men instead of God. In fact, Jeremiah says, not only should we not substitute other people's advice for God's advice, we shouldn't even trust our *own* advice (17:5–9). His summarizing argument is that the heart is deceitful and wicked. Since the concept of the heart is central to this important argument, and since the heart is referred to throughout Scripture, we must try to understand what Jeremiah and others are talking about when they refer to "the heart."

1. *"The heart" refers to the mental process.* Solomon urged his son to "apply [his] heart to understanding" as an essential step in gaining wisdom (Proverbs 2:2). In Proverbs 4:4, he wrote that his father "taught me and said 'Lay hold of my words with all your heart.'" In Psalm 19:14 David prayed, "May the . . . meditation of my heart be pleasing in your sight, O LORD." So the mental process of acquiring or laying hold of words is done with the heart. The discerning, mental process of *understanding* words is a function of the heart. Musing or meditating on what information means is done in the heart. And wisdom is located in the heart. Jeremiah was serving a warning that the mind can deceive and must be carefully monitored.
2. *"The heart" refers to the emotions.* In Proverbs 3:3 Solomon wrote, "Let love and faithfulness never leave you . . . write them on the tablet of your heart." That's where these vital emotions are stored. In Psalm 119:10–11 David wrote, "I seek you with all my heart . . . I have hidden your word in my heart that I might not sin against you." This passionate statement to God gives us a glimpse of David's heart. In fact, when David did violate his relationship with God and poured out his confession and repentance, he offered God "a broken and contrite heart" (Psalm 51:17). So love is a matter of the heart. Passionate expressions of devotion and commitment are heart issues. Deep sorrow, repentance and contrition are processed in the heart. Jeremiah was warning his readers that the heart—including the emotional process—is deceitful and cannot be fully trusted or understood.
3. *"The heart" is the volitional center.* Proverbs 3:5 urges us to "trust in the LORD with all your heart." The choice to trust is made and sustained in the heart. In Genesis 8:21 God said that "every inclination" of a man's heart is evil. The word translated "inclination" also means intention, and refers to man's volitional desire and choices. So when a man decides to trust or has intentions or inclinations, the heart is at work.
4. *"The heart" is the place we communicate with God.* An example of this fourth element in defining heart is found in 1 Samuel 1:13. There we read that Hannah was praying in her heart. Often we read in Scripture that the heart is where we converse with God, understand God, process God's Word.

In summary, the word translated "heart" in the Old Testament refers to the thinking, feeling, willing process. It is where we interact with God and process our understanding of him. Solomon, in fact, wrote a startling statement in regard to the heart (Proverbs 4:23). With all the critical and life-changing statements contained in Proverbs, Solomon prefaced only *one* statement with the words "above all else." What statement did he want to set up that way? "Guard your heart, for it is the wellspring of life." He described how we do that in verses 20–27. Meditate carefully on those verses.

Jeremiah warned us that this thing he called "the heart" is deceitful and beyond human understanding. This becomes a great problem when we understand what the heart is . . . and does. That's why Jeremiah included the truth contained in verse 10: Only God can help with your heart. Guard it. Protect it. Give it to God. Keep it in his care. It is the wellspring of your life.

For the next Promise 1 reading go to page 829.

Let it now be fulfilled!"[m]
16I have not run away from being
your shepherd;
you know I have not desired the
day of despair.
What passes my lips is open
before you.
17Do not be a terror[n] to me;
you are my refuge[o] in the day
of disaster.
18Let my persecutors be put to
shame,
but keep me from shame;
let them be terrified,
but keep me from terror.
Bring on them the day of disaster;
destroy them with double
destruction.[p]

Keeping the Sabbath Holy

19This is what the LORD said to me:
"Go and stand at the gate of the people,
through which the kings of Judah go
in and out; stand also at all the other
gates of Jerusalem.[q] 20Say to them,
'Hear the word of the LORD, O kings of
Judah and all people of Judah and everyone living in Jerusalem[r] who come
through these gates.[s] 21This is what
the LORD says: Be careful not to carry a
load on the Sabbath[t] day or bring it
through the gates of Jerusalem. 22Do
not bring a load out of your houses or
do any work on the Sabbath, but keep
the Sabbath day holy, as I commanded
your forefathers.[u] 23Yet they did not
listen or pay attention;[v] they were
stiff-necked[w] and would not listen or
respond to discipline.[x] 24But if you are
careful to obey me, declares the LORD,
and bring no load through the gates of
this city on the Sabbath, but keep the
Sabbath day holy by not doing any
work on it, 25then kings who sit on David's throne[y] will come through the
gates of this city with their officials.
They and their officials will come riding in chariots and on horses, accompanied by the men of Judah and those
living in Jerusalem, and this city will be
inhabited forever. 26People will come
from the towns of Judah and the villages around Jerusalem, from the territory of Benjamin and the western foothills, from the hill country and the
Negev,[z] bringing burnt offerings and
sacrifices, grain offerings, incense and
thank offerings to the house of the
LORD. 27But if you do not obey[a] me to
keep the Sabbath day holy by not carrying any load as you come through the
gates of Jerusalem on the Sabbath day,
then I will kindle an unquenchable
fire[b] in the gates of Jerusalem that will
consume her fortresses.' "[c]

At the Potter's House

18 This is the word that came to Jeremiah from the LORD: 2"Go down to
the potter's house, and there I will give
you my message." 3So I went down to
the potter's house, and I saw him
working at the wheel. 4But the pot he
was shaping from the clay was marred
in his hands; so the potter formed it
into another pot, shaping it as seemed
best to him.
5Then the word of the LORD came to
me: 6"O house of Israel, can I not do
with you as this potter does?" declares
the LORD. "Like clay[d] in the hand of
the potter, so are you in my hand, O
house of Israel. 7If at any time I announce that a nation or kingdom is to
be uprooted,[e] torn down and destroyed, 8and if that nation I warned
repents of its evil, then I will relent[f]
and not inflict on it the disaster[g] I had
planned. 9And if at another time I announce that a nation or kingdom is to
be built[h] up and planted, 10and if it
does evil[i] in my sight and does not
obey me, then I will reconsider[j] the
good I had intended to do for it.
11"Now therefore say to the people
of Judah and those living in Jerusalem,
'This is what the LORD says: Look! I am
preparing a disaster[k] for you and de-
vising a plan against you. So turn[l]
from your evil ways,[m] each one of you,
and reform your ways and your actions.' 12But they will reply, 'It's no
use.[n] We will continue with our own
plans; each of us will follow the stubbornness of his evil heart.' "

13Therefore this is what the LORD
says:

"Inquire among the nations:
Who has ever heard anything
like this?[o]
A most horrible[p] thing has been
done
by Virgin Israel.
14Does the snow of Lebanon
ever vanish from its rocky
slopes?
Do its cool waters from distant
sources
ever cease to flow?[a]
15Yet my people have forgotten me;
they burn incense to worthless
idols,[q]
which made them stumble in their
ways
and in the ancient paths.[r]
They made them walk in bypaths
and on roads not built up.[s]

a 14 The meaning of the Hebrew for this sentence is uncertain.

17:15 m Isa 5:19; 2Pe 3:4
17:17 n Ps 88:15-16 o Jer 16:19; Na 1:7
17:18 p Ps 35:1-8
17:19 q Jer 7:2; 26:2
17:20 r Jer 19:3 s Jer 22:2
17:21 t Nu 15:32-36; Ne 13:15-21; Jn 5:10
17:22 u Ex 20:8; 31:13; Isa 56:2-6; Eze 20:12
17:23 v Jer 7:26 w Jer 19:15 x Jer 7:28
17:25 y 2Sa 7:13; Isa 9:7; Jer 22:2,4; Lk 1:32
17:26 z Jer 32:44; 33:13; Zec 7:7
17:27 a Jer 22:5 b Jer 7:20 c 2Ki 25:9; Am 2:5
18:6 d Isa 45:9; Ro 9:20-21
18:7 e Jer 1:10
18:8 f Jer 26:13; Jnh 3:8-10 g Eze 18:21; Hos 11:8-9
18:9 h Jer 1:10; 31:28
18:10 i Eze 33:18 j 1Sa 2:29-30
18:11 k Jer 4:6 l 2Ki 17:13; Isa 1:16-19 m Jer 7:3
18:12 n Isa 57:10; Jer 2:25
18:13 o Isa 66:8; Jer 2:10 p Jer 5:30
18:15 q Jer 10:15 r Jer 6:16 s Isa 57:14; 62:10

16Their land will be laid waste,[t]
an object of lasting scorn;[u]
all who pass by will be appalled
and will shake their heads.[v]
17Like a wind[w] from the east,
I will scatter them before their
enemies;
I will show them my back and not
my face[x]
in the day of their disaster."

18They said, "Come, let's make
plans[y] against Jeremiah; for the
teaching of the law by the priest[z] will
not be lost, nor will counsel from the
wise, nor the word from the prophets.[a] So come, let's attack him with
our tongues[b] and pay no attention to
anything he says."

19Listen to me, O LORD;
hear what my accusers are
saying!
20Should good be repaid with evil?
Yet they have dug a pit[c] for me.
Remember that I stood before you
and spoke in their behalf[d]
to turn your wrath away from
them.
21So give their children over to
famine;[e]
hand them over to the power of
the sword.
Let their wives be made childless
and widows;[f]
let their men be put to death,
their young men slain by the
sword in battle.
22Let a cry[g] be heard from their
houses
when you suddenly bring
invaders against them,
for they have dug a pit to capture
me
and have hidden snares[h] for my
feet.
23But you know, O LORD,
all their plots to kill[i] me.
Do not forgive[j] their crimes
or blot out their sins from your
sight.
Let them be overthrown before
you;
deal with them in the time of
your anger.

19 This is what the LORD says: "Go and
buy a clay jar from a potter.[k] Take
along some of the elders[l] of the people and of the priests 2and go out to the
Valley of Ben Hinnom,[m] near the entrance of the Potsherd Gate. There proclaim the words I tell you, 3and say,
'Hear the word of the LORD, O kings[n]
of Judah and people of Jerusalem. This
is what the LORD Almighty, the God of
Israel, says: Listen! I am going to bring
a disaster[o] on this place that will make
the ears of everyone who hears of it
tingle.[p] 4For they have forsaken[q] me
and made this a place of foreign gods;
they have burned sacrifices[r] in it to
gods that neither they nor their fathers
nor the kings of Judah ever knew, and
they have filled this place with the
blood of the innocent.[s] 5They have
built the high places of Baal to burn
their sons[t] in the fire as offerings to
Baal—something I did not command
or mention, nor did it enter my
mind.[u] 6So beware, the days are coming, declares the LORD, when people
will no longer call this place Topheth
or the Valley of Ben Hinnom,[v] but the
Valley of Slaughter.[w]
7" 'In this place I will ruin[a] the
plans of Judah and Jerusalem. I will
make them fall by the sword before
their enemies,[x] at the hands of those
who seek their lives, and I will give
their carcasses[y] as food[z] to the birds
of the air and the beasts of the earth. 8I
will devastate this city and make it an
object of scorn;[a] all who pass by will
be appalled and will scoff because of all
its wounds. 9I will make them eat[b] the
flesh of their sons and daughters, and
they will eat one another's flesh during
the stress of the siege imposed on them
by the enemies[c] who seek their lives.'
10"Then break the jar[d] while those
who go with you are watching, 11and
say to them, 'This is what the LORD Almighty says: I will smash[e] this nation
and this city just as this potter's jar is
smashed and cannot be repaired. They
will bury[f] the dead in Topheth until
there is no more room. 12This is what I
will do to this place and to those who
live here, declares the LORD. I will make
this city like Topheth. 13The houses[g]
in Jerusalem and those of the kings of
Judah will be defiled like this place,
Topheth—all the houses where they
burned incense on the roofs to all the
starry hosts[h] and poured out drink offerings[i] to other gods.' "
14Jeremiah then returned from Topheth, where the LORD had sent him to
prophesy, and stood in the court[j] of
the LORD's temple and said to all the
people, 15"This is what the LORD Almighty, the God of Israel, says: 'Listen!
I am going to bring on this city and the
villages around it every disaster I pronounced against them, because they
were stiff-necked[k] and would not listen to my words.' "

a 7 The Hebrew for *ruin* sounds like the Hebrew for *jar* (see verses 1 and 10).

18:16 t Jer 25:9 u Jer 19:8 v Ps 22:7
18:17 w Jer 13:24 x Jer 2:27
18:18 y Jer 11:19 z Mal 2:7 a Jer 5:13 b Ps 52:2
18:20 c Ps 35:7; 57:6 d Ps 106:23
18:21 e Jer 11:22 f Ps 109:9
18:22 g Jer 6:26 h Ps 140:5
18:23 i Jer 11:21 j Ps 109:14
19:1 k Jer 18:2 l Nu 11:17
19:2 m Jos 15:8
19:3 n Jer 17:20
o Jer 6:19 p 1Sa 3:11
19:4 q Dt 28:20; Isa 65:11 r Lev 18:21 s 2Ki 21:16; Jer 2:34
19:5 t Lev 18:21; Ps 106:37-38 u Jer 7:31; 32:35
19:6 v Jos 15:8 w Jer 7:32
19:7 x Lev 26:17; Dt 28:25 y Jer 16:4; 34:20 z Ps 79:2
19:8 a Jer 18:16
19:9 b Lev 26:29; Dt 28:49-57; La 4:10 c Isa 9:20
19:10 d ver 1
19:11 e Ps 2:9; Isa 30:14 f Jer 7:32
19:13 g Jer 32:29; 52:13 h Dt 4:19; Ac 7:42 i Jer 7:18; Eze 20:28
19:14 j 2Ch 20:5; Jer 26:2
19:15 k Ne 9:16; Jer 7:26; 17:23

Jeremiah and Pashhur

20 When the priest Pashhur son of
Immer,[l] the chief officer[m] in the
temple of the LORD, heard Jeremiah
prophesying these things, 2he had Jeremiah the prophet beaten[n] and put in
the stocks[o] at the Upper Gate of Benjamin[p] at the LORD's temple. 3The
next day, when Pashhur released him
from the stocks, Jeremiah said to him,
"The LORD's name for you is not Pashhur, but Magor-Missabib.[a][q] 4For this
is what the LORD says: 'I will make you
a terror to yourself and to all your
friends; with your own eyes[r] you will
see them fall by the sword of their enemies. I will hand[s] all Judah over to the
king of Babylon, who will carry[t] them
away to Babylon or put them to the
sword. 5I will hand over to their enemies all the wealth[u] of this city—all its
products, all its valuables and all the
treasures of the kings of Judah. They
will take it away[v] as plunder and carry
it off to Babylon. 6And you, Pashhur,
and all who live in your house will go
into exile to Babylon. There you will die
and be buried, you and all your friends
to whom you have prophesied[w] lies.' "

Jeremiah's Complaint

7O LORD, you deceived[b] me, and I
was deceived[b];
you overpowered me and
prevailed.
I am ridiculed all day long;
everyone mocks me.
8Whenever I speak, I cry out
proclaiming violence and
destruction.[x]
So the word of the LORD has
brought me
insult and reproach[y] all day
long.
9But if I say, "I will not mention
him
or speak any more in his name,"
his word is in my heart like a
fire,[z]
a fire shut up in my bones.
I am weary of holding it in;[a]
indeed, I cannot.
10I hear many whispering,
"Terror[b] on every side!
Report[c] him! Let's report him!"
All my friends[d]
are waiting for me to slip,[e]
saying,
"Perhaps he will be deceived;
then we will prevail[f] over him
and take our revenge on him."
11But the LORD[g] is with me like a
mighty warrior;
so my persecutors[h] will stumble
and not prevail.[i]
They will fail and be thoroughly
disgraced;[j]
their dishonor will never be
forgotten.
12O LORD Almighty, you who examine
the righteous
and probe the heart and mind,[k]
let me see your vengeance[l] upon
them,
for to you I have committed[m]
my cause.
13Sing to the LORD!
Give praise to the LORD!
He rescues[n] the life of the needy
from the hands of the wicked.
14Cursed be the day I was born![o]
May the day my mother bore me
not be blessed!
15Cursed be the man who brought
my father the news,
who made him very glad, saying,
"A child is born to you—a son!"
16May that man be like the towns[p]
the LORD overthrew without pity.
May he hear wailing in the
morning,
a battle cry at noon.
17For he did not kill me in the
womb,[q]
with my mother as my grave,
her womb enlarged forever.
18Why did I ever come out of the
womb

20:7–13

PROMISE 1

CROSSING THE LINE

Many godly Christians are working hard to cross over long-established ethnic, racial, denominational, and economic barriers. In Jeremiah's time, as in ours, there was a legitimate line to observe: the line of God's truth. While appreciating various understandings and applications of God's truth, while learning from various expressions of worship and ministry styles, we must beware of adopting and proclaiming a false gospel. God urgently warned his people not to listen to or embrace those who—in his name—proclaimed a false message.

Carefully read God's Word and ask the Holy Spirit to guide you into the truth that's so richly revealed in its pages. Work hard to embrace various expressions of God's truth; and, at the same time, be cautious to guard your mind against what is not God's truth.

For the next Promise 1 reading go to page 873.

20:1 [l]1Ch 24:14 [m]2Ki 25:18 **20:2** [n]Jer 1:19 [o]Job 13:27 [p]Jer 37:13; 38:7; Zec 14:10 **20:3** [q]ver 10 **20:4** [r]Jer 29:21 [s]Jer 21:10 [t]Jer 52:27 **20:5** [u]Jer 17:3 [v]2Ki 20:17 **20:6** [w]Jer 14:15; La 2:14 **20:8** [x]Jer 6:7 [y]2Ch 36:16; Jer 6:10 **20:9** [z]Ps 39:3 [a]Job 32:18-20; Ac 4:20 **20:10** [b]Ps 31:13; Jer 6:25 [c]Isa 29:21 [d]Ps 41:9 [e]Lk 11:53-54 [f]1Ki 19:2 **20:11** [g]Jer 1:8; Ro 8:31 [h]Jer 17:18 [i]Jer 15:20 [j]Jer 23:40 **20:12** [k]Jer 17:10 [l]Ps 54:7; 59:10 [m]Ps 62:8; Jer 11:20 **20:13** [n]Ps 35:10 **20:14** [o]Job 3:3; Jer 15:10 **20:16** [p]Ge 19:25 **20:17** [q]Job 10:18-19

[a]3 *Magor-Missabib* means *terror on every side.*
[b]7 Or *persuaded*

to see trouble and sorrow
and to end my days in shame?[r]

God Rejects Zedekiah's Request

21 The word came to Jeremiah from the LORD when King Zedekiah[s] sent to him Pashhur[t] son of Malkijah and the priest Zephaniah[u] son of Maaseiah. They said: 2"Inquire[v] now of the LORD for us because Nebuchadnezzar[a][w] king of Babylon is attacking us. Perhaps the LORD will perform wonders[x] for us as in times past so that he will withdraw from us."

3But Jeremiah answered them, "Tell Zedekiah, 4'This is what the LORD, the God of Israel, says: I am about to turn[y] against you the weapons of war that are in your hands, which you are using to fight the king of Babylon and the Babylonians[b] who are outside the wall besieging[z] you. And I will gather them inside this city. 5I myself will fight against you with an outstretched hand[a] and a mighty arm in anger and fury and great wrath. 6I will strike down those who live in this city—both men and animals—and they will die of a terrible plague.[b] 7After that, declares the LORD, I will hand over Zedekiah[c] king of Judah, his officials and the people in this city who survive the plague, sword and famine, to Nebuchadnezzar king of Babylon[d] and to their enemies who seek their lives. He will put them to the sword; he will show them no mercy or pity or compassion.'[e]

8"Furthermore, tell the people, 'This is what the LORD says: See, I am setting before you the way of life and the way of death. 9Whoever stays in this city will die by the sword, famine or plague.[f] But whoever goes out and surrenders to the Babylonians who are besieging you will live; he will escape with his life.[g] 10I have determined to do this city harm[h] and not good, declares the LORD. It will be given into the hands[i] of the king of Babylon, and he will destroy it with fire.'[j]

11"Moreover, say to the royal house[k] of Judah, 'Hear the word of the LORD; 12O house of David, this is what the LORD says:

" 'Administer justice[l] every
morning;
rescue from the hand of his
oppressor
the one who has been robbed,
or my wrath will break out and
burn like fire
because of the evil you have
done—
burn with no one to quench[m] it.
13I am against[n] you, ⌞Jerusalem,⌟

20:18 [r]Ps 90:9
21:1 [s]2Ki 24:18; Jer 52:1 [t]Jer 38:1 [u]2Ki 25:18; Jer 29:25; 37:3
21:2 [v]Jer 37:3,7 [w]2Ki 25:1 [x]Ps 44:1-4; Jer 32:17
21:4 [y]Jer 32:5 [z]Jer 37:8-10
21:5 [a]Jer 6:12
21:6 [b]Jer 14:12
21:7 [c]2Ki 25:7; Jer 52:9 [d]Jer 37:17; 39:5 [e]2Ch 36:17; Eze 7:9; Hab 1:6
21:9 [f]Jer 14:12 [g]Jer 38:2,17; 39:18; 45:5
21:10 [h]Jer 44:11,27; Am 9:4 [i]Jer 32:28; 38:2-3 [j]Jer 52:13
21:11 [k]Jer 13:18
21:12 [l]Jer 22:3 [m]Isa 1:31
21:13 [n]Eze 13:8

[o]Ps 125:2 [p]Jer 49:4; Ob 1:3-4
21:14 [q]Isa 3:10-11 [r]2Ch 36:19; Jer 52:13 [s]Eze 20:47
22:2 [t]Jer 17:25; Lk 1:32 [u]Jer 17:20
22:3 [v]Mic 6:8; Zec 7:9 [w]Ps 72:4; Jer 21:12 [x]Ex 22:22
22:4 [y]Jer 17:25
22:5 [z]Jer 17:27 [a]Heb 6:13
22:6 [b]Mic 3:12
22:7 [c]Jer 4:7 [d]Isa 10:34
22:8 [e]Dt 29:25-26; 1Ki 9:8-9; Jer 16:10-11
22:9 [f]2Ki 22:17; 2Ch 34:25

you who live above this valley[o]
on the rocky plateau,
declares the LORD—
you who say, "Who can come
against us?
Who can enter our refuge?"[p]
14I will punish you as your deeds[q]
deserve,
declares the LORD.
I will kindle a fire[r] in your
forests[s]
that will consume everything
around you.' "

Judgment Against Evil Kings

22 This is what the LORD says: "Go down to the palace of the king of Judah and proclaim this message there: 2'Hear the word of the LORD, O king of Judah, you who sit on David's throne[t]—you, your officials and your people who come through these gates.[u] 3This is what the LORD says: Do what is just[v] and right. Rescue from the hand of his oppressor[w] the one who has been robbed. Do no wrong or violence to the alien, the fatherless or the widow,[x] and do not shed innocent blood in this place. 4For if you are careful to carry out these commands, then kings[y] who sit on David's throne will come through the gates of this palace, riding in chariots and on horses, accompanied by their officials and their people. 5But if you do not obey[z] these commands, declares the LORD, I swear[a] by myself that this palace will become a ruin.' "

7 →PG. 831

6For this is what the LORD says about the palace of the king of Judah:

"Though you are like Gilead to me,
like the summit of Lebanon,
I will surely make you like a
desert,[b]
like towns not inhabited.
7I will send destroyers[c] against
you,
each man with his weapons,
and they will cut[d] up your fine
cedar beams
and throw them into the fire.

8"People from many nations will pass by this city and will ask one another, 'Why has the LORD done such a thing to this great city?'[e] 9And the answer will be: 'Because they have forsaken the covenant of the LORD their God and have worshiped and served other gods.[f]' "

[a] *2* Hebrew *Nebuchadrezzar,* of which *Nebuchadnezzar* is a variant; here and often in Jeremiah and Ezekiel [b] *4* Or *Chaldeans*; also in verse 9

10Do not weep for the dead[g] ⌊king⌋
or mourn[h] his loss;
rather, weep bitterly for him who
is exiled,
because he will never return
nor see his native land again.

11For this is what the LORD says about
Shallum[a][i] son of Josiah, who succeeded his father as king of Judah but
has gone from this place: "He will never return. 12He will die[j] in the place
where they have led him captive; he
will not see this land again."

13"Woe to him who builds[k] his
palace by unrighteousness,
his upper rooms by injustice,
making his countrymen work for
nothing,
not paying[l] them for their
labor.
14He says, 'I will build myself a great
palace[m]
with spacious upper rooms.'
So he makes large windows in it,
panels it with cedar[n]
and decorates it in red.

15"Does it make you a king
to have more and more cedar?
Did not your father have food and
drink?
He did what was right and
just,[o]
so all went well[p] with him.
7 →PG. 901
16He defended the cause of the poor
and needy,[q]
and so all went well.
Is that not what it means to know
me?"
declares the LORD.
17"But your eyes and your heart
are set only on dishonest gain,
on shedding innocent blood[r]
and on oppression and
extortion."

18Therefore this is what the LORD says
about Jehoiakim son of Josiah king of
Judah:

"They will not mourn for him:
'Alas, my brother! Alas, my
sister!'
They will not mourn for him:
'Alas, my master! Alas, his
splendor!'
19He will have the burial of a
donkey—
dragged away and thrown[s]
outside the gates of Jerusalem."

20"Go up to Lebanon and cry out,
let your voice be heard in
Bashan,
cry out from Abarim,[t]
for all your allies are crushed.
21I warned you when you felt secure,
but you said, 'I will not listen!'
This has been your way from your
youth;[u]
you have not obeyed[v] me.
22The wind will drive all your
shepherds away,
and your allies will go into exile.
Then you will be ashamed and
disgraced
because of all your wickedness.
23You who live in 'Lebanon,[b]'
who are nestled in cedar
buildings,
how you will groan when pangs
come upon you,
pain[w] like that of a woman in
labor!

24"As surely as I live," declares the
LORD, "even if you, Jehoiachin[c][x] son
of Jehoiakim king of Judah, were a signet ring on my right hand, I would still
pull you off. 25I will hand you over[y] to
those who seek your life, those you
fear—to Nebuchadnezzar king of Babylon and to the Babylonians.[d] 26I will
hurl[z] you and the mother who gave
you birth into another country, where
neither of you was born, and there you
both will die. 27You will never come
back to the land you long to return to."

28Is this man Jehoiachin a despised,
broken pot,[a]
an object no one wants?
Why will he and his children be
hurled[b] out,
cast into a land[c] they do not
know?
29O land,[d] land, land,
hear the word of the LORD!
30This is what the LORD says:
"Record this man as if childless,[e]
a man who will not prosper[f] in
his lifetime,
for none of his offspring will
prosper,
none will sit on the throne[g] of
David
or rule anymore in Judah."

The Righteous Branch

23 "Woe to the shepherds[h] who are
destroying and scattering[i] the
sheep of my pasture!"[j] declares the
LORD. 2Therefore this is what the LORD,
the God of Israel, says to the shepherds
who tend my people: "Because you
have scattered my flock and driven
them away and have not bestowed care
on them, I will bestow punishment on
you for the evil[k] you have done," de-

22:10 [g]Ecc 4:2 [h]ver 18
22:11 [i]2Ki 23:31
22:12 [j]2Ki 23:34
22:13 [k]Mic 3:10; Hab 2:9 [l]Lev 19:13; Jas 5:4
22:14 [m]Isa 5:8-9 [n]2Sa 7:2
22:15 [o]2Ki 23:25 [p]Ps 128:2; Isa 3:10
22:16 [q]Ps 72:1-4, 12-13
22:17 [r]2Ki 24:4
22:19 [s]Jer 36:30
22:20 [t]Nu 27:12
22:21 [u]Jer 3:25; 32:30 [v]Jer 7:23-28
22:23 [w]Jer 4:31
22:24 [x]2Ki 24:6,8; Jer 37:1
22:25 [y]2Ki 24:16; Jer 34:20
22:26 [z]2Ki 24:8; 2Ch 36:10
22:28 [a]Ps 31:12; Jer 48:38; Hos 8:8 [b]Jer 15:1 [c]Jer 17:4
22:29 [d]Jer 6:19; Mic 1:2
22:30 [e]1Ch 3:18; Mt 1:12 [f]Jer 10:21 [g]Ps 94:20
23:1 [h]Jer 10:21; Eze 34:1-10; Zec 11:15-17 [i]Isa 56:11 [j]Eze 34:31
23:2 [k]Jer 21:12

[a]*11* Also called *Jehoahaz* [b]*23* That is, the palace in Jerusalem (see 1 Kings 7:2)
[c]*24* Hebrew *Coniah,* a variant of *Jehoiachin;* also in verse 28 [d]*25* Or *Chaldeans*

clares the LORD. 3"I myself will gather
the remnant[l] of my flock out of all the
countries where I have driven them
and will bring them back to their pasture, where they will be fruitful and increase in number. 4I will place shepherds[m] over them who will tend them,
and they will no longer be afraid[n] or
terrified, nor will any be missing,[o]"
declares the LORD.

5"The days are coming," declares
the LORD,
"when I will raise up to David[a]
a righteous Branch,[p]
a King who will reign[q] wisely
and do what is just and right[r]
in the land.
6In his days Judah will be saved
and Israel will live in safety.
This is the name[s] by which he will
be called:
The LORD Our Righteousness.[t]

7"So then, the days are coming," declares the LORD, "when people will no
longer say, 'As surely as the LORD lives,
who brought the Israelites up out of
Egypt,'[u] 8but they will say, 'As surely
as the LORD lives, who brought the
descendants of Israel up out of the land
of the north and out of all the countries
where he had banished them.' Then
they will live in their own land."[v]

Lying Prophets

9Concerning the prophets:

My heart is broken within me;
all my bones tremble.
I am like a drunken man,
like a man overcome by wine,
because of the LORD
and his holy words.[w]
10The land is full of adulterers;[x]
because of the curse[b] the land
lies parched[c]
and the pastures[y] in the desert
are withered.[z]
The ⌊prophets⌋ follow an evil
course
and use their power unjustly.

11"Both prophet and priest are
godless;[a]
even in my temple[b] I find their
wickedness,"
declares the LORD.
12"Therefore their path will become
slippery;[c]
they will be banished to darkness
and there they will fall.
I will bring disaster on them
in the year they are punished,[d]"
declares the LORD.

13"Among the prophets of Samaria
I saw this repulsive thing:
They prophesied by Baal[e]
and led my people Israel astray.
14And among the prophets of
Jerusalem
I have seen something
horrible:[f]
They commit adultery and live a
lie.[g]
They strengthen the hands of
evildoers,[h]
so that no one turns from his
wickedness.
They are all like Sodom[i] to me;
the people of Jerusalem are like
Gomorrah."[j]

15Therefore, this is what the LORD Almighty says concerning the prophets:

"I will make them eat bitter food
and drink poisoned water,[k]
because from the prophets of
Jerusalem
ungodliness has spread
throughout the land."

16This is what the LORD Almighty
says:

"Do not listen[l] to what the
prophets are prophesying to
you;
they fill you with false hopes.
They speak visions[m] from their
own minds,
not from the mouth[n] of the
LORD.
17They keep saying to those who
despise me,
'The LORD says: You will have
peace.'[o]
And to all who follow the
stubbornness[p] of their
hearts
they say, 'No harm[q] will come
to you.'
18But which of them has stood in the
council of the LORD
to see or to hear his word?
Who has listened and heard his
word?
19See, the storm[r] of the LORD
will burst out in wrath,
a whirlwind swirling down
on the heads of the wicked.
20The anger[s] of the LORD will not
turn back[t]
until he fully accomplishes
the purposes of his heart.
In days to come
you will understand it clearly.
21I did not send[u] these prophets,
yet they have run with their
message;
I did not speak to them,

23:3 [l]Isa 11:10-12; Jer 32:37; Eze 34:11-16
23:4 [m]Jer 3:15; 31:10; Eze 34:23 [n]Jer 30:10; 46:27-28 [o]Jn 6:39
23:5 [p]Isa 4:2 [q]Isa 9:7 [r]Isa 11:1; Zec 6:12
23:6 [s]Jer 33:16; Mt 1:21-23 [t]Ro 3:21-22; 1Co 1:30
23:7 [u]Jer 16:14
23:8 [v]Isa 43:5-6; Am 9:14-15
23:9 [w]Jer 20:8-9
23:10 [x]Jer 9:2 [y]Ps 107:34; Jer 9:10 [z]Hos 4:2-3
23:11 [a]Jer 6:13; 8:10; Zep 3:4 [b]Jer 7:10
23:12 [c]Ps 35:6; Jer 13:16 [d]Jer 11:23
23:13 [e]Jer 2:8
23:14 [f]Jer 5:30 [g]Jer 29:23 [h]Eze 13:22 [i]Ge 18:20 [j]Isa 1:9-10; Jer 20:16
23:15 [k]Jer 8:14; 9:15
23:16 [l]Jer 27:9-10, 14; Mt 7:15 [m]Jer 14:14 [n]Jer 9:20
23:17 [o]Jer 8:11 [p]Jer 13:10 [q]Jer 5:12; Am 9:10; Mic 3:11
23:19 [r]Jer 25:32; 30:23
23:20 [s]2Ki 23:26 [t]Jer 30:24
23:21 [u]Jer 14:14; 27:15

[a]5 Or *up from David's line* [b]10 Or *because of these things* [c]10 Or *land mourns*

yet they have prophesied.
22But if they had stood in my
council,
they would have proclaimed my
words to my people
and would have turned[v] them
from their evil ways
and from their evil deeds.

23"Am I only a God nearby,[w]"
declares the LORD,
"and not a God far away?
24Can anyone hide[x] in secret places
so that I cannot see him?"
declares the LORD.
"Do not I fill heaven and
earth?"[y]
declares the LORD.

25"I have heard what the prophets
say who prophesy lies[z] in my name.
They say, 'I had a dream![a] I had a
dream!' 26How long will this continue
in the hearts of these lying prophets,
who prophesy the delusions[b] of their
own minds? 27They think the dreams
they tell one another will make my
people forget[c] my name, just as their
fathers forgot[d] my name through Baal
worship. 28Let the prophet who has a
dream tell his dream, but let the one
who has my word speak it faithfully.
For what has straw to do with grain?"
declares the LORD. 29"Is not my word
like fire,"[e] declares the LORD, "and like
a hammer that breaks a rock in pieces?
30"Therefore," declares the LORD, "I
am against[f] the prophets[g] who steal
from one another words supposed-
ly from me. 31Yes," declares the LORD,
"I am against the prophets who wag
their own tongues and yet declare,
'The LORD declares.'[h] 32Indeed, I am
against those who prophesy false
dreams,[i]" declares the LORD. "They
tell them and lead my people astray
with their reckless lies, yet I did not
send or appoint them. They do not
benefit[j] these people in the least," declares the LORD.

False Oracles and False Prophets

33"When these people, or a prophet
or a priest, ask you, 'What is the oracle[a][k] of the LORD?' say to them, 'What
oracle?[b] I will forsake[l] you, declares
the LORD.' 34If a prophet or a priest or
anyone else claims, 'This is the oracle[m] of the LORD,' I will punish[n] that
man and his household. 35This is what
each of you keeps on saying to his
friend or relative: 'What is the LORD's
answer?'[o] or 'What has the LORD spoken?' 36But you must not mention 'the
oracle of the LORD' again, because every man's own word becomes his oracle and so you distort[p] the words of
the living God, the LORD Almighty, our
God. 37This is what you keep saying to
a prophet: 'What is the LORD's answer
to you?' or 'What has the LORD spoken?'
38Although you claim, 'This is the oracle of the LORD,' this is what the LORD
says: You used the words, 'This is the
oracle of the LORD,' even though I told
you that you must not claim, 'This
is the oracle of the LORD.' 39Therefore,
I will surely forget you and cast[q]
you out of my presence along with the
city I gave to you and your fathers.
40I will bring upon you everlasting
disgrace[r]—everlasting shame that
will not be forgotten."

Two Baskets of Figs

24 After Jehoiachin[c][s] son of Jehoiakim king of Judah and the officials,
the craftsmen and the artisans of Judah
were carried into exile from Jerusalem
to Babylon by Nebuchadnezzar king of
Babylon, the LORD showed me two baskets of figs[t] placed in front of the temple of the LORD. 2One basket had very
good figs, like those that ripen early;
the other basket had very poor[u] figs,
so bad they could not be eaten.
3Then the LORD asked me, "What do
you see,[v] Jeremiah?"
"Figs," I answered. "The good ones
are very good, but the poor ones are so
bad they cannot be eaten."
4Then the word of the LORD came to
me: 5"This is what the LORD, the God of
Israel, says: 'Like these good figs, I regard as good the exiles from Judah,
whom I sent away from this place to
the land of the Babylonians.[d] 6My eyes
will watch over them for their good,
and I will bring them back[w] to this
land. I will build[x] them up and not
tear them down; I will plant them and
not uproot them. 7I will give them a
heart to know me, that I am the LORD.
They will be my people,[y] and I will be
their God, for they will return[z] to me
with all their heart.[a]
8" 'But like the poor[b] figs, which are
so bad they cannot be eaten,' says the
LORD, 'so will I deal with Zedekiah king
of Judah, his officials[c] and the survivors[d] from Jerusalem, whether they
remain in this land or live in Egypt.[e] 9I
will make them abhorrent[f] and an offense to all the kingdoms of the earth,
a reproach and a byword,[g] an object
of ridicule and cursing,[h] wherever

23:22 [v]Jer 25:5; Zec 1:4
23:23 [w]Ps 139:1-10
23:24 [x]Job 22:12-14 [y]1Ki 8:27
23:25 [z]Jer 14:14 [a]ver 28,32; Jer 29:8
23:26 [b]1Ti 4:1-2
23:27 [c]Dt 13:1-3; Jer 29:8 [d]Jdg 3:7; 8:33-34
23:29 [e]Jer 5:14
23:30 [f]Ps 34:16 [g]Dt 18:20; Jer 14:15
23:31 [h]ver 17
23:32 [i]ver 25 [j]Jer 7:8; La 2:14
23:33 [k]Mal 1:1 [l]ver 39
23:34 [m]La 2:14 [n]Zec 13:3
23:35 [o]Jer 33:3; 42:4
23:36 [p]Gal 1:7-8; 2Pe 3:16
23:39 [q]Jer 7:15
23:40 [r]Jer 20:11; Eze 5:14-15
24:1 [s]2Ki 24:16; 2Ch 36:9; Jer 29:2 [t]Am 8:1-2
24:2 [u]Isa 5:4
24:3 [v]Jer 1:11; Am 8:2
24:6 [w]Jer 29:10; Eze 11:17 [x]Jer 33:7; 42:10
24:7 [y]Isa 51:16; Jer 31:33; Heb 8:10 [z]Jer 32:40 [a]Eze 11:19
24:8 [b]Jer 29:17 [c]Jer 39:6 [d]Jer 39:9 [e]Jer 44:1,26
24:9 [f]Jer 15:4; 34:17 [g]Dt 28:25; 1Ki 9:7 [h]Jer 29:18

[a] 33 Or *burden* (see Septuagint and Vulgate)
[b] 33 Hebrew; Septuagint and Vulgate *'You are the burden.* (The Hebrew for *oracle* and *burden* is the same.)
[c] 1 Hebrew *Jeconiah,* a variant of *Jehoiachin*
[d] 5 Or *Chaldeans*

I banish[i] them. **10**I will send the
sword,[j] famine and plague[k] against
them until they are destroyed from the
land I gave to them and their fathers.' "

Seventy Years of Captivity

25 The word came to Jeremiah concerning all the people of Judah in
the fourth year of Jehoiakim[l] son of
Josiah king of Judah, which was the
first year of Nebuchadnezzar[m] king of
Babylon. **2**So Jeremiah the prophet said
to all the people of Judah[n] and to all
those living in Jerusalem: **3**For twenty-
three years—from the thirteenth year
of Josiah[o] son of Amon king of Judah
until this very day—the word of the
LORD has come to me and I have spoken to you again and again,[p] but you
have not listened.[q]
4And though the LORD has sent all
his servants the prophets[r] to you
again and again, you have not listened
or paid any attention. **5**They said,
"Turn now, each of you, from your evil
ways and your evil practices, and you
can stay in the land the LORD gave to
you and your fathers for ever and ever.
6Do not follow other gods[s] to serve
and worship them; do not provoke me
to anger with what your hands have
made. Then I will not harm you."
7"But you did not listen to me," declares the LORD, "and you have provoked me with what your hands have
made,[t] and you have brought harm[u]
to yourselves."
8Therefore the LORD Almighty says
this: "Because you have not listened to
my words, **9**I will summon[v] all the
peoples of the north[w] and my servant[x] Nebuchadnezzar king of Babylon," declares the LORD, "and I will
bring them against this land and its inhabitants and against all the surrounding nations. I will completely destroy[a]
them and make them an object of horror and scorn,[y] and an everlasting
ruin. **10**I will banish from them the
sounds[z] of joy and gladness, the
voices of bride and bridegroom,[a]
the sound of millstones[b] and the light
of the lamp.[c] **11**This whole country
will become a desolate wasteland,[d]
and these nations will serve the king of
Babylon seventy years.[e]
12"But when the seventy years[f] are
fulfilled, I will punish the king of Babylon and his nation, the land of the
Babylonians,[b] for their guilt," declares
the LORD, "and will make it desolate[g]
forever. **13**I will bring upon that land all
the things I have spoken against it, all
that are written in this book and
prophesied by Jeremiah against all the

24:9 [i]Dt 28:37
24:10 [j]Isa 51:19 [k]Jer 27:8
25:1 [l]2Ki 24:2; Jer 36:1 [m]2Ki 24:1
25:2 [n]Jer 18:11
25:3 [o]Jer 1:2 [p]Jer 11:7; 26:5 [q]Jer 7:26
25:4 [r]Jer 7:25
25:6 [s]Dt 8:19
25:7 [t]Dt 32:21 [u]2Ki 21:15
25:9 [v]Isa 13:3-5 [w]Jer 1:15 [x]Jer 27:6 [y]Jer 18:16
25:10 [z]Isa 24:8; Eze 26:13 [a]Jer 7:34 [b]Ecc 12:3-4 [c]Rev 18:22-23
25:11 [d]Jer 4:26-27; 12:11-12 [e]2Ch 36:21
25:12 [f]Jer 29:10 [g]Isa 13:19-22; 14:22-23
25:14 [h]Jer 27:7 [i]Jer 50:9; 51:27-28 [j]Jer 51:6
25:15 [k]Isa 51:17; Ps 75:8; Rev 14:10
25:16 [l]Na 3:11 [m]Jer 51:7
25:17 [n]Jer 1:10
25:18 [o]Jer 24:9 [p]Jer 44:22
25:20 [q]Job 1:1 [r]Jer 47:5
25:21 [s]Jer 49:1
25:22 [t]Jer 47:4 [u]Jer 31:10
25:23 [v]Jer 9:26; 49:32
25:24 [w]2Ch 9:14
25:25 [x]Ge 10:22
25:26 [y]Jer 50:3,9 [z]Jer 51:41
25:27 [a]ver 16,28; Hab 2:16 [b]Eze 21:4
25:29 [c]Jer 13:12-14 [d]1Pe 4:17 [e]Pr 11:31 [f]ver 30-31

nations. **14**They themselves will be enslaved[h] by many nations[i] and great
kings; I will repay[j] them according to
their deeds and the work of their
hands."

The Cup of God's Wrath

15This is what the LORD, the God of
Israel, said to me: "Take from my hand
this cup[k] filled with the wine of my
wrath and make all the nations to
whom I send you drink it. **16**When they
drink it, they will stagger[l] and go
mad[m] because of the sword I will send
among them."
17So I took the cup from the LORD's
hand and made all the nations to
whom he sent[n] me drink it: **18**Jerusalem and the towns of Judah, its kings
and officials, to make them a ruin and
an object of horror and scorn and cursing,[o] as they are today;[p] **19**Pharaoh
king of Egypt, his attendants, his officials and all his people, **20**and all the
foreign people there; all the kings of
Uz;[q] all the kings of the Philistines
(those of Ashkelon,[r] Gaza, Ekron, and
the people left at Ashdod); **21**Edom,
Moab and Ammon;[s] **22**all the kings of
Tyre and Sidon;[t] the kings of the
coastlands[u] across the sea; **23**Dedan,
Tema, Buz and all who are in distant
places[c];[v] **24**all the kings of Arabia[w]
and all the kings of the foreign people
who live in the desert; **25**all the kings of
Zimri, Elam[x] and Media; **26**and all the
kings of the north,[y] near and far, one
after the other—all the kingdoms on
the face of the earth. And after all of
them, the king of Sheshach[d][z] will
drink it too.
27"Then tell them, 'This is what the
LORD Almighty, the God of Israel, says:
Drink, get drunk[a] and vomit, and fall
to rise no more because of the sword[b]
I will send among you.' **28**But if they
refuse to take the cup from your hand
and drink, tell them, 'This is what the
LORD Almighty says: You must drink it!
29See, I am beginning to bring disaster[c] on the city that bears my Name,[d]
and will you indeed go unpunished?[e]
You will not go unpunished, for I am
calling down a sword upon all[f] who
live on the earth, declares the LORD Almighty.'
30"Now prophesy all these words
against them and say to them:

a9 The Hebrew term refers to the irrevocable giving over of things or persons to the LORD, often by totally destroying them. **b**12 Or *Chaldeans* **c**23 Or *who clip the hair by their foreheads* **d**26 *Sheshach* is a cryptogram for Babylon.

" 'The LORD will roar[g] from on
high;
he will thunder[h] from his holy
dwelling
and roar mightily against his
land.
He will shout like those who tread
the grapes,
shout against all who live on the
earth.
31The tumult will resound to the
ends of the earth,
for the LORD will bring charges[i]
against the nations;
he will bring judgment on all
mankind
and put the wicked to the
sword,' "
declares the LORD.

32This is what the LORD Almighty
says:

"Look! Disaster is spreading
from nation to nation;[j]
a mighty storm[k] is rising
from the ends of the earth."

33At that time those slain[l] by the LORD
will be everywhere—from one end of
the earth to the other. They will not be
mourned or gathered[m] up or buried,[n]
but will be like refuse lying on the
ground.

34Weep and wail, you shepherds;
roll[o] in the dust, you leaders of
the flock.
For your time to be slaughtered[p]
has come;
you will fall and be shattered like
fine pottery.
35The shepherds will have nowhere
to flee,
the leaders of the flock no place
to escape.[q]
36Hear the cry of the shepherds,
the wailing of the leaders of the
flock,
for the LORD is destroying their
pasture.
37The peaceful meadows will be laid
waste
because of the fierce anger of the
LORD.
38Like a lion[r] he will leave his lair,
and their land will become
desolate
because of the sword[a] of the
oppressor
and because of the LORD's fierce
anger.

Jeremiah Threatened With Death

26 Early in the reign of Jehoiakim[s]
son of Josiah king of Judah, this
word came from the LORD: 2"This is
what the LORD says: Stand in the courtyard[t] of the LORD's house and speak
to all the people of the towns of Judah
who come to worship in the house of
the LORD. Tell[u] them everything I
command you; do not omit[v] a word.
3Perhaps they will listen and each will
turn[w] from his evil way. Then I will
relent[x] and not bring on them the disaster I was planning because of the
evil they have done. 4Say to them, 'This
is what the LORD says: If you do not
listen[y] to me and follow my law,[z]
which I have set before you, 5and if you
do not listen to the words of my servants the prophets, whom I have sent
to you again and again (though you
have not listened[a]), 6then I will make
this house like Shiloh[b] and this city an
object of cursing[c] among all the nations of the earth.' "

7The priests, the prophets and all the
people heard Jeremiah speak these
words in the house of the LORD. 8But as
soon as Jeremiah finished telling all the
people everything the LORD had commanded him to say, the priests, the
prophets and all the people seized him
and said, "You must die! 9Why do you
prophesy in the LORD's name that this
house will be like Shiloh and this city
will be desolate and deserted?"[d] And
all the people crowded around Jeremiah in the house of the LORD.

10When the officials of Judah heard
about these things, they went up from
the royal palace to the house of the
LORD and took their places at the entrance of the New Gate of the LORD's
house. 11Then the priests and the
prophets said to the officials and all
the people, "This man should be sentenced to death[e] because he has
prophesied against this city. You have
heard it with your own ears!"

12Then Jeremiah said to all the officials[f] and all the people: "The LORD
sent me to prophesy[g] against this
house and this city all the things you
have heard.[h] 13Now reform[i] your
ways and your actions and obey the
LORD your God. Then the LORD will relent and not bring the disaster he has
pronounced against you. 14As for me, I
am in your hands;[j] do with me whatever you think is good and right. 15Be
assured, however, that if you put me to
death, you will bring the guilt of innocent blood on yourselves and on this
city and on those who live in it, for in
truth the LORD has sent me to you to
speak all these words in your hearing."

25:30 [g]Isa 16:10; 42:13 [h]Joel 3:16; Am 1:2
25:31 [i]Hos 4:1; Joel 3:2; Mic 6:2
25:32 [j]Isa 34:2 [k]Jer 23:19
25:33 [l]Isa 66:16; Eze 39:17-20 [m]Jer 16:4 [n]Ps 79:3
25:34 [o]Jer 6:26 [p]Isa 34:6; Jer 50:27
25:35 [q]Job 11:20
25:38 [r]Jer 4:7
26:1 [s]2Ki 23:36
26:2 [t]Jer 19:14 [u]Jer 1:17; Mt 28:20; Ac 20:27 [v]Dt 4:2
26:3 [w]Jer 36:7 [x]Jer 18:8
26:4 [y]Lev 26:14 [z]1Ki 9:6
26:5 [a]Jer 25:4
26:6 [b]Jos 18:1 [c]2Ki 22:19
26:9 [d]Jer 9:11
26:11 [e]Dt 18:20; Jer 18:23; 38:4; Mt 26:66; Ac 6:11
26:12 [f]Jer 1:18 [g]Am 7:15; Ac 4:18-20; 5:29 [h]ver 2,15
26:13 [i]Jer 7:5; Joel 2:12-14
26:14 [j]Jer 38:5

[a] *38* Some Hebrew manuscripts and Septuagint (see also Jer. 46:16 and 50:16); most Hebrew manuscripts *anger*

16Then the officials[k] and all the
people said to the priests and the
prophets, "This man should not be
sentenced to death![l] He has spoken to
us in the name of the LORD our God."
17Some of the elders of the land
stepped forward and said to the entire
assembly of people, 18"Micah[m] of Moresheth prophesied in the days of Hezekiah king of Judah. He told all the people of Judah, 'This is what the LORD
Almighty says:

" 'Zion[n] will be plowed like a field,
Jerusalem will become a heap of
rubble,[o]
the temple hill[p] a mound
overgrown with
thickets.'[a][q]

19"Did Hezekiah king of Judah or anyone else in Judah put him to death? Did
not Hezekiah[r] fear the LORD and seek
his favor? And did not the LORD relent,[s] so that he did not bring the disaster[t] he pronounced against them?
We are about to bring a terrible disaster[u] on ourselves!"
20(Now Uriah son of Shemaiah from
Kiriath Jearim[v] was another man who
prophesied in the name of the LORD; he
prophesied the same things against
this city and this land as Jeremiah did.
21When King Jehoiakim[w] and all his
officers and officials heard his words,
the king sought to put him to death.
But Uriah heard of it and fled[x] in fear
to Egypt. 22King Jehoiakim, however,
sent Elnathan[y] son of Acbor to Egypt,
along with some other men. 23They
brought Uriah out of Egypt and took
him to King Jehoiakim, who had him
struck down with a sword and his body
thrown into the burial place of the
common people.)
24Furthermore, Ahikam[z] son of
Shaphan supported Jeremiah, and so
he was not handed over to the people
to be put to death.

Judah to Serve Nebuchadnezzar

27 Early in the reign of Zedekiah[b][a]
son of Josiah king of Judah, this
word came to Jeremiah from the LORD:
2This is what the LORD said to me:
"Make a yoke[b] out of straps and crossbars and put it on your neck. 3Then
send word to the kings of Edom, Moab,
Ammon,[c] Tyre and Sidon through the
envoys who have come to Jerusalem to
Zedekiah king of Judah. 4Give them a
message for their masters and say,
'This is what the LORD Almighty, the
God of Israel, says: "Tell this to your
masters: 5With my great power and
outstretched arm[d] I made the earth
and its people and the animals that are
on it, and I give[e] it to anyone I please.
6Now I will hand all your countries
over to my servant[f] Nebuchadnezzar[g] king of Babylon; I will make even
the wild animals subject to him.[h] 7All
nations will serve[i] him and his son
and his grandson until the time[j] for
his land comes; then many nations and
great kings will subjugate[k] him.
8" ' "If, however, any nation or kingdom will not serve Nebuchadnezzar
king of Babylon or bow its neck under
his yoke, I will punish that nation with
the sword, famine and plague, declares
the LORD, until I destroy it by his hand.
9So do not listen to your prophets, your
diviners, your interpreters of dreams,
your mediums[l] or your sorcerers who
tell you, 'You will not serve the king
of Babylon.' 10They prophesy lies[m] to
you that will only serve to remove you
far from your lands; I will banish you
and you will perish. 11But if any nation
will bow its neck under the yoke[n] of
the king of Babylon and serve him, I
will let that nation remain in its own
land to till it and to live there, declares
the LORD." ' "
12I gave the same message to Zedekiah king of Judah. I said, "Bow your
neck under the yoke of the king of Babylon; serve him and his people, and
you will live. 13Why will you and your
people die[o] by the sword, famine and
plague with which the LORD has threatened any nation that will not serve the
king of Babylon? 14Do not listen to the
words of the prophets who say to you,
'You will not serve the king of Babylon,'
for they are prophesying lies[p] to you.
15'I have not sent[q] them,' declares the
LORD. 'They are prophesying lies in my
name.[r] Therefore, I will banish you
and you will perish,[s] both you and the
prophets who prophesy to you.' "
16Then I said to the priests and all
these people, "This is what the LORD
says: Do not listen to the prophets who
say, 'Very soon now the articles[t] from
the LORD's house will be brought back
from Babylon.' They are prophesying
lies to you. 17Do not listen to them.
Serve the king of Babylon, and you will
live. Why should this city become a
ruin? 18If they are prophets and have
the word of the LORD, let them plead[u]
with the LORD Almighty that the furnishings remaining in the house of the
LORD and in the palace of the king of
Judah and in Jerusalem not be taken to

26:16 [k]Ac 23:9 [l]Ac 5:34-39; 23:29 **26:18** [m]Mic 1:1 [n]Isa 2:3 [o]Ne 4:2; Jer 9:11 [p]Mic 4:1; Zec 8:3 [q]Jer 17:3 **26:19** [r]2Ch 32:24-26; Isa 37:14-20 [s]Ex 32:14; 2Sa 24:16 [t]Jer 44:7 [u]Hab 2:10 **26:20** [v]Jos 9:17 **26:21** [w]1Ki 19:2 [x]Mt 10:23 **26:22** [y]Jer 36:12,25 **26:24** [z]2Ki 22:12 **27:1** [a]2Ch 36:11 **27:2** [b]Jer 28:10,13 **27:3** [c]Jer 25:21 **27:5** [d]Dt 9:29 [e]Ps 115:16 **27:6** [f]Jer 25:9 [g]Jer 21:7; Eze 29:18-20 [h]Jer 28:14; Da 2:37-38 **27:7** [i]2Ch 36:20 [j]Jer 25:12 [k]Jer 25:14; Da 5:28 **27:9** [l]Dt 18:11 **27:10** [m]Jer 23:25 **27:11** [n]Jer 21:9 **27:13** [o]Eze 18:31 **27:14** [p]Jer 14:14 **27:15** [q]Jer 23:21 [r]Jer 29:9 [s]Jer 6:15 **27:16** [t]2Ki 24:13; 2Ch 36:7,10; Jer 28:3; Da 1:2 **27:18** [u]1Sa 7:8

a *18* Micah 3:12 **b** *1* A few Hebrew manuscripts and Syriac (see also Jer. 27:3, 12 and 28:1); most Hebrew manuscripts *Jehoiakim* (Most Septuagint manuscripts do not have this verse.)

Babylon. 19For this is what the LORD Almighty says about the pillars, the Sea,[v] the movable stands and the other furnishings[w] that are left in this city, 20which Nebuchadnezzar king of Babylon did not take away when he carried[x] Jehoiachin[a][y] son of Jehoiakim king of Judah into exile from Jerusalem to Babylon, along with all the nobles of Judah and Jerusalem— 21yes, this is what the LORD Almighty, the God of Israel, says about the things that are left in the house of the LORD and in the palace of the king of Judah and in Jerusalem: 22'They will be taken[z] to Babylon and there they will remain until the day[a] I come for them,' declares the LORD. 'Then I will bring[b] them back and restore them to this place.' "

The False Prophet Hananiah

28 In the fifth month of that same year, the fourth year, early in the reign of Zedekiah[c] king of Judah, the prophet Hananiah son of Azzur, who was from Gibeon,[d] said to me in the house of the LORD in the presence of the priests and all the people: 2"This is what the LORD Almighty, the God of Israel, says: 'I will break the yoke[e] of the king of Babylon. 3Within two years I will bring back to this place all the articles[f] of the LORD's house that Nebuchadnezzar king of Babylon removed from here and took to Babylon. 4I will also bring back to this place Jehoiachin[a][g] son of Jehoiakim king of Judah and all the other exiles from Judah who went to Babylon,' declares the LORD, 'for I will break the yoke of the king of Babylon.' "

5Then the prophet Jeremiah replied to the prophet Hananiah before the priests and all the people who were standing in the house of the LORD. 6He said, "Amen! May the LORD do so! May the LORD fulfill the words you have prophesied by bringing the articles of the LORD's house and all the exiles back to this place from Babylon. 7Nevertheless, listen to what I have to say in your hearing and in the hearing of all the people: 8From early times the prophets who preceded you and me have prophesied war, disaster and plague[h] against many countries and great kingdoms. 9But the prophet who prophesies peace will be recognized as one truly sent by the LORD only if his prediction comes true.[i]"

10Then the prophet Hananiah took the yoke[j] off the neck of the prophet Jeremiah and broke it, 11and he said[k] before all the people, "This is what the LORD says: 'In the same way will I break the yoke of Nebuchadnezzar king of Babylon off the neck of all the nations within two years.' " At this, the prophet Jeremiah went on his way.

12Shortly after the prophet Hananiah had broken the yoke off the neck of the prophet Jeremiah, the word of the LORD came to Jeremiah: 13"Go and tell Hananiah, 'This is what the LORD says: You have broken a wooden yoke, but in its place you will get a yoke of iron. 14This is what the LORD Almighty, the God of Israel, says: I will put an iron yoke[l] on the necks of all these nations to make them serve[m] Nebuchadnezzar king of Babylon, and they will serve him. I will even give him control over the wild animals.[n]' "

15Then the prophet Jeremiah said to Hananiah the prophet, "Listen, Hananiah! The LORD has not sent[o] you, yet you have persuaded this nation to trust in lies.[p] 16Therefore, this is what the LORD says: 'I am about to remove you from the face of the earth.[q] This very year you are going to die, because you have preached rebellion[r] against the LORD.' "

17In the seventh month of that same year, Hananiah the prophet died.

A Letter to the Exiles

29 This is the text of the letter that the prophet Jeremiah sent from Jerusalem to the surviving elders among the exiles and to the priests, the prophets and all the other people Nebuchadnezzar had carried into exile from Jerusalem to Babylon.[s] 2(This was after King Jehoiachin[a][t] and the queen mother, the court officials and the leaders of Judah and Jerusalem, the craftsmen and the artisans had gone into exile from Jerusalem.) 3He entrusted the letter to Elasah son of Shaphan and to Gemariah son of Hilkiah, whom Zedekiah king of Judah sent to King Nebuchadnezzar in Babylon. It said:

4This is what the LORD Almighty, the God of Israel, says to all those I carried[u] into exile from Jerusalem to Babylon: 5"Build[v] houses and settle down; plant gardens and eat what they produce. 6Marry and have sons and daughters; find wives for your sons and give your daughters in marriage, so that they too may have sons and daughters. Increase in number there; do not decrease. 7Also, seek the peace and prosperity of the city to which I have carried

27:19 [v]2Ki 25:13 [w]Jer 52:17-23
27:20 [x]2Ch 36:10; Jer 24:1 [y]Jer 22:24
27:22 [z]2Ki 25:13 [a]2Ch 36:21 [b]Ezr 1:7; 7:19
28:1 [c]Jer 27:1,3 [d]Jos 9:3
28:2 [e]Jer 27:12
28:3 [f]2Ki 24:13
28:4 [g]Jer 22:24-27
28:8 [h]Lev 26:14-17; Isa 5:5-7
28:9 [i]Dt 18:22
28:10 [j]Jer 27:2
28:11 [k]Jer 14:14; 27:10
28:14 [l]Dt 28:48 [m]Jer 25:11 [n]Jer 27:6
28:15 [o]Jer 29:31 [p]Jer 20:6; 29:21; La 2:14; Eze 13:6
28:16 [q]Ge 7:4 [r]Dt 13:5; Jer 29:32
29:1 [s]2Ch 36:10
29:2 [t]2Ki 24:12; Jer 22:24-28
29:4 [u]Jer 24:5
29:5 [v]ver 28

[a] *20,4,2* Hebrew *Jeconiah,* a variant of *Jehoiachin*

you into exile. Pray[w] to the LORD for it, because if it prospers, you too will prosper." 8Yes, this is what the LORD Almighty, the God of Israel, says: "Do not let the prophets and diviners among you deceive[x] you. Do not listen to the dreams you encourage them to have.[y] 9They are prophesying lies[z] to you in my name. I have not sent them," declares the LORD.

10This is what the LORD says: "When seventy years[a] are completed for Babylon, I will come to you and fulfill my gracious promise to bring you back[b] to this place. 11For I know the plans[c] I have for you," declares the LORD, "plans to prosper you and not to harm you, plans to give you hope and a future. 12Then you will call upon me and come and pray to me, and I will listen[d] to you. 13You will seek[e] me and find me when you seek me with all your heart.[f] 14I will be found by you," declares the LORD, "and will bring you back[g] from captivity.[a] I will gather you from all the nations and places where I have banished you," declares the LORD, "and will bring you back to the place from which I carried you into exile."[h]

15You may say, "The LORD has raised up prophets for us in Babylon," 16but this is what the LORD says about the king who sits on David's throne and all the people who remain in this city, your countrymen who did not go with you into exile— 17yes, this is what the LORD Almighty says: "I will send the sword, famine and plague[i] against them and I will make them like poor figs[j] that are so bad they cannot be eaten. 18I will pursue them with the sword, famine and plague and will make them abhorrent[k] to all the kingdoms of the earth and an object of cursing and horror,[l] of scorn and reproach, among all the nations where I drive them. 19For they have not listened to my words,"[m] declares the LORD, "words that I sent to them again and again by my servants the prophets.[n] And you exiles have not listened either," declares the LORD.

20Therefore, hear the word of the LORD, all you exiles whom I have sent[o] away from Jerusalem to Babylon. 21This is what the LORD Almighty, the God of Israel, says about Ahab son of Kolaiah and Zedekiah son of Maaseiah, who are prophesying lies[p] to you in my name: "I will hand them over to Nebuchadnezzar king of Babylon, and he will put them to death before your very eyes. 22Because of them, all the exiles from Judah who are in Babylon will use this curse: 'The LORD treat you like Zedekiah and Ahab, whom the king of Babylon burned[q] in the fire.' 23For they have done outrageous things in Israel; they have committed adultery[r] with their neighbors' wives and in my name have spoken lies, which I did not tell them to do. I know[s] it and am a witness to it," declares the LORD.

Message to Shemaiah

24Tell Shemaiah the Nehelamite, 25"This is what the LORD Almighty, the God of Israel, says: You sent letters in your own name to all the people in Jerusalem, to Zephaniah[t] son of Maaseiah the priest, and to all the other priests. You said to Zephaniah, 26'The LORD has appointed you priest in place of Jehoiada to be in charge of the house of the LORD; you should put any madman[u] who acts like a prophet into the stocks[v] and neck-irons. 27So why have you not reprimanded Jeremiah

29:7 [w]Ezr 6:10; 1Ti 2:1-2 **29:8** [x]Jer 37:9 [y]Jer 23:27 **29:9** [z]Jer 14:14; 27:15 **29:10** [a]2Ch 36:21; Jer 25:12; Da 9:2 [b]Jer 21:22 **29:11** [c]Ps 40:5 **29:12** [d]Ps 145:19 **29:13** [e]Mt 7:7 [f]Dt 4:29; Jer 24:7 **29:14** [g]Dt 30:3; Jer 30:3 [h]Jer 23:3-4

29:17 [i]Jer 27:8 [j]Jer 24:8-10 **29:18** [k]Jer 15:4 [l]Dt 28:25; Jer 42:18 **29:19** [m]Jer 6:19 [n]Jer 25:4 **29:20** [o]Jer 24:5 **29:21** [p]ver 9; Jer 14:14 **29:22** [q]Da 3:6 **29:23** [r]Jer 23:14 [s]Heb 4:13 **29:25** [t]2Ki 25:18; Jer 21:1 **29:26** [u]2Ki 9:11; Hos 9:7; Jn 10:20 [v]Jer 20:2

a 14 Or *will restore your fortunes*

29:11-13

PROMISE OF HOPE

What a promise! God himself was saying he would prosper his people, give them hope and a future. He promised he would hear their prayers and reveal himself to them. This is a great and reassuring promise for any time. But verses 1–10 clue us in to just how great this promise really is. It was written to people who were in exile; to people suffering God's judgment on their many sins. These uprooted people had lost their homes and their nation. Their whole world had been turned upside down. In this terrible darkness, God's words of hope and encouragement brought much-needed light.

God's power and presence is always the godly man's comfort, but in the days when disappointment and despair are strongest, remember this promise from the One who keeps his promises. When you encounter other men's darkness, be the Jeremiah who delivers God's word of hope.

from Anathoth, who poses as a prophet
among you? 28He has sent this message[w] to us in Babylon: It will be a long
time.[x] Therefore build[y] houses and
settle down; plant gardens and eat
what they produce.' "
29Zephaniah the priest, however,
read the letter to Jeremiah the prophet.
30Then the word of the LORD came to
Jeremiah: 31"Send this message to all
the exiles: 'This is what the LORD says
about Shemaiah[z] the Nehelamite: Because Shemaiah has prophesied to
you, even though I did not send[a] him,
and has led you to believe a lie, 32this
is what the LORD says: I will surely punish Shemaiah the Nehelamite and his
descendants.[b] He will have no one left
among this people, nor will he see the
good[c] things I will do for my people,
declares the LORD, because he has
preached rebellion[d] against me.' "

Restoration of Israel

30 This is the word that came to Jeremiah from the LORD: 2"This is what
the LORD, the God of Israel, says:
'Write[e] in a book all the words I have
spoken to you. 3The days are coming,'
declares the LORD, 'when I will bring[f]
my people Israel and Judah back from
captivity[a] and restore[g] them to the
land I gave their forefathers to possess,'
says the LORD."
4These are the words the LORD spoke
concerning Israel and Judah: 5"This is
what the LORD says:

" 'Cries of fear[h] are heard—
terror, not peace.
6Ask and see:
Can a man bear children?
Then why do I see every strong
man
with his hands on his stomach
like a woman in labor,[i]
every face turned deathly pale?
7How awful that day[j] will be!
None will be like it.
It will be a time of trouble[k] for
Jacob,
but he will be saved[l] out of it.

8" 'In that day,' declares the LORD
Almighty,
'I will break the yoke[m] off their
necks
and will tear off their bonds;
no longer will foreigners enslave
them.[n]
9Instead, they will serve the LORD
their God
and David[o] their king,[p]
whom I will raise up for them.

10" 'So do not fear,[q] O Jacob my
servant;[r]
do not be dismayed, O Israel,'
declares the LORD.
'I will surely save[s] you out of a
distant place,
your descendants from the land
of their exile.
Jacob will again have peace and
security,[t]
and no one will make him afraid.
11I am with you and will save you,'
declares the LORD.
'Though I completely destroy all
the nations
among which I scatter you,
I will not completely destroy[u]
you.
I will discipline[v] you but only with
justice;
I will not let you go entirely
unpunished.'[w]

12"This is what the LORD says:

" 'Your wound is incurable,
your injury beyond healing.[x]
13There is no one to plead your
cause,
no remedy for your sore,
no healing[y] for you.
14All your allies[z] have forgotten you;
they care nothing for you.
I have struck you as an enemy[a]
would
and punished you as would the
cruel,[b]
because your guilt is so great
and your sins[c] so many.
15Why do you cry out over your
wound,
your pain that has no cure?
Because of your great guilt and
many sins
I have done these things to you.

16" 'But all who devour[d] you will be
devoured;
all your enemies will go into
exile.[e]
Those who plunder[f] you will be
plundered;
all who make spoil of you I will
despoil.
17But I will restore you to health
and heal your wounds,'
declares the LORD,
'because you are called an
outcast,[g]
Zion for whom no one cares.'

18"This is what the LORD says:

" 'I will restore the fortunes[h] of
Jacob's tents
and have compassion[i] on his
dwellings;

29:28 [w]ver 1 [x]ver 10 [y]ver 5 **29:31** [z]ver 24 [a]Jer 14:14; 28:15 **29:32** [b]1Sa 2:30-33 [c]ver 10 [d]Jer 28:16 **30:2** [e]Isa 30:8 **30:3** [f]Jer 29:14 [g]Jer 16:15 **30:5** [h]Jer 6:25 **30:6** [i]Jer 4:31 **30:7** [j]Isa 2:12; Joel 2:11 [k]Zep 1:15 [l]ver 10 **30:8** [m]Isa 9:4 [n]Eze 34:27 **30:9** [o]Isa 55:3-4; Lk 1:69; Ac 2:30; 13:23 [p]Eze 34:23-24; 37:24; Hos 3:5 **30:10** [q]Isa 43:5; Jer 46:27-28 [r]Isa 44:2

[s]Jer 29:14 [t]Isa 35:9 **30:11** [u]Jer 4:27; 46:28 [v]Jer 10:24 [w]Am 9:8 **30:12** [x]Jer 15:18 **30:13** [y]Jer 8:22; 14:19; 46:11 **30:14** [z]Jer 22:20; La 1:2 [a]Job 13:24 [b]Job 30:21 [c]Jer 5:6 **30:16** [d]Isa 33:1; Jer 2:3; 10:25 [e]Isa 14:2; Joel 3:4-8 [f]Jer 50:10 **30:17** [g]Jer 33:24 **30:18** [h]ver 3; Jer 31:23 [i]Ps 102:13

a 3 Or *will restore the fortunes of my people Israel and Judah*

the city will be rebuilt[j] on her
ruins,
and the palace will stand in its
proper place.
19From them will come songs[k] of
thanksgiving[l]
and the sound of rejoicing.[m]
I will add to their numbers,[n]
and they will not be decreased;
I will bring them honor,[o]
and they will not be disdained.
20Their children[p] will be as in days
of old,
and their community will be
established[q] before me;
I will punish all who oppress
them.
21Their leader[r] will be one of their
own;
their ruler will arise from among
them.
I will bring him near[s] and he will
come close to me,
for who is he who will devote
himself
to be close to me?'
declares the LORD.
22" 'So you will be my people,
and I will be your God.' "
23See, the storm[t] of the LORD
will burst out in wrath,
a driving wind swirling down
on the heads of the wicked.
24The fierce anger[u] of the LORD will
not turn back[v]
until he fully accomplishes
the purposes of his heart.
In days to come
you will understand[w] this.

31 "At that time," declares the LORD, "I
will be the God[x] of all the clans of
Israel, and they will be my people."
2This is what the LORD says:

"The people who survive the sword
will find favor[y] in the desert;
I will come to give rest[z] to
Israel."

3The LORD appeared to us in the
past,[a] saying:
"I have loved[a] you with an
everlasting love;
I have drawn[b] you with
loving-kindness.
4I will build you up again
and you will be rebuilt, O Virgin
Israel.
Again you will take up your
tambourines
and go out to dance with the
joyful.[c]
5Again you will plant vineyards
on the hills of Samaria;[d]
the farmers will plant them
and enjoy their fruit.[e]
6There will be a day when
watchmen cry out
on the hills of Ephraim,
'Come, let us go up to Zion,
to the LORD our God.' "[f]

7This is what the LORD says:

"Sing with joy for Jacob;
shout for the foremost[g] of the
nations.
Make your praises heard, and say,
'O LORD, save[h] your people,
the remnant[i] of Israel.'
8See, I will bring them from the
land of the north[j]
and gather[k] them from the ends
of the earth.
Among them will be the blind[l]
and the lame,[m]
expectant mothers and women
in labor;
a great throng will return.
9They will come with weeping;[n]
they will pray as I bring them
back.
I will lead[o] them beside streams of
water
on a level[p] path where they will
not stumble,
because I am Israel's father,[q]
and Ephraim is my firstborn son.
10"Hear the word of the LORD,
O nations;
proclaim it in distant
coastlands:[r]
'He who scattered Israel will
gather[s] them
and will watch over his flock like
a shepherd.'[t]
11For the LORD will ransom Jacob
and redeem[u] them from the
hand of those stronger[v]
than they.
12They will come and shout for joy
on the heights[w] of Zion;
they will rejoice in the bounty[x]
of the LORD—
the grain, the new wine and the
oil,[y]
the young of the flocks and
herds.
They will be like a well-watered
garden,[z]
and they will sorrow[a] no more.
13Then maidens will dance and be
glad,
young men and old as well.
I will turn their mourning[b] into
gladness;
I will give them comfort and
joy[c] instead of sorrow.

30:18 [j]Jer 31:4,24,38 **30:19** [k]Isa 35:10; 51:11 [l]Isa 51:3 [m]Ps 126:1-2; Jer 31:4 [n]Jer 33:22 [o]Isa 60:9 **30:20** [p]Isa 54:13; Jer 31:17 [q]Isa 54:14 **30:21** [r]ver 9 [s]Nu 16:5 **30:23** [t]Jer 23:19 **30:24** [u]Jer 4:8 [v]Jer 4:28 [w]Jer 23:19-20 **31:1** [x]Jer 30:22 **31:2** [y]Nu 14:20 [z]Ex 33:14 **31:3** [a]Dt 4:37 [b]Hos 11:4 **31:4** [c]Jer 30:19 **31:5** [d]Jer 50:19 [e]Isa 65:21; Am 9:14 **31:6** [f]Isa 2:3; Jer 50:4-5; Mic 4:2 **31:7** [g]Dt 28:13; Isa 61:9 [h]Ps 14:7; 28:9 [i]Isa 37:31 **31:8** [j]Jer 3:18; 23:8 [k]Dt 30:4; Eze 34:12-14 [l]Isa 42:16 [m]Eze 34:16; Mic 4:6 **31:9** [n]Ps 126:5 [o]Isa 63:13 [p]Isa 49:11 [q]Ex 4:22; Jer 3:4 **31:10** [r]Isa 66:19; Jer 25:22 [s]Jer 50:19 [t]Isa 40:11; Eze 34:12 **31:11** [u]Isa 44:23; 48:20 [v]Ps 142:6 **31:12** [w]Eze 17:23; Mic 4:1 [x]Joel 3:18 [y]Hos 2:21-22 [z]Isa 58:11 [a]Isa 65:19; Jn 16:22; Rev 7:17 **31:13** [b]Isa 61:3 [c]Ps 30:11; Isa 51:11

[a]3 Or *LORD has appeared to us from afar*

14I will satisfy[d] the priests with
abundance,
and my people will be filled with
my bounty,"
declares the LORD.

15This is what the LORD says:

"A voice is heard in Ramah,[e]
mourning and great weeping,
Rachel weeping for her children
and refusing to be comforted,[f]
because her children are no
more."[g]

16This is what the LORD says:

"Restrain your voice from weeping
and your eyes from tears,[h]
for your work will be rewarded,[i]"
declares the LORD.
"They will return[j] from the
land of the enemy.
17So there is hope for your future,"
declares the LORD.
"Your children will return to
their own land.

18"I have surely heard Ephraim's
moaning:
'You disciplined[k] me like an
unruly calf,[l]
and I have been disciplined.
Restore[m] me, and I will return,
because you are the LORD my
God.
19After I strayed,[n]
I repented;
after I came to understand,
I beat[o] my breast.
I was ashamed and humiliated
because I bore the disgrace of
my youth.'
20Is not Ephraim my dear son,
the child in whom I delight?
Though I often speak against him,
I still remember[p] him.
Therefore my heart yearns for him;
I have great compassion[q] for
him,"
declares the LORD.

21"Set up road signs;
put up guideposts.
Take note of the highway,[r]
the road that you take.
Return,[s] O Virgin[t] Israel,
return to your towns.
22How long will you wander,[u]
O unfaithful[v] daughter?
The LORD will create a new thing
on earth—
a woman will surround[a] a
man."

23This is what the LORD Almighty, the
God of Israel, says: "When I bring them
back from captivity,[b][w] the people
in the land of Judah and in its towns
will once again use these words: 'The
LORD bless you, O righteous dwelling,[x]
O sacred mountain.'[y] 24People will
live[z] together in Judah and all its
towns—farmers and those who move
about with their flocks. 25I will refresh
the weary and satisfy the faint."[a]

26At this I awoke[b] and looked
around. My sleep had been pleasant
to me.

27"The days are coming," declares
the LORD, "when I will plant[c] the
house of Israel and the house of Judah
with the offspring of men and of animals.
28Just as I watched over them to
uproot and tear down, and to overthrow, destroy and bring disaster,[d] so
I will watch over them to build and to
plant,"[e] declares the LORD. 29"In those
days people will no longer say,

'The fathers[f] have eaten sour
grapes,
and the children's teeth are set
on edge.'[g]

30Instead, everyone will die for his own
sin;[h] whoever eats sour grapes—his
own teeth will be set on edge.

31"The time is coming," declares the
LORD,
"when I will make a new
covenant[i]
with the house of Israel
and with the house of Judah.
32It will not be like the covenant[j]
I made with their forefathers[k]
when I took them by the hand
to lead them out of Egypt,
because they broke my covenant,
though I was a husband to[c]
them,[d]"
declares the LORD.
33"This is the covenant I will make
with the house of Israel
after that time," declares the
LORD.
"I will put my law in their minds
and write it on their hearts.[l]
I will be their God,
and they will be my people.[m]
34No longer will a man teach[n] his
neighbor,
or a man his brother, saying,
'Know the LORD,'
because they will all know[o] me,
from the least of them to the
greatest,"
declares the LORD.
"For I will forgive[p] their
wickedness

31:14 [d]ver 25
31:15 [e]Jos 18:25 [f]Ge 37:35 [g]Jer 10:20; Mt 2:17-18*
31:16 [h]Isa 25:8; 30:19 [i]Ru 2:12 [j]Jer 30:3; Eze 11:17
31:18 [k]Job 5:17 [l]Hos 4:16 [m]Ps 80:3
31:19 [n]Eze 36:31 [o]Eze 21:12; Lk 18:13
31:20 [p]Hos 4:4; 11:8 [q]Isa 55:7; 63:15; Mic 7:18
31:21 [r]Jer 50:5 [s]Isa 52:11 [t]ver 4
31:22 [u]Jer 2:23 [v]Jer 3:6
31:23 [w]Jer 30:18 [x]Isa 1:26 [y]Ps 48:1; Zec 8:3
31:24 [z]Zec 8:4-8
31:25 [a]Jn 4:14
31:26 [b]Zec 4:1
31:27 [c]Eze 36:9-11; Hos 2:23
31:28 [d]Jer 18:8; 44:27 [e]Jer 1:10
31:29 [f]La 5:7 [g]Eze 18:2
31:30 [h]Isa 3:11; Gal 6:7
31:31 [i]Jer 32:40; Eze 37:26; Lk 22:20; Heb 8:8-12*; 10:16-17
31:32 [j]Ex 24:8 [k]Dt 5:3
31:33 [l]2Co 3:3 [m]Jer 24:7; Heb 10:16
31:34 [n]1Jn 2:27 [o]Jn 6:45 [p]Isa 54:13; Jer 33:8; 50:20

[a] 22 Or *will go about* ⌞*seeking*⌟; or *will protect*
[b] 23 Or *I restore their fortunes* [c] 32 Hebrew; Septuagint and Syriac */ and I turned away from*
[d] 32 Or *was their master*

and will remember their sins[q]
no more."

35This is what the LORD says,

he who appoints[r] the sun
to shine by day,
who decrees the moon and stars
to shine by night,[s]
who stirs up the sea
so that its waves roar—
the LORD Almighty is his name:[t]
36"Only if these decrees[u] vanish
from my sight,"
declares the LORD,
"will the descendants[v] of Israel
ever cease
to be a nation before me."

37This is what the LORD says:

"Only if the heavens above can be
measured[w]
and the foundations of the earth
below be searched out
will I reject[x] all the descendants of
Israel
because of all they have done,"
declares the LORD.

38"The days are coming," declares
the LORD, "when this city will be rebuilt[y] for me from the Tower of Hananel[z] to the Corner Gate.[a] 39The measuring line will stretch from there
straight to the hill of Gareb and then
turn to Goah. 40The whole valley[b]
where dead bodies[c] and ashes are
thrown, and all the terraces out to the
Kidron Valley[d] on the east as far as the
corner of the Horse Gate,[e] will be
holy[f] to the LORD. The city will never
again be uprooted or demolished."

31:31–34

PROMISE 6

OUR COVENANT WITH GOD

Even a casual reader of the Old Testament can be amazed at Israel's disobedience. These people had a covenant with God himself. How could they fail? That's a valid question, and one from which we can learn a great deal. But this passage poses a much larger question: How can the church today, living under God's new covenant, do anything but succeed?

Read what God said about his new covenant. He is our God and we are his people. The old covenant was written on stone tablets; the new covenant is written in our hearts and minds. All who are his know him. Our sins are forgiven. The one Holy Spirit now lives in every Christian to teach, guide and unite us. The book of Hebrews teaches that Christians are under this new and better covenant (Hebrews 8:6–13).

Learn from Israel's failure to keep God's covenant and the awful consequences they suffered. Live as children of the new covenant—members of Christ's body, united by one Holy Spirit, guided by the law of God that is written on your hearts and minds.

For the next Promise 6 reading go to page 981.

31:34 [q]Ro 11:27; Mic 7:19; Heb 10:17*
31:35 [r]Ps 136:7-9 [s]Ge 1:16 [t]Jer 10:16
31:36 [u]Isa 54:9-10; Jer 33:20-26 [v]Ps 89:36-37
31:37 [w]Jer 33:22 [x]Jer 33:24-26; Ro 11:1-5
31:38 [y]Jer 30:18 [z]Ne 3:1 [a]2Ki 14:13; Zec 14:10
31:40 [b]Jer 7:31-32 [c]Jer 8:2 [d]2Sa 15:23; Jn 18:1 [e]2Ki 11:16 [f]Joel 3:17; Zec 14:21
32:1 [g]2Ki 25:1 [h]Jer 25:1; 39:1
32:2 [i]Ne 3:25; Jer 37:21
32:3 [j]Jer 26:8-9 [k]ver 28; Jer 34:2-3
32:4 [l]Jer 38:18,23; 39:5-7; 52:9
32:5 [m]Jer 39:7; Eze 12:13 [n]Jer 21:4
32:7 [o]Lev 25:24-25; Ru 4:3-4; Mt 27:10*
32:9 [p]Ge 23:16
32:10 [q]Ru 4:9
32:12 [r]ver 16; Jer 36:4; 43:3, 6; 45:1 [s]Jer 51:59

Jeremiah Buys a Field

32 This is the word that came to Jeremiah from the LORD in the tenth[g]
year of Zedekiah king of Judah, which
was the eighteenth[h] year of Nebuchadnezzar. 2The army of the king of
Babylon was then besieging Jerusalem,
and Jeremiah the prophet was confined in the courtyard of the guard[i] in
the royal palace of Judah.
3Now Zedekiah king of Judah had
imprisoned him there, saying, "Why do
you prophesy[j] as you do? You say,
'This is what the LORD says: I am about
to hand this city over to the king of
Babylon, and he will capture[k] it. 4Zed-
ekiah king of Judah will not escape[l]
out of the hands of the Babylonians[a]
but will certainly be handed over to the
king of Babylon, and will speak with
him face to face and see him with his
own eyes. 5He will take[m] Zedekiah to
Babylon, where he will remain until I
deal with him, declares the LORD. If you
fight against the Babylonians, you will
not succeed.' "[n]
6Jeremiah said, "The word of the
LORD came to me: 7Hanamel son of
Shallum your uncle is going to come to
you and say, 'Buy my field at Anathoth,
because as nearest relative it is your
right and duty[o] to buy it.'
8"Then, just as the LORD had said,
my cousin Hanamel came to me in the
courtyard of the guard and said, 'Buy
my field at Anathoth in the territory of
Benjamin. Since it is your right to redeem it and possess it, buy it for yourself.'
"I knew that this was the word of the
LORD; 9so I bought the field at Anathoth
from my cousin Hanamel and weighed
out for him seventeen shekels[b] of silver.[p] 10I signed and sealed the deed,
had it witnessed,[q] and weighed out
the silver on the scales. 11I took the
deed of purchase—the sealed copy
containing the terms and conditions,
as well as the unsealed copy— 12and I
gave this deed to Baruch[r] son of Neriah,[s] the son of Mahseiah, in the presence of my cousin Hanamel and of the
witnesses who had signed the deed

[a] *4* Or *Chaldeans*; also in verses 5, 24, 25, 28, 29 and 43 [b] *9* That is, about 7 ounces (about 200 grams)

and of all the Jews sitting in the courtyard of the guard.

13“In their presence I gave Baruch these instructions: 14‘This is what the LORD Almighty, the God of Israel, says: Take these documents, both the sealed and unsealed copies of the deed of purchase, and put them in a clay jar so they will last a long time. 15For this is what the LORD Almighty, the God of Israel, says: Houses, fields and vineyards will again be bought in this land.’[t]

16“After I had given the deed of purchase to Baruch son of Neriah, I prayed to the LORD:

17“Ah, Sovereign LORD,[u] you have made the heavens and the earth by your great power and outstretched arm.[v] Nothing is too hard[w] for you. 18You show love[x] to thousands but bring the punishment for the fathers' sins into the laps of their children[y] after them. O great and powerful God, whose name is the LORD Almighty,[z] 19great are your purposes and mighty are your deeds.[a] Your eyes are open to all the ways of men;[b] you reward everyone according to his conduct and as his deeds deserve.[c] 20You performed miraculous signs and wonders in Egypt[d] and have continued them to this day, both in Israel and among all mankind, and have gained the renown that is still yours. 21You brought your people Israel out of Egypt with signs and wonders, by a mighty hand[e] and an outstretched arm and with great terror.[f] 22You gave them this land you had sworn to give their forefathers, a land flowing with milk and honey.[g] 23They came in and took possession[h] of it, but they did not obey you or follow your law;[i] they did not do what you commanded them to do. So you brought all this disaster[j] upon them.

24“See how the siege ramps are built up to take the city. Because of the sword, famine and plague,[k] the city will be handed over to the Babylonians who are attacking it. What you said[l] has happened, as you now see. 25And though the city will be handed over to the Babylonians, you, O Sovereign LORD, say to me, ‘Buy the field with silver and have the transaction witnessed.’ ”

26Then the word of the LORD came to Jeremiah: 27“I am the LORD, the God of all mankind.[m] Is anything too hard for me? 28Therefore, this is what the LORD says: I am about to hand this city over to the Babylonians and to Nebuchadnezzar[n] king of Babylon, who will capture it.[o] 29The Babylonians who are attacking this city will come in and set it on fire; they will burn it down,[p] along with the houses[q] where the people provoked me to anger by burning incense on the roofs to Baal and by pouring out drink offerings[r] to other gods.

30“The people of Israel and Judah have done nothing but evil in my sight from their youth;[s] indeed, the people of Israel have done nothing but provoke[t] me with what their hands have made,[u] declares the LORD. 31From the day it was built until now, this city has so aroused my anger and wrath that I must remove[v] it from my sight. 32The people of Israel and Judah have provoked me by all the evil[w] they have done—they, their kings and officials, their priests and prophets, the men of Judah and the people of Jerusalem. 33They turned their backs[x] to me and not their faces; though I taught[y] them again and again, they would not listen or respond to discipline. 34They set up their abominable idols in the house that bears my Name and defiled[z] it. 35They built high places for Baal in the Valley of Ben Hinnom to sacrifice their sons and daughters**a** to Molech,[a] though I never commanded, nor did it enter my mind,[b] that they should do such a detestable thing and so make Judah sin.

36“You are saying about this city, ‘By the sword, famine and plague[c] it will be handed over to the king of Babylon’; but this is what the LORD, the God of Israel, says: 37I will surely gather[d] them from all the lands where I banish them in my furious anger and great wrath; I will bring them back to this place and let them live in safety.[e] 38They will be my people,[f] and I will be their God. 39I will give them singleness[g] of heart and action, so that they will always fear me for their own good and the good of their children after them. 40I will make an everlasting covenant[h] with them: I will never stop doing good to them, and I will inspire them to fear me, so that they will never turn away from me.[i] 41I will rejoice in doing them good[j] and will assuredly plant[k] them in this land with all my heart and soul.

42“This is what the LORD says: As I

32:15 [t]ver 43-44; Jer 30:18; Am 9:14-15
32:17 [u]Jer 1:6 [v]2Ki 19:15; Ps 102:25 [w]Mt 19:26
32:18 [x]Dt 5:10 [y]Ex 20:5 [z]Jer 10:16
32:19 [a]Isa 28:29 [b]Pr 5:21; Jer 16:17 [c]Jer 17:10; Mt 16:27
32:20 [d]Ex 9:16
32:21 [e]Ex 6:6; 1Ch 17:21; Da 9:15 [f]Dt 26:8
32:22 [g]Ex 3:8; Jer 11:5
32:23 [h]Ps 44:2; 78:54-55 [i]Ne 9:26; Jer 11:8 [j]Da 9:14
32:24 [k]Jer 14:12 [l]Dt 4:25-26; Jos 23:15-16
32:27 [m]Nu 16:22
32:28 [n]2Ch 36:17 [o]ver 3
32:29 [p]2Ch 36:19; Jer 21:10; 37:8, 10; 52:13 [q]Jer 19:13 [r]Jer 44:18
32:30 [s]Jer 22:21 [t]Jer 8:19 [u]Jer 25:7
32:31 [v]2Ki 23:27; 24:3
32:32 [w]Isa 1:4-6; Da 9:8
32:33 [x]Jer 2:27; Eze 8:16 [y]Jer 7:13
32:34 [z]Jer 7:30
32:35 [a]Lev 18:21 [b]Jer 7:31; 19:5
32:36 [c]ver 24
32:37 [d]Jer 23:3,6 [e]Dt 30:3; Eze 34:28
32:38 [f]Jer 24:7; 2Co 6:16*
32:39 [g]Eze 11:19
32:40 [h]Isa 55:3 [i]Jer 24:7
32:41 [j]Dt 30:9 [k]Jer 24:6; 31:28; Am 9:15

a35 Or *to make their sons and daughters pass through ⌞the fire⌟*

have brought all this great calamity on this people, so I will give them all the prosperity I have promised[l] them. 43Once more fields will be bought[m] in this land of which you say, 'It is a desolate waste, without men or animals, for it has been handed over to the Babylonians.' 44Fields will be bought for silver, and deeds[n] will be signed, sealed and witnessed in the territory of Benjamin, in the villages around Jerusalem, in the towns of Judah and in the towns of the hill country, of the western foothills and of the Negev,[o] because I will restore[p] their fortunes,[a] declares the LORD."

Promise of Restoration

33 While Jeremiah was still confined in the courtyard[q] of the guard, the word of the LORD came to him a second time: 2"This is what the LORD says, he who made the earth,[r] the LORD who formed it and established it—the LORD is his name:[s] 3'Call[t] to me and I will answer you and tell you great and unsearchable things you do not know.' 4For this is what the LORD, the God of Israel, says about the houses in this city and the royal palaces of Judah that have been torn down to be used against the siege[u] ramps[v] and the sword 5in the fight with the Babylonians[b]: 'They will be filled with the dead bodies of the men I will slay in my anger and wrath.[w] I will hide my face[x] from this city because of all its wickedness.

6" 'Nevertheless, I will bring health and healing to it; I will heal my people and will let them enjoy abundant peace and security. 7I will bring Judah[y] and Israel back from captivity[c][z] and will rebuild them as they were before.[a] 8I will cleanse[b] them from all the sin they have committed against me and will forgive[c] all their sins of rebellion against me. 9Then this city will bring me renown, joy, praise[d] and honor[e] before all nations on earth that hear of all the good things I do for it; and they will be in awe and will tremble at the abundant prosperity and peace I provide for it.'

10"This is what the LORD says: 'You say about this place, "It is a desolate waste, without men or animals."[f] Yet in the towns of Judah and the streets of Jerusalem that are deserted, inhabited by neither men nor animals, there will be heard once more 11the sounds of joy and gladness,[g] the voices of bride and bridegroom, and the voices of those who bring thank offerings[h] to the house of the LORD, saying,

"Give thanks to the LORD Almighty,
for the LORD is good;[i]
his love endures forever."[j]

For I will restore the fortunes of the land as they were before,' says the LORD.

12"This is what the LORD Almighty says: 'In this place, desolate[k] and without men or animals—in all its towns there will again be pastures for shepherds to rest their flocks.[l] 13In the towns of the hill country, of the western foothills and of the Negev,[m] in the territory of Benjamin, in the villages around Jerusalem and in the towns of Judah, flocks will again pass under the hand[n] of the one who counts them,' says the LORD.

14" 'The days are coming,' declares the LORD, 'when I will fulfill the gracious promise[o] I made to the house of Israel and to the house of Judah.

15" 'In those days and at that time
I will make a righteous[p]
Branch[q] sprout from
David's line;
he will do what is just and right
in the land.
16In those days Judah will be saved[r]
and Jerusalem will live in safety.
This is the name by which it[d] will
be called:
The LORD Our Righteousness.'[s]

17For this is what the LORD says: 'David will never fail[t] to have a man to sit on the throne of the house of Israel, 18nor will the priests, who are Levites,[u] ever fail to have a man to stand before me continually to offer burnt offerings, to burn grain offerings and to present sacrifices.[v]' "

19The word of the LORD came to Jeremiah: 20"This is what the LORD says: 'If you can break my covenant with the day[w] and my covenant with the night, so that day and night no longer come at their appointed time, 21then my covenant[x] with David my servant—and my covenant with the Levites who are

32:42 [l]Jer 31:28
32:43 [m]ver 15
32:44 [n]ver 10 [o]Jer 17:26 [p]Jer 33:7,11,26
33:1 [q]Jer 32:2-3; 37:21; 38:28
33:2 [r]Jer 10:16 [s]Ex 3:15; 15:3
33:3 [t]Isa 55:6; Jer 29:12
33:4 [u]Eze 4:2 [v]Jer 32:24; Hab 1:10
33:5 [w]Jer 21:4-7 [x]Isa 8:17
33:7 [y]Jer 32:44 [z]Jer 30:3; Am 9:14 [a]Isa 1:26
33:8 [b]Heb 9:13-14 [c]Jer 31:34; Mic 7:18; Zec 13:1
33:9 [d]Jer 13:11 [e]Isa 62:7; Jer 3:17
33:10 [f]Jer 32:43
33:11 [g]Isa 51:3 [h]Lev 7:12 [i]1Ch 16:8; Ps 136:1 [j]1Ch 16:34; 2Ch 5:13; Ps 100:4-5
33:12 [k]Jer 32:43 [l]Isa 65:10; Eze 34:11-15
33:13 [m]Jer 17:26 [n]Lev 27:32
33:14 [o]Jer 29:10
33:15 [p]Ps 72:2 [q]Isa 4:2; 11:1; Jer 23:5
33:16 [r]Isa 45:17 [s]1Co 1:30
33:17 [t]2Sa 7:13; 1Ki 2:4; Ps 89:29-37; Lk 1:33
33:18 [u]Dt 18:1 [v]Heb 13:15
33:20 [w]Ps 89:36
33:21 [x]Ps 89:34

[a]44 Or *will bring them back from captivity* [b]5 Or *Chaldeans* [c]7 Or *will restore the fortunes of Judah and Israel* [d]16 Or *he*

33:19–26

PE

ROCK SOLID

How solid are God's promises? Read this passage for some insight. As long as day and night continue, God's promises will still stand.

priests ministering before me—can be
broken and David will no longer have a
descendant to reign on his throne.[y]
22I will make the descendants of David
my servant and the Levites who minister before me as countless[z] as the
stars of the sky and as measureless as
the sand on the seashore.' "
23The word of the LORD came to Jeremiah: 24"Have you not noticed that
these people are saying, 'The LORD has
rejected the two kingdoms[a][a] he
chose'? So they despise[b] my people
and no longer regard them as a nation.[c] 25This is what the LORD says: 'If
I have not established my covenant
with day and night[d] and the fixed laws
of heaven and earth,[e] 26then I will reject[f] the descendants of Jacob[g] and
David my servant and will not choose
one of his sons to rule over the descendants of Abraham, Isaac and Jacob. For
I will restore their fortunes[b][h] and
have compassion on them.' "

Warning to Zedekiah

34 While Nebuchadnezzar king of
Babylon and all his army and all
the kingdoms and peoples[i] in the empire he ruled were fighting against Jerusalem[j] and all its surrounding
towns, this word came to Jeremiah
from the LORD: 2"This is what the LORD,
the God of Israel, says: Go to Zedekiah[k] king of Judah and tell him, 'This is
what the LORD says: I am about to hand
this city over to the king of Babylon,
and he will burn it down.[l] 3You will
not escape from his grasp but will surely be captured and handed over[m] to
him. You will see the king of Babylon
with your own eyes, and he will speak
with you face to face. And you will go
to Babylon.
4" 'Yet hear the promise of the LORD,
O Zedekiah king of Judah. This is what
the LORD says concerning you: You will
not die by the sword; 5you will die
peacefully. As people made a funeral
fire[n] in honor of your fathers, the former kings who preceded you, so they
will make a fire in your honor and
lament, "Alas,[o] O master!" I myself
make this promise, declares the
LORD.' "
6Then Jeremiah the prophet told all
this to Zedekiah king of Judah, in Jerusalem, 7while the army of the king of
Babylon was fighting against Jerusalem
and the other cities of Judah that were
still holding out—Lachish[p] and Azekah.[q] These were the only fortified cities left in Judah.

Freedom for Slaves

8The word came to Jeremiah from
the LORD after King Zedekiah had made
a covenant with all the people[r] in Jerusalem to proclaim freedom[s] for the
slaves. 9Everyone was to free his Hebrew slaves, both male and female; no
one was to hold a fellow Jew in bondage.[t] 10So all the officials and people
who entered into this covenant agreed
that they would free their male and female slaves and no longer hold them in
bondage. They agreed, and set them
free. 11But afterward they changed
their minds and took back the slaves
they had freed and enslaved them
again.
12Then the word of the LORD came to
Jeremiah: 13"This is what the LORD, the
God of Israel, says: I made a covenant
with your forefathers[u] when I brought
them out of Egypt, out of the land of
slavery. I said, 14'Every seventh year
each of you must free any fellow Hebrew who has sold himself to you. After
he has served you six years, you must
let him go free.'[c][v] Your fathers, however, did not listen to me or pay attention[w] to me. 15Recently you repented
and did what is right in my sight: Each
of you proclaimed freedom to his
countrymen.[x] You even made a covenant before me in the house that
bears my Name.[y] 16But now you have
turned around[z] and profaned[a] my
name; each of you has taken back the
male and female slaves you had set free
to go where they wished. You have
forced them to become your slaves
again.
17"Therefore, this is what the LORD
says: You have not obeyed me; you
have not proclaimed freedom for your
fellow countrymen. So I now proclaim
'freedom' for you,[b] declares the
LORD—'freedom' to fall by the sword,
plague and famine. I will make you abhorrent to all the kingdoms of the
earth.[c] 18The men who have violated
my covenant and have not fulfilled the
terms of the covenant they made before me, I will treat like the calf they cut
in two and then walked between its
pieces.[d] 19The leaders of Judah and
Jerusalem, the court officials,[e] the
priests and all the people of the land
who walked between the pieces of the
calf, 20I will hand over[f] to their enemies who seek their lives.[g] Their dead
bodies will become food for the birds
of the air and the beasts of the earth.[h]
21"I will hand Zedekiah[i] king of Ju-

33:21 [y]2Ch 7:18 **33:22** [z]Ge 15:5 **33:24** [a]Eze 37:22 [b]Ne 4:4 [c]Jer 30:17 **33:25** [d]Jer 31:35-36 [e]Ps 74:16-17 **33:26** [f]Jer 31:37 [g]Isa 14:1 [h]ver 7 **34:1** [i]Jer 27:7 [j]2Ki 25:1; Jer 39:1 **34:2** [k]2Ch 36:11 [l]ver 22; Jer 32:29; 37:8 **34:3** [m]2Ki 25:7; Jer 21:7; 32:4 **34:5** [n]2Ch 16:14; 21:19 [o]Jer 22:18 **34:7** [p]Jos 10:3 [q]Jos 10:10; 2Ch 11:9

34:8 [r]2Ki 11:17 [s]Ex 21:2; Lev 25:10, 39-41; Ne 5:5-8 **34:9** [t]Lev 25:39-46 **34:13** [u]Ex 24:8 **34:14** [v]Ex 21:2 [w]Dt 15:12; 2Ki 17:14 **34:15** [x]ver 8 [y]Jer 7:10-11; 32:34 **34:16** [z]Eze 3:20; 18:24 [a]Ex 20:7; Lev 19:12 **34:17** [b]Mt 7:2; Gal 6:7 [c]Dt 28:25,64; Jer 29:18 **34:18** [d]Ge 15:10 **34:19** [e]Zep 3:3-4 **34:20** [f]Jer 21:7 [g]Jer 11:21 [h]Dt 28:26; Jer 7:33; 19:7 **34:21** [i]Jer 32:4

[a]*24* Or *families* [b]*26* Or *will bring them back from captivity* [c]*14* Deut. 15:12

dah and his officials[j] over to their enemies who seek their lives, to the army
of the king of Babylon, which has withdrawn[k] from you. 22I am going to give
the order, declares the LORD, and I will
bring them back to this city. They will
fight against it, take[l] it and burn[m] it
down. And I will lay waste the towns of
Judah so no one can live there."

The Recabites

35 This is the word that came to Jeremiah from the LORD during the
reign of Jehoiakim[n] son of Josiah king
of Judah: 2"Go to the Recabite[o] family
and invite them to come to one of the
side rooms[p] of the house of the LORD
and give them wine to drink."
3So I went to get Jaazaniah son of
Jeremiah, the son of Habazziniah,
and his brothers and all his sons—
the whole family of the Recabites. 4I
brought them into the house of the
LORD, into the room of the sons of Hanan son of Igdaliah the man of God.[q]
It was next to the room of the officials,
which was over that of Maaseiah son of
Shallum[r] the doorkeeper.[s] 5Then I
set bowls full of wine and some cups
before the men of the Recabite family
and said to them, "Drink some wine."
6But they replied, "We do not drink
wine, because our forefather Jonadab[t] son of Recab gave us this command: 'Neither you nor your descendants must ever drink wine.[u] 7Also
you must never build houses, sow seed
or plant vineyards; you must never
have any of these things, but must always live in tents.[v] Then you will live
a long time in the land[w] where you are
nomads.' 8We have obeyed everything
our forefather[x] Jonadab son of Recab
commanded us. Neither we nor our
wives nor our sons and daughters have
ever drunk wine 9or built houses to live
in or had vineyards, fields or crops.[y]
10We have lived in tents and have fully
obeyed everything our forefather Jonadab commanded us. 11But when Nebuchadnezzar king of Babylon invaded[z]
this land, we said, 'Come, we must go
to Jerusalem[a] to escape the Babylonian[a] and Aramean armies.' So we have
remained in Jerusalem."
12Then the word of the LORD came to
Jeremiah, saying: 13"This is what the
LORD Almighty, the God of Israel, says:
Go and tell the men of Judah and the
people of Jerusalem, 'Will you not
learn a lesson[b] and obey my words?'
declares the LORD. 14'Jonadab son of
Recab ordered his sons not to drink
wine and this command has been kept.
To this day they do not drink wine, because they obey their forefather's command. But I have spoken to you again
and again,[c] yet you have not obeyed[d]
me. 15Again and again I sent all my servants the prophets[e] to you. They said,
"Each of you must turn[f] from your
wicked ways and reform[g] your actions; do not follow other gods to serve
them. Then you will live in the land[h]
I have given to you and your fathers."
But you have not paid attention or
listened[i] to me. 16The descendants
of Jonadab son of Recab have carried
out the command their forefather[j]
gave them, but these people have not
obeyed me.'
17"Therefore, this is what the LORD
God Almighty, the God of Israel, says:
'Listen! I am going to bring on Judah
and on everyone living in Jerusalem
every disaster[k] I pronounced against
them. I spoke to them, but they did not
listen;[l] I called to them, but they did
not answer.' "[m]
18Then Jeremiah said to the family of
the Recabites, "This is what the LORD
Almighty, the God of Israel, says: 'You
have obeyed the command of your
forefather Jonadab and have followed
all his instructions and have done
everything he ordered.' 19Therefore,
this is what the LORD Almighty, the
God of Israel, says: 'Jonadab son of
Recab will never fail[n] to have a man
to serve[o] me.' "

Jehoiakim Burns Jeremiah's Scroll

36 In the fourth year of Jehoiakim[p]
son of Josiah king of Judah, this
word came to Jeremiah from the LORD:
2"Take a scroll[q] and write on it all the
words I have spoken to you concerning

34:21 [j]Jer 39:6; 52:24-27 [k]Jer 37:5 **34:22** [l]Jer 39:1-2 [m]Jer 39:8 **35:1** [n]2Ch 36:5 **35:2** [o]2Ki 10:15; 1Ch 2:55 [p]1Ki 6:5 **35:4** [q]Dt 33:1 [r]1Ch 9:19 [s]2Ki 12:9 **35:6** [t]2Ki 10:15 [u]Lev 10:9; Nu 6:2-4; Lk 1:15 **35:7** [v]Heb 11:9 [w]Ex 20:12; Eph 6:2-3 **35:8** [x]Pr 1:8; Col 3:20 **35:9** [y]1Ti 6:6 **35:11** [z]2Ki 24:1 [a]Jer 8:14 **35:13** [b]Jer 6:10; 32:33 **35:14** [c]Jer 7:13; 25:3 [d]Isa 30:9 **35:15** [e]Jer 7:25 [f]Jer 26:3 [g]Isa 1:16-17; Jer 4:1; 18:11; Eze 18:30 [h]Jer 25:5 [i]Jer 7:26 **35:16** [j]Mal 1:6 **35:17** [k]Jos 23:15; Jer 21:4-7 [l]Pr 1:24; Ro 10:21 [m]Isa 65:12; 66:4; Jer 7:13 **35:19** [n]Jer 33:17 [o]Jer 15:19 **36:1** [p]2Ch 36:5 **36:2** [q]Ex 17:14; Jer 30:2; Hab 2:2

[a] *11* Or *Chaldean*

35:12–16 PROMISE 4

A MATTER OF HONOR

Talk about men of their word! The members of this family had promised to honor their forefathers' command that they live a certain lifestyle, and they had kept their vow. God used their example to teach Israel about obedience (vv. 12–16). He honored their honor (vv. 18–19). Recab and Jonadab had taught their sons to be men of their word and God recognized them for that.

Read this story prayerfully and instructively. Ask God to show you how to prepare the next generation of your family to be so honorable they honor God—and God honors them.

For the next Promise 4 reading go to page 951.

Israel, Judah and all the other nations from the time I began speaking to you in the reign of Josiah[r] till now. **3**Perhaps[s] when the people of Judah hear[t] about every disaster I plan to inflict on them, each of them will turn[u] from his wicked way; then I will forgive[v] their wickedness and their sin."

4So Jeremiah called Baruch[w] son of Neriah, and while Jeremiah dictated[x] all the words the LORD had spoken to him, Baruch wrote them on the scroll.[y] **5**Then Jeremiah told Baruch, "I am restricted; I cannot go to the LORD's temple. **6**So you go to the house of the LORD on a day of fasting[z] and read to the people from the scroll the words of the LORD that you wrote as I dictated. Read them to all the people of Judah who come in from their towns. **7**Perhaps they will bring their petition before the LORD, and each will turn[a] from his wicked ways, for the anger[b] and wrath pronounced against this people by the LORD are great."

8Baruch son of Neriah did everything Jeremiah the prophet told him to do; at the LORD's temple he read the words of the LORD from the scroll. **9**In the ninth month[c] of the fifth year of Jehoiakim son of Josiah king of Judah, a time of fasting[d] before the LORD was proclaimed for all the people in Jerusalem and those who had come from the towns of Judah. **10**From the room of Gemariah son of Shaphan the secretary,[e] which was in the upper courtyard at the entrance of the New Gate[f] of the temple, Baruch read to all the people at the LORD's temple the words of Jeremiah from the scroll.

11When Micaiah son of Gemariah, the son of Shaphan, heard all the words of the LORD from the scroll, **12**he went down to the secretary's room in the royal palace, where all the officials were sitting: Elishama the secretary, Delaiah son of Shemaiah, Elnathan[g] son of Acbor, Gemariah son of Shaphan, Zedekiah son of Hananiah, and all the other officials. **13**After Micaiah told them everything he had heard Baruch read to the people from the scroll, **14**all the officials sent Jehudi[h] son of Nethaniah, the son of Shelemiah, the son of Cushi, to say to Baruch, "Bring the scroll from which you have read to the people and come." So Baruch son of Neriah went to them with the scroll in his hand. **15**They said to him, "Sit down, please, and read it to us."

So Baruch read it to them. **16**When they heard all these words, they looked at each other in fear and said to Baruch, "We must report all these words to the king." **17**Then they asked Baruch, "Tell us, how did you come to write all this? Did Jeremiah dictate it?"

18"Yes," Baruch replied, "he dictated[i] all these words to me, and I wrote them in ink on the scroll."

19Then the officials said to Baruch, "You and Jeremiah, go and hide.[j] Don't let anyone know where you are."

20After they put the scroll in the room of Elishama the secretary, they went to the king in the courtyard and reported everything to him. **21**The king sent Jehudi[k] to get the scroll, and Jehudi brought it from the room of Elishama the secretary and read it to the king[l] and all the officials standing beside him. **22**It was the ninth month and the king was sitting in the winter apartment,[m] with a fire burning in the firepot in front of him. **23**Whenever Jehudi had read three or four columns of the scroll, the king cut them off with a scribe's knife and threw them into the firepot, until the entire scroll was burned in the fire.[n] **24**The king and all his attendants who heard all these words showed no fear,[o] nor did they tear their clothes.[p] **25**Even though Elnathan, Delaiah and Gemariah urged the king not to burn the scroll, he would not listen to them. **26**Instead, the king commanded Jerahmeel, a son of the king, Seraiah son of Azriel and Shelemiah son of Abdeel to arrest[q] Baruch the scribe and Jeremiah the prophet. But the LORD had hidden[r] them.

27After the king burned the scroll containing the words that Baruch had written at Jeremiah's dictation,[s] the word of the LORD came to Jeremiah: **28**"Take another scroll and write on it all the words that were on the first scroll, which Jehoiakim king of Judah burned up. **29**Also tell Jehoiakim king of Judah, 'This is what the LORD says: You burned that scroll and said, "Why did you write on it that the king of Babylon would certainly come and destroy this land and cut off both men and animals from it?"[t] **30**Therefore, this is what the LORD says about Jehoiakim king of Judah: He will have no one to sit on the throne of David; his body will be thrown out[u] and exposed to the heat by day and the frost by night. **31**I will punish him and his children and his attendants for their wickedness; I will bring on them and those living in Jerusalem and the people of Judah every disaster[v] I pronounced against them, because they have not listened.' "

32So Jeremiah took another scroll and gave it to the scribe Baruch son of Neriah, and as Jeremiah dictated,[w]

36:2 [r]Jer 1:2; 25:3
36:3 [s]ver 7; Eze 12:3 [t]Mk 4:12 [u]Jer 26:3; Jnh 3:8; Ac 3:19 [v]Jer 18:8
36:4 [w]Jer 32:12 [x]ver 18 [y]Eze 2:9
36:6 [z]ver 9
36:7 [a]Jer 26:3 [b]Dt 31:17
36:9 [c]ver 22 [d]2Ch 20:3
36:10 [e]Jer 52:25 [f]Jer 26:10
36:12 [g]Jer 26:22
36:14 [h]ver 21
36:18 [i]ver 4
36:19 [j]1Ki 17:3
36:21 [k]ver 14 [l]2Ki 22:10
36:22 [m]Am 3:15
36:23 [n]1Ki 22:8
36:24 [o]Ps 36:1 [p]Ge 37:29; 2Ki 22:11; Isa 37:1
36:26 [q]Mt 23:34 [r]Jer 15:21
36:27 [s]ver 4
36:29 [t]Isa 30:10
36:30 [u]Jer 22:19
36:31 [v]Pr 29:1
36:32 [w]ver 4

Baruch wrote[x] on it all the words of
the scroll that Jehoiakim king of Judah
had burned[y] in the fire. And many
similar words were added to them.

Jeremiah in Prison

37 Zedekiah[z] son of Josiah was made
king[a] of Judah by Nebuchadnezzar king of Babylon; he reigned in place
of Jehoiachin[a][b] son of Jehoiakim.
2Neither he nor his attendants nor the
people of the land paid any attention[c]
to the words the LORD had spoken
through Jeremiah the prophet.
3King Zedekiah, however, sent Jehucal son of Shelemiah with the priest
Zephaniah[d] son of Maaseiah to Jeremiah the prophet with this message:
"Please pray[e] to the LORD our God
for us."
4Now Jeremiah was free to come and
go among the people, for he had not
yet been put in prison.[f] 5Pharaoh's
army had marched out of Egypt,[g] and
when the Babylonians[b] who were besieging Jerusalem heard the report
about them, they withdrew[h] from Jerusalem.[i]
6Then the word of the LORD came to
Jeremiah the prophet: 7"This is what
the LORD, the God of Israel, says: Tell
the king of Judah, who sent you to inquire[j] of me, 'Pharaoh's army, which
has marched out to support you, will
go back to its own land, to Egypt.[k]
8Then the Babylonians will return and
attack this city; they will capture it and
burn[l] it down.'
9"This is what the LORD says: Do not
deceive[m] yourselves, thinking, 'The
Babylonians will surely leave us.' They
will not! 10Even if you were to defeat
the entire Babylonian[c] army that is attacking you and only wounded men
were left in their tents, they would
come out and burn this city down."
11After the Babylonian army had
withdrawn[n] from Jerusalem because
of Pharaoh's army, 12Jeremiah started
to leave the city to go to the territory of
Benjamin to get his share of the property[o] among the people there. 13But
when he reached the Benjamin Gate,
the captain of the guard, whose name
was Irijah son of Shelemiah, the son of
Hananiah, arrested him and said, "You
are deserting to the Babylonians!"
14"That's not true!" Jeremiah said. "I
am not deserting to the Babylonians."
But Irijah would not listen to him; instead, he arrested[p] Jeremiah and
brought him to the officials. 15They
were angry with Jeremiah and had
him beaten[q] and imprisoned in the
house[r] of Jonathan the secretary,
which they had made into a prison.
16Jeremiah was put into a vaulted
cell in a dungeon, where he remained
a long time. 17Then King Zedekiah sent
for him and had him brought to the
palace, where he asked[s] him privately,[t] "Is there any word from the
LORD?"
"Yes," Jeremiah replied, "you will be
handed over[u] to the king of Babylon."
18Then Jeremiah said to King Zedekiah, "What crime[v] have I committed
against you or your officials or this
people, that you have put me in prison? 19Where are your prophets who
prophesied to you, 'The king of Babylon will not attack you or this land'?
20But now, my lord the king, please listen. Let me bring my petition before
you: Do not send me back to the house
of Jonathan the secretary, or I will die
there."
21King Zedekiah then gave orders for
Jeremiah to be placed in the courtyard
of the guard and given bread from the
street of the bakers each day until all
the bread[w] in the city was gone.[x] So
Jeremiah remained in the courtyard of
the guard.[y]

Jeremiah Thrown Into a Cistern

38 Shephatiah son of Mattan, Gedaliah son of Pashhur, Jehucal[d][z] son
of Shelemiah, and Pashhur son of Malkijah heard what Jeremiah was telling
all the people when he said, 2"This is
what the LORD says: 'Whoever stays in
this city will die by the sword, famine
or plague,[a] but whoever goes over to
the Babylonians[e] will live. He will escape with his life; he will live.'[b] 3And
this is what the LORD says: 'This city
will certainly be handed over to the
army of the king of Babylon, who will
capture it.' "[c]
4Then the officials[d] said to the king,
"This man should be put to death.[e]
He is discouraging the soldiers who are
left in this city, as well as all the people,
by the things he is saying to them. This
man is not seeking the good of these
people but their ruin."
5"He is in your hands," King Zedekiah answered. "The king can do nothing
to oppose you."
6So they took Jeremiah and put him
into the cistern of Malkijah, the king's
son, which was in the courtyard of the
guard.[f] They lowered Jeremiah by

36:32 x Ex 34:1 y ver 23
37:1 z 2Ki 24:17 a Eze 17:13 b 2Ki 24:8,12; 2Ch 36:10; Jer 22:24
37:2 c 2Ki 24:19; 2Ch 36:12,14
37:3 d Jer 29:25; 52:24 e 1Ki 13:6; Jer 21:1-2; 42:2
37:4 f ver 15; Jer 32:2
37:5 g Eze 17:15 h Jer 34:21 i 2Ki 24:7
37:7 j 2Ki 22:18 k Jer 2:36; La 4:17
37:8 l Jer 34:22; 39:8
37:9 m Jer 29:8
37:11 n ver 5
37:12 o Jer 32:9
37:14 p Jer 40:4
37:15 q Jer 20:2 r Jer 38:26
37:17 s Jer 15:11 t Jer 38:16 u Jer 21:7
37:18 v 1Sa 26:18; Jn 10:32; Ac 25:8
37:21 w Isa 33:16; Jer 38:9 x 2Ki 25:3; Jer 52:6 y Jer 32:2; 38:6, 13,28
38:1 z Jer 37:3
38:2 a Jer 34:17 b Jer 21:9; 39:18; 45:5
38:3 c Jer 21:4,10; 32:3
38:4 d Jer 36:12 e Jer 26:11
38:6 f Jer 37:21

a *1* Hebrew *Coniah,* a variant of *Jehoiachin* **b** *5* Or *Chaldeans;* also in verses 8, 9, 13 and 14 **c** *10* Or *Chaldean;* also in verse 11 **d** *1* Hebrew *Jucal,* a variant of *Jehucal* **e** *2* Or *Chaldeans;* also in verses 18, 19 and 23

ropes into the cistern; it had no water
in it, only mud, and Jeremiah sank
down into the mud.
7But Ebed-Melech,[g] a Cushite,[a] an
official[b][h] in the royal palace, heard
that they had put Jeremiah into the cistern. While the king was sitting in the
Benjamin Gate,[i] 8Ebed-Melech went
out of the palace and said to him, 9"My
lord the king, these men have acted
wickedly in all they have done to Jeremiah the prophet. They have thrown
him into a cistern, where he will starve
to death when there is no longer any
bread[j] in the city."
10Then the king commanded Ebed-
Melech the Cushite, "Take thirty men
from here with you and lift Jeremiah
the prophet out of the cistern before he
dies."
11So Ebed-Melech took the men
with him and went to a room under the
treasury in the palace. He took some
old rags and worn-out clothes from
there and let them down with ropes to
Jeremiah in the cistern. 12Ebed-Melech
the Cushite said to Jeremiah, "Put
these old rags and worn-out clothes
under your arms to pad the ropes." Jeremiah did so, 13and they pulled him up
with the ropes and lifted him out of the
cistern. And Jeremiah remained in the
courtyard of the guard.[k]

Zedekiah Questions Jeremiah Again

14Then King Zedekiah sent for Jeremiah the prophet and had him brought
to the third entrance to the temple of
the LORD. "I am going to ask you something," the king said to Jeremiah. "Do
not hide[l] anything from me."
15Jeremiah said to Zedekiah, "If I
give you an answer, will you not kill
me? Even if I did give you counsel, you
would not listen to me."
16But King Zedekiah swore this oath
secretly[m] to Jeremiah: "As surely as the
LORD lives, who has given us breath,[n]
I will neither kill you nor hand you over
to those who are seeking your life."[o]
17Then Jeremiah said to Zedekiah,
"This is what the LORD God Almighty,
the God of Israel, says: 'If you surrender to the officers of the king of Babylon, your life will be spared and this
city will not be burned down; you and
your family will live.[p] 18But if you will
not surrender to the officers of the king
of Babylon, this city will be handed
over[q] to the Babylonians and they will
burn[r] it down; you yourself will not
escape[s] from their hands.' "
19King Zedekiah said to Jeremiah, "I
am afraid[t] of the Jews who have gone
over[u] to the Babylonians, for the Babylonians may hand me over to them
and they will mistreat me."
20"They will not hand you over," Jeremiah replied. "Obey[v] the LORD by
doing what I tell you. Then it will go
well with you, and your life[w] will be
spared. 21But if you refuse to surrender, this is what the LORD has revealed
to me: 22All the women[x] left in the
palace of the king of Judah will be
brought out to the officials of the king
of Babylon. Those women will say to
you:

" 'They misled you and overcame
you—
those trusted friends of yours.
Your feet are sunk in the mud;
your friends have deserted you.'

23"All your wives and children[y] will
be brought out to the Babylonians. You
yourself will not escape from their
hands but will be captured[z] by the
king of Babylon; and this city will[c] be
burned down."
24Then Zedekiah said to Jeremiah,
"Do not let anyone know about this
conversation, or you may die. 25If the
officials hear that I talked with you, and
they come to you and say, 'Tell us what
you said to the king and what the king
said to you; do not hide it from us or we
will kill you,' 26then tell them, 'I was
pleading with the king not to send me
back to Jonathan's house[a] to die
there.' "
27All the officials did come to Jeremiah and question him, and he told them
everything the king had ordered him to
say. So they said no more to him, for no
one had heard his conversation with
the king.
28And Jeremiah remained in the
courtyard of the guard[b] until the day
Jerusalem was captured.

The Fall of Jerusalem

39 This is how Jerusalem was taken:
1In the ninth year of Zedekiah king
of Judah, in the tenth month, Nebuchadnezzar king of Babylon marched
against Jerusalem with his whole army
and laid siege[c] to it. 2And on the ninth
day of the fourth month of Zedekiah's
eleventh year, the city wall was broken
through. 3Then all the officials[d] of the
king of Babylon came and took seats in
the Middle Gate: Nergal-Sharezer of
Samgar, Nebo-Sarsekim[d] a chief officer, Nergal-Sharezer a high official and
all the other officials of the king of Bab-

38:7 [g]Jer 39:16 [h]Ac 8:27 [i]Job 29:7
38:9 [j]Jer 37:21
38:13 [k]Jer 37:21
38:14 [l]1Sa 3:17
38:16 [m]Jer 37:17 [n]Isa 42:5; 57:16 [o]ver 4
38:17 [p]2Ki 24:12; Jer 21:9
38:18 [q]ver 3; Jer 34:3 [r]Jer 37:8 [s]Jer 24:8; 32:4
38:19 [t]Isa 51:12; Jn 12:42 [u]Jer 39:9
38:20 [v]Jer 11:4 [w]Isa 55:3
38:22 [x]Jer 6:12
38:23 [y]2Ki 25:6 [z]Jer 41:10
38:26 [a]Jer 37:15
38:28 [b]Jer 37:21; 39:14
39:1 [c]2Ki 25:1; Jer 52:4; Eze 24:2
39:3 [d]Jer 21:4

[a] *7* Probably from the upper Nile region
[b] *7* Or *a eunuch*
[c] *23* Or *and you will cause this city to*
[d] *3* Or *Nergal-Sharezer, Samgar-Nebo, Sarsekim*

ylon. 4When Zedekiah king of Judah
and all the soldiers saw them, they fled;
they left the city at night by way of the
king's garden, through the gate between the two walls, and headed toward the Arabah.[a]
5But the Babylonian[b] army pursued
them and overtook Zedekiah[e] in the
plains of Jericho. They captured him
and took him to Nebuchadnezzar king
of Babylon at Riblah[f] in the land of
Hamath, where he pronounced sentence on him. 6There at Riblah the king
of Babylon slaughtered the sons of
Zedekiah before his eyes and also
killed all the nobles of Judah. 7Then he
put out Zedekiah's eyes[g] and bound
him with bronze shackles to take him
to Babylon.[h]
8The Babylonians[c] set fire[i] to the
royal palace and the houses of the people and broke down the walls[j] of Jerusalem. 9Nebuzaradan commander of
the imperial guard carried into exile to
Babylon the people who remained in
the city, along with those who had
gone over to him, and the rest of the
people.[k] 10But Nebuzaradan the commander of the guard left behind in the
land of Judah some of the poor people,
who owned nothing; and at that time
he gave them vineyards and fields.
11Now Nebuchadnezzar king of Babylon had given these orders about
Jeremiah through Nebuzaradan commander of the imperial guard: 12"Take
him and look after him; don't harm[l]
him but do for him whatever he asks."
13So Nebuzaradan the commander of
the guard, Nebushazban a chief officer,
Nergal-Sharezer a high official and all
the other officers of the king of Babylon
14sent and had Jeremiah taken out of
the courtyard of the guard.[m] They
turned him over to Gedaliah son of
Ahikam,[n] the son of Shaphan, to take
him back to his home. So he remained
among his own people.[o]
15While Jeremiah had been confined
in the courtyard of the guard, the word
of the LORD came to him: 16"Go and tell
Ebed-Melech[p] the Cushite, 'This is
what the LORD Almighty, the God of Israel, says: I am about to fulfill my
words against this city through disaster,[q] not prosperity. At that time they
will be fulfilled before your eyes. 17But
I will rescue[r] you on that day, declares
the LORD; you will not be handed over
to those you fear. 18I will save you; you
will not fall by the sword[s] but will escape with your life,[t] because you
trust[u] in me, declares the LORD.' "

Jeremiah Freed

40 The word came to Jeremiah from
the LORD after Nebuzaradan commander of the imperial guard had released him at Ramah. He had found
Jeremiah bound in chains among all
the captives from Jerusalem and Judah
who were being carried into exile to
Babylon. 2When the commander of the
guard found Jeremiah, he said to him,
"The LORD your God decreed this disaster for this place.[v] 3And now the
LORD has brought it about; he has done
just as he said he would. All this happened because you people sinned[w]
against the LORD and did not obey[x]
him. 4But today I am freeing you from
the chains on your wrists. Come with
me to Babylon, if you like, and I will
look after you; but if you do not want
to, then don't come. Look, the whole
country lies before you; go wherever
you please."[y] 5However, before Jeremiah turned to go,[d] Nebuzaradan
added, "Go back to Gedaliah[z] son of
Ahikam, the son of Shaphan, whom the
king of Babylon has appointed over the
towns of Judah, and live with him
among the people, or go anywhere else
you please."[a]
Then the commander gave him provisions and a present and let him go.
6So Jeremiah went to Gedaliah son of

39:1-18

PROMISE 3

NO IMMUNITY

This is one of the truly amazing chapters of the Old Testament. We read of Noah and the flood, Moses and the Red Sea, Jonah and the fish. Our minds try to grasp the magnitude of it all. But this! It seems so simply stated, "This is how Jerusalem was taken," but those six small words speak volumes. God's temple, the epicenter of Israelite worship, was located in Jerusalem. This was God's earthly dwelling place, the capital city of the nation God had established to show his power and holiness to all the earth. How could this wicked gentile nation destroy the temple and carry off the ark of the covenant and the golden altar?

Jeremiah 39 teaches us that no one is immune to the effects of a sinful life. Sin destroys everything it touches. Read those six words again and reflect for a few minutes on their meaning. Even God's beloved Jerusalem fell under sin's destruction. Pray daily that the phrase will never be written: "This was how (you) were taken." Listen to and learn from this sober warning.

For the next Promise 3 reading go to page 876.

39:5 [e]Jer 32:4 [f]2Ki 23:33
39:7 [g]Eze 12:13 [h]Jer 32:5
39:8 [i]Jer 38:18 [j]Ne 1:3
39:9 [k]Jer 40:1
39:12 [l]Pr 16:7; 1Pe 3:13
39:14 [m]Jer 38:28 [n]2Ki 22:12 [o]Jer 40:5
39:16 [p]Jer 38:7 [q]Jer 21:10; Da 9:12
39:17 [r]Ps 41:1-2
39:18 [s]Jer 45:5 [t]Jer 21:9; 38:2 [u]Jer 17:7
40:2 [v]Jer 50:7
40:3 [w]Da 9:11 [x]Dt 29:24-28; Ro 2:5-9
40:4 [y]Ge 13:9; Jer 39:11-12
40:5 [z]2Ki 25:22 [a]Jer 39:14

[a]4 Or *the Jordan Valley* [b]5 Or *Chaldean*
[c]8 Or *Chaldeans* [d]5 Or *Jeremiah answered*

Ahikam at Mizpah[b] and stayed with
him among the people who were left
behind in the land.

Gedaliah Assassinated

7When all the army officers and their
men who were still in the open country
heard that the king of Babylon had appointed Gedaliah son of Ahikam as
governor over the land and had put
him in charge of the men, women and
children who were the poorest[c] in the
land and who had not been carried
into exile to Babylon, **8**they came to
Gedaliah at Mizpah[d]—Ishmael[e] son
of Nethaniah, Johanan and Jonathan
the sons of Kareah, Seraiah son of Tanhumeth, the sons of Ephai the Netophathite,[f] and Jaazaniah[a] the son of the
Maacathite,[g] and their men. **9**Gedaliah son of Ahikam, the son of Shaphan,
took an oath to reassure them and their
men. "Do not be afraid to serve[h] the
Babylonians,[b]" he said. "Settle down
in the land and serve the king of Babylon, and it will go well with you.[i] **10**I
myself will stay at Mizpah[j] to represent you before the Babylonians who
come to us, but you are to harvest the
wine, summer fruit and oil, and put
them in your storage jars, and live in
the towns you have taken over."[k]

11When all the Jews in Moab,[l] Ammon, Edom and all the other countries
heard that the king of Babylon had left
a remnant in Judah and had appointed
Gedaliah son of Ahikam, the son of
Shaphan, as governor over them,
12they all came back to the land of Judah, to Gedaliah at Mizpah, from all
the countries where they had been
scattered.[m] And they harvested an
abundance of wine and summer fruit.

13Johanan son of Kareah and all the
army officers still in the open country
came to Gedaliah at Mizpah[n] **14**and
said to him, "Don't you know that Baa-
lis king of the Ammonites[o] has sent
Ishmael son of Nethaniah to take your
life?" But Gedaliah son of Ahikam did
not believe them.

15Then Johanan son of Kareah said
privately to Gedaliah in Mizpah, "Let
me go and kill Ishmael son of Nethaniah, and no one will know it. Why
should he take your life and cause all
the Jews who are gathered around you
to be scattered and the remnant of Judah to perish?"

16But Gedaliah son of Ahikam said to
Johanan son of Kareah, "Don't do such
a thing! What you are saying about Ishmael is not true."

41 In the seventh month Ishmael[p]
son of Nethaniah, the son of Elishama, who was of royal blood and had
been one of the king's officers, came
with ten men to Gedaliah son of Ahikam at Mizpah. While they were eating
together there, **2**Ishmael[q] son of Nethaniah and the ten men who were with
him got up and struck down Gedaliah
son of Ahikam, the son of Shaphan,
with the sword, killing the one whom
the king of Babylon had appointed[r] as
governor over the land.[s] **3**Ishmael also
killed all the Jews who were with Gedaliah at Mizpah, as well as the Babylonian[c] soldiers who were there.

4The day after Gedaliah's assassina-
tion, before anyone knew about it,
5eighty men who had shaved off their
beards,[t] torn their clothes and cut
themselves came from Shechem,[u]
Shiloh[v] and Samaria,[w] bringing grain
offerings and incense with them to the
house of the LORD.[x] **6**Ishmael son of
Nethaniah went out from Mizpah to
meet them, weeping[y] as he went.
When he met them, he said, "Come to
Gedaliah son of Ahikam." **7**When they
went into the city, Ishmael son of
Nethaniah and the men who were with
him slaughtered them and threw them
into a cistern. **8**But ten of them said to
Ishmael, "Don't kill us! We have wheat
and barley, oil and honey, hidden in a
field."[z] So he let them alone and did
not kill them with the others. **9**Now the
cistern where he threw all the bodies
of the men he had killed along with
Gedaliah was the one King Asa[a] had
made as part of his defense[b] against
Baasha[c] king of Israel. Ishmael son of
Nethaniah filled it with the dead.

10Ishmael made captives of all the
rest of the people[d] who were in
Mizpah—the king's daughters along
with all the others who were left there,
over whom Nebuzaradan commander
of the imperial guard had appointed
Gedaliah son of Ahikam. Ishmael son
of Nethaniah took them captive and set
out to cross over to the Ammonites.[e]

11When Johanan[f] son of Kareah
and all the army officers who were with
him heard about all the crimes Ishmael
son of Nethaniah had committed,
12they took all their men and went to
fight Ishmael son of Nethaniah. They
caught up with him near the great
pool[g] in Gibeon. **13**When all the people[h] Ishmael had with him saw Johanan son of Kareah and the army officers who were with him, they were
glad. **14**All the people Ishmael had tak-
en captive at Mizpah turned and went

40:6 [b]Jdg 20:1; 1Sa 7:5-17
40:7 [c]Jer 39:10
40:8 [d]ver 13 [e]ver 14; Jer 41:1,2 [f]2Sa 23:28 [g]Dt 3:14
40:9 [h]Jer 27:11 [i]Jer 38:20
40:10 [j]ver 6 [k]Dt 1:39
40:11 [l]Nu 25:1
40:12 [m]Jer 43:5
40:13 [n]ver 8
40:14 [o]2Sa 10:1-19; Jer 25:21; 41:10
41:1 [p]Jer 40:8
41:2 [q]Ps 41:9; 109:5 [r]Jer 40:5 [s]2Sa 3:27; 20:9-10
41:5 [t]Lev 19:27 [u]Ge 33:18; Jdg 9:1-57; 1Ki 12:1 [v]Jos 18:1 [w]1Ki 16:24 [x]2Ki 25:9
41:6 [y]2Sa 3:16
41:8 [z]Isa 45:3
41:9 [a]1Ki 15:22; 2Ch 16:6 [b]Jdg 6:2 [c]2Ch 16:1
41:10 [d]Jer 40:7,12 [e]Jer 40:14
41:11 [f]Jer 40:8
41:12 [g]2Sa 2:13
41:13 [h]ver 10

[a] *8* Hebrew *Jezaniah,* a variant of *Jaazaniah*
[b] *9* Or *Chaldeans;* also in verse 10 [c] *3* Or *Chaldean*

over to Johanan son of Kareah. **15**But Ishmael son of Nethaniah and eight of his men escaped[i] from Johanan and fled to the Ammonites.

Flight to Egypt

16Then Johanan son of Kareah and all the army officers who were with him led away all the survivors[j] from Mizpah whom he had recovered from Ishmael son of Nethaniah after he had assassinated Gedaliah son of Ahikam: the soldiers, women, children and court officials he had brought from Gibeon. **17**And they went on, stopping at Geruth Kimham[k] near Bethlehem on their way to Egypt[l] **18**to escape the Babylonians.[a] They were afraid[m] of them because Ishmael son of Nethaniah had killed Gedaliah[n] son of Ahikam, whom the king of Babylon had appointed as governor over the land.

42 Then all the army officers, including Johanan[o] son of Kareah and Jezaniah[b] son of Hoshaiah, and all the people from the least to the greatest[p] approached **2**Jeremiah the prophet and said to him, "Please hear our petition and pray[q] to the LORD your God for this entire remnant.[r] For as you now see, though we were once many, now only a few[s] are left. **3**Pray that the LORD your God will tell us where we should go and what we should do."[t]

4"I have heard you," replied Jeremiah the prophet. "I will certainly pray[u] to the LORD your God as you have requested; I will tell you everything the LORD says and will keep nothing back from you."[v]

5Then they said to Jeremiah, "May the LORD be a true and faithful witness[w] against us if we do not act in accordance with everything the LORD your God sends you to tell us. **6**Whether it is favorable or unfavorable, we will obey the LORD our God, to whom we are sending you, so that it will go well[x] with us, for we will obey[y] the LORD our God."

7Ten days later the word of the LORD came to Jeremiah. **8**So he called together Johanan son of Kareah and all the army officers[z] who were with him and all the people from the least to the greatest. **9**He said to them, "This is what the LORD, the God of Israel, to whom you sent me to present your petition, says:[a] **10**'If you stay in this land, I will build[b] you up and not tear you down; I will plant[c] you and not uproot you,[d] for I am grieved over the disaster I have inflicted on you.[e] **11**Do not be afraid of the king of Babylon,[f] whom you now fear.[g] Do not be afraid of him, declares the LORD, for I am with you and will save[h] you and deliver you from his hands.[i] **12**I will show you compassion so that he will have compassion on you and restore you to your land.'[j]

13"However, if you say, 'We will not stay in this land,' and so disobey[k] the LORD your God, **14**and if you say, 'No, we will go and live in Egypt,[l] where we will not see war or hear the trumpet or be hungry for bread,' **15**then hear the word of the LORD, O remnant of Judah. This is what the LORD Almighty, the God of Israel, says: 'If you are determined to go to Egypt and you do go to settle there, **16**then the sword[m] you fear will overtake you there, and the famine you dread will follow you into Egypt, and there you will die. **17**Indeed, all who are determined to go to Egypt to settle there will die by the sword, famine and plague;[n] not one of them will survive or escape the disaster I will bring on them.' **18**This is what the LORD Almighty, the God of Israel, says: 'As my anger and wrath[o] have been poured out on those who lived in Jerusalem,[p] so will my wrath be poured out on you when you go to Egypt. You will be an object of cursing and horror,[q] of condemnation and reproach; you will never see this place again.'[r]

19"O remnant of Judah, the LORD has told you, 'Do not go to Egypt.'[s] Be sure of this: I warn you today **20**that you made a fatal mistake[c] when you sent me to the LORD your God and said, 'Pray to the LORD our God for us; tell us everything he says and we will do it.'[t] **21**I have told you today, but you still have not obeyed the LORD your God in all he sent me to tell you.[u] **22**So now, be sure of this: You will die by the sword, famine and plague[v] in the place where you want to go to settle."[w]

43 When Jeremiah finished telling the people all the words of the LORD their God—everything the LORD had sent him to tell them[x]— **2**Azariah son of Hoshaiah and Johanan[y] son of Kareah and all the arrogant men said to Jeremiah, "You are lying! The LORD our God has not sent you to say, 'You must not go to Egypt to settle there.' **3**But Baruch son of Neriah is inciting you against us to hand us over to the Babylonians,[a] so they may kill us or carry us into exile to Babylon."[z]

4So Johanan son of Kareah and all the army officers and all the people disobeyed the LORD's command[a] to

41:15 [i]Job 21:30; Pr 28:17
41:16 [j]Jer 43:4
41:17 [k]2Sa 19:37 [l]Jer 42:14
41:18 [m]Isa 51:12; Jer 42:16; Lk 12:4-5 [n]Jer 40:5
42:1 [o]Jer 40:13; 41:11 [p]Jer 6:13; 44:12
42:2 [q]Jer 36:7; Ac 8:24; Jas 5:16 [r]Isa 1:9 [s]Lev 26:22; La 1:1
42:3 [t]Ps 86:11; Pr 3:6
42:4 [u]Ex 8:29; 1Sa 12:23 [v]1Ki 22:14; 1Sa 3:17
42:5 [w]Ge 31:50
42:6 [x]Dt 5:29; 6:3; Jer 7:23 [y]Ex 24:7; Jos 24:24
42:8 [z]ver 1
42:9 [a]2Ki 22:15
42:10 [b]Jer 24:6 [c]Jer 31:28 [d]Eze 36:36 [e]Jer 18:8
42:11 [f]Jer 27:11 [g]Nu 14:9 [h]Isa 43:5 [i]Jer 1:8; Ro 8:31
42:12 [j]Ps 106:44-46
42:13 [k]Jer 44:16
42:14 [l]Nu 11:4-5
42:16 [m]Eze 11:8
42:17 [n]ver 22; Jer 44:13
42:18 [o]Dt 29:18-20; Jer 7:20 [p]2Ch 36:19; Jer 39:1-9 [q]Jer 29:18 [r]Jer 22:10
42:19 [s]Dt 17:16; Isa 30:7
42:20 [t]ver 2
42:21 [u]Eze 2:7; Zec 7:11-12
42:22 [v]ver 17; Eze 6:11 [w]Hos 9:6
43:1 [x]Jer 26:8; 42:9-22
43:2 [y]Jer 42:1
43:3 [z]Jer 38:4
43:4 [a]Jer 42:5-6

[a] *18,3* Or *Chaldeans*
[b] *1* Hebrew; Septuagint (see also 43:2) *Azariah*
[c] *20* Or *you erred in your hearts*

stay in the land of Judah.[b] **5**Instead, Johanan son of Kareah and all the army officers led away all the remnant of Judah who had come back to live in the land of Judah from all the nations where they had been scattered.[c] **6**They also led away all the men, women and children and the king's daughters whom Nebuzaradan commander of the imperial guard had left with Gedaliah son of Ahikam, the son of Shaphan, and Jeremiah the prophet and Baruch son of Neriah. **7**So they entered Egypt in disobedience to the LORD and went as far as Tahpanhes.[d]

8In Tahpanhes[e] the word of the LORD came to Jeremiah: **9**"While the Jews are watching, take some large stones with you and bury them in clay in the brick pavement at the entrance to Pharaoh's palace in Tahpanhes. **10**Then say to them, 'This is what the LORD Almighty, the God of Israel, says: I will send for my servant[f] Nebuchadnezzar king of Babylon, and I will set his throne over these stones I have buried here; he will spread his royal canopy above them. **11**He will come and attack Egypt,[g] bringing death to those destined for death, captivity to those destined for captivity, and the sword to those destined for the sword.[h] **12**He[a] will set fire to the temples of the gods[i] of Egypt; he will burn their temples and take their gods captive. As a shepherd wraps[j] his garment around him, so will he wrap Egypt around himself and depart from there unscathed. **13**There in the temple of the sun[b] in Egypt he will demolish the sacred pillars and will burn down the temples of the gods of Egypt.' "

Disaster Because of Idolatry

44 This word came to Jeremiah concerning all the Jews living in Lower Egypt—in Migdol,[k] Tahpanhes[l] and Memphis[c][m]—and in Upper Egypt[d]:[n] **2**"This is what the LORD Almighty, the God of Israel, says: You saw the great disaster I brought on Jerusalem and on all the towns of Judah. Today they lie deserted and in ruins[o] **3**because of the evil they have done. They provoked me to anger by burning incense and by worshiping other gods[p] that neither they nor you nor your fathers[q] ever knew. **4**Again and again[r] I sent my servants the prophets,[s] who said, 'Do not do this detestable thing that I hate!' **5**But they did not listen or pay attention; they did not turn from their wickedness or stop burning incense to other gods.[t] **6**Therefore, my fierce anger was poured out; it raged against the towns of Judah and the streets of Jerusalem and made them the desolate ruins they are today.

7"Now this is what the LORD God Almighty, the God of Israel, says: Why bring such great disaster[u] on yourselves by cutting off from Judah the men and women,[v] the children and infants, and so leave yourselves without a remnant? **8**Why provoke me to anger with what your hands have made,[w] burning incense to other gods in Egypt, where you have come to live?[x] You will destroy yourselves and make yourselves an object of cursing and reproach[y] among all the nations on earth. **9**Have you forgotten the wickedness committed by your fathers and by the kings and queens of Judah and the wickedness committed by you and your wives in the land of Judah and the streets of Jerusalem?[z] **10**To this day they have not humbled themselves or shown reverence, nor have they followed my law[a] and the decrees I set before you and your fathers.[b]

11"Therefore, this is what the LORD Almighty, the God of Israel, says: I am determined to bring disaster[c] on you and to destroy all Judah. **12**I will take away the remnant[d] of Judah who were determined to go to Egypt to settle there. They will all perish in Egypt; they will fall by the sword or die from famine. From the least to the greatest, they will die by sword or famine.[e] They will become an object of cursing and horror, of condemnation and reproach.[f] **13**I will punish those who live in Egypt with the sword, famine and plague,[g] as I punished Jerusalem. **14**None of the remnant of Judah who have gone to live in Egypt will escape or survive to return to the land of Judah, to which they long to return and live; none will return except a few fugitives."[h]

15Then all the men who knew that their wives were burning incense to other gods, along with all the women who were present—a large assembly—and all the people living in Lower and Upper Egypt,[e] said to Jeremiah, **16**"We will not listen[i] to the message you have spoken to us in the name of the LORD! **17**We will certainly do everything we said we would:[j] We will burn incense to the Queen of Heaven[k] and will pour out drink offerings to her just as we and our fathers, our kings and our officials did in the towns of Judah

43:4 [b]Jer 42:10
43:5 [c]Jer 40:12
43:7 [d]Jer 2:16; 44:1
43:8 [e]Jer 2:16
43:10 [f]Isa 44:28; Jer 25:9; 27:6
43:11 [g]Jer 46:13-26; Eze 29:19-20 [h]Jer 15:2; 44:13; Zec 11:9
43:12 [i]Jer 46:25; Eze 30:13 [j]Ps 104:2; 109:18-19
44:1 [k]Ex 14:2 [l]Jer 43:7,8 [m]Isa 19:13 [n]Isa 11:11; Jer 46:14
44:2 [o]Isa 6:11; Jer 9:11; 34:22
44:3 [p]ver 8; Dt 13:6-11; 29:26 [q]Dt 32:17; Jer 19:4
44:4 [r]Jer 7:13 [s]Jer 7:25; 25:4; 26:5
44:5 [t]Jer 11:8-10
44:7 [u]Jer 26:19 [v]Jer 51:22
44:8 [w]Jer 25:6-7 [x]1Co 10:22 [y]Jer 42:18
44:9 [z]ver 17,21
44:10 [a]Jos 1:7 [b]1Ki 9:6-9
44:11 [c]Jer 21:10; Am 9:4
44:12 [d]ver 7 [e]Isa 1:28 [f]Jer 29:18; 42:15-18
44:13 [g]Jer 42:17
44:14 [h]ver 28; Jer 22:24-27; Ro 9:27
44:16 [i]Jer 11:8-10
44:17 [j]Dt 23:23 [k]ver 25; Jer 7:18

[a]*12* Or *I* [b]*13* Or *in Heliopolis* [c]*1* Hebrew *Noph* [d]*1* Hebrew *in Pathros* [e]*15* Hebrew *in Egypt and Pathros*

and in the streets of Jerusalem. At that
time we had plenty of food and were
well off and suffered no harm.[l] 18But
ever since we stopped burning incense
to the Queen of Heaven and pouring
out drink offerings to her, we have had
nothing and have been perishing by
sword and famine.[m]"
19The women added, "When we
burned incense to the Queen of Heav-
en[n] and poured out drink offerings to
her, did not our husbands know that
we were making cakes like her image
and pouring out drink offerings to
her?"
20Then Jeremiah said to all the people, both men and women, who were
answering him, 21"Did not the LORD remember[o] and think about the incense[p] burned in the towns of Judah
and the streets of Jerusalem[q] by you
and your fathers,[r] your kings and
your officials and the people of the
land? 22When the LORD could no longer
endure your wicked actions and the
detestable things you did, your land
became an object of cursing[s] and a
desolate waste without inhabitants,
as it is today.[t] 23Because you have
burned incense and have sinned
against the LORD and have not obeyed
him or followed his law or his decrees
or his stipulations, this disaster[u] has
come upon you, as you now see."[v]
24Then Jeremiah said to all the people, including the women,[w] "Hear the
word of the LORD, all you people of Judah in Egypt.[x] 25This is what the LORD
Almighty, the God of Israel, says: You
and your wives have shown by your
actions what you promised when you
said, 'We will certainly carry out the
vows we made to burn incense and
pour out drink offerings to the Queen
of Heaven.'[y]
"Go ahead then, do what you promised! Keep your vows![z] 26But hear the
word of the LORD, all Jews living in
Egypt: 'I swear[a] by my great name,'
says the LORD, 'that no one from Judah
living anywhere in Egypt will ever
again invoke my name or swear, "As
surely as the Sovereign LORD lives."[b]
27For I am watching over them for
harm,[c] not for good; the Jews in Egypt
will perish by sword and famine until
they are all destroyed. 28Those who escape the sword and return to the land
of Judah from Egypt will be very few.[d]
Then the whole remnant of Judah who
came to live in Egypt will know whose
word will stand—mine or theirs.[e]
29" 'This will be the sign to you that
I will punish you in this place,' declares
the LORD, 'so that you will know that
my threats of harm against you will
surely stand.'[f] 30This is what the LORD
says: 'I am going to hand Pharaoh[g]
Hophra king of Egypt over to his enemies who seek his life, just as I handed
Zedekiah[h] king of Judah over to Nebuchadnezzar king of Babylon, the enemy who was seeking his life.' "[i]

44:17 [l]Hos 2:5-13 **44:18** [m]Mal 3:13-15 **44:19** [n]Jer 7:18 **44:21** [o]Isa 64:9; Jer 14:10 [p]Jer 11:13 [q]ver 9 [r]Ps 79:8 **44:22** [s]Jer 25:18 [t]Ge 19:13; Ps 107:33-34 **44:23** [u]Jer 40:2 [v]1Ki 9:9; Jer 7:13-15; Da 9:11-12 **44:24** [w]ver 15 [x]Jer 43:7 **44:25** [y]ver 17 [z]Eze 20:39 **44:26** [a]Ge 22:16; Isa 48:1; Heb 6:13-17 [b]Dt 32:40; Ps 50:16 **44:27** [c]Jer 31:28 **44:28** [d]ver 13-14; Isa 10:19 [e]ver 17,25-26 **44:29** [f]Pr 19:21 **44:30** [g]Jer 46:26; Eze 30:21 [h]2Ki 25:1-7 [i]Jer 39:5 **45:1** [j]Jer 32:12; 36:4,18,32 [k]2Ch 36:5 **45:3** [l]Ps 69:3 **45:4** [m]Jer 11:17 [n]Isa 5:5-7; Jer 18:7-10 **45:5** [o]Mt 6:25-27,33 [p]Jer 21:9; 38:2; 39:18 **46:1** [q]Jer 1:10; 25:15-38 **46:2** [r]2Ki 23:29 [s]2Ch 35:20

A Message to Baruch

45 This is what Jeremiah the prophet
told Baruch[j] son of Neriah in the
fourth year of Jehoiakim[k] son of Josiah king of Judah, after Baruch had written on a scroll the words Jeremiah was
then dictating: 2"This is what the LORD,
the God of Israel, says to you, Baruch:
3You said, 'Woe to me! The LORD has
added sorrow to my pain; I am worn
out with groaning[l] and find no rest.' "
4⌊The LORD said,⌋ "Say this to him:
'This is what the LORD says: I will overthrow what I have built and uproot
what I have planted,[m] throughout the
land.[n] 5Should you then seek great
things for yourself? Seek them not.[o]
For I will bring disaster on all people,
declares the LORD, but wherever you go
I will let you escape with your life.' "[p]

A Message About Egypt

46 This is the word of the LORD that
came to Jeremiah the prophet concerning the nations:[q]

2Concerning Egypt:

This is the message against the army
of Pharaoh Neco[r] king of Egypt,
which was defeated at Carchemish[s]
on the Euphrates River by Nebuchad-

46:1–51:64

PROMISE 7

THE GOD OF ALL NATIONS

Israel was God's covenant people. The Israelites were supposed to lead other nations to God, to be a living testimony to his love and power. Most of the Old Testament focuses on Israel because of that fact. These chapters reveal a vital reality, however: they show us that God is concerned for all people and all nations.

The Old Testament's focus on Israel should never lead us to conclude that other peoples didn't matter. Or don't matter. The church's commission to reach all nations (Matthew 28), to be his witnesses to the uttermost parts of the world (Acts 1:8), and to act in love and service to others (Mark 12:30–31) further confirms the fact that God is the Creator and Savior of all humanity.

For the next Promise 7 reading go to page 880.

nezzar king of Babylon in the fourth year of Jehoiakim[t] son of Josiah king of Judah:

3"Prepare your shields,[u] both large
and small,
and march out for battle!
4Harness the horses,
mount the steeds!
Take your positions
with helmets on!
Polish[v] your spears,
put on your armor![w]
5What do I see?
They are terrified,
they are retreating,
their warriors are defeated.
They flee[x] in haste
without looking back,
and there is terror[y] on every
side,"
declares the LORD.
6"The swift cannot flee[z]
nor the strong escape.
In the north by the River Euphrates
they stumble and fall.[a]

7"Who is this that rises like the Nile,
like rivers of surging waters?[b]
8Egypt rises like the Nile,
like rivers of surging waters.
She says, 'I will rise and cover the
earth;
I will destroy cities and their
people.'
9Charge, O horses!
Drive furiously, O charioteers![c]
March on, O warriors—
men of Cush**a** and Put who
carry shields,
men of Lydia[d] who draw the bow.
10But that day[e] belongs to the Lord,
the LORD Almighty—
a day of vengeance, for
vengeance on his foes.
The sword will devour[f] till it is
satisfied,
till it has quenched its thirst with
blood.
For the Lord, the LORD Almighty,
will offer sacrifice[g]
in the land of the north by the
River Euphrates.

11"Go up to Gilead and get balm,[h]
O Virgin[i] Daughter of Egypt.
But you multiply remedies in vain;
there is no healing[j] for you.
12The nations will hear of your
shame;
your cries will fill the earth.
One warrior will stumble over
another;
both will fall[k] down together."

13This is the message the LORD spoke to Jeremiah the prophet about the coming of Nebuchadnezzar king of Babylon to attack Egypt:[l]

14"Announce this in Egypt, and
proclaim it in Migdol;
proclaim it also in Memphis**b**
and Tahpanhes:[m]
'Take your positions and get ready,
for the sword devours those
around you.'
15Why will your warriors be laid low?
They cannot stand, for the LORD
will push them down.[n]
16They will stumble[o] repeatedly;
they will fall[p] over each other.
They will say, 'Get up, let us go
back
to our own people and our
native lands,
away from the sword of the
oppressor.'
17There they will exclaim,
'Pharaoh king of Egypt is only a
loud noise;
he has missed his opportunity.[q]'

18"As surely as I live," declares the
King,[r]
whose name is the LORD
Almighty,
"one will come who is like Tabor[s]
among the mountains,
like Carmel[t] by the sea.
19Pack your belongings for exile,[u]
you who live in Egypt,
for Memphis will be laid waste
and lie in ruins without
inhabitant.

20"Egypt is a beautiful heifer,
but a gadfly is coming
against her from the north.[v]
21The mercenaries[w] in her ranks
are like fattened calves.
They too will turn and flee[x]
together,
they will not stand their ground,
for the day[y] of disaster is coming
upon them,
the time for them to be
punished.
22Egypt will hiss like a fleeing serpent
as the enemy advances in force;
they will come against her with
axes,
like men who cut down trees.
23They will chop down her forest,"
declares the LORD,
"dense though it be.
They are more numerous than
locusts,[z]
they cannot be counted.
24The Daughter of Egypt will be put
to shame,

46:2 [t]Jer 45:1 **46:3** [u]Isa 21:5; Jer 51:11-12 **46:4** [v]Eze 21:9-11 [w]1Sa 17:5,38; 2Ch 26:14; Ne 4:16 **46:5** [x]ver 21 [y]Jer 49:29 **46:6** [z]Isa 30:16 [a]ver 12,16; Da 11:19 **46:7** [b]Jer 47:2 **46:9** [c]Jer 47:3 [d]Isa 66:19 **46:10** [e]Joel 1:15 [f]Dt 32:42 [g]Zep 1:7 **46:11** [h]Jer 8:22 [i]Isa 47:1 [j]Jer 30:13; Mic 1:9 **46:12** [k]Isa 19:4; Na 3:8-10 **46:13** [l]Isa 19:1 **46:14** [m]Jer 43:8 **46:15** [n]Isa 66:15-16 **46:16** [o]Lev 26:37 [p]ver 6 **46:17** [q]Isa 19:11-16 **46:18** [r]Jer 48:15 [s]Jos 19:22 [t]1Ki 18:42 **46:19** [u]Isa 20:4 **46:20** [v]ver 24; Jer 47:2 **46:21** [w]2Ki 7:6 [x]ver 5 [y]Ps 37:13 **46:23** [z]Jdg 7:12

a *9* That is, the upper Nile region
b *14* Hebrew *Noph*; also in verse 19

handed over to the people of the
north.[a]"

25The LORD Almighty, the God of Israel, says: "I am about to bring punishment on Amon god of Thebes,[a][b] on Pharaoh, on Egypt and her gods[c] and her kings, and on those who rely[d] on Pharaoh. 26I will hand them over[e] to those who seek their lives, to Nebuchadnezzar king[f] of Babylon and his officers. Later, however, Egypt will be inhabited[g] as in times past," declares the LORD.

27"Do not fear,[h] O Jacob my
servant;
do not be dismayed, O Israel.
I will surely save you out of a
distant place,
your descendants from the land
of their exile.[i]
Jacob will again have peace and
security,
and no one will make him afraid.
28Do not fear, O Jacob my servant,
for I am with you,"[j] declares
the LORD.
"Though I completely destroy[k] all
the nations
among which I scatter you,
I will not completely destroy you.
I will discipline you but only with
justice;
I will not let you go entirely
unpunished."

A Message About the Philistines

47 This is the word of the LORD that came to Jeremiah the prophet concerning the Philistines before Pharaoh attacked Gaza:[l]

2This is what the LORD says:

"See how the waters are rising in
the north;[m]
they will become an overflowing
torrent.
They will overflow the land and
everything in it,
the towns and those who live in
them.
The people will cry out;
all who dwell in the land will
wail
3at the sound of the hoofs of
galloping steeds,
at the noise of enemy chariots
and the rumble of their wheels.
Fathers will not turn to help their
children;
their hands will hang limp.
4For the day has come
to destroy all the Philistines
and to cut off all survivors
who could help Tyre[n] and
Sidon.[o]
The LORD is about to destroy the
Philistines,[p]
the remnant from the coasts of
Caphtor.[b][q]
5Gaza will shave[r] her head in
mourning;
Ashkelon[s] will be silenced.
O remnant on the plain,
how long will you cut yourselves?

6" 'Ah, sword[t] of the LORD,' ⌞you
cry,⌟
'how long till you rest?
Return to your scabbard;
cease and be still.'
7But how can it rest
when the LORD has commanded
it,
when he has ordered it
to attack Ashkelon and the
coast?"

A Message About Moab

48 Concerning Moab:

This is what the LORD Almighty, the God of Israel, says:

"Woe to Nebo,[u] for it will be
ruined.
Kiriathaim[v] will be disgraced
and captured;
the stronghold[c] will be
disgraced and shattered.
2Moab will be praised[w] no more;
in Heshbon[d][x] men will plot her
downfall:
'Come, let us put an end to that
nation.'
You too, O Madmen,[e] will be
silenced;
the sword will pursue you.
3Listen to the cries from
Horonaim,[y]
cries of great havoc and
destruction.
4Moab will be broken;
her little ones will cry out.[f]
5They go up the way to Luhith,[z]
weeping bitterly as they go;
on the road down to Horonaim
anguished cries over the
destruction are heard.
6Flee! Run for your lives;
become like a bush[g] in the
desert.[a]
7Since you trust in your deeds and
riches,
you too will be taken captive,

46:24 [a]Jer 1:15
46:25 [b]Eze 30:14; Na 3:8 [c]Jer 43:12 [d]Isa 20:6
46:26 [e]Jer 44:30 [f]Eze 32:11 [g]Eze 29:11-16
46:27 [h]Isa 41:13; 43:5 [i]Isa 11:11; Jer 50:19
46:28 [j]Isa 8:9-10 [k]Jer 4:27
47:1 [l]Ge 10:19; Am 1:6; Zec 9:5-7
47:2 [m]Isa 8:7; 14:31
47:4 [n]Am 1:9-10; Zec 9:2-4 [o]Jer 25:22 [p]Ge 10:14; Joel 3:4 [q]Dt 2:23
47:5 [r]Jer 41:5; Mic 1:16 [s]Jer 25:20
47:6 [t]Jer 12:12
48:1 [u]Nu 32:38 [v]Nu 32:37
48:2 [w]Isa 16:14 [x]Nu 21:25
48:3 [y]Isa 15:5
48:5 [z]Isa 15:5
48:6 [a]Jer 17:6

[a]*25* Hebrew *No* [b]*4* That is, Crete [c]*1* Or / *Misgab* [d]*2* The Hebrew for *Heshbon* sounds like the Hebrew for *plot.* [e]*2* The name of the Moabite town Madmen sounds like the Hebrew for *be silenced.* [f]*4* Hebrew; Septuagint / *proclaim it to Zoar* [g]*6* Or *like Aroer*

and Chemosh[b] will go into exile,[c]
together with his priests and
officials.
8The destroyer will come against
every town,
and not a town will escape.
The valley will be ruined
and the plateau destroyed,
because the LORD has spoken.
9Put salt on Moab,
for she will be laid waste[a];
her towns will become desolate,
with no one to live in them.

10"A curse on him who is lax in
doing the LORD's work!
A curse on him who keeps his
sword[d] from bloodshed![e]

11"Moab has been at rest[f] from
youth,
like wine left on its dregs,[g]
not poured from one jar to
another—
she has not gone into exile.
So she tastes as she did,
and her aroma is unchanged.
12But days are coming,"
declares the LORD,
"when I will send men who pour
from jars,
and they will pour her out;
they will empty her jars
and smash her jugs.
13Then Moab will be ashamed[h] of
Chemosh,
as the house of Israel was
ashamed
when they trusted in Bethel.

14"How can you say, 'We are
warriors,[i]
men valiant in battle'?
15Moab will be destroyed and her
towns invaded;
her finest young men will go
down in the slaughter,[j]"
declares the King,[k] whose name
is the LORD Almighty.[l]
16"The fall of Moab is at hand;[m]
her calamity will come quickly.
17Mourn for her, all who live around
her,
all who know her fame;
say, 'How broken is the mighty
scepter,
how broken the glorious staff!'

18"Come down from your glory
and sit on the parched ground,[n]
O inhabitants of the Daughter of
Dibon,[o]
for he who destroys Moab
will come up against you
and ruin your fortified cities.[p]
19Stand by the road and watch,
you who live in Aroer.[q]
Ask the man fleeing and the
woman escaping,
ask them, 'What has happened?'
20Moab is disgraced, for she is
shattered.
Wail[r] and cry out!
Announce by the Arnon[s]
that Moab is destroyed.
21Judgment has come to the
plateau—
to Holon, Jahzah[t] and
Mephaath,[u]
22 to Dibon,[v] Nebo and Beth
Diblathaim,
23 to Kiriathaim, Beth Gamul and
Beth Meon,[w]
24 to Kerioth[x] and Bozrah—
to all the towns of Moab, far and
near.
25Moab's horn[b][y] is cut off;
her arm[z] is broken,"
declares the LORD.

26"Make her drunk,[a]
for she has defied the LORD.
Let Moab wallow in her vomit;
let her be an object of ridicule.
27Was not Israel the object of your
ridicule?[b]
Was she caught among thieves,
that you shake your head[c] in
scorn[d]
whenever you speak of her?
28Abandon your towns and dwell
among the rocks,
you who live in Moab.
Be like a dove[e] that makes its nest
at the mouth of a cave.[f]

29"We have heard of Moab's
pride[g]—
her overweening pride and
conceit,
her pride and arrogance
and the haughtiness of her heart.
30I know her insolence but it is
futile,"
declares the LORD,
"and her boasts accomplish
nothing.
31Therefore I wail[h] over Moab,
for all Moab I cry out,
I moan for the men of Kir
Hareseth.[i]
32I weep for you, as Jazer weeps,
O vines of Sibmah.[j]
Your branches spread as far as the
sea;
they reached as far as the sea of
Jazer.
The destroyer has fallen
on your ripened fruit and grapes.
33Joy and gladness are gone

48:7 [b]Nu 21:29 [c]Isa 46:1-2; Jer 49:3
48:10 [d]Jer 47:6 [e]1Ki 20:42; 2Ki 13:15-19
48:11 [f]Zec 1:15 [g]Zep 1:12
48:13 [h]Hos 10:6
48:14 [i]Ps 33:16
48:15 [j]Jer 50:27 [k]Jer 46:18 [l]Jer 51:57
48:16 [m]Isa 13:22
48:18 [n]Isa 47:1 [o]Nu 21:30; Jos 13:9 [p]ver 8
48:19 [q]Dt 2:36
48:20 [r]Isa 16:7 [s]Nu 21:13
48:21 [t]Nu 21:23; Isa 15:4 [u]Jos 13:18
48:22 [v]Jos 13:9,17
48:23 [w]Jos 13:17
48:24 [x]Am 2:2
48:25 [y]Ps 75:10 [z]Ps 10:15; Eze 30:21
48:26 [a]Jer 25:16,27
48:27 [b]Jer 2:26 [c]Job 16:4; Jer 18:16 [d]Mic 7:8-10
48:28 [e]Ps 55:6-7 [f]Jdg 6:2
48:29 [g]Job 40:12; Isa 16:6
48:31 [h]Isa 15:5-8 [i]2Ki 3:25
48:32 [j]Isa 16:8-9

[a]9 Or *Give wings to Moab, / for she will fly away*
[b]25 *Horn* here symbolizes strength.

from the orchards and fields of
Moab.
I have stopped the flow of wine[k]
from the presses;
no one treads them with shouts
of joy.[l]
Although there are shouts,
they are not shouts of joy.

34"The sound of their cry rises
from Heshbon to Elealeh[m] and
Jahaz,[n]
from Zoar[o] as far as Horonaim[p]
and Eglath Shelishiyah,
for even the waters of Nimrim
are dried up.[q]
35In Moab I will put an end
to those who make offerings on
the high places[r]
and burn incense[s] to their
gods,"
declares the LORD.
36"So my heart laments[t] for Moab
like a flute;
it laments like a flute for the
men of Kir Hareseth.
The wealth they acquired[u] is
gone.
37Every head is shaved[v]
and every beard cut off;
every hand is slashed
and every waist is covered with
sackcloth.[w]
38On all the roofs in Moab
and in the public squares
there is nothing but mourning,
for I have broken Moab
like a jar[x] that no one wants,"
declares the LORD.
39"How shattered she is! How they
wail!
How Moab turns her back in
shame!
Moab has become an object of
ridicule,
an object of horror to all those
around her."

40This is what the LORD says:

"Look! An eagle is swooping[y]
down,
spreading its wings[z] over Moab.
41Kerioth[a] will be captured
and the strongholds taken.
In that day the hearts of Moab's
warriors
will be like the heart of a woman
in labor.[a]
42Moab will be destroyed[b] as a
nation[c]
because she defied[d] the LORD.
43Terror and pit and snare[e] await
you,
O people of Moab,"
declares the LORD.
44"Whoever flees[f] from the terror
will fall into a pit,
whoever climbs out of the pit
will be caught in a snare;
for I will bring upon Moab
the year[g] of her punishment,"
declares the LORD.

45"In the shadow of Heshbon
the fugitives stand helpless,
for a fire has gone out from
Heshbon,
a blaze from the midst of
Sihon;[h]
it burns the foreheads of Moab,
the skulls[i] of the noisy boasters.
46Woe to you, O Moab![j]
The people of Chemosh are
destroyed;
your sons are taken into exile
and your daughters into
captivity.

47"Yet I will restore[k] the fortunes of
Moab
in days to come,"
declares the LORD.

Here ends the judgment on Moab.

A Message About Ammon

49 Concerning the Ammonites:[l]

This is what the LORD says:

"Has Israel no sons?
Has she no heirs?
Why then has Molech[b] taken
possession of Gad?
Why do his people live in its
towns?
2But the days are coming,"
declares the LORD,
"when I will sound the battle cry[m]
against Rabbah[n] of the
Ammonites;
it will become a mound of ruins,
and its surrounding villages will
be set on fire.
Then Israel will drive out
those who drove her out,[o]"
says the LORD.
3"Wail, O Heshbon, for Ai[p] is
destroyed!
Cry out, O inhabitants of
Rabbah!
Put on sackcloth and mourn;
rush here and there inside the
walls,
for Molech will go into exile,[q]
together with his priests and
officials.
4Why do you boast of your valleys,
boast of your valleys so fruitful?
O unfaithful daughter,

48:33 [k]Isa 16:10 [l]Joel 1:12 **48:34** [m]Nu 32:3 [n]Isa 15:4 [o]Ge 13:10 [p]Isa 15:5 [q]Isa 15:6 **48:35** [r]Isa 15:2; 16:12 [s]Jer 11:13 **48:36** [t]Isa 16:11 [u]Isa 15:7 **48:37** [v]Isa 15:2; Jer 41:5 [w]Ge 37:34 **48:38** [x]Jer 22:28 **48:40** [y]Dt 28:49; Hab 1:8 [z]Isa 8:8 **48:41** [a]Isa 21:3 **48:42** [b]Ps 83:4; Isa 16:14 [c]ver 2 [d]ver 26 **48:43** [e]Isa 24:17 **48:44** [f]1Ki 19:17; Isa 24:18 [g]Jer 11:23 **48:45** [h]Nu 21:21, 26-28 [i]Nu 24:17 **48:46** [j]Nu 21:29 **48:47** [k]Jer 12:15; 49:6,39 **49:1** [l]Am 1:13; Zep 2:8-9 **49:2** [m]Jer 4:19 [n]Dt 3:11 [o]Isa 14:2; Eze 21:28-32; 25:2-11 **49:3** [p]Jos 8:28 [q]Jer 48:7

a *41* Or *The cities* b *1* Or *their king;* Hebrew *malcam;* also in verse 3

you trust in your riches[r] and
say,
'Who will attack me?'[s]
5I will bring terror on you
from all those around you,"
declares the Lord,
the LORD Almighty.
"Every one of you will be driven
away,
and no one will gather the
fugitives.
6"Yet afterward, I will restore[t] the
fortunes of the Ammonites,"
declares the LORD.

A Message About Edom

7Concerning Edom:[u]

This is what the LORD Almighty says:

"Is there no longer wisdom in
Teman?[v]
Has counsel perished from the
prudent?
Has their wisdom decayed?
8Turn and flee, hide in deep caves,
you who live in Dedan,[w]
for I will bring disaster on Esau
at the time I punish him.
9If grape pickers came to you,
would they not leave a few
grapes?
If thieves came during the night,
would they not steal only as
much as they wanted?
10But I will strip Esau bare;
I will uncover his hiding places,
so that he cannot conceal
himself.
His children, relatives and
neighbors will perish,
and he will be no more.[x]
11Leave your orphans;[y] I will protect
their lives.
Your widows too can trust in
me."

12This is what the LORD says: "If
those who do not deserve to drink the
cup[z] must drink it, why should you go
unpunished?[a] You will not go unpunished, but must drink it. 13I swear[b] by
myself," declares the LORD, "that Bozrah[c] will become a ruin and an object
of horror, of reproach and of cursing;
and all its towns will be in ruins forever."

14I have heard a message from the
LORD:
An envoy was sent to the nations
to say,
"Assemble yourselves to attack it!
Rise up for battle!"

15"Now I will make you small among
the nations,

49:4 [r]Jer 9:23; 1Ti 6:17 [s]Jer 21:13 **49:6** [t]ver 39; Jer 48:47 **49:7** [u]Ge 25:30; Eze 25:12 [v]Ge 36:11,15, 34 **49:8** [w]Jer 25:23 **49:10** [x]Mal 1:2-5 **49:11** [y]Hos 14:3 **49:12** [z]Jer 25:15 [a]Jer 25:28-29 **49:13** [b]Ge 22:16 [c]Ge 36:33; Isa 34:6

49:16 [d]Job 39:27; Am 9:2 **49:17** [e]ver 13 [f]Jer 50:13; Eze 35:7 **49:18** [g]Ge 19:24; Dt 29:23 [h]ver 33 **49:19** [i]Jer 12:5 [j]Jer 50:44 **49:20** [k]Isa 14:27 [l]Jer 50:45 [m]Mal 1:3-4 **49:21** [n]Eze 26:15 [o]Jer 50:46; Eze 26:18 **49:22** [p]Hos 8:1 [q]Isa 13:8; Jer 48:40-41 **49:23** [r]Ge 14:15; 2Ch 16:2; Ac 9:2 [s]Isa 10:9; Am 6:2; Zec 9:2 [t]2Ki 18:34

despised among men.
16The terror you inspire
and the pride of your heart have
deceived you,
you who live in the clefts of the
rocks,
who occupy the heights of the
hill.
Though you build your nest[d] as
high as the eagle's,
from there I will bring you
down,"
declares the LORD.
17"Edom will become an object of
horror;[e]
all who pass by will be appalled
and will scoff
because of all its wounds.[f]
18As Sodom and Gomorrah[g] were
overthrown,
along with their neighboring
towns,"
says the LORD,
"so no one will live there;
no man will dwell[h] in it.
19"Like a lion coming up from
Jordan's thickets[i]
to a rich pastureland,
I will chase Edom from its land in
an instant.
Who is the chosen one I will
appoint for this?
Who is like me and who can
challenge me?[j]
And what shepherd can stand
against me?"
20Therefore, hear what the LORD has
planned against Edom,
what he has purposed[k] against
those who live in Teman:
The young of the flock[l] will be
dragged away;
he will completely destroy[m]
their pasture because of
them.
21At the sound of their fall the earth
will tremble;[n]
their cry[o] will resound to the
Red Sea.[a]
22Look! An eagle will soar and
swoop[p] down,
spreading its wings over Bozrah.
In that day the hearts of Edom's
warriors
will be like the heart of a woman
in labor.[q]

A Message About Damascus

23Concerning Damascus:[r]

"Hamath[s] and Arpad[t] are
dismayed,
for they have heard bad news.

[a]21 Hebrew *Yam Suph*; that is, Sea of Reeds

They are disheartened,
troubled like[a] the restless sea.[u]
24 Damascus has become feeble,
she has turned to flee
and panic has gripped her;
anguish and pain have seized her,
pain like that of a woman in labor.
25 Why has the city of renown not been abandoned,
the town in which I delight?
26 Surely, her young men will fall in the streets;
all her soldiers will be silenced[v] in that day,"
declares the LORD Almighty.
27 "I will set fire[w] to the walls of Damascus;
it will consume the fortresses of Ben-Hadad.[x]"

A Message About Kedar and Hazor

28 Concerning Kedar[y] and the kingdoms of Hazor, which Nebuchadnezzar king of Babylon attacked:

This is what the LORD says:

"Arise, and attack Kedar
and destroy the people of the East.[z]
29 Their tents and their flocks will be taken;
their shelters will be carried off
with all their goods and camels.
Men will shout to them,
'Terror[a] on every side!'
30 "Flee quickly away!
Stay in deep caves, you who live in Hazor,"
declares the LORD.
"Nebuchadnezzar king of Babylon
has plotted against you;
he has devised a plan against you.
31 "Arise and attack a nation at ease,
which lives in confidence,"
declares the LORD,
"a nation that has neither gates nor bars;[b]
its people live alone.
32 Their camels will become plunder,
and their large herds will be booty.
I will scatter to the winds those
who are in distant places[b][c]
and will bring disaster on them
from every side,"
declares the LORD.
33 "Hazor will become a haunt of jackals,
a desolate[d] place forever.
No one will live there;
no man will dwell[e] in it."

49:23 [u]Ge 49:4; Isa 57:20
49:26 [v]Jer 50:30
49:27 [w]Jer 43:12; Am 1:4 [x]1Ki 15:18
49:28 [y]Ge 25:13 [z]Jdg 6:3
49:29 [a]Jer 6:25; 46:5
49:31 [b]Eze 38:11
49:32 [c]Jer 9:26
49:33 [d]Jer 10:22 [e]ver 18; Jer 51:37

A Message About Elam

34 This is the word of the LORD that came to Jeremiah the prophet concerning Elam,[f] early in the reign of Zedekiah[g] king of Judah:

35 This is what the LORD Almighty says:

"See, I will break the bow[h] of Elam,
the mainstay of their might.
36 I will bring against Elam the four winds[i]
from the four quarters of the heavens;
I will scatter them to the four winds,
and there will not be a nation
where Elam's exiles do not go.
37 I will shatter Elam before their foes,
before those who seek their lives;
I will bring disaster upon them,
even my fierce anger,"[j]
declares the LORD.
"I will pursue them with the sword[k]
until I have made an end of them.
38 I will set my throne in Elam
and destroy her king and officials,"
declares the LORD.

39 "Yet I will restore[l] the fortunes of Elam
in days to come,"
declares the LORD.

A Message About Babylon

50 This is the word the LORD spoke through Jeremiah the prophet concerning Babylon[m] and the land of the Babylonians[c]:

2 "Announce and proclaim[n] among the nations,
lift up a banner and proclaim it;
keep nothing back, but say,
'Babylon will be captured;[o]
Bel[p] will be put to shame,
Marduk[q] filled with terror.
Her images will be put to shame
and her idols filled with terror.'
3 A nation from the north will attack her
and lay waste her land.
No one will live[r] in it;
both men and animals[s] will flee away.

4 "In those days, at that time,"
declares the LORD,

49:34 [f]Ge 10:22 [g]2Ki 24:18
49:35 [h]Isa 22:6
49:36 [i]ver 32
49:37 [j]Jer 30:24 [k]Jer 9:16
49:39 [l]Jer 48:47
50:1 [m]Ge 10:10; Isa 13:1
50:2 [n]Jer 4:16 [o]Jer 51:31 [p]Isa 46:1 [q]Jer 51:47
50:3 [r]ver 13; Isa 14:22-23 [s]Zep 1:3

[a] 23 Hebrew *on* or *by*
[b] 32 Or *who clip the hair by their foreheads*
[c] 1 Or *Chaldeans*; also in verses 8, 25, 35 and 45

"the people of Israel and the
people of Judah together[t]
will go in tears[u] to seek[v] the
LORD their God.
5They will ask the way to Zion
and turn their faces toward it.
They will come[w] and bind
themselves to the LORD
in an everlasting covenant[x]
that will not be forgotten.

6"My people have been lost sheep;[y]
their shepherds have led them
astray
and caused them to roam on the
mountains.
They wandered over mountain and
hill[z]
and forgot their own resting
place.[a]
7Whoever found them devoured
them;
their enemies said, 'We are not
guilty,[b]
for they sinned against the LORD,
their true pasture,
the LORD, the hope[c] of their
fathers.'

8"Flee[d] out of Babylon;
leave the land of the
Babylonians;
and be like the goats that lead
the flock.
9For I will stir up and bring against
Babylon
an alliance of great nations from
the land of the north.
They will take up their positions
against her,
and from the north she will be
captured.
Their arrows will be like skilled
warriors
who do not return
empty-handed.
10So Babylonia[a] will be plundered;
all who plunder her will have
their fill,"
declares the LORD.

11"Because you rejoice and are glad,
you who pillage my
inheritance,[e]
because you frolic like a heifer
threshing grain
and neigh like stallions,
12your mother will be greatly
ashamed;
she who gave you birth will be
disgraced.
She will be the least of the
nations—
a wilderness, a dry land, a desert.
13Because of the LORD's anger she
will not be inhabited
but will be completely desolate.
All who pass Babylon will be
horrified and scoff[f]
because of all her wounds.[g]

14"Take up your positions around
Babylon,
all you who draw the bow.[h]
Shoot at her! Spare no arrows,
for she has sinned against
the LORD.
15Shout[i] against her on every
side!
She surrenders, her towers
fall,
her walls[j] are torn down.
Since this is the vengeance[k]
of the LORD,
take vengeance on her;
do to her[l] as she has done to
others.
16Cut off from Babylon the sower,
and the reaper with his sickle at
harvest.
Because of the sword[m] of the
oppressor
let everyone return to his own
people,[n]
let everyone flee to his own
land.[o]

17"Israel is a scattered flock
that lions[p] have chased away.
The first to devour him
was the king[q] of Assyria;
the last to crush his bones
was Nebuchadnezzar[r] king[s] of
Babylon."

18Therefore this is what the LORD Almighty, the God of Israel, says:

"I will punish the king of Babylon
and his land
as I punished the king[t] of
Assyria.[u]
19But I will bring[v] Israel back to his
own pasture
and he will graze on Carmel and
Bashan;
his appetite will be satisfied
on the hills[w] of Ephraim and
Gilead.
20In those days, at that time,"
declares the LORD,
"search will be made for Israel's
guilt,
but there will be none,
and for the sins[x] of Judah,
but none will be found,
for I will forgive[y] the remnant[z]
I spare.

21"Attack the land of Merathaim
and those who live in Pekod.[a]

50:4 [t]Jer 3:18; Hos 1:11 [u]Ezr 3:12; Jer 31:9 [v]Hos 3:5 **50:5** [w]Jer 33:7 [x]Isa 55:3; Jer 32:40; Heb 8:6-10 **50:6** [y]Isa 53:6; Mt 9:36; 10:6 [z]Jer 3:6; Eze 34:6 [a]ver 19 **50:7** [b]Jer 2:3 [c]Jer 14:8 **50:8** [d]Isa 48:20; Jer 51:6; Rev 18:4 **50:11** [e]Isa 47:6

50:13 [f]Jer 18:16 [g]Jer 49:17 **50:14** [h]ver 29,42 **50:15** [i]Jer 51:14 [j]Jer 51:44,58 [k]Jer 51:6 [l]Ps 137:8; Rev 18:6 **50:16** [m]Jer 25:38 [n]Isa 13:14 [o]Jer 51:9 **50:17** [p]Jer 2:15 [q]2Ki 17:6 [r]2Ki 24:10,14 [s]2Ki 25:7 **50:18** [t]Isa 10:12 [u]Eze 31:3 **50:19** [v]Jer 31:10; Eze 34:13 [w]Jer 31:5; 33:12 **50:20** [x]Mic 7:18,19 [y]Jer 31:34 [z]Isa 1:9 **50:21** [a]Eze 23:23

[a]*10* Or *Chaldea*

Pursue, kill and completely
destroy[a] them,"
declares the LORD.
"Do everything I have
commanded you.
22The noise[b] of battle is in the land,
the noise of great destruction!
23How broken and shattered
is the hammer of the whole
earth!
How desolate[c] is Babylon
among the nations!
24I set a trap[d] for you, O Babylon,
and you were caught before you
knew it;
you were found and captured[e]
because you opposed[f] the
LORD.
25The LORD has opened his arsenal
and brought out the weapons[g]
of his wrath,
for the Sovereign LORD Almighty
has work to do
in the land of the Babylonians.[h]
26Come against her from afar.
Break open her granaries;
pile her up like heaps of grain.
Completely destroy[i] her
and leave her no remnant.
27Kill all her young bulls;
let them go down to the
slaughter!
Woe to them! For their day has
come,
the time for them to be
punished.
28Listen to the fugitives and refugees
from Babylon
declaring in Zion[j]
how the LORD our God has taken
vengeance,[k]
vengeance for his temple.

29"Summon archers against Babylon,
all those who draw the bow.[l]
Encamp all around her;
let no one escape.
Repay[m] her for her deeds;[n]
do to her as she has done.
For she has defied[o] the LORD,
the Holy One of Israel.
30Therefore, her young men[p] will
fall in the streets;
all her soldiers will be silenced in
that day,"
declares the LORD.
31"See, I am against[q] you,
O arrogant one,"
declares the Lord, the LORD
Almighty,
"for your day has come,
the time for you to be punished.
32The arrogant one will stumble and
fall
and no one will help her up;
I will kindle a fire[r] in her towns
that will consume all who are
around her."

33This is what the LORD Almighty
says:

"The people of Israel are
oppressed,[s]
and the people of Judah as well.
All their captors hold them fast,
refusing to let them go.[t]
34Yet their Redeemer is strong;
the LORD Almighty[u] is his name.
He will vigorously defend their
cause[v]
so that he may bring rest[w] to
their land,
but unrest to those who live in
Babylon.

35"A sword[x] against the
Babylonians!"
declares the LORD—
"against those who live in Babylon
and against her officials and
wise[y] men!
36A sword against her false prophets!
They will become fools.
A sword against her warriors![z]
They will be filled with terror.
37A sword against her horses and
chariots[a]
and all the foreigners in her
ranks!
They will become women.[b]
A sword against her treasures!
They will be plundered.
38A drought on[b] her waters!
They will dry[c] up.
For it is a land of idols,[d]
idols that will go mad with
terror.

39"So desert creatures and hyenas
will live there,
and there the owl will dwell.
It will never again be inhabited
or lived in from generation to
generation.[e]
40As God overthrew Sodom and
Gomorrah[f]
along with their neighboring
towns,"
declares the LORD,
"so no one will live there;
no man will dwell in it.

41"Look! An army is coming from the
north;[g]
a great nation and many kings
are being stirred up from the
ends of the earth.[h]
42They are armed with bows[i] and
spears;

50:22 [b]Jer 4:19-21; 51:54 **50:23** [c]Isa 14:16 **50:24** [d]Da 5:30-31 [e]Jer 51:31 [f]Job 9:4 **50:25** [g]Isa 13:5 [h]Jer 51:25,55 **50:26** [i]Isa 14:22-23 **50:28** [j]Isa 48:20; Jer 51:10 [k]ver 15 **50:29** [l]ver 14 [m]Rev 18:6 [n]Jer 51:56 [o]Isa 47:10 **50:30** [p]Isa 13:18; Jer 49:26 **50:31** [q]Jer 21:13 **50:32** [r]Jer 21:14; 49:27

50:33 [s]Isa 58:6 [t]Isa 14:17 **50:34** [u]Jer 51:19 [v]Jer 15:21; 51:36 [w]Isa 14:7 **50:35** [x]Jer 47:6 [y]Da 5:7 **50:36** [z]Jer 49:22 **50:37** [a]Jer 51:21 [b]Jer 51:30; Na 3:13 **50:38** [c]Jer 51:36 [d]ver 2 **50:39** [e]Isa 13:19-22; 34:13-15; Jer 51:37; Rev 18:2 **50:40** [f]Ge 19:24 **50:41** [g]Jer 6:22 [h]Isa 13:4; Jer 51:22-28 **50:42** [i]ver 14

a *21* The Hebrew term refers to the irrevocable giving over of things or persons to the LORD, often by totally destroying them; also in verse 26. **b** *38* Or *A sword against*

they are cruel and without
mercy.[j]
They sound like the roaring sea[k]
as they ride on their horses;
they come like men in battle
formation
to attack you, O Daughter of
Babylon.[l]
43The king of Babylon has heard
reports about them,
and his hands hang limp.
Anguish has gripped him,
pain like that of a woman in
labor.
44Like a lion coming up from
Jordan's thickets
to a rich pastureland,
I will chase Babylon from its land
in an instant.
Who is the chosen[m] one I will
appoint for this?
Who is like me and who can
challenge me?[n]
And what shepherd can stand
against me?"
45Therefore, hear what the LORD has
planned against Babylon,
what he has purposed[o] against
the land of the Babylonians:
The young of the flock will be
dragged away;
he will completely destroy their
pasture because of them.
46At the sound of Babylon's capture
the earth will tremble;
its cry[p] will resound among the
nations.

51 This is what the LORD says:

"See, I will stir up the spirit of a
destroyer
against Babylon and the people
of Leb Kamai.[a]
2I will send foreigners to Babylon
to winnow[q] her and to
devastate her land;
they will oppose her on every side
in the day of her disaster.
3Let not the archer string his bow,[r]
nor let him put on his armor.[s]
Do not spare her young men;
completely destroy[b] her army.
4They will fall[t] down slain in
Babylon,[c]
fatally wounded in her streets.[u]
5For Israel and Judah have not been
forsaken[v]
by their God, the LORD Almighty,
though their land[d] is full of guilt[w]
before the Holy One of Israel.
6"Flee[x] from Babylon!
Run for your lives!
Do not be destroyed because of
her sins.[y]

50:42
[j]Isa 13:18
[k]Isa 5:30
[l]Jer 6:23
50:44
[m]Nu 16:5
[n]Job 41:10; Isa 46:9; Jer 49:19
50:45
[o]Ps 33:11; Isa 14:24; Jer 51:11
50:46
[p]Rev 18:9-10
51:2
[q]Isa 41:16; Jer 15:7; Mt 3:12
51:3
[r]Jer 50:29
[s]Jer 46:4
51:4
[t]Isa 13:15
[u]Jer 49:26; 50:30
51:5
[v]Isa 54:6-8
[w]Hos 4:1
51:6
[x]Jer 50:8
[y]Nu 16:26; Rev 18:4
[z]Jer 50:15
[a]Jer 25:14
51:7
[b]Jer 25:15-16; Rev 14:8-10; 17:4
51:8
[c]Isa 21:9; Rev 14:8
[d]Jer 46:11
51:9
[e]Isa 13:14; Jer 50:16
[f]Rev 18:4-5
51:10
[g]Mic 7:9
[h]Jer 50:28
51:11
[i]Jer 50:9
[j]Jer 46:4
[k]ver 28
[l]Jer 50:45
[m]Jer 50:28
51:13
[n]Rev 17:1,15
[o]Isa 45:3; Hab 2:9
51:14
[p]Am 6:8
[q]ver 27; Na 3:15
[r]Jer 50:15
51:15
[s]Ge 1:1; Job 9:8; Ps 104:2

It is time for the LORD's
vengeance;[z]
he will pay[a] her what she
deserves.
7Babylon was a gold cup[b] in the
LORD's hand;
she made the whole earth drunk.
The nations drank her wine;
therefore they have now gone
mad.
8Babylon will suddenly fall[c] and be
broken.
Wail over her!
Get balm[d] for her pain;
perhaps she can be healed.
9" 'We would have healed Babylon,
but she cannot be healed;
let us leave[e] her and each go to
his own land,
for her judgment[f] reaches to
the skies,
it rises as high as the clouds.'
10" 'The LORD has vindicated[g] us;
come, let us tell in Zion
what the LORD our God has
done.'[h]
11"Sharpen the arrows,[i]
take up the shields![j]
The LORD has stirred up the kings
of the Medes,[k]
because his purpose[l] is to
destroy Babylon.
The LORD will take vengeance,
vengeance for his temple.[m]
12Lift up a banner against the walls
of Babylon!
Reinforce the guard,
station the watchmen,
prepare an ambush!
The LORD will carry out his
purpose,
his decree against the people of
Babylon.
13You who live by many waters[n]
and are rich in treasures,[o]
your end has come,
the time for you to be cut off.
14The LORD Almighty has sworn by
himself:[p]
I will surely fill you with men, as
with a swarm of locusts,[q]
and they will shout[r] in triumph
over you.
15"He made the earth by his power;
he founded the world by his
wisdom
and stretched[s] out the heavens
by his understanding.

a1 *Leb Kamai* is a cryptogram for Chaldea, that is, Babylonia. **b**3 The Hebrew term refers to the irrevocable giving over of things or persons to the LORD, often by totally destroying them. **c**4 Or *Chaldea* **d**5 Or / *and the land* ⌞*of the Babylonians*⌟

16When he thunders,[t] the waters in
the heavens roar;
he makes clouds rise from the
ends of the earth.
He sends lightning with the rain
and brings out the wind from his
storehouses.[u]

17"Every man is senseless and
without knowledge;
every goldsmith is shamed by his
idols.
His images are a fraud;[v]
they have no breath in them.
18They are worthless,[w] the objects of
mockery;
when their judgment comes,
they will perish.
19He who is the Portion of Jacob is
not like these,
for he is the Maker of all things,
including the tribe of his
inheritance—
the LORD Almighty is his name.

20"You are my war club,[x]
my weapon for battle—
with you I shatter[y] nations,
with you I destroy kingdoms,
21with you I shatter horse and
rider,[z]
with you I shatter chariot and
driver,
22with you I shatter man and
woman,
with you I shatter old man and
youth,
with you I shatter young man
and maiden,[a]
23with you I shatter shepherd and
flock,
with you I shatter farmer and
oxen,
with you I shatter governors and
officials.[b]

24"Before your eyes I will repay[c]
Babylon and all who live in Babylonia[a]
for all the wrong they have done in
Zion," declares the LORD.

25"I am against you, O destroying
mountain,
you who destroy the whole
earth,"
declares the LORD.
"I will stretch out my hand against
you,
roll you off the cliffs,
and make you a burned-out
mountain.[d]
26No rock will be taken from you for
a cornerstone,
nor any stone for a foundation,
for you will be desolate[e]
forever,"
declares the LORD.

27"Lift up a banner[f] in the land!
Blow the trumpet among the
nations!
Prepare the nations for battle
against her;
summon against her these
kingdoms:[g]
Ararat,[h] Minni and Ashkenaz.[i]
Appoint a commander against her;
send up horses like a swarm of
locusts.
28Prepare the nations for battle
against her—
the kings of the Medes,[j]
their governors and all their
officials,
and all the countries they rule.
29The land trembles and writhes,
for the LORD's purposes against
Babylon stand—
to lay waste the land of Babylon
so that no one will live there.[k]
30Babylon's warriors[l] have stopped
fighting;
they remain in their strongholds.
Their strength is exhausted;
they have become like women.[m]
Her dwellings are set on fire;
the bars[n] of her gates are
broken.
31One courier[o] follows another
and messenger follows
messenger
to announce to the king of Babylon
that his entire city is captured,
32the river crossings seized,
the marshes set on fire,
and the soldiers terrified.[p]"

33This is what the LORD Almighty, the
God of Israel, says:

"The Daughter of Babylon is like a
threshing floor[q]
at the time it is trampled;
the time to harvest[r] her will
soon come."

34"Nebuchadnezzar[s] king of
Babylon has devoured us,
he has thrown us into confusion,
he has made us an empty jar.
Like a serpent he has swallowed us
and filled his stomach with our
delicacies,
and then has spewed us out.
35May the violence done to our
flesh[b] be upon Babylon,"
say the inhabitants of Zion.
"May our blood be on those who
live in Babylonia,"
says Jerusalem.[t]

36Therefore, this is what the LORD
says:

51:16 [t]Ps 18:11-13 [u]Ps 135:7; Jnh 1:4 **51:17** [v]Isa 44:20; Hab 2:18-19 **51:18** [w]Jer 18:15 **51:20** [x]Isa 10:5 [y]Mic 4:13 **51:21** [z]Ex 15:1 **51:22** [a]2Ch 36:17; Isa 13:17-18 **51:23** [b]ver 57 **51:24** [c]Jer 50:15 **51:25** [d]Zec 4:7 **51:26** [e]ver 29; Isa 13:19-22; Jer 50:12
51:27 [f]Isa 13:2; Jer 50:2 [g]Jer 25:14 [h]Ge 8:4 [i]Ge 10:3 **51:28** [j]ver 11 **51:29** [k]ver 43; Isa 13:20 **51:30** [l]Jer 50:36 [m]Isa 19:16 [n]Isa 45:2; La 2:9; Na 3:13 **51:31** [o]2Sa 18:19-31 **51:32** [p]Jer 50:36 **51:33** [q]Isa 21:10 [r]Isa 17:5; Hos 6:11 **51:34** [s]Jer 50:17 **51:35** [t]ver 24; Ps 137:8

[a]*24* Or *Chaldea;* also in verse 35 [b]*35* Or *done to us and to our children*

"See, I will defend your cause[u]
and avenge[v] you;
I will dry up[w] her sea
and make her springs dry.
37Babylon will be a heap of ruins,
a haunt[x] of jackals,
an object of horror and scorn,
a place where no one lives.[y]
38Her people all roar like young lions,
they growl like lion cubs.
39But while they are aroused,
I will set out a feast for them
and make them drunk,
so that they shout with laughter—
then sleep forever and not awake,"
declares the LORD.[z]
40"I will bring them down
like lambs to the slaughter,
like rams and goats.

41"How Sheshach[a][a] will be captured,[b]
the boast of the whole earth seized!
What a horror Babylon will be
among the nations!
42The sea will rise over Babylon;
its roaring waves[c] will cover her.
43Her towns will be desolate,
a dry and desert land,
a land where no one lives,
through which no man travels.[d]
44I will punish Bel[e] in Babylon
and make him spew out[f] what he has swallowed.
The nations will no longer stream to him.
And the wall[g] of Babylon will fall.
45"Come out[h] of her, my people!
Run[i] for your lives!
Run from the fierce anger of the LORD.
46Do not lose heart or be afraid[j]
when rumors[k] are heard in the land;
one rumor comes this year,
another the next,
rumors of violence in the land
and of ruler against ruler.
47For the time will surely come
when I will punish the idols[l] of Babylon;
her whole land will be disgraced[m]
and her slain will all lie fallen within her.
48Then heaven and earth and all that is in them
will shout[n] for joy over Babylon,
for out of the north[o]
destroyers will attack her,"
declares the LORD.

49"Babylon must fall because of Israel's slain,
just as the slain in all the earth
have fallen because of Babylon.[p]
50You who have escaped the sword,
leave[q] and do not linger!
Remember[r] the LORD in a distant land,
and think on Jerusalem."

51"We are disgraced,[s]
for we have been insulted
and shame covers our faces,
because foreigners have entered
the holy places of the LORD's house."[t]

52"But days are coming," declares the LORD,
"when I will punish her idols,[u]
and throughout her land
the wounded will groan.
53Even if Babylon reaches the sky[v]
and fortifies her lofty stronghold,
I will send destroyers[w] against her,"
declares the LORD.

54"The sound of a cry comes from Babylon,
the sound of great destruction[x]
from the land of the Babylonians.[b]
55The LORD will destroy Babylon;
he will silence her noisy din.
Waves[y] ⌊of enemies⌋ will rage like great waters;
the roar of their voices will resound.
56A destroyer[z] will come against Babylon;
her warriors will be captured,
and their bows will be broken.[a]
For the LORD is a God of retribution;
he will repay[b] in full.
57I will make her officials and wise men drunk,
her governors, officers and warriors as well;
they will sleep[c] forever and not awake,"
declares the King,[d] whose name
is the LORD Almighty.

58This is what the LORD Almighty says:

"Babylon's thick wall[e] will be leveled
and her high gates set on fire;
the peoples[f] exhaust themselves for nothing,
the nations' labor is only fuel for the flames."[g]

51:36 [u]Ps 140:12; Jer 50:34; La 3:58 [v]ver 6; Ro 12:19 [w]Jer 50:38
51:37 [x]Isa 13:22; Rev 18:2 [y]Jer 50:13,39
51:39 [z]ver 57
51:41 [a]Jer 25:26 [b]Isa 13:19
51:42 [c]Isa 8:7
51:43 [d]ver 29,62; Isa 13:20; Jer 2:6
51:44 [e]Isa 46:1 [f]ver 34 [g]ver 58; Jer 50:15
51:45 [h]Rev 18:4 [i]ver 6; Isa 48:20; Jer 50:8
51:46 [j]Jer 46:27 [k]2Ki 19:7
51:47 [l]ver 52; Isa 46:1-2; Jer 50:2 [m]Jer 50:12
51:48 [n]Isa 44:23; Rev 18:20 [o]ver 11
51:49 [p]Ps 137:8; Jer 50:29
51:50 [q]ver 45 [r]Ps 137:6
51:51 [s]Ps 44:13-16; 79:4 [t]La 1:10
51:52 [u]ver 47
51:53 [v]Ge 11:4; Isa 14:13-14 [w]Jer 49:16
51:54 [x]Jer 50:22
51:55 [y]Ps 18:4
51:56 [z]ver 48 [a]Ps 46:9 [b]ver 6; Ps 94:1-2; Hab 2:8
51:57 [c]Ps 76:5; Jer 25:27 [d]Jer 46:18; 48:15
51:58 [e]ver 44 [f]ver 64 [g]Hab 2:13

a *41* *Sheshach* is a cryptogram for Babylon.
b *54* Or *Chaldeans*

59This is the message Jeremiah gave
to the staff officer Seraiah son of Neriah,[h] the son of Mahseiah, when he
went to Babylon with Zedekiah[i] king
of Judah in the fourth[j] year of his
reign. 60Jeremiah had written on a
scroll[k] about all the disasters that
would come upon Babylon—all that
had been recorded concerning Babylon. 61He said to Seraiah, "When you
get to Babylon, see that you read
all these words aloud. 62Then say,
'O LORD, you have said you will destroy
this place, so that neither man nor animal will live in it; it will be desolate[l]
forever.' 63When you finish reading this
scroll, tie a stone to it and throw it into
the Euphrates. 64Then say, 'So will Babylon sink to rise no more because of
the disaster I will bring upon her. And
her people[m] will fall.' "

The words of Jeremiah end[n] here.

The Fall of Jerusalem

52 Zedekiah[o] was twenty-one years
old when he became king, and he
reigned in Jerusalem eleven years. His
mother's name was Hamutal daughter
of Jeremiah; she was from Libnah.[p]
2He did evil in the eyes of the LORD, just
as Jehoiakim[q] had done. 3It was because of the LORD's anger that all this
happened to Jerusalem and Judah,[r]
and in the end he thrust them from his
presence.

Now Zedekiah rebelled[s] against the
king of Babylon.

4So in the ninth year of Zedekiah's
reign, on the tenth[t] day of the tenth
month, Nebuchadnezzar king of Babylon marched against Jerusalem[u] with
his whole army. They camped outside
the city and built siege works all
around it.[v] 5The city was kept under
siege until the eleventh year of King
Zedekiah.

6By the ninth day of the fourth
month the famine in the city had become so severe that there was no food
for the people to eat.[w] 7Then the city
wall was broken through, and the
whole army fled. They left the city at
night through the gate between the two
walls near the king's garden, though
the Babylonians[a] were surrounding
the city. They fled toward the Arabah,[b]
8but the Babylonian[c] army pursued
King Zedekiah and overtook him in the
plains of Jericho. All his soldiers were
separated from him and scattered,
9and he was captured.[x]

He was taken to the king of Babylon
at Riblah[y] in the land of Hamath,[z]
where he pronounced sentence on
him. 10There at Riblah the king of Babylon slaughtered the sons[a] of Zedekiah before his eyes; he also killed all the
officials of Judah. 11Then he put out
Zedekiah's eyes, bound him with
bronze shackles and took him to Babylon, where he put him in prison till
the day of his death.[b]

12On the tenth day of the fifth[c]
month, in the nineteenth year of Nebuchadnezzar king of Babylon, Nebuzaradan[d] commander of the imperial
guard, who served the king of Babylon,
came to Jerusalem. 13He set fire[e] to
the temple[f] of the LORD, the royal palace and all the houses of Jerusalem.
Every important building he burned
down. 14The whole Babylonian army
under the commander of the imperial
guard broke down all the walls[g]
around Jerusalem. 15Nebuzaradan the
commander of the guard carried into
exile some of the poorest people and
those who remained in the city, along
with the rest of the craftsmen[d] and
those who had gone over to the king of
Babylon. 16But Nebuzaradan left behind[h] the rest of the poorest people
of the land to work the vineyards and
fields.

17The Babylonians broke up the
bronze pillars,[i] the movable stands[j]
and the bronze Sea[k] that were at the
temple of the LORD and they carried all
the bronze to Babylon.[l] 18They also
took away the pots, shovels, wick trimmers, sprinkling bowls, dishes and all
the bronze articles used in the temple
service.[m] 19The commander of the imperial guard took away the basins, censers,[n] sprinkling bowls, pots, lampstands, dishes and bowls used for drink
offerings—all that were made of pure
gold or silver.

20The bronze from the two pillars,
the Sea and the twelve bronze bulls under it, and the movable stands, which
King Solomon had made for the temple
of the LORD, was more than could be
weighed.[o] 21Each of the pillars was
eighteen cubits high and twelve cubits
in circumference[e]; each was four fingers thick, and hollow.[p] 22The bronze
capital[q] on top of the one pillar was
five cubits[f] high and was decorated
with a network and pomegranates of
bronze all around. The other pillar,
with its pomegranates, was similar.
23There were ninety-six pomegranates
on the sides; the total number of

51:59 [h]Jer 36:4 [i]Jer 52:1 [j]Jer 28:1
51:60 [k]Jer 30:2; 36:2
51:62 [l]Isa 13:20; Jer 50:13,39
51:64 [m]ver 58 [n]Job 31:40
52:1 [o]2Ki 24:17 [p]Jos 10:29; 2Ki 8:22
52:2 [q]Jer 36:30
52:3 [r]Isa 3:1 [s]Eze 17:12-16
52:4 [t]Zec 8:19 [u]2Ki 25:1-7; Jer 39:1 [v]Eze 24:1-2
52:6 [w]Isa 3:1
52:9 [x]Jer 32:4 [y]Nu 34:11 [z]Nu 13:21
52:10 [a]Jer 22:30
52:11 [b]Eze 12:13
52:12 [c]Zec 7:5; 8:19 [d]Jer 39:9
52:13 [e]2Ch 36:19; Ps 74:8; La 2:6 [f]Ps 79:1; Mic 3:12
52:14 [g]Ne 1:3
52:16 [h]Jer 40:6
52:17 [i]1Ki 7:15 [j]1Ki 7:27-37 [k]1Ki 7:23 [l]Jer 27:19-22
52:18 [m]Ex 27:3; 1Ki 7:45
52:19 [n]1Ki 7:50
52:20 [o]1Ki 7:47
52:21 [p]1Ki 7:15
52:22 [q]1Ki 7:16

a *7* Or *Chaldeans*; also in verse 17 b *7* Or *the Jordan Valley* c *8* Or *Chaldean*; also in verse 14 d *15* Or *populace* e *21* That is, about 27 feet (about 8.1 meters) high and 18 feet (about 5.4 meters) in circumference
f *22* That is, about 7 1/2 feet (about 2.3 meters)

pomegranates[r] above the surrounding network was a hundred.

24The commander of the guard took as prisoners Seraiah[s] the chief priest, Zephaniah[t] the priest next in rank and the three doorkeepers. 25Of those still in the city, he took the officer in charge of the fighting men, and seven royal advisers. He also took the secretary who was chief officer in charge of conscripting the people of the land and sixty of his men who were found in the city. 26Nebuzaradan[u] the commander took them all and brought them to the king of Babylon at Riblah. 27There at Riblah, in the land of Hamath, the king had them executed.

So Judah went into captivity, away[v] from her land. 28This is the number of the people Nebuchadnezzar carried into exile:[w]

in the seventh year, 3,023 Jews;
29in Nebuchadnezzar's eighteenth year,
832 people from Jerusalem;
30in his twenty-third year,
745 Jews taken into exile by Nebuzaradan the commander of the imperial guard.
There were 4,600 people in all.

Jehoiachin Released

31In the thirty-seventh year of the exile of Jehoiachin king of Judah, in the year Evil-Merodach[a] became king of Babylon, he released Jehoiachin king of Judah and freed him from prison on the twenty-fifth day of the twelfth month. 32He spoke kindly to him and gave him a seat of honor higher than those of the other kings who were with him in Babylon. 33So Jehoiachin put aside his prison clothes and for the rest of his life ate regularly at the king's table.[x] 34Day by day the king of Babylon gave Jehoiachin a regular allowance[y] as long as he lived, till the day of his death.

52:23 [r] 1Ki 7:20
52:24 [s] 2Ki 25:18 [t] Jer 21:1; 37:3
52:26 [u] ver 12
52:27 [v] Jer 20:4
52:28 [w] 2Ki 24:14-16; 2Ch 36:20
52:33 [x] 2Sa 9:7
52:34 [y] 2Sa 9:10

[a] *31* Also called *Amel-Marduk*

LAMENTATIONS

AT A GLANCE

Key Principle: Even when our immediate circumstances appear disastrous, God's unchanging character and faithfulness always give us reason to have hope.
Author: Jeremiah
Time and Place: 586–580 B.C. / The remains of Jerusalem
Key Verses: 1:1, 12; 2:5–6, 17; 3:22–24; 5:21

BENEFIT

The sad and mournful set of five poems known as Lamentations is striking in its emotional content, beauty and literary structure. Writing with a broken heart, Jeremiah identifies with his people's sorrow and the apparent destruction of their future, but he also pauses to remember God's faithfulness and compassion. This book is a reminder to us to hold fast to God's character, especially in the distressing times of life.

SETTING

The prophet Jeremiah wrote Lamentations while still feeling the sting of the fulfillment of what he had prophesied. He had warned the people repeatedly about Jerusalem's impending devastation, and now it had come to pass. Jeremiah witnessed Nebuchadnezzar's siege of Jerusalem from January of 588 B.C. until its fall on July 19 of 586 B.C. (Jeremiah 39; 52). Babylonian troops burned the holy city and Solomon's temple on August 15. After this destruction, they killed the city's Jewish leaders and deported the bulk of its inhabitants to Babylon. Jeremiah remained behind, but was eventually forced to go to Egypt by Jewish survivors who refused to listen when he exhorted them to stay in the land of Judah (Jeremiah 43:1–7).

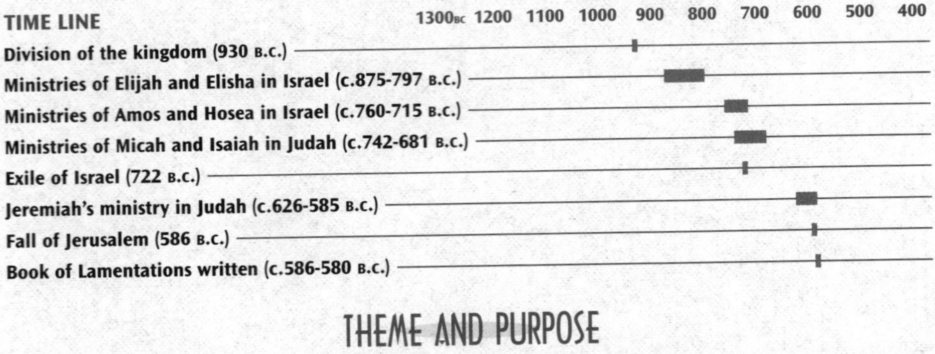

THEME AND PURPOSE

The dominant theme of Lamentations is mourning over the destruction of the once-splendid city of Jerusalem. Instead of gloating over the fact that his prophetic warnings had been fulfilled, Jeremiah grieves over the plight of the same countrymen who had scorned and abused him for so many years. As he writes, Jeremiah not only speaks for himself, but also personifies Jerusalem and all the captives. Another theme acknowledges that God's judgment on Judah was consistent with his righteous and holy character, and that the people's sins warranted the destruction. Finally, in the middle of his sorrow, Jeremiah sounds a note of hope that God will restore his people (3:22–24).

UNIQUE CONTRIBUTION

While Jeremiah anticipates the fall of Jerusalem, Lamentations looks back on this tragic event; the former is a book of warning, the latter a book of mourning. Lamentations is similar to the poetic portions of Jeremiah in that both share the same compassion and anguish over Judah's condition.

This book's literary structure in the Hebrew text is significant. The first four chapters are alphabetic acrostics; they begin with the first letter of the Hebrew alphabet (aleph) and move progressively through the remaining 21 letters. Thus, chapters 1 and 2 have 22 verses, and each verse begins with a different letter of the alphabet. While these chapters have three lines per verse, chapter 3 has only one line per verse, but it has 66 verses, with three verses allocated to each Hebrew letter. Chapter 4 has two lines per verse and is another acrostic of 22 verses. Chapter 5 has one line per verse, but while it has 22 verses, it is not an acrostic. These elegies also use the same mournful rhythm (called "limping meter") that was used in funeral dirges. This complex structure stands in contrast to the flowing emotional content of the book.

LINKS TO THE NEW TESTAMENT

Just as the prophet Jeremiah wept over the fallen city of Jerusalem, so Christ would also weep over the same city as he anticipated its future destruction in A.D. 70 (Matthew 23:37–38). Like Christ, Jeremiah was "despised and rejected by men, a man of sorrows and familiar with suffering" (Isaiah 53:3).

OVERVIEW

FOCUS	Jerusalem Deserted	Jerusalem Destroyed	Jeremiah's Distress	Jerusalem Defeated	Jeremiah's Desire
REFERENCE	1	2	3	4	5
TOPICS	Lament 1	Lament 2	Lament 3	Lament 4	Lament 5
	Desolation and Sorrow of Jerusalem	Indignation of God upon Jerusalem	Lamentation and Prayer of Jeremiah	Description of the Siege of Jerusalem	Prayer for the Restoration of Jerusalem
	God's Chastening and Control				God's Character
	Four Acrostic Laments				Non-acrostic Prayer
LOCATION	The Remains of Jerusalem				
TIME	Soon After the Fall of Jerusalem				

The first lament begins with Jeremiah's mournful elegy (1:1–11) over the recent fall of Jerusalem. It ends with a personification in which Jerusalem acknowledges that she has been left desolate because of her many sins (1:12–22). The second lament describes the extent and grievousness of Jerusalem's destruction, with the loss of its magnificent temple and palace (2). In the third lament, Jeremiah empathizes with his people's anguish, but also finds hope when he considers God's compassion and faithfulness (3). The fourth lament reviews the people's suffering during the siege on Jerusalem, and acknowledges that it was brought about by their sinful trust in human assistance rather than the Lord (4). The fifth lament is an elegiac poem that summarizes the people's grievous condition and prays for their restoration (5).

LAMENTATIONS

1[a] How deserted lies the city,
once so full of people!
How like a widow[a] is she,
who once was great[b] among the nations!
She who was queen among the provinces
has now become a slave.[c]

2 Bitterly she weeps[d] at night,
tears are upon her cheeks.
Among all her lovers[e]
there is none to comfort her.
All her friends have betrayed[f] her;
they have become her enemies.[g]

3 After affliction and harsh labor,
Judah has gone into exile.[h]
She dwells among the nations;
she finds no resting place.[i]
All who pursue her have overtaken her
in the midst of her distress.

4 The roads to Zion mourn,
for no one comes to her appointed feasts.
All her gateways are desolate,[j]
her priests groan,
her maidens grieve,
and she is in bitter anguish.[k]

5 Her foes have become her masters;
her enemies are at ease.
The LORD has brought her grief[l]
because of her many sins.
Her children have gone into exile,[m]
captive before the foe.

6 All the splendor has departed
from the Daughter of Zion.[n]
Her princes are like deer
that find no pasture;
in weakness they have fled
before the pursuer.

7 In the days of her affliction and wandering
Jerusalem remembers all the treasures
that were hers in days of old.
When her people fell into enemy hands,
there was no one to help her.[o]
Her enemies looked at her
and laughed at her destruction.

8 Jerusalem has sinned[p] greatly
and so has become unclean.
All who honored her despise her,
for they have seen her nakedness;[q]
she herself groans[r]
and turns away.

9 Her filthiness clung to her skirts;
she did not consider her future.[s]
Her fall[t] was astounding;
there was none to comfort[u] her.
"Look, O LORD, on my affliction,[v]
for the enemy has triumphed."

10 The enemy laid hands
on all her treasures;[w]
she saw pagan nations
enter her sanctuary[x]—
those you had forbidden[y]
to enter your assembly.

11 All her people groan[z]
as they search for bread;[a]
they barter their treasures for food
to keep themselves alive.
"Look, O LORD, and consider,
for I am despised."

12 "Is it nothing to you, all you who pass by?[b]
Look around and see.
Is any suffering like my suffering[c]
that was inflicted on me,
that the LORD brought on me
in the day of his fierce anger?[d]

13 "From on high he sent fire,
sent it down into my bones.[e]
He spread a net for my feet
and turned me back.
He made me desolate,[f]
faint[g] all the day long.

14 "My sins have been bound into a yoke[b];[h]
by his hands they were woven together.
They have come upon my neck
and the Lord has sapped my strength.
He has handed me over[i]
to those I cannot withstand.

15 "The Lord has rejected
all the warriors in my midst;[j]
he has summoned an army[k] against me
to[c] crush my young men.[l]
In his winepress the Lord has trampled
the Virgin Daughter of Judah.

1:1 [a] Isa 47:8 [b] 1Ki 4:21 [c] Isa 3:26; Jer 40:9
1:2 [d] Ps 6:6 [e] Jer 3:1 [f] Jer 4:30; Mic 7:5 [g] ver 16
1:3 [h] Jer 13:19 [i] Dt 28:65
1:4 [j] Jer 9:11 [k] Joel 1:8-13
1:5 [l] Jer 30:15 [m] Jer 39:9; 52:28-30
1:6 [n] Jer 13:18
1:7 [o] Jer 37:7; La 4:17
1:8 [p] ver 20; Isa 59:2-13 [q] Jer 13:22,26 [r] ver 21,22
1:9 [s] Dt 32:28-29; Isa 47:7; Eze 24:13 [t] Jer 13:18 [u] Ecc 4:1; Jer 16:7 [v] Ps 25:18
1:10 [w] Isa 64:11 [x] Ps 74:7-8; Jer 51:51 [y] Dt 23:3
1:11 [z] Ps 38:8 [a] Jer 52:6
1:12 [b] Jer 18:16 [c] ver 18 [d] Isa 13:13; Jer 30:24
1:13 [e] Job 30:30 [f] Jer 44:6 [g] Hab 3:16
1:14 [h] Dt 28:48; Isa 47:6 [i] Jer 32:5
1:15 [j] Jer 37:10 [k] Isa 41:2 [l] Isa 28:18; Jer 18:21

[a] This chapter is an acrostic poem, the verses of which begin with the successive letters of the Hebrew alphabet. [b] *14* Most Hebrew manuscripts; Septuagint *He kept watch over my sins* [c] *15* Or *has set a time for me / when he will*

16"This is why I weep
and my eyes overflow with tears.[m]
No one is near to comfort[n] me,
no one to restore my spirit.
My children are destitute
because the enemy has prevailed."[o]

17Zion stretches out her hands,[p]
but there is no one to comfort her.
The LORD has decreed for Jacob
that his neighbors become his foes;
Jerusalem has become
an unclean thing among them.

18"The LORD is righteous,
yet I rebelled[q] against his command.
Listen, all you peoples;
look upon my suffering.[r]
My young men and maidens
have gone into exile.[s]

19"I called to my allies
but they betrayed me.
My priests and my elders
perished[t] in the city
while they searched for food
to keep themselves alive.

20"See, O LORD, how distressed[u] I am!
I am in torment[v] within,
and in my heart I am disturbed,
for I have been most rebellious.
Outside, the sword bereaves;
inside, there is only death.[w]

21"People have heard my groaning,[x]
but there is no one to comfort me.[y]
All my enemies have heard of my distress;
they rejoice[z] at what you have done.
May you bring the day[a] you have announced
so they may become like me.

22"Let all their wickedness come before you;
deal with them
as you have dealt with me
because of all my sins.[b]
My groans are many
and my heart is faint."

2[a] How the Lord has covered the Daughter of Zion
with the cloud of his anger[b]![c]
He has hurled down the splendor of Israel
from heaven to earth;
he has not remembered his footstool[d]
in the day of his anger.

2Without pity[e] the Lord has swallowed[f] up
all the dwellings of Jacob;
in his wrath he has torn down
the strongholds[g] of the Daughter of Judah.
He has brought her kingdom and its princes
down to the ground[h] in dishonor.

3In fierce anger he has cut off
every horn[c][i] of Israel.
He has withdrawn his right hand[j]
at the approach of the enemy.
He has burned in Jacob like a flaming fire
that consumes everything around it.[k]

4Like an enemy he has strung his bow;[l]
his right hand is ready.
Like a foe he has slain
all who were pleasing to the eye;[m]
he has poured out his wrath like fire[n]
on the tent of the Daughter of Zion.

5The Lord is like an enemy;[o]
he has swallowed up Israel.
He has swallowed up all her palaces
and destroyed her strongholds.[p]
He has multiplied mourning and lamentation
for the Daughter of Judah.[q]

6He has laid waste his dwelling like a garden;
he has destroyed his place of meeting.[r]
The LORD has made Zion forget
her appointed feasts and her Sabbaths;[s]
in his fierce anger he has spurned
both king and priest.[t]

7The Lord has rejected his altar
and abandoned his sanctuary.
He has handed over to the enemy
the walls of her palaces;[u]
they have raised a shout in the house of the LORD
as on the day of an appointed feast.

8The LORD determined to tear down
the wall around the Daughter of Zion.

1:16 [m]La 2:11,18; 3:48-49 [n]Ps 69:20; Ecc 4:1 [o]ver 2; Jer 13:17; 14:17
1:17 [p]Jer 4:31
1:18 [q]1Sa 12:14 [r]ver 12 [s]Dt 28:32,41
1:19 [t]Jer 14:15; La 2:20
1:20 [u]Jer 4:19 [v]La 2:11 [w]Dt 32:25; Eze 7:15
1:21 [x]ver 8 [y]ver 4 [z]La 2:15 [a]Isa 47:11; Jer 30:16
1:22 [b]Ne 4:5
2:1 [c]La 3:44 [d]Ps 99:5; 132:7
2:2 [e]La 3:43 [f]Ps 21:9 [g]Ps 89:39-40; Mic 5:11 [h]Isa 25:12
2:3 [i]Ps 75:5,10 [j]Ps 74:11 [k]Isa 42:25; Jer 21:4-5,14
2:4 [l]Job 16:13; La 3:12-13 [m]Eze 24:16,25 [n]Isa 42:25; Jer 7:20
2:5 [o]Jer 30:14 [p]ver 2 [q]Jer 9:17-20
2:6 [r]Jer 52:13 [s]La 1:4; Zep 3:18 [t]La 4:16
2:7 [u]Ps 74:7-8; Isa 64:11; Jer 33:4-5

[a]This chapter is an acrostic poem, the verses of which begin with the successive letters of the Hebrew alphabet. [b]*1* Or *How the Lord in his anger / has treated the Daughter of Zion with contempt* [c]*3* Or / *all the strength*; or *every king*; *horn* here symbolizes strength.

He stretched out a measuring
line[v]
and did not withhold his hand
from destroying.
He made ramparts and walls
lament;
together they wasted away.[w]

9Her gates[x] have sunk into the
ground;
their bars he has broken and
destroyed.
Her king and her princes are
exiled[y] among the nations,
the law[z] is no more,
and her prophets no longer find
visions[a] from the LORD.

10The elders of the Daughter of Zion
sit on the ground in silence;
they have sprinkled dust on their
heads[b]
and put on sackcloth.[c]
The young women of Jerusalem
have bowed their heads to the
ground.[d]

11My eyes fail from weeping,[e]
I am in torment within,[f]
my heart is poured out[g] on the
ground
because my people are
destroyed,
because children and infants
faint[h]
in the streets of the city.

12They say to their mothers,
"Where is bread and wine?"
as they faint like wounded men
in the streets of the city,
as their lives ebb away
in their mothers' arms.[i]

13What can I say for you?
With what can I compare you,
O Daughter of Jerusalem?
To what can I liken you,
that I may comfort you,
O Virgin Daughter of Zion?[j]
Your wound is as deep as the
sea.[k]
Who can heal you?

14The visions of your prophets
were false and worthless;
they did not expose your sin
to ward off your captivity.[l]
The oracles they gave you
were false and misleading.[m]

15All who pass your way
clap their hands at you;[n]
they scoff[o] and shake their heads
at the Daughter of Jerusalem:
"Is this the city that was called
the perfection of beauty,[p]
the joy of the whole earth?"[q]

16All your enemies open their
mouths
wide against you;[r]
they scoff and gnash their teeth[s]
and say, "We have swallowed her
up.[t]
This is the day we have waited for;
we have lived to see it."

17The LORD has done what he
planned;
he has fulfilled his word,
which he decreed long ago.[u]
He has overthrown you without
pity,[v]
he has let the enemy gloat over
you,
he has exalted the horn[a] of your
foes.[w]

18The hearts of the people
cry out to the Lord.[x]
O wall of the Daughter of Zion,
let your tears[y] flow like a river
day and night;[z]
give yourself no relief,
your eyes no rest.[a]

19Arise, cry out in the night,
as the watches of the night
begin;
pour out your heart[b] like water
in the presence of the Lord.[c]
Lift up your hands to him
for the lives of your children,
who faint[d] from hunger
at the head of every street.

20"Look, O LORD, and consider:
Whom have you ever treated like
this?
Should women eat their
offspring,[e]
the children they have cared
for?[f]
Should priest and prophet be
killed[g]
in the sanctuary of the Lord?

21"Young and old lie together
in the dust of the streets;
my young men and maidens
have fallen by the sword.[h]
You have slain them in the day of
your anger;
you have slaughtered them
without pity.[i]

22"As you summon to a feast day,
so you summoned against me
terrors[j] on every side.
In the day of the LORD's anger
no one escaped or survived;
those I cared for and reared,[k]
my enemy has destroyed."

2:8 [v]2Ki 21:13; Isa 34:11 [w]Isa 3:26
2:9 [x]Ne 1:3 [y]Dt 28:36; 2Ki 24:15 [z]2Ch 15:3 [a]Jer 14:14
2:10 [b]Job 2:12 [c]Isa 15:3 [d]Job 2:13; Isa 3:26
2:11 [e]La 1:16; 3:48-51 [f]La 1:20 [g]ver 19; Ps 22:14 [h]La 4:4
2:12 [i]La 4:4
2:13 [j]Isa 37:22 [k]Jer 14:17; La 1:12
2:14 [l]Isa 58:1 [m]Jer 2:8; 23:25-32, 33-40; 29:9; Eze 13:3; 22:28
2:15 [n]Eze 25:6 [o]Jer 19:8 [p]Ps 50:2 [q]Ps 48:2
2:16 [r]Ps 56:2; La 3:46 [s]Job 16:9 [t]Ps 35:25
2:17 [u]Dt 28:15-45 [v]ver 2; Eze 5:11 [w]Ps 89:42
2:18 [x]Ps 119:145 [y]La 1:16 [z]Jer 9:1 [a]La 3:49
2:19 [b]1Sa 1:15; Ps 62:8 [c]Isa 26:9 [d]Isa 51:20
2:20 [e]Dt 28:53; Jer 19:9 [f]La 4:10 [g]Ps 78:64; Jer 14:15
2:21 [h]2Ch 36:17; Ps 78:62-63; Jer 6:11 [i]Jer 13:14; La 3:43; Zec 11:6
2:22 [j]Ps 31:13; Jer 6:25 [k]Hos 9:13

[a]17 *Horn* here symbolizes strength.

3 [a] I am the man who has seen
affliction
by the rod of his wrath.[l]
2He has driven me away and made
me walk
in darkness[m] rather than light;
3indeed, he has turned his hand
against me[n]
again and again, all day long.

4He has made my skin and my flesh
grow old
and has broken my bones.[o]
5He has besieged me and
surrounded me
with bitterness[p] and hardship.[q]
6He has made me dwell in darkness
like those long dead.[r]

7He has walled me in so I cannot
escape;[s]
he has weighed me down with
chains.[t]
8Even when I call out or cry for
help,
he shuts out my prayer.[u]
9He has barred my way with blocks
of stone;
he has made my paths
crooked.[v]

10Like a bear lying in wait,
like a lion in hiding,
11he dragged me from the path and
mangled[w] me
and left me without help.
12He drew his bow[x]
and made me the target[y] for his
arrows.[z]

13He pierced my heart
with arrows from his quiver.[a]
14I became the laughingstock[b] of all
my people;
they mock me in song[c] all day
long.
15He has filled me with bitter herbs
and sated me with gall.[d]

16He has broken my teeth with
gravel;[e]
he has trampled me in the dust.
17I have been deprived of peace;
I have forgotten what prosperity
is.
18So I say, "My splendor is gone
and all that I had hoped from
the LORD."[f]

19I remember my affliction and my
wandering,
the bitterness and the gall.
20I well remember them,
and my soul is downcast[g]
within me.[h]
21Yet this I call to mind
and therefore I have hope:

3:1 [l]Job 19:21; Ps 88:7
3:2 [m]Jer 4:23
3:3 [n]Isa 5:25
3:4 [o]Ps 51:8; Isa 38:13; Jer 50:17
3:5 [p]ver 19 [q]Jer 23:15
3:6 [r]Ps 88:5-6
3:7 [s]Job 3:23 [t]Jer 40:4
3:8 [u]Job 30:20; Ps 22:2
3:9 [v]Isa 63:17; Hos 2:6
3:11 [w]Hos 6:1
3:12 [x]La 2:4 [y]Job 7:20 [z]Ps 7:12-13; 38:2
3:13 [a]Job 6:4
3:14 [b]Jer 20:7 [c]Job 30:9
3:15 [d]Jer 9:15
3:16 [e]Pr 20:17
3:18 [f]Job 17:15
3:20 [g]Ps 42:5 [h]Ps 42:11
3:22 [i]Ps 78:38; Mal 3:6
3:23 [j]Zep 3:5
3:24 [k]Ps 16:5
3:25 [l]Isa 25:9; 30:18
3:26 [m]Ps 37:7; 40:1
3:28 [n]Jer 15:17
3:29 [o]Jer 31:17
3:30 [p]Job 16:10; Isa 50:6
3:31 [q]Ps 94:14; Isa 54:7
3:32 [r]Ps 78:38; Hos 11:8

22Because of the LORD's great love we
are not consumed,
for his compassions never fail.[i]
23They are new every morning;
great is your faithfulness.[j]
24I say to myself, "The LORD is my
portion;[k]
therefore I will wait for him."

25The LORD is good to those whose
hope is in him,
to the one who seeks him;[l]
26it is good to wait quietly
for the salvation of the LORD.[m]
27It is good for a man to bear the
yoke
while he is young.

28Let him sit alone in silence,[n]
for the LORD has laid it on him.
29Let him bury his face in the dust—
there may yet be hope.[o]
30Let him offer his cheek to one who
would strike him,[p]
and let him be filled with
disgrace.

31For men are not cast off
by the Lord forever.[q]
32Though he brings grief, he will
show compassion,
so great is his unfailing love.[r]

[a]This chapter is an acrostic poem; the verses of each stanza begin with the successive letters of the Hebrew alphabet, and the verses within each stanza begin with the same letter.

3:20–26

PROMISE 1

COPING WITH DISASTER

The worst possible thing had happened: Jeremiah's prophecies had been fulfilled, as he knew they would be. Jerusalem had been destroyed! Thousands of people had been killed or carried into exile. The temple had been destroyed, and Jerusalem's walls burned down. Jeremiah, sitting in the rubble of this once-proud city, bitterly mourned the destruction (1:1–3:20).

How does a godly man cope with disaster? Verses 20–26 demand a careful reading in this regard. Notice the way Jeremiah's statement of strength begins: "Yet . . ." (v. 21). He didn't minimize the crushing agony he experienced by saying, "Oh, its all right, everything will work out." No! Life was lousy! "Yet . . ." Everything he owned was gone! "Yet . . ." His friends and family had been killed! "Yet . . ." No job! "Yet . . ."

What will you put after the "Yet . . ."? Better read what's on the other side of this "Yet," because Jeremiah's God is your God and he never changes.

For the next Promise 1 reading go to page 887.

33For he does not willingly bring
affliction
or grief to the children of men.[s]

34To crush underfoot
all prisoners in the land,
35to deny a man his rights
before the Most High,
36to deprive a man of justice—
would not the Lord see such
things?[t]

37Who can speak and have it happen
if the Lord has not decreed it?[u]
38Is it not from the mouth of the
Most High
that both calamities and good
things come?[v]
39Why should any living man
complain
when punished for his sins?[w]

40Let us examine our ways and test
them,[x]
and let us return to the LORD.[y]
41Let us lift up our hearts and our
hands
to God in heaven,[z] and say:
42"We have sinned and rebelled[a]
and you have not forgiven.[b]

43"You have covered yourself with
anger and pursued us;
you have slain without pity.[c]
44You have covered yourself with a
cloud[d]
so that no prayer[e] can get
through.
45You have made us scum[f] and
refuse
among the nations.

46"All our enemies have opened their
mouths
wide against us.[g]
47We have suffered terror and
pitfalls,[h]
ruin and destruction.[i]"
48Streams of tears flow from my
eyes[j]
because my people are
destroyed.[k]

49My eyes will flow unceasingly,
without relief,[l]
50until the LORD looks down
from heaven and sees.[m]
51What I see brings grief to my soul
because of all the women of my
city.

52Those who were my enemies
without cause
hunted me like a bird.[n]
53They tried to end my life in a pit[o]
and threw stones at me;
54the waters closed over my head,[p]
and I thought I was about to be
cut off.

55I called on your name, O LORD,
from the depths of the pit.[q]
56You heard my plea:[r] "Do not
close your ears
to my cry for relief."
57You came near when I called you,
and you said, "Do not fear."[s]

58O Lord, you took up my case;[t]
you redeemed my life.[u]
59You have seen, O LORD, the wrong
done to me.[v]
Uphold my cause!
60You have seen the depth of their
vengeance,
all their plots against me.[w]

61O LORD, you have heard their
insults,
all their plots against me—
62what my enemies whisper and
mutter
against me all day long.[x]
63Look at them! Sitting or standing,
they mock me in their songs.

64Pay them back what they deserve,
O LORD,
for what their hands have
done.[y]
65Put a veil over their hearts,[z]
and may your curse be on them!
66Pursue them in anger and destroy
them
from under the heavens of the
LORD.

4

[a] How the gold has lost its luster,
the fine gold become dull!
The sacred gems are scattered
at the head of every street.[a]

2How the precious sons of Zion,
once worth their weight in gold,
are now considered as pots of clay,
the work of a potter's hands!

3Even jackals offer their breasts
to nurse their young,
but my people have become
heartless
like ostriches in the desert.[b]

4Because of thirst the infant's
tongue
sticks to the roof of its mouth;[c]
the children beg for bread,
but no one gives it to them.[d]

5Those who once ate delicacies
are destitute in the streets.
Those nurtured in purple[e]
now lie on ash heaps.[f]

6The punishment of my people
is greater than that of Sodom,[g]

3:33 [s]Eze 33:11
3:36 [t]Jer 22:3; Hab 1:13
3:37 [u]Ps 33:9-11
3:38 [v]Job 2:10; Isa 45:7; Jer 32:42
3:39 [w]Jer 30:15; Mic 7:9
3:40 [x]2Co 13:5 [y]Ps 119:59; 139:23-24
3:41 [z]Ps 25:1; 28:2
3:42 [a]Da 9:5 [b]Jer 5:7-9
3:43 [c]La 2:2,17,21
3:44 [d]Ps 97:2 [e]ver 8
3:45 [f]1Co 4:13
3:46 [g]La 2:16
3:47 [h]Jer 48:43 [i]Isa 24:17-18; 51:19
3:48 [j]La 1:16 [k]La 2:11
3:49 [l]Jer 14:17
3:50 [m]Isa 63:15
3:52 [n]Ps 35:7
3:53 [o]Jer 37:16
3:54 [p]Ps 69:2; Jnh 2:3-5
3:55 [q]Ps 130:1; Jnh 2:2
3:56 [r]Ps 55:1
3:57 [s]Isa 41:10
3:58 [t]Jer 51:36 [u]Ps 34:22; Jer 50:34
3:59 [v]Jer 18:19-20
3:60 [w]Jer 11:20; 18:18
3:62 [x]Eze 36:3
3:64 [y]Ps 28:4
3:65 [z]Isa 6:10
4:1 [a]Eze 7:19
4:3 [b]Job 39:16
4:4 [c]Ps 22:15 [d]La 2:11,12
4:5 [e]Jer 6:2 [f]Am 6:3-7
4:6 [g]Ge 19:25

[a]This chapter is an acrostic poem, the verses of which begin with the successive letters of the Hebrew alphabet.

which was overthrown in a
moment
without a hand turned to help
her.

7Their princes were brighter than
snow
and whiter than milk,
their bodies more ruddy than
rubies,
their appearance like sapphires.[a]

8But now they are blacker[h] than
soot;
they are not recognized in the
streets.
Their skin has shriveled on their
bones;[i]
it has become as dry as a stick.

9Those killed by the sword are
better off
than those who die of famine;
racked with hunger, they waste
away
for lack of food from the field.[j]

10With their own hands
compassionate women
have cooked their own
children,[k]
who became their food
when my people were destroyed.

11The LORD has given full vent to his
wrath;
he has poured out his fierce
anger.
He kindled a fire[l] in Zion
that consumed her
foundations.[m]

12The kings of the earth did not
believe,
nor did any of the world's
people,
that enemies and foes could enter
the gates of Jerusalem.[n]

13But it happened because of the
sins of her prophets
and the iniquities of her
priests,[o]
who shed within her
the blood of the righteous.

14Now they grope through the streets
like men who are blind.[p]
They are so defiled with blood[q]
that no one dares to touch their
garments.

15"Go away! You are unclean!" men
cry to them.
"Away! Away! Don't touch us!"
When they flee and wander about,
people among the nations say,
"They can stay here no
longer."[r]

16The LORD himself has scattered
them;
he no longer watches over
them.[s]
The priests are shown no honor,
the elders[t] no favor.

17Moreover, our eyes failed,
looking in vain[u] for help;[v]
from our towers we watched
for a nation[w] that could not
save us.

18Men stalked us at every step,
so we could not walk in our
streets.
Our end was near, our days were
numbered,
for our end had come.[x]

19Our pursuers were swifter
than eagles[y] in the sky;
they chased us[z] over the
mountains
and lay in wait for us in the
desert.

20The LORD's anointed,[a] our very life
breath,
was caught in their traps.[b]
We thought that under his shadow
we would live among the
nations.

21Rejoice and be glad, O Daughter of
Edom,
you who live in the land of Uz.
But to you also the cup[c] will be
passed;
you will be drunk and stripped
naked.[d]

22O Daughter of Zion, your
punishment will end;[e]
he will not prolong your exile.
But, O Daughter of Edom, he will
punish your sin
and expose your wickedness.[f]

5

Remember, O LORD, what has
happened to us;
look, and see our disgrace.[g]
2Our inheritance[h] has been turned
over to aliens,
our homes[i] to foreigners.
3We have become orphans and
fatherless,
our mothers like widows.[j]
4We must buy the water we drink;
our wood can be had only at a
price.[k]
5Those who pursue us are at our
heels;
we are weary[l] and find no rest.
6We submitted to Egypt and
Assyria[m]
to get enough bread.

4:8 [h]Job 30:28 [i]Ps 102:3-5 **4:9** [j]Jer 15:2; 16:4 **4:10** [k]Lev 26:29; Dt 28:53-57; Jer 19:9; La 2:20; Eze 5:10 **4:11** [l]Jer 17:27 [m]Dt 32:22; Jer 7:20; Eze 22:31 **4:12** [n]1Ki 9:9; Jer 21:13 **4:13** [o]Jer 5:31; 6:13; Eze 22:28; Mic 3:11 **4:14** [p]Isa 59:10 [q]Jer 2:34; 19:4 **4:15** [r]Lev 13:46 **4:16** [s]Isa 9:14-16 [t]La 5:12 **4:17** [u]Isa 20:5; Eze 29:16 [v]La 1:7 [w]Jer 37:7 **4:18** [x]Eze 7:2-12; Am 8:2 **4:19** [y]Dt 28:49 [z]Isa 5:26-28 **4:20** [a]2Sa 19:21 [b]Jer 39:5; Eze 12:12-13; 19:4,8 **4:21** [c]Jer 25:15 [d]Isa 34:6-10; Am 1:11-12; Ob 1:16 **4:22** [e]Isa 40:2; Jer 33:8 [f]Ps 137:7; Mal 1:4 **5:1** [g]Ps 44:13-16; 89:50 **5:2** [h]Ps 79:1 [i]Zep 1:13 **5:3** [j]Jer 15:8; 18:21 **5:4** [k]Isa 3:1 **5:5** [l]Ne 9:37 **5:6** [m]Hos 9:3

[a] 7 Or *lapis lazuli*

7Our fathers sinned and are no
more,
and we bear their punishment.[n]
8Slaves[o] rule over us,
and there is none to free us from
their hands.[p]
9We get our bread at the risk of our
lives
because of the sword in the
desert.
10Our skin is hot as an oven,
feverish from hunger.[q]
11Women have been ravished[r] in
Zion,
and virgins in the towns of
Judah.
12Princes have been hung up by their
hands;
elders are shown no respect.[s]
13Young men toil at the millstones;
boys stagger under loads of
wood.
14The elders are gone from the city
gate;
the young men have stopped
their music.[t]
15Joy is gone from our hearts;
our dancing has turned to
mourning.[u]
16The crown[v] has fallen from our
head.
Woe to us, for we have sinned![w]
17Because of this our hearts[x] are
faint,
because of these things our
eyes[y] grow dim
18for Mount Zion, which lies
desolate,[z]
with jackals prowling over it.

19You, O LORD, reign forever;
your throne endures[a] from
generation to generation.
20Why do you always forget us?[b]
Why do you forsake us so long?
21Restore[c] us to yourself, O LORD,
that we may return;
renew our days as of old
22unless you have utterly rejected us
and are angry with us beyond
measure.[d]

5:7 [n]Jer 14:20; 16:12
5:8 [o]Ne 5:15 [p]Zec 11:6
5:10 [q]La 4:8-9
5:11 [r]Zec 14:2
5:12 [s]La 4:16
5:14 [t]Isa 24:8; Jer 7:34
5:15 [u]Jer 25:10
5:16 [v]Ps 89:39 [w]Isa 3:11
5:17 [x]Isa 1:5 [y]Ps 6:7
5:18 [z]Mic 3:12
5:19 [a]Ps 45:6; 102:12,24-27
5:20 [b]Ps 13:1; 44:24
5:21 [c]Ps 80:3
5:22 [d]Isa 64:9

5:15

PROMISE 3

SWEET, BUT SHORT

In the short run, sin can seem to be more fun—or easier—than righteousness. That's why it's so tempting! We are only lured by what gives us pleasure. God knows that. He gave us the Bible to warn us that sin, in the long run, only hurts, kills, destroys. Hear the haunting statement of this verse as it echoes back from the other side of sin. You might want to read Lamentations regularly as a reminder that sin's short run, though often sweet, is always short; and that its long run is always bitter.

For the next Promise 3 reading go to page 886.

EZEKIEL

AT A GLANCE

Key Principle: God is holy, glorious and sovereign, and those who walk with him must honor him through repentance, trust and obedience.
Author: Ezekiel
Time and Place: 593–571 B.C. / Babylon
Key Verses: 7:3; 36:24–26, 33–35; 37:21

BENEFIT

Ezekiel is an extraordinary book of mystery, visions, symbolism, parables and allegories that stretches our minds about God's glory and his majestic splendor, and invites us to fear and hope in him. This book is a complex and multifaceted collection of prophetic messages, and it offers readers a number of significant keys to grasping God's future program to bring salvation and righteousness upon the earth.

SETTING

The prophet Ezekiel's ministry overlapped the latter portion of Jeremiah's life and the early portion of Daniel's. If "the thirtieth year" in 1:1 refers to Ezekiel's age, he was born in 622 B.C. and deported to Babylon when he was 25 in 597 B.C. His first prophetic oracle took place in 593 B.C., and he prophesied over a period of 22 years until 571 B.C. (1:2; 29:17). Daniel was among the captives in Nebuchadnezzar's first wave of deportation from Jerusalem in 605 B.C., and Ezekiel was taken to Babylon in the second wave along with 10,000 other hostages in 597 B.C. The third and final wave of deportation took place in 586 B.C. when Jerusalem was finally destroyed. Ezekiel lived in Babylon along the Kebar River in a prominent colony of Jewish refugees known as Tel Aviv (1:1; 3:15, 23).

TIME LINE

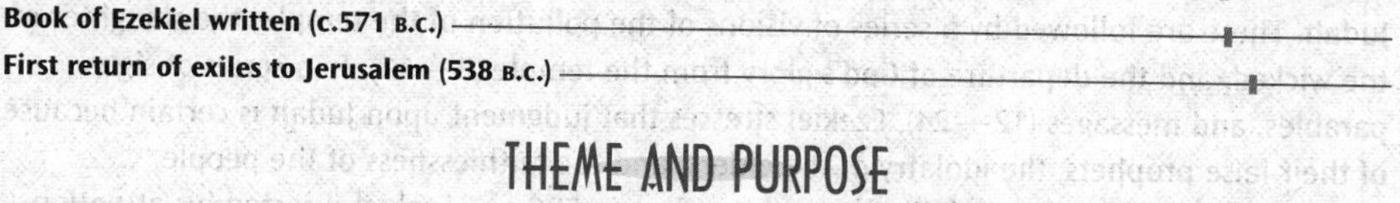

THEME AND PURPOSE

Although Ezekiel prophesied in Babylon and Jeremiah prophesied in Judah, their ministries addressed many of the same issues. Like Jeremiah, Ezekiel tried to convince the Jewish people that the city's impending fall was an inevitable consequence of their idolatry and moral corruption. Both prophets tried to refute false hopes that Jerusalem would not be overthrown, and in both cases, the people refused to respond. Also, after Jerusalem's destruction, both prophets tried to persuade the Jews that the Babylonian captivity would last for a considerable time. Like Jeremiah, Ezekiel incorporated a dual message of condemnation (1—32) and consolation (33—48), but Ezekiel's message of comfort and a future hope for God's people is much more extensive than that of Jeremiah.

Ezekiel's oracles stress the additional themes of God's glory, the temple and God's power and faithfulness.

UNIQUE CONTRIBUTION

Ezekiel's vision of God's glory in chapter 1 is one of the most remarkable passages in Scripture. It's the first of a series of passages that traces the presence of God's glory from its departure from the temple to its return to the new temple (1:28; 3:12, 23; 9:3; 10:4, 18–19; 11:22–23; 43:1–5; 44:4). Ezekiel also provides us with valuable information on the degradation and destruction of Solomon's temple, and gives us a detailed description of a future temple (40—48).

LINKS TO THE NEW TESTAMENT

Ezekiel's description of the "figure like that of a man" (1:25–28) is similar to John's description of the glorified Christ in Revelation 1:12–17. Ezekiel also anticipated the coming of Christ when he prophesied that the kingdom would be overthrown and "not be restored until he comes to whom it rightfully belongs; to him I will give it" (21:27). And Messiah is the tender shoot that "will produce branches and bear fruit and become a splendid cedar" (17:22–24; similarly, Messiah is called the righteous Branch that will sprout from David's line in Jeremiah 23:5; 33:15; Isaiah 11:1; and Zechariah 3:8; 6:12).

OVERVIEW

FOCUS	Judah's Fall	Judah's Foes	Judah's Future
REFERENCE	1 — 24	25 — 32	33 — 48
TOPICS	Condemnation of Judah	Condemnation of the Nations	Consolation for Judah
	Judah's End	Judah's Enemies	Judah's Expectations
	Before the Siege	During the Siege	After the Siege
	592–587 B.C.	586 B.C.	585–570 B.C.
LOCATION	Ezekiel in Babylon		
TIME	22 Years of Prophetic Ministry		

After showing Ezekiel a staggering vision of his glory (1), God commissions Ezekiel as a prophet to the Jewish exiles in Babylon (2—3). The bulk of this book is a prophetic condemnation that focuses first on Judah (4—24) and then on the surrounding nations (25—32). Ezekiel's oracles begin with four signs (4—5) and two sermons (6—7) that forecast coming judgment upon Judah. These are followed by a series of visions of the pollution of the temple, the slaughter of the wicked, and the departure of God's glory from the temple (8—11). In a series of signs, parables, and messages (12—24), Ezekiel stresses that judgment upon Judah is certain because of their false prophets, the idolatry of the elders, and the faithlessness of the people.

When final judgment was falling upon Jerusalem in 586 B.C., Ezekiel directed his attention to God's future judgment upon the surrounding nations of Ammon, Moab, Edom, Philistia, Tyre, Sidon, and Egypt (25—32).

The final section of Ezekiel's prophecy (33—48), delivered after Jerusalem's destruction, turns from the theme of condemnation to a message of consolation. The dramatic vision of the dry bones (37) anticipates the restoration and purification of Israel and Judah, and the book concludes with details of the new temple, the new Jerusalem, and the new land (40—48).

EZEKIEL

The Living Creatures and the Glory of the LORD

1 In the[a] thirtieth year, in the fourth month on the fifth day, while I was among the exiles[a] by the Kebar River, the heavens were opened[b] and I saw visions[c] of God.

2On the fifth of the month—it was the fifth year of the exile of King Jehoiachin[d]— **3**the word of the LORD came to Ezekiel the priest, the son of Buzi,[b] by the Kebar River in the land of the Babylonians.[c] There the hand of the LORD was upon him.[e]

4I looked, and I saw a windstorm coming out of the north[f]—an immense cloud with flashing lightning and surrounded by brilliant light. The center of the fire looked like glowing metal,[g] **5**and in the fire was what looked like four living creatures.[h] In appearance their form was that of a man,[i] **6**but each of them had four faces[j] and four wings. **7**Their legs were straight; their feet were like those of a calf and gleamed like burnished bronze.[k] **8**Under their wings on their four sides they had the hands of a man.[l] All four of them had faces and wings, **9**and their wings touched one another. Each one went straight ahead; they did not turn as they moved.[m]

10Their faces looked like this: Each of the four had the face of a man, and on the right side each had the face of a lion, and on the left the face of an ox; each also had the face of an eagle.[n] **11**Such were their faces. Their wings[o] were spread out upward; each had two wings, one touching the wing of another creature on either side, and two wings covering its body. **12**Each one went straight ahead. Wherever the spirit would go, they would go, without turning as they went. **13**The appearance of the living creatures was like burning coals of fire or like torches. Fire moved back and forth among the creatures; it was bright, and lightning[p] flashed out of it. **14**The creatures sped back and forth like flashes of lightning.[q]

15As I looked at the living creatures, I saw a wheel on the ground beside each creature with its four faces. **16**This was the appearance and structure of the wheels: They sparkled like chrysolite,[r] and all four looked alike. Each appeared to be made like a wheel intersecting a wheel. **17**As they moved, they would go in any one of the four directions the creatures faced; the wheels did not turn[s] about[d] as the creatures went. **18**Their rims were high and awesome, and all four rims were full of eyes[t] all around.

19When the living creatures moved, the wheels beside them moved; and when the living creatures rose from the ground, the wheels also rose. **20**Wherever the spirit would go, they would go,[u] and the wheels would rise along with them, because the spirit of the living creatures was in the wheels. **21**When the creatures moved, they also moved; when the creatures stood still, they also stood still; and when the creatures rose from the ground, the wheels rose along with them, because the spirit of the living creatures was in the wheels.[v]

22Spread out above the heads of the living creatures was what looked like an expanse,[w] sparkling like ice, and awesome. **23**Under the expanse their wings were stretched out one toward the other, and each had two wings covering its body. **24**When the creatures moved, I heard the sound of their wings, like the roar of rushing waters, like the voice[x] of the Almighty,[e] like the tumult of an army.[y] When they stood still, they lowered their wings.

25Then there came a voice from above the expanse over their heads as they stood with lowered wings. **26**Above the expanse over their heads was what looked like a throne of sapphire,[f][z] and high above on the throne was a figure like that of a man.[a] **27**I saw that from what appeared to be his waist up he looked like glowing metal, as if full of fire, and that from there down he looked like fire; and brilliant light surrounded him.[b] **28**Like the appearance of a rainbow[c] in the clouds on a rainy day, so was the radiance around him.[d]

This was the appearance of the likeness of the glory[e] of the LORD. When I saw it, I fell facedown,[f] and I heard the voice of one speaking.

Ezekiel's Call

2 He said to me, "Son of man, stand[g] up on your feet and I will speak to

1:1 *a*Eze 11:24-25 *b*Mt 3:16; Ac 7:56 *c*Ex 24:10
1:2 *d*2Ki 24:15
1:3 *e*2Ki 3:15; Eze 3:14,22
1:4 *f*Jer 1:14 *g*Eze 8:2
1:5 *h*Rev 4:6 *i*ver 26
1:6 *j*Eze 10:14
1:7 *k*Da 10:6; Rev 1:15
1:8 *l*Eze 10:8
1:9 *m*Eze 10:22
1:10 *n*Eze 10:14; Rev 4:7
1:11 *o*Isa 6:2
1:13 *p*Rev 4:5
1:14 *q*Ps 29:7
1:16 *r*Eze 10:9-11; Da 10:6
1:17 *s*ver 9
1:18 *t*Eze 10:12; Rev 4:6
1:20 *u*ver 12
1:21 *v*Eze 10:17
1:22 *w*Eze 10:1
1:24 *x*Eze 10:5; 43:2; Da 10:6; Rev 1:15; 19:6 *y*2Ki 7:6
1:26 *z*Ex 24:10; Eze 10:1 *a*Rev 1:13
1:27 *b*Eze 8:2
1:28 *c*Ge 9:13; Rev 10:1 *d*Rev 4:2 *e*Eze 8:4 *f*Eze 3:23; Da 8:17; Rev 1:17
2:1 *g*Da 10:11

a *1* Or *my* **b** *3* Or *Ezekiel son of Buzi the priest* **c** *3* Or *Chaldeans* **d** *17* Or *aside* **e** *24* Hebrew *Shaddai* **f** *26* Or *lapis lazuli*

you." **2**As he spoke, the Spirit came into
me and raised me[h] to my feet, and I
heard him speaking to me.
3He said: "Son of man, I am sending
you to the Israelites, to a rebellious nation that has rebelled against me; they
and their fathers have been in revolt
against me to this very day.[i] **4**The
people to whom I am sending you are
obstinate and stubborn.[j] Say to them,
'This is what the Sovereign LORD says.'
5And whether they listen or fail to
listen[k]—for they are a rebellious
house[l]—they will know that a prophet has been among them.[m] **6**And you,
son of man, do not be afraid[n] of them
or their words. Do not be afraid,
though briers and thorns[o] are all
around you and you live among scorpions. Do not be afraid of what they say
or terrified by them, though they are a
rebellious house.[p] **7**You must speak
my words to them, whether they listen
or fail to listen, for they are rebellious.[q] **8**But you, son of man, listen to
what I say to you. Do not rebel like that
rebellious house;[r] open your mouth
and eat[s] what I give you."
9Then I looked, and I saw a hand[t]
stretched out to me. In it was a scroll,
10which he unrolled before me. On
both sides of it were written words of
lament and mourning and woe.[u]

3 And he said to me, "Son of man, eat
what is before you, eat this scroll;
then go and speak to the house of Israel." **2**So I opened my mouth, and he
gave me the scroll to eat.
3Then he said to me, "Son of man,
eat this scroll I am giving you and fill
your stomach with it." So I ate[v] it, and
it tasted as sweet as honey[w] in my
mouth.
4He then said to me: "Son of man, go
now to the house of Israel and speak
my words to them. **5**You are not being
sent to a people of obscure speech and
difficult language,[x] but to the house of
Israel— **6**not to many peoples of obscure speech and difficult language,
whose words you cannot understand.
Surely if I had sent you to them, they
would have listened to you.[y] **7**But the
house of Israel is not willing to listen to
you because they are not willing to listen to me, for the whole house of Israel
is hardened and obstinate.[z] **8**But I will
make you as unyielding and hardened
as they are.[a] **9**I will make your forehead like the hardest stone, harder
than flint. Do not be afraid of them or
terrified by them, though they are a rebellious house.[b]"
10And he said to me, "Son of man,
listen carefully and take to heart all the
words I speak to you. **11**Go now to your
countrymen in exile and speak to
them. Say to them, 'This is what the
Sovereign LORD says,' whether they listen or fail to listen.[c]"
12Then the Spirit lifted me up,[d] and
I heard behind me a loud rumbling
sound—May the glory of the LORD be
praised in his dwelling place!— **13**the
sound of the wings of the living creatures brushing against each other and
the sound of the wheels beside them,
a loud rumbling sound.[e] **14**The Spirit
then lifted me up and took me away,
and I went in bitterness and in the anger of my spirit, with the strong hand of
the LORD upon me. **15**I came to the exiles who lived at Tel Abib near the Kebar River.[f] And there, where they
were living, I sat among them for seven
days[g]—overwhelmed.

Warning to Israel

16At the end of seven days the word
of the LORD came to me:[h] **17**"Son of
man, I have made you a watchman[i]
for the house of Israel; so hear the word
I speak and give them warning from
me. **18**When I say to a wicked man,
'You will surely die,' and you do not
warn him or speak out to dissuade him
from his evil ways in order to save his
life, that wicked man will die for[a] his
sin, and I will hold you accountable for
his blood.[j] **19**But if you do warn the
wicked man and he does not turn from
his wickedness or from his evil ways,

2:2 [h] Eze 3:24; Da 8:18
2:3 [i] Jer 3:25; Eze 20:8-24
2:4 [j] Eze 3:7
2:5 [k] Eze 3:11 [l] Eze 3:27 [m] Eze 33:33
2:6 [n] Jer 1:8,17 [o] Isa 9:18; Mic 7:4 [p] Eze 3:9
2:7 [q] Jer 1:7; Eze 3:10-11
2:8 [r] Isa 50:5 [s] Jer 15:16; Rev 10:9
2:9 [t] Eze 8:3
2:10 [u] Rev 8:13
3:3 [v] Jer 15:16 [w] Ps 19:10; Ps 119:103; Rev 10:9-10
3:5 [x] Isa 28:11; Jnh 1:2
3:6 [y] Mt 11:21-23
3:7 [z] Eze 2:4; Jn 15:20-23
3:8 [a] Jer 1:18
3:9 [b] Isa 50:7; Eze 2:6; Mic 3:8
3:11 [c] Eze 2:4-5,7
3:12 [d] Eze 8:3; Ac 8:39
3:13 [e] Eze 1:24; 10:5,16-17
3:15 [f] Ps 137:1 [g] Job 2:13
3:16 [h] Jer 42:7
3:17 [i] Isa 52:8; Jer 6:17; Eze 33:7-9
3:18 [j] ver 20; Eze 33:6

a 18 Or *in*; also in verses 19 and 20

3:7–11 PROMISE 7

FLINT FOREHEAD?

One of life's highest privileges is to lead a person to Christ. Time invested in the Great Commission is high and holy time. But it *can* be discouraging and frustrating. Difficult questions, frontal challenges, even abuse are sometimes involved in the process. But read Ezekiel's call (2:1–8). Involvement in the Great Commission may scare the fainthearted, but read how God reassured Ezekiel and pray for the same courage and tenacity. Go to your place of ministry—the factory, business office, school, construction site, wherever God has placed you—and with God's resolve, you'll have nothing to fear. As you witness for the living Christ through your words and through your godly example, always remember: "'This is what the Sovereign LORD says,' whether they listen or fail to listen" (v. 11).

For the next Promise 7 reading go to page 898.

he will die for his sin; but you will have
saved yourself.[k]
20“Again, when a righteous man
turns from his righteousness and does
evil, and I put a stumbling block before
him, he will die. Since you did not warn
him, he will die for his sin. The righteous things he did will not be remembered, and I will hold you accountable
for his blood.[l] **21**But if you do warn
the righteous man not to sin and he
does not sin, he will surely live because
he took warning, and you will have
saved yourself.[m]”

22The hand of the LORD[n] was upon
me there, and he said to me, “Get up
and go[o] out to the plain,[p] and there
I will speak to you.” **23**So I got up and
went out to the plain. And the glory of
the LORD was standing there, like the
glory I had seen by the Kebar River,[q]
and I fell facedown.[r]
24Then the Spirit came into me and
raised me[s] to my feet. He spoke to me
and said: “Go, shut yourself inside your
house. **25**And you, son of man, they will
tie with ropes; you will be bound so
that you cannot go out among the people.[t] **26**I will make your tongue stick to
the roof of your mouth so that you will
be silent and unable to rebuke them,
though they are a rebellious house.[u]
27But when I speak to you, I will open
your mouth and you shall say to them,
‘This is what the Sovereign LORD
says.’[v] Whoever will listen let him
listen, and whoever will refuse let
him refuse; for they are a rebellious
house.[w]

Siege of Jerusalem Symbolized

4 “Now, son of man, take a clay tablet,
put it in front of you and draw the
city of Jerusalem on it. **2**Then lay siege
to it: Erect siege works against it, build
a ramp[x] up to it, set up camps against
it and put battering rams around it.[y]
3Then take an iron pan, place it as an
iron wall between you and the city and
turn your face toward it. It will be under siege, and you shall besiege it. This
will be a sign[z] to the house of Israel.[a]
4“Then lie on your left side and put
the sin of the house of Israel upon
yourself.**[a]** You are to bear their sin for
the number of days you lie on your
side. **5**I have assigned you the same
number of days as the years of their
sin. So for 390 days you will bear the sin
of the house of Israel.
6“After you have finished this, lie
down again, this time on your right
side, and bear the sin of the house of
Judah. I have assigned you 40 days, a
day for each year.[b] **7**Turn your face
toward the siege of Jerusalem and with
bared arm prophesy against her. **8**I will
tie you up with ropes so that you cannot turn from one side to the other until you have finished the days of your
siege.[c]
9“Take wheat and barley, beans and
lentils, millet and spelt;[d] put them in
a storage jar and use them to make
bread for yourself. You are to eat it during the 390 days you lie on your side.
10Weigh out twenty shekels**[b]** of food to
eat each day and eat it at set times.
11Also measure out a sixth of a hin**[c]** of
water and drink it at set times. **12**Eat the
food as you would a barley cake; bake
it in the sight of the people, using human excrement[e] for fuel.” **13**The LORD
said, “In this way the people of Israel
will eat defiled food among the nations
where I will drive them.”[f]
14Then I said, “Not so, Sovereign
LORD![g] I have never defiled myself.
From my youth until now I have never
eaten anything found dead[h] or torn
by wild animals. No unclean meat has
ever entered my mouth.[i]”
15“Very well,” he said, “I will let you
bake your bread over cow manure instead of human excrement.”
16He then said to me: “Son of man,
I will cut off[j] the supply of food in
Jerusalem. The people will eat rationed
food in anxiety and drink rationed water in despair,[k] **17**for food and water
will be scarce. They will be appalled at
the sight of each other and will waste
away because of**[d]** their sin.[l]

5 “Now, son of man, take a sharp
sword and use it as a barber’s ra-

3:19 [k]2Ki 17:13; Eze 14:14,20; Ac 18:6; 20:26; 1Ti 4:14-16
3:20 [l]Ps 125:5; Eze 18:24; 33:12,18
3:21 [m]Ac 20:31
3:22 [n]Eze 1:3 [o]Ac 9:6 [p]Eze 8:4
3:23 [q]Eze 1:1 [r]Eze 1:28
3:24 [s]Eze 2:2
3:25 [t]Eze 4:8
3:26 [u]Eze 2:5; 24:27; 33:22
3:27 [v]ver 11 [w]Eze 12:3; 24:27; 33:22
4:2 [x]Jer 6:6 [y]Eze 21:22
4:3 [z]Isa 8:18; 20:3; Eze 12:3-6; 24:24,27 [a]Jer 39:1
4:6 [b]Nu 14:34; Da 9:24-26; 12:11-12
4:8 [c]Eze 3:25
4:9 [d]Isa 28:25
4:12 [e]Isa 36:12
4:13 [f]Hos 9:3
4:14 [g]Jer 1:6; Eze 9:8; 20:49 [h]Lev 11:39 [i]Ex 22:31; Dt 14:3; Ac 10:14
4:16 [j]Ps 105:16; Eze 5:16 [k]ver 10-11; Lev 26:26; Isa 3:1; Eze 12:19
4:17 [l]Lev 26:39; Eze 24:23; 33:10

[a] *4* Or *your side* **[b]** *10* That is, about 8 ounces (about 0.2 kilogram) **[c]** *11* That is, about 2/3 quart (about 0.6 liter) **[d]** *17* Or *away in*

3:17–21 PROMISE 2

PERSONAL ACCOUNTABILITY

This is sobering stuff. The Christian’s role in society takes on an added dimension with this truth in focus. God’s witnesses are to warn both the unregenerate person (vv. 18–19) of his or her need to repent, and the righteous person (vv. 20–21) when he or she turns from righteousness.

Think your way through these verses very carefully. They cast a new light on the mission of the church to reach lost people. They also highlight the need for every Christian man to seek out a few vital relationships where Biblical accountability (described in vv. 20–21) can occur. Passages like this one put a new sense of urgency on being a godly man.

For the next Promise 2 reading go to page 1074.

zor[m] to shave[n] your head and your beard.[o] Then take a set of scales and divide up the hair. 2When the days of your siege come to an end, burn a third of the hair with fire inside the city. Take a third and strike it with the sword all around the city. And scatter a third to the wind. For I will pursue them with drawn sword.[p] 3But take a few strands of hair and tuck them away in the folds of your garment.[q] 4Again, take a few of these and throw them into the fire and burn them up. A fire will spread from there to the whole house of Israel.

5"This is what the Sovereign LORD says: This is Jerusalem, which I have set in the center of the nations, with countries all around her. 6Yet in her wickedness she has rebelled against my laws and decrees more than the nations and countries around her. She has rejected my laws and has not followed my decrees.[r]

7"Therefore this is what the Sovereign LORD says: You have been more unruly than the nations around you and have not followed my decrees or kept my laws. You have not even[a] conformed to the standards of the nations around you.[s]

8"Therefore this is what the Sovereign LORD says: I myself am against you, Jerusalem, and I will inflict punishment on you in the sight of the nations.[t] 9Because of all your detestable idols, I will do to you what I have never done before and will never do again.[u] 10Therefore in your midst fathers will eat their children, and children will eat their fathers.[v] I will inflict punishment on you and will scatter all your survivors to the winds.[w] 11Therefore as surely as I live, declares the Sovereign LORD, because you have defiled my sanctuary with all your vile images[x] and detestable practices,[y] I myself will withdraw my favor; I will not look on you with pity or spare you.[z] 12A third of your people will die of the plague or perish by famine inside you; a third will fall by the sword outside your walls; and a third I will scatter to the winds and pursue with drawn sword.[a]

13"Then my anger will cease and my wrath[b] against them will subside, and I will be avenged.[c] And when I have spent my wrath upon them, they will know that I the LORD have spoken in my zeal.

14"I will make you a ruin and a reproach among the nations around you, in the sight of all who pass by.[d] 15You will be a reproach and a taunt, a warning and an object of horror to the nations around you when I inflict punishment on you in anger and in wrath and with stinging rebuke.[e] I the LORD have spoken.[f] 16When I shoot at you with my deadly and destructive arrows of famine, I will shoot to destroy you. I will bring more and more famine upon you and cut off your supply of food.[g] 17I will send famine and wild beasts against you, and they will leave you childless. Plague and bloodshed[h] will sweep through you, and I will bring the sword against you. I the LORD have spoken.[i]"

A Prophecy Against the Mountains of Israel

6 The word of the LORD came to me: 2"Son of man, set your face against the mountains[j] of Israel; prophesy against them 3and say: 'O mountains of Israel, hear the word of the Sovereign LORD. This is what the Sovereign LORD says to the mountains and hills, to the ravines and valleys:[k] I am about to bring a sword against you, and I will destroy your high places.[l] 4Your altars will be demolished and your incense altars[m] will be smashed; and I will slay your people in front of your idols. 5I will lay the dead bodies of the Israelites in front of their idols, and I will scatter your bones[n] around your altars. 6Wherever you live, the towns will be laid waste and the high places demolished, so that your altars will be laid waste and devastated, your idols[o] smashed and ruined, your incense altars[p] broken down, and what you have made wiped out.[q] 7Your people will fall slain among you, and you will know that I am the LORD.

8" 'But I will spare some, for some of you will escape[r] the sword when you are scattered among the lands and nations.[s] 9Then in the nations where they have been carried captive, those who escape will remember me—how I have been grieved[t] by their adulterous hearts, which have turned away from me, and by their eyes, which have lusted after their idols.[u] They will loathe themselves for the evil they have done and for all their detestable practices.[v] 10And they will know that I am the LORD; I did not threaten in vain to bring this calamity on them.

11" 'This is what the Sovereign LORD says: Strike your hands together and stamp your feet and cry out "Alas!" because of all the wicked and detestable practices of the house of Israel, for they will fall by the sword, famine and

5:1 [m]Isa 7:20 [n]Eze 44:20 [o]Lev 21:5
5:2 [p]ver 12; Lev 26:33
5:3 [q]Jer 39:10
5:6 [r]Jer 11:10; Eze 16:47-51; Zec 7:11
5:7 [s]2Ch 33:9; Jer 2:10-11; Eze 16:47
5:8 [t]Eze 15:7
5:9 [u]Da 9:12; Mt 24:21
5:10 [v]Lev 26:29; La 2:20 [w]Lev 26:33; Ps 44:11; Eze 12:14; Zec 2:6
5:11 [x]Eze 7:20 [y]2Ch 36:14; Eze 8:6 [z]Eze 7:4,9
5:12 [a]ver 2,17; Jer 15:2; 21:9; Eze 6:11-12; 12:14
5:13 [b]Eze 21:17; 36:6 [c]Isa 1:24
5:14 [d]Lev 26:32; Ne 2:17; Ps 74:3-10; 79:1-4
5:15 [e]1Ki 9:7; Jer 22:8-9; 24:9 [f]Eze 25:17
5:16 [g]Dt 32:24
5:17 [h]Eze 38:22 [i]Eze 14:21
6:2 [j]Eze 36:1
6:3 [k]Eze 36:4 [l]Lev 26:30
6:4 [m]2Ch 14:5
6:5 [n]Jer 8:1-2
6:6 [o]Mic 1:7; Zec 13:2 [p]Lev 26:30 [q]Isa 6:11; Eze 5:14
6:8 [r]Jer 44:28 [s]Isa 6:13; Jer 44:14; Eze 12:16; 14:22
6:9 [t]Ps 78:40; Isa 7:13 [u]Eze 20:7,24 [v]Eze 20:43; 36:31

a 7 Most Hebrew manuscripts; some Hebrew manuscripts and Syriac *You have*

plague.[w] 12He that is far away will die
of the plague, and he that is near will
fall by the sword, and he that survives
and is spared will die of famine. So will
I spend my wrath upon them.[x] 13And
they will know that I am the LORD,
when their people lie slain among their
idols around their altars, on every high
hill and on all the mountaintops, under
every spreading tree and every leafy
oak[y]—places where they offered fragrant incense to all their idols.[z] 14And
I will stretch out my hand[a] against
them and make the land a desolate
waste from the desert to Diblah**[a]**—
wherever they live. Then they will
know that I am the LORD.[b]' "

The End Has Come

7 The word of the LORD came to me:
2"Son of man, this is what the Sovereign LORD says to the land of Israel: The
end![c] The end has come upon the
four corners[d] of the land. 3The end is
now upon you and I will unleash my
anger against you. I will judge you according to your conduct and repay you
for all your detestable practices. 4I will
not look on you with pity[e] or spare
you; I will surely repay you for your
conduct and the detestable practices
among you. Then you will know that I
am the LORD.
5"This is what the Sovereign LORD
says: Disaster![f] An unheard-of**[b]** disaster is coming. 6The end has come!
The end has come! It has roused itself
against you. It has come! 7Doom has
come upon you—you who dwell in the
land. The time has come, the day is
near;[g] there is panic, not joy, upon the
mountains. 8I am about to pour out my
wrath[h] on you and spend my anger
against you; I will judge you according
to your conduct and repay you for all
your detestable practices.[i] 9I will not
look on you with pity or spare you; I
will repay you in accordance with your
conduct and the detestable practices
among you. Then you will know that it
is I the LORD who strikes the blow.
10"The day is here! It has come!
Doom has burst forth, the rod[j] has
budded, arrogance has blossomed!
11Violence has grown into**[c]** a rod to
punish wickedness; none of the people
will be left, none of that crowd—no
wealth, nothing of value.[k] 12The time
has come, the day has arrived. Let not
the buyer rejoice nor the seller grieve,
for wrath is upon the whole crowd.[l]
13The seller will not recover the land he
has sold as long as both of them live,
for the vision concerning the whole
crowd will not be reversed. Because of
their sins, not one of them will preserve
his life.[m] 14Though they blow the
trumpet and get everything ready, no
one will go into battle, for my wrath is
upon the whole crowd.
15"Outside is the sword, inside are
plague and famine; those in the country will die by the sword, and those in
the city will be devoured by famine and
plague.[n] 16All who survive and escape
will be in the mountains, moaning like
doves[o] of the valleys, each because of
his sins.[p] 17Every hand will go limp,[q]
and every knee will become as weak as
water. 18They will put on sackcloth and
be clothed with terror.[r] Their faces
will be covered with shame and their
heads will be shaved.[s] 19They will
throw their silver into the streets, and
their gold will be an unclean thing.
Their silver and gold will not be able
to save them in the day of the LORD's
wrath.[t] They will not satisfy their
hunger or fill their stomachs with it, for
it has made them stumble[u] into sin.[v]
20They were proud of their beautiful
jewelry and used it to make their detestable idols and vile images.[w] Therefore I will turn these into an unclean
thing for them. 21I will hand it all over
as plunder to foreigners and as loot to
the wicked of the earth, and they will
defile it.[x] 22I will turn my face[y] away
from them, and they will desecrate my
treasured place; robbers will enter it
and desecrate it.
23"Prepare chains, because the land
is full of bloodshed[z] and the city is full
of violence. 24I will bring the most
wicked of the nations to take possession of their houses; I will put an end to
the pride of the mighty, and their sanctuaries[a] will be desecrated.[b] 25When
terror comes, they will seek peace, but
there will be none.[c] 26Calamity upon
calamity[d] will come, and rumor upon
rumor. They will try to get a vision from
the prophet; the teaching of the law by
the priest will be lost, as will the counsel of the elders.[e] 27The king will
mourn, the prince will be clothed with
despair,[f] and the hands of the people
of the land will tremble. I will deal with
them according to their conduct,[g]
and by their own standards I will judge
them. Then they will know that I am
the LORD.[h]"

6:11 [w]Eze 5:12; 21:14,17; 25:6
6:12 [x]Eze 5:12
6:13 [y]Isa 57:5 [z]1Ki 14:23; Jer 2:20; Eze 20:28; Hos 4:13
6:14 [a]Isa 5:25 [b]Eze 14:13
7:2 [c]Am 8:2,10 [d]Rev 7:1; 20:8
7:4 [e]Eze 5:11
7:5 [f]2Ki 21:12
7:7 [g]Eze 12:23; Zep 1:14
7:8 [h]Isa 42:25; Eze 9:8; 14:19; Na 1:6 [i]Eze 20:8,21; 36:19
7:10 [j]Ps 89:32; Isa 10:5
7:11 [k]Jer 16:6; Zep 1:18
7:12 [l]ver 7; Isa 5:13-14; Eze 30:3
7:13 [m]Lev 25:24-28
7:15 [n]Dt 32:25; Jer 14:18; La 1:20; Eze 5:12
7:16 [o]Isa 59:11 [p]Ezr 9:15; Eze 6:8
7:17 [q]Isa 13:7; Eze 21:7; 22:14
7:18 [r]Ps 55:5 [s]Isa 15:2-3; Eze 27:31; Am 8:10
7:19 [t]Eze 13:5; Zep 1:7,18 [u]Eze 14:3 [v]Pr 11:4
7:20 [w]Jer 7:30
7:21 [x]2Ki 24:13
7:22 [y]Eze 39:23-24
7:23 [z]2Ki 21:16
7:24 [a]Eze 24:21 [b]2Ch 7:20; Eze 28:7
7:25 [c]Eze 13:10,16
7:26 [d]Jer 4:20 [e]Isa 47:11; Eze 20:1-3; Mic 3:6
7:27 [f]Ps 109:19; Eze 26:16 [g]Eze 18:20 [h]ver 4

a *14* Most Hebrew manuscripts; a few Hebrew manuscripts *Riblah* **b** *5* Most Hebrew manuscripts; some Hebrew manuscripts and Syriac *Disaster after* **c** *11* Or *The violent one has become*

Idolatry in the Temple

8 In the sixth year, in the sixth month on the fifth day, while I was sitting in my house and the elders[i] of Judah were sitting before[j] me, the hand of the Sovereign LORD came upon me there.[k] 2 I looked, and I saw a figure like that of a man.[a] From what appeared to be his waist down he was like fire, and from there up his appearance was as bright as glowing metal.[l] 3 He stretched out what looked like a hand and took me by the hair of my head. The Spirit lifted me up[m] between earth and heaven and in visions of God he took me to Jerusalem, to the entrance to the north gate of the inner court, where the idol that provokes to jealousy[n] stood. 4 And there before me was the glory[o] of the God of Israel, as in the vision I had seen in the plain.[p]

5 Then he said to me, "Son of man, look toward the north." So I looked, and in the entrance north of the gate of the altar I saw this idol[q] of jealousy.

6 And he said to me, "Son of man, do you see what they are doing—the utterly detestable[r] things the house of Israel is doing here, things that will drive me far from my sanctuary? But you will see things that are even more detestable."

7 Then he brought me to the entrance to the court. I looked, and I saw a hole in the wall. 8 He said to me, "Son of man, now dig into the wall." So I dug into the wall and saw a doorway there.

9 And he said to me, "Go in and see the wicked and detestable things they are doing here." 10 So I went in and looked, and I saw portrayed all over the walls all kinds of crawling things and detestable animals and all the idols of the house of Israel.[s] 11 In front of them stood seventy elders of the house of Israel, and Jaazaniah son of Shaphan was standing among them. Each had a censer[t] in his hand, and a fragrant cloud of incense[u] was rising.

12 He said to me, "Son of man, have you seen what the elders of the house of Israel are doing in the darkness, each at the shrine of his own idol? They say, 'The LORD does not see[v] us; the LORD has forsaken the land.' " 13 Again, he said, "You will see them doing things that are even more detestable."

14 Then he brought me to the entrance to the north gate of the house of the LORD, and I saw women sitting there, mourning for Tammuz. 15 He said to me, "Do you see this, son of man? You will see things that are even more detestable than this."

16 He then brought me into the inner court of the house of the LORD, and there at the entrance to the temple, between the portico and the altar,[w] were about twenty-five men. With their backs toward the temple of the LORD and their faces toward the east, they were bowing down to the sun in the east.[x]

17 He said to me, "Have you seen this, son of man? Is it a trivial matter for the house of Judah to do the detestable things they are doing here? Must they also fill the land with violence[y] and continually provoke me to anger?[z] Look at them putting the branch to their nose! 18 Therefore I will deal with them in anger; I will not look on them with pity[a] or spare them. Although they shout in my ears, I will not listen[b] to them."

Idolaters Killed

9 Then I heard him call out in a loud voice, "Bring the guards of the city here, each with a weapon in his hand." 2 And I saw six men coming from the direction of the upper gate, which faces north, each with a deadly weapon in his hand. With them was a man clothed in linen[c] who had a writing kit at his side. They came in and stood beside the bronze altar.

3 Now the glory[d] of the God of Israel went up from above the cherubim,[e] where it had been, and moved to the threshold of the temple. Then the LORD called to the man clothed in linen who had the writing kit at his side 4 and said to him, "Go throughout the city of Jerusalem and put a mark[f] on the foreheads of those who grieve and lament[g] over all the detestable things that are done in it.[h]"

5 As I listened, he said to the others, "Follow him through the city and kill, without showing pity[i] or compassion. 6 Slaughter old men, young men and maidens, women and children, but do not touch anyone who has the mark. Begin at my sanctuary." So they began with the elders[j] who were in front of the temple.[k]

7 Then he said to them, "Defile the temple and fill the courts with the slain. Go!" So they went out and began killing throughout the city. 8 While they were killing and I was left alone, I fell facedown,[l] crying out, "Ah, Sovereign LORD! Are you going to destroy the entire remnant of Israel in this outpouring of your wrath on Jerusalem?[m]"

9 He answered me, "The sin of the house of Israel and Judah is exceeding-

8:1 i Eze 14:1 j Eze 33:31 k Eze 1:1-3 **8:2** l Eze 1:4,26-27 **8:3** m Eze 3:12; 11:1 n Ex 20:5; Dt 32:16 **8:4** o Eze 1:28 p Eze 3:22 **8:5** q Ps 78:58; Jer 32:34 **8:6** r Eze 5:11 **8:10** s Ex 20:4 **8:11** t Nu 16:17 u Nu 16:35 **8:12** v Ps 10:11; Isa 29:15; Eze 9:9

8:16 w Joel 2:17 x Dt 4:19; 17:3; Job 31:28; Jer 2:27; Eze 11:1,12 **8:17** y Eze 9:9 z Eze 16:26 **8:18** a Eze 9:10; 24:14 b Isa 1:15; Jer 11:11; Mic 3:4; Zec 7:13 **9:2** c Lev 16:4; Eze 10:2; Rev 15:6 **9:3** d Eze 10:4 e Eze 11:22 **9:4** f Ex 12:7; 2Co 1:22; Rev 7:3; 9:4 g Ps 119:136; Jer 13:17; Eze 21:6 h Ps 119:53 **9:5** i Eze 5:11 **9:6** j Eze 8:11-13, 16 k 2Ch 36:17; Jer 25:29; 1Pe 4:17 **9:8** l Jos 7:6 m Eze 11:13; Am 7:1-6

a 2 Or *saw a fiery figure*

ly great; the land is full of bloodshed
and the city is full of injustice.[n] They
say, 'The LORD has forsaken the land;
the LORD does not see.'[o] 10So I will not
look on them with pity[p] or spare
them, but I will bring down on their
own heads what they have done.[q]"
11Then the man in linen with the
writing kit at his side brought back
word, saying, "I have done as you commanded."

The Glory Departs From the Temple

10 I looked, and I saw the likeness of a
throne[r] of sapphire[a][s] above the
expanse[t] that was over the heads of
the cherubim. 2The LORD said to the
man clothed in linen,[u] "Go in among
the wheels[v] beneath the cherubim.
Fill[w] your hands with burning coals
from among the cherubim and scatter
them over the city." And as I watched,
he went in.
3Now the cherubim were standing
on the south side of the temple when
the man went in, and a cloud filled the
inner court. 4Then the glory of the
LORD[x] rose from above the cherubim
and moved to the threshold of the temple. The cloud filled the temple, and
the court was full of the radiance of the
glory of the LORD. 5The sound of the
wings of the cherubim could be heard
as far away as the outer court, like the
voice[y] of God Almighty[b] when he
speaks.
6When the LORD commanded the
man in linen, "Take fire from among
the wheels, from among the cherubim," the man went in and stood beside a wheel. 7Then one of the cherubim reached out his hand to the fire
that was among them. He took up
some of it and put it into the hands of
the man in linen, who took it and went
out. 8(Under the wings of the cherubim
could be seen what looked like the
hands of a man.)[z]
9I looked, and I saw beside the cherubim four wheels, one beside each of
the cherubim; the wheels sparkled like
chrysolite.[a] 10As for their appearance,
the four of them looked alike; each was
like a wheel intersecting a wheel. 11As
they moved, they would go in any one
of the four directions the cherubim
faced; the wheels did not turn about[c]
as the cherubim went. The cherubim
went in whatever direction the head
faced, without turning as they went.
12Their entire bodies, including their
backs, their hands and their wings,
were completely full of eyes,[b] as were
their four wheels.[c] 13I heard the
wheels being called "the whirling
wheels." 14Each of the cherubim[d] had
four faces:[e] One face was that of a
cherub, the second the face of a man,
the third the face of a lion, and the
fourth the face of an eagle.[f]
15Then the cherubim rose upward.
These were the living creatures[g] I had
seen by the Kebar River. 16When the
cherubim moved, the wheels beside
them moved; and when the cherubim
spread their wings to rise from the
ground, the wheels did not leave their
side. 17When the cherubim stood still,
they also stood still; and when the
cherubim rose, they rose with them,
because the spirit of the living creatures was in them.[h]
18Then the glory of the LORD departed from over the threshold of
the temple and stopped above the
cherubim.[i] 19While I watched, the
cherubim spread their wings and rose
from the ground, and as they went,
the wheels went with them.[j] They
stopped at the entrance to the east gate
of the LORD's house, and the glory of
the God of Israel was above them.
20These were the living creatures I
had seen beneath the God of Israel by
the Kebar River,[k] and I realized that
they were cherubim. 21Each had four
faces[l] and four wings,[m] and under
their wings was what looked like the
hands of a man. 22Their faces had the
same appearance as those I had seen
by the Kebar River. Each one went
straight ahead.

Judgment on Israel's Leaders

11 Then the Spirit lifted me up and
brought me to the gate of the house
of the LORD that faces east. There at the
entrance to the gate were twenty-five
men, and I saw among them Jaazaniah
son of Azzur and Pelatiah son of Benaiah, leaders of the people.[n] 2The LORD
said to me, "Son of man, these are the
men who are plotting evil and giving
wicked advice in this city. 3They say,
'Will it not soon be time to build
houses?[d] This city is a cooking pot,[o]
and we are the meat.'[p] 4Therefore
prophesy[q] against them; prophesy,
son of man."
5Then the Spirit of the LORD came
upon me, and he told me to say: "This
is what the LORD says: That is what you
are saying, O house of Israel, but I
know what is going through your
mind.[r] 6You have killed many people
in this city and filled its streets with the
dead.[s]

9:9 [n]Eze 22:29 [o]Job 22:13; Eze 8:12
9:10 [p]Eze 7:4; 8:18 [q]Isa 65:6; Eze 11:21
10:1 [r]Rev 4:2 [s]Ex 24:10 [t]Eze 1:22
10:2 [u]Eze 9:2 [v]Eze 1:15 [w]Rev 8:5
10:4 [x]Eze 1:28; 9:3
10:5 [y]Job 40:9; Eze 1:24
10:8 [z]Eze 1:8
10:9 [a]Eze 1:15-16; Rev 21:20
10:12 [b]Rev 4:6-8 [c]Eze 1:15-21
10:14 [d]1Ki 7:36 [e]Eze 1:6 [f]Eze 1:10; Rev 4:7
10:15 [g]Eze 1:3,5
10:17 [h]Eze 1:20-21
10:18 [i]Ps 18:10
10:19 [j]Eze 11:1,22
10:20 [k]Eze 1:1
10:21 [l]Eze 41:18 [m]Eze 1:6
11:1 [n]Eze 8:16; 10:19; 43:4-5
11:3 [o]Jer 1:13; Eze 24:3 [p]ver 7,11
11:4 [q]Eze 3:4,17
11:5 [r]Jer 17:10
11:6 [s]Eze 7:23; 22:6

a *1* Or *lapis lazuli* **b** *5* Hebrew *El-Shaddai* **c** *11* Or *aside* **d** *3* Or *This is not the time to build houses.*

7 "Therefore this is what the Sovereign LORD says: The bodies you have thrown there are the meat and this city is the pot, but I will drive you out of it.[t] 8 You fear the sword, and the sword is what I will bring against you, declares the Sovereign LORD.[u] 9 I will drive you out of the city and hand you over[v] to foreigners and inflict punishment on you.[w] 10 You will fall by the sword, and I will execute judgment on you at the borders of Israel.[x] Then you will know that I am the LORD. 11 This city will not be a pot[y] for you, nor will you be the meat in it; I will execute judgment on you at the borders of Israel. 12 And you will know that I am the LORD, for you have not followed my decrees[z] or kept my laws but have conformed to the standards of the nations around you.[a]"

13 Now as I was prophesying, Pelatiah[b] son of Benaiah died. Then I fell facedown and cried out in a loud voice, "Ah, Sovereign LORD! Will you completely destroy the remnant of Israel?[c]"

14 The word of the LORD came to me: 15 "Son of man, your brothers—your brothers who are your blood relatives**[a]** and the whole house of Israel—are those of whom the people of Jerusalem have said, 'They are**[b]** far away from the LORD; this land was given to us as our possession.'[d]

Promised Return of Israel

16 "Therefore say: 'This is what the Sovereign LORD says: Although I sent them far away among the nations and scattered them among the countries, yet for a little while I have been a sanctuary[e] for them in the countries where they have gone.'

17 "Therefore say: 'This is what the Sovereign LORD says: I will gather you from the nations and bring you back from the countries where you have been scattered, and I will give you back the land of Israel again.'[f]

18 "They will return to it and remove all its vile images[g] and detestable idols.[h] 19 I will give them an undivided heart[i] and put a new spirit in them; I will remove from them their heart of stone[j] and give them a heart of flesh.[k] 20 Then they will follow my decrees and be careful to keep my laws.[l] They will be my people, and I will be their God.[m] 21 But as for those whose hearts are devoted to their vile images and detestable idols, I will bring down on their own heads what they have done, declares the Sovereign LORD.[n]"

22 Then the cherubim, with the wheels beside them, spread their wings, and the glory of the God of Israel was above them.[o] 23 The glory[p] of the LORD went up from within the city and stopped above the mountain[q] east of it. 24 The Spirit[r] lifted me up and brought me to the exiles in Babylonia**[c]** in the vision[s] given by the Spirit of God.

Then the vision I had seen went up from me, 25 and I told the exiles everything the LORD had shown me.[t]

The Exile Symbolized

12 The word of the LORD came to me: 2 "Son of man, you are living among a rebellious people. They have eyes to see but do not see and ears to hear but do not hear, for they are a rebellious people.[u]

3 "Therefore, son of man, pack your belongings for exile and in the daytime, as they watch, set out and go from where you are to another place. Perhaps[v] they will understand,[w] though they are a rebellious house.[x] 4 During the daytime, while they watch, bring out your belongings packed for exile. Then in the evening, while they are watching, go out like those who go into exile.[y] 5 While they watch, dig through the wall and take your belongings out through it. 6 Put them on your shoulder as they are watching and carry them out at dusk. Cover your face so that you cannot see the land, for I have made you a sign[z] to the house of Israel."

7 So I did as I was commanded.[a] During the day I brought out my things packed for exile. Then in the evening I dug through the wall with my hands. I took my belongings out at dusk, carrying them on my shoulders while they watched.

8 In the morning the word of the LORD came to me: 9 "Son of man, did

11:7 [t]Eze 24:3-13; Mic 3:2-3 **11:8** [u]Pr 10:24 **11:9** [v]Ps 106:41 [w]Dt 28:36; Eze 5:8 **11:10** [x]2Ki 14:25 **11:11** [y]ver 3 **11:12** [z]Lev 18:4; Eze 18:9 [a]Eze 8:10 **11:13** [b]ver 1 [c]Eze 9:8 **11:15** [d]Eze 33:24 **11:16** [e]Ps 90:1; 91:9; Isa 8:14 **11:17** [f]Jer 3:18; 24:5-6; Eze 28:25; 34:13 **11:18** [g]Eze 5:11 [h]Eze 37:23 **11:19** [i]Jer 32:39 [j]Zec 7:12 [k]Eze 18:31; 36:26; 2Co 3:3 **11:20** [l]Ps 105:45 [m]Eze 14:11; 36:26-28 **11:21** [n]Eze 9:10; 16:43

11:22 [o]Eze 10:19 **11:23** [p]Eze 8:4; 10:4 [q]Zec 14:4 **11:24** [r]Eze 8:3 [s]2Co 12:2-4 **11:25** [t]Eze 3:4,11 **12:2** [u]Isa 6:10; Eze 2:6-8; Mt 13:15 **12:3** [v]Jer 36:3 [w]Jer 26:3 [x]2Ti 2:25-26 **12:4** [y]ver 12; Jer 39:4 **12:6** [z]ver 12; Isa 8:18; 20:3; Eze 4:3; 24:24 **12:7** [a]Eze 24:18; 37:10

a *15* Or *are in exile with you* (see Septuagint and Syriac) **b** *15* Or *those to whom the people of Jerusalem have said, 'Stay* **c** *24* Or *Chaldea*

11:18–20

PROMISE 3

QUICK CHECK-UP

What's it look like when it's right? Managers and teachers spend a great deal of time describing roles and activities so people can do their tasks correctly. Ezekiel described the roles and activities required of anyone who wants to walk with God. Work through these phrases one by one and give yourself a quick check-up.

For the next Promise 3 reading go to page 889.

not that rebellious house of Israel ask
you, 'What are you doing?'[b]
10"Say to them, 'This is what the
Sovereign LORD says: This oracle concerns the prince in Jerusalem and the
whole house of Israel who are there.'
11Say to them, 'I am a sign to you.'
"As I have done, so it will be done to
them. They will go into exile as captives.[c]
12"The prince among them will put
his things on his shoulder at dusk[d]
and leave, and a hole will be dug in the
wall for him to go through. He will cover his face so that he cannot see the
land.[e] 13I will spread my net[f] for
him, and he will be caught in my
snare;[g] I will bring him to Babylonia,
the land of the Chaldeans, but he will
not see[h] it, and there he will die.[i] 14I
will scatter to the winds all those
around him—his staff and all his
troops—and I will pursue them with
drawn sword.[j]
15"They will know that I am the
LORD, when I disperse them among the
nations and scatter them through the
countries. 16But I will spare a few of
them from the sword, famine and
plague, so that in the nations where
they go they may acknowledge all their
detestable practices. Then they will
know that I am the LORD.[k]"
17The word of the LORD came to me:
18"Son of man, tremble as you eat your
food,[l] and shudder in fear as you
drink your water. 19Say to the people of
the land: 'This is what the Sovereign
LORD says about those living in Jerusalem and in the land of Israel: They will
eat their food in anxiety and drink their
water in despair, for their land will be
stripped of everything[m] in it because
of the violence of all who live there.[n]
20The inhabited towns will be laid
waste and the land will be desolate.
Then you will know that I am the
LORD.[o]' "
21The word of the LORD came to me:
22"Son of man, what is this proverb you
have in the land of Israel: 'The days go
by and every vision comes to nothing'?[p] 23Say to them, 'This is what the
Sovereign LORD says: I am going to put
an end to this proverb, and they will no
longer quote it in Israel.' Say to them,
'The days are near when every vision
will be fulfilled.[q] 24For there will be no
more false visions or flattering divinations[r] among the people of Israel.
25But I the LORD will speak what I will,
and it shall be fulfilled without delay.
For in your days, you rebellious house,
I will fulfill whatever I say, declares the
Sovereign LORD.[s]' "
26The word of the LORD came to me:
27"Son of man, the house of Israel is
saying, 'The vision he sees is for many
years from now, and he prophesies
about the distant future.'[t]
28"Therefore say to them, 'This is
what the Sovereign LORD says: None of
my words will be delayed any longer;
whatever I say will be fulfilled, declares
the Sovereign LORD.' "

False Prophets Condemned

13 The word of the LORD came to me:
2"Son of man, prophesy against the
prophets of Israel who are now prophesying. Say to those who prophesy out
of their own imagination: 'Hear the
word of the LORD![u] 3This is what the
Sovereign LORD says: Woe to the foolish[a] prophets[v] who follow their own
spirit and have seen nothing![w] 4Your
prophets, O Israel, are like jackals
among ruins. 5You have not gone up to
the breaks in the wall to repair[x] it for
the house of Israel so that it will stand
firm in the battle on the day of the
LORD.[y] 6Their visions are false and
their divinations a lie. They say, "The
LORD declares," when the LORD has not
sent them; yet they expect their words
to be fulfilled.[z] 7Have you not seen
false visions and uttered lying divinations when you say, "The LORD declares," though I have not spoken?
8" 'Therefore this is what the Sovereign LORD says: Because of your false
words and lying visions, I am against
you, declares the Sovereign LORD. 9My
hand will be against the prophets who
see false visions and utter lying divinations. They will not belong to the council of my people or be listed in the

[a] 3 Or *wicked*

12:9 [b]Eze 17:12; 20:49; 24:19 **12:11** [c]2Ki 25:7; Jer 15:2; 52:15 **12:12** [d]Jer 39:4 [e]Jer 52:7 **12:13** [f]Eze 17:20; 19:8; Hos 7:12 [g]Isa 24:17-18 [h]Jer 39:7 [i]Jer 52:11; Eze 17:16 **12:14** [j]2Ki 25:5; Eze 5:10,12 **12:16** [k]Jer 22:8-9; Eze 6:8-10; 14:22 **12:18** [l]La 5:9; Eze 4:16 **12:19** [m]Eze 6:6-14; Mic 7:13; Zec 7:14 [n]Eze 4:16; 23:33 **12:20** [o]Isa 7:23-24; Jer 4:7 **12:22** [p]Eze 11:3; Am 6:3; 2Pe 3:4 **12:23** [q]Ps 37:13; Joel 2:1; Zep 1:14 **12:24** [r]Jer 14:14; Eze 13:23; Zec 13:2-4 **12:25** [s]Isa 14:24; Hab 1:5

12:27 [t]Da 10:14 **13:2** [u]ver 17; Jer 23:16; 37:19 **13:3** [v]La 2:14 [w]Jer 23:25-32 **13:5** [x]Isa 58:12; Eze 22:30 [y]Eze 7:19 **13:6** [z]Jer 28:15; Eze 22:28

12:26–28 PROMISE 1

DON'T PUT OFF UNTIL TOMORROW . . .

Verse 27 is the procrastinator's favorite Bible verse. But what the procrastinator pushes into the future usually demands immediate attention. That's the way it is in the Christian life. Like these Israelites, we find it easy to think we have forever to get ourselves right with God. A wiser approach to life is to treat every word of God as if verse 28 is true instead of verse 27.

Why take that approach? Read these verses one more time and you'll discover the urgency of answering that question correctly.

For the next Promise 1 reading go to page 933.

records[a] of the house of Israel, nor will they enter the land of Israel. Then you will know that I am the Sovereign LORD.[b]

10" 'Because they lead my people astray,[c] saying, "Peace," when there is no peace, and because, when a flimsy wall is built, they cover it with whitewash,[d] 11therefore tell those who cover it with whitewash that it is going to fall. Rain will come in torrents, and I will send hailstones hurtling down, and violent winds will burst forth.[e] 12When the wall collapses, will people not ask you, "Where is the whitewash you covered it with?"

13" 'Therefore this is what the Sovereign LORD says: In my wrath I will unleash a violent wind, and in my anger hailstones[f] and torrents of rain will fall with destructive fury.[g] 14I will tear down the wall you have covered with whitewash and will level it to the ground so that its foundation[h] will be laid bare. When it[a] falls,[i] you will be destroyed in it; and you will know that I am the LORD. 15So I will spend my wrath against the wall and against those who covered it with whitewash. I will say to you, "The wall is gone and so are those who whitewashed it, 16those prophets of Israel who prophesied to Jerusalem and saw visions of peace for her when there was no peace, declares the Sovereign LORD.[j]" '

17"Now, son of man, set your face against the daughters[k] of your people who prophesy out of their own imagination. Prophesy against them[l] 18and say, 'This is what the Sovereign LORD says: Woe to the women who sew magic charms on all their wrists and make veils of various lengths for their heads in order to ensnare people. Will you ensnare the lives of my people but preserve your own? 19You have profaned[m] me among my people for a few handfuls of barley and scraps of bread. By lying to my people, who listen to lies, you have killed those who should not have died and have spared those who should not live.[n]

20" 'Therefore this is what the Sovereign LORD says: I am against your magic charms with which you ensnare people like birds and I will tear them from your arms; I will set free the people that you ensnare like birds. 21I will tear off your veils and save my people from your hands, and they will no longer fall prey to your power. Then you will know that I am the LORD.[o] 22Because you disheartened the righteous with your lies, when I had brought them no grief, and because you encouraged the wicked not to turn from their evil ways and so save their lives,[p] 23therefore you will no longer see false visions or practice divination.[q] I will save my people from your hands. And then you will know that I am the LORD.[r]' "

Idolaters Condemned

14 Some of the elders of Israel came to me and sat down in front of me.[s] 2Then the word of the LORD came to me: 3"Son of man, these men have set up idols in their hearts and put wicked stumbling blocks[t] before their faces. Should I let them inquire of me at all?[u] 4Therefore speak to them and tell them, 'This is what the Sovereign LORD says: When any Israelite sets up idols in his heart and puts a wicked stumbling block before his face and then goes to a prophet, I the LORD will answer him myself in keeping with his great idolatry. 5I will do this to recapture the hearts of the people of Israel, who have all deserted[v] me for their idols.'[w]

6"Therefore say to the house of Israel, 'This is what the Sovereign LORD says: Repent! Turn from your idols and renounce all your detestable practices![x]

7" 'When any Israelite or any alien[y] living in Israel separates himself from me and sets up idols in his heart and puts a wicked stumbling block before his face and then goes to a prophet to inquire of me, I the LORD will answer him myself. 8I will set my face against[z] that man and make him an example and a byword.[a] I will cut him off from my people. Then you will know that I am the LORD.

9" 'And if the prophet[b] is enticed[c] to utter a prophecy, I the LORD have enticed that prophet, and I will stretch out my hand against him and destroy him from among my people Israel.[d] 10They will bear their guilt—the prophet will be as guilty as the one who consults him. 11Then the people of Israel will no longer stray[e] from me, nor will they defile themselves anymore with all their sins. They will be my people, and I will be their God, declares the Sovereign LORD.[f]' "

Judgment Inescapable

12The word of the LORD came to me: 13"Son of man, if a country sins against me by being unfaithful and I stretch out my hand against it to cut off its food supply[g] and send famine upon it and kill its men and their animals,[h] 14even if these three men—Noah,[i]

13:9 [a]Jer 17:13 [b]Eze 20:38
13:10 [c]Jer 50:6 [d]Eze 7:25; 22:28
13:11 [e]Eze 38:22
13:13 [f]Rev 11:19; 16:21 [g]Ex 9:25; Isa 30:30
13:14 [h]Mic 1:6 [i]Jer 6:15
13:16 [j]Isa 57:21; Jer 6:14
13:17 [k]Rev 2:20 [l]ver 2
13:19 [m]Eze 20:39; 22:26 [n]Pr 28:21
13:21 [o]Ps 91:3
13:22 [p]Jer 23:14; Eze 33:14-16
13:23 [q]ver 6; Eze 12:24 [r]Mic 3:6
14:1 [s]Eze 8:1; 20:1
14:3 [t]ver 7; Eze 7:19 [u]Isa 1:15; Eze 20:31
14:5 [v]Zec 11:8 [w]Jer 2:11
14:6 [x]Isa 2:20; 30:22
14:7 [y]Ex 12:48; 20:10
14:8 [z]Eze 15:7 [a]Eze 5:15
14:9 [b]Jer 14:15 [c]Jer 4:10 [d]1Ki 22:23
14:11 [e]Eze 48:11 [f]Eze 11:19-20; 37:23
14:13 [g]Lev 26:26 [h]Eze 5:16; 6:14; 15:8
14:14 [i]Ge 6:8

a 14 Or *the city*

Daniel[a][j] and Job[k]—were in it, they
could save only themselves by their
righteousness,[l] declares the Sovereign LORD.
15"Or if I send wild beasts[m] through
that country and they leave it childless
and it becomes desolate so that no one
can pass through it because of the
beasts,[n] 16as surely as I live, declares
the Sovereign LORD, even if these three
men were in it, they could not save
their own sons or daughters. They
alone would be saved, but the land
would be desolate.[o]
17"Or if I bring a sword[p] against that
country and say, 'Let the sword pass
throughout the land,' and I kill its men
and their animals,[q] 18as surely as I
live, declares the Sovereign LORD, even
if these three men were in it, they could
not save their own sons or daughters.
They alone would be saved.
19"Or if I send a plague into that land
and pour out my wrath[r] upon it
through bloodshed, killing its men and
their animals,[s] 20as surely as I live, declares the Sovereign LORD, even if
Noah, Daniel and Job were in it, they
could save neither son nor daughter.
They would save only themselves by
their righteousness.[t]
21"For this is what the Sovereign
LORD says: How much worse will it be
when I send against Jerusalem my four
dreadful judgments—sword and famine and wild beasts and plague—to kill
its men and their animals![u] 22Yet there
will be some survivors—sons and
daughters who will be brought out of
it.[v] They will come to you, and when
you see their conduct[w] and their
actions, you will be consoled regarding the disaster I have brought
upon Jerusalem—every disaster I have
brought upon it. 23You will be consoled
when you see their conduct and their
actions, for you will know that I have
done nothing in it without cause, declares the Sovereign LORD.[x]"

Jerusalem, A Useless Vine

15 The word of the LORD came to me:
2"Son of man, how is the wood of a
vine[y] better than that of a branch on
any of the trees in the forest? 3Is wood
ever taken from it to make anything
useful? Do they make pegs from it to
hang things on? 4And after it is thrown
on the fire as fuel and the fire burns
both ends and chars the middle, is it
then useful for anything?[z] 5If it was
not useful for anything when it was
whole, how much less can it be made
into something useful when the fire
has burned it and it is charred?
6"Therefore this is what the Sovereign LORD says: As I have given the
wood of the vine among the trees of the
forest as fuel for the fire, so will I treat
the people living in Jerusalem. 7I will
set my face against[a] them. Although
they have come out of the fire, the fire
will yet consume them. And when I set
my face against them, you will know
that I am the LORD.[b] 8I will make the
land desolate[c] because they have
been unfaithful,[d] declares the Sovereign LORD."

An Allegory of Unfaithful Jerusalem

16 The word of the LORD came to me:
2"Son of man, confront Jerusalem
with her detestable practices[e] 3and
say, 'This is what the Sovereign LORD
says to Jerusalem: Your ancestry[f] and
birth were in the land of the Canaanites; your father was an Amorite and
your mother a Hittite.[g] 4On the day
you were born[h] your cord was not cut,
nor were you washed with water to
make you clean, nor were you rubbed
with salt or wrapped in cloths. 5No one
looked on you with pity or had compassion enough to do any of these
things for you. Rather, you were
thrown out into the open field, for on
the day you were born you were despised.
6" 'Then I passed by and saw you

14:12–20 PROMISE 3

GOD IS NO GRANDFATHER

Some sayings become trite because they are so true. However, trite doesn't necessarily negate true. One such statement is "God has no grandchildren." It speaks to the need for each individual to foster a personal relationship with the Creator.

Being a member of a great Christian family or attending a church or Bible study won't, by itself, make anyone right with God. Even if a person could stand before God and say in all honesty that Noah, Daniel and Job were close friends, those relationships would make no difference if he or she had no personal relationship with God.

Every person will give an account for his or her own response to God and his Word. We must diligently pursue an obedient walk with God. Add 18:19–23 and 18:31–32 to get the full impact of how seriously God takes this truth of individual responsibility.

For the next Promise 3 reading go to page 938.

14:14 [j]ver 20; Eze 28:3; Da 1:6; 6:13 [k]Job 1:1 [l]Job 42:9; Jer 15:1; Eze 18:20
14:15 [m]Eze 5:17 [n]Lev 26:22
14:16 [o]Eze 18:20
14:17 [p]Lev 26:25; Eze 5:12; 21:3-4 [q]Eze 25:13; Zep 1:3
14:19 [r]Eze 7:8 [s]Eze 38:22
14:20 [t]ver 14
14:21 [u]Jer 15:3; Eze 5:17; 33:27; Am 4:6-10; Rev 6:8
14:22 [v]Eze 12:16 [w]Eze 20:43
14:23 [x]Jer 22:8-9
15:2 [y]Isa 5:1-7; Jer 2:21; Hos 10:1
15:4 [z]Eze 19:14; Jn 15:6
15:7 [a]Ps 34:16; Eze 14:8 [b]Isa 24:18; Am 9:1-4
15:8 [c]Eze 14:13 [d]Eze 17:20
16:2 [e]Eze 20:4; 22:2
16:3 [f]Eze 21:30 [g]ver 45
16:4 [h]Hos 2:3

[a] 14 Or *Danel*; the Hebrew spelling may suggest a person other than the prophet Daniel; also in verse 20.

kicking about in your blood, and as you lay there in your blood I said to you, "Live!"[a][i] 7I made you grow[j] like a plant of the field. You grew up and developed and became the most beautiful of jewels.[b] Your breasts were formed and your hair grew, you who were naked and bare.[k]

8" 'Later I passed by, and when I looked at you and saw that you were old enough for love, I spread the corner of my garment[l] over you and covered your nakedness. I gave you my solemn oath and entered into a covenant with you, declares the Sovereign LORD, and you became mine.[m]

9" 'I bathed[c] you with water and washed[n] the blood from you and put ointments on you. 10I clothed you with an embroidered[o] dress and put leather sandals on you. I dressed you in fine linen[p] and covered you with costly garments.[q] 11I adorned you with jewelry:[r] I put bracelets[s] on your arms and a necklace[t] around your neck, 12and I put a ring on your nose,[u] earrings on your ears and a beautiful crown[v] on your head. 13So you were adorned with gold and silver; your clothes were of fine linen and costly fabric and embroidered cloth. Your food was fine flour, honey and olive oil.[w] You became very beautiful and rose to be a queen.[x] 14And your fame[y] spread among the nations on account of your beauty,[z] because the splendor I had given you made your beauty perfect, declares the Sovereign LORD.

15" 'But you trusted in your beauty and used your fame to become a prostitute. You lavished your favors on anyone who passed by[a] and your beauty became his.[d][b] 16You took some of your garments to make gaudy high places, where you carried on your prostitution.[c] Such things should not happen, nor should they ever occur. 17You also took the fine jewelry I gave you, the jewelry made of my gold and silver, and you made for yourself male idols and engaged in prostitution with them.[d] 18And you took your embroidered clothes to put on them, and you offered my oil and incense before them. 19Also the food I provided for you—the fine flour, olive oil and honey I gave you to eat—you offered as fragrant incense before them. That is what happened, declares the Sovereign LORD.[e]

20" 'And you took your sons and daughters[f] whom you bore to me[g] and sacrificed them as food to the idols. Was your prostitution not enough?[h] 21You slaughtered my children and sacrificed them[e] to the idols.[i] 22In all your detestable practices and your prostitution you did not remember the days of your youth,[j] when you were naked and bare, kicking about in your blood.[k]

23" 'Woe! Woe to you, declares the Sovereign LORD. In addition to all your other wickedness, 24you built a mound for yourself and made a lofty shrine[l] in every public square.[m] 25At the head of every street you built your lofty shrines and degraded your beauty, offering your body with increasing promiscuity to anyone who passed by.[n] 26You engaged in prostitution with the Egyptians, your lustful neighbors, and provoked[o] me to anger with your increasing promiscuity.[p] 27So I stretched out my hand[q] against you and reduced your territory; I gave you over to the greed of your enemies, the daughters of the Philistines,[r] who were shocked by your lewd conduct. 28You engaged in prostitution with the Assyrians[s] too, because you were insatiable; and even after that, you still were not satisfied. 29Then you increased your promiscuity to include Babylonia,[f][t] a land of merchants, but even with this you were not satisfied.

30" 'How weak-willed you are, declares the Sovereign LORD, when you do all these things, acting like a brazen prostitute![u] 31When you built your mounds at the head of every street and made your lofty shrines[v] in every public square, you were unlike a prostitute, because you scorned payment.

32" 'You adulterous wife! You prefer strangers to your own husband! 33Every prostitute receives a fee, but you give gifts[w] to all your lovers, bribing them to come to you from everywhere for your illicit favors.[x] 34So in your prostitution you are the opposite of others; no one runs after you for your favors. You are the very opposite, for you give payment and none is given to you.

35" 'Therefore, you prostitute, hear the word of the LORD! 36This is what the Sovereign LORD says: Because you poured out your wealth[g] and exposed your nakedness in your promiscuity with your lovers, and because of all your detestable idols, and because you

16:6 [i]Ex 19:4
16:7 [j]Dt 1:10 [k]Ex 1:7
16:8 [l]Ru 3:9 [m]Jer 2:2; Hos 2:7,19-20
16:9 [n]Ru 3:3
16:10 [o]Ex 26:36 [p]Eze 27:16 [q]ver 18
16:11 [r]Eze 23:40 [s]Isa 3:19; Eze 23:42 [t]Ge 41:42
16:12 [u]Isa 3:21 [v]Isa 28:5; Jer 13:18
16:13 [w]1Sa 10:1 [x]Dt 32:13-14; 1Ki 4:21
16:14 [y]1Ki 10:24 [z]La 2:15
16:15 [a]ver 25 [b]Isa 57:8; Jer 2:20; Eze 23:3; 27:3
16:16 [c]2Ki 23:7
16:17 [d]Eze 7:20
16:19 [e]Hos 2:8
16:20 [f]Jer 7:31 [g]Ex 13:2 [h]Ps 106:37-38; Isa 57:5; Eze 23:37
16:21 [i]2Ki 17:17; Jer 19:5
16:22 [j]Jer 2:2; Hos 11:1 [k]ver 6
16:24 [l]ver 31; Isa 57:7 [m]Ps 78:58; Jer 2:20; 3:2; Eze 20:28
16:25 [n]ver 15; Pr 9:14
16:26 [o]Eze 8:17 [p]Eze 20:8; 23:19-21
16:27 [q]Eze 20:33 [r]2Ch 28:18
16:28 [s]2Ki 16:7
16:29 [t]Eze 23:14-17
16:30 [u]Jer 3:3
16:31 [v]ver 24
16:33 [w]Isa 30:6; 57:9 [x]Hos 8:9-10

a *6* A few Hebrew manuscripts, Septuagint and Syriac; most Hebrew manuscripts *"Live!" And as you lay there in your blood I said to you, "Live!"* b *7* Or *became mature* c *9* Or *I had bathed* d *15* Most Hebrew manuscripts; one Hebrew manuscript (see some Septuagint manuscripts) *by. Such a thing should not happen* e *21* Or *and made them pass through ⌊the fire⌋* f *29* Or *Chaldea* g *36* Or *lust*

gave them your children's blood,[y]
37 therefore I am going to gather all
your lovers, with whom you found
pleasure, those you loved as well as
those you hated. I will gather them
against you from all around and will
strip you in front of them, and they will
see all your nakedness.[z] 38 I will sentence you to the punishment of women
who commit adultery and who shed
blood;[a] I will bring upon you the
blood vengeance of my wrath and jealous anger.[b] 39 Then I will hand you
over to your lovers, and they will tear
down your mounds and destroy your
lofty shrines. They will strip you of your
clothes and take your fine jewelry and
leave you naked and bare.[c] 40 They
will bring a mob against you, who will
stone[d] you and hack you to pieces
with their swords. 41 They will burn
down[e] your houses and inflict punishment on you in the sight of many
women.[f] I will put a stop[g] to your
prostitution, and you will no longer
pay your lovers. 42 Then my wrath
against you will subside and my jealous anger will turn away from you; I will
be calm and no longer angry.[h]
43 " 'Because you did not remember[i] the days of your youth but enraged me with all these things, I will
surely bring down[j] on your head what
you have done, declares the Sovereign
LORD. Did you not add lewdness to all
your other detestable practices?[k]
44 " 'Everyone who quotes proverbs
will quote this proverb about you:
"Like mother, like daughter." 45 You are
a true daughter of your mother, who
despised her husband and her children; and you are a true sister of your
sisters, who despised their husbands
and their children. Your mother was a
Hittite and your father an Amorite.[l]
46 Your older sister was Samaria, who
lived to the north of you with her
daughters; and your younger sister,
who lived to the south of you with her
daughters, was Sodom.[m] 47 You not
only walked in their ways and copied
their detestable practices, but in all
your ways you soon became more depraved than they.[n] 48 As surely as I live,
declares the Sovereign LORD, your sister Sodom and her daughters never did
what you and your daughters have
done.[o]
49 " 'Now this was the sin of your sister Sodom:[p] She and her daughters
were arrogant,[q] overfed and unconcerned; they did not help the poor and
needy.[r] 50 They were haughty and did
detestable things before me. Therefore
I did away with them as you have
seen.[s] 51 Samaria did not commit half
the sins you did. You have done more
detestable things than they, and have
made your sisters seem righteous by all
these things you have done.[t] 52 Bear
your disgrace, for you have furnished
some justification for your sisters. Because your sins were more vile than
theirs, they appear more righteous
than you. So then, be ashamed and
bear your disgrace, for you have made
your sisters appear righteous.
53 " 'However, I will restore[u] the fortunes of Sodom and her daughters and
of Samaria and her daughters, and
your fortunes along with them, 54 so
that you may bear your disgrace[v] and
be ashamed of all you have done in
giving them comfort. 55 And your sisters, Sodom with her daughters and Samaria with her daughters, will return to
what they were before; and you and
your daughters will return to what you
were before.[w] 56 You would not even
mention your sister Sodom in the
day of your pride, 57 before your wickedness was uncovered. Even so, you are
now scorned by the daughters of
Edom[a][x] and all her neighbors and the
daughters of the Philistines—all those
around you who despise you. 58 You
will bear the consequences of your
lewdness and your detestable practices, declares the LORD.[y]
59 " 'This is what the Sovereign LORD
says: I will deal with you as you deserve, because you have despised my
oath by breaking the covenant.[z] 60 Yet
I will remember the covenant I made
with you in the days of your youth, and
I will establish an everlasting covenant[a] with you. 61 Then you will remember your ways and be ashamed[b]
when you receive your sisters, both
those who are older than you and those
who are younger. I will give them to
you as daughters, but not on the basis
of my covenant with you. 62 So I will
establish my covenant with you, and
you will know that I am the LORD.[c]
63 Then, when I make atonement[d] for
you for all you have done, you will remember and be ashamed and never
again open your mouth[e] because of
your humiliation, declares the Sovereign LORD.[f]' "

Two Eagles and a Vine

17 The word of the LORD came to me:
2 "Son of man, set forth an allegory
and tell the house of Israel a parable.[g]
3 Say to them, 'This is what the Sovereign LORD says: A great eagle[h] with

16:36 [y]Jer 19:5; Eze 23:10
16:37 [z]Jer 13:22
16:38 [a]Eze 23:45 [b]Lev 20:10; Eze 23:25
16:39 [c]Eze 23:26; Hos 2:3
16:40 [d]Jn 8:5,7
16:41 [e]Dt 13:16 [f]Eze 23:10 [g]Eze 23:27,48
16:42 [h]Isa 54:9; Eze 5:13; 39:29
16:43 [i]Ps 78:42 [j]Eze 22:31 [k]ver 22; Eze 11:21
16:45 [l]Eze 23:2
16:46 [m]Ge 13:10-13; Eze 23:4
16:47 [n]2Ki 21:9; Eze 5:7
16:48 [o]Mt 10:15; 11:23-24
16:49 [p]Ge 13:13 [q]Ps 138:6 [r]Eze 18:7,12, 16; Lk 12:16-20
16:50 [s]Ge 18:20-21; 19:5
16:51 [t]Jer 3:8-11
16:53 [u]Isa 19:24-25
16:54 [v]Jer 2:26; Eze 14:22
16:55 [w]Mal 3:4
16:57 [x]2Ki 16:6
16:58 [y]Eze 23:49
16:59 [z]Eze 17:19
16:60 [a]Jer 32:40; Eze 37:26
16:61 [b]Eze 20:43
16:62 [c]Jer 24:7; Eze 20:37, 43-44; Hos 2:19-20
16:63 [d]Ps 65:3; 79:9 [e]Ro 3:19 [f]Ps 39:9; Da 9:7-8
17:2 [g]Eze 20:49
17:3 [h]Hos 8:1

[a]57 Many Hebrew manuscripts and Syriac; most Hebrew manuscripts, Septuagint and Vulgate *Aram*

powerful wings, long feathers and full
plumage of varied colors came to Lebanon.[i] Taking hold of the top of a cedar, 4he broke off its topmost shoot
and carried it away to a land of merchants, where he planted it in a city of
traders.
5" 'He took some of the seed of your
land and put it in fertile soil. He planted it like a willow by abundant water,[j]
6and it sprouted and became a low,
spreading vine. Its branches turned toward him, but its roots remained under
it. So it became a vine and produced
branches and put out leafy boughs.
7" 'But there was another great eagle
with powerful wings and full plumage.
The vine now sent out its roots toward
him from the plot where it was planted
and stretched out its branches to him
for water.[k] 8It had been planted in
good soil by abundant water so that
it would produce branches, bear fruit
and become a splendid vine.'
9"Say to them, 'This is what the Sovereign LORD says: Will it thrive? Will it
not be uprooted and stripped of its
fruit so that it withers? All its new
growth will wither. It will not take a
strong arm or many people to pull it up
by the roots. 10Even if it[l] is transplant-
ed, will it thrive? Will it not wither completely when the east wind strikes it—
wither away in the plot where it
grew?' "
11Then the word of the LORD came to
me: 12"Say to this rebellious house, 'Do
you not know what these things
mean?[m]' Say to them: 'The king of
Babylon went to Jerusalem and carried
off her king and her nobles,[n] bringing
them back with him to Babylon.[o]
13Then he took a member of the royal
family and made a treaty with him,
putting him under oath.[p] He also
carried away the leading men of the
land, 14so that the kingdom would be
brought low,[q] unable to rise again,
surviving only by keeping his treaty.
15But the king rebelled[r] against him
by sending his envoys to Egypt to get
horses and a large army.[s] Will he succeed? Will he who does such things escape? Will he break the treaty and yet
escape?[t]
16" 'As surely as I live, declares the
Sovereign LORD, he shall die[u] in Babylon, in the land of the king who put
him on the throne, whose oath he despised and whose treaty he broke.[v]
17Pharaoh[w] with his mighty army and
great horde will be of no help to him in
war, when ramps[x] are built and siege
works erected to destroy many lives.[y]
18He despised the oath by breaking the
covenant. Because he had given his
hand in pledge[z] and yet did all these
things, he shall not escape.
19" 'Therefore this is what the Sovereign LORD says: As surely as I live, I will
bring down on his head my oath that
he despised and my covenant that he
broke.[a] 20I will spread my net[b] for
him, and he will be caught in my snare.
I will bring him to Babylon and execute
judgment[c] upon him there because
he was unfaithful to me. 21All his fleeing troops will fall by the sword,[d] and
the survivors[e] will be scattered to the
winds.[f] Then you will know that I the
LORD have spoken.
22" 'This is what the Sovereign LORD
says: I myself will take a shoot from the
very top of a cedar and plant it; I will
break off a tender sprig from its topmost shoots and plant it on a high and
lofty mountain.[g] 23On the mountain
heights of Israel I will plant it; it will
produce branches and bear fruit and
become a splendid cedar. Birds of every kind will nest in it; they will find
shelter in the shade of its branches.[h]
24All the trees of the field[i] will know
that I the LORD bring down the tall tree
and make the low tree grow tall. I dry
up the green tree and make the dry tree
flourish.
" 'I the LORD have spoken, and I will
do it.[j]' "

The Soul Who Sins Will Die

18 The word of the LORD came to me:
2"What do you people mean by
quoting this proverb about the land of
Israel:

" 'The fathers eat sour grapes,
and the children's teeth are set
on edge'?[k]

3"As surely as I live, declares the Sovereign LORD, you will no longer quote
this proverb in Israel. 4For every living
soul belongs to me, the father as well as
the son—both alike belong to me. The
soul who sins is the one who will die.[l]

5"Suppose there is a righteous man
who does what is just and right.
6He does not eat at the mountain[m]
shrines
or look to the idols[n] of the
house of Israel.
He does not defile his neighbor's
wife
or lie with a woman during her
period.
7He does not oppress[o] anyone,
but returns what he took in
pledge[p] for a loan.
He does not commit robbery
but gives his food to the hungry

3 →PG. 930

17:3 [i]Jer 22:23
17:5 [j]Dt 8:7-9; Isa 44:4
17:7 [k]Eze 31:4
17:10 [l]Hos 13:15
17:12 [m]Eze 12:9 [n]2Ki 24:15 [o]Eze 24:19
17:13 [p]2Ch 36:13
17:14 [q]Eze 29:14
17:15 [r]Jer 52:3 [s]Dt 17:16 [t]Jer 34:3; 38:18
17:16 [u]Jer 52:11; Eze 12:13 [v]2Ki 24:17
17:17 [w]Jer 37:7 [x]Eze 4:2 [y]Isa 36:6; Jer 37:5; Eze 29:6-7
17:18 [z]1Ch 29:24
17:19 [a]Eze 16:59
17:20 [b]Eze 12:13; 32:3 [c]Jer 2:35; Eze 20:36
17:21 [d]Eze 12:14 [e]2Ki 25:11 [f]2Ki 25:5
17:22 [g]Jer 23:5; Eze 20:40; 36:1,36; 37:22
17:23 [h]Ps 92:12; Isa 2:2; Eze 31:6; Da 4:12; Hos 14:5-7; Mt 13:32
17:24 [i]Ps 96:12 [j]Eze 19:12; 21:26; 22:14; Am 9:11
18:2 [k]Isa 3:15; Jer 31:29; La 5:7
18:4 [l]ver 20; Isa 42:5; Ro 6:23
18:6 [m]Eze 22:9 [n]Dt 4:19; Eze 6:13; 20:24
18:7 [o]Ex 22:21 [p]Ex 22:26; Dt 24:12

and provides clothing for the
naked.[q]
8He does not lend at usury
or take excessive interest.[a][r]
He withholds his hand from doing
wrong
and judges fairly[s] between man
and man.
9He follows my decrees
and faithfully keeps my laws.
That man is righteous;[t]
he will surely live,[u]
declares the Sovereign LORD.

10"Suppose he has a violent son,
who sheds blood[v] or does any of these
other things[b] 11(though the father has
done none of them):

"He eats at the mountain shrines.
He defiles his neighbor's wife.
12He oppresses the poor[w] and
needy.
He commits robbery.
He does not return what he took in
pledge.
He looks to the idols.
He does detestable things.[x]
13He lends at usury and takes
excessive interest.[y]

Will such a man live? He will not! Because he has done all these detestable things, he will surely be put to death and his blood will be on his own head.[z]

14"But suppose this son has a son
who sees all the sins his father commits, and though he sees them, he does not do such things:[a]

15"He does not eat at the mountain
shrines
or look to the idols of the house
of Israel.
He does not defile his neighbor's
wife.
16He does not oppress anyone
or require a pledge for a loan.
He does not commit robbery
but gives his food to the hungry
and provides clothing for the
naked.[b]
17He withholds his hand from sin[c]
and takes no usury or excessive
interest.
He keeps my laws and follows my
decrees.

He will not die for his father's sin; he
will surely live. 18But his father will die
for his own sin, because he practiced extortion, robbed his brother and did what was wrong among his people.

19"Yet you ask, 'Why does the son
not share the guilt of his father?' Since the son has done what is just and right and has been careful to keep all my decrees, he will surely live.[c]
20The soul who sins is the one who will die. The son will not share the guilt of the father, nor will the father share the guilt of the son. The righteousness of the righteous man will be credited to him, and the wickedness of the wicked will be charged against him.[d]

21"But if a wicked man turns away from all the sins he has committed and keeps all my decrees and does what is just and right, he will surely live; he will not die.[e]
22None of the offenses he has committed will be remembered against him. Because of the righteous things he has done, he will live.[f]
23Do I take any pleasure in the death of the wicked? declares the Sovereign LORD. Rather, am I not pleased[g] when they turn from their ways and live?[h]

24"But if a righteous man turns from his righteousness and commits sin and does the same detestable things the wicked man does, will he live? None of the righteous things he has done will be remembered. Because of the unfaithfulness he is guilty of and because of the sins he has committed, he will die.[i]

25"Yet you say, 'The way of the Lord is not just.' Hear, O house of Israel: Is my way unjust?[j] Is it not your ways that are unjust?
26If a righteous man turns from his righteousness and commits sin, he will die for it; because of the sin he has committed he will die.
27But if a wicked man turns away from the wickedness he has committed and does what is just and right, he will save his life.[k]
28Because he considers all the offenses he has committed and turns away from them, he will surely live; he will not die.
29Yet the house of Israel says, 'The way of the Lord is not just.' Are my ways unjust, O house of Israel? Is it not your ways that are unjust?

30"Therefore, O house of Israel, I will judge you, each one according to his ways, declares the Sovereign LORD. Repent![l] Turn away from all your offenses; then sin will not be your downfall.[m]
31Rid yourselves of all the offenses you have committed, and get a new heart[n] and a new spirit. Why will you die, O house of Israel?[o]
32For I take no pleasure in the death of anyone, declares the Sovereign LORD. Repent and live![p]

18:7 [q]Dt 15:11; Mt 25:36
18:8 [r]Ex 22:25; Lev 25:35-37; Dt 23:19-20 [s]Zec 8:16
18:9 [t]Hab 2:4 [u]Lev 18:5; Eze 20:11; Am 5:4
18:10 [v]Ex 21:12
18:12 [w]Am 4:1 [x]2Ki 21:11; Isa 59:6-7; Jer 22:17; Eze 8:6,17
18:13 [y]Ex 22:25 [z]Eze 33:4-5
18:14 [a]2Ch 34:21; Pr 23:24
18:16 [b]Ps 41:1; Isa 58:10
18:19 [c]Ex 20:5; Dt 5:9; Jer 15:4; Zec 1:3-6
18:20 [d]Dt 24:16; 1Ki 8:32; 2Ki 14:6; Isa 3:11; Mt 16:27; Ro 2:9
18:21 [e]Eze 33:12,19
18:22 [f]Ps 18:20-24; Isa 43:25; Mic 7:19
18:23 [g]Ps 147:11 [h]Eze 33:11; 1Ti 2:4
18:24 [i]1Sa 15:11; 2Ch 24:17-20; Eze 3:20; 20:27; 2Pe 2:20-22
18:25 [j]Ge 18:25; Jer 12:1; Eze 33:17; Zep 3:5; Mal 2:17; 3:13-15
18:27 [k]Isa 1:18
18:30 [l]Mt 3:2 [m]Eze 7:3; 33:20; Hos 12:6
18:31 [n]Ps 51:10 [o]Isa 1:16-17; Eze 11:19; 36:26
18:32 [p]Eze 33:11

[a] *8* Or *take interest*; similarly in verses 13 and 17
[b] *10* Or *things to a brother*
[c] *17* Septuagint (see also verse 8); Hebrew *from the poor*

A Lament for Israel's Princes

19 "Take up a lament[q] concerning the princes[r] of Israel 2and say:

" 'What a lioness was your mother
among the lions!
She lay down among the young
lions
and reared her cubs.
3She brought up one of her cubs,
and he became a strong lion.
He learned to tear the prey
and he devoured men.
4The nations heard about him,
and he was trapped in their pit.
They led him with hooks
to the land of Egypt.[s]

5" 'When she saw her hope
unfulfilled,
her expectation gone,
she took another of her cubs
and made him a strong lion.[t]
6He prowled among the lions,
for he was now a strong lion.
He learned to tear the prey
and he devoured men.[u]
7He broke down[a] their strongholds
and devastated[v] their towns.
The land and all who were in it
were terrified by his roaring.
8Then the nations[w] came against
him,
those from regions round about.
They spread their net for him,
and he was trapped in their
pit.[x]
9With hooks they pulled him into a
cage
and brought him to the king of
Babylon.[y]
They put him in prison,
so his roar was heard no longer
on the mountains of Israel.[z]
10" 'Your mother was like a vine in
your vineyard[b]
planted by the water;
it was fruitful and full of branches
because of abundant water.[a]
11Its branches were strong,
fit for a ruler's scepter.
It towered high
above the thick foliage,
conspicuous for its height
and for its many branches.[b]
12But it was uprooted[c] in fury
and thrown to the ground.
The east wind made it shrivel,
it was stripped of its fruit;
its strong branches withered
and fire consumed them.[d]
13Now it is planted in the desert,[e]
in a dry and thirsty land.[f]
14Fire spread from one of its main[c]
branches
and consumed[g] its fruit.
No strong branch is left on it
fit for a ruler's scepter.'[h]

This is a lament and is to be used as a lament."

Rebellious Israel

20 In the seventh year, in the fifth
month on the tenth day, some of
the elders of Israel came to inquire of
the LORD, and they sat down in front
of me.[i]
2Then the word of the LORD came to
me: 3"Son of man, speak to the elders
of Israel and say to them, 'This is what
the Sovereign LORD says: Have you
come to inquire[j] of me? As surely as I
live, I will not let you inquire of me,
declares the Sovereign LORD.[k]'
4"Will you judge them? Will you
judge them, son of man? Then confront them with the detestable practices of their fathers[l] 5and say to
them: 'This is what the Sovereign LORD
says: On the day I chose[m] Israel, I
swore with uplifted hand to the
descendants of the house of Jacob and
revealed myself to them in Egypt. With
uplifted hand I said to them, "I am the
LORD your God."[n] 6On that day I swore
to them that I would bring them out of
Egypt into a land I had searched out for
them, a land flowing with milk and
honey,[o] the most beautiful of all
lands.[p] 7And I said to them, "Each of
you, get rid of the vile images[q] you
have set your eyes on, and do not defile
yourselves with the idols of Egypt. I am
the LORD your God.[r]"
8" 'But they rebelled against me and
would not listen to me; they did not get
rid of the vile images they had set their
eyes on, nor did they forsake the idols
of Egypt.[s] So I said I would pour out
my wrath on them and spend my anger
against them in Egypt.[t] 9But for the
sake of my name I did what would keep
it from being profaned in the eyes of
the nations they lived among and in
whose sight I had revealed myself to
the Israelites by bringing them out of
Egypt.[u] 10Therefore I led them out
of Egypt and brought them into the
desert.[v] 11I gave them my decrees
and made known to them my laws, for
the man who obeys them will live
by them.[w] 12Also I gave them my Sabbaths as a sign[x] between us, so they
would know that I the LORD made them
holy.
13" 'Yet the people of Israel re-

19:1 [q]Eze 26:17; 27:2,32 [r]2Ki 24:6
19:4 [s]2Ki 23:33-34; 2Ch 36:4
19:5 [t]2Ki 23:34
19:6 [u]2Ki 24:9; 2Ch 36:9
19:7 [v]Eze 30:12
19:8 [w]2Ki 24:2 [x]2Ki 24:11
19:9 [y]2Ch 36:6 [z]2Ki 24:15
19:10 [a]Ps 80:8-11
19:11 [b]Eze 31:3; Da 4:11
19:12 [c]Eze 17:10 [d]Isa 27:11; Eze 28:17; Hos 13:15
19:13 [e]Eze 20:35 [f]Hos 2:3
19:14 [g]Eze 20:47 [h]Eze 15:4
20:1 [i]Eze 8:1
20:3 [j]Eze 14:3 [k]Mic 3:7
20:4 [l]Eze 16:2; 22:2; Mt 23:32
20:5 [m]Dt 7:6 [n]Ex 6:7
20:6 [o]Ex 3:8; Jer 32:22 [p]Dt 8:7; Ps 48:2; Da 8:9
20:7 [q]Ex 20:4 [r]Ex 20:2; Lev 18:3; Dt 29:18
20:8 [s]Eze 7:8 [t]Isa 63:10
20:9 [u]Eze 36:22; 39:7
20:10 [v]Ex 13:18
20:11 [w]Lev 18:5; Dt 4:7-8; Ro 10:5
20:12 [x]Ex 31:13

a *7* Targum (see Septuagint); Hebrew *He knew*
b *10* Two Hebrew manuscripts; most Hebrew manuscripts *your blood*
c *14* Or *from under its*

belled[y] against me in the desert. They
did not follow my decrees but rejected
my laws—although the man who
obeys them will live by them—and
they utterly desecrated my Sabbaths.
So I said I would pour out my wrath[z]
on them and destroy them in the
desert.[a] 14But for the sake of my name
I did what would keep it from being
profaned in the eyes of the nations in
whose sight I had brought them out.[b]
15Also with uplifted hand I swore to
them in the desert that I would not
bring them into the land I had given
them—a land flowing with milk and
honey, most beautiful of all lands[c]—
16because they rejected my laws and
did not follow my decrees and desecrated my Sabbaths. For their hearts[d]
were devoted to their idols.[e] 17Yet I
looked on them with pity and did not
destroy them or put an end to them in
the desert. 18I said to their children in
the desert, "Do not follow the statutes
of your fathers[f] or keep their laws or
defile yourselves with their idols. 19I
am the LORD your God;[g] follow my decrees and be careful to keep my laws.[h]
20Keep my Sabbaths holy, that they
may be a sign between us. Then you
will know that I am the LORD your
God.[i]"

21" 'But the children rebelled against
me: They did not follow my decrees,
they were not careful to keep my
laws—although the man who obeys
them will live by them—and they desecrated my Sabbaths. So I said I would
pour out my wrath on them and spend
my anger against them in the desert.
22But I withheld[j] my hand, and for
the sake of my name I did what would
keep it from being profaned in the eyes
of the nations in whose sight I had
brought them out. 23Also with uplifted
hand I swore to them in the desert that
I would disperse them among the nations and scatter[k] them through the
countries, 24because they had not
obeyed my laws but had rejected my
decrees and desecrated my Sabbaths,[l] and their eyes ⌊lusted⌋ after[m]
their fathers' idols.[n] 25I also gave them
over[o] to statutes that were not good
and laws they could not live by;[p] 26I let
them become defiled through their
gifts—the sacrifice of every firstborn[a]—that I might fill them with horror so they would know that I am the
LORD.[q]'

27"Therefore, son of man, speak to
the people of Israel and say to them,
'This is what the Sovereign LORD says:
In this also your fathers blasphemed[r]
me by forsaking me:[s] 28When I
brought them into the land[t] I had

20:13 [y]Ps 78:40 [z]Dt 9:8 [a]Nu 14:29; Ps 95:8-10; Isa 56:6
20:14 [b]Eze 36:23
20:15 [c]Ps 95:11; 106:26
20:16 [d]Nu 15:39 [e]Am 5:26
20:18 [f]Zec 1:4
20:19 [g]Ex 20:2 [h]Dt 5:32-33; 6:1-2; 8:1; 11:1; 12:1
20:20 [i]Jer 17:22
20:22 [j]Ps 78:38
20:23 [k]Lev 26:33; Dt 28:64
20:24 [l]ver 13 [m]Eze 6:9 [n]ver 16
20:25 [o]Ps 81:12 [p]2Th 2:11
20:26 [q]2Ki 17:17
20:27 [r]Ro 2:24 [s]Eze 18:24
20:28 [t]Ps 78:55,58 [u]Eze 6:13
20:30 [v]ver 43 [w]Jer 16:12
20:31 [x]Eze 16:20 [y]Ps 106:37-39; Jer 7:31
20:33 [z]Jer 21:5
20:34 [a]2Co 6:17* [b]Isa 27:12-13; S Jer 44:6; La 2:4
20:35 [c]Jer 2:35
20:36 [d]Nu 11:1-35; 1Co 10:5-10
20:37 [e]Lev 27:32; Jer 33:13 [f]Eze 16:62
20:38 [g]Eze 34:17-22; Am 9:9-10 [h]Ps 95:11; Jer 44:14; Eze 13:9; Mal 3:3; Heb 4:3
20:39 [i]Jer 44:25 [j]Isa 1:13; Eze 43:7; Am 4:4
20:40 [k]Isa 60:7

sworn to give them and they saw any
high hill or any leafy tree, there they
offered their sacrifices, made offerings
that provoked me to anger, presented
their fragrant incense and poured out
their drink offerings.[u] 29Then I said to
them: What is this high place you go
to?' " (It is called Bamah[b] to this day.)

Judgment and Restoration

30"Therefore say to the house of Israel: 'This is what the Sovereign LORD
says: Will you defile yourselves[v] the
way your fathers did and lust after their
vile images?[w] 31When you offer your
gifts—the sacrifice of your sons[x] in[c]
the fire—you continue to defile yourselves with all your idols to this day.
Am I to let you inquire of me, O house
of Israel? As surely as I live, declares the
Sovereign LORD, I will not let you inquire of me.[y]

32" 'You say, "We want to be like the
nations, like the peoples of the world,
who serve wood and stone." But what
you have in mind will never happen.
33As surely as I live, declares the Sovereign LORD, I will rule over you with a
mighty hand and an outstretched arm
and with outpoured wrath.[z] 34I will
bring you from the nations[a] and gather you from the countries where you
have been scattered—with a mighty
hand and an outstretched arm and
with outpoured wrath.[b] 35I will bring
you into the desert of the nations and
there, face to face, I will execute judgment[c] upon you. 36As I judged your
fathers in the desert of the land of
Egypt, so I will judge you, declares the
Sovereign LORD.[d] 37I will take note of
you as you pass under my rod,[e] and I
will bring you into the bond of the covenant.[f] 38I will purge[g] you of those
who revolt and rebel against me. Although I will bring them out of the land
where they are living, yet they will not
enter the land of Israel. Then you will
know that I am the LORD.[h]

39" 'As for you, O house of Israel, this
is what the Sovereign LORD says: Go
and serve your idols,[i] every one of
you! But afterward you will surely listen
to me and no longer profane my holy
name with your gifts and idols.[j] 40For
on my holy mountain, the high mountain of Israel, declares the Sovereign
LORD, there in the land the entire house
of Israel will serve me, and there I will
accept them. There I will require your
offerings[k] and your choice gifts,[d]

[a]*26* Or *—making every firstborn pass through ⌊the fire⌋* [b]*29* *Bamah* means *high place.*
[c]*31* Or *—making your sons pass through*
[d]*40* Or *and the gifts of your firstfruits*

along with all your holy sacrifices.[l] 41I
will accept you as fragrant incense
when I bring you out from the nations
and gather you from the countries
where you have been scattered, and I
will show myself holy[m] among you in
the sight of the nations.[n] 42Then you
will know that I am the LORD,[o] when I
bring you into the land of Israel,[p] the
land I had sworn with uplifted hand to
give to your fathers. 43There you will
remember your conduct and all the
actions by which you have defiled
yourselves, and you will loathe yourselves for all the evil you have done.[q]
44You will know that I am the LORD,
when I deal with you for my name's
sake[r] and not according to your evil
ways and your corrupt practices,
O house of Israel, declares the Sovereign LORD.[s]' "

Prophecy Against the South

45The word of the LORD came to me:
46"Son of man, set your face toward the
south; preach against the south and
prophesy against[t] the forest of the
southland.[u] 47Say to the southern forest: 'Hear the word of the LORD. This
is what the Sovereign LORD says: I am
about to set fire to you, and it will consume all your trees, both green and
dry. The blazing flame will not be
quenched, and every face from south
to north will be scorched by it.[v] 48Ev-
eryone will see that I the LORD have
kindled it; it will not be quenched.[w]' "

49Then I said, "Ah, Sovereign LORD!
They are saying of me, 'Isn't he just
telling parables?[x]' "

Babylon, God's Sword of Judgment

21 The word of the LORD came to me:
2"Son of man, set your face against
Jerusalem and preach against the sanctuary. Prophesy against[y] the land of
Israel 3and say to her: 'This is what the
LORD says: I am against you.[z] I will
draw my sword from its scabbard and
cut off from you both the righteous and
the wicked.[a] 4Because I am going to
cut off the righteous and the wicked,
my sword will be unsheathed against
everyone from south to north.[b] 5Then
all people will know that I the LORD
have drawn my sword from its scabbard; it will not return[c] again.'[d]

6"Therefore groan, son of man!
Groan before them with broken heart
and bitter grief.[e] 7And when they ask
you, 'Why are you groaning?' you shall
say, 'Because of the news that is coming. Every heart will melt and every
hand go limp;[f] every spirit will become faint and every knee become as
weak as water.' It is coming! It will
surely take place, declares the Sovereign LORD."

8The word of the LORD came to me:
9"Son of man, prophesy and say, 'This
is what the Lord says:

" 'A sword, a sword,
sharpened and polished—
10sharpened for the slaughter,[g]
polished to flash like lightning!

" 'Shall we rejoice in the scepter of
my son ⌞Judah⌟? The sword despises
every such stick.

11" 'The sword is appointed to be
polished,[h]
to be grasped with the hand;
it is sharpened and polished,
made ready for the hand of the
slayer.
12Cry out and wail, son of man,
for it is against my people;
it is against all the princes of
Israel.
They are thrown to the sword
along with my people.
Therefore beat your breast.[i]

13" 'Testing will surely come. And
what if the scepter ⌞of Judah⌟, which
the sword despises, does not continue?
declares the Sovereign LORD.'

14"So then, son of man, prophesy
and strike your hands[j] together.
Let the sword strike twice,
even three times.
It is a sword for slaughter—
a sword for great slaughter,
closing in on them from every
side.[k]
15So that hearts may melt[l]
and the fallen be many,
I have stationed the sword for
slaughter[a]
at all their gates.
Oh! It is made to flash like
lightning,
it is grasped for slaughter.[m]
16O sword, slash to the right,
then to the left,
wherever your blade is turned.
17I too will strike my hands[n]
together,
and my wrath[o] will subside.
I the LORD have spoken."

18The word of the LORD came to me:
19"Son of man, mark out two roads for
the sword of the king of Babylon to
take, both starting from the same
country. Make a signpost where the
road branches off to the city. 20Mark
out one road for the sword to come

20:40 [l]Isa 56:7; Mal 3:4
20:41 [m]Eze 28:25; 36:23 [n]Eze 11:17
20:42 [o]Eze 38:23 [p]Eze 34:13; 36:24
20:43 [q]Eze 6:9; 16:61; Hos 5:15
20:44 [r]Eze 36:22 [s]Eze 24:24
20:46 [t]Eze 21:2; Am 7:16 [u]Isa 30:6; Jer 13:19
20:47 [v]Isa 9:18-19; 13:8; Jer 21:14
20:48 [w]Jer 7:20
20:49 [x]Mt 13:13; Jn 16:25
21:2 [y]Eze 20:46
21:3 [z]Jer 21:13 [a]ver 9-11; Job 9:22
21:4 [b]Eze 20:47
21:5 [c]ver 30 [d]Na 1:9
21:6 [e]Isa 22:4
21:7 [f]Eze 22:14; 7:17
21:10 [g]Ps 110:5-6; Isa 34:5-6
21:11 [h]Jer 46:4
21:12 [i]Jer 31:19
21:14 [j]Nu 24:10 [k]Eze 6:11; 30:24
21:15 [l]2Sa 17:10 [m]Ps 22:14
21:17 [n]ver 14; Eze 22:13 [o]Eze 5:13

[a] *15* Septuagint; the meaning of the Hebrew for this word is uncertain.

against Rabbah of the Ammonites[p]
and another against Judah and fortified Jerusalem. 21For the king of Babylon will stop at the fork in the road, at
the junction of the two roads, to seek
an omen: He will cast lots[q] with arrows, he will consult his idols, he will
examine the liver.[r] 22Into his right
hand will come the lot for Jerusalem,
where he is to set up battering rams,
to give the command to slaughter, to
sound the battle cry, to set battering
rams against the gates, to build a ramp
and to erect siege works.[s] 23It will
seem like a false omen to those who
have sworn allegiance to him, but he
will remind[t] them of their guilt and
take them captive.

24"Therefore this is what the Sovereign LORD says: 'Because you people
have brought to mind your guilt by
your open rebellion, revealing your
sins in all that you do—because you
have done this, you will be taken captive.

25" 'O profane and wicked prince of
Israel, whose day has come, whose
time of punishment has reached its climax,[u] 26this is what the Sovereign
LORD says: Take off the turban, remove
the crown.[v] It will not be as it was: The
lowly will be exalted and the exalted
will be brought low.[w] 27A ruin! A ruin!
I will make it a ruin! It will not be restored until he comes to whom it rightfully belongs; to him I will give it.'[x]

28"And you, son of man, prophesy
and say, 'This is what the Sovereign
LORD says about the Ammonites[y] and
their insults:

" 'A sword,[z] a sword,
drawn for the slaughter,
polished to consume
and to flash like lightning!
29Despite false visions concerning
you
and lying divinations about you,
it will be laid on the necks
of the wicked who are to be
slain,
whose day has come,
whose time of punishment has
reached its climax.[a]
30Return the sword to its scabbard.[b]
In the place where you were
created,
in the land of your ancestry,[c]
I will judge you.
31I will pour out my wrath upon you
and breathe out my fiery anger[d]
against you;
I will hand you over to brutal men,
men skilled in destruction.[e]
32You will be fuel for the fire,[f]
your blood will be shed in your
land,
you will be remembered[g] no
more;
for I the LORD have spoken.' "

Jerusalem's Sins

22 The word of the LORD came to me:
2"Son of man, will you judge her?
Will you judge this city of bloodshed?[h]
Then confront her with all her detestable practices[i] 3and say: 'This is what
the Sovereign LORD says: O city that
brings on herself doom by shedding
blood[j] in her midst and defiles herself
by making idols, 4you have become
guilty because of the blood you have
shed[k] and have become defiled by the
idols you have made. You have brought
your days to a close, and the end of
your years has come.[l] Therefore I will
make you an object of scorn to the nations and a laughingstock to all the
countries.[m] 5Those who are near and
those who are far away will mock you,
O infamous city, full of turmoil.

6" 'See how each of the princes of
Israel who are in you uses his power to
shed blood.[n] 7In you they have treated
father and mother with contempt;[o] in
you they have oppressed the alien and
mistreated the fatherless and the widow.[p] 8You have despised my holy
things and desecrated my Sabbaths.[q]
9In you are slanderous men[r] bent on
shedding blood; in you are those who
eat at the mountain shrines[s] and
commit lewd acts.[t] 10In you are those
who dishonor their fathers' bed; in you
are those who violate women during
their period, when they are ceremonially unclean.[u] 11In you one man commits a detestable offense with his
neighbor's wife, another shamefully
defiles his daughter-in-law,[v] and another violates his sister,[w] his own father's daughter. 12In you men accept
bribes[x] to shed blood; you take usury
and excessive interest[a] and make unjust gain from your neighbors[y] by extortion. And you have forgotten me,
declares the Sovereign LORD.

13" 'I will surely strike my hands[z]
together at the unjust gain[a] you have
made and at the blood[b] you have shed
in your midst. 14Will your courage endure or your hands be strong in the day
I deal with you? I the LORD have spoken,[c] and I will do it.[d] 15I will disperse you among the nations and scatter[e] you through the countries; and I
will put an end to your uncleanness.[f]
16When you have been defiled[b] in the

a 12 Or *usury and interest* b 16 Or *When I have allotted you your inheritance*

21:20 [p]Dt 3:11; Jer 49:2; Am 1:14
21:21 [q]Pr 16:33 [r]Nu 22:7; 23:23
21:22 [s]Eze 4:2; 26:9
21:23 [t]Nu 5:15
21:25 [u]Eze 35:5
21:26 [v]Jer 13:18 [w]Ps 75:7; Eze 17:24
21:27 [x]Ps 2:6; Jer 23:5-6; Eze 37:24; Hag 2:21-22
21:28 [y]Zep 2:8 [z]Jer 12:12
21:29 [a]ver 25; Eze 22:28; 35:5
21:30 [b]Jer 47:6 [c]Eze 16:3
21:31 [d]Eze 22:20-21 [e]Jer 51:20-23
21:32 [f]Mal 4:1 [g]Eze 25:10
22:2 [h]Eze 24:6,9; Na 3:1 [i]Eze 16:2
22:3 [j]ver 6,13,27; Eze 23:37,45
22:4 [k]2Ki 21:16 [l]Eze 21:25 [m]Eze 5:14
22:6 [n]Isa 1:23
22:7 [o]Dt 5:16; 27:16 [p]Ex 22:21-22
22:8 [q]Eze 23:38-39
22:9 [r]Lev 19:16 [s]Eze 18:11 [t]Hos 4:10,14
22:10 [u]Lev 18:8,19
22:11 [v]Lev 18:15 [w]Lev 18:9; 2Sa 13:14
22:12 [x]Dt 27:25; Mic 7:3 [y]Lev 19:13
22:13 [z]Eze 21:17 [a]Isa 33:15 [b]ver 3
22:14 [c]Eze 24:14 [d]Eze 17:24; 21:7
22:15 [e]Dt 4:27; Zec 7:14 [f]Eze 23:27

eyes of the nations, you will know that I am the LORD.' "

17Then the word of the LORD came to me: **18**"Son of man, the house of Israel has become dross[g] to me; all of them are the copper, tin, iron and lead left inside a furnace. They are but the dross of silver.[h] **19**Therefore this is what the Sovereign LORD says: 'Because you have all become dross, I will gather you into Jerusalem. **20**As men gather silver, copper, iron, lead and tin into a furnace to melt it with a fiery blast, so will I gather you in my anger and my wrath and put you inside the city and melt you.[i] **21**I will gather you and I will blow on you with my fiery wrath, and you will be melted inside her. **22**As silver is melted[j] in a furnace, so you will be melted inside her, and you will know that I the LORD have poured out my wrath upon you.' "[k]

23Again the word of the LORD came to me: **24**"Son of man, say to the land, 'You are a land that has had no rain or showers[a] in the day of wrath.'[l] **25**There is a conspiracy[m] of her princes[b] within her like a roaring lion tearing its prey; they devour people,[n] take treasures and precious things and make many widows[o] within her. **26**Her priests do violence to my law[p] and profane my holy things; they do not distinguish between the holy and the common;[q] they teach that there is no difference between the unclean and the clean;[r] and they shut their eyes to the keeping of my Sabbaths, so that I am profaned among them.[s] **27**Her officials within her are like wolves tearing their prey; they shed blood and kill people to make unjust gain.[t] **28**Her prophets whitewash[u] these deeds for them by false visions and lying divinations. They say, 'This is what the Sovereign LORD says'—when the LORD has not spoken.[v] **29**The people of the land practice extortion and commit robbery; they oppress the poor and needy and mistreat the alien,[w] denying them justice.[x]

30"I looked for a man among them who would build up the wall[y] and stand before me in the gap on behalf of the land so I would not have to destroy it, but I found none.[z] **31**So I will pour out my wrath on them and consume them with my fiery anger, bringing down[a] on their own heads all they have done, declares the Sovereign LORD.[b]"

Two Adulterous Sisters

23 The word of the LORD came to me: **2**"Son of man, there were two women, daughters of the same mother.[c] **3**They became prostitutes in Egypt,[d] engaging in prostitution[e] from their youth. In that land their breasts were fondled and their virgin bosoms caressed. **4**The older was named Oholah, and her sister was Oholibah. They were mine and gave birth to sons and daughters. Oholah is Samaria, and Oholibah is Jerusalem.

5"Oholah engaged in prostitution while she was still mine; and she lusted after her lovers, the Assyrians[f]—warriors[g] **6**clothed in blue, governors and commanders, all of them handsome young men, and mounted horsemen. **7**She gave herself as a prostitute to all the elite of the Assyrians and defiled herself with all the idols of everyone she lusted after.[h] **8**She did not give up the prostitution she began in Egypt,[i] when during her youth men slept with her, caressed her virgin bosom and poured out their lust upon her.[j]

9"Therefore I handed her over[k] to her lovers, the Assyrians, for whom she lusted.[l] **10**They stripped[m] her naked, took away her sons and daughters and killed her with the sword. She became a byword among women,[n] and punishment was inflicted on her.[o]

11"Her sister Oholibah saw this, yet in her lust and prostitution she was more depraved than her sister.[p] **12**She too lusted after the Assyrians—governors and commanders, warriors in full dress, mounted horsemen, all handsome young men.[q] **13**I saw that she too defiled herself; both of them went the same way.

14"But she carried her prostitution

22:18 [g]Ps 119:119; Isa 1:22 [h]Jer 6:28-30
22:20 [i]Mal 3:2
22:22 [j]Isa 1:25 [k]Eze 20:8,33
22:24 [l]Eze 24:13
22:25 [m]Jer 11:9 [n]Hos 6:9 [o]Jer 15:8
22:26 [p]Mal 2:7-8 [q]Eze 44:23 [r]Lev 10:10 [s]1Sa 2:12-17; Jer 2:8,26; Hag 2:11-14
22:27 [t]Isa 1:23
22:28 [u]Eze 13:10 [v]Eze 13:2,6-7
22:29 [w]Ex 22:21; 23:9 [x]Isa 5:7
22:30 [y]Eze 13:5 [z]Ps 106:23; Jer 5:1
22:31 [a]Eze 16:43 [b]Eze 7:8-9; 9:10; Ro 2:8
23:2 [c]Jer 3:7; Eze 16:45
23:3 [d]Jos 24:14 [e]Lev 17:7
23:5 [f]2Ki 16:7; Hos 5:13 [g]Hos 8:9
23:7 [h]Hos 5:3; 6:10
23:8 [i]Ex 32:4 [j]Eze 16:15
23:9 [k]2Ki 18:11 [l]Hos 11:5
23:10 [m]Hos 2:10 [n]Eze 16:41 [o]Eze 16:36
23:11 [p]Jer 3:8-11; Eze 16:51
23:12 [q]2Ki 16:7-15; 2Ch 28:16

[a]*24* Septuagint; Hebrew *has not been cleansed or rained on* [b]*25* Septuagint; Hebrew *prophets*

22:30

PROMISE 7

ARE YOU GOD'S MAN?

God has always looked for a few good men. This verse is a mighty challenge to any man who cares about the people around him. God may not use that man to save a nation or a city—but then again, he may! How widely God chooses to "build a man's wall" is God's choice, but he always starts with a man who will be used. Think of your family, your workplace, your church: Will you be God's man in your sphere of influence? In what ways can you "stand in the gap," pray for, and communicate God's message of love to others around you?

For the next Promise 7 reading go to page 909.

still further. She saw men portrayed on
a wall,[r] figures of Chaldeans[a] portrayed in red,[s] 15with belts around
their waists and flowing turbans on
their heads; all of them looked like
Babylonian chariot officers, natives of
Chaldea.[b] 16As soon as she saw them,
she lusted after them and sent messengers to them in Chaldea. 17Then the
Babylonians came to her, to the bed of
love, and in their lust they defiled her.
After she had been defiled by them, she
turned away from them in disgust.
18When she carried on her prostitution
openly and exposed her nakedness, I
turned away[t] from her in disgust, just
as I had turned away from her sister.[u]
19Yet she became more and more promiscuous as she recalled the days of
her youth, when she was a prostitute in
Egypt. 20There she lusted after her lovers, whose genitals were like those of
donkeys and whose emission was like
that of horses. 21So you longed for the
lewdness of your youth, when in Egypt
your bosom was caressed and your
young breasts fondled.[c][v]

22"Therefore, Oholibah, this is what
the Sovereign LORD says: I will stir up
your lovers against you, those you
turned away from in disgust, and I will
bring them against you from every
side[w]— 23the Babylonians[x] and all
the Chaldeans, the men of Pekod[y] and
Shoa and Koa, and all the Assyrians
with them, handsome young men, all
of them governors and commanders,
chariot officers and men of high rank,
all mounted on horses.[z] 24They will
come against you with weapons,[d]
chariots and wagons[a] and with a
throng of people; they will take up positions against you on every side with
large and small shields and with helmets. I will turn you over to them for
punishment,[b] and they will punish
you according to their standards. 25I
will direct my jealous anger against
you, and they will deal with you in fury.
They will cut off your noses and your
ears, and those of you who are left will
fall by the sword. They will take away
your sons and daughters,[c] and those
of you who are left will be consumed by
fire.[d] 26They will also strip[e] you of
your clothes and take your fine jewelry.[f] 27So I will put a stop[g] to the
lewdness and prostitution you began
in Egypt. You will not look on these
things with longing or remember Egypt
anymore.

28"For this is what the Sovereign
LORD says: I am about to hand you
over[h] to those you hate, to those you
turned away from in disgust. 29They
will deal with you in hatred and take
away everything you have worked for.
They will leave you naked and bare,
and the shame of your prostitution will
be exposed. Your lewdness and promiscuity[i] 30have brought this upon
you, because you lusted after the nations and defiled yourself with their
idols.[j] 31You have gone the way of
your sister; so I will put her cup[k] into
your hand.[l]

32"This is what the Sovereign LORD
says:

"You will drink your sister's cup,
a cup large and deep;
it will bring scorn and derision,
for it holds so much.[m]
33You will be filled with drunkenness
and sorrow,
the cup of ruin and desolation,
the cup of your sister Samaria.[n]
34You will drink it[o] and drain it dry;
you will dash it to pieces
and tear your breasts.

I have spoken, declares the Sovereign
LORD.

35"Therefore this is what the Sovereign LORD says: Since you have forgotten[p] me and thrust me behind your
back,[q] you must bear the consequences of your lewdness and prostitution."

36The LORD said to me: "Son of man,
will you judge Oholah and Oholibah?
Then confront[r] them with their detestable practices,[s] 37for they have
committed adultery and blood is on
their hands. They committed adultery
with their idols; they even sacrificed
their children, whom they bore to
me,[e] as food for them.[t] 38They have
also done this to me: At that same time
they defiled my sanctuary and desecrated my Sabbaths. 39On the very day
they sacrificed their children to their
idols, they entered my sanctuary and
desecrated[u] it. That is what they did in
my house.[v]

40"They even sent messengers for
men who came from far away,[w] and
when they arrived you bathed yourself
for them, painted your eyes[x] and put
on your jewelry.[y] 41You sat on an elegant couch,[z] with a table[a] spread before it on which you had placed the
incense and oil that belonged to me.

42"The noise of a carefree crowd was
around her; Sabeans[f] were brought
from the desert along with men from

23:14 [r]Eze 8:10 [s]Jer 22:14
23:18 [t]Ps 78:59; 106:40; Jer 6:8 [u]Jer 12:8; Am 5:21
23:21 [v]Eze 16:26
23:22 [w]Eze 16:37
23:23 [x]2Ki 20:14-18 [y]Jer 50:21 [z]2Ki 24:2
23:24 [a]Jer 47:3; Eze 26:7,10; Na 2:4 [b]Jer 39:5-6
23:25 [c]ver 47 [d]Eze 20:47-48
23:26 [e]Jer 13:22 [f]Isa 3:18-23; Eze 16:39
23:27 [g]Eze 16:41
23:28 [h]Jer 34:20
23:29 [i]Dt 28:48
23:30 [j]Eze 6:9
23:31 [k]Jer 25:15 [l]2Ki 21:13
23:32 [m]Ps 60:3; Isa 51:17; Jer 25:15
23:33 [n]Jer 25:15-16
23:34 [o]Ps 75:8; Isa 51:17
23:35 [p]Isa 17:10; Jer 3:21 [q]1Ki 14:9
23:36 [r]Eze 16:2 [s]Isa 58:1; Eze 22:2; Mic 3:8
23:37 [t]Eze 16:36
23:39 [u]2Ki 21:4 [v]Jer 7:10
23:40 [w]Isa 57:9 [x]2Ki 9:30 [y]Jer 4:30; Eze 16:13-19
23:41 [z]Est 1:6; Pr 7:17; Am 6:4 [a]Isa 65:11; Eze 44:16

a *14* Or *Babylonians* **b** *15* Or *Babylonia*; also in verse 16 **c** *21* Syriac (see also verse 3); Hebrew *caressed because of your young breasts* **d** *24* The meaning of the Hebrew for this word is uncertain. **e** *37* Or *even made the children they bore to me pass through* ⌊*the fire*⌋ **f** *42* Or *drunkards*

the rabble, and they put bracelets[b] on
the arms of the woman and her sister
and beautiful crowns on their heads.[c]
43Then I said about the one worn out
by adultery, 'Now let them use her as a
prostitute,[d] for that is all she is.' 44And
they slept with her. As men sleep with
a prostitute, so they slept with those
lewd women, Oholah and Oholibah.
45But righteous men will sentence
them to the punishment of women
who commit adultery and shed blood,
because they are adulterous and blood
is on their hands.[e]

46"This is what the Sovereign LORD
says: Bring a mob[f] against them and
give them over to terror and plunder.
47The mob will stone them and cut
them down with their swords; they will
kill their sons and daughters and
burn[g] down their houses.[h]

48"So I will put an end to lewdness
in the land, that all women may take
warning and not imitate you.[i] 49You
will suffer the penalty for your lewdness and bear the consequences of
your sins of idolatry. Then you will
know that I am the Sovereign LORD.[j]"

The Cooking Pot

24 In the ninth year, in the tenth
month on the tenth day, the word
of the LORD came to me:[k] 2"Son of
man, record this date, this very date,
because the king of Babylon has laid
siege to Jerusalem this very day.[l] 3Tell
this rebellious house[m] a parable[n] and
say to them: 'This is what the Sovereign LORD says:

" 'Put on the cooking pot;[o] put it
on
and pour water into it.
4Put into it the pieces of meat,
all the choice pieces—the leg
and the shoulder.
Fill it with the best of these bones;
5 take the pick of the flock.[p]
Pile wood beneath it for the bones;
bring it to a boil
and cook the bones in it.[q]

6" 'For this is what the Sovereign LORD
says:

" 'Woe to the city of bloodshed,[r]
to the pot now encrusted,
whose deposit will not go away!
Empty it piece by piece
without casting lots[s] for them.

7" 'For the blood she shed is in her
midst:
She poured it on the bare rock;
she did not pour it on the ground,
where the dust would cover it.[t]
8To stir up wrath and take revenge
I put her blood on the bare rock,
so that it would not be covered.

9" 'Therefore this is what the Sovereign
LORD says:

" 'Woe to the city of bloodshed!
I, too, will pile the wood high.
10So heap on the wood
and kindle the fire.
Cook the meat well,
mixing in the spices;
and let the bones be charred.
11Then set the empty pot on the
coals
till it becomes hot and its copper
glows
so its impurities may be melted
and its deposit burned away.[u]
12It has frustrated all efforts;
its heavy deposit has not been
removed,
not even by fire.

13" 'Now your impurity is lewdness.
Because I tried to cleanse you but you
would not be cleansed from your impurity, you will not be clean again until
my wrath against you has subsided.[v]

14" 'I the LORD have spoken. The
time has come for me to act. I will not
hold back; I will not have pity, nor will
I relent. You will be judged according
to your conduct and your actions,[w]
declares the Sovereign LORD.[x]' "

Ezekiel's Wife Dies

15The word of the LORD came to me:
16"Son of man, with one blow I am
about to take away from you the delight of your eyes. Yet do not lament or
weep or shed any tears.[y] 17Groan quietly; do not mourn for the dead. Keep
your turban fastened and your sandals
on your feet; do not cover the lower
part of your face or eat the customary
food ⌞of mourners⌟.[z]"

18So I spoke to the people in the
morning, and in the evening my wife
died. The next morning I did as I had
been commanded.

19Then the people asked me, "Won't
you tell us what these things have to do
with us?[a]"

20So I said to them, "The word of the
LORD came to me: 21Say to the house of
Israel, 'This is what the Sovereign LORD
says: I am about to desecrate my
sanctuary—the stronghold in which
you take pride, the delight of your
eyes,[b] the object of your affection.
The sons and daughters[c] you left behind will fall by the sword.[d] 22And you
will do as I have done. You will not
cover the lower part of your face or eat
the customary food ⌞of mourners⌟.[e]

23:42 [b]Ge 24:30 [c]Eze 16:11-12
23:43 [d]ver 3
23:45 [e]Lev 20:10; Eze 16:38; Hos 6:5
23:46 [f]Eze 16:40
23:47 [g]2Ch 36:19 [h]2Ch 36:17; Eze 16:40-41
23:48 [i]2Pe 2:6
23:49 [j]Eze 7:4; 9:10; 20:38
24:1 [k]Eze 8:1
24:2 [l]2Ki 25:1; Jer 39:1; 52:4
24:3 [m]Isa 1:2; Eze 2:3,6 [n]Eze 17:2; 20:49
[o]Jer 1:13; Eze 11:3
24:5 [p]Jer 52:10 [q]Jer 52:24-27
24:6 [r]Eze 22:2 [s]Ob 1:11; Na 3:10
24:7 [t]Lev 17:13
24:11 [u]Jer 21:10; Eze 22:15
24:13 [v]Jer 6:28-30; Eze 16:42; 22:24
24:14 [w]Eze 36:19 [x]Eze 18:30
24:16 [y]Jer 13:17; 16:5; 22:10
24:17 [z]Jer 16:7
24:19 [a]Eze 12:9; 37:18
24:21 [b]Ps 27:4 [c]Eze 23:25 [d]Jer 7:14,15; Eze 23:47
24:22 [e]Jer 16:7

23You will keep your turbans on your
heads and your sandals on your feet.
You will not mourn[f] or weep but will
waste away because of[a] your sins and
groan among yourselves.[g] 24Ezekiel
will be a sign[h] to you; you will do just
as he has done. When this happens,
you will know that I am the Sovereign
LORD.'

7 →PG. 933

25"And you, son of man, on the day
I take away their stronghold, their joy
and glory, the delight of their eyes,
their heart's desire, and their sons
and daughters[i] as well— 26on that day
a fugitive will come to tell you[j] the
news. 27At that time your mouth will be
opened; you will speak with him and
will no longer be silent. So you will be
a sign to them, and they will know that
I am the LORD.[k]"

A Prophecy Against Ammon

25 The word of the LORD came to me:
2"Son of man, set your face against
the Ammonites[l] and prophesy
against them.[m] 3Say to them, 'Hear the
word of the Sovereign LORD. This is
what the Sovereign LORD says: Because
you said "Aha![n]" over my sanctuary
when it was desecrated and over the
land of Israel when it was laid waste
and over the people of Judah when
they went into exile,[o] 4therefore I am
going to give you to the people of the
East[p] as a possession. They will set
up their camps and pitch their tents
among you; they will eat your fruit
and drink your milk.[q] 5I will turn
Rabbah[r] into a pasture for camels
and Ammon into a resting place for
sheep.[s] Then you will know that I am
the LORD. 6For this is what the Sovereign LORD says: Because you have
clapped your hands and stamped your
feet, rejoicing with all the malice of
your heart against the land of Israel,[t]
7therefore I will stretch out my hand[u]
against you and give you as plunder to
the nations. I will cut you off from the
nations and exterminate you from the
countries. I will destroy[v] you, and you
will know that I am the LORD.[w]' "

A Prophecy Against Moab

8"This is what the Sovereign LORD
says: 'Because Moab[x] and Seir said,
"Look, the house of Judah has become
like all the other nations," 9therefore
I will expose the flank of Moab, beginning at its frontier towns—Beth
Jeshimoth[y], Baal Meon[z] and Kiriathaim[a]—the glory of that land. 10I
will give Moab along with the Ammonites to the people of the East as a
possession, so that the Ammonites will
not be remembered[b] among the nations; 11and I will inflict punishment
on Moab. Then they will know that I
am the LORD.' "

A Prophecy Against Edom

12"This is what the Sovereign LORD
says: 'Because Edom[c] took revenge
on the house of Judah and became very
guilty by doing so, 13therefore this is
what the Sovereign LORD says: I will
stretch out my hand against Edom and
kill its men and their animals.[d] I will
lay it waste, and from Teman to Dedan[e] they will fall by the sword. 14I
will take vengeance on Edom by the
hand of my people Israel, and they will
deal with Edom in accordance with my
anger[f] and my wrath; they will know
my vengeance, declares the Sovereign
LORD.' "

A Prophecy Against Philistia

15"This is what the Sovereign LORD
says: 'Because the Philistines[g] acted
in vengeance and took revenge with
malice in their hearts, and with ancient
hostility sought to destroy Judah,
16therefore this is what the Sovereign
LORD says: I am about to stretch out my
hand against the Philistines,[h] and I
will cut off the Kerethites[i] and destroy
those remaining along the coast. 17I
will carry out great vengeance on them
and punish them in my wrath. Then
they will know that I am the LORD,
when I take vengeance on them.' "

A Prophecy Against Tyre

26 In the eleventh year, on the first
day of the month, the word of the
LORD came to me: 2"Son of man, because Tyre[j] has said of Jerusalem,
'Aha![k] The gate to the nations is broken, and its doors have swung open to
me; now that she lies in ruins I will
prosper,' 3therefore this is what the
Sovereign LORD says: I am against you,
O Tyre, and I will bring many nations
against you, like the sea[l] casting up its
waves. 4They will destroy[m] the walls of
Tyre[n] and pull down her towers; I will
scrape away her rubble and make her a
bare rock. 5Out in the sea[o] she will
become a place to spread fishnets, for
I have spoken, declares the Sovereign
LORD. She will become plunder[p] for
the nations, 6and her settlements on
the mainland will be ravaged by the
sword. Then they will know that I am
the LORD.

7"For this is what the Sovereign LORD
says: From the north I am going to

24:23 [f]Job 27:15 [g]Ps 78:64 **24:24** [h]Isa 20:3; Eze 4:3; 12:11 **24:25** [i]Jer 11:22 **24:26** [j]1Sa 4:12; Job 1:15-19 **24:27** [k]Eze 3:26; 33:22 **25:2** [l]Eze 21:28; Zep 2:8-9 [m]Jer 49:1-6 **25:3** [n]Eze 26:2; 36:2 [o]Pr 17:5 **25:4** [p]Jdg 6:3 [q]Dt 28:33,51; Jdg 6:33 **25:5** [r]Dt 3:11; Eze 21:20 [s]Isa 17:2 **25:6** [t]Ob 1:12; Zep 2:8 **25:7** [u]Zep 1:4 [v]Eze 21:31 [w]Am 1:14-15 **25:8** [x]Jer 48:1; Am 2:1 **25:9** [y]Nu 33:49 [z]Nu 32:3; Jos 13:17 [a]Nu 32:37; Jos 13:19

25:10 [b]Eze 21:32 **25:12** [c]2Ch 28:17 **25:13** [d]Eze 29:8 [e]Jer 25:23 **25:14** [f]Eze 35:11 **25:15** [g]2Ch 28:18 **25:16** [h]Jer 47:1-7 [i]1Sa 30:14; Zep 2:4-5 **26:2** [j]2Sa 5:11; Isa 23 [k]Eze 25:3 **26:3** [l]Isa 5:30; Jer 50:42; 51:42 **26:4** [m]Isa 23:1,11 [n]Am 1:10 **26:5** [o]Eze 27:32 [p]Eze 29:19

a 23 Or *away in*

bring against Tyre Nebuchadnezzar[a][q] king of Babylon, king of
kings,[r] with horses and chariots,[s]
with horsemen and a great army. **8**He
will ravage your settlements on the
mainland with the sword; he will set
up siege works[t] against you, build a
ramp[u] up to your walls and raise his
shields against you. **9**He will direct the
blows of his battering rams against
your walls and demolish your towers
with his weapons. **10**His horses will be
so many that they will cover you with
dust. Your walls will tremble at the
noise of the war horses, wagons and
chariots[v] when he enters your gates as
men enter a city whose walls have been
broken through. **11**The hoofs[w] of his
horses will trample all your streets; he
will kill your people with the sword,
and your strong pillars[x] will fall to the
ground.[y] **12**They will plunder your
wealth and loot your merchandise;
they will break down your walls and
demolish your fine houses and throw
your stones, timber and rubble into the
sea.[z] **13**I will put an end[a] to your
noisy songs, and the music of your
harps[b] will be heard no more.[c] **14**I
will make you a bare rock, and you will
become a place to spread fishnets. You
will never be rebuilt,[d] for I the LORD
have spoken, declares the Sovereign
LORD.

15"This is what the Sovereign LORD
says to Tyre: Will not the coastlands[e]
tremble[f] at the sound of your fall,
when the wounded groan and the
slaughter takes place in you? **16**Then all
the princes of the coast will step down
from their thrones and lay aside their
robes and take off their embroidered
garments. Clothed[g] with terror, they
will sit on the ground, trembling[h] every moment, appalled[i] at you. **17**Then
they will take up a lament[j] concerning you and say to you:

" 'How you are destroyed, O city of
renown,
peopled by men of the sea!
You were a power on the seas,
you and your citizens;
you put your terror
on all who lived there.[k]
18Now the coastlands tremble
on the day of your fall;
the islands in the sea
are terrified at your collapse.'[l]

19"This is what the Sovereign LORD
says: When I make you a desolate city,
like cities no longer inhabited, and
when I bring the ocean depths over
you and its vast waters cover you,[m]
20then I will bring you down with those
who go down to the pit,[n] to the people
of long ago. I will make you dwell in the
earth below, as in ancient ruins, with
those who go down to the pit, and you
will not return or take your place[b] in
the land of the living.[o] **21**I will bring
you to a horrible end and you will be
no more. You will be sought, but you
will never again be found, declares the
Sovereign LORD."[p]

A Lament for Tyre

27 The word of the LORD came to me:
2"Son of man, take up a lament
concerning Tyre. **3**Say to Tyre, situated
at the gateway to the sea,[q] merchant
of peoples on many coasts, 'This is
what the Sovereign LORD says:

" 'You say, O Tyre,
"I am perfect in beauty.[r]"
4Your domain was on the high seas;
your builders brought your
beauty to perfection.
5They made all your timbers
of pine trees from Senir[c];[s]
they took a cedar from Lebanon
to make a mast for you.
6Of oaks[t] from Bashan
they made your oars;
of cypress wood[d] from the coasts
of Cyprus[e][u]
they made your deck, inlaid with
ivory.
7Fine embroidered linen from Egypt
was your sail
and served as your banner;
your awnings were of blue and
purple[v]
from the coasts of Elishah.
8Men of Sidon and Arvad[w] were
your oarsmen;
your skilled men, O Tyre, were
aboard as your seamen.[x]
9Veteran craftsmen of Gebal[f][y]
were on board
as shipwrights to caulk your
seams.
All the ships of the sea and their
sailors
came alongside to trade for your
wares.

10" 'Men of Persia,[z] Lydia and Put[a]
served as soldiers in your army.
They hung their shields and
helmets on your walls,
bringing you splendor.
11Men of Arvad and Helech
manned your walls on every
side;

26:7 [q]Jer 27:6 [r]Ezr 7:12; Da 2:37 [s]Eze 23:24; Na 2:3-4
26:8 [t]Jer 6:6 [u]Eze 21:22
26:10 [v]Jer 4:13
26:11 [w]Isa 5:28 [x]Jer 43:13 [y]Isa 26:5
26:12 [z]Isa 23:8; Eze 27:3-27; 28:8
26:13 [a]Jer 7:34 [b]Isa 14:11 [c]Jer 25:10; Rev 18:22
26:14 [d]Job 12:14; Mal 1:4
26:15 [e]Eze 27:35 [f]Jer 49:21
26:16 [g]Job 8:22 [h]Hos 11:10 [i]Eze 32:10
26:17 [j]Eze 19:1; 27:32 [k]Isa 14:12
26:18 [l]Isa 23:5; 41:5; Eze 27:35
26:19 [m]Isa 8:7-8
26:20 [n]Eze 32:18; Am 9:2; Jnh 2:2,6 [o]Eze 32:24,30
26:21 [p]Eze 27:36; 28:19; Rev 18:21
27:3 [q]ver 33 [r]Eze 28:2
27:5 [s]Dt 3:9
27:6 [t]Nu 21:33; Jer 22:20; Zec 11:2 [u]Ge 10:4; Isa 23:12
27:7 [v]Ex 25:4; Jer 10:9
27:8 [w]Ge 10:18 [x]1Ki 9:27
27:9 [y]Jos 13:5; 1Ki 5:18
27:10 [z]Eze 38:5 [a]Eze 30:5

a7 Hebrew *Nebuchadrezzar,* of which *Nebuchadnezzar* is a variant; here and often in Ezekiel and Jeremiah **b**20 Septuagint; Hebrew *return, and I will give glory* **c**5 That is, Hermon **d**6 Targum; the Masoretic Text has a different division of the consonants. **e**6 Hebrew *Kittim* **f**9 That is, Byblos

men of Gammad
were in your towers.
They hung their shields around
your walls;
they brought your beauty to
perfection.

12 " 'Tarshish[b] did business with
you because of your great wealth of
goods;[c] they exchanged silver, iron,
tin and lead for your merchandise.
13 " 'Greece, Tubal and Meshech[d]
traded with you; they exchanged
slaves[e] and articles of bronze for your
wares.
14 " 'Men of Beth Togarmah[f] exchanged work horses, war horses and
mules for your merchandise.
15 " 'The men of Rhodes[a][g] traded
with you, and many coastlands[h] were
your customers; they paid you with
ivory[i] tusks and ebony.
16 " 'Aram[b][j] did business with you
because of your many products; they
exchanged turquoise,[k] purple fabric,
embroidered work, fine linen, coral
and rubies for your merchandise.
17 " 'Judah and Israel traded with
you; they exchanged wheat from Minnith[l] and confections,[c] honey, oil
and balm for your wares.
18 " 'Damascus,[m] because of your
many products and great wealth of
goods, did business with you in wine
from Helbon and wool from Zahar.
19 " 'Danites and Greeks from Uzal
bought your merchandise; they exchanged wrought iron, cassia and calamus for your wares.
20 " 'Dedan traded in saddle blankets
with you.
21 " 'Arabia and all the princes of Kedar[n] were your customers; they did
business with you in lambs, rams and
goats.
22 " 'The merchants of Sheba[o] and
Raamah traded with you; for your merchandise they exchanged the finest of
all kinds of spices[p] and precious
stones, and gold.
23 " 'Haran,[q] Canneh and Eden[r]
and merchants of Sheba, Asshur and
Kilmad traded with you. 24 In your marketplace they traded with you beautiful
garments, blue fabric, embroidered
work and multicolored rugs with cords
twisted and tightly knotted.

25 " 'The ships of Tarshish[s] serve
as carriers for your wares.
You are filled with heavy cargo
in the heart of the sea.
26 Your oarsmen take you
out to the high seas.
But the east wind[t] will break you
to pieces
in the heart of the sea.
27 Your wealth,[u] merchandise and
wares,
your mariners, seamen and
shipwrights,
your merchants and all your
soldiers,
and everyone else on board
will sink into the heart of the sea
on the day of your shipwreck.
28 The shorelands will quake[v]
when your seamen cry out.
29 All who handle the oars
will abandon their ships;
the mariners and all the seamen
will stand on the shore.
30 They will raise their voice
and cry bitterly over you;
they will sprinkle dust[w] on their
heads
and roll[x] in ashes.[y]
31 They will shave their heads because
of you
and will put on sackcloth.
They will weep[z] over you with
anguish of soul
and with bitter mourning.[a]
32 As they wail and mourn over you,
they will take up a lament[b]
concerning you:
"Who was ever silenced like Tyre,
surrounded by the sea?"
33 When your merchandise went out
on the seas,
you satisfied many nations;
with your great wealth[c] and your
wares
you enriched the kings of the
earth.
34 Now you are shattered by the sea
in the depths of the waters;
your wares and all your company
have gone down with you.[d]
35 All who live in the coastlands[e]
are appalled at you;
their kings shudder with horror
and their faces are distorted with
fear.
36 The merchants among the nations
hiss at you;[f]
you have come to a horrible end
and will be no more.[g]' "

A Prophecy Against the King of Tyre

28 The word of the LORD came to me:
2 "Son of man, say to the ruler of
Tyre, 'This is what the Sovereign LORD
says:

" 'In the pride of your heart
you say, "I am a god;
I sit on the throne[h] of a god
in the heart of the seas."

27:12 [b] Ge 10:4 [c] ver 18,33 **27:13** [d] Ge 10:2; Isa 66:19; Eze 38:2 [e] Rev 18:13 **27:14** [f] Ge 10:3; Eze 38:6 **27:15** [g] Ge 10:7 [h] Jer 25:22 [i] 1Ki 10:22; Rev 18:12 **27:16** [j] Jdg 10:6; Isa 7:1-8 [k] Eze 28:13 **27:17** [l] Jdg 11:33 **27:18** [m] Ge 14:15; Eze 47:16-18 **27:21** [n] Ge 25:13; Isa 60:7 **27:22** [o] Ge 10:7,28; 1Ki 10:1-2; Isa 60:6 [p] Ge 43:11 **27:23** [q] 2Ki 19:12 [r] Isa 37:12 **27:25** [s] Isa 2:16 *fn* **27:26** [t] Ps 48:7; Jer 18:17 **27:27** [u] Pr 11:4 **27:28** [v] Eze 26:15 **27:30** [w] 2Sa 1:2 [x] Jer 6:26 [y] Rev 18:18-19 **27:31** [z] Isa 16:9 [a] Isa 22:12; Eze 7:18 **27:32** [b] Eze 26:17 **27:33** [c] ver 12; Eze 28:4-5 **27:34** [d] Zec 9:4 **27:35** [e] Eze 26:15 **27:36** [f] Jer 18:16; 19:8; 49:17; 50:13; Zep 2:15 [g] Ps 37:10,36; Eze 26:21 **28:2** [h] Isa 14:13

a *15* Septuagint; Hebrew *Dedan* **b** *16* Most Hebrew manuscripts; some Hebrew manuscripts and Syriac *Edom* **c** *17* The meaning of the Hebrew for this word is uncertain.

But you are a man and not a god,
though you think you are as wise
as a god.[i]
3Are you wiser than Daniel[a]?[j]
Is no secret hidden from you?
4By your wisdom and understanding
you have gained wealth for
yourself
and amassed gold and silver
in your treasuries.[k]
5By your great skill in trading
you have increased your wealth,
and because of your wealth
your heart has grown proud.[l]

6" 'Therefore this is what the Sovereign LORD says:

" 'Because you think you are wise,
as wise as a god,
7I am going to bring foreigners
against you,
the most ruthless of nations;[m]
they will draw their swords against
your beauty and wisdom
and pierce your shining
splendor.
8They will bring you down to the
pit,[n]
and you will die a violent death
in the heart of the seas.[o]
9Will you then say, "I am a god,"
in the presence of those who kill
you?
You will be but a man, not a god,
in the hands of those who slay
you.
10You will die the death of the
uncircumcised[p]
at the hands of foreigners.

I have spoken, declares the Sovereign LORD.' "

11The word of the LORD came to me:
12"Son of man, take up a lament[q] concerning the king of Tyre and say to him:
'This is what the Sovereign LORD says:

" 'You were the model of
perfection,
full of wisdom and perfect in
beauty.[r]
13You were in Eden,[s]
the garden of God;[t]
every precious stone adorned you:
ruby, topaz and emerald,
chrysolite, onyx and jasper,
sapphire,[b] turquoise[u] and
beryl.[c]
Your settings and mountings[d]
were made of gold;
on the day you were created they
were prepared.
14You were anointed[v] as a guardian
cherub,[w]
for so I ordained you.
You were on the holy mount of
God;
you walked among the fiery
stones.
15You were blameless in your ways
from the day you were created
till wickedness was found in you.
16Through your widespread trade
you were filled with violence,[x]
and you sinned.
So I drove you in disgrace from the
mount of God,
and I expelled you, O guardian
cherub,[y]
from among the fiery stones.
17Your heart became proud[z]
on account of your beauty,
and you corrupted your wisdom
because of your splendor.
So I threw you to the earth;
I made a spectacle of you before
kings.
18By your many sins and dishonest
trade
you have desecrated your
sanctuaries.
So I made a fire come out from
you,
and it consumed you,
and I reduced you to ashes[a] on
the ground
in the sight of all who were
watching.
19All the nations who knew you
are appalled at you;
you have come to a horrible end
and will be no more.[b]' "

A Prophecy Against Sidon

20The word of the LORD came to me:
21"Son of man, set your face against[c]
Sidon;[d] prophesy against her 22and
say: 'This is what the Sovereign LORD
says:

" 'I am against you, O Sidon,
and I will gain glory[e] within
you.
They will know that I am the LORD,
when I inflict punishment[f] on
her
and show myself holy within her.
23I will send a plague upon her
and make blood flow in her
streets.
The slain will fall within her,
with the sword against her on
every side.
Then they will know that I am the
LORD.[g]

[a]3 Or *Danel*; the Hebrew spelling may suggest a person other than the prophet Daniel.
[b]13 Or *lapis lazuli* [c]13 The precise identification of some of these precious stones is uncertain. [d]13 The meaning of the Hebrew for this phrase is uncertain.

28:2 [i]Ps 9:20; 82:6-7; Isa 31:3; 2Th 2:4
28:3 [j]Da 1:20; 5:11-12
28:4 [k]Zec 9:3
28:5 [l]Job 31:25; Ps 52:7; 62:10; Hos 12:8; 13:6
28:7 [m]Eze 30:11; 31:12; 32:12; Hab 1:6
28:8 [n]Eze 32:30 [o]Eze 27:27
28:10 [p]Eze 31:18; 32:19,24
28:12 [q]Eze 19:1 [r]Eze 27:2-4
28:13 [s]Ge 2:8 [t]Eze 31:8-9 [u]Eze 27:16
28:14 [v]Ex 30:26; 40:9 [w]Ex 25:17-20
28:16 [x]Hab 2:17 [y]Ge 3:24
28:17 [z]Eze 31:10
28:18 [a]Mal 4:3
28:19 [b]Jer 51:64; Eze 26:21; 27:36
28:21 [c]Eze 6:2 [d]Ge 10:15; Jer 25:22
28:22 [e]Eze 39:13 [f]Eze 30:19
28:23 [g]Eze 38:22

24“ ‘No longer will the people of Israel have malicious neighbors who are
painful briers and sharp thorns.[h]
Then they will know that I am the Sovereign LORD.
25“ ‘This is what the Sovereign LORD
says: When I gather[i] the people of Israel from the nations where they have
been scattered,[j] I will show myself
holy[k] among them in the sight of the
nations. Then they will live in their
own land, which I gave to my servant
Jacob.[l] 26They will live there in safety[m] and will build houses and plant
vineyards; they will live in safety when
I inflict punishment on all their neighbors who maligned them. Then they
will know that I am the LORD their
God.[n]’ ”

A Prophecy Against Egypt

29 In the tenth year, in the tenth
month on the twelfth day, the
word of the LORD came to me:[o] 2“Son
of man, set your face against Pharaoh
king of Egypt[p] and prophesy against
him and against all Egypt.[q] 3Speak to
him and say: ‘This is what the Sovereign LORD says:

“ ‘I am against you, Pharaoh[r] king
of Egypt,
you great monster[s] lying among
your streams.
You say, “The Nile is mine;
I made it for myself.”
4But I will put hooks[t] in your jaws
and make the fish of your
streams stick to your scales.
I will pull you out from among
your streams,
with all the fish sticking to your
scales.[u]
5I will leave you in the desert,
you and all the fish of your
streams.
You will fall on the open field
and not be gathered or picked
up.
I will give you as food
to the beasts of the earth and
the birds of the air.[v]

6Then all who live in Egypt will know
that I am the LORD.

“ ‘You have been a staff of reed[w] for
the house of Israel. 7When they
grasped you with their hands, you
splintered[x] and you tore open their
shoulders; when they leaned on you,
you broke and their backs were
wrenched.[a][y]
8“ ‘Therefore this is what the Sovereign LORD says: I will bring a sword
against you and kill your men and their
animals.[z] 9Egypt will become a desolate wasteland. Then they will know
that I am the LORD.
“ ‘Because you said, “The Nile is
mine; I made it,[a]” 10therefore I am
against you and against your streams,
and I will make the land of Egypt a ruin
and a desolate waste from Migdol to
Aswan,[b] as far as the border of Cush.[b]
11No foot of man or animal will pass
through it; no one will live there for
forty years.[c] 12I will make the land of
Egypt desolate among devastated
lands, and her cities will lie desolate
forty years among ruined cities. And I
will disperse the Egyptians among the
nations and scatter them through the
countries.[d]
13“ ‘Yet this is what the Sovereign
LORD says: At the end of forty years I
will gather the Egyptians from the nations where they were scattered. 14I will
bring them back from captivity and return them to Upper Egypt,[c][e] the land
of their ancestry. There they will be a
lowly[f] kingdom. 15It will be the lowliest of kingdoms and will never again
exalt itself above the other nations.[g] I
will make it so weak that it will never
again rule over the nations. 16Egypt will
no longer be a source of confidence[h]
for the people of Israel but will be a
reminder of their sin in turning to her
for help. Then they will know that I am
the Sovereign LORD.[i]’ ”
17In the twenty-seventh year, in the
first month on the first day, the word of
the LORD came to me:[j] 18“Son of man,
Nebuchadnezzar[k] king of Babylon
drove his army in a hard campaign
against Tyre; every head was rubbed
bare[l] and every shoulder made raw.
Yet he and his army got no reward from
the campaign he led against Tyre.
19Therefore this is what the Sovereign
LORD says: I am going to give Egypt to
Nebuchadnezzar king of Babylon, and
he will carry off its wealth. He will loot
and plunder the land as pay for his
army.[m] 20I have given him Egypt as a
reward for his efforts because he and
his army did it for me, declares the Sovereign LORD.[n]
21“On that day I will make a horn[d][o]
grow for the house of Israel, and I will
open your mouth[p] among them. Then
they will know that I am the LORD.[q]”

A Lament for Egypt

30 The word of the LORD came to me:
2“Son of man, prophesy and say:

28:24 [h]Nu 33:55; Jos 23:13; Eze 2:6
28:25 [i]Ps 106:47; Jer 32:37 [j]Isa 11:12 [k]Eze 20:41 [l]Jer 23:8; Eze 11:17; 34:27; 37:25
28:26 [m]Jer 23:6 [n]Isa 65:21; Jer 32:15; Eze 38:8; Am 9:14-15
29:1 [o]ver 17; Eze 26:1
29:2 [p]Jer 25:19 [q]Isa 19:1-17; Jer 46:2; Eze 30:1-26; 31:1-18; 32:1-32
29:3 [r]Jer 44:30 [s]Ps 74:13; Isa 27:1; Eze 32:2
29:4 [t]2Ki 19:28 [u]Eze 38:4
29:5 [v]Jer 7:33; 34:20; Eze 32:4-6; 39:4
29:6 [w]2Ki 18:21; Isa 36:6
29:7 [x]Isa 36:6 [y]Eze 17:15-17
29:8 [z]Eze 14:17; 32:11-13
29:9 [a]Eze 30:7-8, 13-19
29:10 [b]Eze 30:6
29:11 [c]Eze 32:13
29:12 [d]Jer 46:19; Eze 30:7,23,26
29:14 [e]Eze 30:14 [f]Eze 17:14
29:15 [g]Zec 10:11
29:16 [h]Isa 36:4,6 [i]Isa 30:2; Hos 8:13
29:17 [j]Eze 24:1
29:18 [k]Jer 27:6; Eze 26:7-8 [l]Jer 48:37
29:19 [m]Jer 43:10-13; Eze 30:4,10, 24-25
29:20 [n]Isa 10:6-7; 45:1; Jer 25:9
29:21 [o]Ps 132:17 [p]Eze 33:22 [q]Eze 24:27

a *7* Syriac (see also Septuagint and Vulgate); Hebrew *and you caused their backs to stand*
b *10* That is, the upper Nile region
c *14* Hebrew *to Pathros*
d *21* *Horn* here symbolizes strength.

'This is what the Sovereign LORD says:

" 'Wail[r] and say,
"Alas for that day!"
3 For the day is near,[s]
the day of the LORD[t] is near—
a day of clouds,
a time of doom for the nations.
4 A sword will come against Egypt,
and anguish will come upon
Cush.[a]
When the slain fall in Egypt,
her wealth will be carried away
and her foundations torn
down.[u]

5 Cush and Put,[v] Lydia and all Arabia,
Libya[b] and the people[w] of the covenant land will fall by the sword along
with Egypt.

6 " 'This is what the LORD says:

" 'The allies of Egypt will fall
and her proud strength will fail.
From Migdol to Aswan[x]
they will fall by the sword within
her,
declares the Sovereign LORD.
7 " 'They will be desolate
among desolate lands,
and their cities will lie
among ruined cities.[y]
8 Then they will know that I am the
LORD,
when I set fire to Egypt
and all her helpers are crushed.

9 " 'On that day messengers will go
out from me in ships to frighten
Cush[z] out of her complacency. Anguish[a] will take hold of them on the
day of Egypt's doom, for it is sure to
come.[b]

10 " 'This is what the Sovereign LORD
says:

" 'I will put an end to the hordes of
Egypt
by the hand of Nebuchadnezzar
king of Babylon.[c]
11 He and his army—the most
ruthless of nations[d]—
will be brought in to destroy the
land.
They will draw their swords against
Egypt
and fill the land with the slain.
12 I will dry up[e] the streams of the
Nile[f]
and sell the land to evil men;
by the hand of foreigners
I will lay waste the land and
everything in it.

I the LORD have spoken.

13 " 'This is what the Sovereign LORD
says:

" 'I will destroy the idols[g]
and put an end to the images in
Memphis.[c][h]
No longer will there be a prince in
Egypt,[i]
and I will spread fear throughout
the land.
14 I will lay[j] waste Upper Egypt,[d]
set fire to Zoan[k]
and inflict punishment on
Thebes.[e][l]
15 I will pour out my wrath on
Pelusium,[f]
the stronghold of Egypt,
and cut off the hordes of Thebes.
16 I will set fire to Egypt;
Pelusium will writhe in agony.
Thebes will be taken by storm;
Memphis will be in constant
distress.
17 The young men of Heliopolis[g][m]
and Bubastis[h]
will fall by the sword,
and the cities themselves will go
into captivity.
18 Dark will be the day at Tahpanhes
when I break the yoke of
Egypt;[n]
there her proud strength will
come to an end.
She will be covered with clouds,
and her villages will go into
captivity.[o]
19 So I will inflict punishment on
Egypt,
and they will know that I am the
LORD.' "

20 In the eleventh year, in the first
month on the seventh day, the word of
the LORD came to me:[p] 21 "Son of man,
I have broken the arm[q] of Pharaoh
king of Egypt. It has not been bound up
for healing[r] or put in a splint so as
to become strong enough to hold a
sword. 22 Therefore this is what the Sovereign LORD says: I am against Pharaoh
king of Egypt.[s] I will break both his
arms, the good arm as well as the broken one, and make the sword fall from
his hand.[t] 23 I will disperse the Egyptians among the nations and scatter
them through the countries.[u] 24 I will
strengthen[v] the arms of the king of
Babylon and put my sword[w] in his
hand, but I will break the arms of Pharaoh, and he will groan before him like
a mortally wounded man. 25 I will
strengthen the arms of the king of Babylon, but the arms of Pharaoh will fall

30:2 [r]Isa 13:6
30:3 [s]Eze 7:7; Joel 2:1,11; Ob 1:15 [t]ver 18; Eze 7:12,19
30:4 [u]Eze 29:19
30:5 [v]Eze 27:10 [w]Jer 25:20
30:6 [x]Eze 29:10
30:7 [y]Eze 29:12
30:9 [z]Isa 18:1-2 [a]Isa 23:5 [b]Eze 32:9-10
30:10 [c]Eze 29:19
30:11 [d]Eze 28:7
30:12 [e]Isa 19:6 [f]Eze 29:9
30:13 [g]Jer 43:12 [h]Isa 19:13 [i]Zec 10:11
30:14 [j]Eze 29:14 [k]Ps 78:12,43 [l]Jer 46:25
30:17 [m]Ge 41:45
30:18 [n]Lev 26:13 [o]ver 3
30:20 [p]Eze 26:1; 29:17; 31:1
30:21 [q]Jer 48:25 [r]Jer 30:13; 46:11
30:22 [s]Jer 46:25 [t]Ps 37:17
30:23 [u]Eze 29:12
30:24 [v]Zec 10:6,12 [w]Eze 21:14; Zep 2:12

[a] *4* That is, the upper Nile region; also in verses 5 and 9 [b] *5* Hebrew *Cub* [c] *13* Hebrew *Noph*; also in verse 16 [d] *14* Hebrew *waste Pathros* [e] *14* Hebrew *No*; also in verses 15 and 16 [f] *15* Hebrew *Sin*; also in verse 16 [g] *17* Hebrew *Awen* (or *On*) [h] *17* Hebrew *Pi Beseth*

limp. Then they will know that I am the
LORD, when I put my sword into the
hand of the king of Babylon and he
brandishes it against Egypt. 26 I will disperse the Egyptians among the nations
and scatter them through the countries. Then they will know that I am the
LORD.[x]"

A Cedar in Lebanon

31 In the eleventh year,[y] in the third
month on the first day, the word of
the LORD came to me:[z] 2 "Son of man,
say to Pharaoh king of Egypt and to his
hordes:

" 'Who can be compared with you
in majesty?
3 Consider Assyria, once a cedar in
Lebanon,
with beautiful branches
overshadowing the forest;
it towered on high,
its top above the thick foliage.[a]
4 The waters nourished it,
deep springs made it grow tall;
their streams flowed
all around its base
and sent their channels
to all the trees of the field.
5 So it towered higher
than all the trees of the field;
its boughs increased
and its branches grew long,
spreading because of abundant
waters.[b]
6 All the birds of the air
nested in its boughs,
all the beasts of the field
gave birth under its branches;
all the great nations
lived in its shade.[c]
7 It was majestic in beauty,
with its spreading boughs,
for its roots went down
to abundant waters.
8 The cedars[d] in the garden of God
could not rival it,
nor could the pine trees
equal its boughs,
nor could the plane trees
compare with its branches—
no tree in the garden of God
could match its beauty.[e]
9 I made it beautiful
with abundant branches,
the envy of all the trees of Eden[f]
in the garden of God.[g]

10 " 'Therefore this is what the Sovereign LORD says: Because it towered on
high, lifting its top above the thick foliage, and because it was proud[h] of its
height, 11 I handed it over to the ruler of
the nations, for him to deal with according to its wickedness. I cast it
aside,[i] 12 and the most ruthless of foreign nations[j] cut it down and left it.
Its boughs fell on the mountains and in
all the valleys;[k] its branches lay broken in all the ravines of the land. All the
nations of the earth came out from under its shade and left it.[l] 13 All the
birds of the air settled on the fallen
tree, and all the beasts of the field were
among its branches.[m] 14 Therefore no
other trees by the waters are ever to
tower proudly on high, lifting their tops
above the thick foliage. No other trees
so well-watered are ever to reach such
a height; they are all destined for
death,[n] for the earth below, among
mortal men, with those who go down
to the pit.[o]

15 " 'This is what the Sovereign LORD
says: On the day it was brought down
to the grave[a] I covered the deep
springs with mourning for it; I held
back its streams, and its abundant waters were restrained. Because of it I
clothed Lebanon with gloom, and all
the trees of the field withered away. 16 I
made the nations tremble[p] at the
sound of its fall when I brought it down
to the grave with those who go down
to the pit. Then all the trees[q] of Eden,
the choicest and best of Lebanon,
all the trees that were well-watered,
were consoled[r] in the earth below.[s]
17 Those who lived in its shade, its allies
among the nations, had also gone
down to the grave with it, joining those
killed by the sword.[t]

18 " 'Which of the trees of Eden can
be compared with you in splendor and
majesty? Yet you, too, will be brought
down with the trees of Eden to the
earth below; you will lie among the uncircumcised,[u] with those killed by the
sword.

" 'This is Pharaoh and all his hordes,
declares the Sovereign LORD.' "

A Lament for Pharaoh

32 In the twelfth year, in the twelfth
month on the first day, the word of
the LORD came to me:[v] 2 "Son of man,
take up a lament[w] concerning Pharaoh king of Egypt and say to him:

" 'You are like a lion[x] among the
nations;
you are like a monster in the
seas
thrashing about in your streams,
churning the water with your
feet
and muddying the streams.[y]

30:26 [x]Eze 29:12
31:1 [y]Jer 52:5 [z]Eze 30:20
31:3 [a]Isa 10:34
31:5 [b]Eze 17:5
31:6 [c]Eze 17:23; Mt 13:32
31:8 [d]Ps 80:10 [e]Ge 2:8-9
31:9 [f]Ge 2:8 [g]Ge 13:10; Eze 28:13
31:10 [h]Isa 14:13-14; Eze 28:17
31:11 [i]Da 5:20
31:12 [j]Eze 28:7 [k]Eze 32:5; 35:8 [l]Eze 32:11-12; Da 4:14
31:13 [m]Isa 18:6; Eze 29:5; 32:4
31:14 [n]Ps 82:7 [o]Ps 63:9; Eze 26:20; 32:24
31:16 [p]Eze 26:15 [q]Isa 14:8 [r]Eze 14:22; 32:31 [s]Isa 14:15; Eze 32:18
31:17 [t]Ps 9:17
31:18 [u]Jer 9:26; Eze 32:19,21
32:1 [v]Eze 31:1; 33:21
32:2 [w]Eze 19:1; 27:2 [x]Eze 19:3,6; Na 2:11-13 [y]Eze 29:3; 34:18

[a] 15 Hebrew *Sheol*; also in verses 16 and 17

3" 'This is what the Sovereign LORD says:

" 'With a great throng of people
I will cast my net over you,
and they will haul you up in my net.[z]
4I will throw you on the land
and hurl you on the open field.
I will let all the birds of the air
settle on you
and all the beasts of the earth
gorge themselves on you.[a]
5I will spread your flesh on the mountains
and fill the valleys[b] with your remains.
6I will drench the land with your flowing blood[c]
all the way to the mountains,
and the ravines will be filled with your flesh.
7When I snuff you out, I will cover the heavens
and darken their stars;
I will cover the sun with a cloud,
and the moon will not give its light.[d]
8All the shining lights in the heavens
I will darken over you;
I will bring darkness over your land,
declares the Sovereign LORD.
9I will trouble the hearts of many peoples
when I bring about your destruction among the nations,
among[a] lands you have not known.
10I will cause many peoples to be appalled at you,
and their kings will shudder with horror because of you
when I brandish my sword before them.
On the day[e] of your downfall
each of them will tremble
every moment for his life.[f]

11" 'For this is what the Sovereign LORD says:

" 'The sword of the king of Babylon[g]
will come against you.
12I will cause your hordes to fall
by the swords of mighty men—
the most ruthless of all nations.[h]
They will shatter the pride of Egypt,
and all her hordes will be overthrown.[i]
13I will destroy all her cattle
from beside abundant waters
no longer to be stirred by the foot of man
or muddied by the hoofs of cattle.[j]
14Then I will let her waters settle
and make her streams flow like oil,
declares the Sovereign LORD.
15When I make Egypt desolate
and strip the land of everything in it,
when I strike down all who live there,
then they will know that I am the LORD.[k]'

16"This is the lament[l] they will
chant for her. The daughters of the nations will chant it; for Egypt and all her
hordes they will chant it, declares the
Sovereign LORD."

17In the twelfth year, on the fifteenth
day of the month, the word of the LORD
came to me:[m] 18"Son of man, wail for
the hordes of Egypt and consign[n] to
the earth below both her and the
daughters of mighty nations, with
those who go down to the pit.[o] 19Say
to them, 'Are you more favored than
others? Go down and be laid among
the uncircumcised.'[p] 20They will fall
among those killed by the sword. The
sword is drawn; let her be dragged[q]
off with all her hordes. 21From within
the grave[b][r] the mighty leaders will
say of Egypt and her allies, 'They have
come down and they lie with the uncircumcised, with those killed by the
sword.'

22"Assyria is there with her whole
army; she is surrounded by the graves
of all her slain, all who have fallen by
the sword. 23Their graves are in the
depths of the pit[s] and her army lies
around her grave. All who had spread
terror in the land of the living are slain,
fallen by the sword.

24"Elam[t] is there, with all her
hordes around her grave. All of them
are slain, fallen by the sword.[u] All who
had spread terror in the land of the
living[v] went down uncircumcised to
the earth below. They bear their shame
with those who go down to the pit.[w]
25A bed is made for her among the
slain, with all her hordes around her
grave. All of them are uncircumcised,
killed by the sword. Because their terror had spread in the land of the living,
they bear their shame with those who
go down to the pit; they are laid among
the slain.

26"Meshech and Tubal[x] are there,
with all their hordes around their

32:3 [z]Eze 12:13 **32:4** [a]Isa 18:6; Eze 31:12-13 **32:5** [b]Eze 31:12 **32:6** [c]Isa 34:3 **32:7** [d]Isa 13:10; 34:4; Eze 30:3; Joel 2:2,31; 3:15; Mt 24:29; Rev 8:12 **32:10** [e]Jer 46:10 [f]Eze 26:16; 27:35 **32:11** [g]Jer 46:26 **32:12** [h]Eze 28:7 [i]Eze 31:11-12 **32:13** [j]Eze 29:8,11 **32:15** [k]Ex 7:5; 14:4, 18; Ps 107:33-34; Eze 6:7 **32:16** [l]2Sa 1:17; 2Ch 35:25; Eze 26:17 **32:17** [m]ver 1 **32:18** [n]Jer 1:10 [o]Eze 31:14,16; Mic 1:8 **32:19** [p]ver 29-30; Eze 28:10; 31:18 **32:20** [q]Ps 28:3 **32:21** [r]Isa 14:9 **32:23** [s]Isa 14:15 **32:24** [t]Ge 10:22 [u]Jer 49:37 [v]Job 28:13 [w]Eze 26:20 **32:26** [x]Ge 10:2; Eze 27:13

a 9 Hebrew; Septuagint *bring you into captivity among the nations, / to* **b** *21* Hebrew *Sheol*; also in verse 27

graves. All of them are uncircumcised,
killed by the sword because they
spread their terror in the land of the
living. 27 Do they not lie with the other
uncircumcised warriors who have fall-
en, who went down to the grave with
their weapons of war, whose swords
were placed under their heads? The
punishment for their sins rested on
their bones, though the terror of these
warriors had stalked through the land
of the living.
28 "You too, O Pharaoh, will be broken and will lie among the uncircumcised, with those killed by the sword.
29 "Edom[y] is there, her kings and all
her princes; despite their power, they
are laid with those killed by the sword.
They lie with the uncircumcised, with
those who go down to the pit.[z]
30 "All the princes of the north[a] and
all the Sidonians[b] are there; they went
down with the slain in disgrace despite
the terror caused by their power. They
lie uncircumcised with those killed by
the sword and bear their shame with
those who go down to the pit.
31 "Pharaoh—he and all his army—
will see them and he will be consoled[c]
for all his hordes that were killed by the
sword, declares the Sovereign LORD.
32 Although I had him spread terror in
the land of the living, Pharaoh and all
his hordes will be laid among the uncircumcised, with those killed by the
sword, declares the Sovereign LORD."

Ezekiel a Watchman

33 The word of the LORD came to me:
2 "Son of man, speak to your countrymen and say to them: 'When I bring
the sword[d] against a land, and the
people of the land choose one of their
men and make him their watchman,[e]
3 and he sees the sword coming against
the land and blows the trumpet[f] to
warn the people, 4 then if anyone hears
the trumpet but does not take warning[g] and the sword comes and takes
his life, his blood will be on his own
head.[h] 5 Since he heard the sound of
the trumpet but did not take warning,
his blood will be on his own head. If
he had taken warning, he would have
saved himself. 6 But if the watchman
sees the sword coming and does not
blow the trumpet to warn the people
and the sword comes and takes the life
of one of them, that man will be taken
away because of his sin, but I will hold
the watchman accountable for his
blood.'[i]
7 "Son of man, I have made you a
watchman for the house of Israel; so
hear the word I speak and give them
warning from me.[j] 8 When I say to the
wicked, 'O wicked man, you will surely
die,[k]' and you do not speak out to dissuade him from his ways, that wicked
man will die for[a] his sin, and I will
hold you accountable for his blood.[l]
9 But if you do warn the wicked man to
turn from his ways and he does not do
so, he will die for his sin, but you will
have saved yourself.[m]
10 "Son of man, say to the house of
Israel, 'This is what you are saying:
"Our offenses and sins weigh us down,
and we are wasting away[n] because
of[b] them. How then can we live?[o]"'
11 Say to them, 'As surely as I live, declares the Sovereign LORD, I take no
pleasure in the death of the wicked, but
rather that they turn from their ways
and live.[p] Turn! Turn from your evil
ways! Why will you die, O house of Israel?'[q]
12 "Therefore, son of man, say to
your countrymen, 'The righteousness
of the righteous man will not save him
when he disobeys, and the wickedness
of the wicked man will not cause him
to fall when he turns from it. The righteous man, if he sins, will not be allowed to live because of his former
righteousness.'[r] 13 If I tell the righteous man that he will surely live, but
then he trusts in his righteousness and
does evil, none of the righteous things
he has done will be remembered; he
will die for the evil he has done.[s]
14 And if I say to the wicked man, 'You
will surely die,' but he then turns away
from his sin and does what is just[t]
and right— 15 if he gives back what he
took in pledge for a loan, returns what
he has stolen,[u] follows the decrees

32:29 [y]Isa 34:5-15; Jer 49:7; Eze 35:15; Ob 1:1 [z]Eze 25:12-14 **32:30** [a]Jer 25:26; Eze 38:6; 39:2 [b]Jer 25:22; Eze 28:21 **32:31** [c]Eze 14:22; 31:16 **33:2** [d]Jer 12:12 [e]Eze 3:11 **33:3** [f]Hos 8:1 **33:4** [g]2Ch 25:16 [h]Jer 6:17; Eze 18:13; Zec 1:4; Ac 18:6 **33:6** [i]Eze 3:18 **33:7** [j]Jer 26:2; Eze 3:17 **33:8** [k]ver 14 [l]Eze 18:4 **33:9** [m]Eze 3:17-19 **33:10** [n]Eze 24:23 [o]Lev 26:39; Eze 4:17 **33:11** [p]Eze 18:32; 2Pe 3:9 [q]Eze 18:23 **33:12** [r]2Ch 7:14; Eze 3:20 **33:13** [s]Eze 18:24; Heb 10:38; 2Pe 2:20-21 **33:14** [t]Eze 18:27 **33:15** [u]Ex 22:1-4; Lev 6:2-5

[a] *8* Or *in*; also in verse 9 [b] *10* Or *away in*

33:7–11

PROMISE 7

THE WATCHMAN

God compares his witness to a watchman on a city wall. This man's sworn duty was to warn people of coming disaster (33:1–6). It is impossible to know essential truth and not be responsible to share it. Ezekiel's watchman image catapults the carrier of truth to a new level of importance.

Christ's Great Commission to his followers takes on an added dimension when we include the watchman imagery. If you know the gospel well enough to be a Christian, you know it well enough to be a watchman. Read these verses again—as a watchman!

For the next Promise 7 reading go to page 964.

that give life, and does no evil, he will surely live; he will not die.[v] **16**None of the sins he has committed will be remembered against him. He has done what is just and right; he will surely live.[w]

17"Yet your countrymen say, 'The way of the Lord is not just.' But it is their way that is not just. **18**If a righteous man turns from his righteousness and does evil, he will die for it.[x] **19**And if a wicked man turns away from his wickedness and does what is just and right, he will live by doing so. **20**Yet, O house of Israel, you say, 'The way of the Lord is not just.' But I will judge each of you according to his own ways."

Jerusalem's Fall Explained

21In the twelfth year of our exile, in the tenth month on the fifth day, a man who had escaped[y] from Jerusalem came to me and said, "The city has fallen![z]" **22**Now the evening before the man arrived, the hand of the LORD was upon me,[a] and he opened my mouth[b] before the man came to me in the morning. So my mouth was opened and I was no longer silent.[c]

23Then the word of the LORD came to me: **24**"Son of man, the people living in those ruins[d] in the land of Israel are saying, 'Abraham was only one man, yet he possessed the land. But we are many; surely the land has been given to us as our possession.'[e] **25**Therefore say to them, 'This is what the Sovereign LORD says: Since you eat meat with the blood[f] still in it and look to your idols and shed blood, should you then possess the land?[g] **26**You rely on your sword, you do detestable things, and each of you defiles his neighbor's wife.[h] Should you then possess the land?'

27"Say this to them: 'This is what the Sovereign LORD says: As surely as I live, those who are left in the ruins will fall by the sword, those out in the country I will give to the wild animals to be devoured, and those in strongholds and caves will die of a plague.[i] **28**I will make the land a desolate waste, and her proud strength will come to an end, and the mountains of Israel will become desolate so that no one will cross them. **29**Then they will know that I am the LORD, when I have made the land a desolate waste because of all the detestable things they have done.'

30"As for you, son of man, your countrymen are talking together about you by the walls and at the doors of the houses, saying to each other, 'Come and hear the message that has come from the LORD.' **31**My people come to you, as they usually do, and sit before[j] you to listen to your words, but they do not put them into practice. With their mouths they express devotion, but their hearts are greedy for unjust gain.[k] **32**Indeed, to them you are nothing more than one who sings love songs with a beautiful voice and plays an instrument well, for they hear your words but do not put them into practice.[l]

33"When all this comes true—and it surely will—then they will know that a prophet has been among them.[m]"

Shepherds and Sheep

34 The word of the LORD came to me: **2**"Son of man, prophesy against the shepherds of Israel; prophesy and say to them: 'This is what the Sovereign LORD says: Woe to the shepherds of Israel who only take care of themselves! Should not shepherds take care of the flock?[n] **3**You eat the curds, clothe yourselves with the wool and slaughter the choice animals, but you do not take care of the flock.[o] **4**You have not strengthened the weak or healed the sick or bound up the injured. You have not brought back the strays or searched for the lost. You have ruled them harshly and brutally.[p] **5**So they were scattered because there was no shepherd,[q] and when they were scattered they became food for all the wild animals.[r] **6**My sheep wandered over all the mountains and on every high hill. They were scattered over the whole earth, and no one searched or looked for them.[s]

7" 'Therefore, you shepherds, hear the word of the LORD: **8**As surely as I live, declares the Sovereign LORD, because my flock lacks a shepherd and so has been plundered and has become food for all the wild animals, and because my shepherds did not search for my flock but cared for themselves rather than for my flock, **9**therefore, O shepherds, hear the word of the LORD: **10**This is what the Sovereign LORD says: I am against[t] the shepherds and will hold them accountable for my flock. I will remove them from tending the flock so that the shepherds can no longer feed themselves. I will rescue[u] my flock from their mouths, and it will no longer be food for them.[v]

11" 'For this is what the Sovereign LORD says: I myself will search for my sheep and look after them. **12**As a shepherd[w] looks after his scattered flock

33:15 [v]Eze 20:11; Lk 19:8
33:16 [w]Isa 43:25; Eze 18:22
33:18 [x]Eze 3:20; Eze 18:26
33:21 [y]Eze 24:26 [z]2Ki 25:4,10; Jer 39:1-2; Eze 32:1
33:22 [a]Eze 1:3 [b]Lk 1:64 [c]Eze 3:26-27; 24:27
33:24 [d]Eze 36:4 [e]Isa 51:2; Jer 40:7; Eze 11:15; Ac 7:5
33:25 [f]Ge 9:4; Dt 12:16 [g]Jer 7:9-10; Eze 22:6,27
33:26 [h]Eze 22:11
33:27 [i]1Sa 13:6; Isa 2:19; Jer 42:22; Eze 39:4
33:31 [j]Eze 8:1 [k]Ps 78:36-37; Isa 29:13; Eze 22:27; Mt 13:22; 1Jn 3:18
33:32 [l]Mk 6:20
33:33 [m]1Sa 3:20; Jer 28:9; Eze 2:5
34:2 [n]Ps 78:70-72; Isa 40:11; Jer 3:15; 23:1; Mic 3:11; Jn 10:11; 21:15-17
34:3 [o]Isa 56:11; Eze 22:27; Zec 11:16
34:4 [p]Zec 11:15-17
34:5 [q]Nu 27:17 [r]ver 28; Isa 56:9
34:6 [s]Ps 142:4; 1Pe 2:25
34:10 [t]Jer 21:13 [u]Ps 72:14 [v]1Sa 2:29-30; Zec 10:3
34:12 [w]Isa 40:11; Jer 31:10; Lk 19:10

when he is with them, so will I look after my sheep. I will rescue them from all the places where they were scattered on a day of clouds and darkness.[x] 13 I will bring them out from the nations and gather them from the countries, and I will bring them into their own land. I will pasture them on the mountains of Israel, in the ravines and in all the settlements in the land.[y] 14 I will tend them in a good pasture, and the mountain heights of Israel[z] will be their grazing land. There they will lie down in good grazing land, and there they will feed in a rich pasture[a] on the mountains of Israel.[b] 15 I myself will tend my sheep and have them lie down, declares the Sovereign LORD.[c] 16 I will search for the lost and bring back the strays. I will bind up the injured and strengthen the weak,[d] but the sleek and the strong I will destroy. I will shepherd the flock with justice.[e]

17 " 'As for you, my flock, this is what the Sovereign LORD says: I will judge between one sheep and another, and between rams and goats.[f] 18 Is it not enough for you to feed on the good pasture? Must you also trample the rest of your pasture with your feet? Is it not enough for you to drink clear water? Must you also muddy the rest with your feet? 19 Must my flock feed on what you have trampled and drink what you have muddied with your feet?

20 " 'Therefore this is what the Sovereign LORD says to them: See, I myself will judge between the fat sheep and the lean sheep. 21 Because you shove with flank and shoulder, butting all the weak sheep with your horns[g] until you have driven them away, 22 I will save my flock, and they will no longer be plundered. I will judge between one sheep and another.[h] 23 I will place over them one shepherd, my servant David, and he will tend[i] them; he will tend them and be their shepherd. 24 I the LORD will be their God,[j] and my servant David will be prince among them. I the LORD have spoken.[k]

25 " 'I will make a covenant of peace with them and rid the land of wild beasts[l] so that they may live in the desert and sleep in the forests in safety.[m] 26 I will bless[n] them and the places surrounding my hill.[a] I will send down showers in season;[o] there will be showers of blessing.[p] 27 The trees of the field will yield their fruit and the ground will yield its crops; the people will be secure in their land. They will know that I am the LORD, when I break the bars of their yoke[q] and rescue them from the hands of those who enslaved them.[r] 28 They will no longer be plundered by the nations, nor will wild animals devour them. They will live in safety, and no one will make them afraid.[s] 29 I will provide for them a land renowned[t] for its crops, and they will no longer be victims of famine[u] in the land or bear the scorn[v] of the nations.[w] 30 Then they will know that I, the LORD their God, am with them and that they, the house of Israel, are my people, declares the Sovereign LORD.[x] 31 You my sheep, the sheep of my pasture,[y] are people, and I am your God, declares the Sovereign LORD.' "

A Prophecy Against Edom

35 The word of the LORD came to me: 2 "Son of man, set your face against Mount Seir; prophesy against it 3 and say: 'This is what the Sovereign LORD says: I am against you, Mount Seir, and I will stretch out my hand[z] against you and make you a desolate waste.[a] 4 I will turn your towns into ruins and you will be desolate. Then you will know that I am the LORD.[b]

5 " 'Because you harbored an ancient hostility and delivered the Israelites over to the sword at the time of their calamity, the time their punishment reached its climax,[c] 6 therefore as surely as I live, declares the Sovereign LORD, I will give you over to bloodshed and it will pursue you.[d] Since you did not hate bloodshed, bloodshed will pursue you. 7 I will make Mount Seir a desolate waste and cut off from it all who come and go. 8 I will fill your mountains with the slain; those killed by the sword will fall on your hills and in your valleys and in all your ravines.[e] 9 I will make you desolate forever; your towns will not be inhabited. Then you will know that I am the LORD.[f]

10 " 'Because you have said, "These two nations and countries will be ours and we will take possession[g] of them," even though I the LORD was there, 11 therefore as surely as I live, declares the Sovereign LORD, I will treat you in accordance with the anger[h] and jealousy you showed in your hatred of them and I will make myself known among them when I judge you.[i] 12 Then you will know that I the LORD have heard all the contemptible things you have said against the mountains of Israel. You said, "They have been laid waste and have been given over to us to devour.[j]" 13 You boasted against me and spoke against me without re-

34:12 [x] Eze 30:3
34:13 [y] Jer 23:3
34:14 [z] Eze 20:40 [a] Ps 23:2 [b] Eze 36:29-30
34:15 [c] Ps 23:1-2
34:16 [d] Mic 4:6 [e] Isa 10:16; Lk 5:32
34:17 [f] Mt 25:32-33
34:21 [g] Dt 33:17
34:22 [h] Ps 72:12-14; Jer 23:2-3
34:23 [i] Isa 40:11
34:24 [j] Eze 36:28 [k] Jer 30:9
34:25 [l] Lev 26:6 [m] Isa 11:6-9; Hos 2:18
34:26 [n] Ge 12:2 [o] Ps 68:9 [p] Dt 11:13-15; Isa 44:3
34:27 [q] Lev 26:13 [r] Jer 30:8
34:28 [s] Jer 30:10; Eze 39:26
34:29 [t] Isa 4:2 [u] Eze 36:29 [v] Eze 36:6 [w] Eze 36:15
34:30 [x] Eze 14:11; 37:27
34:31 [y] Ps 100:3; Jer 23:1
35:3 [z] Jer 6:12 [a] Eze 25:12-14
35:4 [b] ver 9
35:5 [c] Ps 137:7; Eze 21:29
35:6 [d] Isa 63:2-6
35:8 [e] Eze 31:12
35:9 [f] Jer 49:13
35:10 [g] Ps 83:12; Eze 36:2,5
35:11 [h] Eze 25:14 [i] Ps 9:16; Mt 7:2
35:12 [j] Jer 50:7

[a] 26 Or *I will make them and the places surrounding my hill a blessing*

straint, and I heard it.[k] **14**This is what
the Sovereign LORD says: While the
whole earth rejoices, I will make you
desolate.[l] **15**Because you rejoiced[m]
when the inheritance of the house of
Israel became desolate, that is how I
will treat you. You will be desolate,
O Mount Seir,[n] you and all of
Edom.[o] Then they will know that I am
the LORD.' "

A Prophecy to the Mountains of Israel

36 "Son of man, prophesy to the
mountains of Israel and say,
'O mountains of Israel, hear the word
of the LORD. **2**This is what the Sovereign
LORD says: The enemy said of you,
"Aha![p] The ancient heights[q] have become our possession.[r]" ' **3**Therefore
prophesy and say, 'This is what the
Sovereign LORD says: Because they ravaged and hounded you from every side
so that you became the possession of
the rest of the nations and the object of
people's malicious talk and slander,[s]
4therefore, O mountains of Israel, hear
the word of the Sovereign LORD: This is
what the Sovereign LORD says to the
mountains and hills, to the ravines and
valleys,[t] to the desolate ruins and the
deserted towns that have been plundered and ridiculed by the rest of the
nations around you[u]— **5**this is what
the Sovereign LORD says: In my burning
zeal I have spoken against the rest of
the nations, and against all Edom, for
with glee and with malice in their
hearts they made my land their own
possession so that they might plunder
its pastureland.'[v] **6**Therefore prophesy concerning the land of Israel and say
to the mountains and hills, to the ravines and valleys: 'This is what the Sovereign LORD says: I speak in my jealous
wrath because you have suffered the
scorn of the nations.[w] **7**Therefore this
is what the Sovereign LORD says: I
swear with uplifted hand that the nations around you will also suffer scorn.
8" 'But you, O mountains of Israel,
will produce branches and fruit[x] for
my people Israel, for they will soon
come home. **9**I am concerned for you
and will look on you with favor; you
will be plowed and sown, **10**and I will
multiply the number of people upon
you, even the whole house of Israel.
The towns will be inhabited and the
ruins rebuilt.[y] **11**I will increase the
number of men and animals upon you,
and they will be fruitful and become
numerous. I will settle people on you
as in the past[z] and will make you
prosper more than before.[a] Then
you will know that I am the LORD. **12**I
will cause people, my people Israel, to
walk upon you. They will possess you,
and you will be their inheritance;[b] you
will never again deprive them of their
children.
13" 'This is what the Sovereign LORD
says: Because people say to you, "You
devour men[c] and deprive your nation
of its children," **14**therefore you will no
longer devour men or make your nation childless, declares the Sovereign
LORD. **15**No longer will I make you hear
the taunts of the nations, and no longer
will you suffer the scorn of the peoples
or cause your nation to fall, declares
the Sovereign LORD.[d]' "
16Again the word of the LORD came
to me: **17**"Son of man, when the people
of Israel were living in their own land,
they defiled it by their conduct and
their actions. Their conduct was like a
woman's monthly uncleanness in my
sight.[e] **18**So I poured out[f] my wrath
on them because they had shed blood
in the land and because they had defiled it with their idols. **19**I dispersed
them among the nations, and they
were scattered[g] through the countries; I judged them according to their
conduct and their actions.[h] **20**And
wherever they went among the nations
they profaned[i] my holy name, for it
was said of them, 'These are the LORD's
people, and yet they had to leave his
land.'[j] **21**I had concern for my holy
name, which the house of Israel profaned among the nations where they
had gone.[k]
22"Therefore say to the house of Israel, 'This is what the Sovereign LORD
says: It is not for your sake, O house
of Israel, that I am going to do these
things, but for the sake of my holy
name, which you have profaned[l]
among the nations where you have
gone.[m] **23**I will show the holiness of my
great name, which has been profaned
among the nations, the name you have
profaned among them. Then the nations will know that I am the LORD, declares the Sovereign LORD, when I show
myself holy[n] through you before their
eyes.[o]
24" 'For I will take you out of the nations; I will gather you from all the
countries and bring you back into your
own land.[p] **25**I will sprinkle[q] clean
water on you, and you will be clean; I
will cleanse[r] you from all your impurities and from all your idols.[s] **26**I will
give you a new heart[t] and put a new
spirit in you; I will remove from you
your heart of stone and give you a heart
of flesh.[u] **27**And I will put my Spirit[v]
in you and move you to follow my decrees and be careful to keep my laws.

35:13 [k]Da 11:36
35:14 [l]Jer 51:48
35:15 [m]Ob 1:12 [n]ver 3 [o]Isa 34:5-6,11; Jer 50:11-13; La 4:21
36:2 [p]Eze 25:3 [q]Dt 32:13 [r]Eze 35:10
36:3 [s]Ps 44:13-14
36:4 [t]Eze 6:3 [u]Dt 11:11; Ps 79:4; Eze 34:28
36:5 [v]Jer 50:11; Eze 25:12-14; 35:10,15
36:6 [w]Ps 123:3-4; Eze 34:29
36:8 [x]Isa 27:6
36:10 [y]ver 33; Isa 49:17-23
36:11 [z]Mic 7:14 [a]Jer 31:28; Eze 16:55
36:12 [b]Eze 47:14,22
36:13 [c]Nu 13:32
36:15 [d]Ps 89:50-51; Eze 34:29
36:17 [e]Jer 2:7
36:18 [f]2Ch 34:21
36:19 [g]Dt 28:64 [h]Eze 39:24
36:20 [i]Ro 2:24 [j]Isa 52:5; Jer 33:24; Eze 12:16
36:21 [k]Ps 74:18; Isa 48:9
36:22 [l]Ro 2:24* [m]Ps 106:8
36:23 [n]Eze 20:41 [o]Ps 126:2; Isa 5:16
36:24 [p]Eze 34:13; 37:21
36:25 [q]Heb 9:13; 10:22 [r]Ps 51:2,7 [s]Zec 13:2
36:26 [t]Jer 24:7 [u]Ps 51:10; Eze 11:19
36:27 [v]Eze 37:14

[28]You will live in the land I gave your
forefathers; you will be my people,[w]
and I will be your God.[x] [29]I will save
you from all your uncleanness. I will
call for the grain and make it plentiful
and will not bring famine[y] upon you.
[30]I will increase the fruit of the trees
and the crops of the field, so that you
will no longer suffer disgrace among
the nations because of famine.[z]
[31]Then you will remember your evil
ways and wicked deeds, and you will
loathe yourselves for your sins and detestable practices.[a] [32]I want you to
know that I am not doing this for your
sake, declares the Sovereign LORD. Be
ashamed and disgraced for your conduct, O house of Israel![b]
[33]" 'This is what the Sovereign LORD
says: On the day I cleanse you from all
your sins, I will resettle your towns,
and the ruins will be rebuilt. [34]The desolate land will be cultivated instead of
lying desolate in the sight of all who
pass through it. [35]They will say, "This
land that was laid waste has become
like the garden of Eden;[c] the cities
that were lying in ruins, desolate and
destroyed, are now fortified and inhabited.[d]" [36]Then the nations around you
that remain will know that I the LORD
have rebuilt what was destroyed and
have replanted what was desolate. I the
LORD have spoken, and I will do it.'[e]
[37]"This is what the Sovereign LORD
says: Once again I will yield to the plea
of the house of Israel and do this for
them: I will make their people as numerous as sheep, [38]as numerous as the
flocks for offerings[f] at Jerusalem during her appointed feasts. So will the
ruined cities be filled with flocks of
people. Then they will know that I am
the LORD."

The Valley of Dry Bones

37 The hand of the LORD was upon
me,[g] and he brought me out by
the Spirit[h] of the LORD and set me in
the middle of a valley;[i] it was full of
bones.[j] [2]He led me back and forth
among them, and I saw a great many
bones on the floor of the valley, bones
that were very dry. [3]He asked me, "Son
of man, can these bones live?"
I said, "O Sovereign LORD, you alone
know.[k]"
[4]Then he said to me, "Prophesy to
these bones and say to them, 'Dry
bones, hear the word of the LORD![l]
[5]This is what the Sovereign LORD says
to these bones: I will make breath[a] enter you, and you will come to life.[m] [6]I
will attach tendons to you and make
flesh come upon you and cover you
with skin; I will put breath in you, and
you will come to life. Then you will
know that I am the LORD.[n]' "
[7]So I prophesied as I was commanded. And as I was prophesying, there
was a noise, a rattling sound, and the
bones came together, bone to bone. [8]I
looked, and tendons and flesh appeared on them and skin covered
them, but there was no breath in them.
[9]Then he said to me, "Prophesy to
the breath;[o] prophesy, son of man,
and say to it, 'This is what the Sovereign LORD says: Come from the four
winds, O breath, and breathe into
these slain, that they may live.' " [10]So I
prophesied as he commanded me, and
breath entered them; they came to life
and stood up on their feet—a vast
army.[p]
[11]Then he said to me: "Son of man,
these bones are the whole house of Israel. They say, 'Our bones are dried up
and our hope is gone; we are cut off.'[q]
[12]Therefore prophesy and say to them:
'This is what the Sovereign LORD says:
O my people, I am going to open your
graves and bring you up from them; I
will bring you back to the land of Israel.[r] [13]Then you, my people, will know
that I am the LORD, when I open your
graves and bring you up from them. [14]I
will put my Spirit[s] in you and you will
live, and I will settle you in your own
land. Then you will know that I the
LORD have spoken, and I have done it,
declares the LORD.[t]' "

One Nation Under One King

[15]The word of the LORD came to me:
[16]"Son of man, take a stick of wood and

36:28 [w]Jer 30:22 [x]Eze 14:11; 37:14,27
36:29 [y]Eze 34:29
36:30 [z]Lev 26:4-5; Eze 34:27; Hos 2:21-22
36:31 [a]Eze 6:9; 20:43
36:32 [b]Dt 9:5
36:35 [c]Joel 2:3 [d]Isa 51:3
36:36 [e]Eze 17:22; 22:14; 37:14; 39:27-28
36:38 [f]1Ki 8:63; 2Ch 35:7-9
37:1 [g]Eze 1:3; 8:3 [h]Eze 11:24; Lk 4:1; Ac 8:39 [i]Jer 7:32 [j]Jer 8:2; Eze 40:1
37:3 [k]Dt 32:39; 1Sa 2:6; Isa 26:19
37:4 [l]Jer 22:29
37:5 [m]Ge 2:7; Ps 104:29-30
37:6 [n]Eze 38:23; Joel 2:27; 3:17
37:9 [o]Ps 104:30
37:10 [p]Rev 11:11
37:11 [q]La 3:54
37:12 [r]Dt 32:39; 1Sa 2:6; Isa 26:19; Hos 13:14; Am 9:14-15
37:14 [s]Joel 2:28-29 [t]Eze 36:27-28, 36

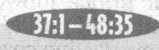

[a]5 The Hebrew for this word can also mean *wind* or *spirit* (see verses 6-14).

37:1–48:35 **PE**

GOD STILL RULES

This final section of Ezekiel was a vision of encouragement for God's people Israel. Ezekiel's first Hebrew readers were living in exile under God's judgment for their sins of idolatry and rebellion against God. But they were still God's people. They were defeated, so God gave them this vision of victory; discouraged, so he encouraged; hopeless, so he gave them hope.

Even flipping through these pages and reading random passages will serve as a great reminder that, no matter how grim things get, God still reigns over this universe and he always acts in love.

write on it, 'Belonging to Judah and the Israelites[u] associated with him.'[v] Then take another stick of wood, and write on it, 'Ephraim's stick, belonging to Joseph and all the house of Israel associated with him.' 17Join them together into one stick so that they will become one in your hand.[w]

18"When your countrymen ask you, 'Won't you tell us what you mean by this?'[x] 19say to them, 'This is what the Sovereign LORD says: I am going to take the stick of Joseph—which is in Ephraim's hand—and of the Israelite tribes associated with him, and join it to Judah's stick, making them a single stick of wood, and they will become one in my hand.'[y] 20Hold before their eyes the sticks you have written on 21and say to them, 'This is what the Sovereign LORD says: I will take the Israelites out of the nations where they have gone. I will gather them from all around and bring them back into their own land.[z] 22I will make them one nation in the land, on the mountains of Israel. There will be one king over all of them and they will never again be two nations or be divided into two kingdoms.[a] 23They will no longer defile[b] themselves with their idols and vile images or with any of their offenses, for I will save them from all their sinful backsliding,[a] and I will cleanse them. They will be my people, and I will be their God.[c]

24" 'My servant David[d] will be king over them, and they will all have one shepherd.[e] They will follow my laws and be careful to keep my decrees.[f] 25They will live in the land I gave to my servant Jacob, the land where your fathers lived.[g] They and their children and their children's children will live there forever,[h] and David my servant will be their prince forever.[i] 26I will make a covenant of peace[j] with them; it will be an everlasting covenant. I will establish them and increase their numbers,[k] and I will put my sanctuary among them forever.[l] 27My dwelling place[m] will be with them; I will be their God, and they will be my people.[n] 28Then the nations will know that I the LORD make Israel holy,[o] when my sanctuary is among them forever.' "

A Prophecy Against Gog

38 The word of the LORD came to me: 2"Son of man, set your face against Gog, of the land of Magog,[p] the chief prince of[b] Meshech and Tubal;[q] prophesy against him 3and say: 'This is what the Sovereign LORD says: I am against you, O Gog, chief prince of[c] Meshech and Tubal.[r] 4I will turn you around, put hooks[s] in your jaws and bring you out with your whole army—your horses, your horsemen fully armed, and a great horde with large and small shields, all of them brandishing their swords.[t] 5Persia, Cush[d][u] and Put[v] will be with them, all with shields and helmets, 6also Gomer[w] with all its troops, and Beth Togarmah[x] from the far north with all its troops—the many nations with you.

7" 'Get ready; be prepared,[y] you and all the hordes gathered about you, and take command of them. 8After many days[z] you will be called to arms. In future years you will invade a land that has recovered from war, whose people were gathered from many nations[a] to the mountains of Israel, which had long been desolate. They had been brought out from the nations, and now all of them live in safety.[b] 9You and all your troops and the many nations with you will go up, advancing like a storm;[c] you will be like a cloud[d] covering the land.

10" 'This is what the Sovereign LORD says: On that day thoughts will come into your mind and you will devise an evil scheme.[e] 11You will say, "I will invade a land of unwalled villages; I will attack a peaceful and unsuspecting people—all of them living without walls and without gates and bars.[f] 12I will plunder and loot and turn my hand against the resettled ruins and the people gathered from the nations, rich in livestock and goods, living at the center of the land." 13Sheba[g] and Dedan and the merchants of Tarshish and all her villages[e] will say to you, "Have you come to plunder? Have you gathered your hordes to loot, to carry off silver and gold, to take away livestock and goods and to seize much plunder?[h]" '

14"Therefore, son of man, prophesy and say to Gog: 'This is what the Sovereign LORD says: In that day, when my people Israel are living in safety,[i] will you not take notice of it? 15You will come from your place in the far north, you and many nations with you, all of them riding on horses, a great horde, a mighty army.[j] 16You will advance against my people Israel like a cloud[k] that covers the land. In days to come, O Gog, I will bring you against my land, so that the nations may know me when

[a] *23* Many Hebrew manuscripts (see also Septuagint); most Hebrew manuscripts *all their dwelling places where they sinned* [b] *2* Or *the prince of Rosh,* [c] *3* Or *Gog, prince of Rosh,* [d] *5* That is, the upper Nile region [e] *13* Or *her strong lions*

37:16 [u] 1Ki 12:20; 2Ch 10:17-19 [v] Nu 17:2-3; 2Ch 15:9
37:17 [w] ver 24; Isa 11:13; Jer 50:4; Hos 1:11
37:18 [x] Eze 24:19
37:19 [y] Zec 10:6
37:21 [z] Isa 43:5-6; Eze 36:24; 39:27
37:22 [a] Isa 11:13; Jer 3:18; Hos 1:11
37:23 [b] Eze 36:25; 43:7 [c] Eze 11:18; 36:28
37:24 [d] Hos 3:5 [e] Isa 40:11; Eze 34:23 [f] Ps 78:70-71
37:25 [g] Eze 28:25 [h] Am 9:15 [i] Isa 11:1
37:26 [j] Isa 55:3 [k] Jer 30:19 [l] Eze 16:62
37:27 [m] Lev 26:11; Jn 1:14 [n] 2Co 6:16*
37:28 [o] Ex 31:13; Eze 20:12
38:2 [p] Ge 10:2 [q] Rev 20:8
38:3 [r] Eze 39:1
38:4 [s] 2Ki 19:28 [t] Eze 29:4; Da 11:40
38:5 [u] Ge 10:6 [v] Eze 27:10
38:6 [w] Ge 10:2 [x] Eze 27:14
38:7 [y] Isa 8:9
38:8 [z] Isa 24:22 [a] Isa 11:11 [b] Jer 23:6
38:9 [c] Isa 28:2 [d] Jer 4:13; Joel 2:2
38:10 [e] Ps 36:4; Mic 2:1
38:11 [f] Jer 49:31; Zec 2:4
38:13 [g] Eze 27:22 [h] Isa 10:6; Jer 15:13
38:14 [i] ver 8; Zec 2:5
38:15 [j] Eze 39:2
38:16 [k] ver 9

I show myself holy through you before
their eyes.[l]
17" 'This is what the Sovereign LORD
says: Are you not the one I spoke of in
former days by my servants the prophets of Israel? At that time they prophesied for years that I would bring you
against them. 18This is what will happen in that day: When Gog attacks the
land of Israel, my hot anger will be
aroused, declares the Sovereign LORD.
19In my zeal and fiery wrath I declare
that at that time there shall be a great
earthquake in the land of Israel.[m]
20The fish of the sea, the birds of the
air, the beasts of the field, every creature that moves along the ground, and
all the people on the face of the earth
will tremble at my presence. The
mountains will be overturned, the cliffs
will crumble and every wall will fall
to the ground.[n] 21I will summon a
sword[o] against Gog on all my mountains, declares the Sovereign LORD. Every man's sword will be against his
brother.[p] 22I will execute judgment[q]
upon him with plague and bloodshed;
I will pour down torrents of rain, hailstones[r] and burning sulfur on him
and on his troops and on the many
nations with him. 23And so I will show
my greatness and my holiness, and I
will make myself known in the sight of
many nations. Then they will know
that I am the LORD.[s]'

39 "Son of man, prophesy against Gog
and say: 'This is what the Sovereign LORD says: I am against you,
O Gog, chief prince of[a] Meshech and
Tubal.[t] 2I will turn you around and
drag you along. I will bring you from
the far north and send you against the
mountains of Israel. 3Then I will strike
your bow[u] from your left hand and
make your arrows[v] drop from your
right hand. 4On the mountains of Israel
you will fall, you and all your troops
and the nations with you. I will give
you as food to all kinds of carrion birds
and to the wild animals.[w] 5You will fall
in the open field, for I have spoken,
declares the Sovereign LORD. 6I will
send fire[x] on Magog and on those
who live in safety in the coastlands,[y]
and they will know that I am the LORD.
7" 'I will make known my holy name
among my people Israel. I will no longer let my holy name be profaned,[z] and
the nations will know that I the LORD
am the Holy One in Israel.[a] 8It is coming! It will surely take place, declares
the Sovereign LORD. This is the day I
have spoken of.
9" 'Then those who live in the towns
of Israel will go out and use the weapons for fuel and burn them up—the
small and large shields, the bows and
arrows, the war clubs and spears. For
seven years they will use them for
fuel.[b] 10They will not need to gather
wood from the fields or cut it from the
forests, because they will use the weapons for fuel. And they will plunder
those who plundered them and loot
those who looted them, declares the
Sovereign LORD.[c]
11" 'On that day I will give Gog a
burial place in Israel, in the valley of
those who travel east toward[b] the
Sea.[c] It will block the way of travelers,
because Gog and all his hordes will be
buried there. So it will be called the
Valley of Hamon Gog.[d][d]
12" 'For seven months the house of
Israel will be burying them in order to
cleanse the land.[e] 13All the people of
the land will bury them, and the day I
am glorified[f] will be a memorable day
for them, declares the Sovereign LORD.
14" 'Men will be regularly employed
to cleanse the land. Some will go
throughout the land and, in addition to
them, others will bury those that remain on the ground. At the end of the
seven months they will begin their
search. 15As they go through the land
and one of them sees a human bone,
he will set up a marker beside it until
the gravediggers have buried it in the
Valley of Hamon Gog. 16(Also a town
called Hamonah[e] will be there.) And
so they will cleanse the land.'
17"Son of man, this is what the Sovereign LORD says: Call out to every kind
of bird[g] and all the wild animals: 'Assemble and come together from all
around to the sacrifice I am preparing
for you, the great sacrifice on the
mountains of Israel. There you will eat
flesh and drink blood. 18You will eat
the flesh of mighty men and drink the
blood of the princes of the earth as if
they were rams and lambs, goats and
bulls—all of them fattened animals
from Bashan.[h] 19At the sacrifice I am
preparing for you, you will eat fat till
you are glutted and drink blood till you
are drunk. 20At my table you will eat
your fill of horses and riders, mighty
men and soldiers of every kind,' declares the Sovereign LORD.[i]
21"I will display my glory among the
nations, and all the nations will see the
punishment I inflict and the hand I lay
upon them.[j] 22From that day forward
the house of Israel will know that I am
the LORD their God. 23And the nations

a 1 Or *Gog, prince of Rosh,* b 11 Or *of* c 11 That is, the Dead Sea d 11 *Hamon Gog* means *hordes of Gog.* e 16 *Hamonah* means *horde.*

38:16 l Isa 29:23; Eze 39:21
38:19 m Ps 18:7; Eze 5:13; Hag 2:6,21
38:20 n Hos 4:3; Na 1:5
38:21 o Eze 14:17 p 1Sa 14:20; 2Ch 20:23; Hag 2:22
38:22 q Isa 66:16; Jer 25:31 r Ps 18:12; Rev 16:21
38:23 s Eze 36:23
39:1 t Eze 38:2,3
39:3 u Hos 1:5 v Ps 76:3
39:4 w ver 17-20; Eze 29:5; 33:27
39:6 x Eze 30:8; Am 1:4 y Jer 25:22
39:7 z Ex 20:7 a Isa 12:6; Eze 36:16,23
39:9 b Ps 46:9
39:10 c Isa 14:2; 33:1; Hab 2:8
39:11 d Eze 38:2
39:12 e Dt 21:23
39:13 f Eze 28:22
39:17 g Rev 19:17
39:18 h Ps 22:12; Jer 51:40
39:20 i Rev 19:17-18
39:21 j Ex 9:16; Isa 37:20; Eze 38:16

will know that the people of Israel went
into exile for their sin, because they
were unfaithful to me. So I hid my face
from them and handed them over to
their enemies, and they all fell by the
sword.[k] 24I dealt with them according
to their uncleanness and their offenses,
and I hid my face from them.[l]

25"Therefore this is what the Sovereign LORD says: I will now bring Jacob
back from captivity[a][m] and will have
compassion[n] on all the people of Israel, and I will be zealous for my holy
name.[o] 26They will forget their shame
and all the unfaithfulness they showed
toward me when they lived in safety[p]
in their land with no one to make them
afraid.[q] 27When I have brought them
back from the nations and have gathered them from the countries of their
enemies, I will show myself holy
through them in the sight of many nations.[r] 28Then they will know that I
am the LORD their God, for though I
sent them into exile among the nations, I will gather them to their own
land, not leaving any behind. 29I will no
longer hide my face from them, for I
will pour out my Spirit[s] on the house
of Israel, declares the Sovereign LORD."

The New Temple Area

40 In the twenty-fifth year of our exile, at the beginning of the year, on
the tenth of the month, in the fourteenth year after the fall of the city[t]—
on that very day the hand of the LORD
was upon me[u] and he took me there.
2In visions[v] of God he took me to the
land of Israel and set me on a very high
mountain,[w] on whose south side were
some buildings that looked like a city.
3He took me there, and I saw a man
whose appearance was like bronze;[x]
he was standing in the gateway with a
linen cord and a measuring rod[y] in his
hand. 4The man said to me, "Son of
man, look with your eyes and hear with
your ears and pay attention to everything I am going to show you, for that
is why you have been brought here.
Tell[z] the house of Israel everything
you see.[a]"

The East Gate to the Outer Court

5I saw a wall completely surrounding the temple area. The length of the
measuring rod in the man's hand was
six long cubits, each of which was a
cubit[b] and a handbreadth.[c] He measured[b] the wall; it was one measuring
rod thick and one rod high.

6Then he went to the gate facing
east.[c] He climbed its steps and measured the threshold of the gate; it was
one rod deep.[d] 7The alcoves[d] for the
guards were one rod long and one rod
wide, and the projecting walls between
the alcoves were five cubits thick. And
the threshold of the gate next to the
portico facing the temple was one rod
deep.

8Then he measured the portico of
the gateway; 9it[e] was eight cubits deep
and its jambs were two cubits thick.
The portico of the gateway faced the
temple.

10Inside the east gate were three alcoves on each side; the three had the
same measurements, and the faces of
the projecting walls on each side had
the same measurements. 11Then he
measured the width of the entrance to
the gateway; it was ten cubits and its
length was thirteen cubits. 12In front of
each alcove was a wall one cubit high,
and the alcoves were six cubits square.
13Then he measured the gateway from
the top of the rear wall of one alcove to
the top of the opposite one; the distance was twenty-five cubits from one
parapet opening to the opposite one.
14He measured along the faces of the
projecting walls all around the inside of
the gateway—sixty cubits. The measurement was up to the portico[f] facing the courtyard.[g][e] 15The distance
from the entrance of the gateway to the
far end of its portico was fifty cubits.
16The alcoves and the projecting walls
inside the gateway were surmounted
by narrow parapet openings all
around, as was the portico; the openings all around faced inward. The faces
of the projecting walls were decorated
with palm trees.[f]

The Outer Court

17Then he brought me into the outer
court.[g] There I saw some rooms and a
pavement that had been constructed
all around the court; there were thirty
rooms[h] along the pavement.[i] 18It
abutted the sides of the gateways and
was as wide as they were long; this was
the lower pavement. 19Then he measured the distance from the inside of
the lower gateway to the outside of the
inner court;[j] it was a hundred cu-

39:23 [k]Isa 1:15; 59:2; Jer 22:8-9; 44:23
39:24 [l]Jer 2:17,19; 4:18; Eze 36:19
39:25 [m]Jer 33:7; Eze 34:13 [n]Jer 30:18 [o]Isa 27:12-13
39:26 [p]1Ki 4:25 [q]Isa 17:2; Eze 34:28; Mic 4:4
39:27 [r]Eze 36:23-24; 37:21; 38:16
39:29 [s]Joel 2:28; Ac 2:17
40:1 [t]2Ki 25:7; Jer 39:1-10; 52:4-11; Eze 33:21 [u]Eze 1:3
40:2 [v]Da 7:1,7 [w]Eze 17:22; Rev 21:10
40:3 [x]Eze 1:7; Da 10:6; Rev 1:15 [y]Eze 47:3; Zec 2:1-2; Rev 11:1; 21:15
40:4 [z]Jer 26:2 [a]Eze 44:5
40:5 [b]Eze 42:20
40:6 [c]Eze 8:16
40:7 [d]ver 36
40:14 [e]Ex 27:9
40:16 [f]ver 21-22; 2Ch 3:5; Eze 41:26
40:17 [g]Rev 11:2 [h]Eze 41:6 [i]Eze 42:1
40:19 [j]Eze 46:1

[a] 25 Or *now restore the fortunes of Jacob*
[b] 5 The common cubit was about 1 1/2 feet (about 0.5 meter). [c] 5 That is, about 3 inches (about 8 centimeters) [d] 6 Septuagint; Hebrew *deep, the first threshold, one rod deep*
[e] 8,9 Many Hebrew manuscripts, Septuagint, Vulgate and Syriac; most Hebrew manuscripts *gateway facing the temple; it was one rod deep. 9Then he measured the portico of the gateway; it*
[f] 14 Septuagint; Hebrew *projecting wall*
[g] 14 The meaning of the Hebrew for this verse is uncertain.

bits[k] on the east side as well as on the north.

The North Gate

20 Then he measured the length and width of the gate facing north, leading into the outer court. 21 Its alcoves[l]—three on each side—its projecting walls and its portico had the same measurements as those of the first gateway. It was fifty cubits long and twenty-five cubits wide. 22 Its openings, its portico[m] and its palm tree decorations had the same measurements as those of the gate facing east. Seven steps led up to it, with its portico opposite them. 23 There was a gate to the inner court facing the north gate, just as there was on the east. He measured from one gate to the opposite one; it was a hundred cubits.[n]

The South Gate

24 Then he led me to the south side and I saw a gate facing south. He measured its jambs and its portico, and they had the same measurements as the others. 25 The gateway and its portico had narrow openings all around, like the openings of the others. It was fifty cubits long and twenty-five cubits wide.[o] 26 Seven steps led up to it, with its portico opposite them; it had palm tree decorations on the faces of the projecting walls on each side.[p] 27 The inner court[q] also had a gate facing south, and he measured from this gate to the outer gate on the south side; it was a hundred cubits.

Gates to the Inner Court

28 Then he brought me into the inner court through the south gate, and he measured the south gate; it had the same measurements[r] as the others. 29 Its alcoves, its projecting walls and its portico had the same measurements as the others. The gateway and its portico had openings all around. It was fifty cubits long and twenty-five cubits wide. 30 (The porticoes[s] of the gateways around the inner court were twenty-five cubits wide and five cubits deep.) 31 Its portico[t] faced the outer court; palm trees decorated its jambs, and eight steps led up to it.

32 Then he brought me to the inner court on the east side, and he measured the gateway; it had the same measurements as the others. 33 Its alcoves, its projecting walls and its portico had the same measurements as the others. The gateway and its portico had openings all around. It was fifty cubits long and twenty-five cubits wide. 34 Its portico[u] faced the outer court; palm trees decorated the jambs on either side, and eight steps led up to it.

35 Then he brought me to the north gate[v] and measured it. It had the same measurements as the others, 36 as did its alcoves,[w] its projecting walls and its portico, and it had openings all around. It was fifty cubits long and twenty-five cubits wide. 37 Its portico[a] faced the outer court; palm trees decorated the jambs on either side, and eight steps led up to it.

The Rooms for Preparing Sacrifices

38 A room with a doorway was by the portico in each of the inner gateways, where the burnt offerings[x] were washed. 39 In the portico of the gateway were two tables on each side, on which the burnt offerings,[y] sin offerings[z] and guilt offerings[a] were slaughtered. 40 By the outside wall of the portico of the gateway, near the steps at the entrance to the north gateway were two tables, and on the other side of the steps were two tables. 41 So there were four tables on one side of the gateway and four on the other—eight tables in all—on which the sacrifices were slaughtered. 42 There were also four tables of dressed stone[b] for the burnt offerings, each a cubit and a half long, a cubit and a half wide and a cubit high. On them were placed the utensils for slaughtering the burnt offerings and the other sacrifices.[c] 43 And double-pronged hooks, each a handbreadth long, were attached to the wall all around. The tables were for the flesh of the offerings.

Rooms for the Priests

44 Outside the inner gate, within the inner court, were two rooms, one[b] at the side of the north gate and facing south, and another at the side of the south[c] gate and facing north. 45 He said to me, "The room facing south is for the priests who have charge of the temple,[d] 46 and the room facing north[e] is for the priests who have charge of the altar.[f] These are the sons of Zadok,[g] who are the only Levites who may draw near to the LORD to minister before him.[h]"

47 Then he measured the court: It was square—a hundred cubits long and a hundred cubits wide. And the altar was in front of the temple.

40:19 [k]ver 23,27
40:21 [l]ver 7
40:22 [m]ver 49
40:23 [n]ver 19
40:25 [o]ver 33
40:26 [p]ver 22
40:27 [q]ver 32
40:28 [r]ver 35
40:30 [s]ver 21
40:31 [t]ver 22
40:34 [u]ver 22
40:35 [v]Eze 44:4; 47:2
40:36 [w]ver 7
40:38 [x]2Ch 4:6; Eze 42:13
40:39 [y]Eze 46:2 [z]Lev 4:3,28 [a]Lev 7:1
40:42 [b]Ex 20:25 [c]ver 39
40:45 [d]1Ch 9:23
40:46 [e]Eze 42:13 [f]Nu 18:5 [g]1Ki 2:35 [h]Nu 16:5; Eze 43:19; 44:15; 45:4; 48:11

[a] *37* Septuagint (see also verses 31 and 34); Hebrew *jambs* [b] *44* Septuagint; Hebrew *were rooms for singers, which were* [c] *44* Septuagint; Hebrew *east*

The Temple

48He brought me to the portico of the temple[i] and measured the jambs of the portico; they were five cubits wide on either side. The width of the entrance was fourteen cubits and its projecting walls were[a] three cubits wide on either side. 49The portico[j] was twenty cubits wide, and twelve[b] cubits from front to back. It was reached by a flight of stairs,[c] and there were pillars[k] on each side of the jambs.

41 Then the man brought me to the outer sanctuary[l] and measured the jambs; the width of the jambs was six cubits[d] on each side.[e] 2The entrance was ten cubits wide, and the projecting walls on each side of it were five cubits wide. He also measured the outer sanctuary; it was forty cubits long and twenty cubits wide.[m]

3Then he went into the inner sanctuary and measured the jambs of the entrance; each was two cubits wide. The entrance was six cubits wide, and the projecting walls on each side of it were seven cubits wide. 4And he measured the length of the inner sanctuary; it was twenty cubits, and its width was twenty cubits across the end of the outer sanctuary.[n] He said to me, "This is the Most Holy Place.[o]"

5Then he measured the wall of the temple; it was six cubits thick, and each side room around the temple was four cubits wide. 6The side rooms were on three levels, one above another, thirty[p] on each level. There were ledges all around the wall of the temple to serve as supports for the side rooms, so that the supports were not inserted into the wall of the temple.[q] 7The side rooms all around the temple were wider at each successive level. The structure surrounding the temple was built in ascending stages, so that the rooms widened as one went upward. A stairway[r] went up from the lowest floor to the top floor through the middle floor.

8I saw that the temple had a raised base all around it, forming the foundation of the side rooms. It was the length of the rod, six long cubits. 9The outer wall of the side rooms was five cubits thick. The open area between the side rooms of the temple 10and the ⌞priests'⌟ rooms was twenty cubits wide all around the temple. 11There were entrances to the side rooms from the open area, one on the north and another on the south; and the base adjoining the open area was five cubits wide all around.

12The building facing the temple courtyard on the west side was seventy cubits wide. The wall of the building was five cubits thick all around, and its length was ninety cubits.

13Then he measured the temple; it was a hundred cubits long, and the temple courtyard and the building with its walls were also a hundred cubits long. 14The width of the temple courtyard on the east, including the front of the temple, was a hundred cubits.[s]

15Then he measured the length of the building facing the courtyard at the rear of the temple, including its galleries[t] on each side; it was a hundred cubits.

The outer sanctuary, the inner sanctuary and the portico facing the court, 16as well as the thresholds and the narrow windows[u] and galleries around the three of them—everything beyond and including the threshold was covered with wood. The floor, the wall up to the windows, and the windows were covered.[v] 17In the space above the outside of the entrance to the inner sanctuary and on the walls at regular intervals all around the inner and outer sanctuary 18were carved[w] cherubim[x] and palm trees.[y] Palm trees alternated with cherubim. Each cherub had two faces:[z] 19the face of a man toward the palm tree on one side and the face of a lion toward the palm tree on the other. They were carved all around the whole temple.[a] 20From the floor to the area above the entrance, cherubim and palm trees were carved on the wall of the outer sanctuary.

21The outer sanctuary[b] had a rectangular doorframe, and the one at the front of the Most Holy Place was similar. 22There was a wooden altar[c] three cubits high and two cubits square[f]; its corners, its base[g] and its sides were of wood. The man said to me, "This is the table[d] that is before the LORD." 23Both the outer sanctuary[e] and the Most Holy Place had double doors.[f] 24Each door had two leaves—two hinged leaves[g] for each door. 25And on the doors of the outer sanctuary were carved cherubim and palm trees like those carved on the walls, and there was a wooden overhang on the front of the portico. 26On the sidewalls of the portico were narrow windows with palm trees carved on each side. The

40:48 [i]1Ki 6:2 **40:49** [j]ver 22; 1Ki 6:3 [k]1Ki 7:15 **41:1** [l]ver 23 **41:2** [m]2Ch 3:3 **41:4** [n]1Ki 6:20 [o]Ex 26:33; Heb 9:3-8 **41:6** [p]Eze 40:17 [q]1Ki 6:5 **41:7** [r]1Ki 6:8

41:14 [s]Eze 40:47 **41:15** [t]Eze 42:3 **41:16** [u]1Ki 6:4 [v]ver 25-26; 1Ki 6:15; Eze 42:3 **41:18** [w]1Ki 6:18 [x]Ex 37:7; 2Ch 3:7 [y]1Ki 6:29; 7:36 [z]Eze 10:21 **41:19** [a]Eze 10:14 **41:21** [b]ver 1 **41:22** [c]Ex 30:1 [d]Ex 25:23; Eze 23:41; 44:16; Mal 1:7, 12 **41:23** [e]ver 1 [f]1Ki 6:32 **41:24** [g]1Ki 6:34

a *48* Septuagint; Hebrew *entrance was* **b** *49* Septuagint; Hebrew *eleven* **c** *49* Hebrew; Septuagint *Ten steps led up to it* **d** *1* The common cubit was about 1 1/2 feet (about 0.5 meter). **e** *1* One Hebrew manuscript and Septuagint; most Hebrew manuscripts *side, the width of the tent* **f** *22* Septuagint; Hebrew *long* **g** *22* Septuagint; Hebrew *length*

side rooms of the temple also had over-
hangs.[h]

Rooms for the Priests

42 Then the man led me northward
into the outer court and brought
me to the rooms[i] opposite the temple
courtyard[j] and opposite the outer
wall on the north side.[k] 2The building
whose door faced north was a hundred
cubits[a] long and fifty cubits wide.
3Both in the section twenty cubits from
the inner court and in the section opposite the pavement of the outer court,
gallery[l] faced gallery at the three levels.[m] 4In front of the rooms was an
inner passageway ten cubits wide and
a hundred cubits[b] long. Their doors
were on the north.[n] 5Now the upper
rooms were narrower, for the galleries
took more space from them than from
the rooms on the lower and middle
floors of the building. 6The rooms on
the third floor had no pillars, as the
courts had; so they were smaller in
floor space than those on the lower and
middle floors. 7There was an outer wall
parallel to the rooms and the outer
court; it extended in front of the rooms
for fifty cubits. 8While the row of rooms
on the side next to the outer court was
fifty cubits long, the row on the side
nearest the sanctuary was a hundred
cubits long. 9The lower rooms had an
entrance[o] on the east side as one enters them from the outer court.
10On the south side[c] along the
length of the wall of the outer court,
adjoining the temple courtyard and
opposite the outer wall, were rooms[p]
11with a passageway in front of them.
These were like the rooms on the
north; they had the same length and
width, with similar exits and dimensions. Similar to the doorways on the
north 12were the doorways of the
rooms on the south. There was a doorway at the beginning of the passageway that was parallel to the corresponding wall extending eastward, by
which one enters the rooms.
13Then he said to me, "The north[q]
and south rooms facing the temple
courtyard are the priests' rooms, where
the priests who approach the LORD will
eat the most holy offerings. There they
will put the most holy offerings—the
grain offerings, the sin offerings[r] and
the guilt offerings[s]—for the place is
holy.[t] 14Once the priests enter the
holy precincts, they are not to go into
the outer court until they leave behind
the garments[u] in which they minister,
for these are holy. They are to put on
other clothes before they go near the
places that are for the people.[v]"
15When he had finished measuring
what was inside the temple area, he led
me out by the east gate[w] and measured the area all around: 16He measured the east side with the measuring
rod; it was five hundred cubits.[d] 17He
measured the north side; it was five
hundred cubits[e] by the measuring
rod. 18He measured the south side; it
was five hundred cubits by the measuring rod. 19Then he turned to the west
side and measured; it was five hundred
cubits by the measuring rod. 20So he
measured[x] the area on all four sides.
It had a wall around it,[y] five hundred
cubits long and five hundred cubits
wide,[z] to separate the holy from the
common.[a]

The Glory Returns to the Temple

43 Then the man brought me to the
gate facing east,[b] 2and I saw the
glory of the God of Israel coming from
the east. His voice was like the roar of
rushing waters,[c] and the land was radiant with his glory.[d] 3The vision I saw
was like the vision I had seen when
he[f] came to destroy the city and like
the visions I had seen by the Kebar River, and I fell facedown. 4The glory[e] of
the LORD entered the temple through
the gate facing east.[f] 5Then the Spirit[g] lifted me up[h] and brought me into
the inner court, and the glory of the
LORD filled the temple.
6While the man was standing beside
me, I heard someone speaking to me
from inside the temple. 7He said: "Son
of man, this is the place of my throne
and the place for the soles of my feet.
This is where I will live among the Israelites forever. The house of Israel will
never again defile my holy name—
neither they nor their kings—by their
prostitution[g] and the lifeless idols[h] of
their kings at their high places.[i]
8When they placed their threshold next
to my threshold and their doorposts
beside my doorposts, with only a wall
between me and them, they defiled my
holy name by their detestable practices. So I destroyed them in my anger.
9Now let them put away from me their
prostitution and the lifeless idols of

41:26 [h]ver 15-16; Eze 40:16 **42:1** [i]ver 13 [j]Eze 41:12-14 [k]Eze 40:17 **42:3** [l]Eze 41:15 [m]Eze 41:16 **42:4** [n]Eze 46:19 **42:9** [o]Eze 44:5; 46:19 **42:10** [p]ver 1 **42:13** [q]Eze 40:46 [r]Lev 10:17; 6:25 [s]Lev 14:13 [t]Ex 29:31; Lev 6:29; 7:6; 10:12-13; Nu 18:9-10 **42:14** [u]Eze 44:19 [v]Ex 29:9; Lev 8:7-9 **42:15** [w]Eze 43:1 **42:20** [x]Eze 40:5 [y]Zec 2:5 [z]Eze 45:2; Rev 21:16 [a]Eze 22:26 **43:1** [b]Eze 10:19; 42:15; 44:1; 46:1 **43:2** [c]Rev 1:15 [d]Isa 6:3; Eze 11:23; Rev 18:1 **43:4** [e]Eze 1:28 [f]Eze 10:19 **43:5** [g]Eze 11:24 [h]Eze 3:12; 8:3 **43:7** [i]Lev 26:30

[a] *2* The common cubit was about 1 1/2 feet (about 0.5 meter). [b] *4* Septuagint and Syriac; Hebrew *and one cubit* [c] *10* Septuagint; Hebrew *Eastward* [d] *16* See Septuagint of verse 17; Hebrew *rods*; also in verses 18 and 19. [e] *17* Septuagint; Hebrew *rods* [f] *3* Some Hebrew manuscripts and Vulgate; most Hebrew manuscripts *I* [g] *7* Or *their spiritual adultery*; also in verse 9 [h] *7* Or *the corpses*; also in verse 9

their kings, and I will live among them forever.[j]

10"Son of man, describe the temple to the people of Israel, that they may be ashamed[k] of their sins. Let them consider the plan, 11and if they are ashamed of all they have done, make known to them the design of the temple—its arrangement, its exits and entrances—its whole design and all its regulations[a] and laws. Write these down before them so that they may be faithful to its design and follow all its regulations.[l]

12"This is the law of the temple: All the surrounding area[m] on top of the mountain will be most holy. Such is the law of the temple.

The Altar

13"These are the measurements of the altar[n] in long cubits, that cubit being a cubit[b] and a handbreadth[c]: Its gutter is a cubit deep and a cubit wide, with a rim of one span[d] around the edge. And this is the height of the altar: 14From the gutter on the ground up to the lower ledge it is two cubits high and a cubit wide, and from the smaller ledge up to the larger ledge it is four cubits high and a cubit wide. 15The altar hearth is four cubits high, and four horns[o] project upward from the hearth. 16The altar hearth is square, twelve cubits long and twelve cubits wide. 17The upper ledge also is square, fourteen cubits long and fourteen cubits wide, with a rim of half a cubit and a gutter of a cubit all around. The steps[p] of the altar face east."

18Then he said to me, "Son of man, this is what the Sovereign LORD says: These will be the regulations for sacrificing burnt offerings[q] and sprinkling blood[r] upon the altar when it is built: 19You are to give a young bull[s] as a sin offering to the priests, who are Levites, of the family of Zadok,[t] who come near[u] to minister before me, declares the Sovereign LORD. 20You are to take some of its blood and put it on the four horns of the altar and on the four corners of the upper ledge[v] and all around the rim, and so purify the altar[w] and make atonement for it. 21You are to take the bull for the sin offering and burn it in the designated part of the temple area outside the sanctuary.[x]

22"On the second day you are to offer a male goat without defect for a sin offering, and the altar is to be purified as it was purified with the bull. 23When you have finished purifying it, you are to offer a young bull and a ram from the flock, both without defect.[y] 24You are to offer them before the LORD, and the priests are to sprinkle salt[z] on them and sacrifice them as a burnt offering to the LORD.

25"For seven days[a] you are to provide a male goat daily for a sin offering; you are also to provide a young bull and a ram from the flock, both without defect.[b] 26For seven days they are to make atonement for the altar and cleanse it; thus they will dedicate it. 27At the end of these days, from the eighth day[c] on, the priests are to present your burnt offerings and fellowship offerings[e][d] on the altar. Then I will accept you, declares the Sovereign LORD."

The Prince, the Levites, the Priests

44 Then the man brought me back to the outer gate of the sanctuary, the

43:9 [j]Eze 37:26-28
43:10 [k]Eze 16:61
43:11 [l]Eze 44:5
43:12 [m]Eze 40:2
43:13 [n]2Ch 4:1
43:15 [o]Ex 27:2
43:17 [p]Ex 20:26
43:18 [q]Ex 40:29 [r]Lev 1:5,11; Heb 9:21-22
43:19 [s]Lev 4:3; Eze 45:18-19 [t]Eze 44:15 [u]Nu 16:40; Eze 40:46
43:20 [v]ver 17 [w]Lev 16:19
43:21 [x]Ex 29:14; Heb 13:11
43:23 [y]Ex 29:1
43:24 [z]Lev 2:13; Mk 9:49-50
43:25 [a]Lev 8:33 [b]Ex 29:37
43:27 [c]Lev 9:1 [d]Lev 17:5

a *11* Some Hebrew manuscripts and Septuagint; most Hebrew manuscripts *regulations and its whole design* b *13* The common cubit was about 1 1/2 feet (about 0.5 meter). c *13* That is, about 3 inches (about 8 centimeters) d *13* That is, about 9 inches (about 22 centimeters) e *27* Traditionally *peace offerings*

43:1–27

PE

FILLED TEMPLES

What's unique about God's people, either in Ezekiel's time or today? For ancient Israel, it wasn't the law or the land or even the temple. It wasn't the religious ritual or the lingo. It wasn't the name "Israel" (or, for us, "church"). Ezekiel 43:1–8 highlights the one thing that made Israel unique; it's the same thing that makes Christians Christian: God's presence.

We need the Bible, we need and enjoy relationships with godly people, we appreciate beautiful buildings and are moved by great worship. But if God isn't present in these things, they are not uniquely Christian. Why? Because without God's presence these things don't match what's inside of us. Paul wrote, "Do you not know that your body is a temple of the Holy Spirit, who is in you, whom you have received from God?" (1 Corinthians 6:19).

Do you see how serious God is about your life? He gave you the one thing that marks you as his. Ezekiel wrote that "the glory of the LORD filled the temple" (43:5). This same God has also filled you through his Spirit.

Read Ezekiel 43:1–5 and 1 Corinthians 6:19 together. Then thank our Lord for filling you with his presence.

one facing east,[e] and it was shut. **2**The
LORD said to me, "This gate is to remain
shut. It must not be opened; no one
may enter through it.[f] It is to remain
shut because the LORD, the God of Israel, has entered through it. **3**The prince
himself is the only one who may sit
inside the gateway to eat in the presence[g] of the LORD. He is to enter by
way of the portico of the gateway and
go out the same way.[h]"
4Then the man brought me by way
of the north gate to the front of the
temple. I looked and saw the glory of
the LORD filling the temple[i] of the
LORD, and I fell facedown.[j]
5The LORD said to me, "Son of man,
look carefully, listen closely and give
attention to everything I tell you concerning all the regulations regarding
the temple of the LORD. Give attention
to the entrance of the temple and all
the exits of the sanctuary.[k] **6**Say to the
rebellious house[l] of Israel, 'This is
what the Sovereign LORD says: Enough
of your detestable practices, O house
of Israel! **7**In addition to all your other
detestable practices, you brought foreigners uncircumcised in heart[m] and
flesh into my sanctuary, desecrating
my temple while you offered me food,
fat and blood, and you broke my covenant.[n] **8**Instead of carrying out your
duty in regard to my holy things, you
put others in charge of my sanctuary.[o]
9This is what the Sovereign LORD says:
No foreigner uncircumcised in heart
and flesh is to enter my sanctuary, not
even the foreigners who live among the
Israelites.[p]
10" 'The Levites who went far from
me when Israel went astray[q] and who
wandered from me after their idols
must bear the consequences of their
sin.[r] **11**They may serve in my sanctuary, having charge of the gates of the
temple and serving in it; they may
slaughter the burnt offerings[s] and
sacrifices for the people and stand before the people and serve them.[t]
12But because they served them in the
presence of their idols and made the
house of Israel fall into sin, therefore I
have sworn with uplifted hand[u] that
they must bear the consequences of
their sin, declares the Sovereign
LORD.[v] **13**They are not to come near to
serve me as priests or come near any of
my holy things or my most holy offerings; they must bear the shame[w] of
their detestable practices.[x] **14**Yet I will
put them in charge of the duties of the
temple and all the work that is to be
done in it.[y]
15" 'But the priests, who are Levites
and descendants of Zadok and who
faithfully carried out the duties of my
sanctuary when the Israelites went
astray from me, are to come near to
minister before me; they are to stand
before me to offer sacrifices of fat and
blood, declares the Sovereign LORD.[z]
16They alone are to enter my sanctuary;
they alone are to come near my table[a]
to minister before me and perform my
service.[b]
17" 'When they enter the gates of the
inner court, they are to wear linen
clothes;[c] they must not wear any
woolen garment while ministering at
the gates of the inner court or inside
the temple. **18**They are to wear linen
turbans[d] on their heads and linen
undergarments[e] around their waists.
They must not wear anything that
makes them perspire.[f] **19**When they
go out into the outer court where the
people are, they are to take off the
clothes they have been ministering in
and are to leave them in the sacred
rooms, and put on other clothes, so
that they do not consecrate[g] the people by means of their garments.[h]
20" 'They must not shave their heads
or let their hair grow long, but they are
to keep the hair of their heads
trimmed.[i] **21**No priest is to drink wine
when he enters the inner court.[j]
22They must not marry widows or divorced women; they may marry only
virgins of Israelite descent or widows of
priests.[k] **23**They are to teach my people the difference between the holy
and the common[l] and show them
how to distinguish between the unclean and the clean.[m]
24" 'In any dispute, the priests are to
serve as judges[n] and decide it according to my ordinances. They are to keep
my laws and my decrees for all my appointed feasts, and they are to keep my
Sabbaths holy.[o]
25" 'A priest must not defile himself
by going near a dead person; however,
if the dead person was his father or
mother, son or daughter, brother or
unmarried sister, then he may defile
himself.[p] **26**After he is cleansed, he
must wait seven days.[q] **27**On the day
he goes into the inner court of the
sanctuary to minister in the sanctuary,
he is to offer a sin offering for himself,
declares the Sovereign LORD.
28" 'I am to be the only inheritance[r]
the priests have. You are to give them
no possession in Israel; I will be their
possession. **29**They will eat the grain offerings, the sin offerings and the guilt
offerings; and everything in Israel

44:1 [e]Eze 43:1
44:2 [f]Eze 43:4-5
44:3 [g]Ex 24:9-11 [h]Eze 46:2,8
44:4 [i]Isa 6:4; Rev 15:8 [j]Eze 1:28; 3:23
44:5 [k]Eze 40:4; 43:10-11
44:6 [l]Eze 3:9
44:7 [m]Lev 26:41 [n]Ge 17:14; Ex 12:48; Lev 22:25
44:8 [o]Lev 22:2; Nu 18:7
44:9 [p]Joel 3:17; Zec 14:21
44:10 [q]2Ki 23:8 [r]Nu 18:23
44:11 [s]2Ch 29:34 [t]Nu 3:5-37; 16:9; 1Ch 26:12-19
44:12 [u]Ps 106:26 [v]2Ki 16:10-16
44:13 [w]Eze 16:61 [x]Nu 18:3
44:14 [y]Nu 18:4; 1Ch 23:28-32
44:15 [z]Jer 33:18; Eze 40:46; Zec 3:7
44:16 [a]Eze 41:22 [b]Nu 18:5
44:17 [c]Ex 39:27-28; Rev 19:8
44:18 [d]Ex 28:39; Isa 3:20 [e]Ex 28:42 [f]Lev 16:4
44:19 [g]Lev 6:27; Eze 46:20 [h]Lev 6:10-11; Eze 42:14
44:20 [i]Lev 21:5; Nu 6:5
44:21 [j]Lev 10:9
44:22 [k]Lev 21:7
44:23 [l]Eze 22:26 [m]Mal 2:7
44:24 [n]Dt 17:8-9; 1Ch 23:4 [o]2Ch 19:8
44:25 [p]Lev 21:1-4
44:26 [q]Nu 19:14
44:28 [r]Nu 18:20; Dt 10:9; 18:1-2; Jos 13:33

devoted[a] to the LORD[s] will belong to
them.[t] 30 The best of all the firstfruits[u] and of all your special gifts will
belong to the priests. You are to give
them the first portion of your ground
meal[v] so that a blessing[w] may rest on
your household.[x] 31 The priests must
not eat anything, bird or animal, found
dead or torn by wild animals.[y]

Division of the Land

45 "'When you allot the land as an
inheritance,[z] you are to present to
the LORD a portion of the land as a sacred district, 25,000 cubits long and
20,000[b] cubits wide; the entire area
will be holy.[a] 2 Of this, a section 500
cubits square[b] is to be for the sanctuary, with 50 cubits around it for open
land. 3 In the sacred district, measure
off a section 25,000 cubits[c] long and
10,000 cubits[d] wide. In it will be the
sanctuary, the Most Holy Place. 4 It will
be the sacred portion of the land for
the priests,[c] who minister in the sanctuary and who draw near to minister
before the LORD. It will be a place for
their houses as well as a holy place for
the sanctuary.[d] 5 An area 25,000 cubits
long and 10,000 cubits wide will belong
to the Levites, who serve in the temple,
as their possession for towns to live
in.[e][e]

6 "'You are to give the city as its
property an area 5,000 cubits wide and
25,000 cubits long, adjoining the sacred portion; it will belong to the whole
house of Israel.[f]

7 "'The prince will have the land
bordering each side of the area formed
by the sacred district and the property
of the city. It will extend westward from
the west side and eastward from the
east side, running lengthwise from the
western to the eastern border parallel
to one of the tribal portions.[g] 8 This
land will be his possession in Israel.
And my princes will no longer oppress
my people but will allow the house of
Israel to possess the land according to
their tribes.[h]

9 "'This is what the Sovereign LORD
says: You have gone far enough,
O princes of Israel! Give up your violence and oppression and do what is
just and right.[i] Stop dispossessing my
people, declares the Sovereign LORD.
10 You are to use accurate scales,[j] an
accurate ephah[f][k] and an accurate
bath.[g] 11 The ephah[l] and the bath are
to be the same size, the bath containing a tenth of a homer[h] and the ephah
a tenth of a homer; the homer is to be
the standard measure for both. 12 The
shekel[i] is to consist of twenty gerahs.[m] Twenty shekels plus twenty-
five shekels plus fifteen shekels equal
one mina.[j]

Offerings and Holy Days

13 "'This is the special gift you are to
offer: a sixth of an ephah from each
homer of wheat and a sixth of an ephah
from each homer of barley. 14 The prescribed portion of oil, measured by the
bath, is a tenth of a bath from each cor
(which consists of ten baths or one homer, for ten baths are equivalent to a
homer). 15 Also one sheep is to be taken
from every flock of two hundred from
the well-watered pastures of Israel.
These will be used for the grain offerings, burnt offerings[n] and fellowship
offerings[k] to make atonement[o] for
the people, declares the Sovereign
LORD. 16 All the people of the land will
participate in this special gift for the
use of the prince in Israel. 17 It will be
the duty of the prince to provide the
burnt offerings, grain offerings and
drink offerings at the festivals, the New
Moons and the Sabbaths[p]—at all the
appointed feasts of the house of Israel.
He will provide the sin offerings, grain
offerings, burnt offerings and fellowship offerings to make atonement for
the house of Israel.[q]

18 "'This is what the Sovereign LORD
says: In the first month[r] on the first
day you are to take a young bull without defect[s] and purify the sanctuary.[t] 19 The priest is to take some of
the blood of the sin offering and put it
on the doorposts of the temple, on the
four corners of the upper ledge[u] of the
altar[v] and on the gateposts of the inner court. 20 You are to do the same on
the seventh day of the month for anyone who sins unintentionally[w] or
through ignorance; so you are to make
atonement for the temple.

21 "'In the first month on the fourteenth day you are to observe the Passover,[x] a feast lasting seven days, during which you shall eat bread made
without yeast. 22 On that day the prince
is to provide a bull as a sin offering for
himself and for all the people of the

44:29 [s]Lev 27:21 [t]Nu 18:9,14
44:30 [u]Nu 18:12-13 [v]Nu 15:18-21 [w]Mal 3:10 [x]Ne 10:35-37
44:31 [y]Ex 22:31; Lev 22:8
45:1 [z]Eze 47:21-22 [a]Eze 48:8-9,29
45:2 [b]Eze 42:20
45:4 [c]Eze 40:46 [d]Eze 48:10-11
45:5 [e]Eze 48:13
45:6 [f]Eze 48:15-18
45:7 [g]Eze 48:21
45:8 [h]Nu 26:53; Eze 46:18
45:9 [i]Jer 22:3; Zec 7:9-10; 8:16
45:10 [j]Dt 25:15; Pr 11:1; Am 8:4-6; Mic 6:10-11 [k]Lev 19:36
45:11 [l]Isa 5:10
45:12 [m]Ex 30:13; Lev 27:25; Nu 3:47
45:15 [n]Lev 1:4 [o]Lev 6:30
45:17 [p]Lev 23:38; Isa 66:23 [q]1Ki 8:62; 2Ch 31:3; Eze 46:4-12
45:18 [r]Ex 12:2 [s]Lev 22:20; Heb 9:14 [t]Lev 16:16,33
45:19 [u]Eze 43:17 [v]Lev 16:18-19; Eze 43:20
45:20 [w]Lev 4:27
45:21 [x]Ex 12:11; Lev 23:5-6

[a] *29* The Hebrew term refers to the irrevocable giving over of things or persons to the LORD.
[b] *1* Septuagint (see also verses 3 and 5 and 48:9); Hebrew *10,000*
[c] *3* That is, about 7 miles (about 12 kilometers)
[d] *3* That is, about 3 miles (about 5 kilometers)
[e] *5* Septuagint; Hebrew *temple; they will have as their possession 20 rooms*
[f] *10* An ephah was a dry measure.
[g] *10* A bath was a liquid measure.
[h] *11* A homer was a dry measure.
[i] *12* A shekel weighed about 2/5 ounce (about 11.5 grams).
[j] *12* That is, 60 shekels; the common mina was 50 shekels.
[k] *15* Traditionally *peace offerings*; also in verse 17

land.[y] **23**Every day during the seven days of the Feast he is to provide seven bulls and seven rams[z] without defect as a burnt offering to the LORD, and a male goat for a sin offering.[a] **24**He is to provide as a grain offering[b] an ephah for each bull and an ephah for each ram, along with a hin[a] of oil for each ephah.[c]

25" 'During the seven days of the Feast,[d] which begins in the seventh month on the fifteenth day, he is to make the same provision for sin offerings, burnt offerings, grain offerings and oil.[e]

46 " 'This is what the Sovereign LORD says: The gate of the inner court[f] facing east[g] is to be shut on the six working days, but on the Sabbath day and on the day of the New Moon[h] it is to be opened. **2**The prince is to enter from the outside through the portico[i] of the gateway and stand by the gatepost. The priests are to sacrifice his burnt offering and his fellowship offerings.[b] He is to worship at the threshold of the gateway and then go out, but the gate will not be shut until evening.[j] **3**On the Sabbaths and New Moons the people of the land are to worship in the presence of the LORD at the entrance to that gateway.[k] **4**The burnt offering the prince brings to the LORD on the Sabbath day is to be six male lambs and a ram, all without defect. **5**The grain offering given with the ram is to be an ephah,[c] and the grain offering with the lambs is to be as much as he pleases, along with a hin[a] of oil for each ephah.[l] **6**On the day of the New Moon[m] he is to offer a young bull, six lambs and a ram, all without defect. **7**He is to provide as a grain offering one ephah with the bull, one ephah with the ram, and with the lambs as much as he wants to give, along with a hin of oil with each ephah.[n] **8**When the prince enters, he is to go in through the portico[o] of the gateway, and he is to come out the same way.[p]

9" 'When the people of the land come before the LORD at the appointed feasts,[q] whoever enters by the north gate to worship is to go out the south gate; and whoever enters by the south gate is to go out the north gate. No one is to return through the gate by which he entered, but each is to go out the opposite gate. **10**The prince is to be among them, going in when they go in and going out when they go out.[r]

11" 'At the festivals and the appointed feasts, the grain offering is to be an ephah with a bull, an ephah with a ram, and with the lambs as much as one pleases, along with a hin of oil for each ephah.[s] **12**When the prince provides[t] a freewill offering[u] to the LORD—whether a burnt offering or fellowship offerings—the gate facing east is to be opened for him. He shall offer his burnt offering or his fellowship offerings as he does on the Sabbath day. Then he shall go out, and after he has gone out, the gate will be shut.[v]

13" 'Every day you are to provide a year-old lamb without defect for a burnt offering to the LORD; morning by morning you shall provide it.[w] **14**You are also to provide with it morning by morning a grain offering, consisting of a sixth of an ephah with a third of a hin of oil to moisten the flour. The presenting of this grain offering to the LORD is a lasting ordinance.[x] **15**So the lamb and the grain offering and the oil shall be provided morning by morning for a regular[y] burnt offering.[z]

16" 'This is what the Sovereign LORD says: If the prince makes a gift from his inheritance to one of his sons, it will also belong to his descendants; it is to be their property by inheritance.[a] **17**If, however, he makes a gift from his inheritance to one of his servants, the servant may keep it until the year of freedom;[b] then it will revert to the prince. His inheritance belongs to his sons only; it is theirs. **18**The prince must not take any of the inheritance[c] of the people, driving them off their property. He is to give his sons their inheritance out of his own property, so that none of my people will be separated from his property.' "

19Then the man brought me through the entrance[d] at the side of the gate to the sacred rooms facing north, which belonged to the priests, and showed me a place at the western end. **20**He said to me, "This is the place where the priests will cook the guilt offering and the sin offering and bake the grain offering, to avoid bringing them into the outer court and consecrating[e] the people."[f]

21He then brought me to the outer court and led me around to its four corners, and I saw in each corner another court. **22**In the four corners of the outer court were enclosed[d] courts, forty cubits long and thirty cubits wide; each of the courts in the four corners was the same size. **23**Around the inside of each of the four courts was a ledge of stone, with places for fire built all

45:22 [y]Lev 4:14
45:23 [z]Job 42:8 [a]Nu 28:16-25
45:24 [b]Nu 28:12-13 [c]Eze 46:5-7
45:25 [d]Dt 16:13 [e]Lev 23:34-43; Nu 29:12-38
46:1 [f]Eze 40:19 [g]1Ch 9:18 [h]ver 6; Isa 66:23
46:2 [i]ver 8 [j]ver 12; Eze 44:3
46:3 [k]Lk 1:10
46:5 [l]ver 11; Eze 45:24
46:6 [m]ver 1; Nu 10:10
46:7 [n]Eze 45:24
46:8 [o]ver 2 [p]Eze 44:3
46:9 [q]Ex 23:14; 34:20
46:10 [r]2Sa 6:14-15; Ps 42:4
46:11 [s]ver 5
46:12 [t]Eze 45:17 [u]Lev 7:16 [v]ver 2
46:13 [w]Ex 29:38; Nu 28:3
46:14 [x]Da 8:11
46:15 [y]Ex 29:42 [z]Ex 29:38; Nu 28:5-6
46:16 [a]2Ch 21:3
46:17 [b]Lev 25:10
46:18 [c]Lev 25:23; Eze 45:8; Mic 2:1-2
46:19 [d]Eze 42:9
46:20 [e]Lev 6:27 [f]Zec 14:20

[a] *24,5* That is, probably about 4 quarts (about 4 liters) [b] *2* Traditionally *peace offerings;* also in verse 12 [c] *5* That is, probably about 3/5 bushel (about 22 liters) [d] *22* The meaning of the Hebrew for this word is uncertain.

around under the ledge. 24He said to me, "These are the kitchens where those who minister at the temple will cook the sacrifices of the people."

The River From the Temple

47 The man brought me back to the entrance of the temple, and I saw water[g] coming out from under the threshold of the temple toward the east (for the temple faced east). The water was coming down from under the south side of the temple, south of the altar.[h] 2He then brought me out through the north gate and led me around the outside to the outer gate facing east, and the water was flowing from the south side.

3As the man went eastward with a measuring line[i] in his hand, he measured off a thousand cubits[a] and then led me through water that was ankle-deep. 4He measured off another thousand cubits and led me through water that was knee-deep. He measured off another thousand and led me through water that was up to the waist. 5He measured off another thousand, but now it was a river that I could not cross, because the water had risen and was deep enough to swim in—a river that no one could cross.[j] 6He asked me, "Son of man, do you see this?"

Then he led me back to the bank of the river. 7When I arrived there, I saw a great number of trees on each side of the river.[k] 8He said to me, "This water flows toward the eastern region and goes down into the Arabah,[b][l] where it enters the Sea.[c] When it empties into the Sea,[c] the water there becomes fresh.[m] 9Swarms of living creatures will live wherever the river flows. There will be large numbers of fish, because this water flows there and makes the salt water fresh; so where the river flows everything will live.[n] 10Fishermen[o] will stand along the shore; from En Gedi[p] to En Eglaim there will be places for spreading nets.[q] The fish will be of many kinds[r]—like the fish of the Great Sea.[d][s] 11But the swamps and marshes will not become fresh; they will be left for salt.[t] 12Fruit trees of all kinds will grow on both banks of the river.[u] Their leaves will not wither, nor will their fruit[v] fail. Every month they will bear, because the water from the sanctuary flows to them. Their fruit will serve for food and their leaves for healing.[w]"

The Boundaries of the Land

13This is what the Sovereign LORD says: "These are the boundaries[x] by which you are to divide the land for an inheritance among the twelve tribes of Israel, with two portions for Joseph.[y] 14You are to divide it equally among them. Because I swore with uplifted hand to give it to your forefathers, this land will become your inheritance.[z]

15"This is to be the boundary of the land:

"On the north side it will run from the Great Sea by the Hethlon road[a] past Lebo[e] Hamath to Zedad, 16Berothah[f][b] and Sibraim (which lies on the border between Damascus and Hamath),[c] as far as Hazer Hatticon, which is on the border of Hauran. 17The boundary will extend from the sea to Hazar Enan,[g] along the northern border of Damascus, with the border of Hamath to the north. This will be the north boundary.[d]

18"On the east side the boundary will run between Hauran and Damascus, along the Jordan between Gilead and the land of Israel, to the eastern sea and as far as Tamar.[h] This will be the east boundary.

19"On the south side it will run from Tamar as far as the waters of Meribah Kadesh,[e] then along the Wadi ⌊of Egypt⌋[f] to the Great Sea.[g] This will be the south boundary.

20"On the west side, the Great Sea will be the boundary to a point opposite Lebo[i] Hamath.[h] This will be the west boundary.[i]

21"You are to distribute this land among yourselves according to the tribes of Israel. 22You are to allot it as an inheritance for yourselves and for the aliens[j] who have settled among you and who have children. You are to consider them as native-born Israelites; along with you they are to be allotted an inheritance among the tribes of Israel.[k] 23In whatever tribe the alien settles, there you are to give him his inheritance," declares the Sovereign LORD.

The Division of the Land

48 "These are the tribes, listed by name: At the northern frontier,

47:1 [g]Isa 55:1 [h]Ps 46:4; Joel 3:18; Rev 22:1
47:3 [i]Eze 40:3
47:5 [j]Isa 11:9; Hab 2:14
47:7 [k]ver 12; Rev 22:2
47:8 [l]Dt 3:17; Jos 3:16 [m]Isa 41:18
47:9 [n]Isa 12:3; 55:1; Jn 4:14; 7:37-38
47:10 [o]Mt 4:19 [p]Jos 15:62 [q]Eze 26:5 [r]Ps 104:25; Mt 13:47 [s]Nu 34:6
47:11 [t]Dt 29:23
47:12 [u]ver 7; Rev 22:2 [v]Ps 1:3 [w]Ge 2:9; Jer 17:8
47:13 [x]Nu 34:2-12 [y]Ge 48:5
47:14 [z]Ge 12:7; Dt 1:8; Eze 20:5-6
47:15 [a]Eze 48:1
47:16 [b]2Sa 8:8 [c]Nu 13:21; Eze 48:1
47:17 [d]Eze 48:1
47:19 [e]Dt 32:51 [f]Isa 27:12 [g]Eze 48:28
47:20 [h]Eze 48:1 [i]Nu 34:6
47:22 [j]Isa 14:1 [k]Nu 26:55-56; Isa 56:6-7; Ro 10:12; Eph 2:12-16; 3:6; Col 3:11

[a] *3* That is, about 1,500 feet (about 450 meters)
[b] *8* Or *the Jordan Valley*
[c] *8* That is, the Dead Sea
[d] *10* That is, the Mediterranean; also in verses 15, 19 and 20
[e] *15* Or *past the entrance to*
[f] *15,16* See Septuagint and Ezekiel 48:1; Hebrew *road to go into Zedad, 16Hamath, Berothah*
[g] *17* Hebrew *Enon,* a variant of *Enan*
[h] *18* Septuagint and Syriac; Hebrew *Israel. You will measure to the eastern sea*
[i] *20* Or *opposite the entrance to*

Dan[l] will have one portion; it will follow the Hethlon road[m] to Lebo[a] Hamath;[n] Hazar Enan and the northern border of Damascus next to Hamath will be part of its border from the east side to the west side.

2"Asher[o] will have one portion; it will border the territory of Dan from east to west.

3"Naphtali[p] will have one portion; it will border the territory of Asher from east to west.

4"Manasseh[q] will have one portion; it will border the territory of Naphtali from east to west.

5"Ephraim[r] will have one portion; it will border the territory of Manasseh[s] from east to west.[t]

6"Reuben[u] will have one portion; it will border the territory of Ephraim from east to west.

7"Judah[v] will have one portion; it will border the territory of Reuben from east to west.

8"Bordering the territory of Judah from east to west will be the portion you are to present as a special gift. It will be 25,000 cubits[b] wide, and its length from east to west will equal one of the tribal portions; the sanctuary will be in the center of it.[w]

9"The special portion you are to offer to the LORD will be 25,000 cubits long and 10,000 cubits[c] wide.[x] 10This will be the sacred portion for the priests. It will be 25,000 cubits long on the north side, 10,000 cubits wide on the west side, 10,000 cubits wide on the east side and 25,000 cubits long on the south side. In the center of it will be the sanctuary of the LORD.[y] 11This will be for the consecrated priests, the Zadokites,[z] who were faithful in serving me[a] and did not go astray as the Levites did when the Israelites went astray.[b] 12It will be a special gift to them from the sacred portion of the land, a most holy portion, bordering the territory of the Levites.

13"Alongside the territory of the priests, the Levites will have an allotment 25,000 cubits long and 10,000 cubits wide. Its total length will be 25,000 cubits and its width 10,000 cubits.[c] 14They must not sell or exchange any of it. This is the best of the land and must not pass into other hands, because it is holy to the LORD.[d]

15"The remaining area, 5,000 cubits wide and 25,000 cubits long, will be for the common use of the city, for houses and for pastureland. The city will be in the center of it 16and will have these measurements: the north side 4,500 cubits, the south side 4,500 cubits, the east side 4,500 cubits, and the west side 4,500 cubits.[e] 17The pastureland for the city will be 250 cubits on the north, 250 cubits on the south, 250 cubits on the east, and 250 cubits on the west. 18What remains of the area, bordering on the sacred portion and running the length of it, will be 10,000 cubits on the east side and 10,000 cubits on the west side. Its produce will supply food for the workers of the city.[f] 19The workers from the city who farm it will come from all the tribes of Israel. 20The entire portion will be a square, 25,000 cubits on each side. As a special gift you will set aside the sacred portion, along with the property of the city.

21"What remains on both sides of the area formed by the sacred portion and the city property will belong to the prince. It will extend eastward from the 25,000 cubits of the sacred portion to the eastern border, and westward from the 25,000 cubits to the western border. Both these areas running the length of the tribal portions will belong to the prince, and the sacred portion with the temple sanctuary will be in the center of them.[g] 22So the property of the Levites and the property of the city will lie in the center of the area that belongs to the prince. The area belonging to the prince will lie between the border of Judah and the border of Benjamin.

23"As for the rest of the tribes: Benjamin[h] will have one portion; it will extend from the east side to the west side.

24"Simeon[i] will have one portion; it will border the territory of Benjamin from east to west.

25"Issachar[j] will have one portion; it will border the territory of Simeon from east to west.

26"Zebulun[k] will have one portion; it will border the territory of Issachar from east to west.

27"Gad[l] will have one portion; it will border the territory of Zebulun from east to west.

28"The southern boundary of Gad will run south from Tamar[m] to the waters of Meribah Kadesh, then along the Wadi ⌊of Egypt⌋ to the Great Sea.[d][n]

29"This is the land you are to allot as an inheritance to the tribes of Israel, and these will be their portions," declares the Sovereign LORD.

The Gates of the City

30"These will be the exits of the city:

48:1 [l] Ge 30:6 [m] Eze 47:15-17 [n] Eze 47:20
48:2 [o] Jos 19:24-31
48:3 [p] Jos 19:32-39
48:4 [q] Jos 17:1-11
48:5 [r] Jos 16:5-9 [s] Jos 17:7-10 [t] Jos 17:17
48:6 [u] Jos 13:15-21
48:7 [v] Jos 15:1-63
48:8 [w] ver 21
48:9 [x] Eze 45:1
48:10 [y] ver 21; Eze 45:3-4
48:11 [z] 2Sa 8:17 [a] Lev 8:35 [b] Eze 14:11; 44:15
48:13 [c] Eze 45:5
48:14 [d] Lev 25:34; 27:10,28
48:16 [e] Rev 21:16
48:18 [f] Eze 45:6
48:21 [g] ver 8,10; Eze 45:7
48:23 [h] Jos 18:11-28
48:24 [i] Ge 29:33; Jos 19:1-9
48:25 [j] Jos 19:17-23
48:26 [k] Jos 19:10-16
48:27 [l] Jos 13:24-28
48:28 [m] Ge 14:7 [n] Eze 47:19

a *1* Or *to the entrance to* **b** *8* That is, about 7 miles (about 12 kilometers) **c** *9* That is, about 3 miles (about 5 kilometers) **d** *28* That is, the Mediterranean

Beginning on the north side, which is
4,500 cubits long, 31the gates of the city
will be named after the tribes of Israel.
The three gates on the north side will
be the gate of Reuben, the gate of Judah and the gate of Levi.

32"On the east side, which is 4,500
cubits long, will be three gates: the gate
of Joseph, the gate of Benjamin and the
gate of Dan.

33"On the south side, which measures 4,500 cubits, will be three gates:
the gate of Simeon, the gate of Issachar
and the gate of Zebulun.

34"On the west side, which is 4,500
cubits long, will be three gates: the gate
of Gad, the gate of Asher and the gate
of Naphtali.

35"The distance all around will be
18,000 cubits.

"And the name of the city from that
time on will be:

THE LORD IS THERE.[o]"

48:35
[o] Isa 12:6; 24:23; Jer 3:17; 14:9; 33:16; Joel 3:21; Zec 2:10; Rev 21:3

DANIEL

AT A GLANCE

Key Principle: The affairs of men and of nations may appear at times to be outside of God's divine control, but regardless of how people rebel against God's plans and purposes, the Most High is sovereign over the kingdoms of the earth.
Author: Daniel
Time and Place: 605–536 B.C. / Babylonia and Persia
Key Verses: 2:20–22, 44; 4:17, 25, 32

BENEFIT

Daniel is an extraordinary book for three main reasons: First, it gives a sweeping overview of the rise and fall of earthly kingdoms; second, it anticipates the kingdom ruled by Messiah that will never fall; third, it gives a detailed account of the character of the prophet himself. Daniel's remarkable life in captivity illustrates a variety of Biblical principles that are relevant to our lives as men who live in a culture that is hostile to spiritual growth and commitment.

SETTING

Over a century after the Assyrians overthrew the northern kingdom of Israel (722 B.C.), the Babylonians captured the Assyrian capital of Nineveh (612 B.C.). Under Nebuchadnezzar's rule, the Babylonians continued to conquer the Middle East. In their first of three assaults on Jerusalem (605 B.C.), they took a select group of Jewish captives to Babylon, including youths from noble families who would be trained for positions in the king's service. Daniel (who was about 16 years old at the time) and his three friends were among those youths. They were renamed and reeducated during a three-year training period. Daniel served as a government official throughout the entire 70-year Babylonian captivity of the Jews, and continued his ministry after the Medes and Persians defeated Babylon in 539 B.C. Daniel's prophetic vocation influenced the Babylonian court of Nebuchadnezzar and Belshazzar and the Persian court of Darius and Cyrus, and his ministry extended at least until the third year of Cyrus in 536 B.C. (10:1).

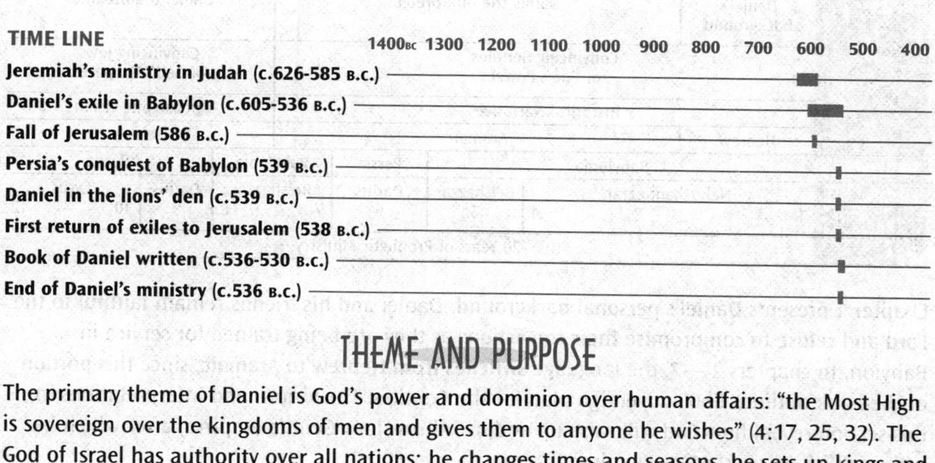

THEME AND PURPOSE

The primary theme of Daniel is God's power and dominion over human affairs: "the Most High is sovereign over the kingdoms of men and gives them to anyone he wishes" (4:17, 25, 32). The God of Israel has authority over all nations; he changes times and seasons, he sets up kings and deposes them, he gives wisdom to the wise and knowledge to the discerning (2:20–22). This book was written to encourage the Jews of the Babylonian captivity by giving them a divine perspective on God's plans—both for the Gentile kingdoms and also for Israel's future when Messiah will establish a kingdom without end. "In the time of those kings, the God of heaven will set up a kingdom that will never be destroyed, nor will it be left to another people. It will crush all those kingdoms and bring them to an end, but it will itself endure forever" (2:44).

UNIQUE CONTRIBUTION

The consistency, quality and character of Daniel's life set him apart from most of the men in the Bible. Unlike other significant Old Testament figures, this book records nothing negative about him. His life was characterized by faithfulness, conviction, trustworthiness, endurance, compassion, courage and dignity, and he was "highly esteemed" (9:23; 10:11, 19). His contemporary Ezekiel used him as an example of righteousness (along with Noah and Job; Ezekiel 14:14, 20) and of wisdom (Ezekiel 28:3).

While Ezekiel focused on the spiritual restoration of Israel, Daniel focused on the political restoration of his people. In the Hebrew Bible, Daniel was placed among the Writings rather than the Prophets, since Daniel, though a bona fide prophet, did not make prophetic addresses to the people as did other prophets such as Jeremiah and Ezekiel. Instead, Daniel interpreted dreams (2—7) and had visions of his own that required angelic interpretation (8—12).

LINKS TO THE NEW TESTAMENT

Christ is portrayed in Daniel as the rock that will bring the kingdoms of the world to an end and establish a kingdom that will endure forever (2:24–35, 44). He is also the "son of man" to whom the Ancient of Days gives authority, glory and sovereign power (7:13–14). And he is evidently the awesome man before whom Daniel was overwhelmed in 10:5–9 (compare Revelation 1:12–17).

OVERVIEW

<table>
<tr><th>FOCUS</th><th>God's Prophet</th><th colspan="4">God's Plan for the Gentiles</th><th colspan="3">God's Plan for Israel</th></tr>
<tr><td>REFERENCE</td><td>1</td><td colspan="4">2 — 7</td><td colspan="3">8 — 12</td></tr>
<tr><td rowspan="4">TOPICS</td><td>Daniel's Background</td><td colspan="4">Daniel the Interpreter</td><td colspan="3">Daniel the Dreamer</td></tr>
<tr><td colspan="5">Convincing Gentiles of God's Power</td><td colspan="3">Convincing Jews of God's Purposes</td></tr>
<tr><td colspan="5">Historical Narratives</td><td colspan="3">Apocalyptic Visions</td></tr>
<tr><td>Hebrew</td><td colspan="4">Aramaic</td><td colspan="3">Hebrew</td></tr>
<tr><td>LOCATION</td><td colspan="3">Babylonia</td><td>Persia</td><td colspan="2">Babylonia</td><td colspan="2">Persia</td></tr>
<tr><td>RULERS</td><td colspan="2">Nebuchadnezzar
1 — 4</td><td>Belshazzar
5</td><td>Darius
6</td><td colspan="2">Belshazzar
7 — 8</td><td>Darius
9</td><td>Cyrus
10 — 12</td></tr>
<tr><td>TIME</td><td colspan="8">70 Years of Prophetic Ministry</td></tr>
</table>

Chapter 1 presents Daniel's personal background. Daniel and his friends remain faithful to the Lord and refuse to compromise their convictions as they are being trained for service in Babylon. In chapters 2—7, the language switches from Hebrew to Aramaic, since this portion of the book outlines God's sovereign plan for the Gentiles. The visions and interpretations in this section reveal how God will raise up and overthrow four Gentile empires, after which he will establish an everlasting kingdom.

In chapters 8—12, the language switches back to Hebrew, since this section overviews God's prophetic plan for Israel. These chapters describe Israel under the Medo-Persian and Grecian empires and detail the coming kings of Persia and Greece. They also describe the wars between the Ptolemies of Egypt and the Seleucids of Syria, and the persecution under Antiochus Epiphanes. Daniel ends with a prophecy that God's people will be delivered from tribulation and raised from the dead (12).

DANIEL

Daniel's Training in Babylon

1 In the third year of the reign of Jehoiakim king of Judah, Nebuchadnezzar[a] king of Babylon came to Jerusalem and besieged it.[b] 2And the Lord delivered Jehoiakim king of Judah into his hand, along with some of the articles from the temple of God. These he carried off to the temple of his god in Babylonia[a] and put in the treasure house of his god.[c]

3Then the king ordered Ashpenaz, chief of his court officials, to bring in some of the Israelites from the royal family and the nobility[d]— 4young men without any physical defect, handsome, showing aptitude for every kind of learning, well informed, quick to understand, and qualified to serve in the king's palace. He was to teach them the language and literature of the Babylonians.[b] 5The king assigned them a daily amount of food and wine[e] from the king's table. They were to be trained for three years, and after that they were to enter the king's service.[f]

6Among these were some from Judah: Daniel,[g] Hananiah, Mishael and Azariah. 7The chief official gave them new names: to Daniel, the name Belteshazzar;[h] to Hananiah, Shadrach; to Mishael, Meshach; and to Azariah, Abednego.[i]

3 →PG. 974

8But Daniel resolved not to defile[j] himself with the royal food and wine, and he asked the chief official for permission not to defile himself this way. 9Now God had caused the official to show favor[k] and sympathy[l] to Daniel, 10but the official told Daniel, "I am afraid of my lord the king, who has assigned your[c] food and drink. Why should he see you looking worse than the other young men your age? The king would then have my head because of you."

11Daniel then said to the guard whom the chief official had appointed over Daniel, Hananiah, Mishael and Azariah, 12"Please test your servants for ten days: Give us nothing but vegetables to eat and water to drink. 13Then compare our appearance with that of the young men who eat the royal food, and treat your servants in accordance with what you see." 14So he agreed to this and tested them for ten days.

15At the end of the ten days they looked healthier and better nourished than any of the young men who ate the royal food.[m] 16So the guard took away their choice food and the wine they were to drink and gave them vegetables instead.[n]

17To these four young men God gave knowledge and understanding[o] of all kinds of literature and learning.[p] And Daniel could understand visions and dreams of all kinds.[q]

18At the end of the time[r] set by the king to bring them in, the chief official presented them to Nebuchadnezzar. 19The king talked with them, and he found none equal to Daniel, Hananiah, Mishael and Azariah; so they entered the king's service.[s] 20In every matter of wisdom and understanding about which the king questioned them, he found them ten times better than all the magicians and enchanters in his whole kingdom.[t]

21And Daniel remained there until the first year of King Cyrus.[u]

Nebuchadnezzar's Dream

2 In the second year of his reign, Nebuchadnezzar had dreams;[v] his mind was troubled[w] and he could not sleep.[x] 2So the king summoned the magicians,[y] enchanters, sorcerers[z] and astrologers[d][a] to tell him what he had dreamed.[b] When they came in and stood before the king, 3he said to them, "I have had a dream that troubles[c] me and I want to know what it means.[e]"

4Then the astrologers answered the king in Aramaic,[f][d] "O king, live forever![e] Tell your servants the dream, and we will interpret it."

5The king replied to the astrologers, "This is what I have firmly decided: If you do not tell me what my dream was and interpret it, I will have you cut into pieces[f] and your houses turned into piles of rubble.[g] 6But if you tell me the dream and explain it, you will receive from me gifts and rewards and great honor.[h] So tell me the dream and interpret it for me."

7Once more they replied, "Let the king tell his servants the dream, and we will interpret it."

8Then the king answered, "I am cer-

1:1 [a]2Ki 24:1 [b]2Ch 36:6 **1:2** [c]2Ch 36:7; Jer 27:19-20; Zec 5:5-11 **1:3** [d]2Ki 20:18; 24:15; Isa 39:7 **1:5** [e]ver 8,10 [f]ver 19 **1:6** [g]Eze 14:14 **1:7** [h]Da 4:8; 5:12 [i]Da 2:49; 3:12 **1:8** [j]Eze 4:13-14 **1:9** [k]Ge 39:21; Pr 16:7 [l]1Ki 8:50; Ps 106:46 **1:15** [m]Ex 23:25 **1:16** [n]ver 12-13 **1:17** [o]1Ki 3:12 [p]Da 2:23; Jas 1:5 [q]Da 2:19,30; 7:1; 8:1 **1:18** [r]ver 5 **1:19** [s]Ge 41:46 **1:20** [t]1Ki 4:30; Da 2:13,28 **1:21** [u]Da 6:28; 10:1 **2:1** [v]Job 33:15,18; Da 4:5 [w]Ge 41:8 [x]Est 6:1; Da 6:18 **2:2** [y]Ge 41:8 [z]Ex 7:11 [a]ver 10; Da 5:7 [b]Da 4:6 **2:3** [c]Da 4:5 **2:4** [d]Ezr 4:7 [e]Da 3:9; 5:10 **2:5** [f]ver 12 [g]Ezr 6:11; Da 3:29 **2:6** [h]ver 48; Da 5:7,16

[a] *2* Hebrew *Shinar* [b] *4* Or *Chaldeans* [c] *10* The Hebrew for *your* and *you* in this verse is plural. [d] *2* Or *Chaldeans*; also in verses 4, 5 and 10 [e] *3* Or *was* [f] *4* The text from here through chapter 7 is in Aramaic.

tain that you are trying to gain time, because you realize that this is what I have firmly decided: 9If you do not tell me the dream, there is just one penalty[i] for you. You have conspired to tell me misleading and wicked things, hoping the situation will change. So then, tell me the dream, and I will know that you can interpret it for me."[j]

10The astrologers answered the king, "There is not a man on earth who can do what the king asks! No king, however great and mighty, has ever asked such a thing of any magician or enchanter or astrologer.[k] 11What the king asks is too difficult. No one can reveal it to the king except the gods,[l] and they do not live among men."

12This made the king so angry and furious[m] that he ordered the execution[n] of all the wise men of Babylon. 13So the decree was issued to put the wise men to death, and men were sent to look for Daniel and his friends to put them to death.[o]

14When Arioch, the commander of the king's guard, had gone out to put to death the wise men of Babylon, Daniel spoke to him with wisdom and tact. 15He asked the king's officer, "Why did the king issue such a harsh decree?" Arioch then explained the matter to Daniel. 16At this, Daniel went in to the king and asked for time, so that he might interpret the dream for him.

2 →PG. 936

17Then Daniel returned to his house and explained the matter to his friends Hananiah, Mishael and Azariah.[p] 18He urged them to plead for mercy[q] from the God of heaven concerning this mystery,[r] so that he and his friends might not be executed with the rest of the wise men of Babylon. 19During the night the mystery[s] was revealed to Daniel in a vision.[t] Then Daniel praised the God of heaven 20and said:

"Praise be to the name of God for
ever and ever;[u]
wisdom and power[v] are his.
21He changes times and seasons;[w]
he sets up kings and deposes[x]
them.
He gives wisdom[y] to the wise
and knowledge to the discerning.
22He reveals deep and hidden
things;[z]
he knows what lies in
darkness,[a]
and light[b] dwells with him.
23I thank and praise you, O God of
my fathers:[c]
You have given me wisdom[d]
and power,
you have made known to me what
we asked of you,
you have made known to us the
dream of the king."

Daniel Interprets the Dream

24Then Daniel went to Arioch,[e] whom the king had appointed to execute the wise men of Babylon, and said to him, "Do not execute the wise men of Babylon. Take me to the king, and I will interpret his dream for him."

25Arioch took Daniel to the king at once and said, "I have found a man among the exiles from Judah[f] who can tell the king what his dream means."

26The king asked Daniel (also called Belteshazzar),[g] "Are you able to tell me what I saw in my dream and interpret it?"

27Daniel replied, "No wise man, enchanter, magician or diviner can explain to the king the mystery he has asked about,[h] 28but there is a God in heaven who reveals mysteries.[i] He has shown King Nebuchadnezzar what will happen in days to come.[j] Your dream and the visions that passed through your mind[k] as you lay on your bed are these:

29"As you were lying there, O king, your mind turned to things to come, and the revealer of mysteries showed you what is going to happen. 30As for me, this mystery has been revealed[l] to me, not because I have greater wisdom than other living men, but so that you, O king, may know the interpretation and that you may understand what went through your mind.

31"You looked, O king, and there before you stood a large statue—an enormous, dazzling statue,[m] awesome in appearance. 32The head of the statue was made of pure gold, its chest and arms of silver, its belly and thighs of bronze, 33its legs of iron, its feet partly of iron and partly of baked clay. 34While you were watching, a rock was cut out, but not by human hands.[n] It struck the statue on its feet of iron and clay and smashed them.[o] 35Then the iron, the clay, the bronze, the silver and the gold were broken to pieces at the same time and became like chaff on a threshing floor in the summer. The wind swept them away[p] without leaving a trace. But the rock that struck the statue became a huge mountain[q] and filled the whole earth.

36"This was the dream, and now we will interpret it to the king. 37You, O king, are the king of kings.[r] The God of heaven has given you domin-

2:9 [i]Est 4:11 [j]Isa 41:22-24
2:10 [k]ver 27
2:11 [l]Da 5:11
2:12 [m]Da 3:13,19 [n]ver 5
2:13 [o]Da 1:20
2:17 [p]Da 1:6
2:18 [q]Isa 37:4 [r]Jer 33:3
2:19 [s]ver 28 [t]Job 33:15; Da 1:17
2:20 [u]Ps 113:2; 145:1-2 [v]Jer 32:19
2:21 [w]Da 7:25 [x]Job 12:19; Ps 75:6-7 [y]Jas 1:5
2:22 [z]Job 12:22; Ps 25:14; Da 5:11 [a]Ps 139:11-12; Jer 23:24; Heb 4:13 [b]Isa 45:7; Jas 1:17
2:23 [c]Ex 3:15 [d]Da 1:17
2:24 [e]ver 14
2:25 [f]Da 1:6; 5:13; 6:13
2:26 [g]Da 1:7
2:27 [h]ver 10
2:28 [i]Ge 40:8; Am 4:13 [j]Ge 49:1; Da 10:14 [k]Da 4:5
2:30 [l]Isa 45:3; Da 1:17; Am 4:13
2:31 [m]Hab 1:7
2:34 [n]Zec 4:6 [o]ver 44-45; Ps 2:9; Isa 60:12; Da 8:25
2:35 [p]Ps 1:4; 37:10; Isa 17:13 [q]Isa 2:3; Mic 4:1
2:37 [r]Eze 26:7

DANIEL

A Man Who Took a Stand

Only a strong man can maintain his commitments if he knows those commitments may cost him something important. That's why many men admire sprinter Eric Lidell, a man who stayed true to his commitments.

At the 1924 Olympic Games, Lidell refused to run in a 100-meter qualifying heat. The race was scheduled for Sunday and Lidell, a committed Christian, felt that racing on Sunday would be a violation of his conscience. Although he went on to win a gold medal in the 400-meter race, Lidell's commitment cost him the chance to find out if he could have also been the fastest sprinter in the world.

Long before the 1924 Olympics, another man and his friends also took a stand for what they believed in. Taken from their homeland by the invading Babylonian army, Daniel, Hananiah, Mishael and Azariah found themselves in the palace of King Nebuchadnezzar. Surrounded by pagan ideas and practices, these young men knew that to preserve their identity as God's people, they would have to make a stand. Maintaining their commitment to God would be tough. The cost could be their lives.

Daring to Be Different—Together

To the casual reader, these four men may have seemed absolutely powerless. They were captives of a pagan, foreign government, living in its mighty capital city. But these men possessed the hidden power of a committed spirit. Surrounded by Babylon's polytheistic environment, they held fast to their faith in God—whose power absolutely eclipsed Babylon's—and practiced a few simple principles.

First, they continued in their dedication to God and in their commitment to their values. The Babylonians believed in many, many gods. These four men believed only in the true God. While only Daniel is specifically mentioned, all of the men no doubt shared his resolve to maintain their religious commitments, no matter what happened (Daniel 1:8).

These men also recognized that their education in the king's court involved exposure to values that ran contrary to their beliefs as Hebrews. Even something as simple as eating from the king's table was a violation of their religious commitments. Mosaic law strictly outlined what the four men could and could not eat. Also, eating from the king's table would provide a strong signal to others in the court that these four young men had given themselves over to the king's rule, that they had conformed to the king's way. Daniel and his friends refused to eat the king's food and stood by their commitment to God in the midst of pressure to conform to another set of values.

Second, these men demonstrated sensitivity to the potential impact of their decision on others around them. The official in charge of the four men was concerned that he would be punished if their health suffered in any way by refusing the king's food. Daniel listened to this man's complaint and recognized his fears, but was unswerving in his dedication to God. He stood by his convictions and suggested a plan that would allow Daniel and his companions to continue to honor God by their diet. The four men were sensitive to the impact their commitments might have on the official, but they still exercised their faith—faith that God would bless them through their diet, and faith that neither the official nor his guard would force them to eat what was forbidden (1:8).

Third, these men stuck together through the ordeal. The text makes it clear that these four men acted as a team—as brothers. Later, Daniel would face life-threatening tests alone, and his three companions would encounter danger without Daniel's presence. But in this story we find the four together. No doubt their companionship enabled them to pass this test and strengthened them for the tests they would later face.

Standing Strong

Like these four young men, we need to learn to live in the world without becoming like it, without absorbing its values. That's tough to do in isolation. Daniel, Hananiah, Mishael and Azariah had each other to help them through this tough time. So also, we need to be part of a team of committed men that regularly meet together to encourage one another.

If you don't have such friends, pray for some. Gather together regularly and discuss with them how you can help each other stand strong in your convictions. Dare to stand together for your Christian commitments, even if the cost for doing so may be high. Dare to stand alone in the midst of a society that doesn't necessarily share your religious and personal values. Dare to make a stand for God. Dare to be a Daniel.

—*Bill Perkins*

ion[s] and power and might and glory; [38]in your hands he has placed mankind and the beasts of the field and the birds of the air. Wherever they live, he has made you ruler over them all.[t] You are that head of gold.

[39]"After you, another kingdom will rise, inferior to yours. Next, a third kingdom, one of bronze, will rule over the whole earth. [40]Finally, there will be a fourth kingdom, strong as iron—for iron breaks and smashes everything—and as iron breaks things to pieces, so it will crush and break all the others.[u] [41]Just as you saw that the feet and toes were partly of baked clay and partly of iron, so this will be a divided kingdom; yet it will have some of the strength of iron in it, even as you saw iron mixed with clay. [42]As the toes were partly iron and partly clay, so this kingdom will be partly strong and partly brittle. [43]And just as you saw the iron mixed with baked clay, so the people will be a mixture and will not remain united, any more than iron mixes with clay.

[44]"In the time of those kings, the God of heaven will set up a kingdom that will never be destroyed, nor will it be left to another people. It will crush[v] all those kingdoms[w] and bring them to an end, but it will itself endure forever.[x] [45]This is the meaning of the vision of the rock[y] cut out of a mountain, but not by human hands[z]—a rock that broke the iron, the bronze, the clay, the silver and the gold to pieces.

"The great God has shown the king what will take place in the future. The dream is true and the interpretation is trustworthy."

7 →PG. 988

[46]Then King Nebuchadnezzar fell prostrate[a] before Daniel and paid him honor and ordered that an offering[b] and incense be presented to him. [47]The king said to Daniel, "Surely your God is the God of gods[c] and the Lord of kings[d] and a revealer of mysteries,[e] for you were able to reveal this mystery."

[48]Then the king placed Daniel in a high position and lavished many gifts on him. He made him ruler over the entire province of Babylon and placed him in charge of all its wise men.[f] [49]Moreover, at Daniel's request the king appointed Shadrach, Meshach and Abednego administrators over the province of Babylon,[g] while Daniel himself remained at the royal court.

The Image of Gold and the Fiery Furnace

3 King Nebuchadnezzar made an image[h] of gold, ninety feet high and nine feet[a] wide, and set it up on the plain of Dura in the province of Babylon. [2]He then summoned the satraps, prefects, governors, advisers, treasurers, judges, magistrates and all the other provincial officials[i] to come to the dedication of the image he had set up. [3]So the satraps, prefects, governors, advisers, treasurers, judges, magistrates and all the other provincial officials assembled for the dedication of the image that King Nebuchadnezzar had set up, and they stood before it.

[4]Then the herald loudly proclaimed, "This is what you are commanded to do, O peoples, nations and men of every language:[j] [5]As soon as you hear

2:37 [s]Jer 27:7 **2:38** [t]Jer 27:6; Da 4:21-22 **2:40** [u]Da 7:7,23 **2:44** [v]Ps 2:9; 1Co 15:24 [w]Isa 60:12 [x]Ps 145:13; Isa 9:7; Da 4:34; 6:26; 7:14,27; Mic 4:7,13; Lk 1:33 **2:45** [y]Isa 28:16 [z]Da 8:25
2:46 [a]Da 8:17; Ac 10:25 [b]Ac 14:13 **2:47** [c]Da 11:36 [d]Da 4:25 [e]ver 22,28 **2:48** [f]ver 6; Da 4:9; 5:11 **2:49** [g]Da 1:7 **3:1** [h]Isa 46:6; Jer 16:20; Hab 2:19 **3:2** [i]ver 27; Da 6:7 **3:4** [j]Da 4:1; 6:25

[a]1 Aramaic *sixty cubits high and six cubits wide* (about 27 meters high and 2.7 meters wide)

3:1–30

PROMISE 1

VIBRANT FAITH

Someone once said the difference between vibrant and weak faith is most evident in how a man responds to hardship. Those who have an active, vibrant faith trust in God even when they're faced with an uncertain future. This story shows us that Shadrach, Meshach and Abednego had what it takes when it came to faith and trust in God.

Faced with Nebuchadnezzar's dire threats for refusing to bow down to his golden idol, these three men stood firm in their commitment not to worship anything or anyone but God. In the face of their defiance, Nebuchadnezzar breathed out his threats, saying "What god will be able to rescue you from my hand?" (v. 15). But Shadrach, Meshach, and Abednego had a ready answer for this arrogant question: "The God we serve will be able to save us." Then they went one step further. "Even if he does not," they said, "we will not . . . worship the image you have set up" (vv. 17–18). Dead or alive, these three men had stolen Nebuchadnezzar's victory. Their commitment to God silenced the king, and God rewarded their dedication by rescuing them from the flames.

Think about it: Guards led Shadrach, Meshach and Abednego to the furnace. These three men smelled the acrid smoke, heard the roar of the fire, saw the inferno, felt the heat. They had no idea whether or not they'd live to see another day, and for the moment their prospects looked bleak. Still these men trusted in God—their faith was strong, vibrant and active. Like those three men, we want to exercise the kind of faith that trusts in God even when the heat is on and the future seems dismal.

For the next Promise 1 reading go to page 941.

the sound of the horn, flute, zither, lyre, harp, pipes and all kinds of music, you must fall down and worship the image of gold that King Nebuchadnezzar has set up.[k] 6Whoever does not fall down and worship will immediately be thrown into a blazing furnace."[l]

7Therefore, as soon as they heard the sound of the horn, flute, zither, lyre, harp and all kinds of music, all the peoples, nations and men of every language fell down and worshiped the image of gold that King Nebuchadnezzar had set up.[m]

8At this time some astrologers[a][n] came forward and denounced the Jews. 9They said to King Nebuchadnezzar, "O king, live forever![o] 10You have issued a decree,[p] O king, that everyone who hears the sound of the horn, flute, zither, lyre, harp, pipes and all kinds of music must fall down and worship the image of gold,[q] 11and that whoever does not fall down and worship will be thrown into a blazing furnace. 12But there are some Jews whom you have set over the affairs of the province of Babylon—Shadrach, Meshach and Abednego[r]—who pay no attention[s] to you, O king. They neither serve your gods nor worship the image of gold you have set up."[t]

13Furious[u] with rage, Nebuchadnezzar summoned Shadrach, Meshach and Abednego. So these men were brought before the king, 14and Nebuchadnezzar said to them, "Is it true, Shadrach, Meshach and Abednego, that you do not serve my gods[v] or worship the image[w] of gold I have set up? 15Now when you hear the sound of the horn, flute, zither, lyre, harp, pipes and all kinds of music, if you are ready to fall down and worship the image I made, very good. But if you do not worship it, you will be thrown immediately into a blazing furnace. Then what god[x] will be able to rescue[y] you from my hand?"

1 →PG. 938

16Shadrach, Meshach and Abednego[z] replied to the king, "O Nebuchadnezzar, we do not need to defend ourselves before you in this matter. 17If we are thrown into the blazing furnace, the God we serve is able to save[a] us from it, and he will rescue[b] us from your hand, O king. 18But even if he does not, we want you to know, O king, that we will not serve your gods or worship the image of gold you have set up.[c]"

19Then Nebuchadnezzar was furious with Shadrach, Meshach and Abednego, and his attitude toward them changed. He ordered the furnace heated seven[d] times hotter than usual 20and commanded some of the strongest soldiers in his army to tie up Shadrach, Meshach and Abednego and throw them into the blazing furnace. 21So these men, wearing their robes, trousers, turbans and other clothes, were bound and thrown into the blazing furnace. 22The king's command was so urgent and the furnace so hot that the flames of the fire killed the soldiers who took up Shadrach, Meshach and Abednego,[e] 23and these three men, firmly tied, fell into the blazing furnace.

24Then King Nebuchadnezzar leaped to his feet in amazement and asked his advisers, "Weren't there three men that we tied up and threw into the fire?"

They replied, "Certainly, O king."

25He said, "Look! I see four men walking around in the fire, unbound and unharmed, and the fourth looks like a son of the gods."

26Nebuchadnezzar then approached the opening of the blazing furnace and shouted, "Shadrach, Meshach and Abednego, servants of the Most High God,[f] come out! Come here!"

So Shadrach, Meshach and Abednego came out of the fire, 27and the satraps, prefects, governors and royal advisers[g] crowded around them.[h] They saw that the fire[i] had not harmed their bodies, nor was a hair of their heads singed; their robes were not scorched, and there was no smell of fire on them.

28Then Nebuchadnezzar said, "Praise be to the God of Shadrach, Meshach and Abednego, who has sent his angel[j] and rescued his servants! They trusted[k] in him and defied the king's command and were willing to give up their lives rather than serve or worship any god except their own God.[l] 29Therefore I decree[m] that the people of any nation or language who say anything against the God of Shadrach, Meshach and Abednego be cut into pieces and their houses be turned into piles of rubble,[n] for no other god can save[o] in this way."

30Then the king promoted Shadrach, Meshach and Abednego in the province of Babylon.[p]

Nebuchadnezzar's Dream of a Tree

4 King Nebuchadnezzar,

To the peoples, nations and men of every language,[q] who live in all the world:

3:5 [k]ver 10,15
3:6 [l]ver 11,15,21; Jer 29:22; Da 6:7; Mt 13:42,50; Rev 13:15
3:7 [m]ver 5
3:8 [n]Da 2:10
3:9 [o]Ne 2:3; Da 5:10; 6:6
3:10 [p]Da 6:12 [q]ver 4-6
3:12 [r]Da 2:49 [s]Da 6:13 [t]Est 3:3
3:13 [u]Da 2:12
3:14 [v]Isa 46:1; Jer 50:2 [w]ver 1
3:15 [x]Isa 36:18-20 [y]Ex 5:2; 2Ch 32:15
3:16 [z]Da 1:7
3:17 [a]Ps 27:1-2 [b]Job 5:19; Jer 1:8
3:18 [c]ver 28; Jos 24:15
3:19 [d]Lev 26:18-28
3:22 [e]Da 1:7
3:26 [f]Da 4:2,34
3:27 [g]ver 2 [h]Isa 43:2; Heb 11:32-34 [i]Da 6:23
3:28 [j]Ps 34:7; Da 6:22; Ac 5:19 [k]Job 13:15; Ps 26:1; 84:12; Jer 17:7 [l]ver 18
3:29 [m]Da 6:26 [n]Ezr 6:11 [o]Da 6:27
3:30 [p]Da 2:49
4:1 [q]Da 3:4

[a]*8* Or *Chaldeans*

May you prosper greatly![r]

2 It is my pleasure to tell you
about the miraculous signs[s] and
wonders that the Most High
God[t] has performed for me.

3 How great are his signs,
how mighty his wonders![u]
His kingdom is an eternal
kingdom;
his dominion endures[v]
from generation to
generation.

4 I, Nebuchadnezzar, was at
home in my palace, contented[w]
and prosperous. 5 I had a dream[x]
that made me afraid. As I was lying in my bed, the images and visions that passed through my
mind[y] terrified me. 6 So I commanded that all the wise men of
Babylon be brought before me to
interpret[z] the dream for me.
7 When the magicians,[a] enchanters, astrologers[a] and diviners[b]
came, I told them the dream, but
they could not interpret it for
me.[c] 8 Finally, Daniel came into
my presence and I told him the
dream. (He is called Belteshazzar,[d] after the name of my god,
and the spirit of the holy gods[e] is
in him.)
9 I said, "Belteshazzar, chief[f] of
the magicians, I know that the
spirit of the holy gods[g] is in you,
and no mystery is too difficult for
you. Here is my dream; interpret it
for me. 10 These are the visions I
saw while lying in my bed:[h] I
looked, and there before me stood
a tree in the middle of the land. Its
height was enormous.[i] 11 The
tree grew large and strong and its
top touched the sky; it was visible
to the ends of the earth. 12 Its
leaves were beautiful, its fruit
abundant, and on it was food for
all. Under it the beasts of the field
found shelter, and the birds of the
air lived in its branches;[j] from it
every creature was fed.
13 "In the visions I saw while lying in my bed,[k] I looked, and
there before me was a messenger,[b] a holy one,[l] coming down
from heaven. 14 He called in a loud
voice: 'Cut down the tree and trim
off its branches; strip off its leaves
and scatter its fruit. Let the animals flee from under it and the
birds from its branches.[m] 15 But
let the stump and its roots, bound
with iron and bronze, remain in
the ground, in the grass of the
field.
" 'Let him be drenched with the
dew of heaven, and let him live
with the animals among the
plants of the earth. 16 Let his mind
be changed from that of a man
and let him be given the mind of
an animal, till seven times[c] pass
by for him.[n]
17 " 'The decision is announced
by messengers, the holy ones declare the verdict, so that the living
may know that the Most High[o] is
sovereign[p] over the kingdoms of
men and gives them to anyone he
wishes and sets over them the
lowliest[q] of men.'
18 "This is the dream that I, King
Nebuchadnezzar, had. Now, Belteshazzar, tell me what it means,
for none of the wise men in my
kingdom can interpret it for me.[r]
But you can,[s] because the spirit
of the holy gods is in you."[t]

Daniel Interprets the Dream

19 Then Daniel (also called Belteshazzar) was greatly perplexed
for a time, and his thoughts terrified[u] him. So the king said, "Belteshazzar, do not let the dream or
its meaning alarm you."
Belteshazzar answered, "My
lord, if only the dream applied to
your enemies and its meaning to
your adversaries! 20 The tree you
saw, which grew large and strong,
with its top touching the sky, visible to the whole earth, 21 with
beautiful leaves and abundant
fruit, providing food for all, giving
shelter to the beasts of the field,
and having nesting places in its
branches for the birds of the air—
22 you, O king, are that tree![v] You
have become great and strong;
your greatness has grown until it
reaches the sky, and your dominion extends to distant parts of the
earth.[w]
23 "You, O king, saw a messenger, a holy one,[x] coming down
from heaven and saying, 'Cut
down the tree and destroy it, but
leave the stump, bound with iron
and bronze, in the grass of the
field, while its roots remain in the
ground. Let him be drenched with
the dew of heaven; let him live like
the wild animals, until seven
times pass by for him.'[y]

4:1 [r]Da 6:25
4:2 [s]Ps 74:9 [t]Da 3:26
4:3 [u]Ps 105:27; Da 6:27 [v]Da 2:44
4:4 [w]Ps 30:6
4:5 [x]Da 2:1 [y]Da 2:28
4:6 [z]Da 2:2
4:7 [a]Ge 41:8 [b]Isa 44:25; Da 2:2 [c]Da 2:10
4:8 [d]Da 1:7 [e]Da 5:11,14
4:9 [f]Da 2:48 [g]Da 5:11-12
4:10 [h]ver 5 [i]Eze 31:3-4
4:12 [j]Eze 17:23; Mt 13:32
4:13 [k]Da 7:1 [l]ver 23; Dt 33:2; Da 8:13
4:14 [m]Eze 31:12; Mt 3:10
4:16 [n]ver 23,32
4:17 [o]ver 2,25; Ps 83:18 [p]Jer 27:5-7; Da 2:21; 5:18-21 [q]Da 11:21
4:18 [r]Ge 41:8; Da 5:8,15 [s]Ge 41:15 [t]ver 7-9
4:19 [u]Da 7:15,28; 8:27; 10:16-17
4:22 [v]2Sa 12:7 [w]Jer 27:7; Da 2:37-38; 5:18-19
4:23 [x]ver 13 [y]Da 5:21

[a] *7* Or *Chaldeans*; also in verses 17 and 23
[b] *13* Or *watchman*; also in verses 17 and 23
[c] *16* Or *years*; also in verses 23, 25 and 32

2 →PG. 1051

24"This is the interpretation, O king, and this is the decree[z] the Most High has issued against my lord the king: 25You will be driven away from people and will live with the wild animals; you will eat grass like cattle and be drenched with the dew of heaven. Seven times will pass by for you until you acknowledge that the Most High[a] is sovereign over the kingdoms of men and gives them to anyone he wishes.[b] 26The command to leave the stump of the tree with its roots[c] means that your kingdom will be restored to you when you acknowledge that Heaven rules.[d] 27Therefore, O king, be pleased to accept my advice: Renounce your sins by doing what is right, and your wickedness by being kind to the oppressed.[e] It may be that then your prosperity will continue.[f]"

The Dream Is Fulfilled

28All this happened[g] to King Nebuchadnezzar. 29Twelve months later, as the king was walking on the roof of the royal palace of Babylon, 30he said, "Is not this the great Babylon I have built as the royal residence, by my mighty power and for the glory of my majesty?"[h]

31The words were still on his lips when a voice came from heaven, "This is what is decreed for you, King Nebuchadnezzar: Your royal authority has been taken from you. 32You will be driven away from people and will live with the wild animals; you will eat grass like cattle. Seven times will pass by for you until you acknowledge that the Most High is sovereign over the kingdoms of men and gives them to anyone he wishes."

33Immediately what had been said about Nebuchadnezzar was fulfilled. He was driven away from people and ate grass like cattle. His body was drenched with the dew of heaven until his hair grew like the feathers of an eagle and his nails like the claws of a bird.[i]

34At the end of that time, I, Nebuchadnezzar, raised my eyes toward heaven, and my sanity was restored. Then I praised the Most High; I honored and glorified him who lives forever.[j]

His dominion is an eternal
    dominion;
  his kingdom endures from
    generation to generation.[k]
35All the peoples of the earth
  are regarded as nothing.[l]
He does as he pleases[m]
  with the powers of heaven
  and the peoples of the earth.
No one can hold back his hand
  or say to him: "What have you
  done?"[n]

36At the same time that my sanity was restored, my honor and splendor were returned to me for the glory of my kingdom.[o] My advisers and nobles sought me out, and I was restored to my throne and became even greater than before. 37Now I, Nebuchadnezzar, praise and exalt and glorify the King of heaven, because everything he does is right and all his ways are just.[p] And those who walk in pride he is able to humble.[q]

The Writing on the Wall

5 King Belshazzar gave a great banquet[r] for a thousand of his nobles and drank wine with them. 2While Belshazzar was drinking his wine, he gave orders to bring in the gold and silver goblets[s] that Nebuchadnezzar his father**a** had taken from the temple in Jerusalem, so that the king and his nobles, his wives and his concubines might drink from them.[t] 3So they brought in the gold goblets that had been taken from the temple of God in Jerusalem, and the king and his nobles, his wives and his concubines drank from them. 4As they drank the wine, they praised the gods of gold and silver, of bronze, iron, wood and stone.[u]

5Suddenly the fingers of a human hand appeared and wrote on the plaster of the wall, near the lampstand in the royal palace. The king watched the hand as it wrote. 6His face turned pale and he was so frightened[v] that his knees knocked together and his legs gave way.[w]

7The king called out for the enchanters, astrologers**b** and diviners[x] to be brought and said to these wise[y] men of Babylon, "Whoever reads this writing and tells me what it means will be clothed in purple and have a gold chain placed around his neck,[z] and he will be made the third highest ruler in the kingdom."[a]

a*2* Or *ancestor;* or *predecessor;* also in verses 11, 13 and 18 **b***7* Or *Chaldeans;* also in verse 11

4:24 [z]Job 40:12; Ps 107:40
4:25 [a]ver 17; Ps 83:18 [b]Jer 27:5; Da 5:21
4:26 [c]ver 15 [d]Da 2:37
4:27 [e]Isa 55:6-7 [f]1Ki 21:29; Ps 41:3; Eze 18:22
4:28 [g]Nu 23:19
4:30 [h]Isa 37:24-25; Da 5:20; Hab 2:4
4:33 [i]Da 5:20-21
4:34 [j]Da 12:7; Rev 4:10 [k]Ps 145:13; Da 2:44; 5:21; 6:26; Lk 1:33
4:35 [l]Isa 40:17 [m]Ps 115:3; 135:6 [n]Isa 45:9; Ro 9:20
4:36 [o]Pr 22:4
4:37 [p]Dt 32:4; Ps 33:4-5 [q]Ex 18:11; Job 40:11-12; Da 5:20,23
5:1 [r]Est 1:3
5:2 [s]2Ki 24:13; Jer 52:19 [t]Est 1:7; Da 1:2
5:4 [u]Ps 135:15-18; Hab 2:19; Rev 9:20
5:6 [v]Da 4:5 [w]Eze 7:17
5:7 [x]Isa 44:25 [y]Da 4:6-7 [z]Ge 41:42 [a]Da 2:5-6,48; 6:2-3

8Then all the king's wise men came
in, but they could not read the writing
or tell the king what it meant.[b] 9So
King Belshazzar became even more
terrified[c] and his face grew more pale.
His nobles were baffled.
10The queen,[a] hearing the voices of
the king and his nobles, came into the
banquet hall. "O king, live forever!"[d]
she said. "Don't be alarmed! Don't look
so pale! 11There is a man in your kingdom who has the spirit of the holy
gods[e] in him. In the time of your father he was found to have insight and
intelligence and wisdom[f] like that of
the gods. King Nebuchadnezzar your
father—your father the king, I say—
appointed him chief of the magicians,
enchanters, astrologers and diviners.[g]
12This man Daniel, whom the king
called Belteshazzar,[h] was found to
have a keen mind and knowledge and
understanding, and also the ability to
interpret dreams, explain riddles and
solve difficult problems.[i] Call for
Daniel, and he will tell you what the
writing means."
13So Daniel was brought before the
king, and the king said to him, "Are you
Daniel, one of the exiles my father the
king brought from Judah?[j] 14I have
heard that the spirit of the gods is in
you and that you have insight, intelligence and outstanding wisdom. 15The
wise men and enchanters were
brought before me to read this writing
and tell me what it means, but they
could not explain it. 16Now I have
heard that you are able to give interpretations and to solve difficult problems. If you can read this writing and
tell me what it means, you will be
clothed in purple and have a gold
chain placed around your neck, and
you will be made the third highest ruler
in the kingdom."
17Then Daniel answered the king,
"You may keep your gifts for yourself
and give your rewards to someone
else.[k] Nevertheless, I will read the
writing for the king and tell him what it
means.
18"O king, the Most High God gave
your father Nebuchadnezzar sovereignty and greatness and glory and
splendor.[l] 19Because of the high position he gave him, all the peoples and
nations and men of every language
dreaded and feared him. Those the
king wanted to put to death, he put to
death;[m] those he wanted to spare, he
spared; those he wanted to promote,
he promoted; and those he wanted to
humble, he humbled. 20But when his
heart became arrogant and hardened
with pride,[n] he was deposed from his
royal throne and stripped[o] of his glory.[p] 21He was driven away from people and given the mind of an animal;
he lived with the wild donkeys and ate
grass like cattle; and his body was
drenched with the dew of heaven, until
he acknowledged that the Most High
God is sovereign[q] over the kingdoms
of men and sets over them anyone he
wishes.[r]
22"But you his son,[b] O Belshazzar,
have not humbled[s] yourself, though
you knew all this. 23Instead, you have
set yourself up against[t] the Lord of
heaven. You had the goblets from his
temple brought to you, and you and
your nobles, your wives and your concubines drank wine from them. You
praised the gods of silver and gold, of
bronze, iron, wood and stone, which
cannot see or hear or understand.[u]
But you did not honor the God who
holds in his hand your life[v] and all
your ways.[w] 24Therefore he sent the
hand that wrote the inscription.
25"This is the inscription that was
written:

MENE, MENE, TEKEL, PARSIN[c]

26"This is what these words mean:

Mene[d]: God has numbered
the days[x] of your reign
and brought it to an
end.[y]
27*Tekel*[e]: You have been weighed
on the scales and found
wanting.[z]
28*Peres*[f]: Your kingdom is
divided and given to
the Medes[a] and Per-
sians."[b]

29Then at Belshazzar's command,
Daniel was clothed in purple, a gold
chain was placed around his neck, and
he was proclaimed the third highest
ruler in the kingdom.
30That very night Belshazzar,[c] king
of the Babylonians,[g] was slain,[d]
31and Darius[e] the Mede took over the
kingdom, at the age of sixty-two.

Daniel in the Den of Lions

6 It pleased Darius[f] to appoint 120
satraps[g] to rule throughout the
kingdom, 2with three administrators
over them, one of whom was Daniel.[h]
The satraps were made accountable[i]
to them so that the king might not suf-

5:8 [b]Da 2:10,27 **5:9** [c]Isa 21:4 **5:10** [d]Da 3:9 **5:11** [e]Da 4:8-9,19 [f]ver 14; Da 1:17 [g]Da 2:47-48 **5:12** [h]Da 1:7 [i]ver 14-16; Da 6:3 **5:13** [j]Da 6:13 **5:17** [k]2Ki 5:16 **5:18** [l]Jer 27:7; Da 2:37-38 **5:19** [m]Da 2:12-13; 3:6 **5:20** [n]Da 4:30 [o]Jer 13:18 [p]Job 40:12; Isa 14:13-15 **5:21** [q]Eze 17:24 [r]Da 4:16-17,35 **5:22** [s]Ex 10:3; 2Ch 33:23 **5:23** [t]Jer 50:29 [u]Ps 115:4-8; Hab 2:19 [v]Job 12:10 [w]Job 31:4; Jer 10:23 **5:26** [x]Jer 27:7 [y]Isa 13:6 **5:27** [z]Ps 62:9 **5:28** [a]Isa 13:17 [b]Da 6:28 **5:30** [c]ver 1 [d]Isa 21:9; Jer 51:31 **5:31** [e]Da 6:1; 9:1 **6:1** [f]Da 5:31 [g]Est 1:1 **6:2** [h]Da 2:48-49 [i]Ezr 4:22

[a]10 Or *queen mother* [b]22 Or *descendant*; or *successor* [c]25 Aramaic *UPARSIN* (that is, *AND PARSIN*) [d]26 *Mene* can mean *numbered* or *mina* (a unit of money). [e]27 *Tekel* can mean *weighed* or *shekel*. [f]28 *Peres* (the singular of *Parsin*) can mean *divided* or *Persia* or *a half mina* or *a half shekel*. [g]30 Or *Chaldeans*

fer loss. 3 Now Daniel so distinguished himself among the administrators and the satraps by his exceptional qualities that the king planned to set him over the whole kingdom.[j] 4 At this, the administrators and the satraps tried to find grounds for charges against Daniel in his conduct of government affairs, but they were unable to do so. They could find no corruption in him, because he was trustworthy and neither corrupt nor negligent. 5 Finally these men said, "We will never find any basis for charges against this man Daniel unless it has something to do with the law of his God."[k]

6 So the administrators and the satraps went as a group to the king and said: "O King Darius, live forever![l] 7 The royal administrators, prefects, satraps, advisers and governors[m] have all agreed that the king should issue an edict and enforce the decree that anyone who prays to any god or man during the next thirty days, except to you, O king, shall be thrown into the lions' den.[n] 8 Now, O king, issue the decree and put it in writing so that it cannot be altered—in accordance with the laws of the Medes and Persians, which cannot be repealed."[o] 9 So King Darius put the decree in writing.

1 →PG. 962

10 Now when Daniel learned that the decree had been published, he went home to his upstairs room where the windows opened toward[p] Jerusalem. Three times a day he got down on his knees[q] and prayed, giving thanks to his God, just as he had done before.[r] 11 Then these men went as a group and found Daniel praying and asking God for help. 12 So they went to the king and spoke to him about his royal decree: "Did you not publish a decree that during the next thirty days anyone who prays to any god or man except to you, O king, would be thrown into the lions' den?"

The king answered, "The decree stands—in accordance with the laws of the Medes and Persians, which cannot be repealed."[s]

13 Then they said to the king, "Daniel, who is one of the exiles from Judah,[t] pays no attention[u] to you, O king, or to the decree you put in writing. He still prays three times a day." 14 When the king heard this, he was greatly distressed;[v] he was determined to rescue Daniel and made every effort until sundown to save him.

15 Then the men went as a group to the king and said to him, "Remember, O king, that according to the law of the Medes and Persians no decree or edict that the king issues can be changed."[w]

16 So the king gave the order, and they brought Daniel and threw him into the lions' den.[x] The king said to Daniel, "May your God, whom you serve continually, rescue[y] you!"

17 A stone was brought and placed over the mouth of the den, and the king sealed[z] it with his own signet ring and with the rings of his nobles, so that Daniel's situation might not be changed. 18 Then the king returned to his palace and spent the night without eating[a] and without any entertainment being brought to him. And he could not sleep.[b]

19 At the first light of dawn, the king got up and hurried to the lions' den. 20 When he came near the den, he called to Daniel in an anguished voice, "Daniel, servant of the living God, has

6:3 [j] Ge 41:41; Est 10:3; Da 5:12-14 **6:5** [k] Ac 24:13-16 **6:6** [l] Ne 2:3; Da 2:4 **6:7** [m] Da 3:2 [n] Ps 59:3; 64:2-6; Da 3:6 **6:8** [o] Est 1:19 **6:10** [p] 1Ki 8:48-49 [q] Ps 95:6 [r] Ac 5:29 **6:12** [s] Est 1:19; Da 3:8-12 **6:13** [t] Da 2:25; 5:13 [u] Est 3:8; Da 3:12 **6:14** [v] Mk 6:26 **6:15** [w] Est 8:8 **6:16** [x] ver 7 [y] Job 5:19; Ps 37:39-40 **6:17** [z] Mt 27:66 **6:18** [a] 2Sa 12:17 [b] Est 6:1; Da 2:1

6:1–28

SPIRITUAL CONSISTENCY

PROMISE 3

If ever a man had to stand for his beliefs against intense opposition, it was Daniel. His enemies had successfully carried out a clever plot aimed at his ultimate demise. King Darius sympathized with Daniel, but the law that he himself had enacted wouldn't allow him to help his friend (vv. 8–9).

Yet Daniel knew he wasn't alone. Although this chapter makes no mention of his friends, we know from the earlier stories in Daniel that he had a few like-minded brothers with him in Babylon. But most importantly, Daniel had God as his constant companion; he spent untold hours cultivating a relationship with God through prayer.

Daniel was a man of great spiritual consistency. He simply refused to allow anyone or anything to stop him from praying. He could have easily postponed his prayer sessions—even for a brief time—to save his skin. Instead, "when Daniel learned that the decree had been published, he went home . . . and prayed, giving thanks to God, just as he had done before" (v. 10). It's as if the thought of putting God off never occurred to this man. This is what makes Daniel such a wonderful model of spiritual integrity, consistency and purity for us today.

While it's unlikely that any one of us will ever be thrown into a lions' den, there are times when we'll be called on to stand for what's right. The best preparation for such a test is prayer. Like Daniel, if we want to do what's right when we're under fire, we must do what's right every day.

For the next Promise 3 reading go to page 958.

your God, whom you serve continually,
been able to rescue you from the lions?"[c]
21 Daniel answered, "O king, live forever![d] 22 My God sent his angel,[e] and
he shut the mouths of the lions.[f] They
have not hurt me, because I was found
innocent in his sight.[g] Nor have I ever
done any wrong before you, O king."
23 The king was overjoyed and gave
orders to lift Daniel out of the den. And
when Daniel was lifted from the den,
no wound[h] was found on him, because he had trusted[i] in his God.
24 At the king's command, the men
who had falsely accused Daniel were
brought in and thrown into the lions'
den,[j] along with their wives and children.[k] And before they reached the
floor of the den, the lions overpowered
them and crushed all their bones.[l]
25 Then King Darius wrote to all the
peoples, nations and men of every language throughout the land:

"May you prosper greatly![m]

26 "I issue a decree that in every
part of my kingdom people must
fear and reverence the God of
Daniel.[n]

"For he is the living God
and he endures forever;
his kingdom will not be destroyed,
his dominion will never end.[o]
27 He rescues and he saves;
he performs signs and wonders[p]
in the heavens and on the earth.
He has rescued Daniel
from the power of the lions."[q]

28 So Daniel prospered during the
reign of Darius and the reign of Cyrus[a][r] the Persian.

Daniel's Dream of Four Beasts

7 In the first year of Belshazzar[s] king
of Babylon, Daniel had a dream, and
visions passed through his mind[t] as
he was lying on his bed. He wrote[u]
down the substance of his dream.
2 Daniel said: "In my vision at night I
looked, and there before me were the
four winds of heaven[v] churning up
the great sea. 3 Four great beasts,[w]
each different from the others, came
up out of the sea.
4 "The first was like a lion,[x] and it
had the wings of an eagle.[y] I watched
until its wings were torn off and it was
lifted from the ground so that it stood
on two feet like a man, and the heart of
a man was given to it.
5 "And there before me was a second
beast, which looked like a bear. It was
raised up on one of its sides, and it had
three ribs in its mouth between its
teeth. It was told, 'Get up and eat your
fill of flesh!'[z]
6 "After that, I looked, and there before me was another beast, one that
looked like a leopard.[a] And on its back
it had four wings like those of a bird.
This beast had four heads, and it was
given authority to rule.
7 "After that, in my vision at night I
looked, and there before me was a
fourth beast—terrifying and frightening and very powerful. It had large
iron[b] teeth; it crushed and devoured
its victims and trampled underfoot
whatever was left. It was different from
all the former beasts, and it had ten
horns.[c]
8 "While I was thinking about the
horns, there before me was another
horn, a little[d] one, which came up
among them; and three of the first
horns were uprooted before it. This
horn had eyes like the eyes of a man[e]
and a mouth that spoke boastfully.[f]
9 "As I looked,

"thrones were set in place,
and the Ancient of Days took his
seat.
His clothing was as white as snow;
the hair of his head was white
like wool.[g]
His throne was flaming with fire,
and its wheels[h] were all ablaze.
10 A river of fire[i] was flowing,
coming out from before him.[j]
Thousands upon thousands
attended him;
ten thousand times ten thousand
stood before him.
The court was seated,
and the books[k] were opened.

11 "Then I continued to watch because of the boastful words the horn
was speaking. I kept looking until the
beast was slain and its body destroyed
and thrown into the blazing fire.[l]
12 (The other beasts had been stripped
of their authority, but were allowed to
live for a period of time.)
13 "In my vision at night I looked, and
there before me was one like a son of
man,[m] coming with the clouds of
heaven.[n] He approached the Ancient
of Days and was led into his presence.
14 He was given authority,[o] glory and
sovereign power; all peoples, nations
and men of every language worshiped
him.[p] His dominion is an everlasting
dominion that will not pass away, and
his kingdom is one that will never be
destroyed.[q]

6:20 [c]Da 3:17
6:21 [d]Da 2:4
6:22 [e]Da 3:28 [f]Ps 91:11-13; Heb 11:33 [g]Ac 12:11; 2Ti 4:17
6:23 [h]Da 3:27 [i]1Ch 5:20
6:24 [j]Dt 19:18-19; Est 7:9-10; Ps 54:5 [k]Dt 24:16; 2Ki 14:6 [l]Isa 38:13
6:25 [m]Da 4:1
6:26 [n]Ps 99:1-3; Da 3:29 [o]Da 2:44; 4:34
6:27 [p]Da 4:3 [q]ver 22
6:28 [r]2Ch 36:22; Da 1:21
7:1 [s]Da 5:1 [t]Da 1:17 [u]Jer 36:4
7:2 [v]Rev 7:1
7:3 [w]Rev 13:1
7:4 [x]Jer 4:7 [y]Eze 17:3
7:5 [z]Da 2:39
7:6 [a]Rev 13:2
7:7 [b]Da 2:40 [c]Rev 12:3
7:8 [d]Da 8:9 [e]Rev 9:7 [f]Ps 12:3; Rev 13:5-6
7:9 [g]Rev 1:14 [h]Eze 1:15; 10:6
7:10 [i]Ps 50:3; 97:3; Isa 30:27 [j]Dt 33:2; Ps 68:17; Rev 5:11 [k]Rev 20:11-15
7:11 [l]Rev 19:20
7:13 [m]Mt 8:20*; Rev 1:13* [n]Mt 24:30; Rev 1:7
7:14 [o]Mt 28:18 [p]Ps 72:11; 102:22; 1Co 15:27; Eph 1:22 [q]Da 2:44; Heb 12:28; Rev 11:15

[a] 28 Or *Darius, that is, the reign of Cyrus*

The Interpretation of the Dream

[15]"I, Daniel, was troubled in spirit, and the visions that passed through my mind disturbed me.[r] [16]I approached one of those standing there and asked him the true meaning of all this.

"So he told me and gave me the interpretation[s] of these things: [17]'The four great beasts are four kingdoms that will rise from the earth. [18]But the saints of the Most High will receive the kingdom and will possess it forever—yes, for ever and ever.'[t]

[19]"Then I wanted to know the true meaning of the fourth beast, which was different from all the others and most terrifying, with its iron teeth and bronze claws—the beast that crushed and devoured its victims and trampled underfoot whatever was left. [20]I also wanted to know about the ten horns on its head and about the other horn that came up, before which three of them fell—the horn that looked more imposing than the others and that had eyes and a mouth that spoke boastfully. [21]As I watched, this horn was waging war against the saints and defeating them,[u] [22]until the Ancient of Days came and pronounced judgment in favor of the saints of the Most High, and the time came when they possessed the kingdom.

[23]"He gave me this explanation: 'The fourth beast is a fourth kingdom that will appear on earth. It will be different from all the other kingdoms and will devour the whole earth, trampling it down and crushing it.[v] [24]The ten horns[w] are ten kings who will come from this kingdom. After them another king will arise, different from the earlier ones; he will subdue three kings. [25]He will speak against the Most High[x] and oppress his saints and try to change the set times[y] and the laws. The saints will be handed over to him for a time, times and half a time.[a][z]

[26]" 'But the court will sit, and his power will be taken away and completely destroyed forever. [27]Then the sovereignty, power and greatness of the kingdoms under the whole heaven will be handed over to the saints, the people of the Most High. His kingdom will be an everlasting[a] kingdom, and all rulers will worship[b] and obey him.'

[28]"This is the end of the matter. I, Daniel, was deeply troubled[c] by my thoughts, and my face turned pale, but I kept the matter to myself."

Daniel's Vision of a Ram and a Goat

8 In the third year of King Belshazzar's reign, I, Daniel, had a vision, after the one that had already appeared to me. [2]In my vision I saw myself in the citadel of Susa[d] in the province of Elam;[e] in the vision I was beside the Ulai Canal. [3]I looked up,[f] and there before me was a ram with two horns, standing beside the canal, and the horns were long. One of the horns was longer than the other but grew up later. [4]I watched the ram as he charged toward the west and the north and the south. No animal could stand against him, and none could rescue from his power. He did as he pleased[g] and became great.

[5]As I was thinking about this, suddenly a goat with a prominent horn between his eyes came from the west, crossing the whole earth without touching the ground. [6]He came toward the two-horned ram I had seen standing beside the canal and charged at him in great rage. [7]I saw him attack the ram furiously, striking the ram and shattering his two horns. The ram was powerless to stand against him; the goat knocked him to the ground and trampled on him,[h] and none could rescue the ram from his power. [8]The goat became very great, but at the height of his power his large horn was broken off,[i] and in its place four prominent horns grew up toward the four winds of heaven.[j]

[9]Out of one of them came another horn, which started small but grew in power to the south and to the east and toward the Beautiful Land.[k] [10]It grew until it reached[l] the host of the heavens, and it threw some of the starry host down to the earth[m] and trampled[n] on them. [11]It set itself up to be as great as the Prince of the host;[o] it took away the daily sacrifice[p] from him, and the place of his sanctuary was brought low.[q] [12]Because of rebellion, the host ⌞of the saints⌟[b] and the daily sacrifice were given over to it. It prospered in everything it did, and truth was thrown to the ground.

[13]Then I heard a holy one[r] speaking, and another holy one said to him, "How long will it take for the vision to be fulfilled[s]—the vision concerning the daily sacrifice, the rebellion that causes desolation, and the surrender of the sanctuary and of the host that will be trampled[t] underfoot?"

[14]He said to me, "It will take 2,300 evenings and mornings; then the sanctuary will be reconsecrated."[u]

7:15 [r]Da 4:19
7:16 [s]Da 8:16; 9:22; Zec 1:9
7:18 [t]Isa 60:12-14; Rev 2:26; 20:4
7:21 [u]Rev 13:7
7:23 [v]Da 2:40
7:24 [w]Rev 17:12
7:25 [x]Isa 37:23; Da 11:36 [y]Da 2:21 [z]Da 8:24; 12:7; Rev 12:14
7:27 [a]Da 2:44; 4:34; Lk 1:33; Rev 11:15; 22:5 [b]Ps 22:27; 72:11; 86:9
7:28 [c]Da 4:19
8:2 [d]Est 1:2 [e]Ge 10:22
8:3 [f]Da 10:5
8:4 [g]Da 11:3,16
8:7 [h]Da 7:7
8:8 [i]2Ch 26:16-21; Da 5:20 [j]Da 7:2; Rev 7:1
8:9 [k]Da 11:16
8:10 [l]Isa 14:13 [m]Rev 12:4 [n]Da 7:7
8:11 [o]Da 11:36-37 [p]Eze 46:13-14 [q]Da 11:31; 12:11
8:13 [r]Da 4:23 [s]Da 12:6 [t]Lk 21:24; Rev 11:2
8:14 [u]Da 12:11-12

[a]25 Or *for a year, two years and half a year*
[b]12 Or *rebellion, the armies*

The Interpretation of the Vision

15While I, Daniel, was watching the
vision[v] and trying to understand it,
there before me stood one who looked
like a man.[w] 16And I heard a man's
voice from the Ulai calling, "Gabriel,[x]
tell this man the meaning of the vision."
17As he came near the place where I
was standing, I was terrified and fell
prostrate.[y] "Son of man," he said to
me, "understand that the vision concerns the time of the end."[z]
18While he was speaking to me, I was
in a deep sleep, with my face to the
ground.[a] Then he touched me and
raised me to my feet.[b]
19He said: "I am going to tell you
what will happen later in the time of
wrath, because the vision concerns the
appointed time of the end.[a][c] 20The
two-horned ram that you saw represents the kings of Media and Persia.
21The shaggy goat is the king of
Greece,[d] and the large horn between
his eyes is the first king.[e] 22The four
horns that replaced the one that was
broken off represent four kingdoms
that will emerge from his nation but
will not have the same power.
23"In the latter part of their reign,
when rebels have become completely
wicked, a stern-faced king, a master of
intrigue, will arise. 24He will become
very strong, but not by his own power.
He will cause astounding devastation
and will succeed in whatever he does.
He will destroy the mighty men and the
holy people.[f] 25He will cause deceit to
prosper, and he will consider himself
superior. When they feel secure, he will
destroy many and take his stand
against the Prince of princes.[g] Yet he
will be destroyed, but not by human
power.[h]
26"The vision of the evenings and
mornings that has been given you is
true,[i] but seal[j] up the vision, for it
concerns the distant future."[k]
27I, Daniel, was exhausted and lay
ill for several days. Then I got up and
went about the king's business.[l] I was
appalled[m] by the vision; it was beyond
understanding.

Daniel's Prayer

9 In the first year of Darius[n] son of
Xerxes[b] (a Mede by descent), who
was made ruler over the Babylonian[c]
kingdom— 2in the first year of his
reign, I, Daniel, understood from the
Scriptures, according to the word of
the LORD given to Jeremiah the prophet, that the desolation of Jerusalem
would last seventy[o] years. 3So I turned
to the Lord God and pleaded with him
in prayer and petition, in fasting, and
in sackcloth and ashes.[p]
4I prayed to the LORD my God and
confessed:

"O Lord, the great and awesome God,[q] who keeps his covenant of love[r] with all who love
him and obey his commands, 5we
have sinned and done wrong.[s]
We have been wicked and have
rebelled; we have turned away[t]
from your commands and laws.[u]
6We have not listened to your ser-

8:15 [v]ver 1 [w]Da 10:16-18 **8:16** [x]Da 9:21; Lk 1:19 **8:17** [y]Eze 1:28; Da 2:46; Rev 1:17 [z]Hab 2:3 **8:18** [a]Da 10:9 [b]Eze 2:2; Da 10:16-18 **8:19** [c]Hab 2:3 **8:21** [d]Da 10:20 [e]Da 11:3 **8:24** [f]Da 7:25; 11:36 **8:25** [g]Da 11:36 [h]Da 2:34; 11:21 **8:26** [i]Da 10:1 [j]Rev 22:10 [k]Da 10:14 **8:27** [l]Da 2:48 [m]Da 7:28 **9:1** [n]Da 5:31 **9:2** [o]2Ch 36:21; Jer 29:10; Zec 7:5 **9:3** [p]Ne 1:4; Jer 29:12 **9:4** [q]Dt 7:21 [r]Dt 7:9 **9:5** [s]Ps 106:6 [t]Isa 53:6 [u]ver 11; La 1:20

[a] *19* Or *because the end will be at the appointed time* [b] *1* Hebrew *Ahasuerus* [c] *1* Or *Chaldean*

9:1-19

PROMISE 1

PRAYER FOR A NATION

Make no mistake about it: Life is difficult, and there are no detours to get us around life's trials. We'll all encounter them. So the question of our lives is not, "How can we avoid hardship?" The question should be, "How can we hold on to God when times get tough?" In the face of great adversity Daniel grabbed hold of God and refused to let go. How did he do it? Daniel prayed. And within his prayer we find an example that we'll do well to follow.

First, Daniel's prayer flowed from his knowledge of God and God's Word. As Daniel examined the Scripture he discovered that the desolation of Jerusalem would last seventy years. The realization that this time would soon be completed drove the prophet to his knees.

Second, Daniel's prayer was filled with confession and repentance. Notice that he prayed not only for his own sins, but for those of the nation. God had disciplined Israel because of its sins. The only way the nation could move forward was for each individual to turn from his or her sin in this same confession and repentance. Realizing that, Daniel poured out his heart to God.

Third, Daniel pled for mercy. He didn't demand. Instead, he humbly asked God to extend mercy to a people who didn't deserve it.

The church today needs men who will pray as Daniel did. Indeed, prayer is our only hope. We need men who are devoted to praying for themselves, for their families, for their church communities, and for their country.

For the next Promise 1 reading go to page 954.

vants the prophets,[v] who spoke
in your name to our kings, our
princes and our fathers, and to all
the people of the land.
7“Lord, you are righteous, but
this day we are covered with
shame[w]—the men of Judah and
people of Jerusalem and all Israel,
both near and far, in all the countries where you have scattered[x]
us because of our unfaithfulness
to you.[y] **8**O LORD, we and our
kings, our princes and our fathers
are covered with shame because
we have sinned against you. **9**The
Lord our God is merciful and forgiving,[z] even though we have rebelled against him;[a] **10**we have
not obeyed the LORD our God or
kept the laws he gave us through
his servants the prophets.[b] **11**All
Israel has transgressed your law
and turned away, refusing to obey
you.
“Therefore the curses and
sworn judgments written in the
Law of Moses, the servant of God,
have been poured out on us, because we have sinned[c] against
you. **12**You have fulfilled[d] the
words spoken against us and
against our rulers by bringing
upon us great disaster. Under the
whole heaven nothing has ever
been done like what has been
done to Jerusalem.[e] **13**Just as it is
written in the Law of Moses, all
this disaster has come upon us,
yet we have not sought the favor
of the LORD our God by turning
from our sins and giving attention
to your truth.[f] **14**The LORD did
not hesitate to bring the disaster[g]
upon us, for the LORD our God is
righteous in everything he does;
yet we have not obeyed him.[h]
15“Now, O Lord our God, who
brought your people out of Egypt
with a mighty hand[i] and who
made for yourself a name[j] that
endures to this day, we have
sinned, we have done wrong.
16O Lord, in keeping with all your
righteous acts,[k] turn away your
anger and your wrath from Jerusalem,[l] your city, your holy
hill.[m] Our sins and the iniquities
of our fathers have made Jerusalem and your people an object of
scorn[n] to all those around us.
17“Now, our God, hear the
prayers and petitions of your servant. For your sake, O Lord, look
with favor[o] on your desolate
sanctuary. **18**Give ear, O God, and
hear; open your eyes and see[p]
the desolation of the city that
bears your Name.[q] We do not
make requests of you because we
are righteous, but because of your
great mercy. **19**O Lord, listen!
O Lord, forgive![r] O Lord, hear
and act! For your sake, O my God,
do not delay, because your city
and your people bear your
Name.”

The Seventy "Sevens"

20While I was speaking and praying,
confessing my sin and the sin of my
people Israel and making my request
to the LORD my God for his holy
hill[s]— **21**while I was still in prayer,
Gabriel,[t] the man I had seen in the
earlier vision, came to me in swift flight
about the time of the evening sacrifice.[u] **22**He instructed me and said to
me, “Daniel, I have now come to give
you insight and understanding. **23**As
soon as you began to pray, an answer
was given, which I have come to tell
you, for you are highly esteemed.[v]
Therefore, consider the message and
understand the vision:[w]
24“Seventy ‘sevens’[a] are decreed for
your people and your holy city to finish[b] transgression, to put an end to
sin, to atone[x] for wickedness, to bring
in everlasting righteousness,[y] to seal
up vision and prophecy and to anoint
the most holy.[c]
25“Know and understand this: From
the issuing of the decree[d] to restore
and rebuild[z] Jerusalem until the
Anointed One,[e][a] the ruler, comes,
there will be seven ‘sevens,’ and sixty-
two ‘sevens.’ It will be rebuilt with
streets and a trench, but in times of
trouble. **26**After the sixty-two ‘sevens,’
the Anointed One will be cut off[b] and
will have nothing.[f] The people of the
ruler who will come will destroy the
city and the sanctuary. The end will
come like a flood:[c] War will continue
until the end, and desolations have
been decreed. **27**He will confirm a covenant with many for one ‘seven.’[g] In
the middle of the ‘seven’[g] he will put
an end to sacrifice and offering. And on
a wing ⌞of the temple⌟ he will set up an
abomination that causes desolation,

9:6 [v]2Ch 36:16; Jer 44:5
9:7 [w]Ps 44:15 [x]Dt 4:27; Am 9:9 [y]Jer 3:25
9:9 [z]Ps 130:4 [a]Ne 9:17; Jer 14:7
9:10 [b]2Ki 17:13-15; 18:12
9:11 [c]Isa 1:4-6; Jer 8:5-10
9:12 [d]Isa 44:26; Zec 1:6 [e]Jer 44:2-6; Eze 5:9
9:13 [f]Isa 9:13; Jer 2:30
9:14 [g]Jer 44:27 [h]Ne 9:33
9:15 [i]Jer 32:21 [j]Ne 9:10
9:16 [k]Ps 31:1 [l]Jer 32:32 [m]Zec 8:3 [n]Eze 5:14
9:17 [o]Nu 6:24-26; Ps 80:19
9:18 [p]Ps 80:14 [q]Isa 37:17; Jer 7:10-12; 25:29
9:19 [r]Ps 44:23
9:20 [s]ver 3; Ps 145:18; Isa 58:9
9:21 [t]Da 8:16; Lk 1:19 [u]Ex 29:39
9:23 [v]Da 10:19; Lk 1:28 [w]Da 10:11-12; Mt 24:15
9:24 [x]Isa 53:10 [y]Isa 56:1
9:25 [z]Ezr 4:24 [a]Jn 4:25
9:26 [b]Isa 53:8 [c]Na 1:8

[a] *24* Or *'weeks'*; also in verses 25 and 26
[b] *24* Or *restrain* [c] *24* Or *Most Holy Place*; or *most holy One* [d] *25* Or *word* [e] *25* Or *an anointed one*; also in verse 26 [f] *26* Or *off and will have no one*; or *off, but not for himself*
[g] *27* Or *'week'*

until the end that is decreed[d] is poured out on him.[a]"[b]

Daniel's Vision of a Man

10 In the third year of Cyrus[e] king of Persia, a revelation was given to Daniel (who was called Belteshazzar).[f] Its message was true[g] and it concerned a great war.[c] The understanding of the message came to him in a vision.

2At that time I, Daniel, mourned[h] for three weeks. 3I ate no choice food; no meat or wine touched my lips; and I used no lotions at all until the three weeks were over.

4On the twenty-fourth day of the first month, as I was standing on the bank of the great river, the Tigris,[i] 5I looked up and there before me was a man dressed in linen,[j] with a belt of the finest gold[k] around his waist. 6His body was like chrysolite, his face like lightning,[l] his eyes like flaming torches,[m] his arms and legs like the gleam of burnished bronze,[n] and his voice like the sound of a multitude.

7I, Daniel, was the only one who saw the vision; the men with me did not see it,[o] but such terror overwhelmed them that they fled and hid themselves. 8So I was left alone,[p] gazing at this great vision; I had no strength left,[q] my face turned deathly pale and I was helpless.[r] 9Then I heard him speaking, and as I listened to him, I fell into a deep sleep, my face to the ground.[s]

10A hand touched me[t] and set me trembling on my hands and knees.[u] 11He said, "Daniel, you who are highly esteemed,[v] consider carefully the words I am about to speak to you, and stand up,[w] for I have now been sent to you." And when he said this to me, I stood up trembling.

12Then he continued, "Do not be afraid, Daniel. Since the first day that you set your mind to gain understanding and to humble[x] yourself before your God, your words were heard, and I have come in response to them.[y] 13But the prince of the Persian kingdom resisted me twenty-one days. Then Michael,[z] one of the chief princes, came to help me, because I was detained there with the king of Persia. 14Now I have come to explain[a] to you what will happen to your people in the future, for the vision concerns a time yet to come.[b]"

15While he was saying this to me, I bowed with my face toward the ground and was speechless.[c] 16Then one who looked like a man[d] touched my lips, and I opened my mouth and began to speak.[d] I said to the one standing before me, "I am overcome with anguish[e] because of the vision, my lord, and I am helpless. 17How can I, your servant, talk with you, my lord? My strength is gone and I can hardly breathe."[f]

18Again the one who looked like a man touched[g] me and gave me strength. 19"Do not be afraid, O man highly esteemed," he said. "Peace![h] Be strong now; be strong."[i]

When he spoke to me, I was strengthened and said, "Speak, my lord, since you have given me strength."[j]

20So he said, "Do you know why I have come to you? Soon I will return to fight against the prince of Persia, and when I go, the prince of Greece[k] will come; 21but first I will tell you what is written in the Book of Truth.[l] (No one supports me against them except Michael,[m] your prince. **11** 1And in the first year of Darius[n] the Mede, I took my stand to support and protect him.)

The Kings of the South and the North

2"Now then, I tell you the truth:[o] Three more kings will appear in Persia, and then a fourth, who will be far richer than all the others. When he has gained power by his wealth, he will stir up everyone against the kingdom of Greece.[p] 3Then a mighty king will appear, who will rule with great power and do as he pleases.[q] 4After he has appeared, his empire will be broken up and parceled out toward the four winds of heaven.[r] It will not go to his descendants, nor will it have the power he exercised, because his empire will be uprooted and given to others.

5"The king of the South will become strong, but one of his commanders will become even stronger than he and will rule his own kingdom with great power. 6After some years, they will become allies. The daughter of the king of the South will go to the king of the North to make an alliance, but she will not retain her power, and he and his power[e] will not last. In those days she will be handed over, together with her royal

9:27 [d]Isa 10:22
10:1 [e]Da 1:21 [f]Da 1:7 [g]Da 8:26
10:2 [h]Ezr 9:4
10:4 [i]Ge 2:14
10:5 [j]Eze 9:2; Rev 15:6 [k]Jer 10:9
10:6 [l]Mt 17:2 [m]Rev 19:12 [n]Rev 1:15
10:7 [o]2Ki 6:17-20; Ac 9:7
10:8 [p]Ge 32:24 [q]Da 8:27 [r]Hab 3:16
10:9 [s]Da 8:18
10:10 [t]Jer 1:9 [u]Rev 1:17
10:11 [v]Da 9:23 [w]Eze 2:1
10:12 [x]Da 9:3 [y]Da 9:20
10:13 [z]ver 21; Da 12:1; Jude 1:9
10:14 [a]Da 9:22 [b]Da 2:28; 8:26; Hab 2:3
10:15 [c]Eze 24:27; Lk 1:20
10:16 [d]Isa 6:7; Jer 1:9; Da 8:15-18 [e]Isa 21:3
10:17 [f]Da 4:19
10:18 [g]ver 16
10:19 [h]Jdg 6:23; Isa 35:4 [i]Jos 1:9 [j]Isa 6:1-8
10:20 [k]Da 8:21; 11:2
10:21 [l]Da 11:2 [m]ver 13; Jude 1:9
11:1 [n]Da 5:31
11:2 [o]Da 10:21 [p]Da 10:20
11:3 [q]Da 8:4,21
11:4 [r]Da 7:2; 8:22

[a] *27* Or *it* [b] *27* Or *And one who causes desolation will come upon the pinnacle of the abominable ⌞temple⌟, until the end that is decreed is poured out on the desolated ⌞city⌟* [c] *1* Or *true and burdensome* [d] *16* Most manuscripts of the Masoretic Text; one manuscript of the Masoretic Text, Dead Sea Scrolls and Septuagint *Then something that looked like a man's hand* [e] *6* Or *offspring*

escort and her father[a] and the one who supported her.

[7]"One from her family line will arise to take her place. He will attack the forces of the king of the North[s] and enter his fortress; he will fight against them and be victorious. [8]He will also seize their gods,[t] their metal images and their valuable articles of silver and gold and carry them off to Egypt.[u] For some years he will leave the king of the North alone. [9]Then the king of the North will invade the realm of the king of the South but will retreat to his own country. [10]His sons will prepare for war and assemble a great army, which will sweep on like an irresistible flood[v] and carry the battle as far as his fortress.

[11]"Then the king of the South will march out in a rage and fight against the king of the North, who will raise a large army, but it will be defeated.[w] [12]When the army is carried off, the king of the South will be filled with pride and will slaughter many thousands, yet he will not remain triumphant. [13]For the king of the North will muster another army, larger than the first; and after several years, he will advance with a huge army fully equipped.

[14]"In those times many will rise against the king of the South. The violent men among your own people will rebel in fulfillment of the vision, but without success. [15]Then the king of the North will come and build up siege ramps[x] and will capture a fortified city. The forces of the South will be powerless to resist; even their best troops will not have the strength to stand. [16]The invader will do as he pleases;[y] no one will be able to stand against him.[z] He will establish himself in the Beautiful Land and will have the power to destroy it.[a] [17]He will determine to come with the might of his entire kingdom and will make an alliance with the king of the South. And he will give him a daughter in marriage in order to overthrow the kingdom, but his plans[b] will not succeed[b] or help him. [18]Then he will turn his attention to the coastlands[c] and will take many of them, but a commander will put an end to his insolence and will turn his insolence back upon him.[d] [19]After this, he will turn back toward the fortresses of his own country but will stumble and fall,[e] to be seen no more.[f]

[20]"His successor will send out a tax collector to maintain the royal splendor.[g] In a few years, however, he will be destroyed, yet not in anger or in battle.

[21]"He will be succeeded by a contemptible[h] person who has not been given the honor of royalty.[i] He will invade the kingdom when its people feel secure, and he will seize it through intrigue. [22]Then an overwhelming army will be swept away before him; both it and a prince of the covenant will be destroyed.[j] [23]After coming to an agreement with him, he will act deceitfully,[k] and with only a few people he will rise to power. [24]When the richest provinces feel secure, he will invade them and will achieve what neither his fathers nor his forefathers did. He will distribute plunder, loot and wealth among his followers.[l] He will plot the overthrow of fortresses—but only for a time.

[25]"With a large army he will stir up his strength and courage against the king of the South. The king of the South will wage war with a large and very powerful army, but he will not be able to stand because of the plots devised against him. [26]Those who eat from the king's provisions will try to destroy him; his army will be swept away, and many will fall in battle. [27]The two kings, with their hearts bent on evil,[m] will sit at the same table and lie[n] to each other, but to no avail, because an end will still come at the appointed time.[o] [28]The king of the North will return to his own country with great wealth, but his heart will be set against the holy covenant. He will take action against it and then return to his own country.

[29]"At the appointed time he will invade the South again, but this time the outcome will be different from what it was before. [30]Ships of the western coastlands[c][p] will oppose him, and he will lose heart. Then he will turn back and vent his fury against the holy covenant. He will return and show favor to those who forsake the holy covenant.

[31]"His armed forces will rise up to desecrate the temple fortress and will abolish the daily sacrifice. Then they will set up the abomination that causes desolation.[q] [32]With flattery he will corrupt those who have violated the covenant, but the people who know their God will firmly resist[r] him.

[33]"Those who are wise will instruct[s] many, though for a time they will fall by the sword or be burned or captured or plundered.[t] [34]When they fall, they will receive a little help, and many who are not sincere[u] will join them. [35]Some of the wise will stumble,

11:7 [s]ver 6
11:8 [t]Isa 37:19; 46:1-2 [u]Jer 43:12
11:10 [v]Isa 8:8; Jer 46:8; Da 9:26
11:11 [w]Da 8:7-8
11:15 [x]Eze 4:2
11:16 [y]Da 8:4 [z]Jos 1:5; Da 8:7 [a]Da 8:9
11:17 [b]Ps 20:4
11:18 [c]Isa 66:19; Jer 25:22 [d]Hos 12:14
11:19 [e]Ps 27:2 [f]Ps 37:36; Eze 26:21
11:20 [g]Isa 60:17
11:21 [h]Da 4:17 [i]Da 8:25
11:22 [j]Da 8:10-11
11:23 [k]Da 8:25
11:24 [l]Ne 9:25
11:27 [m]Ps 64:6 [n]Ps 12:2; Jer 9:5 [o]Hab 2:3
11:30 [p]Ge 10:4
11:31 [q]Da 8:11-13; 9:27; Mt 24:15*; Mk 13:14*
11:32 [r]Mic 5:7-9
11:33 [s]Mal 2:7 [t]Mt 24:9; Jn 16:2; Heb 11:32-38
11:34 [u]Mt 7:15; Ro 16:18

[a]6 Or *child* (see Vulgate and Syriac) [b]17 Or *but she* [c]30 Hebrew *of Kittim*

so that they may be refined,[v] purified
and made spotless until the time of the
end, for it will still come at the appointed time.

The King Who Exalts Himself

36“The king will do as he pleases. He
will exalt and magnify himself above
every god and will say unheard-of
things[w] against the God of gods.[x] He
will be successful until the time of
wrath[y] is completed, for what has
been determined must take place. 37He
will show no regard for the gods of his
fathers or for the one desired by wom-
en, nor will he regard any god, but will
exalt himself above them all. 38Instead
of them, he will honor a god of fortresses; a god unknown to his fathers
he will honor with gold and silver, with
precious stones and costly gifts. 39He
will attack the mightiest fortresses with
the help of a foreign god and will greatly honor those who acknowledge him.
He will make them rulers over many
people and will distribute the land at a
price.[a]

40“At the time of the end the king of
the South[z] will engage him in battle,
and the king of the North will storm[a]
out against him with chariots and cavalry and a great fleet of ships. He will
invade many countries and sweep
through them like a flood.[b] 41He will
also invade the Beautiful Land. Many
countries will fall, but Edom,[c] Moab[d]
and the leaders of Ammon will be delivered from his hand. 42He will extend
his power over many countries; Egypt
will not escape. 43He will gain control
of the treasures of gold and silver and
all the riches of Egypt,[e] with the Libyans[f] and Nubians in submission.
44But reports from the east and the
north will alarm him, and he will set
out in a great rage to destroy and annihilate many. 45He will pitch his royal
tents between the seas at[b] the beautiful holy mountain. Yet he will come to
his end, and no one will help him.

The End Times

12 “At that time Michael,[g] the great
prince who protects your people,
will arise. There will be a time of
distress[h] such as has not happened
from the beginning of nations until
then. But at that time your people—
everyone whose name is found written
in the book[i]—will be delivered.[j]
2Multitudes who sleep in the dust of
the earth will awake: some to everlasting life, others to shame and everlasting contempt.[k] 3Those who are
wise[c][l] will shine[m] like the brightness
of the heavens, and those who lead
many to righteousness, like the stars
for ever and ever.[n] 4But you, Daniel,
close up and seal[o] the words of the
scroll until the time of the end.[p] Many
will go here and there to increase
knowledge.”

5Then I, Daniel, looked, and there
before me stood two others, one on
this bank of the river and one on the
opposite bank.[q] 6One of them said to
the man clothed in linen,[r] who was
above the waters of the river, “How
long will it be before these astonishing
things are fulfilled?”[s]

7The man clothed in linen, who was
above the waters of the river, lifted his
right hand and his left hand toward
heaven, and I heard him swear by him
who lives forever,[t] saying, “It will be
for a time, times and half a time.[d][u]
When the power of the holy people[v]
has been finally broken, all these things
will be completed.[w]”

8I heard, but I did not understand.
So I asked, “My lord, what will the outcome of all this be?”

9He replied, “Go your way, Daniel,
because the words are closed up and
sealed until the time of the end.[x]
10Many will be purified, made spotless
and refined,[y] but the wicked will continue to be wicked.[z] None of the wicked will understand, but those who are
wise will understand.[a]

11“From the time that the daily sacrifice is abolished and the abomination
that causes desolation[b] is set up, there
will be 1,290 days. 12Blessed is the one
who waits[c] for and reaches the end of
the 1,335 days.[d]

13“As for you, go your way till the
end. You will rest,[e] and then at the
end of the days you will rise to receive
your allotted inheritance.[f]”

11:35 [v]Ps 78:38; Da 12:10; Zec 13:9; Jn 15:2 **11:36** [w]Rev 13:5-6 [x]Dt 10:17; Isa 14:13-14; Da 7:25; 8:11-12,25; 2Th 2:4 [y]Isa 10:25; 26:20 **11:40** [z]Isa 21:1 [a]Isa 5:28 [b]Eze 38:4 **11:41** [c]Isa 11:14 [d]Jer 48:47 **11:43** [e]Eze 30:4 [f]2Ch 12:3; Na 3:9 **12:1** [g]Da 10:13 [h]Da 9:12; Mt 24:21; Mk 13:19; Rev 16:18 [i]Ex 32:32; Ps 56:8 [j]Jer 30:7 **12:2** [k]Isa 26:19; Mt 25:46; Jn 5:28-29 **12:3** [l]Da 11:33 [m]Mt 13:43; Jn 5:35 [n]1Co 15:42 **12:4** [o]Isa 8:16 [p]ver 9,13; Rev 22:10 **12:5** [q]Da 10:4 **12:6** [r]Eze 9:2 [s]Da 8:13 **12:7** [t]Rev 10:5-6 [u]Da 7:25 [v]Da 8:24 [w]Lk 21:24; Rev 10:7 **12:9** [x]ver 4 **12:10** [y]Da 11:35 [z]Isa 32:7; Rev 22:11 [a]Hos 14:9 **12:11** [b]Da 8:11; 9:27; Mt 24:15*; Mk 13:14* **12:12** [c]Isa 30:18 [d]Da 8:14 **12:13** [e]Isa 57:2 [f]Ps 16:5; Rev 14:13

[a]39 Or *land for a reward* [b]45 Or *the sea and* [c]3 Or *who impart wisdom* [d]7 Or *a year, two years and half a year*

HOSEA

AT A GLANCE

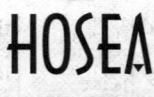

Key Principle: Even when we are faithless, God faithfully keeps his covenant with his people; he lovingly calls us to return to his care when we turn our backs on him.

Author: Hosea

Time and Place: ~753 B.C. to ~715 B.C. / Northern kingdom of Israel

Key Verses: 6:4–6; 11:7–9; 13:6; 14:1, 4

BENEFIT

The book of Hosea offers a profound illustration of God's love for us. This love is unconditional, but it is also marked by his holiness. Because of this, God seeks better things for us than the things we choose for ourselves. This book reminds us of our need to turn back to God, the Lover of our souls, whenever we have strayed from him.

SETTING

Hosea (whose name means "salvation") was a prophet to the northern kingdom of Israel (often called "Ephraim" after its largest tribe; 5:3–13) in the days of its last six kings. His ministry began near the end of the reign of Jeroboam II (793–753 B.C.) and continued beyond the reign of Israel's last king, Hoshea (732–722 B.C.). Hosea's lengthy time of service (from about 753 B.C. to about 715 B.C.) made him a contemporary of Isaiah and Micah, and a younger contemporary of Amos, who also prophesied to the northern kingdom.

In the days of Jeroboam II, Israel experienced a short-lived time of economic and political prosperity, but after this period it sunk into a decline from which it never recovered. None of the kings of Israel were godly men, and Israel's descent into idolatry and wickedness continued unabated until God used the Assyrians to sweep the nation away in 722 B.C.

TIME LINE 1300BC 1200 1100 1000 900 800 700 600 500 400

- **Division of the kingdom (930 B.C.)**
- **Ministries of Elijah and Elisha in Israel (c.875-797 B.C.)**
- **Amos's ministry in Israel (c.760-750 B.C.)**
- **Hosea's ministry in Israel (c.753-715 B.C.)**
- **Ministries of Micah and Isaiah in Judah (c.742-681 B.C.)**
- **Exile of Israel (722 B.C.)**
- **Book of Hosea written (c.715 B.C.)**
- **Fall of Jerusalem (586 B.C.)**

THEME AND PURPOSE

Hosea centers around the triple theme of sin in view of God's holiness, punishment in view of God's justice and restoration in view of God's loyal love. The adultery of Hosea's wife Gomer (1) led to her degradation (2), but Hosea's love led to her redemption (3). Similarly, the spiritual adultery of Yahweh's wife Israel (4—7) would lead her to the degradation of judgment (8—10), but God's love for Israel would lead to her future restoration (11—14). The lack of good kings in Israel, the pervasiveness of idolatry and injustice and the people's hardness of heart stand in radical contrast to God's holiness, justice and compassion.

UNIQUE CONTRIBUTION

In the English Bible, the five major prophets (Isaiah through Daniel) are followed by the 12 minor prophets (Hosea through Malachi). The minor prophets are designated as such because of their average size, and not because of their relative importance. In the Hebrew Bible, "The Twelve" were joined together to make a single scroll of 67 chapters, about equal in length to Isaiah.

More than any other prophet, Hosea's personal experiences communicated and illustrated his prophetic burden. While some critics regard his relationship to Gomer as fictional allegory, no internal evidence in the book supports this view. God instructed him to marry "an adulterous wife" (1:2; this does not necessarily mean that she was a harlot before he married her) as a visible analogy of God's relationship to Israel. A number of New Testament passages quote several of the key truths in Hosea.

LINKS TO THE NEW TESTAMENT

The way Hosea redeemed his wayward wife from slavery beautifully illustrates Christ's loving initiative and willingness to redeem us from our slavery to sin. Matthew 2:15 applies the prophecy in Hosea 11:1, "When Israel was a child, I loved him, and out of Egypt I called my son" to Christ's sojourn in Egypt. The parallel meaning includes both the people of Israel, whom God called out of slavery in Egypt, and Israel's Messiah, who as a child also returned to Israel from Egypt.

OVERVIEW

FOCUS	Illustration of God and Israel	Israel's Sin and God's Holiness	Israel's Suffering and God's Justice	Israel's Salvation and God's Love
REFERENCE	1 3	4 7	8 10	11 14
TOPICS	Sin, Judgment, and Restoration	Sin	Judgment	Restoration
	Faithless Wife and Forgiving Husband	Faithless Nation and Forgiving Lord		
	The Marriage of Hosea	The Message of Hosea		
	Narrative	Sermons		
LOCATION	Northern Kingdom in Israel			
TIME	About 45 Years of Prophetic Ministry			

Hosea's prophetic appeals are addressed to the northern kingdom of Israel in its last days. One observer summarized this book in these terms: "What we see in the prophecy of Hosea are the last few swirls as the kingdom of Israel goes down the drain." In spite of the Lord's loving appeals through his prophet, Israel steadfastly refused to listen to the last-hour warnings.

Hosea's personal affliction (1—3) illustrates Israel's coming national catastrophe (4—14). After bearing him three children, Gomer abandons Hosea and becomes an adulteress. When she is reduced to slavery, Hosea publicly redeems and restores her. In the same way, Israel has committed spiritual adultery through corruption, injustice and willful idolatry, and resolutely refuses to repent (4—7). Because of Israel's hardness of heart, it will be brought into a judgment of dispersion and destruction (8—10). God's holiness and justice requires him to discipline Israel, but because of his steadfast love and compassion, he will restore Israel in the future (11—14).

HOSEA

1 The word of the LORD that came to
Hosea son of Beeri during the reigns
of Uzziah, Jotham, Ahaz and Hezekiah,
kings of Judah,[a] and during the reign
of Jeroboam[b] son of Jehoash[a] king of
Israel:[c]

Hosea's Wife and Children

2When the LORD began to speak
through Hosea, the LORD said to him,
"Go, take to yourself an adulterous[d]
wife and children of unfaithfulness,
because the land is guilty of the
vilest adultery[e] in departing from the
LORD." 3So he married Gomer daughter
of Diblaim, and she conceived and
bore him a son.
4Then the LORD said to Hosea, "Call
him Jezreel,[f] because I will soon punish the house of Jehu for the massacre
at Jezreel, and I will put an end to the
kingdom of Israel. 5In that day I will
break Israel's bow in the Valley of Jezreel.[g]"
6Gomer[h] conceived again and gave
birth to a daughter. Then the LORD said
to Hosea, "Call her Lo-Ruhamah,[b] for
I will no longer show love to the house
of Israel,[i] that I should at all forgive
them. 7Yet I will show love to the house
of Judah; and I will save them—not by
bow,[j] sword or battle, or by horses
and horsemen, but by the LORD their
God.[k]"
8After she had weaned Lo-
Ruhamah, Gomer had another son.
9Then the LORD said, "Call him Lo-
Ammi,[c] for you are not my people,
and I am not your God.
10"Yet the Israelites will be like the
sand on the seashore, which cannot be
measured or counted.[l] In the place
where it was said to them, 'You are not
my people,' they will be called 'sons of
the living God.'[m] 11The people of Judah and the people of Israel will be
reunited,[n] and they will appoint one
leader[o] and will come up out of the
land,[p] for great will be the day of Jezreel.

2 "Say of your brothers, 'My people,'
and of your sisters, 'My loved one.'[q]

Israel Punished and Restored

2"Rebuke your mother,[r] rebuke
her,
for she is not my wife,
and I am not her husband.
Let her remove the adulterous[s]
look from her face
and the unfaithfulness from
between her breasts.
3Otherwise I will strip her naked
and make her as bare as on the
day she was born;[t]
I will make her like a desert,[u]
turn her into a parched land,
and slay her with thirst.
4I will not show my love to her
children,[v]
because they are the children of
adultery.
5Their mother has been unfaithful
and has conceived them in
disgrace.
She said, 'I will go after my
lovers,[w]
who give me my food and my
water,
my wool and my linen, my oil
and my drink.'[x]
6Therefore I will block her path with
thornbushes;
I will wall her in so that she
cannot find her way.[y]
7She will chase after her lovers but
not catch them;
she will look for them but not
find them.[z]
Then she will say,
'I will go back to my husband as
at first,[a]
for then I was better off[b] than
now.'
8She has not acknowledged[c] that I
was the one
who gave her the grain, the new
wine and oil,
who lavished on her the silver and
gold—
which they used for Baal.[d]
9"Therefore I will take away my
grain[e] when it ripens,
and my new wine[f] when it is
ready.
I will take back my wool and my
linen,
intended to cover her nakedness.
10So now I will expose her lewdness
before the eyes of her lovers;
no one will take her out of my
hands.[g]
11I will stop[h] all her celebrations:
her yearly festivals, her New
Moons,

1:1 [a]Isa 1:1; Mic 1:1 [b]2Ki 13:13 [c]Am 1:1
1:2 [d]Jer 3:1; Hos 2:2,5; 3:1 [e]Dt 31:16; Jer 3:14; Eze 23:3-21; Hos 5:3
1:4 [f]2Ki 10:1-14; Hos 2:22
1:5 [g]2Ki 15:29
1:6 [h]ver 3 [i]Hos 2:4
1:7 [j]Ps 44:6 [k]Zec 4:6
1:10 [l]Ge 22:17; Jer 33:22 [m]ver 9; Ro 9:26*
1:11 [n]Isa 11:12,13 [o]Jer 23:5-8 [p]Eze 37:15-28
2:1 [q]ver 23
2:2 [r]ver 5; Isa 50:1; Hos 1:2 [s]Eze 23:45
2:3 [t]Eze 16:4,22 [u]Isa 32:13-14
2:4 [v]Eze 8:18
2:5 [w]Jer 3:6 [x]Jer 44:17-18
2:6 [y]Job 3:23; 19:8; La 3:9
2:7 [z]Hos 5:13 [a]Jer 2:2; 3:1 [b]Eze 16:8
2:8 [c]Isa 1:3 [d]Eze 16:15-19; Hos 8:4
2:9 [e]Hos 8:7 [f]Hos 9:2
2:10 [g]Eze 16:37
2:11 [h]Jer 7:34

a *1* Hebrew *Joash,* a variant of *Jehoash*
b *6* *Lo-Ruhamah* means *not loved.*
c *9* *Lo-Ammi* means *not my people.*

her Sabbath days—all her
appointed feasts.[i]
12I will ruin her vines[j] and her fig
trees,
which she said were her pay
from her lovers;
I will make them a thicket,[k]
and wild animals will devour
them.[l]
13I will punish her for the days
she burned incense to the
Baals;[m]
she decked herself with rings and
jewelry,[n]
and went after her lovers,[o]
but me she forgot,[p]"
declares the LORD.

14"Therefore I am now going to
allure her;
I will lead her into the desert
and speak tenderly to her.
15There I will give her back her
vineyards,
and will make the Valley of
Achor[a][q] a door of hope.
There she will sing[b][r] as in the
days of her youth,[s]
as in the day she came up out of
Egypt.[t]

16"In that day," declares the LORD,
"you will call me 'my husband';
you will no longer call me 'my
master.[c]'
17I will remove the names of the
Baals from her lips;[u]
no longer will their names be
invoked.[v]
18In that day I will make a covenant
for them
with the beasts of the field and
the birds of the air
and the creatures that move
along the ground.[w]
Bow and sword and battle
I will abolish[x] from the land,
so that all may lie down in
safety.[y]
19I will betroth[z] you to me forever;
I will betroth you in[d]
righteousness and justice,[a]
in[e] love and compassion.
20I will betroth you in faithfulness,
and you will acknowledge[b] the
LORD.

21"In that day I will respond,"
declares the LORD—
"I will respond[c] to the skies,
and they will respond to the
earth;
22and the earth will respond to the
grain,
the new wine and oil,[d]
and they will respond to
Jezreel.[f]

2:11 [i]Isa 1:14; Jer 16:9; Hos 3:4; Am 8:10
2:12 [j]Isa 7:23; Jer 8:13 [k]Isa 5:6 [l]Hos 13:8
2:13 [m]Hos 11:2 [n]Eze 16:17 [o]Hos 4:13 [p]Hos 4:6; 8:14; 13:6
2:15 [q]Jos 7:24,26 [r]Ex 15:1-18 [s]Jer 2:2 [t]Hos 12:9
2:17 [u]Ex 23:13; Ps 16:4 [v]Jos 23:7
2:18 [w]Job 5:22 [x]Isa 2:4 [y]Jer 23:6; Eze 34:25
2:19 [z]Isa 62:4 [a]Isa 1:27
2:20 [b]Jer 31:34; Hos 6:6; 13:4
2:21 [c]Isa 55:10; Zec 8:12
2:22 [d]Jer 31:12; Joel 2:19
2:23 [e]Jer 31:27 [f]Hos 1:6 [g]Hos 1:10 [h]Ro 9:25*; 1Pe 2:10
3:1 [i]Hos 1:2 [j]2Sa 6:19
3:4 [k]Hos 13:11 [l]Da 11:31; Hos 2:11 [m]Jdg 17:5-6; Zec 10:2
3:5 [n]Eze 34:23-24 [o]Jer 50:4-5
4:1 [p]Jer 7:28
4:2 [q]Hos 7:3; 10:4 [r]Hos 6:9 [s]Hos 7:1
4:3 [t]Jer 4:28 [u]Isa 33:9

23I will plant[e] her for myself in the
land;
I will show my love to the one I
called 'Not my loved
one.[g][f]'
I will say to those called 'Not my
people,[h]' 'You are my
people';[g]
and they will say, 'You are my
God.[h]'"

Hosea's Reconciliation With His Wife

3 The LORD said to me, "Go, show your
love to your wife again, though she
is loved by another and is an adulteress.[i] Love her as the LORD loves
the Israelites, though they turn to other gods and love the sacred raisin
cakes.[j]"
2So I bought her for fifteen shekels[i]
of silver and about a homer and a
lethek[j] of barley. 3Then I told her,
"You are to live with[k] me many days;
you must not be a prostitute or be intimate with any man, and I will live
with[k] you."
4For the Israelites will live many
days without king or prince,[k] without
sacrifice[l] or sacred stones, without
ephod or idol.[m] 5Afterward the Israelites will return and seek the LORD their
God and David their king.[n] They will
come trembling to the LORD and to his
blessings in the last days.[o]

The Charge Against Israel

4 Hear the word of the LORD, you
Israelites,
because the LORD has a charge to
bring
against you who live in the land:
"There is no faithfulness, no love,
no acknowledgment[p] of God in
the land.
2There is only cursing,[l] lying[q] and
murder,[r]
stealing[s] and adultery;
they break all bounds,
and bloodshed follows
bloodshed.
3Because of this the land
mourns,[m][t]
and all who live in it waste
away;[u]

[a]15 *Achor* means *trouble.* [b]15 Or *respond* [c]16 Hebrew *baal* [d]19 Or *with*; also in verse 20 [e]19 Or *with* [f]22 *Jezreel* means *God plants.* [g]23 Hebrew *Lo-Ruhamah* [h]23 Hebrew *Lo-Ammi* [i]2 That is, about 6 ounces (about 170 grams) [j]2 That is, probably about 10 bushels (about 330 liters) [k]3 Or *wait for* [l]2 That is, to pronounce a curse upon [m]3 Or *dries up*

HOSEA

A Man of Love and Loyalty

Few things hurt more deeply than a spouse's infidelity. The sense of loss and failure and the violation of intimacy can be overwhelming. Such must have been the case with Hosea, a prophet whom God called to demonstrate, through his own life, God's love for his unfaithful people Israel. Even though Hosea's wife had sunk to this extreme level of unfaithfulness, God asked Hosea to demonstrate a higher quality of love, the same love he had shown to Israel—and has shown to us—over and over again.

God called Hosea to deliver this challenge of love and loyalty to the people of Israel. In God's eyes the Israelites had committed "spiritual adultery." God called upon Hosea to tell his people how it feels to be betrayed in this way, and to remind them of the divine love that was still available for the asking. And no one knew better than Hosea the hurt and betrayal that God felt in the face of Israel's unfaithfulness.

Love Isn't Always Easy

God had chosen Israel to be his own people, but they had rejected his love and worshiped false gods. God had also blessed the Israelites with many children and material things, yet they turned from him and committed horrible sins of immorality. In spite of their unfaithfulness, God still loved them and repeatedly told them so. He promised that if the people of Israel would reject their false "lovers" and return to God, he would welcome them back and love them even more.

Hosea had "married Gomer, daughter of Diblaim" (Hosea 1:3). She bore him three children—two sons and a daughter. But, as a prophet, Hosea knew even before their wedding day that Gomer would be unfaithful, just as God knew the Israelites would be unfaithful to him when he claimed them as his chosen people centuries before.

Gomer did indeed commit adultery. Yet God told Hosea to redeem her, bring her back and reassure her of his devoted love (3:1). Hosea's words ring with the intensity of one who knows what it feels like to have an unfaithful spouse. His personal experiences eloquently communicated to the Israelites an undying love—a godly love—that was available for the Israelites if they would turn back to God.

A Parable with a Punch

This, of course, was an unusual situation. God does not ordinarily ask us to enter a marriage that we know is heading for disaster. However, he does ask us to love our enemies and forgive those who sin against us (Matthew 5:44; 6:14). And God willingly forgives us for our sins of infidelity against him.

In a remarkable display of obedience to God and loyal love for Gomer, Hosea rescued his wife from a life of degradation. He went searching for her and then literally had to buy her back from this sinful lifestyle (Hosea 3:2).

According to the law of Moses an unfaithful wife was to be killed, stoned by her family and neighbors. When Hosea offered Gomer forgiveness and loyal love rather than the punishment the law allowed, those in Israel who heard about it sat up and took notice. Hosea's example helped them understand more fully God's grace in forgiving them for their spiritual adultery. They deserved judgment too, but God was offering love.

The Quality of Your Love

Are you like Hosea when it comes to love? How do you respond when someone you love turns away from you, deserts you or repeatedly tries your patience? When your devotion is pushed to the limit in a severe test like Hosea's, what happens to the endurance and quality of your love? Can you pass the loyal love test?

Hosea showed a degree of loyal love that can only come from God. The Bible says love is an aspect of the fruit of the Holy Spirit in our lives (Galatians 5:22). The apostle Paul reminds us that love "keeps no record of wrongs" and that "love never fails" (1 Corinthians 13:5, 8). Does your love measure up to those standards?

It's not easy to love that way—in fact, it's impossible to love that way in our own strength. But as we submit our wills to the power of the Holy Spirit and allow his love to work in our lives, we can follow Hosea's example. We can model God's love by loving others with a depth and a loyalty that will make the world around us sit up, take notice and give glory to God. —*Dr. Gene Getz*

the beasts of the field and the birds
of the air
and the fish of the sea are
dying.[v]

4"But let no man bring a charge,
let no man accuse another,
for your people are like those
who bring charges against a
priest.[w]
5You stumble[x] day and night,
and the prophets stumble with
you.
So I will destroy your mother[y]—
6 my people are destroyed from
lack of knowledge.[z]

"Because you have rejected
knowledge,
I also reject you as my priests;
because you have ignored the
law[a] of your God,
I also will ignore your children.
7The more the priests increased,
the more they sinned against
me;
they exchanged[a] their[b] Glory[b]
for something disgraceful.[c]
8They feed on the sins of my people
and relish their wickedness.[d]
9And it will be: Like people, like
priests.[e]
I will punish both of them for
their ways
and repay them for their
deeds.[f]

10"They will eat but not have
enough;[g]
they will engage in prostitution
but not increase,
because they have deserted[h] the
LORD
to give themselves 11to
prostitution,[i]
to old wine and new,
which take away the
understanding[j] 12of my
people.
They consult a wooden idol[k]
and are answered by a stick of
wood.[l]
A spirit of prostitution leads them
astray;[m]
they are unfaithful to their God.
13They sacrifice on the mountaintops
and burn offerings on the hills,
under oak,[n] poplar and terebinth,
where the shade is pleasant.[o]
Therefore your daughters turn to
prostitution[p]
and your daughters-in-law to
adultery.[q]

14"I will not punish your daughters
when they turn to prostitution,
nor your daughters-in-law
when they commit adultery,
because the men themselves
consort with harlots[r]
and sacrifice with shrine
prostitutes—
a people without understanding
will come to ruin!

15"Though you commit adultery,
O Israel,
let not Judah become guilty.

"Do not go to Gilgal;[s]
do not go up to Beth Aven.[c]
And do not swear, 'As surely as
the LORD lives!'
16The Israelites are stubborn,
like a stubborn heifer.

4:3 [v]Jer 4:25; Zep 1:3
4:4 [w]Dt 17:12; Eze 3:26
4:5 [x]Eze 14:7 [y]Hos 2:2
4:6 [z]Hos 2:13; Mal 2:7-8 [a]Hos 8:1,12
4:7 [b]Hab 2:16 [c]Hos 10:1,6; 13:6
4:8 [d]Isa 56:11; Mic 3:11
4:9 [e]Isa 24:2 [f]Jer 5:31; Hos 8:13; 9:9, 15
4:10 [g]Lev 26:26; Mic 6:14 [h]Hos 7:14; 9:17
4:11 [i]Hos 5:4 [j]Pr 20:1
4:12 [k]Jer 2:27 [l]Hab 2:19 [m]Isa 44:20
4:13 [n]Isa 1:29 [o]Jer 3:6; Hos 11:2 [p]Jer 2:20; Am 7:17 [q]Hos 2:13
4:14 [r]ver 11
4:15 [s]Hos 9:15; 12:11; Am 4:4

[a]*7* Syriac and an ancient Hebrew scribal tradition; Masoretic Text *I will exchange*
[b]*7* Masoretic Text; an ancient Hebrew scribal tradition *my*
[c]*15 Beth Aven* means *house of wickedness* (a name for Bethel, which means *house of God*).

4:4-6

PROMISE 4

THE MORAL COMPASS

What was Israel's basic problem? What allowed her to play the role of the wife-become-prostitute that chapters 1–3 describe? The simple explanation in verse 6 is, "My people are destroyed from lack of knowledge." Israel's priests were responsible to teach and model God's truth to the people (Deuteronomy 31:9–13). They not only failed to teach the law, they also failed to follow it themselves. The teachers were so corrupt they couldn't teach others or rebuke the people when they engaged in godless activity (4:1–5). The people had no knowledge because the moral teachers had eliminated themselves from the role by their own immorality. These leaders had lost their sense of direction; their corrupted moral compasses had turned them from God's way.

Our families need men whose moral compasses are in line and who live and teach God's truth. Our churches, our businesses, our society needs men who can speak powerfully as moral models. God called every Christian a priest (1 Peter 2:5), every father a teacher (Ephesians 6:1, 4), every spiritual man a restorer of the fallen saint (Galatians 6:1) and every believer a discipler (Matthew 28:18–20).

Each generation needs godly men who sense God's call to be teachers. Never let it be said of your sphere of influence that "people are destroyed from lack of knowledge." And never let it be said of you that you couldn't teach others because your lifestyle annulled your message.

For the next Promise 4 reading go to page 961.

How then can the LORD pasture
them
like lambs[t] in a meadow?
17 Ephraim is joined to idols;
leave him alone!
18 Even when their drinks are gone,
they continue their prostitution;
their rulers dearly love shameful
ways.
19 A whirlwind[u] will sweep them
away,
and their sacrifices will bring
them shame.[v]

Judgment Against Israel

5 "Hear this, you priests!
Pay attention, you Israelites!
Listen, O royal house!
This judgment is against you:
You have been a snare[w] at
Mizpah,
a net spread out on Tabor.
2 The rebels are deep in slaughter.[x]
I will discipline all of them.[y]
3 I know all about Ephraim;
Israel is not hidden from me.
Ephraim, you have now turned to
prostitution;
Israel is corrupt.[z]

4 "Their deeds do not permit them
to return to their God.
A spirit of prostitution[a] is in their
heart;
they do not acknowledge[b] the
LORD.
5 Israel's arrogance testifies[c] against
them;
the Israelites, even Ephraim,
stumble in their sin;
Judah also stumbles with them.
6 When they go with their flocks and
herds
to seek the LORD,[d]
they will not find him;
he has withdrawn[e] himself from
them.
7 They are unfaithful[f] to the LORD;
they give birth to illegitimate[g]
children.
Now their New Moon festivals
will devour[h] them and their
fields.

8 "Sound the trumpet in Gibeah,[i]
the horn in Ramah.[j]
Raise the battle cry in Beth
Aven[a];[k]
lead on, O Benjamin.
9 Ephraim will be laid waste
on the day of reckoning.[l]
Among the tribes of Israel
I proclaim what is certain.[m]
10 Judah's leaders are like those
who move boundary stones.[n]
I will pour out my wrath[o] on them
like a flood of water.
11 Ephraim is oppressed,
trampled in judgment,
intent on pursuing idols.[b][p]
12 I am like a moth[q] to Ephraim,
like rot to the people of Judah.

13 "When Ephraim saw his sickness,
and Judah his sores,
then Ephraim turned to Assyria,[r]
and sent to the great king for
help.[s]
But he is not able to cure[t] you,
not able to heal your sores.[u]
14 For I will be like a lion[v] to
Ephraim,
like a great lion to Judah.
I will tear them to pieces and go
away;
I will carry them off, with no one
to rescue them.[w]
15 Then I will go back to my place
until they admit their guilt.
And they will seek my face;[x]
in their misery[y] they will
earnestly seek me.[z]"

Israel Unrepentant

6 "Come, let us return to the LORD.
He has torn us to pieces[a]
but he will heal us;
he has injured us
but he will bind up our
wounds.[b]
2 After two days he will revive us;[c]
on the third day he will restore
us,
that we may live in his presence.
3 Let us acknowledge the LORD;
let us press on to acknowledge
him.
As surely as the sun rises,
he will appear;
he will come to us like the winter
rains,[d]
like the spring rains that water
the earth.[e]"

4 "What can I do with you,
Ephraim?[f]
What can I do with you, Judah?
Your love is like the morning mist,
like the early dew that
disappears.[g]
5 Therefore I cut you in pieces with
my prophets,
I killed you with the words of my
mouth;[h]
my judgments flashed like
lightning upon you.[i]
6 For I desire mercy, not sacrifice,[j]

4:16 [t]Isa 5:17; 7:25 **4:19** [u]Hos 12:1; 13:15 [v]Isa 1:29 **5:1** [w]Hos 6:9; 9:8 **5:2** [x]Hos 4:2 [y]Hos 9:15 **5:3** [z]Hos 6:10 **5:4** [a]Hos 4:11 [b]Hos 4:6 **5:5** [c]Hos 7:10 **5:6** [d]Mic 6:6-7 [e]Pr 1:28; Isa 1:15; Eze 8:6 **5:7** [f]Hos 6:7 [g]Hos 2:4 [h]Hos 2:11-12 **5:8** [i]Hos 9:9; 10:9 [j]Isa 10:29 [k]Hos 4:15 **5:9** [l]Isa 37:3; Hos 9:11-17 [m]Isa 46:10; Zec 1:6 **5:10** [n]Dt 19:14 [o]Eze 7:8 **5:11** [p]Hos 9:16; Mic 6:16 **5:12** [q]Isa 51:8 **5:13** [r]Hos 7:11; 8:9 [s]Hos 10:6 [t]Hos 14:3 [u]Jer 30:12 **5:14** [v]Am 3:4 [w]Mic 5:8 **5:15** [x]Hos 3:5 [y]Jer 2:27 [z]Isa 64:9 **6:1** [a]Hos 5:14 [b]Dt 32:39; Jer 30:17; Hos 14:4 **6:2** [c]Ps 30:5 **6:3** [d]Joel 2:23 [e]Ps 72:6 **6:4** [f]Hos 11:8 [g]Hos 7:1; 13:3 **6:5** [h]Jer 1:9-10; 23:29 [i]Heb 4:12 **6:6** [j]Isa 1:11; Mt 9:13*; 12:7*

a *8 Beth Aven* means *house of wickedness* (a name for Bethel, which means *house of God*).
b *11* The meaning of the Hebrew for this word is uncertain.

and acknowledgment[k] of God
rather than burnt offerings.
7 Like Adam,[a] they have broken the
covenant[l]—
they were unfaithful[m] to me
there.
8 Gilead is a city of wicked men,
stained with footprints of blood.
9 As marauders lie in ambush for a
man,
so do bands of priests;
they murder on the road to
Shechem,
committing shameful crimes.[n]
10 I have seen a horrible[o] thing
in the house of Israel.
There Ephraim is given to
prostitution
and Israel is defiled.[p]

11 "Also for you, Judah,
a harvest[q] is appointed.

"Whenever I would restore the
fortunes of my people,
7 1 whenever I would heal Israel,
the sins of Ephraim are exposed
and the crimes of Samaria
revealed.[r]
They practice deceit,[s]
thieves break into houses,[t]
bandits rob in the streets;
2 but they do not realize
that I remember[u] all their evil
deeds.
Their sins engulf them;[v]
they are always before me.

3 "They delight the king with their
wickedness,
the princes with their lies.[w]
4 They are all adulterers,[x]
burning like an oven
whose fire the baker need not stir
from the kneading of the dough
till it rises.
5 On the day of the festival of our
king
the princes become inflamed
with wine,[y]
and he joins hands with the
mockers.
6 Their hearts are like an oven;[z]
they approach him with intrigue.
Their passion smolders all night;
in the morning it blazes like a
flaming fire.
7 All of them are hot as an oven;
they devour their rulers.
All their kings fall,
and none of them calls[a] on me.

8 "Ephraim mixes[b] with the nations;
Ephraim is a flat cake not turned
over.
9 Foreigners sap his strength,[c]
but he does not realize it.
His hair is sprinkled with gray,
but he does not notice.
10 Israel's arrogance testifies against
him,[d]
but despite all this
he does not return to the LORD his
God
or search[e] for him.

11 "Ephraim is like a dove,[f]
easily deceived and senseless—
now calling to Egypt,
now turning to Assyria.[g]
12 When they go, I will throw my
net[h] over them;
I will pull them down like birds
of the air.
When I hear them flocking
together,
I will catch them.
13 Woe[i] to them,
because they have strayed[j]
from me!
Destruction to them,
because they have rebelled
against me!
I long to redeem them
but they speak lies against me.[k]
14 They do not cry out to me from
their hearts[l]
but wail upon their beds.
They gather together[b] for grain
and new wine[m]
but turn away from me.[n]
15 I trained them and strengthened
them,
but they plot evil[o] against me.
16 They do not turn to the Most High;
they are like a faulty bow.[p]
Their leaders will fall by the sword
because of their insolent words.
For this they will be ridiculed[q]
in the land of Egypt.[r]

Israel to Reap the Whirlwind

8 "Put the trumpet to your lips!
An eagle[s] is over the house of
the LORD
because the people have broken
my covenant
and rebelled against my law.[t]
2 Israel cries out to me,
'O our God, we acknowledge
you!'
3 But Israel has rejected what is
good;
an enemy will pursue him.
4 They set up kings without my
consent;
they choose princes without my
approval.[u]
With their silver and gold
they make idols[v] for themselves

6:6 [k]Hos 2:20 **6:7** [l]Hos 8:1 [m]Hos 5:7 **6:9** [n]Jer 7:9-10; Eze 22:9; Hos 7:1 **6:10** [o]Jer 5:30 [p]Hos 5:3 **6:11** [q]Jer 51:33; Joel 3:13 **7:1** [r]Hos 6:4 [s]ver 13 [t]Hos 4:2 **7:2** [u]Jer 14:10; Hos 8:13 [v]Jer 2:19 **7:3** [w]Hos 4:2; Mic 7:3 **7:4** [x]Jer 9:2 **7:5** [y]Isa 28:1,7 **7:6** [z]Ps 21:9 **7:7** [a]ver 16 **7:8** [b]ver 11; Ps 106:35; Hos 5:13 **7:9** [c]Isa 1:7; Hos 8:7 **7:10** [d]Hos 5:5 [e]Isa 9:13 **7:11** [f]Hos 11:11 [g]Hos 5:13; 12:1 **7:12** [h]Eze 12:13 **7:13** [i]Hos 9:12 [j]Jer 14:10; Eze 34:4-6; Hos 9:17 [k]ver 1; Mt 23:37 **7:14** [l]Jer 3:10 [m]Am 2:8 [n]Hos 13:16 **7:15** [o]Na 1:9,11 **7:16** [p]Ps 78:9,57 [q]Eze 23:32 [r]Hos 9:3 **8:1** [s]Dt 28:49; Jer 4:13 [t]Hos 4:6; 6:7 **8:4** [u]Hos 13:10 [v]Hos 2:8

[a] 7 Or *As at Adam*; or *Like men* [b] 14 Most Hebrew manuscripts; some Hebrew manuscripts and Septuagint *They slash themselves*

to their own destruction.
5Throw out your calf-idol,
O Samaria![w]
My anger burns against them.
How long will they be incapable of
purity?[x]
6 They are from Israel!
This calf—a craftsman has made it;
it is not God.
It will be broken in pieces,
that calf of Samaria.

7"They sow the wind
and reap the whirlwind.[y]
The stalk has no head;
it will produce no flour.
Were it to yield grain,
foreigners would swallow it up.[z]
8Israel is swallowed up;[a]
now she is among the nations
like a worthless[b] thing.
9For they have gone up to Assyria
like a wild donkey wandering
alone.
Ephraim has sold herself to
lovers.
10Although they have sold themselves
among the nations,
I will now gather them
together.[c]
They will begin to waste away[d]
under the oppression of the
mighty king.

11"Though Ephraim built many altars
for sin offerings,
these have become altars for
sinning.[e]
12I wrote for them the many things
of my law,
but they regarded them as
something alien.
13They offer sacrifices given to me
and they eat[f] the meat,
but the LORD is not pleased with
them.
Now he will remember[g] their
wickedness
and punish their sins:[h]
They will return to Egypt.[i]
14Israel has forgotten[j] his Maker
and built palaces;
Judah has fortified many towns.
But I will send fire upon their cities
that will consume their
fortresses."[k]

Punishment for Israel

9 Do not rejoice, O Israel;
do not be jubilant[l] like the
other nations.
For you have been unfaithful[m] to
your God;
you love the wages of a
prostitute
at every threshing floor.

8:5 [w]Hos 10:5 [x]Jer 13:27
8:7 [y]Pr 22:8; Isa 66:15; Hos 10:12-13; Na 1:3 [z]Hos 2:9
8:8 [a]Jer 51:34 [b]Jer 22:28
8:10 [c]Eze 16:37; 22:20 [d]Jer 42:2
8:11 [e]Hos 10:1; 12:11
8:13 [f]Jer 7:21 [g]Hos 7:2 [h]Hos 4:9 [i]Hos 9:3,6
8:14 [j]Dt 32:18; Hos 2:13 [k]Jer 17:27
9:1 [l]Isa 22:12-13 [m]Hos 10:5

9:2 [n]Hos 2:9
9:3 [o]Lev 25:23 [p]Hos 8:13 [q]Eze 4:13; Hos 7:11
9:4 [r]Jer 6:20; Hos 8:13 [s]Hag 2:13-14
9:5 [t]Isa 10:3; Jer 5:31 [u]Hos 2:11
9:6 [v]Isa 19:13 [w]Isa 5:6; Hos 10:8
9:7 [x]Isa 34:8; Jer 10:15; Mic 7:4 [y]Jer 16:18 [z]Isa 44:25; La 2:14; Eze 14:9-10

2Threshing floors and winepresses
will not feed the people;
the new wine[n] will fail them.
3They will not remain[o] in the
LORD's land;
Ephraim will return to Egypt[p]
and eat unclean[a] food in
Assyria.[q]
4They will not pour out wine
offerings to the LORD,
nor will their sacrifices please[r]
him.
Such sacrifices will be to them like
the bread of mourners;
all who eat them will be
unclean.[s]
This food will be for themselves;
it will not come into the temple
of the LORD.

5What will you do[t] on the day of
your appointed feasts,[u]
on the festival days of the LORD?
6Even if they escape from
destruction,
Egypt will gather them,
and Memphis[v] will bury them.
Their treasures of silver will be
taken over by briers,
and thorns[w] will overrun their
tents.
7The days of punishment[x] are
coming,
the days of reckoning are at
hand.
Let Israel know this.
Because your sins[y] are so many
and your hostility so great,
the prophet is considered a fool,[z]
the inspired man a maniac.

a *3* That is, ceremonially unclean

8:14

PROMISE 1

FORGETTING GOD

"Israel has forgotten his Maker." Could there be any worse indictment on a nation—or on a person? Notice what happened when God's people forgot him. Israel "built palaces" and Judah "fortified many towns." Both nations spent their resources trying to artificially create what God had long ago promised to supply. Instead of trusting God, Israel chose to trust what it could build on its own—an exercise in futility if ever there was one.

Imagine how much we can accomplish if we trust God for what he has promised and spend our time and energy doing what he has given us to do! As we work and save and build and invest for our future and for our family, we must never "forget our Maker" in the process.

For the next Promise 1 reading go to page 963.

8The prophet, along with my God,
is the watchman over Ephraim,[a]
yet snares[a] await him on all his paths,
and hostility in the house of his God.
9They have sunk deep into corruption,
as in the days of Gibeah.[b]
God will remember[c] their wickedness
and punish them for their sins.

10"When I found Israel,
it was like finding grapes in the desert;
when I saw your fathers,
it was like seeing the early fruit on the fig tree.
But when they came to Baal Peor,[d]
they consecrated themselves to that shameful idol[e]
and became as vile as the thing they loved.
11Ephraim's glory will fly away like a bird[f]—
no birth, no pregnancy, no conception.[g]
12Even if they rear children,
I will bereave them of every one.
Woe[h] to them
when I turn away from them![i]
13I have seen Ephraim, like Tyre,
planted in a pleasant place.[j]
But Ephraim will bring out
their children to the slayer."

14Give them, O LORD—
what will you give them?
Give them wombs that miscarry
and breasts that are dry.[k]

15"Because of all their wickedness in Gilgal,[l]
I hated them there.
Because of their sinful deeds,[m]
I will drive them out of my house.
I will no longer love them;
all their leaders are rebellious.[n]
16Ephraim[o] is blighted,
their root is withered,
they yield no fruit.[p]
Even if they bear children,
I will slay[q] their cherished offspring."
17My God will reject them
because they have not obeyed[r] him;
they will be wanderers among the nations.[s]

10 Israel was a spreading vine;[t]
he brought forth fruit for himself.
As his fruit increased,
he built more altars;[u]
as his land prospered,
he adorned his sacred stones.[v]
2Their heart is deceitful,[w]
and now they must bear their guilt.[x]
The LORD will demolish their altars[y]
and destroy their sacred stones.[z]

3Then they will say, "We have no king
because we did not revere the LORD.
But even if we had a king,
what could he do for us?"
4They make many promises,
take false oaths[a]
and make agreements;[b]
therefore lawsuits spring up
like poisonous weeds in a plowed field.
5The people who live in Samaria fear
for the calf-idol of Beth Aven.[b][c]
Its people will mourn over it,
and so will its idolatrous priests,[d]
those who had rejoiced over its splendor,
because it is taken from them into exile.[e]
6It will be carried to Assyria[f]
as tribute for the great king.[g]
Ephraim will be disgraced;[h]
Israel will be ashamed of its wooden idols.[c]
7Samaria and its king will float away[i]
like a twig on the surface of the waters.
8The high places of wickedness[d][j]
will be destroyed—
it is the sin of Israel.
Thorns[k] and thistles will grow up
and cover their altars.[l]
Then they will say to the mountains, "Cover us!"
and to the hills, "Fall on us!"[m]

9"Since the days of Gibeah,[n] you have sinned, O Israel,
and there you have remained.[e]
Did not war overtake
the evildoers in Gibeah?
10When I please, I will punish[o] them;
nations will be gathered against them

9:8 [a]Hos 5:1 **9:9** [b]Jdg 19:16-30; Hos 5:8; 10:9 [c]Hos 8:13 **9:10** [d]Nu 25:1-5; Ps 106:28-29 [e]Jer 11:13; Hos 4:14 **9:11** [f]Hos 4:7; 10:5 [g]ver 14 **9:12** [h]Hos 7:13 [i]Dt 31:17 **9:13** [j]Eze 27:3 **9:14** [k]ver 11; Lk 23:29 **9:15** [l]Hos 4:15 [m]Hos 7:2 [n]Isa 1:23; Hos 4:9; 5:2 **9:16** [o]Hos 5:11 [p]Hos 8:7 [q]ver 12 **9:17** [r]Hos 4:10 [s]Dt 28:65; Hos 7:13 **10:1** [t]Eze 15:2 [u]1Ki 14:23 [v]Hos 8:11; 12:11 **10:2** [w]1Ki 18:21 [x]Hos 13:16 [y]ver 8 [z]Mic 5:13 **10:4** [a]Hos 4:2 [b]Eze 17:19; Am 5:7 **10:5** [c]Hos 5:8 [d]2Ki 23:5 [e]Hos 8:5; 9:1, 3,11 **10:6** [f]Hos 11:5 [g]Hos 5:13 [h]Isa 30:3; Hos 4:7 **10:7** [i]Hos 13:11 **10:8** [j]1Ki 12:28-30; Hos 4:13 [k]Hos 9:6 [l]ver 2; Isa 32:13 [m]Lk 23:30*; Rev 6:16 **10:9** [n]Hos 5:8 **10:10** [o]Eze 5:13; Hos 4:9

[a]8 Or *The prophet is the watchman over Ephraim, / the people of my God* [b]5 *Beth Aven* means *house of wickedness* (a name for Bethel, which means *house of God*). [c]6 Or *its counsel* [d]8 Hebrew *aven,* a reference to Beth Aven (a derogatory name for Bethel) [e]9 Or *there a stand was taken*

to put them in bonds for their
double sin.
11Ephraim is a trained heifer
that loves to thresh;
so I will put a yoke
on her fair neck.
I will drive Ephraim,
Judah must plow,
and Jacob must break up the
ground.
12Sow for yourselves righteousness,[p]
reap the fruit of unfailing love,
and break up your unplowed
ground;[q]
for it is time to seek[r] the LORD,
until he comes
and showers righteousness[s] on
you.
13But you have planted wickedness,
you have reaped evil,[t]
you have eaten the fruit of
deception.
Because you have depended on
your own strength
and on your many warriors,[u]
14the roar of battle will rise against
your people,
so that all your fortresses will be
devastated[v]—
as Shalman devastated Beth Arbel
on the day of battle,
when mothers were dashed to
the ground with their
children.[w]
15Thus will it happen to you,
O Bethel,
because your wickedness is
great.
When that day dawns,
the king of Israel will be
completely destroyed.[x]

God's Love for Israel

11 "When Israel was a child, I loved
him,
and out of Egypt I called my
son.[y]
2But the more I[a] called Israel,
the further they went from me.[b]
They sacrificed to the Baals[z]
and they burned incense to
images.[a]
3It was I who taught Ephraim to
walk,
taking them by the arms;[b]
but they did not realize
it was I who healed[c] them.
4I led them with cords of human
kindness,
with ties of love;[d]
I lifted the yoke[e] from their neck
and bent down to feed[f] them.

5"Will they not return to Egypt[g]
and will not Assyria[h] rule over
them
because they refuse to repent?
6Swords[i] will flash in their cities,
will destroy the bars of their
gates
and put an end to their plans.
7My people are determined to turn
from me.[j]
Even if they call to the Most
High,
he will by no means exalt them.

8"How can I give you up,
Ephraim?[k]
How can I hand you over, Israel?
How can I treat you like Admah?
How can I make you like
Zeboiim?[l]
My heart is changed within me;
all my compassion is aroused.
9I will not carry out my fierce
anger,[m]
nor will I turn and devastate[n]
Ephraim.
For I am God, and not man[o]—
the Holy One among you.
I will not come in wrath.[c]
10They will follow the LORD;
he will roar like a lion.
When he roars,
his children will come trembling
from the west.[p]
11They will come trembling
like birds from Egypt,
like doves from Assyria.[q]
I will settle them in their homes,"[r]
declares the LORD.

Israel's Sin

12Ephraim has surrounded me with
lies,[s]

10:12 [p]Pr 11:18 [q]Jer 4:3 [r]Hos 12:6 [s]Isa 45:8
10:13 [t]Job 4:8; Hos 7:3; 11:12; Gal 6:7-8 [u]Ps 33:16
10:14 [v]Isa 17:3 [w]Hos 13:16
10:15 [x]ver 7
11:1 [y]Ex 4:22; Hos 12:9,13; 13:4; Mt 2:15*
11:2 [z]Hos 2:13 [a]2Ki 17:15; Isa 65:7; Jer 18:15
11:3 [b]Dt 1:31; Hos 7:15 [c]Jer 30:17
11:4 [d]Jer 31:2-3 [e]Lev 26:13 [f]Ex 16:32; Ps 78:25
11:5 [g]Hos 7:16 [h]Hos 10:6
11:6 [i]Hos 13:16
11:7 [j]Jer 3:6-7; 8:5
11:8 [k]Hos 6:4 [l]Ge 14:8
11:9 [m]Dt 13:17; Jer 30:11 [n]Mal 3:6 [o]Nu 23:19
11:10 [p]Hos 6:1-3
11:11 [q]Isa 11:11 [r]Eze 28:26
11:12 [s]Hos 4:2

[a]*2* Some Septuagint manuscripts; Hebrew *they*
[b]*2* Septuagint; Hebrew *them*
[c]*9* Or *come against any city*

11:1-4

PE

GOD'S TOUGH LOVE

Prophets call people to God. They warn and they rebuke. They threaten with judgment and proclaim God's anger at sin. Why? What is God's basic motivation for such a message? This passage reminds us that God loves his people. He knows the destructive power of sin and stops at nothing to protect people from its consequences.

Heed God's warnings and believe his threats, but never lose sight of his motives. "I led them with cords of human kindness, with ties of love" (v. 4). The story of Hosea is, at its most basic level, a story of love's great strength.

the house of Israel with deceit.
And Judah is unruly against God,
even against the faithful Holy One.

12 [1]Ephraim feeds on the wind;[t]
he pursues the east wind all day
and multiplies lies and violence.
He makes a treaty with Assyria
and sends olive oil to Egypt.[u]
[2]The LORD has a charge[v] to bring against Judah;
he will punish Jacob[a] according to his ways
and repay him according to his deeds.[w]
[3]In the womb he grasped his brother's heel;[x]
as a man he struggled[y] with God.
[4]He struggled with the angel and overcame him;
he wept and begged for his favor.
He found him at Bethel[z]
and talked with him there—
[5]the LORD God Almighty,
the LORD is his name[a] of renown!
[6]But you must return to your God;
maintain love and justice,[b]
and wait for your God always.[c]

[7]The merchant uses dishonest scales;[d]
he loves to defraud.
[8]Ephraim boasts,
"I am very rich; I have become wealthy.[e]
With all my wealth they will not find in me
any iniquity or sin."

[9]"I am the LORD your God,
⌞who brought you⌟ out of[b] Egypt;[f]
I will make you live in tents[g] again,
as in the days of your appointed feasts.
[10]I spoke to the prophets,
gave them many visions
and told parables[h] through them."[i]

[11]Is Gilead wicked?[j]
Its people are worthless!
Do they sacrifice bulls in Gilgal?[k]
Their altars will be like piles of stones
on a plowed field.[l]
[12]Jacob fled to the country of Aram[c];[m]
Israel served to get a wife,
and to pay for her he tended sheep.[n]
[13]The LORD used a prophet to bring Israel up from Egypt,
by a prophet he cared for him.[o]
[14]But Ephraim has bitterly provoked him to anger;
his Lord will leave upon him the guilt of his bloodshed[p]
and will repay him for his contempt.[q]

The LORD's Anger Against Israel

13 When Ephraim spoke, men trembled;[r]
he was exalted[s] in Israel.
But he became guilty of Baal worship[t] and died.
[2]Now they sin more and more;
they make idols for themselves from their silver,[u]
cleverly fashioned images,
all of them the work of craftsmen.
It is said of these people,
"They offer human sacrifice
and kiss[d] the calf-idols.[v]"
[3]Therefore they will be like the morning mist,
like the early dew that disappears,[w]
like chaff[x] swirling from a threshing floor,[y]
like smoke[z] escaping through a window.

[4]"But I am the LORD your God,
⌞who brought you⌟ out of[b] Egypt.[a]
You shall acknowledge no God but me,[b]
no Savior[c] except me.
[5]I cared for you in the desert,
in the land of burning heat.
[6]When I fed them, they were satisfied;
when they were satisfied, they became proud;
then they forgot me.[d]
[7]So I will come upon them like a lion,
like a leopard I will lurk by the path.
[8]Like a bear robbed of her cubs,[e]
I will attack them and rip them open.
Like a lion I will devour them;
a wild animal will tear them apart.[f]

[9]"You are destroyed, O Israel,
because you are against me,[g]
against your helper.[h]
[10]Where is your king,[i] that he may save you?

12:1 [t]Eze 17:10 [u]2Ki 17:4 **12:2** [v]Mic 6:2 [w]Hos 4:9 **12:3** [x]Ge 25:26 [y]Ge 32:24-29 **12:4** [z]Ge 28:12-15; 35:15 **12:5** [a]Ex 3:15 **12:6** [b]Mic 6:8 [c]Hos 6:1-3; 10:12; Mic 7:7 **12:7** [d]Am 8:5 **12:8** [e]Ps 62:10; Rev 3:17 **12:9** [f]Lev 23:43; Hos 11:1 [g]Ne 8:17 **12:10** [h]Eze 20:49 [i]2Ki 17:13; Jer 7:25 **12:11** [j]Hos 6:8 [k]Hos 4:15 [l]Hos 8:11 **12:12** [m]Ge 28:5 [n]Ge 29:18 **12:13** [o]Ex 13:3; Isa 63:11-14 **12:14** [p]Eze 18:13 [q]Da 11:18 **13:1** [r]Jdg 12:1 [s]Jdg 8:1 [t]Hos 11:2 **13:2** [u]Isa 46:6; Jer 10:4 [v]Isa 44:17-20 **13:3** [w]Hos 6:4 [x]Isa 17:13 [y]Da 2:35 [z]Ps 68:2 **13:4** [a]Hos 12:9 [b]Ex 20:3 [c]Isa 43:11; 45:21-22 **13:6** [d]Dt 32:12-15; Hos 2:13 **13:8** [e]2Sa 17:8 [f]Ps 50:22 **13:9** [g]Jer 2:17-19 [h]Dt 33:29 **13:10** [i]2Ki 17:4

a *2 Jacob* means *he grasps the heel* (figuratively, *he deceives*). **b** *9,4* Or *God / ever since you were in* **c** *12* That is, Northwest Mesopotamia **d** *2* Or *"Men who sacrifice / kiss*

Where are your rulers in all your
towns,
of whom you said,
'Give me a king and princes'?[j]
11So in my anger I gave you a king,
and in my wrath I took him
away.[k]
12The guilt of Ephraim is stored up,
his sins are kept on record.[l]
13Pains as of a woman in childbirth[m]
come to him,
but he is a child without
wisdom;
when the time arrives,
he does not come to the opening
of the womb.[n]

14"I will ransom them from the
power of the grave[a];[o]
I will redeem them from death.
Where, O death, are your plagues?
Where, O grave,[a] is your
destruction?[p]

"I will have no compassion,
15 even though he thrives[q] among
his brothers.
An east wind[r] from the LORD will
come,
blowing in from the desert;
his spring will fail
and his well dry up.[s]
His storehouse will be plundered[t]
of all its treasures.
16The people of Samaria must bear
their guilt,[u]
because they have rebelled[v]
against their God.
They will fall by the sword;[w]
their little ones will be dashed[x]
to the ground,
their pregnant women[y] ripped
open."

Repentance to Bring Blessing

14 Return, O Israel, to the LORD your
God.
Your sins have been your
downfall![z]
2Take words with you
and return to the LORD.
Say to him:
"Forgive all our sins
and receive us graciously,[a]
that we may offer the fruit of our
lips.[b][b]
3Assyria cannot save us;
we will not mount war-horses.[c]
We will never again say 'Our
gods'[d]
to what our own hands have
made,
for in you the fatherless[e] find
compassion."

4"I will heal[f] their waywardness
and love them freely,[g]
for my anger has turned away
from them.
5I will be like the dew to Israel;
he will blossom like a lily.[h]
Like a cedar of Lebanon[i]
he will send down his roots;[j]
6 his young shoots will grow.
His splendor will be like an olive
tree,[k]
his fragrance like a cedar of
Lebanon.[l]
7Men will dwell again in his
shade.[m]
He will flourish like the grain.
He will blossom like a vine,
and his fame will be like the
wine[n] from Lebanon.[o]
8O Ephraim, what more have I[c] to
do with idols?[p]
I will answer him and care for
him.
I am like a green pine tree;
your fruitfulness comes from
me."

9Who is wise?[q] He will realize these
things.
Who is discerning? He will
understand them.[r]
The ways of the LORD are right;[s]
the righteous walk[t] in them,
but the rebellious stumble in
them.

[a]14 Hebrew *Sheol* [b]2 Or *offer our lips as sacrifices of bulls* [c]8 Or *What more has Ephraim*

13:10 [j]1Sa 8:6; Hos 8:4
13:11 [k]1Ki 14:10; Hos 10:7
13:12 [l]Dt 32:34
13:13 [m]Isa 13:8; Mic 4:9-10 [n]Isa 66:9
13:14 [o]Ps 49:15; Eze 37:12-13 [p]1Co 15:55*
13:15 [q]Hos 10:1 [r]Eze 19:12 [s]Jer 51:36 [t]Jer 20:5
13:16 [u]Hos 10:2 [v]Hos 7:14 [w]Hos 11:6 [x]2Ki 8:12; Hos 10:14 [y]2Ki 15:16; Isa 13:16
14:1 [z]Hos 5:5
14:2 [a]Mic 7:18-19 [b]Heb 13:15
14:3 [c]Ps 33:17; Isa 31:1 [d]Hos 8:6 [e]Ps 10:14; 68:5
14:4 [f]Hos 6:1 [g]Zep 3:17
14:5 [h]SS 2:1 [i]Isa 35:2 [j]Job 29:19
14:6 [k]Ps 52:8; Jer 11:16 [l]SS 4:11
14:7 [m]Ps 91:1-4 [n]Hos 2:22 [o]Eze 17:23
14:8 [p]ver 3
14:9 [q]Ps 107:43 [r]Pr 10:29; Isa 1:28 [s]Ps 111:7-8; Zep 3:5; Ac 13:10 [t]Isa 26:7

14:9

PROMISE 3

SIN EXPOSED

The sinful heart looks better with make-up. In his book, Hosea washed it down and gave us a look at stark, exposed evil. The picture is not pretty. It is, in fact, scary, shocking and repulsive. Hosea's portrayal of sinful Israel as an adulterous wife is something we would rather not deal with. As Israel did, so do we sin against God and against one another. These images of deception and betrayal make us feel filthy and corrupt.

But how does this shocking book conclude? Don't pass quickly over God's final invitation to learn from this graphic story. Hosea painted sin as God sees it, but he offered the alternative only God can offer (see 14:1–2). Then he closed the book with a simple challenge (14:9). Read it and realize that it's your choice—will you be righteous or rebellious?

For the next Promise 3 reading go to page 973.

JOEL

AT A GLANCE

Key Principle: God is the Ruler of nature and nations; he sometimes uses the realm of nature to get our attention and draw us to him.
Author: Joel
Time and Place: ~835 B.C. / Southern kingdom of Judah
Key Verses: 1:15; 2:11–13, 28–29, 32; 3:17

BENEFIT

The book of Joel is striking in its use of a natural disaster to communicate spiritual truth. He uses a disastrous locust plague as an analogy of a far greater spiritual catastrophe that will come if Judah does not repent and return to the Lord. This book helps us to see how God uses the natural realm to point us to truths in the spiritual realm.

SETTING

Joel's frequent allusions to "the house of the Lord" and "Zion" and "Jerusalem" indicate that he lived near Jerusalem, but it is difficult to date this brief prophecy since it has no specific time references. Commentators are divided as to whether Joel was written in the ninth century B.C. or centuries later, after the Babylonian exile. Those who claim that Joel is postexilic note that there is no reference to a king, or to key countries such as Syria, Assyria, and Babylonia. There is also a reference to the Greeks (3:6) that could indicate a later date.

Those who claim an early date note that Joel's failure to mention a king is inconclusive; other prophets such as Jonah, Nahum and Habakkuk do the same. And its emphasis on the priests and silence concerning the king would fit this setting if this book was written when the young Joash was being protected by Jehoiada the priest (841–835 B.C.). In addition, Joel's references to Phoenicia, Philistia, Egypt and Edom and failure to mention Syria, Assyria and Babylonia would also fit well against a ninth-century background. Finally, Joel's style fits that of Hosea and Amos better than the postexilic writers, and it appears likely that the eighth-century prophet Amos borrowed from Joel (compare 3:16 with Amos 1:2 and 3:18 with Amos 9:13).

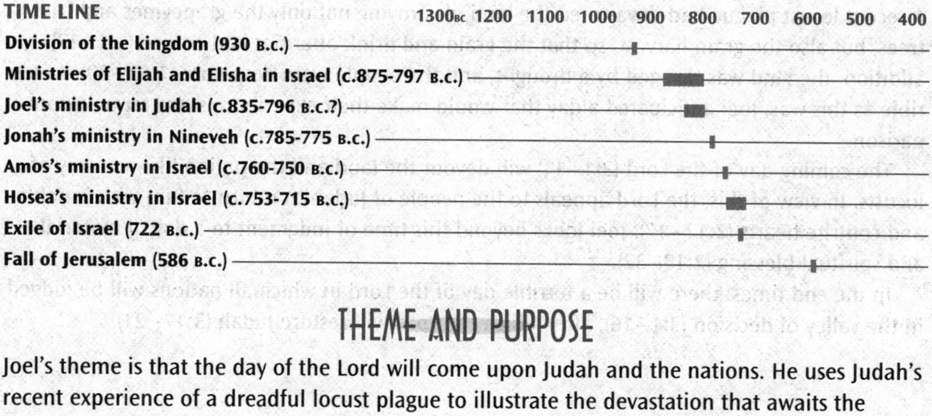

THEME AND PURPOSE

Joel's theme is that the day of the Lord will come upon Judah and the nations. He uses Judah's recent experience of a dreadful locust plague to illustrate the devastation that awaits the nation if they do not humbly turn to the Lord in repentance and obedience. God, through the prophet, appeals to the people to "return to me with all your heart, with fasting and weeping and mourning" (2:12). Images of disaster run through this book, including locust plagues, famine, fires, invading armies and phenomena in the heavens. After their judgment is completed, the people of Judah and all who call on the name of the Lord will be saved (2:32).

UNIQUE CONTRIBUTION

Joel was the first prophet to develop the theme of the coming day of the Lord as a day of judgment not only on God's covenant people, but also upon the nations (1:15; 2:1–2, 11, 31; 3:14–18). Thus, the day of the Lord combines a past aspect, fulfilled with the destruction of Judah and the exile in Babylon, with a future aspect that still awaits fulfillment. Peter quoted Joel 2:28–32 in his sermon on the day of Pentecost (Acts 2:16–21), and Jesus associated the events in Joel 2:10, 31 and 3:15 with the signs of his second coming in his Olivet Discourse (Matthew 24:29). Second Thessalonians 2:2 and 2 Peter 3:10 also view the day of the Lord as a future event.

LINKS TO THE NEW TESTAMENT

Jesus told his disciples that he would send the Holy Spirit after he ascended to the Father (John 16:7–15; Acts 1:8), and Peter announced that God's gift of the Holy Spirit on the day of Pentecost was the fulfillment of Jesus' promise as anticipated by the prophet Joel. He said, "this is what was spoken by the prophet Joel" and proceeded to quote Joel 2:28–32a (Acts 2:16–21). Christ will also fulfill Joel's prophecy of the Lord's judgment of the nations in the Valley of Jehoshaphat (which means "the Lord judges"; 3:2, 12).

OVERVIEW

FOCUS	The Day of the Locust	The Day of the Lord	The Day of Deliverance	
REFERENCE	1:1 — 1:20	2:1 — 2:17	2:18-32	3:1-21
TOPICS	Historic Invasion	Prophetic Invasion	Promised Blessing	Final Triumph
	Destruction		Restoration	
	God's Dealings in Nature	God's Dealings with Israel and the Nations		
	History	Prophecy		
LOCATION	Southern Kingdom of Judah			
TIME	~835 B.C.			

A recent locust plague had devastated the land, destroying not only the grapevines and fruit trees, but also the grain harvest, so that the grain and drink offerings had ceased (1:1–12). In addition, the land was ravaged by a drought, and the people were desperate (1:13–20). As terrible as this was, Joel anticipated a day that would make their experience seem tame in comparison.

The coming day of the Lord (2:1–11) will devour the land and the nation like an army of locusts. In view of this, the Lord appeals to the people of Judah to return to him with humble and contrite hearts (2:12–17). Joel looks beyond this time of judgment to a day of material and spiritual blessing (2:18–32).

In the end times, there will be a terrible day of the Lord in which all nations will be judged in the valley of decision (3:1–16), after which the Lord will restore Judah (3:17–21).

JOEL

1 The word of the LORD that came[a] to
Joel[b] son of Pethuel.

An Invasion of Locusts

4 →PG. 1038

2Hear this,[c] you elders;
listen, all who live in the land.[d]
Has anything like this ever
happened in your days
or in the days of your
forefathers?[e]
3Tell it to your children,[f]
and let your children tell it to
their children,
and their children to the next
generation.
4What the locust swarm has left
the great locusts have eaten;
what the great locusts have left
the young locusts have eaten;
what the young locusts have left
other locusts[a] have eaten.[g]
5Wake up, you drunkards, and
weep!
Wail, all you drinkers of wine;[h]
wail because of the new wine,
for it has been snatched from
your lips.
6A nation has invaded my land,
powerful and without number;[i]
it has the teeth[j] of a lion,
the fangs of a lioness.
7It has laid waste[k] my vines
and ruined my fig trees.[l]
It has stripped off their bark
and thrown it away,
leaving their branches white.
8Mourn like a virgin[b] in sackcloth[m]
grieving for the husband[c] of her
youth.
9Grain offerings and drink
offerings[n]
are cut off from the house of the
LORD.
The priests are in mourning,
those who minister before the
LORD.
10The fields are ruined,
the ground is dried up[d];[o]
the grain is destroyed,
the new wine[p] is dried up,
the oil fails.
11Despair, you farmers,[q]
wail, you vine growers;
grieve for the wheat and the barley,
because the harvest of the field
is destroyed.[r]
12The vine is dried up
and the fig tree is withered;
the pomegranate, the palm and the
apple tree—
all the trees of the field—are
dried up.[s]
Surely the joy of mankind
is withered away.

A Call to Repentance

13Put on sackcloth,[t] O priests, and
mourn;
wail, you who minister[u] before
the altar.
Come, spend the night in
sackcloth,
you who minister before my
God;
for the grain offerings and drink
offerings[v]
are withheld from the house of
your God.
14Declare a holy fast;[w]
call a sacred assembly.
Summon the elders
and all who live in the land
to the house of the LORD your God,
and cry out[x] to the LORD.

1:3

PROMISE 4

HISTORY AS TEACHER

If God's people had learned this lesson they would have succeeded, not suffered. Joel instructed the Israelites to learn from history and to teach their children to do the same. Notice Joel's call to the people: "Hear this" (v. 2) and "Wake up" (v. 5). The prophet's fear was that the people were so dull in their souls that they would see the locust plague and the drought only as natural disasters. He was afraid that God's own people would miss God's hand at work.

Man, do we need to wake up and hear this! Our God is always at work. Events don't just happen—God is in control of everything that goes on in this world. Teach your children to see God at work in their lives. Consistently teach these Old Testament passages to your children (and review them yourself) to develop an unshakable conviction that God works in world events to teach and to warn.

What happens when people see God at work? Read verses 13–15.

For the next Promise 4 reading go to page 1026.

1:1 [a]Jer 1:2 [b]Ac 2:16 **1:2** [c]Hos 5:1 [d]Hos 4:1 [e]Joel 2:2 **1:3** [f]Ex 10:2; Ps 78:4 **1:4** [g]Dt 28:39; Na 3:15 **1:5** [h]Joel 3:3 **1:6** [i]Joel 2:2,11,25 [j]Rev 9:8 **1:7** [k]Isa 5:6 [l]Am 4:9 **1:8** [m]ver 13; Isa 22:12; Am 8:10 **1:9** [n]Hos 9:4; Joel 2:14,17 **1:10** [o]Isa 24:4 [p]Hos 9:2 **1:11** [q]Jer 14:3-4; Am 5:16 [r]Isa 17:11 **1:12** [s]Hag 2:19 **1:13** [t]Jer 4:8 [u]Joel 2:17 [v]ver 9 **1:14** [w]2Ch 20:3 [x]Jnh 3:8

---

a *4* The precise meaning of the four Hebrew words used here for locusts is uncertain.
b *8* Or *young woman* c *8* Or *betrothed*
d *10* Or *ground mourns*

15Alas for that[y] day!
For the day of the LORD[z] is near;
it will come like destruction from the Almighty.[a]
16Has not the food been cut off[a]
before our very eyes—
joy and gladness
from the house of our God?[b]
17The seeds are shriveled
beneath the clods.[b][c]
The storehouses are in ruins,
the granaries have been broken down,
for the grain has dried up.
18How the cattle moan!
The herds mill about
because they have no pasture;
even the flocks of sheep are suffering.
19To you, O LORD, I call,[d]
for fire[e] has devoured the open pastures[f]
and flames have burned up all the trees of the field.
20Even the wild animals pant for you;[g]
the streams of water have dried up[h]
and fire has devoured the open pastures.

An Army of Locusts

2 Blow the trumpet[i] in Zion;[j]
sound the alarm on my holy hill.
Let all who live in the land tremble,
for the day of the LORD[k] is coming.
It is close at hand[l]—
2 a day of darkness[m] and gloom,[n]
a day of clouds and blackness.
Like dawn spreading across the mountains
a large and mighty army[o] comes,
such as never was of old[p]
nor ever will be in ages to come.
3Before them fire devours,
behind them a flame blazes.
Before them the land is like the garden of Eden,[q]
behind them, a desert waste[r]—
nothing escapes them.
4They have the appearance of horses;[s]
they gallop along like cavalry.
5With a noise like that of chariots[t]
they leap over the mountaintops,
like a crackling fire[u] consuming stubble,
like a mighty army drawn up for battle.

6At the sight of them, nations are in anguish;[v]
every face turns pale.[w]
7They charge like warriors;
they scale walls like soldiers.
They all march in line,
not swerving[x] from their course.
8They do not jostle each other;
each marches straight ahead.
They plunge through defenses
without breaking ranks.
9They rush upon the city;
they run along the wall.
They climb into the houses;
like thieves they enter through the windows.[y]
10Before them the earth shakes,[z]
the sky trembles,
the sun and moon are darkened,[a]
and the stars no longer shine.[b]
11The LORD[c] thunders
at the head of his army;
his forces are beyond number,
and mighty are those who obey his command.
The day of the LORD is great;[d]
it is dreadful.
Who can endure it?[e]

Rend Your Heart

1 →PG. 994

12"Even now," declares the LORD,
"return[f] to me with all your heart,
with fasting and weeping and mourning."
13Rend your heart[g]
and not your garments.[h]
Return to the LORD your God,
for he is gracious and compassionate,
slow to anger and abounding in love,[i]
and he relents from sending calamity.[j]
14Who knows? He may turn[k] and have pity
and leave behind a blessing[l]—
grain offerings and drink offerings[m]
for the LORD your God.
15Blow the trumpet[n] in Zion,
declare a holy fast,[o]
call a sacred assembly.[p]
16Gather the people,
consecrate[q] the assembly;
bring together the elders,
gather the children,
those nursing at the breast.
Let the bridegroom[r] leave his room
and the bride her chamber.

1:15 [y]Jer 30:7 [z]Isa 13:6,9; Joel 2:1,11,31 **1:16** [a]Isa 3:7 [b]Dt 12:7 **1:17** [c]Isa 17:10-11 **1:19** [d]Ps 50:15 [e]Am 7:4 [f]Jer 9:10 **1:20** [g]Ps 104:21 [h]1Ki 17:7 **2:1** [i]Jer 4:5 [j]ver 15 [k]Joel 1:15; Zep 1:14-16 [l]Ob 1:15 **2:2** [m]Am 5:18 [n]Da 9:12 [o]Joel 1:6 [p]Joel 1:2 **2:3** [q]Ge 2:8 [r]Ps 105:34-35 **2:4** [s]Rev 9:7 **2:5** [t]Rev 9:9 [u]Isa 5:24; 30:30 **2:6** [v]Isa 13:8 [w]Na 2:10 **2:7** [x]Isa 5:27 **2:9** [y]Jer 9:21 **2:10** [z]Ps 18:7 [a]Mt 24:29 [b]Isa 13:10; Eze 32:8 **2:11** [c]Joel 1:15 [d]Zep 1:14; Rev 18:8 [e]Eze 22:14 **2:12** [f]Jer 4:1; Hos 12:6 **2:13** [g]Ps 34:18; Isa 57:15 [h]Job 1:20 [i]Ex 34:6 [j]Jer 18:8 **2:14** [k]Jer 26:3 [l]Hag 2:19 [m]Joel 1:13 **2:15** [n]Nu 10:2 [o]Jer 36:9 [p]Joel 1:14 **2:16** [q]Ex 19:10,22 [r]Ps 19:5

a *15* Hebrew *Shaddai* b *17* The meaning of the Hebrew for this word is uncertain.

17Let the priests, who minister before
the LORD,
weep between the temple porch
and the altar.[s]
Let them say, "Spare your people,
O LORD.
Do not make your inheritance an
object of scorn,[t]
a byword among the nations.
Why should they say among the
peoples,
'Where is their God?[u]' "

The LORD's Answer

18Then the LORD will be jealous[v] for
his land
and take pity on his people.
19The LORD will reply[a] to them:

"I am sending you grain, new wine
and oil,[w]
enough to satisfy you fully;
never again will I make you
an object of scorn[x] to the
nations.

20"I will drive the northern army[y]
far from you,
pushing it into a parched and
barren land,
with its front columns going into
the eastern[z] sea[b]
and those in the rear into the
western sea.[c]
And its stench[a] will go up;
its smell will rise."

Surely he has done great things.[d]

2:12-13

PROMISE 1

HOLDING OFF DISASTER

God had sent a warning to his people. The swarm of locusts was a picture of an invading army that would destroy everything Israel had built. What would hold off the coming disaster? A simple statement made in verses 12 and 13 (and developed in verses 14–17) tells us. The command "Rend your heart and not your garments" (v. 13) calls for genuine repentance. God said to forget the appearance of repentance (the tradition of tearing clothes as a sign of sorrow); he wanted the people to turn to God in genuine repentance for sin.

Joel called people to holiness and repentance. He urged a return to God, who is "gracious and compassionate, slow to anger and abounding in love" (v. 13). This is an invitation to anyone who has sinned against God. Meditate on this dual emphasis of God's judgment and compassion, warning and invitation.

For the next Promise 1 reading go to page 974.

21 Be not afraid,[b] O land;
be glad and rejoice.
Surely the LORD has done great
things.[c]
22 Be not afraid, O wild animals,
for the open pastures are
becoming green.[d]
The trees are bearing their fruit;
the fig tree and the vine yield
their riches.[e]
23Be glad, O people of Zion,
rejoice[f] in the LORD your God,
for he has given you
the autumn rains in
righteousness.[e]
He sends you abundant showers,
both autumn and spring rains,[g]
as before.
24The threshing floors will be filled
with grain;
the vats will overflow[h] with new
wine[i] and oil.

25"I will repay you for the years the
locusts have eaten—
the great locust and the young
locust,
the other locusts and the locust
swarm[f]—
my great army that I sent among
you.
26You will have plenty to eat, until
you are full,[j]
and you will praise[k] the name
of the LORD your God,
who has worked wonders[l] for
you;
never again will my people be
shamed.
27Then you will know that I am in
Israel,
that I am the LORD[m] your God,
and that there is no other;
never again will my people be
shamed.

The Day of the LORD

28"And afterward,
I will pour out my Spirit[n] on all
people.
Your sons and daughters will
prophesy,
your old men will dream dreams,
your young men will see visions.
29Even on my servants,[o] both men
and women,
I will pour out my Spirit in those
days.

2:17 [s]Eze 8:16; Mt 23:35 [t]Dt 9:26-29; Ps 44:13 [u]Ps 42:3
2:18 [v]Zec 1:14
2:19 [w]Jer 31:12 [x]Eze 34:29
2:20 [y]Jer 1:14-15 [z]Zec 14:8 [a]Isa 34:3
2:21 [b]Isa 54:4; Zep 3:16-17 [c]Ps 126:3
2:22 [d]Ps 65:12 [e]Joel 1:18-20
2:23 [f]Ps 149:2; Isa 12:6; 41:16; Hab 3:18; Zec 10:7 [g]Lev 26:4
2:24 [h]Lev 26:10; Mal 3:10 [i]Am 9:13
2:26 [j]Lev 26:5 [k]Isa 62:9 [l]Ps 126:3; Isa 25:1
2:27 [m]Joel 3:17
2:28 [n]Eze 39:29
2:29 [o]1Co 12:13; Gal 3:28

[a]*18,19* Or *LORD was jealous . . . / and took pity . . . / 19The LORD replied* [b]*20* That is, the Dead Sea [c]*20* That is, the Mediterranean
[d]*20* Or *rise. / Surely it has done great things."*
[e]*23* Or / *the teacher for righteousness:*
[f]*25* The precise meaning of the four Hebrew words used here for locusts is uncertain.

[30]I will show wonders in the
heavens[p]
and on the earth,[q]
blood and fire and billows of
smoke.
[31]The sun will be turned to
darkness[r]
and the moon to blood
before the coming of the great
and dreadful day of the
LORD.[s]
[32]And everyone who calls
on the name of the LORD will be
saved;[t]
for on Mount Zion[u] and in
Jerusalem
there will be deliverance,[v]
as the LORD has said,
among the survivors[w]
whom the LORD calls.

The Nations Judged

3 "In those days and at that time,
when I restore the fortunes[x] of
Judah and Jerusalem,
[2]I will gather all nations
and bring them down to the
Valley of Jehoshaphat.[a]
There I will enter into judgment[y]
against them
concerning my inheritance, my
people Israel,
for they scattered my people
among the nations
and divided up my land.
[3]They cast lots for my people
and traded boys for prostitutes;
they sold girls for wine[z]
that they might drink.

[4]"Now what have you against me,
O Tyre and Sidon[a] and all you regions
of Philistia? Are you repaying me for
something I have done? If you are paying me back, I will swiftly and speedily
return on your own heads what you
have done.[b] [5]For you took my silver
and my gold and carried off my finest
treasures to your temples.[c] [6]You sold
the people of Judah and Jerusalem to
the Greeks, that you might send them
far from their homeland.
[7]"See, I am going to rouse them out
of the places to which you sold them,[d]
and I will return on your own heads
what you have done. [8]I will sell your
sons[e] and daughters to the people of
Judah,[f] and they will sell them to the
Sabeans, a nation far away." The LORD
has spoken.

[9]Proclaim this among the nations:
Prepare for war![g]
Rouse the warriors![h]
Let all the fighting men draw
near and attack.
[10]Beat your plowshares into swords
and your pruning hooks[i] into
spears.
Let the weakling[j] say,
"I am strong!"
[11]Come quickly, all you nations from
every side,
and assemble[k] there.

Bring down your warriors,[l]
O LORD!

[12]"Let the nations be roused;
let them advance into the Valley
of Jehoshaphat,
for there I will sit
to judge[m] all the nations on
every side.
[13]Swing the sickle,
for the harvest[n] is ripe.
Come, trample the grapes,
for the winepress[o] is full
and the vats overflow—
so great is their wickedness!"

[14]Multitudes, multitudes
in the valley of decision!
For the day of the LORD[p] is near
in the valley of decision.
[15]The sun and moon will be
darkened,
and the stars no longer shine.
[16]The LORD will roar from Zion
and thunder from Jerusalem;[q]
the earth and the sky will
tremble.[r]
But the LORD will be a refuge for
his people,

[a]2 *Jehoshaphat* means *the LORD judges*; also in verse 12.

2:30 [p]Lk 21:11 [q]Mk 13:24-25 **2:31** [r]Mt 24:29 [s]Isa 13:9-10; Mal 4:1,5 **2:32** [t]Ac 2:17-21*; Ro 10:13* [u]Isa 46:13 [v]Ob 1:17 [w]Isa 11:11; Mic 4:7; Ro 9:27 **3:1** [x]Jer 16:15 **3:2** [y]Eze 36:5 **3:3** [z]Am 2:6

3:4 [a]Mt 11:21 [b]Isa 34:8 **3:5** [c]2Ch 21:16-17 **3:7** [d]Isa 43:5-6; Jer 23:8 **3:8** [e]Isa 60:14 [f]Isa 14:2 **3:9** [g]Isa 8:9 [h]Jer 46:4 **3:10** [i]Isa 2:4; Mic 4:3 [j]Zec 12:8 **3:11** [k]Eze 38:15-16; Zep 3:8 [l]Isa 13:3 **3:12** [m]Isa 2:4 **3:13** [n]Hos 6:11; Mt 13:39; Rev 14:15-19 [o]Rev 14:20 **3:14** [p]Isa 34:2-8; Joel 1:15 **3:16** [q]Am 1:2 [r]Eze 38:19

2:28–32

PROMISE 7

GOD'S WORLDWIDE CALL

This passage reveals an amazing and wonderful hope! Even in this book of rebuke and warning, God reminds us that he calls all people to himself. Peter quoted this passage (Acts 2:17–21) to explain what God was doing when people from every nation miraculously heard the message of God's love and forgiveness in their own language. Joel, in his warnings about locusts and drought and invading armies, never lost sight of God's saving hand stretched out to anyone who would reach for it.

Every modern-day Christian is called to proclaim this same message of salvation. In our troubled times, the Great Commission (Matthew 28:18–20) and the Great Commandment (Mark 12:30–31) repeat Joel's invitation to *everyone*!

For the next Promise 7 reading go to page 968.

a stronghold[s] for the people of
Israel.

Blessings for God's People

17"Then you will know that I, the
LORD your God,[t]
dwell in Zion,[u] my holy hill.
Jerusalem will be holy;
never again will foreigners
invade her.

18"In that day the mountains will
drip new wine,
and the hills will flow with
milk;[v]
all the ravines of Judah will run
with water.[w]
A fountain will flow out of the
LORD's house[x]
and will water the valley of
acacias.[a][y]
19But Egypt will be desolate,
Edom a desert waste,
because of violence[z] done to the
people of Judah,
in whose land they shed
innocent blood.
20Judah will be inhabited forever[a]
and Jerusalem through all
generations.
21Their bloodguilt, which I have not
pardoned,
I will pardon.[b]"

The LORD dwells in Zion!

3:16 [s]Jer 16:19 **3:17** [t]Joel 2:27 [u]Isa 4:3 **3:18** [v]Ex 3:8 [w]Isa 30:25; 35:6 [x]Rev 22:1-2 [y]Eze 47:1; Am 9:13 **3:19** [z]Ob 1:10 **3:20** [a]Am 9:15 **3:21** [b]Eze 36:25

[a] 18 Or *Valley of Shittim*

AMOS

AT A GLANCE

Key Principle: Times of prosperity in a culture can foster a growth in materialism, immorality and injustice, making it more difficult for people to hear and respond to God's words.
Author: Amos
Time and Place: ~760 to ~750 B.C. / Northern kingdom of Israel
Key Verses: 1:2; 3:2; 4:12; 5:4, 24, 27; 8:11–12

BENEFIT

Amos, like James in the New Testament, does not mince his words, but delivers a series of sharp and incisive declarations and images that stir up the conscience and require a response. This book is relevant to our times because Amos addressed a materialistic culture that fostered greed, injustice and arrogance. It is a word of warning that such a culture cannot continue for long without being diminished by divine judgment.

SETTING

Although Amos lived in Judah (Tekoa was 12 miles south of Jerusalem), God sent him as a prophet to the northern kingdom of Israel. "I was neither a prophet nor a prophet's son, but I was a shepherd, and I also took care of sycamore-fig trees. But the LORD took me from tending the flock and said to me, 'Go, prophesy to my people Israel' " (7:14–15). Bethel, a center for idolatrous calf-worship and the residence of the king, was the focus of Amos's ministry. Amos prophesied "when Uzziah was king of Judah and Jeroboam son of Jehoash was king of Israel" (1:1). A solar eclipse occurred in Israel on June 15, 763 B.C., and Amos's statement in 8:9 probably reminded his hearers of it. The earthquake he mentioned in 1:1 is referred to over two centuries later in Zechariah 14:5. Amos was a contemporary of Jonah and was the first of two writing prophets whose ministry focused on the northern kingdom of Israel. The other was Hosea, who came a few years later.

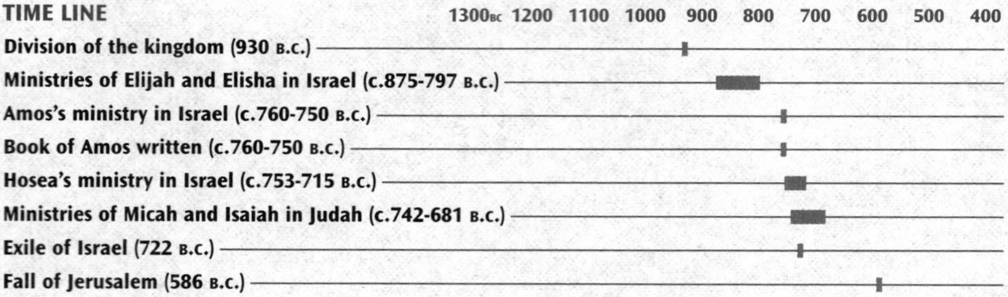

THEME AND PURPOSE

Like other prophets, Amos has a dual theme of condemnation and consolation, but the proportion of the judgment section (1:1—9:10) relative to the comfort section (9:11–15) in Amos is greater than most. Amos particularly addresses the social injustice practiced by the people of Israel. He rebukes their oppression of poor people, their greed and materialism, their arrogance and hypocrisy and their indifference to the plight of others. In the days of Jeroboam II, Israel enjoyed a prosperous economy and relative freedom from foreign oppression. In this context, the people had no interest in hearing a message about coming doom. Amos's words, "prepare to meet your God, O Israel" (4:12) were met with complete scorn and callousness. In spite of this, God still presented his people with a gracious offer of deliverance from impending judgment and disaster.

UNIQUE CONTRIBUTION

Amos is an extraordinarily concise and penetrating book. The prophet multiplies oracles (revelations) and striking images to hammer home the solemn theme of inescapable judgment. Only in the last five verses do we find a message of hope and promise. Throughout the rest of the book, Amos unflinchingly delivers a series of oracles that are so countercultural, it is no surprise when he is told to go back to Judah and stay away from Israel (7:10–17).

LINKS TO THE NEW TESTAMENT

Amos 9:11–15 beautifully anticipates the coming Messianic kingdom in which the effects of the curse will be reversed. The earth will be so fertile that "the reaper will be overtaken by the plowman and the planter by the one treading grapes" (9:13). Messiah will be the judge of all the earth (1:1—9:10) but he will also usher in an everlasting kingdom of blessedness and righteousness.

OVERVIEW

FOCUS	Prediction of Judgment	Purposes for Judgment	Pictures of Judgment	Promises after Judgment
REFERENCE	1 — 2	3 — 6	7 — 9:10	9:11 — 9:15
TOPICS	Eight Oracles	Three Sermons	Five Visions	Three Promises
	"This is what the LORD says"	"Hear this word"	"This is what the Sovereign LORD showed me"	"'I will'...declares the LORD"
	Sentences	Sermons	Scenes	Securities
	Vengeance	Vindication	Visions	Victory
LOCATION	Surrounding Nations	Northern Kingdom of Israel		
TIME	~760 to ~750 B.C.			

The book of Amos begins with a series of eight prophetic oracles that pronounce judgment on the nations that surround Israel (1—2). The word "fire," a symbol of judgment, often appears in this section. A study of an ancient map will show that the sequence of the seven nations gradually spirals in on the last nation, Israel. This figurative "funnel of fire" demonstrates that the sins of these countries have reached the breaking point and that judgment is unavoidable. In three sermons, each beginning with the phrase, "Hear this word" (3:1; 4:1; 5:1), Amos outlines the reasons for Israel's coming judgment. In spite of all that God has done, he tells them, "yet you have not returned to me" (4:6, 8–11). Because they refuse to turn to him, God will send them into exile beyond Damascus (5:27).

In a series of five visions (7:1—9:10), Amos pictures the coming judgment on the northern kingdom of Israel. Because of Amos's intercession, the first two judgments of locusts and fire will not take place. The vision of the plumb line pictures Israel as a leaning wall; the vision of the basket of ripe fruit pictures Israel as rotten and overripe for judgment.

The three promises at the end of the book (9:11–15) are that God will restore the line of David, rebuild the nation and renew the people.

AMOS

1 The words of Amos, one of the shepherds of Tekoa[a]—what he saw concerning Israel two years before the
earthquake,[b] when Uzziah[c] was king
of Judah and Jeroboam[d] son of Jehoash[a] was king of Israel.[e]
2He said:

"The LORD roars[f] from Zion
and thunders from Jerusalem;[g]
the pastures of the shepherds dry
up,[b]
and the top of Carmel[h]
withers."[i]

Judgment on Israel's Neighbors

3This is what the LORD says:

"For three sins of Damascus,[j]
even for four, I will not turn
back ⌊my wrath⌋.[k]
Because she threshed Gilead
with sledges having iron teeth,
4I will send fire[l] upon the house of
Hazael
that will consume the
fortresses[m] of
Ben-Hadad.[n]
5I will break down the gate[o] of
Damascus;
I will destroy the king who is in[c]
the Valley of Aven[d]
and the one who holds the scepter
in Beth Eden.
The people of Aram will go into
exile to Kir,[p]"
says the LORD.

6This is what the LORD says:

"For three sins of Gaza,[q]
even for four, I will not turn
back ⌊my wrath⌋.
Because she took captive whole
communities
and sold them to Edom,[r]
7I will send fire upon the walls of
Gaza
that will consume her fortresses.
8I will destroy the king[e] of
Ashdod[s]
and the one who holds the
scepter in Ashkelon.
I will turn my hand[t] against
Ekron,
till the last of the Philistines[u] is
dead,"
says the Sovereign LORD.[v]

9This is what the LORD says:

"For three sins of Tyre,[w]
even for four, I will not turn
back ⌊my wrath⌋.
Because she sold whole
communities of captives to
Edom,
disregarding a treaty of
brotherhood,
10I will send fire upon the walls of
Tyre
that will consume her
fortresses.[x]"

11This is what the LORD says:

"For three sins of Edom,[y]
even for four, I will not turn
back ⌊my wrath⌋.
Because he pursued his brother
with a sword,
stifling all compassion,[f]
because his anger raged continually
and his fury flamed
unchecked,[z]
12I will send fire upon Teman[a]
that will consume the fortresses
of Bozrah."

13This is what the LORD says:

"For three sins of Ammon,[b]

1:1; 7:14–15 — PROMISE 7

WORKING MAN'S PROPHET

You know what's great about Amos? He never stopped being a farmer. God calls some to be full-time ministers to "prepare God's people for works of service" (Ephesians 4:12). But he calls most of us to be farmers (and teachers and factory workers and business people and . . .) as he did Amos.

It was through Amos the farmer that the "Lord roar[ed] from Zion and thunder[ed] from Jerusalem" (1:2). You too can "thunder and roar" for God in places where a preacher could never go without putting people on their guard. The church's great need today is for men in the marketplace who minister as God's prophets. Whatever your occupation, God calls you to transform your job into a place where his truth is proclaimed through your words and actions.

For the next Promise 7 reading go to page 977.

1:1 [a] 2Sa 14:2 [b] Zec 14:5 [c] 2Ch 26:23 [d] 2Ki 14:23 [e] Hos 1:1
1:2 [f] Isa 42:13 [g] Joel 3:16 [h] Am 9:3 [i] Jer 12:4
1:3 [j] Isa 8:4; 17:1-3 [k] Am 2:6
1:4 [l] Jer 49:27 [m] Jer 17:27 [n] 1Ki 20:1; 2Ki 6:24
1:5 [o] Jer 51:30 [p] 2Ki 16:9
1:6 [q] 1Sa 6:17; Zep 2:4 [r] Ob 1:11
1:8 [s] 2Ch 26:6 [t] Ps 81:14 [u] Eze 25:16 [v] Isa 14:28-32; Zep 2:4-7
1:9 [w] 1Ki 5:1; 9:11-14; Isa 23:1-18; Jer 25:22; Joel 3:4; Mt 11:21
1:10 [x] Zec 9:1-4
1:11 [y] Nu 20:14-21; 2Ch 28:17; Jer 49:7-22 [z] Eze 25:12-14
1:12 [a] Ob 1:9-10
1:13 [b] Jer 49:1-6; Eze 21:28; 25:2-7

---

[a] *1* Hebrew *Joash,* a variant of *Jehoash* [b] *2* Or *shepherds mourn* [c] *5* Or *the inhabitants of* [d] *5* *Aven* means *wickedness.* [e] *8* Or *inhabitants* [f] *11* Or *sword / and destroyed his allies*

even for four, I will not turn
back ⌞my wrath⌟.
Because he ripped open the
pregnant women[c] of Gilead
in order to extend his borders,
14I will set fire to the walls of
Rabbah[d]
that will consume her fortresses
amid war cries[e] on the day of
battle,
amid violent winds on a stormy
day.
15Her king[a] will go into exile,
he and his officials together,"
says the LORD.

2 This is what the LORD says:

"For three sins of Moab,
even for four, I will not turn
back ⌞my wrath⌟.
Because he burned, as if to lime,
the bones of Edom's king,
2I will send fire upon Moab
that will consume the fortresses
of Kerioth.[b]
Moab will go down in great tumult
amid war cries and the blast of
the trumpet.
3I will destroy her ruler[f]
and kill all her officials with
him,"[g]
says the LORD.

4This is what the LORD says:

"For three sins of Judah,[h]
even for four, I will not turn
back ⌞my wrath⌟.
Because they have rejected the
law[i] of the LORD
and have not kept his decrees,[j]
because they have been led
astray[k] by false gods,[c][l]
the gods[d] their ancestors
followed,[m]
5I will send fire upon Judah
that will consume the fortresses
of Jerusalem.[n]"

Judgment on Israel

6This is what the LORD says:

"For three sins of Israel,
even for four, I will not turn
back ⌞my wrath⌟.
They sell the righteous for silver,
and the needy for a pair of
sandals.[o]
7They trample on the heads of the
poor
as upon the dust of the ground
and deny justice to the
oppressed.
Father and son use the same girl
and so profane my holy name.[p]
8They lie down beside every altar
on garments taken in pledge.[q]
In the house of their god
they drink wine[r] taken as fines.

9"I destroyed the Amorite[s] before
them,
though he was tall as the cedars
and strong as the oaks.
I destroyed his fruit above
and his roots[t] below.
10"I brought you up out of Egypt,[u]
and I led you forty years in the
desert[v]
to give you the land of the
Amorites.[w]
11I also raised up prophets[x] from
among your sons
and Nazirites[y] from among your
young men.
Is this not true, people of Israel?"
declares the LORD.
12"But you made the Nazirites drink
wine
and commanded the prophets
not to prophesy.[z]

13"Now then, I will crush you
as a cart crushes when loaded
with grain.
14The swift will not escape,
the strong[a] will not muster their
strength,
and the warrior will not save his
life.[b]
15The archer[c] will not stand his
ground,
the fleet-footed soldier will not
get away,
and the horseman will not save
his life.
16Even the bravest warriors[d]
will flee naked on that day,"
declares the LORD.

Witnesses Summoned Against Israel

3 Hear this word the LORD has spoken against you, O people of Israel—against the whole family I brought up out of Egypt:[e]

2"You only have I chosen[f]
of all the families of the earth;
therefore I will punish you
for all your sins.[g]"

3Do two walk together
unless they have agreed to do
so?
4Does a lion roar in the thicket
when he has no prey?[h]
Does he growl in his den
when he has caught nothing?
5Does a bird fall into a trap on the
ground

1:13 [c]Hos 13:16
1:14 [d]Dt 3:11 [e]Am 2:2
2:3 [f]Ps 2:10 [g]Isa 40:23
2:4 [h]2Ki 17:19; Hos 12:2 [i]Jer 6:19 [j]Eze 20:24 [k]Isa 9:16 [l]Isa 28:15 [m]2Ki 22:13; Jer 16:12
2:5 [n]Jer 17:27; Hos 8:14
2:6 [o]Joel 3:3; Am 8:6
2:7 [p]Am 5:11-12; 8:4
2:8 [q]Ex 22:26 [r]Am 4:1; 6:6
2:9 [s]Nu 21:23-26; Jos 10:12 [t]Eze 17:9; Mal 4:1
2:10 [u]Ex 20:2; Am 3:1 [v]Dt 2:7 [w]Ex 3:8; Am 9:7
2:11 [x]Dt 18:18; Jer 7:25 [y]Nu 6:2-3; Jdg 13:5
2:12 [z]Isa 30:10; Jer 11:21; Am 7:12-13; Mic 2:6
2:14 [a]Jer 9:23 [b]Ps 33:16; Isa 30:16-17
2:15 [c]Eze 39:3
2:16 [d]Jer 48:41
3:1 [e]Am 2:10
3:2 [f]Dt 7:6; Lk 12:47 [g]Jer 14:10
3:4 [h]Ps 104:21; Hos 5:14

[a]15 Or / *Molech;* Hebrew *malcam* [b]2 Or *of her cities* [c]4 Or *by lies* [d]4 Or *lies*

AMOS

A Shepherd Turned Prophet

It's a fact of ministry that sometimes a non-professional preacher can connect with an audience better than a seminary-trained pastor. This was true of Amos, a man who was "neither a prophet nor a prophet's son" (7:14). He was just a regular guy whom God chose to deliver a message of judgment, particularly to the northern kingdom of Israel.

Amos lived in Tekoa, a small village located about ten miles south of Jerusalem. There he operated a sheep farm. In his spare time, he also cared for sycamore trees (Amos 1:1; 7:14). His use of the Hebrew language suggests that he was well-educated, and he knew firsthand the corruption that existed among God's people.

Bad for Business

When God called Amos to preach against the sins of Israel, he faced a serious challenge. He had to bring God's message of judgment to the very people with whom he did business. That meant he had a choice to make, one that sometimes cost him. In fact, Amaziah, the priest at Bethel, misjudged Amos and even turned King Jeroboam against him saying, "Amos is raising a conspiracy against you in the very heart of Israel" (7:10). In spite of Amaziah's threats, and even though he would probably lose business, Amos responded with characteristic conviction and boldness: "But the LORD took me from tending the flock and said to me, 'Go, prophesy to my people Israel.' Now then, hear the word of the LORD" (7:15–16).

Amos was doing God's business. He had not asked for the job, nor did he enjoy the task. But because he loved God, he chose to be faithful and obedient. His message to Israel was very specific. Amos did not couch it in spiritual language, but rather used a powerful metaphor from everyday life to get their attention. He began by saying that he saw the Lord "standing by a wall that had been built true to plumb"—a straight wall, a wall that would not buckle or topple—and the Lord had a "plumb line in his hand." God had set that "plumb line" among his people, and they did not measure up to his standard (7:7–8). They were not true to plumb. No priest would talk like that.

Amos compared the people of Israel to a tilted wall that was ready to collapse because they had violated God's laws. He further spelled out the specifics so there could be no denial: They had trampled "on the heads of the poor" and had committed horrible immorality (2:7). They had oppressed the righteous and had taken bribes (5:12). They had worshiped idols and even elevated their king to a position greater than God himself (5:26). Consequently, God told Amos to tell the people he would "spare them no longer" (7:8). They would all be captured and taken "into exile" (7:17). Amos's message proved true; Israel was scattered to the ends of the earth, and the Babylonian army took the southern kingdom of Judah into captivity.

Compelled to Speak

Amos carried out this difficult task because he had submitted himself to God. Again and again he referred to his "Sovereign LORD" (1:8; 3:7, 11; 4:2; 6:8; 7:1, 4, 5; 8:3, 9). Amos knew God's hand was on him and on Israel. He had to speak, no matter what the personal consequences.

God used Amos to proclaim a serious message. This kind of confrontation is always difficult, especially if you're not "credentialed" for the task. But this is exactly what made Amos so effective. He communicated clearly in a language everyone could understand. He had credibility. He was a "regular guy," a laborer. He himself was not poor, so his message of condemnation for those who mistreated the poor could not be interpreted as "sour grapes."

However, a large measure of his credibility also can be attributed to his lifestyle. Amos was a man of integrity. He took God's plumb line seriously in his own life. Unlike so many of his peers, he did not worship idols or deify the king of Israel. He did not commit adultery and other forms of immorality. Though just a layman, he didn't mince words with the priests in Israel to gain their approval. When he gave his tithes and offerings, they came from his heart. He was not a hypocrite who put up a good facade by performing meaningless rituals.

What About You?

God will always have a use for men like Amos. The church today may not be in the same moral and spiritual condition overall as was Israel in Amos's day, but all of these sins *do* exist in some measure. We need godly laymen—lots of them—who will hear God's voice and boldly deliver a message of exhortation.

Like Amos, you may have more credibility than the average pastor. People expect to hear an exhortation to repentance from their professional spiritual leaders. However, when they hear it from God-fearing businessmen, the message is often more powerful.

God certainly wants to use you. Can you risk your business interests for him if he asks it of you? Will you allow him to be your sovereign Lord, as did Amos?

—*Dr. Gene Getz*

where no snare has been set?
Does a trap spring up from the earth
when there is nothing to catch?
6When a trumpet sounds in a city,
do not the people tremble?
When disaster comes to a city,
has not the LORD caused it?[i]

7Surely the Sovereign LORD does nothing
without revealing his plan[j]
to his servants the prophets.[k]

8The lion has roared—
who will not fear?
The Sovereign LORD has spoken—
who can but prophesy?[l]

9Proclaim to the fortresses of Ashdod
and to the fortresses of Egypt:
"Assemble yourselves on the mountains of Samaria;[m]
see the great unrest within her
and the oppression among her people."

10"They do not know how to do right,[n]" declares the LORD,
"who hoard plunder[o] and loot
in their fortresses."[p]

11Therefore this is what the Sovereign LORD says:

"An enemy will overrun the land;
he will pull down your strongholds
and plunder your fortresses.[q]"

12This is what the LORD says:

"As a shepherd saves from the lion's[r] mouth
only two leg bones or a piece of an ear,
so will the Israelites be saved,
those who sit in Samaria
on the edge of their beds
and in Damascus on their couches.[a][s]"

13"Hear this and testify[t] against the house of Jacob," declares the Lord, the LORD God Almighty.

14"On the day I punish Israel for her sins,
I will destroy the altars of Bethel;[u]
the horns of the altar will be cut off
and fall to the ground.
15I will tear down the winter house[v]
along with the summer house;[w]
the houses adorned with ivory[x]
will be destroyed
and the mansions will be demolished,"
declares the LORD.

3:6 [i]Isa 14:24-27; 45:7
3:7 [j]Ge 18:17; Da 9:22; Jn 15:15; Rev 10:7 [k]Jer 23:22
3:8 [l]Jer 20:9; Jnh 1:1-3; 3:1-3; Ac 4:20
3:9 [m]Am 4:1; 6:1
3:10 [n]Jer 4:22; Am 5:7; 6:12 [o]Hab 2:8 [p]Zep 1:9
3:11 [q]Am 2:5; 6:14
3:12 [r]1Sa 17:34 [s]Am 6:4
3:13 [t]Eze 2:7
3:14 [u]Am 5:5-6
3:15 [v]Jer 36:22 [w]Jdg 3:20 [x]1Ki 22:39
4:1 [y]Ps 22:12; Eze 39:18 [z]Am 3:9 [a]Am 2:8; 5:11; 8:6
4:2 [b]Am 6:8
4:3 [c]Eze 12:5
4:4 [d]Hos 4:15 [e]Nu 28:3 [f]Dt 14:28 [g]Eze 20:39; Am 5:21-22
4:5 [h]Lev 7:13 [i]Lev 22:18-21
4:6 [j]Isa 3:1; Jer 5:3; Hag 2:17
4:7 [k]Ex 9:4,26; Dt 11:17; 2Ch 7:13
4:8 [l]Eze 4:16-17 [m]Jer 3:7 [n]Jer 14:4
4:9 [o]Dt 28:22 [p]Joel 1:7

Israel Has Not Returned to God

4 Hear this word, you cows of Bashan[y] on Mount Samaria,[z]
you women who oppress the poor and crush the needy
and say to your husbands, "Bring us some drinks![a]"
2The Sovereign LORD has sworn by his holiness:
"The time will surely come
when you will be taken away[b] with hooks,
the last of you with fishhooks.
3You will each go straight out
through breaks in the wall,[c]
and you will be cast out toward Harmon,[b]"
declares the LORD.

4"Go to Bethel and sin;
go to Gilgal[d] and sin yet more.
Bring your sacrifices every morning,[e]
your tithes[f] every three years.[c][g]
5Burn leavened bread[h] as a thank offering
and brag about your freewill offerings[i]—
boast about them, you Israelites,
for this is what you love to do,"
declares the Sovereign LORD.

6"I gave you empty stomachs[d] in every city
and lack of bread in every town,
yet you have not returned to me,"
declares the LORD.[j]

7"I also withheld rain from you
when the harvest was still three months away.
I sent rain on one town,
but withheld it from another.[k]
One field had rain;
another had none and dried up.
8People staggered from town to town for water[l]
but did not get enough to drink,
yet you have not returned[m] to me,"
declares the LORD.[n]

9"Many times I struck your gardens and vineyards,
I struck them with blight and mildew.[o]
Locusts devoured your fig and olive trees,[p]

a *12* The meaning of the Hebrew for this line is uncertain. b *3* Masoretic Text; with a different word division of the Hebrew (see Septuagint) *out, O mountain of oppression* c *4* Or *tithes on the third day* d *6* Hebrew *you cleanness of teeth*

yet you have not returned[q] to
me,"
declares the LORD.

10 "I sent plagues[r] among you
as I did to Egypt.
I killed your young men with the
sword,
along with your captured horses.
I filled your nostrils with the stench
of your camps,
yet you have not returned to
me,"
declares the LORD.[s]

11 "I overthrew some of you
as I[a] overthrew Sodom and
Gomorrah.[t]
You were like a burning stick
snatched from the fire,
yet you have not returned to
me,"
declares the LORD.

12 "Therefore this is what I will do to
you, Israel,
and because I will do this to you,
prepare to meet your God,
O Israel."

13 He who forms the mountains,[u]
creates the wind,
and reveals his thoughts[v] to
man,
he who turns dawn to darkness,
and treads the high places of the
earth[w]—
the LORD God Almighty is his
name.[x]

A Lament and Call to Repentance

5 Hear this word, O house of Israel, this lament[y] I take up concerning you:

2 "Fallen is Virgin[z] Israel,
never to rise again,
deserted in her own land,
with no one to lift her up.[a]"

3 This is what the Sovereign LORD says:

"The city that marches out a
thousand strong for Israel
will have only a hundred left;
the town that marches out a
hundred strong
will have only ten left.[b]"

4 This is what the LORD says to the house of Israel:

"Seek me and live;[c]
5 do not seek Bethel,
do not go to Gilgal,[d]
do not journey to Beersheba.[e]
For Gilgal will surely go into exile,
and Bethel will be reduced to
nothing.[b][f]"

6 Seek[g] the LORD and live,[h]
or he will sweep through the
house of Joseph like a fire;[i]
it will devour,
and Bethel[j] will have no one to
quench it.
7 You who turn justice into
bitterness[k]
and cast righteousness to the
ground
8 (he who made the Pleiades and
Orion,[l]
who turns blackness into dawn[m]
and darkens day into night,[n]
who calls for the waters of the sea
and pours them out over the
face of the land—
the LORD is his name[o]—
9 he flashes destruction on the
stronghold
and brings the fortified city to
ruin),[p]

4:9 [q]Jer 3:10; Hag 2:17 **4:10** [r]Ex 9:3; Dt 28:27 [s]Isa 9:13 **4:11** [t]Ge 19:24; Jer 23:14 **4:13** [u]Ps 65:6 [v]Da 2:28 [w]Mic 1:3 [x]Isa 47:4; Am 5:8,27; 9:6 **5:1** [y]Eze 19:1 **5:2** [z]Jer 14:17 [a]Jer 50:32; Am 8:14 **5:3** [b]Isa 6:13; Am 6:9 **5:4** [c]Isa 55:3; Jer 29:13 **5:5** [d]1Sa 11:14; Am 4:4 [e]Am 8:14 [f]1Sa 7:16 **5:6** [g]Isa 55:6 [h]ver 14 [i]Dt 4:24 [j]Am 3:14 **5:7** [k]Am 6:12 **5:8** [l]Job 9:9 [m]Isa 42:16 [n]Ps 104:20; Am 8:9 [o]Ps 104:6-9; Am 4:13 **5:9** [p]Mic 5:11

[a] *11* Hebrew *God* [b] *5* Or *grief*; or *wickedness*; Hebrew *aven*, a reference to Beth Aven (a derogatory name for Bethel)

4:12–13

PROMISE 3

MEET YOUR MAKER

"Prepare to meet your maker." That's a line we've all heard in old gangster and suspense movies. Amos is quoted as saying this to the people of Israel not as a threat, but as a last-ditch attempt at getting God's people to turn back to him in repentance.

Amos's plea comes after he outlines a series of catastrophes that will result if the people refuse to return to God and serve him. One can almost sense the desperation in the prophet's voice as he urges the people to turn and avoid the coming events. Why is God going to exercise judgment on his people? Verse 13 gives us an idea. In it Amos outlines God's perfect nature. He's the powerful Creator who—unbelievably—reveals himself and his commands to people, the God whose power and vision far exceed ours. He can see beyond our sin to its inevitable result, and urges us to turn from the path that will lead us to destruction.

God's judgment may seem severe; Amos's audience certainly thought so. But God's holy, divine nature simply cannot tolerate sin. That's why he sent his Son to pay the price for our sin (John 3:16), and why Amos and other prophets urged the ancient Israelites—and through them, us as well—to avoid sin at all costs.

Someday, each one of us will meet the God who "forms the mountains" and "creates the wind." Will you be ready?

For the next Promise 3 reading go to page 993.

10you hate the one who reproves in court[q]
and despise him who tells the truth.[r]
11You trample on the poor[s]
and force him to give you grain.
Therefore, though you have built stone mansions,[t]
you will not live in them;
though you have planted lush vineyards,
you will not drink their wine.[u]
12For I know how many are your offenses
and how great your sins.

You oppress the righteous and take bribes
and you deprive the poor of justice in the courts.[v]
13Therefore the prudent man keeps quiet in such times,
for the times are evil.

3 →PG. 996
14Seek good, not evil,
that you may live.
Then the LORD God Almighty will be with you,
just as you say he is.
15Hate evil,[w] love good;
maintain justice in the courts.
Perhaps the LORD God Almighty will have mercy[x]
on the remnant[y] of Joseph.

16Therefore this is what the Lord, the LORD God Almighty, says:

"There will be wailing[z] in all the streets
and cries of anguish in every public square.
The farmers[a] will be summoned to weep
and the mourners to wail.
17There will be wailing in all the vineyards,
for I will pass through[b] your midst,"
says the LORD.[c]

The Day of the LORD

18Woe to you who long
for the day of the LORD![d]
Why do you long for the day of the LORD?
That day will be darkness,[e] not light.[f]
19It will be as though a man fled from a lion
only to meet a bear,
as though he entered his house
and rested his hand on the wall
only to have a snake bite him.[g]
20Will not the day of the LORD be darkness, not light—
pitch-dark, without a ray of brightness?[h]

21"I hate, I despise your religious feasts;[i]
I cannot stand your assemblies.[j]
22Even though you bring me burnt offerings and grain offerings,
I will not accept them.
Though you bring choice fellowship offerings,[a]
I will have no regard for them.[k l]
23Away with the noise of your songs!

5:10 [q]Isa 29:21 [r]1Ki 22:8
5:11 [s]Am 8:6 [t]Am 3:15 [u]Mic 6:15
5:12 [v]Isa 5:23; Am 2:6-7
5:15 [w]Ps 97:10; Ro 12:9 [x]Joel 2:14 [y]Mic 5:7,8
5:16 [z]Jer 9:17 [a]Joel 1:11
5:17 [b]Ex 12:12 [c]Isa 16:10; Jer 48:33
5:18 [d]Joel 1:15 [e]Joel 2:2 [f]Isa 5:19,30; Jer 30:7
5:19 [g]Job 20:24; Isa 24:17-18; Jer 15:2-3; 48:44
5:20 [h]Isa 13:10; Zep 1:15
5:21 [i]Lev 26:31 [j]Isa 1:11-16
5:22 [k]Am 4:4; Mic 6:6-7 [l]Isa 66:3

[a] 22 Traditionally *peace offerings*

5:21

PROMISE 1

PAYING GOD OFF?

Ever thought of bribing your local police chief?

Imagine setting up a meeting in which you sit down with the chief in his or her office, lay down a stack of cash and propose that you be allowed to do whatever you want without fear of prosecution. Chances are good that you'd soon find yourself in a holding cell, deliberating about which friend or family member to call. Not a very good idea, is it? But that's what Amos said Israel was trying to do with God.

God introduced a system of sacrifices (Leviticus 4:1–7:10) that allowed repentant people to express grief over their sin. But what God intended as a way to help people stop sinning, the people turned into a way to pay God off and make sinning easier. Amos (and Isaiah, and Jeremiah) pointed out Israel's hypocrisy and said that God detested the very act he had commanded. Israel treated the sacrifice as a bribe that gave them permission to sin.

Today we face a similar danger. We think we're pleasing God by what we say and do, but sometimes our hearts aren't in the right place. God has offered us eternal salvation, and all he asks in return is obedience, holiness, purity and justice. When we blow it (and God knows we will), he makes provision for us to repair our relationship with him: "If we confess our sins, [God] is faithful and just and will forgive us our sins" (1 John 1:9). But God's provision of forgiveness should *never* be seen as permission for us to continue in sin.

Avoid this subtle trap. When you sin, repent and confess it; but don't ever think of God's provision as God's permission.

For the next Promise 1 reading go to page 988.

I will not listen to the music of
your harps.[m]
24But let justice[n] roll on like a river,
righteousness like a never-failing
stream![o]
25"Did you bring me sacrifices[p] and
offerings
forty years[q] in the desert,
O house of Israel?
26You have lifted up the shrine of
your king,
the pedestal of your idols,
the star of your god[a]—
which you made for yourselves.
27Therefore I will send you into exile
beyond Damascus,"
says the LORD, whose name is
God Almighty.[r]

Woe to the Complacent

6 Woe to you[s] who are complacent
in Zion,
and to you who feel secure on
Mount Samaria,
you notable men of the foremost
nation,
to whom the people of Israel
come![t]
2Go to Calneh[u] and look at it;
go from there to great Hamath,[v]
and then go down to Gath[w] in
Philistia.
Are they better off than[x] your two
kingdoms?
Is their land larger than yours?
3You put off the evil day
and bring near a reign of
terror.[y]
4You lie on beds inlaid with ivory
and lounge on your couches.
You dine on choice lambs
and fattened calves.[z]
5You strum away on your harps[a]
like David
and improvise on musical
instruments.[b]
6You drink wine[c] by the bowlful
and use the finest lotions,
but you do not grieve[d] over the
ruin of Joseph.
7Therefore you will be among the
first to go into exile;
your feasting and lounging will
end.

The LORD Abhors the Pride of Israel

8The Sovereign LORD has sworn by
himself[e]—the LORD God Almighty declares:

"I abhor[f] the pride of Jacob[g]
and detest his fortresses;
I will deliver up[h] the city
and everything in it.[i]"
9If ten[j] men are left in one house,
they too will die. 10And if a relative who
is to burn the bodies[k] comes to carry
them out of the house and asks anyone
still hiding there, "Is anyone with you?"
and he says, "No," then he will say,
"Hush![l] We must not mention the
name of the LORD."

11For the LORD has given the
command,
and he will smash the great
house[m] into pieces
and the small house into bits.[n]

12Do horses run on the rocky crags?
Does one plow there with oxen?
But you have turned justice into
poison[o]
and the fruit of righteousness
into bitterness[p]—
13you who rejoice in the conquest of
Lo Debar[b]
and say, "Did we not take
Karnaim[c] by our own
strength?[q]"

14For the LORD God Almighty
declares,
"I will stir up a nation[r] against
you, O house of Israel,
that will oppress you all the way
from Lebo[d] Hamath[s] to the
valley of the Arabah.[t]"

Locusts, Fire and a Plumb Line

7 This is what the Sovereign LORD
showed me:[u] He was preparing
swarms of locusts[v] after the king's
share had been harvested and just as
the second crop was coming up.
2When they had stripped the land
clean,[w] I cried out, "Sovereign LORD,
forgive! How can Jacob survive?[x] He is
so small![y]"
3So the LORD relented.[z]
"This will not happen," the LORD
said.[a]
4This is what the Sovereign LORD
showed me: The Sovereign LORD was
calling for judgment by fire;[b] it dried
up the great deep and devoured[c] the
land. 5Then I cried out, "Sovereign
LORD, I beg you, stop! How can Jacob
survive? He is so small![d]"
6So the LORD relented.[e]
"This will not happen either," the
Sovereign LORD said.

7This is what he showed me: The
Lord was standing by a wall that had
been built true to plumb, with a plumb

5:23 [m]Am 6:5
5:24 [n]Jer 22:3 [o]Mic 6:8
5:25 [p]Isa 43:23 [q]Dt 32:17
5:27 [r]Am 4:13; Ac 7:42-43*
6:1 [s]Lk 6:24 [t]Isa 32:9-11
6:2 [u]Ge 10:10 [v]2Ki 18:34 [w]2Ch 26:6 [x]Na 3:8
6:3 [y]Isa 56:12; Am 9:10
6:4 [z]Eze 34:2-3; Am 3:12
6:5 [a]Isa 5:12; Am 5:23 [b]1Ch 15:16
6:6 [c]Am 2:8 [d]Eze 9:4
6:8 [e]Ge 22:16; Heb 6:13 [f]Lev 26:30 [g]Ps 47:4 [h]Am 4:2 [i]Dt 32:19
6:9 [j]Am 5:3
6:10 [k]1Sa 31:12 [l]Am 8:3
6:11 [m]Am 3:15 [n]Isa 55:11
6:12 [o]Hos 10:4 [p]Am 5:7
6:13 [q]Job 8:15; Isa 28:14-15
6:14 [r]Jer 5:15 [s]1Ki 8:65 [t]Am 3:11
7:1 [u]Am 8:1 [v]Joel 1:4
7:2 [w]Ex 10:15 [x]Isa 37:4 [y]Eze 11:13
7:3 [z]Dt 32:36; Jer 26:19; Jnh 3:10 [a]Hos 11:8
7:4 [b]Isa 66:16 [c]Dt 32:22
7:5 [d]ver 1-2; Joel 2:17
7:6 [e]Jnh 3:10

[a]26 Or *lifted up Sakkuth your king / and Kaiwan your idols, / your star-gods;* Septuagint *lifted up the shrine of Molech / and the star of your god Rephan, / their idols* [b]13 *Lo Debar* means *nothing.* [c]13 *Karnaim* means *horns; horn* here symbolizes strength. [d]14 Or *from the entrance to*

line in his hand. 8 And the LORD asked
me, "What do you see,[f] Amos?[g]"
"A plumb line,[h]" I replied.
Then the Lord said, "Look, I am set-
ting a plumb line among my people
Israel; I will spare them no longer.[i]

9 "The high places of Isaac will be
destroyed
and the sanctuaries[j] of Israel
will be ruined;
with my sword I will rise against
the house of Jeroboam.[k]"

Amos and Amaziah

10 Then Amaziah the priest of Bethel[l] sent a message to Jeroboam[m] king
of Israel: "Amos is raising a conspiracy[n] against you in the very heart of
Israel. The land cannot bear all his
words.[o] 11 For this is what Amos is saying:

" 'Jeroboam will die by the sword,
and Israel will surely go into
exile,
away from their native land.' "

12 Then Amaziah said to Amos, "Get
out, you seer! Go back to the land of
Judah. Earn your bread there and do
your prophesying there.[p] 13 Don't
prophesy anymore at Bethel, because
this is the king's sanctuary and the
temple of the kingdom.[q]"
14 Amos answered Amaziah, "I was
neither a prophet[r] nor a prophet's
son, but I was a shepherd, and I also
took care of sycamore-fig trees. 15 But
the LORD took me from tending the
flock[s] and said to me, 'Go, prophesy
to my people Israel.'[t] 16 Now then,
hear the word of the LORD. You say,

" 'Do not prophesy against[u] Israel,
and stop preaching against the
house of Isaac.'

17 "Therefore this is what the LORD
says:

" 'Your wife will become a
prostitute[v] in the city,
and your sons and daughters will
fall by the sword.
Your land will be measured and
divided up,
and you yourself will die in a
pagan[a] country.
And Israel will certainly go into
exile,
away from their native land.[w]' "

A Basket of Ripe Fruit

8 This is what the Sovereign LORD
showed me: a basket of ripe fruit.
2 "What do you see,[x] Amos?[y]" he
asked.

"A basket of ripe fruit," I answered.
Then the LORD said to me, "The time
is ripe for my people Israel; I will spare
them no longer.[z]
3 "In that day," declares the Sovereign LORD, "the songs in the temple
will turn to wailing.[b][a] Many, many
bodies—flung everywhere! Silence![b]"

4 Hear this, you who trample the
needy
and do away with the poor[c] of
the land,[d]

5 saying,

"When will the New Moon be over
that we may sell grain,
and the Sabbath be ended
that we may market wheat?"—
skimping the measure,
boosting the price
and cheating with dishonest
scales,[e]
6 buying the poor with silver
and the needy for a pair of
sandals,
selling even the sweepings with
the wheat.[f]

7 The LORD has sworn by the Pride of
Jacob:[g] "I will never forget[h] anything
they have done.

8 "Will not the land tremble[i] for
this,
and all who live in it mourn?
The whole land will rise like the
Nile;
it will be stirred up and then
sink
like the river of Egypt.[j]

9 "In that day," declares the Sovereign LORD,

"I will make the sun go down at
noon
and darken the earth in broad
daylight.[k]
10 I will turn your religious feasts into
mourning
and all your singing into
weeping.
I will make all of you wear
sackcloth[l]
and shave your heads.
I will make that time like mourning
for an only son[m]
and the end of it like a bitter
day.[n]

11 "The days are coming," declares
the Sovereign LORD,
"when I will send a famine
through the land—

7:8 [f]Jer 1:11,13 [g]Isa 28:17; La 2:8; Am 8:2 [h]2Ki 21:13 [i]Jer 15:6; Eze 7:2-9
7:9 [j]Lev 26:31 [k]2Ki 15:9; Isa 63:18; Hos 10:8
7:10 [l]1Ki 12:32 [m]2Ki 14:23 [n]Jer 38:4 [o]Jer 26:8-11
7:12 [p]Mt 8:34
7:13 [q]Am 2:12; Ac 4:18
7:14 [r]2Ki 2:5; 4:38
7:15 [s]2Sa 7:8 [t]Jer 7:1-2; Eze 2:3-4
7:16 [u]Eze 20:46; Mic 2:6
7:17 [v]Hos 4:13 [w]2Ki 17:6; Eze 4:13; Hos 9:3
8:2 [x]Jer 24:3 [y]Am 7:8 [z]Eze 7:2-9
8:3 [a]Am 5:16 [b]Am 5:23; 6:10
8:4 [c]Pr 30:14 [d]Ps 14:4; Am 2:7
8:5 [e]2Ki 4:23; Ne 13:15-16; Hos 12:7; Mic 6:10-11
8:6 [f]Am 2:6
8:7 [g]Am 6:8 [h]Hos 8:13
8:8 [i]Hos 4:3 [j]Ps 18:7; Jer 46:8; Am 9:5
8:9 [k]Job 5:14; Isa 59:9-10; Jer 15:9; Am 5:8; Mic 3:6
8:10 [l]Jer 48:37 [m]Jer 6:26; Zec 12:10 [n]Eze 7:18

a *17* Hebrew *an unclean* b *3* Or *"the temple singers will wail*

not a famine of food or a thirst for water,
but a famine of hearing the words of the LORD.[o]
12Men will stagger from sea to sea
and wander from north to east,
searching for the word of the LORD,
but they will not find it.[p]

13"In that day

"the lovely young women and strong young men
will faint because of thirst.[q]
14They who swear by the shame[a] of Samaria,
or say, 'As surely as your god lives, O Dan,'[r]
or, 'As surely as the god[b] of Beersheba[s] lives'—
they will fall,
never to rise again.[t]"

Israel to Be Destroyed

9 I saw the Lord standing by the altar, and he said:

"Strike the tops of the pillars
so that the thresholds shake.
Bring them down on the heads[u] of all the people;
those who are left I will kill with the sword.
Not one will get away,
none will escape.
2Though they dig down to the depths of the grave,[c][v]
from there my hand will take them.
Though they climb up to the heavens,[w]
from there I will bring them down.[x]
3Though they hide themselves on the top of Carmel,[y]
there I will hunt them down and seize them.[z]
Though they hide from me at the bottom of the sea,
there I will command the serpent to bite them.[a]
4Though they are driven into exile by their enemies,
there I will command the sword[b] to slay them.
I will fix my eyes upon them
for evil[c] and not for good.[d]"[e]

5The Lord, the LORD Almighty,
he who touches the earth and it melts,[f]
and all who live in it mourn—
the whole land rises like the Nile,
then sinks like the river of Egypt[g]—
6he who builds his lofty palace[d] in the heavens
and sets its foundation[e] on the earth,
who calls for the waters of the sea
and pours them out over the face of the land—
the LORD is his name.[h]

7"Are not you Israelites
the same to me as the Cushites[f]?"[i]
declares the LORD.
"Did I not bring Israel up from Egypt,
the Philistines from Caphtor[g][j]
and the Arameans from Kir?[k]
8"Surely the eyes of the Sovereign LORD
are on the sinful kingdom.
I will destroy it
from the face of the earth—
yet I will not totally destroy
the house of Jacob,"
declares the LORD.[l]
9"For I will give the command,
and I will shake the house of Israel
among all the nations
as grain[m] is shaken in a sieve,[n]
and not a pebble will reach the ground.
10All the sinners among my people
will die by the sword,
all those who say,

8:11 [o]1Sa 3:1; 2Ch 15:3; Eze 7:26 **8:12** [p]Eze 20:3,31 **8:13** [q]Isa 41:17; Hos 2:3 **8:14** [r]1Ki 12:29 [s]Am 5:5 [t]Am 5:2 **9:1** [u]Ps 68:21 **9:2** [v]Ps 139:8 [w]Jer 51:53 [x]Ob 1:4 **9:3** [y]Am 1:2 [z]Ps 139:8-10 [a]Jer 16:16-17 **9:4** [b]Lev 26:33; Eze 5:12 [c]Jer 21:10 [d]Jer 39:16 [e]Jer 44:11 **9:5** [f]Ps 46:2; Mic 1:4 [g]Am 8:8 **9:6** [h]Ps 104:1-3, 5-6,13; Am 5:8 **9:7** [i]Isa 20:4; 43:3 [j]Dt 2:23; Jer 47:4 [k]2Ki 16:9; Isa 22:6; Am 1:5; 2:10 **9:8** [l]Jer 44:27 **9:9** [m]Lk 22:31 [n]Isa 30:28

a *14* Or *by Ashima*; or *by the idol* b *14* Or *power* c *2* Hebrew *to Sheol*
d *6* The meaning of the Hebrew for this phrase is uncertain. e *6* The meaning of the Hebrew for this word is uncertain. f *7* That is, people from the upper Nile region g *7* That is, Crete

9:13–15

PROMISE 7

THERE'S ALWAYS HOPE

God's prophets told the truth. They never softened God's anger toward sin. They knew about sin's destructive power and they knew it must be stopped. But the prophets always provided a way out; they always provided hope.

The Great Commission (Matthew 28:18–20) is about salvation. As a godly man you must—as Amos did—call people to repentance. But reflect on the ending of this message from Amos. This prophet's purpose was not to talk about sin. He talked about sin to achieve his purpose—restoration, salvation, hope and the promise of a relationship with God. Both in Amos's time and in ours, that's the prophet's commission. That is also your great commission: to proclaim a better way and tell lost people that God always offers the hope of salvation.

For the next Promise 7 reading go to page 985.

'Disaster will not overtake or
meet us.'[o]

Israel's Restoration

11 "In that day I will restore
David's fallen tent.
I will repair its broken places,
restore its ruins,
and build it as it used to be,[p]
12 so that they may possess the
remnant of Edom[q]
and all the nations that bear my
name,[a][r]"
declares the LORD,
who will do these things.[s]

13 "The days are coming," declares
the LORD,
"when the reaper will be overtaken
by the plowman[t]
and the planter by the one
treading grapes.
New wine will drip from the
mountains
and flow from all the hills.[u]
14 I will bring back my exiled[b] people
Israel;
they will rebuild the ruined
cities[v] and live in them.
They will plant vineyards and drink
their wine;
they will make gardens and eat
their fruit.[w]
15 I will plant[x] Israel in their own
land,
never again to be uprooted
from the land I have given
them,"
says the LORD your God.[y]

9:10 [o]Am 6:3
9:11 [p]Ps 80:12
9:12 [q]Nu 24:18 [r]Isa 43:7 [s]Ac 15:16-17*
9:13 [t]Lev 26:5 [u]Joel 3:18
9:14 [v]Isa 61:4 [w]Jer 30:18; 31:28; Eze 28:25-26
9:15 [x]Isa 60:21 [y]Jer 24:6; Eze 34:25-28; 37:12,25

[a] *12* Hebrew; Septuagint *so that the remnant of men / and all the nations that bear my name may seek ⌊the Lord⌋*
[b] *14* Or *will restore the fortunes of my*

OBADIAH

AT A GLANCE

Key Principle: The things we do to other people eventually come back to us; we can either sow to please our sinful nature and reap corruption, or we can sow to please the Spirit and reap blessing.
Author: Obadiah
Time and Place: ~840 B.C. / Edom and Israel
Key Verses: 10, 15, 21

BENEFIT

Unlike the other prophetical books, Obadiah has no message of consolation for its target audience. The Edomites, because of their treachery against the Israelites, faced certain doom. A nation can rebel against God's purposes to the point of no return, and Edom's fate can be a lesson for us today.

SETTING

Obadiah's personal background is unknown, though he likely lived in the southern kingdom of Judah because of his concern with the fate of Jerusalem. The only historical detail we can use to date the book is the foreign invasion of Jerusalem mentioned in verses 11–14. This could be a reference to many different invasions, but the most likely candidate is during the time of Jehoram (848–841 B.C.) when the Philistines and Arabians plundered the palace (2 Chronicles 21:16–17). Dating the book in this way fits best with Obadiah 11–14, and if this is correct, Obadiah wrote this prophecy against Edom around 840 B.C.

The original struggle between Esau and Jacob continued on as a struggle between their descendants, the Edomites and the Israelites. The Edomites refused to allow Israel to pass through their land on their way to Canaan; this act began a centuries-long state of enmity between the two nations. Because of their failure to help Jacob's descendants in their time of need, Obadiah prophesied that they would be "destroyed forever" (10). In the fourth century B.C., the Edomites were forced to leave their territory and resettled in southern Palestine. There they became known as Idumeans, and were never heard of again after they joined in the Jewish rebellion against Rome and were defeated in A.D. 70 by Titus of Rome.

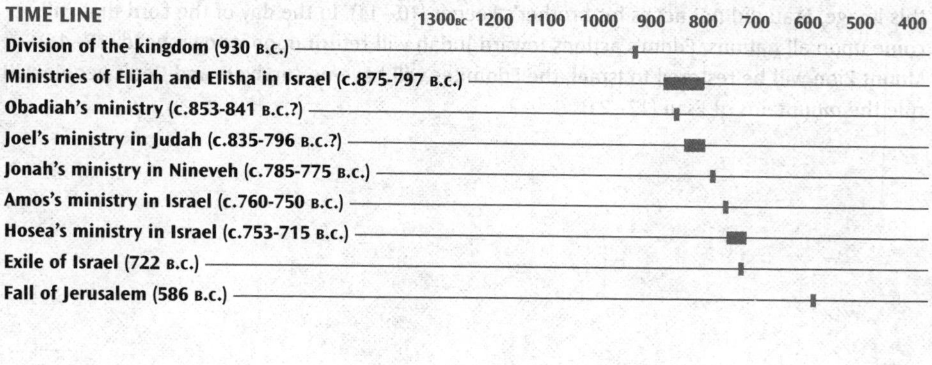

THEME AND PURPOSE

Obadiah pronounced inescapable doom upon the Edomites (Esau) because they looked down on their brother Judah (Jacob) in the day of misfortune and rejoiced over the people of Judah in the day of disaster (12–14). Obadiah proclaimed that the Edomites' pride would be brought low (3–4), and they would be ransacked (6), terrified (9) and obliterated (10). Israel, on the other hand, would be restored, and it would possess its inheritance (17–21).

UNIQUE CONTRIBUTION

With only 21 verses, Obadiah is the shortest book in the Old Testament. Yet, it is a complete message with its twin prophetic themes of condemnation (1–16) and consolation (17–21; the consolation portion concerns Judah, not Edom). While other prophets (Isaiah, Jeremiah, Ezekiel, Joel, Amos and Malachi) speak of God's judgment on Edom, Obadiah is the only Biblical book that is exclusively concerned with Edom's downfall. Obadiah is possibly the earliest of the writing prophets if verses 11–14 refer to the invasion of Jerusalem in the time of Jehoram (see "Setting," above). It appears that Joel, Amos and Jeremiah alluded to portions of Obadiah.

LINKS TO THE NEW TESTAMENT

We see in Obadiah an illustration of Christ as the Judge of the nations in the day of the Lord (15–16), the Deliverer of Israel and Judah (17–20) and the Lord of the coming kingdom (21).

OVERVIEW

FOCUS	Condemnation	Cause	Consummation	
REFERENCE	1 ... 9	10 ... 14	15 ... 16	17 ... 21
TOPICS	Arrogance of Edom	Antagonism of Edom	Annihilation of Edom	
	Arraignment	Indictment	Sentence	
	Destruction of Edom		Day of the Lord	Deliverance of Judah
	Security on the Mountain of Esau (v. 3)		Sentence on the Mountain of Esau (v. 21)	
LOCATION	Edom		All Nations	Israel and Judah
TIME	~840 B.C.			

Obadiah's vision begins with a message of irreversible condemnation against the pride of the Edomites (1–9). They have grown arrogant because of their secure position in the mountainous region south of the Dead Sea, but God declares that they will be ransacked and pillaged. Their doom is sealed because of their violence and treachery against the descendants of Jacob; in this image, Esau did not act as his brother's keeper (10–14). In the day of the Lord that will come upon all nations, Edom's actions toward Judah will return upon its own head (15–16). Mount Zion will be restored to Israel, the Edomites will have no survivors and God's people will rule the mountains of Esau (17–21).

OBADIAH

1 The vision of Obadiah.

This is what the Sovereign LORD says about Edom[a]—

We have heard a message from the LORD:
An envoy[b] was sent to the nations to say,
"Rise, and let us go against her for battle"[c]—
2 "See, I will make you small among the nations;
you will be utterly despised.
3 The pride[d] of your heart has deceived you,
you who live in the clefts of the rocks[a]
and make your home on the heights,
you who say to yourself,
'Who can bring me down to the ground?'[e]
4 Though you soar like the eagle
and make your nest[f] among the stars,
from there I will bring you down,"[g]
declares the LORD.[h]
5 "If thieves came to you,
if robbers in the night—
Oh, what a disaster awaits you—
would they not steal only as much as they wanted?
If grape pickers came to you,
would they not leave a few grapes?[i]
6 But how Esau will be ransacked,
his hidden treasures pillaged!
7 All your allies[j] will force you to the border;
your friends will deceive and overpower you;
those who eat your bread[k] will set a trap for you,[b]
but you will not detect it.

8 "In that day," declares the LORD,
"will I not destroy[l] the wise men of Edom,
men of understanding in the mountains of Esau?
9 Your warriors, O Teman,[m] will be terrified,
and everyone in Esau's mountains
will be cut down in the slaughter.
10 Because of the violence[n] against your brother Jacob,[o]
you will be covered with shame;
you will be destroyed forever.[p]
11 On the day you stood aloof
while strangers carried off his wealth
and foreigners entered his gates
and cast lots[q] for Jerusalem,
you were like one of them.
12 You should not look down on your brother
in the day of his misfortune,
nor rejoice[r] over the people of Judah
in the day of their destruction,[s]
nor boast so much
in the day of their trouble.[t]
13 You should not march through the gates of my people
in the day of their disaster,
nor look down on them in their calamity[u]
in the day of their disaster,
nor seize their wealth
in the day of their disaster.

1:1 [a] Isa 63:1-6; Jer 49:7-22; Eze 25:12-14; Am 1:11-12 [b] Isa 18:2 [c] Jer 6:4-5 **1:3** [d] Isa 16:6 [e] Isa 14:13-15; Rev 18:7 **1:4** [f] Hab 2:9 [g] Isa 14:13 [h] Job 20:6 **1:5** [i] Dt 24:21 **1:7** [j] Jer 30:14 [k] Ps 41:9 **1:8** [l] Job 5:12; Isa 29:14 **1:9** [m] Ge 36:11,34 **1:10** [n] Joel 3:19 [o] Ps 137:7; Am 1:11-12 [p] Eze 35:9 **1:11** [q] Na 3:10 **1:12** [r] Eze 35:15 [s] Pr 17:5 [t] Mic 4:11 **1:13** [u] Eze 35:5

a *3* Or *of Sela* **b** *7* The meaning of the Hebrew for this clause is uncertain.

12

PROMISE **6**

BROTHER'S KEEPER

Judah and Edom had a long history of hostility. The people of Edom descended directly from Esau, and the people of Judah from his twin brother Jacob. (You can read about the beginnings of this hostility in Genesis 25:19–34 and 27:1–45.) But God told the people of Edom not to gloat over their enemies' destruction. In Judah's day of trouble, God promised he would hold Edom accountable for giving Judah no compassion or support. Verses 8–11 give the running start into this important conclusion. Notice the word "because" in verse 10, and the warning that word begins.

If God expects godless, Gentile nations to treat their enemies as brothers, how much more will he expect of those who follow him! Too often Christian brothers get short-sighted; the competitive nature takes over, and one man inwardly gloats over the failure of another. This happens all too often in business, sports, family relations, and even on some church councils. As you relate to your brothers in Christ, make it a point to demonstrate the power of Biblical unity. Be your brother's (or sister's) keeper.

For the next Promise 6 reading go to page 988.

14 You should not wait at the
crossroads
to cut down their fugitives,
nor hand over their survivors
in the day of their trouble.

15 "The day of the LORD is near[v]
for all nations.
As you have done, it will be done
to you;
your deeds[w] will return upon
your own head.
16 Just as you drank on my holy hill,
so all the nations will drink[x]
continually;
they will drink and drink
and be as if they had never
been.
17 But on Mount Zion will be
deliverance;[y]
it will be holy,[z]
and the house of Jacob
will possess its inheritance.
18 The house of Jacob will be a fire
and the house of Joseph a flame;
the house of Esau will be stubble,
and they will set it on fire and
consume[a] it.
There will be no survivors
from the house of Esau."
The LORD has spoken.

19 People from the Negev will occupy
the mountains of Esau,
and people from the foothills will
possess
the land of the Philistines.[b]
They will occupy the fields of
Ephraim and Samaria,[c]
and Benjamin will possess
Gilead.
20 This company of Israelite exiles
who are in Canaan
will possess ⌞the land⌟ as far as
Zarephath;[d]
the exiles from Jerusalem who are
in Sepharad
will possess the towns of the
Negev.[e]
21 Deliverers will go up on[a] Mount
Zion
to govern the mountains of Esau.
And the kingdom will be the
LORD's.[f]

1:15 [v]Eze 30:3 [w]Jer 50:29; Hab 2:8 **1:16** [x]Jer 25:15; 49:12 **1:17** [y]Am 9:11-15 [z]Isa 4:3 **1:18** [a]Zec 12:6
1:19 [b]Isa 11:14 [c]Jer 31:5 **1:20** [d]1Ki 17:9-10 [e]Jer 33:13 **1:21** [f]Ps 22:28; Zec 14:9,16; Rev 11:15

a *21* Or *from*

JONAH

AT A GLANCE

Key Principle: The God of Israel is the Lord of nature and the Lord of nations, and his compassion and grace extend beyond national boundaries.
Author: Jonah
Time and Place: ~785–750 B.C. / The Mediterranean Sea and the city of Nineveh
Key Verses: 2:8–9; 4:2, 10–11

BENEFIT

We typically want God to treat us with grace and to treat our enemies with justice, and Jonah is no exception. Jonah resisted God's call to prophesy to the capital city of Israel's archenemy, Assyria. He was afraid that if he prophesied to the people of Nineveh, they would repent and God would avert the disaster that was due to come upon them in 40 days. This book teaches us about the folly of resenting God's grace when it is extended to people we think should not receive it. We can be thankful that God's mercy moves beyond national borders.

SETTING

According to 2 Kings 14:25, Jonah son of Amittai (1:1) came from Gath Hepher in lower Galilee and prophesied during the reign of Jeroboam II of Israel (793–753 B.C.). Thus, he lived in the northern kingdom after the time of Elisha and near the time of Amos and Hosea. During Jeroboam's reign, Israel enjoyed a brief time of prosperity and relative safety, but Jonah knew that Assyria was the power that would eventually overthrow his nation. Since Jonah ministered during the reign of Jeroboam, Nineveh's repentance likely took place in the reign of Ashurdan III (773–755 B.C.). It was during his reign that Assyria experienced two plagues (765 B.C. and 759 B.C.) and a solar eclipse (763 B.C.), and these may have contributed to the Ninevites' response to Jonah's preaching.

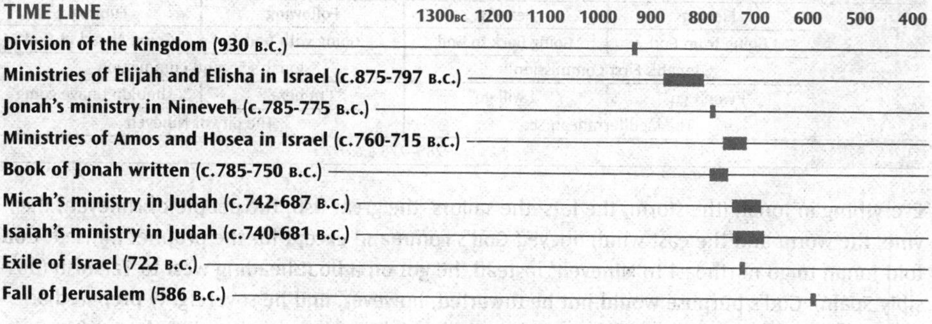

THEME AND PURPOSE

Jonah demonstrates that Yahweh is not the God of Jews only, but also the God of Gentiles (Romans 3:29). As the apostle Peter observed when he went to the house of Cornelius, "I now realize how true it is that God does not show favoritism but accepts men from every nation who fear him and do what is right" (Acts 10:34). Jonah's nationalistic fervor kept him from wanting God's grace and mercy to reach beyond Israel's boundaries. This was especially true of his attitude toward the Assyrians, a people with a reputation for extreme military savagery and brutality toward their captives. In this book, Jonah learns that "Salvation comes from the Lord" (2:9), and that God's compassion is greater and wider than he previously thought.

UNIQUE CONTRIBUTION

More than any other Old Testament book, Jonah reveals God's universal concern for people in all nations. Significantly, Nineveh's response to Jonah's brief message is greater than was Israel and Judah's response to the prophets whom God sent to them.

The Pharisees were mistaken when they said, "Look into it, and you will find that a prophet does not come out of Galilee" (John 7:52), since Jonah was from Gath Hepher, a village that was three miles north of Nazareth in Galilee (2 Kings 14:25). Although he lived in the northern kingdom of Israel, his book focuses exclusively on the great city of Nineveh, the capital of the Assyrian Empire. Another unique feature of Jonah is its stress on the messenger rather than the prophetic message (the message itself is summed up in this single statement: "Forty more days and Nineveh will be overturned").

LINKS TO THE NEW TESTAMENT

Christ used Jonah's experience of being engulfed by the deep, swallowed by a great fish and later deposited alive on land as an illustration of his death, burial and resurrection. "A wicked and adulterous generation asks for a miraculous sign! But none will be given it except the sign of the prophet Jonah. For as Jonah was three days and three nights in the belly of a huge fish, so the Son of Man will be three days and three nights in the heart of the earth. The men of Nineveh will stand up at the judgment with this generation and condemn it; for they repented at the preaching of Jonah, and now one greater than Jonah is here" (Matthew 12:39–41). Here it is important to note that only a portion of the first and third days are necessary to fulfill the Hebrew idiom, "three days and three nights."

OVERVIEW

FOCUS	Disobedience of Jonah	Distress of Jonah	Declaration of Jonah	Displeasure of Jonah
REFERENCE	1	2	3	4
TOPICS	Fleeing	Fearing	Following	Fuming
	Going from God	Going Back to God	Going with God	Going Ahead of God
	Jonah's First Commission		Jonah's Second Commission	
	"I won't go"	"I will go"	"I'm here"	"I shouldn't have come"
LOCATION	The Mediterranean Sea		The City of Nineveh	
TIME	~785–775 B.C.			

Everything in Jonah (the storm, the lots, the sailors, the great fish, the people of Nineveh, the vine, the worm and the east wind) obeyed God's command except for the prophet himself. God told Jonah to go northeast to Nineveh; instead, he got on a boat heading west to Tarshish (possibly Spain). God's purpose would not be thwarted, however, and he sovereignly prepared a great fish to deliver the disobedient prophet to his original destination and to change his perspective (1).

After Jonah prayed a prayer of praise to God for delivering him from a watery grave (2), God recommissioned him to preach to the people of Nineveh. When the Ninevites responded with repentance and fasting (3), Jonah reacted with anger rather than rejoicing, because he resented God's willingness to show mercy to his enemies. The Lord then taught Jonah a lesson on compassion by using a vine as an object lesson (4).

JONAH

Jonah Flees From the LORD

1 The word of the LORD came to Jonah[a] son of Amittai:[b] 2"Go to the
great city of Nineveh[c] and preach
against it, because its wickedness has
come up before me."
3But Jonah ran[d] away from the
LORD and headed for Tarshish. He went
down to Joppa,[e] where he found a
ship bound for that port. After paying
the fare, he went aboard and sailed for
Tarshish to flee from the LORD.
4Then the LORD sent a great wind on
the sea, and such a violent storm arose
that the ship threatened to break up.[f]
5All the sailors were afraid and each
cried out to his own god. And they
threw the cargo into the sea to lighten
the ship.[g]
But Jonah had gone below deck,
where he lay down and fell into a deep
sleep. 6The captain went to him and
said, "How can you sleep? Get up and
call[h] on your god! Maybe he will take
notice of us, and we will not perish."[i]
7Then the sailors said to each other,
"Come, let us cast lots to find out
who is responsible for this calamity."[j]
They cast lots and the lot fell on Jonah.
8So they asked him, "Tell us, who is
responsible for making all this trouble
for us? What do you do? Where do you
come from? What is your country?
From what people are you?"
9He answered, "I am a Hebrew
and I worship the LORD, the God of
heaven,[k] who made the sea and the
land.[l]"
10This terrified them and they asked,
"What have you done?" (They knew he
was running away from the LORD, because he had already told them so.)
11The sea was getting rougher and
rougher. So they asked him, "What
should we do to you to make the sea
calm down for us?"
12"Pick me up and throw me into the
sea," he replied, "and it will become
calm. I know that it is my fault that this
great storm has come upon you."[m]
13Instead, the men did their best to
row back to land. But they could not,
for the sea grew even wilder than before.[n] 14Then they cried to the LORD,
"O LORD, please do not let us die for
taking this man's life. Do not hold us
accountable for killing an innocent
man,[o] for you, O LORD, have done as
you pleased."[p] 15Then they took Jonah and threw him overboard, and the
raging sea grew calm.[q] 16At this the
men greatly feared[r] the LORD, and
they offered a sacrifice to the LORD and
made vows to him.
17But the LORD provided a great fish
to swallow Jonah,[s] and Jonah was inside the fish three days and three
nights.

Jonah's Prayer

2 From inside the fish Jonah prayed to
the LORD his God. 2He said:

"In my distress I called to the
LORD,[t]
and he answered me.
From the depths of the grave[a] I
called for help,
and you listened to my cry.
3You hurled me into the deep,[u]
into the very heart of the seas,
and the currents swirled about
me;
all your waves and breakers
swept over me.[v]

1:1–3 PROMISE 7

RUNNING THE OTHER WAY

How amazing is this? A prophet, a "word of the LORD" (v. 1), and a direct act of disobedience. Don't miss the power of the phrase "But Jonah" in verse 3. That phrase holds the seed of this prophet's rebellion.

God sent Jonah to Nineveh; Jonah turned tail and went in the opposite direction to Tarshish. Such blatant disobedience to God's direct command leaves us slack-jawed. It seems impossible that a man of God could ever hope to get away with such an action.

But guess what? Subtle disobedience is just as destructive. Jonah jumped on a ship to escape his commission. Many Christian men today simply ignore theirs. Is going through life ignoring our Great Commission and the Great Commandment any different than Jonah running in this situation? More subtle, yes. Less disobedient, no! Read the rest of Jonah 1 and see how serious God is about his great commissions.

Don't let your life contain one of the "But Jonah" phrases. Remember, walking away from God's plan for your life is no less disobedient than running.

For the next Promise 7 reading go to page 1029.

1:1 [a]Mt 12:39-41 [b]2Ki 14:25 **1:2** [c]Ge 10:11 **1:3** [d]Ps 139:7 [e]Jos 19:46; Ac 9:36,43 **1:4** [f]Ps 107:23-26 **1:5** [g]Ac 27:18-19 **1:6** [h]Jnh 3:8 [i]Ps 107:28 **1:7** [j]Jos 7:10-18; 1Sa 14:42 **1:9** [k]Ac 17:24 [l]Ps 146:6 **1:12** [m]2Sa 24:17; 1Ch 21:17 **1:13** [n]Pr 21:30 **1:14** [o]Dt 21:8 [p]Ps 115:3 **1:15** [q]Ps 107:29; Lk 8:24 **1:16** [r]Mk 4:41 **1:17** [s]Mt 12:40; 16:4; Lk 11:30 **2:2** [t]Ps 18:6; 120:1 **2:3** [u]Ps 88:6 [v]Ps 42:7

[a]*2* Hebrew *Sheol*

JONAH

Prejudice Personified

The seeds of war find their origin in the personal prejudice and the hatred one man holds for another. A casual glance through history books—or through the daily newspaper—shows the destruction that prejudice has brought to our world. Prejudice is like an infectious disease that colors our perceptions of other people without any rational basis, and hinders our ministry as God's ambassadors to a sinful world. As was the case with the prophet Jonah, prejudice can also color our acceptance of God's will in the lives of others.

Jonah felt the Ninevites were completely unworthy of God's news of forgiveness, and exceptionally worthy of his judgment. After all, Assyria was Israel's hated enemy. Jonah knew the Lord wasn't pleased to see anyone perish, but this angry prophet couldn't transcend his own prejudiced heart to see the potential that God saw in such an evil people.

The Price of Disobedience

The Lord's assignment to Jonah was unique. While most of God's prophets spoke to the children of Israel, God commanded Jonah to preach to the non-Jewish city of Nineveh. Jonah, however, did not display a heart for lost souls. He was angry, because he knew that God might have compassion on Assyria. So "Jonah ran away from the LORD" and boarded a ship that was going in the opposite direction (Jonah 1:3). Shortly after leaving port, a storm threatened to sink the ship. Since violent storms didn't normally occur at that time of year, the sailors sensed something was very wrong. They decided to cast lots to find out who was responsible for the horrible storm. When they did, "the lot fell on Jonah" (1:7).

Jonah couldn't hide it now. He openly admitted he was the culprit. He even advised the sailors to throw him overboard. It seems Jonah was so resistant to God's plan that he was willing to die for his own prejudice. The sailors were reluctant to comply with his radical suggestion, and tried to row the ship to land. But the storm only became more violent. Finally, the sailors decided they had no other choice. With a prayer to Jonah's God asking him not to hold them responsible for Jonah's inevitable death, the sailors threw the prophet overboard. As soon as Jonah plunged into the depths of the sea, the wind died down and everything became calm.

That would have been the end of Jonah if the Lord had not "provided a great fish to swallow Jonah, and Jonah was inside the fish three days and three nights" (1:17). While in the fish's belly, Jonah finally cried out in anguish to the Lord. He realized that God had saved him from a horrible death, and he promised to serve God if he had another chance. The Lord heard Jonah's heartfelt prayer. He "commanded the fish, and it vomited Jonah onto dry land" (2:10).

Jonah got the second chance he prayed for. And the Lord once again told Jonah to go to Nineveh. This time, Jonah obeyed and preached a message of coming judgment and destruction (3:4). Jonah did as the Lord commanded, walking through the city proclaiming God's judgment on the city's inhabitants. Amazingly, the Ninevites repented. This was *not* what Jonah expected.

Personal Prejudice Condemns the Lost

Who would have predicted that the wicked Ninevites would listen? Yet everyone, including the king, gave up their evil ways and asked for mercy (3:8). God's heart was touched with compassion. But Jonah's was not. In fact, he "was greatly displeased and became angry" (4:1). He had known God would show mercy and compassion to repentant hearts. The potential redemption of the Ninevites had been his main concern from the start. These evil people were God's enemies. Their military power and cruelty were legendary, and they worshiped many false gods. In Jonah's eyes they did not deserve compassion, they deserved annihilation.

Jonah could have been rejoicing about the Ninevites' change of heart. Instead his prejudice robbed him of his own well-being. He was so disturbed and depressed that he asked God to take his life (4:3). As was the case when he ran from God's initial call, he wanted his will to be done above God's will—even to the point of becoming a martyr for his own prejudices.

But more importantly, Jonah's hatred for Nineveh blinded him to the implications of what he was witnessing—God's miraculous grace at work in evil hearts. Only God's power can change a pagan culture into redeemed people of God. Jonah missed the miracle because he chose to cling to his own perceptions and harden his heart to God's grace.

God Saves the Lost

God desires to show mercy to all people who sincerely repent and turn to him. He accepts all who do so, regardless of past sins. This profound message was lost on the prophet Jonah. We, as men of God, must search our hearts, minds, and attitudes for personal prejudices that can cause us to respond like Jonah and miss God's greater plan. God is not willing that anyone should perish, even those who are evil and spiteful to us. May we be challenged by Jonah's life to wipe our hearts and minds clean from personal prejudice, and bring God's good news to our fallen and sinful world. When people respond to that good news, we can rejoice once again in the miracle of God's love for all who fall short of his will for their lives—including each one of us.

—Dr. Gene Getz

4I said, 'I have been banished
from your sight;[w]
yet I will look again
toward your holy temple.'
5The engulfing waters threatened
me,[a]
the deep surrounded me;
seaweed was wrapped around
my head.[x]
6To the roots of the mountains I
sank down;
the earth beneath barred me in
forever.
But you brought my life up from
the pit,
O LORD my God.

7"When my life was ebbing
away,
I remembered[y] you, LORD,
and my prayer[z] rose to you,
to your holy temple.[a]

8"Those who cling to worthless
idols[b]
forfeit the grace that could be
theirs.
9But I, with a song of thanksgiving,
will sacrifice[c] to you.
What I have vowed[d] I will make
good.
Salvation[e] comes from the
LORD."

10And the LORD commanded the
fish, and it vomited Jonah onto dry
land.

1:17; 3:1

PROMISE 1

GOD OF THE SECOND CHANCE

You may be surprised to find that many people have a problem believing Jonah's story. Oh, it's not the fish! Such a miracle is a piece of cake for God. The statement that many have trouble believing is this: "Then the word of the LORD came to Jonah a second time." Even after Jonah's blatant disobedience, God gave him a second chance. God was willing to forgive, restore, trust and use someone who had so obviously rebelled against God and failed in his mission. God still used a coward, a quitter.

We read Jonah's story as a diary of a prophet's disobedience. But more importantly, we must read this story as a portrait of the Lord's patience. Do you need a second chance? Have you failed God, perhaps in harboring personal rebellion against him or in hurting another person in some way? Read Jonah 3:1 and thank God that he is the God of the second chance.

For the next Promise 1 reading go to page 992.

2:4 [w]Ps 31:22
2:5 [x]Ps 69:1-2
2:7 [y]Ps 77:11-12 [z]2Ch 30:27 [a]Ps 11:4; 18:6
2:8 [b]2Ki 17:15; Jer 10:8
2:9 [c]Ps 50:14,23; Hos 14:2 [d]Ecc 5:4-5 [e]Ps 3:8

Jonah Goes to Nineveh

3 Then the word of the LORD came to
Jonah[f] a second time: 2"Go to the 7 →PG. 1029
great city of Nineveh and proclaim to it
the message I give you."
3Jonah obeyed the word of the LORD
and went to Nineveh. Now Nineveh
was a very important city—a visit
required three days. 4On the first day,
Jonah started into the city. He proclaimed: "Forty more days and Nineveh will be overturned." 5The Ninevites believed God. They declared a
fast, and all of them, from the greatest
to the least, put on sackcloth.[g]
6When the news reached the king of
Nineveh, he rose from his throne, took
off his royal robes, covered himself
with sackcloth and sat down in the
dust.[h] 7Then he issued a proclamation in Nineveh:

"By the decree of the king and his nobles:

> Do not let any man or beast,
> herd or flock, taste anything; do
> not let them eat or drink.[i] 8But
> let man and beast be covered with
> sackcloth. Let everyone call[j] urgently on God. Let them give up
> their evil ways and their violence.
> 9Who knows?[k] God may yet relent and with compassion turn[l]
> from his fierce anger so that we
> will not perish."

10When God saw what they did and
how they turned from their evil ways,
he had compassion[m] and did not
bring upon them the destruction[n] he
had threatened.[o]

Jonah's Anger at the LORD's Compassion

4 But Jonah was greatly displeased
and became angry.[p] 2He prayed to
the LORD, "O LORD, is this not what I
said when I was still at home? That is
why I was so quick to flee to Tarshish.

[a]5 Or *waters were at my throat*

3:1 [f]Jnh 1:1
3:5 [g]Da 9:3; Lk 11:32
3:6 [h]Job 2:8,13; Eze 27:30-31
3:7 [i]2Ch 20:3
3:8 [j]Ps 130:1; Jnh 1:6
3:9 [k]2Sa 12:22 [l]Joel 2:14
3:10 [m]Am 7:6 [n]Jer 18:8 [o]Ex 32:14
4:1 [p]ver 4; Lk 15:28

4:1-3

PROMISE 6

JONAH'S HATE, GOD'S LOVE

Why did Jonah disobey God? Because he despised the Ninevites. Why did God send Jonah to Nineveh? Because he loved the Ninevites. Reaching beyond racial, cultural, gender and ethnic barriers to demonstrate the power of Biblical unity is more than a nice idea. It is God's will and command. To miss this fact is to miss the message of Jonah's story.

For the next Promise 6 reading go to page 994.

I knew[q] that you are a gracious and
compassionate God, slow to anger
and abounding in love,[r] a God who
relents from sending calamity.[s] **3**Now,
O LORD, take away my life,[t] for it is
better for me to die[u] than to live."
4But the LORD replied, "Have you
any right to be angry?"[v]
5Jonah went out and sat down at a
place east of the city. There he made
himself a shelter, sat in its shade and
waited to see what would happen to
the city. **6**Then the LORD God provided
a vine and made it grow up over Jonah
to give shade for his head to ease his
discomfort, and Jonah was very happy
about the vine. **7**But at dawn the next
day God provided a worm, which
chewed the vine so that it withered.[w]
8When the sun rose, God provided a
scorching east wind, and the sun
blazed on Jonah's head so that he grew
faint. He wanted to die, and said, "It
would be better for me to die than to
live."
9But God said to Jonah, "Do you
have a right to be angry about the
vine?"
"I do," he said. "I am angry enough
to die."
10But the LORD said, "You have been
concerned about this vine, though you
did not tend it or make it grow. It
sprang up overnight and died overnight. **11**But Nineveh[x] has more than a
hundred and twenty thousand people
who cannot tell their right hand from
their left, and many cattle as well.
Should I not be concerned[y] about
that great city?"

4:2 [q] Jer 20:7-8 [r] Ex 34:6; Ps 86:5,15 [s] Joel 2:13
4:3 [t] 1Ki 19:4 [u] Job 7:15
4:4 [v] Mt 20:11-15
4:7 [w] Joel 1:12
4:11 [x] Jnh 1:2; 3:2 [y] Jnh 3:10

MICAH

AT A GLANCE

Key Principle: True spirituality (our vertical relationship with God) should always lead to social ethics (our horizontal relationship with others).
Author: Micah
Time and Place:~740 B.C. to ~710 B.C. / Judah and Israel
Key Verses: 6:8; 7:18

BENEFIT

Micah's particular concern is with the social sins of exploitation and injustice. Two problems permeated the kingdoms of Israel and Judah: political corruption, greed and arrogance among religious leaders, and false prophets who were more interested in personal gain than in corporate goodness. As the prophet of the poor and the downtrodden, Micah has particular relevance to the conditions we face in our own culture.

SETTING

The prophet Micah lived southwest of Jerusalem during the time of Hosea in Israel and Isaiah in Judah. His prophetic visions occurred during the reigns of Jotham (750–732 B.C.), Ahaz (735–715 B.C.) and Hezekiah (715–686 B.C.). Micah's visions had probably concluded prior to the widespread religious reforms under the godly King Hezekiah.

While Jotham is listed among the good kings, he did not remove the high places in Judah. The Assyrians and Syrians threatened Judah in the days of the idolatrous King Ahaz, but God honored the faith of Hezekiah; as a result of his prayers, God delivered Judah from the Assyrians.

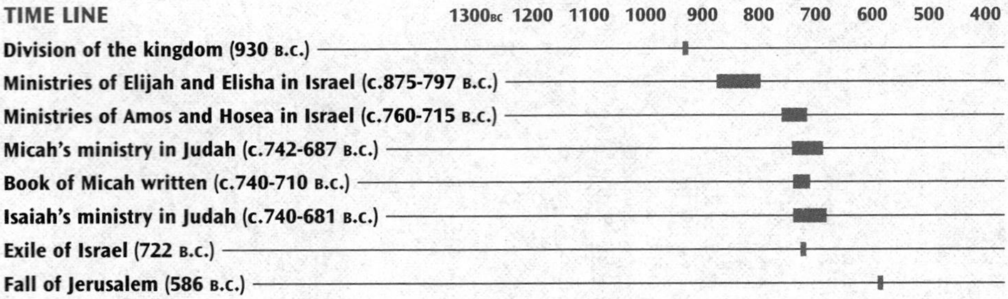

THEME AND PURPOSE

The book of Micah had a three-fold purpose: First, to indict both the northern kingdom of Israel and the southern kingdom of Judah for their sins; second, to reveal the judgment that was coming as a consequence; third, to offer a message of hope in spite of this judgment. The three major sections begin with an exhortation to hear what the Lord is saying (1:2; 3:1; 6:1) followed by words of condemnation (1:3—2:11; 3:2–12; 6:2–16) and words of consolation (2:12–13; 4:1–5:15; 7:1–20).

This book builds a case that instead of acting justly, loving mercy and walking in humility before God (6:8), the people had done just the opposite. The princes, priests, prophets and judges—in short, virtually all the leadership of Israel and Judah in Micah's time—had succumbed to corruption, greed, oppression, exploitation, bribery, violence, cheating and arrogance. God's judgment was inevitable, but the prophet makes it clear that there is still a future hope for God's people—Messiah's coming reign will be marked by righteousness, justice and peace.

UNIQUE CONTRIBUTION

Unlike other prophets, Micah is equally concerned with both Israel and Judah; therefore, much of his ministry occurred before the Assyrian captivity of Israel in 722 B.C. Old Testament prophets typically engaged in both forthtelling (exhorting the people and applying God's standards to the times) and foretelling (anticipating future judgment and blessing), but the proportion of foretelling in Micah is unusually high.

LINKS TO THE NEW TESTAMENT

A good proportion of the book of Micah is devoted to the advent and reign of Israel's coming Messiah. Micah 5:2, quoted in Matthew 2:5–6, is one of the most significant Old Testament prophecies concerning the coming of Christ: "But you, Bethlehem Ephrathah, though you are small among the clans of Judah, out of you will come for me one who will be ruler over Israel, whose origins are from of old, from ancient times." This is a very specific prophecy about the birthplace of the Messiah that was given some seven centuries before Christ's incarnation. Micah also anticipates Christ's worldwide reign of righteousness in 2:12–13; 4:1–8 and 5:4–5.

OVERVIEW

FOCUS	Retribution	Restoration	Repentance
REFERENCE	1 — 2	3 — 5	6 — 7
TOPICS	"Hear, O peoples, all of you" (1:2)	"Listen, you leaders of Jacob" (3:1)	"Listen to what the Lord says" (6:1)
	Judgment (1:2–2:11) and Hope (2:12-13)	Judgment (3:1-12) and Hope (4:1–5:15)	Judgment (6:1-16) and Hope (7:1-20)
	Day of Condemnation	Day of Consolation	Day in Court
	Message of Punishment	Message of Promise	Message of Pardon
LOCATION	Judah and Israel		
TIME	About 25 Years of Prophetic Ministry		

Micah's prophecy opens with a declaration of coming judgment upon the northern kingdom of Israel (Samaria) and the southern kingdom of Judah (Jerusalem). The cause of this judgment is listed as premeditated crime, covetousness, fraud and lying prophets (1:1—2:11). Nevertheless, there is a word of hope in God's promises of regathering and deliverance (2:12–13).

Micah next focuses his prophetic barbs on the ungodly rulers and false prophets of Israel and Judah and predicts a coming disaster (3). He follows this word of condemnation by announcing the future restoration they would experience when the kingdom was reinstituted under Messiah's rule (4—5).

In the concluding section of this book (6—7), God calls the people into court and summons the whole earth to witness against them (6:1–2; cf. 1:2). In spite of God's gracious acts of deliverance, his people have rejected him and walked in dishonesty, injustice and treachery. Still, Micah closes with a series of promises that God will restore the remnant and pardon their transgressions (7:7–20).

MICAH

1 The word of the LORD that came to
Micah of Moresheth[a] during the
reigns of Jotham,[b] Ahaz[c] and Hezekiah, kings of Judah[d]—the vision[e] he
saw concerning Samaria and Jerusalem.

2Hear, O peoples, all of you,[f]
listen, O earth[g] and all who are in it,
that the Sovereign LORD may witness[h] against you,
the Lord from his holy temple.[i]

Judgment Against Samaria and Jerusalem

3Look! The LORD is coming from his dwelling[j] place;
he comes down and treads the high places of the earth.[k]
4The mountains melt[l] beneath him
and the valleys split apart,[m]
like wax before the fire,
like water rushing down a slope.
5All this is because of Jacob's transgression,
because of the sins of the house of Israel.
What is Jacob's transgression?
Is it not Samaria?[n]
What is Judah's high place?
Is it not Jerusalem?

6"Therefore I will make Samaria a heap of rubble,
a place for planting vineyards.
I will pour her stones[o] into the valley
and lay bare her foundations.[p]
7All her idols[q] will be broken to pieces;
all her temple gifts will be burned with fire;
I will destroy all her images.[r]
Since she gathered her gifts from the wages of prostitutes,[s]
as the wages of prostitutes they will again be used."

Weeping and Mourning

8Because of this I will weep[t] and wail;
I will go about barefoot and naked.
I will howl like a jackal
and moan like an owl.
9For her wound[u] is incurable;
it has come to Judah.[v]
It[a] has reached the very gate[w] of my people,
even to Jerusalem itself.
10Tell it not in Gath[b];
weep not at all.[c]
In Beth Ophrah[d]
roll in the dust.
11Pass on in nakedness[x] and shame,
you who live in Shaphir.[e]
Those who live in Zaanan[f]
will not come out.
Beth Ezel is in mourning;
its protection is taken from you.
12Those who live in Maroth[g] writhe in pain,
waiting for relief,[y]
because disaster has come from the LORD,
even to the gate of Jerusalem.
13You who live in Lachish,[h][z]
harness the team to the chariot.
You were the beginning of sin
to the Daughter of Zion,
for the transgressions of Israel
were found in you.
14Therefore you will give parting gifts[a]
to Moresheth Gath.
The town of Aczib[i][b] will prove deceptive[c]
to the kings of Israel.
15I will bring a conqueror against you
who live in Mareshah.[j][d]
He who is the glory of Israel
will come to Adullam.[e]
16Shave[f] your heads in mourning
for the children in whom you delight;

1:1 [a]Jer 26:18 [b]1Ch 3:12 [c]1Ch 3:13 [d]Hos 1:1 [e]Isa 1:1
1:2 [f]Ps 50:7 [g]Jer 6:19 [h]Ge 31:50; Dt 4:26; Isa 1:2 [i]Ps 11:4
1:3 [j]Isa 18:4 [k]Am 4:13
1:4 [l]Ps 46:2,6 [m]Nu 16:31; Na 1:5
1:5 [n]Am 8:14
1:6 [o]Am 5:11 [p]Eze 13:14
1:7 [q]Eze 6:6 [r]Dt 9:21 [s]Dt 23:17-18
1:8 [t]Isa 15:3
1:9 [u]Jer 46:11 [v]2Ki 18:13 [w]Isa 3:26
1:11 [x]Eze 23:29
1:12 [y]Jer 14:19
1:13 [z]Jos 10:3
1:14 [a]2Ki 16:8 [b]Jos 15:44 [c]Jer 15:18
1:15 [d]Jos 15:44 [e]Jos 12:15
1:16 [f]Job 1:20

1:2–3

THE BEGINNING — PROMISE 1

Micah began his message where we must all begin. Life—its obedience and glory; its disobedience and agony—begins and ends right here. Reflect for a few minutes on the awesome power of the truth Micah proclaimed in this short introduction. Do you listen to the Sovereign Lord? What might God say about you?

For the next Promise 1 reading go to page 1002.

[a] *9* Or *He* [b] *10 Gath* sounds like the Hebrew for *tell.* [c] *10* Hebrew; Septuagint may suggest *not in Acco.* The Hebrew for *in Acco* sounds like the Hebrew for *weep.* [d] *10 Beth Ophrah* means *house of dust.* [e] *11 Shaphir* means *pleasant.* [f] *11 Zaanan* sounds like the Hebrew for *come out.* [g] *12 Maroth* sounds like the Hebrew for *bitter.* [h] *13 Lachish* sounds like the Hebrew for *team.* [i] *14 Aczib* means *deception.* [j] *15 Mareshah* sounds like the Hebrew for *conqueror.*

make yourselves as bald as the
vulture,
for they will go from you into
exile.

Man's Plans and God's

2 Woe to those who plan iniquity,
to those who plot evil on their
beds![g]
At morning's light they carry it out
because it is in their power to do
it.
2They covet fields[h] and seize them,
and houses, and take them.
They defraud[i] a man of his home,
a fellowman of his inheritance.
3Therefore, the LORD says:

"I am planning disaster[j] against
this people,
from which you cannot save
yourselves.
You will no longer walk proudly,[k]
for it will be a time of calamity.
4In that day men will ridicule you;
they will taunt you with this
mournful song:
'We are utterly ruined;[l]
my people's possession is
divided up.
He takes it from me!
He assigns our fields to
traitors.' "

5Therefore you will have no one in
the assembly of the LORD
to divide the land[m] by lot.

False Prophets

6"Do not prophesy," their prophets
say.
"Do not prophesy about these
things;
disgrace[n] will not overtake
us.[o]"
7Should it be said, O house of Jacob:
"Is the Spirit of the LORD angry?
Does he do such things?"

"Do not my words do good[p]
to him whose ways are
upright?[q]
8Lately my people have risen up
like an enemy.
You strip off the rich robe
from those who pass by without
a care,
like men returning from battle.
9You drive the women of my people
from their pleasant homes.[r]
You take away my blessing
from their children forever.
10Get up, go away!
For this is not your resting
place,[s]
because it is defiled,[t]
it is ruined, beyond all remedy.
11If a liar and deceiver[u] comes and
says,
'I will prophesy for you plenty of
wine and beer,'
he would be just the prophet for
this people![v]

Deliverance Promised

12"I will surely gather all of you,
O Jacob;
I will surely bring together the
remnant[w] of Israel.
I will bring them together like
sheep in a pen,
like a flock in its pasture;
the place will throng with
people.
13One who breaks open the way will
go up before[x] them;
they will break through the gate
and go out.
Their king will pass through before
them,
the LORD at their head."

Leaders and Prophets Rebuked

3 Then I said,

"Listen, you leaders[y] of Jacob,
you rulers of the house of Israel.
Should you not know justice,
2 you who hate good and love evil;
who tear the skin from my people
and the flesh from their bones;[z]
3who eat my people's flesh,[a]
strip off their skin
and break their bones in
pieces;[b]
who chop them up like meat for
the pan,
like flesh for the pot?[c]"

2:1 [g]Ps 36:4
2:2 [h]Isa 5:8 [i]Jer 22:17
2:3 [j]Jer 18:11; Am 3:1-2 [k]Isa 2:12
2:4 [l]Jer 4:13
2:5 [m]Jos 18:4
2:6 [n]Mic 6:16 [o]Am 2:12
2:7 [p]Ps 119:65 [q]Ps 15:2; 84:11
2:9 [r]Jer 10:20
2:10 [s]Dt 12:9 [t]Lev 18:25-29; Ps 106:38-39
2:11 [u]Jer 5:31 [v]Isa 30:10
2:12 [w]Mic 4:7; 5:7; 7:18
2:13 [x]Isa 52:12
3:1 [y]Jer 5:5
3:2 [z]Ps 53:4; Eze 22:27
3:3 [a]Ps 14:4 [b]Zep 3:3 [c]Eze 11:7

2:1–5 PROMISE 3

GOD OF THE WORK WEEK

God attends our business conferences. He taps our phones. He observes how we fill out our tax returns and balance our books. He sits with our families at dinner after work and school. God doesn't simply show up on Sunday morning and go back to heaven on Monday. He stays around for the business week.

Isn't it wonderful to know that we worship God and witness for him in our business transactions as much as we do in singing our hymns and teaching or participating in our Sunday school classes? Micah reminds us that God governs every area of his people's lives, every day.

Now that's comforting! Isn't it?

For the next Promise 3 reading go to page 996.

4Then they will cry out to the LORD,
but he will not answer them.[d]
At that time he will hide his face[e]
from them
because of the evil they have
done.

5This is what the LORD says:

"As for the prophets
who lead my people astray,[f]
if one feeds them,
they proclaim 'peace';
if he does not,
they prepare to wage war against
him.
6Therefore night will come over you,
without visions,
and darkness, without
divination.[g]
The sun will set for the prophets,[h]
and the day will go dark for
them.
7The seers will be ashamed[i]
and the diviners disgraced.[j]
They will all cover their faces
because there is no answer from
God."
8But as for me, I am filled with
power,
with the Spirit of the LORD,
and with justice and might,
to declare to Jacob his
transgression,
to Israel his sin.[k]
9Hear this, you leaders of the house
of Jacob,
you rulers of the house of Israel,
who despise justice
and distort all that is right;[l]
10who build[m] Zion with
bloodshed,[n]
and Jerusalem with
wickedness.[o]
11Her leaders judge for a bribe,
her priests teach for a price,
and her prophets tell fortunes for
money.[p]
Yet they lean upon the LORD and
say,
"Is not the LORD among us?
No disaster will come upon
us."[q]
12Therefore because of you,
Zion will be plowed like a field,
Jerusalem will become a heap of
rubble,[r]
the temple hill a mound
overgrown with thickets.

The Mountain of the LORD

1 →PG. 1055

4 In the last days

the mountain[s] of the LORD's
temple will be established
as chief among the mountains;
it will be raised above the hills,[t]
and peoples will stream to it.[u]

2Many nations will come and say,

"Come, let us go up to the
mountain of the LORD,[v]
to the house of the God of
Jacob.[w]
He will teach us his ways,[x]
so that we may walk in his
paths."
The law will go out from Zion,
the word of the LORD from
Jerusalem.
3He will judge between many
peoples
and will settle disputes for strong
nations far and wide.[y]
They will beat their swords into
plowshares
and their spears into pruning
hooks.[z]
Nation will not take up sword
against nation,
nor will they train for war
anymore.[a]
4Every man will sit under his own
vine
and under his own fig tree,[b]
and no one will make them
afraid,[c]
for the LORD Almighty has
spoken.[d]
5All the nations may walk
in the name of their gods;[e]
we will walk in the name of the
LORD
our God for ever and ever.[f]

The LORD's Plan

6"In that day," declares the LORD,

"I will gather the lame;
I will assemble the exiles[g]
and those I have brought to
grief.[h]
7I will make the lame a remnant,[i]

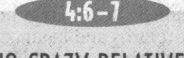

3:4 [d]Ps 18:41; Isa 1:15 [e]Dt 31:17
3:5 [f]Isa 3:12; 9:16
3:6 [g]Isa 8:19-22 [h]Isa 29:10
3:7 [i]Mic 7:16 [j]Isa 44:25
3:8 [k]Isa 58:1
3:9 [l]Ps 58:1-2; Isa 1:23
3:10 [m]Jer 22:13 [n]Hab 2:12 [o]Eze 22:27
3:11 [p]Isa 1:23; Jer 6:13; Hos 4:8,18 [q]Jer 7:4
3:12 [r]Jer 26:18
4:1 [s]Zec 8:3 [t]Eze 17:22 [u]Ps 22:27; 86:9; Jer 3:17
4:2 [v]Jer 31:6 [w]Zec 2:11; 14:16 [x]Ps 25:8-9; Isa 54:13
4:3 [y]Isa 11:4 [z]Joel 3:10 [a]Isa 2:4
4:4 [b]1Ki 4:25 [c]Lev 26:6 [d]Isa 1:20; Zec 3:10
4:5 [e]2Ki 17:29 [f]Jos 24:14-15; Isa 26:8; Zec 10:12
4:6 [g]Ps 147:2 [h]Eze 34:13,16; 37:21; Zep 3:19
4:7 [i]Mic 2:12

4:6–7

PROMISE 6

NO CRAZY RELATIVES

Who makes up God's family? Whom do we include and exclude? In God's family do we have cranky in-laws we can ignore? Crazy aunts with whom we choose not to associate? Obnoxious cousins we don't invite to family reunions? Micah reminds us that God's family is all-inclusive. The racially, denominationally, economically and behaviorally acceptable lines we draw are superficial and artificial. Most tragically, they grieve God.

For the next Promise 6 reading go to page 1017.

those driven away a strong
nation.
The LORD will rule over them in
Mount Zion
from that day and forever.[j]
8 As for you, O watchtower of the
flock,
O stronghold[a] of the Daughter
of Zion,
the former dominion will be
restored[k] to you;
kingship will come to the
Daughter of Jerusalem."

9 Why do you now cry aloud—
have you no king?[l]
Has your counselor perished,
that pain seizes you like that of a
woman in labor?[m]
10 Writhe in agony, O Daughter of
Zion,
like a woman in labor,
for now you must leave the city
to camp in the open field.
You will go to Babylon;[n]
there you will be rescued.
There the LORD will redeem[o] you
out of the hand of your enemies.

11 But now many nations
are gathered against you.
They say, "Let her be defiled,
let our eyes gloat[p] over Zion!"
12 But they do not know
the thoughts of the LORD;
they do not understand his plan,[q]
he who gathers them like
sheaves to the threshing
floor.
13 "Rise and thresh, O Daughter of
Zion,
for I will give you horns of iron;
I will give you hoofs of bronze
and you will break to pieces
many nations."[r]
You will devote their ill-gotten
gains to the LORD,
their wealth to the Lord of all the
earth.

A Promised Ruler From Bethlehem

5 Marshal your troops, O city of
troops,[b]
for a siege is laid against us.
They will strike Israel's ruler
on the cheek[s] with a rod.

2 "But you, Bethlehem[t]
Ephrathah,[u]
though you are small among the
clans[c] of Judah,
out of you will come for me
one who will be ruler over Israel,
whose origins[d] are from of old,[v]
from ancient times.[e]"[w]

3 Therefore Israel will be abandoned
until the time when she who is
in labor gives birth
and the rest of his brothers return
to join the Israelites.

4 He will stand and shepherd his
flock[x]
in the strength of the LORD,
in the majesty of the name of
the LORD his God.
And they will live securely, for then
his greatness[y]
will reach to the ends of the
earth.
5 And he will be their peace.[z]

Deliverance and Destruction

When the Assyrian invades[a] our
land
and marches through our
fortresses,
we will raise against him seven
shepherds,
even eight leaders of men.[b]
6 They will rule[f] the land of Assyria
with the sword,
the land of Nimrod[c] with drawn
sword.[g][d]
He will deliver us from the Assyrian
when he invades our land
and marches into our borders.[e]

7 The remnant[f] of Jacob will be
in the midst of many peoples
like dew from the LORD,
like showers on the grass,[g]
which do not wait for man
or linger for mankind.
8 The remnant of Jacob will be
among the nations,
in the midst of many peoples,
like a lion among the beasts of the
forest,[h]
like a young lion among flocks of
sheep,
which mauls and mangles[i] as it
goes,
and no one can rescue.[j]
9 Your hand will be lifted up[k] in
triumph over your enemies,
and all your foes will be
destroyed.

10 "In that day," declares the LORD,

"I will destroy your horses from
among you
and demolish your chariots.[l]
11 I will destroy the cities[m] of your
land
and tear down all your
strongholds.[n]

4:7 [j]Da 7:14; Lk 1:33; Rev 11:15
4:8 [k]Isa 1:26
4:9 [l]Jer 8:19 [m]Jer 30:6
4:10 [n]2Ki 20:18; Isa 43:14 [o]Isa 48:20
4:11 [p]La 2:16; Ob 1:12
4:12 [q]Isa 55:8; Ro 11:33-34
4:13 [r]Da 2:44
5:1 [s]La 3:30
5:2 [t]Jn 7:42 [u]Ge 48:7 [v]Ps 102:25 [w]Mt 2:6*
5:4 [x]Isa 40:11; 49:9; Eze 34:11-15, 23; Mic 7:14 [y]Isa 52:13; Lk 1:32
5:5 [z]Isa 9:6; Lk 2:14; Col 1:19-20 [a]Isa 8:7 [b]Isa 10:24-27
5:6 [c]Ge 10:8 [d]Zep 2:13 [e]Na 2:11-13
5:7 [f]Mic 2:12 [g]Isa 44:4
5:8 [h]Ge 49:9 [i]Mic 4:13; Zec 10:5 [j]Ps 50:22; Hos 5:14
5:9 [k]Ps 10:12
5:10 [l]Hos 14:3; Zec 9:10
5:11 [m]Isa 6:11 [n]Hos 10:14; Am 5:9

[a] 8 Or *hill* [b] 1 Or *Strengthen your walls, O walled city* [c] 2 Or *rulers* [d] 2 Hebrew *goings out* [e] 2 Or *from days of eternity* [f] 6 Or *crush* [g] 6 Or *Nimrod in its gates*

12I will destroy your witchcraft
and you will no longer cast
spells.[o]
13I will destroy your carved images
and your sacred stones from
among you;
you will no longer bow down
to the work of your hands.[p]
14I will uproot from among you your
Asherah poles[a][q]
and demolish your cities.
15I will take vengeance[r] in anger
and wrath
upon the nations that have not
obeyed me."

The LORD's Case Against Israel

6 Listen to what the LORD says:

"Stand up, plead your case before
the mountains;[s]
let the hills hear what you have
to say.
2Hear,[t] O mountains, the LORD's
accusation;[u]
listen, you everlasting
foundations of the earth.
For the LORD has a case against his
people;
he is lodging a charge[v] against
Israel.

3"My people, what have I done to
you?
How have I burdened[w] you?
Answer me.
4I brought you up out of Egypt
and redeemed you from the land
of slavery.[x]
I sent Moses[y] to lead you,
also Aaron[z] and Miriam.[a]
5My people, remember
what Balak[b] king of Moab
counseled
and what Balaam son of Beor
answered.
Remember ⌞your journey⌟ from
Shittim[c] to Gilgal,[d]
that you may know the righteous
acts[e] of the LORD."

3 →PG. 1029

6With what shall I come before the
LORD
and bow down before the
exalted God?
Shall I come before him with burnt
offerings,
with calves a year old?[f]
7Will the LORD be pleased with
thousands of rams,[g]
with ten thousand rivers of oil?[h]
Shall I offer my firstborn[i] for my
transgression,
the fruit of my body for the sin
of my soul?[j]

5:12 [o]Dt 18:10-12; Isa 2:6; 8:19
5:13 [p]Eze 6:9; Zec 13:2
5:14 [q]Ex 34:13
5:15 [r]Isa 65:12
6:1 [s]Ps 50:1; Eze 6:2
6:2 [t]Dt 32:1 [u]Hos 12:2 [v]Ps 50:7
6:3 [w]Jer 2:5
6:4 [x]Dt 7:8 [y]Ex 4:16 [z]Ps 77:20 [a]Ex 15:20
6:5 [b]Nu 22:5-6 [c]Nu 25:1 [d]Jos 5:9-10 [e]Jdg 5:11; 1Sa 12:7
6:6 [f]Ps 40:6-8; 51:16-17
6:7 [g]Isa 40:16 [h]Ps 50:8-10 [i]Lev 18:21 [j]2Ki 16:3
6:8 [k]Isa 1:17; Jer 22:3 [l]Isa 57:15 [m]Dt 10:12-13; 1Sa 15:22; Hos 6:6
6:10 [n]Eze 45:9-10; Am 3:10; 8:4-6
6:11 [o]Lev 19:36; Hos 12:7
6:12 [p]Isa 1:23 [q]Isa 3:8 [r]Jer 9:3
6:13 [s]Isa 1:7; 6:11
6:14 [t]Isa 9:20 [u]Isa 30:6
6:15 [v]Dt 28:38; Jer 12:13 [w]Am 5:11; Zep 1:13
6:16 [x]1Ki 16:25 [y]1Ki 16:29-33 [z]Jer 7:24

8He has showed you, O man, what
is good.
And what does the LORD require
of you?
To act justly[k] and to love mercy
and to walk humbly[l] with your
God.[m]

Israel's Guilt and Punishment

9Listen! The LORD is calling to the
city—
and to fear your name is
wisdom—
"Heed the rod and the One who
appointed it.[b]
10Am I still to forget, O wicked
house,
your ill-gotten treasures
and the short ephah,[c] which is
accursed?[n]
11Shall I acquit a man with dishonest
scales,[o]
with a bag of false weights?
12Her rich men are violent;[p]
her people are liars[q]
and their tongues speak
deceitfully.[r]
13Therefore, I have begun to
destroy[s] you,
to ruin you because of your sins.
14You will eat but not be satisfied;[t]
your stomach will still be
empty.[d]
You will store up but save
nothing,[u]
because what you save I will give
to the sword.
15You will plant but not harvest;[v]
you will press olives but not use
the oil on yourselves,
you will crush grapes but not
drink the wine.[w]
16You have observed the statutes of
Omri[x]
and all the practices of Ahab's[y]
house,
and you have followed their
traditions.[z]

a *14* That is, symbols of the goddess Asherah **b** *9* The meaning of the Hebrew for this line is uncertain. **c** *10* An ephah was a dry measure. **d** *14* The meaning of the Hebrew for this word is uncertain.

6:8

PROMISE 3

GOD'S REQUIREMENTS

Don't miss this statement. How does a Christian man please God? Micah tells us in simple, straightforward language. Nothing confusing here!

For the next Promise 3 reading go to page 1010.

Therefore I will give you over to
ruin[a]
and your people to derision;
you will bear the scorn[b] of the
nations.[a]"

Israel's Misery

7 What misery is mine!
I am like one who gathers summer
fruit
at the gleaning of the vineyard;
there is no cluster of grapes to eat,
none of the early figs that I
crave.
2The godly have been swept from
the land;[c]
not one upright man remains.
All men lie in wait to shed blood;[d]
each hunts his brother with a
net.[e]
3Both hands are skilled in doing
evil;[f]
the ruler demands gifts,
the judge accepts bribes,
the powerful dictate what they
desire—
they all conspire together.
4The best of them is like a brier,[g]
the most upright worse than a
thorn hedge.
The day of your watchmen has
come,
the day God visits you.
Now is the time of their
confusion.[h]
5Do not trust a neighbor;
put no confidence in a friend.[i]
Even with her who lies in your
embrace
be careful of your words.
6For a son dishonors his father,
a daughter rises up against her
mother,[j]
a daughter-in-law against her
mother-in-law—
a man's enemies are the
members of his own
household.[k]

7But as for me, I watch in hope[l]
for the LORD,
I wait for God my Savior;
my God will hear[m] me.

Israel Will Rise

8Do not gloat over me,[n] my enemy!
Though I have fallen, I will
rise.[o]
Though I sit in darkness,
the LORD will be my light.[p]
9Because I have sinned against him,
I will bear the LORD's wrath,[q]
until he pleads my case
and establishes my right.
He will bring me out into the light;
I will see his righteousness.[r]

10Then my enemy will see it
and will be covered with shame,[s]
she who said to me,
"Where is the LORD your God?"
My eyes will see her downfall;[t]
even now she will be trampled[u]
underfoot
like mire in the streets.
11The day for building your walls[v]
will come,
the day for extending your
boundaries.
12In that day people will come to
you
from Assyria and the cities of
Egypt,
even from Egypt to the Euphrates
and from sea to sea
and from mountain to
mountain.[w]
13The earth will become desolate
because of its inhabitants,
as the result of their deeds.[x]

Prayer and Praise

14Shepherd[y] your people with your
staff,[z]
the flock of your inheritance,
which lives by itself in a forest,
in fertile pasturelands.[b]
Let them feed in Bashan and
Gilead[a]
as in days long ago.

15"As in the days when you came out
of Egypt,
I will show them my wonders.[b]"

16Nations will see and be ashamed,[c]
deprived of all their power.

6:16 [a]Jer 25:9 [b]Jer 51:51 **7:2** [c]Ps 12:1 [d]Mic 3:10 [e]Jer 5:26 **7:3** [f]Pr 4:16 **7:4** [g]Eze 2:6 [h]Isa 22:5; Hos 9:7 **7:5** [i]Jer 9:4 **7:6** [j]Eze 22:7 [k]Mt 10:35-36* **7:7** [l]Ps 130:5; Isa 25:9 [m]Ps 4:3 **7:8** [n]Pr 24:17 [o]Ps 37:24; Am 9:11 [p]Isa 9:2 **7:9** [q]La 3:39-40 [r]Isa 46:13
7:10 [s]Ps 35:26 [t]Isa 51:23 [u]Zec 10:5 **7:11** [v]Isa 54:11 **7:12** [w]Isa 19:23-25 **7:13** [x]Isa 3:10-11 **7:14** [y]Mic 5:4 [z]Ps 23:4 [a]Jer 50:19 **7:15** [b]Ex 3:20; Ps 78:12 **7:16** [c]Isa 26:11

a *16* Septuagint; Hebrew *scorn due my people*
b *14* Or *in the middle of Carmel*

7:18–19

PE

MERCY

This passage claims that God loves you and wants you to have the best. That's sometimes difficult to understand when we read Moses' list of laws and restrictions or the prophets' threats of judgment and doom. Such passages may make us think that God is mean-spirited.

But in these verses, Micah joins the other prophets in painting a more accurate picture of God. Like a father who forbids his child to eat garbage or play with a loaded gun, a father who may use strong measures to keep a determined child from harm, God protects us from dangerous and destructive behavior. Does he do all this because he's a grouch? Read these verses again for your answer.

They will lay their hands on their mouths
and their ears will become deaf.
17They will lick dust like a snake,
like creatures that crawl on the ground.
They will come trembling out of their dens;
they will turn in fear[d] to the LORD our God
and will be afraid of you.
18Who is a God like you,
who pardons sin[e] and forgives[f] the transgression
of the remnant[g] of his inheritance?[h]
You do not stay angry[i] forever
but delight to show mercy.[j]
19You will again have compassion on us;
you will tread our sins underfoot
and hurl all our iniquities[k] into the depths of the sea.[l]
20You will be true to Jacob,
and show mercy to Abraham,
as you pledged on oath to our fathers[m]
in days long ago.

7:17 [d]Isa 25:3; 49:23; 59:19
7:18 [e]Isa 43:25; Jer 50:20 [f]Ps 103:8-13 [g]Mic 2:12 [h]Ex 34:9 [i]Ps 103:9 [j]Jer 32:41
7:19 [k]Isa 43:25 [l]Jer 31:34
7:20 [m]Dt 7:8; Lk 1:72

NAHUM

AT A GLANCE

Key Principle: Humility and repentance (Nineveh in the time of Jonah) leads to deliverance, but arrogance and cruelty (Nineveh in the time of Nahum) leads to destruction.
Author: Nahum
Time and Place: ~660 B.C. / Directed from Judah against Nineveh, capital of Assyria
Key Verses: 1:2–3, 7–8; 2:13; 3:5–7

BENEFIT

Nahum illustrates the truth that each generation needs to respond to the Lord. The Ninevites repented as a result of Jonah's prophecy, but their attitude of repentance did not last. It was certainly not passed on to the next generation. We cannot inherit the spiritual life; each one of us must make a personal decision to accept Christ and commit our lives to him.

SETTING

Around 760 B.C., the prophet Jonah preached a message of destruction to the people of Nineveh. As a result, the whole city responded in repentance. Because they humbled themselves before the Lord, the city was spared from the promised disaster. But as the years passed, the Assyrians grew in power and returned to their proud, violent and cruel ways. Thus, a century after Jonah's preaching, the Lord raised up Nahum, a prophet from Elkosh (1:1), to deliver to Nineveh this message of unqualified condemnation.

When Nahum wrote this prophecy, the Babylonian overthrow of Nineveh (612 B.C.) was a future event. Nahum also refers to the fall of Thebes as a recent event, and since Thebes fell in 663 B.C. and was rebuilt a decade later, it is likely that Nahum's prophecy was written around 660 B.C. before Thebes was rebuilt. By this time, the Assyrian Empire had reached its greatest extent under Ashurbanipal (669–633 B.C.).

The capital city of Nineveh seemed unconquerable, with walls 100 feet high and huge towers scattered around the walls that were an additional 100 feet in height. The city was surrounded by a moat that was 150 feet wide and 60 feet deep, and it could withstand a 20-year siege. Yet it was "with an overwhelming flood" that the Lord made an end of Nineveh (1:8)—the Tigris River overflowed its banks, destroying enough of the wall to allow the invading Babylonian army to go through the breach, sack the city and burn it to the ground. The city was so completely devastated that its ruins were not identified until 1842.

TIME LINE

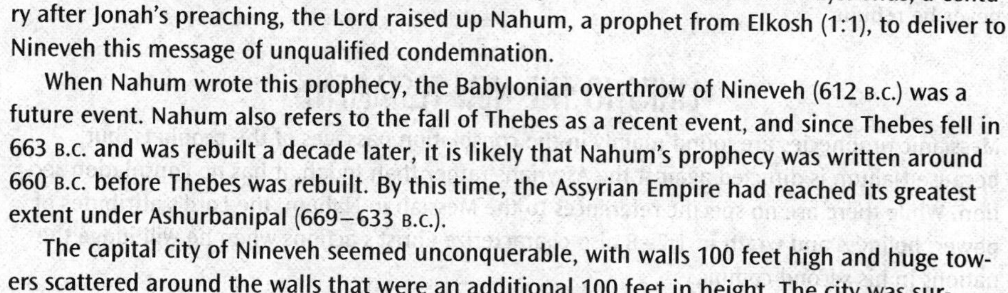

THEME AND PURPOSE

The bulk of Nahum is concerned with God's future judgment of Nineveh for its arrogance, cruelty and idolatry. The first eight verses present God's holiness, power, wrath and righteous indignation against his enemies, and the rest of the book deals exclusively with the overthrow of Nineveh. Unlike Jonah, who was personally sent to Nineveh to deliver his message, Nahum wrote this prophecy to comfort the people of Judah decades after the kingdom of Israel was scattered by the Assyrians. For those in Judah who trusted in the Lord, Nahum's message was greatly reassuring: "Celebrate your festivals, O Judah, and fulfill your vows. No more will the wicked invade you; they will be completely destroyed" (1:15; cf. 2:2). God had delayed his wrath against the violence and arrogance of the Assyrians, but it was certain to come, and Nineveh's end would be sudden and final.

UNIQUE CONTRIBUTION

As was Obadiah's prophecy against Edom and Habakkuk's prophecy against Babylonia, the primary thrust of Nahum was against the enemies of Judah. God raised up other prophets like Zephaniah and Jeremiah to deal with Judah's own idolatry and immorality, but Nahum's purpose in this book was to announce the future devastation of Nineveh, the capital of Judah's enemy, Assyria. Nineveh was hardened against God; Nahum's message contains no appeal to repentance and no words of consolation for its inhabitants. In contrast to Jonah's mission a century earlier, the people of Nineveh were beyond the possibility of repentance, and judgment was certain. Nahum describes this judgment in detail, including the coming flood, the plundering of its temples and idols, the destruction of the city by fire and the fact that it would never be rebuilt.

LINKS TO THE NEW TESTAMENT

Messianic prophecies are found mainly in the consolation passages of the prophets, but because Nahum is directed against the Assyrians rather than Judah, it has no consolation section. While there are no specific references to the Messiah in Nahum, the Lord's attributes of power, holiness and wrath in 1:2–8 also characterize Christ's actions when he will judge the nations in his second coming.

OVERVIEW

FOCUS	Devastation Decreed	Devastation Described	Devastation Deserved
REFERENCE	1	2	3
TOPICS	Proclamation of God's Displeasure	Prediction of Nineveh's Doom	Portrait of Nineveh's Downfall
	What	How	Why
	Declaration	Details	
	God's Justice	God's Judgment	
LOCATION	Directed from Judah Against Nineveh, Capital of Assyria		
TIME	~660 B.C.		

Nahum's prophecy opens with a description of Yahweh's righteous character. He is "a jealous and avenging God" who "maintains his wrath against his enemies" (1:2). God's power is unlimited; no one can endure his anger (1:3–6). Those who trust in him discover his goodness and grace, but he overcomes his foes (1:7–8). Because of his holiness, God condemns the wickedness of Nineveh (1:9–14) and comforts those who are righteous in Judah (1:15).

Using vivid imagery, Nahum describes the siege and the plundering of Nineveh after the invading warriors move through the breach in its wall (2). As the chariots and charging cavalry invade, the city is thrown into chaos and there is no one to mourn for it (3:1–7). Just as the Assyrians overthrew Thebes, Egypt's proud capital, so Assyria's capital will also be destroyed in spite of its many fortifications (3:8–18). Because of Assyria's cruelty, everyone will rejoice at its fall (3:19).

NAHUM

1 An oracle[a] concerning Nineveh.[b] The book of the vision of Nahum the Elkoshite.

The LORD's Anger Against Nineveh

2 The LORD is a jealous[c] and avenging God;
the LORD takes vengeance[d] and is filled with wrath.
The LORD takes vengeance on his foes
and maintains his wrath against his enemies.
3 The LORD is slow to anger[e] and great in power;
the LORD will not leave the guilty unpunished.[f]
His way is in the whirlwind and the storm,
and clouds[g] are the dust of his feet.
4 He rebukes the sea and dries it up;
he makes all the rivers run dry.
Bashan and Carmel[h] wither
and the blossoms of Lebanon fade.
5 The mountains quake[i] before him
and the hills melt away.[j]
The earth trembles at his presence,
the world and all who live in it.
6 Who can withstand his indignation?
Who can endure[k] his fierce anger?
His wrath is poured out like fire;[l]
the rocks are shattered[m] before him.

7 The LORD is good,[n]
a refuge in times of trouble.
He cares for[o] those who trust in him,
8 but with an overwhelming flood
he will make an end of ⌞Nineveh⌟;
he will pursue his foes into darkness.

9 Whatever they plot against the LORD
he[a] will bring to an end;
trouble will not come a second time.
10 They will be entangled among thorns[p]
and drunk from their wine;
they will be consumed like dry stubble.[b][q]
11 From you, ⌞O Nineveh,⌟ has one come forth
who plots evil against the LORD
and counsels wickedness.

12 This is what the LORD says:

"Although they have allies and are numerous,
they will be cut off[r] and pass away.
Although I have afflicted you, ⌞O Judah,⌟
I will afflict you no more.[s]
13 Now I will break their yoke[t] from your neck
and tear your shackles away."

14 The LORD has given a command concerning you, ⌞Nineveh⌟:
"You will have no descendants to bear your name.[u]
I will destroy the carved images[v] and cast idols
that are in the temple of your gods.
I will prepare your grave,[w]
for you are vile."

15 Look, there on the mountains,
the feet of one who brings good news,[x]
who proclaims peace![y]
Celebrate your festivals,[z] O Judah,
and fulfill your vows.
No more will the wicked invade you;[a]
they will be completely destroyed.

Nineveh to Fall

2 An attacker[b] advances against you, ⌞Nineveh⌟.
Guard the fortress,
watch the road,
brace yourselves,

1:7–8

PROMISE 1

THIS OR THAT

This passage takes our lives here on earth and boils them down to the basics. We're either This or That—a person who trusts God, or one who doesn't.

Obedience results in God's care; he is a refuge to those who trust him. But an overwhelming flood, an end and darkness await those who oppose God. This passage tells us it *really is* that simple.

For the next Promise 1 reading go to page 1008.

1:1 [a]Isa 13:1; 19:1; Jer 23:33-34 [b]Jnh 1:2; Na 2:8; Zep 2:13 **1:2** [c]Ex 20:5 [d]Dt 32:41; Ps 94:1 **1:3** [e]Ne 9:17 [f]Ex 34:7 [g]Ps 104:3 **1:4** [h]Isa 33:9 **1:5** [i]Ex 19:18 [j]Mic 1:4 **1:6** [k]Mal 3:2 [l]Jer 10:10 [m]1Ki 19:11 **1:7** [n]Jer 33:11 [o]Ps 1:6 **1:10** [p]2Sa 23:6 [q]Isa 5:24; Mal 4:1 **1:12** [r]Isa 10:34 [s]Isa 54:6-8; La 3:31-32 **1:13** [t]Isa 9:4 **1:14** [u]Isa 14:22 [v]Mic 5:13 [w]Eze 32:22-23 **1:15** [x]Isa 40:9; Ro 10:15 [y]Isa 52:7 [z]Lev 23:2-4 [a]Isa 52:1 **2:1** [b]Jer 51:20

[a] 9 Or *What do you foes plot against the LORD? / He* [b] 10 The meaning of the Hebrew for this verse is uncertain.

marshal all your strength!

2The LORD will restore[c] the
splendor[d] of Jacob
like the splendor of Israel,
though destroyers have laid them
waste
and have ruined their vines.

3The shields of his soldiers are red;
the warriors are clad in scarlet.[e]
The metal on the chariots flashes
on the day they are made ready;
the spears of pine are
brandished.[a]
4The chariots[f] storm through the
streets,
rushing back and forth through
the squares.
They look like flaming torches;
they dart about like lightning.

5He summons his picked troops,
yet they stumble[g] on their way.
They dash to the city wall;
the protective shield is put in
place.
6The river gates[h] are thrown open
and the palace collapses.
7It is decreed[b] that ⌞the city⌟
be exiled and carried away.
Its slave girls moan[i] like doves
and beat upon their breasts.[j]
8Nineveh is like a pool,
and its water is draining away.
"Stop! Stop!" they cry,
but no one turns back.
9Plunder the silver!
Plunder the gold!
The supply is endless,
the wealth from all its treasures!
10She is pillaged, plundered, stripped!
Hearts melt, knees give way,
bodies tremble, every face grows
pale.[k]

11Where now is the lions' den,[l]
the place where they fed their
young,
where the lion and lioness went,
and the cubs, with nothing to
fear?
12The lion killed[m] enough for his
cubs
and strangled the prey for his
mate,
filling his lairs with the kill
and his dens with the prey.

13"I am against[n] you,"
declares the LORD Almighty.
"I will burn up your chariots in
smoke,[o]
and the sword will devour your
young lions.
I will leave you no prey on the
earth.
The voices of your messengers
will no longer be heard."

Woe to Nineveh

3 Woe to the city of blood,[p]
full of lies,
full of plunder,
never without victims!
2The crack of whips,
the clatter of wheels,
galloping horses
and jolting chariots!
3Charging cavalry,
flashing swords
and glittering spears!
Many casualties,
piles of dead,
bodies without number,
people stumbling over the
corpses[q]—
4all because of the wanton lust of a
harlot,
alluring, the mistress of
sorceries,[r]
who enslaved nations by her
prostitution[s]
and peoples by her witchcraft.

5"I am against[t] you," declares the
LORD Almighty.
"I will lift your skirts[u] over your
face.
I will show the nations your
nakedness[v]
and the kingdoms your shame.
6I will pelt you with filth,[w]
I will treat you with contempt[x]
and make you a spectacle.[y]
7All who see you will flee from you
and say,
'Nineveh[z] is in ruins—who will
mourn for her?'[a]
Where can I find anyone to
comfort[b] you?"

8Are you better than[c] Thebes,[c d]
situated on the Nile,[e]
with water around her?
The river was her defense,
the waters her wall.
9Cush[d f] and Egypt were her
boundless strength;
Put[g] and Libya[h] were among
her allies.
10Yet she was taken captive[i]
and went into exile.
Her infants were dashed[j] to
pieces
at the head of every street.
Lots were cast for her nobles,

2:2 [c]Eze 37:23 [d]Isa 60:15 **2:3** [e]Eze 23:14-15 **2:4** [f]Jer 4:13 **2:5** [g]Jer 46:12 **2:6** [h]Na 3:13 **2:7** [i]Isa 59:11 [j]Isa 32:12 **2:10** [k]Isa 29:22 **2:11** [l]Isa 5:29 **2:12** [m]Jer 51:34 **2:13** [n]Jer 21:13; Na 3:5 [o]Ps 46:9

3:1 [p]Eze 22:2; Mic 3:10 **3:3** [q]2Ki 19:35; Isa 34:3 **3:4** [r]Isa 47:9 [s]Isa 23:17; Eze 16:25-29 **3:5** [t]Na 2:13 [u]Jer 13:22 [v]Isa 47:3 **3:6** [w]Job 9:31 [x]1Sa 2:30; Jer 51:37 [y]Isa 14:16 **3:7** [z]Na 1:1 [a]Jer 15:5 [b]Isa 51:19 **3:8** [c]Am 6:2 [d]Jer 46:25 [e]Isa 19:6-9 **3:9** [f]2Ch 12:3 [g]Eze 27:10 [h]Eze 30:5 **3:10** [i]Isa 20:4 [j]Isa 13:16; Hos 13:16

[a]3 Hebrew; Septuagint and Syriac / *the horsemen rush to and fro* [b]7 The meaning of the Hebrew for this word is uncertain. [c]8 Hebrew *No Amon* [d]9 That is, the upper Nile region

and all her great men were put
in chains.
11You too will become drunk;[k]
you will go into hiding[l]
and seek refuge from the enemy.

12All your fortresses are like fig trees
with their first ripe fruit;
when they are shaken,
the figs[m] fall into the mouth of
the eater.
13Look at your troops—
they are all women![n]
The gates[o] of your land
are wide open to your enemies;
fire has consumed their bars.[p]

14Draw water for the siege,[q]
strengthen your defenses![r]
Work the clay,
tread the mortar,
repair the brickwork!
15There the fire will devour you;
the sword will cut you down
and, like grasshoppers, consume
you.
Multiply like grasshoppers,
multiply like locusts![s]
16You have increased the number of
your merchants
till they are more than the stars
of the sky,
but like locusts they strip the land
and then fly away.
17Your guards are like locusts,[t]
your officials like swarms of
locusts
that settle in the walls on a cold
day—
but when the sun appears they fly
away,
and no one knows where.

18O king of Assyria, your shepherds[a]
slumber;[u]
your nobles lie down to rest.[v]
Your people are scattered[w] on the
mountains
with no one to gather them.
19Nothing can heal your wound;[x]
your injury is fatal.
Everyone who hears the news
about you
claps his hands[y] at your fall,
for who has not felt
your endless cruelty?

3:11 [k]Isa 49:26 [l]Isa 2:10
3:12 [m]Isa 28:4
3:13 [n]Isa 19:16; Jer 50:37 [o]Na 2:6 [p]Isa 45:2
3:14 [q]2Ch 32:4 [r]Na 2:1
3:15 [s]Joel 1:4
3:17 [t]Jer 51:27
3:18 [u]Ps 76:5-6 [v]Isa 56:10 [w]1Ki 22:17
3:19 [x]Jer 30:13; Mic 1:9 [y]Job 27:23; La 2:15; Zep 2:15

[a]18 Or *rulers*

HABAKKUK

AT A GLANCE

Key Principle: The better we know the divine Planner, the more we can trust his plans; as we confide in God's wisdom, we will acknowledge his ways.
Author: Habakkuk
Time and Place: ~607 B.C. / Kingdom of Judah
Key Verses: 1:13; 2:1, 4, 20; 3:17–19

BENEFIT

Habakkuk's openness and honesty in his relationship with God is refreshing. Like Job, Habakkuk brings his complaints and questions directly to the Lord. He not only talks about God, but he also talks to God. All of us struggle at times with the problem of evil and injustice. The perspectives provided in this book help with these issues since they affirm God's perfect goodness (1:13) as well as his plan to punish all iniquity (2:2–20).

SETTING

The phrase "Habakkuk the prophet" appears twice in this book (1:1; 3:1), and it concludes with the words, "For the director of music. On my stringed instruments" (3:19). This may suggest that Habakkuk was a professional prophet who may also have been involved in Judah's temple worship, possibly as a priest. Habakkuk wrote at a time when injustice and corruption abounded in Judah; soon it would be invaded by the Babylonians (also known as the Chaldeans; 1:6–11; 3:16).

The Babylonian Empire became dominant in the time of Nabopolassar (626–605 B.C.). In 612 B.C. it overthrew the Assyrians by defeating Nineveh. Nebuchadnezzar succeeded Nabopolassar in 605 B.C. and in that year swept through Palestine and carried off most of Judah's nobles (including Daniel and his friends) to Babylon. It appears likely that Habakkuk ministered during the time when the Babylonians were Judah's greatest threat, and this would be after they had defeated the Assyrians. In addition, Habakkuk probably received this oracle after the time of Judah's last good king, Josiah (640–609 B.C.), since Josiah's spiritual and moral reforms were not in evidence (1:2–4). Thus, Habakkuk was most likely written in the early days of Judah's ungodly King Jehoiakim (609–598 B.C.) before Nebuchadnezzar's invasion in 605 B.C.

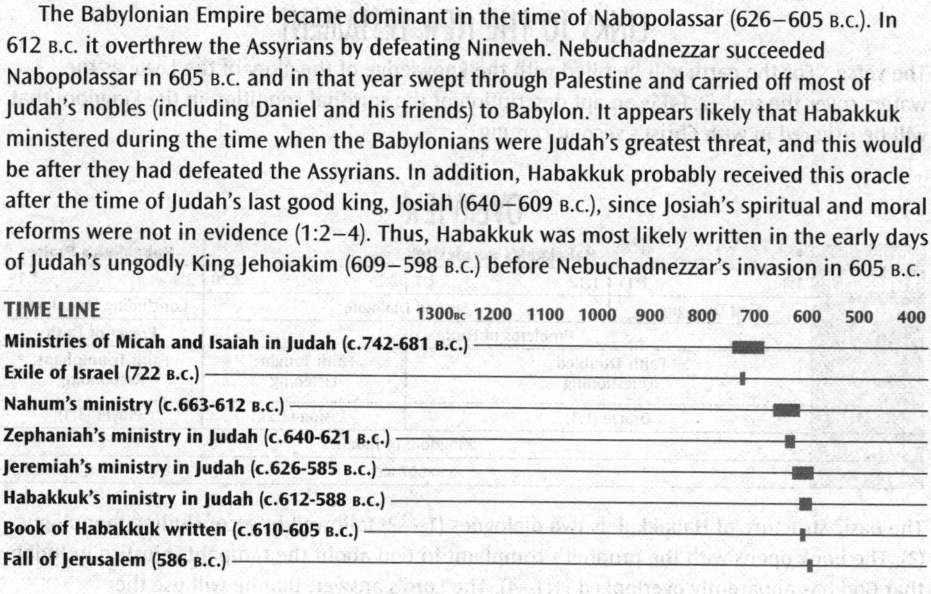

THEME AND PURPOSE

When Habakkuk saw his countrymen shamelessly disobeying God's laws and openly distorting justice on every level, he wondered how God could allow this to go on without bringing Judah to judgment. God answered that he was raising up the Babylonians as his rod of judgment on Judah, but this answer only increased Habakkuk's confusion. The Babylonians were even more violent and depraved than the people of Judah—how could God allow this?

God's second answer helped Habakkuk better understand the goodness, perfection, wisdom and power of Yahweh. With a clearer grasp of God's person, he had a greater capacity to trust God's purposes. Thus, Habakkuk could conclude his book with confidence rather than complaint, and with praise rather than perplexity.

UNIQUE CONTRIBUTION

Like the book of Jonah, Habakkuk deals with the personal experiences and emotions of the prophet himself. But while Jonah tried to run from God, Habakkuk ran to God; God called on Jonah, but Habakkuk called on God; Jonah concluded with folly, but Habakkuk concluded with faith. A significant portion of Habakkuk concerns two dialogues between the prophet and God. This structure is very different from most of the other prophets, whose books deliver a series of messages proclaiming condemnation and consolation to the people. In the case of Habakkuk, the message is first delivered for the benefit of the prophet and then given to the people.

This book moves from problems to praise, from challenge to confidence and from confusion to worship. The key phrase of the book is "the righteous will live by his faith" (2:4); this crucial truth was of great significance to Paul (Romans 1:17; Galatians 3:11) and the author of Hebrews (10:38) and also to Augustine, Martin Luther and John Wesley. In addition, chapter 3 is one of the most beautiful psalms of praise in the Old Testament (compare Psalm 18; 68).

LINKS TO THE NEW TESTAMENT

The verse, "For the earth will be filled with the knowledge of the glory of the LORD, as the waters cover the sea" (2:14) is an apt description of the spiritual condition in the kingdom that will be ushered in with Christ's second coming.

OVERVIEW

FOCUS	Habakkuk's Perplexity			Habakkuk's Praise
REFERENCE	1:1 1:11	1:12 2:1	2:2 2:20	3:1 3:19
TOPICS	First Dialogue	Second Dialogue		Concluding Monologue
	Problems of Faith			Prayer of Faith
	Faith Troubled: Questioning		Faith Taught: Listening	Faith Triumphant: Responding
	Oracle (1:1)		Vision (2:2)	Prayer (3:1)
LOCATION	Kingdom of Judah			
TIME	~607 B.C.			

The basic structure of Habakkuk is two dialogues (1—2) followed by a concluding monologue (3). The book opens with the prophet's complaint to God about the rampant injustice in Judah that God has apparently overlooked (1:1–4). The Lord's answer, that he will use the Babylonians to overthrow Judah (1:5–11), leaves Habakkuk even more perplexed than before. The people of Judah may be wicked, but they're righteous when compared with the Babylonians. So in his second complaint, Habakkuk asks how God can be just in allowing the wicked to swallow up those more righteous than themselves (1:12–17). Habakkuk stands on a watchtower to await God's reply (2:1), and God responds by saying that the Babylonians will not escape divine retribution (2:2–3). He underscores this statement with a set of five woes (2:4–8, 9–11, 12–14, 15–17, 18–20) directed at Babylon's sins of arrogance, greed, extortion, injustice, violence, lewdness and idolatry.

As a result of his encounter with God, Habakkuk concludes his prophecy with a psalm of praise that extols the Lord's awesome person (3:1–3), majestic power (3:4–12) and trustworthy plan (3:13–19). No matter what ills might come, Habakkuk promises, he will rejoice in the Lord and continue to trust in him (3:17–19).

HABAKKUK

1 The oracle[a] that Habakkuk the prophet received.

Habakkuk's Complaint

2How long, O LORD, must I call for help,
but you do not listen?[b]
Or cry out to you, "Violence!"
but you do not save?[c]
3Why do you make me look at injustice?
Why do you tolerate[d] wrong?
Destruction and violence[e] are before me;
there is strife,[f] and conflict abounds.
4Therefore the law[g] is paralyzed,
and justice never prevails.
The wicked hem in the righteous,
so that justice is perverted.[h]

The LORD's Answer

5"Look at the nations and watch—
and be utterly amazed.[i]
For I am going to do something in your days
that you would not believe,
even if you were told.[j]
6I am raising up the Babylonians,[a][k]
that ruthless and impetuous people,
who sweep across the whole earth
to seize dwelling places not their own.[l]
7They are a feared and dreaded people;[m]
they are a law to themselves
and promote their own honor.
8Their horses are swifter[n] than leopards,
fiercer than wolves at dusk.
Their cavalry gallops headlong;
their horsemen come from afar.
They fly like a vulture swooping to devour;
9 they all come bent on violence.
Their hordes[b] advance like a desert wind
and gather prisoners[o] like sand.
10They deride kings
and scoff at rulers.[p]
They laugh at all fortified cities;
they build earthen ramps and capture them.
11Then they sweep past like the wind[q] and go on—
guilty men, whose own strength is their god."[r]

Habakkuk's Second Complaint

12O LORD, are you not from everlasting?
My God, my Holy One,[s] we will not die.
O LORD, you have appointed[t] them to execute judgment;
O Rock, you have ordained them to punish.
13Your eyes are too pure to look on evil;
you cannot tolerate wrong.[u]
Why then do you tolerate the treacherous?
Why are you silent while the wicked
swallow up those more righteous than themselves?
14You have made men like fish in the sea,

[a]6 Or *Chaldeans* [b]9 The meaning of the Hebrew for this word is uncertain.

1:1 [a]Na 1:1 **1:2** [b]Ps 13:1-2; 22:1-2 [c]Jer 14:9 **1:3** [d]ver 13 [e]Jer 20:8 [f]Ps 55:9 **1:4** [g]Ps 119:126 [h]Job 19:7; Isa 1:23; 5:20; Eze 9:9 **1:5** [i]Isa 29:9 [j]Ac 13:41* **1:6** [k]2Ki 24:2 [l]Jer 13:20 **1:7** [m]Isa 18:7; Jer 39:5-9 **1:8** [n]Jer 4:13 **1:9** [o]Hab 2:5 **1:10** [p]2Ch 36:6 **1:11** [q]Jer 4:11-12 [r]Da 4:30 **1:12** [s]Isa 31:1 [t]Isa 10:6 **1:13** [u]La 3:34-36

1:2–4, 12–13

PROMISE 1

COMPLAINT DEPARTMENT

What does a man do when he's angry at God? Habakkuk was upset that God didn't judge sin in Judah (vv. 2–4). When God told him he would judge Judah with a Babylonian invasion (vv. 5–11), Habakkuk grew even angrier (vv. 12–13). Notice the basis of Habakkuk's complaint—he was jealous for God's name and reputation. In this prophet's day as in ours, the wicked seemed to get ahead while people who followed God suffered abuse and injustice.

What people get angry about (and what they *don't* get angry about) provides a clear commentary on their values. Do you ever want to complain when people violate God's will and seem to get away with it? If such violation doesn't frustrate you, learn from Habakkuk. Also as you read these verses, notice that even in his frustration and complaint, Habakkuk expressed respect and worship as he addressed God.

How we use God's name in our anger and complaining reveals our view of God. What upsets you? How do you approach God when you are frustrated? Habakkuk serves as a great model of a questioning, yet reverent heart. Read his words carefully.

For the next Promise 1 reading go to page 1010.

like sea creatures that have no
ruler.
15 The wicked foe pulls all of them up
with hooks,[v]
he catches them in his net,[w]
he gathers them up in his dragnet;
and so he rejoices and is glad.
16 Therefore he sacrifices to his net
and burns incense[x] to his
dragnet,
for by his net he lives in luxury
and enjoys the choicest food.
17 Is he to keep on emptying his net,
destroying nations without
mercy?[y]

2 I will stand at my watch[z]
and station myself on the
ramparts;[a]
I will look to see what he will say[b]
to me,
and what answer I am to give to
this complaint.[a][c]

The LORD's Answer

2 Then the LORD replied:

"Write[d] down the revelation
and make it plain on tablets
so that a herald[b] may run with
it.
3 For the revelation awaits an
appointed time;
it speaks of the end[e]
and will not prove false.
Though it linger, wait[f] for it;
it[c] will certainly come and will
not delay.[g]

4 "See, he is puffed up;
his desires are not upright—
but the righteous will live by his
faith[d][h]—
5 indeed, wine[i] betrays him;
he is arrogant and never at rest.
Because he is as greedy as the
grave[e]
and like death is never
satisfied,[j]
he gathers to himself all the
nations
and takes captive all the peoples.

6 "Will not all of them taunt[k] him
with ridicule and scorn, saying,

" 'Woe to him who piles up stolen
goods
and makes himself wealthy by
extortion![l]
How long must this go on?'
7 Will not your debtors[f] suddenly
arise?
Will they not wake up and make
you tremble?
Then you will become their
victim.[m]
8 Because you have plundered many
nations,
the peoples who are left will
plunder you.[n]
For you have shed man's blood;[o]
you have destroyed lands and
cities and everyone in them.

9 "Woe to him who builds[p] his
realm by unjust gain
to set his nest on high,
to escape the clutches of ruin!
10 You have plotted the ruin[q] of
many peoples,
shaming[r] your own house and
forfeiting your life.
11 The stones[s] of the wall will cry
out,
and the beams of the woodwork
will echo it.

12 "Woe to him who builds a city with
bloodshed[t]
and establishes a town by crime!
13 Has not the LORD Almighty
determined
that the people's labor is only
fuel for the fire,[u]
that the nations exhaust
themselves for nothing?[v]
14 For the earth will be filled with the
knowledge of the glory[w] of
the LORD,
as the waters cover the sea.[x]

15 "Woe to him who gives drink to his
neighbors,
pouring it from the wineskin till
they are drunk,
so that he can gaze on their
naked bodies.
16 You will be filled with shame[y]
instead of glory.
Now it is your turn! Drink and
be exposed[g]![z]
The cup[a] from the LORD's right
hand is coming around to
you,
and disgrace will cover your
glory.
17 The violence[b] you have done to
Lebanon will overwhelm
you,
and your destruction of animals
will terrify you.[c]
For you have shed man's blood;[d]
you have destroyed lands and
cities and everyone in them.

18 "Of what value is an idol,[e] since a
man has carved it?

1:15 [v]Isa 19:8 [w]Jer 16:16
1:16 [x]Jer 44:8
1:17 [y]Isa 14:6; 19:8
2:1 [z]Isa 21:8 [a]Ps 48:13 [b]Ps 85:8 [c]Ps 5:3
2:2 [d]Rev 1:19
2:3 [e]Da 8:17; 10:14 [f]Ps 27:14 [g]Eze 12:25; Heb 10:37-38
2:4 [h]Ro 1:17*; Gal 3:11*; Heb 10:37-38*
2:5 [i]Pr 20:1 [j]Pr 27:20; 30:15-16
2:6 [k]Isa 14:4 [l]Am 2:8
2:7 [m]Pr 29:1
2:8 [n]Isa 33:1; Zec 2:8-9 [o]ver 17
2:9 [p]Jer 22:13
2:10 [q]Jer 26:19 [r]ver 16
2:11 [s]Jos 24:27; Lk 19:40
2:12 [t]Mic 3:10
2:13 [u]Isa 50:11 [v]Isa 47:13
2:14 [w]Nu 14:21 [x]Isa 11:9
2:16 [y]ver 10 [z]La 4:21 [a]Isa 51:22
2:17 [b]Jer 51:35 [c]Jer 50:15 [d]ver 8
2:18 [e]Jer 5:21

[a] *1* Or *and what to answer when I am rebuked* [b] *2* Or *so that whoever reads it* [c] *3* Or *Though he linger, wait for him; / he* [d] *4* Or *faithfulness* [e] *5* Hebrew *Sheol* [f] *7* Or *creditors* [g] *16* Masoretic Text; Dead Sea Scrolls, Aquila, Vulgate and Syriac (see also Septuagint) *and stagger*

Or an image that teaches lies?
For he who makes it trusts in his
own creation;
he makes idols that cannot
speak.[f]
19 Woe to him who says to wood,
'Come to life!'
Or to lifeless stone, 'Wake up!'[g]
Can it give guidance?
It is covered with gold and
silver;[h]
there is no breath in it.
20 But the LORD is in his holy
temple;[i]
let all the earth be silent[j] before
him."

Habakkuk's Prayer

3 A prayer of Habakkuk the prophet.
On *shigionoth.*[a]

2 LORD, I have heard[k] of your fame;
I stand in awe[l] of your deeds,
O LORD.
Renew[m] them in our day,
in our time make them known;
in wrath remember mercy.[n]

3 God came from Teman,
the Holy One from Mount Paran.
Selah[b]
His glory covered the heavens
and his praise filled the earth.[o]
4 His splendor was like the sunrise;
rays flashed from his hand,
where his power was hidden.
5 Plague went before him;
pestilence followed his steps.

2:18–3:2

PROMISE 3

DON'T PRAY FOR JUSTICE

The verdict was in: Judah was about to be destroyed because the people listened to gods who couldn't speak and followed idols who couldn't lead. Now the God who *can* speak commanded silence. He heard the prophet's complaint, but the time for complaining was over. Habakkuk's only security was his knowledge of God's mercy. Because he had no defense—he knew the destruction was deserved—Habakkuk prayed before God his only hope: "In wrath remember mercy" (3:2).

Every man on earth must come to the same place. We *never* want to demand justice for ourselves before God; we all have sinned and deserve death (Romans 3:23). Each one of us stands in silent worship and accepts God's great mercy. Were it not for God's saving grace through Jesus Christ, Christians would be without hope and above all to be pitied (1 Corinthians 15:19).

For the next Promise 3 reading go to page 1052.

2:18 [f] Ps 115:4-5; Jer 10:14
2:19 [g] 1Ki 18:27 [h] Jer 10:4
2:20 [i] Ps 11:4 [j] Isa 41:1
3:2 [k] Ps 44:1 [l] Ps 119:120 [m] Ps 85:6 [n] Isa 54:8
3:3 [o] Ps 48:10
3:6 [p] Ps 114:1-6
3:7 [q] Jdg 7:24-25 [r] Ex 15:14
3:8 [s] Ex 7:20 [t] Ps 68:17
3:9 [u] Ps 7:12-13
3:10 [v] Ps 98:7 [w] Ps 93:3
3:11 [x] Jos 10:13 [y] Ps 18:14

6 He stood, and shook the earth;
he looked, and made the nations
tremble.
The ancient mountains crumbled
and the age-old hills collapsed.[p]
His ways are eternal.
7 I saw the tents of Cushan in
distress,
the dwellings of Midian[q] in
anguish.[r]

8 Were you angry with the rivers,[s]
O LORD?
Was your wrath against the
streams?
Did you rage against the sea
when you rode with your horses
and your victorious chariots?[t]
9 You uncovered your bow,
you called for many arrows.[u]
Selah
You split the earth with rivers;
10 the mountains saw you and
writhed.
Torrents of water swept by;
the deep roared[v]
and lifted its waves[w] on high.
11 Sun and moon stood still[x] in the
heavens
at the glint of your flying
arrows,[y]
at the lightning of your flashing
spear.
12 In wrath you strode through the
earth

a *1* Probably a literary or musical term
b *3* A word of uncertain meaning; possibly a musical term; also in verses 9 and 13

3:17–19

PROMISE 1

INSIDE-OUT JOY

The prophet Habakkuk learned that joy works from the inside out, not from the outside in. Read these amazing verses again! Most men say, "When the fig tree buds, and the olive crop comes in . . . then I will rejoice in the Lord, I will be joyful in God."

What was Habakkuk's secret? The prophet himself tells us: "The Sovereign LORD is my strength" (v. 19). The kind of joy Habakkuk talked about isn't a response to what's outside of a man; it's a response to what's inside of him.

Meditate on the messages these prophets proclaim about the incredible God you serve. The better you know God, the more consistently you can say the words in this passage sincerely. And you really do *need* to say the words of this passage sincerely.

For the next Promise 1 reading go to page 1021.

and in anger you threshed[z] the
nations.
13You came out to deliver[a] your
people,
to save your anointed one.
You crushed[b] the leader of the
land of wickedness,
you stripped him from head to
foot. *Selah*
14With his own spear you pierced his
head
when his warriors stormed out to
scatter us,[c]
gloating as though about to devour
the wretched[d] who were in
hiding.
15You trampled the sea with your
horses,
churning the great waters.[e]
16I heard and my heart pounded,
my lips quivered at the sound;
decay crept into my bones,
and my legs trembled.
Yet I will wait patiently for the day
of calamity
to come on the nation invading
us.
17Though the fig tree does not bud
and there are no grapes on the
vines,
though the olive crop fails
and the fields produce no
food,[f]
though there are no sheep in the
pen
and no cattle in the stalls,[g]
18yet I will rejoice in the LORD,[h]
I will be joyful in God my Savior.

19The Sovereign LORD is my
strength;[i]
he makes my feet like the feet of
a deer,
he enables me to go on the
heights.[j]

For the director of music. On my
stringed instruments.

3:12 [z]Isa 41:15
3:13 [a]Ps 20:6; 28:8 [b]Ps 68:21; 110:6
3:14 [c]Jdg 7:22 [d]Ps 64:2-5
3:15 [e]Ex 15:8; Ps 77:19
3:17 [f]Joel 1:10-12, 18 [g]Jer 5:17
3:18 [h]Isa 61:10; Php 4:4
3:19 [i]Dt 33:29; Ps 46:1-5 [j]Dt 32:13; 2Sa 22:34; Ps 18:33

ZEPHANIAH

AT A GLANCE

Key Principle: Yahweh is the Lord of all the earth, and all nations are accountable to him; he promises a time of universal judgment followed by worldwide rejoicing.
Author: Zephaniah
Time and Place: ~635–630 B.C. / Judah and the Nations
Key Verses: 1:14–15; 2:3

BENEFIT

Zephaniah is a book of warning, not only about judgments that were fulfilled in ancient times against Judah, Philistia, Moab, Ammon, Cush (Ethiopia) and Assyria (1:4–2:15), but also about a judgment that has yet to take place upon the entire earth (1:2–3; 3:8). Nevertheless, this prophecy also ends with a message of hope. It points ahead to a time after this judgment when all nations will call on the name of the Lord "and serve him shoulder to shoulder" (3:9–10). Without pulling any punches, Zephaniah gives a concise and powerful portrait of God's severity and his mercy in the day of judgment.

SETTING

Zephaniah's familiarity with the features and people of Jerusalem (1:9–10; 3:1–7), as well as his reference to it as "this place" (1:4), make it likely that he lived in Judah's capital. He prophesied "during the reign of Josiah son of Amon king of Judah" (1:1), between 640 and 609 B.C. Since he spoke of the fall of Nineveh as a future event (2:13), he wrote this message before 612 B.C. Two reforms took place in the days of King Josiah: the first in 628 B.C. when he did away with Judah's idolatrous images, altars and priests (2 Chronicles 34:3–7); the second in 622 B.C. when the book of the Law was discovered in the temple (2 Chronicles 34:8—35:19).

In view of the sins of idolatry and corruption that Zephaniah lists (1:4–13; 3:1–7), this prophecy was probably delivered early in Josiah's reign prior to the first reform in his twelfth year (~630 B.C.). Unfortunately, the wickedness of Manasseh and Amon had taken their toll, and Josiah's reforms were reversed immediately after his death. Judah's last godly king only slowed the inevitable collapse of the kingdom that occurred under the series of four evil kings who followed him.

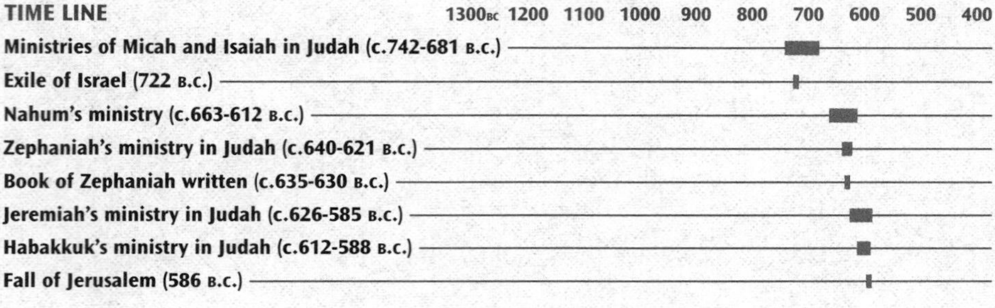

THEME AND PURPOSE

As with the majority of Old Testament prophets, Zephaniah develops the twin themes of condemnation (1:1—3:8) and consolation (3:9–20). The bulk of the book concerns God's judgment on Judah, and like Joel before him, Zephaniah's central image of judgment is "the day of the LORD." This image appears 23 times in different forms in this book's three chapters. It refers to a judgment that is universal (1:2–3; 3:8), imminent (1:14) and wrathful (1:15–17). But there is also another side of the day of the Lord that points to restoration (3:9–13) and blessing (3:14–20).

UNIQUE CONTRIBUTION

Unlike other prophets, Zephaniah traces four generations of his ancestry. Assuming that the Hezekiah of 1:1 is King Hezekiah, Zephaniah is the only known prophet of royal descent. Zephaniah was a contemporary of Habakkuk and Jeremiah, and God sent all three as eleventh-hour prophets to Judah with a call to repent in view of his imminent judgment. Habakkuk prophesied just before the fall of Jerusalem (~607 B.C.), and Jeremiah ministered both before and after Jerusalem's destruction (~626–585 B.C.).

Zephaniah is a very powerful and condensed book that uses vivid and gripping imagery to communicate an unrelenting message of judgment. This prophet said that God's wrath would be poured out not only on Judah and the nations that surrounded Judah, but also in the future on all the nations of the earth. The message of this book is directed to Judah, but it also makes a significant statement in 3:9–10 about God's intention that the Gentiles worship him as well.

LINKS TO THE NEW TESTAMENT

Jesus alluded to Zephaniah 1:3 in Matthew 13:41 and to Zephaniah 1:15 in Matthew 24:29 when he spoke of the judgment at the end of the age. Christ will fulfill the universal aspects of Zephaniah's prophecies about the day of the Lord as a time of worldwide judgment (1:2–3; 3:8) followed by great blessing and joy (3:9–20). He is the king who will restore and preserve his people Israel: "The LORD has taken away your punishment, he has turned back your enemy. The LORD, the King of Israel, is with you; never again will you fear any harm" (3:15).

OVERVIEW

FOCUS	Day of the Lord: Judgment		Deliverance of the Lord: Joy
REFERENCE	1:1 — 2:3	2:4 — 3:8	3:9 — 3:20
TOPICS	Judgment of Sin		Joy of Salvation
	Judgment upon Judah	Judgment upon the Nations	Blessings after Judgment
	Retribution in the Day of the Lord		Salvation in the Day of the Lord
	"I will sweep away everything" (1:2)		"I will restore your fortunes" (3:20)
LOCATION	Judah and the Nations		
TIME	~630 B.C.		

Zephaniah focuses on two aspects of the day of the Lord—it is a day of wrath, but it is also a day of blessing. This book is structured around three movements from the general to the specific. The first is from worldwide judgment (1:1–3) to judgment on Judah (1:4—2:3). Because of Judah's corruption and idolatry, it will soon encounter distress and terror on the day of the Lord. Zephaniah calls his people to repent and seek the Lord before this disaster comes upon them (2:1–3).

The second movement is from judgment on the nations around Judah (2:4–15) to judgment on Jerusalem (3:1–7). The surrounding nations from the west (Philistia), to the east (Moab and Ammon), to the south (Ethiopia) and to the north (Assyria) will encounter God's indignation, and rebellious Jerusalem will not escape desolation.

The third movement is from the judgment and purification of the Gentiles (3:8–10) to the renewal and blessing of Israel (3:11–20). Gentiles will serve the Lord, and the remnant of Israel will be gathered together and restored.

ZEPHANIAH

1 The word of the LORD that came to Zephaniah son of Cushi, the son of Gedaliah, the son of Amariah, the son of Hezekiah, during the reign of Josiah[a] son of Amon king of Judah:

Warning of Coming Destruction

2"I will sweep away everything
from the face of the earth,"[b]
declares the LORD.
3"I will sweep away both men and animals;
I will sweep away the birds of the air[c]
and the fish of the sea.
The wicked will have only heaps of rubble[a]
when I cut off man from the face of the earth,"[d]
declares the LORD.

Against Judah

4"I will stretch out my hand[e]
against Judah
and against all who live in Jerusalem.
I will cut off from this place every remnant of Baal,[f]
the names of the pagan and the idolatrous priests[g]—
5those who bow down on the roofs
to worship the starry host,
those who bow down and swear by the LORD
and who also swear by Molech,[b][h]
6those who turn back from following[i] the LORD
and neither seek[j] the LORD nor inquire[k] of him.
7Be silent[l] before the Sovereign LORD,
for the day of the LORD[m] is near.
The LORD has prepared a sacrifice;[n]
he has consecrated those he has invited.
8On the day of the LORD's sacrifice
I will punish[o] the princes
and the king's sons[p]
and all those clad
in foreign clothes.
9On that day I will punish
all who avoid stepping on the threshold,[c]
who fill the temple of their gods
with violence and deceit.[q]
10"On that day," declares the LORD,
"a cry will go up from the Fish Gate,[r]
wailing from the New Quarter,
and a loud crash from the hills.
11Wail,[s] you who live in the market district[d];
all your merchants will be wiped out,
all who trade with[e] silver will be ruined.[t]
12At that time I will search Jerusalem with lamps
and punish those who are complacent,[u]
who are like wine left on its dregs,[v]
who think, 'The LORD will do nothing,[w]
either good or bad.'
13Their wealth will be plundered,[x]
their houses demolished.
They will build houses
but not live in them;
they will plant vineyards
but not drink the wine.[y]

The Great Day of the LORD

14"The great day of the LORD[z] is near[a]—
near and coming quickly.
Listen! The cry on the day of the LORD will be bitter,
the shouting of the warrior there.
15That day will be a day of wrath,
a day of distress and anguish,
a day of trouble and ruin,
a day of darkness and gloom,
a day of clouds and blackness,[b]
16a day of trumpet and battle cry[c]
against the fortified cities
and against the corner towers.[d]
17I will bring distress on the people
and they will walk like blind[e] men,
because they have sinned against the LORD.
Their blood will be poured out[f] like dust
and their entrails like filth.[g]
18Neither their silver nor their gold
will be able to save them
on the day of the LORD's wrath.[h]
In the fire of his jealousy
the whole world will be consumed,[i]
for he will make a sudden end

1:1 [a]2Ki 22:1; 2Ch 34:1-35:25 **1:2** [b]Ge 6:7 **1:3** [c]Jer 4:25 [d]Hos 4:3 **1:4** [e]Jer 6:12 [f]Mic 5:13 [g]Hos 10:5 **1:5** [h]Jer 5:7 **1:6** [i]Isa 1:4; Jer 2:13 [j]Isa 9:13 [k]Hos 7:7 **1:7** [l]Hab 2:20; Zec 2:13 [m]ver 14; Isa 13:6 [n]Isa 34:6; Jer 46:10 **1:8** [o]Isa 24:21 [p]Jer 39:6 **1:9** [q]Am 3:10 **1:10** [r]2Ch 33:14 **1:11** [s]Jas 5:1 [t]Hos 9:6 **1:12** [u]Am 6:1 [v]Jer 48:11 [w]Eze 8:12 **1:13** [x]Jer 15:13 [y]Dt 28:30,39; Am 5:11; Mic 6:15 **1:14** [z]ver 7; Joel 1:15 [a]Eze 7:7 **1:15** [b]Isa 22:5; Joel 2:2 **1:16** [c]Jer 4:19 [d]Isa 2:15 **1:17** [e]Isa 59:10 [f]Ps 79:3 [g]Jer 9:22 **1:18** [h]Eze 7:19 [i]ver 2-3; Zep 3:8

[a]3 The meaning of the Hebrew for this line is uncertain. [b]5 Hebrew *Malcam,* that is, Milcom [c]9 See 1 Samuel 5:5. [d]11 Or *the Mortar* [e]11 Or *in*

of all who live in the earth.[j]"

2 Gather together,[k] gather together,
O shameful[l] nation,
2 before the appointed time arrives
and that day sweeps on like chaff,[m]
before the fierce anger[n] of the LORD comes upon you,
before the day of the LORD's wrath comes upon you.
3 Seek[o] the LORD, all you humble of the land,
you who do what he commands.
Seek righteousness, seek humility;[p]
perhaps you will be sheltered[q]
on the day of the LORD's anger.

Against Philistia

4 Gaza[r] will be abandoned
and Ashkelon left in ruins.
At midday Ashdod will be emptied
and Ekron uprooted.
5 Woe to you who live by the sea,
O Kerethite[s] people;
the word of the LORD is against you,[t]
O Canaan, land of the Philistines.

"I will destroy you,
and none will be left."[u]

6 The land by the sea, where the Kerethites[a] dwell,
will be a place for shepherds and sheep pens.[v]
7 It will belong to the remnant of the house of Judah;
there they will find pasture.
In the evening they will lie down
in the houses of Ashkelon.
The LORD their God will care for them;
he will restore their fortunes.[b][w]

Against Moab and Ammon

8 "I have heard the insults[x] of Moab
and the taunts of the Ammonites,
who insulted[y] my people
and made threats against their land.
9 Therefore, as surely as I live,"
declares the LORD Almighty, the God of Israel,
"surely Moab[z] will become like Sodom,[a]
the Ammonites[b] like Gomorrah—
a place of weeds and salt pits,
a wasteland forever.
The remnant of my people will plunder[c] them;
the survivors of my nation will inherit their land.[d]"

10 This is what they will get in return for their pride,[e]
for insulting[f] and mocking the people of the LORD Almighty.
11 The LORD will be awesome[g] to them
when he destroys all the gods[h] of the land.
The nations on every shore will worship him,[i]
every one in its own land.

Against Cush

12 "You too, O Cushites,[c][j]
will be slain by my sword.[k]"

Against Assyria

13 He will stretch out his hand against the north
and destroy Assyria,
leaving Nineveh[l] utterly desolate
and dry as the desert.[m]
14 Flocks and herds will lie down there,
creatures of every kind.
The desert owl[n] and the screech owl
will roost on her columns.
Their calls will echo through the windows,
rubble will be in the doorways,
the beams of cedar will be exposed.
15 This is the carefree[o] city
that lived in safety.[p]
She said to herself,
"I am, and there is none besides me."[q]
What a ruin she has become,
a lair for wild beasts!
All who pass by her scoff[r]
and shake their fists.

The Future of Jerusalem

3 Woe to the city of oppressors,[s]
rebellious and defiled![t]
2 She obeys[u] no one,
she accepts no correction.[v]
She does not trust in the LORD,
she does not draw near[w] to her God.
3 Her officials are roaring lions,
her rulers are evening wolves,[x]
who leave nothing for the morning.
4 Her prophets are arrogant;
they are treacherous[y] men.
Her priests profane the sanctuary
and do violence to the law.[z]
5 The LORD within her is righteous;

1:18 [j]Ge 6:7
2:1 [k]2Ch 20:4; Joel 1:14 [l]Jer 3:3; 6:15
2:2 [m]Isa 17:13; Hos 13:3 [n]La 4:11
2:3 [o]Am 5:6 [p]Ps 45:4; Am 5:14-15 [q]Ps 57:1
2:4 [r]Am 1:6,7-8; Zec 9:5-7
2:5 [s]Eze 25:16 [t]Am 3:1 [u]Isa 14:30
2:6 [v]Isa 5:17
2:7 [w]Ps 126:4; Jer 32:44
2:8 [x]Jer 48:27 [y]Eze 25:3
2:9 [z]Isa 15:1-16:14; Jer 48:1-47 [a]Dt 29:23 [b]Jer 49:1-6; Eze 25:1-7 [c]Isa 11:14 [d]Am 2:1-3
2:10 [e]Isa 16:6 [f]Jer 48:27
2:11 [g]Joel 2:11 [h]Zep 1:4 [i]Zep 3:9
2:12 [j]Isa 18:1; 20:4 [k]Jer 46:10
2:13 [l]Na 1:1 [m]Mic 5:6
2:14 [n]Isa 14:23
2:15 [o]Isa 32:9 [p]Isa 47:8 [q]Eze 28:2 [r]Na 3:19
3:1 [s]Jer 6:6 [t]Eze 23:30
3:2 [u]Jer 22:21 [v]Jer 7:28 [w]Ps 73:28; Jer 5:3
3:3 [x]Eze 22:27
3:4 [y]Jer 9:4 [z]Eze 22:26

[a]6 The meaning of the Hebrew for this word is uncertain. [b]7 Or *will bring back their captives* [c]12 That is, people from the upper Nile region

he does no wrong.[a]
Morning by morning he dispenses
his justice,
and every new day he does not
fail,
yet the unrighteous know no
shame.

6"I have cut off nations;
their strongholds are demolished.
I have left their streets deserted,
with no one passing through.
Their cities are destroyed;[b]
no one will be left—no one at
all.
7I said to the city,
'Surely you will fear me
and accept correction!'
Then her dwelling would not be
cut off,
nor all my punishments come
upon her.
But they were still eager
to act corruptly[c] in all they did.
8Therefore wait[d] for me," declares
the LORD,
"for the day I will stand up to
testify.[a]
I have decided to assemble the
nations,[e]
to gather the kingdoms
and to pour out my wrath on
them—
all my fierce anger.
The whole world will be
consumed[f]
by the fire of my jealous anger.

9"Then will I purify the lips of the
peoples,
that all of them may call[g] on
the name of the LORD
and serve[h] him shoulder to
shoulder.

3:9–20

PROMISE 6

GOD'S FUTURE KINGDOM NOW

Two features stand out in this prophecy about God's reign on earth. First, God said all peoples will serve him "shoulder to shoulder" (vv. 9–10). Second, he said the proud and arrogant will be removed and the humble and meek who trust in God's name will be preserved (vv. 11–20).

This passage describes life as God intends it to be, with all people serving him together. God calls for an absence of pride and arrogance; he wants followers to become people characterized by humility and trust in him. Within your own sphere of influence, work to make this true of you and the people with whom you come into contact.

For the next Promise 6 reading go to page 1027.

3:5 [a]Dt 32:4
3:6 [b]Lev 26:31
3:7 [c]Hos 9:9
3:8 [d]Ps 27:14 [e]Joel 3:2 [f]Zep 1:18
3:9 [g]Zep 2:11 [h]Isa 19:18
3:10 [i]Ps 68:31 [j]Isa 60:7
3:11 [k]Joel 2:26-27
3:12 [l]Isa 14:32 [m]Na 1:7
3:13 [n]Isa 10:21; Mic 4:7 [o]Ps 119:3 [p]Rev 14:5 [q]Eze 34:15; Zep 2:7 [r]Eze 34:25-28
3:14 [s]Zec 2:10 [t]Isa 12:6
3:15 [u]Eze 37:26-28 [v]Isa 54:14
3:16 [w]Job 4:3; Isa 35:3-4; Heb 12:12
3:17 [x]Isa 63:1 [y]Isa 62:4
3:19 [z]Eze 34:16; Mic 4:6 [a]Isa 60:18

10From beyond the rivers of Cush[b][i]
my worshipers, my scattered
people,
will bring me offerings.[j]
11On that day you will not be put to
shame[k]
for all the wrongs you have done
to me,
because I will remove from this city
those who rejoice in their pride.
Never again will you be haughty
on my holy hill.
12But I will leave within you
the meek[l] and humble,
who trust[m] in the name of the
LORD.
13The remnant[n] of Israel will do no
wrong;[o]
they will speak no lies,[p]
nor will deceit be found in their
mouths.
They will eat and lie down[q]
and no one will make them
afraid.[r]"

14Sing, O Daughter of Zion;[s]
shout aloud,[t] O Israel!
Be glad and rejoice with all your
heart,
O Daughter of Jerusalem!
15The LORD has taken away your
punishment,
he has turned back your enemy.
The LORD, the King of Israel, is with
you;[u]
never again will you fear[v] any
harm.
16On that day they will say to
Jerusalem,
"Do not fear, O Zion;
do not let your hands hang
limp.[w]
17The LORD your God is with you,
he is mighty to save.[x]
He will take great delight[y] in you,
he will quiet you with his love,
he will rejoice over you with
singing."

18"The sorrows for the appointed
feasts
I will remove from you;
they are a burden and a
reproach to you.[c]
19At that time I will deal
with all who oppressed you;
I will rescue the lame
and gather those who have been
scattered.[z]
I will give them praise[a] and honor
in every land where they were
put to shame.

[a]*8* Septuagint and Syriac; Hebrew *will rise up to plunder* [b]*10* That is, the upper Nile region [c]*18* Or *"I will gather you who mourn for the appointed feasts; / your reproach is a burden to you*

20At that time I will gather you;
at that time I will bring[b] you home.
I will give you honor[c] and praise
among all the peoples of the earth
when I restore your fortunes[a][d]
before your very eyes,"
says the LORD.

3:20
[b]Jer 29:14; Eze 37:12
[c]Isa 56:5; 66:22
[d]Joel 3:1

[a]*20* Or *I bring back your captives*

HAGGAI

AT A GLANCE

Key Principle: When we place God's interests above ours, we have more joy and satisfaction in life than when we place our own interests above God's.
Author: Haggai
Time and Place: 520 B.C. / Jerusalem
Key Verses: 1:7–8; 2:7–9

BENEFIT

Haggai spoke to a people whose spiritual lives were in decline because they had misplaced their priorities. In a series of sharp exhortations, Haggai encouraged them to consider their ways, to take action and to take heart. This little book provides a strong word to us when we find ourselves discouraged and despondent because of spiritual lethargy.

SETTING

The name "Haggai" appears nine times in the two chapters of this book, and the prophet Haggai is also mentioned in Ezra 5:1 and 6:14 in association with the rebuilding of the temple. He was a part of the first return of the Jews from Babylon to their homeland under Zerubbabel's leadership in 538 B.C., and he ministered along with the younger prophet Zechariah to the Jewish remnant in Jerusalem. Work began on the second temple in 536 B.C., but stopped in 534 B.C. due to opposition by the Samaritans, crop failure and general hardships in a land that had become desolate (see Ezra 4—6 for more background for the book of Haggai). A few of the people were old enough to see that the new temple's foundations were small when compared to the scale of Solomon's temple. In 520 B.C. God called Haggai to encourage the people to see that God had a significant purpose for the new temple (2:3–9).

Haggai and Zechariah ministered during the reign of King Darius I of Persia (521–486 B.C.), and their prophecies can be dated precisely because they are chronologically linked to Darius's reign.

TIME LINE

1300BC 1200 1100 1000 900 800 700 600 500 400

Fall of Jerusalem (586 B.C.)
First return of exiles to Jerusalem (538 B.C.)
Ministries of Haggai and Zechariah (c.520-480 B.C.)
Book of Haggai written (c.520 B.C.)
Completion of temple (516 B.C.)
Second return to Jerusalem under Ezra (458 B.C.)
Third return to Jerusalem under Nehemiah (445 B.C.)
Malachi's ministry (c.440-430 B.C.)

THEME AND PURPOSE

Haggai's theme is that the Jewish remnant needs to adjust its priorities from the material to the spiritual by honoring God first. Instead of completing the temple reconstruction, they let the work stop for 14 years while they built their own paneled houses and attempted to enhance their tangible assets (1:3). As a result, God withheld his blessing from their efforts:

They planted much, but harvested little; they worked hard, but their wages went into a purse with holes in it (1:5–6). The people thought that they had to avoid distraction and work harder to overcome their hardships, even to the point of abandoning the temple project. Instead, Haggai called them to see that God had actually increased their hardships to get their attention, and that they were to look to God, not to themselves, to meet their needs. If they sought him first and honored him by finishing the temple, God would bless them and provide for their material needs.

UNIQUE CONTRIBUTION

Of all the Old Testament books, Haggai is second only to Obadiah in brevity. The four brief sermons in this book go straight to the point; they lack the vivid poetic imagery of other prophets like Isaiah and Jeremiah. Nevertheless, these concise messages met with a surprisingly enthusiastic response. The people had not worked on the second temple for 14 years, but they resumed construction within 23 days after Haggai's first message, and by 516 B.C. had completed the temple (Ezra 6:15). Haggai was able to shift his audience's perspective. When they responded to Haggai's message, God told the people, "From this day on I will bless you" (2:19).

Now that Israel lacked a king on the throne of David, the temple was especially critical to Israel's spiritual identity. It was the visible manifestation of God's presence among his people, and the central sanctuary where the whole Mosaic system of the priesthood, sacrifices and worship converged.

LINKS TO THE NEW TESTAMENT

"'On that day,' declares the LORD Almighty, 'I will take you, my servant Zerubbabel son of Shealtiel,' declares the LORD, 'and I will make you like my signet ring, for I have chosen you,' declares the LORD Almighty" (2:23). Zerubbabel was a descendant of both Solomon and Nathan, and like a signet ring, he seals both branches of the Messianic line together. Jesus was the legal heir to David's throne through Solomon, Zerubbabel (Matthew 1:12) and Joseph. Jesus was the physical heir to David's throne through Nathan, Zerubbabel (Luke 3:27) and Mary.

OVERVIEW

FOCUS	A Call to Completion	A Call to Courage	A Call to Cleansing	A Call to the Chosen
REFERENCE	1:1 — 1:15	2:1 — 2:9	2:10 — 2:19	2:20 — 2:23
TOPICS	Sermon 1: Priorities	Sermon 2: Perspective	Sermon 3: Purity	Sermon 4: Promises
	Arousing	Assuring	Affirming	Anticipating
	Rebuke	Encouragement	Rebuke	Encouragement
	Finishing God's Building		Finding God's Blessing	
LOCATION	Jerusalem			
TIME	August 29, 520 B.C.	October 17, 520 B.C.	December 18, 520 B.C.	

In his first sermon to the Jewish remnant, Haggai told the people that they needed to reorder their priorities. They were more concerned with their own comfort than with their spiritual well-being, and as a consequence, God withheld his material blessing. Zerubbabel the governor of Judah, Joshua the high priest, and the whole remnant responded to Haggai's message, and they resumed temple construction (1:1–15). Haggai's second sermon encouraged the people that, despite its smaller scale, the glory of this new temple would be greater than the former temple, and that it would be a place of peace (2:1–9). The third message of this book is addressed to the priests and concerns purification from the contamination of sin and the need for obedience (2:10–19). The final message reaffirms God's plan to overthrow the nations of the earth (2:20–23; cf. 2:6–7).

HAGGAI

A Call to Build the House of the LORD

1 In the second year of King Darius,[a]
on the first day of the sixth month,
the word of the LORD came through the
prophet Haggai[b] to Zerubbabel[c] son
of Shealtiel, governor[d] of Judah, and
to Joshua[a][e] son of Jehozadak,[f] the
high priest:
2This is what the LORD Almighty
says: "These people say, 'The time has
not yet come for the LORD's house to be
built.' "
3Then the word of the LORD came
through the prophet Haggai:[g] 4"Is it a
time for you yourselves to be living in
your paneled houses,[h] while this
house remains a ruin?[i]"
5Now this is what the LORD Almighty
says: "Give careful thought[j] to your
ways. 6You have planted much, but
have harvested little.[k] You eat, but
never have enough. You drink, but never have your fill. You put on clothes,
but are not warm. You earn wages,[l]
only to put them in a purse with
holes in it."

1:1 [a]Ezr 4:24 [b]Ezr 5:1 [c]Mt 1:12-13 [d]Ezr 5:3 [e]Ezr 2:2 [f]1Ch 6:15; Ezr 3:2 **1:3** [g]Ezr 5:1 **1:4** [h]2Sa 7:2 [i]ver 9; Jer 33:12 **1:5** [j]La 3:40 **1:6** [k]Dt 28:38 [l]Hag 2:16; Zec 8:10 **1:8** [m]Ps 132:13-14 **1:9** [n]ver 4 **1:10** [o]Lev 26:19; Dt 28:23 **1:11** [p]Dt 28:22; 1Ki 17:1 [q]Hag 2:17 **1:12** [r]ver 1 [s]ver 14; Isa 1:9; Hag 2:2 [t]Isa 50:10

7This is what the LORD Almighty
says: "Give careful thought to your
ways. 8Go up into the mountains and
bring down timber and build the
house, so that I may take pleasure[m]
in it and be honored," says the LORD.
9"You expected much, but see, it
turned out to be little. What you
brought home, I blew away. Why?" declares the LORD Almighty. "Because of
my house, which remains a ruin,[n]
while each of you is busy with his own
house. 10Therefore, because of you the
heavens have withheld their dew and
the earth its crops.[o] 11I called for a
drought[p] on the fields and the mountains, on the grain, the new wine, the
oil and whatever the ground produces,
on men and cattle, and on the labor of
your hands.[q]"

12Then Zerubbabel[r] son of Shealtiel, Joshua son of Jehozadak, the high
priest, and the whole remnant[s] of the
people obeyed[t] the voice of the LORD
their God and the message of the

a *1* A variant of *Jeshua;* here and elsewhere in Haggai

1:2-11

PROMISE 1

NO SATISFACTION

The people whom Haggai addressed had so much stuff and so little satisfaction—sort of like a culture that advertises food and diet plans in the same magazine.

God had brought his people back to Jerusalem from their exile in Babylon. Essential to their way of life was a temple, and God had provided the resources to build it. But read verses 2–4—God's people used material he provided for *his* house to build *their* houses. Their attitude was, "After we take care of ourselves, we will invest in God's work." Wow! Ponder the question in verse 4, because it is timeless. The people thought they didn't have enough resources to cover God's plans and their own. They had to make a choice: Do we satisfy God or ourselves? Haggai tells us that they made the wrong choice.

Verses 5–6 and 9–11 address the basic issues of appetite and satisfaction at their root. Twice Haggai repeated the sentence: "This is what the LORD Almighty says: Give careful thought to your ways" (vv. 5, 7). That kind of repetition demands attention, so let's "give careful thought" together for a few moments.

Notice the contrasts: The people planted much / harvested little; ate / never had enough; drank / were never full; put on clothes / were not warm; earned wages / put them in a bag with holes (v. 6). They expected much / received little; brought home / God blew away (v. 9). No dew, no crops. They experienced drought on fields, mountains, grain, fruit, oil, men, cattle and the work of their hands (vv. 10–11).

These people worked, brought home, consumed . . . and starved. They had abandoned God and scattered their resources in a feeding frenzy, spending everything trying to satisfy the urge only he could fulfill. God's people had not discovered two facts: (1) They couldn't buy enough junk to fill up their empty lives; (2) God ultimately gives or withholds everything we want or need.

When prophets bring problems to the surface, prophets also provide solutions. Haggai told his readers how to satisfy the soul: Use God's resources to accomplish God's will. Men will never satisfy themselves by trying to satisfy themselves. God lives and rules over this earth; he will not be ignored. Verse 7 relates this timeless principle: A man is only satisfied when his life is lived "'so that I may take pleasure in it and be honored' says the LORD."

For the next Promise 1 reading go to page 1039.

prophet Haggai, because the LORD their God had sent him. And the people feared[u] the LORD.

13 Then Haggai, the LORD's messenger, gave this message of the LORD to the people: "I am with[v] you," declares the LORD. 14 So the LORD stirred up the spirit of Zerubbabel[w] son of Shealtiel, governor of Judah, and the spirit of Joshua son of Jehozadak, the high priest, and the spirit of the whole remnant[x] of the people. They came and began to work on the house of the LORD Almighty, their God, 15 on the twenty-fourth day of the sixth month[y] in the second year of King Darius.

The Promised Glory of the New House

2 On the twenty-first day of the seventh month, the word of the LORD came through the prophet Haggai: 2 "Speak to Zerubbabel son of Shealtiel, governor of Judah, to Joshua son of Jehozadak, the high priest, and to the remnant of the people. Ask them, 3 'Who of you is left who saw this house[z] in its former glory? How does it look to you now? Does it not seem to you like nothing?[a] 4 But now be strong, O Zerubbabel,' declares the LORD. 'Be strong,[b] O Joshua son of Jehozadak, the high priest. Be strong, all you people of the land,' declares the LORD, 'and work. For I am with[c] you,' declares the LORD Almighty. 5 'This is what I covenanted with you when you came out of Egypt.[d] And my Spirit[e] remains among you. Do not fear.'

6 "This is what the LORD Almighty says: 'In a little while[f] I will once more shake the heavens and the earth,[g] the sea and the dry land. 7 I will shake all nations, and the desired of all nations will come, and I will fill this house[h] with glory,' says the LORD Almighty. 8 'The silver is mine and the gold is mine,' declares the LORD Almighty. 9 'The glory[i] of this present house will be greater than the glory of the former house,' says the LORD Almighty. 'And in this place I will grant peace,' declares the LORD Almighty."

Blessings for a Defiled People

10 On the twenty-fourth day of the ninth month,[j] in the second year of Darius, the word of the LORD came to the prophet Haggai: 11 "This is what the LORD Almighty says: 'Ask the priests[k] what the law says: 12 If a person carries consecrated meat in the fold of his garment, and that fold touches some bread or stew, some wine, oil or other food, does it become consecrated?[l]' "

The priests answered, "No."

13 Then Haggai said, "If a person defiled by contact with a dead body touches one of these things, does it become defiled?"

"Yes," the priests replied, "it becomes defiled.[m]"

14 Then Haggai said, " 'So it is with this people and this nation in my sight,' declares the LORD. 'Whatever they do and whatever they offer[n] there is defiled.

15 " 'Now give careful thought[o] to this from this day on[a]—consider how things were before one stone was laid[p] on another in the LORD's temple.[q] 16 When anyone came to a heap of twenty measures, there were only ten. When anyone went to a wine vat to draw fifty measures, there were only twenty.[r] 17 I struck all the work of your hands[s] with blight,[t] mildew and hail, yet you did not turn to me,' declares the LORD.[u] 18 'From this day on, from this twenty-fourth day of the ninth month, give careful thought to the day when the foundation[v] of the LORD's temple was laid. Give careful thought: 19 Is there yet any seed left in the barn? Until now, the vine and the fig tree, the pomegranate and the olive tree have not borne fruit.

" 'From this day on I will bless you.' "

Zerubbabel the LORD's Signet Ring

20 The word of the LORD came to Haggai a second time on the twenty-fourth day of the month: 21 "Tell Zerubbabel[w] governor of Judah that I will shake the heavens and the earth. 22 I will overturn royal thrones and shatter the power of the foreign kingdoms.[x] I will overthrow chariots[y] and their drivers; horses and their riders will fall, each by the sword of his brother.[z]

23 " 'On that day,' declares the LORD Almighty, 'I will take you, my servant[a] Zerubbabel son of Shealtiel,' declares the LORD, 'and I will make you like my signet ring, for I have chosen you,' declares the LORD Almighty."

1:12 [u]Dt 31:12
1:13 [v]Mt 28:20; Ro 8:31
1:14 [w]Ezr 5:2 [x]ver 12
1:15 [y]ver 1
2:3 [z]Ezr 3:12 [a]Zec 4:10
2:4 [b]1Ch 28:20; Zec 8:9; Eph 6:10 [c]2Sa 5:10; Ac 7:9
2:5 [d]Ex 29:46 [e]Ne 9:20; Isa 63:11
2:6 [f]Isa 10:25 [g]Heb 12:26*
2:7 [h]Isa 60:7
2:9 [i]Ps 85:9
2:10 [j]ver 1
2:11 [k]Lev 10:10-11; Dt 17:8-11; Mal 2:7
2:12 [l]Lev 6:27; Mt 23:19
2:13 [m]Lev 22:4-6
2:14 [n]Isa 1:13
2:15 [o]Hag 1:5 [p]Ezr 3:10 [q]Ezr 4:24
2:16 [r]Hag 1:6
2:17 [s]Hag 1:11 [t]Dt 28:22; 1Ki 8:37; Am 4:9 [u]Am 4:6
2:18 [v]Zec 8:9
2:21 [w]Ezr 5:2
2:22 [x]Da 2:44 [y]Mic 5:10 [z]Jdg 7:22
2:23 [a]Isa 43:10

a *15* Or *to the days past*

ZECHARIAH

AT A GLANCE

Key Principle: God gives his people the hope of glory so they can press on in present obedience, realizing that their labor is not in vain.
Author: Zechariah
Time and Place: 520 B.C. to ~480 B.C. / Jerusalem
Key Verses: 8:3; 9:9

BENEFIT

This book fills in a number of important details about the Messiah's humiliation and exaltation. It gives us insight into God's plan to transform history from Gentile domination to the Messianic kingdom. It also encourages us to realize that, regardless of our present difficulties, God's good and gracious purposes will be fulfilled, and we are a part of those purposes.

SETTING

Some 29 Old Testament characters share the name Zechariah, which means "God remembers." The Zechariah who recorded the visions and oracles in this book was born in Babylonia during the Jewish exile. Like Jeremiah and Ezekiel, he was part of the priestly line. His grandfather Iddo brought him to Palestine with the remnant who returned under Zerubbabel (Ezra 5:1; 6:14; Nehemiah 12:4, 16). If Zechariah was the "young man" of 2:4, his prophetic ministry began at an early age in 520 B.C.

As a younger contemporary of Haggai the prophet, Zerubbabel the governor and Joshua the high priest, Zechariah's initial concern (1—8) was that Israel's second temple in Jerusalem be completed. There is evidence that God gave the latter portion of this book to Zechariah some years later, around 480 B.C. If this is so, his early ministry was in the time of the Persian King Darius I (521–486 B.C.) and his latter ministry was in the time of Xerxes (486–464 B.C.), the king who made Esther his queen in Persia. According to Matthew 23:35, Zechariah was murdered between the temple and the altar in the same way that an earlier Zechariah was stoned to death in the courtyard of the temple in the time of King Joash (2 Chronicles 24:20–21).

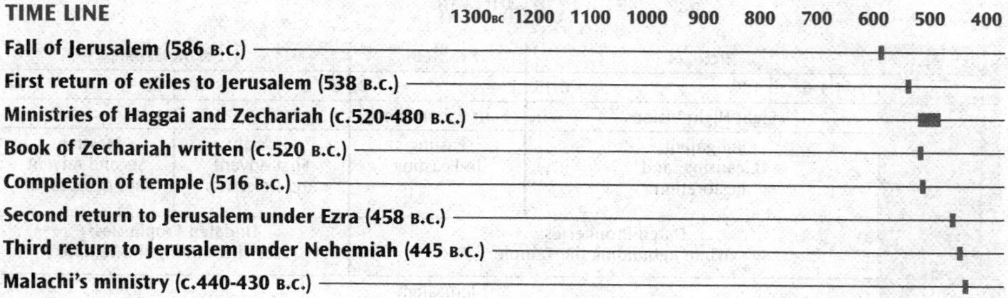

THEME AND PURPOSE

Chapters 1—8 record the visions and exhortations God gave Zechariah in Jerusalem. One purpose of this portion of the book, dated from November of 520 B.C. to December of 518 B.C., was to encourage the people to complete the new central sanctuary. Another purpose was to help them realize that this new temple was not simply a building, but a key to their spiritual identity. The Messiah would appear in this very temple when he came to bring salvation to his people.

Zechariah evidently received the two oracles of chapters 9—14 a few decades after the temple was completed in 516 B.C.; they are directly concerned with the coming Messiah and Israel's restoration after the time of the Gentiles. These oracles were meant to comfort and reassure the remnant that despite the uncertainty and hardship of their lives, the Lord had regathered them for a purpose and promised a glorious future for them in the Messianic kingdom.

UNIQUE CONTRIBUTION

Zechariah has been called "the major minor prophet" because its 14 chapters make it the longest of the minor prophets. In addition, this book has more Messianic prophecies than any other Old Testament book except Isaiah.

Although Haggai and Zechariah both ministered to the Jewish remnant as they were rebuilding the temple, the older prophet Haggai was a reformer who exhorted the people to take action, while the younger prophet Zechariah was a visionary who encouraged the people to take heart. Zechariah's book is marked by a wide variety of visions, messages and oracles about God's plans for the future.

LINKS TO THE NEW TESTAMENT

Zechariah's two apocalyptic oracles clearly present the person and work of Israel's coming Messiah. The first oracle (9—11) concerns Messiah's first advent in which he will appear as the Servant who will come in humility. The second oracle (12—14) concerns Messiah's second advent in which he will come in power and glory as the Ruler of the everlasting kingdom. Christ is also seen as the angel of Yahweh (3:1–2), the Branch and the stone (3:8–9), the priest who will reign as king (6:13), the humble king who rides to Jerusalem on the back of a donkey (9:9–10), the cornerstone, tent peg, and battle bow (10:4), the shepherd who will be sold for 30 pieces of silver (11:4–13), the one who was pierced by the inhabitants of Jerusalem (12:10), the fountain that cleanses from sin and impurity (13:1) and the shepherd who is struck and abandoned (13:7). He is also the Lord who will defeat and judge the nations, stand on the Mount of Olives, split it in two and reign over the whole earth from Jerusalem (14:2–15).

OVERVIEW

FOCUS	Pictures		Problems	Predictions	
REFERENCE	1:1-6	1:7 6:15	7 8	9 11	12 14
TOPICS	Eight Night Visions		Four Exhortations	Two Oracles	
	Judgment, Cleansing, and Restoration		Fasting to Feasting	Messiah: First Advent and Rejection	Messiah: Second Advent and Acceptance
	Dated Prophecies: While Rebuilding the Temple			Undated Prophecies: After Rebuilding the Temple	
LOCATION	Jerusalem				
TIME	November, 520 B.C.	February 15, 519 B.C.	December 7, 518 B.C.	~480–470 B.C.	

Zechariah opens with a brief exhortation to the remnant to return to the Lord (1:1–6). This is followed by a series of eight visions, evidently given on the same night, that symbolically depict

God restoring and cleansing his people (1:7—6:15). God will rebuild Jerusalem, judge those who have oppressed Judah and Israel, protect the future Jerusalem without walls, empower her leaders and judge the sins of Israel and the nations.

In a set of four exhortations the Lord denounces empty ritual, reminds the people of their fathers' disobedience, promises future blessing on Judah and Israel and announces that the nations of the earth will come to worship him in Jerusalem (7—8).

In the first of two oracles, God promises to overthrow Israel's neighbors and preserve Jerusalem until her king comes (9). The people will later be scattered among the nations, but the Lord will bring them back to the land and bless them (10). Zechariah predicts that Israel will reject the true Shepherd and will be led away by false shepherds (11). In the second oracle Zechariah says that the nations will attack Jerusalem, but will be destroyed. The inhabitants of Jerusalem will mourn for the One they pierced (12). The Jews who survive will be cleansed of impurity (13) and the Messiah will judge the nations and rule in Jerusalem (14).

ZECHARIAH

A Call to Return to the LORD

1 In the eighth month of the second
year of Darius,[a] the word of the
LORD came to the prophet Zechariah[b]
son of Berekiah,[c] the son of Iddo:[d]
2"The LORD was very angry[e] with
your forefathers. 3Therefore tell the
people: This is what the LORD Almighty
says: 'Return to me,' declares the LORD
Almighty, 'and I will return to you,'[f]
says the LORD Almighty. 4Do not be like
your forefathers,[g] to whom the earlier
prophets proclaimed: This is what the
LORD Almighty says: 'Turn from your
evil ways[h] and your evil practices.' But
they would not listen or pay attention
to me,[i] declares the LORD. 5Where are
your forefathers now? And the prophets, do they live forever? 6But did not
my words and my decrees, which I
commanded my servants the prophets,
overtake your forefathers?
"Then they repented and said, 'The
LORD Almighty has done to us what our
ways and practices deserve,[j] just as
he determined to do.' "

The Man Among the Myrtle Trees

7On the twenty-fourth day of the
eleventh month, the month of Shebat,
in the second year of Darius, the word
of the LORD came to the prophet Zechariah son of Berekiah, the son of Iddo.
8During the night I had a vision—
and there before me was a man riding a red[k] horse! He was standing
among the myrtle trees in a ravine. Behind him were red, brown and white
horses.[l]
9I asked, "What are these, my lord?"
The angel[m] who was talking with
me answered, "I will show you what
they are."
10Then the man standing among the
myrtle trees explained, "They are the
ones the LORD has sent to go throughout the earth."[n]
11And they reported to the angel of
the LORD, who was standing among the
myrtle trees, "We have gone throughout the earth and found the whole
world at rest and in peace."[o]
12Then the angel of the LORD said,
"LORD Almighty, how long will you
withhold mercy from Jerusalem and
from the towns of Judah, which you
have been angry with these seventy[p]
years?" 13So the LORD spoke kind and
comforting words to the angel who
talked with me.[q]
14Then the angel who was speaking
to me said, "Proclaim this word: This
is what the LORD Almighty says: 'I am
very jealous[r] for Jerusalem and Zion,
15but I am very angry with the nations
that feel secure.[s] I was only a little
angry, but they added to the calamity.'[t]
16"Therefore, this is what the LORD
says: 'I will return[u] to Jerusalem with
mercy, and there my house will be rebuilt. And the measuring line[v] will be
stretched out over Jerusalem,' declares
the LORD Almighty.
17"Proclaim further: This is what the
LORD Almighty says: 'My towns will
again overflow with prosperity, and the
LORD will again comfort[w] Zion and
choose[x] Jerusalem.' "[y]

Four Horns and Four Craftsmen

18Then I looked up—and there before me were four horns! 19I asked the
angel who was speaking to me, "What
are these?"
He answered me, "These are the
horns[z] that scattered Judah, Israel
and Jerusalem."
20Then the LORD showed me four
craftsmen. 21I asked, "What are these
coming to do?"
He answered, "These are the horns
that scattered Judah so that no one
could raise his head, but the craftsmen
have come to terrify them and throw
down these horns of the nations who
lifted up their horns[a] against the land
of Judah to scatter its people."[b]

1:1 [a]Ezr 4:24; 6:15 [b]Ezr 5:1 [c]Mt 23:35; Lk 11:51 [d]ver 7; Ne 12:4
1:2 [e]2Ch 36:16
1:3 [f]Mal 3:7; Jas 4:8
1:4 [g]2Ch 36:15 [h]Ps 106:6 [i]2Ch 24:19; Ps 78:8; Jer 6:17
1:6 [j]Jer 12:14-17; La 2:17
1:8 [k]Rev 6:4 [l]Zec 6:2-7
1:9 [m]Zec 4:1,4-5
1:10 [n]Zec 6:5-8
1:11 [o]Isa 14:7
1:12 [p]Da 9:2
1:13 [q]Zec 4:1
1:14 [r]Joel 2:18; Zec 8:2
1:15 [s]Jer 48:11 [t]Ps 123:3-4; Am 1:11
1:16 [u]Zec 8:3 [v]Zec 2:1-2
1:17 [w]Isa 51:3 [x]Isa 14:1 [y]Zec 2:12
1:19 [z]Am 6:13
1:21 [a]Ps 75:4 [b]Ps 75:10

1:2–6 PROMISE 4

LEGACY

What legacy are you writing for your life? Seven times in these five verses, Zechariah referred to "your forefathers" (four direct and three indirect references). Imagine God talking to your children ten years from now. Change the word "forefathers" to "father" and the word "they" to "he" in this passage and read it as if God were speaking to your kids.

Scary, isn't it? Want to rewrite the passage? You can, starting now. Ten years from now you may not be able to. That's Zechariah's challenging message to God's people from every age.

For the next Promise 4 reading go to page 1049.

A Man With a Measuring Line

2 Then I looked up—and there before
me was a man with a measuring line
in his hand! 2 I asked, "Where are you
going?"
He answered me, "To measure Jerusalem, to find out how wide and how
long it is."[c]
3 Then the angel who was speaking
to me left, and another angel came to
meet him 4 and said to him: "Run, tell
that young man, 'Jerusalem will be a
city without walls[d] because of the
great number[e] of men and livestock
in it. 5 And I myself will be a wall[f] of
fire around it,' declares the LORD, 'and
I will be its glory[g] within.'
6 "Come! Come! Flee from the land of
the north," declares the LORD, "for I
have scattered you to the four winds of
heaven,"[h] declares the LORD.
7 "Come, O Zion! Escape, you who
live in the Daughter of Babylon!"[i]
8 For this is what the LORD Almighty
says: "After he has honored me and has
sent me against the nations that have
plundered you—for whoever touches
you touches the apple of his eye[j]— 9 I
will surely raise my hand against them
so that their slaves will plunder
them.[a][k] Then you will know that the
LORD Almighty has sent me.[l]
10 "Shout and be glad, O Daughter of
Zion.[m] For I am coming,[n] and I will
live among you,"[o] declares the LORD.
11 "Many nations will be joined with the
LORD in that day and will become my
people. I will live among you and you
will know that the LORD Almighty has
sent me to you. 12 The LORD will inherit[p] Judah as his portion in the holy
land and will again choose[q] Jerusalem. 13 Be still[r] before the LORD, all
mankind, because he has roused himself from his holy dwelling."

Clean Garments for the High Priest

3 Then he showed me Joshua[b][s] the
high priest standing before the angel
of the LORD, and Satan[c][t] standing at

2:10–13

PROMISE **6**

DRAWN TOGETHER

A consistent theme of prophecies that describe the Lord's return and his kingdom is repeated here in verse 11: "Many nations will be joined with the LORD in that day and will become my people." Two characteristics of God's work are reconciliation and unity. God's presence draws people together.

For the next Promise 6 reading go to page 1054.

2:2 [c]Eze 40:3; Rev 21:15
2:4 [d]Eze 38:11 [e]Isa 49:20; Jer 30:19; 33:22
2:5 [f]Isa 26:1 [g]Rev 21:23
2:6 [h]Eze 17:21
2:7 [i]Isa 48:20
2:8 [j]Dt 32:10
2:9 [k]Isa 14:2 [l]Zec 4:9
2:10 [m]Zep 3:14 [n]Zec 9:9 [o]Lev 26:12; Zec 8:3
2:12 [p]Dt 32:9; Ps 33:12; Jer 10:16 [q]Zec 1:17
2:13 [r]Hab 2:20
3:1 [s]Hag 1:1; Zec 6:11 [t]Ps 109:6
3:2 [u]Jude 1:9 [v]Isa 14:1 [w]Am 4:11; Jude 1:23
3:4 [x]Eze 36:25; Mic 7:18 [y]Isa 52:1; Rev 19:8
3:5 [z]Ex 29:6
3:7 [a]Dt 17:8-11; Eze 44:15-16
3:8 [b]Eze 12:11 [c]Isa 4:2
3:9 [d]Isa 28:16 [e]Jer 50:20
3:10 [f]1Ki 4:25; Mic 4:4
4:1 [g]Da 8:18 [h]Jer 31:26
4:2 [i]Jer 1:13 [j]Ex 25:31; Rev 1:12 [k]Rev 4:5
4:3 [l]ver 11; Rev 11:4
4:5 [m]Zec 1:9
4:6 [n]Ezr 5:2

his right side to accuse him. 2 The LORD
said to Satan, "The LORD rebuke you,[u]
Satan! The LORD, who has chosen[v] Jerusalem, rebuke you! Is not this man
a burning stick snatched from the
fire?"[w]
3 Now Joshua was dressed in filthy
clothes as he stood before the angel.
4 The angel said to those who were
standing before him, "Take off his
filthy clothes."
Then he said to Joshua, "See, I have
taken away your sin,[x] and I will put
rich garments[y] on you."
5 Then I said, "Put a clean turban[z]
on his head." So they put a clean turban on his head and clothed him, while
the angel of the LORD stood by.
6 The angel of the LORD gave this
charge to Joshua: 7 "This is what the
LORD Almighty says: 'If you will walk in
my ways and keep my requirements,
then you will govern my house[a] and
have charge of my courts, and I will
give you a place among these standing
here.
8 " 'Listen, O high priest Joshua and
your associates seated before you, who
are men symbolic[b] of things to come:
I am going to bring my servant, the
Branch.[c] 9 See, the stone I have set in
front of Joshua! There are seven eyes[d]
on that one stone,[d] and I will engrave
an inscription on it,' says the LORD Almighty, 'and I will remove the sin[e] of
this land in a single day.
10 " 'In that day each of you will invite his neighbor to sit under his vine
and fig tree,[f]' declares the LORD Almighty."

The Gold Lampstand and the Two Olive Trees

4 Then the angel who talked with me
returned and wakened[g] me, as a
man is wakened from his sleep.[h] 2 He
asked me, "What do you see?"[i]
I answered, "I see a solid gold lampstand[j] with a bowl at the top and sev-
en lights[k] on it, with seven channels
to the lights. 3 Also there are two olive
trees[l] by it, one on the right of the
bowl and the other on its left."
4 I asked the angel who talked with
me, "What are these, my lord?"
5 He answered, "Do you not know
what these are?"
"No, my lord," I replied.[m]
6 So he said to me, "This is the word
of the LORD to Zerubbabel:[n] 'Not by

[a] *8,9* Or *says after . . . eye:* *9"I . . . plunder them."*
[b] *1* A variant of *Jeshua;* here and elsewhere in Zechariah [c] *1* *Satan* means *accuser.* [d] *9* Or *facets*

might nor by power, but by my Spirit,'[o] says the LORD Almighty.

7"What[a] are you, O mighty mountain? Before Zerubbabel you will become level ground.[p] Then he will bring out the capstone[q] to shouts of 'God bless it! God bless it!' "

8Then the word of the LORD came to me: 9"The hands of Zerubbabel have laid the foundation[r] of this temple; his hands will also complete it.[s] Then you will know that the LORD Almighty has sent me[t] to you.

10"Who despises the day of small things?[u] Men will rejoice when they see the plumb line in the hand of Zerubbabel.

"(These seven are the eyes[v] of the LORD, which range throughout the earth.)"

11Then I asked the angel, "What are these two olive trees[w] on the right and the left of the lampstand?"

12Again I asked him, "What are these two olive branches beside the two gold pipes that pour out golden oil?"

13He replied, "Do you not know what these are?"

"No, my lord," I said.

14So he said, "These are the two who are anointed[x] to[b] serve the Lord of all the earth."

The Flying Scroll

5 I looked again—and there before me was a flying scroll![y]

2He asked me, "What do you see?"

I answered, "I see a flying scroll, thirty feet long and fifteen feet wide.[c] "

3And he said to me, "This is the curse[z] that is going out over the whole land; for according to what it says on one side, every thief[a] will be banished, and according to what it says on the other, everyone who swears falsely[b] will be banished. 4The LORD Almighty declares, 'I will send it out, and it will enter the house of the thief and the house of him who swears falsely by my name. It will remain in his house and destroy it, both its timbers and its stones.[c]' "

The Woman in a Basket

5Then the angel who was speaking to me came forward and said to me, "Look up and see what this is that is appearing."

6I asked, "What is it?"

He replied, "It is a measuring basket.[d]" And he added, "This is the iniquity[e] of the people throughout the land."

7Then the cover of lead was raised, and there in the basket sat a woman! 8He said, "This is wickedness," and he pushed her back into the basket and pushed the lead cover down over its mouth.[d]

9Then I looked up—and there before me were two women, with the wind in their wings! They had wings like those of a stork,[e] and they lifted up the basket between heaven and earth.

10"Where are they taking the basket?" I asked the angel who was speaking to me.

11He replied, "To the country of Babylonia[f][f] to build a house[g] for it. When it is ready, the basket will be set there in its place."[h]

Four Chariots

6 I looked up again—and there before me were four chariots[i] coming out from between two mountains—mountains of bronze! 2The first chariot had red horses, the second black,[j] 3the third white,[k] and the fourth dappled—all of them powerful. 4I asked the angel who was speaking to me, "What are these, my lord?"

5The angel answered me, "These are the four spirits[g][l] of heaven, going out from standing in the presence of the Lord of the whole world. 6The one with the black horses is going toward the north country, the one with the white horses toward the west,[h] and the one with the dappled horses toward the south."

7When the powerful horses went out, they were straining to go throughout the earth.[m] And he said, "Go throughout the earth!" So they went throughout the earth.

8Then he called to me, "Look, those going toward the north country have given my Spirit[i] rest[n] in the land of the north."

A Crown for Joshua

9The word of the LORD came to me: 10"Take ⌞silver and gold⌟ from the exiles Heldai, Tobijah and Jedaiah, who have arrived from Babylon.[o] Go the same day to the house of Josiah son of Zephaniah. 11Take the silver and gold and make a crown,[p] and set it on the head of the high priest, Joshua[q] son of Jehozadak.[r] 12Tell him this is what the LORD Almighty says: 'Here is the man whose name is the Branch,[s] and he

4:6 [o]Isa 11:2-4; Hos 1:7
4:7 [p]Jer 51:25 [q]Ps 118:22
4:9 [r]Ezr 3:11 [s]Ezr 3:8; 6:15; Zec 6:12 [t]Zec 2:9
4:10 [u]Hag 2:3 [v]Zec 3:9; Rev 5:6
4:11 [w]ver 3; Rev 11:4
4:14 [x]Ex 29:7; 40:15; Da 9:24-26; Zec 3:1-7
5:1 [y]Eze 2:9; Rev 5:1
5:3 [z]Isa 24:6; 43:28; Mal 3:9; 4:6 [a]Ex 20:15; Mal 3:8 [b]Isa 48:1
5:4 [c]Lev 14:34-45; Hab 2:9-11; Mal 3:5
5:8 [d]Mic 6:11
5:9 [e]Lev 11:19
5:11 [f]Ge 10:10 [g]Jer 29:5,28 [h]Da 1:2
6:1 [i]ver 5
6:2 [j]Rev 6:5
6:3 [k]Rev 6:2
6:5 [l]Eze 37:9; Mt 24:31; Rev 7:1
6:7 [m]Zec 1:10
6:8 [n]Eze 5:13; 24:13
6:10 [o]Ezr 7:14-16; Jer 28:6
6:11 [p]Ps 21:3 [q]Zec 3:1 [r]Ezr 3:2
6:12 [s]Isa 4:2; Zec 3:8

a 7 Or *Who*
b 14 Or *two who bring oil and*
c 2 Hebrew *twenty cubits long and ten cubits wide* (about 9 meters long and 4.5 meters wide)
d 6 Hebrew *an ephah*; also in verses 7-11
e 6 Or *appearance*
f 11 Hebrew *Shinar*
g 5 Or *winds*
h 6 Or *horses after them*
i 8 Or *spirit*

will branch out from his place and build the temple of the LORD.[t] 13It is he who will build the temple of the LORD, and he will be clothed with majesty and will sit and rule on his throne. And he will be a priest[u] on his throne. And there will be harmony between the two.' 14The crown will be given to Heldai,[a] Tobijah, Jedaiah and Hen[b] son of Zephaniah as a memorial in the temple of the LORD. 15Those who are far away will come and help to build the temple of the LORD,[v] and you will know that the LORD Almighty has sent me to you.[w] This will happen if you diligently obey[x] the LORD your God."

Justice and Mercy, Not Fasting

7 In the fourth year of King Darius, the word of the LORD came to Zechariah on the fourth day of the ninth month, the month of Kislev.[y] 2The people of Bethel had sent Sharezer and Regem-Melech, together with their men, to entreat[z] the LORD 3by asking the priests of the house of the LORD Almighty and the prophets, "Should I mourn[a] and fast in the fifth[b] month, as I have done for so many years?"

4Then the word of the LORD Almighty came to me: 5"Ask all the people of the land and the priests, 'When you fasted[c] and mourned in the fifth and seventh months for the past seventy years, was it really for me that you fasted? 6And when you were eating and drinking, were you not just feasting for yourselves? 7Are these not the words the LORD proclaimed through the earlier prophets[d] when Jerusalem and its surrounding towns were at rest[e] and prosperous, and the Negev and the western foothills[f] were settled?' "

3 →PG. 1052
7 →PG. 1053

8And the word of the LORD came again to Zechariah: 9"This is what the LORD Almighty says: 'Administer true justice;[g] show mercy and compassion to one another. 10Do not oppress the widow or the fatherless, the alien[h] or the poor. In your hearts do not think evil of each other.'[i]

11"But they refused to pay attention; stubbornly they turned their backs and stopped up their ears.[j] 12They made their hearts as hard as flint[k] and would not listen to the law or to the words that the LORD Almighty had sent by his Spirit through the earlier prophets.[l] So the LORD Almighty was very angry.[m]

13" 'When I called, they did not listen;[n] so when they called, I would not listen,'[o] says the LORD Almighty.[p] 14'I scattered[q] them with a whirlwind[r] among all the nations, where they were strangers. The land was left so desolate behind them that no one could come or go. This is how they made the pleasant land desolate.[s]' "

The LORD Promises to Bless Jerusalem

8 Again the word of the LORD Almighty came to me. 2This is what the LORD Almighty says: "I am very jealous for Zion; I am burning with jealousy for her."

3This is what the LORD says: "I will return[t] to Zion and dwell in Jerusalem.[u] Then Jerusalem will be called the City of Truth, and the mountain of the LORD Almighty will be called the Holy Mountain."

4This is what the LORD Almighty says: "Once again men and women of ripe old age will sit in the streets of Jerusalem,[v] each with cane in hand because of his age. 5The city streets will be filled with boys and girls playing there.[w]"

6This is what the LORD Almighty says: "It may seem marvelous to the remnant of this people at that time,[x] but will it seem marvelous to me?[y]" declares the LORD Almighty.

6:12 [t]Ezr 3:8-10; Zec 4:6-9
6:13 [u]Ps 110:4
6:15 [v]Isa 60:10 [w]Zec 2:9-11 [x]Isa 58:12; Jer 7:23; Zec 3:7
7:1 [y]Ne 1:1
7:2 [z]Jer 26:19; Zec 8:21
7:3 [a]Zec 12:12-14 [b]Jer 52:12-14; Zec 8:19
7:5 [c]Isa 58:5
7:7 [d]Zec 1:4 [e]Jer 22:21 [f]Jer 17:26
7:9 [g]Zec 8:16
7:10 [h]Ex 22:21 [i]Ex 22:22; Isa 1:17
7:11 [j]Jer 8:5; 11:10; 17:23
7:12 [k]Jer 17:1; Eze 11:19 [l]Ne 9:29 [m]Da 9:12
7:13 [n]Pr 1:24 [o]Isa 1:15; Jer 11:11; 14:12; Mic 3:4 [p]Pr 1:28
7:14 [q]Dt 4:27; 28:64-67 [r]Jer 23:19 [s]Jer 44:6
8:3 [t]Zec 1:16 [u]Zec 2:10
8:4 [v]Isa 65:20
8:5 [w]Jer 30:20; 31:13
8:6 [x]Ps 118:23; 126:1-3 [y]Jer 32:17,27

[a]14 Syriac; Hebrew *Helem* [b]14 Or *and the gracious one, the*

7:8–14

PROMISE 7

AM I GENUINE?

Most men can't stand a phony and don't want to be known as one. So how do we know if our devotion to God is genuine? Zechariah identified some signs here that Moses recorded in Deuteronomy 24:17–18 as part of God's law. James 1:27 calls these things "pure and faultless" religion. Jesus' parable of the good Samaritan also taught the importance of these signs (Luke 10:25–37). At the final judgment they will be the basis of knowing who has genuinely accepted Jesus as Savior and lived a Christian life (Matthew 25:31–46).

The signs of genuine devotion to God are not what most people think. As important as it is to attend church, pray and quote Scripture, those things aren't the ticket. Moses, the prophets, Jesus and the apostles all agree: Mercy, compassion and generosity *to those who cannot repay you* is a fundamental sign of godliness. After all, our relationship with God is based on that very principle.

God meets the needs of those who cannot possibly repay him. A godly man acts like God. Think about how you can live out these signs and show your genuine commitment to God.

For the next Promise 7 reading go to page 1085.

7 This is what the LORD Almighty
says: "I will save my people from the
countries of the east and the west.[z] 8 I
will bring them back[a] to live in Jerusalem; they will be my people,[b] and I
will be faithful and righteous to them
as their God."
9 This is what the LORD Almighty
says: "You who now hear these words
spoken by the prophets[c] who were
there when the foundation was laid for
the house of the LORD Almighty, let
your hands be strong[d] so that the
temple may be built. 10 Before that time
there were no wages[e] for man or
beast. No one could go about his business safely because of his enemy, for
I had turned every man against his
neighbor. 11 But now I will not deal
with the remnant of this people as I
did in the past,"[f] declares the LORD
Almighty.
12 "The seed will grow well, the vine
will yield its fruit,[g] the ground will
produce its crops,[h] and the heavens
will drop their dew.[i] I will give all
these things as an inheritance[j] to the
remnant of this people. 13 As you have
been an object of cursing[k] among the
nations, O Judah and Israel, so will I
save you, and you will be a blessing.[l]
Do not be afraid, but let your hands be
strong."
14 This is what the LORD Almighty
says: "Just as I had determined to bring
disaster[m] upon you and showed no
pity when your fathers angered me,"
says the LORD Almighty, 15 "so now I
have determined to do good[n] again to
Jerusalem and Judah. Do not be afraid.
16 These are the things you are to do:
Speak the truth[o] to each other, and
render true and sound judgment in
your courts;[p] 17 do not plot evil[q]
against your neighbor, and do not love
to swear falsely.[r] I hate all this," declares the LORD.
18 Again the word of the LORD Almighty came to me. 19 This is what the
LORD Almighty says: "The fasts of the
fourth,[s] fifth,[t] seventh[u] and tenth[v]
months will become joyful[w] and
glad occasions and happy festivals for
Judah. Therefore love truth[x] and
peace."
20 This is what the LORD Almighty
says: "Many peoples and the inhabitants of many cities will yet come,
21 and the inhabitants of one city will go
to another and say, 'Let us go at once
to entreat[y] the LORD and seek the
LORD Almighty. I myself am going.'
22 And many peoples and powerful
nations will come to Jerusalem to seek
the LORD Almighty and to entreat
him."[z]
23 This is what the LORD Almighty
says: "In those days ten men from all
languages and nations will take firm
hold of one Jew by the hem of his robe
and say, 'Let us go with you, because
we have heard that God is with
you.' "[a]

8:7 [z]Ps 107:3; Isa 11:11; 43:5 **8:8** [a]Zec 10:10 [b]Eze 11:19-20; 36:28; Zec 2:11 **8:9** [c]Ezr 5:1 [d]Hag 2:4 **8:10** [e]Hag 1:6 **8:11** [f]Isa 12:1 **8:12** [g]Joel 2:22 [h]Ps 67:6 [i]Ge 27:28 [j]Ob 1:17 **8:13** [k]Jer 42:18 [l]Ge 12:2 **8:14** [m]Jer 31:28; Eze 24:14 **8:15** [n]ver 13; Jer 29:11; Mic 7:18-20 **8:16** [o]Ps 15:2; Eph 4:25 [p]Zec 7:9 **8:17** [q]Pr 3:29 [r]Pr 6:16-19 **8:19** [s]Jer 39:2 [t]Jer 52:12 [u]2Ki 25:25 [v]Jer 52:4 [w]Ps 30:11 [x]ver 16 **8:21** [y]Zec 7:2 **8:22** [z]Ps 117:1; Isa 60:3; Zec 2:11

8:23 [a]Isa 45:14; 1Co 14:25 **9:1** [b]Isa 17:1 **9:2** [c]Jer 49:23 [d]Eze 28:1-19 **9:3** [e]Job 27:16; Eze 28:4 **9:4** [f]Isa 23:1; Eze 26:3-5; 28:18

Judgment on Israel's Enemies

An Oracle

9 The word of the LORD is against
the land of Hadrach
and will rest upon
Damascus[b]—
for the eyes of men and all the
tribes of Israel
are on the LORD—[a]
2 and upon Hamath[c] too, which
borders on it,
and upon Tyre[d] and Sidon,
though they are very skillful.
3 Tyre has built herself a stronghold;
she has heaped up silver like
dust,
and gold like the dirt of the
streets.[e]
4 But the Lord will take away her
possessions
and destroy her power on the
sea,
and she will be consumed by
fire.[f]
5 Ashkelon will see it and fear;
Gaza will writhe in agony,
and Ekron too, for her hope will
wither.
Gaza will lose her king
and Ashkelon will be deserted.
6 Foreigners will occupy Ashdod,
and I will cut off the pride of the
Philistines.
7 I will take the blood from their
mouths,
the forbidden food from between
their teeth.
Those who are left will belong to
our God

[a] *1* Or *Damascus. / For the eye of the LORD is on all mankind, / as well as on the tribes of Israel,*

9:1—14:21

PE

CHRIST PREDICTED

This section of Zechariah contains two extended prophecies about Jesus Christ. Chapters 9—11 refer primarily to his first coming and 12—14 to his second coming. These passages build our confidence in God's direction for his creation. Read them not only to see how the Old Testament prophet predicted Christ's coming, but also to appreciate the wonder of God.

and become leaders in Judah,
and Ekron will be like the Jebusites.
[8]But I will defend my house
against marauding forces.
Never again will an oppressor
overrun my people,
for now I am keeping watch.[g]

The Coming of Zion's King

[9]Rejoice greatly, O Daughter of Zion!
Shout, Daughter of Jerusalem!
See, your king[a] comes to you,
righteous and having salvation,[h]
gentle and riding on a donkey,
on a colt, the foal of a donkey.[i]
[10]I will take away the chariots from Ephraim
and the war-horses from Jerusalem,
and the battle bow will be broken.[j]
He will proclaim peace to the nations.
His rule will extend from sea to sea
and from the River[b] to the ends of the earth.[c][k]
[11]As for you, because of the blood of my covenant[l] with you,
I will free your prisoners[m] from the waterless pit.
[12]Return to your fortress,[n]
O prisoners of hope;
even now I announce that I will restore twice as much to you.
[13]I will bend Judah as I bend my bow
and fill it with Ephraim.[o]
I will rouse your sons, O Zion,
against your sons, O Greece,[p]
and make you like a warrior's sword.[q]

The LORD Will Appear

[14]Then the LORD will appear over them;[r]
his arrow will flash like lightning.[s]
The Sovereign LORD will sound the trumpet;
he will march in the storms[t] of the south,
[15] and the LORD Almighty will shield[u] them.
They will destroy
and overcome with slingstones.
They will drink and roar as with wine;
they will be full like a bowl
used for sprinkling[d] the corners[v] of the altar.
[16]The LORD their God will save them on that day
as the flock of his people.
They will sparkle in his land
like jewels in a crown.[w]
[17]How attractive and beautiful they will be!
Grain will make the young men thrive,
and new wine the young women.

The LORD Will Care for Judah

10 Ask the LORD for rain in the springtime;
it is the LORD who makes the storm clouds.
He gives showers of rain to men,
and plants of the field to everyone.
[2]The idols[x] speak deceit,
diviners see visions that lie;
they tell dreams that are false,
they give comfort in vain.
Therefore the people wander like sheep
oppressed for lack of a shepherd.[y]
[3]"My anger burns against the shepherds,
and I will punish the leaders;[z]
for the LORD Almighty will care
for his flock, the house of Judah,
and make them like a proud horse in battle.
[4]From Judah will come the cornerstone,
from him the tent peg,[a]
from him the battle bow,[b]
from him every ruler.
[5]Together they[e] will be like mighty men
trampling the muddy streets in battle.[c]
Because the LORD is with them,
they will fight and overthrow the horsemen.[d]
[6]"I will strengthen the house of Judah
and save the house of Joseph.
I will restore them
because I have compassion on them.[e]
They will be as though
I had not rejected them,
for I am the LORD their God
and I will answer[f] them.
[7]The Ephraimites will become like mighty men,
and their hearts will be glad as with wine.[g]
Their children will see it and be joyful;

9:8 [g]Isa 52:1; 54:14 **9:9** [h]Isa 9:6-7; 43:3-11; Jer 23:5-6; Zep 3:14-15; Zec 2:10 [i]Mt 21:5*; Jn 12:15* **9:10** [j]Hos 1:7; 2:18; Mic 4:3; 5:10; Zec 10:4 [k]Ps 72:8 **9:11** [l]Ex 24:8 [m]Isa 42:7 **9:12** [n]Joel 3:16 **9:13** [o]Isa 49:2 [p]Joel 3:6 [q]Jer 51:20 **9:14** [r]Isa 31:5 [s]Ps 18:14; Hab 3:11 [t]Isa 21:1; 66:15 **9:15** [u]Isa 37:35; Zec 12:8 [v]Ex 27:2

9:16 [w]Isa 62:3; Jer 31:11 **10:2** [x]Eze 21:21 [y]Eze 34:5; Hos 3:4; Mt 9:36 **10:3** [z]Jer 25:34 **10:4** [a]Isa 22:23 [b]Zec 9:10 **10:5** [c]2Sa 22:43 [d]Am 2:15; Hag 2:22 **10:6** [e]Zec 8:7-8 [f]Zec 13:9 **10:7** [g]Zec 9:15

[a]9 Or *King* [b]10 That is, the Euphrates
[c]10 Or *the end of the land* [d]15 Or *bowl, / like* [e]4,5 Or *ruler, all of them together. / 5They*

their hearts will rejoice in the
LORD.
8I will signal[h] for them
and gather them in.
Surely I will redeem them;
they will be as numerous[i] as
before.
9Though I scatter them among the
peoples,
yet in distant lands they will
remember me.[j]
They and their children will
survive,
and they will return.
10I will bring them back from Egypt
and gather them from Assyria.[k]
I will bring them to Gilead[l] and
Lebanon,
and there will not be room[m]
enough for them.
11They will pass through the sea of
trouble;
the surging sea will be subdued
and all the depths of the Nile
will dry up.[n]
Assyria's pride[o] will be brought
down
and Egypt's scepter[p] will pass
away.
12I will strengthen them in the LORD
and in his name they will
walk,[q]"
declares the LORD.

11 Open your doors, O Lebanon,[r]
so that fire may devour your
cedars!
2Wail, O pine tree, for the cedar has
fallen;
the stately trees are ruined!
Wail, oaks of Bashan;
the dense forest[s] has been cut
down!
3Listen to the wail of the shepherds;
their rich pastures are destroyed!
Listen to the roar of the lions;
the lush thicket of the Jordan is
ruined![t]

Two Shepherds

4This is what the LORD my God says:
"Pasture the flock marked for slaughter. 5Their buyers slaughter them and
go unpunished. Those who sell them
say, 'Praise the LORD, I am rich!' Their
own shepherds do not spare them.[u]
6For I will no longer have pity on the
people of the land," declares the LORD.
"I will hand everyone over to his neighbor[v] and his king. They will oppress
the land, and I will not rescue them
from their hands."[w]
7So I pastured the flock marked for
slaughter, particularly the oppressed of
the flock. Then I took two staffs and
called one Favor and the other Union,

10:8 [h]Isa 5:26 [i]Jer 33:22; Eze 36:11 **10:9** [j]Eze 6:9 **10:10** [k]Isa 11:11 [l]Jer 50:19 [m]Isa 49:19 **10:11** [n]Isa 19:5-7; 51:10 [o]Zep 2:13 [p]Eze 30:13 **10:12** [q]Mic 4:5 **11:1** [r]Eze 31:3 **11:2** [s]Isa 32:19 **11:3** [t]Jer 2:15; 50:44 **11:5** [u]Jer 50:7; Eze 34:2-3 **11:6** [v]Zec 14:13 [w]Isa 9:19-21; Jer 13:14; Mic 5:8; 7:2-6

11:9 [x]Jer 15:2; 43:11 **11:10** [y]ver 7 [z]Ps 89:39; Jer 14:21 **11:12** [a]Ex 21:32; Mt 26:15 **11:13** [b]Mt 27:9-10*; Ac 1:18-19 **11:17** [c]Jer 23:1 [d]Eze 30:21-22 [e]Jer 23:1 **12:1** [f]Isa 42:5; Jer 51:15 [g]Ps 102:25; Heb 1:10 [h]Isa 57:16 **12:2** [i]Ps 75:8 [j]Isa 51:23 [k]Zec 14:14 **12:3** [l]Zec 14:2 [m]Da 2:34-35 [n]Mt 21:44 **12:4** [o]Ps 76:6

and I pastured the flock. 8In one month
I got rid of the three shepherds.
The flock detested me, and I grew
weary of them 9and said, "I will not be
your shepherd. Let the dying die, and
the perishing perish.[x] Let those who
are left eat one another's flesh."
10Then I took my staff called Favor[y]
and broke it, revoking[z] the covenant I
had made with all the nations. 11It was
revoked on that day, and so the afflicted of the flock who were watching me
knew it was the word of the LORD.
12I told them, "If you think it best,
give me my pay; but if not, keep it." So
they paid me thirty pieces of silver.[a]
13And the LORD said to me, "Throw it
to the potter"—the handsome price at
which they priced me! So I took the
thirty pieces of silver and threw them
into the house of the LORD to the potter.[b]
14Then I broke my second staff
called Union, breaking the brotherhood between Judah and Israel.
15Then the LORD said to me, "Take
again the equipment of a foolish shepherd. 16For I am going to raise up a
shepherd over the land who will not
care for the lost, or seek the young, or
heal the injured, or feed the healthy,
but will eat the meat of the choice
sheep, tearing off their hoofs.

17"Woe to the worthless shepherd,[c]
who deserts the flock!
May the sword strike his arm[d] and
his right eye!
May his arm be completely
withered,
his right eye totally blinded!"[e]

Jerusalem's Enemies to Be Destroyed

An Oracle

12 This is the word of the LORD concerning Israel. The LORD, who
stretches out the heavens,[f] who lays
the foundation of the earth,[g] and
who forms the spirit of man[h] within
him, declares: 2"I am going to make
Jerusalem a cup[i] that sends all the
surrounding peoples reeling.[j] Judah[k]
will be besieged as well as Jerusalem.
3On that day, when all the nations[l] of
the earth are gathered against her, I
will make Jerusalem an immovable
rock[m] for all the nations. All who try to
move it will injure[n] themselves. 4On
that day I will strike every horse with
panic and its rider with madness," declares the LORD. "I will keep a watchful
eye over the house of Judah, but I will
blind all the horses of the nations.[o]
5Then the leaders of Judah will say in
their hearts, 'The people of Jerusalem

are strong, because the LORD Almighty is their God.’

6“On that day I will make the leaders of Judah like a firepot[p] in a woodpile, like a flaming torch among sheaves. They will consume[q] right and left all the surrounding peoples, but Jerusalem will remain intact in her place.

7“The LORD will save the dwellings of Judah first, so that the honor of the house of David and of Jerusalem’s inhabitants may not be greater than that of Judah.[r] 8On that day the LORD will shield[s] those who live in Jerusalem, so that the feeblest among them will be like David, and the house of David will be like God,[t] like the Angel of the LORD going before[u] them. 9On that day I will set out to destroy all the nations that attack Jerusalem.[v]

Mourning for the One They Pierced

10“And I will pour out on the house of David and the inhabitants of Jerusalem a spirit[a] of grace and supplication.[w] They will look on[b] me, the one they have pierced,[x] and they will mourn for him as one mourns for an only child, and grieve bitterly for him as one grieves for a firstborn son. 11On that day the weeping in Jerusalem will be great, like the weeping of Hadad Rimmon in the plain of Megiddo.[y] 12The land will mourn,[z] each clan by itself, with their wives by themselves: the clan of the house of David and their wives, the clan of the house of Nathan and their wives, 13the clan of the house of Levi and their wives, the clan of Shimei and their wives, 14and all the rest of the clans and their wives.

Cleansing From Sin

13 “On that day a fountain[a] will be opened to the house of David and the inhabitants of Jerusalem, to cleanse[b] them from sin and impurity.

2“On that day, I will banish the names of the idols[c] from the land, and they will be remembered no more,” declares the LORD Almighty. “I will remove both the prophets[d] and the spirit of impurity from the land. 3And if anyone still prophesies, his father and mother, to whom he was born, will say to him, ‘You must die, because you have told lies in the LORD’s name.’ When he prophesies, his own parents will stab him.[e]

4“On that day every prophet will be ashamed[f] of his prophetic vision. He will not put on a prophet’s garment[g] of hair[h] in order to deceive. 5He will say, ‘I am not a prophet. I am a farmer; the land has been my livelihood since my youth.[c][i] 6If someone asks him, ‘What are these wounds on your body[d]?’ he will answer, ‘The wounds I was given at the house of my friends.’

The Shepherd Struck, the Sheep Scattered

7“Awake, O sword,[j] against my
shepherd,[k]
against the man who is close to
me!”
declares the LORD Almighty.
“Strike the shepherd,
and the sheep will be
scattered,[l]
and I will turn my hand against
the little ones.
8In the whole land,” declares the
LORD,
“two-thirds will be struck down
and perish;
yet one-third will be left in it.[m]
9This third I will bring into the
fire;[n]
I will refine them like silver[o]
and test them like gold.
They will call[p] on my name
and I will answer[q] them;
I will say, ‘They are my people,’[r]
and they will say, ‘The LORD is
our God.[s]’ ”

The LORD Comes and Reigns

14 A day of the LORD[t] is coming when your plunder will be divided among you.

2I will gather all the nations to Jerusalem to fight against it; the city will be captured, the houses ransacked, and the women raped. Half of the city will go into exile, but the rest of the people will not be taken from the city.[u]

3Then the LORD will go out and fight[v] against those nations, as he fights in the day of battle. 4On that day his feet will stand on the Mount of Olives,[w] east of Jerusalem, and the Mount of Olives will be split in two from east to west, forming a great valley, with half of the mountain moving north and half moving south. 5You will flee by my mountain valley, for it will extend to Azel. You will flee as you fled from the earthquake[e][x] in the days of Uzziah king of Judah. Then the LORD my God will come,[y] and all the holy ones with him.[z]

6On that day there will be no light,[a] no cold or frost. 7It will be a unique[b] day, without daytime or nighttime[c]—

12:6 [p]Isa 10:17-18; Zec 11:1 [q]Ob 1:18
12:7 [r]Jer 30:18; Am 9:11
12:8 [s]Joel 3:16; Zec 9:15 [t]Ps 82:6 [u]Mic 7:8
12:9 [v]Zec 14:2-3
12:10 [w]Isa 44:3; Eze 39:29; Joel 2:28-29 [x]Jn 19:34,37*; Rev 1:7
12:11 [y]2Ki 23:29
12:12 [z]Mt 24:30; Rev 1:7
13:1 [a]Jer 17:13 [b]Ps 51:2; Heb 9:14
13:2 [c]Ex 23:13; Eze 36:25; Hos 2:17 [d]1Ki 22:22; Jer 23:14-15
13:3 [e]Dt 13:6-11; 18:20; Jer 23:34; Eze 14:9
13:4 [f]Jer 6:15; Mic 3:6-7 [g]Mt 3:4 [h]2Ki 1:8; Isa 20:2
13:5 [i]Am 7:14
13:7 [j]Jer 47:6 [k]Isa 40:11; 53:4; Eze 37:24 [l]Mt 26:31*; Mk 14:27*
13:8 [m]Eze 5:2-4,12
13:9 [n]Mal 3:2 [o]Isa 48:10; 1Pe 1:6-7 [p]Ps 50:15 [q]Zec 10:6 [r]Jer 30:22 [s]Jer 29:12
14:1 [t]Isa 13:9; Mal 4:1
14:2 [u]Isa 13:6; Zec 13:8
14:3 [v]Zec 9:14-15
14:4 [w]Eze 11:23
14:5 [x]Am 1:1 [y]Isa 29:6; 66:15-16 [z]Mt 16:27; 25:31
14:6 [a]Isa 13:10; Jer 4:23
14:7 [b]Jer 30:7 [c]Rev 21:23-25; 22:5

a *10* Or *the Spirit* **b** *10* Or *to* **c** *5* Or *farmer; a man sold me in my youth* **d** *6* Or *wounds between your hands* **e** *5* Or *5My mountain valley will be blocked and will extend to Azel. It will be blocked as it was blocked because of the earthquake*

a day known to the LORD. When evening comes, there will be light.[d]

8On that day living water[e] will flow out from Jerusalem, half to the eastern[f] sea[a] and half to the western sea,[b] in summer and in winter.

9The LORD will be king over the whole earth.[g] On that day there will be one LORD, and his name the only name.[h]

10The whole land, from Geba[i] to Rimmon, south of Jerusalem, will become like the Arabah. But Jerusalem will be raised up[j] and remain in its place,[k] from the Benjamin Gate to the site of the First Gate, to the Corner Gate, and from the Tower of Hananel to the royal winepresses. 11It will be inhabited; never again will it be destroyed. Jerusalem will be secure.[l]

12This is the plague with which the LORD will strike all the nations that fought against Jerusalem: Their flesh will rot while they are still standing on their feet, their eyes will rot in their sockets, and their tongues will rot in their mouths.[m] 13On that day men will be stricken by the LORD with great panic. Each man will seize the hand of another, and they will attack each other.[n] 14Judah[o] too will fight at Jerusalem. The wealth of all the surrounding nations will be collected[p]—great quantities of gold and silver and clothing. 15A similar plague[q] will strike the horses and mules, the camels and donkeys, and all the animals in those camps.

16Then the survivors from all the nations that have attacked Jerusalem will go up year after year to worship the King, the LORD Almighty, and to celebrate the Feast of Tabernacles.[r] 17If any of the peoples of the earth do not go up to Jerusalem to worship the King, the LORD Almighty, they will have no rain.[s] 18If the Egyptian people do not go up and take part, they will have no rain. The LORD[c] will bring on them the plague he inflicts on the nations that do not go up to celebrate the Feast of Tabernacles.[t] 19This will be the punishment of Egypt and the punishment of all the nations that do not go up to celebrate the Feast of Tabernacles.

20On that day HOLY TO THE LORD will be inscribed on the bells of the horses, and the cooking pots[u] in the LORD's house will be like the sacred bowls[v] in front of the altar. 21Every pot in Jerusalem and Judah will be holy[w] to the LORD Almighty, and all who come to sacrifice will take some of the pots and cook in them. And on that day[x] there will no longer be a Canaanite[d][y] in the house of the LORD Almighty.[z]

14:7 [d]Isa 30:26
14:8 [e]Eze 47:1-12; Jn 7:38; Rev 22:1-2 [f]Joel 2:20
14:9 [g]Dt 6:4; Isa 45:24; Rev 11:15 [h]Eph 4:5-6
14:10 [i]1Ki 15:22 [j]Jer 30:18; Am 9:11 [k]Zec 12:6
14:11 [l]Eze 34:25-28
14:12 [m]Lev 26:16; Dt 28:22
14:13 [n]Zec 11:6
14:14 [o]Zec 12:2 [p]Isa 23:18
14:15 [q]ver 12
14:16 [r]Isa 60:6-9
14:17 [s]Jer 14:4; Am 4:7
14:18 [t]ver 12
14:20 [u]Eze 46:20 [v]Zec 9:15
14:21 [w]Ro 14:6-7; 1Co 10:31 [x]Ne 8:10 [y]Zec 9:8 [z]Eze 44:9

[a] *8* That is, the Dead Sea [b] *8* That is, the Mediterranean [c] *18* Or *part, then the LORD* [d] *21* Or *merchant*

MALACHI

AT A GLANCE

Key Principle: Our religious observances become stale and meaningless when they are not accompanied by a wholehearted desire to honor and trust the Lord.
Author: Malachi
Time and Place: ~440–430 B.C. / Jerusalem
Key Verses: 1:2; 3:1, 14; 4:5

BENEFIT

In this book, God uses a series of questions and answers to expose the real attitudes of his people. We, as God's people, face an ever-present danger of being more concerned about the veneer of our lives than about the underlying motives and intentions of our hearts. Malachi is a helpful diagnostic tool that can illuminate problems in our own attitudes toward serving and worshiping God—especially when we place ourselves in the position of the accused Israel and consider whether we have dishonored or robbed God.

SETTING

Internal evidence suggests that Malachi lived in Nehemiah's time and prophesied to the Jewish remnant in Jerusalem several decades after the second temple was completed (516 B.C.). The priests had grown weary of administrating the offerings and sacrifices in the temple; they had also grown increasingly hardened and corrupt. Other problems that are addressed in Malachi—such as intermarriage with pagan wives, hypocrisy and neglect in worship—are the same as those Nehemiah faced after his return from Persia to Jerusalem in 425 B.C. Since Nehemiah first came to Jerusalem in 445 B.C. and returned to Persia in 432 B.C., it may be that Malachi prophesied while Nehemiah was away. When Nehemiah returned again to Jerusalem, he dealt with the sins addressed in this book.

The problems of concern about external issues and materialism that resulted from religious hypocrisy and indifference in Malachi's time gradually grew into a settled disposition that typified the Pharisees and Sadducees of later years.

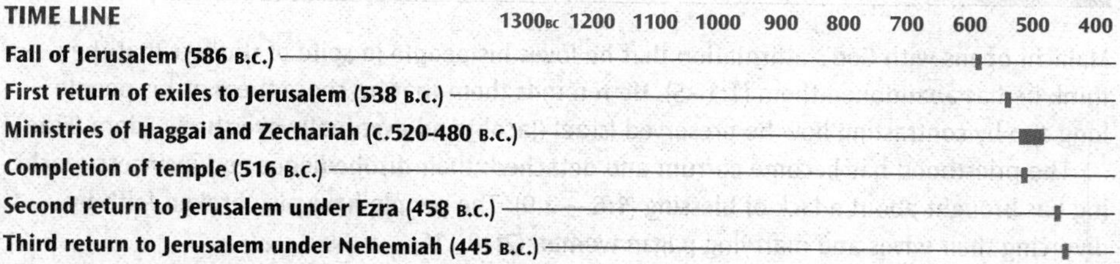

THEME AND PURPOSE

Malachi delivers this oracle as a dialogue between God and his people. In it God seeks to penetrate the barriers that the priests and people have erected between themselves and their God. The people's religious and moral corruption reveal a condition of spiritual lethargy, marked by an attitude that "it doesn't pay" to serve the Lord. The people are convinced that in spite of their religious practices, God still hasn't removed their difficult circumstances. God tells them that their lack of blessing is not due to divine indifference, but to their hypocrisy, lack of sincerity and disobedience to God's moral law. When they repent and return to God, God will return to them (3:7) and bless their labors.

UNIQUE CONTRIBUTION

The series of accusations and responses in Malachi set this book apart from the other prophets, and the proportion of the prophecy that God directly speaks (47 out of 55 verses) is the highest among the prophets. Another distinct aspect of Malachi is that it concludes on a note of judgment rather than one of hope and future blessing. It emphasizes the curse of the human condition and our need for the salvation that the Messiah brings.

LINKS TO THE NEW TESTAMENT

Malachi anticipates the coming of the Lord's messenger who will prepare the way for the Messiah. "See, I will send my messenger, who will prepare the way before me . . . See, I will send you the prophet Elijah before that great and dreadful day of the Lord comes" (3:1; 4:5; cf. Isaiah 40:3). One aspect of this was fulfilled by John the Baptist (Matthew 3:3; 11:10–14; 17:9–13; Mark 1:2–3; 9:10–13; Luke 1:17; 3:4–6; John 1:23). But another aspect awaits for Elijah himself to appear before the second advent of Christ (3:2–3). The last of the Old Testament prophets anticipates the coming of the first of the New Testament prophets, John the Baptist; between the two stands a 400-year prophetic silence.

OVERVIEW

FOCUS	Prized by the Lord	Pollution of the Priests	Problems of the People	Promise of the Lord
REFERENCE	1:1 — 1:5	1:6 — 2:9	2:10 — 3:15	3:16 — 4:6
TOPICS	God Still Loves Israel	Obstacles to Divine Blessing		Future of the Righteous and Wicked
	Past	Present		Future
	The Condemnation of the Lord		The Coming of the Lord	
	Repent: Prevailing Sins		Repent: Promise of Judgment	
LOCATION	Jerusalem			
TIME	~440–430 B.C.			

Malachi opens with God's affirmation that he loves his people in spite of the fact that they think he has abandoned them (1:1–5). He reminds them that he chose them as his people long ago by contrasting how he preserved Israel (Jacob) and eventually overthrew Edom (Esau).

The priesthood has become corrupt and detached; their disobedience and insincere teaching has brought about a lack of blessing (1:6—2:9). The people have also broken faith by divorcing their wives and marrying pagan women (2:10–16).

The people question God's justice, and God responds by announcing that the Messiah will purify his people (2:17—3:6). God promises that when the people stop robbing God in their tithes and offerings and begin to put him first, he will bless them with abundance (3:7–12).

The Jews have questioned God's justice (3:13–15), and the Lord assures them that a day of justice and retribution will come (3:16—4:6). Serving God is not a futile activity, as some people claim (3:14)—those who fear the Lord will be blessed, and the wicked will be judged.

MALACHI

1 An oracle:[a] The word[b] of the LORD to Israel through Malachi.[a]

Jacob Loved, Esau Hated

2"I have loved[c] you," says the LORD.

"But you ask, 'How have you loved us?'

"Was not Esau Jacob's brother?" the LORD says. "Yet I have loved Jacob,[d] **3**but Esau I have hated, and I have turned his mountains into a wasteland[e] and left his inheritance to the desert jackals.[f]"

4Edom may say, "Though we have been crushed, we will rebuild[g] the ruins."

But this is what the LORD Almighty says: "They may build, but I will demolish. They will be called the Wicked Land, a people always under the wrath of the LORD.[h] **5**You will see it with your own eyes and say, 'Great[i] is the LORD—even beyond the borders of Israel!'[j]

Blemished Sacrifices

6"A son honors his father, and a servant his master. If I am a father, where is the honor due me? If I am a master, where is the respect[k] due me?" says the LORD Almighty.[l] "It is you, O priests, who show contempt for my name.

"But you ask, 'How have we shown contempt for your name?'

7"You place defiled food[m] on my altar.

"But you ask, 'How have we defiled you?'

"By saying that the LORD's table is contemptible. **8**When you bring blind animals for sacrifice, is that not wrong? When you sacrifice crippled or diseased animals,[n] is that not wrong? Try offering them to your governor! Would he be pleased with you? Would he accept you?" says the LORD Almighty.[o]

9"Now implore God to be gracious to us. With such offerings[p] from your hands, will he accept you?"—says the LORD Almighty.

10"Oh, that one of you would shut the temple doors, so that you would not light useless fires on my altar! I am not pleased[q] with you," says the LORD Almighty, "and I will accept no offering[r] from your hands. **11**My name will be great among the nations, from the rising to the setting of the sun. In every place incense[s] and pure offerings will be brought to my name, because my name will be great among the nations," says the LORD Almighty.

12"But you profane it by saying of the Lord's table, 'It is defiled,' and of its food,[t] 'It is contemptible.' **13**And you say, 'What a burden!'[u] and you sniff at it contemptuously," says the LORD Almighty.

"When you bring injured, crippled or diseased animals and offer them as sacrifices, should I accept them from your hands?" says the LORD. **14**"Cursed is the cheat who has an acceptable male in his flock and vows to give it, but then sacrifices a blemished animal[v] to the Lord. For I am a great king,[w]" says the LORD Almighty, "and my name is to be feared among the nations.

Admonition for the Priests

2 "And now this admonition is for you, O priests.[x] **2**If you do not listen, and if you do not set your heart to honor my name," says the LORD Almighty, "I will send a curse[y] upon you, and I will curse your blessings. Yes, I have already cursed them, because you have not set your heart to honor me.

3"Because of you I will rebuke[b] your descendants[c]; I will spread on your faces the offal[z] from your festival sacrifices, and you will be carried off with it.[a] **4**And you will know that I have sent you this admonition so that my

1:1 [a]Na 1:1 [b]1Pe 4:11 **1:2** [c]Dt 4:37 [d]Ro 9:13* **1:3** [e]Isa 34:10 [f]Eze 35:3-9 **1:4** [g]Isa 9:10 [h]Eze 25:12-14 **1:5** [i]Ps 35:27; Mic 5:4 [j]Am 1:11-12 **1:6** [k]Isa 1:2 [l]Job 5:17 **1:7** [m]ver 12; Lev 21:6

1:8 [n]Lev 22:22; Dt 15:21 [o]Isa 43:23 **1:9** [p]Lev 23:33-44 **1:10** [q]Hos 5:6 [r]Isa 1:11-14; Jer 14:12 **1:11** [s]Isa 60:6-7; Rev 8:3 **1:12** [t]ver 7 **1:13** [u]Isa 43:22-24 **1:14** [v]Lev 22:18-21 [w]1Ti 6:15 **2:1** [x]ver 7 **2:2** [y]Dt 28:20 **2:3** [z]Ex 29:14 [a]1Ki 14:10

1:6-14 PROMISE **5**

ONLY THE BEST

What does God want from you? He wants what he gave to you: the very best! Israel was bringing its cast-off, worthless animals and offering them as sacrifices to God. God was insulted. After you read this heartbreaking passage, examine your schedule and your checkbook to see what your gifts to God look like. Are they blemished, blind, lame, insignificant? Or do they reflect the very best of what you have?

Honor God with your offerings. Don't insult him.

For the next Promise 5 reading go to page 1038.

---

[a]*1 Malachi* means *my messenger.* [b]*3* Or *cut off* (see Septuagint) [c]*3* Or *will blight your grain*

covenant with Levi[b] may continue,"
says the LORD Almighty. 5"My covenant
was with him, a covenant[c] of life and
peace,[d] and I gave them to him; this
called for reverence and he revered me
and stood in awe of my name. 6True
instruction[e] was in his mouth and
nothing false was found on his lips. He
walked with me in peace and uprightness, and turned many from sin.[f]

5 →PG. 1039

7"For the lips of a priest[g] ought
to preserve knowledge, and from
his mouth men should seek instruction[h]—because he is the messenger[i] of the LORD Almighty. 8But
you have turned from the way and by
your teaching have caused many to
stumble;[j] you have violated the covenant with Levi," says the LORD Almighty. 9"So I have caused you to be
despised[k] and humiliated before all
the people, because you have not followed my ways but have shown partiality in matters of the law."

Judah Unfaithful

6 →PG. 1053

10Have we not all one Father[a]?[l]
Did not one God create us? Why do we
profane the covenant[m] of our fathers
by breaking faith with one another?
11Judah has broken faith. A detestable thing has been committed in Israel and in Jerusalem: Judah has desecrated the sanctuary the LORD loves, by
marrying[n] the daughter of a foreign
god.[o] 12As for the man who does this,
whoever he may be, may the LORD cut
him off[p] from the tents of Jacob[b]—
even though he brings offerings[q] to
the LORD Almighty.
13Another thing you do: You flood
the LORD's altar with tears. You weep
and wail because he no longer pays attention[r] to your offerings or accepts
them with pleasure from your hands.
14You ask, "Why?" It is because the
LORD is acting as the witness between
you and the wife of your youth,[s] because you have broken faith with her,
though she is your partner, the wife of
your marriage covenant.

4 →PG. 1040

15Has not ⌊the LORD⌋ made them
one?[t] In flesh and spirit they are his.
And why one? Because he was seeking
godly offspring.[c][u] So guard yourself
in your spirit, and do not break faith
with the wife of your youth.
16"I hate divorce,[v]" says the LORD
God of Israel, "and I hate a man's covering himself[d] with violence as well as
with his garment," says the LORD Almighty.
So guard yourself in your spirit, and
do not break faith.

The Day of Judgment

17You have wearied[w] the LORD with
your words.
"How have we wearied him?" you
ask.
By saying, "All who do evil are good
in the eyes of the LORD, and he is
pleased with them" or "Where is the
God of justice?"
3 "See, I will send my messenger, who
will prepare the way before me.[x]
Then suddenly the Lord you are seeking will come to his temple; the
messenger of the covenant, whom
you desire, will come," says the LORD
Almighty.
2But who can endure[y] the day of his
coming? Who can stand when he appears? For he will be like a refiner's
fire[z] or a launderer's soap. 3He will sit
as a refiner and purifier of silver;[a] he
will purify[b] the Levites and refine
them like gold and silver. Then the
LORD will have men who will bring offerings in righteousness, 4and the offerings[c] of Judah and Jerusalem will
be acceptable to the LORD, as in days
gone by, as in former years.[d]
5"So I will come near to you for judgment. I will be quick to testify against
sorcerers, adulterers and perjurers,[e]
against those who defraud laborers of
their wages,[f] who oppress the widows[g] and the fatherless, and deprive
aliens of justice, but do not fear me,"
says the LORD Almighty.

2:4 [b]Nu 3:12 **2:5** [c]Dt 33:9 [d]Nu 25:12 **2:6** [e]Dt 33:10 [f]Jer 23:22; Jas 5:19-20 **2:7** [g]Jer 18:18 [h]Lev 10:11 [i]Nu 27:21 **2:8** [j]Jer 18:15 **2:9** [k]1Sa 2:30 **2:10** [l]1Co 8:6 [m]Ex 19:5 **2:11** [n]Ne 13:23 [o]Ezr 9:1; Jer 3:7-9 **2:12** [p]Eze 24:21 [q]Mal 1:10

2:13 [r]Jer 14:12 **2:14** [s]Pr 5:18 **2:15** [t]Ge 2:24; Mt 19:4-6 [u]1Co 7:14 **2:16** [v]Dt 24:1; Mt 5:31-32; 19:4-9 **2:17** [w]Isa 43:24 **3:1** [x]Isa 40:3; Mt 11:10*; Mk 1:2*; Lk 7:27* **3:2** [y]Eze 22:14; Rev 6:17 [z]Zec 13:9; Mt 3:10-12 **3:3** [a]Da 12:10 [b]Isa 1:25 **3:4** [c]2Ch 7:12; Ps 51:19; Mal 1:11 [d]2Ch 7:3 **3:5** [e]Jer 7:9 [f]Lev 19:13; Jas 5:4 [g]Ex 22:22

2:7

PROMISE 5

MESSENGER

What do you look for when you choose a church to attend? Malachi presents one critical issue here. While a pastor is not a priest like Israel's priests, there is one similarity: Both instruct people to follow God based on guidelines found in God's Word. Whatever else is or is not happening in a church, this one question is essential: Is the pastor a faithful "messenger of the LORD Almighty"?

The only church worth considering is one that maintains a basic commitment to understand and follow God's Word. When you find such a place, get involved. Encourage and support that pastor as he teaches from the Bible (1 Timothy 5:17). He is God's messenger to you.

For the next Promise 5 reading go to page 1055.

---

[a]*10* Or *father* [b]*12* Or *12May the LORD cut off from the tents of Jacob anyone who gives testimony in behalf of the man who does this*
[c]*15* Or *15But the one ⌊who is our father⌋ did not do this, not as long as life remained in him. And what was he seeking? An offspring from God*
[d]*16* Or *his wife*

Robbing God

6 “I the LORD do not change.[h] So
you, O descendants of Jacob, are not
destroyed. 7 Ever since the time of your
forefathers you have turned away[i]
from my decrees and have not kept
them. Return to me, and I will return to
you,”[j] says the LORD Almighty.
“But you ask, ‘How are we to return?’
8 “Will a man rob God? Yet you
rob me.
“But you ask, ‘How do we rob you?’
“In tithes[k] and offerings. 9 You are
under a curse—the whole nation of
you—because you are robbing me.
5 →PG. 1080
10 Bring the whole tithe into the storehouse,[l] that there may be food in my
house. Test me in this,” says the LORD
Almighty, “and see if I will not throw
open the floodgates[m] of heaven and
pour out so much blessing that you will
not have room enough for it. 11 I will
prevent pests from devouring your
crops, and the vines in your fields will
not cast their fruit,” says the LORD Almighty. 12 “Then all the nations will call
you blessed,[n] for yours will be a delightful land,”[o] says the LORD Almighty.
13 “You have said harsh things[p]
against me,” says the LORD.
“Yet you ask, ‘What have we said
against you?’
14 “You have said, ‘It is futile[q] to
serve God. What did we gain by carrying out his requirements and going
about like mourners[r] before the LORD
Almighty? 15 But now we call the arrogant blessed. Certainly the evildoers[s]
prosper, and even those who challenge
God escape.’ ”
16 Then those who feared the LORD
talked with each other, and the LORD
listened and heard.[t] A scroll[u] of remembrance was written in his presence concerning those who feared the
LORD and honored his name.
17 “They will be mine,” says the LORD
Almighty, “in the day when I make up
my treasured possession.[a][v] I will
spare[w] them, just as in compassion a
man spares his son who serves him.
18 And you will again see the distinction
between the righteous[x] and the wicked, between those who serve God and
those who do not.

The Day of the LORD

4 “Surely the day is coming;[y] it will
burn like a furnace. All the arrogant
and every evildoer will be stubble,[z]
and that day that is coming will set
them on fire,” says the LORD Almighty.
“Not a root or a branch will be left to
them. 2 But for you who revere my
name, the sun of righteousness[a] will
rise with healing[b] in its wings. And
you will go out and leap[c] like calves

3:6 [h] Nu 23:19; Jas 1:17 **3:7** [i] Jer 7:26; Ac 7:51 [j] Zec 1:3 **3:8** [k] Ne 13:10-12 **3:10** [l] Ne 13:12 [m] 2Ki 7:2 **3:12** [n] Isa 61:9 [o] Isa 62:4 **3:13** [p] Mal 2:17 **3:14** [q] Ps 73:13 [r] Isa 58:3 **3:15** [s] Jer 7:10 **3:16** [t] Ps 34:15 [u] Ps 56:8 **3:17** [v] Dt 7:6 [w] Ps 103:13; Isa 26:20 **3:18** [x] Ge 18:25 **4:1** [y] Joel 2:31 [z] Isa 5:24; Ob 1:18 **4:2** [a] Lk 1:78; Eph 5:14 [b] Isa 30:26 [c] Isa 35:6

[a] 17 Or *Almighty, “my treasured possession, in the day when I act*

3:8–12

PROMISE 1

TRUE REALITY

Prophets always saw the Reality behind the reality. The Jews in Malachi’s day were not giving their gifts and offerings to God, and what they did give were leftovers and cast-offs (1:6–14). These people felt the financial squeeze and decided to cut out their giving to God. Their reality was: “We’re not giving because we need to make ends meet. God won’t mind.” God’s Reality was different. He called their actions “robbing God.” He saw their strategy for financial gain leading to their financial disaster (vv. 9–12), and made an astounding offer: “Test me in this . . .” (v. 10).

The great advantage of reading the Bible is that it deals with Reality and not just reality. God sees beyond the immediate and the obvious. And he instructs men from his view. Do you see Reality or reality?

For the next Promise 1 reading go to page 1039.

4:4–6

PROMISE 1

THE BIBLE’S CORE ISSUES

The Old Testament closes with a reminder of God’s ultimate rule. Cultures change and technology advances, but right and wrong, sin and righteousness don’t change. God himself defines these core issues (v. 4). Shifting attention from the beginning of the law (v. 4) to the end of time (v. 5) changes nothing. We will be accountable for our obedience to God’s revealed will at that time as well.

As always, when people come to God and obey him, they also come to each other. When God is at work, he turns “the hearts of the fathers to their children, and the hearts of the children to their fathers” (v. 6).

God’s timeless truth never changes. The fundamental issues are always understanding of and obedience to what God has revealed in Scripture. Live by them and the land experiences peace and harmony. Violate them and the land is struck with a curse. The Bible is more than interesting information. It is the key to living life as God intended. Read it. Meditate on it. Live it.

For the next Promise 1 reading go to page 1053.

released from the stall. 3Then you will
trample[d] down the wicked; they will
be ashes[e] under the soles of your feet
on the day when I do these things,"
says the LORD Almighty.
4"Remember the law[f] of my servant Moses, the decrees and laws I
gave him at Horeb for all Israel.
4 5"See, I will send you the prophet
→PG. 1071
Elijah[g] before that great and dreadful
day of the LORD comes.[h] 6He will turn
the hearts of the fathers to their children,[i] and the hearts of the children
to their fathers; or else I will come and
strike[j] the land with a curse."[k]

4:3 [d] Job 40:12 [e] Eze 28:18
4:4 [f] Ps 147:19
4:5 [g] Mt 11:14; Lk 1:17 [h] Joel 2:31
4:6 [i] Lk 1:17 [j] Isa 11:4; Rev 19:15 [k] Zec 5:3

JESUS IN THE OLD TESTAMENT

After his resurrection, Jesus met two men on the road to Emmaus, "And beginning with Moses and all the Prophets, he explained to them what was said in all the Scriptures concerning himself" (Luke 24:27). How we wish we could have a transcript of that conversation! The disciples testified that their hearts "burned" with wonder and new insight as Jesus explained how all of Scripture pointed directly to himself, the Messiah.

Jesus is the central figure in Scripture. Much of Israel's religious practice given in the Mosaic Law pictured his life and his death (see the notes on the Day of Atonement at Leviticus 16 and the Passover at Exodus 12). Other Old Testament authors, under God's inspiration, wrote of the coming Savior in the Book of Psalms and in some of the books of prophecy.

To see Jesus in the Old Testament, work through the passages listed below. There isn't room to include every reference, but these will illustrate how Jesus the Messiah was the fulfillment of ancient prophecy and ritual. Enjoy a small taste of what Jesus revealed to these men on the road to Emmaus. Then take some time to worship your Lord as he is presented in his Older Testament.

PROPHECIES ABOUT HIS BIRTH

THE OT PASSAGE	THE PROPHECY	THE NT FULFILLMENT
Micah 5:2	To be born in Bethlehem	Matthew 2:1; Luke 2:4-7
Genesis 49:10	From the tribe of Judah	Matthew 1:2,3; Luke 3:33
Isaiah 7:14	Born to a virgin	Matthew 1:18-23; Luke 1:26-35
Jeremiah 31:15	The murder of the babies	Matthew 2:16-18
Hosea 11:1	He would be taken to Egypt	Matthew 2:13-15
Isaiah 9:7	Heir to David's throne	Matthew 1:1

JESUS IN THE PSALMS

Many of the Psalms present pictures of Jesus. While they are not prophecies, and they were written to describe an immediate situation in the psalmist's life, we can read them in reference to Jesus and gain insight into his life.

- Psalm 110 may be the only purely prophetic psalm, as it refers to a future Davidic king. Matthew tells us that Jesus used a portion of this psalm to prove that the king of Psalm 110 is none other than the Christ (Matthew 22:41–46).
- Psalms 96–99 are called the "enthronement psalms" and refer to Christ's second coming. Read these psalms as your own expression of praise for Jesus' ultimate victory and glory.
- David wrote Psalm 22 as his anguished prayer to God for deliverance from his enemies. The Gospel writers, especially Matthew and John, quoted this psalm often in their descriptions of Jesus' suffering and death (Matthew 27:35, 39, 43, 46; John 19:23–24, 28). The writer of Hebrews also informs us that Jesus quoted from this psalm on Calvary (Hebrews 2:12). Read this psalm with deep gratitude for Jesus' willingness to pay for your sin.
- Psalms 2, 45 and 72 were written for actual kings of Israel and Judah, but will only be completely fulfilled in Christ. These psalms lead us to worship and rejoice in the eternal reign of Jesus the Messiah. They instill hope and confidence that regardless of how things sometimes appear, Jesus is still ultimately the King of kings and Lord of lords.
- Some other psalms that refer to Jesus are: 16:10; 24:7, 8; 40:6–10; 41:9; 68:18; 69:9; 72:17; 89:27; 118:22.

PROPHECIES ABOUT JESUS IN ISAIAH THE PROPHET

Many of the Old Testament prophets make reference to Jesus Christ, but none as frequently and as clearly as Isaiah. Be bolstered in your faith as you see how one prophet, writing 700 years before Jesus' birth, was led by the Holy Spirit to write of him.

Isaiah's prophecies about:

Jesus' birth:	7:14; 9:6
Jesus' life on earth:	7:15; 11:1–2; 53:2
Jesus as the Son of his Father:	42:1; 50:4–5
Jesus' miracles:	35:5–6
Jesus' ministry:	9:2; 42:1–3
Jesus' message:	61:1, 2
Jesus' substitutionary death:	53
Jesus' eternal kingdom:	9:7; 11:3–5; 32:1; 33:22; 49:1–12; 59:18–21

NEW TESTAMENT

MATTHEW

AT A GLANCE

Key Principle: Just as Jesus presented himself to Israel as her rightful Messiah and King, so he offers himself to us as our Savior and Lord.
Author: Matthew (Levi)
Time and Place: ~6–4 B.C. to A.D. 33 / Galilee and Judea
Key Verses: 1:1; 4:17; 16:16–19; 21:5; 27:22; 28:18–20

BENEFIT

Matthew is the first of the five historical books (the Gospels and Acts) that together make up 60 percent of the New Testament. These books, the foundation on which the epistles are built, provide a historical context for the life of Jesus Christ and the acts of the apostles. Emphasizing that Jesus is Lord and the perfect fulfillment of many Old Testament Messianic passages, the Gospel of Matthew invites us to respond humbly and obediently to his loving authority.

SETTING

The Greek word *euaggelion* speaks of the "good news" of Jesus Christ, and the word "gospel" comes from the Anglo-Saxon *godspell*, meaning "God story" or "good story." The early churches quickly accepted Matthew's Gospel, and while some scholars challenge the view that Jesus' disciple Matthew (also known as Levi; Luke 5:27–28) wrote it, there is still good reason to accept his authorship. Although the phrases "to this day" (27:8) and "to this very day" (28:15) suggest the book was written several years after the time of Christ, they do support a date of origin before Jerusalem's destruction in A.D. 70.

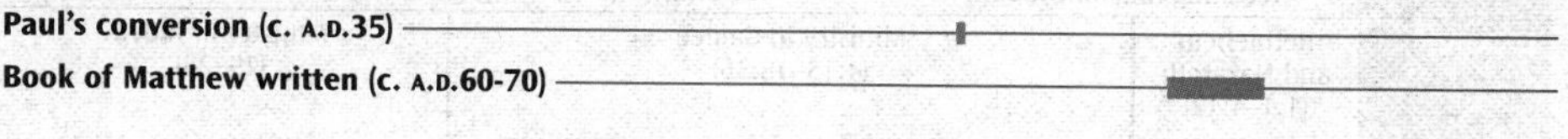

THEME AND PURPOSE

The four Gospels are not biographies of Jesus Christ but rather thematic portraits, each addressed to a particular audience and stressing particular aspects of his life. Together these unique portraits create a composite picture in which the whole is greater than the sum of its parts.

Matthew addresses a Jewish audience and uses extensive Old Testament quotations to demonstrate that Jesus is, in fact, Israel's long-awaited Messiah and King. Like the other Gospels, Matthew was written in part to help readers make a well-informed decision about Jesus in light of his person and works. Because Matthew develops Christ's unique claims and credentials so well, we are asked to either reject or accept him—to ignore him is essentially to reject him. This Gospel also answers objections and misconceptions about Jesus and instructs its readers in his ethical and theological teachings.

UNIQUE CONTRIBUTION

More than the other Gospels, Matthew emphasizes the Jewish background of Christ's life; further, it assumes readers know in detail the Hebrew Bible as well as Jewish customs and religious traditions. Matthew also stresses the teachings of Jesus, and 60 percent of its 1,071 verses contain his spoken words. These include two of the three major discourses of our Lord: The Sermon on the Mount (5—7) and the Olivet Discourse (24—25; the third is the Upper Room Discourse in John 13—17). Through thematically arranged sections, this Gospel clearly presents Jesus' miracles, parables, questions, and discourses, as well as introduces a central theme—the mounting opposition to Jesus. His offer to the religious leaders, and their subsequent rejection, lead to the climax of the book—Jesus' death, burial and resurrection.

CHRIST IN MATTHEW

Matthew builds a solid case that Jesus fulfills the qualifications for Israel's Messiah in his lineage, his healing ministry, and his teachings. He does this by using more Old Testament quotations and allusions than any other New Testament book (almost 130). The expression, "what was said through the prophet was fulfilled" recurs nine times in this Gospel, but does not appear in the other three Gospels. This is a book of fulfillment in which Jesus as the Christ or Messiah uniquely fulfills the Messianic prophecies of the Hebrew Bible and offers himself to Israel as her King. The phrase "kingdom of heaven," repeated 32 times in this book and found nowhere else in the New Testament, reveals an important theme—the type of kingdom Christ came to establish. Without this critical phrase, the Jewish reader might wonder why, if he was indeed Israel's Messiah, Jesus did not overthrow the Romans and establish an earthly kingdom.

OVERVIEW

FOCUS	Presentation of Israel's Messiah		Rejection of Israel's Messiah			
REFERENCE	1 4	5 10	11 16a	16b 20	21 25	26 28
TOPICS	Credentials of the King	Words and Works	Initial Opposition	Preparation of Disciples	Presentation and Preaching	Rejection and Resurrection
	Growing Reception		Growing Rejection			
	Chronological	Topical	Chronological			
	Teaching the Multitudes			Teaching the Disciples		
LOCATION	Bethlehem and Nazareth (1:1–4:12)	Ministry in Galilee (4:13–18:35)			Ministry in Judea (19–28)	
TIME	~6–4 B.C. to A.D. 33					

Matthew begins his account of the presentation and rejection of Israel's Messiah and King by unveiling Jesus' credentials: He is the direct descendant of David, the King of the Jews sought by the Magi, the fulfillment of John the Baptist's preaching and the sinless One who overcame the satanic temptations in the wilderness (1—4). The matchless Sermon on the Mount (5—7) shows that God looks on the heart and not merely on our actions. A collection of miracles follows, revealing Jesus' authority over nature, disease, demons, and death. His words are thereby authenticated by his works (8—10).

As the people hear Jesus' words and see his works, their religious leaders begin to oppose

him. This theme of mounting rejection finally culminates in the crucifixion. In response to this opposition, Jesus begins to speak in parables and to spend more time with his disciples, preparing them for his coming death and resurrection (11—20). After his triumphal entry into Jerusalem, Jesus primarily addresses those who have rejected their rightful King as he predicts the city's downfall and the Jewish people's dispersion among the nations. He also predicts the events surrounding his second coming as Judge and Lord. The Gospel of Matthew culminates in the crucifixion, humanity's supreme act of rejection (26—27), and the resurrection, God's supreme act of vindication and exaltation (28).

MATTHEW

The Genealogy of Jesus

›See Ruth 4:18–22; 1 Chronicles 3:10–17; Luke 3:23–38

1 A record of the genealogy of Jesus Christ the son of David,[a] the son of Abraham:[b]

2 Abraham was the father of Isaac,[c]
Isaac the father of Jacob,[d]
Jacob the father of Judah and his brothers,[e]
3 Judah the father of Perez and Zerah, whose mother was Tamar,[f]
Perez the father of Hezron,
Hezron the father of Ram,
4 Ram the father of Amminadab,
Amminadab the father of Nahshon,
Nahshon the father of Salmon,
5 Salmon the father of Boaz, whose mother was Rahab,
Boaz the father of Obed, whose mother was Ruth,
Obed the father of Jesse,
6 and Jesse the father of King David.[g]

David was the father of Solomon, whose mother had been Uriah's wife,[h]
7 Solomon the father of Rehoboam,
Rehoboam the father of Abijah,
Abijah the father of Asa,
8 Asa the father of Jehoshaphat,
Jehoshaphat the father of Jehoram,
Jehoram the father of Uzziah,
9 Uzziah the father of Jotham,
Jotham the father of Ahaz,
Ahaz the father of Hezekiah,
10 Hezekiah the father of Manasseh,[i]
Manasseh the father of Amon,
Amon the father of Josiah,
11 and Josiah the father of Jeconiah[a] and his brothers at the time of the exile to Babylon.[j]

12 After the exile to Babylon:
Jeconiah was the father of Shealtiel,[k]
Shealtiel the father of Zerubbabel,[l]
13 Zerubbabel the father of Abiud,
Abiud the father of Eliakim,
Eliakim the father of Azor,
14 Azor the father of Zadok,
Zadok the father of Akim,
Akim the father of Eliud,
15 Eliud the father of Eleazar,
Eleazar the father of Matthan,
Matthan the father of Jacob,
16 and Jacob the father of Joseph, the husband of Mary,[m] of whom was born Jesus, who is called Christ.[n]

17 Thus there were fourteen generations in all from Abraham to David, fourteen from David to the exile to Babylon, and fourteen from the exile to the Christ.[b]

The Birth of Jesus Christ

18 This is how the birth of Jesus
Christ came about: His mother Mary
was pledged to be married to Joseph,
but before they came together, she
was found to be with child through
the Holy Spirit.[o] 19 Because Joseph her
husband was a righteous man and did
not want to expose her to public disgrace, he had in mind to divorce[p] her
quietly.
20 But after he had considered this,
an angel of the Lord appeared to him in
a dream and said, "Joseph son of David, do not be afraid to take Mary home
as your wife, because what is conceived in her is from the Holy Spirit.
21 She will give birth to a son, and you
are to give him the name Jesus,[c][q] because he will save his people from their
sins."[r]
22 All this took place to fulfill what
the Lord had said through the prophet:
23 "The virgin will be with child and
will give birth to a son, and they will
call him Immanuel"[d][s]—which means,
"God with us."
24 When Joseph woke up, he did what
the angel of the Lord had commanded
him and took Mary home as his wife.
25 But he had no union with her until
she gave birth to a son. And he gave
him the name Jesus.[t]

The Visit of the Magi

2 After Jesus was born in Bethlehem
in Judea,[u] during the time of King
Herod,[v] Magi[e] from the east came to

1:1 [a] 2Sa 7:12-16; Isa 9:6,7; 11:1; Jer 23:5,6; 2Mt 9:27; Lk 1:32,69; Ro 1:3; Rev 22:16 [b] Ge 22:18; Gal 3:16
1:2 [c] Ge 21:3,12 [d] Ge 25:26 [e] Ge 29:35
1:3 [f] Ge 38:27-30
1:6 [g] 1Sa 16:1; 17:12 [h] 2Sa 12:24
1:10 [i] 2Ki 20:21
1:11 [j] 2Ki 24:14-16; Jer 27:20; Da 1:1,2
1:12 [k] 1Ch 3:17 [l] 1Ch 3:19; Ezr 3:2
1:16 [m] Lk 1:27 [n] Mt 27:17
1:18 [o] Lk 1:35
1:19 [p] Dt 24:1
1:21 [q] Lk 1:31 [r] Lk 2:11; Ac 5:31; 13:23, 28
1:23 [s] Isa 7:14; 8:8, 10
1:25 [t] ver 21
2:1 [u] Lk 2:4-7 [v] Lk 1:5

[a] *11* That is, Jehoiachin; also in verse 12
[b] *17* Or *Messiah.* "The Christ" (Greek) and "the Messiah" (Hebrew) both mean "the Anointed One."
[c] *21* *Jesus* is the Greek form of *Joshua,* which means *the LORD saves.*
[d] *23* Isaiah 7:14
[e] *1* Traditionally *Wise Men*

Jerusalem 2 and asked, "Where is the
one who has been born king of the
Jews?[w] We saw his star[x] in the east[a]
and have come to worship him."
3 When King Herod heard this he was
disturbed, and all Jerusalem with him.
4 When he had called together all the
people's chief priests and teachers of
the law, he asked them where the
Christ[b] was to be born. 5 "In Bethlehem[y] in Judea," they replied, "for this
is what the prophet has written:

6 " 'But you, Bethlehem, in the land
of Judah,
are by no means least among the
rulers of Judah;
for out of you will come a ruler
who will be the shepherd of my
people Israel.'[c] "[z]

7 Then Herod called the Magi secretly and found out from them the exact
time the star had appeared. 8 He sent
them to Bethlehem and said, "Go and
make a careful search for the child. As
soon as you find him, report to me, so
that I too may go and worship him."
9 After they had heard the king, they
went on their way, and the star they
had seen in the east[d] went ahead of
them until it stopped over the place
where the child was. 10 When they saw
the star, they were overjoyed. 11 On
coming to the house, they saw the
child with his mother Mary, and they
bowed down and worshiped him.[a]
Then they opened their treasures and
presented him with gifts[b] of gold and
of incense and of myrrh. 12 And having
been warned[c] in a dream[d] not to go
back to Herod, they returned to their
country by another route.

The Escape to Egypt

13 When they had gone, an angel[e]
of the Lord appeared to Joseph in a
dream.[f] "Get up," he said, "take the
child and his mother and escape to
Egypt. Stay there until I tell you, for
Herod is going to search for the child to
kill him."
14 So he got up, took the child and his
mother during the night and left for
Egypt, 15 where he stayed until the
death of Herod. And so was fulfilled
what the Lord had said through the
prophet: "Out of Egypt I called my
son."[e][g]
16 When Herod realized that he had
been outwitted by the Magi, he was furious, and he gave orders to kill all the
boys in Bethlehem and its vicinity who
were two years old and under, in accordance with the time he had learned
from the Magi. 17 Then what was said
through the prophet Jeremiah was fulfilled:

18 "A voice is heard in Ramah,
weeping and great mourning,
Rachel weeping for her children
and refusing to be comforted,
because they are no more."[f][h]

The Return to Nazareth

19 After Herod died, an angel of the
Lord appeared in a dream[i] to Joseph
in Egypt 20 and said, "Get up, take the
child and his mother and go to the land
of Israel, for those who were trying to
take the child's life are dead."
21 So he got up, took the child and his
mother and went to the land of Israel.
22 But when he heard that Archelaus
was reigning in Judea in place of his
father Herod, he was afraid to go there.
Having been warned in a dream,[j] he
withdrew to the district of Galilee,[k]
23 and he went and lived in a town
called Nazareth.[l] So was fulfilled[m]
what was said through the prophets:
"He will be called a Nazarene."[n]

John the Baptist Prepares the Way

›See Mark 1:3–8; Luke 3:2–17

3 In those days John the Baptist[o]
came, preaching in the Desert of Judea 2 and saying, "Repent, for the kingdom of heaven[p] is near." 3 This is he

2:2 [w] Jer 23:5; Mt 27:11; Mk 15:2; Jn 1:49; 18:33-37 [x] Nu 24:17
2:5 [y] Jn 7:42
2:6 [z] Mic 5:2; 2Sa 5:2
2:11 [a] Isa 60:3 [b] Ps 72:10
2:12 [c] Heb 11:7 [d] ver 13,19,22; Mt 27:19
2:13 [e] Ac 5:19 [f] ver 12,19,22
2:15 [g] Hos 11:1; Ex 4:22,23
2:18 [h] Jer 31:15
2:19 [i] ver 12,13,22
2:22 [j] ver 12,13,19; Mt 27:19 [k] Lk 2:39
2:23 [l] Lk 1:26; Jn 1:45,46 [m] Mt 1:22 [n] Mk 1:24
3:1 [o] Lk 1:13, 57-66; 3:2-19
3:2 [p] Da 2:44; Mt 4:17; 6:10; Lk 11:20; 21:31; Jn 3:3,5; Ac 1:3,6

a *2* Or *star when it rose* b *4* Or *Messiah*
c *6* Micah 5:2 d *9* Or *seen when it rose*
e *15* Hosea 11:1 f *18* Jer. 31:15

2:13–15

PROMISE 4

IMMEDIATE OBEDIENCE

"So he got up." Those four short words communicate volumes about the character of Joseph, Jesus' earthly father. Upon receiving a command from God concerning the protection of his family, he immediately obeyed. No debating. No delaying. Just immediate and complete obedience.

Would Joseph's obedience bring hardship? Probably. And danger? No doubt. But still he obeyed. And so must every man who commits to listening to God and following his commands. The Bible has much to say about fathers and their families (check the PromiseFinder index for a listing of passages addressing Promise 4 in this Bible). Make it a personal goal each day to find one command from the Bible that you can diligently obey, whether the command be about family or another aspect of your life. And, like Joseph, make your obedience immediate and complete.

For the next Promise 4 reading go to page 1072.

JOSEPH

A Good Husband and Father

What was it about Joseph that makes him so special, that sets him apart as a good example for husbands and fathers? By looking closely at his life, we can find several aspects of Joseph's character to model in our own lives.

Joseph was caring and sensitive. According to the Mosaic law, a man and woman's pledge to be married was as binding as the marriage ceremony itself (Deuteronomy 22:24). When Joseph discovered Mary was pregnant before they were married, he could have publicly disgraced her and her whole family. He could have even had her stoned for the sin of adultery (22:21). The baby in her womb was all the evidence he needed to demonstrate that she had been promiscuous.

However, Joseph chose not to exercise those rights. Though he probably had difficulty at first believing her story about her encounter with the angel Gabriel (Luke 1:26–38), he dearly loved this young woman. He wanted to protect her from shame and "did not want to expose her to public disgrace" (Matthew 1:19). Consequently, he suggested that he break their engagement quietly and attempt to make the best of a troublesome situation.

Joseph was righteous and spiritual. He was committed to keeping God's laws (1:19). He firmly believed Mary held the same convictions. When an angel appeared to him and told him the child Mary was carrying was conceived by the Holy Spirit, Joseph responded in faith, accepted the angel's message, and "took Mary home as his wife" (1:24).

Joseph was a loyal man. When he made his decision to wed Mary, Joseph knew he would face public ridicule. After all, how could he explain the situation? And who would believe the story anyway? But Joseph was willing to face the critics. If people condemned Mary, they would have to condemn him as well.

Joseph was morally protective. Though Joseph was Mary's legal husband, the Bible records that Joseph had no intimate relationship with Mary until after Jesus was born (1:25). Though it would not have been immoral to have sexual relations with his pregnant wife, it seems as though Joseph didn't want to risk interfering with any aspect of this holy, supernatural pregnancy. Joseph was also careful to take Mary with him when he went to Bethlehem to register and pay his tax (Luke 2:5). He could have gone alone; her presence wasn't required. But Joseph knew that if he left her behind he would not be able to protect her from further ridicule.

Joseph was a responsible man. Joseph knew the requirements of the Mosaic law concerning the firstborn male. He made sure that the baby was circumcised and given the name Jesus, just as the angel had instructed. Joseph also took the lead in making the journey to Jerusalem to present the infant Jesus to God and to make a sacrifice for him (Luke 2:21–24).

Joseph was an obedient man. In every instance when Joseph discerned the will of God, he responded positively. When warned in a dream by an angel of the Lord to move to Egypt to protect Jesus from King Herod, Joseph immediately obeyed (Matthew 2:13–14). And when the angel again appeared to him following King Herod's death and told him to return to Israel, Joseph obeyed again. Obedience to God's direction was a way of life for Joseph.

Measuring Up

Even if you never had a positive role model while you were growing up to show you how to be a good husband and father, you can follow Joseph's example and make some positive changes in your own life. Begin by asking yourself the following questions:

Am I caring and sensitive? Do I only look out for myself, or am I concerned about the needs of others?

Am I righteous and spiritual? Do I seek after the things of God?

Am I loyal? Do I stick by my family and friends through tough times? Am I willing to suffer ridicule for their sakes?

Am I morally protective? Do I watch out for those who are weaker than I am? Do I live by a positive moral code?

Am I responsible? Do I take care of the obligations that are mine as a husband and father?

Am I obedient—to God? To my superiors? To the laws of the land?

Learning to be a good husband and father will take work. By following Joseph's example and asking God every day for his wisdom and strength, you can be the husband and father that God wants and your family needs.

—*Dr. Gene Getz*

who was spoken of through the prophet Isaiah:

"A voice of one calling in the
desert,
'Prepare the way for the Lord,
make straight paths for
him.' "[a][q]

4John's clothes were made of camel's hair, and he had a leather belt around his waist.[r] His food was locusts[s] and wild honey. 5People went out to him from Jerusalem and all Judea and the whole region of the Jordan. 6Confessing their sins, they were baptized by him in the Jordan River.

7But when he saw many of the Pharisees and Sadducees coming to where he was baptizing, he said to them: "You brood of vipers![t] Who warned you to flee from the coming wrath?[u] 8Produce fruit in keeping with repentance.[v] 9And do not think you can say to yourselves, 'We have Abraham as our father.' I tell you that out of these stones God can raise up children for Abraham. 10The ax is already at the root of the trees, and every tree that does not produce good fruit will be cut down and thrown into the fire.[w]

11"I baptize you with[b] water for repentance. But after me will come one who is more powerful than I, whose sandals I am not fit to carry. He will baptize you with the Holy Spirit[x] and with fire.[y] 12His winnowing fork is in his hand, and he will clear his threshing floor, gathering his wheat into the barn and burning up the chaff with unquenchable fire."[z]

The Baptism of Jesus

›See Mark 1:9–11; Luke 3:21–22; John 1:31–34

13Then Jesus came from Galilee to the Jordan to be baptized by John.[a] 14But John tried to deter him, saying, "I need to be baptized by you, and do you come to me?"

15Jesus replied, "Let it be so now; it is proper for us to do this to fulfill all righteousness." Then John consented.

16As soon as Jesus was baptized, he went up out of the water. At that moment heaven was opened, and he saw the Spirit of God[b] descending like a dove and lighting on him. 17And a voice from heaven[c] said, "This is my Son,[d] whom I love; with him I am well pleased."[e]

The Temptation of Jesus

›See Mark 1:12–13; Luke 4:1–13

4 Then Jesus was led by the Spirit into the desert to be tempted by the devil. 2After fasting forty days and forty nights,[f] he was hungry. 3The tempter[g] came to him and said, "If you are the Son of God,[h] tell these stones to become bread."

4Jesus answered, "It is written: 'Man does not live on bread alone, but on every word that comes from the mouth of God.'[c]"[i]

5Then the devil took him to the holy city[j] and had him stand on the highest point of the temple. 6"If you are the Son of God," he said, "throw yourself down. For it is written:

" 'He will command his angels
concerning you,
and they will lift you up in their
hands,
so that you will not strike your foot
against a stone.'[d]"[k]

7Jesus answered him, "It is also written: 'Do not put the Lord your God to the test.'[e]"[l]

8Again, the devil took him to a very high mountain and showed him all the kingdoms of the world and their splendor. 9"All this I will give you," he said, "if you will bow down and worship me."

10Jesus said to him, "Away from me, Satan![m] For it is written: 'Worship the Lord your God, and serve him only.'[f]"[n]

11Then the devil left him, and angels came and attended him.[o]

Jesus Begins to Preach

12When Jesus heard that John had been put in prison,[p] he returned to Galilee.[q] 13Leaving Nazareth, he went and lived in Capernaum,[r] which was by the lake in the area of Zebulun and Naphtali— 14to fulfill what was said through the prophet Isaiah:

15"Land of Zebulun and land of
Naphtali,
the way to the sea, along the
Jordan,
Galilee of the Gentiles—
16the people living in darkness
have seen a great light;
on those living in the land of the
shadow of death
a light has dawned."[g][s]

17From that time on Jesus began to preach, "Repent, for the kingdom of heaven[t] is near."

The Calling of the First Disciples

›See Mark 1:16–20; Luke 5:2–11; John 1:35–42

18As Jesus was walking beside the

2 →PG. 1056

3:3 [q]Isa 40:3; Mal 3:1; Lk 1:76; Jn 1:23
3:4 [r]2Ki 1:8 [s]Lev 11:22
3:7 [t]Mt 12:34; 23:33 [u]Ro 1:18; 1Th 1:10
3:8 [v]Ac 26:20
3:10 [w]Mt 7:19; Lk 13:6-9; Jn 15:2,6
3:11 [x]Mk 1:8 [y]Isa 4:4; Ac 2:3,4
3:12 [z]Mt 13:30
3:13 [a]Mk 1:4
3:16 [b]Isa 11:2; 42:1
3:17 [c]Mt 17:5; Jn 12:28 [d]Ps 2:7; 2Pe 1:17,18 [e]Isa 42:1; Mt 12:18; 17:5; Mk 1:11; 9:7; Lk 9:35
4:2 [f]Ex 34:28; 1Ki 19:8
4:3 [g]1Th 3:5 [h]Mt 3:17; Jn 5:25; Ac 9:20
4:4 [i]Dt 8:3
4:5 [j]Ne 11:1; Da 9:24; Mt 27:53
4:6 [k]Ps 91:11,12
4:7 [l]Dt 6:16
4:10 [m]1Ch 21:1 [n]Dt 6:13
4:11 [o]Mt 26:53; Lk 22:43; Heb 1:14
4:12 [p]Mt 14:3 [q]Mk 1:14
4:13 [r]Mk 1:21; Lk 4:23,31; Jn 2:12; 4:46, 47
4:16 [s]Isa 9:1,2; Lk 2:32
4:17 [t]Mt 3:2

a *3* Isaiah 40:3 **b** *11* Or *in* **c** *4* Deut. 8:3
d *6* Psalm 91:11,12 **e** *7* Deut. 6:16
f *10* Deut. 6:13 **g** *16* Isaiah 9:1,2

Sea of Galilee,[u] he saw two brothers,
Simon called Peter[v] and his brother
Andrew. They were casting a net
into the lake, for they were fishermen.
19"Come, follow me,"[w] Jesus said,
"and I will make you fishers of men."
20At once they left their nets and followed him.
21Going on from there, he saw two
other brothers, James son of Zebedee
and his brother John.[x] They were in a
boat with their father Zebedee, preparing their nets. Jesus called them, 22and
immediately they left the boat and
their father and followed him.

Jesus Heals the Sick

23Jesus went throughout Galilee,[y]
teaching in their synagogues,[z] preaching the good news[a] of the kingdom,[b]
and healing every disease and sickness among the people.[c] 24News
about him spread all over Syria,[d] and
people brought to him all who were ill
with various diseases, those suffering
severe pain, the demon-possessed,[e]
those having seizures,[f] and the paralyzed,[g] and he healed them. 25Large
crowds from Galilee, the Decapolis,[a]
Jerusalem, Judea and the region across
the Jordan followed him.[h]

4:18 [u]Mt 15:29; Mk 7:31; Jn 6:1 [v]Mt 16:17,18 **4:19** [w]Mk 10:21,28, 52 **4:21** [x]Mt 20:20 **4:23** [y]Mk 1:39; Lk 4:15,44 [z]Mt 9:35; 13:54; Mk 1:21; Lk 4:15; Jn 6:59 [a]Mk 1:14 [b]Mt 3:2; Ac 20:25 [c]Mt 8:16; 15:30; Ac 10:38 **4:24** [d]Lk 2:2 [e]Mt 8:16,28; 9:32; 15:22; Mk 1:32; 5:15, 16,18 [f]Mt 17:15 [g]Mt 8:6; 9:2; Mk 2:3

The Beatitudes

›See Luke 6:20–23

5 Now when he saw the crowds, he
went up on a mountainside and sat
down. His disciples came to him, 2and
he began to teach them, saying:

3"Blessed are the poor in spirit,
for theirs is the kingdom of
heaven.[i]
4Blessed are those who mourn,

3 →PG. 1054

[a]25 That is, the Ten Cities

4:25 [h]Mk 3:7,8; Lk 6:17 **5:3** [i]ver 10,19; Mt 25:34

4:1–11

PROMISE 3

BATTLING TEMPTATION

Temptation: No enemy you face is more persistent. Just about the time you think you've outrun it, temptation shows up around the next corner. When you think you've finally delivered a knock-out punch, it gets back up.

Temptation is not only persistent; it's also pervasive. It winks at you from a billboard. It entices you from the TV set. It calls alluringly over a radio. It lives in newspapers, magazines and books. It's as comfortable in your office as it is in your home.

No wonder the apostle Paul told the Corinthians, "If you think you are standing firm, be careful that you don't fall" (1 Corinthians 10:12). Temptation will sucker-punch you in the blink of an eye, and it will do so without an ounce of remorse.

Jesus himself faced—and overcame—temptation while he walked this earth. You can defeat temptation as well, if you'll depend on the Spirit to help you follow Jesus' example. How did Jesus defeat this powerful adversary? First, Jesus recognized the reality of his enemy. The Lord knew that Satan was a real being who was intent on luring him into sin. Be assured that your opponent is no phantom. He's a real being who will urge you to satisfy healthy appetites in sinful ways.

Second, Jesus recognized that Satan deceives by mixing the truth of Scripture with a lie. Satan did this with Jesus, and he'll do it with you. For instance, the Bible promises that God will forgive a believer for any sin that he or she confesses (1 John 1:9). Satan will take that truth and whisper in your ear, "Go ahead and lie, or steal, or fornicate. It doesn't matter. God will forgive you." Jesus knew the Scriptures so well he could combat such distortions with the truth (verses 4, 7, 10). And so must we.

James, Jesus' half-brother, provided some additional guidance for us in our battle by showing us that temptation sometimes comes in a four-step process. "Each one is tempted when, by his own evil desire, he is dragged away and enticed. Then, after desire has conceived, it gives birth to sin; and sin, when it is full-grown, gives birth to death" (James 1:14–15).

The four stages of temptation are enticement, conception, birth, and death. The key to resisting temptation occurs at the enticement and conception stages. We avoid enticement by meditating on Scripture rather than fantasizing about something that appeals to our sinful nature. We're guarded from conception by identifying and avoiding those situations that trigger our sinful appetites. Understand, however, that the Spirit plays a role in this. We can pray to him for the strength we need to avoid thoughts and places that tempt us to sin.

If you want to guard yourself from temptation, take these steps today. First, begin by praying for the Spirit to empower your resolve and resistance to temptation. Next, make a list of the situations in which you're most frequently tempted and devise a strategy to physically avoid them. If you want to see some real progress, share that list with your small group and ask them to check up on you. You might also want to select a pertinent Bible verse to meditate on that will help you keep your mind on the things of the Lord. Write it on a card and carry it with you.

Temptation is a formidable enemy. But the Lord is an invincible ally. The next time temptation mounts an attack, execute a battle plan that will keep you close to God's side.

For the next Promise 3 reading go to page 1075.

for they will be comforted.[j]
5Blessed are the meek,
for they will inherit the earth.[k]
6Blessed are those who hunger and
thirst for righteousness,
for they will be filled.[l]
7Blessed are the merciful,
for they will be shown mercy.
8Blessed are the pure in heart,[m]
for they will see God.[n]
9Blessed are the peacemakers,
for they will be called sons of
God.[o]
10Blessed are those who are
persecuted because of
righteousness,[p]
for theirs is the kingdom of
heaven.

11"Blessed are you when people insult you,[q] persecute you and falsely
say all kinds of evil against you because
of me. 12Rejoice and be glad,[r] because
great is your reward in heaven, for in
the same way they persecuted the
prophets who were before you.[s]

Salt and Light

7 →PG. 1054
13"You are the salt of the earth. But
if the salt loses its saltiness, how can
it be made salty again? It is no longer
good for anything, except to be thrown
out and trampled by men.[t]
14"You are the light of the world.[u] A
city on a hill cannot be hidden. 15Nei-
ther do people light a lamp and put it
under a bowl. Instead they put it on its
stand, and it gives light to everyone in
the house.[v] 16In the same way, let
your light shine before men, that they
may see your good deeds and praise[w]
your Father in heaven.

The Fulfillment of the Law

17"Do not think that I have come to
abolish the Law or the Prophets; I have
not come to abolish them but to fulfill
them.[x] 18I tell you the truth, until
heaven and earth disappear, not the
smallest letter, not the least stroke of a
pen, will by any means disappear from
the Law until everything is accomplished.[y] 19Anyone who breaks one of
the least of these commandments[z]
and teaches others to do the same will
be called least in the kingdom of heav-
en, but whoever practices and teaches
these commands will be called great in
the kingdom of heaven. 20For I tell you
that unless your righteousness surpasses that of the Pharisees and the
teachers of the law, you will certainly
not enter the kingdom of heaven.

Murder

21"You have heard that it was said
to the people long ago, 'Do not murder,[a][a] and anyone who murders will
be subject to judgment.' 22But I tell 6 →PG. 1065
you that anyone who is angry with
his brother[b] will be subject to judgment.[b] Again, anyone who says to his
brother, 'Raca,[c]' is answerable to the

[a] 21 Exodus 20:13 [b] 22 Some manuscripts *brother without cause* [c] 22 An Aramaic term of contempt

5:4 [j] Isa 61:2,3; Rev 7:17
5:5 [k] Ps 37:11; Ro 4:13
5:6 [l] Isa 55:1,2
5:8 [m] Ps 24:3,4 [n] Heb 12:14; Rev 22:4
5:9 [o] ver 44,45; Ro 8:14
5:10 [p] 1Pe 3:14
5:11 [q] 1Pe 4:14
5:12 [r] Ac 5:41; 1Pe 4:13,16 [s] Mt 23:31,37; Ac 7:52; 1Th 2:15
5:13 [t] Mk 9:50; Lk 14:34,35
5:14 [u] Jn 8:12
5:15 [v] Mk 4:21; Lk 8:16
5:16 [w] Mt 9:8
5:17 [x] Ro 3:31
5:18 [y] Lk 16:17
5:19 [z] Jas 2:10
5:21 [a] Ex 20:13; Dt 5:17
5:22 [b] 1Jn 3:15

5:1–7:29

PE

JESUS' KEYNOTE ADDRESS

These three chapters contain perhaps the most well-known words of Jesus. These words spell out the qualities and conduct that should characterize a godly man. As you read these chapters you'll realize that you can't measure up to such a high standard. Fortunately, Jesus has a solution for that problem. He not only shows us how to live, he offers us his power. Read the Sermon on the Mount prayerfully. Meditate on the Lord's words, and ask that the Spirit will give you new insight as you learn about being a godly man through these chapters.

5:3–10

PROMISE 1

THE "BE ATTITUDES"

The Pharisees, the ruling Jewish religious leaders during New Testament times, were busy men. They believed a man's spirituality could be measured by outward acts of righteousness—acts that would win the approval of other people. And they worked hard to ensure that those under their supervision held fast to a laundry list of rigorous rules for living.

Jesus turned the Pharisees' world upside down. As the promised King, Jesus alone knew that people could enter the kingdom of God only through accepting God's forgiveness through him. He stressed that such acceptance was evidenced in inner attitudes, not outward actions. He said that the man who was truly blessed and happy, the man who was truly to be envied, was the one who possessed such character traits as humility, remorse, mercy and purity. Jesus' stress on personal godliness stood in sharp contrast to the false outward righteousness that the Pharisees demanded.

Ask God to help turn these Beatitudes into your "be attitudes." As you allow him to work through you, you'll discover the blessedness that comes from cultivating inner attitudes that reflect Jesus' own character.

For the next Promise 1 reading go to page 1066.

Sanhedrin.[c] But anyone who says, 'You fool!' will be in danger of the fire of hell.[d]

23 "Therefore, if you are offering your gift at the altar and there remember that your brother has something against you, 24 leave your gift there in front of the altar. First go and be reconciled to your brother; then come and offer your gift.

25 "Settle matters quickly with your adversary who is taking you to court. Do it while you are still with him on the way, or he may hand you over to the judge, and the judge may hand you over to the officer, and you may be thrown into prison. 26 I tell you the truth, you will not get out until you have paid the last penny.[a]

Adultery

3 →PG. 1055

27 "You have heard that it was said, 'Do not commit adultery.'[b][e] 28 But I tell you that anyone who looks at a woman lustfully has already committed adultery with her in his heart.[f] 29 If your right eye causes you to sin,[g] gouge it out and throw it away. It is better for you to lose one part of your body than for your whole body to be thrown into hell. 30 And if your right hand causes you to sin, cut it off and throw it away. It is better for you to lose one part of your body than for your whole body to go into hell.

Divorce

31 "It has been said, 'Anyone who divorces his wife must give her a certificate of divorce.'[c][h] 32 But I tell you that anyone who divorces his wife, except for marital unfaithfulness, causes her to become an adulteress, and anyone who marries the divorced woman commits adultery.[i]

Oaths

33 "Again, you have heard that it was said to the people long ago, 'Do not break your oath,[j] but keep the oaths you have made to the Lord.'[k] 34 But I tell you, Do not swear at all:[l] either by heaven, for it is God's throne;[m] 35 or by the earth, for it is his footstool; or by Jerusalem, for it is the city of the Great King.[n] 36 And do not swear by your head, for you cannot make even one hair white or black. 37 Simply let your 'Yes' be 'Yes,' and your 'No,' 'No';[o] anything beyond this comes from the evil one.[p]

An Eye for an Eye

38 "You have heard that it was said, 'Eye for eye, and tooth for tooth.'[d][q] 39 But I tell you, Do not resist an evil person. If someone strikes you on the right cheek, turn to him the other also.[r] 40 And if someone wants to sue you and take your tunic, let him have your cloak as well. 41 If someone forces you to go one mile, go with him two miles. 42 Give to the one who asks you, and do not turn away from the one who wants to borrow from you.[s]

Love for Enemies

7 →PG. 1055

43 "You have heard that it was said, 'Love your neighbor[e][t] and hate your enemy.'[u] 44 But I tell you: Love your enemies[f] and pray for those who persecute you,[v] 45 that you may be sons[w] of your Father in heaven. He causes his sun to rise on the evil and the good, and sends rain on the righteous and the unrighteous.[x] 46 If you love those who love you, what reward will you get?[y] Are not even the tax collectors doing that? 47 And if you greet only your brothers, what are you doing more than others? Do not even pagans do

[a] *26* Greek *kodrantes* [b] *27* Exodus 20:14 [c] *31* Deut. 24:1 [d] *38* Exodus 21:24; Lev. 24:20; Deut. 19:21 [e] *43* Lev. 19:18 [f] *44* Some late manuscripts *enemies, bless those who curse you, do good to those who hate you*

5:22 [c] Mt 26:59 [d] Jas 3:6
5:27 [e] Ex 20:14; Dt 5:18
5:28 [f] Pr 6:25
5:29 [g] Mt 18:6,8,9; Mk 9:42-47
5:31 [h] Dt 24:1-4
5:32 [i] Lk 16:18
5:33 [j] Lev 19:12 [k] Nu 30:2; Dt 23:21; Mt 23:16-22
5:34 [l] Jas 5:12 [m] Isa 66:1; Mt 23:22
5:35 [n] Ps 48:2
5:37 [o] Jas 5:12 [p] Mt 6:13; 13:19,38; Jn 17:15; 2Th 3:3; 1Jn 2:13,14; 3:12; 5:18,19
5:38 [q] Ex 21:24; Lev 24:20; Dt 19:21
5:39 [r] Lk 6:29; Ro 12:17,19; 1Co 6:7; 1Pe 3:9
5:42 [s] Dt 15:8; Lk 6:30
5:43 [t] Lev 19:18 [u] Dt 23:6
5:44 [v] Lk 6:27,28; 23:34; Ac 7:60; Ro 12:14; 1Co 4:12; 1Pe 2:23
5:45 [w] ver 9 [x] Job 25:3
5:46 [y] Lk 6:32

5:21–26

PROMISE 6

BECOMING A PEACEMAKER

How important is it for you to be at peace with other people? It's crucial! In fact, Jesus said that if you're at odds with someone, it's your responsibility to go to them right away and do all you can to make peace. That means approaching people in your family, at work and at church, regardless of their ethnic, socio-economic or educational background.

How important is it for you to become a peacemaker? In verses 24 and 25 Jesus urges you to pursue peace before you approach God for worship, whether that's in a church or in your personal prayer time. Why? Because a broken human relationship is a roadblock that stands between you and a proper relationship with God.

Is there someone you need to talk with today? Do you need to extend a hand of forgiveness? If so, pick up your phone right now and make that call. Reconciliation is one of the key principles of Scripture; a man can't be in a growing relationship with God unless he is actively forgiving his brothers and sisters (see 1 John 2:9–11).

For the next Promise 6 reading go to page 1091.

that? 48Be perfect, therefore, as your heavenly Father is perfect.[z]

Giving to the Needy

7 →PG. 1061

6 "Be careful not to do your 'acts of righteousness' before men, to be seen by them.[a] If you do, you will have no reward from your Father in heaven.

2"So when you give to the needy, do not announce it with trumpets, as the hypocrites do in the synagogues and on the streets, to be honored by men. I tell you the truth, they have received their reward in full. 3But when you give to the needy, do not let your left hand know what your right hand is doing, 4so that your giving may be in secret. Then your Father, who sees what is done in secret, will reward you.[b]

Prayer

›See Luke 11:2–4

1 →PG. 1056

5"And when you pray, do not be like the hypocrites, for they love to pray standing[c] in the synagogues and on the street corners to be seen by men. I tell you the truth, they have received their reward in full. 6But when you pray, go into your room, close the door and pray to your Father,[d] who is unseen. Then your Father, who sees what is done in secret, will reward you. 7And when you pray, do not keep on babbling[e] like pagans, for they think they will be heard because of their many words.[f] 8Do not be like them, for your Father knows what you need[g] before you ask him.

9"This, then, is how you should pray:

" 'Our Father in heaven,
hallowed be your name,
10your kingdom[h] come,
your will be done[i]
on earth as it is in heaven.
11Give us today our daily bread.[j]
12Forgive us our debts,
as we also have forgiven our debtors.[k]
13And lead us not into temptation,[l]
but deliver us from the evil one.[a]'[m]

14For if you forgive men when they sin against you, your heavenly Father will also forgive you.[n] 15But if you do not forgive men their sins, your Father will not forgive your sins.[o]

Fasting

16"When you fast, do not look somber[p] as the hypocrites do, for they disfigure their faces to show men they are fasting. I tell you the truth, they have received their reward in full. 17But when you fast, put oil on your head and wash your face, 18so that it will not be obvious to men that you are fasting, but only to your Father, who is unseen; and your Father, who sees what is done in secret, will reward you.[q]

Treasures in Heaven

19"Do not store up for yourselves treasures on earth,[r] where moth and rust destroy,[s] and where thieves break in and steal. 20But store up for yourselves treasures in heaven,[t] where moth and rust do not destroy, and where thieves do not break in and steal.[u] 21For where your treasure is, there your heart will be also.[v]

22"The eye is the lamp of the body. If your eyes are good, your whole body will be full of light. 23But if your eyes are bad, your whole body will be full of darkness. If then the light within you is darkness, how great is that darkness!

24"No one can serve two masters. Either he will hate the one and love the other, or he will be devoted to the one and despise the other. You cannot serve both God and Money.[w]

3 →PG. 1061

5:48 [z]Lev 19:2; 1Pe 1:16
6:1 [a]Mt 23:5
6:4 [b]ver 6,18; Col 3:23,24
6:5 [c]Mk 11:25; Lk 18:10-14
6:6 [d]2Ki 4:33
6:7 [e]Ecc 5:2 [f]1Ki 18:26-29
6:8 [g]ver 32
6:10 [h]Mt 3:2 [i]Mt 26:39
6:11 [j]Pr 30:8
6:12 [k]Mt 18:21-35
6:13 [l]Jas 1:13 [m]Mt 5:37
6:14 [n]Mt 18:21-35; Mk 11:25,26; Eph 4:32; Col 3:13
6:15 [o]Mt 18:35
6:16 [p]Isa 58:5
6:18 [q]ver 4,6
6:19 [r]Pr 23:4; Heb 13:5 [s]Jas 5:2,3
6:20 [t]Mt 19:21; Lk 12:33; 18:22; 1Ti 6:19 [u]Lk 12:33
6:21 [v]Lk 12:34
6:24 [w]Lk 16:13

[a]13 Or *from evil*; some late manuscripts *one, / for yours is the kingdom and the power and the glory forever. Amen.*

6:19–24

PROMISE 5

CHECKBOOK GUT-CHECK

Every man wants to know that his life matters, that he has invested himself in something that will make a difference. Jesus understood that need. That's why he urged every man to invest his life in the kingdom of God. How can you know if you're doing that? Jesus gave a foolproof test. Pull out your checkbook and look at where you spend your money.

The Lord didn't pull any punches when he said that we spend our money on what's important to us. As your eye moves down the ledger of your checkbook, what do you see? If you really want your life to matter, then invest in God's kingdom. Give to your local church and to other ministries that spread God's Word and expand his kingdom.

Make it a personal goal to review your checkbook every month to see where you're investing your resources. And make up your mind today that every month you'll see evidence that you're investing in something that's eternal—something that will give your life meaning.

For the next Promise 5 reading go to page 1197.

Do Not Worry

>See Luke 12:22–31

25“Therefore I tell you, do not worry[x] about your life, what you will eat or drink; or about your body, what you will wear. Is not life more important than food, and the body more important than clothes? 26Look at the birds of the air; they do not sow or reap or store away in barns, and yet your heavenly Father feeds them.[y] Are you not much more valuable than they?[z] 27Who of you by worrying can add a single hour to his life[a]?[a]

28“And why do you worry about clothes? See how the lilies of the field grow. They do not labor or spin. 29Yet I tell you that not even Solomon in all his splendor[b] was dressed like one of these. 30If that is how God clothes the grass of the field, which is here today and tomorrow is thrown into the fire, will he not much more clothe you, O you of little faith?[c] 31So do not worry, saying, ‘What shall we eat?’ or ‘What shall we drink?’ or ‘What shall we wear?’ 32For the pagans run after all these things, and your heavenly Father knows that you need them.[d] 33But seek first his kingdom and his righteousness, and all these things will be given to you as well.[e] 34Therefore do not worry about tomorrow, for tomorrow will worry about itself. Each day has enough trouble of its own.

Judging Others

>See Luke 6:41–42

2 →PG. 1071

7 “Do not judge, or you too will be judged.[f] 2For in the same way you judge others, you will be judged, and with the measure you use, it will be measured to you.[g]

3“Why do you look at the speck of sawdust in your brother’s eye and pay no attention to the plank in your own eye? 4How can you say to your brother, ‘Let me take the speck out of your eye,’ when all the time there is a plank in your own eye? 5You hypocrite, first take the plank out of your own eye, and then you will see clearly to remove the speck from your brother’s eye.

6“Do not give dogs what is sacred; do not throw your pearls to pigs. If you do, they may trample them under their feet, and then turn and tear you to pieces.

Ask, Seek, Knock

>See Luke 11:9–13

7“Ask and it will be given to you;[h] seek and you will find; knock and the door will be opened to you. 8For everyone who asks receives; he who seeks finds;[i] and to him who knocks, the door will be opened.

1 →PG. 1056

9“Which of you, if his son asks for bread, will give him a stone? 10Or if he asks for a fish, will give him a snake? 11If you, then, though you are evil, know how to give good gifts to your children, how much more will your Father in heaven give good gifts to those who ask him! 12So in everything, do to others what you would have them do to you,[j] for this sums up the Law and the Prophets.[k]

The Narrow and Wide Gates

13“Enter through the narrow gate.[l] For wide is the gate and broad is the road that leads to destruction, and many enter through it. 14But small is the gate and narrow the road that leads to life, and only a few find it.

A Tree and Its Fruit

15“Watch out for false prophets.[m] They come to you in sheep’s clothing, but inwardly they are ferocious wolves.[n] 16By their fruit you will recognize them.[o] Do people pick grapes from thornbushes, or figs from thistles?[p] 17Likewise every good tree bears good fruit, but a bad tree bears bad fruit. 18A good tree cannot bear bad fruit, and a bad tree cannot bear good fruit. 19Every tree that does not bear good fruit is cut down and thrown into the fire.[q] 20Thus, by their fruit you will recognize them.

1 →PG. 1062

21“Not everyone who says to me, ‘Lord, Lord,’[r] will enter the kingdom of heaven, but only he who does the will of my Father who is in heaven.[s] 22Many will say to me on that day,[t] ‘Lord, Lord, did we not prophesy in your name, and in your name drive out demons and perform many miracles?’[u] 23Then I will tell them plainly, ‘I never knew you. Away from me, you evildoers!’[v]

The Wise and Foolish Builders

>See Luke 6:47–49

24“Therefore everyone who hears these words of mine and puts them into practice[w] is like a wise man who built his house on the rock. 25The rain came down, the streams rose, and the winds blew and beat against that house; yet it did not fall, because it had its foundation on the rock. 26But everyone who hears these words of mine and does not put them into practice is like a foolish man who built his house

6:25 [x]ver 27,28,31, 34; Lk 10:41; 12:11,22; Php 4:6; 1Pe 5:7
6:26 [y]Job 38:41; Ps 147:9 [z]Mt 10:29-31
6:27 [a]Ps 39:5
6:29 [b]1Ki 10:4-7
6:30 [c]Mt 8:26; 14:31; 16:8
6:32 [d]ver 8
6:33 [e]Mt 19:29; Mk 10:29-30
7:1 [f]Lk 6:37; Ro 14:4,10,13; 1Co 4:5; Jas 4:11,12
7:2 [g]Mk 4:24; Lk 6:38
7:7 [h]Mt 21:22; Mk 11:24; Jn 14:13,14; 15:7,16; 16:23, 24; Jas 1:5-8; 4:2,3; 1Jn 3:22; 5:14,15
7:8 [i]Pr 8:17; Jer 29:12,13
7:12 [j]Lk 6:31 [k]Ro 13:8-10; Gal 5:14
7:13 [l]Lk 13:24
7:15 [m]Jer 23:16; Mt 24:24; Mk 13:22; Lk 6:26; 2Pe 2:1; 1Jn 4:1; Rev 16:13 [n]Ac 20:29
7:16 [o]Mt 12:33; Lk 6:44 [p]Jas 3:12
7:19 [q]Mt 3:10
7:21 [r]Hos 8:2; Mt 25:11 [s]Ro 2:13; Jas 1:22
7:22 [t]Mt 10:15 [u]1Co 13:1-3
7:23 [v]Ps 6:8; Mt 25:12,41; Lk 13:25-27
7:24 [w]Jas 1:22-25

[a] 27 Or *single cubit to his height*

on sand. 27The rain came down, the streams rose, and the winds blew and beat against that house, and it fell with a great crash."

28When Jesus had finished saying these things,[x] the crowds were amazed at his teaching,[y] 29because he taught as one who had authority, and not as their teachers of the law.

The Man With Leprosy

›See Mark 1:40–44; Luke 5:12–14

8 When he came down from the mountainside, large crowds followed him. 2A man with leprosy[a][z] came and knelt before him[a] and said, "Lord, if you are willing, you can make me clean."

3Jesus reached out his hand and touched the man. "I am willing," he said. "Be clean!" Immediately he was cured[b] of his leprosy. 4Then Jesus said to him, "See that you don't tell anyone.[b] But go, show yourself to the priest and offer the gift Moses commanded,[c] as a testimony to them."

The Faith of the Centurion

›See Luke 7:1–10

5When Jesus had entered Capernaum, a centurion came to him, asking for help. 6"Lord," he said, "my servant lies at home paralyzed and in terrible suffering."

7Jesus said to him, "I will go and heal him."

8The centurion replied, "Lord, I do not deserve to have you come under my roof. But just say the word, and my servant will be healed.[d] 9For I myself am a man under authority, with soldiers under me. I tell this one, 'Go,' and he goes; and that one, 'Come,' and he comes. I say to my servant, 'Do this,' and he does it."

10When Jesus heard this, he was astonished and said to those following him, "I tell you the truth, I have not found anyone in Israel with such great faith.[e] 11I say to you that many will come from the east and the west,[f] and will take their places at the feast with Abraham, Isaac and Jacob in the kingdom of heaven.[g] 12But the subjects of the kingdom[h] will be thrown outside, into the darkness, where there will be weeping and gnashing of teeth."[i]

13Then Jesus said to the centurion, "Go! It will be done just as you believed it would."[j] And his servant was healed at that very hour.

7:28 *x*Mt 11:1; 13:53; 19:1; 26:1 *y*Mt 13:54; Mk 1:22; 6:2; Lk 4:32; Jn 7:46
8:2 *z*Lk 5:12 *a*Mt 9:18; 15:25; 18:26; 20:20
8:4 *b*Mt 9:30; Mk 5:43; 7:36; 8:30 *c*Lev 14:2-32
8:8 *d*Ps 107:20
8:10 *e*Mt 15:28
8:11 *f*Ps 107:3; Isa 49:12; 59:19; Mal 1:11 *g*Lk 13:29
8:12 *h*Mt 13:38 *i*Mt 13:42,50; 22:13; 24:51; 25:30; Lk 13:28
8:13 *j*Mt 9:22
8:16 *k*Mt 4:23,24
8:17 *l*Mt 1:22 *m*Isa 53:4
8:18 *n*Mk 4:35
8:20 *o*Da 7:13; Mt 12:8,32,40; 16:13,27,28; 17:9; 19:28; Mk 2:10; 8:31
8:22 *p*Mt 4:19
8:26 *q*Mt 6:30 *r*Ps 65:7; 89:9; 107:29
8:28 *s*Mt 4:24

Jesus Heals Many

›See Mark 1:29–34; Luke 4:38–41

14When Jesus came into Peter's house, he saw Peter's mother-in-law lying in bed with a fever. 15He touched her hand and the fever left her, and she got up and began to wait on him.

16When evening came, many who were demon-possessed were brought to him, and he drove out the spirits with a word and healed all the sick.[k] 17This was to fulfill[l] what was spoken through the prophet Isaiah:

"He took up our infirmities
and carried our diseases."[c][m]

The Cost of Following Jesus

›See Luke 9:57–60

18When Jesus saw the crowd around him, he gave orders to cross to the other side of the lake.[n] 19Then a teacher of the law came to him and said, "Teacher, I will follow you wherever you go."

20Jesus replied, "Foxes have holes and birds of the air have nests, but the Son of Man[o] has no place to lay his head."

21Another disciple said to him, "Lord, first let me go and bury my father."

22But Jesus told him, "Follow me,[p] and let the dead bury their own dead."

Jesus Calms the Storm

›See Mark 4:36–41; Luke 8:22–25

23Then he got into the boat and his disciples followed him. 24Without warning, a furious storm came up on the lake, so that the waves swept over the boat. But Jesus was sleeping. 25The disciples went and woke him, saying, "Lord, save us! We're going to drown!"

26He replied, "You of little faith,[q] why are you so afraid?" Then he got up and rebuked the winds and the waves, and it was completely calm.[r]

27The men were amazed and asked, "What kind of man is this? Even the winds and the waves obey him!"

The Healing of Two Demon-possessed Men

›See Mark 5:1–17; Luke 8:26–37

28When he arrived at the other side in the region of the Gadarenes,[d] two demon-possessed[s] men coming from the tombs met him. They were so vio-

a *2* The Greek word was used for various diseases affecting the skin—not necessarily leprosy. **b** *3* Greek *made clean*
c *17* Isaiah 53:4 **d** *28* Some manuscripts *Gergesenes*; others *Gerasenes*

lent that no one could pass that way.
29"What do *you want with us,*[t] *Son of*
God?" they shouted. "Have you come
here to torture us before the appointed
time?"[u]
30Some distance from them a large
herd of pigs was feeding. 31The demons begged Jesus, "If you drive us
out, send us into the herd of pigs."
32He said to them, "Go!" So they
came out and went into the pigs, and
the whole herd rushed down the steep
bank into the lake and died in the water. 33Those tending the pigs ran off,
went into the town and reported all
this, including what had happened to
the demon-possessed men. 34Then the
whole town went out to meet Jesus.
And when they saw him, they pleaded
with him to leave their region.[v]

Jesus Heals a Paralytic

›See Mark 2:3–12; Luke 5:18–26

9 Jesus stepped into a boat, crossed
over and came to his own town.[w]
2Some men brought to him a paralytic,[x] lying on a mat. When Jesus saw
their faith,[y] he said to the paralytic,
"Take heart,[z] son; your sins are forgiven."[a]
3At this, some of the teachers of the
law said to themselves, "This fellow is
blaspheming!"[b]
4Knowing their thoughts,[c] Jesus
said, "Why do you entertain evil
thoughts in your hearts? 5Which is easier: to say, 'Your sins are forgiven,' or
to say, 'Get up and walk'? 6But so that
you may know that the Son of Man[d]
has authority on earth to forgive
sins . . ." Then he said to the paralytic,
"Get up, take your mat and go home."
7And the man got up and went home.
8When the crowd saw this, they were
filled with awe; and they praised God,[e]
who had given such authority to men.

The Calling of Matthew

›See Mark 2:14–17; Luke 5:27–32

9As Jesus went on from there, he saw
a man named Matthew sitting at the
tax collector's booth. "Follow me," he
told him, and Matthew got up and followed him.
10While Jesus was having dinner at
Matthew's house, many tax collectors
and "sinners" came and ate with him
and his disciples. 11When the Pharisees
saw this, they asked his disciples, "Why
does your teacher eat with tax collectors and 'sinners'?"[f]
12On hearing this, Jesus said, "It is
not the healthy who need a doctor, but
the sick. 13But go and learn what this
means: 'I desire mercy, not sacrifice.'[a][g] For I have not come to call the
righteous, but sinners."[h]

Jesus Questioned About Fasting

›See Mark 2:18–22; Luke 5:33–39

14Then John's disciples came and
asked him, "How is it that we and the
Pharisees fast,[i] but your disciples do
not fast?"
15Jesus answered, "How can the
guests of the bridegroom mourn while
he is with them?[j] The time will come
when the bridegroom will be taken
from them; then they will fast.[k]
16"No one sews a patch of unshrunk
cloth on an old garment, for the patch
will pull away from the garment, making the tear worse. 17Neither do men
pour new wine into old wineskins. If
they do, the skins will burst, the wine
will run out and the wineskins will be
ruined. No, they pour new wine into
new wineskins, and both are preserved."

A Dead Girl and a Sick Woman

›See Mark 5:22–43; Luke 8:41–56

18While he was saying this, a ruler
came and knelt before him[l] and said,
"My daughter has just died. But come
and put your hand on her,[m] and she
will live." 19Jesus got up and went with
him, and so did his disciples.
20Just then a woman who had been
subject to bleeding for twelve years
came up behind him and touched the
edge of his cloak.[n] 21She said to herself, "If I only touch his cloak, I will be
healed."
22Jesus turned and saw her. "Take
heart, daughter," he said, "your faith
has healed you."[o] And the woman was
healed from that moment.[p]
23When Jesus entered the ruler's
house and saw the flute players and the
noisy crowd,[q] 24he said, "Go away.
The girl is not dead[r] but asleep."[s]
But they laughed at him. 25After the
crowd had been put outside, he went
in and took the girl by the hand, and
she got up. 26News of this spread
through all that region.[t]

Jesus Heals the Blind and Mute

27As Jesus went on from there, two
blind men followed him, calling out,
"Have mercy on us, Son of David!"[u]
28When he had gone indoors, the
blind men came to him, and he asked
them, "Do you believe that I am able to
do this?"
"Yes, Lord," they replied.
29Then he touched their eyes and

8:29 [t]Jdg 11:12; 2Sa 16:10; 1Ki 17:18; Mk 1:24; Lk 4:34; Jn 2:4 [u]2Pe 2:4
8:34 [v]Lk 5:8; Ac 16:39
9:1 [w]Mt 4:13
9:2 [x]Mt 4:24 [y]ver 22 [z]Jn 16:33 [a]Lk 7:48
9:3 [b]Mt 26:65; Jn 10:33
9:4 [c]Ps 94:11; Mt 12:25; Lk 6:8; 9:47; 11:17
9:6 [d]Mt 8:20
9:8 [e]Mt 5:16; 15:31; Lk 7:16; 13:13; 17:15; 23:47; Jn 15:8; Ac 4:21; 11:18; 21:20
9:11 [f]Mt 11:19; Lk 5:30; 15:2; Gal 2:15
9:13 [g]Hos 6:6; Mic 6:6-8; Mt 12:7 [h]1Ti 1:15
9:14 [i]Lk 18:12
9:15 [j]Jn 3:29 [k]Ac 13:2,3; 14:23
9:18 [l]Mt 8:2 [m]Mk 5:23
9:20 [n]Mt 14:36; Mk 3:10
9:22 [o]Mk 10:52; Lk 7:50; 17:19; 18:42 [p]Mt 15:28
9:23 [q]2Ch 35:25; Jer 9:17,18
9:24 [r]Ac 20:10 [s]Jn 11:11-14
9:26 [t]Mt 4:24
9:27 [u]Mt 15:22; Mk 10:47; Lk 18:38-39

a 13 Hosea 6:6

MATTHEW

The Spoiler

Matthew knew he was the odd man out, the spoiler with a bad reputation. Jesus' decision to include him as one of the disciples was a strange one. Up to now the group had been so compatible: two sets of brothers, all fishermen, all disciples of John the Baptist, now following the carpenter's son. These men were compatible on a number of levels, and must have been comfortable in each other's company.

But Matthew spoiled the group. He knew that apart from Jesus' invitation to join this tight-knit band, these guys wouldn't have taken the time to spit on his grave. He was a tax collector, a publican, a Jewish turncoat who worked for the Roman empire. He extorted, cheated and chiseled the Jews out of their money. No respectable Jew would think of a publican as an equal.

From Despised to Essential

Yet it was vitally important that Matthew be included in this company of disciples. These very men would one day take Jesus' message of redemption and reconciliation to the despised Samaritans and the hated Gentiles. He had to bring about an enormous change in their thinking by teaching the disciples to tolerate . . . no, accept . . . no, *love* those they now despised. Going through that very process with Matthew was an essential first step. They would have to learn to accept, trust and even love a man they initially suspected, despised and hated.

It was also a huge risk for Matthew to accept Jesus' invitation. He walked away from his job and income. If all this failed, Peter and his buddies could go back to fishing, but Matthew had burned some very important bridges to become one of Jesus' disciples. He had abandoned his tax collecting business and his tight-knit support system of publican colleagues. The other disciples trusted each other, but Matthew was viewed with suspicion, held at a distance until he proved himself. More than likely, some of the disciples silently hoped he never would.

It may have been a strategic blunder in the eyes of some for Jesus to include Matthew in his band of followers. But how enormous Matthew's gratitude to Jesus must have been. Jesus was willing to upset his comfortable little clan. He was willing to deal with the additional hassles that would inevitably come from having a man like Matthew as a follower. That had to make an enormous statement of acceptance and love to Matthew.

And Christ's acceptance and love changes things. Perhaps of all Jesus' disciples, Matthew matured the most from what he was when Jesus called him to what he was when Jesus finished with him. Formerly, the things that mattered to God and his people meant little or nothing to Matthew. But after being touched by Jesus, Matthew's perspective and priorities were turned upside down. What was important to God had become important to him. What mattered to God's people, now mattered to Matthew. What he formerly despised, he now loved. And much of what he formerly loved, he now despised.

This change in values and commitment is seen clearly in Matthew's gospel. It was Matthew, after all, who gave us the most complete rendition of the Beatitudes (Matthew 5). Matthew listened closely as Jesus praised the meek, the humble, those who hunger and thirst for righteousness. Jesus' statement, "He who has ears, let him hear" revealed Matthew's understanding that a man hears what he wants to hear (11:15). Matthew met Jesus and wanted to hear it all. What's more, Matthew also gave us the clearest picture of Jesus Christ as the long-awaited Messiah of the Jews. His Jewish heritage, and the religious tradition that accompanied it, became a key focal point of his gospel message.

Liabilities and Assets

But initially, Matthew was a spoiler. The comfortable group of buddies who followed Jesus treated the inside circle of his attention as their own private playground. That is, until Matthew showed up. He wasn't the kind of person you wanted to join your cause. We probably wouldn't have included him either. We exclude many from our churches today because they are different, make us feel uncomfortable, come from questionable backgrounds. In our minds, these "spoilers" are liabilities to our work for the Lord.

At times, Matthew probably felt like a liability to Jesus' ministry too. Yet there are those like Matthew whose background, though at one time contrary to God's will, becomes a great asset to Christ's cause. God used Matthew without regard for his background, employment history or former way of life. And God can use you too. What you perceive as liabilities to God's work in you are merely the same excuses that Matthew could have spouted as reasons why he shouldn't have been trained as a disciple. Yet God often turns the things we consider liabilities into assets for his kingdom. Only

God can accomplish this great feat. He will take any life, regardless of background, success or failur and turn it into something useful for his kingdom.

Today, God still uses Matthew to upset people's neat little view of how things ought to be. Matthew's life shows that any man who follows Jesus can be significantly used by the Master. So do yourself a favor. Let Matthew spoil your excuses and prejudices. Learn to love all those who work with you to build God's kingdom. Follow the Master willingly, and he'll also take your own personal liabilities and turn them into assets, your failures into successes for his kingdom.

—Dr. Sid Buzz

said, "According to your faith will it be
done to you";[v] 30and their sight was
restored. Jesus warned them sternly,
"See that no one knows about this."[w]
31But they went out and spread the
news about him all over that region.[x]
32While they were going out, a
man who was demon-possessed[y] and
could not talk[z] was brought to Jesus.
33And when the demon was driven out,
the man who had been mute spoke.
The crowd was amazed and said,
"Nothing like this has ever been seen
in Israel."[a]
34But the Pharisees said, "It is by the
prince of demons that he drives out
demons."[b]

The Workers Are Few

35Jesus went through all the towns
and villages, teaching in their synagogues, preaching the good news of
the kingdom and healing every dis-
7 →PG. 1062
ease and sickness.[c] 36When he saw
the crowds, he had compassion on
them,[d] because they were harassed
and helpless, like sheep without a
shepherd.[e] 37Then he said to his disciples, "The harvest[f] is plentiful but the
workers are few.[g] 38Ask the Lord of the
harvest, therefore, to send out workers
into his harvest field."

Jesus Sends Out the Twelve

›See Mark 6:8–11; Luke 9:3–5; 10:4–12

10 He called his twelve disciples to
him and gave them authority to
drive out evil[a] spirits[h] and to heal every disease and sickness.
2These are the names of the twelve
apostles: first, Simon (who is called Peter) and his brother Andrew; James son
of Zebedee, and his brother John;
3Philip and Bartholomew; Thomas and
Matthew the tax collector; James son of
Alphaeus, and Thaddaeus; 4Simon the
Zealot and Judas Iscariot, who betrayed him.[i]
5These twelve Jesus sent out with the
following instructions: "Do not go
among the Gentiles or enter any town
of the Samaritans.[j] 6Go rather to the
lost sheep of Israel.[k] 7As you go,
preach this message: 'The kingdom of
heaven[l] is near.' 8Heal the sick, raise
the dead, cleanse those who have leprosy,[b] drive out demons. Freely you
have received, freely give. 9Do not take
along any gold or silver or copper in
your belts;[m] 10take no bag for the journey, or extra tunic, or sandals or a staff;
for the worker is worth his keep.[n]
11"Whatever town or village you enter, search for some worthy person
there and stay at his house until you
leave. 12As you enter the home, give it
your greeting.[o] 13If the home is deserving, let your peace rest on it; if it is
not, let your peace return to you. 14If
anyone will not welcome you or listen
to your words, shake the dust off your
feet[p] when you leave that home or
town. 15I tell you the truth, it will be
more bearable for Sodom and Gomorrah[q] on the day of judgment[r] than
for that town.[s] 16I am sending you out
like sheep among wolves.[t] Therefore
be as shrewd as snakes and as innocent
as doves.[u]
17"Be on your guard against men;
they will hand you over to the local
councils[v] and flog you in their synagogues.[w] 18On my account you will be
brought before governors and kings[x]
as witnesses to them and to the Gentiles. 19But when they arrest you, do
not worry about what to say or how to
say it.[y] At that time you will be given
what to say, 20for it will not be you
speaking, but the Spirit of your Father[z] speaking through you.
21"Brother will betray brother to 3 →PG. 1065
death, and a father his child; children
will rebel against their parents[a] and
have them put to death. 22All men will
hate you because of me, but he who
stands firm to the end will be saved.[b]
23When you are persecuted in one
place, flee to another. I tell you the
truth, you will not finish going through
the cities of Israel before the Son of
Man comes.
24"A student is not above his teacher, nor a servant above his master.[c]
25It is enough for the student to be like
his teacher, and the servant like his
master. If the head of the house has
been called Beelzebub,[c][d] how much
more the members of his household!
26"So do not be afraid of them. There
is nothing concealed that will not be
disclosed, or hidden that will not be
made known.[e] 27What I tell you in the
dark, speak in the daylight; what is
whispered in your ear, proclaim from
the roofs. 28Do not be afraid of those
who kill the body but cannot kill the
soul. Rather, be afraid of the One[f]
who can destroy both soul and body in
hell. 29Are not two sparrows sold for a
penny[d]? Yet not one of them will fall
to the ground apart from the will of
your Father. 30And even the very hairs
of your head are all numbered.[g] 31So

9:29 [v] ver 22
9:30 [w] Mt 8:4
9:31 [x] ver 26; Mk 7:36
9:32 [y] Mt 4:24 [z] Mt 12:22-24
9:33 [a] Mk 2:12
9:34 [b] Mt 12:24; Lk 11:15
9:35 [c] Mt 4:23
9:36 [d] Mt 14:14 [e] Nu 27:17; Eze 34:5,6; Zec 10:2; Mk 6:34
9:37 [f] Jn 4:35 [g] Lk 10:2
10:1 [h] Mk 3:13-15; Lk 9:1
10:4 [i] Mt 26:14-16, 25,47; Jn 13:2, 26,27
10:5 [j] 2Ki 17:24; Lk 9:52; Jn 4:4-26,39, 40; Ac 8:5,25
10:6 [k] Jer 50:6; Mt 15:24
10:7 [l] Mt 3:2
10:9 [m] Lk 22:35
10:10 [n] 1Ti 5:18
10:12 [o] 1Sa 25:6
10:14 [p] Ne 5:13; Lk 10:11; Ac 13:51
10:15 [q] 2Pe 2:6 [r] Mt 12:36; 2Pe 2:9; 1Jn 4:17 [s] Mt 11:22,24
10:16 [t] Lk 10:3 [u] Ro 16:19
10:17 [v] Mt 5:22 [w] Mt 23:34; Mk 13:9; Ac 5:40; 26:11
10:18 [x] Ac 25:24-26
10:19 [y] Ex 4:12
10:20 [z] Ac 4:8
10:21 [a] ver 35,36; Mic 7:6
10:22 [b] Mt 24:13; Mk 13:13
10:24 [c] Lk 6:40; Jn 13:16; 15:20
10:25 [d] Mk 3:22
10:26 [e] Mk 4:22; Lk 8:17
10:28 [f] Isa 8:12,13; Heb 10:31
10:30 [g] 1Sa 14:45; 2Sa 14:11; Lk 21:18; Ac 27:34

a *1* Greek *unclean* b *8* The Greek word was used for various diseases affecting the skin—not necessarily leprosy. c *25* Greek *Beezeboul* or *Beelzeboul* d *29* Greek *an assarion*

don't be afraid; you are worth more than many sparrows.[h]

7 →PG. 1073

32"Whoever acknowledges me before men,[i] I will also acknowledge him before my Father in heaven. 33But whoever disowns me before men, I will disown him before my Father in heaven.[j]

34"Do not suppose that I have come to bring peace to the earth. I did not come to bring peace, but a sword. 35For I have come to turn

" 'a man against his father,
a daughter against her mother,
a daughter-in-law against her mother-in-law[k]—
36 a man's enemies will be the members of his own household.'[a][l]

1 →PG. 1070

37"Anyone who loves his father or mother more than me is not worthy of me; anyone who loves his son or daughter more than me is not worthy of me;[m] 38and anyone who does not take his cross and follow me is not worthy of me.[n] 39Whoever finds his life will lose it, and whoever loses his life for my sake will find it.[o]

40"He who receives you receives me,[p] and he who receives me receives the one who sent me.[q] 41Anyone who receives a prophet because he is a prophet will receive a prophet's reward, and anyone who receives a righteous man because he is a righteous man will receive a righteous man's reward. 42And if anyone gives even a cup of cold water to one of these little ones because he is my disciple, I tell you the truth, he will certainly not lose his reward."[r]

Jesus and John the Baptist

›See Luke 7:18–35

11 After Jesus had finished instructing his twelve disciples,[s] he went on from there to teach and preach in the towns of Galilee.[b]

2When John heard in prison[t] what Christ was doing, he sent his disciples 3to ask him, "Are you the one who was to come,[u] or should we expect someone else?"

4Jesus replied, "Go back and report to John what you hear and see: 5The blind receive sight, the lame walk, those who have leprosy[c] are cured, the deaf hear, the dead are raised, and the good news is preached to the poor.[v] 6Blessed is the man who does not fall away on account of me."[w]

7As John's[x] disciples were leaving, Jesus began to speak to the crowd about John: "What did you go out into the desert to see? A reed swayed by the wind? 8If not, what did you go out to see? A man dressed in fine clothes? No, those who wear fine clothes are in kings' palaces. 9Then what did you go out to see? A prophet?[y] Yes, I tell you, and more than a prophet. 10This is the one about whom it is written:

" 'I will send my messenger ahead of you,
who will prepare your way before you.'[d][z]

11I tell you the truth: Among those born of women there has not risen anyone greater than John the Baptist; yet he who is least in the kingdom of heaven is greater than he. 12From the days of John the Baptist until now, the kingdom of heaven has been forcefully advancing, and forceful men lay hold of it. 13For all the Prophets and the Law prophesied until John. 14And if you are willing to accept it, he is the Elijah who was to come.[a] 15He who has ears, let him hear.[b]

16"To what can I compare this generation? They are like children sitting in the marketplaces and calling out to others:

17" 'We played the flute for you,
and you did not dance;
we sang a dirge,
and you did not mourn.'

18For John came neither eating[c] nor drinking,[d] and they say, 'He has a demon.' 19The Son of Man came eating and drinking, and they say, 'Here is a glutton and a drunkard, a friend of tax collectors and "sinners." '[e] But wisdom is proved right by her actions."

Woe on Unrepentant Cities

›See Luke 10:13–15

20Then Jesus began to denounce the cities in which most of his miracles had been performed, because they did not repent. 21"Woe to you, Korazin! Woe to you, Bethsaida![f] If the miracles that were performed in you had been performed in Tyre and Sidon,[g] they would have repented long ago in sackcloth and ashes.[h] 22But I tell you, it will be more bearable for Tyre and Sidon on the day of judgment than for you.[i] 23And you, Capernaum,[j] will you be lifted up to the skies? No, you will go down to the depths.[e][k] If the miracles that were performed in you had been performed in Sodom, it

10:31 [h]Mt 12:12
10:32 [i]Ro 10:9
10:33 [j]Mk 8:38; 2Ti 2:12
10:35 [k]ver 21
10:36 [l]Mic 7:6
10:37 [m]Lk 14:26
10:38 [n]Mt 16:24; Lk 14:27
10:39 [o]Lk 17:33; Jn 12:25
10:40 [p]Mt 18:5; Gal 4:14 [q]Lk 9:48; Jn 12:44; 13:20
10:42 [r]Mt 25:40; Mk 9:41; Heb 6:10
11:1 [s]Mt 7:28
11:2 [t]Mt 14:3
11:3 [u]Ps 118:26; Jn 11:27; Heb 10:37
11:5 [v]Isa 35:4-6; 61:1; Lk 4:18, 19
11:6 [w]Mt 13:21
11:7 [x]Mt 3:1
11:9 [y]Mt 21:26; Lk 1:76
11:10 [z]Mal 3:1; Mk 1:2
11:14 [a]Mal 4:5; Mt 17:10-13; Mk 9:11-13; Lk 1:17; Jn 1:21
11:15 [b]Mt 13:9,43; Mk 4:23; Lk 14:35; Rev 2:7
11:18 [c]Mt 3:4 [d]Lk 1:15
11:19 [e]Mt 9:11
11:21 [f]Mk 6:45; Lk 9:10; Jn 12:21 [g]Mt 15:21; Lk 6:17; Ac 12:20 [h]Jnh 3:5-9
11:22 [i]ver 24; Mt 10:15
11:23 [j]Mt 4:13 [k]Isa 14:13-15

[a]*36* Micah 7:6 [b]*1* Greek *in their towns*
[c]*5* The Greek word was used for various diseases affecting the skin—not necessarily leprosy. [d]*10* Mal. 3:1 [e]*23* Greek *Hades*

JOHN THE BAPTIST

A Man Who Put God First

John the Baptist was one of the most remarkable men who ever lived. His birth was a miracle, his life was devoted to service, and he died a martyr's death. Yet the most outstanding thing about John the Baptist may simply have been the way he submitted himself to God.

John was born long after his parents had given up hope of ever having a child since his mother "Elizabeth was barren, and they were well along in years" (Luke 1:7). God sent the angel Gabriel to John's father Zechariah to announce the news that they would have a son. Zechariah was afraid when he saw the angel, but Gabriel assured him that this long-awaited son would be a joy to his parents and a blessing to the people of Israel. "Many of the people of Israel will he bring back to the Lord their God," Gabriel said. "And he will go before the Lord . . . to make ready a people prepared for the Lord" (1:16, 17).

The angel's prophecy was fulfilled when "Elizabeth became pregnant" and "gave birth to a son" (1:24, 57). John grew strong and, as an adult, fulfilled the second half of the angel's prophecy by preaching a message of repentance to the people of Israel. He condemned the hypocrisy of the religious leaders and warned them to "produce fruit in keeping with repentance" (Matthew 3:8).

In this way, John's ministry prepared the people for the message of the Messiah, Jesus Christ. Some of the people who came to hear John began wondering if *he* might be the Messiah. But John told them, "I baptize you with water. But one more powerful than I will come, the thongs of whose sandals I am not worthy to untie. He will baptize you with the Holy Spirit and with fire" (Luke 3:16). Though many prophets in the Old Testament had pointed to the coming Messiah, John the Baptist had the unique privilege of personally introducing Christ to the world.

Relinquishing Himself to God

In the course of his ministry, John attracted many followers who recognized him as a prophet of God. But when Jesus began teaching and preaching, many of those people left John to follow Jesus. This concerned John's closest disciples. They worried that John was "losing out" to this other preacher. However, John knew his place in God's plan. He knew where his position was in relation to Jesus. He reassured his disciples and said, "He must become greater; I must become less" (John 3:30). With that statement, John demonstrated how completely he had relinquished his life to God. He sought nothing for himself—no wealth, no fame, no glory—but instead wanted only to fulfill his calling of preparing the hearts of men and women for the Lord's Messiah.

John didn't fully understand everything about his role, nor, apparently, did he fully comprehend the nature of Jesus' ministry. When Herod put John in prison for publicly condemning Herod's immorality, John sent a message to Jesus asking, "Are you the one who was to come, or should we expect someone else?" (Matthew 11:3). John seemed unsure of Jesus' public ministry, yet he was willing to accept whatever God had set in motion. He never hesitated to do what God asked of him, no matter what the consequences. Because of that, Jesus said, "I tell you the truth: Among those born of women there has not risen anyone greater than John the Baptist" (Matthew 11:11).

Jesus later told his disciples that "if anyone wants to be first, he must be the very last, and the servant of all" (Mark 9:35). He illustrated the servant's role beautifully when he washed the disciples feet and told them to do the same for one another (John 13:1–17). That's exactly the kind of self-denying service John the Baptist gave to God throughout his lifetime.

Relinquishing Ourselves to God

John's ministry was a one-time-in-history calling to prepare the way for the Messiah, the Savior, Jesus Christ. But the heart attitude that motivated John's service is a timeless example for all people. God is always looking for men who will say sincerely, "He must become greater; I must become less."

Is there any part of your life that you haven't relinquished to God and the authority of his Word? What about your marriage? Your family? Your career? Your time? Your finances? Your thoughts? Examine yourself prayerfully in each of these areas, asking the Holy Spirit to help you understand your heart and motives. Don't hesitate to relinquish whatever God asks of you, no matter what the consequences. May John's words to let Christ become greater than personal desires and goals become your testimony as well.

—Dr. Gene Getz

would have remained to this day. [24]But I tell you that it will be more bearable for Sodom on the day of judgment than for you."[l]

Rest for the Weary

›See Luke 10:21–22

[25]At that time Jesus said, "I praise you, Father,[m] Lord of heaven and earth, because you have hidden these things from the wise and learned, and revealed them to little children.[n] [26]Yes, Father, for this was your good pleasure.

[27]"All things have been committed to me[o] by my Father.[p] No one knows the Son except the Father, and no one knows the Father except the Son and those to whom the Son chooses to reveal him.[q]

[28]"Come to me,[r] all you who are weary and burdened, and I will give you rest. [29]Take my yoke upon you and learn from me,[s] for I am gentle and humble in heart, and you will find rest for your souls.[t] [30]For my yoke is easy and my burden is light."[u]

Lord of the Sabbath

›See Mark 2:23—3:6; Luke 6:1–11

12 At that time Jesus went through the grainfields on the Sabbath. His disciples were hungry and began to pick some heads of grain[v] and eat them. [2]When the Pharisees saw this, they said to him, "Look! Your disciples are doing what is unlawful on the Sabbath."[w]

[3]He answered, "Haven't you read what David did when he and his companions were hungry?[x] [4]He entered the house of God, and he and his companions ate the consecrated bread—which was not lawful for them to do, but only for the priests.[y] [5]Or haven't you read in the Law that on the Sabbath the priests in the temple desecrate the day[z] and yet are innocent? [6]I tell you that one[a] greater than the temple is here.[a] [7]If you had known what these words mean, 'I desire mercy, not sacrifice,'[b][b] you would not have condemned the innocent. [8]For the Son of Man[c] is Lord of the Sabbath."

[9]Going on from that place, he went into their synagogue, [10]and a man with a shriveled hand was there. Looking for a reason to accuse Jesus, they asked him, "Is it lawful to heal on the Sabbath?"[d]

[11]He said to them, "If any of you has a sheep and it falls into a pit on the Sabbath, will you not take hold of it and lift it out?[e] [12]How much more valuable is a man than a sheep![f] Therefore it is lawful to do good on th[e] Sabbath."

[13]Then he said to the man, "Stretc[h] out your hand." So he stretched it ou[t] and it was completely restored, just a[s] sound as the other. [14]But the Pharisee[s] went out and plotted how they migh[t] kill Jesus.[g]

God's Chosen Servant

[15]Aware of this, Jesus withdrew fro[m] that place. Many followed him, and h[e] healed all their sick,[h] [16]warning the[m] not to tell who he was.[i] [17]This was t[o] fulfill what was spoken through th[e] prophet Isaiah:

[18]"Here is my servant whom I have
chosen,
the one I love, in whom I
delight;[j]
I will put my Spirit on him,
and he will proclaim justice to
the nations.
[19]He will not quarrel or cry out;
no one will hear his voice in the
streets.
[20]A bruised reed he will not break,
and a smoldering wick he will
not snuff out,
till he leads justice to victory.
[21] In his name the nations will put
their hope."[c][k]

Jesus and Beelzebub

›See Mark 3:23–27; Luke 11:17–22

[22]Then they brought him a demon-possessed man who was blind an[d] mute, and Jesus healed him, so that h[e] could both talk and see.[l] [23]All th[e] people were astonished and sai[d], "Could this be the Son of David?"[m]

[24]But when the Pharisees heard thi[s] they said, "It is only by Beelzebub,[d] the prince of demons, that this fello[w] drives out demons."[o]

[25]Jesus knew their thoughts[p] an[d] said to them, "Every kingdom divide[d] against itself will be ruined, and ever[y] city or household divided against itse[lf] will not stand. [26]If Satan[q] drives ou[t] Satan, he is divided against himsel[f]. How then can his kingdom stan[d]? [27]And if I drive out demons by Beelze[bub], by whom do your people[r] dri[ve] them out? So then, they will be yo[ur] judges. [28]But if I drive out demons b[y] the Spirit of God, then the kingdom [of] God has come upon you.

[29]"Or again, how can anyone enter [a] strong man's house and carry off h[is] possessions unless he first ties up th[e]

a *6* Or *something*; also in verses 41 and 42
b *7* Hosea 6:6 **c** *21* Isaiah 42:1-4 **d** *24* Greek *Beezeboul* or *Beelzeboul*; also in verse 27

11:24 [l]Mt 10:15
11:25 [m]Lk 22:42; Jn 11:41 [n]1Co 1:26-29
11:27 [o]Mt 28:18 [p]Jn 3:35; 13:3; 17:2 [q]Jn 10:15
11:28 [r]Jn 7:37
11:29 [s]Jn 13:15; Php 2:5; 1Pe 2:21; 1Jn 2:6 [t]Jer 6:16
11:30 [u]1Jn 5:3
12:1 [v]Dt 23:25
12:2 [w]ver 10; Lk 13:14; 14:3; Jn 5:10; 7:23; 9:16
12:3 [x]1Sa 21:6
12:4 [y]Lev 24:5,9
12:5 [z]Nu 28:9,10; Jn 7:22,23
12:6 [a]ver 41,42
12:7 [b]Hos 6:6; Mic 6:6-8; Mt 9:13
12:8 [c]Mt 8:20
12:10 [d]ver 2; Lk 13:14; 14:3; Jn 9:16
12:11 [e]Lk 14:5
12:12 [f]Mt 10:31
12:14 [g]Mt 26:4; 27:1; Mk 3:6; Lk 6:11; Jn 5:18; 11:53
12:15 [h]Mt 4:23
12:16 [i]Mt 8:4
12:18 [j]Mt 3:17
12:21 [k]Isa 42:1-4
12:22 [l]Mt 4:24; 9:32-33
12:23 [m]Mt 9:27
12:24 [n]Mk 3:22 [o]Mt 9:34
12:25 [p]Mt 9:4
12:26 [q]Mt 4:10
12:27 [r]Ac 19:13

strong man? Then he can rob his house.

[30]"He who is not with me is against me, and he who does not gather with me scatters.[s] [31]And so I tell you, every sin and blasphemy will be forgiven men, but the blasphemy against the Spirit will not be forgiven.[t] [32]Anyone who speaks a word against the Son of Man will be forgiven, but anyone who speaks against the Holy Spirit will not be forgiven, either in this age[u] or in the age to come.[v]

3 →PG. 1071

[33]"Make a tree good and its fruit will be good, or make a tree bad and its fruit will be bad, for a tree is recognized by its fruit.[w] [34]You brood of vipers,[x] how can you who are evil say anything good? For out of the overflow of the heart the mouth speaks.[y] [35]The good man brings good things out of the good stored up in him, and the evil man brings evil things out of the evil stored up in him. [36]But I tell you that men will have to give account on the day of judgment for every careless word they have spoken. [37]For by your words you will be acquitted, and by your words you will be condemned."

The Sign of Jonah

›See Luke 11:29–32

[38]Then some of the Pharisees and teachers of the law said to him, "Teacher, we want to see a miraculous sign from you."[z]

[39]He answered, "A wicked and adulterous generation asks for a miraculous sign! But none will be given it except the sign of the prophet Jonah.[a] [40]For as Jonah was three days and three nights in the belly of a huge fish,[b] so the Son of Man[c] will be three days and three nights in the heart of the earth.[d] [41]The men of Nineveh[e] will stand up at the judgment with this generation and condemn it; for they repented at the preaching of Jonah,[f] and now one**[a]** greater than Jonah is here. [42]The Queen of the South will rise at the judgment with this generation and condemn it; for she came[g] from the ends of the earth to listen to Solomon's wisdom, and now one greater than Solomon is here.

[43]"When an evil**[b]** spirit comes out of a man, it goes through arid places seeking rest and does not find it. [44]Then it says, 'I will return to the house I left.' When it arrives, it finds the house unoccupied, swept clean and put in order. [45]Then it goes and takes with it seven other spirits more wicked than itself, and they go in and live there. And the final condition of that man is worse than the first.[h] That is how it will be with this wicked generation."

Jesus' Mother and Brothers

›See Mark 3:31–35; Luke 8:19–21

6 →PG. 1072

[46]While Jesus was still talking to the crowd, his mother[i] and brothers[j] stood outside, wanting to speak to him. [47]Someone told him, "Your mother and brothers are standing outside, wanting to speak to you."**[c]**

[48]He replied to him, "Who is my mother, and who are my brothers?" [49]Pointing to his disciples, he said, "Here are my mother and my brothers. [50]For whoever does the will of my Father in heaven[k] is my brother and sister and mother."

The Parable of the Sower

›See Mark 4:1–20; Luke 8:4–15

13 That same day Jesus went out of the house[l] and sat by the lake. [2]Such large crowds gathered around him that he got into a boat[m] and sat in it, while all the people stood on the shore. [3]Then he told them many things in parables, saying: "A farmer went out to sow his seed. [4]As he was scattering the seed, some fell along the path, and the birds came and ate it up. [5]Some fell on rocky places, where it did not have much soil. It sprang up quickly, because the soil was shallow. [6]But when the sun came up, the plants were scorched, and they withered because they had no root. [7]Other seed fell among thorns, which grew up and choked the plants. [8]Still other seed fell on good soil, where it produced a crop—a hundred,[n] sixty or thirty times what was sown. [9]He who has ears, let him hear."[o]

[10]The disciples came to him and asked, "Why do you speak to the people in parables?"

[11]He replied, "The knowledge of the secrets of the kingdom of heaven has been given to you,[p] but not to them. [12]Whoever has will be given more, and he will have an abundance. Whoever does not have, even what he has will be taken from him.[q] [13]This is why I speak to them in parables:

"Though seeing, they do not see;
  though hearing, they do not hear
    or understand.[r]

[14]In them is fulfilled the prophecy of Isaiah:

12:30 [s]Mk 9:40; Lk 11:23
12:31 [t]Mk 3:28,29; Lk 12:10
12:32 [u]Tit 2:12 [v]Mk 10:30; Lk 20:34,35; Eph 1:21; Heb 6:5
12:33 [w]Mt 7:16,17; Lk 6:43,44
12:34 [x]Mt 3:7; 23:33 [y]Mt 15:18; Lk 6:45
12:38 [z]Mt 16:1; Mk 8:11,12; Lk 11:16; Jn 2:18; 6:30; 1Co 1:22
12:39 [a]Mt 16:4; Lk 11:29
12:40 [b]Jnh 1:17 [c]Mt 8:20 [d]Mt 16:21
12:41 [e]Jnh 1:2 [f]Jnh 3:5
12:42 [g]1Ki 10:1; 2Ch 9:1
12:45 [h]2Pe 2:20
12:46 [i]Mt 1:18; 2:11, 13,14,20; Lk 1:43; 2:33, 34,48,51; Jn 2:1,5; 19:25, 26 [j]Mt 13:55; Jn 2:12; 7:3,5; Ac 1:14; 1Co 9:5; Gal 1:19
12:50 [k]Jn 15:14
13:1 [l]ver 36; Mt 9:28
13:2 [m]Lk 5:3
13:8 [n]Ge 26:12
13:9 [o]Mt 11:15
13:11 [p]Mt 11:25; 16:17; 19:11; Jn 6:65; 1Co 2:10,14; Col 1:27; 1Jn 2:20,27
13:12 [q]Mt 25:29; Lk 19:26
13:13 [r]Dt 29:4; Jer 5:21; Eze 12:2

a *41* Or *something;* also in verse 42 **b** *43* Greek *unclean* **c** *47* Some manuscripts do not have verse 47.

" 'You will be ever hearing but
never understanding;
you will be ever seeing but never
perceiving.
15 For this people's heart has become
calloused;
they hardly hear with their ears,
and they have closed their eyes.
Otherwise they might see with their
eyes,
hear with their ears,
understand with their hearts
and turn, and I would heal
them.'[a][s]

16 But blessed are your eyes because
they see, and your ears because they
hear.[t] 17 For I tell you the truth, many
prophets and righteous men longed to
see what you see[u] but did not see it,
and to hear what you hear but did not
hear it.

18 "Listen then to what the parable
of the sower means: 19 When anyone
hears the message about the kingdom[v] and does not understand it, the
evil one[w] comes and snatches away
what was sown in his heart. This is the
seed sown along the path. 20 The one
who received the seed that fell on rocky
places is the man who hears the word
and at once receives it with joy. 21 But
since he has no root, he lasts only a
short time. When trouble or persecution comes because of the word, he
quickly falls away.[x] 22 The one who received the seed that fell among the
thorns is the man who hears the word,
but the worries of this life and the deceitfulness of wealth[y] choke it, making it unfruitful. 23 But the one who received the seed that fell on good soil is
the man who hears the word and understands it. He produces a crop, yielding a hundred, sixty or thirty times
what was sown."[z]

The Parable of the Weeds

24 Jesus told them another parable:
"The kingdom of heaven is like[a] a
man who sowed good seed in his field.
25 But while everyone was sleeping, his
enemy came and sowed weeds among
the wheat, and went away. 26 When the
wheat sprouted and formed heads,
then the weeds also appeared.

27 "The owner's servants came to
him and said, 'Sir, didn't you sow good
seed in your field? Where then did the
weeds come from?'

28 " 'An enemy did this,' he replied.

"The servants asked him, 'Do you
want us to go and pull them up?'

29 " 'No,' he answered, 'because
while you are pulling the weeds, you
may root up the wheat with them. 30 Let
both grow together until the harvest. At
that time I will tell the harvesters: First
collect the weeds and tie them in bundles to be burned; then gather the
wheat and bring it into my barn.' "[b]

The Parables of the Mustard Seed and the Yeast

›See Mark 4:30–32; Luke 13:18–21

31 He told them another parable:
"The kingdom of heaven is like[c] a
mustard seed,[d] which a man took and
planted in his field. 32 Though it is the
smallest of all your seeds, yet when
it grows, it is the largest of garden
plants and becomes a tree, so that the
birds of the air come and perch in its
branches."[e]

33 He told them still another parable:
"The kingdom of heaven is like[f] yeast
that a woman took and mixed into

[a] 15 Isaiah 6:9,10

13:15 [s] Isa 6:9,10; Jn 12:40; Ac 28:26,27; Ro 11:8
13:16 [t] Mt 16:17
13:17 [u] Jn 8:56; Heb 11:13; 1Pe 1:10-12
13:19 [v] Mt 4:23 [w] Mt 5:37
13:21 [x] Mt 11:6
13:22 [y] Mt 19:23; 1Ti 6:9,10,17
13:23 [z] ver 8
13:24 [a] ver 31,33,45, 47; Mt 18:23; 20:1; 22:2; 25:1; Mk 4:26, 30
13:30 [b] Mt 3:12
13:31 [c] ver 24 [d] Mt 17:20; Lk 17:6
13:32 [e] Ps 104:12; Eze 17:23; 31:6; Da 4:12
13:33 [f] ver 24

13:1–23

PROMISE 1

ETERNAL INVESTMENT RETURNS—GUARANTEED

In this story, Jesus told the crowd about an investment opportunity that would produce a guaranteed profit of up to 100 percent. How can you get in on this? The deal is simple. If you'll just prepare the soil of your heart so that the Word of God will find fertile ground, it will yield a massive spiritual harvest in your life.

How do you prepare the soil of your heart for the seed? By following the example of a farmer. He has to set aside time to plow, weed, fertilize and water the soil. A farmer knows that good soil doesn't just appear out of nowhere. It requires planning, nurturing, cultivating—and a good measure of effort.

The same is true in the spiritual realm. A follower of Jesus Christ must set aside a daily time to examine his heart and weed out every thought and attitude that will choke the effectiveness of God's Word. He must cultivate his heart through prayer and water it by meditating on God's purposes for his life. When the soil is prepared in this way, the seed will be ready to germinate; that's when the Scriptures will take root in the believer's life and begin to produce an abundant harvest.

Do your best to set aside time every day for prayer and Scripture reading. And remember, it will be time well invested. In fact, it will bring a huge spiritual profit—guaranteed!

For the next Promise 1 reading go to page 1082.

a large amount[a] of flour[g] until it
worked all through the dough."[h]
34 Jesus spoke all these things to the
crowd in parables; he did not say anything to them without using a parable.[i] 35 So was fulfilled what was spoken through the prophet:

"I will open my mouth in parables,
I will utter things hidden since
the creation of the
world."[b][j]

The Parable of the Weeds Explained

36 Then he left the crowd and went
into the house. His disciples came to
him and said, "Explain to us the parable[k] of the weeds in the field."
37 He answered, "The one who
sowed the good seed is the Son of
Man.[l] 38 The field is the world, and the
good seed stands for the sons of the
kingdom. The weeds are the sons of
the evil one,[m] 39 and the enemy who
sows them is the devil. The harvest[n] is
the end of the age,[o] and the harvesters
are angels.[p]
40 "As the weeds are pulled up and
burned in the fire, so it will be at the
end of the age. 41 The Son of Man[q] will
send out his angels,[r] and they will
weed out of his kingdom everything
that causes sin and all who do evil.
42 They will throw them into the fiery
furnace, where there will be weeping
and gnashing of teeth.[s] 43 Then the
righteous will shine like the sun[t] in
the kingdom of their Father. He who
has ears, let him hear.[u]

The Parables of the Hidden Treasure and the Pearl

44 "The kingdom of heaven is like[v]
treasure hidden in a field. When a man
found it, he hid it again, and then in
his joy went and sold all he had and
bought that field.[w]
45 "Again, the kingdom of heaven is
like[x] a merchant looking for fine
pearls. 46 When he found one of great
value, he went away and sold everything he had and bought it.

The Parable of the Net

47 "Once again, the kingdom of heav-
en is like[y] a net that was let down into
the lake and caught all kinds[z] of fish.
48 When it was full, the fishermen
pulled it up on the shore. Then they sat
down and collected the good fish in
baskets, but threw the bad away. 49 This
is how it will be at the end of the age.
The angels will come and separate the
wicked from the righteous[a] 50 and
throw them into the fiery furnace,
where there will be weeping and
gnashing of teeth.[b]
51 "Have you understood all these
things?" Jesus asked.
"Yes," they replied.
52 He said to them, "Therefore every
teacher of the law who has been instructed about the kingdom of heaven
is like the owner of a house who brings
out of his storeroom new treasures as
well as old."

A Prophet Without Honor

›See Mark 6:1–6

53 When Jesus had finished these
parables,[c] he moved on from there.
54 Coming to his hometown, he began
teaching the people in their synagogue,[d] and they were amazed.[e]
"Where did this man get this wisdom
and these miraculous powers?" they
asked. 55 "Isn't this the carpenter's
son?[f] Isn't his mother's[g] name Mary,
and aren't his brothers James, Joseph,
Simon and Judas? 56 Aren't all his sisters with us? Where then did this man
get all these things?" 57 And they took
offense[h] at him.
But Jesus said to them, "Only in his
hometown and in his own house is a
prophet without honor."[i]
58 And he did not do many miracles
there because of their lack of faith.

John the Baptist Beheaded

›See Mark 6:14–29

14 At that time Herod[j] the tetrarch
heard the reports about Jesus,[k]
2 and he said to his attendants, "This is
John the Baptist;[l] he has risen from
the dead! That is why miraculous powers are at work in him."
3 Now Herod had arrested John and
bound him and put him in prison[m]
because of Herodias, his brother Philip's wife,[n] 4 for John had been saying
to him: "It is not lawful for you to have
her."[o] 5 Herod wanted to kill John, but
he was afraid of the people, because
they considered him a prophet.[p]
6 On Herod's birthday the daughter
of Herodias danced for them and
pleased Herod so much 7 that he promised with an oath to give her whatever
she asked. 8 Prompted by her mother,
she said, "Give me here on a platter the
head of John the Baptist." 9 The king
was distressed, but because of his
oaths and his dinner guests, he ordered
that her request be granted 10 and had
John beheaded[q] in the prison. 11 His
head was brought in on a platter and

13:33 [g]Ge 18:6 [h]Gal 5:9
13:34 [i]Mk 4:33; Jn 16:25
13:35 [j]Ps 78:2; Ro 16:25,26; 1Co 2:7; Eph 3:9; Col 1:26
13:36 [k]Mt 15:15
13:37 [l]Mt 8:20
13:38 [m]Jn 8:44,45; 1Jn 3:10
13:39 [n]Joel 3:13 [o]Mt 24:3; 28:20 [p]Rev 14:15
13:41 [q]Mt 8:20 [r]Mt 24:31
13:42 [s]ver 50; Mt 8:12
13:43 [t]Da 12:3 [u]Mt 11:15
13:44 [v]ver 24 [w]Isa 55:1; Php 3:7,8
13:45 [x]ver 24
13:47 [y]ver 24 [z]Mt 22:10
13:49 [a]Mt 25:32
13:50 [b]Mt 8:12
13:53 [c]Mt 7:28
13:54 [d]Mt 4:23 [e]Mt 7:28
13:55 [f]Lk 3:23; Jn 6:42 [g]Mt 12:46
13:57 [h]Jn 6:61 [i]Lk 4:24; Jn 4:44
14:1 [j]Mk 8:15; Lk 3:1,19; 13:31; 23:7,8; Ac 4:27; 12:1 [k]Lk 9:7-9
14:2 [l]Mt 3:1
14:3 [m]Mt 4:12; 11:2 [n]Lk 3:19,20
14:4 [o]Lev 18:16; 20:21
14:5 [p]Mt 11:9
14:10 [q]Mt 17:12

[a] *33* Greek *three satas* (probably about 1/2 bushel or 22 liters) [b] *35* Psalm 78:2

given to the girl, who carried it to her mother. 12John's disciples came and took his body and buried it.[r] Then they went and told Jesus.

Jesus Feeds the Five Thousand

›See Mark 6:32–44; Luke 9:10–17; John 6:1–13

13When Jesus heard what had happened, he withdrew by boat privately to a solitary place. Hearing of this, the crowds followed him on foot from the towns. 14When Jesus landed and saw a large crowd, he had compassion on them[s] and healed their sick.[t]

15As evening approached, the disciples came to him and said, "This is a remote place, and it's already getting late. Send the crowds away, so they can go to the villages and buy themselves some food."

16Jesus replied, "They do not need to go away. You give them something to eat."

17"We have here only five loaves[u] of bread and two fish," they answered.

18"Bring them here to me," he said. 19And he directed the people to sit down on the grass. Taking the five loaves and the two fish and looking up to heaven, he gave thanks and broke the loaves.[v] Then he gave them to the disciples, and the disciples gave them to the people. 20They all ate and were satisfied, and the disciples picked up twelve basketfuls of broken pieces that were left over. 21The number of those who ate was about five thousand men, besides women and children.

Jesus Walks on the Water

›See Mark 6:45–51; John 6:15–21

22Immediately Jesus made the disciples get into the boat and go on ahead of him to the other side, while he dismissed the crowd. 23After he had dismissed them, he went up on a mountainside by himself to pray.[w] When evening came, he was there alone, 24but the boat was already a considerable distance[a] from land, buffeted by the waves because the wind was against it.

25During the fourth watch of the night Jesus went out to them, walking on the lake. 26When the disciples saw him walking on the lake, they were terrified. "It's a ghost,"[x] they said, and cried out in fear.

27But Jesus immediately said to them: "Take courage![y] It is I. Don't be afraid."[z]

28"Lord, if it's you," Peter replied, "tell me to come to you on the water."

29"Come," he said.

Then Peter got down out of the boat, walked on the water and came toward Jesus. 30But when he saw the wind, he was afraid and, beginning to sink, cried out, "Lord, save me!"

31Immediately Jesus reached out his hand and caught him. "You of little faith,"[a] he said, "why did you doubt?"

32And when they climbed into the boat, the wind died down. 33Then those who were in the boat worshiped him, saying, "Truly you are the Son of God."[b]

34When they had crossed over, they landed at Gennesaret. 35And when the men of that place recognized Jesus, they sent word to all the surrounding country. People brought all their sick to him 36and begged him to let the sick just touch the edge of his cloak,[c] and all who touched him were healed.

Clean and Unclean

›See Mark 7:1–23

15 Then some Pharisees and teachers of the law came to Jesus from Jerusalem and asked, 2"Why do your disciples break the tradition of the elders? They don't wash their hands before they eat!"[d]

3Jesus replied, "And why do you break the command of God for the sake of your tradition? 4For God said, 'Honor your father and mother'[b][e] and 'Anyone who curses his father or mother must be put to death.'[c][f] 5But you say that if a man says to his father or mother, 'Whatever help you might otherwise have received from me is a gift devoted to God,' 6he is not to 'honor his father[d]' with it. Thus you nullify the word of God for the sake of your tradition. 7You hypocrites! Isaiah was right when he prophesied about you:

8" 'These people honor me with
their lips,
but their hearts are far from me.
9They worship me in vain;
their teachings are but rules
taught by men.[g]'[e][h]"

10Jesus called the crowd to him and said, "Listen and understand. 11What goes into a man's mouth does not make him 'unclean,'[i] but what comes out of his mouth, that is what makes him 'unclean.' "[j]

12Then the disciples came to him and asked, "Do you know that the Pharisees were offended when they heard this?"

13He replied, "Every plant that my

14:12 [r]Ac 8:2
14:14 [s]Mt 9:36 [t]Mt 4:23
14:17 [u]Mt 16:9
14:19 [v]1Sa 9:13; Mt 26:26; Mk 8:6; Lk 24:30; Ac 2:42; 27:35; 1Ti 4:4
14:23 [w]Lk 3:21
14:26 [x]Lk 24:37
14:27 [y]Mt 9:2; Ac 23:11 [z]Da 10:12; Mt 17:7; 28:10; Lk 1:13,30; 2:10; Ac 18:9; 23:11; Rev 1:17
14:31 [a]Mt 6:30
14:33 [b]Ps 2:7; Mt 4:3
14:36 [c]Mt 9:20
15:2 [d]Lk 11:38
15:4 [e]Ex 20:12; Dt 5:16; Eph 6:2 [f]Ex 21:17; Lev 20:9
15:9 [g]Col 2:20-22 [h]Isa 29:13; Mal 2:2
15:11 [i]Ac 10:14,15 [j]ver 18

a 24 Greek *many stadia* b 4 Exodus 20:12; Deut. 5:16 c 4 Exodus 21:17; Lev. 20:9
d 6 Some manuscripts *father or his mother*
e 9 Isaiah 29:13

heavenly Father has not planted[k] will
be pulled up by the roots. 14 Leave
them; they are blind guides.[a][l] If a
blind man leads a blind man, both will
fall into a pit."[m]
15 Peter said, "Explain the parable
to us."[n]
16 "Are you still so dull?"[o] Jesus
asked them. 17 "Don't you see that
whatever enters the mouth goes into
the stomach and then out of the body?
18 But the things that come out of the
mouth come from the heart,[p] and
these make a man 'unclean.' 19 For out
of the heart come evil thoughts, murder, adultery, sexual immorality, theft,
false testimony, slander.[q] 20 These are
what make a man 'unclean';[r] but eating with unwashed hands does not
make him 'unclean.' "

The Faith of the Canaanite Woman

›See Mark 7:24–30

21 Leaving that place, Jesus withdrew
to the region of Tyre and Sidon.[s] 22 A
Canaanite woman from that vicinity
came to him, crying out, "Lord, Son
of David,[t] have mercy on me! My
daughter is suffering terribly from
demon-possession."[u]
23 Jesus did not answer a word. So his
disciples came to him and urged him,
"Send her away, for she keeps crying
out after us."
24 He answered, "I was sent only to
the lost sheep of Israel."[v]
25 The woman came and knelt before
him.[w] "Lord, help me!" she said.
26 He replied, "It is not right to take
the children's bread and toss it to their
dogs."
27 "Yes, Lord," she said, "but even the
dogs eat the crumbs that fall from their
masters' table."
28 Then Jesus answered, "Woman,
you have great faith![x] Your request is
granted." And her daughter was healed
from that very hour.

Jesus Feeds the Four Thousand

›See Mark 8:1–10

29 Jesus left there and went along the
Sea of Galilee. Then he went up on a
mountainside and sat down. 30 Great
crowds came to him, bringing the
lame, the blind, the crippled, the mute
and many others, and laid them at his
feet; and he healed them.[y] 31 The people were amazed when they saw the
mute speaking, the crippled made well,
the lame walking and the blind seeing.
And they praised the God of Israel.[z]
32 Jesus called his disciples to him
and said, "I have compassion for these
people;[a] they have already been with
me three days and have nothing to eat.
I do not want to send them away hungry, or they may collapse on the way."
33 His disciples answered, "Where
could we get enough bread in this remote place to feed such a crowd?"
34 "How many loaves do you have?"
Jesus asked.
"Seven," they replied, "and a few
small fish."
35 He told the crowd to sit down on
the ground. 36 Then he took the seven
loaves and the fish, and when he had
given thanks, he broke them[b] and
gave them to the disciples, and they in
turn to the people. 37 They all ate and
were satisfied. Afterward the disciples
picked up seven basketfuls of broken
pieces that were left over.[c] 38 The
number of those who ate was four
thousand, besides women and children. 39 After Jesus had sent the crowd
away, he got into the boat and went to
the vicinity of Magadan.

The Demand for a Sign

›See Mark 8:11–21

16 The Pharisees and Sadducees[d]
came to Jesus and tested him by
asking him to show them a sign from
heaven.[e]
2 He replied,[b] "When evening comes,
you say, 'It will be fair weather, for
the sky is red,' 3 and in the morning,
'Today it will be stormy, for the sky is
red and overcast.' You know how to
interpret the appearance of the sky,
but you cannot interpret the signs of
the times.[f] 4 A wicked and adulterous
generation looks for a miraculous sign,
but none will be given it except the sign
of Jonah."[g] Jesus then left them and
went away.

The Yeast of the Pharisees and Sadducees

5 When they went across the lake, the
disciples forgot to take bread. 6 "Be
careful," Jesus said to them. "Be on
your guard against the yeast of the
Pharisees and Sadducees."[h]
7 They discussed this among themselves and said, "It is because we didn't
bring any bread."
8 Aware of their discussion, Jesus
asked, "You of little faith,[i] why are
you talking among yourselves about
having no bread? 9 Do you still not understand? Don't you remember the five
loaves for the five thousand, and how
many basketfuls you gathered?[j] 10 Or
the seven loaves for the four thousand,
and how many basketfuls you gath-

15:13 k Isa 60:21; 61:3; Jn 15:2
15:14 l Mt 23:16,24; Ro 2:19 m Lk 6:39
15:15 n Mt 13:36
15:16 o Mt 16:9
15:18 p Mt 12:34; Lk 6:45; Jas 3:6
15:19 q Gal 5:19-21
15:20 r Ro 14:14
15:21 s Mt 11:21
15:22 t Mt 9:27 u Mt 4:24
15:24 v Mt 10:6,23; Ro 15:8
15:25 w Mt 8:2
15:28 x Mt 9:22
15:30 y Mt 4:23
15:31 z Mt 9:8
15:32 a Mt 9:36
15:36 b Mt 14:19
15:37 c Mt 16:10
16:1 d Ac 4:1 e Mt 12:38
16:3 f Lk 12:54-56
16:4 g Mt 12:39
16:6 h Lk 12:1
16:8 i Mt 6:30
16:9 j Mt 14:17-21

a 14 Some manuscripts *guides of the blind*
b 2 Some early manuscripts do not have the rest of verse 2 and all of verse 3.

ered?[k] 11How is it you don't understand that I was not talking to you
about bread? But be on your guard
against the yeast of the Pharisees and
Sadducees." 12Then they understood
that he was not telling them to guard
against the yeast used in bread, but
against the teaching of the Pharisees
and Sadducees.[l]

Peter's Confession of Christ

›See Mark 8:27–29; Luke 9:18–20

13When Jesus came to the region of
Caesarea Philippi, he asked his disciples, "Who do people say the Son of
Man is?"
14They replied, "Some say John the
Baptist;[m] others say Elijah; and still
others, Jeremiah or one of the prophets."[n]
15"But what about you?" he asked.
"Who do you say I am?"
16Simon Peter answered, "You are
the Christ,[a] the Son of the living
God."[o]
17Jesus replied, "Blessed are you, Simon son of Jonah, for this was not revealed to you by man,[p] but by my Father in heaven. 18And I tell you that you
are Peter,[b][q] and on this rock I will
build my church,[r] and the gates of
Hades[c] will not overcome it.[d] 19I will
give you the keys[s] of the kingdom of
heaven; whatever you bind on earth
will be[e] bound in heaven, and whatever you loose on earth will be[e] loosed
in heaven."[t] 20Then he warned his
disciples not to tell anyone[u] that he
was the Christ.

Jesus Predicts His Death

›See Mark 8:31—9:1; Luke 9:22–27

21From that time on Jesus began to
explain to his disciples that he must go
to Jerusalem and suffer many things[v]
at the hands of the elders, chief priests
and teachers of the law, and that he
must be killed and on the third day[w]
be raised to life.[x]
22Peter took him aside and began to
rebuke him. "Never, Lord!" he said.
"This shall never happen to you!"
23Jesus turned and said to Peter,
"Get behind me, Satan![y] You are a
stumbling block to me; you do not
have in mind the things of God, but the
things of men."

1 →PG. 1071

24Then Jesus said to his disciples, "If
anyone would come after me, he must
deny himself and take up his cross and
follow me.[z] 25For whoever wants to
save his life[f] will lose it, but whoever
loses his life for me will find it.[a]
26What good will it be for a man if he
gains the whole world, yet forfeits his
soul? Or what can a man give in exchange for his soul? 27For the Son of
Man[b] is going to come[c] in his Father's glory with his angels, and then
he will reward each person according
to what he has done.[d] 28I tell you the
truth, some who are standing here will
not taste death before they see the Son
of Man coming in his kingdom."

The Transfiguration

›See Mark 9:2–13; Luke 9:28–36

17 After six days Jesus took with him
Peter, James and John the brother
of James, and led them up a high
mountain by themselves. 2There he
was transfigured before them. His face
shone like the sun, and his clothes became as white as the light. 3Just then
there appeared before them Moses and
Elijah, talking with Jesus.
4Peter said to Jesus, "Lord, it is good
for us to be here. If you wish, I will put
up three shelters—one for you, one for
Moses and one for Elijah."
5While he was still speaking, a bright
cloud enveloped them, and a voice
from the cloud said, "This is my Son,
whom I love; with him I am well
pleased.[e] Listen to him!"[f]
6When the disciples heard this, they
fell facedown to the ground, terrified.
7But Jesus came and touched them.
"Get up," he said. "Don't be afraid."[g]
8When they looked up, they saw no one
except Jesus.
9As they were coming down the
mountain, Jesus instructed them,
"Don't tell anyone[h] what you have
seen, until the Son of Man[i] has been
raised from the dead."[j]
10The disciples asked him, "Why
then do the teachers of the law say that
Elijah must come first?"
11Jesus replied, "To be sure, Elijah
comes and will restore all things.[k]
12But I tell you, Elijah has already
come,[l] and they did not recognize
him, but have done to him everything
they wished.[m] In the same way the Son
of Man is going to suffer[n] at their
hands." 13Then the disciples understood that he was talking to them
about John the Baptist.

The Healing of a Boy With a Demon

›See Mark 9:14–28; Luke 9:37–42

14When they came to the crowd, a
man approached Jesus and knelt before him. 15"Lord, have mercy on my

16:10 [k]Mt 15:34-38
16:12 [l]Ac 4:1
16:14 [m]Mt 3:1; 14:2 [n]Mk 6:15; Jn 1:21
16:16 [o]Mt 4:3; Ps 42:2; Jn 11:27; Ac 14:15; 2Co 6:16; 1Th 1:9; 1Ti 3:15; Heb 10:31; 12:22
16:17 [p]1Co 15:50; Gal 1:16; Eph 6:12; Heb 2:14
16:18 [q]Jn 1:42 [r]Eph 2:20
16:19 [s]Isa 22:22; Rev 3:7 [t]Mt 18:18; Jn 20:23
16:20 [u]Mk 8:30
16:21 [v]Mk 10:34; Lk 17:25 [w]Jn 2:19 [x]Mt 17:22,23; 27:63; Mk 9:31; Lk 9:22; 18:31-33; 24:6,7
16:23 [y]Mt 4:10
16:24 [z]Mt 10:38; Lk 14:27
16:25 [a]Jn 12:25
16:27 [b]Mt 8:20 [c]Ac 1:11 [d]Job 34:11; Ps 62:12; Jer 17:10; Ro 2:6; 2Co 5:10; Rev 22:12
17:5 [e]Mt 3:17; 2Pe 1:17 [f]Ac 3:22,23
17:7 [g]Mt 14:27
17:9 [h]Mk 8:30 [i]Mt 8:20 [j]Mt 16:21
17:11 [k]Mal 4:6; Lk 1:16,17
17:12 [l]Mt 11:14 [m]Mt 14:3,10 [n]Mt 16:21

a *16* Or *Messiah*; also in verse 20 b *18* *Peter* means *rock.* c *18* Or *hell* d *18* Or *not prove stronger than it* e *19* Or *have been*
f *25* The Greek word means either *life* or *soul*; also in verse 26.

son," he said. "He has seizures[o] and is suffering greatly. He often falls into the fire or into the water. 16I brought him to your disciples, but they could not heal him."

17"O unbelieving and perverse generation," Jesus replied, "how long shall I stay with you? How long shall I put up with you? Bring the boy here to me." 18Jesus rebuked the demon, and it came out of the boy, and he was healed from that moment.

19Then the disciples came to Jesus in private and asked, "Why couldn't we drive it out?"

1 →PG. 1071

20He replied, "Because you have so little faith. I tell you the truth, if you have faith[p] as small as a mustard seed,[q] you can say to this mountain, 'Move from here to there' and it will move.[r] Nothing will be impossible for you.[a]"

22When they came together in Galilee, he said to them, "The Son of Man[s] is going to be betrayed into the hands of men. 23They will kill him,[t] and on the third day[u] he will be raised to life."[v] And the disciples were filled with grief.

The Temple Tax

3 →PG. 1071

24After Jesus and his disciples arrived in Capernaum, the collectors of the two-drachma tax[w] came to Peter and asked, "Doesn't your teacher pay the temple tax[b]?"

25"Yes, he does," he replied.

When Peter came into the house, Jesus was the first to speak. "What do you think, Simon?" he asked. "From whom do the kings of the earth collect duty and taxes[x]—from their own sons or from others?"

26"From others," Peter answered.

"Then the sons are exempt," Jesus said to him. 27"But so that we may not offend[y] them, go to the lake and throw out your line. Take the first fish you catch; open its mouth and you will find a four-drachma coin. Take it and give it to them for my tax and yours."

The Greatest in the Kingdom of Heaven

›See Mark 9:33–37; Luke 9:46–48

18 At that time the disciples came to Jesus and asked, "Who is the greatest in the kingdom of heaven?"

4 →PG. 1071

2He called a little child and had him stand among them. 3And he said: "I tell you the truth, unless you change and become like little children,[z] you will never enter the kingdom of heaven.[a] 4Therefore, whoever humbles himself like this child is the greatest in the kingdom of heaven.[b]

17:15 [o]Mt 4:24 **17:20** [p]Mt 21:21 [q]Mt 13:31; Mk 11:23; Lk 17:6 [r]1Co 13:2 **17:22** [s]Mt 8:20 **17:23** [t]Ac 2:23; 3:13 [u]Mt 16:21 [v]Mt 16:21 **17:24** [w]Ex 30:13 **17:25** [x]Mt 22:17-21; Ro 13:7 **17:27** [y]Jn 6:61 **18:3** [z]Mt 19:14; 1Pe 2:2 [a]Mt 3:2 **18:4** [b]Mk 9:35

18:5 [c]Mt 10:40 **18:6** [d]Mt 5:29 [e]Mk 9:42; Lk 17:2 **18:7** [f]Lk 17:1 **18:8** [g]Mt 5:29; Mk 9:43,45 **18:9** [h]Mt 5:29 [i]Mt 5:22 **18:10** [j]Ge 48:16; Ps 34:7; Ac 12:11,15; Heb 1:14 **18:15** [k]Lev 19:17; Lk 17:3; Gal 6:1; Jas 5:19,20 **18:16** [l]Nu 35:30; Dt 17:6; 19:15; Jn 8:17; 2Co 13:1; 1Ti 5:19; Heb 10:28 **18:17** [m]1Co 6:1-6 [n]Ro 16:17; 2Th 3:6,14 **18:18** [o]Mt 16:19; Jn 20:23

5"And whoever welcomes a little child like this in my name welcomes me.[c] 6But if anyone causes one of these little ones who believe in me to sin,[d] it would be better for him to have a large millstone hung around his neck and to be drowned in the depths of the sea.[e]

7"Woe to the world because of the things that cause people to sin! Such things must come, but woe to the man through whom they come![f] 8If your hand or your foot causes you to sin,[g] cut it off and throw it away. It is better for you to enter life maimed or crippled than to have two hands or two feet and be thrown into eternal fire. 9And if your eye causes you to sin,[h] gouge it out and throw it away. It is better for you to enter life with one eye than to have two eyes and be thrown into the fire of hell.[i]

3 →PG. 1080

The Parable of the Lost Sheep

›See Luke 15:4–7

10"See that you do not look down on one of these little ones. For I tell you that their angels[j] in heaven always see the face of my Father in heaven.[c]

4 →PG. 1072

12"What do you think? If a man owns a hundred sheep, and one of them wanders away, will he not leave the ninety-nine on the hills and go to look for the one that wandered off? 13And if he finds it, I tell you the truth, he is happier about that one sheep than about the ninety-nine that did not wander off. 14In the same way your Father in heaven is not willing that any of these little ones should be lost.

A Brother Who Sins Against You

15"If your brother sins against you,[d] go and show him his fault,[k] just between the two of you. If he listens to you, you have won your brother over.

2 →PG. 1082

16But if he will not listen, take one or two others along, so that 'every matter may be established by the testimony of two or three witnesses.'[e][l] 17If he refuses to listen to them, tell it to the church;[m] and if he refuses to listen even to the church, treat him as you would a pagan or a tax collector.[n]

18"I tell you the truth, whatever you bind on earth will be[f] bound in heaven, and whatever you loose on earth will be[f] loosed in heaven.[o]

19"Again, I tell you that if two of you

[a] *20* Some manuscripts *you. 21But this kind does not go out except by prayer and fasting.*
[b] *24* Greek *the two drachmas*
[c] *10* Some manuscripts *heaven. 11The Son of Man came to save what was lost.*
[d] *15* Some manuscripts do not have *against you.*
[e] *16* Deut. 19:15
[f] *18* Or *have been*

1 →PG. 1075

on earth agree about anything you ask for, it will be done for you[p] by my Father in heaven. 20 For where two or three come together in my name, there am I with them."

The Parable of the Unmerciful Servant

6 →PG. 1094

21 Then Peter came to Jesus and asked, "Lord, how many times shall I forgive my brother when he sins against me?[q] Up to seven times?"[r]

22 Jesus answered, "I tell you, not seven times, but seventy-seven times.[a][s]

23 "Therefore, the kingdom of heaven is like[t] a king who wanted to settle accounts[u] with his servants. 24 As he began the settlement, a man who owed him ten thousand talents[b] was brought to him. 25 Since he was not able to pay,[v] the master ordered that he and his wife and his children and all that he had be sold[w] to repay the debt.

26 "The servant fell on his knees before him.[x] 'Be patient with me,' he begged, 'and I will pay back everything.' 27 The servant's master took pity on him, canceled the debt and let him go.

28 "But when that servant went out, he found one of his fellow servants who owed him a hundred denarii.[c] He grabbed him and began to choke him. 'Pay back what you owe me!' he demanded.

29 "His fellow servant fell to his knees and begged him, 'Be patient with me, and I will pay you back.'

30 "But he refused. Instead, he went off and had the man thrown into prison until he could pay the debt. 31 When the other servants saw what had happened, they were greatly distressed and went and told their master everything that had happened.

32 "Then the master called the servant in. 'You wicked servant,' he said, 'I canceled all that debt of yours because you begged me to. 33 Shouldn't you have had mercy on your fellow servant just as I had on you?' 34 In anger his master turned him over to the jailers to be tortured, until he should pay back all he owed.

35 "This is how my heavenly Father will treat each of you unless you forgive your brother from your heart."[y]

Divorce

›See Mark 10:1–12

19 When Jesus had finished saying these things,[z] he left Galilee and went into the region of Judea to the other side of the Jordan. 2 Large crowds followed him, and he healed them[a] there.

3 Some Pharisees came to him to test him. They asked, "Is it lawful for a man to divorce his wife[b] for any and every reason?"

4 →PG. 1073

4 "Haven't you read," he replied, "that at the beginning the Creator 'made them male and female,'[d][c] 5 and said, 'For this reason a man will leave his father and mother and be united to his wife, and the two will become one flesh'[e]?[d] 6 So they are no longer two, but one. Therefore what God has joined together, let man not separate."

7 "Why then," they asked, "did Moses command that a man give his wife a certificate of divorce and send her away?"[e]

8 Jesus replied, "Moses permitted you to divorce your wives because your hearts were hard. But it was not this way from the beginning. 9 I tell you that anyone who divorces his wife, except for marital unfaithfulness, and marries another woman commits adultery."[f]

18:19 [p]Mt 7:7
18:21 [q]Mt 6:14 [r]Lk 17:4
18:22 [s]Ge 4:24
18:23 [t]Mt 13:24 [u]Mt 25:19
18:25 [v]Lk 7:42 [w]Lev 25:39; 2Ki 4:1; Ne 5:5,8
18:26 [x]Mt 8:2
18:35 [y]Mt 6:14; Jas 2:13
19:1 [z]Mt 7:28
19:2 [a]Mt 4:23
19:3 [b]Mt 5:31
19:4 [c]Ge 1:27; 5:2
19:5 [d]Ge 2:24; 1Co 6:16; Eph 5:31
19:7 [e]Dt 24:1-4; Mt 5:31
19:9 [f]Mt 5:32; Lk 16:18

[a] *22* Or *seventy times seven* [b] *24* That is, millions of dollars [c] *28* That is, a few dollars
[d] *4* Gen. 1:27 [e] *5* Gen. 2:24

19:1–12

PROMISE 4

GOD'S NEW MATH

1+1=1. Now, any third grader could tell you that that little mathematical equation is clearly incorrect. There is, however, one exception to this rule. God designed marriage so that 1 man + 1 woman = 1 flesh. The coming together of a man and woman in marriage forms a new creation.

In this passage, the Pharisees tried to trip Jesus up on a technicality. In asking this question, they hoped to capitalize on the conflict between two schools of Jewish thought that created controversy over Moses' pronouncements on divorce in Deuteronomy 24:1–4. The teacher Shammai allowed a man to divorce his wife only on the grounds of marital unfaithfulness; another teacher, Hillel, argued that divorce was allowable for reasons as simple as, for example, burning dinner. But Jesus chose to emphasize the permanent aspects of God's plan for marriage. Knowing that divorce came about as the result of sin in people's hearts, Jesus pointed the scheming Pharisees back to the words of Genesis (vv. 4–6)—the place where God's perfect plan for marriage is revealed.

If you're married, ask God for the grace you need to keep your vows as diligently today as you did on the day you made them.

For the next Promise 4 reading go to page 1104.

10 The disciples said to him, "If this is
the situation between a husband and
wife, it is better not to marry."
11 Jesus replied, "Not everyone can
accept this word, but only those to
whom it has been given.[g] 12 For some
are eunuchs because they were born
that way; others were made that way by
men; and others have renounced marriage[a] because of the kingdom of
heaven. The one who can accept this
should accept it."

The Little Children and Jesus

›See Mark 10:13–16; Luke 18:15–17

4 →PG. 1074
13 Then little children were brought
to Jesus for him to place his hands on
them[h] and pray for them. But the disciples rebuked those who brought
them.
14 Jesus said, "Let the little children
come to me, and do not hinder them,
for the kingdom of heaven belongs[i]
to such as these."[j] 15 When he had
placed his hands on them, he went on
from there.

The Rich Young Man

›See Mark 10:17–30; Luke 18:18–30

16 Now a man came up to Jesus and
asked, "Teacher, what good thing must
I do to get eternal life[k]?"[l]
17 "Why do you ask me about what
is good?" Jesus replied. "There is only
One who is good. If you want to enter
life, obey the commandments."[m]
18 "Which ones?" the man inquired.
Jesus replied, " 'Do not murder, do
not commit adultery,[n] do not steal, do
not give false testimony, 19 honor your
father and mother,'[b][o] and 'love your
neighbor as yourself.'[c]"[p]
20 "All these I have kept," the young
man said. "What do I still lack?"
7 →PG. 1074
21 Jesus answered, "If you want to be
perfect,[q] go, sell your possessions and
give to the poor,[r] and you will have
treasure in heaven.[s] Then come, follow me."
22 When the young man heard this,
he went away sad, because he had
great wealth.
23 Then Jesus said to his disciples, "I
tell you the truth, it is hard for a rich
man[t] to enter the kingdom of heaven.
24 Again I tell you, it is easier for a camel
to go through the eye of a needle than
for a rich man to enter the kingdom of
God."
25 When the disciples heard this, they
were greatly astonished and asked,
"Who then can be saved?"
26 Jesus looked at them and said,
"With man this is impossible, but with
God all things are possible."[u]
27 Peter answered him, "We have left
everything to follow you![v] What then
will there be for us?"
28 Jesus said to them, "I tell you the
truth, at the renewal of all things, when
the Son of Man sits on his glorious
throne,[w] you who have followed me
will also sit on twelve thrones, judging
the twelve tribes of Israel.[x] 29 And everyone who has left houses or brothers
or sisters or father or mother[d] or children or fields for my sake will receive a
hundred times as much and will inherit eternal life.[y] 30 But many who are
first will be last, and many who are last
will be first.[z]

The Parable of the Workers in the Vineyard

20 "For the kingdom of heaven is
like[a] a landowner who went out
early in the morning to hire men to
work in his vineyard.[b] 2 He agreed to
pay them a denarius for the day and
sent them into his vineyard.
3 "About the third hour he went out
and saw others standing in the marketplace doing nothing. 4 He told them,
'You also go and work in my vineyard,
and I will pay you whatever is right.'
5 So they went.
"He went out again about the sixth
hour and the ninth hour and did the
same thing. 6 About the eleventh hour
he went out and found still others
standing around. He asked them, 'Why
have you been standing here all day
long doing nothing?'
7 " 'Because no one has hired us,'
they answered.
"He said to them, 'You also go and
work in my vineyard.'
8 "When evening came,[c] the owner
of the vineyard said to his foreman,
'Call the workers and pay them their
wages, beginning with the last ones
hired and going on to the first.'
9 "The workers who were hired about
the eleventh hour came and each received a denarius. 10 So when those
came who were hired first, they expected to receive more. But each one of
them also received a denarius. 11 When
they received it, they began to grumble[d] against the landowner. 12 'These
men who were hired last worked only
one hour,' they said, 'and you have
made them equal to us who have borne
the burden of the work and the heat[e]
of the day.'
13 "But he answered one of them,

19:11 [g]Mt 13:11; 1Co 7:7-9,17
19:13 [h]Mk 5:23
19:14 [i]Mt 25:34 [j]Mt 18:3; 1Pe 2:2
19:16 [k]Mt 25:46 [l]Lk 10:25
19:17 [m]Lev 18:5
19:18 [n]Jas 2:11
19:19 [o]Ex 20:12-16; Dt 5:16-20 [p]Lev 19:18; Mt 5:43
19:21 [q]Mt 5:48 [r]Lk 12:33; Ac 2:45; 4:34-35 [s]Mt 6:20
19:23 [t]Mt 13:22; 1Ti 6:9,10
19:26 [u]Ge 18:14; Job 42:2; Jer 32:17; Zec 8:6; Lk 1:37; 18:27; Ro 4:21
19:27 [v]Mt 4:19
19:28 [w]Mt 20:21; 25:31 [x]Lk 22:28-30; Rev 3:21; 4:4; 20:4
19:29 [y]Mt 6:33; 25:46
19:30 [z]Mt 20:16; Mk 10:31; Lk 13:30
20:1 [a]Mt 13:24 [b]Mt 21:28,33
20:8 [c]Lev 19:13; Dt 24:15
20:11 [d]Jnh 4:1
20:12 [e]Jnh 4:8; Lk 12:55; Jas 1:11

[a] *12* Or *have made themselves eunuchs*
[b] *19* Exodus 20:12-16; Deut. 5:16-20
[c] *19* Lev. 19:18
[d] *29* Some manuscripts *mother or wife*

'Friend,[f] I am not being unfair to you.
Didn't you agree to work for a denarius? 14Take your pay and go. I want to
give the man who was hired last the
same as I gave you. 15Don't I have the
right to do what I want with my own
money? Or are you envious because I
am generous?'[g]
16"So the last will be first, and the
first will be last."[h]

Jesus Again Predicts His Death

›See Mark 10:32–34; Luke 18:31–33

17Now as Jesus was going up to Jerusalem, he took the twelve disciples
aside and said to them, 18"We are going up to Jerusalem,[i] and the Son of
Man[j] will be betrayed to the chief
priests and the teachers of the law.[k]
They will condemn him to death 19and
will turn him over to the Gentiles to be
mocked and flogged[l] and crucified.[m]
On the third day[n] he will be raised to
life!"[o]

A Mother's Request

›See Mark 10:35–45

20Then the mother of Zebedee's
sons[p] came to Jesus with her sons
and, kneeling down,[q] asked a favor of
him.
21"What is it you want?" he asked.
She said, "Grant that one of these
two sons of mine may sit at your right
and the other at your left in your kingdom."[r]
22"You don't know what you are asking," Jesus said to them. "Can you
drink the cup[s] I am going to drink?"
"We can," they answered.
23Jesus said to them, "You will indeed drink from my cup,[t] but to sit at
my right or left is not for me to grant.
These places belong to those for whom
they have been prepared by my Father."
24When the ten heard about this,
they were indignant[u] with the two
brothers. 25Jesus called them together
and said, "You know that the rulers of
the Gentiles lord it over them, and their
high officials exercise authority over
them. 26Not so with you. Instead, whoever wants to become great among you
must be your servant,[v] 27and whoever
wants to be first must be your slave—
28just as the Son of Man[w] did not
come to be served, but to serve,[x] and
to give his life as a ransom[y] for many."

4 →PG. 1078
7 →PG. 1079

Two Blind Men Receive Sight

›See Mark 10:46–52; Luke 18:35–43

29As Jesus and his disciples were
leaving Jericho, a large crowd followed
him. 30Two blind men were sitting by
the roadside, and when they heard that
Jesus was going by, they shouted,
"Lord, Son of David,[z] have mercy
on us!"
31The crowd rebuked them and told
them to be quiet, but they shouted all
the louder, "Lord, Son of David, have
mercy on us!"
32Jesus stopped and called them.
"What do you want me to do for you?"
he asked.
33"Lord," they answered, "we want
our sight."
34Jesus had compassion on them
and touched their eyes. Immediately
they received their sight and followed
him.

The Triumphal Entry

›See Mark 11:1–10; Luke 19:29–38;
John 12:12–15

21 As they approached Jerusalem and
came to Bethphage on the Mount
of Olives,[a] Jesus sent two disciples,
2saying to them, "Go to the village
ahead of you, and at once you will find
a donkey tied there, with her colt by
her. Untie them and bring them to me.
3If anyone says anything to you, tell
him that the Lord needs them, and he
will send them right away."
4This took place to fulfill what was
spoken through the prophet:

5"Say to the Daughter of Zion,
'See, your king comes to you,
gentle and riding on a donkey,

20:20–28

PROMISE 2

GREATNESS COMES BY SERVING

Men often find it hard to get close to other men. Why? One reason is because men tend to view each other as competitors, as rivals. Most men think that opening up to other men will put them at a disadvantage and give the others some kind of an edge.

That's probably why the disciples were "indignant" when they heard about the request of James and John's mother. If this woman succeeded in her behind-the-scenes lobbying, the rest of them would be on the bottom of the ladder looking up at their rivals.

But Jesus turned their thinking upside down. He told them that the key to true greatness isn't in climbing over others, but in helping them up and serving them. From Jesus' perspective, men aren't rivals who need to compete; they're allies who need to help each other along on the journey of life.

For the next Promise 2 reading go to page 1174.

20:13 [f]Mt 22:12; 26:50
20:15 [g]Dt 15:9; Mk 7:22
20:16 [h]Mt 19:30
20:18 [i]Lk 9:51 [j]Mt 8:20 [k]Mt 16:21; 27:1,2
20:19 [l]Mt 16:21 [m]Ac 2:23 [n]Mt 16:21 [o]Mt 16:21
20:20 [p]Mt 4:21 [q]Mt 8:2
20:21 [r]Mt 19:28
20:22 [s]Isa 51:17,22; Jer 49:12; Mt 26:39,42; Mk 14:36; Lk 22:42; Jn 18:11
20:23 [t]Ac 12:2; Rev 1:9
20:24 [u]Lk 22:24,25
20:26 [v]Mt 23:11; Mk 9:35
20:28 [w]Mt 8:20 [x]Lk 22:27; Jn 13:13-16; 2Co 8:9; Php 2:7 [y]Isa 53:10; Mt 26:28; 1Ti 2:6; Tit 2:14; Heb 9:28; 1Pe 1:18,19
20:30 [z]Mt 9:27
21:1 [a]Mt 24:3; 26:30; Mk 14:26; Lk 19:37; 21:37; 22:39; Jn 8:1; Ac 1:12

on a colt, the foal of a
donkey.' "[a][b]

6The disciples went and did as Jesus
had instructed them. 7They brought
the donkey and the colt, placed their
cloaks on them, and Jesus sat on them.
8A very large crowd spread their
cloaks[c] on the road, while others cut
branches from the trees and spread
them on the road. 9The crowds that
went ahead of him and those that followed shouted,

"Hosanna[b] to the Son of David!"[d]

"Blessed is he who comes in the
name of the Lord!"[c][e]

"Hosanna[b] in the highest!"[f]

10When Jesus entered Jerusalem, the
whole city was stirred and asked, "Who
is this?"
11The crowds answered, "This is
Jesus, the prophet[g] from Nazareth in
Galilee."

Jesus at the Temple

›See Mark 11:15–18; Luke 19:45–47

12Jesus entered the temple area
and drove out all who were buying[h]
and selling there. He overturned the
tables of the money changers[i] and
the benches of those selling doves.[j]
13"It is written," he said to them,
" 'My house will be called a house of
prayer,'[d][k] but you are making it a
'den of robbers.'[e] "[l]
14The blind and the lame came to
him at the temple, and he healed
them.[m] 15But when the chief priests
and the teachers of the law saw the
wonderful things he did and the children shouting in the temple area,
"Hosanna to the Son of David,"[n] they
were indignant.[o]
16"Do you hear what these children
are saying?" they asked him.

"Yes," replied Jesus, "have you never
read,

" 'From the lips of children and
infants
you have ordained praise'[f]?"[p]

17And he left them and went out of
the city to Bethany,[q] where he spent
the night.

The Fig Tree Withers

›See Mark 11:12–14,20–24

18Early in the morning, as he was on
his way back to the city, he was hungry.
19Seeing a fig tree by the road, he went
up to it but found nothing on it except
leaves. Then he said to it, "May you
never bear fruit again!" Immediately
the tree withered.[r]
20When the disciples saw this, they
were amazed. "How did the fig tree
wither so quickly?" they asked.
21Jesus replied, "I tell you the truth,
if you have faith and do not doubt,[s]
not only can you do what was done to
the fig tree, but also you can say to this
mountain, 'Go, throw yourself into the
sea,' and it will be done. 22If you believe, you will receive whatever you ask
for[t] in prayer."

1 →PG. 1082

The Authority of Jesus Questioned

›See Mark 11:27–33; Luke 20:1–8

23Jesus entered the temple courts,
and, while he was teaching, the chief
priests and the elders of the people
came to him. "By what authority[u] are
you doing these things?" they asked.
"And who gave you this authority?"
24Jesus replied, "I will also ask you
one question. If you answer me, I will

21:5 [b]Zec 9:9; Isa 62:11 **21:8** [c]2Ki 9:13 **21:9** [d]ver 15; Mt 9:27 [e]Ps 118:26; Mt 23:39 [f]Lk 2:14 **21:11** [g]Lk 7:16,39; 24:19; Jn 1:21, 25; 6:14; 7:40 **21:12** [h]Dt 14:26 [i]Ex 30:13 [j]Lev 1:14 **21:13** [k]Isa 56:7 [l]Jer 7:11 **21:14** [m]Mt 4:23 **21:15** [n]ver 9; Mt 9:27 [o]Lk 19:39 **21:16** [p]Ps 8:2 **21:17** [q]Mt 26:6; Mk 11:1; Lk 24:50; Jn 11:1,18; 12:1 **21:19** [r]Isa 34:4; Jer 8:13 **21:21** [s]Mt 17:20; Lk 17:6; 1Co 13:2; Jas 1:6 **21:22** [t]Mt 7:7 **21:23** [u]Ac 4:7; 7:27

[a]*5* Zech. 9:9 [b]*9* A Hebrew expression meaning "Save!" which became an exclamation of praise; also in verse 15 [c]*9* Psalm 118:26 [d]*13* Isaiah 56:7 [e]*13* Jer. 7:11 [f]*16* Psalm 8:2

21:12–17

PROMISE 3

POSITIVELY FURIOUS

We're living in an angry age. The morning newspaper and the nightly news are grisly reminders to the fact that ugliness, random anger, short tempers and bad manners are as much a part of life in our world as are traffic jams and telephone calls. Hardly an hour goes by without a reminder of the seething rage that exists in our society.

As this emotion is so prevalent and so surrounded by negativity in our world, it's easy for us to make the assumption that all anger is wrong. But the problem isn't with anger. It's with anger that's inappropriately expressed. In this passage we see that Jesus felt anger that was justified. He then expressed it appropriately. In the process, the Lord gave us a model we are to follow. The next time you're angry, think about where that anger comes from. Ask yourself, "Is my anger justified in God's eyes?" Next, determine to express your anger in a way that addresses what's wrong and honors God.

How we express anger varies according to our temperament. Some of us need to walk away when we're mad. We need time to work through our anger before we express it. Others need to talk with a friend. Regardless of your unique temperament, ask God for grace to deal with your anger in a way that pleases him.

For the next Promise 3 reading go to page 1099.

tell you by what authority I am doing
these things. 25John's baptism—where
did it come from? Was it from heaven,
or from men?"
They discussed it among themselves
and said, "If we say, 'From heaven,' he
will ask, 'Then why didn't you believe
him?' 26But if we say, 'From men'—we
are afraid of the people, for they all
hold that John was a prophet."[v]
27So they answered Jesus, "We don't
know."
Then he said, "Neither will I tell you
by what authority I am doing these
things.

The Parable of the Two Sons

28"What do you think? There was a
man who had two sons. He went to the
first and said, 'Son, go and work today
in the vineyard.'[w]
29" 'I will not,' he answered, but later
he changed his mind and went.
30"Then the father went to the other
son and said the same thing. He answered, 'I will, sir,' but he did not go.
31"Which of the two did what his father wanted?"
"The first," they answered.
Jesus said to them, "I tell you the
truth, the tax collectors[x] and the prostitutes[y] are entering the kingdom of
God ahead of you. 32For John came to
you to show you the way of righteousness,[z] and you did not believe him,
but the tax collectors[a] and the prostitutes[b] did. And even after you saw
this, you did not repent[c] and believe
him.

The Parable of the Tenants

›See Mark 12:1–12; Luke 20:9–19

33"Listen to another parable: There
was a landowner who planted[d] a vineyard. He put a wall around it, dug a
winepress in it and built a watchtower.[e] Then he rented the vineyard to
some farmers and went away on a journey.[f] 34When the harvest time approached, he sent his servants[g] to the
tenants to collect his fruit.
35"The tenants seized his servants;
they beat one, killed another, and
stoned a third.[h] 36Then he sent other
servants[i] to them, more than the first
time, and the tenants treated them the
same way. 37Last of all, he sent his son
to them. 'They will respect my son,' he
said.
38"But when the tenants saw the
son, they said to each other, 'This is the
heir.[j] Come, let's kill him[k] and take
his inheritance.'[l] 39So they took him
and threw him out of the vineyard and
killed him.
40"Therefore, when the owner of the
vineyard comes, what will he do to
those tenants?"
41"He will bring those wretches to a
wretched end,"[m] they replied, "and he
will rent the vineyard to other tenants,[n] who will give him his share of
the crop at harvest time."
42Jesus said to them, "Have you never read in the Scriptures:

" 'The stone the builders rejected
has become the capstone[a];
the Lord has done this,
and it is marvelous in our
eyes'[b]?[o]

43"Therefore I tell you that the kingdom of God will be taken away from
you[p] and given to a people who will
produce its fruit. 44He who falls on this
stone will be broken to pieces, but he
on whom it falls will be crushed."[c][q]
45When the chief priests and the
Pharisees heard Jesus' parables, they
knew he was talking about them.
46They looked for a way to arrest him,
but they were afraid of the crowd because the people held that he was a
prophet.[r]

The Parable of the Wedding Banquet

22 Jesus spoke to them again in parables, saying: 2"The kingdom of
heaven is like[s] a king who prepared a
wedding banquet for his son. 3He sent
his servants[t] to those who had been
invited to the banquet to tell them to
come, but they refused to come.
4"Then he sent some more servants[u] and said, 'Tell those who have
been invited that I have prepared my
dinner: My oxen and fattened cattle
have been butchered, and everything is
ready. Come to the wedding banquet.'
5"But they paid no attention and
went off—one to his field, another to
his business. 6The rest seized his servants, mistreated them and killed
them. 7The king was enraged. He sent
his army and destroyed those murderers[v] and burned their city.
8"Then he said to his servants, 'The
wedding banquet is ready, but those I
invited did not deserve to come. 9Go to
the street corners[w] and invite to the
banquet anyone you find.' 10So the servants went out into the streets and
gathered all the people they could find,
both good and bad,[x] and the wedding
hall was filled with guests.
11"But when the king came in to see
the guests, he noticed a man there who
was not wearing wedding clothes.

21:26 v Mt 11:9; Mk 6:20
21:28 w ver 33; Mt 20:1
21:31 x Lk 7:29 y Lk 7:50
21:32 z Mt 3:1-12 a Lk 3:12,13; 7:29 b Lk 7:36-50 c Lk 7:30
21:33 d Ps 80:8 e Isa 5:1-7 f Mt 25:14,15
21:34 g Mt 22:3
21:35 h 2Ch 24:21; Mt 23:34,37; Heb 11:36,37
21:36 i Mt 22:4
21:38 j Heb 1:2 k Mt 12:14 l Ps 2:8
21:41 m Mt 8:11,12 n Ac 13:46; 18:6; 28:28
21:42 o Ps 118:22,23; Ac 4:11; 1Pe 2:7
21:43 p Mt 8:12
21:44 q Lk 2:34
21:46 r ver 11,26
22:2 s Mt 13:24
22:3 t Mt 21:34
22:4 u Mt 21:36
22:7 v Lk 19:27
22:9 w Eze 21:21
22:10 x Mt 13:47,48

a *42* Or *cornerstone* b *42* Psalm 118:22,23
c *44* Some manuscripts do not have verse 44.

12‘Friend,’[y] he asked, ‘how did you get
in here without wedding clothes?’ The
man was speechless.
13“Then the king told the attendants,
‘Tie him hand and foot, and throw
him outside, into the darkness, where
there will be weeping and gnashing
of teeth.’[z]
14“For many are invited, but few are
chosen.”[a]

Paying Taxes to Caesar

›See Mark 12:13–17; Luke 20:20–26

15Then the Pharisees went out and
laid plans to trap him in his words.
16They sent their disciples to him along
with the Herodians.[b] “Teacher,” they
said, “we know you are a man of integrity and that you teach the way of God
in accordance with the truth. You
aren’t swayed by men, because you
pay no attention to who they are. 17Tell
us then, what is your opinion? Is it right
to pay taxes[c] to Caesar or not?”
18But Jesus, knowing their evil intent, said, “You hypocrites, why are
you trying to trap me? 19Show me the
coin used for paying the tax.” They
brought him a denarius, 20and he
asked them, “Whose portrait is this?
And whose inscription?”
21“Caesar’s,” they replied.
Then he said to them, “Give to Caesar what is Caesar’s,[d] and to God what
is God’s.”
22When they heard this, they were
amazed. So they left him and went
away.[e]

Marriage at the Resurrection

›See Mark 12:18–27; Luke 20:27–40

23That same day the Sadducees,[f]
who say there is no resurrection,[g] came
to him with a question. 24“Teacher,”
they said, “Moses told us that if
a man dies without having children,
his brother must marry the widow
and have children for him.[h] 25Now
there were seven brothers among us.
The first one married and died, and
since he had no children, he left his
wife to his brother. 26The same thing
happened to the second and third
brother, right on down to the seventh.
27Finally, the woman died. 28Now then,
at the resurrection, whose wife will she
be of the seven, since all of them were
married to her?”
29Jesus replied, “You are in error because you do not know the Scriptures[i] or the power of God. 30At the
resurrection people will neither marry
nor be given in marriage;[j] they will be
like the angels in heaven. 31But about
the resurrection of the dead—have you
not read what God said to you, 32‘I am
the God of Abraham, the God of Isaac,
and the God of Jacob’[a]?[k] He is not
the God of the dead but of the living.”
33When the crowds heard this, they
were astonished at his teaching.[l]

The Greatest Commandment

›See Mark 12:28–31

34Hearing that Jesus had silenced
the Sadducees,[m] the Pharisees got together. 35One of them, an expert in the
law,[n] tested him with this question:
36“Teacher, which is the greatest commandment in the Law?”
37Jesus replied: “ ‘Love the Lord your
God with all your heart and with all
your soul and with all your mind.’[b][o]
38This is the first and greatest commandment. 39And the second is like it:
‘Love your neighbor as yourself.’[c][p]
40All the Law and the Prophets hang on
these two commandments.”[q]

Whose Son Is the Christ?

›See Mark 12:35–37; Luke 20:41–44

41While the Pharisees were gathered
together, Jesus asked them, 42“What do
you think about the Christ[d]? Whose
son is he?”
“The son of David,”[r] they replied.
43He said to them, “How is it then
that David, speaking by the Spirit, calls
him ‘Lord’? For he says,

44“ ‘The Lord said to my Lord:
“Sit at my right hand
until I put your enemies
under your feet.” ’[e][s]

45If then David calls him ‘Lord,’ how
can he be his son?” 46No one could say
a word in reply, and from that day on
no one dared to ask him any more
questions.[t]

Seven Woes

›See Mark 12:38–39; Luke 20:45–46

23 Then Jesus said to the crowds and
to his disciples: 2“The teachers of
the law[u] and the Pharisees sit in Moses’ seat. 3So you must obey them and
do everything they tell you. But do not
do what they do, for they do not practice what they preach. 4They tie up
heavy loads and put them on men’s
shoulders, but they themselves are not
willing to lift a finger to move them.[v]
5“Everything they do is done for
men to see:[w] They make their phylacteries[f][x] wide and the tassels on their

22:12 [y]Mt 20:13; 26:50 **22:13** [z]Mt 8:12 **22:14** [a]Rev 17:14 **22:16** [b]Mk 3:6 **22:17** [c]Mt 17:25 **22:21** [d]Ro 13:7 **22:22** [e]Mk 12:12 **22:23** [f]Ac 4:1 [g]Ac 23:8; 1Co 15:12 **22:24** [h]Dt 25:5,6 **22:29** [i]Jn 20:9 **22:30** [j]Mt 24:38 **22:32** [k]Ex 3:6; Ac 7:32 **22:33** [l]Mt 7:28 **22:34** [m]Ac 4:1 **22:35** [n]Lk 7:30; 10:25; 11:45; 14:3 **22:37** [o]Dt 6:5 **22:39** [p]Lev 19:18; Mt 5:43; 19:19; Gal 5:14 **22:40** [q]Mt 7:12 **22:42** [r]Mt 9:27 **22:44** [s]Ps 110:1; Ac 2:34,35; 1Co 15:25; Heb 1:13; 10:13 **22:46** [t]Mk 12:34; Lk 20:40 **23:2** [u]Ezr 7:6,25; Ne 8:4 **23:4** [v]Lk 11:46; Ac 15:10; Gal 6:13 **23:5** [w]Mt 6:1,2,5,16 [x]Ex 13:9; Dt 6:8

[a] *32* Exodus 3:6 [b] *37* Deut. 6:5
[c] *39* Lev. 19:18 [d] *42* Or *Messiah*
[e] *44* Psalm 110:1 [f] *5* That is, boxes containing Scripture verses, worn on forehead and arm

garments[y] long; **6**they love the place
of honor at banquets and the most important seats in the synagogues;[z]
7they love to be greeted in the marketplaces and to have men call them
'Rabbi.'[a]
8"But you are not to be called 'Rabbi,' for you have only one Master and
you are all brothers. **9**And do not call
anyone on earth 'father,' for you have
one Father,[b] and he is in heaven.
10Nor are you to be called 'teacher,' for
you have one Teacher, the Christ.[a]
4 →PG. 1096
11The greatest among you will be your
servant.[c] **12**For whoever exalts himself
will be humbled, and whoever humbles himself will be exalted.[d]
13"Woe to you, teachers of the law
and Pharisees, you hypocrites![e] You
shut the kingdom of heaven in men's
faces. You yourselves do not enter, nor
will you let those enter who are trying
to.[b][f]
15"Woe to you, teachers of the law
and Pharisees, you hypocrites! You
travel over land and sea to win a single
convert,[g] and when he becomes one,
you make him twice as much a son of
hell[h] as you are.
16"Woe to you, blind guides![i] You
say, 'If anyone swears by the temple, it
means nothing; but if anyone swears
by the gold of the temple, he is bound
by his oath.'[j] **17**You blind fools! Which
is greater: the gold, or the temple that
makes the gold sacred?[k] **18**You also
say, 'If anyone swears by the altar, it
means nothing; but if anyone swears
by the gift on it, he is bound by his
oath.' **19**You blind men! Which is greater: the gift, or the altar that makes the
gift sacred?[l] **20**Therefore, he who
swears by the altar swears by it and by
everything on it. **21**And he who swears
by the temple swears by it and by the
one who dwells[m] in it. **22**And he who
swears by heaven swears by God's
throne and by the one who sits on it.[n]
23"Woe to you, teachers of the law
and Pharisees, you hypocrites! You give
a tenth[o] of your spices—mint, dill and
cummin. But you have neglected the
more important matters of the law—
justice, mercy and faithfulness.[p] You
should have practiced the latter, without neglecting the former. **24**You blind
guides![q] You strain out a gnat but
swallow a camel.
25"Woe to you, teachers of the law
and Pharisees, you hypocrites! You
clean the outside of the cup and dish,[r]
but inside they are full of greed and
self-indulgence.[s] **26**Blind Pharisee!
First clean the inside of the cup and
dish, and then the outside also will be
clean.
27"Woe to you, teachers of the law
and Pharisees, you hypocrites! You are
like whitewashed tombs,[t] which look
beautiful on the outside but on the inside are full of dead men's bones and
everything unclean. **28**In the same way,
on the outside you appear to people as
righteous but on the inside you are full
of hypocrisy and wickedness.
29"Woe to you, teachers of the law
and Pharisees, you hypocrites! You
build tombs for the prophets[u] and
decorate the graves of the righteous.
30And you say, 'If we had lived in the
days of our forefathers, we would not
have taken part with them in shedding
the blood of the prophets.' **31**So you
testify against yourselves that you are
the descendants of those who murdered the prophets.[v] **32**Fill up, then,
the measure[w] of the sin of your forefathers!
33"You snakes! You brood of vipers![x] How will you escape being condemned to hell?[y] **34**Therefore I am
sending you prophets and wise men
and teachers. Some of them you will
kill and crucify;[z] others you will flog in
your synagogues[a] and pursue from
town to town.[b] **35**And so upon you will
come all the righteous blood that has
been shed on earth, from the blood of
righteous Abel[c] to the blood of Zechariah son of Berekiah,[d] whom you murdered between the temple and the al-
tar.[e] **36**I tell you the truth, all this will
come upon this generation.[f]
37"O Jerusalem, Jerusalem, you who
kill the prophets and stone those sent
to you,[g] how often I have longed to
gather your children together, as a hen
gathers her chicks under her wings, but
you were not willing. **38**Look, your
house is left to you desolate.[h] **39**For I
tell you, you will not see me again until
you say, 'Blessed is he who comes in
the name of the Lord.'[c]"[i]

Signs of the End of the Age

›See Mark 13:1–37; Luke 21:5–36

24 Jesus left the temple and was walking away when his disciples came
up to him to call his attention to its
buildings. **2**"Do you see all these
things?" he asked. "I tell you the truth,
not one stone here will be left on another;[j] every one will be thrown
down."
3As Jesus was sitting on the Mount of
Olives,[k] the disciples came to him pri-

23:5 [y]Nu 15:38; Dt 22:12
23:6 [z]Lk 11:43; 14:7; 20:46
23:7 [a]ver 8; Mk 9:5; 10:51; Jn 1:38, 49
23:9 [b]Mal 1:6; Mt 7:11
23:11 [c]Mt 20:26; Mk 9:35
23:12 [d]Lk 14:11
23:13 [e]ver 15,23,25, 27,29 [f]Lk 11:52
23:15 [g]Ac 2:11; 6:5; 13:43 [h]Mt 5:22
23:16 [i]ver 24; Mt 15:14 [j]Mt 5:33-35
23:17 [k]Ex 30:29
23:19 [l]Ex 29:37
23:21 [m]1Ki 8:13; Ps 26:8
23:22 [n]Ps 11:4; Mt 5:34
23:23 [o]Lev 27:30 [p]Mic 6:8; Lk 11:42
23:24 [q]ver 16
23:25 [r]Mk 7:4 [s]Lk 11:39
23:27 [t]Lk 11:44; Ac 23:3
23:29 [u]Lk 11:47,48
23:31 [v]Ac 7:51-52
23:32 [w]1Th 2:16
23:33 [x]Mt 3:7; 12:34 [y]Mt 5:22
23:34 [z]2Ch 36:15,16; Lk 11:49 [a]Mt 10:17 [b]Mt 10:23
23:35 [c]Ge 4:8; Heb 11:4 [d]Zec 1:1 [e]2Ch 24:21
23:36 [f]Mt 10:23; 24:34
23:37 [g]2Ch 24:21; Mt 5:12
23:38 [h]1Ki 9:7,8; Jer 22:5
23:39 [i]Ps 118:26; Mt 21:9
24:2 [j]Lk 19:44
24:3 [k]Mt 21:1

[a] *10* Or *Messiah* [b] *13* Some manuscripts *to. 14Woe to you, teachers of the law and Pharisees, you hypocrites! You devour widows' houses and for a show make lengthy prayers. Therefore you will be punished more severely.* [c] *39* Psalm 118:26

vately. "Tell us," they said, "when will this happen, and what will be the sign of your coming and of the end of the age?"

4Jesus answered: "Watch out that no one deceives you. 5For many will come in my name, claiming, 'I am the Christ,[a]' and will deceive many.[l] 6You will hear of wars and rumors of wars, but see to it that you are not alarmed. Such things must happen, but the end is still to come. 7Nation will rise against nation, and kingdom against kingdom.[m] There will be famines[n] and earthquakes in various places. 8All these are the beginning of birth pains.

9"Then you will be handed over to be persecuted[o] and put to death,[p] and you will be hated by all nations because of me. 10At that time many will turn away from the faith and will betray and hate each other, 11and many false prophets[q] will appear and deceive many people. 12Because of the increase of wickedness, the love of

7 →PG. 1081

most will grow cold, 13but he who stands firm to the end will be saved.[r] 14And this gospel of the kingdom[s] will be preached in the whole world[t] as a testimony to all nations, and then the end will come.

15"So when you see standing in the holy place[u] 'the abomination that causes desolation,'[b][v] spoken of through the prophet Daniel—let the reader understand— 16then let those who are in Judea flee to the mountains. 17Let no one on the roof of his house[w] go down to take anything out of the house. 18Let no one in the field go back to get his cloak. 19How dreadful it will be in those days for pregnant women and nursing mothers![x] 20Pray that your flight will not take place in winter or on the Sabbath. 21For then there will be great distress, unequaled from the beginning of the world until now—and never to be equaled again.[y] 22If those days had not been cut short, no one would survive, but for the sake of the elect[z] those days will be shortened. 23At that time if anyone says to you, 'Look, here is the Christ!' or, 'There he is!' do not believe it.[a] 24For false Christs and false prophets will appear and perform great signs and miracles[b] to deceive even the elect—if that were possible. 25See, I have told you ahead of time.

26"So if anyone tells you, 'There he is, out in the desert,' do not go out; or, 'Here he is, in the inner rooms,' do not believe it. 27For as lightning[c] that comes from the east is visible even in the west, so will be the coming of the Son of Man.[d] 28Wherever there is a carcass, there the vultures will gather.[e]

29"Immediately after the distress of those days

" 'the sun will be darkened,
and the moon will not give its light;
the stars will fall from the sky,
and the heavenly bodies will be shaken.'[c][f]

30"At that time the sign of the Son of Man will appear in the sky, and all the nations of the earth will mourn. They will see the Son of Man coming on the clouds of the sky,[g] with power and great glory. 31And he will send his angels[h] with a loud trumpet call,[i] and they will gather his elect from the four winds, from one end of the heavens to the other.

32"Now learn this lesson from the fig tree: As soon as its twigs get tender and its leaves come out, you know that summer is near. 33Even so, when you see all these things, you know that it[d] is near, right at the door.[j] 34I tell you the truth, this generation[e] will certainly not pass away until all these things have happened.[k] 35Heaven and earth will pass away, but my words will never pass away.[l]

The Day and Hour Unknown

›See Luke 12:42–46; 17:26–27

36"No one knows about that day or hour, not even the angels in heaven, nor the Son,[f] but only the Father.[m] 37As it was in the days of Noah,[n] so it will be at the coming of the Son of Man. 38For in the days before the flood, people were eating and drinking, marrying and giving in marriage,[o] up to the day Noah entered the ark; 39and they knew nothing about what would happen until the flood came and took them all away. That is how it will be at the coming of the Son of Man. 40Two men will be in the field; one will be taken and the other left.[p] 41Two women will be grinding with a hand mill; one will be taken and the other left.[q]

42"Therefore keep watch, because you do not know on what day your Lord will come.[r] 43But understand this: If the owner of the house had known at what time of night the thief was coming,[s] he would have kept watch and would not have let his house

24:5 [l]ver 11,23,24; 1Jn 2:18
24:7 [m]Isa 19:2 [n]Ac 11:28
24:9 [o]Mt 10:17 [p]Jn 16:2
24:11 [q]Mt 7:15
24:13 [r]Mt 10:22
24:14 [s]Mt 4:23 [t]Ro 10:18; Col 1:6,23; Lk 2:1; 4:5; Ac 11:28; 17:6; Rev 3:10; 16:14
24:15 [u]Ac 6:13 [v]Da 9:27; 11:31; 12:11
24:17 [w]1Sa 9:25; Mt 10:27; Lk 12:3; Ac 10:9
24:19 [x]Lk 23:29
24:21 [y]Da 12:1; Joel 2:2
24:22 [z]ver 24,31
24:23 [a]Lk 17:23; 21:8
24:24 [b]2Th 2:9-11; Rev 13:13
24:27 [c]Lk 17:24 [d]Mt 8:20
24:28 [e]Lk 17:37
24:29 [f]Isa 13:10; 34:4; Eze 32:7; Joel 2:10,31; Zep 1:15; Rev 6:12,13; 8:12
24:30 [g]Da 7:13; Rev 1:7
24:31 [h]Mt 13:41 [i]Isa 27:13; Zec 9:14; 1Co 15:52; 1Th 4:16; Rev 8:2; 10:7; 11:15
24:33 [j]Jas 5:9
24:34 [k]Mt 16:28; 23:36
24:35 [l]Mt 5:18
24:36 [m]Ac 1:7
24:37 [n]Ge 6:5; 7:6-23
24:38 [o]Mt 22:30
24:40 [p]Lk 17:34
24:41 [q]Lk 17:35
24:42 [r]Mt 25:13; Lk 12:40
24:43 [s]Lk 12:39

a *5* Or *Messiah*; also in verse 23 **b** *15* Daniel 9:27; 11:31; 12:11 **c** *29* Isaiah 13:10; 34:4 **d** *33* Or *he* **e** *34* Or *race* **f** *36* Some manuscripts do not have *nor the Son.*

be broken into. **44**So you also must be ready,[t] because the Son of Man will come at an hour when you do not expect him.

3 →PG. 1109

45"Who then is the faithful and wise servant,[u] whom the master has put in charge of the servants in his household to give them their food at the proper time? **46**It will be good for that servant whose master finds him doing so when he returns.[v] **47**I tell you the truth, he will put him in charge of all his possessions.[w] **48**But suppose that servant is wicked and says to himself, 'My master is staying away a long time,' **49**and he then begins to beat his fellow servants and to eat and drink with drunkards.[x] **50**The master of that servant will come on a day when he does not expect him and at an hour he is not aware of. **51**He will cut him to pieces and assign him a place with the hypocrites, where there will be weeping and gnashing of teeth.[y]

The Parable of the Ten Virgins

25 "At that time the kingdom of heaven will be like[z] ten virgins who took their lamps[a] and went out to meet the bridegroom.[b] **2**Five of them were foolish and five were wise.[c] **3**The foolish ones took their lamps but did not take any oil with them. **4**The wise, however, took oil in jars along with their lamps. **5**The bridegroom was a long time in coming, and they all became drowsy and fell asleep.[d]

6"At midnight the cry rang out: 'Here's the bridegroom! Come out to meet him!'

7"Then all the virgins woke up and trimmed their lamps. **8**The foolish ones said to the wise, 'Give us some of your oil; our lamps are going out.'[e]

9" 'No,' they replied, 'there may not be enough for both us and you. Instead, go to those who sell oil and buy some for yourselves.'

10"But while they were on their way to buy the oil, the bridegroom arrived. The virgins who were ready went in with him to the wedding banquet.[f] And the door was shut.

11"Later the others also came. 'Sir! Sir!' they said. 'Open the door for us!'

12"But he replied, 'I tell you the truth, I don't know you.'

13"Therefore keep watch, because you do not know the day or the hour.[g]

The Parable of the Talents

5 →PG. 1105

14"Again, it will be like a man going on a journey,[h] who called his servants and entrusted his property to them. **15**To one he gave five talents[a] of money, to another two talents, and to another one talent, each according to his ability.[i] Then he went on his journey. **16**The man who had received the five talents went at once and put his money to work and gained five more. **17**So also, the one with the two talents gained two more. **18**But the man who had received the one talent went off, dug a hole in the ground and hid his master's money.

19"After a long time the master of those servants returned and settled accounts with them.[j] **20**The man who had received the five talents brought the other five. 'Master,' he said, 'you entrusted me with five talents. See, I have gained five more.'

21"His master replied, 'Well done, good and faithful servant! You have been faithful with a few things; I will put you in charge of many things.[k] Come and share your master's happiness!'

22"The man with the two talents also came. 'Master,' he said, 'you entrusted me with two talents; see, I have gained two more.'

23"His master replied, 'Well done, good and faithful servant! You have been faithful with a few things; I will put you in charge of many things.[l] Come and share your master's happiness!'

24"Then the man who had received the one talent came. 'Master,' he said, 'I knew that you are a hard man, harvesting where you have not sown and gathering where you have not scattered seed. **25**So I was afraid and went out and hid your talent in the ground. See, here is what belongs to you.'

26"His master replied, 'You wicked, lazy servant! So you knew that I harvest where I have not sown and gather where I have not scattered seed? **27**Well then, you should have put my money on deposit with the bankers, so that when I returned I would have received it back with interest.

28" 'Take the talent from him and give it to the one who has the ten talents. **29**For everyone who has will be given more, and he will have an abundance. Whoever does not have, even what he has will be taken from him.[m] **30**And throw that worthless servant outside, into the darkness, where there will be weeping and gnashing of teeth.'[n]

The Sheep and the Goats

31"When the Son of Man comes[o] in

24:44 [t]1Th 5:6
24:45 [u]Mt 25:21,23
24:46 [v]Rev 16:15
24:47 [w]Mt 25:21,23
24:49 [x]Lk 21:34
24:51 [y]Mt 8:12
25:1 [z]Mt 13:24 [a]Lk 12:35-38; Ac 20:8; Rev 4:5 [b]Rev 19:7; 21:2
25:2 [c]Mt 24:45
25:5 [d]1Th 5:6
25:8 [e]Lk 12:35
25:10 [f]Rev 19:9
25:13 [g]Mt 24:42,44; Mk 13:35; Lk 12:40
25:14 [h]Mt 21:33; Lk 19:12
25:15 [i]Mt 18:24,25
25:19 [j]Mt 18:23
25:21 [k]ver 23; Mt 24:45,47; Lk 16:10
25:23 [l]ver 21
25:29 [m]Mt 13:12; Mk 4:25; Lk 8:18; 19:26
25:30 [n]Mt 8:12
25:31 [o]Mt 16:27; Lk 17:30

[a] *15* A talent was worth more than a thousand dollars.

his glory, and all the angels with him,
he will sit on his throne[p] in heavenly
glory. 32All the nations will be gathered
before him, and he will separate[q] the
people one from another as a shepherd
separates the sheep from the goats.[r]
33He will put the sheep on his right and
the goats on his left.
34"Then the King will say to those on
his right, 'Come, you who are blessed
by my Father; take your inheritance,
the kingdom[s] prepared for you since
the creation of the world.[t] 35For I was
hungry and you gave me something to
eat, I was thirsty and you gave me
something to drink, I was a stranger
and you invited me in,[u] 36I needed
clothes and you clothed me,[v] I was
sick and you looked after me,[w] I was in
prison and you came to visit me.'[x]
37"Then the righteous will answer
him, 'Lord, when did we see you hungry and feed you, or thirsty and give
you something to drink? 38When did
we see you a stranger and invite you in,
or needing clothes and clothe you?
39When did we see you sick or in prison
and go to visit you?'
40"The King will reply, 'I tell you the
truth, whatever you did for one of the
least of these brothers of mine, you did
for me.'[y]
41"Then he will say to those on his
left, 'Depart from me,[z] you who are
cursed, into the eternal fire[a] prepared
for the devil and his angels.[b] 42For I
was hungry and you gave me nothing
to eat, I was thirsty and you gave me
nothing to drink, 43I was a stranger and
you did not invite me in, I needed
clothes and you did not clothe me, I
was sick and in prison and you did not
look after me.'
44"They also will answer, 'Lord,
when did we see you hungry or thirsty
or a stranger or needing clothes or sick
or in prison, and did not help you?'
45"He will reply, 'I tell you the truth,
whatever you did not do for one of the
least of these, you did not do for me.'[c]
46"Then they will go away to eternal
punishment, but the righteous to eternal life.[d]"[e]

7 →PG. 1087

The Plot Against Jesus

›See Mark 14:1–2; Luke 22:1–2

26 When Jesus had finished saying all
these things,[f] he said to his disciples, 2"As you know, the Passover[g] is
two days away—and the Son of Man
will be handed over to be crucified."
3Then the chief priests and the elders of the people assembled[h] in the
palace of the high priest, whose name
was Caiaphas,[i] 4and they plotted to
arrest Jesus in some sly way and kill
him.[j] 5"But not during the Feast,"
they said, "or there may be a riot[k]
among the people."

Jesus Anointed at Bethany

›See Mark 14:3–9

6While Jesus was in Bethany[l] in the
home of a man known as Simon the
Leper, 7a woman came to him with an
alabaster jar of very expensive perfume, which she poured on his head as
he was reclining at the table.
8When the disciples saw this, they
were indignant. "Why this waste?" they
asked. 9"This perfume could have been
sold at a high price and the money giv-
en to the poor."
10Aware of this, Jesus said to them,
"Why are you bothering this woman?
She has done a beautiful thing to me.
11The poor you will always have with
you,[m] but you will not always have me.
12When she poured this perfume on
my body, she did it to prepare me for
burial.[n] 13I tell you the truth, wherever
this gospel is preached throughout the
world, what she has done will also be
told, in memory of her."

Judas Agrees to Betray Jesus

›See Mark 14:10–11; Luke 22:3–6

14Then one of the Twelve—the one
called Judas Iscariot[o]—went to the
chief priests 15and asked, "What are
you willing to give me if I hand him
over to you?" So they counted out for
him thirty silver coins.[p] 16From then
on Judas watched for an opportunity to
hand him over.

The Lord's Supper

›See Mark 14:12–25; Luke 22:7–13

17On the first day of the Feast of Unleavened Bread,[q] the disciples came
to Jesus and asked, "Where do you
want us to make preparations for you
to eat the Passover?"
18He replied, "Go into the city to a
certain man and tell him, 'The Teacher
says: My appointed time[r] is near. I am
going to celebrate the Passover with
my disciples at your house.'" 19So the
disciples did as Jesus had directed
them and prepared the Passover.
20When evening came, Jesus was reclining at the table with the Twelve.
21And while they were eating, he said,
"I tell you the truth, one of you will
betray me."[s]
22They were very sad and began to
say to him one after the other, "Surely
not I, Lord?"
23Jesus replied, "The one who has
dipped his hand into the bowl with me

25:31 [p]Mt 19:28
25:32 [q]Mal 3:18 [r]Eze 34:17,20
25:34 [s]Mt 3:2; 5:3, 10,19; 19:14; Ac 20:32; 1Co 15:50; Gal 5:21; Jas 2:5 [t]Heb 4:3; 9:26; Rev 13:8; 17:8
25:35 [u]Job 31:32; Isa 58:7; Eze 18:7; Heb 13:2
25:36 [v]Isa 58:7; Eze 18:7; Jas 2:15,16 [w]Jas 1:27 [x]2Ti 1:16
25:40 [y]Pr 19:17; Mt 10:40,42; Heb 6:10; 13:2
25:41 [z]Mt 7:23 [a]Isa 66:24; Mt 3:12; 5:22; Mk 9:43,48; Lk 3:17; Jude 7 [b]2Pe 2:4
25:45 [c]Pr 14:31; 17:5
25:46 [d]Mt 19:29; Jn 3:15,16,36; 17:2,3; Ro 2:7; Gal 6:8; 5:11, 13,20 [e]Da 12:2; Jn 5:29; Ac 24:15; Ro 2:7,8; Gal 6:8
26:1 [f]Mt 7:28
26:2 [g]Jn 11:55; 13:1
26:3 [h]Ps 2:2 [i]ver 57; Jn 11:47-53; 18:13,14,24,28
26:4 [j]Mt 12:14
26:5 [k]Mt 27:24
26:6 [l]Mt 21:17
26:11 [m]Dt 15:11
26:12 [n]Jn 19:40
26:14 [o]ver 25,47; Mt 10:4
26:15 [p]Ex 21:32; Zec 11:12
26:17 [q]Ex 12:18-20
26:18 [r]Jn 7:6,8,30; 12:23; 13:1; 17:1
26:21 [s]Lk 22:21-23; Jn 13:21

will betray me.[t] 24 The Son of Man will go just as it is written about him.[u] But woe to that man who betrays the Son of Man! It would be better for him if he had not been born."

25 Then Judas, the one who would betray him, said, "Surely not I, Rabbi?"[v]

Jesus answered, "Yes, it is you."[a]

26 While they were eating, Jesus took bread, gave thanks and broke it,[w] and gave it to his disciples, saying, "Take and eat; this is my body."

27 Then he took the cup, gave thanks and offered it to them, saying, "Drink from it, all of you. 28 This is my blood of the[b] covenant,[x] which is poured out for many for the forgiveness of sins.[y] 29 I tell you, I will not drink of this fruit of the vine from now on until that day when I drink it anew with you[z] in my Father's kingdom."

30 When they had sung a hymn, they went out to the Mount of Olives.[a]

Jesus Predicts Peter's Denial

›See Mark 14:27–31; Luke 22:31–34

31 Then Jesus told them, "This very night you will all fall away on account of me,[b] for it is written:

" 'I will strike the shepherd,
and the sheep of the flock will
be scattered.'[c][c]

32 But after I have risen, I will go ahead of you into Galilee."[d]

33 Peter replied, "Even if all fall away on account of you, I never will."

34 "I tell you the truth," Jesus answered, "this very night, before the rooster crows, you will disown me three times."[e]

35 But Peter declared, "Even if I have to die with you,[f] I will never disown you." And all the other disciples said the same.

Gethsemane

›See Mark 14:32–42; Luke 22:40–46

36 Then Jesus went with his disciples to a place called Gethsemane, and he said to them, "Sit here while I go over there and pray." 37 He took Peter and the two sons of Zebedee[g] along with him, and he began to be sorrowful and troubled. 38 Then he said to them, "My soul is overwhelmed with sorrow[h] to the point of death. Stay here and keep watch with me."[i]

39 Going a little farther, he fell with his face to the ground and prayed, "My Father, if it is possible, may this cup[j] be taken from me. Yet not as I will, but as you will."[k]

40 Then he returned to his disciples and found them sleeping. "Could you men not keep watch with me[l] for one hour?" he asked Peter. 41 "Watch and pray so that you will not fall into temptation.[m] The spirit is willing, but the body is weak."

1 →PG. 1087
2 →PG. 1110

42 He went away a second time and prayed, "My Father, if it is not possible for this cup to be taken away unless I drink it, may your will be done."

a 25 Or *"You yourself have said it"* b 28 Some manuscripts *the new* c 31 Zech. 13:7

26:23 [t]Ps 41:9; Jn 13:18
26:24 [u]Isa 53; Da 9:26; Mk 9:12; Lk 24:25-27, 46; Ac 17:2,3; 26:22,23
26:25 [v]Mt 23:7
26:26 [w]Mt 14:19; 1Co 10:16
26:28 [x]Ex 24:6-8; Heb 9:20 [y]Mt 20:28; Mk 1:4
26:29 [z]Ac 10:41
26:30 [a]Mt 21:1; Mk 14:26
26:31 [b]Mt 11:6 [c]Zec 13:7; Jn 16:32
26:32 [d]Mt 28:7,10,16
26:34 [e]ver 75; Jn 13:38
26:35 [f]Jn 13:37
26:37 [g]Mt 4:21
26:38 [h]Jn 12:27 [i]ver 40,41
26:39 [j]Mt 20:22 [k]ver 42; Ps 40:6-8; Isa 50:5; Jn 5:30; 6:38
26:40 [l]ver 38
26:41 [m]Mt 6:13

26:36–46 PROMISE 1

WHERE'S YOUR GETHSEMANE?

How do you handle situations where God wants you to do something you don't want to do? Perhaps God is calling you to hang in there and work hard to preserve a marriage that is on the rocks. Or perhaps he's asking you to do your job with excellence when the pay is low and the appreciation is lower. Whatever your situation in life, God calls you—and all of us—to face situations where obedience is the hardest route. On such occasions we often look for a detour, a way around the hard parts of life.

So did Jesus. Does that surprise you? It shouldn't. Even though he was fully God, he was a man, just like you. His crisis point had a name: Gethsemane. In that garden, just outside of Jerusalem, Jesus prayed two things. He first asked if the "cup," the figurative goblet that contained the sins of the world and their consequences, could be taken away. This symbol of deep sorrow and suffering represented the weight of sin that Jesus would pay for through his crucifixion on our behalf. Second, he agreed to submit to his Father's will.

While there is no comparison between the tough times we face today and the one-of-a-kind agony and separation from God that awaited Jesus Christ on the cross, we can learn a crucial lesson in submission to God's will from Jesus' prayer and actions in his darkest hour. Is there a Gethsemane in your life today? Is there something of vital concern or hope that God has asked you to die to, or completely surrender to him? Whatever the challenge, remember that Jesus has already been there. He knew the difficulty that was coming and prayed earnestly about it; but when the time came, he completely surrendered to God's will. As you prayerfully consider what this means for you, know that as the Father was with his Son in that garden, so he is with you now, ready and willing to help you through your own personal Gethsemane.

For the next Promise 1 reading go to page 1091.

43 When he came back, he again
found them sleeping, because their
eyes were heavy. 44 So he left them and
went away once more and prayed the
third time, saying the same thing.
45 Then he returned to the disciples
and said to them, "Are you still sleeping and resting? Look, the hour[n] is
near, and the Son of Man is betrayed
into the hands of sinners. 46 Rise, let us
go! Here comes my betrayer!"

Jesus Arrested

›See Mark 14:43–50; Luke 22:47–53

47 While he was still speaking, Judas,
one of the Twelve, arrived. With him
was a large crowd armed with swords
and clubs, sent from the chief priests
and the elders of the people. 48 Now the
betrayer had arranged a signal with
them: "The one I kiss is the man; arrest
him." 49 Going at once to Jesus, Judas
said, "Greetings, Rabbi!"[o] and kissed
him.
50 Jesus replied, "Friend,[p] do what
you came for."[a]
Then the men stepped forward,
seized Jesus and arrested him. 51 With
that, one of Jesus' companions reached
for his sword,[q] drew it out and struck
the servant of the high priest, cutting
off his ear.[r]
52 "Put your sword back in its place,"
Jesus said to him, "for all who draw the
sword will die by the sword.[s] 53 Do you
think I cannot call on my Father, and
he will at once put at my disposal more
than twelve legions of angels?[t] 54 But
how then would the Scriptures be fulfilled[u] that say it must happen in this
way?"
55 At that time Jesus said to the
crowd, "Am I leading a rebellion, that
you have come out with swords and
clubs to capture me? Every day I sat in
the temple courts teaching,[v] and you
did not arrest me. 56 But this has all tak-
en place that the writings of the prophets might be fulfilled."[w] Then all the
disciples deserted him and fled.

Before the Sanhedrin

›See Mark 14:53–65; John 18:12–13,19–24

57 Those who had arrested Jesus took
him to Caiaphas,[x] the high priest,
where the teachers of the law and the
elders had assembled. 58 But Peter followed him at a distance, right up to the
courtyard of the high priest.[y] He entered and sat down with the guards[z]
to see the outcome.
59 The chief priests and the whole
Sanhedrin[a] were looking for false evidence against Jesus so that they could
put him to death. 60 But they did not
find any, though many false witnesses[b] came forward.
Finally two[c] came forward 61 and
declared, "This fellow said, 'I am able
to destroy the temple of God and rebuild it in three days.' "[d]
62 Then the high priest stood up and
said to Jesus, "Are you not going to answer? What is this testimony that these
men are bringing against you?" 63 But
Jesus remained silent.[e]
The high priest said to him, "I charge
you under oath[f] by the living God:[g]
Tell us if you are the Christ,[b] the Son
of God."
64 "Yes, it is as you say," Jesus replied.
"But I say to all of you: In the future
you will see the Son of Man sitting at
the right hand of the Mighty One[h] and
coming on the clouds of heaven."[i]
65 Then the high priest tore his
clothes[j] and said, "He has spoken
blasphemy! Why do we need any more
witnesses? Look, now you have heard
the blasphemy. 66 What do you think?"
"He is worthy of death,"[k] they answered.
67 Then they spit in his face and
struck him with their fists.[l] Others
slapped him 68 and said, "Prophesy to
us, Christ. Who hit you?"[m]

Peter Disowns Jesus

›See Mark 14:66–72; Luke 22:52–62;
John 18:16–18,25–27

69 Now Peter was sitting out in the
courtyard, and a servant girl came to
him. "You also were with Jesus of Galilee," she said.
70 But he denied it before them all. "I
don't know what you're talking about,"
he said.
71 Then he went out to the gateway,
where another girl saw him and said to
the people there, "This fellow was with
Jesus of Nazareth."
72 He denied it again, with an oath: "I
don't know the man!"
73 After a little while, those standing
there went up to Peter and said, "Surely you are one of them, for your accent
gives you away."
74 Then he began to call down curses
on himself and he swore to them, "I
don't know the man!"
Immediately a rooster crowed.
75 Then Peter remembered the word
Jesus had spoken: "Before the rooster
crows, you will disown me three
times."[n] And he went outside and
wept bitterly.

26:45 [n] ver 18
26:49 [o] ver 25
26:50 [p] Mt 20:13; 22:12
26:51 [q] Lk 22:36,38 [r] Jn 18:10
26:52 [s] Ge 9:6; Rev 13:10
26:53 [t] 2Ki 6:17; Da 7:10; Mt 4:11
26:54 [u] ver 24
26:55 [v] Mk 12:35; Lk 21:37; Jn 7:14,28; 18:20
26:56 [w] ver 24
26:57 [x] ver 3
26:58 [y] Jn 18:15 [z] Jn 7:32,45,46
26:59 [a] Mt 5:22
26:60 [b] Ps 27:12; 35:11; Ac 6:13 [c] Dt 19:15
26:61 [d] Jn 2:19
26:63 [e] Mt 27:12,14 [f] Lev 5:1 [g] Mt 16:16
26:64 [h] Ps 110:1 [i] Da 7:13; Rev 1:7
26:65 [j] Mk 14:63
26:66 [k] Lev 24:16; Jn 19:7
26:67 [l] Mt 16:21; 27:30
26:68 [m] Lk 22:63-65
26:75 [n] ver 34; Jn 13:38

[a] *50* Or *"Friend, why have you come?"* [b] *63* Or *Messiah;* also in verse 68

Judas Hangs Himself

27 Early in the morning, all the chief priests and the elders of the people came to the decision to put Jesus to death.[o] 2They bound him, led him away and handed him over[p] to Pilate, the governor.[q]

3When Judas, who had betrayed him,[r] saw that Jesus was condemned, he was seized with remorse and returned the thirty silver coins[s] to the chief priests and the elders. 4"I have sinned," he said, "for I have betrayed innocent blood."

"What is that to us?" they replied. "That's your responsibility."[t]

5So Judas threw the money into the temple[u] and left. Then he went away and hanged himself.[v]

6The chief priests picked up the coins and said, "It is against the law to put this into the treasury, since it is blood money." 7So they decided to use the money to buy the potter's field as a burial place for foreigners. 8That is why it has been called the Field of Blood[w] to this day. 9Then what was spoken by Jeremiah the prophet was fulfilled:[x] "They took the thirty silver coins, the price set on him by the people of Israel, 10and they used them to buy the potter's field, as the Lord commanded me."[a][y]

Jesus Before Pilate

›See Mark 15:2–15; Luke 23:2–3,18–25; John 18:29—19:16

11Meanwhile Jesus stood before the governor, and the governor asked him, "Are you the king of the Jews?"[z]

"Yes, it is as you say," Jesus replied.

12When he was accused by the chief priests and the elders, he gave no answer.[a] 13Then Pilate asked him, "Don't you hear the testimony they are bringing against you?"[b] 14But Jesus made no reply,[c] not even to a single charge—to the great amazement of the governor.

15Now it was the governor's custom at the Feast to release a prisoner[d] chosen by the crowd. 16At that time they had a notorious prisoner, called Barabbas. 17So when the crowd had gathered, Pilate asked them, "Which one do you want me to release to you: Barabbas, or Jesus who is called Christ?"[e] 18For he knew it was out of envy that they had handed Jesus over to him.

19While Pilate was sitting on the judge's seat,[f] his wife sent him this message: "Don't have anything to do with that innocent[g] man, for I have suffered a great deal today in a dream[h] because of him."

20But the chief priests and the elders persuaded the crowd to ask for Barabbas and to have Jesus executed.[i]

21"Which of the two do you want me to release to you?" asked the governor.

"Barabbas," they answered.

22"What shall I do, then, with Jesus who is called Christ?"[j] Pilate asked.

They all answered, "Crucify him!"

23"Why? What crime has he committed?" asked Pilate.

But they shouted all the louder, "Crucify him!"

24When Pilate saw that he was getting nowhere, but that instead an uproar[k] was starting, he took water and washed his hands[l] in front of the crowd. "I am innocent of this man's blood,"[m] he said. "It is your responsibility!"[n]

25All the people answered, "Let his blood be on us and on our children!"[o]

26Then he released Barabbas to them. But he had Jesus flogged,[p] and handed him over to be crucified.

The Soldiers Mock Jesus

›See Mark 15:16–20

27Then the governor's soldiers took Jesus into the Praetorium[q] and gathered the whole company of soldiers around him. 28They stripped him and put a scarlet robe on him,[r] 29and then twisted together a crown of thorns and set it on his head. They put a staff in his right hand and knelt in front of him and mocked him. "Hail, king of the Jews!" they said.[s] 30They spit on him, and took the staff and struck him on the head again and again.[t] 31After they had mocked him, they took off the robe and put his own clothes on him. Then they led him away to crucify him.[u]

The Crucifixion

›See Mark 15:22–32; Luke 23:33–43; John 19:17–24

32As they were going out,[v] they met a man from Cyrene,[w] named Simon, and they forced him to carry the cross.[x] 33They came to a place called Golgotha (which means The Place of the Skull).[y] 34There they offered Jesus wine to drink, mixed with gall;[z] but after tasting it, he refused to drink it. 35When they had crucified him, they divided up his clothes by casting lots.[b][a] 36And sitting down, they kept watch[b] over him there. 37Above his

27:1 [o]Mt 12:14; Mk 15:1; Lk 22:66
27:2 [p]Mt 20:19 [q]Mk 15:1; Lk 13:1; Ac 3:13; 1Ti 6:13
27:3 [r]Mt 10:4 [s]Mt 26:14,15
27:4 [t]ver 24
27:5 [u]Lk 1:9,21 [v]Ac 1:18
27:8 [w]Ac 1:19
27:9 [x]Mt 1:22
27:10 [y]Zec 11:12,13; Jer 32:6-9
27:11 [z]Mt 2:2
27:12 [a]Mt 26:63; Mk 14:61; Jn 19:9
27:13 [b]Mt 26:62
27:14 [c]Mk 14:61
27:15 [d]Jn 18:39
27:17 [e]ver 22; Mt 1:16
27:19 [f]Jn 19:13 [g]ver 24 [h]Ge 20:6; Nu 12:6; 1Ki 3:5; Job 33:14-16; Mt 1:20; 2:12, 13,19,22
27:20 [i]Ac 3:14
27:22 [j]Mt 1:16
27:24 [k]Mt 26:5 [l]Ps 26:6 [m]Dt 21:6-8 [n]ver 4
27:25 [o]Jos 2:19; Ac 5:28
27:26 [p]Isa 53:5; Jn 19:1
27:27 [q]Jn 18:28,33; 19:9
27:28 [r]Jn 19:2
27:29 [s]Isa 53:3; Jn 19:2,3
27:30 [t]Mt 16:21; 26:67
27:31 [u]Isa 53:7
27:32 [v]Heb 13:12 [w]Ac 2:10; 6:9; 11:20; 13:1 [x]Mk 15:21; Lk 23:26
27:33 [y]Jn 19:17
27:34 [z]ver 48; Ps 69:21
27:35 [a]Ps 22:18
27:36 [b]ver 54

[a] *10* See Zech. 11:12,13; Jer. 19:1-13; 32:6-9.
[b] *35* A few late manuscripts *lots that the word spoken by the prophet might be fulfilled: "They divided my garments among themselves and cast lots for my clothing"* (Psalm 22:18)

27:31–50

PROMISE 7

THE ULTIMATE PRICE

After enduring the clamor of the trial and the jeers of the crowd, Jesus reached the summit of the hill where he would be crucified. The Roman guards assigned to execution duty that day stretched Jesus out on the ground, pinning his arms roughly against a wooden crossbeam. Then one of the guards found the soft spot on Jesus' wrist and placed the point of a spike against his flesh. The sound of the hammer striking the spike rang out over the din of the crowd. He repeated the process on the other arm. Two guards then lifted Jesus up and secured the crossbeam on an upright pole. Grabbing one of Jesus' feet and placing it over the other, the powerful Roman drove another spike through both feet, securing them to the base of the cross. Jesus, the sinless one, God's own Son, hung there in the burning Palestinian sun. There he also felt the full heat of the crowd's scorn and mocking.

While nailed to the cross, Jesus had to lift himself on the spike in his feet in order to breathe. When the pain in his feet became unbearable, he would slump and hang by his wrists. As his head hung heavy, his windpipe was cut off, making breathing impossible. That's why death by crucifixion was so horrible—it was a slow, desperate kind of death, with the urge to breathe battling constantly against the white-hot pain presented by the spikes embedded in the victim's flesh. The Lord spoke only seven times during the hours he hung on the cross—three times before the darkness, once during it, and three times after.

"Father, forgive them, for they do not know what they are doing" (Luke 23:34). Jesus was resolute in the face of his death, knowing that his purpose on earth would now be fulfilled. He asked God to forgive the crowd—the very ones who had condemned him unjustly; who had spat on, mocked and jeered at him; even the ones who had nailed him to the cross and now gambled for his clothes. He asked the Father to forgive those who did not deserve it—a true picture of his work on the cross for all of us.

"I tell you the truth, today you will be with me in paradise" (Luke 23:43). Originally both thieves mocked Jesus (Matthew 27:39–44). But one changed his mind and asked Jesus to remember him when he entered his heavenly kingdom. From his pathetic position on the cross, that lawless man received the unexpected, free gift of eternal life. Had he done anything to earn such a gift? Of course not. He simply changed his mind about Jesus and placed his faith in him.

"Dear woman, here is your son . . . Here is your mother" (John 19:26–27). Upon seeing his mother and one of his disciples (probably John) standing close to the cross, Jesus fulfilled his role as Mary's oldest son and made provision for her future care. She was now to consider John her son, and John was to treat Mary as his own mother.

"My God, my God, why have you forsaken me?" (Matthew 27:46). When darkness covered the land, Jesus cried out in a loud voice. The blackness signified Jesus' separation from God. In these hours he took the punishment for sin that was meant for all of us. He carried the guilt of our own sins, even though he was perfect. That's what was happening here—nothing short of the most awesome and most significant event in all of human history.

"I am thirsty" (John 19:28). Moments before the end of his earthly life, Jesus was aware of his swollen and parched tongue. As his craving for water demanded a response, he uttered this statement. In doing so, Jesus fulfilled a prophecy made hundreds of years earlier by King David (Psalm 69:21).

"It is finished" (John 19:30). With these words, Jesus declared victory. In the original language, this phrase was a legal term. Common practice dictated that when a man was convicted of a crime, his punishment was written on a scroll. The scroll was then rolled up and nailed over his jail cell. When he had served his sentence, the scroll was taken down and had the phrase "It is finished" written across it. Never again would that man be punished for that crime; complete restitution had been made.

In Jesus' person, a scroll carrying the crimes of all mankind had been nailed to a cross (see Colossians 2:13–15). When he had paid in full for the sins of the world, Jesus cried out, "It is finished!" Never again would humans have to suffer eternal condemnation for their sins. Jesus has paid our debt to our Creator in full, and offers us the gift of his payment in place of ours if we will but choose to accept it.

"Father, into your hands I commit my spirit" (Luke 23:46). With these words Jesus handed his life over to his Father. Neither the Jewish religious rulers, nor Pilate, nor the crowds, nor even the guards themselves took away Jesus' life; he willingly gave it up.

Jesus' crucifixion was the greatest act of love in human history. Reflect on the seven sentences he uttered from the cross. Which of the statements leaves the greatest impression? Take a moment and thank God for giving his Son as the perfect sacrifice for our sins. Then thank Jesus himself for paying the ultimate price and for dying in your place.

For the next Promise 7 reading go to page 1087.

head they placed the written charge against him: THIS IS JESUS, THE KING OF THE JEWS. 38 Two robbers were crucified with him,[c] one on his right and one on his left. 39 Those who passed by hurled insults at him, shaking their heads[d] 40 and saying, "You who are going to destroy the temple and build it in three days,[e] save yourself![f] Come down from the cross, if you are the Son of God!"[g]

41 In the same way the chief priests, the teachers of the law and the elders mocked him. 42 "He saved others," they said, "but he can't save himself! He's the King of Israel![h] Let him come down now from the cross, and we will believe[i] in him. 43 He trusts in God. Let God rescue him[j] now if he wants him, for he said, 'I am the Son of God.' " 44 In the same way the robbers who were crucified with him also heaped insults on him.

The Death of Jesus

›See Mark 15:33–41; Luke 23:44–49; John 19:29–30

45 From the sixth hour until the ninth hour darkness[k] came over all the land. 46 About the ninth hour Jesus cried out in a loud voice, *"Eloi, Eloi,*[a] *lama sabachthani?"*—which means, "My God, my God, why have you forsaken me?"[b][l]

47 When some of those standing there heard this, they said, "He's calling Elijah."

48 Immediately one of them ran and got a sponge. He filled it with wine vinegar,[m] put it on a stick, and offered it to Jesus to drink. 49 The rest said, "Now leave him alone. Let's see if Elijah comes to save him."

50 And when Jesus had cried out again in a loud voice, he gave up his spirit.[n]

51 At that moment the curtain of the temple[o] was torn in two from top to bottom. The earth shook and the rocks split.[p] 52 The tombs broke open and the bodies of many holy people who had died were raised to life. 53 They came out of the tombs, and after Jesus' resurrection they went into the holy city[q] and appeared to many people.

54 When the centurion and those with him who were guarding[r] Jesus saw the earthquake and all that had happened, they were terrified, and exclaimed, "Surely he was the Son[c] of God!"[s]

55 Many women were there, watching from a distance. They had followed Jesus from Galilee to care for his needs.[t] 56 Among them were Mary Magdalene, Mary the mother of James and Joses, and the mother of Zebedee's sons.[u]

The Burial of Jesus

›See Mark 15:42–47; Luke 23:50–56; John 19:38–42

57 As evening approached, there came a rich man from Arimathea, named Joseph, who had himself become a disciple of Jesus. 58 Going to Pilate, he asked for Jesus' body, and Pilate ordered that it be given to him. 59 Joseph took the body, wrapped it in a clean linen cloth, 60 and placed it in his own new tomb[v] that he had cut out of the rock. He rolled a big stone in front of the entrance to the tomb and went away. 61 Mary Magdalene and the other Mary were sitting there opposite the tomb.

The Guard at the Tomb

62 The next day, the one after Preparation Day, the chief priests and the Pharisees went to Pilate. 63 "Sir," they said, "we remember that while he was still alive that deceiver said, 'After three days I will rise again.'[w] 64 So give the order for the tomb to be made secure until the third day. Otherwise, his disciples may come and steal the body and tell the people that he has been raised from the dead. This last deception will be worse than the first."

65 "Take a guard,"[x] Pilate answered. "Go, make the tomb as secure as you know how." 66 So they went and made the tomb secure by putting a seal[y] on the stone[z] and posting the guard.[a]

The Resurrection

›See Mark 16:1–8; Luke 24:1–10; John 20:1–8

28 After the Sabbath, at dawn on the first day of the week, Mary Magdalene and the other Mary[b] went to look at the tomb.

2 There was a violent earthquake,[c] for an angel[d] of the Lord came down from heaven and, going to the tomb, rolled back the stone and sat on it. 3 His appearance was like lightning, and his clothes were white as snow.[e] 4 The guards were so afraid of him that they shook and became like dead men.

5 The angel said to the women, "Do not be afraid,[f] for I know that you are looking for Jesus, who was crucified. 6 He is not here; he has risen, just as he said.[g] Come and see the place where he lay. 7 Then go quickly and tell his disciples: 'He has risen from the dead

27:38 [c]Isa 53:12
27:39 [d]Ps 22:7; 109:25; La 2:15
27:40 [e]Mt 26:61; Jn 2:19 [f]ver 42 [g]Mt 4:3,6
27:42 [h]Jn 1:49; 12:13 [i]Jn 3:15
27:43 [j]Ps 22:8
27:45 [k]Am 8:9
27:46 [l]Ps 22:1
27:48 [m]ver 34; Ps 69:21
27:50 [n]Jn 19:30
27:51 [o]Ex 26:31-33; Heb 9:3,8 [p]ver 54
27:53 [q]Mt 4:5
27:54 [r]ver 36 [s]Mt 4:3; 17:5
27:55 [t]Lk 8:2,3
27:56 [u]Mk 15:47; Lk 24:10; Jn 19:25
27:60 [v]Mt 27:66; 28:2; Mk 16:4
27:63 [w]Mt 16:21
27:65 [x]ver 66; Mt 28:11
27:66 [y]Da 6:17 [z]ver 60; Mt 28:2 [a]Mt 28:11
28:1 [b]Mt 27:56
28:2 [c]Mt 27:51 [d]Jn 20:12
28:3 [e]Da 10:6; Mk 9:3; Jn 20:12
28:5 [f]ver 10; Mt 14:27
28:6 [g]Mt 16:21

[a] *46* Some manuscripts *Eli, Eli*
[b] *46* Psalm 22:1
[c] *54* Or *a son*

and is going ahead of you into Galilee.[h] There you will see him.' Now I
have told you."
1 →PG. 1090
8So the women hurried away from
the tomb, afraid yet filled with joy, and
ran to tell his disciples. 9Suddenly
Jesus met them.[i] "Greetings," he said.
They came to him, clasped his feet and
worshiped him. 10Then Jesus said to
them, "Do not be afraid. Go and tell my
brothers[j] to go to Galilee; there they
will see me."

The Guards' Report

11While the women were on their
way, some of the guards[k] went into
the city and reported to the chief
priests everything that had happened.
12When the chief priests had met with
the elders and devised a plan, they
gave the soldiers a large sum of money,
13telling them, "You are to say, 'His disciples came during the night and stole
him away while we were asleep.' 14If
this report gets to the governor,[l] we
will satisfy him and keep you out of
trouble." 15So the soldiers took the
money and did as they were instructed.
And this story has been widely circulated among the Jews to this very day.

The Great Commission

16Then the eleven disciples went to
Galilee, to the mountain where Jesus
had told them to go.[m] 17When they
saw him, they worshiped him; but
some doubted. 18Then Jesus came to
them and said, "All authority in heaven
and on earth has been given to me.[n]
7 →PG. 1095
19Therefore go and make disciples of
all nations,[o] baptizing them in[a] the
name of the Father and of the Son and
of the Holy Spirit,[p] 20and teaching[q]
them to obey everything I have commanded you. And surely I am with
you[r] always, to the very end of the
age."[s]

[a] *19* Or *into*; see Acts 8:16; 19:5; Romans 6:3; 1 Cor. 1:13; 10:2 and Gal. 3:27.

28:7 [h] ver 10,16; Mt 26:32
28:9 [i] Jn 20:14-18
28:10 [j] Jn 20:17; Ro 8:29; Heb 2:11-13, 17
28:11 [k] Mt 27:65,66
28:14 [l] Mt 27:2
28:16 [m] ver 7,10; Mt 26:32
28:18 [n] Da 7:13,14; Lk 10:22; Jn 3:35; 17:2; 1Co 15:27; Eph 1:20-22; Php 2:9,10
28:19 [o] Mk 16:15,16; Lk 24:47; Ac 1:8; 14:21 [p] Ac 2:38; 8:16; Ro 6:3,4
28:20 [q] Ac 2:42 [r] Mt 18:20; Ac 18:10 [s] Mt 13:39

28:18–20

PROMISE 7

GLOBAL VISION

If you've ever wondered what God wants you to do with your life, these verses paint a clear picture. The Lord commands everyone who commits to follow him to "make disciples of all nations." Our vision is to be global. Our eyes are to be on reaching the world for Jesus Christ.

Obeying such a command may seem beyond our reach; and, in fact, it is. But keep in mind that it's not beyond the Lord's reach. Here Jesus promises to be with us as we begin, even in the smallest way within our own sphere of influence, to affect positive change in the world for him.

If you'd like to have your vision expanded, pray that God will show you the way that he would like you to begin "making disciples." Perhaps you could pray about changing your attitude and being more of a positive force at work, spending more time influencing the lives of your children or of a person who doesn't yet know the Lord, or even participating in a short- or long-term missions trip.

For the next Promise 7 reading go to page 1096.

MARK

AT A GLANCE

Key Principle: Those who follow Christ are called to take up their cross and live in service to him and to others.
Author: Mark
Time and Place: A.D. 29–33 / Galilee, Perea, and Judea
Key Verses: 8:34–37; 10:43–45

BENEFIT

The Gospel of Mark is the most clear and concise of the four Gospels. Its fast-paced narrative tells the story of the suffering Servant who constantly engaged in other-centered ministry through healing, teaching and preaching. This book stresses the power of servanthood and the reality of finding our life by losing it for Christ's sake, just as he gave his life for our sake. Like the other Gospels, Mark disproportionately emphasizes Christ's final week on earth; Jesus' last eight days comprise 40 percent of the book.

SETTING

The early church fathers attested that Mark, a cousin of Barnabas (Colossians 4:10) and a close associate of Peter (1 Peter 5:13) and Paul (Colossians 4:10; Philemon 24; 2 Timothy 4:11) wrote this Gospel. He wrote this Gospel before the temple was destroyed (13:2); the likely range of authorship is A.D. 55–65. Early tradition points to a Roman origin and readership, which the text itself supports. For example, Mark uses several Latin terms rather than their Greek equivalents, explains the meanings of Aramaic words, and omits many details that would not have been meaningful to a Gentile audience (e.g. the genealogy of Jesus, reference to the Mosaic law and Jewish customs that appear in other Gospels, and Christ's fulfillment of Old Testament prophecies).

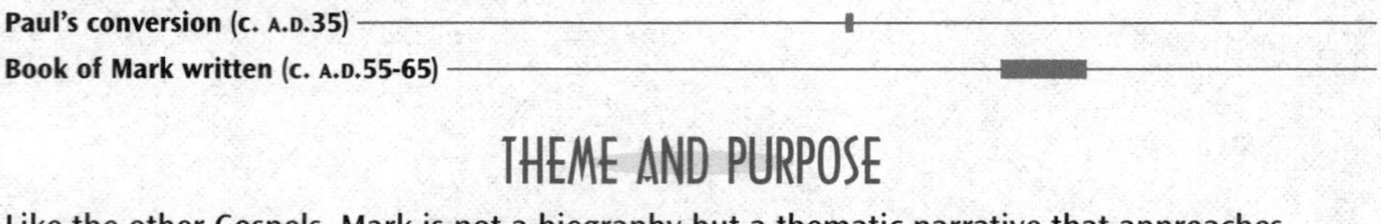

THEME AND PURPOSE

Like the other Gospels, Mark is not a biography but a thematic narrative that approaches Christ's life from a specific perspective. This Gospel's theme is conveyed in Christ's clear purpose statement in 10:45: "For even the Son of Man did not come to be served, but to serve, and to give his life as a ransom for many." Mark presents Jesus as the Servant and Redeemer of his people (compare Philippians 2:5–11) and develops this theme by using a large number of miracles, 18 in all, to illustrate how Jesus ministered to others. Demonstrating not only the

Lord's compassion but also his power and authority, these miracles also authenticate his teachings, which are dispersed throughout. This Gospel was written to reveal to Gentiles the person and claims of Christ and to instruct believers in the early church.

UNIQUE CONTRIBUTION

Apart from only two extended discourses (4:1–34; 13:3–37), Mark's Gospel moves at a lively, vigorous pace. Such practicality and emphasis on action would have appealed to the Roman mind, which may be why Mark presents over half of Christ's 35 recorded miracles, as opposed to only 18 out of the 70 known parables. Mark's simple and straightforward style is ideally suited to present the life of the divine Servant. Its unvarnished language, including colloquialisms and broken sentence structure, may reflect Peter's influence, a possibility consistent with the tradition that Peter was Mark's primary resource. This Gospel also richly depicts a wide range of emotional reactions in Jesus' audience, and in his own life as well.

CHRIST IN MARK

Mark presents Christ as an active and other-centered Servant who continually ministers to those he encounters. The servant motif, as well as the intended Gentile audience, explain why this Gospel provides no account of his ancestry and birth. His radical obedience to the Father and his compassionate concern for the physical and spiritual needs of others are clearly evident throughout, but Mark also emphasizes that this service is borne by the authoritative and powerful Son of God (1:1, 11; 3:11; 5:7; 9:7; 13:32; 14:61–62; 15:39).

OVERVIEW

FOCUS	Servant to the Israelites		Sacrifice for the World
REFERENCE	1 — 8:26	8:27 — 10:52	11 — 16
TOPICS	Ministry to the Multitudes	Ministry to the Disciples	Rejection by the Rulers
	"For even the Son of Man did not come to be served, but to serve, . . ."		"and to give his life as a ransom for many."
	Sayings and Signs of the Servant		Suffering of the Servant
LOCATION	Galilee and Perea		Judea and Jerusalem
TIME	Three Years	Six Months	Eight Days
	A.D. 29–33		

Mark's Gospel overlooks Jesus' birth and early life. He launches his narrative with Jesus' baptism by his forerunner John and Jesus' temptation in the wilderness (1:1–13). Mark continues his account with a series of miracle stories, interspersing teachings in such a way that the words and the works of Jesus are mutually supportive (1:14—8:26). In his miracles, Jesus demonstrates his authority over nature, disease, demons, and death.

Jesus responds to mounting opposition by intensifying his preaching and by preparing his disciples for his departure. In the approximate six-month period between Mark 8:27 and 10:52, Jesus more and more frequently speaks to his disciples of his coming death and resurrection as he turns his steps toward Jerusalem.

Jesus' triumphal entry into Jerusalem and his cleansing of the temple are met with opposition; during the last week of his ministry the Pharisees, Sadducees, chief priests, scribes and Herodians all rebuke him. Jesus refutes their arguments and announces the coming destruction of the city (11—13). Jesus is arrested, tried before the civil and religious authorities and crucified (14—15)—but he is raised from the dead as he had promised (16).

MARK

John the Baptist Prepares the Way

›See Matthew 3:1–11; Luke 3:2–16

1 The beginning of the gospel about
Jesus Christ, the Son of God.[a][a]

2 It is written in Isaiah the prophet:

"I will send my messenger ahead of
you,
who will prepare your
way"[b][b]—
3 "a voice of one calling in the
desert,
'Prepare the way for the Lord,
make straight paths for
him.' "[c][c]

4 And so John[d] came, baptizing in the
desert region and preaching a baptism
of repentance[e] for the forgiveness of
sins.[f] 5 The whole Judean countryside
and all the people of Jerusalem went
out to him. Confessing their sins, they
were baptized by him in the Jordan
River. 6 John wore clothing made of
camel's hair, with a leather belt around
his waist, and he ate locusts[g] and wild
honey. 7 And this was his message: "After me will come one more powerful
than I, the thongs of whose sandals I
am not worthy to stoop down and untie.[h] 8 I baptize you with[d] water, but
he will baptize you with the Holy
Spirit."[i]

The Baptism and Temptation of Jesus

›See Matthew 3:13–17; 4:1–11; Luke 3:21–22;
4:1–13

9 At that time Jesus came from Nazareth[j] in Galilee and was baptized by
John in the Jordan. 10 As Jesus was coming up out of the water, he saw heaven
being torn open and the Spirit descending on him like a dove.[k] 11 And a
voice came from heaven: "You are my
Son,[l] whom I love; with you I am well
pleased."

12 At once the Spirit sent him out into
the desert, 13 and he was in the desert
forty days, being tempted by Satan.[m]
He was with the wild animals, and angels attended him.

The Calling of the First Disciples

›See Matthew 4:18–22; Luke 5:2–11;
John 1:35–42

14 After John was put in prison, Jesus
went into Galilee,[n] proclaiming the
good news of God.[o] 15 "The time has
come,"[p] he said. "The kingdom of
God is near. Repent and believe the
good news!"[q]

16 As Jesus walked beside the Sea of
Galilee, he saw Simon and his brother
Andrew casting a net into the lake, for
they were fishermen. 17 "Come, follow
me," Jesus said, "and I will make you
fishers of men." 18 At once they left their
nets and followed him.

19 When he had gone a little farther,
he saw James son of Zebedee and his
brother John in a boat, preparing their
nets. 20 Without delay he called them,
and they left their father Zebedee in
the boat with the hired men and followed him.

Jesus Drives Out an Evil Spirit

›See Luke 4:31–37

21 They went to Capernaum, and
when the Sabbath came, Jesus went
into the synagogue and began to
teach.[r] 22 The people were amazed at
his teaching, because he taught them
as one who had authority, not as the
teachers of the law.[s] 23 Just then a man
in their synagogue who was possessed
by an evil[e] spirit cried out, 24 "What do
you want with us,[t] Jesus of Nazareth?[u] Have you come to destroy us? I
know who you are—the Holy One of
God!"[v]

1 →PG. 1098

25 "Be quiet!" said Jesus sternly.
"Come out of him!"[w] 26 The evil spirit
shook the man violently and came out
of him with a shriek.[x]

27 The people were all so amazed[y]
that they asked each other, "What is
this? A new teaching—and with authority! He even gives orders to evil
spirits and they obey him." 28 News
about him spread quickly over the
whole region[z] of Galilee.

Jesus Heals Many

›See Matthew 8:14–17; Luke 4:38–41

29 As soon as they left the synagogue,[a] they went with James and
John to the home of Simon and Andrew. 30 Simon's mother-in-law was in
bed with a fever, and they told Jesus
about her. 31 So he went to her, took her
hand and helped her up.[b] The fever
left her and she began to wait on them.
32 That evening after sunset the

1:1 [a] Mt 4:3
1:2 [b] Mal 3:1; Mt 11:10; Lk 7:27
1:3 [c] Isa 40:3; Jn 1:23
1:4 [d] Mt 3:1 [e] Ac 13:24 [f] Lk 1:77
1:6 [g] Lev 11:22
1:7 [h] Ac 13:25
1:8 [i] Isa 44:3; Joel 2:28; Ac 1:5; 2:4; 11:16; 19:4-6
1:9 [j] Mt 2:23
1:10 [k] Jn 1:32
1:11 [l] Mt 3:17
1:13 [m] Mt 4:10
1:14 [n] Mt 4:12 [o] Mt 4:23
1:15 [p] Gal 4:4; Eph 1:10 [q] Ac 20:21
1:21 [r] Mt 4:23; Mk 10:1
1:22 [s] Mt 7:28,29
1:24 [t] Mt 8:29 [u] Mt 2:23; Lk 24:19; Ac 24:5 [v] Lk 1:35; Jn 6:69; Ac 3:14
1:25 [w] ver 34
1:26 [x] Mk 9:20
1:27 [y] Mk 10:24,32
1:28 [z] Mt 9:26
1:29 [a] ver 21,23
1:31 [b] Lk 7:14

[a] *1* Some manuscripts do not have *the Son of God.* [b] *2* Mal. 3:1 [c] *3* Isaiah 40:3
[d] *8* Or *in* [e] *23* Greek *unclean*; also in verses 26 and 27

people brought to Jesus all the sick
and demon-possessed.[c] 33The whole
town gathered at the door, 34and Jesus
healed many who had various diseases.[d] He also drove out many demons, but he would not let the demons
speak because they knew who he
was.[e]

Jesus Prays in a Solitary Place

›See Luke 4:42–43

35Very early in the morning, while
it was still dark, Jesus got up, left the
house and went off to a solitary place,
where he prayed.[f] 36Simon and his
companions went to look for him,
37and when they found him, they exclaimed: "Everyone is looking for you!"
38Jesus replied, "Let us go somewhere else—to the nearby villages—
so I can preach there also. That is
why I have come."[g] 39So he traveled
throughout Galilee, preaching in their
synagogues[h] and driving out demons.[i]

A Man With Leprosy

›See Matthew 8:2–4; Luke 5:12–14

40A man with leprosy[a] came to him
and begged him on his knees,[j] "If you
are willing, you can make me clean."
41Filled with compassion, Jesus
reached out his hand and touched
the man. "I am willing," he said. "Be
clean!" 42Immediately the leprosy left
him and he was cured.
43Jesus sent him away at once with a
strong warning: 44"See that you don't
tell this to anyone.[k] But go, show
yourself to the priest[l] and offer the
sacrifices that Moses commanded for
your cleansing,[m] as a testimony to
them." 45Instead he went out and began to talk freely, spreading the news.
As a result, Jesus could no longer enter
a town openly but stayed outside in
lonely places.[n] Yet the people still
came to him from everywhere.[o]

Jesus Heals a Paralytic

›See Matthew 9:2–8; Luke 5:18–26

2 A few days later, when Jesus again
entered Capernaum, the people
heard that he had come home. 2So
many[p] gathered that there was no
room left, not even outside the door,
and he preached the word to them.
3Some men came, bringing to him a
paralytic,[q] carried by four of them.
4Since they could not get him to Jesus
because of the crowd, they made an
opening in the roof above Jesus and,
after digging through it, lowered the
mat the paralyzed man was lying on.
5When Jesus saw their faith, he said to
the paralytic, "Son, your sins are forgiven."[r]
6Now some teachers of the law were
sitting there, thinking to themselves,
7"Why does this fellow talk like that?

1:32 [c]Mt 4:24 **1:34** [d]Mt 4:23 [e]Mk 3:12; Ac 16:17,18 **1:35** [f]Lk 3:21 **1:38** [g]Isa 61:1 **1:39** [h]Mt 4:23 [i]Mt 4:24 **1:40** [j]Mk 10:17 **1:44** [k]Mt 8:4 [l]Lev 13:49 [m]Lev 14:1-32 **1:45** [n]Lk 5:15,16 [o]Mk 2:13; Lk 5:17; Jn 6:2 **2:2** [p]ver 13; Mk 1:45 **2:3** [q]Mt 4:24 **2:5** [r]Lk 7:48

[a]*40* The Greek word was used for various diseases affecting the skin—not necessarily leprosy.

1:35

PROMISE 1

PRIORITIES

Have you ever noticed that some well-known sayings rub us the wrong way because they're so true? For instance, "You always have time to do the things that you consider important." Those words have a way of reminding us that we choose to do some things that we want to do while avoiding others that we probably should do.

That's what makes Jesus' early-morning meeting with his Father so impressive. Jesus could have slept in, or he could have risen early to get a jump on the day's activities. But Jesus knew something that each of us must learn: Nothing is more important than time spent alone with God.

For the next Promise 1 reading go to page 1109.

1:40–44

PROMISE 6

TOUCHED BY THE MASTER

In this passage, we see Jesus do something that most people of his day would have considered unthinkable. He reaches out his hand, touches a leper, and then heals him.

Think about that for a moment. Jesus touched the leper *first,* and *then* healed him. Most of us, if we had the power within us, would have healed the leper first, and then touched him. But not Jesus. Why? Because he knew that, as a leper, this man probably hadn't felt the touch of a human hand in months, perhaps even years. Jesus knew that this man needed to experience God's unconditional love in a concrete, physical way.

The life of Jesus in us makes it possible to for us to follow his example. We can love the unlovely. We can reach out and touch people who might feel out of place in our company—people unlike ourselves, those whom we in our pride may consider "unclean." Every time we break through the barrier of racism, favoritism or prejudice, we show the love of Jesus in the most practical way possible.

For the next Promise 6 reading go to page 1128.

He's blaspheming! Who can forgive sins but God alone?"[s]

8 Immediately Jesus knew in his spirit that this was what they were thinking in their hearts, and he said to them, "Why are you thinking these things? 9 Which is easier: to say to the paralytic, 'Your sins are forgiven,' or to say, 'Get up, take your mat and walk'? 10 But that you may know that the Son of Man[t] has authority on earth to forgive sins . . ." He said to the paralytic, 11 "I tell you, get up, take your mat and go home." 12 He got up, took his mat and walked out in full view of them all. This amazed everyone and they praised God,[u] saying, "We have never seen anything like this!"[v]

The Calling of Levi

›See Matthew 9:9–13; Luke 5:27–32

13 Once again Jesus went out beside the lake. A large crowd came to him,[w] and he began to teach them. 14 As he walked along, he saw Levi son of Alphaeus sitting at the tax collector's booth. "Follow me,"[x] Jesus told him, and Levi got up and followed him.

15 While Jesus was having dinner at Levi's house, many tax collectors and "sinners" were eating with him and his disciples, for there were many who followed him. 16 When the teachers of the law who were Pharisees[y] saw him eating with the "sinners" and tax collectors, they asked his disciples: "Why does he eat with tax collectors and 'sinners'?"[z]

17 On hearing this, Jesus said to them, "It is not the healthy who need a doctor, but the sick. I have not come to call the righteous, but sinners."[a]

Jesus Questioned About Fasting

›See Matthew 9:14–17; Luke 5:33–38

18 Now John's disciples and the Pharisees were fasting.[b] Some people came and asked Jesus, "How is it that John's disciples and the disciples of the Pharisees are fasting, but yours are not?"

19 Jesus answered, "How can the guests of the bridegroom fast while he is with them? They cannot, so long as they have him with them. 20 But the time will come when the bridegroom will be taken from them,[c] and on that day they will fast.

21 "No one sews a patch of unshrunk cloth on an old garment. If he does, the new piece will pull away from the old, making the tear worse. 22 And no one pours new wine into old wineskins. If he does, the wine will burst the skins, and both the wine and the wineskins will be ruined. No, he pours new wine into new wineskins."

Lord of the Sabbath

›See Matthew 12:1–14; Luke 6:1–11

23 One Sabbath Jesus was going through the grainfields, and as his disciples walked along, they began to pick some heads of grain.[d] 24 The Pharisees said to him, "Look, why are they doing what is unlawful on the Sabbath?"[e]

25 He answered, "Have you never read what David did when he and his companions were hungry and in need? 26 In the days of Abiathar the high priest,[f] he entered the house of God and ate the consecrated bread, which is lawful only for priests to eat.[g] And he also gave some to his companions."[h]

27 Then he said to them, "The Sabbath was made for man,[i] not man for the Sabbath.[j] 28 So the Son of Man[k] is Lord even of the Sabbath."

3 Another time he went into the synagogue,[l] and a man with a shriveled hand was there. 2 Some of them were looking for a reason to accuse Jesus, so they watched him closely[m] to see if he would heal him on the Sabbath.[n] 3 Jesus said to the man with the shriveled hand, "Stand up in front of everyone."

4 Then Jesus asked them, "Which is lawful on the Sabbath: to do good or to do evil, to save life or to kill?" But they remained silent.

5 He looked around at them in anger and, deeply distressed at their stubborn hearts, said to the man, "Stretch out your hand." He stretched it out, and his hand was completely restored. 6 Then the Pharisees went out and began to plot with the Herodians[o] how they might kill Jesus.[p]

Crowds Follow Jesus

›See Matthew 12:15–16; Luke 6:17–19

7 Jesus withdrew with his disciples to the lake, and a large crowd from Galilee followed.[q] 8 When they heard all he was doing, many people came to him from Judea, Jerusalem, Idumea, and the regions across the Jordan and around Tyre and Sidon.[r] 9 Because of the crowd he told his disciples to have a small boat ready for him, to keep the people from crowding him. 10 For he had healed many,[s] so that those with diseases were pushing forward to touch him.[t] 11 Whenever the evil[a] spirits saw him, they fell down before him and cried out, "You are the Son of

2:7 [s]Isa 43:25
2:10 [t]Mt 8:20
2:12 [u]Mt 9:8 [v]Mt 9:33
2:13 [w]Mk 1:45; Lk 5:15; Jn 6:2
2:14 [x]Mt 4:19
2:16 [y]Ac 23:9 [z]Mt 9:11
2:17 [a]Lk 19:10; 1Ti 1:15
2:18 [b]Mt 6:16-18; Ac 13:2
2:20 [c]Lk 17:22
2:23 [d]Dt 23:25
2:24 [e]Mt 12:2
2:26 [f]1Ch 24:6; 2Sa 8:17 [g]Lev 24:5-9 [h]1Sa 21:1-6
2:27 [i]Ex 23:12; Dt 5:14 [j]Col 2:16
2:28 [k]Mt 8:20
3:1 [l]Mt 4:23; Mk 1:21
3:2 [m]Mt 12:10 [n]Lk 14:1
3:6 [o]Mt 22:16; Mk 12:13 [p]Mt 12:14
3:7 [q]Mt 4:25
3:8 [r]Mt 11:21
3:10 [s]Mt 4:23 [t]Mt 9:20

a *11* Greek *unclean*; also in verse 30

MARK

A Failure Restored

Suppose you heard the gospel and responded in faith, believing in Jesus as your Savior. When someone offered you an opportunity for Christian service, you jumped at the chance. Things went fine for a while. You were learning and growing. But after a time, for some reason, you dropped out. Others pushed ahead, but you quit. And you've been feeling a little guilty ever since. Would God ever be able to use you in his service again?

Mark, the Gospel writer, could certainly identify with that scenario and those questions. He earned the reputation of being unreliable after dropping out of his first significant ministry opportunity. But he also learned the blessing of a second chance and God's restoration.

From Failure to Second Chance

We first read of Mark in Acts, when Peter went to "the house of Mary the mother of John, also called Mark" after Peter's miraculous release from Herod's prison (Acts 12:12). Believers in Jerusalem would often meet at Mary's home to pray. Mark must have demonstrated some useful abilities and gifts, as well as a willing spirit, as he accompanied them (12:25), for when Paul and Barnabas left on their first missionary journey, they took Mark with them as their assistant (13:5).

This was a great opportunity for the young man, living and working alongside the great apostle and his cousin Barnabas (Colossians 4:10). But not too far into the trip, Mark deserted Paul and his companions and returned to Jerusalem (13:13). We aren't given any reasons for his turning back, but it may well have been that things just got too tough for him. In any event, Paul was bothered by Mark's decision and came to regard him as unreliable.

When Paul decided to take another missionary journey, Barnabas wanted to give Mark another chance to prove himself, but Paul was unwilling (15:37–38). Paul chose Silas as a companion in his work instead, and "Barnabas took Mark and sailed for Cyprus" (15:39). Barnabas became Mark's mentor and encourager. He knew Mark's heart and had faith in him.

Complete Restoration

Barnabas's confidence in Mark paid off. Approximately ten years later Paul wrote a letter from prison to a man named Philemon. Paul sent greetings from several men, including Mark, whom Paul referred to as his "fellow worker" (Philemon 24). During Paul's second imprisonment in Rome, Paul wrote to Timothy and asked him to "get Mark and bring him with you, because he is helpful to me in my ministry" (2 Timothy 4:11). At this point, Paul had so much confidence in Mark that he actually requested the assistance of this one-time deserter. Barnabas's second chance, God's restoring work, and Mark's faithful response had led Paul to regain his confidence in Mark.

What a change! What a turnaround! The apostle Peter gives a strong indication that Mark did indeed make that journey to Rome to be with Paul during his final days. And it is very possible that Mark developed a close relationship with Peter as well since Peter later referred to him as his son (1 Peter 5:13).

Hope for Us Today

In our day, Mark's story stands as a beacon of hope. Though Mark failed at a key point to be the devoted disciple he wanted to be, he was given a second chance and was fully restored. If Mark could fail the apostle Paul but later be restored to a position as a valued cominister, we can be restored from failure as well. Mark proves that failure isn't final. Most of us will need many second chances over the course of a lifetime. Some things can never be undone or redone, but we can pick up from where we failed and move forward.

Maybe someone has failed you. Maybe you share Paul's view that that person is unreliable and a failure. Think what might have happened to Mark if Barnabas had not come to his rescue and offered him a second chance. Mark might have become so consumed by guilt and self-doubt that his future effectiveness in ministry would have been greatly impaired. Jesus Christ always sees the potential in us, and he's always willing—and waiting—to offer us a second chance. We all need someone to believe in us. Can you hold out a second chance to that one who has failed you?

Jesus touched Mark's life forever with a second chance, and Mark finished his life as a faithful servant rather than a failure. With God working in us, may we be willing to grant second chances, as well as admit our need for them, as we become the men God wants us to be!

—*Dr. Gene Getz*

God."[u] 12But he gave them strict orders not to tell who he was.[v]

The Appointing of the Twelve Apostles

13Jesus went up on a mountainside and called to him those he wanted,
and they came to him.[w] 14He appointed twelve—designating them
apostles[a][x]—that they might be with
him and that he might send them out
to preach 15and to have authority to
drive out demons.[y] 16These are the
twelve he appointed: Simon (to whom
he gave the name Peter);[z] 17James son
of Zebedee and his brother John (to
them he gave the name Boanerges,
which means Sons of Thunder); 18An-
drew, Philip, Bartholomew, Matthew,
Thomas, James son of Alphaeus, Thaddaeus, Simon the Zealot 19and Judas
Iscariot, who betrayed him.

Jesus and Beelzebub

›See Matthew 12:25–29; Luke 11:17–22

20Then Jesus entered a house, and
again a crowd gathered,[a] so that he
and his disciples were not even able to
eat.[b] 21When his family heard about
this, they went to take charge of him,
for they said, "He is out of his mind."[c]
22And the teachers of the law who
came down from Jerusalem[d] said, "He
is possessed by Beelzebub[b]![e] By the
prince of demons he is driving out demons."[f]
23So Jesus called them and spoke to
them in parables:[g] "How can Satan[h]
drive out Satan? 24If a kingdom is divided against itself, that kingdom cannot
stand. 25If a house is divided against
itself, that house cannot stand. 26And if
Satan opposes himself and is divided,
he cannot stand; his end has come.
27In fact, no one can enter a strong
man's house and carry off his possessions unless he first ties up the strong
man. Then he can rob his house.[i] 28I
tell you the truth, all the sins and blasphemies of men will be forgiven them.
29But whoever blasphemes against the
Holy Spirit will never be forgiven; he is
guilty of an eternal sin."[j]
30He said this because they were
saying, "He has an evil spirit."

Jesus' Mother and Brothers

›See Matthew 12:46–50; Luke 8:19–21

31Then Jesus' mother and brothers
arrived.[k] Standing outside, they sent
someone in to call him. 32A crowd was
sitting around him, and they told him,
"Your mother and brothers are outside
looking for you."
33"Who are my mother and my
brothers?" he asked.

6 →PG. 1133

34Then he looked at those seated in
a circle around him and said, "Here are
my mother and my brothers! 35Who-
ever does God's will is my brother and
sister and mother."

The Parable of the Sower

›See Matthew 13:1–15,18–23; Luke 8:4–15

4 Again Jesus began to teach by the
lake.[l] The crowd that gathered
around him was so large that he got
into a boat and sat in it out on the lake,
while all the people were along the
shore at the water's edge. 2He taught
them many things by parables,[m] and
in his teaching said: 3"Listen! A farmer
went out to sow his seed.[n] 4As he was
scattering the seed, some fell along the
path, and the birds came and ate it up.
5Some fell on rocky places, where it did
not have much soil. It sprang up quickly, because the soil was shallow. 6But
when the sun came up, the plants were
scorched, and they withered because
they had no root. 7Other seed fell
among thorns, which grew up and
choked the plants, so that they did not
bear grain. 8Still other seed fell on good
soil. It came up, grew and produced a
crop, multiplying thirty, sixty, or even a
hundred times."[o]
9Then Jesus said, "He who has ears
to hear, let him hear."[p]
10When he was alone, the Twelve
and the others around him asked him
about the parables. 11He told them,
"The secret of the kingdom of God[q]
has been given to you. But to those on
the outside[r] everything is said in parables 12so that,

" 'they may be ever seeing but
never perceiving,
and ever hearing but never
understanding;
otherwise they might turn and be
forgiven!'[c] "[s]

13Then Jesus said to them, "Don't
you understand this parable? How
then will you understand any parable?
14The farmer sows the word.[t] 15Some
people are like seed along the path,
where the word is sown. As soon as
they hear it, Satan[u] comes and takes
away the word that was sown in them.
16Others, like seed sown on rocky
places, hear the word and at once receive it with joy. 17But since they have
no root, they last only a short time.
When trouble or persecution comes
because of the word, they quickly fall
away. 18Still others, like seed sown

3:11 [u]Mt 4:3; Mk 1:23,24
3:12 [v]Mt 8:4; Mk 1:24,25,34; Ac 16:17,18
3:13 [w]Mt 5:1
3:14 [x]Mk 6:30
3:15 [y]Mt 10:1
3:16 [z]Jn 1:42
3:20 [a]ver 7 [b]Mk 6:31
3:21 [c]Jn 10:20; Ac 26:24
3:22 [d]Mt 15:1 [e]Mt 10:25; 11:18; 12:24; Jn 7:20; 8:48, 52; 10:20 [f]Mt 9:34
3:23 [g]Mk 4:2 [h]Mt 4:10
3:27 [i]Isa 49:24,25
3:29 [j]Mt 12:31,32; Lk 12:10
3:31 [k]ver 21
4:1 [l]Mk 2:13; 3:7
4:2 [m]ver 11; Mk 3:23
4:3 [n]ver 26
4:8 [o]Jn 15:5; Col 1:6
4:9 [p]ver 23; Mt 11:15
4:11 [q]Mt 3:2 [r]1Co 5:12,13; Col 4:5; 1Th 4:12; 1Ti 3:7
4:12 [s]Isa 6:9,10; Mt 13:13-15
4:14 [t]Mk 16:20; Lk 1:2; Ac 4:31; 8:4; 16:6; 17:11; Php 1:14
4:15 [u]Mt 4:10

a *14* Some manuscripts do not have *designating them apostles.* **b** *22* Greek *Beezeboul* or *Beelzeboul* **c** *12* Isaiah 6:9,10

among thorns, hear the word; 19but the
worries of this life, the deceitfulness
of wealth[v] and the desires for other
things come in and choke the word,
making it unfruitful. 20Others, like seed
sown on good soil, hear the word, accept it, and produce a crop—thirty,
sixty or even a hundred times what was
sown."

A Lamp on a Stand

7 →PG. 1096

21He said to them, "Do you bring in
a lamp to put it under a bowl or a bed?
Instead, don't you put it on its stand?[w]
22For whatever is hidden is meant to be
disclosed, and whatever is concealed
is meant to be brought out into the
open.[x] 23If anyone has ears to hear, let
him hear."[y]

24"Consider carefully what you
hear," he continued. "With the measure you use, it will be measured to
you—and even more.[z] 25Whoever has
will be given more; whoever does not
have, even what he has will be taken
from him."[a]

The Parable of the Growing Seed

26He also said, "This is what the
kingdom of God is like.[b] A man scatters seed on the ground. 27Night and
day, whether he sleeps or gets up, the
seed sprouts and grows, though he
does not know how. 28All by itself the
soil produces grain—first the stalk,
then the head, then the full kernel in
the head. 29As soon as the grain is ripe,
he puts the sickle to it, because the harvest has come."[c]

The Parable of the Mustard Seed

›See Matthew 13:31–32; Luke 13:18–19

30Again he said, "What shall we say
the kingdom of God is like,[d] or what
parable shall we use to describe it? 31It
is like a mustard seed, which is the
smallest seed you plant in the ground.
32Yet when planted, it grows and becomes the largest of all garden plants,
with such big branches that the birds
of the air can perch in its shade."

33With many similar parables Jesus
spoke the word to them, as much as
they could understand.[e] 34He did not
say anything to them without using a
parable.[f] But when he was alone with
his own disciples, he explained everything.

Jesus Calms the Storm

›See Matthew 8:18,23–27; Luke 8:22–25

35That day when evening came, he
said to his disciples, "Let us go over to
the other side." 36Leaving the crowd
behind, they took him along, just as he
was, in the boat.[g] There were also other boats with him. 37A furious squall
came up, and the waves broke over the
boat, so that it was nearly swamped.
38Jesus was in the stern, sleeping on a
cushion. The disciples woke him and
said to him, "Teacher, don't you care if
we drown?"

39He got up, rebuked the wind and
said to the waves, "Quiet! Be still!"
Then the wind died down and it was
completely calm.

40He said to his disciples, "Why are
you so afraid? Do you still have no
faith?"[h]

41They were terrified and asked each
other, "Who is this? Even the wind and
the waves obey him!"

The Healing of a Demon-possessed Man

›See Matthew 8:28–34; Luke 8:26–39

5 They went across the lake to the
region of the Gerasenes.[a] 2When
Jesus got out of the boat,[i] a man with
an evil[b] spirit[j] came from the tombs
to meet him. 3This man lived in the
tombs, and no one could bind him any
more, not even with a chain. 4For he
had often been chained hand and foot,
but he tore the chains apart and broke
the irons on his feet. No one was strong
enough to subdue him. 5Night and day
among the tombs and in the hills he
would cry out and cut himself with
stones.

6When he saw Jesus from a distance,
he ran and fell on his knees in front
of him. 7He shouted at the top of his
voice, "What do you want with me,[k]
Jesus, Son of the Most High God?[l]
Swear to God that you won't torture
me!" 8For Jesus had said to him, "Come
out of this man, you evil spirit!"

9Then Jesus asked him, "What is
your name?"

"My name is Legion,"[m] he replied,
"for we are many." 10And he begged
Jesus again and again not to send them
out of the area.

11A large herd of pigs was feeding
on the nearby hillside. 12The demons
begged Jesus, "Send us among the pigs;
allow us to go into them." 13He gave
them permission, and the evil spirits
came out and went into the pigs. The
herd, about two thousand in number,
rushed down the steep bank into the
lake and were drowned.

14Those tending the pigs ran off and
reported this in the town and countryside, and the people went out to see

4:19 [v]Mt 19:23; 1Ti 6:9,10,17; 1Jn 2:15-17
4:21 [w]Mt 5:15
4:22 [x]Jer 16:17; Mt 10:26; Lk 8:17; 12:2
4:23 [y]ver 9; Mt 11:15
4:24 [z]Mt 7:2; Lk 6:38
4:25 [a]Mt 13:12; 25:29
4:26 [b]Mt 13:24
4:29 [c]Rev 14:15
4:30 [d]Mt 13:24
4:33 [e]Jn 16:12
4:34 [f]Jn 16:25
4:36 [g]ver 1; Mk 3:9; 5:2,21; 6:32,45
4:40 [h]Mt 14:31; Mk 16:14
5:2 [i]Mk 4:1 [j]Mk 1:23
5:7 [k]Mt 8:29 [l]Mt 4:3; Lk 1:32; 6:35; Ac 16:17; Heb 7:1
5:9 [m]ver 15

[a] *1* Some manuscripts *Gadarenes;* other manuscripts *Gergesenes* [b] *2* Greek *unclean;* also in verses 8 and 13

what had happened. 15When they
came to Jesus, they saw the man who
had been possessed by the legion[n] of
demons,[o] sitting there, dressed and in
his right mind; and they were afraid.
16Those who had seen it told the people what had happened to the demon-
possessed man—and told about the
pigs as well. 17Then the people began
to plead with Jesus to leave their region.

7 →PG. 1102

18As Jesus was getting into the boat,
the man who had been demon-
possessed begged to go with him.
19Jesus did not let him, but said, "Go
home to your family and tell them[p]
how much the Lord has done for you,
and how he has had mercy on you."
20So the man went away and began to
tell in the Decapolis[a][q] how much
Jesus had done for him. And all the
people were amazed.

A Dead Girl and a Sick Woman

›See Matthew 9:18–26; Luke 8:41–56

21When Jesus had again crossed over
by boat to the other side of the lake,[r]
a large crowd gathered around him

4 →PG. 1102

while he was by the lake.[s] 22Then one
of the synagogue rulers,[t] named Jairus, came there. Seeing Jesus, he fell
at his feet 23and pleaded earnestly
with him, "My little daughter is dying.
Please come and put your hands on[u]
her so that she will be healed and live."
24So Jesus went with him.

A large crowd followed and pressed
around him. 25And a woman was there
who had been subject to bleeding[v] for
twelve years. 26She had suffered a great
deal under the care of many doctors
and had spent all she had, yet instead
of getting better she grew worse.
27When she heard about Jesus, she
came up behind him in the crowd
and touched his cloak, 28because she
thought, "If I just touch his clothes,[w]
I will be healed." 29Immediately her
bleeding stopped and she felt in her
body that she was freed from her suffering.[x]

30At once Jesus realized that power[y] had gone out from him. He turned
around in the crowd and asked, "Who
touched my clothes?"

31"You see the people crowding
against you," his disciples answered,
"and yet you can ask, 'Who touched
me?' "

32But Jesus kept looking around to
see who had done it. 33Then the woman, knowing what had happened to
her, came and fell at his feet and, trembling with fear, told him the whole
truth. 34He said to her, "Daughter, your
faith has healed you.[z] Go in peace[a]
and be freed from your suffering."

35While Jesus was still speaking,
some men came from the house of
Jairus, the synagogue ruler.[b] "Your
daughter is dead," they said. "Why
bother the teacher any more?"
36Ignoring what they said, Jesus told
the synagogue ruler, "Don't be afraid;
just believe."

37He did not let anyone follow him
except Peter, James and John the
brother of James.[c] 38When they came
to the home of the synagogue ruler,[d]
Jesus saw a commotion, with people
crying and wailing loudly. 39He went in
and said to them, "Why all this commotion and wailing? The child is not
dead but asleep."[e] 40But they laughed
at him.

5:15 [n] ver 9 [o] ver 16,18; Mt 4:24
5:19 [p] Mt 8:4
5:20 [q] Mt 4:25; Mk 7:31
5:21 [r] Mt 9:1 [s] Mk 4:1
5:22 [t] ver 35,36,38; Lk 13:14; Ac 13:15; 18:8, 17
5:23 [u] Mt 19:13; Mk 6:5; 7:32; 8:23; 16:18; Lk 4:40; 13:13; Ac 6:6
5:25 [v] Lev 15:25-30
5:28 [w] Mt 9:20
5:29 [x] ver 34
5:30 [y] Lk 5:17; 6:19
5:34 [z] Mt 9:22 [a] Ac 15:33
5:35 [b] ver 22
5:37 [c] Mt 4:21
5:38 [d] ver 22
5:39 [e] Mt 9:24

[a] *20* That is, the Ten Cities

5:1–20

AN AMAZING TRANSFORMATION

PROMISE 7

Isolation and terror had been this man's closest companions. For years he had lived in dark, dusty, putrid tombs—small caves in the side of a hill. Hated and feared by the local townspeople, they had tried on several occasions to control and imprison him. But the evil spirits that tormented him gave him fearful and supernatural strength, and he broke free. In his misery he cried out day and night and ripped at his flesh with stones.

Society, it seemed, had given up on this man. He'd been branded a hopeless case. But Jesus didn't label him that way. Instead of trying to control or restrain this tormented man, Jesus dealt with the cause of his condition. Jesus cast out the demons that had invaded and had for so long inhabited this man's spirit. And in that moment, this anguished man found freedom. No longer exiled to the place of the dead, he would once again be able to rejoin society. And after his encounter with Jesus, that's exactly what he did, telling anyone who would listen about what the Lord had done for him (v. 20).

Perhaps you know someone who seems like a hopeless case—a lost cause. Imagine the difference Jesus could make in his or her life. When you have the opportunity, tell this person what the Lord has done for you. And then pray that Jesus will perform this same amazing transformation in the life of that individual.

For the next Promise 7 reading go to page 1130.

After he put them all out, he took the
child's father and mother and the disciples who were with him, and went in
where the child was. 41He took her by
the hand[f] and said to her, *"Talitha
koum!"* (which means, "Little girl, I say
to you, get up!").[g] 42Immediately the
girl stood up and walked around (she
was twelve years old). At this they were
completely astonished. 43He gave strict
orders not to let anyone know about
this,[h] and told them to give her something to eat.

A Prophet Without Honor

>See Matthew 13:54–58

6 Jesus left there and went to his
hometown,[i] accompanied by his
disciples. 2When the Sabbath came,[j]
he began to teach in the synagogue,[k]
and many who heard him were
amazed.[l]

"Where did this man get these
things?" they asked. "What's this wisdom that has been given him, that he
even does miracles! 3Isn't this the carpenter? Isn't this Mary's son and the
brother of James, Joseph,[a] Judas and
Simon?[m] Aren't his sisters here with
us?" And they took offense at him.[n]

4Jesus said to them, "Only in his
hometown, among his relatives and in
his own house is a prophet without
honor."[o] 5He could not do any miracles there, except lay his hands on[p] a
few sick people and heal them. 6And
he was amazed at their lack of faith.

Jesus Sends Out the Twelve

>See Matthew 10:1,9–14; Luke 9:1,3–5

Then Jesus went around teaching
from village to village.[q] 7Calling the
Twelve to him,[r] he sent them out two
by two[s] and gave them authority over
evil[b] spirits.[t]

8These were his instructions: "Take
nothing for the journey except a staff—
no bread, no bag, no money in your
belts. 9Wear sandals but not an extra
tunic. 10Whenever you enter a house,
stay there until you leave that town.
11And if any place will not welcome
you or listen to you, shake the dust off
your feet[u] when you leave, as a testimony against them."

12They went out and preached that
people should repent.[v] 13They drove
out many demons and anointed many
sick people with oil[w] and healed them.

John the Baptist Beheaded

>See Matthew 14:1–12

14King Herod heard about this, for
Jesus' name had become well known.
Some were saying,[c] "John the Baptist[x] has been raised from the dead,
and that is why miraculous powers are
at work in him."

15Others said, "He is Elijah."[y]

And still others claimed, "He is a
prophet,[z] like one of the prophets of
long ago."[a]

16But when Herod heard this, he
said, "John, the man I beheaded, has
been raised from the dead!"

17For Herod himself had given orders to have John arrested, and he had
him bound and put in prison.[b] He did
this because of Herodias, his brother
Philip's wife, whom he had married.
18For John had been saying to Herod, "It is not lawful for you to have
your brother's wife."[c] 19So Herodias
nursed a grudge against John and
wanted to kill him. But she was not
able to, 20because Herod feared John
and protected him, knowing him to be
a righteous and holy man.[d] When
Herod heard John, he was greatly puzzled[d]; yet he liked to listen to him.

21Finally the opportune time came.
On his birthday Herod gave a banquet[e] for his high officials and military commanders and the leading men
of Galilee.[f] 22When the daughter of
Herodias came in and danced, she
pleased Herod and his dinner guests.

The king said to the girl, "Ask me for
anything you want, and I'll give it to
you." 23And he promised her with an
oath, "Whatever you ask I will give you,
up to half my kingdom."[g]

24She went out and said to her mother, "What shall I ask for?"

"The head of John the Baptist," she
answered.

25At once the girl hurried in to the
king with the request: "I want you to
give me right now the head of John the
Baptist on a platter."

26The king was greatly distressed,
but because of his oaths and his dinner
guests, he did not want to refuse her.
27So he immediately sent an execu-
tioner with orders to bring John's head.
The man went, beheaded John in the
prison, 28and brought back his head
on a platter. He presented it to the
girl, and she gave it to her mother.
29On hearing of this, John's disciples
came and took his body and laid it in a
tomb.

5:41 [f]Mk 1:31 [g]Lk 7:14; Ac 9:40
5:43 [h]Mt 8:4
6:1 [i]Mt 2:23
6:2 [j]Mk 1:21 [k]Mt 4:23 [l]Mt 7:28
6:3 [m]Mt 12:46 [n]Mt 11:6; Jn 6:61
6:4 [o]Lk 4:24; Jn 4:44
6:5 [p]Mk 5:23
6:6 [q]Mt 9:35; Mk 1:39; Lk 13:22
6:7 [r]Mk 3:13 [s]Dt 17:6; Lk 10:1 [t]Mt 10:1
6:11 [u]Mt 10:14
6:12 [v]Lk 9:6
6:13 [w]Jas 5:14
6:14 [x]Mt 3:1
6:15 [y]Mal 4:5 [z]Mt 21:11 [a]Mt 16:14; Mk 8:28
6:17 [b]Mt 4:12; 11:2; Lk 3:19,20
6:18 [c]Lev 18:16; 20:21
6:20 [d]Mt 11:9; 21:26
6:21 [e]Est 1:3; 2:18 [f]Lk 3:1
6:23 [g]Est 5:3,6; 7:2

[a] *3* Greek *Joses,* a variant of *Joseph* [b] *7* Greek *unclean* [c] *14* Some early manuscripts *He was saying* [d] *20* Some early manuscripts *he did many things*

Jesus Feeds the Five Thousand

›See Matthew 14:13–21; Luke 9:10–17; John 6:5–13

30The apostles[h] gathered around Jesus and reported to him all they had done and taught.[i] 31Then, because so many people were coming and going that they did not even have a chance to eat,[j] he said to them, "Come with me by yourselves to a quiet place and get some rest."

32So they went away by themselves in a boat[k] to a solitary place. 33But many who saw them leaving recognized them and ran on foot from all the towns and got there ahead of them. 34When Jesus landed and saw a large crowd, he had compassion on them, because they were like sheep without a shepherd.[l] So he began teaching them many things.

35By this time it was late in the day, so his disciples came to him. "This is a remote place," they said, "and it's already very late. 36Send the people away so they can go to the surrounding countryside and villages and buy themselves something to eat."

37But he answered, "You give them something to eat."[m]

They said to him, "That would take eight months of a man's wages[a]! Are we to go and spend that much on bread and give it to them to eat?"

38"How many loaves do you have?" he asked. "Go and see."

When they found out, they said, "Five—and two fish."[n]

39Then Jesus directed them to have all the people sit down in groups on the green grass. 40So they sat down in groups of hundreds and fifties. 41Taking the five loaves and the two fish and looking up to heaven, he gave thanks and broke the loaves.[o] Then he gave them to his disciples to set before the people. He also divided the two fish among them all. 42They all ate and were satisfied, 43and the disciples picked up twelve basketfuls of broken pieces of bread and fish. 44The number of the men who had eaten was five thousand.

Jesus Walks on the Water

›See Matthew 14:22–32; John 6:15–21

1 →PG. 1105

45Immediately Jesus made his disciples get into the boat[p] and go on ahead of him to Bethsaida,[q] while he dismissed the crowd. 46After leaving them, he went up on a mountainside to pray.[r]

47When evening came, the boat was in the middle of the lake, and he was alone on land. 48He saw the disciples straining at the oars, because the wind was against them. About the fourth watch of the night he went out to them, walking on the lake. He was about to pass by them, 49but when they saw him walking on the lake, they thought he was a ghost.[s] They cried out, 50because they all saw him and were terrified.

Immediately he spoke to them and said, "Take courage! It is I. Don't be afraid."[t] 51Then he climbed into the boat[u] with them, and the wind died down.[v] They were completely amazed, 52for they had not understood about the loaves; their hearts were hardened.[w]

53When they had crossed over, they landed at Gennesaret and anchored there.[x] 54As soon as they got out of the boat, people recognized Jesus. 55They ran throughout that whole region and carried the sick on mats to wherever they heard he was. 56And wherever he went—into villages, towns or countryside—they placed the sick in the marketplaces. They begged him to let them touch even the edge of his cloak,[y] and all who touched him were healed.

Clean and Unclean

›See Matthew 15:1–20

7 The Pharisees and some of the teachers of the law who had come from Jerusalem gathered around Jesus and 2saw some of his disciples eating food with hands that were "unclean,"[z] that is, unwashed. 3(The Pharisees and all the Jews do not eat unless they give their hands a ceremonial washing, holding to the tradition of the elders.[a] 4When they come from the marketplace they do not eat unless they wash. And they observe many other traditions, such as the washing of cups, pitchers and kettles.[b])[b]

5So the Pharisees and teachers of the law asked Jesus, "Why don't your disciples live according to the tradition of the elders[c] instead of eating their food with 'unclean' hands?"

6He replied, "Isaiah was right when he prophesied about you hypocrites; as it is written:

" 'These people honor me with
their lips,
but their hearts are far from me.
7They worship me in vain;
their teachings are but rules
taught by men.'[c][d]

6:30 [h]Mt 10:2; Lk 9:10; 17:5; 22:14; 24:10; Ac 1:2,26 [i]Lk 9:10
6:31 [j]Mk 3:20
6:32 [k]ver 45; Mk 4:36
6:34 [l]Mt 9:36
6:37 [m]2Ki 4:42-44
6:38 [n]Mt 15:34; Mk 8:5
6:41 [o]Mt 14:19
6:45 [p]ver 32 [q]Mt 11:21
6:46 [r]Lk 3:21
6:49 [s]Lk 24:37
6:50 [t]Mt 14:27
6:51 [u]ver 32 [v]Mk 4:39
6:52 [w]Mk 8:17-21
6:53 [x]Jn 6:24,25
6:56 [y]Mt 9:20
7:2 [z]Ac 10:14,28; 11:8; Ro 14:14
7:3 [a]ver 5,8,9,13; Lk 11:38
7:4 [b]Mt 23:25; Lk 11:39
7:5 [c]ver 3; Gal 1:14; Col 2:8
7:7 [d]Isa 29:13

[a]37 Greek *take two hundred denarii*
[b]4 Some early manuscripts *pitchers, kettles and dining couches*
[c]6,7 Isaiah 29:13

8You have let go of the commands of
God and are holding on to the traditions of men."[e]
9And he said to them: "You have a
fine way of setting aside the commands
of God in order to observe[a] your own
traditions![f] 10For Moses said, 'Honor
your father and your mother,'[b][g] and,
'Anyone who curses his father or mother must be put to death.'[c][h] 11But you
say[i] that if a man says to his father or
mother: 'Whatever help you might otherwise have received from me is Cor-
ban' (that is, a gift devoted to God),
12then you no longer let him do anything for his father or mother. 13Thus
you nullify the word of God[j] by your
tradition[k] that you have handed
down. And you do many things like
that."
14Again Jesus called the crowd to
him and said, "Listen to me, everyone,
and understand this. 15Nothing outside
a man can make him 'unclean' by going into him. Rather, it is what comes
out of a man that makes him 'unclean.'[d]"
17After he had left the crowd and entered the house, his disciples asked
him[l] about this parable. 18"Are you so
dull?" he asked. "Don't you see that
nothing that enters a man from the
outside can make him 'unclean'? 19For
it doesn't go into his heart but into his
stomach, and then out of his body." (In
saying this, Jesus declared all foods[m]
"clean.")[n]
20He went on: "What comes out of
a man is what makes him 'unclean.'
21For from within, out of men's hearts,
come evil thoughts, sexual immorality,
theft, murder, adultery, 22greed,[o] malice, deceit, lewdness, envy, slander, arrogance and folly. 23All these evils
come from inside and make a man 'unclean.' "

The Faith of a Syrophoenician Woman

›See Matthew 15:21–28

24Jesus left that place and went to
the vicinity of Tyre.[e][p] He entered a
house and did not want anyone to
know it; yet he could not keep his presence secret. 25In fact, as soon as she
heard about him, a woman whose little
daughter was possessed by an evil[f]
spirit[q] came and fell at his feet. 26The
woman was a Greek, born in Syrian
Phoenicia. She begged Jesus to drive
the demon out of her daughter.
27"First let the children eat all they
want," he told her, "for it is not right to
take the children's bread and toss it to
their dogs."
28"Yes, Lord," she replied, "but even
the dogs under the table eat the children's crumbs."
29Then he told her, "For such a reply, you may go; the demon has left
your daughter."
30She went home and found her
child lying on the bed, and the demon
gone.

The Healing of a Deaf and Mute Man

›See Matthew 15:29–31

31Then Jesus left the vicinity of
Tyre[r] and went through Sidon, down
to the Sea of Galilee[s] and into the
region of the Decapolis.[g][t] 32There
some people brought to him a man
who was deaf and could hardly talk,[u]
and they begged him to place his hand
on[v] the man.
33After he took him aside, away from
the crowd, Jesus put his fingers into
the man's ears. Then he spit[w] and
touched the man's tongue. 34He looked
up to heaven[x] and with a deep sigh[y]
said to him, *"Ephphatha!"* (which
means, "Be opened!"). 35At this, the
man's ears were opened, his tongue
was loosened and he began to speak
plainly.[z]
36Jesus commanded them not to tell
anyone.[a] But the more he did so, the
more they kept talking about it. 37Peo-

7:8 [e]ver 3 **7:9** [f]ver 3 **7:10** [g]Ex 20:12; Dt 5:16 [h]Ex 21:17; Lev 20:9 **7:11** [i]Mt 23:16,18 **7:13** [j]Heb 4:12 [k]ver 3 **7:17** [l]Mk 9:28 **7:19** [m]Ro 14:1-12; Col 2:16; 1Ti 4:3-5 [n]Ac 10:15 **7:22** [o]Mt 20:15 **7:24** [p]Mt 11:21 **7:25** [q]Mt 4:24 **7:31** [r]ver 24; Mt 11:21 [s]Mt 4:18 [t]Mt 4:25; Mk 5:20 **7:32** [u]Mt 9:32; Lk 11:14 [v]Mk 5:23 **7:33** [w]Mk 8:23 **7:34** [x]Mk 6:41; Jn 11:41 [y]Mk 8:12 **7:35** [z]Isa 35:5,6 **7:36** [a]Mt 8:4

[a]9 Some manuscripts *set up* [b]*10* Exodus 20:12; Deut. 5:16 [c]*10* Exodus 21:17; Lev. 20:9 [d]*15* Some early manuscripts *'unclean.' 16If anyone has ears to hear, let him hear.* [e]*24* Many early manuscripts *Tyre and Sidon* [f]*25* Greek *unclean* [g]*31* That is, the Ten Cities

7:17–23

PROMISE 3

CLEAN ON THE INSIDE

No one can take a rotten apple and make it edible again by washing it. In the same way, an impure spirit can't be made pure by performing superficial activities. Not even religious rituals and activities, by themselves, can make a person pure. Why? Because purity before God comes from the heart.

The implication of this truth is profound: Men of integrity, those who choose to follow God, have pure minds. And pure minds, like clean hands, don't just happen. A man who commits himself to purity works to flush out the dirt of impure thoughts through confession and meditation on God's Word. This is a painstaking, lifelong process; there really is no shortcut to purity. But resolving and acting to become a man of integrity and purity pleases the heart of God.

For the next Promise 3 reading go to page 1126.

ple were overwhelmed with amazement. "He has done everything well," they said. "He even makes the deaf hear and the mute speak."

Jesus Feeds the Four Thousand

›See Matthew 15:32–39

8 During those days another large crowd gathered. Since they had nothing to eat, Jesus called his disciples to him and said, 2"I have compassion for these people;[b] they have already been with me three days and have nothing to eat. 3If I send them home hungry, they will collapse on the way, because some of them have come a long distance."

4His disciples answered, "But where in this remote place can anyone get enough bread to feed them?"

5"How many loaves do you have?" Jesus asked.

"Seven," they replied.

6He told the crowd to sit down on the ground. When he had taken the seven loaves and given thanks, he broke them and gave them to his disciples to set before the people, and they did so. 7They had a few small fish as well; he gave thanks for them also and told the disciples to distribute them.[c] 8The people ate and were satisfied. Afterward the disciples picked up seven basketfuls of broken pieces that were left over.[d] 9About four thousand men were present. And having sent them away, 10he got into the boat with his disciples and went to the region of Dalmanutha.

11The Pharisees came and began to question Jesus. To test him, they asked him for a sign from heaven.[e] 12He sighed deeply[f] and said, "Why does this generation ask for a miraculous sign? I tell you the truth, no sign will be given to it." 13Then he left them, got back into the boat and crossed to the other side.

The Yeast of the Pharisees and Herod

14The disciples had forgotten to bring bread, except for one loaf they had with them in the boat. 15"Be careful," Jesus warned them. "Watch out for the yeast[g] of the Pharisees[h] and that of Herod."[i]

16They discussed this with one another and said, "It is because we have no bread."

17Aware of their discussion, Jesus asked them: "Why are you talking about having no bread? Do you still not see or understand? Are your hearts hardened?[j] 18Do you have eyes but fail to see, and ears but fail to hear? And don't you remember? 19When I broke the five loaves for the five thousand, how many basketfuls of pieces did you pick up?"

"Twelve,"[k] they replied.

20"And when I broke the seven loaves for the four thousand, how many basketfuls of pieces did you pick up?"

They answered, "Seven."[l]

21He said to them, "Do you still not understand?"[m]

The Healing of a Blind Man at Bethsaida

22They came to Bethsaida,[n] and some people brought a blind man[o] and begged Jesus to touch him. 23He took the blind man by the hand and led him outside the village. When he had spit[p] on the man's eyes and put his hands on[q] him, Jesus asked, "Do you see anything?"

24He looked up and said, "I see people; they look like trees walking around."

25Once more Jesus put his hands on the man's eyes. Then his eyes were opened, his sight was restored, and he saw everything clearly. 26Jesus sent him home, saying, "Don't go into the village.[a]"

Peter's Confession of Christ

›See Matthew 16:13–16; Luke 9:18–20

27Jesus and his disciples went on to the villages around Caesarea Philippi. On the way he asked them, "Who do people say I am?"

28They replied, "Some say John the Baptist;[r] others say Elijah;[s] and still others, one of the prophets."

29"But what about you?" he asked. "Who do you say I am?"

Peter answered, "You are the Christ.[b]"[t]

30Jesus warned them not to tell anyone about him.[u]

Jesus Predicts His Death

›See Matthew 16:21–28; Luke 9:22–27

31He then began to teach them that the Son of Man[v] must suffer many things[w] and be rejected by the elders, chief priests and teachers of the law,[x] and that he must be killed[y] and after three days[z] rise again.[a] 32He spoke plainly[b] about this, and Peter took him aside and began to rebuke him.

33But when Jesus turned and looked at his disciples, he rebuked Peter. "Get behind me, Satan!"[c] he said. "You do

8:2 [b]Mt 9:36
8:7 [c]Mt 14:19
8:8 [d]ver 20
8:11 [e]Mt 12:38
8:12 [f]Mk 7:34
8:15 [g]1Co 5:6-8 [h]Lk 12:1 [i]Mt 14:1; Mk 12:13
8:17 [j]Isa 6:9,10; Mk 6:52
8:19 [k]Mt 14:20; Mk 6:41-44; Lk 9:17; Jn 6:13
8:20 [l]ver 6-9; Mt 15:37
8:21 [m]Mk 6:52
8:22 [n]Mt 11:21 [o]Mk 10:46; Jn 9:1
8:23 [p]Mk 7:33 [q]Mk 5:23
8:28 [r]Mt 3:1 [s]Mal 4:5
8:29 [t]Jn 6:69; 11:27
8:30 [u]Mt 8:4; 16:20; 17:9; Mk 9:9; Lk 9:21
8:31 [v]Mt 8:20 [w]Mt 16:21 [x]Mt 27:1,2 [y]Ac 2:23; 3:13 [z]Mt 16:21 [a]Mt 16:21
8:32 [b]Jn 18:20
8:33 [c]Mt 4:10

[a]26 Some manuscripts *Don't go and tell anyone in the village* [b]29 Or *Messiah.* "The Christ" (Greek) and "the Messiah" (Hebrew) both mean "the Anointed One."

not have in mind the things of God, but the things of men."

34 Then he called the crowd to him along with his disciples and said: "If anyone would come after me, he must deny himself and take up his cross and follow me.[d] 35 For whoever wants to save his life[a] will lose it, but whoever loses his life for me and for the gospel will save it.[e] 36 What good is it for a man to gain the whole world, yet forfeit his soul? 37 Or what can a man give in exchange for his soul? 38 If anyone is ashamed of me and my words in this adulterous and sinful generation, the Son of Man[f] will be ashamed of him[g] when he comes[h] in his Father's glory with the holy angels."

9 And he said to them, "I tell you the truth, some who are standing here will not taste death before they see the kingdom of God come[i] with power."[j]

The Transfiguration

›See Matthew 17:1–13; Luke 9:28–36

2 After six days Jesus took Peter, James and John[k] with him and led them up a high mountain, where they were all alone. There he was transfigured before them. 3 His clothes became dazzling white,[l] whiter than anyone in the world could bleach them. 4 And there appeared before them Elijah and Moses, who were talking with Jesus.

5 Peter said to Jesus, "Rabbi,[m] it is good for us to be here. Let us put up three shelters—one for you, one for Moses and one for Elijah." 6 (He did not know what to say, they were so frightened.)

7 Then a cloud appeared and enveloped them, and a voice came from the cloud:[n] "This is my Son, whom I love. Listen to him!"[o]

8 Suddenly, when they looked around, they no longer saw anyone with them except Jesus.

9 As they were coming down the mountain, Jesus gave them orders not to tell anyone[p] what they had seen until the Son of Man[q] had risen from the dead. 10 They kept the matter to themselves, discussing what "rising from the dead" meant.

11 And they asked him, "Why do the teachers of the law say that Elijah must come first?"

12 Jesus replied, "To be sure, Elijah does come first, and restores all things. Why then is it written that the Son of Man[r] must suffer much[s] and be rejected?[t] 13 But I tell you, Elijah has come,[u] and they have done to him everything they wished, just as it is written about him."

8:34 [d]Mt 10:38; Lk 14:27 **8:35** [e]Jn 12:25 **8:38** [f]Mt 8:20 [g]Mt 10:33; Lk 12:9 [h]1Th 2:19 **9:1** [i]Mk 13:30; Lk 22:18 [j]Mt 24:30; 25:31 **9:2** [k]Mt 4:21 **9:3** [l]Mt 28:3 **9:5** [m]Mt 23:7 **9:7** [n]Ex 24:16 [o]Mt 3:17 **9:9** [p]Mk 8:30 [q]Mt 8:20 **9:12** [r]Mt 8:20 [s]Mt 16:21 [t]Lk 23:11 **9:13** [u]Mt 11:14

The Healing of a Boy With an Evil Spirit

›See Matthew 17:14–19,22–23; Luke 9:37–45

14 When they came to the other disciples, they saw a large crowd around them and the teachers of the law arguing with them. 15 As soon as all the people saw Jesus, they were overwhelmed with wonder and ran to greet him.

16 "What are you arguing with them about?" he asked.

17 A man in the crowd answered, "Teacher, I brought you my son, who is possessed by a spirit that has robbed him of speech. 18 Whenever it seizes him, it throws him to the ground. He foams at the mouth, gnashes his teeth and becomes rigid. I asked your disciples to drive out the spirit, but they could not."

19 "O unbelieving generation," Jesus replied, "how long shall I stay with you? How long shall I put up with you? Bring the boy to me."

20 So they brought him. When the spirit saw Jesus, it immediately threw the boy into a convulsion. He fell to the ground and rolled around, foaming at the mouth.[v]

21 Jesus asked the boy's father, "How long has he been like this?"

"From childhood," he answered. 22 "It has often thrown him into fire or water to kill him. But if you can do anything, take pity on us and help us."

23 " 'If you can'?" said Jesus. "Everything is possible for him who believes."[w]

24 Immediately the boy's father exclaimed, "I do believe; help me overcome my unbelief!"

25 When Jesus saw that a crowd was running to the scene,[x] he rebuked the evil[b] spirit. "You deaf and mute spirit," he said, "I command you, come out of him and never enter him again."

26 The spirit shrieked, convulsed him violently and came out. The boy looked so much like a corpse that many said, "He's dead." 27 But Jesus took him by the hand and lifted him to his feet, and he stood up.

28 After Jesus had gone indoors, his disciples asked him privately,[y] "Why couldn't we drive it out?"

29 He replied, "This kind can come out only by prayer.[c]"

30 They left that place and passed through Galilee. Jesus did not want anyone to know where they were, 31 be-

9:20 [v]Mk 1:26 **9:23** [w]Mt 21:21; Mk 11:23; Jn 11:40 **9:25** [x]ver 15 **9:28** [y]Mk 7:17

[a] *35* The Greek word means either *life* or *soul*; also in verse 36. [b] *25* Greek *unclean*
[c] *29* Some manuscripts *prayer and fasting*

cause he was teaching his disciples. He said to them, "The Son of Man[z] is going to be betrayed into the hands of men. They will kill him,[a] and after three days[b] he will rise."[c] **32**But they did not understand what he meant[d] and were afraid to ask him about it.

Who Is the Greatest?

›See Matthew 18:1–5; Luke 9:46–48

33They came to Capernaum.[e] When he was in the house,[f] he asked them, "What were you arguing about on the road?" **34**But they kept quiet because on the way they had argued about who was the greatest.[g]

4 →PG. 1102
7 →PG. 1104

35Sitting down, Jesus called the Twelve and said, "If anyone wants to be first, he must be the very last, and the servant of all."[h]

36He took a little child and had him stand among them. Taking him in his arms,[i] he said to them, **37**"Whoever welcomes one of these little children in my name welcomes me; and whoever welcomes me does not welcome me but the one who sent me."[j]

Whoever Is Not Against Us Is for Us

›See Luke 9:49–50

38"Teacher," said John, "we saw a man driving out demons in your name and we told him to stop, because he was not one of us."[k]

39"Do not stop him," Jesus said. "No one who does a miracle in my name can in the next moment say anything bad about me, **40**for whoever is not against us is for us.[l] **41**I tell you the truth, anyone who gives you a cup of water in my name because you belong to Christ will certainly not lose his reward.[m]

Causing to Sin

42"And if anyone causes one of these little ones who believe in me to sin,[n] it would be better for him to be thrown into the sea with a large millstone tied around his neck.[o] **43**If your hand causes you to sin,[p] cut it off. It is better for you to enter life maimed than with two hands to go into hell,[q] where the fire never goes out.[a][r] **45**And if your foot causes you to sin,[s] cut it off. It is better for you to enter life crippled than to have two feet and be thrown into hell.[b][t] **47**And if your eye causes you to sin,[u] pluck it out. It is better for you to enter the kingdom of God with one eye than to have two eyes and be thrown into hell,[v] **48**where

" 'their worm does not die,
and the fire is not quenched.'[c][w]

9:31 [z]Mt 8:20 [a]ver 12; Ac 2:23; 3:13 [b]Mt 16:21 [c]Mt 16:21
9:32 [d]Lk 2:50; 9:45; 18:34; Jn 12:16
9:33 [e]Mt 4:13 [f]Mk 1:29
9:34 [g]Lk 22:24
9:35 [h]Mt 18:4; 20:26; Mk 10:43; Lk 22:26
9:36 [i]Mk 10:16
9:37 [j]Mt 10:40
9:38 [k]Nu 11:27-29
9:40 [l]Mt 12:30; Lk 11:23
9:41 [m]Mt 10:42
9:42 [n]Mt 5:29 [o]Mt 18:6; Lk 17:2
9:43 [p]Mt 5:29 [q]Mt 5:30; 18:8 [r]Mt 25:41
9:45 [s]Mt 5:29 [t]Mt 18:8
9:47 [u]Mt 5:29 [v]Mt 5:29; 18:9
9:48 [w]Isa 66:24; Mt 25:41
9:49 [x]Lev 2:13
9:50 [y]Mt 5:13; Lk 14:34,35 [z]Col 4:6 [a]Ro 12:18; 2Co 13:11; 1Th 5:13
10:1 [b]Mk 1:5; Jn 10:40; 11:7 [c]Mt 4:23; Mk 2:13; 4:2; 6:6,34
10:2 [d]Mk 2:16
10:4 [e]Dt 24:1-4; Mt 5:31
10:5 [f]Ps 95:8; Heb 3:15
10:6 [g]Ge 1:27; 5:2
10:8 [h]Ge 2:24; 1Co 6:16
10:11 [i]Mt 5:32; Lk 16:18
10:12 [j]Ro 7:3; 1Co 7:10,11
10:14 [k]Mt 25:34
10:15 [l]Mt 18:3
10:16 [m]Mk 9:36

49Everyone will be salted[x] with fire. **50**"Salt is good, but if it loses its saltiness, how can you make it salty again?[y] Have salt in yourselves,[z] and be at peace with each other."[a]

Divorce

›See Matthew 19:1–9

10 Jesus then left that place and went into the region of Judea and across the Jordan.[b] Again crowds of people came to him, and as was his custom, he taught them.[c]

2Some Pharisees[d] came and tested him by asking, "Is it lawful for a man to divorce his wife?"

3"What did Moses command you?" he replied.

4They said, "Moses permitted a man to write a certificate of divorce and send her away."[e]

5"It was because your hearts were hard[f] that Moses wrote you this law," Jesus replied. **6**"But at the beginning of creation God 'made them male and female.'[d][g] **7**'For this reason a man will leave his father and mother and be united to his wife,[e] **8**and the two will become one flesh.'[f][h] So they are no longer two, but one. **9**Therefore what God has joined together, let man not separate."

4 →PG. 1102

10When they were in the house again, the disciples asked Jesus about this. **11**He answered, "Anyone who divorces his wife and marries another woman commits adultery against her.[i] **12**And if she divorces her husband and marries another man, she commits adultery."[j]

The Little Children and Jesus

›See Matthew 19:13–15; Luke 18:15–17

4 →PG. 1105

13People were bringing little children to Jesus to have him touch them, but the disciples rebuked them. **14**When Jesus saw this, he was indignant. He said to them, "Let the little children come to me, and do not hinder them, for the kingdom of God belongs to such as these.[k] **15**I tell you the truth, anyone who will not receive the kingdom of God like a little child will never enter it."[l] **16**And he took the children in his arms,[m] put his hands on them and blessed them.

a *43* Some manuscripts *out,* *44where / " 'their worm does not die, / and the fire is not quenched.'* **b** *45* Some manuscripts *hell,* *46where / " 'their worm does not die, / and the fire is not quenched.'* **c** *48* Isaiah 66:24
d *6* Gen. 1:27 **e** *7* Some early manuscripts do not have *and be united to his wife.*
f *8* Gen. 2:24

JOHN

A Self-centered Man Learns to Love

Jesus called him one of the "Sons of Thunder" (Mark 3:17). He was bombastic, self-centered, insensitive and power hungry. Yet, John's name and his writings would one day become synonymous with the message of love. What a transformation!

Two Times in the Spotlight

The Bible tells us that at one point in the disciples' ministry, an unidentified man was driving out demons in Christ's name. Several of the apostles issued an order for him to stop. John told Jesus that they had silenced this man because he was not a part of their elite group (Mark 9:38).

But John didn't anticipate Jesus' rebuke. Rather than being complimented for such behavior, Jesus saw right through this attitude of false superiority and let John know that this man was not doing anything wrong (Mark 9:39). Rather, it was John who was out of order for his attitude of pride.

What makes John's behavior even more inappropriate are the events that happened earlier. All of the disciples had been arguing about "which of them would be the greatest" in Jesus' kingdom (Luke 9:46). When the argument broke out, John and his brother James were probably square in the middle of the squabble. Very disappointed in this childish behavior, Jesus taught them about humility, making it clear that if anyone "wants to be first, he must be the very last, and the servant of all" (Mark 9:35).

The Bible also records another time that John was the center of attention. But this time the circumstances were totally different. This time John stood beneath the cross of Christ.

Among those kneeling at the foot of the cross was Mary, Jesus' mother. It was her son who hung there, blood dripping from his open wounds, as he instructed John to take care of her. We can only assume, because of these instructions, that Jesus' earthly father had already died. As a widow, Mary would have been left without husband or son; in that era, such a woman faced poverty, hardship, disaster. Imagine how John must have felt, in spite of his previous selfish and irresponsible antics, to be entrusted with this very personal and intimate responsibility of caring for Jesus' own mother. What an amazing example of Jesus' love and forgiveness.

God's Love Changes People

This rough, outspoken, insensitive man held a special place in the Savior's heart. It was John who sat next to Jesus at the Passover meal. It was John who was called "the disciple whom Jesus loved" (John 13:23). It was John who leaned "back against Jesus" and asked which one of them would betray him (13:25).

Though Jesus loved all the apostles—including Judas—he had a special love for John because he saw what John could become, not merely what he was. Jesus knew that once this bombastic, rough-edged man understood and experienced the "new birth," he would become a humble and caring man. And, indeed, John eventually found he no longer needed to be first. He no longer yielded to the temptation of jealousy or desire for power and prestige. He had only one goal in mind—to be like Jesus, to serve rather than be served, to build *Christ's* kingdom by showing love to others.

John never forgot the lesson that Jesus taught at the Passover meal when he humbled himself and washed the disciples' dirty feet. And he never forgot Jesus' command following that humbling experience: "As I have loved you, so you must love one another" (John 13:34). Nearly sixty years later, John reiterated Jesus' command to "love one another" five times in his first letter (1 John 3:11, 23; 4:7, 11, 12) and used the word "love" in the same letter over thirty times. John remembered that "Jesus Christ laid down his life for us. And we ought to lay down our lives for our brothers" (3:16).

Revolutionized by Love

John's transformation from an egotistical, power-hungry disciple to a man with a servant's heart demonstrates what is possible for one who is revolutionized by God's love. When we receive Jesus Christ as our Savior and experience the new birth he offers, we begin to reflect Jesus' life in our lives (1 John 3:1–6). Our minds are renewed when we focus on God's Word and hide his truth in our hearts. And, through the power of God's Spirit within us, we become more like Christ as we "grasp how wide and long and high and deep is the love of Christ, and . . . know this love that surpasses knowledge" (Ephesians 3:18–19).

Through the Spirit of Christ who lives within us, it *is* possible to become more and more like Jesus. John's life is proof of that. Your life can be too.

—*Dr. Gene Getz*

The Rich Young Man

›See Matthew 19:16–30; Luke 18:18–30

17 As Jesus started on his way, a man ran up to him and fell on his knees[n] before him. "Good teacher," he asked, "what must I do to inherit eternal life?"[o]

18 "Why do you call me good?" Jesus answered. "No one is good—except God alone. 19 You know the commandments: 'Do not murder, do not commit adultery, do not steal, do not give false testimony, do not defraud, honor your father and mother.'[a]"[p]

20 "Teacher," he declared, "all these I have kept since I was a boy."

7 →PG. 1105

21 Jesus looked at him and loved him. "One thing you lack," he said. "Go, sell everything you have and give to the poor,[q] and you will have treasure in heaven.[r] Then come, follow me."[s]

22 At this the man's face fell. He went away sad, because he had great wealth.

23 Jesus looked around and said to his disciples, "How hard it is for the rich[t] to enter the kingdom of God!"

24 The disciples were amazed at his words. But Jesus said again, "Children, how hard it is[b] to enter the kingdom of God![u] 25 It is easier for a camel to go through the eye of a needle than for a rich man to enter the kingdom of God."[v]

26 The disciples were even more amazed, and said to each other, "Who then can be saved?"

27 Jesus looked at them and said, "With man this is impossible, but not with God; all things are possible with God."[w]

28 Peter said to him, "We have left everything to follow you!"[x]

29 "I tell you the truth," Jesus replied, "no one who has left home or brothers

10:17 [n]Mk 1:40 [o]Lk 10:25; Ac 20:32
10:19 [p]Ex 20:12-16; Dt 5:16-20
10:21 [q]Ac 2:45 [r]Mt 6:20; Lk 12:33 [s]Mt 4:19
10:23 [t]Ps 52:7; 62:10; 1Ti 6:9, 10,17
10:24 [u]Mt 7:13,14
10:25 [v]Lk 12:16-20
10:27 [w]Mt 19:26
10:28 [x]Mt 4:19

[a] 19 Exodus 20:12-16; Deut. 5:16-20
[b] 24 Some manuscripts *is for those who trust in riches*

10:13-16

PROMISE 4

THE GIFT OF A BLESSING

A number of years ago, University of Southern California football coach John McKay had the privilege of coaching his son, John. During a television interview a reporter commented on the athletic ability of young John. Coach McKay responded in an impressive way. "Yes, I'm pleased that John had a good season last year," he said. "He does a fine job and I'm proud of him. But I would be just as proud if he never played the game."

What a statement! McKay's son knew that he didn't have to excel on the football field to be loved by his dad. That means that neither a knee injury nor a season on the bench would have made him any less worthy of his dad's love. And John could look to the future and know that his dad would love him even if he didn't make it big in the business world. It's that kind of parental encouragement that motivates young men like John to excel. Parents who provide a nurturing environment instead of a competitive, pressure-packed climate for their children give them the chance to make their parents proud of them for all the right reasons.

One of the most important needs a child has is the need for a father's approval. If you're a dad, this means that one of your greatest responsibilities is to pass on to your children an awareness of your love, an awareness that each child in your family is important to you. And if you're not a father, you probably have the chance to influence the younger generation through family, church, work or social ties. Your responsibility, then, is to set the proper example of godliness for those under your influence to follow.

While Jesus wasn't a father, he understood children, and he realized their need to be blessed. Since Jesus is our ultimate example, let's look at his blessing in this short passage.

This blessing had two aspects. First, it involved *verbal affirmation.* When Jesus opened his mouth and blessed the children, he spoke words that praised and built them up. Through this we learn that it is not enough for a father to love and appreciate his children from a distance. A father must verbally express his love and affection to make it real to his children.

Second, Jesus' blessing involved *physical affirmation.* Notice that Jesus "took the children in his arms" and "put his hands on them." Jesus could have stood over the children and lectured to them. He could have had them sit at his feet. Instead, he wrapped his arms around them and placed his hands on their heads and shoulders. Jesus knew that nothing communicates love and acceptance like physical touch.

If you're a dad, rivet that truth in your mind. Even if you're a "hands off" kind of a man, try to discover how you could communicate more through words and through touch as a means of blessing your children. Talk to other men who seem to have a good relationship with their children to find out what their method of "blessing" is, and then act on it. If you're not a dad, reflect on how you could be a blessing to the young people with whom you relate as an uncle, a brother, a church member, or even as an employer. God has given us the responsibility of influencing the young people of today for his purposes and for the expansion of his kingdom.

For the next Promise 4 reading go to page 1140.

or sisters or mother or father or children or fields for me and the gospel 30will fail to receive a hundred times as much[y] in this present age (homes, brothers, sisters, mothers, children and fields—and with them, persecutions) and in the age to come,[z] eternal life.[a] 31But many who are first will be last, and the last first."[b]

Jesus Again Predicts His Death

›See Matthew 20:17–19; Luke 18:31–33

32They were on their way up to Jerusalem, with Jesus leading the way, and the disciples were astonished, while those who followed were afraid. Again he took the Twelve[c] aside and told them what was going to happen to him. 33"We are going up to Jerusalem,"[d] he said, "and the Son of Man[e] will be betrayed to the chief priests and teachers of the law.[f] They will condemn him to death and will hand him over to the Gentiles, 34who will mock him and spit on him, flog him[g] and kill him.[h] Three days later[i] he will rise."[j]

The Request of James and John

›See Matthew 20:20–28

35Then James and John, the sons of Zebedee, came to him. "Teacher," they said, "we want you to do for us whatever we ask."

36"What do you want me to do for you?" he asked.

37They replied, "Let one of us sit at your right and the other at your left in your glory."[k]

38"You don't know what you are asking,"[l] Jesus said. "Can you drink the cup[m] I drink or be baptized with the baptism I am baptized with?"[n]

39"We can," they answered.

Jesus said to them, "You will drink the cup I drink and be baptized with the baptism I am baptized with,[o] 40but to sit at my right or left is not for me to grant. These places belong to those for whom they have been prepared."

41When the ten heard about this, they became indignant with James and John. 42Jesus called them together and said, "You know that those who are regarded as rulers of the Gentiles lord it over them, and their high officials exercise authority over them. 43Not so with you. Instead, whoever wants to become great among you must be your servant,[p] 44and whoever wants to be first must be slave of all. 45For even the Son of Man did not come to be served, but to serve,[q] and to give his life as a ransom for many."[r]

4 →PG. 1121
5 →PG. 1127
7 →PG. 1107

10:30 [y]Mt 6:33 [z]Mt 12:32 [a]Mt 25:46
10:31 [b]Mt 19:30
10:32 [c]Mk 3:16-19
10:33 [d]Lk 9:51 [e]Mt 8:20 [f]Mt 27:1,2
10:34 [g]Mt 16:21 [h]Ac 2:23; 3:13 [i]Mt 16:21 [j]Mt 16:21
10:37 [k]Mt 19:28
10:38 [l]Job 38:2 [m]Mt 20:22 [n]Lk 12:50
10:39 [o]Ac 12:2; Rev 1:9
10:43 [p]Mk 9:35
10:45 [q]Mt 20:28 [r]Mt 20:28
10:47 [s]Mk 1:24 [t]Mt 9:27
10:51 [u]Mt 23:7
10:52 [v]Mt 9:22 [w]Mt 4:19
11:1 [x]Mt 21:17 [y]Mt 21:1
11:2 [z]Nu 19:2; Dt 21:3; 1Sa 6:7
11:4 [a]Mk 14:16
11:9 [b]Ps 118:25,26; Mt 23:39

Blind Bartimaeus Receives His Sight

›See Matthew 20:29–34; Luke 18:35–43

46Then they came to Jericho. As Jesus and his disciples, together with a large crowd, were leaving the city, a blind man, Bartimaeus (that is, the Son of Timaeus), was sitting by the roadside begging. 47When he heard that it was Jesus of Nazareth,[s] he began to shout, "Jesus, Son of David,[t] have mercy on me!"

48Many rebuked him and told him to be quiet, but he shouted all the more, "Son of David, have mercy on me!"

49Jesus stopped and said, "Call him."

So they called to the blind man, "Cheer up! On your feet! He's calling you." 50Throwing his cloak aside, he jumped to his feet and came to Jesus.

51"What do you want me to do for you?" Jesus asked him.

The blind man said, "Rabbi,[u] I want to see."

52"Go," said Jesus, "your faith has healed you."[v] Immediately he received his sight and followed[w] Jesus along the road.

1 →PG. 1106

The Triumphal Entry

›See Matthew 21:1–9; Luke 19:29–38; John 12:12–15

11 As they approached Jerusalem and came to Bethphage and Bethany[x] at the Mount of Olives,[y] Jesus sent two of his disciples, 2saying to them, "Go to the village ahead of you, and just as you enter it, you will find a colt tied there, which no one has ever ridden.[z] Untie it and bring it here. 3If anyone asks you, 'Why are you doing this?' tell him, 'The Lord needs it and will send it back here shortly.' "

4They went and found a colt outside in the street, tied at a doorway.[a] As they untied it, 5some people standing there asked, "What are you doing, untying that colt?" 6They answered as Jesus had told them to, and the people let them go. 7When they brought the colt to Jesus and threw their cloaks over it, he sat on it. 8Many people spread their cloaks on the road, while others spread branches they had cut in the fields. 9Those who went ahead and those who followed shouted,

"Hosanna![a]"

"Blessed is he who comes in the
name of the Lord!"[b][b]

[a]9 A Hebrew expression meaning "Save!" which became an exclamation of praise; also in verse 10 [b]9 Psalm 118:25,26

10"Blessed is the coming kingdom of
our father David!"

"Hosanna in the highest!"[c]

11Jesus entered Jerusalem and went to the temple. He looked around at everything, but since it was already late, he went out to Bethany with the Twelve.[d]

Jesus Clears the Temple

›See Matthew 21:12–16; Luke 19:45–47; John 2:13–16

12The next day as they were leaving Bethany, Jesus was hungry. 13Seeing in the distance a fig tree in leaf, he went to find out if it had any fruit. When he reached it, he found nothing but leaves, because it was not the season for figs.[e] 14Then he said to the tree, "May no one ever eat fruit from you again." And his disciples heard him say it.

15On reaching Jerusalem, Jesus entered the temple area and began driving out those who were buying and selling there. He overturned the tables of the money changers and the benches of those selling doves, 16and would not allow anyone to carry merchandise through the temple courts. 17And as he taught them, he said, "Is it not written:

" 'My house will be called
a house of prayer for all
nations'[a]?[f]

But you have made it 'a den of robbers.'[b]"[g]

18The chief priests and the teachers of the law heard this and began looking for a way to kill him, for they feared him,[h] because the whole crowd was amazed at his teaching.[i]

19When evening came, they[c] went out of the city.[j]

The Withered Fig Tree

›See Matthew 21:19–22

20In the morning, as they went along, they saw the fig tree withered from the roots. 21Peter remembered and said to Jesus, "Rabbi,[k] look! The fig tree you cursed has withered!"

1 →PG. 1110

22"Have[d] faith in God," Jesus answered. 23"I tell you the truth, if anyone says to this mountain, 'Go, throw yourself into the sea,' and does not doubt in his heart but believes that what he says will happen, it will be done for him.[l] 24Therefore I tell you, whatever you ask for in prayer, believe that you have received it, and it will be yours.[m] 25And when you stand praying, if you hold anything against anyone, forgive him, so that your Father in heaven may forgive you your sins.[e]"[n]

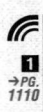

The Authority of Jesus Questioned

›See Matthew 21:23–27; Luke 20:1–8

27They arrived again in Jerusalem, and while Jesus was walking in the temple courts, the chief priests, the teachers of the law and the elders came to him. 28"By what authority are you doing these things?" they asked. "And who gave you authority to do this?"

29Jesus replied, "I will ask you one question. Answer me, and I will tell you by what authority I am doing these things. 30John's baptism—was it from heaven, or from men? Tell me!"

31They discussed it among themselves and said, "If we say, 'From heaven,' he will ask, 'Then why didn't you believe him?' 32But if we say, 'From men' . . . ." (They feared the people, for everyone held that John really was a prophet.)[o]

33So they answered Jesus, "We don't know."

Jesus said, "Neither will I tell you by what authority I am doing these things."

The Parable of the Tenants

›See Matthew 21:33–46; Luke 20:9–19

12 He then began to speak to them in parables: "A man planted a vineyard.[p] He put a wall around it, dug a pit for the winepress and built a watchtower. Then he rented the vineyard to some farmers and went away on a journey. 2At harvest time he sent a servant to the tenants to collect from them some of the fruit of the vineyard. 3But they seized him, beat him and sent him away empty-handed. 4Then he sent another servant to them; they struck this man on the head and treated him shamefully. 5He sent still another, and that one they killed. He sent many others; some of them they beat, others they killed.

6"He had one left to send, a son, whom he loved. He sent him last of all,[q] saying, 'They will respect my son.'

7"But the tenants said to one another, 'This is the heir. Come, let's kill him, and the inheritance will be ours.' 8So they took him and killed him, and threw him out of the vineyard.

9"What then will the owner of the

11:10 [c]Lk 2:14
11:11 [d]Mt 21:12,17
11:13 [e]Lk 13:6-9
11:17 [f]Isa 56:7 [g]Jer 7:11
11:18 [h]Mt 21:46; Mk 12:12; Lk 20:19 [i]Mt 7:28
11:19 [j]Lk 21:37
11:21 [k]Mt 23:7
11:23 [l]Mt 21:21
11:24 [m]Mt 7:7
11:25 [n]Mt 6:14
11:32 [o]Mt 11:9
12:1 [p]Isa 5:1-7
12:6 [q]Heb 1:1-3

[a]*17* Isaiah 56:7 [b]*17* Jer. 7:11 [c]*19* Some early manuscripts *he* [d]*22* Some early manuscripts *If you have* [e]*25* Some manuscripts *sins.* [26]*But if you do not forgive, neither will your Father who is in heaven forgive your sins.*

vineyard do? He will come and kill
those tenants and give the vineyard to
others. 10 Haven't you read this scripture:

" 'The stone the builders rejected
has become the capstone[a]; [r]
11 the Lord has done this,
and it is marvelous in our
eyes'[b]?" [s]

12 Then they looked for a way to arrest him because they knew he had
spoken the parable against them. But
they were afraid of the crowd; [t] so they
left him and went away. [u]

Paying Taxes to Caesar

›See Matthew 22:15–22; Luke 20:20–26

13 Later they sent some of the Pharisees and Herodians [v] to Jesus to catch
him [w] in his words. 14 They came to
him and said, "Teacher, we know you
are a man of integrity. You aren't
swayed by men, because you pay no
attention to who they are; but you
teach the way of God in accordance
with the truth. Is it right to pay taxes
to Caesar or not? 15 Should we pay or
shouldn't we?"
But Jesus knew their hypocrisy.
"Why are you trying to trap me?" he
asked. "Bring me a denarius and let me
look at it." 16 They brought the coin,
and he asked them, "Whose portrait is
this? And whose inscription?"
"Caesar's," they replied.
17 Then Jesus said to them, "Give to
Caesar what is Caesar's and to God
what is God's." [x]
And they were amazed at him.

Marriage at the Resurrection

›See Matthew 22:23–33; Luke 20:27–38

18 Then the Sadducees, [y] who say
there is no resurrection, [z] came to him
with a question. 19 "Teacher," they said,
"Moses wrote for us that if a man's
brother dies and leaves a wife but no
children, the man must marry the widow and have children for his brother. [a]
20 Now there were seven brothers. The
first one married and died without
leaving any children. 21 The second one
married the widow, but he also died,
leaving no child. It was the same with
the third. 22 In fact, none of the seven
left any children. Last of all, the woman
died too. 23 At the resurrection[c] whose
wife will she be, since the seven were
married to her?"
24 Jesus replied, "Are you not in error
because you do not know the Scriptures [b] or the power of God? 25 When
the dead rise, they will neither marry
nor be given in marriage; they will be
like the angels in heaven. [c] 26 Now
about the dead rising—have you not
read in the book of Moses, in the account of the bush, how God said to
him, 'I am the God of Abraham, the
God of Isaac, and the God of Jacob'[d]? [d] 27 He is not the God of the
dead, but of the living. You are badly
mistaken!"

The Greatest Commandment

›See Matthew 22:34–40

28 One of the teachers of the law [e]
came and heard them debating. Noticing that Jesus had given them a good
answer, he asked him, "Of all the commandments, which is the most important?"
29 "The most important one," answered Jesus, "is this: 'Hear, O Israel,
the Lord our God, the Lord is one.[e]
30 Love the Lord your God with all
your heart and with all your soul and
with all your mind and with all
your strength.'[f] [f] 31 The second is this:
'Love your neighbor as yourself.'[g] [g]
There is no commandment greater
than these."

7 →PG. 1113

32 "Well said, teacher," the man replied. "You are right in saying that God
is one and there is no other but him. [h]
33 To love him with all your heart, with
all your understanding and with all
your strength, and to love your neighbor as yourself is more important than
all burnt offerings and sacrifices." [i]
34 When Jesus saw that he had answered wisely, he said to him, "You are
not far from the kingdom of God." [j]
And from then on no one dared ask
him any more questions. [k]

Whose Son Is the Christ?

›See Matthew 22:41–46; Luke 20:41–47

35 While Jesus was teaching in the
temple courts, [l] he asked, "How is it
that the teachers of the law say that the
Christ[h] is the son of David? [m] 36 David
himself, speaking by the Holy Spirit, [n]
declared:

" 'The Lord said to my Lord:
"Sit at my right hand
until I put your enemies
under your feet." '[i] [o]

37 David himself calls him 'Lord.' How
then can he be his son?"
The large crowd [p] listened to him
with delight.

12:10 [r] Ac 4:11 **12:11** [s] Ps 118:22,23 **12:12** [t] Mk 11:18 [u] Mt 22:22 **12:13** [v] Mt 22:16; Mk 3:6 [w] Mt 12:10 **12:17** [x] Ro 13:7 **12:18** [y] Ac 4:1 [z] Ac 23:8; 1Co 15:12 **12:19** [a] Dt 25:5 **12:24** [b] 2Ti 3:15-17 **12:25** [c] 1Co 15:42,49, 52 **12:26** [d] Ex 3:6 **12:28** [e] Lk 10:25-28; 20:39 **12:30** [f] Dt 6:4,5 **12:31** [g] Lev 19:18; Mt 5:43 **12:32** [h] Dt 4:35,39; Isa 45:6,14; 46:9 **12:33** [i] 1Sa 15:22; Hos 6:6; Mic 6:6-8; Heb 10:8 **12:34** [j] Mt 3:2 [k] Mt 22:46; Lk 20:40 **12:35** [l] Mt 26:55 [m] Mt 9:27 **12:36** [n] 2Sa 23:2 [o] Ps 110:1; Mt 22:44 **12:37** [p] Jn 12:9

[a] *10* Or *cornerstone* [b] *11* Psalm 118:22,23 [c] *23* Some manuscripts *resurrection, when men rise from the dead,* [d] *26* Exodus 3:6 [e] *29* Or *the Lord our God is one Lord* [f] *30* Deut. 6:4,5 [g] *31* Lev. 19:18 [h] *35* Or *Messiah* [i] *36* Psalm 110:1

38 As he taught, Jesus said, "Watch
out for the teachers of the law. They
like to walk around in flowing robes
and be greeted in the marketplaces,
39 and have the most important seats in
the synagogues and the places of hon-
or at banquets.[q] 40 They devour widows' houses and for a show make
lengthy prayers. Such men will be punished most severely."

The Widow's Offering

›See Luke 21:1–4

41 Jesus sat down opposite the place
where the offerings were put[r] and
watched the crowd putting their money into the temple treasury. Many rich
people threw in large amounts. 42 But
a poor widow came and put in two
very small copper coins,[a] worth only
a fraction of a penny.[b]
43 Calling his disciples to him, Jesus
said, "I tell you the truth, this poor widow has put more into the treasury than
all the others. 44 They all gave out of
their wealth; but she, out of her poverty, put in everything—all she had to
live on."[s]

Signs of the End of the Age

›See Matthew 24:1–51; Luke 21:5–36

13 As he was leaving the temple, one
of his disciples said to him, "Look,
Teacher! What massive stones! What
magnificent buildings!"
2 "Do you see all these great buildings?" replied Jesus. "Not one stone
here will be left on another; every one
will be thrown down."[t]
3 As Jesus was sitting on the Mount of
Olives[u] opposite the temple, Peter,
James, John[v] and Andrew asked him
privately, 4 "Tell us, when will these
things happen? And what will be the
sign that they are all about to be fulfilled?"
5 Jesus said to them: "Watch out that
no one deceives you.[w] 6 Many will
come in my name, claiming, 'I am he,'
and will deceive many. 7 When you
hear of wars and rumors of wars, do
not be alarmed. Such things must happen, but the end is still to come. 8 Nation will rise against nation, and kingdom against kingdom. There will be
earthquakes in various places, and
famines. These are the beginning of
birth pains.
9 "You must be on your guard. You
will be handed over to the local councils and flogged in the synagogues.[x]
On account of me you will stand before
governors and kings as witnesses to
them. 10 And the gospel must first be
preached to all nations. 11 Whenever
you are arrested and brought to trial,
do not worry beforehand about what to
say. Just say whatever is given you at
the time, for it is not you speaking, but
the Holy Spirit.[y]
12 "Brother will betray brother to
death, and a father his child. Children
will rebel against their parents and
have them put to death.[z] 13 All men
will hate you because of me,[a] but he
who stands firm to the end will be
saved.[b]
14 "When you see 'the abomination
that causes desolation'[c][c] standing
where it[d] does not belong—let the
reader understand—then let those
who are in Judea flee to the mountains.
15 Let no one on the roof of his house go
down or enter the house to take anything out. 16 Let no one in the field go
back to get his cloak. 17 How dreadful
it will be in those days for pregnant
women and nursing mothers![d] 18 Pray
that this will not take place in winter,
19 because those will be days of distress
unequaled from the beginning, when
God created the world,[e] until now—
and never to be equaled again.[f] 20 If
the Lord had not cut short those days,
no one would survive. But for the sake
of the elect, whom he has chosen, he
has shortened them. 21 At that time if
anyone says to you, 'Look, here is the
Christ[e]!' or, 'Look, there he is!' do not
believe it.[g] 22 For false Christs and
false prophets[h] will appear and perform signs and miracles[i] to deceive
the elect—if that were possible. 23 So be
on your guard;[j] I have told you everything ahead of time.
24 "But in those days, following that
distress,

" 'the sun will be darkened,
and the moon will not give its
light;
25 the stars will fall from the sky,
and the heavenly bodies will be
shaken.'[f][k]

26 "At that time men will see the Son
of Man coming in clouds[l] with great
power and glory. 27 And he will send his
angels and gather his elect from the
four winds, from the ends of the earth
to the ends of the heavens.[m]
28 "Now learn this lesson from the fig
tree: As soon as its twigs get tender and
its leaves come out, you know that
summer is near. 29 Even so, when you
see these things happening, you know
that it is near, right at the door. 30 I tell

12:39 [q]Lk 11:43
12:41 [r]2Ki 12:9; Jn 8:20
12:44 [s]2Co 8:12
13:2 [t]Lk 19:44
13:3 [u]Mt 21:1 [v]Mt 4:21
13:5 [w]ver 22; Jer 29:8; Eph 5:6; 2Th 2:3,10-12; 1Ti 4:1; 2Ti 3:13; 1Jn 4:6
13:9 [x]Mt 10:17
13:11 [y]Mt 10:19,20; Lk 12:11,12
13:12 [z]Mic 7:6; Mt 10:21; Lk 12:51-53
13:13 [a]Jn 15:21 [b]Mt 10:22
13:14 [c]Da 9:27; 11:31; 12:11
13:17 [d]Lk 23:29
13:19 [e]Mk 10:6 [f]Da 9:26; 12:1; Joel 2:2
13:21 [g]Lk 17:23; 21:8
13:22 [h]Mt 7:15 [i]Jn 4:48; 2Th 2:9,10
13:23 [j]2Pe 3:17
13:25 [k]Isa 13:10; 34:4; Mt 24:29
13:26 [l]Da 7:13; Mt 16:27; Rev 1:7
13:27 [m]Zec 2:6

[a] *42* Greek *two lepta* [b] *42* Greek *kodrantes*
[c] *14* Daniel 9:27; 11:31; 12:11 [d] *14* Or *he*; also in verse 29 [e] *21* Or *Messiah*
[f] *25* Isaiah 13:10; 34:4

you the truth, this generation[a][n] will certainly not pass away until all these things have happened.[o] [31]Heaven and earth will pass away, but my words will never pass away.[p]

The Day and Hour Unknown

[32]"No one knows about that day or hour, not even the angels in heaven, nor the Son, but only the Father.[q]

3 →PG. 1123

[33]Be on guard! Be alert[b]![r] You do not know when that time will come. [34]It's like a man going away: He leaves his house and puts his servants[s] in charge, each with his assigned task, and tells the one at the door to keep watch.

[35]"Therefore keep watch because you do not know when the owner of the house will come back—whether in the evening, or at midnight, or when the rooster crows, or at dawn. [36]If he comes suddenly, do not let him find you sleeping. [37]What I say to you, I say to everyone: 'Watch!' "[t]

Jesus Anointed at Bethany

›See Matthew 26:2–16; Luke 22:1–6

14 Now the Passover[u] and the Feast of Unleavened Bread were only two days away, and the chief priests and the teachers of the law were looking for some sly way to arrest Jesus and kill him.[v] [2]"But not during the Feast," they said, "or the people may riot."

[3]While he was in Bethany,[w] reclining at the table in the home of a man known as Simon the Leper, a woman came with an alabaster jar of very expensive perfume, made of pure nard. She broke the jar and poured the perfume on his head.[x]

[4]Some of those present were saying indignantly to one another, "Why this waste of perfume? [5]It could have been sold for more than a year's wages[c] and the money given to the poor." And they rebuked her harshly.

[6]"Leave her alone," said Jesus. "Why are you bothering her? She has done a beautiful thing to me. [7]The poor you will always have with you, and you can help them any time you want.[y] But you will not always have me. [8]She did what she could. She poured perfume on my body beforehand to prepare for my burial.[z] [9]I tell you the truth, wherever the gospel is preached throughout the world,[a] what she has done will also be told, in memory of her."

[10]Then Judas Iscariot, one of the Twelve,[b] went to the chief priests to betray Jesus to them.[c] [11]They were delighted to hear this and promised to give him money. So he watched for an opportunity to hand him over.

The Lord's Supper

›See Matthew 26:17–30; Luke 22:7–23

[12]On the first day of the Feast of Unleavened Bread, when it was customary to sacrifice the Passover lamb,[d] Jesus' disciples asked him, "Where do you want us to go and make preparations for you to eat the Passover?"

[13]So he sent two of his disciples, telling them, "Go into the city, and a man carrying a jar of water will meet you. Follow him. [14]Say to the owner of the house he enters, 'The Teacher asks: Where is my guest room, where I may eat the Passover with my disciples?' [15]He will show you a large upper room,[e] furnished and ready. Make preparations for us there."

[16]The disciples left, went into the city and found things just as Jesus had told them. So they prepared the Passover.

[17]When evening came, Jesus arrived with the Twelve. [18]While they were reclining at the table eating, he said, "I tell you the truth, one of you will betray me—one who is eating with me."

13:30 [n]Lk 17:25 [o]Mk 9:1
13:31 [p]Mt 5:18
13:32 [q]Ac 1:7; 1Th 5:1,2
13:33 [r]1Th 5:6
13:34 [s]Mt 25:14
13:37 [t]Lk 12:35-40
14:1 [u]Jn 11:55; 13:1 [v]Mt 12:14
14:3 [w]Mt 21:17 [x]Lk 7:37-39
14:7 [y]Dt 15:11
14:8 [z]Jn 19:40
14:9 [a]Mt 24:14; Mk 16:15
14:10 [b]Mk 3:16-19 [c]Mt 10:4
14:12 [d]Ex 12:1-11; Dt 16:1-4; 1Co 5:7
14:15 [e]Ac 1:13

a 30 Or *race* b 33 Some manuscripts *alert and pray* c 5 Greek *than three hundred denarii*

13:32–37

PROMISE 1

BE PREPARED

The best way to deal with the unexpected is to always be prepared. People such as airline pilots, ship captains, fire fighters, police officers and business and sports professionals know firsthand how true this statement is. And, as this passage shows, it's true in the spiritual realm as well.

Before his death, Jesus clearly stated that he would return. He also emphasized that nobody would know the exact time of his appearance. So he urged his followers to always be alert and prepared for his return. We do that by living with a conscious awareness that he could return at any moment.

This isn't to say that we should do right simply to avoid being caught red-handed. As men of integrity, we must seek to follow Jesus' example and live godly lives at all times. True, Jesus could physically return at any moment. But at *every* moment, he is present with us through his Spirit at work in our lives. Make a commitment to live in the power of the Spirit, and you'll never have to worry about being caught off guard.

For the next Promise 1 reading go to page 1117.

19They were saddened, and one by one they said to him, "Surely not I?"

20"It is one of the Twelve," he replied, "one who dips bread into the bowl with me.[f] 21The Son of Man[g] will go just as it is written about him. But woe to that man who betrays the Son of Man! It would be better for him if he had not been born."

22While they were eating, Jesus took bread, gave thanks and broke it,[h] and gave it to his disciples, saying, "Take it; this is my body."

23Then he took the cup, gave thanks and offered it to them, and they all drank from it.[i]

24"This is my blood of the[a] covenant,[j] which is poured out for many," he said to them. 25"I tell you the truth, I will not drink again of the fruit of the vine until that day when I drink it anew in the kingdom of God."[k]

26When they had sung a hymn, they went out to the Mount of Olives.[l]

Jesus Predicts Peter's Denial

›See Matthew 26:31–35

27"You will all fall away," Jesus told them, "for it is written:

" 'I will strike the shepherd,
and the sheep will be
scattered.'[b][m]

> **14:27**
>
> **PE**
>
> ### BAD NEWS IS GOOD NEWS?
>
> This must have been the worst possible news for Jesus' disciples. Jesus here predicted that he would be killed and that his followers would be scattered. These must have been abrupt and shocking words for men who had been together for over three years, men who had given up careers and sacrificed family commitments to follow Jesus.
>
> But Jesus also spoke words that seem to have slipped past the disciples. He said, "But after I have risen, I will go ahead of you" (v. 28). Those few short words have forever transformed bad news into good news. Jesus' resurrection pulls together scattered men. It gives hope and life. It infects people with the miraculous.
>
> Don't let his words slip past you. Believing them could affect your struggles, your perspective, your life. If you haven't yet decided to accept these words, make an effort to discuss them with a small group. If you have accepted them and believe in Jesus' resurrection power, talk to another person who remains unconvinced. It could be the most important conversation you'll ever have with that individual.

28But after I have risen, I will go ahead of you into Galilee."[n]

29Peter declared, "Even if all fall away, I will not."

30"I tell you the truth," Jesus answered, "today—yes, tonight—before the rooster crows twice[c] you yourself will disown me three times."[o]

31But Peter insisted emphatically, "Even if I have to die with you,[p] I will never disown you." And all the others said the same.

Gethsemane

›See Matthew 26:36–46; Luke 22:40–46

32They went to a place called Gethsemane, and Jesus said to his disciples, "Sit here while I pray." 33He took Peter, James and John[q] along with him, and he began to be deeply distressed and troubled. 34"My soul is overwhelmed with sorrow to the point of death,"[r] he said to them. "Stay here and keep watch." 2 →PG. 1126

35Going a little farther, he fell to the ground and prayed that if possible the hour[s] might pass from him. 36"*Abba*,[d] Father,"[t] he said, "everything is possible for you. Take this cup[u] from me. Yet not what I will, but what you will."[v]

37Then he returned to his disciples and found them sleeping. "Simon," he said to Peter, "are you asleep? Could you not keep watch for one hour? 38Watch and pray so that you will not fall into temptation.[w] The spirit is willing, but the body is weak."[x] 1 →PG. 1131

39Once more he went away and prayed the same thing. 40When he came back, he again found them sleeping, because their eyes were heavy. They did not know what to say to him.

41Returning the third time, he said to them, "Are you still sleeping and resting? Enough! The hour[y] has come. Look, the Son of Man is betrayed into the hands of sinners. 42Rise! Let us go! Here comes my betrayer!"

Jesus Arrested

›See Matthew 26:47–56; Luke 22:47–50; John 18:3–11

43Just as he was speaking, Judas,[z] one of the Twelve, appeared. With him was a crowd armed with swords and clubs, sent from the chief priests, the teachers of the law, and the elders.

44Now the betrayer had arranged a signal with them: "The one I kiss is the man; arrest him and lead him away under guard." 45Going at once to Jesus,

14:20 [f]Jn 13:18-27
14:21 [g]Mt 8:20
14:22 [h]Mt 14:19
14:23 [i]1Co 10:16
14:24 [j]Mt 26:28
14:25 [k]Mt 3:2
14:26 [l]Mt 21:1
14:27 [m]Zec 13:7
14:28 [n]Mk 16:7
14:30 [o]ver 66-72; Lk 22:34; Jn 13:38
14:31 [p]Lk 22:33; Jn 13:37
14:33 [q]Mt 4:21
14:34 [r]Jn 12:27
14:35 [s]ver 41; Mt 26:18
14:36 [t]Ro 8:15; Gal 4:6 [u]Mt 20:22 [v]Mt 26:39
14:38 [w]Mt 6:13 [x]Ro 7:22,23
14:41 [y]ver 35; Mt 26:18
14:43 [z]Mt 10:4

[a]*24* Some manuscripts *the new*
[b]*27* Zech. 13:7
[c]*30* Some early manuscripts do not have *twice.*
[d]*36* Aramaic for *Father*

Judas said, "Rabbi!"[a] and kissed him.
46The men seized Jesus and arrested
him. **47**Then one of those standing near
drew his sword and struck the servant
of the high priest, cutting off his ear.
48"Am I leading a rebellion," said
Jesus, "that you have come out with
swords and clubs to capture me? **49**Every day I was with you, teaching in the
temple courts,[b] and you did not arrest
me. But the Scriptures must be fulfilled."[c] **50**Then everyone deserted
him and fled.[d]
51A young man, wearing nothing but
a linen garment, was following Jesus.
When they seized him, **52**he fled naked,
leaving his garment behind.

Before the Sanhedrin

›See Matthew 26:57–68; John 18:12–13,19–24

53They took Jesus to the high priest,
and all the chief priests, elders and
teachers of the law came together.
54Peter followed him at a distance,
right into the courtyard of the high
priest.[e] There he sat with the guards
and warmed himself at the fire.[f]
55The chief priests and the whole
Sanhedrin[g] were looking for evidence
against Jesus so that they could put
him to death, but they did not find any.
56Many testified falsely against him,
but their statements did not agree.
57Then some stood up and gave this
false testimony against him: **58**"We
heard him say, 'I will destroy this man-
made temple and in three days will
build another,[h] not made by man.' "
59Yet even then their testimony did not
agree.
60Then the high priest stood up before them and asked Jesus, "Are you
not going to answer? What is this testimony that these men are bringing
against you?" **61**But Jesus remained silent and gave no answer.[i]
Again the high priest asked him,
"Are you the Christ,[a] the Son of the
Blessed One?"[j]
62"I am," said Jesus. "And you will
see the Son of Man sitting at the right
hand of the Mighty One and coming on
the clouds of heaven."[k]
63The high priest tore his clothes.[l]
"Why do we need any more witnesses?" he asked. **64**"You have heard
the blasphemy. What do you think?"
They all condemned him as worthy
of death.[m] **65**Then some began to spit
at him; they blindfolded him, struck
him with their fists, and said, "Prophesy!" And the guards took him and beat
him.[n]

14:45 [a]Mt 23:7 **14:49** [b]Mt 26:55 [c]Isa 53:7-12; Mt 1:22 **14:50** [d]ver 27 **14:54** [e]Mt 26:3 [f]Jn 18:18 **14:55** [g]Mt 5:22 **14:58** [h]Mk 15:29; Jn 2:19 **14:61** [i]Isa 53:7; Mt 27:12,14; Mk 15:5; Lk 23:9; Jn 19:9 [j]Mt 16:16; Jn 4:25,26 **14:62** [k]Rev 1:7 **14:63** [l]Lev 10:6; 21:10; Nu 14:6; Ac 14:14 **14:64** [m]Lev 24:16 **14:65** [n]Mt 16:21

14:66 [o]ver 54 **14:67** [p]ver 54 [q]Mk 1:24 **14:68** [r]ver 30,72 **14:70** [s]ver 30,68,72 [t]Ac 2:7 **14:71** [u]ver 30,72 **14:72** [v]ver 30,68 **15:1** [w]Mt 27:1; Lk 22:66 [x]Mt 5:22 [y]Mt 27:2 **15:2** [z]ver 9,12,18, 26; Mt 2:2 **15:5** [a]Mk 14:61 **15:9** [b]ver 2

Peter Disowns Jesus

›See Matthew 26:69–75; Luke 22:56–62; John 18:16–18,25–27

66While Peter was below in the
courtyard,[o] one of the servant girls of
the high priest came by. **67**When she
saw Peter warming himself,[p] she
looked closely at him.
"You also were with that Nazarene,
Jesus,"[q] she said.
68But he denied it. "I don't know
or understand what you're talking
about,"[r] he said, and went out into
the entryway.[b]
69When the servant girl saw him
there, she said again to those standing
around, "This fellow is one of them."
70Again he denied it.[s]
After a little while, those standing
near said to Peter, "Surely you are one
of them, for you are a Galilean."[t]
71He began to call down curses on
himself, and he swore to them, "I don't
know this man you're talking about."[u]
72Immediately the rooster crowed
the second time.[c] Then Peter remembered the word Jesus had spoken to
him: "Before the rooster crows twice[d]
you will disown me three times."[v] And
he broke down and wept.

Jesus Before Pilate

›See Matthew 27:11–26; Luke 23:2–3,18–25; John 18:29—19:16

15 Very early in the morning, the chief
priests, with the elders, the teachers of the law[w] and the whole Sanhedrin,[x] reached a decision. They bound
Jesus, led him away and handed him
over to Pilate.[y]
2"Are you the king of the Jews?"[z]
asked Pilate.
"Yes, it is as you say," Jesus replied.
3The chief priests accused him of
many things. **4**So again Pilate asked
him, "Aren't you going to answer? See
how many things they are accusing
you of."
5But Jesus still made no reply,[a] and
Pilate was amazed.
6Now it was the custom at the Feast
to release a prisoner whom the people
requested. **7**A man called Barabbas was
in prison with the insurrectionists who
had committed murder in the uprising.
8The crowd came up and asked Pilate
to do for them what he usually did.
9"Do you want me to release to you
the king of the Jews?"[b] asked Pilate,
10knowing it was out of envy that the
chief priests had handed Jesus over to

[a] *61* Or *Messiah* [b] *68* Some early manuscripts *entryway and the rooster crowed* [c] *72* Some early manuscripts do not have *the second time.* [d] *72* Some early manuscripts do not have *twice.*

him. **11**But the chief priests stirred up
the crowd to have Pilate release Barabbas[c] instead.
12"What shall I do, then, with the
one you call the king of the Jews?" Pilate asked them.
13"Crucify him!" they shouted.
14"Why? What crime has he committed?" asked Pilate.

But they shouted all the louder,
"Crucify him!"
15Wanting to satisfy the crowd, Pilate released Barabbas to them. He had
Jesus flogged,[d] and handed him over
to be crucified.

The Soldiers Mock Jesus

›See Matthew 27:27–31

16The soldiers led Jesus away into
the palace[e] (that is, the Praetorium)
and called together the whole company of soldiers. **17**They put a purple robe
on him, then twisted together a crown
of thorns and set it on him. **18**And they
began to call out to him, "Hail, king of
the Jews!"[f] **19**Again and again they
struck him on the head with a staff and
spit on him. Falling on their knees,
they paid homage to him. **20**And when
they had mocked him, they took off the
purple robe and put his own clothes on
him. Then they led him out[g] to crucify
him.

The Crucifixion

›See Matthew 27:33–44; Luke 23:33–43;
John 19:17–24

21A certain man from Cyrene,[h] Simon, the father of Alexander and Rufus,[i] was passing by on his way in
from the country, and they forced him
to carry the cross.[j] **22**They brought
Jesus to the place called Golgotha
(which means The Place of the Skull).
23Then they offered him wine mixed
with myrrh,[k] but he did not take it.
24And they crucified him. Dividing up
his clothes, they cast lots[l] to see what
each would get.
25It was the third hour when they
crucified him. **26**The written notice of
the charge against him read: THE KING
OF THE JEWS.[m] **27**They crucified two robbers with him, one on his right and one
on his left.[a] **29**Those who passed by
hurled insults at him, shaking their
heads[n] and saying, "So! You who are
going to destroy the temple and build
it in three days,[o] **30**come down from
the cross and save yourself!"
31In the same way the chief priests
and the teachers of the law mocked
him[p] among themselves. "He saved
others," they said, "but he can't save
himself! **32**Let this Christ,[b][q] this King
of Israel,[r] come down now from the
cross, that we may see and believe."
Those crucified with him also heaped
insults on him.

The Death of Jesus

›See Matthew 27:45–56; Luke 23:44–49;
John 19:29–30

33At the sixth hour darkness came
over the whole land until the ninth
hour.[s] **34**And at the ninth hour Jesus
cried out in a loud voice, *"Eloi, Eloi,
lama sabachthani?"*—which means,
"My God, my God, why have you forsaken me?"[c][t]
35When some of those standing near
heard this, they said, "Listen, he's calling Elijah."
36One man ran, filled a sponge with
wine vinegar,[u] put it on a stick, and
offered it to Jesus to drink. "Now leave
him alone. Let's see if Elijah comes to
take him down," he said.
37With a loud cry, Jesus breathed his
last.[v]
38The curtain of the temple was torn
in two from top to bottom.[w] **39**And
when the centurion,[x] who stood there
in front of Jesus, heard his cry and[d]
saw how he died, he said, "Surely this
man was the Son[e] of God!"[y]
40Some women were watching from
a distance.[z] Among them were Mary
Magdalene, Mary the mother of James
the younger and of Joses, and Salome.[a] **41**In Galilee these women had
followed him and cared for his needs.
Many other women who had come up
with him to Jerusalem were also
there.[b]

The Burial of Jesus

›See Matthew 27:57–61; Luke 23:50–56;
John 19:38–42

42It was Preparation Day (that is, the
day before the Sabbath).[c] So as evening approached, **43**Joseph of Arimathea, a prominent member of the
Council,[d] who was himself waiting for
the kingdom of God,[e] went boldly to
Pilate and asked for Jesus' body. **44**Pilate was surprised to hear that he was
already dead. Summoning the centurion, he asked him if Jesus had already
died. **45**When he learned from the centurion[f] that it was so, he gave the
body to Joseph. **46**So Joseph bought
some linen cloth, took down the body,
wrapped it in the linen, and placed it in
a tomb cut out of rock. Then he rolled

15:11 [c]Ac 3:14
15:15 [d]Isa 53:6
15:16 [e]Jn 18:28,33; 19:9
15:18 [f]ver 2
15:20 [g]Heb 13:12
15:21 [h]Mt 27:32 [i]Ro 16:13 [j]Mt 27:32; Lk 23:26
15:23 [k]ver 36; Ps 69:21; Pr 31:6
15:24 [l]Ps 22:18
15:26 [m]ver 2
15:29 [n]Ps 22:7; 109:25 [o]Mk 14:58; Jn 2:19
15:31 [p]Ps 22:7
15:32 [q]Mk 14:61 [r]ver 2
15:33 [s]Am 8:9
15:34 [t]Ps 22:1
15:36 [u]ver 23; Ps 69:21
15:37 [v]Jn 19:30
15:38 [w]Heb 10:19,20
15:39 [x]ver 45 [y]Mk 1:1,11; 9:7; Mt 4:3
15:40 [z]Ps 38:11 [a]Mk 16:1; Lk 24:10; Jn 19:25
15:41 [b]Mt 27:55,56; Lk 8:2,3
15:42 [c]Mt 27:62; Jn 19:31
15:43 [d]Mt 5:22 [e]Mt 3:2; Lk 2:25,38
15:45 [f]ver 39

[a]*27* Some manuscripts *left,* [28]*and the scripture was fulfilled which says, "He was counted with the lawless ones"* (Isaiah 53:12) [b]*32* Or *Messiah* [c]*34* Psalm 22:1 [d]*39* Some manuscripts do not have *heard his cry and* [e]*39* Or *a son*

a stone against the entrance of the
tomb.[g] 47Mary Magdalene and Mary
the mother of Joses[h] saw where he
was laid.

The Resurrection

›See Matthew 28:1–8; Luke 24:1–10

16 When the Sabbath was over, Mary
Magdalene, Mary the mother of
James, and Salome bought spices[i] so
that they might go to anoint Jesus'
body. 2Very early on the first day of the
week, just after sunrise, they were on
their way to the tomb 3and they asked
each other, "Who will roll the stone
away from the entrance of the
tomb?"[j]

4But when they looked up, they saw
that the stone, which was very large,
had been rolled away. 5As they entered
the tomb, they saw a young man
dressed in a white robe[k] sitting on the
right side, and they were alarmed.

6"Don't be alarmed," he said. "You
are looking for Jesus the Nazarene,[l]
who was crucified. He has risen! He is
not here. See the place where they laid
him. 7But go, tell his disciples and Peter, 'He is going ahead of you into Galilee. There you will see him,[m] just as he
told you.' "[n]

8Trembling and bewildered, the
women went out and fled from the
tomb. They said nothing to anyone, because they were afraid.

[The earliest manuscripts and some other ancient witnesses do not have Mark 16:9–20.]

9When Jesus rose early on the first
day of the week, he appeared first to
Mary Magdalene,[o] out of whom he
had driven seven demons. 10She went
and told those who had been with him
and who were mourning and weeping.
11When they heard that Jesus was alive
and that she had seen him, they did not
believe it.[p]

12Afterward Jesus appeared in a different form to two of them while they
were walking in the country.[q] 13These
returned and reported it to the rest; but
they did not believe them either.

14Later Jesus appeared to the Eleven
as they were eating; he rebuked them
for their lack of faith and their stubborn refusal to believe those who had
seen him after he had risen.[r]

15He said to them, "Go into all the
world and preach the good news to all
creation.[s] 16Whoever believes and is
baptized will be saved, but whoever
does not believe will be condemned.[t]
17And these signs will accompany
those who believe: In my name they
will drive out demons;[u] they will
speak in new tongues;[v] 18they will
pick up snakes[w] with their hands; and
when they drink deadly poison, it will
not hurt them at all; they will place
their hands on[x] sick people, and they
will get well."

19After the Lord Jesus had spoken to
them, he was taken up into heaven[y]
and he sat at the right hand of God.[z]
20Then the disciples went out and
preached everywhere, and the Lord
worked with them and confirmed his
word by the signs that accompanied it.

7 →PG. 1122

15:46 [g] Mk 16:3
15:47 [h] ver 40
16:1 [i] Lk 23:56; Jn 19:39,40
16:3 [j] Mk 15:46
16:5 [k] Jn 20:12
16:6 [l] Mk 1:24
16:7 [m] Jn 21:1-23 [n] Mk 14:28
16:9 [o] Jn 20:11-18
16:11 [p] ver 13,14; Lk 24:11
16:12 [q] Lk 24:13-32
16:14 [r] Lk 24:36-43
16:15 [s] Mt 28:18-20; Lk 24:47,48
16:16 [t] Jn 3:16,18,36; Ac 16:31
16:17 [u] Mk 9:38; Lk 10:17; Ac 5:16; 8:7; 16:18; 19:13-16 [v] Ac 2:4; 10:46; 19:6; 1Co 12:10,28, 30
16:18 [w] Lk 10:19; Ac 28:3-5 [x] Ac 6:6
16:19 [y] Lk 24:50,51; Jn 6:62; Ac 1:9-11; 1Ti 3:16 [z] Ps 110:1; Ro 8:34; Col 3:1; Heb 1:3; 12:2

LUKE

AT A GLANCE

Key Principle: The Son of Man came to seek and to save what was lost so that we could be delivered from the bondage and penalty of sin and given new hope and life in him.

Author: Luke

Time and Place: ~6–4 B.C. to A.D. 33 / Judea, Galilee, and Jerusalem

Key Verses: 1:3–4; 19:10

BENEFIT

Luke, the most comprehensive of the Gospels, is marked by careful chronological development and accurate historical details. Together with Acts, it begins the first of a lengthy two-part narrative that opens by foretelling John the Baptist's birth and ends with Paul's first Roman imprisonment. Luke is a beautifully written Gospel, documenting the perfect humanity of Jesus and presenting him as the Son of Man who seeks us out and makes a life-giving relationship with him possible for us.

SETTING

Luke, a physician and a beloved friend and traveling companion of Paul (Colossians 4:14; 2 Timothy 4:11; Philemon 24), may have been the only Gentile contributor to the New Testament. While he was not an eyewitness of the events he recorded in this Gospel, he carefully collected and investigated a number of written and oral eyewitness accounts (1:1–4). He arranged his material in such a way that Christ's life would be accessible to what was probably an originally Greek readership. Luke assumes his readers are unfamiliar with Aramaic terms and Jewish customs and geography, and therefore explains these Jewish details. He addressed both Luke and Acts to a "most excellent Theophilus" (meaning "Friend of God") who was probably a man of prominent social standing. This Gospel was probably written in the A.D. 60s, prior to the destruction of the Jerusalem temple in A.D. 70.

TIME LINE 10BC AD1 10 20 30 40 50 60 70 80 90 100

- **Herod the Great's reign (c.37-4 B.C.)**
- **Jesus' birth (c.6/5 B.C.)**
- **Jesus' flight to Egypt (c.5/4 B.C.)**
- **Jesus' visit to the temple (c. A.D.5)**
- **Beginning of John the Baptist's ministry (c. A.D.26)**
- **Beginning of Jesus' ministry (c. A.D.26)**
- **Jesus' death, resurrection and ascension (c. A.D.30)**
- **Paul's conversion (c. A.D.35)**
- **Book of Luke written (c. A.D.59-63)**

THEME AND PURPOSE

The theme of Luke is captured by Jesus' statement in Luke 19:10: "For the Son of Man came to seek and to save what was lost." The first portion of this Gospel presents the works and words of the Son of Man, and depicts twin responses to Jesus—growing belief and growing opposition. Luke captures Christ's ministry of saving the lost by using vivid accounts of his trials, his death and burial, and his resurrection. Having "carefully investigated everything from the beginning," Luke wrote this Gospel to "write an orderly account" of the life of the Lord "so that you may know the certainty of the things you have been taught" (1:3–4).

UNIQUE CONTRIBUTION

Not only is Luke the longest of the four Gospels, but it is also the longest book in the New Testament. When this Gospel is combined with Luke's other book, Acts, it constitutes 28 percent of the New Testament. Luke is also the most historically detailed of the Gospels. Finally, the four hymns in chapters 1 and 2 have added immensely to Christian worship (these are the *Magnificat* of Mary in 1:46–55, the *Benedictus* of Zechariah in 1:67–79, the *Gloria in Excelsis Deo* of the heavenly host in 2:14, and the *Nunc Dimittis* of Simeon in 2:28–32).

CHRIST IN LUKE

Luke emphasizes Christ's perfect humanity as well as his kindness and compassion. His account delves into Jesus' ancestry, birth and early life more than the other Gospels, thus providing a wealth of details about Christ's life and ministry that otherwise would have been lost. Jesus' concern for all classes and conditions of people (poor and wealthy, women, Jews, Samaritans, Gentiles, tax collectors and religious leaders) is especially evident in this book. Luke reveals Christ's solidarity with the human condition by relating how he identified with our sorrowful, sinful plight, and he shows how Jesus has satisfied our need for salvation by his sacrificial death and glorious resurrection.

OVERVIEW

FOCUS	Seeking the Lost		Saving the Lost
REFERENCE	1:1 9:50	9:51 19:27	19:28 24:53
TOPICS	Advent and Activities	Antagonism and Admonitions	Affliction and Authentication
	Presentation	Preaching	Passion
	Miracles of the Son of Man	Parables and Teaching of the Son of Man	
LOCATION	Judea and Galilee	On the Way to Jerusalem	Jerusalem
TIME	~6–4 B.C. to A.D. 33		

Luke begins by intertwining the infancy narratives of John the Baptist and Jesus (1—2). After a one-verse transition (2:52), he skips to John's early ministry and to Jesus' baptism, genealogy and temptation (3:1—4:13). Next come a series of narratives depicting Jesus' miraculous ministry of exorcism, healing and teaching, as well as his calling and instruction of his disciples (4:14—9:50).

As Christ encounters increasing antagonism, he spends proportionately more time with his disciples. He teaches them about such practical issues as prayer, repentance, hypocrisy, anxiety, watchfulness, the kingdom, salvation, humility, the cost of discipleship, evangelism, stewardship, faith, persistence and wealth (9:51—19:27).

After Jesus' triumphal entry into Jerusalem, the religious leaders question his authority. Jesus refutes their arguments and predicts the destruction of Jerusalem (19:28—21:38). Jesus has his last supper with his disciples, is betrayed and abandoned in Gethsemane, suffers abuse at his trials, and is crucified and buried (22—23). Luke concludes with the empty tomb and a series of post-resurrection appearances, including the marvelous story of Jesus' encounter with two disciples on the road to Emmaus (24).

LUKE

Introduction

1 Many have undertaken to draw up an account of the things that have been fulfilled[a] among us, **2**just as they were handed down to us by those who from the first[a] were eyewitnesses[b] and servants of the word.[c] **3**Therefore, since I myself have carefully investigated everything from the beginning, it seemed good also to me to write an orderly account[d] for you, most excellent[e] Theophilus,[f] **4**so that you may know the certainty of the things you have been taught.[g]

The Birth of John the Baptist Foretold

5In the time of Herod king of Judea[h] there was a priest named Zechariah, who belonged to the priestly division of Abijah;[i] his wife Elizabeth was also a descendant of Aaron. **6**Both of them were upright in the sight of God, observing all the Lord's commandments and regulations blamelessly.[j] **7**But they had no children, because Elizabeth was barren; and they were both well along in years.

8Once when Zechariah's division was on duty and he was serving as priest before God,[k] **9**he was chosen by lot, according to the custom of the priesthood, to go into the temple of the Lord and burn incense.[l] **10**And when the time for the burning of incense came, all the assembled worshipers were praying outside.[m]

11Then an angel[n] of the Lord appeared to him, standing at the right side of the altar of incense.[o] **12**When Zechariah saw him, he was startled and was gripped with fear.[p] **13**But the angel said to him: "Do not be afraid,[q] Zechariah; your prayer has been heard. Your wife Elizabeth will bear you a son, and you are to give him the name John.[r] **14**He will be a joy and delight to you, and many will rejoice because of his birth,[s] **15**for he will be great in the sight of the Lord. He is never to take wine or other fermented drink,[t] and he will be filled with the Holy Spirit even from birth.[b][u] **16**Many of the people of Israel will he bring back to the Lord their God. **17**And he will go on before the Lord,[v] in the spirit and power of Elijah,[w] to turn the hearts of the fathers to their children[x] and the disobedient to the wisdom of the righteous—to make ready a people prepared for the Lord."

18Zechariah asked the angel, "How can I be sure of this? I am an old man and my wife is well along in years."[y]

19The angel answered, "I am Gabriel.[z] I stand in the presence of God, and I have been sent to speak to you and to tell you this good news. **20**And now you will be silent and not able to speak[a] until the day this happens, because you did not believe my words, which will come true at their proper time."

21Meanwhile, the people were waiting for Zechariah and wondering why he stayed so long in the temple. **22**When he came out, he could not speak to them. They realized he had seen a vision in the temple, for he kept making signs[b] to them but remained unable to speak.

23When his time of service was completed, he returned home. **24**After this his wife Elizabeth became pregnant and for five months remained in seclusion. **25**"The Lord has done this for me," she said. "In these days he has shown his favor and taken away my disgrace[c] among the people."

The Birth of Jesus Foretold

26In the sixth month, God sent the angel Gabriel[d] to Nazareth,[e] a town in Galilee, **27**to a virgin pledged to be married to a man named Joseph,[f] a descendant of David. The virgin's name was Mary. **28**The angel went to her and said, "Greetings, you who are highly favored! The Lord is with you."

29Mary was greatly troubled at his words and wondered what kind of greeting this might be. **30**But the angel said to her, "Do not be afraid,[g] Mary, you have found favor with God. **31**You will be with child and give birth to a son, and you are to give him the name Jesus.[h] **32**He will be great and will be called the Son of the Most High.[i] The Lord God will give him the throne of his father David, **33**and he will reign over the house of Jacob forever; his kingdom[j] will never end."[k]

34"How will this be," Mary asked the angel, "since I am a virgin?"

35The angel answered, "The Holy

1:2 [a]Mk 1:1; Jn 15:27; Ac 1:21,22 [b]Heb 2:3; 1Pe 5:1; 2Pe 1:16; 1Jn 1:1 [c]Mk 4:14
1:3 [d]Ac 11:4 [e]Ac 24:3; 26:25 [f]Ac 1:1
1:4 [g]Jn 20:31
1:5 [h]Mt 2:1 [i]1Ch 24:10
1:6 [j]Ge 7:1; 1Ki 9:4
1:8 [k]1Ch 24:19; 2Ch 8:14
1:9 [l]Ex 30:7,8; 1Ch 23:13; 2Ch 29:11
1:10 [m]Lev 16:17
1:11 [n]Ac 5:19 [o]Ex 30:1-10
1:12 [p]Jdg 6:22,23; 13:22
1:13 [q]ver 30; Mt 14:27 [r]ver 60,63
1:14 [s]ver 58
1:15 [t]Nu 6:3; Jdg 13:4; Lk 7:33 [u]Jer 1:5; Gal 1:15
1:17 [v]ver 76 [w]Mt 11:14 [x]Mal 4:5,6
1:18 [y]ver 34; Ge 17:17
1:19 [z]ver 26; Mt 18:10; Da 8:16; 9:21
1:20 [a]Eze 3:26
1:22 [b]ver 62
1:25 [c]Ge 30:23; Isa 4:1
1:26 [d]ver 19 [e]Mt 2:23
1:27 [f]Mt 1:16,18,20; Lk 2:4
1:30 [g]ver 13; Mt 14:27
1:31 [h]Isa 7:14; Mt 1:21,25; Lk 2:21
1:32 [i]ver 35,76; Mk 5:7
1:33 [j]Mt 28:18 [k]Da 2:44; 7:14,27; Mic 4:7; Heb 1:8

a *1* Or *been surely believed* **b** *15* Or *from his mother's womb*

Spirit will come upon you,[l] and the
power of the Most High[m] will over-
shadow you. So the holy one[n] to be
born will be called[a] the Son of God.[o]
36 Even Elizabeth your relative is going
to have a child in her old age, and she
who was said to be barren is in her
sixth month. 37 For nothing is impossible with God."[p]
38 "I am the Lord's servant," Mary
answered. "May it be to me as you have
said." Then the angel left her.

Mary Visits Elizabeth

39 At that time Mary got ready and
hurried to a town in the hill country of
Judea,[q] 40 where she entered Zechariah's home and greeted Elizabeth.
41 When Elizabeth heard Mary's greeting, the baby leaped in her womb, and
Elizabeth was filled with the Holy Spirit. 42 In a loud voice she exclaimed:
"Blessed are you among women,[r] and
blessed is the child you will bear! 43 But
why am I so favored, that the mother of
my Lord should come to me? 44 As soon
as the sound of your greeting reached
my ears, the baby in my womb leaped
for joy. 45 Blessed is she who has believed that what the Lord has said to
her will be accomplished!"

Mary's Song

›See 1 Samuel 2:1–10

46 And Mary said:

"My soul glorifies the Lord[s]
47 and my spirit rejoices in God my
Savior,[t]
48 for he has been mindful
of the humble state of his
servant.[u]
From now on all generations will
call me blessed,[v]
49 for the Mighty One has done
great things[w] for me—
holy is his name.[x]
50 His mercy extends to those who
fear him,
from generation to generation.[y]
51 He has performed mighty deeds
with his arm;[z]
he has scattered those who are
proud in their inmost
thoughts.
52 He has brought down rulers from
their thrones
but has lifted up the humble.
53 He has filled the hungry with good
things[a]
but has sent the rich away
empty.
54 He has helped his servant Israel,
remembering to be merciful[b]
55 to Abraham and his descendants[c]
forever,
even as he said to our fathers."

56 Mary stayed with Elizabeth for
about three months and then returned
home.

The Birth of John the Baptist

57 When it was time for Elizabeth to
have her baby, she gave birth to a son.
58 Her neighbors and relatives heard
that the Lord had shown her great mercy, and they shared her joy.
59 On the eighth day they came to

1:35 [l] Mt 1:18 [m] ver 32,76 [n] Mk 1:24 [o] Mt 4:3 **1:37** [p] Mt 19:26 **1:39** [q] ver 65 **1:42** [r] Jdg 5:24 **1:46** [s] Ps 34:2,3 **1:47** [t] 1Ti 1:1; 2:3 **1:48** [u] Ps 138:6 [v] Lk 11:27 **1:49** [w] Ps 71:19 [x] Ps 111:9 **1:50** [y] Ex 20:6; Ps 103:17 **1:51** [z] Ps 98:1; Isa 40:10 **1:53** [a] Ps 107:9 **1:54** [b] Ps 98:3 **1:55** [c] Ge 17:19; Ps 132:11; Gal 3:16

[a] 35 Or *So the child to be born will be called holy,*

1:5–25

PROMISE 1

MIRACULOUS INVASION

How would you respond if the miraculous invaded your life? That theoretical question became a reality for Zechariah. One day while he was carrying out his job as a priest, an angel of the Lord suddenly appeared before him. How did Zechariah respond? He was "startled and was gripped with fear" (v. 12). Wouldn't you be?

Zechariah listened to the angel's promise that he and his wife would have a son, one who would become a blessing to the nation of Israel. Being a priest, old Zechariah knew about the ancient teaching that one like Elijah would precede the Messiah's coming (Malachi 4:5–6). So when the angel spoke of this boy in terms of the "spirit and power of Elijah," Zechariah knew that this one short phrase summarized his son's career as the precursor to the Savior of the world.

Overcome with doubt, Zechariah asked for proof (v. 18). He got it, but it wasn't the kind of proof that he expected. The elderly priest completely lost his speech until his son, the child of this promise, was born. Once the child arrived, Zechariah opened his mouth wide and gave praise to God (v. 64).

Look at Zechariah's progression; he moved from fear to doubt to faith. We've all known fear and doubt, and most of us have found out that it's easy to get stuck there. Faith can follow fear and doubt for us as it did for Zechariah. But, as Zechariah eventually was, we need to be receptive to truth.

God may not send an angel to speak to you or take away your speech to prove himself. But he will give you all the evidence you need to believe in his promises for your life. As you read God's Word and discover his promises, ask him to move you beyond fear and doubt and into faith.

For the next Promise 1 reading go to page 1135.

MARY

She Knew What to Treasure

When you read Luke 1:46–55, you are probably amazed at this detailed analysis of the Messiah's ministry. Who utters such profound ideas? Who has such a grasp of life's complicated realities? In this case, it was a 14-year-old peasant girl.

We know tantalizingly little about her. She had no formal education. She was, after all, a girl. Living in Israel. In the region of Galilee. In the days when Rome ruled the world. One can hardly imagine a person with less worldly power or importance than this young girl.

God's Chosen Vessel

But the Gospel writer Luke, ever the detailed historian, hints at her status in her world (Luke 1:26–27). Notice the path we take in finding out about this girl: "*God* sent an angel named *Gabriel* to *Nazareth* in *Galilee*, to a virgin pledged to be married to *Joseph*, son of *David*." Mixed in with all this important information is a key detail: The virgin's name is Mary. Certainly, no one would accuse Luke of treating Mary as unimportant. But in the grand scheme of things, we have to work down from God, through Gabriel, through Joseph the son of David before we find that the virgin had a name, and that it was Mary.

That's just how things were in Mary's world. Teenage virgins didn't get first, or second, or even third billing. Little girls just didn't matter all that much in a Roman man's world. Each part of Luke's statement diminishes her chance of being someone significant. Rome ruled and she wasn't Roman. She wasn't even Greek. She was one of those mysterious people called Jews. For centuries they had been pushed around by one empire after another. The Babylonians, then the Persians, then the Greeks and now the Romans. The Jews' survival depended on their ability to keep Gentile influence, education and culture out of their closed community. Even Jerusalem, the most cosmopolitan of their cities, was a bastion against Greek and Roman culture.

But Mary didn't live in Jerusalem. No, she lived in Nazareth, a little hamlet in the remote, rural province of Galilee. She lived 88 miles north of the closest thing the Jews had to a center for culture and learning. Her education prepared her mainly for home and motherhood. Her reading skills would have been minimal. Her understanding of the Mosaic law was more utilitarian than philosophical. There was little intentional education for girls. They learned what they picked up by watching, listening, asking. Boys were taught to read and to study the law. Girls learned where they could.

So Mary probably didn't influence Caesar Augustus or King Herod as they ruled their empires. Her world was remote and small and dusty and boring. But Gabriel catapulted her into eternal significance with eleven words: "Greetings you who are highly favored! The Lord is with you" (Luke 1:28). And then Gabriel added, "You have found favor with God" (v. 30).

Mary would soon become the focal point of all heaven's host. Her womb would generate, protect and nourish the One who is the center of time and space. What produces a person like Mary, one who can be trusted by God with the most important responsibility ever delegated to anyone?

A Heart for God

Luke describes an event that helps us understand her. Having believed and submitted to God's will without regard for how it would affect her personally, Mary carried this miracle baby in her womb. Then, nine months pregnant, she traveled for days on a donkey's back over rough terrain. Her journey to Bethlehem complete, she gave birth to the baby in a stable, of all places. Finally, the shepherds showed up with their fantastic story about the angels and the heavenly host (Luke 2:1–18).

In the middle of all this noise and activity, Luke dropped, almost as an aside, a statement that proclaims volumes about this young virgin-mother. "But Mary treasured all these things, and pondered them in her heart" (Luke 2:19). Luke used particular language to suggest a higher act than "remembering" these things. He informed us that Mary *treasured* them. She guarded them in a safe place, these important events. And then she meditated on them. She turned them over, pondered them, made sense of them in her heart. Though she was nothing in the world's eyes, and though her society did not appreciate her for her understanding, God honors her in this and in other passages for having a heart for the things of God.

This very special young lady was hungry to grow in her awareness and understanding. Her senses were always sharp to learn more about God, his creation, his will and his ways. She watched and listened and sorted through what went on around her. She, like the rest of us, rejected some of the data as not worth storing. And what counted, what mattered, she *treasured* and *pondered*. She learned to understand which was which.

Do you see her profound understanding of what God was doing with her? Read Luke 1:46–55

again and notice the references to salvation, to equality and to social justice. This is Mary's interpretation of the Messianic Hope that was growing in her womb. First, this teenage girl understood God's call: "Mary, you are the one I have chosen to carry my Child. Together, you and I are going to bring hope and light into a dark world." Second, she believed that God could do this great thing through her, though she was as obscure and as powerless as she could possibly be in the world's eyes. Finally, she submitted to God's will completely and without hesitation.

—Dr. Sid Buzzell

circumcise[d] the child, and they were
going to name him after his father
Zechariah, 60but his mother spoke up
and said, "No! He is to be called John."[e]
61They said to her, "There is no one
among your relatives who has that
name."
62Then they made signs[f] to his father, to find out what he would like to
name the child. 63He asked for a writing tablet, and to everyone's astonishment he wrote, "His name is John."[g]
64Immediately his mouth was opened
and his tongue was loosed, and he began to speak,[h] praising God. 65The
neighbors were all filled with awe, and
throughout the hill country of Judea[i]
people were talking about all these
things. 66Everyone who heard this
wondered about it, asking, "What then
is this child going to be?" For the Lord's
hand was with him.[j]

Zechariah's Song

67His father Zechariah was filled
with the Holy Spirit and prophesied:[k]

68"Praise be to the Lord, the God of
Israel,[l]
because he has come and has
redeemed his people.[m]
69He has raised up a horn[a][n] of
salvation for us
in the house of his servant
David[o]
70(as he said through his holy
prophets of long ago),[p]
71salvation from our enemies
and from the hand of all who
hate us—
72to show mercy to our fathers[q]
and to remember his holy
covenant,[r]
73 the oath he swore to our father
Abraham:[s]
74to rescue us from the hand of our
enemies,
and to enable us to serve him[t]
without fear
75 in holiness and righteousness[u]
before him all our days.

76And you, my child, will be called a
prophet[v] of the Most
High;[w]
for you will go on before the
Lord to prepare the way for
him,[x]
77to give his people the knowledge of
salvation
through the forgiveness of their
sins,[y]
78because of the tender mercy of our
God,
by which the rising sun[z] will
come to us from heaven
79to shine on those living in darkness
and in the shadow of death,[a]
to guide our feet into the path of
peace."

80And the child grew and became
strong in spirit;[b] and he lived in the
desert until he appeared publicly to Israel.

The Birth of Jesus

2 In those days Caesar Augustus[c] issued a decree that a census should
be taken of the entire Roman world.[d]
2(This was the first census that took
place while Quirinius was governor of
Syria.)[e] 3And everyone went to his
own town to register.
4So Joseph also went up from the
town of Nazareth in Galilee to Judea, to
Bethlehem[f] the town of David, because he belonged to the house and
line of David. 5He went there to register
with Mary, who was pledged to be
married to him and was expecting a
child. 6While they were there, the time
came for the baby to be born, 7and she
gave birth to her firstborn, a son. She
wrapped him in cloths and placed him
in a manger, because there was no
room for them in the inn.

The Shepherds and the Angels

8And there were shepherds living
out in the fields nearby, keeping watch
over their flocks at night. 9An angel[g]
of the Lord appeared to them, and the
glory of the Lord shone around them,
and they were terrified. 10But the angel
said to them, "Do not be afraid.[h] I
bring you good news of great joy that
will be for all the people. 11Today in the
town of David a Savior[i] has been born
to you; he is Christ[b][j] the Lord. 12This
will be a sign[k] to you: You will find a
baby wrapped in cloths and lying in a
manger."
13Suddenly a great company of the
heavenly host appeared with the angel,
praising God and saying,

14"Glory to God in the highest,
and on earth peace[l] to men on
whom his favor rests."

15When the angels had left them and
gone into heaven, the shepherds said
to one another, "Let's go to Bethlehem
and see this thing that has happened,
which the Lord has told us about."
16So they hurried off and found
Mary and Joseph, and the baby, who

1:59 [d]Ge 17:12; Lev 12:3; Lk 2:21; Php 3:5
1:60 [e]ver 13,63
1:62 [f]ver 22
1:63 [g]ver 13,60
1:64 [h]ver 20
1:65 [i]ver 39
1:66 [j]Ge 39:2; Ac 11:21
1:67 [k]Joel 2:28
1:68 [l]Ps 72:18 [m]Ps 111:9; Lk 7:16
1:69 [n]1Sa 2:1,10; Ps 18:2; 89:17; 132:17; Eze 29:21 [o]Mt 1:1
1:70 [p]Jer 23:5
1:72 [q]Mic 7:20 [r]Ps 105:8,9; 106:45; Eze 16:60
1:73 [s]Ge 22:16-18
1:74 [t]Heb 9:14
1:75 [u]Eph 4:24
1:76 [v]Mt 11:9 [w]ver 32,35 [x]ver 17; Mal 3:1
1:77 [y]Jer 31:34; Mk 1:4
1:78 [z]Mal 4:2
1:79 [a]Isa 9:2; 59:9; Mt 4:16; Ac 26:18
1:80 [b]Lk 2:40,52
2:1 [c]Lk 3:1; Mt 22:17 [d]Mt 24:14
2:2 [e]Mt 4:24
2:4 [f]Jn 7:42
2:9 [g]Lk 1:11; Ac 5:19
2:10 [h]Mt 14:27
2:11 [i]Mt 1:21; Jn 4:42; Ac 5:31 [j]Mt 1:16; 16:16,20; Jn 11:27; Ac 2:36
2:12 [k]1Sa 2:34; 2Ki 19:29; Isa 7:14
2:14 [l]Lk 1:79; Ro 5:1; Eph 2:14,17

[a] *69 Horn* here symbolizes strength. [b] *11* Or *Messiah.* "The Christ" (Greek) and "the Messiah" (Hebrew) both mean "the Anointed One"; also in verse 26.

was lying in the manger. **17**When they had seen him, they spread the word concerning what had been told them about this child, **18**and all who heard it were amazed at what the shepherds said to them. **19**But Mary treasured up all these things and pondered them in her heart.[m] **20**The shepherds returned, glorifying and praising God[n] for all the things they had heard and seen, which were just as they had been told.

Jesus Presented in the Temple

21On the eighth day, when it was time to circumcise him,[o] he was named Jesus, the name the angel had given him before he had been conceived.[p]

22When the time of their purification according to the Law of Moses[q] had been completed, Joseph and Mary took him to Jerusalem to present him to the Lord **23**(as it is written in the Law of the Lord, "Every firstborn male is to be consecrated to the Lord"[a]),[r] **24**and to offer a sacrifice in keeping with what is said in the Law of the Lord: "a pair of doves or two young pigeons."[b][s]

25Now there was a man in Jerusalem called Simeon, who was righteous and devout.[t] He was waiting for the consolation of Israel,[u] and the Holy Spirit was upon him. **26**It had been revealed to him by the Holy Spirit that he would not die before he had seen the Lord's Christ. **27**Moved by the Spirit, he went into the temple courts. When the parents brought in the child Jesus to do for him what the custom of the Law required,[v] **28**Simeon took him in his arms and praised God, saying:

29"Sovereign Lord, as you have
promised,[w]
you now dismiss[c] your servant
in peace.[x]
30For my eyes have seen your
salvation,[y]
31 which you have prepared in the
sight of all people,
32a light for revelation to the Gentiles
and for glory to your people
Israel."[z]

33The child's father and mother marveled at what was said about him. **34**Then Simeon blessed them and said to Mary, his mother:[a] "This child is destined to cause the falling[b] and rising of many in Israel, and to be a sign that will be spoken against, **35**so that the thoughts of many hearts will be revealed. And a sword will pierce your own soul too."

36There was also a prophetess,[c] Anna, the daughter of Phanuel, of the tribe of Asher. She was very old; she had lived with her husband seven years after her marriage, **37**and then was a widow until she was eighty-four.[d][d] She never left the temple but worshiped night and day, fasting and praying.[e] **38**Coming up to them at that very moment, she gave thanks to God and spoke about the child to all who were looking forward to the redemption of Jerusalem.[f]

39When Joseph and Mary had done everything required by the Law of the Lord, they returned to Galilee to their own town of Nazareth.[g] **40**And the child grew and became strong; he was filled with wisdom, and the grace of God was upon him.[h]

The Boy Jesus at the Temple

41Every year his parents went to Jerusalem for the Feast of the Passover.[i] **42**When he was twelve years old, they went up to the Feast, according to the custom. **43**After the Feast was over, while his parents were returning home, the boy Jesus stayed behind in Jerusalem, but they were unaware of it. **44**Thinking he was in their company, they traveled on for a day. Then they began looking for him among their relatives and friends. **45**When they did not find him, they went back to Jerusalem to look for him. **46**After three days they found him in the temple courts, sitting among the teachers, listening to them and asking them questions. **47**Everyone who heard him was amazed[j] at his understanding and his answers. **48**When his parents saw him, they were astonished. His mother[k] said to him, "Son, why have you treated us like this? Your father[l] and I have been anxiously searching for you."

49"Why were you searching for me?" he asked. "Didn't you know I had to be in my Father's house?"[m] **50**But they did not understand what he was saying to them.[n]

51Then he went down to Nazareth with them[o] and was obedient to them. But his mother treasured all these things in her heart.[p] **52**And Jesus grew in wisdom and stature, and in favor with God and men.[q]

4 →PG. 1141

John the Baptist Prepares the Way

›See Matthew 3:1–10; Mark 1:3–5

3 In the fifteenth year of the reign of Tiberius Caesar—when Pontius Pilate[r] was governor of Judea, Herod[s] tetrarch of Galilee, his brother Philip

2:19 [m]ver 51
2:20 [n]Mt 9:8
2:21 [o]Lk 1:59 [p]Lk 1:31
2:22 [q]Lev 12:2-8
2:23 [r]Ex 13:2,12,15; Nu 3:13
2:24 [s]Lev 12:8
2:25 [t]Lk 1:6 [u]ver 38; Isa 52:9; Lk 23:51
2:27 [v]ver 22
2:29 [w]ver 26 [x]Ac 2:24
2:30 [y]Isa 52:10; Lk 3:6
2:32 [z]Isa 42:6; 49:6; Ac 13:47; 26:23
2:34 [a]Mt 12:46 [b]Isa 8:14; Mt 21:44; 1Co 1:23; 2Co 2:16; 1Pe 2:7,8
2:36 [c]Ac 21:9
2:37 [d]1Ti 5:9 [e]Ac 13:3; 14:23; 1Ti 5:5
2:38 [f]ver 25; Isa 40:2; Lk 1:68; 24:21
2:39 [g]ver 51; Mt 2:23
2:40 [h]ver 52; Lk 1:80
2:41 [i]Ex 23:15; Dt 16:1-8
2:47 [j]Mt 7:28
2:48 [k]Mt 12:46 [l]Lk 3:23; 4:22
2:49 [m]Jn 2:16
2:50 [n]Mk 9:32
2:51 [o]ver 39; Mt 2:23 [p]ver 19
2:52 [q]ver 40; 1Sa 2:26; Lk 1:80
3:1 [r]Mt 27:2 [s]Mt 14:1

[a]*23* Exodus 13:2,12 [b]*24* Lev. 12:8 [c]*29* Or *promised, / now dismiss* [d]*37* Or *widow for eighty-four years*

tetrarch of Iturea and Traconitis, and Lysanias tetrarch of Abilene— 2during the high priesthood of Annas and Caiaphas,[t] the word of God came to John[u] son of Zechariah[v] in the desert. 3He went into all the country around the Jordan, preaching a baptism of repentance for the forgiveness of sins.[w] 4As is written in the book of the words of Isaiah the prophet:

"A voice of one calling in the desert,
'Prepare the way for the Lord,
make straight paths for him.
5Every valley shall be filled in,
every mountain and hill made low.
The crooked roads shall become straight,
the rough ways smooth.
6And all mankind will see God's salvation.' "[a][x]

7John said to the crowds coming out to be baptized by him, "You brood of vipers![y] Who warned you to flee from the coming wrath?[z] 8Produce fruit in keeping with repentance. And do not begin to say to yourselves, 'We have Abraham as our father.'[a] For I tell you that out of these stones God can raise up children for Abraham. 9The ax is already at the root of the trees, and every tree that does not produce good fruit will be cut down and thrown into the fire."[b]

10"What should we do then?"[c] the crowd asked.

7 →PG. 1126

11John answered, "The man with two tunics should share with him who has none, and the one who has food should do the same."[d]

12Tax collectors also came to be baptized.[e] "Teacher," they asked, "what should we do?"

13"Don't collect any more than you are required to,"[f] he told them.

14Then some soldiers asked him, "And what should we do?"

He replied, "Don't extort money and don't accuse people falsely[g]—be content with your pay."

15The people were waiting expectantly and were all wondering in their hearts if John[h] might possibly be the Christ.[b][i] 16John answered them all, "I baptize you with[c] water.[j] But one more powerful than I will come, the thongs of whose sandals I am not worthy to untie. He will baptize you with the Holy Spirit and with fire.[k] 17His winnowing fork[l] is in his hand to clear his threshing floor and to gather the wheat into his barn, but he will burn up the chaff with unquenchable fire."[m] 18And with many other words John exhorted the people and preached the good news to them.

19But when John rebuked Herod[n] the tetrarch because of Herodias, his brother's wife, and all the other evil things he had done, 20Herod added this to them all: He locked John up in prison.[o]

The Baptism and Genealogy of Jesus

›See Matthew 1:1–17; 3:13–17; Mark 1:9–11

21When all the people were being baptized, Jesus was baptized too. And as he was praying,[p] heaven was opened 22and the Holy Spirit descended on him[q] in bodily form like a dove. And a voice came from heaven: "You are my Son,[r] whom I love; with you I am well pleased."[s]

23Now Jesus himself was about thirty years old when he began his ministry.[t] He was the son, so it was thought, of Joseph,[u]

the son of Heli, 24the son of Matthat,
the son of Levi, the son of Melki,
the son of Jannai, the son of Joseph,
25the son of Mattathias, the son of Amos,
the son of Nahum, the son of Esli,
the son of Naggai, 26the son of Maath,
the son of Mattathias, the son of Semein,
the son of Josech, the son of Joda,
27the son of Joanan, the son of Rhesa,
the son of Zerubbabel,[v] the son of Shealtiel,
the son of Neri, 28the son of Melki,
the son of Addi, the son of Cosam,
the son of Elmadam, the son of Er,
29the son of Joshua, the son of Eliezer,
the son of Jorim, the son of Matthat,
the son of Levi, 30the son of Simeon,
the son of Judah, the son of Joseph,
the son of Jonam, the son of Eliakim,
31the son of Melea, the son of Menna,
the son of Mattatha, the son of Nathan,[w]
the son of David, 32the son of Jesse,

3:2 [t]Mt 26:3; Jn 18:13; Ac 4:6 [u]Mt 3:1 [v]Lk 1:13
3:3 [w]ver 16; Mk 1:4
3:6 [x]Isa 40:3-5; Ps 98:2; Isa 42:16; 52:10; Lk 2:30
3:7 [y]Mt 12:34; 23:33 [z]Ro 1:18
3:8 [a]Isa 51:2; Lk 19:9; Jn 8:33,39; Ac 13:26; Ro 4:1,11,12, 16,17; Gal 3:7
3:9 [b]Mt 3:10
3:10 [c]ver 12,14; Ac 2:37; 16:30
3:11 [d]Isa 58:7
3:12 [e]Lk 7:29
3:13 [f]Lk 19:8
3:14 [g]Ex 23:1; Lev 19:11
3:15 [h]Mt 3:1 [i]Jn 1:19,20; Ac 13:25
3:16 [j]ver 3; Mk 1:4 [k]Jn 1:26,33; Ac 1:5; 11:16; 19:4
3:17 [l]Isa 30:24 [m]Mt 13:30; 25:41
3:19 [n]ver 1
3:20 [o]Mt 14:3,4; Mk 6:17-18
3:21 [p]Mt 14:23; Mk 1:35; 6:46; Lk 5:16; 6:12; 9:18,28; 11:1
3:22 [q]Isa 42:1; Jn 1:32,33; Ac 10:38 [r]Mt 3:17 [s]Mt 3:17
3:23 [t]Mt 4:17; Ac 1:1 [u]Lk 1:27
3:27 [v]Mt 1:12
3:31 [w]2Sa 5:14; 1Ch 3:5

[a]*6* Isaiah 40:3-5 [b]*15* Or *Messiah*
[c]*16* Or *in*

the son of Obed, the son of Boaz,
the son of Salmon,[a] the son of Nahshon,
33 the son of Amminadab, the son of Ram,[b]
the son of Hezron, the son of Perez,[x]
the son of Judah, 34 the son of Jacob,
the son of Isaac, the son of Abraham,
the son of Terah, the son of Nahor,[y]
35 the son of Serug, the son of Reu,
the son of Peleg, the son of Eber,
the son of Shelah, 36 the son of Cainan,
the son of Arphaxad,[z] the son of Shem,
the son of Noah, the son of Lamech,[a]
37 the son of Methuselah, the son of Enoch,
the son of Jared, the son of Mahalalel,
the son of Kenan, 38 the son of Enosh,
the son of Seth, the son of Adam,
the son of God.[b]

The Temptation of Jesus

›See Matthew 4:1–11; Mark 1:12–13

3 →PG. 1127

4 Jesus, full of the Holy Spirit,[c] returned from the Jordan[d] and was led by the Spirit[e] in the desert, 2 where for forty days[f] he was tempted by the devil. He ate nothing during those days, and at the end of them he was hungry.

3 The devil said to him, "If you are the Son of God, tell this stone to become bread."

4 Jesus answered, "It is written: 'Man does not live on bread alone.'[c]"[g]

5 The devil led him up to a high place and showed him in an instant all the kingdoms of the world.[h] 6 And he said to him, "I will give you all their authority and splendor, for it has been given to me,[i] and I can give it to anyone I want to. 7 So if you worship me, it will all be yours."

8 Jesus answered, "It is written: 'Worship the Lord your God and serve him only.'[d]"[j]

9 The devil led him to Jerusalem and had him stand on the highest point of the temple. "If you are the Son of God," he said, "throw yourself down from here. 10 For it is written:

" 'He will command his angels
concerning you
to guard you carefully;
11 they will lift you up in their hands,
so that you will not strike your
foot against a stone.'[e]"[k]

12 Jesus answered, "It says: 'Do not put the Lord your God to the test.'[f]"[l]

13 When the devil had finished all this tempting,[m] he left him[n] until an opportune time.

Jesus Rejected at Nazareth

14 Jesus returned to Galilee[o] in the power of the Spirit, and news about him spread through the whole countryside.[p] 15 He taught in their synagogues,[q] and everyone praised him.

16 He went to Nazareth,[r] where he had been brought up, and on the Sabbath day he went into the synagogue,[s] as was his custom. And he stood up to read. 17 The scroll of the prophet Isaiah was handed to him. Unrolling it, he found the place where it is written:

18 "The Spirit of the Lord is on me,[t]
because he has anointed me
to preach good news to the poor.
He has sent me to proclaim
freedom for the prisoners
and recovery of sight for the
blind,
to release the oppressed,
19 to proclaim the year of the
Lord's favor."[g][u]

20 Then he rolled up the scroll, gave it back to the attendant and sat down.[v] The eyes of everyone in the synagogue were fastened on him, 21 and he began by saying to them, "Today this scripture is fulfilled in your hearing."

22 All spoke well of him and were amazed at the gracious words that came from his lips. "Isn't this Joseph's son?" they asked.[w]

23 Jesus said to them, "Surely you will quote this proverb to me: 'Physician, heal yourself! Do here in your hometown[x] what we have heard that you did in Capernaum.' "[y]

24 "I tell you the truth," he continued, "no prophet is accepted in his hometown.[z] 25 I assure you that there were many widows in Israel in Elijah's time, when the sky was shut for three and a half years and there was a severe famine throughout the land.[a] 26 Yet Elijah was not sent to any of them, but to a widow in Zarephath in the region of Sidon.[b] 27 And there were many in Israel with leprosy[h] in the time of Elisha

3:33 [x] Ru 4:18-22; 1Ch 2:10-12
3:34 [y] Ge 11:24,26
3:36 [z] Ge 11:12 [a] Ge 5:28-32
3:38 [b] Ge 5:1,2,6-9
4:1 [c] ver 14,18 [d] Lk 3:3,21 [e] Lk 2:27
4:2 [f] Ex 34:28; 1Ki 19:8
4:4 [g] Dt 8:3
4:5 [h] Mt 24:14
4:6 [i] Jn 12:31; 14:30; 1Jn 5:19
4:8 [j] Dt 6:13
4:11 [k] Ps 91:11,12
4:12 [l] Dt 6:16
4:13 [m] Heb 4:15 [n] Jn 14:30
4:14 [o] Mt 4:12 [p] Mt 9:26
4:15 [q] Mt 4:23
4:16 [r] Mt 2:23 [s] Mt 13:54
4:18 [t] Jn 3:34
4:19 [u] Isa 61:1,2; Lev 25:10
4:20 [v] ver 17; Mt 26:55
4:22 [w] Mt 13:54,55; Jn 6:42; 7:15
4:23 [x] ver 16 [y] Mk 1:21-28; 2:1-12
4:24 [z] Mt 13:57; Jn 4:44
4:25 [a] 1Ki 17:1; 18:1; Jas 5:17, 18
4:26 [b] 1Ki 17:8-16; Mt 11:21

a *32* Some early manuscripts *Sala* b *33* Some manuscripts *Amminadab, the son of Admin, the son of Arni*; other manuscripts vary widely.
c *4* Deut. 8:3 d *8* Deut. 6:13
e *11* Psalm 91:11,12 f *12* Deut. 6:16
g *19* Isaiah 61:1,2 h *27* The Greek word was used for various diseases affecting the skin—not necessarily leprosy.

the prophet, yet not one of them was cleansed—only Naaman the Syrian."[c]

28 All the people in the synagogue were furious when they heard this. 29 They got up, drove him out of the town,[d] and took him to the brow of the hill on which the town was built, in order to throw him down the cliff. 30 But he walked right through the crowd and went on his way.[e]

Jesus Drives Out an Evil Spirit

31 Then he went down to Capernaum,[f] a town in Galilee, and on the Sabbath began to teach the people. 32 They were amazed at his teaching,[g] because his message had authority.[h]

33 In the synagogue there was a man possessed by a demon, an evil[a] spirit. He cried out at the top of his voice, 34 "Ha! What do you want with us,[i] Jesus of Nazareth?[j] Have you come to destroy us? I know who you are[k]—the Holy One of God!"[l]

35 "Be quiet!" Jesus said sternly.[m] "Come out of him!" Then the demon threw the man down before them all and came out without injuring him.

36 All the people were amazed[n] and said to each other, "What is this teaching? With authority[o] and power he gives orders to evil spirits and they come out!" 37 And the news about him spread throughout the surrounding area.[p]

Jesus Heals Many

›See Matthew 8:14–17; Mark 1:29–38

38 Jesus left the synagogue and went to the home of Simon. Now Simon's mother-in-law was suffering from a high fever, and they asked Jesus to help her. 39 So he bent over her and rebuked[q] the fever, and it left her. She got up at once and began to wait on them.

40 When the sun was setting, the people brought to Jesus all who had various kinds of sickness, and laying his hands on each one,[r] he healed them.[s] 41 Moreover, demons came out of many people, shouting, "You are the Son of God!"[t] But he rebuked[u] them and would not allow them to speak,[v] because they knew he was the Christ.[b]

42 At daybreak Jesus went out to a solitary place. The people were looking for him and when they came to where he was, they tried to keep him from leaving them. 43 But he said, "I must preach the good news of the kingdom of God[w] to the other towns also, because that is why I was sent." 44 And he kept on preaching in the synagogues of Judea.[c][x]

4:27 [c]2Ki 5:1-14
4:29 [d]Nu 15:35; Ac 7:58; Heb 13:12
4:30 [e]Jn 8:59; 10:39
4:31 [f]ver 23; Mt 4:13
4:32 [g]Mt 7:28 [h]ver 36; Mt 7:29
4:34 [i]Mt 8:29 [j]Mk 1:24 [k]Jas 2:19 [l]ver 41; Mk 1:24
4:35 [m]ver 39,41; Mt 8:26; Lk 8:24
4:36 [n]Mt 7:28 [o]ver 32; Mt 7:29; Mt 10:1
4:37 [p]ver 14; Mt 9:26
4:39 [q]ver 35,41
4:40 [r]Mk 5:23 [s]Mt 4:23
4:41 [t]Mt 4:3 [u]ver 35 [v]Mt 8:4
4:43 [w]Mt 3:2
4:44 [x]Mt 4:23
5:1 [y]Mk 4:14; Heb 4:12
5:3 [z]Mt 13:2
5:4 [a]Jn 21:6
5:5 [b]Lk 8:24,45; 9:33,49; 17:13 [c]Jn 21:3
5:6 [d]Jn 21:11
5:8 [e]Ge 18:27; Job 42:6; Isa 6:5
5:10 [f]Mt 14:27
5:11 [g]ver 28; Mt 4:19
5:12 [h]Mt 8:2
5:14 [i]Mt 8:4 [j]Lev 14:2-32

The Calling of the First Disciples

›See Matthew 4:18–22; Mark 1:16–20; John 1:40–42

5 One day as Jesus was standing by the Lake of Gennesaret,[d] with the people crowding around him and listening to the word of God,[y] 2 he saw at the water's edge two boats, left there by the fishermen, who were washing their nets. 3 He got into one of the boats, the one belonging to Simon, and asked him to put out a little from shore. Then he sat down and taught the people from the boat.[z]

4 When he had finished speaking, he said to Simon, "Put out into deep water, and let down[e] the nets for a catch."[a]

5 Simon answered, "Master,[b] we've worked hard all night and haven't caught anything.[c] But because you say so, I will let down the nets."

6 When they had done so, they caught such a large number of fish that their nets began to break.[d] 7 So they signaled their partners in the other boat to come and help them, and they came and filled both boats so full that they began to sink.

8 When Simon Peter saw this, he fell at Jesus' knees and said, "Go away from me, Lord; I am a sinful man!"[e] 9 For he and all his companions were astonished at the catch of fish they had taken, 10 and so were James and John, the sons of Zebedee, Simon's partners.

Then Jesus said to Simon, "Don't be afraid;[f] from now on you will catch men." 11 So they pulled their boats up on shore, left everything and followed him.[g]

The Man With Leprosy

›See Matthew 8:2–4; Mark 1:40–44

12 While Jesus was in one of the towns, a man came along who was covered with leprosy.[f][h] When he saw Jesus, he fell with his face to the ground and begged him, "Lord, if you are willing, you can make me clean."

13 Jesus reached out his hand and touched the man. "I am willing," he said. "Be clean!" And immediately the leprosy left him.

14 Then Jesus ordered him, "Don't tell anyone,[i] but go, show yourself to the priest and offer the sacrifices that Moses commanded[j] for your cleansing, as a testimony to them."

[a] *33* Greek *unclean*; also in verse 36 [b] *41* Or *Messiah* [c] *44* Or *the land of the Jews*; some manuscripts *Galilee* [d] *1* That is, Sea of Galilee [e] *4* The Greek verb is plural. [f] *12* The Greek word was used for various diseases affecting the skin—not necessarily leprosy.

15Yet the news about him spread all the more,[k] so that crowds of people came to hear him and to be healed of their sicknesses. 16But Jesus often withdrew to lonely places and prayed.[l]

Jesus Heals a Paralytic

›See Matthew 9:2–8; Mark 2:3–12

17One day as he was teaching, Pharisees and teachers of the law,[m] who had come from every village of Galilee and from Judea and Jerusalem, were sitting there. And the power of the Lord was present for him to heal the sick.[n] 18Some men came carrying a paralytic on a mat and tried to take him into the house to lay him before Jesus. 19When they could not find a way to do this because of the crowd, they went up on the roof and lowered him on his mat through the tiles into the middle of the crowd, right in front of Jesus.

20When Jesus saw their faith, he said, "Friend, your sins are forgiven."[o]

21The Pharisees and the teachers of the law began thinking to themselves, "Who is this fellow who speaks blasphemy? Who can forgive sins but God alone?"[p]

22Jesus knew what they were thinking and asked, "Why are you thinking these things in your hearts? 23Which is easier: to say, 'Your sins are forgiven,' or to say, 'Get up and walk'? 24But that you may know that the Son of Man[q] has authority on earth to forgive sins . . ." He said to the paralyzed man, "I tell you, get up, take your mat and go home." 25Immediately he stood up in front of them, took what he had been lying on and went home praising God. 26Everyone was amazed and gave praise to God.[r] They were filled with awe and said, "We have seen remarkable things today."

The Calling of Levi

›See Matthew 9:9–13; Mark 2:14–17

27After this, Jesus went out and saw a tax collector by the name of Levi sitting at his tax booth. "Follow me,"[s] Jesus said to him, 28and Levi got up, left everything and followed him.[t]

29Then Levi held a great banquet for Jesus at his house, and a large crowd of tax collectors[u] and others were eating with them. 30But the Pharisees and the teachers of the law who belonged to their sect[v] complained to his disciples, "Why do you eat and drink with tax collectors and 'sinners'?"[w]

31Jesus answered them, "It is not the healthy who need a doctor, but the sick. 32I have not come to call the righteous, but sinners to repentance."[x]

5:15 [k]Mt 9:26 **5:16** [l]Mt 14:23; Lk 3:21 **5:17** [m]Mt 15:1; Lk 2:46 [n]Mk 5:30; Lk 6:19 **5:20** [o]Lk 7:48,49 **5:21** [p]Isa 43:25 **5:24** [q]Mt 8:20 **5:26** [r]Mt 9:8 **5:27** [s]Mt 4:19 **5:28** [t]ver 11; Mt 4:19 **5:29** [u]Lk 15:1 **5:30** [v]Ac 23:9 [w]Mt 9:11 **5:32** [x]Jn 3:17

5:33 [y]Lk 7:18; Jn 1:35; 3:25, 26 **5:34** [z]Jn 3:29 **5:35** [a]Lk 9:22; 17:22; Jn 16:5-7 **6:1** [b]Dt 23:25 **6:2** [c]Mt 12:2 **6:3** [d]1Sa 21:6 **6:4** [e]Lev 24:5,9 **6:5** [f]Mt 8:20 **6:6** [g]ver 1 **6:7** [h]Mt 12:10 [i]Mt 12:2 **6:8** [j]Mt 9:4

Jesus Questioned About Fasting

›See Matthew 9:14–17; Mark 2:18–22

33They said to him, "John's disciples[y] often fast and pray, and so do the disciples of the Pharisees, but yours go on eating and drinking."

34Jesus answered, "Can you make the guests of the bridegroom[z] fast while he is with them? 35But the time will come when the bridegroom will be taken from them;[a] in those days they will fast."

36He told them this parable: "No one tears a patch from a new garment and sews it on an old one. If he does, he will have torn the new garment, and the patch from the new will not match the old. 37And no one pours new wine into old wineskins. If he does, the new wine will burst the skins, the wine will run out and the wineskins will be ruined. 38No, new wine must be poured into new wineskins. 39And no one after drinking old wine wants the new, for he says, 'The old is better.' "

Lord of the Sabbath

›See Matthew 12:1–14; Mark 2:23—3:6

6 One Sabbath Jesus was going through the grainfields, and his disciples began to pick some heads of grain, rub them in their hands and eat the kernels.[b] 2Some of the Pharisees asked, "Why are you doing what is unlawful on the Sabbath?"[c]

3Jesus answered them, "Have you never read what David did when he and his companions were hungry?[d] 4He entered the house of God, and taking the consecrated bread, he ate what is lawful only for priests to eat.[e] And he also gave some to his companions." 5Then Jesus said to them, "The Son of Man[f] is Lord of the Sabbath."

6On another Sabbath[g] he went into the synagogue and was teaching, and a man was there whose right hand was shriveled. 7The Pharisees and the teachers of the law were looking for a reason to accuse Jesus, so they watched him closely[h] to see if he would heal on the Sabbath.[i] 8But Jesus knew what they were thinking[j] and said to the man with the shriveled hand, "Get up and stand in front of everyone." So he got up and stood there.

9Then Jesus said to them, "I ask you, which is lawful on the Sabbath: to do good or to do evil, to save life or to destroy it?"

10He looked around at them all, and then said to the man, "Stretch out your hand." He did so, and his hand was completely restored. 11But they were furious[k] and began to discuss with one another what they might do to Jesus.

The Twelve Apostles

›See Matthew 10:2–4; Mark 3:16–19; Acts 1:13

2 →PG. 1150

12One of those days Jesus went out to a mountainside to pray, and spent the night praying to God.[l] 13When morning came, he called his disciples to him and chose twelve of them, whom he also designated apostles:[m] 14Simon (whom he named Peter), his brother Andrew, James, John, Philip, Bartholomew, 15Matthew,[n] Thomas, James son of Alphaeus, Simon who was called the Zealot, 16Judas son of James, and Judas Iscariot, who became a traitor.

Blessings and Woes

›See Matthew 5:3–12

17He went down with them and stood on a level place. A large crowd of his disciples was there and a great number of people from all over Judea, from Jerusalem, and from the coast of Tyre and Sidon,[o] 18who had come to hear him and to be healed of their diseases. Those troubled by evil[a] spirits were cured, 19and the people all tried to touch him,[p] because power was coming from him and healing them all.[q]

7 →PG. 1126

20Looking at his disciples, he said:

"Blessed are you who are poor,
for yours is the kingdom of God.[r]
21Blessed are you who hunger now,
for you will be satisfied.[s]
Blessed are you who weep now,
for you will laugh.[t]
22Blessed are you when men hate you,
when they exclude you[u] and insult you[v]
and reject your name as evil,
because of the Son of Man.[w]

23"Rejoice in that day and leap for joy,[x] because great is your reward in heaven. For that is how their fathers treated the prophets.[y]

24"But woe to you who are rich,[z]
for you have already received your comfort.[a]
25Woe to you who are well fed now,
for you will go hungry.[b]
Woe to you who laugh now,
for you will mourn and weep.[c]
26Woe to you when all men speak well of you,
for that is how their fathers treated the false prophets.[d]

Love for Enemies

27"But I tell you who hear me: Love your enemies, do good to those who hate you,[e] 28bless those who curse you, pray for those who mistreat you.[f] 29If someone strikes you on one cheek, turn to him the other also. If someone takes your cloak, do not stop him from taking your tunic. 30Give to everyone who asks you, and if anyone takes what belongs to you, do not demand it back.[g] 31Do to others as you would have them do to you.[h]

32"If you love those who love you, what credit is that to you?[i] Even 'sinners' love those who love them. 33And if you do good to those who are good to you, what credit is that to you? Even 'sinners' do that. 34And if you lend to those from whom you expect repayment, what credit is that to you?[j] Even 'sinners' lend to 'sinners,' expecting to be repaid in full. 35But love your enemies, do good to them,[k] and lend to them without expecting to get anything back. Then your reward will be great, and you will be sons[l] of the Most High,[m] because he is kind to the ungrateful and wicked. 36Be merciful,[n] just as your Father[o] is merciful. 7 →PG. 1129

6:11 [k] Jn 5:18
6:12 [l] Lk 3:21
6:13 [m] Mk 6:30
6:15 [n] Mt 9:9
6:17 [o] Mt 4:25; Mt 11:21; Mk 3:7,8
6:19 [p] Mt 9:20 [q] Mt 14:36; Mk 5:30; Lk 5:17
6:20 [r] Mt 25:34
6:21 [s] Isa 55:1,2; Mt 5:6 [t] Isa 61:2,3; Mt 5:4; Rev 7:17
6:22 [u] Jn 9:22; 16:2 [v] Isa 51:7 [w] Jn 15:21
6:23 [x] Mt 5:12 [y] Mt 5:12
6:24 [z] Jas 5:1 [a] Lk 16:25
6:25 [b] Isa 65:13 [c] Pr 14:13
6:26 [d] Mt 7:15
6:27 [e] ver 35; Mt 5:44; Ro 12:20
6:28 [f] Mt 5:44
6:30 [g] Dt 15:7,8,10; Pr 21:26
6:31 [h] Mt 7:12
6:32 [i] Mt 5:46
6:34 [j] Mt 5:42
6:35 [k] ver 27 [l] Ro 8:14 [m] Mk 5:7
6:36 [n] Jas 2:13 [o] Mt 5:48; 6:1; Lk 11:2; 12:32; Ro 8:15; Eph 4:6; 1Pe 1:17; 1Jn 1:3; 3:1

[a] *18* Greek *unclean*

6:27–36 PROMISE 3

TURN THE OTHER CHEEK?

When Jesus told his followers, "If someone strikes you on the cheek, turn to him the other also," he wasn't telling us not to defend ourselves. Instead, he was urging us to live our lives under God's control.

Our natural reaction to an attack is to strike back when struck. However, when we react and angrily strike back at someone, we're allowing that person to control us. Jesus here explains that men who live under God's control hold that natural impulse in check. They respond gently and rationally when treated abrasively. In a nutshell, they treat others as they want to be treated.

Make it a personal goal to obey the Lord this week. Instead of lashing out at those who wrong you and falling under their control, seek God's control in handling the situation positively and constructively.

For the next Promise 3 reading go to page 1143.

Judging Others

›See Matthew 7:1–5

37“Do not judge, and you will not be judged.[p] Do not condemn, and you will not be condemned. Forgive, and you will be forgiven.[q] 38Give, and it will be given to you. A good measure, pressed down, shaken together and running over, will be poured into your lap.[r] For with the measure you use, it will be measured to you.”[s]

5 →PG. 1140

39He also told them this parable: “Can a blind man lead a blind man? Will they not both fall into a pit?[t] 40A student is not above his teacher, but everyone who is fully trained will be like his teacher.[u]

41“Why do you look at the speck of sawdust in your brother’s eye and pay no attention to the plank in your own eye? 42How can you say to your brother, ‘Brother, let me take the speck out of your eye,’ when you yourself fail to see the plank in your own eye? You hypocrite, first take the plank out of your eye, and then you will see clearly to remove the speck from your brother’s eye.

A Tree and Its Fruit

›See Matthew 7:16,18,20

43“No good tree bears bad fruit, nor does a bad tree bear good fruit. 44Each tree is recognized by its own fruit.[v] People do not pick figs from thornbushes, or grapes from briers. 45The good man brings good things out of the good stored up in his heart, and the evil man brings evil things out of the evil stored up in his heart. For out of the overflow of his heart his mouth speaks.[w]

3 →PG. 1137

The Wise and Foolish Builders

›See Matthew 7:24–27

46“Why do you call me, ‘Lord, Lord,’[x] and do not do what I say?[y] 47I will show you what he is like who comes to me and hears my words and puts them into practice.[z] 48He is like a man building a house, who dug down deep and laid the foundation on rock. When a flood came, the torrent struck that house but could not shake it, because it was well built. 49But the one who hears my words and does not put them into practice is like a man who built a house on the ground without a foundation. The moment the torrent struck that house, it collapsed and its destruction was complete.”

6:37 [p]Mt 7:1 [q]Mt 6:14
6:38 [r]Ps 79:12; Isa 65:6,7 [s]Mt 7:2; Mk 4:24
6:39 [t]Mt 15:14
6:40 [u]Mt 10:24; Jn 13:16
6:44 [v]Mt 12:33
6:45 [w]Pr 4:23; Mt 12:34,35; Mk 7:20
6:46 [x]Jn 13:13 [y]Mal 1:6; Mt 7:21
6:47 [z]Lk 8:21; 11:28; Jas 1:22-25

The Faith of the Centurion

›See Matthew 8:5–13

7 When Jesus had finished saying all this[a] in the hearing of the people, he entered Capernaum. 2There a centurion’s servant, whom his master valued highly, was sick and about to die. 3The centurion heard of Jesus and sent some elders of the Jews to him, asking him to come and heal his servant. 4When they came to Jesus, they pleaded earnestly with him, “This man deserves to have you do this, 5because he loves our nation and has built our synagogue.” 6So Jesus went with them.

He was not far from the house when the centurion sent friends to say to him: “Lord, don’t trouble yourself, for I do not deserve to have you come under my roof. 7That is why I did not even consider myself worthy to come to you. But say the word, and my servant will be healed.[b] 8For I myself am a man under authority, with soldiers under me. I tell this one, ‘Go,’ and he goes; and that one, ‘Come,’ and he comes. I say to my servant, ‘Do this,’ and he does it.”

9When Jesus heard this, he was amazed at him, and turning to the crowd following him, he said, “I tell you, I have not found such great faith even in Israel.” 10Then the men who had been sent returned to the house and found the servant well.

Jesus Raises a Widow’s Son

11Soon afterward, Jesus went to a town called Nain, and his disciples and a large crowd went along with him. 12As he approached the town gate, a dead person was being carried out—the only son of his mother, and she was a widow. And a large crowd from the town was with her. 13When the Lord[c] saw her, his heart went out to her and he said, “Don’t cry.”

14Then he went up and touched the coffin, and those carrying it stood still. He said, “Young man, I say to you, get up!”[d] 15The dead man sat up and began to talk, and Jesus gave him back to his mother.

16They were all filled with awe[e] and praised God.[f] “A great prophet[g] has appeared among us,” they said. “God has come to help his people.”[h] 17This news about Jesus spread throughout Judea[a] and the surrounding country.[i]

7:1 [a]Mt 7:28
7:7 [b]Ps 107:20
7:13 [c]ver 19; Lk 10:1; 13:15; 17:5; 22:61; 24:34; Jn 11:2
7:14 [d]Mt 9:25; Mk 1:31; Lk 8:54; Jn 11:43; Ac 9:40
7:16 [e]Lk 1:65 [f]Mt 9:8 [g]ver 39; Mt 21:11 [h]Lk 1:68
7:17 [i]Mt 9:26

[a]17 Or *the land of the Jews*

Jesus and John the Baptist

›See Matthew 11:2–19

18John's[j] disciples[k] told him about
all these things. Calling two of them,
19he sent them to the Lord to ask,
"Are you the one who was to come, or
should we expect someone else?"
20When the men came to Jesus, they
said, "John the Baptist sent us to you to
ask, 'Are you the one who was to come,
or should we expect someone else?' "
21At that very time Jesus cured many
who had diseases, sicknesses[l] and
evil spirits, and gave sight to many who
were blind. 22So he replied to the messengers, "Go back and report to John
what you have seen and heard: The
blind receive sight, the lame walk,
those who have leprosy[a] are cured,
the deaf hear, the dead are raised, and
the good news is preached to the
poor.[m] 23Blessed is the man who does
not fall away on account of me."
24After John's messengers left, Jesus
began to speak to the crowd about
John: "What did you go out into the
desert to see? A reed swayed by the
wind? 25If not, what did you go out to
see? A man dressed in fine clothes? No,
those who wear expensive clothes and
indulge in luxury are in palaces. 26But
what did you go out to see? A prophet?[n] Yes, I tell you, and more than a
prophet. 27This is the one about whom
it is written:

" 'I will send my messenger ahead
of you,
who will prepare your way
before you.'[b][o]

28I tell you, among those born of wom-
en there is no one greater than John;
yet the one who is least in the kingdom
of God[p] is greater than he."
29(All the people, even the tax collectors, when they heard Jesus' words, acknowledged that God's way was right,
because they had been baptized by
John.[q] 30But the Pharisees and experts
in the law[r] rejected God's purpose for
themselves, because they had not been
baptized by John.)
31"To what, then, can I compare the
people of this generation? What are
they like? 32They are like children sitting in the marketplace and calling out
to each other:

" 'We played the flute for you,
and you did not dance;
we sang a dirge,
and you did not cry.'

33For John the Baptist came neither
eating bread nor drinking wine,[s] and
you say, 'He has a demon.' 34The Son
of Man came eating and drinking, and
you say, 'Here is a glutton and a drunkard, a friend of tax collectors and "sinners." '[t] 35But wisdom is proved right
by all her children."

Jesus Anointed by a Sinful Woman

36Now one of the Pharisees invited
Jesus to have dinner with him, so he
went to the Pharisee's house and reclined at the table. 37When a woman
who had lived a sinful life in that town
learned that Jesus was eating at the
Pharisee's house, she brought an alabaster jar of perfume, 38and as she
stood behind him at his feet weeping,

7:18 [j]Mt 3:1 [k]Lk 5:33
7:21 [l]Mt 4:23
7:22 [m]Isa 29:18,19; 35:5,6; 61:1,2; Lk 4:18
7:26 [n]Mt 11:9
7:27 [o]Mal 3:1; Mt 11:10; Mk 1:2
7:28 [p]Mt 3:2
7:29 [q]Mt 21:32; Mk 1:5; Lk 3:12
7:30 [r]Mt 22:35
7:33 [s]Lk 1:15
7:34 [t]Lk 5:29,30; 15:1,2

[a] *22* The Greek word was used for various diseases affecting the skin—not necessarily leprosy. [b] *27* Mal. 3:1

7:36–50

PROMISE 6

BEYOND FIRST IMPRESSIONS

It's easy to reject someone because they appear different from us. To the Pharisee who hosted Jesus in this story, the woman who anointed the Lord's feet was a sinner, a degenerate. Her reputation in the town had been sullied; her past was littered with one-night stands. Nobody of high reputation, especially not this religious leader, would want to be seen with her. Yet Jesus allowed her to anoint his feet with perfume, cover them with tears and wipe them with her hair.

Why did Jesus do this? Because he looked beyond this woman's past and saw her future. He knew she "loved much" because she had been forgiven much. His parable and his sharp rebuke of the Pharisee (vv. 41–47) bring his actions—and the lesson we're to learn through them—into razor-sharp focus.

How would you have responded if you had been present that evening? Or, to be more pointed, how do you respond to people who are different than yourself—people with lighter or darker skin, people who speak with a different accent, people whose bad reputation precedes them? Remember, Jesus loved and accepted love from someone just like that. And today he wants those who follow him to show the same kind of love. Jesus looked beyond appearances. He shunned stereotypes. Just as Jesus did, look beyond such a person's past or his or her differences. Look toward that person's bright potential future—complete forgiveness of sins and eternity with Jesus Christ (v. 50).

For the next Promise 6 reading go to page 1185.

she began to wet his feet with her tears. Then she wiped them with her hair, kissed them and poured perfume on them.

39When the Pharisee who had invited him saw this, he said to himself, "If this man were a prophet,[u] he would know who is touching him and what kind of woman she is—that she is a sinner."

40Jesus answered him, "Simon, I have something to tell you."

"Tell me, teacher," he said.

41"Two men owed money to a certain moneylender. One owed him five hundred denarii,[a] and the other fifty. **42**Neither of them had the money to pay him back, so he canceled the debts of both. Now which of them will love him more?"

43Simon replied, "I suppose the one who had the bigger debt canceled."

"You have judged correctly," Jesus said.

44Then he turned toward the woman and said to Simon, "Do you see this woman? I came into your house. You did not give me any water for my feet,[v] but she wet my feet with her tears and wiped them with her hair. **45**You did not give me a kiss,[w] but this woman, from the time I entered, has not stopped kissing my feet. **46**You did not put oil on my head,[x] but she has poured perfume on my feet. **47**Therefore, I tell you, her many sins have been forgiven—for she loved much. But he who has been forgiven little loves little."

48Then Jesus said to her, "Your sins are forgiven."[y]

49The other guests began to say among themselves, "Who is this who even forgives sins?"

50Jesus said to the woman, "Your faith has saved you;[z] go in peace."[a]

The Parable of the Sower

›See Matthew 13:2–23; Mark 4:1–20

8 After this, Jesus traveled about from one town and village to another, proclaiming the good news of the kingdom of God.[b] The Twelve were with him, **2**and also some women who had been cured of evil spirits and diseases: Mary (called Magdalene)[c] from whom seven demons had come out; **3**Joanna the wife of Cuza, the manager of Herod's[d] household; Susanna; and many others. These women were helping to support them out of their own means.

4While a large crowd was gathering and people were coming to Jesus from town after town, he told this parable: **5**"A farmer went out to sow his seed. As he was scattering the seed, some fell along the path; it was trampled on, and the birds of the air ate it up. **6**Some fell on rock, and when it came up, the plants withered because they had no moisture. **7**Other seed fell among thorns, which grew up with it and choked the plants. **8**Still other seed fell on good soil. It came up and yielded a crop, a hundred times more than was sown."

When he said this, he called out, "He who has ears to hear, let him hear."[e]

9His disciples asked him what this parable meant. **10**He said, "The knowledge of the secrets of the kingdom of God has been given to you,[f] but to others I speak in parables, so that,

" 'though seeing, they may not see;
though hearing, they may not
understand.'[b][g]

11"This is the meaning of the parable: The seed is the word of God.[h] **12**Those along the path are the ones who hear, and then the devil comes and takes away the word from their hearts, so that they may not believe and be saved. **13**Those on the rock are the ones who receive the word with joy when they hear it, but they have no root. They believe for a while, but in the time of testing they fall away.[i] **14**The seed that fell among thorns stands for those who hear, but as they go on their way they are choked by life's worries, riches[j] and pleasures, and they do not mature. **15**But the seed on good soil stands for those with a noble and good heart, who hear the word, retain it, and by persevering produce a crop.

A Lamp on a Stand

16"No one lights a lamp and hides it in a jar or puts it under a bed. Instead, he puts it on a stand, so that those who come in can see the light.[k] **17**For there is nothing hidden that will not be disclosed, and nothing concealed that will not be known or brought out into the open.[l] **18**Therefore consider carefully how you listen. Whoever has will be given more; whoever does not have, even what he thinks he has will be taken from him."[m]

7 →PG. 1130

Jesus' Mother and Brothers

›See Matthew 12:46–50; Mark 3:31–35

19Now Jesus' mother and brothers came to see him, but they were not able to get near him because of the

7:39 [u]ver 16; Mt 21:11
7:44 [v]Ge 18:4; 19:2; 43:24; Jdg 19:21; Jn 13:4-14; 1Ti 5:10
7:45 [w]Lk 22:47,48; Ro 16:16
7:46 [x]Ps 23:5; Ecc 9:8
7:48 [y]Mt 9:2
7:50 [z]Mt 9:22; Mk 5:34; Lk 8:48 [a]Ac 15:33
8:1 [b]Mt 4:23
8:2 [c]Mt 27:55,56
8:3 [d]Mt 14:1
8:8 [e]Mt 11:15
8:10 [f]Mt 13:11 [g]Isa 6:9; Mt 13:13,14
8:11 [h]Heb 4:12
8:13 [i]Mt 11:6
8:14 [j]Mt 19:23; 1Ti 6:9,10,17
8:16 [k]Mt 5:15; Mk 4:21; Lk 11:33
8:17 [l]Mt 10:26; Mk 4:22; Lk 12:2
8:18 [m]Mt 13:12; 25:29; Lk 19:26

a *41* A denarius was a coin worth about a day's wages. b *10* Isaiah 6:9

crowd. 20Someone told him, "Your mother and brothers[n] are standing outside, wanting to see you."

21He replied, "My mother and brothers are those who hear God's word and put it into practice."[o]

Jesus Calms the Storm

›See Matthew 8:23–27; Mark 4:36–41

22One day Jesus said to his disciples, "Let's go over to the other side of the lake." So they got into a boat and set out. 23As they sailed, he fell asleep. A squall came down on the lake, so that the boat was being swamped, and they were in great danger.

24The disciples went and woke him, saying, "Master, Master,[p] we're going to drown!"

He got up and rebuked[q] the wind and the raging waters; the storm subsided, and all was calm.[r] 25"Where is your faith?" he asked his disciples.

In fear and amazement they asked one another, "Who is this? He commands even the winds and the water, and they obey him."

The Healing of a Demon-possessed Man

›See Matthew 8:28–34; Mark 5:1–20

26They sailed to the region of the Gerasenes,[a] which is across the lake from Galilee. 27When Jesus stepped ashore, he was met by a demon-possessed man from the town. For a long time this man had not worn clothes or lived in a house, but had lived in the tombs. 28When he saw Jesus, he cried out and fell at his feet, shouting at the top of his voice, "What do you want with me,[s] Jesus, Son of the Most High God?[t] I beg you, don't torture me!" 29For Jesus had commanded the evil[b] spirit to come out of the man. Many times it had seized him, and though he was chained hand and foot and kept under guard, he had broken his chains and had been driven by the demon into solitary places.

30Jesus asked him, "What is your name?"

"Legion," he replied, because many demons had gone into him. 31And they begged him repeatedly not to order them to go into the Abyss.[u]

32A large herd of pigs was feeding there on the hillside. The demons begged Jesus to let them go into them, and he gave them permission. 33When the demons came out of the man, they went into the pigs, and the herd rushed down the steep bank into the lake[v] and was drowned.

34When those tending the pigs saw what had happened, they ran off and reported this in the town and countryside, 35and the people went out to see what had happened. When they came to Jesus, they found the man from whom the demons had gone out, sitting at Jesus' feet,[w] dressed and in his right mind; and they were afraid. 36Those who had seen it told the people how the demon-possessed[x] man had been cured. 37Then all the people of the region of the Gerasenes asked Jesus to leave them,[y] because they were overcome with fear. So he got into the boat and left.

38The man from whom the demons had gone out begged to go with him, but Jesus sent him away, saying, 39"Return home and tell how much God has done for you." So the man went away and told all over town how much Jesus had done for him.

7 →PG. 1131

A Dead Girl and a Sick Woman

›See Matthew 9:18–26; Mark 5:22–43

40Now when Jesus returned, a crowd welcomed him, for they were all expecting him. 41Then a man named Jairus, a ruler of the synagogue,[z] came and fell at Jesus' feet, pleading with him to come to his house 42because his only daughter, a girl of about twelve, was dying.

As Jesus was on his way, the crowds almost crushed him. 43And a woman was there who had been subject to bleeding[a] for twelve years,[c] but no one could heal her. 44She came up behind him and touched the edge of his cloak,[b] and immediately her bleeding stopped.

45"Who touched me?" Jesus asked.

When they all denied it, Peter said,

8:20 [n]Jn 7:5 **8:21** [o]Lk 6:47; 11:28; Jn 14:21 **8:24** [p]Lk 5:5 [q]Lk 4:35,39,41 [r]Ps 107:29; Jnh 1:15 **8:28** [s]Mt 8:29 [t]Mk 5:7 **8:31** [u]Rev 9:1,2,11; 11:7; 17:8; 20:1,3 **8:33** [v]ver 22,23 **8:35** [w]Lk 10:39 **8:36** [x]Mt 4:24 **8:37** [y]Ac 16:39 **8:41** [z]ver 49; Mk 5:22 **8:43** [a]Lev 15:25-30 **8:44** [b]Mt 9:20

a *26* Some manuscripts *Gadarenes*; other manuscripts *Gergesenes*; also in verse 37
b *29* Greek *unclean*
c *43* Many manuscripts *years, and she had spent all she had on doctors*

8:38–39

PROMISE 7

GO AND TELL

The Lord's command to the demon-possessed man still applies today. If God has done a transforming work in your life, go and tell others about it. After all, nothing creates a thirst for Christ like evidence of a changed life. If you're uncertain what you'd say to another person, take a moment and jot down what you were like before you knew Christ, how you met him, and how he has changed you. After you've done that, pray for a chance to tell someone else the good news.

For the next Promise 7 reading go to page 1141.

"Master,[c] the people are crowding and pressing against you."

46 But Jesus said, "Someone touched me;[d] I know that power has gone out from me."[e]

47 Then the woman, seeing that she could not go unnoticed, came trembling and fell at his feet. In the presence of all the people, she told why she had touched him and how she had been instantly healed. 48 Then he said to her, "Daughter, your faith has healed you.[f] Go in peace."[g]

49 While Jesus was still speaking, someone came from the house of Jairus, the synagogue ruler.[h] "Your daughter is dead," he said. "Don't bother the teacher any more."

50 Hearing this, Jesus said to Jairus, "Don't be afraid; just believe, and she will be healed."

51 When he arrived at the house of Jairus, he did not let anyone go in with him except Peter, John and James,[i] and the child's father and mother. 52 Meanwhile, all the people were wailing and mourning[j] for her. "Stop wailing," Jesus said. "She is not dead but asleep."[k]

53 They laughed at him, knowing that she was dead. 54 But he took her by the hand and said, "My child, get up!"[l] 55 Her spirit returned, and at once she stood up. Then Jesus told them to give her something to eat. 56 Her parents were astonished, but he ordered them not to tell anyone what had happened.[m]

Jesus Sends Out the Twelve

›See Matthew 10:9–15; Mark 6:8–11

7 →PG. 1133

9 When Jesus had called the Twelve together, he gave them power and authority to drive out all demons[n] and to cure diseases,[o] 2 and he sent them out to preach the kingdom of God[p] and to heal the sick. 3 He told them: "Take nothing for the journey—no staff, no bag, no bread, no money, no extra tunic.[q] 4 Whatever house you enter, stay there until you leave that town. 5 If people do not welcome you, shake the dust off your feet when you leave their town, as a testimony against them."[r] 6 So they set out and went from village to village, preaching the gospel and healing people everywhere.

7 Now Herod[s] the tetrarch heard about all that was going on. And he was perplexed, because some were saying that John[t] had been raised from the dead,[u] 8 others that Elijah had appeared,[v] and still others that one of the prophets of long ago had come back to life.[w] 9 But Herod said, "I beheaded John. Who, then, is this I hear such things about?" And he tried to see him.[x]

Jesus Feeds the Five Thousand

›See Matthew 14:13–21; Mark 6:32–44; John 6:5–13

10 When the apostles[y] returned, they reported to Jesus what they had done. Then he took them with him and they withdrew by themselves to a town called Bethsaida,[z] 11 but the crowds learned about it and followed him. He welcomed them and spoke to them about the kingdom of God,[a] and healed those who needed healing.

12 Late in the afternoon the Twelve came to him and said, "Send the crowd away so they can go to the surrounding villages and countryside and find food and lodging, because we are in a remote place here."

13 He replied, "You give them something to eat."

They answered, "We have only five loaves of bread and two fish—unless we go and buy food for all this crowd." 14 (About five thousand men were there.)

But he said to his disciples, "Have them sit down in groups of about fifty each." 15 The disciples did so, and everybody sat down. 16 Taking the five loaves and the two fish and looking up to heaven, he gave thanks and broke them.[b] Then he gave them to the disciples to set before the people. 17 They all ate and were satisfied, and the disciples picked up twelve basketfuls of broken pieces that were left over.

Peter's Confession of Christ

›See Matthew 16:13–16; Mark 8:27–29

18 Once when Jesus was praying[c] in private and his disciples were with him, he asked them, "Who do the crowds say I am?"

19 They replied, "Some say John the Baptist;[d] others say Elijah; and still others, that one of the prophets of long ago has come back to life."[e]

20 "But what about you?" he asked. "Who do you say I am?"

Peter answered, "The Christ[a] of God."[f]

21 Jesus strictly warned them not to tell this to anyone.[g] 22 And he said, "The Son of Man[h] must suffer many things[i] and be rejected by the elders, chief priests and teachers of the law,[j] and he must be killed[k] and on the third day[l] be raised to life."[m]

23 Then he said to them all: "If any-

1 →PG. 1134

8:45 [c] Lk 5:5
8:46 [d] Mt 14:36; Mk 3:10 [e] Lk 5:17; 6:19
8:48 [f] Mt 9:22 [g] Ac 15:33
8:49 [h] ver 41
8:51 [i] Mt 4:21
8:52 [j] Lk 23:27 [k] Mt 9:24; Jn 11:11,13
8:54 [l] Lk 7:14
8:56 [m] Mt 8:4
9:1 [n] Mt 10:1 [o] Mt 4:23; Lk 5:17
9:2 [p] Mt 3:2
9:3 [q] Lk 10:4; 22:35
9:5 [r] Mt 10:14
9:7 [s] Mt 14:1 [t] Mt 3:1 [u] ver 19
9:8 [v] Mt 11:14 [w] ver 19; Jn 1:21
9:9 [x] Lk 23:8
9:10 [y] Mk 6:30 [z] Mt 11:21
9:11 [a] ver 2; Mt 3:2
9:16 [b] Mt 14:19
9:18 [c] Lk 3:21
9:19 [d] Mt 3:1 [e] ver 7,8
9:20 [f] Jn 1:49; 6:66-69; 11:27
9:21 [g] Mt 16:20; Mk 8:30
9:22 [h] Mt 8:20 [i] Mt 16:21 [j] Mt 27:1,2 [k] Ac 2:23; 3:13 [l] Mt 16:21 [m] Mt 16:21

a 20 Or *Messiah*

one would come after me, he must
deny himself and take up his cross daily and follow me.[n] 24For whoever
wants to save his life will lose it, but
whoever loses his life for me will save
it.[o] 25What good is it for a man to gain
the whole world, and yet lose or forfeit
his very self? 26If anyone is ashamed of
me and my words, the Son of Man will
be ashamed of him[p] when he comes
in his glory and in the glory of the Father and of the holy angels.[q] 27I tell
you the truth, some who are standing
here will not taste death before they
see the kingdom of God."

The Transfiguration

›See Matthew 17:1–8; Mark 9:2–8

28About eight days after Jesus said
this, he took Peter, John and James[r]
with him and went up onto a mountain
to pray.[s] 29As he was praying, the appearance of his face changed, and his
clothes became as bright as a flash of
lightning. 30Two men, Moses and Elijah, 31appeared in glorious splendor,
talking with Jesus. They spoke about
his departure,[t] which he was about to
bring to fulfillment at Jerusalem. 32Pe-
ter and his companions were very
sleepy,[u] but when they became fully
awake, they saw his glory and the two
men standing with him. 33As the men
were leaving Jesus, Peter said to him,
"Master,[v] it is good for us to be here.
Let us put up three shelters—one for
you, one for Moses and one for Elijah."
(He did not know what he was saying.)
34While he was speaking, a cloud appeared and enveloped them, and they
were afraid as they entered the cloud.
35A voice came from the cloud, saying, "This is my Son, whom I have
chosen;[w] listen to him."[x] 36When the
voice had spoken, they found that
Jesus was alone. The disciples kept this
to themselves, and told no one at that
time what they had seen.[y]

The Healing of a Boy With an Evil Spirit

›See Matthew 17:14–18,22–23;
Mark 9:14–27,30–32

37The next day, when they came
down from the mountain, a large
crowd met him. 38A man in the crowd
called out, "Teacher, I beg you to look
at my son, for he is my only child. 39A
spirit seizes him and he suddenly
screams; it throws him into convul-
sions so that he foams at the mouth. It
scarcely ever leaves him and is destroying him. 40I begged your disciples to
drive it out, but they could not."
41"O unbelieving and perverse generation,"[z] Jesus replied, "how long
shall I stay with you and put up with
you? Bring your son here."
42Even while the boy was coming,
the demon threw him to the ground in
a convulsion. But Jesus rebuked the
evil[a] spirit, healed the boy and gave
him back to his father. 43And they were
all amazed at the greatness of God.
While everyone was marveling at all
that Jesus did, he said to his disciples,
44"Listen carefully to what I am about
to tell you: The Son of Man is going to
be betrayed into the hands of men."[a]
45But they did not understand what
this meant. It was hidden from them,
so that they did not grasp it,[b] and they
were afraid to ask him about it.

Who Will Be the Greatest?

›See Matthew 18:1–5; Mark 9:33–40

46An argument started among the
disciples as to which of them would be
the greatest.[c] 47Jesus, knowing their
thoughts,[d] took a little child and had
him stand beside him. 48Then he said
to them, "Whoever welcomes this little
child in my name welcomes me; and
whoever welcomes me welcomes the
one who sent me.[e] For he who is least
among you all—he is the greatest."[f]
49"Master,"[g] said John, "we saw a
man driving out demons in your name
and we tried to stop him, because he is
not one of us."
50"Do not stop him," Jesus said, "for
whoever is not against you is for
you."[h]

Samaritan Opposition

51As the time approached for him to
be taken up to heaven,[i] Jesus resolutely set out for Jerusalem.[j] 52And he
sent messengers on ahead, who went
into a Samaritan[k] village to get things
ready for him; 53but the people there
did not welcome him, because he was
heading for Jerusalem. 54When the disciples James and John[l] saw this, they
asked, "Lord, do you want us to call
fire down from heaven to destroy
them[b]?"[m] 55But Jesus turned and rebuked them, 56and[c] they went to another village.

The Cost of Following Jesus

›See Matthew 8:19–22

57As they were walking along the
road,[n] a man said to him, "I will follow
you wherever you go."

9:23 [n]Mt 10:38; Lk 14:27
9:24 [o]Jn 12:25
9:26 [p]Mt 10:33; Lk 12:9; 2Ti 2:12 [q]Mt 16:27
9:28 [r]Mt 4:21 [s]Lk 3:21
9:31 [t]2Pe 1:15
9:32 [u]Mt 26:43
9:33 [v]Lk 5:5
9:35 [w]Isa 42:1 [x]Mt 3:17
9:36 [y]Mt 17:9
9:41 [z]Dt 32:5
9:44 [a]ver 22
9:45 [b]Mk 9:32
9:46 [c]Lk 22:24
9:47 [d]Mt 9:4
9:48 [e]Mt 10:40 [f]Mk 9:35
9:49 [g]Lk 5:5
9:50 [h]Mt 12:30; Lk 11:23
9:51 [i]Mk 16:19 [j]Lk 13:22; 17:11; 18:31; 19:28
9:52 [k]Mt 10:5
9:54 [l]Mt 4:21 [m]2Ki 1:10,12
9:57 [n]ver 51

a *42* Greek *unclean* **b** *54* Some manuscripts *them, even as Elijah did* **c** *55,56* Some manuscripts *them. And he said, "You do not know what kind of spirit you are of, for the Son of Man did not come to destroy men's lives, but to save them."* 56And

58Jesus replied, "Foxes have holes and birds of the air have nests, but the Son of Man[o] has no place to lay his head."

59He said to another man, "Follow me."[p]

But the man replied, "Lord, first let me go and bury my father."

60Jesus said to him, "Let the dead bury their own dead, but you go and proclaim the kingdom of God."[q]

61Still another said, "I will follow you, Lord; but first let me go back and say good-by to my family."[r]

62Jesus replied, "No one who puts his hand to the plow and looks back is fit for service in the kingdom of God."

Jesus Sends Out the Seventy-two

›See Luke 9:3–5

10 After this the Lord[s] appointed seventy-two[a] others[t] and sent them two by two[u] ahead of him to every town and place where he was about to go.[v] 2He told them, "The harvest is plentiful, but the workers are few. Ask the Lord of the harvest, therefore, to send out workers into his harvest field.[w] 3Go! I am sending you out like lambs among wolves.[x] 4Do not take a purse or bag or sandals; and do not greet anyone on the road.

5"When you enter a house, first say, 'Peace to this house.' 6If a man of peace is there, your peace will rest on him; if not, it will return to you. 7Stay in that house, eating and drinking whatever they give you, for the worker deserves his wages.[y] Do not move around from house to house.

8"When you enter a town and are welcomed, eat what is set before you.[z] 9Heal the sick who are there and tell them, 'The kingdom of God[a] is near you.' 10But when you enter a town and are not welcomed, go into its streets and say, 11'Even the dust of your town that sticks to our feet we wipe off against you.[b] Yet be sure of this: The kingdom of God is near.'[c] 12I tell you, it will be more bearable on that day for Sodom[d] than for that town.[e]

13"Woe to you,[f] Korazin! Woe to you, Bethsaida! For if the miracles that were performed in you had been performed in Tyre and Sidon, they would have repented long ago, sitting in sackcloth[g] and ashes. 14But it will be more bearable for Tyre and Sidon at the judgment than for you. 15And you, Capernaum,[h] will you be lifted up to the skies? No, you will go down to the depths.[b]

16"He who listens to you listens to me; he who rejects you rejects me; but he who rejects me rejects him who sent me."[i]

17The seventy-two[j] returned with joy and said, "Lord, even the demons submit to us in your name."[k]

18He replied, "I saw Satan[l] fall like lightning from heaven.[m] 19I have given you authority to trample on snakes[n] and scorpions and to overcome all the power of the enemy; nothing will harm you. 20However, do not rejoice that the spirits submit to you, but rejoice that your names are written in heaven."[o]

21At that time Jesus, full of joy through the Holy Spirit, said, "I praise you, Father, Lord of heaven and earth, because you have hidden these things from the wise and learned, and revealed them to little children.[p] Yes, Father, for this was your good pleasure.

22"All things have been committed to me by my Father.[q] No one knows who the Son is except the Father, and no one knows who the Father is except the Son and those to whom the Son chooses to reveal him."[r]

23Then he turned to his disciples and said privately, "Blessed are the eyes that see what you see. 24For I tell you that many prophets and kings wanted to see what you see but did not see it, and to hear what you hear but did not hear it."[s]

The Parable of the Good Samaritan

›See Matthew 22:34–40; Mark 12:28–31

25On one occasion an expert in the law stood up to test Jesus. "Teacher," he asked, "what must I do to inherit eternal life?"[t]

26"What is written in the Law?" he replied. "How do you read it?"

27He answered: " 'Love the Lord your God with all your heart and with all your soul and with all your strength and with all your mind'[c];[u] and, 'Love your neighbor as yourself.'[d]"[v] 7 →PG. 1133

28"You have answered correctly," Jesus replied. "Do this and you will live."[w]

29But he wanted to justify himself,[x] so he asked Jesus, "And who is my neighbor?" 6 →PG. 1163

30In reply Jesus said: "A man was going down from Jerusalem to Jericho, when he fell into the hands of robbers. They stripped him of his clothes, beat him and went away, leaving him half dead. 31A priest happened to be going down the same road, and when he saw the man, he passed by on the other side.[y] 32So too, a Levite, when he 7 →PG. 1136

9:58 [o]Mt 8:20
9:59 [p]Mt 4:19
9:60 [q]Mt 3:2
9:61 [r]1Ki 19:20
10:1 [s]Lk 7:13 [t]Lk 9:1,2,51,52 [u]Mk 6:7 [v]Mt 10:1
10:2 [w]Mt 9:37,38; Jn 4:35
10:3 [x]Mt 10:16
10:7 [y]Mt 10:10; 1Co 9:14; 1Ti 5:18
10:8 [z]1Co 10:27
10:9 [a]Mt 3:2; 10:7
10:11 [b]Mt 10:14; Mk 6:11 [c]ver 9
10:12 [d]Mt 10:15 [e]Mt 11:24
10:13 [f]Lk 6:24-26 [g]Rev 11:3
10:15 [h]Mt 4:13
10:16 [i]Mt 10:40; Jn 13:20
10:17 [j]ver 1 [k]Mk 16:17
10:18 [l]Mt 4:10 [m]Isa 14:12; Rev 9:1; 12:8,9
10:19 [n]Mk 16:18; Ac 28:3-5
10:20 [o]Ex 32:32; Ps 69:28; Da 12:1; Php 4:3; Heb 12:23; Rev 13:8; 20:12; 21:27
10:21 [p]1Co 1:26-29
10:22 [q]Mt 28:18 [r]Jn 1:18
10:24 [s]1Pe 1:10-12
10:25 [t]Mt 19:16; Lk 18:18
10:27 [u]Dt 6:5 [v]Lev 19:18; Mt 5:43
10:28 [w]Lev 18:5; Ro 7:10
10:29 [x]Lk 16:15
10:31 [y]Lev 21:1-3

a *1* Some manuscripts *seventy;* also in verse 17
b *15* Greek *Hades*
c *27* Deut. 6:5
d *27* Lev. 19:18

came to the place and saw him, passed by on the other side. 33But a Samaritan,[z] as he traveled, came where the man was; and when he saw him, he took pity on him. 34He went to him and bandaged his wounds, pouring on oil and wine. Then he put the man on his own donkey, took him to an inn and took care of him. 35The next day he took out two silver coins[a] and gave them to the innkeeper. 'Look after him,' he said, 'and when I return, I will reimburse you for any extra expense you may have.'

36"Which of these three do you think was a neighbor to the man who fell into the hands of robbers?"

37The expert in the law replied, "The one who had mercy on him."

Jesus told him, "Go and do likewise."

At the Home of Martha and Mary

1 →PG. 1134

38As Jesus and his disciples were on their way, he came to a village where a woman named Martha[a] opened her home to him. 39She had a sister called Mary,[b] who sat at the Lord's feet[c] listening to what he said. 40But Martha was distracted by all the preparations that had to be made. She came to him and asked, "Lord, don't you care[d] that my sister has left me to do the work by myself? Tell her to help me!"

41"Martha, Martha," the Lord answered, "you are worried[e] and upset about many things, 42but only one thing is needed.[b][f] Mary has chosen what is better, and it will not be taken away from her."

Jesus' Teaching on Prayer

›See Matthew 6:9–13; 7:7–11

1 →PG. 1154

11 One day Jesus was praying[g] in a certain place. When he finished, one of his disciples said to him, "Lord,[h] teach us to pray, just as John taught his disciples."

2He said to them, "When you pray, say:

" 'Father,[c]
hallowed be your name,
your kingdom[i] come.[d]
3Give us each day our daily bread.
4Forgive us our sins,
for we also forgive everyone who sins against us.[e][j]
And lead us not into temptation.[f]' "[k]

5Then he said to them, "Suppose one of you has a friend, and he goes to him at midnight and says, 'Friend, lend me three loaves of bread, 6because a friend of mine on a journey has come to me, and I have nothing to set before him.'

7"Then the one inside answers, 'Don't bother me. The door is already locked, and my children are with me in bed. I can't get up and give you anything.' 8I tell you, though he will not get up and give him the bread because he is his friend, yet because of the man's boldness[g] he will get up and give him as much as he needs.[l]

9"So I say to you: Ask and it will be given to you;[m] seek and you will find; knock and the door will be opened to you. 10For everyone who asks receives; he who seeks finds; and to him who knocks, the door will be opened.

11"Which of you fathers, if your son asks for[h] a fish, will give him a snake instead? 12Or if he asks for an egg, will give him a scorpion? 13If you then, though you are evil, know how to give good gifts to your children, how much more will your Father in heaven give the Holy Spirit to those who ask him!"

Jesus and Beelzebub

›See Matthew 12:22,24–29,43–45; Mark 3:23–27

14Jesus was driving out a demon that was mute. When the demon left, the man who had been mute spoke, and the crowd was amazed.[n] 15But some of them said, "By Beelzebub,[i][o] the prince of demons, he is driving out demons."[p] 16Others tested him by asking for a sign from heaven.[q]

17Jesus knew their thoughts[r] and said to them: "Any kingdom divided against itself will be ruined, and a house divided against itself will fall. 18If Satan[s] is divided against himself, how can his kingdom stand? I say this because you claim that I drive out demons by Beelzebub. 19Now if I drive out demons by Beelzebub, by whom do your followers drive them out? So then, they will be your judges. 20But if I drive out demons by the finger of God,[t] then the kingdom of God[u] has come to you.

21"When a strong man, fully armed, guards his own house, his possessions are safe. 22But when someone stronger attacks and overpowers him, he takes away the armor in which the man trusted and divides up the spoils.

10:33 [z]Mt 10:5
10:38 [a]Jn 11:1; 12:2
10:39 [b]Jn 11:1; 12:3 [c]Lk 8:35
10:40 [d]Mk 4:38
10:41 [e]Mt 6:25-34; Lk 12:11,22
10:42 [f]Ps 27:4
11:1 [g]Lk 3:21 [h]Jn 13:13
11:2 [i]Mt 3:2
11:4 [j]Mt 18:35; Mk 11:25 [k]Mt 26:41; Jas 1:13
11:8 [l]Lk 18:1-6
11:9 [m]Mt 7:7
11:14 [n]Mt 9:32,33
11:15 [o]Mk 3:22 [p]Mt 9:34
11:16 [q]Mt 12:38
11:17 [r]Mt 9:4
11:18 [s]Mt 4:10
11:20 [t]Ex 8:19 [u]Mt 3:2

[a]35 Greek *two denarii* [b]42 Some manuscripts *but few things are needed—or only one* [c]2 Some manuscripts *Our Father in heaven* [d]2 Some manuscripts *come. May your will be done on earth as it is in heaven.* [e]4 Greek *everyone who is indebted to us* [f]4 Some manuscripts *temptation but deliver us from the evil one* [g]8 Or *persistence* [h]11 Some manuscripts *for bread, will give him a stone; or if he asks for* [i]15 Greek *Beezeboul* or *Beelzeboul*; also in verses 18 and 19

23“He who is not with me is against
me, and he who does not gather with
me, scatters.[v]
24“When an evil[a] spirit comes out of
a man, it goes through arid places seeking rest and does not find it. Then it
says, ‘I will return to the house I left.’
25When it arrives, it finds the house
swept clean and put in order. 26Then
it goes and takes seven other spirits
more wicked than itself, and they go
in and live there. And the final condition of that man is worse than the
first.”[w]
27As Jesus was saying these things,
a woman in the crowd called out,
“Blessed is the mother who gave you
birth and nursed you.”[x]
28He replied, “Blessed rather are
those who hear the word of God[y] and
obey it.”[z]

11:23 [v]Mt 12:30; Mk 9:40; Lk 9:50
11:26 [w]2Pe 2:20
11:27 [x]Lk 23:29
11:28 [y]Heb 4:12 [z]Pr 8:32; Lk 6:47; 8:21; Jn 14:21
11:29 [a]ver 16; Mt 12:38 [b]Jnh 1:17; Mt 16:4
11:31 [c]1Ki 10:1; 2Ch 9:1

The Sign of Jonah

›See Matthew 12:39–42

29As the crowds increased, Jesus
said, “This is a wicked generation. It
asks for a miraculous sign,[a] but none
will be given it except the sign of Jonah.[b] 30For as Jonah was a sign to the
Ninevites, so also will the Son of Man
be to this generation. 31The Queen of
the South will rise at the judgment with
the men of this generation and condemn them; for she came from the
ends of the earth to listen to Solomon’s
wisdom,[c] and now one[b] greater than
Solomon is here. 32The men of Nineveh will stand up at the judgment with
this generation and condemn it; for
they repented at the preaching of Jo-

[a] *24* Greek *unclean*   [b] *31* Or *something*; also in verse 32

11:2-4

PROMISE 1

A PATTERN FOR PRAYER

One thing was clear to the disciples: Jesus had a prayer life the likes of which they had never seen before. Realizing that his communication with God created the deepest, most intense connection they had ever seen, they asked Jesus to teach them how to pray. Jesus responded by giving them a model prayer, the one we read in this short passage. Jesus didn’t intend that this “Lord’s Prayer” be something for his followers to thoughtlessly recite. Instead, through this prayer Jesus taught his followers about the basic elements we should include in all of our prayers to God.

First, because he is our heavenly Father, we have no need that God can’t meet. His resources are unlimited and his power is infinite. As a father cares for a child, so God cares for his people.

Second, we should pray that God’s name will be revered and esteemed. While God is our heavenly Father, Jesus wants us to realize that he also is almighty God and that he must be revered. That is, we should pray that our lives will honor God’s person and works. We do that when we trust him (Romans 4:20), give him thanks (Psalm 50:23), obey him (1 Corinthians 10:31) and are constantly aware of his presence (Psalm 16:8).

Third, as followers of Jesus we should pray that God’s kingdom will come in us *and* on the earth. We need to live in such a way that the kingdom of God will be seen in our words and actions. At the same time, we need to live in anticipation of Jesus’ return and the establishment of his kingdom on earth. Remember, Jesus did promise to come back again (Matthew 24:30–44).

Fourth, we should ask God to meet our daily needs and the needs of those around us. This directive brings the realm of prayer into the real world. Having prayed about God’s kingdom, we’re to look around us and see people’s needs. Only God can supply what we and other people need, and he does so in response to prayer. In the Greek language the word for “give” is a present imperative, indicating that we’re to ask God to continually meet our daily needs. When we realize that all we are and have and do comes directly from God’s hand and as a result of his blessing in our lives, this prayer becomes a natural part of our daily conversation with God.

Fifth, because sin creates a barrier between us and God, it’s imperative that we seek God’s forgiveness every single day. That means we must first confess to him the sins we’ve committed, realizing that we have failed many times during the day to live up to his standard for our lives. And, as we request God’s forgiveness, we also need to consciously extend forgiveness to those who have wronged us.

Sixth, our prayers should involve a request that God protect us from temptation. Of course, God never leads us into temptation; that’s a result of our own sinful inclinations (see James 1:13–14). Jesus’ statement here means that we need to ask for God’s help in leading us away from temptation. A good prayer in this instance is this: “Lord, keep me from the inclination to sin when I have the opportunity, and from the opportunity to sin when I have the inclination.” Taking this prayer a step further, it’s helpful to identify the specific areas where we’re weak and ask God for the grace we need to stand strong against temptation in those areas.

After giving his disciples this model prayer, Jesus told them that the key to answered prayer was in the asking (Luke 11:9–10). God delights in meeting the needs of his children, but we must first ask. To help you follow the Lord’s model, jot down the six parts of the “Lord’s Prayer” in a small notebook; make it your prayer journal. Each day as you pray, allow these six points to guide your prayers to God.

For the next Promise 1 reading go to page 1137.

nah,[d] and now one greater than Jonah is here.

The Lamp of the Body

›See Matthew 6:22–23

7 →PG. 1136

33"No one lights a lamp and puts it in a place where it will be hidden, or under a bowl. Instead he puts it on its stand, so that those who come in may see the light.[e] 34Your eye is the lamp of your body. When your eyes are good, your whole body also is full of light. But when they are bad, your body also is full of darkness. 35See to it, then, that the light within you is not darkness. 36Therefore, if your whole body is full of light, and no part of it dark, it will be completely lighted, as when the light of a lamp shines on you."

Six Woes

37When Jesus had finished speaking, a Pharisee invited him to eat with him; so he went in and reclined at the table.[f] 38But the Pharisee, noticing that Jesus did not first wash before the meal,[g] was surprised.

39Then the Lord[h] said to him, "Now then, you Pharisees clean the outside of the cup and dish, but inside you are full of greed and wickedness.[i] 40You foolish people![j] Did not the one who made the outside make the inside also? 41But give what is inside ⌞the dish⌟[a] to the poor,[k] and everything will be clean for you.[l]

42"Woe to you Pharisees, because you give God a tenth[m] of your mint, rue and all other kinds of garden herbs, but you neglect justice and the love of God.[n] You should have practiced the latter without leaving the former undone.[o]

43"Woe to you Pharisees, because you love the most important seats in the synagogues and greetings in the marketplaces.[p]

44"Woe to you, because you are like unmarked graves,[q] which men walk over without knowing it."

45One of the experts in the law[r] answered him, "Teacher, when you say these things, you insult us also."

46Jesus replied, "And you experts in the law, woe to you, because you load people down with burdens they can hardly carry, and you yourselves will not lift one finger to help them.[s]

47"Woe to you, because you build tombs for the prophets, and it was your forefathers who killed them. 48So you testify that you approve of what your forefathers did; they killed the prophets, and you build their tombs.[t] 49Because of this, God in his wisdom[u] said, 'I will send them prophets and apostles, some of whom they will kill and others they will persecute.'[v] 50Therefore this generation will be held responsible for the blood of all the prophets that has been shed since the beginning of the world, 51from the blood of Abel[w] to the blood of Zechariah,[x] who was killed between the altar and the sanctuary. Yes, I tell you, this generation will be held responsible for it all.[y]

52"Woe to you experts in the law, because you have taken away the key to knowledge. You yourselves have not entered, and you have hindered those who were entering."[z]

53When Jesus left there, the Pharisees and the teachers of the law began to oppose him fiercely and to besiege him with questions, 54waiting to catch him in something he might say.[a]

Warnings and Encouragements

›See Matthew 10:26–33

12 Meanwhile, when a crowd of many thousands had gathered, so that they were trampling on one another, Jesus began to speak first to his disciples, saying: "Be on your guard against the yeast of the Pharisees, which is hypocrisy.[b] 2There is nothing concealed that will not be disclosed, or hidden that will not be made known.[c] 3What you have said in the dark will be heard in the daylight, and what you have whispered in the ear in the inner rooms will be proclaimed from the roofs.

4"I tell you, my friends,[d] do not be afraid of those who kill the body and after that can do no more. 5But I will show you whom you should fear: Fear him who, after the killing of the body, has power to throw you into hell. Yes, I tell you, fear him.[e] 6Are not five sparrows sold for two pennies[b]? Yet not one of them is forgotten by God. 7Indeed, the very hairs of your head are all numbered.[f] Don't be afraid; you are worth more than many sparrows.[g]

7 →PG. 1137

8"I tell you, whoever acknowledges me before men, the Son of Man will also acknowledge him before the angels of God.[h] 9But he who disowns me before men will be disowned[i] before the angels of God. 10And everyone who speaks a word against the Son of Man[j] will be forgiven, but anyone who blasphemes against the Holy Spirit will not be forgiven.[k]

11"When you are brought before synagogues, rulers and authorities, do

11:32 [d]Jnh 3:5
11:33 [e]Mt 5:15; Mk 4:21; Lk 8:16
11:37 [f]Lk 7:36; 14:1
11:38 [g]Mk 7:3,4
11:39 [h]Lk 7:13 [i]Mt 23:25,26; Mk 7:20-23
11:40 [j]Lk 12:20; 1Co 15:36
11:41 [k]Lk 12:33 [l]Ac 10:15
11:42 [m]Lk 18:12 [n]Dt 6:5; Mic 6:8 [o]Mt 23:23
11:43 [p]Mt 23:6,7; Mk 12:38-39; Lk 14:7; 20:46
11:44 [q]Mt 23:27
11:45 [r]Mt 22:35
11:46 [s]Mt 23:4
11:48 [t]Mt 23:29-32; Ac 7:51-53
11:49 [u]1Co 1:24,30; Col 2:3 [v]Mt 23:34
11:51 [w]Ge 4:8 [x]2Ch 24:20,21 [y]Mt 23:35,36
11:52 [z]Mt 23:13
11:54 [a]Mt 12:10; Mk 12:13
12:1 [b]Mt 16:6,11,12; Mk 8:15
12:2 [c]Mk 4:22; Lk 8:17
12:4 [d]Jn 15:14,15
12:5 [e]Heb 10:31
12:7 [f]Mt 10:30 [g]Mt 12:12
12:8 [h]Lk 15:10
12:9 [i]Mk 8:38; 2Ti 2:12
12:10 [j]Mt 8:20 [k]Mt 12:31,32; Mk 3:28-29; 1Jn 5:16

a 41 Or *what you have* b 6 Greek *two assaria*

not worry about how you will defend yourselves or what you will say,[l] [12]for the Holy Spirit will teach you at that time what you should say."[m]

The Parable of the Rich Fool

[13]Someone in the crowd said to him, "Teacher, tell my brother to divide the inheritance with me."

[14]Jesus replied, "Man, who appointed me a judge or an arbiter between you?" [15]Then he said to them, "Watch out! Be on your guard against all kinds of greed; a man's life does not consist in the abundance of his possessions."[n]

3 →PG. 1137

[16]And he told them this parable: "The ground of a certain rich man produced a good crop. [17]He thought to himself, 'What shall I do? I have no place to store my crops.'

[18]"Then he said, 'This is what I'll do. I will tear down my barns and build bigger ones, and there I will store all my grain and my goods. [19]And I'll say to myself, "You have plenty of good things laid up for many years. Take life easy; eat, drink and be merry." '

[20]"But God said to him, 'You fool![o] This very night your life will be demanded from you.[p] Then who will get what you have prepared for yourself?'[q]

[21]"This is how it will be with anyone who stores up things for himself but is not rich toward God."[r]

Do Not Worry

›See Matthew 6:25–33

[22]Then Jesus said to his disciples: "Therefore I tell you, do not worry about your life, what you will eat; or about your body, what you will wear. [23]Life is more than food, and the body more than clothes. [24]Consider the ravens: They do not sow or reap, they have no storeroom or barn; yet God feeds them.[s] And how much more valuable you are than birds! [25]Who of you by worrying can add a single hour to his life[a]? [26]Since you cannot do this very little thing, why do you worry about the rest?

[27]"Consider how the lilies grow. They do not labor or spin. Yet I tell you, not even Solomon in all his splendor[t] was dressed like one of these. [28]If that is how God clothes the grass of the field, which is here today, and tomorrow is thrown into the fire, how much more will he clothe you, O you of little faith![u] [29]And do not set your heart on what you will eat or drink; do not worry about it. [30]For the pagan world runs after all such things, and your Father[v] knows that you need them.[w] [31]But seek his kingdom,[x] and these things will be given to you as well.[y]

[32]"Do not be afraid,[z] little flock, for your Father has been pleased to give you the kingdom.[a] [33]Sell your possessions and give to the poor.[b] Provide purses for yourselves that will not wear out, a treasure in heaven[c] that will not be exhausted, where no thief comes near and no moth destroys.[d] [34]For where your treasure is, there your heart will be also.[e]

7 →PG. 1140

Watchfulness

›See Matthew 24:43–51; Mark 13:33–37

[35]"Be dressed ready for service and keep your lamps burning, [36]like men waiting for their master to return from a wedding banquet, so that when he comes and knocks they can immediately open the door for him. [37]It will be good for those servants whose master finds them watching when he comes.[f] I tell you the truth, he will dress himself

3 →PG. 1138

[a]25 Or *single cubit to his height*

12:11 [l]Mt 10:17,19; Mk 13:11; Lk 21:12,14 **12:12** [m]Ex 4:12; Mt 10:20; Mk 13:11; Lk 21:15 **12:15** [n]Job 20:20; 31:24; Ps 62:10 **12:20** [o]Jer 17:11; Lk 11:40 [p]Job 27:8 [q]Ps 39:6; 49:10 **12:21** [r]ver 33 **12:24** [s]Job 38:41; Ps 147:9 **12:27** [t]1Ki 10:4-7 **12:28** [u]Mt 6:30 **12:30** [v]Lk 6:36 [w]Mt 6:8 **12:31** [x]Mt 3:2 [y]Mt 19:29 **12:32** [z]Mt 14:27 [a]Mt 25:34 **12:33** [b]Mt 19:21; Ac 2:45 [c]Mt 6:20 [d]Jas 5:2 **12:34** [e]Mt 6:21 **12:37** [f]Mt 24:42,46; 25:13

12:22–34

PROMISE 1

WHY WORRY?

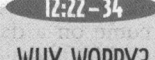

Worry infects all members of society. In today's turbulent culture, people worry about their health, their wealth, their jobs, their families and their futures. Jesus understood our tendency to worry. That's why he addressed the issue head on. The Lord not only commanded us not to worry, he told us why we shouldn't. Consider the following points:

Worry ignores God's faithfulness (vv. 22–24). If God feeds the birds and clothes the flowers, doesn't it make sense that he'll provide for us?

Worry ignores its own limitations (vv. 25–26). Has anything ever changed for the better because we worried about it? Of course not! Yet we worry as though the mere act of worrying will somehow make a difference.

Worry ignores God's love (vv. 27–31). Unbelievers, like fatherless orphans, worry about the future. But God's children don't need to worry. The God who gives life also cares for his own.

Worry ignores the present (v. 32). When we worry about the future, we miss out on the blessings of today.

The next time you find yourself worrying, turn to this passage. If you're still anxious after reading it, then ask yourself which of these four things you're ignoring. Consider how different your perspective might be if you didn't ignore them.

For the next Promise 1 reading go to page 1144.

to serve, will have them recline at the table and will come and wait on them.[g] 38It will be good for those servants whose master finds them ready, even if he comes in the second or third watch of the night. 39But understand this: If the owner of the house had known at what hour the thief[h] was coming, he would not have let his house be broken into. 40You also must be ready,[i] because the Son of Man will come at an hour when you do not expect him."

41Peter asked, "Lord, are you telling this parable to us, or to everyone?"

3 →PG. 1142

42The Lord[j] answered, "Who then is the faithful and wise manager, whom the master puts in charge of his servants to give them their food allowance at the proper time? 43It will be good for that servant whom the master finds doing so when he returns. 44I tell you the truth, he will put him in charge of all his possessions. 45But suppose the servant says to himself, 'My master is taking a long time in coming,' and he then begins to beat the menservants and maidservants and to eat and drink and get drunk. 46The master of that servant will come on a day when he does not expect him and at an hour he is not aware of.[k] He will cut him to pieces and assign him a place with the unbelievers.

47"That servant who knows his master's will and does not get ready or does not do what his master wants will be beaten with many blows.[l] 48But the one who does not know and does things deserving punishment will be beaten with few blows.[m] From everyone who has been given much, much will be demanded; and from the one who has been entrusted with much, much more will be asked.

Not Peace but Division

›See Matthew 10:34–36

49"I have come to bring fire on the earth, and how I wish it were already kindled! 50But I have a baptism[n] to undergo, and how distressed I am until it is completed![o] 51Do you think I came to bring peace on earth? No, I tell you, but division. 52From now on there will be five in one family divided against each other, three against two and two against three. 53They will be divided, father against son and son against father, mother against daughter and daughter against mother, mother-in-law against daughter-in-law and daughter-in-law against mother-in-law."[p]

12:37 [g]Mt 20:28
12:39 [h]Mt 6:19; 1Th 5:2; 2Pe 3:10; Rev 3:3; 16:15
12:40 [i]Mk 13:33; Lk 21:36
12:42 [j]Lk 7:13
12:46 [k]ver 40
12:47 [l]Dt 25:2
12:48 [m]Lev 5:17; Nu 15:27-30
12:50 [n]Mk 10:38 [o]Jn 19:30
12:53 [p]Mic 7:6; Mt 10:21
12:54 [q]Mt 16:2
12:56 [r]Mt 16:3
12:58 [s]Mt 5:25
12:59 [t]Mt 5:26; Mk 12:42
13:1 [u]Mt 27:2
13:2 [v]Jn 9:2,3
13:4 [w]Jn 9:7,11
13:5 [x]Mt 3:2; Ac 2:38
13:6 [y]Isa 5:2; Jer 8:13; Mt 21:19
13:7 [z]Mt 3:10
13:10 [a]Mt 4:23
13:11 [b]ver 16

Interpreting the Times

54He said to the crowd: "When you see a cloud rising in the west, immediately you say, 'It's going to rain,' and it does.[q] 55And when the south wind blows, you say, 'It's going to be hot,' and it is. 56Hypocrites! You know how to interpret the appearance of the earth and the sky. How is it that you don't know how to interpret this present time?[r]

57"Why don't you judge for yourselves what is right? 58As you are going with your adversary to the magistrate, try hard to be reconciled to him on the way, or he may drag you off to the judge, and the judge turn you over to the officer, and the officer throw you into prison.[s] 59I tell you, you will not get out until you have paid the last penny.[a]"[t]

Repent or Perish

13 Now there were some present at that time who told Jesus about the Galileans whose blood Pilate[u] had mixed with their sacrifices. 2Jesus answered, "Do you think that these Galileans were worse sinners than all the other Galileans because they suffered this way?[v] 3I tell you, no! But unless you repent, you too will all perish. 4Or those eighteen who died when the tower in Siloam[w] fell on them—do you think they were more guilty than all the others living in Jerusalem? 5I tell you, no! But unless you repent,[x] you too will all perish."

6Then he told this parable: "A man had a fig tree, planted in his vineyard, and he went to look for fruit on it, but did not find any.[y] 7So he said to the man who took care of the vineyard, 'For three years now I've been coming to look for fruit on this fig tree and haven't found any. Cut it down![z] Why should it use up the soil?'

8" 'Sir,' the man replied, 'leave it alone for one more year, and I'll dig around it and fertilize it. 9If it bears fruit next year, fine! If not, then cut it down.' "

A Crippled Woman Healed on the Sabbath

10On a Sabbath Jesus was teaching in one of the synagogues,[a] 11and a woman was there who had been crippled by a spirit for eighteen years.[b] She was bent over and could not straighten up at all. 12When Jesus saw her, he called her forward and said to

[a] 59 Greek *lepton*

her, "Woman, you are set free from your infirmity." 13 Then he put his hands on her,[c] and immediately she straightened up and praised God.

14 Indignant because Jesus had healed on the Sabbath,[d] the synagogue ruler[e] said to the people, "There are six days for work.[f] So come and be healed on those days, not on the Sabbath."

15 The Lord answered him, "You hypocrites! Doesn't each of you on the Sabbath untie his ox or donkey from the stall and lead it out to give it water?[g] 16 Then should not this woman, a daughter of Abraham,[h] whom Satan[i] has kept bound for eighteen long years, be set free on the Sabbath day from what bound her?"

17 When he said this, all his opponents were humiliated,[j] but the people were delighted with all the wonderful things he was doing.

The Parables of the Mustard Seed and the Yeast

›See Matthew 13:31–33; Mark 4:30–32

18 Then Jesus asked, "What is the kingdom of God[k] like?[l] What shall I compare it to? 19 It is like a mustard seed, which a man took and planted in his garden. It grew and became a tree,[m] and the birds of the air perched in its branches."[n]

20 Again he asked, "What shall I compare the kingdom of God to? 21 It is like yeast that a woman took and mixed into a large amount[a] of flour until it worked all through the dough."[o]

The Narrow Door

22 Then Jesus went through the towns and villages, teaching as he made his way to Jerusalem.[p] 23 Someone asked him, "Lord, are only a few people going to be saved?"

He said to them, 24 "Make every effort to enter through the narrow door,[q] because many, I tell you, will try to enter and will not be able to. 25 Once the owner of the house gets up and closes the door, you will stand outside knocking and pleading, 'Sir, open the door for us.'

"But he will answer, 'I don't know you or where you come from.'[r]

26 "Then you will say, 'We ate and drank with you, and you taught in our streets.'

27 "But he will reply, 'I don't know you or where you come from. Away from me, all you evildoers!'[s]

28 "There will be weeping there, and gnashing of teeth,[t] when you see Abraham, Isaac and Jacob and all the prophets in the kingdom of God, but you yourselves thrown out. 29 People will come from east and west[u] and north and south, and will take their places at the feast in the kingdom of God. 30 Indeed there are those who are last who will be first, and first who will be last."[v]

Jesus' Sorrow for Jerusalem

›See Matthew 23:37–39

31 At that time some Pharisees came to Jesus and said to him, "Leave this place and go somewhere else. Herod[w] wants to kill you."

32 He replied, "Go tell that fox, 'I will drive out demons and heal people today and tomorrow, and on the third day I will reach my goal.'[x] 33 In any case, I must keep going today and tomorrow and the next day—for surely no prophet[y] can die outside Jerusalem!

34 "O Jerusalem, Jerusalem, you who kill the prophets and stone those sent to you, how often I have longed to gather your children together, as a hen gathers her chicks under her wings,[z] but you were not willing! 35 Look, your house is left to you desolate.[a] I tell you, you will not see me again until you say, 'Blessed is he who comes in the name of the Lord.'[b]"[b]

Jesus at a Pharisee's House

14 One Sabbath, when Jesus went to eat in the house of a prominent Pharisee,[c] he was being carefully watched.[d] 2 There in front of him was a man suffering from dropsy. 3 Jesus asked the Pharisees and experts in the law,[e] "Is it lawful to heal on the Sabbath or not?"[f] 4 But they remained silent. So taking hold of the man, he healed him and sent him away.

5 Then he asked them, "If one of you has a son[c] or an ox that falls into a well on the Sabbath day, will you not immediately pull him out?"[g] 6 And they had nothing to say.

7 When he noticed how the guests picked the places of honor at the table,[h] he told them this parable: 8 "When someone invites you to a wedding feast, do not take the place of honor, for a person more distinguished than you may have been invited. 9 If so, the host who invited both of you will come and say to you, 'Give this man your seat.' Then, humiliated, you will have to take the least important place. 10 But when you are invited, take the

13:13 [c] Mk 5:23
13:14 [d] Mt 12:2; Lk 14:3 [e] Mk 5:22 [f] Ex 20:9
13:15 [g] Lk 14:5
13:16 [h] Lk 3:8; 19:9 [i] Mt 4:10
13:17 [j] Isa 66:5
13:18 [k] Mt 3:2 [l] Mt 13:24
13:19 [m] Lk 17:6 [n] Mt 13:32
13:21 [o] 1Co 5:6
13:22 [p] Lk 9:51
13:24 [q] Mt 7:13
13:25 [r] Mt 7:23; 25:10-12
13:27 [s] Mt 7:23; 25:41
13:28 [t] Mt 8:12
13:29 [u] Mt 8:11
13:30 [v] Mt 19:30
13:31 [w] Mt 14:1
13:32 [x] Heb 2:10
13:33 [y] Mt 21:11
13:34 [z] Mt 23:37
13:35 [a] Jer 12:17; 22:5 [b] Ps 118:26; Mt 21:9; Lk 19:38
14:1 [c] Lk 7:36; 11:37 [d] Mt 12:10
14:3 [e] Mt 22:35 [f] Mt 12:2
14:5 [g] Lk 13:15
14:7 [h] Lk 11:43

a *21* Greek *three satas* (probably about 1/2 bushel or 22 liters) b *35* Psalm 118:26
c *5* Some manuscripts *donkey*

lowest place, so that when your host
comes, he will say to you, 'Friend,
move up to a better place.' Then you
will be honored in the presence of all
your fellow guests. 11For everyone who
exalts himself will be humbled, and
he who humbles himself will be exalted."[i]

7 →PG. 1145

12Then Jesus said to his host, "When
you give a luncheon or dinner, do not
invite your friends, your brothers or
relatives, or your rich neighbors; if you
do, they may invite you back and so
you will be repaid. 13But when you give
a banquet, invite the poor, the crippled, the lame, the blind,[j] 14and you
will be blessed. Although they cannot
repay you, you will be repaid at the
resurrection of the righteous."[k]

The Parable of the Great Banquet

15When one of those at the table
with him heard this, he said to Jesus,
"Blessed is the man who will eat at the
feast[l] in the kingdom of God."[m]
16Jesus replied: "A certain man was
preparing a great banquet and invited
many guests. 17At the time of the banquet he sent his servant to tell those
who had been invited, 'Come, for everything is now ready.'
18"But they all alike began to make
excuses. The first said, 'I have just
bought a field, and I must go and see it.
Please excuse me.'
19"Another said, 'I have just bought
five yoke of oxen, and I'm on my way to
try them out. Please excuse me.'
20"Still another said, 'I just got married, so I can't come.'
21"The servant came back and reported this to his master. Then the
owner of the house became angry and
ordered his servant, 'Go out quickly
into the streets and alleys of the town
and bring in the poor, the crippled, the
blind and the lame.'[n]
22" 'Sir,' the servant said, 'what you
ordered has been done, but there is
still room.'
23"Then the master told his servant,
'Go out to the roads and country lanes
and make them come in, so that my
house will be full. 24I tell you, not one
of those men who were invited will get
a taste of my banquet.' "[o]

The Cost of Being a Disciple

25Large crowds were traveling with
Jesus, and turning to them he said:

5 →PG. 1148

26"If anyone comes to me and does not
hate his father and mother, his wife
and children, his brothers and sisters—
yes, even his own life—he cannot be
my disciple.[p] 27And anyone who does
not carry his cross and follow me cannot be my disciple.[q]
28"Suppose one of you wants to
build a tower. Will he not first sit down
and estimate the cost to see if he has
enough money to complete it? 29For if
he lays the foundation and is not able
to finish it, everyone who sees it will
ridicule him, 30saying, 'This fellow began to build and was not able to finish.'
31"Or suppose a king is about to go
to war against another king. Will he not
first sit down and consider whether he
is able with ten thousand men to oppose the one coming against him with
twenty thousand? 32If he is not able, he
will send a delegation while the other
is still a long way off and will ask for
terms of peace. 33In the same way, any
of you who does not give up everything
he has cannot be my disciple.[r]
34"Salt is good, but if it loses its saltiness, how can it be made salty again?[s]
35It is fit neither for the soil nor for the
manure pile; it is thrown out.[t]
"He who has ears to hear, let him
hear."[u]

The Parable of the Lost Sheep

›See Matthew 18:12–14

15 Now the tax collectors[v] and "sinners" were all gathering around to
hear him. 2But the Pharisees and the
teachers of the law muttered, "This
man welcomes sinners and eats with
them."[w]
3Then Jesus told them this parable:[x] 4"Suppose one of you has a hundred sheep and loses one of them.

14:25–35

PROMISE 4

JESUS ENCOURAGES HATE?

To many readers this passage seems confusing. Hating self and family seems like the opposite of God's ideal for his people today. But Jesus wasn't telling his followers they were to hate their families and themselves. Instead, Jesus used this vivid imagery so his hearers would realize that all earthly commitments and affections were to pale in comparison to their love for him.

Amazingly, when we love Jesus above everything else, everything else takes on more meaning. A man who is completely devoted to Christ will allow a Christlike attitude to permeate all of his relationships—even his relationship to himself. This man will soon discover that he's more devoted to his wife, his children, his work, and his brothers and sisters in Christ.

For the next Promise 4 reading go to page 1179.

14:11 [i]Mt 23:12; Lk 18:14
14:13 [j]ver 21
14:14 [k]Ac 24:15
14:15 [l]Isa 25:6; Mt 26:29; Lk 13:29; Rev 19:9 [m]Mt 3:2
14:21 [n]ver 13
14:24 [o]Mt 21:43; Ac 13:46
14:26 [p]Mt 10:37; Jn 12:25
14:27 [q]Mt 10:38; Lk 9:23
14:33 [r]Php 3:7,8
14:34 [s]Mk 9:50
14:35 [t]Mt 5:13 [u]Mt 11:15
15:1 [v]Lk 5:29
15:2 [w]Mt 9:11
15:3 [x]Mt 13:3

Does he not leave the ninety-nine in
the open country and go after the lost
sheep until he finds it?[y] 5And when he
finds it, he joyfully puts it on his shoulders 6and goes home. Then he calls his
friends and neighbors together and
says, 'Rejoice with me; I have found my
lost sheep.'[z] 7I tell you that in the
same way there will be more rejoicing
in heaven over one sinner who repents
than over ninety-nine righteous persons who do not need to repent.[a]

The Parable of the Lost Coin

8"Or suppose a woman has ten silver
coins[a] and loses one. Does she not
light a lamp, sweep the house and
search carefully until she finds it? 9And
when she finds it, she calls her friends
and neighbors together and says, 'Rejoice with me; I have found my lost
coin.'[b] 10In the same way, I tell you,
there is rejoicing in the presence of the
angels of God over one sinner who repents."[c]

The Parable of the Lost Son

11Jesus continued: "There was a
man who had two sons.[d] 12The younger one said to his father, 'Father, give
me my share of the estate.'[e] So he divided his property[f] between them.

4 →PG. 1150

15:4 [y] Ps 23; 119:176; Jer 31:10; Eze 34:11-16; Lk 5:32; 19:10 **15:6** [z] ver 9 **15:7** [a] ver 10 **15:9** [b] ver 6 **15:10** [c] ver 7 **15:11** [d] Mt 21:28 **15:12** [e] Dt 21:17 [f] ver 30

[a] 8 Greek *ten drachmas,* each worth about a day's wages

15:4-7

PROMISE 7

THE PROBLEM WITH JESUS

The ancient religious leaders had a problem with Jesus. A big problem. They believed that God hated sinners, and were convinced that God wanted them to avoid such people. That's why they struggled with Jesus' behavior. He regularly hung around with dishonest businessmen, crooked politicians and prostitutes. From the religious community's perspective, Jesus must have been a sinner himself. Otherwise, why would he associate with such people?

Jesus knew how the Pharisees and the teachers of the law felt. In order to correct their perception of God and how he feels about sinners, Jesus told three parables. The first one was targeted at working men, the second at women, and the third at fathers. But through these three different stories, the one message Jesus communicated was clear: *God loves lost people and seeks them out.* What a powerful lesson for those religious leaders, and for us today: God doesn't hate sinners, he loves them! Consider the characteristics of each parable and what it says about God.

Every person is important to God. The shepherd in the first parable had a hundred sheep. You might think he would hardly miss one. He might have considered leaving the others behind and searching for the one an inconvenience, a hassle. After all, this shepherd was a business owner, and as such had to figure in loss as part of his operating cost. But God, as the shepherd in this story, never considers abandoning even one soul without searching after it. This shepherd immediately went after the sheep, and didn't stop searching until he found it. Further, when he found the sheep, he didn't scold the sheep for walking away from his protection. He joyfully scooped it up into his arms and carried it home.

God celebrates when a lost person is found. Each of these three parables ended with a party. The shepherd, woman and father all rejoiced with their friends after they'd found what they'd lost. All of the people who listened to Jesus tell this story had probably participated in a celebration similar to the ones he described. And because Jesus had come down from heaven, he had seen similar rejoicing there. Jesus wanted his listeners to know that every time a lost person is found, all of heaven rejoices.

While we may turn our backs on God, he never turns his back on us. At the beginning of the final parable the young man asked for, and received, his share of his father's estate. In taking his inheritance before his father had died, this young man implied, "I wish you were dead. I want your money more than I want you in my life." So when this young man reached a point of despair and decided to go home, he wasn't expecting a warm welcome. While he hoped his father would forgive him, he wasn't sure he would be forgiven completely. And he certainly didn't expect to be restored to the family with all the privileges of a son.

What the lost son didn't know was that his father had never stopped looking for him. The moment the father saw his son approaching, he ran to greet him and the celebration began. Even though his son had completely turned away, the father never turned his back on the straying son.

God has compassion for the lost. Again in the third parable, Jesus specifically said that the father felt "compassion" for his son (v. 20). He understood how miserable the boy must have become. He realized how hard it must have been for the son to come home. Prompted by compassion, the father extended his love and acceptance.

Jesus intended that these three parables not only inform, but also tug at the emotions of his listeners. Think through each story and put it in a contemporary setting. Imagine those situations where you've lost something of value, searched for it and then recovered it. Then ask God to give you his heart when it comes to lost people. Pray that he'll enable you to search for them as diligently as you would look for a cherished item that's lost.

For the next Promise 7 reading go to page 1163.

13"Not long after that, the younger son got together all he had, set off for a distant country and there squandered his wealth[g] in wild living. 14After he had spent everything, there was a severe famine in that whole country, and he began to be in need. 15So he went and hired himself out to a citizen of that country, who sent him to his fields to feed pigs.[h] 16He longed to fill his stomach with the pods that the pigs were eating, but no one gave him anything.

17"When he came to his senses, he said, 'How many of my father's hired men have food to spare, and here I am starving to death! 18I will set out and go back to my father and say to him: Father, I have sinned[i] against heaven and against you. 19I am no longer worthy to be called your son; make me like one of your hired men.' 20So he got up and went to his father.

"But while he was still a long way off, his father saw him and was filled with compassion for him; he ran to his son, threw his arms around him and kissed him.[j]

21"The son said to him, 'Father, I have sinned against heaven and against you.[k] I am no longer worthy to be called your son.[a]'

22"But the father said to his servants, 'Quick! Bring the best robe[l] and put it on him. Put a ring on his finger[m] and sandals on his feet. 23Bring the fattened calf and kill it. Let's have a feast and celebrate. 24For this son of mine was dead and is alive again;[n] he was lost and is found.' So they began to celebrate.[o]

25"Meanwhile, the older son was in the field. When he came near the house, he heard music and dancing. 26So he called one of the servants and asked him what was going on. 27'Your brother has come,' he replied, 'and your father has killed the fattened calf because he has him back safe and sound.'

28"The older brother became angry[p] and refused to go in. So his father went out and pleaded with him. 29But he answered his father, 'Look! All these years I've been slaving for you and never disobeyed your orders. Yet you never gave me even a young goat so I could celebrate with my friends. 30But when this son of yours who has squandered your property[q] with prostitutes[r] comes home, you kill the fattened calf for him!'

31" 'My son,' the father said, 'you are always with me, and everything I have is yours. 32But we had to celebrate and be glad, because this brother of yours was dead and is alive again; he was lost and is found.' "[s]

The Parable of the Shrewd Manager

16 Jesus told his disciples: "There was a rich man whose manager was accused of wasting his possessions.[t] 2So he called him in and asked him, 'What is this I hear about you? Give an account of your management, because you cannot be manager any longer.'

3"The manager said to himself, 'What shall I do now? My master is taking away my job. I'm not strong enough to dig, and I'm ashamed to beg— 4I know what I'll do so that, when I lose my job here, people will welcome me into their houses.'

5"So he called in each one of his master's debtors. He asked the first, 'How much do you owe my master?'

6" 'Eight hundred gallons[b] of olive oil,' he replied.

"The manager told him, 'Take your bill, sit down quickly, and make it four hundred.'

7"Then he asked the second, 'And how much do you owe?'

" 'A thousand bushels[c] of wheat,' he replied.

"He told him, 'Take your bill and make it eight hundred.'

8"The master commended the dishonest manager because he had acted shrewdly. For the people of this world[u] are more shrewd[v] in dealing with their own kind than are the people of the light.[w] 9I tell you, use worldly wealth[x] to gain friends for yourselves, so that when it is gone, you will be welcomed into eternal dwellings.[y]

10"Whoever can be trusted with very little can also be trusted with much,[z] and whoever is dishonest with very little will also be dishonest with much. 11So if you have not been trustworthy in handling worldly wealth,[a] who will trust you with true riches? 12And if you have not been trustworthy with someone else's property, who will give you property of your own?

13"No servant can serve two masters. Either he will hate the one and love the other, or he will be devoted to the one and despise the other. You cannot serve both God and Money."[b]

3 →PG. 1146

14The Pharisees, who loved money,[c] heard all this and were sneering at Jesus.[d] 15He said to them, "You are the ones who justify yourselves[e] in the

15:13 [g]ver 30; Lk 16:1
15:15 [h]Lev 11:7
15:18 [i]Lev 26:40; Mt 3:2
15:20 [j]Ge 45:14,15; 46:29; Ac 20:37
15:21 [k]Ps 51:4
15:22 [l]Zec 3:4; Rev 6:11 [m]Ge 41:42
15:24 [n]Eph 2:1,5; 5:14; 1Ti 5:6 [o]ver 32
15:28 [p]Jnh 4:1
15:30 [q]ver 12,13 [r]Pr 29:3
15:32 [s]ver 24; Mal 3:17
16:1 [t]Lk 15:13,30
16:8 [u]Ps 17:14 [v]Ps 18:26 [w]Jn 12:36; Eph 5:8; 1Th 5:5
16:9 [x]ver 11,13 [y]Mt 19:21; Lk 12:33
16:10 [z]Mt 25:21,23; Lk 19:17
16:11 [a]ver 9,13
16:13 [b]ver 9,11; Mt 6:24
16:14 [c]1Ti 3:3 [d]Lk 23:35
16:15 [e]Lk 10:29

a *21* Some early manuscripts *son. Make me like one of your hired men.* **b** *6* Greek *one hundred batous* (probably about 3 kiloliters) **c** *7* Greek *one hundred korous* (probably about 35 kiloliters)

eyes of men, but God knows your
hearts.[f] What is highly valued among
men is detestable in God's sight.

Additional Teachings

16“The Law and the Prophets were
proclaimed until John.[g] Since that
time, the good news of the kingdom of
God is being preached,[h] and everyone
is forcing his way into it. 17It is easier
for heaven and earth to disappear than
for the least stroke of a pen to drop out
of the Law.[i]
18“Anyone who divorces his wife and
marries another woman commits
adultery, and the man who marries a
divorced woman commits adultery.[j]

The Rich Man and Lazarus

19“There was a rich man who was
dressed in purple and fine linen and
lived in luxury every day.[k] 20At his
gate was laid a beggar[l] named Lazarus, covered with sores 21and longing
to eat what fell from the rich man's
table.[m] Even the dogs came and licked
his sores.
22“The time came when the beggar
died and the angels carried him to
Abraham's side. The rich man also died
and was buried. 23In hell,[a] where he
was in torment, he looked up and saw
Abraham far away, with Lazarus by his
side. 24So he called to him, ‘Father
Abraham,[n] have pity on me and send
Lazarus to dip the tip of his finger in
water and cool my tongue, because I
am in agony in this fire.’[o]
25“But Abraham replied, ‘Son, remember that in your lifetime you received your good things, while Lazarus
received bad things,[p] but now he is
comforted here and you are in agony.[q] 26And besides all this, between us
and you a great chasm has been fixed,
so that those who want to go from here
to you cannot, nor can anyone cross
over from there to us.’
27“He answered, ‘Then I beg you,
father, send Lazarus to my father's
house, 28for I have five brothers. Let
him warn them,[r] so that they will not
also come to this place of torment.’
29“Abraham replied, ‘They have Moses[s] and the Prophets;[t] let them listen to them.’
30“ ‘No, father Abraham,’[u] he said,
‘but if someone from the dead goes to
them, they will repent.’
31“He said to him, ‘If they do not
listen to Moses and the Prophets, they
will not be convinced even if someone
rises from the dead.’ ”

Sin, Faith, Duty

17 Jesus said to his disciples: “Things
that cause people to sin[v] are
bound to come, but woe to that person
through whom they come.[w] 2It would
be better for him to be thrown into the
sea with a millstone tied around his
neck than for him to cause one of these
little ones[x] to sin.[y] 3So watch yourselves.
“If your brother sins, rebuke him,[z]
and if he repents, forgive him.[a] 4If he
sins against you seven times in a day,
and seven times comes back to you
and says, ‘I repent,’ forgive him.”[b]
5The apostles[c] said to the Lord,[d]
“Increase our faith!”
6He replied, “If you have faith as
small as a mustard seed,[e] you can say
to this mulberry tree, ‘Be uprooted and
planted in the sea,’ and it will obey
you.[f]
7“Suppose one of you had a servant
plowing or looking after the sheep.
Would he say to the servant when he
comes in from the field, ‘Come along
now and sit down to eat’? 8Would he
not rather say, ‘Prepare my supper, get
yourself ready and wait on me[g] while
I eat and drink; after that you may eat
and drink’? 9Would he thank the servant because he did what he was told
to do? 10So you also, when you have
done everything you were told to do,
should say, ‘We are unworthy servants;
we have only done our duty.’ ”[h]

[a]23 Greek *Hades*

16:15 [f]1Sa 16:7; Rev 2:23
16:16 [g]Mt 11:12,13 [h]Mt 4:23
16:17 [i]Mt 5:18
16:18 [j]Mt 5:31,32; 19:9; Mk 10:11; Ro 7:2,3; 1Co 7:10,11
16:19 [k]Eze 16:49
16:20 [l]Ac 3:2
16:21 [m]Mt 15:27
16:24 [n]ver 30; Lk 3:8 [o]Mt 5:22
16:25 [p]Ps 17:14 [q]Lk 6:21,24,25
16:28 [r]Ac 2:40; 20:23; 1Th 4:6
16:29 [s]Lk 24:27,44; Jn 5:45-47; Ac 15:21 [t]Lk 4:17; Jn 1:45
16:30 [u]ver 24; Lk 3:8
17:1 [v]Mt 5:29 [w]Mt 18:7
17:2 [x]Mk 10:24; Lk 10:21 [y]Mt 5:29
17:3 [z]Mt 18:15 [a]Eph 4:32; Col 3:13
17:4 [b]Mt 18:21,22
17:5 [c]Mk 6:30 [d]Lk 7:13
17:6 [e]Mt 13:31; 17:20; Lk 13:19 [f]Mt 21:21; Mk 9:23
17:8 [g]Lk 12:37
17:10 [h]1Co 9:16

16:13

PROMISE 3

LOVE OF MONEY

God never says that money itself is evil. Indeed, some of the greatest men in the Bible were extremely wealthy (Abraham, Jacob, David, Solomon—to name a few). But God does warn us about the danger of loving money. Because a person's personal worth is often measured by annual income and personal assets, it's easy for us to develop a fondness for money.

But we need to beware. Money is a tool to be used, not an entity to be loved over all else. In this passage Jesus clearly states that, as Christians, we're to love and serve our true Master—God himself—first and use our money for his kingdom work. One of the best ways to overcome a love of money is to give generously to the Lord's work and to the needy. To keep this area of your life in balance, be sure that your financial plan involves regular and generous giving.

For the next Promise 3 reading go to page 1237.

Ten Healed of Leprosy

11Now on his way to Jerusalem,[i]
Jesus traveled along the border between Samaria and Galilee.[j] **12**As he
was going into a village, ten men who
had leprosy[a][k] met him. They stood at
a distance[l] **13**and called out in a loud
voice, "Jesus, Master,[m] have pity
on us!"
14When he saw them, he said, "Go,
show yourselves to the priests."[n] And
as they went, they were cleansed.
15One of them, when he saw he was
healed, came back, praising God[o] in a
loud voice. **16**He threw himself at Jesus'
feet and thanked him—and he was a
Samaritan.[p]
17Jesus asked, "Were not all ten
cleansed? Where are the other nine?
18Was no one found to return and give
praise to God except this foreigner?"
19Then he said to him, "Rise and go;
your faith has made you well."[q]

The Coming of the Kingdom of God

20Once, having been asked by the
Pharisees when the kingdom of God
would come,[r] Jesus replied, "The
kingdom of God does not come with
your careful observation, **21**nor will
people say, 'Here it is,' or 'There it
is,'[s] because the kingdom of God is
within[b] you."
22Then he said to his disciples, "The
time is coming when you will long to
see one of the days of the Son of
Man,[t] but you will not see it.[u] **23**Men
will tell you, 'There he is!' or 'Here he
is!' Do not go running off after them.[v]
24For the Son of Man in his day[c] will
be like the lightning,[w] which flashes
and lights up the sky from one end to
the other. **25**But first he must suffer
many things[x] and be rejected[y] by
this generation.[z]
26"Just as it was in the days of
Noah,[a] so also will it be in the days of
the Son of Man. **27**People were eating,
drinking, marrying and being given in
marriage up to the day Noah entered
the ark. Then the flood came and destroyed them all.
28"It was the same in the days of
Lot.[b] People were eating and drinking, buying and selling, planting and
building. **29**But the day Lot left Sodom,
fire and sulfur rained down from heav-
en and destroyed them all.
30"It will be just like this on the day
the Son of Man is revealed.[c] **31**On that
day no one who is on the roof of his
house, with his goods inside, should go
down to get them. Likewise, no one in
the field should go back for anything.[d]
32Remember Lot's wife![e] **33**Whoever
tries to keep his life will lose it, and
whoever loses his life will preserve it.[f]
34I tell you, on that night two people
will be in one bed; one will be taken
and the other left. **35**Two women will
be grinding grain together; one will be
taken and the other left.[d] "[g]
37"Where, Lord?" they asked.
He replied, "Where there is a dead
body, there the vultures will gather."[h]

The Parable of the Persistent Widow

18 Then Jesus told his disciples a parable to show them that they should
always pray and not give up.[i] **2**He
said: "In a certain town there was a
judge who neither feared God nor
cared about men. **3**And there was a
widow in that town who kept coming
to him with the plea, 'Grant me justice[j] against my adversary.'
4"For some time he refused. But finally he said to himself, 'Even though
I don't fear God or care about men,
5yet because this widow keeps bothering me, I will see that she gets justice,
so that she won't eventually wear me
out with her coming!' "[k]
6And the Lord[l] said, "Listen to
what the unjust judge says. **7**And will
not God bring about justice for his chosen ones, who cry out[m] to him day and
night? Will he keep putting them off? **8**I

17:11 [i]Lk 9:51; [j]Lk 9:51,52; Jn 4:3,4
17:12 [k]Mt 8:2; [l]Lev 13:45,46
17:13 [m]Lk 5:5
17:14 [n]Lev 14:2; Mt 8:4
17:15 [o]Mt 9:8
17:16 [p]Mt 10:5
17:19 [q]Mt 9:22
17:20 [r]Mt 3:2
17:21 [s]ver 23
17:22 [t]Mt 8:20; [u]Mt 9:15; Lk 5:35
17:23 [v]Mt 24:23; Mk 13:21; Lk 21:8
17:24 [w]Mt 24:27
17:25 [x]Mt 16:21; [y]Lk 9:22; 18:32; [z]Mk 13:30; Lk 21:32
17:26 [a]Ge 7:6-24
17:28 [b]Ge 19:1-28
17:30 [c]Mt 10:23; 16:27; 24:3,27, 37,39; 25:31; 1Co 1:7; 1Th 2:19; 2Th 1:7; 2:8; 2Pe 3:4; Rev 1:7
17:31 [d]Mt 24:17,18; Mk 13:15-16
17:32 [e]Ge 19:26
17:33 [f]Jn 12:25
17:35 [g]Mt 24:41
17:37 [h]Mt 24:28
18:1 [i]Isa 40:31; Lk 11:5-8; Ac 1:14; Ro 12:12; Eph 6:18; Col 4:2; 1Th 5:17
18:3 [j]Isa 1:17
18:5 [k]Lk 11:8
18:6 [l]Lk 7:13
18:7 [m]Ex 22:23; Ps 88:1; Rev 6:10

a *12* The Greek word was used for various diseases affecting the skin—not necessarily leprosy. **b** *21* Or *among* **c** *24* Some manuscripts do not have *in his day.*
d *35* Some manuscripts *left.* *36Two men will be in the field; one will be taken and the other left.*

18:1-8

PROMISE **1**

PERSISTENCE PAYS OFF

How are you to respond when you've prayed for something and God hasn't answered? With this parable, Jesus urges us to keep on praying.

Jesus sets up the comparison between God and this unjust judge to prove a point, and to encourage his listeners. God, the almighty being who knows us from before birth and who cares for us as his own children, is infinitely more inclined to hear and answer us than this judge, who "neither feared God nor cared about man."

God is not like the judge in this parable. He is not, as some religious philosophers have asserted, an uncaring, apathetic entity who sits in his heaven and looks down on us with contempt. Rather, God hears and answers prayer in his time, and his answers are always a part of his master plan for our lives.

For the next Promise 1 reading go to page 1151.

tell you, he will see that they get justice, and quickly. However, when the Son of Man[n] comes,[o] will he find faith on the earth?"

The Parable of the Pharisee and the Tax Collector

9To some who were confident of their own righteousness[p] and looked down on everybody else,[q] Jesus told this parable: **10**"Two men went up to the temple to pray,[r] one a Pharisee and the other a tax collector. **11**The Pharisee stood up[s] and prayed about[a] himself: 'God, I thank you that I am not like other men—robbers, evildoers, adulterers—or even like this tax collector. **12**I fast[t] twice a week and give a tenth[u] of all I get.'

13"But the tax collector stood at a distance. He would not even look up to heaven, but beat his breast[v] and said, 'God, have mercy on me, a sinner.'[w]

14"I tell you that this man, rather than the other, went home justified before God. For everyone who exalts himself will be humbled, and he who humbles himself will be exalted."[x]

The Little Children and Jesus

›See Matthew 19:13–15; Mark 10:13–16

15People were also bringing babies to Jesus to have him touch them. When the disciples saw this, they rebuked them. **16**But Jesus called the children to him and said, "Let the little children come to me, and do not hinder them, for the kingdom of God belongs to such as these. **17**I tell you the truth, anyone who will not receive the kingdom of God like a little child[y] will never enter it."

The Rich Ruler

›See Matthew 19:16–29; Mark 10:17–30

18A certain ruler asked him, "Good teacher, what must I do to inherit eternal life?"[z]

19"Why do you call me good?" Jesus answered. "No one is good—except God alone. **20**You know the commandments: 'Do not commit adultery, do not murder, do not steal, do not give false testimony, honor your father and mother.'[b]"[a]

21"All these I have kept since I was a boy," he said.

7 →PG. 1150

22When Jesus heard this, he said to him, "You still lack one thing. Sell everything you have and give to the poor,[b] and you will have treasure in heaven.[c] Then come, follow me."

23When he heard this, he became very sad, because he was a man of great wealth. **24**Jesus looked at him and said, "How hard it is for the rich to enter the kingdom of God![d] **25**Indeed, it is easier for a camel to go through the eye of a needle than for a rich man to enter the kingdom of God."

26Those who heard this asked, "Who then can be saved?"

27Jesus replied, "What is impossible with men is possible with God."[e]

28Peter said to him, "We have left all we had to follow you!"[f]

29"I tell you the truth," Jesus said to them, "no one who has left home or wife or brothers or parents or children for the sake of the kingdom of God **30**will fail to receive many times as much in this age and, in the age to come,[g] eternal life."[h]

Jesus Again Predicts His Death

›See Matthew 20:17–19; Mark 10:32–34

31Jesus took the Twelve aside and told them, "We are going up to Jerusalem,[i] and everything that is written by the prophets[j] about the Son of Man[k] will be fulfilled. **32**He will be handed over to the Gentiles.[l] They will mock him, insult him, spit on him, flog him[m] and kill him.[n] **33**On the third day[o] he will rise again."[p]

34The disciples did not understand any of this. Its meaning was hidden from them, and they did not know what he was talking about.[q]

A Blind Beggar Receives His Sight

›See Matthew 20:29–34; Mark 10:46–52

35As Jesus approached Jericho,[r] a blind man was sitting by the roadside begging. **36**When he heard the crowd going by, he asked what was happening. **37**They told him, "Jesus of Nazareth is passing by."[s]

38He called out, "Jesus, Son of David,[t] have mercy[u] on me!"

39Those who led the way rebuked him and told him to be quiet, but he shouted all the more, "Son of David, have mercy on me!"[v]

40Jesus stopped and ordered the man to be brought to him. When he came near, Jesus asked him, **41**"What do you want me to do for you?"

"Lord, I want to see," he replied.

42Jesus said to him, "Receive your sight; your faith has healed you."[w] **43**Immediately he received his sight and followed Jesus, praising God. When all the people saw it, they also praised God.[x]

18:8 [n]Mt 8:20 [o]Mt 16:27
18:9 [p]Lk 16:15 [q]Isa 65:5
18:10 [r]Ac 3:1
18:11 [s]Mt 6:5; Mk 11:25
18:12 [t]Isa 58:3; Mt 9:14 [u]Mal 3:8; Lk 11:42
18:13 [v]Isa 66:2; Jer 31:19; Lk 23:48 [w]Lk 5:32; 1Ti 1:15
18:14 [x]Mt 23:12; Lk 14:11
18:17 [y]Mt 11:25; 18:3
18:18 [z]Lk 10:25
18:20 [a]Ex 20:12-16; Dt 5:16-20; Ro 13:9
18:22 [b]Ac 2:45 [c]Mt 6:20
18:24 [d]Pr 11:28
18:27 [e]Mt 19:26
18:28 [f]Mt 4:19
18:30 [g]Mt 12:32 [h]Mt 25:46
18:31 [i]Lk 9:51 [j]Ps 22; Isa 53 [k]Mt 8:20
18:32 [l]Lk 23:1 [m]Mt 16:21 [n]Ac 2:23
18:33 [o]Mt 16:21 [p]Mt 16:21
18:34 [q]Mk 9:32; Lk 9:45
18:35 [r]Lk 19:1
18:37 [s]Lk 19:4
18:38 [t]ver 39; Mt 9:27 [u]Mt 17:15; Lk 18:13
18:39 [v]ver 38
18:42 [w]Mt 9:22
18:43 [x]Mt 9:8; Lk 13:17

[a]*11* Or *to* [b]*20* Exodus 20:12-16; Deut. 5:16-20

Zacchaeus the Tax Collector

19 Jesus entered Jericho[y] and was passing through. 2A man was there by the name of Zacchaeus; he was a chief tax collector and was wealthy. 3He wanted to see who Jesus was, but being a short man he could not, because of the crowd. 4So he ran ahead and climbed a sycamore-fig[z] tree to see him, since Jesus was coming that way.[a]

5When Jesus reached the spot, he looked up and said to him, "Zacchaeus, come down immediately. I must stay at your house today." 6So he came down at once and welcomed him gladly.

3 →PG. 1149

7All the people saw this and began to mutter, "He has gone to be the guest of a 'sinner.' "[b]

8But Zacchaeus stood up and said to the Lord,[c] "Look, Lord! Here and now I give half of my possessions to the poor, and if I have cheated anybody out of anything,[d] I will pay back four times the amount."[e]

9Jesus said to him, "Today salvation has come to this house, because this man, too, is a son of Abraham.[f] 10For the Son of Man came to seek and to save what was lost."[g]

The Parable of the Ten Minas

11While they were listening to this, he went on to tell them a parable, because he was near Jerusalem and the people thought that the kingdom of God[h] was going to appear at once.[i] 12He said: "A man of noble birth went to a distant country to have himself appointed king and then to return. 13So he called ten of his servants[j] and gave them ten minas.[a] 'Put this money to work,' he said, 'until I come back.'

14"But his subjects hated him and sent a delegation after him to say, 'We don't want this man to be our king.'

15"He was made king, however, and returned home. Then he sent for the servants to whom he had given the money, in order to find out what they had gained with it.

16"The first one came and said, 'Sir, your mina has earned ten more.'

17" 'Well done, my good servant!'[k] his master replied. 'Because you have been trustworthy in a very small matter, take charge of ten cities.'[l]

18"The second came and said, 'Sir, your mina has earned five more.'

19"His master answered, 'You take charge of five cities.'

20"Then another servant came and said, 'Sir, here is your mina; I have kept it laid away in a piece of cloth. 21I was afraid of you, because you are a hard man. You take out what you did not put in and reap what you did not sow.'[m]

22"His master replied, 'I will judge you by your own words,[n] you wicked servant! You knew, did you, that I am a hard man, taking out what I did not put in, and reaping what I did not sow?[o] 23Why then didn't you put my money on deposit, so that when I came back, I could have collected it with interest?'

24"Then he said to those standing by, 'Take his mina away from him and give it to the one who has ten minas.'

25" 'Sir,' they said, 'he already has ten!'

26"He replied, 'I tell you that to everyone who has, more will be given, but as for the one who has nothing, even what he has will be taken away.[p] 27But those enemies of mine who did not want me to be king over them—bring them here and kill them in front of me.' "

The Triumphal Entry

>See Matthew 21:1–9; Mark 11:1–10; John 12:12–15

28After Jesus had said this, he went on ahead, going up to Jerusalem.[q] 29As he approached Bethphage and Bethany[r] at the hill called the Mount of Olives,[s] he sent two of his disciples, saying to them, 30"Go to the village ahead of you, and as you enter it, you will find a colt tied there, which no one has ever ridden. Untie it and bring it here. 31If anyone asks you, 'Why are you untying it?' tell him, 'The Lord needs it.' "

32Those who were sent ahead went and found it just as he had told them.[t] 33As they were untying the colt, its owners asked them, "Why are you untying the colt?"

34They replied, "The Lord needs it."

35They brought it to Jesus, threw their cloaks on the colt and put Jesus on it. 36As he went along, people spread their cloaks[u] on the road.

37When he came near the place where the road goes down the Mount of Olives,[v] the whole crowd of disciples began joyfully to praise God in loud voices for all the miracles they had seen:

38"Blessed is the king who comes in
the name of the Lord!"[b][w]

"Peace in heaven and glory in the
highest!"[x]

a *13* A mina was about three months' wages.
b *38* Psalm 118:26

19:1 y Lk 18:35 **19:4** z 1Ki 10:27; 1Ch 27:28; Isa 9:10 a Lk 18:37 **19:7** b Mt 9:11 **19:8** c Lk 7:13 d Lk 3:12,13 e Ex 22:1; Lev 6:4,5; Nu 5:7; 2Sa 12:6 **19:9** f Lk 3:8; 13:16; Ro 4:16; Gal 3:7 **19:10** g Eze 34:12,16; Jn 3:17 **19:11** h Mt 3:2 i Lk 17:20; Ac 1:6 **19:13** j Mk 13:34 **19:17** k Pr 27:18 l Lk 16:10 **19:21** m Mt 25:24 **19:22** n 2Sa 1:16; Job 15:6 o Mt 25:26 **19:26** p Mt 13:12; 25:29; Lk 8:18 **19:28** q Mk 10:32; Lk 9:51 **19:29** r Mt 21:17 s Mt 21:1 **19:32** t Lk 22:13 **19:36** u 2Ki 9:13 **19:37** v Mt 21:1 **19:38** w Ps 118:26; Lk 13:35 x Lk 2:14

39 Some of the Pharisees in the crowd
said to Jesus, "Teacher, rebuke your
disciples!"[y]
40 "I tell you," he replied, "if they
keep quiet, the stones will cry out."[z]
41 As he approached Jerusalem and
saw the city, he wept over it[a] 42 and
said, "If you, even you, had only known
on this day what would bring you
peace—but now it is hidden from your
eyes. 43 The days will come upon you
when your enemies will build an em-
bankment against you and encircle
you and hem you in on every side.[b]
44 They will dash you to the ground, you
and the children within your walls.[c]
They will not leave one stone on another,[d] because you did not recognize the
time of God's coming[e] to you."

Jesus at the Temple

›See Matthew 21:12–16; Mark 11:15–18; John 2:13–16

45 Then he entered the temple area
and began driving out those who were
selling. 46 "It is written," he said to
them, " 'My house will be a house of
prayer'[a];[f] but you have made it 'a
den of robbers.'[b] "[g]
47 Every day he was teaching at the
temple.[h] But the chief priests, the
teachers of the law and the leaders
among the people were trying to kill
him.[i] 48 Yet they could not find any
way to do it, because all the people
hung on his words.

The Authority of Jesus Questioned

›See Matthew 21:23–27; Mark 11:27–33

20 One day as he was teaching the
people in the temple courts[j] and
preaching the gospel,[k] the chief
priests and the teachers of the law, together with the elders, came up to him.
2 "Tell us by what authority you are doing these things," they said. "Who gave
you this authority?"[l]
3 He replied, "I will also ask you a
question. Tell me, 4 John's baptism[m]—
was it from heaven, or from men?"
5 They discussed it among themselves and said, "If we say, 'From heav-
en,' he will ask, 'Why didn't you believe
him?' 6 But if we say, 'From men,' all
the people[n] will stone us, because
they are persuaded that John was a
prophet."[o]
7 So they answered, "We don't know
where it was from."
8 Jesus said, "Neither will I tell you
by what authority I am doing these
things."

19:39 [y]Mt 21:15,16 **19:40** [z]Hab 2:11 **19:41** [a]Isa 22:4; Lk 13:34,35 **19:43** [b]Isa 29:3; Jer 6:6; Eze 4:2; 26:8; Lk 21:20 **19:44** [c]Ps 137:9 [d]Mt 24:2; Mk 13:2; Lk 21:6 [e]1Pe 2:12 **19:46** [f]Isa 56:7 [g]Jer 7:11 **19:47** [h]Mt 26:55 [i]Mt 12:14; Mk 11:18 **20:1** [j]Mt 26:55 [k]Lk 8:1 **20:2** [l]Jn 2:18; Ac 4:7; 7:27 **20:4** [m]Mk 1:4 **20:6** [n]Lk 7:29 [o]Mt 11:9

The Parable of the Tenants

›See Matthew 21:33–46; Mark 12:1–12

9 He went on to tell the people this
parable: "A man planted a vineyard,[p]
rented it to some farmers and went
away for a long time.[q] 10 At harvest
time he sent a servant to the tenants
so they would give him some of the
fruit of the vineyard. But the tenants
beat him and sent him away empty-
handed. 11 He sent another servant, but
that one also they beat and treated
shamefully and sent away empty-
handed. 12 He sent still a third, and they
wounded him and threw him out.
13 "Then the owner of the vineyard
said, 'What shall I do? I will send my
son, whom I love;[r] perhaps they will
respect him.'
14 "But when the tenants saw him,
they talked the matter over. 'This is the
heir,' they said. 'Let's kill him, and the
inheritance will be ours.' 15 So they
threw him out of the vineyard and
killed him.
"What then will the owner of the
vineyard do to them? 16 He will come
and kill those tenants[s] and give the
vineyard to others."
When the people heard this, they
said, "May this never be!"
17 Jesus looked directly at them and
asked, "Then what is the meaning of
that which is written:

" 'The stone the builders rejected
has become the capstone[c]'[d]?[t]

18 Everyone who falls on that stone will
be broken to pieces, but he on whom it
falls will be crushed."[u]
19 The teachers of the law and the
chief priests looked for a way to arrest
him[v] immediately, because they knew
he had spoken this parable against
them. But they were afraid of the people.[w]

Paying Taxes to Caesar

›See Matthew 22:15–22; Mark 12:13–17

20 Keeping a close watch on him,
they sent spies, who pretended to be
honest. They hoped to catch Jesus in
something he said[x] so that they might
hand him over to the power and authority of the governor.[y] 21 So the spies
questioned him: "Teacher, we know
that you speak and teach what is right,
and that you do not show partiality but
teach the way of God in accordance
with the truth.[z] 22 Is it right for us to
pay taxes to Caesar or not?"
23 He saw through their duplicity and

20:9 [p]Isa 5:1-7 [q]Mt 25:14 **20:13** [r]Mt 3:17 **20:16** [s]Lk 19:27 **20:17** [t]Ps 118:22; Ac 4:11 **20:18** [u]Isa 8:14,15 **20:19** [v]Lk 19:47 [w]Mk 11:18 **20:20** [x]Mt 12:10 [y]Mt 27:2 **20:21** [z]Jn 3:2

a *46* Isaiah 56:7 b *46* Jer. 7:11 c *17* Or *cornerstone* d *17* Psalm 118:22

said to them, 24“Show me a denarius. Whose portrait and inscription are on it?”

25“Caesar’s,” they replied.

He said to them, “Then give to Caesar what is Caesar’s,[a] and to God what is God’s.”

26They were unable to trap him in what he had said there in public. And astonished by his answer, they became silent.

The Resurrection and Marriage

›See Matthew 22:23–33; Mark 12:18–27

27Some of the Sadducees,[b] who say there is no resurrection,[c] came to Jesus with a question. 28“Teacher,” they said, “Moses wrote for us that if a man’s brother dies and leaves a wife but no children, the man must marry the widow and have children for his brother.[d] 29Now there were seven brothers. The first one married a woman and died childless. 30The second 31and then the third married her, and in the same way the seven died, leaving no children. 32Finally, the woman died too. 33Now then, at the resurrection whose wife will she be, since the seven were married to her?”

34Jesus replied, “The people of this age marry and are given in marriage. 35But those who are considered worthy of taking part in that age[e] and in the resurrection from the dead will neither marry nor be given in marriage, 36and they can no longer die; for they are like the angels. They are God’s children,[f] since they are children of the resurrection. 37But in the account of the bush, even Moses showed that the dead rise, for he calls the Lord ‘the God of Abraham, and the God of Isaac, and the God of Jacob.’[a][g] 38He is not the God of the dead, but of the living, for to him all are alive.”

39Some of the teachers of the law responded, “Well said, teacher!” 40And no one dared to ask him any more questions.[h]

Whose Son Is the Christ?

›See Matthew 22:41—23:7; Mark 12:35–40

41Then Jesus said to them, “How is it that they say the Christ[b] is the Son of David?[i] 42David himself declares in the Book of Psalms:

“ ‘The Lord said to my Lord:
“Sit at my right hand
43until I make your enemies
a footstool for your feet.” ’[c][j]

44David calls him ‘Lord.’ How then can he be his son?”

45While all the people were listening, Jesus said to his disciples, 46“Beware of the teachers of the law. They like to walk around in flowing robes and love to be greeted in the marketplaces and have the most important seats in the synagogues and the places of honor at banquets.[k] 47They devour widows’ houses and for a show make lengthy prayers. Such men will be punished most severely.”

The Widow’s Offering

›See Mark 12:41–44

21 As he looked up, Jesus saw the rich putting their gifts into the temple treasury.[l] 2He also saw a poor widow put in two very small copper coins.[d] 3“I tell you the truth,” he said, “this poor widow has put in more than all the others. 4All these people gave their gifts out of their wealth; but she out of her poverty put in all she had to live on.”[m]

5 →PG. 1164

Signs of the End of the Age

›See Matthew 24; Mark 13

5Some of his disciples were remarking about how the temple was adorned with beautiful stones and with gifts dedicated to God. But Jesus said, 6“As for what you see here, the time will come when not one stone will be left on another;[n] every one of them will be thrown down.”

7“Teacher,” they asked, “when will these things happen? And what will be the sign that they are about to take place?”

8He replied: “Watch out that you are not deceived. For many will come in my name, claiming, ‘I am he,’ and, ‘The time is near.’ Do not follow them.[o] 9When you hear of wars and revolutions, do not be frightened. These things must happen first, but the end will not come right away.”

10Then he said to them: “Nation will rise against nation, and kingdom against kingdom.[p] 11There will be great earthquakes, famines and pestilences in various places, and fearful events and great signs from heaven.[q]

12“But before all this, they will lay hands on you and persecute you. They will deliver you to synagogues and prisons, and you will be brought before kings and governors, and all on account of my name. 13This will result in your being witnesses to them.[r] 14But make up your mind not to worry beforehand how you will defend yourselves.[s] 15For I will give you[t] words

20:25 [a]Lk 23:2; Ro 13:7
20:27 [b]Ac 4:1 [c]Ac 23:8; 1Co 15:12
20:28 [d]Dt 25:5
20:35 [e]Mt 12:32
20:36 [f]Jn 1:12; 1Jn 3:1-2
20:37 [g]Ex 3:6
20:40 [h]Mt 22:46; Mk 12:34
20:41 [i]Mt 1:1
20:43 [j]Ps 110:1; Mt 22:44
20:46 [k]Lk 11:43
21:1 [l]Mt 27:6; Jn 8:20
21:4 [m]2Co 8:12
21:6 [n]Lk 19:44
21:8 [o]Lk 17:23
21:10 [p]2Ch 15:6; Isa 19:2
21:11 [q]Isa 29:6; Joel 2:30
21:13 [r]Php 1:12
21:14 [s]Lk 12:11
21:15 [t]Lk 12:12

a37 Exodus 3:6
b41 Or *Messiah*
c43 Psalm 110:1
d2 Greek *two lepta*

and wisdom that none of your adversaries will be able to resist or con-
tradict. 16You will be betrayed even
by parents, brothers, relatives and
friends,[u] and they will put some of
you to death. 17All men will hate you
because of me.[v] 18But not a hair of
your head will perish.[w] 19By standing
firm you will gain life.[x]

20"When you see Jerusalem being
surrounded by armies,[y] you will know
that its desolation is near. 21Then let
those who are in Judea flee to the
mountains, let those in the city get out,
and let those in the country not enter
the city.[z] 22For this is the time of punishment[a] in fulfillment[b] of all that
has been written. 23How dreadful it will
be in those days for pregnant women
and nursing mothers! There will be
great distress in the land and wrath
against this people. 24They will fall by
the sword and will be taken as prisoners to all the nations. Jerusalem will be
trampled[c] on by the Gentiles until the
times of the Gentiles are fulfilled.

25"There will be signs in the sun,
moon and stars. On the earth, nations
will be in anguish and perplexity at the
roaring and tossing of the sea.[d] 26Men
will faint from terror, apprehensive of
what is coming on the world, for the
heavenly bodies will be shaken.[e] 27At
that time they will see the Son of
Man[f] coming in a cloud[g] with power
and great glory. 28When these things
begin to take place, stand up and lift up
your heads, because your redemption
is drawing near."[h]

29He told them this parable: "Look at
the fig tree and all the trees. 30When
they sprout leaves, you can see for
yourselves and know that summer is
near. 31Even so, when you see these
things happening, you know that the
kingdom of God[i] is near.

32"I tell you the truth, this generation[a][j] will certainly not pass away
until all these things have happened.
3 →PG. 1162
33Heaven and earth will pass away, but
my words will never pass away.[k]

34"Be careful, or your hearts will be
weighed down with dissipation, drunkenness and the anxieties of life,[l] and
that day will close on you unexpectedly[m] like a trap. 35For it will come upon
all those who live on the face of the
whole earth. 36Be always on the watch,
and pray[n] that you may be able to escape all that is about to happen, and
that you may be able to stand before
the Son of Man."

37Each day Jesus was teaching at the
temple,[o] and each evening he went
out[p] to spend the night on the hill
called the Mount of Olives,[q] 38and all
the people came early in the morning
to hear him at the temple.[r]

Judas Agrees to Betray Jesus

›See Matthew 26:2–5; Mark 14:1–2,10–11

22 Now the Feast of Unleavened
Bread, called the Passover, was approaching,[s] 2and the chief priests and
the teachers of the law were looking for
some way to get rid of Jesus,[t] for they
were afraid of the people. 3Then Satan[u] entered Judas, called Iscariot,[v]
one of the Twelve. 4And Judas went
to the chief priests and the officers of
the temple guard[w] and discussed with
them how he might betray Jesus. 5They
were delighted and agreed to give him
money.[x] 6He consented, and watched
for an opportunity to hand Jesus over
to them when no crowd was present.

The Last Supper

›See Matthew 26:17–19,26–29;
Mark 14:12–16,22–25

7Then came the day of Unleavened
Bread on which the Passover lamb had
to be sacrificed.[y] 8Jesus sent Peter and
John,[z] saying, "Go and make preparations for us to eat the Passover."

9"Where do you want us to prepare
for it?" they asked.

10He replied, "As you enter the city,
a man carrying a jar of water will meet
you. Follow him to the house that he
enters, 11and say to the owner of the
house, 'The Teacher asks: Where is the
guest room, where I may eat the Passover with my disciples?' 12He will show
you a large upper room, all furnished.
Make preparations there."

13They left and found things just as
Jesus had told them.[a] So they prepared the Passover.

14When the hour came, Jesus and
his apostles[b] reclined at the table.[c]
15And he said to them, "I have eagerly
desired to eat this Passover with you
before I suffer.[d] 16For I tell you, I will
not eat it again until it finds fulfillment
in the kingdom of God."[e]

17After taking the cup, he gave
thanks and said, "Take this and divide
it among you. 18For I tell you I will not
drink again of the fruit of the vine until
the kingdom of God comes."

19And he took bread, gave thanks
and broke it,[f] and gave it to them,
saying, "This is my body given for you;
do this in remembrance of me."

20In the same way, after the supper
he took the cup, saying, "This cup is
the new covenant[g] in my blood,
which is poured out for you. 21But the

21:16 [u]Lk 12:52,53
21:17 [v]Jn 15:21
21:18 [w]Mt 10:30
21:19 [x]Mt 10:22
21:20 [y]Lk 19:43
21:21 [z]Lk 17:31
21:22 [a]Isa 63:4; Da 9:24-27; Hos 9:7 [b]Mt 1:22
21:24 [c]Isa 5:5; 63:18; Da 8:13; Rev 11:2
21:25 [d]2Pe 3:10,12
21:26 [e]Mt 24:29
21:27 [f]Mt 8:20 [g]Rev 1:7
21:28 [h]Lk 18:7
21:31 [i]Mt 3:2
21:32 [j]Lk 11:50; 17:25
21:33 [k]Mt 5:18
21:34 [l]Mk 4:19 [m]Lk 12:40,46; 1Th 5:2-7
21:36 [n]Mt 26:41
21:37 [o]Mt 26:55 [p]Mk 11:19 [q]Mt 21:1
21:38 [r]Jn 8:2
22:1 [s]Jn 11:55
22:2 [t]Mt 12:14
22:3 [u]Mt 4:10; Jn 13:2 [v]Mt 10:4
22:4 [w]ver 52; Ac 4:1; 5:24
22:5 [x]Zec 11:12
22:7 [y]Ex 12:18-20; Dt 16:5-8; Mk 14:12
22:8 [z]Ac 3:1,11; 4:13,19; 8:14
22:13 [a]Lk 19:32
22:14 [b]Mk 6:30 [c]Mt 26:20; Mk 14:17,18
22:15 [d]Mt 16:21
22:16 [e]Lk 14:15; Rev 19:9
22:19 [f]Mt 14:19
22:20 [g]Ex 24:8; Isa 42:6; Jer 31:31-34; Zec 9:11; 2Co 3:6; Heb 8:6; 9:15

[a]32 Or *race*

hand of him who is going to betray me is with mine on the table.[h] 22 The Son of Man[i] will go as it has been decreed,[j] but woe to that man who betrays him." 23 They began to question among themselves which of them it might be who would do this.

24 Also a dispute arose among them as to which of them was considered to be greatest.[k] 25 Jesus said to them, "The kings of the Gentiles lord it over them; and those who exercise authority over them call themselves Benefactors. 26 But you are not to be like that. Instead, the greatest among you should be like the youngest,[l] and the one who rules like the one who serves.[m] 27 For who is greater, the one who is at the table or the one who serves? Is it not the one who is at the table? But I am among you as one who serves.[n] 28 You are those who have stood by me in my trials. 29 And I confer on you a kingdom,[o] just as my Father conferred one on me, 30 so that you may eat and drink at my table in my kingdom[p] and sit on thrones, judging the twelve tribes of Israel.[q]

4 →PG. 1160
7 →PG. 1154

31 "Simon, Simon, Satan has asked[r] to sift you[a] as wheat.[s] 32 But I have prayed for you,[t] Simon, that your faith may not fail. And when you have turned back, strengthen your brothers."[u]

2 →PG. 1153

33 But he replied, "Lord, I am ready to go with you to prison and to death."[v]

34 Jesus answered, "I tell you, Peter, before the rooster crows today, you will deny three times that you know me."

35 Then Jesus asked them, "When I sent you without purse, bag or sandals,[w] did you lack anything?"

"Nothing," they answered.

36 He said to them, "But now if you have a purse, take it, and also a bag; and if you don't have a sword, sell your cloak and buy one. 37 It is written: 'And he was numbered with the transgressors'[b];[x] and I tell you that this must be fulfilled in me. Yes, what is written about me is reaching its fulfillment."

38 The disciples said, "See, Lord, here are two swords."

"That is enough," he replied.

Jesus Prays on the Mount of Olives

›See Matthew 26:36–46; Mark 14:32–42

39 Jesus went out as usual[y] to the Mount of Olives,[z] and his disciples followed him. 40 On reaching the place, he said to them, "Pray that you will not fall into temptation."[a] 41 He withdrew about a stone's throw beyond them, knelt down[b] and prayed, 42 "Father, if you are willing, take this cup[c] from me; yet not my will, but yours be done."[d] 43 An angel from heaven appeared to him and strengthened him.[e] 44 And being in anguish, he prayed more earnestly, and his sweat was like drops of blood falling to the ground.[c]

45 When he rose from prayer and went back to the disciples, he found them asleep, exhausted from sorrow. 46 "Why are you sleeping?" he asked them. "Get up and pray so that you will not fall into temptation."[f]

Jesus Arrested

›See Matthew 26:47–56; Mark 14:43–50; John 18:3–11

47 While he was still speaking a crowd came up, and the man who was called Judas, one of the Twelve, was leading them. He approached Jesus to kiss him, 48 but Jesus asked him, "Judas, are you betraying the Son of Man with a kiss?"

49 When Jesus' followers saw what was going to happen, they said, "Lord, should we strike with our swords?"[g] 50 And one of them struck the servant of the high priest, cutting off his right ear.

51 But Jesus answered, "No more of this!" And he touched the man's ear and healed him.

52 Then Jesus said to the chief priests, the officers of the temple guard,[h] and the elders, who had come for him, "Am I leading a rebellion, that you have come with swords and clubs? 53 Every day I was with you in the temple courts,[i] and you did not lay a hand on me. But this is your hour[j]—when darkness reigns."[k]

Peter Disowns Jesus

›See Matthew 26:69–75; Mark 14:66–72; John 18:16–18,25–27

54 Then seizing him, they led him away and took him into the house of the high priest.[l] Peter followed at a distance.[m] 55 But when they had kindled a fire in the middle of the courtyard and had sat down together, Peter sat down with them. 56 A servant girl saw him seated there in the firelight. She looked closely at him and said, "This man was with him."

57 But he denied it. "Woman, I don't know him," he said.

58 A little later someone else saw him and said, "You also are one of them."

"Man, I am not!" Peter replied.

59 About an hour later another as-

22:21 [h]Ps 41:9
22:22 [i]Mt 8:20 [j]Ac 2:23; 4:28
22:24 [k]Mk 9:34; Lk 9:46
22:26 [l]1Pe 5:5 [m]Mk 9:35; Lk 9:48
22:27 [n]Mt 20:28; Lk 12:37
22:29 [o]Mt 25:34; 2Ti 2:12
22:30 [p]Lk 14:15 [q]Mt 19:28
22:31 [r]Job 1:6-12 [s]Am 9:9
22:32 [t]Jn 17:9,15; Ro 8:34 [u]Jn 21:15-17
22:33 [v]Jn 11:16
22:35 [w]Mt 10:9,10; Lk 9:3; 10:4
22:37 [x]Isa 53:12
22:39 [y]Lk 21:37 [z]Mt 21:1
22:40 [a]Mt 6:13
22:41 [b]Lk 18:11
22:42 [c]Mt 20:22 [d]Mt 26:39
22:43 [e]Mt 4:11; Mk 1:13
22:46 [f]ver 40
22:49 [g]ver 38
22:52 [h]ver 4
22:53 [i]Mt 26:55 [j]Jn 12:27 [k]Mt 8:12; Jn 1:5; 3:20
22:54 [l]Mt 26:57; Mk 14:53 [m]Mt 26:58; Mk 14:54; Jn 18:15

a *31* The Greek is plural. b *37* Isaiah 53:12
c *44* Some early manuscripts do not have verses 43 and 44.

serted, "Certainly this fellow was with
him, for he is a Galilean."[n]
60 Peter replied, "Man, I don't know
what you're talking about!" Just as
he was speaking, the rooster crowed.
61 The Lord[o] turned and looked
straight at Peter. Then Peter remembered the word the Lord had spoken to
him: "Before the rooster crows today,
you will disown me three times."[p]
62 And he went outside and wept bitterly.

The Guards Mock Jesus

›See Matthew 26:67–68; Mark 14:65; John 18:22–23

63 The men who were guarding Jesus
began mocking and beating him.
64 They blindfolded him and demanded, "Prophesy! Who hit you?" 65 And
they said many other insulting things
to him.[q]

Jesus Before Pilate and Herod

›See Matthew 26:63–66; Mark 14:61–63; John 18:19–21

66 At daybreak the council[r] of the
elders of the people, both the chief
priests and teachers of the law, met together,[s] and Jesus was led before
them. 67 "If you are the Christ,[a]" they
said, "tell us."
Jesus answered, "If I tell you, you
will not believe me, 68 and if I asked
you, you would not answer.[t] 69 But
from now on, the Son of Man will be
seated at the right hand of the mighty
God."[u]
70 They all asked, "Are you then the
Son of God?"[v]
He replied, "You are right in saying
I am."[w]
71 Then they said, "Why do we need
any more testimony? We have heard it
from his own lips."

23 Then the whole assembly rose and
led him off to Pilate.[x] 2 And they
began to accuse him, saying, "We have
found this man subverting our nation.[y] He opposes payment of taxes to
Caesar[z] and claims to be Christ,[b] a
king."[a]
3 So Pilate asked Jesus, "Are you the
king of the Jews?"
"Yes, it is as you say," Jesus replied.
4 Then Pilate announced to the chief
priests and the crowd, "I find no basis
for a charge against this man."[b]
5 But they insisted, "He stirs up the
people all over Judea[c] by his teaching.
He started in Galilee[c] and has come
all the way here."
6 On hearing this, Pilate asked if the
man was a Galilean.[d] 7 When he
learned that Jesus was under Herod's
jurisdiction, he sent him to Herod,[e]
who was also in Jerusalem at that time.
8 When Herod saw Jesus, he was
greatly pleased, because for a long time
he had been wanting to see him.[f]
From what he had heard about him, he

22:59 [n]Lk 23:6
22:61 [o]Lk 7:13 [p]ver 34
22:65 [q]Mt 16:21
22:66 [r]Mt 5:22 [s]Mt 27:1; Mk 15:1
22:68 [t]Lk 20:3-8
22:69 [u]Mk 16:19
22:70 [v]Mt 4:3 [w]Mt 27:11; Lk 23:3
23:1 [x]Mt 27:2; Mk 15:1; Jn 18:28
23:2 [y]ver 14 [z]Lk 20:22 [a]Jn 19:12
23:4 [b]ver 14,22,41; Mt 27:23; Jn 18:38; 1Ti 6:13; 2Co 5:21
23:5 [c]Mk 1:14
23:6 [d]Lk 22:59
23:7 [e]Mt 14:1; Lk 3:1
23:8 [f]Lk 9:9

a 67 Or *Messiah* b 2 Or *Messiah;* also in verses 35 and 39 c 5 Or *over the land of the Jews*

22:54–62

PROMISE 1

PETER DOES THE UNTHINKABLE

It was the sin Peter thought he would never commit (Matthew 26:31–35). Yet, in direct opposition to his bold and self-confident oath, in this passage Peter denied that he ever even knew who Jesus was. And in this scene, one that has gone down through the years as one of history's most unthinkable, Peter disavowed his Lord not once, not twice, but three times over.

Have you ever wondered what Peter thought after the first denial? Did he look around hoping none of his friends had heard him lie? Did he promise himself it wouldn't happen again?

Of course, he did deny that he knew the Lord two more times. But the third and final denial was different from the others. Aside from being Peter's most emphatic denial, this one was accompanied by a rooster's crow and a look from Jesus. From across the courtyard, the eyes of these two men locked. While Jesus' gaze was probably short-lived, it was long enough to send Peter's world crashing down around him. In that instant Peter not only saw the emotion in Jesus' eyes, but he also became convicted of the gravity of his sin. Overcome with grief, Peter walked away from the crowd, went outside the courtyard and "wept bitterly."

Have you ever found yourself committing a sin you thought you were incapable of committing? Have you ever done something that you believe God could never forgive you for? Let Peter's story be your guide for responding to such sins. The process of forgiveness begins with realizing that you've sinned and confessing that sin to God.

Jesus not only forgave Peter, he continued to use him greatly (see John 21:15–19 and Acts 2:14–41). Each one of us is guilty of sinning against God, but that doesn't make us worthless in his sight. God sent his Son Jesus to come to earth, to die and to be raised again so that sin would no longer have any power over us. There's no sin that can disable God's love for us or his desire that we turn to him in repentance.

For the next Promise 1 reading go to page 1158.

hoped to see him perform some miracle. 9He plied him with many questions, but Jesus gave him no answer.[g]
10The chief priests and the teachers of
the law were standing there, vehemently accusing him. 11Then Herod
and his soldiers ridiculed and mocked
him. Dressing him in an elegant
robe,[h] they sent him back to Pilate.
12That day Herod and Pilate became
friends[i]—before this they had been
enemies.

13Pilate called together the chief
priests, the rulers and the people,
14and said to them, "You brought me
this man as one who was inciting the
people to rebellion. I have examined
him in your presence and have found
no basis for your charges against
him.[j] 15Neither has Herod, for he sent
him back to us; as you can see, he
has done nothing to deserve death.
16Therefore, I will punish him[k] and
then release him.[a]"

18With one voice they cried out,
"Away with this man! Release Barabbas
to us!"[l] 19(Barabbas had been thrown
into prison for an insurrection in the
city, and for murder.)

20Wanting to release Jesus, Pilate appealed to them again. 21But they kept
shouting, "Crucify him! Crucify him!"

22For the third time he spoke to
them: "Why? What crime has this man
committed? I have found in him no
grounds for the death penalty. Therefore I will have him punished and then
release him."[m]

23But with loud shouts they insis-
tently demanded that he be crucified,
and their shouts prevailed. 24So Pilate
decided to grant their demand. 25He
released the man who had been
thrown into prison for insurrection
and murder, the one they asked for,
and surrendered Jesus to their will.

The Crucifixion

›See Matthew 27:33–44; Mark 15:22–32;
John 19:17–24

26As they led him away, they seized
Simon from Cyrene,[n] who was on his
way in from the country, and put the
cross on him and made him carry it
behind Jesus.[o] 27A large number of
people followed him, including women
who mourned and wailed[p] for him.
28Jesus turned and said to them,
"Daughters of Jerusalem, do not weep
for me; weep for yourselves and for
your children.[q] 29For the time will
come when you will say, 'Blessed are
the barren women, the wombs that
never bore and the breasts that never
nursed!'[r] 30Then

" 'they will say to the mountains,
"Fall on us!"
and to the hills, "Cover us!" '[b][s]

31For if men do these things when the
tree is green, what will happen when it
is dry?"[t]

32Two other men, both criminals,
were also led out with him to be executed.[u] 33When they came to the
place called the Skull, there they crucified him, along with the criminals—
one on his right, the other on his left.
34Jesus said, "Father,[v] forgive them,
for they do not know what they are doing."[c][w] And they divided up his
clothes by casting lots.[x]

35The people stood watching, and
the rulers even sneered at him.[y] They
said, "He saved others; let him save
himself if he is the Christ of God, the
Chosen One."[z]

36The soldiers also came up and
mocked him.[a] They offered him wine
vinegar[b] 37and said, "If you are the
king of the Jews,[c] save yourself."

38There was a written notice above
him, which read: THIS IS THE KING OF THE
JEWS.[d]

39One of the criminals who hung
there hurled insults at him: "Aren't you
the Christ? Save yourself and us!"[e]

40But the other criminal rebuked
him. "Don't you fear God," he said,
"since you are under the same sentence? 41We are punished justly, for we
are getting what our deeds deserve. But
this man has done nothing wrong."[f]

42Then he said, "Jesus, remember
me when you come into your kingdom.[d]"[g]

43Jesus answered him, "I tell you the
truth, today you will be with me in paradise."[h]

Jesus' Death

›See Matthew 27:45–56; Mark 15:33–41;
John 19:29–30

44It was now about the sixth hour,
and darkness came over the whole
land until the ninth hour,[i] 45for the
sun stopped shining. And the curtain
of the temple[j] was torn in two.[k]
46Jesus called out with a loud voice,[l]
"Father, into your hands I commit my
spirit."[m] When he had said this, he
breathed his last.[n]

47The centurion, seeing what had
happened, praised God[o] and said,
"Surely this was a righteous man."
48When all the people who had gath-

23:9 [g]Mk 14:61
23:11 [h]Mk 15:17-19; Jn 19:2,3
23:12 [i]Ac 4:27
23:14 [j]ver 4
23:16 [k]ver 22; Mt 27:26; Jn 19:1; Ac 16:37; 2Co 11:23,24
23:18 [l]Ac 3:13,14
23:22 [m]ver 16
23:26 [n]Mt 27:32 [o]Mk 15:21; Jn 19:17
23:27 [p]Lk 8:52
23:28 [q]Lk 19:41-44; 21:23,24
23:29 [r]Mt 24:19
23:30 [s]Hos 10:8; Isa 2:19; Rev 6:16
23:31 [t]Eze 20:47
23:32 [u]Isa 53:12; Mt 27:38; Mk 15:27; Jn 19:18
23:34 [v]Mt 11:25 [w]Mt 5:44 [x]Ps 22:18
23:35 [y]Ps 22:17 [z]Isa 42:1
23:36 [a]Ps 22:7 [b]Ps 69:21; Mt 27:48
23:37 [c]Lk 4:3,9
23:38 [d]Mt 2:2
23:39 [e]ver 35,37
23:41 [f]ver 4
23:42 [g]Mt 16:27
23:43 [h]2Co 12:3,4; Rev 2:7
23:44 [i]Am 8:9
23:45 [j]Ex 26:31-33; Heb 9:3,8 [k]Heb 10:19,20
23:46 [l]Mt 27:50 [m]Ps 31:5; 1Pe 2:23 [n]Jn 19:30
23:47 [o]Mt 9:8

a *16* Some manuscripts *him." 17Now he was obliged to release one man to them at the Feast.*
b *30* Hosea 10:8
c *34* Some early manuscripts do not have this sentence.
d *42* Some manuscripts *come with your kingly power*

ered to witness this sight saw what took
place, they beat their breasts[p] and
went away. **49**But all those who knew
him, including the women who had
followed him from Galilee,[q] stood at a
distance,[r] watching these things.

Jesus' Burial

›See Matthew 27:57–61; Mark 15:42–47;
John 19:38–42

50Now there was a man named Joseph, a member of the Council, a good
and upright man, **51**who had not consented to their decision and action. He
came from the Judean town of Arimathea and he was waiting for the kingdom of God.[s] **52**Going to Pilate, he
asked for Jesus' body. **53**Then he took it
down, wrapped it in linen cloth and
placed it in a tomb cut in the rock, one
in which no one had yet been laid. **54**It
was Preparation Day,[t] and the Sabbath was about to begin.

55The women who had come with
Jesus from Galilee[u] followed Joseph
and saw the tomb and how his body
was laid in it. **56**Then they went home
and prepared spices and perfumes.[v]
But they rested on the Sabbath in obedience to the commandment.[w]

The Resurrection

›See Matthew 28:1–8; Mark 16:1–8; John 20:1–8

24 On the first day of the week, very
early in the morning, the women
took the spices they had prepared[x]
and went to the tomb. **2**They found the
stone rolled away from the tomb, **3**but
when they entered, they did not find
the body of the Lord Jesus.[y] **4**While
they were wondering about this, suddenly two men in clothes that gleamed
like lightning[z] stood beside them. **5**In
their fright the women bowed down
with their faces to the ground, but the
men said to them, "Why do you look
for the living among the dead? **6**He is
not here; he has risen! Remember how
he told you, while he was still with you
in Galilee:[a] **7**'The Son of Man[b] must
be delivered into the hands of sinful
men, be crucified and on the third day
be raised again.' "[c] **8**Then they remembered his words.[d]

9When they came back from the
tomb, they told all these things to the
Eleven and to all the others. **10**It was
Mary Magdalene, Joanna, Mary the
mother of James, and the others with
them[e] who told this to the apostles.[f]
11But they did not believe[g] the wom-
en, because their words seemed to
them like nonsense. **12**Peter, however,
got up and ran to the tomb. Bending
over, he saw the strips of linen lying by
themselves,[h] and he went away,[i]
wondering to himself what had happened.

On the Road to Emmaus

13Now that same day two of them
were going to a village called Emmaus,
about seven miles[a] from Jerusalem.[j]
14They were talking with each other
about everything that had happened.
15As they talked and discussed these
things with each other, Jesus himself
came up and walked along with
them;[k] **16**but they were kept from recognizing him.[l]

17He asked them, "What are you discussing together as you walk along?"

They stood still, their faces downcast. **18**One of them, named Cleopas,[m]
asked him, "Are you only a visitor to
Jerusalem and do not know the things
that have happened there in these
days?"

19"What things?" he asked.

"About Jesus of Nazareth,"[n] they
replied. "He was a prophet,[o] powerful
in word and deed before God and all
the people. **20**The chief priests and our
rulers[p] handed him over to be sentenced to death, and they crucified
him; **21**but we had hoped that he was
the one who was going to redeem Israel.[q] And what is more, it is the third
day[r] since all this took place. **22**In addition, some of our women amazed
us.[s] They went to the tomb early this
morning **23**but didn't find his body.
They came and told us that they had
seen a vision of angels, who said he
was alive. **24**Then some of our companions went to the tomb and found it just
as the women had said, but him they
did not see."[t]

25He said to them, "How foolish you
are, and how slow of heart to believe all
that the prophets have spoken! **26**Did
not the Christ[b] have to suffer these
things and then enter his glory?"[u]
27And beginning with Moses[v] and all
the Prophets,[w] he explained to them
what was said in all the Scriptures concerning himself.[x]

2 →PG. 1159

28As they approached the village to
which they were going, Jesus acted as if
he were going farther. **29**But they urged
him strongly, "Stay with us, for it is
nearly evening; the day is almost over."
So he went in to stay with them.

30When he was at the table with
them, he took bread, gave thanks,
broke it[y] and began to give it to them.
31Then their eyes were opened and
they recognized him,[z] and he disap-

23:48 [p]Lk 18:13
23:49 [q]Lk 8:2 [r]Ps 38:11
23:51 [s]Lk 2:25,38
23:54 [t]Mt 27:62
23:55 [u]ver 49
23:56 [v]Mk 16:1; Lk 24:1 [w]Ex 12:16; 20:10
24:1 [x]Lk 23:56
24:3 [y]ver 23,24
24:4 [z]Jn 20:12
24:6 [a]Mt 17:22,23; Mk 9:30-31; Lk 9:22; 24:44
24:7 [b]Mt 8:20 [c]Mt 16:21
24:8 [d]Jn 2:22
24:10 [e]Lk 8:1-3 [f]Mk 6:30
24:11 [g]Mk 16:11
24:12 [h]Jn 20:3-7 [i]Jn 20:10
24:13 [j]Mk 16:12
24:15 [k]ver 36
24:16 [l]Jn 20:14; 21:4
24:18 [m]Jn 19:25
24:19 [n]Mk 1:24 [o]Mt 21:11
24:20 [p]Lk 23:13
24:21 [q]Lk 1:68; 2:38; 21:28 [r]Mt 16:21
24:22 [s]ver 1-10
24:24 [t]ver 12
24:26 [u]Heb 2:10; 1Pe 1:11
24:27 [v]Ge 3:15; Nu 21:9; Dt 18:15 [w]Isa 7:14; 9:6; 40:10,11; 53; Eze 34:23; Da 9:24; Mic 7:20; Mal 3:1 [x]Jn 1:45
24:30 [y]Mt 14:19
24:31 [z]ver 16

a *13* Greek *sixty stadia* (about 11 kilometers)
b *26* Or *Messiah*; also in verse 46

peared from their sight. 32They asked
each other, "Were not our hearts burning within us[a] while he talked with
us on the road and opened the Scriptures[b] to us?"
33They got up and returned at once
to Jerusalem. There they found the
Eleven and those with them, assembled together 34and saying, "It is true!
The Lord has risen and has appeared to
Simon."[c] 35Then the two told what
had happened on the way, and how
Jesus was recognized by them when he
broke the bread.[d]

Jesus Appears to the Disciples

36While they were still talking about
this, Jesus himself stood among them
and said to them, "Peace be with
you."[e]
37They were startled and frightened,
thinking they saw a ghost.[f] 38He said
to them, "Why are you troubled, and
why do doubts rise in your minds?
39Look at my hands and my feet. It is I
myself! Touch me and see;[g] a ghost
does not have flesh and bones, as you
see I have."
40When he had said this, he showed
them his hands and feet. 41And while
they still did not believe it because of
joy and amazement, he asked them,
"Do you have anything here to eat?"
42They gave him a piece of broiled fish,
43and he took it and ate it in their presence.[h]
44He said to them, "This is what I
told you while I was still with you:[i]
Everything must be fulfilled[j] that is
written about me in the Law of Moses,[k] the Prophets and the Psalms."[l]
45Then he opened their minds so
they could understand the Scriptures.
46He told them, "This is what is written: The Christ will suffer and rise from
the dead on the third day, 47and repentance and forgiveness of sins will be
preached in his name[m] to all nations,[n] beginning at Jerusalem. 48You
are witnesses[o] of these things. 49I am
going to send you what my Father has
promised;[p] but stay in the city until
you have been clothed with power
from on high."

7 →PG. 1159

The Ascension

50When he had led them out to the
vicinity of Bethany,[q] he lifted up his
hands and blessed them. 51While he
was blessing them, he left them and
was taken up into heaven.[r] 52Then
they worshiped him and returned to
Jerusalem with great joy. 53And they
stayed continually at the temple,[s]
praising God.

1 →PG. 1160

24:32 [a]Ps 39:3 [b]ver 27,45
24:34 [c]1Co 15:5
24:35 [d]ver 30,31
24:36 [e]Jn 20:19,21, 26; 14:27
24:37 [f]Mk 6:49
24:39 [g]Jn 20:27; 1Jn 1:1
24:43 [h]Ac 10:41
24:44 [i]Lk 9:45; 18:34 [j]Mt 16:21; Lk 9:22,44; 18:31-33; 22:37 [k]ver 27 [l]Ps 2; 16; 22; 69; 72; 110; 118
24:47 [m]Ac 5:31; 10:43; 13:38 [n]Mt 28:19
24:48 [o]Ac 1:8; 2:32; 5:32; 13:31; 1Pe 5:1
24:49 [p]Jn 14:16; Ac 1:4
24:50 [q]Mt 21:17
24:51 [r]2Ki 2:11
24:53 [s]Ac 2:46

JOHN

AT A GLANCE

Key Principle: The eternal Word has taken on flesh to become the Lamb of God who takes away the sin of the world; those who receive him become children of God and enjoy the gift of eternal life.

Author: John

Time and Place: ~6–4 B.C. to A.D. 33 / Perea, Galilee, Samaria, and Judea

Key Verses: 1:10–14; 3:16; 20:30–31

BENEFIT

Matthew, Mark and Luke are known collectively as the Synoptic ("seeing together") Gospels; they share a common viewpoint and similar material. John, on the other hand, is a supplemental gospel, providing a wealth of stories about and teachings of Jesus not found in the Synoptic Gospels. For example, the Synoptic Gospels focus on Christ's Galilean ministry, while John develops his Judean ministry.

John is, at the same time, the simplest and the most profound of the Gospels, and is the greatest evangelistic tool ever written. Rich in insights and application, this book rewards repeated reading and reflection.

SETTING

The two sons of Zebedee, John and James, together with Peter, formed the inner circle of Jesus' disciples. John was evidently "the disciple whom Jesus loved" (13:23; 20:2; 21:7, 20). He was also an eyewitness of the things recorded decades later in this Gospel, as evidenced by his detailed knowledge of Palestinian geography and his careful attention to names and to numbers (e.g., 2:6; 6:13, 19; 21:11). The author explicitly claims to be an eyewitness in 1:14, 19:35 and 21:24–25. As an apostle, John was one of the pillars of the church in Jerusalem; he spent his later years in Asia Minor. He evidently wrote this Gospel after the Synoptic Gospels, but before his three epistles and Revelation. If that is so, John probably wrote this book in the late 60s to the early 90s. Irenaeus, a second-century disciple of Polycarp who was in turn a disciple of John, was one of the many church fathers who attested that John authored this Gospel. Irenaeus also wrote that John lived until the time of the emperor Trajan (A.D. 98–117).

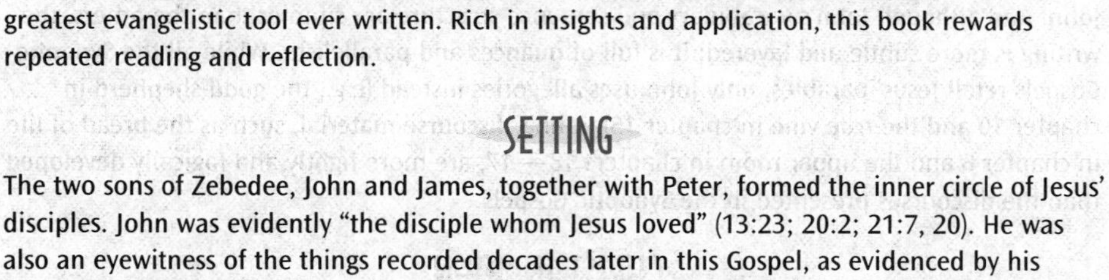

THEME AND PURPOSE

As topical narratives, each of the four Gospels approaches Christ's life from a different angle. Matthew presents him to Jewish readers as Israel's Messiah-King; Mark presents him to Roman readers as the Servant-Redeemer; Luke presents him to Greek readers as the perfect man. John, evidently written after the three Synoptic Gospels, presents Christ to a universal readership as the Son of God.

John's purpose statement is the clearest in Scripture: "But these are written that you may believe that Jesus is the Christ, the Son of God, and that by believing you may have life in his name" (20:31). He selected the seven miraculous signs in 1—12 and the resurrection in 20—21 to help readers understand who Jesus is, and to elicit a response of personal trust in him. In his narratives, John shows symbolically how those who were exposed to Jesus' words and works responded by either accepting or rejecting him. Those who receive him have eternal life (1:12; 3:16; 5:24; 10:27–29), while those who reject his offer remain under God's condemnation (3:36; 5:25–29; 8:24).

UNIQUE CONTRIBUTION

While all of the Gospels offer thematic portraits, John is by far the most theological and selective. It also contains the most unique material: 42 percent of Matthew, 7 percent of Mark, and 59 percent of Luke is content unique to these Gospels, but 92 percent of John is unique to John. And although John's vocabulary and sentence structure are simpler than the others, the writing is more subtle and layered; it is full of nuances and parallelism. While all the Synoptic Gospels retell Jesus' parables, only John uses allegories instead (e.g., the good shepherd in chapter 10 and the true vine in chapter 15). John's discourse material, such as the bread of life in chapter 6 and the upper room in chapters 13—17, are more tightly and logically developed than the discourses presented in the Synoptic Gospels.

CHRIST IN JOHN

John's presentation of Jesus as the incarnate Son of God is the clearest in Scripture, but this Gospel also unmistakably shows that Jesus was, at the same time, fully human. Jesus got weary and thirsty; he experienced grief, anguish of soul and death (4:6–7; 11:35; 12:27; 19:1–42). The seven "I am" statements combine to provide a profound portrait of the Lord Jesus: "I am the bread of life" (6:35); "I am the light of the world" (8:12; 9:5); "I am the gate" (10:7, 9); "I am the good shepherd" (10:11, 14); "I am the resurrection and the life" (11:25); "I am the way and the truth and the life" (14:6); "I am the true vine" (15:1–5). John also uses the seven miraculous signs in 1—12 and the five witnesses in 5:30–40 to present Christ's authority and deity.

The prologue (1:1–18) is one of the richest theological texts in Scripture, for it reveals the eternality and divinity of the Word, as well as the incarnation of the Word. John also records occasions in which Jesus associated himself with the divine I AM of the Old Testament (4:25–26; 8:24, 28, 58; 13:19; 18:5–6, 8).

OVERVIEW

FOCUS	Seven Miracles	Upper Room Discourse	Crucifixion and Resurrection
REFERENCE	1 — 12	13 — 17	18 — 21
TOPICS	Revelation and Rejection of the Son of God	Instruction and Intercession of the Son of God	Suffering, Resurrection, and Appearances of the Son of God
	Coming and Confrontation	Comfort	Crucifixion and Climax
	"that you may believe"	"that you may have life in his name"	
LOCATION	Perea, Galilee, Judea, Samaria	Judea	Galilee
TIME	Years	Hours	Weeks
	~6–4 B.C. to A.D. 33		

After a magnificent prologue that proclaims the incarnation of the eternal Word (1:1–18), this Gospel gives eyewitness accounts of Jesus from John the Baptist and from Jesus' first disciples (1:19–51). Chapters 2—12 present seven signs that point to the person and life-giving power of Jesus: (1) turning water into wine (2:1–11); (2) healing the royal official's son (4:46–54); (3) healing the invalid (5:1–15); (4) feeding the multitude (6:1–14); (5) walking on water (6:16–21); (6) giving sight to the man born blind (9:1–41); and (7) raising Lazarus from the dead (11:1–44). In most cases, John follows these signs by describing people reacting in either belief or disbelief.

In view of increasing hostility to his words and works, Jesus sees that his final hour has come. At his last supper with the disciples, he prepares them for his imminent departure (13—16) and intercedes for them before God (17). The upper room discourse, recorded only in John and the most complete of Jesus' messages, contains the "seed themes" contained in the spiritual life that later New Testament books develop.

After a gripping account of Jesus' arrest, trials and crucifixion (18—19), John provides a vivid narrative of several post-resurrection encounters between the Lord and his disciples (20—21).

JOHN

The Word Became Flesh

1 In the beginning was the Word,[a]
and the Word was with God,[b] and
the Word was God.[c] 2He was with God
in the beginning.[d]
3Through him all things were made;
without him nothing was made that
has been made.[e] 4In him was life,[f]
and that life was the light[g] of men.
5The light shines in the darkness,
but the darkness has not understood[a] it.[h]
6There came a man who was sent
from God; his name was John.[i] 7He
came as a witness to testify[j] concerning that light, so that through him all
men might believe.[k] 8He himself was
not the light; he came only as a witness
to the light. 9The true light[l] that gives
light to every man[m] was coming into
the world.[b]
10He was in the world, and though
the world was made through him,[n]
the world did not recognize him. 11He
came to that which was his own, but
his own did not receive him. 12Yet to all
who received him, to those who believed[o] in his name,[p] he gave the
right to become children of God[q]—
13children born not of natural descent,[c] nor of human decision or a
husband's will, but born of God.[r]
14The Word became flesh[s] and
made his dwelling among us. We have
seen his glory, the glory of the One and
Only,[d] who came from the Father, full
of grace and truth.[t]
15John testifies[u] concerning him.
He cries out, saying, "This was he of
whom I said, 'He who comes after
me has surpassed me because he was
before me.' "[v] 16From the fullness[w]
of his grace we have all received one
blessing after another. 17For the law

1:1 [a]Rev 19:13 [b]Jn 17:5; 1Jn 1:2 [c]Php 2:6 **1:2** [d]Ge 1:1 **1:3** [e]1Co 8:6; Col 1:16; Heb 1:2 **1:4** [f]Jn 5:26; 11:25; 14:6 [g]Jn 8:12 **1:5** [h]Jn 3:19 **1:6** [i]Mt 3:1 **1:7** [j]ver 15,19,32 [k]ver 12 **1:9** [l]1Jn 2:8 [m]Isa 49:6 **1:10** [n]Heb 1:2 **1:12** [o]ver 7 [p]1Jn 3:23 [q]Gal 3:26 **1:13** [r]Jn 3:6; Jas 1:18; 1Pe 1:23; 1Jn 3:9 **1:14** [s]Gal 4:4; Php 2:7,8; 1Ti 3:16; Heb 2:14 [t]Jn 14:6 **1:15** [u]ver 7 [v]ver 30; Mt 3:11 **1:16** [w]Eph 1:23; Col 1:19

a 5 Or *darkness, and the darkness has not overcome* **b** 9 Or *This was the true light that gives light to every man who comes into the world* **c** 13 Greek *of bloods* **d** 14 Or *the Only Begotten*

1:1–3 PROMISE 1

JESUS, THE GOD-MAN

John, the writer of this Gospel, wants to make one thing perfectly clear: Jesus is more than a mere man—he is the God-Man. To accomplish this, John opens his Gospel by linking Jesus with the creation. The first verse of Genesis reads, "In the beginning God . . ." John picks up on that language and begins his Gospel, "In the beginning was the Word."

To the ancient Greeks, the term "Word" referred to the all-pervasive Mind, the entity that ruled the universe and gave meaning to all things. John understood the term. That's why he used it. He wanted his readers to know that Jesus was—and is—more than a mere man; he's God in the flesh.

If the sky outside is clear tonight, do some star-gazing. You might go for a short walk, or perhaps simply sit on a chair in your back yard. As you look up at the stars, contemplate the power and might of the Creator. And thank God that while he's as big as the universe, he clothed himself in flesh so that you could know him. Jesus, the Word, the One who was "with God," the One who indeed "was God," walked the surface of this earth in human form. For you. For all of humanity. Praise God for his indescribable goodness!

For the next Promise 1 reading go to page 1158.

1:12–13 PROMISE 1

GOD'S CHILDREN

The apostle John was a man of contrasts. He saw things as black or white, good or evil, light or dark. And when, at the beginning of his Gospel, he contemplated the entrance of the Word into the world, he saw another contrast—those who accepted Jesus, the Word, and those who rejected him.

Amazingly, many of Jesus and John's own people rejected Jesus. Most didn't recognize who he was, and refused to believe when Jesus showed them who he was. But others believed his words and accepted all that his name stood for. They saw Jesus as their Savior and Shepherd. They believed he was both God and man. These people received the greatest of all gifts—they became children of God.

While all people are God's creation, not all people are his children. That privilege is reserved only for believers. As God's children, believers possess his Spirit—his life.

Think for a minute about the differences between being just a part of God's creation and being God's own child. Have you accepted this privileged status? Are you a child of God? How is that special status revealed in your daily life?

For the next Promise 1 reading go to page 1162.

was given through Moses;[x] grace and truth came through Jesus Christ.[y] 18 No one has ever seen God,[z] but God the One and Only,[a,b][a] who is at the Father's side, has made him known.

John the Baptist Denies Being the Christ

19 Now this was John's testimony when the Jews[b] of Jerusalem sent priests and Levites to ask him who he was. 20 He did not fail to confess, but confessed freely, "I am not the Christ.[c]"[c]

21 They asked him, "Then who are you? Are you Elijah?"[d]

He said, "I am not."

"Are you the Prophet?"[e]

He answered, "No."

22 Finally they said, "Who are you? Give us an answer to take back to those who sent us. What do you say about yourself?"

23 John replied in the words of Isaiah the prophet, "I am the voice of one calling in the desert,[f] 'Make straight the way for the Lord.' "[d][g]

24 Now some Pharisees who had been sent 25 questioned him, "Why then do you baptize if you are not the Christ, nor Elijah, nor the Prophet?"

26 "I baptize with[e] water," John replied, "but among you stands one you do not know. 27 He is the one who comes after me,[h] the thongs of whose sandals I am not worthy to untie."

28 This all happened at Bethany on the other side of the Jordan,[i] where John was baptizing.

Jesus the Lamb of God

29 The next day John saw Jesus coming toward him and said, "Look, the Lamb of God,[j] who takes away the sin of the world! 30 This is the one I meant when I said, 'A man who comes after me has surpassed me because he was before me.'[k] 31 I myself did not know him, but the reason I came baptizing with water was that he might be revealed to Israel."

32 Then John gave this testimony: "I saw the Spirit come down from heaven as a dove and remain on him.[l] 33 I would not have known him, except that the one who sent me to baptize with water[m] told me, 'The man on whom you see the Spirit come down and remain is he who will baptize with the Holy Spirit.'[n] 34 I have seen and I testify that this is the Son of God."[o]

Jesus' First Disciples

35 The next day John[p] was there again with two of his disciples. 36 When he saw Jesus passing by, he said, "Look, the Lamb of God!"[q]

37 When the two disciples heard him say this, they followed Jesus. 38 Turning around, Jesus saw them following and asked, "What do you want?"

They said, "Rabbi"[r] (which means Teacher), "where are you staying?"

39 "Come," he replied, "and you will see."

So they went and saw where he was staying, and spent that day with him. It was about the tenth hour.

40 Andrew, Simon Peter's brother, was one of the two who heard what John had said and who had followed Jesus. 41 The first thing Andrew did was to find his brother Simon and tell him, "We have found the Messiah" (that is, the Christ).[s] 42 And he brought him to Jesus.

Jesus looked at him and said, "You are Simon son of John. You will be called[t] Cephas" (which, when translated, is Peter[f]).[u]

2 →PG. 1182
7 →PG. 1162

Jesus Calls Philip and Nathanael

43 The next day Jesus decided to leave for Galilee. Finding Philip,[v] he said to him, "Follow me."[w]

44 Philip, like Andrew and Peter, was from the town of Bethsaida.[x] 45 Philip found Nathanael[y] and told him, "We have found the one Moses wrote about in the Law,[z] and about whom the prophets also wrote[a]—Jesus of Nazareth,[b] the son of Joseph."[c]

46 "Nazareth! Can anything good come from there?"[d] Nathanael asked.

"Come and see," said Philip.

47 When Jesus saw Nathanael approaching, he said of him, "Here is a true Israelite,[e] in whom there is nothing false."[f]

48 "How do you know me?" Nathanael asked.

Jesus answered, "I saw you while you were still under the fig tree before Philip called you."

49 Then Nathanael declared, "Rabbi,[g] you are the Son of God;[h] you are the King of Israel."[i]

50 Jesus said, "You believe[g] because I told you I saw you under the fig tree. You shall see greater things than that." 51 He then added, "I tell you[h] the truth, you[h] shall see heaven open,[j] and the

1:17 [x] Jn 7:19; [y] ver 14
1:18 [z] Ex 33:20; Jn 6:46; Col 1:15; 1Ti 6:16; [a] Jn 3:16,18; 1Jn 4:9
1:19 [b] Jn 2:18; 5:10,16; 6:41,52
1:20 [c] Jn 3:28; Lk 3:15,16
1:21 [d] Mt 11:14; [e] Dt 18:15
1:23 [f] Mt 3:1; [g] Isa 40:3
1:27 [h] ver 15,30
1:28 [i] Jn 3:26; 10:40
1:29 [j] ver 36; Isa 53:7; 1Pe 1:19; Rev 5:6
1:30 [k] ver 15,27
1:32 [l] Mt 3:16; Mk 1:10
1:33 [m] Mk 1:4; [n] Mt 3:11; Mk 1:8
1:34 [o] ver 49; Mt 4:3
1:35 [p] Mt 3:1
1:36 [q] ver 29
1:38 [r] ver 49; Mt 23:7
1:41 [s] Jn 4:25
1:42 [t] Ge 17:5,15; [u] Mt 16:18
1:43 [v] Mt 10:3; Jn 6:5-7; 12:21,22; 14:8,9; [w] Mt 4:19
1:44 [x] Mt 11:21; Jn 12:21
1:45 [y] Jn 21:2; [z] Lk 24:27; [a] Lk 24:27; [b] Mt 2:23; Mk 1:24; [c] Lk 3:23
1:46 [d] Jn 7:41,42,52
1:47 [e] Ro 9:4,6; [f] Ps 32:2
1:49 [g] ver 38; Mt 23:7; [h] ver 34; Mt 4:3; [i] Mt 2:2; 27:42; Jn 12:13
1:51 [j] Mt 3:16

a *18* Or *the Only Begotten* **b** *18* Some manuscripts *but the only* (or *only begotten*) *Son* **c** *20* Or *Messiah.* "The Christ" (Greek) and "the Messiah" (Hebrew) both mean "the Anointed One"; also in verse 25. **d** *23* Isaiah 40:3 **e** *26* Or *in;* also in verses 31 and 33 **f** *42* Both *Cephas* (Aramaic) and *Peter* (Greek) mean *rock.* **g** *50* Or *Do you believe . . . ?* **h** *51* The Greek is plural.

angels of God ascending and descending[k] on the Son of Man."[l]

Jesus Changes Water to Wine

4 →PG. 1178

2 On the third day a wedding took place at Cana in Galilee.[m] Jesus' mother[n] was there, **2**and Jesus and his disciples had also been invited to the wedding. **3**When the wine was gone, Jesus' mother said to him, "They have no more wine."

4"Dear woman,[o] why do you involve me?"[p] Jesus replied. "My time[q] has not yet come."

5His mother said to the servants, "Do whatever he tells you."[r]

6Nearby stood six stone water jars, the kind used by the Jews for ceremonial washing,[s] each holding from twenty to thirty gallons.[a]

7Jesus said to the servants, "Fill the jars with water"; so they filled them to the brim.

8Then he told them, "Now draw some out and take it to the master of the banquet."

They did so, **9**and the master of the banquet tasted the water that had been turned into wine.[t] He did not realize where it had come from, though the servants who had drawn the water knew. Then he called the bridegroom aside **10**and said, "Everyone brings out the choice wine first and then the cheaper wine after the guests have had too much to drink; but you have saved the best till now."

11This, the first of his miraculous signs,[u] Jesus performed at Cana in Galilee. He thus revealed his glory,[v] and his disciples put their faith in him.[w]

Jesus Clears the Temple

›See Matthew 21:12–13; Mark 11:15–17; Luke 19:45–46

12After this he went down to Capernaum[x] with his mother and brothers[y] and his disciples. There they stayed for a few days.

13When it was almost time for the Jewish Passover,[z] Jesus went up to Jerusalem.[a] **14**In the temple courts he found men selling cattle, sheep and doves, and others sitting at tables exchanging money. **15**So he made a whip out of cords, and drove all from the temple area, both sheep and cattle; he scattered the coins of the money changers and overturned their tables. **16**To those who sold doves he said, "Get these out of here! How dare you turn my Father's house[b] into a market!"

17His disciples remembered that it is written: "Zeal for your house will consume me."[b][c]

18Then the Jews demanded of him, "What miraculous sign can you show us to prove your authority to do all this?"[d]

19Jesus answered them, "Destroy this temple, and I will raise it again in three days."[e]

20The Jews replied, "It has taken forty-six years to build this temple, and you are going to raise it in three days?" **21**But the temple he had spoken of was his body.[f] **22**After he was raised from the dead, his disciples recalled what he had said.[g] Then they believed the Scripture and the words that Jesus had spoken.

23Now while he was in Jerusalem at the Passover Feast,[h] many people saw the miraculous signs he was doing and believed in his name.[c] **24**But Jesus would not entrust himself to them, for he knew all men. **25**He did not need man's testimony about man, for he knew what was in a man.[i]

Jesus Teaches Nicodemus

1 →PG. 1164

3 Now there was a man of the Pharisees named Nicodemus,[j] a member of the Jewish ruling council.[k] **2**He came to Jesus at night and said, "Rabbi, we know you are a teacher who has come from God. For no one could perform the miraculous signs[l] you are doing if God were not with him."[m]

3In reply Jesus declared, "I tell you the truth, no one can see the kingdom of God unless he is born again.[d]"[n]

4"How can a man be born when he is old?" Nicodemus asked. "Surely he cannot enter a second time into his mother's womb to be born!"

5Jesus answered, "I tell you the truth, no one can enter the kingdom of God unless he is born of water and the Spirit.[o] **6**Flesh gives birth to flesh, but the Spirit[e] gives birth to spirit.[p] **7**You should not be surprised at my saying, 'You[f] must be born again.' **8**The wind blows wherever it pleases. You hear its sound, but you cannot tell where it comes from or where it is going. So it is with everyone born of the Spirit."

9"How can this be?"[q] Nicodemus asked.

10"You are Israel's teacher,"[r] said Jesus, "and do you not understand these things? **11**I tell you the truth, we speak of what we know,[s] and we testi-

1:51 [k]Ge 28:12 [l]Mt 8:20
2:1 [m]Jn 4:46; 21:2 [n]Mt 12:46
2:4 [o]Jn 19:26 [p]Mt 8:29 [q]Mt 26:18; Jn 7:6
2:5 [r]Ge 41:55
2:6 [s]Mk 7:3,4; Jn 3:25
2:9 [t]Jn 4:46
2:11 [u]ver 23; Jn 3:2; 4:48; 6:2,14,26,30; 12:37; 20:30 [v]Jn 1:14 [w]Ex 14:31
2:12 [x]Mt 4:13 [y]Mt 12:46
2:13 [z]Jn 11:55 [a]Dt 16:1-6; Lk 2:41
2:16 [b]Lk 2:49
2:17 [c]Ps 69:9
2:18 [d]Mt 12:38
2:19 [e]Mt 26:61; 27:40; Mk 14:58; 15:29
2:21 [f]1Co 6:19
2:22 [g]Lk 24:5-8; Jn 12:16; 14:26
2:23 [h]ver 13
2:25 [i]Mt 9:4; Jn 6:61,64; 13:11
3:1 [j]Jn 7:50; 19:39 [k]Lk 23:13
3:2 [l]Jn 9:16,33 [m]Ac 2:22; 10:38
3:3 [n]Jn 1:13; 1Pe 1:23
3:5 [o]Tit 3:5
3:6 [p]Jn 1:13; 1Co 15:50
3:9 [q]Jn 6:52,60
3:10 [r]Lk 2:46
3:11 [s]Jn 1:18; 7:16,17

a *6* Greek *two to three metretes* (probably about 75 to 115 liters) b *17* Psalm 69:9 c *23* Or *and believed in him* d *3* Or *born from above*; also in verse 7 e *6* Or *but spirit*
f *7* The Greek is plural.

NICODEMUS

A Religious Man Who Needed a Savior

When we first meet Nicodemus in John 3, we find that he was a member of the Sanhedrin, the Jewish ruling council (John 3:1). Only the well-educated, wealthy and highly respected in the community served on this council. Nicodemus was also a Pharisee, a member of a religious group known for its strict adherence to the laws of ritual purity. Pharisees were the teachers of the Mosaic law, and were well versed with the traditions surrounding it. In short, Nicodemus was a good man, a religious man, a model of moral behavior, a pillar of the community.

When Nicodemus came to see Jesus one night, it was to talk about spiritual matters. This pious man had been listening to Jesus' teachings. Nicodemus was impressed with the miracles that Jesus performed. He believed Jesus was a teacher who had "come from God. For no one could perform the miraculous signs you are doing if God were not with him" (3:2).

Jesus knew that Nicodemus was open to the things of God. He was a devout man whose life was exemplary in many ways. If it were possible for a man to earn God's approval by righteous living, Nicodemus would have come close. But Jesus knew that earning God's approval by outward signs was impossible. He knew Nicodemus needed to learn that the only way to win God's favor was through an inward change of heart. Jesus told Nicodemus that "no one can see the kingdom of God unless he is born again" (3:3).

Nicodemus was confused. He wanted to know how someone could be born from his mother's womb a second time. So Jesus expanded on his initial words and told him that he was not referring to natural birth, but rather a rebirth of the spirit (3:7–8). Nicodemus still didn't understand (3:9).

Jesus gently but powerfully replied, "God so loved the world that he gave his one and only Son, that whoever believes in him shall not perish but have eternal life" (3:16). Simple words—the best-known words in Scripture—that tell how sinful human beings can be reconciled to a holy God. We must be born again, born of the Spirit, by believing in the reality behind these words.

In those few words, Jesus totally upset Nicodemus's theological world. At the same time, he also gave him the most incredible hope anyone will ever know. Jesus never said anything about being good or earning God's favor. Instead, Jesus said Nicodemus only needed to believe in him as God's Son and his Savior. If Nicodemus would do that, he would have the promise of eternal life in heaven.

What an incredible offer from a loving God! What a gospel! No one could ever be good enough to warrant God's forgiveness. So God the Father gave his only Son, and Jesus the Son gave his life willingly on the cross to pay the penalty for our sins. Simply believe it, and we are acceptable in God's sight.

A Public Stand for Christ

Did Nicodemus, the religious man of good works, ever come to this simple belief in Jesus? We aren't told directly one way or the other, but we can draw some conclusions from the Bible's references to him.

At one point, Nicodemus defended Jesus before his peers in the Sanhedrin (7:51).

After Jesus was crucified, a man named Joseph of Arimathea secured Pilate's permission to give Jesus a decent burial. But notice the man who helped Joseph accomplish this dangerous task—none other than our friend Nicodemus, "the man who earlier had visited Jesus at night" (19:39). The two men tenderly and deliberately prepared Jesus' body for burial and laid him in "a new tomb, in which no one had ever been laid" (19:41).

If Nicodemus had not become a believer in Jesus, why would he accompany a secret disciple on such a risky mission? In this sense, Nicodemus was bolder in his faith than the apostles. After all, Nicodemus was a member of the Sanhedrin—not a fisherman or tax collector. He would have to pay a much greater price for taking a public stand for Jesus Christ.

Saved by Faith

Nicodemus came to understand that being right with God meant he needed to "gain Christ and be found in him, not having a righteousness of [his] own that comes from the law, but that which is through faith in Christ" (Philippians 3:8–9). Nicodemus wasn't good enough to earn his way into heaven. And neither are we. That's the bad news. But the good news is that God has made a way into heaven through the work of Jesus Christ. Will you simply believe in him, gain eternal life and be born again—as did Nicodemus?

—Dr. Gene Getz

fy to what we have seen, but still you
people do not accept our testimony.[t]
12I have spoken to you of earthly things
and you do not believe; how then will
you believe if I speak of heavenly
things? **13**No one has ever gone into
heaven[u] except the one who came
from heaven[v]—the Son of Man.[a]
14Just as Moses lifted up the snake in
the desert,[w] so the Son of Man must
be lifted up,[x] **15**that everyone who
believes[y] in him may have eternal
life.[b]
16"For God so loved[z] the world that
he gave his one and only Son,[c] that
whoever believes in him shall not perish but have eternal life.[a] **17**For God
did not send his Son into the world[b]
to condemn the world, but to save
the world through him.[c] **18**Whoever
believes in him is not condemned,[d]
but whoever does not believe stands
condemned already because he has not
believed in the name of God's one
and only Son.[d e] **19**This is the verdict:
Light[f] has come into the world, but
men loved darkness instead of light because their deeds were evil. **20**Everyone
who does evil hates the light, and will
not come into the light for fear that his
deeds will be exposed.[g] **21**But whoever
lives by the truth comes into the light,
so that it may be seen plainly that what
he has done has been done through
God."[e]

7 →PG. 1164

3 →PG. 1238

3:11 [t]ver 32
3:13 [u]Pr 30:4; Ac 2:34; Eph 4:8-10 [v]Jn 6:38,42
3:14 [w]Nu 21:8,9 [x]Jn 8:28; 12:32
3:15 [y]ver 16,36
3:16 [z]Ro 5:8; Eph 2:4; 1Jn 4:9,10 [a]ver 36; Jn 6:29,40; 11:25,26
3:17 [b]Jn 6:29,57; 10:36; 11:42; 17:8,21; 20:21 [c]Jn 12:47; 1Jn 4:14
3:18 [d]Jn 5:24 [e]1Jn 4:9
3:19 [f]Jn 1:4; 8:12
3:20 [g]Eph 5:11,13

[a] *13* Some manuscripts *Man, who is in heaven* [b] *15* Or *believes may have eternal life in him* [c] *16* Or *his only begotten Son* [d] *18* Or *God's only begotten Son* [e] *21* Some interpreters end the quotation after verse 15.

3:16–18

PROMISE 1

THE ONE MOST IMPORTANT ISSUE YOU FACE

This passage addresses the most important issue of a person's life. Indeed, it's so important that a person's response will define life here on earth and for eternity. That issue: Discovering who Jesus is and either accepting or rejecting his words and his identity as truth. Yet many people, just like Nicodemus in this passage, fail to address this pivotal issue.

Nicodemus was a member of the Jewish ruling class. As such, we might expect him to immediately and publicly engage Jesus in a lively theological debate. After all, in chapter 2 we read that Jesus had publicly performed a miracle—his first—for the benefit of many people (2:1–11). He then made an unmistakable statement about his beliefs in the sanctity of the temple when he drove out the money changers (2:12–25). But Nicodemus chose to approach Jesus under the cover of night. And instead of cutting to the chase and engaging in a discourse about the real issues of life, Nicodemus began the conversation with small talk (3:2).

Nicodemus may have wanted to stick with this line of conversation, but Jesus didn't. The Lord moved past the superficial and got to the heart of the matter. He saw past this man's status as a member of the ruling council, past the rich robes, past his image as an expert interpreter of the Scriptures. He saw Nicodemus as a man who needed to hear how to get into the kingdom of God.

To our ears, the concept of being "born again" isn't foreign. Nowadays this term has been applied to everything from life transformation (as Jesus spoke of it) to a piece of furniture that's been refurbished. But these simple words puzzled Nicodemus. So Jesus boiled the concept down to its basic parts, and in so doing summarized the whole plan of redemption for all of us (3:16).

First, God loves us infinitely and unconditionally. Regardless of what we may have done in the past, no matter how much we have rebelled against him, God still seeks us in love.

Second, God demonstrated his love by giving his Son for us. That's a profound truth. It's possible that we would consider giving our own life for a friend, but few of us would sacrifice our own children to save a friend. Yet God did this for us while we were in sinful rebellion against him, while we were still his enemies (Romans 5:6–8).

The idea of Jesus dying for us requires serious thought. He didn't die simply as an example of sacrificial love. Nor did he die simply as a martyr. Rather, Jesus died as our substitute. Because we've sinned against God (Romans 3:23), we deserve physical and spiritual death (Romans 6:23). No matter how good we may try to be, we can't possibly be good enough to avoid the consequences of our sins (James 2:10).

When Jesus died he carried upon himself the guilt and punishment for all of our sins. As God, he could bear all of our sins and pay their eternal consequences in a matter of hours while hanging on the cross. Because Jesus paid for our sins, we no longer have to suffer for them. We do, however, have a responsibility in the face of Jesus' sacrifice, which leads to the next point.

Third, we must believe in Jesus in order to receive God's forgiveness and enter his kingdom. Jesus said those who believe in him will have "eternal life" (3:16). He made it clear that the basis for forgiveness is faith and the basis for condemnation is unbelief (3:18). Believing in Jesus means trusting in him for forgiveness and eternal life. It means accepting that through his death he paid in full the debt of your sins and that by his resurrection he assures you of eternal life.

For the next Promise 1 reading go to page 1180.

John the Baptist's Testimony About Jesus

22After this, Jesus and his disciples
went out into the Judean countryside,
where he spent some time with them,
and baptized.[h] 23Now John also was
baptizing at Aenon near Salim, because there was plenty of water, and
people were constantly coming to be
baptized. 24(This was before John was
put in prison.)[i] 25An argument developed between some of John's disciples
and a certain Jew**[a]** over the matter of
ceremonial washing.[j] 26They came to
John and said to him, "Rabbi,[k] that
man who was with you on the other
side of the Jordan—the one you testified[l] about—well, he is baptizing,
and everyone is going to him."

27To this John replied, "A man can
receive only what is given him from
heaven. 28You yourselves can testify
that I said, 'I am not the Christ**[b]** but
am sent ahead of him.'[m] 29The bride
belongs to the bridegroom.[n] The
friend who attends the bridegroom
waits and listens for him, and is full of
joy when he hears the bridegroom's
voice. That joy is mine, and it is now
complete.[o] 30He must become greater; I must become less.

31"The one who comes from
above[p] is above all; the one who is
from the earth belongs to the earth,
and speaks as one from the earth.[q]
The one who comes from heaven is
above all. 32He testifies to what he has
seen and heard,[r] but no one accepts
his testimony.[s] 33The man who has
accepted it has certified that God is
truthful. 34For the one whom God has
sent[t] speaks the words of God, for
God**[c]** gives the Spirit[u] without limit.
35The Father loves the Son and has
placed everything in his hands.[v]
36Whoever believes in the Son has eternal life,[w] but whoever rejects the Son
will not see life, for God's wrath remains on him."**[d]**

Jesus Talks With a Samaritan Woman

4 The Pharisees heard that Jesus was
gaining and baptizing more disciples than John,[x] 2although in fact it
was not Jesus who baptized, but his
disciples. 3When the Lord learned of
this, he left Judea[y] and went back
once more to Galilee.

4Now he had to go through Samaria.
5So he came to a town in Samaria
called Sychar, near the plot of ground
Jacob had given to his son Joseph.[z]
6Jacob's well was there, and Jesus, tired
as he was from the journey, sat down
by the well. It was about the sixth hour.

7When a Samaritan woman came to
draw water, Jesus said to her, "Will you
give me a drink?" 8(His disciples had
gone into the town[a] to buy food.)

9The Samaritan woman said to him,
"You are a Jew and I am a Samaritan[b]
woman. How can you ask me for a
drink?" (For Jews do not associate with
Samaritans.**[e]**)

10Jesus answered her, "If you knew
the gift of God and who it is that asks
you for a drink, you would have asked
him and he would have given you living water."[c]

11"Sir," the woman said, "you have
nothing to draw with and the well is
deep. Where can you get this living water? 12Are you greater than our father
Jacob, who gave us the well[d] and
drank from it himself, as did also his
sons and his flocks and herds?"

13Jesus answered, "Everyone who
drinks this water will be thirsty again,
14but whoever drinks the water I give
him will never thirst.[e] Indeed, the water I give him will become in him a
spring of water[f] welling up to eternal
life."[g]

15The woman said to him, "Sir, give
me this water so that I won't get

3:22 [h]Jn 4:2
3:24 [i]Mt 4:12; 14:3
3:25 [j]Jn 2:6
3:26 [k]Mt 23:7 [l]Jn 1:7
3:28 [m]Jn 1:20,23
3:29 [n]Mt 9:15 [o]Jn 16:24; 17:13; Php 2:2; 1Jn 1:4; 2Jn 12
3:31 [p]ver 13 [q]Jn 8:23; 1Jn 4:5
3:32 [r]Jn 8:26; 15:15 [s]ver 11
3:34 [t]ver 17 [u]Mt 12:18; Lk 4:18; Ac 10:38
3:35 [v]Mt 28:18; Jn 5:20,22; 17:2
3:36 [w]ver 15; Jn 5:24; 6:47
4:1 [x]Jn 3:22,26
4:3 [y]Jn 3:22
4:5 [z]Ge 33:19; 48:22; Jos 24:32
4:8 [a]ver 5,39
4:9 [b]Mt 10:5; Lk 9:52,53
4:10 [c]Isa 44:3; Jer 2:13; Zec 14:8; Jn 7:37,38; Rev 21:6; 22:1, 17
4:12 [d]ver 6
4:14 [e]Jn 6:35 [f]Jn 7:38 [g]Mt 25:46

a *25* Some manuscripts *and certain Jews*
b *28* Or *Messiah*
c *34* Greek *he*
d *36* Some interpreters end the quotation after verse 30.
e *9* Or *do not use dishes Samaritans have used*

4:1–26

PROMISE **7**

BUILDING BRIDGES

Have you ever wondered how to build a bridge to an unbeliever? In this passage Jesus provides us with an excellent model for reaching out to those who are different from us.

As you talk with unbelieving individuals about your faith, follow Jesus' example. First, accept them for who they are and for where they are in their spiritual life. One way you can demonstrate this acceptance is by letting them meet *your* needs. Jesus did that when he asked for a drink. Such acceptance not only deepens friendships, it makes people more willing to let you meet their spiritual needs. Second, meet *their* needs. Jesus did as much when he promised her what she most needed—water—as an illustration of "living water." Third, reveal Jesus to them as the Messiah, the Savior of the world. When they foster a relationship with Jesus, they will soon declare what the townspeople did: "We no longer believe just because of what you said; now we have heard for ourselves, and we know that this man really is the Savior of the world" (v. 42).

For the next Promise 7 reading go to page 1195.

6 →PG. 1164

thirsty[h] and have to keep coming here to draw water."

16 He told her, "Go, call your husband and come back."

17 "I have no husband," she replied.

Jesus said to her, "You are right when you say you have no husband. 18 The fact is, you have had five husbands, and the man you now have is not your husband. What you have just said is quite true."

19 "Sir," the woman said, "I can see that you are a prophet.[i] 20 Our fathers worshiped on this mountain,[j] but you Jews claim that the place where we must worship is in Jerusalem."[k]

21 Jesus declared, "Believe me, woman, a time is coming[l] when you will worship the Father neither on this mountain nor in Jerusalem.[m] 22 You Samaritans worship what you do not know;[n] we worship what we do know,

1 →PG. 1170

for salvation is from the Jews.[o] 23 Yet a time is coming and has now come[p] when the true worshipers will worship the Father in spirit[q] and truth, for they are the kind of worshipers the Father seeks. 24 God is spirit,[r] and his worshipers must worship in spirit and in truth."

25 The woman said, "I know that Messiah" (called Christ)[s] "is coming. When he comes, he will explain everything to us."

26 Then Jesus declared, "I who speak to you am he."[t]

The Disciples Rejoin Jesus

6 →PG. 1172

27 Just then his disciples returned[u] and were surprised to find him talking with a woman. But no one asked, "What do you want?" or "Why are you talking with her?"

28 Then, leaving her water jar, the woman went back to the town and said to the people, 29 "Come, see a man who told me everything I ever did.[v] Could this be the Christ[a]?"[w] 30 They came out of the town and made their way toward him.

31 Meanwhile his disciples urged him, "Rabbi,[x] eat something."

32 But he said to them, "I have food to eat[y] that you know nothing about."

33 Then his disciples said to each other, "Could someone have brought him food?"

34 "My food," said Jesus, "is to do the will[z] of him who sent me and to finish

5 →PG. 1175

7 →PG. 1172

his work.[a] 35 Do you not say, 'Four months more and then the harvest'? I tell you, open your eyes and look at the fields! They are ripe for harvest.[b] 36 Even now the reaper draws his wages, even now he harvests[c] the crop for eternal life,[d] so that the sower and the reaper may be glad together. 37 Thus the saying 'One sows and another reaps'[e] is true. 38 I sent you to reap what you have not worked for. Others have done the hard work, and you have reaped the benefits of their labor."

Many Samaritans Believe

39 Many of the Samaritans from that town[f] believed in him because of the woman's testimony, "He told me everything I ever did."[g] 40 So when the Samaritans came to him, they urged him to stay with them, and he stayed two days. 41 And because of his words many more became believers.

42 They said to the woman, "We no longer believe just because of what you said; now we have heard for ourselves, and we know that this man really is the Savior of the world."[h]

Jesus Heals the Official's Son

43 After the two days[i] he left for Galilee. 44 (Now Jesus himself had pointed out that a prophet has no honor in his own country.)[j] 45 When he arrived in Galilee, the Galileans welcomed him. They had seen all that he had done in Jerusalem at the Passover Feast,[k] for they also had been there.

46 Once more he visited Cana in Galilee, where he had turned the water into wine.[l] And there was a certain royal official whose son lay sick at Capernaum. 47 When this man heard that Jesus had arrived in Galilee from Judea,[m] he went to him and begged him to come and heal his son, who was close to death.

48 "Unless you people see miraculous signs and wonders,"[n] Jesus told him, "you will never believe."

49 The royal official said, "Sir, come down before my child dies."

50 Jesus replied, "You may go. Your son will live."

The man took Jesus at his word and departed. 51 While he was still on the way, his servants met him with the news that his boy was living. 52 When he inquired as to the time when his son got better, they said to him, "The fever left him yesterday at the seventh hour."

53 Then the father realized that this was the exact time at which Jesus had said to him, "Your son will live." So he and all his household[o] believed.

54 This was the second miraculous sign[p] that Jesus performed, having come from Judea to Galilee.

4:15 [h] Jn 6:34
4:19 [i] Mt 21:11
4:20 [j] Dt 11:29; Jos 8:33 [k] Lk 9:53
4:21 [l] Jn 5:28; 16:2 [m] Mal 1:11; 1Ti 2:8
4:22 [n] 2Ki 17:28-41 [o] Isa 2:3; Ro 3:1,2; 9:4,5
4:23 [p] Jn 5:25; 16:32 [q] Php 3:3
4:24 [r] Php 3:3
4:25 [s] Mt 1:16
4:26 [t] Jn 8:24; 9:35-37
4:27 [u] ver 8
4:29 [v] ver 17,18 [w] Mt 12:23; Jn 7:26,31
4:31 [x] Mt 23:7
4:32 [y] Job 23:12; Mt 4:4; Jn 6:27
4:34 [z] Mt 26:39; Jn 6:38; 17:4; 19:30 [a] Jn 19:30
4:35 [b] Mt 9:37; Lk 10:2
4:36 [c] Ro 1:13 [d] Mt 25:46
4:37 [e] Job 31:8; Mic 6:15
4:39 [f] ver 5 [g] ver 29
4:42 [h] Lk 2:11; 1Jn 4:14
4:43 [i] ver 40
4:44 [j] Mt 13:57; Lk 4:24
4:45 [k] Jn 2:23
4:46 [l] Jn 2:1-11
4:47 [m] ver 3,54
4:48 [n] Da 4:2,3; Jn 2:11; Ac 2:43; 14:3; Ro 15:19; 2Co 12:12; Heb 2:4
4:53 [o] Ac 11:14
4:54 [p] ver 48; Jn 2:11

[a] 29 Or *Messiah*

The Healing at the Pool

5 Some time later, Jesus went up to
Jerusalem for a feast of the Jews.
2Now there is in Jerusalem near the
Sheep Gate[q] a pool, which in Aramaic[r] is called Bethesda[a] and which is
surrounded by five covered colon-
nades. **3**Here a great number of disabled people used to lie—the blind,
the lame, the paralyzed.[b] **5**One who
was there had been an invalid for
thirty-eight years. **6**When Jesus saw
him lying there and learned that he
had been in this condition for a long
time, he asked him, "Do you want to
get well?"
7"Sir," the invalid replied, "I have no
one to help me into the pool when the
water is stirred. While I am trying to get
in, someone else goes down ahead
of me."
8Then Jesus said to him, "Get up!
Pick up your mat and walk."[s] **9**At once
the man was cured; he picked up his
mat and walked.
The day on which this took place
was a Sabbath,[t] **10**and so the Jews[u]
said to the man who had been healed,
"It is the Sabbath; the law forbids you
to carry your mat."[v]
11But he replied, "The man who
made me well said to me, 'Pick up your
mat and walk.' "
12So they asked him, "Who is this
fellow who told you to pick it up and
walk?"
13The man who was healed had no
idea who it was, for Jesus had slipped
away into the crowd that was there.
14Later Jesus found him at the temple and said to him, "See, you are well
again. Stop sinning[w] or something
worse may happen to you." **15**The man
went away and told the Jews[x] that it
was Jesus who had made him well.

Life Through the Son

16So, because Jesus was doing these
things on the Sabbath, the Jews persecuted him. **17**Jesus said to them, "My
Father is always at his work[y] to this
very day, and I, too, am working." **18**For
this reason the Jews tried all the harder
to kill him;[z] not only was he breaking
the Sabbath, but he was even calling
God his own Father, making himself
equal with God.[a]
19Jesus gave them this answer: "I tell
you the truth, the Son can do nothing
by himself;[b] he can do only what he
sees his Father doing, because whatever the Father does the Son also does.
20For the Father loves the Son[c] and
shows him all he does. Yes, to your
amazement he will show him even
greater things than these.[d] **21**For just
as the Father raises the dead and gives
them life,[e] even so the Son gives life[f]
to whom he is pleased to give it.
22Moreover, the Father judges no one,
but has entrusted all judgment to the
Son,[g] **23**that all may honor the Son
just as they honor the Father. He who
does not honor the Son does not honor
the Father, who sent him.[h]
24"I tell you the truth, whoever hears
my word and believes him who sent
me has eternal life and will not be condemned;[i] he has crossed over from
death to life.[j] **25**I tell you the truth, a
time is coming and has now come[k]
when the dead will hear[l] the voice of
the Son of God and those who hear will
live. **26**For as the Father has life in himself, so he has granted the Son to have
life in himself. **27**And he has given him
authority to judge[m] because he is the
Son of Man.
28"Do not be amazed at this, for a
time is coming[n] when all who are in
their graves will hear his voice **29**and
come out—those who have done good
will rise to live, and those who have
done evil will rise to be condemned.[o]
30By myself I can do nothing;[p] I judge
only as I hear, and my judgment is
just,[q] for I seek not to please myself
but him who sent me.[r]

Testimonies About Jesus

31"If I testify about myself, my testimony is not valid.[s] **32**There is another
who testifies in my favor,[t] and I know
that his testimony about me is valid.
33"You have sent to John and he has
testified[u] to the truth. **34**Not that I accept human testimony;[v] but I mention it that you may be saved. **35**John
was a lamp that burned and gave
light,[w] and you chose for a time to enjoy his light.
36"I have testimony weightier than
that of John.[x] For the very work that
the Father has given me to finish, and
which I am doing,[y] testifies that the
Father has sent me.[z] **37**And the Father
who sent me has himself testified concerning me.[a] You have never heard
his voice nor seen his form,[b] **38**nor
does his word dwell in you,[c] for you
do not believe the one he sent.[d] **39**You
diligently study[c] the Scriptures[e] be-

a2 Some manuscripts *Bethzatha;* other manuscripts *Bethsaida* **b**3 Some less important manuscripts *paralyzed—and they waited for the moving of the waters.* 4*From time to time an angel of the Lord would come down and stir up the waters. The first one into the pool after each such disturbance would be cured of whatever disease he had.* **c**39 Or *Study diligently* (the imperative)

5:2 q Ne 3:1; 12:39 r Jn 19:13,17, 20; 20:16; Ac 21:40; 22:2; 26:14
5:8 s Mt 9:5,6; Mk 2:11; Lk 5:24
5:9 t Jn 9:14
5:10 u ver 16 v Ne 13:15-22; Jer 17:21; Mt 12:2
5:14 w Mk 2:5; Jn 8:11
5:15 x Jn 1:19
5:17 y Jn 9:4; 14:10
5:18 z Jn 7:1 a Jn 10:30,33; 19:7
5:19 b ver 30; Jn 8:28
5:20 c Jn 3:35 d Jn 14:12
5:21 e Ro 4:17; 8:11 f Jn 11:25
5:22 g ver 27; Jn 9:39; Ac 10:42; 17:31
5:23 h Lk 10:16; 1Jn 2:23
5:24 i Jn 3:18 j 1Jn 3:14
5:25 k Jn 4:23 l Jn 8:43,47
5:27 m ver 22; Ac 10:42; 17:31
5:28 n Jn 4:21
5:29 o Da 12:2; Mt 25:46
5:30 p ver 19 q Jn 8:16 r Mt 26:39; Jn 4:34; 6:38
5:31 s Jn 8:14
5:32 t ver 37; Jn 8:18
5:33 u Jn 1:7
5:34 v 1Jn 5:9
5:35 w 2Pe 1:19
5:36 x 1Jn 5:9 y Jn 14:11; 15:24 z Jn 3:17; 10:25
5:37 a Jn 8:18 b Dt 4:12; 1Ti 1:17; Jn 1:18
5:38 c 1Jn 2:14 d Jn 3:17
5:39 e Ro 2:17,18

cause you think that by them you possess eternal life. These are the Scriptures that testify about me,[f] **40**yet you
refuse to come to me to have life.
41"I do not accept praise from
men,[g] **42**but I know you. I know that
you do not have the love of God in your
hearts. **43**I have come in my Father's
name, and you do not accept me; but
if someone else comes in his own
name, you will accept him. **44**How can
you believe if you accept praise from
one another, yet make no effort to obtain the praise that comes from the
only God[a]?[h]
45"But do not think I will accuse you
before the Father. Your accuser is Moses,[i] on whom your hopes are set.[j]
46If you believed Moses, you would believe me, for he wrote about me.[k]
47But since you do not believe what he
wrote, how are you going to believe
what I say?"[l]

Jesus Feeds the Five Thousand

>See Matthew 14:13–21; Mark 6:32–44; Luke 9:10–17

6 Some time after this, Jesus crossed
to the far shore of the Sea of Galilee
(that is, the Sea of Tiberias), **2**and a
great crowd of people followed him because they saw the miraculous signs[m]
he had performed on the sick. **3**Then
Jesus went up on a mountainside[n]
and sat down with his disciples. **4**The
Jewish Passover Feast[o] was near.
5When Jesus looked up and saw a
great crowd coming toward him, he
said to Philip,[p] "Where shall we buy
bread for these people to eat?" **6**He
asked this only to test him, for he already had in mind what he was going
to do.
7Philip answered him, "Eight months'
wages[b] would not buy enough bread
for each one to have a bite!"
8Another of his disciples, Andrew,
Simon Peter's brother,[q] spoke up,
9"Here is a boy with five small barley
loaves and two small fish, but how far
will they go among so many?"[r]
10Jesus said, "Have the people sit
down." There was plenty of grass in
that place, and the men sat down,
about five thousand of them. **11**Jesus
then took the loaves, gave thanks,[s]
and distributed to those who were
seated as much as they wanted. He did
the same with the fish.
12When they had all had enough to
eat, he said to his disciples, "Gather the
pieces that are left over. Let nothing be
wasted." **13**So they gathered them and
filled twelve baskets with the pieces of
the five barley loaves left over by those
who had eaten.
14After the people saw the miraculous sign[t] that Jesus did, they began
to say, "Surely this is the Prophet who
is to come into the world."[u] **15**Jesus,
knowing that they intended to come
and make him king[v] by force, withdrew again to a mountain by himself.[w]

Jesus Walks on the Water

>See Matthew 14:22–33; Mark 6:47–51

16When evening came, his disciples
went down to the lake, **17**where they
got into a boat and set off across the
lake for Capernaum. By now it was
dark, and Jesus had not yet joined
them. **18**A strong wind was blowing and
the waters grew rough. **19**When they
had rowed three or three and a half
miles,[c] they saw Jesus approaching
the boat, walking on the water;[x] and
they were terrified. **20**But he said to
them, "It is I; don't be afraid."[y] **21**Then
they were willing to take him into
the boat, and immediately the boat
reached the shore where they were
heading.
22The next day the crowd that had
stayed on the opposite shore of the
lake[z] realized that only one boat had
been there, and that Jesus had not entered it with his disciples, but that they
had gone away alone.[a] **23**Then some
boats from Tiberias[b] landed near the
place where the people had eaten
the bread after the Lord had given
thanks.[c] **24**Once the crowd realized
that neither Jesus nor his disciples
were there, they got into the boats and
went to Capernaum in search of Jesus.

Jesus the Bread of Life

25When they found him on the other
side of the lake, they asked him, "Rabbi,[d] when did you get here?"
26Jesus answered, "I tell you the
truth, you are looking for me,[e] not because you saw miraculous signs[f] but
because you ate the loaves and had
your fill. **27**Do not work for food that
spoils, but for food that endures[g] to
eternal life,[h] which the Son of Man[i]
will give you. On him God the Father
has placed his seal[j] of approval."
28Then they asked him, "What must
we do to do the works God requires?"
29Jesus answered, "The work of God
is this: to believe[k] in the one he has
sent."[l]
30So they asked him, "What miracu-

5:39 [f]Lk 24:27,44; Ac 13:27
5:41 [g]ver 44
5:44 [h]Ro 2:29
5:45 [i]Jn 9:28 [j]Ro 2:17
5:46 [k]Ge 3:15; Lk 24:27,44; Ac 26:22
5:47 [l]Lk 16:29,31
6:2 [m]Jn 2:11
6:3 [n]ver 15
6:4 [o]Jn 2:13; 11:55
6:5 [p]Jn 1:43
6:8 [q]Jn 1:40
6:9 [r]2Ki 4:43
6:11 [s]ver 23; Mt 14:19
6:14 [t]Jn 2:11 [u]Dt 18:15,18; Mt 11:3; 21:11
6:15 [v]Jn 18:36 [w]Mt 14:23; Mk 6:46
6:19 [x]Job 9:8
6:20 [y]Mt 14:27
6:22 [z]ver 2 [a]ver 15-21
6:23 [b]ver 1 [c]ver 11
6:25 [d]Mt 23:7
6:26 [e]ver 24 [f]ver 30; Jn 2:11
6:27 [g]Isa 55:2 [h]ver 54; Mt 25:46; Jn 4:14 [i]Mt 8:20 [j]Ro 4:11; 1Co 9:2; 2Co 1:22; Eph 1:13; 4:30; 2Ti 2:19; Rev 7:3
6:29 [k]1Jn 3:23 [l]Jn 3:17

a *44* Some early manuscripts *the Only One*
b *7* Greek *two hundred denarii*
c *19* Greek *rowed twenty-five or thirty stadia* (about 5 or 6 kilometers)

lous sign[m] then will you give that we may see it and believe you?[n] What will you do? 31Our forefathers ate the manna[o] in the desert; as it is written: 'He gave them bread from heaven to eat.'[a]"[p]

32Jesus said to them, "I tell you the truth, it is not Moses who has given you the bread from heaven, but it is my Father who gives you the true bread from heaven. 33For the bread of God is he who comes down from heaven[q] and gives life to the world."

34"Sir," they said, "from now on give us this bread."[r]

35Then Jesus declared, "I am the bread of life.[s] He who comes to me will never go hungry, and he who believes in me will never be thirsty.[t] 36But as I told you, you have seen me and still you do not believe. 37All that the Father gives me[u] will come to me, and whoever comes to me I will never drive away. 38For I have come down from heaven not to do my will but to do the will of him who sent me.[v] 39And this is the will of him who sent me, that I shall lose none of all that he has given me,[w] but raise them up at the last day.[x] 40For my Father's will is that everyone who looks to the Son and believes in him shall have eternal life,[y] and I will raise him up at the last day."

41At this the Jews began to grumble about him because he said, "I am the bread that came down from heaven." 42They said, "Is this not Jesus, the son of Joseph,[z] whose father and mother we know?[a] How can he now say, 'I came down from heaven'?"[b]

43"Stop grumbling among yourselves," Jesus answered. 44"No one can come to me unless the Father who sent me draws him,[c] and I will raise him up at the last day. 45It is written in the Prophets: 'They will all be taught by God.'[b][d] Everyone who listens to the Father and learns from him comes to me. 46No one has seen the Father except the one who is from God;[e] only he has seen the Father. 47I tell you the truth, he who believes has everlasting life. 48I am the bread of life.[f] 49Your forefathers ate the manna in the desert, yet they died.[g] 50But here is the bread that comes down from heaven,[h] which a man may eat and not die. 51I am the living bread that came down from heaven. If anyone eats of this bread, he will live forever. This bread is my flesh, which I will give for the life of the world."[i]

52Then the Jews began to argue sharply among themselves,[j] "How can this man give us his flesh to eat?"

53Jesus said to them, "I tell you the truth, unless you eat the flesh of the Son of Man[k] and drink his blood, you have no life in you. 54Whoever eats my flesh and drinks my blood has eternal life, and I will raise him up at the last day.[l] 55For my flesh is real food and my blood is real drink. 56Whoever eats my flesh and drinks my blood remains in me, and I in him.[m] 57Just as the living Father sent me[n] and I live because of the Father, so the one who feeds on me will live because of me. 58This is the bread that came down from heaven. Your forefathers ate manna and died, but he who feeds on this bread will live forever."[o] 59He said this while teaching in the synagogue in Capernaum.

Many Disciples Desert Jesus

60On hearing it, many of his disciples[p] said, "This is a hard teaching. Who can accept it?"

61Aware that his disciples were grumbling about this, Jesus said to them, "Does this offend you?[q] 62What if you see the Son of Man ascend to where he was before![r] 63The Spirit gives life;[s] the flesh counts for nothing. The words I have spoken to you are spirit[c] and they are life. 64Yet there are some of you who do not believe." For Jesus had known[t] from the beginning which of them did not believe and who would betray him. 65He went on to say, "This is why I told you that no one can come to me unless the Father has enabled him."[u]

66From this time many of his disciples[v] turned back and no longer followed him.

67"You do not want to leave too, do you?" Jesus asked the Twelve.[w]

68Simon Peter answered him,[x] "Lord, to whom shall we go? You have the words of eternal life. 69We believe and know that you are the Holy One of God."[y]

70Then Jesus replied, "Have I not chosen you,[z] the Twelve? Yet one of you is a devil!"[a] 71(He meant Judas, the son of Simon Iscariot, who, though one of the Twelve, was later to betray him.)

Jesus Goes to the Feast of Tabernacles

7 After this, Jesus went around in Galilee, purposely staying away from Judea because the Jews[b] there were waiting to take his life.[c] 2But when the Jewish Feast of Tabernacles[d] was near, 3Jesus' brothers[e] said to him,

6:30 [m]Jn 2:11 [n]Mt 12:38
6:31 [o]Nu 11:7-9 [p]Ex 16:4,15; Ne 9:15; Ps 78:24; 105:40
6:33 [q]ver 50
6:34 [r]Jn 4:15
6:35 [s]ver 48,51 [t]Jn 4:14
6:37 [u]ver 39; Jn 17:2,6,9,24
6:38 [v]Jn 4:34; 5:30
6:39 [w]Jn 10:28; 17:12; 18:9 [x]ver 40,44,54
6:40 [y]Jn 3:15,16
6:42 [z]Lk 4:22 [a]Jn 7:27,28 [b]ver 38,62
6:44 [c]ver 65; Jer 31:3; Jn 12:32
6:45 [d]Isa 54:13; Jer 31:33,34; Heb 8:10,11; 10:16
6:46 [e]Jn 1:18; 5:37; 7:29
6:48 [f]ver 35,51
6:49 [g]ver 31,58
6:50 [h]ver 33
6:51 [i]Heb 10:10
6:52 [j]Jn 7:43; 9:16; 10:19
6:53 [k]Mt 8:20
6:54 [l]ver 39
6:56 [m]Jn 15:4-7; 1Jn 3:24; 4:15
6:57 [n]Jn 3:17
6:58 [o]ver 49-51; Jn 3:36
6:60 [p]ver 66
6:61 [q]Mt 11:6
6:62 [r]Mk 16:19; Jn 3:13; 17:5
6:63 [s]2Co 3:6
6:64 [t]Jn 2:25
6:65 [u]ver 37,44
6:66 [v]ver 60
6:67 [w]Mt 10:2
6:68 [x]Mt 16:16
6:69 [y]Mk 8:29; Lk 9:20
6:70 [z]Jn 15:16,19 [a]Jn 13:27
7:1 [b]Jn 1:19 [c]Jn 5:18

[a] *31* Exodus 16:4; Neh. 9:15; Psalm 78:24,25
[b] *45* Isaiah 54:13 [c] *63* Or *Spirit*

7:2 [d]Lev 23:34; Dt 16:16 **7:3** [e]Mt 12:46

"You ought to leave here and go to Judea, so that your disciples may see the
miracles you do. 4No one who wants to
become a public figure acts in secret.
Since you are doing these things, show
yourself to the world." 5For even his
own brothers did not believe in him.[f]
6Therefore Jesus told them, "The
right time[g] for me has not yet come;
for you any time is right. 7The world
cannot hate you, but it hates me[h] because I testify that what it does is evil.[i]
8You go to the Feast. I am not yet[a]
going up to this Feast, because for me
the right time[j] has not yet come."
9Having said this, he stayed in Galilee.
10However, after his brothers had
left for the Feast, he went also, not
publicly, but in secret. 11Now at the
Feast the Jews were watching for him[k]
and asking, "Where is that man?"
12Among the crowds there was widespread whispering about him. Some
said, "He is a good man."

Others replied, "No, he deceives the
people."[l] 13But no one would say anything publicly about him for fear of the
Jews.[m]

Jesus Teaches at the Feast

14Not until halfway through the
Feast did Jesus go up to the temple
courts and begin to teach.[n] 15The
Jews[o] were amazed and asked, "How
did this man get such learning[p] without having studied?"[q]
16Jesus answered, "My teaching is
not my own. It comes from him who
sent me.[r] 17If anyone chooses to do
God's will, he will find out[s] whether
my teaching comes from God or
whether I speak on my own. 18He who
speaks on his own does so to gain hon-
or for himself,[t] but he who works for
the honor of the one who sent him is
a man of truth; there is nothing false
about him. 19Has not Moses given you
the law?[u] Yet not one of you keeps the
law. Why are you trying to kill me?"[v]
20"You are demon-possessed,"[w] the
crowd answered. "Who is trying to kill
you?"
21Jesus said to them, "I did one miracle, and you are all astonished. 22Yet,
because Moses gave you circumcision[x] (though actually it did not come
from Moses, but from the patriarchs),[y] you circumcise a child on the
Sabbath. 23Now if a child can be circumcised on the Sabbath so that the
law of Moses may not be broken, why
are you angry with me for healing the
whole man on the Sabbath? 24Stop
judging by mere appearances, and
make a right judgment."[z]

7:5 [f]Mk 3:21
7:6 [g]Mt 26:18
7:7 [h]Jn 15:18,19 [i]Jn 3:19,20
7:8 [j]ver 6
7:11 [k]Jn 11:56
7:12 [l]ver 40,43
7:13 [m]Jn 9:22; 12:42; 19:38
7:14 [n]ver 28; Mt 26:55
7:15 [o]Jn 1:19 [p]Ac 26:24 [q]Mt 13:54
7:16 [r]Jn 3:11; 14:24
7:17 [s]Ps 25:14; Jn 8:43
7:18 [t]Jn 5:41; 8:50, 54
7:19 [u]Jn 1:17 [v]ver 1; Mt 12:14
7:20 [w]Jn 8:48; 10:20
7:22 [x]Lev 12:3 [y]Ge 17:10-14
7:24 [z]Isa 11:3,4; Jn 8:15
7:26 [a]ver 48
7:27 [b]Mt 13:55; Lk 4:22
7:28 [c]ver 14 [d]Jn 8:14 [e]Jn 8:26,42
7:29 [f]Mt 11:27
7:30 [g]ver 32,44; Jn 10:39
7:31 [h]Jn 8:30 [i]Jn 2:11
7:33 [j]Jn 13:33; 16:16 [k]Jn 16:5,10,17, 28
7:34 [l]Jn 8:21; 13:33
7:35 [m]Jas 1:1 [n]Jn 12:20; 1Pe 1:1
7:37 [o]Lev 23:36 [p]Isa 55:1; Rev 22:17
7:38 [q]Isa 58:11 [r]Jn 4:10 [s]Jn 4:14
7:39 [t]Joel 2:28; Ac 2:17,33 [u]Jn 20:22 [v]Jn 12:23; 13:31,32
7:40 [w]Mt 21:11; Jn 1:21
7:41 [x]ver 52; Jn 1:46

Is Jesus the Christ?

25At that point some of the people of
Jerusalem began to ask, "Isn't this the
man they are trying to kill? 26Here he is,
speaking publicly, and they are not
saying a word to him. Have the authorities[a] really concluded that he is the
Christ[b]? 27But we know where this
man is from;[b] when the Christ comes,
no one will know where he is from."
28Then Jesus, still teaching in the
temple courts,[c] cried out, "Yes, you
know me, and you know where I am
from.[d] I am not here on my own, but
he who sent me is true.[e] You do not
know him, 29but I know him[f] because
I am from him and he sent me."
30At this they tried to seize him, but
no one laid a hand on him,[g] because
his time had not yet come. 31Still, many
in the crowd put their faith in him.[h]
They said, "When the Christ comes,
will he do more miraculous signs[i]
than this man?"
32The Pharisees heard the crowd
whispering such things about him.
Then the chief priests and the Pharisees sent temple guards to arrest him.
33Jesus said, "I am with you for only
a short time,[j] and then I go to the one
who sent me.[k] 34You will look for me,
but you will not find me; and where I
am, you cannot come."[l]
35The Jews said to one another,
"Where does this man intend to go that
we cannot find him? Will he go where
our people live scattered[m] among
the Greeks,[n] and teach the Greeks?
36What did he mean when he said,
'You will look for me, but you will not
find me,' and 'Where I am, you cannot
come'?"
37On the last and greatest day of the
Feast,[o] Jesus stood and said in a loud
voice, "If anyone is thirsty, let him
come to me and drink.[p] 38Whoever
believes in me, as[c] the Scripture has
said,[q] streams of living water[r] will
flow from within him."[s] 39By this he
meant the Spirit,[t] whom those who
believed in him were later to receive.[u]
Up to that time the Spirit had not been
given, since Jesus had not yet been glorified.[v]
40On hearing his words, some of the
people said, "Surely this man is the
Prophet."[w]
41Others said, "He is the Christ."

Still others asked, "How can the
Christ come from Galilee?[x] 42Does

a *8* Some early manuscripts do not have *yet.*
b *26* Or *Messiah*; also in verses 27, 31, 41 and 42
c *37,38* Or / *If anyone is thirsty, let him come to me. / And let him drink, 38who believes in me. / As*

not the Scripture say that the Christ will come from David's family[a][y] and from Bethlehem,[z] the town where David lived?" **43**Thus the people were divided[a] because of Jesus. **44**Some wanted to seize him, but no one laid a hand on him.[b]

Unbelief of the Jewish Leaders

45Finally the temple guards went back to the chief priests and Pharisees, who asked them, "Why didn't you bring him in?"

46"No one ever spoke the way this man does,"[c] the guards declared.

47"You mean he has deceived you also?"[d] the Pharisees retorted. **48**"Has any of the rulers or of the Pharisees believed in him?[e] **49**No! But this mob that knows nothing of the law—there is a curse on them."

50Nicodemus,[f] who had gone to Jesus earlier and who was one of their own number, asked, **51**"Does our law condemn anyone without first hearing him to find out what he is doing?"

52They replied, "Are you from Galilee, too? Look into it, and you will find that a prophet[b] does not come out of Galilee."[g]

[The earliest manuscripts and many other ancient witnesses do not have John 7:53–8:11.]

53Then each went to his own home.

8 But Jesus went to the Mount of Olives.[h] **2**At dawn he appeared again in the temple courts, where all the people gathered around him, and he sat down to teach them.[i] **3**The teachers of the law and the Pharisees brought in a woman caught in adultery. They made her stand before the group **4**and said to Jesus, "Teacher, this woman was caught in the act of adultery. **5**In the Law Moses commanded us to stone such women.[j] Now what do you say?" **6**They were using this question as a trap,[k] in order to have a basis for accusing him.[l]

But Jesus bent down and started to write on the ground with his finger. **7**When they kept on questioning him, he straightened up and said to them, "If any one of you is without sin, let him be the first to throw a stone[m] at her."[n] **8**Again he stooped down and wrote on the ground.

9At this, those who heard began to go away one at a time, the older ones first, until only Jesus was left, with the woman still standing there. **10**Jesus straightened up and asked her, "Woman, where are they? Has no one condemned you?"

11"No one, sir," she said.

"Then neither do I condemn you,"[o] Jesus declared. "Go now and leave your life of sin."[p]

The Validity of Jesus' Testimony

12When Jesus spoke again to the people, he said, "I am[q] the light of the world.[r] Whoever follows me will never walk in darkness, but will have the light of life."[s]

13The Pharisees challenged him, "Here you are, appearing as your own witness; your testimony is not valid."[t]

14Jesus answered, "Even if I testify on my own behalf, my testimony is valid, for I know where I came from and where I am going.[u] But you have no idea where I come from[v] or where I am going. **15**You judge by human standards;[w] I pass judgment on no one.[x] **16**But if I do judge, my decisions are right, because I am not alone. I stand with the Father, who sent me.[y] **17**In your own Law it is written that the testimony of two men is valid.[z] **18**I am one who testifies for myself; my other witness is the Father, who sent me."[a]

19Then they asked him, "Where is your father?"

"You do not know me or my Father,"[b] Jesus replied. "If you knew me, you would know my Father also."[c] **20**He spoke these words while teaching[d] in the temple area near the place

7:42 [y]Mt 1:1 [z]Mic 5:2; Mt 2:5,6; Lk 2:4
7:43 [a]Jn 9:16; 10:19
7:44 [b]ver 30
7:46 [c]Mt 7:28
7:47 [d]ver 12
7:48 [e]Jn 12:42
7:50 [f]Jn 3:1; 19:39
7:52 [g]ver 41
8:1 [h]Mt 21:1
8:2 [i]ver 20; Mt 26:55
8:5 [j]Lev 20:10; Dt 22:22
8:6 [k]Mt 22:15,18 [l]Mt 12:10
8:7 [m]Dt 17:7 [n]Ro 2:1,22
8:11 [o]Jn 3:17 [p]Jn 5:14
8:12 [q]Jn 6:35 [r]Jn 1:4; 12:35 [s]Pr 4:18; Mt 5:14
8:13 [t]Jn 5:31
8:14 [u]Jn 13:3; 16:28 [v]Jn 7:28; 9:29
8:15 [w]Jn 7:24 [x]Jn 3:17
8:16 [y]Jn 5:30
8:17 [z]Dt 17:6; Mt 18:16
8:18 [a]Jn 5:37
8:19 [b]Jn 16:3 [c]Jn 14:7; 1Jn 2:23
8:20 [d]Mt 26:55

a 42 Greek *seed* b 52 Two early manuscripts *the Prophet*

7:37–39

THIRSTY FOR THE SPIRIT

What a promise! Jesus told his followers that after his resurrection from the dead, God's Spirit would permanently dwell inside of them. The longing for lasting meaning and eternal significance inside every man can't be satisfied with external things like money, fame, power, position or even religious activity. But those who know Jesus will find internal—and eternal—fulfillment. Here Jesus promises that the indwelling Holy Spirit will be like a spring of water that quenches their greatest thirst.

Thank God for giving you his Spirit. Ask him to give you the wisdom you need to draw on the Spirit's power when you're weak and on his comfort when you're down.

where the offerings were put.[e] Yet no one seized him, because his time had not yet come.[f]

21Once more Jesus said to them, "I am going away, and you will look for me, and you will die[g] in your sin. Where I go, you cannot come."[h]

22This made the Jews ask, "Will he kill himself? Is that why he says, 'Where I go, you cannot come'?"

23But he continued, "You are from below; I am from above. You are of this world; I am not of this world.[i] 24I told you that you would die in your sins; if you do not believe that I am ⌞the one I claim to be⌟,[a][j] you will indeed die in your sins."

25"Who are you?" they asked.

"Just what I have been claiming all along," Jesus replied. 26"I have much to say in judgment of you. But he who sent me is reliable,[k] and what I have heard from him I tell the world."[l]

27They did not understand that he was telling them about his Father. 28So Jesus said, "When you have lifted up the Son of Man,[m] then you will know that I am ⌞the one I claim to be⌟ and that I do nothing on my own but speak just what the Father has taught me. 29The one who sent me is with me; he has not left me alone,[n] for I always do what pleases him."[o] 30Even as he spoke, many put their faith in him.[p]

The Children of Abraham

1 →PG. 1175

31To the Jews who had believed him, Jesus said, "If you hold to my teaching,[q] you are really my disciples. 32Then you will know the truth, and the truth will set you free."[r]

33They answered him, "We are Abraham's descendants[b][s] and have never been slaves of anyone. How can you say that we shall be set free?"

34Jesus replied, "I tell you the truth, everyone who sins is a slave to sin.[t] 35Now a slave has no permanent place in the family, but a son belongs to it forever.[u] 36So if the Son sets you free, you will be free indeed. 37I know you are Abraham's descendants. Yet you are ready to kill me,[v] because you have no room for my word. 38I am telling you what I have seen in the Father's presence,[w] and you do what you have heard from your father.[c]"

39"Abraham is our father," they answered.

"If you were Abraham's children,"[x] said Jesus, "then you would[d] do the things Abraham did. 40As it is, you are determined to kill me, a man who has told you the truth that I heard from God.[y] Abraham did not do such things. 41You are doing the things your own father does."[z]

"We are not illegitimate children," they protested. "The only Father we have is God himself."[a]

The Children of the Devil

42Jesus said to them, "If God were your Father, you would love me,[b] for I came from God[c] and now am here. I have not come on my own;[d] but he sent me.[e] 43Why is my language not clear to you? Because you are unable to hear what I say. 44You belong to your father, the devil,[f] and you want to carry out your father's desire.[g] He was a murderer from the beginning, not holding to the truth, for there is no truth in him. When he lies, he speaks his native language, for he is a liar and the father of lies.[h] 45Yet because I tell the truth,[i] you do not believe me! 46Can any of you prove me guilty of sin? If I am telling the truth, why don't you believe me? 47He who belongs to God hears what God says.[j] The reason you do not hear is that you do not belong to God."

8:20 [e]Mk 12:41 [f]Mt 26:18; Jn 7:30
8:21 [g]Eze 3:18 [h]Jn 7:34; 13:33
8:23 [i]Jn 3:31; 17:14
8:24 [j]Jn 4:26; 13:19
8:26 [k]Jn 7:28 [l]Jn 3:32; 15:15
8:28 [m]Jn 3:14; 5:19; 12:32
8:29 [n]ver 16; Jn 16:32 [o]Jn 4:34; 5:30; 6:38
8:30 [p]Jn 7:31
8:31 [q]Jn 15:7; 2Jn 9
8:32 [r]Ro 8:2; Jas 2:12
8:33 [s]ver 37,39; Mt 3:9
8:34 [t]Ro 6:16; 2Pe 2:19
8:35 [u]Gal 4:30
8:37 [v]ver 39,40
8:38 [w]Jn 5:19,30; 14:10,24
8:39 [x]ver 37; Ro 9:7; Gal 3:7
8:40 [y]ver 26
8:41 [z]ver 38,44 [a]Isa 63:16; 64:8
8:42 [b]1Jn 5:1 [c]Jn 16:27; 17:8 [d]Jn 7:28 [e]Jn 3:17
8:44 [f]1Jn 3:8 [g]ver 38,41 [h]Ge 3:4
8:45 [i]Jn 18:37
8:47 [j]Jn 18:37; 1Jn 4:6

[a]24 Or *I am he*; also in verse 28 [b]33 Greek *seed*; also in verse 37 [c]38 Or *presence. Therefore do what you have heard from the Father.* [d]39 Some early manuscripts *"If you are Abraham's children," said Jesus, "then*

8:31–32

TRUE FREEDOM

Freedom. People write and sing about it. They fight and die for it. Every person wants to be free from slavery, poverty and ignorance.

Jesus spoke of another kind of freedom. He referred to a freedom from the power of sin, a freedom to know and serve God. That freedom isn't found through any religious activity. Nor is it obtained as a birthright—as some ancient Jews thought. Instead, true freedom comes through a relationship with the One who is the embodiment of the true path to salvation—Jesus Christ. When Jesus lives within a person, he liberates that person from enslavement to sin and death.

If you've struggled with sin, and we all have, you know about its tyrannical hold. You've felt its tight, vise-like grip on your soul. In this passage Jesus offers freedom from sin's oppression in our lives. All we need to do is to "hold to his teaching" through the power of the Holy Spirit and become his true disciples in thought, word and deed.

The Claims of Jesus About Himself

48The Jews answered him, "Aren't we right in saying that you are a Samaritan[k] and demon-possessed?"[l]

49"I am not possessed by a demon," said Jesus, "but I honor my Father and you dishonor me. 50I am not seeking glory for myself;[m] but there is one who seeks it, and he is the judge. 51I tell you the truth, if anyone keeps my word, he will never see death."[n]

52At this the Jews exclaimed, "Now we know that you are demon-possessed! Abraham died and so did the prophets, yet you say that if anyone keeps your word, he will never taste death. 53Are you greater than our father Abraham?[o] He died, and so did the prophets. Who do you think you are?"

54Jesus replied, "If I glorify myself,[p] my glory means nothing. My Father, whom you claim as your God, is the one who glorifies me.[q] 55Though you do not know him,[r] I know him.[s] If I said I did not, I would be a liar like you, but I do know him and keep his word.[t] 56Your father Abraham[u] rejoiced at the thought of seeing my day; he saw it[v] and was glad."

57"You are not yet fifty years old," the Jews said to him, "and you have seen Abraham!"

58"I tell you the truth," Jesus answered, "before Abraham was born,[w] I am!"[x] 59At this, they picked up stones to stone him,[y] but Jesus hid himself,[z] slipping away from the temple grounds.

Jesus Heals a Man Born Blind

9 As he went along, he saw a man blind from birth. 2His disciples asked him, "Rabbi,[a] who sinned,[b] this man[c] or his parents,[d] that he was born blind?"

3"Neither this man nor his parents sinned," said Jesus, "but this happened so that the work of God might be displayed in his life.[e] 4As long as it is day,[f] we must do the work of him who sent me. Night is coming, when no one can work. 5While I am in the world, I am the light of the world."[g]

6Having said this, he spit[h] on the ground, made some mud with the saliva, and put it on the man's eyes. 7"Go," he told him, "wash in the Pool of Siloam"[i] (this word means Sent). So the man went and washed, and came home seeing.[j]

8His neighbors and those who had formerly seen him begging asked, "Isn't this the same man who used to sit and beg?"[k] 9Some claimed that he was.

Others said, "No, he only looks like him."

But he himself insisted, "I am the man."

10"How then were your eyes opened?" they demanded.

11He replied, "The man they call Jesus made some mud and put it on my eyes. He told me to go to Siloam and wash. So I went and washed, and then I could see."[l]

12"Where is this man?" they asked him.

"I don't know," he said.

The Pharisees Investigate the Healing

13They brought to the Pharisees the man who had been blind. 14Now the day on which Jesus had made the mud and opened the man's eyes was a Sabbath.[m] 15Therefore the Pharisees also asked him how he had received his sight.[n] "He put mud on my eyes," the man replied, "and I washed, and now I see."

16Some of the Pharisees said, "This man is not from God, for he does not keep the Sabbath."[o]

But others asked, "How can a sinner do such miraculous signs?" So they were divided.[p]

17Finally they turned again to the blind man, "What have you to say about him? It was your eyes he opened."

The man replied, "He is a prophet."[q]

18The Jews[r] still did not believe that he had been blind and had received his sight until they sent for the man's parents. 19"Is this your son?" they asked. "Is this the one you say was born blind? How is it that now he can see?"

20"We know he is our son," the parents answered, "and we know he was born blind. 21But how he can see now, or who opened his eyes, we don't know. Ask him. He is of age; he will speak for himself." 22His parents said this because they were afraid of the Jews,[s] for already the Jews had decided that anyone who acknowledged that Jesus was the Christ[a] would be put out[t] of the synagogue.[u] 23That was why his parents said, "He is of age; ask him."[v]

24A second time they summoned the man who had been blind. "Give glory to God,[b]"[w] they said. "We know this man is a sinner."[x]

25He replied, "Whether he is a sinner

8:48 [k] Mt 10:5 [l] ver 52; Jn 7:20
8:50 [m] ver 54; Jn 5:41
8:51 [n] Jn 11:26
8:53 [o] Jn 4:12
8:54 [p] ver 50 [q] Jn 16:14; 17:1,5
8:55 [r] ver 19 [s] Jn 7:28,29 [t] Jn 15:10
8:56 [u] ver 37,39 [v] Mt 13:17; Heb 11:13
8:58 [w] Jn 1:2; 17:5, 24 [x] Ex 3:14
8:59 [y] Lev 24:16; Jn 10:31; 11:8 [z] Jn 12:36
9:2 [a] Mt 23:7 [b] ver 34; Lk 13:2; Ac 28:4 [c] Eze 18:20 [d] Ex 20:5; Job 21:19
9:3 [e] Jn 11:4
9:4 [f] Jn 11:9; 12:35
9:5 [g] Jn 1:4; 8:12; 12:46
9:6 [h] Mk 7:33; 8:23
9:7 [i] ver 11; 2Ki 5:10; Lk 13:4 [j] Isa 35:5; Jn 11:37
9:8 [k] Ac 3:2,10
9:11 [l] ver 7
9:14 [m] Jn 5:9
9:15 [n] ver 10
9:16 [o] Mt 12:2 [p] Jn 6:52; 7:43; 10:19
9:17 [q] Mt 21:11
9:18 [r] Jn 1:19
9:22 [s] Jn 7:13 [t] ver 34; Lk 6:22 [u] Jn 12:42; 16:2
9:23 [v] ver 21
9:24 [w] Jos 7:19 [x] ver 16

[a] 22 Or *Messiah* [b] 24 A solemn charge to tell the truth (see Joshua 7:19)

or not, I don't know. One thing I do
know. I was blind but now I see!"
26 Then they asked him, "What did
he do to you? How did he open your
eyes?"
27 He answered, "I have told you already[y] and you did not listen. Why do
you want to hear it again? Do you want
to become his disciples, too?"
28 Then they hurled insults at him
and said, "You are this fellow's disciple!
We are disciples of Moses![z] 29 We
know that God spoke to Moses, but as
for this fellow, we don't even know
where he comes from."[a]
30 The man answered, "Now that is
remarkable! You don't know where he
comes from, yet he opened my eyes.
31 We know that God does not listen to
sinners. He listens to the godly man
who does his will.[b] 32 Nobody has ever
heard of opening the eyes of a man
born blind. 33 If this man were not from
God,[c] he could do nothing."
34 To this they replied, "You were
steeped in sin at birth;[d] how dare you
lecture us!" And they threw him out.[e]

Spiritual Blindness

35 Jesus heard that they had thrown
him out, and when he found him, he
said, "Do you believe in the Son of
Man?"
36 "Who is he, sir?" the man asked.
"Tell me so that I may believe in
him."[f]
37 Jesus said, "You have now seen
him; in fact, he is the one speaking with
you."[g]
38 Then the man said, "Lord, I believe," and he worshiped him.[h]
39 Jesus said, "For judgment[i] I have
come into this world,[j] so that the
blind will see[k] and those who see will
become blind."[l]
40 Some Pharisees who were with
him heard him say this and asked,
"What? Are we blind too?"[m]
41 Jesus said, "If you were blind, you
would not be guilty of sin; but now that
you claim you can see, your guilt remains.[n]

The Shepherd and His Flock

10 "I tell you the truth, the man who
does not enter the sheep pen by the
gate, but climbs in by some other way,
is a thief and a robber. 2 The man who
enters by the gate is the shepherd of
his sheep.[o] 3 The watchman opens the
gate for him, and the sheep listen to his
voice.[p] He calls his own sheep by
name and leads them out. 4 When he
has brought out all his own, he goes on
ahead of them, and his sheep follow
him because they know his voice. 5 But
they will never follow a stranger; in
fact, they will run away from him because they do not recognize a stranger's voice." 6 Jesus used this figure of
speech,[q] but they did not understand
what he was telling them.
7 Therefore Jesus said again, "I tell
you the truth, I am the gate for the
sheep. 8 All who ever came before me[r]
were thieves and robbers, but the
sheep did not listen to them. 9 I am the
gate; whoever enters through me will
be saved.[a] He will come in and go out,
and find pasture. 10 The thief comes
only to steal and kill and destroy; I have
come that they may have life, and have
it to the full.
11 "I am the good shepherd.[s] The
good shepherd lays down his life for
the sheep.[t] 12 The hired hand is not
the shepherd who owns the sheep. So
when he sees the wolf coming, he
abandons the sheep and runs away.[u]
Then the wolf attacks the flock and
scatters it. 13 The man runs away because he is a hired hand and cares
nothing for the sheep.
14 "I am the good shepherd;[v] I know
my sheep[w] and my sheep know me—
15 just as the Father knows me and I
know the Father[x]—and I lay down my
life for the sheep. 16 I have other
sheep[y] that are not of this sheep pen.
I must bring them also. They too will
listen to my voice, and there shall be
one flock[z] and one shepherd.[a] 17 The
reason my Father loves me is that I lay
down my life[b]—only to take it up
again. 18 No one takes it from me, but I
lay it down of my own accord.[c] I have
authority to lay it down and authority
to take it up again. This command I
received from my Father."[d]
19 At these words the Jews were again
divided.[e] 20 Many of them said, "He
is demon-possessed[f] and raving
mad.[g] Why listen to him?"
21 But others said, "These are not the
sayings of a man possessed by a demon.[h] Can a demon open the eyes of
the blind?"[i]

6 →PG. 1182
7 →PG. 1178

The Unbelief of the Jews

22 Then came the Feast of Dedication[b] at Jerusalem. It was winter,
23 and Jesus was in the temple area
walking in Solomon's Colonnade.[j]
24 The Jews[k] gathered around him,
saying, "How long will you keep us in
suspense? If you are the Christ,[c] tell us
plainly."[l]
25 Jesus answered, "I did tell you,[m]

9:27 [y]ver 15
9:28 [z]Jn 5:45
9:29 [a]Jn 8:14
9:31 [b]Ge 18:23-32; Ps 34:15,16; 66:18; 145:19, 20; Pr 15:29; Isa 1:15; 59:1, 2; Jn 15:7; Jas 5:16-18; 1Jn 5:14,15
9:33 [c]ver 16; Jn 3:2
9:34 [d]ver 2 [e]ver 22,35; Isa 66:5
9:36 [f]Ro 10:14
9:37 [g]Jn 4:26
9:38 [h]Mt 28:9
9:39 [i]Jn 5:22 [j]Jn 3:19 [k]Lk 4:18 [l]Mt 13:13
9:40 [m]Ro 2:19
9:41 [n]Jn 15:22,24
10:2 [o]ver 11,14
10:3 [p]ver 4,5,14,16, 27
10:6 [q]Jn 16:25
10:8 [r]Jer 23:1,2
10:11 [s]ver 14; Isa 40:11; Eze 34:11-16, 23; Heb 13:20; 1Pe 5:4; Rev 7:17 [t]Jn 15:13; 1Jn 3:16
10:12 [u]Zec 11:16,17
10:14 [v]ver 11 [w]ver 27
10:15 [x]Mt 11:27
10:16 [y]Isa 56:8 [z]Jn 11:52; Eph 2:11-19 [a]Eze 37:24; 1Pe 2:25
10:17 [b]ver 11,15,18
10:18 [c]Mt 26:53 [d]Jn 15:10; Php 2:8; Heb 5:8
10:19 [e]Jn 7:43; 9:16
10:20 [f]Jn 7:20 [g]Mk 3:21
10:21 [h]Mt 4:24 [i]Ex 4:11; Jn 9:32,33
10:23 [j]Ac 3:11; 5:12
10:24 [k]Jn 1:19 [l]Jn 16:25,29
10:25 [m]Jn 8:58

a 9 Or *kept safe*
b 22 That is, Hanukkah
c 24 Or *Messiah*

but you do not believe. The miracles
I do in my Father's name speak for
me,[n] 26but you do not believe because
you are not my sheep.[o] 27My sheep
listen to my voice; I know them,[p] and
they follow me.[q] 28I give them eternal
life, and they shall never perish; no one
can snatch them out of my hand.[r]
29My Father, who has given them to
me,[s] is greater than all[a];[t] no one
can snatch them out of my Father's
hand. 30I and the Father are one."[u]
31Again the Jews picked up stones to
stone him,[v] 32but Jesus said to them,
"I have shown you many great miracles
from the Father. For which of these do
you stone me?"
33"We are not stoning you for any of
these," replied the Jews, "but for blasphemy, because you, a mere man,
claim to be God."[w]
34Jesus answered them, "Is it not
written in your Law,[x] 'I have said you
are gods'[b]?[y] 35If he called them
'gods,' to whom the word of God
came—and the Scripture cannot be
broken— 36what about the one whom
the Father set apart[z] as his very own[a]
and sent into the world?[b] Why then do
you accuse me of blasphemy because I
said, 'I am God's Son'?[c] 37Do not believe me unless I do what my Father
does.[d] 38But if I do it, even though you
do not believe me, believe the miracles,
that you may know and understand
that the Father is in me, and I in the
Father."[e] 39Again they tried to seize
him,[f] but he escaped their grasp.[g]
40Then Jesus went back across the
Jordan[h] to the place where John had
been baptizing in the early days. Here
he stayed 41and many people came to
him. They said, "Though John never
performed a miraculous sign,[i] all that
John said about this man was true."[j]
42And in that place many believed in
Jesus.[k]

The Death of Lazarus

11 Now a man named Lazarus was
sick. He was from Bethany,[l] the
village of Mary and her sister Martha.[m]
2This Mary, whose brother Lazarus
now lay sick, was the same one who
poured perfume on the Lord and
wiped his feet with her hair.[n] 3So the
sisters sent word to Jesus, "Lord, the
one you love[o] is sick."
4When he heard this, Jesus said,
"This sickness will not end in death.
No, it is for God's glory[p] so that God's
Son may be glorified through it." 5Jesus
loved Martha and her sister and Lazarus. 6Yet when he heard that Lazarus
was sick, he stayed where he was two
more days.
7Then he said to his disciples, "Let
us go back to Judea."[q]
8"But Rabbi,"[r] they said, "a short
while ago the Jews tried to stone you,[s]
and yet you are going back there?"
9Jesus answered, "Are there not
twelve hours of daylight? A man who
walks by day will not stumble, for he
sees by this world's light.[t] 10It is when
he walks by night that he stumbles, for
he has no light."
11After he had said this, he went on
to tell them, "Our friend[u] Lazarus has
fallen asleep;[v] but I am going there to
wake him up."
12His disciples replied, "Lord, if he
sleeps, he will get better." 13Jesus had
been speaking of his death, but his disciples thought he meant natural
sleep.[w]
14So then he told them plainly, "Lazarus is dead, 15and for your sake I am
glad I was not there, so that you may
believe. But let us go to him."
16Then Thomas[x] (called Didymus)
said to the rest of the disciples, "Let us
also go, that we may die with him."

10:25 [n]Jn 5:36 **10:26** [o]Jn 8:47 **10:27** [p]ver 14 [q]ver 4 **10:28** [r]Jn 6:39 **10:29** [s]Jn 17:2,6,24 [t]Jn 14:28 **10:30** [u]Jn 17:21-23 **10:31** [v]Jn 8:59 **10:33** [w]Lev 24:16; Jn 5:18 **10:34** [x]Jn 8:17; Ro 3:19 [y]Ps 82:6 **10:36** [z]Jer 1:5 [a]Jn 6:69 [b]Jn 3:17 [c]Jn 5:17,18 **10:37** [d]ver 25; Jn 15:24 **10:38** [e]Jn 14:10,11, 20; 17:21 **10:39** [f]Jn 7:30 [g]Lk 4:30; Jn 8:59 **10:40** [h]Jn 1:28 **10:41** [i]Jn 2:11; 3:30 [j]Jn 1:26,27,30, 34 **10:42** [k]Jn 7:31 **11:1** [l]Mt 21:17 [m]Lk 10:38 **11:2** [n]Mk 14:3; Lk 7:38; Jn 12:3 **11:3** [o]ver 5,36 **11:4** [p]ver 40; Jn 9:3 **11:7** [q]Jn 10:40 **11:8** [r]Mt 23:7 [s]Jn 8:59; 10:31 **11:9** [t]Jn 9:4; 12:35 **11:11** [u]ver 3 [v]Ac 7:60 **11:13** [w]Mt 9:24 **11:16** [x]Mt 10:3; Jn 14:5; 20:24-28; 21:2; Ac 1:13

10:27–30

JESUS, OUR SHEPHERD

When Jesus compared himself to a shepherd, he evoked an image that every man who heard his words understood. These men were either shepherds themselves, or knew people who were. They understood the devotion that shepherds had for their sheep. Jesus not only said he was the good shepherd, but he also told the men standing around him that they were his sheep—if they followed him. He promised to give his sheep eternal life. That was a promise he could keep because Jesus and his Father were one (v. 30).

You would think such tender language would endear Jesus to his listeners. Instead, the people picked up stones to kill him. Why? Because they understood that through these bold promises, Jesus was claiming to be God himself.

Occasionally you may meet someone who claims that Jesus never said he was God. But why would people accuse him of blasphemy if he had never made such a claim? And why did they threaten to stone him?

Think for a few moments about the implications of having a divine shepherd watch over you. Read Psalm 23 for some additional insight into this idea of Jesus being our Shepherd.

[a] *29* Many early manuscripts *What my Father has given me is greater than all*
[b] *34* Psalm 82:6

Jesus Comforts the Sisters

17On his arrival, Jesus found that
Lazarus had already been in the tomb
for four days.[y] 18Bethany[z] was less
than two miles[a] from Jerusalem, 19and
many Jews had come to Martha and
Mary to comfort them in the loss of
their brother.[a] 20When Martha heard
that Jesus was coming, she went out to
meet him, but Mary stayed at home.[b]
21"Lord," Martha said to Jesus, "if
you had been here, my brother would
not have died.[c] 22But I know that even
now God will give you whatever you
ask."[d]
23Jesus said to her, "Your brother
will rise again."
24Martha answered, "I know he will
rise again in the resurrection[e] at the
last day."
25Jesus said to her, "I am the resurrection and the life.[f] He who believes
in me will live, even though he dies;
26and whoever lives and believes in me
will never die. Do you believe this?"
27"Yes, Lord," she told him, "I believe that you are the Christ,[b][g] the
Son of God,[h] who was to come into
the world."[i]
28And after she had said this, she
went back and called her sister Mary
aside. "The Teacher[j] is here," she
said, "and is asking for you." 29When
Mary heard this, she got up quickly and
went to him. 30Now Jesus had not yet
entered the village, but was still at the
place where Martha had met him.[k]
31When the Jews who had been with
Mary in the house, comforting her,[l]
noticed how quickly she got up and
went out, they followed her, supposing
she was going to the tomb to mourn
there.
32When Mary reached the place
where Jesus was and saw him, she fell
at his feet and said, "Lord, if you had
been here, my brother would not have
died."[m]
33When Jesus saw her weeping, and
the Jews who had come along with her
also weeping, he was deeply moved[n]
in spirit and troubled.[o] 34"Where have
you laid him?" he asked.
"Come and see, Lord," they replied.
35Jesus wept.[p]
36Then the Jews said, "See how he
loved him!"[q]
37But some of them said, "Could not
he who opened the eyes of the blind
man[r] have kept this man from dying?"[s]

Jesus Raises Lazarus From the Dead

38Jesus, once more deeply moved,[t]
came to the tomb. It was a cave with
a stone laid across the entrance.[u]
39"Take away the stone," he said.
"But, Lord," said Martha, the sister
of the dead man, "by this time there is
a bad odor, for he has been there four
days."[v]
40Then Jesus said, "Did I not tell you
that if you believed,[w] you would see
the glory of God?"[x]
41So they took away the stone. Then
Jesus looked up[y] and said, "Father,[z]
I thank you that you have heard me. 42I
knew that you always hear me, but I
said this for the benefit of the people
standing here,[a] that they may believe
that you sent me."[b]
43When he had said this, Jesus called
in a loud voice, "Lazarus, come out!"[c]
44The dead man came out, his hands
and feet wrapped with strips of linen,[d]
and a cloth around his face.[e]
Jesus said to them, "Take off the
grave clothes and let him go."

The Plot to Kill Jesus

45Therefore many of the Jews who
had come to visit Mary,[f] and had seen
what Jesus did,[g] put their faith in
him.[h] 46But some of them went to the
Pharisees and told them what Jesus

[a] 18 Greek *fifteen stadia* (about 3 kilometers)
[b] 27 Or *Messiah*

11:17 [y] ver 6,39
11:18 [z] ver 1
11:19 [a] ver 31; Job 2:11
11:20 [b] Lk 10:38-42
11:21 [c] ver 32,37
11:22 [d] ver 41,42; Jn 9:31
11:24 [e] Da 12:2; Jn 5:28,29; Ac 24:15
11:25 [f] Jn 1:4
11:27 [g] Lk 2:11 [h] Mt 16:16 [i] Jn 6:14
11:28 [j] Mt 26:18; Jn 13:13
11:30 [k] ver 20
11:31 [l] ver 19
11:32 [m] ver 21
11:33 [n] ver 38 [o] Jn 12:27
11:35 [p] Lk 19:41
11:36 [q] ver 3
11:37 [r] Jn 9:6,7 [s] ver 21,32
11:38 [t] ver 33 [u] Mt 27:60; Lk 24:2; Jn 20:1
11:39 [v] ver 17
11:40 [w] ver 23-25 [x] ver 4
11:41 [y] Jn 17:1 [z] Mt 11:25
11:42 [a] Jn 12:30 [b] Jn 3:17
11:43 [c] Lk 7:14
11:44 [d] Jn 19:40 [e] Jn 20:7
11:45 [f] ver 19 [g] Jn 2:23 [h] Ex 14:31; Jn 7:31

11:35

PROMISE 2

REAL MEN WEEP

"Jesus wept." Those two words comprise the shortest verse in the Bible. Yet, they say volumes about real manhood, don't they? They tell us that real men love deeply (see 11:5 and 36), real men cry when they're in pain, and real men allow others to see their pain (see v. 38).

Most men find it difficult to openly share their pain. After all, if they should cry, others might think they're weak or inadequate. For most men in our society, crying as Jesus did leaves a sense of being uncomfortably vulnerable. Yet Jesus, during this time of intense emotion, wept. His display was such that others who saw him weeping could openly see the love that he had for Lazarus and his two sisters.

Crying can bring healing and much-needed emotional release. In a sense, it cleanses the soul. It also places us in a position where others can express their love to us. They can comfort us during our times of deep pain, and in so doing reinforce the emotional connections that are imperative to strengthening the bond of friendship.

For the next Promise 2 reading go to page 1190.

had done. 47Then the chief priests and the Pharisees[i] called a meeting[j] of the Sanhedrin.[k]

"What are we accomplishing?" they asked. "Here is this man performing many miraculous signs.[l] 48If we let him go on like this, everyone will believe in him, and then the Romans will come and take away both our place[a] and our nation."

49Then one of them, named Caiaphas,[m] who was high priest that year,[n] spoke up, "You know nothing at all! 50You do not realize that it is better for you that one man die for the people than that the whole nation perish."[o]

51He did not say this on his own, but as high priest that year he prophesied that Jesus would die for the Jewish nation, 52and not only for that nation but also for the scattered children of God, to bring them together and make them one.[p] 53So from that day on they plotted to take his life.[q]

54Therefore Jesus no longer moved about publicly among the Jews.[r] Instead he withdrew to a region near the desert, to a village called Ephraim, where he stayed with his disciples.

55When it was almost time for the Jewish Passover,[s] many went up from the country to Jerusalem for their ceremonial cleansing[t] before the Passover. 56They kept looking for Jesus,[u] and as they stood in the temple area they asked one another, "What do you think? Isn't he coming to the Feast at all?" 57But the chief priests and Pharisees had given orders that if anyone found out where Jesus was, he should report it so that they might arrest him.

Jesus Anointed at Bethany

1 →PG. 1180
5 →PG. 1182

12 Six days before the Passover,[v] Jesus arrived at Bethany,[w] where Lazarus lived, whom Jesus had raised from the dead. 2Here a dinner was given in Jesus' honor. Martha served,[x] while Lazarus was among those reclining at the table with him. 3Then Mary took about a pint[b] of pure nard, an expensive perfume;[y] she poured it on Jesus' feet and wiped his feet with her hair.[z] And the house was filled with the fragrance of the perfume.

4But one of his disciples, Judas Iscariot, who was later to betray him,[a] objected, 5"Why wasn't this perfume sold and the money given to the poor? It was worth a year's wages.[c]" 6He did not say this because he cared about the poor but because he was a thief; as keeper of the money bag,[b] he used to help himself to what was put into it.

7"Leave her alone," Jesus replied. "⌞It was intended⌟ that she should save this perfume for the day of my burial.[c] 8You will always have the poor among you,[d] but you will not always have me."

9Meanwhile a large crowd of Jews found out that Jesus was there and came, not only because of him but also to see Lazarus, whom he had raised from the dead.[e] 10So the chief priests made plans to kill Lazarus as well, 11for on account of him[f] many of the Jews were going over to Jesus and putting their faith in him.[g]

The Triumphal Entry

›See Matthew 21:4–9; Mark 11:7–10; Luke 19:35–38

12The next day the great crowd that had come for the Feast heard that Jesus was on his way to Jerusalem. 13They took palm branches and went out to meet him, shouting,

"Hosanna![d]"

"Blessed is he who comes in the
name of the Lord!"[e][h]

"Blessed is the King of Israel!"[i]

14Jesus found a young donkey and sat upon it, as it is written,

15"Do not be afraid, O Daughter of
Zion;
see, your king is coming,
seated on a donkey's colt."[f][j]

16At first his disciples did not understand all this.[k] Only after Jesus was glorified[l] did they realize that these things had been written about him and that they had done these things to him.

17Now the crowd that was with him[m] when he called Lazarus from the tomb and raised him from the dead continued to spread the word. 18Many people, because they had heard that he had given this miraculous sign,[n] went out to meet him. 19So the Pharisees said to one another, "See, this is getting us nowhere. Look how the whole world has gone after him!"[o]

Jesus Predicts His Death

20Now there were some Greeks[p] among those who went up to worship at the Feast. 21They came to Philip, who was from Bethsaida[q] in Galilee, with a request. "Sir," they said, "we would like to see Jesus." 22Philip went

11:47 [i]ver 57 [j]Mt 26:3 [k]Mt 5:22 [l]Jn 2:11 **11:49** [m]Mt 26:3 [n]ver 51; Jn 18:13,14 **11:50** [o]Jn 18:14 **11:52** [p]Isa 49:6; Jn 10:16 **11:53** [q]Mt 12:14 **11:54** [r]Jn 7:1 **11:55** [s]Ex 12:13,23, 27; Mt 26:1,2; Mk 14:1; Jn 13:1 [t]2Ch 30:17,18 **11:56** [u]Jn 7:11 **12:1** [v]Jn 11:55 [w]Mt 21:17 **12:2** [x]Lk 10:38-42 **12:3** [y]Mk 14:3 [z]Jn 11:2 **12:4** [a]Mt 10:4 **12:6** [b]Jn 13:29

12:7 [c]Jn 19:40 **12:8** [d]Dt 15:11 **12:9** [e]Jn 11:43,44 **12:11** [f]ver 17,18; Jn 11:45 [g]Jn 7:31 **12:13** [h]Ps 118:25,26 [i]Jn 1:49 **12:15** [j]Zec 9:9 **12:16** [k]Mk 9:32 [l]Jn 2:22; 7:39; 14:26 **12:17** [m]Jn 11:42 **12:18** [n]ver 11 **12:19** [o]Jn 11:47,48 **12:20** [p]Jn 7:35; Ac 11:20 **12:21** [q]Mt 11:21; Jn 1:44

a *48* Or *temple* **b** *3* Greek *a litra* (probably about 0.5 liter) **c** *5* Greek *three hundred denarii* **d** *13* A Hebrew expression meaning "Save!" which became an exclamation of praise **e** *13* Psalm 118:25, 26 **f** *15* Zech. 9:9

PHILIP

A Man of Faith, Wisdom and Service

If you have ever wanted to meet an enthusiastic witness for Christ, Philip is your man. When some Greeks approached him and said, "We would like to see Jesus," Philip went running to find Andrew (John 12:21). Together they brought these non-Jewish men to Jesus. That's all it took. Philip "the evangelist, one of the Seven" (Acts 21:8) was anxious to share the gospel with these searching foreigners. Yet Philip was also willing "to wait on tables" in service to the Grecian widows in the early church (6:2–3). Philip was faithful—whether feeding hungry hearts or hungry mouths.

Preaching to the Multitudes

Though numerous believers left Jerusalem to preach the good news to Jews throughout Judea, Philip went "to a city in Samaria and proclaimed the Christ there" (8:5). Many of the believers considered the Samaritans unfit for the gospel message. In fact, most of the Jews in Philip's day would have nothing to do with the Samaritans. Samaritans were not "true" Jews, but a mixed race resulting from Jewish intermarriages with Gentiles. There was such strong tension between these two peoples that most Jews traveling from Judea to Galilee would cross the Jordan River and use the road along its eastern bank in order to avoid traveling through Samaria.

Philip did not share this animosity toward the Samaritans; he willingly shared the gospel message with them. God richly blessed Philip's ministry, so that "when the crowds heard Philip and saw the miraculous signs he did, they all paid close attention to what he said" (Acts 8:6). Many people were healed and delivered from evil spirits, "so there was great joy in that city" (8:8). In this way, God demonstrated through Philip that the gospel was not an exclusive message for "pure Jews," but was extended to the Samaritans as well.

Preaching to Only One

You might think that because of Philip's successful ministry among the crowds of Samaria, he would be tempted after that to minister exclusively to large gatherings. In our own society we tend to view bigger as better. If Philip were ministering today to an assembly of hundreds, he should, in our minds, plan to move up and preach to a gathering of thousands.

Yet Philip was not motivated by prestige or the need to appear successful. Whether with large or small audiences, Philip willingly ministered wherever and to whomever God wanted. He had overcome the barriers of prejudice and exclusivity with the crowds in Samaria. The Lord now arranged a special assignment, a command performance, for an Ethiopian eunuch. This encounter with one man on a desert road would make Philip a witness "to the ends of the earth" (1:8).

Note that the eunuch was from an African nation—he was a black Gentile—and was "an important official in charge of all the treasury of Candace, Queen of the Ethiopians" (8:27). This man differed from Philip in class, race and religion, yet Philip didn't shy away from this wealthy, prominent individual; he showed no sign of questioning God's assignment. This was a one-of-a-kind situation for him, but Philip had a firm grasp on the Holy Spirit's leading. He listened and obeyed when the Spirit told him to approach the Ethiopian's chariot (8:29).

As Philip approached the chariot he could hear the eunuch reading from the prophet Isaiah. With wisdom and tact Philip took his cue from what he saw and began to converse with the Ethiopian, asking, "Do you understand what you are reading?" (8:30). With the Ethiopian's permission, Philip explained the prophecy, led this man to Christ, baptized him and ultimately sent this man "on his way rejoicing" in his new faith (8:39).

Our Faithfulness to Our Calling

Philip's ministry to this man illustrates important principles for sharing Christ with others. God gives us all "divine opportunities"—people whose hearts he has prepared to hear the gospel message. We must be sensitive to the Holy Spirit's leading when these opportunities occur, whether we are ministering to the multitudes or to individuals. No doubt the Ethiopian eunuch, because of his powerful position, was able to share the message of Christ with many influential people in his own country. We, too, may have an opportunity to share the Good News with those who could lead others to Christ in ways that we never could. We must look for these moments and be willing to respond by sharing our witness.

Philip was unusually gifted to serve Jesus Christ. His humble attitudes and faithful witness for Christ in every circumstance are instructive for us all. But we don't need the same kind of extraordinary experiences that Philip had in order to validate our service to the Lord. God may choose to

have us witness to unbelievers under the direction of the Holy Spirit. Or he may choose to have us do menial tasks to meet the needs of others, helping to feed hungry mouths as well as hungry hearts. We must not limit what the Holy Spirit wants to do through us, but rather acknowledge God's presence and power in our lives and make ourselves available to God in every circumstance. Then we will prove faithful in both big and little things—as did Philip.

—Dr. Gene Getz

to tell Andrew; Andrew and Philip in turn told Jesus.

23 Jesus replied, "The hour has come for the Son of Man to be glorified.[r] 24 I tell you the truth, unless a kernel of wheat falls to the ground and dies,[s] it remains only a single seed. But if it dies, it produces many seeds. 25 The man who loves his life will lose it, while the man who hates his life in this world will keep it[t] for eternal life. 26 Whoever serves me must follow me; and where I am, my servant also will be.[u] My Father will honor the one who serves me.

27 "Now my heart is troubled,[v] and what shall I say? 'Father,[w] save me from this hour'?[x] No, it was for this very reason I came to this hour. 28 Father, glorify your name!"

Then a voice came from heaven,[y] "I have glorified it, and will glorify it again." 29 The crowd that was there and heard it said it had thundered; others said an angel had spoken to him.

30 Jesus said, "This voice was for your benefit,[z] not mine. 31 Now is the time for judgment on this world;[a] now the prince of this world[b] will be driven out. 32 But I, when I am lifted up from the earth,[c] will draw all men to myself."[d] 33 He said this to show the kind of death he was going to die.[e]

34 The crowd spoke up, "We have heard from the Law that the Christ**[a]** will remain forever,[f] so how can you say, 'The Son of Man[g] must be lifted up'?[h] Who is this 'Son of Man'?"

35 Then Jesus told them, "You are going to have the light[i] just a little while longer. Walk while you have the light,[j] before darkness overtakes you.[k] The man who walks in the dark does not know where he is going. 36 Put your trust in the light while you have it, so that you may become sons of light."[l] When he had finished speaking, Jesus left and hid himself from them.[m]

The Jews Continue in Their Unbelief

37 Even after Jesus had done all these miraculous signs[n] in their presence, they still would not believe in him. 38 This was to fulfill the word of Isaiah the prophet:

> "Lord, who has believed our
> message
> and to whom has the arm of the
> Lord been revealed?"**[b]**[o]

39 For this reason they could not believe, because, as Isaiah says elsewhere:

> 40 "He has blinded their eyes
> and deadened their hearts,
> so they can neither see with their
> eyes,
> nor understand with their hearts,
> nor turn—and I would heal
> them."**[c]**[p]

41 Isaiah said this because he saw Jesus' glory[q] and spoke about him.[r]

42 Yet at the same time many even among the leaders believed in him.[s] But because of the Pharisees[t] they would not confess their faith for fear they would be put out of the synagogue;[u] 43 for they loved praise from men more than praise from God.[v]

44 Then Jesus cried out, "When a man believes in me, he does not believe in me only, but in the one who sent me.[w] 45 When he looks at me, he sees the one who sent me.[x] 46 I have come into the world as a light,[y] so that no one who believes in me should stay in darkness.

47 "As for the person who hears my words but does not keep them, I do not judge him. For I did not come to judge the world, but to save it.[z] 48 There is a judge for the one who rejects me and does not accept my words; that very word which I spoke will condemn him[a] at the last day. 49 For I did not speak of my own accord, but the Father who sent me commanded me[b] what to say and how to say it. 50 I know that his command leads to eternal life. So whatever I say is just what the Father has told me to say."

Jesus Washes His Disciples' Feet

13 It was just before the Passover Feast.[c] Jesus knew that the time had come[d] for him to leave this world and go to the Father.[e] Having loved his own who were in the world, he now showed them the full extent of his love.**[d]**

4 →PG. 1206
7 →PG. 1180

2 The evening meal was being served, and the devil had already prompted Judas Iscariot, son of Simon, to betray Jesus. 3 Jesus knew that the Father had put all things under his power,[f] and that he had come from God[g] and was returning to God; 4 so he got up from the meal, took off his outer clothing, and wrapped a towel around his waist. 5 After that, he poured water into a basin and began to wash his disciples' feet,[h] drying them with the towel that was wrapped around him.

6 He came to Simon Peter, who said to him, "Lord, are you going to wash my feet?"

12:23 [r] Jn 13:32; 17:1
12:24 [s] 1Co 15:36
12:25 [t] Mt 10:39; Mk 8:35; Lk 14:26
12:26 [u] Jn 14:3; 17:24; 2Co 5:8; 1Th 4:17
12:27 [v] Mt 26:38,39; Jn 11:33,38; 13:21 [w] Mt 11:25 [x] ver 23
12:28 [y] Mt 3:17
12:30 [z] Jn 11:42
12:31 [a] Jn 16:11 [b] Jn 14:30; 16:11; 2Co 4:4; Eph 2:2; 1Jn 4:4
12:32 [c] ver 34; Jn 3:14; 8:28 [d] Jn 6:44
12:33 [e] Jn 18:32
12:34 [f] Ps 110:4; Isa 9:7; Eze 37:25; Da 7:14 [g] Mt 8:20 [h] Jn 3:14
12:35 [i] ver 46 [j] Eph 5:8 [k] 1Jn 2:11
12:36 [l] Lk 16:8 [m] Jn 8:59
12:37 [n] Jn 2:11
12:38 [o] Isa 53:1; Ro 10:16
12:40 [p] Isa 6:10; Mt 13:13,15
12:41 [q] Isa 6:1-4 [r] Lk 24:27
12:42 [s] ver 11; Jn 7:48 [t] Jn 7:13 [u] Jn 9:22
12:43 [v] Jn 5:44
12:44 [w] Mt 10:40; Jn 5:24
12:45 [x] Jn 14:9
12:46 [y] Jn 1:4; 3:19; 8:12; 9:5
12:47 [z] Jn 3:17
12:48 [a] Jn 5:45
12:49 [b] Jn 14:31
13:1 [c] Jn 11:55 [d] Jn 12:23 [e] Jn 16:28
13:3 [f] Mt 28:18 [g] Jn 8:42; 16:27,28,30
13:5 [h] Lk 7:44

a *34* Or *Messiah* **b** *38* Isaiah 53:1
c *40* Isaiah 6:10 **d** *1* Or *he loved them to the last*

7 Jesus replied, "You do not realize
now what I am doing, but later you will
understand."[i]
8 "No," said Peter, "you shall never
wash my feet."
Jesus answered, "Unless I wash you,
you have no part with me."
9 "Then, Lord," Simon Peter replied,
"not just my feet but my hands and my
head as well!"
10 Jesus answered, "A person who
has had a bath needs only to wash his
feet; his whole body is clean. And you
are clean,[j] though not every one of
you." 11 For he knew who was going to
betray him, and that was why he said
not every one was clean.
12 When he had finished washing
their feet, he put on his clothes and
returned to his place. "Do you understand what I have done for you?" he
asked them. 13 "You call me 'Teacher'[k]
and 'Lord,'[l] and rightly so, for that is
what I am. 14 Now that I, your Lord and
Teacher, have washed your feet, you
also should wash one another's feet.[m]
15 I have set you an example that you
should do as I have done for you.[n] 16 I
tell you the truth, no servant is greater
than his master,[o] nor is a messenger
greater than the one who sent him.
17 Now that you know these things, you
will be blessed if you do them.[p]

Jesus Predicts His Betrayal

18 "I am not referring to all of you;[q]
I know those I have chosen.[r] But this
is to fulfill the scripture: 'He who
shares my bread[s] has lifted up his
heel[t] against me.'[a][u]
19 "I am telling you now before it
happens, so that when it does happen
you will believe[v] that I am He.[w] 20 I
tell you the truth, whoever accepts
anyone I send accepts me; and whoever accepts me accepts the one who
sent me."[x]
21 After he had said this, Jesus was
troubled in spirit[y] and testified, "I tell
you the truth, one of you is going to
betray me."[z]
22 His disciples stared at one another,
at a loss to know which of them he
meant. 23 One of them, the disciple
whom Jesus loved,[a] was reclining next
to him. 24 Simon Peter motioned to this
disciple and said, "Ask him which one
he means."
25 Leaning back against Jesus, he
asked him, "Lord, who is it?"[b]
26 Jesus answered, "It is the one to
whom I will give this piece of bread
when I have dipped it in the dish."
Then, dipping the piece of bread, he
gave it to Judas Iscariot, son of Simon.
27 As soon as Judas took the bread, Satan entered into him.[c]
"What you are about to do, do quickly," Jesus told him, 28 but no one at the
meal understood why Jesus said this to
him. 29 Since Judas had charge of the
money,[d] some thought Jesus was telling him to buy what was needed for the
Feast, or to give something to the poor.
30 As soon as Judas had taken the bread,
he went out. And it was night.[e]

13:7 [i]ver 12
13:10 [j]Jn 15:3
13:13 [k]Jn 11:28 [l]Lk 6:46; 1Co 12:3; Php 2:11
13:14 [m]1Pe 5:5
13:15 [n]Mt 11:29
13:16 [o]Mt 10:24; Lk 6:40; Jn 15:20
13:17 [p]Mt 7:24,25; Lk 11:28; Jas 1:25
13:18 [q]ver 10 [r]Jn 15:16,19 [s]Mt 26:23 [t]Jn 6:70 [u]Ps 41:9
13:19 [v]Jn 14:29; 16:4 [w]Jn 8:24
13:20 [x]Mt 10:40; Lk 10:16
13:21 [y]Jn 12:27 [z]Mt 26:21
13:23 [a]Jn 19:26; 20:2; 21:7,20
13:25 [b]Jn 21:20
13:27 [c]Lk 22:3
13:29 [d]Jn 12:6
13:30 [e]Lk 22:53

[a] *18* Psalm 41:9

13:1–17

PROMISE 4

CEO OR SERVANT?

Just about every work situation has a "gopher." That's the guy who does the odd jobs, runs the errands and cleans up the messes. He's usually underpaid and overworked. It's a job with little hope for advancement and less affirmation. It's the job nobody wants.

At the time of Jesus nobody wanted to be a slave. Especially demeaning was the job of foot washing—a role assigned to the lowest slave in the Oriental home. Foot washing was traditionally observed at times like this, before an intimate meal or banquet. In this dry and dusty region, sandaled feet were quickly soiled. Having washed and prepared themselves for the meal earlier, the attendees would only need their feet washed to be completely clean and ready for the festivities.

As the disciples and Jesus gathered for this Passover dinner, they had also prepared in this manner. But there was no servant present to wash their feet, and nobody was about to volunteer. The disciples wanted to be served, not serve. They wanted to rule, not be ruled.

Imagine the disciples' shock when Jesus took off his outer garment, wrapped a towel around his waist and washed their dirty feet! The master became a servant. The CEO became a gopher. He even washed the feet of Judas, who would betray him into the hands of the Jews who wanted him silenced (v. 11); and of Peter, who would later deny that he even knew who Jesus was (v. 38).

When he finished cleaning the disciples' feet, Jesus told them to follow his example of humble service. We too need to follow his example in our family and work lives. We should serve our wives, children, coworkers, bosses, friends and even enemies. Take a few minutes and identify some jobs or chores that you don't normally perform and volunteer to do them.

For the next Promise 4 reading go to page 1260.

Jesus Predicts Peter's Denial

›See Matthew 26:33–35; Mark 14:29–31;
Luke 22:33–34

31When he was gone, Jesus said,
"Now is the Son of Man glorified[f] and
God is glorified in him.[g] 32If God is
glorified in him,[a] God will glorify the
Son in himself,[h] and will glorify him at
once.

33"My children, I will be with you
only a little longer. You will look for
me, and just as I told the Jews, so I tell
you now: Where I am going, you cannot come.[i]

7 →PG. 1181

34"A new command[j] I give you:
Love one another.[k] As I have loved
you, so you must love one another.[l]
35By this all men will know that you
are my disciples, if you love one another."[m]

36Simon Peter asked him, "Lord,
where are you going?"

Jesus replied, "Where I am going,
you cannot follow now,[n] but you will
follow later."[o]

37Peter asked, "Lord, why can't I follow you now? I will lay down my life for
you."

38Then Jesus answered, "Will you
really lay down your life for me? I tell
you the truth, before the rooster crows,
you will disown me three times![p]

Jesus Comforts His Disciples

14 "Do not let your hearts be troubled.[q] Trust in God[b]; trust also in
me. 2In my Father's house are many
rooms; if it were not so, I would have
told you. I am going there[r] to prepare
a place for you. 3And if I go and prepare
a place for you, I will come back and
take you to be with me that you also
may be where I am.[s] 4You know the
way to the place where I am going."

Jesus the Way to the Father

5Thomas[t] said to him, "Lord, we
don't know where you are going, so
how can we know the way?"

6Jesus answered, "I am the way[u]
and the truth and the life.[v] No one
comes to the Father except through
me. 7If you really knew me, you would
know[c] my Father as well.[w] From now
on, you do know him and have seen
him."

8Philip said, "Lord, show us the Father and that will be enough for us."

9Jesus answered: "Don't you know
me, Philip, even after I have been
among you such a long time? Anyone
who has seen me has seen the Father.[x] How can you say, 'Show us the
Father'? 10Don't you believe that I am
in the Father, and that the Father is in
me?[y] The words I say to you are not
just my own.[z] Rather, it is the Father,
living in me, who is doing his work.
11Believe me when I say that I am in the
Father and the Father is in me; or at
least believe on the evidence of the
miracles themselves.[a] 12I tell you the
truth, anyone who has faith[b] in me
will do what I have been doing.[c] He
will do even greater things than these,
because I am going to the Father.
13And I will do whatever you ask[d] in
my name, so that the Son may bring
glory to the Father. 14You may ask me
for anything in my name, and I will
do it.

Jesus Promises the Holy Spirit

1 →PG. 1182

15"If you love me, you will obey what
I command.[e] 16And I will ask the Father, and he will give you another
Counselor[f] to be with you forever—
17the Spirit of truth.[g] The world cannot accept him,[h] because it neither
sees him nor knows him. But you know
him, for he lives with you and will be[d]
in you. 18I will not leave you as orphans; I will come to you.[i] 19Before
long, the world will not see me anymore, but you will see me.[j] Because I
live, you also will live.[k] 20On that day
you will realize that I am in my Fa-

13:31 [f]Jn 7:39 [g]Jn 14:13; 17:4; 1Pe 4:11
13:32 [h]Jn 17:1
13:33 [i]Jn 7:33,34
13:34 [j]1Jn 2:7-11; 3:11 [k]Lev 19:18; 1Th 4:9; 1Pe 1:22 [l]Jn 15:12; Eph 5:2; 1Jn 4:10,11
13:35 [m]1Jn 3:14; 4:20
13:36 [n]ver 33; Jn 14:2 [o]Jn 21:18,19; 2Pe 1:14
13:38 [p]Jn 18:27
14:1 [q]ver 27
14:2 [r]Jn 13:33,36
14:3 [s]Jn 12:26
14:5 [t]Jn 11:16
14:6 [u]Jn 10:9 [v]Jn 11:25
14:7 [w]Jn 8:19
14:9 [x]Jn 12:45; Col 1:15; Heb 1:3
14:10 [y]Jn 10:38 [z]Jn 5:19
14:11 [a]Jn 5:36; 10:38
14:12 [b]Mt 21:21 [c]Lk 10:17
14:13 [d]Mt 7:7
14:15 [e]ver 21,23; Jn 15:10; 1Jn 5:3
14:16 [f]Jn 15:26; 16:7
14:17 [g]Jn 15:26; 16:13; 1Jn 4:6 [h]1Co 2:14
14:18 [i]ver 3,28
14:19 [j]Jn 7:33,34; 16:16 [k]Jn 6:57

a 32 Many early manuscripts do not have *If God is glorified in him.* b 1 Or *You trust in God* c 7 Some early manuscripts *If you really have known me, you will know* d 17 Some early manuscripts *and is*

14:6

PROMISE 1

ONLY ONE WAY

Is belief and trust in Jesus really the *only* way to know God? Christians are sometimes accused of being narrow-minded and exclusive for claiming to have inside information on the one and only way to know God. Yet we as Christians take our cue from Jesus himself.

Why did he make this claim? Because only Jesus lived a sinless life. Only Jesus died for our sins. And only Jesus rose from the dead. As God's Son, only Jesus can bring us into a relationship with his Father.

Jesus did declare that the path to God is narrow. But most truth is narrow. In a sense, Jesus is like a mathematics teacher helping a student find the correct solution to an equation. In stating that "No one comes to the Father except by me," Jesus helps us arrive at the truth and keeps us from making incorrect conclusions.

For the next Promise 1 reading go to page 1182.

ther,[l] and you are in me, and I am in
you. **21**Whoever has my commands and
obeys them, he is the one who loves
me.[m] He who loves me will be loved by
my Father,[n] and I too will love him
and show myself to him."
22Then Judas[o] (not Judas Iscariot)
said, "But, Lord, why do you intend to
show yourself to us and not to the
world?"[p]
23Jesus replied, "If anyone loves me,
he will obey my teaching.[q] My Father
will love him, and we will come to him
and make our home with him.[r] **24**He
who does not love me will not obey my
teaching. These words you hear are not
my own; they belong to the Father who
sent me.[s]
25"All this I have spoken while still
with you. **26**But the Counselor,[t] the
Holy Spirit, whom the Father will send
in my name,[u] will teach you all
things[v] and will remind you of everything I have said to you.[w] **27**Peace I
leave with you; my peace I give you.[x]
I do not give to you as the world gives.
Do not let your hearts be troubled and
do not be afraid.
28"You heard me say, 'I am going
away and I am coming back to you.'[y]
If you loved me, you would be glad
that I am going to the Father,[z] for the
Father is greater than I.[a] **29**I have
told you now before it happens, so
that when it does happen you will
believe.[b] **30**I will not speak with you
much longer, for the prince of this
world[c] is coming. He has no hold on
me, **31**but the world must learn that I
love the Father and that I do exactly
what my Father has command-
ed me.[d]
"Come now; let us leave.

The Vine and the Branches

15 "I am the true vine,[e] and my Father is the gardener. **2**He cuts off
every branch in me that bears no fruit,
while every branch that does bear fruit

7 →PG. 1195

14:20 [l]Jn 10:38
14:21 [m]1Jn 5:3 [n]1Jn 2:5
14:22 [o]Lk 6:16; Ac 1:13 [p]Ac 10:41
14:23 [q]ver 15 [r]1Jn 2:24; Rev 3:20
14:24 [s]Jn 7:16
14:26 [t]Jn 15:26; 16:7 [u]Ac 2:33 [v]Jn 16:13; 1Jn 2:20,27 [w]Jn 2:22
14:27 [x]Jn 16:33; Php 4:7; Col 3:15
14:28 [y]ver 2-4,18 [z]Jn 5:18 [a]Jn 10:29; Php 2:6
14:29 [b]Jn 13:19; 16:4
14:30 [c]Jn 12:31
14:31 [d]Jn 10:18; 12:49 **15:1** [e]Isa 5:1-7

15:1–8

PE

WISDOM FROM THE GRAPEVINE

Many men ask, "How can I live the Christian life?" Others want to know, "How can I please God?" In this passage, Jesus provides us with a model to follow.

The night prior to his crucifixion, Jesus knew he would soon leave his disciples. He also realized that his disciples would feel alone and powerless after he left. As Jesus and his disciples left the upper room, the Lord let them know that while he would be physically absent, their relationship would continue. Perhaps he and his disciples passed by a vineyard as Jesus spoke these words. At any rate, Jesus' analogy in this passage describes the future of the relationship between him and his disciples. And it also helps us to know how we can become godly men.

First, Jesus told his disciples that they would have a new union with him (vv. 1–4). How close would their union be? Just as close as a branch and a grapevine. The branch that holds the grape cluster gets all of its water and all of its nourishment—in short, it draws its life—from the grapevine. In the same way, the disciples would draw spiritual life and nourishment from Jesus. As Jesus stated, a branch separated from a vine can't bear fruit; it only bears fruit because of its union with the vine. Remember, a vine produces fruit, a branch bears it. Similarly, God produces the fruit of the Spirit in our lives, and we bear it.

Second, Jesus said his disciples would be cleansed by the Father. As a gardener prunes a vine, so God the Father prunes us. A gardener uses a knife. God uses adversity and his Word. Why? So we will be fruitful. Here Jesus may have referred to two kinds of fruit: The fruit of the Spirit (Galatians 5:22–23) and new converts (John 4:36). God wants every believer to bear the fruit of the Spirit and see others come to Jesus Christ. As you consider what this means for your life, remember that the divine Gardener is at work in you to help you be fruitful. You're not on your own.

Third, Jesus said the disciples would have a new responsibility (vv. 5–8). What was it? Simply to "remain in him." As branches, we're to "remain" in the vine. The word "remain" means to "dwell." We're to dwell or abide in the Lord, just like a branch remains in a vine. As a branch draws sap from the roots and trunk, so we're to rest in the Lord and draw our strength from him.

Have you ever walked by a grapevine and heard a branch grunting and groaning as it tries to bear fruit? Or have you ever seen a tomato plant thrashing about wildly trying to bear fruit? Of course not! Every fruit-bearing branch has a single job: to remain in the vine. As long as it remains in the vine it can relax and enjoy the sunshine and rain. The vine will produce the fruit. This means that being a godly man, and pleasing God, is something Jesus does through us as we abide in him.

Of course, that raises another question: "How does a follower of Jesus go about abiding in him?" Jesus gave us a hint. He related remaining in him to having his Word remain in us (v. 7). It's not enough to casually read the Bible on occasion. It will remain in our minds only when we read it often, meditate on it and memorize it. The more we do that, the more we'll bear spiritual fruit.

he prunes[a] so that it will be even more fruitful. 3You are already clean because of the word I have spoken to you.[f] 4Remain in me, and I will remain in you.[g] No branch can bear fruit by itself; it must remain in the vine. Neither can you bear fruit unless you remain in me.

5"I am the vine; you are the branches. If a man remains in me and I in him, he will bear much fruit;[h] apart from me you can do nothing. 6If anyone does not remain in me, he is like a branch that is thrown away and withers; such branches are picked up, thrown into the fire and burned.[i] 7If you remain in me and my words remain in you, ask whatever you wish, and it will be given you.[j] 8This is to my Father's glory,[k] that you bear much fruit, showing yourselves to be my disciples.[l]

1 →PG. 1183
5 →PG. 1182

9"As the Father has loved me,[m] so have I loved you. Now remain in my love. 10If you obey my commands,[n] you will remain in my love, just as I have obeyed my Father's commands and remain in his love. 11I have told you this so that my joy may be in you and that your joy may be complete.[o] 12My command is this: Love each other as I have loved you.[p] 13Greater love has no one than this, that he lay down his life for his friends.[q] 14You are my friends[r] if you do what I command.[s] 15I no longer call you servants, because a servant does not know his master's business. Instead, I have called you friends, for everything that I learned from my Father I have made known to you.[t] 16You did not choose me, but I chose you and appointed you[u] to go and bear fruit—fruit that will last. Then the Father will give you whatever you ask in my name. 17This is my command: Love each other.[v]

2 →PG. 1190
6 →PG. 1184
5 →PG. 1184

The World Hates the Disciples

18"If the world hates you,[w] keep in mind that it hated me first. 19If you belonged to the world, it would love you as its own. As it is, you do not belong to the world, but I have chosen you[x] out of the world. That is why the world hates you.[y] 20Remember the words I spoke to you: 'No servant is greater than his master.'[b][z] If they persecuted me, they will persecute you also.[a] If they obeyed my teaching, they will obey yours also. 21They will treat you this way because of my name,[b] for they do not know the One who sent me.[c] 22If I had not come and spoken to them, they would not be guilty of sin. Now, however, they have no excuse for their sin.[d] 23He who hates me hates my Father as well. 24If I had not done among them what no one else did,[e] they would not be guilty of sin. But now they have seen these miracles, and yet they have hated both me and my Father. 25But this is to fulfill what is written in their Law: 'They hated me without reason.'[c][f]

26"When the Counselor[g] comes, whom I will send to you from the Father,[h] the Spirit of truth[i] who goes out from the Father, he will testify about me.[j] 27And you also must testify,[k] for you have been with me from the beginning.[l]

16 "All this[m] I have told you so that you will not go astray.[n] 2They will put you out of the synagogue;[o] in fact, a time is coming when anyone who kills you will think he is offering a service to God.[p] 3They will do such things because they have not known the Father or me.[q] 4I have told you this, so that when the time comes you will remember[r] that I warned you. I did not tell you this at first because I was with you.

The Work of the Holy Spirit

5"Now I am going to him who sent me,[s] yet none of you asks me, 'Where are you going?'[t] 6Because I have said these things, you are filled with grief.

[a]*2* The Greek for *prunes* also means *cleans.*
[b]*20* John 13:16 [c]*25* Psalms 35:19; 69:4

15:3 [f]Jn 13:10; 17:17; Eph 5:26
15:4 [g]Jn 6:56; 1Jn 2:6
15:5 [h]ver 16
15:6 [i]ver 2
15:7 [j]Mt 7:7
15:8 [k]Mt 5:16 [l]Jn 8:31
15:9 [m]Jn 17:23,24, 26
15:10 [n]Jn 14:15
15:11 [o]Jn 17:13
15:12 [p]Jn 13:34
15:13 [q]Jn 10:11; Ro 5:7,8
15:14 [r]Lk 12:4 [s]Mt 12:50
15:15 [t]Jn 8:26
15:16 [u]Jn 6:70; 13:18
15:17 [v]ver 12
15:18 [w]1Jn 3:13
15:19 [x]ver 16 [y]Jn 17:14
15:20 [z]Jn 13:16 [a]2Ti 3:12
15:21 [b]Mt 10:22 [c]Jn 16:3
15:22 [d]Jn 9:41; Ro 1:20
15:24 [e]Jn 5:36
15:25 [f]Ps 35:19; 69:4
15:26 [g]Jn 14:16 [h]Jn 14:26 [i]Jn 14:17 [j]1Jn 5:7
15:27 [k]Lk 24:48; 1Jn 1:2; 4:14 [l]Lk 1:2
16:1 [m]Jn 15:18-27 [n]Mt 11:6
16:2 [o]Jn 9:22 [p]Isa 66:5; Ac 26:9,10; Rev 6:9
16:3 [q]Jn 15:21; 17:25; 1Jn 3:1
16:4 [r]Jn 13:19
16:5 [s]Jn 7:33 [t]Jn 13:36; 14:5

16:5–15

PROMISE 1

OUR COUNSELOR

For over three years the disciples traveled with Jesus, listening to his words and witnessing his miracles. As his death approached, Jesus told the disciples his departure would actually be good for them. Such words sound like the stuff of which fairy tales are made. How could the absence of Jesus be good for his followers?

The Lord had an answer to that question. As long as he was physically present, the Holy Spirit couldn't come to them. Jesus refers to the Holy Spirit as "the Counselor" (v. 7). The term means "one called alongside to help." While Jesus was on earth, he only taught a few people at one time. But the Spirit given to the disciples comes alongside every believer. That same Spirit will personally guide us all into truth. Remember that the next time you read the Bible. Since the Spirit is available to teach you, ask him to guide you into truth as you read God's Word.

For the next Promise 1 reading go to page 1215.

7But I tell you the truth: It is for your good that I am going away. Unless I go away, the Counselor[u] will not come to you; but if I go, I will send him to you.[v] **8**When he comes, he will convict the world of guilt[a] in regard to sin and righteousness and judgment: **9**in regard to sin,[w] because men do not believe in me; **10**in regard to righteousness,[x] because I am going to the Father, where you can see me no longer; **11**and in regard to judgment, because the prince of this world[y] now stands condemned.

12"I have much more to say to you, more than you can now bear.[z] **13**But when he, the Spirit of truth,[a] comes, he will guide you into all truth.[b] He will not speak on his own; he will speak only what he hears, and he will tell you what is yet to come. **14**He will bring glory to me by taking from what is mine and making it known to you. **15**All that belongs to the Father is mine.[c] That is why I said the Spirit will take from what is mine and make it known to you.

16"In a little while[d] you will see me no more, and then after a little while you will see me."[e]

The Disciples' Grief Will Turn to Joy

17Some of his disciples said to one another, "What does he mean by saying, 'In a little while you will see me no more, and then after a little while you will see me,'[f] and 'Because I am going to the Father'?"[g] **18**They kept asking, "What does he mean by 'a little while'? We don't understand what he is saying."

19Jesus saw that they wanted to ask him about this, so he said to them, "Are you asking one another what I meant when I said, 'In a little while you will see me no more, and then after a little while you will see me'? **20**I tell you the truth, you will weep and mourn[h] while the world rejoices. You will grieve, but your grief will turn to joy.[i] **21**A woman giving birth to a child has pain[j] because her time has come; but when her baby is born she forgets the anguish because of her joy that a child is born into the world. **22**So with you: Now is your time of grief,[k] but I will see you again[l] and you will rejoice, and no one will take away your joy. **23**In that day you will no longer ask me anything. I tell you the truth, my Father will give you whatever you ask in my name.[m] **24**Until now you have not asked for anything in my name. Ask and you will receive, and your joy will be complete.[n]

1 →PG. 1196

25"Though I have been speaking figuratively,[o] a time is coming[p] when I will no longer use this kind of language but will tell you plainly about my Father. **26**In that day you will ask in my name.[q] I am not saying that I will ask the Father on your behalf. **27**No, the Father himself loves you because you have loved me[r] and have believed that I came from God. **28**I came from the Father and entered the world; now I am leaving the world and going back to the Father."[s]

29Then Jesus' disciples said, "Now you are speaking clearly and without figures of speech.[t] **30**Now we can see that you know all things and that you do not even need to have anyone ask you questions. This makes us believe that you came from God."

31"You believe at last!"[b] Jesus answered. **32**"But a time is coming,[u] and has come, when you will be scattered,[v] each to his own home. You will leave me all alone. Yet I am not alone, for my Father is with me.[w]

33"I have told you these things, so that in me you may have peace.[x] In this world you will have trouble.[y] But take heart! I have overcome[z] the world."

Jesus Prays for Himself

17 After Jesus said this, he looked toward heaven[a] and prayed:

"Father, the time has come. Glorify your Son, that your Son may glorify you.[b] **2**For you granted him authority over all people that he might give eternal life to all those you have given him.[c] **3**Now this is eternal life: that they may know you, the only true God, and Jesus Christ, whom you have sent.[d] **4**I have brought you glory[e] on earth by completing the work you gave me to do.[f] **5**And now, Father, glorify me in your presence with the glory I had with you[g] before the world began.[h]

Jesus Prays for His Disciples

6"I have revealed you[c][i] to those whom you gave me[j] out of the world. They were yours; you gave them to me and they have obeyed your word. **7**Now they know that everything you have given me comes from you. **8**For I gave them the words you gave me[k] and they accepted them.

16:7 [u]Jn 14:16,26; 15:26 [v]Jn 7:39
16:9 [w]Jn 15:22
16:10 [x]Ac 3:14; 7:52; 1Pe 3:18
16:11 [y]Jn 12:31
16:12 [z]Mk 4:33
16:13 [a]Jn 14:17 [b]Jn 14:26
16:15 [c]Jn 17:10
16:16 [d]Jn 7:33 [e]Jn 14:18-24
16:17 [f]ver 16 [g]ver 5
16:20 [h]Lk 23:27 [i]Jn 20:20
16:21 [j]Isa 26:17; 1Th 5:3
16:22 [k]ver 6 [l]ver 16
16:23 [m]Mt 7:7; Jn 15:16
16:24 [n]Jn 3:29; 15:11
16:25 [o]Mt 13:34; Jn 10:6 [p]ver 2
16:26 [q]ver 23,24
16:27 [r]Jn 14:21,23
16:28 [s]Jn 13:3
16:29 [t]ver 25
16:32 [u]ver 2,25 [v]Mt 26:31 [w]Jn 8:16,29
16:33 [x]Jn 14:27 [y]Jn 15:18-21 [z]Ro 8:37; 1Jn 4:4
17:1 [a]Jn 11:41 [b]Jn 12:23; 13:31,32
17:2 [c]ver 6,9,24; Da 7:14; Jn 6:37,39
17:3 [d]ver 8,18,21, 23,25; Jn 3:17
17:4 [e]Jn 13:31 [f]Jn 4:34
17:5 [g]Php 2:6 [h]Jn 1:2
17:6 [i]ver 26 [j]ver 2; Jn 6:37, 39
17:8 [k]ver 14,26

[a] 8 Or *will expose the guilt of the world*
[b] 31 Or *"Do you now believe?"*
[c] 6 Greek *your name*; also in verse 26

They knew with certainty that I came from you,[l] and they believed that you sent me.[m] **9**I pray for them.[n] I am not praying for the world, but for those you have given me, for they are yours. **10**All I have is yours, and all you have is mine.[o] And glory has come to me through them. **11**I will remain in the world no longer, but they are still in the world,[p] and I am coming to you.[q] Holy Father, protect them by the power of your name—the name you gave me—so that they may be one[r] as we are one.[s] **12**While I was with them, I protected them and kept them safe by that name you gave me. None has been lost[t] except the one doomed to destruction[u] so that Scripture would be fulfilled.

13"I am coming to you now, but I say these things while I am still in the world, so that they may have the full measure of my joy[v] within them. **14**I have given them your word and the world has hated them,[w] for they are not of the world any more than I am of the world.[x]

5 →PG. 1197

15My prayer is not that you take them out of the world but that you protect them from the evil one.[y] **16**They are not of the world, even as I am not of it.[z] **17**Sanctify[a] them by the truth; your word is truth.[a] **18**As you sent me into the world,[b] I have sent them into the world.[c] **19**For them I sanctify myself, that they too may be truly sanctified.

Jesus Prays for All Believers

6 →PG. 1199

20"My prayer is not for them alone. I pray also for those who will believe in me through their message, **21**that all of them may be one, Father, just as you are in me and I am in you.[d] May they also be in us so that the world may believe that you have sent me.[e] **22**I have given them the glory that you gave me, that they may be one as we are one:[f] **23**I in them and you in me. May they be brought to complete unity to let the world know that you sent me[g] and have loved them[h] even as you have loved me.

24"Father, I want those you have given me to be with me where I am,[i] and to see my glory,[j] the glory you have given me because you loved me before the creation of the world.[k]

25"Righteous Father, though the world does not know you,[l] I know you, and they know that you have sent me.[m] **26**I have made you known to them,[n] and will continue to make you known in order that the love you have for me may be in them[o] and that I myself may be in them."

Jesus Arrested

›See Matthew 26:47–56; Mark 14:43–50; Luke 22:47–53

18 When he had finished praying, Jesus left with his disciples and crossed the Kidron Valley.[p] On the other side there was an olive grove,[q] and he and his disciples went into it.[r]

2Now Judas, who betrayed him, knew the place, because Jesus had often met there with his disciples.[s] **3**So Judas came to the grove, guiding[t] a detachment of soldiers and some officials from the chief priests and Pharisees.[u] They were carrying torches, lanterns and weapons.

4Jesus, knowing all that was going to happen to him,[v] went out and asked them, "Who is it you want?"[w]

5"Jesus of Nazareth," they replied.

"I am he," Jesus said. (And Judas the traitor was standing there with them.) **6**When Jesus said, "I am he," they drew back and fell to the ground.

7Again he asked them, "Who is it you want?"[x]

And they said, "Jesus of Nazareth."

8"I told you that I am he," Jesus answered. "If you are looking for me, then let these men go." **9**This happened so that the words he had spoken would be fulfilled: "I have not lost one of those you gave me."[b][y]

10Then Simon Peter, who had a sword, drew it and struck the high priest's servant, cutting off his right ear. (The servant's name was Malchus.)

11Jesus commanded Peter, "Put your sword away! Shall I not drink the cup[z] the Father has given me?"

Jesus Taken to Annas

›See Matthew 26:57

12Then the detachment of soldiers with its commander and the Jewish officials[a] arrested Jesus. They bound him **13**and brought him first to Annas, who was the father-in-law of Caiaphas,[b] the high priest that year. **14**Caiaphas was the one who had advised the Jews that it would be good if one man died for the people.[c]

a *17* Greek *hagiazo (set apart for sacred use* or *make holy)*; also in verse 19 **b** *9* John 6:39

17:8 [l]Jn 16:27 [m]ver 3,18,21, 23,25; Jn 3:17
17:9 [n]Lk 22:32
17:10 [o]Jn 16:15
17:11 [p]Jn 13:1 [q]Jn 7:33 [r]ver 21-23 [s]Jn 10:30
17:12 [t]Jn 6:39 [u]Jn 6:70
17:13 [v]Jn 3:29
17:14 [w]Jn 15:19 [x]Jn 8:23
17:15 [y]Mt 5:37
17:16 [z]ver 14
17:17 [a]Jn 15:3
17:18 [b]ver 3,8,21,23, 25 [c]Jn 20:21
17:21 [d]Jn 10:38 [e]ver 3,8,18,23, 25; Jn 3:17
17:22 [f]Jn 14:20
17:23 [g]Jn 3:17 [h]Jn 16:27
17:24 [i]Jn 12:26 [j]Jn 1:14 [k]ver 5; Mt 25:34
17:25 [l]Jn 15:21; 16:3 [m]ver 3,8,18,21, 23; Jn 3:17; 7:29; 16:27
17:26 [n]ver 6 [o]Jn 15:9
18:1 [p]2Sa 15:23 [q]ver 26 [r]Mt 26:36
18:2 [s]Lk 21:37; 22:39
18:3 [t]Ac 1:16 [u]ver 12
18:4 [v]Jn 6:64; 13:1, 11 [w]ver 7
18:7 [x]ver 4
18:9 [y]Jn 17:12
18:11 [z]Mt 20:22
18:12 [a]ver 3
18:13 [b]ver 24; Mt 26:3
18:14 [c]Jn 11:49-51

Peter's First Denial

›See Matthew 26:69–70; Mark 14:66–68; Luke 22:55–57

15Simon Peter and another disciple
were following Jesus. Because this disciple was known to the high priest,[d]
he went with Jesus into the high
priest's courtyard,[e] 16but Peter had to
wait outside at the door. The other disciple, who was known to the high
priest, came back, spoke to the girl on
duty there and brought Peter in.
17"You are not one of his disciples,
are you?" the girl at the door asked Peter.
He replied, "I am not."[f]
18It was cold, and the servants and
officials stood around a fire[g] they had
made to keep warm. Peter also was
standing with them, warming himself.[h]

18:15 [d]Mt 26:3 [e]Mt 26:58; Mk 14:54; Lk 22:54 **18:17** [f]ver 25 **18:18** [g]Jn 21:9 [h]Mk 14:54,67 **18:20** [i]Mt 4:23 [j]Mt 26:55 [k]Jn 7:26 **18:22** [l]ver 3 [m]Mt 16:21; Jn 19:3 **18:23** [n]Mt 5:39; Ac 23:2-5

The High Priest Questions Jesus

›See Matthew 26:59–68; Mark 14:55–65; Luke 22:63–71

19Meanwhile, the high priest questioned Jesus about his disciples and his
teaching.
20"I have spoken openly to the
world," Jesus replied. "I always taught
in synagogues[i] or at the temple,[j]
where all the Jews come together. I said
nothing in secret.[k] 21Why question
me? Ask those who heard me. Surely
they know what I said."
22When Jesus said this, one of the
officials[l] nearby struck him in the
face.[m] "Is this the way you answer
the high priest?" he demanded.
23"If I said something wrong," Jesus
replied, "testify as to what is wrong.
But if I spoke the truth, why did you
strike me?"[n] 24Then Annas sent him,

17:20–21

PROMISE 6

BEATING IN UNISON

A biologist cracks the shell of an egg containing a fully developed chicken. He then extracts a few living muscle cells from the chick's tiny heart and drops them in a saline solution. Even though the cells are isolated from the body, each heart cell beats out an incessant rhythm.

When he gazes at them under a microscope, he sees each cell tapping out a rhythm approximate to the 350 beats a minute normal to a chick. But over the hours something astonishing occurs. Instead of several independent cells contracting at their own pace, first two, then three, then all of the cells pulse in unison. There are no longer any independent cells beating out their own rhythm. Instead of several different beats, there is one.

Why does this happen? It occurs because those heart cells sense an innate rightness about playing the same note at the same time. Each heart cell has a sense of belonging that causes it to work in unison with the others. While they are each separate, they are also one. (Taken from *Fearfully & Wonderfully Made* by Dr. Paul Brand and Philip Yancey [Grand Rapids, MI: Zondervan Publishing House, 1980, pp. 45–46].)

As followers of Jesus Christ, we are unique individuals, akin to those independent cells. Yet we've been called to live in unity, to function as one body. That's what Jesus prayed for in this passage as he considered all the people who would come to know him through the work of his followers. That means he prayed for us today—for me and for you and for each person who calls on Jesus' name in our time.

Among other things, Jesus prayed for our unity. He asked that "all" future believers would be one as he and the Father are one. Jesus wasn't asking for uniformity. He didn't mean all believers should look alike, think alike and talk alike. Nor was he asking for organizational unity. The sum total of all the world's believers will never organize their churches alike or worship alike. While we can agree on certain Biblical standards of approaching God and preaching the gospel, Jesus wasn't praying for a lack of diversity in worship.

Jesus prayed that all future believers would have a unity of relationship, as he has with his Father. This unity already exists, and we as believers are called to "make every effort to keep the unity of the Spirit through the bond of peace" (Ephesians 4:3). Such unity rests on mutual acceptance of differences, and is based upon our faith in God and the truth of God's Word. The unity that Christ prayed for here includes all people who confess Jesus Christ as Lord, and is intended to be a foretaste and sign of the kind of love, unity, and community that will be present in Christ's coming kingdom (Acts 2:42–27; 1 Peter 2:9–10).

Jesus said that when such unity occurs among his believers, it validates his mission to outsiders and proves that he came from God (John 13:34–35). And he said it demonstrates something else, something that defies human comprehension. Our unity proves that God the Father loves us as much as he loves Jesus. Love unites the members of the Godhead. And love unites believers. When we live in unity with believers of a different color and creed, we reveal the supernatural love of God.

As a Christian, you have a high calling to live in unity with your fellow believers. Make it a personal goal to build a friendship with a man of a different color or from a different church. Focus on that which you have in common in Christ. Like the cells from the heart of that chick, let's beat to the same tune. After all, we do belong to the same body.

For the next Promise 6 reading go to page 1206.

still bound, to Caiaphas[o] the high priest.[a]

Peter's Second and Third Denials

›See Matthew 26:71–75; Mark 14:69–72; Luke 22:58–62

25As Simon Peter stood warming himself,[p] he was asked, "You are not one of his disciples, are you?"

He denied it, saying, "I am not."[q]

26One of the high priest's servants, a relative of the man whose ear Peter had cut off,[r] challenged him, "Didn't I see you with him in the olive grove?"[s] 27Again Peter denied it, and at that moment a rooster began to crow.[t]

Jesus Before Pilate

›See Matthew 27:11–18,20–23; Mark 15:2–15; Luke 23:2–3,18–25

28Then the Jews led Jesus from Caiaphas to the palace of the Roman governor.[u] By now it was early morning, and to avoid ceremonial uncleanness the Jews did not enter the palace;[v] they wanted to be able to eat the Passover.[w] 29So Pilate came out to them and asked, "What charges are you bringing against this man?"

30"If he were not a criminal," they replied, "we would not have handed him over to you."

31Pilate said, "Take him yourselves and judge him by your own law."

"But we have no right to execute anyone," the Jews objected. 32This happened so that the words Jesus had spoken indicating the kind of death he was going to die[x] would be fulfilled.

33Pilate then went back inside the palace,[y] summoned Jesus and asked him, "Are you the king of the Jews?"[z]

34"Is that your own idea," Jesus asked, "or did others talk to you about me?"

35"Am I a Jew?" Pilate replied. "It was your people and your chief priests who handed you over to me. What is it you have done?"

36Jesus said, "My kingdom[a] is not of this world. If it were, my servants would fight to prevent my arrest by the Jews.[b] But now my kingdom is from another place."[c]

37"You are a king, then!" said Pilate.

Jesus answered, "You are right in saying I am a king. In fact, for this reason I was born, and for this I came into the world, to testify to the truth.[d] Everyone on the side of truth listens to me."[e]

38"What is truth?" Pilate asked. With this he went out again to the Jews and said, "I find no basis for a charge against him.[f] 39But it is your custom for me to release to you one prisoner at the time of the Passover. Do you want me to release 'the king of the Jews'?"

40They shouted back, "No, not him! Give us Barabbas!" Now Barabbas had taken part in a rebellion.[g]

Jesus Sentenced to Be Crucified

›See Matthew 27:27–31; Mark 15:16–20

19 Then Pilate took Jesus and had him flogged.[h] 2The soldiers twisted together a crown of thorns and put it on his head. They clothed him in a purple robe 3and went up to him again and again, saying, "Hail, king of the Jews!"[i] And they struck him in the face.[j]

4Once more Pilate came out and said to the Jews, "Look, I am bringing him out[k] to you to let you know that I find no basis for a charge against him."[l] 5When Jesus came out wearing the crown of thorns and the purple robe,[m] Pilate said to them, "Here is the man!"

6As soon as the chief priests and their officials saw him, they shouted, "Crucify! Crucify!"

But Pilate answered, "You take him and crucify him.[n] As for me, I find no basis for a charge against him."[o]

7The Jews insisted, "We have a law, and according to that law he must die,[p] because he claimed to be the Son of God."[q]

8When Pilate heard this, he was even more afraid, 9and he went back inside the palace.[r] "Where do you come from?" he asked Jesus, but Jesus gave him no answer.[s] 10"Do you refuse to speak to me?" Pilate said. "Don't you realize I have power either to free you or to crucify you?"

11Jesus answered, "You would have no power over me if it were not given to you from above.[t] Therefore the one who handed me over to you[u] is guilty of a greater sin."

12From then on, Pilate tried to set Jesus free, but the Jews kept shouting, "If you let this man go, you are no friend of Caesar. Anyone who claims to be a king[v] opposes Caesar."

13When Pilate heard this, he brought Jesus out and sat down on the judge's seat[w] at a place known as the Stone Pavement (which in Aramaic[x] is Gabbatha). 14It was the day of Preparation[y] of Passover Week, about the sixth hour.[z]

"Here is your king,"[a] Pilate said to the Jews.

[a]*24* Or *(Now Annas had sent him, still bound, to Caiaphas the high priest.)*

18:24 [o]ver 13; Mt 26:3
18:25 [p]ver 18 [q]ver 17
18:26 [r]ver 10 [s]ver 1
18:27 [t]Jn 13:38
18:28 [u]Mt 27:2; Mk 15:1; Lk 23:1 [v]ver 33; Jn 19:9 [w]Jn 11:55
18:32 [x]Mt 20:19; 26:2; Jn 3:14; 8:28; 12:32,33
18:33 [y]ver 28,29; Jn 19:9 [z]Lk 23:3; Mt 2:2
18:36 [a]Mt 3:2 [b]Mt 26:53 [c]Lk 17:21; Jn 6:15
18:37 [d]Jn 3:32 [e]Jn 8:47; 1Jn 4:6
18:38 [f]Lk 23:4; Jn 19:4,6
18:40 [g]Ac 3:14
19:1 [h]Dt 25:3; Isa 50:6; 53:5; Mt 27:26
19:3 [i]Mt 27:29 [j]Jn 18:22
19:4 [k]Jn 18:38 [l]ver 6; Lk 23:4
19:5 [m]ver 2
19:6 [n]Ac 3:13 [o]ver 4; Lk 23:4
19:7 [p]Lev 24:16 [q]Mt 26:63-66; Jn 5:18; 10:33
19:9 [r]Jn 18:33 [s]Mk 14:61
19:11 [t]Ro 13:1 [u]Jn 18:28-30; Ac 3:13
19:12 [v]Lk 23:2
19:13 [w]Mt 27:19 [x]Jn 5:2
19:14 [y]Mt 27:62 [z]Mk 15:25 [a]ver 19,21

15But they shouted, "Take him away! Take him away! Crucify him!"

"Shall I crucify your king?" Pilate asked.

"We have no king but Caesar," the chief priests answered.

16Finally Pilate handed him over to them to be crucified.[b]

The Crucifixion

›See Matthew 27:33–44; Mark 15:22–32; Luke 23:33–43

So the soldiers took charge of Jesus. 17Carrying his own cross,[c] he went out to the place of the Skull[d] (which in Aramaic[e] is called Golgotha). 18Here they crucified him, and with him two others[f]—one on each side and Jesus in the middle.

19Pilate had a notice prepared and fastened to the cross. It read: JESUS OF NAZARETH,[g] THE KING OF THE JEWS.[h] 20Many of the Jews read this sign, for the place where Jesus was crucified was near the city,[i] and the sign was written in Aramaic, Latin and Greek. 21The chief priests of the Jews protested to Pilate, "Do not write 'The King of the Jews,' but that this man claimed to be king of the Jews."[j]

22Pilate answered, "What I have written, I have written."

23When the soldiers crucified Jesus, they took his clothes, dividing them into four shares, one for each of them, with the undergarment remaining. This garment was seamless, woven in one piece from top to bottom.

24"Let's not tear it," they said to one another. "Let's decide by lot who will get it."

This happened that the scripture might be fulfilled[k] which said,

"They divided my garments among
them
and cast lots for my
clothing."[a][l]

So this is what the soldiers did.

25Near the cross[m] of Jesus stood his mother,[n] his mother's sister, Mary the wife of Clopas, and Mary Magdalene.[o] 26When Jesus saw his mother[p] there, and the disciple whom he loved[q] standing nearby, he said to his mother, "Dear woman, here is your son," 27and to the disciple, "Here is your mother." From that time on, this disciple took her into his home.

The Death of Jesus

›See Matthew 27:48,50; Mark 15:36–37; Luke 23:36

28Later, knowing that all was now completed,[r] and so that the Scripture would be fulfilled,[s] Jesus said, "I am thirsty." 29A jar of wine vinegar[t] was there, so they soaked a sponge in it, put the sponge on a stalk of the hyssop plant, and lifted it to Jesus' lips. 30When he had received the drink, Jesus said, "It is finished."[u] With that, he bowed his head and gave up his spirit.

31Now it was the day of Preparation,[v] and the next day was to be a special Sabbath. Because the Jews did not want the bodies left on the crosses[w] during the Sabbath, they asked Pilate to have the legs broken and the bodies taken down. 32The soldiers therefore came and broke the legs of the first man who had been crucified with Jesus, and then those of the other.[x] 33But when they came to Jesus and found that he was already dead, they did not break his legs. 34Instead, one of the soldiers pierced[y] Jesus' side with a spear, bringing a sudden flow of blood and water.[z] 35The man who saw it[a] has given testimony, and his testimony is true.[b] He knows that he tells the truth, and he testifies so that you also may believe. 36These things happened so that the scripture would be fulfilled:[c] "Not one of his bones will be broken,"[b][d] 37and, as another scripture says, "They will look on the one they have pierced."[c][e]

The Burial of Jesus

›See Matthew 27:57–61; Mark 15:42–47; Luke 23:50–56

38Later, Joseph of Arimathea asked Pilate for the body of Jesus. Now Joseph was a disciple of Jesus, but secretly because he feared the Jews. With Pilate's permission, he came and took the body away. 39He was accompanied by Nicodemus,[f] the man who earlier had visited Jesus at night. Nicodemus brought a mixture of myrrh and aloes, about seventy-five pounds.[d] 40Taking Jesus' body, the two of them wrapped it, with the spices, in strips of linen.[g] This was in accordance with Jewish burial customs.[h] 41At the place where Jesus was crucified, there was a garden, and in the garden a new tomb, in which no one had ever been laid. 42Because it was the Jewish day of Preparation[i] and since the tomb was nearby,[j] they laid Jesus there.

19:16 [b]Mt 27:26; Mk 15:15; Lk 23:25
19:17 [c]Ge 22:6; Lk 14:27; 23:26 [d]Lk 23:33 [e]Jn 5:2
19:18 [f]Lk 23:32
19:19 [g]Mk 1:24 [h]ver 14,21
19:20 [i]Heb 13:12
19:21 [j]ver 14
19:24 [k]ver 28,36,37; Mt 1:22 [l]Ps 22:18
19:25 [m]Mt 27:55,56; Mk 15:40,41; Lk 23:49 [n]Mt 12:46 [o]Lk 24:18
19:26 [p]Mt 12:46 [q]Jn 13:23
19:28 [r]ver 30; Jn 13:1 [s]ver 24,36,37
19:29 [t]Ps 69:21
19:30 [u]Lk 12:50; Jn 17:4
19:31 [v]ver 14,42 [w]Dt 21:23; Jos 8:29; 10:26,27
19:32 [x]ver 18
19:34 [y]Zec 12:10 [z]1Jn 5:6,8
19:35 [a]Lk 24:48 [b]Jn 15:27; 21:24
19:36 [c]ver 24,28,37; Mt 1:22 [d]Ex 12:46; Nu 9:12; Ps 34:20
19:37 [e]Zec 12:10; Rev 1:7
19:39 [f]Jn 3:1; 7:50
19:40 [g]Lk 24:12; Jn 11:44; 20:5,7 [h]Mt 26:12
19:42 [i]ver 14,31 [j]ver 20,41

a *24* Psalm 22:18 **b** *36* Exodus 12:46; Num. 9:12; Psalm 34:20 **c** *37* Zech. 12:10
d *39* Greek *a hundred litrai* (about 34 kilograms)

The Empty Tomb

›See Matthew 28:1–8; Mark 16:1–8; Luke 24:1–10

20 Early on the first day of the week, while it was still dark, Mary Magdalene[k] went to the tomb and saw that the stone had been removed from the entrance.[l] 2 So she came running to Simon Peter and the other disciple, the one Jesus loved,[m] and said, "They have taken the Lord out of the tomb, and we don't know where they have put him!"[n]

3 So Peter and the other disciple started for the tomb.[o] 4 Both were running, but the other disciple outran Peter and reached the tomb first. 5 He bent over and looked in[p] at the strips of linen[q] lying there but did not go in. 6 Then Simon Peter, who was behind him, arrived and went into the tomb. He saw the strips of linen lying there, 7 as well as the burial cloth that had been around Jesus' head.[r] The cloth was folded up by itself, separate from the linen. 8 Finally the other disciple, who had reached the tomb first,[s] also went inside. He saw and believed. 9 (They still did not understand from Scripture[t] that Jesus had to rise from the dead.)[u]

Jesus Appears to Mary Magdalene

10 Then the disciples went back to their homes, 11 but Mary stood outside the tomb crying. As she wept, she bent over to look into the tomb[v] 12 and saw two angels in white,[w] seated where Jesus' body had been, one at the head and the other at the foot.

13 They asked her, "Woman, why are you crying?"[x]

"They have taken my Lord away," she said, "and I don't know where they have put him."[y] 14 At this, she turned around and saw Jesus standing there,[z] but she did not realize that it was Jesus.[a]

15 "Woman," he said, "why are you crying?[b] Who is it you are looking for?"

Thinking he was the gardener, she said, "Sir, if you have carried him away, tell me where you have put him, and I will get him."

16 Jesus said to her, "Mary."

She turned toward him and cried out in Aramaic,[c] "Rabboni!"[d] (which means Teacher).

17 Jesus said, "Do not hold on to me, for I have not yet returned to the Father. Go instead to my brothers[e] and tell them, 'I am returning to my Father[f] and your Father, to my God and your God.'"

18 Mary Magdalene[g] went to the disciples[h] with the news: "I have seen the Lord!" And she told them that he had said these things to her.

Jesus Appears to His Disciples

19 On the evening of that first day of the week, when the disciples were together, with the doors locked for fear of the Jews,[i] Jesus came and stood among them and said, "Peace[j] be with you!"[k] 20 After he said this, he showed them his hands and side.[l] The disciples were overjoyed[m] when they saw the Lord.

21 Again Jesus said, "Peace be with you![n] As the Father has sent me,[o] I am sending you."[p] 22 And with that he breathed on them and said, "Receive the Holy Spirit.[q] 23 If you forgive anyone his sins, they are forgiven; if you do not forgive them, they are not forgiven."[r]

Jesus Appears to Thomas

24 Now Thomas[s] (called Didymus), one of the Twelve, was not with the disciples when Jesus came. 25 So the other disciples told him, "We have seen the Lord!"

But he said to them, "Unless I see the nail marks in his hands and put my finger where the nails were, and put my hand into his side,[t] I will not believe it."[u]

26 A week later his disciples were in the house again, and Thomas was with them. Though the doors were locked, Jesus came and stood among them and said, "Peace[v] be with you!"[w] 27 Then he said to Thomas, "Put your finger here; see my hands. Reach out your hand and put it into my side. Stop doubting and believe."[x]

28 Thomas said to him, "My Lord and my God!"

29 Then Jesus told him, "Because you have seen me, you have believed;[y] blessed are those who have not seen and yet have believed."[z]

30 Jesus did many other miraculous signs[a] in the presence of his disciples, which are not recorded in this book.[b] 31 But these are written that you may[a] believe[c] that Jesus is the Christ, the Son of God,[d] and that by believing you may have life in his name.[e]

Jesus and the Miraculous Catch of Fish

21 Afterward Jesus appeared again to his disciples,[f] by the Sea of Tiberias.[b][g] It happened this way: 2 Simon

20:1 [k] ver 18; Jn 19:25 [l] Mt 27:60,66
20:2 [m] Jn 13:23 [n] ver 13
20:3 [o] Lk 24:12
20:5 [p] ver 11 [q] Jn 19:40
20:7 [r] Jn 11:44
20:8 [s] ver 4
20:9 [t] Mt 22:29; Jn 2:22 [u] Lk 24:26,46
20:11 [v] ver 5
20:12 [w] Mt 28:2,3; Mk 16:5; Lk 24:4; Ac 5:19
20:13 [x] ver 15 [y] ver 2
20:14 [z] Mt 28:9; Mk 16:9 [a] Lk 24:16; Jn 21:4
20:15 [b] ver 13
20:16 [c] Jn 5:2 [d] Mt 23:7
20:17 [e] Mt 28:10 [f] Jn 7:33
20:18 [g] ver 1 [h] Lk 24:10,22, 23
20:19 [i] Jn 7:13 [j] Jn 14:27 [k] ver 21,26; Lk 24:36-39
20:20 [l] Lk 24:39,40; Jn 19:34 [m] Jn 16:20,22
20:21 [n] ver 19 [o] Jn 3:17 [p] Mt 28:19; Jn 17:18
20:22 [q] Jn 7:39; Ac 2:38; 8:15-17; 19:2; Gal 3:2
20:23 [r] Mt 16:19; 18:18
20:24 [s] Jn 11:16
20:25 [t] ver 20 [u] Mk 16:11
20:26 [v] Jn 14:27 [w] ver 21
20:27 [x] ver 25; Lk 24:40
20:29 [y] Jn 3:15 [z] 1Pe 1:8
20:30 [a] Jn 2:11 [b] Jn 21:25
20:31 [c] Jn 3:15; 19:35 [d] Mt 4:3 [e] Mt 25:46
21:1 [f] Jn 20:19,26 [g] Jn 6:1

a *31* Some manuscripts *may continue to*
b *1* That is, Sea of Galilee

THOMAS

A Transformed Pessimist

Have you ever met someone who always sees the glass as "half empty" rather than "half full"? That person is more of a pessimist than an optimist! Thomas was certainly a pessimist. Even when he heard eyewitness accounts of the greatest news in history, his negativity distorted his perspective and almost caused him to miss an encounter with the risen Lord.

Courage Versus Faith

Thomas was a courageous disciple, one who was zealously devoted to Jesus. At one point in his career as a disciple, word had come to Jesus that his friend Lazarus was seriously ill. After a delay of two days, Jesus informed his disciples that he was going to return to Judea and go to Bethany to see Lazarus. The disciples were shocked and fearful. "'But Rabbi,' they said, 'a short while ago the Jews tried to stone you, and yet you are going back there?'" (John 11:8).

Jesus responded affirmatively. And while the others may still have been a bit frightened, Thomas had the courage and devotion to declare "to the rest of the disciples 'Let us also go, that we may die with him'" (11:16). Thomas was committed to following Jesus Christ even though it meant he might have to sacrifice his own life. No other apostle had been so courageous up to that point.

But Thomas's faith did not match his bravery. After Jesus' death, Thomas and the other disciples heard from Mary Magdalene that she had seen the risen Christ (20:18). How could this be so? The one who claimed to be "the way and the truth and the life" (14:6) had just been crucified as a criminal. Thomas likely turned his back and walked away in disgust, believing he had been duped into following an impostor.

Jesus Is Risen!

Tension and fear permeated Jerusalem and the surrounding area. Several of the apostles gathered together in someone's home "with the doors locked for fear of the Jews" (20:19). Imagine their surprise when Jesus suddenly appeared, standing in the room with them. Calming their fears, "he showed them his hands and side" (20:20). The disciples' anxiety turned to joy as they realized they were face to face with the risen Christ!

For some reason, Thomas "was not with the disciples when Jesus came" (20:24). So the other disciples quickly informed him about their encounter with Jesus, telling him he had missed an incredible experience. But it's obvious from Thomas's response that he had already made up his mind. He would not be deceived by some ghost! He would not trust his fellow disciples' report. He chose not to believe. Jesus was dead, and that was that (20:25).

One week later, the disciples were all together again in the same house. This time, "Thomas was with them" (20:26). The disciples were afraid; reports were circulating that they had stolen Jesus' body and were only spreading a myth that he had risen from the dead (Matthew 28:13–15). But as before, Jesus suddenly appeared in their midst. He immediately walked over to Thomas and said, "Put your finger here; see my hands. Reach out your hand and put it into my side. Stop doubting and believe" (John 20:27).

Remember that none of the disciples had seen Jesus since his last appearance a week earlier. Who could have told Jesus about Thomas's challenge? No one! For Jesus to know Thomas's words of unbelief meant only one thing to Thomas—Jesus Christ was who he had claimed to be all along! Thomas immediately went from disbelief and cynicism to complete faith in Jesus Christ as he exclaimed with amazement, "My Lord and my God!" (20:28).

The Thomas in Us All

We all have the same tendency to cynicism and doubt as our friend Thomas. God certainly wants us to use the critical and objective thinking abilities he has given us to make decisions and judgments. But when all is said and done, we must ultimately trust God more than we trust ourselves. If we don't, our God is no bigger than our limited capacity to reason and comprehend the infinite.

Don't misunderstand. This does not mean that God will not reveal himself to us unless we are standing on a dynamic faith. When Philip first met Jesus, he challenged his friend Nathanael to explore Christ's claims for himself. "Come and see," he said (1:46). Jesus honored Nathanael's willingness to at least explore the possibility that Jesus was the Son of God. If you are struggling with doubt and disillusionment, he'll do the same for you. Will you remain a doubting, cynical Thomas, or will you "come and see" for yourself? That was the challenge for Thomas; and it's the challenge for you too.

—Dr. Gene Getz

Peter, Thomas[h] (called Didymus), Nathanael[i] from Cana in Galilee,[j] the sons of Zebedee,[k] and two other disciples were together. 3"I'm going out to fish," Simon Peter told them, and they said, "We'll go with you." So they went out and got into the boat, but that night they caught nothing.[l]

4Early in the morning, Jesus stood on the shore, but the disciples did not realize that it was Jesus.[m]

5He called out to them, "Friends, haven't you any fish?"

"No," they answered.

6He said, "Throw your net on the right side of the boat and you will find some." When they did, they were unable to haul the net in because of the large number of fish.[n]

7Then the disciple whom Jesus loved[o] said to Peter, "It is the Lord!" As soon as Simon Peter heard him say, "It is the Lord," he wrapped his outer garment around him (for he had taken it off) and jumped into the water. 8The other disciples followed in the boat, towing the net full of fish, for they were not far from shore, about a hundred yards.[a] 9When they landed, they saw a fire[p] of burning coals there with fish on it,[q] and some bread.

10Jesus said to them, "Bring some of the fish you have just caught."

11Simon Peter climbed aboard and dragged the net ashore. It was full of large fish, 153, but even with so many the net was not torn. 12Jesus said to them, "Come and have breakfast." None of the disciples dared ask him, "Who are you?" They knew it was the Lord. 13Jesus came, took the bread and gave it to them, and did the same with the fish.[r] 14This was now the third time Jesus appeared to his disciples[s] after he was raised from the dead.

Jesus Reinstates Peter

2 →PG. 1195

15When they had finished eating, Jesus said to Simon Peter, "Simon son of John, do you truly love me more than these?"

"Yes, Lord," he said, "you know that I love you."[t]

Jesus said, "Feed my lambs."[u]

16Again Jesus said, "Simon son of John, do you truly love me?"

He answered, "Yes, Lord, you know that I love you."

Jesus said, "Take care of my sheep."[v]

17The third time he said to him, "Simon son of John, do you love me?"

Peter was hurt because Jesus asked him the third time, "Do you love me?"[w] He said, "Lord, you know all things;[x] you know that I love you."

Jesus said, "Feed my sheep.[y] 18I tell you the truth, when you were younger you dressed yourself and went where you wanted; but when you are old you will stretch out your hands, and someone else will dress you and lead you where you do not want to go." 19Jesus said this to indicate the kind of death[z] by which Peter would glorify God.[a] Then he said to him, "Follow me!"

20Peter turned and saw that the disciple whom Jesus loved[b] was following them. (This was the one who had leaned back against Jesus at the supper and had said, "Lord, who is going to betray you?")[c] 21When Peter saw him, he asked, "Lord, what about him?"

22Jesus answered, "If I want him to remain alive until I return,[d] what is that to you? You must follow me."[e] 23Because of this, the rumor spread

21:2 [h]Jn 11:16 [i]Jn 1:45 [j]Jn 2:1 [k]Mt 4:21
21:3 [l]Lk 5:5
21:4 [m]Lk 24:16; Jn 20:14
21:6 [n]Lk 5:4-7
21:7 [o]Jn 13:23
21:9 [p]Jn 18:18 [q]ver 10,13
21:13 [r]ver 9
21:14 [s]Jn 20:19,26
21:15 [t]Mt 26:33,35; Jn 13:37 [u]Lk 12:32
21:16 [v]Mt 2:6; Ac 20:28; 1Pe 5:2,3
21:17 [w]Jn 13:38 [x]Jn 16:30 [y]ver 16
21:19 [z]Jn 12:33; 18:32 [a]2Pe 1:14
21:20 [b]ver 7; Jn 13:23 [c]Jn 13:25
21:22 [d]Mt 16:27; 1Co 4:5; Rev 2:25 [e]ver 19

[a] 8 Greek *about two hundred cubits* (about 90 meters)

21:19–22

PROMISE 2

"WHAT ABOUT HIM?"

Comparisons are odious. When we compare ourselves with another person, one of two things happens: either we feel good or bad about ourselves. In either case, we lose. And so does the other person. Yet we all get trapped in the game of comparisons. We compare our income, our house, our car, our children, even our wife to those of other men. And even if we win, we lose.

Peter struggled with this problem. After the resurrection, as Peter and the Lord were walking along the shore of the Sea of Galilee, Peter affirmed his love for the Lord three times. The fisherman's words were fitting, especially in light of his three previous denials. But as the two walked, Peter glanced over his shoulder and saw John walking behind them. In that moment only one thing mattered to Peter—what Jesus had planned for John. "What about him?" Peter asked.

The Lord's answer is fitting for everyone who plays the game of comparisons. Jesus told Peter not to worry about John. Instead, Jesus told Peter to do one thing: "You must follow me." What an answer! And what a cure for the problem of comparisons. Instead of seeing how you measure up to another man, check out how closely you're walking to Jesus.

For the next Promise 2 reading go to page 1274.

among the brothers[f] that this disciple
would not die. But Jesus did not say
that he would not die; he only said, "If
I want him to remain alive until I return, what is that to you?"
24This is the disciple who testifies to
these things[g] and who wrote them
down. We know that his testimony is
true.[h]
25Jesus did many other things as
well.[i] If every one of them were written down, I suppose that even the
whole world would not have room for
the books that would be written.

21:23 [f] Ac 1:16
21:24 [g] Jn 15:27 [h] Jn 19:35
21:25 [i] Jn 20:30

ACTS

AT A GLANCE

Key Principle: God calls his children to be ambassadors who bear witness to Jesus Christ, in the power of the Holy Spirit, to people in their circle of influence.
Author: Luke
Time and Place: A.D. 30–62 / Jerusalem, Judea, Samaria, the Roman Empire
Key Verses: 1:8; 2:42–47

BENEFIT

Acts continues the story of the birth of Christianity from the ascension of Christ to the time of Paul's first imprisonment in Rome. A crucial historical narrative, Acts provides the backdrop to most of the other New Testament letters. It develops the exciting story of the birth and expansion of the early church, which begins in Jerusalem, the city of the empty tomb (1—7), spreads into the provinces of Judea and Samaria (8—12) and finally reaches throughout the Roman Empire (13—28). This book challenges us to be engaged in the process of lifestyle evangelism. Just as the good news of Jesus Christ has spread in an unbroken succession from one changed life to another for nearly twenty centuries, so our task is to continue to pass it on until Christ returns.

SETTING

Acts is the second volume of a two-part work by Luke written to pick up the story where his Gospel left off. An associate of Paul, Luke was an eyewitness to several of the events recorded in this history; this is evident in the "we" sections where Luke includes himself as a fellow traveler (16:10–17; 20:5–21:18; 27:1—28:16). Elsewhere in the book, Luke uses the same careful investigative techniques he employed in writing his Gospel, relying on eyewitness accounts and written documents (15:23–29; 23:26–30).

Luke includes a wealth of geographical and narrative details in Acts, and archaeological discoveries have confirmed Luke's trustworthiness as a historian. Luke probably completed this account in A.D. 62, since he makes no mention of the outcome of the trial Paul had been waiting to face for two years. If, in fact, he knew what happened at Paul's trial, Luke probably would not have cut his story short in chapter 28 with Paul still in prison. In addition, he says nothing about Nero's persecution in A.D. 64, of Paul's execution in A.D. 68, or of the devastation of Jerusalem in A.D. 70.

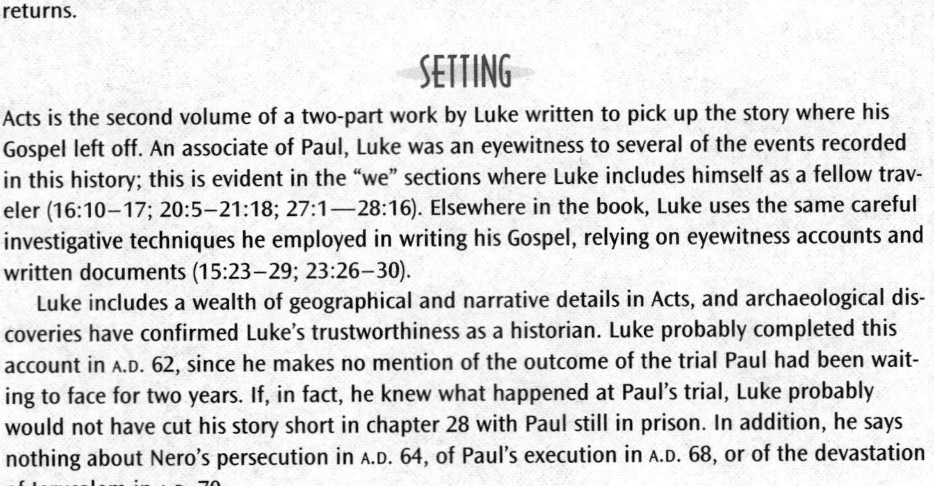

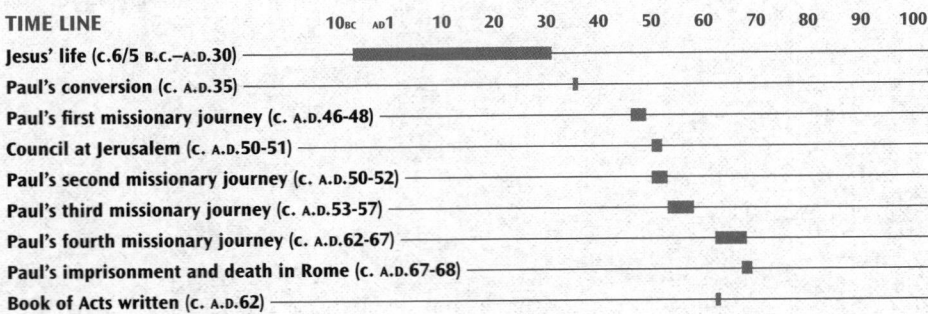

THEME AND PURPOSE

The Great Commission in Matthew 28:19–20 to "go and make disciples of all nations" is supplemented by Christ's last words to his disciples before his ascension into heaven: "But you will receive power when the Holy Spirit comes on you; and you will be my witnesses in Jerusalem, and in all Judea and Samaria, and to the ends of the earth" (1:8). Luke wrote Acts to provide a historical link between the Gospels and the epistles. He also wrote to chronicle the key events that brought about the birth and rapid spread of the church, which began in Jerusalem and moved beyond Israel's borders to the Roman Empire's other provinces. This is a highly selective historical account, and though it is sometimes called "The Acts of the Apostles," it is predominantly a series of important acts of Peter (1—12) and of Paul (13—28). Acts is a transitional book that explains how the early church changed from being entirely Jewish (1—7) to including Samaritans and Gentiles (8—12). By the end the of time period covered by this book, Gentiles comprised the majority of believers in Christ.

UNIQUE CONTRIBUTION

While the four Gospels chronicle the life of our Lord, only one book continues their story line, describing the movement of the Holy Spirit in the lives of the apostles through the decades that followed. Without the book of Acts, many events that the other New Testament books mention would be obscure and confusing. As historical treatises, Luke and Acts together provide an extensive and impressive portrait of the foundation and early development of Christianity. Both books are characterized by the same refined literary quality, and both books designate names, places and events with careful attention to historical precision. In these two books, Luke uses over 700 Greek words not found anywhere else in the New Testament, and in Acts alone he includes some 80 geographical references and over 100 personal references. Speeches and sermons also play an unusually prominent role in this book, with 24 messages in the course of its 28 chapters.

CHRIST IN ACTS

All the sermons and defenses in Acts point to Jesus Christ as the resurrected Savior of the world. In his sermon on the day of Pentecost, Peter builds upon Jesus' fulfillment of several Old Testament passages and uses the fact and example of the empty tomb to convince his listeners that Jesus is both Lord and Christ (2:36). The resurrected Christ "is the one whom God appointed as judge of the living and the dead. All the prophets testify about him that everyone who believes in him receives forgiveness of sins through his name" (10:42–43). There is no hope of salvation apart from the work of Christ: "Salvation is found in no one else, for there is no other name under heaven given to men by which we must be saved" (4:12). It is through Jesus Christ that all men will be judged: "[God] has set a day when he will judge the world with justice by the man he has appointed. He has given proof of this to all men by raising him from the dead" (17:31).

OVERVIEW

FOCUS	The Gospel in Jerusalem	The Gospel in Judea and Samaria	The Gospel to the Ends of the Earth	
REFERENCE	1 7	8 12	13 21:26	21:27 28
TOPICS	Establishment	Extension	Expansion	Explanation
	Triumph	Transition	Travels	Trials
	Jews	Samaritans	Gentiles	
	Peter	Philip	Paul	
LOCATION	Jerusalem	Judea and Samaria	The Roman Empire	
TIME	2 years	13 Years	14 Years	
	A.D. 33–35	A.D. 35–48	A.D. 48–62	

Just before being taken up into heaven, Jesus instructs his disciples to wait for the gift of the Holy Spirit to empower them to be his witnesses (1). The Holy Spirit comes at Pentecost and empowers Peter to deliver a sermon about the resurrected Christ that leads to the conversion of 3,000 listeners (2). After healing a man who had been lame from birth, Peter delivers a persuasive message to the people and another to the Sanhedrin (3—4). The church continues to grow, but the apostles are persecuted because of their message (5). The apostles appoint deacons to assist them (6); one of the deacons, Stephen, is martyred for his powerful testimony (7).

God uses another deacon, Philip, to bring the gospel to the Samaritans and to minister to an Ethiopian eunuch (8). The resurrected Christ appears to Saul, a key persecutor of the church; meanwhile Peter continues his miraculous ministry (9). Peter's presence at the conversion of Cornelius' household opens the gospel to the Gentiles, and Peter convinces Jewish believers that God has granted Gentiles repentance unto life (10—11).

In chapters 13—28, Luke shifts his attention from Peter to Paul, giving an account of Paul's three missionary journeys and his trials and expedition to Rome. In the first missionary journey in A.D. 46–48 (13:1—14:28), Paul ministers in the province of Galatia. After this journey, a church council in Jerusalem determines that Gentile converts are not required to submit to the Mosaic Law (15). During his second missionary journey in A.D. 50–52 (15:36—18:22), Paul returns to Galatia and proceeds beyond to Macedonia and Greece. In his third missionary journey in A.D. 53–57 (18:23—21:16), Paul spends almost three years in Ephesus and revisits Macedonia and Greece. He is later arrested in Jerusalem, defends himself in three trials in Caesarea and travels by ship to Rome where he is placed under house arrest while he awaits trial before Caesar (21:17—28:31).

ACTS

Jesus Taken Up Into Heaven

1 In my former book,[a] Theophilus, I wrote about all that Jesus began to do and to teach[b] **2**until the day he was taken up to heaven,[c] after giving instructions[d] through the Holy Spirit to the apostles[e] he had chosen.[f] **3**After his suffering, he showed himself to these men and gave many convincing proofs that he was alive. He appeared to them[g] over a period of forty days and spoke about the kingdom of God. **4**On one occasion, while he was eating with them, he gave them this command: "Do not leave Jerusalem, but wait for the gift my Father promised, which you have heard me speak about.[h] **5**For John baptized with[a] water, but in a few days you will be baptized with the Holy Spirit."

6So when they met together, they asked him, "Lord, are you at this time going to restore[i] the kingdom to Israel?"

7 →PG. 1200

7He said to them: "It is not for you to know the times or dates the Father has set by his own authority.[j] **8**But you will receive power when the Holy Spirit comes on you;[k] and you will be my witnesses[l] in Jerusalem, and in all Judea and Samaria,[m] and to the ends of the earth."[n]

9After he said this, he was taken up[o] before their very eyes, and a cloud hid him from their sight.

10They were looking intently up into the sky as he was going, when suddenly two men dressed in white[p] stood beside them. **11**"Men of Galilee,"[q] they said, "why do you stand here looking into the sky? This same Jesus, who has been taken from you into heaven, will come back[r] in the same way you have seen him go into heaven."

Matthias Chosen to Replace Judas

2 →PG. 1204

12Then they returned to Jerusalem[s] from the hill called the Mount of Olives,[t] a Sabbath day's walk[b] from the city. **13**When they arrived, they went upstairs to the room[u] where they were staying. Those present were Peter, John, James and Andrew; Philip and Thomas, Bartholomew and Matthew; James son of Alphaeus and Simon the Zealot, and Judas son of James.[v] **14**They all joined together constantly in prayer,[w] along with the women[x] and Mary the mother of Jesus, and with his brothers.[y]

15In those days Peter stood up among the believers[c] (a group numbering about a hundred and twenty) **16**and said, "Brothers, the Scripture had to be fulfilled[z] which the Holy Spirit spoke long ago through the mouth of David concerning Judas,[a] who served as guide for those who arrested Jesus— **17**he was one of our number[b] and shared in this ministry."[c]

18(With the reward[d] he got for his wickedness, Judas bought a field;[e] there he fell headlong, his body burst open and all his intestines spilled out. **19**Everyone in Jerusalem heard about this, so they called that field in their language Akeldama, that is, Field of Blood.)

20"For," said Peter, "it is written in the book of Psalms,

" 'May his place be deserted;

1:1 [a]Lk 1:1-4 [b]Lk 3:23
1:2 [c]ver 9,11; Mk 16:19 [d]Mt 28:19,20 [e]Mk 6:30 [f]Jn 13:18
1:3 [g]Mt 28:17; Lk 24:34,36; Jn 20:19,26; 21:1,14; 1Co 15:5-7
1:4 [h]Lk 24:49; Jn 14:16; Ac 2:33
1:6 [i]Mt 17:11
1:7 [j]Mt 24:36
1:8 [k]Ac 2:1-4 [l]Lk 24:48 [m]Ac 8:1-25 [n]Mt 28:19
1:9 [o]ver 2
1:10 [p]Lk 24:4; Jn 20:12
1:11 [q]Ac 2:7 [r]Mt 16:27
1:12 [s]Lk 24:52 [t]Mt 21:1
1:13 [u]Ac 9:37; 20:8 [v]Mt 10:2-4; Mk 3:16-19; Lk 6:14-16
1:14 [w]Ac 2:42; 6:4 [x]Lk 23:49,55 [y]Mt 12:46
1:16 [z]ver 20 [a]Jn 13:18
1:17 [b]Jn 6:70,71 [c]ver 25
1:18 [d]Mt 26:14,15 [e]Mt 27:3-10

[a]*5* Or *in* [b]*12* That is, about 3/4 mile (about 1,100 meters) [c]*15* Greek *brothers*

1:8

PROMISE 7

JESUS' FINAL WORDS

In this passage, Jesus spoke of a progression of steps the disciples would take in service to him. First, Jesus said they would receive power from God. This power would flow from the Holy Spirit, who would dwell within them. Second, Jesus said they would tell the world about him, beginning in Jerusalem and spreading outward from there.

As you read this passage, think about the men who heard Jesus speak these words. Most of the disciples were ordinary, working-class men; none of them had the power within themselves to spread the word about Jesus. Their power came from above, and God used them to influence their culture for Jesus.

This same Holy Spirit can empower you to do God's work in the world. Through this passage, Jesus calls all people who believe in him to witness to his power and saving grace. As you meditate on Jesus' words, think of ways you can shape your personal ministry around this verse. Then pray for the Spirit to open up opportunities so that you can influence your world for Jesus Christ.

For the next Promise 7 reading go to page 1205.

let there be no one to dwell in
it,'[a][f]

and,

" 'May another take his place of
leadership.'[b][g]

21 Therefore it is necessary to choose one of the men who have been with us the whole time the Lord Jesus went in and out among us, 22 beginning from John's baptism[h] to the time when Jesus was taken up from us. For one of these must become a witness[i] with us of his resurrection."

23 So they proposed two men: Joseph called Barsabbas (also known as Justus) and Matthias. 24 Then they prayed,[j] "Lord, you know everyone's heart.[k] Show us which of these two you have chosen 25 to take over this apostolic ministry, which Judas left to go where he belongs." 26 Then they cast lots, and the lot fell to Matthias; so he was added to the eleven apostles.[l]

The Holy Spirit Comes at Pentecost

2 When the day of Pentecost[m] came, they were all together[n] in one place. 2 Suddenly a sound like the blowing of a violent wind came from heaven and filled the whole house where they were sitting.[o] 3 They saw what seemed to be tongues of fire that separated and came to rest on each of them. 4 All of them were filled with the Holy Spirit and began to speak in other tongues[c][p] as the Spirit enabled them.

5 Now there were staying in Jerusalem God-fearing[q] Jews from every nation under heaven. 6 When they heard this sound, a crowd came together in bewilderment, because each one heard them speaking in his own language. 7 Utterly amazed,[r] they asked: "Are not all these men who are speaking Galileans?[s] 8 Then how is it that each of us hears them in his own native language? 9 Parthians, Medes and Elamites; residents of Mesopotamia, Judea and Cappadocia,[t] Pontus[u] and Asia,[v] 10 Phrygia[w] and Pamphylia,[x] Egypt and the parts of Libya near Cyrene;[y] visitors from Rome 11 (both Jews and converts to Judaism); Cretans and Arabs—we hear them declaring the wonders of God in our own tongues!" 12 Amazed and perplexed, they asked one another, "What does this mean?"

13 Some, however, made fun of them and said, "They have had too much wine.[d]"[z]

Peter Addresses the Crowd

14 Then Peter stood up with the Eleven, raised his voice and addressed the crowd: "Fellow Jews and all of you who live in Jerusalem, let me explain this to you; listen carefully to what I say. 15 These men are not drunk, as you suppose. It's only nine in the morning![a] 16 No, this is what was spoken by the prophet Joel:

17 " 'In the last days, God says,
I will pour out my Spirit on all
people.[b]
Your sons and daughters will
prophesy,[c]
your young men will see visions,
your old men will dream dreams.
18 Even on my servants, both men
and women,
I will pour out my Spirit in those
days,
and they will prophesy.[d]
19 I will show wonders in the heaven
above
and signs on the earth below,
blood and fire and billows of
smoke.
20 The sun will be turned to darkness
and the moon to blood[e]
before the coming of the great
and glorious day of the
Lord.
21 And everyone who calls
on the name of the Lord will be
saved.'[e][f]

1 →PG. 1197

22 "Men of Israel, listen to this: Jesus of Nazareth was a man accredited by God to you by miracles, wonders and signs,[g] which God did among you through him,[h] as you yourselves know. 23 This man was handed over to you by God's set purpose and foreknowledge;[i] and you, with the help of wicked men,[f] put him to death by nailing him to the cross.[j] 24 But God raised him from the dead,[k] freeing him from the agony of death, because it was impossible for death to keep its hold on him.[l] 25 David said about him:

" 'I saw the Lord always before me.
Because he is at my right hand,
I will not be shaken.
26 Therefore my heart is glad and my
tongue rejoices;
my body also will live in hope,
27 because you will not abandon me
to the grave,
nor will you let your Holy One
see decay.[m]
28 You have made known to me the
paths of life;
you will fill me with joy in your
presence.'[g]

1:20 [f]Ps 69:25 [g]Ps 109:8 **1:22** [h]Mk 1:4 [i]ver 8 **1:24** [j]Ac 6:6; 14:23 [k]1Sa 16:7; Jer 17:10; Ac 15:8; Rev 2:23 **1:26** [l]Ac 2:14 **2:1** [m]Lev 23:15,16; Ac 20:16 [n]Ac 1:14 **2:2** [o]Ac 4:31 **2:4** [p]Mk 16:17; 1Co 12:10 **2:5** [q]Ac 8:2 **2:7** [r]ver 12 [s]Ac 1:11 **2:9** [t]1Pe 1:1 [u]Ac 18:2 [v]Ac 16:6; Ro 16:5; 1Co 16:19; 2Co 1:8 **2:10** [w]Ac 16:6; 18:23 [x]Ac 13:13; 15:38 [y]Mt 27:32 **2:13** [z]1Co 14:23

2:15 [a]1Th 5:7 **2:17** [b]Isa 44:3; Jn 7:37-39; Ac 10:45 [c]Ac 21:9 **2:18** [d]Ac 21:9-12 **2:20** [e]Mt 24:29 **2:21** [f]Ro 10:13 **2:22** [g]Jn 4:48; Ac 10:38 [h]Jn 3:2 **2:23** [i]Lk 22:22; Ac 3:18; 4:28 [j]Lk 24:20; Ac 3:13 **2:24** [k]ver 32; 1Co 6:14; 2Co 4:14; Eph 1:20; Col 2:12; Heb 13:20; 1Pe 1:21 [l]Jn 20:9 **2:27** [m]ver 31; Ac 13:35

[a] *20* Psalm 69:25 [b] *20* Psalm 109:8 [c] *4* Or *languages;* also in verse 11 [d] *13* Or *sweet wine* [e] *21* Joel 2:28-32 [f] *23* Or *of those not having the law* (that is, Gentiles) [g] *28* Psalm 16:8-11

29"Brothers, I can tell you confidently that the patriarch[n] David died and
was buried,[o] and his tomb is here[p] to
this day. 30But he was a prophet and
knew that God had promised him on
oath that he would place one of his
descendants on his throne.[q] 31Seeing
what was ahead, he spoke of the resurrection of the Christ,[a] that he was
not abandoned to the grave, nor did
his body see decay.[r] 32God has raised
this Jesus to life,[s] and we are all witnesses[t] of the fact. 33Exalted[u] to the
right hand of God,[v] he has received
from the Father[w] the promised Holy
Spirit[x] and has poured out[y] what you
now see and hear. 34For David did not
ascend to heaven, and yet he said,

> " 'The Lord said to my Lord:
> "Sit at my right hand
> 35until I make your enemies
> a footstool for your feet." '[b][z]

36"Therefore let all Israel be assured
of this: God has made this Jesus, whom
you crucified, both Lord and Christ."[a]

37When the people heard this, they
were cut to the heart and said to Peter
and the other apostles, "Brothers, what
shall we do?"[b]

1 →PG. 1213

38Peter replied, "Repent and be baptized,[c] every one of you, in the name
of Jesus Christ for the forgiveness of
your sins.[d] And you will receive the
gift of the Holy Spirit. 39The promise is
for you and your children[e] and for all
who are far off[f]—for all whom the
Lord our God will call."

40With many other words he warned
them; and he pleaded with them, "Save
yourselves from this corrupt generation."[g] 41Those who accepted his
message were baptized, and about
three thousand were added to their
number that day.

The Fellowship of the Believers

5 →PG. 1199

42They devoted themselves to the
apostles' teaching and to the fellowship, to the breaking of bread and to
prayer.[h] 43Everyone was filled with
awe, and many wonders and miraculous signs were done by the apostles.[i]
44All the believers were together and
had everything in common.[j] 45Selling
their possessions and goods, they gave
to anyone as he had need.[k] 46Every
day they continued to meet together
in the temple courts.[l] They broke
bread[m] in their homes and ate together with glad and sincere hearts, 47prais-
ing God and enjoying the favor of all
the people.[n] And the Lord added to
their number[o] daily those who were
being saved.

2:29 [n]Ac 7:8,9 [o]Ac 13:36; 1Ki 2:10 [p]Ne 3:16
2:30 [q]2Sa 7:12; Ps 132:11
2:31 [r]Ps 16:10
2:32 [s]ver 24 [t]Ac 1:8
2:33 [u]Php 2:9 [v]Mk 16:19 [w]Ac 1:4 [x]Jn 7:39; 14:26 [y]Ac 10:45
2:35 [z]Ps 110:1; Mt 22:44
2:36 [a]Lk 2:11
2:37 [b]Lk 3:10,12,14
2:38 [c]Ac 8:12,16,36, 38; 22:16 [d]Lk 24:47; Ac 3:19
2:39 [e]Isa 44:3 [f]Ac 10:45; Eph 2:13
2:40 [g]Dt 32:5
2:42 [h]Ac 1:14
2:43 [i]Ac 5:12
2:44 [j]Ac 4:32
2:45 [k]Mt 19:21
2:46 [l]Lk 24:53; Ac 5:21,42 [m]Ac 20:7
2:47 [n]Ro 14:18 [o]ver 41; Ac 5:14

Peter Heals the Crippled Beggar

3 One day Peter and John[p] were going up to the temple[q] at the time of
prayer—at three in the afternoon.[r]
2Now a man crippled from birth[s] was
being carried to the temple gate[t]
called Beautiful, where he was put every day to beg[u] from those going into
the temple courts. 3When he saw Peter
and John about to enter, he asked them
for money. 4Peter looked straight at
him, as did John. Then Peter said,
"Look at us!" 5So the man gave them
his attention, expecting to get something from them.

6Then Peter said, "Silver or gold I do
not have, but what I have I give you. In
the name of Jesus Christ of Nazareth,[v]
walk." 7Taking him by the right hand,
he helped him up, and instantly the
man's feet and ankles became strong.
8He jumped to his feet and began to
walk. Then he went with them into the
temple courts, walking and jumping,[w]

3:1 [p]Lk 22:8 [q]Ac 2:46 [r]Ps 55:17
3:2 [s]Ac 14:8 [t]Lk 16:20 [u]Jn 9:8
3:6 [v]ver 16; Ac 4:10
3:8 [w]Ac 14:10

[a] *31* Or *Messiah.* "The Christ" (Greek) and "the Messiah" (Hebrew) both mean "the Anointed One"; also in verse 36. [b] *35* Psalm 110:1

2:42–44

PROMISE 5

THE YOUNG CHURCH

The source of power unleashed on the day of Pentecost (vv. 1–4) will never fail. On the day the church was born, the greatest spiritual renewal in world history occurred. The early church grew because, under the direction of the Holy Spirit, believers devoted themselves to four things:

1. *The apostle's teaching.* A growing church is one that's grounded in God's Word.
2. *Fellowship.* These believers spent time together in corporate worship. They cared for each other.
3. *The breaking of bread.* Early believers ate and celebrated the sacrament of the Lord's Supper together. Each one shared his or her resources for the benefit of the group.
4. *Prayer.* These growing believers prayed together. Both personal and corporate prayer are crucial for spiritual growth.

How does your church incorporate these four activities into your congregational life? Or, to make it more personal, how much do you incorporate these activities into your own life? Think of some creative ways you can continue to pursue these four activities in your personal life, and ways you can encourage your pastoral staff as they carry these activities out in your church life.

For the next Promise 5 reading go to page 1201.

and praising God. 9When all the people[x] saw him walking and praising God, 10they recognized him as the same man who used to sit begging at the temple gate called Beautiful,[y] and they were filled with wonder and amazement at what had happened to him.

Peter Speaks to the Onlookers

11While the beggar held on to Peter and John,[z] all the people were astonished and came running to them in the place called Solomon's Colonnade.[a] 12When Peter saw this, he said to them: "Men of Israel, why does this surprise you? Why do you stare at us as if by our own power or godliness we had made this man walk? 13The God of Abraham, Isaac and Jacob, the God of our fathers,[b] has glorified his servant Jesus. You handed him over to be killed, and you disowned him before Pilate,[c] though he had decided to let him go.[d] 14You disowned the Holy[e] and Righteous One[f] and asked that a murderer be released to you.[g] 15You killed the author of life, but God raised him from the dead.[h] We are witnesses of this. 16By faith in the name of Jesus, this man whom you see and know was made strong. It is Jesus' name and the faith that comes through him that has given this complete healing to him, as you can all see.

17"Now, brothers, I know that you acted in ignorance,[i] as did your leaders.[j] 18But this is how God fulfilled what he had foretold[k] through all the prophets,[l] saying that his Christ[a] would suffer.[m] 19Repent, then, and turn to God, so that your sins may be wiped out,[n] that times of refreshing may come from the Lord, 20and that he may send the Christ, who has been appointed for you—even Jesus. 21He must remain in heaven[o] until the time comes for God to restore everything,[p] as he promised long ago through his holy prophets.[q] 22For Moses said, 'The Lord your God will raise up for you a prophet like me from among your own people; you must listen to everything he tells you.[r] 23Anyone who does not listen to him will be completely cut off from among his people.'[b][s]

24"Indeed, all the prophets[t] from Samuel on, as many as have spoken, have foretold these days. 25And you are heirs[u] of the prophets and of the covenant[v] God made with your fathers. He said to Abraham, 'Through your offspring all peoples on earth will be blessed.'[c][w] 26When God raised up[x] his servant, he sent him first[y] to you to bless you by turning each of you from your wicked ways."

Peter and John Before the Sanhedrin

4 The priests and the captain of the temple guard[z] and the Sadducees[a] came up to Peter and John while they were speaking to the people. 2They were greatly disturbed because the apostles were teaching the people and proclaiming in Jesus the resurrection of the dead.[b] 3They seized Peter and John, and because it was evening, they put them in jail[c] until the next day. 4But many who heard the message believed, and the number of men grew[d] to about five thousand.

5The next day the rulers,[e] elders and teachers of the law met in Jerusalem. 6Annas the high priest was there, and so were Caiaphas,[f] John, Alexander and the other men of the high priest's family. 7They had Peter and John brought before them and began to question them: "By what power or what name did you do this?"

8Then Peter, filled with the Holy Spirit, said to them: "Rulers and elders of the people![g] 9If we are being called to account today for an act of kindness shown to a cripple[h] and are asked how he was healed, 10then know this, you and all the people of Israel: It is by the name of Jesus Christ of Nazareth, whom you crucified but whom God raised from the dead,[i] that this man stands before you healed. 11He is

" 'the stone you builders rejected,
which has become the
capstone.[d]'[e][j]

12Salvation is found in no one else, for there is no other name under heaven given to men by which we must be saved."[k]

13When they saw the courage of Peter and John[l] and realized that they were unschooled, ordinary men,[m] they were astonished and they took note that these men had been with Jesus. 14But since they could see the man who had been healed standing there with them, there was nothing they could say. 15So they ordered them to withdraw from the Sanhedrin[n] and then conferred together. 16"What are we going to do with these men?"[o] they asked. "Everybody living in Jerusalem knows they have done an outstanding miracle,[p] and we cannot deny it. 17But to stop this thing from spreading any

3:9 [x]Ac 4:16,21 **3:10** [y]ver 2 **3:11** [z]Lk 22:8 [a]Jn 10:23; Ac 5:12 **3:13** [b]Ac 5:30 [c]Mt 27:2 [d]Lk 23:4 **3:14** [e]Mk 1:24; Ac 4:27 [f]Ac 7:52 [g]Mk 15:11; Lk 23:18-25 **3:15** [h]Ac 2:24 **3:17** [i]Lk 23:34 [j]Ac 13:27 **3:18** [k]Ac 2:23 [l]Lk 24:27 [m]Ac 17:2,3; 26:22,23 **3:19** [n]Ac 2:38 **3:21** [o]Ac 1:11 [p]Mt 17:11 [q]Lk 1:70 **3:22** [r]Dt 18:15,18; Ac 7:37 **3:23** [s]Dt 18:19 **3:24** [t]Lk 24:27 **3:25** [u]Ac 2:39 [v]Ro 9:4,5 [w]Ge 12:3; 22:18; 26:4; 28:14 **3:26** [x]ver 22; Ac 2:24 [y]Ac 13:46; Ro 1:16 **4:1** [z]Lk 22:4 [a]Mt 3:7 **4:2** [b]Ac 17:18 **4:3** [c]Ac 5:18 **4:4** [d]Ac 2:41 **4:5** [e]Lk 23:13 **4:6** [f]Mt 26:3; Lk 3:2 **4:8** [g]ver 5; Lk 23:13 **4:9** [h]Ac 3:6 **4:10** [i]Ac 2:24 **4:11** [j]Ps 118:22; Isa 28:16; Mt 21:42 **4:12** [k]Mt 1:21; Ac 10:43; 1Ti 2:5 **4:13** [l]Lk 22:8 [m]Mt 11:25 **4:15** [n]Mt 5:22 **4:16** [o]Jn 11:47 [p]Ac 3:6-10

a *18* Or *Messiah*; also in verse 20
b *23* Deut. 18:15,18,19 c *25* Gen. 22:18; 26:4
d *11* Or *cornerstone* e *11* Psalm 118:22

further among the people, we must warn these men to speak no longer to anyone in this name."

18Then they called them in again and commanded them not to speak or teach at all in the name of Jesus.[q] 19But Peter and John replied, "Judge for yourselves whether it is right in God's sight to obey you rather than God.[r] 20For we cannot help speaking about what we have seen and heard."

21After further threats they let them go. They could not decide how to punish them, because all the people[s] were praising God[t] for what had happened. 22For the man who was miraculously healed was over forty years old.

The Believers' Prayer

23On their release, Peter and John went back to their own people and reported all that the chief priests and elders had said to them. 24When they heard this, they raised their voices together in prayer to God. "Sovereign Lord," they said, "you made the heaven and the earth and the sea, and everything in them. 25You spoke by the Holy Spirit through the mouth of your servant, our father David:[u]

" 'Why do the nations rage
and the peoples plot in vain?
26The kings of the earth take their
stand
and the rulers gather together
against the Lord
and against his Anointed
One.[a]'[b][v]

27Indeed Herod[w] and Pontius Pilate[x] met together with the Gentiles and the people[c] of Israel in this city to conspire against your holy servant Jesus,[y] whom you anointed. 28They did what your power and will had decided beforehand should happen.[z] 29Now, Lord, consider their threats and enable your servants to speak your word with great boldness.[a] 30Stretch out your hand to heal and perform miraculous signs and wonders[b] through the name of your holy servant Jesus."[c]

31After they prayed, the place where they were meeting was shaken.[d] And they were all filled with the Holy Spirit and spoke the word of God boldly.[e]

The Believers Share Their Possessions

5 →PG. 1199
6 →PG. 1203

32All the believers were one in heart and mind. No one claimed that any of his possessions was his own, but they shared everything they had.[f] 33With great power the apostles continued to testify[g] to the resurrection[h] of the Lord Jesus, and much grace was upon them all. 34There were no needy persons among them. For from time to time those who owned lands or houses sold them,[i] brought the money from the sales 35and put it at the apostles' feet,[j] and it was distributed to anyone as he had need.[k]

36Joseph, a Levite from Cyprus, whom the apostles called Barnabas[l] (which means Son of Encouragement), 37sold a field he owned and brought the money and put it at the apostles' feet.[m]

Ananias and Sapphira

5 Now a man named Ananias, together with his wife Sapphira, also sold a piece of property. 2With his wife's full knowledge he kept back part of the money for himself, but brought the rest and put it at the apostles' feet.[n]

3Then Peter said, "Ananias, how is it that Satan[o] has so filled your heart[p] that you have lied to the Holy Spirit[q] and have kept for yourself some of the money you received for the land? 4Didn't it belong to you before it was sold? And after it was sold, wasn't the money at your disposal? What made you think of doing such a thing? You have not lied to men but to God."

5When Ananias heard this, he fell down and died.[r] And great fear[s] seized all who heard what had happened. 6Then the young men came forward, wrapped up his body,[t] and carried him out and buried him.

7About three hours later his wife came in, not knowing what had happened. 8Peter asked her, "Tell me, is this the price you and Ananias got for the land?"

"Yes," she said, "that is the price."[u]

9Peter said to her, "How could you agree to test the Spirit of the Lord?[v] Look! The feet of the men who buried your husband are at the door, and they will carry you out also."

10At that moment she fell down at his feet and died.[w] Then the young men came in and, finding her dead, carried her out and buried her beside her husband. 11Great fear[x] seized the whole church and all who heard about these events.

The Apostles Heal Many

12The apostles performed many miraculous signs and wonders[y] among the people. And all the believers used to meet together[z] in Solomon's Colonnade.[a] 13No one else dared join

5 →PG. 1200

4:18 [q]Ac 5:40
4:19 [r]Ac 5:29
4:21 [s]Ac 5:26 [t]Mt 9:8
4:25 [u]Ac 1:16
4:26 [v]Ps 2:1,2; Da 9:25; Lk 4:18; Ac 10:38; Heb 1:9
4:27 [w]Mt 14:1 [x]Mt 27:2; Lk 23:12 [y]ver 30
4:28 [z]Ac 2:23
4:29 [a]ver 13,31; Ac 9:27; 14:3; Php 1:14
4:30 [b]Jn 4:48 [c]ver 27
4:31 [d]Ac 2:2 [e]ver 29
4:32 [f]Ac 2:44
4:33 [g]Lk 24:48 [h]Ac 1:22
4:34 [i]Mt 19:21; Ac 2:45
4:35 [j]ver 37; Ac 5:2 [k]Ac 2:45; 6:1
4:36 [l]Ac 9:27; 1Co 9:6
4:37 [m]ver 35; Ac 5:2
5:2 [n]Ac 4:35,37
5:3 [o]Mt 4:10 [p]Jn 13:2,27 [q]ver 9
5:5 [r]ver 10 [s]ver 11
5:6 [t]Jn 19:40
5:8 [u]ver 2
5:9 [v]ver 3
5:10 [w]ver 5
5:11 [x]ver 5; Ac 19:17
5:12 [y]Ac 2:43 [z]Ac 4:32 [a]Ac 3:11

[a]26 That is, Christ or Messiah
[b]26 Psalm 2:1,2
[c]27 The Greek is plural.

them, even though they were highly regarded by the people.[b] **14**Nevertheless, more and more men and women believed in the Lord and were added to their number. **15**As a result, people brought the sick into the streets and laid them on beds and mats so that at least Peter's shadow might fall on some of them as he passed by.[c] **16**Crowds gathered also from the towns around Jerusalem, bringing their sick and those tormented by evil[a] spirits, and all of them were healed.[d]

The Apostles Persecuted

17Then the high priest and all his associates, who were members of the party[e] of the Sadducees,[f] were filled with jealousy. **18**They arrested the apostles and put them in the public jail.[g] **19**But during the night an angel[h] of the Lord opened the doors of the jail[i] and brought them out. **20**"Go, stand in the temple courts," he said, "and tell the people the full message of this new life."[j]

7 →PG. 1203

21At daybreak they entered the temple courts, as they had been told, and began to teach the people.

When the high priest and his associates[k] arrived, they called together the Sanhedrin[l]—the full assembly of the elders of Israel—and sent to the jail for the apostles. **22**But on arriving at the jail, the officers did not find them there. So they went back and reported, **23**"We found the jail securely locked, with the guards standing at the doors; but when we opened them, we found no one inside." **24**On hearing this report, the captain of the temple guard and the chief priests[m] were puzzled, wondering what would come of this.

25Then someone came and said, "Look! The men you put in jail are standing in the temple courts teaching the people." **26**At that, the captain went with his officers and brought the apostles. They did not use force, because they feared that the people[n] would stone them.

27Having brought the apostles, they made them appear before the Sanhedrin[o] to be questioned by the high priest. **28**"We gave you strict orders not to teach in this name,"[p] he said. "Yet you have filled Jerusalem with your teaching and are determined to make us guilty of this man's blood."[q]

29Peter and the other apostles replied: "We must obey God rather than men![r] **30**The God of our fathers[s] raised Jesus from the dead[t]—whom you had killed by hanging him on a tree.[u] **31**God exalted him to his own right hand[v] as Prince and Savior[w] that he might give repentance and forgiveness of sins to Israel.[x] **32**We are witnesses of these things,[y] and so is the Holy Spirit,[z] whom God has given to those who obey him."

33When they heard this, they were furious[a] and wanted to put them to death. **34**But a Pharisee named Gamaliel,[b] a teacher of the law,[c] who was honored by all the people, stood up in the Sanhedrin and ordered that the men be put outside for a little while. **35**Then he addressed them: "Men of Israel, consider carefully what you intend to do to these men. **36**Some time ago Theudas appeared, claiming to be somebody, and about four hundred men rallied to him. He was killed, all his followers were dispersed, and it all came to nothing. **37**After him, Judas the Galilean appeared in the days of the census[d] and led a band of people in revolt. He too was killed, and all his followers were scattered. **38**Therefore, in the present case I advise you: Leave these men alone! Let them go! For if their purpose or activity is of human origin, it will fail.[e] **39**But if it is from God, you will not be able to stop these men; you will only find yourselves fighting against God."[f]

40His speech persuaded them. They called the apostles in and had them flogged.[g] Then they ordered them not to speak in the name of Jesus, and let them go.

41The apostles left the Sanhedrin, rejoicing[h] because they had been counted worthy of suffering disgrace for the Name.[i] **42**Day after day, in the temple courts[j] and from house to house, they never stopped teaching and proclaiming the good news that Jesus is the Christ.[b]

The Choosing of the Seven

6 In those days when the number of disciples was increasing,[k] the Grecian Jews[l] among them complained against the Hebraic Jews because their widows[m] were being overlooked in the daily distribution of food.[n] **2**So the Twelve gathered all the disciples together and said, "It would not be right for us to neglect the ministry of the word of God in order to wait on tables. **3**Brothers,[o] choose seven men from among you who are known to be full of the Spirit and wisdom. We will turn this responsibility over to them **4**and will give our attention to prayer[p] and the ministry of the word."

5 →PG. 1209

5:13 [b]Ac 2:47; 4:21
5:15 [c]Ac 19:12
5:16 [d]Mk 16:17
5:17 [e]Ac 15:5 [f]Ac 4:1
5:18 [g]Ac 4:3
5:19 [h]Mt 1:20; Lk 1:11; Ac 8:26; 27:23 [i]Ac 16:26
5:20 [j]Jn 6:63,68
5:21 [k]Ac 4:5,6 [l]ver 27,34,41; Mt 5:22
5:24 [m]Ac 4:1
5:26 [n]Ac 4:21
5:27 [o]Mt 5:22
5:28 [p]Ac 4:18 [q]Mt 23:35; 27:25; Ac 2:23,36; 3:14,15; 7:52
5:29 [r]Ac 4:19
5:30 [s]Ac 3:13 [t]Ac 2:24 [u]Ac 10:39; 13:29; Gal 3:13; 1Pe 2:24
5:31 [v]Ac 2:33 [w]Lk 2:11 [x]Mt 1:21; Lk 24:47; Ac 2:38
5:32 [y]Lk 24:48 [z]Jn 15:26
5:33 [a]Ac 2:37; 7:54
5:34 [b]Ac 22:3 [c]Lk 2:46
5:37 [d]Lk 2:1,2
5:38 [e]Mt 15:13
5:39 [f]Pr 21:30; Ac 7:51; 11:17
5:40 [g]Mt 10:17
5:41 [h]Mt 5:12 [i]Jn 15:21
5:42 [j]Ac 2:46
6:1 [k]Ac 2:41 [l]Ac 9:29 [m]Ac 9:39,41 [n]Ac 4:35
6:3 [o]Ac 1:16
6:4 [p]Ac 1:14

[a] 16 Greek *unclean* [b] 42 Or *Messiah*

5This proposal pleased the whole
group. They chose Stephen,[q] a man
full of faith and of the Holy Spirit;[r]
also Philip,[s] Procorus, Nicanor, Ti-
mon, Parmenas, and Nicolas from
Antioch, a convert to Judaism. **6**They
presented these men to the apostles,
who prayed[t] and laid their hands on
them.[u]
7So the word of God spread.[v] The
number of disciples in Jerusalem increased rapidly, and a large number of
priests became obedient to the faith.

Stephen Seized

8Now Stephen, a man full of God's
grace and power, did great wonders
and miraculous signs[w] among the
people. **9**Opposition arose, however,
from members of the Synagogue of the
Freedmen (as it was called)—Jews
of Cyrene[x] and Alexandria as well as
the provinces of Cilicia[y] and Asia.[z]
These men began to argue with Stephen, **10**but they could not stand up
against his wisdom or the Spirit by
whom he spoke.[a]
11Then they secretly[b] persuaded
some men to say, "We have heard
Stephen speak words of blasphemy
against Moses and against God."[c]
12So they stirred up the people and
the elders and the teachers of the law.
They seized Stephen and brought him
before the Sanhedrin.[d] **13**They produced false witnesses, who testified,
"This fellow never stops speaking
against this holy place[e] and against

> **6:1–5**
>
> **PROMISE 5**
>
> ### SERVING MINISTRY
>
> This passage speaks to those of us who have not been called to pursue a seminary degree or engage in full-time ministry. The early church's leaders found themselves so caught up with the day-to-day demands of the new believers that they had little time to devote to prayer and teaching about God's Word. They chose men to help them with those tasks, which included distributing food to widows. These men were dedicated to serving God together with the apostles in a different, but no less important, ministry.
>
> Most of us should see a reflection of ourselves in these men. Today's churches and pastors have the same need for dedicated, Spirit-filled men to join them in ministry to their communities. How can you participate in the life of your church? One phone call to your pastor should provide you with a wealth of opportunities.
>
> *For the next Promise 5 reading go to page 1269.*

6:5 [q]ver 8; Ac 11:19 [r]Ac 11:24 [s]Ac 8:5-40; 21:8
6:6 [t]Ac 1:24; 8:17; 13:3; 2Ti 1:6 [u]Nu 8:10; Ac 9:17; 1Ti 4:14
6:7 [v]Ac 12:24; 19:20
6:8 [w]Jn 4:48
6:9 [x]Mt 27:32 [y]Ac 15:23,41; 22:3; 23:34 [z]Ac 2:9
6:10 [a]Lk 21:15
6:11 [b]1Ki 21:10 [c]Mt 26:59-61
6:12 [d]Mt 5:22
6:13 [e]Ac 21:28
6:14 [f]Ac 15:1; 21:21; 26:3; 28:17
6:15 [g]Mt 5:22
7:2 [h]Ac 22:1 [i]Ps 29:3 [j]Ge 11:31; 15:7
7:3 [k]Ge 12:1
7:4 [l]Ge 12:5
7:5 [m]Ge 12:7; 17:8; 26:3
7:6 [n]Ex 12:40
7:7 [o]Ex 3:12
7:8 [p]Ge 17:9-14 [q]Ge 21:2-4 [r]Ge 25:26 [s]Ge 29:31-35; 30:5-13,17-24; 35:16-18,22-26
7:9 [t]Ge 37:4,11 [u]Ge 37:28; Ps 105:17 [v]Ge 39:2,21,23
7:10 [w]Ge 41:37-43
7:11 [x]Ge 41:54
7:12 [y]Ge 42:1,2
7:13 [z]Ge 45:1-4
7:14 [a]Ge 45:9,10 [b]Ge 46:26,27; Ex 1:5; Dt 10:22

the law. **14**For we have heard him say
that this Jesus of Nazareth will destroy
this place and change the customs Moses handed down to us."[f]
15All who were sitting in the Sanhedrin[g] looked intently at Stephen, and
they saw that his face was like the face
of an angel.

Stephen's Speech to the Sanhedrin

7 Then the high priest asked him, "Are
these charges true?"
2To this he replied: "Brothers and fathers,[h] listen to me! The God of glory[i] appeared to our father Abraham
while he was still in Mesopotamia, before he lived in Haran.[j] **3**'Leave your
country and your people,' God said,
'and go to the land I will show you.'[a][k]
4"So he left the land of the Chaldeans and settled in Haran. After the
death of his father, God sent him to this
land where you are now living.[l] **5**He
gave him no inheritance here, not even
a foot of ground. But God promised
him that he and his descendants after
him would possess the land,[m] even
though at that time Abraham had no
child. **6**God spoke to him in this way:
'Your descendants will be strangers in
a country not their own, and they will
be enslaved and mistreated four hundred years.[n] **7**But I will punish the nation they serve as slaves,' God said,
'and afterward they will come out of
that country and worship me in this
place.'[b][o] **8**Then he gave Abraham the
covenant of circumcision.[p] And Abraham became the father of Isaac and
circumcised him eight days after his
birth.[q] Later Isaac became the father
of Jacob,[r] and Jacob became the father of the twelve patriarchs.[s]
9"Because the patriarchs were jealous of Joseph,[t] they sold him as a
slave into Egypt.[u] But God was with
him[v] **10**and rescued him from all his
troubles. He gave Joseph wisdom and
enabled him to gain the goodwill of
Pharaoh king of Egypt; so he made him
ruler over Egypt and all his palace.[w]
11"Then a famine struck all Egypt
and Canaan, bringing great suffering,
and our fathers could not find food.[x]
12When Jacob heard that there was
grain in Egypt, he sent our fathers on
their first visit.[y] **13**On their second visit, Joseph told his brothers who he
was,[z] and Pharaoh learned about Joseph's family. **14**After this, Joseph sent
for his father Jacob and his whole family,[a] seventy-five in all.[b] **15**Then Jacob
went down to Egypt, where he and

[a] 3 Gen. 12:1 [b] 7 Gen. 15:13,14

our fathers died.[c] **16**Their bodies were brought back to Shechem and placed in the tomb that Abraham had bought from the sons of Hamor at Shechem for a certain sum of money.[d]

17"As the time drew near for God to fulfill his promise to Abraham, the number of our people in Egypt greatly increased.[e] **18**Then another king, who knew nothing about Joseph, became ruler of Egypt.[f] **19**He dealt treacherously with our people and oppressed our forefathers by forcing them to throw out their newborn babies so that they would die.[g]

20"At that time Moses was born, and he was no ordinary child.[a] For three months he was cared for in his father's house.[h] **21**When he was placed outside, Pharaoh's daughter took him and brought him up as her own son.[i] **22**Moses was educated in all the wisdom of the Egyptians[j] and was powerful in speech and action.

23"When Moses was forty years old, he decided to visit his fellow Israelites. **24**He saw one of them being mistreated by an Egyptian, so he went to his defense and avenged him by killing the Egyptian. **25**Moses thought that his own people would realize that God was using him to rescue them, but they did not. **26**The next day Moses came upon two Israelites who were fighting. He tried to reconcile them by saying, 'Men, you are brothers; why do you want to hurt each other?'

27"But the man who was mistreating the other pushed Moses aside and said, 'Who made you ruler and judge over us? **28**Do you want to kill me as you killed the Egyptian yesterday?'[b] **29**When Moses heard this, he fled to Midian, where he settled as a foreigner and had two sons.[k]

30"After forty years had passed, an angel appeared to Moses in the flames of a burning bush in the desert near Mount Sinai. **31**When he saw this, he was amazed at the sight. As he went over to look more closely, he heard the Lord's voice:[l] **32**'I am the God of your fathers, the God of Abraham, Isaac and Jacob.'[c] Moses trembled with fear and did not dare to look.[m]

33"Then the Lord said to him, 'Take off your sandals; the place where you are standing is holy ground.[n] **34**I have indeed seen the oppression of my people in Egypt. I have heard their groaning and have come down to set them free. Now come, I will send you back to Egypt.'[d][o]

35"This is the same Moses whom they had rejected with the words, 'Who made you ruler and judge?'[p] He was sent to be their ruler and deliverer by God himself, through the angel who appeared to him in the bush. **36**He led them out of Egypt[q] and did wonders and miraculous signs in Egypt, at the Red Sea[e][r] and for forty years in the desert.

37"This is that Moses who told the Israelites, 'God will send you a prophet like me from your own people.'[f][s] **38**He was in the assembly in the desert, with the angel[t] who spoke to him on Mount Sinai, and with our fathers;[u] and he received living words[v] to pass on to us.[w]

39"But our fathers refused to obey him. Instead, they rejected him and in their hearts turned back to Egypt.[x] **40**They told Aaron, 'Make us gods who will go before us. As for this fellow Moses who led us out of Egypt—we don't know what has happened to him!'[g][y] **41**That was the time they made an idol in the form of a calf. They brought sacrifices to it and held a celebration in honor of what their hands had made.[z] **42**But God turned away[a] and gave them over to the worship of the heavenly bodies.[b] This agrees with what is written in the book of the prophets:

" 'Did you bring me sacrifices and
offerings
forty years in the desert, O house
of Israel?
43You have lifted up the shrine of
Molech
and the star of your god Rephan,
the idols you made to worship.
Therefore I will send you into
exile'[h][c] beyond Babylon.

44"Our forefathers had the tabernacle of the Testimony[d] with them in the desert. It had been made as God directed Moses, according to the pattern he had seen.[e] **45**Having received the tabernacle, our fathers under Joshua brought it with them when they took the land from the nations God drove out before them.[f] It remained in the land until the time of David, **46**who enjoyed God's favor and asked that he might provide a dwelling place for the God of Jacob.[i][g] **47**But it was Solomon who built the house for him.

48"However, the Most High does not live in houses made by men.[h] As the prophet says:

49" 'Heaven is my throne,

7:15 [c]Ge 46:5-7; 49:33; Ex 1:6
7:16 [d]Ge 23:16-20; 33:18,19; 50:13; Jos 24:32
7:17 [e]Ex 1:7; Ps 105:24
7:18 [f]Ex 1:8
7:19 [g]Ex 1:10-22
7:20 [h]Ex 2:2; Heb 11:23
7:21 [i]Ex 2:3-10
7:22 [j]1Ki 4:30; Isa 19:11
7:29 [k]Ex 2:11-15
7:31 [l]Ex 3:1-4
7:32 [m]Ex 3:6
7:33 [n]Ex 3:5; Jos 5:15
7:34 [o]Ex 3:7-10
7:35 [p]ver 27
7:36 [q]Ex 12:41; 33:1 [r]Ex 14:21
7:37 [s]Dt 18:15,18; Ac 3:22
7:38 [t]ver 53 [u]Ex 19:17 [v]Dt 32:45-47; Heb 4:12 [w]Ro 3:2
7:39 [x]Nu 14:3,4
7:40 [y]Ex 32:1,23
7:41 [z]Ex 32:4-6; Ps 106:19,20; Rev 9:20
7:42 [a]Jos 24:20; Isa 63:10 [b]Jer 19:13
7:43 [c]Am 5:25-27
7:44 [d]Ex 38:21 [e]Ex 25:8,9,40
7:45 [f]Jos 3:14-17; 18:1; 23:9; 24:18; Ps 44:2
7:46 [g]2Sa 7:8-16; Ps 132:1-5
7:48 [h]1Ki 8:27; 2Ch 2:6

a *20* Or *was fair in the sight of God*
b *28* Exodus 2:14 **c** *32* Exodus 3:6
d *34* Exodus 3:5,7,8,10 **e** *36* That is, Sea of Reeds **f** *37* Deut. 18:15 **g** *40* Exodus 32:1
h *43* Amos 5:25-27 **i** *46* Some early manuscripts *the house of Jacob*

and the earth is my footstool.[i]
What kind of house will you build
for me?
says the Lord.
Or where will my resting place
be?
50Has not my hand made all these
things?'[a][j]

51"You stiff-necked people,[k] with uncircumcised hearts[l] and ears! You are just like your fathers: You always resist the Holy Spirit! 52Was there ever a prophet your fathers did not persecute?[m] They even killed those who predicted the coming of the Righteous One. And now you have betrayed and murdered him[n]— 53you who have received the law that was put into effect through angels[o] but have not obeyed it."

The Stoning of Stephen

54When they heard this, they were furious[p] and gnashed their teeth at him. 55But Stephen, full of the Holy Spirit, looked up to heaven and saw the glory of God, and Jesus standing at the right hand of God.[q] 56"Look," he said, "I see heaven open[r] and the Son of Man[s] standing at the right hand of God."

57At this they covered their ears and, yelling at the top of their voices, they all rushed at him, 58dragged him out of the city[t] and began to stone him.[u] Meanwhile, the witnesses laid their clothes[v] at the feet of a young man named Saul.[w]

59While they were stoning him, Stephen prayed, "Lord Jesus, receive my spirit."[x] 60Then he fell on his knees[y] and cried out, "Lord, do not hold this sin against them."[z] When he had said this, he fell asleep.

8 And Saul[a] was there, giving approval to his death.

The Church Persecuted and Scattered

On that day a great persecution broke out against the church at Jerusalem, and all except the apostles were scattered[b] throughout Judea and Samaria.[c] 2Godly men buried Stephen and mourned deeply for him. 3But Saul[d] began to destroy the church.[e] Going from house to house, he dragged off men and women and put them in prison.

Philip in Samaria

7 →PG. 1223
4Those who had been scattered[f] preached the word wherever they went.[g] 5Philip[h] went down to a city in Samaria and proclaimed the Christ[b]

7:49 [i]Mt 5:34,35
7:50 [j]Isa 66:1,2
7:51 [k]Ex 32:9; 33:3,5 [l]Lev 26:41; Dt 10:16; Jer 4:4; 9:26
7:52 [m]2Ch 36:16; Mt 5:12 [n]Ac 3:14; 1Th 2:15
7:53 [o]ver 38; Gal 3:19; Heb 2:2
7:54 [p]Ac 5:33
7:55 [q]Mk 16:19
7:56 [r]Mt 3:16 [s]Mt 8:20
7:58 [t]Lk 4:29 [u]Lev 24:14,16; Dt 13:9 [v]Ac 22:20 [w]Ac 8:1
7:59 [x]Ps 31:5; Lk 23:46
7:60 [y]Ac 9:40 [z]Mt 5:44
8:1 [a]Ac 7:58 [b]Ac 11:19 [c]Ac 9:31
8:3 [d]Ac 7:58 [e]Ac 22:4,19; 26:10,11; 1Co 15:9; Gal 1:13,23; Php 3:6; 1Ti 1:13
8:4 [f]ver 1 [g]Ac 15:35
8:5 [h]Ac 6:5
8:7 [i]Mk 16:17 [j]Mt 4:24
8:9 [k]Ac 13:6 [l]Ac 5:36
8:10 [m]Ac 14:11; 28:6
8:12 [n]Ac 1:3 [o]Ac 2:38
8:13 [p]ver 6; Ac 19:11
8:14 [q]ver 1 [r]Lk 22:8
8:15 [s]Ac 2:38
8:16 [t]Ac 19:2 [u]Mt 28:19; Ac 2:38
8:17 [v]Ac 6:6
8:20 [w]2Ki 5:16; Da 5:17; Mt 10:8; Ac 2:38
8:21 [x]Ps 78:37
8:24 [y]Ex 8:8; Nu 21:7; 1Ki 13:6

there. 6When the crowds heard Philip and saw the miraculous signs he did, they all paid close attention to what he said. 7With shrieks, evil[c] spirits came out of many,[i] and many paralytics and cripples were healed.[j] 8So there was great joy in that city.

Simon the Sorcerer

9Now for some time a man named Simon had practiced sorcery[k] in the city and amazed all the people of Samaria. He boasted that he was someone great,[l] 10and all the people, both high and low, gave him their attention and exclaimed, "This man is the divine power known as the Great Power."[m] 11They followed him because he had amazed them for a long time with his magic. 12But when they believed Philip as he preached the good news of the kingdom of God[n] and the name of Jesus Christ, they were baptized,[o] both men and women. 13Simon himself believed and was baptized. And he followed Philip everywhere, astonished by the great signs and miracles[p] he saw.

14When the apostles in Jerusalem heard that Samaria[q] had accepted the word of God, they sent Peter and John[r] to them. 15When they arrived, they prayed for them that they might receive the Holy Spirit,[s] 16because the Holy Spirit had not yet come upon any of them;[t] they had simply been baptized into[d] the name of the Lord Jesus.[u] 17Then Peter and John placed their hands on them,[v] and they received the Holy Spirit.

18When Simon saw that the Spirit was given at the laying on of the apostles' hands, he offered them money 19and said, "Give me also this ability so that everyone on whom I lay my hands may receive the Holy Spirit."

20Peter answered: "May your money perish with you, because you thought you could buy the gift of God with money![w] 21You have no part or share in this ministry, because your heart is not right[x] before God. 22Repent of this wickedness and pray to the Lord. Perhaps he will forgive you for having such a thought in your heart. 23For I see that you are full of bitterness and captive to sin."

24Then Simon answered, "Pray to the Lord for me[y] so that nothing you have said may happen to me."

25When they had testified and proclaimed the word of the Lord, Peter and John returned to Jerusalem, 6 →PG. 1206

[a] *50* Isaiah 66:1,2 [b] *5* Or *Messiah* [c] *7* Greek *unclean* [d] *16* Or *in*

preaching the gospel in many Samaritan villages.[z]

Philip and the Ethiopian

26Now an angel[a] of the Lord said to Philip, "Go south to the road—the desert road—that goes down from Jerusalem to Gaza." **27**So he started out, and on his way he met an Ethiopian[a][b] eunuch,[c] an important official in charge of all the treasury of Candace, queen of the Ethiopians. This man had gone to Jerusalem to worship,[d] **28**and on his way home was sitting in his chariot reading the book of Isaiah the prophet. **29**The Spirit told[e] Philip, "Go to that chariot and stay near it."

30Then Philip ran up to the chariot and heard the man reading Isaiah the prophet. "Do you understand what you are reading?" Philip asked.

31"How can I," he said, "unless someone explains it to me?" So he invited Philip to come up and sit with him.

32The eunuch was reading this passage of Scripture:

"He was led like a sheep to the
 slaughter,
and as a lamb before the shearer
 is silent,
so he did not open his mouth.
33In his humiliation he was deprived
 of justice.
Who can speak of his
 descendants?
For his life was taken from the
 earth."[b][f]

34The eunuch asked Philip, "Tell me, please, who is the prophet talking about, himself or someone else?" **35**Then Philip began[g] with that very passage of Scripture[h] and told him the good news about Jesus.

36As they traveled along the road, they came to some water and the eunuch said, "Look, here is water. Why shouldn't I be baptized?"[c][i] **38**And he gave orders to stop the chariot. Then both Philip and the eunuch went down into the water and Philip baptized him. **39**When they came up out of the water, the Spirit of the Lord suddenly took Philip away,[j] and the eunuch did not see him again, but went on his way rejoicing. **40**Philip, however, appeared at Azotus and traveled about, preaching the gospel in all the towns[k] until he reached Caesarea.[l]

Saul's Conversion

9 Meanwhile, Saul was still breathing out murderous threats against the Lord's disciples.[m] He went to the high priest **2**and asked him for letters to the synagogues in Damascus, so that if he found any there who belonged to the Way,[n] whether men or women, he might take them as prisoners to Jerusalem. **3**As he neared Damascus on his journey, suddenly a light from heaven flashed around him.[o] **4**He fell to the ground and heard a voice say to him, "Saul, Saul, why do you persecute me?"

5"Who are you, Lord?" Saul asked.

"I am Jesus, whom you are persecuting," he replied. **6**"Now get up and go into the city, and you will be told what you must do."[p]

7The men traveling with Saul stood there speechless; they heard the sound[q] but did not see anyone.[r] **8**Saul got up from the ground, but when he opened his eyes he could see nothing. So they led him by the hand into Damascus. **9**For three days he was blind, and did not eat or drink anything.

10In Damascus there was a disciple named Ananias. The Lord called to him in a vision,[s] "Ananias!"

"Yes, Lord," he answered.

11The Lord told him, "Go to the house of Judas on Straight Street and ask for a man from Tarsus[t] named Saul, for he is praying. **12**In a vision he has seen a man named Ananias come and place his hands on[u] him to restore his sight."

13"Lord," Ananias answered, "I have heard many reports about this man and all the harm he has done to your saints[v] in Jerusalem.[w] **14**And he has come here with authority from the chief priests[x] to arrest all who call on your name."

15But the Lord said to Ananias, "Go! This man is my chosen instrument[y] to carry my name before the Gentiles[z] and their kings[a] and before the people of Israel. **16**I will show him how much he must suffer for my name."[b]

2 →PG. 1216

17Then Ananias went to the house and entered it. Placing his hands on[c] Saul, he said, "Brother Saul, the Lord—Jesus, who appeared to you on the road as you were coming here—has sent me so that you may see again and be filled with the Holy Spirit." **18**Immediately, something like scales fell from Saul's eyes, and he could see again. He got up and was baptized, **19**and after taking some food, he regained his strength.

8:25 [z]ver 40
8:26 [a]Ac 5:19
8:27 [b]Ps 68:31; 87:4; Zep 3:10 [c]Isa 56:3-5 [d]1Ki 8:41-43; Jn 12:20
8:29 [e]Ac 10:19; 11:12; 13:2; 20:23; 21:11
8:33 [f]Isa 53:7,8
8:35 [g]Mt 5:2 [h]Lk 24:27; Ac 17:2; 18:28; 28:23
8:36 [i]Ac 10:47
8:39 [j]1Ki 18:12; 2Ki 2:16; Eze 3:12,14; 8:3; 11:1,24; 43:5; 2Co 12:2
8:40 [k]ver 25 [l]Ac 10:1,24; 12:19; 21:8,16; 23:23,33; 25:1, 4,6,13
9:1 [m]Ac 8:3
9:2 [n]Ac 19:9,23; 22:4; 24:14,22
9:3 [o]1Co 15:8
9:6 [p]ver 16
9:7 [q]Jn 12:29 [r]Da 10:7; Ac 22:9
9:10 [s]Ac 10:3,17,19
9:11 [t]ver 30; Ac 21:39; 22:3
9:12 [u]Mk 5:23
9:13 [v]ver 32; Ro 1:7; 16:2,15 [w]Ac 8:3
9:14 [x]ver 2,21
9:15 [y]Ac 13:2; Ro 1:1; Gal 1:15 [z]Ro 11:13; 15:15,16; Gal 2:7,8; Eph 3:7,8 [a]Ac 25:22,23; 26:1
9:16 [b]Ac 20:23; 21:11; 2Co 11:23-27
9:17 [c]Ac 6:6

a *27* That is, from the upper Nile region
b *33* Isaiah 53:7,8 c *36* Some late manuscripts *baptized?" 37Philip said, "If you believe with all your heart, you may." The eunuch answered, "I believe that Jesus Christ is the Son of God."*

Saul in Damascus and Jerusalem

Saul spent several days with the disciples[d] in Damascus.[e] **20**At once he began to preach in the synagogues[f] that Jesus is the Son of God.[g] **21**All those who heard him were astonished and asked, "Isn't he the man who raised havoc in Jerusalem among those who call on this name?[h] And hasn't he come here to take them as prisoners to the chief priests?"[i] **22**Yet Saul grew more and more powerful and baffled the Jews living in Damascus by proving that Jesus is the Christ.[a][j]

23After many days had gone by, the Jews conspired to kill him, **24**but Saul learned of their plan.[k] Day and night they kept close watch on the city gates in order to kill him. **25**But his followers took him by night and lowered him in a basket through an opening in the wall.[l]

26When he came to Jerusalem,[m] he tried to join the disciples, but they were all afraid of him, not believing that he really was a disciple. **27**But Barnabas[n] took him and brought him to the apostles. He told them how Saul on his journey had seen the Lord and that the Lord had spoken to him,[o] and how in Damascus he had preached fearlessly in the name of Jesus.[p] **28**So Saul stayed with them and moved about freely in Jerusalem, speaking boldly in the name of the Lord. **29**He talked and debated with the Grecian Jews,[q] but they tried to kill him.[r] **30**When the brothers[s] learned of this, they took him down to Caesarea[t] and sent him off to Tarsus.[u]

31Then the church throughout Judea, Galilee and Samaria[v] enjoyed a time of peace. It was strengthened; and encouraged by the Holy Spirit, it grew

9:19 [d]Ac 11:26 [e]Ac 26:20
9:20 [f]Ac 13:5,14 [g]Mt 4:3
9:21 [h]Ac 8:3 [i]Gal 1:13,23
9:22 [j]Ac 18:5,28
9:24 [k]Ac 20:3,19
9:25 [l]1Sa 19:12; 2Co 11:32,33
9:26 [m]Ac 22:17; 26:20; Gal 1:17,18
9:27 [n]Ac 4:36 [o]ver 3-6 [p]ver 20,22
9:29 [q]Ac 6:1 [r]2Co 11:26
9:30 [s]Ac 1:16 [t]Ac 8:40 [u]ver 11
9:31 [v]Ac 8:1

[a]*22* Or *Messiah*

9:1–31

PROMISE 7

DIAMONDS AT YOUR FEET

Russell H. Conwell, in a speech entitled "Acres of Diamonds," told a story about a Persian farmer named Al Hafed whose ambition reached far beyond the plot of ground he tilled. Although this farmer possessed a productive plot of land and enjoyed great wealth, he dreamed of owning a diamond mine. So one day he sold his farm, gathered his belongings, and set off on a worldwide search for diamonds. But the drive and determination with which he began his quest faded over the months and years. Eventually Hafed died—dejected, alone and penniless—in a far-away land. This once-prosperous farmer had thrown away his life in search of an elusive dream.

As Hafed searched for diamonds in foreign countries, a man from Hafed's home territory watered a camel in one of the clear pools on his property. In the brightness of the midday sun, he noticed a shimmer in the white sand. What this fortunate man discovered that day turned out to be the backbone of the world's richest diamond mine, located in the Persian region of Golconda—on the back side of Hafed's old farm.

Like Al Hafed, it's easy for people to overlook the diamonds that are directly at their feet. And Saul of Tarsus was no exception. Convinced that Jesus was a false Messiah, he rejected the spiritual treasure that Jesus offered. Saul not only refused to consider Jesus' claims, but he also refused to allow others to look in the right place. He doggedly hunted down Christians and had them thrown in jail.

But God had a different plan for Saul. He forced this man to look at the truth. Several points about Saul's conversion are impressive.

First, after Saul met Jesus, his beliefs about him were radically transformed. He began to see Jesus as the true Messiah, the fulfillment of Jewish prophecy. Before his encounter with Jesus Christ, Saul was sincere and moral and deeply religious—and also deeply wrong. In the burst of light that surrounded him, Saul, the religious zealot, learned he was a sinner in need of a Savior.

Second, an obscure Jewish believer had the privilege of helping move Saul along the path to faith in Jesus. Ananias was understandably reluctant to meet with Saul. After all, he had heard about this Jewish zealot's treatment of Christians. But, in obedience to Jesus, Ananias spoke the words that Saul so desperately needed to hear. In a wonderfully symbolic moment, Saul's blindness was removed and he received the Holy Spirit.

Finally, Saul's confession of faith in Jesus was immediate and bold. He wasted no time in telling others that he had been looking for spiritual truth in the wrong places. And when he finally recognized the spiritual treasure that Jesus offered, he didn't horde what he had found. He shared it with others.

If you already know Jesus, contemplate the fact that you're surrounded by men who are looking for life in the wrong places. Also realize that you are the keeper of an immense spiritual treasure that grows when it's given away. Like Ananias, be available for God to use you to lead others to his Son. If that idea frightens you, that's okay. But don't let your fear control you. Go ahead and tell others what God has done for you. Show them the diamonds at their feet. And the same Lord who prepared the way for Ananias to serve him will prepare the way for you.

For the next Promise 7 reading go to page 1219.

in numbers, living in the fear of the Lord.

Aeneas and Dorcas

32 As Peter traveled about the country, he went to visit the saints[w] in Lydda. 33 There he found a man named Aeneas, a paralytic who had been bedridden for eight years. 34 "Aeneas," Peter said to him, "Jesus Christ heals you.[x] Get up and take care of your mat." Immediately Aeneas got up. 35 All those who lived in Lydda and Sharon[y] saw him and turned to the Lord.[z]

36 In Joppa[a] there was a disciple named Tabitha (which, when translated, is Dorcas[a]), who was always doing good[b] and helping the poor. 37 About that time she became sick and died, and her body was washed and placed in an upstairs room.[c] 38 Lydda was near Joppa; so when the disciples[d] heard that Peter was in Lydda, they sent two men to him and urged him, "Please come at once!"

39 Peter went with them, and when he arrived he was taken upstairs to the room. All the widows[e] stood around him, crying and showing him the robes and other clothing that Dorcas had made while she was still with them.

40 Peter sent them all out of the room;[f] then he got down on his knees[g] and prayed. Turning toward the dead woman, he said, "Tabitha, get up." She opened her eyes, and seeing Peter she sat up. 41 He took her by the hand and helped her to her feet. Then he called the believers and the widows and presented her to them alive. 42 This became known all over Joppa, and many people believed in the Lord. 43 Peter stayed in Joppa for some time with a tanner named Simon.[h]

Cornelius Calls for Peter

4 →PG. 1217

10 At Caesarea[i] there was a man named Cornelius, a centurion in what was known as the Italian Regiment. 2 He and all his family were devout and God-fearing;[j] he gave generously to those in need and prayed to God regularly. 3 One day at about three in the afternoon[k] he had a vision.[l] He distinctly saw an angel[m] of God, who came to him and said, "Cornelius!"

4 Cornelius stared at him in fear. "What is it, Lord?" he asked.

The angel answered, "Your prayers and gifts to the poor have come up as a memorial offering[n] before God.[o] 5 Now send men to Joppa[p] to bring back a man named Simon who is called Peter. 6 He is staying with Simon the tanner,[q] whose house is by the sea."

7 When the angel who spoke to him had gone, Cornelius called two of his servants and a devout soldier who was one of his attendants. 8 He told them everything that had happened and sent them to Joppa.[r]

Peter's Vision

6 →PG. 1208

9 About noon the following day as they were on their journey and approaching the city, Peter went up on the roof[s] to pray. 10 He became hungry and wanted something to eat, and while the meal was being prepared, he fell into a trance.[t] 11 He saw heaven opened and something like a large sheet being let down to earth by its four corners. 12 It contained all kinds of four-footed animals, as well as reptiles of the earth and birds of the air. 13 Then a voice told him, "Get up, Peter. Kill and eat."

14 "Surely not, Lord!"[u] Peter replied.

9:32 [w] ver 13
9:34 [x] Ac 3:6,16; 4:10
9:35 [y] 1Ch 5:16; 27:29; Isa 33:9; 35:2; 65:10 [z] Ac 11:21
9:36 [a] Jos 19:46; 2Ch 2:16; Ezr 3:7; Jnh 1:3; Ac 10:5 [b] 1Ti 2:10; Tit 3:8
9:37 [c] Ac 1:13
9:38 [d] Ac 11:26
9:39 [e] Ac 6:1
9:40 [f] Mt 9:25 [g] Lk 22:41; Ac 7:60
9:43 [h] Ac 10:6
10:1 [i] Ac 8:40
10:2 [j] ver 22,35; Ac 13:16,26
10:3 [k] Ac 3:1 [l] Ac 9:10 [m] Ac 5:19
10:4 [n] Mt 26:13 [o] Rev 8:4
10:5 [p] Ac 9:36
10:6 [q] Ac 9:43
10:8 [r] Ac 9:36
10:9 [s] Mt 24:17
10:10 [t] Ac 22:17
10:14 [u] Ac 9:5

[a] *36* Both *Tabitha* (Aramaic) and *Dorcas* (Greek) mean *gazelle.*

10:9–20

PROMISE 6

VISION OF UNITY

Prejudice is defined in *Webster's Ninth New Collegiate Dictionary* as "an irrational attitude of hostility directed against an individual, a group, a race, or their supposed characteristics." That definition describes an attitude from which we'd all like to be free. Tragically, we're not. Even the spiritually mature struggle with this malady, such as Peter did in this passage.

Peter had agreed to preach to Gentiles. But he wouldn't eat with them or accept them into the Christian family as brothers. As a Jew, Peter believed the touch of a Gentile could defile him. He found their culture and customs repulsive.

God saw Peter's prejudice and corrected it with this vision. Some of the animals Peter saw in the sheet let down from heaven were ceremonially clean and fit to eat, others were not. Yet three times a heavenly voice told Peter to eat. Why? Because God had cleansed what had been unclean.

The object lesson was clear: Peter was no longer to avoid contact with men of other races; he was not to consider unclean what God had made clean. As a member of God's worldwide family, he has called you to follow Peter's example and proactively seek fellowship with people from all other races and backgrounds.

For the next Promise 6 reading go to page 1209.

CORNELIUS

Tough Guys Can Be Nice Guys

Roman soldiers were tough guys. They survived by the sword, facing their enemies in hand-to-hand combat. They fought close enough to see their enemies' eyes and smell their breath. Only the tough survived, and those who commanded them were the toughest. Cornelius was a Roman centurion. At least 100 Roman soldiers looked to him as their commander. No doubt about it; Cornelius was one tough guy.

Luke gives us a wallet-sized snapshot of Cornelius, but even the small space given to this man is a "jaw-dropper." We read that he was a centurion in the Italian Regiment, a devout man with a God-fearing family, and that "he gave generously to those in need and prayed to God regularly" (Acts 10:1–2). Wait a minute! This tough guy has a family, loves God, drops money in the Salvation Army bucket of his day and prays to God? That can't be. The stereotypes clash. Can tough guys really be nice guys too?

Shattering Conventional Thinking

Conventional wisdom suggests that one has to compromise one's commitment to God in order to stay on the company promotion list. Not so! That myth takes a severe beating around Cornelius. Cornelius didn't sacrifice his soldiering to be godly. Soldiers who neglected the emperor's business weren't promoted to centurion. As a godly man, Cornelius built toughness and discipline in his troops without being harsh, crude and nasty. But his leadership style didn't overwhelm his love for God or godly matters.

Cornelius was a Gentile who lived a righteous life. His faith was so great that God entrusted him with an angelic visit (10:3). The angel told Cornelius to send messengers to fetch Peter. Can you picture the conversation afterwards between this Roman centurion and his servants? Do you think the servants had a problem with the centurion talking about angels? Probably not. God's presence in Cornelius's life allowed him to be both tough and tender.

Peter and Cornelius

The scene changes to Peter's residence. Peter had been struggling with his attitude toward "unclean" things—certain foods, people, places and activities that were forbidden by Jewish custom and law. Cornelius's servants showed up on his doorstep. Note their commentary about their boss: "He is a righteous and God-fearing man, who is respected by all the Jewish people" (10:22). What? Cornelius the Gentile, respected by the Jews? It was against their laws for "a Jew to associate with a Gentile or visit him" (10:28).

But God was doing something new. God was working on Peter's life-long prejudice toward "unclean" Gentiles because God wanted the church—which up until now had been filled with only Jewish converts—to receive Gentiles into their fellowship. Part of God's strategy to bring reconciliation in the church between Jew and Gentile was to prepare one man, Peter, to deal with one Gentile, Cornelius, a centurion in an army known for force, brutality and cruelty. Yet the servants' description of Cornelius kicked Peter's curiosity into overdrive. He set off with the servants for Cornelius's home.

When Peter arrived at Cornelius's house, a crowd was waiting. Cornelius "was expecting them and had called together his relatives and close friends" (10:24). As Peter entered the house, "Cornelius met him and fell at his feet in reverence" (10:25). The only thing Cornelius's guests knew about Peter was that he was Jewish. Period. They probably had their own ideas about Jews and religious fanatics. Prejudice, unfortunately, is a double-edged sword. But Cornelius put the social and professional pecking order aside and showed great honor and respect to this guest from God. God's presence in his life gave him a security that didn't need superiority.

That day, as Peter preached in Cornelius's Gentile house, the fledgling church leaped over an enormous racial and social barrier. God placed the right man in the right place at the right time. Cornelius represented what the Romans admired and respected. He was a tough guy. But he also represented what God produces in a man through the Holy Spirit—love, compassion, goodness and all the other fruit of God's Spirit (Galatians 5:22–23).

Tough Guys for God

Cornelius demonstrated that when God is at work in a man, the balance between tough and tender takes care of itself. We know from Cornelius that if God is allowed to shape a man, to make him a real man, a complete man, tough guys can be nice guys too.

—Dr. Sid Buzzell

"I have never eaten anything impure or unclean."[v]

15 The voice spoke to him a second time, "Do not call anything impure that God has made clean."[w]

16 This happened three times, and immediately the sheet was taken back to heaven.

17 While Peter was wondering about the meaning of the vision, the men sent by Cornelius[x] found out where Simon's house was and stopped at the gate. 18 They called out, asking if Simon who was known as Peter was staying there.

19 While Peter was still thinking about the vision, the Spirit said[y] to him, "Simon, three[a] men are looking for you. 20 So get up and go downstairs. Do not hesitate to go with them, for I have sent them."[z]

21 Peter went down and said to the men, "I'm the one you're looking for. Why have you come?"

22 The men replied, "We have come from Cornelius the centurion. He is a righteous and God-fearing man,[a] who is respected by all the Jewish people. A holy angel told him to have you come to his house so that he could hear what you have to say."[b] 23 Then Peter invited the men into the house to be his guests.

Peter at Cornelius' House

The next day Peter started out with them, and some of the brothers[c] from Joppa went along.[d] 24 The following day he arrived in Caesarea.[e] Cornelius was expecting them and had called together his relatives and close friends. 25 As Peter entered the house, Cornelius met him and fell at his feet in reverence. 26 But Peter made him get up. "Stand up," he said, "I am only a man myself."[f]

6 →PG. 1208

27 Talking with him, Peter went inside and found a large gathering of people. 28 He said to them: "You are well aware that it is against our law for a Jew to associate with a Gentile or visit him.[g] But God has shown me that I should not call any man impure or unclean.[h] 29 So when I was sent for, I came without raising any objection. May I ask why you sent for me?"

30 Cornelius answered: "Four days ago I was in my house praying at this hour, at three in the afternoon. Suddenly a man in shining clothes stood before me 31 and said, 'Cornelius, God has heard your prayer and remembered your gifts to the poor. 32 Send to Joppa for Simon who is called Peter. He is a guest in the home of Simon the tanner, who lives by the sea.' 33 So I sent for you immediately, and it was good of you to come. Now we are all here in the presence of God to listen to everything the Lord has commanded you to tell us."

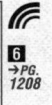

6 →PG. 1208

34 Then Peter began to speak: "I now realize how true it is that God does not show favoritism[i] 35 but accepts men from every nation who fear him and do what is right.[j] 36 You know the message God sent to the people of Israel, telling the good news[k] of peace[l] through Jesus Christ, who is Lord of all.[m] 37 You know what has happened throughout Judea, beginning in Galilee after the baptism that John preached— 38 how God anointed[n] Jesus of Nazareth with the Holy Spirit and power, and how he went around doing good and healing[o] all who were under the power of the devil, because God was with him.[p]

39 "We are witnesses[q] of everything he did in the country of the Jews and in Jerusalem. They killed him by hanging him on a tree,[r] 40 but God raised him from the dead[s] on the third day and caused him to be seen. 41 He was not seen by all the people,[t] but by witnesses whom God had already chosen—by us who ate[u] and drank with him after he rose from the dead. 42 He commanded us to preach to the people[v] and to testify that he is the one whom God appointed as judge of the living and the dead.[w] 43 All the prophets testify about him[x] that everyone[y] who believes in him receives forgiveness of sins through his name."

6 →PG. 1215

44 While Peter was still speaking these words, the Holy Spirit came on[z] all who heard the message. 45 The circumcised believers who had come with Peter[a] were astonished that the gift of the Holy Spirit had been poured out[b] even on the Gentiles.[c] 46 For they heard them speaking in tongues[b][d] and praising God.

Then Peter said, 47 "Can anyone keep these people from being baptized with water?[e] They have received the Holy Spirit just as we have."[f] 48 So he ordered that they be baptized in the name of Jesus Christ.[g] Then they asked Peter to stay with them for a few days.

Peter Explains His Actions

11 The apostles and the brothers[h] throughout Judea heard that the Gentiles also had received the word of

10:14 [v]Lev 11:4-8, 13-20; 20:25; Dt 14:3-20; Eze 4:14
10:15 [w]Mt 15:11; Ro 14:14,17, 20; 1Co 10:25; 1Ti 4:3,4; Tit 1:15
10:17 [x]ver 7,8
10:19 [y]Ac 8:29
10:20 [z]Ac 15:7-9
10:22 [a]ver 2 [b]Ac 11:14
10:23 [c]Ac 1:16 [d]ver 45; Ac 11:12
10:24 [e]Ac 8:40
10:26 [f]Ac 14:15; Rev 19:10
10:28 [g]Jn 4:9; 18:28; Ac 11:3 [h]Ac 15:8,9
10:34 [i]Dt 10:17; 2Ch 19:7; Job 34:19; Ro 2:11; Gal 2:6; Eph 6:9; Col 3:25; 1Pe 1:17
10:35 [j]Ac 15:9
10:36 [k]Ac 13:32 [l]Lk 2:14 [m]Mt 28:18; Ro 10:12
10:38 [n]Ac 4:26 [o]Mt 4:23 [p]Jn 3:2
10:39 [q]Lk 24:48 [r]Ac 5:30
10:40 [s]Ac 2:24
10:41 [t]Jn 14:17,22 [u]Lk 24:43; Jn 21:13
10:42 [v]Mt 28:19,20 [w]Jn 5:22; Ac 17:31; Ro 14:9; 2Co 5:10; 2Ti 4:1; 1Pe 4:5
10:43 [x]Isa 53:11 [y]Ac 15:9
10:44 [z]Ac 8:15,16; 11:15; 15:8
10:45 [a]ver 23 [b]Ac 2:33,38 [c]Ac 11:18
10:46 [d]Mk 16:17
10:47 [e]Ac 8:36 [f]Ac 11:17
10:48 [g]Ac 2:38; 8:16
11:1 [h]Ac 1:16

[a] *19* One early manuscript *two*; other manuscripts do not have the number.
[b] *46* Or *other languages*

God. **2**So when Peter went up to Jerusalem, the circumcised believers[i] criticized him **3**and said, "You went into the house of uncircumcised men and ate with them."[j]

4Peter began and explained everything to them precisely as it had happened: **5**"I was in the city of Joppa praying, and in a trance I saw a vision.[k] I saw something like a large sheet being let down from heaven by its four corners, and it came down to where I was. **6**I looked into it and saw four-footed animals of the earth, wild beasts, reptiles, and birds of the air. **7**Then I heard a voice telling me, 'Get up, Peter. Kill and eat.'

8"I replied, 'Surely not, Lord! Nothing impure or unclean has ever entered my mouth.'

9"The voice spoke from heaven a second time, 'Do not call anything impure that God has made clean.'[l] **10**This happened three times, and then it was all pulled up to heaven again.

11"Right then three men who had been sent to me from Caesarea stopped at the house where I was staying. **12**The Spirit told[m] me to have no hesitation about going with them.[n] These six brothers also went with me, and we entered the man's house. **13**He told us how he had seen an angel appear in his house and say, 'Send to Joppa for Simon who is called Peter. **14**He will bring you a message through which you and all your household[o] will be saved.'

15"As I began to speak, the Holy Spirit came on[p] them as he had come on us at the beginning.[q] **16**Then I remembered what the Lord had said: 'John baptized with[a] water, but you will be baptized with the Holy Spirit.'[r] **17**So if God gave them the same gift as he gave us,[s] who believed in the Lord Jesus Christ, who was I to think that I could oppose God?"

18When they heard this, they had no further objections and praised God, saying, "So then, God has granted even the Gentiles repentance unto life."[t]

The Church in Antioch

19Now those who had been scattered by the persecution in connection with Stephen[u] traveled as far as Phoenicia, Cyprus and Antioch,[v] telling the message only to Jews. **20**Some of them, however, men from Cyprus[w] and Cyrene,[x] went to Antioch and began to speak to Greeks also, telling them the good news about the Lord Jesus. **21**The Lord's hand was with them,[y] and a great number of people believed and turned to the Lord.[z]

22News of this reached the ears of the church at Jerusalem, and they sent Barnabas[a] to Antioch. **23**When he arrived and saw the evidence of the grace of God,[b] he was glad and encouraged them all to remain true to the Lord with all their hearts.[c] **24**He was a good man, full of the Holy Spirit and faith, and a great number of people were brought to the Lord.[d]

25Then Barnabas went to Tarsus[e] to look for Saul, **26**and when he found him, he brought him to Antioch. So for a whole year Barnabas and Saul met with the church and taught great numbers of people. The disciples[f] were called Christians first[g] at Antioch.

27During this time some prophets[h] came down from Jerusalem to Antioch. **28**One of them, named Agabus,[i] stood up and through the Spirit predicted that a severe famine would spread over the entire Roman world.[j] (This happened during the reign of Claudius.)[k] **29**The disciples,[l] each according to his ability, decided to provide help[m] for the brothers[n] living in Judea. **30**This they did, sending their gift to the elders[o] by Barnabas and Saul.[p]

5 →PG. 1214

Peter's Miraculous Escape From Prison

12 It was about this time that King Herod arrested some who belonged to the church, intending to persecute them. **2**He had James, the brother of John,[q] put to death with the sword. **3**When he saw that this pleased the Jews,[r] he proceeded to seize Peter also. This happened during the Feast of Unleavened Bread.[s] **4**After arresting him, he put him in prison, handing him over to be guarded by four squads of four soldiers each. Herod intended

11:2 [i]Ac 10:45 **11:3** [j]Ac 10:25,28; Gal 2:12 **11:5** [k]Ac 10:9-32; 9:10 **11:9** [l]Ac 10:15 **11:12** [m]Ac 8:29 [n]Ac 15:9; Ro 3:22 **11:14** [o]Jn 4:53; Ac 16:15, 31-34; 1Co 1:11,16 **11:15** [p]Ac 10:44 [q]Ac 2:4 **11:16** [r]Mk 1:8; Ac 1:5 **11:17** [s]Ac 10:45,47 **11:18** [t]Ro 10:12,13; 2Co 7:10 **11:19** [u]Ac 8:1,4 [v]ver 26,27; Ac 13:1; 18:22; Gal 2:11 **11:20** [w]Ac 4:36 [x]Mt 27:32 **11:21** [y]Lk 1:66 [z]Ac 2:47 **11:22** [a]Ac 4:36 **11:23** [b]Ac 13:43; 14:26; 20:24 [c]Ac 14:22 **11:24** [d]ver 21; Ac 5:14 **11:25** [e]Ac 9:11 **11:26** [f]Ac 6:1,2; 13:52 [g]Ac 26:28; 1Pe 4:16 **11:27** [h]Ac 13:1; 15:32; 1Co 12:28,29; Eph 4:11 **11:28** [i]Ac 21:10 [j]Mt 24:14 [k]Ac 18:2 **11:29** [l]ver 26 [m]Ro 15:26; 2Co 9:2 [n]Ac 1:16 **11:30** [o]Ac 14:23 [p]Ac 12:25 **12:2** [q]Mt 4:21 **12:3** [r]Ac 24:27 [s]Ex 12:15; 23:15

[a]*16* Or *in*

11:18 PROMISE 6

THE CHURCH EXPANDS

The first Christians were almost all Jews who had accepted Jesus as their Messiah. But God's desire was (and is) that all nations should hear about the salvation available through Jesus Christ. When the members of the early church discovered this wonderful truth, they celebrated. Take a moment right now and thank God that he is Lord of all men—regardless of their culture, race, religious tradition or economic background.

For the next Promise 6 reading go to page 1250.

BARNABAS

Son of Encouragement

In one episode of "Peanuts," the comic strip by Charles Schultz, Linus has just written a comic strip of his own and wants his sister Lucy's opinion. He tentatively hands it to Lucy and says, "Lucy, would you read this and tell me if you think it's funny?"

Lucy taps her foot, and a bit of a grin comes across her face. "Well, Linus, who wrote this?"

Linus, with his chest heaved out and a great big grin says, "Lucy, I wrote that."

Lucy wads it up, throws it aside, and says, "Well, then, I don't think it's very funny."

In the final frame, Linus picks up his comic strip, throws his blanket over his shoulder and says to Lucy, "Big sisters are the crab grass in the lawn of life."

It's very likely if we thought hard enough, we'd probably remember occasions when we acted like the crab grass on somebody else's lawn of life. None of us wants to be like that. Yet, if we're not careful, we find ourselves being more pessimistic than optimistic, more discouraging than encouraging.

God has given us a Biblical role model for encouragement in the life of a New Testament believer. He was a Levite from Cyprus, and his real name was Joseph. But his friends called him Barnabas, "which means Son of Encouragement" (Acts 4:36). Whenever the apostles saw Joe coming, they would say, "Here comes Barnabas, that old Son of Encouragement." What was it about this man that earned him that nickname?

Encouragers Grant Acceptance

Acts 9 details Paul's conversion—Paul's change from being a persecutor of the faith to a promoter of the gospel. When Paul went to Jerusalem to join the disciples, they were afraid of him. They thought he was pretending to be a believer so that he could continue his persecution of the Christians. Who came to his rescue? None other than our friend, Barnabas. Barnabas stood up for Paul and told the disciples "how in Damascus he had preached fearlessly in the name of Jesus" (9:27).

Encouragers like Barnabas realize that none of us comes to Christ with an advantage. All are sinners. Yet all who accept Christ are new creations. Having repented, there is no blame, no shame; only the possibility of a fresh start. Encouragers recognize that and foster acceptance of all who claim this new life.

Encouragers Rejoice in Progress

Because of God's Spirit at work, the message of the gospel was spreading. Groups of believers were springing up "as far as Phoenecia, Cyprus and Antioch" (11:19). The church in Jerusalem, seeing the need to strengthen these new Gentile believers, decided to send Barnabas to Antioch.

Good choice! What does a new believer need more than anything when he or she first starts to walk with God? Encouragement! When he got to Antioch, Barnabas "saw the evidence of the grace of God" in their lives, and he "encouraged them all to remain true to the Lord with all their hearts" (11:23). Barnabas rejoiced with them. He got excited about their progress. And he urged them to keep on going.

That's what encouragers do. When they see someone growing in the Lord, they rejoice. Encouragers don't envy such people; they don't get jealous, they get excited!

Encouragers Meet Current Needs

Encouragers also recognize that their possessions belong to God and should be used to meet the needs of others. After Barnabas came to Christ, he "sold a field he owned and brought the money and put it at the apostles' feet" (4:37). He saw a financial need and freely gave every last penny.

But many needs that encouragers meet are not monetary. As Barnabas ministered in Antioch, he perceived a spiritual need that he could not fill. So "Barnabas went to Tarsus to look for [Paul], and when he found him, he brought him to Antioch" (11:25–26). Though Barnabas was in charge of the ministry at Antioch, he knew that Paul had gifts that this growing church could use, so he put the two together. Sometimes a true encourager must look for another person who will best fit the needs of a particular situation. It may mean that the encourager himself will sit in the back seat and let somebody else drive, if that's what will bring God glory.

Encouragers also meet the needs of those who have failed. Paul and Barnabas wanted to go back and visit the young churches they had helped to establish, but there was a problem: John Mark. "Barnabas wanted to take John, also called Mark, with them, but Paul did not think it wise to take him, because he had deserted them in Pamphylia" (15:37–38). Eventually Paul chose Silas to go with him, and Barnabas took John Mark and sailed for Cyprus. Barnabas was willing to give John Mark a second chance. As an encourager, he realized that one failure in life doesn't mean a life of total failure.

Encouragers for Today

Encouragement is vital for all of life's relationships. Like a cool breeze on a hot summer day, encouragement revives and refreshes. It renews and gives strength. Encouragement helps us overcome when we feel overwhelmed. It helps us soar rather than sink. Encouragement makes us victors rather than victims.

How can you become a Barnabas, an encourager, in the life of another person today?

—Dr. Rod Cooper

to bring him out for public trial after
the Passover.
5So Peter was kept in prison, but the
church was earnestly praying to God
for him.[t]
6The night before Herod was to
bring him to trial, Peter was sleeping
between two soldiers, bound with two
chains,[u] and sentries stood guard at
the entrance. 7Suddenly an angel[v] of
the Lord appeared and a light shone in
the cell. He struck Peter on the side and
woke him up. "Quick, get up!" he said,
and the chains fell off Peter's wrists.[w]
8Then the angel said to him, "Put on
your clothes and sandals." And Peter
did so. "Wrap your cloak around you
and follow me," the angel told him.
9Peter followed him out of the prison,
but he had no idea that what the angel
was doing was really happening; he
thought he was seeing a vision.[x]
10They passed the first and second
guards and came to the iron gate leading to the city. It opened for them by
itself,[y] and they went through it.
When they had walked the length of
one street, suddenly the angel left him.
11Then Peter came to himself[z] and
said, "Now I know without a doubt that
the Lord sent his angel and rescued
me[a] from Herod's clutches and from
everything the Jewish people were anticipating."
12When this had dawned on him, he
went to the house of Mary the mother
of John, also called Mark,[b] where
many people had gathered and were
praying.[c] 13Peter knocked at the outer
entrance, and a servant girl named
Rhoda came to answer the door.[d]
14When she recognized Peter's voice,
she was so overjoyed[e] she ran back
without opening it and exclaimed, "Peter is at the door!"
15"You're out of your mind," they
told her. When she kept insisting that it
was so, they said, "It must be his angel."[f]
16But Peter kept on knocking, and
when they opened the door and
saw him, they were astonished. 17Peter
motioned with his hand[g] for them
to be quiet and described how the
Lord had brought him out of prison.
"Tell James[h] and the brothers[i] about
this," he said, and then he left for another place.
18In the morning, there was no small
commotion among the soldiers as to
what had become of Peter. 19After Herod had a thorough search made for
him and did not find him, he cross-
examined the guards and ordered that
they be executed.[j]

12:5 [t]Eph 6:18
12:6 [u]Ac 21:33
12:7 [v]Ac 5:19 [w]Ac 16:26
12:9 [x]Ac 9:10
12:10 [y]Ac 5:19; 16:26
12:11 [z]Lk 15:17 [a]Ps 34:7; Da 3:28; 6:22; 2Co 1:10; 2Pe 2:9
12:12 [b]ver 25; Ac 15:37,39; Col 4:10; Phm 24; 1Pe 5:13 [c]ver 5
12:13 [d]Jn 18:16,17
12:14 [e]Lk 24:41
12:15 [f]Mt 18:10
12:17 [g]Ac 13:16; 19:33; 21:40 [h]Ac 15:13 [i]Ac 1:16
12:19 [j]Ac 16:27

Herod's Death

Then Herod went from Judea to
Caesarea[k] and stayed there a while.
20He had been quarreling with the people of Tyre and Sidon;[l] they now
joined together and sought an audience with him. Having secured the
support of Blastus, a trusted personal
servant of the king, they asked for
peace, because they depended on the
king's country for their food supply.[m]
21On the appointed day Herod,
wearing his royal robes, sat on his
throne and delivered a public address
to the people. 22They shouted, "This is
the voice of a god, not of a man." 23Im-
mediately, because Herod did not give
praise to God, an angel of the Lord
struck him down,[n] and he was eaten
by worms and died.
24But the word of God continued to
increase and spread.[o]
25When Barnabas[p] and Saul had
finished their mission,[q] they returned
from[a] Jerusalem, taking with them
John, also called Mark.[r]

Barnabas and Saul Sent Off

13 In the church at Antioch[s] there
were prophets[t] and teachers: Barnabas,[u] Simeon called Niger, Lucius
of Cyrene, Manaen (who had been
brought up with Herod[v] the tetrarch)
and Saul. 2While they were worshiping
the Lord and fasting, the Holy Spirit
said,[w] "Set apart for me Barnabas and
Saul for the work[x] to which I have
called them."[y] 3So after they had fasted and prayed, they placed their hands
on them[z] and sent them off.[a]

On Cyprus

4The two of them, sent on their way
by the Holy Spirit,[b] went down to Se-
leucia and sailed from there to Cyprus.[c] 5When they arrived at Salamis,
they proclaimed the word of God in the
Jewish synagogues.[d] John[e] was with
them as their helper.
6They traveled through the whole island until they came to Paphos. There
they met a Jewish sorcerer[f] and false
prophet[g] named Bar-Jesus, 7who was
an attendant of the proconsul,[h] Sergi-
us Paulus. The proconsul, an intelligent man, sent for Barnabas and Saul
because he wanted to hear the word of
God. 8But Elymas the sorcerer[i] (for
that is what his name means) opposed
them and tried to turn the proconsul[j]
from the faith.[k] 9Then Saul, who was
also called Paul, filled with the Holy
Spirit,[l] looked straight at Elymas and

[k]Ac 8:40
12:20 [l]Mt 11:21 [m]1Ki 5:9,11; Eze 27:17
12:23 [n]1Sa 25:38; 2Sa 24:16,17
12:24 [o]Ac 6:7; 19:20
12:25 [p]Ac 4:36 [q]Ac 11:30 [r]ver 12
13:1 [s]Ac 11:19 [t]Ac 11:27 [u]Ac 4:36; 11:22-26 [v]Mt 14:1
13:2 [w]Ac 8:29 [x]Ac 14:26 [y]Ac 22:21
13:3 [z]Ac 6:6 [a]Ac 14:26
13:4 [b]ver 2,3 [c]Ac 4:36
13:5 [d]Ac 9:20 [e]Ac 12:12
13:6 [f]Ac 8:9 [g]Mt 7:15
13:7 [h]ver 8,12; Ac 19:38
13:8 [i]Ac 8:9 [j]ver 7 [k]Ac 6:7
13:9 [l]Ac 4:8

[a]25 Some manuscripts *to*

said, 10“You are a child of the devil[m] and an enemy of everything that is right! You are full of all kinds of deceit and trickery. Will you never stop perverting the right ways of the Lord?[n] 11Now the hand of the Lord is against you.[o] You are going to be blind, and for a time you will be unable to see the light of the sun.”

Immediately mist and darkness came over him, and he groped about, seeking someone to lead him by the hand. 12When the proconsul[p] saw what had happened, he believed, for he was amazed at the teaching about the Lord.

In Pisidian Antioch

13From Paphos,[q] Paul and his companions sailed to Perga in Pamphylia, where John[r] left them to return to Jerusalem. 14From Perga they went on to Pisidian Antioch.[s] On the Sabbath[t] they entered the synagogue[u] and sat down. 15After the reading from the Law[v] and the Prophets, the synagogue rulers sent word to them, saying, “Brothers, if you have a message of encouragement for the people, please speak.”

16Standing up, Paul motioned with his hand[w] and said: “Men of Israel and you Gentiles who worship God, listen to me! 17The God of the people of Israel chose our fathers; he made the people prosper during their stay in Egypt, with mighty power he led them out of that country,[x] 18he endured their conduct[a][y] for about forty years in the desert,[z] 19he overthrew seven nations in Canaan[a] and gave their land to his people[b] as their inheritance. 20All this took about 450 years.

“After this, God gave them judges[c] until the time of Samuel the prophet.[d] 21Then the people asked for a king,[e] and he gave them Saul[f] son of Kish, of the tribe of Benjamin,[g] who ruled forty years. 22After removing Saul,[h] he made David their king.[i] He testified concerning him: ‘I have found David son of Jesse a man after my own heart;[j] he will do everything I want him to do.’

23“From this man’s descendants[k] God has brought to Israel the Savior[l] Jesus,[m] as he promised.[n] 24Before the coming of Jesus, John preached repentance and baptism to all the people of Israel.[o] 25As John was completing his work,[p] he said: ‘Who do you think I am? I am not that one.[q] No, but he is coming after me, whose sandals I am not worthy to untie.’[r]

26“Brothers, children of Abraham, and you God-fearing Gentiles, it is to us that this message of salvation[s] has been sent. 27The people of Jerusalem and their rulers did not recognize Jesus,[t] yet in condemning him they fulfilled the words of the prophets[u] that are read every Sabbath. 28Though they found no proper ground for a death sentence, they asked Pilate to have him executed.[v] 29When they had carried out all that was written about him,[w] they took him down from the tree[x] and laid him in a tomb.[y] 30But God raised him from the dead,[z] 31and for many days he was seen by those who had traveled with him from Galilee to Jerusalem.[a] They are now his witnesses[b] to our people.

32“We tell you the good news:[c] What God promised our fathers[d] 33he has fulfilled for us, their children, by raising up Jesus. As it is written in the second Psalm:

> “ ‘You are my Son;
> today I have become your
> Father.[b]’[c][e]

1 →PG. 1218

34The fact that God raised him from the dead, never to decay, is stated in these words:

> “ ‘I will give you the holy and sure
> blessings promised to
> David.’[d][f]

35So it is stated elsewhere:

> “ ‘You will not let your Holy One
> see decay.’[e][g]

36“For when David had served God’s purpose in his own generation, he fell asleep; he was buried with his fathers[h] and his body decayed. 37But the one whom God raised from the dead did not see decay.

38“Therefore, my brothers, I want you to know that through Jesus the forgiveness of sins is proclaimed to you.[i] 39Through him everyone who believes is justified from everything you could not be justified from by the law of Moses.[j] 40Take care that what the prophets have said does not happen to you:

> 41“ ‘Look, you scoffers,
> wonder and perish,
> for I am going to do something in
> your days
> that you would never believe,
> even if someone told you.’[f]”[k]

42As Paul and Barnabas were leaving

13:10 [m]Mt 13:38; Jn 8:44 [n]Hos 14:9
13:11 [o]Ex 9:3; 1Sa 5:6,7; Ps 32:4
13:12 [p]ver 7
13:13 [q]ver 6 [r]Ac 12:12
13:14 [s]Ac 14:19,21 [t]Ac 16:13 [u]Ac 9:20
13:15 [v]Ac 15:21
13:16 [w]Ac 12:17
13:17 [x]Ex 6:6,7; Dt 7:6-8
13:18 [y]Dt 1:31 [z]Ac 7:36
13:19 [a]Dt 7:1 [b]Jos 19:51
13:20 [c]Jdg 2:16 [d]1Sa 3:19,20
13:21 [e]1Sa 8:5,19 [f]1Sa 10:1 [g]1Sa 9:1,2
13:22 [h]1Sa 15:23,26 [i]1Sa 16:13; Ps 89:20 [j]1Sa 13:14
13:23 [k]Mt 1:1 [l]Lk 2:11 [m]Mt 1:21 [n]ver 32
13:24 [o]Mk 1:4
13:25 [p]Ac 20:24 [q]Jn 1:20 [r]Mt 3:11; Jn 1:27
13:26 [s]Ac 4:12
13:27 [t]Ac 3:17 [u]Lk 24:27
13:28 [v]Mt 27:20-25; Ac 3:14
13:29 [w]Lk 18:31 [x]Ac 5:30 [y]Lk 23:53
13:30 [z]Mt 28:6; Ac 2:24
13:31 [a]Mt 28:16 [b]Lk 24:48
13:32 [c]Ac 5:42 [d]Ac 26:6; Ro 4:13
13:33 [e]Ps 2:7
13:34 [f]Isa 55:3
13:35 [g]Ps 16:10; Ac 2:27
13:36 [h]1Ki 2:10; Ac 2:29
13:38 [i]Lk 24:47; Ac 2:38
13:39 [j]Ro 3:28
13:41 [k]Hab 1:5

a 18 Some manuscripts *and cared for them*
b 33 Or *have begotten you* c 33 Psalm 2:7
d 34 Isaiah 55:3 e 35 Psalm 16:10
f 41 Hab. 1:5

the synagogue,[l] the people invited them to speak further about these things on the next Sabbath. 43When the congregation was dismissed, many of the Jews and devout converts to Judaism followed Paul and Barnabas, who talked with them and urged them to continue in the grace of God.[m]

44On the next Sabbath almost the whole city gathered to hear the word of the Lord. 45When the Jews saw the crowds, they were filled with jealousy and talked abusively[n] against what Paul was saying.[o]

46Then Paul and Barnabas answered them boldly: "We had to speak the word of God to you first.[p] Since you reject it and do not consider yourselves worthy of eternal life, we now turn to the Gentiles.[q] 47For this is what the Lord has commanded us:

" 'I have made you[a] a light for the
Gentiles,[r]
that you[a] may bring salvation to
the ends of the earth.'[b] "[s]

48When the Gentiles heard this, they were glad and honored the word of the Lord; and all who were appointed for eternal life believed.

49The word of the Lord spread through the whole region. 50But the Jews incited the God-fearing women of high standing and the leading men of the city. They stirred up persecution against Paul and Barnabas, and expelled them from their region.[t] 51So they shook the dust from their feet[u] in protest against them and went to Iconium.[v] 52And the disciples were filled with joy and with the Holy Spirit.

In Iconium

14 At Iconium[w] Paul and Barnabas went as usual into the Jewish synagogue. There they spoke so effectively that a great number of Jews and Gentiles believed. 2But the Jews who refused to believe stirred up the Gentiles and poisoned their minds against the brothers. 3So Paul and Barnabas spent considerable time there, speaking boldly[x] for the Lord, who confirmed the message of his grace by enabling them to do miraculous signs and wonders.[y] 4The people of the city were divided; some sided with the Jews, others with the apostles.[z] 5There was a plot afoot among the Gentiles and Jews, together with their leaders, to mistreat them and stone them.[a] 6But they found out about it and fled[b] to the Lycaonian cities of Lystra and Derbe and to the surrounding country, 7where they continued to preach[c] the good news.[d]

In Lystra and Derbe

8In Lystra there sat a man crippled in his feet, who was lame from birth[e] and had never walked. 9He listened to Paul as he was speaking. Paul looked directly at him, saw that he had faith to be healed[f] 10and called out, "Stand up on your feet!" At that, the man jumped up and began to walk.[g]

11When the crowd saw what Paul had done, they shouted in the Lycaonian language, "The gods have come down to us in human form!"[h] 12Barnabas they called Zeus, and Paul they called Hermes because he was the chief speaker. 13The priest of Zeus, whose temple was just outside the city, brought bulls and wreaths to the city gates because he and the crowd wanted to offer sacrifices to them.

14But when the apostles Barnabas and Paul heard of this, they tore their clothes[i] and rushed out into the crowd, shouting: 15"Men, why are you doing this? We too are only men,[j] human like you. We are bringing you good news,[k] telling you to turn from these worthless things[l] to the living God,[m] who made heaven and earth[n] and sea and everything in them.[o] 16In the past, he let[p] all nations go their own way.[q] 17Yet he has not left himself without testimony:[r] He has shown kindness by giving you rain from heaven and crops in their seasons;[s] he provides you with plenty of food and fills your hearts with joy." 18Even with these words, they had difficulty keeping the crowd from sacrificing to them.

19Then some Jews[t] came from Antioch and Iconium[u] and won the crowd over. They stoned Paul[v] and dragged him outside the city, thinking he was dead. 20But after the disciples[w] had gathered around him, he got up and went back into the city. The next day he and Barnabas left for Derbe.

The Return to Antioch in Syria

21They preached the good news in that city and won a large number of disciples. Then they returned to Lystra, Iconium[x] and Antioch, 22strengthening the disciples and encouraging them to remain true to the faith.[y] "We must go through many hardships[z] to enter the kingdom of God," they said. 23Paul and Barnabas appointed el-

5 →PG. 1216

13:42 [l] ver 14
13:43 [m] Ac 11:23; 14:22
13:45 [n] Ac 18:6; 1Pe 4:4; Jude 10 [o] 1Th 2:16
13:46 [p] ver 26; Ac 3:26 [q] Ac 18:6; 22:21; 28:28
13:47 [r] Lk 2:32 [s] Isa 49:6
13:50 [t] 1Th 2:16
13:51 [u] Mt 10:14; Ac 18:6 [v] Ac 14:1,19,21; 2Ti 3:11
14:1 [w] Ac 13:51
14:3 [x] Ac 4:29 [y] Jn 4:48; Heb 2:4
14:4 [z] Ac 17:4,5
14:5 [a] ver 19
14:6 [b] Mt 10:23
14:7 [c] Ac 16:10 [d] ver 15,21
14:8 [e] Ac 3:2
14:9 [f] Mt 9:28,29
14:10 [g] Ac 3:8
14:11 [h] Ac 8:10; 28:6
14:14 [i] Mk 14:63
14:15 [j] Ac 10:26; Jas 5:17 [k] ver 7,21; Ac 13:32 [l] 1Sa 12:21; 1Co 8:4; 1Th 1:9 [m] Mt 16:16 [n] Ge 1:1; Jer 14:22 [o] Ps 146:6; Rev 14:7
14:16 [p] Ac 17:30 [q] Ps 81:12; Mic 4:5
14:17 [r] Ac 17:27; Ro 1:20 [s] Dt 11:14; Job 5:10; Ps 65:10
14:19 [t] Ac 13:45 [u] Ac 13:51 [v] 2Co 11:25; 2Ti 3:11
14:20 [w] ver 22,28; Ac 11:26
14:21 [x] Ac 13:51
14:22 [y] Ac 11:23; 13:43 [z] Jn 16:33; 1Th 3:3; 2Ti 3:12

[a] *47* The Greek is singular. [b] *47* Isaiah 49:6

ders[a][a] for them in each church and, with prayer and fasting,[b] committed them to the Lord,[c] in whom they had put their trust. **24**After going through Pisidia, they came into Pamphylia, **25**and when they had preached the word in Perga, they went down to Attalia.

26From Attalia they sailed back to Antioch,[d] where they had been committed to the grace of God[e] for the work they had now completed.[f] **27**On arriving there, they gathered the church together and reported all that God had done through them[g] and how he had opened the door[h] of faith to the Gentiles. **28**And they stayed there a long time with the disciples.

The Council at Jerusalem

15 Some men[i] came down from Judea to Antioch and were teaching the brothers: "Unless you are circumcised,[j] according to the custom taught by Moses,[k] you cannot be saved." **2**This brought Paul and Barnabas into sharp dispute and debate with them. So Paul and Barnabas were appointed, along with some other believers, to go up to Jerusalem[l] to see the apostles and elders[m] about this question. **3**The church sent them on their way, and as they traveled through Phoenicia and Samaria, they told how the Gentiles had been converted.[n] This news made all the brothers very glad. **4**When they came to Jerusalem, they were welcomed by the church and the apostles and elders, to whom they reported everything God had done through them.[o]

6 →PG. 1240

5Then some of the believers who belonged to the party of the Pharisees stood up and said, "The Gentiles must be circumcised and required to obey the law of Moses."

6The apostles and elders met to consider this question. **7**After much discussion, Peter got up and addressed them: "Brothers, you know that some time ago God made a choice among you that the Gentiles might hear from my lips the message of the gospel and believe. **8**God, who knows the heart,[p] showed that he accepted them by giving the Holy Spirit to them,[q] just as he did to us. **9**He made no distinction between us and them,[r] for he purified their hearts by faith.[s] **10**Now then, why do you try to test God by putting on the necks of the disciples a yoke[t] that neither we nor our fathers have been able to bear? **11**No! We believe it is through the grace[u] of our Lord Jesus that we are saved, just as they are."

12The whole assembly became silent as they listened to Barnabas and Paul telling about the miraculous signs and wonders[v] God had done among the Gentiles through them.[w] **13**When they finished, James[x] spoke up: "Brothers, listen to me. **14**Simon[b] has described to us how God at first showed his concern by taking from the Gentiles a people for himself. **15**The words of the prophets are in agreement with this, as it is written:

16" 'After this I will return
and rebuild David's fallen tent.
Its ruins I will rebuild,
and I will restore it,
17that the remnant of men may seek the Lord,
and all the Gentiles who bear my name,
says the Lord, who does these things'[c][y]
18 that have been known for ages.[d]

19"It is my judgment, therefore, that we should not make it difficult for the Gentiles who are turning to God. **20**Instead we should write to them, telling them to abstain from food polluted

14:23 [a]Ac 11:30; Tit 1:5 [b]Ac 13:3 [c]Ac 20:32
14:26 [d]Ac 11:19 [e]Ac 15:40 [f]Ac 13:1,3
14:27 [g]Ac 15:4,12; 21:19 [h]1Co 16:9; 2Co 2:12; Col 4:3; Rev 3:8
15:1 [i]ver 24; Gal 2:12 [j]ver 5; Gal 5:2,3 [k]Ac 6:14
15:2 [l]Gal 2:2 [m]Ac 11:30
15:3 [n]Ac 14:27
15:4 [o]ver 12; Ac 14:27
15:8 [p]Ac 1:24 [q]Ac 10:44,47
15:9 [r]Ac 10:28,34; 11:12 [s]Ac 10:43
15:10 [t]Mt 23:4; Gal 5:1
15:11 [u]Ro 3:24; Eph 2:5-8
15:12 [v]Jn 4:48 [w]Ac 14:27
15:13 [x]Ac 12:17
15:17 [y]Am 9:11,12

[a] *23* Or *Barnabas ordained elders*; or *Barnabas had elders elected* [b] *14* Greek *Simeon*, a variant of *Simon*; that is, Peter [c] *17* Amos 9:11,12 [d] *17,18* Some manuscripts *things'— / 18known to the Lord for ages is his work*

15:7–11

PROMISE 1

BY FAITH ALONE

The message Paul preached was simple: Salvation is by faith alone. What could be clearer? But some of the ancient Jews thought Gentile believers had to do more than believe to be saved. They believed a person must also keep the law of Moses—that system of dietary restrictions and behavioral directives that governed Jewish life in Old Testament times.

Like those Jews, some Christians today try to add to the gospel message. They insist that certain religious practices and other good deeds are necessary for salvation. But Paul would vehemently disagree. He insisted that people were saved by faith in Jesus Christ alone, not faith combined with pious activities. And he argued that God had validated the Gentiles' faith by giving them the Holy Spirit.

Paul's words are as appropriate for us today as they were back then. Salvation isn't about you doing something for God. It's about accepting what God has done for you. (For more insight on how to become a Christian, turn to the notes on John 3:16.)

For the next Promise 1 reading go to page 1217.

by idols,[z] from sexual immorality,[a] from the meat of strangled animals and from blood.[b] 21For Moses has been preached in every city from the earliest times and is read in the synagogues on every Sabbath."[c]

The Council's Letter to Gentile Believers

22Then the apostles and elders, with the whole church, decided to choose some of their own men and send them to Antioch with Paul and Barnabas. They chose Judas (called Barsabbas) and Silas,[d] two men who were leaders among the brothers. 23With them they sent the following letter:

> The apostles and elders, your brothers,
>
> To the Gentile believers in Antioch,[e] Syria and Cilicia:[f]
>
> Greetings.[g]
>
> 24We have heard that some went out from us without our authorization and disturbed you, troubling your minds by what they said.[h] 25So we all agreed to choose some men and send them to you with our dear friends Barnabas and Paul— 26men who have risked their lives[i] for the name of our Lord Jesus Christ. 27Therefore we are sending Judas and Silas to confirm by word of mouth what we are writing. 28It seemed good to the Holy Spirit[j] and to us not to burden you with anything beyond the following requirements: 29You are to abstain from food sacrificed to idols, from blood, from the meat of strangled animals and from sexual immorality.[k] You will do well to avoid these things.
>
> Farewell.

2 →PG. 1223

30The men were sent off and went down to Antioch, where they gathered the church together and delivered the letter. 31The people read it and were glad for its encouraging message. 32Judas and Silas, who themselves were prophets, said much to encourage and strengthen the brothers. 33After spending some time there, they were sent off by the brothers with the blessing of peace[l] to return to those who had sent them.[a] 35But Paul and Barnabas remained in Antioch, where they and many others taught and preached[m] the word of the Lord.

Disagreement Between Paul and Barnabas

36Some time later Paul said to Barnabas, "Let us go back and visit the brothers in all the towns[n] where we preached the word of the Lord and see how they are doing." 37Barnabas wanted to take John, also called Mark,[o] with them, 38but Paul did not think it wise to take him, because he had deserted them[p] in Pamphylia and had not continued with them in the work. 39They had such a sharp disagreement that they parted company. Barnabas took Mark and sailed for Cyprus, 40but Paul chose Silas[q] and left, commended by the brothers to the grace of the Lord.[r] 41He went through Syria[s] and Cilicia,[t] strengthening the churches.[u]

Timothy Joins Paul and Silas

16 He came to Derbe and then to Lystra,[v] where a disciple named Timothy[w] lived, whose mother was a Jewess and a believer, but whose father was a Greek. 2The brothers[x] at Lystra and Iconium[y] spoke well of him. 3Paul wanted to take him along on the journey, so he circumcised him because of the Jews who lived in that area, for they all knew that his father was a Greek.[z] 4As they traveled from town to town, they delivered the decisions reached by the apostles and elders[a] in Jerusalem[b] for the people to obey.[c] 5So the churches were strengthened[d] in the faith and grew daily in numbers.

5 →PG. 1217

Paul's Vision of the Man of Macedonia

6Paul and his companions traveled throughout the region of Phrygia[e] and Galatia,[f] having been kept by the Holy Spirit from preaching the word in the province of Asia.[g] 7When they came to the border of Mysia, they tried to enter Bithynia, but the Spirit of Jesus[h] would not allow them to. 8So they passed by Mysia and went down to Troas.[i] 9During the night Paul had a vision[j] of a man of Macedonia[k] standing and begging him, "Come over to Macedonia and help us." 10After Paul had seen the vision, we[l] got ready at once to leave for Macedonia, concluding that God had called us to preach the gospel[m] to them.

Lydia's Conversion in Philippi

11From Troas[n] we put out to sea and sailed straight for Samothrace, and the next day on to Neapolis. 12From

15:20 [z] 1Co 8:7-13; 10:14-28; Rev 2:14,20 [a] 1Co 10:7,8 [b] ver 29; Ge 9:4; Lev 3:17; Dt 12:16,23
15:21 [c] Ac 13:15; 2Co 3:14,15
15:22 [d] ver 27,32,40
15:23 [e] ver 1 [f] ver 41 [g] Ac 23:25,26; Jas 1:1
15:24 [h] ver 1; Gal 1:7; 5:10
15:26 [i] Ac 9:23-25; 14:19
15:28 [j] Ac 5:32
15:29 [k] ver 20; Ac 21:25
15:33 [l] Mk 5:34; Ac 16:36; 1Co 16:11
15:35 [m] Ac 8:4
15:36 [n] Ac 13:4,13, 14,51; 14:1,6, 24,25
15:37 [o] Ac 12:12
15:38 [p] Ac 13:13
15:40 [q] ver 22 [r] Ac 11:23
15:41 [s] ver 23 [t] Ac 6:9 [u] Ac 16:5
16:1 [v] Ac 14:6 [w] Ac 17:14; 18:5; 19:22; Ro 16:21; 1Co 4:17; 2Co 1:1,19; 1Th 3:2,6; 1Ti 1:2,18; 2Ti 1:2,5,6
16:2 [x] ver 40 [y] Ac 13:51
16:3 [z] Gal 2:3
16:4 [a] Ac 11:30 [b] Ac 15:2 [c] Ac 15:28,29
16:5 [d] Ac 9:31; 15:41
16:6 [e] Ac 18:23 [f] Ac 18:23; Gal 1:2; 3:1 [g] Ac 2:9
16:7 [h] Ro 8:9; Gal 4:6
16:8 [i] ver 11; 2Co 2:12; 2Ti 4:13
16:9 [j] Ac 9:10 [k] Ac 20:1,3
16:10 [l] ver 10-17 [m] Ac 14:7
16:11 [n] ver 8

[a] *33* Some manuscripts *them,* *34but Silas decided to remain there*

there we traveled to Philippi,[o] a Roman colony and the leading city of that district of Macedonia.[p] And we stayed there several days.

13On the Sabbath[q] we went outside the city gate to the river, where we expected to find a place of prayer. We sat down and began to speak to the women who had gathered there. **14**One of those listening was a woman named Lydia, a dealer in purple cloth from the city of Thyatira,[r] who was a worshiper of God. The Lord opened her heart[s] to respond to Paul's message. **15**When she and the members of her household[t] were baptized, she invited us to her home. "If you consider me a believer in the Lord," she said, "come and stay at my house." And she persuaded us.

4 →PG. 1217
5 →PG. 1217

Paul and Silas in Prison

16Once when we were going to the place of prayer,[u] we were met by a slave girl who had a spirit[v] by which she predicted the future. She earned a great deal of money for her owners by fortune-telling. **17**This girl followed Paul and the rest of us, shouting, "These men are servants of the Most High God,[w] who are telling you the way to be saved." **18**She kept this up for many days. Finally Paul became so troubled that he turned around and said to the spirit, "In the name of Jesus Christ I command you to come out of her!" At that moment the spirit left her.[x]

19When the owners of the slave girl realized that their hope of making money[y] was gone, they seized Paul and Silas[z] and dragged[a] them into the marketplace to face the authorities. **20**They brought them before the magistrates and said, "These men are Jews, and are throwing our city into an uproar[b] **21**by advocating customs unlawful for us Romans[c] to accept or practice."[d]

22The crowd joined in the attack against Paul and Silas, and the magistrates ordered them to be stripped and beaten.[e] **23**After they had been severely flogged, they were thrown into prison, and the jailer[f] was commanded to guard them carefully. **24**Upon receiving such orders, he put them in the inner cell and fastened their feet in the stocks.[g]

25About midnight Paul and Silas were praying and singing hymns[h] to God, and the other prisoners were listening to them. **26**Suddenly there was such a violent earthquake that the foundations of the prison were shaken.[i] At once all the prison doors flew open,[j] and everybody's chains came loose.[k] **27**The jailer woke up, and when he saw the prison doors open, he drew his sword and was about to kill himself because he thought the prisoners had escaped.[l] **28**But Paul shouted, "Don't harm yourself! We are all here!"

29The jailer called for lights, rushed in and fell trembling before Paul and Silas. **30**He then brought them out and asked, "Sirs, what must I do to be saved?"[m]

31They replied, "Believe in the Lord Jesus, and you will be saved—you and your household."[n] **32**Then they spoke the word of the Lord to him and to all the others in his house. **33**At that hour of the night[o] the jailer took them and washed their wounds; then immediately he and all his family were baptized. **34**The jailer brought them into his house and set a meal before them; he[p] was filled with joy because he had come to believe in God—he and his whole family.

4 →PG. 1219
5 →PG. 1221

35When it was daylight, the magistrates sent their officers to the jailer with the order: "Release those men." **36**The jailer[q] told Paul, "The magistrates have ordered that you and Silas be released. Now you can leave. Go in peace."[r]

37But Paul said to the officers: "They beat us publicly without a trial, even though we are Roman citizens,[s] and threw us into prison. And now do they want to get rid of us quietly? No! Let

16:12 [o]Ac 20:6; Php 1:1; 1Th 2:2 [p]ver 9
16:13 [q]Ac 13:14
16:14 [r]Rev 1:11 [s]Lk 24:45
16:15 [t]Ac 11:14
16:16 [u]ver 13 [v]Dt 18:11; 1Sa 28:3,7
16:17 [w]Mk 5:7
16:18 [x]Mk 16:17
16:19 [y]ver 16; Ac 19:25,26 [z]Ac 15:22 [a]Ac 8:3; 17:6; 21:30; Jas 2:6
16:20 [b]Ac 17:6
16:21 [c]ver 12 [d]Est 3:8
16:22 [e]2Co 11:25; 1Th 2:2
16:23 [f]ver 27,36
16:24 [g]Job 13:27; 33:11; Jer 20:2,3; 29:26
16:25 [h]Eph 5:19
16:26 [i]Ac 4:31 [j]Ac 12:10 [k]Ac 12:7
16:27 [l]Ac 12:19
16:30 [m]Ac 2:37
16:31 [n]Ac 11:14
16:33 [o]ver 25
16:34 [p]Ac 11:14
16:36 [q]ver 23,27 [r]Ac 15:33
16:37 [s]Ac 22:25-29

16:25–34

PROMISE 1

DESPAIR LEADING TO GRACE

Nobody likes to face a personal crisis. Yet God can use hard times in our lives to bring us to a point of despair so we'll turn to him. That's what happened to the Philippian jailer in this story. The events the writer describes brought this man to the brink of suicide.

Despairing, broken and helpless, the jailer asked Paul and Silas, "What must I do to be saved?" Paul told the jailer to go to Jesus, believe in him, trust in him, rely on him. In Jesus, this man began a new life (v. 34).

Has God used some personal crisis in your life as a "wake-up call" to bring you back to him? The challenge for men today is to learn from the jailer's example. We need to maintain our relationship with Jesus so that when life's inevitable trials do come, we're prepared to look to him for help.

For the next Promise 1 reading go to page 1239.

them come themselves and escort us out."

38 The officers reported this to the magistrates, and when they heard that Paul and Silas were Roman citizens, they were alarmed.[t] 39 They came to appease them and escorted them from the prison, requesting them to leave the city.[u] 40 After Paul and Silas came out of the prison, they went to Lydia's house,[v] where they met with the brothers[w] and encouraged them. Then they left.

In Thessalonica

17 When they had passed through Amphipolis and Apollonia, they came to Thessalonica,[x] where there was a Jewish synagogue. 2 As his custom was, Paul went into the synagogue,[y] and on three Sabbath[z] days he reasoned with them from the Scriptures,[a] 3 explaining and proving that the Christ[a] had to suffer[b] and rise from the dead.[c] "This Jesus I am proclaiming to you is the Christ,[a]"[d] he said. 4 Some of the Jews were persuaded and joined Paul and Silas,[e] as did a large number of God-fearing Greeks and not a few prominent women.

5 But the Jews were jealous; so they rounded up some bad characters from the marketplace, formed a mob and started a riot in the city.[f] They rushed to Jason's[g] house in search of Paul and Silas in order to bring them out to the crowd.[b] 6 But when they did not find them, they dragged[h] Jason and some other brothers before the city officials, shouting: "These men who have caused trouble all over the world[i] have now come here,[j] 7 and Jason has welcomed them into his house. They are all defying Caesar's decrees, saying that there is another king, one called Jesus."[k] 8 When they heard this, the crowd and the city officials were thrown into turmoil. 9 Then they made Jason[l] and the others post bond and let them go.

In Berea

10 As soon as it was night, the brothers sent Paul and Silas away to Berea.[m] On arriving there, they went to the Jewish synagogue. 11 Now the Bereans were of more noble character than the Thessalonians,[n] for they received the message with great eagerness and examined the Scriptures[o] every day to see if what Paul said was true. 12 Many of the Jews believed, as did also a number of prominent Greek women and many Greek men.

13 When the Jews in Thessalonica learned that Paul was preaching the word of God at Berea, they went there too, agitating the crowds and stirring them up. 14 The brothers immediately sent Paul to the coast, but Silas[p] and Timothy[q] stayed at Berea. 15 The men who escorted Paul brought him to Athens[r] and then left with instructions for Silas and Timothy to join him as soon as possible.[s]

In Athens

16 While Paul was waiting for them in Athens, he was greatly distressed to see that the city was full of idols. 17 So he reasoned in the synagogue[t] with the Jews and the God-fearing Greeks, as well as in the marketplace day by day with those who happened to be there. 18 A group of Epicurean and Stoic philosophers began to dispute with him. Some of them asked, "What is this babbler trying to say?" Others remarked, "He seems to be advocating foreign gods." They said this because Paul was preaching the good news about Jesus and the resurrection.[u] 19 Then they took him and brought him to a meeting of the Areopagus,[v] where they said to him, "May we know what this new teaching[w] is that you are presenting? 20 You are bringing some strange ideas to our ears, and we want to know what they mean." 21 (All the Athenians and the foreigners who lived there spent their time doing nothing but talking about and listening to the latest ideas.)

22 Paul then stood up in the meeting of the Areopagus and said: "Men of Athens! I see that in every way you are very religious. 23 For as I walked around and looked carefully at your objects of worship, I even found an altar with this inscription: TO AN UNKNOWN GOD. Now what you worship as something unknown[x] I am going to proclaim to you.

24 "The God who made the world and everything in it[y] is the Lord of heaven and earth[z] and does not live in temples built by hands.[a] 25 And he is not served by human hands, as if he needed anything, because he himself gives all men life and breath and everything else.[b] 26 From one man he made every nation of men, that they should inhabit the whole earth; and he determined the times set for them and the exact places where they should live.[c] 27 God did this so that men would seek him and perhaps reach out for him and find him, though he is not far from each one of us.[d] 28 'For in him we live and

1 →PG. 1237

16:38 [t]Ac 22:29 **16:39** [u]Mt 8:34 **16:40** [v]ver 14 [w]ver 2; Ac 1:16 **17:1** [x]ver 11,13; Php 4:16; 1Th 1:1; 2Th 1:1; 2Ti 4:10 **17:2** [y]Ac 9:20 [z]Ac 13:14 [a]Ac 8:35 **17:3** [b]Lk 24:26; Ac 3:18 [c]Lk 24:46 [d]Ac 9:22; 18:28 **17:4** [e]Ac 15:22 **17:5** [f]ver 13; 1Th 2:16 [g]Ro 16:21 **17:6** [h]Ac 16:19 [i]Mt 24:14 [j]Ac 16:20 **17:7** [k]Lk 23:2; Jn 19:12 **17:9** [l]ver 5 **17:10** [m]ver 13; Ac 20:4 **17:11** [n]ver 1 [o]Lk 16:29; Jn 5:39

17:14 [p]Ac 15:22 [q]Ac 16:1 **17:15** [r]ver 16,21,22; Ac 18:1; 1Th 3:1 [s]Ac 18:5 **17:17** [t]Ac 9:20 **17:18** [u]ver 31,32; Ac 4:2 **17:19** [v]ver 22 [w]Mk 1:27 **17:23** [x]Jn 4:22 **17:24** [y]Isa 42:5; Ac 14:15 [z]Dt 10:14; Mt 11:25 [a]Ac 7:48 **17:25** [b]Ps 50:10-12; Isa 42:5 **17:26** [c]Dt 32:8; Job 12:23 **17:27** [d]Dt 4:7; Jer 23:23,24; Ac 14:17

[a] 3 Or *Messiah* [b] 5 Or *the assembly of the people*

move and have our being.'[e] As some of your own poets have said, 'We are his offspring.'

29"Therefore since we are God's offspring, we should not think that the divine being is like gold or silver or stone—an image made by man's design and skill.[f] 30In the past God overlooked[g] such ignorance,[h] but now he commands all people everywhere to repent.[i] 31For he has set a day when he will judge[j] the world with justice[k] by the man he has appointed.[l] He has given proof of this to all men by raising him from the dead."[m]

32When they heard about the resurrection of the dead,[n] some of them sneered, but others said, "We want to hear you again on this subject." 33At that, Paul left the Council. 34A few men became followers of Paul and believed. Among them was Dionysius, a member of the Areopagus,[o] also a woman named Damaris, and a number of others.

In Corinth

18 After this, Paul left Athens[p] and went to Corinth.[q] 2There he met a Jew named Aquila, a native of Pontus, who had recently come from Italy with his wife Priscilla,[r] because Claudius[s] had ordered all the Jews to leave Rome. Paul went to see them, 3and because he was a tentmaker as they were, he stayed and worked with them.[t] 4Every Sabbath[u] he reasoned in the synagogue, trying to persuade Jews and Greeks.

5When Silas[v] and Timothy[w] came from Macedonia,[x] Paul devoted himself exclusively to preaching, testifying to the Jews that Jesus was the Christ.[a][y] 6But when the Jews opposed Paul and became abusive,[z] he shook out his clothes in protest and said to them, "Your blood be on your own heads![a] I am clear of my responsibility.[b] From now on I will go to the Gentiles."[c]

7Then Paul left the synagogue and went next door to the house of Titius Justus, a worshiper of God.[d] 8Cris-

4 →PG. 1259

17:28 [e]Job 12:10; Da 5:23 **17:29** [f]Isa 40:18-20; Ro 1:23 **17:30** [g]Ac 14:16; Ro 3:25 [h]ver 23; 1Pe 1:14 [i]Lk 24:47; Tit 2:11,12 **17:31** [j]Mt 10:15 [k]Ps 9:8; 96:13; 98:9 [l]Ac 10:42 [m]Ac 2:24 **17:32** [n]ver 18,31 **17:34** [o]ver 19,22 **18:1** [p]Ac 17:15 [q]Ac 19:1; 1Co 1:2; 2Co 1:1,23; 2Ti 4:20 **18:2** [r]Ro 16:3; 1Co 16:19; 2Ti 4:19 [s]Ac 11:28 **18:3** [t]Ac 20:34; 1Co 4:12; 1Th 2:9; 2Th 3:8 **18:4** [u]Ac 13:14

[a]5 Or *Messiah;* also in verse 28

18:5 [v]Ac 15:22 [w]Ac 16:1 [x]Ac 16:9; 17:14,15 [y]ver 28; Ac 17:3 **18:6** [z]Ac 13:45 [a]2Sa 1:16; Eze 18:13; 33:4 [b]Ac 20:26 [c]Ac 13:46 **18:7** [d]Ac 16:14

17:24–31

PROMISE 7

OUT OF DARKNESS

It was a miner's worst nightmare. What began as a typical working day in March of 1977 ended tragically when a crushing torrent of water slammed into the Kosher Coal Company mine in Tower City, Pennsylvania. The flash flood wrecked the mining operation and buried nine miners alive. Amazingly, one man survived. For 29 hours Ronald Adley sat trapped in a cold, wet and dark tomb. Surrounded by darkness and silence, Adley's only companion was his imagination. And it ran wild as he stared into the blackness.

After all those hours of silence and darkness, Adley suddenly thought he heard something. He tilted his head and listened. Again he heard the sound, like a tapping on the stone wall behind him. In the darkness, Adley groped for a rock and began tapping back. Time and again he hit the wall, hoping he would be heard.

One minute passed. And then another. All of a sudden a drill burst through the wall, flooding the dark cavern with light and life-giving fresh air! Adley's friends had pulled through; they had done all they could to get him out of that dark place.

In a sense, the men of ancient Athens were like Ronald Adley. They were surrounded by darkness—spiritual darkness. And, like Adley, they needed someone to bring them light and life.

Notice how Paul brought light into their dark world. First, Paul spoke courteously (v. 22), showing an awareness of and appreciation for their religious quest. Second, he used an example from their own religious culture as a means of introducing them to the true God (v. 23). Third, Paul gently pointed out the fallacies of their belief system (vv. 24–25). He declared that God, the Creator and Ruler of the universe, isn't distant or uncaring. On the contrary, he is a personal God who wants all men to know him. Again Paul made reference to something they would find familiar in making a theological point (vv. 26–28). Finally, Paul urged his listeners to repent and embrace God's Son, whom God had raised from the dead (v. 31). Repentance was a fitting response because God would one day judge all men.

Notice how Paul identified something he could affirm in these men and then gently told them about their need for a Savior. And how did they respond? Some of his listeners saw the light and were delivered from darkness. Others chose to stay in the darkness; they simply walked away from the good news of the gospel.

God has called us to see unbelievers as victims of the enemy, the devil, not as the enemy. They are trapped in darkness and need someone to bring them the message of light and life. Ask God to allow you to see your unbelieving friends in that way. And ask God to help you to gently point them to Jesus Christ.

For the next Promise 7 reading go to page 1226.

AQUILA AND PRISCILLA

Teamwork in Ministry

Have you ever thought about how you and your wife might work together in a ministry for Jesus Christ? The opportunities—and the benefits—are many, and you might end up making a significant impact. Just look at the example of the couple introduced in this passage.

Aquila and Priscilla were marriage partners in the early years of the church. They were Jews who had been living in Italy when an anti-Semitic Roman emperor named Claudius ordered them and "all the Jews to leave Rome" (Acts 18:2). Consequently, they moved to the Greek city of Corinth and set up their tentmaking business.

Shortly after their arrival, Paul came to Corinth to preach the gospel. Since Paul needed to provide for his own physical needs while doing his missionary work, he linked up with Aquila and Priscilla in the tentmaking trade (18:3–4).

We're not told when Aquila and Priscilla responded to the gospel and became Christians. It may have happened while Paul toiled alongside them, making tents. He certainly would have described his dramatic experience on the road to Damascus—his own conversion to Christ (9:1–19).

More likely, they believed in Jesus as their Messiah while listening to Paul expound the Old Testament Scriptures as he "reasoned in the synagogue" each Sabbath, "trying to persuade" both "Jews and Greeks" (18:4). But one thing is certain: At some point, they became convinced that Jesus is the Son of God and the Savior of the world (John 3:16).

Serving Together

While ministering in Corinth, Paul planted a church. He stayed there a year and a half before moving on to Ephesus (Acts 18:11). By that time, Aquila and Priscilla had developed such a deep relationship with Paul that they decided to join him on his journey into Asia.

When they arrived in Ephesus, Paul stayed a while, once again entering the synagogue each Sabbath to discuss the gospel "with the Jews" (18:19). The Ephesian Jews' response was positive, but the Holy Spirit led Paul to leave that city, while Aquila and Priscilla remained to continue the work Paul had begun.

One of this couple's most significant accomplishments in Ephesus was to help a dynamic fellow Jew named Apollos understand more fully the gospel of God's grace. Sensing that Apollos was theologically confused since he was still preaching "the baptism of John," they "invited him to their home," not only to demonstrate hospitality, but also to share the same Good News they had heard from their friend Paul. Apollos responded and became a great apologetic preacher and defender of the gospel message (18:24–28).

Willing to Risk

We're not told how long Aquila and Priscilla stayed in Ephesus. However, when Paul wrote his letter to the Roman Christians, he again greeted the two of them warmly, along with "the church" that was meeting "at their house" (Romans 16:5). That means they had returned to Rome—probably after Claudius had been poisoned by his wife, Agrippina.

Then Paul let us in on an important character quality Aquila and Priscilla possessed. They were incredibly loyal to Paul and, more importantly, to Jesus Christ. Not only had they helped Paul preach the gospel and disciple new believers, but they had also "risked their lives" for Paul and for the cause of the gospel (Romans 16:4).

That may have happened when Paul returned to Ephesus, where his teaching precipitated a sharp decline in business for those who crafted and sold the silver shrines of the goddess Artemis (19:23–24). The ensuing riot almost cost Paul his own life (Acts 19:1—20:1). Aquila and Priscilla would have become objects of persecution along with Paul, since they certainly would not have stood idly by while their friend, brother, and mentor in Christ stood "under fire."

Couples Serving Together

Today as then, God is looking for couples who have a heart to minister and can effectively work together in presenting the gospel and building his church. There is so much you and your mate could do in your local church if you would make your time and energy available to your pastor and other church leaders. Prayerfully consider the options, and then discuss how God might want to use the two of you as a ministry team.

—Dr. Gene Getz

pus,[e] the synagogue ruler,[f] and his entire household[g] believed in the Lord; and many of the Corinthians who heard him believed and were baptized.

9One night the Lord spoke to Paul in a vision: "Do not be afraid; keep on speaking, do not be silent. 10For I am with you,[h] and no one is going to attack and harm you, because I have many people in this city." 11So Paul stayed for a year and a half, teaching them the word of God.

12While Gallio was proconsul of Achaia,[i] the Jews made a united attack on Paul and brought him into court. 13"This man," they charged, "is persuading the people to worship God in ways contrary to the law."

14Just as Paul was about to speak, Gallio said to the Jews, "If you Jews were making a complaint about some misdemeanor or serious crime, it would be reasonable for me to listen to you. 15But since it involves questions about words and names and your own law[j]—settle the matter yourselves. I will not be a judge of such things." 16So he had them ejected from the court. 17Then they all turned on Sosthenes[k] the synagogue ruler and beat him in front of the court. But Gallio showed no concern whatever.

Priscilla, Aquila and Apollos

18Paul stayed on in Corinth for some time. Then he left the brothers[l] and sailed for Syria, accompanied by Priscilla and Aquila. Before he sailed, he had his hair cut off at Cenchrea[m] because of a vow he had taken.[n] 19They arrived at Ephesus,[o] where Paul left Priscilla and Aquila. He himself went into the synagogue and reasoned with the Jews. 20When they asked him to spend more time with them, he declined. 21But as he left, he promised, "I will come back if it is God's will."[p] Then he set sail from Ephesus. 22When he landed at Caesarea,[q] he went up and greeted the church and then went down to Antioch.[r]

23After spending some time in Antioch, Paul set out from there and traveled from place to place throughout the region of Galatia[s] and Phrygia, strengthening all the disciples.[t]

24Meanwhile a Jew named Apollos,[u] a native of Alexandria, came to Ephesus. He was a learned man, with a thorough knowledge of the Scriptures. 25He had been instructed in the way of the Lord, and he spoke with great fervor[a][v] and taught about Jesus accurately, though he knew only the baptism of John.[w] 26He began to speak boldly in the synagogue. When Priscilla and Aquila heard him, they invited him to their home and explained to him the way of God more adequately.

27When Apollos wanted to go to Achaia,[x] the brothers[y] encouraged him and wrote to the disciples there to welcome him. On arriving, he was a great help to those who by grace had believed. 28For he vigorously refuted the Jews in public debate, proving from the Scriptures[z] that Jesus was the Christ.[a]

5 →PG. 1223

Paul in Ephesus

19 While Apollos was at Corinth,[b] Paul took the road through the interior and arrived at Ephesus.[c] There he found some disciples 2and asked them, "Did you receive the Holy Spirit when[b] you believed?"

They answered, "No, we have not even heard that there is a Holy Spirit."

3So Paul asked, "Then what baptism did you receive?"

"John's baptism," they replied.

4Paul said, "John's baptism was a baptism of repentance. He told the people to believe in the one coming after him, that is, in Jesus."[d] 5On hearing this, they were baptized into[c] the name of the Lord Jesus. 6When Paul placed his hands on them,[e] the Holy Spirit came on them,[f] and they spoke in tongues[d][g] and prophesied. 7There were about twelve men in all.

8Paul entered the synagogue[h] and spoke boldly there for three months, arguing persuasively about the kingdom of God.[i] 9But some of them[j] became obstinate; they refused to believe and publicly maligned the Way.[k] So Paul left them. He took the disciples[l] with him and had discussions daily in the lecture hall of Tyrannus. 10This went on for two years,[m] so that all the Jews and Greeks who lived in the province of Asia[n] heard the word of the Lord.

11God did extraordinary miracles[o] through Paul, 12so that even handkerchiefs and aprons that had touched him were taken to the sick, and their illnesses were cured[p] and the evil spirits left them.

13Some Jews who went around driving out evil spirits[q] tried to invoke the name of the Lord Jesus over those who were demon-possessed. They would say, "In the name of Jesus,[r] whom Paul preaches, I command you to come out." 14Seven sons of Sceva, a Jewish chief priest, were doing this.

18:8 [e] 1Co 1:14 [f] Mk 5:22 [g] Ac 11:14
18:10 [h] Mt 28:20
18:12 [i] ver 27
18:15 [j] Ac 23:29; 25:11,19
18:17 [k] 1Co 1:1
18:18 [l] Ac 1:16 [m] Ro 16:1 [n] Nu 6:2,5,18; Ac 21:24
18:19 [o] ver 21,24; 1Co 15:32
18:21 [p] Ro 1:10; 1Co 4:19; Jas 4:15
18:22 [q] Ac 8:40 [r] Ac 11:19
18:23 [s] Ac 16:6 [t] Ac 14:22; 15:32,41
18:24 [u] Ac 19:1; 1Co 1:12; 3:5, 6,22; 4:6; 16:12; Tit 3:13
18:25 [v] Ro 12:11 [w] Ac 19:3
18:27 [x] ver 12 [y] ver 18
18:28 [z] Ac 17:2 [a] ver 5; Ac 9:22
19:1 [b] Ac 18:1 [c] Ac 18:19
19:4 [d] Jn 1:7; Ac 13:24,25
19:6 [e] Ac 6:6; 8:17 [f] Ac 2:4 [g] Mk 16:17; Ac 10:46
19:8 [h] Ac 9:20 [i] Ac 1:3; 28:23
19:9 [j] Ac 14:4 [k] ver 23; Ac 9:2 [l] ver 30; Ac 11:26
19:10 [m] Ac 20:31 [n] ver 22,26,27
19:11 [o] Ac 8:13
19:12 [p] Ac 5:15
19:13 [q] Mt 12:27 [r] Mk 9:38

[a] 25 Or *with fervor in the Spirit* [b] 2 Or *after*
[c] 5 Or *in* [d] 6 Or *other languages*

15⌊One day⌋ the evil spirit answered
them, "Jesus I know, and I know about
Paul, but who are you?" 16Then the
man who had the evil spirit jumped on
them and overpowered them all. He
gave them such a beating that they ran
out of the house naked and bleeding.
17When this became known to the
Jews and Greeks living in Ephesus,[s]
they were all seized with fear,[t] and
the name of the Lord Jesus was held in
high honor. 18Many of those who believed now came and openly confessed
their evil deeds. 19A number who had
practiced sorcery brought their scrolls
together and burned them publicly.
When they calculated the value of the
scrolls, the total came to fifty thousand
drachmas.[a] 20In this way the word of
the Lord spread widely and grew in
power.[u]
21After all this had happened, Paul
decided to go to Jerusalem,[v] passing
through Macedonia[w] and Achaia.[x]
"After I have been there," he said, "I
must visit Rome also."[y] 22He sent two
of his helpers,[z] Timothy[a] and Erastus,[b] to Macedonia, while he stayed in
the province of Asia[c] a little longer.

The Riot in Ephesus

23About that time there arose a great
disturbance about the Way.[d] 24A silversmith named Demetrius, who made
silver shrines of Artemis, brought in no
little business for the craftsmen. 25He
called them together, along with the
workmen in related trades, and said:
"Men, you know we receive a good income from this business.[e] 26And you
see and hear how this fellow Paul has
convinced and led astray large numbers of people here in Ephesus[f] and
in practically the whole province of
Asia. He says that man-made gods are
no gods at all.[g] 27There is danger not
only that our trade will lose its good
name, but also that the temple of the
great goddess Artemis will be discredited, and the goddess herself, who is
worshiped throughout the province of
Asia and the world, will be robbed of
her divine majesty."
28When they heard this, they were
furious and began shouting: "Great is
Artemis of the Ephesians!"[h] 29Soon
the whole city was in an uproar. The
people seized Gaius[i] and Aristarchus,[j] Paul's traveling companions
from Macedonia,[k] and rushed as one
man into the theater. 30Paul wanted to
appear before the crowd, but the disciples would not let him. 31Even some of
the officials of the province, friends of
Paul, sent him a message begging him
not to venture into the theater.
32The assembly was in confusion:
Some were shouting one thing, some
another.[l] Most of the people did not
even know why they were there. 33The
Jews pushed Alexander to the front,
and some of the crowd shouted instructions to him. He motioned[m] for
silence in order to make a defense before the people. 34But when they realized he was a Jew, they all shouted in
unison for about two hours: "Great is
Artemis of the Ephesians!"
35The city clerk quieted the crowd
and said: "Men of Ephesus,[n] doesn't
all the world know that the city of Ephesus is the guardian of the temple of
the great Artemis and of her image,
which fell from heaven? 36Therefore,
since these facts are undeniable, you
ought to be quiet and not do anything
rash. 37You have brought these men
here, though they have neither robbed
temples[o] nor blasphemed our goddess. 38If, then, Demetrius and his fellow craftsmen have a grievance against
anybody, the courts are open and there
are proconsuls.[p] They can press
charges. 39If there is anything further
you want to bring up, it must be settled
in a legal assembly. 40As it is, we are in
danger of being charged with rioting
because of today's events. In that case
we would not be able to account for
this commotion, since there is no reason for it." 41After he had said this, he
dismissed the assembly.

Through Macedonia and Greece

20 When the uproar had ended, Paul
sent for the disciples[q] and, after
encouraging them, said good-by and
set out for Macedonia.[r] 2He traveled
through that area, speaking many
words of encouragement to the people,
and finally arrived in Greece, 3where he
stayed three months. Because the Jews
made a plot against him[s] just as he
was about to sail for Syria, he decided
to go back through Macedonia.[t] 4He
was accompanied by Sopater son of
Pyrrhus from Berea, Aristarchus[u] and
Secundus from Thessalonica,[v] Gaius[w] from Derbe, Timothy[x] also, and
Tychicus[y] and Trophimus[z] from the
province of Asia. 5These men went on
ahead and waited for us[a] at Troas.[b]
6But we sailed from Philippi[c] after the
Feast of Unleavened Bread, and five
days later joined the others at Troas,[d]
where we stayed seven days.

19:17 [s]Ac 18:19 [t]Ac 5:5,11
19:20 [u]Ac 6:7; 12:24
19:21 [v]Ac 20:16,22; Ro 15:25 [w]Ac 16:9 [x]Ac 18:12 [y]Ro 15:24,28
19:22 [z]Ac 13:5 [a]Ac 16:1 [b]Ro 16:23; 2Ti 4:20 [c]ver 10,26,27
19:23 [d]Ac 9:2
19:25 [e]Ac 16:16,19, 20
19:26 [f]Ac 18:19 [g]Dt 4:28; Ps 115:4; Isa 44:10-20; Jer 10:3-5; Ac 17:29; 1Co 8:4; Rev 9:20
19:28 [h]Ac 18:19
19:29 [i]Ac 20:4; Ro 16:23; 1Co 1:14 [j]Ac 20:4; 27:2; Col 4:10; Phm 24 [k]Ac 16:9
19:32 [l]Ac 21:34
19:33 [m]Ac 12:17
19:35 [n]Ac 18:19
19:37 [o]Ro 2:22
19:38 [p]Ac 13:7,8,12
20:1 [q]Ac 11:26 [r]Ac 16:9
20:3 [s]ver 19; Ac 9:23,24; 23:12,15,30; 25:3; 2Co 11:26 [t]Ac 16:9
20:4 [u]Ac 19:29 [v]Ac 17:1 [w]Ac 19:29 [x]Ac 16:1 [y]Eph 6:21; Col 4:7; 2Ti 4:12; Tit 3:12 [z]Ac 21:29; 2Ti 4:20
20:5 [a]Ac 16:10 [b]Ac 16:8
20:6 [c]Ac 16:12 [d]Ac 16:8

[a] *19* A drachma was a silver coin worth about a day's wages.

Eutychus Raised From the Dead at Troas

7On the first day of the week[e] we
came together to break bread. Paul
spoke to the people and, because he
intended to leave the next day, kept on
talking until midnight. 8There were
many lamps in the upstairs room[f]
where we were meeting. 9Seated in a
window was a young man named Euty-
chus, who was sinking into a deep
sleep as Paul talked on and on. When
he was sound asleep, he fell to the
ground from the third story and was
picked up dead. 10Paul went down,
threw himself on the young man[g] and
put his arms around him. "Don't
be alarmed," he said. "He's alive!"[h]
11Then he went upstairs again and
broke bread[i] and ate. After talking
until daylight, he left. 12The people
took the young man home alive and
were greatly comforted.

Paul's Farewell to the Ephesian Elders

13We went on ahead to the ship and
sailed for Assos, where we were going
to take Paul aboard. He had made this
arrangement because he was going
there on foot. 14When he met us at Assos, we took him aboard and went on
to Mitylene. 15The next day we set sail
from there and arrived off Kios. The
day after that we crossed over to Sa-
mos, and on the following day arrived
at Miletus.[j] 16Paul had decided to sail
past Ephesus[k] to avoid spending time
in the province of Asia, for he was in a
hurry to reach Jerusalem,[l] if possible,
by the day of Pentecost.[m]
17From Miletus, Paul sent to Ephesus for the elders[n] of the church.
18When they arrived, he said to them:
"You know how I lived the whole time
I was with you,[o] from the first day I
came into the province of Asia. 19I
served the Lord with great humility
and with tears, although I was severely
tested by the plots of the Jews.[p] 20You
know that I have not hesitated to
preach anything[q] that would be helpful to you but have taught you publicly
and from house to house. 21I have declared to both Jews[r] and Greeks that
they must turn to God in repentance[s]
and have faith in our Lord Jesus.[t]
22"And now, compelled by the Spirit,
I am going to Jerusalem,[u] not knowing what will happen to me there. 23I
only know that in every city the Holy
Spirit warns me[v] that prison and
hardships are facing me.[w] 24However,
I consider my life worth nothing to
me,[x] if only I may finish the race and
complete the task[y] the Lord Jesus has
given me[z]—the task of testifying to
the gospel of God's grace.
25"Now I know that none of you
among whom I have gone about
preaching the kingdom will ever see
me again.[a] 26Therefore, I declare to
you today that I am innocent of the
blood of all men.[b] 27For I have not
hesitated to proclaim to you the whole
will of God.[c] 28Keep watch over yourselves and all the flock of which the
Holy Spirit has made you overseers.[a][d] Be shepherds of the church
of God,[b] which he bought with his
own blood. 29I know that after I leave,
savage wolves[e] will come in among
you and will not spare the flock.[f]
30Even from your own number men
will arise and distort the truth in order
to draw away disciples[g] after them.
31So be on your guard! Remember that
for three years[h] I never stopped warning each of you night and day with
tears.[i]
32"Now I commit you to God[j] and
to the word of his grace, which can
build you up and give you an inheritance[k] among all those who are sanctified.[l] 33I have not coveted anyone's
silver or gold or clothing.[m] 34You yourselves know that these hands of mine
have supplied my own needs and the
needs of my companions.[n] 35In everything I did, I showed you that by this
kind of hard work we must help the
weak, remembering the words the Lord
Jesus himself said: 'It is more blessed
to give than to receive.' "
36When he had said this, he knelt
down with all of them and prayed.[o]
37They all wept as they embraced him
and kissed him.[p] 38What grieved them
most was his statement that they
would never see his face again.[q] Then
they accompanied him to the ship.

On to Jerusalem

21 After we[r] had torn ourselves away
from them, we put out to sea and
sailed straight to Cos. The next day we
went to Rhodes and from there to Pata-
ra. 2We found a ship crossing over to
Phoenicia,[s] went on board and set
sail. 3After sighting Cyprus and passing
to the south of it, we sailed on to Syria.
We landed at Tyre, where our ship was
to unload its cargo. 4Finding the disciples[t] there, we stayed with them sev-
en days. Through the Spirit[u] they
urged Paul not to go on to Jerusalem.
5But when our time was up, we left and
continued on our way. All the disciples
and their wives and children accompa-

5 →PG. 1223
2 →PG. 1231
7 →PG. 1229
5 →PG. 1231

20:7 [e]1Co 16:2; Rev 1:10
20:8 [f]Ac 1:13
20:10 [g]1Ki 17:21; 2Ki 4:34 [h]Mt 9:23,24
20:11 [i]ver 7
20:15 [j]ver 17; 2Ti 4:20
20:16 [k]Ac 18:19 [l]Ac 19:21 [m]Ac 2:1; 1Co 16:8
20:17 [n]Ac 11:30
20:18 [o]Ac 18:19-21; 19:1-41
20:19 [p]ver 3
20:20 [q]ver 27
20:21 [r]Ac 18:5 [s]Ac 2:38 [t]Ac 24:24; 26:18; Eph 1:15; Col 2:5; Phm 5
20:22 [u]ver 16
20:23 [v]Ac 21:4 [w]Ac 9:16
20:24 [x]Ac 21:13 [y]2Co 4:1 [z]Gal 1:1; Tit 1:3
20:25 [a]ver 38
20:26 [b]Ac 18:6
20:27 [c]ver 20
20:28 [d]1Pe 5:2
20:29 [e]Mt 7:15 [f]ver 28
20:30 [g]Ac 11:26
20:31 [h]Ac 19:10 [i]ver 19
20:32 [j]Ac 14:23 [k]Eph 1:14; Col 1:12; 3:24; Heb 9:15; 1Pe 1:4 [l]Ac 26:18
20:33 [m]1Sa 12:3; 1Co 9:12; 2Co 7:2; 11:9; 12:14-17
20:34 [n]Ac 18:3
20:36 [o]Lk 22:41; Ac 21:5
20:37 [p]Lk 15:20
20:38 [q]ver 25
21:1 [r]Ac 16:10
21:2 [s]Ac 11:19
21:4 [t]Ac 11:26 [u]ver 11; Ac 20:23

[a]28 Traditionally *bishops* [b]28 Many manuscripts *of the Lord*

nied us out of the city, and there on the beach we knelt to pray.[v] **6**After saying good-by to each other, we went aboard the ship, and they returned home.

7We continued our voyage from Tyre[w] and landed at Ptolemais, where we greeted the brothers[x] and stayed with them for a day. **8**Leaving the next day, we reached Caesarea[y] and stayed at the house of Philip[z] the evangelist,[a] one of the Seven. **9**He had four unmarried daughters who prophesied.[b]

10After we had been there a number of days, a prophet named Agabus[c] came down from Judea. **11**Coming over to us, he took Paul's belt, tied his own hands and feet with it and said, "The Holy Spirit says, 'In this way the Jews of Jerusalem will bind[d] the owner of this belt and will hand him over to the Gentiles.' "[e]

12When we heard this, we and the people there pleaded with Paul not to go up to Jerusalem. **13**Then Paul answered, "Why are you weeping and breaking my heart? I am ready not only to be bound, but also to die[f] in Jerusalem for the name of the Lord Jesus."[g] **14**When he would not be dissuaded, we gave up and said, "The Lord's will be done."

15After this, we got ready and went up to Jerusalem. **16**Some of the disciples from Caesarea[h] accompanied us and brought us to the home of Mnason, where we were to stay. He was a man from Cyprus[i] and one of the early disciples.

Paul's Arrival at Jerusalem

17When we arrived at Jerusalem, the brothers received us warmly.[j] **18**The next day Paul and the rest of us went to see James,[k] and all the elders[l] were present. **19**Paul greeted them and reported in detail what God had done among the Gentiles[m] through his ministry.[n]

20When they heard this, they praised God. Then they said to Paul: "You see, brother, how many thousands of Jews have believed, and all of them are zealous[o] for the law.[p] **21**They have been informed that you teach all the Jews who live among the Gentiles to turn away from Moses,[q] telling them not to circumcise their children[r] or live according to our customs.[s] **22**What shall we do? They will certainly hear that you have come, **23**so do what we tell you. There are four men with us who have made a vow.[t] **24**Take these men, join in their purification rites[u] and pay their expenses, so that they can have their heads shaved.[v] Then everybody will know there is no truth in these reports about you, but that you yourself are living in obedience to the law. **25**As for the Gentile believers, we have written to them our decision that they should abstain from food sacrificed to idols, from blood, from the meat of strangled animals and from sexual immorality."[w]

26The next day Paul took the men and purified himself along with them. Then he went to the temple to give notice of the date when the days of purification would end and the offering would be made for each of them.[x]

Paul Arrested

27When the seven days were nearly over, some Jews from the province of Asia saw Paul at the temple. They stirred up the whole crowd and seized him,[y] **28**shouting, "Men of Israel, help us! This is the man who teaches all men everywhere against our people and our law and this place. And besides, he has brought Greeks into the temple area and defiled this holy place."[z] **29**(They had previously seen Trophimus[a] the Ephesian[b] in the city with Paul and assumed that Paul had brought him into the temple area.)

30The whole city was aroused, and the people came running from all directions. Seizing Paul,[c] they dragged him[d] from the temple, and immediately the gates were shut. **31**While they were trying to kill him, news reached the commander of the Roman troops that the whole city of Jerusalem was in an uproar. **32**He at once took some officers and soldiers and ran down to the crowd. When the rioters saw the commander and his soldiers, they stopped beating Paul.[e]

33The commander came up and arrested him and ordered him to be bound[f] with two[g] chains.[h] Then he asked who he was and what he had done. **34**Some in the crowd shouted one thing and some another,[i] and since the commander could not get at the truth because of the uproar, he ordered that Paul be taken into the barracks.[j] **35**When Paul reached the steps,[k] the violence of the mob was so great he had to be carried by the soldiers. **36**The crowd that followed kept shouting, "Away with him!"[l]

Paul Speaks to the Crowd

37As the soldiers were about to take Paul into the barracks,[m] he asked the commander, "May I say something to you?"

21:5 [v]Ac 20:36
21:7 [w]Ac 12:20 [x]Ac 1:16
21:8 [y]Ac 8:40 [z]Ac 6:5; 8:5-40 [a]Eph 4:11; 2Ti 4:5
21:9 [b]Lk 2:36; Ac 2:17
21:10 [c]Ac 11:28
21:11 [d]ver 33 [e]1Ki 22:11
21:13 [f]Ac 20:24 [g]Ac 9:16
21:16 [h]Ac 8:40 [i]ver 3,4
21:17 [j]Ac 15:4
21:18 [k]Ac 15:13 [l]Ac 11:30
21:19 [m]Ac 14:27 [n]Ac 1:17
21:20 [o]Ac 22:3; Ro 10:2; Gal 1:14 [p]Ac 15:1,5
21:21 [q]ver 28 [r]Ac 15:19-21; 1Co 7:18,19 [s]Ac 6:14
21:23 [t]Ac 18:18
21:24 [u]ver 26; Ac 24:18 [v]Ac 18:18
21:25 [w]Ac 15:20,29
21:26 [x]Nu 6:13-20; Ac 24:18
21:27 [y]Ac 24:18; 26:21
21:28 [z]Mt 24:15; Ac 24:5,6
21:29 [a]Ac 20:4 [b]Ac 18:19
21:30 [c]Ac 26:21 [d]Ac 16:19
21:32 [e]Ac 23:27
21:33 [f]ver 11 [g]Ac 12:6 [h]Ac 20:23; Eph 6:20; 2Ti 2:9
21:34 [i]Ac 19:32 [j]ver 37; Ac 23:10,16,32
21:35 [k]ver 40
21:36 [l]Lk 23:18; Jn 19:15; Ac 22:22
21:37 [m]ver 34

"Do you speak Greek?" he replied.
38"Aren't you the Egyptian who started
a revolt and led four thousand terror-
ists out into the desert[n] some time
ago?"[o]
39Paul answered, "I am a Jew, from
Tarsus[p] in Cilicia,[q] a citizen of no ordinary city. Please let me speak to the
people."
40Having received the commander's
permission, Paul stood on the steps
and motioned[r] to the crowd. When
they were all silent, he said to them
22 in Aramaic[a]:[s] **1**"Brothers and fathers,[t] listen now to my defense."
2When they heard him speak to
them in Aramaic,[u] they became very
quiet.
Then Paul said: **3**"I am a Jew,[v] born
in Tarsus[w] of Cilicia, but brought up
in this city. Under[x] Gamaliel[y] I was
thoroughly trained in the law of our
fathers[z] and was just as zealous[a] for
God as any of you are today. **4**I persecuted[b] the followers of this Way to
their death, arresting both men and
women and throwing them into pris-
on,[c] **5**as also the high priest and all the
Council[d] can testify. I even obtained
letters from them to their brothers[e] in
Damascus,[f] and went there to bring
these people as prisoners to Jerusalem
to be punished.
6"About noon as I came near Damascus, suddenly a bright light from
heaven flashed around me.[g] **7**I fell to
the ground and heard a voice say to
me, 'Saul! Saul! Why do you persecute me?'
8" 'Who are you, Lord?' I asked.
" 'I am Jesus of Nazareth, whom you
are persecuting,' he replied. **9**My companions saw the light,[h] but they did
not understand the voice[i] of him who
was speaking to me.
10" 'What shall I do, Lord?' I asked.
" 'Get up,' the Lord said, 'and go into
Damascus. There you will be told all
that you have been assigned to do.'[j]
11My companions led me by the hand
into Damascus, because the brilliance
of the light had blinded me.[k]
12"A man named Ananias came to
see me.[l] He was a devout observer of
the law and highly respected by all the
Jews living there.[m] **13**He stood beside
me and said, 'Brother Saul, receive
your sight!' And at that very moment I
was able to see him.
14"Then he said: 'The God of our fathers[n] has chosen you to know his will
and to see[o] the Righteous One[p] and
to hear words from his mouth. **15**You
will be his witness[q] to all men of what
you have seen and heard. **16**And now
what are you waiting for? Get up, be
baptized[r] and wash your sins away,[s]
calling on his name.'[t]
17"When I returned to Jerusalem[u]
and was praying at the temple, I fell
into a trance[v] **18**and saw the Lord
speaking. 'Quick!' he said to me. 'Leave
Jerusalem immediately, because they
will not accept your testimony
about me.'
19" 'Lord,' I replied, 'these men
know that I went from one synagogue
to another to imprison[w] and beat[x]
those who believe in you. **20**And when
the blood of your martyr[b] Stephen
was shed, I stood there giving my approval and guarding the clothes of
those who were killing him.'[y]
21"Then the Lord said to me, 'Go; I
will send you far away to the Gentiles.' "[z]

Paul the Roman Citizen

22The crowd listened to Paul until he
said this. Then they raised their voices
and shouted, "Rid the earth of him![a]
He's not fit to live!"[b]
23As they were shouting and throwing off their cloaks[c] and flinging dust
into the air,[d] **24**the commander ordered Paul to be taken into the barracks.[e] He directed[f] that he be
flogged and questioned in order to find
out why the people were shouting at
him like this. **25**As they stretched him
out to flog him, Paul said to the centurion standing there, "Is it legal for you
to flog a Roman citizen who hasn't
even been found guilty?"[g]
26When the centurion heard this, he
went to the commander and reported
it. "What are you going to do?" he
asked. "This man is a Roman citizen."
27The commander went to Paul and
asked, "Tell me, are you a Roman citizen?"
"Yes, I am," he answered.
28Then the commander said, "I had
to pay a big price for my citizenship."
"But I was born a citizen," Paul replied.
29Those who were about to question
him withdrew immediately. The commander himself was alarmed when he
realized that he had put Paul, a Roman
citizen,[h] in chains.

Before the Sanhedrin

30The next day, since the commander wanted to find out exactly why Paul
was being accused by the Jews,[i] he
released him[j] and ordered the chief
priests and all the Sanhedrin[k] to as-

21:38 [n]Mt 24:26 [o]Ac 5:36
21:39 [p]Ac 9:11 [q]Ac 22:3
21:40 [r]Ac 12:17 [s]Jn 5:2
22:1 [t]Ac 7:2
22:2 [u]Ac 21:40
22:3 [v]Ac 21:39 [w]Ac 9:11 [x]Lk 10:39 [y]Ac 5:34 [z]Ac 26:5 [a]Ac 21:20
22:4 [b]Ac 8:3 [c]ver 19,20
22:5 [d]Lk 22:66 [e]Ac 13:26 [f]Ac 9:2
22:6 [g]Ac 9:3
22:9 [h]Ac 26:13 [i]Ac 9:7
22:10 [j]Ac 16:30
22:11 [k]Ac 9:8
22:12 [l]Ac 9:17 [m]Ac 10:22
22:14 [n]Ac 3:13 [o]1Co 9:1; 15:8 [p]Ac 7:52
22:15 [q]Ac 23:11; 26:16
22:16 [r]Ac 2:38 [s]Heb 10:22 [t]Ro 10:13
22:17 [u]Ac 9:26 [v]Ac 10:10
22:19 [w]ver 4; Ac 8:3 [x]Mt 10:17
22:20 [y]Ac 7:57-60; 8:1
22:21 [z]Ac 9:15; 13:46
22:22 [a]Ac 21:36 [b]Ac 25:24
22:23 [c]Ac 7:58 [d]2Sa 16:13
22:24 [e]Ac 21:34 [f]ver 29
22:25 [g]Ac 16:37
22:29 [h]ver 24,25; Ac 16:38
22:30 [i]Ac 23:28 [j]Ac 21:33 [k]Mt 5:22

a *40* Or possibly *Hebrew*; also in 22:2 **b** *20* Or *witness*

semble. Then he brought Paul and had
him stand before them.

23 Paul looked straight at the Sanhedrin[l] and said, "My brothers,[m]
I have fulfilled my duty to God in
all good conscience[n] to this day." 2At
this the high priest Ananias[o] ordered
those standing near Paul to strike him
on the mouth.[p] 3Then Paul said to
him, "God will strike you, you whitewashed wall![q] You sit there to judge
me according to the law, yet you yourself violate the law by commanding
that I be struck!"[r]

4Those who were standing near Paul
said, "You dare to insult God's high
priest?"

5Paul replied, "Brothers, I did not realize that he was the high priest; for it
is written: 'Do not speak evil about the
ruler of your people.'[a]"[s]

6Then Paul, knowing that some of
them were Sadducees and the others
Pharisees, called out in the Sanhedrin,
"My brothers,[t] I am a Pharisee,[u] the
son of a Pharisee. I stand on trial because of my hope in the resurrection of
the dead."[v] 7When he said this, a dispute broke out between the Pharisees
and the Sadducees, and the assembly
was divided. 8(The Sadducees say that
there is no resurrection,[w] and that
there are neither angels nor spirits,
but the Pharisees acknowledge them
all.)

9There was a great uproar, and some
of the teachers of the law who were
Pharisees[x] stood up and argued vigorously. "We find nothing wrong with
this man,"[y] they said. "What if a spirit
or an angel has spoken to him?"[z]
10The dispute became so violent that
the commander was afraid Paul would
be torn to pieces by them. He ordered
the troops to go down and take him
away from them by force and bring
him into the barracks.[a]

11The following night the Lord stood
near Paul and said, "Take courage![b]
As you have testified about me in Jerusalem, so you must also testify in
Rome."[c]

The Plot to Kill Paul

12The next morning the Jews formed
a conspiracy and bound themselves
with an oath not to eat or drink until
they had killed Paul.[d] 13More than forty men were involved in this plot.
14They went to the chief priests and
elders and said, "We have taken a solemn oath not to eat anything until we
have killed Paul.[e] 15Now then, you
and the Sanhedrin[f] petition the commander to bring him before you on the
pretext of wanting more accurate information about his case. We are ready
to kill him before he gets here."

16But when the son of Paul's sister
heard of this plot, he went into the barracks[g] and told Paul.

17Then Paul called one of the centu-
rions and said, "Take this young man
to the commander; he has something
to tell him." 18So he took him to the
commander.

The centurion said, "Paul, the prisoner,[h] sent for me and asked me to
bring this young man to you because
he has something to tell you."

19The commander took the young
man by the hand, drew him aside and
asked, "What is it you want to tell me?"

20He said: "The Jews have agreed to
ask you to bring Paul before the Sanhedrin[i] tomorrow on the pretext of
wanting more accurate information
about him.[j] 21Don't give in to them,
because more than forty[k] of them are
waiting in ambush for him. They have
taken an oath not to eat or drink until
they have killed him.[l] They are ready
now, waiting for your consent to their
request."

22The commander dismissed the
young man and cautioned him, "Don't

23:1–27:44

BEFORE KINGS AND PRISONERS

PROMISE 7

These chapters read like an exciting adventure novel. They chronicle Paul's arrest, imprisonment, and the chain of events that led this man to Rome which was, in Paul's day, the undisputed power center of the known world. This ordeal, summarized in Acts 28:17–20, shows Paul as God's faithful servant in every situation—whether rotting in a prison cell (24:27) or preaching before kings (26:1–32).

God doesn't always call his servants to work for him in the spotlight. He even allowed Paul, the fiery apostle, to cool his heels in prison for months on end. While we don't know what Paul's prison experiences were, we can be assured that God used him to further his kingdom among Paul's fellow prisoners. We do know that letters he wrote, under God's inspiration, and sent to the churches while in prison have edified God's people for centuries.

Do you have the same passion for the gospel? God may not be calling you to preach before kings, but he is calling you to influence and serve those with whom you associate every day.

For the next Promise 7 reading go to page 1248.

23:1 [l]Ac 22:30 [m]Ac 22:5 [n]Ac 24:16; 1Co 4:4; 2Co 1:12; 2Ti 1:3; Heb 13:18 **23:2** [o]Ac 24:1 [p]Jn 18:22 **23:3** [q]Mt 23:27 [r]Lev 19:15; Dt 25:1,2; Jn 7:51 **23:5** [s]Ex 22:28 **23:6** [t]Ac 22:5 [u]Ac 26:5; Php 3:5 [v]Ac 24:15,21; 26:8 **23:8** [w]Mt 22:23 **23:9** [x]Mk 2:16 [y]ver 29; Ac 25:25; 26:31 [z]Ac 22:7,17,18 **23:10** [a]Ac 21:34 **23:11** [b]Ac 18:9 [c]Ac 19:21; 28:23 **23:12** [d]ver 14,21,30; Ac 25:3 **23:14** [e]ver 12 **23:15** [f]ver 1; Ac 22:30 **23:16** [g]ver 10; Ac 21:34 **23:18** [h]Eph 3:1 **23:20** [i]ver 1 [j]ver 14,15 **23:21** [k]ver 13 [l]ver 12,14

[a]5 Exodus 22:28

tell anyone that you have reported this
to me."

Paul Transferred to Caesarea

23Then he called two of his centuri-
ons and ordered them, "Get ready a
detachment of two hundred soldiers,
seventy horsemen and two hundred
spearmen[a] to go to Caesarea[m] at nine
tonight.[n] 24Provide mounts for Paul so
that he may be taken safely to Governor Felix."[o]
25He wrote a letter as follows:

26Claudius Lysias,

To His Excellency,[p] Governor Felix:

Greetings.[q]

27This man was seized by the
Jews and they were about to kill
him,[r] but I came with my troops
and rescued him,[s] for I had
learned that he is a Roman citizen.[t] 28I wanted to know why
they were accusing him, so I
brought him to their Sanhedrin.[u]
29I found that the accusation had
to do with questions about their
law,[v] but there was no charge
against him[w] that deserved death
or imprisonment. 30When I was
informed[x] of a plot[y] to be carried out against the man, I sent
him to you at once. I also ordered
his accusers[z] to present to you
their case against him.

31So the soldiers, carrying out their
orders, took Paul with them during the
night and brought him as far as An-
tipatris. 32The next day they let the
cavalry[a] go on with him, while they
returned to the barracks.[b] 33When
the cavalry[c] arrived in Caesarea,[d] they
delivered the letter to the governor[e]
and handed Paul over to him. 34The
governor read the letter and asked
what province he was from. Learning
that he was from Cilicia,[f] 35he said, "I
will hear your case when your accusers[g] get here." Then he ordered that
Paul be kept under guard[h] in Herod's
palace.

The Trial Before Felix

24 Five days later the high priest Ananias[i] went down to Caesarea with
some of the elders and a lawyer named
Tertullus, and they brought their
charges[j] against Paul before the governor.[k] 2When Paul was called in, Tertullus presented his case before Felix:
"We have enjoyed a long period of
peace under you, and your foresight
has brought about reforms in this nation. 3Everywhere and in every way,
most excellent[l] Felix, we acknowledge this with profound gratitude. 4But
in order not to weary you further, I
would request that you be kind enough
to hear us briefly.
5"We have found this man to be
a troublemaker, stirring up riots[m]
among the Jews[n] all over the world.
He is a ringleader of the Nazarene[o]
sect[p] 6and even tried to desecrate the
temple;[q] so we seized him. 8By[b] examining him yourself you will be able
to learn the truth about all these
charges we are bringing against him."
9The Jews joined in the accusation,[r] asserting that these things were
true.
10When the governor[s] motioned for
him to speak, Paul replied: "I know
that for a number of years you have
been a judge over this nation; so I gladly make my defense. 11You can easily
verify that no more than twelve days[t]
ago I went up to Jerusalem to worship.
12My accusers did not find me arguing
with anyone at the temple,[u] or stirring
up a crowd[v] in the synagogues or anywhere else in the city. 13And they cannot prove to you the charges they are
now making against me.[w] 14However,
I admit that I worship the God of our
fathers[x] as a follower of the Way,[y]
which they call a sect.[z] I believe everything that agrees with the Law and that
is written in the Prophets,[a] 15and I
have the same hope in God as these
men, that there will be a resurrection[b]
of both the righteous and the wicked.[c]
16So I strive always to keep my conscience clear[d] before God and man.
17"After an absence of several years,
I came to Jerusalem to bring my people
gifts for the poor[e] and to present offerings. 18I was ceremonially clean[f]
when they found me in the temple
courts doing this. There was no crowd
with me, nor was I involved in any disturbance.[g] 19But there are some Jews
from the province of Asia, who ought
to be here before you and bring
charges if they have anything against
me.[h] 20Or these who are here should
state what crime they found in me
when I stood before the Sanhedrin—
21unless it was this one thing I shouted

23:23 [m]Ac 8:40 [n]ver 33 **23:24** [o]ver 26,33; Ac 24:1-3,10; 25:14 **23:26** [p]Lk 1:3; Ac 24:3; 26:25 [q]Ac 15:23 **23:27** [r]Ac 21:32 [s]Ac 21:33 [t]Ac 22:25-29 **23:28** [u]Ac 22:30 **23:29** [v]Ac 18:15; 25:19 [w]ver 9; Ac 26:31 **23:30** [x]ver 20,21 [y]Ac 20:3 [z]ver 35; Ac 24:19; 25:16 **23:32** [a]ver 23 [b]Ac 21:34 **23:33** [c]ver 23,24 [d]Ac 8:40 [e]ver 26 **23:34** [f]Ac 6:9; 21:39 **23:35** [g]ver 30; Ac 24:19; 25:16 [h]Ac 24:27 **24:1** [i]Ac 23:2 [j]Ac 23:30,35 [k]Ac 23:24

24:3 [l]Lk 1:3; Ac 23:26; 26:25 **24:5** [m]Ac 16:20; 17:6 [n]Ac 21:28 [o]Mk 1:24 [p]ver 14; Ac 26:5; 28:22 **24:6** [q]Ac 21:28 **24:9** [r]1Th 2:16 **24:10** [s]Ac 23:24 **24:11** [t]Ac 21:27; ver 1 **24:12** [u]Ac 25:8; 28:17 [v]ver 18 **24:13** [w]Ac 25:7 **24:14** [x]Ac 3:13 [y]Ac 9:2 [z]ver 5 [a]Ac 26:6,22; 28:23 **24:15** [b]Ac 23:6; 28:20 [c]Da 12:2; Jn 5:28,29 **24:16** [d]Ac 23:1 **24:17** [e]Ac 11:29,30; Ro 15:25-28, 31; 1Co 16:1-4,15; 2Co 8:1-4; Gal 2:10 **24:18** [f]Ac 21:26 [g]ver 12 **24:19** [h]Ac 23:30

[a]*23* The meaning of the Greek for this word is uncertain. [b]*6-8* Some manuscripts *him and wanted to judge him according to our law. 7But the commander, Lysias, came and with the use of much force snatched him from our hands 8and ordered his accusers to come before you. By*

as I stood in their presence: 'It is concerning the resurrection of the dead that I am on trial before you today.' "[i]

[22]Then Felix, who was well acquainted with the Way, adjourned the proceedings. "When Lysias the commander comes," he said, "I will decide your case." [23]He ordered the centurion to keep Paul under guard[j] but to give him some freedom[k] and permit his friends to take care of his needs.[l]

[24]Several days later Felix came with his wife Drusilla, who was a Jewess. He sent for Paul and listened to him as he spoke about faith in Christ Jesus.[m] [25]As Paul discoursed on righteousness, self-control[n] and the judgment[o] to come, Felix was afraid and said, "That's enough for now! You may leave. When I find it convenient, I will send for you." [26]At the same time he was hoping that Paul would offer him a bribe, so he sent for him frequently and talked with him.

[27]When two years had passed, Felix was succeeded by Porcius Festus,[p] but because Felix wanted to grant a favor to the Jews,[q] he left Paul in prison.[r]

The Trial Before Festus

25 Three days after arriving in the province, Festus went up from Caesarea[s] to Jerusalem, [2]where the chief priests and Jewish leaders appeared before him and presented the charges against Paul.[t] [3]They urgently requested Festus, as a favor to them, to have Paul transferred to Jerusalem, for they were preparing an ambush to kill him along the way. [4]Festus answered, "Paul is being held[u] at Caesarea, and I myself am going there soon. [5]Let some of your leaders come with me and press charges against the man there, if he has done anything wrong."

[6]After spending eight or ten days with them, he went down to Caesarea, and the next day he convened the court[v] and ordered that Paul be brought before him. [7]When Paul appeared, the Jews who had come down from Jerusalem stood around him, bringing many serious charges against him,[w] which they could not prove.[x]

[8]Then Paul made his defense: "I have done nothing wrong against the law of the Jews or against the temple[y] or against Caesar."

[9]Festus, wishing to do the Jews a favor,[z] said to Paul, "Are you willing to go up to Jerusalem and stand trial before me there on these charges?"[a]

[10]Paul answered: "I am now standing before Caesar's court, where I ought to be tried. I have not done any wrong to the Jews, as you yourself know very well. [11]If, however, I am guilty of doing anything deserving death, I do not refuse to die. But if the charges brought against me by these Jews are not true, no one has the right to hand me over to them. I appeal to Caesar!"[b]

[12]After Festus had conferred with his council, he declared: "You have appealed to Caesar. To Caesar you will go!"

Festus Consults King Agrippa

[13]A few days later King Agrippa and Bernice arrived at Caesarea[c] to pay their respects to Festus. [14]Since they were spending many days there, Festus discussed Paul's case with the king. He said: "There is a man here whom Felix left as a prisoner.[d] [15]When I went to Jerusalem, the chief priests and elders of the Jews brought charges against him[e] and asked that he be condemned.

[16]"I told them that it is not the Roman custom to hand over any man before he has faced his accusers and has had an opportunity to defend himself against their charges.[f] [17]When they came here with me, I did not delay the case, but convened the court the next day and ordered the man to be brought in.[g] [18]When his accusers got up to speak, they did not charge him with any of the crimes I had expected. [19]Instead, they had some points of dispute[h] with him about their own religion[i] and about a dead man named Jesus who Paul claimed was alive. [20]I was at a loss how to investigate such matters; so I asked if he would be willing to go to Jerusalem and stand trial there on these charges.[j] [21]When Paul made his appeal to be held over for the Emperor's decision, I ordered him held until I could send him to Caesar."[k]

[22]Then Agrippa said to Festus, "I would like to hear this man myself."

He replied, "Tomorrow you will hear him."[l]

Paul Before Agrippa

[23]The next day Agrippa and Bernice[m] came with great pomp and entered the audience room with the high ranking officers and the leading men of the city. At the command of Festus, Paul was brought in. [24]Festus said: "King Agrippa, and all who are present with us, you see this man! The whole Jewish community[n] has petitioned me about him in Jerusalem and here in Caesarea, shouting that he ought not

24:21 [i]Ac 23:6
24:23 [j]Ac 23:35 [k]Ac 28:16 [l]Ac 23:16; 27:3
24:24 [m]Ac 20:21
24:25 [n]Gal 5:23; 2Pe 1:6 [o]Ac 10:42
24:27 [p]Ac 25:1,4,9, 14 [q]Ac 12:3; 25:9 [r]Ac 23:35; 25:14
25:1 [s]Ac 8:40
25:2 [t]ver 15; Ac 24:1
25:4 [u]Ac 24:23
25:6 [v]ver 17
25:7 [w]Mk 15:3; Lk 23:2,10; Ac 24:5,6 [x]Ac 24:13
25:8 [y]Ac 6:13; 24:12; 28:17
25:9 [z]Ac 24:27 [a]ver 20
25:11 [b]ver 21,25; Ac 26:32; 28:19
25:13 [c]Ac 8:40
25:14 [d]Ac 24:27
25:15 [e]ver 2; Ac 24:1
25:16 [f]ver 4,5; Ac 23:30
25:17 [g]ver 6,10
25:19 [h]Ac 18:15; 23:29 [i]Ac 17:22
25:20 [j]ver 9
25:21 [k]ver 11,12
25:22 [l]Ac 9:15
25:23 [m]ver 13; Ac 26:30
25:24 [n]ver 2,3,7

to live any longer.[o] 25I found he had
done nothing deserving of death,[p] but
because he made his appeal to the Emperor[q] I decided to send him to Rome.
26But I have nothing definite to write
to His Majesty about him. Therefore I
have brought him before all of you, and
especially before you, King Agrippa, so
that as a result of this investigation
I may have something to write. 27For
I think it is unreasonable to send
on a prisoner without specifying the
charges against him."

26 Then Agrippa said to Paul, "You
have permission to speak for yourself."[r]

So Paul motioned with his hand and
began his defense: 2"King Agrippa, I
consider myself fortunate to stand before you today as I make my defense
against all the accusations of the Jews,
3and especially so because you are well
acquainted with all the Jewish customs[s] and controversies.[t] Therefore,
I beg you to listen to me patiently.

4"The Jews all know the way I have
lived ever since I was a child,[u] from
the beginning of my life in my own
country, and also in Jerusalem. 5They
have known me for a long time[v] and
can testify, if they are willing, that according to the strictest sect of our religion, I lived as a Pharisee.[w] 6And now
it is because of my hope[x] in what God
has promised our fathers[y] that I am
on trial today. 7This is the promise our
twelve tribes[z] are hoping to see fulfilled as they earnestly serve God day
and night.[a] O king, it is because of
this hope that the Jews are accusing
me.[b] 8Why should any of you consider
it incredible that God raises the
dead?[c]

9"I too was convinced[d] that I ought
to do all that was possible to oppose[e]
the name of Jesus of Nazareth.[f] 10And
that is just what I did in Jerusalem. On
the authority of the chief priests I put
many of the saints[g] in prison,[h] and
when they were put to death, I cast my
vote against them.[i] 11Many a time I
went from one synagogue to another to
have them punished,[j] and I tried to
force them to blaspheme. In my obsession against them, I even went to foreign cities to persecute them.

12"On one of these journeys I was
going to Damascus with the authority
and commission of the chief priests.
13About noon, O king, as I was on the
road, I saw a light from heaven, brighter than the sun, blazing around me and
my companions. 14We all fell to the
ground, and I heard a voice[k] saying to
me in Aramaic,[a] 'Saul, Saul, why do
you persecute me? It is hard for you to
kick against the goads.'

15"Then I asked, 'Who are you,
Lord?'

" 'I am Jesus, whom you are persecuting,' the Lord replied. 16'Now get up
and stand on your feet.[l] I have appeared to you to appoint you as a servant and as a witness of what you have
seen of me and what I will show you.[m]
17I will rescue you[n] from your own
people and from the Gentiles.[o] I am
sending you to them 18to open their
eyes[p] and turn them from darkness to
light,[q] and from the power of Satan to
God, so that they may receive forgiveness of sins[r] and a place among those
who are sanctified by faith in me.'[s]

19"So then, King Agrippa, I was not
disobedient to the vision from heaven.
20First to those in Damascus,[t] then to
those in Jerusalem[u] and in all Judea,
and to the Gentiles[v] also, I preached
that they should repent[w] and turn to
God and prove their repentance by
their deeds.[x] 21That is why the Jews
seized me[y] in the temple courts and
tried to kill me.[z] 22But I have had
God's help to this very day, and so I
stand here and testify to small and
great alike. I am saying nothing beyond
what the prophets and Moses said
would happen[a]— 23that the Christ[b]
would suffer and, as the first to rise
from the dead,[b] would proclaim light
to his own people and to the Gentiles."[c]

24At this point Festus interrupted
Paul's defense. "You are out of your
mind,[d] Paul!" he shouted. "Your great
learning[e] is driving you insane."

25"I am not insane, most excellent[f]
Festus," Paul replied. "What I am saying is true and reasonable. 26The king is
familiar with these things,[g] and I can
speak freely to him. I am convinced
that none of this has escaped his notice, because it was not done in a corner. 27King Agrippa, do you believe the
prophets? I know you do."

28Then Agrippa said to Paul, "Do
you think that in such a short time you
can persuade me to be a Christian?"[h]

29Paul replied, "Short time or long—
I pray God that not only you but all
who are listening to me today may become what I am, except for these
chains."[i]

30The king rose, and with him the
governor and Bernice[j] and those sitting with them. 31They left the room,
and while talking with one another,
they said, "This man is not doing any-

25:24 [o]Ac 22:22
25:25 [p]Ac 23:9 [q]ver 11
26:1 [r]Ac 9:15; 25:22
26:3 [s]ver 7; Ac 6:14 [t]Ac 25:19
26:4 [u]Gal 1:13,14; Php 3:5
26:5 [v]Ac 22:3 [w]Ac 23:6; Php 3:5
26:6 [x]Ac 23:6; 24:15; 28:20 [y]Ac 13:32; Ro 15:8
26:7 [z]Jas 1:1 [a]1Th 3:10; 1Ti 5:5 [b]ver 2
26:8 [c]Ac 23:6
26:9 [d]1Ti 1:13 [e]Jn 16:2 [f]Jn 15:21
26:10 [g]Ac 9:13 [h]Ac 8:3; 9:2, 14,21 [i]Ac 22:20
26:11 [j]Mt 10:17
26:14 [k]Ac 9:7
26:16 [l]Eze 2:1; Da 10:11 [m]Ac 22:14,15
26:17 [n]Jer 1:8,19 [o]Ac 9:15
26:18 [p]Isa 35:5 [q]Isa 42:7,16; Eph 5:8; Col 1:13; 1Pe 2:9 [r]Lk 24:47; Ac 2:38 [s]Ac 20:21,32
26:20 [t]Ac 9:19-25 [u]Ac 9:26-29; 22:17-20 [v]Ac 9:15; 13:46 [w]Ac 3:19 [x]Mt 3:8; Lk 3:8
26:21 [y]Ac 21:27,30 [z]Ac 21:31
26:22 [a]Lk 24:27,44; Ac 10:43; 24:14
26:23 [b]1Co 15:20,23; Col 1:18; Rev 1:5 [c]Lk 2:32
26:24 [d]Jn 10:20; 1Co 4:10 [e]Jn 7:15
26:25 [f]Ac 23:26
26:26 [g]ver 3
26:28 [h]Ac 11:26
26:29 [i]Ac 21:33
26:30 [j]Ac 25:23

7 →PG. 1246

[a]14 Or *Hebrew* [b]23 Or *Messiah*

thing that deserves death or imprisonment."[k]
32Agrippa said to Festus, "This man
could have been set free[l] if he had not
appealed to Caesar."[m]

Paul Sails for Rome

27 When it was decided that we[n]
would sail for Italy,[o] Paul and
some other prisoners were handed
over to a centurion named Julius, who
belonged to the Imperial Regiment.[p]
2We boarded a ship from Adramyttium
about to sail for ports along the coast of
the province of Asia,[q] and we put out
to sea. Aristarchus,[r] a Macedonian[s]
from Thessalonica,[t] was with us.
3The next day we landed at Sidon;[u]
and Julius, in kindness to Paul,[v] allowed him to go to his friends so they
might provide for his needs.[w] 4From
there we put out to sea again and
passed to the lee of Cyprus because the
winds were against us.[x] 5When we
had sailed across the open sea off the
coast of Cilicia[y] and Pamphylia, we
landed at Myra in Lycia. 6There the
centurion found an Alexandrian ship[z]
sailing for Italy[a] and put us on board.
7We made slow headway for many
days and had difficulty arriving off
Cnidus. When the wind did not allow
us to hold our course,[b] we sailed to the
lee of Crete,[c] opposite Salmone. 8We
moved along the coast with difficulty
and came to a place called Fair Havens,
near the town of Lasea.
9Much time had been lost, and sailing had already become dangerous because by now it was after the Fast.[a][d]
So Paul warned them, 10"Men, I can
see that our voyage is going to be disastrous and bring great loss to ship and
cargo, and to our own lives also."[e]
11But the centurion, instead of listening to what Paul said, followed the advice of the pilot and of the owner of the
ship. 12Since the harbor was unsuitable
to winter in, the majority decided that
we should sail on, hoping to reach
Phoenix and winter there. This was a
harbor in Crete, facing both southwest
and northwest.

The Storm

13When a gentle south wind began
to blow, they thought they had obtained what they wanted; so they
weighed anchor and sailed along the
shore of Crete. 14Before very long, a
wind of hurricane force,[f] called the
"northeaster," swept down from the island. 15The ship was caught by the
storm and could not head into the
wind; so we gave way to it and were
driven along. 16As we passed to the lee
of a small island called Cauda, we were
hardly able to make the lifeboat secure.
17When the men had hoisted it aboard,
they passed ropes under the ship itself
to hold it together. Fearing that they
would run aground[g] on the sandbars
of Syrtis, they lowered the sea anchor
and let the ship be driven along. 18We
took such a violent battering from the
storm that the next day they began to
throw the cargo overboard.[h] 19On the
third day, they threw the ship's tackle
overboard with their own hands.
20When neither sun nor stars appeared
for many days and the storm continued raging, we finally gave up all hope
of being saved.
21After the men had gone a long time
without food, Paul stood up before
them and said: "Men, you should have
taken my advice[i] not to sail from
Crete;[j] then you would have spared
yourselves this damage and loss. 22But
now I urge you to keep up your courage,[k] because not one of you will be
lost; only the ship will be destroyed.
23Last night an angel[l] of the God
whose I am and whom I serve[m] stood
beside me[n] 24and said, 'Do not be
afraid, Paul. You must stand trial before Caesar;[o] and God has graciously
given you the lives of all who sail with
you.'[p] 25So keep up your courage,[q]
men, for I have faith in God that it will
happen just as he told me.[r] 26Never-
theless, we must run aground[s] on
some island."[t]

The Shipwreck

27On the fourteenth night we were
still being driven across the Adriatic[b]
Sea, when about midnight the sailors
sensed they were approaching land.
28They took soundings and found that
the water was a hundred and twenty
feet[c] deep. A short time later they took
soundings again and found it was
ninety feet[d] deep. 29Fearing that we
would be dashed against the rocks,
they dropped four anchors from the
stern and prayed for daylight. 30In an
attempt to escape from the ship, the
sailors let the lifeboat[u] down into the
sea, pretending they were going to lower some anchors from the bow. 31Then
Paul said to the centurion and the soldiers, "Unless these men stay with the
ship, you cannot be saved."[v] 32So the

26:31 [k]Ac 23:9
26:32 [l]Ac 28:18 [m]Ac 25:11
27:1 [n]Ac 16:10 [o]Ac 18:2; 25:12,25 [p]Ac 10:1
27:2 [q]Ac 2:9 [r]Ac 19:29 [s]Ac 16:9 [t]Ac 17:1
27:3 [u]Mt 11:21 [v]ver 43 [w]Ac 24:23; 28:16
27:4 [x]ver 7
27:5 [y]Ac 6:9
27:6 [z]Ac 28:11 [a]ver 1
27:7 [b]ver 4 [c]ver 12,13,21
27:9 [d]Lev 16:29-31; 23:27-29; Nu 29:7
27:10 [e]ver 21
27:14 [f]Mk 4:37
27:17 [g]ver 26,39
27:18 [h]ver 19,38; Jnh 1:5
27:21 [i]ver 10 [j]ver 7
27:22 [k]ver 25,36
27:23 [l]Ac 5:19 [m]Ro 1:9 [n]Ac 18:9; 23:11; 2Ti 4:17
27:24 [o]Ac 23:11 [p]ver 44
27:25 [q]ver 22,36 [r]Ro 4:20,21
27:26 [s]ver 17,39 [t]Ac 28:1
27:30 [u]ver 16
27:31 [v]ver 24

a *9* That is, the Day of Atonement (Yom Kippur)
b *27* In ancient times the name referred to an area extending well south of Italy.
c *28* Greek *twenty orguias* (about 37 meters)
d *28* Greek *fifteen orguias* (about 27 meters)

soldiers cut the ropes that held the lifeboat and let it fall away.
33Just before dawn Paul urged them
all to eat. "For the last fourteen days,"
he said, "you have been in constant
suspense and have gone without
food—you haven't eaten anything.
34Now I urge you to take some food.
You need it to survive. Not one of you
will lose a single hair from his head."[w]
35After he said this, he took some bread
and gave thanks to God in front of
them all. Then he broke it[x] and began
to eat. **36**They were all encouraged[y]
and ate some food themselves. **37**Altogether there were 276 of us on board.
38When they had eaten as much as they
wanted, they lightened the ship by
throwing the grain into the sea.[z]
39When daylight came, they did not
recognize the land, but they saw a bay
with a sandy beach,[a] where they decided to run the ship aground if they
could. **40**Cutting loose the anchors,[b]
they left them in the sea and at the
same time untied the ropes that held
the rudders. Then they hoisted the
foresail to the wind and made for the
beach. **41**But the ship struck a sandbar
and ran aground. The bow stuck fast
and would not move, and the stern was
broken to pieces by the pounding of
the surf.[c]
42The soldiers planned to kill the
prisoners to prevent any of them from
swimming away and escaping. **43**But
the centurion wanted to spare Paul's
life[d] and kept them from carrying out
their plan. He ordered those who could
swim to jump overboard first and get
to land. **44**The rest were to get there on
planks or on pieces of the ship. In this
way everyone reached land in safety.[e]

Ashore on Malta

28 Once safely on shore, we[f] found
out that the island[g] was called
Malta. **2**The islanders showed us unusual kindness. They built a fire and
welcomed us all because it was raining
and cold. **3**Paul gathered a pile of
brushwood and, as he put it on the fire,
a viper, driven out by the heat, fastened
itself on his hand. **4**When the islanders
saw the snake hanging from his
hand,[h] they said to each other, "This
man must be a murderer; for though
he escaped from the sea, Justice has
not allowed him to live."[i] **5**But Paul
shook the snake off into the fire and
suffered no ill effects.[j] **6**The people
expected him to swell up or suddenly
fall dead, but after waiting a long time
and seeing nothing unusual happen to
him, they changed their minds and
said he was a god.[k]
7There was an estate nearby that belonged to Publius, the chief official of
the island. He welcomed us to his
home and for three days entertained us
hospitably. **8**His father was sick in bed,
suffering from fever and dysentery.
Paul went in to see him and, after
prayer,[l] placed his hands on him and
healed him.[m] **9**When this had happened, the rest of the sick on the island
came and were cured. **10**They honored
us in many ways and when we were
ready to sail, they furnished us with the
supplies we needed.

5 →PG. 1247

Arrival at Rome

11After three months we put out to
sea in a ship that had wintered in the
island. It was an Alexandrian ship[n]
with the figurehead of the twin gods
Castor and Pollux. **12**We put in at Syra-
cuse and stayed there three days.
13From there we set sail and arrived at
Rhegium. The next day the south wind
came up, and on the following day
we reached Puteoli. **14**There we found
some brothers[o] who invited us to
spend a week with them. And so we
came to Rome. **15**The brothers[p] there
had heard that we were coming, and
they traveled as far as the Forum of
Appius and the Three Taverns to meet
us. At the sight of these men Paul
thanked God and was encouraged.
16When we got to Rome, Paul was allowed to live by himself, with a soldier
to guard him.[q]

2 →PG. 1247

Paul Preaches at Rome Under Guard

17Three days later he called together
the leaders of the Jews.[r] When they
had assembled, Paul said to them: "My
brothers,[s] although I have done nothing against our people[t] or against the
customs of our ancestors,[u] I was arrested in Jerusalem and handed over to
the Romans. **18**They examined me[v]
and wanted to release me,[w] because
I was not guilty of any crime deserving death.[x] **19**But when the Jews objected, I was compelled to appeal to
Caesar[y]—not that I had any charge to
bring against my own people. **20**For
this reason I have asked to see you and
talk with you. It is because of the hope
of Israel[z] that I am bound with this
chain."[a]
21They replied, "We have not received any letters from Judea concerning you, and none of the brothers[b]
who have come from there has reported or said anything bad about you.
22But we want to hear what your views

27:34 [w] Mt 10:30
27:35 [x] Mt 14:19
27:36 [y] ver 22,25
27:38 [z] ver 18; Jnh 1:5
27:39 [a] Ac 28:1
27:40 [b] ver 29
27:41 [c] 2Co 11:25
27:43 [d] ver 3
27:44 [e] ver 22,31
28:1 [f] Ac 16:10 [g] Ac 27:26,39
28:4 [h] Mk 16:18 [i] Lk 13:2,4
28:5 [j] Lk 10:19
28:6 [k] Ac 14:11
28:8 [l] Jas 5:14,15 [m] Ac 9:40
28:11 [n] Ac 27:6
28:14 [o] Ac 1:16
28:15 [p] Ac 1:16
28:16 [q] Ac 24:23; 27:3
28:17 [r] Ac 25:2 [s] Ac 22:5 [t] Ac 25:8 [u] Ac 6:14
28:18 [v] Ac 22:24 [w] Ac 26:31,32 [x] Ac 23:9
28:19 [y] Ac 25:11
28:20 [z] Ac 26:6,7 [a] Ac 21:33
28:21 [b] Ac 22:5

are, for we know that people everywhere are talking against this sect."[c]
23They arranged to meet Paul on a
certain day, and came in even larger
numbers to the place where he was
staying. From morning till evening he
explained and declared to them the
kingdom of God[d] and tried to convince them about Jesus[e] from the Law
of Moses and from the Prophets.[f]
24Some were convinced by what he
said, but others would not believe.[g]
25They disagreed among themselves
and began to leave after Paul had made
this final statement: "The Holy Spirit
spoke the truth to your forefathers
when he said through Isaiah the
prophet:

26" 'Go to this people and say,
"You will be ever hearing but never
understanding;
you will be ever seeing but never
perceiving."

28:22 [c]Ac 24:5,14
28:23 [d]Ac 19:8 [e]Ac 17:3 [f]Ac 8:35
28:24 [g]Ac 14:4
28:27 [h]Ps 119:70 [i]Isa 6:9,10
28:28 [j]Lk 2:30 [k]Ac 13:46
28:31 [l]ver 23; Mt 4:23

27For this people's heart has become
calloused;[h]
they hardly hear with their ears,
and they have closed their eyes.
Otherwise they might see with their
eyes,
hear with their ears,
understand with their hearts
and turn, and I would heal
them.'[a][i]

28"Therefore I want you to know that
God's salvation[j] has been sent to the
Gentiles,[k] and they will listen!"[b]
30For two whole years Paul stayed
there in his own rented house and welcomed all who came to see him.
31Boldly and without hindrance he
preached the kingdom of God[l] and
taught about the Lord Jesus Christ.

[a] *27* Isaiah 6:9,10 [b] *28* Some manuscripts *listen!" 29After he said this, the Jews left, arguing vigorously among themselves.*

ROMANS

AT A GLANCE

Key Principle: In spite of human sin, God offers his righteousness to us through the redemptive work of Jesus Christ, his Son, so that we can be justified by faith.
Author: Paul
Time and Place: A.D. 57 / Sent from Corinth to Rome
Key Verses: 1:16–17; 3:21–26; 10:9–10

BENEFIT

While the Gospels portray Jesus Christ's words and works, Romans develops the profound implications of Jesus' life, death and resurrection for those who trust in him. Romans is the Bible's most systematic and comprehensive theological treatise. In it Paul presents, more clearly than perhaps any other author in Scripture, the powerful themes of salvation, righteousness, faith, justification, redemption, atonement, reconciliation and Christ taking our sin upon himself. Romans 6—8 provides the supreme definition for the meaning of the spiritual life, and Romans 12—14 is crucial to our understanding of how our spirituality works in our everyday lives.

SETTING

During his stay in Corinth near the end of his third missionary journey in A.D. 57, Paul wrote this magnificent letter to the well-known and influential church in Rome. Although he had not yet visited that church, Paul had already met some of the believers in his travels (16:1–15). He spoke of his plan to visit this church after delivering a monetary offering from the churches of Macedonia and Achaia to the poor among the saints in Jerusalem (15:20–29). Paul was staying with Gaius of Corinth (16:23; 1 Corinthians 1:14) when he dictated this letter to Tertius (16:22) and gave it to Phoebe to deliver to Rome (16:1–2).

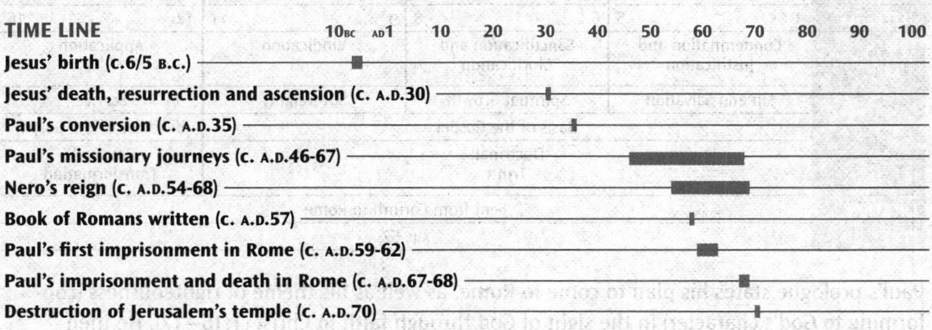

THEME AND PURPOSE

The theme of Romans, spelled out in chapter 1:16–17, is that the gospel "is the power of God for the salvation of everyone who believes" and has faith in Jesus Christ. In chapters 1—8 Paul unfolds God's sovereign plan of salvation, and in chapters 9—11 discusses God's relationship to Israel now that the Gentiles have the same access as the Jews to Israel's Messiah. Chapters 9—16 focus on how believers apply their life in Christ to various everyday situations.

Paul wrote this letter to prepare the Romans for his planned visit to them (which was delayed by a two-year imprisonment in Caesarea) and to ground them in the knowledge of the faith. He also wanted to encourage the Jews and Gentiles in the church in Rome to develop a spirit of unity in Christ. Finally, Paul wanted to solicit their prayer support at a transitional point in his ministry—he had completed his task of laying the foundation for the gospel in the eastern provinces, and was now hoping to do the same in the western provinces.

UNIQUE CONTRIBUTION

Romans is placed first in the list of Paul's letters because it is the longest and most foundational of his writings. It has been called "the cathedral of the Christian faith" because of its magnificent structure and sweeping scope. Romans contains the most complete and systematic treatment of the doctrines of sin and of salvation in Scripture, and its debate-like question-and-answer format and formal structure give it an eloquence and logical precision that has shaped Christian theology more than any other book. At the same time, Paul's clear and practical appeals to his readers make Romans a life-transforming book.

CHRIST IN ROMANS

Romans presents Christ as the Savior and Redeemer whose atoning work on the cross has made it possible for God "to be just and the one who justifies those who have faith in Jesus" (3:26). Jesus is the second Adam; his obedience has overcome the sin and separation established by the disobedience of the first Adam (5:12–20). It is through identification with Christ in his death, burial and resurrection that believers enjoy freedom from the power of sin and newness of life (6:1–18). In Christ, we have been delivered from the fear of condemnation to the joy of peace with God. Jesus is the basis for our redemption, justification, reconciliation, sanctification and glorification.

OVERVIEW

FOCUS	Problem and Provision of Righteousness	Power of Righteousness	Program of Righteousness	Practice of Righteousness
REFERENCE	1 — 5	6 — 8	9 — 11	12 — 16
TOPICS	Condemnation and Justification	Sanctification and Glorification	Vindication	Application
	Sin and Salvation	Spiritual Growth	Sovereignty	Service
	Basis of the Gospel			Behavior of the Gospel
	Doctrinal: Truth			Practical: Transformation
LOCATION	Sent from Corinth to Rome			
TIME	A.D. 57			

Paul's prologue states his plan to come to Rome, as well as his theme of righteousness (conforming to God's character) in the sight of God through faith in Christ (1:16–17). He then moves on to describe our sinful human condition, and the perfect right that God has to condemn both Gentiles and Jews because we've fallen so short of God's righteousness (1:18—3:20). But God's solution to this human dilemma is not found in condemnation; rather, he has provided a way out for us in Jesus Christ's redemptive and atoning work. Through faith in Christ, not by our own works, we accept his offer to be justified (declared righteous) by God

(3:21–31). Paul uses Abraham to illustrate this principle of justification by faith apart from works of the law (4). He then explains that God's love for us, even while we were in our sinful state, led to the obedient sacrifice of his Son, Jesus Christ. When we accept Christ's great work on our behalf, his righteousness is imputed (credited) to our account (5).

Paul says that people who accept Christ have been "united with him in his death." That's the basis for our new identity and destiny with him. We must acknowledge by faith that in Christ we have been brought from death to life, just as he was, and that we are no longer under the power of sin (6). Even though we continue to struggle with the pull of sin (7), God has given us the power of his indwelling Holy Spirit to accomplish in us what we could not do ourselves. Ultimately, our struggle with sin will end when we are glorified in resurrected bodies (8). Chapters 9—11 deal with the question of God's relationship to Israel now that the Gentiles have the same access to salvation in Christ.

Having developed the believer's position in Christ, Paul concludes his letter by addressing practical issues. Belief (1—11) is the foundation for behavior (12—16). Paul applies the dynamic of faith in Christ to relationships in the body of Christ (12), to submission to authority and to the needs of others (13) and to the principles and practice of Christian liberty (14:1—15:13). After stating his plans (15:14–33), Paul closes with a series of personal greetings and an admonition (16).

ROMANS

1 Paul, a servant of Christ Jesus, called to be an apostle[a] and set apart[b] for the gospel of God[c]— **2**the gospel he promised beforehand through his prophets in the Holy Scriptures[d] **3**regarding his Son, who as to his human nature[e] was a descendant of David, **4**and who through the Spirit**[a]** of holiness was declared with power to be the Son of God**[b]** by his resurrection from the dead: Jesus Christ our Lord. **5**Through him and for his name's sake, we received grace and apostleship to call people from among all the Gentiles[f] to the obedience that comes from faith.[g] **6**And you also are among those who are called to belong to Jesus Christ.[h]

7To all in Rome who are loved by God[i] and called to be saints:

Grace and peace to you from God our Father and from the Lord Jesus Christ.[j]

Paul's Longing to Visit Rome

8First, I thank my God through Jesus Christ for all of you,[k] because your faith is being reported all over the world.[l] **9**God, whom I serve[m] with my whole heart in preaching the gospel of his Son, is my witness[n] how constantly I remember you **10**in my prayers at all times; and I pray that now at last by God's will the way may be opened for me to come to you.[o]

11I long to see you[p] so that I may impart to you some spiritual gift to make you strong— **12**that is, that you and I may be mutually encouraged by each other's faith. **13**I do not want you to be unaware, brothers, that I planned many times to come to you (but have been prevented from doing so until now)[q] in order that I might have a harvest among you, just as I have had among the other Gentiles.

14I am obligated[r] both to Greeks and non-Greeks, both to the wise and the foolish. **15**That is why I am so eager to preach the gospel also to you who are at Rome.[s]

16I am not ashamed of the gospel,[t] because it is the power of God[u] for the salvation of everyone who believes: first for the Jew,[v] then for the Gentile.[w] **17**For in the gospel a righteousness from God is revealed,[x] a righteousness that is by faith from first to last,**[c]** just as it is written: "The righteous will live by faith."**[d]**[y]

God's Wrath Against Mankind

18The wrath of God[z] is being revealed from heaven against all the godlessness and wickedness of men who suppress the truth by their wickedness, **19**since what may be known about God is plain to them, because God has made it plain to them.[a] **20**For since the creation of the world God's invisible qualities—his eternal power and divine nature—have been clearly seen, being understood from what has been made,[b] so that men are without excuse.

21For although they knew God, they neither glorified him as God nor gave thanks to him, but their thinking became futile and their foolish hearts were darkened.[c] **22**Although they claimed to be wise, they became fools[d] **23**and exchanged the glory of the immortal God for images[e] made to look like mortal man and birds and animals and reptiles.

24Therefore God gave them over[f] in the sinful desires of their hearts to sexual impurity for the degrading of their bodies with one another.[g] **25**They exchanged the truth of God for a lie,[h] and worshiped and served created things[i] rather than the Creator—who is forever praised.[j] Amen.

26Because of this, God gave them over[k] to shameful lusts.[l] Even their women exchanged natural relations for unnatural ones.[m] **27**In the same way the men also abandoned natural relations with women and were inflamed with lust for one another. Men committed indecent acts with other men, and received in themselves the due penalty for their perversion.[n]

28Furthermore, since they did not think it worthwhile to retain the knowledge of God, he gave them over[o] to a depraved mind, to do what ought not to be done. **29**They have become filled with every kind of wickedness, evil, greed and depravity. They are full of envy, murder, strife, deceit and malice. They are gossips,[p] **30**slanderers, God-haters, insolent, arrogant and boastful; they invent ways of doing evil; they disobey their parents;[q] **31**they are

1:1 *a* 1Co 1:1 *b* Ac 9:15 *c* 2Co 11:7
1:2 *d* Gal 3:8
1:3 *e* Jn 1:14
1:5 *f* Ac 9:15 *g* Ac 6:7
1:6 *h* Rev 17:14
1:7 *i* Ro 8:39 *j* 1Co 1:3
1:8 *k* 1Co 1:4 *l* Ro 16:19
1:9 *m* 2Ti 1:3 *n* Php 1:8
1:10 *o* Ro 15:32
1:11 *p* Ro 15:23
1:13 *q* Ro 15:22,23
1:14 *r* 1Co 9:16
1:15 *s* Ro 15:20
1:16 *t* 2Ti 1:8 *u* 1Co 1:18 *v* Ac 3:26 *w* Ro 2:9,10
1:17 *x* Ro 3:21 *y* Hab 2:4; Gal 3:11; Heb 10:38
1:18 *z* Eph 5:6; Col 3:6
1:19 *a* Ac 14:17
1:20 *b* Ps 19:1-6
1:21 *c* Jer 2:5; Eph 4:17,18
1:22 *d* 1Co 1:20,27
1:23 *e* Ps 106:20; Jer 2:11; Ac 17:29
1:24 *f* Eph 4:19 *g* 1Pe 4:3
1:25 *h* Isa 44:20 *i* Jer 10:14 *j* Ro 9:5
1:26 *k* ver 24,28 *l* 1Th 4:5 *m* Lev 18:22,23
1:27 *n* Lev 18:22; 20:13
1:28 *o* ver 24,26
1:29 *p* 2Co 12:20
1:30 *q* 2Ti 3:2

a 4 Or *who as to his spirit* **b** 4 Or *was appointed to be the Son of God with power* **c** 17 Or *is from faith to faith* **d** 17 Hab. 2:4

senseless, faithless, heartless,[r] ruthless.
32 Although they know God's righteous
decree that those who do such things
deserve death,[s] they not only continue to do these very things but also approve[t] of those who practice them.

God's Righteous Judgment

2 You, therefore, have no excuse,[u]
you who pass judgment on someone
else, for at whatever point you judge
the other, you are condemning yourself, because you who pass judgment
do the same things.[v] 2 Now we know
that God's judgment against those who
do such things is based on truth. 3 So
when you, a mere man, pass judgment
on them and yet do the same things, do
you think you will escape God's judgment? 4 Or do you show contempt
for the riches[w] of his kindness,[x] tolerance[y] and patience,[z] not realizing
that God's kindness leads you toward
repentance?[a]

5 But because of your stubbornness
and your unrepentant heart, you are
storing up wrath against yourself for
the day of God's wrath, when his righteous judgment[b] will be revealed.
6 God "will give to each person accord-

1:31
[r] 2Ti 3:3
1:32
[s] Ro 6:23
[t] Ps 50:18; Lk 11:48; Ac 8:1; 22:20
2:1
[u] Ro 1:20
[v] 2Sa 12:5-7; Mt 7:1,2
2:4
[w] Ro 9:23; Eph 1:7,18; 2:7
[x] Ro 11:22
[y] Ro 3:25
[z] Ex 34:6
[a] 2Pe 3:9
2:5
[b] Jude 6
2:6
[c] Ps 62:12; Mt 16:27
2:7
[d] ver 10
[e] 1Co 15:53,54
2:8
[f] 2Th 2:12
2:9
[g] 1Pe 4:17
2:10
[h] ver 9
2:11
[i] Ac 10:34
2:12
[j] Ro 3:19; 1Co 9:20,21
2:13
[k] Jas 1:22,23,25
2:14
[l] Ac 10:35

ing to what he has done."[a][c] 7 To those
who by persistence in doing good seek
glory, honor[d] and immortality,[e] he
will give eternal life. 8 But for those who
are self-seeking and who reject the
truth and follow evil,[f] there will be
wrath and anger. 9 There will be trouble
and distress for every human being
who does evil: first for the Jew, then for
the Gentile;[g] 10 but glory, honor and
peace for everyone who does good:
first for the Jew, then for the Gentile.[h]
11 For God does not show favoritism.[i]

12 All who sin apart from the law will
also perish apart from the law, and all
who sin under the law[j] will be judged
by the law. 13 For it is not those who 1 →PG. 1240
hear the law who are righteous in
God's sight, but it is those who obey[k]
the law who will be declared righteous.
14 (Indeed, when Gentiles, who do not
have the law, do by nature things required by the law,[l] they are a law for
themselves, even though they do not
have the law, 15 since they show that
the requirements of the law are written
on their hearts, their consciences also
bearing witness, and their thoughts
now accusing, now even defending

[a] 6 Psalm 62:12; Prov. 24:12

1:18–32

PROMISE 3

UNCONTROLLED APPETITE

God has revealed himself to humanity through creation. If people respond to that revelation by turning away from God, they'll experience God's judgment. But that judgment won't come in the way they might expect. God seldom strikes people with a bolt of lightning or makes the earth open up to swallow a person. His wrath, or judgment, comes as he allows their uncontrolled and distorted appetites to consume them.

These appetites are part of the sinful nature; unless held in check through the power of God's Spirit, they inevitably lead to physical and spiritual destruction. But notice where this passage begins: The people Paul describes know God, yet they deliberately cover the truth with their own wickedness (v. 18). This kind of denial and betrayal begins deep in the heart, and is eventually evidenced in the body and the soul.

Paul says that God will hand such people over to their sinful desires (vv. 24–25). Without God's Spirit and law to restrain them, their impure appetites will sweep them into an immoral lifestyle. To justify their behavior they'll have to find a religious system that permits immorality. If they can't find one, they'll create one.

God will also give them over to "shameful lusts" (v. 26). They'll do those things they once considered abnormal and degrading and will indulge in activities that, in the past, they would have hidden from others. Ultimately, their own unbridled passions will destroy them.

Finally, God will hand them over to a "depraved mind" (v. 28). Once that happens, they won't be able to tell right from wrong. Paul lists 21 examples of such thinking. He concludes his discussion with a shocking statement. Those with a depraved mind *know* their behavior displeases God. They're *aware* that God's judgment will fall upon them. Yet, not only do they continue in their lifestyle, they also applaud others who live the same way.

In the context of Paul's letter to the Romans, the apostle wants us to know that sin is serious. It's progressive. It's deadly. But as the rest of the letter points out, there is forgiveness and freedom in Jesus Christ.

As you look at our society, doesn't it seem as though God's judgment is already falling upon it? Maybe you've been feeding your sensual appetites in a sinful way. If so, put on the brakes now—it's never to late to repent and turn back to God. Allow your character to be molded constructively by God, not destroyed by your sinful appetites.

For the next Promise 3 reading go to page 1241.

them.) 16 This will take place on the day
when God will judge men's secrets[m]
through Jesus Christ,[n] as my gospel[o]
declares.

The Jews and the Law

17 Now you, if you call yourself a Jew;
if you rely on the law and brag about
your relationship to God;[p] 18 if you
know his will and approve of what is
superior because you are instructed by
the law; 19 if you are convinced that you
are a guide for the blind, a light for
those who are in the dark, 20 an instructor of the foolish, a teacher of infants,
because you have in the law the embodiment of knowledge and truth—
21 you, then, who teach others, do you
not teach yourself? You who preach
against stealing, do you steal?[q] 22 You
who say that people should not commit adultery, do you commit adultery?
You who abhor idols, do you rob temples?[r] 23 You who brag about the
law,[s] do you dishonor God by breaking the law? 24 As it is written: "God's
name is blasphemed among the Gentiles because of you."[a][t]

25 Circumcision has value if you observe the law,[u] but if you break the
law, you have become as though you
had not been circumcised.[v] 26 If those
who are not circumcised keep the law's
requirements,[w] will they not be regarded as though they were circumcised?[x] 27 The one who is not circumcised physically and yet obeys the law
will condemn you[y] who, even though
you have the[b] written code and circumcision, are a lawbreaker.

3 →PG. 1241
28 A man is not a Jew if he is only one
outwardly,[z] nor is circumcision merely outward and physical.[a] 29 No, a man
is a Jew if he is one inwardly; and circumcision is circumcision of the heart,
by the Spirit,[b] not by the written
code.[c] Such a man's praise is not from
men, but from God.[d]

God's Faithfulness

3 What advantage, then, is there in being a Jew, or what value is there in
circumcision? 2 Much in every way!
First of all, they have been entrusted
with the very words of God.[e]

3 What if some did not have faith?[f]
Will their lack of faith nullify God's
faithfulness?[g] 4 Not at all! Let God be
true,[h] and every man a liar.[i] As it is
written:

"So that you may be proved right
when you speak
and prevail when you judge."[c][j]

5 But if our unrighteousness brings
out God's righteousness more clearly,
what shall we say? That God is unjust
in bringing his wrath on us? (I am using
a human argument.)[k] 6 Certainly not!
If that were so, how could God judge
the world?[l] 7 Someone might argue,
"If my falsehood enhances God's
truthfulness and so increases his glory,[m] why am I still condemned as a
sinner?" 8 Why not say—as we are being slanderously reported as saying
and as some claim that we say—"Let
us do evil that good may result"?[n]
Their condemnation is deserved.

No One Is Righteous

9 What shall we conclude then? Are
we any better[d]? Not at all! We have
already made the charge that Jews and
Gentiles alike are all under sin.[o] 10 As it
is written:

"There is no one righteous, not
even one;
11 there is no one who understands,
no one who seeks God.
12 All have turned away,

2:16 [m]Ecc 12:14 [n]Ac 10:42 [o]Ro 16:25
2:17 [p]ver 23; Mic 3:11; Ro 9:4
2:21 [q]Mt 23:3,4
2:22 [r]Ac 19:37
2:23 [s]ver 17
2:24 [t]Isa 52:5; Eze 36:22
2:25 [u]Gal 5:3 [v]Jer 4:4
2:26 [w]Ro 8:4 [x]1Co 7:19
2:27 [y]Mt 12:41,42
2:28 [z]Mt 3:9; Jn 8:39; Ro 9:6,7 [a]Gal 6:15
2:29 [b]Php 3:3; Col 2:11 [c]Ro 7:6 [d]Jn 5:44; 1Co 4:5; 2Co 10:18; 1Th 2:4; 1Pe 3:4
3:2 [e]Dt 4:8; Ps 147:19
3:3 [f]Heb 4:2 [g]2Ti 2:13
3:4 [h]Jn 3:33 [i]Ps 116:11 [j]Ps 51:4
3:5 [k]Ro 6:19; Gal 3:15
3:6 [l]Ge 18:25
3:7 [m]ver 4
3:8 [n]Ro 6:1
3:9 [o]ver 19,23; Gal 3:22

a *24* Isaiah 52:5; Ezek. 36:22 b *27* Or *who, by means of a* c *4* Psalm 51:4 d *9* Or *worse*

3:21–31

JUSTIFIED BY GOD

Paul makes one thing clear in the first three chapters of Romans: All people are guilty before God and deserving of his judgment. Not one person alive can do anything to earn God's favor.

How, then, do we find salvation? Paul says we are "justified" by God's "grace." The word "justification" refers to the act by which God, the righteous Judge, declares guilty sinners "not guilty." God freely gives us this forgiveness; it isn't something we earn.

Does God overlook sin? No. He demands payment. In Old Testament times God temporarily accepted the blood of animals as payment for sin. However, the death of goats and lambs ultimately could not pay the price for the sins of a human. Those sacrifices were only a symbol of the perfect sacrifice that God's Son would one day offer.

Through his death on the cross, Jesus offered his life as a blood sacrifice to satisfy God's demand that the sin of the world be paid for. Now, because of Jesus' blood, God can declare us righteous. But there is a condition: We must believe that Jesus' death has satisfied God's demand that payment be made for our sins. We must also trust Jesus to provide us with God's forgiveness.

they have together become
worthless;
there is no one who does good,
not even one."[a][p]
13"Their throats are open graves;
their tongues practice
deceit."[b][q]
"The poison of vipers is on their
lips."[c][r]
14 "Their mouths are full of cursing
and bitterness."[d][s]
15"Their feet are swift to shed blood;
16 ruin and misery mark their ways,
17and the way of peace they do not
know."[e]
18 "There is no fear of God before
their eyes."[f][t]

19Now we know that whatever the
law says,[u] it says to those who are under the law,[v] so that every mouth may
be silenced and the whole world held
accountable to God. 20Therefore no
one will be declared righteous in his
sight by observing the law;[w] rather,
through the law we become conscious
of sin.[x]

Righteousness Through Faith

21But now a righteousness from
God,[y] apart from law, has been made
known, to which the Law and the
Prophets testify.[z] 22This righteousness from God comes through faith[a]
in Jesus Christ to all who believe. There
is no difference,[b] 23for all have sinned
and fall short of the glory of God, 24and
are justified freely by his grace[c]
through the redemption[d] that came
by Christ Jesus. 25God presented him
as a sacrifice of atonement,[g][e] through
faith in his blood.[f] He did this to demonstrate his justice, because in his
forbearance he had left the sins committed beforehand unpunished[g]—
26he did it to demonstrate his justice
at the present time, so as to be just and
the one who justifies those who have
faith in Jesus.

27Where, then, is boasting?[h] It is excluded. On what principle? On that of
observing the law? No, but on that of
faith. 28For we maintain that a man is
justified by faith apart from observing
the law.[i] 29Is God the God of Jews
only? Is he not the God of Gentiles
too? Yes, of Gentiles too,[j] 30since there
is only one God, who will justify the
circumcised by faith and the uncircumcised through that same faith.[k]
31Do we, then, nullify the law by this
faith? Not at all! Rather, we uphold
the law.

3:12 [p]Ps 14:1-3
3:13 [q]Ps 5:9 [r]Ps 140:3
3:14 [s]Ps 10:7
3:18 [t]Ps 36:1
3:19 [u]Jn 10:34 [v]Ro 2:12
3:20 [w]Ac 13:39; Gal 2:16 [x]Ro 7:7
3:21 [y]Ro 1:17; 9:30 [z]Ac 10:43
3:22 [a]Ro 9:30 [b]Ro 10:12; Gal 3:28; Col 3:11
3:24 [c]Ro 4:16; Eph 2:8 [d]Eph 1:7,14; Col 1:14; Heb 9:12
3:25 [e]1Jn 4:10 [f]Heb 9:12,14 [g]Ac 17:30
3:27 [h]Ro 2:17,23; 4:2; 1Co 1:29-31; Eph 2:9
3:28 [i]ver 20,21; Ac 13:39; Eph 2:9
3:29 [j]Ro 9:24
3:30 [k]Gal 3:8

Abraham Justified by Faith

4 What then shall we say that Abraham, our forefather, discovered in
this matter? 2If, in fact, Abraham was
justified by works, he had something to
boast about—but not before God.[l]
3What does the Scripture say? "Abraham believed God, and it was credited
to him as righteousness."[h][m]
4Now when a man works, his wages
are not credited to him as a gift,[n] but
as an obligation. 5However, to the man
who does not work but trusts God who
justifies the wicked, his faith is credited
as righteousness. 6David says the same
thing when he speaks of the blessedness of the man to whom God credits
righteousness apart from works:

7"Blessed are they
whose transgressions are forgiven,
whose sins are covered.
8Blessed is the man
whose sin the Lord will never
count against him."[i][o]

9Is this blessedness only for the circumcised, or also for the uncircumcised?[p] We have been saying that
Abraham's faith was credited to him
as righteousness.[q] 10Under what circumstances was it credited? Was it after he was circumcised, or before? It
was not after, but before! 11And he received the sign of circumcision, a seal

4:2 [l]1Co 1:31
4:3 [m]ver 5,9,22; Ge 15:6; Gal 3:6; Jas 2:23
4:4 [n]Ro 11:6
4:8 [o]Ps 32:1,2; 2Co 5:19
4:9 [p]Ro 3:30 [q]ver 3

a *12* Psalms 14:1-3; 53:1-3; Eccles. 7:20
b *13* Psalm 5:9 c *13* Psalm 140:3
d *14* Psalm 10:7 e *17* Isaiah 59:7,8
f *18* Psalm 36:1 g *25* Or *as the one who would turn aside his wrath, taking away sin*
h *3* Gen. 15:6; also in verse 22 i *8* Psalm 32:1,2

4:1-25

PROMISE 1

JUSTIFIED BY FAITH

Must a person participate in any religious ritual to be saved from the penalty of sin?

Paul teaches that all people are made right with God by faith in Jesus Christ apart from anything they might do to win God's favor. He validates this statement by reminding them that God declared Abraham, the father of the Jewish people, righteous *before* he received the rite of circumcision. Abraham wasn't justified by keeping God's law, but by believing God's promise (vv. 13–22).

If you want to be a godly man, remember that neither rituals nor good deeds will help you win God's favor. Salvation isn't based on something you do for God; it involves accepting what God has already done for you through his Son, Jesus Christ.

For the next Promise 1 reading go to page 1240.

of the righteousness that he had by faith while he was still uncircumcised.[r] So then, he is the father[s] of all who believe[t] but have not been circumcised, in order that righteousness might be credited to them. **12**And he is also the father of the circumcised who not only are circumcised but who also walk in the footsteps of the faith that our father Abraham had before he was circumcised.

13It was not through law that Abraham and his offspring received the promise[u] that he would be heir of the world,[v] but through the righteousness that comes by faith. **14**For if those who live by law are heirs, faith has no value and the promise is worthless,[w] **15**because law brings wrath.[x] And where there is no law there is no transgression.[y]

16Therefore, the promise comes by faith, so that it may be by grace[z] and may be guaranteed[a] to all Abraham's offspring—not only to those who are of the law but also to those who are of the faith of Abraham. He is the father of us all. **17**As it is written: "I have made you a father of many nations."[a][b] He is our father in the sight of God, in whom he believed—the God who gives life[c] to the dead and calls[d] things that are not[e] as though they were.

1 →PG. 1243

18Against all hope, Abraham in hope believed and so became the father of many nations,[f] just as it had been said to him, "So shall your offspring be."[b][g] **19**Without weakening in his faith, he faced the fact that his body was as good as dead[h]—since he was about a hundred years old[i]—and that Sarah's womb was also dead.[j] **20**Yet he did not waver through unbelief regarding the promise of God, but was strengthened in his faith and gave glory to God,[k] **21**being fully persuaded that God had power to do what he had promised.[l] **22**This is why "it was credited to him as righteousness."[m] **23**The words "it was credited to him" were written not for him alone, **24**but also for us,[n] to whom God will credit righteousness—for us who believe in him[o] who raised Jesus our Lord from the dead.[p] **25**He was delivered over to death for our sins[q] and was raised to life for our justification.

Peace and Joy

5 Therefore, since we have been justified through faith,[r] we[c] have peace with God through our Lord Jesus Christ, **2**through whom we have gained access[s] by faith into this grace in which we now stand.[t] And we[c] rejoice in the hope[u] of the glory of God. **3**Not only so, but we[c] also rejoice in our sufferings,[v] because we know that suffering produces perseverance;[w] **4**perseverance, character; and character, hope. **5**And hope[x] does not disappoint us, because God has poured out his love into our hearts by the Holy Spirit,[y] whom he has given us.

6You see, at just the right time,[z] when we were still powerless, Christ died for the ungodly.[a] **7**Very rarely will anyone die for a righteous man, though for a good man someone might possibly dare to die. **8**But God demonstrates his own love for us in this: While we were still sinners, Christ died for us.[b]

6 →PG. 1245

9Since we have now been justified by his blood,[c] how much more shall we be saved from God's wrath[d] through him! **10**For if, when we were God's enemies,[e] we were reconciled[f] to him through the death of his Son, how much more, having been reconciled, shall we be saved through his life![g] **11**Not only is this so, but we also rejoice in God through our Lord Jesus Christ, through whom we have now received reconciliation.

Death Through Adam, Life Through Christ

12Therefore, just as sin entered the world through one man,[h] and death through sin,[i] and in this way death came to all men, because all sinned—**13**for before the law was given, sin was in the world. But sin is not taken into account when there is no law.[j] **14**Nev-

a *17* Gen. 17:5 b *18* Gen. 15:5 c *1,2,3* Or *let us*

4:11 [r]Ge 17:10,11 [s]ver 16,17; Lk 19:9 [t]Ro 3:22
4:13 [u]Gal 3:16,29 [v]Ge 17:4-6
4:14 [w]Gal 3:18
4:15 [x]Ro 7:7-25; 1Co 15:56; 2Co 3:7; Gal 3:10; Ro 7:12 [y]Ro 3:20; 7:7
4:16 [z]Ro 3:24 [a]Ro 15:8
4:17 [b]Ge 17:5 [c]Jn 5:21 [d]Isa 48:13 [e]1Co 1:28
4:18 [f]ver 17 [g]Ge 15:5
4:19 [h]Heb 11:11,12 [i]Ge 17:17 [j]Ge 18:11
4:20 [k]Mt 9:8
4:21 [l]Ge 18:14; Heb 11:19
4:22 [m]ver 3
4:24 [n]Ro 15:4; 1Co 9:10; 10:11 [o]Ro 10:9 [p]Ac 2:24
4:25 [q]Isa 53:5,6; Ro 5:6,8
5:1 [r]Ro 3:28
5:2 [s]Eph 2:18 [t]1Co 15:1 [u]Heb 3:6
5:3 [v]Mt 5:12 [w]Jas 1:2,3
5:5 [x]Php 1:20 [y]Ac 2:33
5:6 [z]Gal 4:4 [a]Ro 4:25
5:8 [b]Jn 15:13; 1Pe 3:18
5:9 [c]Ro 3:25 [d]Ro 1:18
5:10 [e]Ro 11:28; Col 1:21 [f]2Co 5:18,19; Col 1:20,22 [g]Ro 8:34
5:12 [h]ver 15,16,17; 1Co 15:21,22 [i]Ge 2:17; 3:19; Ro 6:23
5:13 [j]Ro 4:15

5:1-5

PROMISE 1

PEACE, HOPE, AND LOVE

At one time or another, most men search for happiness in the wrong way. We try to find it in seeking money, power, pleasure and fame. But Paul tells us where we can find the most sought-after things in life. He lists three practical benefits of following Christ: peace with God (v. 1), hope in affliction (v. 3), and love that's unconditional (v. 5).

Look over your life and identify the places, things or experiences you go to in search of happiness. Do they actually produce happiness? Does that happiness last? Now consider the three benefits of knowing Christ that Paul mentions. These benefits hold considerable power to change your whole outlook on life (and death!). They go far beyond any search for temporary happiness.

For the next Promise 1 reading go to page 1244.

ertheless, death reigned from the time of Adam to the time of Moses, even over those who did not sin by breaking a command, as did Adam, who was a pattern of the one to come.[k]

15But the gift is not like the trespass. For if the many died by the trespass of the one man,[l] how much more did God's grace and the gift that came by the grace of the one man, Jesus Christ,[m] overflow to the many! 16Again, the gift of God is not like the result of the one man's sin: The judgment followed one sin and brought condemnation, but the gift followed many trespasses and brought justification. 17For if, by the trespass of the one man, death[n] reigned through that one man, how much more will those who receive God's abundant provision of grace and of the gift of righteousness reign in life through the one man, Jesus Christ.

18Consequently, just as the result of one trespass was condemnation for all men,[o] so also the result of one act of righteousness was justification[p] that brings life for all men. 19For just as through the disobedience of the one man[q] the many were made sinners, so also through the obedience[r] of the one man the many will be made righteous.

20The law was added so that the trespass might increase.[s] But where sin increased, grace increased all the more,[t] 21so that, just as sin reigned in death,[u] so also grace might reign through righteousness to bring eternal life through Jesus Christ our Lord.

Dead to Sin, Alive in Christ

3 →PG. 1242

6 What shall we say, then? Shall we go on sinning so that grace may increase?[v] 2By no means! We died to sin;[w] how can we live in it any longer? 3Or don't you know that all of us who were baptized[x] into Christ Jesus were baptized into his death? 4We were therefore buried with him through baptism into death in order that, just as Christ was raised from the dead[y] through the glory of the Father, we too may live a new life.[z]

5If we have been united with him like this in his death, we will certainly also be united with him in his resurrection.[a] 6For we know that our old self[b] was crucified with him[c] so that the body of sin[d] might be done away with,[a] that we should no longer be slaves to sin— 7because anyone who has died has been freed from sin.

8Now if we died with Christ, we believe that we will also live with him. 9For we know that since Christ was raised from the dead,[e] he cannot die again; death no longer has mastery over him.[f] 10The death he died, he died to sin[g] once for all; but the life he lives, he lives to God.

11In the same way, count yourselves dead to sin[h] but alive to God in Christ Jesus. 12Therefore do not let sin reign in your mortal body so that you obey its evil desires. 13Do not offer the parts of your body to sin, as instruments of wickedness,[i] but rather offer yourselves to God, as those who have been brought from death to life; and offer the parts of your body to him as instruments of righteousness.[j] 14For sin shall not be your master, because you are not under law,[k] but under grace.[l]

Slaves to Righteousness

15What then? Shall we sin because we are not under law but under grace? By no means! 16Don't you know that when you offer yourselves to someone to obey him as slaves, you are slaves to

5:14 [k]1Co 15:22,45 **5:15** [l]ver 12,18,19 [m]Ac 15:11 **5:17** [n]ver 12 **5:18** [o]ver 12 [p]Ro 4:25 **5:19** [q]ver 12 [r]Php 2:8 **5:20** [s]Ro 7:7,8; Gal 3:19 [t]1Ti 1:13,14 **5:21** [u]ver 12,14 **6:1** [v]ver 15; Ro 3:5,8 **6:2** [w]Col 3:3,5; 1Pe 2:24 **6:3** [x]Mt 28:19 **6:4** [y]Col 2:12 [z]Ro 7:6; Gal 6:15; Eph 4:22-24; Col 3:10 **6:5** [a]2Co 4:10; Php 3:10,11 **6:6** [b]Eph 4:22; Col 3:9 [c]Gal 2:20; Col 2:12,20 [d]Ro 7:24 **6:9** [e]Ac 2:24 [f]Rev 1:18 **6:10** [g]ver 2 **6:11** [h]ver 2 **6:13** [i]ver 16,19; Ro 7:5 [j]Ro 12:1; 1Pe 2:24 **6:14** [k]Gal 5:18 [l]Ro 3:24

[a]6 Or *be rendered powerless*

6:1–14

PROMISE 3

WHY NOT SIN?

"If salvation is a gift, what's to keep me from sinning?" Perhaps you've asked that question yourself a time or two, or perhaps someone has asked it of you. Fortunately, Paul anticipated that question and gave a pointed answer. Why not sin? Because as a believer, you are spiritually identified with Jesus in his death and resurrection. And because sin has no power over Jesus, it has no power over you or over others who are united with him.

So, then, are Jesus' followers free from sinful appetites? No (although they wish they could be!), but those appetites no longer have unbridled power over them. Think of sin and its effects as a motorcycle with a disconnected chain. The engine (sin) still has great power, but it can't turn the wheels (action). Similarly, for followers of Jesus, the chain that drives their sinful activity has been disconnected. Their sinful motor is still there, and at times they may re-engage the chain. But the more they realize they're liberated from sin's power, the more they find themselves living free of its appetites.

If you've accepted Jesus' resurrection, you no longer have to pray for power over sin. You already have that. Instead, pray that you'll utilize the power you have. Ask for the grace you need to stand in the freedom Jesus has given you.

For the next Promise 3 reading go to page 1243.

the one whom you obey—whether you are slaves to sin,[m] which leads to death,[n] or to obedience, which leads to righteousness? **17**But thanks be to God[o] that, though you used to be slaves to sin, you wholeheartedly obeyed the form of teaching[p] to which you were entrusted. **18**You have been set free from sin[q] and have become slaves to righteousness.

19I put this in human terms[r] because you are weak in your natural selves. Just as you used to offer the parts of your body in slavery to impurity and to ever-increasing wickedness, so now offer them in slavery to righteousness[s] leading to holiness. **20**When you were slaves to sin,[t] you were free from the control of righteousness. **21**What benefit did you reap at that time from the things you are now ashamed of? Those things result in death![u] **22**But now that you have been set free from sin[v] and have become slaves to God,[w] the benefit you reap leads to holiness, and the result is eternal life. **23**For the wages of sin is death,[x] but the gift of God is eternal life[y] in[a] Christ Jesus our Lord.

An Illustration From Marriage

7 Do you not know, brothers[z]—for I am speaking to men who know the law—that the law has authority over a man only as long as he lives? **2**For example, by law a married woman is bound to her husband as long as he is alive, but if her husband dies, she is released from the law of marriage.[a] **3**So then, if she marries another man while her husband is still alive, she is called an adulteress. But if her husband dies, she is released from that law and is not an adulteress, even though she marries another man.

3 →PG. 1243

4So, my brothers, you also died to the law[b] through the body of Christ,[c] that you might belong to another, to him who was raised from the dead, in order that we might bear fruit to God. **5**For when we were controlled by the sinful nature,[b] the sinful passions aroused by the law[d] were at work in our bodies,[e] so that we bore fruit for death. **6**But now, by dying to what once bound us, we have been released from the law so that we serve in the new way of the Spirit, and not in the old way of the written code.[f]

Struggling With Sin

7What shall we say, then? Is the law sin? Certainly not! Indeed I would not have known what sin was except through the law.[g] For I would not have known what coveting really was if the law had not said, "Do not covet."[c][h] **8**But sin, seizing the opportunity afforded by the commandment,[i] produced in me every kind of covetous desire. For apart from law, sin is dead.[j] **9**Once I was alive apart from law; but when the commandment came, sin sprang to life and I died. **10**I found that the very commandment that was intended to bring life[k] actually brought death. **11**For sin, seizing the opportunity afforded by the commandment, deceived me,[l] and through the commandment put me to death. **12**So then, the law is holy, and the commandment is holy, righteous and good.[m]

13Did that which is good, then, become death to me? By no means! But in order that sin might be recognized as sin, it produced death in me through what was good, so that through the commandment sin might become utterly sinful.

14We know that the law is spiritual; but I am unspiritual,[n] sold[o] as a slave to sin. **15**I do not understand what I do. For what I want to do I do not do, but what I hate I do.[p] **16**And if I do what I do not want to do, I agree that the law is good.[q] **17**As it is, it is no longer I myself who do it, but it is sin living in me.[r] **18**I know that nothing good lives in me, that is, in my sinful nature.[d][s] For I have the desire to do what is good, but I cannot carry it out. **19**For what I do is not the good I want to do; no, the evil I do not want to do—this I keep on doing.[t] **20**Now if I do what I do not want to do, it is no longer I who do it, but it is sin living in me that does it.[u]

21So I find this law at work:[v] When I want to do good, evil is right there with me. **22**For in my inner being[w] I delight in God's law;[x] **23**but I see another law at work in the members of my body, waging war[y] against the law of my mind and making me a prisoner of the law of sin at work within my members. **24**What a wretched man I am! Who will rescue me from this body of death?[z] **25**Thanks be to God—through Jesus Christ our Lord!

So then, I myself in my mind am a slave to God's law, but in the sinful nature a slave to the law of sin.

Life Through the Spirit

8 Therefore, there is now no condemnation[a] for those who are in Christ

6:16 [m]Jn 8:34; 2Pe 2:19 [n]ver 23
6:17 [o]Ro 1:8; 2Co 2:14 [p]2Ti 1:13
6:18 [q]ver 7,22; Ro 8:2
6:19 [r]Ro 3:5 [s]ver 13
6:20 [t]ver 16
6:21 [u]ver 23
6:22 [v]ver 18 [w]1Co 7:22; 1Pe 2:16
6:23 [x]Ge 2:17; Ro 5:12; Gal 6:7,8; Jas 1:15 [y]Mt 25:46
7:1 [z]Ro 1:13
7:2 [a]1Co 7:39
7:4 [b]Ro 8:2; Gal 2:19 [c]Col 1:22
7:5 [d]Ro 7:7-11 [e]Ro 6:13
7:6 [f]Ro 2:29; 2Co 3:6
7:7 [g]Ro 3:20; 4:15 [h]Ex 20:17; Dt 5:21
7:8 [i]ver 11 [j]Ro 4:15; 1Co 15:56
7:10 [k]Lev 18:5; Lk 10:26-28; Ro 10:5; Gal 3:12
7:11 [l]Ge 3:13
7:12 [m]1Ti 1:8
7:14 [n]1Co 3:1 [o]1Ki 21:20,25; 2Ki 17:17
7:15 [p]ver 19; Gal 5:17
7:16 [q]ver 12
7:17 [r]ver 20
7:18 [s]ver 25
7:19 [t]ver 15
7:20 [u]ver 17
7:21 [v]ver 23,25
7:22 [w]Eph 3:16 [x]Ps 1:2
7:23 [y]Gal 5:17; Jas 4:1; 1Pe 2:11
7:24 [z]Ro 6:6; 8:2
8:1 [a]ver 34

[a]*23* Or *through* [b]*5* Or *the flesh*; also in verse 25 [c]*7* Exodus 20:17; Deut. 5:21
[d]*18* Or *my flesh*

Jesus,[a][b] [2]because through Christ Jesus the law of the Spirit of life[c] set me free[d] from the law of sin[e] and death. [3]For what the law was powerless[f] to do in that it was weakened by the sinful nature,[b] God did by sending his own Son in the likeness of sinful man[g] to be a sin offering.[c][h] And so he condemned sin in sinful man,[d] [4]in order that the righteous requirements of the law might be fully met in us, who do not live according to the sinful nature but according to the Spirit.[i]

1 →PG. 1243

[5]Those who live according to the sinful nature have their minds set on what that nature desires;[j] but those who live in accordance with the Spirit have their minds set on what the Spirit desires.[k] [6]The mind of sinful man[e] is death, but the mind controlled by the Spirit is life[l] and peace; [7]the sinful mind[f] is hostile to God.[m] It does not submit to God's law, nor can it do so. [8]Those controlled by the sinful nature cannot please God.

[9]You, however, are controlled not by the sinful nature but by the Spirit, if the Spirit of God lives in you.[n] And if anyone does not have the Spirit of Christ,[o] he does not belong to Christ. [10]But if Christ is in you,[p] your body is dead because of sin, yet your spirit is alive because of righteousness. [11]And if the Spirit of him who raised Jesus from the dead[q] is living in you, he who raised Christ from the dead will also give life to your mortal bodies[r] through his Spirit, who lives in you.

[12]Therefore, brothers, we have an obligation—but it is not to the sinful nature, to live according to it. [13]For if you live according to the sinful nature, you will die; but if by the Spirit you put to death the misdeeds of the body, you will live,[s] [14]because those who are led by the Spirit of God[t] are sons of God.[u] [15]For you did not receive a spirit that makes you a slave again to fear,[v] but you received the Spirit of sonship.[g] And by him we cry, *"Abba,*[h] Father."[w] [16]The Spirit himself testifies with our spirit[x] that we are God's children. [17]Now if we are children, then we are heirs[y]—heirs of God and co-heirs with Christ, if indeed we share in his sufferings in order that we may also share in his glory.[z]

1 →PG. 1243
3 →PG. 1247

Future Glory

[18]I consider that our present sufferings are not worth comparing with the glory that will be revealed in us.[a] [19]The creation waits in eager expectation for the sons of God to be revealed. [20]For the creation was subjected to frustration, not by its own choice, but by the will of the one who subjected it,[b] in hope [21]that[i] the creation itself will be liberated from its bondage to decay[c] and brought into the glorious freedom of the children of God.

[22]We know that the whole creation has been groaning[d] as in the pains of childbirth right up to the present time. [23]Not only so, but we ourselves, who have the firstfruits of the Spirit,[e] groan[f] inwardly as we wait eagerly[g] for our adoption as sons, the redemption of our bodies. [24]For in this hope we were saved.[h] But hope that is seen is no hope at all. Who hopes for what he already has? [25]But if we hope for what we do not yet have, we wait for it patiently.

[26]In the same way, the Spirit helps us in our weakness. We do not know what we ought to pray for, but the Spirit himself intercedes for us[i] with groans that words cannot express. [27]And he who searches our hearts[j] knows the

1 →PG. 1245

8:1–4 PROMISE 3

FREED BY THE SPIRIT

Do you sometimes feel as though you're fighting a losing battle against sin? Just about the time you think you've got things under control you lose your temper or your lust runs wild.

When Paul spoke of the "law of sin and death" (v. 2), he wasn't referring to a rule or regulation. Instead, he was speaking of a principle that says sin and death always pull us down. They always compel us to do wrong. No matter how long a man knows Jesus Christ, he'll feel sin trying to pull him away from God.

But that doesn't mean defeat is inevitable. Jesus not only promises us victory, he assures it. Just as the principle of sin states that sin always pulls us down, so the principle of the Spirit of life states that the Spirit always lifts us up.

As the laws of aerodynamics liberate airplanes from the downward pull of gravity, so God's Spirit frees us from the downward pull of sin. The next time you're tempted to sin, turn to God's Spirit. Ask for his help to lift you above the power of sin.

For the next Promise 3 reading go to page 1249.

8:1 [b]ver 39; Ro 16:3
8:2 [c]1Co 15:45 [d]Ro 6:18 [e]Ro 7:4
8:3 [f]Ac 13:39; Heb 7:18 [g]Php 2:7 [h]Heb 2:14,17
8:4 [i]Gal 5:16
8:5 [j]Gal 5:19-21 [k]Gal 5:22-25
8:6 [l]Gal 6:8
8:7 [m]Jas 4:4
8:9 [n]1Co 6:19; Gal 4:6 [o]Jn 14:17; 1Jn 4:13
8:10 [p]Gal 2:20; Eph 3:17; Col 1:27
8:11 [q]Ac 2:24 [r]Jn 5:21
8:13 [s]Gal 6:8
8:14 [t]Gal 5:18 [u]Jn 1:12; Rev 21:7
8:15 [v]2Ti 1:7; Heb 2:15 [w]Mk 14:36; Gal 4:5,6
8:16 [x]Eph 1:13
8:17 [y]Ac 20:32; Gal 4:7 [z]1Pe 4:13
8:18 [a]2Co 4:17; 1Pe 4:13
8:20 [b]Ge 3:17-19
8:21 [c]Ac 3:21; 2Pe 3:13; Rev 21:1
8:22 [d]Jer 12:4
8:23 [e]2Co 5:5 [f]2Co 5:2,4 [g]Gal 5:5
8:24 [h]1Th 5:8
8:26 [i]Eph 6:18
8:27 [j]Rev 2:23

---

a *1* Some later manuscripts *Jesus, who do not live according to the sinful nature but according to the Spirit,* **b** *3* Or *the flesh*; also in verses 4, 5, 8, 9, 12 and 13 **c** *3* Or *man, for sin* **d** *3* Or *in the flesh* **e** *6* Or *mind set on the flesh* **f** *7* Or *the mind set on the flesh* **g** *15* Or *adoption* **h** *15* Aramaic for *Father* **i** *20,21* Or *subjected it in hope.* [21]*For*

mind of the Spirit, because the Spirit
intercedes for the saints in accordance
with God's will.

More Than Conquerors

28And we know that in all things God
works for the good of those who love
him,[a] who[b] have been called[k] according to his purpose. **29**For those
God foreknew[l] he also predestined[m]
to be conformed to the likeness of his
Son,[n] that he might be the firstborn
among many brothers. **30**And those he
predestined,[o] he also called; those he
called, he also justified;[p] those he justified, he also glorified.[q]
31What, then, shall we say in response to this?[r] If God is for us, who
can be against us?[s] **32**He who did not
spare his own Son,[t] but gave him up
for us all—how will he not also, along
with him, graciously give us all things?
33Who will bring any charge[u] against
those whom God has chosen? It is
God who justifies. **34**Who is he that
condemns? Christ Jesus, who died[v]—
more than that, who was raised to
life—is at the right hand of God[w] and
is also interceding for us.[x] **35**Who shall
separate us from the love of Christ?
Shall trouble or hardship or persecution or famine or nakedness or danger
or sword?[y] **36**As it is written:

"For your sake we face death all
day long;
we are considered as sheep to be
slaughtered."[c][z]

37No, in all these things we are more
than conquerors[a] through him who
loved us.[b] **38**For I am convinced that
neither death nor life, neither angels
nor demons,[d] neither the present nor
the future, nor any powers,[c] **39**neither
height nor depth, nor anything else in
all creation, will be able to separate us
from the love of God[d] that is in Christ
Jesus our Lord.

God's Sovereign Choice

9 I speak the truth in Christ—I am not
lying,[e] my conscience confirms[f] it
in the Holy Spirit— **2**I have great sorrow and unceasing anguish in my
heart. **3**For I could wish that I myself[g]
were cursed[h] and cut off from Christ
for the sake of my brothers, those of
my own race,[i] **4**the people of Israel.
Theirs is the adoption as sons;[j] theirs
the divine glory, the covenants,[k] the
receiving of the law,[l] the temple worship[m] and the promises.[n] **5**Theirs are
the patriarchs, and from them is traced
the human ancestry of Christ,[o] who
is God over all,[p] forever praised![e][q]
Amen.
6It is not as though God's word had
failed. For not all who are descended
from Israel are Israel.[r] **7**Nor because
they are his descendants are they all
Abraham's children. On the contrary,
"It is through Isaac that your offspring
will be reckoned."[f][s] **8**In other words,
it is not the natural children who are
God's children,[t] but it is the children
of the promise who are regarded as
Abraham's offspring. **9**For this was how
the promise was stated: "At the appointed time I will return, and Sarah
will have a son."[g][u]
10Not only that, but Rebekah's children had one and the same father, our
father Isaac.[v] **11**Yet, before the twins
were born or had done anything good
or bad—in order that God's purpose[w]
in election might stand: **12**not by works
but by him who calls—she was told,
"The older will serve the younger."[h][x]
13Just as it is written: "Jacob I loved,
but Esau I hated."[i][y]

[a] *28* Some manuscripts *And we know that all things work together for good to those who love God* [b] *28* Or *works together with those who love him to bring about what is good—with those who* [c] *36* Psalm 44:22 [d] *38* Or *nor heavenly rulers* [e] *5* Or *Christ, who is over all. God be forever praised!* Or *Christ. God who is over all be forever praised!* [f] *7* Gen. 21:12 [g] *9* Gen. 18:10,14 [h] *12* Gen. 25:23 [i] *13* Mal. 1:2,3

8:28 [k]1Co 1:9; 2Ti 1:9
8:29 [l]Ro 11:2 [m]Eph 1:5,11 [n]1Co 15:49; 2Co 3:18; Php 3:21; 1Jn 3:2
8:30 [o]Eph 1:5,11 [p]1Co 6:11 [q]Ro 9:23
8:31 [r]Ro 4:1 [s]Ps 118:6
8:32 [t]Jn 3:16; Ro 4:25; 5:8
8:33 [u]Isa 50:8,9
8:34 [v]Ro 5:6-8 [w]Mk 16:19 [x]Heb 7:25; 9:24; 1Jn 2:1
8:35 [y]1Co 4:11
8:36 [z]Ps 44:22; 2Co 4:11
8:37 [a]1Co 15:57 [b]Gal 2:20; Rev 1:5; 3:9
8:38 [c]Eph 1:21; 1Pe 3:22
8:39 [d]Ro 5:8
9:1 [e]2Co 11:10; Gal 1:20; 1Ti 2:7 [f]Ro 1:9
9:3 [g]Ex 32:32 [h]1Co 12:3; 16:22 [i]Ro 11:14
9:4 [j]Ex 4:22 [k]Ge 17:2; Ac 3:25; Eph 2:12 [l]Ps 147:19 [m]Heb 9:1 [n]Ac 13:32
9:5 [o]Mt 1:1-16 [p]Jn 1:1 [q]Ro 1:25
9:6 [r]Ro 2:28,29; Gal 6:16
9:7 [s]Ge 21:12; Heb 11:18
9:8 [t]Ro 8:14
9:9 [u]Ge 18:10,14
9:10 [v]Ge 25:21
9:11 [w]Ro 8:28
9:12 [x]Ge 25:23
9:13 [y]Mal 1:2,3

8:28–30

PROMISE 1

WHY ME?

"Why this? Why now? Why me?"

All of us have asked these questions at times. And they seem to come most readily when something goes wrong in our lives. When we lose a job, break off a relationship, or hear bad news from the doctor, it's only natural to wonder if life has any rhyme or reason.

Fortunately, Paul has a response to our "Whys?" He says that "in *all* things" God works for the good of those who love him (v. 28). Paul doesn't say, "in some things," or "in most things." He says "in *all* things." That means God will use difficulties in your life to accomplish something good. Can you see what the end result is? Perhaps not right away, but you might be able to at a later date.

So what do you do in the meantime? Trust that because you know God, he will fit every piece of your life's puzzle together to form a beautiful picture. Memorize Romans 8:28 if you haven't done so before. Then take time to carefully read this entire chapter. It's one of the most comforting passages in the Bible.

For the next Promise 1 reading go to page 1255.

14 What then shall we say? Is God unjust? Not at all![z] 15 For he says to Moses,

> "I will have mercy on whom I have mercy,
> and I will have compassion on whom I have compassion."[a][a]

16 It does not, therefore, depend on man's desire or effort, but on God's mercy.[b] 17 For the Scripture says to Pharaoh: "I raised you up for this very purpose, that I might display my power in you and that my name might be proclaimed in all the earth."[b][c] 18 Therefore God has mercy on whom he wants to have mercy, and he hardens whom he wants to harden.[d]

19 One of you will say to me:[e] "Then why does God still blame us? For who resists his will?"[f] 20 But who are you, O man, to talk back to God? "Shall what is formed say to him who formed it,[g] 'Why did you make me like this?' "[c][h] 21 Does not the potter have the right to make out of the same lump of clay some pottery for noble purposes and some for common use?[i]

22 What if God, choosing to show his wrath and make his power known, bore with great patience[j] the objects of his wrath—prepared for destruction? 23 What if he did this to make the riches of his glory[k] known to the objects of his mercy, whom he prepared in advance for glory[l]— 24 even us, whom he also called,[m] not only from the Jews but also from the Gentiles?[n] 25 As he says in Hosea:

> "I will call them 'my people' who are not my people;
> and I will call her 'my loved one' who is not my loved one,"[d][o]

26 and,

> "It will happen that in the very place where it was said to them,
> 'You are not my people,'
> they will be called 'sons of the living God.' "[e][p]

27 Isaiah cries out concerning Israel:

> "Though the number of the Israelites be like the sand by the sea,[q]
> only the remnant will be saved.[r]

28 For the Lord will carry out
> his sentence on earth with speed and finality."[f][s]

29 It is just as Isaiah said previously:

> "Unless the Lord Almighty[t]
> had left us descendants,
> we would have become like Sodom,
> we would have been like Gomorrah."[g][u]

Israel's Unbelief

30 What then shall we say? That the Gentiles, who did not pursue righteousness, have obtained it, a righteousness that is by faith;[v] 31 but Israel, who pursued a law of righteousness,[w] has not attained it.[x] 32 Why not? Because they pursued it not by faith but as if it were by works. They stumbled over the "stumbling stone."[y] 33 As it is written:

> "See, I lay in Zion a stone that causes men to stumble
> and a rock that makes them fall,
> and the one who trusts in him will never be put to shame."[h][z]

10 Brothers, my heart's desire and prayer to God for the Israelites is that they may be saved. 2 For I can testify about them that they are zealous[a] for God, but their zeal is not based on knowledge. 3 Since they did not know the righteousness that comes from God and sought to establish their own, they did not submit to God's righteousness.[b] 4 Christ is the end of the law[c] so that there may be righteousness for everyone who believes.[d]

5 Moses describes in this way the righteousness that is by the law: "The man who does these things will live by them."[i][e] 6 But the righteousness that is by faith[f] says: "Do not say in your heart, 'Who will ascend into heaven?'[j]"[g] (that is, to bring Christ down) 7 "or 'Who will descend into the deep?'[k]" (that is, to bring Christ up from the dead). 8 But what does it say? "The word is near you; it is in your mouth and in your heart,"[l][h] that is, the word of faith we are proclaiming: 9 That if you confess[i] with your mouth, "Jesus is Lord," and believe in your heart that God raised him from the dead,[j] you will be saved. 10 For it is with your heart that you believe and are justified, and it is with your mouth that you confess and are saved. 11 As the Scripture says, "Anyone who trusts in him will never be put to shame."[m][k]
1 →PG. 1247

12 For there is no difference between Jew and Gentile[l]—the same Lord is Lord of all[m] and richly blesses all who
6 →PG. 1247

9:14 [z] 2Ch 19:7
9:15 [a] Ex 33:19
9:16 [b] Eph 2:8
9:17 [c] Ex 9:16
9:18 [d] Ex 4:21
9:19 [e] Ro 11:19 [f] 2Ch 20:6; Da 4:35
9:20 [g] Isa 64:8 [h] Isa 29:16
9:21 [i] 2Ti 2:20
9:22 [j] Ro 2:4
9:23 [k] Ro 2:4 [l] Ro 8:30
9:24 [m] Ro 8:28 [n] Ro 3:29
9:25 [o] Hos 2:23; 1Pe 2:10
9:26 [p] Hos 1:10
9:27 [q] Ge 22:17; Hos 1:10 [r] Ro 11:5
9:28 [s] Isa 10:22,23
9:29 [t] Jas 5:4 [u] Isa 1:9; Dt 29:23; Isa 13:19; Jer 50:40
9:30 [v] Ro 1:17; 10:6; Gal 2:16; Php 3:9; Heb 11:7
9:31 [w] Isa 51:1; Ro 10:2,3 [x] Gal 5:4
9:32 [y] 1Pe 2:8
9:33 [z] Isa 28:16; Ro 10:11
10:2 [a] Ac 21:20
10:3 [b] Ro 1:17
10:4 [c] Gal 3:24; Ro 7:1-4 [d] Ro 3:22
10:5 [e] Lev 18:5; Ne 9:29; Eze 20:11,13, 21; Ro 7:10
10:6 [f] Ro 9:30 [g] Dt 30:12
10:8 [h] Dt 30:14
10:9 [i] Mt 10:32; Lk 12:8 [j] Ac 2:24
10:11 [k] Isa 28:16; Ro 9:33
10:12 [l] Ro 3:22,29 [m] Ac 10:36

a *15* Exodus 33:19 b *17* Exodus 9:16
c *20* Isaiah 29:16; 45:9 d *25* Hosea 2:23
e *26* Hosea 1:10 f *28* Isaiah 10:22,23
g *29* Isaiah 1:9 h *33* Isaiah 8:14; 28:16
i *5* Lev. 18:5 j *6* Deut. 30:12 k *7* Deut. 30:13
l *8* Deut. 30:14 m *11* Isaiah 28:16

call on him, 13for, "Everyone who calls
on the name of the Lord[n] will be
saved."[a][o]

7 →PG. 1247

14How, then, can they call on the
one they have not believed in? And
how can they believe in the one
of whom they have not heard? And
how can they hear without someone preaching to them? 15And how can
they preach unless they are sent? As it
is written, "How beautiful are the feet
of those who bring good news!"[b][p]

16But not all the Israelites accepted
the good news. For Isaiah says, "Lord,
who has believed our message?"[c][q]
17Consequently, faith comes from
hearing the message,[r] and the message is heard through the word of
Christ.[s] 18But I ask: Did they not hear?
Of course they did:

> "Their voice has gone out into all
> the earth,
> their words to the ends of the
> world."[d][t]

19Again I ask: Did Israel not understand? First, Moses says,

> "I will make you envious[u] by
> those who are not a nation;
> I will make you angry by a
> nation that has no
> understanding."[e][v]

20And Isaiah boldly says,

> "I was found by those who did not
> seek me;
> I revealed myself to those who
> did not ask for me."[f][w]

21But concerning Israel he says,

> "All day long I have held out my
> hands
> to a disobedient and obstinate
> people."[g][x]

The Remnant of Israel

11 I ask then: Did God reject his people? By no means![y] I am an Israelite myself, a descendant of Abraham,[z]
from the tribe of Benjamin.[a] 2God did
not reject his people, whom he foreknew.[b] Don't you know what the
Scripture says in the passage about
Elijah—how he appealed to God
against Israel: 3"Lord, they have killed
your prophets and torn down your altars; I am the only one left, and they are
trying to kill me"[h]?[c] 4And what was
God's answer to him? "I have reserved
for myself seven thousand who have
not bowed the knee to Baal."[i][d] 5So
too, at the present time there is a remnant[e] chosen by grace. 6And if by
grace, then it is no longer by works;[f]
if it were, grace would no longer be
grace.[j]

7What then? What Israel sought so
earnestly it did not obtain,[g] but the
elect did. The others were hardened,[h]
8as it is written:

> "God gave them a spirit of stupor,
> eyes so that they could not see
> and ears so that they could not
> hear,[i]
> to this very day."[k][j]

9And David says:

> "May their table become a snare
> and a trap,
> a stumbling block and a
> retribution for them.
> 10May their eyes be darkened so they
> cannot see,
> and their backs be bent
> forever."[l][k]

Ingrafted Branches

11Again I ask: Did they stumble so as
to fall beyond recovery? Not at all![l]
Rather, because of their transgression,
salvation has come to the Gentiles[m] to
make Israel envious.[n] 12But if their
transgression means riches for the
world, and their loss means riches for
the Gentiles,[o] how much greater
riches will their fullness bring!

13I am talking to you Gentiles. Inas-
much as I am the apostle to the Gentiles,[p] I make much of my ministry
14in the hope that I may somehow
arouse my own people to envy[q] and
save[r] some of them. 15For if their
rejection is the reconciliation[s] of the
world, what will their acceptance be
but life from the dead?[t] 16If the part
of the dough offered as firstfruits[u] is
holy, then the whole batch is holy; if
the root is holy, so are the branches.

17If some of the branches have been
broken off,[v] and you, though a wild
olive shoot, have been grafted in
among the others[w] and now share in
the nourishing sap from the olive root,
18do not boast over those branches. If
you do, consider this: You do not support the root, but the root supports
you.[x] 19You will say then, "Branches
were broken off so that I could be grafted in." 20Granted. But they were broken off because of unbelief, and you
stand by faith.[y] Do not be arrogant,[z]
but be afraid.[a] 21For if God did not

10:13 [n]Ac 2:21 [o]Joel 2:32
10:15 [p]Isa 52:7; Na 1:15
10:16 [q]Isa 53:1; Jn 12:38
10:17 [r]Gal 3:2,5 [s]Col 3:16
10:18 [t]Ps 19:4; Mt 24:14; Col 1:6,23; 1Th 1:8
10:19 [u]Ro 11:11,14 [v]Dt 32:21
10:20 [w]Isa 65:1; Ro 9:30
10:21 [x]Isa 65:2
11:1 [y]1Sa 12:22; Jer 31:37 [z]2Co 11:22 [a]Php 3:5
11:2 [b]Ro 8:29
11:3 [c]1Ki 19:10,14
11:4 [d]1Ki 19:18
11:5 [e]Ro 9:27
11:6 [f]Ro 4:4
11:7 [g]Ro 9:31 [h]ver 25; Ro 9:18
11:8 [i]Mt 13:13-15 [j]Dt 29:4; Isa 29:10
11:10 [k]Ps 69:22,23
11:11 [l]ver 1 [m]Ac 13:46 [n]Ro 10:19
11:12 [o]ver 25
11:13 [p]Ac 9:15
11:14 [q]ver 11; Ro 10:19 [r]1Co 1:21; 1Ti 2:4; Tit 3:5
11:15 [s]Ro 5:10 [t]Lk 15:24,32
11:16 [u]Lev 23:10,17; Nu 15:18-21
11:17 [v]Jer 11:16; Jn 15:2 [w]Ac 2:39; Eph 2:11-13
11:18 [x]Jn 4:22
11:20 [y]1Co 10:12; 2Co 1:24 [z]Ro 12:16; 1Ti 6:17 [a]1Pe 1:17

a *13* Joel 2:32 b *15* Isaiah 52:7
c *16* Isaiah 53:1 d *18* Psalm 19:4
e *19* Deut. 32:21 f *20* Isaiah 65:1
g *21* Isaiah 65:2 h *3* 1 Kings 19:10,14
i *4* 1 Kings 19:18 j *6* Some manuscripts *by grace. But if by works, then it is no longer grace; if it were, work would no longer be work.*
k *8* Deut. 29:4; Isaiah 29:10 l *10* Psalm 69:22,23

spare the natural branches, he will not
spare you either.
22 Consider therefore the kindness[b]
and sternness of God: sternness to
those who fell, but kindness to you,
provided that you continue[c] in his
kindness. Otherwise, you also will be
cut off.[d] 23 And if they do not persist in
unbelief, they will be grafted in, for
God is able to graft them in again.[e]
24 After all, if you were cut out of an
olive tree that is wild by nature, and
contrary to nature were grafted into a
cultivated olive tree, how much more
readily will these, the natural branches,
be grafted into their own olive tree!

All Israel Will Be Saved

25 I do not want you to be ignorant[f]
of this mystery,[g] brothers, so that you
may not be conceited:[h] Israel has experienced
a hardening[i] in part until
the full number of the Gentiles has
come in.[j] 26 And so all Israel will be
saved, as it is written:

> "The deliverer will come from Zion;
> he will turn godlessness away
> from Jacob.

27 And this is[a] my covenant with
them
when I take away their sins."[b] [k]

28 As far as the gospel is concerned,
they are enemies[l] on your account;
but as far as election is concerned, they
are loved on account of the patriarchs,[m]
29 for God's gifts and his call[n]
are irrevocable.[o] 30 Just as you who
were at one time disobedient[p] to God
have now received mercy as a result of
their disobedience, 31 so they too have
now become disobedient in order that
they too may now[c] receive mercy as a
result of God's mercy to you. 32 For God
has bound all men over to disobedience[q]
so that he may have mercy on
them all.

Doxology

33 Oh, the depth of the riches[r] of the
wisdom and[d] knowledge of
God![s]
How unsearchable his
judgments,
and his paths beyond tracing
out![t]
34 "Who has known the mind of the
Lord?
Or who has been his
counselor?"[e] [u]
35 "Who has ever given to God,
that God should repay him?"[f] [v]
36 For from him and through him and
to him are all things.[w]

11:22 [b] Ro 2:4 [c] 1Co 15:2; Heb 3:6 [d] Jn 15:2 **11:23** [e] 2Co 3:16 **11:25** [f] Ro 1:13 [g] Ro 16:25 [h] Ro 12:16 [i] ver 7; Ro 9:18 [j] Lk 21:24 **11:27** [k] Isa 27:9; Heb 8:10,12 **11:28** [l] Ro 5:10 [m] Dt 7:8; 10:15; Ro 9:5 **11:29** [n] Ro 8:28 [o] Heb 7:21 **11:30** [p] Eph 2:2 **11:32** [q] Ro 3:9 **11:33** [r] Ro 2:4 [s] Ps 92:5 [t] Job 11:7 **11:34** [u] Isa 40:13,14; Job 15:8; 36:22; 1Co 2:16 **11:35** [v] Job 35:7 **11:36** [w] 1Co 8:6; Col 1:16; Heb 2:10

[x] Ro 16:27 **12:1** [y] Eph 4:1 [z] Ro 6:13,16, 19; 1Pe 2:5 **12:2** [a] 1Pe 1:14 [b] 1Jn 2:15 [c] Eph 4:23 [d] Eph 5:17 **12:3** [e] Ro 15:15; Gal 2:9; Eph 4:7 **12:4** [f] 1Co 12:12-14; Eph 4:16 **12:5** [g] 1Co 10:17 **12:6** [h] 1Co 7:7; 12:4, 8-10 [i] 1Pe 4:10,11 **12:7** [j] Eph 4:11 **12:8** [k] Ac 15:32 [l] 2Co 9:5-13 **12:9** [m] 1Ti 1:5 **12:10** [n] Heb 13:1 [o] Php 2:3 **12:11** [p] Ac 18:25 **12:12** [q] Ro 5:2 [r] Heb 10:32,36 **12:13** [s] 1Ti 3:2 **12:14** [t] Mt 5:44 **12:15** [u] Job 30:25 **12:16** [v] Ro 15:5 [w] Jer 45:5; Ro 11:25 **12:17** [x] Pr 20:22 [y] 2Co 8:21

To him be the glory forever!
Amen.[x]

Living Sacrifices

12 Therefore, I urge you,[y] brothers, 1 →PG. 1249
in view of God's mercy, to offer
your bodies as living sacrifices,[z] holy
and pleasing to God—this is your spiritual[g] 3 →PG. 1248
act of worship. 2 Do not conform[a]
any longer to the pattern of this
world,[b] but be transformed by the renewing
of your mind.[c] Then you will
be able to test and approve what God's
will is[d]—his good, pleasing and perfect
will.
3 For by the grace given me[e] I say to
every one of you: Do not think of yourself
more highly than you ought, but
rather think of yourself with sober
judgment, in accordance with the
measure of faith God has given you.
4 Just as each of us has one body with 5 →PG. 1251
many members, and these members
do not all have the same function,[f]
5 so in Christ we who are many form 7 →PG. 1248
one body,[g] and each member belongs
to all the others. 6 We have different
gifts,[h] according to the grace given us.
If a man's gift is prophesying, let him
use it in proportion to his[h] faith.[i] 7 If
it is serving, let him serve; if it is teaching,
let him teach;[j] 8 if it is encouraging,
let him encourage;[k] if it is contributing
to the needs of others, let him
give generously;[l] if it is leadership, let
him govern diligently; if it is showing
mercy, let him do it cheerfully.

Love

9 Love must be sincere.[m] Hate what 2 →PG. 1251
is evil; cling to what is good. 10 Be devoted
to one another in brotherly
love.[n] Honor one another above yourselves.[o]
11 Never be lacking in zeal, but
keep your spiritual fervor,[p] serving
the Lord. 12 Be joyful in hope,[q] patient
in affliction,[r] faithful in prayer.
13 Share with God's people who are in
need. Practice hospitality.[s]
14 Bless those who persecute you;[t] 6 →PG. 1249
bless and do not curse. 15 Rejoice with
those who rejoice; mourn with those
who mourn.[u] 16 Live in harmony with
one another.[v] Do not be proud, but be
willing to associate with people of low
position.[i] Do not be conceited.[w]
17 Do not repay anyone evil for evil.[x]
Be careful to do what is right in the
eyes of everybody.[y] 18 If it is possible,

[a] *27* Or *will be* [b] *27* Isaiah 59:20,21; 27:9; Jer. 31:33,34 [c] *31* Some manuscripts do not have *now.* [d] *33* Or *riches and the wisdom and the* [e] *34* Isaiah 40:13 [f] *35* Job 41:11 [g] *1* Or *reasonable* [h] *6* Or *in agreement with the* [i] *16* Or *willing to do menial work*

as far as it depends on you, live at peace with everyone.[z] 19Do not take revenge,[a] my friends, but leave room for God's wrath, for it is written: "It is mine to avenge; I will repay,"[a][b] says the Lord. 20On the contrary:

"If your enemy is hungry, feed him;
 if he is thirsty, give him
  something to drink.
In doing this, you will heap
  burning coals on his
  head."[b][c]

21Do not be overcome by evil, but overcome evil with good.

Submission to the Authorities

3 →PG. 1249

13 Everyone must submit himself to the governing authorities,[d] for there is no authority except that which God has established.[e] The authorities that exist have been established by God. 2Consequently, he who rebels against the authority is rebelling against what God has instituted, and those who do so will bring judgment on themselves. 3For rulers hold no terror for those who do right, but for those who do wrong. Do you want to be free from fear of the one in authority? Then do what is right and he will commend you.[f] 4For he is God's servant to do you good. But if you do wrong, be afraid, for he does not bear the sword for nothing. He is God's servant, an agent of wrath to bring punishment on the wrongdoer.[g] 5Therefore, it is necessary to submit to the authorities, not only because of possible punishment but also because of conscience.

6This is also why you pay taxes, for the authorities are God's servants, who give their full time to governing. 7Give everyone what you owe him: If you owe taxes, pay taxes;[h] if revenue, then revenue; if respect, then respect; if honor, then honor.

Love, for the Day Is Near

7 →PG. 1250

8Let no debt remain outstanding, except the continuing debt to love one another, for he who loves his fellowman has fulfilled the law.[i] 9The commandments, "Do not commit adultery," "Do not murder," "Do not steal,"

12:18 [z]Mk 9:50; Ro 14:19
12:19 [a]Lev 19:18; Pr 20:22; 24:29 [b]Dt 32:35
12:20 [c]Pr 25:21,22; Mt 5:44; Lk 6:27
13:1 [d]Tit 3:1; 1Pe 2:13,14 [e]Da 2:21; Jn 19:11
13:3 [f]1Pe 2:14
13:4 [g]1Th 4:6
13:7 [h]Mt 17:25; 22:17,21; Lk 23:2
13:8 [i]ver 10; Jn 13:34; Gal 5:14; Col 3:14

a*19* Deut. 32:35 b*20* Prov. 25:21,22

12:1–21

PROMISE 7

WHO NEEDS INSTRUCTIONS?

If you've ever assembled something with more than five parts, then you know the importance of instructions. One small misstep can make the difference between an item not quite functioning and that same item functioning smoothly. That's true of machines, buildings and toys, and it's also true of our spiritual life. Of course it's easy, and maybe even a bit natural, for men to overlook the instructions. Growing spiritually doesn't seem all that complicated. But it's impossible to make progress without some guidance.

After explaining the essential doctrinal truths of our relationship with God (Romans 1—11), Paul spends the remainder of this letter fleshing out our walk with God. He gives us some specific instructions concerning how we as believers can put our spiritual lives together. Romans 12 provides some of the most important steps in Paul's instruction booklet.

Step One: Devote yourselves completely to God (vv. 1–2). Such a commitment to God may seem like a lot to ask. But that commitment pales in comparison to all Paul has said in the first eleven chapters of Romans. The same God who rescued us from sin, gave us his power, and protects our relationship with him wants to spur us on to this one great act. This act of dedication is *voluntary*. It's also serious, like making wedding vows. And while it occurs only once, it can be renewed. As we commit ourselves to God, our minds become transformed. No longer are our thoughts shaped by the sinful world's ideas and standards. Instead, they are reshaped by God himself.

Step Two: Serve others (vv. 3–8). People who are committed to God are easy to spot. Their humble service gives them away. They know God has given them specific talents, interests and abilities, and they use those gifts to serve others. They also recognize that every person is different. God has placed within the body of Christ a wide variety of people with complementary gifts and talents.

Step Three: Love others (vv. 9–21). People who are committed to God sincerely love those around them. Paul describes that honest, sacrificial love in these few verses. Christians are called to treat both believers and unbelievers with such kindness that our relationship to Jesus is evident through our actions. We should do all we can to bring peace to every relationship. In all things, we should "overcome evil with good." That's an exhortation that allows for a lot of positive creative action on our part!

Read Romans 12 thoughtfully. As you review Paul's instructions, ask God for the grace you need to follow them. And then put your love into action by investing some time serving in your community or helping out in your church. The instructions for being a spiritual man aren't complicated, but they do require diligence. Remember, trusting and imitating Jesus over the long haul involves trusting and imitating him one day at a time.

For the next Promise 7 reading go to page 1274.

"Do not covet,"[a][j] and whatever other commandment there may be, are summed up in this one rule: "Love your neighbor as yourself."[b][k] 10 Love does no harm to its neighbor. Therefore love is the fulfillment of the law.[l]

11 And do this, understanding the present time. The hour has come[m] for you to wake up from your slumber,[n] because our salvation is nearer now than when we first believed. 12 The night is nearly over; the day is almost here.[o] So let us put aside the deeds of darkness[p] and put on the armor[q] of light. 13 Let us behave decently, as in the daytime, not in orgies and drunkenness, not in sexual immorality and debauchery, not in dissension and jealousy.[r] 14 Rather, clothe yourselves with the Lord Jesus Christ,[s] and do not think about how to gratify the desires of the sinful nature.[c]

3 →PG. 1251

The Weak and the Strong

14 Accept him whose faith is weak,[t] without passing judgment on disputable matters. 2 One man's faith allows him to eat everything, but another man, whose faith is weak, eats only vegetables. 3 The man who eats everything must not look down on[u] him who does not, and the man who does not eat everything must not condemn[v] the man who does, for God has accepted him. 4 Who are you to judge someone else's servant?[w] To his own master he stands or falls. And he will stand, for the Lord is able to make him stand.

5 One man considers one day more sacred than another;[x] another man considers every day alike. Each one should be fully convinced in his own mind. 6 He who regards one day as special, does so to the Lord. He who eats meat, eats to the Lord, for he gives thanks to God;[y] and he who abstains, does so to the Lord and gives thanks to God. 7 For none of us lives to himself alone[z] and none of us dies to himself alone. 8 If we live, we live to the Lord; and if we die, we die to the Lord. So, whether we live or die, we belong to the Lord.[a]

1 →PG. 1250

9 For this very reason, Christ died and returned to life[b] so that he might be the Lord of both the dead and the living.[c] 10 You, then, why do you judge your brother? Or why do you look down on your brother? For we will all stand before God's judgment seat.[d] 11 It is written:

> " 'As surely as I live,' says the Lord,
> 'every knee will bow before me;
> every tongue will confess to
> God.' "[d][e]

12 So then, each of us will give an account of himself to God.[f]

13 Therefore let us stop passing judgment[g] on one another. Instead, make up your mind not to put any stumbling block or obstacle in your brother's way. 14 As one who is in the Lord Jesus, I am fully convinced that no food[e] is unclean in itself.[h] But if anyone regards something as unclean, then for him it is unclean.[i] 15 If your brother is distressed because of what you eat, you are no longer acting in love.[j] Do not by your eating destroy your brother for whom Christ died.[k] 16 Do not allow what you consider good to be spoken of as evil.[l] 17 For the kingdom of God is not a matter of eating and drinking,[m] but of righteousness, peace and joy in the Holy Spirit,[n] 18 because anyone who serves Christ in this way is pleasing to God and approved by men.[o]

6 →PG. 1250

19 Let us therefore make every effort to do what leads to peace[p] and to mutual edification.[q] 20 Do not destroy the work of God for the sake of food.[r] All food is clean, but it is wrong for a man to eat anything that causes someone else to stumble.[s] 21 It is better not to eat meat or drink wine or to do anything else that will cause your brother to fall.[t]

22 So whatever you believe about these things keep between yourself and God. Blessed is the man who does not condemn[u] himself by what he approves. 23 But the man who has

13:9 [j] Ex 20:13-15,17; Dt 5:17-19,21 [k] Lev 19:18; Mt 19:19 **13:10** [l] ver 8; Mt 22:39,40 **13:11** [m] 1Co 7:29-31; 10:11 [n] Eph 5:14; 1Th 5:5,6 **13:12** [o] 1Jn 2:8 [p] Eph 5:11 [q] Eph 6:11,13 **13:13** [r] Gal 5:20,21 **13:14** [s] Gal 3:27; 5:16; Eph 4:24 **14:1** [t] Ro 15:1; 1Co 8:9-12 **14:3** [u] Lk 18:9 [v] Col 2:16 **14:4** [w] Jas 4:12 **14:5** [x] Gal 4:10

14:6 [y] Mt 14:19; 1Co 10:30,31; 1Ti 4:3,4 **14:7** [z] 2Co 5:15; Gal 2:20 **14:8** [a] Php 1:20 **14:9** [b] Rev 1:18 [c] 2Co 5:15 **14:10** [d] 2Co 5:10 **14:11** [e] Isa 45:23; Php 2:10,11 **14:12** [f] Mt 12:36; 1Pe 4:5 **14:13** [g] Mt 7:1 **14:14** [h] Ac 10:15 [i] 1Co 8:7 **14:15** [j] Eph 5:2 [k] 1Co 8:11 **14:16** [l] 1Co 10:30 **14:17** [m] 1Co 8:8 [n] Ro 15:13 **14:18** [o] 2Co 8:21 **14:19** [p] Ps 34:14; Ro 12:18; Heb 12:14 [q] Ro 15:2; 2Co 12:19 **14:20** [r] ver 15 [s] 1Co 8:9-12 **14:21** [t] 1Co 8:13 **14:22** [u] 1Jn 3:21

[a] 9 Exodus 20:13-15,17; Deut. 5:17-19,21
[b] 9 Lev. 19:18
[c] 14 Or *the flesh*
[d] 11 Isaiah 45:23
[e] 14 Or *that nothing*

13:1–7 PROMISE 3

RESPECT YOUR MAIL CARRIER

While followers of Jesus may not agree with everything government does, they will submit to governmental authority. Why? Because, as this passage says, governmental authority has been established by God. Christians are called to resist such authority only if asked to do something that violates God's teaching in the Bible (see Acts 5:27–29).

Generally speaking, submitting to governing authorities is a visible way for Christians to show their submission to God. With that in mind, be sure to treat all government officials with respect—whether they're delivering your mail or a speeding ticket.

For the next Promise 3 reading go to page 1257.

doubts[v] is condemned if he eats, because his eating is not from faith; and everything that does not come from faith is sin.

7 →PG. 1257

15 We who are strong ought to bear with the failings of the weak[w] and not to please ourselves. 2Each of us should please his neighbor for his good,[x] to build him up.[y] 3For even Christ did not please himself[z] but, as it is written: "The insults of those who insult you have fallen on me."[a][a] 4For

1 →PG. 1255

everything that was written in the past was written to teach us,[b] so that through endurance and the encouragement of the Scriptures we might have hope.

6 →PG. 1255

5May the God who gives endurance and encouragement give you a spirit of unity[c] among yourselves as you follow Christ Jesus, 6so that with one heart and mouth you may glorify the God and Father[d] of our Lord Jesus Christ.

7Accept one another,[e] then, just as Christ accepted you, in order to bring praise to God. 8For I tell you that Christ has become a servant of the Jews[b][f] on behalf of God's truth, to confirm the promises[g] made to the patriarchs 9so that the Gentiles[h] may glorify God[i] for his mercy, as it is written:

"Therefore I will praise you among
the Gentiles;
I will sing hymns to your
name."[c][j]

10Again, it says,

"Rejoice, O Gentiles, with his
people."[d][k]

11And again,

"Praise the Lord, all you Gentiles,
and sing praises to him, all you
peoples."[e][l]

12And again, Isaiah says,

"The Root of Jesse[m] will spring up,
one who will arise to rule over
the nations;
the Gentiles will hope in him."[f][n]

13May the God of hope fill you with all joy and peace[o] as you trust in him, so that you may overflow with hope by the power of the Holy Spirit.[p]

Paul the Minister to the Gentiles

14I myself am convinced, my brothers, that you yourselves are full of goodness,[q] complete in knowledge[r] and competent to instruct one another. 15I have written you quite boldly on some points, as if to remind you of them again, because of the grace God gave me[s] 16to be a minister of Christ Jesus to the Gentiles[t] with the priestly duty of proclaiming the gospel of God,[u] so that the Gentiles might become an offering[v] acceptable to God, sanctified by the Holy Spirit.

17Therefore I glory in Christ Jesus[w] in my service to God.[x] 18I will not venture to speak of anything except what Christ has accomplished through me in leading the Gentiles[y] to obey God[z] by what I have said and done— 19by the power of signs and miracles,[a] through the power of the Spirit.[b] So from Jerusalem[c] all the way around to Illyricum, I have fully proclaimed the gospel of Christ. 20It has always been my ambition to preach the gospel where Christ was not known, so that I would not be building on someone else's foundation.[d] 21Rather, as it is written:

"Those who were not told about
him will see,
and those who have not heard
will understand."[g][e]

22This is why I have often been hindered from coming to you.[f]

Paul's Plan to Visit Rome

23But now that there is no more place for me to work in these regions, and since I have been longing for many years to see you,[g] 24I plan to do so when I go to Spain.[h] I hope to visit you while passing through and to have you assist me on my journey there, after I have enjoyed your company for a

---

15:1–3

PROMISE 6

PEACE AND EDIFICATION

What do others want to see in a man who claims to be a Christian? Chances are they want to see a man who reflects the life of Jesus Christ.

Paul's admonition for us in this passage is that we must treat Christian brothers of all backgrounds with respect, not criticism. The apostle acknowledges that people have different beliefs in regard to "disputable matters" of the Christian faith (14:1). He then summarizes what should be the godly man's attitude in this regard: "Let us therefore make every effort to do what leads to peace and to mutual edification" (14:19).

For the next Promise 6 reading go to page 1265.

14:23 [v]ver 5
15:1 [w]Ro 14:1; Gal 6:1,2; 1Th 5:14
15:2 [x]1Co 10:33 [y]Ro 14:19
15:3 [z]2Co 8:9 [a]Ps 69:9
15:4 [b]Ro 4:23,24
15:5 [c]Ro 12:16; 1Co 1:10
15:6 [d]Rev 1:6
15:7 [e]Ro 14:1
15:8 [f]Mt 15:24; Ac 3:25,26 [g]2Co 1:20
15:9 [h]Ro 3:29 [i]Mt 9:8 [j]2Sa 22:50; Ps 18:49
15:10 [k]Dt 32:43
15:11 [l]Ps 117:1
15:12 [m]Rev 5:5 [n]Isa 11:10; Mt 12:21
15:13 [o]Ro 14:17 [p]ver 19; 1Co 2:4; 1Th 1:5
15:14 [q]Eph 5:9 [r]2Pe 1:12
15:15 [s]Ro 12:3
15:16 [t]Ac 9:15; Ro 11:13 [u]Ro 1:1 [v]Isa 66:20
15:17 [w]Php 3:3 [x]Heb 2:17
15:18 [y]Ac 15:12; 21:19; Ro 1:5 [z]Ro 16:26
15:19 [a]Jn 4:48; Ac 19:11 [b]ver 13 [c]Ac 22:17-21
15:20 [d]2Co 10:15,16
15:21 [e]Isa 52:15
15:22 [f]Ro 1:13
15:23 [g]Ac 19:21; Ro 1:10,11
15:24 [h]ver 28

---

a *3* Psalm 69:9 b *8* Greek *circumcision*
c *9* 2 Samuel 22:50; Psalm 18:49
d *10* Deut. 32:43 e *11* Psalm 117:1
f *12* Isaiah 11:10 g *21* Isaiah 52:15

while. 25Now, however, I am on my way to Jerusalem[i] in the service[j] of the saints there. 26For Macedonia[k] and Achaia[l] were pleased to make a contribution for the poor among the saints in Jerusalem. 27They were pleased to do it, and indeed they owe it to them. For if the Gentiles have shared in the Jews' spiritual blessings, they owe it to the Jews to share with them their material blessings.[m] 28So after I have completed this task and have made sure that they have received this fruit, I will go to Spain and visit you on the way. 29I know that when I come to you,[n] I will come in the full measure of the blessing of Christ.

5 →PG. 1257

30I urge you, brothers, by our Lord Jesus Christ and by the love of the Spirit,[o] to join me in my struggle by praying to God for me.[p] 31Pray that I may be rescued[q] from the unbelievers in Judea and that my service in Jerusalem may be acceptable to the saints there, 32so that by God's will[r] I may come to you[s] with joy and together with you be refreshed.[t] 33The God of peace[u] be with you all. Amen.

2 →PG. 1281

Personal Greetings

16 I commend[v] to you our sister Phoebe, a servant[a] of the church in Cenchrea.[w] 2I ask you to receive her in the Lord[x] in a way worthy of the saints and to give her any help she may need from you, for she has been a great help to many people, including me.

3Greet Priscilla[b] and Aquila,[y] my fellow workers in Christ Jesus.[z] 4They risked their lives for me. Not only I but all the churches of the Gentiles are grateful to them.

5Greet also the church that meets at their house.[a]

Greet my dear friend Epenetus, who was the first convert[b] to Christ in the province of Asia.

6Greet Mary, who worked very hard for you.

7Greet Andronicus and Junias, my relatives[c] who have been in prison with me. They are outstanding among the apostles, and they were in Christ before I was.

8Greet Ampliatus, whom I love in the Lord.

9Greet Urbanus, our fellow worker in Christ,[d] and my dear friend Stachys.

10Greet Apelles, tested and approved in Christ.

Greet those who belong to the household of Aristobulus.

11Greet Herodion, my relative.[e]

Greet those in the household of Narcissus who are in the Lord.

12Greet Tryphena and Tryphosa, those women who work hard in the Lord.

Greet my dear friend Persis, another woman who has worked very hard in the Lord.

13Greet Rufus, chosen in the Lord, and his mother, who has been a mother to me, too.

14Greet Asyncritus, Phlegon, Hermes, Patrobas, Hermas and the brothers with them.

15Greet Philologus, Julia, Nereus and his sister, and Olympas and all the saints[f] with them.[g]

16Greet one another with a holy kiss.[h]

All the churches of Christ send greetings.

17I urge you, brothers, to watch out for those who cause divisions and put obstacles in your way that are contrary to the teaching you have learned.[i] Keep away from them.[j] 18For such people are not serving our Lord Christ, but their own appetites.[k] By smooth talk and flattery they deceive[l] the minds of naive people. 19Everyone has heard[m] about your obedience, so I am full of joy over you; but I want you to be wise about what is good, and innocent about what is evil.[n]

3 →PG. 1257

20The God of peace[o] will soon crush[p] Satan under your feet.

The grace of our Lord Jesus be with you.[q]

21Timothy,[r] my fellow worker, sends his greetings to you, as do Lucius,[s] Jason[t] and Sosipater, my relatives.[u]

22I, Tertius, who wrote down this letter, greet you in the Lord.

23Gaius, whose hospitality I and the whole church here enjoy, sends you his greetings.

Erastus,[v] who is the city's director of public works, and our brother Quartus send you their greetings.[c]

25Now to him who is able[w] to establish you by my gospel[x] and the proclamation of Jesus Christ, according to the revelation of the mystery[y] hidden for long ages past, 26but now revealed and made known through the prophetic writings by the command of the eternal God, so that all nations might believe and obey him— 27to the only wise God be glory forever through Jesus Christ! Amen.[z]

15:25 [i]Ac 19:21 [j]Ac 24:17
15:26 [k]Ac 16:9; 2Co 8:1 [l]Ac 18:12
15:27 [m]1Co 9:11
15:29 [n]Ro 1:10,11
15:30 [o]Gal 5:22 [p]2Co 1:11; Col 4:12
15:31 [q]2Th 3:2
15:32 [r]Ac 18:21 [s]Ro 1:10,13 [t]1Co 16:18
15:33 [u]Ro 16:20; 2Co 13:11; Php 4:9; 1Th 5:23; Heb 13:20
16:1 [v]2Co 3:1 [w]Ac 18:18
16:2 [x]Php 2:29
16:3 [y]Ac 18:2 [z]ver 7,9,10
16:5 [a]1Co 16:19; Col 4:15; Phm 2 [b]1Co 16:15
16:7 [c]ver 11,21
16:9 [d]ver 3
16:11 [e]ver 7,21
16:15 [f]ver 2 [g]ver 14
16:16 [h]1Co 16:20; 2Co 13:12; 1Th 5:26
16:17 [i]Gal 1:8,9; 1Ti 1:3; 6:3 [j]2Th 3:6,14; 2Jn 10
16:18 [k]Php 3:19 [l]Col 2:4
16:19 [m]Ro 1:8 [n]Mt 10:16; 1Co 14:20
16:20 [o]Ro 15:33 [p]Ge 3:15 [q]1Th 5:28
16:21 [r]Ac 16:1 [s]Ac 13:1 [t]Ac 17:5 [u]ver 7,11
16:23 [v]Ac 19:22
16:25 [w]Eph 3:20 [x]Ro 2:16 [y]Eph 1:9; Col 1:26,27
16:27 [z]Ro 11:36

a *1* Or *deaconess* **b** *3* Greek *Prisca,* a variant of *Priscilla* **c** *23* Some manuscripts *their greetings. 24May the grace of our Lord Jesus Christ be with all of you. Amen.*

1 CORINTHIANS

AT A GLANCE

Key Principle: Knowledge of Christ should transform believers, both personally and in community, so that their character and conduct are clearly different from those who do not know Christ.

Author: Paul

Time and Place: A.D. 55 / Sent from Ephesus to Corinth

Key Verses: 6:19–20; 10:12–13, 31; 13:4–7

BENEFIT

In this letter, Paul gives very practical instruction on how to apply Biblical principles to a wide variety of personal and communal issues, including the need for unity rather than divisiveness in the body of believers, church discipline for sexual immorality, the problem of lawsuits between believers. He also gives advice about marriage and the believer's liberty regarding doubtful things, and instructs his readers about the use of spiritual gifts in public worship and the nature of the resurrection.

SETTING

Corinth was a thriving commercial center in Greece; it was strategically located on a narrow isthmus between the Aegean and the Adriatic Seas. Corinth was also a center of idolatry and immorality, travelers and pleasure seekers came here to be entertained. It boasted many temples and shrines, the most prominent of which was the Temple of Aphrodite, the goddess of love. She was worshiped by means of religious prostitution, and at one time 1,000 cult prostitutes served in her temple.

During his second missionary journey, Paul established a church in this corrupt city and taught the Scriptures there for 18 months. Years later he wrote this epistle to the church at Corinth (5:9 indicates that he had written at least one previous letter to them) while on his third missionary journey near the end of his years of ministry in Ephesus (16:5–8).

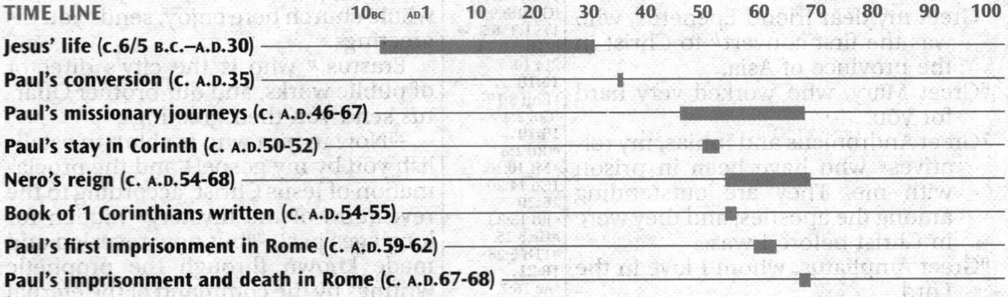

THEME AND PURPOSE

A delegation of three men from Corinth came to visit Paul in Ephesus (16:17). They delivered a letter that requested his discernment on a number of issues (7:1). Paul wrote this epistle not only to respond to this request, but also to deal with disturbing reports from Chloe's household about quarrels in the church (1:11). In this corrective letter, Paul rebukes the Corinthian church for problems of disunity, immorality, lack of discipline, selfishness, abuse of the Lord's Supper and of spiritual gifts and disbelief in the resurrection. The church was entrenched at Corinth, but the problem was that Corinth was becoming entrenched in the church. As Paul answers the believers' specific questions, he uses the expression "Now about" or "Now . . ." to delineate these subjects (7:1, 25; 8:1; 11:3; 12:1; 16:1). The theme of 1 Corinthians is that believers need to demonstrate a lifestyle of Christlike love and purity, both in their personal relationships and in the church body as a whole.

UNIQUE CONTRIBUTION

1 Corinthians is the most practical of Paul's epistles; it's full of specific counsel that relates to a wide range of personal and corporate issues. Among Paul's letters to the church it is second only to Romans in length, but in contrast to his eloquent, systematic, formal and preventive focus in Romans, 1 Corinthians is plain, unvarnished, informal and corrective. In spite of its urgency and intense practicality, this letter contributes a number of significant doctrinal insights, particularly in the areas of ecclesiology (the doctrine of the church) and eschatology (the doctrine of end times; chapter 15 contributes greatly to our understanding of the resurrection). Chapter 7 is one of the central Biblical passages on marriage, and chapters 12—14 are critical to the church's understanding of the nature and use of spiritual gifts. This epistle also provides more insight into the problems and conditions of the first-century church than any other biblical book.

CHRIST IN 1 CORINTHIANS

First Corinthians presents Christ as the source of true unity, other-centered love, godly moral conduct and character and spiritual wisdom and maturity. Christ Jesus "has become for us wisdom from God—that is, our righteousness, holiness and redemption" (1:30). He is our exemplar (11:1) and our hope. Because of his resurrection, all who have faith in him will also be resurrected (15).

OVERVIEW

FOCUS	Reproofs to the Church		Replies to the Church	
REFERENCE	1 — 4	5 — 6	7 — 11:1	11:2 — 16
TOPICS	Divisions	Discipline	Discussion	Disorder and Disbelief
	Condemnation		Counsel	
	Four Problems: Factions, Incest, Lawsuits, Sexual Immorality		Four Perspectives: Marriage, Food Offered to Idols, Public Worship, Resurrection	
LOCATION	Sent from Ephesus to Corinth			
TIME	A.D. 55			

First, Paul addresses the problem of false pride and divisiveness that comes by focusing on people rather than the Lord (1:1–17). Human wisdom is totally inadequate; only God's power and wisdom can bring salvation (1:18–31). The spiritual truth of the gospel must be spiritually discerned (2), and the divisions in the Corinthian church flow from a lack of such discernment (3). God raises up human leaders as his servants; however, it is not these people, but *Christ* who should be the believer's source of pride (4).

Second, Paul turns to the problem of incest between a church member and his stepmother, exhorting the church to exercise corporate discipline by removing the offender from their fellowship until he repents (5). Third, regarding the problem of lawsuits between believers, Paul instructs them to settle their differences among themselves without resorting to the civil courts (6:1–8). Fourth, Paul addresses sexual immorality (6:9–20).

In chapters 7—16, Paul discusses the specific questions raised and offers spiritual perspectives on four areas. First, he takes up the issues of marriage, celibacy, divorce and remarriage (7). Second, he turns to the problem of food offered to idols and develops the principles of liberty in Christ and limiting this liberty out of love and concern for the weaker believer (8—11:1). Third, the apostle focuses on public worship and deals with selfish abuses of the Lord's Supper and of spiritual gifts (11:2—14:40). Fourth, Paul corrects misunderstandings concerning the resurrection (15). He concludes his epistle with personal requests and greetings (16).

1 CORINTHIANS

1 Paul, called to be an apostle[a] of Christ Jesus by the will of God,[b] and our brother Sosthenes,[c]

2 To the church of God in Corinth,[d] to those sanctified in Christ Jesus and called[e] to be holy, together with all those everywhere who call on the name of our Lord Jesus Christ—their Lord and ours:

3 Grace and peace to you from God our Father and the Lord Jesus Christ.[f]

Thanksgiving

1 →PG. 1277

4 I always thank God for you[g] because of his grace given you in Christ Jesus. 5 For in him you have been enriched[h] in every way—in all your speaking and in all your knowledge[i]— 6 because our testimony[j] about Christ was confirmed in you. 7 Therefore you do not lack any spiritual gift as you eagerly wait for our Lord Jesus Christ to be revealed.[k] 8 He will keep you strong to the end, so that you will be blameless[l] on the day of our Lord Jesus Christ. 9 God, who has called you into fellowship with his Son Jesus Christ our Lord,[m] is faithful.[n]

Divisions in the Church

6 →PG. 1256

10 I appeal to you, brothers, in the name of our Lord Jesus Christ, that all of you agree with one another so that there may be no divisions among you and that you may be perfectly united in mind and thought. 11 My brothers, some from Chloe's household have informed me that there are quarrels among you. 12 What I mean is this: One of you says, "I follow Paul";[o] another, "I follow Apollos";[p] another, "I follow Cephas**a**";[q] still another, "I follow Christ."

13 Is Christ divided? Was Paul crucified for you? Were you baptized into**b** the name of Paul?[r] 14 I am thankful that I did not baptize any of you except Crispus[s] and Gaius,[t] 15 so no one can say that you were baptized into my name. 16 (Yes, I also baptized the household of Stephanas;[u] beyond that, I don't remember if I baptized anyone else.) 17 For Christ did not send me to baptize,[v] but to preach the gospel—not with words of human wisdom,[w] lest the cross of Christ be emptied of its power.

1:1 [a]Ro 1:1; Eph 1:1 [b]2Co 1:1 [c]Ac 18:17
1:2 [d]Ac 18:1 [e]Ro 1:7
1:3 [f]Ro 1:7
1:4 [g]Ro 1:8
1:5 [h]2Co 9:11 [i]2Co 8:7
1:6 [j]Rev 1:2
1:7 [k]Php 3:20; Tit 2:13; 2Pe 3:12
1:8 [l]1Th 3:13
1:9 [m]1Jn 1:3 [n]Isa 49:7; 1Th 5:24
1:12 [o]1Co 3:4,22 [p]Ac 18:24 [q]Jn 1:42
1:13 [r]Mt 28:19
1:14 [s]Ac 18:8; Ro 16:23 [t]Ac 19:29
1:16 [u]1Co 16:15
1:17 [v]Jn 4:2 [w]1Co 2:1,4,13
1:18 [x]2Co 2:15 [y]Ro 1:16
1:19 [z]Isa 29:14
1:20 [a]Isa 19:11,12 [b]Job 12:17; Ro 1:22
1:22 [c]Mt 12:38
1:23 [d]Lk 2:34; Gal 5:11 [e]1Co 2:14
1:24 [f]Ro 8:28

Christ the Wisdom and Power of God

18 For the message of the cross is foolishness to those who are perishing,[x] but to us who are being saved it is the power of God.[y] 19 For it is written:

"I will destroy the wisdom of the
wise;
the intelligence of the intelligent
I will frustrate."**c**[z]

20 Where is the wise man?[a] Where is the scholar? Where is the philosopher of this age? Has not God made foolish[b] the wisdom of the world? 21 For since in the wisdom of God the world through its wisdom did not know him, God was pleased through the foolishness of what was preached to save those who believe. 22 Jews demand miraculous signs[c] and Greeks look for wisdom, 23 but we preach Christ crucified: a stumbling block[d] to Jews and foolishness[e] to Gentiles, 24 but to those whom God has called,[f] both

a *12* That is, Peter **b** *13* Or *in*; also in verse 15
c *19* Isaiah 29:14

1:18–25

PROMISE 1

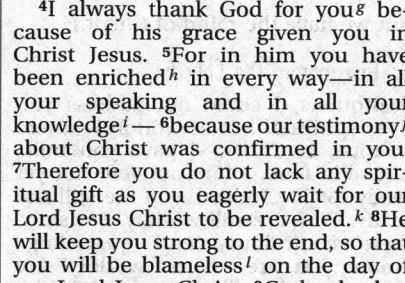

SOMETHING FOR NOTHING

Some people simply refuse to believe in God if his existence can't be proven by scientific, intellectual means. But God offers mankind a message that goes beyond the grasp of rational human intellect. While believers throughout the centuries have testified that faith in Jesus is reasonable, Paul reflects the fact that to most people, the message of salvation seems utterly foolish. Why? Because its only requirement is faith. Men don't like that. Most men feel like they want or need to *do* something to earn God's favor.

But for a believer, the gospel isn't foolish. On the contrary, it demonstrates both the wisdom and power of God. It shows God's wisdom by providing the only possible basis for forgiveness—a sinless sacrifice. It shows God's power because Jesus secured something through his death and resurrection that man was unable to produce: namely, our salvation.

One thing is clear, the gospel message came from God. Men would never have dreamed up something so amazing and wonderful—and so completely free.

For the next Promise 1 reading go to page 1256.

Jews and Greeks, Christ the power of God and the wisdom of God.[g] 25For the foolishness[h] of God is wiser than man's wisdom, and the weakness[i] of God is stronger than man's strength.

6 →PG. 1264

26Brothers, think of what you were when you were called. Not many of you were wise by human standards; not many were influential; not many were of noble birth. 27But God chose[j] the foolish[k] things of the world to shame the wise; God chose the weak things of the world to shame the strong. 28He chose the lowly things of this world and the despised things—and the things that are not[l]—to nullify the things that are, 29so that no one may boast before him.[m] 30It is because of him that you are in Christ Jesus, who has become for us wisdom from God—that is, our righteousness,[n] holiness and redemption.[o] 31Therefore, as it is written: "Let him who boasts boast in the Lord."[a][p]

2 When I came to you, brothers, I did not come with eloquence or superior wisdom[q] as I proclaimed to you the testimony about God.[b] 2For I resolved to know nothing while I was with you except Jesus Christ and him crucified.[r] 3I came to you[s] in weakness and fear, and with much trembling. 4My message and my preaching were not with wise and persuasive words, but with a demonstration of the Spirit's power,[t] 5so that your faith might not rest on men's wisdom, but on God's power.[u]

Wisdom From the Spirit

6We do, however, speak a message of wisdom among the mature,[v] but not the wisdom of this age[w] or of the rulers of this age, who are coming to nothing. 7No, we speak of God's secret wisdom, a wisdom that has been hidden and that God destined for our glory before time began. 8None of the rulers of this age understood it, for if they had, they would not have crucified the Lord of glory.[x] 9However, as it is written:

"No eye has seen,
  no ear has heard,
no mind has conceived
  what God has prepared for those
    who love him"[c][y]—

10but God has revealed[z] it to us by his Spirit.[a]

The Spirit searches all things, even the deep things of God. 11For who among men knows the thoughts of a man[b] except the man's spirit[c] within him? In the same way no one knows the thoughts of God except the Spirit of God. 12We have not received the spirit[d] of the world[e] but the Spirit who is from God, that we may understand what God has freely given us. 13This is what we speak, not in words taught us by human wisdom[f] but in words taught by the Spirit, expressing spiritual truths in spiritual words.[d] 14The man without the Spirit does not accept the things that come from the Spirit of God, for they are foolishness[g] to him, and he cannot understand them, because they are spiritually discerned. 15The spiritual man makes judgments about all things, but he himself is not subject to any man's judgment:

16"For who has known the mind of
    the Lord
  that he may instruct him?"[e][h]

But we have the mind of Christ.[i]

On Divisions in the Church

3 Brothers, I could not address you as spiritual[j] but as worldly[k]—mere infants[l] in Christ. 2I gave you milk, not solid food,[m] for you were not yet ready for it.[n] Indeed, you are still not ready. 3You are still worldly. For since there is jealousy and quarreling[o] among you, are you not worldly? Are you not acting like mere men? 4For

1:24 g ver 30; Col 2:3 **1:25** h ver 18 i 2Co 13:4 **1:27** j Jas 2:5 k ver 20 **1:28** l Ro 4:17 **1:29** m Eph 2:9 **1:30** n Jer 23:5,6; 2Co 5:21 o Ro 3:24; Eph 1:7,14 **1:31** p Jer 9:23,24; 2Co 10:17 **2:1** q 1Co 1:17 **2:2** r Gal 6:14; 1Co 1:23 **2:3** s Ac 18:1-18 **2:4** t Ro 15:19 **2:5** u 2Co 4:7; 6:7 **2:6** v Eph 4:13; Php 3:15; Heb 5:14 w 1Co 1:20 **2:8** x Ac 7:2; Jas 2:1 **2:9** y Isa 64:4; 65:17 **2:10** z Mt 13:11; Eph 3:3,5 a Jn 14:26 **2:11** b Jer 17:9 c Pr 20:27 **2:12** d Ro 8:15 e 1Co 1:20,27 **2:13** f 1Co 1:17 **2:14** g 1Co 1:18 **2:16** h Isa 40:13 i Jn 15:15 **3:1** j 1Co 2:15 k Ro 7:14; 1Co 2:14 l Heb 5:13 **3:2** m Heb 5:12-14; 1Pe 2:2 n Jn 16:12 **3:3** o 1Co 1:11; Gal 5:20

a *31* Jer. 9:24 **b** *1* Some manuscripts *as I proclaimed to you God's mystery*
c *9* Isaiah 64:4 **d** *13* Or *Spirit, interpreting spiritual truths to spiritual men*
e *16* Isaiah 40:13

2:9–3:4

PROMISE 1

GUIDED BY GOD'S SPIRIT

While Paul makes it clear that only the Spirit of God can tell us about God, not all men can comprehend what the Spirit says.

The apostle describes three kinds of men. The first man is "spiritual"; he is a believer who is sensitive to and allows the Spirit to direct his life. The second man is "worldly"; he is a believer, but he is controlled by his sinful appetites and desires rather than by God's Spirit. The third man is "without the Spirit"; he rejects whatever spiritual truth he is exposed to as complete foolishness.

As followers of Jesus Christ we possess God's Spirit. That means we can choose to have him direct our thoughts and actions while leading us into spiritual truth. But that's a choice we have to make, combined with prayer for the Spirit's power to do so, throughout every day.

For the next Promise 1 reading go to page 1276.

when one says, "I follow Paul," and another, "I follow Apollos,"[p] are you not mere men?

5What, after all, is Apollos? And what is Paul? Only servants, through whom you came to believe—as the Lord has assigned to each his task. 6I planted the seed,[q] Apollos watered it, but God made it grow. 7So neither he who plants nor he who waters is anything, but only God, who makes things grow. 8The man who plants and the man who waters have one purpose, and each will be rewarded according to his own labor.[r] 9For we are God's fellow workers;[s] you are God's field,[t] God's building.[u]

7 →PG. 1258

10By the grace God has given me,[v] I laid a foundation[w] as an expert builder, and someone else is building on it. But each one should be careful how he builds. 11For no one can lay any foundation other than the one already laid, which is Jesus Christ.[x] 12If any man builds on this foundation using gold, silver, costly stones, wood, hay or straw, 13his work will be shown for what it is,[y] because the Day[z] will bring it to light. It will be revealed with fire, and the fire will test the quality of each man's work. 14If what he has built survives, he will receive his reward. 15If it is burned up, he will suffer loss; he himself will be saved, but only as one escaping through the flames.[a]

5 →PG. 1263

16Don't you know that you yourselves are God's temple[b] and that God's Spirit lives in you? 17If anyone destroys God's temple, God will destroy him; for God's temple is sacred, and you are that temple.

3 →PG. 1257

18Do not deceive yourselves. If any one of you thinks he is wise[c] by the standards of this age, he should become a "fool" so that he may become wise. 19For the wisdom of this world is foolishness[d] in God's sight. As it is written: "He catches the wise in their craftiness"[a];[e] 20and again, "The Lord knows that the thoughts of the wise are futile."[b][f] 21So then, no more boasting about men![g] All things are yours,[h] 22whether Paul or Apollos or Cephas[c][i] or the world or life or death or the present or the future[j]—all are yours, 23and you are of Christ,[k] and Christ is of God.

Apostles of Christ

3 →PG. 1258

4 So then, men ought to regard us as servants of Christ and as those entrusted[l] with the secret things[m] of God. 2Now it is required that those who have been given a trust must prove faithful. 3I care very little if I am judged by you or by any human court; indeed, I do not even judge myself. 4My conscience is clear, but that does not make me innocent.[n] It is the Lord who judges me. 5Therefore judge nothing[o] before the appointed time; wait till the Lord comes. He will bring to light what is hidden in darkness and will expose the motives of men's hearts. At that time each will receive his praise from God.[p]

6Now, brothers, I have applied these things to myself and Apollos for your benefit, so that you may learn from us the meaning of the saying, "Do not go beyond what is written."[q] Then you will not take pride in one man over against another.[r] 7For who makes you different from anyone else? What do you have that you did not receive?[s] And if you did receive it, why do you boast as though you did not?

8Already you have all you want! Already you have become rich![t] You have become kings—and that without us! How I wish that you really had become kings so that we might be kings with you! 9For it seems to me that God has put us apostles on display at the end of the procession, like men condemned to die[u] in the arena. We have been made a spectacle[v] to the whole universe, to angels as well as to men. 10We are fools for Christ,[w] but you are so wise in Christ![x] We are weak, but you are strong![y] You are honored, we are dishonored! 11To this very hour we go hungry and thirsty, we are in rags, we are brutally treated, we are homeless.[z] 12We work hard with our own hands.[a] When we are cursed, we bless;[b] when we are persecuted, we endure it; 13when we are slandered, we answer kindly. Up to this moment

3:4 [p]1Co 1:12
3:6 [q]Ac 18:4-11
3:8 [r]Ps 62:12
3:9 [s]2Co 6:1 [t]Isa 61:3 [u]Eph 2:20-22; 1Pe 2:5
3:10 [v]Ro 12:3 [w]Ro 15:20
3:11 [x]Isa 28:16; Eph 2:20
3:13 [y]1Co 4:5 [z]2Th 1:7-10
3:15 [a]Jude 23
3:16 [b]1Co 6:19; 2Co 6:16
3:18 [c]Isa 5:21; 1Co 8:2
3:19 [d]1Co 1:20,27 [e]Job 5:13
3:20 [f]Ps 94:11
3:21 [g]1Co 4:6 [h]Ro 8:32
3:22 [i]1Co 1:12 [j]Ro 8:38
3:23 [k]1Co 15:23; 2Co 10:7; Gal 3:29
4:1 [l]1Co 9:17; Tit 1:7 [m]Ro 16:25
4:4 [n]Ro 2:13
4:5 [o]Mt 7:1,2; Ro 2:1 [p]Ro 2:29
4:6 [q]1Co 1:19,31; 3:19,20 [r]1Co 1:12
4:7 [s]Jn 3:27; Ro 12:3,6
4:8 [t]Rev 3:17,18
4:9 [u]Ro 8:36 [v]Heb 10:33
4:10 [w]1Co 1:18; Ac 17:18 [x]1Co 3:18 [y]1Co 2:3
4:11 [z]Ro 8:35; 2Co 11:23-27
4:12 [a]Ac 18:3 [b]1Pe 3:9

[a] *19* Job 5:13 [b] *20* Psalm 94:11 [c] *22* That is, Peter

4:1-4

PROMISE 3

ARE YOU SUCCESSFUL?

We tend to measure our success as men by our personal wealth or influence. Paul said success, in God's eyes, is measured by our faithfulness. As Christians we've all been given access to the mystery of salvation and are charged with living in the joy of that hope and letting others know about it.

The one thing God wants from you is to be a good steward, to do the best you can with what you have. No more. No less.

For the next Promise 3 reading go to page 1259.

we have become the scum of the earth, the refuse[c] of the world.

14I am not writing this to shame you, but to warn you, as my dear children.[d] 15Even though you have ten thousand guardians in Christ, you do not have many fathers, for in Christ Jesus I became your father through the gospel.[e]

7 →PG. 1262

16Therefore I urge you to imitate me.[f] 17For this reason I am sending to you Timothy, my son[g] whom I love, who is faithful in the Lord. He will remind you of my way of life in Christ Jesus, which agrees with what I teach everywhere in every church.[h]

18Some of you have become arrogant, as if I were not coming to you. 19But I will come to you very soon,[i] if the Lord is willing,[j] and then I will find out not only how these arrogant people are talking, but what power they have. 20For the kingdom of God is not a matter of talk but of power. 21What do you prefer? Shall I come to you with a whip,[k] or in love and with a gentle spirit?

Expel the Immoral Brother!

5 It is actually reported that there is sexual immorality among you, and of a kind that does not occur even among pagans: A man has his father's wife.[l] 2And you are proud! Shouldn't you rather have been filled with grief[m] and have put out of your fellowship the man who did this? 3Even though I am not physically present, I am with you in spirit.[n] And I have already passed judgment on the one who did this, just as if I were present. 4When you are assembled in the name of our Lord Jesus[o] and I am with you in spirit, and the power of our Lord Jesus is present, 5hand this man over[p] to Satan, so that the sinful nature[a] may be destroyed and his spirit saved on the day of the Lord.

6Your boasting is not good.[q] Don't you know that a little yeast[r] works through the whole batch of dough?[s]

3 →PG. 1258

7Get rid of the old yeast that you may be a new batch without yeast—as you really are. For Christ, our Passover lamb, has been sacrificed.[t] 8Therefore let us keep the Festival, not with the old yeast, the yeast of malice and wickedness, but with bread without yeast,[u] the bread of sincerity and truth.

9I have written you in my letter not to associate[v] with sexually immoral people— 10not at all meaning the people of this world[w] who are immoral, or the greedy and swindlers, or idolaters. In that case you would have to leave this world. 11But now I am writing you that you must not associate with anyone who calls himself a brother but is sexually immoral or greedy, an idolater[x] or a slanderer, a drunkard or a swindler. With such a man do not even eat.

12What business is it of mine to judge those outside[y] the church? Are you not to judge those inside?[z] 13God will judge those outside. "Expel the wicked man from among you."[b][a]

Lawsuits Among Believers

6 If any of you has a dispute with another, dare he take it before the ungodly for judgment instead of before the saints?[b] 2Do you not know that the saints will judge the world?[c] And if you are to judge the world, are you not competent to judge trivial cases? 3Do you not know that we will judge angels? How much more the things of this life! 4Therefore, if you have disputes about such matters, appoint as judges even men of little account in the church![c] 5I say this to shame you.[d] Is it possible that there is nobody among you wise enough to judge a dispute between believers?[e] 6But instead, one brother goes to law against another—and this in front of unbelievers![f]

7The very fact that you have lawsuits among you means you have been completely defeated already. Why not rather be wronged? Why not rather be cheated?[g] 8Instead, you yourselves cheat and do wrong, and you do this to your brothers.[h]

9Do you not know that the wicked will not inherit the kingdom of God?[i] Do not be deceived:[j] Neither the sexually immoral nor idolaters nor adulterers nor male prostitutes nor homosexual offenders 10nor thieves nor the greedy nor drunkards nor slanderers nor swindlers will inherit the kingdom of God. 11And that is what some of you were.[k] But you were washed,[l] you were sanctified,[m] you were justified in the name of the Lord Jesus Christ and by the Spirit of our God.

Sexual Immorality

12"Everything is permissible for me"—but not everything is beneficial.[n] "Everything is permissible for me"—but I will not be mastered by anything.

3 →PG. 1262

13"Food for the stomach and the stomach for food"—but God will destroy them both.[o] The body is not meant for sexual immorality, but for

a *5* Or *that his body;* or *that the flesh*
b *13* Deut. 17:7; 19:19; 21:21; 22:21,24; 24:7
c *4* Or *matters, do you appoint as judges men of little account in the church?*

4:13 c La 3:45
4:14 d 1Th 2:11
4:15 e 1Co 9:12,14, 18,23
4:16 f 1Co 11:1; Php 3:17; 1Th 1:6; 2Th 3:7,9
4:17 g 1Ti 1:2 h 1Co 7:17
4:19 i 2Co 1:15,16 j Ac 18:21
4:21 k 2Co 1:23; 13:2,10
5:1 l Lev 18:8; Dt 22:30
5:2 m 2Co 7:7-11
5:3 n Col 2:5
5:4 o 2Th 3:6
5:5 p 1Ti 1:20
5:6 q Jas 4:16 r Mt 16:6,12 s Gal 5:9
5:7 t Mk 14:12; 1Pe 1:19
5:8 u Ex 12:14,15; Dt 16:3
5:9 v Eph 5:11; 2Th 3:6,14
5:10 w 1Co 10:27
5:11 x 1Co 10:7,14
5:12 y Mk 4:11 z ver 3-5; 1Co 6:1-4
5:13 a Dt 13:5
6:1 b Mt 18:17
6:2 c Mt 19:28; Lk 22:30
6:5 d 1Co 4:14 e Ac 1:15
6:6 f 2Co 6:14,15
6:7 g Mt 5:39,40
6:8 h 1Th 4:6
6:9 i Gal 5:21 j 1Co 15:33; Jas 1:16
6:11 k Eph 2:2 l Ac 22:16 m 1Co 1:2
6:12 n 1Co 10:23
6:13 o Col 2:22

the Lord, and the Lord for the body. 14 By his power God raised the Lord from the dead, and he will raise us also.[p] 15 Do you not know that your bodies are members of Christ himself?[q] Shall I then take the members of Christ and unite them with a prostitute? Never! 16 Do you not know that he who unites himself with a prostitute is one with her in body? For it is said, "The two will become one flesh."[a][r] 17 But he who unites himself with the Lord is one with him in spirit.[s]

18 Flee from sexual immorality.[t] All other sins a man commits are outside his body, but he who sins sexually sins against his own body.[u] 19 Do you not know that your body is a temple[v] of the Holy Spirit, who is in you, whom you have received from God? You are not your own;[w] 20 you were bought at a price.[x] Therefore honor God with your body.

Marriage

4 →PG. 1259

7 Now for the matters you wrote about: It is good for a man not to marry.[b][y] 2 But since there is so much immorality, each man should have his own wife, and each woman her own husband. 3 The husband should fulfill his marital duty to his wife,[z] and likewise the wife to her husband. 4 The wife's body does not belong to her alone but also to her husband. In the same way, the husband's body does not belong to him alone but also to his wife. 5 Do not deprive each other except by mutual consent and for a time,[a] so that you may devote yourselves to prayer. Then come together again so that Satan[b] will not tempt you[c] because of your lack of self-control. 6 I say this as a concession, not as a command.[d] 7 I wish that all men were as I am.[e] But each man has his own gift from God; one has this gift, another has that.[f]

8 Now to the unmarried and the widows I say: It is good for them to stay unmarried, as I am.[g] 9 But if they cannot control themselves, they should marry,[h] for it is better to marry than to burn with passion.

4 →PG. 1263

10 To the married I give this command (not I, but the Lord): A wife must not separate from her husband.[i] 11 But if she does, she must remain unmarried or else be reconciled to her husband. And a husband must not divorce his wife.

12 To the rest I say this (I, not the Lord):[j] If any brother has a wife who is not a believer and she is willing to live with him, he must not divorce her. 13 And if a woman has a husband who is not a believer and he is willing to live with her, she must not divorce him. 14 For the unbelieving husband has been sanctified through his wife, and the unbelieving wife has been sanctified through her believing husband. Otherwise your children would be unclean, but as it is, they are holy.[k]

15 But if the unbeliever leaves, let him do so. A believing man or woman is not bound in such circumstances; God has called us to live in peace.[l] 16 How do you know, wife, whether you will save[m] your husband?[n] Or, how do you know, husband, whether you will save your wife?

17 Nevertheless, each one should retain the place in life that the Lord assigned to him and to which God has called him.[o] This is the rule I lay down in all the churches.[p] 18 Was a man already circumcised when he was called? He should not become uncircumcised. Was a man uncircumcised when he

6:14 [p]Ro 6:5; Eph 1:19,20
6:15 [q]Ro 12:5
6:16 [r]Ge 2:24; Mt 19:5; Eph 5:31
6:17 [s]Jn 17:21-23; Gal 2:20
6:18 [t]2Co 12:21; 1Th 4:3,4; Heb 13:4 [u]Ro 6:12
6:19 [v]Jn 2:21 [w]Ro 14:7,8
6:20 [x]Ac 20:28; 1Co 7:23; 1Pe 1:18,19; Rev 5:9
7:1 [y]ver 8,26
7:3 [z]Ex 21:10; 1Pe 3:7
7:5 [a]Ex 19:15; 1Sa 21:4,5 [b]Mt 4:10 [c]1Th 3:5
7:6 [d]2Co 8:8
7:7 [e]ver 8; 1Co 9:5 [f]Mt 19:11,12; Ro 12:6; 1Co 12:4,11
7:8 [g]ver 1,26
7:9 [h]1Ti 5:14
7:10 [i]Mal 2:14-16; Mt 5:32; 19:3-9; Mk 10:11; Lk 16:18
7:12 [j]ver 6,10; 2Co 11:17
7:14 [k]Mal 2:15
7:15 [l]Ro 14:19; 1Co 14:33
7:16 [m]Ro 11:14 [n]1Pe 3:1
7:17 [o]Ro 12:3 [p]1Co 4:17; 14:33; 2Co 8:18; 11:28

[a] 16 Gen. 2:24 [b] 1 Or *"It is good for a man not to have sexual relations with a woman."*

6:12–20

PROMISE 3

TEMPTATION CALLING

When a television reporter once asked a group of Christian men about the difficulties of managing their lives, they identified moral purity as the number one challenge. Most men would probably respond as these men did, especially in our modern era when we're bombarded by so much sexual stimulation. Paul's words to the believers in Corinth are as timely today as in any other era in the church's history.

Paul outlines the first step in maintaining moral purity: "Flee from sexual immorality" (v. 18). We're all aware of situations that fuel our lust. Paul's word picture here is of an individual literally *running away* from such a situation. Take Paul's advice to heart: Identify those specific situations where you're sexually tempted, and chart out a game plan that will enable you to avoid temptation. Once you've got it, share the plan with a close friend or with your men's group. Keep reminding each other to send Jesus to the door when temptation knocks.

All Christian men should make a daily, conscious decision to turn from all forms of sexual immorality. Why? See verses 19–20 for Paul's summary. We've been called to live a life that's compatible with our new identity in Jesus Christ, and to choose to avoid such sin out of gratitude for what he's done for us.

For the next Promise 3 reading go to page 1262.

was called? He should not be circumcised.[q] 19Circumcision is nothing and
uncircumcision is nothing.[r] Keeping
God's commands is what counts.
20Each one should remain in the situation which he was in when God called
him.[s] 21Were you a slave when you
were called? Don't let it trouble you—
although if you can gain your freedom,
do so. 22For he who was a slave when
he was called by the Lord is the Lord's
freedman;[t] similarly, he who was a
free man when he was called is Christ's
slave.[u] 23You were bought at a price;[v]
do not become slaves of men. 24Broth-
ers, each man, as responsible to God,
should remain in the situation God
called him to.[w]

25Now about virgins: I have no command from the Lord,[x] but I give a
judgment as one who by the Lord's
mercy[y] is trustworthy. 26Because of
the present crisis, I think that it is good
for you to remain as you are.[z] 27Are
you married? Do not seek a divorce.
Are you unmarried? Do not look for a
wife. 28But if you do marry, you have
not sinned; and if a virgin marries, she
has not sinned. But those who marry
will face many troubles in this life, and
I want to spare you this.

29What I mean, brothers, is that the
time is short.[a] From now on those
who have wives should live as if they
had none; 30those who mourn, as if
they did not; those who are happy, as
if they were not; those who buy something, as if it were not theirs to keep;
31those who use the things of the
world, as if not engrossed in them. For

7:18 [q] Ac 15:1,2
7:19 [r] Ro 2:25-27; Gal 5:6; 6:15; Col 3:11
7:20 [s] ver 24
7:22 [t] Jn 8:32,36; Phm 16 [u] Eph 6:6
7:23 [v] 1Co 6:20
7:24 [w] ver 20
7:25 [x] ver 6; 2Co 8:8 [y] 2Co 4:1; 1Ti 1:13,16
7:26 [z] ver 1,8
7:29 [a] ver 31; Ro 13:11,12

7:1-7

PROMISE 4

HAPPILY EVER AFTER?

Four-year-old Suzi had just heard the story of *Snow White and the Seven Dwarfs* for the first time. When she got home, she retold the fairy tale with wide-eyed excitement. After telling her dad how Prince Charming had arrived on his beautiful white horse and brought Snow White back to life with a kiss, Suzi asked, "And daddy, do you know what happened next?"

"Yes," he said, "they lived happily ever after."

"No!" she replied with a frown. "They got married."

In childlike innocence that little girl spoke an in-depth truth without realizing it. Getting married doesn't necessarily mean the same thing as living happily ever after. Marriages require hard work and devotion in order to be strong. One other important factor in a healthy and happy marriage is a commitment to moral purity. In this passage, Paul gives us guidance toward that end. Underlying his instructions is an assumption that the husband and wife are in a committed, exclusive relationship—that they look only to each other to meet their needs for intimacy.

First, Paul says, the husband and wife are to meet each other's sexual needs. Notice how Paul's instructions exhort the couple to focus attention on the other's needs, not their own. A man whose sexual appetite is greater than his wife's might find such instructions a bit unsettling. After all, if he focuses on his wife, his sexual needs might go unmet. The sacrificial nature of the marriage relationship may call for this at times. But Paul's instructions not to "deprive each other" stand equally for both marriage partners.

Second, the husband is to regard his body as belonging to his wife, and the wife is to do likewise. Sometimes men make the costly mistake of getting this backwards, thinking that this passage calls their wives to be there for them. But look at Paul's instructions again: Neither the husband nor the wife is to think of the other as being there for them. Instead, they're both to view themselves as being there for their mate.

Third, a husband and wife need to take time to devote themselves to prayer. Paul lays out the ground rules for this time period: It should be mutually agreed upon. Its focus should be on prayer, not abstinence. It should also be short, so that the increased sexual energy won't provide Satan with an opportunity to tempt either spouse.

The idea of voluntary abstinence from sex within marriage may be new to you. Indeed, you may wonder why Paul would urge couples to periodically abstain from physical intimacy. Many couples find that following Paul's instructions helps to develop spiritual and emotional intimacy between partners. They see this as an exhortation for married couples to maintain a balance in their lives. They find that the transparency of prayer links them together on a number of levels, helping them find and maintain that delicate balance.

The God-honoring marriage relationship encompasses all aspects of the couple's lives—physical, emotional, spiritual, intellectual, and so on. Prayer between marriage partners dissolves barriers. It creates emotional intimacy. It strengthens the relationship, and in so doing brings partners closer together on all levels.

Paul's instructions leave no room for spouses to ignore the needs of their partners. They urge husbands to put their wives' needs before their own, and vice versa. A couple who demonstrates such sacrificial love will have made a good start on the journey toward living "happily ever after."

For the next Promise 4 reading go to page 1300.

this world in its present form is passing
away.[b]
32I would like you to be free from
concern. An unmarried man is concerned about the Lord's affairs[c]—
how he can please the Lord. **33**But a
married man is concerned about the
affairs of this world—how he can
please his wife— **34**and his interests are
divided. An unmarried woman or virgin is concerned about the Lord's affairs: Her aim is to be devoted to the
Lord in both body and spirit.[d] But a
married woman is concerned about
the affairs of this world—how she can
please her husband. **35**I am saying this
for your own good, not to restrict you,
but that you may live in a right way in
undivided[e] devotion to the Lord.
36If anyone thinks he is acting im-
properly toward the virgin he is engaged to, and if she is getting along in
years and he feels he ought to marry,
he should do as he wants. He is not
sinning.[f] They should get married.
37But the man who has settled the matter in his own mind, who is under no
compulsion but has control over his
own will, and who has made up his
mind not to marry the virgin—this
man also does the right thing. **38**So
then, he who marries the virgin does
right,[g] but he who does not marry her
does even better.[a]
39A woman is bound to her husband
as long as he lives.[h] But if her husband
dies, she is free to marry anyone she
wishes, but he must belong to the
Lord.[i] **40**In my judgment,[j] she is
happier if she stays as she is—and I
think that I too have the Spirit of God.

Food Sacrificed to Idols

8 Now about food sacrificed to
idols:[k] We know that we all possess
knowledge.[b][l] Knowledge puffs up,
but love builds up. **2**The man who
thinks he knows something[m] does not
yet know as he ought to know.[n] **3**But
the man who loves God is known by
God.[o]
4So then, about eating food sacrificed to idols:[p] We know that an idol is
nothing at all in the world[q] and that
there is no God but one.[r] **5**For even if
there are so-called gods,[s] whether in
heaven or on earth (as indeed there are
many "gods" and many "lords"), **6**yet
for us there is but one God, the Father,[t] from whom all things came[u]
and for whom we live; and there is but
one Lord,[v] Jesus Christ, through
whom all things came[w] and through
whom we live.
7But not everyone knows this. Some
people are still so accustomed to idols
that when they eat such food they
think of it as having been sacrificed to
an idol, and since their conscience is
weak,[x] it is defiled. **8**But food does not
bring us near to God;[y] we are no
worse if we do not eat, and no better if
we do.
9Be careful, however, that the exercise of your freedom does not become
a stumbling block[z] to the weak.[a]
10For if anyone with a weak conscience
sees you who have this knowledge eating in an idol's temple, won't he be
emboldened to eat what has been sacrificed to idols? **11**So this weak brother,
for whom Christ died, is destroyed[b]
by your knowledge. **12**When you sin
against your brothers[c] in this way and
wound their weak conscience, you sin
against Christ. **13**Therefore, if what I eat
causes my brother to fall into sin, I will
never eat meat again, so that I will not
cause him to fall.[d]

The Rights of an Apostle

9 Am I not free? Am I not an apostle?[e] Have I not seen Jesus our
Lord?[f] Are you not the result of my
work in the Lord?[g] **2**Even though I
may not be an apostle to others, surely
I am to you! For you are the seal[h] of
my apostleship in the Lord.
3This is my defense to those who sit
in judgment on me. **4**Don't we have the
right to food and drink?[i] **5**Don't we
have the right to take a believing wife[j]
along with us, as do the other apostles
and the Lord's brothers[k] and Cephas[c]? **6**Or is it only I and Barnabas[l]
who must work for a living?
7Who serves as a soldier at his own
expense? Who plants a vineyard[m] and
does not eat of its grapes? Who tends a
flock and does not drink of the milk?
8Do I say this merely from a human
point of view? Doesn't the Law say the
same thing? **9**For it is written in the Law
of Moses: "Do not muzzle an ox while
it is treading out the grain."[d][n] Is it
about oxen that God is concerned?[o]
10Surely he says this for us, doesn't he?
Yes, this was written for us,[p] because

7:31 [b]1Jn 2:17
7:32 [c]1Ti 5:5
7:34 [d]Lk 2:37
7:35 [e]Ps 86:11
7:36 [f]ver 28
7:38 [g]Heb 13:4
7:39 [h]Ro 7:2,3 [i]2Co 6:14
7:40 [j]ver 25
8:1 [k]Ac 15:20 [l]Ro 15:14
8:2 [m]1Co 3:18 [n]1Co 13:8,9, 12; 1Ti 6:4
8:3 [o]Ro 8:29; Gal 4:9
8:4 [p]ver 1,7,10 [q]1Co 10:19 [r]Dt 6:4; Eph 4:6
8:5 [s]2Th 2:4
8:6 [t]Mal 2:10 [u]Ro 11:36 [v]Eph 4:5 [w]Jn 1:3
8:7 [x]Ro 14:14; 1Co 10:28
8:8 [y]Ro 14:17
8:9 [z]Gal 5:13 [a]Ro 14:1
8:11 [b]Ro 14:15,20
8:12 [c]Mt 18:6
8:13 [d]Ro 14:21
9:1 [e]2Co 12:12 [f]1Co 15:8 [g]1Co 3:6; 4:15
9:2 [h]2Co 3:2,3
9:4 [i]1Th 2:6
9:5 [j]1Co 7:7,8 [k]Mt 12:46
9:6 [l]Ac 4:36
9:7 [m]Dt 20:6; Pr 27:18
9:9 [n]Dt 25:4; 1Ti 5:18 [o]Dt 22:1-4
9:10 [p]Ro 4:23,24

[a] *36-38* Or *36If anyone thinks he is not treating his daughter properly, and if she is getting along in years, and he feels she ought to marry, he should do as he wants. He is not sinning. He should let her get married. 37But the man who has settled the matter in his own mind, who is under no compulsion but has control over his own will, and who has made up his mind to keep the virgin unmarried—this man also does the right thing. 38So then, he who gives his virgin in marriage does right, but he who does not give her in marriage does even better.*
[b] *1* Or *"We all possess knowledge," as you say*
[c] *5* That is, Peter
[d] *9* Deut. 25:4

when the plowman plows and the thresher threshes, they ought to do so in the hope of sharing in the harvest.[q] 11If we have sown spiritual seed among you, is it too much if we reap a material harvest from you?[r] 12If others have this right of support from you, shouldn't we have it all the more?

But we did not use this right.[s] On the contrary, we put up with anything rather than hinder[t] the gospel of Christ. 13Don't you know that those who work in the temple get their food from the temple, and those who serve at the altar share in what is offered on the altar?[u] 14In the same way, the Lord has commanded that those who preach the gospel should receive their living from the gospel.[v]

15But I have not used any of these rights.[w] And I am not writing this in the hope that you will do such things for me. I would rather die than have anyone deprive me of this boast.[x] 16Yet when I preach the gospel, I cannot boast, for I am compelled to preach.[y] Woe to me if I do not preach the gospel! 17If I preach voluntarily, I have a reward;[z] if not voluntarily, I am simply discharging the trust committed to me.[a] 18What then is my reward? Just this: that in preaching the gospel I may offer it free of charge,[b] and so not make use of my rights in preaching it.

7 →PG. 1263

19Though I am free[c] and belong to no man, I make myself a slave to everyone,[d] to win as many as possible.[e] 20To the Jews I became like a Jew, to win the Jews.[f] To those under the law I became like one under the law (though I myself am not under the law), so as to win those under the law. 21To those not having the law I became like one not having the law[g] (though I am not free from God's law but am under Christ's law), so as to win those not having the law. 22To the weak I became weak, to win the weak. I have become all things to all men[h] so that by all possible means I might save some.[i] 23I do all this for the sake of the gospel, that I may share in its blessings.

3 →PG. 1263

24Do you not know that in a race all the runners run, but only one gets the prize? Run[j] in such a way as to get the prize. 25Everyone who competes in the games goes into strict training. They do it to get a crown that will not last; but we do it to get a crown that will last forever.[k] 26Therefore I do not run like a man running aimlessly; I do not fight like a man beating the air. 27No, I beat my body[l] and make it my slave so that after I have preached to others, I myself will not be disqualified for the prize.

9:10 [q]2Ti 2:6 **9:11** [r]Ro 15:27 **9:12** [s]Ac 18:3 [t]2Co 11:7-12 **9:13** [u]Lev 6:16,26; Dt 18:1 **9:14** [v]Mt 10:10; 1Ti 5:18 **9:15** [w]Ac 18:3 [x]2Co 11:9,10 **9:16** [y]Ro 1:14; Ac 9:15 **9:17** [z]1Co 3:8,14 [a]Gal 2:7; Col 1:25 **9:18** [b]2Co 11:7; 12:13 **9:19** [c]ver 1 [d]Gal 5:13 [e]Mt 18:15; 1Pe 3:1 **9:20** [f]Ac 16:3; 21:20-26; Ro 11:14 **9:21** [g]Ro 2:12,14 **9:22** [h]1Co 10:33 [i]Ro 11:14 **9:24** [j]Gal 2:2; 2Ti 4:7; Heb 12:1 **9:25** [k]Jas 1:12; Rev 2:10 **9:27** [l]Ro 8:13

10:1 [m]Ex 13:21 [n]Ex 14:22,29 **10:4** [o]Ex 17:6; Nu 20:11; Ps 78:15 **10:5** [p]Nu 14:29; Heb 3:17 **10:7** [q]ver 14 [r]Ex 32:4,6,19 **10:8** [s]Nu 25:1-9 **10:9** [t]Nu 21:5,6

Warnings From Israel's History

10 For I do not want you to be ignorant of the fact, brothers, that our forefathers were all under the cloud[m] and that they all passed through the sea.[n] 2They were all baptized into Moses in the cloud and in the sea. 3They all ate the same spiritual food 4and drank the same spiritual drink; for they drank from the spiritual rock[o] that accompanied them, and that rock was Christ. 5Nevertheless, God was not pleased with most of them; their bodies were scattered over the desert.[p]

6Now these things occurred as examples[a] to keep us from setting our hearts on evil things as they did. 7Do not be idolaters,[q] as some of them were; as it is written: "The people sat down to eat and drink and got up to indulge in pagan revelry."[b][r] 8We should not commit sexual immorality, as some of them did—and in one day twenty-three thousand of them died.[s] 9We should not test the Lord, as some of them did—and were killed by snakes.[t] 10And do not grumble, as

[a]6 Or *types*; also in verse 11 [b]7 Exodus 32:6

9:24–27

WINNING THE PRIZE

PROMISE 3

Olympic champions earn their medals the hard way—they work for them. On an average day, the U.S. Olympic Training Center in Colorado Springs, Colorado, has 350 athletes training in different events. These young people have given up full-time studies and family time and have dedicated themselves to one thing: winning in national and international competition.

Most of us will never have the privilege of participating in the Olympics. But as believers, we're called to train for a prize that will shine long after an Olympic gold medal has lost its luster. Right now God has a prize waiting for us—eternal life. It will be our reward for running the race of life in a way that pleases God.

A dedicated athlete has to carefully chart out his training routine. So does a dedicated Christian. What activities would be on a godly man's spiritual training regimen? What activities would such a man avoid? Paul responded to the challenge of "running the race" with discipline, devotion and direction. He kept the finish line in mind at all times. Can you think of ways that will help you maintain that kind of eternal perspective?

For the next Promise 3 reading go to page 1278.

some of them did[u]—and were killed[v] by the destroying angel.[w]

11These things happened to them as examples and were written down as warnings for us, on whom the fulfillment of the ages has come.[x] **12**So, if you think you are standing firm,[y] be careful that you don't fall! **13**No temptation has seized you except what is common to man. And God is faithful;[z] he will not let you be tempted beyond what you can bear.[a] But when you are tempted, he will also provide a way out so that you can stand up under it.

3 →PG. 1275

Idol Feasts and the Lord's Supper

14Therefore, my dear friends, flee from idolatry. **15**I speak to sensible people; judge for yourselves what I say. **16**Is not the cup of thanksgiving for which we give thanks a participation in the blood of Christ? And is not the bread that we break a participation in the body of Christ?[b] **17**Because there is one loaf, we, who are many, are one body,[c] for we all partake of the one loaf.

5 →PG. 1264

18Consider the people of Israel: Do not those who eat the sacrifices[d] participate in the altar? **19**Do I mean then that a sacrifice offered to an idol is anything, or that an idol is anything?[e] **20**No, but the sacrifices of pagans are offered to demons,[f] not to God, and I do not want you to be participants with demons. **21**You cannot drink the cup of the Lord and the cup of demons too; you cannot have a part in both the Lord's table and the table of demons.[g] **22**Are we trying to arouse the Lord's jealousy?[h] Are we stronger than he?[i]

The Believer's Freedom

23"Everything is permissible"—but not everything is beneficial.[j] "Everything is permissible"—but not everything is constructive. **24**Nobody should seek his own good, but the good of others.[k]

25Eat anything sold in the meat market without raising questions of conscience,[l] **26**for, "The earth is the Lord's, and everything in it."[a][m]

27If some unbeliever invites you to a meal and you want to go, eat whatever is put before you[n] without raising questions of conscience. **28**But if anyone says to you, "This has been offered in sacrifice," then do not eat it, both for the sake of the man who told you and for conscience' sake[b][o]— **29**the other man's conscience, I mean, not yours. For why should my freedom[p] be judged by another's conscience? **30**If I take part in the meal with thankfulness, why am I denounced because of something I thank God for?[q]

31So whether you eat or drink or whatever you do, do it all for the glory of God.[r] **32**Do not cause anyone to stumble,[s] whether Jews, Greeks or the church of God[t]— **33**even as I try to please everybody in every way.[u] For I am not seeking my own good but the good of many, so that they may be saved.[v]

11 **1**Follow my example,[w] as I follow the example of Christ.

7 →PG. 1265

Propriety in Worship

2I praise you[x] for remembering me in everything[y] and for holding to the teachings,[c] just as I passed them on to you.[z]

3Now I want you to realize that the head of every man is Christ,[a] and the head of the woman is man,[b] and the head of Christ is God.[c] **4**Every man who prays or prophesies with his head covered dishonors his head. **5**And every woman who prays or prophesies[d] with her head uncovered dishonors her head—it is just as though her head were shaved.[e] **6**If a woman does not cover her head, she should have her hair cut off; and if it is a disgrace for a woman to have her hair cut or shaved off, she should cover her head. **7**A man ought not to cover his head,[d] since he is the image[f] and glory of God; but the woman is the glory of man. **8**For man did not come from woman, but woman from man;[g] **9**neither was man created for woman, but woman for man.[h] **10**For this reason, and because of the angels, the woman ought to have a sign of authority on her head.

11In the Lord, however, woman is not independent of man, nor is man independent of woman. **12**For as woman came from man, so also man is born of woman. But everything comes from God.[i] **13**Judge for yourselves: Is it proper for a woman to pray to God with her head uncovered? **14**Does not the very nature of things teach you that if a man has long hair, it is a disgrace to him, **15**but that if a woman has long hair, it is her glory? For long hair is given to her as a covering. **16**If anyone wants to be contentious about this, we

4 →PG. 1300

- **10:10** [u]Nu 16:41 [v]Nu 16:49 [w]Ex 12:23
- **10:11** [x]Ro 13:11
- **10:12** [y]Ro 11:20
- **10:13** [z]1Co 1:9 [a]2Pe 2:9
- **10:16** [b]Mt 26:26-28
- **10:17** [c]Ro 12:5; 1Co 12:27
- **10:18** [d]Lev 7:6,14,15
- **10:19** [e]1Co 8:4
- **10:20** [f]Dt 32:17; Ps 106:37; Rev 9:20
- **10:21** [g]2Co 6:15,16
- **10:22** [h]Dt 32:16,21 [i]Ecc 6:10; Isa 45:9
- **10:23** [j]1Co 6:12
- **10:24** [k]ver 33; Ro 15:1,2; 1Co 13:5; Php 2:4,21
- **10:25** [l]Ac 10:15; 1Co 8:7
- **10:26** [m]Ps 24:1
- **10:27** [n]Lk 10:7
- **10:28** [o]1Co 8:7,10-12
- **10:29** [p]Ro 14:16; 1Co 9:1,19
- **10:30** [q]Ro 14:6
- **10:31** [r]Col 3:17; 1Pe 4:11
- **10:32** [s]Ac 24:16 [t]Ac 20:28
- **10:33** [u]Ro 15:2; 1Co 9:22 [v]Ro 11:14
- **11:1** [w]1Co 4:16
- **11:2** [x]ver 17,22 [y]1Co 4:17 [z]1Co 15:2,3; 2Th 2:15
- **11:3** [a]Eph 1:22 [b]Ge 3:16; Eph 5:23 [c]1Co 3:23
- **11:5** [d]Ac 21:9 [e]Dt 21:12
- **11:7** [f]Ge 1:26; Jas 3:9
- **11:8** [g]Ge 2:21-23; 1Ti 2:13
- **11:9** [h]Ge 2:18
- **11:12** [i]Ro 11:36

a *26* Psalm 24:1 **b** *28* Some manuscripts *conscience' sake, for "the earth is the Lord's and everything in it"* **c** *2* Or *traditions* **d** *4-7* Or *4Every man who prays or prophesies with long hair dishonors his head. 5And every woman who prays or prophesies with no covering ⌊of hair⌋ on her head dishonors her head—she is just like one of the "shorn women." 6If a woman has no covering, let her be for now with short hair, but since it is a disgrace for a woman to have her hair shorn or shaved, she should grow it again. 7A man ought not to have long hair*

have no other practice—nor do the churches of God.[j]

The Lord's Supper

17 In the following directives I have no praise for you,[k] for your meetings do more harm than good. 18 In the first place, I hear that when you come together as a church, there are divisions[l] among you, and to some extent I believe it. 19 No doubt there have to be differences among you to show which of you have God's approval.[m] 20 When you come together, it is not the Lord's Supper you eat, 21 for as you eat, each of you goes ahead without waiting for anybody else.[n] One remains hungry, another gets drunk. 22 Don't you have homes to eat and drink in? Or do you despise the church of God[o] and humiliate those who have nothing?[p] What shall I say to you? Shall I praise you[q] for this? Certainly not!

23 For I received from the Lord[r] what I also passed on to you:[s] The Lord Jesus, on the night he was betrayed, took bread, 24 and when he had given thanks, he broke it and said, "This is my body, which is for you; do this in remembrance of me." 25 In the same way, after supper he took the cup, saying, "This cup is the new covenant[t] in my blood;[u] do this, whenever you drink it, in remembrance of me." 26 For whenever you eat this bread and drink this cup, you proclaim the Lord's death until he comes.

27 Therefore, whoever eats the bread or drinks the cup of the Lord in an unworthy manner will be guilty of sinning against the body and blood of the Lord.[v] 28 A man ought to examine himself[w] before he eats of the bread and drinks of the cup. 29 For anyone who eats and drinks without recognizing the body of the Lord eats and drinks judgment on himself. 30 That is why many among you are weak and sick, and a number of you have fallen asleep. 31 But if we judged ourselves, we would not come under judgment.[x] 32 When we are judged by the Lord, we are being disciplined[y] so that we will not be condemned with the world.

33 So then, my brothers, when you come together to eat, wait for each other. 34 If anyone is hungry,[z] he should eat at home,[a] so that when you meet together it may not result in judgment.

And when I come[b] I will give further directions.

Spiritual Gifts

12 Now about spiritual gifts,[c] brothers, I do not want you to be ignorant. 2 You know that when you were pagans,[d] somehow or other you were influenced and led astray to mute idols.[e] 3 Therefore I tell you that no one who is speaking by the Spirit of God says, "Jesus be cursed,"[f] and no one can say, "Jesus is Lord,"[g] except by the Holy Spirit.[h]

4 There are different kinds of gifts, but the same Spirit.[i] 5 There are different kinds of service, but the same Lord. 6 There are different kinds of working, but the same God[j] works all of them in all men.

5 →PG. 1265
6 →PG. 1276

7 Now to each one the manifestation of the Spirit is given for the common good.[k] 8 To one there is given through the Spirit the message of wisdom,[l] to another the message of knowledge[m] by means of the same Spirit, 9 to another faith[n] by the same Spirit, to another gifts of healing[o] by that one Spirit, 10 to another miraculous powers,[p] to another prophecy, to another distinguishing between spirits,[q] to another speaking in different kinds of tongues,[a][r] and to still another the interpretation of tongues.[a] 11 All these are the work of one and the same Spirit,[s] and he gives them to each one, just as he determines.

One Body, Many Parts

12 The body is a unit, though it is made up of many parts; and though all its parts are many, they form one body.[t] So it is with Christ.[u] 13 For we were all baptized by[b] one Spirit[v] into one body—whether Jews or Greeks, slave or free[w]—and we were all given the one Spirit to drink.[x]

14 Now the body is not made up of one part but of many. 15 If the foot should say, "Because I am not a hand, I do not belong to the body," it would not for that reason cease to be part of the body. 16 And if the ear should say, "Because I am not an eye, I do not belong to the body," it would not for that reason cease to be part of the body. 17 If the whole body were an eye, where would the sense of hearing be? If the whole body were an ear, where would the sense of smell be? 18 But in fact God has arranged[y] the parts in the body, every one of them, just as he wanted them to be.[z] 19 If they were all one part, where would the body be? 20 As it is, there are many parts, but one body.[a]

21 The eye cannot say to the hand, "I don't need you!" And the head cannot say to the feet, "I don't need you!" 22 On

11:16 [j]1Co 7:17
11:17 [k]ver 2,22
11:18 [l]1Co 1:10-12; 3:3
11:19 [m]1Jn 2:19
11:21 [n]2Pe 2:13; Jude 12
11:22 [o]1Co 10:32 [p]Jas 2:6 [q]ver 2,17
11:23 [r]Gal 1:12 [s]1Co 15:3
11:25 [t]Lk 22:20 [u]1Co 10:16
11:27 [v]Heb 10:29
11:28 [w]2Co 13:5
11:31 [x]Ps 32:5; 1Jn 1:9
11:32 [y]Ps 94:12; Heb 12:7-10; Rev 3:19
11:34 [z]ver 21 [a]ver 22 [b]1Co 4:19
12:1 [c]Ro 1:11; 1Co 14:1,37
12:2 [d]Eph 2:11,12; 1Pe 4:3 [e]Ps 115:5; Jer 10:5; Hab 2:18,19; 1Th 1:9
12:3 [f]Ro 9:3 [g]Jn 13:13 [h]1Jn 4:2,3
12:4 [i]Ro 12:4-8; Eph 4:11; Heb 2:4
12:6 [j]Eph 4:6
12:7 [k]Eph 4:12
12:8 [l]1Co 2:6 [m]2Co 8:7
12:9 [n]Mt 17:19,20; 2Co 4:13 [o]ver 28,30
12:10 [p]Gal 3:5 [q]1Jn 4:1 [r]Mk 16:17
12:11 [s]ver 4
12:12 [t]Ro 12:5 [u]ver 27
12:13 [v]Eph 2:18 [w]Gal 3:28; Col 3:11 [x]Jn 7:37-39
12:18 [y]ver 28 [z]ver 11
12:20 [a]ver 12,14

a *10* Or *languages*; also in verse 28 **b** *13* Or *with*; or *in*

the contrary, those parts of the body
that seem to be weaker are indispensable, **23**and the parts that we think are
less honorable we treat with special
honor. And the parts that are unpre-
sentable are treated with special mod-
esty, **24**while our presentable parts
need no special treatment. But God
has combined the members of the
body and has given greater honor to
the parts that lacked it, **25**so that there
should be no division in the body, but
that its parts should have equal concern for each other. **26**If one part suffers, every part suffers with it; if one
part is honored, every part rejoices
with it.
5 →PG. 1268
27Now you are the body of Christ,[b]
and each one of you is a part of it.[c]
28And in the church[d] God has appointed first of all apostles,[e] second
prophets, third teachers, then workers
of miracles, also those having gifts of
healing,[f] those able to help others,
those with gifts of administration,[g]
and those speaking in different kinds
of tongues.[h] **29**Are all apostles? Are all
prophets? Are all teachers? Do all work
miracles? **30**Do all have gifts of healing? Do all speak in tongues[a]?[i] Do all

12:27 [b]Eph 1:23; 4:12; Col 1:18, 24 [c]Ro 12:5 **12:28** [d]1Co 10:32 [e]Eph 4:11 [f]ver 9 [g]Ro 12:6-8 [h]ver 10 **12:30** [i]ver 10 **12:31** [j]1Co 14:1,39 **13:1** [k]ver 8 **13:2** [l]1Co 14:2 [m]1Co 12:9 [n]Mt 17:20; 21:21 **13:3** [o]Mt 6:2 [p]Da 3:28 **13:4** [q]1Th 5:14 **13:5** [r]1Co 10:24 **13:6** [s]2Th 2:12 [t]2Jn 4; 3Jn 3,4

interpret? **31**But eagerly desire[b][j] the
greater gifts.

Love

And now I will show you the most
excellent way.

13 If I speak in the tongues[c][k] of men
and of angels, but have not love, I
am only a resounding gong or a clanging cymbal. **2**If I have the gift of prophecy and can fathom all mysteries[l] and
all knowledge, and if I have a faith[m]
that can move mountains,[n] but have
not love, I am nothing. **3**If I give all I
possess to the poor[o] and surrender
my body to the flames,[d][p] but have
not love, I gain nothing.
4Love is patient,[q] love is kind. It
does not envy, it does not boast, it is
not proud. **5**It is not rude, it is not self-
seeking,[r] it is not easily angered, it
keeps no record of wrongs. **6**Love does
not delight in evil[s] but rejoices with
the truth.[t] **7**It always protects, always
trusts, always hopes, always perseveres.
7 →PG. 1276

[a]*30* Or *other languages* [b]*31* Or *But you are eagerly desiring* [c]*1* Or *languages* [d]*3* Some early manuscripts *body that I may boast*

12:12–31

BODY PARTS

PROMISE 6

Paul liked to use the human body as an illustration of the relationship believers have with one another. As members of the body of Christ, God lives in every believer; his presence links believers together. Just as each cell in your body is attuned to every other cell and receives direction from one brain, so also in Christ's body (the church) the Spirit establishes a connection between each cell and the Head, and among all the cells of his body. God has called you as a Christian to join a body that binds you together with other diverse cells.

Paul points out three things we must realize about the parts of the body of Christ. First, we need each other. Disputes in the church at Corinth had discouraged some members whose gifts weren't as publicly visible. They wondered whether they had any right to belong to a church with such impressive spiritual gifts. And apparently those whose gifts were more publicly visible felt superior to those with less spectacular gifts. But Paul set the record straight by making it clear that every part of the body needs every other part, regardless of the parts' respective functions. God doesn't value one type of gift more highly than another.

The implication is profound. No matter what church or denomination you're involved in, your bond in the Spirit links you together with every other Christian in the world. Without each committed Christian, Christ's body would be incomplete.

Second, we must honor each other. This step follows naturally from the previous one. Regardless of a man or woman's spiritual gifts, race, denominational affiliation, economic position, or any other variable, we need to honor our Christian brothers and sisters for who they are and what they contribute to the worldwide body of Christ.

Third, we must care for each other. For instance, the presence of pain in one member of the body means the whole body is involved. Just think of the last time you smashed your finger with a hammer. Your mouth opened. Your lungs and vocal cords responded with a yell. Your arm shook up and down and brought the damaged finger to your mouth. Your legs and feet helped you to jump around. Then your brain assessed the damage and decided on an appropriate treatment. Every part of your body acted to help you cope with the pain. Similarly, we can't disassociate ourselves from the trials—or the triumphs—of other devoted followers of Jesus Christ.

Paul's message provides a challenge to all of us to live in unity with other believers. Take this message as an encouragement to promote the health of the church, Christ's body, whenever and wherever you can.

For the next Promise 6 reading go to page 1289.

8Love never fails. But where there are prophecies,[u] they will cease; where there are tongues,[v] they will be stilled; where there is knowledge, it will pass away. 9For we know in part[w] and we prophesy in part, 10but when perfection comes,[x] the imperfect disappears. 11When I was a child, I talked like a child, I thought like a child, I reasoned like a child. When I became a man, I put childish ways behind me. 12Now we see but a poor reflection as in a mirror; then we shall see face to face.[y] Now I know in part; then I shall know fully, even as I am fully known.[z]

13And now these three remain: faith, hope and love.[a] But the greatest of these is love.[b]

Gifts of Prophecy and Tongues

14 Follow the way of love[c] and eagerly desire[d] spiritual gifts,[e] especially the gift of prophecy. 2For anyone who speaks in a tongue[a][f] does not speak to men but to God. Indeed, no one understands him; he utters mysteries[g] with his spirit.[b] 3But everyone who prophesies speaks to men for their strengthening,[h] encouragement and comfort. 4He who speaks in a tongue[i] edifies himself, but he who prophesies[j] edifies the church. 5I would like every one of you to speak in tongues,[c] but I would rather have you prophesy.[k] He who prophesies is greater than one who speaks in tongues,[c] unless he interprets, so that the church may be edified.

6Now, brothers, if I come to you and speak in tongues, what good will I be to you, unless I bring you some revelation[l] or knowledge or prophecy or word of instruction?[m] 7Even in the case of lifeless things that make sounds, such as the flute or harp, how will anyone know what tune is being played unless there is a distinction in the notes? 8Again, if the trumpet does not sound a clear call, who will get ready for battle?[n] 9So it is with you. Unless you speak intelligible words with your tongue, how will anyone know what you are saying? You will just be speaking into the air. 10Undoubtedly there are all sorts of languages in the world, yet none of them is without meaning. 11If then I do not grasp the meaning of what someone is saying, I am a foreigner to the speaker, and he is a foreigner to me. 12So it is with you. Since you are eager to have spiritual gifts, try to excel in gifts that build up the church.

13For this reason anyone who speaks in a tongue should pray that he may interpret what he says. 14For if I pray in a tongue, my spirit prays, but my mind is unfruitful. 15So what shall I do? I will pray with my spirit, but I will also pray with my mind; I will sing[o] with my spirit, but I will also sing with my mind. 16If you are praising God with your spirit, how can one who finds himself among those who do not understand[d] say "Amen"[p] to your thanksgiving,[q] since he does not know what you are saying? 17You may be giving thanks well enough, but the other man is not edified.

18I thank God that I speak in tongues more than all of you. 19But in the church I would rather speak five intelligible words to instruct others than ten thousand words in a tongue.

20Brothers, stop thinking like children.[r] In regard to evil be infants,[s] but in your thinking be adults. 21In the Law[t] it is written:

"Through men of strange tongues
 and through the lips of foreigners
I will speak to this people,
 but even then they will not listen to me,"[e][u]
says the Lord.

22Tongues, then, are a sign, not for believers but for unbelievers; prophecy,[v] however, is for believers, not for unbelievers. 23So if the whole church comes together and everyone speaks in tongues, and some who do not understand[f] or some unbelievers come in, will they not say that you are out of your mind?[w] 24But if an unbeliever or someone who does not understand[g] comes in while everybody is prophesying, he will be convinced by all that he is a sinner and will be judged by all, 25and the secrets of his heart will be laid bare. So he will fall down and worship God, exclaiming, "God is really among you!"[x]

Orderly Worship

26What then shall we say, brothers? When you come together, everyone[y] has a hymn,[z] or a word of instruction,[a] a revelation, a tongue or an interpretation. All of these must be done for the strengthening[b] of the church. 27If anyone speaks in a tongue, two—or at the most three—should speak, one at a time, and someone must interpret. 28If there is no interpreter, the

13:8 [u]ver 2 [v]ver 1
13:9 [w]ver 12; 1Co 8:2
13:10 [x]Php 3:12
13:12 [y]Ge 32:30; 2Co 5:7; 1Jn 3:2 [z]1Co 8:3
13:13 [a]Gal 5:5,6 [b]1Co 16:14
14:1 [c]1Co 16:14 [d]ver 39; 1Co 12:31 [e]1Co 12:1
14:2 [f]Mk 16:17 [g]1Co 13:2
14:3 [h]ver 4,5,12,17, 26; Ro 14:19
14:4 [i]Mk 16:17 [j]1Co 13:2
14:5 [k]Nu 11:29
14:6 [l]ver 26; Eph 1:17 [m]Ro 6:17
14:8 [n]Nu 10:9; Jer 4:19
14:15 [o]Eph 5:19; Col 3:16
14:16 [p]Dt 27:15-26; 1Ch 16:36; Ne 8:6; Ps 106:48; Rev 5:14; 7:12 [q]1Co 11:24
14:20 [r]Eph 4:14; Heb 5:12,13; 1Pe 2:2 [s]Ro 16:19
14:21 [t]Jn 10:34 [u]Isa 28:11,12
14:22 [v]ver 1
14:23 [w]Ac 2:13
14:25 [x]Isa 45:14; Zec 8:23
14:26 [y]1Co 12:7-10 [z]Eph 5:19 [a]ver 6 [b]Ro 14:19

[a] *2* Or *another language*; also in verses 4, 13, 14, 19, 26 and 27 [b] *2* Or *by the Spirit* [c] *5* Or *other languages*; also in verses 6, 18, 22, 23 and 39 [d] *16* Or *among the inquirers* [e] *21* Isaiah 28:11,12 [f] *23* Or *some inquirers* [g] *24* Or *or some inquirer*

speaker should keep quiet in the
church and speak to himself and God.
29Two or three prophets should
speak, and the others should weigh
carefully what is said.[c] **30**And if a revelation comes to someone who is sitting
down, the first speaker should stop.
31For you can all prophesy in turn so
that everyone may be instructed and
encouraged. **32**The spirits of prophets
are subject to the control of prophets.[d] **33**For God is not a God of disorder[e] but of peace.
As in all the congregations of the
saints,[f] **34**women should remain silent in the churches. They are not allowed to speak, but must be in submission,[g] as the Law[h] says. **35**If they want
to inquire about something, they
should ask their own husbands at
home; for it is disgraceful for a woman
to speak in the church.
36Did the word of God originate with
you? Or are you the only people it has
reached? **37**If anybody thinks he is a
prophet[i] or spiritually gifted, let him
acknowledge that what I am writing
to you is the Lord's command.[j] **38**If
he ignores this, he himself will be ignored.[a]
39Therefore, my brothers, be eager[k]
to prophesy, and do not forbid speaking in tongues. **40**But everything should
be done in a fitting and orderly[l] way.

The Resurrection of Christ

15 Now, brothers, I want to remind
you of the gospel[m] I preached to
you, which you received and on which
you have taken your stand. **2**By this
gospel you are saved,[n] if you hold
firmly[o] to the word I preached to you.
Otherwise, you have believed in vain.
3For what I received[p] I passed on
to you[q] as of first importance[b]: that
Christ died for our sins[r] according to
the Scriptures,[s] **4**that he was buried,
that he was raised[t] on the third day[u]
according to the Scriptures,[v] **5**and
that he appeared to Peter,[c][w] and then
to the Twelve.[x] **6**After that, he appeared to more than five hundred of
the brothers at the same time, most
of whom are still living, though some
have fallen asleep. **7**Then he appeared
to James, then to all the apostles,[y]
8and last of all he appeared to me
also,[z] as to one abnormally born.
9For I am the least of the apostles[a]
and do not even deserve to be called an
apostle, because I persecuted[b] the
church of God. **10**But by the grace of
God I am what I am, and his grace to
me[c] was not without effect. No, I
worked harder than all of them[d]—yet
not I, but the grace of God that was
with me.[e] **11**Whether, then, it was I or
they, this is what we preach, and this is
what you believed.

The Resurrection of the Dead

12But if it is preached that Christ has
been raised from the dead, how can
some of you say that there is no resurrection of the dead?[f] **13**If there is no
resurrection of the dead, then not even
Christ has been raised. **14**And if Christ
has not been raised,[g] our preaching
is useless and so is your faith. **15**More
than that, we are then found to be false
witnesses about God, for we have testified about God that he raised Christ
from the dead.[h] But he did not raise
him if in fact the dead are not raised.
16For if the dead are not raised, then
Christ has not been raised either.
17And if Christ has not been raised,
your faith is futile; you are still in your
sins.[i] **18**Then those also who have fall-
en asleep in Christ are lost. **19**If only for
this life we have hope in Christ, we are
to be pitied more than all men.[j]
20But Christ has indeed been raised
from the dead,[k] the firstfruits[l] of
those who have fallen asleep.[m] **21**For
since death came through a man,[n]
the resurrection of the dead comes
also through a man. **22**For as in Adam
all die, so in Christ all will be made

14:29 [c] 1Co 12:10
14:32 [d] 1Jn 4:1
14:33 [e] ver 40 [f] Ac 9:13
14:34 [g] 1Ti 2:11,12 [h] Ge 3:16
14:37 [i] 2Co 10:7 [j] 1Jn 4:6
14:39 [k] 1Co 12:31
14:40 [l] ver 33
15:1 [m] Ro 2:16
15:2 [n] Ro 1:16 [o] Ro 11:22
15:3 [p] Gal 1:12 [q] 1Co 11:23 [r] Isa 53:5; 1Pe 2:24 [s] Lk 24:27; Ac 26:22,23
15:4 [t] Ac 2:24 [u] Mt 16:21 [v] Ac 2:25,30,31
15:5 [w] Lk 24:34 [x] Mk 16:14
15:7 [y] Lk 24:33,36, 37; Ac 1:3,4
15:8 [z] Ac 9:3-6,17; 1Co 9:1
15:9 [a] Eph 3:8; 1Ti 1:15 [b] Ac 8:3
15:10 [c] Ro 12:3 [d] 2Co 11:23 [e] Php 2:13
15:12 [f] Ac 17:32; 23:8; 2Ti 2:18
15:14 [g] 1Th 4:14
15:15 [h] Ac 2:24
15:17 [i] Ro 4:25
15:19 [j] 1Co 4:9
15:20 [k] 1Pe 1:3 [l] ver 23; Ac 26:23; Rev 1:5 [m] ver 6,18
15:21 [n] Ro 5:12

[a] 38 Some manuscripts *If he is ignorant of this, let him be ignorant* [b] 3 Or *you at the first* [c] 5 Greek *Cephas*

15:3–20

PE

EYEWITNESS ACCOUNT

There's no better proof that an event occurred than the testimony of an eyewitness. When Paul wanted to substantiate the resurrection of Jesus, he didn't refer to one credible witness; he referred to hundreds, including himself. At the time Paul wrote to the Corinthians, many of those eyewitnesses were still living. If someone wanted definitive evidence of the resurrection, it was available.

The resurrection isn't the stuff of fables. It's historical fact. Paul considered this truth of "first importance"; so much so that he said the entire ministry of the gospel hinged on it. If, as some in Corinth believed, resurrection from the dead was impossible, then Jesus was just another murdered dreamer and all of his followers were pitiably deluded (vv. 17–18).

Paul presented enough witnesses to convince an unbiased jury. Along with providing us with the heart of the gospel message (vv. 3–5), this passage can encourage us and strengthen our faith.

alive.[o] 23But each in his own turn: Christ, the firstfruits;[p] then, when he comes,[q] those who belong to him. 24Then the end will come, when he hands over the kingdom[r] to God the Father after he has destroyed all dominion, authority and power.[s] 25For he must reign until he has put all his enemies under his feet.[t] 26The last enemy to be destroyed is death.[u] 27For he "has put everything under his feet."[a][v] Now when it says that "everything" has been put under him, it is clear that this does not include God himself, who put everything under Christ.[w] 28When he has done this, then the Son himself will be made subject to him who put everything under him,[x] so that God may be all in all.[y]

29Now if there is no resurrection, what will those do who are baptized for the dead? If the dead are not raised at all, why are people baptized for them? 30And as for us, why do we endanger ourselves every hour?[z] 31I die every day[a]—I mean that, brothers—just as surely as I glory over you in Christ Jesus our Lord. 32If I fought wild beasts[b] in Ephesus[c] for merely human reasons, what have I gained? If the dead are not raised,

"Let us eat and drink,
for tomorrow we die."[b][d]

33Do not be misled: "Bad company corrupts good character." 34Come back to your senses as you ought, and stop sinning; for there are some who are ignorant of God—I say this to your shame.

The Resurrection Body

35But someone may ask,[e] "How are the dead raised? With what kind of body will they come?"[f] 36How foolish![g] What you sow does not come to life unless it dies.[h] 37When you sow, you do not plant the body that will be, but just a seed, perhaps of wheat or of something else. 38But God gives it a body as he has determined, and to each kind of seed he gives its own body.[i] 39All flesh is not the same: Men have one kind of flesh, animals have another, birds another and fish another. 40There are also heavenly bodies and there are earthly bodies; but the splendor of the heavenly bodies is one kind, and the splendor of the earthly bodies is another. 41The sun has one kind of splendor, the moon another and the stars another; and star differs from star in splendor.

42So will it be[j] with the resurrection of the dead. The body that is sown is perishable, it is raised imperishable; 43it is sown in dishonor, it is raised in glory;[k] it is sown in weakness, it is raised in power; 44it is sown a natural body, it is raised a spiritual body.[l]

If there is a natural body, there is also a spiritual body. 45So it is written: "The first man Adam became a living being"[c];[m] the last Adam,[n] a life-giving spirit.[o] 46The spiritual did not come first, but the natural, and after that the spiritual. 47The first man was of the dust of the earth,[p] the second man from heaven.[q] 48As was the earthly man, so are those who are of the earth; and as is the man from heaven, so also are those who are of heaven.[r] 49And just as we have borne the likeness of the earthly man,[s] so shall we[d] bear the likeness of the man from heaven.[t]

50I declare to you, brothers, that flesh and blood[u] cannot inherit the kingdom of God, nor does the perishable inherit the imperishable. 51Listen, I tell you a mystery:[v] We will not all sleep, but we will all be changed[w]— 52in a flash, in the twinkling of an eye, at the last trumpet. For the trumpet will sound,[x] the dead[y] will be raised imperishable, and we will be changed. 53For the perishable must clothe itself with the imperishable,[z] and the mortal with immortality. 54When the perishable has been clothed with the imperishable, and the mortal with immortality, then the saying that is written will come true: "Death has been swallowed up in victory."[e][a]

55"Where, O death, is your victory?
Where, O death, is your
sting?"[f][b]

56The sting of death is sin,[c] and the power of sin is the law.[d] 57But thanks be to God![e] He gives us the victory through our Lord Jesus Christ.[f]

58Therefore, my dear brothers, stand firm. Let nothing move you. Always give yourselves fully to the work of the Lord,[g] because you know that your labor in the Lord is not in vain.

The Collection for God's People

16 Now about the collection[h] for God's people:[i] Do what I told the Galatian[j] churches to do. 2On the first day of every week,[k] each one of you should set aside a sum of money in keeping with his income, saving it up, so that when I come no collections will have to be made.[l] 3Then, when I ar-

5 →PG. 1269

15:22 [o]Ro 5:14-18
15:23 [p]ver 20 [q]ver 52
15:24 [r]Da 7:14,27 [s]Ro 8:38
15:25 [t]Ps 110:1; Mt 22:44
15:26 [u]2Ti 1:10; Rev 20:14; 21:4
15:27 [v]Ps 8:6 [w]Mt 28:18
15:28 [x]Php 3:21 [y]1Co 3:23
15:30 [z]2Co 11:26
15:31 [a]Ro 8:36
15:32 [b]2Co 1:8 [c]Ac 18:19 [d]Isa 22:13; Lk 12:19
15:35 [e]Ro 9:19 [f]Eze 37:3
15:36 [g]Lk 11:40 [h]Jn 12:24
15:38 [i]Ge 1:11
15:42 [j]Da 12:3; Mt 13:43
15:43 [k]Php 3:21; Col 3:4
15:44 [l]ver 50
15:45 [m]Ge 2:7 [n]Ro 5:14 [o]Jn 5:21; Ro 8:2
15:47 [p]Ge 2:7; 3:19 [q]Jn 3:13,31
15:48 [r]Php 3:20,21
15:49 [s]Ge 5:3 [t]Ro 8:29
15:50 [u]Jn 3:3,5
15:51 [v]1Co 13:2 [w]Php 3:21
15:52 [x]Mt 24:31 [y]Jn 5:25
15:53 [z]2Co 5:2,4
15:54 [a]Isa 25:8; Rev 20:14
15:55 [b]Hos 13:14
15:56 [c]Ro 5:12 [d]Ro 4:15
15:57 [e]2Co 2:14 [f]Ro 8:37
15:58 [g]1Co 16:10
16:1 [h]Ac 24:17 [i]Ac 9:13 [j]Ac 16:6
16:2 [k]Ac 20:7 [l]2Co 9:4,5

[a]27 Psalm 8:6 [b]32 Isaiah 22:13 [c]45 Gen. 2:7 [d]49 Some early manuscripts *so let us* [e]54 Isaiah 25:8 [f]55 Hosea 13:14

rive, I will give letters of introduction to the men you approve[m] and send them with your gift to Jerusalem. 4If it seems advisable for me to go also, they will accompany me.

Personal Requests

5After I go through Macedonia, I will come to you[n]—for I will be going through Macedonia.[o] 6Perhaps I will stay with you awhile, or even spend the winter, so that you can help me on my journey,[p] wherever I go. 7I do not want to see you now and make only a passing visit; I hope to spend some time with you, if the Lord permits.[q] 8But I will stay on at Ephesus[r] until Pentecost,[s] 9because a great door for effective work has opened to me,[t] and there are many who oppose me.

10If Timothy[u] comes, see to it that he has nothing to fear while he is with you, for he is carrying on the work of the Lord,[v] just as I am. 11No one, then, should refuse to accept him.[w] Send him on his way in peace[x] so that he may return to me. I am expecting him along with the brothers.

12Now about our brother Apollos:[y] I strongly urged him to go to you with the brothers. He was quite unwilling to go now, but he will go when he has the opportunity.

13Be on your guard; stand firm[z] in the faith; be men of courage; be strong.[a] 14Do everything in love.[b]

15You know that the household of Stephanas[c] were the first converts[d] in Achaia,[e] and they have devoted themselves to the service of the saints. I urge you, brothers, 16to submit[f] to such as these and to everyone who joins in the work, and labors at it. 17I was glad when Stephanas, Fortunatus and Achaicus arrived, because they have supplied what was lacking from you.[g] 18For they refreshed[h] my spirit and yours also. Such men deserve recognition.[i]

5 →PG. 1278

Final Greetings

19The churches in the province of Asia send you greetings. Aquila and Priscilla[a][j] greet you warmly in the Lord, and so does the church that meets at their house.[k] 20All the brothers here send you greetings. Greet one another with a holy kiss.[l]

21I, Paul, write this greeting in my own hand.[m]

22If anyone does not love the Lord[n]—a curse[o] be on him. Come, O Lord[b]![p]

23The grace of the Lord Jesus be with you.[q]

24My love to all of you in Christ Jesus. Amen.[c]

[a] 19 Greek *Prisca,* a variant of *Priscilla*
[b] 22 In Aramaic the expression *Come, O Lord* is *Marana tha.* [c] 24 Some manuscripts do not have *Amen.*

16:3 [m] 2Co 8:18,19 **16:5** [n] 1Co 4:19 [o] Ac 19:21 **16:6** [p] Ro 15:24 **16:7** [q] Ac 18:21 **16:8** [r] Ac 18:19 [s] Ac 2:1 **16:9** [t] Ac 14:27 **16:10** [u] Ac 16:1 [v] 1Co 15:58 **16:11** [w] 1Ti 4:12 [x] Ac 15:33 **16:12** [y] Ac 18:24; 1Co 1:12 **16:13** [z] Gal 5:1; Php 1:27; 1Th 3:8; 2Th 2:15 [a] Eph 6:10 **16:14** [b] 1Co 14:1 **16:15** [c] 1Co 1:16 [d] Ro 16:5 [e] Ac 18:12 **16:16** [f] Heb 13:17 **16:17** [g] 2Co 11:9; Php 2:30 **16:18** [h] Phm 7 [i] Php 2:29 **16:19** [j] Ac 18:2 [k] Ro 16:5 **16:20** [l] Ro 16:16 **16:21** [m] Gal 6:11; Col 4:18 **16:22** [n] Eph 6:24 [o] Ro 9:3 [p] Rev 22:20 **16:23** [q] Ro 16:20

16:1–2

PROMISE 5

GENEROUS DEVOTION

Giving to the Lord is to be a planned part of our lives, not something that happens haphazardly. In this passage Paul said our giving should be characterized by two things. First, It should be regular. He urged believers to give set aside money on a weekly basis. Second, it should be in keeping with our income. The more a man earns, the more he should give to the Lord.

As believers, our financial gifts may not be equal, but they should represent equal sacrifice. Ask God how much he wants you to budget for your church's ministry and for the work of God's kingdom. And then obediently respond to his leading.

For the next Promise 5 reading go to page 1279.

2 CORINTHIANS

AT A GLANCE

Key Principle: We have been entrusted with a ministry of reconciliation, and our ability to fulfill our calling comes from the power of the indwelling Spirit of Christ, not from us.

Author: Paul

Time and Place: A.D. 55 / Sent from Macedonia (or possibly Philippi) to Corinth

Key Verses: 4:5–6; 5:10, 17–21; 10:5

BENEFIT

Second Corinthians is an intensely personal epistle that reveals the apostle Paul's heart, his motives for ministry and the way he conducted himself in service to others. He defends the integrity of his ministry with the Corinthians in the face of attacks and wrongful allegations by false teachers. This defense gives us a model for the way we should pursue integrity, so that even if we are challenged, we will have a clear conscience before God and a faithful record before men.

SETTING

Not long after Paul wrote 1 Corinthians, false teachers began to attack his apostolic authority, claiming that he was proud, undependable, dishonest and that "he is unimpressive and his speaking amounts to nothing" (10:10). Timothy evidently reported this opposition to Paul (1 Corinthians 16:10–11), and Paul made a brief but "painful visit" (2:1) to Corinth to deal with problems in the church (12:14; 13:1–2). After returning to Ephesus, he sent Titus with a sorrowful letter urging the Corinthian church to discipline the opposition's leader (2:1–11; 7:8).

Paul went to Troas and then to Macedonia to meet Titus on his return trip (2:12–13; 7:5–16). When Titus met him with the good news that the majority of the Corinthians had repented of their rebellion against Paul's authority, the apostle responded with this letter. He sent it from Macedonia (or possibly Philippi) with Titus and another brother (8:16–24). Paul then made his third trip to Corinth (12:14; 13:1–2; Acts 20:1–3) where he wrote his letter to the Romans.

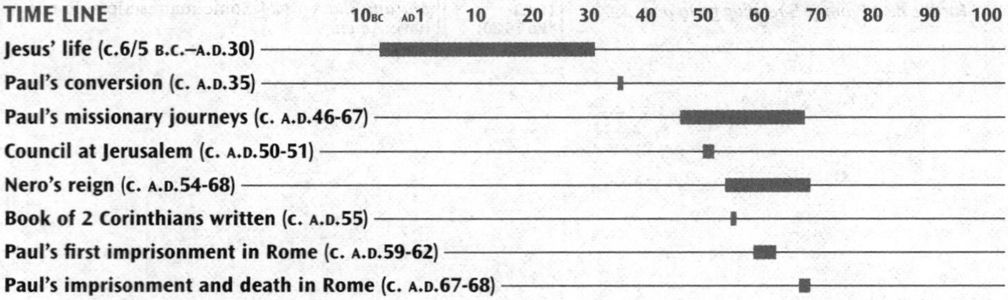

THEME AND PURPOSE

Although the majority of Corinthian believers had repented from opposing Paul's apostolic authority, an unrepentant minority, evidently led by a group of Judaizers (10—13), still continued to challenge him. Paul wrote this letter, therefore, to defend his conduct, character and apostolic calling. That primary theme ties this letter together, even in the portion that was addressed to the repentant majority (1—9).

Paul was glad to hear that the gospel of grace had triumphed (2:14) and that the people's "godly sorrow" (7:10) had led to repentance. Jewish activists (11:22) who claimed to be apostles (11:5, 13; 12:11) but who preached a different Jesus and "a different gospel" (11:4), exploited the opposing minority (11:20). Paul wrote the second part of this epistle (10—13) to refute these "false apostles, deceitful workmen" (11:13) and to defend his true calling as God's apostle. A secondary purpose surfaces in chapters 8—9. The Corinthians had promised to contribute to the collection Paul was making for the Jewish believers in Judea, and Paul encouraged them to fulfill this promise.

UNIQUE CONTRIBUTION

This is the most autobiographical of Paul's epistles, and it reveals a wealth of details about his personal life that would otherwise be unknown. These include a number of his persecutions and hardships (11:23–27) and his vision of paradise (12:1–7). Second Corinthians is also the most emotional of Paul's epistles as evidenced not only in the content, but also in the broken sentence structure, stylistic shifts, mixed metaphors and digressions. If Romans is Paul's most systematic letter, this epistle is his least. But it does make a number of important theological contributions, including the spiritual dynamic of resistance to the gospel (3:7—4:18), the resurrection and judgment of believers (5:1–10), the meaning and ministry of reconciliation (5:11–21), key principles of Christian stewardship (8—9) and insights on spiritual warfare (2:10–11; 4:4; 11:3, 13–15; 12:7).

CHRIST IN 2 CORINTHIANS

Jesus Christ is the Lord of all, and the new covenant points to him and is brought about by him (3—4). He is the judge of all, and all believers must appear before his judgment seat to give an account (5:6–10). Because of his indescribable gift (9:15), Jesus is the source of reconciliation between man and God—he bore our sin and gave us his righteousness (5:21). When we come to him, we become a new creation (5:17) and are sent out as his ambassadors of reconciliation (5:20). He comforts us in all our troubles (1:4–5) and shares his triumph with us (2:14).

OVERVIEW

FOCUS	Paul's Conduct and Character	Paul's Collection	Paul's Credentials
REFERENCE	1 — 7	8 — 9	10 — 13
TOPICS	Explanation	Exhortation	Vindication
	Testimonial	Practical	Defense
	Account	Appeal	Answer
	Addressed to the Repentant Majority		Addressed to the Rebellious Minority
LOCATION	Sent from Macedonia (Possibly Philippi) to Corinth		
TIME	A.D. 55		

Paul begins this epistle with thanksgiving for God's comfort in his hardships (1:1–11) and then explains that his delay in visiting the Corinthians was not due to wavering, but to giving them sufficient time to repent (1:12—2:4). He asks them to restore the repentant offender (2:5–13) and goes on to defend the conduct, content, and motivation of his ministry among them

(2:14—6:10). After instructing them not to defile themselves (6:11—7:1), Paul describes the encouragement he received from Titus' report (7:2–16).

The apostle then appeals to the Corinthians to follow the Macedonians' example of generosity. He asks them to keep their promise to contribute to the collection he was planning to bring to the believers in Judea (8—9).

Turning his attention to the unrepentant minority who continued to challenge his authority, Paul defends his apostolic calling and credentials (10—13). His meekness in their presence does not minimize his authority (10) and though he hates to boast about them, his knowledge, honesty, achievements, persecutions, visions and miraculous signs all vindicate his apostolic claims (11–12:13). He concludes by telling of his plans for a third visit, and warns them to repent before he comes (12:14—13:14).

2 CORINTHIANS

1 Paul, an apostle of Christ Jesus by
the will of God,[a] and Timothy our
brother,

To the church of God[b] in Corinth,
together with all the saints throughout
Achaia:[c]

2Grace and peace to you from God
our Father and the Lord Jesus Christ.[d]

The God of All Comfort

3Praise be to the God and Father of
our Lord Jesus Christ,[e] the Father of
compassion and the God of all comfort, 4who comforts us[f] in all our troubles, so that we can comfort those in
any trouble with the comfort we ourselves have received from God. 5For
just as the sufferings of Christ flow over
into our lives,[g] so also through Christ
our comfort overflows. 6If we are distressed, it is for your comfort and salvation;[h] if we are comforted, it is for
your comfort, which produces in you
patient endurance of the same sufferings we suffer. 7And our hope for you is
firm, because we know that just as you
share in our sufferings,[i] so also you
share in our comfort.

8We do not want you to be unin-
formed, brothers, about the hardships
we suffered[j] in the province of Asia.
We were under great pressure, far beyond our ability to endure, so that we
despaired even of life. 9Indeed, in our
hearts we felt the sentence of death.
But this happened that we might not
rely on ourselves but on God,[k] who
raises the dead. 10He has delivered us
from such a deadly peril,[l] and he will
deliver us. On him we have set our
hope that he will continue to deliver
us, 11as you help us by your prayers.[m]
Then many will give thanks[n] on our**[a]**
behalf for the gracious favor granted us
in answer to the prayers of many.

Paul's Change of Plans

12Now this is our boast: Our conscience[o] testifies that we have conducted ourselves in the world, and
especially in our relations with you,
in the holiness and sincerity[p] that are
from God. We have done so not according to worldly wisdom[q] but according to God's grace. 13For we do not
write you anything you cannot read or
understand. And I hope that, 14as you
have understood us in part, you will
come to understand fully that you can
boast of us just as we will boast of you
in the day of the Lord Jesus.[r]

15Because I was confident of this, I
planned to visit you[s] first so that you
might benefit twice.[t] 16I planned to
visit you on my way[u] to Macedonia
and to come back to you from Macedonia, and then to have you send me on
my way to Judea. 17When I planned
this, did I do it lightly? Or do I make my
plans in a worldly manner[v] so that in
the same breath I say, "Yes, yes" and
"No, no"?

18But as surely as God is faithful,[w]
our message to you is not "Yes" and
"No." 19For the Son of God, Jesus
Christ, who was preached among you
by me and Silas**[b]** and Timothy, was
not "Yes" and "No," but in him it has
always[x] been "Yes." 20For no matter
how many promises[y] God has made,
they are "Yes" in Christ. And so
through him the "Amen"[z] is spoken
by us to the glory of God. 21Now it is
God who makes both us and you stand
firm in Christ. He anointed[a] us, 22set
his seal of ownership on us, and put his
Spirit in our hearts as a deposit, guaranteeing what is to come.[b]

23I call God as my witness[c] that it
was in order to spare you[d] that I did
not return to Corinth. 24Not that we
lord it over[e] your faith, but we work
with you for your joy, because it is by
2 faith you stand firm.[f] 1So I made up
my mind that I would not make another painful visit to you.[g] 2For if I
grieve you,[h] who is left to make me
glad but you whom I have grieved? 3I
wrote as I did[i] so that when I came
I should not be distressed[j] by those
who ought to make me rejoice. I had
confidence[k] in all of you, that you
would all share my joy. 4For I wrote
you[l] out of great distress and anguish
of heart and with many tears, not to
grieve you but to let you know the
depth of my love for you.

Forgiveness for the Sinner

5If anyone has caused grief,[m] he has
not so much grieved me as he has
grieved all of you, to some extent—not
to put it too severely. 6The punishment[n] inflicted on him by the majority is sufficient for him. 7Now instead,
you ought to forgive and comfort

1:1 [a]1Co 1:1; Eph 1:1; Col 1:1; 2Ti 1:1 [b]1Co 10:32 [c]Ac 18:12
1:2 [d]Ro 1:7
1:3 [e]Eph 1:3; 1Pe 1:3
1:4 [f]2Co 7:6,7,13
1:5 [g]2Co 4:10; Col 1:24
1:6 [h]2Co 4:15
1:7 [i]Ro 8:17
1:8 [j]1Co 15:32
1:9 [k]Jer 17:5,7
1:10 [l]Ro 15:31
1:11 [m]Ro 15:30; Php 1:19 [n]2Co 4:15
1:12 [o]Ac 23:1 [p]2Co 2:17 [q]1Co 2:1,4,13
1:14 [r]1Co 1:8
1:15 [s]1Co 4:19 [t]Ro 1:11,13; 15:29
1:16 [u]1Co 16:5-7
1:17 [v]2Co 10:2,3
1:18 [w]1Co 1:9
1:19 [x]Heb 13:8
1:20 [y]Ro 15:8 [z]1Co 14:16
1:21 [a]1Jn 2:20,27
1:22 [b]2Co 5:5
1:23 [c]Ro 1:9; Gal 1:20 [d]1Co 4:21; 2Co 2:1,3; 13:2,10
1:24 [e]1Pe 5:3 [f]Ro 11:20; 1Co 15:1
2:1 [g]2Co 1:23
2:2 [h]2Co 7:8
2:3 [i]2Co 7:8,12 [j]2Co 12:21 [k]2Co 8:22; Gal 5:10
2:4 [l]2Co 7:8,12
2:5 [m]1Co 5:1,2
2:6 [n]1Co 5:4,5

a *11* Many manuscripts *your*
b *19* Greek *Silvanus,* a variant of *Silas*

him,[o] so that he will not be overwhelmed by excessive sorrow. **8**I urge
you, therefore, to reaffirm your love for
him. **9**The reason I wrote you was to
see if you would stand the test and be
obedient in everything.[p] **10**If you forgive anyone, I also forgive him. And
what I have forgiven—if there was anything to forgive—I have forgiven in the
sight of Christ for your sake, **11**in order
that Satan[q] might not outwit us. For
we are not unaware of his schemes.[r]

Ministers of the New Covenant

12Now when I went to Troas[s] to
preach the gospel of Christ[t] and
found that the Lord had opened a
door[u] for me, **13**I still had no peace
of mind,[v] because I did not find my
brother Titus[w] there. So I said good-
by to them and went on to Macedonia.
14But thanks be to God,[x] who always leads us in triumphal procession
in Christ and through us spreads everywhere the fragrance[y] of the knowledge of him. **15**For we are to God the
aroma of Christ among those who are
being saved and those who are perishing.[z] **16**To the one we are the smell of
death;[a] to the other, the fragrance of
life. And who is equal to such a task?[b]
17Unlike so many, we do not peddle
the word of God for profit.[c] On the
contrary, in Christ we speak before
God with sincerity,[d] like men sent
from God.[e]

3 Are we beginning to commend ourselves[f] again? Or do we need, like
some people, letters of recommendation[g] to you or from you? **2**You yourselves are our letter, written on our
hearts, known and read by everybody.[h] **3**You show that you are a letter from Christ, the result of our ministry, written not with ink but with the
Spirit of the living God, not on tablets
of stone[i] but on tablets of human
hearts.[j]
4Such confidence[k] as this is ours
through Christ before God. **5**Not that
we are competent in ourselves to claim
anything for ourselves, but our competence comes from God.[l] **6**He has
made us competent as ministers of a
new covenant[m]—not of the letter but
of the Spirit; for the letter kills, but the
Spirit gives life.[n]

The Glory of the New Covenant

7Now if the ministry that brought
death, which was engraved in letters
on stone, came with glory, so that the
Israelites could not look steadily at the
face of Moses because of its glory,[o]
fading though it was, **8**will not the ministry of the Spirit be even more glorious? **9**If the ministry that condemns
men[p] is glorious, how much more glo-

2:7 [o]Gal 6:1; Eph 4:32
2:9 [p]2Co 10:6
2:11 [q]Mt 4:10 [r]Lk 22:31; 2Co 4:4; 1Pe 5:8,9
2:12 [s]Ac 16:8 [t]Ro 1:1 [u]Ac 14:27
2:13 [v]2Co 7:5 [w]2Co 7:6,13; 12:18
2:14 [x]Ro 6:17 [y]Eph 5:2; Php 4:18
2:15 [z]1Co 1:18
2:16 [a]Lk 2:34 [b]2Co 3:5,6
2:17 [c]2Co 4:2 [d]1Co 5:8 [e]2Co 1:12
3:1 [f]2Co 5:12; 12:11 [g]Ac 18:27
3:2 [h]1Co 9:2
3:3 [i]Ex 24:12 [j]Pr 3:3; Jer 31:33; Eze 11:19
3:4 [k]Eph 3:12
3:5 [l]1Co 15:10
3:6 [m]Lk 22:20 [n]Jn 6:63
3:7 [o]Ex 34:29-35
3:9 [p]ver 7

2:5–11

PROMISE **2**

CONFRONTING SIN

It's one thing to see a brother caught in a sin; it's another thing to confront him. The church members in Corinth had done both. They had followed Paul's instructions and dealt with another member who was guilty of sin (see 1 Corinthians 5:1–5 for a possible reference to this incident).

So the hard part was over—or so it seemed. After they confronted the man with his sin face-to-face, the unexpected happened—this man's heart softened and he repented. Faced with the need to forgive and restore him to the church fellowship, the Corinthian believers balked.

Paul wanted these church members to take the next step. He told them to forgive the man and restore the relationship. Paul knew about Satan's schemes (v. 11) and didn't want this issue to become divisive.

There's a time to confront sin in our Christian brothers and a time to forgive. Ask God for the courage you need to do both, and the wisdom to know when.

For the next Promise 2 reading go to page 1292.

3:1–6

PROMISE **7**

LIVING LETTERS

Has anyone ever challenged your credibility? If so, then you can identify with the apostle Paul. False teachers had infiltrated the church at Corinth with phony letters of authority, and accused Paul of having no such written commendation. Paul's response was brilliant. He said *the Corinthians themselves* were his letter of recommendation, waiting to be known and read by everyone.

Just to set the record straight, Paul made it clear that whatever he had accomplished in the ministry, Christ had done through him. What a statement! And what an attitude.

The same Christ who gave Paul competence is there for you too. He is the one who will enable you to carry out a ministry in the lives of other people. But, like Paul, you need to be available for God to use. If you're discouraged by your present ministry, don't be. God may be working to produce Christlikeness in you today, so he can use you more effectively in the future. Thank God that whatever gifts you have, or will have, come from him.

For the next Promise 7 reading go to page 1275.

rious is the ministry that brings righteousness![q] 10For what was glorious has no glory now in comparison with the surpassing glory. 11And if what was fading away came with glory, how much greater is the glory of that which lasts!

12Therefore, since we have such a hope, we are very bold.[r] 13We are not like Moses, who would put a veil over his face[s] to keep the Israelites from gazing at it while the radiance was fading away. 14But their minds were made dull,[t] for to this day the same veil remains when the old covenant[u] is read.[v] It has not been removed, because only in Christ is it taken away. 15Even to this day when Moses is read, a veil covers their hearts. 16But whenever anyone turns to the Lord,[w] the veil is taken away.[x] 17Now the Lord is the Spirit,[y] and where the Spirit of the Lord is, there is freedom.[z] 18And we, who with unveiled faces all reflect[a][a] the Lord's glory,[b] are being transformed into his likeness[c] with ever-increasing glory, which comes from the Lord, who is the Spirit.

Treasures in Jars of Clay

4 Therefore, since through God's mercy[d] we have this ministry, we do not lose heart. 2Rather, we have renounced secret and shameful ways;[e] we do not use deception, nor do we distort the word of God.[f] On the contrary, by setting forth the truth plainly we commend ourselves to every man's conscience[g] in the sight of God. 3And even if our gospel[h] is veiled,[i] it is veiled to those who are perishing.[j] 4The god[k] of this age has blinded[l] the minds of unbelievers, so that they cannot see the light of the gospel of the glory of Christ, who is the image of God. 5For we do not preach ourselves,[m] but Jesus Christ as Lord, and ourselves as your servants[n] for Jesus' sake. 6For God, who said, "Let light shine out of darkness,"[b][o] made his light shine in our hearts[p] to give us the light of the knowledge of the glory of God in the face of Christ.

3 →PG. 1277

7But we have this treasure in jars of clay[q] to show that this all-surpassing power is from God[r] and not from us. 8We are hard pressed on every side,[s] but not crushed; perplexed, but not in despair; 9persecuted,[t] but not abandoned;[u] struck down, but not destroyed.[v] 10We always carry around in our body the death of Jesus, so that the life of Jesus may also be revealed in our body.[w] 11For we who are alive are always being given over to death for Jesus' sake,[x] so that his life may be revealed in our mortal body. 12So then, death is at work in us, but life is at work in you.[y]

13It is written: "I believed; therefore I have spoken."[c][z] With that same spirit of faith we also believe and therefore speak, 14because we know that the one who raised the Lord Jesus from the dead will also raise us with Jesus[a] and present us with you in his presence.[b] 15All this is for your benefit, so that the grace that is reaching more and more people may cause thanksgiving[c] to overflow to the glory of God.

16Therefore we do not lose heart. Though outwardly we are wasting away, yet inwardly[d] we are being renewed[e] day by day. 17For our light and momentary troubles are achieving for us an eternal glory that far outweighs them all.[f] 18So we fix our eyes not on what is seen, but on what is unseen.[g] For what is seen is temporary, but what is unseen is eternal.

Our Heavenly Dwelling

5 Now we know that if the earthly[h] tent[i] we live in is destroyed, we have a building from God, an eternal house in heaven, not built by human hands. 2Meanwhile we groan,[j] longing to be clothed with our heavenly dwelling,[k] 3because when we are clothed, we will not be found naked. 4For while we are in this tent, we groan and are burdened, because we do not wish to be unclothed but to be clothed with our heavenly dwelling,[l] so that what is mortal may be swallowed up by

[a] *18* Or *contemplate* [b] *6* Gen. 1:3
[c] *13* Psalm 116:10

3:9 [q]Ro 1:17; 3:21, 22
3:12 [r]Eph 6:19
3:13 [s]ver 7; Ex 34:33
3:14 [t]Ro 11:7,8 [u]Ac 13:15 [v]ver 6
3:16 [w]Ro 11:23 [x]Ex 34:34
3:17 [y]Isa 61:1,2 [z]Jn 8:32
3:18 [a]1Co 13:12 [b]2Co 4:4,6 [c]Ro 8:29
4:1 [d]1Co 7:25
4:2 [e]1Co 4:5 [f]2Co 2:17 [g]2Co 5:11
4:3 [h]2Co 2:12 [i]2Co 3:14 [j]1Co 1:18
4:4 [k]Jn 12:31 [l]2Co 3:14
4:5 [m]1Co 1:13 [n]1Co 9:19
4:6 [o]Ge 1:3 [p]2Pe 1:19
4:7 [q]Job 4:19; 2Co 5:1 [r]1Co 2:5
4:8 [s]2Co 7:5
4:9 [t]Jn 15:20 [u]Heb 13:5 [v]Ps 37:24
4:10 [w]Ro 6:5
4:11 [x]Ro 8:36
4:12 [y]2Co 13:9
4:13 [z]Ps 116:10
4:14 [a]1Th 4:14 [b]Eph 5:27
4:15 [c]2Co 1:11
4:16 [d]Ro 7:22 [e]Col 3:10
4:17 [f]Ro 8:18; 1Pe 1:6,7
4:18 [g]Ro 8:24; Heb 11:1
5:1 [h]1Co 15:47 [i]2Pe 1:13,14
5:2 [j]ver 4; Ro 8:23 [k]1Co 15:53,54
5:4 [l]1Co 15:53,54

4:3-7

PROMISE 7

GOD OPENS EYES

Evangelism is a spiritual activity. People reject Jesus because they don't see him. They're spiritually blind. Indeed, Satan has blinded them so they can't see the truth of the gospel.

The next time you share Christ with an unbelieving friend, remember that you're talking with someone who is spiritually blind. *Your* role is to gently and clearly share the gospel. *God's* role is to "open that person's eyes" to the truth of the gospel and reveal its relevance to his or her life. Ask God for the courage you need to do your job so he can do his job through you.

For the next Promise 7 reading go to page 1306.

life. 5Now it is God who has made us
for this very purpose and has given us
the Spirit as a deposit, guaranteeing
what is to come.[m]
6Therefore we are always confident
and know that as long as we are at
home in the body we are away from the
Lord. 7We live by faith, not by sight.[n]
8We are confident, I say, and would
prefer to be away from the body and at
home with the Lord.[o] 9So we make it
our goal to please him,[p] whether we
are at home in the body or away from
it. 10For we must all appear before the
judgment seat of Christ, that each one
may receive what is due him[q] for the
things done while in the body, whether
good or bad.

The Ministry of Reconciliation

11Since, then, we know what it is to
fear the Lord,[r] we try to persuade
men. What we are is plain to God, and
I hope it is also plain to your conscience.[s] 12We are not trying to commend ourselves to you again,[t] but are
giving you an opportunity to take pride
in us,[u] so that you can answer those
who take pride in what is seen rather
than in what is in the heart. 13If we are
out of our mind,[v] it is for the sake of
God; if we are in our right mind, it is for
you. 14For Christ's love compels us, because we are convinced that one died
for all, and therefore all died.[w] 15And
he died for all, that those who live
should no longer live for themselves[x]
but for him who died for them and was
raised again.
16So from now on we regard no one
from a worldly[y] point of view. Though
we once regarded Christ in this way, we
do so no longer. 17Therefore, if anyone
is in Christ, he is a new creation;[z] the
old has gone, the new has come![a] 18All
this is from God, who reconciled us to
himself through Christ[b] and gave us
the ministry of reconciliation: 19that
God was reconciling the world to himself in Christ, not counting men's sins
against them.[c] And he has committed
to us the message of reconciliation.
20We are therefore Christ's ambassadors,[d] as though God were making his
appeal through us. We implore you on
Christ's behalf: Be reconciled to God.
21God made him who had no sin[e] to

6 →PG. 1278
7 →PG. 1280

5:5 [m]Ro 8:23; 2Co 1:22 **5:7** [n]1Co 13:12 **5:8** [o]Php 1:23 **5:9** [p]Ro 14:18 **5:10** [q]Mt 16:27; Ro 14:10; Eph 6:8 **5:11** [r]Heb 10:31; Jude 23 [s]2Co 4:2 **5:12** [t]2Co 3:1 [u]2Co 1:14 **5:13** [v]2Co 11:1,16, 17 **5:14** [w]Gal 2:20 **5:15** [x]Ro 14:7-9 **5:16** [y]2Co 11:18 **5:17** [z]Gal 6:15 [a]Isa 65:17; Rev 21:4,5 **5:18** [b]Ro 5:10; Col 1:20 **5:19** [c]Ro 4:8 **5:20** [d]2Co 6:1; Eph 6:20 **5:21** [e]Heb 4:15; 1Pe 2:22,24; 1Jn 3:5

4:16–18

PROMISE 1

TEMPORARY PAIN, ETERNAL PERSPECTIVE

At times, we all experience emotional, physical or psychological pain as we stand for Christ in this world. At such times we may wonder if anything good could come from our suffering. But Paul insisted that good things come from bad situations.

As he boldly proclaimed Christ's message of salvation, Paul experienced severe persecution and suffered greatly. Yet in the midst of those hardships he saw that his suffering always had an eternal benefit. That eternal perspective affected his attitude about suffering for Christ, and turned it into something for which Paul thanked God.

Whenever believers suffer for the cause of Christ, they're making deposits in an eternal account. Can they see the account grow? No, usually not. Can they make early withdrawals? Again, the answer is no. But Paul promises suffering Christians that the eternal benefits far outweigh any present suffering they're experiencing.

While this truth may not relieve a person's immediate pain, it will give hope. And the hope that something good can come from something bad helps us trust God during tough times. If your faith has brought you hardship that hasn't yet passed, ask God for a new sense of the hope of which Paul spoke.

For the next Promise 1 reading go to page 1276.

5:1–10

PROMISE 1

GETTING AWAY FROM IT ALL

We've all had times when we've longed to get away from the pressure and stress of everyday life to go to some quiet place—a library, a stream or a twisting trail in the woods. But, in moments of quiet reflection, have you ever yearned to be with the Lord? Have you ever dreamed about getting away from the pull of sin and the attraction of the world once and for all?

The apostle Paul did. While he didn't necessarily want to leave his earthly body, he did long to be with the Lord. And his yearning wasn't some form of escapism. On the contrary, his desire to share eternity with the Lord spurred him on to please Christ even more in his life on earth.

As Christians, we must imitate Paul in keeping this eternal perspective on our lives. He challenges us to live in a way that will win the Lord's praise. To bring this home, think through your schedule for the next week and ask yourself how well it reflects your commitment to eternal things. Ask for the grace you need to remember that everything you do, even the smallest things, have eternal value.

For the next Promise 1 reading go to page 1301.

be sin[a] for us, so that in him we might
become the righteousness of God.[f]
6 As God's fellow workers[g] we urge
you not to receive God's grace in
vain. 2For he says,

"In the time of my favor I heard
you,
and in the day of salvation I
helped you."[b][h]

I tell you, now is the time of God's favor, now is the day of salvation.

Paul's Hardships

3We put no stumbling block in anyone's path,[i] so that our ministry will
3 →PG. 1277
not be discredited. 4Rather, as servants
of God we commend ourselves in every
way: in great endurance; in troubles,
hardships and distresses; 5in beatings,
imprisonments[j] and riots; in hard
work, sleepless nights and hunger;[k]
6in purity, understanding, patience
and kindness; in the Holy Spirit[l] and
in sincere love; 7in truthful speech[m]
and in the power of God; with weapons
of righteousness[n] in the right hand
and in the left; 8through glory and dishonor,[o] bad report and good report;
genuine, yet regarded as impostors;[p]
9known, yet regarded as unknown; dying,[q] and yet we live on;[r] beaten, and
yet not killed; 10sorrowful, yet always
rejoicing;[s] poor, yet making many
rich;[t] having nothing, and yet possessing everything.[u]

11We have spoken freely to you,
Corinthians, and opened wide our
hearts to you.[v] 12We are not withholding our affection from you, but you
are withholding yours from us. 13As
a fair exchange—I speak as to my
children[w]—open wide your hearts
also.

5:21 [f]Ro 1:17
6:1 [g]1Co 3:9; 2Co 5:20
6:2 [h]Isa 49:8
6:3 [i]Ro 14:13,20; 1Co 9:12; 10:32
6:5 [j]2Co 11:23-25 [k]1Co 4:11
6:6 [l]1Th 1:5
6:7 [m]2Co 4:2 [n]2Co 10:4; Eph 6:10-18
6:8 [o]1Co 4:10 [p]Mt 27:63
6:9 [q]Ro 8:36 [r]2Co 1:8-10; 4:10,11
6:10 [s]2Co 7:4 [t]2Co 8:9 [u]Ro 8:32; 1Co 3:21
6:11 [v]2Co 7:3
6:13 [w]1Co 4:14
6:14 [x]1Co 5:9,10 [y]Eph 5:7,11; 1Jn 1:6
6:15 [z]Ac 5:14
6:16 [a]1Co 3:16 [b]Lev 26:12; Jer 32:38; Eze 37:27
6:17 [c]Rev 18:4 [d]Isa 52:11
6:18 [e]Isa 43:6
7:1 [f]2Co 6:17,18
7:2 [g]2Co 6:12,13
7:3 [h]2Co 6:11,12

Do Not Be Yoked With Unbelievers

14Do not be yoked together[x] with
1 →PG. 1288
unbelievers. For what do righteousness
and wickedness have in common? Or
3 →PG. 1282
what fellowship can light have with
darkness?[y] 15What harmony is there
between Christ and Belial[c]? What
does a believer[z] have in common with
an unbeliever? 16What agreement is
there between the temple of God and
idols? For we are the temple[a] of the
living God. As God has said: "I will live
with them and walk among them, and
I will be their God, and they will be my
people."[d][b]

17"Therefore come out from them[c]
and be separate,
says the Lord.
Touch no unclean thing,
and I will receive you."[e][d]
18"I will be a Father to you,
and you will be my sons and
daughters,[e]
says the Lord Almighty."[f]

7 Since we have these promises,[f]
dear friends, let us purify ourselves
from everything that contaminates
body and spirit, perfecting holiness out
of reverence for God.

Paul's Joy

2Make room for us in your hearts.[g]
We have wronged no one, we have corrupted no one, we have exploited no
one. 3I do not say this to condemn you;
I have said before that you have such a
place in our hearts[h] that we would live
or die with you. 4I have great confidence in you; I take great pride in

[a]*21* Or *be a sin offering* [b]*2* Isaiah 49:8
[c]*15* Greek *Beliar,* a variant of *Belial*
[d]*16* Lev.26:12; Jer. 32:38; Ezek. 37:27
[e]*17* Isaiah 52:11; Ezek. 20:34,41,
[f]*18* 2 Samuel 7:14; 7:8

5:16–21

PE

RECONCILED TO GOD

For those of us who have trusted Jesus Christ as our personal Savior, being a disciple isn't a matter of trying harder to be a better person. Instead, it's a matter of recognizing the work Christ has done *in* us and then allowing him to work *through* us.

God works through us because we have been *reconciled* to him. The term "reconciliation" describes the act by which God brings into his family people who should be his enemies—sinful people like us. Because of our sin, we would have no right to approach God and ask for forgiveness on our own. So God took the first step. He placed our sins on his sinless Son, and then punished Jesus in our place.

But that's only half the story. After taking away our sins, God offered us the righteousness of his Son. Through Jesus, God collected on a debt that we could never have paid by ourselves. Then he turned around and offered us the untold riches of his love and the promise of eternal life. On an infinitely smaller scale, it's as though we owed a million-dollar debt to someone who not only paid it, but also deposited ten million tax-free dollars into our savings account.

Because we've received such an incredible gift, we'll want to tell others where they too can find it. We're to carry this message of reconciliation to others as we follow Paul's example and urge others to "be reconciled to God."

you. I am greatly encouraged; in all
our troubles my joy knows no bounds.[i]
5For when we came into Macedo-
nia,[j] this body of ours had no rest, but
we were harassed at every turn[k]—
conflicts on the outside, fears within.[l]
6But God, who comforts the downcast,[m] comforted us by the coming of
Titus,[n] 7and not only by his coming
but also by the comfort you had given
him. He told us about your longing for
me, your deep sorrow, your ardent
concern for me, so that my joy was
greater than ever.
8Even if I caused you sorrow by my
letter,[o] I do not regret it. Though I did
regret it—I see that my letter hurt you,
but only for a little while— 9yet now I
am happy, not because you were made
sorry, but because your sorrow led you
to repentance. For you became sorrowful as God intended and so were
not harmed in any way by us. 10Godly
sorrow brings repentance that leads
to salvation[p] and leaves no regret,
but worldly sorrow brings death. 11See
what this godly sorrow has produced in
you: what earnestness, what eagerness
to clear yourselves, what indignation,
what alarm, what longing, what concern,[q] what readiness to see justice
done. At every point you have proved
yourselves to be innocent in this matter. 12So even though I wrote to you,[r]
it was not on account of the one who
did the wrong[s] or of the injured party,
but rather that before God you could
see for yourselves how devoted to us
you are. 13By all this we are encouraged.
In addition to our own encouragement, we were especially delighted to
see how happy Titus[t] was, because
his spirit has been refreshed by all of
you. 14I had boasted to him about
you,[u] and you have not embarrassed
me. But just as everything we said to
you was true, so our boasting about
you to Titus[v] has proved to be true as
well. 15And his affection for you is all
the greater when he remembers that
you were all obedient,[w] receiving him
with fear and trembling.[x] 16I am glad
I can have complete confidence in
you.[y]

Generosity Encouraged

8 And now, brothers, we want you
to know about the grace that God
has given the Macedonian[z] churches.
2Out of the most severe trial, their
overflowing joy and their extreme poverty welled up in rich generosity. 3For
I testify that they gave as much as they
were able,[a] and even beyond their
ability. Entirely on their own, 4they
urgently pleaded with us for the privilege of sharing in this service[b] to the
saints.[c] 5And they did not do as we
expected, but they gave themselves
first to the Lord and then to us in keeping with God's will. 6So we urged[d] Titus,[e] since he had earlier made a beginning, to bring also to completion[f]
this act of grace on your part. 7But just
as you excel in everything[g]—in faith,
in speech, in knowledge,[h] in complete
earnestness and in your love for us[a]—
see that you also excel in this grace of
giving.
8I am not commanding you,[i] but I
want to test the sincerity of your love
by comparing it with the earnestness of
others. 9For you know the grace of our
Lord Jesus Christ,[j] that though he was
rich, yet for your sakes he became
poor,[k] so that you through his poverty
might become rich.
10And here is my advice[l] about
what is best for you in this matter: Last
year you were the first not only to give
but also to have the desire to do so.[m]
11Now finish the work, so that your
eager willingness[n] to do it may be
matched by your completion of it, according to your means. 12For if the willingness is there, the gift is acceptable

5 →PG. 1280
6 →PG. 1278
6 →PG. 1283

a 7 Some manuscripts *in our love for you*

6:14–7:1

PROMISE 3

CONTAMINATION ALERT

If you've ever had a bad cold or the flu, then you know what contamination is all about. Just as a single flu germ can infect a healthy person, so a little evil can contaminate a spiritually healthy person.

Paul warns us to guard against the power of evil to contaminate good. His message about the dangers of alliances between believers and unbelievers (vv. 14–16) refers not only to marriage, but also to business, religious and other personal relationships. Notice that Paul emphasizes both a negative and a positive duty of every believer. First, we must avoid being corrupted by the influence of unbelievers, keeping both body and spirit clean from anything that might defile us. Second, we're to continually seek to please God with our lives out of reverence and awe for him.

Paul raises five questions in this passage. Take a moment to read and answer them for yourself as you think about your relationships. How can you go about avoiding spiritual contamination? What steps can you take to pursue holiness?

For the next Promise 3 reading go to page 1287.

7:4 [i] 2Co 6:10
7:5 [j] 2Co 2:13 [k] 2Co 4:8 [l] Dt 32:25
7:6 [m] 2Co 1:3,4 [n] ver 13; 2Co 2:13
7:8 [o] 2Co 2:2,4
7:10 [p] Ac 11:18
7:11 [q] ver 7
7:12 [r] ver 8; 2Co 2:3,9 [s] 1Co 5:1,2
7:13 [t] ver 6; 2Co 2:13
7:14 [u] ver 4 [v] ver 6
7:15 [w] 2Co 2:9 [x] Php 2:12
7:16 [y] 2Co 2:3
8:1 [z] Ac 16:9
8:3 [a] 1Co 16:2
8:4 [b] Ac 24:17 [c] Ro 15:25; 2Co 9:1
8:6 [d] ver 17; 2Co 12:18 [e] ver 16,23 [f] ver 10,11
8:7 [g] 2Co 9:8 [h] 1Co 1:5
8:8 [i] 1Co 7:6
8:9 [j] 2Co 13:14 [k] Mt 20:28; Php 2:6-8
8:10 [l] 1Co 7:25,40 [m] 1Co 16:2,3; 2Co 9:2
8:11 [n] 2Co 9:2

according to what one has,[o] not according to what he does not have.
[13]Our desire is not that others might
be relieved while you are hard pressed,
but that there might be equality. [14]At
the present time your plenty will supply what they need,[p] so that in turn
their plenty will supply what you need.
Then there will be equality, [15]as it is
written: "He who gathered much did
not have too much, and he who gathered little did not have too little."[a][q]

Titus Sent to Corinth

[16]I thank God,[r] who put into the
heart[s] of Titus[t] the same concern I
have for you. [17]For Titus not only welcomed our appeal, but he is coming to
you with much enthusiasm and on his
own initiative.[u] [18]And we are sending
along with him the brother[v] who is
praised by all the churches[w] for his
service to the gospel.[x] [19]What is more,
he was chosen by the churches to accompany us[y] as we carry the offering,
which we administer in order to honor
the Lord himself and to show our eagerness to help.[z] [20]We want to avoid
any criticism of the way we administer
this liberal gift. [21]For we are taking
pains to do what is right, not only in
the eyes of the Lord but also in the eyes
of men.[a]
[22]In addition, we are sending with
them our brother who has often
proved to us in many ways that he is
zealous, and now even more so because of his great confidence in you.
[23]As for Titus, he is my partner[b] and
fellow worker[c] among you; as for our
brothers,[d] they are representatives of
the churches and an honor to Christ.
[24]Therefore show these men the proof
of your love and the reason for our
pride in you,[e] so that the churches
can see it.

9 There is no need[f] for me to write
to you about this service to the
saints.[g] [2]For I know your eagerness to
help, and I have been boasting[h] about

8:12 [o]Mk 12:43,44; Lk 21:3
8:14 [p]2Co 9:12
8:15 [q]Ex 16:18
8:16 [r]2Co 2:14 [s]Rev 17:17 [t]2Co 2:13
8:17 [u]ver 6
8:18 [v]2Co 12:18 [w]1Co 7:17 [x]2Co 2:12
8:19 [y]1Co 16:3,4 [z]ver 11,12
8:21 [a]Ro 12:17; 14:18
8:23 [b]Phm 17 [c]Php 2:25 [d]ver 18,22
8:24 [e]2Co 7:4,14; 9:2
9:1 [f]1Th 4:9 [g]2Co 8:4
9:2 [h]2Co 7:4,14

[a] *15* Exodus 16:18

8:1–9:14

PROMISE 5

A CHEERFUL GIVER

As followers of Jesus Christ, the way we handle our money should reflect our faith. That's what Paul's instructions in this passage are all about. In providing us with the Bible's most extensive discussion of financial stewardship, Paul offers several helpful insights.

First, *generosity is prompted by God's grace* (8:1–2). The Macedonian Christians were destitute. Yet when they heard about the financial needs of their Christian brothers in Jerusalem, they begged for the chance to give—and did so beyond what they could afford. Were the Macedonians somehow different from us? Hardly. They were just as concerned about paying their bills and feeding their kids as we are today. But they gave out of gratitude to God for the forgiveness and salvation he had given them. Generosity doesn't come naturally to most people. But gratitude for God's grace frees us from the tendency to keep a chokehold on our checkbooks.

Second, *before we give our money to the Lord, we should give him ourselves* (8:5). Once the Macedonians had given themselves to God, giving away their money was easy. In fact, they considered it a privilege. Never forget: God wants you before he wants yours. In fact, when God has you, he'll also have all you possess.

Third, *when we give, we're following Jesus' example* (8:9). Jesus chose to lay aside his divine glory, clothe himself with flesh and blood and live on earth in relative poverty. And then, with incomprehensible generosity, he gave his life for us. Jesus did this so we who were spiritually poor could become rich beyond our wildest imagination. When you give your resources to help others, you're reflecting Jesus' sacrificial love and generosity to you. Paul commended the Macedonians for doing just that.

Fourth, *God enables us to give generously* (9:6–11). The principle is simple: "As you sow, so shall you reap." Unfortunately, some people twist this passage and believe Paul is promising that if we give money to the Lord, he will give us more money back—as if God is some sort of celestial investment counselor. While God may grant you financial prosperity in life, the Bible doesn't promise that he will or say that he must do so. Rather, Paul says here that if we give generously, God will make his *grace* abound to us (v. 8). God is able and willing to provide for us so we can give generously to his work (9:8, 11).

Finally, *the amount of your gift doesn't matter—it's your attitude that counts* (9:7). While the size of your gift should be guided by the resources you have, the Lord doesn't measure his approval of that gift by its dollar amount. Rather, he looks at your desire to give from what you have. God applauds an attitude of sacrificial giving, not necessarily the act of giving large gifts. (See Mark 12:41–44 for an excellent illustration of this principle.)

Ultimately, financial stewardship is an issue of submission to God and obedience to his will. Review these five principles again, and learn to live in such a way that your checkbook ledger reflects a life that's devoted to God.

For the next Promise 5 reading go to page 1324.

it to the Macedonians, telling them that since last year[i] you in Achaia[j] were ready to give; and your enthusiasm has stirred most of them to action. 3But I am sending the brothers in order that our boasting about you in this matter should not prove hollow, but that you may be ready, as I said you would be.[k] 4For if any Macedonians[l] come with me and find you unprepared, we—not to say anything about you—would be ashamed of having been so confident. 5So I thought it necessary to urge the brothers to visit you in advance and finish the arrangements for the generous gift you had promised. Then it will be ready as a generous gift,[m] not as one grudgingly given.[n]

Sowing Generously

5 →PG. 1291
7 →PG. 1291

6Remember this: Whoever sows sparingly will also reap sparingly, and whoever sows generously will also reap generously.[o] 7Each man should give what he has decided in his heart to give,[p] not reluctantly or under compulsion,[q] for God loves a cheerful giver.[r] 8And God is able[s] to make all grace abound to you, so that in all things at all times, having all that you need,[t] you will abound in every good work. 9As it is written:

"He has scattered abroad his gifts
to the poor;
his righteousness endures
forever."[a][u]

10Now he who supplies seed to the sower and bread for food[v] will also supply and increase your store of seed and will enlarge the harvest of your righteousness.[w] 11You will be made rich[x] in every way so that you can be generous on every occasion, and through us your generosity will result in thanksgiving to God.[y]

12This service that you perform is not only supplying the needs[z] of God's people but is also overflowing in many expressions of thanks to God.[a] 13Because of the service[b] by which you have proved yourselves, men will praise God[c] for the obedience that accompanies your confession of the gospel of Christ,[d] and for your generosity in sharing with them and with everyone else. 14And in their prayers for you their hearts will go out to you, because of the surpassing grace God has given you. 15Thanks be to God[e] for his indescribable gift![f]

9:2 [i]2Co 8:10 [j]Ac 18:12
9:3 [k]1Co 16:2
9:4 [l]Ro 15:26
9:5 [m]Php 4:17 [n]2Co 12:17,18
9:6 [o]Pr 11:24,25; 22:9; Gal 6:7,9
9:7 [p]Ex 25:2; 2Co 8:12 [q]Dt 15:10 [r]Ro 12:8
9:8 [s]Eph 3:20 [t]Php 4:19
9:9 [u]Ps 112:9
9:10 [v]Isa 55:10 [w]Hos 10:12
9:11 [x]1Co 1:5 [y]2Co 1:11
9:12 [z]2Co 8:14 [a]2Co 1:11
9:13 [b]2Co 8:4 [c]Mt 9:8 [d]2Co 2:12
9:15 [e]2Co 2:14 [f]Ro 5:15,16

Paul's Defense of His Ministry

10 By the meekness and gentleness[g] of Christ, I appeal to you—I, Paul,[h] who am "timid" when face to face with you, but "bold" when away! 2I beg you that when I come I may not have to be as bold[i] as I expect to be toward some people who think that we live by the standards of this world. 3For though we live in the world, we do not wage war as the world does. 4The weapons we fight with[j] are not the weapons of the world. On the contrary, they have divine power[k] to demolish strongholds.[l] 5We demolish arguments and every pretension that sets itself up against the knowledge of God,[m] and we take captive every thought to make it obedient[n] to Christ. 6And we will be ready to punish every act of disobedience, once your obedience is complete.[o]

7You are looking only on the surface of things.[b][p] If anyone is confident that he belongs to Christ,[q] he should consider again that we belong to Christ just as much as he.[r] 8For even if I boast somewhat freely about the authority the Lord gave us for building you up rather than pulling you down,[s] I will not be ashamed of it. 9I do not want to seem to be trying to frighten you with my letters. 10For some say, "His letters are weighty and forceful, but in person he is unimpressive[t] and his speaking amounts to nothing."[u] 11Such people should realize that what we are in our letters when we are absent, we will be in our actions when we are present.

12We do not dare to classify or compare ourselves with some who commend themselves.[v] When they measure themselves by themselves and compare themselves with themselves, they are not wise. 13We, however, will not boast beyond proper limits, but will confine our boasting to the field God has assigned to us,[w] a field that reaches even to you. 14We are not going too far in our boasting, as would be the case if we had not come to you, for we did get as far as you[x] with the gospel of Christ.[y] 15Neither do we go beyond our limits by boasting of work done by others.[c][z] Our hope is that, as your faith continues to grow,[a] our

10:1 [g]Mt 11:29 [h]Gal 5:2
10:2 [i]1Co 4:21; 2Co 13:2,10
10:4 [j]2Co 6:7 [k]1Co 2:5 [l]Jer 1:10; 2Co 13:10
10:5 [m]Isa 2:11,12; 1Co 1:19 [n]2Co 9:13
10:6 [o]2Co 2:9; 7:15
10:7 [p]Jn 7:24 [q]1Co 1:12; 3:23; 14:37 [r]2Co 11:23
10:8 [s]2Co 13:10
10:10 [t]1Co 2:3; Gal 4:13,14 [u]1Co 1:17
10:12 [v]2Co 3:1
10:13 [w]ver 15,16
10:14 [x]1Co 3:6 [y]2Co 2:12
10:15 [z]Ro 15:20 [a]2Th 1:3

a 9 Psalm 112:9 **b** 7 Or *Look at the obvious facts* **c** 13-15 Or 13*We, however, will not boast about things that cannot be measured, but we will boast according to the standard of measurement that the God of measure has assigned us—a measurement that relates even to you.* 14 . . . . 15*Neither do we boast about things that cannot be measured in regard to the work done by others.*

area of activity among you will greatly
expand, 16so that we can preach the
gospel in the regions beyond you.[b]
For we do not want to boast about
work already done in another man's
territory. 17But, "Let him who boasts
boast in the Lord."[a][c] 18For it is not
the one who commends himself[d] who
is approved, but the one whom the
Lord commends.[e]

Paul and the False Apostles

11 I hope you will put up with[f] a little
of my foolishness;[g] but you are already doing that. 2I am jealous for you
with a godly jealousy. I promised you
to one husband,[h] to Christ, so that I
might present you[i] as a pure virgin to
him. 3But I am afraid that just as Eve
was deceived by the serpent's cunning,[j] your minds may somehow be
led astray from your sincere and pure
devotion to Christ. 4For if someone
comes to you and preaches a Jesus other than the Jesus we preached,[k] or if
you receive a different spirit[l] from the
one you received, or a different gospel[m] from the one you accepted, you
put up with it easily enough. 5But I do
not think I am in the least inferior to
those "super-apostles."[n] 6I may not
be a trained speaker,[o] but I do have
knowledge.[p] We have made this perfectly clear to you in every way.

7Was it a sin[q] for me to lower myself
in order to elevate you by preaching
the gospel of God to you free of
charge?[r] 8I robbed other churches by
receiving support from them[s] so as to
serve you. 9And when I was with you
and needed something, I was not a
burden to anyone, for the brothers who
came from Macedonia supplied what I
needed. I have kept myself from being
a burden to you[t] in any way, and will
continue to do so. 10As surely as the
truth of Christ is in me,[u] nobody in
the regions of Achaia[v] will stop this
boasting[w] of mine. 11Why? Because I
do not love you? God knows I do![x]
12And I will keep on doing what I am
doing in order to cut the ground from
under those who want an opportunity
to be considered equal with us in the
things they boast about.

13For such men are false apostles,[y]
deceitful[z] workmen, masquerading as
apostles of Christ.[a] 14And no wonder,
for Satan himself masquerades as an
angel of light. 15It is not surprising,
then, if his servants masquerade as servants of righteousness. Their end will
be what their actions deserve.[b]

2 →PG. 1291

Paul Boasts About His Sufferings

16I repeat: Let no one take me for a
fool.[c] But if you do, then receive me
just as you would a fool, so that I may
do a little boasting. 17In this self-
confident boasting I am not talking
as the Lord would,[d] but as a fool.
18Since many are boasting in the way
the world does, I too will boast.[e] 19You
gladly put up with fools since you
are so wise![f] 20In fact, you even put
up with anyone who enslaves you[g]
or exploits you or takes advantage of
you or pushes himself forward or
slaps you in the face. 21To my shame
I admit that we were too weak[h] for
that!

What anyone else dares to boast
about—I am speaking as a fool—I also
dare to boast about.[i] 22Are they Hebrews? So am I.[j] Are they Israelites?
So am I.[k] Are they Abraham's descendants? So am I. 23Are they servants of
Christ? (I am out of my mind to talk like
this.) I am more. I have worked much
harder,[l] been in prison more frequently,[m] been flogged more severely,
and been exposed to death again and
again. 24Five times I received from the
Jews the forty lashes[n] minus one.
25Three times I was beaten with rods,[o]
once I was stoned,[p] three times I was
shipwrecked, I spent a night and a day
in the open sea, 26I have been constantly on the move. I have been in
danger from rivers, in danger from
bandits, in danger from my own countrymen,[q] in danger from Gentiles; in
danger in the city,[r] in danger in the
country, in danger at sea; and in danger from false brothers.[s] 27I have labored and toiled and have often gone
without sleep; I have known hunger
and thirst and have often gone without
food;[t] I have been cold and naked.
28Besides everything else, I face daily
the pressure of my concern for all the
churches. 29Who is weak, and I do not
feel weak? Who is led into sin, and I do
not inwardly burn?

30If I must boast, I will boast of the
things that show my weakness.[u] 31The
God and Father of the Lord Jesus, who
is to be praised forever,[v] knows that I
am not lying. 32In Damascus the governor under King Aretas had the city of
the Damascenes guarded in order to
arrest me.[w] 33But I was lowered in a
basket from a window in the wall and
slipped through his hands.[x]

[a] *17* Jer. 9:24

10:16 [b]Ac 19:21 **10:17** [c]Jer 9:24; 1Co 1:31 **10:18** [d]ver 12 [e]Ro 2:29; 1Co 4:5 **11:1** [f]ver 4,19,20; Mt 17:17 [g]ver 16,17,21; 2Co 5:13 **11:2** [h]Hos 2:19; Eph 5:26,27 [i]2Co 4:14 **11:3** [j]Ge 3:1-6,13; Jn 8:44; 1Ti 2:14; Rev 12:9 **11:4** [k]1Co 3:11 [l]Ro 8:15 [m]Gal 1:6-9 **11:5** [n]2Co 12:11; Gal 2:6 **11:6** [o]1Co 1:17 [p]Eph 3:4 **11:7** [q]2Co 12:13 [r]1Co 9:18 **11:8** [s]Php 4:15,18 **11:9** [t]2Co 12:13,14, 16 **11:10** [u]Ro 9:1 [v]Ac 18:12 [w]1Co 9:15 **11:11** [x]2Co 12:15 **11:13** [y]2Pe 2:1 [z]Tit 1:10 [a]Rev 2:2 **11:15** [b]Php 3:19

11:16 [c]ver 1 **11:17** [d]1Co 7:12,25 **11:18** [e]Php 3:3,4 **11:19** [f]1Co 4:10 **11:20** [g]Gal 2:4 **11:21** [h]2Co 10:1,10 [i]Php 3:4 **11:22** [j]Php 3:5 [k]Ro 9:4 **11:23** [l]1Co 15:10 [m]Ac 16:23; 2Co 6:4,5 **11:24** [n]Dt 25:3 **11:25** [o]Ac 16:22 [p]Ac 14:19 **11:26** [q]Ac 9:23; 14:5 [r]Ac 21:31 [s]Gal 2:4 **11:27** [t]1Co 4:11,12; 2Co 6:5 **11:30** [u]1Co 2:3

11:31 [v]Ro 9:5 **11:32** [w]Ac 9:24 **11:33** [x]Ac 9:25

Paul's Vision and His Thorn

12 I must go on boasting.[y] Although
there is nothing to be gained, I will
go on to visions and revelations[z] from
the Lord. 2I know a man in Christ who
fourteen years ago was caught up[a] to
the third heaven.[b] Whether it was in
the body or out of the body I do not
know—God knows.[c] 3And I know that
this man—whether in the body or
apart from the body I do not know, but
God knows— 4was caught up to paradise.[d] He heard inexpressible things,
things that man is not permitted to tell.
5I will boast about a man like that, but
I will not boast about myself, except
about my weaknesses. 6Even if I should
choose to boast, I would not be a
fool,[e] because I would be speaking
the truth. But I refrain, so no one will
think more of me than is warranted by
what I do or say.

7To keep me from becoming conceited because of these surpassingly
great revelations, there was given me a
thorn in my flesh,[f] a messenger of Satan, to torment me. 8Three times I
pleaded with the Lord to take it away
from me.[g] 9But he said to me, "My
grace is sufficient for you, for my
power[h] is made perfect in weakness."
Therefore I will boast all the more
gladly about my weaknesses, so that
Christ's power may rest on me. 10That
is why, for Christ's sake, I delight in
weaknesses, in insults, in hardships,[i]
in persecutions,[j] in difficulties. For
when I am weak, then I am strong.[k]

3 →PG. 1288

Paul's Concern for the Corinthians

11I have made a fool of myself,[l]
but you drove me to it. I ought to
have been commended by you, for I
am not in the least inferior to the
"super-apostles,"[m] even though I am
nothing.[n] 12The things that mark
an apostle—signs, wonders and miracles[o]—were done among you with
great perseverance. 13How were you
inferior to the other churches, except
that I was never a burden to you?[p]
Forgive me this wrong![q]

14Now I am ready to visit you for the
third time,[r] and I will not be a burden
to you, because what I want is not your
possessions but you. After all, children
should not have to save up for their
parents,[s] but parents for their children.[t] 15So I will very gladly spend for
you everything I have and expend myself as well.[u] If I love you more, will
you love me less? 16Be that as it may, I
have not been a burden to you.[v] Yet,
crafty fellow that I am, I caught you by
trickery! 17Did I exploit you through
any of the men I sent you? 18I urged[w]
Titus to go to you and I sent our brother[x] with him. Titus did not exploit
you, did he? Did we not act in the same
spirit and follow the same course?

19Have you been thinking all along
that we have been defending ourselves
to you? We have been speaking in the
sight of God[y] as those in Christ; and
everything we do, dear friends, is for
your strengthening.[z] 20For I am afraid
that when I come[a] I may not find you
as I want you to be, and you may not
find me as you want me to be.[b] I fear
that there may be quarreling,[c] jealousy, outbursts of anger, factions,[d] slander, gossip,[e] arrogance and disorder.[f] 21I am afraid that when I come
again my God will humble me before
you, and I will be grieved[g] over many
who have sinned earlier[h] and have
not repented of the impurity, sexual sin
and debauchery in which they have in-
dulged.

Final Warnings

13 This will be my third visit to you.[i]
"Every matter must be established
by the testimony of two or three witnesses."[a][j] 2I already gave you a
warning when I was with you the second time. I now repeat it while absent:

[a] 1 Deut. 19:15

12:1 [y]2Co 11:16,30 [z]ver 7
12:2 [a]Ac 8:39 [b]Eph 4:10 [c]2Co 11:11
12:4 [d]Lk 23:43; Rev 2:7
12:6 [e]2Co 11:16
12:7 [f]Nu 33:55
12:8 [g]Mt 26:39,44
12:9 [h]Php 4:13
12:10 [i]2Co 6:4 [j]Ro 5:3; 2Th 1:4 [k]2Co 13:4
12:11 [l]2Co 11:1 [m]2Co 11:5 [n]1Co 15:9,10
12:12 [o]Jn 4:48
12:13 [p]1Co 9:12,18 [q]2Co 11:7
12:14 [r]2Co 13:1 [s]1Co 4:14,15 [t]Pr 19:14
12:15 [u]Php 2:17; 1Th 2:8
12:16 [v]2Co 11:9
12:18 [w]2Co 8:6,16 [x]2Co 8:18
12:19 [y]Ro 9:1 [z]2Co 10:8
12:20 [a]2Co 2:1-4 [b]1Co 4:21 [c]1Co 1:11; 3:3 [d]Gal 5:20 [e]Ro 1:29 [f]1Co 14:33
12:21 [g]2Co 2:1,4 [h]2Co 13:2
13:1 [i]2Co 12:14 [j]Dt 19:15; Mt 18:16

12:7–10 PE

"MY GRACE IS SUFFICIENT"

We've all faced situations in which we've called out to God for help and nothing seemed to happen. That was exactly Paul's experience here. While we don't know what Paul's "thorn" was, we do know it was a source of great pain. From his testimony we know that he prayed sincerely to have this hardship removed, but God chose not to do so. Instead, God gave Paul what he most needed—an extra measure of his grace to cope with his pain.

Through this trial, Paul realized that God's power is actually perfected during our times of greatest need. If God doesn't choose to take away our suffering, he'll give us the strength we need to get through it.

If you're presently suffering from some kind of "thorn in your flesh," you're probably looking for a way to get rid of it. There's nothing wrong with that. But if God doesn't choose to remove the cause of your suffering, don't despair. Instead, ask God to help you learn, as Paul did, to experience his power during your difficulty.

On my return I will not spare[k] those
who sinned earlier[l] or any of the others, **3**since you are demanding proof
that Christ is speaking through me.[m]
He is not weak in dealing with you, but
is powerful among you. **4**For to be sure,
he was crucified in weakness,[n] yet he
lives by God's power.[o] Likewise, we
are weak[p] in him, yet by God's power
we will live with him to serve you.

5Examine yourselves[q] to see whether you are in the faith; test yourselves.[r] Do you not realize that Christ
Jesus is in you[s]—unless, of course,
you fail the test? **6**And I trust that you
will discover that we have not failed the
test. **7**Now we pray to God that you will
not do anything wrong. Not that people will see that we have stood the test
but that you will do what is right even
though we may seem to have failed.
8For we cannot do anything against the
truth, but only for the truth. **9**We are
glad whenever we are weak but you are
strong; and our prayer is for your perfection.[t] **10**This is why I write these
things when I am absent, that when I
come I may not have to be harsh in my
use of authority—the authority the
Lord gave me for building you up, not
for tearing you down.[u]

Final Greetings

11Finally, brothers,[v] good-by. Aim
for perfection, listen to my appeal, be
of one mind, live in peace.[w] And the
God of love and peace[x] will be with
you.

6 →PG. 1288

12Greet one another with a holy
kiss.[y] **13**All the saints send their greetings.[z]

14May the grace of the Lord Jesus
Christ,[a] and the love of God,[b] and
the fellowship of the Holy Spirit[c] be
with you all.

13:2 [k] 2Co 1:23 [l] 2Co 12:21
13:3 [m] Mt 10:20; 1Co 5:4
13:4 [n] Php 2:7,8; 1Pe 3:18 [o] Ro 1:4; 6:4 [p] ver 9
13:5 [q] 1Co 11:28 [r] Jn 6:6 [s] Ro 8:10
13:9 [t] ver 11
13:10 [u] 2Co 10:8
13:11 [v] 1Th 4:1; 2Th 3:1 [w] Mk 9:50 [x] Ro 15:33; Eph 6:23
13:12 [y] Ro 16:16
13:13 [z] Php 4:22
13:14 [a] Ro 16:20; 2Co 8:9 [b] Ro 5:5; Jude 21 [c] Php 2:1

GALATIANS

AT A GLANCE

Key Principle: Just as we were justified (in God's eyes, as if we had never sinned) by grace through faith in Jesus Christ, so we are also sanctified (through the Spirit's power, conformed into Christ's image) by grace through faith in him.

Author: Paul

Time and Place: South Galatian Theory: A.D. 49 / Probably written in Syrian Antioch; North Galatian Theory: A.D. 53–55 / Probably written in Ephesus or Macedonia

Key Verses: 2:20–21; 3:3, 13–14; 5:1, 22–23

BENEFIT

Galatians contains the clearest explanation of the gospel of grace as opposed to the trap of works-based religious practice. There is a natural human tendency to suppose that we can or must earn God's approval, acceptance, love, or forgiveness through our own efforts and achievements. Even those who understand salvation as a gift of God's grace slip into the error of thinking that spiritual growth is a matter of human effort and merit. Galatians seeks to correct this error by stressing that the same principle that brings about our justification also brings about our sanctification.

SETTING

There are two theories concerning the setting and date of this epistle. (1) The North Galatian Theory argues that Paul was using "Galatia" to refer to the territory in central Asia Minor in which the Celtic tribes settled after their conflicts with the Romans and Macedonians. If this is true, this letter would not have been addressed to the southern cities of Pisidian Antioch, Iconium, Lystra and Derbe that Paul visited during his first missionary journey. During his second missionary journey (A.D. 50–53) Paul visited the northern ethnographic Galatian area, and established churches there. At the outset of his third missionary journey, Paul revisited these Galatian churches (Acts 18:23) before arriving at Ephesus in A.D. 53. He addressed this epistle to the Galatian churches during his time in Ephesus (A.D. 53–55) or in Macedonia (A.D. 55).

(2) The South Galatian Theory holds that Paul was using "Galatia" in its later political sense as a province of Rome which included the southern cities he visited during his first missionary journey (A.D. 46–48). Paul then would have sent this epistle to these cities after returning to Syrian Antioch in A.D. 48–49 prior to the Jerusalem Council in A.D. 50–51. This view is preferable for several reasons, including the fact that it fits against the background of Acts 13–14.

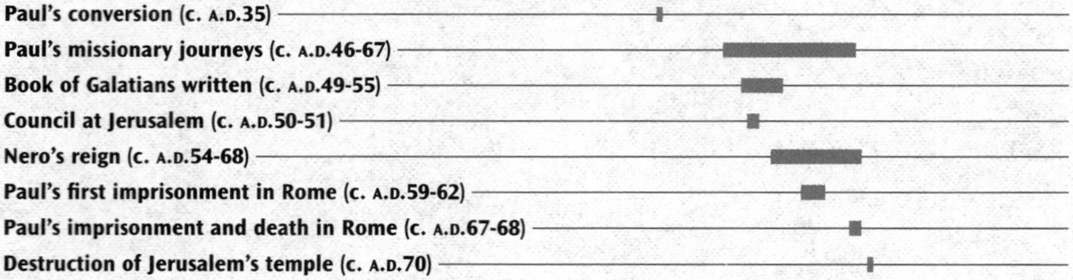

THEME AND PURPOSE

Paul had received a report that false teachers in the Galatian churches were claiming that Gentile converts to faith in Jesus must also submit to the requirements of the Mosaic law. Paul wrote this epistle to correct this error, and to demonstrate that justification by faith in Christ sets believers free to enjoy true liberty in him. He defends his apostolic authority and gospel message in chapters 1—2, and in chapters 3—4 uses the Old Testament to develop a multifaceted case for justification by faith. He then argues that liberty from the law does not mean lawlessness; instead, the indwelling power of the Holy Spirit makes it possible for believers to fulfill the law of love (5—6).

UNIQUE CONTRIBUTION

Galatians has been described as "the Magna Carta of Christian liberty" because it stresses justification by faith and liberty in Christ from bondage to the Mosaic Law. Galatians clearly contrasts faith and works and the principles of grace and law. In doing so, it incorporates a variety of persuasive arguments, including rebuke, personal experience, logical implications, exegesis of several Old Testament passages, allegory and warnings. While this epistle has much in common with Romans, it is far more corrective and confrontational.

CHRIST IN GALATIANS

Personal faith in the person and work of Christ is the key to righteousness before God; if righteousness could be gained through the law, Christ died needlessly (2:21). Christ frees those who trust in him from bondage to the law and from the futile quest to please God in our own power. His indwelling life and power makes it possible for us to be rightly related to God and to fulfill the requirements of the law (2:20; 5:16, 22–23, 25). Through his cross we are rescued from the present evil age, from the curse of sin, from enslavement to the law and from the works of the flesh (1:4; 3:13; 4:5; 5:24; 6:14).

OVERVIEW

FOCUS	Biographical Argument	Theological Argument	Moral Argument
REFERENCE	1 — 2	3 — 4	5 — 6
TOPICS	Defense of Justification by Faith	Explanation of Justification by Faith	Application of Justification by Faith
	Personal Explanation	Doctrinal Exposition	Practical Exhortation
	Validity of the Gospel: Apostleship	Vindication of the Gospel: Appeal	Victory of the Gospel: Application
	Legalism Versus Liberty		Life of Liberty
LOCATION	South Galatian Theory: Probably Written in Syrian Antioch North Galatian Theory: Probably Written in Ephesus or Macedonia		
TIME	South Galatian Theory: A.D. 49 North Galatian Theory: A.D. 53–55		

Paul begins this epistle with a biographical argument (1—2) that contrasts the divine origin of his apostleship and his message of the gospel of grace (1:1–5) with the distortion of the gospel by false teachers (1:6–10). He recounts how God gave him the message of justification by faith in Christ (1:11–24) and how the apostles confirmed that message (2:1–10). He even had to correct Peter on the issue of freedom from the law (2:11–21).

Paul uses several Old Testament references as he launches into a theological argument (3—4) in defense of justification by faith. He contends that the law was given not to save people, but to bring them to faith. He also uses Abraham's example to present the principle of faith, which leads to liberty, as superior to the principle of law, which leads to bondage.

Galatians concludes with a moral argument (5—6) that anticipates the objection that the liberty of grace could degenerate into license and lawlessness. Paul insists that faith, expressing itself through love and empowered by the Holy Spirit, will overcome sinful desires of the flesh and fulfill the law's requirements.

GALATIANS

1 Paul, an apostle—sent not from men
nor by man, but by Jesus Christ[a]
and God the Father, who raised him
from the dead[b]— 2and all the brothers with me,[c]

To the churches in Galatia:[d]

3Grace and peace to you from God
our Father and the Lord Jesus Christ,[e]
4who gave himself for our sins[f] to rescue us from the present evil age, according to the will of our God and Father,[g] 5to whom be glory for ever and
ever. Amen.[h]

No Other Gospel

6I am astonished that you are so
quickly deserting the one who called[i]
you by the grace of Christ and are turning to a different gospel[j]— 7which is
really no gospel at all. Evidently some
people are throwing you into confusion[k] and are trying to pervert the
gospel of Christ. 8But even if we or an
angel from heaven should preach a
gospel other than the one we preached
to you,[l] let him be eternally condemned![m] 9As we have already said, so
now I say again: If anybody is preaching to you a gospel other than what you
accepted,[n] let him be eternally condemned!

10Am I now trying to win the approval of men, or of God? Or am I trying to please men?[o] If I were still trying to please men, I would not be a
servant of Christ.

1:1 [a]Ac 9:15 [b]Ac 2:24 **1:2** [c]Php 4:21 [d]Ac 16:6; 1Co 16:1 **1:3** [e]Ro 1:7 **1:4** [f]Mt 20:28; Ro 4:25; Gal 2:20 [g]Php 4:20 **1:5** [h]Ro 11:36 **1:6** [i]Gal 5:8 [j]2Co 11:4 **1:7** [k]Ac 15:24; Gal 5:10 **1:8** [l]2Co 11:4 [m]Ro 9:3 **1:9** [n]Ro 16:17 **1:10** [o]Ro 2:29; 1Th 2:4

1:6–10

PROMISE **3**

PASSION FOR A PURE GOSPEL

Suppose someone tried to put a few drops of cyanide in your milk or in your aspirin bottle. Or suppose someone offered to pour a gallon of water into your car's gas tank or oil reservoir. How much of each substance would you be willing to tolerate?

No doubt your response to that question is quick and sure: "None!" No man would drink poisoned milk or take cyanide-laced aspirin. And even a little water in your car's gas tank or engine oil would put your car out of commission, at least temporarily. In such a situation, you'd diligently protect your health and your car.

In this book, Paul urges believers to show the same diligence in guarding the gospel against corruption and perversion. After all, a perverted gospel can do more damage than killing a body or ruining a car's engine. It can destroy a person spiritually and prevent him or her from finding the One who offers eternal life.

Paul provides us with an excellent example of someone who guarded the purity of the gospel. A group of "agitators" in the Galatian church distorted the gospel message and tried to lead the members into legalistic religious practices. They talked about Jesus, but added numerous elements of Jewish law to the message of salvation. Paul set the record straight with some pointed insights.

First, *there is only one true gospel* (vv. 6–7). While the false teachers said they proclaimed the true gospel, their message wasn't good news at all. Instead of stressing God's free gift of salvation, they urged men and women to believe in Jesus Christ *plus* perform good deeds to win God's favor. Any message that adds anything to faith in Christ isn't the true gospel.

Paul's hard-line attitude about the gospel should cause us to sit up and take notice. The gospel is simple: "For it is by grace you have been saved, through faith—and this not from yourselves, it is the gift of God—not by works, so that no one can boast" (Ephesians 2:8–9). As you seek to determine if a person's gospel message is truly Biblical, ask that person what he or she believes one must to do be saved. Listen carefully to the answer. It will tell you if he or she is adding cyanide to the pure milk of the gospel.

Second, *don't be impressed with appearances; look for truth.* Most of us would be awed if an "angel of light" suddenly appeared before us. We'd marvel if that dazzling personage told us how we could know God. But Paul cuts no corners. In essence, he tells us not to be impressed with a person's superficial appearance, but rather to find out where that person stands on the gospel. Paul saw through appearances. He saw those false teachers standing by the gas tank, gallon of water in hand, waiting to disable the engine of the Galatian church.

Don't allow someone's religious pedigree or position get in the way of the truth. It doesn't matter who he or she is; what matters is what he or she teaches. To make his point, Paul said even *his* message should be rejected if it added anything to the gospel message (v. 8).

Paul's message is clear, and so should yours be as you bring the gospel to others: Salvation comes by faith alone.

For the next Promise 3 reading go to page 1291.

Paul Called by God

11I want you to know, brothers,[p]
that the gospel I preached is not something that man made up. 12I did not
receive it from any man,[q] nor was I
taught it; rather, I received it by revelation[r] from Jesus Christ.
13For you have heard of my previous
way of life in Judaism,[s] how intensely
I persecuted the church of God and
tried to destroy it.[t] 14I was advancing
in Judaism beyond many Jews of my
own age and was extremely zealous for
the traditions of my fathers.[u] 15But
when God, who set me apart from
birth[a][v] and called me[w] by his grace,
was pleased 16to reveal his Son in me
so that I might preach him among the
Gentiles,[x] I did not consult any
man,[y] 17nor did I go up to Jerusalem
to see those who were apostles before
I was, but I went immediately into Arabia and later returned to Damascus.
18Then after three years,[z] I went
up to Jerusalem[a] to get acquainted
with Peter[b] and stayed with him fifteen days. 19I saw none of the other apostles—only James,[b] the Lord's
brother. 20I assure you before God that
what I am writing you is no lie.[c] 21Lat-
er I went to Syria and Cilicia.[d] 22I was
personally unknown to the churches
of Judea[e] that are in Christ. 23They
only heard the report: "The man who
formerly persecuted us is now preaching the faith[f] he once tried to destroy." 24And they praised God[g] because of me.

Paul Accepted by the Apostles

2 Fourteen years later I went up again
to Jerusalem,[h] this time with Barnabas. I took Titus along also. 2I went
in response to a revelation and set before them the gospel that I preach
among the Gentiles.[i] But I did this
privately to those who seemed to be
leaders, for fear that I was running or
had run my race[j] in vain. 3Yet not
even Titus,[k] who was with me, was
compelled to be circumcised, even
though he was a Greek.[l] 4⌞This matter
arose⌟ because some false brothers[m]
had infiltrated our ranks to spy on[n]
the freedom[o] we have in Christ Jesus
and to make us slaves. 5We did not
give in to them for a moment, so that
the truth of the gospel[p] might remain
with you.
6 →PG. 1289
6As for those who seemed to be
important[q]—whatever they were
makes no difference to me; God does
not judge by external appearance[r]—
those men added nothing to my message. 7On the contrary, they saw that I
had been entrusted with the task[s] of
preaching the gospel to the Gentiles,[c][t] just as Peter[u] had been to the
Jews.[d] 8For God, who was at work in
the ministry of Peter as an apostle[v] to
the Jews, was also at work in my ministry as an apostle to the Gentiles.
9James, Peter[e][w] and John, those re-
puted to be pillars,[x] gave me and Barnabas[y] the right hand of fellowship
when they recognized the grace given
to me.[z] They agreed that we should go
to the Gentiles, and they to the Jews.
10All they asked was that we should
continue to remember the poor,[a] the
very thing I was eager to do.

Paul Opposes Peter

11When Peter[b] came to Antioch,[c] I
opposed him to his face, because he
was clearly in the wrong. 12Before certain men came from James, he used to
eat with the Gentiles.[d] But when they
arrived, he began to draw back and
separate himself from the Gentiles because he was afraid of those who belonged to the circumcision group.[e]
13The other Jews joined him in his hypocrisy, so that by their hypocrisy even
Barnabas[f] was led astray.
14When I saw that they were not acting in line with the truth of the gospel,[g] I said to Peter[h] in front of them
all, "You are a Jew, yet you live like a
Gentile and not like a Jew.[i] How is it,
then, that you force Gentiles to follow
Jewish customs?
15"We who are Jews by birth[j] and
not 'Gentile sinners'[k] 16know that a
man is not justified by observing the
law, but by faith in Jesus Christ.[l] So
we, too, have put our faith in Christ
Jesus that we may be justified by faith
in Christ and not by observing the law,
because by observing the law no one
will be justified.
17"If, while we seek to be justified in 3 →PG. 1291
Christ, it becomes evident that we ourselves are sinners,[m] does that mean
that Christ promotes sin? Absolutely
not![n] 18If I rebuild what I destroyed,
I prove that I am a lawbreaker. 19For
through the law I died to the law[o] so
that I might live for God.[p] 20I have
been crucified with Christ[q] and I no 1 →PG. 1292
longer live, but Christ lives in me.[r]
The life I live in the body, I live by faith

a *15* Or *from my mother's womb* **b** *18* Greek *Cephas* **c** *7* Greek *uncircumcised* **d** *7* Greek *circumcised*; also in verses 8 and 9 **e** *9* Greek *Cephas*; also in verses 11 and 14

1:11 [p] 1Co 15:1
1:12 [q] ver 1 [r] ver 16
1:13 [s] Ac 26:4,5 [t] Ac 8:3
1:14 [u] Mt 15:2
1:15 [v] Isa 49:1,5; Jer 1:5 [w] Ac 9:15
1:16 [x] Gal 2:9 [y] Mt 16:17
1:18 [z] Ac 9:22,23 [a] Ac 9:26,27
1:19 [b] Mt 13:55
1:20 [c] Ro 9:1
1:21 [d] Ac 6:9
1:22 [e] 1Th 2:14
1:23 [f] Ac 6:7
1:24 [g] Mt 9:8
2:1 [h] Ac 15:2
2:2 [i] Ac 15:4,12 [j] 1Co 9:24; Php 2:16
2:3 [k] 2Co 2:13 [l] Ac 16:3; 1Co 9:21
2:4 [m] 2Co 11:26 [n] Jude 4 [o] Ac 15:1; Gal 5:1,13
2:5 [p] ver 14
2:6 [q] Gal 6:3 [r] Ac 10:34
2:7 [s] 1Th 2:4; 1Ti 1:11 [t] Ac 9:15 [u] ver 9,11,14
2:8 [v] Ac 1:25
2:9 [w] ver 7,11,14 [x] 1Ti 3:15 [y] Ac 4:36 [z] Ro 12:3
2:10 [a] Ac 24:17
2:11 [b] ver 7,9,14 [c] Ac 11:19
2:12 [d] Ac 11:3 [e] Ac 11:2
2:13 [f] ver 1; Ac 4:36
2:14 [g] ver 5 [h] ver 7,9,11 [i] Ac 10:28
2:15 [j] Php 3:4,5 [k] 1Sa 15:18
2:16 [l] Ac 13:39; Ro 9:30
2:17 [m] ver 15 [n] Gal 3:21
2:19 [o] Ro 7:4 [p] Ro 6:10,11, 14; 2Co 5:15
2:20 [q] Ro 6:6 [r] 1Pe 4:2

in the Son of God,[s] who loved me[t] and gave himself for me.[u] 21I do not set aside the grace of God, for if righteousness could be gained through the law,[v] Christ died for nothing!"[a]

Faith or Observance of the Law

3 You foolish Galatians! Who has bewitched you?[w] Before your very eyes Jesus Christ was clearly portrayed as crucified.[x] 2I would like to learn just one thing from you: Did you receive the Spirit by observing the law, or by believing what you heard?[y] 3Are you so foolish? After beginning with the Spirit, are you now trying to attain your goal by human effort? 4Have you suffered so much for nothing—if it really was for nothing? 5Does God give you his Spirit and work miracles[z] among you because you observe the law, or because you believe what you heard?

6Consider Abraham: "He believed God, and it was credited to him as righteousness."[b][a] 7Understand, then, that those who believe[b] are children of Abraham. 8The Scripture foresaw that God would justify the Gentiles by faith, and announced the gospel in advance to Abraham: "All nations will be blessed through you."[c][c] 9So those who have faith[d] are blessed along with Abraham, the man of faith.

10All who rely on observing the law are under a curse, for it is written: "Cursed is everyone who does not continue to do everything written in the Book of the Law."[d][e] 11Clearly no one is justified before God by the law, because, "The righteous will live by faith."[e][f] 12The law is not based on faith; on the contrary, "The man who does these things will live by them."[f][g] 13Christ redeemed us from the curse of the law[h] by becoming a curse for us, for it is written: "Cursed is everyone who is hung on a tree."[g][i] 14He redeemed us in order that the blessing given to Abraham might come to the Gentiles through Christ Jesus,[j] so that by faith we might receive the promise of the Spirit.[k]

The Law and the Promise

15Brothers, let me take an example from everyday life. Just as no one can set aside or add to a human covenant that has been duly established, so it is in this case. 16The promises were spoken to Abraham and to his seed.[l] The Scripture does not say "and to seeds," meaning many people, but "and to your seed,"[h] meaning one person, who is Christ. 17What I mean is this: The law, introduced 430 years[m] later, does not set aside the covenant previously established by God and thus do away with the promise. 18For if the inheritance depends on the law, then it no longer depends on a promise;[n] but God in his grace gave it to Abraham through a promise.

19What, then, was the purpose of the law? It was added because of transgressions[o] until the Seed[p] to whom the promise referred had come. The law was put into effect through angels[q] by a mediator.[r] 20A mediator,[s] however, does not represent just one party; but God is one.

21Is the law, therefore, opposed to the promises of God? Absolutely not![t] For if a law had been given that could impart life, then righteousness would certainly have come by the law.[u] 22But the Scripture declares that the whole world is a prisoner of sin,[v] so that what was promised, being given through faith in Jesus Christ, might be given to those who believe.

23Before this faith came, we were held prisoners[w] by the law, locked up until faith should be revealed. 24So the law was put in charge to lead us to Christ[i][x] that we might be justified by faith.[y] 25Now that faith has come, we are no longer under the supervision of the law.

Sons of God

26You are all sons of God[z] through faith in Christ Jesus, 27for all of you who were baptized into Christ[a] have clothed yourselves with Christ.[b] 28There is neither Jew nor Greek, slave nor free,[c] male nor female, for you are all one in Christ Jesus.[d] 29If you belong to Christ,[e] then you are Abra-

6 →PG. 1297

2:20 [s]Mt 4:3 [t]Ro 8:37 [u]Gal 1:4
2:21 [v]Gal 3:21
3:1 [w]Gal 5:7 [x]1Co 1:23
3:2 [y]Ro 10:17
3:5 [z]1Co 12:10
3:6 [a]Ge 15:6; Ro 4:3
3:7 [b]ver 9
3:8 [c]Ge 12:3; Ac 3:25
3:9 [d]ver 7; Ro 4:16
3:10 [e]Dt 27:26; Jer 11:3
3:11 [f]Hab 2:4; Gal 2:16; Heb 10:38
3:12 [g]Lev 18:5; Ro 10:5
3:13 [h]Gal 4:5 [i]Dt 21:23; Ac 5:30
3:14 [j]Ro 4:9,16 [k]ver 2; Joel 2:28; Ac 2:33
3:16 [l]Lk 1:55; Ro 4:13,16
3:17 [m]Ge 15:13,14; Ex 12:40
3:18 [n]Ro 4:14
3:19 [o]Ro 5:20 [p]ver 16 [q]Ac 7:53 [r]Ex 20:19
3:20 [s]Heb 8:6; 9:15; 12:24
3:21 [t]Gal 2:17 [u]Gal 2:21
3:22 [v]Ro 3:9-19; 11:32
3:23 [w]Ro 11:32
3:24 [x]Ro 10:4 [y]Gal 2:16
3:26 [z]Ro 8:14
3:27 [a]Mt 28:19; Ro 6:3 [b]Ro 13:14
3:28 [c]Col 3:11 [d]Jn 10:16; 17:11; Eph 2:14,15
3:29 [e]1Co 3:23

[a] *21* Some interpreters end the quotation after verse 14. [b] *6* Gen. 15:6 [c] *8* Gen. 12:3; 18:18; 22:18 [d] *10* Deut. 27:26 [e] *11* Hab. 2:4 [f] *12* Lev. 18:5 [g] *13* Deut. 21:23 [h] *16* Gen. 12:7; 13:15; 24:7 [i] *24* Or *charge until Christ came*

3:23–29

PROMISE 6

BEYOND LAW TO FAITH

These verses constitute one of Paul's strongest calls for unity among Christians. Because all believers are heirs of God's promise of eternal life, we'll be together forever in heaven. The next time you're with Christian brothers who are somehow different from you, rejoice together over the promise of eternal life that you share.

For the next Promise 6 reading go to page 1297.

ham's seed, and heirs according to the promise.[f]

4 What I am saying is that as long as the heir is a child, he is no different from a slave, although he owns the whole estate. 2He is subject to guardians and trustees until the time set by his father. 3So also, when we were children, we were in slavery[g] under the basic principles of the world.[h] 4But when the time had fully come,[i] God sent his Son, born of a woman,[j] born under law,[k] 5to redeem those under law, that we might receive the full rights[l] of sons. 6Because you are sons, God sent the Spirit of his Son into our hearts,[m] the Spirit who calls out, *"Abba,*[a] Father."[n] 7So you are no longer a slave, but a son; and since you are a son, God has made you also an heir.[o]

Paul's Concern for the Galatians

8Formerly, when you did not know God,[p] you were slaves to those who by nature are not gods.[q] 9But now that you know God—or rather are known by God[r]—how is it that you are turning back to those weak and miserable principles? Do you wish to be enslaved[s] by them all over again?[t] 10You are observing special days and months and seasons and years![u] 11I fear for you, that somehow I have wasted my efforts on you.[v]

12I plead with you, brothers,[w] become like me, for I became like you. You have done me no wrong. 13As you know, it was because of an illness[x] that I first preached the gospel to you. 14Even though my illness was a trial to you, you did not treat me with contempt or scorn. Instead, you welcomed me as if I were an angel of God, as if I were Christ Jesus himself.[y] 15What has happened to all your joy? I can testify that, if you could have done so, you would have torn out your eyes and given them to me. 16Have I now become your enemy by telling you the truth?[z]

17Those people are zealous to win you over, but for no good. What they want is to alienate you ⌊from us⌋, so that you may be zealous for them. 18It is fine to be zealous, provided the purpose is good, and to be so always and not just when I am with you.[a] 19My dear children,[b] for whom I am again in the pains of childbirth until Christ is formed in you,[c] 20how I wish I could be with you now and change my tone, because I am perplexed about you!

Hagar and Sarah

21Tell me, you who want to be under the law, are you not aware of what the law says? 22For it is written that Abraham had two sons, one by the slave woman[d] and the other by the free woman.[e] 23His son by the slave woman was born in the ordinary way;[f] but his son by the free woman was born as the result of a promise.[g]

24These things may be taken figuratively, for the women represent two covenants. One covenant is from Mount Sinai and bears children who are to be slaves: This is Hagar. 25Now Hagar stands for Mount Sinai in Arabia and corresponds to the present city of Jerusalem, because she is in slavery with her children. 26But the Jerusalem that is above[h] is free, and she is our mother. 27For it is written:

"Be glad, O barren woman,
who bears no children;
break forth and cry aloud,
you who have no labor pains;
because more are the children of
the desolate woman
than of her who has a
husband."[b][i]

28Now you, brothers, like Isaac, are children of promise. 29At that time the son born in the ordinary way[j] persecuted the son born by the power of the Spirit.[k] It is the same now. 30But what does the Scripture say? "Get rid of the slave woman and her son, for the slave woman's son will never share in the inheritance with the free woman's son."[c][l] 31Therefore, brothers, we are

4:4

FULLNESS OF TIME

Jesus' birth was a well-planned event. All of the Old Testament prophecies concerning the Messiah's birth, life and death found their fulfillment in Jesus. This inspired Paul to testify that God sent his Son "when the time had fully come." In other words—from an economic, political, social and spiritual standpoint—God so ordered history that Jesus came at the perfect point in human history. Paul's long and earnest practice of the Jewish faith adds perspective to his statement. As a former Pharisee, Paul had joined with his people down the centuries who fervently prayed for the coming of God's Messiah.

This brief testimony serves to remind us that God's timing is not always in line with our own. From his all-seeing and all-powerful position, God moves according to his own eternally trustworthy timeline.

3:29 f ver 16
4:3 g Gal 2:4; h Col 2:8,20
4:4 i Mk 1:15; Eph 1:10; j Jn 1:14; k Lk 2:27
4:5 l Jn 1:12
4:6 m Ro 5:5; n Ro 8:15,16
4:7 o Ro 8:17
4:8 p 1Co 1:21; Eph 2:12; 1Th 4:5; q 2Ch 13:9; Isa 37:19
4:9 r 1Co 8:3; s ver 3; t Col 2:20
4:10 u Ro 14:5
4:11 v 1Th 3:5
4:12 w Gal 6:18
4:13 x 1Co 2:3
4:14 y Mt 10:40
4:16 z Am 5:10
4:18 a ver 13,14
4:19 b 1Co 4:15; c Eph 4:13
4:22 d Ge 16:15; e Ge 21:2
4:23 f Ro 9:7,8; g Ge 18:10-14; Heb 11:11
4:26 h Heb 12:22; Rev 3:12
4:27 i Isa 54:1
4:29 j ver 23; k Ge 21:9
4:30 l Ge 21:10

a *6* Aramaic for *Father* b *27* Isaiah 54:1
c *30* Gen. 21:10

not children of the slave woman, but of the free woman.

Freedom in Christ

5 It is for freedom that Christ has set us free.[m] Stand firm,[n] then, and do not let yourselves be burdened again by a yoke of slavery.[o]

2Mark my words! I, Paul, tell you that if you let yourselves be circumcised,[p] Christ will be of no value to you at all. **3**Again I declare to every man who lets himself be circumcised that he is obligated to obey the whole law.[q] **4**You who are trying to be justified by law have been alienated from Christ; you have fallen away from grace.[r] **5**But by faith we eagerly await through the Spirit the righteousness for which we hope.[s] **6**For in Christ Jesus neither circumcision nor uncircumcision has any value.[t] The only thing that counts is faith expressing itself through love.[u]

7You were running a good race.[v] Who cut in on you[w] and kept you from obeying the truth? **8**That kind of persuasion does not come from the one who calls you.[x] **9**"A little yeast works through the whole batch of dough."[y] **10**I am confident[z] in the Lord that you will take no other view.[a] The one who is throwing you into confusion[b] will pay the penalty, whoever he may be. **11**Brothers, if I am still preaching circumcision, why am I still being persecuted?[c] In that case the offense[d] of the cross has been abolished. **12**As for those agitators,[e] I wish they would go the whole way and emasculate themselves!

2 →PG. 1291
7 →PG. 1292

13You, my brothers, were called to be free. But do not use your freedom to indulge the sinful nature**a**;[f] rather, serve one another[g] in love. **14**The entire law is summed up in a single command: "Love your neighbor as yourself."**b**[h] **15**If you keep on biting and devouring each other, watch out or you will be destroyed by each other.

Life by the Spirit

3 →PG. 1291

16So I say, live by the Spirit,[i] and you will not gratify the desires of the sinful nature.[j] **17**For the sinful nature desires what is contrary to the Spirit, and the Spirit what is contrary to the sinful nature.[k] They are in conflict with each other, so that you do not do what you want.[l] **18**But if you are led by the Spirit, you are not under law.[m]

19The acts of the sinful nature are obvious: sexual immorality,[n] impurity and debauchery; **20**idolatry and witchcraft; hatred, discord, jealousy, fits of rage, selfish ambition, dissensions, factions **21**and envy; drunkenness, orgies, and the like.[o] I warn you, as I did before, that those who live like this will not inherit the kingdom of God.

22But the fruit[p] of the Spirit is love,[q] joy, peace, patience, kindness, goodness, faithfulness, **23**gentleness and self-control.[r] Against such things there is no law. **24**Those who belong to Christ Jesus have crucified the sinful nature[s] with its passions and desires.[t] **25**Since we live by the Spirit, let us keep in step with the Spirit. **26**Let us not become conceited,[u] provoking and envying each other.

Doing Good to All

2 →PG. 1307
3 →PG. 1298
5 →PG. 1292

6 Brothers, if someone is caught in a sin, you who are spiritual[v] should restore him gently. But watch yourself, or you also may be tempted. **2**Carry each other's burdens, and in this way you will fulfill the law of Christ.[w] **3**If anyone thinks he is something[x] when he is nothing, he deceives himself. **4**Each one should test his own actions.

a *13* Or *the flesh*; also in verses 16, 17, 19 and 24
b *14* Lev. 19:18

5:1 [m] Jn 8:32 [n] 1Co 16:13 [o] Ac 15:10; Gal 2:4
5:2 [p] Ac 15:1
5:3 [q] Gal 3:10
5:4 [r] Heb 12:15; 2Pe 3:17
5:5 [s] Ro 8:23,24
5:6 [t] 1Co 7:19 [u] 1Th 1:3
5:7 [v] 1Co 9:24 [w] Gal 3:1
5:8 [x] Ro 8:28; Gal 1:6
5:9 [y] 1Co 5:6
5:10 [z] 2Co 2:3 [a] Php 3:15 [b] Gal 1:7
5:11 [c] Gal 4:29; 6:12 [d] 1Co 1:23
5:12 [e] ver 10
5:13 [f] 1Co 8:9; 1Pe 2:16 [g] 1Co 9:19; Eph 5:21
5:14 [h] Lev 19:18; Mt 22:39
5:16 [i] Ro 8:2,4-6,9,14 [j] ver 24
5:17 [k] Ro 8:5-8 [l] Ro 7:15-23
5:18 [m] Ro 6:14; 1Ti 1:9
5:19 [n] 1Co 6:18
5:21 [o] Ro 13:13
5:22 [p] Mt 7:16-20; Eph 5:9 [q] Col 3:12-15
5:23 [r] Ac 24:25
5:24 [s] Ro 6:6 [t] ver 16,17
5:26 [u] Php 2:3
6:1 [v] 1Co 2:15
6:2 [w] Ro 15:1; Jas 2:8
6:3 [x] Ro 12:3; 1Co 8:2

5:16–21

PROMISE 3

FEEDING THE GOOD DOG

Someone has said that cultivating our spiritual life begins in earnest when we recognize that we all have what amounts to two dogs living within us—a "good dog" and a "bad dog." The key is feeding the good dog and starving the bad one. Paul described not two dogs, but two forces within us—the sinful nature and the Spirit.

In his discussion about our "bad dog," or sinful nature, the apostle identified four groups of sins: (1) all forms of sexual impurity, (2) sins of superstition, (3) attitudes and actions that flow from a rebellious heart, and (4) sins of excess that flow from a complete lack of self control. As Paul looked back over this list, he noted that people whose lives are given over to such sins will not enter God's kingdom. A life that is characterized by these and other "acts of the sinful nature" reveals a person who isn't at all connected with God.

As followers of Jesus Christ, we need to be sure we don't feed our sinful nature. We can't starve it to death; our sinful nature will be with us until we're with the Lord. But we can weaken it by avoiding situations in which we're tempted to sin, and praying for the Spirit's power to overcome temptation when it does strike.

For the next Promise 3 reading go to page 1315.

Then he can take pride in himself,
without comparing himself to somebody else, 5for each one should carry
his own load.
6Anyone who receives instruction in
the word must share all good things
with his instructor.[y]
7Do not be deceived:[z] God cannot
be mocked. A man reaps what he
sows.[a] 8The one who sows to please
his sinful nature, from that nature[a]
will reap destruction;[b] the one who
sows to please the Spirit, from the Spirit will reap eternal life.[c] 9Let us not
become weary in doing good,[d] for at
the proper time we will reap a harvest
if we do not give up.[e] 10Therefore, as
we have opportunity, let us do good[f]
to all people, especially to those who
belong to the family[g] of believers.

5 →PG. 1298
7 →PG. 1297

Not Circumcision but a New Creation

11See what large letters I use as I
write to you with my own hand![h]
12Those who want to make a good
impression outwardly are trying to
compel you to be circumcised.[i] The
only reason they do this is to avoid being persecuted[j] for the cross of Christ.
13Not even those who are circumcised
obey the law,[k] yet they want you to be
circumcised that they may boast about
your flesh.[l] 14May I never boast except
in the cross of our Lord Jesus Christ,
through which[b] the world has been
crucified to me, and I to the world.[m]
15Neither circumcision nor uncircumcision means anything;[n] what counts is
a new creation.[o] 16Peace and mercy
to all who follow this rule, even to the
Israel of God.
17Finally, let no one cause me trouble, for I bear on my body the marks[p]
of Jesus.
18The grace of our Lord Jesus
Christ[q] be with your spirit,[r] brothers.
Amen.

1 →PG. 1296

[a] 8 Or *his flesh, from the flesh* [b] 14 Or *whom*

6:6 [y] 1Co 9:11,14 **6:7** [z] 1Co 6:9 [a] 2Co 9:6 **6:8** [b] Job 4:8; Hos 8:7 [c] Jas 3:18 **6:9** [d] 1Co 15:58 [e] Rev 2:10 **6:10** [f] Pr 3:27 [g] Eph 2:19 **6:11** [h] 1Co 16:21 **6:12** [i] Ac 15:1 [j] Gal 5:11 **6:13** [k] Ro 2:25 [l] Php 3:3 **6:14** [m] Ro 6:2,6 **6:15** [n] 1Co 7:19 [o] 2Co 5:17 **6:17** [p] Isa 44:5; 2Co 1:5 **6:18** [q] Ro 16:20 [r] 2Ti 4:22

6:1–5

PROMISE 2

THREE STEPS TO RESTORATION

How do you confront someone who is "caught in a sin"? Here Paul gives us some specific guidelines.

1. *Be "spiritual."* Make sure you're properly connected with God so you don't fall as well. Also bathe your upcoming meeting with prayer.
2. *Be gentle.* Deal with the person in the same way you would set a broken bone—with tenderness and care and with a view toward complete healing.
3. *Be humble.* Recognize that you too could be caught in a sin. Let the person know you won't reject him or her because of the sin. And be there to help that person get back up; you'd want the same treatment if the tables were turned.

For the next Promise 2 reading go to page 1320.

5:22–23

PE

THE SPIRIT'S FRUIT

God gives us as believers victory over sin and enables us to be Christlike. He does that by producing the fruit of the Spirit in our lives.

Love tops the list. Paul may have mentioned it first because all the other attributes flow from it.

Joy and peace are the result of our relationship with God. They replace guilt, anger, resentment, and a host of other destructive emotions that characterize our lives when we're not walking with God.

As we deal with other people, the Spirit gives us patience, kindness and goodness. We develop the ability to live with the failings of others; in fact, we are even prompted to lighten their load.

At the same time, the Spirit produces faithfulness, gentleness and self-control in our lives. These three character traits are impossible for a man to experience without the Spirit, whose work in us helps us keep our promises, gives us a gentle touch and tone and enables us to live a disciplined life.

There's no way you can succeed in cultivating these qualities on your own. But by accepting Jesus Christ and becoming a devoted follower, you've opened your heart so that God's Spirit can do the work for you.

Do these attributes characterize your life as a believer in the workplace? At the family reunion? In the middle of a traffic jam? The journey of faith may have its setbacks, but your goal should be to pray for the Spirit's presence and work in your life at all times and in all situations.

EPHESIANS

AT A GLANCE

Key Principle: Our new identity in Christ should be the basis for what we do; our high calling and position before God is the foundation and power source for our holy conduct and practice.
Author: Paul
Time and Place: A.D. 60–62 / Sent from Rome to Ephesus
Key Verses: 1:3; 2:8–10; 4:1–5

BENEFIT

Most believers have only a vague notion of their true identity and spiritual wealth. As a consequence, most live like spiritual paupers, rarely using the marvelous resources that God has placed at their disposal. The first half of Ephesians offers a solution to this dilemma. It exposes us to the treasury of spiritual blessings that are already ours in Christ if we will lay hold of them by faith in his promises. By looking to Jesus for our identity and empowerment, we discover that it is possible—through his grace—to fulfill the commands that Paul develops in the second half of Ephesians.

SETTING

Ephesus was a commercial and religious center in Asia Minor. Paul visited this city during his second missionary journey (Acts 18:18–21) and stayed there for nearly three years on his third missionary journey (Acts 19; 20:30). Ephesus boasted the impressive temple of Diana (Roman name) or Artemis (Greek name), considered to be one of the seven wonders of the ancient world. Paul's ministry began to cut into the profits of those who sold images of Artemis and diminish the practice of sorcery, and this eventually led to an uproar in the giant theater in Ephesus. Paul left for Macedonia, and on the way to Jerusalem met with the Ephesian elders (Acts 20:17–38).

Ephesians is one of what have been called the four Prison Epistles (the others are Philippians, Colossians and Philemon) that Paul wrote during his first imprisonment in Rome (Acts 28:16–31; A.D. 60–62). The fact that many ancient manuscripts omit the words "in Ephesus" in 1:1 has led to the theory that this was originally a circular letter, directed to the churches of Asia, and that it only later became associated with the church in Ephesus. It is also possible, however, that Paul initially directed it to the Ephesians, but wrote it in such a way that it would be relevant to the other Asian churches as well.

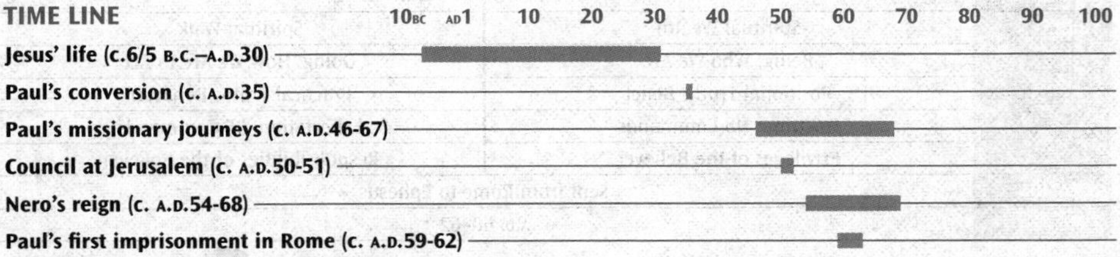

THEME AND PURPOSE

Paul captures the theme of Ephesians in the pivotal verse that links the two major sections together: "As a prisoner for the Lord, then, I urge you to live a life worthy of the calling you have received" (4:1). The believer's calling is in chapters 1—3, and the believer's conduct is in chapters 4—6; the former is the basis for the latter. Paul wrote this epistle to encourage his readers to grow into spiritual maturity by laying hold of the resources they have in Christ, and by building each other up through the use of spiritual gifts and through serving one another out of Christ's love. Like Romans, this is a preventive rather than a corrective epistle.

UNIQUE CONTRIBUTION

Ephesians as a whole—and especially the first three chapters—is full of rich imagery and thought. It develops insights about the believer's position in Christ that are both profound and powerful. The two prayers in this book (1:15–23; 3:14–21) are among the most significant in the Bible, and they can be used with great profit by believers today.

In contrast to the informal and personal nature of 2 Corinthians and Galatians, Ephesians is a formal letter that instructs and encourages readers concerning principles of spiritual growth and practice. Apart from his reference to himself as a prisoner for the Lord and a recipient of God's mystery (3:1–4; 4:1), Paul's only personal allusions are in 6:19–22. Even his benediction is in the third person (6:23–24). This kind of writing would be surprising in a letter directed to people with whom he had spent three years in ministry, and it supports the theory that Paul had a wider audience in mind when he wrote this letter.

CHRIST IN EPHESIANS

Paul's important expression "in Christ" and its equivalent ("in him") appears more often in Ephesians (35 times) than in any other New Testament book. The "in Christ" relationship that is available to every believer is rich and multifaceted: We have received every spiritual blessing in Christ (1:3); we were chosen in Christ (1:4, 11); we were adopted as God's children in Christ (1:5); we have redemption in Christ (1:7); our hope is in Christ (1:12); we were sealed in Christ (1:13); we were made alive in Christ (2:5); we were raised up with Christ and seated with him in the heavenly realms (2:6); we are God's workmanship, created in Christ Jesus to do good works (2:10); we are joined together in Christ (2:21); we share together in the promise in Christ Jesus (3:6); we can approach God with freedom and confidence in Christ (3:12); we are called to strengthen ourselves in Christ's mighty power (6:10).

OVERVIEW

FOCUS	Calling of the Body	Conduct of the Body
REFERENCE	1 — 3	4 — 6
TOPICS	Spiritual Wealth	Spiritual Walk
	Being: Who We Are	Doing: How We Are to Act
	Positional Truth: Belief	Practical Truth: Behavior
	Doctrine: No Commands	Exhortation: 35 Commands
	Privileges of the Believer	Responsibilities of the Believer
LOCATION	Sent from Rome to Ephesus	
TIME	A.D. 60–62	

Our position in Christ (1—3) lays the foundation for our practice in Christ (4—6). After a prologue, Paul praises the triune God for the work of the Father in choosing us (1:3–6), the Son in redeeming us (1:7–12) and the Spirit for sealing us (1:13–14). This marvelous hymn to God's grace is followed by a prayer that we will gain a true knowledge of our calling, inheritance and power (1:15–23). Paul contrasts his readers' former spiritual condition with the life and hope that salvation by grace through faith in Christ has given them (2:1–10). He then shows how Gentiles are now fellow citizens with Jewish believers (2:11–22). This unification of Jew and Gentile in one body was formerly a mystery which had now become a reality (3:1–13). In his second prayer, Paul asks that his readers be strengthened with God's power and with the knowledge of the love of Christ (3:14–21).

Turning from the privileges to the responsibilities of the believer (4—6), Paul exhorts his readers to grow in unity and in maturity as they exercise their spiritual gifts (4:1–16). He calls them to walk in the power of the new self and to practice righteousness, truth, self-control and forgiveness (4:17–32). As God's beloved children, they are to live in the light and avoid the deeds of darkness (5:1–21). Their relationships as wives and husbands (5:22–33), as children and parents (6:1–4) and as slaves and masters (6:5–9) are to be transformed by Christ's love. They are to stand firm as they engage in spiritual warfare and use the weapons of truth, righteousness, peace, faith, salvation, the word of God and prayer (6:10–20).

EPHESIANS

1 Paul, an apostle[a] of Christ Jesus by the will of God,[b]

To the saints in Ephesus,[a] the faithful[b][c] in Christ Jesus:

[2]Grace and peace to you from God our Father and the Lord Jesus Christ.[d]

Spiritual Blessings in Christ

[3]Praise be to the God and Father of our Lord Jesus Christ,[e] who has blessed us in the heavenly realms[f] with every spiritual blessing in Christ. [4]For he chose us in him before the creation of the world to be holy and blameless[g] in his sight. In love[h] [5]he[c] predestined[i] us to be adopted as his sons through Jesus Christ, in accordance with his pleasure[j] and will— [6]to the praise of his glorious grace, which he has freely given us in the One he loves.[k] [7]In him we have redemption[l] through his blood, the forgiveness of sins, in accordance with the riches of God's grace [8]that he lavished on us with all wisdom and understanding. [9]And he[d] made known to us the mystery[m] of his will according to his good pleasure, which he purposed in Christ, [10]to be put into effect when the times will have reached their fulfillment[n]—to bring all things in heaven and on earth together under one head, even Christ.[o]

[11]In him we were also chosen,[e] having been predestined according to the plan of him who works out everything in conformity with the purpose[p] of his will, [12]in order that we, who were the first to hope in Christ, might be for the
1 →PG. 1298
praise of his glory.[q] [13]And you also were included in Christ when you heard the word of truth,[r] the gospel of your salvation. Having believed, you were marked in him with a seal,[s] the promised Holy Spirit, [14]who is a deposit guaranteeing our inheritance[t] until the redemption of those who are God's possession—to the praise of his glory.

Thanksgiving and Prayer

[15]For this reason, ever since I heard about your faith in the Lord Jesus and your love for all the saints,[u] [16]I have not stopped giving thanks for you,[v] remembering you in my prayers. [17]I keep asking that the God of our Lord Jesus Christ, the glorious Father,[w] may give you the Spirit[f] of wisdom[x] and revelation, so that you may know him better. [18]I pray also that the eyes of your heart may be enlightened[y] in order that you may know the hope to which he has called you, the riches of his glorious inheritance in the saints, [19]and his incomparably great power for us who believe. That power[z] is like the working of his mighty strength,[a] [20]which he exerted in Christ when he raised him from the dead[b] and seated him at his right hand in the heavenly realms, [21]far above all rule and authority, power and dominion, and every title[c] that can be given, not only in the present age but also in the one to come. [22]And God placed all things under his feet[d] and appointed him to be head[e] over everything for the church, [23]which is his body, the fullness of him who fills everything in every way.

Made Alive in Christ

2 As for you, you were dead in your transgressions and sins,[f] [2]in which you used to live[g] when you followed the ways of this world and of the ruler of the kingdom of the air,[h] the spirit who is now at work in those who are disobedient.[i] [3]All of us also lived

1:1 [a]1Co 1:1 [b]2Co 1:1 [c]Col 1:2
1:2 [d]Ro 1:7
1:3 [e]2Co 1:3 [f]Eph 2:6; 3:10; 6:12
1:4 [g]Eph 5:27; Col 1:22 [h]Eph 4:2,15,16
1:5 [i]Ro 8:29,30 [j]1Co 1:21
1:6 [k]Mt 3:17
1:7 [l]Ro 3:24
1:9 [m]Ro 16:25
1:10 [n]Gal 4:4 [o]Col 1:20
1:11 [p]Eph 3:11; Heb 6:17
1:12 [q]ver 6,14
1:13 [r]Col 1:5 [s]Eph 4:30
1:14 [t]Ac 20:32
1:15 [u]Col 1:4
1:16 [v]Ro 1:8
1:17 [w]Jn 20:17 [x]Col 1:9
1:18 [y]Ac 26:18; 2Co 4:6
1:19 [z]Col 1:29 [a]Eph 6:10
1:20 [b]Ac 2:24
1:21 [c]Php 2:9,10
1:22 [d]Mt 28:18 [e]Eph 4:15; 5:23
2:1 [f]ver 5; Col 2:13
2:2 [g]Col 3:7 [h]Jn 12:31; Eph 6:12 [i]Eph 5:6

a *1* Some early manuscripts do not have *in Ephesus.* **b** *1* Or *believers who are* **c** *4,5* Or *sight in love. 5He* **d** *8,9* Or *us. With all wisdom and understanding, 9he* **e** *11* Or *were made heirs* **f** *17* Or *a spirit*

1:15–23 **PE**

HIGHER POWER

When Paul prayed for the Ephesians, he didn't ask God to give them anything new. Instead, he prayed they would comprehend the power they already had through Jesus Christ. Specifically, he asked that God would help them understand that they have available to them the same "incomparably great" power God exercised when he raised Jesus from the dead (vv. 19–20).

While men have found ways to split the atom and land on the moon, they haven't—and won't—overcome death. Yet God can and did. And every follower of Jesus can depend on the same power God used to raise Jesus. The next time you're faced with a problem that seems too big for you to handle, don't pray for more power. Instead, ask God to help you use the power you already have in Jesus Christ.

among them at one time, gratifying the cravings of our sinful nature[a][j] and following its desires and thoughts. Like the rest, we were by nature objects of wrath. **4**But because of his great love for us, God, who is rich in mercy, **5**made us alive with Christ even when we were dead in transgressions[k]—it is by grace you have been saved.[l] **6**And God raised us up with Christ and seated us with him[m] in the heavenly realms[n] in Christ Jesus, **7**in order that in the coming ages he might show the incomparable riches of his grace, expressed in his kindness[o] to us in Christ Jesus. **8**For it is by grace you

7 →PG. 1299

have been saved,[p] through faith—and this not from yourselves, it is the gift of God— **9**not by works,[q] so that no one can boast.[r] **10**For we are God's workmanship, created[s] in Christ Jesus to do good works,[t] which God prepared in advance for us to do.

One in Christ

6 →PG. 1298

11Therefore, remember that formerly you who are Gentiles by birth and called "uncircumcised" by those who call themselves "the circumcision" (that done in the body by the hands of men)[u]— **12**remember that at that time you were separate from Christ, excluded from citizenship in Israel and foreigners to the covenants of the promise,[v] without hope[w] and without God in the world. **13**But now in Christ Jesus you who once were far away have been brought near[x] through the blood of Christ.[y]

14For he himself is our peace, who has made the two one[z] and has destroyed the barrier, the dividing wall of hostility, **15**by abolishing in his flesh[a] the law with its commandments and regulations.[b] His purpose was to create in himself one[c] new man out of the two, thus making peace, **16**and in this one body to reconcile both of them to God through the cross,[d] by which he put to death their hostility. **17**He came and preached peace to you who were far away and peace to those who were near.[e] **18**For through him we both have access[f] to the Father[g] by one Spirit.[h]

19Consequently, you are no longer foreigners and aliens,[i] but fellow citi-

[a] 3 Or *our flesh*

2:3 [j]Gal 5:16 **2:5** [k]ver 1 [l]ver 8; Ac 15:11 **2:6** [m]Eph 1:20 [n]Eph 1:3 **2:7** [o]Tit 3:4 **2:8** [p]ver 5 **2:9** [q]2Ti 1:9 [r]1Co 1:29 **2:10** [s]Eph 4:24 [t]Tit 2:14 **2:11** [u]Col 2:11 **2:12** [v]Gal 3:17 [w]1Th 4:13 **2:13** [x]ver 17; Ac 2:39 [y]Col 1:20 **2:14** [z]1Co 12:13 **2:15** [a]Col 1:21,22 [b]Col 2:14 [c]Gal 3:28 **2:16** [d]Col 1:20,22 **2:17** [e]Ps 148:14; Isa 57:19 **2:18** [f]Eph 3:12 [g]Col 1:12 [h]1Co 12:13 **2:19** [i]ver 12

2:8–10

PE

DESTINATION: HEAVEN

A number of years ago researchers in Dallas, Texas, found that a majority of people believed in heaven and thought they would go there after death. When asked what they thought a person had to do to go to heaven, those surveyed gave a wide range of answers. Some said a person only had to believe in God. Others indicated that some sort of religious activity was necessary. The survey revealed that while most people believe in and want to go to heaven, they don't agree about how to get there.

Paul gives us the map in this passage. The experience of salvation and heaven involves two things: grace and faith. "Grace" means that God has done for us what we desperately need, don't deserve and couldn't do for ourselves. Grace prompted Jesus to die for rebels like us. "Faith" involves trusting God to forgive our sins and give us the hope of eternal life in heaven. Grace and faith constitute the complete opposite of hopelessly trying to earn salvation through good works.

When Jesus came to earth, died and rose from the dead, he took what you deserve so you could get what you don't deserve. And you can receive it now by telling God you want to trust Jesus alone for forgiveness and eternal life in heaven. If you have taken that step of faith, read over Romans 8 for a few words of encouragement.

2:14

PROMISE 6

NO BARRIERS

Paul was committed to declaring the message of reconciliation between Jews and Gentiles. He often wrote and spoke about tearing down the barriers that separated Jews and other races. The "wall of hostility" that Paul mentions here is a reference to the ultimate symbol of Jewish / Gentile separation—a barrier that had been erected in the temple courts to separate Jewish and Gentile worshipers.

In his death and resurrection, Jesus Christ destroyed all such walls. But today, as in Paul's time, Christians have often refused to live in the unity he has won for us. Jesus has freely given us reconciliation between God and our fellow believers, but we fail to appropriate the unity that should emerge from that gift. Tragically, we have chosen to highlight differences between ourselves and others. But Christ's power still shatters these flimsy constructions, be they physical, psychological, stereotypical or spiritual. Knowing this, our job is to not only point people to Christ, but, like Paul, to remind believers that in Christ there are no barriers.

That message begins with each individual. What can you do today to begin to live in the unity that Jesus Christ has won?

For the next Promise 6 reading go to page 1315.

zens[j] with God's people and members of God's household,[k] 20built on
the foundation[l] of the apostles and
prophets, with Christ Jesus himself as
the chief cornerstone.[m] 21In him the
whole building is joined together and
rises to become a holy temple[n] in the
Lord. 22And in him you too are being
built together to become a dwelling in
which God lives by his Spirit.

Paul the Preacher to the Gentiles

3 For this reason I, Paul, the prisoner[o] of Christ Jesus for the sake of
you Gentiles—
2Surely you have heard about the
administration of God's grace that was
given to me[p] for you, 3that is, the mystery[q] made known to me by revelation,[r] as I have already written briefly.
4In reading this, then, you will be able
to understand my insight[s] into the
mystery of Christ, 5which was not
made known to men in other generations as it has now been revealed
by the Spirit to God's holy apostles
and prophets.[t] 6This mystery is that
through the gospel the Gentiles are
heirs[u] together with Israel, members
together of one body,[v] and sharers together in the promise in Christ Jesus.
7I became a servant of this gospel[w]
by the gift of God's grace given me
through the working of his power.[x]
8Although I am less than the least of all
God's people,[y] this grace was given
me: to preach to the Gentiles the unsearchable riches of Christ, 9and to
make plain to everyone the administration of this mystery,[z] which for
ages past was kept hidden in God, who
created all things. 10His intent was that
now, through the church, the manifold
wisdom of God[a] should be made
known[b] to the rulers and authorities[c] in the heavenly realms, 11accord-
ing to his eternal purpose which he accomplished in Christ Jesus our Lord.
12In him and through faith in him we
may approach God[d] with freedom
and confidence.[e] 13I ask you, therefore, not to be discouraged because of
my sufferings for you, which are your
glory.

A Prayer for the Ephesians

1 →PG. 1301

14For this reason I kneel[f] before the
Father, 15from whom his whole family[a] in heaven and on earth derives its
name. 16I pray that out of his glorious
riches he may strengthen you with
power[g] through his Spirit in your inner being,[h] 17so that Christ may dwell
in your hearts[i] through faith. And I
pray that you, being rooted[j] and established in love, 18may have power,
together with all the saints, to grasp
how wide and long and high and
deep[k] is the love of Christ, 19and to
know this love that surpasses knowledge—that you may be filled[l] to
the measure of all the fullness of
God.[m]
20Now to him who is able[n] to do
immeasurably more than all we ask or
imagine, according to his power that is
at work within us, 21to him be glory
in the church and in Christ Jesus
throughout all generations, for ever
and ever! Amen.[o]

Unity in the Body of Christ

6 →PG. 1299

4 As a prisoner[p] for the Lord, then, I
urge you to live a life worthy[q] of the
calling you have received. 2Be completely humble and gentle; be patient,
bearing with one another[r] in love.[s]
3Make every effort to keep the unity[t]
of the Spirit through the bond of peace.
4There is one body and one Spirit[u]—
just as you were called to one hope
when you were called— 5one Lord, one
faith, one baptism; 6one God and Father of all, who is over all and through
all and in all.[v]
7But to each one of us[w] grace has
been given[x] as Christ apportioned it.
8This is why it[b] says:

"When he ascended on high,
he led captives[y] in his train
and gave gifts to men."[c][z]

9(What does "he ascended" mean except that he also descended to the lower, earthly regions[d]? 10He who descended is the very one who ascended
higher than all the heavens, in order to
fill the whole universe.) 11It was he who
gave some to be apostles,[a] some to be
prophets, some to be evangelists,[b]
and some to be pastors and teachers,
12to prepare God's people for works of
service, so that the body of Christ[c]
may be built up 13until we all reach
unity[d] in the faith and in the knowledge of the Son of God and become
mature,[e] attaining to the whole measure of the fullness of Christ.

5 →PG. 1299

14Then we will no longer be infants,[f] tossed back and forth by the
waves,[g] and blown here and there by
every wind of teaching and by the cunning and craftiness of men in their deceitful scheming.[h] 15Instead, speaking
the truth in love, we will in all things
grow up into him who is the Head,[i]
that is, Christ. 16From him the whole
body, joined and held together by ev-

3 →PG. 1299

2:19 [j]Php 3:20 [k]Gal 6:10 **2:20** [l]Mt 16:18; Rev 21:14 [m]1Pe 2:4-8 **2:21** [n]1Co 3:16,17 **3:1** [o]Ac 23:18; Eph 4:1 **3:2** [p]Col 1:25 **3:3** [q]Ro 16:25 [r]1Co 2:10 **3:4** [s]2Co 11:6 **3:5** [t]Ro 16:26 **3:6** [u]Gal 3:29 [v]Eph 2:15,16 **3:7** [w]1Co 3:5 [x]Eph 1:19 **3:8** [y]1Co 15:9 **3:9** [z]Ro 16:25 **3:10** [a]1Co 2:7 [b]1Pe 1:12 [c]Eph 1:21 **3:12** [d]Eph 2:18 [e]Heb 4:16 **3:14** [f]Php 2:10 **3:16** [g]Col 1:11 [h]Ro 7:22 **3:17** [i]Jn 14:23 [j]Col 1:23

3:18 [k]Job 11:8,9 **3:19** [l]Col 2:10 [m]Eph 1:23 **3:20** [n]Ro 16:25 **3:21** [o]Ro 11:36 **4:1** [p]Eph 3:1 [q]Php 1:27; Col 1:10 **4:2** [r]Col 3:12,13 [s]Eph 1:4 **4:3** [t]Col 3:14 **4:4** [u]1Co 12:13 **4:6** [v]Ro 11:36 **4:7** [w]1Co 12:7,11 [x]Ro 12:3 **4:8** [y]Col 2:15 [z]Ps 68:18 **4:11** [a]1Co 12:28 [b]Ac 21:8 **4:12** [c]1Co 12:27 **4:13** [d]ver 3,5 [e]Col 1:28 **4:14** [f]1Co 14:20 [g]Jas 1:6 [h]Eph 6:11 **4:15** [i]Eph 1:22

[a] *15* Or *whom all fatherhood* [b] *8* Or *God*
[c] *8* Psalm 68:18 [d] *9* Or *the depths of the earth*

ery supporting ligament, grows[j] and builds itself up in love, as each part does its work.

Living as Children of Light

17So I tell you this, and insist on it in the Lord, that you must no longer live as the Gentiles do, in the futility of their thinking.[k] **18**They are darkened in their understanding[l] and separated from the life of God[m] because of the ignorance that is in them due to the hardening of their hearts.[n] **19**Having lost all sensitivity,[o] they have given themselves over[p] to sensuality[q] so as to indulge in every kind of impurity, with a continual lust for more.

20You, however, did not come to know Christ that way. **21**Surely you heard of him and were taught in him in accordance with the truth that is in

3 →PG. 1299

Jesus. **22**You were taught, with regard to your former way of life, to put off[r] your old self,[s] which is being corrupted by its deceitful desires; **23**to be made new in the attitude of your minds;[t] **24**and to put on the new self,[u] created to be like God in true righteousness and holiness.[v]

5 →PG. 1299

25Therefore each of you must put off falsehood and speak truthfully[w] to his neighbor, for we are all members of one body.[x] **26**"In your anger do not sin"[a]: Do not let the sun go down while you are still angry, **27**and do not give the devil a foothold. **28**He who has been stealing must steal no longer, but must work,[y] doing something useful with his own hands,[z] that he may have something to share with those in need.[a]

29Do not let any unwholesome talk come out of your mouths,[b] but only what is helpful for building others up according to their needs, that it may benefit those who listen. **30**And do not grieve the Holy Spirit of God,[c] with whom you were sealed for the day of

6 →PG. 1305

redemption.[d] **31**Get rid of all bitterness, rage and anger, brawling and slander, along with every form of malice.[e] **32**Be kind and compassionate to one another, forgiving each other, just as in Christ God forgave you.[f]

7 →PG. 1306

5 Be imitators of God,[g] therefore, as dearly loved children **2**and live a life of love, just as Christ loved us and gave himself up for us[h] as a fragrant offering and sacrifice to God.[i]

3 →PG. 1300

3But among you there must not be even a hint of sexual immorality, or of any kind of impurity, or of greed,[j] because these are improper for God's holy people. **4**Nor should there be obscenity, foolish talk or coarse joking,

4:16 [j]Col 2:19
4:17 [k]Ro 1:21
4:18 [l]Ro 1:21 [m]Eph 2:12 [n]2Co 3:14
4:19 [o]1Ti 4:2 [p]Ro 1:24 [q]Col 3:5
4:22 [r]1Pe 2:1 [s]Ro 6:6
4:23 [t]Col 3:10
4:24 [u]Ro 6:4 [v]Eph 2:10
4:25 [w]Zec 8:16 [x]Ro 12:5
4:28 [y]Ac 20:35 [z]1Th 4:11 [a]Lk 3:11
4:29 [b]Col 3:8
4:30 [c]1Th 5:19 [d]Ro 8:23
4:31 [e]Col 3:8
4:32 [f]Mt 6:14,15
5:1 [g]Lk 6:36
5:2 [h]Gal 1:4 [i]2Co 2:15; Heb 7:27
5:3 [j]Col 3:5
5:4 [k]ver 20
5:5 [l]Col 3:5 [m]1Co 6:9
5:6 [n]Ro 1:18
5:8 [o]Eph 2:2 [p]Lk 16:8
5:9 [q]Gal 5:22
5:13 [r]Jn 3:20,21
5:14 [s]Ro 13:11 [t]Jn 5:25 [u]Isa 60:1
5:16 [v]Col 4:5 [w]Eph 6:13
5:17 [x]Ro 12:2; 1Th 4:3
5:18 [y]Pr 20:1 [z]Lk 1:15
5:19 [a]Ac 16:25; Col 3:16
5:20 [b]Ps 34:1
5:21 [c]Gal 5:13
5:22 [d]Ge 3:16; 1Pe 3:1,5,6 [e]Eph 6:5
5:23 [f]1Co 11:3; Eph 1:22
5:25 [g]Col 3:19 [h]ver 2
5:26 [i]Ac 22:16

which are out of place, but rather thanksgiving.[k] **5**For of this you can be sure: No immoral, impure or greedy person—such a man is an idolater[l]—has any inheritance in the kingdom of Christ and of God.[b][m] **6**Let no one deceive you with empty words, for because of such things God's wrath[n] comes on those who are disobedient. **7**Therefore do not be partners with them.

8For you were once[o] darkness, but now you are light in the Lord. Live as children of light[p] **9**(for the fruit[q] of the light consists in all goodness, righteousness and truth) **10**and find out what pleases the Lord. **11**Have nothing to do with the fruitless deeds of darkness, but rather expose them. **12**For it is shameful even to mention what the disobedient do in secret. **13**But everything exposed by the light[r] becomes visible, **14**for it is light that makes everything visible. This is why it is said:

"Wake up, O sleeper,[s]
  rise from the dead,[t]
and Christ will shine on you."[u]

15Be very careful, then, how you live—not as unwise but as wise, **16**making the most of every opportunity,[v] because the days are evil.[w] **17**Therefore do not be foolish, but understand what the Lord's will is.[x] **18**Do not get drunk on wine,[y] which leads to debauchery. Instead, be filled with the Spirit.[z] **19**Speak to one another with psalms, hymns and spiritual songs.[a]

5 →PG. 1301

Sing and make music in your heart to the Lord, **20**always giving thanks[b] to God the Father for everything, in the name of our Lord Jesus Christ.

4 →PG. 1300

21Submit to one another[c] out of reverence for Christ.

Wives and Husbands

22Wives, submit to your husbands[d] as to the Lord.[e] **23**For the husband is the head of the wife as Christ is the head of the church,[f] his body, of which he is the Savior. **24**Now as the church submits to Christ, so also wives should submit to their husbands in everything.

25Husbands, love your wives,[g] just as Christ loved the church and gave himself up for her[h] **26**to make her holy, cleansing[c] her by the washing[i] with water through the word, **27**and to present her to himself as a radiant church, without stain or wrinkle or any other blemish, but holy and blame-

[a] *26* Psalm 4:4 [b] *5* Or *kingdom of the Christ and God* [c] *26* Or *having cleansed*

less.[j] 28In this same way, husbands
ought to love their wives[k] as their own
bodies. He who loves his wife loves
himself. 29After all, no one ever hated
his own body, but he feeds and cares
for it, just as Christ does the church—
30for we are members of his body.[l]
31"For this reason a man will leave
his father and mother and be united
to his wife, and the two will become
one flesh."[a][m] 32This is a profound
mystery—but I am talking about Christ
and the church. 33However, each one
of you also must love his wife[n] as he
loves himself, and the wife must respect her husband.

Children and Parents

4 →PG. 1306

6 Children, obey your parents in the
Lord, for this is right.[o] 2"Honor
your father and mother"—which is the
first commandment with a promise—
3"that it may go well with you and
that you may enjoy long life on the
earth."[b][p]
4Fathers, do not exasperate your
children;[q] instead, bring them up in
the training and instruction of the
Lord.[r]

Slaves and Masters

3 →PG. 1305

5Slaves, obey your earthly masters
with respect[s] and fear, and with sincerity of heart,[t] just as you would
obey Christ.[u] 6Obey them not only to
win their favor when their eye is on
you, but like slaves of Christ, doing the
will of God from your heart. 7Serve
wholeheartedly, as if you were serving
the Lord, not men,[v] 8because you
know that the Lord will reward everyone for whatever good he does,[w]
whether he is slave or free.
9And masters, treat your slaves in
the same way. Do not threaten them,
since you know that he who is both
their Master and yours[x] is in heav-
en, and there is no favoritism with
him.

The Armor of God

10Finally, be strong in the Lord[y]
and in his mighty power.[z] 11Put on

5:27 [j]Eph 1:4; Col 1:22
5:28 [k]ver 25
5:30 [l]1Co 12:27
5:31 [m]Ge 2:24; Mt 19:5; 1Co 6:16
5:33 [n]ver 25
6:1 [o]Col 3:20
6:3 [p]Ex 20:12
6:4 [q]Col 3:21 [r]Ge 18:19; Dt 6:7
6:5 [s]1Ti 6:1 [t]Col 3:22 [u]Eph 5:22
6:7 [v]Col 3:23
6:8 [w]Col 3:24
6:9 [x]Job 31:13,14
6:10 [y]1Co 16:13 [z]Eph 1:19

a *31* Gen. 2:24 b *3* Deut. 5:16

6:1–4

PROMISE 4

A GODLY FATHER

Paul's command to fathers is pointed. He tells dads not to "exasperate" their children, which means surrendering any right they may feel they have to act unreasonably toward their children. Instead, fathers are to train their children, as a coach trains an athlete, in the ways of the Lord.

A godly father always treats his children in a manner that befits their standing as children of God. A child who can see Christ working through his or her father will be more likely to cultivate a personal relationship with Christ.

If you're a dad, do you do things that needlessly frustrate your children? Do you balance correction with affirmation and discipline with play? Do you let Christ's love show through you to your children?

For the next Promise 4 reading go to page 5.

5:21–33

PROMISE 4

MARRIAGE 101

While getting married takes only a few minutes, being a good husband takes a lifetime. God places a premium on a husband's role, and Paul emphasized that fact by giving the Ephesian men a short course in being better husbands.

Unfortunately, some men and women who read Ephesians 5:22–33 get sidetracked on Paul's instructions concerning wives' responsibility to submit to their husbands. Such people make the critical mistake of overlooking verse 21: "Submit to one another out of reverence for Christ." Marriage requires mutual submission, an attitude that doesn't always come naturally.

It's in that context that Paul tells husbands they're to provide their wives with leadership. Not a heavy-handed, domineering, "I'm the boss!" kind of leadership. But the kind of leadership Christ exercises over the church—*servant leadership* (see also Philippians 2:3–11). This powerful image shows the degree of commitment that God requires of husbands. As Christ gave his life for the church, so husbands are to give their lives for their wives and are to always put their wives' needs before their own. In the context of such leadership, following becomes a delight.

Godly leadership begins with a servant's heart. That servant attitude runs the gamut from the daily issues of basic housework and child care, to major issues such as seeking her opinion first when new career opportunities arise. Take a minute to reread this passage and think of some specific, concrete ways you can be a servant to your wife. Determine that, by the grace of God, your love for her will emulate Christ's complete and sacrificial love for the church.

For the next Promise 4 reading go to page 1300.

the full armor of God[a] so that you can
take your stand against the devil's
schemes. **12**For our struggle is not
against flesh and blood, but against
the rulers, against the authorities,[b]
against the powers[c] of this dark world
and against the spiritual forces of evil
in the heavenly realms.[d] **13**Therefore
put on the full armor of God, so that
when the day of evil comes, you may
be able to stand your ground, and after
you have done everything, to stand.
14Stand firm then, with the belt of truth
buckled around your waist,[e] with the
breastplate of righteousness in place,[f]
15and with your feet fitted with the
readiness that comes from the gospel
of peace.[g] **16**In addition to all this, take
up the shield of faith,[h] with which you
can extinguish all the flaming arrows
of the evil one. **17**Take the helmet of salvation[i] and the sword of the Spirit,
which is the word of God.[j] **18**And pray
in the Spirit on all occasions[k] with all
kinds of prayers and requests.[l] With
this in mind, be alert and always keep
on praying for all the saints.

1 →PG. 1305
5 →PG. 1305

19Pray also for me,[m] that whenever I open my mouth, words may be
given me so that I will fearlessly[n]
make known the mystery of the gospel,
20for which I am an ambassador[o]
in chains.[p] Pray that I may declare it
fearlessly, as I should.

Final Greetings

21Tychicus,[q] the dear brother and
faithful servant in the Lord, will tell
you everything, so that you also may
know how I am and what I am doing.
22I am sending him to you for this very
purpose, that you may know how
we are,[r] and that he may encourage
you.

23Peace[s] to the brothers, and love
with faith from God the Father and the
Lord Jesus Christ. **24**Grace to all who
love our Lord Jesus Christ with an undying love.

6:11 [a]Ro 13:12
6:12 [b]Eph 1:21 [c]Ro 8:38 [d]Eph 1:3
6:14 [e]Isa 11:5 [f]Isa 59:17
6:15 [g]Isa 52:7
6:16 [h]1Jn 5:4
6:17 [i]Isa 59:17 [j]Heb 4:12
6:18 [k]Lk 18:1 [l]Mt 26:41; Php 1:4
6:19 [m]1Th 5:25 [n]Ac 4:29; 2Co 3:12
6:20 [o]2Co 5:20 [p]Ac 21:33
6:21 [q]Ac 20:4
6:22 [r]Col 4:7-9
6:23 [s]Gal 6:16; 1Pe 5:14

6:10–18

PROMISE 1

PREPARING FOR BATTLE

Paul uses vivid military imagery in this passage to encourage his readers in their daily Christian walk. Reading through this passage, one can almost envision a warrior putting on his armor piece by piece. But don't miss the main point of this passage: The focus must be on personal preparation, not on the enemy.

How does the godly man prepare to live each day as a follower of Jesus Christ? By paying careful attention to keeping his sword sharp (v. 17) and by praying "on all occasions with all kinds of prayers and requests" (v. 18). God's Word and prayer are the Christian's two greatest weapons against evil. Against these, the enemy's "flaming arrows"—temptation, lust, greed, rebellion and the like—are completely useless.

For the next Promise 1 reading go to page 1307.

PHILIPPIANS

AT A GLANCE

Key Principle: Because we are in Christ and our lives are bound up in his, we can have joy and contentment even in the midst of difficult circumstances.
Author: Paul
Time and Place: A.D. 62 / Sent from Rome to Philippi
Key Verses: 1:21; 2:2, 5–11; 3:10, 20; 4:4–8, 12

BENEFIT

Philippians is an epistle of joy and encouragement that inspires its readers to focus their thoughts and actions on pursuing Jesus Christ. When our joy is threatened by adverse circumstances (1), disunity (2), the quest for accomplishments (3), or anxiety (4), this letter is a powerful tool that can help us get our eyes back on Jesus. Only by pursuing him first will we discover the peace and contentment that comes from God.

SETTING

Philippi, named after King Philip of Macedonia, the father of Alexander the Great, became a Roman colony and a military outpost under Octavian (later Augustus Caesar). Following his Macedonian call in Troas during his second missionary journey (Acts 16:8–10), Paul went with Silas, Timothy and Luke to Philippi in A.D. 51. After Lydia and others believed the gospel message, Paul and Silas were beaten and imprisoned. This led to the conversion of the Philippian jailer and his household (Acts 16:11–40).

Paul revisited the Philippians during his third missionary journey (Acts 20:1, 6), and when they heard of his Roman imprisonment, they sent Epaphroditus with a gift of money (4:16–18; they had helped him this way before). Epaphroditus took ill, and Paul sent him back to Philippi with this letter after he recovered (2:25–30). The apostle wrote this letter in A.D. 62 near the end of his first Roman imprisonment while he was awaiting the verdict of his trial before the Imperial Court (2:20–26).

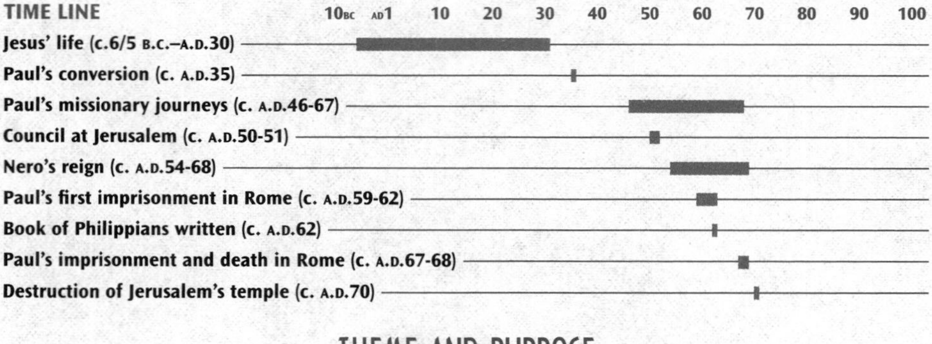

THEME AND PURPOSE

Paul wrote this letter to thank the Philippians for their gift, to convey his warm affection for them and to encourage them to "stand firm in one spirit, contending as one man for the faith of the gospel" (1:27). He argues that joy springs out of unity and that unity springs out of humility; the ultimate example of humility is Jesus' obedience to his Father's will (2:5–11).

Apart from the appeal to deal with disunity in 4:2–3 and a warning about the problem of legalistic influences in 3:3–9, Paul does not seek to correct existing problems. Rather, he encourages the Philippians in their spiritual growth and in their love and service toward one another. He also updates them on his own situation and prospects (1:12–26) and prepares them for Timothy's arrival (2:19–24).

UNIQUE CONTRIBUTION

The tone and content of this very affectionate letter ("I have you in my heart," "my brothers," "my dear friends," "my brothers, you whom I love and long for, my joy and crown") show us that the church at Philippi may have been Paul's favorite. These people were apparently not plagued by the problems of disorder, doctrinal error and lack of discipline that characterized many other churches, and they were the most faithful church in supporting Paul's ministry (4:14–18). Philippians is an informal letter; it does not follow an outline, but quickly moves through a variety of topics. The words "joy" and "rejoice" capture the spirit of this epistle. Paul had learned the secret of being content in any and every situation (4:12), and his single-minded pursuit of personal knowledge of Christ (3:10) and understanding that to live is Christ and to die is gain (1:21) are at the core of his being.

CHRIST IN PHILIPPIANS

While Philippians contains little doctrinal teaching, Paul uses the example of Christ's self-emptying (2:5–11) as a model of other-centered humility. This is one of the most significant passages on the person and work of Christ in the Bible. This is known as the *kenosis* passage; this Greek word speaks of the emptying involved in the incarnation. Christ did not empty himself of his deity, but stripped himself of the full manifestation of his divine rights and attributes during his earthly life. Christ is also seen as the believer's life and identity (1:21), the believer's model (2:5–8), the believer's righteousness (3:7–9), the believer's highest aspiration (3:10), the one who will transform the believer's body at the resurrection (3:20–21) and the believer's source of strength and provision (4:13, 19).

OVERVIEW

FOCUS	Personal Affairs	Practical Appeals	Promised Attainment	Proper Attitudes
REFERENCE	1	2	3	4
TOPICS	Experience	Examples	Exposition	Exhortation
	Circumstances	Call to Unity and Humility	Challenge to Legalism	Counsel and Contentment
	Situation and Suffering	Submission and Service	Safeguard and Salvation	Sanctification and Sharing
	Partakers of Christ	People of Christ	Pursuit of Christ	Power of Christ
LOCATION	Sent from Rome to Philippi			
TIME	A.D. 62			

Paul begins this epistle with a word of thanks for the Philippians and a prayer for their spiritual growth in love and discernment (1:1–11). He then tells them about his imprisonment, the progress of the gospel and his openness to either outcome (life or death) in his trial (1:12–26). After encouraging the church to fight for the gospel in the face of persecution (1:27–30), Paul exhorts them to maintain a spirit of love and unity by having the attitude of Christ, who served others through his incarnation and death (2:1–11). He calls them to cultivate this attitude (2:12–18) and illustrates it through the sacrificial service of Timothy and Epaphroditus (2:19–30).

Turning to the problem of legalistic influences, Paul uses his own life as an example of the futility of attempting to earn righteousness through keeping the law (3:1–9). Having found the true righteousness that comes through faith in Christ, he presses on toward the goal of fulfilling Christ's calling (3:10–16). He warns about those who set their mind on earthly things, and contrasts this with his passion for heavenly things (3:17–21). In the last chapter, Paul exhorts the Philippians to maintain unity, to enjoy God's peace by offering all anxieties to God in prayer and to be content in their circumstances (4:1–13). After thanking them for supporting his ministry, he closes with greetings and a benediction (4:14–23).

PHILIPPIANS

1 Paul and Timothy,[a] servants of
Christ Jesus,

To all the saints[b] in Christ Jesus
at Philippi,[c] together with the overseers[a][d] and deacons:[e]

2Grace and peace to you from God
our Father and the Lord Jesus Christ.[f]

Thanksgiving and Prayer

3I thank my God every time I re-
1 →PG. 1306 member you.[g] 4In all my prayers for
all of you, I always pray[h] with joy 5be-
cause of your partnership[i] in the gospel from the first day[j] until now, 6be-
ing confident of this, that he who
began a good work in you will carry it
on to completion until the day of Christ
Jesus.[k]

7It is right[l] for me to feel this way
about all of you, since I have you in my
heart;[m] for whether I am in chains[n] or
defending[o] and confirming the gospel, all of you share in God's grace with
me. 8God can testify[p] how I long for
all of you with the affection of Christ
Jesus.

3 →PG. 1307 9And this is my prayer: that your
love[q] may abound more and more in
knowledge and depth of insight, 10so
that you may be able to discern what is
best and may be pure and blameless
until the day of Christ,[r] 11filled with
the fruit of righteousness[s] that comes
through Jesus Christ—to the glory and
praise of God.

Paul's Chains Advance the Gospel

12Now I want you to know, brothers,
that what has happened to me has
really served to advance the gospel.
13As a result, it has become clear
throughout the whole palace guard[b]
and to everyone else that I am in
chains[t] for Christ. 14Because of my
chains,[u] most of the brothers in the
Lord have been encouraged to speak
the word of God more courageously
and fearlessly.

15It is true that some preach Christ
out of envy and rivalry, but others out
of goodwill. 16The latter do so in love,
knowing that I am put here for the defense of the gospel.[v] 17The former
preach Christ out of selfish ambition,[w]
not sincerely, supposing that they can
stir up trouble for me while I am in
5 →PG. 1307 chains.[c][x] 18But what does it matter?
The important thing is that in every
way, whether from false motives or
true, Christ is preached. And because
of this I rejoice.

Yes, and I will continue to rejoice,
19for I know that through your
prayers[y] and the help given by the
Spirit of Jesus Christ,[z] what has happened to me will turn out for my deliverance.[d] 20I eagerly expect[a] and hope
that I will in no way be ashamed, but
will have sufficient courage[b] so that
now as always Christ will be exalted
in my body,[c] whether by life or by
death.[d] 21For to me, to live is Christ[e]
and to die is gain. 22If I am to go on
living in the body, this will mean fruitful labor for me. Yet what shall I
choose? I do not know! 23I am torn between the two: I desire to depart[f] and
be with Christ,[g] which is better by far;
24but it is more necessary for you that
I remain in the body. 25Convinced of
this, I know that I will remain, and I will
continue with all of you for your progress and joy in the faith, 26so that
through my being with you again your
joy in Christ Jesus will overflow on account of me.

27Whatever happens, conduct your-
selves in a manner worthy[h] of the gos- 6 →PG. 1306
pel of Christ. Then, whether I come

1:1 [a] Ac 16:1; 2Co 1:1 [b] Ac 9:13 [c] Ac 16:12 [d] 1Ti 3:1 [e] 1Ti 3:8 **1:2** [f] Ro 1:7 **1:3** [g] Ro 1:8 **1:4** [h] Ro 1:10 **1:5** [i] Ac 2:42; Php 4:15 [j] Ac 16:12-40 **1:6** [k] ver 10; 1Co 1:8 **1:7** [l] 2Pe 1:13 [m] 2Co 7:3 [n] ver 13,14,17; Ac 21:33 [o] ver 16 **1:8** [p] Ro 1:9 **1:9** [q] 1Th 3:12 **1:10** [r] ver 6; 1Co 1:8 **1:11** [s] Jas 3:18 **1:13** [t] ver 7,14,17 **1:14** [u] ver 7,13,17 **1:16** [v] ver 7,12 **1:17** [w] Php 2:3 [x] ver 7,13,14 **1:19** [y] 2Co 1:11 [z] Ac 16:7 **1:20** [a] Ro 8:19 [b] ver 14 [c] 1Co 6:20 [d] Ro 14:8 **1:21** [e] Gal 2:20 **1:23** [f] 2Ti 4:6 [g] Jn 12:26; 2Co 5:8 **1:27** [h] Eph 4:1

a *1* Traditionally *bishops* **b** *13* Or *whole palace* **c** *16,17* Some late manuscripts have verses 16 and 17 in reverse order. **d** *19* Or *salvation*

1:21-26

PE

IN LIFE AND IN DEATH

When the apostle Paul referred to his death, he spoke of "departing." That word conjures up images of loosening the moorings of a ship and setting sail; of untying the ropes of a tent, pulling up the stakes and moving on. For Paul death was nothing more than a journey from one place to another, far better, place. While he was here on earth Paul would point others to Jesus Christ. After death he would be in the presence of Jesus. Paul's words give us a glimpse of Paul's passion for his Savior and his intense desire that Jesus would perform kingdom work through him.

What an example! Ask God for the grace you need to have that same passion. To help you cultivate it, try a simple exercise. When your alarm goes off in the morning, after you've cleared away the mental cobwebs, utter this prayer: "Lord, help me point others to you today."

and see you or only hear about you in my absence, I will know that you stand firm[i] in one spirit, contending[j] as one man for the faith of the gospel 28without being frightened in any way by those who oppose you. This is a sign to them that they will be destroyed, but that you will be saved—and that by God. 29For it has been granted to you[k] on behalf of Christ not only to believe on him, but also to suffer[l] for him, 30since you are going through the same struggle[m] you saw[n] I had, and now hear[o] that I still have.

Imitating Christ's Humility

4 →PG. 1316
6 →PG. 1308
7 →PG. 1306

2 If you have any encouragement from being united with Christ, if any comfort from his love, if any fellowship with the Spirit,[p] if any tenderness and compassion,[q] 2then make my joy complete[r] by being like-minded,[s] having the same love, being one[t] in spirit and purpose. 3Do nothing out of selfish ambition or vain conceit,[u] but in humility consider others better than yourselves.[v] 4Each of you should look not only to your own interests, but also to the interests of others.

5Your attitude should be the same as that of Christ Jesus:[w]

6Who, being in very nature[a] God,[x]
did not consider equality with
God[y] something to be
grasped,
7but made himself nothing,
taking the very nature[b] of a
servant,[z]
being made in human likeness.[a]
8And being found in appearance as
a man,
he humbled himself
and became obedient to
death[b]—
even death on a cross!
9Therefore God exalted him[c] to the
highest place
and gave him the name that is
above every name,[d]
10that at the name of Jesus every
knee should bow,[e]
in heaven and on earth and
under the earth,[f]
11and every tongue confess that Jesus
Christ is Lord,[g]
to the glory of God the Father.

1 →PG. 1307

Shining as Stars

12Therefore, my dear friends, as you have always obeyed—not only in my presence, but now much more in my absence—continue to work out your salvation with fear and trembling,[h] 13for it is God who works in you[i] to will and to act according to his good purpose.

7 →PG. 1316

14Do everything without complaining[j] or arguing, 15so that you may become blameless and pure, children of God[k] without fault in a crooked and depraved generation,[l] in which you shine like stars in the universe 16as you hold out[c] the word of life—in order that I may boast on the day of Christ that I did not run or labor for nothing.[m] 17But even if I am being poured out like a drink offering[n] on the sacri-

[a]6 Or *in the form of* [b]7 Or *the form*
[c]16 Or *hold on to*

1:27 [i]1Co 16:13 [j]Jude 3 **1:29** [k]Mt 5:11,12 [l]Ac 14:22 **1:30** [m]Col 2:1; 1Th 2:2 [n]Ac 16:19-40 [o]ver 13 **2:1** [p]2Co 13:14 [q]Col 3:12 **2:2** [r]Jn 3:29 [s]Php 4:2 [t]Ro 12:16 **2:3** [u]Gal 5:26 [v]Ro 12:10; 1Pe 5:5 **2:5** [w]Mt 11:29 **2:6** [x]Jn 1:1 [y]Jn 5:18 **2:7** [z]Mt 20:28 [a]Jn 1:14; Heb 2:17 **2:8** [b]Mt 26:39; Jn 10:18; Heb 5:8 **2:9** [c]Ac 2:33; Heb 2:9 [d]Eph 1:20,21 **2:10** [e]Ro 14:11 [f]Mt 28:18 **2:11** [g]Jn 13:13 **2:12** [h]2Co 7:15 **2:13** [i]Ezr 1:5 **2:14** [j]1Co 10:10; 1Pe 4:9 **2:15** [k]Mt 5:45,48; Eph 5:1 [l]Ac 2:40 **2:16** [m]1Th 2:19 **2:17** [n]2Ti 4:6

2:1-11

PROMISE 7

PUTTING OTHERS FIRST

"Neighbor Braves Flames to Save Family"; "Hundreds of Volunteers Protect Homes from Flood"; "Unknown Man Stops Assailant." When ordinary people do extraordinary tasks, we sit up and take notice. These are the kinds of newspaper headlines that inspire us and give us hope.

But beyond the headlines and beyond the sight of most people are other individuals who also inspire hope. Thousands of people make a career out of putting others ahead of themselves by following the call to full-time Christian service occupations. These people follow the example of Jesus Christ himself, who "made himself nothing, taking the very nature of the servant" (v. 7).

In one of the most profound passages in the Bible, Paul describes the journey Jesus made for us. From the glory of heaven to death on a cross and back again to heaven, Jesus made the ultimate sacrifice to save us from our sins. Paul says that even though Jesus was God, he gave up his heavenly status to save a rebellious and sinful human population. As you read this passage again, absorb the wondrous and amazing nature of Jesus' selfless sacrifice.

As followers of Jesus, we're called on to put others' interests before our own. While such sacrifice may be difficult at times, no amount of human difficulty will ever rival the sacrifice Jesus made for us. Following this call could be as simple as giving up a prime parking spot to an elderly couple or as difficult as giving up a lucrative career to follow Jesus' call to a ministry position. However we live out Paul's call to servanthood, we need to continually "consider others better than [our]selves" as part of a life that's devoted to Jesus Christ, who gave us the ultimate example of selflessness and servanthood.

For the next Promise 7 reading go to page 1316.

fice[o] and service coming from your faith, I am glad and rejoice with all of you. **18**So you too should be glad and rejoice with me.

Timothy and Epaphroditus

2 →PG. 1308
5 →PG. 1308

19I hope in the Lord Jesus to send Timothy to you soon,[p] that I also may be cheered when I receive news about you. **20**I have no one else like him,[q] who takes a genuine interest in your welfare. **21**For everyone looks out for his own interests,[r] not those of Jesus Christ. **22**But you know that Timothy has proved himself, because as a son with his father[s] he has served with me in the work of the gospel. **23**I hope, therefore, to send him as soon as I see how things go with me.[t] **24**And I am confident[u] in the Lord that I myself will come soon.

25But I think it is necessary to send back to you Epaphroditus, my brother, fellow worker[v] and fellow soldier,[w] who is also your messenger, whom you sent to take care of my needs.[x] **26**For he longs for all of you[y] and is distressed because you heard he was ill. **27**Indeed he was ill, and almost died. But God had mercy on him, and not on him only but also on me, to spare me sorrow upon sorrow. **28**Therefore I am all the more eager to send him, so that when you see him again you may be glad and I may have less anxiety. **29**Welcome him in the Lord with great joy, and honor men like him,[z] **30**because he almost died for the work of Christ, risking his life to make up for the help you could not give me.[a]

No Confidence in the Flesh

3 Finally, my brothers, rejoice in the Lord! It is no trouble for me to write the same things to you again, and it is a safeguard for you.

2Watch out for those dogs,[b] those men who do evil, those mutilators of the flesh. **3**For it is we who are the circumcision,[c] we who worship by the Spirit of God, who glory in Christ Jesus, and who put no confidence in the flesh— **4**though I myself have reasons for such confidence.

If anyone else thinks he has reasons to put confidence in the flesh, I have more: **5**circumcised[d] on the eighth day, of the people of Israel,[e] of the tribe of Benjamin,[f] a Hebrew of Hebrews; in regard to the law, a Pharisee;[g] **6**as for zeal, persecuting the church;[h] as for legalistic righteousness,[i] faultless.

2:17 [o]Ro 15:16
2:19 [p]ver 23
2:20 [q]1Co 16:10
2:21 [r]1Co 10:24; 13:5
2:22 [s]1Co 4:17; 1Ti 1:2
2:23 [t]ver 19
2:24 [u]Php 1:25
2:25 [v]Php 4:3 [w]Phm 2 [x]Php 4:18
2:26 [y]Php 1:8
2:29 [z]1Co 16:18; 1Ti 5:17
2:30 [a]1Co 16:17
3:2 [b]Ps 22:16,20
3:3 [c]Ro 2:28,29; Gal 6:15; Col 2:11
3:5 [d]Lk 1:59 [e]2Co 11:22 [f]Ro 11:1 [g]Ac 23:6
3:6 [h]Ac 8:3 [i]Ro 10:5
3:7 [j]Mt 13:44; Lk 14:33
3:8 [k]Eph 4:13; 2Pe 1:2
3:9 [l]Ro 10:5 [m]Ro 9:30
3:10 [n]Ro 8:17 [o]Ro 6:3-5
3:11 [p]Rev 20:5,6
3:12 [q]1Co 13:10 [r]1Ti 6:12 [s]Ac 9:5,6
3:13 [t]Lk 9:62
3:14 [u]Heb 6:1 [v]Ro 8:28

1 →PG. 1308
3 →PG. 1308

7But whatever was to my profit I now consider loss[j] for the sake of Christ. **8**What is more, I consider everything a loss compared to the surpassing greatness of knowing[k] Christ Jesus my Lord, for whose sake I have lost all things. I consider them rubbish, that I may gain Christ **9**and be found in him, not having a righteousness of my own that comes from the law,[l] but that which is through faith in Christ—the righteousness that comes from God and is by faith.[m] **10**I want to know Christ and the power of his resurrection and the fellowship of sharing in his sufferings,[n] becoming like him in his death,[o] **11**and so, somehow, to attain to the resurrection[p] from the dead.

Pressing on Toward the Goal

12Not that I have already obtained all this, or have already been made perfect,[q] but I press on to take hold[r] of that for which Christ Jesus took hold of me.[s] **13**Brothers, I do not consider myself yet to have taken hold of it. But one thing I do: Forgetting what is behind[t] and straining toward what is ahead, **14**I press on[u] toward the goal to win the prize for which God has called[v] me heavenward in Christ Jesus.

3:7–14

PROMISE 1

LAVISH LOVE FOR GOD

Focused living. That's what characterized the apostle Paul. Prior to his conversion he had achieved significant status among the Jews. After his conversion he became one of history's greatest evangelists. But he felt all he possessed and all he had achieved was "rubbish" compared with the value of knowing Jesus and becoming more like him. His intense love for his Savior inspired Paul's words in this passage.

How can we cultivate such a lavish love for God? First, by asking God for the desire to make him first in our hearts. Second, by asking God for the strength and stamina to stand strong in the face of our commitment to him, no matter what happens. Third, by devoting time and energy every day to strengthening our love for Jesus Christ.

As with all relationships, our relationship with Jesus is dynamic—constantly growing and changing. It's a process that continues for as long as we run the race of life. As Paul did, we need to devote our lives to Jesus' service and develop an intense love for him out of gratitude for what he's done for us.

For the next Promise 1 reading go to page 1308.

2 →PG. 1316 5 →PG. 1308 6 →PG. 1308

15All of us who are mature[w] should
take such a view of things.[x] And if on
some point you think differently, that
too God will make clear to you. **16**Only
let us live up to what we have already
attained.
17Join with others in following my
example,[y] brothers, and take note of
those who live according to the pattern
we gave you. **18**For, as I have often told
you before and now say again even
with tears,[z] many live as enemies of
the cross of Christ.[a] **19**Their destiny is
destruction, their god is their stomach,[b] and their glory is in their
shame.[c] Their mind is on earthly
things.[d] **20**But our citizenship[e] is in
heaven.[f] And we eagerly await a Savior from there, the Lord Jesus Christ,[g]
21who, by the power[h] that enables
him to bring everything under his control, will transform our lowly bodies[i]
so that they will be like his glorious
body.[j]

4 Therefore, my brothers, you whom
I love and long for,[k] my joy and
crown, that is how you should stand
firm[l] in the Lord, dear friends!

Exhortations

5 →PG. 1308 6 →PG. 1313

2I plead with Euodia and I plead
with Syntyche to agree with each other[m] in the Lord. **3**Yes, and I ask you,
loyal yokefellow,[a] help these women
who have contended at my side in
the cause of the gospel, along with
Clement and the rest of my fellow
workers, whose names are in the book
of life.
4Rejoice in the Lord always. I will say
it again: Rejoice![n] **5**Let your gentleness
be evident to all. The Lord is near.[o]
6Do not be anxious about anything,[p]
but in everything, by prayer and petition, with thanksgiving, present your
requests to God.[q] **7**And the peace of
God,[r] which transcends all understanding, will guard your hearts and
your minds in Christ Jesus.
8Finally, brothers, whatever is true,
whatever is noble, whatever is right,
whatever is pure, whatever is lovely, whatever is admirable—if anything
is excellent or praiseworthy—think
about such things. **9**Whatever you have
learned or received or heard from me,
or seen in me—put it into practice.[s]
And the God of peace[t] will be with
you.

1 →PG. 1313 3 →PG. 1313

Thanks for Their Gifts

5 →PG. 1316

10I rejoice greatly in the Lord that at
last you have renewed your concern
for me.[u] Indeed, you have been concerned, but you had no opportunity to
show it. **11**I am not saying this because
I am in need, for I have learned to be
content[v] whatever the circumstances.
12I know what it is to be in need, and I
know what it is to have plenty. I have
learned the secret of being content
in any and every situation, whether
well fed or hungry,[w] whether living in
plenty or in want.[x] **13**I can do everything through him who gives me
strength.[y]
14Yet it was good of you to share[z] in
my troubles. **15**Moreover, as you Philippians know, in the early days[a] of your
acquaintance with the gospel, when
I set out from Macedonia, not one
church shared with me in the matter
of giving and receiving, except you
only;[b] **16**for even when I was in Thessalonica,[c] you sent me aid again and
again when I was in need.[d] **17**Not that
I am looking for a gift, but I am looking
for what may be credited to your account.[e] **18**I have received full payment
and even more; I am amply supplied,
now that I have received from Epaphroditus[f] the gifts you sent. They are
a fragrant[g] offering, an acceptable sac-

3:15 [w] 1Co 2:6 [x] Gal 5:10 **3:17** [y] 1Co 4:16; 1Pe 5:3 **3:18** [z] Ac 20:31 [a] Gal 6:12 **3:19** [b] Ro 16:18 [c] Ro 6:21 [d] Ro 8:5,6 **3:20** [e] Eph 2:19 [f] Col 3:1 [g] 1Co 1:7 **3:21** [h] Eph 1:19 [i] 1Co 15:43-53 [j] Col 3:4 **4:1** [k] Php 1:8 [l] 1Co 16:13; Php 1:27 **4:2** [m] Php 2:2 **4:4** [n] Ro 12:12; Php 3:1 **4:5** [o] Heb 10:37; Jas 5:8,9 **4:6** [p] Mt 6:25-34 [q] Eph 6:18 **4:7** [r] Isa 26:3; Jn 14:27; Col 3:15 **4:9** [s] Php 3:17 [t] Ro 15:33 **4:10** [u] 2Co 11:9 **4:11** [v] 1Ti 6:6,8 **4:12** [w] 1Co 4:11 [x] 2Co 11:9 **4:13** [y] 2Co 12:9 **4:14** [z] Php 1:7 **4:15** [a] Php 1:5 [b] 2Co 11:8,9 **4:16** [c] Ac 17:1 [d] 1Th 2:9 **4:17** [e] 1Co 9:11,12 **4:18** [f] Php 2:25 [g] 2Co 2:14

[a] 3 Or *loyal Syzygus*

4:4–9

PROMISE 1

DEEP-DOWN JOY

Paul repeatedly uses the word "joy" in this letter. His attitude is nothing short of supernatural in light of the fact that he wrote this letter while sitting in a prison cell. His joyful attitude is contagious as he urges his readers to "rejoice in the Lord always."

Paul knew that there are no detours around hardship in this life. We will all have a share of suffering. But while we can't control whether or not we experience hardship, we can control our response to it. Instead of being overcome by despair when difficulty strikes, we can choose to be joyful. How? First, by presenting our requests in prayer to God and trusting God to handle the answers in his time. Second, by saturating our minds with "whatever is true, whatever is right, whatever is noble . . . " (v. 8). In doing so we focus on how great God is instead of how difficult our circumstances are. Finally, by following the example of Paul and others who have put their faith into practice and experienced joy in spite of hardships. When we do these things, we'll begin to see both trials and joys as gifts from God.

For the next Promise 1 reading go to page 1313.

rifice, pleasing to God. 19And my God
will meet all your needs[h] according to
his glorious riches[i] in Christ Jesus.
20To our God and Father[j] be glory
for ever and ever. Amen.[k]

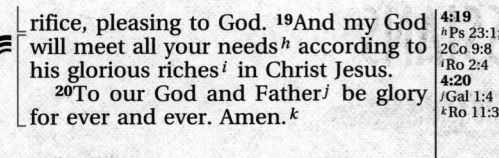

4:19 [h]Ps 23:1; 2Co 9:8 [i]Ro 2:4
4:20 [j]Gal 1:4 [k]Ro 11:36

Final Greetings

21Greet all the saints in Christ Jesus.
The brothers who are with me[l] send
greetings. 22All the saints[m] send you
greetings, especially those who belong
to Caesar's household.
23The grace of the Lord Jesus
Christ[n] be with your spirit. Amen.[a]

4:21 [l]Gal 1:2

[a]23 Some manuscripts do not have *Amen.*

4:22 [m]Ac 9:13 4:23 [n]Ro 16:20

COLOSSIANS

AT A GLANCE

Key Principle: We have been united with Christ in his death, burial and resurrection; this is the basis for our new position and practice as God's holy and beloved children.
Author: Paul
Time and Place: A.D. 60–62 / Sent from Rome to Colosse
Key Verses: 1:28; 2:9–10; 3:1–2, 17

BENEFIT

Colossians may be the most Christ-centered book in Scripture—everything in it lifts the mind and heart to "things above, where Christ is seated at the right hand of God" (3:1). This epistle edifies the mind as it portrays Christ's supremacy and person, and it edifies the heart as it encourages us to pursue him in our conduct and character.

SETTING

During his third missionary journey, Paul ministered in the Asian city of Ephesus for almost three years (A.D. 53–55; Acts 19:10; 20:31). It was probably during this time that Epaphras came to Christ. Epaphras (probably not the Epaphroditus of Philippians 2:25; 4:18) carried the gospel east to the cities of Colosse, Laodicea and Hierpolis in the fertile Lycus Valley (1:4–8; 4:13), and later visited Paul in prison (4:12–13; Philemon 23). Similar names, circumstances and themes between Colossians, Ephesians and Philemon indicate that they were written at the same time (A.D. 60–62) and carried to the Roman province of Asia by Tychicus and the converted slave Onesimus (4:7–9; Ephesians 6:21; Philemon 10–12).

Epaphras' report about the Colossian believers prompted Paul to write this letter to this church, which he had never visited (2:1). The believers in Colosse were predominantly Gentile (1:21, 27; 2:13), and were being influenced by false teaching that denied that faith in Christ alone was sufficient for salvation. The nature of the Colossian heresy can only be reconstructed by the way Paul refuted it in this epistle, but it appears to have been an early form of Gnosticism that combined elements from Greek philosophy (2:4, 8–10), Jewish legalism (2:11–17) and Oriental mysticism (2:18–33). This teaching evidently required circumcision, dietary laws, asceticism, mysticism and the worship of angels as mediators.

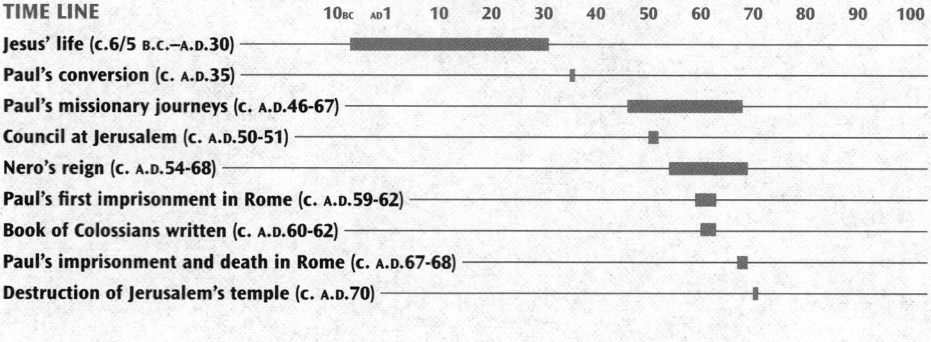

THEME AND PURPOSE

The theme of Colossians is particularly clear: The person and work of Jesus Christ is supreme and sufficient for the believer's salvation and sanctification. Paul knew that the best way to refute error is to focus on a clear presentation of the truth, so he wrote this Christ-centered epistle to combat false teachings that were beginning to take hold in Colosse. He argued that Christ alone holds all the treasures of wisdom and knowledge (2:3); it is unnecessary to turn to other sources to find what he alone can offer.

Paul also wrote this letter to encourage his readers to be established and firm in their faith and to keep their hope fixed on Christ (1:23). As they grew in this hope, their relationships would reflect a quality of holiness that is not based on rules and regulations, but on a growing personal relationship with Jesus Christ (3:1–4:6).

UNIQUE CONTRIBUTION

Colossians contains Paul's most highly developed Christology (doctrine of Christ). Evidently, his two-year imprisonment in Caesarea followed by his Roman imprisonment gave him an opportunity to reflect deeply and prayerfully on the person and work of Christ. The Christology of 1:15–23 compares well with the doctrine of the *logos* (the Word) that is so clearly developed in the prologue to the fourth Gospel (John 1:1–18).

Ephesians and Colossians, written at the same time, are twin epistles that have much in common. Both begin with our position in Christ and end with our practice in him; both deal with similar subjects and stress wisdom, mystery and the true knowledge of Christ. Ephesians focuses on the church as the body of Christ, while Colossians focuses on Christ as the head of the body.

CHRIST IN COLOSSIANS

Christ is the image of the invisible God by whom and for whom all things were created (1:15–16). In him all the fullness of the Deity lives in bodily form (1:15, 19; 2:9), and he sustains the entire cosmos (1:16–17). Paul redefines the terms used by the Colossian heretics by arguing that only in Christ can one discover the true *gnosis* (knowledge) and *pleroma* (fullness); in him are "all the treasures of wisdom and knowledge" (2:3). Jesus Christ is the source of redemption and reconciliation to God (1:14, 20–22; 2:11–15); he is the all-sufficient Savior of those who know him (1:28; 2:10; 3:1–4). Finally Paul writes that Christ is "the head of the body, the church; he is the beginning and the firstborn from among the dead, so that in everything he might have the supremacy" (1:18).

OVERVIEW

FOCUS	The Person of Christ	The Pursuit of Christ
REFERENCE	1 — 2	3 — 4
TOPICS	The Character of Christ	Our Conduct in Christ
	The Supremacy of Christ	Our Submission to Christ
	Belief: Doctrinal	Behavior: Practical
	"the knowledge of his will through all spiritual wisdom and understanding" (1:9)	"that you may live a life worthy of the Lord" (1:10)
LOCATION	Sent from Rome to Colossae	
TIME	A.D. 60–62	

The first half of Colossians presents the person, character and supremacy of Christ. After a brief greeting, Paul thanks God for the Colossians (1:3–8) and prays that they will come to a deeper knowledge of and growth in Christ (1:9–14). He develops his theme of Christ's supremacy by demonstrating his preeminence in the realms of creation (1:15–18) and redemption (1:19–2:3). This teaching is the basis from which Paul refutes the false teachings of deceptive philosophy, legalistic regulations, misguided mysticism and vain asceticism (2:4–23).

The second half of Colossians turns to the believer's pursuit of Christ through submission to him and godly conduct in each area of life. Because of our union with Christ (3:1–4), we are to put to death the sinful manifestations of the old self (3:5–11) and demonstrate the life of the new self in Christ (3:12–17). This inward transformation should be expressed in the outward transformation of our family and marketplace relationships and in proclamation to unbelievers (3:18—4:6). Paul concludes his epistle with instructions and greetings (4:7–18).

COLOSSIANS

1 Paul, an apostle[a] of Christ Jesus by the will of God,[b] and Timothy our brother,

2To the holy and faithful[a] brothers in Christ at Colosse:

Grace[c] and peace to you from God our Father.[b][d]

Thanksgiving and Prayer

3We always thank God,[e] the Father of our Lord Jesus Christ, when we pray for you, **4**because we have heard of your faith in Christ Jesus and of the love[f] you have for all the saints[g]— **5**the faith and love that spring from the hope[h] that is stored up for you in heaven[i] and that you have already heard about in the word of truth, the gospel **6**that has come to you. All over the world[j] this gospel is bearing fruit[k] and growing, just as it has been doing among you since the day you heard it and understood God's grace in all its truth. **7**You learned it from Epaphras,[l] our dear fellow servant, who is a faithful minister[m] of Christ on our[c] behalf, **8**and who also told us of your love in the Spirit.[n]

9For this reason, since the day we heard about you,[o] we have not stopped praying for you and asking God to fill you with the knowledge of his will[p] through all spiritual wisdom and understanding.[q] **10**And we pray this in order that you may live a life worthy[r] of the Lord and may please him in every way: bearing fruit in every good work, growing in the knowledge of God, **11**being strengthened with all power[s] according to his glorious might so that you may have great endurance and patience,[t] and joyfully **12**giving thanks to the Father,[u] who has qualified you[d] to share in the inheritance[v] of the saints in the kingdom of light. **13**For he has rescued us from the dominion of darkness[w] and brought us into the kingdom[x] of the Son he loves,[y] **14**in whom we have redemption,[e][z] the forgiveness of sins.[a]

1 →PG. 1316
3 →PG. 1313

The Supremacy of Christ

15He is the image[b] of the invisible God,[c] the firstborn over all creation. **16**For by him all things were created:[d] things in heaven and on earth, visible and invisible, whether thrones or powers or rulers or authorities;[e] all things were created by him and for him.[f] **17**He is before all things,[g] and in him all things hold together. **18**And he is the head[h] of the body, the church; he is the beginning and the firstborn from among the dead,[i] so that in everything he might have the supremacy. **19**For God was pleased[j] to have all his fullness[k] dwell in him, **20**and through him to reconcile[l] to himself all things, whether things on earth or things in heaven,[m] by making peace through his blood,[n] shed on the cross.

6 →PG. 1316

21Once you were alienated from God and were enemies[o] in your minds[p] because of[f] your evil behavior. **22**But now he has reconciled you by Christ's physical body[q] through death to present you holy in his sight, without blemish and free from accusation[r]— **23**if you continue in your faith, established[s] and firm, not moved from the

3 →PG. 1314

1:1 [a]1Co 1:1 [b]2Co 1:1
1:2 [c]Col 4:18 [d]Ro 1:7
1:3 [e]Ro 1:8
1:4 [f]Gal 5:6 [g]Eph 1:15
1:5 [h]1Th 5:8; Tit 1:2 [i]1Pe 1:4
1:6 [j]Ro 10:18 [k]Jn 15:16
1:7 [l]Phm 23 [m]Col 4:7
1:8 [n]Ro 15:30
1:9 [o]Eph 1:15 [p]Eph 5:17 [q]Eph 1:17
1:10 [r]Eph 4:1
1:11 [s]Eph 3:16 [t]Eph 4:2
1:12 [u]Eph 5:20 [v]Ac 20:32
1:13 [w]Ac 26:18 [x]Eph 6:12; 2Pe 1:11 [y]Mt 3:17
1:14 [z]Ro 3:24 [a]Eph 1:7
1:15 [b]2Co 4:4 [c]Jn 1:18
1:16 [d]Jn 1:3 [e]Eph 1:20,21 [f]Ro 11:36
1:17 [g]Jn 1:2
1:18 [h]Eph 1:22 [i]Ac 26:23; Rev 1:5
1:19 [j]Eph 1:5 [k]Jn 1:16
1:20 [l]2Co 5:18 [m]Eph 1:10 [n]Eph 2:13
1:21 [o]Ro 5:10 [p]Eph 2:3
1:22 [q]Ro 7:4 [r]Eph 5:27
1:23 [s]Eph 3:17

a *2* Or *believing* b *2* Some manuscripts *Father and the Lord Jesus Christ* c *7* Some manuscripts *your* d *12* Some manuscripts *us* e *14* A few late manuscripts *redemption through his blood* f *21* Or *minds, as shown by*

1:9–14

PROMISE 1

PRAYING WITH CONFIDENCE

It's one thing to pray for another believer; it's another thing to pray with confidence. Sometimes we lack confidence because we're not sure exactly what we should pray on behalf of other people. But here Paul gives us an excellent example of intercessory prayer.

Paul prayed that God would give the Colossians a knowledge of God's will, which would result in "all spiritual wisdom and understanding." "Wisdom" means comprehending spiritual truth. "Understanding" refers to the ability to apply that insight to the problems of life. Such wisdom and knowledge is spiritual because it comes from God and not man.

Paul also prayed that they would grow spiritually. This growth would flow from their spiritual understanding and would be characterized by endurance, patience and thankfulness.

Prayer requires disciplined, consistent effort. Don't put off spending time in prayer. Get a notebook, write down the names of your friends and family members, and pray for them. Remember, the more specific your prayers, the more specific will be the answers to look for.

For the next Promise 1 reading go to page 1329.

hope[t] held out in the gospel. This is the gospel that you heard and that has been proclaimed to every creature under heaven,[u] and of which I, Paul, have become a servant.[v]

Paul's Labor for the Church

24Now I rejoice in what was suffered for you, and I fill up in my flesh what is still lacking in regard to Christ's afflictions,[w] for the sake of his body, which is the church. 25I have become its servant[x] by the commission God gave me[y] to present to you the word of God in its fullness— 26the mystery[z] that has been kept hidden for ages and generations, but is now disclosed to the saints. 27To them God has chosen to make known[a] among the Gentiles the glorious riches of this mystery, which is Christ in you, the hope of glory.

28We proclaim him, admonishing[b] and teaching everyone with all wisdom,[c] so that we may present everyone perfect[d] in Christ. 29To this end I labor,[e] struggling[f] with all his energy, which so powerfully works in me.[g]

2 I want you to know how much I am struggling[h] for you and for those at Laodicea,[i] and for all who have not met me personally. 2My purpose is that they may be encouraged in heart[j] and united in love, so that they may have the full riches of complete understanding, in order that they may know the mystery of God, namely, Christ, 3in whom are hidden all the treasures of wisdom and knowledge.[k] 4I tell you this so that no one may deceive you by fine-sounding arguments.[l] 5For though I am absent from you in body, I am present with you in spirit[m] and delight to see how orderly[n] you are and how firm[o] your faith in Christ is.

Freedom From Human Regulations Through Life With Christ

6So then, just as you received Christ Jesus as Lord,[p] continue to live in him, 7rooted[q] and built up in him, strengthened in the faith as you were taught, and overflowing with thankfulness. 3 →PG. 1316

8See to it that no one takes you captive through hollow and deceptive philosophy,[r] which depends on human

1:23 [t]ver 5 [u]Ro 10:18 [v]ver 25; 1Co 3:5
1:24 [w]2Co 1:5
1:25 [x]ver 23 [y]Eph 3:2
1:26 [z]Ro 16:25
1:27 [a]Mt 13:11
1:28 [b]Col 3:16 [c]1Co 2:6,7 [d]Eph 5:27
1:29 [e]1Co 15:10 [f]Col 2:1 [g]Eph 1:19
2:1 [h]Col 1:29; 4:12 [i]Rev 1:11
2:2 [j]Col 4:8
2:3 [k]Ro 11:33; 1Co 1:24,30
2:4 [l]Ro 16:18
2:5 [m]1Th 2:17 [n]1Co 14:40 [o]1Pe 5:9
2:6 [p]Col 1:10
2:7 [q]Eph 3:17
2:8 [r]1Ti 6:20

1:15–22

PE

JESUS IS GOD!

One day you may encounter someone who says to you, "The Bible doesn't teach that Jesus was actually God." On such an occasion there is no better passage to turn to than this one. Here Paul describes Jesus in language that can only be applied to deity—"the image of the invisible God." In the original language the word for "image" means "likeness," just as the image on a coin bears the likeness of the die from which it was made. But Jesus Christ doesn't merely bear a resemblance to God—he possesses the very character and nature of God. Take a moment to reflect on Paul's descriptions of Jesus.

Firstborn over all creation. Paul wasn't saying that God created Jesus. He was using a figure of speech to indicate that Jesus is the first in rank, not in order of creation. In other words, Jesus holds the top spot in all the universe.

Creator. Just to make sure there is no mistake about the deity of Jesus Christ, Paul wrote that Jesus created all things. He is both the architect and builder of everything. That includes earthly seats of power and those who occupy them.

Predecessor. Because Jesus made all things, he must have existed before all things. In making this bold statement, Paul was saying nothing different than what Jesus himself declared: "Before Abraham was born, I am!" (John 8:58).

Sustainer. Jesus Christ is also the "glue" that holds the universe together. Apart from him nothing would exist, and apart from him nothing would stay in place. What an amazing thought! Jesus is literally the sustainer of all creation.

Head of the church. Jesus is not only supreme in the physical world, but also in the spiritual world. He is the leader and chief of the church. He created, directs and unites both the universe and the church. He is supreme over all!

Firstborn from among the dead. Again Paul talks about Jesus' rank among those who have been raised from the dead. While the Bible contains several accounts of people being raised from the dead, Jesus' resurrection was the most important because it symbolized his ultimate authority over sin and death. Because he lives today, Jesus can guarantee the resurrection of all believers, and he is the leader over all people who will be raised.

Redeemer. Only a divine Savior could reconcile the world to himself. He alone could remove all barriers between God and humanity. To accomplish this, he had to pay for our sins. Because he carried our sins to the cross, we can now stand holy and blameless before God, completely free of accusation.

The Lord of creation, the Master of the physical and spiritual world, died so we could be brought close to God. As you reflect on Jesus' role in reconciling us to God, think about the implications of his actions for your life. What will be your role in helping others connect with God?

tradition and the basic principles of
this world[s] rather than on Christ.
9For in Christ all the fullness of the
Deity lives in bodily form, 10and you
have been given fullness in Christ, who
is the head[t] over every power and authority. 11In him you were also circumcised,[u] in the putting off of the sinful nature,[a][v] not with a circumcision
done by the hands of men but with the
circumcision done by Christ, 12having
been buried with him in baptism and
raised with him[w] through your faith in
the power of God, who raised him from
the dead.[x]
13When you were dead in your sins[y]
and in the uncircumcision of your
sinful nature,[b] God made you[c] alive
with Christ. He forgave us all our sins,
14having canceled the written code,
with its regulations,[z] that was against
us and that stood opposed to us; he
took it away, nailing it to the cross.[a]
15And having disarmed the powers and
authorities,[b] he made a public spectacle of them, triumphing over them[c]
by the cross.[d]
16Therefore do not let anyone judge
you[d] by what you eat or drink,[e] or
with regard to a religious festival,[f] a
New Moon celebration[g] or a Sabbath
day.[h] 17These are a shadow of the
things that were to come;[i] the reality,
however, is found in Christ. 18Do not
let anyone who delights in false humility[j] and the worship of angels disqualify you for the prize.[k] Such a person
goes into great detail about what he
has seen, and his unspiritual mind
puffs him up with idle notions. 19He
has lost connection with the Head,[l]
from whom the whole body, supported
and held together by its ligaments
and sinews, grows as God causes it to
grow.[m]
20Since you died with Christ to the
basic principles of this world,[n] why, as
though you still belonged to it, do you
submit to its rules:[o] 21"Do not handle!
Do not taste! Do not touch!"? 22These
are all destined to perish[p] with use,
because they are based on human
commands and teachings.[q] 23Such
regulations indeed have an appearance of wisdom, with their self-imposed worship, their false humility
and their harsh treatment of the body,
but they lack any value in restraining
sensual indulgence.

Rules for Holy Living

3 Since, then, you have been raised
with Christ, set your hearts on things
above, where Christ is seated at the
right hand of God. 2Set your minds on
things above, not on earthly things.[r]
3For you died,[s] and your life is now
hidden with Christ in God. 4When

2:8 [s]Gal 4:3
2:10 [t]Eph 1:22
2:11 [u]Ro 2:29; Php 3:3 [v]Gal 5:24
2:12 [w]Ro 6:5 [x]Ac 2:24
2:13 [y]Eph 2:1,5
2:14 [z]Eph 2:15 [a]1Pe 2:24
2:15 [b]Eph 6:12 [c]Lk 10:18
2:16 [d]Ro 14:3,4 [e]Ro 14:17 [f]Ro 14:5 [g]1Ch 23:31 [h]Gal 4:10
2:17 [i]Heb 8:5
2:18 [j]ver 23 [k]Php 3:14
2:19 [l]Eph 1:22 [m]Eph 4:16
2:20 [n]Gal 4:3,9 [o]ver 14,16
2:22 [p]1Co 6:13 [q]Isa 29:13; Mt 15:9; Tit 1:14
3:2 [r]Php 3:19,20
3:3 [s]Ro 6:2; 2Co 5:14

[a] *11* Or *the flesh* [b] *13* Or *your flesh* [c] *13* Some manuscripts *us* [d] *15* Or *them in him*

2:6–8

PROMISE 3

ROOTED IN CHRIST

Paul encouraged the Colossian believers to hold on to their devotion to Jesus. When they received Jesus, he became the foundation of their faith—just as roots are to a tree and concrete is to a house. That union with Jesus was to continue to be the basis of their spiritual lives, even though some individuals tried to pervert the gospel message.

We also need to be careful that we don't abandon Jesus for something or someone else. The competition for our attention today is fierce—opposing philosophies and a corrupt culture constantly try to lure us away from our Savior. Here Paul calls his readers to sharpen their focus on Jesus, who gives us "fullness" and provides us with everything we need.

For the next Promise 3 reading go to page 1337.

3:1–21

PROMISE 6

NEW CLOTHES

"You have been raised with Christ." What an amazing statement! That means if you know Christ, you're presently seated with him at the right hand of God. That's your spiritual position in Christ.

Since you died with Christ and have been raised with him, Paul exhorts you to put on the virtues that belong to your new life. You've entered into a spiritual realm where distinctions of race, creed, culture and class have lost their importance. Because that's the case, you must maintain attitudes and actions that build peace and unity with other believers—even those who are different from yourself. You're to clothe yourself with attitudes that reflect love and create harmony in your home and at work.

Read over the list of attitudes and actions Paul exhorts you to put on (vv. 12–17) and evaluate how you think you're doing with each one. Rank yourself on a scale of 1 ("I'm blowing it") to 10 ("I'm doing well"). Pick the one that needs the most work. Then ask God to use you as his agent for encouraging unity among your Christian brothers and sisters at home and at work.

For the next Promise 6 reading go to page 1354.

Christ, who is your[a] life, appears,[t] then you also will appear with him in glory.[u]

3 →PG. 1316 **5**Put to death, therefore, whatever belongs to your earthly nature: sexual immorality, impurity, lust, evil desires and greed,[v] which is idolatry.[w] **6**Because of these, the wrath of God[x] is coming.[b] **7**You used to walk in these ways, in the life you once lived.[y] **8**But now you must rid yourselves[z] of all such things as these: anger, rage, malice, slander,[a] and filthy language from your lips.[b] **9**Do not lie to each other,[c] since you have taken off your old self with its practices **10**and have put on the new self, which is being renewed[d] in knowledge in the image of its Creator.[e] **11**Here there is no Greek 6 →PG. 1359 or Jew,[f] circumcised or uncircumcised,[g] barbarian, Scythian, slave or free,[h] but Christ is all,[i] and is in all.

7 →PG. 1316 **12**Therefore, as God's chosen people, holy and dearly loved, clothe yourselves with compassion, kindness, humility,[j] gentleness and patience.[k] **13**Bear with each other[l] and forgive whatever grievances you may have against one another. Forgive as the Lord forgave you.[m] **14**And over all these virtues put on love,[n] which binds them all together in perfect unity.[o]

15Let the peace of Christ[p] rule in your hearts, since as members of one body you were called to peace. And be 1 →PG. 1316 thankful. **16**Let the word of Christ[q] dwell in you richly as you teach and admonish one another with all wis- 5 →PG. 1324 dom,[r] and as you sing psalms, hymns and spiritual songs with gratitude in 7 →PG. 1316 your hearts to God.[s] **17**And whatever you do,[t] whether in word or deed, do it all in the name of the Lord Jesus, giving thanks[u] to God the Father through him.

Rules for Christian Households

4 →PG. 1334 **18**Wives, submit to your husbands,[v] as is fitting in the Lord.

19Husbands, love your wives and do not be harsh with them.

20Children, obey your parents in everything, for this pleases the Lord.

21Fathers, do not embitter your children, or they will become discouraged.

3 →PG. 1320 **22**Slaves, obey your earthly masters in everything; and do it, not only when their eye is on you and to win their favor, but with sincerity of heart and reverence for the Lord. **23**Whatever you do, work at it with all your heart, as working for the Lord, not for men, **24**since you know that you will receive an inheritance[w] from the Lord as a reward. It is the Lord Christ you are serving. **25**Anyone who does wrong will be repaid for his wrong, and there is no favoritism.[x]

4 Masters, provide your slaves with what is right and fair, because you know that you also have a Master in heaven.

Further Instructions

1 →PG. 1320 **2**Devote yourselves to prayer,[y] being watchful and thankful. **3**And pray for us, too, that God may open a door[z] 7 →PG. 1320 for our message, so that we may proclaim the mystery of Christ, for which I am in chains.[a] **4**Pray that I may proclaim it clearly, as I should. **5**Be wise[b] in the way you act toward outsiders;[c] make the most of every opportunity.[d] **6**Let your conversation be always full of grace,[e] seasoned with salt,[f] so that you may know how to answer everyone.[g]

Final Greetings

2 →PG. 1320 **7**Tychicus[h] will tell you all the news

[a] 4 Some manuscripts *our* [b] 6 Some early manuscripts *coming on those who are disobedient*

3:4 [t]1Co 1:7 [u]1Pe 1:13; 1Jn 3:2
3:5 [v]Eph 5:3 [w]Eph 5:5
3:6 [x]Ro 1:18
3:7 [y]Eph 2:2
3:8 [z]Eph 4:22 [a]Eph 4:31 [b]Eph 4:29
3:9 [c]Eph 4:22,25
3:10 [d]Ro 12:2; Eph 4:23 [e]Eph 2:10
3:11 [f]Ro 10:12 [g]1Co 7:19 [h]Gal 3:28 [i]Eph 1:23
3:12 [j]Php 2:3 [k]2Co 6:6; Gal 5:22,23
3:13 [l]Eph 4:2 [m]Eph 4:32
3:14 [n]1Co 13:1-13 [o]Eph 4:3
3:15 [p]Jn 14:27
3:16 [q]Ro 10:17 [r]Col 1:28 [s]Eph 5:19
3:17 [t]1Co 10:31 [u]Eph 5:20
3:18 [v]Eph 5:22
3:24 [w]Ac 20:32
3:25 [x]Ac 10:34
4:2 [y]Lk 18:1
4:3 [z]Ac 14:27 [a]Eph 6:19,20
4:5 [b]Eph 5:15 [c]Mk 4:11 [d]Eph 5:16
4:6 [e]Eph 4:29 [f]Mk 9:50 [g]1Pe 3:15
4:7 [h]Ac 20:4

4:2–6

PROMISE 7

EVANGELISTIC PRAYER

Does the idea of sharing your faith make you a little uneasy? If so, you're not alone. Many men feel that way. Even Paul, one of the boldest evangelists in church history, requested that the Colossians pray for his ministry of evangelism. In his prayer we find insight into how we should pray for others and how they should pray for us as we spread the gospel.

First, we should pray for open doors, asking that God will give us opportunities to share our faith. Second, we should pray that we'll recognize and capitalize on each opportunity. Third, we should pray that the Spirit will give us clarity of mind and speech when we do tell someone about Jesus. Fourth, we should pray for sensitivity in our language. As followers of Jesus we need to tell the gospel story in a way that connects with people on a personal level.

Remember, concepts that are clear for one person can be muddy for another. Ask God to give you the wisdom and sensitivity to know how to adapt your presentation of the gospel so it's clear to each person to whom you speak. And remember, actions can speak even louder than words, so combine your verbal message with a godly example of Jesus' love.

For the next Promise 7 reading go to page 1328.

about me. He is a dear brother, a faithful minister and fellow servant[i] in the
Lord. 8I am sending him to you for the
express purpose that you may know
about our[a] circumstances and that he
may encourage your hearts.[j] 9He is
coming with Onesimus,[k] our faithful
and dear brother, who is one of you.
They will tell you everything that is
happening here.

10My fellow prisoner Aristarchus[l]
sends you his greetings, as does Mark,
the cousin of Barnabas.[m] (You have received instructions about him; if he
comes to you, welcome him.) 11Jesus,
who is called Justus, also sends greetings. These are the only Jews among
my fellow workers for the kingdom of
God, and they have proved a comfort
to me. 12Epaphras,[n] who is one of you
and a servant of Christ Jesus, sends
greetings. He is always wrestling in
prayer for you,[o] that you may stand
firm in all the will of God, mature[p]
and fully assured. 13I vouch for him
that he is working hard for you and for
those at Laodicea[q] and Hierapolis.
14Our dear friend Luke,[r] the doctor,
and Demas[s] send greetings. 15Give
my greetings to the brothers at Laodicea, and to Nympha and the church in
her house.[t]

16After this letter has been read to
you, see that it is also read[u] in the
church of the Laodiceans and that you
in turn read the letter from Laodicea.

17Tell Archippus:[v] "See to it that
you complete the work you have received in the Lord."[w]

18I, Paul, write this greeting in my
own hand.[x] Remember[y] my chains.
Grace be with you.[z]

4:7 [i] Eph 6:21,22
4:8 [j] Eph 6:21,22
4:9 [k] Phm 10
4:10 [l] Ac 19:29 [m] Ac 4:36
4:12 [n] Col 1:7; Phm 23 [o] Ro 15:30 [p] 1Co 2:6
4:13 [q] Col 2:1
4:14 [r] 2Ti 4:11; Phm 24 [s] 2Ti 4:10
4:15 [t] Ro 16:5
4:16 [u] 2Th 3:14
4:17 [v] Phm 2 [w] 2Ti 4:5
4:18 [x] 1Co 16:21 [y] Heb 13:3

[a] 8 Some manuscripts *that he may know about your*

[z] 1Ti 6:21; 2Ti 4:22; Tit 3:15; Heb 13:25

1 THESSALONIANS

AT A GLANCE

Key Principle: The gift of salvation is the beginning, not the end, of our spiritual journey; once we come to know Christ, we are called to grow in faith, hope and love.
Author: Paul
Time and Place: A.D. 51 / Sent from Corinth to Thessalonica
Key Verses: 2:19–20; 3:12–13; 4:13–18; 5:23

BENEFIT

This warm and personal epistle encourages us to remain strong in our faith and to grow in our pursuit of a godly life. Paul gives us a model for relational ministry as he describes the way he worked with and nurtured the Thessalonians, and provides us with an example of the kind of personal concern we should adopt for those we have been privileged to serve. This letter also contains critical insights on Christ's second coming and the nature of "the day of the Lord."

SETTING

By Paul's time, Thessalonica had become the capital city of the Roman province of Macedonia. In this busy seaport lived a substantial number of Jews as well as God-fearing Gentiles who were converts to Judaism. When Paul came to Thessalonica in A.D. 51 during his second missionary journey, a number of Jews and God-fearing Gentiles responded to the gospel. However, opposition from the Jewish leaders led Paul and Silas to depart for Berea (Acts 17:1–10). The same Jewish leaders went to Berea and stirred up the crowds against Paul. Because of this, some of the brothers accompanied Paul to Athens and returned with instructions for Silas and Timothy to join him there (Acts 17:11–16). Not long after they did so, Paul sent Timothy back to the Thessalonians because he was concerned that they might have faltered in their faith (3:1–2); he also sent Silas to Macedonia, probably Philippi (Acts 18:5). By the time Timothy and Silas again returned to Paul, he had moved from Athens to Corinth, where he wrote this letter in response to Timothy's good report (1:1; 3:6).

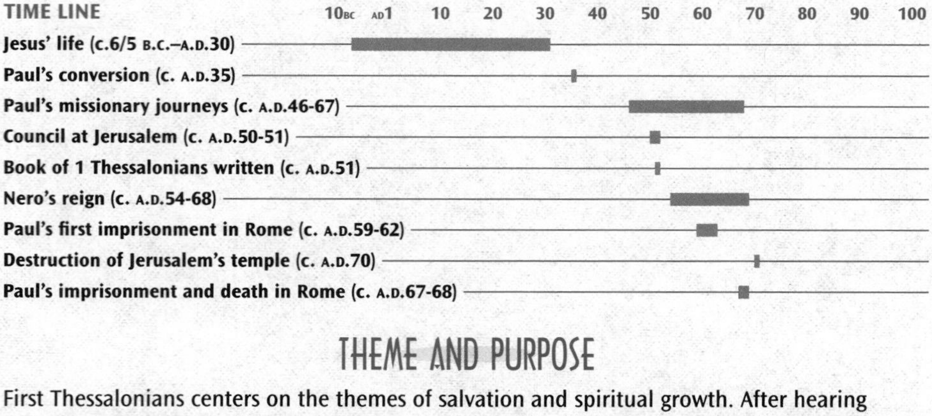

THEME AND PURPOSE

First Thessalonians centers on the themes of salvation and spiritual growth. After hearing Timothy's report about the Thessalonians' strong faith, Paul wrote this epistle to tell them how thankful he was that their faith and love was growing, even in the face of persecution. He responded to the Jewish opposition by reminding his readers of the selfless way he ministered to them and the truth of the message he proclaimed. Paul also wanted to encourage and admonish his readers to stand firm in the face of moral temptation, and to comfort them in view of their concern for those who had died in Christ. Finally, Paul wrote this letter to instruct them in steadfastness, conduct and worship.

UNIQUE CONTRIBUTION

Both of Paul's Thessalonian epistles deal with matters of eschatology (prophecy), and all five chapters of 1 Thessalonians refer to Christ's return (1:10; 2:19; 3:13; 4:13–18; 5:1–11, 23). The prophetic message in 4:13—5:11 is vivid and practical; this is one of the Bible's most important passages concerning Christ's second coming. Paul refers to but does not develop other Biblical doctrines, assuming that they learned a considerable amount of truth from him in spite of the short time (probably a few weeks) he spent with them.

CHRIST IN 1 THESSALONIANS

In this epistle, Christ is shown as the Lord who will return from heaven and rescue his people from the coming wrath (1:10; 5:4–11). The certainty of Jesus' second coming is a great source of hope for those who trust in him, because both the dead in Christ and those who are alive when he comes will be resurrected and united in him (4:13–18). He will sanctify (3:13; 5:23) and reward (2:19–20) all who hope in him.

OVERVIEW

FOCUS	Personal Experiences			Practical Exhortations		
REFERENCE	1:1-10	2:1-16	2:17–3:13	4:1-12	4:13–5:11	5:12-28
TOPICS	Commendation	Character	Concern	Commandments	Consolation	Conduct
	Retrospective			Prospective		
	Salvation of the Thessalonians			Sanctification of the Thessalonians		
	Implantation			Irrigation		
LOCATION	Sent from Corinth to Thessalonica					
TIME	A.D. 51					

Paul begins this epistle of personal reflection, exhortation, encouragement and instruction by giving thanks for the Thessalonians' work produced by faith, their labor prompted by love and their endurance inspired by hope in Christ (1:1–3). He rejoices that their faith has inspired all the believers in Macedonia and Achaia (1:4–10). He then reviews his ministry in their midst and defends his care, concern, motives and message (2:1–16). He explains that, after he left, he was concerned about their spiritual condition, but was profoundly encouraged to hear that their faith and love were continuing to grow (2:17—3:10). Before moving on to a series of exhortations and instructions, Paul pauses to pray for their continued spiritual progress (3:11–13).

Paul's practical exhortations begin with a reminder of his teaching on sexual purity, brotherly love and personal responsibility (4:1–12). In answer to their concern about the destiny of believers who have died in Christ, the apostle comforts them with the hope of resurrection and reunion with Christ at his coming (4:13–18). He continues with a discourse on the future day of the Lord and exhorts the Thessalonians to be alert and self-controlled as people of the light whose destiny is to live together with Christ (5:1–11). The epistle ends with specific admonitions and instructions that relate to their sanctification (5:12–22) and with a benediction and parting thoughts (5:23–28).

1 THESSALONIANS

1 Paul, Silas[a] and Timothy,[a]

To the church of the Thessalonians[b] in God the Father and the Lord
Jesus Christ:

Grace and peace to you.[b][c]

Thanksgiving for the Thessalonians' Faith

7 →PG. 1321

2We always thank God for all of
you,[d] mentioning you in our prayers.
3We continually remember before our
God and Father your work produced
by faith,[e] your labor prompted by
love, and your endurance inspired by
hope in our Lord Jesus Christ.
4For we know, brothers loved by
God, that he has chosen you, 5because
our gospel[f] came to you not simply
with words, but also with power, with
the Holy Spirit and with deep conviction. You know how we lived among

1 →PG. 1325

you for your sake. 6You became imitators of us[g] and of the Lord; in spite of
severe suffering,[h] you welcomed the
message with the joy given by the Holy
Spirit.[i] 7And so you became a model
to all the believers in Macedonia and
Achaia. 8The Lord's message rang out
from you not only in Macedonia and
Achaia—your faith in God has become
known everywhere.[j] Therefore we do
not need to say anything about it, 9for
they themselves report what kind of re-
ception you gave us. They tell how you
turned to God from idols[k] to serve the
living and true God, 10and to wait for
his Son from heaven, whom he raised
from the dead[l]—Jesus, who rescues
us from the coming wrath.[m]

Paul's Ministry in Thessalonica

2 You know, brothers, that our visit to
you[n] was not a failure. 2We had
previously suffered[o] and been insulted in Philippi, as you know, but with
the help of our God we dared to tell you
his gospel in spite of strong opposition.
3For the appeal we make does not
spring from error or impure motives,[p]

3 →PG. 1325

nor are we trying to trick you. 4On the
contrary, we speak as men approved
by God to be entrusted with the gospel.[q] We are not trying to please
men[r] but God, who tests our hearts.
5You know we never used flattery,
nor did we put on a mask to cover
up greed[s]—God is our witness.[t] 6We
were not looking for praise from men,
not from you or anyone else.
As apostles[u] of Christ we could
have been a burden to you, 7but we
were gentle among you, like a mother
caring for her little children.[v] 8We
loved you so much that we were delighted to share with you not only the
gospel of God but our lives as well,[w]
because you had become so dear to us.
9Surely you remember, brothers, our
toil and hardship; we worked[x] night
and day in order not to be a burden to
anyone[y] while we preached the gospel of God to you.

2 →PG. 1321

10You are witnesses,[z] and so is God,
of how holy,[a] righteous and blameless
we were among you who believed.
11For you know that we dealt with each
of you as a father deals with his own
children,[b] 12encouraging, comforting
and urging you to live lives worthy[c] of

1:1 [a]Ac 16:1; 2Th 1:1 [b]Ac 17:1 [c]Ro 1:7
1:2 [d]Ro 1:8
1:3 [e]2Th 1:11
1:5 [f]2Th 2:14
1:6 [g]1Co 4:16 [h]Ac 17:5-10 [i]Ac 13:52
1:8 [j]Ro 1:8; 10:18
1:9 [k]1Co 12:2; Gal 4:8
1:10 [l]Ac 2:24 [m]Ro 5:9
2:1 [n]1Th 1:5,9
2:2 [o]Ac 16:22; Php 1:30
2:3 [p]2Co 2:17
2:4 [q]Gal 2:7 [r]Gal 1:10
2:5 [s]Ac 20:33 [t]Ro 1:9
2:6 [u]1Co 9:1,2
2:7 [v]ver 11
2:8 [w]2Co 12:15; 1Jn 3:16
2:9 [x]Ac 18:3 [y]2Th 3:8
2:10 [z]1Th 1:5 [a]2Co 1:12
2:11 [b]ver 7; 1Co 4:14
2:12 [c]Eph 4:1

a *1* Greek *Silvanus,* a variant of *Silas*
b *1* Some early manuscripts *you from God our Father and the Lord Jesus Christ*

1:6–7 | PROMISE 2

STEPS OF DISCIPLESHIP

Some of us can remember as boys following in Dad's footsteps on a beach or in the snow. He would take a step and we'd put our foot where his had been.

That's a good illustration of discipleship. In this case, Paul, Silas and Timothy followed in Jesus' footsteps (1:1). The Thessalonians followed in the same footsteps, and in turn were leading others along the same path.

What a pattern—and what a legacy. This kind of activity has brought the gospel to people of all times and places who have accepted Jesus as Savior. Jesus' story has extended through history in an unbroken line that went from Jesus himself to the disciples, from the disciples to the early churches, and from those early believers through history to your church, your pastor and you!

Now, many generations later, God wants you to become part of that legacy by helping others to step into the line of believers. Find a man who is following Jesus that you can get behind and learn from. Then look for at least one man who can follow you. Determine that, by the grace of God, you'll reflect Jesus to him and be the kind of mentor he'll be glad he followed.

For the next Promise 2 reading go to page 1333.

God, who calls you into his kingdom and glory.

13And we also thank God continually[d] because, when you received the word of God,[e] which you heard from us, you accepted it not as the word of men, but as it actually is, the word of God, which is at work in you who believe. 14For you, brothers, became imitators of God's churches in Judea,[f] which are in Christ Jesus: You suffered from your own countrymen[g] the same things those churches suffered from the Jews, 15who killed the Lord Jesus[h] and the prophets[i] and also drove us out. They displease God and are hostile to all men 16in their effort to keep us from speaking to the Gentiles[j] so that they may be saved. In this way they always heap up their sins to the limit.[k] The wrath of God has come upon them at last.[a]

Paul's Longing to See the Thessalonians

17But, brothers, when we were torn away from you for a short time (in person, not in thought),[l] out of our intense longing we made every effort to see you.[m] 18For we wanted to come to you—certainly I, Paul, did, again and again—but Satan[n] stopped us.[o] 19For what is our hope, our joy, or the crown[p] in which we will glory[q] in the presence of our Lord Jesus when he comes?[r] Is it not you? 20Indeed, you are our glory[s] and joy.

3 So when we could stand it no longer,[t] we thought it best to be left by ourselves in Athens.[u] 2We sent Timothy, who is our brother and God's fellow worker[b] in spreading the gospel of Christ, to strengthen and encourage you in your faith, 3so that no one would be unsettled by these trials. You know quite well that we were destined for them.[v] 4In fact, when we were with you, we kept telling you that we would be persecuted. And it turned out that way, as you well know.[w] 5For this reason, when I could stand it no longer,[x] I sent to find out about your faith. I was afraid that in some way the tempter[y] might have tempted you and our efforts might have been useless.[z]

Timothy's Encouraging Report

6But Timothy has just now come to us from you[a] and has brought good news about your faith and love.[b] He has told us that you always have pleasant memories of us and that you long to see us, just as we also long to see you. 7Therefore, brothers, in all our distress and persecution we were encouraged about you because of your faith. 8For now we really live, since you are standing firm[c] in the Lord. 9How can we thank God enough for you[d] in return for all the joy we have in the presence of our God because of you? 10Night and day we pray[e] most earnestly that we may see you again[f] and supply what is lacking in your faith.

11Now may our God and Father himself and our Lord Jesus clear the way for us to come to you. 12May the Lord make your love increase and overflow for each other[g] and for everyone else, just as ours does for you. 13May he strengthen your hearts so that you will be blameless[h] and holy in the presence of our God and Father when our Lord Jesus comes[i] with all his holy ones.

Living to Please God

4 Finally, brothers,[j] we instructed you how to live in order to please God,[k] as in fact you are living. Now we ask you and urge you in the Lord Jesus to do this more and more. 2For you know what instructions we gave you by the authority of the Lord Jesus.

3It is God's will that you should be sanctified: that you should avoid sexual immorality;[l] 4that each of you should learn to control his own body[c][m] in a way that is holy and honorable, 5not in passionate lust[n] like the heathen,[o] who do not know God; 6and that in this matter no one should wrong his brother or take advantage of him.[p] The Lord will punish men for all such sins,[q] as we have already told you and warned you. 7For God did not call us to be impure, but to live a holy life.[r] 8Therefore, he who rejects this instruction does not reject man but God, who gives you his Holy Spirit.[s]

9Now about brotherly love[t] we do not need to write to you,[u] for you yourselves have been taught by God to love each other.[v] 10And in fact, you do love all the brothers throughout Macedonia.[w] Yet we urge you, brothers, to do so more and more.[x]

2 →PG. 1324
7 →PG. 1329

11Make it your ambition to lead a quiet life, to mind your own business and to work with your hands,[y] just as we told you, 12so that your daily life may win the respect of outsiders[z] and so that you will not be dependent on anybody.

The Coming of the Lord

13Brothers, we do not want you to be

2:13 [d]1Th 1:2 [e]Heb 4:12
2:14 [f]Gal 1:22 [g]Ac 17:5; 2Th 1:4
2:15 [h]Ac 2:23 [i]Mt 5:12
2:16 [j]Ac 13:45,50 [k]Mt 23:32
2:17 [l]1Co 5:3; Col 2:5 [m]1Th 3:10
2:18 [n]Mt 4:10 [o]Ro 1:13; 15:22
2:19 [p]Php 4:1 [q]2Co 1:14 [r]Mt 16:27; 1Th 3:13
2:20 [s]2Co 1:14
3:1 [t]ver 5 [u]Ac 17:15
3:3 [v]Ac 9:16; 14:22
3:4 [w]1Th 2:14
3:5 [x]ver 1 [y]Mt 4:3 [z]Gal 2:2; Php 2:16
3:6 [a]Ac 18:5 [b]1Th 1:3
3:8 [c]1Co 16:13
3:9 [d]1Th 1:2
3:10 [e]2Ti 1:3 [f]1Th 2:17
3:12 [g]1Th 4:9,10
3:13 [h]1Co 1:8 [i]1Th 2:19
4:1 [j]2Co 13:11 [k]2Co 5:9
4:3 [l]1Co 6:18
4:4 [m]1Co 7:2,9
4:5 [n]Ro 1:26 [o]Eph 4:17
4:6 [p]1Co 6:8 [q]Heb 13:4
4:7 [r]Lev 11:44; 1Pe 1:15
4:8 [s]Ro 5:5; Gal 4:6
4:9 [t]Ro 12:10 [u]1Th 5:1 [v]Jn 13:34
4:10 [w]1Th 1:7 [x]1Th 3:12
4:11 [y]Eph 4:28; 2Th 3:10-12
4:12 [z]Mk 4:11

[a]16 Or *them fully* [b]2 Some manuscripts *brother and fellow worker*; other manuscripts *brother and God's servant* [c]4 Or *learn to live with his own wife*; or *learn to acquire a wife*

SILAS

A Faithful Brother

During the days of intense persecution in the early Christian church, the apostle Peter labeled Silas a "faithful brother" (1 Peter 5:12). This is a simple yet profound description for a man whom the apostles could always count on to be there, no matter what the circumstances.

We first meet Silas in Jerusalem when the church leaders were debating law and grace. After a lengthy discussion, a letter was drafted to the Gentile Christians explaining the leaders' conclusions. To deliver this letter, they enlisted two "of their own men and [sent] them to Antioch with Paul and Barnabas" (Acts 15:22). One of these two men was Silas. He was, quite possibly, like Barnabas, a Grecian Jew. As such, he would have been very familiar with Gentile customs and beliefs. Silas was also a leader "among the brothers" (15:22). As a leader in the early church, Silas would have manifested an outstanding moral, ethical and spiritual reputation in both the Christian and non-Christian communities (1 Timothy 3:2–7).

Paul's Coworker

After Silas had faithfully carried out this first assignment, the unexpected happened. Paul and Barnabas had a disagreement over who should accompany them on their next journey. Because of this disagreement, Barnabas took Mark and sailed for his own country, Cyprus. "Paul chose Silas" and together they went "through Syria and Cilicia, strengthening the churches" (Acts 15:40–41).

Paul knew he needed a reliable assistant on this journey—someone who was highly respected in the church in Jerusalem; someone he could trust. This assistant would have to be a loyal companion, a coworker who understood the Gentile mind. Paul also wanted someone who would not confuse the doctrines of Judaism with those of Christianity, someone who understood God's grace. Silas measured up to all these expectations. So Silas replaced Barnabas as Paul's right-hand man.

Tested and True

Silas's greatest test came in the city of Philippi. He and Paul had been preaching the gospel and were arrested, severely beaten and thrown into the inner prison with their feet placed in stocks (16:24). In spite of this horrible abuse, during the night Paul and Silas began to pray aloud and sing praise to God. While the rest of the prisoners listened, "suddenly there was such a violent earthquake that the foundations of the prison were shaken" (16:26). The prison doors opened, and all the prisoners' chains fell off.

The jailer thought that the prisoners had escaped, and decided to take his own life. As a Roman officer, he would have been accountable for the prison break and put to death anyway. But to his surprise, Paul stopped him and told him that not one prisoner had left. Shocked and shaken, the jailer fell down before Paul and Silas and asked the eternal question: "Sirs, what must I do to be saved?" (16:30). Paul and Silas then led the jailer, along with his whole family, to the Lord and "immediately he and all his family were baptized" (16:33).

Paul and Silas moved on to Thessalonica and Berea. Though Paul was definitely the leader of the team, Silas stood side-by-side with him. Together they faithfully took on any assignment the Holy Spirit gave them. Silas was dedicated to carrying the gospel to the Gentiles with the same forthrightness as Paul. Just as they had faced persecution together in Philippi, they faced it in Thessalonica as well (17:5). And when persecution came, Silas faced it head-on and bore the same burdens as Paul. Silas was truly a faithful brother in the Lord.

A Godly Life

After Paul and Silas's visit to Thessalonica, Paul sent a letter to the new Christians there that tells us a great deal about Paul's traveling companions, "Silas and Timothy" (1 Thessalonians 1:1). Throughout the letter, Paul used the plural pronouns "we" and "our" to refer to their ministry together. Hidden within the words of the letter are hints about what Paul saw in Silas, his coworker:

Silas was not a greedy man-pleaser, but a God-pleaser (2:4–5).
Silas was gentle and loving with the new believers (2:7–8).
Silas was a hard worker who didn't want to be a burden to anyone (2:9).
Silas modeled a holy, righteous and blameless life to the new believers (2:10).
Silas was an encourager who urged the new believers to "live lives worthy of God" (2:12).

After Paul's ministry to the Thessalonians, Silas disappears from the historical record in Acts. Yet, Silas was still busy for the Lord. We find him again, ten or twelve years later, helping Peter when he wrote his first epistle. At that point Peter called Silas his "faithful brother"—a great tribute indeed to one whose life was dedicated to sharing the gospel (1 Peter 5:12).

An Example Worth Following

Though we may never have the experiences that Silas encountered as a New Testament missionary, the way he lived should inspire us all. No matter what our vocation or calling in life, we must evaluate what price we are willing to pay to help others become Christians. Are you willing to stand side-by-side with other godly men, using your time and talents to help others grow in their relationship with God? Are you living your life so that people can describe you as "a faithful brother"? What will it take to reach this goal?

—*Dr. Gene Getz*

ignorant about those who fall asleep,
or to grieve like the rest of men, who
have no hope.[a] 14We believe that
Jesus died and rose again and so we
believe that God will bring with Jesus
those who have fallen asleep in him.[b]
15According to the Lord's own word,
we tell you that we who are still alive,
who are left till the coming of the Lord,
will certainly not precede those who
have fallen asleep.[c] 16For the Lord
himself will come down from heaven,
with a loud command, with the voice
of the archangel and with the trumpet
call of God,[d] and the dead in Christ
will rise first.[e] 17After that, we who are
still alive and are left[f] will be caught
up together with them in the clouds[g]
to meet the Lord in the air. And so
we will be with the Lord[h] forever.
18Therefore encourage each other with
these words.

5 Now, brothers, about times and
dates[i] we do not need to write to
you,[j] 2for you know very well that the
day of the Lord[k] will come like a thief
in the night.[l] 3While people are saying, "Peace and safety," destruction
will come on them suddenly, as labor
pains on a pregnant woman, and they
will not escape.
4But you, brothers, are not in darkness[m] so that this day should surprise
you like a thief. 5You are all sons of the
light and sons of the day. We do not
belong to the night or to the darkness.
6So then, let us not be like others, who
are asleep,[n] but let us be alert and
self-controlled. 7For those who sleep,
sleep at night, and those who get
drunk, get drunk at night.[o] 8But since
we belong to the day, let us be self-
controlled, putting on faith and love as
a breastplate,[p] and the hope of salvation[q] as a helmet.[r] 9For God did
not appoint us to suffer wrath but to
receive salvation through our Lord
Jesus Christ.[s] 10He died for us so that,
whether we are awake or asleep, we
may live together with him.[t] 11There-
fore encourage one another and build
each other up, just as in fact you are
doing.

2 →PG. 1325

Final Instructions

12Now we ask you, brothers, to respect those who work hard among you,
who are over you in the Lord[u] and
who admonish you. 13Hold them in the
highest regard in love because of their
work. Live in peace with each other.[v]
14And we urge you, brothers, warn
those who are idle,[w] encourage the
timid, help the weak,[x] be patient with

5 →PG. 1329

4:13 [a]Eph 2:12
4:14 [b]1Co 15:18
4:15 [c]1Co 15:52
4:16 [d]Mt 24:31 [e]1Co 15:23; 2Th 2:1
4:17 [f]1Co 15:52 [g]Ac 1:9; Rev 11:12 [h]Jn 12:26
5:1 [i]Ac 1:7 [j]1Th 4:9
5:2 [k]1Co 1:8 [l]2Pe 3:10
5:4 [m]Ac 26:18; 1Jn 2:8
5:6 [n]Ro 13:11
5:7 [o]Ac 2:15; 2Pe 2:13
5:8 [p]Eph 6:14 [q]Ro 8:24 [r]Eph 6:17
5:9 [s]2Th 2:13,14
5:10 [t]2Co 5:15
5:12 [u]1Ti 5:17; Heb 13:17
5:13 [v]Mk 9:50
5:14 [w]2Th 3:6,7,11 [x]Ro 14:1

5:12–22

PROMISE 5

GETTING ALONG

How are believers to relate to one another? Paul concludes his remarks to the Thessalonians by giving a series of exhortations aimed at answering that question. They come in rapid-fire succession in these verses, and they apply to us today as well as they did to the Thessalonian church.

Paul's instructions run the gamut from encouraging ministry professionals (v. 12) to being joyful in all circumstances (v. 18) to avoiding false teaching (v. 21). Paul probably could have written a chapter on each of these, but he left them as short, easy-to-remember statements that summarized his teaching to the Thessalonians.

As you read over this list, think about how Paul addressed each of these issues in this short letter. Then think of creative ways that you can implement these positive commands in your own life—at work, in your local church, in your neighborhood and in your own family.

For the next Promise 5 reading go to page 1328.

4:13–18

PE

SLEEP OF DEATH

Each one of us has been touched in some way by death's cold hand. Perhaps it struck a friend, a classmate or a family member unexpectedly. Perhaps it came after a loved one's long illness. While we live on this earth, death is the great equalizer. Young and old, rich and poor are snatched away in an instant. We fear it and fight it, yet death always wins.

But Paul gives us words of comfort in the face of death. He said for a Christian, death is like "sleep." It's temporary. One day, when Jesus comes back to the earth from heaven, living people will be changed in an instant, and dead people will be raised from the grave. The Thessalonian believers were evidently under the impression that all believers would continue to live on earth until Jesus came again, and worried that those who had died already would miss eternity with Jesus. Here Paul reassured his readers that all believers will be with Jesus and with each other for eternity.

Does this mean we shouldn't grieve the death of a loved one? No. Jesus himself wept when a close friend died (John 11:35). But it does mean that we have comfort and hope for the future. While separation tears at our hearts, we know that we will once again see those who knew and trusted Jesus Christ in this life. And what a wonderful reunion that will be! Thank God for this wonderful hope.

everyone. 15 Make sure that nobody
pays back wrong for wrong,[y] but always try to be kind to each other[z] and
to everyone else.
1 →PG. 1329
16 Be joyful always;[a] 17 pray continually; 18 give thanks in all circumstances,
for this is God's will for you in Christ
Jesus.
3 →PG. 1329
19 Do not put out the Spirit's fire;[b]
20 do not treat prophecies[c] with contempt. 21 Test everything.[d] Hold on to
the good. 22 Avoid every kind of evil.
23 May God himself, the God of
peace,[e] sanctify you through and
through. May your whole spirit, soul
and body be kept blameless at the
coming of our Lord Jesus Christ. 24 The
one who calls you is faithful[f] and he
will do it.

2 →PG. 1333
25 Brothers, pray for us.[g] 26 Greet all
the brothers with a holy kiss.[h] 27 I
charge you before the Lord to have this
letter read to all the brothers.[i]
28 The grace of our Lord Jesus Christ
be with you.[j]

5:15 [y] 1Pe 3:9 [z] Gal 6:10; Eph 4:32 **5:16** [a] Php 4:4 **5:19** [b] Eph 4:30 **5:20** [c] 1Co 14:1-40 **5:21** [d] 1Co 14:29; 1Jn 4:1 **5:23** [e] Ro 15:33 **5:24** [f] 1Co 1:9 **5:25** [g] Eph 6:19 **5:26** [h] Ro 16:16 **5:27** [i] Col 4:16 **5:28** [j] Ro 16:20

2 THESSALONIANS

AT A GLANCE

Key Principle: Erroneous thinking leads to erroneous practice; an accurate understanding of Biblical doctrine can lead to a balanced application of truth.
Author: Paul
Time and Place: A.D. 51–52 / Sent from Corinth to Thessalonica
Key Verses: 2:1–3, 13; 3:3–5

BENEFIT

Second Thessalonians illustrates the subtlety of deception that is based on half-truths. False teachers had distorted the truth of Paul's teaching in his first epistle to the Thessalonians, claiming that the day of the Lord was already taking place. This teaching led some believers to become passive and idle as they waited for Christ's second coming. This corrective epistle clarifies the Biblical teaching on the coming day of the Lord, and promotes a positive balance between waiting and working.

SETTING

The "Setting" section in the introduction to 1 Thessalonians provides the background to both of Paul's epistles to this church. This second letter was probably written just a few months after 1 Thessalonians while Paul, Silas and Timothy were still in Corinth (1:1; Acts 18:5). Paul was beginning to encounter growing opposition in his ministry in Corinth (3:2; Acts 18:5–10). The unnamed carrier of Paul's first letter to the Thessalonian church may have returned to Paul in Corinth with news about recent developments in the church, which prompted Paul to respond with this second letter. The Thessalonians were vulnerable to the false teaching that the day of the Lord had already arrived because of the persecution they faced. Some of the believers had stopped working, assuming that Christ's coming was so imminent that earthly labor was now pointless. The preexisting tendency to idleness among some of the believers (1 Thessalonians 4:11–12) was now escalating (3:6–15).

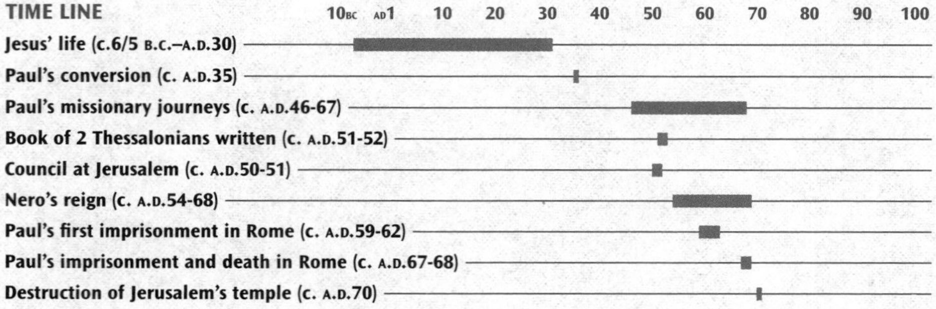

THEME AND PURPOSE

The Thessalonians were experiencing three problems: first, increased persecution for their faith; second, confusion due to false teaching that stemmed either from a prophecy or from a letter attributed to Paul; third, an overreaction to this teaching that was leading to disorder.

The apostle sought to correct these problems with this firm and authoritative letter so the Thessalonian church would continue to grow and be established in the truth. The believers there needed to know that their persecution would be vindicated when Christ returned, that the day of the Lord was still in the future and that they should continue to be diligent while they awaited the coming of the Lord.

The theme of this epistle is comfort and correction in view of practical and doctrinal obstacles to spiritual maturity.

UNIQUE CONTRIBUTION

Second Thessalonians continues the prophetic themes discussed in 1 Thessalonians, and these two epistles, together with Christ's Olivet Discourse in Matthew 24—25 and the book of Revelation, are the key New Testament prophetic texts. In spite of its length, this epistle includes four prayers on behalf of Paul's readers (1:11–12; 2:16–17; 3:5, 16); this underscores the priority of prayer in Paul's life.

CHRIST IN 2 THESSALONIANS

The first two chapters of 2 Thessalonians focus on Christ's return and teach that when he is "revealed from heaven in blazing fire with his powerful angels," those who do not know God and do not obey the gospel of our Lord Jesus will be judged (1:6–10). But Christ will not judge the earth "until the rebellion occurs and the man of lawlessness is revealed" (2:3, 6–12). Paul's teaching is a comfort for believers and a warning to unbelievers.

OVERVIEW

FOCUS	Discouraged Christians	Disturbed Christians	Disobedient Christians
REFERENCE	1:1 — 1:12	2:1 — 2:17	3:1 — 3:18
TOPICS	Commendation and Comfort	Confusion and Correction	Confidence and Comments
	Encouragement to the Persecuted	Explanation to the Perplexed	Exhortation to the Unproductive
	Appreciation	Agitation	Admonition
	Intervention and Intercession	Instructions and Identification	Injunctions and Idleness
LOCATION	Sent from Corinth to Thessalonica		
TIME	A.D. 51–52		

This letter begins with a salutation (1:1–2) and a word of thanks for the Thessalonians' growing faith and perseverance in the face of mounting opposition (1:3–4). Paul encourages them to endure, knowing that their sufferings will be repaid and that God will deal in righteousness with those who have been oppressing them (1:5–10). The first chapter ends with a prayer that God will fulfill his good purposes in their lives (1:11–13).

In view of some prophecy or a report falsely attributed to Paul, the church was being disrupted by the deception that the day of the Lord (1 Thessalonians 5:1–11) had come. Paul shows that this cannot be so until the man of lawlessness is revealed and the one who holds him back is taken out of the way (2:1–12). Paul adds a word of encouragement, tells his readers to stand firm and prays for them (2:13–17).

After a request for prayer on his behalf (3:1–5), Paul admonishes those in the church who have become idle and are living off the resources of others rather than earning their own provisions (3:6–15). Paul says the doctrine of Christ's return should stimulate responsible living rather than laziness. This brief epistle concludes with a benediction and greetings (3:16–18).

2 THESSALONIANS

1 Paul, Silas[a] and Timothy,[a]

To the church of the Thessalonians in God our Father and the Lord Jesus Christ:

2 Grace and peace to you from God the Father and the Lord Jesus Christ.[b]

Thanksgiving and Prayer

3 We ought always to thank God for you, brothers, and rightly so, because your faith is growing more and more, and the love every one of you has for each other is increasing.[c] 4 Therefore, among God's churches we boast[d] about your perseverance and faith[e] in all the persecutions and trials you are enduring.[f]

5 All this is evidence[g] that God's judgment is right, and as a result you will be counted worthy of the kingdom of God, for which you are suffering. 6 God is just: He will pay back trouble to those who trouble you[h] 7 and give relief to you who are troubled, and to us as well. This will happen when the Lord Jesus is revealed from heaven in blazing fire with his powerful angels.[i] 8 He will punish those who do not know God[j] and do not obey the gospel of our Lord Jesus.[k] 9 They will be punished with everlasting destruction[l] and shut out from the presence of the Lord and from the majesty of his power[m] 10 on the day[n] he comes to be glorified[o] in his holy people and to be marveled at among all those who have believed. This includes you, because you believed our testimony to you.[p]

11 With this in mind, we constantly pray for you, that our God may count you worthy[q] of his calling, and that by his power he may fulfill every good purpose of yours and every act prompted by your faith.[r] 12 We pray this so that the name of our Lord Jesus may be glorified in you,[s] and you in him, according to the grace of our God and the Lord Jesus Christ.[b]

The Man of Lawlessness

2 Concerning the coming of our Lord Jesus Christ and our being gathered to him,[t] we ask you, brothers, 2 not to become easily unsettled or alarmed by some prophecy, report or letter[u] supposed to have come from us, saying that the day of the Lord[v] has already come. 3 Don't let anyone deceive you[w] in any way, for ⌊that day will not come⌋ until the rebellion occurs and the man of lawlessness[c] is revealed,[x] the man doomed to destruction. 4 He will oppose and will exalt himself over everything that is called God[y] or is worshiped, so that he sets himself up in God's temple, proclaiming himself to be God.[z]

5 Don't you remember that when I

1:1 [a] Ac 16:1; 1Th 1:1 **1:2** [b] Ro 1:7 **1:3** [c] 1Th 3:12 **1:4** [d] 2Co 7:14 [e] 1Th 1:3 [f] 1Th 2:14 **1:5** [g] Php 1:28 **1:6** [h] Col 3:25; Rev 6:10 **1:7** [i] 1Th 4:16; Jude 14 **1:8** [j] Gal 4:8 [k] Ro 2:8 **1:9** [l] Php 3:19; 2Pe 3:7 [m] 2Th 2:8 **1:10** [n] 1Co 3:13 [o] Jn 17:10 [p] 1Co 1:6 **1:11** [q] ver 5 [r] 1Th 1:3 **1:12** [s] Php 2:9-11 **2:1** [t] Mk 13:27; 1Th 4:15-17 **2:2** [u] 2Th 3:17 [v] 1Co 1:8 **2:3** [w] Eph 5:6-8 [x] Da 7:25; 8:25; 11:36; Rev 13:5,6 **2:4** [y] 1Co 8:5 [z] Isa 14:13,14; Eze 28:2

a *1* Greek *Silvanus,* a variant of *Silas* **b** *12* Or *God and Lord, Jesus Christ* **c** *3* Some manuscripts *sin*

1:3–4

PROMISE 5

ACCENTUATE THE POSITIVE

Sometimes it's hard to know how to affirm others honestly. In the opening lines of his letter to the Thessalonians, Paul gives a great example for us to follow. He obviously considered thanksgiving a duty as well as a privilege—a reflection of God's goodness in the lives of other believers.

Even though Paul wrote this letter to correct the Thessalonian churches on a number of practical and theological matters, he still began by finding and accentuating the positive in the lives of these church members. We'll do well to follow Paul's lead with our Christian brothers and sisters.

For the next Promise 5 reading go to page 1338.

1:5–10

PROMISE 7

SEPARATION

Paul's words to the Thessalonian church in the first two chapters have been interpreted in various ways by sincere and faithful Christians throughout the centuries. One fact that is not open to interpretation, however, is what Paul outlines in these few verses. Make no mistake about it, the day will come when those who have rejected Jesus Christ will be punished and forever separated from the Lord and from those who have believed in Jesus' saving power.

Paul's discussion fills us today with a particular urgency to reach out to those who are lost. On the day of judgment, there will be no middle ground. Are you doing all you can to make sure others know about that?

For the next Promise 7 reading go to page 1345.

was with you I used to tell you these
things? 6And now you know what is
holding him back, so that he may be
revealed at the proper time. 7For the
secret power of lawlessness is already
at work; but the one who now holds it
back will continue to do so till he is
taken out of the way. 8And then the
lawless one will be revealed, whom
the Lord Jesus will overthrow with
the breath of his mouth[a] and destroy
by the splendor of his coming. 9The
coming of the lawless one will be in
accordance with the work of Satan displayed in all kinds of counterfeit miracles, signs and wonders,[b] 10and in every sort of evil that deceives those who
are perishing.[c] They perish because
they refused to love the truth and so be
saved. 11For this reason God sends
them[d] a powerful delusion so that
they will believe the lie 12and so that all
will be condemned who have not believed the truth but have delighted in
wickedness.[e]

Stand Firm

13But we ought always to thank God
for you, brothers loved by the Lord,
because from the beginning God
chose you**a**[f] to be saved[g] through the
sanctifying work of the Spirit[h] and
through belief in the truth. 14He called
you to this through our gospel, that you
might share in the glory of our Lord
Jesus Christ. 15So then, brothers, stand
firm[i] and hold to the teachings**b** we
passed on to you,[j] whether by word of
mouth or by letter.
16May our Lord Jesus Christ himself
and God our Father, who loved us[k]
and by his grace gave us eternal encouragement and good hope, 17en-
courage[l] your hearts and strength-
en[m] you in every good deed and word.

2:16–17

PROMISE 1

POWER SOURCE

In the midst of a sometimes harsh letter to a church that had strayed, Paul prays a blessing of kindness and hope. These words shine in this letter like a ray of sun breaking through clouds on a rainy day.

Paul's letters to the early churches are sprinkled with these brief prayers and words of encouragement. They helped his original readers (and us as well) keep an eternal perspective on their everyday lives. As you continue through Paul's letters, look for these verses and ponder what they mean for your life today.

For the next Promise 1 reading go to page 1334.

2:8 [a]Isa 11:4; Rev 19:15 **2:9** [b]Mt 24:24; Jn 4:48 **2:10** [c]1Co 1:18 **2:11** [d]Ro 1:28 **2:12** [e]Ro 1:32 **2:13** [f]Eph 1:4 [g]1Th 5:9 [h]1Pe 1:2 **2:15** [i]1Co 16:13 [j]1Co 11:2 **2:16** [k]Jn 3:16 **2:17** [l]1Th 3:2 [m]2Th 3:3

3:1 [n]1Th 4:1 [o]1Th 5:25 [p]1Th 1:8 **3:2** [q]Ro 15:31 **3:3** [r]1Co 1:9 [s]Mt 5:37 **3:4** [t]2Co 2:3 **3:5** [u]1Ch 29:18 **3:6** [v]1Co 5:4 [w]Ro 16:17 [x]ver 7,11 [y]1Co 11:2 **3:7** [z]1Co 4:16 **3:8** [a]Ac 18:3; Eph 4:28 **3:9** [b]1Co 9:4-14 [c]ver 7 **3:10** [d]1Th 3:4 [e]1Th 4:11 **3:11** [f]ver 6,7; 1Ti 5:13 **3:12** [g]1Th 4:1 [h]1Th 4:11; Eph 4:28 **3:13** [i]Gal 6:9 **3:14** [j]ver 6 **3:15** [k]Gal 6:1; 1Th 5:14 **3:16** [l]Ro 15:33 [m]Ru 2:4 **3:17** [n]1Co 16:21 **3:18** [o]Ro 16:20

Request for Prayer

3 Finally, brothers,[n] pray for us[o]
that the message of the Lord[p] may
spread rapidly and be honored, just as
it was with you. 2And pray that we may
be delivered from wicked and evil
men,[q] for not everyone has faith. 3But
the Lord is faithful,[r] and he will
strengthen and protect you from the
evil one.[s] 4We have confidence[t] in
the Lord that you are doing and will
continue to do the things we command. 5May the Lord direct your
hearts[u] into God's love and Christ's
perseverance.

1 →PG. 1334
5 →PG. 1338

Warning Against Idleness

6In the name of the Lord Jesus
Christ,[v] we command you, brothers,
to keep away from[w] every brother who
is idle[x] and does not live according
to the teaching**c** you received from
us.[y] 7For you yourselves know how
you ought to follow our example.[z] We
were not idle when we were with you,
8nor did we eat anyone's food without
paying for it. On the contrary, we
worked[a] night and day, laboring and
toiling so that we would not be a burden to any of you. 9We did this, not
because we do not have the right to
such help,[b] but in order to make ourselves a model for you to follow.[c]
10For even when we were with you,[d]
we gave you this rule: "If a man will not
work,[e] he shall not eat."
11We hear that some among you are
idle. They are not busy; they are busybodies.[f] 12Such people we command
and urge in the Lord Jesus Christ[g] to
settle down and earn the bread they
eat.[h] 13And as for you, brothers, never
tire of doing what is right.[i]
14If anyone does not obey our instruction in this letter, take special
note of him. Do not associate with
him,[j] in order that he may feel
ashamed. 15Yet do not regard him as an
enemy, but warn him as a brother.[k]

3 →PG. 1333
7 →PG. 1337

Final Greetings

16Now may the Lord of peace[l] himself give you peace at all times and in
every way. The Lord be with all of
you.[m]
17I, Paul, write this greeting in my
own hand,[n] which is the distinguishing mark in all my letters. This is how
I write.
18The grace of our Lord Jesus Christ
be with you all.[o]

a *13* Some manuscripts *because God chose you as his firstfruits* **b** *15* Or *traditions* **c** *6* Or *tradition*

1 TIMOTHY

AT A GLANCE

Key Principle: Spiritual leadership requires a commitment to sound doctrine, pure living and a determination to have an effective influence on others.
Author: Paul
Time and Place: ~A.D. 63–65 / Sent from Macedonia to Ephesus
Key Verses: 1:18; 3:15–16; 6:11–14

BENEFIT

First Timothy is full of specific principles of leadership and holy living, and is particularly relevant to people who are in positions of spiritual influence. This extremely practical book touches on issues of doctrine, public worship, the problem of false teaching, the treatment of various groups within the church, wealth, contentment and personal integrity.

SETTING

Paul's two letters to Timothy and his letter to Titus are collectively known as the Pastoral Epistles because they deal with issues of overseeing and shepherding local churches. While the authenticity of these three epistles has been challenged by many critics since the nineteenth century, none of the challenges is substantial enough to justify the conclusion that someone other than Paul wrote them. The early church was sensitive to forgeries, and Paul himself was concerned about this problem (2 Thessalonians 2:2; 3:17). These letters are full of personal details and are compatible with the character and teachings of Paul that mark Paul's other epistles.

These letters do not fit against the background of the book of Acts, since they were written after Paul's release from his first Roman imprisonment (Acts 28). The last years of Paul's life must be reconstructed from clues provided in these epistles. It appears that in spite of his statement in Acts 20:25, Paul did return to Ephesus. Timothy joined him there and stayed while Paul moved on to Macedonia (1:3). Paul wrote this letter to Timothy when he realized his return to Ephesus might be delayed (3:14–15).

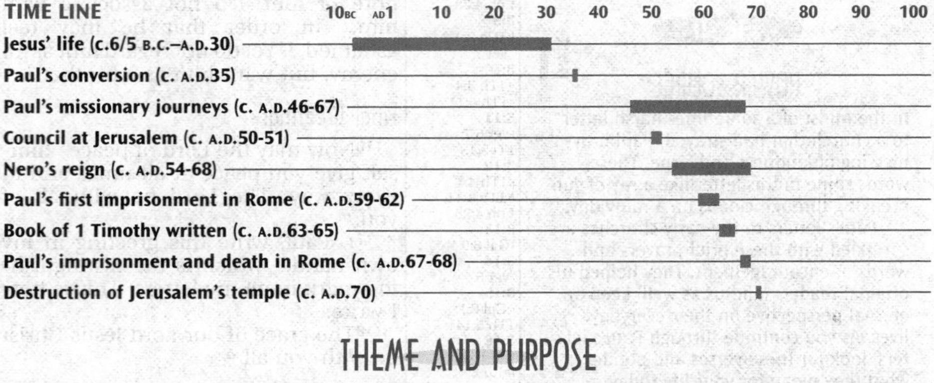

THEME AND PURPOSE

Paul's purpose in writing this epistle to his disciple Timothy is clear in 3:14–15: "Although I hope to come to you soon, I am writing you these instructions so that, if I am delayed, you will know how people ought to conduct themselves in God's household, which is the church of the living God, the pillar and foundation of the truth." This letter is really a leadership manual that Paul designed to guide Timothy on a number of specific issues: personal godliness and development of his spiritual gifts, worship in the churches, defending apostolic doctrine in the face of false teaching, the treatment of widows and elders, the temptations of wealth and faithfulness to his calling.

UNIQUE CONTRIBUTION

The books of 1 Timothy, 2 Timothy and Titus were Paul's only recorded letters to individuals (his letter to Philemon was addressed to several people). As the last of Paul's letters in Scripture, 1 Timothy and Titus were written after his first imprisonment, and 2 Timothy was written during his second imprisonment near the end of his life. While 1 Timothy is a personal letter, it is written in an authoritative tone in light of Timothy's leadership responsibilities during Paul's absence. Since Paul wrote this letter to his trusted and personal associate, it refers to doctrine without developing it and encourages Timothy to stand firm in the truth. This epistle contains the Bible's clearest and most explicit directions for church organization and administration.

The Pastoral Epistles refer to people who are found nowhere else in the New Testament, and the expression, "here is a trustworthy saying" (1:15; 3:1; 4:9; 2 Timothy 2:11; Titus 3:8) is unique to these epistles.

CHRIST IN 1 TIMOTHY

First Timothy presents Christ Jesus as the "one mediator between God and men" who gave himself as a ransom for all people (2:5). Possibly referring to an early confession, Paul summarizes Christ's person and ministry in these words: "Beyond all question, the mystery of godliness is great: He appeared in a body, was vindicated by the Spirit, was seen by angels, was preached among the nations, was believed on in the world, was taken up in glory" (3:16). Christ Jesus came into the world to save sinners, and he is the Savior of all men—especially of those who believe (1:15; 4:10). It is in him that we find strength, mercy, faith, love, salvation, hope, godliness and contentment (1:12–14; 2:3–6; 4:10; 6:6).

OVERVIEW

FOCUS	Reminders	Regulations	Responsibilities		
REFERENCE	1:1-20	2:1–3:16	4:1-16	5:1-25	6:1-21
TOPICS	Doctrine	Directions	Defense	Duties	
	Warning	Worship	Wisdom	Widows	Wealth
	Charge	Church	Counsel and Conduct		
LOCATION	Sent from Macedonia to Ephesus				
TIME	~A.D. 63–65				

Paul begins his letter by warning his young associate about how false teachers misuse the law of Moses (1:3–11). He looks back to his dramatic conversion to Christ and encourages Timothy to fulfill his own God-ordained purpose by fighting the good fight (1:12–20).

Turning to matters of church worship and leadership, Paul stresses that the men of the church should be leaders in prayer (2:1–8) and that the women should be characterized by inner godliness (2:9–15). He then lists the qualifications for overseers in 3:1–7 (in the early church, the titles of bishop and elder referred to the same office; Acts 20:17, 28; Titus 1:5, 7) and the qualifications for deacons in 3:8–13.

In view of the influence that false teachers had, Paul exhorts Timothy to counter error with the truth of the gospel and to set an example of purity in life and doctrine as he continues to use his spiritual gift (4:1–16). Paul then gives specific instructions on how the church should provide for widows and for the elders who direct the affairs of the church (5:1–25). After a word about those who are slaves (6:1–2), Paul condemns the false teaching that godliness is a means to financial gain, affirming instead that contentment is more valuable than material abundance (6:3–10). He concludes this epistle with a charge to Timothy to fight the good fight of the faith (6:11–16) and a final word about those who are rich in this present world (6:17–21).

1 TIMOTHY

1 Paul, an apostle of Christ Jesus by the command of God[a] our Savior and of Christ Jesus our hope,[b]

2To Timothy[c] my true son[d] in the faith:

Grace, mercy and peace from God the Father and Christ Jesus our Lord.

Warning Against False Teachers of the Law

3 →PG. 1337

3As I urged you when I went into Macedonia, stay there in Ephesus[e] so that you may command certain men not to teach false doctrines[f] any longer 4nor to devote themselves to myths[g] and endless genealogies. These promote controversies[h] rather than God's work—which is by faith. 5The goal of this command is love, which comes from a pure heart[i] and a good conscience and a sincere faith.[j] 6Some have wandered away from these and turned to meaningless talk. 7They want to be teachers of the law, but they do not know what they are talking about or what they so confidently affirm.

8We know that the law is good[k] if one uses it properly. 9We also know that law[a] is made not for the righteous but for lawbreakers and rebels,[l] the ungodly and sinful, the unholy and irreligious; for those who kill their fathers or mothers, for murderers, 10for adulterers and perverts, for slave traders and liars and perjurers—and for whatever else is contrary to the sound doctrine[m] 11that conforms to the glorious gospel of the blessed God, which he entrusted to me.[n]

The Lord's Grace to Paul

12I thank Christ Jesus our Lord, who has given me strength,[o] that he considered me faithful, appointing me to his service. 13Even though I was once a blasphemer and a persecutor[p] and a violent man, I was shown mercy because I acted in ignorance and unbelief.[q] 14The grace of our Lord was poured out on me abundantly,[r] along with the faith and love that are in Christ Jesus.[s]

15Here is a trustworthy saying[t] that deserves full acceptance: Christ Jesus came into the world to save sinners—of whom I am the worst. 16But for that very reason I was shown mercy[u] so that in me, the worst of sinners, Christ Jesus might display his unlimited patience as an example for those who would believe on him and receive eternal life. 17Now to the King[v] eternal, immortal, invisible,[w] the only God, be honor and glory for ever and ever. Amen.[x]

2 →PG. 1337

18Timothy, my son, I give you this instruction in keeping with the prophecies once made about you,[y] so that by following them you may fight the good fight,[z] 19holding on to faith and a good conscience. Some have rejected

1:1 [a]Tit 1:3 [b]Col 1:27
1:2 [c]Ac 16:1 [d]2Ti 1:2; Tit 1:4
1:3 [e]Ac 18:19 [f]Gal 1:6,7
1:4 [g]1Ti 4:7; Tit 1:14 [h]1Ti 6:4
1:5 [i]2Ti 2:22 [j]2Ti 1:5
1:8 [k]Ro 7:12
1:9 [l]Gal 3:19
1:10 [m]2Ti 4:3; Tit 1:9
1:11 [n]Gal 2:7
1:12 [o]Php 4:13
1:13 [p]Ac 8:3 [q]Ac 26:9
1:14 [r]Ro 5:20 [s]2Ti 1:13
1:15 [t]1Ti 3:1; 2Ti 2:11; Tit 3:8
1:16 [u]ver 13
1:17 [v]Rev 15:3 [w]Col 1:15 [x]Ro 11:36
1:18 [y]1Ti 4:14 [z]2Ti 2:3

[a] 9 Or *that the law*

1:2

PROMISE 2

FATHER AND SON

While Paul never speaks of having a wife or children, we know that he did have many spiritual children. Both here and in other places Paul refers to Timothy as a "son in the faith" (see 1:18 and 1 Corinthians 4:17). And the faith, encouragement and support Paul provided to this spiritual son would do any biological father proud.

Paul was a wonderful teacher and a mentor to Timothy, a young convert who proved his mettle as he followed Paul wherever the apostle went. Six times Paul mentions that Timothy was with him on his missionary journeys. And when Paul asked him to work at the church in Ephesus, this young man proved himself again.

Timothy's leadership in the church came at a critical time in history. God called Timothy, and others like him, to pick up where Paul and the other apostles left off. Although the task of ministering to a congregation was (and still is) difficult, Timothy faithfully took up the challenge and, through the Spirit's power, the early church flourished.

If you are a single man, consider which role you might be called to fill in your church community. Are there any young men in your circle of influence who are in need of a spiritual mentor? Or are you being called, as Timothy was, to learn from another person in preparation for a position of leadership and ministry?

For the next Promise 2 reading go to page 1343.

these and so have shipwrecked their faith.[a] [20]Among them are Hymenaeus[b] and Alexander,[c] whom I have handed over to Satan[d] to be taught not to blaspheme.

Instructions on Worship

1 →PG. 1345

2 I urge, then, first of all, that requests, prayers, intercession and thanksgiving be made for everyone— [2]for kings and all those in authority,[e] that we may live peaceful and quiet lives in all godliness and holiness. [3]This is good, and pleases God our Savior, [4]who wants[f] all men[g] to be saved and to come to a knowledge of the truth.[h] [5]For there is one God[i] and one mediator[j] between God and men, the man Christ Jesus, [6]who gave himself as a ransom for all men—the testimony[k] given in its proper time.[l] [7]And for this purpose I was appointed a herald and an apostle—I am telling the truth, I am not lying[m]—and a teacher[n] of the true faith to the Gentiles.[o]

[8]I want men everywhere to lift up holy hands[p] in prayer, without anger or disputing.

[9]I also want women to dress modestly, with decency and propriety, not with braided hair or gold or pearls or expensive clothes,[q] [10]but with good deeds, appropriate for women who profess to worship God.

[11]A woman should learn in quietness and full submission.[r] [12]I do not permit a woman to teach or to have authority over a man; she must be silent. [13]For Adam was formed first, then Eve.[s] [14]And Adam was not the one deceived; it was the woman who was deceived and became a sinner.[t] [15]But women[a] will be saved[b] through childbearing—if they continue in faith, love[u] and holiness with propriety.

Overseers and Deacons

3 Here is a trustworthy saying:[v] If anyone sets his heart on being an overseer,[c][w] he desires a noble task. [2]Now the overseer must be above reproach,[x] the husband of but one wife, temperate, self-controlled, respectable, hospitable,[y] able to teach,[z] [3]not given to drunkenness, not violent but gentle, not quarrelsome,[a] not a lover of money.[b] [4]He must manage his own family well and see that his children obey him with proper respect.[c] [5](If anyone does not know how to manage his own family, how can he take care of God's church?)[d] [6]He must not be a recent convert, or he may become conceited[e] and fall under the same judgment as the devil. [7]He must also have a good reputation with outsiders, so that he will not fall into disgrace and into the devil's trap.[f]

[8]Deacons,[g] likewise, are to be men worthy of respect, sincere, not indulging in much wine,[h] and not pursuing dishonest gain. [9]They must keep hold of the deep truths of the faith with a clear conscience.[i] [10]They must first be tested; and then if there is nothing against them, let them serve as deacons.

[11]In the same way, their wives[d] are to be women worthy of respect, not malicious talkers[j] but temperate and trustworthy in everything.

[12]A deacon must be the husband of but one wife and must manage his children and his household well.[k] [13]Those who have served well gain an excellent standing and great assurance in their faith in Christ Jesus. 4 →PG. 1338

[14]Although I hope to come to you

2:1-5

PROMISE 1

BIG PRAYER

When Paul thought of prayer, he didn't think small. He said our prayers should be for "everyone." We should pray for kings (presidents) and other national and local leaders. And yes, this includes those duly elected officials whom we voted against in the last election.

Paul knew that prayer has power to change things—big things. Not in vain do godly men pray for national and world peace. God has control over national and international affairs, and it's in times of peace that followers of Jesus can quietly pursue a life of holiness.

Another prayer that Paul said we should pray is that individuals who don't know Jesus Christ—both those who lead and otherwise—will be saved. Paul emphasized that God wants to see all people come to a saving knowledge of Jesus (see also Ezekiel 18:31–32).

Because you have the privilege of drawing near to God, take some time now and go to him in prayer. And remember to think big. Pray for your local and national government leaders. Pray for peace in this world. Pray that many might come to a saving knowledge of Jesus. Remember, "the prayer of a righteous man is powerful and effective" (James 5:16).

For the next Promise 1 reading go to page 1344.

1:19 [a]1Ti 6:21
1:20 [b]2Ti 2:17 [c]2Ti 4:14 [d]1Co 5:5
2:2 [e]Ezr 6:10; Ro 13:1
2:4 [f]Eze 18:23,32 [g]Tit 2:11 [h]2Ti 2:25
2:5 [i]Ro 3:29,30 [j]Gal 3:20
2:6 [k]1Co 1:6 [l]1Ti 6:15
2:7 [m]Ro 9:1 [n]2Ti 1:11 [o]Ac 9:15; Eph 3:7,8
2:8 [p]Ps 134:2; Lk 24:50
2:9 [q]1Pe 3:3
2:11 [r]1Co 14:34
2:13 [s]Ge 2:7,22; 1Co 11:8
2:14 [t]Ge 3:1-6,13; 2Co 11:3
2:15 [u]1Ti 1:14
3:1 [v]1Ti 1:15 [w]Ac 20:28
3:2 [x]Tit 1:6-8 [y]Ro 12:13 [z]2Ti 2:24
3:3 [a]2Ti 2:24 [b]Heb 13:5; 1Pe 5:2
3:4 [c]Tit 1:6
3:5 [d]1Co 10:32
3:6 [e]1Ti 6:4
3:7 [f]2Ti 2:26
3:8 [g]Php 1:1 [h]Tit 2:3
3:9 [i]1Ti 1:19
3:11 [j]2Ti 3:3; Tit 2:3
3:12 [k]ver 4

---

a 15 Greek *she*   b 15 Or *restored*
c 1 Traditionally *bishop*; also in verse 2
d 11 Or *way, deaconesses*

TIMOTHY

A Man Who Conquered His Fear

NO FEAR! You find this slogan on hats, shirts, bumper stickers—you name it. This has been a popular motto of those who are currently in their twenties and early thirties. Many of these people seem to feel that if they say, "No Fear" loud enough and often enough, they will indeed overcome fear. But in reality, we all have fears that cannot be overcome by mottoes and slogans. Anxieties can immobilize us. Yet, we have an example of someone who made "No Fear" a reality in his life. His name is Timothy.

The Power of the Gospel

Timothy lived in the city of Lystra. Though Lystra and the surrounding regions embraced pagan religions, Timothy had been faithfully reared in the Jewish faith from the time he was a young child (2 Timothy 3:15). When Paul and Barnabas first visited Lystra, Timothy probably saw them and heard the gospel message. The message rang true in Timothy's heart, and he became a believer.

However, not all the people in Lystra accepted Paul's teaching. A group of hostile individuals who had rejected Paul's message in Antioch followed Paul and Barnabas to Lystra. They turned the crowds against these two men. Grabbing Paul, they stoned him and, when they thought he was dead, dragged him to the outskirts of the city (Acts 14:19).

How frightening this experience must have been for young Timothy! He lived among these people, and now he too was a believer. Would his neighbors stone him as well? Timothy was probably tempted to hide his faith and become a "Secret Service Christian."

But the believers gathered around Paul's bruised body, and he was miraculously healed (14:20). In this way, Timothy probably saw firsthand the incredible power of the gospel and witnessed God's ability to sustain the believers even under severe persecution.

The Brothers' Influence

When Paul later returned to Lystra with Silas, Timothy had already developed an outstanding reputation—"the brothers at Lystra and Iconium spoke well of him" (16:2). The term "brothers" probably refers to the elders of the churches in these two cities. As Timothy grew up in his faith, he would have been able to look up to mature Christian men in the church at Lystra as examples. Timothy needed these male role models in his life, since it appears his father was a Gentile unbeliever (16:1).

Timothy needed strong Christian brothers who would be on his team when times got tough, men who would encourage him to face and overcome his fears. Under their leadership, Timothy's faith grew strong. And as Paul prepared to travel to Galatia, he invited Timothy to join him and Silas as their companion in ministry (16:3).

Growth in the Faith

These three men traveled and ministered together in many cities. But after they reached Athens, Paul and Silas decided to send Timothy back to Thessalonica (1 Thessalonians 3:2). They wanted to know how the new believers were doing. And even though Timothy was still a bit unsure of ministering by himself, Paul and Silas were confident of Timothy's spiritual and emotional growth and ability. They believed he was ready for this challenging task, and they sent him off alone.

When Timothy returned from Thessalonica, he brought a glowing report about the Thessalonians' "faith and love" (3:6). But something else had happened. Timothy had handled this assignment well and proved to Paul and Silas—and to himself—that he was now ready for more responsibility.

Later in their travels, Paul challenged Timothy once again. When they arrived in Ephesus, they discovered that certain men were teaching false doctrines and leading the believers astray. Paul needed to travel on to Macedonia, but urged Timothy to stay in Ephesus to correct the problem.

Timothy was hesitant at first to accept this assignment alone. Most of the men who were teaching these false doctrine were older than he was. Knowing Timothy's fear, Paul wrote and encouraged him not to be intimidated by age (1 Timothy 4:12). Timothy accepted Paul's challenge, and once again saw God's power in his life.

Keeping Our Perspective

Many of us struggle with fear, anxiety and intimidation, as did Timothy. Yet Timothy became a man God greatly used. The apostle Paul, his mentor, encouraged Timothy throughout his ministry. This

encouragement built Timothy up in his self-confidence and in his faith in Jesus Christ, which is the source for that self-confidence.

Paul addressed Timothy's fears directly when he reminded him that "God did not give us a spirit of timidity, but a spirit of power, of love and of self-discipline" (2 Timothy 1:7). Paul urged Timothy not to let his fears keep him from being an effective servant of Christ. He encouraged Timothy to rely on God's grace and to stand firm "like a good soldier of Christ Jesus" (2:3).

Do you have an encourager, a mentor like Paul in your own life? As Christian men we all need mentors to remind us that Jesus never fails. We need to relate to others who have overcome their fears through God's help and strength. Are you encouraging and mentoring others? How can you help another brother learn to have "No Fear" through the power of the gospel?

—Dr. Gene Getz

soon, I am writing you these instructions so that, 15if I am delayed, you will
know how people ought to conduct
themselves in God's household, which
is the church[l] of the living God, the
pillar and foundation of the truth.
16Beyond all question, the mystery[m] of
godliness is great:

He[a] appeared in a body,[b n]
  was vindicated by the Spirit,
was seen by angels,
  was preached among the
    nations,[o]
was believed on in the world,
  was taken up in glory.[p]

Instructions to Timothy

4 The Spirit[q] clearly says that in later
times[r] some will abandon the faith
and follow deceiving spirits[s] and
things taught by demons. 2Such teachings come through hypocritical liars,
whose consciences have been seared
as with a hot iron.[t] 3They forbid people to marry[u] and order them to abstain from certain foods,[v] which God
created[w] to be received with thanksgiving[x] by those who believe and who
know the truth. 4For everything God
created is good,[y] and nothing is to be
rejected if it is received with thanksgiving, 5because it is consecrated by the
word of God and prayer.

6If you point these things out to the
brothers, you will be a good minister of
Christ Jesus, brought up in the truths of
the faith[z] and of the good teaching
3 →PG. 1338
that you have followed. 7Have nothing
to do with godless myths and old
wives' tales;[a] rather, train yourself to
7 →PG. 1339
be godly. 8For physical training is of
some value, but godliness has value for
all things,[b] holding promise for both
the present life[c] and the life to come.
9This is a trustworthy saying[d] that
deserves full acceptance 10(and for this
we labor and strive), that we have put
our hope in the living God, who is the
Savior of all men, and especially of
those who believe.

11Command and teach these
things.[e] 12Don't let anyone look down
on you because you are young, but set
an example[f] for the believers in
speech, in life, in love, in faith[g] and in
purity. 13Until I come, devote yourself
to the public reading of Scripture, to
preaching and to teaching. 14Do not
neglect your gift, which was given you
through a prophetic message[h] when
the body of elders laid their hands on
you.[i]

15Be diligent in these matters; give
yourself wholly to them, so that everyone may see your progress. 16Watch
your life and doctrine closely. Persevere in them, because if you do, you
will save both yourself and your hearers.

Advice About Widows, Elders and Slaves

5 Do not rebuke an older man[j]
harshly,[k] but exhort him as if he
2 →PG. 1343
were your father. Treat younger men[l]
as brothers, 2older women as mothers,
and younger women as sisters, with
absolute purity.

3Give proper recognition to those
widows who are really in need.[m] 4But
if a widow has children or grandchildren, these should learn first of all to
put their religion into practice by caring for their own family and so repaying their parents and grandparents,[n]
for this is pleasing to God.[o] 5The widow who is really in need[p] and left all
alone puts her hope in God[q] and continues night and day to pray[r] and to
ask God for help. 6But the widow who
lives for pleasure is dead even while

3:15 [l]ver 5; Eph 2:21
3:16 [m]Ro 16:25 [n]Jn 1:14 [o]Col 1:23 [p]Mk 16:19
4:1 [q]Jn 16:13 [r]2Ti 3:1 [s]2Th 2:3
4:2 [t]Eph 4:19
4:3 [u]Heb 13:4 [v]Col 2:16 [w]Ge 1:29 [x]Ro 14:6
4:4 [y]Ro 14:14-18
4:6 [z]1Ti 1:10
4:7 [a]2Ti 2:16
4:8 [b]1Ti 6:6 [c]Ps 37:9,11; Mk 10:29,30
4:9 [d]1Ti 1:15
4:11 [e]1Ti 5:7; 6:2
4:12 [f]Tit 2:7; 1Pe 5:3 [g]1Ti 1:14
4:14 [h]1Ti 1:18 [i]Ac 6:6; 2Ti 1:6
5:1 [j]Tit 2:2 [k]Lev 19:32 [l]Tit 2:6
5:3 [m]ver 5,16
5:4 [n]Eph 6:1,2 [o]1Ti 2:3
5:5 [p]ver 3,16 [q]1Co 7:34; 1Pe 3:5 [r]Lk 2:37

[a]16 Some manuscripts *God* [b]16 Or *in the flesh*

4:7–15

PROMISE 3

SPIRITUAL WORKOUT

Paul was fond of comparing spiritual discipline to physical discipline. In our fitness-focused age, this comparison is especially effective. Most of us know what it takes for athletes at any level—from high school through professional—to excel in their sports: dedication, discipline, commitment and, of course, practice.

As if he were a spiritual coach, Paul said he expected Timothy to train himself in godly living with this same singular focus. Some might have thought that Timothy's youth (he may have been in his 30s) would limit the scope of his ministry. But Paul believed that Timothy could still be an example to others in "speech, in life, in love, in faith and in purity." As young professional athletes can sometimes teach veteran players a thing or two, so Paul was looking to Timothy to set a positive example for both older and younger believers.

If you're a young man, take Paul's words to heart. Examine how you can pursue discipline and godliness in your spiritual life. Practice often—spend time in prayer and in God's Word. Then go after the unique ministry to which God has called you. And if you're not sure how God wants you to minister, get involved in your church and God will show you.

For the next Promise 3 reading go to page 1339.

4 →PG. 1343

she lives.[s] 7Give the people these instructions,[t] too, so that no one may be open to blame. 8If anyone does not provide for his relatives, and especially for his immediate family, he has denied[u] the faith and is worse than an unbeliever.

9No widow may be put on the list of widows unless she is over sixty, has been faithful to her husband,[a] 10and is well known for her good deeds,[v] such as bringing up children, showing hospitality, washing the feet[w] of the saints, helping those in trouble[x] and devoting herself to all kinds of good deeds.

11As for younger widows, do not put them on such a list. For when their sensual desires overcome their dedication to Christ, they want to marry. 12Thus they bring judgment on themselves, because they have broken their first pledge. 13Besides, they get into the habit of being idle and going about from house to house. And not only do they become idlers, but also gossips and busybodies,[y] saying things they ought not to. 14So I counsel younger widows to marry,[z] to have children, to manage their homes and to give the enemy no opportunity for slander.[a] 15Some have in fact already turned away to follow Satan.[b]

16If any woman who is a believer has widows in her family, she should help them and not let the church be burdened with them, so that the church can help those widows who are really in need.[c]

5 →PG. 1343

17The elders[d] who direct the affairs of the church well are worthy of double honor,[e] especially those whose work is preaching and teaching. 18For the Scripture says, "Do not muzzle the ox while it is treading out the grain,"[b][f] and "The worker deserves his wages."[c][g] 19Do not entertain an accusation against an elder[h] unless it is brought by two or three witnesses.[i] 20Those who sin are to be rebuked[j] publicly, so that the others may take warning.[k]

21I charge you, in the sight of God and Christ Jesus[l] and the elect angels, to keep these instructions without partiality, and to do nothing out of favoritism.

22Do not be hasty in the laying on of hands,[m] and do not share in the sins of others.[n] Keep yourself pure.

23Stop drinking only water, and use a little wine[o] because of your stomach and your frequent illnesses.

24The sins of some men are obvious, reaching the place of judgment ahead of them; the sins of others trail behind them. 25In the same way, good deeds are obvious, and even those that are not cannot be hidden.

3 →PG. 1338

6 All who are under the yoke of slavery should consider their masters worthy of full respect,[p] so that God's name and our teaching may not be slandered.[q] 2Those who have believing masters are not to show less respect for them because they are brothers.[r] Instead, they are to serve them even better, because those who benefit from their service are believers, and dear to them. These are the things you are to teach and urge on them.[s]

Love of Money

3If anyone teaches false doctrines[t] and does not agree to the sound instruction[u] of our Lord Jesus Christ and to godly teaching, 4he is conceited and understands nothing. He has an unhealthy interest in controversies and quarrels about words[v] that result in envy, strife, malicious talk, evil suspicions 5and constant friction between men of corrupt mind, who have been robbed of the truth[w] and who think that godliness is a means to financial gain.

3 →PG. 1343

6But godliness with contentment[x] is great gain.[y] 7For we brought nothing into the world, and we can take nothing out of it.[z] 8But if we have food and clothing, we will be content with that.[a] 9People who want to get rich[b] fall into temptation and a trap[c] and

5:6 [s]Lk 15:24
5:7 [t]1Ti 4:11
5:8 [u]2Pe 2:1; Jude 4; Tit 1:16
5:10 [v]Ac 9:36; 1Ti 6:18; 1Pe 2:12 [w]Lk 7:44 [x]ver 16
5:13 [y]2Th 3:11
5:14 [z]1Co 7:9 [a]1Ti 6:1
5:15 [b]Mt 4:10
5:16 [c]ver 3-5
5:17 [d]Ac 11:30 [e]Php 2:29; 1Th 5:12
5:18 [f]Dt 25:4; 1Co 9:7-9 [g]Lk 10:7; Lev 19:13; Dt 24:14,15; Mt 10:10; 1Co 9:14
5:19 [h]Ac 11:30 [i]Mt 18:16
5:20 [j]2Ti 4:2; Tit 1:13 [k]Dt 13:11
5:21 [l]1Ti 6:13; 2Ti 4:1
5:22 [m]Ac 6:6 [n]Eph 5:11
5:23 [o]1Ti 3:8
6:1 [p]Eph 6:5; Tit 2:9; 1Pe 2:18 [q]Tit 2:5,8
6:2 [r]Phm 16 [s]1Ti 4:11
6:3 [t]1Ti 1:3 [u]1Ti 1:10
6:4 [v]2Ti 2:14
6:5 [w]Tit 1:15
6:6 [x]Php 4:11; Heb 13:5 [y]1Ti 4:8
6:7 [z]Job 1:21; Ecc 5:15
6:8 [a]Heb 13:5
6:9 [b]Pr 15:27 [c]1Ti 3:7

[a]9 Or *has had but one husband*
[b]18 Deut. 25:4 [c]18 Luke 10:7

5:1-3

PROMISE 5

FAMILY LIFE

One of the great gifts God gives believers is a loving family—God's family, the church. Yet, like any family, we as church members sometimes need to be reminded how to properly treat each other. With that in mind, Paul gives special instruction in how believers are to treat in particular younger or older members of the congregation. His exhortation is that we treat all members with courtesy, respect, gentleness and absolute purity as we spur them on to full participation in church life.

Consider Paul's words and evaluate how you regard all the members of your congregation. Determine to express to them the same kindness you would want others to show your own mother, father, brother or sister.

For the next Promise 5 reading go to page 1366.

into many foolish and harmful desires that plunge men into ruin and destruction. [10]For the love of money[d] is a root of all kinds of evil. Some people, eager for money, have wandered from the faith[e] and pierced themselves with many griefs.

Paul's Charge to Timothy

[11]But you, man of God,[f] flee from all this, and pursue righteousness, godliness, faith, love,[g] endurance and gentleness. [12]Fight the good fight[h] of the faith. Take hold of[i] the eternal life to which you were called when you made your good confession in the presence of many witnesses. [13]In the sight of God, who gives life to everything, and of Christ Jesus, who while testifying before Pontius Pilate[j] made the good confession, I charge you[k] [14]to keep this command without spot or blame until the appearing of our Lord Jesus Christ, [15]which God will bring about in his own time—God, the blessed[l] and only Ruler,[m] the King of kings and Lord of lords,[n] [16]who alone is immortal[o] and who lives in unapproachable light, whom no one has seen or can see.[p] To him be honor and might forever. Amen.

7 →PG. 1345

[17]Command those who are rich in this present world not to be arrogant nor to put their hope in wealth,[q] which is so uncertain, but to put their hope in God,[r] who richly provides us with everything for our enjoyment.[s] [18]Command them to do good, to be rich in good deeds,[t] and to be generous and willing to share.[u] [19]In this way they will lay up treasure for themselves[v] as a firm foundation for the coming age, so that they may take hold of the life that is truly life.

[20]Timothy, guard what has been entrusted[w] to your care. Turn away from godless chatter[x] and the opposing ideas of what is falsely called knowledge, [21]which some have professed and in so doing have wandered from the faith.[y]

Grace be with you.[z]

6:10 [d]1Ti 3:3 [e]Jas 5:19
6:11 [f]2Ti 3:17 [g]2Ti 2:22
6:12 [h]1Co 9:25,26; 1Ti 1:18 [i]Php 3:12
6:13 [j]Jn 18:33-37 [k]1Ti 5:21
6:15 [l]1Ti 1:11 [m]1Ti 1:17 [n]Rev 17:14; 19:16
6:16 [o]1Ti 1:17 [p]Jn 1:18
6:17 [q]Lk 12:20,21 [r]1Ti 4:10 [s]Ac 14:17
6:18 [t]1Ti 5:10 [u]Ro 12:8,13
6:19 [v]Mt 6:20
6:20 [w]2Ti 1:12,14 [x]2Ti 2:16
6:21 [y]2Ti 2:18 [z]Col 4:18

6:10

PROMISE 3

SERVANT OR MASTER?

The Bible never says money is evil. Why? Because, in itself, it isn't. Here Paul makes the distinction between money itself and *human love of money,* which he describes as a foundational evil. When we long for money, we run the risk of wandering away from Jesus. Jesus echoed the same idea when he said we can't love both God and Money (Matthew 6:24).

Remember, money is a great servant, but a terrible master.

For the next Promise 3 reading go to page 1346.

2 TIMOTHY

AT A GLANCE

Key Principle: In times of opposition and adversity, we must make full use of our spiritual resources in Christ and endure hardship by depending on the Holy Spirit's power.
Author: Paul
Time and Place: A.D. 67–68 / Sent from Rome to Ephesus
Key Verses: 2:2–4, 15; 3:14–17; 4:2

BENEFIT

Second Timothy contains Paul's parting words to his younger associate, Timothy. By "listening in," we can gain wise and godly counsel that is as relevant to us today as it was to Timothy in the first century. This is a powerful manual for spiritual combat. It encourages us to be diligent and courageous and to make the most of the opportunities that God has given us.

SETTING

The "Setting" section in the introduction to 1 Timothy offers a brief comment on the contemporary challenge to Paul's authorship of the Pastoral Epistles. The assertion that these letters were fabricated in the second century would be especially damaging to 2 Timothy, since it would render this highly personal letter virtually meaningless.

After his release from his first Roman imprisonment, Paul ministered in Macedonia, Asia (Ephesus) and Crete. When he wrote to the Romans years earlier, Paul expressed his intention to go to the western province of Spain (Romans 15:24, 28), and early church tradition supports that he did so during these years of freedom, probably in A.D. 64–66. He returned to Greece and Asia (4:13, 20) and may have been arrested in Troas, where he left his precious scrolls and parchments (4:13, 15).

With the burning of Rome in July of A.D. 64, Nero declared Christianity an illicit religion in the Roman Empire, and Paul's enemies were able to get him arrested (fearing for their own lives, his friends in Asia deserted him; 1:15). His second Roman imprisonment took place in A.D. 67–68; he wrote this epistle to Timothy during the time after his first defense before the Imperial Court (1:8–17; 2:9; 4:16–17). Unlike the Prison Epistles (Ephesians, Philippians, Colossians and Philemon) which he wrote during his first imprisonment, Paul did not expect to be released from this second imprisonment (4:6–8, 18). Therefore, this letter urges Timothy to come quickly before winter (4:9, 21). According to tradition, Paul was beheaded west of Rome on the Ostian Way.

Timothy was evidently converted when Paul came to Lystra on his first missionary journey (Acts 14:8–20), and joined Paul when he visited Lystra again on his second missionary journey (Acts 16:1–3). He was ordained to the ministry (1 Timothy 4:14; 2 Timothy 1:6) and served as a devoted associate with Paul in a number of cities during Paul's second and third missionary journeys. He was with Paul during his first Roman imprisonment, and after his release, Paul sent him to minister in Ephesus (1 Timothy 1:3). Hebrews 13:23 says that Timothy was imprisoned and released, but does not tell us where.

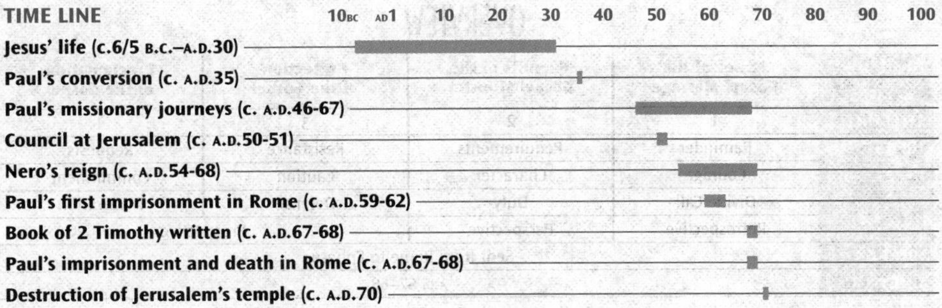

THEME AND PURPOSE

Paul's letters to Timothy indicate that this man was youthful, frequently ill and timid (1 Timothy 4:12; 5:23; 2 Timothy 1:7), but that he was a trustworthy and gifted teacher. Paul wrote this letter to encourage Timothy to remain faithful to his calling and to stand firm in the face of obstacles to the gospel message. Timothy encountered a number of hardships, including external persecution and the problems of false doctrine and dissension within the churches. Paul's instruction was especially urgent in light of the fact that he was nearing the end of his ministry and needed to entrust important areas into Timothy's care. Paul specifically challenged Timothy to boldly proclaim the gospel of Christ Jesus, even if doing so meant increased persecution. Paul's immediate purpose in writing this epistle was to urge Timothy and Mark to join him in Rome and to bring his scrolls, parchments and the cloak that he left in Troas.

UNIQUE CONTRIBUTION

As Paul's last recorded epistle, 2 Timothy serves as his final testament to the world. He reviews Christ's faithfulness in his past, and commissions Timothy to carry on the good work of proclaiming Christ in the present. He also looks ahead to the future when he will be rewarded with the crown of righteousness after being brought safely to the Lord's heavenly kingdom. This letter is full of sharp imperatives that underscore the spiritual conflict Timothy was facing. In this conflict, Timothy must depend upon the Holy Scriptures, and this letter contains the clearest Biblical statement of their inspiration (3:16–17; 4:2). Second Timothy has become a manual for encouraging and equipping Christian workers over the centuries.

CHRIST IN 2 TIMOTHY

"Remember Jesus Christ, raised from the dead, descended from David" (2:8). In Christ, we have been saved and called to a holy life because of his own purpose and grace (1:9). "This grace was given us in Christ Jesus before the beginning of time, but it has now been revealed through the appearing of our Savior, Christ Jesus, who has destroyed death and has brought life and immortality to light through the gospel" (1:9–10). We who have trusted in Christ have died with him, and we will also live with him (2:11). Those who long for his appearing will receive the crown of righteousness (4:8).

OVERVIEW

FOCUS	Power of the Gospel Message	Pursuits of the Gospel Minister	Protection of the Gospel	Proclamation of the Gospel
REFERENCE	1	2	3	4
TOPICS	Reminder	Requirements	Resistance	Requests
	Courage	Character	Caution	Commitment
	Divine Call	Duty	Defense	Declaration
	Retrospective	Perspective	Prospective	
LOCATION	Sent from Rome to Ephesus			
TIME	A.D. 67–68			

After a brief greeting, Paul reviews Timothy's conversion and reminds him to fan into flame the gift he received and to overcome timidity with God's power (1:1–7). He invites Timothy to join with him in suffering for the gospel, knowing that Christ will guard whatever he entrusts to him (1:8–14). Paul commends Onesiphorus, who supported him and sought him out in Rome when other believers abandoned him (1:15–18). He then exhorts Timothy to reproduce the message of Christ and to be disciplined in service, strong in the word of truth and to avoid godless chatter, youthful lusts and fruitless quarrels (2:1–26).

Paul predicts a time of increasing arrogance, rebelliousness and vulnerability to spiritual deception (3:1–9) and warns Timothy that he can expect increased persecution for the sake of following Christ (3:10–13). He reminds Timothy to stay strong in Scripture and to use it effectively in this spiritual combat (3:14–17). Finally, Paul charges Timothy to preach and teach the Word, to correct, rebuke and encourage and to endure hardship and do the work of an evangelist (4:1–5). Paul concludes this epistle with thoughts about his future reward with Christ and with personal remarks and requests (4:6–22).

2 TIMOTHY

1 Paul, an apostle of Christ Jesus by the will of God,[a] according to the promise of life that is in Christ Jesus,[b]

2 To Timothy,[c] my dear son:[d]

Grace, mercy and peace from God the Father and Christ Jesus our Lord.

Encouragement to Be Faithful

3 I thank God,[e] whom I serve, as my forefathers did, with a clear conscience, as night and day I constantly remember you in my prayers.[f] 4 Recalling your tears,[g] I long to see you,[h] so that I may be filled with joy. 5 I have been reminded of your sincere faith,[i] which first lived in your grandmother Lois and in your mother Eunice[j] and, I am persuaded, now lives in you also.

4 →PG. 1370

6 For this reason I remind you to fan into flame the gift of God, which is in you through the laying on of my hands.[k] 7 For God did not give us a spirit of timidity,[l] but a spirit of power, of love and of self-discipline.

8 So do not be ashamed[m] to testify about our Lord, or ashamed of me his prisoner.[n] But join with me in suffering for the gospel,[o] by the power of God, 9 who has saved us and called[p] us to a holy life—not because of anything we have done but because of his own purpose and grace. This grace was given us in Christ Jesus before the beginning of time, 10 but it has now been revealed[q] through the appearing of our Savior, Christ Jesus, who has destroyed death[r] and has brought life and immortality to light through the gospel. 11 And of this gospel I was appointed a herald and an apostle and a teacher.[s] 12 That is why I am suffering as I am. Yet I am not ashamed, because I know whom I have believed, and am convinced that he is able to guard[t] what I have entrusted to him for that day.[u]

13 What you heard from me, keep[v] as the pattern of sound teaching, with faith and love in Christ Jesus.[w] 14 Guard the good deposit that was entrusted to you—guard it with the help of the Holy Spirit who lives in us.[x]

3 →PG. 1344

15 You know that everyone in the province of Asia has deserted me,[y] including Phygelus and Hermogenes.

16 May the Lord show mercy to the household of Onesiphorus,[z] because he often refreshed me and was not ashamed of my chains. 17 On the contrary, when he was in Rome, he searched hard for me until he found me. 18 May the Lord grant that he will find mercy from the Lord on that day! You know very well in how many ways he helped me[a] in Ephesus.

2 You then, my son, be strong[b] in the grace that is in Christ Jesus. 2 And the things you have heard me say[c] in the presence of many witnesses[d] entrust to reliable men who will also be qualified to teach others. 3 Endure hardship with us like a good soldier[e] of Christ Jesus. 4 No one serving as a soldier gets involved in civilian affairs—he wants to please his commanding officer. 5 Similarly, if anyone competes as an athlete, he does not receive the victor's crown[f] unless he competes according to the rules. 6 The hardworking farmer should be the first to receive a share of the crops. 7 Reflect on what I am saying, for the Lord will give you insight into all this.

2 →PG. 1349
5 →PG. 1365

8 Remember Jesus Christ, raised from the dead,[g] descended from David.[h] This is my gospel,[i] 9 for which I am suffering[j] even to the point of being chained like a criminal. But God's word is not chained. 10 Therefore I endure everything[k] for the sake of the elect, that they too may obtain the sal-

1:1 [a] 2Co 1:1 [b] Eph 3:6; 1Ti 6:19
1:2 [c] Ac 16:1 [d] 1Ti 1:2
1:3 [e] Ro 1:8 [f] Ro 1:10
1:4 [g] Ac 20:37 [h] 2Ti 4:9
1:5 [i] 1Ti 1:5 [j] Ac 16:1
1:6 [k] 1Ti 4:14
1:7 [l] Ro 8:15
1:8 [m] Mk 8:38; Ro 1:16 [n] Eph 3:1 [o] 2Ti 2:3,9; 4:5
1:9 [p] Ro 8:28
1:10 [q] Eph 1:9 [r] 1Co 15:26,54
1:11 [s] 1Ti 2:7
1:12 [t] 1Ti 6:20 [u] ver 18
1:13 [v] Tit 1:9 [w] 1Ti 1:14
1:14 [x] Ro 8:9
1:15 [y] 2Ti 4:10,11,16
1:16 [z] 2Ti 4:19
1:18 [a] Heb 6:10
2:1 [b] Eph 6:10
2:2 [c] 2Ti 1:13 [d] 1Ti 6:12
2:3 [e] 1Ti 1:18
2:5 [f] 1Co 9:25
2:8 [g] Ac 2:24 [h] Mt 1:1 [i] Ro 2:16
2:9 [j] Ac 9:16
2:10 [k] Col 1:24

2:2

PROMISE 2

PASSING THE BATON

If you've ever seen or run in a relay race, you know that the most critical part is not the start or the sprint; it's the hand-off. The baton carrier has only a short time to place the baton securely in the next runner's hand. No matter how fast the sprinters run, the race can be lost if the hand-off is bungled.

As Christian men, we're all running in a relay—a spiritual relay. Our job is to hand off Biblical truth to faithful men who will take the truth, apply it to their lives, and then hand it off to others.

It could be you don't feel qualified to run in such a race. Maybe you feel like too slow a learner, or too awkward with Biblical truth. If so, find someone who can hand off that truth to you. After some practice, you'll be ready to pass that truth to others. Remember, you only have to be one step ahead of someone to disciple them.

For the next Promise 2 reading go to page 1360.

vation that is in Christ Jesus, with eternal glory.[l]
11 Here is a trustworthy saying:

If we died with him,
we will also live with him;[m]
12 if we endure,
we will also reign with him.[n]
If we disown him,
he will also disown us;[o]
13 if we are faithless,
he will remain faithful,[p]
for he cannot disown himself.

A Workman Approved by God

14 Keep reminding them of these
things. Warn them before God against
quarreling about words;[q] it is of no
value, and only ruins those who listen.
15 Do your best to present yourself to
God as one approved, a workman who
does not need to be ashamed and who
correctly handles the word of truth.[r]
16 Avoid godless chatter,[s] because
those who indulge in it will become
more and more ungodly. 17 Their teaching will spread like gangrene. Among
them are Hymenaeus[t] and Philetus,
18 who have wandered away from the
truth. They say that the resurrection
has already taken place, and they destroy the faith of some.[u] 19 Nevertheless, God's solid foundation stands

3 →PG. 1345

2:10 [l] 2Co 4:17 **2:11** [m] Ro 6:2-11 **2:12** [n] Ro 8:17; 1Pe 4:13 [o] Mt 10:33 **2:13** [p] Nu 23:19; Ro 3:3 **2:14** [q] 1Ti 6:4 **2:15** [r] Eph 1:13; Jas 1:18 **2:16** [s] Tit 3:9 **2:17** [t] 1Ti 1:20 **2:18** [u] 1Ti 1:19

3:16–17

PROMISE 1

OUR GOD-BREATHED BIBLE

No other document has affected world history more significantly than the Bible. And nothing is more important to your faith development than this book. These pages contain all God has chosen to reveal to humanity about Jesus and the plan of salvation. Because the Bible is fully inspired, you can trust it without question and accept its guidelines without wavering.

In order to underline the absolute reliability of the Bible, the apostle Paul said, "*All* Scripture is God-breathed." Every part of the Bible is dependable because God supervised the human authors who, using their own personalities, recorded without error his revelation to man. Because the Scriptures are the breath of God, they partake of God's nature. Therefore, in the original manuscripts, the Bible is flawless.

There are two kinds of evidence to consider when evaluating the reliability of a historical document: internal and external. Internal evidence deals with what the Bible says about itself. External evidence involves proof outside the Bible that validates its credibility.

The internal evidence of the Bible's inspiration is overwhelming. It was written over hundreds of years by over 40 different authors, yet maintains an amazing internal consistency as it outlines God's plan of redemption for humanity. The Bible's authors believed their writing was inspired by God (2 Peter 1:20–21). Many of the New Testament writers were eyewitnesses who honestly and accurately recorded what they had seen (Luke 1:1–3; 2 Peter 1:16; 1 John 1:3). Those who challenge the nature of Scripture need to consider what Jesus said. When he spoke of the Old Testament, Jesus made it clear he believed every detail of it was inspired (Luke 11:51; 24:44; John 10:31–36).

External evidence also verifies the reliability of the Biblical text. Consider for a moment how the number and quality of the existing New Testament documents, in the original language, compare with other pieces of literature. Take, for instance, the ancient text of Homer's *Illiad*, which in ancient times was read, studied, written about, and memorized much as was the Bible. Researchers comparing the textual variations of the earliest manuscripts of both the New Testament and the *Illiad* have discovered that fully five percent of the text of Homer's work is in dispute. But of the New Testament, they have found that only 400 words of the original manuscript are in question—that comes out to a total of one-half of one percent in text variation throughout the centuries! Of these variations, it has been said that "No fundamental doctrine of the Christian faith rests on a disputed reading" (Josh McDowell, *Evidence that Demands A Verdict*, San Bernardino, CA: Here's Life Publishers, 1972, 1979, p. 45).

Additionally, the *Illiad* was written in about 900 B.C., and the earliest surviving manuscripts are from 400 B.C.—a span of 500 years. On the other hand, archaeologists have discovered portions of the New Testament that date to 125 A.D., only a few decades after the original manuscripts were completed. Finally, only 643 ancient copies of the *Illiad* survive, whereas many thousands of documents support the New Testament's authenticity (*Evidence*, p. 43).

Further, no archaeological discovery has ever disproved something the Bible said. On the contrary, archaeological evidence has confirmed the teaching of the Bible (*Evidence*, p. 68). And on those occasions when the evidence seemed to question the reliability of the Bible, later discoveries validated the Biblical record.

The Bible is not only inspired, it's unlike any other book in every way. Through this book, its Author constantly empowers people according to his purposes. It's a living book because God's Spirit animates it (Hebrews 4:12).

Second Timothy 3:16 is a verse worthy of committing to memory. As you meditate on it, ask God to use his Word to "teach, reprove, correct and train" you in righteousness. One way to evaluate whether you're on track is to ask yourself, "What change is God's Word bringing about in my life today?"

For the next Promise 1 reading go to page 1351.

firm,[v] sealed with this inscription: "The Lord knows those who are his,"[a][w] and, "Everyone who confesses the name of the Lord[x] must turn away from wickedness."

20In a large house there are articles not only of gold and silver, but also of wood and clay; some are for noble purposes and some for ignoble.[y] **21**If a man cleanses himself from the latter, he will be an instrument for noble purposes, made holy, useful to the Master and prepared to do any good work.[z]

7 →PG. 1351

22Flee the evil desires of youth, and pursue righteousness, faith, love[a] and peace, along with those who call on the Lord out of a pure heart.[b] **23**Don't have anything to do with foolish and stupid arguments, because you know they produce quarrels. **24**And the Lord's servant must not quarrel; instead, he must be kind to everyone, able to teach, not resentful.[c] **25**Those who oppose him he must gently instruct, in the hope that God will grant them repentance leading them to a knowledge of the truth,[d] **26**and that they will come to their senses and escape from the trap of the devil,[e] who has taken them captive to do his will.

3 →PG. 1349

Godlessness in the Last Days

3 But mark this: There will be terrible times in the last days.[f] **2**People will be lovers of themselves, lovers of money,[g] boastful, proud,[h] abusive, disobedient to their parents,[i] ungrateful, unholy, **3**without love, unforgiving, slanderous, without self-control, brutal, not lovers of the good, **4**treacherous, rash, conceited,[j] lovers of pleasure rather than lovers of God— **5**having a form of godliness but denying its power. Have nothing to do with them.

6They are the kind who worm their way[k] into homes and gain control over weak-willed women, who are loaded down with sins and are swayed by all kinds of evil desires, **7**always learning but never able to acknowledge the truth. **8**Just as Jannes and Jambres opposed Moses,[l] so also these men oppose[m] the truth—men of depraved minds,[n] who, as far as the faith is concerned, are rejected. **9**But they will not get very far because, as in the case of those men,[o] their folly will be clear to everyone.

Paul's Charge to Timothy

10You, however, know all about my teaching,[p] my way of life, my purpose, faith, patience, love, endurance, **11**persecutions, sufferings—what kinds of things happened to me in Antioch,[q] Iconium and Lystra, the persecutions I endured.[r] Yet the Lord rescued me from all of them.[s] **12**In fact, everyone who wants to live a godly life in Christ Jesus will be persecuted,[t] **13**while evil men and impostors will go from bad to worse,[u] deceiving and being deceived. **14**But as for you, continue in what you have learned and have become convinced of, because you know those from whom you learned it,[v] **15**and how from infancy[w] you have known the holy Scriptures,[x] which are able to make you wise[y] for salvation through faith in Christ Jesus. **16**All Scripture is God-breathed[z] and is useful for teaching,[a] rebuking, correcting and training in righteousness, **17**so that the man of God[b] may be thoroughly equipped for every good work.[c]

1 →PG. 1358

4 In the presence of God and of Christ Jesus, who will judge the living and the dead,[d] and in view of his appearing and his kingdom, I give you this charge:[e] **2**Preach[f] the Word;[g] be prepared in season and out of season; correct, rebuke[h] and encourage—with great patience and careful instruction. **3**For the time will come when men will not put up with sound doctrine.[i] Instead, to suit their own desires, they will gather around them a great number of teachers to say what their itching ears want to hear. **4**They will turn their ears away from the truth and turn aside to myths.[j] **5**But you, keep your head in all situations, en-

2:19 [v]Isa 28:16 [w]Jn 10:14 [x]1Co 1:2 **2:20** [y]Ro 9:21 **2:21** [z]2Ti 3:17 **2:22** [a]1Ti 1:14; 6:11 [b]1Ti 1:5 **2:24** [c]1Ti 3:2,3 **2:25** [d]1Ti 2:4 **2:26** [e]1Ti 3:7 **3:1** [f]1Ti 4:1 **3:2** [g]1Ti 3:3 [h]Ro 1:30 [i]Ro 1:30 **3:4** [j]1Ti 3:6 **3:6** [k]Jude 4 **3:8** [l]Ex 7:11 [m]Ac 13:8 [n]1Ti 6:5 **3:9** [o]Ex 7:12 **3:10** [p]1Ti 4:6 **3:11** [q]Ac 13:14,50 [r]2Co 11:23-27 [s]Ps 34:19 **3:12** [t]Ac 14:22 **3:13** [u]2Ti 2:16 **3:14** [v]2Ti 1:13 **3:15** [w]2Ti 1:5 [x]Jn 5:39 [y]Ps 119:98,99 **3:16** [z]2Pe 1:20,21 [a]Ro 4:23,24 **3:17** [b]1Ti 6:11 [c]2Ti 2:21 **4:1** [d]Ac 10:42 [e]1Ti 5:21 **4:2** [f]1Ti 4:13 [g]Gal 6:6 [h]1Ti 5:20; Tit 1:13; 2:15 **4:3** [i]1Ti 1:10 **4:4** [j]1Ti 1:4

[a]*19* Num. 16:5 (see Septuagint)

4:1–2

PROMISE 7

RIGHT WORD, RIGHT TIME

Paul's words to Timothy in this passage apply to us today as well. We are to be students of God's Word so that in all times and in all situations we'll be ready with well-chosen, Biblically based words of correction, rebuke and encouragement. That doesn't mean we're called to be abrasive and insensitive so that others are turned off to God's truth. Instead, we need to be prepared to honestly and lovingly proclaim the truth of God's Word.

Ask God to help you know what to share from the Bible and when to share it. Remember Paul's exhortation—believers are to preach the Word with "great patience and careful instruction" (v. 2).

For the next Promise 7 reading go to page 1384.

dure hardship,[k] do the work of an evangelist,[l] discharge all the duties of your ministry.

6For I am already being poured out like a drink offering,[m] and the time has come for my departure.[n] **7**I have fought the good fight,[o] I have finished the race,[p] I have kept the faith. **8**Now there is in store for me[q] the crown of righteousness, which the Lord, the righteous Judge, will award to me on that day[r]—and not only to me, but also to all who have longed for his appearing.

Personal Remarks

9Do your best to come to me quickly, **10**for Demas,[s] because he loved this world,[t] has deserted me and has gone to Thessalonica. Crescens has gone to Galatia,[u] and Titus to Dalmatia. **11**Only Luke[v] is with me.[w] Get Mark[x] and bring him with you, because he is helpful to me in my ministry. **12**I sent Tychicus[y] to Ephesus. **13**When you come, bring the cloak that I left with Carpus at Troas, and my scrolls, especially the parchments.

14Alexander[z] the metalworker did me a great deal of harm. The Lord will repay him for what he has done.[a] **15**You too should be on your guard against him, because he strongly opposed our message.

16At my first defense, no one came to my support, but everyone deserted me. May it not be held against them.[b] **17**But the Lord stood at my side[c] and gave me strength, so that through me the message might be fully proclaimed and all the Gentiles might hear it.[d] And I was delivered from the lion's mouth. **18**The Lord will rescue me from every evil attack[e] and will bring me safely to his heavenly kingdom. To him be glory for ever and ever. Amen.[f]

Final Greetings

19Greet Priscilla[a] and Aquila[g] and the household of Onesiphorus. **20**Erastus[h] stayed in Corinth, and I left Trophimus[i] sick in Miletus. **21**Do your best to get here before winter.[j] Eubulus greets you, and so do Pudens, Linus, Claudia and all the brothers.

22The Lord be with your spirit.[k] Grace be with you.[l]

4:6–8

PROMISE 3

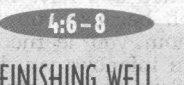

FINISHING WELL

As the apostle Paul faced death, he shared with Timothy how a man of God views his life as it comes to a close. When he said he was being poured out "like a drink offering," he referred to the Old Testament practice of offering gifts of wine to God. Two distinctive characteristics of drink offerings shed light on this metaphor. First, once the ritual began it continued until the entire offering had been made. Second, the drink was poured out until the vessel was empty; nothing was withheld.

Paul knew the process had begun by which he would offer his earthly life to the Lord. Here he indicated that his offering included every last bit of energy and vitality that he possessed. He was confident that he had done God's will to the best of his ability through the enabling of the Holy Spirit. He frequently compared the Christian life to a race; now he looked toward the reward that would come when he crossed that eternal finish line.

Paul finished the race of life well. As you reflect on his closing words to Timothy, contemplate what you might say to a family member, or a close friend, about your life at its end. Ask God for the grace you need to live every day in a way that will allow you to run in Christ's power and, eventually, to finish well.

For the next Promise 3 reading go to page 1349.

4:5 [k]2Ti 1:8 [l]Ac 21:8
4:6 [m]Php 2:17 [n]Php 1:23
4:7 [o]1Ti 1:18 [p]1Co 9:24
4:8 [q]Col 1:5 [r]2Ti 1:12
4:10 [s]Col 4:14 [t]1Jn 2:15 [u]Ac 16:6
4:11 [v]Col 4:14 [w]2Ti 1:15 [x]Ac 12:12
4:12 [y]Ac 20:4
4:14 [z]Ac 19:33 [a]Ro 12:19
4:16 [b]Ac 7:60
4:17 [c]Ac 23:11 [d]Ac 9:15
4:18 [e]Ps 121:7 [f]Ro 11:36
4:19 [g]Ac 18:2
4:20 [h]Ac 19:22 [i]Ac 20:4
4:21 [j]ver 9
4:22 [k]Gal 6:18; Phm 25 [l]Col 4:18

[a] *19* Greek *Prisca,* a variant of *Priscilla*

TITUS

AT A GLANCE

Key Principle: God's gift of salvation in Christ Jesus should transform not only personal character, but also the way believers relate to one another.
Author: Paul
Time and Place: A.D. 63–65 / Sent from Greece (perhaps Corinth) to Crete
Key Verses: 1:5; 2:1; 3:5, 8

BENEFIT

This epistle is a concise manual for how assemblies of brothers and sisters in Christ should conduct themselves. Titus 1 and 1 Timothy 3 are critical to the organization of the local church; they outline God's requirements for the leaders of the body of believers. Titus provides us with instruction on the ordination of elders, dealing with false teachers, the roles of different groups within the church and the relationship between sound doctrine and godly behavior.

SETTING

While Titus is not mentioned in Acts, Paul's epistles tell us that he was a convert (1:4) and trusted associate ("my partner and fellow worker"; 2 Corinthians 8:23). Second Corinthians tells us that Titus accompanied Paul on his third missionary journey, since Paul sent him to Corinth three separate times during that period. After Paul's release from his first Roman imprisonment, Paul took Titus to Crete and left him there for a time to strengthen the ministry (1:5). Paul may have been in Corinth when he wrote this letter to Titus around A.D. 63.

Paul urged Titus to join him in Nicopolis (western Greece) after he sent Artemas or Tychicus to Crete (3:12). Titus evidently did so, and he was later with Paul during his second imprisonment before going from Rome to Dalmatia (2 Timothy 4:10).

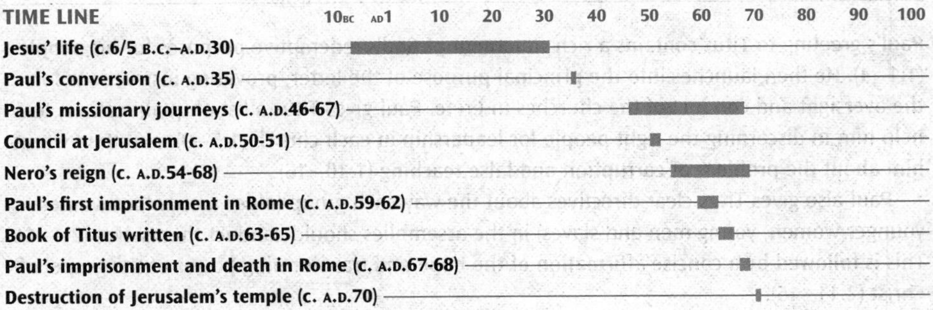

THEME AND PURPOSE

The inhabitants of Crete were notorious in the first century for immorality and deception (1:12–13), and leaders in those churches had to stress godly conduct in the lives of the new converts. This letter, therefore, focuses on proper behavior within the various groups in the churches, and encourages Titus to instruct the people on the truths of the gospel that will lead to spiritual maturity while avoiding "foolish controversies." "The reason I left you in Crete was that you might straighten out what was left unfinished and appoint elders in every town, as I directed you" (1:5). Paul wrote this epistle to follow through on these instructions by giving Titus a list of qualifications to use in this process (1:5–9; compare 1 Timothy 3). He emphasizes the need for sound doctrine and illustrates this with three important summaries of the faith (1:1–3; 2:11–14; 3:3–7).

UNIQUE CONTRIBUTION

Titus is less personal and more official than 1 Timothy, possibly because Titus needed clear instructions more than personal encouragement. In both letters, Paul instructed his associates to establish leadership and to teach sound doctrine in their respective areas (Timothy: Ephesus and other cities in the province of Asia; Titus: the cities on the island of Crete). Both letters discuss doctrine and conduct, but false teaching seemed to be a bigger problem in Ephesus, while immoral conduct was the greater concern on Crete. Nevertheless, the brief theological statements in Titus make a significant contribution to the Biblical teaching on the doctrine of grace.

CHRIST IN TITUS

In Titus, Paul presents Christ as the supreme manifestation of God's grace, mercy and redemptive purposes. It is by his grace that we are justified, and through him we have become heirs who enjoy the hope of eternal life. Our hope is in "the glorious appearing of our great God and Savior, Jesus Christ" (2:13).

OVERVIEW

FOCUS	Protection of Sound Doctrine	Preaching of Sound Doctrine	Practice of Sound Doctrine
REFERENCE	1	2	3
TOPICS	Governing Conduct	Group Conduct	General Conduct
	Organization and Offenders	Operation	Obedience
	Battle	Behavior	Belief
	Elders and Error	Example	Effort
LOCATION	Sent from Greece (perhaps Corinth) to Crete		
TIME	A.D. 63–65		

Paul's greeting to Titus contains a rich statement of God's redemptive purposes for his people (1:1–4). He then launches into the principal purpose of the letter, providing instructions for the oversight and conduct of the churches in Crete. Paul gives Titus a list of qualifications to help him in discerning the right people for leadership in each church (1:5–9), and then warns him about the problem of corruption and false teaching (1:10–16).

Paul also gives Titus clear directives about the way each group (older men, older women, younger women, young men and slaves) in the assemblies should conduct themselves (2:1–10). This is followed by a concise affirmation of the hope and transforming power of the gospel of Christ (2:11–15).

After an exhortation concerning the general conduct of all believers (3:1–2), Paul gives a sublime summary of how God's kindness, love and mercy brought about our salvation through grace and not by works (3:3–7). Good works, however, should follow from this great act of redemption (3:8). This letter closes with instructions on dealing with divisive people (3:9–11) and some final remarks (3:12–15).

TITUS

1 Paul, a servant of God[a] and an apostle of Jesus Christ for the faith of God's elect and the knowledge of the truth[b] that leads to godliness— **2**a faith and knowledge resting on the hope of eternal life,[c] which God, who does not lie, promised before the beginning of time,[d] **3**and at his appointed season[e] he brought his word to light[f] through the preaching entrusted to me[g] by the command of God our Savior,[h]

4To Titus,[i] my true son in our common faith:

Grace and peace from God the Father and Christ Jesus our Savior.

Titus' Task on Crete

5The reason I left you in Crete[j] was that you might straighten out what was left unfinished and appoint[a] elders[k] in every town, as I directed you. **6**An elder must be blameless,[l] the husband of but one wife, a man whose children believe and are not open to the charge of being wild and disobedient. **7**Since an overseer[b][m] is entrusted with God's work,[n] he must be blameless—not overbearing, not quick-tempered, not given to drunkenness, not violent, not pursuing dishonest gain.[o] **8**Rather he must be hospitable,[p] one who loves what is good,[q] who is self-controlled, upright, holy and disciplined. **9**He must hold firmly[r] to the trustworthy message as it has been taught, so that he can encourage others by sound doctrine[s] and refute those who oppose it.

2 →PG. 1354

3 →PG. 1349

10For there are many rebellious people, mere talkers[t] and deceivers, especially those of the circumcision group.[u] **11**They must be silenced, because they are ruining whole households[v] by teaching things they ought not to teach—and that for the sake of dishonest gain. **12**Even one of their own prophets[w] has said, "Cretans[x] are always liars, evil brutes, lazy gluttons." **13**This testimony is true. Therefore, rebuke[y] them sharply, so that they will be sound in the faith[z] **14**and will pay no attention to Jewish myths[a] or to the commands[b] of those who reject the truth. **15**To the pure, all things are pure, but to those who are corrupted and do not believe, nothing is pure.[c] In fact, both their minds and consciences are corrupted. **16**They claim to know God, but by their actions they deny him.[d] They are detestable, disobedient and unfit for doing anything good.

What Must Be Taught to Various Groups

2 You must teach what is in accord with sound doctrine.[e] **2**Teach the older men to be temperate, worthy of respect, self-controlled, and sound in faith,[f] in love and in endurance.

3Likewise, teach the older women to be reverent in the way they live, not to be slanderers or addicted to much wine,[g] but to teach what is good. **4**Then they can train the younger women to love their husbands and children, **5**to be self-controlled and pure, to be busy at home, to be kind, and to be subject to their husbands,[h] so that no one will malign the word of God.[i]

6Similarly, encourage the young men[j] to be self-controlled. **7**In everything set them an example[k] by doing what is good. In your teaching show integrity, seriousness **8**and soundness of speech that cannot be condemned, so that those who oppose you may be ashamed because they have nothing bad to say about us.[l]

3 →PG. 1351

9Teach slaves to be subject to their masters in everything,[m] to try to

[a]5 Or *ordain* [b]7 Traditionally *bishop*

1:1 [a]Ro 1:1 [b]1Ti 2:4
1:2 [c]2Ti 1:1 [d]2Ti 1:9
1:3 [e]1Ti 2:6 [f]2Ti 1:10 [g]1Ti 1:11 [h]Lk 1:47
1:4 [i]2Co 2:13
1:5 [j]Ac 27:7 [k]Ac 11:30
1:6 [l]1Ti 3:2
1:7 [m]1Ti 3:1 [n]1Co 4:1 [o]1Ti 3:3,8
1:8 [p]1Ti 3:2 [q]2Ti 3:3
1:9 [r]1Ti 1:19 [s]1Ti 1:10
1:10 [t]1Ti 1:6 [u]11:2
1:11 [v]2Ti 3:6
1:12 [w]Ac 17:28 [x]Ac 2:11
1:13 [y]2Co 13:10 [z]Tit 2:2
1:14 [a]1Ti 1:4 [b]Col 2:22
1:15 [c]Ro 14:14,23
1:16 [d]1Jn 2:4
2:1 [e]1Ti 1:10
2:2 [f]Tit 1:13
2:3 [g]1Ti 3:8
2:5 [h]Eph 5:22 [i]1Ti 6:1
2:6 [j]1Ti 5:1
2:7 [k]1Ti 4:12
2:8 [l]1Pe 2:12
2:9 [m]Eph 6:5

1:5–9

PROMISE 3

CHARACTER CHECKLIST

What does a devoted Christian look like? You'd be hard pressed to find a better description than the one found here and in 1 Timothy 3:1–13. As you read over the traits of a church leader, remember that these traits describe a man's character as reflected in his lifestyle. Since that's the case, make these traits the target of your personal growth. Review them often and see how you measure up. If an area jumps out at you as one of personal weakness, determine to take the steps necessary to grow in that part of your life.

These qualities would make an excellent topic for discussion with your small group. Take one trait a week and discuss how it could be demonstrated in your life. Be as specific as you can, promise to pray for one another and agree to report back each week on how you're doing.

For the next Promise 3 reading go to page 1376.

TITUS

A Man Who Loved a Challenge

British explorer Sir Ernest Henry Shackleton (1874–1922) conducted an Antarctic expedition in 1900. The following advertisement in the London newspapers preceded this ill-fated journey: *Men Wanted For Hazardous Journey.* Small wages, bitter cold, long months of complete darkness, constant danger, safe return doubtful. Honor and recognition in case of success—Ernest Shackleton. The explorer was amazed by the overwhelming response to his ad.

Those men must have been descendants of Titus, for he was a man who loved a challenge. He appears to have been the type of person who could handle any difficult task. He worked alongside the apostle Paul, helping to confront some of the most troublesome problems any missionary will ever face. And Titus did it all willingly, welcoming and taking on every challenge!

Eager to Do God's Work

The Bible doesn't tell us where Paul first met Titus. However, it seems Paul was instrumental in Titus's conversion, since Paul identified him specifically as his "true son" in their "common faith" (Titus 1:4). At some point thereafter, Titus joined Paul's missionary team.

When Paul assigned Titus his first task, it was a big one. Titus was to hold the church at Corinth accountable for its financial giving. The Corinthians, like many Christians today, had difficulty following through in that area (1 Corinthians 16:1–2). Paul had already confronted them with their negligence. But when they failed to follow through again, Paul sent Titus to straighten them out.

Anyone who has ever raised money and confronted Christians on their financial stewardship knows how defensive people can become when money is the issue. However, Titus apparently thrived on such challenging assignments. In this situation, Titus responded "with much enthusiasm and on his own initiative" (2 Corinthians 8:17). Titus's eagerness helped resolve the stewardship problem in Corinth quickly.

Following Paul's first imprisonment, he again linked up with Titus as his missionary companion. Together, they tackled the pagan island of Crete, which was a difficult area of the world for sharing the gospel. God gave them success—people believed in Jesus for salvation, and churches were established in a number of towns. Paul felt the need to move on, but he left Titus behind to "straighten out what was left unfinished" in those churches (Titus 1:5).

Titus needed to appoint qualified elders and remove unqualified men from leadership positions. These false teachers were "ruining whole households by teaching things they ought not to teach—and that for the sake of dishonest gain" (1:11). Their motives were purely selfish and materialistic. Paul minced no words when he told Titus, "They must be silenced" (1:11). Titus was to give these false teachers only two warnings to stop their divisive teaching. If they refused to listen to his warnings, Titus was to "have nothing to do" with them (3:10).

Paul also instructed Titus to confront those people whose minds and consciences were corrupted (1:15). These were people who claimed to be believers, but their actions proved otherwise. Paul concluded that they were "detestable, disobedient and unfit for doing anything good" (1:16).

Clearly, this was a tough assignment! Only a strong Christian individual who could teach sound doctrine and "encourage and rebuke with all authority" (2:15) could take on this kind of responsibility. Titus was that kind of person, and with God's help, followed through on this confrontation in Crete.

It Takes All Kinds

There may come a time, regardless of your personality type, when you too may have to stand up for the truth. Confronting fellow Christians who are violating God's will is not an easy task, but it is sometimes necessary. Though Titus had to silence certain so-called "believers" because of their evil intentions, God's plan for dealing with people who are self-deceived or deceiving others is for us to always speak "the truth in love" (Ephesians 4:15). We must remember that in all confrontations we must not be quarrelsome, but rather "be kind to everyone, able to teach, not resentful" (2 Timothy 2:24). A servant's heart will dispel the antagonism of a confrontation.

Remember, no matter what your particular passion is in ministry, God has a place for you. Whether you're a Titus—a person who thrives on challenging situations—or someone who prefers to work behind the scenes, God wants to use your talents and gifts in his service. With that in mind, are you building on your strengths and overcoming your weaknesses? With God's help, you can do all things—even the most challenging things—through Christ, who gives you strength (Philippians 4:13).

—*Dr. Gene Getz*

please them, not to talk back to them,
10and not to steal from them, but to
show that they can be fully trusted, so
that in every way they will make the
teaching about God our Savior attractive.[n]

3 →PG. 1351

11For the grace of God that brings
salvation has appeared to all men.[o]
12It teaches us to say "No" to ungodliness and worldly passions,[p] and to
live self-controlled, upright and godly
lives[q] in this present age, **13**while we
wait for the blessed hope—the glorious
appearing of our great God and Savior,
Jesus Christ,[r] **14**who gave himself for
us to redeem us from all wickedness
and to purify for himself a people that
are his very own,[s] eager to do what is
good.[t]
15These, then, are the things you
should teach. Encourage and rebuke
with all authority. Do not let anyone
despise you.

Doing What Is Good

3 Remind the people to be subject
to rulers and authorities,[u] to be
obedient, to be ready to do whatever
is good,[v] **2**to slander no one,[w] to be
peaceable and considerate, and to
show true humility toward all men.
3At one time we too were foolish,
disobedient, deceived and enslaved by
all kinds of passions and pleasures. We
lived in malice and envy, being hated
and hating one another. **4**But when the
kindness[x] and love of God our Savior
appeared,[y] **5**he saved us, not because
of righteous things we had done,[z] but
because of his mercy. He saved us
through the washing of rebirth and renewal[a] by the Holy Spirit, **6**whom he
poured out on us[b] generously through
Jesus Christ our Savior, **7**so that, having
been justified by his grace,[c] we might
become heirs[d] having the hope[e] of
eternal life.[f] **8**This is a trustworthy

3 →PG. 1362

saying.[g] And I want you to stress these
things, so that those who have trusted
in God may be careful to devote them-

7 →PG. 1354

selves to doing what is good.[h] These
things are excellent and profitable for
everyone.
9But avoid foolish controversies and
genealogies and arguments and quarrels[i] about the law, because these are
unprofitable and useless. **10**Warn a divisive person once, and then warn him
a second time. After that, have nothing
to do with him.[j] **11**You may be sure
that such a man is warped and sinful;
he is self-condemned.

Final Remarks

12As soon as I send Artemas or Tychicus[k] to you, do your best to come to
me at Nicopolis, because I have decided to winter there.[l] **13**Do everything
you can to help Zenas the lawyer and
Apollos[m] on their way and see that
they have everything they need. **14**Our
people must learn to devote themselves to doing what is good,[n] in order
that they may provide for daily necessi-
ties and not live unproductive lives.
15Everyone with me sends you greetings. Greet those who love us in the
faith.[o]
Grace be with you all.[p]

2:10 [n]Mt 5:16
2:11 [o]1Ti 2:4
2:12 [p]Tit 3:3 [q]2Ti 3:12
2:13 [r]2Pe 1:1
2:14 [s]Ex 19:5 [t]Eph 2:10
3:1 [u]Ro 13:1 [v]2Ti 2:21
3:2 [w]Eph 4:31; 2Ti 2:24
3:4 [x]Eph 2:7 [y]Tit 2:11
3:5 [z]Eph 2:9 [a]Ro 12:2
3:6 [b]Ro 5:5
3:7 [c]Ro 3:24 [d]Ro 8:17 [e]Ro 8:24 [f]Tit 1:2
3:8 [g]1Ti 1:15 [h]Tit 2:14
3:9 [i]1Ti 1:4; 2Ti 2:14
3:10 [j]Ro 16:17
3:12 [k]Ac 20:4 [l]2Ti 4:9,21
3:13 [m]Ac 18:24
3:14 [n]ver 8
3:15 [o]1Ti 1:2 [p]Col 4:18

3:3–7

PROMISE **1**

180-DEGREE TURN

Here Paul gives us a timeless description of life without and life with Jesus Christ in our lives. He speaks of the kind of radical life transformation that characterizes many who have found Christ after years of living without him. And his words in this passage also challenge believers who have been raised in the faith to reexamine the basic concepts that comprise the foundation of their lives with Christ.

Paul said that Christ's presence in a man's life has the potential to turn him completely around. Make no mistake about it, Paul knew what he was talking about. Before his amazing experience on the road to Damascus (Acts 9:1–19), he had fostered hatred and evil. His life had been directed by a lifeless religious code, rather than by a living relationship with Christ. His example dramatically portrays what new life in Christ is all about; he repeatedly spoke about the freedom and wonder and hope that life includes.

People who follow Christ embark on a journey that takes them away from dedication to self and toward complete dedication to Christ. Make it your goal to prayerfully follow along that path, with the "hope of eternal life" (v. 7) providing perspective and inspiration.

For the next Promise 1 reading go to page 1358.

PHILEMON

AT A GLANCE

Key Principle: Our reconciliation with God should always lead to reconciliation with our brothers and sisters in Christ.
Author: Paul
Time and Place: A.D. 60–62 / Sent from Rome to Colosse
Key Verses: 10–11, 16–17

BENEFIT

Philemon is a brief but powerful testimony to the transforming power of faith, forgiveness and freedom in Christ. Transformation on this vertical level should result in transformation on the horizontal level of our relationships with others. This epistle teaches us that spiritual change produces social change.

SETTING

Philemon was converted by Paul's teaching (1–2), perhaps during a visit to Ephesus during Paul's third missionary journey. He lived in Colosse (1–2), a city Paul had not visited, and was probably a prominent citizen in view of his benevolence (5–7) and his ownership of a house that was large enough to be a meeting place for the church (2). Philemon had a slave named Onesimus who robbed him and escaped to Rome. Onesimus somehow came into contact with Paul during his first imprisonment (Acts 28:16–31). As a result, this runaway slave was converted to Christ and became highly useful to Paul.

When Paul wrote his epistle to the Colossians in A.D. 60–62, he sent Tychicus to deliver the letter and sent Onesimus along with Tychicus (Colossians 4:7–9; Philemon 12) so that the former slave could be restored to his former master. This letter was addressed to other members of the church in Colosse as well as Philemon so that it would have a broad impact.

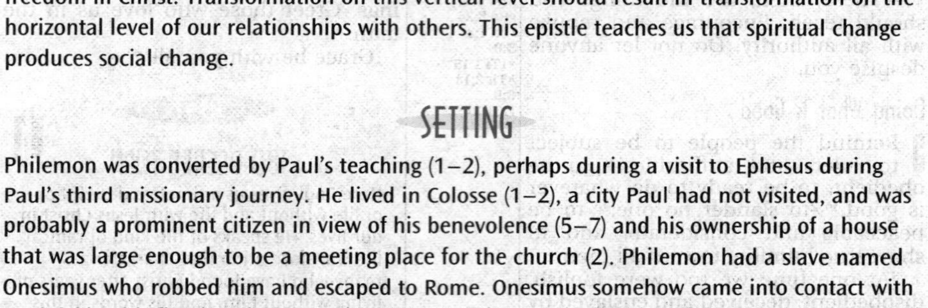

THEME AND PURPOSE

Paul's purpose in writing this letter was to appeal to Philemon on behalf of a man who was previously a useless slave, thief and runaway. Because of Onesimus's conversion, Paul argues that his character has been transformed and that his former master should regard him as a brother rather than a slave. Just as Philemon himself received grace and forgiveness in Christ, so he must extend the same to this new brother in the Lord. Paul urges Philemon to receive Onesimus just as he would receive the apostle himself, and even offers to cover Onesimus's debt.

UNIQUE CONTRIBUTION

Philemon, the shortest of Paul's epistles (334 words in the Greek text), is a masterpiece of tact and diplomacy in the way it approaches a very tense situation. This little note gives us insight into the apostle's courtesy, discretion and other-centered love as he takes up the cause of another brother in Christ. This warm and highly personal letter affirms Paul's relationship with Philemon before going on to make a bold request. He does not minimize the serious nature of Onesimus's offense, but stresses the basis for reconciliation—their joint relationship with Jesus Christ. Another personal and emphatic touch in Philemon is that, unlike his other epistles, Paul wrote this letter entirely in his own hand (19).

Philemon does not teach but does apply doctrine; this brief message of advocacy underscores the gospel's social implications and demonstrates that God does not show partiality (cf. Galatians 3:28; Colossians 3:11). The Biblical principles in this epistle provide a first-century basis for the renunciation of slavery.

CHRIST IN PHILEMON

Paul's letter to Philemon offers an analogy of the love, grace and forgiveness of Christ, and shows how these qualities should be applied to relationships with others. Just as Philemon benefited from forgiveness through the gospel, so he was now being called to forgive Onesimus. And just as Philemon was restored and entered into a new relationship with God through Christ, so he was to enter into a new relationship with Onesimus—no longer as a slave, but as a brother in Christ.

OVERVIEW

FOCUS	Philemon's Character	Onesimus' Conversion	Paul's Confidence
REFERENCE	1 7	8 16	17 25
TOPICS	Faith	Forgiveness	Friendship
	Prayer	Plea	Pledge
	Praise	Petition	Promise
	Gratitude	Grace	Grant
LOCATION	Sent from Rome to Colossae		
TIME	A.D. 60–62		

Paul addresses this epistle not only to Philemon, but also to the other members of the church in Colosse (1–2). As in his other letters, his salutation combines the customary Greek ("grace") and Hebrew ("peace") greetings of his day and ties them to the message of the gospel (3). Paul then expresses his thanksgiving for Philemon's faith, love and ministry (4–7).

Moving into the occasion of the letter, Paul appeals to Philemon on behalf of Onesimus and stresses how difficult it was to send him away (8–16). Paul requests that Philemon welcome Onesimus just as he would welcome himself, and offers any necessary restitution (17–19). Paul expresses his confidence that Philemon will do so, and requests that Philemon prepare a guest room for him after his release from prison (20–22). He concludes this letter with closing greetings and a benediction (23–25).

PHILEMON

1Paul, a prisoner[a] of Christ Jesus, and Timothy our brother,[b]

To Philemon our dear friend and fellow worker,[c] 2to Apphia our sister, to Archippus[d] our fellow soldier[e] and to the church that meets in your home:[f]

3Grace to you and peace from God our Father and the Lord Jesus Christ.

Thanksgiving and Prayer

7 →PG. 1362

4I always thank my God[g] as I remember you in my prayers, 5because I hear about your faith in the Lord Jesus and your love for all the saints.[h] 6I pray that you may be active in sharing your faith, so that you will have a full understanding of every good thing we have in Christ. 7Your love has given me great joy and encouragement,[i] because you, brother, have refreshed[j] the hearts of the saints.

2 →PG. 1354

Paul's Plea for Onesimus

8Therefore, although in Christ I could be bold and order you to do what you ought to do, 9yet I appeal to you on the basis of love. I then, as Paul—an old man and now also a prisoner[k] of Christ Jesus— 10I appeal to you for my son[l] Onesimus,[a][m] who became my son while I was in chains. 11Formerly he was useless to you, but now he has become useful both to you and to me.

2 →PG. 1360

12I am sending him—who is my very heart—back to you. 13I would have liked to keep him with me so that he could take your place in helping me while I am in chains for the gospel. 14But I did not want to do anything without your consent, so that any favor you do will be spontaneous and not forced.[n] 15Perhaps the reason he was separated from you for a little while was that you might have him back for good— 16no longer as a slave, but better than a slave, as a dear brother.[o] He is very dear to me but even dearer to you, both as a man and as a brother in the Lord.

17So if you consider me a partner,[p] welcome him as you would welcome me. 18If he has done you any wrong or owes you anything, charge it to me. 19I, Paul, am writing this with my own hand. I will pay it back—not to mention that you owe me your very self. 20I do wish, brother, that I may have some benefit from you in the Lord; refresh[q] my heart in Christ. 21Confident[r] of your obedience, I write to you, knowing that you will do even more than I ask.

22And one thing more: Prepare a guest room for me, because I hope to be[s] restored to you in answer to your prayers.[t]

23Epaphras,[u] my fellow prisoner in Christ Jesus, sends you greetings. 24And so do Mark,[v] Aristarchus,[w] Demas[x] and Luke, my fellow workers.

25The grace of the Lord Jesus Christ be with your spirit.[y]

a 10 *Onesimus* means *useful.*

1:1 [a] ver 9,23; Eph 3:1 [b] 2Co 1:1 [c] Php 2:25
1:2 [d] Col 4:17 [e] Php 2:25 [f] Ro 16:5
1:4 [g] Ro 1:8
1:5 [h] Eph 1:15; Col 1:4
1:7 [i] 2Co 7:4,13 [j] ver 20
1:9 [k] ver 1,23
1:10 [l] 1Co 4:15 [m] Col 4:9
1:14 [n] 2Co 9:7; 1Pe 5:2
1:16 [o] Mt 23:8; 1Ti 6:2
1:17 [p] 2Co 8:23
1:20 [q] ver 7
1:21 [r] 2Co 2:3
1:22 [s] Php 1:25; 2:24 [t] 2Co 1:11
1:23 [u] Col 1:7
1:24 [v] Ac 12:12 [w] Ac 19:29 [x] Col 4:14
1:25 [y] 2Ti 4:22

15–16

PROMISE 6

SOCIAL DYNAMITE

Paul's letter to his friend and brother Philemon exhorts readers to look beyond external circumstances and focus on identity in Christ. Here Paul stood in the gap between two Christ-followers and asked them to put their faith and theology into action.

In our modern age, some may question why Paul encouraged a runaway slave to go back to his master. Doesn't the slave / master relationship violate basic human rights? But instead of addressing the injustice of a practice that was culturally acceptable at the time, Paul encouraged his readers to look at the timeless issue of their mutual relationship to Jesus Christ. In doing so Paul referred to his own status as a prisoner (vv. 1, 9, 13, 23), acting as a living example of looking beyond circumstances and toward the higher goal of living for Jesus.

Our status as followers of Christ raises us above any physical, theological, cultural or political differences. Paul's message of brother-to-brother reconciliation, carried out to its fullest extent, is the equivalent of social dynamite that blasts through culturally determined walls of hostility.

For the next Promise 6 reading go to page 1375.

HEBREWS

AT A GLANCE

Key Principle: Once we come to Christ, there is no turning back; we must depend on God's grace to help us mature in Christ even when this leads to adversity, since knowing him is better than anything the world can offer.
Author: Unknown
Time and Place: ~A.D. 60–70 / Place of writing unknown
Key Verses: 2:1–3, 9; 4:12–16; 6:1a; 7:25; 10:19–22; 12:1–2

BENEFIT

Hebrews uses a wide variety of Old Testament passages to present a clear case for Christ's superiority over everything that preceded him. This book adds immeasurably to our understanding of Jesus' person and work, and it applies this understanding to the believer's spiritual growth. Hebrews 11 is one of the most extraordinary chapters in Scripture, providing us with the clearest exposition of the meaning and rewards of faith in the Bible.

SETTING

Hebrews is the only New Testament book whose authorship remains a mystery. Despite its anonymity, its spiritual quality and depth overcame early questions about its inclusion in the New Testament. The original readers clearly knew the author (13:18–24) as an associate of Timothy, but no consistent tradition exists as to his identity. Some in the early church attributed it to Paul, others to Barnabas, to Luke and to Clement. While Hebrews bears some similarities to the style and content of Paul's epistles, there are also enough dissimilarities to lead the majority of New Testament scholars to reject the idea that Paul wrote this book. Suggestions in modern scholarship include Apollos, Silas, Luke, Philip and Clement of Rome, but no one knows.

The traditional view is that the original readers were Jewish believers in Jesus who were tempted to revert back to Judaism because of growing persecution against Christians (2:1; 3:12; 12:4–12). This epistle assumes a detailed understanding of Jewish history, the Mosaic covenant, the priesthood, the sanctuary and the sacrificial ritual of the Old Testament. It exclusively uses the Septuagint (the Greek translation of the Old Testament) rather than the Hebrew, and this may indicate that a good portion of its readers were Hellenistic Jews. This and other evidence suggests to modern scholars that the original readers lived not in Jerusalem, but in Rome (this fits well with "Those from Italy send you their greetings" in 13:24). This epistle was directed to believers who had come to faith through the testimony of eyewitnesses of Christ (2:3; 3:1).

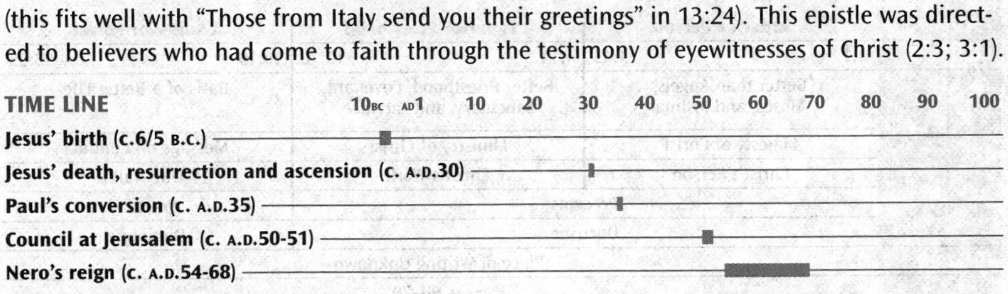

THEME AND PURPOSE

Hebrews builds a cumulative argument to demonstrate Christ's superiority over the old covenant, priesthood and sacrifices. This theme is developed by frequent use of the words "better" or "superior" as well as the terms "heavenly" and "perfect" in comparing Christ's person and work to what was previously revealed. Christ is better than the angels in that they worship him; he is better than Moses in that he created him; he offers a better rest than Joshua, a better priesthood than Levi, a better covenant, a better sanctuary and a better sacrifice; he also provides the power to live a better life. The purpose for this high Christology is to show the folly of moving away from the substance back to the shadow. The author wanted to convince his readers not to revert back to Judaism, and to encourage them to go on to maturity in Christ. As "aliens and strangers on earth" (1 Peter 2:11), believers must realize that their sufferings for Christ are part of God's purpose, and that their reward is in the future.

UNIQUE CONTRIBUTION

This epistle is unique in style and approach; it has no salutation, and apart from the instructions and greetings in 13:18–25, it reads more like a sermonic essay than a letter. It may have been adapted from a sermon or a series of sermons, and its literary elegance, scholarly precision and forceful eloquence are the finest in the New Testament (with the possible exception of Luke). The author skillfully uses an impressive range of Old Testament quotations and allusions to build a careful case for the finality of Christ's priestly sacrifice. Among the book's most important doctrinal contributions are its emphasis on Christ's present priestly ministry, its development of Christ's atonement and its contrast between the old and new covenants and between the earthly and heavenly sanctuaries. Hebrews illumines the typology of the Mosaic Law and the offerings and feasts in Leviticus.

CHRIST IN HEBREWS

Hebrews contrasts the temporary Aaronic priesthood with Christ as our eternal high priest in the order of Melchizedek. Christ is equally divine (1:1–3, 8) and human (2:9, 14, 17–18), and he fulfills the three orders of prophet, priest and king. His perfect and voluntary sacrifice fulfills all that was anticipated, but not realized, in Old Testament animal sacrifices. Unlike those sacrifices, Christ's sacrificial work never needs to be repeated. "The Son is the radiance of God's glory and the exact representation of his being, sustaining all things by his powerful word. After he had provided purification for sins, he sat down at the right hand of the Majesty in heaven" (1:3).

OVERVIEW

FOCUS	A Superior Person	A Superior Priesthood	A Superior Power
REFERENCE	1:1 4:13	4:14 10:18	10:19 13:25
TOPICS	Better than Angels, Moses, and Joshua	Better Priesthood, Covenant, Sanctuary, and Sacrifice	Basis of a Better Life
	Majesty of Christ	Ministry of Christ	Message on Conduct
	Christ's Person	Christ's Work	Our Walk
	Precepts		Practice
	Doctrine		Discipline
LOCATION	Place of Writing Unknown		
TIME	~A.D. 60–70		

Hebrews immediately launches into its main theme by showing that Jesus Christ is the supreme revelation of God (1:1–3). Because he is worshiped by the angels, he is superior to them (1:4–14). Through his incarnation, he understands the human condition: He became the author of our salvation and our merciful and faithful high priest (2:1–18). He is superior to Moses, since Moses was a servant while Christ is the Son (3:1–6). Thus, the author warns of the danger of unbelief and rebellion against Christ (3:7–19). Jesus offers a better rest than Joshua, and this rest is appropriated by faith in him (4:1–13).

As our great high priest in the order of Melchizedek, Christ is able to sympathize with our weaknesses. He suffered to become "the source of eternal salvation for all who obey him" (4:14—5:10). The author urges his readers not to fall away, but to press on to spiritual maturity and to put their hope in God's promises (5:11—6:20). Christ's priesthood is superior to that of the Levites (7:1–28); as such, he is the mediator of a better covenant than the Mosaic covenant (8:1–13). Further, Christ ministers in a heavenly tabernacle, and his blood sacrifice is better than those offered in the earthly sanctuary (9:1—10:18).

Because of all this, the author calls his readers to obey Christ and to persevere in their sufferings for his sake (10:19–39). Like the obedient men and women of the Old Testament, their faith must be in God's character and their hope must be in his promised heavenly rewards (11:1–40). The author tells his readers to expect hardship and discipline for the sake of holiness, and warns them not to refuse God during these difficult times (12:1–29). He concludes this epistle with a series of exhortations to purity, contentment, Christlike character, service and submission (13:1–17) as well as personal instructions and a beautiful benediction (13:18–25).

HEBREWS

The Son Superior to Angels

1 →PG. 1360

1 In the past God spoke[a] to our forefathers through the prophets[b] at
many times and in various ways,[c]
2but in these last days he has spoken
to us by his Son, whom he appointed
heir[d] of all things, and through whom[e]
he made the universe. 3The Son is
the radiance of God's glory[f] and the
exact representation of his being, sustaining all things[g] by his powerful
word. After he had provided purification for sins,[h] he sat down at the
right hand of the Majesty in heaven.[i]
4So he became as much superior to the
angels as the name he has inherited is
superior to theirs.[j]
5For to which of the angels did God
ever say,

"You are my Son;
today I have become your
Father[a]"[b]?[k]

Or again,

"I will be his Father,
and he will be my Son"[c]?[l]

6And again, when God brings his firstborn into the world,[m] he says,

"Let all God's angels worship
him."[d][n]

7In speaking of the angels he says,

"He makes his angels winds,
his servants flames of fire."[e][o]

8But about the Son he says,

"Your throne, O God, will last for
ever and ever,
and righteousness will be the
scepter of your kingdom.
9You have loved righteousness and
hated wickedness;
therefore God, your God, has set
you above your
companions[p]
by anointing you with the oil[q]
of joy."[f]

10He also says,

"In the beginning, O Lord, you laid
the foundations of the earth,
and the heavens are the work of
your hands.
11They will perish, but you remain;
they will all wear out like a
garment.[r]
12You will roll them up like a robe;
like a garment they will be
changed.
But you remain the same,[s]
and your years will never
end."[g][t]

13To which of the angels did God ever
say,

"Sit at my right hand
until I make your enemies
a footstool[u] for your feet"[h]?[v]

1:1 [a]Jn 9:29; Heb 2:2,3 [b]Ac 2:30 [c]Nu 12:6,8 **1:2** [d]Ps 2:8 [e]Jn 1:3 **1:3** [f]Jn 1:14 [g]Col 1:17 [h]Heb 7:27 [i]Mk 16:19 **1:4** [j]Eph 1:21; Php 2:9,10 **1:5** [k]Ps 2:7 [l]2Sa 7:14 **1:6** [m]Heb 10:5 [n]Dt 32:43 (LXX and DSS); Ps 97:7 **1:7** [o]Ps 104:4 **1:9** [p]Php 2:9 [q]Isa 61:1,3 **1:11** [r]Isa 34:4 **1:12** [s]Heb 13:8 [t]Ps 102:25-27 **1:13** [u]Jos 10:24; Heb 10:13 [v]Ps 110:1

a5 Or *have begotten you* b5 Psalm 2:7
c5 2 Samuel 7:14; 1 Chron. 17:13
d6 Deut. 32:43 (see Dead Sea Scrolls and Septuagint) e7 Psalm 104:4
f9 Psalm 45:6,7 g12 Psalm 102:25-27
h13 Psalm 110:1

1:1-4

PROMISE 1

KNOWING GOD

Have you noticed how often self-proclaimed "spiritual gurus" appear on the scene? Many of these people are eager to tell talk-show hosts and book publishers about how they discovered their own "unique" way to know God. Some say each of us is actually a god. Others urge us to find God through meditation, self-denial, pampered indulgence and / or a host of other misdirected practices.

The author of the book of Hebrews says that if we want to know God, then we must know Jesus. Jesus is God's final word to man. He is superior to any prophet—while prophets were God's spokesmen, Jesus is God himself, the Creator of all things. He is greater than any priest—while ancient priests offered sacrifices over and over again, Jesus offered himself as a sacrifice once and for all. Finally, he is greater than any angel—while angels are powerful created beings, only Jesus can claim the title "Son of God."

Jesus Christ is superior to everyone and everything else because he alone is God. Nothing you can buy or build or imagine compares with him. Indeed, everything else in life pales when compared with his glory. And no thing or person or idea is as deserving of our love and devotion as Jesus Christ. Go to the Lord in prayer and offer him your adoration. Praise him as the One who, while being superior to all else, has called you into a relationship with himself.

For the next Promise 1 reading go to page 1367.

14 Are not all angels ministering spirits[w] sent to serve those who will inherit salvation?[x]

Warning to Pay Attention

2 We must pay more careful attention, therefore, to what we have heard, so that we do not drift away. 2 For if the message spoken[y] by angels[z] was binding, and every violation and disobedience received its just punishment,[a] 3 how shall we escape if we ignore such a great salvation?[b] This salvation, which was first announced by the Lord,[c] was confirmed to us by those who heard him.[d] 4 God also testified to it by signs, wonders and various miracles,[e] and gifts of the Holy Spirit[f] distributed according to his will.[g]

Jesus Made Like His Brothers

5 It is not to angels that he has subjected the world to come, about which we are speaking. 6 But there is a place where someone has testified:

"What is man that you are mindful
of him,
the son of man that you care for
him?[h]
7 You made him a little[a] lower than
the angels;
you crowned him with glory and
honor
8 and put everything under his
feet."[b][i]

In putting everything under him, God left nothing that is not subject to him. Yet at present we do not see everything subject to him. 9 But we see Jesus, who was made a little lower than the angels, now crowned with glory and honor[j] because he suffered death,[k] so that by the grace of God he might taste death for everyone.[l]

6 →PG. 1370

10 In bringing many sons to glory, it was fitting that God, for whom and through whom everything exists,[m] should make the author of their salvation perfect through suffering.[n] 11 Both the one who makes men holy and those who are made holy[o] are of the same family. So Jesus is not ashamed to call them brothers.[p] 12 He says,

"I will declare your name to my
brothers;
in the presence of the
congregation I will sing your
praises."[c][q]

13 And again,

"I will put my trust in him."[d][r]

And again he says,

"Here am I, and the children God
has given me."[e][s]

14 Since the children have flesh and blood, he too shared in their humanity[t] so that by his death he might destroy[u] him who holds the power of death—that is, the devil[v]— 15 and free those who all their lives were held in slavery by their fear[w] of death. 16 For surely it is not angels he helps, but Abraham's descendants. 17 For this reason he had to be made like his brothers[x] in every way, in order that he might become a merciful[y] and faithful high priest[z] in service to God,[a] and that he might make atonement for[f] the sins of the people. 18 Because he himself suffered when he was tempted, he is able to help those who are being tempted.[b]

Jesus Greater Than Moses

3 Therefore, holy brothers,[c] who share in the heavenly calling, fix your thoughts on Jesus, the apostle and high priest[d] whom we confess.[e] 2 He was faithful to the one who appointed him, just as Moses was faithful in all God's house.[f] 3 Jesus has been found worthy of greater honor than Moses, just as the builder of a house has greater honor than the house itself. 4 For every house is built by someone, but God is the builder of everything. 5 Moses was faithful as a servant[g] in all God's house,[h] testifying to what would be said in the future. 6 But Christ is faithful as a son[i] over God's house. And we are his house,[j] if we hold on[k] to our courage and the hope[l] of which we boast.

Warning Against Unbelief

7 So, as the Holy Spirit says:[m]

"Today, if you hear his voice,
8 do not harden your hearts
as you did in the rebellion,
during the time of testing in the
desert,
9 where your fathers tested and tried
me
and for forty years saw what I
did.[n]
10 That is why I was angry with that
generation,
and I said, 'Their hearts are
always going astray,

1:14 [w]Ps 103:20 [x]Heb 5:9
2:2 [y]Heb 1:1 [z]Dt 33:2; Ac 7:53 [a]Heb 10:28
2:3 [b]Heb 10:29 [c]Heb 1:2 [d]Lk 1:2
2:4 [e]Jn 4:48 [f]1Co 12:4 [g]Eph 1:5
2:6 [h]Job 7:17
2:8 [i]Ps 8:4-6; 1Co 15:25
2:9 [j]Ac 2:33; 3:13; Php 2:9 [k]Php 2:7-9 [l]Jn 3:16; 2Co 5:15
2:10 [m]Ro 11:36 [n]Lk 24:26; Heb 7:28
2:11 [o]Heb 10:10 [p]Mt 28:10; Jn 20:17
2:12 [q]Ps 22:22
2:13 [r]Isa 8:17 [s]Isa 8:18; Jn 10:29
2:14 [t]Jn 1:14 [u]1Co 15:54-57; 2Ti 1:10 [v]1Jn 3:8
2:15 [w]2Ti 1:7
2:17 [x]Php 2:7 [y]Heb 5:2 [z]Heb 4:14,15; 7:26,28 [a]Heb 5:1
2:18 [b]Heb 4:15
3:1 [c]Heb 2:11 [d]Heb 2:17 [e]Heb 4:14
3:2 [f]Nu 12:7
3:5 [g]Ex 14:31 [h]ver 2; Nu 12:7
3:6 [i]Heb 1:2 [j]1Co 3:16 [k]Ro 11:22 [l]Ro 5:2
3:7 [m]Heb 9:8
3:9 [n]Ac 7:36

a 7 Or *him for a little while,* also in verse 9
b 8 Psalm 8:4-6 c 12 Psalm 22:22
d 13 Isaiah 8:17 e 13 Isaiah 8:18
f 17 Or *and that he might turn aside God's wrath, taking away*

and they have not known my
ways.'
11 So I declared on oath in my anger,
'They shall never enter my
rest.' [o]"[a][p]

2 →PG. 1370

12 See to it, brothers, that none of you has a sinful, unbelieving heart that turns away from the living God. 13 But encourage one another daily,[q] as long as it is called Today, so that none of you may be hardened by sin's deceitfulness.[r] 14 We have come to share in Christ if we hold firmly[s] till the end the confidence we had at first. 15 As has just been said:

"Today, if you hear his voice,
do not harden your hearts
as you did in the rebellion."[b][t]

16 Who were they who heard and rebelled? Were they not all those Moses led out of Egypt?[u] 17 And with whom was he angry for forty years? Was it not with those who sinned, whose bodies fell in the desert?[v] 18 And to whom did God swear that they would never enter his rest[w] if not to those who disobeyed[c]?[x] 19 So we see that they were not able to enter, because of their unbelief.[y]

A Sabbath-Rest for the People of God

4 Therefore, since the promise of entering his rest still stands, let us be careful that none of you be found to have fallen short of it.[z] 2 For we also have had the gospel preached to us, just as they did; but the message they heard was of no value to them, because those who heard did not combine it with faith.[d][a] 3 Now we who have believed enter that rest, just as God has said,

"So I declared on oath in my anger,
'They shall never enter my
rest.' "[e][b]

And yet his work has been finished since the creation of the world. 4 For somewhere he has spoken about the seventh day in these words: "And on the seventh day God rested from all his work."[f][c] 5 And again in the passage above he says, "They shall never enter my rest."[d]

6 It still remains that some will enter that rest, and those who formerly had the gospel preached to them did not go in, because of their disobedience.[e] 7 Therefore God again set a certain day, calling it Today, when a long time later he spoke through David, as was said before:

"Today, if you hear his voice,
do not harden your hearts."[b][f]

8 For if Joshua had given them rest,[g] God would not have spoken[h] later about another day. 9 There remains, then, a Sabbath-rest for the people of God; 10 for anyone who enters God's rest also rests from his own work, just as God did from his.[i] 11 Let us, therefore, make every effort to enter that rest, so that no one will fall by following their example of disobedience.[j]

12 For the word of God[k] is living and active.[l] Sharper than any double-edged sword,[m] it penetrates even to dividing soul and spirit, joints and marrow; it judges the thoughts and attitudes of the heart.[n] 13 Nothing in all creation is hidden from God's sight.[o] Everything is uncovered and laid bare before the eyes of him to whom we must give account.

1 →PG. 1361

3:12-13

PROMISE 2

DAILY ENCOURAGEMENT

This passage is an important one for men in today's culture. It's a call to fellowship and accountability in the face of a society that encourages self-reliance and privacy above all else. Be careful not to simply pass over this verse and miss its direct application and call.

The writer calls on Christians to meet together and encourage one another so that sin doesn't begin to control their lives. It's in this kind of a relationship that believers can open up to each other and share what they've learned.

Men today need to foster positive relationships with other men that go beyond the business world or the playing field. Think about it—who else will be better able to relate to your struggles and joys than another man, one who has had life experiences that parallel your own? If you don't have such a person in your life, ask that God will show you who could be that kind of man. While forming a comfortable level of trust may take time and effort, it will be worth it.

Finally, verse 13 outlines the urgent need to develop and maintain these relationships. If you have a friend to whom you can be accountable, don't let your struggle with sin wait until tomorrow. Talk to him about it and allow him to pray for you in your struggles "Today"—before the clock strikes midnight.

For the next Promise 2 reading go to page 71.

3:11 [o]Heb 4:3,5 [p]Ps 95:7-11
3:13 [q]Heb 10:24,25 [r]Eph 4:22
3:14 [s]ver 6
3:15 [t]ver 7,8; Ps 95:7,8
3:16 [u]Nu 14:2
3:17 [v]Nu 14:29; Ps 106:26
3:18 [w]Nu 14:20-23 [x]Heb 4:6
3:19 [y]Jn 3:36
4:1 [z]Heb 12:15
4:2 [a]1Th 2:13
4:3 [b]Ps 95:11; Heb 3:11
4:4 [c]Ge 2:2,3; Ex 20:11
4:5 [d]Ps 95:11
4:6 [e]Heb 3:18
4:7 [f]Ps 95:7,8; Heb 3:7,8,15
4:8 [g]Jos 22:4 [h]Heb 1:1
4:10 [i]ver 4
4:11 [j]Heb 3:18
4:12 [k]1Pe 1:23 [l]Jer 23:29 [m]Eph 6:17; Rev 1:16 [n]1Co 14:24,25
4:13 [o]Ps 33:13-15

a *11* Psalm 95:7-11 **b** *15,7* Psalm 95:7,8 **c** *18* Or *disbelieved* **d** *2* Many manuscripts *because they did not share in the faith of those who obeyed* **e** *3* Psalm 95:11; also in verse 5 **f** *4* Gen. 2:2

Jesus the Great High Priest

1 →PG. 1365

14Therefore, since we have a great
high priest who has gone through the
heavens,[a][p] Jesus the Son of God, let
us hold firmly to the faith we profess.[q]
15For we do not have a high priest who
is unable to sympathize with our weaknesses, but we have one who has been
tempted in every way, just as we
are[r]—yet was without sin.[s] 16Let us
then approach the throne of grace with
confidence, so that we may receive
mercy and find grace to help us in our
time of need.

5 Every high priest is selected from
among men and is appointed to represent them in matters related to God,
to offer gifts and sacrifices[t] for sins.[u]
2He is able to deal gently with those
who are ignorant and are going
astray,[v] since he himself is subject to
weakness.[w] 3This is why he has to offer sacrifices for his own sins, as well as
for the sins of the people.[x]
4No one takes this honor upon himself; he must be called by God, just as
Aaron was.[y] 5So Christ also did not
take upon himself the glory[z] of becoming a high priest. But God said[a] to
him,

> "You are my Son;
> today I have become your
> Father.[b]"[c]

6And he says in another place,

> "You are a priest forever,
> in the order of Melchizedek."[d][c]

7During the days of Jesus' life on
earth, he offered up prayers and petitions with loud cries and tears[d] to the
one who could save him from death,
and he was heard because of his reverent submission.[e] 8Although he was a
son, he learned obedience from what
he suffered[f] 9and, once made perfect,[g] he became the source of eternal
salvation for all who obey him 10and

4:14 [p]Heb 6:20 [q]Heb 3:1 **4:15** [r]Heb 2:18 [s]2Co 5:21 **5:1** [t]Heb 8:3 [u]Heb 7:27 **5:2** [v]Heb 2:18 [w]Heb 7:28 **5:3** [x]Heb 7:27; 9:7 **5:4** [y]Ex 28:1 **5:5** [z]Jn 8:54 [a]Heb 1:1 [b]Ps 2:7 **5:6** [c]Ps 110:4; Heb 7:17,21 **5:7** [d]Mt 27:46,50 [e]Mk 14:36 **5:8** [f]Php 2:8 **5:9** [g]Heb 2:10

[a] 14 Or *gone into heaven* [b] 5 Or *have begotten you* [c] 5 Psalm 2:7 [d] 6 Psalm 110:4

4:14–16

PE

JESUS KNOWS OUR STRUGGLES

When you think of God, what's your main impression?

Your view of God will influence whether or not you trust him when times are tough. If you think he's weak and disinterested, you won't look to him for help. If you think he's strong but distant and removed, you'll avoid him when you're discouraged.

The author of Hebrews wanted his readers to have a clear picture of God. He wanted them to understand Jesus' role as the ultimate high priest—that Jesus offered his own sinless life as the one-time sacrifice for our sins. By doing so he permanently took away the penalty of our sin and destroyed its power to control our lives.

Maybe you've fallen under a burden that seems too heavy. Discouragement, a broken relationship, a habitual sin or some other circumstance may be turning your heart away from God. If so, this writer offers encouragement.

First, he tells us Jesus is sympathetic to human pain. In Jesus, God took on the soft tissue of human flesh, along with its pain cells, so he could identify with us. Indeed, the purpose of his coming was to make our weaknesses his own in fulfillment of Messianic prophecy (Isaiah 53:4; Matthew 8:17). Jesus has been where we are. He knows what physical, emotional and mental anguish is. And he stands ready to help us cope with our pain through his Spirit.

Second, Jesus has faced and resisted every temptation you ever have or will encounter (see Matthew 4:1–11; 26:36–46). Jesus' entire life on earth involved testing and proving. By facing temptation, Jesus identified with our weaknesses. By overcoming temptation, he broke sin's power.

Although you may feel that no one could ever understand your struggles, there is One who has been there and is always available to help you win. Remember, "No temptation has seized you except what is common to man. And God is faithful; he will not let you be tempted beyond what you can bear. But when you are tempted, he will also provide a way out so that you can stand up under it" (1 Corinthians 10:13). By turning to God in prayer during your times of temptation, you'll be following God's call to purity and living a life that coincides with your new identity in Jesus Christ (2 Corinthians 5:7).

Finally, Jesus is merciful and full of grace. He wants us to look to him in our times of greatest need. The Spirit that dwells in all believers delivers grace and comfort whenever we need it. Jesus' power over sin is there for the taking, if we will just look to him for the strength we need. And even though we can't be completely sinless as long as we live on this earth, we know that, through Jesus, we can receive strength to live in a way that pleases him.

Read over Hebrews 4:15–16 once more. How do these verses affect the way you feel about going to Jesus with your problems? How will his "mercy" and "grace" help you? Go to him when you struggle with pain and temptation. He is ready and able to hear and to help.

was designated by God to be high priest[h] in the order of Melchizedek.[i]

Warning Against Falling Away

11 We have much to say about this, but it is hard to explain because you are slow to learn. 12 In fact, though by this time you ought to be teachers, you need someone to teach you the elementary truths[j] of God's word all over again. You need milk, not solid food![k] 13 Anyone who lives on milk, being still an infant,[l] is not acquainted with the teaching about righteousness. 14 But solid food is for the mature,[m] who by constant use have trained themselves to distinguish good from evil.[n]

6 Therefore let us leave[o] the elementary teachings[p] about Christ and go on to maturity, not laying again the foundation of repentance from acts that lead to death,**[a]**[q] and of faith in God, 2 instruction about baptisms,[r] the laying on of hands,[s] the resurrection of the dead,[t] and eternal judgment. 3 And God permitting,[u] we will do so.

4 It is impossible for those who have once been enlightened,[v] who have tasted the heavenly gift,[w] who have shared in the Holy Spirit,[x] 5 who have tasted the goodness of the word of God and the powers of the coming age, 6 if they fall away, to be brought back to repentance,[y] because**[b]** to their loss they are crucifying the Son of God all over again and subjecting him to public disgrace.

7 Land that drinks in the rain often falling on it and that produces a crop useful to those for whom it is farmed receives the blessing of God. 8 But land that produces thorns and thistles is worthless and is in danger of being cursed.[z] In the end it will be burned.

3 →PG. 1368
7 →PG. 1365

9 Even though we speak like this, dear friends,[a] we are confident of better things in your case—things that accompany salvation. 10 God is not unjust; he will not forget your work and the love you have shown him as you have helped his people and continue to help them.[b] 11 We want each of you to show this same diligence to the very end, in order to make your hope[c] sure. 12 We do not want you to become lazy, but to imitate[d] those who through faith and patience[e] inherit what has been promised.[f]

The Certainty of God's Promise

13 When God made his promise to Abraham, since there was no one greater for him to swear by, he swore by himself,[g] 14 saying, "I will surely bless you and give you many descendants."**[c]**[h] 15 And so after waiting patiently, Abraham received what was promised.[i]

16 Men swear by someone greater than themselves, and the oath confirms what is said and puts an end to all argument.[j] 17 Because God wanted to make the unchanging[k] nature of his purpose very clear to the heirs of what was promised,[l] he confirmed it with an oath. 18 God did this so that, by two unchangeable things in which it is impossible for God to lie,[m] we who have fled to take hold of the hope[n] offered to us may be greatly encouraged. 19 We have this hope as an anchor for the soul, firm and secure. It enters the inner sanctuary behind the curtain,[o] 20 where Jesus, who went before us, has entered on our behalf.[p] He has become a high priest[q] forever, in the order of Melchizedek.[r]

Melchizedek the Priest

7 This Melchizedek was king of Salem and priest of God Most High.[s] He met Abraham returning from the defeat of the kings and blessed him,[t] 2 and Abraham gave him a tenth of everything. First, his name means "king of righteousness"; then also, "king of Salem" means "king of peace." 3 Without father or mother, without genealogy,[u] without beginning of days or end of life, like the Son of God[v] he remains a priest forever.

4 Just think how great he was: Even the patriarch[w] Abraham gave him a tenth of the plunder![x] 5 Now the law requires the descendants of Levi who become priests to collect a tenth from the people[y]—that is, their brothers—even though their brothers are descended from Abraham. 6 This man, however, did not trace his descent from Levi, yet he collected a tenth from Abraham and blessed[z] him who had the promises.[a] 7 And without doubt the lesser person is blessed by the greater. 8 In the one case, the tenth is collected by men who die; but in the other case, by him who is declared to be living.[b] 9 One might even say that Levi, who collects the tenth, paid the tenth through Abraham, 10 because when Melchizedek met Abraham, Levi was still in the body of his ancestor.

Jesus Like Melchizedek

11 If perfection could have been attained through the Levitical priesthood

a *1* Or *from useless rituals* **b** *6* Or *repentance while* **c** *14* Gen. 22:17

5:10 [h]ver 5 [i]ver 6
5:12 [j]Heb 6:1 [k]1Co 3:2; 1Pe 2:2
5:13 [l]1Co 14:20
5:14 [m]1Co 2:6 [n]Isa 7:15
6:1 [o]Php 3:12-14 [p]Heb 5:12 [q]Heb 9:14
6:2 [r]Jn 3:25 [s]Ac 6:6 [t]Ac 17:18,32
6:3 [u]Ac 18:21
6:4 [v]Heb 10:32 [w]Eph 2:8 [x]Gal 3:2
6:6 [y]2Pe 2:21; 1Jn 5:16
6:8 [z]Ge 3:17,18; Isa 5:6
6:9 [a]1Co 10:14
6:10 [b]Mt 10:40,42; 25:40; 1Th 1:3
6:11 [c]Heb 3:6
6:12 [d]Heb 13:7 [e]2Th 1:4; Jas 1:3; Rev 13:10 [f]Heb 10:36
6:13 [g]Ge 22:16; Lk 1:73
6:14 [h]Ge 22:17
6:15 [i]Ge 21:5
6:16 [j]Ex 22:11
6:17 [k]Ps 110:4 [l]Heb 11:9
6:18 [m]Nu 23:19; Tit 1:2 [n]Heb 3:6
6:19 [o]Lev 16:2; Heb 9:2,3,7
6:20 [p]Heb 4:14 [q]Heb 2:17 [r]Heb 5:6
7:1 [s]Mk 5:7 [t]Ge 14:18-20
7:3 [u]ver 6 [v]Mt 4:3
7:4 [w]Ac 2:29 [x]Ge 14:20
7:5 [y]Nu 18:21,26
7:6 [z]Ge 14:19,20 [a]Ro 4:13
7:8 [b]Heb 5:6; 6:20

(for on the basis of it the law was given
to the people),[c] why was there still
need for another priest to come[d]—
one in the order of Melchizedek,[e] not
in the order of Aaron? 12For when there
is a change of the priesthood, there
must also be a change of the law. 13He
of whom these things are said belonged to a different tribe,[f] and no
one from that tribe has ever served at
the altar.[g] 14For it is clear that our
Lord descended from Judah,[h] and in
regard to that tribe Moses said nothing
about priests. 15And what we have said
is even more clear if another priest like
Melchizedek appears, 16one who has
become a priest not on the basis of a
regulation as to his ancestry but on the
basis of the power of an indestructible
life. 17For it is declared:

"You are a priest forever,
in the order of Melchizedek."[a][i]

18The former regulation is set aside
because it was weak and useless[j]
19(for the law made nothing perfect),[k]
and a better hope is introduced, by
which we draw near to God.[l]
20And it was not without an oath!
Others became priests without any
oath, 21but he became a priest with an
oath when God said to him:

"The Lord has sworn
and will not change his mind:[m]
'You are a priest forever.' "[a][n]

22Because of this oath, Jesus has become the guarantee of a better covenant.[o]
23Now there have been many of
those priests, since death prevented
them from continuing in office; 24but
because Jesus lives forever, he has a
permanent priesthood.[p] 25Therefore
he is able to save completely[b] those
who come to God[q] through him, because he always lives to intercede for
them.[r]
26Such a high priest meets our
need—one who is holy, blameless,
pure, set apart from sinners,[s] exalted
above the heavens.[t] 27Unlike the other high priests, he does not need to
offer sacrifices[u] day after day, first for
his own sins,[v] and then for the sins of
the people. He sacrificed for their sins
once for all[w] when he offered himself.[x] 28For the law appoints as high
priests men who are weak;[y] but the
oath, which came after the law, appointed the Son,[z] who has been made
perfect[a] forever.

7:11 [c]ver 18,19; Heb 8:7 [d]Heb 10:1 [e]ver 17
7:13 [f]ver 11 [g]ver 14
7:14 [h]Isa 11:1; Mt 1:3; Lk 3:33
7:17 [i]Ps 110:4; ver 21; Heb 5:6
7:18 [j]Ro 8:3
7:19 [k]Ac 13:39; Ro 3:20; Heb 9:9 [l]Heb 4:16
7:21 [m]1Sa 15:29 [n]Ps 110:4
7:22 [o]Heb 8:6
7:24 [p]ver 28
7:25 [q]ver 19 [r]Ro 8:34
7:26 [s]2Co 5:21 [t]Heb 4:14
7:27 [u]Heb 5:1 [v]Heb 5:3 [w]Heb 9:12,26,28 [x]Eph 5:2; Heb 9:14,28
7:28 [y]Heb 5:2 [z]Heb 1:2 [a]Heb 2:10
8:1 [b]Heb 2:17
8:2 [c]Heb 9:11,24
8:3 [d]Heb 5:1 [e]Heb 9:14
8:4 [f]Heb 5:1
8:5 [g]Heb 9:23 [h]Col 2:17; Heb 10:1 [i]Heb 11:7; 12:25 [j]Ex 25:40
8:6 [k]Lk 22:20 [l]Heb 7:22
8:7 [m]Heb 7:11,18
8:8 [n]Jer 31:31
8:9 [o]Ex 19:5,6
8:10 [p]2Co 3:3; Heb 10:16 [q]Zec 8:8
8:11 [r]Isa 54:13; Jn 6:45

The High Priest of a New Covenant

8 The point of what we are saying is
this: We do have such a high
priest,[b] who sat down at the right
hand of the throne of the Majesty in
heaven, 2and who serves in the sanctuary, the true tabernacle[c] set up by the
Lord, not by man.
3Every high priest is appointed to offer both gifts and sacrifices,[d] and so it
was necessary for this one also to have
something to offer.[e] 4If he were on
earth, he would not be a priest, for
there are already men who offer the
gifts prescribed by the law.[f] 5They
serve at a sanctuary that is a copy[g]
and shadow[h] of what is in heaven.
This is why Moses was warned[i] when
he was about to build the tabernacle:
"See to it that you make everything according to the pattern shown you on
the mountain."[c][j] 6But the ministry
Jesus has received is as superior to
theirs as the covenant[k] of which he is
mediator[l] is superior to the old one,
and it is founded on better promises.
7For if there had been nothing
wrong with that first covenant, no
place would have been sought for another.[m] 8But God found fault with the
people and said[d]:

"The time is coming, declares the
Lord,
when I will make a new
covenant[n]
with the house of Israel
and with the house of Judah.
9It will not be like the covenant
I made with their forefathers[o]
when I took them by the hand
to lead them out of Egypt,
because they did not remain
faithful to my covenant,
and I turned away from them,
declares the Lord.
10This is the covenant I will make
with the house of Israel
after that time, declares the Lord.
I will put my laws in their minds
and write them on their hearts.[p]
I will be their God,
and they will be my people.[q]
11No longer will a man teach his
neighbor,
or a man his brother, saying,
'Know the Lord,'
because they will all know me,[r]
from the least of them to the
greatest.
12For I will forgive their wickedness

[a] *17,21* Psalm 110:4 [b] *25* Or *forever*
[c] *5* Exodus 25:40 [d] *8* Some manuscripts may be translated *fault and said to the people.*

and will remember their sins no
more.[s]"[a][t]

13By calling this covenant "new," he
has made the first one obsolete;[u] and
what is obsolete and aging will soon
disappear.

Worship in the Earthly Tabernacle

9 Now the first covenant had regulations for worship and also an earthly
sanctuary.[v] 2A tabernacle[w] was set
up. In its first room were the lampstand,[x] the table[y] and the consecrated bread;[z] this was called the Holy
Place. 3Behind the second curtain was
a room called the Most Holy Place,[a]
4which had the golden altar of incense[b] and the gold-covered ark of
the covenant.[c] This ark contained the
gold jar of manna,[d] Aaron's staff that
had budded,[e] and the stone tablets of
the covenant. 5Above the ark were the
cherubim of the Glory,[f] overshadowing the atonement cover.[b] But we cannot discuss these things in detail now.
6When everything had been arranged like this, the priests entered
regularly[g] into the outer room to carry
on their ministry. 7But only the high
priest entered[h] the inner room, and
that only once a year,[i] and never
without blood, which he offered for
himself[j] and for the sins the people
had committed in ignorance. 8The
Holy Spirit was showing[k] by this that
the way[l] into the Most Holy Place had
not yet been disclosed as long as
the first tabernacle was still standing.
9This is an illustration for the present
time, indicating that the gifts and sacrifices being offered[m] were not able to
clear the conscience of the worshiper.
10They are only a matter of food[n] and
drink[o] and various ceremonial wash-
ings—external regulations[p] applying
until the time of the new order.

The Blood of Christ

11When Christ came as high priest[q]
of the good things that are already
here,[c][r] he went through the greater
and more perfect tabernacle[s] that is
not man-made, that is to say, not a
part of this creation. 12He did not enter
by means of the blood of goats and
calves;[t] but he entered the Most Holy
Place[u] once for all[v] by his own blood,
having obtained eternal redemption.
13The blood of goats and bulls and the
ashes of a heifer[w] sprinkled on those
who are ceremonially unclean sanctify
them so that they are outwardly clean.
14How much more, then, will the blood
of Christ, who through the eternal
Spirit[x] offered himself unblemished to
God, cleanse our consciences[y] from
acts that lead to death,[d][z] so that we
may serve the living God!
15For this reason Christ is the mediator[a] of a new covenant, that those
who are called may receive the promised eternal inheritance—now that he
has died as a ransom to set them free
from the sins committed under the
first covenant.[b]
16In the case of a will,[e] it is necessary to prove the death of the one who
made it, 17because a will is in force only
when somebody has died; it never
takes effect while the one who made it
is living. 18This is why even the first
covenant was not put into effect without blood.[c] 19When Moses had proclaimed every commandment of the
law to all the people, he took the blood
of calves, together with water, scarlet
wool and branches of hyssop, and
sprinkled the scroll and all the people.[d] 20He said, "This is the blood of
the covenant, which God has commanded you to keep."[f][e] 21In the
same way, he sprinkled with the blood
both the tabernacle and everything
used in its ceremonies. 22In fact, the
law requires that nearly everything be
cleansed with blood,[f] and without the
shedding of blood there is no forgiveness.[g]
23It was necessary, then, for the copies[h] of the heavenly things to be purified with these sacrifices, but the heavenly things themselves with better
sacrifices than these. 24For Christ did
not enter a man-made sanctuary that
was only a copy of the true one;[i] he
entered heaven itself, now to appear
for us in God's presence. 25Nor did he
enter heaven to offer himself again and
again, the way the high priest enters
the Most Holy Place[j] every year with
blood that is not his own.[k] 26Then
Christ would have had to suffer many
times since the creation of the world.[l]
But now he has appeared once for all[m]
at the end of the ages to do away with
sin by the sacrifice of himself. 27Just as
man is destined to die once,[n] and after that to face judgment,[o] 28so Christ
was sacrificed once to take away the
sins of many people; and he will appear a second time,[p] not to bear sin,[q]
but to bring salvation to those who are
waiting for him.[r]

8:12 [s]Heb 10:17 [t]Ro 11:27
8:13 [u]2Co 5:17
9:1 [v]Ex 25:8
9:2 [w]Ex 25:8,9 [x]Ex 25:31-39 [y]Ex 25:23-29 [z]Lev 24:5-8
9:3 [a]Ex 26:31-33
9:4 [b]Ex 30:1-5 [c]Ex 25:10-22 [d]Ex 16:32,33 [e]Nu 17:10
9:5 [f]Ex 25:17-19
9:6 [g]Nu 28:3
9:7 [h]Lev 16:11-19 [i]Lev 16:34 [j]Heb 5:2,3
9:8 [k]Heb 3:7 [l]Jn 14:6; Heb 10:19,20
9:9 [m]Heb 5:1
9:10 [n]Lev 11:2-23 [o]Col 2:16 [p]Heb 7:16
9:11 [q]Heb 2:17 [r]Heb 10:1 [s]Heb 8:2
9:12 [t]Heb 10:4 [u]ver 24 [v]Heb 7:27
9:13 [w]Nu 19:9,17, 18
9:14 [x]1Pe 3:18 [y]Tit 2:14; Heb 10:2,22 [z]Heb 6:1
9:15 [a]1Ti 2:5 [b]Heb 7:22
9:18 [c]Ex 24:6-8
9:19 [d]Ex 24:6-8
9:20 [e]Ex 24:8; Mt 26:28
9:22 [f]Lev 8:15 [g]Lev 17:11
9:23 [h]Heb 8:5
9:24 [i]Heb 8:2
9:25 [j]Heb 10:19 [k]ver 7,8
9:26 [l]Heb 4:3 [m]Heb 7:27
9:27 [n]Ge 3:19 [o]2Co 5:10
9:28 [p]Tit 2:13 [q]1Pe 2:24 [r]1Co 1:7

a *12* Jer. 31:31-34 **b** *5* Traditionally *the mercy seat* **c** *11* Some early manuscripts *are to come* **d** *14* Or *from useless rituals* **e** *16* Same Greek word as *covenant*; also in verse 17
f *20* Exodus 24:8

Christ's Sacrifice Once for All

1 →PG. 1370

10 The law is only a shadow[s] of the
good things[t] that are coming—
not the realities themselves.[u] For this
reason it can never, by the same sacrifices repeated endlessly year after year,
make perfect[v] those who draw near to
worship. 2If it could, would they not
have stopped being offered? For the
worshipers would have been cleansed
once for all, and would no longer have
felt guilty for their sins. 3But those
sacrifices are an annual reminder of
sins,[w] 4because it is impossible for the
blood of bulls and goats[x] to take away
sins.
5Therefore, when Christ came into
the world,[y] he said:

"Sacrifice and offering you did not
desire,
but a body you prepared for
me;[z]
6with burnt offerings and sin
offerings
you were not pleased.
7Then I said, 'Here I am—it is
written about me in the
scroll[a]—
I have come to do your will,
O God.' "[a][b]

8First he said, "Sacrifices and offerings,
burnt offerings and sin offerings you
did not desire, nor were you pleased
with them"[c] (although the law required them to be made). 9Then
he said, "Here I am, I have come to
do your will."[d] He sets aside the
first to establish the second. 10And by
that will, we have been made holy[e]
through the sacrifice of the body[f] of
Jesus Christ once for all.[g]
11Day after day every priest stands
and performs his religious duties;
again and again he offers the same sacrifices,[h] which can never take away
sins.[i] 12But when this priest had offered for all time one sacrifice for sins,
he sat down at the right hand of God.
13Since that time he waits for his enemies to be made his footstool,[j] 14be-
cause by one sacrifice he has made
perfect[k] forever those who are being
made holy.
15The Holy Spirit also testifies[l] to
us about this. First he says:

16"This is the covenant I will make
with them
after that time, says the Lord.
I will put my laws in their hearts,
and I will write them on their
minds."[b][m]

17Then he adds:

"Their sins and lawless acts
I will remember no more."[c][n]

18And where these have been forgiven,
there is no longer any sacrifice for sin.

A Call to Persevere

19Therefore, brothers, since we have
confidence to enter the Most Holy
Place[o] by the blood of Jesus, 20by a
new and living way[p] opened for us
through the curtain,[q] that is, his body,
21and since we have a great priest[r]
over the house of God, 22let us draw
near to God[s] with a sincere heart in
full assurance of faith, having our
hearts sprinkled to cleanse us from a
guilty conscience[t] and having our
bodies washed with pure water. 23Let
us hold unswervingly to the hope[u] we
profess, for he who promised is faithful.[v] 24And let us consider how we
may spur one another on toward love
and good deeds. 25Let us not give up
meeting together,[w] as some are in the
habit of doing, but let us encourage
one another[x]—and all the more as
you see the Day approaching.
26If we deliberately keep on sinning[y] after we have received the
knowledge of the truth, no sacrifice for
sins is left, 27but only a fearful expectation of judgment and of raging fire[z]
that will consume the enemies of God.
28Anyone who rejected the law of Moses died without mercy on the testimony of two or three witnesses.[a] 29How

5 →PG. 1370
7 →PG. 1374

[a] 7 Psalm 40:6-8 (see Septuagint)
[b] 16 Jer. 31:33 [c] 17 Jer. 31:34

10:1 [s]Heb 8:5 [t]Heb 9:11 [u]Heb 9:23 [v]Heb 7:19 **10:3** [w]Heb 9:7 **10:4** [x]Heb 9:12,13 **10:5** [y]Heb 1:6 [z]1Pe 2:24 **10:7** [a]Jer 36:2 [b]Ps 40:6-8 **10:8** [c]ver 5,6; Mk 12:33 **10:9** [d]ver 7 **10:10** [e]Jn 17:19 [f]Heb 2:14; 1Pe 2:24 [g]Heb 7:27 **10:11** [h]Heb 5:1 [i]ver 1,4 **10:13** [j]Heb 1:13 **10:14** [k]ver 1 **10:15** [l]Heb 3:7 **10:16** [m]Jer 31:33; Heb 8:10 **10:17** [n]Heb 8:12 **10:19** [o]Eph 2:18; Heb 9:8,12,25 **10:20** [p]Heb 9:8 [q]Heb 9:3 **10:21** [r]Heb 2:17 **10:22** [s]Heb 7:19 [t]Eze 36:25; Heb 9:14 **10:23** [u]Heb 3:6 [v]1Co 1:9 **10:25** [w]Ac 2:42 [x]Heb 3:13 **10:26** [y]Nu 15:30; 2Pe 2:20 **10:27** [z]Isa 26:11; 2Th 1:7; Heb 9:27 **10:28** [a]Dt 17:6,7; Heb 2:2

9:27–28

ONCE AND FOR ALL TIME

In describing Jesus' death, the author of Hebrews gives us a brief, Biblical perspective. As a person dies only once, so Jesus died only once and took our punishment for us.

Earlier in the chapter the writer compares the inheritance we have through Jesus Christ to a will (vv. 16–17). Just as wealth is passed on only after a person dies, so Jesus had to die so that we could take hold of what God had in store for us: salvation from our sin and eternal life in heaven with him. Along with this assurance comes the promise that Jesus will return and gather all believers to himself (v. 28).

This short passage explains in a nutshell the hope that we have as believers. Our spiritual inheritance goes far beyond any earthly inheritance we might receive. What's more, the One who died to guarantee that treasure is alive today!

much more severely do you think a man deserves to be punished who has trampled the Son of God under foot,[b] who has treated as an unholy thing the blood of the covenant[c] that sanctified him, and who has insulted the Spirit[d] of grace?[e] 30For we know him who said, "It is mine to avenge; I will repay,"[a][f] and again, "The Lord will judge his people."[b][g] 31It is a dreadful thing to fall into the hands of the living God.[h]

32Remember those earlier days after you had received the light,[i] when you stood your ground in a great contest in the face of suffering.[j] 33Sometimes you were publicly exposed to insult and persecution;[k] at other times you stood side by side with those who were so treated.[l] 34You sympathized with those in prison[m] and joyfully accepted the confiscation of your property, because you knew that you yourselves had better and lasting possessions.[n]

35So do not throw away your confidence; it will be richly rewarded. 36You need to persevere[o] so that when you have done the will of God, you will receive what he has promised. 37For in just a very little while,

"He who is coming[p] will come
and will not delay.[q]
38 But my righteous one[c] will live
by faith.[r]
And if he shrinks back,
I will not be pleased with him."[d]

39But we are not of those who shrink back and are destroyed, but of those who believe and are saved.

By Faith

11 Now faith is being sure of what we hope for and certain of what we do not see.[s] 2This is what the ancients were commended for.[t]

3By faith we understand that the universe was formed at God's command,[u] so that what is seen was not made out of what was visible.

4By faith Abel offered God a better sacrifice than Cain did. By faith he was commended as a righteous man, when God spoke well of his offerings.[v] And by faith he still speaks, even though he is dead.[w]

5By faith Enoch was taken from this life, so that he did not experience death; he could not be found, because God had taken him away.[x] For before he was taken, he was commended as one who pleased God. 6And without faith it is impossible to please God, because anyone who comes to him[y] must believe that he exists and that he rewards those who earnestly seek him.

7By faith Noah, when warned about things not yet seen, in holy fear built an ark[z] to save his family.[a] By his faith he condemned the world and became heir of the righteousness that comes by faith.

8By faith Abraham, when called to go to a place he would later receive as his inheritance,[b] obeyed and went,[c] even though he did not know where he was going. 9By faith he made his home in the promised land[d] like a stranger in a foreign country; he lived in tents,[e] as did Isaac and Jacob, who were heirs with him of the same promise.[f] 10For he was looking forward to the city[g] with foundations,[h] whose architect and builder is God.

11By faith Abraham, even though he was past age—and Sarah herself was barren[i]—was enabled to become a father[j] because he[e] considered him faithful who had made the promise. 12And so from this one man, and he as good as dead,[k] came descendants as numerous as the stars in the sky and as countless as the sand on the seashore.[l]

13All these people were still living by faith when they died. They did not re-

10:23–25 PROMISE 5

WORSHIP IN A BASS BOAT?

Is church attendance optional? Many guys think so. Some say they worship just as well on the golf course or in a fishing boat as in a church. While we may be able to commune with God during our leisure hours, church attendance isn't optional—it's imperative.

Just as fish need water to survive, so also believers need the environment of worship with fellow believers to thrive. When we stay away from that fellowship, we can put our faith at risk. We deny ourselves the opportunity to minister to others and be supported and encouraged ourselves.

What's your church attendance record like? If you're there every week, be sure and take the time to encourage others. If you've been slack in this area, determine to make church attendance a priority.

For the next Promise 5 reading go to page 1370.

10:29 [b]Heb 6:6 [c]Mt 26:28 [d]Eph 4:30; Heb 6:4 [e]Heb 2:3 **10:30** [f]Dt 32:35; Ro 12:19 [g]Dt 32:36 **10:31** [h]Mt 16:16 **10:32** [i]Heb 6:4 [j]Php 1:29,30 **10:33** [k]1Co 4:9 [l]Php 4:14; 1Th 2:14 **10:34** [m]Heb 13:3 [n]Heb 11:16 **10:36** [o]Lk 21:19; Heb 12:1 **10:37** [p]Mt 11:3 [q]Rev 22:20 **10:38** [r]Ro 1:17; Gal 3:11

11:1 [s]Ro 8:24; 2Co 4:18 **11:2** [t]ver 4,39 **11:3** [u]Ge 1; Jn 1:3; 2Pe 3:5 **11:4** [v]Ge 4:4; 1Jn 3:12 [w]Heb 12:24 **11:5** [x]Ge 5:21-24 **11:6** [y]Heb 7:19 **11:7** [z]Ge 6:13-22 [a]1Pe 3:20 **11:8** [b]Ge 12:7 [c]Ge 12:1-4; Ac 7:2-4 **11:9** [d]Ac 7:5 [e]Ge 12:8; 18:1,9 [f]Heb 6:17 **11:10** [g]Heb 12:22; 13:14 [h]Rev 21:2,14 **11:11** [i]Ge 17:17-19; 18:11-14 [j]Ge 21:2 **11:12** [k]Ro 4:19 [l]Ge 22:17

[a] *30* Deut. 32:35 [b] *30* Deut. 32:36; Psalm 135:14 [c] *38* One early manuscript *But the righteous* [d] *38* Hab. 2:3,4 [e] *11* Or *By faith even Sarah, who was past age, was enabled to bear children because she*

ceive the things promised;[m] they only
saw them and welcomed them from
a distance.[n] And they admitted that
they were aliens and strangers on
earth.[o] 14People who say such things
show that they are looking for a country of their own. 15If they had been
thinking of the country they had left,
they would have had opportunity to return.[p] 16Instead, they were longing for
a better country—a heavenly one.[q]
Therefore God is not ashamed[r] to be
called their God,[s] for he has prepared
a city[t] for them.

17By faith Abraham, when God tested him, offered Isaac as a sacrifice.[u]
He who had received the promises was
about to sacrifice his one and only son,
18even though God had said to him, "It
is through Isaac that your offspring[a]
will be reckoned."[b][v] 19Abraham reasoned that God could raise the dead,[w]
and figuratively speaking, he did receive Isaac back from death.

20By faith Isaac blessed Jacob and
Esau in regard to their future.[x]

21By faith Jacob, when he was dying,
blessed each of Joseph's sons,[y] and
worshiped as he leaned on the top of
his staff.

22By faith Joseph, when his end was
near, spoke about the exodus of the
Israelites from Egypt and gave instructions about his bones.[z]

23By faith Moses' parents hid him for
three months after he was born,[a] because they saw he was no ordinary
child, and they were not afraid of the
king's edict.[b]

24By faith Moses, when he had
grown up, refused to be known as
the son of Pharaoh's daughter.[c] 25He
chose to be mistreated[d] along with
the people of God rather than to enjoy
the pleasures of sin for a short time.
26He regarded disgrace[e] for the sake
of Christ as of greater value than the
treasures of Egypt, because he was
looking ahead to his reward.[f] 27By
faith he left Egypt,[g] not fearing the
king's anger; he persevered because he
saw him who is invisible. 28By faith he
kept the Passover and the sprinkling of
blood, so that the destroyer of the firstborn would not touch the firstborn of
Israel.[h]

29By faith the people passed through
the Red Sea[c] as on dry land; but when
the Egyptians tried to do so, they were
drowned.[i]

30By faith the walls of Jericho fell,
after the people had marched around
them for seven days.[j]

31By faith the prostitute Rahab, because she welcomed the spies, was not
killed with those who were disobedient.[d][k]

32And what more shall I say? I do
not have time to tell about Gideon,

11:13 [m]ver 39 [n]Mt 13:17 [o]Ge 23:4; Ps 39:12; 1Pe 1:17
11:15 [p]Ge 24:6-8
11:16 [q]2Ti 4:18 [r]Mk 8:38 [s]Ex 3:6,15 [t]Heb 13:14
11:17 [u]Ge 22:1-10; Jas 2:21
11:18 [v]Ge 21:12; Ro 9:7
11:19 [w]Ro 4:21
11:20 [x]Ge 27:27-29, 39,40
11:21 [y]Ge 48:1,8-22
11:22 [z]Ge 50:24,25; Ex 13:19
11:23 [a]Ex 2:2 [b]Ex 1:16,22
11:24 [c]Ex 2:10,11
11:25 [d]ver 37
11:26 [e]Heb 13:13 [f]Heb 10:35
11:27 [g]Ex 12:50,51
11:28 [h]Ex 12:21-23
11:29 [i]Ex 14:21-31
11:30 [j]Jos 6:12-20
11:31 [k]Jos 2:1,9-14; 6:22-25; Jas 2:25

a *18* Greek *seed* **b** *18* Gen. 21:12 **c** *29* That is, Sea of Reeds **d** *31* Or *unbelieving*

11:1-39

PROMISE 1

FAITH-FULL

As followers of Jesus Christ we've been called to a life of faith. When the Bible's writers discussed faith they weren't merely writing about thinking positively, being an optimist or following through on a hunch. They spoke of faith as the rock-solid internal assurance that unseen things are real, and that promises made would come to pass.

The men and women whose names are recorded in Hebrews 11 won God's approval because of their faith. As you read this great chapter, notice that in verses 1–35a those who trusted God saw him provide for them in astounding ways. Reading these fantastic stories, one might easily conclude that faith in God always assures miraculous deliverance out of difficulty.

But verses 35b-38 indicate otherwise. These people trusted God and suffered unimaginable hardship. They endured excruciating pain and suffered unparalleled losses, yet their faith never wavered. They discovered that when God doesn't deliver us out of a difficulty, he still gets us through it. For some, "getting through it" meant entering God's presence through death.

These people demonstrate that our faith is strongest when it's placed in something or someone who has proven trustworthy. If these "heroes of the faith" hadn't found God trustworthy, their faith might have faltered. Despite the circumstances, their trust in God's promises to them remained clear, and their faith pleased God.

Ultimately, the only way we can please God is by faith. Religious activity apart from faith doesn't please God. Neither do good deeds. Only faith and the kind of life that flows from faith pleases God.

The truth is, you already have faith. You exercise it every day when you trust a friend to keep a secret, a pharmacist to fill a prescription or the driver of an oncoming truck to stay on his side of the road. But while these earthly people may—and often do—let you down, God never will. His promises in the Bible are trustworthy and true. A life based on faith in God transcends circumstances—whether good or bad—and gives the believer a rock-solid hope for the future.

For the next Promise 1 reading go to page 1368.

Barak,[l] Samson, Jephthah, David,[m]
Samuel[n] and the prophets, 33who
through faith conquered kingdoms,[o]
administered justice, and gained what
was promised; who shut the mouths
of lions,[p] 34quenched the fury of the
flames, and escaped the edge of the
sword; whose weakness was turned to
strength;[q] and who became powerful
in battle and routed foreign armies.[r]
35Women received back their dead,
raised to life again.[s] Others were tortured and refused to be released, so
that they might gain a better resurrection. 36Some faced jeers and flogging,[t]
while still others were chained and
put in prison.[u] 37They were stoned[a];[v]
they were sawed in two; they were put
to death by the sword.[w] They went
about in sheepskins and goatskins,[x]
destitute, persecuted and mistreated—
38the world was not worthy of them.
They wandered in deserts and mountains, and in caves[y] and holes in the
ground.
39These were all commended[z] for
their faith, yet none of them received
what had been promised.[a] 40God had
planned something better for us so
that only together with us would they
be made perfect.

God Disciplines His Sons

3 →PG. 1368

12 Therefore, since we are surrounded
by such a great cloud of witnesses,
let us throw off everything that hinders
and the sin that so easily entangles,
and let us run[b] with perseverance[c]
the race marked out for us. 2Let us fix
our eyes on Jesus, the author and perfecter of our faith, who for the joy set
before him endured the cross,[d] scorning its shame,[e] and sat down at the
right hand of the throne of God. 3Con-
sider him who endured such opposition from sinful men, so that you will
not grow weary[f] and lose heart.
4In your struggle against sin, you
have not yet resisted to the point of
shedding your blood.[g] 5And you have
forgotten that word of encouragement
that addresses you as sons:

"My son, do not make light of the
Lord's discipline,
and do not lose heart when he
rebukes you,
6because the Lord disciplines those
he loves,[h]
and he punishes everyone he
accepts as a son."[b][i]

3 →PG. 1368

7Endure hardship as discipline; God
is treating you as sons.[j] For what son
is not disciplined by his father? 8If you
are not disciplined (and everyone un-
dergoes discipline),[k] then you are illegitimate children and not true sons.
9Moreover, we have all had human fathers who disciplined us and we respected them for it. How much more
should we submit to the Father of our
spirits[l] and live![m] 10Our fathers disciplined us for a little while as they
thought best; but God disciplines us for
our good, that we may share in his holiness.[n] 11No discipline seems pleasant
at the time, but painful. Later on, however, it produces a harvest of righteousness and peace[o] for those who
have been trained by it.
12Therefore, strengthen your feeble
arms and weak knees.[p] 13"Make level
paths for your feet,"[c][q] so that the
lame may not be disabled, but rather
healed.[r]

Warning Against Refusing God

14Make every effort to live in peace
with all men[s] and to be holy;[t] without holiness no one will see the Lord.[u]
15See to it that no one misses the grace
of God[v] and that no bitter root grows

3 →PG. 1370

11:32 [l]Jdg 4-5 [m]1Sa 16:1,13 [n]1Sa 1:20
11:33 [o]2Sa 7:11; 8:1-3 [p]Da 6:22
11:34 [q]2Ki 20:7 [r]Jdg 15:8
11:35 [s]1Ki 17:22,23
11:36 [t]Jer 20:2 [u]Ge 39:20
11:37 [v]2Ch 24:21 [w]1Ki 19:10 [x]2Ki 1:8
11:38 [y]1Ki 18:4
11:39 [z]ver 2,4 [a]ver 13
12:1 [b]1Co 9:24 [c]Heb 10:36
12:2 [d]Php 2:8,9 [e]Heb 13:13
12:3 [f]Gal 6:9
12:4 [g]Heb 10:32-34
12:6 [h]Ps 94:12; Rev 3:19 [i]Pr 3:11,12
12:7 [j]Dt 8:5
12:8 [k]1Pe 5:9
12:9 [l]Nu 16:22 [m]Isa 38:16
12:10 [n]2Pe 1:4
12:11 [o]Isa 32:17; Jas 3:17,18
12:12 [p]Isa 35:3
12:13 [q]Pr 4:26 [r]Gal 6:1
12:14 [s]Ro 14:19 [t]Ro 6:22 [u]Mt 5:8
12:15 [v]Gal 5:4; Heb 3:12

a37 Some early manuscripts *stoned; they were put to the test;* b6 Prov. 3:11,12 c13 Prov. 4:26

12:1–11

PROMISE 1

LOVING DISCIPLINE

A child undergoing parental discipline may feel unloved. Yet few things demonstrate a father's love more than discipline. Why? Because a dad knows discipline is necessary for his child's growth and maturity.

Sometimes we may feel like that disciplined child. Difficult times may make us feel that God is unconcerned for our welfare. The original readers of this letter felt that way, but the author assured them the exact opposite was true. The very thing that made them feel abandoned by God was proof of his divine love. The tests they experienced were for their benefit, helping them to become stronger, leaner, more able to do God's work. As a coach on the sidelines motivates his team, so the writer of this book brought encouragement to his readers in their struggles.

Take that encouragement to heart. God asks believers to hold on to their faith—no matter what their external circumstances. If you're undergoing hardship, consider the positive lessons you can learn from it. Ask for the grace you need to trust in your heavenly Father, realizing that in and through it all he is seeking your greatest good.

For the next Promise 1 reading go to page 1377.

JAMES

A Man with Godly Ambition

Jesus is looking for men with drive and ambition. But that drive and ambition needs to be redirected away from the desire toward personal gain and toward carrying out God's purposes in this world. Jesus' disciples were all hard-working men who were, as far as we know, successful in what they did. But they were driven by their own motives and ambitions—especially James. Jesus' life and lessons changed all that.

Why Do We Do What We Do?

James, his brother John and Peter formed an "inner circle" of disciples who had a special relationship with Jesus. They shared some of the most powerful moments in Jesus' life. They were there when the Lord healed Jairus's daughter (Luke 8:51); they shared in the glorious "transfiguration" experience (Matthew 17:1–2); and when Jesus entered the Garden of Gethsemane to pour out his agony in prayer, he again chose these three to accompany him—another high but sobering honor (Mark 14:33).

James loved the limelight. He loved the power. From his point of view, he was on his way to the top. He was traveling with the future "King of Israel." The Lord recognized this drive and ambition in James, and was well aware that James's power-grabbing ways needed to be redirected for the Father's glory. But at this point in his life, James was still wrapped up in himself. He couldn't completely understand why Jesus had come into this world. Nor could he handle the prominence and power that came with being one of the Twelve. James was too opportunistic to be selfless.

The Perils of Prominence

James wanted to be "first in line." His mother, Salome, came to Jesus with a very specific request: "Grant that one of these two sons of mine may sit at your right and the other at your left in your kingdom" (Matthew 20:21). No doubt James and John had put their mother up to it, because not long afterward the two brothers spoke up for themselves, asking the same basic question (Mark 10:37). When the other apostles heard what these two men had done, they were livid. We can only imagine the heated shouting match that ensued.

Jesus must have been discouraged by this immature jockeying for position and prestige, especially since these men had been with him for nearly three and a half years. But Jesus took this opportunity to teach the disciples a very important lesson in leadership. Rather than vying for power and ruling over one another, Jesus instructed them to serve one another (Mark 10:42–45).

James eventually became this servant leader. He died a martyr's death approximately five years after the church was born on Pentecost. But, why James? His brother John had become very prominent in Jerusalem as Peter's associate, and had confronted Jewish leaders both publicly and privately. Could it be that James—as the elder brother—was perhaps the most passionate and outspoken of the two sons of Zebedee? Could it be that after he became a true believer, he was even more daring as a witness for Christ than his brother John?

All of this is speculation, for we don't know what ultimately led to James's martyrdom. But from an eternal perspective, there is no need to speculate. James was the first of the apostles to die for his faith. He entered God's presence before any of the other apostles. In that sense James achieved his ambition to be "first in line"—though not in a way he might have originally planned. Yet the apostle Paul understood this same godly ambition when he wrote to the Philippians from a Roman prison: "For to me, to live is Christ and to die is gain" (Philippians 1:21).

Godly Ambition Is Costly

Throughout church history, many soldiers of the cross have given their lives for their faith. Stephen was the first recorded Christian martyr; perhaps his death inspired James to be an even more dynamic believer. The apostles Paul and Peter also died for Christ. In fact, ten of the original disciples were martyred because of their faith. These men paid the ultimate price for their radical obedience. The stories of countless others fill the last portion of Hebrews 11.

We may not have to pay the price of death for being a true believer. But the Lord asks us to pay a price nonetheless. Jesus Christ wants our tough-minded, egocentric, power-hungry selves to be surrendered to him. He wants us to practice love and Biblical Christianity in the ultimate sense by taking on "the very nature of a servant" (2:7). He wants to redirect our drive and ambition away from worldly power and prestige and replace it instead with a godly ambition to carry out his purposes in this world. He wants to do this, and will—if we'll let him. *—Dr. Gene Getz*

up to cause trouble and defile many.
16 See that no one is sexually immoral,
or is godless like Esau, who for a single
meal sold his inheritance rights as the
oldest son.[w] 17 Afterward, as you know,
when he wanted to inherit this blessing, he was rejected. He could bring
about no change of mind, though he
sought the blessing with tears.[x]
18 You have not come to a mountain
that can be touched and that is burning with fire; to darkness, gloom and
storm;[y] 19 to a trumpet blast[z] or to
such a voice speaking words that those
who heard it begged that no further
word be spoken to them,[a] 20 because
they could not bear what was commanded: "If even an animal touches
the mountain, it must be stoned."[a][b]
21 The sight was so terrifying that Moses
said, "I am trembling with fear."[b]
22 But you have come to Mount Zion,
to the heavenly Jerusalem,[c] the city[d]
of the living God. You have come to
thousands upon thousands of angels in
joyful assembly, 23 to the church of the
firstborn, whose names are written
in heaven.[e] You have come to God,
the judge of all men,[f] to the spirits
of righteous men made perfect,[g] 24 to
Jesus the mediator of a new covenant,
and to the sprinkled blood that speaks
a better word than the blood of Abel.[h]
25 See to it that you do not refuse him
who speaks. If they did not escape
when they refused him who warned[i]
them on earth, how much less will we,
if we turn away from him who warns us
from heaven?[j] 26 At that time his voice
shook the earth,[k] but now he has
promised, "Once more I will shake not
only the earth but also the heavens."[c][l] 27 The words "once more" indicate the removing of what can be
shaken[m]—that is, created things—so
that what cannot be shaken may remain.
1 →PG. 1374
28 Therefore, since we are receiving a
kingdom that cannot be shaken,[n] let
us be thankful, and so worship God acceptably with reverence and awe,[o]
29 for our "God is a consuming fire."[d][p]

Concluding Exhortations

2 →PG. 1378
13 Keep on loving each other as brothers.[q] 2 Do not forget to entertain
6 →PG. 1375
strangers,[r] for by so doing some people have entertained angels without
knowing it.[s] 3 Remember those in
prison[t] as if you were their fellow
prisoners, and those who are mistreated as if you yourselves were suffering.
4 →PG. 1384
4 Marriage should be honored by all,
and the marriage bed kept pure, for
God will judge the adulterer and all the
sexually immoral.[u] 5 Keep your lives
free from the love of money and be
content with what you have,[v] because
God has said,
3 →PG. 1374

"Never will I leave you;
never will I forsake you."[e][w]

6 So we say with confidence,

"The Lord is my helper; I will not
be afraid.
What can man do to me?"[f]

7 Remember your leaders,[x] who
5 →PG. 1371
spoke the word of God to you. Consider the outcome of their way of life and
imitate[y] their faith. 8 Jesus Christ is the
same yesterday and today and forever.[z]
9 Do not be carried away by all kinds
of strange teachings.[a] It is good for
our hearts to be strengthened[b] by
grace, not by ceremonial foods,[c]
which are of no value to those who eat
them. 10 We have an altar from which
those who minister at the tabernacle
have no right to eat.[d]
11 The high priest carries the blood of

12:16 [w] Ge 25:29-34
12:17 [x] Ge 27:30-40
12:18 [y] Ex 19:12-22; Dt 4:11
12:19 [z] Ex 20:18 [a] Ex 20:19; Dt 5:5,25
12:20 [b] Ex 19:12,13
12:22 [c] Gal 4:26 [d] Heb 11:10
12:23 [e] Lk 10:20 [f] Ps 94:2 [g] Php 3:12
12:24 [h] Ge 4:10; Heb 11:4
12:25 [i] Heb 8:5; 11:7 [j] Heb 2:2,3
12:26 [k] Ex 19:18 [l] Hag 2:6
12:27 [m] 1Co 7:31; 2Pe 3:10
12:28 [n] Da 2:44 [o] Heb 13:15
12:29 [p] Dt 4:24
13:1 [q] Ro 12:10; 1Pe 1:22
13:2 [r] Mt 25:35 [s] Ge 18:1-33
13:3 [t] Mt 25:36; Col 4:18
13:4 [u] 1Co 6:9
13:5 [v] Php 4:11 [w] Dt 31:6,8; Jos 1:5
13:7 [x] ver 17,24 [y] Heb 6:12
13:8 [z] Heb 1:12
13:9 [a] Eph 4:14 [b] Col 2:7 [c] Col 2:16
13:10 [d] 1Co 9:13; 10:18

[a] *20* Exodus 19:12,13 [b] *21* Deut. 9:19
[c] *26* Haggai 2:6 [d] *29* Deut. 4:24
[e] *5* Deut. 31:6 [f] *6* Psalm 118:6,7

13:17

PROMISE **5**

LIGHTEN THEIR LOAD

We've all heard of people who serve "roast preacher" for Sunday dinner. When individuals work to undermine congregational support for the pastor, the job of being a church leader can become extremely taxing.

But the writer of Hebrews calls his readers to be proactive in making their leaders' jobs easier. In a single verse this writer twice uses the word "obey" and once uses the word "submit." Why should we obey our leaders? First, because those who lead our churches are watching out for our spiritual development. They have an awesome responsibility; one day they'll answer to God for how faithfully they carried out that role. They're looking out for our interests, and we should support their efforts. Second, because our support lightens their load. More than that, it gives them joy. Third, because a believer does himself or herself no good by tearing down his or her church leaders through insubordination. It's to a believer's advantage to support his or her leaders.

As you reflect on this passage, try to identify some specific ways you could demonstrate support for your church leaders. Be sure and include prayer for them on your list.

For the next Promise 5 reading go to page 57.

animals into the Most Holy Place as a
sin offering, but the bodies are burned
outside the camp.[e] 12And so Jesus also
suffered outside the city gate[f] to make
the people holy through his own blood.
13Let us, then, go to him outside the
camp, bearing the disgrace he bore.[g]
14For here we do not have an enduring
city, but we are looking for the city that
is to come.[h]
15Through Jesus, therefore, let us
continually offer to God a sacrifice[i] of
praise—the fruit of lips[j] that confess
his name. 16And do not forget to do
good and to share with others,[k] for
with such sacrifices[l] God is pleased.
5 →PG. 1383
17Obey your leaders and submit to
their authority. They keep watch over
you[m] as men who must give an account. Obey them so that their work
will be a joy, not a burden, for that
would be of no advantage to you.
18Pray for us.[n] We are sure that we
have a clear conscience[o] and desire to
live honorably in every way. 19I particularly urge you to pray so that I may be
restored to you soon.[p]
20May the God of peace,[q] who
through the blood of the eternal covenant[r] brought back from the dead[s]
our Lord Jesus, that great Shepherd of
the sheep,[t] 21equip you with everything good for doing his will, and may
he work in us[u] what is pleasing to
him,[v] through Jesus Christ, to whom
be glory for ever and ever. Amen.[w]

22Brothers, I urge you to bear with
my word of exhortation, for I have written you only a short letter.[x]
23I want you to know that our brother Timothy[y] has been released. If he
arrives soon, I will come with him to
see you.
24Greet all your leaders[z] and all
God's people. Those from Italy[a] send
you their greetings.
25Grace be with you all.[b]

13:11 [e] Ex 29:14; Lev 16:27
13:12 [f] Jn 19:17
13:13 [g] Heb 11:26
13:14 [h] Php 3:20; Heb 12:22
13:15 [i] 1Pe 2:5 [j] Hos 14:2
13:16 [k] Ro 12:13 [l] Php 4:18
13:17 [m] Isa 62:6; Ac 20:28
13:18 [n] 1Th 5:25 [o] Ac 23:1
13:19 [p] Phm 22
13:20 [q] Ro 15:33 [r] Isa 55:3; Eze 37:26; Zec 9:11 [s] Ac 2:24 [t] Jn 10:11
13:21 [u] Php 2:13 [v] 1Jn 3:22 [w] Ro 11:36

13:22 [x] 1Pe 5:12 **13:23** [y] Ac 16:1 **13:24** [z] ver 7,17 [a] Ac 18:2 **13:25** [b] Col 4:18

JAMES

AT A GLANCE

Key Principle: An authentic faith is a faith that works; it is not merely verbal, but visible, and it is manifested in real changes in a believer's conduct and character.
Author: James, the Lord's brother
Time and Place: ~A.D. 40–50 / Probably Jerusalem
Key Verses: 1:19–22; 2:14–17

BENEFIT

James is a powerful and practical manual on applying our faith in Christ to the struggles and relationships we encounter every day. With force, conviction and clarity, this epistle relates Christlike conduct to a wide range of everyday topics.

SETTING

The James who wrote this epistle is evidently not the son of Zebedee and brother of John, since that James was martyred in A.D. 44 (Acts 12:2). Tradition and Biblical evidence point to James, the Lord's brother (Matthew 13:55; Mark 6:3; Galatians 1:19), as the author of this book. He was one of the leaders in the church in Jerusalem (Acts 12:17; 15:13–21; 21:18; Galatians 2:9, 12), and the language of a letter drafted under his leadership in Acts 15:23–29 shares a number of linguistic parallels with this epistle. In addition, this epistle has a strong Jewish orientation (it alludes to 22 Old Testament books) that fits well with the leader of the early church in Jerusalem, since he continued to observe the Mosaic Law as a testimony to other Jews (Acts 21:18–25).

James is addressed to "the twelve tribes scattered among the nations" (1:1)—this refers to the Hebrew Christians who lived outside of Palestine. These Jewish believers in Jesus as Messiah encountered many trials and needed encouragement to persevere in their faith. This epistle doesn't mention Gentile believers, and appears to have been written before the Jerusalem council (Acts 15). According to Josephus, James was martyred in A.D. 62.

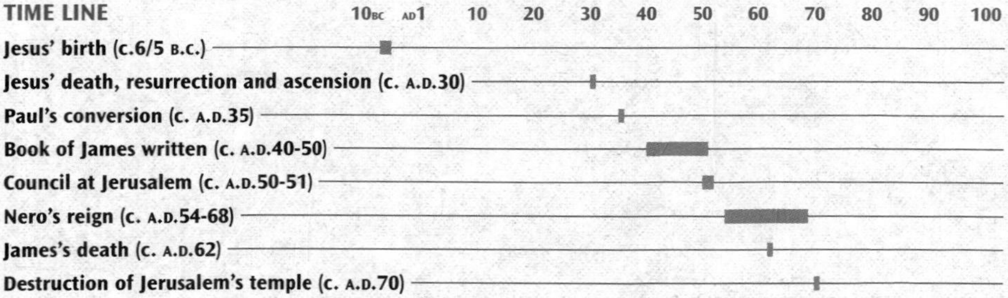

THEME AND PURPOSE

The theme of James is the character of true faith as it is expressed in various situations and relationships. Jewish believers scattered throughout the Roman Empire were struggling with trials and temptations, and needed instruction and correction regarding their problems with spiritual apathy, preferential treatment of the wealthy, disunity and materialism. James wrote this letter to exhort these believers to obey the truth and to apply a living faith in Christ to their attitudes and actions. He warned them that a refusal to change personal character and conduct is symptomatic of a dead faith.

UNIQUE CONTRIBUTION

This epistle is the wisdom literature of the New Testament, and it is strongly influenced by Proverbs (e.g., the material on speech and wisdom in Proverbs 3) and the Sermon on the Mount. It combines the pithy teachings of the Proverbs with the fiery rhetoric of Amos in its relentlessly ethical stance. It is full of vivid imagery and sharp commands (it includes 54 imperatives in its 108 verses). Because it specifically treats so many different life situations, James is the most practical book in the New Testament. Its timeless principles apply just as well to life today as they did in the first century.

CHRIST IN JAMES

James calls himself "a servant of God and of the Lord Jesus Christ" (1:1) and speaks of his readers as brothers who are "believers in our glorious Lord Jesus Christ" (2:1). While he says less than other New Testament writers about Christ's person and work, his words are saturated with allusions to Jesus' teaching (he includes 15 indirect references to the Sermon on the Mount). He anticipates the Lord's coming as the Judge in 5:7–9.

OVERVIEW

FOCUS	Character of Faith	Control of Faith	Conflicts of Faith	Consummation of Faith
REFERENCE	1:1 — 2:26	3:1 — 3:18	4:1 — 5:6	5:7 — 5:20
TOPICS	Word and Works	Words and Wisdom	Worldliness and Wealth	Waiting and Wholeness
	Tests	Tongue	Tensions	Triumph
	"be quick to listen"	"slow to speak"	"and slow to become angry" (1:19)	
LOCATION	Probably Jerusalem			
TIME	~A.D. 40–50			

After a brief greeting (1:1) James speaks of the eternal perspective believers need to cultivate when they face trials so they will be able to persevere when tested and tempted (1:2–18). They must not only listen to the word, but apply it to their actions (1:19–27). James then instructs his readers to love the poor and the rich alike (2:1–13). He contrasts profession of faith with possession of faith, and argues that a genuine faith is expressed in deeds (2:14–26). While faith alone justifies us before God (Romans 4), it is only by the works of faith that we are justified before others (2:24).

The tongue is the hardest thing in nature to control; our speech can lead to blessing or cursing, to life or to death (3:1–12). James contrasts two kinds of wisdom, the heavenly and the earthly and exhorts his readers to turn away from envy and selfish ambition to love, mercy and peace (3:13–18). Selfishness and materialism lead to quarrels, disunity and pride; James counsels us to humble ourselves and submit to God rather than envying and slandering others (4:1–12).

Those who engage in business must submit their plans to God's will and avoid the arrogance of autonomy (4:13–17). Those who depend on their wealth and oppress others will meet with a day of reckoning (5:1–6).

James says that those who are suffering and oppressed must set their hope in the promised coming of the Lord (5:7–12). He concludes his epistle with instruction on the healing and restoration that can be accomplished through prayers offered in faith (5:13–20).

JAMES

1 James,[a] a servant of God[b] and of the Lord Jesus Christ,

To the twelve tribes[c] scattered[d] among the nations:

Greetings.

Trials and Temptations

3 →PG. 1374

2Consider it pure joy, my brothers, whenever you face trials of many kinds,[e] **3**because you know that the testing of your faith develops perseverance. **4**Perseverance must finish its work so that you may be mature and complete, not lacking anything. **5**If any of you lacks wisdom, he should ask God,[f] who gives generously to all without finding fault, and it will be given to him.[g] **6**But when he asks, he must believe and not doubt,[h] because he who doubts is like a wave of the sea, blown and tossed by the wind. **7**That man should not think he will receive anything from the Lord; **8**he is a double-minded man,[i] unstable in all he does.

9The brother in humble circumstances ought to take pride in his high position. **10**But the one who is rich should take pride in his low position, because he will pass away like a wild flower.[j] **11**For the sun rises with scorching heat and withers[k] the plant; its blossom falls and its beauty is destroyed.[l] In the same way, the rich man will fade away even while he goes about his business.

12Blessed is the man who perseveres under trial, because when he has stood the test, he will receive the crown of life[m] that God has promised to those who love him.[n]

13When tempted, no one should say, "God is tempting me." For God cannot be tempted by evil, nor does he tempt anyone; **14**but each one is tempted when, by his own evil desire, he is dragged away and enticed. **15**Then, after desire has conceived, it gives birth to sin;[o] and sin, when it is full-grown, gives birth to death.[p]

16Don't be deceived,[q] my dear brothers.[r] **17**Every good and perfect gift is from above,[s] coming down from the Father of the heavenly lights, who does not change[t] like shifting shadows. **18**He chose to give us birth[u] through the word of truth, that we might be a kind of firstfruits[v] of all he created.

Listening and Doing

3 →PG. 1377

19My dear brothers, take note of this: Everyone should be quick to listen, slow to speak[w] and slow to become angry, **20**for man's anger does not bring about the righteous life that God desires. **21**Therefore, get rid of[x] all moral filth and the evil that is so prevalent and humbly accept the word planted in you,[y] which can save you.

1 →PG. 1377

22Do not merely listen to the word, and so deceive yourselves. Do what it says. **23**Anyone who listens to the word but does not do what it says is like a man who looks at his face in a mirror **24**and, after looking at himself, goes away and immediately forgets what he looks like. **25**But the man who looks intently into the perfect law that gives freedom,[z] and continues to do this, not forgetting what he has heard, but doing it—he will be blessed in what he does.[a]

26If anyone considers himself religious and yet does not keep a tight rein on his tongue,[b] he deceives himself and his religion is worthless. **27**Religion that God our Father accepts as pure and faultless is this: to look after[c] orphans and widows[d] in their distress and to keep oneself from being polluted by the world.[e]

7 →PG. 1375

1:2-4

PE

PURE JOY?

After reading the opening lines of James's letter, the original recipients were probably surprised. Instead of sympathizing with them and offering them comfort in the face of their struggles, James urged them to consider their trials "pure joy." At first glance his words sound insensitive—like someone telling a friend to be glad he or she is unemployed or sick. But James wasn't doing that. Instead, he urged them to rejoice because of what God would accomplish in their spiritual lives through these trials.

As in weight training, trials create pain but are followed by greater strength. Our earthly trials produce perseverance or spiritual endurance, and the outcome of perseverance is spiritual maturity—a stronger relationship with God. Now that's something to be joyful about!

1:1 [a]Ac 15:13 [b]Tit 1:1 [c]Ac 26:7 [d]Dt 32:26; Jn 7:35; 1Pe 1:1
1:2 [e]Mt 5:12; 1Pe 1:6
1:5 [f]1Ki 3:9,10; Pr 2:3-6 [g]Mt 7:7
1:6 [h]Mk 11:24
1:8 [i]Jas 4:8
1:10 [j]1Co 7:31; 1Pe 1:24
1:11 [k]Ps 102:4,11 [l]Isa 40:6-8
1:12 [m]1Co 9:25 [n]Jas 2:5
1:15 [o]Job 15:35; Ps 7:14 [p]Ro 6:23
1:16 [q]1Co 6:9 [r]ver 19
1:17 [s]Jn 3:27 [t]Nu 23:19; Mal 3:6
1:18 [u]Jn 1:13 [v]Eph 1:12; Rev 14:4
1:19 [w]Pr 10:19
1:21 [x]Eph 4:22 [y]Eph 1:13
1:25 [z]Jas 2:12 [a]Jn 13:17
1:26 [b]Ps 34:13; 1Pe 3:10
1:27 [c]Mt 25:36 [d]Isa 1:17,23 [e]Ro 12:2

Favoritism Forbidden

6 →PG. 1377
2 My brothers, as believers in our
glorious[f] Lord Jesus Christ, don't
show favoritism.[g] 2 Suppose a man
comes into your meeting wearing a
gold ring and fine clothes, and a poor
man in shabby clothes also comes in.
3 If you show special attention to the
man wearing fine clothes and say,
"Here's a good seat for you," but say to
the poor man, "You stand there" or "Sit
on the floor by my feet," 4 have you not
discriminated among yourselves and
become judges[h] with evil thoughts?
5 Listen, my dear brothers:[i] Has not
God chosen those who are poor in the
eyes of the world[j] to be rich in faith[k]
and to inherit the kingdom he promised those who love him?[l] 6 But you
have insulted the poor.[m] Is it not the
rich who are exploiting you? Are they
not the ones who are dragging you into
court?[n] 7 Are they not the ones who are
slandering the noble name of him to
whom you belong?
8 If you really keep the royal law
found in Scripture, "Love your neighbor as yourself,"[a][o] you are doing
right. 9 But if you show favoritism,[p]
you sin and are convicted by the law as
lawbreakers.[q] 10 For whoever keeps
the whole law and yet stumbles at
just one point is guilty of breaking all
of it.[r] 11 For he who said, "Do not
commit adultery,"[b][s] also said, "Do
not murder."[c][t] If you do not commit
adultery but do commit murder, you
have become a lawbreaker.
7 →PG. 1376
12 Speak and act as those who are going to be judged by the law that gives
freedom,[u] 13 because judgment without mercy will be shown to anyone
who has not been merciful.[v] Mercy
triumphs over judgment!

Faith and Deeds

14 What good is it, my brothers, if a
man claims to have faith but has no
deeds?[w] Can such faith save him?
15 Suppose a brother or sister is without
clothes and daily food.[x] 16 If one of
you says to him, "Go, I wish you well;

2:1 [f]1Co 2:8 [g]Lev 19:15
2:4 [h]Jn 7:24
2:5 [i]Jas 1:16,19 [j]1Co 1:26-28 [k]Lk 12:21 [l]Jas 1:12
2:6 [m]1Co 11:22 [n]Ac 8:3
2:8 [o]Lev 19:18
2:9 [p]ver 1 [q]Dt 1:17
2:10 [r]Mt 5:19; Gal 3:10
2:11 [s]Ex 20:14; Dt 5:18 [t]Ex 20:13; Dt 5:17
2:12 [u]Jas 1:25
2:13 [v]Mt 5:7; 18:32-35
2:14 [w]Mt 7:26; Jas 1:22-25
2:15 [x]Mt 25:35,36

[a]8 Lev. 19:18 [b]11 Exodus 20:14; Deut. 5:18
[c]11 Exodus 20:13; Deut. 5:17

2:1-13

PROMISE 6

PLAYING FAVORITES

It's a popular game, one we've all played at one time or another. It doesn't require expensive equipment or an elaborate playing field. It can be played at work, school, home or church. In fact, it can be played anywhere people gather.

Some adults play the game with sophistication. With all the effort it takes to make a 6-inch putt, they detect slight social graces that identify someone as acceptable. And with a glance of the eye or an "excuse me," they're able to inform someone they would rather not be around him or her. Others play with brutality. With all the delicacy of a tractor pull, they vocalize loudly about who they want to be around. With no tact and even less concern for personal feelings, they spew degrading names at people whom they'd rather not be around.

By now you've probably guessed the name of the game: *Favoritism.* James says this is a game no follower of Jesus Christ is ever to play.

As followers of Jesus, we're not to be concerned with human ideas about significance. We're to be so absorbed with the excellence of Jesus that all signs of human greatness or weakness fade away. Just as the brightness of the sun drowns out the light of the moon and stars, so the greatness of Jesus Christ drowns out all human differences.

When we play favorites we're allowing ourselves to be consumed with the pursuit of human greatness. Throughout the Bible God condemns such partiality. In Leviticus 19:15 God commands his people to deal fairly with others. In Malachi 2:9 God condemns his people for judging with partiality.

We're not to treat anybody better or worse because of the clothes they wear or the car they drive. Why? Because when we play favorites we're making value judgments about someone else's worth. That unfounded judgment translates into unfair and sometimes harsh treatment of individuals. We believe that somehow a person's wealth, popularity or influence will rub off on us, so we want to be around him or her. Conversely, we believe those people who are poor or unattractive can't help us.

But God values everyone equally—both people who are rich and those who are poor. Indeed, people who have less may be more inclined to see their need for God. For that reason, they're often rich in faith. When we show partiality to people who are rich, we demonstrate that our values are different than God's.

As believers, we're to think and act like people who have been liberated from the internal power of sin. God will judge us by how well we allow the love of Jesus to live through us, moving us to show mercy to the needy. Because Jesus Christ is the governing force in our lives, we're to love all believers as brothers and sisters in the Lord. And for those who have yet to believe in Jesus, we're to show them the love of Jesus in all we say and do.

For the next Promise 6 reading go to page 1420.

keep warm and well fed," but does nothing about his physical needs, what good is it?[y] 17In the same way, faith by itself, if it is not accompanied by action, is dead.

18But someone will say, "You have faith; I have deeds."

Show me your faith without deeds,[z] and I will show you my faith by what I do.[a] 19You believe that there is one God.[b] Good! Even the demons believe that[c]—and shudder.

20You foolish man, do you want evidence that faith without deeds is useless[a]?[d] 21Was not our ancestor Abraham considered righteous for what he did when he offered his son Isaac on the altar?[e] 22You see that his faith and his actions were working together,[f] and his faith was made complete by what he did.[g] 23And the scripture was fulfilled that says, "Abraham believed God, and it was credited to him as righteousness,"[b][h] and he was called God's friend.[i] 24You see that a person is justified by what he does and not by faith alone.

25In the same way, was not even Rahab the prostitute considered righteous for what she did when she gave lodging to the spies and sent them off in a different direction?[j] 26As the body without the spirit is dead, so faith without deeds is dead.[k]

Taming the Tongue

3 Not many of you should presume to be teachers, my brothers, because you know that we who teach will be judged more strictly. 2We all stumble[l] in many ways. If anyone is never at fault in what he says,[m] he is a perfect man,[n] able to keep his whole body in check.[o]

3When we put bits into the mouths of horses to make them obey us, we can turn the whole animal.[p] 4Or take ships as an example. Although they are so large and are driven by strong winds, they are steered by a very small rudder wherever the pilot wants to go. 5Likewise the tongue is a small part of the body, but it makes great boasts.[q] Consider what a great forest is set on fire by a small spark. 6The tongue also is a fire,[r] a world of evil among the parts of the body. It corrupts the whole person,[s] sets the whole course of his life on fire, and is itself set on fire by hell.

7All kinds of animals, birds, reptiles and creatures of the sea are being tamed and have been tamed by man, 8but no man can tame the tongue. It is a restless evil, full of deadly poison.[t]

9With the tongue we praise our Lord and Father, and with it we curse men, who have been made in God's likeness.[u] 10Out of the same mouth come praise and cursing. My brothers, this should not be. 11Can both fresh water and salt[c] water flow from the same spring? 12My brothers, can a fig tree bear olives, or a grapevine bear figs?[v] Neither can a salt spring produce fresh water.

Two Kinds of Wisdom

13Who is wise and understanding among you? Let him show it[w] by his good life, by deeds done in the humility that comes from wisdom. 14But if you harbor bitter envy and selfish ambition[x] in your hearts, do not boast about it or deny the truth.[y] 15Such "wisdom" does not come down from heaven[z] but is earthly, unspiritual, of the devil.[a] 16For where you have envy

7 →PG. 1378

2:16 [y]1Jn 3:17,18
2:18 [z]Ro 3:28 [a]Jas 3:13
2:19 [b]Dt 6:4 [c]Mt 8:29; Lk 4:34
2:20 [d]ver 17,26
2:21 [e]Ge 22:9,12
2:22 [f]Heb 11:17 [g]1Th 1:3
2:23 [h]Ge 15:6; Ro 4:3 [i]2Ch 20:7; Isa 41:8
2:25 [j]Heb 11:31
2:26 [k]ver 17,20
3:2 [l]1Ki 8:46; Jas 2:10 [m]1Pe 3:10 [n]Mt 12:37 [o]Jas 1:26
3:3 [p]Ps 32:9
3:5 [q]Ps 12:3,4
3:6 [r]Pr 16:27 [s]Mt 15:11,18,19
3:8 [t]Ps 140:3; Ro 3:13
3:9 [u]Ge 1:26,27; 1Co 11:7
3:12 [v]Mt 7:16
3:13 [w]Jas 2:18
3:14 [x]ver 16 [y]Jas 5:19
3:15 [z]Jas 1:17 [a]1Ti 4:1

[a]20 Some early manuscripts *dead*
[b]23 Gen. 15:6 [c]11 Greek *bitter* (see also verse 14)

3:3–12

PROMISE 3

TAMING THE TONGUE

In this short passage, James bluntly addresses the issue of our speech. Read over this passage again to catch the metaphors he uses to describe the tongue. Have you ever realized what a potentially wicked thing that little muscle in your mouth is?

Make no mistake about it—the words you speak are powerful beyond imagination. They expand or limit your friendships. They can make or break your career opportunities. If you're married, they'll help determine the quality of your marriage. If you're a father, they'll shape your children.

A godly man recognizes the tongue's power to build up or to tear down. But the tongue only shapes the words that originate in our hearts and minds. Hearts that are controlled by the Spirit's power will produce speech that builds others up instead of tearing them down. In other words, if we want to control our tongues, we must ask God to help us control our hearts.

The book of Proverbs is filled with verses that address a person's speech. Turn to that book and take an hour or so to read through it. As you do, highlight in some way every verse that addresses this subject. Allow the Bible's wisdom and the Spirit to direct your heart—and your tongue.

For the next Promise 3 reading go to page 1382.

and selfish ambition, there you find disorder and every evil practice.

3 →PG. 1377 6 →PG. 1384

17But the wisdom that comes from heaven[b] is first of all pure; then peace-loving, considerate, submissive, full of mercy[c] and good fruit, impartial and sincere.[d] 18Peacemakers who sow in peace raise a harvest of righteousness.[e]

Submit Yourselves to God

4 What causes fights and quarrels[f] among you? Don't they come from your desires that battle[g] within you? 1 →PG. 1378 2You want something but don't get it. You kill and covet, but you cannot have what you want. You quarrel and fight. You do not have, because you do not ask God. 3When you ask, you do not receive,[h] because you ask with wrong motives,[i] that you may spend what you get on your pleasures.

4You adulterous people, don't you know that friendship with the world[j] is hatred toward God?[k] Anyone who chooses to be a friend of the world becomes an enemy of God.[l] 5Or do you think Scripture says without reason that the spirit he caused to live in us envies intensely?[a] 6But he gives us more grace. That is why Scripture says:

> "God opposes the proud
> but gives grace to the humble."[b][m]

3 →PG. 1378

7Submit yourselves, then, to God. Resist the devil,[n] and he will flee from you. 8Come near to God and he will come near to you.[o] Wash your hands,[p] you sinners, and purify your hearts, you double-minded.[q] 9Grieve, mourn and wail. Change your laughter to mourning and your joy to gloom.[r] 10Humble yourselves before the Lord, and he will lift you up.

11Brothers, do not slander one another.[s] Anyone who speaks against his brother or judges him[t] speaks against the law and judges it. When you judge the law, you are not keeping it,[u] but sitting in judgment on it. 12There is only one Lawgiver and Judge, the one who is able to save and destroy.[v] But you—who are you to judge your neighbor?[w]

Boasting About Tomorrow

13Now listen, you who say, "Today or tomorrow we will go to this or that city, spend a year there, carry on business and make money."[x] 14Why, you do not even know what will happen tomorrow. What is your life? You are a mist that appears for a little while and then vanishes.[y] 15Instead, you ought to say, "If it is the Lord's will,[z] we will live and do this or that." 16As it is, you boast and brag. All such boasting is evil.[a] 17Anyone, then, who knows the good he ought to do and doesn't do it, sins.[b]

Warning to Rich Oppressors

5 Now listen, you rich people,[c] weep and wail because of the misery that is coming upon you. 2Your wealth has rotted, and moths have eaten your clothes.[d] 3Your gold and silver are corroded. Their corrosion will testify against you and eat your flesh like fire. You have hoarded wealth in the last days.[e] 4Look! The wages you failed to pay the workmen[f] who mowed your fields are crying out against you. The cries[g] of the harvesters have reached the ears of the Lord Almighty.[h] 5You have lived on earth in luxury and self-indulgence. You have fattened yourselves[i] in the day of slaughter.[c][j] 6You have condemned and murdered innocent men,[k] who were not opposing you.

3:17 [b]1Co 2:6 [c]Lk 6:36 [d]Ro 12:9
3:18 [e]Pr 11:18; Isa 32:17
4:1 [f]Tit 3:9 [g]Ro 7:23
4:3 [h]Ps 18:41 [i]1Jn 3:22; 5:14
4:4 [j]Jas 1:27 [k]1Jn 2:15 [l]Jn 15:19
4:6 [m]Ps 138:6; Pr 3:34; Mt 23:12
4:7 [n]Eph 4:27; 1Pe 5:6-9
4:8 [o]2Ch 15:2 [p]Isa 1:16 [q]Jas 1:8
4:9 [r]Lk 6:25
4:11 [s]1Pe 2:1 [t]Mt 7:1 [u]Jas 1:22
4:12 [v]Mt 10:28 [w]Ro 14:4
4:13 [x]Pr 27:1
4:14 [y]Job 7:7; Ps 102:3
4:15 [z]Ac 18:21
4:16 [a]1Co 5:6
4:17 [b]Lk 12:47; Jn 9:41
5:1 [c]Lk 6:24
5:2 [d]Job 13:28; Mt 6:19,20
5:3 [e]ver 7,8
5:4 [f]Lev 19:13 [g]Dt 24:15 [h]Ro 9:29
5:5 [i]Am 6:1 [j]Jer 12:3; 25:34
5:6 [k]Heb 10:38

[a]5 Or *that God jealously longs for the spirit that he made to live in us;* or *that the Spirit he caused to live in us longs jealously*
[b]6 Prov. 3:34 [c]5 Or *yourselves as in a day of feasting*

4:13–17

PROMISE 1

PLANNING AHEAD?

James's advice in this passage flies in the face of corporate and personal planning efforts. When he addresses his readers in verse 13, he's talking to virtually all of us. Does James mean that planning for the future is evil?

No. Planning for the future is great. Doing so helps us become good stewards of our time and other resources. But when we plan, we must begin at the beginning: by asking God what he would have us do. We must never forget that God holds the future in his hands. No matter how many detailed quarterly projections we produce, no matter how carefully controlled our personal five-year plans may be, God is the One who controls what will happen.

How should we respond to that truth? By submitting all of our hopes, dreams and plans to the Lord, asking that his will be worked out in our lives. James urged us to acknowledge God's ultimate rule by saying, "If the Lord wills." Make that the first sentence in your next planning session.

For the next Promise 1 reading go to page 1378.

Patience in Suffering

7 Be patient, then, brothers, until the
Lord's coming. See how the farmer
waits for the land to yield its valuable
crop and how patient he is for the autumn and spring rains.[l] 8 You too, be
patient and stand firm, because the
Lord's coming is near.[m] 9 Don't grumble against each other, brothers,[n] or
you will be judged. The Judge[o] is
standing at the door![p]

5:1–13 PROMISE 1

PATIENCE: SCARCE COMMODITY

We've all heard the phrase "Patience is a virtue." And in a culture that seems to run on fast food, 24-hour-a-day banking machines, up-to-the-minute news coverage and instantaneous digital internet access, that virtue seems to be in short supply.

James urged believers to cultivate patience in their lives, just as a farmer does who waits for his crops to come up. Make no mistake about it, planting the seed and allowing patience to grow takes a great deal of self-control and trust in God. The Bible is filled with people who waited on God for weeks, months, even years.

Whatever our circumstances, we must calmly wait for God to do his work in people and events. When you think about it, it only makes sense—God works according to his own divine timeline, not an earthly one. The choice, then, is ours: We can either develop an ulcer by wondering, waiting and worrying, or we can lay our fears and anxieties before the Lord and let him work.

For the next Promise 1 reading go to page 1387.

10 Brothers, as an example of pa- 3 →PG. 1382
tience in the face of suffering, take the
prophets[q] who spoke in the name of
the Lord. 11 As you know, we consider
blessed[r] those who have persevered.
You have heard of Job's perseverance[s] and have seen what the Lord
finally brought about.[t] The Lord is full
of compassion and mercy.[u]

12 Above all, my brothers, do not
swear—not by heaven or by earth or by
anything else. Let your "Yes" be yes,
and your "No," no, or you will be condemned.[v]

The Prayer of Faith

13 Is any one of you in trouble? He 1 →PG. 1383
should pray.[w] Is anyone happy? Let
him sing songs of praise.[x] 14 Is any one
of you sick? He should call the elders of
the church to pray over him and anoint
him with oil[y] in the name of the Lord.
15 And the prayer offered in faith will
make the sick person well; the Lord
will raise him up. If he has sinned,
he will be forgiven. 16 Therefore con-
fess your sins[z] to each other and pray 2 →PG. 1378
for each other so that you may be
healed.[a] The prayer of a righteous
man is powerful and effective.[b]

17 Elijah was a man just like us.[c] He
prayed earnestly that it would not rain,
and it did not rain on the land for three
and a half years.[d] 18 Again he prayed,
and the heavens gave rain, and the
earth produced its crops.[e]

19 My brothers, if one of you should 2 →PG. 1383
wander from the truth[f] and someone
should bring him back,[g] 20 remember
this: Whoever turns a sinner from the 7 →PG. 1383
error of his way will save[h] him from
death and cover over a multitude of
sins.[i]

5:7 [l] Dt 11:14; Jer 5:24
5:8 [m] Ro 13:11; 1Pe 4:7
5:9 [n] Jas 4:11 [o] 1Co 4:5; 1Pe 4:5 [p] Mt 24:33
5:10 [q] Mt 5:12
5:11 [r] Mt 5:10 [s] Job 1:21,22; 2:10 [t] Job 42:10, 12-17 [u] Nu 14:18
5:12 [v] Mt 5:34-37
5:13 [w] Ps 50:15 [x] Col 3:16
5:14 [y] Mk 6:13
5:16 [z] Mt 3:6 [a] 1Pe 2:24 [b] Jn 9:31
5:17 [c] Ac 14:15 [d] 1Ki 17:1; Lk 4:25
5:18 [e] 1Ki 18:41-45
5:19 [f] Jas 3:14 [g] Mt 18:15
5:20 [h] Ro 11:14 [i] 1Pe 4:8

1 PETER

AT A GLANCE

Key Principle: As people who have the hope of salvation, we are called to a lifestyle of submission and service, and are encouraged to see suffering as part of a growth process as we follow in Christ's steps.
Author: Peter
Time and Place: ~A.D. 60–64 / Probably Rome
Key Verses: 1:3, 10–12; 2:21; 4:12–13

BENEFIT

First Peter gives us a divine perspective on living as strangers in a world that is increasingly hostile to Christ's gospel. Each of its five chapters alludes to suffering as a very real part of the Christian experience. This letter counsels and comforts us in times of adversity and affliction by pointing us to the living hope we have in our relationship with Christ.

SETTING

The apostle Peter wrote this letter with the help of Silas (5:12). Clear similarities exist between phrases in this epistle and Peter's sermons in Acts. Peter addresses "God's elect, strangers in the world" who are scattered throughout the Roman provinces of Asia Minor. Apparently, many of these people were Gentiles who had come to faith in Christ (2:9–10) and were being maligned by their countrymen for abstaining from pagan debauchery (4:3–4). Christians in Asia Minor were facing growing suspicion and hostility because of their new way of living and their talk about another kingdom; before long, Christianity would be officially banned. Peter wrote this epistle in "Babylon" (5:13), which is probably a reference to Rome as a center of idolatry (cf. Revelation 17—18). Early tradition says that Peter spent the last years of his life in Rome, and this is also supported by the presence of Mark (5:13) who was in Rome during Paul's first imprisonment (Colossians 4:10). Peter probably wrote this letter not long before the outbreak of Roman persecution under Nero in A.D. 64.

Peter played a key role in forming the early church and in spreading the gospel from the Jews to both the Samaritans and the Gentiles. Peter apparently traveled extensively with his wife (1 Corinthians 9:5) and ministered in various Roman provinces. According to tradition, he was crucified upside down in Rome prior to Nero's death in A.D. 68.

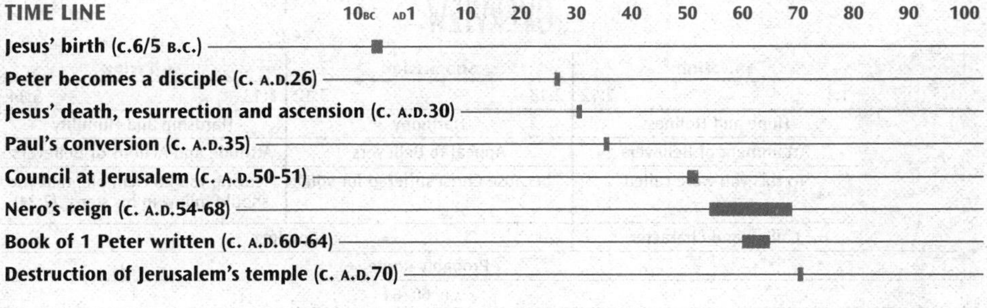

THEME AND PURPOSE

First Peter develops the theme of a Biblical response to suffering. Peter anticipated a growing wave of persecution against followers of Christ; it appears that he wrote this epistle not long before Christianity was outlawed. He wanted to prepare his readers to persevere under adversity and not to be surprised at the painful trials they were suffering, as though something strange were happening to them (4:12). Peter encouraged his readers to rejoice that they were participating in the sufferings of Christ, because they would be "overjoyed when his glory is revealed" (4:13). They also needed to know that their brothers and sisters throughout the world were also experiencing the same kind of sufferings (5:9). Peter encouraged them to submit to God's loving purposes for their lives, and to draw on his strength in the present while maintaining a clear hope in their heavenly future. The more they realized that they were strangers and aliens in the world, the better they would be able to stand fast in the true grace of God (5:12).

UNIQUE CONTRIBUTION

First Peter is a warm and compassionate letter that demonstrates a sympathetic concern for the plight of its readers. But it is also firm and forceful—there are 34 imperatives (commands) from 1:13 to 5:9, and these underscore the apostle's authority and the urgency of the situation he was addressing. This epistle has been called "the Job of the New Testament" because it stresses suffering and submission to God's sovereign will. First Peter contributes significantly to the areas of soteriology (the doctrine of salvation) and Christology (the doctrine of Christ) (1:2–12, 18–20; 2:21–25; 3:18–22; 4:12–19). This book shares a number of similarities with some of Paul's epistles, since both men interacted with each other and held apostolic doctrine in common.

CHRIST IN 1 PETER

The resurrected Christ is the source of our new birth and eternal inheritance; our hope in him can give us the power to rejoice even in times of trials and suffering (1:3–7). We can love him even though we have not yet seen him (1:8), and we can share his joy now as well as anticipating the glories to come (1:9–11). Christ is the cornerstone of God's living temple; through his suffering and death, he purchased redemption for us "so that we might die to sins and live for righteousness" (2:24; 1:18–19; 3:18). Christ's example of suffering sinlessly, silently and as our substitute is a model for us to follow (2:21–24). He is the Chief Shepherd and Overseer of our souls (2:25; 5:4), and we can cast all our anxieties on him, knowing that we have been called to share his eternal glory (5:6, 10).

OVERVIEW

FOCUS	Salvation		Submission		Suffering	
REFERENCE	1:1	2:12	2:13	3:12	3:13	5:14
TOPICS	Hope and Holiness		Harmony		Hardship and Humility	
	Attainment of Believers		Appeal to Believers		Attitude and Actions of Believers	
	"To this you were called"		"because Christ suffered for you"		"leaving you an example, that you should follow in his steps" (2:21)	
	Calling and Character		Conduct			
LOCATION	Probably Rome					
TIME	~A.D. 60–64					

This epistle uses God's grace in our salvation as the foundation for an attitude of submission when suffering for Christ's sake. It begins by portraying salvation in terms of the believer's future hope in an imperishable inheritance (1:3–5), the joy that is available in spite of present trials (1:6–9) and the past predictions of this salvation (1:10–12). In view of our salvation, Peter urges believers to grow in holiness and to purify themselves in obedience to the truth (1:13—2:12). As "a chosen people, a royal priesthood, a holy nation, a people belonging to God" (2:9), they should mature in their salvation and manifest a new quality of life to a watching world.

This gift of salvation is best expressed on a relational level by an attitude of submission and service to others (2:13—3:12). Believers should submit for the Lord's sake to those in government and to those who personally have authority over them (2:13–20). This attitude of submission to God's purposes is best illustrated in Christ's undeserved suffering (2:21–25). Peter extends this theme of submission to the marital relationship (3:1–7) and to the pursuit of harmonious relationships with others (3:8–12).

While submission to Christ's lordship may lead to suffering for his sake, Peter encourages his readers to order their lives so that those who slander them will be ashamed (3:13–17). Peter points to Christ's work in bringing about their salvation (3:18–22) and urges believers to live in Christ's power and in service to one another (4:1–11). If they suffer for Christ's sake, they should commit themselves to the Lord and continue in his service (4:12–19). Peter exhorts spiritual leaders to serve as examples to their flocks, and calls all of his readers to a lifestyle of humility and hope (5:1–11).

1 PETER

1 Peter, an apostle of Jesus Christ,[a]
To God's elect,[b] strangers in the
world, scattered throughout Pontus,
Galatia, Cappadocia, Asia and Bithynia,[c] **2**who have been chosen according to the foreknowledge[d] of God the
Father, through the sanctifying work
of the Spirit,[e] for obedience to Jesus
Christ and sprinkling by his blood:[f]

Grace and peace be yours in abundance.

Praise to God for a Living Hope

3Praise be to the God and Father of
our Lord Jesus Christ![g] In his great
mercy[h] he has given us new birth into
a living hope through the resurrection
of Jesus Christ from the dead,[i] **4**and
into an inheritance that can never perish, spoil or fade—kept in heaven for
you,[j] **5**who through faith are shielded
by God's power[k] until the coming of
the salvation that is ready to be revealed in the last time. **6**In this you
greatly rejoice,[l] though now for a little
while[m] you may have had to suffer
grief in all kinds of trials.[n] **7**These have
come so that your faith—of great-
er worth than gold, which perishes
even though refined by fire[o]—may be
proved genuine[p] and may result in
praise, glory and honor when Jesus
Christ is revealed.[q] **8**Though you have
not seen him, you love him; and even
though you do not see him now, you
believe in him[r] and are filled with an
inexpressible and glorious joy, **9**for you
are receiving the goal of your faith, the
salvation of your souls.[s]
10Concerning this salvation, the
prophets, who spoke[t] of the grace
that was to come to you, searched intently and with the greatest care,[u]
11trying to find out the time and circumstances to which the Spirit of
Christ[v] in them was pointing when he
predicted the sufferings of Christ and
the glories that would follow. **12**It was
revealed to them that they were not
serving themselves but you, when they
spoke of the things that have now been
told you by those who have preached
the gospel to you[w] by the Holy Spirit
sent from heaven. Even angels long to
look into these things.

Be Holy

13Therefore, prepare your minds for 3 →PG. 1383
action; be self-controlled; set your
hope fully on the grace to be given you
when Jesus Christ is revealed. **14**As obedient children, do not conform[x] to the
evil desires you had when you lived
in ignorance.[y] **15**But just as he who
called you is holy, so be holy in all you
do;[z] **16**for it is written: "Be holy, because I am holy."[a][a]
17Since you call on a Father who
judges each man's work impartially,[b]
live your lives as strangers here in reverent fear.[c] **18**For you know that it was
not with perishable things such as silver or gold that you were redeemed[d]
from the empty way of life handed
down to you from your forefathers,
19but with the precious blood of Christ,
a lamb[e] without blemish or defect.[f]
20He was chosen before the creation of
the world,[g] but was revealed in these
last times[h] for your sake. **21**Through

[a]*16* Lev. 11:44,45; 19:2; 20:7

1:1 [a]2Pe 1:1 [b]Mt 24:22 [c]Ac 16:7
1:2 [d]Ro 8:29 [e]2Th 2:13 [f]Heb 10:22; 12:24
1:3 [g]2Co 1:3; Eph 1:3 [h]Tit 3:5; Jas 1:18 [i]1Co 15:20
1:4 [j]Col 1:5
1:5 [k]Jn 10:28
1:6 [l]Ro 5:2 [m]1Pe 5:10 [n]Jas 1:2
1:7 [o]Job 23:10; Ps 66:10; Pr 17:3 [p]Jas 1:3 [q]Ro 2:7
1:8 [r]Jn 20:29
1:9 [s]Ro 6:22
1:10 [t]Mt 26:24 [u]Mt 13:17
1:11 [v]2Pe 1:21
1:12 [w]ver 25
1:14 [x]Ro 12:2 [y]Eph 4:18
1:15 [z]2Co 7:1; 1Th 4:7
1:16 [a]Lev 11:44,45
1:17 [b]Ac 10:34 [c]Heb 12:28
1:18 [d]Mt 20:28; 1Co 6:20
1:19 [e]Jn 1:29 [f]Ex 12:5
1:20 [g]Eph 1:4 [h]Heb 9:26

1:1–2

PROMISE 3

STRANGERS

What did Peter mean when he called his readers "strangers in the world"? Aren't Christians part of God's family, called to associate with one another and work toward furthering God's kingdom in the world? How then can they be called strangers?

Peter's readers were "strangers" in the sense that they refused to be a part of pagan Roman political and religious culture. They stood out from the norm, and they were persecuted for their beliefs. Like warriors in hostile enemy territory, these people experienced political and personal oppression. They desperately needed advice from Peter on how to respond in the face of such suffering.

While people may be more tolerant of Christianity in our own society, we are still called on to reflect Christ to a culture that actively works against Christian values and beliefs. In the process, we can experience various forms of persecution from our coworkers, neighbors and others who refuse to accept Christ's work in their lives. In the face of such opposition, verses 3 and 4 provide the ultimate hope.

These words shone like a beacon to Peter's original readers. Allow them to illuminate your life as well as you live as a "stranger" in this world.

For the next Promise 3 reading go to page 1383.

him you believe in God,[i] who raised him from the dead and glorified him, and so your faith and hope are in God.

2 →PG. 1386

22Now that you have purified[j] yourselves by obeying the truth so that you have sincere love for your brothers, love one another deeply,[k] from the heart.[a] 23For you have been born

7 →PG. 1383

again,[l] not of perishable seed, but of imperishable, through the living and enduring word of God.[m] 24For,

"All men are like grass,
and all their glory is like the flowers of the field;
the grass withers and the flowers fall,
25 but the word of the Lord stands forever."[b][n]

And this is the word that was preached to you.

3 →PG. 1383

2 Therefore, rid yourselves[o] of all malice and all deceit, hypocrisy, envy, and slander[p] of every kind. 2Like

1 →PG. 1383

newborn babies, crave pure spiritual milk,[q] so that by it you may grow up[r] in your salvation, 3now that you have tasted that the Lord is good.[s]

The Living Stone and a Chosen People

5 →PG. 1386

4As you come to him, the living Stone[t]—rejected by men but chosen by God and precious to him— 5you also, like living stones, are being built[u] into a spiritual house[v] to be a holy priesthood,[w] offering spiritual sacrifices acceptable to God through Jesus Christ.[x] 6For in Scripture it says:

"See, I lay a stone in Zion,
a chosen and precious cornerstone,[y]
and the one who trusts in him
will never be put to shame."[c][z]

7Now to you who believe, this stone is precious. But to those who do not believe,[a]

"The stone the builders rejected
has become the capstone,[d]"[e][b]

8and,

"A stone that causes men to stumble
and a rock that makes them fall."[f][c]

They stumble because they disobey the message—which is also what they were destined for.[d]

1 →PG. 1384

9But you are a chosen people,[e] a royal priesthood, a holy nation,[f] a people belonging to God, that you may declare the praises of him who called you out of darkness into his wonderful light.[g] 10Once you were not a people, but now you are the people of God;[h] once you had not received mercy, but now you have received mercy.

7 →PG. 1383

11Dear friends, I urge you, as aliens and strangers in the world, to abstain from sinful desires,[i] which war against your soul.[j] 12Live such good lives among the pagans that, though they accuse you of doing wrong, they may see your good deeds[k] and glorify God[l] on the day he visits us.

Submission to Rulers and Masters

3 →PG. 1386

7 →PG. 1384

13Submit yourselves for the Lord's sake to every authority[m] instituted among men: whether to the king, as the supreme authority, 14or to governors, who are sent by him to punish those who do wrong[n] and to commend those who do right.[o] 15For it is God's will[p] that by doing good you should silence the ignorant talk of foolish men.[q] 16Live as free men,[r] but do not use your freedom as a cover-up for evil; live as servants of God.[s] 17Show proper respect to everyone: Love the brotherhood of believers,[t] fear God, honor the king.[u]

18Slaves, submit yourselves to your masters with all respect,[v] not only to those who are good and considerate,[w] but also to those who are harsh. 19For it is commendable if a man bears up under the pain of unjust suffering because he is conscious of God.[x] 20But how is it to your credit if you receive a beating for doing wrong and endure it? But if you suffer for doing good and you endure it, this is commendable before God.[y] 21To this[z] you were called, because Christ suffered for you, leaving you an example,[a] that you should follow in his steps.

1:21 [i]Ro 4:24
1:22 [j]Jas 4:8 [k]Jn 13:34; Heb 13:1
1:23 [l]Jn 1:13 [m]Heb 4:12
1:25 [n]Isa 40:6-8
2:1 [o]Eph 4:22 [p]Jas 4:11
2:2 [q]1Co 3:2 [r]Eph 4:15,16
2:3 [s]Heb 6:5
2:4 [t]ver 7
2:5 [u]1Co 3:9 [v]1Ti 3:15 [w]Isa 61:6 [x]Php 4:18; Heb 13:15
2:6 [y]Eph 2:20 [z]Isa 28:16
2:7 [a]2Co 2:16 [b]Ps 118:22
2:8 [c]Isa 8:14; 1Co 1:23 [d]Ro 9:22
2:9 [e]Dt 10:15 [f]Isa 62:12 [g]Ac 26:18
2:10 [h]Hos 1:9,10
2:11 [i]Gal 5:16 [j]Jas 4:1
2:12 [k]Php 2:15; 1Pe 3:16 [l]Mt 5:16; 9:8
2:13 [m]Ro 13:1
2:14 [n]Ro 13:4 [o]Ro 13:3
2:15 [p]1Pe 3:17 [q]ver 12
2:16 [r]Jn 8:32 [s]Ro 6:22
2:17 [t]Ro 12:10 [u]Ro 13:7
2:18 [v]Eph 6:5 [w]Jas 3:17
2:19 [x]1Pe 3:14,17
2:20 [y]1Pe 3:17
2:21 [z]Ac 14:22 [a]Mt 16:24

[a]22 Some early manuscripts *from a pure heart*
[b]25 Isaiah 40:6-8 [c]6 Isaiah 28:16 [d]7 Or *cornerstone* [e]7 Psalm 118:22 [f]8 Isaiah 8:14

2:11–12

PROMISE 3

THE IMPORTANCE OF EXAMPLE

This advice was very practical for the original recipients of this letter, and it remains so for us today. Here Peter speaks of setting an example that is beyond reproach as part of a life that is devoted to Jesus Christ. If others then choose to criticize us for our beliefs and practices, their words will ring hollow in the face of our actions and activities. Such a life requires devotion to God and a passion for his Word, but the results of that discipline will be evident to all.

For the next Promise 3 reading go to page 1386.

[22]"He committed no sin,
and no deceit was found in his
mouth."[a][b]

[23]When they hurled their insults at
him, he did not retaliate; when he suffered, he made no threats.[c] Instead,
he entrusted himself[d] to him who
1 judges justly. [24]He himself bore our
→PG. 1386 sins[e] in his body on the tree, so that
we might die to sins[f] and live for righteousness; by his wounds you have
been healed.[g] [25]For you were like
sheep going astray,[h] but now you
have returned to the Shepherd[i] and
Overseer of your souls.

Wives and Husbands

3 Wives, in the same way be submissive[j] to your husbands[k] so that, if
any of them do not believe the word,
they may be won over[l] without words
by the behavior of their wives, [2]when
they see the purity and reverence of
your lives. [3]Your beauty should not
come from outward adornment, such
as braided hair and the wearing of gold
jewelry and fine clothes.[m] [4]Instead, it
should be that of your inner self,[n] the
unfading beauty of a gentle and quiet
spirit, which is of great worth in God's
sight. [5]For this is the way the holy
women of the past who put their hope
in God[o] used to make themselves
beautiful. They were submissive to
their own husbands, [6]like Sarah, who
obeyed Abraham and called him her
master.[p] You are her daughters if you
do what is right and do not give way to
fear.

4 [7]Husbands,[q] in the same way be
→PG. 4 considerate as you live with your wives,
and treat them with respect as the
weaker partner and as heirs with you of
the gracious gift of life, so that nothing
will hinder your prayers.

Suffering for Doing Good

6 [8]Finally, all of you, live in harmony
→PG. 1397 with one another; be sympathetic, love
as brothers,[r] be compassionate and
humble.[s] [9]Do not repay evil with
evil[t] or insult with insult,[u] but with
blessing, because to this[v] you were
called so that you may inherit a blessing.[w] [10]For,

"Whoever would love life
and see good days
must keep his tongue from evil
and his lips from deceitful
speech.
[11]He must turn from evil and do
good;
he must seek peace and pursue
it.
[12]For the eyes of the Lord are on the
righteous
and his ears are attentive to their
prayer,
but the face of the Lord is against
those who do evil."[b][x]

[13]Who is going to harm you if you
are eager to do good?[y] [14]But even if
you should suffer for what is right, you
are blessed.[z] "Do not fear what they
fear[c]; do not be frightened."[d][a] [15]But
in your hearts set apart Christ as Lord. 7
Always be prepared to give an an- →PG. 1386
swer[b] to everyone who asks you to
give the reason for the hope that
you have. But do this with gentleness
and respect, [16]keeping a clear conscience,[c] so that those who speak maliciously against your good behavior in
Christ may be ashamed of their slan-
der.[d] [17]It is better, if it is God's will,[e]
to suffer for doing good[f] than for doing evil. [18]For Christ died for sins[g]
once for all, the righteous for the unrighteous, to bring you to God. He was
put to death in the body[h] but made
alive by the Spirit,[i] [19]through whom[e]
also he went and preached to the spirits in prison[j] [20]who disobeyed long
ago when God waited patiently in the
days of Noah while the ark was being
built.[k] In it only a few people, eight
in all, were saved[l] through water,
[21]and this water symbolizes baptism
that now saves you[m] also—not the removal of dirt from the body but the

a *22* Isaiah 53:9 b *12* Psalm 34:12-16
c *14* Or *not fear their threats* d *14* Isaiah 8:12
e *18,19* Or *alive in the spirit, 19through which*

2:22 [b]Isa 53:9 **2:23** [c]Isa 53:7 [d]Lk 23:46 **2:24** [e]Heb 9:28 [f]Ro 6:2 [g]Isa 53:5; Heb 12:13; Jas 5:16 **2:25** [h]Isa 53:6 [i]Jn 10:11 **3:1** [j]1Pe 2:18 [k]Eph 5:22 [l]1Co 7:16; 9:19 **3:3** [m]Isa 3:18-23; 1Ti 2:9 **3:4** [n]Ro 7:22 **3:5** [o]1Ti 5:5 **3:6** [p]Ge 18:12 **3:7** [q]Eph 5:25-33 **3:8** [r]Ro 12:10 [s]1Pe 5:5 **3:9** [t]Ro 12:17 [u]1Pe 2:23 [v]1Pe 2:21 [w]Heb 6:14

3:12 [x]Ps 34:12-16 **3:13** [y]Pr 16:7 **3:14** [z]1Pe 2:19,20; 4:15,16 [a]Isa 8:12,13 **3:15** [b]Col 4:6 **3:16** [c]Heb 13:18 [d]1Pe 2:12,15 **3:17** [e]1Pe 2:15 [f]1Pe 2:20 **3:18** [g]1Pe 2:21 [h]Col 1:22; 1Pe 4:1 [i]1Pe 4:6 **3:19** [j]1Pe 4:6 **3:20** [k]Ge 6:3,5,13,14 [l]Heb 11:7 **3:21** [m]Tit 3:5

3:13-16

PROMISE 7

BE PREPARED

If someone asked you to explain what this "Christianity thing" was all about, what would you say? Would you be able to explain clearly and completely why your relationship with Jesus Christ gives you hope? Peter encouraged his readers to live in such a way that their faith would draw out such questions. And he encouraged them to have a ready answer for anyone and everyone who asked.

For us today, questions like these can come at various times and places—at the company party, on a long airline flight or when riding on the mass transit system. A student of God's Word will always be ready to explain the hope that others see in his or her life. Think about, and perhaps write out and memorize, your answer to this question. Then when it comes, you won't be caught off guard.

For the next Promise 7 reading go to page 1398.

PETER

A Man Who Never Stopped Learning

Imagine for a moment that you are the apostle John and you've just been handed Peter's first letter. To the rest of the church, this is a timely letter from a great apostle. But to you it is a letter from a dear old friend.

As you read, a great laugh begins to form in your belly and bubble up through your throat. You don't laugh because the words are comical. Rather it is a laugh of affection and respect because you know where Peter learned these timeless truths he wrote about. His words remind you of his enthusiastic, headlong leaps into whatever situation presented itself. You chuckle a little as you realize that this great man has never stopped learning. What you are reading Peter learned, and is still learning, in the crucible of real life.

John's Remembrances of Peter

Many years had passed since Peter, James and John were raw recruits in Jesus' band of disciples. Now Peter held a prominent position in the church. He had performed many miracles. He had opened the church to the Samaritans and Gentiles in the face of great prejudice. He was deeply respected and honored by the believers in Jerusalem and throughout the world.

Peter wrote this letter to a group of believers who were suffering for their faith. This letter might have been sent on to John. Though it was a serious letter dealing with a serious subject, John would have read Peter's statement about suffering silently and would have laughed aloud (1 Peter 2:20). John knew that keeping silent was the last thing Peter ever did. When Peter, James and John were on the mountain where Jesus was transfigured, Peter started babbling about building some tents to mark the spot. God himself essentially told Peter to shut up and listen to Jesus (Matthew 17:4–5). So often Peter seemed to speak at the wrong time and say the wrong thing. Now he was telling others about the value of silence.

John would have laughed again when he read the words, "set your hope fully on the grace to be given you when Jesus Christ is revealed" (1:13). John would never forget when he and the other disciples pulled Peter, soaking wet, out of the Sea of Galilee. He had jumped out of the boat and tried to walk to Jesus on the water (Matthew 14:25–29). Peter's unbridled enthusiasm embarrassed his fellow disciples; he believed he could do whatever the Lord was doing. Peter learned that day that anyone who wants to follow Jesus had better have their hope fully set on him. Although Peter learned his lesson the hard way, he obviously learned it well. Now he was able to teach it to others.

But the statement that would have grabbed John most deeply comes near the end of the letter. Peter encouraged the pastors of these suffering churches to "be shepherds of God's flock" (5:2). The word "shepherds" was the key. After the resurrection the disciples had come in from an all-night fishing expedition to find Jesus, sitting on the shoreline, with breakfast prepared. After breakfast, Jesus zeroed in on Peter. He asked Peter three times if he loved him. Each time, Peter assured Jesus that he did, in fact, love him. By the third time Jesus asked the same question, Peter was really feeling uncomfortable.

John would have remembered that each time Peter affirmed his love for Jesus, Peter was told to get involved in service for him: "Feed my lambs . . . Take care of my sheep . . . Feed my sheep" (John 21:15, 16, 17). The moment was so powerful. Jesus was assuring Peter that even though he had miserably failed and denied Jesus three times, he was forgiven and being given a second chance. Jesus' words meant that Peter "the denier" was being recommissioned as Peter "the shepherd." Now, these years later, Peter referred to these pastors as Jesus had referred to him that morning on the beach—as shepherd to the sheep.

John's Words to You

Peter filled his letter with truths that were hammered out on the anvil of his own life, truths that included failure and forgiveness. But Peter was also a learner. He was a grower. His letter carried the power of one who never stopped learning and growing as a godly man, even when blowing it became a part of the curriculum.

If John were alive today, he would certainly challenge every man, "Read Peter. And read him well. As you read his words, never forget that this truth pours out of a man who has learned it first-hand. You can trust that when Peter tells you how to live, he knows what he's talking about. Peter never stopped learning. Learn that lesson from him. Grow on!"

—Dr. Sid Buzzell

pledge[a] of a good conscience toward God. It saves you by the resurrection of Jesus Christ,[n] 22who has gone into heaven and is at God's right hand[o]—with angels, authorities and powers in submission to him.[p]

Living for God

3 →PG. 1390

4 Therefore, since Christ suffered in his body, arm yourselves also with the same attitude, because he who has suffered in his body is done with sin. 2As a result, he does not live the rest of his earthly life for evil human desires,[q] but rather for the will of God. 3For you have spent enough time in the past[r] doing what pagans choose to do—living in debauchery, lust, drunkenness, orgies, carousing and detestable idolatry. 4They think it strange that you do not plunge with them into the same flood of dissipation, and they heap abuse on you.[s] 5But they will have to give account to him who is ready to judge the living and the dead.[t] 6For this is the reason the gospel was preached even to those who are now dead,[u] so that they might be judged according to men in regard to the body, but live according to God in regard to the spirit.

1 →PG. 1386

7The end of all things is near.[v] Therefore be clear minded and self-controlled so that you can pray. 8Above all, love each other deeply,[w] because love covers over a multitude of sins.[x] 9Offer hospitality to one another without grumbling.[y] 10Each one should use whatever gift he has received to serve others,[z] faithfully[a] administering God's grace in its various forms. 11If anyone speaks, he should do it as one speaking the very words of God. If anyone serves, he should do it with the strength God provides,[b] so that in all things God may be praised[c] through Jesus Christ. To him be the glory and the power for ever and ever. Amen.

5 →PG. 1406

7 →PG. 1398

Suffering for Being a Christian

12Dear friends, do not be surprised at the painful trial you are suffering,[d] as though something strange were happening to you. 13But rejoice that you participate in the sufferings of Christ, so that you may be overjoyed when his glory is revealed.[e] 14If you are insulted because of the name of Christ, you are blessed,[f] for the Spirit of glory and of God rests on you. 15If you suffer, it should not be as a murderer or thief or any other kind of criminal, or even as a meddler. 16However, if you suffer as a Christian, do not be ashamed, but praise God that you bear that name.[g] 17For it is time for judgment to begin with the family of God;[h] and if it begins with us, what will the outcome be for those who do not obey the gospel of God?[i] 18And,

"If it is hard for the righteous to be saved,
what will become of the ungodly and the sinner?"[a][j]

19So then, those who suffer according to God's will should commit themselves to their faithful Creator and continue to do good.

To Elders and Young Men

5 To the elders among you, I appeal as a fellow elder,[k] a witness[l] of Christ's sufferings and one who also will share in the glory to be revealed:[m] 2Be shepherds of God's flock[n] that is under your care, serving as overseers—not because you must, but because you are willing, as God wants you to be; not greedy for money,[o] but eager to serve; 3not lording it over[p] those entrusted to you, but being examples[q] to the flock. 4And when the Chief Shepherd appears, you will receive the crown of glory[r] that will never fade away.

1 →PG. 1390

5Young men, in the same way be submissive[s] to those who are older.

2 →PG. 1398

[a]21 Or *response*

3:21 [n]1Pe 1:3 **3:22** [o]Mk 16:19 [p]Ro 8:38 **4:2** [q]Ro 6:2 **4:3** [r]Eph 2:2 **4:4** [s]1Pe 3:16 **4:5** [t]Ac 10:42; 2Ti 4:1 **4:6** [u]1Pe 3:19 **4:7** [v]Ro 13:11 **4:8** [w]1Pe 1:22 [x]Pr 10:12 **4:9** [y]Php 2:14 **4:10** [z]Ro 12:6,7 [a]1Co 4:2 **4:11** [b]Eph 6:10 [c]1Co 10:31 **4:12** [d]1Pe 1:6,7 **4:13** [e]Ro 8:17 **4:14** [f]Mt 5:11 **4:16** [g]Ac 5:41 **4:17** [h]Jer 25:29 [i]2Th 1:8 **4:18** [j]Pr 11:31; Lk 23:31 **5:1** [k]Ac 11:30 [l]Lk 24:48 [m]1Pe 1:5,7; Rev 1:9 **5:2** [n]Jn 21:16 [o]1Ti 3:3 **5:3** [p]Eze 34:4 [q]Php 3:17 **5:4** [r]1Co 9:25 **5:5** [s]Eph 5:21

4:1–6 PROMISE 3

DONE WITH SIN?

Verses 1 and 2 sum up the main reason why we need to resist temptation. Peter says that when we accept Christ's suffering on our behalf, our life's perspective is transformed. We then live to do God's will instead of our own.

This may involve some significant life change for believers who come to Christ as adults. They may find that old friends drag them down and take them away from their new purpose in Christ. Those friends may also criticize them for not participating in the same activities they had before they accepted Christ. That's exactly the difference Peter is talking about here.

Obviously, the Christian's first goal is to lead his or her closest friends to Christ. When that doesn't happen, the lifestyle differences will become obvious, and separating from old friends and old habits may be painful. But, as night is different from day, so people who have accepted Christ are different from people who have not.

For the next Promise 3 reading go to page 1390.

All of you, clothe yourselves with humility toward one another, because,

> "God opposes the proud
> but gives grace to the
> humble."[b][t]

6Humble yourselves, therefore, under
God's mighty hand, that he may lift
you up in due time.[u] **7**Cast all your
anxiety on him[v] because he cares for
you.[w]

8Be self-controlled and alert. Your
enemy the devil prowls around[x] like a
roaring lion looking for someone to devour. **9**Resist him,[y] standing firm in
the faith,[z] because you know that
your brothers throughout the world are
undergoing the same kind of sufferings.[a]

10And the God of all grace, who
called you to his eternal glory[b] in
Christ, after you have suffered a little
while, will himself restore you and
make you strong,[c] firm and steadfast.
11To him be the power for ever and
ever. Amen.[d]

Final Greetings

12With the help of Silas,[c][e] whom I
regard as a faithful brother, I have written to you briefly,[f] encouraging you
and testifying that this is the true grace
of God. Stand fast in it.

13She who is in Babylon, chosen together with you, sends you her greetings, and so does my son Mark.[g]
14Greet one another with a kiss of
love.[h]

Peace[i] to all of you who are in
Christ.

5:5 [t]Pr 3:34; Jas 4:6
5:6 [u]Jas 4:10
5:7 [v]Ps 37:5; Mt 6:25 [w]Heb 13:5
5:8 [x]Job 1:7
5:9 [y]Jas 4:7 [z]Col 2:5 [a]Ac 14:22
5:10 [b]2Co 4:17 [c]2Th 2:17
5:11 [d]Ro 11:36
5:12 [e]2Co 1:19 [f]Heb 13:22
5:13 [g]Ac 12:12
5:14 [h]Ro 16:16 [i]Eph 6:23

a *18* Prov. 11:31 **b** *5* Prov. 3:34 **c** *12* Greek *Silvanus,* a variant of *Silas*

5:8–11

PROMISE 1

PLEASE DON'T FEED THE LION

What a vivid picture Peter paints of the devil! Make no mistake about it, Satan is a living, moving being who is intent on inflicting pain and making life difficult for believers. His weapons against us in the face of suffering include discouragement, anxiety, impatience and despair. How do we stay alert so we can resist his attacks?

Scripture tells us that resisting the devil begins with submitting ourselves to God (James 4:7). By standing firm in the Lord's strength and not our own, we will be sensitive to the Spirit's promptings in our lives. We'll also look to others to encourage us through our suffering, no matter what form it may take (1 Peter 5:9).

Just as a person wouldn't willingly battle a lion without a weapon and a group of others to back him up, so we should take advantage of the resources at our disposal (God's Word, the Holy Spirit and the encouragement of others) when we ward off the devil's claws.

For the next Promise 1 reading go to page 1392.

2 PETER

AT A GLANCE

Key Principle: A firm grasp of Biblical truth and continued growth in the personal knowledge of our Lord and Savior Jesus Christ is the best defense against heretical teachings and spiritual counterfeits.

Author: Peter

Time and Place: ~A.D. 64–68 / Probably Rome

Key Verses: 1:19–21; 3:9–11, 18

BENEFIT

While 1 Peter deals with the problem of external opposition to the gospel, 2 Peter confronts the insidious problem of internal opposition to the truth by teachers who distort the gospel. These false teachers "secretly introduce destructive heresies" (2:1) even to the point of denying Christ, and their teachings seduce believers into error and immorality. This letter tells us how to deal with the problem of false teaching. In our day, when spiritual counterfeits confront us from every imaginable media, this message is more relevant than ever before.

SETTING

Over the centuries, scholars have challenged the authenticity of this letter more than any other New Testament book. Churchwide recognition of this book as being an inspired work of the apostle Peter didn't come until the fourth century. Part of this was due to slow circulation, the letter's brevity, stylistic differences between this epistle and 1 Peter and the fact that it had to compete with other works that falsely claimed to have been written by Peter, such as the Apocalypse of Peter. Many scholars continue to raise questions about stylistic differences, because the Greek of this epistle is more awkward than that of 1 Peter. These differences, however, can be explained by the fact that Silas assisted Paul with the first epistle (1 Peter 5:12), but not with the second epistle. In light of the spiritually penetrating and apostolic content of this epistle, other arguments used to claim that this is a second-century forgery are far less convincing than the traditional position.

See the "Setting" section in the introduction to 1 Peter for more on the background of this epistle. Peter probably wrote this letter in Rome not long after he wrote 1 Peter and shortly before his death (1:13–15). He wrote this to counteract a number of heretical teachings that were distorting Christian truth and practice and gaining a foothold in various assemblies. Tradition tells us that Peter was crucified upside down in Rome before Nero's death in A.D. 68.

TIME LINE

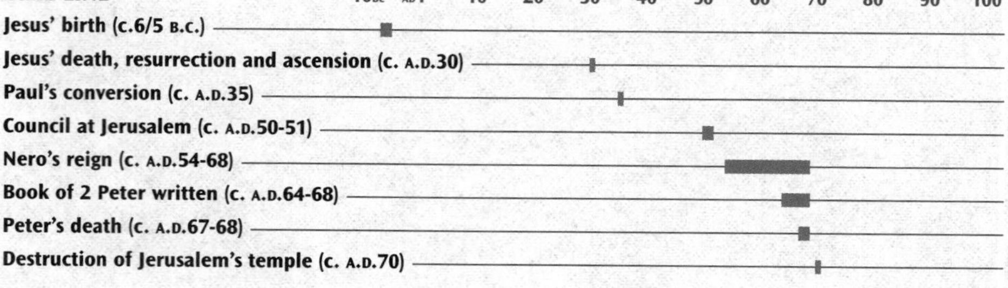

THEME AND PURPOSE

In this second letter to believers, Peter addresses the internal dangers of false teachers that threatened to corrupt the body of believers in both doctrine and practice. His message is that application and conformity to Scriptural truth is the best defense against spiritual counterfeits. Peter wrote this epistle as a lasting reminder to his readers to remain faithful to the foundations of their faith and to urge believers to live holy and godly lives in view of the certain coming of the Lord Jesus.

UNIQUE CONTRIBUTION

The focus of 1 Peter is suffering for the sake of commitment to Christ; the focus of 2 Peter is knowledge of the truth in a context of misleading teachings. Peter's first epistle deals with the implications of spiritual birth, and his second epistle stresses the importance of spiritual growth. This growth in the truth is not based merely on intellectual assent, but on a living and growing relational knowledge of Christ through faith, obedience and the pursuit of godliness.

CHRIST IN 2 PETER

With one exception (1:1), Peter uses the title "Lord" each time he refers to Jesus Christ in this letter. Through Christ's divine power we have been given "everything we need for life and godliness" (1:3), and a personal knowledge of him is the goal of our conduct (1:8). Through his "power and coming" (1:16) we have been given hope of an eternal future with God (3:11–12) as we look forward to "a new heaven and a new earth, the home of righteousness" (3:13). In this epistle, Peter recalls the transfiguration that revealed Christ's true power and glory, which had been veiled by his flesh (1:17–18), and anticipates the full revelation of his glory at his *parousia*, his "coming" (3:3–13), when the whole world will see him.

OVERVIEW

FOCUS	Holiness	Heresy	Hope
REFERENCE	1	2	3
TOPICS	Development in the Truth	Denunciation of Error	Day of the Lord
	Confidence	Conflict	Consummation
	Walking and Witnessing	Warning	Waiting
	Progress	Peril	Promised Coming
LOCATION	Probably Rome		
TIME	~A.D. 64–68		

After a brief greeting that mentions his theme of the knowledge of Jesus Christ (1:1–2), Peter speaks of Christ's "great and precious promises" and the life of faith, goodness, knowledge, self-control, perseverance, godliness, kindness and love that these promises should produce in us (1:3–11). Peter, knowing that his martyrdom was imminent, wanted to stir up his readers to remember and hold fast to the prophetic word (1:12–21).

Next, Peter warns his readers of the danger of false teachers who deny the truths of the gospel and seek to captivate others (2:1–22). He not only denounces their teachings and conduct, but also anticipates the divine judgment they will receive.

The promised coming of Christ will happen suddenly and certainly, and Peter refers back to the creation and the flood to refute those who deny that the day of the Lord will arrive (3:1–10). In view of the fact that the earth will be destroyed, Peter urges his readers to live holy and blameless lives as they look forward to a new heaven and a new earth (3:11–18).

2 PETER

1 Simon Peter, a servant[a] and apostle
of Jesus Christ,[b]

To those who through the righteousness[c] of our God and Savior Jesus
Christ[d] have received a faith as precious as ours:

2Grace and peace be yours in abundance through the knowledge of God
and of Jesus our Lord.[e]

Making One's Calling and Election Sure

1 →PG. 1390
3 →PG. 1391

3His divine power[f] has given us everything we need for life and godliness
through our knowledge of him who
called us[g] by his own glory and goodness. **4**Through these he has given us
his very great and precious promises,[h]
so that through them you may participate in the divine nature[i] and escape
the corruption in the world caused by
evil desires.[j]
5For this very reason, make every effort to add to your faith goodness; and
to goodness, knowledge;[k] **6**and to
knowledge, self-control;[l] and to self-
control, perseverance; and to perseverance, godliness;[m] **7**and to godliness,
brotherly kindness; and to brotherly
kindness, love.[n] **8**For if you possess
these qualities in increasing measure,
they will keep you from being ineffective and unproductive[o] in your
knowledge of our Lord Jesus Christ.
9But if anyone does not have them, he
is nearsighted and blind,[p] and has forgotten that he has been cleansed from
his past sins.[q]
10Therefore, my brothers, be all the
more eager to make your calling and
election sure. For if you do these
things, you will never fall,[r] **11**and you
will receive a rich welcome into the
eternal kingdom of our Lord and Savior
Jesus Christ.

Prophecy of Scripture

12So I will always remind you of
these things,[s] even though you know
them and are firmly established in the
truth you now have. **13**I think it is right
to refresh your memory as long as I live
in the tent of this body,[t] **14**because I
know that I will soon put it aside,[u] as
our Lord Jesus Christ has made clear to
me.[v] **15**And I will make every effort to
see that after my departure[w] you will
always be able to remember these
things.
16We did not follow cleverly invented stories when we told you about the
power and coming of our Lord Jesus
Christ, but we were eyewitnesses of his
majesty.[x] **17**For he received honor and
glory from God the Father when the
voice came to him from the Majestic
Glory, saying, "This is my Son, whom I
love; with him I am well pleased."[a][y]
18We ourselves heard this voice that
came from heaven when we were with
him on the sacred mountain.[z]

1 →PG. 1396

19And we have the word of the
prophets made more certain, and you
will do well to pay attention to it, as to
a light[a] shining in a dark place, until
the day dawns and the morning star[b]
rises in your hearts. **20**Above all, you
must understand that no prophecy of
Scripture came about by the prophet's
own interpretation. **21**For prophecy
never had its origin in the will of man,
but men spoke from God[c] as they
were carried along by the Holy Spirit.[d]

False Teachers and Their Destruction

2 But there were also false prophets[e]
among the people, just as there will
be false teachers among you.[f] They
will secretly introduce destructive
heresies, even denying the sovereign Lord[g] who bought them[h]—bringing swift destruction on themselves.

1:5-11 PROMISE 3

DRIVING LESSONS

Power steering makes driving a car a lot easier, but it doesn't take away the driver's responsibility. He or she still has to hold on to the steering wheel and direct the car.

In a similar sense, God has given us the power to live a life that pleases him, but we have to steer the wheel. We have an obligation to live our lives in a way that pleases God. In this passage Peter outlines the character traits we need to build into our lives to keep us on the right road.

As you review these traits, think about how you could integrate each one into your life. How important are these qualities? Peter said if they're growing in a man's life, then he's growing in his relationship with Jesus Christ—the One who makes them possible.

For the next Promise 3 reading go to page 1397.

1:1 [a]Ro 1:1 [b]1Pe 1:1 [c]Ro 3:21-26 [d]Tit 2:13
1:2 [e]Php 3:8
1:3 [f]1Pe 1:5 [g]1Th 2:12
1:4 [h]2Co 7:1 [i]Eph 4:24; Heb 12:10; 1Jn 3:2 [j]2Pe 2:18-20
1:5 [k]Col 2:3
1:6 [l]Ac 24:25 [m]ver 3
1:7 [n]1Th 3:12
1:8 [o]Jn 15:2; Tit 3:14
1:9 [p]1Jn 2:11 [q]Eph 5:26
1:10 [r]2Pe 3:17
1:12 [s]Php 3:1; 1Jn 2:21
1:13 [t]2Co 5:1,4
1:14 [u]2Ti 4:6 [v]Jn 21:18,19
1:15 [w]Lk 9:31
1:16 [x]Mt 17:1-8
1:17 [y]Mt 3:17
1:18 [z]Mt 17:6
1:19 [a]Ps 119:105 [b]Rev 22:16
1:21 [c]2Ti 3:16 [d]2Sa 23:2; Ac 1:16; 1Pe 1:11
2:1 [e]Dt 13:1-3 [f]1Ti 4:1 [g]Jude 4 [h]1Co 6:20

[a]*17* Matt. 17:5; Mark 9:7; Luke 9:35

2 Many will follow their shameful ways and will bring the way of truth into disrepute. 3 In their greed these teachers will exploit you[i] with stories they have made up. Their condemnation has long been hanging over them, and their destruction has not been sleeping.

4 For if God did not spare angels when they sinned, but sent them to hell,[a] putting them into gloomy dungeons[b] to be held for judgment;[j] 5 if he did not spare the ancient world[k] when he brought the flood on its ungodly people, but protected Noah, a preacher of righteousness, and seven others;[l] 6 if he condemned the cities of Sodom and Gomorrah by burning them to ashes,[m] and made them an example[n] of what is going to happen to the ungodly; 7 and if he rescued Lot,[o] a righteous man, who was distressed by the filthy lives of lawless men[p] 8 (for that righteous man, living among them day after day, was tormented in his righteous soul by the lawless deeds he saw and heard)— 9 if this is so, then the Lord knows how to rescue godly men from trials[q] and to hold the unrighteous for the day of judgment, while continuing their punishment.[c] 10 This is especially true of those who follow the corrupt desire[r] of the sinful nature[d] and despise authority.

Bold and arrogant, these men are not afraid to slander celestial beings;[s] 11 yet even angels, although they are stronger and more powerful, do not bring slanderous accusations against such beings in the presence of the Lord.[t] 12 But these men blaspheme in matters they do not understand. They are like brute beasts, creatures of instinct, born only to be caught and destroyed, and like beasts they too will perish.[u]

13 They will be paid back with harm for the harm they have done. Their idea of pleasure is to carouse in broad daylight.[v] They are blots and blemishes, reveling in their pleasures while they feast with you.[e][w] 14 With eyes full of adultery, they never stop sinning; they seduce[x] the unstable; they are experts in greed[y]—an accursed brood![z] 15 They have left the straight way and wandered off to follow the way of Balaam[a] son of Beor, who loved the wages of wickedness. 16 But he was rebuked for his wrongdoing by a donkey—a beast without speech—who spoke with a man's voice and restrained the prophet's madness.[b]

17 These men are springs without water[c] and mists driven by a storm. Blackest darkness is reserved for them.[d] 18 For they mouth empty, boastful words[e] and, by appealing to the lustful desires of sinful human nature, they entice people who are just escaping from those who live in error. 19 They promise them freedom, while they themselves are slaves of depravity—for a man is a slave to whatever has mastered him.[f] 20 If they have escaped the corruption of the world by knowing[g] our Lord and Savior Jesus Christ and are again entangled in it and overcome, they are worse off at the end than they were at the beginning.[h] 21 It would have been better for them not to have known the way of righteousness, than to have known it and then to turn their backs on the sacred command that was passed on to them.[i] 22 Of them the proverbs are true: "A dog returns to its vomit,"[f][j] and, "A sow that is washed goes back to her wallowing in the mud."

The Day of the Lord

3 Dear friends, this is now my second letter to you. I have written both of them as reminders[k] to stimulate you to wholesome thinking. 2 I want you to recall the words spoken in the past by the holy prophets and the command given by our Lord and Savior through your apostles.

3 First of all, you must understand that in the last days[l] scoffers will come, scoffing and following their own evil desires.[m] 4 They will say, "Where is this 'coming' he promised?[n] Ever since our fathers died, everything goes on as it has since the beginning of creation."[o] 5 But they deliberately forget that long ago by God's word[p] the heavens existed and the earth was formed out of water and by water.[q] 6 By these waters also the world of that time was deluged and destroyed.[r] 7 By the same word the present heavens and earth are reserved for fire,[s] being kept for the day of judgment and destruction of ungodly men.

8 But do not forget this one thing, dear friends: With the Lord a day is like a thousand years, and a thousand years are like a day.[t] 9 The Lord is not slow in keeping his promise,[u] as some understand slowness. He is patient[v] with you, not wanting anyone to perish, but everyone to come to repentance.[w]

10 But the day of the Lord will come

3 →PG. 1396

2:3 [i] 2Co 2:17; 1Th 2:5
2:4 [j] Jude 6; Rev 20:1,2
2:5 [k] 2Pe 3:6 [l] Heb 11:7; 1Pe 3:20
2:6 [m] Ge 19:24,25 [n] Nu 26:10; Jude 7
2:7 [o] Ge 19:16 [p] 2Pe 3:17
2:9 [q] 1Co 10:13
2:10 [r] 2Pe 3:3 [s] Jude 8
2:11 [t] Jude 9
2:12 [u] Jude 10
2:13 [v] Ro 13:13 [w] 1Co 11:20, 21; Jude 12
2:14 [x] ver 18 [y] ver 3 [z] Eph 2:3
2:15 [a] Nu 22:4-20; Jude 11
2:16 [b] Nu 22:21-30
2:17 [c] Jude 12 [d] Jude 13
2:18 [e] Jude 16
2:19 [f] Jn 8:34; Ro 6:16
2:20 [g] 2Pe 1:2 [h] Mt 12:45
2:21 [i] Heb 6:4-6
2:22 [j] Pr 26:11
3:1 [k] 2Pe 1:13
3:3 [l] 1Ti 4:1 [m] 2Pe 2:10; Jude 18
3:4 [n] Isa 5:19; Eze 12:22; Mt 24:48 [o] Mk 10:6
3:5 [p] Ge 1:6,9; Heb 11:3 [q] Ps 24:2
3:6 [r] Ge 7:21,22
3:7 [s] ver 10,12; 2Th 1:7
3:8 [t] Ps 90:4
3:9 [u] Hab 2:3; Heb 10:37 [v] Ro 2:4 [w] 1Ti 2:4

[a] *4* Greek *Tartarus* [b] *4* Some manuscripts *into chains of darkness* [c] *9* Or *unrighteous for punishment until the day of judgment* [d] *10* Or *the flesh* [e] *13* Some manuscripts *in their love feasts* [f] *22* Prov. 26:11

like a thief.[x] The heavens will disappear with a roar; the elements will be
destroyed by fire, and the earth and
everything in it will be laid bare.[a][y]
11Since everything will be destroyed
in this way, what kind of people ought
you to be? You ought to live holy and
godly lives 12as you look forward[z] to
the day of God and speed its coming.[b][a] That day will bring about the
destruction of the heavens by fire, and
the elements will melt in the heat.[b]
13But in keeping with his promise we
are looking forward to a new heaven
and a new earth,[c] the home of righteousness.
14So then, dear friends, since you are
looking forward to this, make every effort to be found spotless, blameless[d]
and at peace with him. 15Bear in mind
that our Lord's patience[e] means salvation,[f] just as our dear brother Paul
also wrote you with the wisdom that
God gave him.[g] 16He writes the same
way in all his letters, speaking in them
of these matters. His letters contain
some things that are hard to understand, which ignorant and unstable[h]
people distort, as they do the other
Scriptures,[i] to their own destruction.
17Therefore, dear friends, since you
already know this, be on your guard[j]
so that you may not be carried away by
the error[k] of lawless men and fall from
your secure position.[l] 18But grow in
the grace and knowledge of our Lord
and Savior Jesus Christ.[m] To him be
glory both now and forever! Amen.

3:10 [x]Lk 12:39; 1Th 5:2 [y]Mt 24:35; Rev 21:1
3:12 [z]1Co 1:7 [a]Ps 50:3 [b]ver 10
3:13 [c]Isa 65:17; 66:22; Rev 21:1
3:14 [d]1Th 3:13
3:15 [e]Ro 2:4 [f]ver 9 [g]Eph 3:3
3:16 [h]2Pe 2:14 [i]ver 2
3:17 [j]1Co 10:12 [k]2Pe 2:18 [l]Rev 2:5
3:18 [m]2Pe 1:11

[a]10 Some manuscripts *be burned up* [b]12 Or *as you wait eagerly for the day of God to come*

3:11

PROMISE 1

PERMANENCE

If you've ever survived or observed the results of a natural disaster such as an earthquake or a flood, you know how impermanent life on this earth can be. A house that has stood for a hundred years can be wiped away in an instant. The very ground on which we stand can shift and crack, making us question our most basic assumptions. People who we loved and who impacted our lives profoundly are forgotten in the space of a few generations. Is there anything in life that's permanent?

The only thing that lasts is our identity in Jesus Christ. This passage makes clear that after God comes in judgment and wipes this earth away, the only thing left standing will be those who have dedicated their lives to Jesus.

In what are you investing your life? Take a few moments to think about your answer to Peter's question in verse 11.

For the next Promise 1 reading go to page 1396.

1 JOHN

AT A GLANCE

Key Principle: Those who have fellowship with God must walk in his light, love one another and receive the life of his Son.
Author: The apostle John
Time and Place: ~A.D. 85–95 / Probably written in Ephesus
Key Verses: 1:3; 2:28; 3:1; 4:1; 5:11–13

BENEFIT

This simple but profound epistle urges us to live out what we profess and to enjoy true fellowship with God by walking in his light, love and life. It contains a perfect blend of truth and love, firmness and graciousness, exhortation and consolation, warning against false teaching and witness to what is genuine. This brief but powerful letter both encourages us and challenges us in our faith.

SETTING

The ancient church testified that the apostle John is the author of this epistle. This assertion is supported by strong stylistic similarities between 1 John and the fourth Gospel, and by the terms "we" (apostles) "you" (readers) and "they" (false teachers) that place this epistle among the apostolic witnesses (e.g., 1:1–4; 2:19; 4:14). John was one of the "pillars" of the church in Jerusalem (Galatians 2:9). Early tradition tells us that he left Jerusalem before it was destroyed in A.D. 70 and went to Ephesus, where he ministered by overseeing the churches in the Roman province of Asia. These churches included the seven churches of Revelation 2—3.

The aged apostle probably wrote this epistle in Ephesus shortly after he wrote his gospel, sometime around A.D. 85–95. His frequent use of the terms "dear children" and "dear friends" indicates a warm and personal relationship with his readers. John was particularly concerned that they hold fast to the truth in the face of increasingly influential Gnostic heresy. This false system taught that matter is evil, and that a divine being could not take on human flesh (cf. 4:2–3). The Gnostics claimed a distinction between the human Jesus and the spiritual Christ who came upon Jesus at his baptism but departed before his crucifixion. They also regarded themselves as part of the spiritual elite who had arrived at a hidden knowledge that set them apart from others and above commonly accepted ethical standards.

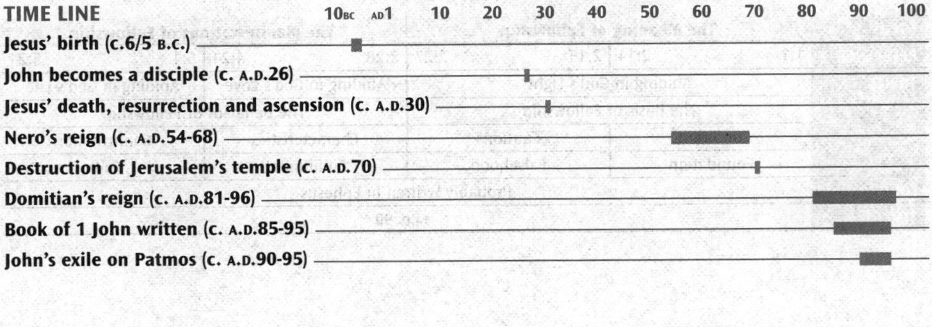

THEME AND PURPOSE

First John develops the theme of fellowship with God in belief and in practice. This epistle argues that belief in Jesus as the Christ becomes evident when expressed in love and service to others. John encouraged his readers to obey God's command to "believe in the name of his Son, Jesus Christ, and to love one another as he commanded us" (3:23) so that they would enjoy the assurance of Christ's life in them. "I write these things to you who believe in the name of the Son of God so that you may know that you have eternal life" (5:13). John also urged his readers to hold fast to apostolic doctrine in the face of Gnostic teaching on the person and work of Christ. The true believer acknowledges that Jesus Christ has come in the flesh, practices righteousness and demonstrates loving concern for others. The false teachers John had in mind failed all three of these tests.

UNIQUE CONTRIBUTION

First John is different from most of the other New Testament epistles in that it lacks the usual components of a salutation, an address, greetings and a benediction. It does, however, have a specific audience and historical situation in mind ("I write to you," 1:4; 2:1, 7–8, 12–14, 21, 26; 5:13), and it is therefore not a transcribed sermon, as some have suggested. In this letter John uses a disarmingly simple vocabulary and style as he subtly interweaves and develops various themes such as light, love, life, truth and righteousness. He also presents several profound and antithetical ideas in this epistle: light and darkness, love and hatred, truth and error, love of the world and love of God's will, righteousness and sin, the children of God and the children of the devil, the Spirit of God and the spirit of the antichrist, life and death.

CHRIST IN 1 JOHN

John stresses the incarnation of Jesus Christ as he refutes Gnosticism in this letter: "Every spirit that acknowledges that Jesus Christ has come in the flesh is from God, but every spirit that does not acknowledge Jesus is not from God" (4:2–3). One who denies that Jesus is the Christ denies both the Father and the Son (2:22). Jesus is the Christ who "came by water and blood" (5:6)—he was the same indivisible person from his baptism to his crucifixion. John emphasizes the need for belief in Jesus Christ (the Greek word translated "believe" involves personal trust and not merely intellectual assent), and says that this is how individuals receive eternal life (3:23; 5:10–13). Jesus Christ, the righteous One, is our advocate before the Father. He is "the atoning sacrifice for our sins, and not only for ours but also for the sins of the whole world" (2:1–2).

OVERVIEW

FOCUS	The Meaning of Fellowship		The Manifestations of Fellowship	
REFERENCE	1:1 — 2:14	2:15 — 2:27	2:28 — 4:21	5:1 — 5:21
TOPICS	Abiding in God's Light		Abiding in God's Love	Abiding in God's Life
	The Basis of Fellowship		The Behavior of Fellowship	
	Conditions	Cautions	Characteristics	Confirmation
	Foundation	Falsehood	Fulfillment	Faith
LOCATION	Probably Written in Ephesus			
TIME	~A.D. 90			

In his prologue, John remembers the apostles' fellowship with Christ and expresses his desire to share the joy of that fellowship with his readers (1:1–4). This fellowship comes by walking in the light and is made possible by the blood of Jesus (1:5–10). Christ is the believer's advocate with the Father, and those who know him must do what he commands—love one another (2:1–11). John wants his readers mature in the Word and to overcome the evil one (2:12–14). He cautions them against the lures of the world system (2:15–17) and against the false teachers who deny that Jesus is the Christ (2:18–27).

John says that believers must abide in God's love as well as in God's light (2:28—4:21). Doing so requires practicing righteousness, since practicing sin is incompatible with the believer's new nature (2:28—3:10). When believers sin, they do not reflect the regenerate new person, but the works of the devil. Regeneration produces righteousness, and righteousness is expressed in sacrificial love for others (3:11–24). Those who have the Spirit of God not only acknowledge the incarnate Christ and the doctrine of the apostles (4:1–6), but also manifest God's love in their relationships with other believers (4:7–21). To trust in Jesus as the Christ is to abide in God's life and to enjoy the assurance of eternal life in Christ (5:1–13). This assurance leads us to confidently access God in prayer (5:14–17) and gives us the power to overcome the evil one (5:18–21).

1 JOHN

The Word of Life

1 That which was from the beginning,[a] which we have heard, which we have seen with our eyes,[b] which we have looked at and our hands have touched[c]—this we proclaim concerning the Word of life.
2The life appeared;[d] we have seen it and testify to it, and we proclaim to you the eternal life, which was with the Father and has appeared to us.
3We proclaim to you what we have seen and heard, so that you also may have fellowship with us. And our fellowship is with the Father and with his Son, Jesus Christ.[e]
4We write this[f] to make our[a] joy complete.[g]

Walking in the Light

5This is the message we have heard[h] from him and declare to you: God is light; in him there is no darkness at all.
6If we claim to have fellowship with him yet walk in the darkness,[i] we lie and do not live by the truth.[j]
7But if we walk in the light, as he is in the light, we have fellowship with one another, and the blood of Jesus, his Son, purifies us from all[b] sin.[k]
8If we claim to be without sin,[l] we deceive ourselves and the truth is not in us.[m]
9If we confess our sins, he is faithful and just and will forgive us our sins[n] and purify us from all unrighteousness.
10If we claim we have not sinned, we make him out to be a liar[o] and his word has no place in our lives.[p]

2 My dear children,[q] I write this to you so that you will not sin. But if anybody does sin, we have one who speaks to the Father in our defense[r]—Jesus Christ, the Righteous One.
2He is the atoning sacrifice for our sins,[s] and not only for ours but also for[c] the sins of the whole world.
3We know that we have come to know him if we obey his commands.[t]
4The man who says, "I know him," but does not do what he commands is a liar, and the truth is not in him.[u]
5But if anyone obeys his word,[v] God's love[d] is truly made complete in him.[w] This is how we know we are in him:

1 →PG. 1396

3 →PG. 1397

1 →PG. 1397

1:1 [a]Jn 1:2 [b]Jn 1:14; 2Pe 1:16 [c]Jn 20:27 **1:2** [d]Jn 1:1-4; 1Ti 3:16 **1:3** [e]1Co 1:9 **1:4** [f]1Jn 2:1 [g]Jn 3:29 **1:5** [h]1Jn 3:11 **1:6** [i]2Co 6:14 [j]Jn 3:19-21 **1:7** [k]Heb 9:14; Rev 1:5 **1:8** [l]Pr 20:9; Jas 3:2 [m]1Jn 2:4 **1:9** [n]Ps 32:5; 51:2 **1:10** [o]1Jn 5:10 [p]1Jn 2:14 **2:1** [q]ver 12,13,28 [r]Ro 8:34; Heb 7:25 **2:2** [s]Ro 3:25 **2:3** [t]Jn 14:15 **2:4** [u]1Jn 1:6,8 **2:5** [v]Jn 14:21,23 [w]1Jn 4:12

[a] *4* Some manuscripts *your* [b] *7* Or *every* [c] *2* Or *He is the one who turns aside God's wrath, taking away our sins, and not only ours but also* [d] *5* Or *word, love for God*

1:1-4

PROMISE 1

CALLED TO FRIENDSHIP

The Jesus John proclaimed wasn't a mythological figure or a ghostlike phantom. John testified that Jesus was God in the flesh. He had known Jesus, walked with him, followed him and listened to his teaching. He had seen Jesus miraculously heal people and had even stood at the foot of the cross when Jesus died (John 19:25–27). Finally, Jesus appeared to John and the other disciples after his resurrection (John 20:19–20).

But John was more than just an eyewitness to Jesus' life, death and resurrection—he was Jesus' close friend, carrying the nickname "the disciple whom [Jesus] loved" (John 19:26). John's testimony about Jesus in these first four verses is completely reliable.

In this passage John extends an invitation for us to enjoy "fellowship . . . with the Father and with his Son." John didn't just want us to intellectually grasp that Jesus is God in the flesh; he wanted us to be in relationship with Jesus, as he was. He wanted his readers to experience Jesus as a friend.

Think about that for a few minutes. You can participate in the same kind of relationship with Jesus that John and the other disciples had. Learn about his life from the Bible. Talk to him in prayer. Enjoy fellowship with others who know and love him. You'll find out firsthand how wonderful a Friend he truly is.

For the next Promise 1 reading go to page 1399.

2:1-2

PE

OUR MEDIATOR

John tells us that Jesus Christ speaks to the Father on our behalf. Similar to a lawyer in front of a courtroom judge, Jesus pleads our case with the Father. And his qualifications as our Mediator are impeccable—he has already paid the penalty for our sins in his death and resurrection. Therefore there's no reason for God to condemn us.

Since Christ died for your sins, God is eager and ready to forgive and restore your relationship with him. In light of that wonderful truth, how should you respond the next time you've sinned and shame is preventing you from turning to God?

[6]Whoever claims to live in him must walk as Jesus did.[x]

[7]Dear friends, I am not writing you a
new command but an old one, which
you have had since the beginning.[y]
This old command is the message you
have heard. [8]Yet I am writing you a
new command;[z] its truth is seen in
him and you, because the darkness
is passing[a] and the true light[b] is already shining.[c]

6 →PG. 1398

[9]Anyone who claims to be in the
light but hates his brother is still in the
darkness. [10]Whoever loves his brother
lives in the light,[d] and there is nothing
in him[a] to make him stumble. [11]But
whoever hates his brother is in the
darkness and walks around in the darkness; he does not know where he is
going, because the darkness has blinded him.[e]

[12]I write to you, dear children,
because your sins have been
forgiven on account of his
name.
[13]I write to you, fathers,
because you have known him
who is from the beginning.
I write to you, young men,
because you have overcome the
evil one.[f]
I write to you, dear children,
because you have known the
Father.
[14]I write to you, fathers,
because you have known him
who is from the beginning.
I write to you, young men,
because you are strong,[g]
and the word of God lives in
you,[h]
and you have overcome the evil
one.[i]

Do Not Love the World

1 →PG. 1397

[15]Do not love the world or anything
in the world.[j] If anyone loves the
world, the love of the Father is not in
him.[k] [16]For everything in the world—
the cravings of sinful man,[l] the lust of
his eyes[m] and the boasting of what he
has and does—comes not from the Father but from the world. [17]The world
and its desires pass away,[n] but the
man who does the will of God lives forever.

Warning Against Antichrists

[18]Dear children, this is the last hour;
and as you have heard that the antichrist is coming,[o] even now many antichrists have come.[p] This is how we
know it is the last hour. [19]They went
out from us,[q] but they did not really
belong to us. For if they had belonged
to us, they would have remained with
us; but their going showed that none of
them belonged to us.[r]

[20]But you have an anointing[s] from
the Holy One,[t] and all of you know
the truth.[b][u] [21]I do not write to you
because you do not know the truth, but
because you do know it[v] and because
no lie comes from the truth. [22]Who is
the liar? It is the man who denies that
Jesus is the Christ. Such a man is the
antichrist—he denies the Father and
the Son.[w] [23]No one who denies the
Son has the Father; whoever acknowledges the Son has the Father also.[x]
[24]See that what you have heard from
the beginning remains in you. If it
does, you also will remain in the Son
and in the Father.[y] [25]And this is what
he promised us—even eternal life.

[26]I am writing these things to you
about those who are trying to lead you
astray.[z] [27]As for you, the anointing[a]
you received from him remains in you,
and you do not need anyone to teach
you. But as his anointing teaches you
about all things and as that anointing
is real, not counterfeit—just as it has
taught you, remain in him.

Children of God

1 →PG. 1398

[28]And now, dear children,[b] continue in him, so that when he appears[c]
we may be confident[d] and unashamed before him at his coming.[e]
[29]If you know that he is righteous,[f]
you know that everyone who does
what is right has been born of him.

3 →PG. 1406

3 How great is the love[g] the Father
has lavished on us, that we should
be called children of God![h] And that is
what we are! The reason the world does
not know us is that it did not know
him.[i] [2]Dear friends, now we are children of God, and what we will be has
not yet been made known. But we
know that when he appears,[c] we shall
be like him,[j] for we shall see him as
he is.[k] [3]Everyone who has this hope
in him purifies himself,[l] just as he is
pure.

[4]Everyone who sins breaks the law;

[a] *10* Or *it* [b] *20* Some manuscripts *and you know all things* [c] *2* Or *when it is made known*

2:6 [x]Mt 11:29; 1Pe 2:21 **2:7** [y]1Jn 3:11,23; 2Jn 5,6 **2:8** [z]Jn 13:34 [a]Ro 13:12 [b]Jn 1:9 [c]Eph 5:8; 1Th 5:5 **2:10** [d]1Jn 3:14 **2:11** [e]Jn 12:35 **2:13** [f]ver 14 **2:14** [g]Eph 6:10 [h]Jn 5:38; 1Jn 1:10 [i]ver 13 **2:15** [j]Ro 12:2 [k]Jas 4:4 **2:16** [l]Ro 13:14 [m]Pr 27:20 **2:17** [n]1Co 7:31 **2:18** [o]ver 22; 1Jn 4:3; 2Jn 7 [p]1Jn 4:1 **2:19** [q]Ac 20:30 [r]1Co 11:19 **2:20** [s]2Co 1:21 [t]Mk 1:24 [u]Jn 14:26 **2:21** [v]2Pe 1:12; Jude 5 **2:22** [w]2Jn 7 **2:23** [x]Jn 8:19; 1Jn 4:15 **2:24** [y]Jn 14:23 **2:26** [z]2Jn 7 **2:27** [a]ver 20 **2:28** [b]ver 1 [c]1Jn 3:2 [d]1Jn 4:17 [e]1Th 2:19 **2:29** [f]1Jn 3:7 **3:1** [g]Jn 3:16 [h]Jn 1:12 [i]Jn 16:3 **3:2** [j]Ro 8:29; 2Pe 1:4 [k]2Co 3:18 **3:3** [l]2Co 7:1; 2Pe 3:13,14

2:17 PROMISE 3

GOD COMES FIRST

In this one brief statement, John provides us with a perspective that should direct all of our thoughts and actions in this life.

For the next Promise 3 reading go to page 1403.

in fact, sin is lawlessness.[m] 5But you
know that he appeared so that he
might take away our sins. And in him
is no sin.[n] 6No one who lives in him
keeps on sinning.[o] No one who continues to sin has either seen him[p] or
known him.[q]
7Dear children,[r] do not let anyone
lead you astray.[s] He who does what
is right is righteous, just as he is righteous.[t] 8He who does what is sinful is
of the devil,[u] because the devil has
been sinning from the beginning. The
reason the Son of God appeared was to
1 →PG. 1398
destroy the devil's work. 9No one who
is born of God[v] will continue to sin,[w]
because God's seed[x] remains in him;
he cannot go on sinning, because he
has been born of God. 10This is how we
know who the children of God are and
who the children of the devil are: Anyone who does not do what is right is
not a child of God; nor is anyone who
does not love[y] his brother.

Love One Another

1 →PG. 1399
2 →PG. 1399
6 →PG. 1399
7 →PG. 1398

11This is the message you heard[z]
from the beginning: We should love
one another.[a] 12Do not be like Cain,
who belonged to the evil one and murdered his brother.[b] And why did he
murder him? Because his own actions
were evil and his brother's were righteous. 13Do not be surprised, my brothers, if the world hates you.[c] 14We
know that we have passed from death
to life,[d] because we love our brothers.
Anyone who does not love remains
in death.[e] 15Anyone who hates his
brother is a murderer,[f] and you know
that no murderer has eternal life in
him.[g]
16This is how we know what love is:
Jesus Christ laid down his life for us.
And we ought to lay down our lives for
our brothers.[h] 17If anyone has material possessions and sees his brother in
need but has no pity on him,[i] how
can the love of God be in him?[j] 18Dear
children,[k] let us not love with words
or tongue but with actions and in
truth.[l] 19This then is how we know
that we belong to the truth, and how
we set our hearts at rest in his presence
20whenever our hearts condemn us.
For God is greater than our hearts, and
he knows everything.
21Dear friends, if our hearts do not
condemn us, we have confidence before God[m] 22and receive from him
anything we ask,[n] because we obey
his commands and do what pleases
him.[o] 23And this is his command: to
believe[p] in the name of his Son, Jesus
Christ, and to love one another as he
commanded us.[q] 24Those who obey
his commands live in him,[r] and he in
them. And this is how we know that he
lives in us: We know it by the Spirit he
gave us.[s]

Test the Spirits

4 Dear friends, do not believe every
spirit, but test the spirits to see
whether they are from God, because
many false prophets have gone out
into the world.[t] 2This is how you can
recognize the Spirit of God: Every spirit
that acknowledges that Jesus Christ
has come in the flesh[u] is from God,[v]
3but every spirit that does not acknowledge Jesus is not from God. This is the
spirit of the antichrist,[w] which you
have heard is coming and even now is
already in the world.
4You, dear children, are from God
and have overcome them, because the
one who is in you[x] is greater than the
one who is in the world.[y] 5They are
from the world[z] and therefore speak
from the viewpoint of the world, and
the world listens to them. 6We are from
God, and whoever knows God listens
to us; but whoever is not from God
does not listen to us.[a] This is how we
recognize the Spirit[a] of truth[b] and
the spirit of falsehood.

God's Love and Ours

7 →PG. 1403

7Dear friends, let us love one another,[c] for love comes from God. Everyone who loves has been born of God
and knows God.[d] 8Whoever does not
love does not know God, because God
is love.[e] 9This is how God showed his
love among us: He sent his one and
only Son[b] into the world that we
might live through him.[f] 10This is

[a] 6 Or *spirit* [b] 9 Or *his only begotten Son*

3:4 m1Jn 5:17
3:5 n2Co 5:21
3:6 over 9 p3Jn 11 q1Jn 2:4
3:7 r1Jn 2:1 s1Jn 2:26 t1Jn 2:29
3:8 uJn 8:44
3:9 vJn 1:13 w1Jn 5:18 x1Pe 1:23
3:10 y1Jn 4:8
3:11 z1Jn 1:5 aJn 13:34,35; 2Jn 5
3:12 bGe 4:8
3:13 cJn 15:18,19; 17:14
3:14 dJn 5:24 e1Jn 2:9
3:15 fMt 5:21,22; Jn 8:44 gGal 5:20,21
3:16 hJn 15:13
3:17 iDt 15:7,8 j1Jn 4:20
3:18 k1Jn 2:1 lEze 33:31; Ro 12:9
3:21 m1Jn 5:14
3:22 nMt 7:7 oJn 8:29
3:23 pJn 6:29 qJn 13:34
3:24 r1Jn 2:6 s1Jn 4:13
4:1 t2Pe 2:1; 1Jn 2:18
4:2 uJn 1:14; 1Jn 2:23 v1Co 12:3
4:3 w1Jn 2:22; 2Jn 7
4:4 xRo 8:31 yJn 12:31
4:5 zJn 15:19
4:6 aJn 8:47 bJn 14:17
4:7 c1Jn 3:11 d1Jn 2:4
4:8 ever 7,16
4:9 fJn 3:16,17; 1Jn 5:11

3:16–20

PROMISE 7

LOVE IN ACTION

The kind of love that John talks about here is the kind that gets up off the couch and does something. It's the kind of love that sees a need and immediately acts to fill it. It's the kind of love that puts others in front of self. It's the kind of love that can act as a gauge of our commitment to Jesus Christ. It's the kind of love that Jesus himself exhibited when he was on earth.

Is this the kind of love you exhibit in your church life and in your community? Whatever your skills, talents or resources, God wants to use them in the service of his kingdom.

For the next Promise 7 reading go to page 1406.

love: not that we loved God, but that he
loved us[g] and sent his Son as an atoning sacrifice for[a] our sins.[h] **11**Dear
friends, since God so loved us,[i] we
also ought to love one another. **12**No
one has ever seen God;[j] but if we love
one another, God lives in us and his
love is made complete in us.[k]

13We know that we live in him and
he in us, because he has given us of his
Spirit.[l] **14**And we have seen and testify[m] that the Father has sent his Son to
be the Savior of the world.[n] **15**If anyone acknowledges that Jesus is the Son
of God,[o] God lives in him and he in
God. **16**And so we know and rely on the
love God has for us.

God is love.[p] Whoever lives in love
lives in God, and God in him.[q] **17**In
this way, love is made complete[r]
among us so that we will have confidence on the day of judgment, because
in this world we are like him. **18**There is
no fear in love. But perfect love drives
out fear,[s] because fear has to do with
punishment. The one who fears is not
made perfect in love.

2 →PG. 1406
19We love because he first loved
us.[t] **20**If anyone says, "I love God," yet
hates his brother,[u] he is a liar.[v] For
6 →PG. 20
anyone who does not love his brother,
whom he has seen,[w] cannot love God,
whom he has not seen.[x] **21**And he has
given us this command: Whoever loves
God must also love his brother.[y]

Faith in the Son of God

5 Everyone who believes that Jesus is
the Christ[z] is born of God,[a] and
everyone who loves the father loves his
child as well.[b] **2**This is how we know
that we love the children of God: by
loving God and carrying out his commands. **3**This is love for God: to obey
his commands.[c] And his commands
are not burdensome,[d] **4**for everyone
born of God overcomes[e] the world.
This is the victory that has overcome
the world, even our faith. **5**Who is it
that overcomes the world? Only he
who believes that Jesus is the Son of
God.

6This is the one who came by water
and blood[f]—Jesus Christ. He did not
come by water only, but by water and
blood. And it is the Spirit who testifies,
because the Spirit is the truth.[g] **7**For
there are three[h] that testify: **8**the[b]
Spirit, the water and the blood; and the
three are in agreement. **9**We accept
man's testimony,[i] but God's testimony is greater because it is the testimony
of God,[j] which he has given about his
Son. **10**Anyone who believes in the Son
of God has this testimony in his
heart.[k] Anyone who does not believe
God has made him out to be a liar,[l]
because he has not believed the testimony God has given about his Son.
11And this is the testimony: God has
given us eternal life, and this life is in
his Son.[m] **12**He who has the Son has
life; he who does not have the Son of
God does not have life.[n]

Concluding Remarks

13I write these things to you who believe in the name of the Son of God[o]
so that you may know that you have
eternal life.[p] **14**This is the confidence[q] we have in approaching God:
that if we ask anything according to his
will, he hears us.[r] **15**And if we know
that he hears us—whatever we ask—
we know[s] that we have what we asked
of him.

1 →PG. 1403

16If anyone sees his brother commit
a sin that does not lead to death, he
should pray and God will give him
life.[t] I refer to those whose sin does
not lead to death. There is a sin that

4:10 [g]Ro 5:8,10 [h]1Jn 2:2
4:11 [i]Jn 3:16
4:12 [j]Jn 1:18; 1Ti 6:16 [k]1Jn 2:5
4:13 [l]1Jn 3:24
4:14 [m]Jn 15:27 [n]Jn 3:17
4:15 [o]Ro 10:9
4:16 [p]ver 8 [q]1Jn 3:24
4:17 [r]1Jn 2:5
4:18 [s]Ro 8:15
4:19 [t]ver 10
4:20 [u]1Jn 2:9 [v]1Jn 2:4 [w]1Jn 3:17 [x]ver 12
4:21 [y]Mt 5:43
5:1 [z]1Jn 2:22 [a]Jn 1:13; 1Jn 2:23 [b]Jn 8:42
5:3 [c]Jn 14:15; 2Jn 6 [d]Mt 11:30
5:4 [e]Jn 16:33
5:6 [f]Jn 19:34 [g]Jn 14:17
5:7 [h]Mt 18:16
5:9 [i]Jn 5:34 [j]Mt 3:16,17; Jn 8:17,18
5:10 [k]Ro 8:16; Gal 4:6 [l]Jn 3:33
5:11 [m]Jn 1:4; 1Jn 2:25
5:12 [n]Jn 3:15,16,36
5:13 [o]1Jn 3:23 [p]Jn 20:31; 1Jn 1:1,2
5:14 [q]1Jn 3:21 [r]Mt 7:7
5:15 [s]ver 18,19,20
5:16 [t]Jas 5:15

[a] *10* Or *as the one who would turn aside his wrath, taking away* [b] *7,8* Late manuscripts of the Vulgate *testify in heaven: the Father, the Word and the Holy Spirit, and these three are one. 8And there are three that testify on earth: the* (not found in any Greek manuscript before the sixteenth century)

5:14–15

PROMISE **1**

PRAYER: IT'S NOT WHAT YOU MAY THINK

It's easy to think of prayer as a matter of God bending his will to fill our requests. But you may be surprised to know that prayer is really the exact opposite of that. Prayer involves bringing our will into compliance with God's.

As believers we can approach God with confidence (1 John 3:21), knowing he will hear our prayers. It's by prayer that we seek God's will, embrace it and align ourselves with it. And the condition of answered prayer depends on whether or not our requests are in line with his divine will.

While we should never hesitate to ask God for something (Philippians 4:6–7), we should do so with an attitude of submission. That's what Jesus did in Gethsemane. He brought his request before God and then said, "Yet not as I will, but as you will" (Matthew 26:39). Our prayer should be the same. As you go to God in prayer this week, ask him to enable you to find his will and to give you the strength to submit your life to it.

For the next Promise 1 reading go to page 1415.

leads to death.[u] I am not saying that
he should pray about that.[v] 17All
wrongdoing is sin,[w] and there is sin
that does not lead to death.[x]
18We know that anyone born of God
does not continue to sin; the one who
was born of God keeps him safe, and
the evil one cannot harm him.[y] 19We
know that we are children of God,[z]
and that the whole world is under the
control of the evil one.[a] 20We know
also that the Son of God has come and
has given us understanding,[b] so that
we may know him who is true.[c] And
we are in him who is true—even in his
Son Jesus Christ. He is the true God
and eternal life.[d]
21Dear children, keep yourselves
from idols.[e]

5:16 [u]Heb 6:4-6; 10:26 [v]Jer 7:16
5:17 [w]1Jn 3:4 [x]1Jn 2:1
5:18 [y]Jn 14:30
5:19 [z]1Jn 4:6 [a]Gal 1:4
5:20 [b]Lk 24:45 [c]Jn 17:3 [d]ver 11
5:21 [e]1Co 10:14; 1Th 1:9

2 JOHN

AT A GLANCE

Key Principle: Walking in the truth means not only loving one another, but also avoiding fellowship with deceivers.
Author: The apostle John
Time and Place: ~A.D. 90 / Probably written in Ephesus
Key Verses: 6, 9–10

BENEFIT

Second John encourages us to walk in God's way by loving and serving one another. It also warns us to be aware of spiritual counterfeits that distort the truth of the gospel of the incarnate Christ. We are to love, but we are also to show discernment; truth without love leads to harshness and severity, while love without truth produces sloppy sentimentality.

SETTING

While the early church disputed the inclusion of both 2 John and 3 John in the New Testament canon, the second-century church fathers Irenaeus and Clement of Alexandria recognized these epistles as authentic writings of the apostle John, and they eventually won universal acceptance. John called himself "the elder" in both of these letters, assuming that his readers knew his identity. The style, vocabulary and content are similar in all three of John's letters. These letters, in turn, are also similar in style and content to the fourth Gospel.

The apostle John evidently wrote his second and third epistles at about the same time as his first epistle (around A.D. 85–95), and like the other two, he probably wrote this letter in Ephesus. Some scholars have suggested that John originally wrote his second and third letters as personal supplements to his first letter, but it seems more likely that these concise letters stood on their own. First John states that several false teachers had departed from the church in Ephesus (2:19), and some of these were spreading their message to other churches by traveling to other cities.

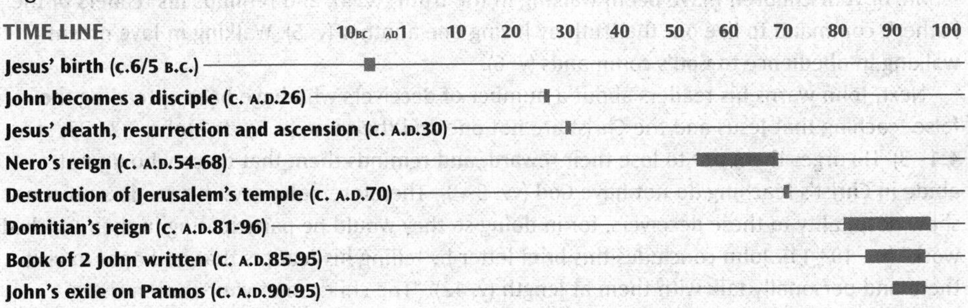

THEME AND PURPOSE

This pithy epistle advocates "speaking the truth in love" (Ephesians 4:15); its original readers had been "walking in the truth" (v. 4) by obeying the Father's command to "walk in love" (v. 6). John wrote to encourage them to hold firm to the apostolic doctrine and practice what they "have heard from the beginning" (v. 6), and also to warn them to avoid false teachers. He said that they must love one another in the truth while practicing discernment so that they do not fall prey to deceptive influences.

UNIQUE CONTRIBUTION

Apart from 3 John, this is the shortest book in the Bible. The first half of 2 John is a positive exhortation (verses 1–6 mention "truth" five times and "love" four times), and the second half is a negative warning (verses 7–13 do not mention either of these words). All three of John's epistles deal with the theme of fellowship—first with God (1 John), then with false teachers (2 John) and finally with those who proclaim the truth (3 John).

CHRIST IN 2 JOHN

Like 1 John, this epistle stresses that Christ's incarnation was real. He wrote this letter to counteract false teachers who denied that Christ came in the flesh. "Many deceivers, who do not acknowledge Jesus Christ as coming in the flesh, have gone out into the world" (v. 7). Anyone "who . . . does not continue in the teaching of Christ does not have God; whoever continues in the teaching has both the Father and the Son" (v. 9). John stresses that the doctrine of Christ is absolutely crucial; it affects every other area of theology.

OVERVIEW

FOCUS	Fellowship with God: Abide		Fellowship with False Teachers: Avoid	
REFERENCE	1 — 3	4 — 6	7 — 11	12 — 13
TOPICS	Commendation and Commandment		Caution	Conclusion
	Preliminary Thoughts	Practicing the Truth	Protecting the Truth	Parting Thoughts
	Walking with Christ		Watching for Counterfeits	
	Abiding in the Truth	Applying God's Love	Avoiding False Teachers	Anticipated Visit
LOCATION	Probably Written in Ephesus			
TIME	~A.D. 90			

John uses the word "truth" four times in the beginning of this letter to emphasize the importance of abiding in the truth of the gospel of Jesus Christ (vv. 1–3). He rejoices in the fact that "some of your children [have been] walking in the truth" (v. 4), and reminds his readers of the Father's command to live out the truth by loving one another (v. 5). Walking in love means walking in obedience to God's commands (v. 6).

Next, John warns his readers about a number of deceivers who have been spreading the false teaching that Jesus and the Christ are not one and the same (v. 7; cf. 1 John 2:2–23; 4:1–3). He urges them not to lose their reward, and reminds them that those who do not abide in Christ's teaching do not have God (vv. 8–9). Therefore, John says, his readers must not show hospitality to these deceivers, for in doing so they would be participating in their "wicked work" (vv. 10–11). John concludes this brief letter by telling his readers that he hopes to visit them and personally talk with them at length (v. 12). "The children of your chosen sister" (v. 13) is probably an indirect reference to the members of a sister congregation.

2 JOHN

1The elder,[a]

To the chosen[b] lady and her children, whom I love in the truth—and
not I only, but also all who know
the truth[c]— 2because of the truth,[d]
which lives in us[e] and will be with us
forever:

3Grace, mercy and peace from God
the Father and from Jesus Christ,[f] the
Father's Son, will be with us in truth
and love.

7 →PG. 1423
4It has given me great joy to find
some of your children walking in the
truth,[g] just as the Father commanded
us. 5And now, dear lady, I am not writing you a new command but one we
have had from the beginning.[h] I ask
that we love one another. 6And this is
love:[i] that we walk in obedience to his
commands. As you have heard from
the beginning, his command is that
you walk in love.

7Many deceivers, who do not acknowledge Jesus Christ[j] as coming
in the flesh, have gone out into the
world.[k] Any such person is the deceiver and the antichrist.[l] 8Watch out that
you do not lose what you have worked
for, but that you may be rewarded fully.[m] 9Anyone who runs ahead and
does not continue in the teaching of
Christ does not have God; whoever
continues in the teaching has both
the Father and the Son.[n] 10If anyone
comes to you and does not bring this
teaching, do not take him into your
house or welcome him.[o] 11Anyone
who welcomes him shares[p] in his
wicked work.

12I have much to write to you, but I
do not want to use paper and ink. Instead, I hope to visit you and talk with
you face to face,[q] so that our joy may
be complete.

13The children of your chosen[r] sister send their greetings.

1 →PG. 1411

1:1 [a] 3Jn 1 [b] Ro 16:13 [c] Jn 8:32 **1:2** [d] 2Pe 1:12 [e] 1Jn 1:8 **1:3** [f] Ro 1:7 **1:4** [g] 3Jn 3,4 **1:5** [h] 1Jn 2:7; 3:11 **1:6** [i] 1Jn 2:5 **1:7** [j] 1Jn 2:22; 4:2,3 [k] 1Jn 4:1 [l] 1Jn 2:18 **1:8** [m] 1Co 3:8 **1:9** [n] 1Jn 2:23 **1:10** [o] Ro 16:17 **1:11** [p] 1Ti 5:22 **1:12** [q] 3Jn 13,14 **1:13** [r] ver 1

7-13

PROMISE 3

SPIRITUAL PURITY

John's call to spiritual purity is as applicable to us today as it was to his original readers. Our pluralistic age values freedom of thought and speech above all things. And that's good, for without such freedoms we would not be able to worship Jesus in the way we do. But we need to be careful to differentiate false teaching from true.

In a day when acceptance and tolerance is the popular way of dealing with disagreement, we need to make it clear we neither accept nor support teachers whose message strays from Biblical truth.

For the next Promise 3 reading go to page 1410.

3 JOHN

AT A GLANCE

Key Principle: Fellowship with Christian brothers and sisters is essential to growing in the truth.
Author: The apostle John
Time and Place: ~A.D. 85–95 / Probably written in Ephesus
Key Verses: 4–5, 11

BENEFIT

This letter reminds us that we have a responsibility to support and encourage those who have been sent to teach and equip us in the truth.

SETTING

See the "Setting" section in the introduction of 2 John for a word concerning the authorship of this epistle.

In the latter part of his ministry, the apostle John used Ephesus, the most important city of the Roman province of Asia, as his base of operations. Apparently, the apostle commissioned several traveling teachers to evangelize, encourage and equip believers in this province. These traveling teachers lived on the hospitality of believers who benefited from their teaching. Evidently, many church members joyfully received these missionaries. Word had reached John, however, that in one of the churches a man named Diotrephes rejected a previous letter from John and arrogantly challenged the apostle's authority. Wishing to seize control of the church himself, Diotrephes sought to expel anyone who showed hospitality to the teachers whom John had sent. Gaius, the man to whom this letter is addressed, demonstrated his godliness and generosity by supporting these teachers.

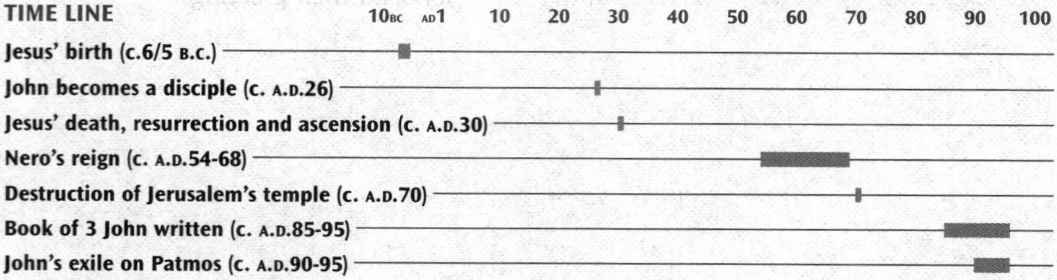

THEME AND PURPOSE

This epistle stresses the importance of maintaining fellowship and undergirding the ministries of people who have committed their lives to sharing the message of new life in Christ. John wrote this brief letter to commend Gaius as a fellow worker in the truth because of his hospitality and support of missionaries who taught and equipped believers in the churches of Asia Minor. At the same time, this letter rebukes the pride and misconduct of Diotrephes, who rejected these teachers. John also commends Demetrius (who may have delivered this letter) to the church and informs Gaius of his plan to visit the church and settle the difficulties.

UNIQUE CONTRIBUTION

Third John is the shortest book in the Bible, but it paints a clear portrait of two radically different kinds of men. The apostle starkly contrasts a man who wants others to look to him, and another man who wants others to look to Jesus. One is the embodiment of selfishness, the other is the embodiment of servanthood.

CHRIST IN 3 JOHN

In contrast to 1 John and 2 John, the apostle does not specifically mention the name of Jesus Christ in this third epistle. However, he indirectly refers to Christ in verse 7 when he writes: "It was for the sake of the Name that they went out" (compare Acts 5:40–41). Christ is also the embodiment of "the truth" that John emphasizes throughout this letter.

OVERVIEW

FOCUS	Commendation of Gaius		Condemnation of Diotrephes		
REFERENCE	1 — 4	5 — 8	9 — 11	12	13 — 14
TOPICS	Fellowship	Faithfulness	Faithlessness	Faithfulness	Farewell
	Servanthood		Selfishness		
	Walking in the Truth		Walking in Error		
	Praise of Hospitality		Problem of Haughtiness		
LOCATION	Probably Written in Ephesus				
TIME	~A.D. 90				

John writes to commend Gaius for his faithfulness and generosity in supporting those who have been sent to teach the truth (vv. 1–4), and encourages Gaius to continue to provide such hospitality (vv. 5–8). By contrast, John sternly rebukes the conduct of Diotrephes, who sought preeminence for himself and opposed these teachers of the truth (vv. 9–11). After recommending Demetrius as a man of good testimony (v. 12), the apostle writes of his hope to visit this Asian church in person (vv. 13–14).

3 JOHN

1 The elder,[a]

To my dear friend Gaius, whom I love in the truth.

2 Dear friend, I pray that you may enjoy good health and that all may go well with you, even as your soul is getting along well. 3 It gave me great joy to have some brothers[b] come and tell about your faithfulness to the truth and how you continue to walk in the truth.[c] 4 I have no greater joy than to hear that my children[d] are walking in the truth.

2 →PG. 20
3 →PG. 1416

5 Dear friend, you are faithful in what you are doing for the brothers, even though they are strangers to you.[e] 6 They have told the church about your love. You will do well to send them on their way in a manner worthy of God. 7 It was for the sake of the Name[f] that they went out, receiving no help from the pagans.[g] 8 We ought therefore to show hospitality to such men so that we may work together for the truth.

5 →PG. 106

9 I wrote to the church, but Diotrephes, who loves to be first, will have nothing to do with us. 10 So if I come,[h] I will call attention to what he is doing, gossiping maliciously about us. Not satisfied with that, he refuses to welcome the brothers.[i] He also stops those who want to do so and puts them out of the church.[j]

11 Dear friend, do not imitate what is evil but what is good.[k] Anyone who does what is good is from God.[l] Anyone who does what is evil has not seen God.[m] 12 Demetrius is well spoken of by everyone[n]—and even by the truth itself. We also speak well of him, and you know that our testimony is true.[o]

13 I have much to write you, but I do not want to do so with pen and ink. 14 I hope to see you soon, and we will talk face to face.[p]

Peace to you. The friends here send their greetings. Greet the friends there by name.[q]

1:1 a 2Jn 1
1:3 b ver 5,10; c 2Jn 4
1:4 d 1Co 4:15; 1Jn 2:1
1:5 e Ro 12:13; Heb 13:2
1:7 f Jn 15:21; g Ac 20:33,35
1:10 h 2Jn 12; i ver 5; j Jn 9:22,34
1:11 k Ps 37:27; l 1Jn 2:29; m 1Jn 3:6,9,10
1:12 n 1Ti 3:7; o Jn 21:24
1:14 p 2Jn 12; q Jn 10:3

5–8

PROMISE **7**

HOSPITALITY

Here the apostle John touches on an aspect of service to others that we may not often think about: *hospitality.* In the original language the word meant, "a love for strangers." John praised Gaius for opening his home to traveling teachers whom he didn't know.

The Great Commission (Matthew 28:19–20) and Great Commandment (Mark 12:30–31) call us to act in service and love for God and for our brothers and sisters. One fantastic and rewarding way to do that is to open our homes to others. The intimate setting of the home and the fellowship around a meal is perfect for showing God's love to other people. By doing so you can bless them and bring God into their lives.

Showing this kind of hospitality is one way the whole family can come together in service to others. It allows families to minister to families, from the oldest parent to the youngest child. Also, if young children prohibit you from spending much time away from home, inviting others into the home to enjoy your family is a fun and creative way to act on Jesus' commandment. But this command isn't only for families! Gaius himself may have been a single man, and he has been remembered down the centuries for his gracious hospitality to strangers.

The call to hospitality is a call to build and foster relationships in the name of our Lord. And isn't that one of the Christian's main responsibilities?

For the next Promise 7 reading go to page 4.

JUDE

AT A GLANCE

Key Principle: We are engaged in a spiritual warfare with deception, heresy and immorality, and we can only stand firm in the truth by being built up in our faith in the Lord Jesus Christ.
Author: Jude, the Lord's brother
Time and Place: ~A.D. 60–65 / Place of writing unknown
Key Verses: 3, 20–21

BENEFIT

Jude combines the style of his brother James and the theme of 2 Peter in writing this brief but powerful word of warning and exhortation. While many of the New Testament writers confront the problem of spiritual counterfeits, Jude is perhaps the most passionate in his denunciation of their teachings and practices. Jude reminds us of the reality of the spiritual warfare that is all about us, and teaches us that complacency leads to surrendered territory, while commitment to the person and cause of Christ will keep us from stumbling.

SETTING

The early church fathers recognized Jude's epistle as authentic revelation, but its place in the New Testament canon was disputed for a time in some parts of the church because it quotes from certain Apocryphal writings. "Jude, a servant of Jesus Christ and a brother of James" (v. 1) should not be confused with the apostle "Judas son of James" (Luke 6:16; Acts 1:13). The ancient church understood the author as the Judas who is mentioned along with James, Joseph and Simon as the sons of Mary and Joseph in Matthew 13:55 and Mark 6:3. Neither Jude nor his brothers believed in Jesus prior to his resurrection (John 7:1–9).

Jude's address in verse 1 is not specific to a group or a location, and his description of the false teachers does not provide enough information to determine the situation he had in mind. The deceivers he warns against were arrogant moral libertines who infiltrated the love feasts of believers and used flattery as a means of influence (vv. 12, 16). Jude's characterization of these heretics in verses 4–18 is similar to Peter's description of false teachers in his second epistle (2:1–3:4), but there are also enough differences to ensure that one is not a mere copy of the other. Due to the lack of internal detail and external tradition, the date and location of this epistle are unknown.

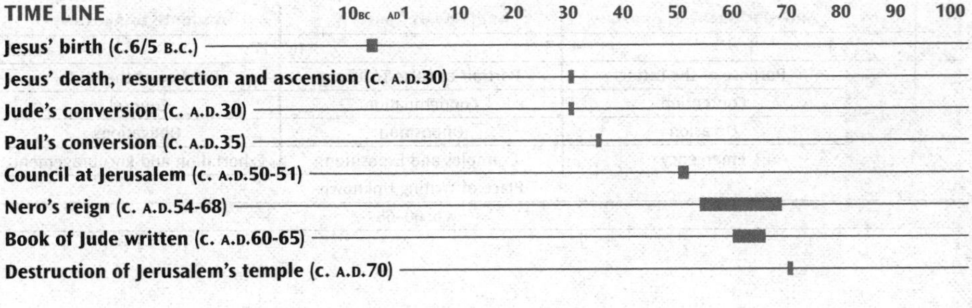

THEME AND PURPOSE

Although his initial intention was to write "about the salvation we share" (v. 3), Jude realized that he had to urge his readers "to contend for the faith that was once for all entrusted to the saints" in view of the growing threat of heretical teachers. His primary purpose, therefore, was to expose the character and tactics of ungodly deceivers who were infiltrating the churches and seducing believers to follow in their immoral path. Jude describes the character, tactics and divine judgment of these false teachers, but he says little about the nature of their teachings. It is possible that these moral libertines were promoting a Gnostic heresy (see "Setting" in the introduction to 1 John).

Jude urged his readers to stand firm in the truth and to grow in their faith and confidence in God's power to keep them from falling.

UNIQUE CONTRIBUTION

In spite of its brevity, Jude makes a number of references to the Old Testament and also appears to refer to two first-century pseudepigraphal (books falsely attributed to Biblical characters). Verse 9 evidently alludes to the Assumption of Moses, and verses 14–15 quote from the Book of Enoch 1:9. While these references have caused concern, Jude did not affirm the authority of these books in quoting from them. Instead, he used them to illustrate his argument in the same way that Paul used the Greek poets Aratus in Acts 17:28, Menander in 1 Corinthians 15:33 and Epimenides in Titus 1:12.

Jude's style is similar to that of his brother James: he vividly describes those who compromise the truth, is very concise, uses natural imagery, stresses moral purity and demonstrates personal concern for his readers' welfare. Another interesting feature in Jude's letter is his use of triads of thought: Jude, servant, brother (v. 1); called, loved, kept (v. 1); mercy, peace, love (v. 2); people, angels, those who did not believe (vv. 5–7); Cain, Balaam, Korah (v. 11); those, others, others (vv. 22–23); before, now, forevermore (v. 25). Even the epistle itself naturally divides into three sections (vv. 1–4, 5–16, 17–25).

CHRIST IN JUDE

Those who have been called are kept by Jesus Christ (v. 1); those who "change the grace of our God into a license for immorality and deny Jesus Christ our only Sovereign and Lord" (v. 4) are under divine condemnation. The mercy of our Lord Jesus Christ will bring us to eternal life (v. 21). He will keep us from falling and present us before his glorious presence without fault and with great joy (vv. 24–25).

OVERVIEW

FOCUS	Announcement of Apostasy	Anatomy of Apostasy	Antidote to Apostasy
REFERENCE	1 — 4	5 — 16	17 — 25
TOPICS	Purpose of the Letter	Portrait of False Teachers	Practice of the Truth
	Contention	Condemnation	Counsel
	Occasion	Opposition	Obligations
	Emergency	Examples and Exposition	Exhortation and Encouragement
LOCATION	Place of Writing Unknown		
TIME	~A.D. 60–65		

Jude addresses this epistle to believers who have been called, loved and kept by Jesus Christ (v. 1). He informs them that he changed his original intention to write about "the salvation we share" in view of the threat of heretical teachers who had infiltrated the churches, and urges them to "contend for the faith that was once for all entrusted to the saints" (vv. 2–4).

The bulk of Jude is an exposition of the character, conduct and condemnation of these deceivers (vv. 5–16). He vividly illustrates the divine punishment that awaits these heretics (vv. 5–7). These teachers foolishly "pollute their own bodies, reject authority and slander celestial beings"; like the rebellious Cain, Balaam and Korah, they are under God's condemnation (vv. 8–11). Jude exposes their deceptiveness, selfishness and instability (vv. 12–15) and denounces their behavior (v. 16).

Turning from a negative warning to a positive exhortation, Jude encourages his readers to "build yourselves up in your most holy faith and pray in the Holy Spirit" (vv. 17–20). By keeping themselves in God's love and anticipating his reward of eternal life, they can mercifully correct and minister to those who have been ensnared by error (vv. 21–23). Jude concludes with a beautiful and powerful doxology that portrays Christ's power to keep those who hope in him from stumbling (vv. 24–25).

JUDE

1Jude,[a] a servant of Jesus Christ and
a brother of James,

To those who have been called,[b]
who are loved by God the Father and
kept by[a] Jesus Christ:[c]

2Mercy, peace and love be yours in
abundance.[d]

The Sin and Doom of Godless Men

3Dear friends, although I was very
eager to write to you about the salvation we share,[e] I felt I had to write and
urge you to contend[f] for the faith that
was once for all entrusted to the saints.
4For certain men whose condemnation
was written about[b] long ago have secretly slipped in among you.[g] They
are godless men, who change the grace
of our God into a license for immorality
and deny Jesus Christ our only Sovereign and Lord.[h]
5Though you already know all this,
I want to remind you that the Lord[c]
delivered his people out of Egypt, but
later destroyed those who did not believe.[i] 6And the angels who did not
keep their positions of authority but
abandoned their own home—these he
has kept in darkness, bound with everlasting chains for judgment on the
great Day.[j] 7In a similar way, Sodom
and Gomorrah and the surrounding
towns[k] gave themselves up to sexual
immorality and perversion. They serve
as an example of those who suffer the
punishment of eternal fire.[l]
8In the very same way, these dreamers pollute their own bodies, reject authority and slander celestial beings.[m]
9But even the archangel Michael,[n]
when he was disputing with the devil
about the body of Moses, did not
dare to bring a slanderous accusation
against him, but said, "The Lord rebuke you!"[o] 10Yet these men speak
abusively against whatever they do not
understand; and what things they do
understand by instinct, like unreason-
ing animals—these are the very things
that destroy them.[p]
11Woe to them! They have taken the
way of Cain;[q] they have rushed for
profit into Balaam's error;[r] they have
been destroyed in Korah's rebellion.[s]
12These men are blemishes at your
love feasts,[t] eating with you without
the slightest qualm—shepherds who
feed only themselves. They are clouds
without rain,[u] blown along by the
wind;[v] autumn trees, without fruit and
uprooted[w]—twice dead. 13They are
wild waves of the sea,[x] foaming up
their shame;[y] wandering stars, for
whom blackest darkness has been reserved forever.[z]
14Enoch,[a] the seventh from Adam,
prophesied about these men: "See,
the Lord is coming with thousands
upon thousands of his holy ones[b] 15to
judge[c] everyone, and to convict all the
ungodly of all the ungodly acts they
have done in the ungodly way, and of
all the harsh words ungodly sinners
have spoken against him."[d] 16These
men are grumblers and faultfinders;
they follow their own evil desires; they
boast[e] about themselves and flatter
others for their own advantage.

A Call to Persevere

17But, dear friends, remember what
the apostles of our Lord Jesus Christ
foretold.[f] 18They said to you, "In the
last times[g] there will be scoffers who
will follow their own ungodly desires."[h] 19These are the men who divide you, who follow mere natural in-
stincts and do not have the Spirit.[i]

1:1 [a]Mt 13:55; Ac 1:13 [b]Ro 1:6,7 [c]Jn 17:12
1:2 [d]2Pe 1:2
1:3 [e]Tit 1:4 [f]1Ti 6:12
1:4 [g]Gal 2:4 [h]Tit 1:16; 2Pe 2:1
1:5 [i]Nu 14:29; Ps 106:26
1:6 [j]2Pe 2:4,9
1:7 [k]Dt 29:23 [l]2Pe 2:6
1:8 [m]2Pe 2:10
1:9 [n]Da 10:13,21 [o]Zec 3:2
1:10 [p]2Pe 2:12
1:11 [q]Ge 4:3-8; 1Jn 3:12 [r]2Pe 2:15 [s]Nu 16:1-3, 31-35
1:12 [t]2Pe 2:13; 1Co 11:20-22 [u]Pr 25:14; 2Pe 2:17 [v]Eph 4:14 [w]Mt 15:13
1:13 [x]Isa 57:20 [y]Php 3:19 [z]2Pe 2:17
1:14 [a]Ge 5:18,21-24 [b]Dt 33:2; Da 7:10
1:15 [c]2Pe 2:6-9 [d]1Ti 1:9
1:16 [e]2Pe 2:18
1:17 [f]2Pe 3:2
1:18 [g]1Ti 4:1 [h]2Pe 2:1
1:19 [i]1Co 2:14,15

a *1* Or *for*; or *in* **b** *4* Or *men who were marked out for condemnation* **c** *5* Some early manuscripts *Jesus*

17-24

PROMISE 3

SPIRITUAL COUNTERFEITS

If an employer fails to recognize an untrustworthy employee, he may lose money. But if we fail to recognize a false teacher, we could lose far more. Jude's description of these false teachers gives us good insight into their character. Although he spoke about people of his own time, such individuals have been creating division and strife in the church since its inception.

What should our response to such people be? Vigilance. We need to be careful to separate false teaching from true and help others who may fall under the power of a false teacher. While doing so in our own power would be impossible, we have God on our side. He is the One who is able to protect us from deception through the power of his Spirit.

For the next Promise 3 reading go to page 50.

1 →PG. 1415

20But you, dear friends, build yourselves up[j] in your most holy faith and
pray in the Holy Spirit.[k] 21Keep yourselves in God's love as you wait[l] for
the mercy of our Lord Jesus Christ to
bring you to eternal life.

22Be merciful to those who doubt;
23snatch others from the fire and save
them;[m] to others show mercy, mixed
with fear—hating even the clothing
stained by corrupted flesh.[n]

1:20 [j]Col 2:7 [k]Eph 6:18
1:21 [l]Tit 2:13; 2Pe 3:12
1:23 [m]Am 4:11; Zec 3:2-5 [n]Rev 3:4
1:24 [o]Ro 16:25 [p]2Co 4:14 [q]Col 1:22

Doxology

24To him who is able[o] to keep you
from falling and to present you before
his glorious presence[p] without fault[q]
and with great joy— 25to the only
God[r] our Savior be glory, majesty,
power and authority, through Jesus
Christ our Lord, before all ages, now
and forevermore![s] Amen.[t]

1:25 [r]Jn 5:44; 1Ti 1:17 [s]Heb 13:8 [t]Ro 11:36

REVELATION

AT A GLANCE

Key Principle: The Lord Jesus Christ has all power and authority to judge the world in righteousness, to bring human history to a consummation and to create a new heaven and a new earth that will display his glory and perfection.
Author: The apostle John
Time and Place: ~A.D. 90–96 / The island of Patmos
Key Verses: 1:1, 19; 5:13; 11:15; 19:11–15; 22:20

BENEFIT

Genesis reaches back and portrays the beginning of all things; Revelation reaches ahead and portrays the consummation of all things as it describes God's judgment of humanity and creation of a new cosmos. This powerful Apocalypse (this word means "unveiling," "disclosure," "revelation") gives us a prophetic look at the completion of God's purposes for human history. It elevates our minds and hearts to the sovereignty, majesty, wisdom, power, holiness and dominion of the eternal Alpha and Omega.

SETTING

Roman authorities exiled the apostle John to the small island of Patmos in the Aegean Sea (1:9) because of his witness for Christ. According to Irenaeus (a disciple of Polycarp who was a disciple of John), this occurred during a wave of persecution near the end of the reign of the emperor Domitian (A.D. 81–96). While on Patmos, John received this prophetic vision and was instructed to direct it to seven churches in the province of Asia where he had previously ministered. John was probably allowed to return to Ephesus after the death of Domitian in A.D. 96, and from there this letter was circulated to the churches in the province of Asia.

The early church quickly accepted Revelation as the apostle John's authentic writing and as a legitimate part of the New Testament canon. However, in the middle of the third century a writer named Dionysius challenged its authorship; he argued that grammatical and stylistic differences between Revelation and the other Johannine writings pointed to a different John. While these differences do exist, significant similarities also exist; the differences can be explained by the radically different subject matter and the conditions under which Revelation was written.

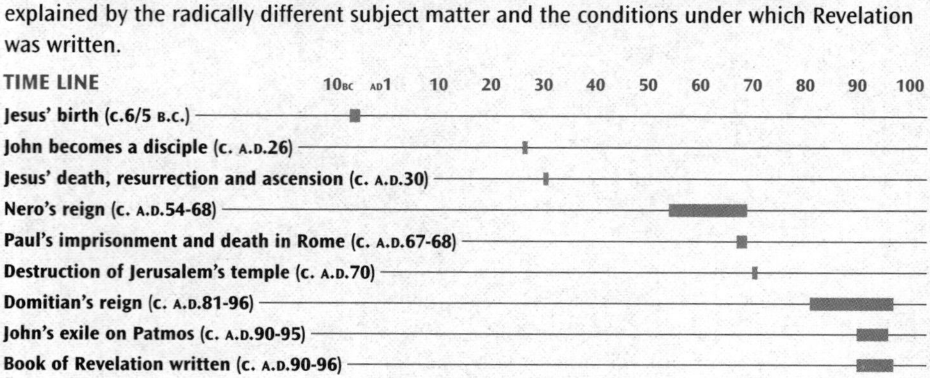

THEME AND PURPOSE

There are four primary approaches to the interpretation of the Apocalypse: (1) The *symbolic* or *idealist* view argues that this book is not prophetic, but that it symbolically portrays the cosmic conflict between the spiritual forces of good and evil. (2) The *preterist* view (from the Latin word for "past") holds that Revelation symbolically refers to events that took place in the first-century Roman empire. (3) The *historicist* view interprets Revelation as an allegorical overview of the history of Christendom—from its inception to Christ's second coming. (4) The *futurist* view sees first-century Roman persecution and emperor worship as an illustration of a far greater future conflict. Based on the fourth view, Revelation 6—19 portrays a coming seven-year tribulation that will end with the second advent of Christ.

Generally speaking, those who hold the first three views are amillennial (Christ's kingdom is taking place now in a spiritual sense) or postmillennial (Christ will return after the church establishes his kingdom by evangelizing society). Those who hold the fourth view are premillennial. (The kingdom has already come in a spiritual sense, but that after Christ's second coming he will also establish a geopolitical kingdom that will last for a thousand years. This activity will be followed by the creation of a new heaven and a new earth.) Thus, John's purpose for writing Revelation depends on which interpretive approach one takes. However, all would agree that one purpose of this book was to encourage its original readers in a time of persecution by assuring them that God would ultimately triumph over evil. Another purpose was to challenge believers to persevere and to hold fast to the truth, because God will reward those who love his Son.

UNIQUE CONTRIBUTION

Because it is highly symbolic, many who have read the Apocalypse have slipped into one of two extremes: they either conclude that it is inexplicable and therefore unfruitful to study, or speculate about every nuance in the book. It is more profitable to take a middle course—much of the symbolism of Revelation is explained in the book itself and in other books, such as Ezekiel and Daniel; however, a number of things remain mysterious in Revelation, and we should not be overconfident in supposing that we can decode every part.

Revelation blends apocalyptic, prophetic and epistolary literature into a unique whole that uses ecstatic visions, admonitions, figurative language, graphic images of worldwide judgments and sublime descriptions of God's glorious character and reign. Many parallels exist between the original beginning—the first three chapters of Genesis—and the new beginning—the last three chapters of Revelation.

CHRIST IN REVELATION

John's vision of the glorified Christ in chapter 1 is unparalleled in Scripture. Christ is portrayed in Revelation as the sovereign Ruler and Judge, and his might, majesty, power and dominion are evidenced throughout this book. The titles ascribed to him in the Apocalypse include: the faithful witness, the firstborn from the dead, the ruler of the kings of the earth (1:5), the First and the Last (1:17), the Living One (1:18), the Son of God (2:18), him who is holy and true, who holds the key of David (3:7), the Amen, the faithful and true witness, the ruler of God's creation (3:14), the Lion of the tribe of Judah, the Root of David (5:5), the Lamb (5:6ff.), Faithful and True (19:11), the Word of God (19:13), King of Kings and Lord of Lords (19:16), the Alpha and the Omega, the First and the Last, the Beginning and the End (22:13), the Root and the Offspring of David, the bright Morning Star (22:16) and the Lord Jesus (22:21).

OVERVIEW

FOCUS	Theophany		Tribulation	Triumph	
REFERENCE	1	2 3	4 18	19 20	21 22
TOPICS	Christ and the Churches		Cosmic Conflict	Consummation	
	"what you have seen"	"what is now"	"and what will take place later" (1:19)		
	Judge		Judgment		Jubilation
	Heavenly Vision on Earth		Heaven and Earth		New Heaven and New Earth
LOCATION	The Island of Patmos				
TIME	~A.D. 90–96				

The Revelation of Jesus Christ begins with a prologue (1:1–3), a salutation that portrays the triune God (1:4–8) and a theophany (a visible manifestation of God) of the omnipotent and omniscient Christ who will conquer and rule all things (1:9–20). This vision is followed by Christ's messages to the seven churches (2—3).

John is given a vision of the majesty of God the Creator (4) and of the Lion / Lamb who as the Redeemer is worthy to judge all creation (5). Chapters 6—18 portray a time of earthly tribulation and heavenly conflict that centers around three cycles of seven judgments: seven seals (6:1—8:5), seven trumpets (8:6—11:1) and seven bowls (15:1—19:6). There are prophetic inserts between the sixth and seventh seal and trumpet judgments, as well as a lengthy supplement between the trumpet and bowl judgments. In addition, chapters 17—18 describe the overthrow of the great prostitute and of Babylon the Great.

After the three cycles of judgment and the wedding supper of the Lamb, the Lord Jesus Christ returns to the earth in power and glory to overthrow the beast and the kings of the earth (19). The Lord confines Satan and reigns on the earth for a thousand years, defeats Satan and his forces in a final conflict and judges the dead (20). Chapters 21—22 depict the new heaven, the new earth and the new Jerusalem that reflect the glory of God. Revelation concludes with an epilogue that assures the readers that Christ will come soon (22:6–21).

REVELATION

Prologue

1 The revelation of Jesus Christ, which
God gave him to show his servants
what must soon take place. He made it
known by sending his angel[a] to his
servant John, 2who testifies to everything he saw—that is, the word of God
and the testimony of Jesus Christ.[b]
3Blessed is the one who reads the
words of this prophecy, and blessed
are those who hear it and take to heart
what is written in it,[c] because the time
is near.

1 →PG. 1418

Greetings and Doxology

4John,

To the seven churches in the province of Asia:

Grace and peace to you from him
who is, and who was, and who is to
come, and from the seven spirits[a][d]
before his throne, 5and from Jesus
Christ, who is the faithful witness,[e]
the firstborn from the dead,[f] and the
ruler of the kings of the earth.[g]

To him who loves us and has freed
us from our sins by his blood, 6and has
made us to be a kingdom and priests[h]
to serve his God and Father—to him
be glory and power for ever and ever!
Amen.[i]

7Look, he is coming with the
clouds,[j]
and every eye will see him,
even those who pierced him;
and all the peoples of the earth
will mourn[k] because of
him.
So shall it be! Amen.

8"I am the Alpha and the Omega,"[l]
says the Lord God, "who is, and who
was, and who is to come, the Almighty."[m]

One Like a Son of Man

9I, John, your brother and companion in the suffering[n] and kingdom and
patient endurance[o] that are ours in
Jesus, was on the island of Patmos because of the word of God and the testimony of Jesus. 10On the Lord's Day I
was in the Spirit,[p] and I heard behind
me a loud voice like a trumpet,[q]
11which said: "Write on a scroll what
you see and send it to the seven
churches:[r] to Ephesus, Smyrna, Pergamum, Thyatira, Sardis,[s] Philadelphia and Laodicea."

12I turned around to see the voice
that was speaking to me. And when
I turned I saw seven golden lampstands,[t] 13and among the lampstands
was someone "like a son of man,"[b][u]
dressed in a robe reaching down to his
feet and with a golden sash around
his chest.[v] 14His head and hair were

1:1 [a]Rev 22:16 **1:2** [b]1Co 1:6; Rev 12:17 **1:3** [c]Lk 11:28 **1:4** [d]Rev 3:1; 4:5 **1:5** [e]Rev 3:14 [f]Col 1:18 [g]Rev 17:14 **1:6** [h]1Pe 2:5 [i]Ro 11:36 **1:7** [j]Da 7:13 [k]Zec 12:10 **1:8** [l]Rev 21:6 [m]Rev 4:8 **1:9** [n]Php 4:14 [o]2Ti 2:12 **1:10** [p]Rev 4:2 [q]Rev 4:1 **1:11** [r]ver 4,20 [s]Rev 3:1 **1:12** [t]Ex 25:31-40; Zec 4:2 **1:13** [u]Eze 1:26; Da 7:13; 10:16 [v]Da 10:5; Rev 15:6

[a] 4 Or *the sevenfold Spirit* [b] 13 Daniel 7:13

1:7–18

PROMISE 1

JESUS, THE ALL-POWERFUL

While John was banished to the rocky island of Patmos for his beliefs and ministry, God showed the elderly apostle what would happen at the end of this age. This book delivers a dramatic and detailed—albeit often symbolic and mysterious—picture of God's judgment and the ultimate salvation of his people.

As John was involved in worship one Lord's Day, he heard a loud voice. Was it recognizable as the voice of Jesus, the God-Man with whom John walked while he lived on the earth? We don't know. What we do know, however, is that when John saw Jesus in his glorified state, he "fell at his feet as though dead."

John's description of the glorified Jesus is stunning and awesome. Jesus' different features symbolize different aspects of his being. His hair suggests wisdom and dignity; his eyes, penetrating insight; his feet represent his earthly suffering; his voice, power and authority. And in this vision Jesus appeared as a priest and a judge, symbolizing his ultimate holiness and spiritual authority.

How would you have responded in such a situation? Does this awesome figure represent the God you serve? As you read through this passage and consider the different aspects of Jesus' power and holiness, let them seep into your soul and fill you with a new awe and reverence for Jesus, your majestic Savior.

For the next Promise 1 reading go to page 1425.

white like wool, as white as snow, and his eyes were like blazing fire.[w] 15His feet were like bronze glowing in a furnace,[x] and his voice was like the sound of rushing waters.[y] 16In his right hand he held seven stars,[z] and out of his mouth came a sharp double-edged sword.[a] His face was like the sun shining in all its brilliance.

17When I saw him, I fell at his feet[b] as though dead. Then he placed his right hand on me and said: "Do not be afraid. I am the First and the Last.[c] 18I am the Living One; I was dead,[d] and behold I am alive for ever and ever![e] And I hold the keys of death and Hades.[f]

19"Write, therefore, what you have seen, what is now and what will take place later. 20The mystery of the seven stars that you saw in my right hand and of the seven golden lampstands[g] is this: The seven stars are the angels[a] of the seven churches,[h] and the seven lampstands are the seven churches.[i]

To the Church in Ephesus

2 "To the angel[b] of the church in Ephesus write:

These are the words of him who holds the seven stars in his right hand[j] and walks among the seven golden lampstands:[k] 2I know your deeds,[l] your hard work and your perseverance. I know that you cannot tolerate wicked men, that you have tested[m] those who claim to be apostles but are not, and have found them false.[n] 3You have persevered and have endured hardships for my name,[o] and have not grown weary.

4Yet I hold this against you: You have forsaken your first love.[p] 5Remember the height from which you have fallen! Repent[q] and do the things you did at first. If you do not repent, I will come to you and remove your lampstand[r] from its place. 6But you have this in your favor: You hate the practices of the Nicolaitans,[s] which I also hate.

7He who has an ear, let him hear[t] what the Spirit says to the churches. To him who overcomes, I will give the right to eat from the tree of life,[u] which is in the paradise[v] of God.

To the Church in Smyrna

8"To the angel of the church in Smyrna[w] write:

These are the words of him who is the First and the Last,[x] who died and came to life again.[y] 9I know your afflictions and your poverty—yet you are rich![z] I know the slander of those who say they are Jews and are not,[a] but are a synagogue of Satan.[b] 10Do not be afraid of what you are about to suffer. I tell you, the devil will put some of you in prison to test you,[c] and you will suffer persecution for ten days.[d] Be faithful,[e] even to the point of death, and I will give you the crown of life.

3 →PG. 1424

11He who has an ear, let him hear what the Spirit says to the churches. He who overcomes will not be hurt at all by the second death.[f]

To the Church in Pergamum

12"To the angel of the church in Pergamum[g] write:

These are the words of him who has the sharp, double-edged sword.[h] 13I know where you live—where Satan has his throne. Yet you remain true to my name. You did not renounce your faith in me,[i] even in the days of Antipas, my faithful witness, who was put to death in your city—where Satan lives.[j]

14Nevertheless, I have a few things against you:[k] You have people there who hold to the teaching of Balaam,[l] who taught Balak to entice the Israelites to sin by eating food sacrificed to idols and by committing sexual immorality.[m] 15Likewise you also have those who hold to the teaching of the Nicolaitans.[n] 16Repent therefore! Otherwise, I will soon come to you and will fight against them with the sword of my mouth.[o]

17He who has an ear, let him hear what the Spirit says to the churches. To him who overcomes, I will give some of the hidden manna.[p] I will also give him a white stone with a new name[q] written on it, known only to him who receives it.[r]

To the Church in Thyatira

18"To the angel of the church in Thyatira[s] write:

These are the words of the Son of God, whose eyes are like

1:14 [w]Da 7:9; 10:6; Rev 19:12
1:15 [x]Da 10:6 [y]Eze 43:2; Rev 14:2
1:16 [z]Rev 2:1; 3:1 [a]Isa 49:2; Heb 4:12; Rev 2:12,16
1:17 [b]Eze 1:28; Da 8:17,18 [c]Isa 41:4; 44:6; 48:12; Rev 22:13
1:18 [d]Ro 6:9 [e]Rev 4:9,10 [f]Rev 20:1
1:20 [g]Zec 4:2 [h]ver 4,11 [i]Mt 5:14,15
2:1 [j]Rev 1:16 [k]Rev 1:12,13
2:2 [l]Rev 3:1,8,15 [m]1Jn 4:1 [n]2Co 11:13
2:3 [o]Jn 15:21
2:4 [p]Mt 24:12
2:5 [q]ver 16,22 [r]Rev 1:20
2:6 [s]ver 15
2:7 [t]Mt 11:15; Rev 3:6,13,22 [u]Ge 2:9; Rev 22:2,14,19 [v]Lk 23:43
2:8 [w]Rev 1:11
[x]Rev 1:17 [y]Rev 1:18
2:9 [z]Jas 2:5 [a]Rev 3:9 [b]Mt 4:10
2:10 [c]Rev 3:10 [d]Da 1:12,14 [e]ver 13
2:11 [f]Rev 20:6,14; 21:8
2:12 [g]Rev 1:11 [h]Rev 1:16
2:13 [i]Rev 14:12 [j]ver 9,24
2:14 [k]ver 20 [l]2Pe 2:15 [m]1Co 6:13
2:15 [n]ver 6
2:16 [o]2Th 2:8; Rev 1:16
2:17 [p]Jn 6:49,50 [q]Isa 62:2 [r]Rev 19:12
2:18 [s]Rev 1:11

[a] *20* Or *messengers* [b] *1* Or *messenger*; also in verses 8, 12 and 18

blazing fire and whose feet are like burnished bronze.[t] 19I know your deeds,[u] your love and faith, your service and perseverance, and that you are now doing more than you did at first.

20Nevertheless, I have this against you: You tolerate that woman Jezebel,[v] who calls herself a prophetess. By her teaching she misleads my servants into sexual immorality and the eating of food sacrificed to idols. 21I have given her time[w] to repent of her immorality, but she is unwilling.[x] 22So I will cast her on a bed of suffering, and I will make those who commit adultery[y] with her suffer intensely, unless they repent of her ways. 23I will strike her children dead. Then all the churches will know that I am he who searches hearts and minds,[z] and I will repay each of you according to your deeds. 24Now I say to the rest of you in Thyatira, to you who do not hold to her teaching and have not learned Satan's so-called deep secrets (I will not impose any other burden on you):[a] 25Only hold on to what you have[b] until I come.

26To him who overcomes and does my will to the end, I will give authority over the nations[c]—

27'He will rule them with an
iron scepter;[d]
he will dash them to
pieces like pottery'[a][e]—

just as I have received authority from my Father. 28I will also give him the morning star.[f] 29He who has an ear, let him hear[g] what the Spirit says to the churches.

To the Church in Sardis

3 "To the angel[b] of the church in Sardis write:

These are the words of him who holds the seven spirits[c][h] of God and the seven stars.[i] I know your deeds;[j] you have a reputation of being alive, but you are dead.[k] 2Wake up! Strengthen what remains and is about to die, for I have not found your deeds complete in the sight of my God. 3Remember, therefore, what you have received and heard; obey it, and repent.[l] But if you do not wake up, I will come like a thief,[m] and you will not know at what time I will come to you.

4Yet you have a few people in Sardis who have not soiled their clothes.[n] They will walk with me, dressed in white,[o] for they are worthy. 5He who overcomes will, like them, be dressed in white. I will never blot out his name from the book of life,[p] but will acknowledge his name before my Father[q] and his angels. 6He who has an ear, let him hear[r] what the Spirit says to the churches.

To the Church in Philadelphia

7"To the angel of the church in Philadelphia[s] write:

These are the words of him who is holy and true,[t] who holds the key of David.[u] What he opens no one can shut, and what he shuts no one can open. 8I know your deeds. See, I have placed before you an open door[v] that no one can shut. I know that you have little strength, yet you have kept my word and have not denied my name.[w] 9I will make those who are of the synagogue of Satan,[x] who claim to be Jews though they are not, but are liars—I will make them come and fall down at your feet[y] and acknowledge that I have loved you.[z] 10Since you have kept my command to endure patiently, I will also keep you[a] from the hour of trial that is going to come upon the whole world to test[b] those who live on the earth.[c]

11I am coming soon. Hold on to what you have,[d] so that no one will take your crown.[e] 12Him who overcomes I will make a pillar[f] in the temple of my God. Never again will he leave it. I will write on him the name of my God[g] and the name of the city of my God, the new Jerusalem,[h] which is coming down out of heaven from my God; and I will also write on him my new name. 13He who has an ear, let him hear what the Spirit says to the churches.

To the Church in Laodicea

14"To the angel of the church in Laodicea write:

These are the words of the Amen, the faithful and true witness, the ruler of God's creation.[i] 15I know your deeds, that you are

2:18 [t]Rev 1:14,15
2:19 [u]ver 2
2:20 [v]1Ki 16:31; 21:25; 2Ki 9:7
2:21 [w]Ro 2:4 [x]Rev 9:20
2:22 [y]Rev 17:2; 18:9
2:23 [z]1Sa 16:7; Jer 11:20; Ac 1:24; Ro 8:27
2:24 [a]Ac 15:28
2:25 [b]Rev 3:11
2:26 [c]Ps 2:8; Rev 3:21
2:27 [d]Rev 12:5 [e]Isa 30:14; Jer 19:11
2:28 [f]Rev 22:16
2:29 [g]ver 7
3:1 [h]Rev 1:4 [i]Rev 1:16 [j]Rev 2:2 [k]1Ti 5:6
3:3 [l]Rev 2:5 [m]2Pe 3:10
3:4 [n]Jude 23 [o]Rev 4:4; 6:11; 7:9,13,14
3:5 [p]Rev 20:12 [q]Mt 10:32
3:6 [r]Rev 2:7
3:7 [s]Rev 1:11 [t]1Jn 5:20 [u]Isa 22:22; Mt 16:19
3:8 [v]Ac 14:27 [w]Rev 2:13
3:9 [x]Rev 2:9 [y]Isa 49:23 [z]Isa 43:4
3:10 [a]2Pe 2:9 [b]Rev 2:10 [c]Rev 6:10; 17:8
3:11 [d]Rev 2:25 [e]Rev 2:10
3:12 [f]Gal 2:9 [g]Rev 14:1; 22:4 [h]Rev 21:2,10
3:14 [i]Col 1:16,18

a *27* Psalm 2:9 b *1* Or *messenger*; also in verses 7 and 14 c *1* Or *the sevenfold Spirit*

neither cold nor hot.[j] I wish you
were either one or the other! 16So,
because you are lukewarm—
neither hot nor cold—I am about
to spit you out of my mouth.
17You say, 'I am rich; I have acquired wealth and do not need a
thing.'[k] But you do not realize
that you are wretched, pitiful,
poor, blind and naked. 18I counsel
you to buy from me gold refined
in the fire, so you can become
rich; and white clothes to wear, so
you can cover your shameful nakedness;[l] and salve to put on
your eyes, so you can see.
19Those whom I love I rebuke
and discipline.[m] So be earnest,
and repent.[n] 20Here I am! I stand
at the door[o] and knock. If anyone
hears my voice and opens the
door,[p] I will come in[q] and eat
with him, and he with me.
21To him who overcomes, I will
give the right to sit with me on my
throne,[r] just as I overcame[s] and
sat down with my Father on his
throne. 22He who has an ear, let
him hear[t] what the Spirit says to
the churches."

The Throne in Heaven

4 After this I looked, and there before
me was a door standing open in
heaven. And the voice I had first heard
speaking to me like a trumpet[u] said,
"Come up here,[v] and I will show you
what must take place after this."[w] 2At
once I was in the Spirit,[x] and there
before me was a throne in heaven[y]
with someone sitting on it. 3And the
one who sat there had the appearance
of jasper and carnelian. A rainbow,[z]
resembling an emerald, encircled the
throne. 4Surrounding the throne were
twenty-four other thrones, and seated
on them were twenty-four elders.[a]
They were dressed in white[b] and had
crowns of gold on their heads. 5From
the throne came flashes of lightning,
rumblings and peals of thunder.[c] Before the throne, seven lamps[d] were
blazing. These are the seven spirits[a][e]
of God. 6Also before the throne there
was what looked like a sea of glass,[f]
clear as crystal.

In the center, around the throne,
were four living creatures,[g] and they
were covered with eyes, in front and in
back. 7The first living creature was like
a lion, the second was like an ox, the
third had a face like a man, the fourth
was like a flying eagle.[h] 8Each of the
four living creatures had six wings[i]
and was covered with eyes all around,
even under his wings. Day and night
they never stop saying:

"Holy, holy, holy
is the Lord God Almighty,[j]
who was, and is, and is to come."[k]

9Whenever the living creatures give
glory, honor and thanks to him who
sits on the throne[l] and who lives for
ever and ever, 10the twenty-four elders[m] fall down before him[n] who sits
on the throne,[o] and worship him who
lives for ever and ever. They lay their
crowns before the throne and say:

11"You are worthy, our Lord and
God,
to receive glory and honor and
power,[p]
for you created all things,
and by your will they were
created
and have their being."[q]

1 →PG. 1419

3:15 [j]Ro 12:11 **3:17** [k]Hos 12:8; 1Co 4:8 **3:18** [l]Rev 16:15 **3:19** [m]Pr 3:12; Heb 12:5,6 [n]Rev 2:5 **3:20** [o]Mt 24:33 [p]Lk 12:36 [q]Jn 14:23 **3:21** [r]Mt 19:28 [s]Rev 5:5 **3:22** [t]Rev 2:7 **4:1** [u]Rev 1:10 [v]Rev 11:12 [w]Rev 1:19 **4:2** [x]Rev 1:10 [y]Isa 6:1; Eze 1:26-28; Da 7:9 **4:3** [z]Eze 1:28 **4:4** [a]Rev 11:16 [b]Rev 3:4,5 **4:5** [c]Rev 8:5; 16:18 [d]Zec 4:2 [e]Rev 1:4 **4:6** [f]Rev 15:2 [g]Eze 1:5 **4:7** [h]Eze 1:10; 10:14 **4:8** [i]Isa 6:2 [j]Isa 6:3; Rev 1:8 [k]Rev 1:4 **4:9** [l]Ps 47:8 **4:10** [m]ver 4 [n]Rev 5:8,14 [o]ver 2 **4:11** [p]Rev 5:12 [q]Rev 10:6

[a]5 Or *the sevenfold Spirit*

4:1–5:14

PE

THE GLORY OF HEAVEN

Most of us have a photo album that carries snapshots of our loved ones, images of special events, and the like. By thumbing through it we can almost relive those moments. As this fourth chapter of Revelation opens, we find ourselves looking at a spiritual "photo album" prepared by the apostle John. This one, however, contains glimpses of heaven.

It's fitting that John would be allowed to enter a door into heaven where he would be given a glimpse of its wonder. Soon he would also see the terrible judgments to be poured out on the earth. As you read about John's vision, however, realize that his words can't begin to express the glory and beauty that we'll see in heaven, the place where God lives.

While the pictures are filled with symbols of God's faithfulness, power and glory, perhaps the most vivid images are at the ends of chapters 4 and 5. These pictures show us the kind of all-out praise that exists in heaven for God and for his holy will, for it's only because of God's will that we even exist. They also show us that only God and Jesus, the Lamb of God, are worthy of praise.

This series of "photos" gives us a dimly lit glimpse of what heaven will be like. One day all believers will join the angels in offering praise to the Lamb of God, Jesus Christ. Are you ready to experience the awesome glory of heaven?

The Scroll and the Lamb

5 Then I saw in the right hand of him who sat on the throne[r] a scroll with writing on both sides[s] and sealed[t] with seven seals. 2And I saw a mighty angel proclaiming in a loud voice, "Who is worthy to break the seals and open the scroll?" 3But no one in heaven or on earth or under the earth could open the scroll or even look inside it. 4I wept and wept because no one was found who was worthy to open the scroll or look inside. 5Then one of the elders said to me, "Do not weep! See, the Lion[u] of the tribe of Judah, the Root of David,[v] has triumphed. He is able to open the scroll and its seven seals."

6Then I saw a Lamb,[w] looking as if it had been slain, standing in the center of the throne, encircled by the four living creatures and the elders. He had seven horns and seven eyes,[x] which are the seven spirits**a** of God sent out into all the earth. 7He came and took the scroll from the right hand of him who sat on the throne.[y] 8And when he had taken it, the four living creatures and the twenty-four elders fell down before the Lamb. Each one had a harp[z] and they were holding golden bowls full of incense, which are the prayers[a] of the saints. 9And they sang a new song:[b]

1 →PG. 1420

"You are worthy[c] to take the scroll
and to open its seals,
because you were slain,
and with your blood[d] you
purchased[e] men for God
from every tribe and language
and people and nation.
10You have made them to be a
kingdom and priests[f] to
serve our God,
and they will reign on the earth."

11Then I looked and heard the voice of many angels, numbering thousands upon thousands, and ten thousand times ten thousand.[g] They encircled the throne and the living creatures and the elders. 12In a loud voice they sang:

"Worthy is the Lamb, who was
slain,
to receive power and wealth and
wisdom and strength
and honor and glory and praise!"[h]

13Then I heard every creature in heaven and on earth and under the earth[i] and on the sea, and all that is in them, singing:

"To him who sits on the throne
and to the Lamb[j]
be praise and honor and glory and
power,
for ever and ever!"[k]

14The four living creatures said, "Amen,"[l] and the elders fell down and worshiped.[m]

The Seals

6 I watched as the Lamb[n] opened the first of the seven seals.[o] Then I heard one of the four living creatures[p] say in a voice like thunder,[q] "Come!" 2I looked, and there before me was a white horse![r] Its rider held a bow, and he was given a crown,[s] and he rode out as a conqueror bent on conquest.[t]

3When the Lamb opened the second seal, I heard the second living creature[u] say, "Come!" 4Then another horse came out, a fiery red one.[v] Its rider was given power to take peace from the earth[w] and to make men slay each other. To him was given a large sword.

5When the Lamb opened the third seal, I heard the third living creature[x] say, "Come!" I looked, and there before me was a black horse![y] Its rider was holding a pair of scales in his hand. 6Then I heard what sounded like a voice among the four living creatures,[z] saying, "A quart**b** of wheat for a day's wages,**c** and three quarts of barley for a day's wages,**c** and do not damage[a] the oil and the wine!"

7When the Lamb opened the fourth seal, I heard the voice of the fourth living creature[b] say, "Come!" 8I looked, and there before me was a pale horse![c] Its rider was named Death, and Hades[d] was following close behind him. They were given power over a fourth of the earth to kill by sword, famine and plague, and by the wild beasts of the earth.[e]

9When he opened the fifth seal, I saw under the altar[f] the souls of those who had been slain[g] because of the word of God and the testimony they had maintained. 10They called out in a loud voice, "How long,[h] Sovereign Lord, holy and true,[i] until you judge the inhabitants of the earth and avenge our blood?"[j] 11Then each of them was given a white robe,[k] and they were told to wait a little longer, until the number of their fellow servants and brothers who were to be killed as they had been was completed.[l]

12I watched as he opened the sixth seal. There was a great earthquake.[m] The sun turned black[n] like sackcloth

5:1 [r]ver 7,13 [s]Eze 2:9,10 [t]Isa 29:11; Da 12:4 **5:5** [u]Ge 49:9 [v]Isa 11:1,10; Ro 15:12; Rev 22:16 **5:6** [w]Jn 1:29 [x]Zec 4:10 **5:7** [y]ver 1 **5:8** [z]Rev 14:2 [a]Ps 141:2 **5:9** [b]Ps 40:3 [c]Rev 4:11 [d]Heb 9:12 [e]1Co 6:20 **5:10** [f]1Pe 2:5 **5:11** [g]Da 7:10; Heb 12:22 **5:12** [h]Rev 4:11 **5:13** [i]ver 3; Php 2:10 [j]Rev 6:16 [k]1Ch 29:11 **5:14** [l]Rev 4:9 [m]Rev 4:10; 19:4 **6:1** [n]Rev 5:6 [o]Rev 5:1 [p]Rev 4:6,7 [q]Rev 14:2; 19:6 **6:2** [r]Zec 6:3; Rev 19:11 [s]Zec 6:11; Rev 14:14 [t]Ps 45:4 **6:3** [u]Rev 4:7 **6:4** [v]Zec 6:2 [w]Mt 10:34 **6:5** [x]Rev 4:7 [y]Zec 6:2 **6:6** [z]Rev 4:6,7 [a]Rev 9:4 **6:7** [b]Rev 4:7 **6:8** [c]Zec 6:3 [d]Hos 13:14 [e]Jer 15:2,3; Eze 5:12,17 **6:9** [f]Rev 14:18; 16:7 [g]Rev 20:4 **6:10** [h]Zec 1:12 [i]Rev 3:7 [j]Rev 19:2 **6:11** [k]Rev 3:4 [l]Heb 11:40 **6:12** [m]Rev 16:18 [n]Mt 24:29

a6 Or *the sevenfold Spirit* **b**6 Greek *a choinix* (probably about a liter) **c**6 Greek *a denarius*

made of goat hair, the whole moon
turned blood red, 13and the stars in the
sky fell to earth,[o] as late figs drop from
a fig tree[p] when shaken by a strong
wind. 14The sky receded like a scroll,
rolling up, and every mountain and island was removed from its place.[q]
15Then the kings of the earth, the
princes, the generals, the rich, the
mighty, and every slave and every free
man hid in caves and among the rocks
of the mountains.[r] 16They called to
the mountains and the rocks, "Fall on
us[s] and hide us from the face of him
who sits on the throne and from the
wrath of the Lamb! 17For the great
day[t] of their wrath has come, and
who can stand?"[u]

144,000 Sealed

7 After this I saw four angels standing
at the four corners of the earth, holding back the four winds[v] of the earth
to prevent any wind from blowing on
the land or on the sea or on any tree.
2Then I saw another angel coming up
from the east, having the seal of the
living God. He called out in a loud
voice to the four angels who had been
given power to harm the land and the
sea: 3"Do not harm[w] the land or the
sea or the trees until we put a seal on
the foreheads[x] of the servants of our
God." 4Then I heard the number[y] of
those who were sealed: 144,000[z] from
all the tribes of Israel.

5From the tribe of Judah 12,000
were sealed,
from the tribe of Reuben 12,000,
from the tribe of Gad 12,000,
6from the tribe of Asher 12,000,
from the tribe of Naphtali 12,000,
from the tribe of Manasseh
12,000,
7from the tribe of Simeon 12,000,
from the tribe of Levi 12,000,
from the tribe of Issachar 12,000,
8from the tribe of Zebulun 12,000,
from the tribe of Joseph 12,000,
from the tribe of Benjamin
12,000.

The Great Multitude in White Robes

9After this I looked and there before
me was a great multitude that no one
could count, from every nation, tribe,
people and language,[a] standing before the throne[b] and in front of the
Lamb. They were wearing white robes
and were holding palm branches in
their hands. 10And they cried out in a
loud voice:

"Salvation belongs to our God,[c]
who sits on the throne,
and to the Lamb."

11All the angels were standing around
the throne and around the elders[d]
and the four living creatures.[e] They
fell down on their faces[f] before the
throne and worshiped God, 12saying:

1 →PG. 1424

"Amen!
Praise and glory
and wisdom and thanks and honor
and power and strength
be to our God for ever and ever.
Amen!"[g]

13Then one of the elders asked me,
"These in white robes—who are they,
and where did they come from?"
14I answered, "Sir, you know."
And he said, "These are they who
have come out of the great tribulation;
they have washed their robes[h] and
made them white in the blood of the
Lamb.[i] 15Therefore,

"they are before the throne of
God[j]
and serve him[k] day and night in
his temple;[l]
and he who sits on the throne will
spread his tent over them.[m]
16Never again will they hunger;
never again will they thirst.
The sun will not beat upon them,
nor any scorching heat.[n]
17For the Lamb at the center of the
throne will be their
shepherd;[o]
he will lead them to springs of
living water.
And God will wipe away every tear
from their eyes."[p]

6:13 [o]Mt 24:29; Rev 8:10; 9:1 [p]Isa 34:4
6:14 [q]Jer 4:24; Rev 16:20
6:15 [r]Isa 2:10,19,21
6:16 [s]Hos 10:8; Lk 23:30
6:17 [t]Zep 1:14,15; Rev 16:14 [u]Ps 76:7
7:1 [v]Da 7:2
7:3 [w]Rev 6:6 [x]Eze 9:4; Rev 22:4
7:4 [y]Rev 9:16 [z]Rev 14:1,3
7:9 [a]Rev 5:9 [b]ver 15
7:10 [c]Ps 3:8; Rev 12:10; 19:1
7:11 [d]Rev 4:4 [e]Rev 4:6 [f]Rev 4:10
7:12 [g]Rev 5:12-14
7:14 [h]Rev 22:14 [i]Heb 9:14; 1Jn 1:7
7:15 [j]ver 9 [k]Rev 22:3 [l]Rev 11:19 [m]Isa 4:5,6; Rev 21:3
7:16 [n]Isa 49:10
7:17 [o]Ps 23:1; Jn 10:11 [p]Isa 25:8; Rev 21:4

7:9

PROMISE 6

HEAVEN'S MULTICULTURAL CROWD

The image in this verse bears out Paul's statement about how Jesus' work on earth eliminates the barriers that separate people: "You are all sons of God through faith in Christ Jesus, for all of you who were baptized into Christ have clothed yourselves with Christ. There is neither Jew nor Greek, slave nor free, male nor female, for you are all one in Christ Jesus" (Galatians 3:26–28). This picture of the multitude before the throne fills us with hope that one day God's church on earth will embrace the unity and singular purpose that we have in Christ Jesus. As you relate to your Christian brothers and sisters, remember that the body of Christ has many members, but only one Head.

For the next Promise 6 reading go to page 16.

The Seventh Seal and the Golden Censer

8 When he opened the seventh seal,[q]
there was silence in heaven for
about half an hour.
2And I saw the seven angels[r] who
stand before God, and to them were
given seven trumpets.
3Another angel,[s] who had a golden
censer, came and stood at the altar. He
was given much incense to offer, with
the prayers of all the saints,[t] on the
golden altar[u] before the throne. 4The
smoke of the incense, together with the
prayers of the saints, went up before
God[v] from the angel's hand. 5Then
the angel took the censer, filled it with
fire from the altar,[w] and hurled it on
the earth; and there came peals of
thunder,[x] rumblings, flashes of lightning and an earthquake.[y]

The Trumpets

6Then the seven angels who had the
seven trumpets[z] prepared to sound
them.
7The first angel sounded his trumpet, and there came hail and fire[a]
mixed with blood, and it was hurled
down upon the earth. A third[b] of the
earth was burned up, a third of the
trees were burned up, and all the green
grass was burned up.[c]
8The second angel sounded his
trumpet, and something like a huge
mountain,[d] all ablaze, was thrown
into the sea. A third[e] of the sea turned
into blood,[f] 9a third[g] of the living
creatures in the sea died, and a third of
the ships were destroyed.
10The third angel sounded his trumpet, and a great star, blazing like a
torch, fell from the sky[h] on a third
of the rivers and on the springs of
water[i]— 11the name of the star is
Wormwood.**[a]** A third[j] of the waters
turned bitter, and many people died
from the waters that had become bitter.[k]
12The fourth angel sounded his
trumpet, and a third of the sun was
struck, a third of the moon, and a third
of the stars, so that a third[l] of them
turned dark.[m] A third of the day was
without light, and also a third of the
night.
13As I watched, I heard an eagle that
was flying in midair[n] call out in a loud
voice: "Woe! Woe! Woe[o] to the inhabitants of the earth, because of the trumpet blasts about to be sounded by the
other three angels!"
9 The fifth angel sounded his trumpet,
and I saw a star that had fallen from
the sky to the earth.[p] The star was giv-
en the key to the shaft of the Abyss.[q]
2When he opened the Abyss, smoke
rose from it like the smoke from a gi-
gantic furnace.[r] The sun and sky were
darkened[s] by the smoke from the
Abyss. 3And out of the smoke locusts[t]
came down upon the earth and were
given power like that of scorpions[u]
of the earth. 4They were told not to
harm[v] the grass of the earth or any
plant or tree,[w] but only those people
who did not have the seal of God on
their foreheads.[x] 5They were not giv-
en power to kill them, but only to torture them for five months.[y] And the
agony they suffered was like that of the
sting of a scorpion[z] when it strikes a
man. 6During those days men will seek
death, but will not find it; they will long
to die, but death will elude them.[a]
7The locusts looked like horses prepared for battle.[b] On their heads they
wore something like crowns of gold,
and their faces resembled human
faces.[c] 8Their hair was like women's
hair, and their teeth were like lions'
teeth.[d] 9They had breastplates like
breastplates of iron, and the sound of
their wings was like the thundering of
many horses and chariots rushing into
battle.[e] 10They had tails and stings
like scorpions, and in their tails they
had power to torment people for five
months.[f] 11They had as king over
them the angel of the Abyss,[g] whose
name in Hebrew is Abaddon, and in
Greek, Apollyon.**[b]**
12The first woe is past; two other
woes are yet to come.[h]
13The sixth angel sounded his trumpet, and I heard a voice coming from
the horns**[c]**[i] of the golden altar that is
before God.[j] 14It said to the sixth angel who had the trumpet, "Release the
four angels who are bound at the great
river Euphrates."[k] 15And the four angels who had been kept ready for this
very hour and day and month and year
were released to kill a third of mankind.[l] 16The number of the mounted
troops was two hundred million. I
heard their number.[m]
17The horses and riders I saw in my
vision looked like this: Their breastplates were fiery red, dark blue, and
yellow as sulfur. The heads of the
horses resembled the heads of lions,
and out of their mouths[n] came fire,
smoke and sulfur.[o] 18A third of mankind was killed[p] by the three plagues
of fire, smoke and sulfur[q] that came

a *11* That is, Bitterness **b** *11* *Abaddon* and *Apollyon* mean *Destroyer.* **c** *13* That is, projections

8:1 [q]Rev 6:1 **8:2** [r]ver 6-13; Rev 9:1,13; 11:15 **8:3** [s]Rev 7:2 [t]Rev 5:8 [u]Ex 30:1-6; Heb 9:4; Rev 9:13 **8:4** [v]Ps 141:2 **8:5** [w]Lev 16:12,13 [x]Rev 4:5 [y]Rev 6:12 **8:6** [z]ver 2 **8:7** [a]Eze 38:22 [b]ver 7-12; Rev 9:15,18; 12:4 [c]Rev 9:4 **8:8** [d]Jer 51:25 [e]ver 7 [f]Rev 16:3 **8:9** [g]ver 7 **8:10** [h]Isa 14:12; Rev 6:13; 9:1 [i]Rev 14:7; 16:4 **8:11** [j]ver 7 [k]Jer 9:15; 23:15 **8:12** [l]ver 7 [m]Ex 10:21-23; Rev 6:12,13 **8:13** [n]Rev 14:6; 19:17 [o]Rev 9:12; 11:14 **9:1** [p]Rev 8:10 [q]ver 2,11; Lk 8:31

9:2 [r]Ge 19:28; Ex 19:18 [s]Joel 2:2,10 **9:3** [t]Ex 10:12-15 [u]ver 5,10 **9:4** [v]Rev 6:6 [w]Rev 8:7 [x]Rev 7:2,3 **9:5** [y]ver 10 [z]ver 3 **9:6** [a]Job 3:21; Jer 8:3; Rev 6:16 **9:7** [b]Joel 2:4 [c]Da 7:8 **9:8** [d]Joel 1:6 **9:9** [e]Joel 2:5 **9:10** [f]ver 3,5,19 **9:11** [g]ver 1,2 **9:12** [h]Rev 8:13 **9:13** [i]Ex 30:1-3 [j]Rev 8:3 **9:14** [k]Rev 16:12 **9:15** [l]ver 18 **9:16** [m]Rev 5:11; 7:4

9:17 [n]Rev 11:5 [o]ver 18 **9:18** [p]ver 15 [q]ver 17

out of their mouths. 19 The power of the horses was in their mouths and in their tails; for their tails were like snakes, having heads with which they inflict injury.

20 The rest of mankind that were not killed by these plagues still did not repent of the work of their hands;[r] they did not stop worshiping demons,[s] and idols of gold, silver, bronze, stone and wood—idols that cannot see or hear or walk.[t] 21 Nor did they repent[u] of their murders, their magic arts,[v] their sexual immorality[w] or their thefts.

The Angel and the Little Scroll

10 Then I saw another mighty angel[x] coming down from heaven. He was robed in a cloud, with a rainbow above his head; his face was like the sun,[y] and his legs were like fiery pillars.[z] 2 He was holding a little scroll, which lay open in his hand. He planted his right foot on the sea and his left foot on the land, 3 and he gave a loud shout like the roar of a lion. When he shouted, the voices of the seven thunders[a] spoke. 4 And when the seven thunders spoke, I was about to write; but I heard a voice from heaven say, "Seal up what the seven thunders have said and do not write it down."[b]

5 Then the angel I had seen standing on the sea and on the land raised his right hand to heaven.[c] 6 And he swore by him who lives for ever and ever, who created the heavens and all that is in them, the earth and all that is in it, and the sea and all that is in it,[d] and said, "There will be no more delay![e] 7 But in the days when the seventh angel is about to sound his trumpet, the mystery[f] of God will be accomplished, just as he announced to his servants the prophets."

8 Then the voice that I had heard from heaven[g] spoke to me once more: "Go, take the scroll that lies open in the hand of the angel who is standing on the sea and on the land."

9 So I went to the angel and asked him to give me the little scroll. He said to me, "Take it and eat it. It will turn your stomach sour, but in your mouth it will be as sweet as honey."[h] 10 I took the little scroll from the angel's hand and ate it. It tasted as sweet as honey in my mouth, but when I had eaten it, my stomach turned sour. 11 Then I was told, "You must prophesy[i] again about many peoples, nations, languages and kings."

The Two Witnesses

11 I was given a reed like a measuring rod[j] and was told, "Go and measure the temple of God and the altar, and count the worshipers there. 2 But exclude the outer court;[k] do not measure it, because it has been given to the Gentiles.[l] They will trample on the holy city[m] for 42 months.[n] 3 And I will give power to my two witnesses,[o] and they will prophesy for 1,260 days, clothed in sackcloth."[p] 4 These are the two olive trees[q] and the two lampstands that stand before the Lord of the earth.[r] 5 If anyone tries to harm them, fire comes from their mouths and devours their enemies.[s] This is how anyone who wants to harm them must die.[t] 6 These men have power to shut up the sky so that it will not rain during the time they are prophesying; and they have power to turn the waters into blood[u] and to strike the earth with every kind of plague as often as they want.

7 Now when they have finished their testimony, the beast[v] that comes up from the Abyss will attack them,[w] and overpower and kill them. 8 Their bodies will lie in the street of the great city, which is figuratively called Sodom[x] and Egypt, where also their Lord was crucified.[y] 9 For three and a half days men from every people, tribe, language and nation will gaze on their bodies and refuse them burial.[z] 10 The inhabitants of the earth[a] will gloat over them and will celebrate by sending each other gifts,[b] because these two prophets had tormented those who live on the earth.

11 But after the three and a half days a breath of life from God entered them,[c] and they stood on their feet, and terror struck those who saw them. 12 Then they heard a loud voice from heaven saying to them, "Come up here."[d] And they went up to heaven in a cloud,[e] while their enemies looked on.

13 At that very hour there was a severe earthquake[f] and a tenth of the city collapsed. Seven thousand people were killed in the earthquake, and the survivors were terrified and gave glory[g] to the God of heaven.[h]

14 The second woe has passed; the third woe is coming soon.[i]

The Seventh Trumpet

15 The seventh angel sounded his trumpet,[j] and there were loud voices[k] in heaven, which said:

9:20 [r]Dt 31:29 [s]1Co 10:20 [t]Ps 115:4-7; 135:15-17; Da 5:23
9:21 [u]Rev 2:21 [v]Rev 18:23 [w]Rev 17:2,5
10:1 [x]Rev 5:2 [y]Mt 17:2; Rev 1:16 [z]Rev 1:15
10:3 [a]Rev 4:5
10:4 [b]Da 8:26; 12:4, 9; Rev 22:10
10:5 [c]Da 12:7
10:6 [d]Rev 4:11; 14:7 [e]Rev 16:17
10:7 [f]Ro 16:25
10:8 [g]ver 4
10:9 [h]Jer 15:16; Eze 2:8-3:3
10:11 [i]Eze 37:4,9
11:1 [j]Eze 40:3; Rev 21:15
11:2 [k]Eze 40:17,20 [l]Lk 21:24 [m]Rev 21:2 [n]Da 7:25; Rev 13:5
11:3 [o]Rev 1:5 [p]Ge 37:34
11:4 [q]Ps 52:8; Jer 11:16; Zec 4:3,11 [r]Zec 4:14
11:5 [s]2Ki 1:10; Jer 5:14 [t]Nu 16:29,35
11:6 [u]Ex 7:17,19
11:7 [v]Rev 13:1-4 [w]Da 7:21
11:8 [x]Isa 1:9 [y]Heb 13:12
11:9 [z]Ps 79:2,3
11:10 [a]Rev 3:10 [b]Est 9:19,22
11:11 [c]Eze 37:5,9,10, 14
11:12 [d]Rev 4:1 [e]2Ki 2:11; Ac 1:9
11:13 [f]Rev 6:12 [g]Rev 14:7 [h]Rev 16:11
11:14 [i]Rev 8:13
11:15 [j]Rev 10:7 [k]Rev 16:17; 19:1

"The kingdom of the world has
become the kingdom of our
Lord and of his Christ,[l]
and he will reign for ever and
ever."[m]

16 And the twenty-four elders,[n] who
were seated on their thrones before
God, fell on their faces and worshiped
God, 17 saying:

"We give thanks to you, Lord God
Almighty,[o]
the One who is and who was,
because you have taken your great
power
and have begun to reign.[p]
18 The nations were angry;[q]
and your wrath has come.
The time has come for judging the
dead,
and for rewarding your servants
the prophets[r]
and your saints and those who
reverence your name,
both small and great[s]—
and for destroying those who
destroy the earth."

19 Then God's temple[t] in heaven
was opened, and within his temple was
seen the ark of his covenant. And there
came flashes of lightning, rumblings,
peals of thunder, an earthquake and a
great hailstorm.[u]

The Woman and the Dragon

12 A great and wondrous sign appeared in heaven: a woman clothed
with the sun, with the moon under her
feet and a crown of twelve stars on
her head. 2 She was pregnant and cried
out in pain[v] as she was about to give
birth. 3 Then another sign appeared in
heaven: an enormous red dragon with
seven heads and ten horns[w] and seven
crowns[x] on his heads. 4 His tail swept
a third[y] of the stars out of the sky and
flung them to the earth.[z] The dragon
stood in front of the woman who was
about to give birth, so that he might
devour her child[a] the moment it was
born. 5 She gave birth to a son, a male
child, who will rule all the nations with
an iron scepter.[b] And her child was
snatched up to God and to his throne.
6 The woman fled into the desert to a
place prepared for her by God, where
she might be taken care of for 1,260
days.[c]
7 And there was war in heaven. Michael and his angels fought against
the dragon,[d] and the dragon and his
angels fought back. 8 But he was not
strong enough, and they lost their
place in heaven. 9 The great dragon was
hurled down—that ancient serpent[e]
called the devil,[f] or Satan, who leads
the whole world astray.[g] He was
hurled to the earth,[h] and his angels
with him.
10 Then I heard a loud voice in heav-
en[i] say:

"Now have come the salvation and
the power and the kingdom
of our God,
and the authority of his Christ.
For the accuser of our brothers,[j]
who accuses them before our
God day and night,
has been hurled down.
11 They overcame him
by the blood of the Lamb[k]
and by the word of their
testimony;[l]
they did not love their lives so
much
as to shrink from death.[m]
12 Therefore rejoice, you heavens[n]
and you who dwell in them!
But woe[o] to the earth and the
sea,[p]
because the devil has gone down
to you!
He is filled with fury,
because he knows that his time
is short."

7 →PG. 1424

13 When the dragon[q] saw that he
had been hurled to the earth, he pursued the woman who had given birth
to the male child.[r] 14 The woman was
given the two wings of a great eagle,[s]
so that she might fly to the place prepared for her in the desert, where she
would be taken care of for a time, times
and half a time,[t] out of the serpent's
reach. 15 Then from his mouth the serpent spewed water like a river, to overtake the woman and sweep her away
with the torrent. 16 But the earth helped
the woman by opening its mouth and
swallowing the river that the dragon
had spewed out of his mouth. 17 Then
the dragon was enraged at the woman
and went off to make war[u] against
the rest of her offspring[v]—those who
obey God's commandments[w] and hold
to the testimony of Jesus.[x] 13 1 And
the dragon[a] stood on the shore of
the sea.

The Beast out of the Sea

And I saw a beast coming out of the
sea.[y] He had ten horns and seven
heads,[z] with ten crowns on his horns,
and on each head a blasphemous
name.[a] 2 The beast I saw resembled a
leopard,[b] but had feet like those of
a bear[c] and a mouth like that of

11:15 [l]Rev 12:10 [m]Da 2:44; 7:14,27
11:16 [n]Rev 4:4
11:17 [o]Rev 1:8 [p]Rev 19:6
11:18 [q]Ps 2:1 [r]Rev 10:7 [s]Rev 19:5
11:19 [t]Rev 15:5,8 [u]Rev 16:21
12:2 [v]Gal 4:19
12:3 [w]Da 7:7,20; Rev 13:1 [x]Rev 19:12
12:4 [y]Rev 8:7 [z]Da 8:10 [a]Mt 2:16
12:5 [b]Ps 2:9; Rev 2:27
12:6 [c]Rev 11:2
12:7 [d]ver 3
12:9 [e]Ge 3:1-7 [f]Mt 25:41 [g]Rev 20:3,8,10 [h]Lk 10:18; Jn 12:31
12:10 [i]Rev 11:15 [j]Job 1:9-11; Zec 3:1
12:11 [k]Rev 7:14 [l]Rev 6:9 [m]Lk 14:26
12:12 [n]Ps 96:11; Isa 49:13; Rev 18:20 [o]Rev 8:13 [p]Rev 10:6
12:13 [q]ver 3 [r]ver 5
12:14 [s]Ex 19:4 [t]Da 7:25
12:17 [u]Rev 11:7 [v]Ge 3:15 [w]Rev 14:12 [x]Rev 1:2
13:1 [y]Da 7:1-6; Rev 15:2 [z]Rev 12:3 [a]Da 11:36; Rev 17:3
13:2 [b]Da 7:6 [c]Da 7:5

a 1 Some late manuscripts *And I*

a lion.[d] The dragon gave the beast his power and his throne and great authority.[e] 3One of the heads of the beast seemed to have had a fatal wound, but the fatal wound had been healed.[f] The whole world was astonished[g] and followed the beast. 4Men worshiped the dragon because he had given authority to the beast, and they also worshiped the beast and asked, "Who is like[h] the beast? Who can make war against him?"

5The beast was given a mouth to utter proud words and blasphemies[i] and to exercise his authority for forty-two months.[j] 6He opened his mouth to blaspheme God, and to slander his name and his dwelling place and those who live in heaven.[k] 7He was given power to make war[l] against the saints and to conquer them. And he was given authority over every tribe, people, language and nation.[m] 8All inhabitants of the earth[n] will worship the beast—all whose names have not been written in the book of life[o] belonging to the Lamb that was slain from the creation of the world.[a][p]

9He who has an ear, let him hear.[q]

10If anyone is to go into captivity,
into captivity he will go.
If anyone is to be killed[b] with the sword,
with the sword he will be killed.[r]

This calls for patient endurance and faithfulness[s] on the part of the saints.[t]

The Beast out of the Earth

11Then I saw another beast, coming out of the earth. He had two horns like a lamb, but he spoke like a dragon. 12He exercised all the authority[u] of the first beast on his behalf,[v] and made the earth and its inhabitants worship the first beast,[w] whose fatal wound had been healed.[x] 13And he performed great and miraculous signs,[y] even causing fire to come down from heaven[z] to earth in full view of men. 14Because of the signs[a] he was given power to do on behalf of the first beast, he deceived[b] the inhabitants of the earth. He ordered them to set up an image in honor of the beast who was wounded by the sword and yet lived. 15He was given power to give breath to the image of the first beast, so that it could speak and cause all who refused to worship the image to be killed.[c] 16He also forced everyone, small and great,[d] rich and poor, free and slave, to receive a mark on his right hand or on his forehead,[e] 17so that no one could buy or sell unless he had the mark,[f] which is the name of the beast or the number of his name.[g]

18This calls for wisdom.[h] If anyone has insight, let him calculate the number of the beast, for it is man's number.[i] His number is 666.

The Lamb and the 144,000

14 Then I looked, and there before me was the Lamb,[j] standing on Mount Zion,[k] and with him 144,000[l] who had his name and his Father's name[m] written on their foreheads. 2And I heard a sound from heaven like the roar of rushing waters[n] and like a loud peal of thunder. The sound I heard was like that of harpists playing their harps.[o] 3And they sang a new song[p] before the throne and before the four living creatures and the elders. No one could learn the song except the 144,000[q] who had been redeemed from the earth. 4These are those who did not defile themselves with women, for they kept themselves pure.[r] They follow the Lamb wherever he goes. They were purchased from among men[s] and offered as firstfruits[t] to God and the Lamb. 5No lie was found in their mouths;[u] they are blameless.[v]

3 →PG. 1428

The Three Angels

6Then I saw another angel flying in midair,[w] and he had the eternal gospel to proclaim to those who live on the earth[x]—to every nation, tribe, language and people.[y] 7He said in a loud voice, "Fear God[z] and give him glory,[a] because the hour of his judgment has come. Worship him who made the heavens, the earth, the sea and the springs of water."[b]

1 →PG. 1425
7 →PG. 24

8A second angel followed and said, "Fallen! Fallen is Babylon the Great,[c] which made all the nations drink the maddening wine of her adulteries."[d]

9A third angel followed them and said in a loud voice: "If anyone worships the beast and his image[e] and receives his mark on the forehead or on the hand, 10he, too, will drink of the wine of God's fury,[f] which has been poured full strength into the cup of his wrath.[g] He will be tormented with burning sulfur in the presence of the holy angels and of the Lamb. 11And the smoke of their torment rises for ever

13:2 [d]Da 7:4 [e]Rev 16:10
13:3 [f]ver 12,14 [g]Rev 17:8
13:4 [h]Ex 15:11
13:5 [i]Da 7:8,11,20, 25; 11:36; 2Th 2:4 [j]Rev 11:2
13:6 [k]Rev 12:12
13:7 [l]Da 7:21; Rev 11:7 [m]Rev 5:9
13:8 [n]Rev 3:10 [o]Rev 3:5; 20:12 [p]Mt 25:34
13:9 [q]Rev 2:7
13:10 [r]Jer 15:2; 43:11 [s]Heb 6:12 [t]Rev 14:12
13:12 [u]ver 4 [v]ver 14 [w]Rev 14:9,11 [x]ver 3
13:13 [y]Mt 24:24 [z]1Ki 18:38; Rev 20:9
13:14 [a]2Th 2:9,10 [b]Rev 12:9
13:15 [c]Da 3:3-6
13:16 [d]Rev 19:5
[e]Rev 14:9
13:17 [f]Rev 14:9 [g]Rev 14:11; 15:2
13:18 [h]Rev 17:9 [i]Rev 15:2; 21:17
14:1 [j]Rev 5:6 [k]Ps 2:6 [l]Rev 7:4 [m]Rev 3:12
14:2 [n]Rev 1:15 [o]Rev 5:8
14:3 [p]Rev 5:9 [q]ver 1
14:4 [r]2Co 11:2; Rev 3:4 [s]Rev 5:9 [t]Jas 1:18
14:5 [u]Ps 32:2; Zep 3:13 [v]Eph 5:27
14:6 [w]Rev 8:13 [x]Rev 3:10 [y]Rev 13:7
14:7 [z]Rev 15:4 [a]Rev 11:13 [b]Rev 8:10
14:8 [c]Isa 21:9; Jer 51:8 [d]Rev 17:2,4; 18:3,9
14:9 [e]Rev 13:14
14:10 [f]Isa 51:17; Jer 25:15 [g]Rev 18:6

[a] *8* Or *written from the creation of the world in the book of life belonging to the Lamb that was slain* [b] *10* Some manuscripts *anyone kills*

and ever.[h] There is no rest day or night for those who worship the beast and his image, or for anyone who receives the mark of his name." **12**This calls for patient endurance on the part of the saints[i] who obey God's commandments and remain faithful to Jesus.

13Then I heard a voice from heaven say, "Write: Blessed are the dead who die in the Lord[j] from now on."

"Yes," says the Spirit, "they will rest from their labor, for their deeds will follow them."

The Harvest of the Earth

14I looked, and there before me was a white cloud, and seated on the cloud was one "like a son of man"[a][k] with a crown[l] of gold on his head and a sharp sickle in his hand. **15**Then another angel came out of the temple and called in a loud voice to him who was sitting on the cloud, "Take your sickle[m] and reap, because the time to reap has come, for the harvest[n] of the earth is ripe." **16**So he who was seated on the cloud swung his sickle over the earth, and the earth was harvested.

17Another angel came out of the temple in heaven, and he too had a sharp sickle. **18**Still another angel, who had charge of the fire, came from the altar and called in a loud voice to him who had the sharp sickle, "Take your sharp sickle and gather the clusters of grapes from the earth's vine, because its grapes are ripe." **19**The angel swung his sickle on the earth, gathered its grapes and threw them into the great winepress of God's wrath.[o] **20**They were trampled in the winepress[p] outside the city,[q] and blood flowed out of the press, rising as high as the horses' bridles for a distance of 1,600 stadia.[b]

Seven Angels With Seven Plagues

15 I saw in heaven another great and marvelous sign:[r] seven angels[s] with the seven last plagues[t]—last, because with them God's wrath is completed. **2**And I saw what looked like a sea of glass[u] mixed with fire and, standing beside the sea, those who had been victorious over the beast and his image[v] and over the number of his name. They held harps given them by God **3**and sang the song of Moses[w] the servant of God and the song of the Lamb:

"Great and marvelous are your
deeds,[x]
Lord God Almighty.
Just and true are your ways,[y]
King of the ages.
4Who will not fear you, O Lord,[z]
and bring glory to your name?
For you alone are holy.
All nations will come
and worship before you,[a]
for your righteous acts have been
revealed."

1 →PG. 1428

5After this I looked and in heaven the temple,[b] that is, the tabernacle of the Testimony,[c] was opened. **6**Out of the temple[d] came the seven angels with the seven plagues.[e] They were dressed in clean, shining linen and wore golden sashes around their chests.[f] **7**Then one of the four living creatures[g] gave to the seven angels seven golden bowls filled with the wrath of God, who lives for ever and ever. **8**And the temple was filled with smoke[h] from the glory of God and from his power, and no one could enter the temple[i] until the seven plagues of the seven angels were completed.

The Seven Bowls of God's Wrath

16 Then I heard a loud voice from the temple saying to the seven an-

14:11 [h]Isa 34:10; Rev 19:3
14:12 [i]Rev 13:10
14:13 [j]1Co 15:18; 1Th 4:16
14:14 [k]Da 7:13; Rev 1:13 [l]Rev 6:2
14:15 [m]Joel 3:13 [n]Jer 51:33
14:19 [o]Rev 19:15
14:20 [p]Isa 63:3 [q]Heb 13:12; Rev 11:8
15:1 [r]Rev 12:1,3 [s]Rev 16:1 [t]Lev 26:21
15:2 [u]Rev 4:6 [v]Rev 13:14
15:3 [w]Ex 15:1; Dt 32:4 [x]Ps 111:2 [y]Ps 145:17
15:4 [z]Jer 10:7 [a]Isa 66:23
15:5 [b]Rev 11:19 [c]Nu 1:50
15:6 [d]Rev 14:15 [e]ver 1 [f]Rev 1:13
15:7 [g]Rev 4:6
15:8 [h]Isa 6:4 [i]Ex 40:34,35; 1Ki 8:10,11; 2Ch 5:13,14

a *14* Daniel 7:13 b *20* That is, about 180 miles (about 300 kilometers)

15:1–4

PROMISE 1

A NEW PERSPECTIVE ON DEATH

As God pours out his judgments, death and destruction cover the earth. In the face of such human loss, it appears as if evil has won and defeated God's agents on the earth. But God sees things differently. He says these martyred followers of Jesus Christ have victory over the beast (12:11).

As chapter 15 opens, it reveals a joyous, though solemn, scene in heaven. Believers who died resisting the beast are worshiping God. They sing the song of Moses and the Lamb, praising God for his mighty acts (see Exodus 15 and Deuteronomy 32). They praise God for a number of reasons, which are outlined in their song (vv. 3–4). Far from defeating these believers, death has ushered them into the presence of God where they can worship him.

Because you will spend eternity praising God with other believers, how should you respond to his greatness now? Look back over the reasons the saints in heaven praised God. Consider how their reasons for praising God could be incorporated into your own devotional time.

For the next Promise 1 reading go to page 1429.

gels,[j] "Go, pour out the seven bowls
of God's wrath on the earth."
2The first angel went and poured out
his bowl on the land,[k] and ugly and
painful sores[l] broke out on the people
who had the mark of the beast and
worshiped his image.[m]
3The second angel poured out his
bowl on the sea, and it turned into
blood like that of a dead man, and every living thing in the sea died.[n]
4The third angel poured out his bowl
on the rivers and springs of water,[o]
and they became blood.[p] **5**Then I
heard the angel in charge of the waters
say:

"You are just in these judgments,[q]
you who are and who were,[r]
the Holy One,[s]
because you have so judged;
6for they have shed the blood of
your saints and prophets,
and you have given them blood
to drink[t] as they deserve."

7And I heard the altar[u] respond:

"Yes, Lord God Almighty,
true and just are your
judgments."[v]

8The fourth angel[w] poured out his
bowl on the sun, and the sun was given
power to scorch people with fire.[x]
9They were seared by the intense heat
and they cursed the name of God,[y]
who had control over these plagues,
but they refused to repent[z] and glorify
him.[a]
10The fifth angel poured out his bowl
on the throne of the beast,[b] and his
kingdom was plunged into darkness.[c]
Men gnawed their tongues in agony
11and cursed[d] the God of heaven[e]
because of their pains and their
sores,[f] but they refused to repent of
what they had done.[g]
12The sixth angel poured out his
bowl on the great river Euphrates,[h]
and its water was dried up to prepare
the way for the kings from the East.[i]
13Then I saw three evil[a] spirits that
looked like frogs; they came out of
the mouth of the dragon,[j] out of the
mouth of the beast[k] and out of the
mouth of the false prophet.[l] **14**They
are spirits of demons[m] performing
miraculous signs, and they go out
to the kings of the whole world, to
gather them for the battle[n] on the
great day of God Almighty.
15"Behold, I come like a thief!
Blessed is he who stays awake[o] and
keeps his clothes with him, so that he
may not go naked and be shamefully
exposed."
16Then they gathered the kings together to the place that in Hebrew[p] is
called Armageddon.[q]
17The seventh angel poured out
his bowl into the air,[r] and out of the
temple[s] came a loud voice[t] from the
throne, saying, "It is done!"[u] **18**Then
there came flashes of lightning, rumblings, peals of thunder[v] and a severe
earthquake.[w] No earthquake like it
has ever occurred since man has been
on earth,[x] so tremendous was the
quake. **19**The great city[y] split into
three parts, and the cities of the nations collapsed. God remembered[z]
Babylon the Great[a] and gave her the
cup filled with the wine of the fury
of his wrath.[b] **20**Every island fled
away and the mountains could not
be found.[c] **21**From the sky huge hailstones[d] of about a hundred pounds
each fell upon men. And they cursed
God on account of the plague of hail,[e]
because the plague was so terrible.

The Woman on the Beast

17 One of the seven angels[f] who had
the seven bowls[g] came and said to
me, "Come, I will show you the punishment[h] of the great prostitute,[i] who
sits on many waters.[j] **2**With her the
kings of the earth committed adultery
and the inhabitants of the earth were
intoxicated with the wine of her adulteries."[k]
3Then the angel carried me away in
the Spirit into a desert.[l] There I saw
a woman sitting on a scarlet beast
that was covered with blasphemous
names[m] and had seven heads and
ten horns.[n] **4**The woman was dressed
in purple and scarlet, and was glittering with gold, precious stones and
pearls.[o] She held a golden cup[p] in
her hand, filled with abominable
things and the filth of her adulteries.
5This title was written on her forehead:

MYSTERY
BABYLON THE GREAT[q]
THE MOTHER OF PROSTITUTES
AND OF THE ABOMINATIONS OF THE EARTH.

6I saw that the woman was drunk with
the blood of the saints,[r] the blood of
those who bore testimony to Jesus.
When I saw her, I was greatly astonished. **7**Then the angel said to me:
"Why are you astonished? I will explain
to you the mystery[s] of the woman and
of the beast she rides, which has the
seven heads and ten horns.[t] **8**The
beast, which you saw, once was, now is
not, and will come up out of the Abyss

16:1 [j]Rev 15:1
16:2 [k]Rev 8:7 [l]Ex 9:9-11 [m]Rev 13:15-17
16:3 [n]Ex 7:17-21; Rev 8:8,9
16:4 [o]Rev 8:10 [p]Ex 7:17-21
16:5 [q]Rev 15:3 [r]Rev 1:4 [s]Rev 15:4
16:6 [t]Isa 49:26; Rev 17:6
16:7 [u]Rev 6:9 [v]Rev 15:3; 19:2
16:8 [w]Rev 8:12 [x]Rev 14:18
16:9 [y]ver 11,21 [z]Rev 2:21 [a]Rev 11:13
16:10 [b]Rev 13:2 [c]Rev 9:2
16:11 [d]ver 9,21 [e]Rev 11:13 [f]ver 2 [g]Rev 2:21
16:12 [h]Rev 9:14 [i]Isa 41:2
16:13 [j]Rev 12:3 [k]Rev 13:1 [l]Rev 19:20
16:14 [m]1Ti 4:1 [n]Rev 17:14
16:15 [o]Lk 12:37
16:16 [p]Rev 9:11 [q]2Ki 23:29,30
16:17 [r]Eph 2:2 [s]Rev 14:15 [t]Rev 11:15 [u]Rev 21:6
16:18 [v]Rev 4:5 [w]Rev 6:12 [x]Da 12:1
16:19 [y]Rev 17:18 [z]Rev 18:5 [a]Rev 14:8 [b]Rev 14:10
16:20 [c]Rev 6:14
16:21 [d]Rev 11:19 [e]Ex 9:23-25
17:1 [f]Rev 15:1 [g]Rev 21:9 [h]Rev 16:19 [i]Rev 19:2 [j]Jer 51:13
17:2 [k]Rev 14:8; 18:3
17:3 [l]Rev 12:6,14 [m]Rev 13:1 [n]Rev 12:3
17:4 [o]Rev 18:16 [p]Jer 51:7; Rev 18:6
17:5 [q]Rev 14:8
17:6 [r]Rev 18:24
17:7 [s]ver 5 [t]ver 3

[a] *13* Greek *unclean*

and go to his destruction.[u] The inhabitants of the earth[v] whose names have
not been written in the book of life[w]
from the creation of the world will be
astonished[x] when they see the beast,
because he once was, now is not, and
yet will come.
9“This calls for a mind with wisdom.[y] The seven heads are seven hills
on which the woman sits. 10They are
also seven kings. Five have fallen, one
is, the other has not yet come; but
when he does come, he must remain
for a little while. 11The beast who once
was, and now is not,[z] is an eighth
king. He belongs to the seven and is
going to his destruction.
12“The ten horns[a] you saw are ten
kings who have not yet received a kingdom, but who for one hour[b] will receive authority as kings along with the
beast. 13They have one purpose and
will give their power and authority to
the beast.[c] 14They will make war[d]
against the Lamb, but the Lamb will
overcome them because he is Lord of
lords and King of kings[e]—and with
him will be his called, chosen[f] and
faithful followers.”
15Then the angel said to me, “The
waters[g] you saw, where the prostitute
sits, are peoples, multitudes, nations
and languages.[h] 16The beast and the
ten horns you saw will hate the prostitute. They will bring her to ruin[i] and
leave her naked;[j] they will eat her
flesh[k] and burn her with fire.[l] 17For
God has put it into their hearts to accomplish his purpose by agreeing to
give the beast their power to rule, until
God’s words are fulfilled.[m] 18The
woman you saw is the great city[n] that
rules over the kings of the earth.”

The Fall of Babylon

18 After this I saw another angel[o]
coming down from heaven.[p] He
had great authority, and the earth was
illuminated by his splendor.[q] 2With a
mighty voice he shouted:

“Fallen! Fallen is Babylon the
Great![r]
She has become a home for
demons
and a haunt for every evil[a] spirit,
a haunt for every unclean and
detestable bird.[s]
3For all the nations have drunk
the maddening wine of her
adulteries.[t]
The kings of the earth committed
adultery with her,[u]
and the merchants of the earth
grew rich[v] from her
excessive luxuries.”[w]

4Then I heard another voice from
heaven say:

“Come out of her, my people,[x]
so that you will not share in her
sins,
so that you will not receive any
of her plagues;
5for her sins are piled up to
heaven,[y]
and God has remembered[z] her
crimes.
6Give back to her as she has given;
pay her back[a] double for what
she has done.
Mix her a double portion from
her own cup.[b]
7Give her as much torture and grief
as the glory and luxury she gave
herself.[c]
In her heart she boasts,
‘I sit as queen; I am not a
widow,
and I will never mourn.’[d]
8Therefore in one day[e] her plagues
will overtake her:
death, mourning and famine.
She will be consumed by fire,[f]
for mighty is the Lord God who
judges her.

9“When the kings of the earth who
committed adultery with her[g] and
shared her luxury see the smoke of her
burning,[h] they will weep and mourn
over her.[i] 10Terrified at her torment,
they will stand far off[j] and cry:

“ ‘Woe! Woe, O great city,[k]
O Babylon, city of power!
In one hour[l] your doom has
come!’

11“The merchants[m] of the earth will
weep and mourn over her because no
one buys their cargoes any more[n]—
12cargoes of gold, silver, precious
stones and pearls; fine linen, purple,
silk and scarlet cloth; every sort of cit-
ron wood, and articles of every kind
made of ivory, costly wood, bronze,
iron and marble;[o] 13cargoes of cinnamon and spice, of incense, myrrh and
frankincense, of wine and olive oil, of
fine flour and wheat; cattle and sheep;
horses and carriages; and bodies and
souls of men.[p]
14“They will say, ‘The fruit you
longed for is gone from you. All your
riches and splendor have vanished,
never to be recovered.’ 15The merchants who sold these things and
gained their wealth from her[q] will
stand far off, terrified at her torment.
They will weep and mourn[r] 16and cry
out:

17:8 [u]Rev 13:10 [v]Rev 3:10 [w]Rev 13:8 [x]Rev 13:3
17:9 [y]Rev 13:18
17:11 [z]ver 8
17:12 [a]Rev 12:3 [b]Rev 18:10,17, 19
17:13 [c]ver 17
17:14 [d]Rev 16:14 [e]1Ti 6:15; Rev 19:16 [f]Mt 22:14
17:15 [g]Isa 8:7 [h]Rev 13:7
17:16 [i]Rev 18:17,19 [j]Eze 16:37,39 [k]Rev 19:18 [l]Rev 18:8
17:17 [m]Rev 10:7
17:18 [n]Rev 16:19
18:1 [o]Rev 17:1 [p]Rev 10:1 [q]Eze 43:2
18:2 [r]Rev 14:8 [s]Isa 13:21,22; Jer 50:39
18:3 [t]Rev 14:8 [u]Rev 17:2 [v]Eze 27:9-25 [w]ver 7,9
18:4 [x]Isa 48:20; Jer 50:8; 2Co 6:17
18:5 [y]Jer 51:9 [z]Rev 16:19
18:6 [a]Ps 137:8; Jer 50:15,29 [b]Rev 14:10; 16:19
18:7 [c]Eze 28:2-8 [d]Isa 47:7,8; Zep 2:15
18:8 [e]ver 10; Isa 47:9; Jer 50:31,32 [f]Rev 17:16
18:9 [g]Rev 17:2,4 [h]ver 18; Rev 19:3 [i]Eze 26:17,18
18:10 [j]ver 15,17 [k]ver 16,19 [l]Rev 17:12
18:11 [m]Eze 27:27 [n]ver 3
18:12 [o]Rev 17:4
18:13 [p]Eze 27:13; 1Ti 1:10
18:15 [q]ver 3 [r]Eze 27:31

[a]2 Greek *unclean*

" 'Woe! Woe, O great city,
dressed in fine linen, purple and
scarlet,
and glittering with gold, precious
stones and pearls![s]
17In one hour[t] such great wealth
has been brought to ruin!'[u]

"Every sea captain, and all who travel by ship, the sailors, and all who earn
their living from the sea,[v] will stand
far off. 18When they see the smoke
of her burning, they will exclaim,
'Was there ever a city like this great
city?'[w] 19They will throw dust on their
heads,[x] and with weeping and mourning cry out:

" 'Woe! Woe, O great city,
where all who had ships on the
sea
became rich through her wealth!
In one hour she has been brought
to ruin![y]
20Rejoice over her, O heaven![z]
Rejoice, saints and apostles and
prophets!
God has judged her for the way she
treated you.' "[a]

21Then a mighty angel[b] picked up a
boulder the size of a large millstone
and threw it into the sea,[c] and said:

"With such violence
the great city of Babylon will be
thrown down,
never to be found again.
22The music of harpists and
musicians, flute players and
trumpeters,
will never be heard in you
again.[d]
No workman of any trade
will ever be found in you again.
The sound of a millstone
will never be heard in you
again.[e]
23The light of a lamp
will never shine in you again.
The voice of bridegroom and bride
will never be heard in you
again.[f]
Your merchants were the world's
great men.[g]
By your magic spell[h] all the
nations were led astray.
24In her was found the blood of
prophets and of the
saints,[i]
and of all who have been killed
on the earth."[j]

Hallelujah!

19 After this I heard what sounded like
the roar of a great multitude[k] in
heaven shouting:

"Hallelujah!
Salvation[l] and glory and power[m]
belong to our God,
2 for true and just are his
judgments.
He has condemned the great
prostitute
who corrupted the earth by her
adulteries.
He has avenged on her the blood
of his servants."[n]

3And again they shouted:

"Hallelujah!
The smoke from her goes up for
ever and ever."[o]

4The twenty-four elders[p] and the
four living creatures[q] fell down[r] and
worshiped God, who was seated on the
throne. And they cried:

1 →PG. 29
3 →PG. 50

"Amen, Hallelujah!"

5Then a voice came from the throne,
saying:

"Praise our God,
all you his servants,[s]
you who fear him,
both small and great!"[t]

6Then I heard what sounded like a
great multitude,[u] like the roar of rushing waters and like loud peals of thunder, shouting:

"Hallelujah!
For our Lord God Almighty
reigns.
7Let us rejoice and be glad
and give him glory!
For the wedding of the Lamb[v] has
come,
and his bride[w] has made herself
ready.
8Fine linen, bright and clean,
was given her to wear."
(Fine linen stands for the righteous
acts[x] of the saints.)

9Then the angel said to me,[y]
"Write:[z] 'Blessed are those who are
invited to the wedding supper of the
Lamb!' "[a] And he added, "These are
the true words of God."[b]
10At this I fell at his feet to worship
him.[c] But he said to me, "Do not do it!
I am a fellow servant with you and with
your brothers who hold to the testimony of Jesus. Worship God![d] For the
testimony of Jesus[e] is the spirit of
prophecy."

The Rider on the White Horse

11I saw heaven standing open and
there before me was a white horse,
whose rider[f] is called Faithful and

18:16 [s]Rev 17:4 **18:17** [t]ver 10 [u]Rev 17:16 [v]Eze 27:28-30 **18:18** [w]Eze 27:32; Rev 13:4 **18:19** [x]Jos 7:6; Eze 27:30 [y]Rev 17:16 **18:20** [z]Jer 51:48; Rev 12:12 [a]Rev 19:2 **18:21** [b]Rev 5:2 [c]Jer 51:63 **18:22** [d]Isa 24:8; Eze 26:13 [e]Jer 25:10 **18:23** [f]Jer 7:34; 16:9; 25:10 [g]Isa 23:8 [h]Na 3:4 **18:24** [i]Rev 16:6; 17:6 [j]Jer 51:49 **19:1** [k]Rev 11:15

[l]Rev 7:10 [m]Rev 4:11 **19:2** [n]Dt 32:43; Rev 6:10 **19:3** [o]Isa 34:10; Rev 14:11 **19:4** [p]Rev 4:4 [q]Rev 4:6 [r]Rev 5:14 **19:5** [s]Ps 134:1 [t]Rev 11:18; 20:12 **19:6** [u]Rev 11:15 **19:7** [v]Mt 22:2; 25:10; Eph 5:32 [w]Rev 21:2,9 **19:8** [x]Rev 15:4 **19:9** [y]ver 10 [z]Rev 1:19 [a]Lk 14:15 [b]Rev 21:5; 22:6 **19:10** [c]Rev 22:8 [d]Ac 10:25,26; Rev 22:9 [e]Rev 12:17 **19:11** [f]Rev 6:2

True.[g] With justice he judges and
makes war.[h] 12His eyes are like blazing fire,[i] and on his head are many
crowns.[j] He has a name written on
him that no one knows but he himself.[k] 13He is dressed in a robe dipped
in blood,[l] and his name is the Word of
God.[m] 14The armies of heaven were
following him, riding on white horses
and dressed in fine linen,[n] white and
clean. 15Out of his mouth comes a
sharp sword[o] with which to strike
down[p] the nations. "He will rule them
with an iron scepter."[a][q] He treads the
winepress[r] of the fury of the wrath of
God Almighty. 16On his robe and on his
thigh he has this name written:[s]

KING OF KINGS AND LORD OF LORDS.[t]

17And I saw an angel standing in the
sun, who cried in a loud voice to all the
birds[u] flying in midair,[v] "Come,[w]
gather together for the great supper of
God, 18so that you may eat the flesh of
kings, generals, and mighty men,
of horses and their riders, and the flesh
of all people,[x] free and slave, small
and great."

19Then I saw the beast and the kings
of the earth[y] and their armies gathered together to make war against the
rider on the horse and his army. 20But
the beast was captured, and with him
the false prophet[z] who had performed the miraculous signs on his behalf.[a] With these signs he had deluded
those who had received the mark of the
beast and worshiped his image. The
two of them were thrown alive into
the fiery lake[b] of burning sulfur.[c]
21The rest of them were killed with the
sword[d] that came out of the mouth
of the rider on the horse,[e] and all
the birds[f] gorged themselves on their
flesh.

The Thousand Years

20 And I saw an angel coming down
out of heaven,[g] having the key[h]
to the Abyss and holding in his hand a
great chain. 2He seized the dragon, that
ancient serpent, who is the devil, or
Satan,[i] and bound him for a thousand years.[j] 3He threw him into the
Abyss, and locked and sealed[k] it over
him, to keep him from deceiving the
nations[l] anymore until the thousand
years were ended. After that, he must
be set free for a short time.

4I saw thrones[m] on which were seated those who had been given authority
to judge. And I saw the souls of those
who had been beheaded[n] because of
their testimony for Jesus and because
of the word of God. They had not worshiped the beast[o] or his image and
had not received his mark on their
foreheads or their hands.[p] They came
to life and reigned with Christ a thousand years. 5(The rest of the dead did
not come to life until the thousand
years were ended.) This is the first resurrection.[q] 6Blessed[r] and holy are
those who have part in the first resurrection. The second death[s] has no
power over them, but they will be
priests[t] of God and of Christ and will
reign with him[u] for a thousand years.

Satan's Doom

7When the thousand years are
over,[v] Satan will be released from his
prison 8and will go out to deceive the

[a] *15* Psalm 2:9

19:11 [g]Rev 3:14 [h]Isa 11:4 **19:12** [i]Rev 1:14 [j]Rev 6:2 [k]Rev 2:17 **19:13** [l]Isa 63:2,3 [m]Jn 1:1 **19:14** [n]ver 8 **19:15** [o]Rev 1:16 [p]Isa 11:4; 2Th 2:8 [q]Ps 2:9; Rev 2:27 [r]Rev 14:20 **19:16** [s]ver 12 [t]Rev 17:14 **19:17** [u]ver 21 [v]Rev 8:13 [w]Eze 39:17 **19:18** [x]Eze 39:18-20 **19:19** [y]Rev 16:14,16 **19:20** [z]Rev 16:13 [a]Rev 13:12 [b]Da 7:11; Rev 20:10,14, 15; 21:8 [c]Rev 14:10 **19:21** [d]ver 15 [e]ver 11,19 [f]ver 17 **20:1** [g]Rev 10:1 [h]Rev 1:18 **20:2** [i]Rev 12:9 [j]2Pe 2:4 **20:3** [k]Da 6:17 [l]Rev 12:9 **20:4** [m]Da 7:9 [n]Rev 6:9 [o]Rev 13:12 [p]Rev 13:16 **20:5** [q]Lk 14:14; Php 3:11 **20:6** [r]Rev 14:13 [s]Rev 2:11 [t]Rev 1:6 [u]ver 4 **20:7** [v]ver 2

19:9

PROMISE 1

BE THERE!

Here John describes a celestial wedding ceremony filled with joyful noise, pageantry and color. It's a picture of total celebration. His use of the wedding party to describe the intimate, trusting relationship of God to his people is one that occurs several times in both the Old and the New Testaments (see Isaiah 54:5–7; Hosea 2:19; Matthew 22:2–14; Ephesians 5:32).

Jesus, the groom, is the center of attention at this event. The church is his bride, and is represented as one who has prepared herself for the wedding by wearing fine and clean linen. This image is of marriage perfected, of people purified with the blood of Jesus. The "righteous acts of the saints" mentioned in this passage speaks of the church's members accepting Jesus' blood on their behalf. The bride herself has been cleansed of sin by the groom.

What an amazing picture of God's grace to us through Jesus! Although we're not worthy of his love (see Isaiah 64:6), Jesus has chosen to love and accept us. As you read through this passage, allow yourself to get caught up in the excitement of this riotous praise and worship of Jesus Christ. Don't you want to be there? What do you have to do to get ready for this glorious party? Is there anything in your life that's hindering your relationship with him now? If so, bring it before him. Seek his forgiveness and cleansing so you can enjoy his fellowship, both now and later.

For the next Promise 1 reading go to page 9.

nations[w] in the four corners of the
earth—Gog and Magog[x]—to gather
them for battle.[y] In number they are
like the sand on the seashore.[z] 9They
marched across the breadth of the
earth and surrounded[a] the camp of
God's people, the city he loves. But fire
came down from heaven[b] and devoured them. 10And the devil, who deceived them,[c] was thrown into the
lake of burning sulfur, where the beast
and the false prophet had been
thrown. They will be tormented day
and night for ever and ever.[d]

The Dead Are Judged

11Then I saw a great white throne[e]
and him who was seated on it. Earth
and sky fled from his presence, and
there was no place for them. 12And I
saw the dead, great and small, standing
before the throne, and books were
opened.[f] Another book was opened,
which is the book of life.[g] The dead
were judged according to what they
had done[h] as recorded in the books.
13The sea gave up the dead that were in
it, and death and Hades[i] gave up the
dead[j] that were in them, and each
person was judged according to what
he had done. 14Then death[k] and Hades were thrown into the lake of fire.
The lake of fire is the second death. 15If
anyone's name was not found written
in the book of life,[l] he was thrown
into the lake of fire.

The New Jerusalem

21 Then I saw a new heaven and a new
earth,[m] for the first heaven and the
first earth had passed away, and there
was no longer any sea. 2I saw the Holy
City, the new Jerusalem, coming down
out of heaven from God,[n] prepared as
a bride beautifully dressed for her husband. 3And I heard a loud voice from
the throne saying, "Now the dwelling
of God is with men, and he will live
with them. They will be his people, and
God himself will be with them and be
their God.[o] 4He will wipe every tear
from their eyes.[p] There will be no
more death[q] or mourning or crying or
pain,[r] for the old order of things has
passed away."

5He who was seated on the throne[s]
said, "I am making everything new!"
Then he said, "Write this down, for
these words are trustworthy and
true."[t]

6He said to me: "It is done.[u] I am
the Alpha and the Omega,[v] the Beginning and the End. To him who is thirsty
I will give to drink without cost from
the spring of the water of life.[w] 7He
who overcomes will inherit all this, and
I will be his God and he will be my son.
8But the cowardly, the unbelieving,
the vile, the murderers, the sexually
immoral, those who practice magic
arts, the idolaters and all liars[x]—their
place will be in the fiery lake of burning
sulfur. This is the second death."[y]

9One of the seven angels who had
the seven bowls full of the seven last
plagues[z] came and said to me,
"Come, I will show you the bride,[a] the
wife of the Lamb." 10And he carried me
away[b] in the Spirit[c] to a mountain
great and high, and showed me the
Holy City, Jerusalem, coming down out
of heaven from God. 11It shone with
the glory of God,[d] and its brilliance
was like that of a very precious jewel,
like a jasper, clear as crystal.[e] 12It had
a great, high wall with twelve gates,
and with twelve angels at the gates. On
the gates were written the names of the
twelve tribes of Israel.[f] 13There were
three gates on the east, three on the
north, three on the south and three on
the west. 14The wall of the city had
twelve foundations, and on them were

20:8 [w]ver 3,10 [x]Eze 38:2; 39:1 [y]Rev 16:14 [z]Heb 11:12
20:9 [a]Eze 38:9,16 [b]Eze 38:22; 39:6
20:10 [c]Rev 19:20 [d]Rev 14:10,11
20:11 [e]Rev 4:2
20:12 [f]Da 7:10 [g]Rev 3:5 [h]Jer 17:10; Mt 16:27; Rev 2:23
20:13 [i]Rev 6:8 [j]Isa 26:19
20:14 [k]1Co 15:26
20:15 [l]ver 12
21:1 [m]Isa 65:17; 2Pe 3:13
21:2 [n]Heb 11:10; 12:22; Rev 3:12
21:3 [o]2Co 6:16
21:4 [p]Rev 7:17 [q]1Co 15:26; Rev 20:14 [r]Isa 35:10; 65:19
21:5 [s]Rev 4:9; 20:11 [t]Rev 19:9
21:6 [u]Rev 16:17 [v]Rev 1:8; 22:13 [w]Jn 4:10
21:8 [x]1Co 6:9 [y]Rev 2:11
21:9 [z]Rev 15:1,6,7 [a]Rev 19:7
21:10 [b]Rev 17:3 [c]Rev 1:10
21:11 [d]Rev 15:8; 22:5 [e]Rev 4:6
21:12 [f]Eze 48:30-34

21:10–27

OUR FINAL DESTINATION

Put on your construction hat for a moment and consider your dream house. What kind of place would you build if you had unlimited access to the finest materials? What location would you choose for this wonderful place? What would it look like on the outside and on the inside?

God has already built a home for all believers that makes even the most magnificent earthly home look like a dilapidated refrigerator box. As you read this amazing chapter, consider the kinds of construction materials God has used. Again, we can't imagine the beauty and glory of heaven (see note on 4:1–5:14). But we can use John's descriptions to prompt our wonder and praise to God for his amazing love.

The best aspects of heaven, however, are described earlier in the chapter. Read verses 1–7 and allow them to inspire your praise.

What will believers do in heaven? John tells us in this book that they will reign with Christ (22:5); they will enjoy their relationship with God and with people from past ages (7:9); they'll serve God without time demands, frustration or exhaustion (21:3–4); they'll enjoy the beauty of heaven for eternity (21:22–27).

Everything Adam and Eve lost in the Garden of Eden will be restored. What a promise! What a hope!

the names of the twelve apostles of the
Lamb.
15 The angel who talked with me had
a measuring rod[g] of gold to measure
the city, its gates and its walls. 16 The
city was laid out like a square, as long
as it was wide. He measured the city
with the rod and found it to be 12,000
stadia[a] in length, and as wide and
high as it is long. 17 He measured its
wall and it was 144 cubits[b] thick,[c] by
man's measurement, which the angel
was using. 18 The wall was made of jasper,[h] and the city of pure gold, as pure
as glass.[i] 19 The foundations of the city
walls were decorated with every kind of
precious stone.[j] The first foundation
was jasper, the second sapphire, the
third chalcedony, the fourth emerald,
20 the fifth sardonyx, the sixth carnelian,[k] the seventh chrysolite, the
eighth beryl, the ninth topaz, the tenth
chrysoprase, the eleventh jacinth, and
the twelfth amethyst.[d] 21 The twelve
gates were twelve pearls, each gate
made of a single pearl. The great street
of the city was of pure gold, like trans-
parent glass.[l]
22 I did not see a temple[m] in the city,
because the Lord God Almighty[n] and
the Lamb[o] are its temple. 23 The city
does not need the sun or the moon to
shine on it, for the glory of God gives it
light,[p] and the Lamb is its lamp. 24 The
nations will walk by its light, and the
kings of the earth will bring their splendor into it.[q] 25 On no day will its gates
ever be shut,[r] for there will be no
night there.[s] 26 The glory and honor
of the nations will be brought into it.
27 Nothing impure will ever enter it, nor
will anyone who does what is shameful
or deceitful,[t] but only those whose
names are written in the Lamb's book
of life.

The River of Life

22 Then the angel showed me the river of the water of life, as clear as
crystal,[u] flowing[v] from the throne of
God and of the Lamb 2 down the middle of the great street of the city. On
each side of the river stood the tree
of life,[w] bearing twelve crops of fruit,
yielding its fruit every month. And the
leaves of the tree are for the healing of
the nations.[x] 3 No longer will there be
any curse.[y] The throne of God and of
the Lamb will be in the city, and his
servants will serve him.[z] 4 They will
see his face,[a] and his name will be on
their foreheads.[b] 5 There will be no
more night.[c] They will not need the
light of a lamp or the light of the sun,
for the Lord God will give them light.[d]
And they will reign for ever and ever.[e]
6 The angel said to me,[f] "These
words are trustworthy and true.[g] The
Lord, the God of the spirits of the
prophets,[h] sent his angel[i] to show
his servants the things that must soon
take place."

Jesus Is Coming

7 "Behold, I am coming soon![j]
Blessed[k] is he who keeps the words of
the prophecy in this book."
8 I, John, am the one who heard and
saw these things.[l] And when I had
heard and seen them, I fell down to
worship at the feet[m] of the angel who
had been showing them to me. 9 But he
said to me, "Do not do it! I am a fellow
servant with you and with your brothers the prophets and of all who keep
the words of this book.[n] Worship
God!"[o]
10 Then he told me, "Do not seal up[p]
the words of the prophecy of this book,
because the time is near.[q] 11 Let him
who does wrong continue to do wrong;
let him who is vile continue to be vile;
let him who does right continue to do

21:15 [g] Rev 11:1 **21:18** [h] ver 11 [i] ver 21 **21:19** [j] Isa 54:11,12 **21:20** [k] Rev 4:3 **21:21** [l] ver 18 **21:22** [m] Jn 4:21,23 [n] Rev 1:8 [o] Rev 5:6 **21:23** [p] Isa 24:23; 60:19,20; Rev 22:5 **21:24** [q] Isa 60:3,5 **21:25** [r] Isa 60:11 [s] Zec 14:7; Rev 22:5 **21:27** [t] Isa 52:1; Joel 3:17; Rev 22:14,15 **22:1** [u] Rev 4:6 [v] Eze 47:1; Zec 14:8 **22:2** [w] Rev 2:7 [x] Eze 47:12 **22:3** [y] Zec 14:11 [z] Rev 7:15 **22:4** [a] Mt 5:8 [b] Rev 14:1 **22:5** [c] Rev 21:25 [d] Rev 21:23

[e] Da 7:27; Rev 20:4 **22:6** [f] Rev 1:1 [g] Rev 19:9; 21:5 [h] Heb 12:9 [i] ver 16 **22:7** [j] Rev 3:11 [k] Rev 1:3 **22:8** [l] Rev 1:1 [m] Rev 19:10 **22:9** [n] ver 10,18,19 [o] Rev 19:10 **22:10** [p] Da 8:26; Rev 10:4 [q] Rev 1:3

[a] *16* That is, about 1,400 miles (about 2,200 kilometers) [b] *17* That is, about 200 feet (about 65 meters) [c] *17* Or *high*
[d] *20* The precise identification of some of these precious stones is uncertain.

22:7, 12–20

JESUS' LAST WORDS

Through the apostle John, Jesus directly addresses all who read the words of this prophecy. His final words to believers makes one thing very clear: He will return. And when he returns, Jesus will bring rewards for his followers and establish his eternal kingdom.

Of course, nobody knows when Jesus will return (see 1 Thessalonians 5:1–5). He could come back tomorrow as you're commuting to work. He could come tonight as you sleep. He could come before you finish reading this note.

Because his return is both certain and imminent, every believer needs to be on constant alert, always ready to meet his or her Maker. As you consider what this might mean for your life today, ask yourself, "How would I live if I knew Jesus would return in one week?" What changes would you make in your life? Ask God for the grace you need to get ready for the Lord's return. As you do that, you'll begin to echo John's words, which have been the confident and hopeful prayer of the church for centuries: "Amen. Come, Lord Jesus" (v. 20).

right; and let him who is holy continue to be holy."[r]

[12]"Behold, I am coming soon![s] My reward is with me,[t] and I will give to everyone according to what he has done. [13]I am the Alpha and the Omega,[u] the First and the Last,[v] the Beginning and the End.[w]

[14]"Blessed are those who wash their robes, that they may have the right to the tree of life[x] and may go through the gates[y] into the city.[z] [15]Outside[a] are the dogs,[b] those who practice magic arts, the sexually immoral, the murderers, the idolaters and everyone who loves and practices falsehood.

[16]"I, Jesus,[c] have sent my angel to give you[a] this testimony for the churches.[d] I am the Root[e] and the Offspring of David, and the bright Morning Star."[f]

[17]The Spirit[g] and the bride say, "Come!" And let him who hears say, "Come!" Whoever is thirsty, let him come; and whoever wishes, let him take the free gift of the water of life.

[18]I warn everyone who hears the words of the prophecy of this book: If anyone adds anything to them,[h] God will add to him the plagues described in this book.[i] [19]And if anyone takes words away[j] from this book of prophecy, God will take away from him his share in the tree of life and in the holy city, which are described in this book.

[20]He who testifies to these things[k] says, "Yes, I am coming soon."

Amen. Come, Lord Jesus.[l]

[21]The grace of the Lord Jesus be with God's people.[m] Amen.

22:11 [r]Eze 3:27; Da 12:10
22:12 [s]ver 7,20 [t]Isa 40:10
22:13 [u]Rev 1:8 [v]Rev 1:17 [w]Rev 21:6
22:14 [x]Rev 2:7 [y]Rev 21:12 [z]Rev 21:27
22:15 [a]1Co 6:9,10; Gal 5:19-21; Col 3:5,6 [b]Php 3:2
22:16 [c]Rev 1:1 [d]Rev 1:4 [e]Rev 5:5 [f]2Pe 1:19; Rev 2:28
22:17 [g]Rev 2:7
22:18 [h]Dt 4:2; Pr 30:6 [i]Rev 15:6-16:21
22:19 [j]Dt 4:2 **22:20** [k]Rev 1:2 [l]1Co 16:22 **22:21** [m]Ro 16:20

[a]*16* The Greek is plural.

WEIGHTS & MEASURES

		BIBLICAL UNIT	APPROXIMATE AMERICAN EQUIVALENT	APPROXIMATE METRIC EQUIVALENT
WEIGHTS	talent	(60 minas)	75 pounds	34 kilograms
	mina	(50 shekels)	1¼ pounds	0.6 kilogram
	shekel	(2 bekas)	⅖ ounce	11.5 grams
	pim	(⅔ shekel)	⅓ ounce	7.6 grams
	beka	(10 gerahs)	⅕ ounce	5.5 grams
	gerah		1/50 ounce	0.6 gram
LENGTH	cubit		18 inches	0.5 meter
	span		9 inches	23 centimeters
	handbreadth		3 inches	8 centimeters
CAPACITY				
Dry Measure	cor [homer]	(10 ephahs)	6 bushels	220 liters
	lethek	(5 ephahs)	3 bushels	110 liters
	ephah	(10 omers)	⅗ bushel	22 liters
	seah	(⅓ ephah)	7 quarts	7.3 liters
	omer	(1/10 ephah)	2 quarts	2 liters
	cab	(1/18 ephah)	1 quart	1 liter
Liquid Measure	bath	(1 ephah)	6 gallons	22 liters
	hin	(⅙ bath)	4 quarts	4 liters
	log	(1/72 bath)	⅓ quart	0.3 liter

The figures of the table are calculated on the basis of a shekel equaling 11.5 grams, a cubit equaling 18 inches and an ephah equaling 22 liters. The quart referred to is either a dry quart (slightly smaller than a liter) or a liquid quart (slightly larger than a liter), whichever is applicable. The ton referred to in the footnotes is the American ton of 2,000 pounds.

This table is based upon the best available information, but it is not intended to be mathematically precise; like the measurement equivalents in the footnotes, it merely gives approximate amounts and distances. Weights and measures differed somewhat at various times and places in the ancient world. There is uncertainty particularly about the ephah and the bath; further discoveries may shed more light on these units of capacity.

STUDY HELPS

PROMISEFINDER INDEX

This PromiseFinder Index is intended to help you target your study. It shows the Scripture location and page number of every reference to each of the Seven Promises that we have targeted throughout the Bible. Those in *italic* indicate in-text notes that comment on the promise as it relates to Scripture, and those in regular indicate side-column, Scripture-only promise references.

Promise 1

Promise 2

Promise 4

Promise 5

Promise 6

(God's Promises)

DICTIONARY OF NIV TERMS

This dictionary will give you a better understanding of many of the names, words, phrases and place names found in the text of the New International Version.

A

Abba
An Aramaic word best translated *Daddy* (Mark 14:36). *Abba* was a deeply personal and affectionate word, that most of Jesus' contemporaries would have considered disrespectful to use in addressing God.

Abomination
That which is repugnant or detestable to God or his people, such as idolatry or immorality (Isaiah 66:3).

Abyss
A bottomless pit where, at the end of the age, Satan will be banished for a time (Rev. 20:3). The Greeks used this word to describe the underworld of spirits, suggesting a place so deep it is unfathomable (Luke 8:31).

Acacia
A durable wood readily available in the Sinai Desert and used in the Old Testament tabernacle. Today the gum of the acacia tree is used for commercial and medicinal uses.

Afflict
See *Affliction*.

Affliction
Hardships, calamities and suffering, often lasting a long time. Sometimes imposed by others, sometimes self-imposed and at other times divinely imposed.

Alien
In the Old Testament, a non-Israelite living in Israel, typically in poverty. Later, a stranger away from home.

Anoint
The symbolic act of pouring oil on objects or individuals as a sign of consecration. The name *Messiah* means *the Anointed One*.

Antichrist
Anyone who opposes or rejects God has, to some degree, the spirit of antichrist (1 John 2:18). Also, at the end of the age, the figure who will embody the worst of the spirit of antichrist but who will finally be defeated.

Apostle
Someone sent to represent another; in the New Testament someone who had seen Jesus and been commissioned by him to teach others about him.

Aramaic
The common language in Palestine at the time of Jesus and the early church.

Asherah poles
See *Poles, Asherah*.

Ashtoreth
Female consort of the chief Canaanite god, Baal. The goddess of love, fertility and war. Also known as Ishtar to Babylonians, Aphrodite to Greeks and Venus to Romans. Also called Asherah.

Assembly, Sacred
The gathering of the entire Israelite community for common worship, celebration or repentance.

Atonement
Act by which sinners are made "at one" with God—when barriers of sin between God and sinners are removed. The Day of Atonement was an Old Testament annual fast when the high priest entered the Most Holy Place to atone for the sins of the people (Lev. 16). Sacrifices on the Day of Atonement cleansed the whole nation of sin—even unknown transgressions. Later Christ's death made the final atonement for believers, making further sacrifices unnecessary (Heb. 9:23–28).

Avenge
To get back at or punish someone who has done wrong.

B

Baal
The Canaanite fertility god believed to be responsible for germinating crops, increasing flocks and adding children to the community. Best known of the Canaanite gods.

Backsliding
To turn or move away from a relationship with God.

Baptism
A Christian rite symbolizing cleansing from sin and identification with Jesus. Sprinkling, immersion and pouring are three ways Christians today practice water baptism.

Beelzebub
Satan, the prince of demons. In the Old Testament, Baal was a Canaanite deity, whose name was expanded to Beelzebul (meaning *Exalted* or *Prince Baal*).

Birthright
In the Old Testament, special rights given to the first-born son, including the authority as leader of the family.

Blaspheme
To speak about God or holy things in a careless, false or insulting way.

Blasphemy
See *Blaspheme*.

Block, Stumbling
Anything or anyone that causes someone to sin.

Bloodguilt
The verdict on a person for crimes deserving death.

Breastpiece
A colorful pouch nine inches square, attached to the attire of the Old Testament high priest. Twelve precious stones on the pouch represented the 12 tribes of Israel—so when it hung around the priest's neck, the people could be close to his heart. Inside the breast-

piece were the Urim and Thummim (Exodus 28:15,30; See ***Urim;*** See ***Thummim***).

Burnt offering
See *Offering, Burnt.*

Byword
An object of scorn and ridicule, a term of verbal abuse (Job 17:6).

C

Calamus
An aromatic spice cane; its juice was an ingredient in incense offerings (Isaiah 43:24).

Capstone
Either the bottom corner of a building (a foundation stone) or the keystone of an archway (Mark 12:10). It can cause a person to stumble (1 Peter 2:8), or it can fall on someone (Matt. 21:44).

Censer
A container used for burning incense (Rev. 8:3).

Centurion
A Roman army officer in charge of 100 soldiers.

Chaff
(1) After wheat was harvested, the chaff (the seed covering, straw and dust) was blown away from the grain in a process called winnowing. See ***Fork, Winnowing.***
(2) A word used to describe the wicked who would be separated from the righteous at judgment (Psalm 1:4).

Cherub
A winged, angelic being who exists primarily to glorify God and to vindicate God's holiness against the presumptuous pride of fallen humans. Symbolic attendant marking the place of God's enthronement in his earthly kingdom (Exodus 25:18). The plural of *cherub* is *cherubim.*

Circumcise
See *Circumcision*.

Circumcision
Cutting off the foreskin of the penis—usually on the eighth day after birth (Gen. 17:10–14). It was a physical reminder of the special, spiritual relationship between God and his chosen people.

Cistern
Covered pits cut into rock or clay to catch and store rainwater (Jer. 14:3). Critical to life in an arid climate, cisterns symbolize security.

Citadel
A tower or building equipped for war, especially one in a city, often thought of as the city's final defense unit.

Collectors, Tax
Those employed by Roman authorities to collect taxes for them. They were notorious for imposing more taxes than were required, skimming off the top to line their own pockets. They were despised by the Jews for collaborating with the Roman government that ruled over them.

Concubine
A woman who belonged to a man in a relationship inferior to that of a wife. Commonly found in ancient cultures where polygamy was practiced, a concubine was often one of the spoils of war—with the primary purpose of bearing children for the man.

Consecrate
To set aside or dedicate for God's use (Exodus 13:2).

Covenant
A mutually binding agreement between two parties. In the Old Testament, God entered into a covenant with Israel. But God alone set the conditions to the agreement. In return for their loyalty and obedience, God promised to protect and love Israel and to give them his presence. The *new covenant* (Heb. 8:7) brought salvation to God's people through the shedding of Jesus' blood.

Cows, Sea
Dugongs (see NIV text note on Exodus 25:5)—marine animals abounding on the coral banks of the Red Sea and in other tropical waters. A dugong can grow to be 11 feet long, with a round head, fish-like tail and flippers for forelimbs. Their appearance is similar to seals.

Cubit
A unit of measurement 18 to 21 inches in length—from the elbow to the tip of the middle finger.

Cyrus
The founder of the Persian empire, Cyrus the Great ruled Persia from 559 to 530 B.C.

D

Day of the Lord
An Old Testament concept describing the time when God would intervene to vindicate the righteous and judge the wicked (Isaiah 2:12). The New Testament links it more specifically to Jesus' second coming (1 Cor. 1:8). The *Day of the Lord* was both a time of salvation and of judgment.

Death
The end of physical life. Spiritual death means separation from God (Eph. 2:1–5). Other uses of the word include: the end of a sinful way of life (Romans 6:4–8) and the final and irreversible separation from God after judgment (Rev. 20:11–15).

Decapolis
The name of the confederation of ten Gentile cities wrenched from Jewish control by the Roman general Pompey in 63 B.C. All but one were east of the Jordan River.

Desecrate
To treat without respect or reverence (Lev. 21:12).

Disciple
A student or follower; an adherent to the teachings of a particular teacher or school of thought. In the New Testament, *disciple* usually refers to a follower of Jesus.

Dissipation
Living only for your own pleasure; wasting your life on foolish or evil pleasures.

Divination
Using a human intermediary or inanimate objects, such as the examination of animal entrails, to receive messages from the spirit world.

Dregs
Sediment that forms during the fermentation of wine.

When not separated from the wine, dregs caused bitter tasting wine. Used as a picture of undesirable characteristics and the bitterness of God's wrath on the wicked (Psalm 75:8).

Drink offering
See *Offering, Drink*.

Dross
The worthless by-product left over and thrown out after refining precious metals like gold or silver ore. A picture of how those who stray are treated (Psalm 119:119).

E

Edict
An order made by someone with power to enforce it.

Edom
The nation of descendants of Esau, the twin brother of Jacob (Gen. 25:23–28). Located south of the Dead Sea amid the reddish sandstone of the Rift Valley, Edom was often hostile to Israel (Obad. v. 1).

Elect
Those chosen for a particular relationship or function. The people of God chosen in Christ before the foundation of the world (Eph. 1:4).

Ephod
One of six articles of clothing specified for Israelite priests' uniforms (Exodus 28:4–8), the ephod consisted of a sleeveless garment made of finely twisted linen. In some instances in the Old Testament, the word is used to describe an object of worship (Judges 8:27).

Eternal life
See *Life, Eternal*.

Eunuch
A castrated male who in the ancient Near East was often employed in a governmental position. The term came to designate an officer, whether physically a eunuch or not.

Exile
One who is banished from his or her own country and taken captive to a foreign land. One of the means God used in the Old Testament to punish his people, purging them of their sinful and rebellious ways.

Extol
To praise highly, to glorify, to laud (Psalm 34:1).

Extortion
Gaining something from someone by force or by some other illegal means.

F

Fear of the Lord
See *Lord, Fear of the*.

Fellowship offering
See *Offering, Fellowship*.

Festival, New Moon
Both a religious and a civil Old Testament festival (1 Samuel 20:5), the New Moon festival was celebrated at the beginning of each month and is often mentioned in the Old Testament together with the Sabbath (Isaiah 1:13).

Firstborn
Oldest son and the possessor of special privileges. In the Old Testament the term often described the privilege and favor God granted to Israel (Exodus 4:22). In the New Testament, Jesus is called the *firstborn* of the Father, the one who rules over all (Heb. 1:6).

Firstfruits
The first crops of the season that ripened. The offering of the firstfruits was a gift of the first and best part of the harvest, signifying that all of Israel's sustenance came from God (Exodus 23:19). In the New Testament, the term is applied to Jesus (1 Cor. 15:20) and to believers (James 1:18).

Footstool
A stool for supporting the feet of someone sitting on a throne (2 Chron. 9:18). The Bible depicts God's *footstool* as (1) the earth (Isaiah 66:1), (2) the ark of the covenant (which in the Old Testament represented God's presence among the Israelites [1 Chron. 28:2]), (3) the temple (Psalm 99:5) and (4) the defeated enemies of the Messiah (Psalm 110:1).

Fork, Winnowing
A large, wooden fork used in Bible times to toss the threshed grain into the air so the wind would blow away the lighter chaff while the heavier grain dropped back to the ground.

G

Gabriel
An angel whose name means *man of God* or *God is powerful*. He heralded the coming births of John the Baptist (Luke 1:11–20) and Jesus (Luke 1:26–28).

Genealogy
A list of a person's ancestors or descendants.

Gentile
A term for anyone who is not an Israelite. Jews and Gentiles have been reconciled to God and to each other through Christ (Eph. 2:11–22).

Glory
An essential quality of God's character (Psalm 63:2), his glory is his worthiness. Everything about him testifies that he is worthy to receive praise, honor and respect. In the New Testament, Jesus is revealed to be the *Lord of glory* (1 Cor. 2:8). In the Bible, glory is often associated with brightness or splendor (Luke 2:9).

Glutton
A person who habitually eats too much.

God, Kingdom of
God's rule on earth. Both present and still future. Began with the arrival of Christ and will be consummated when Christ comes back to earth for the second time.

Gospel
Good news—specifically, the good news of salvation through Jesus Christ, who died for our sins and rose again. *Gospel* describes the message of Christianity, as well as the first four books of the New Testament (Matthew, Mark, Luke and John) in which the record of Jesus' life and teaching is found.

Grace
Unmerited favor, unearned benefit, undeserved kindness. God's amazing gift of forgiveness of sins and power to live with dignity in the present and with hope for the future.

Grain offering
See *Offering, Grain*.

Guilt offering
See *Offering, Guilt*.

H

Hades
Greek word referring to the place of the dead, akin to the Hebrew *Sheol*.

Hallelujah
Occurring only four times in the New Testament, *hallelujah* comes from two Hebrew words that mean *praise the* L*ORD* (Rev. 19:1).

Hebrew
(1) The language in which most of the Old Testament was written. (2) Another name for an Israelite; a descendant of Abraham. (3) Sometimes refers to a broader group, including non-Israelites descended from Eber (Gen. 10:21–32)—such as Arameans (descendants of Nahor) and Moabites and Ammonites (descendants of Lot).

Hell
Place of final punishment for the wicked. In the New Testament, the word *hell* typically translates the Greek word *ge[h]enna.* and is used as a metaphor to picture hell. *Ge[h]enna* comes from a Hebrew expression meaning *the Valley of Ben Hinnom,* a deep ravine outside Jerusalem where human sacrifices had at one time been offered to the pagan god, Molech (2 Kings 23:10). See ***Topheth.***

Herodians
A group of Jews who opposed Jesus and supported the Herods, a line of Judean kings during Jesus' lifetime. They were supporters of Rome, from which the Herods received their authority.

High places
See *Places, High*.

Holy kiss
See *Kiss, Holy*.

Holy Place
See *Place, Holy*.

Hosts, Starry
The stars and other heavenly bodies, the worship of which is warned against in the Bible (Deut. 4:19).

Hyssop
A plant used in a ritual cleansing ceremony. Its hairy branches were dipped in sacrificial blood, which was then brushed or sprinkled on the object or person being cleansed (Exodus 12:22), symbolizing spiritual cleansing from sin.

I

Idol
Image of a god (Exodus 20:3–4). Anything that takes the place of God or steals our affections from him—often things like our relationships, work or hobbies.

Idolatry
The worship of false gods, sometimes by means of images. Anything that takes us away from the worship of the one true God (Romans 1:18–25).

Incense
Aromatic substances such as frankincense and myrrh burned to make a fragrant smoke. Used as an offering in worship. Can symbolize either prayers (Psalm 141:2) or the presence of God (Exodus 30:1–10).

Intercede
To pray for another person, usually to obtain God's help.

J

Jericho
An ancient city situated several miles west of the Jordan River and north of the Dead Sea.

Jerusalem
(1) The capital of Israel before it split into two kingdoms in 930 B.C. After the split, it was the capital of the southern kingdom of Judah. (2) The place where Solomon built the temple. (3) Captured by the Babylonians in 597 B.C. and then destroyed by them in 586 B.C., Jerusalem was rebuilt between 538 and 445 B.C. (4) Jewish center of worship during the time of Jesus. See ***Zion.***

Jew
Derived from *Judah,* the term originally denoted one belonging to the tribe of Judah and later was applied to all the descendants of Abraham. Other names: Israelites and Hebrews.

Joppa
A seaport located about 35 miles northwest of Jerusalem, known today as Jaffa.

Jubilee
An Old Testament celebration held every 50 years (Lev. 25:10). During the 49th and 50th years, the land would have lain idle for two consecutive years (Isaiah 37:30), enslaved Israelites were freed and property was returned to its original owners.

Justification
That act of God whereby he places us in a right relationship with him (Romans 5:16); a declaration of innocence or righteousness, a freeing from guilt or blame.

Justify
To erase someone's sins; to declare righteous.

K

Kidron Valley
See *Valley, Kidron*.

Kingdom of God
See *God, Kingdom of*.

Kiss, Holy
A sign of mutual respect and trust; the equivalent of a handshake or hug (2 Cor. 13:12).

L

Lament
A musical or poetic dirge—a song of sorrow, a cry of grief (often a recognition of judgment). The Bible book of Lamentations is composed of five laments.

Legion
A very large number (Mark 5:9). The name of a Roman army division of 6,000 soldiers.

Leprosy
Known today as "Hansen's disease," although the Biblical term included other types of skin diseases as well. Can cause paralysis, deformity and gangrene.

Leviathan
(1) A great marine mammal—possibly a crocodile (see NIV text note on Job 41:1) or a sea serpent. (2) Thought by some to be an ancient mythological dragon that caused eclipses by twisting itself around the sun (Job 3:8). (3) A creature said by ancient mythology to represent the chaotic waters overcome by God at creation (Psalm 74:14; 89:10; See ***Rahab***).

Levite
The name given to the descendants of Levi. Given a place of privilege and responsibility among God's people in overseeing worship and in caring for the tabernacle. Only Levites could become priests, but not all Levites were priests.

Life, Eternal
A quality of life that begins the moment someone trusts in Jesus for salvation (John 3:36) and continues after physical death through fellowship with God in life that will never end (Jude v. 21).

Line, Measuring
(1) A rope, string or cord of a specific length used for measuring. (2) Sometimes used to picture God's thorough and calculated punishment of Judah and other nations (2 Kings 21:13), but also used as a symbol of restoration (Zech. 1:16).

Locust
An insect similar to the grasshopper but more aggressive. An army of these insects can devastate entire fields of crops within minutes.

Lord, Fear of the
An attitude of reverence or worship in the presence of God—an attitude of humility and awe more than dread and fright (Prov. 1:7).

Lyre
A harplike instrument made of wood and distinguished by its number of strings (historians say the lyre had about ten strings). Lyres typically had a sound board over which the vibrating strings could resonate.

M

Magicians
Ancient wise men who were expected to foretell the future and influence such events as harvests, droughts and battles (Daniel 2:2). Many claimed to possess occult knowledge.

Man, Son of
An expression found in the Old Testament and used as a self-description of Jesus in the New Testament. Over 90 times Ezekiel is called *son of man* to emphasize his humanity in the presence of Almighty God (Ezek. 2:1). Jesus used this name to show he was the Messiah prophesied by Daniel (Daniel 7:13).

Mandrake
A fragrant flowering plant that grew wild in desert areas. Thought by ancients to possess magical powers, it was used for medicinal purposes and as a charm against evil spirits; it was also credited with aphrodisiac qualities.

Manna
The food God miraculously supplied during the Israelites' 40 years of wilderness wandering (the manna stopped at the time of their first Passover in Canaan). Israelites described its appearance as *white like coriander seed* and its taste as *wafers made with honey* (Exodus 16:31).

Measuring line
See *Line, Measuring*.

Medium
Someone believed to be able to consult with ghosts or spirits; a person through whom the spirit of a dead person would communicate with the living (Isaiah 8:19). The practice was condemned and prohibited in the Old Testament (Deut. 18:10–11).

Meeting, Tent of
Another name for the tabernacle, for it was the place where God showed his presence and met with his people.

Mercy
Compassion or kindness shown to someone instead of severity, especially to someone who doesn't deserve it.

Midwife
A person who helps with the birth of a baby (Gen. 35:17).

Millstone
One of a pair of stones used to crush grain for flour.

Molech
Traditionally understood as the name of a pagan god to whom children were burned in sacrifice (Lev. 18:21).

Most Holy Place
See *Place, Most Holy*.

Myrrh
A fragrant gum extracted from a small tree growing in certain areas of the Middle East. Its oil was used as a spice, as a medicine and as a cosmetic; myrrh was applied to Jesus' body after his burial (John 19:39–40). One of the gifts of the Magi to Jesus after his birth (Matt. 2:11).

Mystery
Among the Greeks, a secret imparted only to the initiated. For Paul in the New Testament, a divine truth once hidden but now revealed in the gospel. The Christian mystery is God's strategy to redeem people through Christ (Eph. 3:2–9)—Jews and Gentiles united in Christ.

N

Nazirite
One who demonstrated total consecration to the Lord by taking a vow of separation and abstinence for the

purpose of some special service; the three standard prohibitions were abstaining from grape products, from haircuts and from contact with dead bodies (Num. 6:2–8).

Negev
The area stretching southward from Beersheba in southern Palestine. It is usually desertlike, but at times there are seasons of rain that leave pools of water (Psalm 126:4).

New Moon festival
See *Festival, New Moon*.

New wine
See *Wine, New*.

O

Offal
The entrails of an animal burned as part of a sin offering (Exodus 29:14).

Offering, Burnt
The most frequent of the sacrifices at the Old Testament sanctuary—offered morning and evening of every day. To make payment for sins, a worshiper voluntarily brought an unblemished animal to the priest and laid his hand on the animal's head to express identification. The priest then killed it and burned it up completely, symbolizing the person's total devotion to God (Lev. 1).

Offering, Drink
Usually a wine or oil poured out as a sacrifice of dedication to God—part of the regular offerings made every day in connection with the grain offering (Exodus 29:38–41). In the New Testament, it is a picture of expending one's life for the cause of Christ (Phil. 2:17).

Offering, Fellowship
To express gratitude to God, a worshiper sacrificed an unblemished animal on the altar. Part of it was burned, and a portion of it was eaten by the worshiper, symbolizing peace and fellowship with God (Lev. 3). Traditionally called *peace offerings*.

Offering, Grain
An offering presented as an act of worship (Lev. 2). It was intended simply to remember God's favor and, by remembering, to please him. The worshiper who offered the sacrifice brought prepared loaves of bread, wafers or small cakes to the sanctuary; a portion was consumed by fire and the rest of the offering was eaten by the priests.

Offering, Guilt
An offering that absolved the worshiper in instances where restitution was required—in cases of theft or cheating, for example. A ram was offered (no substitutes allowed), and complete restitution plus 20 percent was to be paid, satisfying both God and the person wronged. Only guilt offerings eased guilty consciences with restitution for sin.

Offering, Sin
The Old Testament blood sacrifice required for unintentional sins (Lev. 4:1–35). Sin offerings were made for the whole congregation on all feast days and especially on the Day of Atonement, and they were prescribed for individuals in a number of instances that demanded payment of the penalty for sins.

Offering, Thank
A type of fellowship offering, the thank offering expressed gratitude to God for deliverance from trouble, healing of sickness, answers to prayer or some other blessing received (Lev. 7:12).

Offering, Wave
A ceremony whereby offerings are dedicated to the Lord—most likely by lifting the object up before the Lord. A number of objects could be the subject of the wave offering, including the breast portion of the fellowship offering (Lev. 7:30).

Oracle
An announcement or message from God. The word often suggests unwelcome news or judgment.

Ordination
An Old Testament ritual signifying the responsibilities and privileges of the Levitical priesthood (Lev. 8:22). The Hebrew word translated *ordination* literally meant *to fill the hand* and probably referred to offerings placed in their hands. Ordination of ministers today has its roots in this Old Testament practice.

P

Parable
A saying or story that drives home a point using illustrations from everyday life; a comparison of two objects for the purpose of teaching. Jesus told many parables during the course of his life on earth.

Patriarch
The father of a family or head of a tribe or race; a forefather of the Israelites (Heb. 7:4).

Peace
The Biblical concept of peace has at its root the meaning of "totality," or "completeness." Important nuances of meaning include such things as "fulfillment," "maturity," "soundness," "wholeness," "harmony," "security," "well-being" and "prosperity." Also connotes absence of war and freedom from disturbance.

Pharisees
A powerful branch of the Jewish religious community during Jesus' time. Considered to be religious experts, this group believed that the oral law of the Jewish faith was as equally authoritative and inspired by God as the Torah, or written law. Consequently, they obeyed very strictly God's laws and all the tradition of interpretation they had established. Jesus reserved some of his harshest criticism for them (Matt. 23).

Place, Holy
Part of the Israelite sanctuaries (tabernacle and temple), located just outside the Most Holy Place. Contained the altar of incense, the table for the bread of the Presence and the lampstand.

Place, Most Holy
The inner sanctuary of both the Old Testament tabernacle and the temple, containing the ark of the covenant, the symbol of God's presence. The high priest alone was allowed to enter it once each year on the Day of Atonement (Lev. 16).

Places, High
Places of worship often associated with pagan religious practices, immorality and human sacrifice. Religious ob-

jects were placed on the tops of hills to appease pagan gods (Num. 33:52). Generally, Israelites were forbidden to worship God there, and God commanded them to destroy these areas.

Plunder
To rob or loot as an act of war. Used as a noun, plunder refers to the spoils gained through the act of looting.

Poles, Asherah
Wooden poles, perhaps carved in the image of Asherah, Canaanite goddess of love and war, set up in her honor and placed near the altars in Canaanite worship.

Precepts
Commands, usually divine injunctions setting forth human obligations.

Priest
The person appointed to act on behalf of men and women in relation to God. The Old Testament group of male leaders descended from Aaron, who performed religious duties in the temple. The New Testament calls Jesus the great high priest (Heb. 4:14) and the body of Christ a holy priesthood (1 Peter 2:5).

Profane
To make a holy thing impure or defiled by treating it with disrespect or irreverence.

Prophecy
The message of a prophet. Also, a spiritual gift, a supernatural empowering to build up God's family. Those with this gift either proclaimed to God's people new truth from God or challenged them with existing Scriptural truths (1 Cor. 14:1–5).

Prophet
A mouthpiece for God, one who receives a message from God and proclaims it to a specific audience.

Prophetess
A female prophet (Exodus 15:20).

Prostitute, Shrine
A special class of ancient Middle Eastern prostitutes (male and female) used in the fertility cults. They performed sexual acts in the temple of their god as acts of religious devotion (Deut. 23:17).

Purify
To make clean or pure. To be ceremonially pure means to be free from defects that would disqualify someone or something from holy uses or holy acts. To be ethically pure means to show oneself, in thought and conduct, to be a person chosen by God.

Purple
A symbol of wealth and royalty. The most highly prized dye in the ancient world, purple dye was obtained from various shellfish common to Phoenicia (a name that means *land of purple*).

Q

Quail
A small spotted bird similar to the partridge; quail migrated from North Africa through Egypt, Sinai and Palestine. God provided quail along with manna (See ***Manna***) as food to sustain the Israelites in their desert wanderings (Exodus 16:13).

R

Rabbi
A title of respect meaning *my master* or *my teacher,* given to teachers of the law (Matt. 23:2–7). Jesus was also addressed as *Rabbi* (Mark 9:5).

Rahab
(1) Old Testament prostitute from Jericho who hid two Hebrew spies and helped them escape danger (Joshua 2:1). (2) A name symbolizing a mythical sea monster that allegedly ruled over the chaos at the time of creation (Psalm 89:10; Isaiah 51:9). See ***Leviathan.*** (3) A nickname for Egypt (Psalm 87:4; Isaiah 30:7). (4) A symbol of hostility toward God's people.

Redeem
To obtain release by paying a price, to buy back.

Redeemer
One who delivers from bondage or trouble. Applied to family situations where a *kinsman-redeemer* was responsible to protect the interests of needy members of the extended family (Ruth 3:9). Applied to God as the protector and deliverer of Israel (Isaiah 41:14). Though Jesus is not specifically called "Redeemer" in the New Testament, he is the one in whom believers have redemption (Eph. 1:7).

Redemption
Deliverance and freedom—described in the New Testament as freedom from the penalty of sin by payment of a ransom. Through his death on the cross Jesus paid the ransom for us (Romans 3:24) and set us free.

Remnant
(1) The remaining part or group after destruction or dispersal (2 Kings 19:30–31). (2) Those who escape God's judgment because of God's grace (Romans 11:5). (3) A symbol of hope pointing toward the great multitude that one day will stand saved before God (Rev. 7).

Repent
To consciously turn from sin to God; to be sorry for what you have done and to resolve not to do it again.

Repentance
A profound change of mind from sin-centeredness to God-centeredness. Though repentance may represent only regret or remorse over a past thought or action, in its fullest sense it connotes a change of orientation involving a deliberate redirection for the future (Acts 26:20).

Reproach
To rebuke or chide, to blame or accuse. Used as a noun, a source of disgrace or shame, an expression of disapproval or rebuke (Psalm 79:4).

Resurrection
The act of coming back to life after being dead. Described as applying to both the righteous and the wicked (Daniel 12:2). Jesus' resurrection (Matt. 28:1–10), along with his death, is considered essential to the salvation of believers (Romans 4:25) and guarantees our resurrection (1 Cor. 15:12–19).

Retribution
Deserved punishment for doing wrong, but also deserved reward for doing good.

Revelation
The act of disclosure or making known; more particularly, God's self-unveiling, his deliberate disclosure of true knowledge of himself and his purposes and actions on our behalf (Eph. 1:17).

Revere
See *Reverence*.

Reverence
An attitude of deep respect, honor and deference. Our worthy response to God's majesty and holiness. From an attitude of reverence naturally flow obedient actions (2 Cor. 7:1). See ***Lord, Fear of the.***

Righteous
See *Righteousness*.

Righteousness
The fulfillment of the demands of a relationship. God brings believers into a right relation with him, erasing their guilt and crediting righteousness to them (Romans 3:21–22) and helping them to be devoted to the service of what God says is right (Romans 6:11–13).

Ring, Signet
A ring containing a design or a name of someone in authority and used to make an impression in soft clay or wax. Used to authorize official documents. A symbol of authority (Gen. 41:42).

S

Sabbath
The Hebrew weekly day of rest and worship observed on the seventh day of the week. It began at sunset on Friday and ended at sunset on Saturday.

Sackcloth
A coarse material, dark in color, usually made of goat's hair. Worn especially during times of mourning or social protest. A symbol of grief and mourning.

Sacred assembly
See *Assembly, Sacred*.

Sacred stones
See *Stones, Sacred*.

Sacrifice
A gift or offering to God (Exodus 12:27). Something offered to God to atone for sin. Jesus is the ultimate sacrifice, which satisfies God's wrath toward humankind (1 John 4:10). Believers are to live in such a way that they offer themselves to God as *living sacrifices* (Romans 12:1).

Saddulees
A group of leaders in the Jewish religious community opposed to the teachings of both the Pharisees and Jesus. During the first century A.D. they held considerable political power and controlled the highest Jewish court in the land, the Sanhedrin. They denied the doctrine of the resurrection of the body (Mark 12:18) and the existence of angels and spirits (Acts 23:8).

Saints
Those dedicated to God and set apart for his service (Phil. 1:1). All who believe in Jesus, regardless of their character or spiritual maturity.

Salvation
Deliverance from danger or death; especially deliverance from all that separates people from God (Titus 2:12).

Sanctification
Act of God by which believers become more and more conformed to Christ's image (1 Thess. 4:3).

Sanctify
To make holy; to set apart (John 17:17).

Sanhedrin
The highest Jewish authority in Palestine prior to A.D. 70. This court, composed of 70 members and the high priest as president, had complete control over the religious affairs of Israel and had the final say-so in the interpretation of Mosaic Law. It also governed civil affairs and tried certain criminal cases under the authority of the Romans; it could not, however, impose capital punishment (John 18:31).

Satrap
An official who ruled over a major division of the Persian empire (Ezra 8:36).

Scepter
A staff or pole the king held as a symbol of his royal authority.

Sea Cows
See *Cows, Sea*.

Seer
A person who prophesies future events. A prophet. One who speaks the word of God (1 Samuel 9:9). See ***Prophet.***

Selah
Generally believed to be a musical cue or instruction for the performer. Some think it may have been a call for a pause or interlude or for a brief liturgical response by the congregation.

Shekel
The basic weight used in ancient Semitic systems of measurement. The exact weight of a shekel is not known. Some estimate it weighed between 11.3 and 11.47 grams.

Shrine prostitute
See *Prostitute, Shrine*.

Siege works
See *Works, Siege*.

Signet ring
See *Ring, Signet*.

Sin offering
See *Offering, Sin*.

Son of man
See *Man, Son of*.

Sorcery
The use of means believed to have supernatural power to produce or prevent a particular result; the craft of controlling or using such means of supernatural powers. Included in the list of magical arts condemned and prohibited in the Old Testament (Deut. 18:10).

Soul
Represents primarily the life force of the person; also the inner life, encompassing desires and emotions. The part of a person that does not die (Rev. 6:9).

Starry hosts
See *Hosts, starry.*

Stones, Sacred
Stone monuments used in idol worship, often engraved with writing and likely intended to be representations of the pagan deity (2 Kings 3:2). Explicitly forbidden to the Israelites (Lev. 26:1–2).

Stronghold
A place of refuge or defense, such as a tower, fortress or fortified hilltop from which an enemy could be resisted. A metaphor for refuge and security (Psalm 27:1).

Stumbling block
See *Block, Stumbling.*

T

Tabernacle
A tent used by the Israelites as a place of worship while they were on the move in the desert (Exodus 25:9). Its basic structure was 15 feet wide by 45 feet long by 15 feet high, a space about half the size of a football field. The holy place of God's presence among his people, the tabernacle was also called the *Tent of Meeting* (See ***Meeting, Tent of***).

Tax collectors
See *Collectors, Tax.*

Tent of Meeting
See *Meeting, Tent of.*

Tetrarch
Originally a ruler over a fourth of a region; later used of a number of rulers (lower in rank than kings) who depended on Rome for power to govern land conquered by the Romans.

Thank offering
See *Offering, Thank.*

Thummim
Together with Urim, some sort of devices by which an Old Testament priest could discern God's will (Exodus 28:30). They were possibly sacred lots or stones cast like dice to determine a yes or no answer from God.

Tithe
One-tenth of one's income. The dedication of a tenth of agricultural products, livestock or other goods to the worship of a deity or to the persons who served in the worship of the deity. In the Old Testament, the Israelites devoted a tithe to support the Levites (Num. 18:21), freeing them to serve the Lord. Some suggest that the New Testament standard for giving for the Lord's work is an amount proportionate to one's income (1 Cor. 16:2).

Topheth
A place in the Valley of Ben Hinnom just outside Jerusalem, where apostate Israelites sacrificed children to the pagan god, Molech (Jer. 7:31). Used as a trash dump with perpetual fires that symbolized judgment. Topheth may derive from the Aramaic word for *fireplace.* See ***Hell.***

U

Uncircumcised
(1) Males who have not had a circle of skin cut off at the front end of the penis (Gen. 17:14). See ***Circumcision.*** (2) Figuratively, a heart that is unresponsive is said to be *uncircumcised* (Acts 7:51), that is, not consecrated to the Lord. (3) Gentiles were called *uncircumcised* (Eph. 2:11), but Paul said real circumcision is *circumcision of the heart* (Romans 2:29).

Unclean
Ritually defiled or polluted, for which various rituals of cleansing were prescribed (Lev. 5:2). By the blood of Jesus, *unclean* sinners are cleansed (Heb. 10:22) and enabled to live a fruitful Christian life (2 Peter 1:5–9).

Uncleanness
See *Unclean.*

Urim
Together with Thummim, some sort of devices by which an Old Testament priest could discern God's will (Exodus 28:30). They were possibly sacred lots or stones cast like dice to determine a yes or no answer from God.

Usury
Interest, often excessive, charged on money lent (Psalm 15:5).

V

Valley, Kidron
Just east of Jerusalem, between the city and the Mount of Olives. Pagan relics were destroyed there under Asa, Hezekiah and Josiah (2 Kings 23:4–6).

Vision
A supernatural revelation, message or insight communicated through images seen only within a person's mind or spirit. The pictures seen in a vision may illustrate spiritual truths or future events (Isaiah 1:1).

Vow
A solemn, voluntary promise made to God to perform some action or refrain from performing some action in return for some hoped-for benefits (Judges 11:30–31).

W

Watchman
Someone on a tower or a high point entrusted to watch for approaching messengers or enemies (Ezek. 3:17).

Watchtower
A tower where guards could watch for danger or where a group of people could find protection from invaders.

Wave offering
See *Offering, Wave.*

Wine, New
The newly pressed juice of the grape. It contains less flavor and less alcohol because of the short aging process.

Winepress
A large vat or trough where several people could work together stomping on grapes to squeeze out the juice so it could be drained off and collected.

Wineskin
A leather container used to store wine (Matt. 9:17).

Winnowing fork
See *Fork, Winnowing.*

Witchcraft
A title linked with the practice of predicting the future by interpreting omens, examining livers of sacrificed animals, and contacting the dead—among other techniques. The Old Testament law prohibited these occultic and magical practices (Deut. 18:9–12).

Works, Siege
Military equipment used in capturing a walled city. Assyrian art shows wheeled battering rams and huge, wheeled towers packed with archers. Soldiers pushed these towers against the wall and used them as protected ladders.

Y

Yeast
(1) A substance that causes bread to rise—often by putting a bit of dough from an earlier batch in the flour, which fermented the entire loaf of bread. (2) A symbol of the pervasiveness of the kingdom of heaven (Matt. 13:33). (3) A symbol of undesirable teaching (Matt. 16:6). (4) A symbol of the pervasiveness of evil (1 Cor. 5:6–7).

Yoke
(1) A piece of timber or a heavy wooden pole formed to fit over the necks of animals (often two oxen) and connected to a plow or cart. (2) A figurative description of slavery and oppression (1 Kings 12:4); in contrast to the heavy "yoke" of the law (Gal. 5:1), the *yoke* of Jesus is easy to bear (Matt. 11:29–30).

Z

Zeal
Impassioned devotion to a person or a cause.

Zion
One of the hills on which Jerusalem stood. Often used to refer to the temple or Jerusalem as a whole (Psalm 48).

INDEX TO SUBJECTS

The Index to Subjects will lead you to key Scripture texts on a wide variety of subjects.

A

B

E

F

G

J

T

Y

Z

NIV CONCORDANCE
INTRODUCTION

This *NIV Concordance* is a condensation of the *NIV Complete Concordance.* It indexes more than 2,000 words from the New International Version Bible and contains over 13,000 references which we have carefully selected as the most helpful for the average Bible student or layperson.

When determining whether or not to include a verse reference, we gave careful consideration to the passage in which the verse is located. We also encourage you to always consider the larger context of the passage, giving special attention to the flow of the thought from beginning to end. Whenever you look up a verse, your goal should be to discover the intended meaning of the verse in context. Do not use this concordance, or any concordance, merely as a *verse-finder;* it should also be used as a *passage-finder.* The contexts surrounding each entry are longer than those usually found in concordances; but even so, the context excerpts are too brief for study purposes. They serve only to help you locate familiar verses.

In some cases the usual short contextual phrases are ineffective in helping you locate a passage. This is especially true in studying key events in a Bible character's life. Therefore, we have incorporated 134 "block entries" in which we use descriptive phrases that mark the breadth of a passage containing episodes of that person's life. The descriptive phrases replace the brief context surrounding each occurrence of the name.

Often more than one Bible character has the same name. For example, there are more than thirty Zechariahs in the Bible. In these cases we have given the name a block entry, assigning each person a number (1), (2), etc., and have included a descriptive phrase to distinguish each. Insignificant names are not included.

In this concordance there are 223 key word entries that have an exhaustive list of every appearance of that word. When this occurs, the word or block entry is marked with an asterisk (*).

It is our hope that this concordance will become the most useful feature of your Bible. Through its use you should become more familiar with God's Word by finding favorite or key passages and by exploring new words and people of the Old and New Testaments.

John R. Kohlenberger III
Edward W. Goodrick

NIV CONCORDANCE

AARON

Priesthood of (Ex 28:1; Nu 17; Heb 5:1-4; 7), garments (Ex 28; 39), consecration (Ex 29), ordination (Lev 8).

Spokesman for Moses (Ex 4:14-16, 27-31; 7:1-2). Supported Moses' hands in battle (Ex 17:8-13). Built golden calf (Ex 32; Dt 9:20). Talked against Moses (Nu 12). Priesthood opposed (Nu 16); staff budded (Nu 17). Forbidden to enter land (Nu 20:1-12). Death (Nu 20:22-29; 33:38-39).

ABANDON
Dt 4:31 he will not *a* or destroy you
1Ti 4: 1 in later times some will *a* the faith

ABBA
Ro 8:15 And by him we cry, *"A,* Father."
Gal 4: 6 the Spirit who calls out, *"A,* Father

ABEL

Second son of Adam (Ge 4:2). Offered proper sacrifice (Ge 4:4; Heb 11:4). Murdered by Cain (Ge 4:8; Mt 23:35; Lk 11:51; 1Jn 3:12).

ABHORS
Pr 11: 1 The LORD *a* dishonest scales,

ABIGAIL

Wife of Nabal (1Sa 25:30); pled for his life with David (1Sa 25:14-35). Became David's wife (1Sa 25:36-42).

ABIJAH

Son of Rehoboam; king of Judah (1Ki 14:31-15:8; 2Ch 12:16-14:1).

ABILITY (ABLE)
Ezr 2:69 According to their *a* they gave
2Co 1: 8 far beyond our *a* to endure,
8: 3 were able, and even beyond their *a.*

ABIMELECH

1. King of Gerar who took Abraham's wife Sarah, believing her to be his sister (Ge 20). Later made a covenant with Abraham (Ge 21:22-33).

2. King of Gerar who took Isaac's wife Rebekah, believing her to be his sister (Ge 26:1-11). Later made a covenant with Isaac (Ge 26:12-31).

ABLE (ABILITY ENABLE ENABLED ENABLES)
Eze 7:19 and gold will not be *a* to save them
Da 3:17 the God we serve is *a* to save us
Ro 8:39 will be *a* to separate us
14: 4 for the Lord is *a* to make him stand
16:25 to him who is *a* to establish you
2Co 9: 8 God is *a* to make all grace abound
Eph 3:20 him who is *a* to do immeasurably
2Ti 1:12 and am convinced that he is *a*
3:15 which are *a* to make you wise
Heb 7:25 he is *a* to save completely
Jude :24 To him who is *a* to keep you
Rev 5: 5 He is *a* to open the scroll

ABOLISH
Mt 5:17 that I have come to *a* the Law

ABOMINATION
Da 11:31 set up the *a* that causes desolation.

ABOUND (ABOUNDING)
2Co 9: 8 able to make all grace *a* to you,
Php 1: 9 that your love may *a* more

ABOUNDING (ABOUND)
Ex 34: 6 slow to anger, *a* in love
Ps 86: 5 *a* in love to all who call to you.

ABRAHAM

Covenant relation with the LORD (Ge 12:1-3; 13:14-17; 15; 17; 22:15-18; Ex 2:24; Ne 9:8; Ps 105; Mic 7:20; Lk 1:68-75; Ro 4; Heb 6:13-15).

Called from Ur, via Haran, to Canaan (Ge 12:1; Ac 7:2-4; Heb 11:8-10). Moved to Egypt, nearly lost Sarah to Pharaoh (Ge 12:10-20). Divided the land with Lot (Ge 13). Saved Lot from four kings (Ge 14:1-16); blessed by Melchizedek (Ge 14:17-20; Heb 7:1-20). Declared righteous by faith (Ge 15:6; Ro 4:3; Gal 3:6-9). Fathered Ishmael by Hagar (Ge 16).

Name changed from Abram (Ge 17:5; Ne 9:7). Circumcised (Ge 17; Ro 4:9-12). Entertained three visitors (Ge 18); promised a son by Sarah (Ge 18:9-15; 17:16). Moved to Gerar; nearly lost Sarah to Abimelech (Ge 20). Fathered Isaac by Sarah (Ge 21:1-7; Ac 7:8; Heb 11:11-12); sent away Hagar and Ishmael (Ge 21:8-21; Gal 4:22-30). Tested by offering Isaac (Ge 22; Heb 11:17-19; Jas 2:21-24). Sarah died; bought field of Ephron for burial (Ge 23). Secured wife for Isaac (Ge 24). Death (Ge 25:7-11).

ABSALOM

Son of David by Maacah (2Sa 3:3; 1Ch 3:2). Killed Amnon for rape of his sister Tamar; banished by David (2Sa 13). Returned to Jerusalem; received by David (2Sa 14). Rebelled against David; seized kingdom (2Sa 15-17). Killed (2Sa 18).

ABSTAIN (ABSTAINS)
1Pe 2:11 to *a* from sinful desires,

ABSTAINS* (ABSTAIN)
Ro 14: 6 thanks to God; and he who *a,*

ABUNDANCE (ABUNDANT)
Lk 12:15 consist in the *a* of his possessions."
Jude : 2 peace and love be yours in *a.*

ABUNDANT (ABUNDANCE)
Dt 28:11 will grant you *a* prosperity—
Ps 145: 7 will celebrate your *a* goodness
Pr 28:19 works his land will have *a* food,
Ro 5:17 who receive God's *a* provision

ACCEPT (ACCEPTED ACCEPTS)
Ex 23: 8 "Do not *a* a bribe,
Pr 10: 8 The wise in heart *a* commands,
19:20 Listen to advice and *a* instruction,
Ro 15: 7 *A* one another, then, just
Jas 1:21 humbly *a* the word planted in you,

ACCEPTED (ACCEPT)
Lk 4:24 "no prophet is *a* in his hometown.

ACCEPTS (ACCEPT)
Ps 6: 9 the LORD *a* my prayer.
Jn 13:20 whoever *a* anyone I send *a* me;

ACCOMPANY
Mk 16:17 these signs will *a* those who believe
Heb 6: 9 your case—things that *a* salvation.

ACCOMPLISH
Isa 55:11 but will *a* what I desire

ACCORD
Nu 24:13 not do anything of my own *a,*
Jn 10:18 but I lay it down of my own *a.*
12:49 For I did not speak of my own *a,*

ACCOUNT (ACCOUNTABLE)
Mt 12:36 to give *a* on the day of judgment
Ro 14:12 each of us will give an *a* of himself
Heb 4:13 of him to whom we must give *a.*

ACCOUNTABLE (ACCOUNT)
Eze 33: 6 but I will hold the watchman *a*
Ro 3:19 and the whole world held *a* to God.

ACCUSATION (ACCUSE)
1Ti 5:19 Do not entertain an *a*

ACCUSATIONS (ACCUSE)
2Pe 2:11 do not bring slanderous *a*

ACCUSE (ACCUSATION ACCUSATIONS)
Pr 3:30 Do not *a* a man for no reason—
Lk 3:14 and don't *a* people falsely—

ACHAN*

Sin at Jericho caused defeat at Ai; stoned (Jos 7; 22:20; 1Ch 2:7).

ACHE*
Pr 14:13 Even in laughter the heart may *a,*

ACKNOWLEDGE
Mt 10:32 *a* him before my Father in heaven.
1Jn 4: 3 spirit that does not *a* Jesus is not

ACQUIT
Ex 23: 7 to death, for I will not *a* the guilty.

ACTION (ACTIONS ACTIVE ACTS)
Jas 2:17 if it is not accompanied by *a,*
1Pe 1:13 minds for *a;* be self-controlled;

ACTIONS (ACTION)
Mt 11:19 wisdom is proved right by her *a.*"

Gal 6: 4 Each one should test his own *a*.
Tit 1:16 but by their *a* they deny him.

ACTIVE (ACTION)
Heb 4:12 For the word of God is living and *a*

ACTS (ACTION)
Ps 145:12 all men may know of your mighty *a*
150: 2 Praise him for his *a* of power;
Isa 64: 6 all our righteous *a* are like filthy
Mt 6: 1 not to do your '*a* of righteousness'

ADAM
First man (Ge 1:26-2:25; Ro 5:14; 1Ti 2:13). Sin of (Ge 3; Hos 6:7; Ro 5:12-21). Children of (Ge 4:1-5:5). Death of (Ge 5:5; Ro 5:12-21; 1Co 15:22).

ADD
Dt 12:32 do not *a* to it or take away from it.
Pr 30: 6 Do not *a* to his words,
Lk 12:25 by worrying can *a* a single hour
Rev 22:18 God will *a* to him the plagues

ADMIRABLE*
Php 4: 8 whatever is lovely, whatever is *a*—

ADMONISH
Col 3:16 and *a* one another with all wisdom,

ADOPTED (ADOPTION)
Eph 1: 5 In love he predestined us to be *a*

ADOPTION (ADOPTED)
Ro 8:23 as we wait eagerly for our *a* as sons,

ADORE*
SS 1: 4 How right they are to *a* you!

ADORNMENT* (ADORNS)
1Pe 3: 3 should not come from outward *a*,

ADORNS (ADORNMENT)
Ps 93: 5 holiness *a* your house

ADULTERY
Ex 20:14 "You shall not commit *a*.
Mt 5:27 that it was said, 'Do not commit *a*.'
5:28 lustfully has already committed *a*
5:32 the divorced woman commits *a*.
15:19 murder, *a*, sexual immorality, theft

ADULTS*
1Co 14:20 but in your thinking be *a*.

ADVANCED
Job 32: 7 *a* years should teach wisdom.'

ADVANTAGE
Ex 22:22 "Do not take *a* of a widow
Dt 24:14 Do not take *a* of a hired man who is
1Th 4: 6 should wrong his brother or take *a*

ADVERSITY
Pr 17:17 and a brother is born for *a*.

ADVICE
1Ki 12: 8 rejected the *a* the elders
1Ki 12:14 he followed the *a* of the young men
Pr 12: 5 but the *a* of the wicked is deceitful.
12:15 but a wise man listens to *a*.
19:20 Listen to *a* and accept instruction,
20:18 Make plans by seeking *a*;

AFFLICTION
Ro 12:12 patient in *a*, faithful in prayer.

AFRAID (FEAR)
Ge 26:24 Do not be *a*, for I am with you;
Ex 3: 6 because he was *a* to look at God.
Ps 27: 1 of whom shall I be *a*?
56: 3 When I am *a*, / I will trust in you.
Pr 3:24 lie down, you will not be *a*;
Jer 1: 8 Do not be *a* of them, for I am
Mt 8:26 You of little faith, why are you so *a*
10:28 be *a* of the One who can destroy
10:31 So don't be *a*; you are worth more
Mk 5:36 "Don't be *a*; just believe."
Jn 14:27 hearts be troubled and do not be *a*.
Heb 13: 6 Lord is my helper; I will not be *a*.

AGED
Job 12:12 Is not wisdom found among the *a*?
Pr 17: 6 children are a crown to the *a*,

AGREE
Mt 18:19 on earth *a* about anything you ask
Ro 7:16 want to do, I *a* that the law is good.
Php 4: 2 with Syntyche to *a* with each other

AHAB
Son of Omri; king of Israel (1Ki 16:28-22:40), husband of Jezebel (1Ki 16:31). Promoted Baal worship (1Ki 16:31-33); opposed by Elijah (1Ki 17:1; 18; 21), a prophet (1Ki 20:35-43), Micaiah (1Ki 22:1-28). Defeated Ben-Hadad (1Ki 20). Killed for failing to kill Ben-Hadad and for murder of Naboth (1Ki 20:35-21:40).

AHAZ
Son of Jotham; king of Judah, (2Ki 16; 2Ch 28; Isa 7).

AHAZIAH
1. Son of Ahab; king of Israel (1Ki 22:51-2Ki 1:18; 2Ch 20:35-37).
2. Son of Jehoram; king of Judah (2Ki 8:25-29; 9:14-29), also called Jehoahaz (2Ch 21:17-22:9; 25:23).

AIM
1Co 7:34 Her *a* is to be devoted to the Lord
2Co 13:11 *A* for perfection, listen

AIR
Mt 8:20 and birds of the *a* have nests,
1Co 9:26 not fight like a man beating the *a*.
Eph 2: 2 of the ruler of the kingdom of the *a*,
1Th 4:17 clouds to meet the Lord in the *a*.

ALABASTER
Mt 26: 7 came to him with an *a* jar

ALERT
Jos 8: 4 All of you be on the *a*.
Mk 13:33 Be *a*! You do not know
Eph 6:18 be *a* and always keep on praying
1Th 5: 6 but let us be *a* and self-controlled.

ALIEN (ALIENATED)
Ex 22:21 "Do not mistreat an *a*

ALIENATED (ALIEN)
Gal 5: 4 by law have been *a* from Christ;

ALIVE (LIVE)
Ac 1: 3 convincing proofs that he was *a*.
Ro 6:11 but *a* to God in Christ Jesus.
1Co 15:22 so in Christ all will be made *a*.

ALMIGHTY (MIGHT)
Ge 17: 1 "I am God *A*; walk before me
Job 11: 7 Can you probe the limits of the *A*?
33: 4 the breath of the *A* gives me life.
Ps 91: 1 will rest in the shadow of the *A*.
Isa 6: 3 "Holy, holy, holy is the LORD *A*;

ALTAR
Ge 22: 9 his son Isaac and laid him on the *a*,
Ex 27: 1 "Build an *a* of acacia wood,
1Ki 18:30 and he repaired the *a* of the LORD
2Ch 4: 1 made a bronze *a* twenty cubits
4:19 the golden *a*; the tables

ALWAYS
Ps 16: 8 I have set the LORD *a* before me.
51: 3 and my sin is *a* before me.
Mt 26:11 The poor you will *a* have with you,
28:20 And surely I will be with you *a*,
1Co 13: 7 *a* protects, *a* trusts, *a* hopes, *a*
Php 4: 4 Rejoice in the Lord *a*.
1Pe 3:15 *A* be prepared to give an answer

AMAZIAH
Son of Joash; king of Judah (2Ki 14; 2Ch 25).

AMBASSADORS
2Co 5:20 We are therefore Christ's *a*,

AMBITION
Ro 15:20 It has always been my *a*
1Th 4:11 Make it your *a* to lead a quiet life,

AMON
Son of Manasseh; king of Judah (2Ki 21:18-26; 1Ch 3:14; 2Ch 33:21-25).

ANANIAS
1. Husband of Sapphira; died for lying to God (Ac 5:1-11).
2. Disciple who baptized Saul (Ac 9:10-19).
3. High priest at Paul's arrest (Ac 22:30-24:1).

ANCHOR
Heb 6:19 We have this hope as an *a*

ANCIENT
Da 7: 9 and the *A* of Days took his seat.

ANDREW*
Apostle; brother of Simon Peter (Mt 4:18; 10:2; Mk 1:16-18, 29; 3:18; 13:3; Lk 6:14; Jn 1:35-44; 6:8-9; 12:22; Ac 1:13).

ANGEL (ANGELS ARCHANGEL)
Ps 34: 7 The *a* of the LORD encamps
Ac 6:15 his face was like the face of an *a*.
2Co 11:14 Satan himself masquerades as an *a*
Gal 1: 8 or an *a* from heaven should preach

ANGELS (ANGEL)
Ps 91:11 command his *a* concerning you
Mt 18:10 For I tell you that their *a*
25:41 prepared for the devil and his *a*.
Lk 20:36 for they are like the *a*.
1Co 6: 3 you not know that we will judge *a*?
Heb 1: 4 as much superior to the *a*
1:14 Are not all *a* ministering spirits
2: 7 made him a little lower than the *a*;
13: 2 some people have entertained *a*
1Pe 1:12 Even *a* long to look
2Pe 2: 4 For if God did not spare *a*

ANGER (ANGERED ANGRY)
Ex 32:10 alone so that my *a* may burn
34: 6 slow to *a*, abounding in love
Dt 29:28 In furious *a* and in great wrath
2Ki 22:13 Great is the LORD's *a* that burns
Ps 30: 5 For his *a* lasts only a moment,
Pr 15: 1 but a harsh word stirs up *a*.
29:11 A fool gives full vent to his *a*,

ANGERED (ANGER)
Pr 22:24 do not associate with one easily *a*,
1Co 13: 5 it is not easily *a*, it keeps no record

ANGRY (ANGER)
Ps 2:12 Kiss the Son, lest he be *a*
Pr 29:22 An *a* man stirs up dissension,
Jas 1:19 slow to speak and slow to become *a*

ANGUISH
Ps 118: 5 In my *a* I cried to the LORD,

ANOINT
Ps 23: 5 You *a* my head with oil;
Jas 5:14 and *a* him with oil in the name

ANT*
Pr 6: 6 Go to the *a*, you sluggard;

ANTICHRIST
1Jn 2:18 have heard that the *a* is coming,
2Jn : 7 person is the deceiver and the *a*.

ANTIOCH
Ac 11:26 were called Christians first at *A*.

ANXIETY (ANXIOUS)
1Pe 5: 7 Cast all your *a* on him

ANXIOUS (ANXIETY)
Pr 12:25 An *a* heart weighs a man down,
Php 4: 6 Do not be *a* about anything,

APOLLOS*
Christian from Alexandria, learned in the Scriptures; instructed by Aquila and Priscilla (Ac 18:24-28). Ministered at Corinth (Ac 19:1; 1Co 1:12; 3; Tit 3:13).

APOSTLES
See also Andrew, Bartholomew, James, John, Judas, Matthew, Nathanael, Paul, Peter, Philip, Simon, Thaddaeus, Thomas.
Mk 3:14 twelve—designating them *a*—
Ac 1:26 so he was added to the eleven *a*.
2:43 signs were done by the *a*.
1Co 12:28 God has appointed first of all *a*,
15: 9 For I am the least of the *a*
2Co 11:13 masquerading as *a* of Christ.
Eph 2:20 built on the foundation of the *a*

APPEAR (APPEARANCE APPEARING)
Mk 13:22 false prophets will *a* and perform
2Co 5:10 we must all *a* before the judgment
Col 3: 4 also will *a* with him in glory.
Heb 9:24 now to *a* for us in God's presence.
9:28 and he will *a* a second time,

APPEARANCE (APPEAR)
1Sa 16: 7 Man looks at the outward *a*,
Gal 2: 6 God does not judge by external *a*—

APPEARING (APPEAR)
2Ti 4: 8 to all who have longed for his *a*.
Tit 2:13 the glorious *a* of our great God

APPLY
Pr 22:17 *a* your heart to what I teach,
23:12 *A* your heart to instruction

APPROACH
Eph 3:12 in him we may *a* God with freedom
Heb 4:16 Let us then *a* the throne of grace

APPROVED
2Ti 2:15 to present yourself to God as one *a*,

AQUILA*
Husband of Priscilla; co-worker with Paul, instructor of Apollos (Ac 18; Ro 16:3; 1Co 16:19; 2Ti 4:19).

ARARAT
Ge 8: 4 came to rest on the mountains of *A*.

ARCHANGEL* (ANGEL)
1Th 4:16 with the voice of the *a*
Jude : 9 *a* Michael, when he was disputing

ARCHITECT*
Heb 11:10 whose *a* and builder is God.

ARK
Ge 6:14 So make yourself an *a*
Dt 10: 5 put the tablets in the *a* I had made,
2Ch 35: 3 "Put the sacred *a* in the temple that
Heb 9: 4 This *a* contained the gold jar

ARM (ARMY)
Nu 11:23 "Is the LORD's *a* too short?
1Pe 4: 1 *a* yourselves also with the same

ARMAGEDDON*
Rev 16:16 that in Hebrew is called *A*.

ARMOR (ARMY)
1Ki 20:11 on his *a* should not boast like one
Eph 6:11 Put on the full *a* of God
6:13 Therefore put on the full *a* of God,

ARMS (ARMY)
Dt 33:27 underneath are the everlasting *a*.
Ps 18:32 It is God who *a* me with strength
Pr 31:20 She opens her *a* to the poor
Isa 40:11 He gathers the lambs in his *a*
Mk 10:16 And he took the children in his *a*,

ARMY (ARM ARMOR ARMS)
Ps 33:16 No king is saved by the size of his *a*
Rev 19:19 the rider on the horse and his *a*.

AROMA
2Co 2:15 For we are to God the *a* of Christ

ARRAYED*
Ps 110: 3 *A* in holy majesty,
Isa 61:10 and *a* me in a robe of righteousness

ARROGANT
Ro 11:20 Do not be *a*, but be afraid.

ARROWS
Eph 6:16 you can extinguish all the flaming *a*

ASA
King of Judah (1Ki 15:8-24; 1Ch 3:10; 2Ch 14-16).

ASCENDED
Eph 4: 8 "When he *a* on high,

ASCRIBE
1Ch 16:28 *a* to the LORD glory and strength,
Job 36: 3 I will *a* justice to my Maker.
Ps 29: 2 *A* to the LORD the glory due his

ASHAMED (SHAME)
Lk 9:26 If anyone is *a* of me and my words,
Ro 1:16 I am not *a* of the gospel,
2Ti 1: 8 So do not be *a* to testify about our
2:15 who does not need to be *a*

ASSIGNED
Mk 13:34 with his *a* task, and tells the one
1Co 3: 5 as the Lord has *a* to each his task.
7:17 place in life that the Lord *a* to him

ASSOCIATE
Pr 22:24 do not *a* with one easily angered,
Ro 12:16 but be willing to *a* with people
1Co 5:11 am writing you that you must not *a*
2Th 3:14 Do not *a* with him,

ASSURANCE
Heb 10:22 with a sincere heart in full *a* of faith

ASTRAY
Pr 10:17 ignores correction leads others *a*.

Isa 53: 6 We all, like sheep, have gone *a*,
Jer 50: 6 their shepherds have led them *a*
Jn 16: 1 you so that you will not go *a*.
1Pe 2:25 For you were like sheep going *a*,
1Jn 3: 7 do not let anyone lead you *a*.

ATHALIAH
Evil queen of Judah (2Ki 11; 2Ch 23).

ATHLETE*
2Ti 2: 5 if anyone competes as an *a*,

ATONEMENT
Ex 25:17 "Make an *a* cover of pure gold—
30:10 Once a year Aaron shall make *a*
Lev 17:11 it is the blood that makes *a*
23:27 this seventh month is the Day of *A*.
Nu 25:13 and made *a* for the Israelites."
Ro 3:25 presented him as a sacrifice of *a*,
Heb 2:17 that he might make *a* for the sins

ATTENTION
Pr 4: 1 pay *a* and gain understanding.
5: 1 My son, pay *a* to my wisdom,
22:17 Pay *a* and listen to the sayings
Tit 1:14 and will pay no *a* to Jewish myths

ATTITUDE (ATTITUDES)
Eph 4:23 new in the *a* of your minds;
Php 2: 5 Your *a* should be the same
1Pe 4: 1 yourselves also with the same *a*,

ATTITUDES (ATTITUDE)
Heb 4:12 it judges the thoughts and *a*

ATTRACTIVE
Tit 2:10 teaching about God our Savior *a*.

AUTHORITIES (AUTHORITY)
Ro 13: 5 it is necessary to submit to the *a*,
13: 6 for the *a* are God's servants,
Tit 3: 1 people to be subject to rulers and *a*,
1Pe 3:22 *a* and powers in submission to him.

AUTHORITY (AUTHORITIES)
Mt 7:29 because he taught as one who had *a*
9: 6 the Son of Man has *a* on earth
28:18 "All *a* in heaven and on earth has
Ro 13: 1 for there is no *a* except that which
13: 2 rebels against the *a* is rebelling
1Co 11:10 to have a sign of *a* on her head.
1Ti 2: 2 for kings and all those in *a*,
2:12 to teach or to have *a* over a man;
Heb 13:17 your leaders and submit to their *a*.

AVENGE (VENGEANCE)
Dt 32:35 It is mine to *a*; I will repay.

AVOID
Pr 20: 3 It is to a man's honor to *a* strife,
20:19 so *a* a man who talks too much.
1Th 4: 3 you should *a* sexual immorality;
5:22 *A* every kind of evil.
2Ti 2:16 *A* godless chatter, because those
Tit 3: 9 But *a* foolish controversies

AWAKE
Ps 17:15 when I *a*, I will be satisfied

AWE (AWESOME)
Job 25: 2 "Dominion and *a* belong to God;
Ps 119:120 I stand in *a* of your laws.
Ecc 5: 7 Therefore stand in *a* of God.
Isa 29:23 will stand in *a* of the God of Israel.
Jer 33: 9 they will be in *a* and will tremble
Hab 3: 2 I stand in *a* of your deeds,
Mal 2: 5 and stood in *a* of my name.
Mt 9: 8 they were filled with *a*;
Lk 7:16 They were all filled with *a*
Ac 2:43 Everyone was filled with *a*,
Heb 12:28 acceptably with reverence and *a*,

AWESOME (AWE)
Ge 28:17 and said, "How *a* is this place!
Ex 15:11 *a* in glory,
Dt 7:21 is among you, is a great and *a* God.
10:17 the great God, mighty and *a*,
28:58 revere this glorious and *a* name—
Jdg 13: 6 like an angel of God, very *a*.
Ne 1: 5 of heaven, the great and *a* God,
9:32 the great, mighty and *a* God,
Job 10:16 again display your *a* power
37:22 God comes in *a* majesty.
Ps 45: 4 let your right hand display *a* deeds.
47: 2 How *a* is the LORD Most High,
66: 5 how *a* his works in man's behalf!
68:35 You are *a*, O God,
89: 7 he is more *a* than all who surround
99: 3 praise your great and *a* name—
111: 9 holy and *a* is his name.
145: 6 of the power of your *a* works,
Da 9: 4 "O Lord, the great and *a* God,

BAAL
1Ki 18:25 Elijah said to the prophets of *B*,

BAASHA
King of Israel (1Ki 15:16-16:7; 2Ch 16:1-6).

BABIES (BABY)
Lk 18:15 also bringing *b* to Jesus
1Pe 2: 2 Like newborn *b*, crave pure

BABY (BABIES)
Isa 49:15 "Can a mother forget the *b*
Lk 1:44 the *b* in my womb leaped for joy.
2:12 You will find a *b* wrapped in strips
Jn 16:21 but when her *b* is born she forgets

BABYLON
Ps 137: 1 By the rivers of *B* we sat and wept

BACKSLIDING
Jer 3:22 I will cure you of *b*."
14: 7 For our *b* is great;
Eze 37:23 them from all their sinful *b*,

BALAAM
Prophet who attempted to curse Israel (Nu 22-24; Dt 23:4-5; 2Pe 2:15; Jude 11). Killed (Nu 31:8; Jos 13:22).

BALM
Jer 8:22 Is there no *b* in Gilead?

BANISH
Jer 25:10 I will *b* from them the sounds of joy

BANQUET
SS 2: 4 He has taken me to the *b* hall,
Lk 14:13 when you give a *b*, invite the poor,

BAPTIZE (BAPTIZED)
Mt 3:11 He will *b* you with the Holy Spirit
Mk 1: 8 he will *b* you with the Holy Spirit."
1Co 1:17 For Christ did not send me to *b*,

BAPTIZED (BAPTIZE)
Mt 3: 6 they were *b* by him in the Jordan
Mk 1: 9 and was *b* by John in the Jordan.
10:38 or be *b* with the baptism I am
16:16 believes and is *b* will be saved,
Jn 4: 2 in fact it was not Jesus who *b*,
Ac 1: 5 but in a few days you will be *b*

BARABBAS
Mt 27:26 Then he released *B* to them.

BARBS*
Nu 33:55 allow to remain will become *b*

BARE
Heb 4:13 and laid *b* before the eyes of him

BARNABAS*
Disciple, originally Joseph (Ac 4:36), prophet (Ac 13:1), apostle (Ac 14:14). Brought Paul to apostles (Ac 9:27), Antioch (Ac 11:22-29; Gal 2:1-13), on the first missionary journey (Ac 13-14). Together at Jerusalem Council, they separated over John Mark (Ac 15). Later co-workers (1Co 9:6; Col 4:10).

BARREN
Ps 113: 9 He settles the *b* woman

BARTHOLOMEW*
Apostle (Mt 10:3; Mk 3:18; Lk 6:14; Ac 1:13). Possibly also known as Nathanael (Jn 1:45-49; 21:2).

BATH
Jn 13:10 person who has had a *b* needs only

BATHSHEBA
Wife of Uriah who committed adultery with and became wife of David (2Sa 11), mother of Solomon (2Sa 12:24; 1Ki 1-2; 1Ch 3:5).

BATTLE
2Ch 20:15 For the *b* is not yours, but God's.
Ps 24: 8 the LORD mighty in *b*.
Ecc 9:11 or the *b* to the strong,

BEAR (BEARING BIRTH BIRTHRIGHT BORN FIRSTBORN NEWBORN)
Ge 4:13 punishment is more than I can *b*.

Ps 38: 4 like a burden too heavy to *b.*
Isa 53:11 and he will *b* their iniquities.
Da 7: 5 beast, which looked like a *b.*
Mt 7:18 A good tree cannot *b* bad fruit,
Jn 15: 2 branch that does *b* fruit he prunes
15:16 and appointed you to go and *b* fruit—
Ro 15: 1 ought to *b* with the failings
1Co 10:13 tempted beyond what you can *b.*
Col 3:13 *B* with each other and forgive

BEARING (BEAR)
Eph 4: 2 *b* with one another in love.
Col 1:10 *b* fruit in every good work,

BEAST
Rev 13:18 him calculate the number of the *b,*

BEAT (BEATING)
Isa 2: 4 They will *b* their swords
Joel 3:10 *B* your plowshares into swords
1Co 9:27 I *b* my body and make it my slave

BEATING (BEAT)
1Co 9:26 I do not fight like a man *b* the air.
1Pe 2:20 if you receive a *b* for doing wrong

BEAUTIFUL (BEAUTY)
Ge 6: 2 that the daughters of men were *b,*
12:11 "I know what a *b* woman you are.
12:14 saw that she was a very *b* woman.
24:16 The girl was very *b,* a virgin;
26: 7 of Rebekah, because she is *b."*
29:17 Rachel was lovely in form, and *b.*
Job 38:31 "Can you bind the *b* Pleiades?
Pr 11:22 is a *b* woman who shows no
Ecc 3:11 He has made everything *b*
Isa 4: 2 of the LORD will be *b*
52: 7 How *b* on the mountains
Eze 20: 6 and honey, the most *b* of all lands.
Zec 9:17 How attractive and *b* they will be!
Mt 23:27 which look *b* on the outside
26:10 She has done a *b* thing to me.
Ro 10:15 "How *b* are the feet
1Pe 3: 5 in God used to make themselves *b.*

BEAUTY (BEAUTIFUL)
Ps 27: 4 to gaze upon the *b* of the LORD
45:11 The king is enthralled by your *b;*
Pr 31:30 is deceptive, and *b* is fleeting;
Isa 33:17 Your eyes will see the king in his *b*
53: 2 He had no *b* or majesty
61: 3 to bestow on them a crown of *b*
Eze 28:12 full of wisdom and perfect in *b.*
1Pe 3: 4 the unfading *b* of a gentle

BED
Heb 13: 4 and the marriage *b* kept pure,

BEELZEBUB
Lk 11:15 "By *B,* the prince of demons,

BEER
Pr 20: 1 Wine is a mocker and *b* a brawler;

BEERSHEBA
Jdg 20: 1 all the Israelites from Dan to *B*

BEGINNING
Ge 1: 1 In the *b* God created the heavens
Ps 102: 25 In the *b* you laid the foundations
111: 10 of the LORD is the *b* of wisdom;
Pr 1: 7 of the LORD is the *b* of knowledge
Jn 1: 1 In the *b* was the Word,
1Jn 1: 1 That which was from the *b,*
Rev 21: 6 and the Omega, the *B* and the End.

BEHAVE
Ro 13:13 Let us *b* decently, as in the daytime

BELIEVE (BELIEVED BELIEVER BELIEVERS BELIEVES BELIEVING)
Mt 18: 6 one of these little ones who *b* in me
21:22 If you *b,* you will receive whatever
Mk 1:15 Repent and *b* the good news!"
9:24 "I do *b;* help me overcome my
16:17 signs will accompany those who *b:*
Lk 8:50 just *b,* and she will be healed."
24:25 to *b* all that the prophets have
Jn 1: 7 that through him all men might *b.*
3:18 does not *b* stands condemned
6:29 to *b* in the one he has sent."
10:38 you do not *b* me, *b* the miracles,
11:27 "I *b* that you are the Christ,
14:11 *B* me when I say that I am
16:30 This makes us *b* that you came
16:31 "You *b* at last!" Jesus answered.
17:21 that the world may *b* that you have
20:27 Stop doubting and *b."*
20:31 written that you may *b* that Jesus is
Ac 16:31 They replied, "*B* in the Lord Jesus,
24:14 I *b* everything that agrees
Ro 3:22 faith in Jesus Christ to all who *b.*
4:11 he is the father of all who *b*
10: 9 *b* in your heart that God raised him
10:14 And how can they *b* in the one
16:26 so that all nations might *b*
1Th 4:14 We *b* that Jesus died and rose again
2Th 2:11 delusion so that they will *b* the lie
1Ti 4:10 and especially of those who *b.*
Tit 1: 6 a man whose children *b*
Heb 11: 6 comes to him must *b* that he exists
Jas 2:19 Even the demons *b* that—
1Jn 4: 1 Dear friends, do not *b* every spirit,

BELIEVED (BELIEVE)
Ge 15: 6 Abram *b* the LORD, and he
Jnh 3: 5 The Ninevites *b* God.
Jn 1:12 to those who *b* in his name,
2:22 Then they *b* the Scripture
3:18 because he has not *b* in the name
20: 8 He saw and *b.*
20:29 who have not seen and yet have *b."*
Ac 13:48 were appointed for eternal life *b.*
Ro 4: 3 Scripture say? "Abraham *b* God,
10:14 call on the one they have not *b* in?
1Co 15: 2 Otherwise, you have *b* in vain.
Gal 3: 6 Consider Abraham: "He *b* God,
2Ti 1:12 because I know whom I have *b,*
Jas 2:23 that says, "Abraham *b* God,

BELIEVER (BELIEVE)
1Co 7:12 brother has a wife who is not a *b*
2Co 6:15 What does a *b* have in common

BELIEVERS (BELIEVE)
Ac 4:32 All the *b* were one in heart
5:12 And all the *b* used to meet together
1Co 6: 5 to judge a dispute between *b?*
1Ti 4:12 set an example for the *b* in speech,
1Pe 2:17 Love the brotherhood of *b,*

BELIEVES (BELIEVE)
Pr 14:15 A simple man *b* anything,
Mk 9:23 is possible for him who *b."*
11:23 *b* that what he says will happen,
16:16 Whoever *b* and is baptized will be
Jn 3:16 that whoever *b* in him shall not
3:36 Whoever *b* in the Son has eternal
5:24 *b* him who sent me has eternal life
6:35 and he who *b* in me will never be
6:40 and *b* in him shall have eternal life,
6:47 he who *b* has everlasting life.
7:38 Whoever *b* in me, as the Scripture
11:26 and *b* in me will never die.
Ro 1:16 for the salvation of everyone who *b*
10: 4 righteousness for everyone who *b.*
1Jn 5: 1 Everyone who *b* that Jesus is
5: 5 Only he who *b* that Jesus is the Son

BELIEVING (BELIEVE)
Jn 20:31 and that by *b* you may have life

BELONG (BELONGS)
Dt 29:29 The secret things *b*
Job 25: 2 "Dominion and awe *b* to God;
Ps 47: 9 for the kings of the earth *b* to God;
95: 4 and the mountain peaks *b* to him.
Jn 8:44 You *b* to your father, the devil,
15:19 As it is, you do not *b* to the world,
Ro 1: 6 called to *b* to Jesus Christ.

Ro 7: 4 that you might *b* to another,
14: 8 we live or die, we *b* to the Lord.
Gal 5:24 Those who *b* to Christ Jesus have
1Th 5: 8 But since we *b* to the day, let us be

BELONGS (BELONG)
Job 41:11 Everything under heaven *b* to me.
Ps 111: 10 To him *b* eternal praise.
Eze 18: 4 For every living soul *b* to me,
Jn 8:47 He who *b* to God hears what God
Ro 12: 5 each member *b* to all the others.

BELOVED (LOVE)
Dt 33:12 "Let the *b* of the LORD rest secure

BELT
Isa 11: 5 Righteousness will be his *b*
Eph 6:14 with the *b* of truth buckled

BENEFIT (BENEFITS)
Ro 6:22 the *b* you reap leads to holiness,
2Co 4:15 All this is for your *b*,

BENEFITS (BENEFIT)
Ps 103: 2 and forget not all his *b*.
Jn 4:38 you have reaped the *b* of their labor

BENJAMIN
Twelfth son of Jacob by Rachel (Ge 35:16-24; 46:19-21; 1Ch 2:2). Jacob refused to send him to Egypt, but relented (Ge 42-45).

BEREANS*
Ac 17:11 the *B* were of more noble character

BESTOWS
Ps 84:11 the LORD *b* favor and honor;

BETHLEHEM
Mt 2: 1 After Jesus was born in *B* in Judea,

BETRAY
Pr 25: 9 do not *b* another man's confidence,

BIND (BINDS)
Dt 6: 8 and *b* them on your foreheads.
Pr 6:21 *B* them upon your heart forever;
Isa 61: 1 me to *b* up the brokenhearted,
Mt 16:19 whatever you *b* on earth will be

BINDS (BIND)
Ps 147: 3 and *b* up their wounds.
Isa 30:26 when the LORD *b* up the bruises

BIRDS
Mt 8:20 and *b* of the air have nests,

BIRTH (BEAR)
Ps 58: 3 Even from *b* the wicked go astray;
Mt 1:18 This is how the *b* of Jesus Christ
1Pe 1: 3 great mercy he has given us new *b*

BIRTHRIGHT (BEAR)
Ge 25:34 So Esau despised his *b*.

BLAMELESS
Ge 17: 1 walk before me and be *b*.
Job 1: 1 This man was *b* and upright;
Ps 84:11 from those whose walk is *b*.
119: 1 Blessed are they whose ways are *b*,
Pr 19: 1 Better a poor man whose walk is *b*
1Co 1: 8 so that you will be *b* on the day
Eph 5:27 any other blemish, but holy and *b*.
Php 2:15 so that you may become *b* and pure
1Th 3:13 hearts so that you will be *b*
5:23 and body be kept *b* at the coming
Tit 1: 6 An elder must be *b*, the husband of
Heb 7:26 *b*, pure, set apart from sinners,
2Pe 3:14 effort to be found spotless, *b*

BLASPHEMES
Mk 3:29 whoever *b* against the Holy Spirit

BLEMISH
1Pe 1:19 a lamb without *b* or defect.

BLESS (BLESSED BLESSING BLESSINGS)
Ge 12: 3 I will *b* those who *b* you,
Ro 12:14 Bless those who persecute you; *b*

BLESSED (BLESS)
Ge 1:22 God *b* them and said, "Be fruitful
2: 3 And God *b* the seventh day
22:18 nations on earth will be *b*,
Ps 1: 1 *B* is the man
2:12 *B* are all who take refuge in him.
33:12 *B* is the nation whose God is
41: 1 *B* is he who has regard for the weak
84: 5 *B* are those whose strength is
106: 3 *B* are they who maintain justice,
112: 1 *B* is the man who fears the LORD,
118: 26 *B* is he who comes in the name
Pr 29:18 but *b* is he who keeps the law.
31:28 Her children arise and call her *b*;
Mt 5: 3 saying: "*B* are the poor in spirit,
5: 4 *B* are those who mourn,
5: 5 *B* are the meek,
5: 6 *B* are those who hunger
5: 7 *B* are the merciful,
5: 8 *B* are the pure in heart,
5: 9 *B* are the peacemakers,
5:10 *B* are those who are persecuted
5:11 "*B* are you when people insult you,
Lk 1:48 on all generations will call me *b*,
Jn 12:13 "*B* is he who comes in the name
Ac 20:35 'It is more *b* to give than to receive
Tit 2:13 while we wait for the *b* hope—
Jas 1:12 *B* is the man who perseveres
Rev 1: 3 *B* is the one who reads the words
22:14 "*B* are those who wash their robes,

BLESSING (BLESS)
Eze 34:26 there will be showers of *b*.

BLESSINGS (BLESS)
Pr 10: 6 *B* crown the head of the righteous,

BLIND
Mt 15:14 a *b* man leads a *b* man, both will fall
23:16 "Woe to you, *b* guides! You say,
Jn 9:25 I was *b* but now I see!"

BLOOD
Ge 9: 6 "Whoever sheds the *b* of man,
Ex 12:13 and when I see the *b*, I will pass
24: 8 "This is the *b* of the covenant that
Lev 17:11 For the life of a creature is in the *b*,
Ps 72:14 for precious is their *b* in his sight.
Pr 6:17 hands that shed innocent *b*,
Mt 26:28 This is my *b* of the covenant,
Ro 3:25 of atonement, through faith in his *b*
5: 9 have now been justified by his *b*,
1Co 11:25 cup is the new covenant in my *b*;
Eph 1: 7 we have redemption through his *b*,
2:13 near through the *b* of Christ.
Col 1:20 by making peace through his *b*,
Heb 9:12 once for all by his own *b*,
9:22 of *b* there is no forgiveness.
1Pe 1:19 but with the precious *b* of Christ,
1Jn 1: 7 and the *b* of Jesus, his Son,
Rev 1: 5 has freed us from our sins by his *b*,
5: 9 with your *b* you purchased men
7:14 white in the *b* of the Lamb.
12:11 him by the *b* of the Lamb

BLOT (BLOTS)
Ex 32:32 then *b* me out of the book you have
Ps 51: 1 *b* out my transgressions.
Rev 3: 5 I will never *b* out his name

BLOTS (BLOT)
Isa 43:25 "I, even I, am he who *b* out

BLOWN
Eph 4:14 and *b* here and there by every wind
Jas 1: 6 doubts is like a wave of the sea, *b*

BOAST
1Ki 20:11 armor should not *b* like one who
Ps 34: 2 My soul will *b* in the LORD;
44: 8 In God we make our *b* all day long,
Pr 27: 1 Do not *b* about tomorrow,
1Co 1:31 Let him who boasts *b* in the Lord."
Gal 6:14 May I never *b* except in the cross
Eph 2: 9 not by works, so that no one can *b*.

BOAZ
Wealthy Bethlehemite who showed favor to Ruth (Ru 2), married her (Ru 4). Ancestor of David (Ru 4:18-22; 1Ch 2:12-15), Jesus (Mt 1:5-16; Lk 3:23-32).

BODIES (BODY)
Ro 12: 1 to offer your *b* as living sacrifices,
1Co 6:15 not know that your *b* are members

Eph 5:28 to love their wives as their own *b*.

BODY (BODIES)
Zec 13: 6 What are these wounds on your *b*?'
Mt 10:28 afraid of those who kill the *b*
26:26 saying, "Take and eat; this is my *b*
26:41 spirit is willing, but the *b* is weak."
Jn 13:10 wash his feet; his whole *b* is clean.
Ro 6:13 Do not offer the parts of your *b*
12: 4 us has one *b* with many members,
1Co 6:19 not know that your *b* is a temple
11:24 "This is my *b*, which is for you;
12:12 The *b* is a unit, though it is made up
Eph 5:30 for we are members of his *b*.

BOLD (BOLDNESS)
Ps 138: 3 you made me *b* and stouthearted.
Pr 21:29 A wicked man puts up a *b* front,
28: 1 but the righteous are as *b* as a lion.

BOLDNESS* (BOLD)
Ac 4:29 to speak your word with great *b*.

BONDAGE
Ezr 9: 9 God has not deserted us in our *b*.

BOOK (BOOKS)
Jos 1: 8 Do not let this *B* of the Law depart
Ne 8: 8 They read from the *B* of the Law
Jn 20:30 which are not recorded in this *b*.
Php 4: 3 whose names are in the *b* of life.
Rev 21:27 written in the Lamb's *b* of life.

BOOKS (BOOK)
Ecc 12:12 Of making many *b* there is no end,

BORN (BEAR)
Isa 9: 6 For to us a child is *b*,
Jn 3: 7 at my saying, 'You must be *b* again
1Pe 1:23 For you have been *b* again,
1Jn 4: 7 Everyone who loves has been *b*
5: 1 believes that Jesus is the Christ is *b*

BORROWER
Pr 22: 7 and the *b* is servant to the lender.

BOUGHT
Ac 20:28 which he *b* with his own blood.
1Co 6:20 You are not your own; you were *b*
7:23 You were *b* at a price; do not
2Pe 2: 1 the sovereign Lord who *b* them—

BOW
Ps 95: 6 Come, let us *b* down in worship,
Isa 45:23 Before me every knee will *b*;
Ro 14:11 'every knee will *b* before me;
Php 2:10 name of Jesus every knee should *b*,

BRANCH (BRANCHES)
Isa 4: 2 In that day the *B* of the LORD will
Jer 33:15 I will make a righteous *B* sprout

BRANCHES (BRANCH)
Jn 15: 5 "I am the vine; you are the *b*.

BRAVE
2Sa 2: 7 Now then, be strong and *b*,

BREAD
Dt 8: 3 that man does not live on *b* alone
Pr 30: 8 but give me only my daily *b*.
Ecc 11: 1 Cast your *b* upon the waters,
Isa 55: 2 Why spend money on what is not *b*
Mt 4: 4 'Man does not live on *b* alone,
6:11 Give us today our daily *b*.
Jn 6:35 Jesus declared, "I am the *b* of life.
21:13 took the *b* and gave it to them,
1Co 11:23 took *b*, and when he had given

BREAK (BREAKING BROKEN)
Nu 30: 2 he must not *b* his word
Jdg 2: 1 'I will never *b* my covenant
Isa 42: 3 A bruised reed he will not *b*,
Mt 12:20 A bruised reed he will not *b*,

BREAKING (BREAK)
Jas 2:10 at just one point is guilty of *b* all

BREASTPIECE (BREASTPLATE)
Ex 28:15 Fashion a *b* for making decisions—

BREASTPLATE* (BREASTPIECE)
Isa 59:17 He put on righteousness as his *b*,
Eph 6:14 with the *b* of righteousness in place
1Th 5: 8 putting on faith and love as a *b*,

BREATHED (GOD-BREATHED)
Ge 2: 7 *b* into his nostrils the breath of life,
Jn 20:22 And with that he *b* on them

BREEDS*
Pr 13:10 Pride only *b* quarrels,

BRIBE
Ex 23: 8 "Do not accept a *b*,
Pr 6:35 will refuse the *b*, however great it

BRIDE
Rev 19: 7 and his *b* has made herself ready,

BRIGHTER (BRIGHTNESS)
Pr 4:18 shining ever *b* till the full light

BRIGHTNESS (BRIGHTER)
2Sa 22:13 Out of the *b* of his presence
Da 12: 3 who are wise will shine like the *b*

BROAD
Mt 7:13 and *b* is the road that leads

BROKEN (BREAK)
Ps 51:17 The sacrifices of God are a *b* spirit;
Ecc 4:12 of three strands is not quickly *b*.
Jn 10:35 and the Scripture cannot be *b*—

BROKENHEARTED* (HEART)
Ps 34:18 The LORD is close to the *b*
109: 16 and the needy and the *b*.
147: 3 He heals the *b*
Isa 61: 1 He has sent me to bind up the *b*,

BROTHER (BROTHER'S BROTHERS)
Pr 17:17 and a *b* is born for adversity.
18:24 a friend who sticks closer than a *b*.
27:10 neighbor nearby than a *b* far away.
Mt 5:24 and be reconciled to your *b*;
18:15 "If your *b* sins against you,
Mk 3:35 Whoever does God's will is my *b*
Lk 17: 3 "If your *b* sins, rebuke him,
1Co 8:13 if what I eat causes my *b* to fall
1Jn 2:10 Whoever loves his *b* lives
4:21 loves God must also love his *b*.

BROTHER'S (BROTHER)
Ge 4: 9 "Am I my *b* keeper?" The LORD

BROTHERS (BROTHER)
Ps 133: 1 is when *b* live together in unity!
Pr 6:19 who stirs up dissension among *b*.
Mt 25:40 one of the least of these *b* of mine,
Mk 10:29 or *b* or sisters or mother or father
Heb 13: 1 Keep on loving each other as *b*.
1Pe 3: 8 be sympathetic, love as *b*,
1Jn 3:14 death to life, because we love our *b*.

BUILD (BUILDING BUILDS BUILT)
Mt 16:18 and on this rock I will *b* my church,
Ac 20:32 which can *b* you up and give you
1Co 14:12 excel in gifts that *b* up the church.
1Th 5:11 one another and *b* each other up,

BUILDING (BUILD)
1Co 3: 9 you are God's field, God's *b*.
2Co 10: 8 us for *b* you up rather
Eph 4:29 helpful for *b* others up according

BUILDS (BUILD)
Ps 127: 1 Unless the LORD *b* the house,
1Co 3:10 one should be careful how he *b*.
8: 1 Knowledge puffs up, but love *b* up.

BUILT (BUILD)
Mt 7:24 is like a wise man who *b* his house
Eph 2:20 *b* on the foundation of the apostles
4:12 the body of Christ may be *b* up

BURDEN (BURDENED BURDENS)
Ps 38: 4 like a *b* too heavy to bear.
Mt 11:30 my yoke is easy and my *b* is light."

BURDENED (BURDEN)
Gal 5: 1 do not let yourselves be *b* again

BURDENS (BURDEN)
Ps 68:19 who daily bears our *b*.
Gal 6: 2 Carry each other's *b*,

BURIED
Ro 6: 4 *b* with him through baptism
1Co 15: 4 that he was *b*, that he was raised

BURNING
Lev 6: 9 the fire must be kept *b* on the altar.
Ro 12:20 you will heap *b* coals on his head."

BUSINESS
Da 8:27 and went about the king's *b*.
1Th 4:11 to mind your own *b* and to work

BUSY
1Ki 20:40 While your servant was *b* here
2Th 3:11 They are not *b*; they are
Tit 2: 5 to be *b* at home, to be kind,

CAESAR
Mt 22:21 "Give to *C* what is Caesar's,

CAIN
Firstborn of Adam (Ge 4:1), murdered brother Abel (Ge 4:1-16; 1Jn 3:12).

CALEB
Judahite who spied out Canaan (Nu 13:6); allowed to enter land because of faith (Nu 13:30-14:38; Dt 1:36). Possessed Hebron (Jos 14:6-15:19).

CALF
Ex 32: 4 into an idol cast in the shape of a *c*,
Lk 15:23 Bring the fattened *c* and kill it.

CALL (CALLED CALLING CALLS)
Ps 105: 1 to the LORD, *c* on his name;
145: 18 near to all who *c* on him,
Pr 31:28 children arise and *c* her blessed;
Isa 5:20 Woe to those who *c* evil good
55: 6 *c* on him while he is near.
65:24 Before they *c* I will answer;
Jer 33: 3 '*C* to me and I will answer you
Mt 9:13 come to *c* the righteous,
Ro 10:12 and richly blesses all who *c* on him,
11:29 gifts and his *c* are irrevocable.
1Th 4: 7 For God did not *c* us to be impure,

CALLED (CALL)
1Sa 3: 5 and said, "Here I am; you *c* me."
2Ch 7:14 if my people, who are *c*
Ps 34: 6 This poor man *c*, and the LORD
Mt 21:13 " 'My house will be *c* a house
Ro 8:30 And those he predestined, he also *c*
1Co 7:15 God has *c* us to live in peace.
Gal 5:13 You, my brothers, were *c* to be free
1Pe 2: 9 of him who *c* you out of darkness

CALLING (CALL)
Jn 1:23 I am the voice of one *c* in the desert
Ac 22:16 wash your sins away, *c* on his name
Eph 4: 1 worthy of the *c* you have received.
2Pe 1:10 all the more eager to make your *c*

CALLS (CALL)
Joel 2:32 And everyone who *c*
Jn 10: 3 He *c* his own sheep by name
Ro 10:13 "Everyone who *c* on the name

CAMEL
Mt 19:24 it is easier for a *c* to go
23:24 strain out a gnat but swallow a *c*.

CANAAN
1Ch 16:18 "To you I will give the land of *C*

CANCELED
Lk 7:42 so he *c* the debts of both.
Col 2:14 having *c* the written code,

CAPITAL
Dt 21:22 guilty of a *c* offense is put to death

CAPSTONE (STONE)
Ps 118: 22 has become the *c*;
1Pe 2: 7 has become the *c*,"

CARE (CAREFUL CARES CARING)
Ps 8: 4 the son of man that you *c* for him?
Pr 29: 7 The righteous *c* about justice
Lk 10:34 him to an inn and took *c* of him.
Jn 21:16 Jesus said, "Take *c* of my sheep."
Heb 2: 6 the son of man that you *c* for him?
1Pe 5: 2 of God's flock that is under your *c*,

CAREFUL (CARE)
Ex 23:13 "Be *c* to do everything I have said
Dt 6: 3 be *c* to obey so that it may go well
Jos 23: 6 be *c* to obey all that is written
23:11 be very *c* to love the LORD your
Pr 13:24 he who loves him is *c*
Mt 6: 1 "Be *c* not to do your 'acts
Ro 12:17 Be *c* to do what is right in the eyes
1Co 3:10 each one should be *c* how he builds
8: 9 Be *c*, however, that the exercise
Eph 5:15 Be very *c*, then, how you live—

CARELESS
Mt 12:36 for every *c* word they have spoken.

CARES (CARE)
Ps 55:22 Cast your *c* on the LORD
Na 1: 7 He *c* for those who trust in him,
Eph 5:29 but he feeds and *c* for it, just
1Pe 5: 7 on him because he *c* for you.

CARING* (CARE)
1Th 2: 7 like a mother *c* for her little
1Ti 5: 4 practice by *c* for their own family

CARRIED (CARRY)
Ex 19: 4 and how I *c* you on eagles' wings
Isa 53: 4 and *c* our sorrows,
Heb 13: 9 Do not be *c* away by all kinds
2Pe 1:21 as they were *c* along by the Holy

CARRIES (CARRY)
Dt 32:11 and *c* them on its pinions.
Isa 40:11 and *c* them close to his heart;

CARRY (CARRIED CARRIES)
Lk 14:27 anyone who does not *c* his cross
Gal 6: 2 *C* each other's burdens,
6: 5 for each one should *c* his own load.

CAST
Ps 22:18 and *c* lots for my clothing.
55:22 *C* your cares on the LORD
Ecc 11: 1 *C* your bread upon the waters,
Jn 19:24 and *c* lots for my clothing."
1Pe 5: 7 *C* all your anxiety on him

CATCH (CAUGHT)
Lk 5:10 from now on you will *c* men."

CATTLE
Ps 50:10 and the *c* on a thousand hills.

CAUGHT (CATCH)
1Th 4:17 and are left will be *c* up together

CAUSE (CAUSES)
Pr 24:28 against your neighbor without *c*,
Ecc 8: 3 Do not stand up for a bad *c*,
Mt 18: 7 of the things that *c* people to sin!
Ro 14:21 else that will *c* your brother
1Co 10:32 Do not *c* anyone to stumble,

CAUSES (CAUSE)
Isa 8:14 a stone that *c* men to stumble
Mt 18: 6 if anyone *c* one of these little ones

CAUTIOUS*
Pr 12:26 A righteous man is *c* in friendship,

CEASE
Ps 46: 9 He makes wars *c* to the ends

CENSER
Lev 16:12 is to take a *c* full of burning coals

CENTURION
Mt 8: 5 had entered Capernaum, a *c* came

CERTAIN (CERTAINTY)
2Pe 1:19 word of the prophets made more *c*,

CERTAINTY* (CERTAIN)
Lk 1: 4 so that you may know the *c*
Jn 17: 8 They knew with *c* that I came

CHAFF
Ps 1: 4 They are like *c*

CHAINED
2Ti 2: 9 But God's word is not *c*.

CHAMPION
Ps 19: 5 like a *c* rejoicing to run his course.

CHANGE (CHANGED)
1Sa 15:29 of Israel does not lie or *c* his mind;

Ps 110: 4 and will not *c* his mind:
Jer 7: 5 If you really *c* your ways
Mal 3: 6 "I the LORD do not *c*.
Mt 18: 3 unless you *c* and become like little
Heb 7:21 and will not *c* his mind:
Jas 1:17 who does not *c* like shifting

CHANGED (CHANGE)
1Co 15:51 but we will all be *c*— in a flash,

CHARACTER
Ru 3:11 that you are a woman of noble *c*.
Pr 31:10 A wife of noble *c* who can find?
Ro 5: 4 perseverance, *c*; and *c*, hope.
1Co 15:33 "Bad company corrupts good *c*."

CHARGE
Ro 8:33 Who will bring any *c*
2Co 11: 7 the gospel of God to you free of *c*?
2Ti 4: 1 I give you this *c*: Preach the Word;

CHARIOTS
2Ki 6:17 and *c* of fire all around Elisha.
Ps 20: 7 Some trust in *c* and some in horses,

CHARM
Pr 31:30 *C* is deceptive, and beauty is

CHASES
Pr 12:11 he who *c* fantasies lacks judgment.

CHATTER* (CHATTERING)
1Ti 6:20 Turn away from godless *c*
2Ti 2:16 Avoid godless *c*, because those

CHATTERING* (CHATTER)
Pr 10: 8 but a *c* fool comes to ruin.
10:10 and a *c* fool comes to ruin.

CHEAT* (CHEATED)
Mal 1:14 "Cursed is the *c* who has
1Co 6: 8 you yourselves *c* and do wrong,

CHEATED (CHEAT)
Lk 19: 8 if I have *c* anybody out of anything,
1Co 6: 7 Why not rather be *c*? Instead,

CHEEK
Mt 5:39 someone strikes you on the right *c*,

CHEERFUL* (CHEERS)
Pr 15:13 A happy heart makes the face *c*,
15:15 but the *c* heart has a continual feast
15:30 A *c* look brings joy to the heart,
17:22 A *c* heart is good medicine,
2Co 9: 7 for God loves a *c* giver.

CHEERS (CHEERFUL)
Pr 12:25 but a kind word *c* him up.

CHILD (CHILDISH CHILDREN)
Pr 20:11 Even a *c* is known by his actions,
22: 6 Train a *c* in the way he should go,
22:15 Folly is bound up in the heart of a *c*
23:13 not withhold discipline from a *c*;
29:15 *c* left to himself disgraces his mother.
Isa 7:14 The virgin will be with *c*
9: 6 For to us a *c* is born,
11: 6 and a little *c* will lead them.
66:13 As a mother comforts her *c*,
Mt 1:23 "The virgin will be with *c*
18: 2 He called a little *c* and had him
Lk 1:42 and blessed is the *c* you will bear!
1:80 And the *c* grew and became strong
1Co 13:11 When I was a *c*, I talked like a *c*,
1Jn 5: 1 who loves the father loves his *c*

CHILDISH* (CHILD)
1Co 13:11 When I became a man, I put *c* ways

CHILDREN (CHILD)
Dt 4: 9 Teach them to your *c*
11:19 them to your *c*, talking about them
Ps 8: 2 From the lips of *c* and infants
Pr 17: 6 Children's *c* are a crown
31:28 Her *c* arise and call her blessed;
Mt 7:11 how to give good gifts to your *c*,
11:25 and revealed them to little *c*.
18: 3 you change and become like little *c*
19:14 "Let the little *c* come to me,
21:16 " 'From the lips of *c* and infants
Mk 9:37 one of these little *c* in my name
10:14 "Let the little *c* come to me,
10:16 And he took the *c* in his arms,
13:12 *C* will rebel against their parents
Lk 10:21 and revealed them to little *c*.
18:16 "Let the little *c* come to me,
Ro 8:16 with our spirit that we are God's *c*.
2Co 12:14 parents, but parents for their *c*.
Eph 6: 1 *C*, obey your parents in the Lord,
6: 4 do not exasperate your *c*; instead,
Col 3:20 *C*, obey your parents in everything,
3:21 Fathers, do not embitter your *c*,
1Ti 3: 4 and see that his *c* obey him
3:12 and must manage his *c* and his
5:10 bringing up *c*, showing hospitality,
1Jn 3: 1 that we should be called *c* of God!

CHOOSE (CHOOSES CHOSE CHOSEN)
Dt 30:19 Now *c* life, so that you
Jos 24:15 then *c* for yourselves this day
Pr 8:10 *C* my instruction instead of silver,
16:16 to *c* understanding rather
Jn 15:16 You did not *c* me, but I chose you

CHOOSES (CHOOSE)
Jn 7:17 If anyone *c* to do God's will,

CHOSE (CHOOSE)
Ge 13:11 So Lot *c* for himself the whole plain
Ps 33:12 the people he *c* for his inheritance.
Jn 15:16 but I *c* you and appointed you to go
1Co 1:27 But God *c* the foolish things
Eph 1: 4 he *c* us in him before the creation
2Th 2:13 from the beginning God *c* you

CHOSEN (CHOOSE)
Isa 41: 8 Jacob, whom I have *c*,
Mt 22:14 For many are invited, but few are *c*
Lk 10:42 Mary has *c* what is better,
23:35 the Christ of God, the *C* One."
Jn 15:19 but I have *c* you out of the world.
1Pe 1:20 He was *c* before the creation
2: 9 But you are a *c* people, a royal

CHRIST (CHRIST'S CHRISTIAN CHRISTS)
Mt 1:16 was born Jesus, who is called *C*.
16:16 Peter answered, "You are the *C*,
22:42 "What do you think about the *C*?
Jn 1:41 found the Messiah" (that is, the *C*).
20:31 you may believe that Jesus is the *C*,
Ac 2:36 you crucified, both Lord and *C*."
5:42 the good news that Jesus is the *C*.
9:22 by proving that Jesus is the *C*.
17: 3 proving that the *C* had to suffer
18:28 the Scriptures that Jesus was the *C*.
26:23 that the *C* would suffer and,
Ro 3:22 comes through faith in Jesus *C*
5: 6 we were still powerless, *C* died
5: 8 While we were still sinners, *C* died
5:17 life through the one man, Jesus *C*.
6: 4 as *C* was raised from the dead
8: 1 for those who are in *C* Jesus,
8: 9 Spirit of *C*, he does not belong to *C*.
8:35 us from the love of *C*?
10: 4 *C* is the end of the law
14: 9 *C* died and returned to life
15: 3 For even *C* did not please himself
1Co 1:23 but we preach *C* crucified:
2: 2 except Jesus *C* and him crucified.
3:11 one already laid, which is Jesus *C*.
5: 7 For *C*, our Passover lamb,
8: 6 and there is but one Lord, Jesus *C*,
10: 4 them, and that rock was *C*.
11: 1 as I follow the example of *C*.
11: 3 the head of every man is *C*,
12:27 Now you are the body of *C*,
15: 3 that *C* died for our sins according
15:14 And if *C* has not been raised,
15:22 so in *C* all will be made alive.
15:57 victory through our Lord Jesus *C*.
2Co 3: 3 show that you are a letter from *C*,
4: 5 not preach ourselves, but Jesus *C*
5:10 before the judgment seat of *C*,

2Co 5:17 Therefore, if anyone is in *C*,
11: 2 you to one husband, to *C*,
Gal 2:20 I have been crucified with *C*
3:13 *C* redeemed us from the curse
6:14 in the cross of our Lord Jesus *C*,
Eph 1: 3 with every spiritual blessing in *C*.
3: 8 the unsearchable riches of *C*,
4:13 measure of the fullness of *C*.
5: 2 as *C* loved us and gave himself up
5:23 as *C* is the head of the church,
5:25 just as *C* loved the church
Php 1:21 to live is *C* and to die is gain.
1:27 worthy of the gospel of *C*.
4:19 to his glorious riches in *C* Jesus.
Col 1:27 which is *C* in you, the hope of glory
1:28 may present everyone perfect in *C*.
2: 6 as you received *C* Jesus as Lord,
2:17 the reality, however, is found in *C*.
3:15 Let the peace of *C* rule
2Th 2: 1 the coming of our Lord Jesus *C*
1Ti 1:15 *C* Jesus came into the world
2: 5 the man *C* Jesus, who gave himself
2Ti 2: 3 us like a good soldier of *C* Jesus.
3:15 salvation through faith in *C* Jesus.
Tit 2:13 our great God and Savior, Jesus *C*,
Heb 3:14 to share in *C* if we hold firmly
9:14 more, then, will the blood of *C*,
9:15 For this reason *C* is the mediator
9:28 so *C* was sacrificed once
10:10 of the body of Jesus *C* once for all.
13: 8 Jesus *C* is the same yesterday
1Pe 1:19 but with the precious blood of *C*,
2:21 because *C* suffered for you,
3:18 For *C* died for sins once for all,
4:14 insulted because of the name of *C*,
1Jn 2:22 man who denies that Jesus is the *C*.
3:16 Jesus *C* laid down his life for us.
5: 1 believes that Jesus is the *C* is born
Rev 20: 4 reigned with *C* a thousand years.

CHRIST'S (CHRIST)
2Co 5:14 For *C* love compels us,
5:20 We are therefore *C* ambassadors,
12: 9 so that *C* power may rest on me.

CHRISTIAN (CHRIST)
1Pe 4:16 as a *C*, do not be ashamed,

CHRISTS (CHRIST)
Mt 24:24 For false *C* and false prophets will

CHURCH
Mt 16:18 and on this rock I will build my *c*,
18:17 if he refuses to listen even to the *c*,
Ac 20:28 Be shepherds of the *c* of God,
1Co 5:12 of mine to judge those outside the *c*
14: 4 but he who prophesies edifies the *c*.
14:12 to excel in gifts that build up the *c*.
14:26 done for the strengthening of the *c*.
Eph 5:23 as Christ is the head of the *c*,
Col 1:24 the sake of his body, which is the *c*.

CIRCUMCISED
Ge 17:10 Every male among you shall be *c*.

CIRCUMSTANCES
Php 4:11 to be content whatever the *c*.
1Th 5:18 continually; give thanks in all *c*,

CITIZENS (CITIZENSHIP)
Eph 2:19 but fellow *c* with God's people

CITIZENSHIP (CITIZENS)
Php 3:20 But our *c* is in heaven.

CITY
Mt 5:14 A *c* on a hill cannot be hidden.
Heb 13:14 here we do not have an enduring *c*,

CIVILIAN*
2Ti 2: 4 a soldier gets involved in *c* affairs—

CLAIM (CLAIMS)
Pr 25: 6 do not *c* a place among great men;
1Jn 1: 6 If we *c* to have fellowship
1: 8 If we *c* to be without sin, we
1:10 If we *c* we have not sinned,

CLAIMS (CLAIM)
Jas 2:14 if a man *c* to have faith
1Jn 2: 6 Whoever *c* to live in him must walk
2: 9 Anyone who *c* to be in the light

CLAP
Ps 47: 1 *C* your hands, all you nations;
Isa 55:12 will *c* their hands.

CLAY
Isa 45: 9 Does the *c* say to the potter,
64: 8 We are the *c*, you are the potter;
Jer 18: 6 "Like *c* in the hand of the potter,
La 4: 2 are now considered as pots of *c*,
Da 2:33 partly of iron and partly of baked *c*.
Ro 9:21 of the same lump of *c* some pottery
2Co 4: 7 we have this treasure in jars of *c*
2Ti 2:20 and *c*; some are for noble purposes

CLEAN
Lev 16:30 you will be *c* from all your sins.
Ps 24: 4 He who has *c* hands and a pure
Mt 12:44 the house unoccupied, swept *c*
23:25 You *c* the outside of the cup
Mk 7:19 Jesus declared all foods "*c*.")
Jn 13:10 to wash his feet; his whole body is *c*
15: 3 are already *c* because of the word
Ac 10:15 impure that God has made *c*."
Ro 14:20 All food is *c*, but it is wrong

CLING (CLINGS)
Ro 12: 9 Hate what is evil; *c* to what is good.

CLINGS (CLING)
Ps 63: 8 My soul *c* to you;

CLOAK
2Ki 4:29 "Tuck your *c* into your belt,

CLOSE (CLOSER)
Ps 34:18 LORD is *c* to the brokenhearted
Isa 40:11 and carries them *c* to his heart;
Jer 30:21 himself to be *c* to me?'

CLOSER (CLOSE)
Ex 3: 5 "Do not come any *c*," God said.
Pr 18:24 there is a friend who sticks *c*

CLOTHE (CLOTHED CLOTHES CLOTHING)
Ps 45: 3 *c* yourself with splendor
Isa 52: 1 *c* yourself with strength.
Ro 13:14 *c* yourselves with the Lord Jesus
Col 3:12 *c* yourselves with compassion,
1Pe 5: 5 *c* yourselves with humility

CLOTHED (CLOTHE)
Ps 30:11 removed my sackcloth and *c* me
Pr 31:25 She is *c* with strength and dignity;
Lk 24:49 until you have been *c* with power

CLOTHES (CLOTHE)
Mt 6:25 the body more important than *c*?
6:28 "And why do you worry about *c*?
Jn 11:44 Take off the grave *c* and let him go

CLOTHING (CLOTHE)
Dt 22: 5 A woman must not wear men's *c*,
Mt 7:15 They come to you in sheep's *c*,

CLOUD (CLOUDS)
Ex 13:21 them in a pillar of *c* to guide them
Isa 19: 1 See, the LORD rides on a swift *c*
Lk 21:27 of Man coming in a *c* with power
Heb 12: 1 by such a great *c* of witnesses,

CLOUDS (CLOUD)
Ps 104: 3 He makes the *c* his chariot
Da 7:13 coming with the *c* of heaven.
Mk 13:26 coming in *c* with great power
1Th 4:17 with them in the *c* to meet the Lord

CO-HEIRS* (INHERIT)
Ro 8:17 heirs of God and *c* with Christ,

COALS
Pr 25:22 you will heap burning *c* on his head

Ro 12:20 you will heap burning *c* on his head

COLD
Pr 25:25 Like *c* water to a weary soul
Mt 10:42 if anyone gives even a cup of *c* water
24:12 the love of most will grow *c,*

COMFORT (COMFORTED COMFORTS)
Ps 23: 4 rod and your staff, they *c* me.
119: 52 and I find *c* in them.
119: 76 May your unfailing love be my *c,*
Zec 1:17 and the LORD will again *c* Zion
1Co 14: 3 encouragement and *c.*
2Co 1: 4 so that we can *c* those
2: 7 you ought to forgive and *c* him,

COMFORTED (COMFORT)
Mt 5: 4 for they will be *c.*

COMFORTS* (COMFORT)
Job 29:25 I was like one who *c* mourners.
Isa 49:13 For the LORD *c* his people
51:12 "I, even I, am he who *c* you.
66:13 As a mother *c* her child,
2Co 1: 4 who *c* us in all our troubles,
7: 6 But God, who *c* the downcast,

COMMAND (COMMANDED COMMANDING COMMANDMENT COMMANDMENTS COMMANDS)
Ex 7: 2 You are to say everything I *c* you,
Nu 24:13 to go beyond the *c* of the LORD—
Dt 4: 2 Do not add to what I *c* you
30:16 For I *c* you today to love
32:46 so that you may *c* your children
Ps 91:11 For he will *c* his angels concerning
Pr 13:13 but he who respects a *c* is rewarded
Ecc 8: 2 Obey the king's *c,* I say,
Joel 2:11 mighty are those who obey his *c.*
Jn 14:15 love me, you will obey what I *c.*
15:12 My *c* is this: Love each other
1Co 14:37 writing to you is the Lord's *c.*
Gal 5:14 law is summed up in a single *c:*
1Ti 1: 5 goal of this *c* is love, which comes
Heb 11: 3 universe was formed at God's *c,*
1Jn 3:23 this is his *c:* to believe in the name
2Jn : 6 his *c* is that you walk in love.

COMMANDED (COMMAND)
Ps 33: 9 he *c,* and it stood firm.
148: 5 for he *c* and they were created.
Mt 28:20 to obey everything I have *c* you.
1Co 9:14 Lord has *c* that those who preach
1Jn 3:23 and to love one another as he *c* us.

COMMANDING (COMMAND)
2Ti 2: 4 he wants to please his *c* officer.

COMMANDMENT (COMMAND)
Jos 22: 5 But be very careful to keep the *c*
Mt 22:38 This is the first and greatest *c.*
Jn 13:34 "A new *c* I give you: Love one
Ro 7:12 and the *c* is holy, righteous
Eph 6: 2 which is the first *c* with a promise

COMMANDMENTS (COMMAND)
Ex 20: 6 who love me and keep my *c.*
34:28 of the covenant—the Ten *C.*
Ecc 12:13 Fear God and keep his *c,*
Mt 5:19 one of the least of these *c*
22:40 the Prophets hang on these two *c."*

COMMANDS (COMMAND)
Dt 7: 9 those who love him and keep his *c.*
11:27 the blessing if you obey the *c*
Ps 112: 1 who finds great delight in his *c.*
119: 47 for I delight in your *c*
119: 86 All your *c* are trustworthy;
119: 98 Your *c* make me wiser
119:127 Because I love your *c*
119:143 but your *c* are my delight.
119:172 for all your *c* are righteous.
Pr 3: 1 but keep my *c* in your heart,
6:23 For these *c* are a lamp,
10: 8 The wise in heart accept *c,*
Da 9: 4 all who love him and obey his *c,*
Mt 5:19 teaches these *c* will be called great
Jn 14:21 Whoever has my *c* and obeys them,
Ac 17:30 but now he *c* all people everywhere
1Co 7:19 Keeping God's *c* is what counts.
1Jn 5: 3 And his *c* are not burdensome,
5: 3 This is love for God: to obey his *c.*

COMMEND (COMMENDED COMMENDS)
Ecc 8:15 So I *c* the enjoyment of life,
Ro 13: 3 do what is right and he will *c* you.
1Pe 2:14 and to *c* those who do right.

COMMENDED (COMMEND)
Heb 11:39 These were all *c* for their faith,

COMMENDS (COMMEND)
2Co 10:18 not the one who *c* himself who is

COMMIT (COMMITS COMMITTED)
Ex 20:14 "You shall not *c* adultery.
Ps 37: 5 *C* your way to the LORD;
Mt 5:27 that it was said, 'Do not *c* adultery.'
Lk 23:46 into your hands I *c* my spirit."
Ac 20:32 I *c* you to God and to the word
1Co 10: 8 We should not *c* sexual immorality,
1Pe 4:19 to God's will should *c* themselves

COMMITS (COMMIT)
Pr 6:32 man who *c* adultery lacks
29:22 a hot-tempered one *c* many sins.
Mt 19: 9 marries another woman *c* adultery

COMMITTED (COMMIT)
Nu 5: 7 and must confess the sin he has *c.*
1Ki 8:61 But your hearts must be fully *c*
2Ch 16: 9 those whose hearts are fully *c*
Mt 5:28 lustfully has already *c* adultery
2Co 5:19 And he has *c* to us the message
1Pe 2:22 "He *c* no sin,

COMMON
Pr 22: 2 Rich and poor have this in *c:*
1Co 10:13 has seized you except what is *c*
2Co 6:14 and wickedness have in *c?*

COMPANION (COMPANIONS)
Pr 13:20 but a *c* of fools suffers harm.
28: 7 a *c* of gluttons disgraces his father.
29: 3 *c* of prostitutes squanders his

COMPANIONS (COMPANION)
Pr 18:24 A man of many *c* may come to ruin

COMPANY
Pr 24: 1 do not desire their *c;*
Jer 15:17 I never sat in the *c* of revelers,
1Co 15:33 "Bad *c* corrupts good character."

COMPARED (COMPARING)
Eze 31: 2 Who can be *c* with you in majesty?
Php 3: 8 I consider everything a loss *c*

COMPARING* (COMPARED)
Ro 8:18 present sufferings are not worth *c*
2Co 8: 8 the sincerity of your love by *c* it
Gal 6: 4 without *c* himself to somebody else

COMPASSION (COMPASSIONATE COMPASSIONS)
Ex 33:19 I will have *c* on whom I will have *c.*
Ne 9:19 of your great *c* you did not
9:28 in your *c* you delivered them time
Ps 51: 1 according to your great *c*
103: 4 and crowns you with love and *c.*
103: 13 As a father has *c* on his children,
145: 9 he has *c* on all he has made.
Isa 49:13 and will have *c* on his afflicted ones
49:15 and have no *c* on the child she has
Hos 2:19 in love and *c.*
11: 8 all my *c* is aroused.
Jnh 3: 9 with *c* turn from his fierce anger
Mt 9:36 When he saw the crowds, he had *c*
Mk 8: 2 "I have *c* for these people;
Ro 9:15 and I will have *c* on whom I have *c*
Col 3:12 clothe yourselves with *c,* kindness,
Jas 5:11 The Lord is full of *c* and mercy.

COMPASSIONATE (COMPASSION)
Ne 9:17 gracious and *c,* slow to anger
Ps 103: 8 The LORD is *c* and gracious,
112: 4 the gracious and *c* and righteous
Eph 4:32 Be kind and *c* to one another,

1Pe 3: 8 love as brothers, be *c* and humble.

COMPASSIONS* (COMPASSION)
La 3:22 for his *c* never fail.

COMPELLED (COMPELS)
Ac 20:22 "And now, *c* by the Spirit,
1Co 9:16 I cannot boast, for I am *c* to preach.

COMPELS (COMPELLED)
2Co 5:14 For Christ's love *c* us, because we

COMPETENCE* (COMPETENT)
2Co 3: 5 but our *c* comes from God.

COMPETENT* (COMPETENCE)
Ro 15:14 and *c* to instruct one another.
1Co 6: 2 are you not *c* to judge trivial cases?
2Co 3: 5 Not that we are *c* in ourselves
3: 6 He has made us *c* as ministers

COMPETES*
1Co 9:25 Everyone who *c* in the games goes
2Ti 2: 5 Similarly, if anyone *c* as an athlete,
2: 5 unless he *c* according to the rules.

COMPLACENT
Am 6: 1 Woe to you who are *c* in Zion,

COMPLAINING*
Php 2:14 Do everything without *c* or arguing

COMPLETE
Jn 15:11 and that your joy may be *c*.
16:24 will receive, and your joy will be *c*.
17:23 May they be brought to *c* unity
Ac 20:24 *c* the task the Lord Jesus has given
Php 2: 2 then make my joy *c*
Col 4:17 to it that you *c* the work you have
Jas 1: 4 so that you may be mature and *c*,
2:22 his faith was made *c* by what he did

CONCEAL (CONCEALED CONCEALS)
Ps 40:10 I do not *c* your love and your truth
Pr 25: 2 It is the glory of God to *c* a matter;

CONCEALED (CONCEAL)
Jer 16:17 nor is their sin *c* from my eyes.
Mt 10:26 There is nothing *c* that will not be
Mk 4:22 and whatever is *c* is meant

CONCEALS (CONCEAL)
Pr 28:13 He who *c* his sins does not prosper,

CONCEITED
Ro 12:16 Do not be *c*.
Gal 5:26 Let us not become *c*, provoking
1Ti 6: 4 he is *c* and understands nothing.

CONCEIVED
Mt 1:20 what is *c* in her is from the Holy
1Co 2: 9 no mind has *c*

CONCERN (CONCERNED)
Eze 36:21 I had *c* for my holy name, which
1Co 7:32 I would like you to be free from *c*.
12:25 that its parts should have equal *c*
2Co 11:28 of my *c* for all the churches.

CONCERNED (CONCERN)
Jnh 4:10 "You have been *c* about this vine,
1Co 7:32 An unmarried man is *c* about

CONDEMN (CONDEMNATION CONDEMNED CONDEMNING CONDEMNS)
Job 40: 8 Would you *c* me to justify yourself?
Isa 50: 9 Who is he that will *c* me?
Lk 6:37 Do not *c*, and you will not be
Jn 3:17 Son into the world to *c* the world,
12:48 very word which I spoke will *c* him
Ro 2:27 yet obeys the law will *c* you who,
1Jn 3:20 presence whenever our hearts *c* us.

CONDEMNATION (CONDEMN)
Ro 5:18 of one trespass was *c* for all men,
8: 1 there is now no *c* for those who are

CONDEMNED (CONDEMN)
Ps 34:22 no one will be *c* who takes refuge
Mt 12:37 and by your words you will be *c*."
23:33 How will you escape being *c* to hell
Jn 3:18 Whoever believes in him is not *c*,
5:24 has eternal life and will not be *c*;
16:11 prince of this world now stands *c*.
Ro 14:23 But the man who has doubts is *c*
1Co 11:32 disciplined so that we will not be *c*
Heb 11: 7 By his faith he *c* the world

CONDEMNING (CONDEMN)
Pr 17:15 the guilty and *c* the innocent—
Ro 2: 1 judge the other, you are *c* yourself,

CONDEMNS (CONDEMN)
Ro 8:34 Who is he that *c*? Christ Jesus,
2Co 3: 9 the ministry that *c* men is glorious,

CONDUCT
Pr 10:23 A fool finds pleasure in evil *c*,
20:11 by whether his *c* is pure and right.
21: 8 but the *c* of the innocent is upright.
Ecc 6: 8 how to *c* himself before others?
Jer 4:18 "Your own *c* and actions
17:10 to reward a man according to his *c*,
Eze 7: 3 I will judge you according to your *c*
Php 1:27 *c* yourselves in a manner worthy
1Ti 3:15 to *c* themselves in God's household

CONFESS (CONFESSION)
Lev 16:21 and *c* over it all the wickedness
26:40 " 'But if they will *c* their sins
Nu 5: 7 must *c* the sin he has committed.
Ps 38:18 I *c* my iniquity;
Ro 10: 9 That if you *c* with your mouth,
Php 2:11 every tongue *c* that Jesus Christ is
Jas 5:16 Therefore *c* your sins to each other
1Jn 1: 9 If we *c* our sins, he is faithful

CONFESSION (CONFESS)
Ezr 10:11 Now make *c* to the LORD,
2Co 9:13 obedience that accompanies your *c*

CONFIDENCE
Ps 71: 5 my *c* since my youth.
Pr 3:26 for the LORD will be your *c*
11:13 A gossip betrays a *c*,
25: 9 do not betray another man's *c*,
31:11 Her husband has full *c* in her
Isa 32:17 will be quietness and *c* forever.
Jer 17: 7 whose *c* is in him.
Php 3: 3 and who put no *c* in the flesh—
Heb 3:14 till the end the *c* we had at first.
4:16 the throne of grace with *c*,
10:19 since we have *c* to enter the Most
10:35 So do not throw away your *c*;
1Jn 5:14 This is the *c* we have

CONFORM* (CONFORMED)
Ro 12: 2 Do not *c* any longer to the pattern
1Pe 1:14 do not *c* to the evil desires you had

CONFORMED (CONFORM)
Ro 8:29 predestined to be *c* to the likeness

CONQUERORS
Ro 8:37 than *c* through him who loved us.

CONSCIENCE (CONSCIENCES)
Ro 13: 5 punishment but also because of *c*.
1Co 8: 7 since their *c* is weak, it is defiled.
8:12 in this way and wound their weak *c*
10:25 without raising questions of *c*,
10:29 freedom be judged by another's *c*?
Heb 10:22 to cleanse us from a guilty *c*
1Pe 3:16 and respect, keeping a clear *c*,

CONSCIENCES* (CONSCIENCE)
Ro 2:15 their *c* also bearing witness,
1Ti 4: 2 whose *c* have been seared
Tit 1:15 their minds and *c* are corrupted.
Heb 9:14 cleanse our *c* from acts that lead

CONSCIOUS*
Ro 3:20 through the law we become *c* of sin
1Pe 2:19 of unjust suffering because he is *c*

CONSECRATE (CONSECRATED)
Ex 13: 2 "*C* to me every firstborn male.
Lev 20: 7 " '*C* yourselves and be holy,

CONSECRATED (CONSECRATE)
Ex 29:43 and the place will be *c* by my glory.
1Ti 4: 5 because it is *c* by the word of God

CONSIDER (CONSIDERATE CONSIDERED CONSIDERS)
1Sa 12:24 *c* what great things he has done
Job 37:14 stop and *c* God's wonders.
Ps 8: 3 When I *c* your heavens,
107: 43 and *c* the great love of the LORD.
143: 5 and *c* what your hands have done.
Lk 12:24 *C* the ravens: They do not sow
12:27 about the rest? "*C* how the lilies
Php 2: 3 but in humility *c* others better
3: 8 I *c* everything a loss compared
Heb 10:24 And let us *c* how we may spur one
Jas 1: 2 *C* it pure joy, my brothers,

CONSIDERATE* (CONSIDER)
Tit 3: 2 to be peaceable and *c*,
Jas 3:17 then peace-loving, *c*, submissive,
1Pe 2:18 only to those who are good and *c*,
3: 7 in the same way be *c* as you live

CONSIDERED (CONSIDER)
Job 1: 8 "Have you *c* my servant Job?
2: 3 "Have you *c* my servant Job?
Ps 44:22 we are *c* as sheep to be slaughtered.
Isa 53: 4 yet we *c* him stricken by God,
Ro 8:36 we are *c* as sheep to be slaughtered

CONSIDERS (CONSIDER)
Pr 31:16 She *c* a field and buys it;
Ro 14: 5 One man *c* one day more sacred
Jas 1:26 If anyone *c* himself religious

CONSIST
Lk 12:15 a man's life does not *c*

CONSOLATION
Ps 94:19 your *c* brought joy to my soul.

CONSTRUCTIVE*
1Co 10:23 but not everything is *c*.

CONSUME (CONSUMING)
Jn 2:17 "Zeal for your house will *c* me."

CONSUMING (CONSUME)
Dt 4:24 For the LORD your God is a *c* fire,
Heb 12:29 and awe, for our "God is a *c* fire."

CONTAIN
1Ki 8:27 the highest heaven, cannot *c* you.
2Pe 3:16 His letters *c* some things that are

CONTAMINATES*
2Co 7: 1 from everything that *c* body

CONTEMPT
Pr 14:31 He who oppresses the poor shows *c*
17: 5 He who mocks the poor shows *c*
18: 3 When wickedness comes, so does *c*
Da 12: 2 others to shame and everlasting *c*.
Ro 2: 4 Or do you show *c* for the riches
Gal 4:14 you did not treat me with *c*
1Th 5:20 do not treat prophecies with *c*.

CONTEND (CONTENDING)
Jude : 3 you to *c* for the faith that was once

CONTENDING* (CONTEND)
Php 1:27 *c* as one man for the faith

CONTENT (CONTENTMENT)
Pr 13:25 The righteous eat to their hearts' *c*,
Php 4:11 to be *c* whatever the circumstances
4:12 I have learned the secret of being *c*
1Ti 6: 8 and clothing, we will be *c* with that.
Heb 13: 5 and be *c* with what you have,

CONTENTMENT (CONTENT)
1Ti 6: 6 But godliness with *c* is great gain.

CONTINUAL (CONTINUE)
Pr 15:15 but the cheerful heart has a *c* feast.

CONTINUE (CONTINUAL)
Php 2:12 *c* to work out your salvation
2Ti 3:14 *c* in what you have learned
1Jn 5:18 born of God does not *c* to sin;
Rev 22:11 and let him who is holy *c* to be holy
22:11 let him who does right *c* to do right;

CONTRITE*
Ps 51:17 a broken and *c* heart,
Isa 57:15 also with him who is *c* and lowly
57:15 and to revive the heart of the *c*.
66: 2 he who is humble and *c* in spirit,

CONTROL (CONTROLLED SELF-CONTROL SELF-CONTROLLED)
Pr 29:11 a wise man keeps himself under *c*.
1Co 7: 9 But if they cannot *c* themselves,
7:37 but has *c* over his own will,
1Th 4: 4 you should learn to *c* his own body

CONTROLLED (CONTROL)
Ps 32: 9 but must be *c* by bit and bridle
Ro 8: 6 but the mind *c* by the Spirit is life
8: 8 Those *c* by the sinful nature cannot

CONTROVERSIES
Tit 3: 9 But avoid foolish *c* and genealogies

CONVERSATION
Col 4: 6 Let your *c* be always full of grace,

CONVERT
1Ti 3: 6 He must not be a recent *c*,

CONVICT
Jn 16: 8 he will *c* the world of guilt in regard

CONVINCED (CONVINCING)
Ro 8:38 For I am *c* that neither death
2Ti 1:12 and am *c* that he is able
3:14 have learned and have become *c*

CONVINCING* (CONVINCED)
Ac 1: 3 and gave many *c* proofs that he was

CORNELIUS*
Roman to whom Peter preached; first Gentile Christian (Ac 10).

CORNERSTONE (STONE)
Isa 28:16 a precious *c* for a sure foundation;
Eph 2:20 Christ Jesus himself as the chief *c*.
1Pe 2: 6 a chosen and precious *c*,

CORRECT (CORRECTING CORRECTION CORRECTS)
2Ti 4: 2 *c*, rebuke and encourage—

CORRECTING* (CORRECT)
2Ti 3:16 *c* and training in righteousness,

CORRECTION (CORRECT)
Pr 10:17 whoever ignores *c* leads others
12: 1 but he who hates *c* is stupid.
15: 5 whoever heeds *c* shows prudence.
15:10 he who hates *c* will die.
29:15 The rod of *c* imparts wisdom,

CORRECTS* (CORRECT)
Job 5:17 "Blessed is the man whom God *c*;
Pr 9: 7 Whoever *c* a mocker invites insult;

CORRUPT (CORRUPTS)
Ge 6:11 Now the earth was *c* in God's sight

CORRUPTS* (CORRUPT)
Ecc 7: 7 and a bribe *c* the heart.
1Co 15:33 "Bad company *c* good character."
Jas 3: 6 It *c* the whole person, sets

COST
Pr 4: 7 Though it *c* all you have, get
Isa 55: 1 milk without money and without *c*.
Rev 21: 6 to drink without *c* from the spring

COUNSEL (COUNSELOR)
1Ki 22: 5 "First seek the *c* of the LORD."
Pr 15:22 Plans fail for lack of *c*,
Rev 3:18 I *c* you to buy from me gold refined

COUNSELOR (COUNSEL)
Isa 9: 6 Wonderful *C*, Mighty God,
Jn 14:16 he will give you another *C* to be
14:26 But the *C*, the Holy Spirit,

COUNT (COUNTING COUNTS)
Ro 4: 8 whose sin the Lord will never *c*
6:11 *c* yourselves dead to sin

COUNTING (COUNT)
2Co 5:19 not *c* men's sins against them.

COUNTRY
Jn 4:44 prophet has no honor in his own *c*.)

COUNTS (COUNT)
Jn 6:63 The Spirit gives life; the flesh *c*

1Co 7:19 God's commands is what *c.*
Gal 5: 6 only thing that *c* is faith expressing

COURAGE (COURAGEOUS)
Ac 23:11 "Take *c!* As you have testified
1Co 16:13 stand firm in the faith; be men of *c;*

COURAGEOUS (COURAGE)
Dt 31: 6 Be strong and *c.*
Jos 1: 6 and *c,* because you will lead these

COURSE
Ps 19: 5 a champion rejoicing to run his *c.*
Pr 15:21 of understanding keeps a straight *c.*

COURTS
Ps 84:10 Better is one day in your *c*
100: 4 and his *c* with praise;

COVENANT (COVENANTS)
Ge 9: 9 "I now establish my *c* with you
Ex 19: 5 if you obey me fully and keep my *c,*
1Ch 16:15 He remembers his *c* forever,
Job 31: 1 "I made a *c* with my eyes
Jer 31:31 "when I will make a new *c*
1Co 11:25 "This cup is the new *c* in my blood;
Gal 4:24 One *c* is from Mount Sinai
Heb 9:15 Christ is the mediator of a new *c,*

COVENANTS (COVENANT)
Ro 9: 4 theirs the divine glory, the *c,*
Gal 4:24 for the women represent two *c.*

COVER (COVER-UP COVERED COVERS)
Ps 91: 4 He will *c* you with his feathers,
Jas 5:20 and *c* over a multitude of sins.

COVER-UP (COVER)
1Pe 2:16 but do not use your freedom as a *c*

COVERED (COVER)
Ps 32: 1 whose sins are *c.*
Isa 6: 2 With two wings they *c* their faces,
Ro 4: 7 whose sins are *c.*
1Co 11: 4 with his head *c* dishonors his head.

COVERS (COVER)
Pr 10:12 but love *c* over all wrongs.
1Pe 4: 8 love *c* over a multitude of sins.

COVET
Ex 20:17 You shall not *c* your neighbor's
Ro 13: 9 "Do not steal," "Do not *c,*"

COWARDLY*
Rev 21: 8 But the *c,* the unbelieving, the vile,

CRAFTINESS (CRAFTY)
1Co 3:19 "He catches the wise in their *c*";

CRAFTY (CRAFTINESS)
Ge 3: 1 the serpent was more *c* than any
2Co 12:16 *c* fellow that I am, I caught you

CRAVE
Pr 23: 3 Do not *c* his delicacies,

1Pe 2: 2 newborn babies, *c* pure spiritual

CREATE (CREATED CREATION CREATOR)
Ps 51:10 *C* in me a pure heart, O God,
Isa 45:18 he did not *c* it to be empty,

CREATED (CREATE)
Ge 1: 1 In the beginning God *c* the heavens
1:21 God *c* the great creatures of the sea
1:27 So God *c* man in his own image,
Ps 148: 5 for he commanded and they were *c*
Isa 42: 5 he who *c* the heavens and stretched
Ro 1:25 and served *c* things rather
1Co 11: 9 neither was man *c* for woman,
Col 1:16 For by him all things were *c:*
1Ti 4: 4 For everything God *c* is good,
Rev 10: 6 who *c* the heavens and all that is

CREATION (CREATE)
Mk 16:15 and preach the good news to all *c.*
Jn 17:24 me before the *c* of the world.
Ro 8:19 The *c* waits in eager expectation
8:39 depth, nor anything else in all *c,*
2Co 5:17 he is a new *c;* the old has gone,
Col 1:15 God, the firstborn over all *c.*
1Pe 1:20 chosen before the *c* of the world,
Rev 13: 8 slain from the *c* of the world.

CREATOR (CREATE)
Ge 14:22 God Most High, *C* of heaven
Ro 1:25 created things rather than the *C*—

CREATURE (CREATURES)
Lev 17:11 For the life of a *c* is in the blood,

CREATURES (CREATURE)
Ge 6:19 bring into the ark two of all living *c,*
Ps 104: 24 the earth is full of your *c.*

CREDIT (CREDITED)
Ro 4:24 to whom God will *c* righteousness
1Pe 2:20 it to your *c* if you receive a beating

CREDITED (CREDIT)
Ge 15: 6 and he *c* it to him as righteousness.
Ro 4: 5 his faith is *c* as righteousness.
Gal 3: 6 and it was *c* to him as righteousness
Jas 2:23 and it was *c* to him as righteousness

CRIED (CRY)
Ps 18: 6 I *c* to my God for help.

CRIMSON
Isa 1:18 though they are red as *c,*

CRIPPLED
Mk 9:45 better for you to enter life *c*

CRITICISM
2Co 8:20 We want to avoid any *c*

CROOKED
Pr 10: 9 he who takes *c* paths will be found

Php 2:15 children of God without fault in a *c*

CROSS
Mt 10:38 and anyone who does not take his *c*
Lk 9:23 take up his *c* daily and follow me.
Ac 2:23 to death by nailing him to the *c.*
1Co 1:17 lest the *c* of Christ be emptied
Gal 6:14 in the *c* of our Lord Jesus Christ,
Php 2: 8 even death on a *c!*
Col 1:20 through his blood, shed on the *c.*
2:14 he took it away, nailing it to the *c.*
2:15 triumphing over them by the *c.*
Heb 12: 2 set before him endured the *c,*

CROWD
Ex 23: 2 Do not follow the *c* in doing wrong.

CROWN (CROWNED CROWNS)
Pr 4: 9 present you with a *c* of splendor."
10: 6 Blessings *c* the head
12: 4 noble character is her husband's *c,*
17: 6 Children's children are a *c*
Isa 61: 3 to bestow on them a *c* of beauty
Zec 9:16 like jewels in a *c.*
Mt 27:29 then twisted together a *c* of thorns
1Co 9:25 it to get a *c* that will last forever.
2Ti 4: 8 store for me the *c* of righteousness,
Rev 2:10 and I will give you the *c* of life.

CROWNED (CROWN)
Ps 8: 5 and *c* him with glory and honor.
Pr 14:18 the prudent are *c* with knowledge.
Heb 2: 7 you *c* him with glory and honor

CROWNS (CROWN)
Rev 4:10 They lay their *c* before the throne
19:12 and on his head are many *c.*

CRUCIFIED (CRUCIFY)
Mt 20:19 to be mocked and flogged and *c.*
27:38 Two robbers were *c* with him,
Lk 24: 7 be *c* and on the third day be raised
Jn 19:18 Here they *c* him, and with him two
Ac 2:36 whom you *c,* both Lord and Christ
Ro 6: 6 For we know that our old self was *c*
1Co 1:23 but we preach Christ *c:* a stumbling
2: 2 except Jesus Christ and him *c.*
Gal 2:20 I have been *c* with Christ
5:24 Christ Jesus have *c* the sinful

CRUCIFY (CRUCIFIED CRUCIFYING)
Mt 27:22 They all answered, "*C* him!" "Why
27:31 Then they led him away to *c* him.

CRUCIFYING* (CRUCIFY)
Heb 6: 6 to their loss they are *c* the Son

CRUSH (CRUSHED)
Ge 3:15 he will *c* your head,
Isa 53:10 it was the LORD's will to *c* him
Ro 16:20 The God of peace will soon *c* Satan

CRUSHED (CRUSH)
Ps 34:18 and saves those who are *c* in spirit.
Isa 53: 5 he was *c* for our iniquities;
2Co 4: 8 not *c;* perplexed, but not in despair;

CRY (CRIED)
Ps 34:15 and his ears are attentive to their *c;*
40: 1 he turned to me and heard my *c.*
130: 1 Out of the depths I *c* to you,

CUP
Ps 23: 5 my *c* overflows.
Mt 10:42 if anyone gives even a *c* of cold water
23:25 You clean the outside of the *c*
26:39 may this *c* be taken from me.
1Co 11:25 after supper he took the *c,* saying,

CURSE (CURSED)
Dt 11:26 before you today a blessing and a *c*
21:23 hung on a tree is under God's *c.*
Lk 6:28 bless those who *c* you, pray
Gal 3:13 of the law by becoming a *c* for us,
Rev 22: 3 No longer will there be any *c.*

CURSED (CURSE)
Ge 3:17 "*C* is the ground because of you;
Dt 27:15 "*C* is the man who carves an image
27:16 "*C* is the man who dishonors his
27:17 "*C* is the man who moves his
27:18 "*C* is the man who leads the blind
27:19 *C* is the man who withholds justice
27:20 "*C* is the man who sleeps
27:21 "*C* is the man who has sexual
27:22 "*C* is the man who sleeps
27:23 "*C* is the man who sleeps
27:24 "*C* is the man who kills his
27:25 "*C* is the man who accepts a bribe
27:26 "*C* is the man who does not uphold
Ro 9: 3 I could wish that I myself were *c*
Gal 3:10 "*C* is everyone who does not

CURTAIN
Ex 26:33 The *c* will separate the Holy Place
Lk 23:45 the *c* of the temple was torn in two.
Heb 10:20 opened for us through the *c,*

CYMBAL*
1Co 13: 1 a resounding gong or a clanging *c.*

DANCE (DANCING)
Ecc 3: 4 a time to mourn and a time to *d,*
Mt 11:17 and you did not *d;*

DANCING (DANCE)
Ps 30:11 You turned my wailing into *d;*
149: 3 Let them praise his name with *d*

DANGER
Pr 27:12 The prudent see *d* and take refuge,
Ro 8:35 famine or nakedness or *d* or sword?

DANIEL
Hebrew exile to Babylon, name changed to Belteshazzar (Da 1:6-7). Refused to eat unclean food (Da 1:8-21). Interpreted Nebuchadnezzar's dreams (Da 2; 4), writing on the wall (Da 5). Thrown into lion's den (Da 6). Visions of (Da 7-12).

DARK (DARKNESS)
Job 34:22 There is no *d* place, no deep
Pr 31:15 She gets up while it is still *d;*
Ro 2:19 a light for those who are in the *d,*
2Pe 1:19 as to a light shining in a *d* place,

DARKNESS (DARK)
Ge 1: 4 he separated the light from the *d.*
2Sa 22:29 the LORD turns my *d* into light.
Jn 3:19 but men loved *d* instead of light
2Co 6:14 fellowship can light have with *d?*
Eph 5: 8 For you were once *d,* but now you
1Pe 2: 9 out of *d* into his wonderful light.
1Jn 1: 5 in him there is no *d* at all.
2: 9 but hates his brother is still in the *d.*

DAUGHTERS
Joel 2:28 sons and *d* will prophesy,

DAVID
Son of Jesse (Ru 4:17-22; 1Ch 2:13-15), ancestor of Jesus (Mt 1:1-17; Lk 3:31).
Anointed king by Samuel (1Sa 16:1-13). Musician to Saul (1Sa 16:14-23; 18:10). Killed Goliath (1Sa 17). Relation with Jonathan (1Sa 18:1-4; 19-20; 23:16-18; 2Sa 1). Disfavor of Saul (1Sa 18:6-23:29). Spared Saul's life (1Sa 24; 26). Among Philistines (1Sa 21:10-14; 27-30). Lament for Saul and Jonathan (2Sa 1).
Anointed king of Judah (2Sa 2:1-11); of Israel (2Sa 5:1-4; 1Ch 11:1-3). Promised eternal dynasty (2Sa 7; 1Ch 17; Ps 132). Adultery with Bathsheba (2Sa 11-12). Absalom's revolt (2Sa 14-18). Last words (2Sa 23:1-7). Death (1Ki 2:10-12; 1Ch 29:28).

DAWN
Ps 37: 6 your righteousness shine like the *d,*
Pr 4:18 is like the first gleam of *d,*

DAY (DAYS)
Ge 1: 5 God called the light "*d,*"
Ex 20: 8 "Remember the Sabbath *d*
Lev 23:28 because it is the *D* of Atonement,
Nu 14:14 before them in a pillar of cloud by *d*
Jos 1: 8 meditate on it *d* and night,
Ps 84:10 Better is one *d* in your courts
96: 2 proclaim his salvation *d* after *d.*
118: 24 This is the *d* the LORD has made;
Pr 27: 1 not know what a *d* may bring forth.
Joel 2:31 and dreadful *d* of the LORD.
Ob :15 The *d* of the LORD is near
Lk 11: 3 Give us each *d* our daily bread.
Ac 17:11 examined the Scriptures every *d*
2Co 4:16 we are being renewed *d* by *d.*
1Th 5: 2 for you know very well that the *d*
2Pe 3: 8 With the Lord a *d* is like

DAYS (DAY)
Dt 17:19 he is to read it all the *d,* of his life
Ps 23: 6 all the *d* of my life,
90:10 The length of our *d* is seventy years
Ecc 12: 1 Creator in the *d* of your youth,
Joel 2:29 I will pour out my Spirit in those *d.*
Mic 4: 1 In the last *d*
Heb 1: 2 in these last *d* he has spoken to us
2Pe 3: 3 that in the last *d* scoffers will come,

DEACONS
1Ti 3: 8 *D,* likewise, are to be men worthy

DEAD (DIE)
Dt 18:11 or spiritist or who consults the *d.*
Mt 28: 7 'He has risen from the *d*
Ro 6:11 count yourselves *d* to sin
Eph 2: 1 you were *d* in your transgressions
1Th 4:16 and the *d* in Christ will rise first.
Jas 2:17 is not accompanied by action, is *d.*
2:26 so faith without deeds is *d.*

DEATH (DIE)
Nu 35:16 the murderer shall be put to *d.*
Ps 23: 4 the valley of the shadow of *d,*
116: 15 is the *d* of his saints.
Pr 8:36 all who hate me love *d.*"
14:12 but in the end it leads to *d.*
Ecc 7: 2 for *d* is the destiny of every man;
Isa 25: 8 he will swallow up *d* forever.
53:12 he poured out his life unto *d,*
Jn 5:24 he has crossed over from *d* to life.
Ro 5:12 and in this way *d* came to all men,
6:23 For the wages of sin is *d,*
8:13 put to *d* the misdeeds of the body,
1Co 15:21 For since *d* came through a man,
15:55 Where, O *d,* is your sting?"
Rev 1:18 And I hold the keys of *d* and Hades
20: 6 The second *d* has no power
20:14 The lake of fire is the second *d.*
21: 4 There will be no more *d*

DEBAUCHERY
Ro 13:13 not in sexual immorality and *d,*
Eph 5:18 drunk on wine, which leads to *d.*

DEBORAH
Prophetess who led Israel to victory over Canaanites (Jdg 4-5).

DEBT (DEBTORS DEBTS)
Ro 13: 8 Let no *d* remain outstanding,

Ro 13: 8 continuing *d* to love one another,

DEBTORS (DEBT)
Mt 6:12 as we also have forgiven our *d*.

DEBTS (DEBT)
Dt 15: 1 seven years you must cancel *d*.
Mt 6:12 Forgive us our *d*,

DECAY
Ps 16:10 will you let your Holy One see *d*.
Ac 2:27 will you let your Holy One see *d*.

DECEIT (DECEIVE)
Mk 7:22 greed, malice, *d*, lewdness, envy,
1Pe 2: 1 yourselves of all malice and all *d*,
2:22 and no *d* was found in his mouth."

DECEITFUL (DECEIVE)
Jer 17: 9 The heart is *d* above all things
2Co 11:13 men are false apostles, *d* workmen,

DECEITFULNESS (DECEIVE)
Mk 4:19 the *d* of wealth and the desires
Heb 3:13 of you may be hardened by sin's *d*.

DECEIVE (DECEIT DECEITFUL DECEITFULNESS DECEIVED DECEIVES DECEPTIVE)
Lev 19:11 " 'Do not *d* one another.
Pr 14: 5 A truthful witness does not *d*,
Mt 24: 5 'I am the Christ,' and will *d* many.
Ro 16:18 and flattery they *d* the minds
1Co 3:18 Do not *d* yourselves.
Eph 5: 6 Let no one *d* you with empty words
Jas 1:22 to the word, and so *d* yourselves.
1Jn 1: 8 we *d* ourselves and the truth is not

DECEIVED (DECEIVE)
Ge 3:13 "The serpent *d* me, and I ate."
Gal 6: 7 Do not be *d*: God cannot be
1Ti 2:14 And Adam was not the one *d*;
2Ti 3:13 to worse, deceiving and being *d*.
Jas 1:16 Don't be *d*, my dear brothers.

DECEIVES (DECEIVE)
Gal 6: 3 when he is nothing, he *d* himself.
Jas 1:26 he *d* himself and his religion is

DECENCY*
1Ti 2: 9 women to dress modestly, with *d*

DECEPTIVE (DECEIVE)
Pr 31:30 Charm is *d*, and beauty is fleeting;
Col 2: 8 through hollow and *d* philosophy,

DECLARE (DECLARED DECLARING)
1Ch 16:24 *D* his glory among the nations,
Ps 19: 1 The heavens *d* the glory of God;
96: 3 *D* his glory among the nations,
Isa 42: 9 and new things I *d*;

DECLARED (DECLARE)
Mk 7:19 Jesus *d* all foods "clean.")
Ro 2:13 the law who will be *d* righteous.
3:20 no one will be *d* righteous

DECLARING (DECLARE)
Ps 71: 8 *d* your splendor all day long.
Ac 2:11 we hear them *d* the wonders

DECREED (DECREES)
La 3:37 happen if the Lord has not *d* it?
Lk 22:22 Son of Man will go as it has been *d*,

DECREES (DECREED)
Lev 10:11 Israelites all the *d* the LORD has
Ps 119:112 My heart is set on keeping your *d*

DEDICATE (DEDICATION)
Nu 6:12 He must *d* himself to the LORD
Pr 20:25 for a man to *d* something rashly

DEDICATION (DEDICATE)
1Ti 5:11 sensual desires overcome their *d*

DEED (DEEDS)
Col 3:17 you do, whether in word or *d*,

DEEDS (DEED)
1Sa 2: 3 and by him *d* are weighed.
Ps 65: 5 with awesome *d* of righteousness,
66: 3 "How awesome are your *d*!
78: 4 the praiseworthy *d* of the LORD,
86:10 you are great and do marvelous *d*;
92: 4 For you make me glad by your *d*,
111: 3 Glorious and majestic are his *d*,
Hab 3: 2 I stand in awe of your *d*, O LORD.
Mt 5:16 that they may see your good *d*
Ac 26:20 prove their repentance by their *d*.
Jas 2:14 claims to have faith but has no *d*?
2:20 faith without *d* is useless?
1Pe 2:12 they may see your good *d*

DEEP (DEPTH)
1Co 2:10 all things, even the *d* things
1Ti 3: 9 hold of the *d* truths of the faith

DEER
Ps 42: 1 As the *d* pants for streams of water,

DEFEND (DEFENSE)
Ps 74:22 Rise up, O God, and *d* your cause;
Pr 31: 9 *d* the rights of the poor and needy
Jer 50:34 He will vigorously *d* their cause

DEFENSE (DEFEND)
Ps 35:23 Awake, and rise to my *d*!
Php 1:16 here for the *d* of the gospel.
1Jn 2: 1 speaks to the Father in our *d*—

DEFERRED*
Pr 13:12 Hope *d* makes the heart sick,

DEFILE (DEFILED)
Da 1: 8 Daniel resolved not to *d* himself

DEFILED (DEFILE)
Isa 24: 5 The earth is *d* by its people;

DEFRAUD
Lev 19:13 Do not *d* your neighbor or rob him.

DEITY*
Col 2: 9 of the *D* lives in bodily form,

DELIGHT (DELIGHTS)
1Sa 15:22 "Does the LORD *d*
Ps 1: 2 But his *d* is in the law of the LORD
16: 3 in whom is all my *d*.
35: 9 and *d* in his salvation.
37: 4 *D* yourself in the LORD
43: 4 to God, my joy and my *d*.
51:16 You do not *d* in sacrifice,
119: 77 for your law is my *d*.
Pr 29:17 he will bring *d* to your soul.
Isa 42: 1 my chosen one in whom I *d*;
55: 2 and your soul will *d* in the richest
61:10 I *d* greatly in the LORD;
Jer 9:24 for in these I *d*,"
15:16 they were my joy and my heart's *d*,
Mic 7:18 but *d* to show mercy.
Zep 3:17 He will take great *d* in you,
Mt 12:18 the one I love, in whom I *d*;
1Co 13: 6 Love does not *d* in evil
2Co 12:10 for Christ's sake, I *d* in weaknesses,

DELIGHTS (DELIGHT)
Ps 22: 8 since he *d* in him."
35:27 who *d* in the well-being
36: 8 from your river of *d*.
37:23 if the LORD *d* in a man's way,
Pr 3:12 as a father the son he *d* in.
12:22 but he *d* in men who are truthful.
23:24 he who has a wise son *d* in him.

DELILAH*
Woman who betrayed Samson (Jdg 16:4-22).

DELIVER (DELIVERANCE DELIVERED DELIVERER DELIVERS)
Ps 72:12 For he will *d* the needy who cry out
79: 9 *d* us and forgive our sins
Mt 6:13 but *d* us from the evil one.'
2Co 1:10 hope that he will continue to *d* us,

DELIVERANCE (DELIVER)
Ps 3: 8 From the LORD comes *d*.
32: 7 and surround me with songs of *d*.
33:17 A horse is a vain hope for *d*;

DELIVERED (DELIVER)
Ps 34: 4 he *d* me from all my fears.
Ro 4:25 He was *d* over to death for our sins

DELIVERER (DELIVER)
Ps 18: 2 is my rock, my fortress and my *d*;
40:17 You are my help and my *d*;
140: 7 O Sovereign LORD, my strong *d*,
144: 2 my stronghold and my *d*,

DELIVERS (DELIVER)
Ps 34:17 he *d* them from all their troubles.
34:19 but the LORD *d* him from them all
37:40 The LORD helps them and *d* them
37:40 he *d* them from the wicked

DEMANDED
Lk 12:20 This very night your life will be *d*
12:48 been given much, much will be *d;*

DEMONS
Mt 12:27 And if I drive out *d* by Beelzebub,
Mk 5:15 possessed by the legion of *d,*
Ro 8:38 neither angels nor *d,* neither
Jas 2:19 Good! Even the *d* believe that—

DEMONSTRATE (DEMONSTRATES)
Ro 3:26 he did it to *d* his justice

DEMONSTRATES* (DEMONSTRATE)
Ro 5: 8 God *d* his own love for us in this:

DEN
Da 6:16 and threw him into the lions' *d.*
Mt 21:13 you are making it a '*d* of robbers.' "

DENARIUS
Mk 12:15 Bring me a *d* and let me look at it."

DENIED (DENY)
1Ti 5: 8 he has *d* the faith and is worse

DENIES (DENY)
1Jn 2:23 No one who *d* the Son has

DENY (DENIED DENIES DENYING)
Ex 23: 6 "Do not *d* justice to your poor
Job 27: 5 till I die, I will not *d* my integrity.
La 3:35 to *d* a man his rights
Lk 9:23 he must *d* himself and take up his
Tit 1:16 but by their actions they *d* him.

DENYING* (DENY)
Eze 22:29 mistreat the alien, *d* them justice.
2Ti 3: 5 a form of godliness but *d* its power.
2Pe 2: 1 *d* the sovereign Lord who bought

DEPART (DEPARTED)
Ge 49:10 The scepter will not *d* from Judah,
Job 1:21 and naked I will *d.*
Mt 25:41 '*D* from me, you who are cursed,
Php 1:23 I desire to *d* and be with Christ,

DEPARTED (DEPART)
1Sa 4:21 "The glory has *d* from Israel"—
Ps 119:102 I have not *d* from your laws,

DEPOSIT
2Co 1:22 put his Spirit in our hearts as a *d,*
5: 5 and has given us the Spirit as a *d,*
Eph 1:14 who is a *d* guaranteeing our
2Ti 1:14 Guard the good *d* that was

DEPRAVED (DEPRAVITY)
Ro 1:28 he gave them over to a *d* mind,
Php 2:15 fault in a crooked and *d* generation,

DEPRAVITY (DEPRAVED)
Ro 1:29 of wickedness, evil, greed and *d.*

DEPRIVE
Dt 24:17 Do not *d* the alien or the fatherless
Pr 18: 5 or to *d* the innocent of justice.
Isa 10: 2 to *d* the poor of their rights
29:21 with false testimony *d* the innocent
1Co 7: 5 Do not *d* each other

DEPTH (DEEP)
Ro 8:39 any powers, neither height nor *d,*
11:33 the *d* of the riches of the wisdom

DESERT
Nu 32:13 wander in the *d* forty years,
Ne 9:19 you did not abandon them in the *d.*
Ps 78:19 "Can God spread a table in the *d?*
78:52 led them like sheep through the *d.*
Mk 1:13 and he was in the *d* forty days,

DESERTED (DESERTS)
Ezr 9: 9 our God has not *d* us
Mt 26:56 all the disciples *d* him and fled.
2Ti 1:15 in the province of Asia has *d* me,

DESERTING (DESERTS)
Gal 1: 6 are so quickly *d* the one who called

DESERTS (DESERTED DESERTING)
Zec 11:17 who *d* the flock!

DESERVE (DESERVES)
Ps 103: 10 he does not treat us as our sins *d*
Jer 21:14 I will punish you as your deeds *d,*
Mt 22: 8 those I invited did not *d* to come.
Ro 1:32 those who do such things *d* death,

DESERVES (DESERVE)
2Sa 12: 5 the man who did this *d* to die!
Lk 10: 7 for the worker *d* his wages.
1Ti 5:18 and "The worker *d* his wages."

DESIRABLE (DESIRE)
Pr 22: 1 A good name is more *d*

DESIRE (DESIRABLE DESIRES)
Ge 3:16 Your *d* will be for your husband,
Dt 5:21 You shall not set your *d*
1Ch 29:18 keep this *d* in the hearts
Ps 40: 6 Sacrifice and offering you did not *d*
40: 8 I *d* to do your will, O my God;
73:25 earth has nothing I *d* besides you
Pr 3:15 nothing you *d* can compare
10:24 what the righteous *d* will be
11:23 The *d* of the righteous ends only
Isa 26: 8 are the *d* of our hearts.
53: 2 appearance that we should *d* him.
Isa 55:11 but will accomplish what I *d*
Hos 6: 6 For I *d* mercy, not sacrifice,
Mt 9:13 learn what this means: 'I *d* mercy,
Ro 7:18 For I have the *d* to do what is good,
1Co 12:31 But eagerly *d* the greater gifts.
14: 1 and eagerly *d* spiritual gifts,
Php 1:23 I *d* to depart and be with Christ,
Heb 13:18 *d* to live honorably in every way.
Jas 1:15 Then, after *d* has conceived,

DESIRES (DESIRE)
Ge 4: 7 at your door; it *d* to have you,
Ps 34:12 and *d* to see many good days,
37: 4 he will give you the *d* of your heart.
103: 5 satisfies your *d* with good things,
145: 19 He fulfills the *d* of those who fear
Pr 11: 6 the unfaithful are trapped by evil *d.*
19:22 What a man *d* is unfailing love;
Mk 4:19 and the *d* for other things come in
Ro 8: 5 set on what that nature *d;*
13:14 to gratify the *d* of the sinful nature.
Gal 5:16 and you will not gratify the *d*
5:17 the sinful nature *d* what is contrary
1Ti 3: 1 an overseer, he *d* a noble task.
6: 9 and harmful *d* that plunge men
2Ti 2:22 Flee the evil *d* of youth,
Jas 1:20 about the righteous life that God *d.*
4: 1 from your *d* that battle within you?
1Pe 2:11 to abstain from sinful *d,* which war
1Jn 2:17 The world and its *d* pass away,

DESOLATE
Isa 54: 1 are the children of the *d* woman

DESPAIR
Isa 61: 3 instead of a spirit of *d.*
2Co 4: 8 perplexed, but not in *d;* persecuted,

DESPISE (DESPISED DESPISES)
Job 42: 6 Therefore I *d* myself
Pr 1: 7 but fools *d* wisdom and discipline.
3:11 do not *d* the LORD's discipline
23:22 do not *d* your mother
Lk 16:13 devoted to the one and *d* the other.
Tit 2:15 Do not let anyone *d* you.

DESPISED (DESPISE)
Ge 25:34 So Esau *d* his birthright.
Isa 53: 3 He was *d* and rejected by men,
1Co 1:28 of this world and the *d* things—

DESPISES (DESPISE)
Pr 14:21 He who *d* his neighbor sins,
15:20 but a foolish man *d* his mother.
15:32 who ignores discipline *d* himself,
Zec 4:10 "Who *d* the day of small things?

DESTINED (DESTINY)
Lk 2:34 “This child is *d* to cause the falling

DESTINY (DESTINED PREDESTINED)
Ps 73:17 then I understood their final *d*.
Ecc 7: 2 for death is the *d* of every man;

DESTITUTE
Pr 31: 8 for the rights of all who are *d*.
Heb 11:37 *d*, persecuted and mistreated—

DESTROY (DESTROYED DESTROYS DESTRUCTION)
Pr 1:32 complacency of fools will *d* them;
Mt 10:28 of the One who can *d* both soul

DESTROYED (DESTROY)
Job 19:26 And after my skin has been *d*,
Isa 55:13 which will not be *d*.”
1Co 8:11 for whom Christ died, is *d*
15:26 The last enemy to be *d* is death.
2Co 5: 1 if the earthly tent we live in is *d*,
Heb 10:39 of those who shrink back and are *d*,
2Pe 3:10 the elements will be *d* by fire,

DESTROYS (DESTROY)
Pr 6:32 whoever does so *d* himself.
11: 9 mouth the godless *d* his neighbor,
18: 9 is brother to one who *d*.
28:24 he is partner to him who *d*.
Ecc 9:18 but one sinner *d* much good.
1Co 3:17 If anyone *d* God's temple,

DESTRUCTION (DESTROY)
Pr 16:18 Pride goes before *d*,
Hos 13:14 Where, O grave, is your *d*?
Mt 7:13 broad is the road that leads to *d*,
Gal 6: 8 from that nature will reap *d*;
2Th 1: 9 punished with everlasting *d*
1Ti 6: 9 that plunge men into ruin and *d*.
2Pe 2: 1 bringing swift *d* on themselves.
3:16 other Scriptures, to their own *d*.

DETERMINED (DETERMINES)
Job 14: 5 Man's days are *d*;
Isa 14:26 This is the plan *d* for the whole
Da 11:36 for what has been *d* must take place
Ac 17:26 and he *d* the times set for them

DETERMINES* (DETERMINED)
Ps 147: 4 He *d* the number of the stars
Pr 16: 9 but the LORD *d* his steps.
1Co 12:11 them to each one, just as he *d*.

DETESTABLE (DETESTS)
Pr 21:27 The sacrifice of the wicked is *d*—
28: 9 even his prayers are *d*.
Isa 1:13 Your incense is *d* to me.
Lk 16:15 among men is *d* in God's sight.
Tit 1:16 They are *d*, disobedient

DETESTS (DETESTABLE)
Dt 22: 5 LORD your God *d* anyone who
23:18 the LORD your God *d* them both.
25:16 LORD your God *d* anyone who
Pr 12:22 The LORD *d* lying lips,
15: 8 The LORD *d* the sacrifice
15: 9 The LORD *d* the way
15:26 The LORD *d* the thoughts
16: 5 The LORD *d* all the proud of heart
17:15 the LORD *d* them both.
20:23 The LORD *d* differing weights,

DEVIL (DEVIL'S)
Mt 13:39 the enemy who sows them is the *d*.
25:41 the eternal fire prepared for the *d*
Lk 4: 2 forty days he was tempted by the *d*.
8:12 then the *d* comes and takes away
Eph 4:27 and do not give the *d* a foothold.
2Ti 2:26 and escape from the trap of the *d*,
Jas 4: 7 Resist the *d*, and he will flee
1Pe 5: 8 Your enemy the *d* prowls
1Jn 3: 8 who does what is sinful is of the *d*,
Rev 12: 9 that ancient serpent called the *d*

DEVIL'S* (DEVIL)
Eph 6:11 stand against the *d* schemes.
1Ti 3: 7 into disgrace and into the *d* trap.
1Jn 3: 8 was to destroy the *d* work.

DEVOTE (DEVOTED DEVOTING DEVOTION DEVOUT)
Job 11:13 “Yet if you *d* your heart to him
Jer 30:21 for who is he who will *d* himself
Col 4: 2 *D* yourselves to prayer, being
1Ti 4:13 *d* yourself to the public reading
Tit 3: 8 may be careful to *d* themselves

DEVOTED (DEVOTE)
Ezr 7:10 For Ezra had *d* himself to the study
Ac 2:42 They *d* themselves
Ro 12:10 Be *d* to one another
1Co 7:34 Her aim is to be *d* to the Lord

DEVOTING (DEVOTE)
1Ti 5:10 *d* herself to all kinds of good deeds.

DEVOTION (DEVOTE)
1Ch 28: 9 and serve him with wholehearted *d*
Eze 33:31 With their mouths they express *d*,
1Co 7:35 way in undivided *d* to the Lord.
2Co 11: 3 from your sincere and pure *d*

DEVOUR
2Sa 2:26 “Must the sword *d* forever?
Mk 12:40 They *d* widows' houses
1Pe 5: 8 lion looking for someone to *d*.

DEVOUT (DEVOTE)
Lk 2:25 Simeon, who was righteous and *d*.

DIE (DEAD DEATH DIED DIES)
Ge 2:17 when you eat of it you will surely *d*
Ex 11: 5 Every firstborn son in Egypt will *d*,
Ru 1:17 Where you *d* I will *d*, and there I
2Ki 14: 6 each is to *d* for his own sins.”
Pr 5:23 He will *d* for lack of discipline,
10:21 but fools *d* for lack of judgment.
15:10 he who hates correction will *d*.
23:13 with the rod, he will not *d*.
Ecc 3: 2 a time to be born and a time to *d*,
Isa 66:24 their worm will not *d*, nor will their
Eze 3:18 that wicked man will *d* for his sin,
18: 4 soul who sins is the one who will *d*.
33: 8 ‘O wicked man, you will surely *d*,’
Mt 26:52 “for all who draw the sword will *d*
Jn 11:26 and believes in me will never *d*.
Ro 5: 7 Very rarely will anyone *d*
14: 8 and if we *d*, we *d* to the Lord.
1Co 15:22 in Adam all *d*, so in Christ all will
15:31 I *d* every day—I mean that,
Php 1:21 to live is Christ and to *d* is gain.
Heb 9:27 Just as man is destined to *d* once,
Rev 14:13 Blessed are the dead who *d*

DIED (DIE)
Ro 5: 6 we were still powerless, Christ *d*
6: 2 By no means! We *d* to sin;
6: 8 if we *d* with Christ, we believe that
14:15 brother for whom Christ *d*.
1Co 8:11 for whom Christ *d*, is destroyed
15: 3 that Christ *d* for our sins according
2Co 5:14 *d* for all, and therefore all *d*.
Col 3: 3 For you *d*, and your life is now
1Th 5:10 He *d* for us so that, whether we are
2Ti 2:11 If we *d* with him,
Heb 9:15 now that he has *d* as a ransom
1Pe 3:18 For Christ *d* for sins once for all,
Rev 2: 8 who *d* and came to life again.

DIES (DIE)
Job 14:14 If a man *d*, will he live again?
Pr 11: 7 a wicked man *d*, his hope perishes;
Jn 11:25 in me will live, even though he *d*;
1Co 15:36 does not come to life unless it *d*.

DIFFERENCE (DIFFERENT)
Ro 10:12 For there is no *d* between Jew

DIFFERENT (DIFFERENCE)
1Co 12: 4 There are *d* kinds of gifts,
2Co 11: 4 or a *d* gospel from the one you

DIGNITY
Pr 31:25 She is clothed with strength and *d*;

DIGS
Pr 26:27 If a man *d* a pit, he will fall into it;

DILIGENCE (DILIGENT)
Heb 6:11 to show this same *d* to the very end

DILIGENT (DILIGENCE)
Pr 21: 5 The plans of the *d* lead to profit
1Ti 4:15 Be *d* in these matters; give yourself

DIRECT (DIRECTS)
Ps 119: 35 *D* me in the path of your
119:133 *D* my footsteps according
Jer 10:23 it is not for man to *d* his steps.
2Th 3: 5 May the Lord *d* your hearts

DIRECTS (DIRECT)
Ps 42: 8 By day the LORD *d* his love,
Isa 48:17 who *d* you in the way you should

DIRGE
Mt 11:17 we sang a *d,*

DISAPPEAR
Mt 5:18 will by any means *d* from the Law
Lk 16:17 earth to *d* than for the least stroke

DISAPPOINT* (DISAPPOINTED)
Ro 5: 5 And hope does not *d* us,

DISAPPOINTED (DISAPPOINT)
Ps 22: 5 in you they trusted and were not *d.*

DISASTER
Ps 57: 1 wings until the *d* has passed.
Pr 3:25 Have no fear of sudden *d*
17: 5 over *d* will not go unpunished.
Isa 45: 7 I bring prosperity and create *d;*
Eze 7: 5 An unheard-of *d* is coming.

DISCERN (DISCERNING DISCERNMENT)
Ps 19:12 Who can *d* his errors?
139: 3 You *d* my going out and my lying
Php 1:10 you may be able to *d* what is best

DISCERNING (DISCERN)
Pr 14: 6 knowledge comes easily to the *d.*
15:14 The *d* heart seeks knowledge,
17:24 A *d* man keeps wisdom in view,
17:28 and *d* if he holds his tongue.
19:25 rebuke a *d* man, and he will gain

DISCERNMENT (DISCERN)
Pr 17:10 A rebuke impresses a man of *d*
28:11 a poor man who has *d* sees

DISCIPLE (DISCIPLES)
Mt 10:42 these little ones because he is my *d,*
Lk 14:27 and follow me cannot be my *d.*

DISCIPLES (DISCIPLE)
Mt 28:19 Therefore go and make *d*
Jn 8:31 to my teaching, you are really my *d*
13:35 men will know that you are my *d*
Ac 11:26 The *d* were called Christians first

DISCIPLINE (DISCIPLINED DISCIPLINES)
Ps 38: 1 or *d* me in your wrath.
39:11 You rebuke and *d* men for their sin;
94:12 Blessed is the man you *d,* O LORD
Pr 1: 7 but fools despise wisdom and *d.*
3:11 do not despise the LORD's *d*
5:12 You will say, "How I hated *d!*
5:23 He will die for lack of *d,*
6:23 and the corrections of *d*
10:17 He who heeds *d* shows the way
12: 1 Whoever loves *d* loves knowledge,
13:18 He who ignores *d* comes to poverty
13:24 who loves him is careful to *d* him.
15: 5 A fool spurns his father's *d,*
15:32 He who ignores *d* despises himself,
19:18 *D* your son, for in that there is hope
22:15 the rod of *d* will drive it far
23:13 Do not withhold *d* from a child;
29:17 *D* your son, and he will give you
Heb 12: 5 do not make light of the Lord's *d,*
12: 7 as *d;* God is treating you
12:11 No *d* seems pleasant at the time,
Rev 3:19 Those whom I love I rebuke and *d.*

DISCIPLINED (DISCIPLINE)
Pr 1: 3 for acquiring a *d* and prudent life,
Jer 31:18 'You *d* me like an unruly calf,
1Co 11:32 we are being *d* so that we will not
Tit 1: 8 upright, holy and *d.*
Heb 12: 7 For what son is not *d* by his father?

DISCIPLINES (DISCIPLINE)
Dt 8: 5 your heart that as a man *d* his son,
Pr 3:12 the LORD *d* those he loves,
Heb 12: 6 because the Lord *d* those he loves,
12:10 but God *d* us for our good,

DISCLOSED
Lk 8:17 is nothing hidden that will not be *d,*

DISCOURAGED
Jos 1: 9 Do not be terrified; do not be *d,*
10:25 "Do not be afraid; do not be *d.*
1Ch 28:20 or *d,* for the LORD God,
Isa 42: 4 he will not falter or be *d*
Col 3:21 children, or they will become *d.*

DISCREDITED
2Co 6: 3 so that our ministry will not be *d.*

DISCRETION*
1Ch 22:12 May the LORD give you *d*
Pr 1: 4 knowledge and *d* to the young—
2:11 *D* will protect you,
5: 2 that you may maintain *d*
8:12 I possess knowledge and *d.*
11:22 a beautiful woman who shows no *d.*

DISCRIMINATED*
Jas 2: 4 have you not *d* among yourselves

DISFIGURED
Isa 52:14 his appearance was so *d*

DISGRACE (DISGRACEFUL DISGRACES)
Pr 11: 2 When pride comes, then comes *d,*
14:34 but sin is a *d* to any people.
19:26 is a son who brings shame and *d.*
Ac 5:41 of suffering *d* for the Name.
Heb 13:13 the camp, bearing the *d* he bore.

DISGRACEFUL (DISGRACE)
Pr 10: 5 during harvest is a *d* son.
17: 2 wise servant will rule over a *d* son,

DISGRACES (DISGRACE)
Pr 28: 7 of gluttons *d* his father.
29:15 but a child left to itself *d* his mother

DISHONEST
Pr 11: 1 The LORD abhors *d* scales,
29:27 The righteous detest the *d;*
Lk 16:10 whoever is *d* with very little will
1Ti 3: 8 wine, and not pursuing *d* gain.

DISHONOR (DISHONORS)
Lev 18: 7 " 'Do not *d* your father
Pr 30: 9 and so *d* the name of my God.
1Co 15:43 it is sown in *d,* it is raised in glory;

DISHONORS (DISHONOR)
Dt 27:16 Cursed is the man who *d* his father

DISMAYED
Isa 28:16 the one who trusts will never be *d.*
41:10 do not be *d,* for I am your God.

DISOBEDIENCE (DISOBEY)
Ro 5:19 as through the *d* of the one man
11:32 to *d* so that he may have mercy
Heb 2: 2 and *d* received its just punishment,
4: 6 go in, because of their *d.*
4:11 fall by following their example of *d.*

DISOBEDIENT (DISOBEY)
2Ti 3: 2 proud, abusive, *d* to their parents,
Tit 1: 6 to the charge of being wild and *d.*
1:16 *d* and unfit for doing anything

DISOBEY (DISOBEDIENCE DISOBEDIENT)
Dt 11:28 the curse if you *d* the commands
2Ch 24:20 'Why do you *d* the LORD's
Ro 1:30 they *d* their parents; they are

DISORDER
1Co 14:33 For God is not a God of *d*
2Co 12:20 slander, gossip, arrogance and *d.*
Jas 3:16 there you find *d* and every evil

DISOWN
Pr 30: 9 I may have too much and *d* you
Mt 10:33 I will *d* him before my Father
26:35 to die with you, I will never *d* you."
2Ti 2:12 If we *d* him,

DISPLAY (DISPLAYS)
Eze 39:21 I will *d* my glory among the nations
1Ti 1:16 Christ Jesus might *d* his unlimited

DISPLAYS (DISPLAY)
Isa 44:23 he *d* his glory in Israel.

DISPUTE (DISPUTES)
Pr 17:14 before a *d* breaks out.
1Co 6: 1 If any of you has a *d* with another,

DISPUTES (DISPUTE)
Pr 18:18 Casting the lot settles *d*

DISQUALIFIED
1Co 9:27 I myself will not be *d* for the prize.

DISREPUTE*
2Pe 2: 2 will bring the way of truth into *d.*

DISSENSION*
Pr 6:14 he always stirs up *d.*
6:19 and a man who stirs up *d*
10:12 Hatred stirs up *d,*
15:18 A hot-tempered man stirs up *d,*
16:28 A perverse man stirs up *d,*
28:25 A greedy man stirs up *d,*
29:22 An angry man stirs up *d,*
Ro 13:13 debauchery, not in *d* and jealousy.

DISSIPATION*
Lk 21:34 will be weighed down with *d,*
1Pe 4: 4 with them into the same flood of *d,*

DISTINGUISH
1Ki 3: 9 and to *d* between right and wrong.
Heb 5:14 themselves to *d* good from evil.

DISTORT
2Co 4: 2 nor do we *d* the word of God.
2Pe 3:16 ignorant and unstable people *d,*

DISTRESS (DISTRESSED)
Ps 18: 6 In my *d* I called to the LORD;
Jnh 2: 2 "In my *d* I called to the LORD,
Jas 1:27 after orphans and widows in their *d*

DISTRESSED (DISTRESS)
Ro 14:15 If your brother is *d*

DIVIDED (DIVISION)
Mt 12:25 household *d* against itself will not
Lk 23:34 they *d* up his clothes by casting lots
1Co 1:13 Is Christ *d?* Was Paul crucified

DIVINATION
Lev 19:26 " 'Do not practice *d* or sorcery.

DIVINE
Ro 1:20 his eternal power and *d* nature—
2Co 10: 4 they have *d* power
2Pe 1: 4 you may participate in the *d* nature

DIVISION (DIVIDED DIVISIONS DIVISIVE)
Lk 12:51 on earth? No, I tell you, but *d.*
1Co 12:25 so that there should be no *d*

DIVISIONS (DIVISION)
Ro 16:17 to watch out for those who cause *d*
1Co 1:10 another so that there may be no *d*
11:18 there are *d* among you,

DIVISIVE* (DIVISION)
Tit 3:10 Warn a *d* person once,

DIVORCE
Mal 2:16 "I hate *d,*" says the LORD God
Mt 19: 3 for a man to *d* his wife for any
1Co 7:11 And a husband must not *d* his wife.
7:27 Are you married? Do not seek a *d.*

DOCTOR
Mt 9:12 "It is not the healthy who need a *d,*

DOCTRINE
1Ti 4:16 Watch your life and *d* closely.
Tit 2: 1 is in accord with sound *d.*

DOMINION
Ps 22:28 for *d* belongs to the LORD

DOOR
Ps 141: 3 keep watch over the *d* of my lips.
Mt 6: 6 close the *d* and pray to your Father
7: 7 and the *d* will be opened to you.
Rev 3:20 I stand at the *d* and knock.

DOORKEEPER
Ps 84:10 I would rather be a *d* in the house

DOUBLE-EDGED
Heb 4:12 Sharper than any *d* sword,
Rev 1:16 of his mouth came a sharp *d* sword.
2:12 of him who has the sharp, *d* sword.

DOUBLE-MINDED (MIND)
Ps 119:113 I hate *d* men,
Jas 1: 8 he is a *d* man, unstable

DOUBT
Mt 14:31 he said, "why did you *d?*"
21:21 if you have faith and do not *d,*
Mk 11:23 and does not *d* in his heart
Jas 1: 6 he must believe and not *d,*
Jude :22 Be merciful to those who *d;*

DOWNCAST
Ps 42: 5 Why are you *d,* O my soul?
2Co 7: 6 But God, who comforts the *d,*

DRAW (DRAWING DRAWS)
Mt 26:52 "for all who *d* the sword will die
Jn 12:32 up from the earth, will *d* all men
Heb 10:22 let us *d* near to God

DRAWING (DRAW)
Lk 21:28 because your redemption is *d* near

DRAWS (DRAW)
Jn 6:44 the Father who sent me *d* him,

DREADFUL
Heb 10:31 It is a *d* thing to fall into the hands

DRESS
1Ti 2: 9 I also want women to *d* modestly,

DRINK (DRUNK DRUNKARDS DRUNKENNESS)
Pr 5:15 *D* water from your own cistern,
Lk 12:19 Take life easy; eat, *d* and be merry
Jn 7:37 let him come to me and *d.*
1Co 12:13 were all given the one Spirit to *d.*
Rev 21: 6 to *d* without cost from the spring

DRIVES
1Jn 4:18 But perfect love *d* out fear,

DROP
Pr 17:14 so *d* the matter before a dispute
Isa 40:15 Surely the nations are like a *d*

DRUNK (DRINK)
Eph 5:18 Do not get *d* on wine, which leads

DRUNKARDS (DRINK)
Pr 23:21 for *d* and gluttons become poor,
1Co 6:10 nor the greedy nor *d* nor slanderers

DRUNKENNESS (DRINK)
Lk 21:34 weighed down with dissipation, *d*
Ro 13:13 and *d,* not in sexual immorality
Gal 5:21 factions and envy; *d,* orgies,
1Pe 4: 3 living in debauchery, lust, *d,* orgies,

DRY
Isa 53: 2 and like a root out of *d* ground.
Eze 37: 4 *'D* bones, hear the word

DUST
Ge 2: 7 man from the *d* of the ground
Ps 103: 14 he remembers that we are *d.*
Ecc 3:20 all come from *d,* and to *d* all return.

DUTY
Ecc 12:13 for this is the whole *d* of man.
Ac 23: 1 I have fulfilled my *d* to God
1Co 7: 3 husband should fulfill his marital *d*

DWELL (DWELLING)
1Ki 8:27 "But will God really *d* on earth?
Ps 23: 6 I will *d* in the house of the LORD
Isa 43:18 do not *d* on the past.
Eph 3:17 so that Christ may *d* in your hearts
Col 1:19 to have all his fullness *d* in him,
3:16 the word of Christ *d* in you richly

DWELLING (DWELL)
Eph 2:22 to become a *d* in which God lives

EAGER
Pr 31:13 and works with *e* hands.
1Pe 5: 2 greedy for money, but *e* to serve;

EAGLE'S (EAGLES)
Ps 103: 5 your youth is renewed like the *e.*

EAGLES (EAGLE'S)
Isa 40:31 They will soar on wings like *e;*

EAR (EARS)
1Co 2: 9 no *e* has heard,
12:16 if the *e* should say, "Because I am

EARNED
Pr 31:31 Give her the reward she has *e,*

EARS (EAR)
Job 42: 5 My *e* had heard of you
Ps 34:15 and his *e* are attentive to their cry;
Pr 21:13 If a man shuts his *e* to the cry
2Ti 4: 3 to say what their itching *e* want

EARTH (EARTHLY)
Ge 1: 1 God created the heavens and the *e.*
Ps 24: 1 *e* is the LORD's, and everything
108: 5 and let your glory be over all the *e.*
Isa 6: 3 the whole *e* is full of his glory."
51: 6 the *e* will wear out like a garment
55: 9 the heavens are higher than the *e,*
66: 1 and the *e* is my footstool.
Jer 23:24 "Do not I fill heaven and *e?"*
Hab 2:20 let all the *e* be silent before him."
Mt 6:10 done on *e* as it is in heaven.
16:19 bind on *e* will be bound
24:35 Heaven and *e* will pass away,
28:18 and on *e* has been given to me.
Lk 2:14 on *e* peace to men
1Co 10:26 The *e* is the Lord's, and everything
Php 2:10 in heaven and on *e* and under the *e,*
2Pe 3:13 to a new heaven and a new *e,*

EARTHLY (EARTH)
Php 3:19 Their mind is on *e* things.
Col 3: 2 on things above, not on *e* things.

EAST
Ps 103: 12 as far as the *e* is from the west,

EASY
Mt 11:30 For my yoke is *e* and my burden is

EAT (EATING)
Ge 2:17 but you must not *e* from the tree
Isa 55: 1 come, buy and *e!*
65:25 and the lion will *e* straw like the ox,
Mt 26:26 "Take and *e;* this is my body."
Ro 14: 2 faith allows him to *e* everything,
1Co 8:13 if what I *e* causes my brother to fall
10:31 So whether you *e* or drink
2Th 3:10 man will not work, he shall not *e."*

EATING (EAT)
Ro 14:17 kingdom of God is not a matter of *e*

EDICT
Heb 11:23 they were not afraid of the king's *e.*

EDIFIES
1Co 14: 4 but he who prophesies *e* the church

EFFECT
Isa 32:17 *e* of righteousness will be quietness
Heb 9:18 put into *e* without blood.

EFFORT
Lk 13:24 "Make every *e* to enter
Ro 9:16 depend on man's desire or *e,*
14:19 make every *e* to do what leads
Eph 4: 3 Make every *e* to keep the unity
Heb 4:11 make every *e* to enter that rest,
12:14 Make every *e* to live in peace
2Pe 1: 5 make every *e* to add
3:14 make every *e* to be found spotless,

ELAH
Son of Baasha; king of Israel (1Ki 16:6-14).

ELDERLY* (ELDERS)
Lev 19:32 show respect for the *e*

ELDERS (ELDERLY)
1Ti 5:17 The *e* who direct the affairs

ELECTION
Ro 9:11 God's purpose in *e* might stand:
2Pe 1:10 to make your calling and *e* sure.

ELI
High priest in youth of Samuel (1Sa 1-4). Blessed Hannah (1Sa 1:12-18); raised Samuel (1Sa 2:11-26).

ELIJAH
Prophet; predicted famine in Israel (1Ki 17:1; Jas 5:17). Fed by ravens (1Ki 17:2-6). Raised Sidonian widow's son (1Ki 17:7-24). Defeated prophets of Baal at Carmel (1Ki 18:16-46). Ran from Jezebel (1Ki 19:1-9). Prophesied death of Azariah (2Ki 1). Succeeded by Elishah (1Ki 19:19-21; 2Ki 2:1-18). Taken to heaven in whirlwind (2Ki 2:11-12).
Return prophesied (Mal 4:5-6); equated with John the Baptist (Mt 17:9-13; Mk 9:9-13; Lk 1:17). Appeared with Moses in transfiguration of Jesus (Mt 17:1-8; Mk 9:1-8).

ELISHA
Prophet; successor of Elijah (1Ki 19:16-21); inherited his cloak (2Ki 2:1-18). Miracles of (2Ki 2-6).

ELIZABETH*
Mother of John the Baptist, relative of Mary (Lk 1:5-58).

EMBITTER*
Col 3:21 Fathers, do not *e* your children,

EMPTY
Eph 5: 6 no one deceive you with *e* words,
1Pe 1:18 from the *e* way of life handed

ENABLE (ABLE)
Lk 1:74 to *e* us to serve him without fear
Ac 4:29 *e* your servants to speak your word

ENABLED (ABLE)
Lev 26:13 *e* you to walk with heads held high.
Jn 6:65 unless the Father has *e* him."

ENABLES (ABLE)
Php 3:21 by the power that *e* him

ENCAMPS*
Ps 34: 7 The angel of the LORD *e*

ENCOURAGE (ENCOURAGEMENT)
Ps 10:17 you *e* them, and you listen
Isa 1:17 *e* the oppressed.
Ac 15:32 to *e* and strengthen the brothers.
Ro 12: 8 if it is encouraging, let him *e;*
1Th 4:18 Therefore *e* each other
2Ti 4: 2 rebuke and *e*—with great patience
Tit 2: 6 *e* the young men to be
Heb 3:13 But *e* one another daily, as long
10:25 but let us *e* one another—

ENCOURAGEMENT (ENCOURAGE)
Ac 4:36 Barnabas (which means Son of *E),*
Ro 15: 4 *e* of the Scriptures we might have
15: 5 and *e* give you a spirit of unity
1Co 14: 3 to men for their strengthening, *e*
Heb 12: 5 word of *e* that addresses you

END
Ps 119: 33 then I will keep them to the *e.*
Pr 14:12 but in the *e* it leads to death.
19:20 and in the *e* you will be wise.
23:32 In the *e* it bites like a snake
Ecc 12:12 making many books there is no *e,*
Mt 10:22 firm to the *e* will be saved.
Lk 21: 9 but the *e* will not come right away
Ro 10: 4 Christ is the *e* of the law
1Co 15:24 the *e* will come, when he hands

ENDURANCE (ENDURE)
Ro 15: 4 through *e* and the encouragement
15: 5 May the God who gives *e*
2Co 1: 6 which produces in you patient *e*
Col 1:11 might so that you may have great *e*
1Ti 6:11 faith, love, *e* and gentleness.
Tit 2: 2 and sound in faith, in love and in *e.*

ENDURE (ENDURANCE ENDURES)
Ps 72:17 May his name *e* forever;
Pr 12:19 Truthful lips *e* forever,
27:24 for riches do not *e* forever,
Ecc 3:14 everything God does will *e* forever;
Mal 3: 2 who can *e* the day of his coming?
2Ti 2: 3 *E* hardship with us like a good
2:12 if we *e,* / we will also reign
Heb 12: 7 *E* hardship as discipline; God is
Rev 3:10 kept my command to *e* patiently,

ENDURES (ENDURE)
Ps 112: 9 his righteousness *e* forever;
136: 1 *His love e forever.*
Da 9:15 made for yourself a name that *e*

ENEMIES (ENEMY)
Ps 23: 5 in the presence of my *e.*
Mic 7: 6 a man's *e* are the members
Mt 5:44 Love your *e* and pray
Lk 20:43 hand until I make your *e*

ENEMY (ENEMIES ENMITY)
Pr 24:17 Do not gloat when your *e* falls;

Pr 25:21 If your *e* is hungry, give him food
27: 6 but an *e* multiplies kisses.
1Co 15:26 The last *e* to be destroyed is death.
1Ti 5:14 and to give the *e* no opportunity

ENJOY (JOY)
Dt 6: 2 and so that you may *e* long life.
Eph 6: 3 and that you may *e* long life
Heb 11:25 rather than to *e* the pleasures of sin

ENJOYMENT (JOY)
Ecc 4: 8 and why am I depriving myself of *e*
1Ti 6:17 us with everything for our *e*.

ENLIGHTENED* (LIGHT)
Eph 1:18 that the eyes of your heart may be *e*
Heb 6: 4 for those who have once been *e*,

ENMITY* (ENEMY)
Ge 3:15 And I will put *e*

ENOCH
Walked with God and taken by him (Ge 5:18-24; Heb 11:5). Prophet (Jude 14).

ENTANGLED (ENTANGLES)
2Pe 2:20 and are again *e* in it and overcome,

ENTANGLES* (ENTANGLED)
Heb 12: 1 and the sin that so easily *e*,

ENTER (ENTERED ENTERS ENTRANCE)
Ps 100: 4 *E* his gates with thanksgiving
Mt 5:20 will certainly not *e* the kingdom
7:13 *"E* through the narrow gate.
18: 8 It is better for you to *e* life maimed
Mk 10:15 like a little child will never *e* it."
10:23 is for the rich to *e* the kingdom

ENTERED (ENTER)
Ro 5:12 as sin *e* the world through one man,
Heb 9:12 but he *e* the Most Holy Place once

ENTERS (ENTER)
Mk 7:18 you see that nothing that *e* a man
Jn 10: 2 The man who *e* by the gate is

ENTERTAIN
1Ti 5:19 Do not *e* an accusation
Heb 13: 2 Do not forget to *e* strangers,

ENTHRALLED*
Ps 45:11 The king is *e* by your beauty;

ENTHRONED (THRONE)
1Sa 4: 4 who is *e* between the cherubim.
Ps 2: 4 The One *e* in heaven laughs;
102: 12 But you, O LORD, sit *e* forever;
Isa 40:22 He sits *e* above the circle

ENTICE
Pr 1:10 My son, if sinners *e* you,
2Pe 2:18 they *e* people who are just escaping

ENTIRE
Gal 5:14 The *e* law is summed up

ENTRUSTED (TRUST)
1Ti 6:20 guard what has been *e* to your care.
2Ti 1:12 able to guard what I have *e* to him
1:14 Guard the good deposit that was *e*
Jude : 3 once for all *e* to the saints.

ENVY
Pr 3:31 Do not *e* a violent man
14:30 but *e* rots the bones.
1Co 13: 4 It does not *e*, it does not boast,

EPHRAIM
1. Second son of Joseph (Ge 41:52; 46:20). Blessed as firstborn by Jacob (Ge 48).
2. Synonymous with Northern Kingdom (Isa 7:17; Hos 5).

EQUAL
Isa 40:25 who is my *e?"* says the Holy One.
Jn 5:18 making himself *e* with God.
1Co 12:25 that its parts should have *e* concern

EQUIP* (EQUIPPED)
Heb 13:21 *e* you with everything good

EQUIPPED (EQUIP)
2Ti 3:17 man of God may be thoroughly *e*

ERROR
Jas 5:20 Whoever turns a sinner from the *e*

ESAU
Firstborn of Isaac, twin of Jacob (Ge 25:21-26). Also called Edom (Ge 25:30). Sold Jacob his birthright (Ge 25:29-34); lost blessing (Ge 27). Reconciled to Jacob (Gen 33).

ESCAPE (ESCAPING)
Ro 2: 3 think you will *e* God's judgment?
Heb 2: 3 how shall we *e* if we ignore such

ESCAPING (ESCAPE)
1Co 3:15 only as one *e* through the flames.

ESTABLISH
Ge 6:18 But I will *e* my covenant with you,
1Ch 28: 7 I will *e* his kingdom forever
Ro 10: 3 God and sought to *e* their own,

ESTEEMED
Pr 22: 1 to be *e* is better than silver or gold.
Isa 53: 3 he was despised, and we *e* him not.

ESTHER
Jewess who lived in Persia; cousin of Mordecai (Est 2:7). Chosen queen of Xerxes (Est 2:8-18). Foiled Haman's plan to exterminate the Jews (Est 3-4; 7-9).

ETERNAL (ETERNALLY ETERNITY)
Ps 16:11 with *e* pleasures at your right hand.
111: 10 To him belongs *e* praise.
119: 89 Your word, O LORD, is *e*;
Isa 26: 4 LORD, the LORD, is the Rock *e*.
Mt 19:16 good thing must I do to get *e* life?"
25:41 into the *e* fire prepared for the devil
25:46 they will go away to *e* punishment,
Jn 3:15 believes in him may have *e* life.
3:16 him shall not perish but have *e* life.
Jn 3:36 believes in the Son has *e* life,
4:14 spring of water welling up to *e* life."
5:24 believes him who sent me has *e* life
6:68 You have the words of *e* life.
10:28 I give them *e* life, and they shall
17: 3 this is *e* life: that they may know
Ro 1:20 his *e* power and divine nature—
6:23 but the gift of God is *e* life
2Co 4:17 for us an *e* glory that far outweighs
4:18 temporary, but what is unseen is *e*.
1Ti 1:16 believe on him and receive *e* life.
1:17 Now to the King *e*, immortal,
Heb 9:12 having obtained *e* redemption.
1Jn 5:11 God has given us *e* life,
5:13 you may know that you have *e* life.

ETERNALLY (ETERNAL)
Gal 1: 8 let him be *e* condemned! As we

ETERNITY (ETERNAL)
Ps 93: 2 you are from all *e*.
Ecc 3:11 also set *e* in the hearts of men;

ETHIOPIAN
Jer 13:23 Can the *E* change his skin

EUNUCHS
Mt 19:12 For some are *e* because they were

EVANGELIST (EVANGELISTS)
2Ti 4: 5 hardship, do the work of an *e*,

EVANGELISTS* (EVANGELIST)
Eph 4:11 some to be prophets, some to be *e*,

EVE
2Co 11: 3 as *E* was deceived by the serpent's
1Ti 2:13 For Adam was formed first, then *E*

EVEN-TEMPERED*
Pr 17:27 and a man of understanding is *e*.

EVER (EVERLASTING FOREVER)
Ex 15:18 LORD will reign for *e* and *e*."
Dt 8:19 If you *e* forget the LORD your
Ps 5:11 let them *e* sing for joy.
10:16 The LORD is King for *e* and *e*;
25: 3 will *e* be put to shame,
26: 3 for your love is *e* before me,
45: 6 O God, will last for *e* and *e*;
52: 8 God's unfailing love for *e* and *e*.
89:33 nor will I *e* betray my faithfulness.
145: 1 I will praise your name for *e* and *e*.
Pr 4:18 shining *e* brighter till the full light
5:19 may you *e* be captivated
Isa 66: 8 Who has *e* heard of such a thing?
Jer 31:36 the descendants of Israel *e* cease
Da 7:18 it forever—yes, for *e* and *e*.'
12: 3 like the stars for *e* and *e*.
Mk 4:12 *e* hearing but never understanding;
Jn 1:18 No one has *e* seen God,

Rev 1:18 and behold I am alive for *e* and *e*!
22: 5 And they will reign for *e* and *e*.

EVER-INCREASING* (INCREASE)
Ro 6:19 to impurity and to *e* wickedness,
2Co 3:18 into his likeness with *e* glory,

EVERLASTING (EVER)
Dt 33:27 and underneath are the *e* arms.
Ne 9: 5 your God, who is from *e* to *e*."
Ps 90: 2 from *e* to *e* you are God.
139: 24 and lead me in the way *e*.
Isa 9: 6 *E* Father, Prince of Peace.
33:14 Who of us can dwell with *e* burning
35:10 *e* joy will crown their heads.
45:17 the LORD with an *e* salvation;
54: 8 but with *e* kindness
55: 3 I will make an *e* covenant with you,
63:12 to gain for himself *e* renown,
Jer 31: 3 "I have loved you with an *e* love;
Da 9:24 to bring in *e* righteousness,
12: 2 some to *e* life, others to shame
Jn 6:47 the truth, he who believes has *e* life.
2Th 1: 9 punished with *e* destruction
Jude : 6 bound with *e* chains for judgment

EVER-PRESENT*
Ps 46: 1 an *e* help in trouble

EVIDENCE (EVIDENT)
Jn 14:11 on the *e* of the miracles themselves.

EVIDENT (EVIDENCE)
Php 4: 5 Let your gentleness be *e* to all.

EVIL
Ge 2: 9 of the knowledge of good and *e*.
Job 1: 1 he feared God and shunned *e*.
1: 8 a man who fears God and shuns *e*."
34:10 Far be it from God to do *e*,
Ps 23: 4 I will fear no *e*,
34:14 Turn from *e* and do good;
51: 4 and done what is *e* in your sight,
97:10 those who love the LORD hate *e*,
101: 4 I will have nothing to do with *e*.
Pr 8:13 To fear the LORD is to hate *e*;
10:23 A fool finds pleasure in *e* conduct,
11:27 *e* comes to him who searches for it.
24:19 Do not fret because of *e* men
24:20 for the *e* man has no future hope,
Isa 5:20 Woe to those who call *e* good
13:11 I will punish the world for its *e*,
55: 7 and the *e* man his thoughts.
Hab 1:13 Your eyes are too pure to look on *e*;
Mt 5:45 He causes his sun to rise on the *e*
6:13 but deliver us from the *e* one.'
7:11 If you, then, though you are *e*,
12:35 and the *e* man brings *e* things out
Jn 17:15 you protect them from the *e* one.
Ro 2: 9 for every human being who does *e*:
12: 9 Hate what is *e*; cling
12:17 Do not repay anyone *e* for *e*.
16:19 and innocent about what is *e*.
1Co 13: 6 Love does not delight in *e*
14:20 In regard to *e* be infants,
Eph 6:16 all the flaming arrows of the *e* one.
1Th 5:22 Avoid every kind of *e*.
1Ti 6:10 of money is a root of all kinds of *e*.
2Ti 2:22 Flee the *e* desires of youth,
Jas 1:13 For God cannot be tempted by *e*,
1Pe 2:16 your freedom as a cover-up for *e*;
3: 9 Do not repay *e* with *e* or insult

EXACT
Heb 1: 3 the *e* representation of his being,

EXALT (EXALTED EXALTS)
Ps 30: 1 I will *e* you, O LORD,
34: 3 let us *e* his name together.
118: 28 you are my God, and I will *e* you.
Isa 24:15 *e* the name of the LORD, the God

EXALTED (EXALT)
2Sa 22:47 *E* be God, the Rock, my Savior!
1Ch 29:11 you are *e* as head over all.
Ne 9: 5 and may it be *e* above all blessing
Ps 21:13 Be *e*, O LORD, in your strength;
46:10 I will be *e* among the nations,
57: 5 Be *e*, O God, above the heavens;
97: 9 you are *e* far above all gods.
99: 2 he is *e* over all the nations.
108: 5 Be *e*, O God, above the heavens,
148: 13 for his name alone is *e*;
Isa 6: 1 *e*, and the train of his robe filled
12: 4 and proclaim that his name is *e*.
33: 5 The LORD is *e*, for he dwells
Eze 21:26 The lowly will be *e* and the *e* will be
Mt 23:12 whoever humbles himself will be *e*.
Php 1:20 always Christ will be *e* in my body,
2: 9 Therefore God *e* him

EXALTS (EXALT)
Ps 75: 7 He brings one down, he *e* another.
Pr 14:34 Righteousness *e* a nation,
Mt 23:12 For whoever *e* himself will be

EXAMINE (EXAMINED)
Ps 26: 2 *e* my heart and my mind;
Jer 17:10 and *e* the mind,
La 3:40 Let us *e* our ways and test them,
1Co 11:28 A man ought to *e* himself
2Co 13: 5 *E* yourselves to see whether you

EXAMINED (EXAMINE)
Ac 17:11 *e* the Scriptures every day to see

EXAMPLE (EXAMPLES)
Jn 13:15 have set you an *e* that you should
1Co 11: 1 Follow my *e*, as I follow
1Ti 4:12 set an *e* for the believers in speech,
Tit 2: 7 In everything set them an *e*
1Pe 2:21 leaving you an *e*, that you should

EXAMPLES* (EXAMPLE)
1Co 10: 6 Now these things occurred as *e*
10:11 as *e* and were written down
1Pe 5: 3 to you, but being *e* to the flock.

EXASPERATE*
Eph 6: 4 Fathers, do not *e* your children;

EXCEL (EXCELLENT)
1Co 14:12 to *e* in gifts that build up the church
2Co 8: 7 But just as you *e* in everything—

EXCELLENT (EXCEL)
1Co 12:31 now I will show you the most *e* way
Php 4: 8 if anything is *e* or praiseworthy—
1Ti 3:13 have served well gain an *e* standing
Tit 3: 8 These things are *e* and profitable

EXCHANGED
Ro 1:23 *e* the glory of the immortal God
1:25 They *e* the truth of God for a lie,

EXCUSE (EXCUSES)
Jn 15:22 they have no *e* for their sin.
Ro 1:20 so that men are without *e*.

EXCUSES* (EXCUSE)
Lk 14:18 "But they all alike began to make *e*.

EXISTS
Heb 2:10 and through whom everything *e*,
11: 6 to him must believe that he *e*

EXPECT (EXPECTATION)
Mt 24:44 at an hour when you do not *e* him.

EXPECTATION (EXPECT)
Ro 8:19 waits in eager *e* for the sons
Heb 10:27 but only a fearful *e* of judgment

EXPEL*
1Co 5:13 *E* the wicked man from among you

EXPENSIVE
1Ti 2: 9 or gold or pearls or *e* clothes,

EXPLOIT
Pr 22:22 Do not *e* the poor because they are
2Co 12:17 Did I *e* you through any

EXPOSE
1Co 4: 5 will *e* the motives of men's hearts.
Eph 5:11 of darkness, but rather *e* them.

EXTENDS
Pr 31:20 and *e* her hands to the needy.
Lk 1:50 His mercy *e* to those who fear him,

EXTINGUISHED
2Sa 21:17 the lamp of Israel will not be *e.*"

EXTOL*
Job 36:24 Remember to *e* his work,
Ps 34: 1 I will *e* the LORD at all times;
68: 4 *e* him who rides on the clouds—
95: 2 and *e* him with music and song.
109: 30 mouth I will greatly *e* the LORD;
111: 1 I will *e* the LORD with all my heart
115: 18 it is we who *e* the LORD,
117: 1 *e* him, all you peoples.
145: 2 and *e* your name for ever and ever.
145: 10 your saints will *e* you.
147: 12 *E* the LORD, O Jerusalem;

EXTORT*
Lk 3:14 "Don't *e* money and don't accuse

EYE (EYES)
Ex 21:24 you are to take life for life, *e* for *e*,
Ps 94: 9 Does he who formed the *e* not see?
Mt 5:29 If your right *e* causes you to sin,
5:38 '*E* for *e*, and tooth for tooth.'
7: 3 of sawdust in your brother's *e*
1Co 2: 9 "No *e* has seen,
Col 3:22 not only when their *e* is on you
Rev 1: 7 and every *e* will see him,

EYES (EYE)
Nu 33:55 remain will become barbs in your *e*
Jos 23:13 on your backs and thorns in your *e*,
2Ch 16: 9 For the *e* of the LORD range
Job 31: 1 "I made a covenant with my *e*
36: 7 He does not take his *e*
Ps 119: 18 Open my *e* that I may see
121: 1 I lift up my *e* to the hills—
141: 8 But my *e* are fixed on you,
Pr 3: 7 Do not be wise in your own *e*;
4:25 Let your *e* look straight ahead,
15: 3 The *e* of the LORD are everywhere
Isa 6: 5 and my *e* have seen the King,
Hab 1:13 Your *e* are too pure to look on evil;
Jn 4:35 open your *e* and look at the fields!
2Co 4:18 So we fix our *e* not on what is seen,
Heb 12: 2 Let us fix our *e* on Jesus, the author
Jas 2: 5 poor in the *e* of the world to be rich
1Pe 3:12 For the *e* of the Lord are
Rev 7:17 wipe away every tear from their *e*."
21: 4 He will wipe every tear from their *e*

EZEKIEL
Priest called to be prophet to the exiles (Eze 1-3).

EZRA
Priest and teacher of the Law who led a return of exiles to Israel to reestablish temple and worship (Ezr 7-8). Corrected intermarriage of priests (Ezr 9-10). Read Law at celebration of Feast of Tabernacles (Neh 8).

FACE (FACES)
Ge 32:30 "It is because I saw God *f* to *f*,
Ex 34:29 was not aware that his *f* was radiant
Nu 6:25 the LORD make his *f* shine
1Ch 16:11 seek his *f* always.
2Ch 7:14 and seek my *f* and turn
Ps 4: 6 Let the light of your *f* shine upon us
27: 8 Your *f*, LORD, I will seek.
31:16 Let your *f* shine on your servant;
105: 4 seek his *f* always.
119:135 Make your *f* shine
Isa 50: 7 Therefore have I set my *f* like flint,
Mt 17: 2 His *f* shone like the sun,
1Co 13:12 mirror; then we shall see *f* to *f*.
2Co 4: 6 the glory of God in the *f* of Christ.
1Pe 3:12 but the *f* of the Lord is
Rev 1:16 His *f* was like the sun shining

FACES (FACE)
2Co 3:18 who with unveiled *f* all reflect

FACTIONS
Gal 5:20 selfish ambition, dissensions, *f*

FADE
1Pe 5: 4 of glory that will never *f* away.

FAIL (FAILING FAILINGS FAILS)
1Ch 28:20 He will not *f* you or forsake you
2Ch 34:33 they did not *f* to follow the LORD,
Ps 89:28 my covenant with him will never *f*.
Pr 15:22 Plans *f* for lack of counsel,
Isa 51: 6 my righteousness will never *f*.
La 3:22 for his compassions never *f*.
2Co 13: 5 unless, of course, you *f* the test?

FAILING (FAIL)
1Sa 12:23 sin against the LORD by *f* to pray

FAILINGS (FAIL)
Ro 15: 1 ought to bear with the *f* of the weak

FAILS (FAIL)
1Co 13: 8 Love never *f*.

FAINT
Isa 40:31 they will walk and not be *f*.

FAIR
Pr 1: 3 doing what is right and just and *f*;
Col 4: 1 slaves with what is right and *f*,

FAITH (FAITHFUL FAITHFULLY FAITHFULNESS FAITHLESS)
2Ch 20:20 Have *f* in the LORD your God
Hab 2: 4 but the righteous will live by his *f*—
Mt 9:29 According to your *f* will it be done
17:20 if you have *f* as small as a mustard
24:10 many will turn away from the *f*
Mk 11:22 "Have *f* in God," Jesus answered.
Lk 7: 9 I have not found such great *f*
12:28 will he clothe you, O you of little *f*!
17: 5 "Increase our *f*!" He replied,
18: 8 will he find *f* on the earth?"
Ac 14: 9 saw that he had *f* to be healed
14:27 the door of *f* to the Gentiles.
Ro 1:12 encouraged by each other's *f*.
1:17 is by *f* from first to last,
1:17 "The righteous will live by *f*."
3: 3 What if some did not have *f*?
3:22 comes through *f* in Jesus Christ
3:25 a sacrifice of atonement, through *f*
4: 5 his *f* is credited as righteousness.
5: 1 we have been justified through *f*,
10:17 *f* comes from hearing the message,
14: 1 Accept him whose *f* is weak,
14:23 that does not come from *f* is sin.
1Co 13: 2 and if I have a *f* that can move
13:13 And now these three remain: *f*,
16:13 stand firm in the *f*; be men
2Co 5: 7 We live by *f*, not by sight.
13: 5 to see whether you are in the *f*;
Gal 2:16 Jesus that we may be justified by *f*
2:20 I live by *f* in the Son of God,
3:11 "The righteous will live by *f*."
3:24 that we might be justified by *f*.
Eph 2: 8 through *f*— and this not
4: 5 one Lord, one *f*, one baptism;
6:16 to all this, take up the shield of *f*,
Col 1:23 continue in your *f*, established
1Th 5: 8 on *f* and love as a breastplate,
1Ti 2:15 if they continue in *f*, love
4: 1 later times some will abandon the *f*
5: 8 he has denied the *f* and is worse
6:12 Fight the good fight of the *f*.
2Ti 3:15 wise for salvation through *f*
4: 7 finished the race, I have kept the *f*.
Phm : 6 may be active in sharing your *f*,
Heb 10:38 But my righteous one will live by *f*.
11: 1 *f* is being sure of what we hope for
11: 3 By *f* we understand that
11: 5 By *f* Enoch was taken from this life
11: 6 And without *f* it is impossible
11: 7 By *f* Noah, when warned about
11: 8 By *f* Abraham, when called to go
11:17 By *f* Abraham, when God tested
11:20 By *f* Isaac blessed Jacob
11:21 By *f* Jacob, when he was dying,
11:22 By *f* Joseph, when his end was near

Heb 11:24 By *f* Moses, when he had grown up
11:31 By *f* the prostitute Rahab,
12: 2 the author and perfecter of our *f*,
Jas 2:14 if a man claims to have *f*
2:17 In the same way, *f* by itself,
2:26 so *f* without deeds is dead.
2Pe 1: 5 effort to add to your *f* goodness;
1Jn 5: 4 overcome the world, even our *f*.
Jude : 3 to contend for the *f* that was once

FAITHFUL (FAITH)
Nu 12: 7 he is *f* in all my house.
Dt 7: 9 your God is God; he is the *f* God,
32: 4 A *f* God who does no wrong,
2Sa 22:26 "To the *f* you show yourself *f*,
Ps 25:10 of the LORD are loving and *f*
31:23 The LORD preserves the *f*,
33: 4 he is *f* in all he does.
37:28 and will not forsake his *f* ones.
97:10 for he guards the lives of his *f* ones
145: 13 The LORD is *f* to all his promises
146: 6 the LORD, who remains *f* forever.
Pr 31:26 and *f* instruction is on her tongue.
Mt 25:21 'Well done, good and *f* servant!
Ro 12:12 patient in affliction, *f* in prayer.
1Co 4: 2 been given a trust must prove *f*.
10:13 And God is *f*; he will not let you be
1Th 5:24 The one who calls you is *f*
2Ti 2:13 he will remain *f*,
Heb 3: 6 But Christ is *f* as a son
10:23 for he who promised is *f*.
1Pe 4:19 themselves to their *f* Creator
1Jn 1: 9 he is *f* and just and will forgive us
Rev 1: 5 who is the *f* witness, the firstborn
2:10 Be *f*, even to the point of death,
19:11 whose rider is called *F* and True.

FAITHFULLY (FAITH)
Dt 11:13 if you *f* obey the commands I am
1Sa 12:24 and serve him *f* with all your heart;
1Ki 2: 4 and if they walk *f* before me
1Pe 4:10 *f* administering God's grace

FAITHFULNESS (FAITH)
Ps 57:10 your *f* reaches to the skies.
85:10 Love and *f* meet together;
86:15 to anger, abounding in love and *f*.
89: 1 mouth I will make your *f* known
89:14 love and *f* go before you.
91: 4 his *f* will be your shield
117: 2 the *f* of the LORD endures forever.
119: 75 and in *f* you have afflicted me.
Pr 3: 3 Let love and *f* never leave you;
Isa 11: 5 and *f* the sash around his waist.
La 3:23 great is your *f*.
Ro 3: 3 lack of faith nullify God's *f*?
Gal 5:22 patience, kindness, goodness, *f*,

FAITHLESS (FAITH)
Ps 119:158 I look on the *f* with loathing,
Jer 3:22 "Return, *f* people;
Ro 1:31 they are senseless, *f*, heartless,
2Ti 2:13 if we are *f*,

FALL (FALLEN FALLING FALLS)
Ps 37:24 though he stumble, he will not *f*,
55:22 he will never let the righteous *f*.
69: 9 of those who insult you *f* on me.
Pr 11:28 Whoever trusts in his riches will *f*,
Lk 11:17 a house divided against itself will *f*.
Ro 3:23 and *f* short of the glory of God,
Heb 6: 6 if they *f* away, to be brought back

FALLEN (FALL)
2Sa 1:19 How the mighty have *f*!
Isa 14:12 How you have *f* from heaven,
1Co 15:20 of those who have *f* asleep.
Gal 5: 4 you have *f* away from grace.
1Th 4:15 precede those who have *f* asleep.

FALLING (FALL)
Jude :24 able to keep you from *f*

FALLS (FALL)
Pr 24:17 Do not gloat when your enemy *f*;
Jn 12:24 a kernel of wheat *f* to the ground
Ro 14: 4 To his own master he stands or *f*.

FALSE (FALSEHOOD FALSELY)
Ex 20:16 "You shall not give *f* testimony
23: 1 "Do not spread *f* reports.
Pr 13: 5 The righteous hate what is *f*,
19: 5 A *f* witness will not go unpunished,
Mt 7:15 "Watch out for *f* prophets.
19:18 not steal, do not give *f* testimony,
24:11 and many *f* prophets will appear
Php 1:18 whether from *f* motives or true,
1Ti 1: 3 not to teach *f* doctrines any longer
2Pe 2: 1 there will be *f* teachers among you.

FALSEHOOD (FALSE)
Ps 119:163 I hate and abhor *f*
Pr 30: 8 Keep *f* and lies far from me;
Eph 4:25 each of you must put off *f*

FALSELY (FALSE)
Lev 19:12 " 'Do not swear *f* by my name
Lk 3:14 and don't accuse people *f*—
1Ti 6:20 ideas of what is *f* called knowledge,

FALTER*
Pr 24:10 If you *f* in times of trouble,
Isa 42: 4 he will not *f* or be discouraged

FAMILIES (FAMILY)
Ps 68: 6 God sets the lonely in *f*,

FAMILY (FAMILIES)
Pr 15:27 greedy man brings trouble to his *f*,
31:15 she provides food for her *f*

Lk 9:61 go back and say good-by to my *f*."
12:52 in one *f* divided against each other,
1Ti 3: 4 He must manage his own *f* well
3: 5 how to manage his own *f*,
5: 4 practice by caring for their own *f*
5: 8 and especially for his immediate *f*,

FAMINE
Ge 41:30 seven years of *f* will follow them.
Am 8:11 but a *f* of hearing the words
Ro 8:35 or persecution or *f* or nakedness

FAN*
2Ti 1: 6 you to *f* into flame the gift of God,

FAST
Dt 13: 4 serve him and hold *f* to him.
Jos 22: 5 to hold *f* to him and to serve him
23: 8 to hold *f* to the LORD your God,
Ps 119: 31 I hold *f* to your statutes, O LORD;
139: 10 your right hand will hold me *f*.
Mt 6:16 "When you *f*, do not look somber
1Pe 5:12 Stand *f* in it.

FATHER (FATHER'S FATHERLESS FATHERS FOREFATHERS)
Ge 2:24 this reason a man will leave his *f*
17: 4 You will be the *f* of many nations.
Ex 20:12 "Honor your *f* and your mother,
21:15 "Anyone who attacks his *f*
21:17 "Anyone who curses his *f*
Lev 18: 7 " 'Do not dishonor your *f*
19: 3 you must respect his mother and *f*,
Dt 5:16 "Honor your *f* and your mother,
21:18 son who does not obey his *f*
Ps 27:10 Though my *f* and mother forsake
68: 5 A *f* to the fatherless, a defender
Pr 10: 1 A wise son brings joy to his *f*,
17:21 there is no joy for the *f* of a fool.
23:22 Listen to your *f*, who gave you life,
23:24 *f* of a righteous man has great joy;
28: 7 of gluttons disgraces his *f*.
29: 3 loves wisdom brings joy to his *f*,
Isa 9: 6 Everlasting *F*, Prince of Peace.
Mt 6: 9 " 'Our *F* in heaven,
10:37 "Anyone who loves his *f*
15: 4 'Honor your *f* and mother'
19: 5 this reason a man will leave his *f*
Lk 12:53 *f* against son and son against *f*,
23:34 Jesus said, "*F*, forgive them,
Jn 6:44 the *F* who sent me draws him,
6:46 No one has seen the *F*
8:44 You belong to your *f*, the devil,
10:30 I and the *F* are one."
14: 6 No one comes to the *F*
14: 9 who has seen me has seen the *F*.

Ro 4:11 he is the *f* of all who believe
2Co 6:18 "I will be a *F* to you,
Eph 6:2 "Honor your *f* and mother"—
Heb 12:7 what son is not disciplined by his *f*?

FATHER'S (FATHER)
Pr 13:1 A wise son heeds his *f* instruction,
15:5 A fool spurns his *f* discipline,
19:13 A foolish son is his *f* ruin,
Lk 2:49 had to be in my *F* house?"
Jn 2:16 How dare you turn my *F* house
10:29 can snatch them out of my *F* hand.
14:2 In my *F* house are many rooms;

FATHERLESS (FATHER)
Dt 10:18 He defends the cause of the *f*
24:17 Do not deprive the alien or the *f*
24:19 Leave it for the alien, the *f*
Ps 68:5 A father to the *f*, a defender
Pr 23:10 or encroach on the fields of the *f*,

FATHERS (FATHER)
Ex 20:5 for the sin of the *f* to the third
Lk 11:11 "Which of you *f*, if your son asks
Eph 6:4 *F*, do not exasperate your children;
Col 3:21 *F*, do not embitter your children,

FATHOM*
Job 11:7 "Can you *f* the mysteries of God?
Ps 145:3 his greatness no one can *f*.
Ecc 3:11 yet they cannot *f* what God has
Isa 40:28 and his understanding no one can *f*
1Co 13:2 and can *f* all mysteries and all

FAULT (FAULTS)
Mt 18:15 and show him his *f*, just
Php 2:15 of God without *f* in a crooked
Jas 1:5 generously to all without finding *f*,
Jude :24 his glorious presence without *f*

FAULTFINDERS*
Jude :16 These men are grumblers and *f*;

FAULTS (FAULT)
Ps 19:12 Forgive my hidden *f*.

FAVORITISM*
Ex 23:3 and do not show *f* to a poor man
Lev 19:15 to the poor or *f* to the great,
Ac 10:34 true it is that God does not show *f*
Ro 2:11 For God does not show *f*.
Eph 6:9 and there is no *f* with him.
Col 3:25 for his wrong, and there is no *f*.
1Ti 5:21 and to do nothing out of *f*.
Jas 2:1 Lord Jesus Christ, don't show *f*.
2:9 But if you show *f*, you sin

FEAR (AFRAID FEARS)
Dt 6:13 *F* the LORD your God, serve him
10:12 but to *f* the LORD your God,
31:12 and learn to *f* the LORD your God
Ps 19:9 The *f* of the LORD is pure,
23:4 I will *f* no evil,
27:1 whom shall I *f*?
91:5 You will not *f* the terror of night,
111:10 *f* of the LORD is the beginning
Pr 8:13 To *f* the LORD is to hate evil;
9:10 *f* of the LORD is the beginning
10:27 The *f* of the LORD adds length
14:27 The *f* of the LORD is a fountain
15:33 *f* of the LORD teaches a man
16:6 through the *f* of the LORD a man
19:23 The *f* of the LORD leads to life:
29:25 *F* of man will prove to be a snare,
Isa 11:3 delight in the *f* of the LORD.
41:10 So do not *f*, for I am with you;
Lk 12:5 I will show you whom you should *f*:
Php 2:12 to work out your salvation with *f*
1Jn 4:18 But perfect love drives out *f*,

FEARS (FEAR)
Job 1:8 a man who *f* God and shuns evil."
Ps 34:4 he delivered me from all my *f*.
Pr 31:30 a woman who *f* the LORD is
1Jn 4:18 The one who *f* is not made perfect

FEED
Jn 21:15 Jesus said, "*F* my lambs."
21:17 Jesus said, "*F* my sheep.
Ro 12:20 "If your enemy is hungry, *f* him;
Jude :12 shepherds who *f* only themselves.

FEET (FOOT)
Ps 8:6 you put everything under his *f*:
22:16 have pierced my hands and my *f*.
40:2 he set my *f* on a rock
110:1 a footstool for your *f*."
119:105 Your word is a lamp to my *f*
Ro 10:15 "How beautiful are the *f*
1Co 12:21 And the head cannot say to the *f*,
15:25 has put all his enemies under his *f*.
Heb 12:13 "Make level paths for your *f*,"

FELLOWSHIP
2Co 6:14 what *f* can light have with darkness
13:14 and the *f* of the Holy Spirit be
Php 3:10 the *f* of sharing in his sufferings,
1Jn 1:6 claim to have *f* with him yet walk
1:7 we have *f* with one another,

FEMALE
Ge 1:27 male and *f* he created them.
Gal 3:28 *f*, for you are all one in Christ Jesus

FERVOR
Ro 12:11 but keep your spiritual *f*, serving

FIELD (FIELDS)
Mt 6:28 See how the lilies of the *f* grow.
13:38 *f* is the world, and the good seed
1Co 3:9 you are God's *f*, God's building.

FIELDS (FIELD)
Lk 2:8 were shepherds living out in the *f*
Jn 4:35 open your eyes and look at the *f*!

FIG (FIGS)
Ge 3:7 so they sewed *f* leaves together

FIGHT (FOUGHT)
Ex 14:14 The LORD will *f* for you; you need
Dt 1:30 going before you, will *f* for you,
3:22 the LORD your God himself will *f*
Ne 4:20 Our God will *f* for us!"
Ps 35:1 *f* against those who *f* against me.
Jn 18:36 my servants would *f*
1Co 9:26 I do not *f* like a man beating the air.
2Co 10:4 The weapons we *f*
1Ti 1:18 them you may *f* the good *f*,
6:12 Fight the good *f* of the faith.
2Ti 4:7 fought the good *f*, I have finished

FIGS (FIG)
Lk 6:44 People do not pick *f*

FILL (FILLED FILLS FULL FULLNESS FULLY)
Ge 1:28 and increase in number; *f* the earth
Ps 16:11 you will *f* me with joy
81:10 wide your mouth and I will *f* it.
Pr 28:19 who chases fantasies will have his *f*
Hag 2:7 and I will *f* this house with glory,'
Jn 6:26 you ate the loaves and had your *f*.
Ac 2:28 you will *f* me with joy
Ro 15:13 the God of hope *f* you with all joy

FILLED (FILL)
Ps 72:19 may the whole earth be *f*
119:64 The earth is *f* with your love,
Eze 43:5 the glory of the LORD *f* the temple
Hab 2:14 For the earth will be *f*
Lk 1:15 and he will be *f* with the Holy Spirit
1:41 and Elizabeth was *f* with the Holy
Jn 12:3 the house was *f* with the fragrance
Ac 2:4 All of them were *f*
4:8 Then Peter, *f* with the Holy Spirit,
9:17 and be *f* with the Holy Spirit."
13:9 called Paul, *f* with the Holy Spirit,
Eph 5:18 Instead, be *f* with the Spirit.
Php 1:11 *f* with the fruit of righteousness

FILLS (FILL)
Nu 14:21 of the LORD *f* the whole earth,
Ps 107:9 and *f* the hungry with good things.

Eph 1:23 fullness of him who *f* everything

FILTHY
Isa 64: 6 all our righteous acts are like *f* rags;
Col 3: 8 and *f* language from your lips.
2Pe 2: 7 by the *f* lives of lawless men

FIND (FINDS FOUND)
Nu 32:23 be sure that your sin will *f* you out.
Dt 4:29 you will *f* him if you look for him
1Sa 23:16 and helped him *f* strength in God.
Ps 36: 7 *f* refuge in the shadow
91: 4 under his wings you will *f* refuge;
Pr 14:22 those who plan what is good *f* love
31:10 A wife of noble character who can *f*
Jer 6:16 and you will *f* rest for your souls.
Mt 7: 7 seek and you will *f*; knock
11:29 and you will *f* rest for your souls.
16:25 loses his life for me will *f* it.
Lk 18: 8 will he *f* faith on the earth?"
Jn 10: 9 come in and go out, and *f* pasture.

FINDS (FIND)
Ps 62: 1 My soul *f* rest in God alone;
112: 1 who *f* great delight
119:162 like one who *f* great spoil.
Pr 18:22 He who *f* a wife *f* what is good
Mt 7: 8 he who seeks *f*; and to him who
10:39 Whoever *f* his life will lose it,
Lk 12:37 whose master *f* them watching
15: 4 go after the lost sheep until he *f* it?

FINISH (FINISHED)
Jn 4:34 him who sent me and to *f* his work.
5:36 that the Father has given me to *f*,
Ac 20:24 if only I may *f* the race
2Co 8:11 Now *f* the work, so that your eager
Jas 1: 4 Perseverance must *f* its work

FINISHED (FINISH)
Ge 2: 2 seventh day God had *f* the work he
Jn 19:30 the drink, Jesus said, "It is *f*."
2Ti 4: 7 I have *f* the race, I have kept

FIRE
Ex 13:21 in a pillar of *f* to give them light,
Lev 6:12 *f* on the altar must be kept burning;
Isa 30:27 and his tongue is a consuming *f*.
Jer 23:29 my word like *f*," declares
Mt 3:11 you with the Holy Spirit and with *f*.
5:22 will be in danger of the *f* of hell.
25:41 into the eternal *f* prepared
Mk 9:43 where the *f* never goes out.
Ac 2: 3 to be tongues of *f* that separated
1Co 3:13 It will be revealed with *f*,
1Th 5:19 Do not put out the Spirit's *f*;
Heb 12:29 for our "God is a consuming *f*."
Jas 3: 5 set on *f* by a small spark.
2Pe 3:10 the elements will be destroyed by *f*,
Jude :23 snatch others from the *f*
Rev 20:14 The lake of *f* is the second death.

FIRM
Ex 14:13 Stand *f* and you will see
2Ch 20:17 stand *f* and see the deliverance
Ps 33:11 of the LORD stand *f* forever,
37:23 he makes his steps *f*;
40: 2 and gave me a *f* place to stand.
89: 2 that your love stands *f* forever,
119: 89 it stands *f* in the heavens.
Pr 4:26 and take only ways that are *f*.
Zec 8:23 nations will take *f* hold of one Jew
Mk 13:13 he who stands *f* to the end will be
1Co 16:13 on your guard; stand *f* in the faith;
2Co 1:24 because it is by faith you stand *f*.
Eph 6:14 Stand *f* then, with the belt
Col 4:12 that you may stand *f* in all the will
2Th 2:15 stand *f* and hold to the teachings
2Ti 2:19 God's solid foundation stands *f*,
Heb 6:19 an anchor for the soul, *f* and secure
1Pe 5: 9 Resist him, standing *f* in the faith,

FIRST
Isa 44: 6 I am the *f* and I am the last;
48:12 I am the *f* and I am the last.
Mt 5:24 *F* go and be reconciled
6:33 But seek *f* his kingdom
7: 5 *f* take the plank out
20:27 wants to be *f* must be your slave—
22:38 This is the *f* and greatest
23:26 *F* clean the inside of the cup
Mk 13:10 And the gospel must *f* be preached
Ac 11:26 disciples were called Christians *f*
Ro 1:16 *f* for the Jew, then for the Gentile.
1Co 12:28 in the church God has appointed *f*
2Co 8: 5 they gave themselves *f* to the Lord
1Ti 2:13 For Adam was formed *f*, then Eve.
Jas 3:17 comes from heaven is *f* of all pure;
1Jn 4:19 We love because he *f* loved us.
3Jn : 9 but Diotrephes, who loves to be *f*,
Rev 1:17 I am the *F* and the Last.
2: 4 You have forsaken your *f* love.

FIRSTBORN (BEAR)
Ex 11: 5 Every *f* son in Egypt will die,

FIRSTFRUITS
Ex 23:19 "Bring the best of the *f* of your soil

FISHERS
Mk 1:17 "and I will make you *f* of men."

FITTING*
Ps 33: 1 it is *f* for the upright to praise him.
147: 1 how pleasant and *f* to praise him!
Pr 10:32 of the righteous know what is *f*,
19:10 It is not *f* for a fool to live in luxury
26: 1 honor is not *f* for a fool.
1Co 14:40 everything should be done in a *f*
Col 3:18 to your husbands, as is *f* in the Lord
Heb 2:10 sons to glory, it was *f* that God,

FIX
Dt 11:18 *F* these words of mine
Pr 4:25 *f* your gaze directly before you.
2Co 4:18 we *f* our eyes not on what is seen,
Heb 3: 1 heavenly calling, *f* your thoughts
12: 2 Let us *f* our eyes on Jesus,

FLAME (FLAMES FLAMING)
2Ti 1: 6 you to fan into *f* the gift of God,

FLAMES (FLAME)
1Co 3:15 only as one escaping through the *f*.
13: 3 and surrender my body to the *f*,

FLAMING (FLAME)
Eph 6:16 you can extinguish all the *f* arrows

FLASH
1Co 15:52 in a *f*, in the twinkling of an eye,

FLATTER (FLATTERING FLATTERY)
Job 32:21 nor will I *f* any man;
Jude :16 *f* others for their own advantage.

FLATTERING (FLATTER)
Ps 12: 2 their *f* lips speak with deception.
12: 3 May the LORD cut off all *f* lips
Pr 26:28 and a *f* mouth works ruin.

FLATTERY (FLATTER)
Ro 16:18 and *f* they deceive the minds
1Th 2: 5 You know we never used *f*,

FLAWLESS*
2Sa 22:31 the word of the LORD is *f*.
Job 11: 4 You say to God, 'My beliefs are *f*
Ps 12: 6 And the words of the LORD are *f*,
18:30 the word of the LORD is *f*.
Pr 30: 5 "Every word of God is *f*;
SS 5: 2 my dove, my *f* one.

FLEE
Ps 139: 7 Where can I *f* from your presence?
1Co 6:18 *F* from sexual immorality.
10:14 my dear friends, *f* from idolatry.
1Ti 6:11 But you, man of God, *f* from all this
2Ti 2:22 *F* the evil desires of youth,
Jas 4: 7 Resist the devil, and he will *f*

FLEETING
Ps 89:47 Remember how *f* is my life.
Pr 31:30 Charm is deceptive, and beauty is *f*

FLESH
Ge 2:23 and *f* of my *f*;
2:24 and they will become one *f*.
Job 19:26 yet in my *f* I will see God;
Eze 11:19 of stone and give them a heart of *f*.
36:26 of stone and give you a heart of *f*.
Mk 10: 8 and the two will become one *f*.'
Jn 1:14 The Word became *f* and made his
6:51 This bread is my *f*, which I will give
1Co 6:16 "The two will become one *f*."
Eph 5:31 and the two will become one *f*."
6:12 For our struggle is not against *f*

FLOCK (FLOCKS)
Isa 40:11 He tends his *f* like a shepherd:
Eze 34: 2 not shepherds take care of the *f*?
Zec 11:17 who deserts the *f*!
Mt 26:31 the sheep of the *f* will be scattered.'
Ac 20:28 all the *f* of which the Holy Spirit
1Pe 5: 2 Be shepherds of God's *f* that is

FLOCKS (FLOCK)
Lk 2: 8 keeping watch over their *f* at night.

FLOG
Ac 22:25 to *f* a Roman citizen who hasn't

FLOODGATES
Mal 3:10 see if I will not throw open the *f*

FLOURISHING
Ps 52: 8 *f* in the house of God;

FLOW (FLOWING)
Nu 13:27 and it does *f* with milk and honey!
Jn 7:38 streams of living water will *f*

FLOWERS
Isa 40: 7 The grass withers and the *f* fall,

FLOWING (FLOW)
Ex 3: 8 a land *f* with milk and honey—

FOLDING
Pr 6:10 a little *f* of the hands to rest—

FOLLOW (FOLLOWING FOLLOWS)
Ex 23: 2 Do not *f* the crowd in doing wrong.
Lev 18: 4 and be careful to *f* my decrees.
Dt 5: 1 Learn them and be sure to *f* them.
Ps 23: 6 Surely goodness and love will *f* me
Mt 16:24 and take up his cross and *f* me.
Jn 10: 4 his sheep *f* him because they know
1Co 14: 1 *F* the way of love and eagerly
Rev 14: 4 They *f* the Lamb wherever he goes.

FOLLOWING (FOLLOW)
1Ti 1:18 by *f* them you may fight the good

FOLLOWS (FOLLOW)
Jn 8:12 Whoever *f* me will never walk

FOOD (FOODS)
Pr 20:13 you will have *f* to spare.
22: 9 for he shares his *f* with the poor.
25:21 If your enemy is hungry, give him *f*
31:15 she provides *f* for her family
Da 1: 8 to defile himself with the royal *f*
Jn 6:27 Do not work for *f* that spoils,
Ro 14:14 fully convinced that no *f* is unclean
1Co 8: 8 But *f* does not bring us near to God
1Ti 6: 8 But if we have *f* and clothing,
Jas 2:15 sister is without clothes and daily *f*.

FOODS (FOOD)
Mk 7:19 Jesus declared all *f* "clean.")

FOOL (FOOLISH FOOLISHNESS FOOLS)
Ps 14: 1 The *f* says in his heart,
Pr 15: 5 A *f* spurns his father's discipline,
17:28 Even a *f* is thought wise
18: 2 A *f* finds no pleasure
26: 5 Answer a *f* according to his folly,
28:26 He who trusts in himself is a *f*,
Mt 5:22 But anyone who says, 'You *f*!'

FOOLISH (FOOL)
Pr 10: 1 but a *f* son grief to his mother.
17:25 A *f* son brings grief to his father
Mt 7:26 practice is like a *f* man who built
25: 2 of them were *f* and five were wise.
1Co 1:27 God chose the *f* things of the world

FOOLISHNESS (FOOL)
1Co 1:18 of the cross is *f* to those who are
1:25 For the *f* of God is wiser
2:14 for they are *f* to him, and he cannot
3:19 of this world is *f* in God's sight.

FOOLS (FOOL)
Pr 14: 9 *F* mock at making amends for sin,
1Co 4:10 We are *f* for Christ, but you are

FOOT (FEET FOOTHOLD)
Jos 1: 3 every place where you set your *f*,
Isa 1: 6 From the sole of your *f* to the top
1Co 12:15 If the *f* should say, "Because I am

FOOTHOLD (FOOT)
Eph 4:27 and do not give the devil a *f*.

FORBEARANCE*
Ro 3:25 because in his *f* he had left the sins

FORBID
1Co 14:39 and do not *f* speaking in tongues.

FOREFATHERS (FATHER)
Heb 1: 1 spoke to our *f* through the prophets

FOREKNEW* (KNOW)
Ro 8:29 For those God *f* he
11: 2 not reject his people, whom he *f*.

FOREVER (EVER)
1Ch 16:15 He remembers his covenant *f*,
16:34 his love endures *f*.
Ps 9: 7 The LORD reigns *f*;
23: 6 dwell in the house of the LORD *f*.
33:11 the plans of the LORD stand firm *f*
86:12 I will glorify your name *f*.
92: 8 But you, O LORD, are exalted *f*.
110: 4 "You are a priest *f*,
119:111 Your statutes are my heritage *f*;
Jn 6:51 eats of this bread, he will live *f*.
14:16 Counselor to be with you *f*—
1Co 9:25 it to get a crown that will last *f*.
1Th 4:17 And so we will be with the Lord *f*.
Heb 13: 8 same yesterday and today and *f*.
1Pe 1:25 but the word of the Lord stands *f*."
1Jn 2:17 who does the will of God lives *f*.

FORFEIT
Lk 9:25 and yet lose or *f* his very self?

FORGAVE (FORGIVE)
Ps 32: 5 and you *f*
Eph 4:32 just as in Christ God *f* you.
Col 2:13 He *f* us all our sins, having
3:13 Forgive as the Lord *f* you.

FORGET (FORGETS FORGETTING)
Dt 6:12 that you do not *f* the LORD,
Ps 103: 2 and *f* not all his benefits.
137: 5 may my right hand *f* ⌊its skill⌋.
Isa 49:15 "Can a mother *f* the baby
Heb 6:10 he will not *f* your work

FORGETS (FORGET)
Jn 16:21 her baby is born she *f* the anguish
Jas 1:24 immediately *f* what he looks like.

FORGETTING (FORGET)
Php 3:13 *F* what is behind and straining

FORGIVE (FORGAVE FORGIVENESS FORGIVING)
2Ch 7:14 will *f* their sin and will heal their
Ps 19:12 *F* my hidden faults.
Mt 6:12 *F* us our debts,
6:14 For if you *f* men when they sin
18:21 many times shall I *f* my brother
Mk 11:25 in heaven may *f* you your sins."
Lk 11: 4 *F* us our sins,
23:34 Jesus said, "Father, *f* them,
Col 3:13 *F* as the Lord forgave you.
1Jn 1: 9 and just and will *f* us our sins

FORGIVENESS (FORGIVE)
Ps 130: 4 But with you there is *f*;
Ac 10:43 believes in him receives *f* of sins
Eph 1: 7 through his blood, the *f* of sins,
Col 1:14 in whom we have redemption, the *f*
Heb 9:22 the shedding of blood there is no *f*.

FORGIVING (FORGIVE)
Ne 9:17 But you are a *f* God, gracious
Eph 4:32 to one another, *f* each other,

FORMED
Ge 2: 7 And the LORD God *f* man
Ps 103: 14 for he knows how we are *f,*
Isa 45:18 but *f* it to be inhabited—
Ro 9:20 "Shall what is *f* say to him who *f* it,
1Ti 2:13 For Adam was *f* first, then Eve.
Heb 11: 3 understand that the universe was *f*

FORSAKE (FORSAKEN)
Jos 1: 5 I will never leave you nor *f* you.
24:16 "Far be it from us to *f* the LORD
2Ch 15: 2 but if you *f* him, he will *f* you.
Ps 27:10 Though my father and mother *f* me
Isa 55: 7 Let the wicked *f* his way
Heb 13: 5 never will I *f* you."

FORSAKEN (FORSAKE)
Ps 22: 1 my God, why have you *f* me?
37:25 I have never seen the righteous *f*
Mt 27:46 my God, why have you *f* me?"
Rev 2: 4 You have *f* your first love.

FORTRESS
Ps 18: 2 The LORD is my rock, my *f*
71: 3 for you are my rock and my *f.*

FOUGHT (FIGHT)
2Ti 4: 7 I have *f* the good fight, I have

FOUND (FIND)
1Ch 28: 9 If you seek him, he will be *f* by you;
Isa 55: 6 Seek the LORD while he may be *f;*
Da 5:27 on the scales and *f* wanting.
Lk 15: 6 with me; I have *f* my lost sheep.'
15: 9 with me; I have *f* my lost coin.'
Ac 4:12 Salvation is *f* in no one else,

FOUNDATION
Isa 28:16 a precious cornerstone for a sure *f;*
1Co 3:11 For no one can lay any *f* other
Eph 2:20 built on the *f* of the apostles
2Ti 2:19 God's solid *f* stands firm,

FOXES
Mt 8:20 "*F* have holes and birds

FRAGRANCE
2Co 2:16 of death; to the other, the *f* of life.

FREE (FREED FREEDOM FREELY)
Ps 146: 7 The LORD sets prisoners *f,*
Jn 8:32 and the truth will set you *f.*"
Ro 6:18 You have been set *f* from sin
Gal 3:28 slave nor *f,* male nor female,
1Pe 2:16 *f* men, but do not use your freedom

FREED (FREE)
Rev 1: 5 has *f* us from our sins by his blood,

FREEDOM (FREE)
Ro 8:21 into the glorious *f* of the children
2Co 3:17 the Spirit of the Lord is, there is *f.*
Gal 5:13 But do not use your *f* to indulge
1Pe 2:16 but do not use your *f* as a cover-up

FREELY (FREE)
Isa 55: 7 and to our God, for he will *f* pardon
Mt 10: 8 Freely you have received, *f* give.
Ro 3:24 and are justified *f* by his grace
Eph 1: 6 which he has *f* given us

FRIEND (FRIENDS)
Ex 33:11 as a man speaks with his *f.*
Pr 17:17 A *f* loves at all times,
18:24 there is a *f* who sticks closer
27: 6 Wounds from a *f* can be trusted,
27:10 Do not forsake your *f* and the *f*
Jas 4: 4 Anyone who chooses to be a *f*

FRIENDS (FRIEND)
Pr 16:28 and a gossip separates close *f.*
Zec 13: 6 given at the house of my *f.*'
Jn 15:13 that he lay down his life for his *f.*

FRUIT (FRUITFUL)
Ps 1: 3 which yields its *f* in season
Pr 11:30 The *f* of the righteous is a tree
Mt 7:16 By their *f* you will recognize them.
Jn 15: 2 branch in me that bears no *f,*
Gal 5:22 But the *f* of the Spirit is love, joy,
Rev 22: 2 of *f,* yielding its *f* every month.

FRUITFUL (FRUIT)
Ge 1:22 "Be *f* and increase in number
Ps 128: 3 Your wife will be like a *f* vine
Jn 15: 2 prunes so that it will be even more *f.*

FULFILL (FULFILLED FULFILLMENT)
Ps 116: 14 I will *f* my vows to the LORD
Mt 5:17 come to abolish them but to *f* them.
1Co 7: 3 husband should *f* his marital duty

FULFILLED (FULFILL)
Pr 13:19 A longing *f* is sweet to the soul,
Mk 14:49 But the Scriptures must be *f.*"
Ro 13: 8 loves his fellowman has *f* the law.

FULFILLMENT (FULFILL)
Ro 13:10 Therefore love is the *f* of the law.

FULL (FILL)
Ps 127: 5 whose quiver is *f* of them.
Pr 31:11 Her husband has *f* confidence
Isa 6: 3 the whole earth is *f* of his glory."
11: 9 for the earth will be *f*
Jn 10:10 may have life, and have it to the *f.*
Ac 6: 3 known to be *f* of the Spirit

FULLNESS (FILL)
Col 1:19 to have all his *f* dwell in him,
2: 9 in Christ all the *f* of the Deity lives

FULLY (FILL)
1Ki 8:61 your hearts must be *f* committed
2Ch 16: 9 whose hearts are *f* committed
Ps 119: 4 that are to be *f* obeyed.
119:138 they are *f* trustworthy.
1Co 15:58 Always give yourselves *f*

FUTURE
Ps 37:37 there is a *f* for the man of peace.
Pr 23:18 There is surely a *f* hope for you,
Ro 8:38 neither the present nor the *f,*

GABRIEL*
Angel who interpreted Daniel's visions (Da 8:16-26; 9:20-27); announced births of John (Lk 1:11-20), Jesus (Lk 1:26-38).

GAIN (GAINED)
Ps 60:12 With God we will *g* the victory,
Mk 8:36 it for a man to *g* the whole world,
1Co 13: 3 but have not love, I *g* nothing.
Php 1:21 to live is Christ and to die is *g.*
3: 8 that I may *g* Christ and be found
1Ti 6: 6 with contentment is great *g.*

GAINED (GAIN)
Ro 5: 2 through whom we have *g* access

GALILEE
Isa 9: 1 but in the future he will honor *G*

GALL
Mt 27:34 mixed with *g;* but after tasting it,

GAP
Eze 22:30 stand before me in the *g* on behalf

GARDENER
Jn 15: 1 true vine, and my Father is the *g.*

GARMENT (GARMENTS)
Ps 102: 26 they will all wear out like a *g.*
Mt 9:16 of unshrunk cloth on an old *g,*
Jn 19:23 This *g* was seamless, woven

GARMENTS (GARMENT)
Ge 3:21 The LORD God made *g* of skin
Isa 61:10 me with *g* of salvation
63: 1 with his *g* stained crimson?
Jn 19:24 "They divided my *g* among them

GATE (GATES)
Mt 7:13 For wide is the *g* and broad is
Jn 10: 9 I am the *g;* whoever enters

GATES (GATE)
Ps 100: 4 Enter his *g* with thanksgiving
Mt 16:18 the *g* of Hades will not overcome it

GATHER (GATHERS)
Zec 14: 2 I will *g* all the nations to Jerusalem

Mt 12:30 he who does not *g* with me scatters
23:37 longed to *g* your children together,

GATHERS (GATHER)
Isa 40:11 He *g* the lambs in his arms
Mt 23:37 a hen *g* her chicks under her wings,

GAVE (GIVE)
Ezr 2:69 According to their ability they *g*
Job 1:21 LORD *g* and the LORD has taken
Jn 3:16 so loved the world that he *g* his one
2Co 8: 5 they *g* themselves first to the Lord
Gal 2:20 who loved me and *g* himself for me
1Ti 2: 6 who *g* himself as a ransom

GAZE
Ps 27: 4 to *g* upon the beauty of the LORD
Pr 4:25 fix your *g* directly before you.

GENEALOGIES
1Ti 1: 4 themselves to myths and endless *g*.

GENERATIONS
Ps 22:30 future *g* will be told about the Lord
102: 12 your renown endures through all *g*.
145: 13 dominion endures through all *g*.
Lk 1:48 now on all *g* will call me blessed,
Eph 3: 5 not made known to men in other *g*

GENEROUS
Ps 112: 5 Good will come to him who is *g*
Pr 22: 9 A *g* man will himself be blessed,
2Co 9: 5 Then it will be ready as a *g* gift,
1Ti 6:18 and to be *g* and willing to share.

GENTILE (GENTILES)
Ro 1:16 first for the Jew, then for the *G*.
10:12 difference between Jew and *G*—

GENTILES (GENTILE)
Isa 42: 6 and a light for the *G*,
Ro 3: 9 and *G* alike are all under sin.
11:13 as I am the apostle to the *G*,
1Co 1:23 block to Jews and foolishness to *G*,

GENTLE (GENTLENESS)
Pr 15: 1 A *g* answer turns away wrath,
Zec 9: 9 *g* and riding on a donkey,
Mt 11:29 for I am *g* and humble in heart,
21: 5 *g* and riding on a donkey,
1Co 4:21 or in love and with a *g* spirit?
1Pe 3: 4 the unfading beauty of a *g*

GENTLENESS* (GENTLE)
2Co 10: 1 By the meekness and *g* of Christ,
Gal 5:23 faithfulness, *g* and self-control.
Php 4: 5 Let your *g* be evident to all.
Col 3:12 kindness, humility, *g* and patience.

1Ti 6:11 faith, love, endurance and *g*.
1Pe 3:15 But do this with *g* and respect,

GETHSEMANE
Mt 26:36 disciples to a place called *G*,

GIDEON*
Judge, also called Jerub-Baal; freed Israel from Midianites (Jdg 6-8; Heb 11:32). Given sign of fleece (Jdg 8:36-40).

GIFT (GIFTS)
Pr 21:14 A *g* given in secret soothes anger,
Mt 5:23 if you are offering your *g*
Ac 2:38 And you will receive the *g*
Ro 6:23 but the *g* of God is eternal life
1Co 7: 7 each man has his own *g* from God;
2Co 8:12 the *g* is acceptable according
9:15 be to God for his indescribable *g!*
Eph 2: 8 it is the *g* of God—not by works,
1Ti 4:14 not neglect your *g*, which was
2Ti 1: 6 you to fan into flame the *g* of God,
Jas 1:17 and perfect *g* is from above,
1Pe 4:10 should use whatever *g* he has

GIFTS (GIFT)
Ro 11:29 for God's *g* and his call are
12: 6 We have different *g*, according
1Co 12: 4 There are different kinds of *g*,
12:31 But eagerly desire the greater *g*.
14: 1 and eagerly desire spiritual *g*,
14:12 excel in *g* that build up the church.

GILEAD
Jer 8:22 Is there no balm in *G?*

GIVE (GAVE GIVEN GIVER GIVES GIVING)
Nu 6:26 and *g* you peace." '
1Sa 1:11 then I will *g* him to the LORD
2Ch 15: 7 be strong and do not *g* up,
Pr 21:26 but the righteous *g* without sparing
23:26 My son, *g* me your heart
30: 8 but *g* me only my daily bread.
31:31 *G* her the reward she has earned,
Isa 42: 8 I will not *g* my glory to another
Eze 36:26 I will *g* you a new heart
Mt 6:11 *G* us today our daily bread.
10: 8 Freely you have received, freely *g*.
22:21 "*G* to Caesar what is Caesar's,
Mk 8:37 Or what can a man *g* in exchange
Lk 6:38 *G*, and it will be given to you.
11:13 Father in heaven *g* the Holy Spirit
Jn 10:28 I *g* them eternal life, and they shall
13:34 "A new commandment I *g* you:
Ac 20:35 blessed to *g* than to receive.' "
Ro 12: 8 let him *g* generously;
13: 7 *G* everyone what you owe him:
14:12 each of us will *g* an account

2Co 9: 7 Each man should *g* what he has
Rev 14: 7 "Fear God and *g* him glory,

GIVEN (GIVE)
Nu 8:16 are to be *g* wholly to me.
Ps 115: 16 but the earth he has *g* to man.
Isa 9: 6 to us a son is *g*,
Mt 6:33 and all these things will be *g* to you
7: 7 "Ask and it will be *g* to you;
Lk 22:19 saying, "This is my body *g* for you;
Jn 3:27 man can receive only what is *g* him
Ro 5: 5 the Holy Spirit, whom he has *g* us.
1Co 4: 2 those who have been *g* a trust must
12:13 we were all *g* the one Spirit to drink
Eph 4: 7 to each one of us grace has been *g*

GIVER* (GIVE)
Pr 18:16 A gift opens the way for the *g*
2Co 9: 7 for God loves a cheerful *g*.

GIVES (GIVE)
Ps 119:130 The unfolding of your words *g* light;
Pr 14:30 A heart at peace *g* life to the body,
15:30 good news *g* health to the bones.
28:27 He who *g* to the poor will lack
Isa 40:29 He *g* strength to the weary
Mt 10:42 if anyone *g* even a cup of cold water
Jn 6:63 The Spirit *g* life; the flesh counts
1Co 15:57 He *g* us the victory
2Co 3: 6 the letter kills, but the Spirit *g* life.

GIVING (GIVE)
Ne 8: 8 *g* the meaning so that the people
Ps 19: 8 *g* joy to the heart.
Mt 6: 4 so that your *g* may be in secret.
2Co 8: 7 also excel in this grace of *g*.

GLAD (GLADNESS)
Ps 31: 7 I will be *g* and rejoice in your love,
46: 4 whose streams make *g* the city
97: 1 LORD reigns, let the earth be *g;*
118: 24 let us rejoice and be *g* in it.
Pr 23:25 May your father and mother be *g;*
Zec 2:10 and be *g*, O Daughter of Zion.
Mt 5:12 be *g*, because great is your reward

GLADNESS (GLAD)
Ps 45:15 They are led in with joy and *g;*
51: 8 Let me hear joy and *g;*
100: 2 Serve the LORD with *g;*
Jer 31:13 I will turn their mourning into *g;*

GLORIFIED (GLORY)
Jn 13:31 Son of Man *g* and God is *g* in him.
Ro 8:30 those he justified, he also *g*.
2Th 1:10 comes to be *g* in his holy people

GLORIFY (GLORY)
Ps 34: 3 *G* the LORD with me;

Ps 86:12 I will *g* your name forever.
Jn 13:32 God will *g* the Son in himself,
17: 1 *G* your Son, that your Son may

GLORIOUS (GLORY)
Ps 45:13 All *g* is the princess
111: 3 *G* and majestic are his deeds,
145: 5 of the *g* splendor of your majesty,
Isa 4: 2 the LORD will be beautiful and *g*,
12: 5 for he has done *g* things;
42:21 to make his law great and *g*.
63:15 from your lofty throne, holy and *g*.
Mt 19:28 the Son of Man sits on his *g* throne,
Lk 9:31 appeared in *g* splendor, talking
Ac 2:20 of the great and *g* day of the Lord.
2Co 3: 8 of the Spirit be even more *g*?
Php 3:21 so that they will be like his *g* body.
4:19 to his *g* riches in Christ Jesus.
Tit 2:13 the *g* appearing of our great God
Jude :24 before his *g* presence without fault

GLORY (GLORIFIED GLORIFY GLORIOUS)
Ex 15:11 awesome in *g*,
33:18 Moses said, "Now show me your *g*
1Sa 4:21 "The *g* has departed from Israel"—
1Ch 16:24 Declare his *g* among the nations,
16:28 ascribe to the LORD *g*
29:11 and the *g* and the majesty
Ps 8: 5 and crowned him with *g* and honor
19: 1 The heavens declare the *g* of God;
24: 7 that the King of *g* may come in.
29: 1 ascribe to the LORD *g*
72:19 the whole earth be filled with his *g*.
96: 3 Declare his *g* among the nations,
Pr 19:11 it is to his *g* to overlook an offense.
25: 2 It is the *g* of God to conceal
Isa 6: 3 the whole earth is full of his *g*."
48:11 I will not yield my *g* to another.
Eze 43: 2 and the land was radiant with his *g*.
Mt 24:30 of the sky, with power and great *g*.
25:31 the Son of Man comes in his *g*,
Mk 8:38 in his Father's *g* with the holy
13:26 in clouds with great power and *g*.
Lk 2: 9 and the *g* of the Lord shone
2:14 saying, "*G* to God in the highest,
Jn 1:14 We have seen his *g*, the *g* of the One
17: 5 presence with the *g* I had with you
17:24 to see my *g*, the *g* you have given
Ac 7: 2 The God of *g* appeared
Ro 1:23 exchanged the *g* of the immortal
3:23 and fall short of the *g* of God,
8:18 with the *g* that will be revealed
9: 4 theirs the divine *g*, the covenants,
1Co 10:31 whatever you do, do it all for the *g*
11: 7 but the woman is the *g* of man.
15:43 it is raised in *g*; it is sown
2Co 3:10 comparison with the surpassing *g*.
3:18 faces all reflect the Lord's *g*,
4:17 us an eternal *g* that far outweighs
Col 1:27 Christ in you, the hope of *g*.
3: 4 also will appear with him in *g*.
1Ti 3:16 was taken up in *g*.
Heb 1: 3 The Son is the radiance of God's *g*
2: 7 you crowned him with *g* and honor
1Pe 1:24 and all their *g* is like the flowers
Rev 4:11 to receive *g* and honor and power,
21:23 for the *g* of God gives it light,

GLUTTONS
Tit 1:12 always liars, evil brutes, lazy *g*."

GNASHING
Mt 8:12 where there will be weeping and *g*

GNAT*
Mt 23:24 You strain out a *g* but swallow

GOAL
2Co 5: 9 So we make it our *g* to please him,
Gal 3: 3 to attain your *g* by human effort?
Php 3:14 on toward the *g* to win the prize

GOAT (GOATS SCAPEGOAT)
Isa 11: 6 the leopard will lie down with the *g*

GOATS (GOAT)
Nu 7:17 five male *g* and five male lambs

GOD (GOD'S GODLINESS GODLY GODS)
Ge 1: 1 In the beginning *G* created
1: 2 and the Spirit of *G* was hovering
1:26 Then *G* said, "Let us make man
1:27 So *G* created man in his own image
1:31 *G* saw all that he had made,
2: 3 And *G* blessed the seventh day
2:22 Then the LORD *G* made a woman
3:21 The LORD *G* made garments
3:23 So the LORD *G* banished him
5:22 Enoch walked with *G* 300 years
6: 2 sons of *G* saw that the daughters
9:16 everlasting covenant between *G*
17: 1 "I am *G* Almighty; walk before me
21:33 name of the LORD, the Eternal *G*.
22: 8 "*G* himself will provide the lamb
28:12 and the angels of *G* were ascending
32:28 because you have struggled with *G*
32:30 "It is because I saw *G* face to face,
35:10 *G* said to him, "Your name is Jacob
41:51 *G* has made me forget all my
50:20 but *G* intended it for good
Ex 2:24 *G* heard their groaning
3: 6 because he was afraid to look at *G*.
6: 7 own people, and I will be your *G*.
8:10 is no one like the LORD our *G*.
13:18 So *G* led the people
15: 2 He is my *G*, and I will praise him,
17: 9 with the staff of *G* in my hands."
19: 3 Then Moses went up to *G*,
20: 2 the LORD your *G*, who brought
20: 5 the LORD your *G*, am a jealous *G*,
20:19 But do not have *G* speak to us
22:28 "Do not blaspheme *G*
31:18 inscribed by the finger of *G*.
34: 6 the compassionate and gracious *G*,
34:14 name is Jealous, is a jealous *G*.
Lev 18:21 not profane the name of your *G*.
19: 2 the LORD your *G*, am holy.
26:12 walk among you and be your *G*,
Nu 22:38 I must speak only what *G* puts
23:19 *G* is not a man, that he should lie,
Dt 1:17 for judgment belongs to *G*.
3:22 LORD your *G* himself will fight
3:24 For what *g* is there in heaven
4:24 is a consuming fire, a jealous *G*.
4:31 the LORD your *G* is a merciful *G*;
4:39 heart this day that the LORD is *G*
5:11 the name of the LORD your *G*,
5:14 a Sabbath to the LORD your *G*.
5:26 of the living *G* speaking out of fire,
6: 4 LORD our *G*, the LORD is one.
6: 5 Love the LORD your *G*
6:13 the LORD your *G*, serve him only
6:16 Do not test the LORD your *G*
7: 9 your *G* is *G*; he is the faithful *G*,
7:12 the LORD your *G* will keep his
7:21 is a great and awesome *G*.
8: 5 the LORD your *G* disciplines you.
10:12 but to fear the LORD your *G*,
10:14 the LORD your *G* belong
10:17 For the LORD your *G* is *G* of gods
11:13 to love the LORD your *G*
13: 3 The LORD your *G* is testing you
13: 4 the LORD your *G* you must
15: 6 the LORD your *G* will bless you
19: 9 to love the LORD your *G*
25:16 the LORD your *G* detests anyone
29:29 belong to the LORD our *G*,
30: 2 return to the LORD your *G*
30:16 today to love the LORD your *G*,

Dt 30:20 you may love the LORD your G,
31: 6 for the LORD your G goes
32: 3 Oh, praise the greatness of our G!
32: 4 A faithful G who does no wrong,
33:27 The eternal G is your refuge,
Jos 1: 9 for the LORD your G will be
14: 8 the LORD my G wholeheartedly.
22: 5 to love the LORD your G,
22:34 Between Us that the LORD is G.
23:11 careful to love the LORD your G.
23:14 the LORD your G gave you has
Jdg 16:28 O G, please strengthen me just
Ru 1:16 be my people and your G my G.
1Sa 2: 2 there is no Rock like our G.
2: 3 for the LORD is a G who knows,
2:25 another man, G may mediate
10:26 men whose hearts G had touched.
12:12 the LORD your G was your king.
17:26 defy the armies of the living G?"
17:46 world will know that there is a G
30: 6 strength in the LORD his G.
2Sa 14:14 But G does not take away life;
22: 3 my G is my rock, in whom I take
22:31 "As for G, his way is perfect;
1Ki 4:29 G gave Solomon wisdom
8:23 there is no G like you in heaven
8:27 "But will G really dwell on earth?
8:61 committed to the LORD our G,
18:21 If the LORD is G, follow him;
18:37 are G, and that you are turning
20:28 a g of the hills and not a g
2Ki 19:15 G of Israel, enthroned
1Ch 16:35 Cry out, "Save us, O G our Savior;
28: 2 for the footstool of our G,
28: 9 acknowledge the G of your father,
29:10 G of our father Israel,
29:17 my G, that you test the heart
2Ch 2: 4 for the Name of the LORD my G
5:14 of the LORD filled the temple of G
6:18 "But will G really dwell on earth
18:13 I can tell him only what my G says
20: 6 are you not the G who is in heaven?
25: 8 for G has the power to help
30: 9 for the LORD your G is gracious
33:12 the favor of the LORD his G
Ezr 8:22 "The good hand of our G is
9: 6 "O my G, I am too ashamed
9:13 our G, you have punished us less
Ne 1: 5 the great and awesome G,
8: 8 from the Book of the Law of G,
9:17 But you are a forgiving G,
9:32 the great, mighty and awesome G,
Job 1: 1 he feared G and shunned evil.
Job 2:10 Shall we accept good from G,
4:17 a mortal be more righteous than G?
5:17 is the man whom G corrects;
11: 7 Can you fathom the mysteries of G
19:26 yet in my flesh I will see G;
22:13 Yet you say, 'What does G know?
25: 4 can a man be righteous before G?
33:14 For G does speak—now one way,
34:12 is unthinkable that G would do
36:26 is G— beyond our understanding!
37:22 G comes in awesome majesty.
Ps 18: 2 my G is my rock, in whom I take
18:28 my G turns my darkness into light.
19: 1 The heavens declare the glory of G;
22: 1 G, my G, why have you forsaken
29: 3 the G of glory thunders,
31:14 I say, "You are my G."
40: 3 a hymn of praise to our G.
40: 8 I desire to do your will, O my G;
42: 2 thirsts for G, for the living G.
42:11 Put your hope in G,
45: 6 O G, will last for ever and ever;
46: 1 G is our refuge and strength,
46:10 "Be still, and know that I am G;
47: 7 For G is the King of all the earth;
50: 3 Our G comes and will not be silent;
51: 1 Have mercy on me, O G,
51:10 Create in me a pure heart, O G,
51:17 O G, you will not despise.
62: 7 my honor depend on G;
65: 5 O G our Savior,
66: 1 Shout with joy to G, all the earth!
66:16 listen, all you who fear G;
68: 6 G sets the lonely in families,
71:17 my youth, O G, you have taught
71:19 reaches to the skies, O G,
71:22 harp for your faithfulness, O my G;
73:26 but G is the strength of my heart
77:13 What g is so great as our God?
78:19 Can G spread a table in the desert?
81: 1 Sing for joy to G our strength;
84: 2 out for the living G.
84:10 a doorkeeper in the house of my G
86:12 O Lord my G, with all my heart;
89: 7 of the holy ones G is greatly feared;
90: 2 to everlasting you are G.
91: 2 my G, in whom I trust."
95: 7 for he is our G
100: 3 Know that the LORD is G.
108: 1 My heart is steadfast, O G;
113: 5 Who is like the LORD our G,
139: 23 Search me, O G, and know my
Pr 3: 4 in the sight of G and man.
25: 2 of G to conceal a matter;
Pr 30: 5 "Every word of G is flawless;
Ecc 3:11 cannot fathom what G has done
11: 5 cannot understand the work of G,
12:13 Fear G and keep his
Isa 9: 6 Wonderful Counselor, Mighty G,
37:16 you alone are G over all
40: 3 a highway for our G.
40: 8 the word of our G stands forever."
40:28 The LORD is the everlasting G,
41:10 not be dismayed, for I am your G.
44: 6 apart from me there is no G.
52: 7 "Your G reigns!"
55: 7 to our G, for he will freely pardon.
57:21 says my G, "for the wicked."
59: 2 you from your G;
61:10 my soul rejoices in my G.
62: 5 so will your G rejoice over you.
Jer 23:23 "Am I only a G nearby,"
31:33 I will be their G,
32:27 "I am the LORD, the G
Eze 28:13 the garden of G;
Da 3:17 the G we serve is able to save us
9: 4 O Lord, the great and awesome G,
Hos 12: 6 and wait for your G always.
Joel 2:13 Return to the LORD your G,
Am 4:12 prepare to meet your G, O Israel."
Mic 6: 8 and to walk humbly with your G.
Na 1: 2 LORD is a jealous and avenging G;
Zec 14: 5 Then the LORD my G will come,
Mal 3: 8 Will a man rob G? Yet you rob me.
Mt 1:23 which means, "G with us."
5: 8 for they will see G.
6:24 You cannot serve both G
19: 6 Therefore what G has joined
19:26 but with G all things are possible."
22:21 and to G what is God's."
22:37 " 'Love the Lord your G
27:46 which means, "My G, my G,
Mk 12:29 the Lord our G, the Lord is one.
16:19 and he sat at the right hand of G.
Lk 1:37 For nothing is impossible with G."
1:47 my spirit rejoices in G my Savior,
10: 9 'The kingdom of G is near you.'
10:27 " 'Love the Lord your G
18:19 "No one is good—except G alone.
Jn 1: 1 was with G, and the Word was G.
1:18 seen G, but G the One and Only,
3:16 "For G so loved the world that he
4:24 G is spirit, and his worshipers must
14: 1 Trust in G; trust also in me.
20:28 "My Lord and my G!"
Ac 2:24 But G raised him from the dead,
5: 4 You have not lied to men but to G
5:29 "We must obey G rather than men!
7:55 to heaven and saw the glory of G,
17:23 TO AN UNKNOWN G.

Ac 20:27 to you the whole will of *G*.
20:32 "Now I commit you to *G*
Ro 1:17 a righteousness from *G* is revealed,
2:11 For *G* does not show favoritism.
3: 4 Let *G* be true, and every man a liar.
3:23 and fall short of the glory of *G*,
4:24 to whom *G* will credit
5: 8 *G* demonstrates his own love for us
6:23 but the gift of *G* is eternal life
8:28 in all things *G* works for the good
11:22 the kindness and sternness of *G*:
14:12 give an account of himself to *G*.
1Co 1:20 Has not *G* made foolish
2: 9 what *G* has prepared
3: 6 watered it, but *G* made it grow.
6:20 Therefore honor *G* with your body.
7:24 each man, as responsible to *G*,
8: 8 food does not bring us near to *G*;
10:13 *G* is faithful; he will not let you be
10:31 do it all for the glory of *G*.
14:33 For *G* is not a *G* of disorder
15:28 so that *G* may be all in all.
2Co 1: 9 rely on ourselves but on *G*,
2:14 be to *G*, who always leads us
3: 5 but our competence comes from *G*.
4: 7 this all-surpassing power is from *G*
5:19 that *G* was reconciling the world
5:21 *G* made him who had no sin
6:16 we are the temple of the living *G*.
9: 7 for *G* loves a cheerful giver.
9: 8 *G* is able to make all grace abound
Gal 2: 6 *G* does not judge by external
6: 7 not be deceived: *G* cannot be
Eph 2:10 which *G* prepared in advance for us
4: 6 one baptism; one *G* and Father
5: 1 Be imitators of *G*, therefore,
Php 2: 6 Who, being in very nature *G*,
4:19 And my *G* will meet all your needs
1Th 2: 4 trying to please men but *G*,
4: 7 For *G* did not call us to be impure,
4: 9 taught by *G* to love each other.
5: 9 For *G* did not appoint us
1Ti 2: 5 one mediator between *G* and men,
4: 4 For everything *G* created is good,
5: 4 for this is pleasing to *G*.
Tit 2:13 glorious appearing of our great *G*
Heb 1: 1 In the past *G* spoke
4:12 For the word of *G* is living
6:10 *G* is not unjust; he will not forget
10:31 to fall into the hands of the living *G*
11: 6 faith it is impossible to please *G*,
Heb 12:10 but *G* disciplines us for our good,
12:29 for our "*G* is a consuming fire."
13:15 offer to *G* a sacrifice of praise—
Jas 1:13 For *G* cannot be tempted by evil,
2:19 You believe that there is one *G*.
2:23 "Abraham believed *G*,
4: 4 the world becomes an enemy of *G*.
4: 8 Come near to *G* and he will come
1Pe 4:11 it with the strength *G* provides,
2Pe 1:21 but men spoke from *G*
1Jn 1: 5 *G* is light; in him there is no
3:20 For *G* is greater than our hearts,
4: 7 for love comes from *G*.
4: 9 This is how *G* showed his love
4:11 Dear friends, since *G* so loved us,
4:12 No one has ever seen *G*;
4:16 *G* is love.
Rev 4: 8 holy is the Lord *G* Almighty,
7:17 *G* will wipe away every tear
19: 6 For our Lord *G* Almighty reigns.

GOD-BREATHED* (BREATHED)
2Ti 3:16 All Scripture is *G* and is useful

GOD'S (GOD)
2Ch 20:15 For the battle is not yours, but *G*.
Job 37:14 stop and consider *G* wonders.
Ps 52: 8 I trust in *G* unfailing love
69:30 I will praise *G* name in song
Mk 3:35 Whoever does *G* will is my brother
Jn 7:17 If anyone chooses to do *G* will,
10:36 'I am *G* Son'? Do not believe me
Ro 2: 3 think you will escape *G* judgment?
2: 4 not realizing that *G* kindness leads
3: 3 lack of faith nullify *G* faithfulness?
7:22 in my inner being I delight in *G* law
9:16 or effort, but on *G* mercy.
11:29 for *G* gifts and his call are
12: 2 and approve what *G* will is—
12:13 Share with *G* people who are
13: 6 for the authorities are *G* servants,
1Co 7:19 Keeping *G* commands is what
2Co 6: 2 now is the time of *G* favor,
Eph 1: 7 riches of *G* grace that he lavished
1Th 4: 3 It is *G* will that you should be
5:18 for this is *G* will for you
1Ti 6: 1 so that *G* name and our teaching
2Ti 2:19 *G* solid foundation stands firm,
Tit 1: 7 overseer is entrusted with *G* work,
Heb 1: 3 The Son is the radiance of *G* glory
9:24 now to appear for us in *G* presence.
11: 3 was formed at *G* command,
1Pe 2:15 For it is *G* will that
3: 4 which is of great worth in *G* sight.
1Jn 2: 5 *G* love is truly made complete

GODLINESS (GOD)
1Ti 2: 2 and quiet lives in all *g* and holiness.
4: 8 but *g* has value for all things,
6: 6 *g* with contentment is great gain.
6:11 and pursue righteousness, *g*, faith,

GODLY (GOD)
Ps 4: 3 that the LORD has set apart the *g*
2Co 7:10 *G* sorrow brings repentance that
11: 2 jealous for you with a *g* jealousy.
2Ti 3:12 everyone who wants to live a *g* life
2Pe 3:11 You ought to live holy and *g* lives

GODS (GOD)
Ex 20: 3 "You shall have no other *g*
Ac 19:26 He says that man-made *g* are no *g*

GOLD
Job 23:10 tested me, I will come forth as *g*.
Ps 19:10 They are more precious than *g*,
119:127 more than *g*, more than pure *g*,
Pr 22: 1 esteemed is better than silver or *g*.

GOLGOTHA
Jn 19:17 (which in Aramaic is called *G*).

GOLIATH
Philistine giant killed by David (1Sa 17; 21:9).

GOOD
Ge 1: 4 God saw that the light was *g*,
1:31 he had made, and it was very *g*.
2:18 "It is not *g* for the man to be alone.
50:20 but God intended it for *g*
Job 2:10 Shall we accept *g* from God,
Ps 14: 1 there is no one who does *g*.
34: 8 Taste and see that the LORD is *g*;
37: 3 Trust in the LORD and do *g*;
84:11 no *g* thing does he withhold
86: 5 You are forgiving and *g*, O Lord
103: 5 satisfies your desires with *g* things,
119: 68 You are *g*, and what you do is *g*;
133: 1 How *g* and pleasant it is
147: 1 How *g* it is to sing praises
Pr 3: 4 you will win favor and a *g* name
11:27 He who seeks *g* finds *g* will,
17:22 A cheerful heart is *g* medicine,
18:22 He who finds a wife finds what is *g*
22: 1 A *g* name is more desirable
31:12 She brings him *g*, not harm,
Isa 5:20 Woe to those who call evil *g*
52: 7 the feet of those who bring *g* news,
Jer 6:16 ask where the *g* way is,
32:39 the *g* of their children after them.
Mic 6: 8 has showed you, O man, what is *g*.

Mt 5:45 sun to rise on the evil and the *g*,
7:17 Likewise every *g* tree bears *g* fruit,
12:35 The *g* man brings *g* things out
19:17 "There is only One who is *g*.
25:21 'Well done, *g* and faithful servant!
Mk 3: 4 lawful on the Sabbath: to do *g*
8:36 What *g* is it for a man
Lk 6:27 do *g* to those who hate you,
Jn 10:11 "I am the *g* shepherd.
Ro 8:28 for the *g* of those who love him,
10:15 feet of those who bring *g* news!"
12: 9 Hate what is evil; cling to what is *g*.
1Co 10:24 should seek his own *g*, but the *g*
15:33 Bad company corrupts *g* character
2Co 9: 8 you will abound in every *g* work.
Gal 6: 9 us not become weary in doing *g*,
6:10 as we have opportunity, let us do *g*
Eph 2:10 in Christ Jesus to do *g* works,
Php 1: 6 that he who began a *g* work
1Th 5:21 Hold on to the *g*.
1Ti 3: 7 have a *g* reputation with outsiders,
4: 4 For everything God created is *g*,
6:12 Fight the *g* fight of the faith.
6:18 them to do *g*, to be rich in *g* deeds,
2Ti 3:17 equipped for every *g* work.
4: 7 I have fought the *g* fight, I have
Heb 12:10 but God disciplines us for our *g*,
1Pe 2: 3 you have tasted that the Lord is *g*.
2:12 Live such *g* lives among the pagans

GOSPEL
Ro 1:16 I am not ashamed of the *g*,
15:16 duty of proclaiming the *g* of God,
1Co 1:17 to preach the *g*— not with words
9:16 Woe to me if I do not preach the *g!*
15: 1 you of the *g* I preached to you,
Gal 1: 7 a different *g*— which is really no *g*
Php 1:27 in a manner worthy of the *g*

GOSSIP
Pr 11:13 A *g* betrays a confidence,
16:28 and a *g* separates close friends.
18: 8 of a *g* are like choice morsels;
26:20 without *g* a quarrel dies down.
2Co 12:20 slander, *g*, arrogance and disorder.

GRACE (GRACIOUS)
Ps 45: 2 lips have been anointed with *g*,
Jn 1:17 *g* and truth came through Jesus
Ac 20:32 to God and to the word of his *g*,
Ro 3:24 and are justified freely by his *g*
5:15 came by the *g* of the one man,
5:17 God's abundant provision of *g*
5:20 where sin increased, *g* increased all
6:14 you are not under law, but under *g*.
11: 6 if by *g*, then it is no longer by works
2Co 6: 1 not to receive God's *g* in vain.
8: 9 For you know the *g*
9: 8 able to make all *g* abound to you,
12: 9 "My *g* is sufficient for you,
Gal 2:21 I do not set aside the *g* of God,
5: 4 you have fallen away from *g*.
Eph 1: 7 riches of God's *g* that he lavished
2: 5 it is by *g* you have been saved.
2: 7 the incomparable riches of his *g*,
2: 8 For it is by *g* you have been saved,
Php 1: 7 all of you share in God's *g* with me.
Col 4: 6 conversation be always full of *g*,
2Th 2:16 and by his *g* gave us eternal
2Ti 2: 1 be strong in the *g* that is
Tit 2:11 For the *g* of God that brings
3: 7 having been justified by his *g*,
Heb 2: 9 that by the *g* of God he might taste
4:16 find *g* to help us in our time of need
4:16 the throne of *g* with confidence,
Jas 4: 6 but gives *g* to the humble."
2Pe 3:18 But grow in the *g* and knowledge

GRACIOUS (GRACE)
Nu 6:25 and be *g* to you;
Pr 22:11 a pure heart and whose speech is *g*
Isa 30:18 Yet the LORD longs to be *g* to you

GRAIN
1Co 9: 9 ox while it is treading out the *g*."

GRANTED
Php 1:29 For it has been *g* to you on behalf

GRASS
Ps 103: 15 As for man, his days are like *g*,
1Pe 1:24 "All men are like *g*,

GRAVE (GRAVES)
Pr 7:27 Her house is a highway to the *g*,
Hos 13:14 Where, O *g*, is your destruction?

GRAVES (GRAVE)
Jn 5:28 are in their *g* will hear his voice
Ro 3:13 "Their throats are open *g*;

GREAT (GREATER GREATEST GREATNESS)
Ge 12: 2 "I will make you into a *g* nation
Dt 10:17 the *g* God, mighty and awesome,
2Sa 22:36 you stoop down to make me *g*.
Ps 19:11 in keeping them there is *g* reward.
89: 1 of the LORD's *g* love forever;
103: 11 so *g* is his love for those who fear
Ps 107: 43 consider the *g* love of the LORD.
108: 4 For *g* is your love, higher
119:165 *G* peace have they who love your
145: 3 *G* is the LORD and most worthy
Pr 23:24 of a righteous man has *g* joy;
Isa 42:21 to make his law *g* and glorious.
La 3:23 *g* is your faithfulness.
Mk 10:43 whoever wants to become *g*
Lk 21:27 in a cloud with power and *g* glory.
1Ti 6: 6 with contentment is *g* gain.
Tit 2:13 glorious appearing of our *g* God
Heb 2: 3 if we ignore such a *g* salvation?
1Jn 3: 1 How *g* is the love the Father has

GREATER (GREAT)
Mk 12:31 There is no commandment *g*
Jn 1:50 You shall see *g* things than that."
15:13 *G* love has no one than this,
1Co 12:31 But eagerly desire the *g* gifts.
Heb 11:26 as of *g* value than the treasures
1Jn 3:20 For God is *g* than our hearts,
4: 4 is in you is *g* than the one who is

GREATEST (GREAT)
Mt 22:38 is the first and *g* commandment.
Lk 9:48 least among you all—he is the *g*."
1Co 13:13 But the *g* of these is love.

GREATNESS (GREAT)
Ps 145: 3 his *g* no one can fathom.
150: 2 praise him for his surpassing *g*.
Isa 63: 1 forward in the *g* of his strength?
Php 3: 8 compared to the surpassing *g*

GREED (GREEDY)
Lk 12:15 on your guard against all kinds of *g*
Ro 1:29 kind of wickedness, evil, *g*
Eph 5: 3 or of any kind of impurity, or of *g*,
Col 3: 5 evil desires and *g*, which is idolatry
2Pe 2:14 experts in *g*— an accursed brood!

GREEDY (GREED)
Pr 15:27 A *g* man brings trouble
1Co 6:10 nor thieves nor the *g* nor drunkards
Eph 5: 5 No immoral, impure or *g* person—
1Pe 5: 2 not *g* for money, but eager to serve;

GREEN
Ps 23: 2 makes me lie down in *g* pastures,

GREW (GROW)
Lk 2:52 And Jesus *g* in wisdom and stature,
Ac 16: 5 in the faith and *g* daily in numbers.

GRIEF (GRIEVE)
Ps 10:14 O God, do see trouble and *g*;
Pr 14:13 and joy may end in *g*.

La 3:32 Though he brings *g*, he will show
Jn 16:20 but your *g* will turn to joy.
1Pe 1: 6 had to suffer *g* in all kinds of trials.

GRIEVE (GRIEF)
Eph 4:30 do not *g* the Holy Spirit of God,
1Th 4:13 or to *g* like the rest of men,

GROUND
Ge 3:17 "Cursed is the *g* because of you;
Ex 3: 5 where you are standing is holy *g*."
Eph 6:13 you may be able to stand your *g*,

GROW (GREW)
Pr 13:11 by little makes it *g*.
1Co 3: 6 watered it, but God made it *g*.
2Pe 3:18 But *g* in the grace and knowledge

GRUMBLE (GRUMBLING)
1Co 10:10 And do not *g*, as some of them did
Jas 5: 9 Don't *g* against each other,

GRUMBLING (GRUMBLE)
Jn 6:43 "Stop *g* among yourselves,"
1Pe 4: 9 to one another without *g*.

GUARANTEE (GUARANTEEING)
Heb 7:22 Jesus has become the *g*

GUARANTEEING (GUARANTEE)
2Co 1:22 as a deposit, *g* what is to come.
Eph 1:14 who is a deposit *g* our inheritance

GUARD (GUARDS)
Ps 141: 3 Set a *g* over my mouth, O LORD;
Pr 4:23 Above all else, *g* your heart,
Isa 52:12 the God of Israel will be your rear *g*
Mk 13:33 Be on *g*! Be alert! You do not know
1Co 16:13 Be on your *g*; stand firm in the faith
Php 4: 7 will *g* your hearts and your minds
1Ti 6:20 *g* what has been entrusted

GUARDS (GUARD)
Pr 13: 3 He who *g* his lips *g* his life,
19:16 who obeys instructions *g* his life,
21:23 He who *g* his mouth and his tongue
22: 5 he who *g* his soul stays far

GUIDE
Ex 13:21 of cloud to *g* them on their way
15:13 In your strength you will *g* them
Ne 9:19 cease to *g* them on their path,
Ps 25: 5 *g* me in your truth and teach me,
43: 3 let them *g* me;
48:14 he will be our *g* even to the end.
67: 4 and *g* the nations of the earth.
73:24 You *g* me with your counsel,
139: 10 even there your hand will *g* me,
Pr 4:11 I *g* you in the way of wisdom
6:22 When you walk, they will *g* you;
Isa 58:11 The LORD will *g* you always;
Jn 16:13 comes, he will *g* you into all truth.

GUILTY
Ex 34: 7 does not leave the *g* unpunished;
Jn 8:46 Can any of you prove me *g* of sin?
Heb 10:22 to cleanse us from a *g* conscience
Jas 2:10 at just one point is *g* of breaking all

HADES
Mt 16:18 the gates of *H* will not overcome it.

HAGAR
Servant of Sarah, wife of Abraham, mother of Ishmael (Ge 16:1-6; 25:12). Driven away by Sarah while pregnant (Ge 16:5-16); after birth of Isaac (Ge 21:9-21; Gal 4:21-31).

HAGGAI*
Post-exilic prophet who encouraged rebuilding of the temple (Ezr 5:1; 6:14; Hag 1-2).

HAIR (HAIRS)
Lk 21:18 But not a *h* of your head will perish
1Co 11: 6 for a woman to have her *h* cut

HAIRS (HAIR)
Mt 10:30 even the very *h* of your head are all

HALLELUJAH*
Rev 19: 1 *H!*

HALLOWED (HOLY)
Mt 6: 9 *h* be your name,

HAND (HANDS)
Ps 16: 8 Because he is at my right *h*,
37:24 the LORD upholds him with his *h*.
139: 10 even there your *h* will guide me,
Ecc 9:10 Whatever your *h* finds to do,
Mt 6: 3 know what your right *h* is doing,
Jn 10:28 one can snatch them out of my *h*.
1Co 12:15 I am not a *h*, I do not belong

HANDS (HAND)
Ps 22:16 they have pierced my *h*
24: 4 He who has clean *h* and a pure
31: 5 Into your *h* I commit my spirit;
31:15 My times are in your *h*;
Pr 10: 4 Lazy *h* make a man poor,
31:20 and extends her *h* to the needy.
Isa 55:12 will clap their *h*.
65: 2 All day long I have held out my *h*
Lk 23:46 into your *h* I commit my spirit."
1Th 4:11 and to work with your *h*,
1Ti 2: 8 to lift up holy *h* in prayer,
5:22 hasty in the laying on of *h*,

HANNAH*
Wife of Elkanah, mother of Samuel (1Sa 1). Prayer at dedication of Samuel (1Sa 2:1-10). Blessed (1Sa 2:18-21).

HAPPY
Ps 68: 3 may they be *h* and joyful.
Pr 15:13 A *h* heart makes the face cheerful,
Ecc 3:12 better for men than to be *h*
Jas 5:13 Is anyone *h*? Let him sing songs

HARD (HARDEN HARDSHIP)
Ge 18:14 Is anything too *h* for the LORD?
Mt 19:23 it is *h* for a rich man
1Co 4:12 We work *h* with our own hands.
1Th 5:12 to respect those who work *h*

HARDEN (HARD)
Ro 9:18 he hardens whom he wants to *h*.
Heb 3: 8 do not *h* your hearts

HARDHEARTED* (HEART)
Dt 15: 7 do not be *h* or tightfisted

HARDSHIP (HARD)
Ro 8:35 Shall trouble or *h* or persecution
2Ti 2: 3 Endure *h* with us like a good
4: 5 endure *h*, do the work
Heb 12: 7 Endure *h* as discipline; God is

HARM
Ps 121: 6 the sun will not *h* you by day,
Pr 3:29 not plot *h* against your neighbor,
31:12 She brings him good, not *h*,
Ro 13:10 Love does no *h* to its neighbor.
1Jn 5:18 and the evil one cannot *h* him.

HARMONY
Ro 12:16 Live in *h* with one another.
2Co 6:15 What *h* is there between Christ
1Pe 3: 8 live in *h* with one another;

HARVEST
Mt 9:37 *h* is plentiful but the workers are
Jn 4:35 at the fields! They are ripe for *h*.
Gal 6: 9 at the proper time we will reap a *h*
Heb 12:11 it produces a *h* of righteousness

HASTE (HASTY)
Pr 21: 5 as surely as *h* leads to poverty.
29:20 Do you see a man who speaks in *h*?

HASTY* (HASTE)
Pr 19: 2 nor to be *h* and miss the way.
Ecc 5: 2 do not be *h* in your heart
1Ti 5:22 Do not be *h* in the laying

HATE (HATED HATES HATRED)
Lev 19:17 " 'Do not *h* your brother
Ps 5: 5 you *h* all who do wrong.
45: 7 righteousness and *h* wickedness;
97:10 those who love the LORD *h* evil,
139: 21 Do I not *h* those who *h* you,
Pr 8:13 To fear the LORD is to *h* evil;
Am 5:15 *H* evil, love good;
Mal 2:16 "I *h* divorce," says the LORD God
Mt 5:43 your neighbor and *h* your enemy.'
10:22 All men will *h* you because of me,
Lk 6:27 do good to those who *h* you,
Ro 12: 9 *H* what is evil; cling to what is good

HATED (HATE)
Ro 9:13 “Jacob I loved, but Esau I *h*.”
Eph 5:29 no one ever *h* his own body,
Heb 1: 9 righteousness and *h* wickedness;

HATES (HATE)
Pr 6:16 There are six things the LORD *h*,
13:24 He who spares the rod *h* his son,
Jn 3:20 Everyone who does evil *h* the light,
1Jn 2: 9 *h* his brother is still in the darkness.

HATRED (HATE)
Pr 10:12 *H* stirs up dissension,
Jas 4: 4 with the world is *h* toward God?

HAUGHTY
Pr 16:18 a *h* spirit before a fall.

HAY
1Co 3:12 costly stones, wood, *h* or straw,

HEAD (HEADS HOTHEADED)
Ge 3:15 he will crush your *h*,
Ps 23: 5 You anoint my *h* with oil;
Pr 25:22 will heap burning coals on his *h*,
Isa 59:17 and the helmet of salvation on his *h*
Mt 8:20 of Man has no place to lay his *h*.”
Ro 12:20 will heap burning coals on his *h*.”
1Co 11: 3 and the *h* of Christ is God.
12:21 And the *h* cannot say to the feet,
Eph 5:23 For the husband is the *h* of the wife
2Ti 4: 5 keep your *h* in all situations,
Rev 19:12 and on his *h* are many crowns.

HEADS (HEAD)
Lev 26:13 you to walk with *h* held high.
Isa 35:10 everlasting joy will crown their *h*.

HEAL (HEALED HEALING HEALS)
2Ch 7:14 their sin and will *h* their land.
Ps 41: 4 *h* me, for I have sinned against you
Mt 10: 8 *H* the sick, raise the dead,
Lk 4:23 to me: ‘Physician, *h* yourself!
5:17 present for him to *h* the sick.

HEALED (HEAL)
Isa 53: 5 and by his wounds we are *h*.
Mt 9:22 he said, “your faith has *h* you.”
14:36 and all who touched him were *h*.
Ac 4:10 this man stands before you *h*.
14: 9 saw that he had faith to be *h*
Jas 5:16 for each other so that you may be *h*
1Pe 2:24 by his wounds you have been *h*.

HEALING (HEAL)
Eze 47:12 for food and their leaves for *h*.”
Mal 4: 2 rise with *h* in its wings.
1Co 12: 9 to another gifts of *h*
12:30 Do all have gifts of *h*? Do all speak
Rev 22: 2 are for the *h* of the nations.

HEALS (HEAL)
Ex 15:26 for I am the LORD, who *h* you.”
Ps 103: 3 and *h* all your diseases;
147: 3 He *h* the brokenhearted

HEALTH (HEALTHY)
Pr 3: 8 This will bring *h* to your body
15:30 and good news gives *h* to the bones

HEALTHY (HEALTH)
Mk 2:17 “It is not the *h* who need a doctor,

HEAR (HEARD HEARING HEARS)
Dt 6: 4 *H*, O Israel: The LORD our God,
31:13 must *h* it and learn
2Ch 7:14 then will I *h* from heaven
Ps 94: 9 he who implanted the ear not *h*?
Isa 29:18 that day the deaf will *h* the words
65:24 while they are still speaking I will *h*
Mt 11:15 He who has ears, let him *h*.
Jn 8:47 reason you do not *h* is that you do
2Ti 4: 3 what their itching ears want to *h*.

HEARD (HEAR)
Job 42: 5 My ears had *h* of you
Isa 66: 8 Who has ever *h* of such a thing?
Mt 5:21 “You have *h* that it was said
5:27 “You have *h* that it was said,
5:33 you have *h* that it was said
5:38 “You have *h* that it was said,
5:43 “You have *h* that it was said,
1Co 2: 9 no ear has *h*,
1Th 2:13 word of God, which you *h* from us,
2Ti 1:13 What you *h* from me, keep
Jas 1:25 not forgetting what he has *h*,

HEARING (HEAR)
Ro 10:17 faith comes from *h* the message,

HEARS (HEAR)
Jn 5:24 whoever *h* my word and believes
1Jn 5:14 according to his will, he *h* us.
Rev 3:20 If anyone *h* my voice and opens

HEART (BROKENHEARTED HARDHEARTED HEARTS WHOLEHEARTEDLY)
Ex 25: 2 each man whose *h* prompts him
Lev 19:17 Do not hate your brother in your *h*.
Dt 4:29 if you look for him with all your *h*
6: 5 LORD your God with all your *h*
10:12 LORD your God with all your *h*
15:10 and do so without a grudging *h*;
30: 6 you may love him with all your *h*
30:10 LORD your God with all your *h*
Jos 22: 5 and to serve him with all your *h*
1Sa 13:14 sought out a man after his own *h*
16: 7 but the LORD looks at the *h*.”
2Ki 23: 3 with all his *h* and all his soul,
1Ch 28: 9 for the LORD searches every *h*
2Ch 7:16 and my *h* will always be there.
Job 22:22 and lay up his words in your *h*.
37: 1 “At this my *h* pounds
Ps 14: 1 The fool says in his *h*,
19:14 and the meditation of my *h*
37: 4 will give you the desires of your *h*.
45: 1 My *h* is stirred by a noble theme
51:10 Create in me a pure *h*, O God,
51:17 a broken and contrite *h*,
66:18 If I had cherished sin in my *h*,
86:11 give me an undivided *h*,
119: 11 I have hidden your word in my *h*
119: 32 for you have set my *h* free.
139: 23 Search me, O God, and know my *h*
Pr 3: 5 Trust in the LORD with all your *h*
4:21 keep them within your *h*;
4:23 Above all else, guard your *h*,
7: 3 write them on the tablet of your *h*.
13:12 Hope deferred makes the *h* sick,
14:13 Even in laughter the *h* may ache,
15:30 A cheerful look brings joy to the *h*,
17:22 A cheerful *h* is good medicine,
24:17 stumbles, do not let your *h* rejoice,
27:19 so a man's *h* reflects the man.
Ecc 8: 5 wise *h* will know the proper time
SS 4: 9 You have stolen my *h*, my sister,
Isa 40:11 and carries them close to his *h*;
57:15 and to revive the *h* of the contrite.
Jer 17: 9 The *h* is deceitful above all things
29:13 when you seek me with all your *h*.
Eze 36:26 I will give you a new *h*
Mt 5: 8 Blessed are the pure in *h*,
6:21 treasure is, there your *h* will be
12:34 of the *h* the mouth speaks.
22:37 the Lord your God with all your *h*
Lk 6:45 overflow of his *h* his mouth speaks.
Ro 2:29 is circumcision of the *h*,
10:10 is with your *h* that you believe
1Co 14:25 the secrets of his *h* will be laid bare.
Eph 5:19 make music in your *h* to the Lord,
6: 6 doing the will of God from your *h*.
Col 3:23 work at it with all your *h*,
1Pe 1:22 one another deeply, from the *h*.

HEARTS (HEART)
Dt 11:18 Fix these words of mine in your *h*
1Ki 8:39 for you alone know the *h* of all men

1Ki 8:61 your *h* must be fully committed
Ps 62: 8 pour out your *h* to him,
Ecc 3:11 also set eternity in the *h* of men;
Jer 31:33 and write it on their *h*.
Lk 16:15 of men, but God knows your *h*.
24:32 "Were not our *h* burning within us
Jn 14: 1 "Do not let your *h* be troubled.
Ac 15: 9 for he purified their *h* by faith.
Ro 2:15 of the law are written on their *h*,
2Co 3: 2 written on our *h*, known
3: 3 but on tablets of human *h*.
4: 6 shine in our *h* to give us the light
Eph 3:17 dwell in your *h* through faith.
Col 3: 1 set your *h* on things above,
Heb 3: 8 do not harden your *h*
10:16 I will put my laws in their *h*,
1Jn 3:20 For God is greater than our *h*,

HEAT
2Pe 3:12 and the elements will melt in the *h*.

HEAVEN (HEAVENLY HEAVENS)
Ge 14:19 Creator of *h* and earth.
1Ki 8:27 the highest *h*, cannot contain you.
2Ki 2: 1 up to *h* in a whirlwind,
2Ch 7:14 then will I hear from *h*
Isa 14:12 How you have fallen from *h*,
66: 1 "*H* is my throne,
Da 7:13 coming with the clouds of *h*.
Mt 6: 9 " 'Our Father in *h*,
6:20 up for yourselves treasures in *h*,
16:19 bind on earth will be bound in *h*,
19:23 man to enter the kingdom of *h*.
24:35 *H* and earth will pass away,
26:64 and coming on the clouds of *h*."
28:18 "All authority in *h*
Mk 16:19 he was taken up into *h*
Lk 15: 7 in *h* over one sinner who repents
18:22 and you will have treasure in *h*.
Ro 10: 6 'Who will ascend into *h*?' " (that is,
2Co 5: 1 an eternal house in *h*, not built
12: 2 ago was caught up to the third *h*.
Php 2:10 *h* and on earth and under the earth,
3:20 But our citizenship is in *h*.
1Th 1:10 and to wait for his Son from *h*,
Heb 8: 5 and shadow of what is in *h*.
9:24 he entered *h* itself, now to appear
2Pe 3:13 we are looking forward to a new *h*
Rev 21: 1 Then I saw a new *h* and a new earth

HEAVENLY (HEAVEN)
Ps 8: 5 him a little lower than the *h* beings
2Co 5: 2 to be clothed with our *h* dwelling,
Eph 1: 3 in the *h* realms with every spiritual
1:20 at his right hand in the *h* realms,

2Ti 4:18 bring me safely to his *h* kingdom.
Heb 12:22 to the *h* Jerusalem, the city

HEAVENS (HEAVEN)
Ge 1: 1 In the beginning God created the *h*
1Ki 8:27 The *h*, even the highest heaven,
2Ch 2: 6 since the *h*, even the highest
Ps 8: 3 When I consider your *h*,
19: 1 The *h* declare the glory of God;
102: 25 the *h* are the work of your hands.
108: 4 is your love, higher than the *h*;
119: 89 it stands firm in the *h*.
139: 8 If I go up to the *h*, you are there;
Isa 51: 6 Lift up your eyes to the *h*,
55: 9 "As the *h* are higher than the earth,
65:17 new *h* and a new earth.
Joel 2:30 I will show wonders in the *h*
Eph 4:10 who ascended higher than all the *h*,
2Pe 3:10 The *h* will disappear with a roar;

HEBREW
Ge 14:13 and reported this to Abram the *H*.

HEEDS
Pr 13: 1 wise son *h* his father's instruction,
13:18 whoever *h* correction is honored.
15: 5 whoever *h* correction shows
15:32 whoever *h* correction gains

HEEL
Ge 3:15 and you will strike his *h*."

HEIRS (INHERIT)
Ro 8:17 then we are *h*— *h* of God
Gal 3:29 and *h* according to the promise.
Eph 3: 6 gospel the Gentiles are *h* together
1Pe 3: 7 as *h* with you of the gracious gift

HELL
Mt 5:22 will be in danger of the fire of *h*.
Lk 16:23 In *h*, where he was in torment,
2Pe 2: 4 but sent them to *h*, putting them

HELMET
Isa 59:17 and the *h* of salvation on his head;
Eph 6:17 Take the *h* of salvation
1Th 5: 8 and the hope of salvation as a *h*.

HELP (HELPED HELPER HELPING HELPS)
Ps 18: 6 I cried to my God for *h*.
30: 2 my God, I called to you for *h*
46: 1 an ever-present *h* in trouble.
79: 9 *H* us, O God our Savior,
121: 1 where does my *h* come from?
Isa 41:10 I will strengthen you and *h* you;
Jnh 2: 2 depths of the grave I called for *h*,
Mk 9:24 *h* me overcome my unbelief!"
Ac 16: 9 Come over to Macedonia and *h* us

1Co 12:28 those able to *h* others, those

HELPED (HELP)
1Sa 7:12 "Thus far has the LORD *h* us."

HELPER (HELP)
Ge 2:18 I will make a *h* suitable for him."
Ps 10:14 you are the *h* of the fatherless.
Heb 13: 6 Lord is my *h*; I will not be afraid.

HELPING (HELP)
Ac 9:36 always doing good and *h* the poor.
1Ti 5:10 *h* those in trouble and devoting

HELPS (HELP)
Ro 8:26 the Spirit *h* us in our weakness.

HEN
Mt 23:37 as a *h* gathers her chicks

HERITAGE (INHERIT)
Ps 127: 3 Sons are a *h* from the LORD,

HEROD
1. King of Judea who tried to kill Jesus (Mt 2; Lk 1:5).
2. Son of 1. Tetrarch of Galilee who arrested and beheaded John the Baptist (Mt 14:1-12; Mk 6:14-29; Lk 3:1, 19-20; 9:7-9); tried Jesus (Lk 23:6-15).
3. Grandson of 1. King of Judea who killed James (Ac 12:2); arrested Peter (Ac 12:3-19). Death (Ac 12:19-23).

HERODIAS
Wife of Herod the Tetrarch who persuaded her daughter to ask for John the Baptist's head (Mt 14:1-12; Mk 6:14-29).

HEZEKIAH
King of Judah. Restored the temple and worship (2Ch 29-31). Sought the LORD for help against Assyria (2Ki 18-19; 2Ch 32:1-23; Isa 36-37). Illness healed (2Ki 20:1-11; 2Ch 32:24-26; Isa 38). Judged for showing Babylonians his treasures (2Ki 20:12-21; 2Ch 32:31; Isa 39).

HID (HIDE)
Ge 3: 8 and they *h* from the LORD God
Ex 2: 2 she *h* him for three months.
Jos 6:17 because she *h* the spies we sent.
Heb 11:23 By faith Moses' parents *h* him

HIDDEN (HIDE)
Ps 19:12 Forgive my *h* faults.
119: 11 I have *h* your word in my heart
Pr 2: 4 and search for it as for *h* treasure,
Isa 59: 2 your sins have *h* his face from you,
Mt 5:14 A city on a hill cannot be *h*.
13:44 of heaven is like treasure *h*
Col 1:26 the mystery that has been kept *h*
2: 3 in whom are *h* all the treasures
3: 3 and your life is now *h* with Christ

HIDE (HID HIDDEN)
Ps 17: 8 *h* me in the shadow of your wings
143: 9 for I *h* myself in you.

HILL (HILLS)
Mt 5:14 A city on a *h* cannot be hidden.

HILLS (HILL)
Ps 50:10 and the cattle on a thousand *h.*
121: 1 I lift up my eyes to the *h*—

HINDER (HINDERS)
1Sa 14: 6 Nothing can *h* the LORD
Mt 19:14 come to me, and do not *h* them,
1Co 9:12 anything rather than *h* the gospel
1Pe 3: 7 so that nothing will *h* your prayers.

HINDERS (HINDER)
Heb 12: 1 let us throw off everything that *h*

HINT*
Eph 5: 3 even a *h* of sexual immorality,

HOLD
Ex 20: 7 LORD will not *h* anyone guiltless
Lev 19:13 " 'Do not *h* back the wages
Jos 22: 5 to *h* fast to him and to serve him
Ps 73:23 you *h* me by my right hand.
Pr 4: 4 "Lay *h* of my words
Isa 54: 2 do not *h* back;
Mk 11:25 if you *h* anything against anyone,
Php 2:16 as you *h* out the word of life—
3:12 but I press on to take *h* of that
Col 1:17 and in him all things *h* together.
1Th 5:21 *H* on to the good.
1Ti 6:12 Take *h* of the eternal life
Heb 10:23 Let us *h* unswervingly

HOLINESS (HOLY)
Ex 15:11 majestic in *h,*
Ps 29: 2 in the splendor of his *h.*
96: 9 in the splendor of his *h;*
Ro 6:19 to righteousness leading to *h.*
2Co 7: 1 perfecting *h* out of reverence
Eph 4:24 God in true righteousness and *h.*
Heb 12:10 that we may share in his *h.*
12:14 without *h* no one will see the Lord.

HOLY (HALLOWED HOLINESS)
Ex 19: 6 kingdom of priests and a *h* nation.'
20: 8 the Sabbath day by keeping it *h.*
Lev 11:44 and be *h,* because I am *h.*
20: 7 " 'Consecrate yourselves and be *h,*
20:26 You are to be *h* to me because I,
21: 8 Consider them *h,* because I
22:32 Do not profane my *h* name.
Ps 16:10 will you let your *H* One see decay.
24: 3 Who may stand in his *h* place?
77:13 Your ways, O God, are *h.*
99: 3 he is *h.*
99: 5 he is *h.*
99: 9 for the LORD our God is *h.*
111: 9 *h* and awesome is his name.
Isa 5:16 the *h* God will show himself *h*
6: 3 *H, h, h* is the LORD Almighty;
40:25 who is my equal?" says the *H* One.
57:15 who lives forever, whose name is *h:*
Eze 28:25 I will show myself *h* among them
Da 9:24 prophecy and to anoint the most *h.*
Hab 2:20 But the LORD is in his *h* temple;
Ac 2:27 will you let your *H* One see decay.
Ro 7:12 and the commandment is *h,*
12: 1 as living sacrifices, *h* and pleasing
Eph 5: 3 improper for God's *h* people.
2Th 1:10 to be glorified in his *h* people
2Ti 1: 9 saved us and called us to a *h* life—
3:15 you have known the *h* Scriptures,
Tit 1: 8 upright, *h* and disciplined.
1Pe 1:15 But just as he who called you is *h,*
1:16 is written: "Be *h,* because I am *h.*"
2: 9 a royal priesthood, a *h* nation,
2Pe 3:11 You ought to live *h* and godly lives
Rev 4: 8 *"H, h, h* is the Lord God

HOME (HOMES)
Dt 6: 7 Talk about them when you sit at *h*
Ps 84: 3 Even the sparrow has found a *h,*
Pr 3:33 but he blesses the *h* of the righteous
Mk 10:29 "no one who has left *h* or brothers
Jn 14:23 to him and make our *h* with him.
Tit 2: 5 to be busy at *h,* to be kind,

HOMES (HOME)
Ne 4:14 daughters, your wives and your *h.*"
1Ti 5:14 to manage their *h* and to give

HOMOSEXUAL*
1Co 6: 9 male prostitutes nor *h* offenders

HONEST
Lev 19:36 Use *h* scales and *h* weights,
Dt 25:15 and *h* weights and measures,
Job 31: 6 let God weigh me in *h* scales
Pr 12:17 truthful witness gives *h* testimony,

HONEY
Ex 3: 8 a land flowing with milk and *h*—
Ps 19:10 than *h* from the comb.
119:103 sweeter than *h* to my mouth!

HONOR (HONORABLE HONORABLY HONORED HONORS)
Ex 20:12 *"H* your father and your mother,
Nu 25:13 he was zealous for the *h* of his God
Dt 5:16 *"H* your father and your mother,
1Sa 2:30 Those who *h* me I will *h,*
Ps 8: 5 and crowned him with glory and *h.*
Pr 3: 9 *H* the LORD with your wealth,
15:33 and humility comes before *h.*
20: 3 It is to a man's *h* to avoid strife,
Mt 15: 4 *'H* your father and mother'
Ro 12:10 *H* one another above yourselves.
1Co 6:20 Therefore *h* God with your body.
Eph 6: 2 *"H* your father and mother"—
1Ti 5:17 well are worthy of double *h,*
Heb 2: 7 you crowned him with glory and *h*
Rev 4: 9 *h* and thanks to him who sits

HONORABLE (HONOR)
1Th 4: 4 body in a way that is holy and *h,*

HONORABLY (HONOR)
Heb 13:18 and desire to live *h* in every way.

HONORED (HONOR)
Ps 12: 8 when what is vile is *h* among men.
Pr 13:18 but whoever heeds correction is *h.*
1Co 12:26 if one part is *h,* every part rejoices
Heb 13: 4 Marriage should be *h* by all,

HONORS (HONOR)
Ps 15: 4 but *h* those who fear the LORD,
Pr 14:31 to the needy *h* God.

HOOKS
Isa 2: 4 and their spears into pruning *h.*
Joel 3:10 and your pruning *h* into spears.

HOPE (HOPES)
Job 13:15 Though he slay me, yet will I *h*
Ps 42: 5 Put your *h* in God,
62: 5 my *h* comes from him.
119: 74 for I have put my *h* in your word.
130: 7 O Israel, put your *h* in the LORD,
147: 11 who put their *h* in his unfailing love
Pr 13:12 *H* deferred makes the heart sick,
Isa 40:31 but those who *h* in the LORD
Ro 5: 4 character; and character, *h.*
8:24 But *h* that is seen is no *h* at all.
12:12 Be joyful in *h,* patient in affliction,
15: 4 of the Scriptures we might have *h.*
1Co 13:13 now these three remain: faith, *h*
15:19 for this life we have *h* in Christ,
Col 1:27 Christ in you, the *h* of glory.
1Th 5: 8 and the *h* of salvation as a helmet.
1Ti 6:17 but to put their *h* in God,
Tit 2:13 while we wait for the blessed *h*—
Heb 6:19 We have this *h* as an anchor
11: 1 faith is being sure of what we *h* for
1Jn 3: 3 Everyone who has this *h*

HOPES (HOPE)
1Co 13: 7 always *h,* always perseveres.

HORSE
Ps 147: 10 not in the strength of the *h,*
Pr 26: 3 A whip for the *h,* a halter
Zec 1: 8 before me was a man riding a red *h*
Rev 6: 2 and there before me was a white *h!*
6: 4 Come!" Then another *h* came out,
6: 5 and there before me was a black *h!*

Rev 6: 8 and there before me was a pale *h!*
19:11 and there before me was a white *h,*

HOSANNA
Mt 21: 9 "*H* in the highest!"

HOSHEA
Last king of Israel (2Ki 15:30; 17:1-6).

HOSPITABLE* (HOSPITALITY)
1Ti 3: 2 self-controlled, respectable, *h,*
Tit 1: 8 Rather he must be *h,* one who loves

HOSPITALITY (HOSPITABLE)
Ro 12:13 Practice *h.*
1Ti 5:10 as bringing up children, showing *h,*
1Pe 4: 9 Offer *h* to one another

HOSTILE
Ro 8: 7 the sinful mind is *h* to God.

HOT
1Ti 4: 2 have been seared as with a *h* iron.
Rev 3:15 that you are neither cold nor *h.*

HOT-TEMPERED
Pr 15:18 A *h* man stirs up dissension,
19:19 A *h* man must pay the penalty;
22:24 Do not make friends with a *h* man,
29:22 and a *h* one commits many sins.

HOTHEADED (HEAD)
Pr 14:16 but a fool is *h* and reckless.

HOUR
Ecc 9:12 knows when his *h* will come:
Mt 6:27 you by worrying can add a single *h*
Lk 12:40 the Son of Man will come at an *h*
Jn 12:23 The *h* has come for the Son of Man
12:27 for this very reason I came to this *h*

HOUSE (HOUSEHOLD STOREHOUSE)
Ex 20:17 shall not covet your neighbor's *h.*
Ps 23: 6 I will dwell in the *h* of the LORD
84:10 a doorkeeper in the *h* of my God
122: 1 "Let us go to the *h* of the LORD."
127: 1 Unless the LORD builds the *h,*
Pr 7:27 Her *h* is a highway to the grave,
21: 9 than share a *h* with a quarrelsome
Isa 56: 7 a *h* of prayer for all nations."
Zec 13: 6 given at the *h* of my friends.'
Mt 7:24 is like a wise man who built his *h*
12:29 can anyone enter a strong man's *h*
21:13 My *h* will be called a *h* of prayer,'
Mk 3:25 If a *h* is divided against itself,
Lk 11:17 a *h* divided against itself will fall.
Jn 2:16 How dare you turn my Father's *h*
12: 3 the *h* was filled with the fragrance
14: 2 In my Father's *h* are many rooms;
Heb 3: 3 the builder of a *h* has greater honor

HOUSEHOLD (HOUSE)
Jos 24:15 my *h,* we will serve the LORD."
Mic 7: 6 are the members of his own *h.*
Mt 10:36 will be the members of his own *h.'*
12:25 or *h* divided against itself will not
1Ti 3:12 manage his children and his *h* well.
3:15 to conduct themselves in God's *h,*

HUMAN (HUMANITY)
Gal 3: 3 to attain your goal by *h* effort?

HUMANITY* (HUMAN)
Heb 2:14 he too shared in their *h* so that

HUMBLE (HUMBLED HUMBLES HUMILIATE HUMILITY)
2Ch 7:14 will *h* themselves and pray
Ps 25: 9 He guides the *h* in what is right
Pr 3:34 but gives grace to the *h.*
Isa 66: 2 he who is *h* and contrite in spirit,
Mt 11:29 for I am gentle and *h* in heart,
Eph 4: 2 Be completely *h* and gentle;
Jas 4:10 *H* yourselves before the Lord,
1Pe 5: 6 *H* yourselves,

HUMBLED (HUMBLE)
Mt 23:12 whoever exalts himself will be *h,*
Php 2: 8 he *h* himself

HUMBLES (HUMBLE)
Mt 18: 4 whoever *h* himself like this child is
23:12 whoever *h* himself will be exalted.

HUMILIATE* (HUMBLE)
Pr 25: 7 than for him to *h* you
1Co 11:22 and *h* those who have nothing?

HUMILITY (HUMBLE)
Pr 11: 2 but with *h* comes wisdom.
15:33 and *h* comes before honor.
Php 2: 3 but in *h* consider others better
Tit 3: 2 and to show true *h* toward all men.
1Pe 5: 5 clothe yourselves with *h*

HUNGRY
Ps 107: 9 and fills the *h* with good things.
146: 7 and gives food to the *h.*
Pr 25:21 If your enemy is *h,* give him food
Eze 18: 7 but gives his food to the *h*
Mt 25:35 For I was *h* and you gave me
Lk 1:53 He has filled the *h* with good things
Jn 6:35 comes to me will never go *h,*
Ro 12:20 "If your enemy is *h,* feed him;

HURT (HURTS)
Ecc 8: 9 it over others to his own *h.*
Mk 16:18 deadly poison, it will not *h* them
Rev 2:11 He who overcomes will not be *h*

HURTS* (HURT)
Ps 15: 4 even when it *h,*
Pr 26:28 A lying tongue hates those it *h,*

HUSBAND (HUSBAND'S HUSBANDS)
1Co 7: 3 The *h* should fulfill his marital duty
7:10 wife must not separate from her *h.*
7:11 And a *h* must not divorce his wife.
7:13 And if a woman has a *h* who is not
7:39 A woman is bound to her *h* as long
2Co 11: 2 I promised you to one *h,* to Christ,
Eph 5:23 For the *h* is the head of the wife
5:33 and the wife must respect her *h.*
1Ti 3: 2 the *h* of but one wife, temperate,

HUSBAND'S (HUSBAND)
Pr 12: 4 of noble character is her *h* crown,
1Co 7: 4 the *h* body does not belong

HUSBANDS (HUSBAND)
Eph 5:22 submit to your *h* as to the Lord.
5:25 *H,* love your wives, just
Tit 2: 4 the younger women to love their *h*
1Pe 3: 1 same way be submissive to your *h*
3: 7 *H,* in the same way be considerate

HYMN
1Co 14:26 everyone has a *h,* or a word

HYPOCRISY (HYPOCRITE HYPOCRITES)
Mt 23:28 but on the inside you are full of *h*
1Pe 2: 1 *h,* envy, and slander of every kind.

HYPOCRITE (HYPOCRISY)
Mt 7: 5 You *h,* first take the plank out

HYPOCRITES (HYPOCRISY)
Ps 26: 4 nor do I consort with *h;*
Mt 6: 5 when you pray, do not be like the *h*

HYSSOP
Ps 51: 7 with *h,* and I will be clean;

IDLE (IDLENESS)
1Th 5:14 those who are *i,* encourage
2Th 3: 6 away from every brother who is *i*
1Ti 5:13 they get into the habit of being *i*

IDLENESS* (IDLE)
Pr 31:27 and does not eat the bread of *i.*

IDOL (IDOLATRY IDOLS)
Isa 44:17 From the rest he makes a god, his *i;*
1Co 8: 4 We know that an *i* is nothing at all

IDOLATRY (IDOL)
Col 3: 5 evil desires and greed, which is *i.*

IDOLS (IDOL)
1Co 8: 1 Now about food sacrificed to *i:*

IGNORANT (IGNORE)
1Co 15:34 for there are some who are *i* of God

Heb 5: 2 to deal gently with those who are *i*
1Pe 2:15 good you should silence the *i* talk
2Pe 3:16 which *i* and unstable people distort

IGNORE (IGNORANT IGNORES)
Dt 22: 1 do not *i* it but be sure
Ps 9:12 he does not *i* the cry of the afflicted
Heb 2: 3 if we *i* such a great salvation?

IGNORES (IGNORE)
Pr 10:17 whoever *i* correction leads others
15:32 He who *i* discipline despises

ILLUMINATED*
Rev 18: 1 and the earth was *i* by his splendor.

IMAGE
Ge 1:26 "Let us make man in our *i*,
1:27 So God created man in his own *i*,
1Co 11: 7 since he is the *i* and glory of God;
Col 1:15 He is the *i* of the invisible God,
3:10 in knowledge in the *i* of its Creator.

IMAGINE
Eph 3:20 more than all we ask or *i*,

IMITATE (IMITATORS)
1Co 4:16 Therefore I urge you to *i* me.
Heb 6:12 but to *i* those who through faith
13: 7 of their way of life and *i* their faith.
3Jn :11 do not *i* what is evil but what is

IMITATORS* (IMITATE)
Eph 5: 1 Be *i* of God, therefore,
1Th 1: 6 You became *i* of us and of the Lord
2:14 became *i* of God's churches

IMMANUEL
Isa 7:14 birth to a son, and will call him *I*.
Mt 1:23 and they will call him *I*"—

IMMORAL* (IMMORALITY)
Pr 6:24 keeping you from the *i* woman,
1Co 5: 9 to associate with sexually *i* people
5:10 the people of this world who are *i*,
5:11 but is sexually *i* or greedy,
6: 9 Neither the sexually *i* nor idolaters
Eph 5: 5 No *i*, impure or greedy person—
Heb 12:16 See that no one is sexually *i*,
13: 4 the adulterer and all the sexually *i*.
Rev 21: 8 the murderers, the sexually *i*,
22:15 the sexually *i*, the murderers,

IMMORALITY (IMMORAL)
1Co 6:13 The body is not meant for sexual *i*,
6:18 Flee from sexual *i*.
10: 8 We should not commit sexual *i*,
Gal 5:19 sexual *i*, impurity and debauchery;
Eph 5: 3 must not be even a hint of sexual *i*,
1Th 4: 3 that you should avoid sexual *i*;
Jude : 4 grace of our God into a license for *i*

IMMORTAL* (IMMORTALITY)
Ro 1:23 glory of the *i* God for images made
1Ti 1:17 Now to the King eternal, *i*,
6:16 who alone is *i* and who lives

IMMORTALITY (IMMORTAL)
Ro 2: 7 honor and *i*, he will give eternal life
1Co 15:53 and the mortal with *i*.
2Ti 1:10 and *i* to light through the gospel.

IMPERISHABLE
1Pe 1:23 not of perishable seed, but of *i*,

IMPORTANCE* (IMPORTANT)
1Co 15: 3 passed on to you as of first *i*:

IMPORTANT (IMPORTANCE)
Mt 6:25 Is not life more *i* than food,
23:23 have neglected the more *i* matters
Mk 12:29 "The most *i* one," answered Jesus,
12:33 as yourself is more *i* than all burnt
Php 1:18 The *i* thing is that in every way,

IMPOSSIBLE
Mt 17:20 Nothing will be *i* for you."
Lk 1:37 For nothing is *i* with God."
18:27 "What is *i* with men is possible
Heb 6:18 things in which it is *i* for God to lie,
11: 6 without faith it is *i* to please God,

IMPROPER*
Eph 5: 3 these are *i* for God's holy people.

IMPURE (IMPURITY)
Ac 10:15 not call anything *i* that God has
Eph 5: 5 No immoral, *i* or greedy person—
1Th 4: 7 For God did not call us to be *i*,
Rev 21:27 Nothing *i* will ever enter it,

IMPURITY (IMPURE)
Ro 1:24 hearts to sexual *i* for the degrading
Eph 5: 3 or of any kind of *i*, or of greed,

INCENSE
Ex 40: 5 Place the gold altar of *i* in front
Ps 141: 2 my prayer be set before you like *i*;
Mt 2:11 him with gifts of gold and of *i*

INCOME
Ecc 5:10 wealth is never satisfied with his *i*.
1Co 16: 2 sum of money in keeping with his *i*,

INCOMPARABLE*
Eph 2: 7 ages he might show the *i* riches

INCREASE (EVER-INCREASING INCREASED INCREASES INCREASING)
Ge 1:22 "Be fruitful and *i* in number
Ps 62:10 though your riches *i*,
Isa 9: 7 Of the *i* of his government
Lk 17: 5 said to the Lord, "*I* our faith!"
1Th 3:12 May the Lord make your love *i*

INCREASED (INCREASE)
Ac 6: 7 of disciples in Jerusalem *i* rapidly,
Ro 5:20 But where sin *i*, grace *i* all the more

INCREASES (INCREASE)
Pr 24: 5 and a man of knowledge *i* strength;

INCREASING (INCREASE)
Ac 6: 1 when the number of disciples was *i*,
2Th 1: 3 one of you has for each other is *i*.
2Pe 1: 8 these qualities in *i* measure,

INDEPENDENT*
1Co 11:11 however, woman is not *i* of man,
11:11 of man, nor is man *i* of woman.

INDESCRIBABLE*
2Co 9:15 Thanks be to God for his *i* gift!

INDISPENSABLE*
1Co 12:22 seem to be weaker are *i*,

INEFFECTIVE*
2Pe 1: 8 they will keep you from being *i*

INEXPRESSIBLE*
2Co 12: 4 He heard *i* things, things that man
1Pe 1: 8 are filled with an *i* and glorious joy,

INFANTS
Mt 21:16 " 'From the lips of children and *i*
1Co 14:20 In regard to evil be *i*,

INFIRMITIES
Isa 53: 4 Surely he took up our *i*

INHERIT (CO-HEIRS HEIRS HERITAGE INHERITANCE)
Ps 37:11 But the meek will *i* the land
37:29 the righteous will *i* the land
Mt 5: 5 for they will *i* the earth.
Mk 10:17 "what must I do to *i* eternal life?"
1Co 15:50 blood cannot *i* the kingdom of God

INHERITANCE (INHERIT)
Dt 4:20 to be the people of his *i*,
Pr 13:22 A good man leaves an *i*
Eph 1:14 who is a deposit guaranteeing our *i*
5: 5 has any *i* in the kingdom of Christ
Heb 9:15 receive the promised eternal *i*—
1Pe 1: 4 and into an *i* that can never perish,

INIQUITIES (INIQUITY)
Ps 78:38 he forgave their *i*
103: 10 or repay us according to our *i*.
Isa 59: 2 But your *i* have separated
Mic 7:19 and hurl all our *i* into the depths

INIQUITY (INIQUITIES)
Ps 51: 2 Wash away all my *i*
Isa 53: 6 the *i* of us all.

INJUSTICE
2Ch 19: 7 the LORD our God there is no *i*

INNOCENT
Pr 17:26 It is not good to punish an *i* man,
Mt 10:16 shrewd as snakes and as *i* as doves.
27: 4 "for I have betrayed *i* blood."
1Co 4: 4 but that does not make me *i*.

INSCRIPTION
Mt 22:20 And whose *i*?" "Caesar's,"

INSOLENT
Ro 1:30 God-haters, *i*, arrogant

INSTITUTED
Ro 13: 2 rebelling against what God has *i*,
1Pe 2:13 to every authority *i* among men:

INSTRUCT (INSTRUCTION)
Ps 32: 8 I will *i* you and teach you
Pr 9: 9 *I* a wise man and he will be wiser
Ro 15:14 and competent to *i* one another.
2Ti 2:25 who oppose him he must gently *i*,

INSTRUCTION (INSTRUCT)
Pr 1: 8 Listen, my son, to your father's *i*
4: 1 Listen, my sons, to a father's *i*;
4:13 Hold on to *i*, do not let it go;
8:10 Choose my *i* instead of silver,
8:33 Listen to my *i* and be wise;
13: 1 A wise son heeds his father's *i*,
13:13 He who scorns *i* will pay for it,
16:20 Whoever gives heed to *i* prospers,
16:21 and pleasant words promote *i*.
19:20 Listen to advice and accept *i*,
23:12 Apply your heart to *i*
1Co 14: 6 or prophecy or word of *i*?
14:26 or a word of *i*, a revelation,
Eph 6: 4 up in the training and *i* of the Lord.
1Th 4: 8 he who rejects this *i* does not reject
2Th 3:14 If anyone does not obey our *i*
1Ti 1:18 I give you this *i* in keeping
6: 3 to the sound *i* of our Lord Jesus
2Ti 4: 2 with great patience and careful *i*.

INSULT
Pr 9: 7 corrects a mocker invites *i*;
12:16 but a prudent man overlooks an *i*.
Mt 5:11 Blessed are you when people *i* you,
Lk 6:22 when they exclude you and *i* you
1Pe 3: 9 evil with evil or *i* with *i*,

INTEGRITY
1Ki 9: 4 if you walk before me in *i* of heart
Job 2: 3 And he still maintains his *i*,
27: 5 till I die, I will not deny my *i*.
Pr 10: 9 The man of *i* walks securely,
11: 3 The *i* of the upright guides them,
29:10 Bloodthirsty men hate a man of *i*

Tit 2: 7 your teaching show *i*, seriousness

INTELLIGENCE
Isa 29:14 the *i* of the intelligent will vanish."
1Co 1:19 *i* of the intelligent I will frustrate."

INTELLIGIBLE
1Co 14:19 I would rather speak five *i* words

INTERCEDE (INTERCEDES INTERCESSION)
Heb 7:25 he always lives to *i* for them.

INTERCEDES (INTERCEDE)
Ro 8:26 but the Spirit himself *i* for us

INTERCESSION* (INTERCEDE)
Isa 53:12 and made *i* for the transgressors.
1Ti 2: 1 *i* and thanksgiving be made

INTERESTS
1Co 7:34 his wife—and his *i* are divided.
Php 2: 4 only to your own *i*, but also to the *i*
2:21 everyone looks out for his own *i*,

INTERMARRY (MARRY)
Dt 7: 3 Do not *i* with them.

INVENTED*
2Pe 1:16 We did not follow cleverly *i* stories

INVESTIGATED
Lk 1: 3 I myself have carefully *i* everything

INVISIBLE
Ro 1:20 of the world God's *i* qualities—
Col 1:15 He is the image of the *i* God,
1Ti 1:17 immortal, *i*, the only God,

INVITE (INVITED INVITES)
Lk 14:13 you give a banquet, *i* the poor,

INVITED (INVITE)
Mt 22:14 For many are *i*, but few are chosen
25:35 I was a stranger and you *i* me in,

INVITES (INVITE)
1Co 10:27 If some unbeliever *i* you to a meal

INVOLVED
2Ti 2: 4 a soldier gets *i* in civilian affairs—

IRON
1Ti 4: 2 have been seared as with a hot *i*.
Rev 2:27 He will rule them with an *i* scepter;

IRREVOCABLE*
Ro 11:29 for God's gifts and his call are *i*.

ISAAC
Son of Abraham by Sarah (Ge 17:19; 21:1-7; 1Ch 1:28). Offered up by Abraham (Ge 22; Heb 11:17-19). Rebekah taken as wife (Ge 24). Fathered Esau and Jacob (Ge 25:19-26; 1Ch 1:34). Tricked into blessing Jacob (Ge 27). Father of Israel (Ex 3:6; Dt 29:13; Ro 9:10).

ISAIAH
Prophet to Judah (Isa 1:1). Called by the LORD (Isa 6).

ISHMAEL
Son of Abraham by Hagar (Ge 16; 1Ch 1:28). Blessed, but not son of covenant (Ge 17:18-21; Gal 4:21-31). Sent away by Sarah (Ge 21:8-21).

ISRAEL (ISRAELITES)
1. Name given to Jacob (see JACOB).
2. Corporate name of Jacob's descendants; often specifically Northern Kingdom.
Dt 6: 4 Hear, O *I*: The LORD our God,
1Sa 4:21 "The glory has departed from *I*"—
Isa 27: 6 *I* will bud and blossom
Jer 31:10 'He who scattered *I* will gather
Eze 39:23 of *I* went into exile for their sin,
Mk 12:29 'Hear, O *I*, the Lord our God,
Lk 22:30 judging the twelve tribes of *I*.
Ro 9: 6 all who are descended from *I* are *I*.
11:26 And so all *I* will be saved,
Eph 3: 6 Gentiles are heirs together with *I*,

ISRAELITES (ISRAEL)
Ex 14:22 and the *I* went through the sea
16:35 The *I* ate manna forty years,
Hos 1:10 "Yet the *I* will be like the sand
Ro 9:27 the number of the *I* be like the sand

ITCHING*
2Ti 4: 3 to say what their *i* ears want to hear

JACOB
Second son of Isaac, twin of Esau (Ge 26:21-26; 1Ch 1:34). Bought Esau's birthright (Ge 26:29-34); tricked Isaac into blessing him (Ge 27:1-37). Abrahamic covenant perpetuated through (Ge 28:13-15; Mal 1:2). Vision at Bethel (Ge 28:10-22). Wives and children (Ge 29:1-30:24; 35:16-26; 1Ch 2-9). Wrestled with God; name changed to Israel (Ge 32:22-32). Sent sons to Egypt during famine (Ge 42-43). Settled in Egypt (Ge 46). Blessed Ephraim and Manasseh (Ge 48). Blessed sons (Ge 49:1-28; Heb 11:21). Death (Ge 49:29-33). Burial (Ge 50:1-14).

JAMES
1. Apostle; brother of John (Mt 4:21-22; 10:2; Mk 3:17; Lk 5:1-10). At transfiguration (Mt 17:1-13; Mk 9:1-13; Lk 9:28-36). Killed by Herod (Ac 12:2).
2. Apostle; son of Alphaeus (Mt 10:3; Mk 3:18; Lk 6:15).
3. Brother of Jesus (Mt 13:55; Mk 6:3; Lk 24:10; Gal 1:19) and Judas (Jude 1). With believers before Pentecost (Ac 1:13). Leader of church at Jerusalem (Ac 12:17; 15; 21:18; Gal 2:9, 12). Author of epistle (Jas 1:1).

JAPHETH
Son of Noah (Ge 5:32; 1Ch 1:4-5). Blessed (Ge 9:18-28).

JARS
2Co 4: 7 we have this treasure in *j* of clay

JEALOUS (JEALOUSY)
Ex 20: 5 the LORD your God, am a *j* God,
34:14 whose name is Jealous, is a *j* God.
Dt 4:24 God is a consuming fire, a *j* God.
Joel 2:18 the LORD will be *j* for his land
Zec 1:14 I am very *j* for Jerusalem and Zion,

2Co 11: 2 I am *j* for you with a godly jealousy

JEALOUSY (JEALOUS)

1Co 3: 3 For since there is *j* and quarreling
2Co 11: 2 I am jealous for you with a godly *j*.
Gal 5:20 hatred, discord, *j*, fits of rage,

JEHOAHAZ

1. Son of Jehu; king of Israel (2Ki 13:1-9).
2. Son of Josiah; king of Judah (2Ki 23:31-34; 2Ch 36:1-4).

JEHOASH

Son of Jehoahaz; king of Israel (2Ki 13-14; 2Ch 25).

JEHOIACHIN

Son of Jehoiakim; king of Judah exiled by Nebuchadnezzar (2Ki 24:8-17; 2Ch 36:8-10; Jer 22:24-30; 24:1). Raised from prisoner status (2Ki 25:27-30; Jer 52:31-34).

JEHOIAKIM

Son of Josiah; king of Judah (2Ki 23:34-24:6; 2Ch 36:4-8; Jer 22:18-23; 36).

JEHORAM

Son of Jehoshaphat; king of Judah (2Ki 8:16-24).

JEHOSHAPHAT

Son of Asa; king of Judah (1Ki 22:41-50; 2Ki 3; 2Ch 17-20).

JEHU

King of Israel (1Ki 19:16-19; 2Ki 9-10).

JEPHTHAH

Judge from Gilead who delivered Israel from Ammon (Jdg 10:6-12:7). Made rash vow concerning his daughter (Jdg 11:30-40).

JEREMIAH

Prophet to Judah (Jer 1:1-3). Called by the LORD (Jer 1). Put in stocks (Jer 20:1-3). Threatened for prophesying (Jer 11:18-23; 26). Opposed by Hananiah (Jer 28). Scroll burned (Jer 36). Imprisoned (Jer 37). Thrown into cistern (Jer 38). Forced to Egypt with those fleeing Babylonians (Jer 43).

JEROBOAM

1. Official of Solomon; rebelled to become first king of Israel (1Ki 11:26-40; 12:1-20; 2Ch 10). Idolatry (1Ki 12:25-33); judgment for (1Ki 13-14; 2Ch 13).
2. Son of Jehoash; king of Israel (1Ki 14:23-29).

JERUSALEM

2Ki 23:27 and I will reject *J*, the city I chose,
2Ch 6: 6 now I have chosen *J* for my Name
Ne 2:17 Come, let us rebuild the wall of *J*,
Ps 122: 6 Pray for the peace of *J*:
125: 2 As the mountains surround *J*,
137: 5 If I forget you, O *J*,
Isa 40: 9 You who bring good tidings to *J*,
65:18 for I will create *J* to be a delight
Joel 3:17 *J* will be holy;
Zep 3:16 On that day they will say to *J*,
Zec 2: 4 '*J* will be a city without walls
8: 8 I will bring them back to live in *J*;
14: 8 living water will flow out from *J*,
Mt 23:37 "O *J*, *J*, you who kill the prophets
Lk 13:34 die outside *J*! "O *J*, *J*,
21:24 *J* will be trampled
Jn 4:20 where we must worship is in *J*."
Ac 1: 8 and you will be my witnesses in *J*,
Gal 4:25 corresponds to the present city of *J*
Rev 21: 2 I saw the Holy City, the new *J*,

JESUS

LIFE: Genealogy (Mt 1:1-17; Lk 3:21-37). Birth announced (Mt 1:18-25; Lk 1:26-45). Birth (Mt 2:1-12; Lk 2:1-40). Escape to Egypt (Mt 2:13-23). As a boy in the temple (Lk 2:41-52). Baptism (Mt 3:13-17; Mk 1:9-11; Lk 3:21-22; Jn 1:32-34). Temptation (Mt 4:1-11; Mk 1:12-13; Lk 4:1-13). Ministry in Galilee (Mt 4:12-18:35; Mk 1:14-9:50; Lk 4:14-13:9; Jn 1:35-2:11; 4; 6), Transfiguration (Mt 17:1-8; Mk 9:2-8; Lk 9:28-36), on the way to Jerusalem (Mt 19-20; Mk 10; Lk 13:10-19:27), in Jerusalem (Mt 21-25; Mk 11-13; Lk 19:28-21:38; Jn 2:12-3:36; 5; 7-12). Last supper (Mt 26:17-35; Mk 14:12-31; Lk 22:1-38; Jn 13-17). Arrest and trial (Mt 26:36-27:31; Mk 14:43-15:20; Lk 22:39-23:25; Jn 18:1-19:16). Crucifixion (Mt 27:32-66; Mk 15:21-47; Lk 23:26-55; Jn 19:28-42). Resurrection and appearances (Mt 28; Mk 16; Lk 24; Jn 20-21; Ac 1:1-11; 7:56; 9:3-6; 1Co 15:1-8; Rev 1:1-20).

MIRACLES. Healings: official's son (Jn 4:43-54), demoniac in Capernaum (Mk 1:23-26; Lk 4:33-35), Peter's mother-in-law (Mt 8:14-17; Mk 1:29-31; Lk 4:38-39), leper (Mt 8:2-4; Mk 1:40-45; Lk 5:12-16), paralytic (Mt 9:1-8; Mk 2:1-12; Lk 5:17-26), cripple (Jn 5:1-9), shriveled hand (Mt 12:10-13; Mk 3:1-5; Lk 6:6-11), centurion's servant (Mt 8:5-13; Lk 7:1-10), widow's son raised (Lk 7:11-17), demoniac (Mt 12:22-23; Lk 11:14), Gadarene demoniacs (Mt 8:28-34; Mk 5:1-20; Lk 8:26-39), woman's bleeding and Jairus' daughter (Mt 9:18-26; Mk 5:21-43; Lk 8:40-56), blind man (Mt 9:27-31), mute man (Mt 9:32-33), Canaanite woman's daughter (Mt 15:21-28; Mk 7:24-30), deaf man (Mk 7:31-37), blind man (Mk 8:22-26), demoniac boy (Mt 17:14-18; Mk 9:14-29; Lk 9:37-43), ten lepers (Lk 17:11-19), man born blind (Jn 9:1-7), Lazarus raised (Jn 11), crippled woman (Lk 13:11-17), man with dropsy (Lk 14:1-6), two blind men (Mt 20:29-34; Mk 10:46-52; Lk 18:35-43), Malchus' ear (Lk 22:50-51). Other Miracles: water to wine (Jn 2:1-11), catch of fish (Lk 5:1-11), storm stilled (Mt 8:23-27; Mk 4:37-41; Lk 8:22-25), 5,000 fed (Mt 14:15-21; Mk 6:35-44; Lk 9:10-17; Jn 6:1-14), walking on water (Mt 14:25-33; Mk 6:48-52; Jn 6:15-21), 4,000 fed (Mt 15:32-39; Mk 8:1-9), money from fish (Mt 17:24-27), fig tree cursed (Mt 21:18-22; Mk 11:12-14), catch of fish (Jn 21:1-14).

MAJOR TEACHING: Sermon on the Mount (Mt 5-7; Lk 6:17-49), to Nicodemus (Jn 3), to Samaritan woman (Jn 4), Bread of Life (Jn 6:22-59), at Feast of Tabernacles (Jn 7-8), woes to Pharisees (Mt 23; Lk 11:37-54), Good Shepherd (Jn 10:1-18), Olivet Discourse (Mt 24-25; Mk 13; Lk 21:5-36), Upper Room Discourse (Jn 13-16).

PARABLES: Sower (Mt 13:3-23; Mk 4:3-25; Lk 8:5-18), seed's growth (Mk 4:26-29), wheat and weeds (Mt 13:24-30, 36-43), mustard seed (Mt 13:31-32; Mk 4:30-32), yeast (Mt 13:33; Lk 13:20-21), hidden treasure (Mt 13:44), valuable pearl (Mt 13:45-46), net (Mt 13:47-51), house owner (Mt 13:52), good Samaritan (Lk 10:25-37), unmerciful servant (Mt 18:15-35), lost sheep (Mt 18:10-14; Lk 15:4-7), lost coin (Lk 15:8-10), prodigal son (Lk 15:11-32), dishonest manager (Lk 16:1-13), rich man and Lazarus (Lk 16:19-31), persistent widow (Lk 18:1-8), Pharisee and tax collector (Lk 18:9-14), payment of workers (Mt 20:1-16), tenants and the vineyard (Mt 21:28-46; Mk 12:1-12; Lk 20:9-19), wedding banquet (Mt 22:1-14), faithful servant (Mt 24:45-51), ten virgins (Mt 25:1-13), talents (Mt 25:1-30; Lk 19:12-27).

DISCIPLES see APOSTLES. Call of (Jn 1:35-51; Mt 4:18-22; 9:9; Mk 1:16-20; 2:13-14; Lk 5:1-11, 27-28). Named Apostles (Mk 3:13-19; Lk 6:12-16). Twelve sent out (Mt 10; Mk 6:7-11; Lk 9:1-5). Seventy sent out (Lk 10:1-24). Defection of (Jn 6:60-71; Mt 26:56; Mk 14:50-52). Final commission (Mt 28:16-20; Jn 21:15-23; Ac 1:3-8).

Ac 2:32 God has raised this *J* to life,
9: 5 "I am *J*, whom you are persecuting
15:11 of our Lord *J* that we are saved,
16:31 "Believe in the Lord *J*,
Ro 3:24 redemption that came by Christ *J*.
5:17 life through the one man, *J* Christ.
8: 1 for those who are in Christ *J*,
1Co 2: 2 except *J* Christ and him crucified.
8: 6 and there is but one Lord, *J* Christ,
12: 3 and no one can say, "*J* is Lord,"
2Co 4: 5 not preach ourselves, but *J* Christ
Gal 2:16 but by faith in *J* Christ.
3:28 for you are all one in Christ *J*.
5: 6 in Christ *J* neither circumcision
Eph 2:10 created in Christ *J*
2:20 with Christ *J* himself as the chief
Php 1: 6 until the day of Christ *J*.
2: 5 be the same as that of Christ *J*:
2:10 name of *J* every knee should bow,
Col 3:17 do it all in the name of the Lord *J*,
2Th 2: 1 the coming of our Lord *J* Christ
1Ti 1:15 Christ *J* came into the world
2Ti 3:12 life in Christ *J* will be persecuted,
Tit 2:13 our great God and Savior, *J* Christ,
Heb 2: 9 But we see *J*, who was made a little
3: 1 fix your thoughts on *J*, the apostle
4:14 through the heavens, *J* the Son
7:22 *J* has become the guarantee
7:24 but because *J* lives forever,
12: 2 Let us fix our eyes on *J*, the author
2Pe 1:16 and coming of our Lord *J* Christ,
1Jn 1: 7 and the blood of *J*, his Son,
2: 1 *J* Christ, the Righteous One.
2: 6 to live in him must walk as *J* did.
4:15 anyone acknowledges that *J* is
Rev 22:20 Come, Lord *J*.

JEW (JEWS JUDAISM)

Zec 8:23 of one *J* by the edge of his robe
Ro 1:16 first for the *J*, then for the Gentile.
10:12 there is no difference between *J*

1Co 9:20 To the Jews I became like a *J*,
Gal 3:28 There is neither *J* nor Greek,

JEWELRY (JEWELS)
1Pe 3: 3 wearing of gold *j* and fine clothes.

JEWELS (JEWELRY)
Isa 61:10 as a bride adorns herself with her *j*.
Zec 9:16 like *j* in a crown.

JEWS (JEW)
Mt 2: 2 who has been born king of the *J*?
27:11 "Are you the king of the *J*?" "Yes,
Jn 4:22 for salvation is from the *J*.
Ro 3:29 Is God the God of *J* only?
1Co 1:22 *J* demand miraculous signs
9:20 To the *J* I became like a Jew,
12:13 whether *J* or Greeks, slave or free
Gal 2: 8 of Peter as an apostle to the *J*,
Rev 3: 9 claim to be *J* though they are not,

JEZEBEL
Sidonian wife of Ahab (1Ki 16:31). Promoted Baal worship (1Ki 16:32-33). Killed prophets of the LORD (1Ki 18:4, 13). Opposed Elijah (1Ki 19:1-2). Had Naboth killed (1Ki 21). Death prophesied (1Ki 21:17-24). Killed by Jehu (2Ki 9:30-37).

JOASH
Son of Ahaziah; king of Judah. Sheltered from Athaliah by Jehoiada (2Ki 11; 2Ch 22:10-23:21). Repaired temple (2Ki 12; 2Ch 24).

JOB
Wealthy man from Uz; feared God (Job 1:1-5). Righteousness tested by disaster (Job 1:6-22), personal affliction (Job 2). Maintained innocence in debate with three friends (Job 3-31), Elihu (Job 32-37). Rebuked by the LORD (Job 38-41). Vindicated and restored to greater stature by the LORD (Job 42). Example of righteousness (Eze 14:14, 20).

JOHN
1. Son of Zechariah and Elizabeth (Lk 1). Called the Baptist (Mt 3:1-12; Mk 1:2-8). Witness to Jesus (Mt 3:11-12; Mk 1:7-8; Lk 3:15-18; Jn 1:6-35; 3:27-30; 5:33-36). Doubts about Jesus (Mt 11:2-6; Lk 7:18-23). Arrest (Mt 4:12; Mk 1:14). Execution (Mt 14:1-12; Mk 6:14-29; Lk 9:7-9). Ministry compared to Elijah (Mt 11:7-19; Mk 9:11-13; Lk 7:24-35).
2. Apostle; brother of James (Mt 4:21-22; 10:2; Mk 3:17; Lk 5:1-10). At transfiguration (Mt 17:1-13; Mk 9:1-13; Lk 9:28-36). Desire to be greatest (Mk 10:35-45). Leader of church at Jerusalem (Ac 4:1-3; Gal 2:9). Elder who wrote epistles (2Jn 1; 3Jn 1). Prophet who wrote Revelation (Rev 1:1; 22:8).
3. Cousin of Barnabas, co-worker with Paul, (Ac 12:12-13:13; 15:37), see MARK.

JOIN (JOINED)
Pr 23:20 Do not *j* those who drink too much
24:21 and do not *j* with the rebellious,
Ro 15:30 to *j* me in my struggle by praying
2Ti 1: 8 *j* with me in suffering for the gospel

JOINED (JOIN)
Mt 19: 6 Therefore what God has *j* together,
Mk 10: 9 Therefore what God has *j* together,
Eph 2:21 him the whole building is *j* together
4:16 *j* and held together

JOINTS
Heb 4:12 even to dividing soul and spirit, *j*

JOKING
Eph 5: 4 or coarse *j*, which are out of place,

JONAH
Prophet in days of Jeroboam II (2Ki 14:25). Called to Nineveh; fled to Tarshish (Jnh 1:1-3). Cause of storm; thrown into sea (Jnh 1:4-16). Swallowed by fish (Jnh 1:17). Prayer (Jnh 2). Preached to Nineveh (Jnh 3). Attitude reproved by the LORD (Jnh 4). Sign of (Mt 12:39-41; Lk 11:29-32).

JONATHAN
Son of Saul (1Sa 13:16; 1Ch 8:33). Valiant warrior (1Sa 13-14). Relation to David (1Sa 18:1-4; 19-20; 23:16-18). Killed at Gilboa (1Sa 31). Mourned by David (2Sa 1).

JORAM
1. Son of Ahab; king of Israel (2Ki 3; 8-9; 2Ch 22).

JORDAN
Nu 34:12 boundary will go down along the *J*
Jos 4:22 Israel crossed the *J* on dry ground.'
Mt 3: 6 baptized by him in the *J* River.

JOSEPH
1. Son of Jacob by Rachel (Ge 30:24; 1Ch 2:2). Favored by Jacob, hated by brothers (Ge 37:3-4). Dreams (Ge 37:5-11). Sold by brothers (Ge 37:12-36). Served Potiphar; imprisoned by false accusation (Ge 39). Interpreted dreams of Pharaoh's servants (Ge 40), of Pharaoh (Ge 41:4-40). Made greatest in Egypt (Ge 41:41-57). Sold grain to brothers (Ge 42-45). Brought Jacob and sons to Egypt (Ge 46-47). Sons Ephraim and Manasseh blessed (Ge 48). Blessed (Ge 49:22-26; Dt 33:13-17). Death (Ge 50:22-26; Ex 13:19; Heb 11:22). 12,000 from (Rev 7:8).
2. Husband of Mary, mother of Jesus (Mt 1:16-24; 2:13-19; Lk 1:27; 2; Jn 1:45).
3. Disciple from Arimathea, who gave his tomb for Jesus' burial (Mt 27:57-61; Mk 15:43-47; Lk 24:50-52).
4. Original name of Barnabas (Ac 4:36).

JOSHUA
1. Son of Nun; name changed from Hoshea (Nu 13:8, 16; 1Ch 7:27). Fought Amalekites under Moses (Ex 17:9-14). Servant of Moses on Sinai (Ex 24:13; 32:17). Spied Canaan (Nu 13). With Caleb, allowed to enter land (Nu 14:6, 30). Succeeded Moses (Dt 1:38; 31:1-8; 34:9).
Charged Israel to conquer Canaan (Jos 1). Crossed Jordan (Jos 3-4). Circumcised sons of wilderness wanderings (Jos 5). Conquered Jericho (Jos 6), Ai (Jos 7-8), five kings at Gibeon (Jos 10:1-28), southern Canaan (Jos 10:29-43), northern Canaan (Jos 11-12). Defeated at Ai (Jos 7). Deceived by Gibeonites (Jos 9). Renewed covenant (Jos 8:30-35; 24:1-27). Divided land among tribes (Jos 13-22). Last words (Jos 23). Death (Jos 24:28-31).
2. High priest during rebuilding of temple (Hag 1-2; Zec 3:1-9; 6:11).

JOSIAH
Son of Amon; king of Judah (2Ki 22-23; 2Ch 34-35).

JOTHAM
Son of Azariah (Uzziah); king of Judah (2Ki 15:32-38; 2Ch 26:21-27:9).

JOY (ENJOY ENJOYMENT JOYFUL OVERJOYED REJOICE REJOICES REJOICING)
Dt 16:15 and your *j* will be complete.
1Ch 16:27 strength and *j* in his dwelling place.
Ne 8:10 for the *j* of the LORD is your
Est 9:22 their sorrow was turned into *j*
Job 38: 7 and all the angels shouted for *j*?
Ps 4: 7 have filled my heart with greater *j*
21: 6 with the *j* of your presence.
30:11 sackcloth and clothed me with *j*,
43: 4 to God, my *j* and my delight.
51:12 to me the *j* of your salvation
66: 1 Shout with *j* to God, all the earth!
96:12 the trees of the forest will sing for *j*;
107: 22 and tell of his works with songs of *j*
119:111 they are the *j* of my heart.
Pr 10: 1 A wise son brings *j* to his father,
10:28 The prospect of the righteous is *j*,
12:20 but *j* for those who promote peace.
Isa 35:10 everlasting *j* will crown their heads
51:11 Gladness and *j* will overtake them,
55:12 You will go out in *j*
Lk 1:44 the baby in my womb leaped for *j*.
2:10 news of great *j* that will be
Jn 15:11 and that your *j* may be complete.
16:20 but your grief will turn to *j*.
2Co 8: 2 their overflowing *j* and their
Php 2: 2 then make my *j* complete
4: 1 and long for, my *j* and crown,
1Th 2:19 For what is our hope, our *j*,
Phm : 7 Your love has given me great *j*
Heb 12: 2 for the *j* set before him endured
Jas 1: 2 Consider it pure *j*, my brothers,
1Pe 1: 8 with an inexpressible and glorious *j*
2Jn : 4 It has given me great *j* to find some
3Jn : 4 I have no greater *j*

JOYFUL (JOY)
Ps 100: 2 come before him with *j* songs.
Hab 3:18 I will be *j* in God my Savior.
1Th 5:16 Be *j* always; pray continually;

JUDAH
1. Son of Jacob by Leah (Ge 29:35; 35:23; 1Ch 2:1). Tribe of blessed as ruling tribe (Ge 49:8-12; Dt 33:7).
2. Name used for people and land of Southern Kingdom.
Jer 13:19 All *J* will be carried into exile,
Zec 10: 4 From *J* will come the cornerstone,
Heb 7:14 that our Lord descended from *J*,

JUDAISM (JEW)
Gal 1:13 of my previous way of life in *J*,

JUDAS

1. Apostle (Lk 6:16; Jn 14:22; Ac 1:13). Probably also called Thaddaeus (Mt 10:3; Mk 3:18).

2. Brother of James and Jesus (Mt 13:55; Mk 6:3), also called Jude (Jude 1).

3. Apostle, also called Iscariot, who betrayed Jesus (Mt 10:4; 26:14-56; Mk 3:19; 14:10-50; Lk 6:16; 22:3-53; Jn 6:71; 12:4; 13:2-30; 18:2-11). Suicide of (Mt 27:3-5; Ac 1:16-25).

JUDGE (JUDGED JUDGES JUDGING JUDGMENT)

Ge 18:25 Will not the *J* of all the earth do
1Ch 16:33 for he comes to *j* the earth.
Ps 9: 8 He will *j* the world in righteousness
Joel 3:12 sit to *j* all the nations on every side.
Mt 7: 1 Do not *j*, or you too will be judged.
Jn 12:47 For I did not come to *j* the world,
Ac 17:31 a day when he will *j* the world
Ro 2:16 day when God will *j* men's secrets
1Co 4: 3 indeed, I do not even *j* myself.
6: 2 that the saints will *j* the world?
Gal 2: 6 not *j* by external appearance—
2Ti 4: 1 who will *j* the living and the dead,
4: 8 which the Lord, the righteous *J*,
Jas 4:12 There is only one Lawgiver and *J*,
4:12 who are you to *j* your neighbor?
Rev 20: 4 who had been given authority to *j*.

JUDGED (JUDGE)

Mt 7: 1 "Do not judge, or you too will be *j*.
1Co 11:31 But if we *j* ourselves, we would not
Jas 3: 1 who teach will be *j* more strictly.
Rev 20:12 The dead were *j* according

JUDGES (JUDGE)

Jdg 2:16 Then the LORD raised up *j*,
Ps 58:11 there is a God who *j* the earth."
Heb 4:12 it *j* the thoughts and attitudes
Rev 19:11 With justice he *j* and makes war.

JUDGING (JUDGE)

Mt 19:28 *j* the twelve tribes of Israel.
Jn 7:24 Stop *j* by mere appearances,

JUDGMENT (JUDGE)

Dt 1:17 of any man, for *j* belongs to God.
Ps 1: 5 the wicked will not stand in the *j*,
119: 66 Teach me knowledge and good *j*,
Pr 6:32 man who commits adultery lacks *j*;
12:11 but he who chases fantasies lacks *j*.
Ecc 12:14 God will bring every deed into *j*,
Isa 66:16 the LORD will execute *j*
Mt 5:21 who murders will be subject to *j*.'
10:15 on the day of *j* than for that town.
12:36 have to give account on the day of *j*
Jn 5:22 but has entrusted all *j* to the Son,
7:24 appearances, and make a right *j*."
16: 8 to sin and righteousness and *j*:
Ro 14:10 stand before God's *j* seat.
14:13 Therefore let us stop passing *j*
1Co 11:29 body of the Lord eats and drinks *j*
2Co 5:10 appear before the *j* seat of Christ,
Heb 9:27 to die once, and after that to face *j*,
10:27 but only a fearful expectation of *j*
1Pe 4:17 For it is time for *j* to begin
Jude : 6 bound with everlasting chains for *j*

JUST (JUSTICE JUSTIFICATION JUSTIFIED JUSTIFY JUSTLY)

Dt 32: 4 and all his ways are *j*.
Ps 37:28 For the LORD loves the *j*
111: 7 of his hands are faithful and *j*;
Pr 1: 3 doing what is right and *j* and fair;
2: 8 for he guards the course of the *j*
Da 4:37 does is right and all his ways are *j*.
Ro 3:26 as to be *j* and the one who justifies
Heb 2: 2 received its *j* punishment,
1Jn 1: 9 and *j* and will forgive us our sins
Rev 16: 7 true and *j* are your judgments."

JUSTICE (JUST)

Ex 23: 2 do not pervert *j* by siding
23: 6 "Do not deny *j* to your poor people
Job 37:23 in his *j* and great righteousness,
Ps 9: 8 he will govern the peoples with *j*.
9:16 The LORD is known by his *j*;
11: 7 he loves *j*;
45: 6 a scepter of *j* will be the scepter
101: 1 I will sing of your love and *j*;
106: 3 Blessed are they who maintain *j*,
Pr 21:15 When *j* is done, it brings joy
28: 5 Evil men do not understand *j*,
29: 4 By *j* a king gives a country stability
29:26 from the LORD that man gets *j*.
Isa 9: 7 it with *j* and righteousness
28:17 I will make *j* the measuring line
30:18 For the LORD is a God of *j*.
42: 1 and he will bring *j* to the nations.
42: 4 till he establishes *j* on earth.
56: 1 "Maintain *j*
61: 8 "For I, the LORD, love *j*;
Jer 30:11 I will discipline you but only with *j*;
Eze 34:16 I will shepherd the flock with *j*.
Am 5:15 maintain *j* in the courts.
5:24 But let *j* roll on like a river,
Zec 7: 9 'Administer true *j*; show mercy
Lk 11:42 you neglect *j* and the love of God.
Ro 3:25 He did this to demonstrate his *j*,

JUSTIFICATION (JUST)

Ro 4:25 and was raised to life for our *j*.
5:18 of righteousness was *j* that brings

JUSTIFIED (JUST)

Ac 13:39 him everyone who believes is *j*
Ro 3:24 and are *j* freely by his grace
3:28 For we maintain that a man is *j*
5: 1 since we have been *j* through faith,
5: 9 Since we have now been *j*
8:30 those he called, he also *j*; those he *j*,
1Co 6:11 you were *j* in the name
Gal 2:16 observing the law no one will be *j*.
3:11 Clearly no one is *j* before God
3:24 to Christ that we might be *j* by faith
Jas 2:24 You see that a person is *j*

JUSTIFY (JUST)

Gal 3: 8 that God would *j* the Gentiles

JUSTLY (JUST)

Mic 6: 8 To act *j* and to love mercy

KEEP (KEEPER KEEPING KEEPS KEPT)

Ge 31:49 "May the LORD *k* watch
Ex 20: 6 and *k* my commandments.
Nu 6:24 and *k* you;
Ps 18:28 You, O LORD, *k* my lamp burning
19:13 *K* your servant also from willful
119: 9 can a young man *k* his way pure?
121: 7 The LORD will *k* you
141: 3 *k* watch over the door of my lips.
Pr 4:24 *k* corrupt talk far from your lips.
Isa 26: 3 You will *k* in perfect peace
Mt 10:10 for the worker is worth his *k*.
Lk 12:35 and *k* your lamps burning,
Gal 5:25 let us *k* in step with the Spirit.
Eph 4: 3 Make every effort to *k* the unity
1Ti 5:22 *K* yourself pure.
2Ti 4: 5 *k* your head in all situations,
Heb 13: 5 *K* your lives free from the love
Jas 1:26 and yet does not *k* a tight rein
2: 8 If you really *k* the royal law found
Jude :24 able to *k* you from falling

KEEPER (KEEP)

Ge 4: 9 I my brother's *k*?" The LORD

KEEPING (KEEP)

Ex 20: 8 the Sabbath day by *k* it holy.
Ps 19:11 in *k* them there is great reward.
Mt 3: 8 Produce fruit in *k* with repentance.
Lk 2: 8 *k* watch over their flocks at night.
1Co 7:19 *K* God's commands is what counts.
2Pe 3: 9 Lord is not slow in *k* his promise,

KEEPS (KEEP)

Pr 17:28 a fool is thought wise if he *k* silent,

Am 5:13 Therefore the prudent man *k* quiet
1Co 13: 5 is not easily angered, it *k* no record
Jas 2:10 For whoever *k* the whole law

KEPT (KEEP)
Ps 130: 3 If you, O LORD, *k* a record of sins,
2Ti 4: 7 finished the race, I have *k* the faith.
1Pe 1: 4 spoil or fade—*k* in heaven for you,

KEYS
Mt 16:19 I will give you the *k* of the kingdom

KILL (KILLS)
Mt 17:23 They will *k* him, and on the third

KILLS (KILL)
Lev 24:21 but whoever *k* a man must be put
2Co 3: 6 for the letter *k,* but the Spirit gives

KIND (KINDNESS KINDS)
Ge 1:24 animals, each according to its *k.*"
2Ch 10: 7 "If you will be *k* to these people
Pr 11:17 A *k* man benefits himself,
12:25 but a *k* word cheers him up.
14:21 blessed is he who is *k* to the needy.
14:31 whoever is *k* to the needy honors
19:17 He who is *k* to the poor lends
Da 4:27 by being *k* to the oppressed.
Lk 6:35 because he is *k* to the ungrateful
1Co 13: 4 Love is patient, love is *k.*
15:35 With what *k* of body will they
Eph 4:32 Be *k* and compassionate
1Th 5:15 but always try to be *k* to each other
2Ti 2:24 instead, he must be *k* to everyone,
Tit 2: 5 to be busy at home, to be *k,*

KINDNESS (KIND)
Ac 14:17 He has shown *k* by giving you rain
Ro 11:22 Consider therefore the *k*
Gal 5:22 peace, patience, *k,* goodness,
Eph 2: 7 expressed in his *k* to us
2Pe 1: 7 brotherly *k;* and to brotherly *k,*

KINDS (KIND)
1Co 12: 4 There are different *k* of gifts,
1Ti 6:10 of money is a root of all *k* of evil.

KING (KINGDOM KINGS)
1. Kings of Judah and Israel: see Saul, David, Solomon.
2. Kings of Judah: see Rehoboam, Abijah, Asa, Jehoshaphat, Jehoram, Ahaziah, Athaliah (Queen), Joash, Amaziah, Uzziah, Jotham, Ahaz, Hezekiah, Manasseh, Amon, Josiah, Jehoahaz, Jehoiakim, Jehoiachin, Zedekiah.
3. Kings of Israel: see Jeroboam I, Nadab, Baasha, Elah, Zimri, Tibni, Omri, Ahab, Ahaziah, Joram, Jehu, Jehoahaz, Jehoash, Jeroboam II, Zechariah, Shallum, Menahem, Pekah, Pekahiah, Hoshea.
Jdg 17: 6 In those days Israel had no *k;*
1Sa 12:12 the LORD your God was your *k.*
Ps 24: 7 that the *K* of glory may come in.
Isa 32: 1 See, a *k* will reign in righteousness
Zec 9: 9 See, your *k* comes to you,
1Ti 6:15 the *K* of kings and Lord of lords,
1Pe 2:17 of believers, fear God, honor the *k.*
Rev 19:16 *k* OF KINGS AND LORD

KINGDOM (KING)
Ex 19: 6 you will be for me a *k* of priests
1Ch 29:11 Yours, O LORD, is the *k;*
Ps 45: 6 justice will be the scepter of your *k.*
Da 4: 3 His *k* is an eternal *k;*
Mt 3: 2 Repent, for the *k* of heaven is near
5: 3 for theirs is the *k* of heaven.
6:10 your *k* come,
6:33 But seek first his *k* and his
7:21 Lord,' will enter the *k* of heaven,
11:11 least in the *k* of heaven is greater
13:24 "The *k* of heaven is like a man who
13:31 *k* of heaven is like a mustard seed,
13:33 "The *k* of heaven is like yeast that
13:44 *k* of heaven is like treasure hidden
13:45 the *k* of heaven is like a merchant
13:47 *k* of heaven is like a net that was let
16:19 the keys of the *k* of heaven;
18:23 the *k* of heaven is like a king who
19:24 for a rich man to enter the *k* of God
24: 7 rise against nation, and *k* against *k.*
24:14 gospel of the *k* will be preached
25:34 the *k* prepared for you
Mk 9:47 better for you to enter the *k* of God
10:14 for the *k* of God belongs to such
10:23 for the rich to enter the *k* of God!"
Lk 10: 9 'The *k* of God is near you.'
12:31 seek his *k,* and these things will be
17:21 because the *k* of God is within you
Jn 3: 5 no one can enter the *k* of God
18:36 "My *k* is not of this world.
1Co 6: 9 the wicked will not inherit the *k*
15:24 hands over the *k* to God the Father
Rev 1: 6 has made us to be a *k* and priests
11:15 of the world has become the *k*

KINGS (KING)
Ps 2: 2 The *k* of the earth take their stand
72:11 All *k* will bow down to him
Da 7:24 ten horns are ten *k* who will come
1Ti 2: 2 for *k* and all those in authority,
Rev 1: 5 and the ruler of the *k* of the earth.

KINSMAN-REDEEMER (REDEEM)
Ru 3: 9 over me, since you are a *k.*"

KISS
Ps 2:12 *K* the Son, lest he be angry
Pr 24:26 is like a *k* on the lips.
Lk 22:48 the Son of Man with a *k?*"

KNEE (KNEES)
Isa 45:23 Before me every *k* will bow;
Ro 14:11 'every *k* will bow before me;
Php 2:10 name of Jesus every *k* should bow,

KNEES (KNEE)
Isa 35: 3 steady the *k* that give way;
Heb 12:12 your feeble arms and weak *k.*

KNEW (KNOW)
Job 23: 3 If only I *k* where to find him;
Jnh 4: 2 I *k* that you are a gracious
Mt 7:23 tell them plainly, 'I never *k* you.

KNOCK
Mt 7: 7 *k* and the door will be opened
Rev 3:20 I am! I stand at the door and *k.*

KNOW (FOREKNEW KNEW KNOWING KNOWLEDGE KNOWN KNOWS)
Dt 18:21 "How can we *k* when a message
Job 19:25 I *k* that my Redeemer lives,
42: 3 things too wonderful for me to *k.*
Ps 46:10 "Be still, and *k* that I am God;
139: 1 and you *k* me.
139: 23 Search me, O God, and *k* my heart;
Pr 27: 1 for you do not *k* what a day may
Jer 24: 7 I will give them a heart to *k* me,
31:34 his brother, saying, '*K* the LORD,'
Mt 6: 3 let your left hand *k* what your right
24:42 you do not *k* on what day your
Lk 1: 4 so that you may *k* the certainty
Jn 3:11 we speak of what we *k,*
4:22 we worship what we do *k,*
9:25 One thing I do *k.*
10:14 I *k* my sheep and my sheep *k* me—
17: 3 that they may *k* you, the only true
21:24 We *k* that his testimony is true.
Ac 1: 7 "It is not for you to *k* the times
Ro 6: 6 For we *k* that our old self was
7:18 I *k* that nothing good lives in me,
8:28 we *k* that in all things God works
1Co 2: 2 For I resolved to *k* nothing
6:15 Do you not *k* that your bodies are
6:19 Do you not *k* that your body is
13:12 Now I *k* in part; then I shall *k* fully,
15:58 because you *k* that your labor
Php 3:10 I want to *k* Christ and the power
2Ti 1:12 because I *k* whom I have believed,
Jas 4:14 *k* what will happen tomorrow.
1Jn 2: 4 The man who says, "I *k* him,"
3:14 We *k* that we have passed

1Jn 3:16 This is how we *k* what love is:
5: 2 This is how we *k* that we love
5:13 so that you may *k* that you have

KNOWING (KNOW)
Ge 3: 5 and you will be like God, *k* good
Php 3: 8 of *k* Christ Jesus my Lord,

KNOWLEDGE (KNOW)
Ge 2: 9 the tree of the *k* of good and evil.
Job 42: 3 obscures my counsel without *k*?'
Ps 19: 2 night after night they display *k*.
73:11 Does the Most High have *k*?"
139: 6 Such *k* is too wonderful for me,
Pr 1: 7 of the LORD is the beginning of *k*,
10:14 Wise men store up *k*,
12: 1 Whoever loves discipline loves *k*,
13:16 Every prudent man acts out of *k*,
19: 2 to have zeal without *k*,
Isa 11: 9 full of the *k* of the LORD
Hab 2:14 filled with the *k* of the glory
Ro 11:33 riches of the wisdom and *k* of God!
1Co 8: 1 *K* puffs up, but love builds up.
8:11 Christ died, is destroyed by your *k*.
13: 2 can fathom all mysteries and all *k*,
2Co 2:14 everywhere the fragrance of the *k*
4: 6 light of the *k* of the glory of God
Eph 3:19 to know this love that surpasses *k*
Col 2: 3 all the treasures of wisdom and *k*.
1Ti 6:20 ideas of what is falsely called *k*,
2Pe 3:18 grow in the grace and *k* of our Lord

KNOWN (KNOW)
Ps 16:11 You have made *k* to me the path
105: 1 make *k* among the nations what he
Isa 46:10 *k* the end from the beginning,
Mt 10:26 or hidden that will not be made *k*.
Ro 1:19 since what may be *k* about God is
11:34 "Who has *k* the mind of the Lord?
15:20 the gospel where Christ was not *k*,
2Co 3: 2 written on our hearts, *k*
2Pe 2:21 than to have *k* it and then

KNOWS (KNOW)
1Sa 2: 3 for the LORD is a God who *k*,
Job 23:10 But he *k* the way that I take;
Ps 44:21 since he *k* the secrets of the heart?
94:11 The LORD *k* the thoughts of man;
Ecc 8: 7 Since no man *k* the future,
Mt 6: 8 for your Father *k* what you need
24:36 "No one *k* about that day or hour,
Ro 8:27 who searches our hearts *k* the mind
1Co 8: 2 who thinks he *k* something does
2Ti 2:19 The Lord *k* those who are his," and

LABAN
Brother of Rebekah (Ge 24:29-51), father of Rachel and Leah (Ge 29-31).

LABOR
Ex 20: 9 Six days you shall *l* and do all your
Isa 55: 2 and your *l* on what does not satisfy
Mt 6:28 They do not *l* or spin.
1Co 3: 8 rewarded according to his own *l*.
15:58 because you know that your *l*

LACK (LACKING LACKS)
Pr 15:22 Plans fail for *l* of counsel,
Ro 3: 3 Will their *l* of faith nullify God's
Col 2:23 *l* any value in restraining sensual

LACKING (LACK)
Ro 12:11 Never be *l* in zeal, but keep your
Jas 1: 4 and complete, not *l* anything.

LACKS (LACK)
Pr 6:32 who commits adultery *l* judgment;
12:11 he who chases fantasies *l* judgment
Jas 1: 5 any of you *l* wisdom, he should ask

LAID (LAY)
Isa 53: 6 and the LORD has *l* on him
1Co 3:11 other than the one already *l*,
1Jn 3:16 Jesus Christ *l* down his life for us.

LAKE
Rev 19:20 into the fiery *l* of burning sulfur.
20:14 The *l* of fire is the second death.

LAMB (LAMB'S LAMBS)
Ge 22: 8 "God himself will provide the *l*
Ex 12:21 and slaughter the Passover *l*.
Isa 11: 6 The wolf will live with the *l*,
53: 7 he was led like a *l* to the slaughter,
Jn 1:29 *L* of God, who takes away the sin
1Co 5: 7 our Passover *l*, has been sacrificed.
1Pe 1:19 a *l* without blemish or defect.
Rev 5: 6 Then I saw a *L*, looking
5:12 "Worthy is the *L*, who was slain,
14: 4 They follow the *L* wherever he

LAMB'S (LAMB)
Rev 21:27 written in the *L* book of life.

LAMBS (LAMB)
Lk 10: 3 I am sending you out like *l*
Jn 21:15 Jesus said, "Feed my *l*."

LAMENT
2Sa 1:17 took up this *l* concerning Saul

LAMP (LAMPS)
2Sa 22:29 You are my *l*, O LORD;
Ps 18:28 You, O LORD, keep my *l* burning;
Ps 119:105 Your word is a *l* to my feet
Pr 31:18 and her *l* does not go out at night.
Lk 8:16 "No one lights a *l* and hides it
Rev 21:23 gives it light, and the Lamb is its *l*.

LAMPS (LAMP)
Mt 25: 1 be like ten virgins who took their *l*
Lk 12:35 for service and keep your *l* burning,

LAND
Ge 1:10 God called the dry ground "*l*,"
1:11 "Let the *l* produce vegetation:
12: 7 To your offspring I will give this *l*."
Ex 3: 8 a *l* flowing with milk and honey—
Nu 35:33 Do not pollute the *l* where you are.
Dt 34: 1 LORD showed him the whole *l*—
Jos 13: 2 "This is the *l* that remains:
14: 4 Levites received no share of the *l*
2Ch 7:14 their sin and will heal their *l*.
7:20 then I will uproot Israel from my *l*,
Eze 36:24 and bring you back into your own *l*.

LANGUAGE
Ge 11: 1 Now the whole world had one *l*
Ps 19: 3 There is no speech or *l*
Jn 8:44 When he lies, he speaks his native *l*
Ac 2: 6 heard them speaking in his own *l*.
Col 3: 8 slander, and filthy *l* from your lips.
Rev 5: 9 from every tribe and *l* and people

LAST (LASTING LASTS LATTER)
2Sa 23: 1 These are the *l* words of David:
Isa 44: 6 I am the first and I am the *l*;
Mt 19:30 But many who are first will be *l*,
Mk 10:31 are first will be *l*, and the *l* first."
Jn 15:16 and bear fruit—fruit that will *l*.
Ro 1:17 is by faith from first to *l*,
2Ti 3: 1 will be terrible times in the *l* days.
2Pe 3: 3 in the *l* days scoffers will come,
Rev 1:17 I am the First and the *L*.
22:13 the First and the *L*, the Beginning

LASTING (LAST)
Ex 12:14 to the LORD—a *l* ordinance.
Lev 24: 8 of the Israelites, as a *l* covenant.
Nu 25:13 have a covenant of a *l* priesthood,
Heb 10:34 had better and *l* possessions.

LASTS (LAST)
Ps 30: 5 For his anger *l* only a moment,
2Co 3:11 greater is the glory of that which *l*!

LATTER (LAST)
Job 42:12 The LORD blessed the *l* part

LAUGH (LAUGHS)
Ecc 3: 4 a time to weep and a time to *l,*

LAUGHS (LAUGH)
Ps 2: 4 The One enthroned in heaven *l;*
37:13 but the Lord *l* at the wicked,

LAVISHED
Eph 1: 8 of God's grace that he *l* on us
1Jn 3: 1 great is the love the Father has *l*

LAW (LAWS)
Dt 31:11 you shall read this *l* before them
31:26 "Take this Book of the *L*
Jos 1: 8 of the *L* depart from your mouth;
Ne 8: 8 from the Book of the *L* of God,
Ps 1: 2 and on his *l* he meditates day
19: 7 The *l* of the LORD is perfect,
119: 18 wonderful things in your *l.*
119: 72 *l* from your mouth is more precious
119: 97 Oh, how I love your *l!*
119:165 peace have they who love your *l,*
Isa 8:20 To the *l* and to the testimony!
Jer 31:33 "I will put my *l* in their minds
Mt 5:17 that I have come to abolish the *L*
7:12 sums up the *L* and the Prophets.
22:40 All the *L* and the Prophets hang
Lk 16:17 stroke of a pen to drop out of the *L.*
Jn 1:17 For the *l* was given through Moses;
Ro 2:12 All who sin apart from the *l* will
2:15 of the *l* are written on their hearts,
5:13 for before the *l* was given,
5:20 *l* was added so that the trespass
6:14 because you are not under *l,*
7: 6 released from the *l* so that we serve
7:12 *l* is holy, and the commandment is
8: 3 For what the *l* was powerless to do
10: 4 Christ is the end of the *l*
13:10 love is the fulfillment of the *l.*
Gal 3:13 curse of the *l* by becoming a curse
3:24 So the *l* was put in charge to lead us
5: 3 obligated to obey the whole *l.*
5: 4 justified by *l* have been alienated
5:14 The entire *l* is summed up
Heb 7:19 (for the *l* made nothing perfect),
10: 1 The *l* is only a shadow
Jas 1:25 intently into the perfect *l* that gives
2:10 For whoever keeps the whole *l*

LAWLESSNESS*
2Th 2: 3 and the man of *l* is revealed,
2: 7 power of *l* is already at work;
1Jn 3: 4 sins breaks the law; in fact, sin is *l.*

LAWS (LAW)
Lev 25:18 and be careful to obey my *l,*
Ps 119: 30 I have set my heart on your *l.*
119:120 I stand in awe of your *l.*
Heb 8:10 I will put my *l* in their minds
10:16 I will put my *l* in their hearts,

LAY (LAID LAYING)
Job 22:22 and *l* up his words in your heart.
Isa 28:16 "See, I *l* a stone in Zion,
Mt 8:20 of Man has no place to *l* his head."
Jn 10:15 and I *l* down my life for the sheep.
15:13 that he *l* down his life
1Co 3:11 no one can *l* any foundation other
1Jn 3:16 And we ought to *l* down our lives
Rev 4:10 They *l* their crowns

LAYING (LAY)
1Ti 5:22 Do not be hasty in the *l* on of hands
Heb 6: 1 not *l* again the foundation

LAZARUS
1. Poor man in Jesus' parable (Lk 16:19-31).
2. Brother of Mary and Martha whom Jesus raised from the dead (Jn 11:1-12:19).

LAZY
Pr 10: 4 *L* hands make a man poor,
Heb 6:12 We do not want you to become *l,*

LEAD (LEADERS LEADERSHIP LEADS LED)
Ex 15:13 "In your unfailing love you will *l*
Ps 27:11 *l* me in a straight path
61: 2 *l* me to the rock that is higher
139: 24 and *l* me in the way everlasting.
143: 10 *l* me on level ground.
Ecc 5: 6 Do not let your mouth *l* you
Isa 11: 6 and a little child will *l* them.
Da 12: 3 those who *l* many to righteousness,
Mt 6:13 And *l* us not into temptation,
1Jn 3: 7 do not let anyone *l* you astray.

LEADERS (LEAD)
Heb 13: 7 Remember your *l,* who spoke
13:17 Obey your *l* and submit

LEADERSHIP (LEAD)
Ro 12: 8 if it is *l,* let him govern diligently;

LEADS (LEAD)
Ps 23: 2 he *l* me beside quiet waters,
Pr 19:23 The fear of the LORD *l* to life:
Isa 40:11 he gently *l* those that have young.
Mt 7:13 and broad is the road that *l*
15:14 If a blind man *l* a blind man,
Jn 10: 3 sheep by name and *l* them out.
Ro 14:19 effort to do what *l* to peace
2Co 2:14 always *l* us in triumphal procession

LEAH
Wife of Jacob (Ge 29:16-30); bore six sons and one daughter (Ge 29:31-30:21; 34:1; 35:23).

LEAN
Pr 3: 5 *l* not on your own understanding;

LEARN (LEARNED LEARNING)
Isa 1:17 *l* to do right!
Mt 11:29 yoke upon you and *l* from me,

LEARNED (LEARN)
Php 4:11 for I have *l* to be content whatever
2Ti 3:14 continue in what you have *l*

LEARNING (LEARN)
Pr 1: 5 let the wise listen and add to their *l,*
2Ti 3: 7 always *l* but never able

LED (LEAD)
Ps 68:18 you *l* captives in your train;
Isa 53: 7 he was *l* like a lamb to the slaughter
Am 2:10 and I *l* you forty years in the desert
Ro 8:14 those who are *l* by the Spirit
Eph 4: 8 he *l* captives in his train

LEFT
Jos 1: 7 turn from it to the right or to the *l,*
Pr 4:27 Do not swerve to the right or the *l;*
Mt 6: 3 do not let your *l* hand know what
25:33 on his right and the goats on his *l.*

LEGION
Mk 5: 9 "My name is *L,*" he replied,

LEND (LENDS)
Dt 15: 8 freely *l* him whatever he needs.
Ps 37:26 are always generous and *l* freely;
Lk 6:34 if you *l* to those from whom you

LENDS (LEND)
Pr 19:17 to the poor *l* to the LORD,

LENGTH (LONG)
Ps 90:10 The *l* of our days is seventy years—
Pr 10:27 The fear of the LORD adds *l* to life

LEPROSY
2Ki 7: 3 men with *l* at the entrance

LETTER (LETTERS)
Mt 5:18 not the smallest *l,* not the least
2Co 3: 2 You yourselves are our *l,* written
3: 6 for the *l* kills, but the Spirit gives
2Th 3:14 not obey our instruction in this *l,*

LETTERS (LETTER)
2Co 3: 7 which was engraved in *l* on stone,
10:10 "His *l* are weighty and forceful,
2Pe 3:16 His *l* contain some things that are

LEVEL
Ps 143: 10 lead me on *l* ground.
Pr 4:26 Make *l* paths for your feet
Isa 26: 7 The path of the righteous is *l;*
Heb 12:13 "Make *l* paths for your feet,"

LEVI (LEVITES)
1. Son of Jacob by Leah (Ge 29:34; 46:11; 1Ch 2:1). Tribe of blessed (Ge 49:5-7; Dt 33:8-11), chosen as priests (Nu 3-4), numbered (Nu 3:39; 26:62), allotted cities, but not land (Nu 18; 35; Dt 10:9; Jos 13:14; 21), land (Eze 48:8-22), 12,000 from (Rev 7:7).
2. See MATTHEW.

LEVITES (LEVI)
Nu 1:53 The *L* are to be responsible
8: 6 "Take the *L* from among the other
18:21 I give to the *L* all the tithes in Israel

LEWDNESS
Mk 7:22 malice, deceit, *l,* envy, slander,

LIAR (LIE)
Pr 19:22 better to be poor than a *l.*
Jn 8:44 for he is a *l* and the father of lies.
Ro 3: 4 Let God be true, and every man a *l.*

LIBERATED*
Ro 8:21 that the creation itself will be *l*

LIE (LIAR LIED LIES LYING)
Lev 19:11 " 'Do not *l.*
Nu 23:19 God is not a man, that he should *l,*
Dt 6: 7 when you *l* down and when you get
Ps 23: 2 me *l* down in green pastures,
Isa 11: 6 leopard will *l* down with the goat,
Eze 34:14 they will *l* down in good grazing
Ro 1:25 exchanged the truth of God for a *l,*
Col 3: 9 Do not *l* to each other,
Heb 6:18 which it is impossible for God to *l,*

LIED (LIE)
Ac 5: 4 You have not *l* to men but to God."

LIES (LIE)
Ps 34:13 and your lips from speaking *l.*
Jn 8:44 for he is a liar and the father of *l.*

LIFE (LIVE)
Ge 2: 7 into his nostrils the breath of *l,*
2: 9 of the garden were the tree of *l*
9:11 Never again will all *l* be cut
Ex 21:23 you are to take *l* for *l,* eye for eye,
Lev 17:14 the *l* of every creature is its blood.
24:18 must make restitution—*l* for *l.*
Dt 30:19 Now choose *l,* so that you
Ps 16:11 known to me the path of *l;*
23: 6 all the days of my *l,*
34:12 Whoever of you loves *l*
39: 4 let me know how fleeting is my *l.*
49: 7 No man can redeem the *l*
104: 33 I will sing to the LORD all my *l;*
Pr 1: 3 a disciplined and prudent *l,*
6:23 are the way to *l,*
7:23 little knowing it will cost him his *l.*
8:35 For whoever finds me finds *l*
11:30 of the righteous is a tree of *l,*
21:21 finds *l,* prosperity and honor.
Jer 10:23 that a man's *l* is not his own;
Eze 37: 5 enter you, and you will come to *l.*
Da 12: 2 some to everlasting *l,* others
Mt 6:25 Is not *l* more important than food,
7:14 and narrow the road that leads to *l,*
10:39 Whoever finds his *l* will lose it,
16:25 wants to save his *l* will lose it,
20:28 to give his *l* as a ransom for many."
Mk 10:45 to give his *l* as a ransom for many."
Lk 12:15 a man's *l* does not consist
12:22 do not worry about your *l,*
14:26 even his own *l*— he cannot be my
Jn 1: 4 In him was *l,* and that *l* was
3:15 believes in him may have eternal *l.*
3:36 believes in the Son has eternal *l,*
4:14 of water welling up to eternal *l."*
5:24 him who sent me has eternal *l*
6:35 Jesus declared, "I am the bread of *l*
6:47 he who believes has everlasting *l.*
6:68 You have the words of eternal *l."*
10:10 I have come that they may have *l,*
10:15 and I lay down my *l* for the sheep.
10:28 I give them eternal *l,* and they shall
11:25 "I am the resurrection and the *l.*
14: 6 am the way and the truth and the *l.*
15:13 lay down his *l* for his friends.
20:31 that by believing you may have *l*
Ac 13:48 appointed for eternal *l* believed.
Ro 4:25 was raised to *l* for our justification.
6:13 have been brought from death to *l;*
6:23 but the gift of God is eternal *l*
8:38 convinced that neither death nor *l,*
1Co 15:19 If only for this *l* we have hope
2Co 3: 6 letter kills, but the Spirit gives *l.*
Gal 2:20 The *l* I live in the body, I live
Eph 4: 1 I urge you to live a *l* worthy
Php 2:16 as you hold out the word of *l*—
Col 1:10 order that you may live a *l* worthy
1Th 4:12 so that your daily *l* may win
1Ti 4: 8 for both the present *l* and the *l*
4:16 Watch your *l* and doctrine closely.
6:19 hold of the *l* that is truly *l.*
2Ti 3:12 to live a godly *l* in Christ Jesus will
Jas 1:12 crown of *l* that God has promised
3:13 Let him show it by his good *l,*
1Pe 3:10 "Whoever would love *l*
2Pe 1: 3 given us everything we need for *l*
1Jn 3:14 we have passed from death to *l,*
5:11 has given us eternal *l,* and this *l* is
Rev 13: 8 written in the book of *l* belonging
20:12 was opened, which is the book of *l.*
21:27 written in the Lamb's book of *l.*
22: 2 side of the river stood the tree of *l,*

LIFT (LIFTED)
Ps 121: 1 I *l* up my eyes to the hills—
134: 2 *L* up your hands in the sanctuary
La 3:41 Let us *l* up our hearts and our
1Ti 2: 8 everywhere to *l* up holy hands

LIFTED (LIFT)
Ps 40: 2 He *l* me out of the slimy pit,
Jn 3:14 Moses *l* up the snake in the desert,
12:32 when I am *l* up from the earth,

LIGHT (ENLIGHTENED)
Ge 1: 3 "Let there be *l,*" and there was *l.*
2Sa 22:29 LORD turns my darkness into *l.*
Job 38:19 "What is the way to the abode of *l?*
Ps 4: 6 Let the *l* of your face shine upon us
19: 8 giving *l* to the eyes.
27: 1 LORD is my *l* and my salvation—
56:13 God in the *l* of life.
76: 4 You are resplendent with *l,*
104: 2 He wraps himself in *l*
119:105 and a *l* for my path.
119:130 The unfolding of your words gives *l;*
Isa 2: 5 let us walk in the *l* of the LORD.
9: 2 have seen a great *l;*
49: 6 also make you a *l* for the Gentiles,
Mt 4:16 have seen a great *l;*
5:16 let your *l* shine before men,
11:30 yoke is easy and my burden is *l."*
Jn 3:19 but men loved darkness instead of *l*
8:12 he said, "I am the *l* of the world.
2Co 4: 6 made his *l* shine in our hearts
6:14 Or what fellowship can *l* have
11:14 masquerades as an angel of *l.*
1Ti 6:16 and who lives in unapproachable *l,*
1Pe 2: 9 of darkness into his wonderful *l.*
1Jn 1: 5 God is *l;* in him there is no
1: 7 But if we walk in the *l,*
Rev 21:23 for the glory of God gives it *l,*

LIGHTNING
Da 10: 6 his face like *l,* his eyes like flaming
Mt 24:27 For as the *l* that comes from the east
28: 3 His appearance was like *l,*

LIKENESS
Ge 1:26 man in our image, in our *l,*

Ps 17:15 I will be satisfied with seeing your *l*
Isa 52:14 his form marred beyond human *l*—
Ro 8: 3 Son in the *l* of sinful man
8:29 to be conformed to the *l* of his Son,
2Co 3:18 his *l* with ever-increasing glory,
Php 2: 7 being made in human *l*.
Jas 3: 9 who have been made in God's *l*.

LILIES
Lk 12:27 "Consider how the *l* grow.

LION
Isa 11: 7 and the *l* will eat straw like the ox.
1Pe 5: 8 around like a roaring *l* looking
Rev 5: 5 See, the *L* of the tribe of Judah,

LIPS
Ps 8: 2 From the *l* of children and infants
34: 1 his praise will always be on my *l*.
119:171 May my *l* overflow with praise,
Pr 13: 3 He who guards his *l* guards his life,
27: 2 someone else, and not your own *l*.
Isa 6: 5 For I am a man of unclean *l*,
Mt 21:16 " 'From the *l* of children
Col 3: 8 and filthy language from your *l*.

LISTEN (LISTENING LISTENS)
Dt 30:20 *l* to his voice, and hold fast to him.
Pr 1: 5 let the wise *l* and add
Jn 10:27 My sheep *l* to my voice; I know
Jas 1:19 Everyone should be quick to *l*,
1:22 Do not merely *l* to the word,

LISTENING (LISTEN)
1Sa 3: 9 Speak, LORD, for your servant is *l*
Pr 18:13 He who answers before *l*—

LISTENS (LISTEN)
Pr 12:15 but a wise man *l* to advice.

LIVE (ALIVE LIFE LIVES LIVING)
Ex 20:12 so that you may *l* long
33:20 for no one may see me and *l*."
Dt 8: 3 to teach you that man does not *l*
Job 14:14 If a man dies, will he *l* again?
Ps 119:175 Let me *l* that I may praise you,
Isa 55: 3 hear me, that your soul may *l*.
Eze 37: 3 can these bones *l*?" I said,
Hab 2: 4 but the righteous will *l* by his faith
Mt 4: 4 'Man does not *l* on bread alone,
Ac 17:24 does not *l* in temples built by hands
17:28 'For in him we *l* and move
Ro 1:17 "The righteous will *l* by faith."
2Co 5: 7 We *l* by faith, not by sight.
Gal 2:20 The life I *l* in the body, I *l* by faith
5:25 Since we *l* by the Spirit, let us keep
Php 1:21 to *l* is Christ and to die is gain.
1Th 5:13 *L* in peace with each other.
2Ti 3:12 who wants to *l* a godly life
Heb 12:14 Make every effort to *l* in peace
1Pe 1:17 *l* your lives as strangers here

LIVES (LIVE)
Job 19:25 I know that my Redeemer *l*,
Isa 57:15 he who *l* forever, whose name is
Da 3:28 to give up their *l* rather than serve
Jn 14:17 for he *l* with you and will be in you.
Ro 7:18 I know that nothing good *l* in me,
14: 7 For none of us *l* to himself alone
1Co 3:16 and that God's Spirit *l* in you?
Gal 2:20 I no longer live, but Christ *l* in me.
Heb 13: 5 Keep your *l* free from the love
2Pe 3:11 You ought to live holy and godly *l*
1Jn 3:16 to lay down our *l* for our brothers.
4:16 Whoever *l* in love *l* in God,

LIVING (LIVE)
Ge 2: 7 and man became a *l* being.
Jer 2:13 the spring of *l* water,
Mt 22:32 the God of the dead but of the *l*."
Jn 7:38 streams of *l* water will flow
Ro 12: 1 to offer your bodies as *l* sacrifices,
Heb 4:12 For the word of God is *l* and active.
10:31 to fall into the hands of the *l* God.
Rev 1:18 I am the *L* One; I was dead,

LOAD
Gal 6: 5 for each one should carry his own *l*.

LOCUSTS
Mt 3: 4 His food was *l* and wild honey.

LOFTY
Ps 139: 6 too *l* for me to attain.
Isa 57:15 is what the high and *l* One says—

LONELY
Ps 68: 6 God sets the *l* in families,

LONG (LENGTH LONGED LONGING LONGS)
1Ki 18:21 "How *l* will you waver
Jn 9: 4 As *l* as it is day, we must do
Eph 3:18 to grasp how wide and *l* and high
1Pe 1:12 Even angels *l* to look

LONGED (LONG)
Mt 13:17 righteous men *l* to see what you see
23:37 how often I have *l*
2Ti 4: 8 to all who have *l* for his appearing.

LONGING (LONG)
Pr 13:19 A *l* fulfilled is sweet to the soul,
2Co 5: 2 *l* to be clothed with our heavenly

LONGS (LONG)
Isa 30:18 Yet the LORD *l* to be gracious

LOOK (LOOKING LOOKS)
Dt 4:29 you will find him if you *l* for him
Job 31: 1 not to *l* lustfully at a girl.
Ps 34: 5 Those who *l* to him are radiant;
Pr 4:25 Let your eyes *l* straight ahead,
Isa 60: 5 Then you will *l* and be radiant,
Hab 1:13 Your eyes are too pure to *l* on evil;
Zec 12:10 They will *l* on me, the one they
Mk 13:21 '*L*, here is the Christ!' or, '*L*,
Lk 24:39 *L* at my hands and my feet.
Jn 1:36 he said, "*L*, the Lamb of God!"
4:35 open your eyes and *l* at the fields!
19:37 "They will *l* on the one they have
Jas 1:27 to *l* after orphans and widows
1Pe 1:12 long to *l* into these things.

LOOKING (LOOK)
2Co 10: 7 You are *l* only on the surface
Rev 5: 6 I saw a Lamb, *l* as if it had been

LOOKS (LOOK)
1Sa 16: 7 Man *l* at the outward appearance,
Lk 9:62 and *l* back is fit for service
Php 2:21 For everyone *l* out

LORD† (LORD'S† LORDING)
Ne 4:14 Remember the *L*, who is great
Job 28:28 'The fear of the *L*— that is wisdom,
Ps 54: 4 the *L* is the one who sustains me.
62:12 and that you, O *L*, are loving.
86: 5 You are forgiving and good, O *L*,
110: 1 The LORD says to my *L*:
147: 5 Great is our *L* and mighty in power
Isa 6: 1 I saw the *L* seated on a throne,
Da 9: 4 "O *L*, the great and awesome God,
Mt 3: 3 'Prepare the way for the *L*,
4: 7 'Do not put the *L* your God
7:21 "Not everyone who says to me, '*L*,
22:37 " 'Love the *L* your God
22:44 For he says, " 'The *L* said to my *L*:
Mk 12:11 the *L* has done this,
12:29 the *L* our God, the *L* is one.
Lk 2: 9 glory of the *L* shone around them,
6:46 "Why do you call me, '*L*, *L*,'
10:27 " 'Love the *L* your God
Ac 2:21 on the name of the *L* will be saved.'
16:31 replied, "Believe in the *L* Jesus,
Ro 10: 9 with your mouth, "Jesus is *L*,"
10:13 on the name of the *L* will be saved
12:11 your spiritual fervor, serving the *L*.
14: 8 we live to the *L*; and if we die,
1Co 1:31 Let him who boasts boast in the *L*."
3: 5 the *L* has assigned to each his task.
7:34 to be devoted to the *L* in both body
10: 9 We should not test the *L*,
11:23 For I received from the *L* what I

1Co 12: 3 "Jesus is *L*," except by the Holy
15:57 victory through our *L* Jesus Christ.
16:22 If anyone does not love the *L*—
2Co 3:17 Now the *L* is the Spirit,
8: 5 they gave themselves first to the *L*
10:17 Let him who boasts boast in the *L*."
Gal 6:14 in the cross of our *L* Jesus Christ,
Eph 4: 5 one *L*, one faith, one baptism;
5:10 and find out what pleases the *L*.
5:19 make music in your heart to the *L*,
Php 2:11 confess that Jesus Christ is *L*,
3: 1 my brothers, rejoice in the *L*!
4: 4 Rejoice in the *L* always.
Col 2: 6 as you received Christ Jesus as *L*,
3:17 do it all in the name of the *L* Jesus,
3:23 as working for the *L*, not for men,
4:17 work you have received in the *L*."
1Th 3:12 May the *L* make your love increase
5: 2 day of the *L* will come like a thief
5:23 at the coming of our *L* Jesus Christ.
2Th 2: 1 the coming of our *L* Jesus Christ
2Ti 2:19 "The *L* knows those who are his,"
Heb 12:14 holiness no one will see the *L*.
13: 6 *L* is my helper; I will not be afraid.
Jas 4:10 Humble yourselves before the *L*,
1Pe 1:25 the word of the *L* stands forever."
2: 3 you have tasted that the *L* is good.
3:15 in your hearts set apart Christ as *L*.
2Pe 1:16 and coming of our *L* Jesus Christ,
2: 1 the sovereign *L* who bought
3: 9 The *L* is not slow in keeping his
Jude :14 the *L* is coming with thousands
Rev 4: 8 holy, holy is the *L* God Almighty,
4:11 "You are worthy, our *L* and God,
17:14 he is *L* of lords and King of kings—
22:20 Come, *L* Jesus.

LORD'S† (LORD†)
Ac 21:14 and said, "The *L* will be done."
1Co 10:26 "The earth is the *L*, and everything
11:26 you proclaim the *L* death
2Co 3:18 faces all reflect the *L* glory,
2Ti 2:24 And the *L* servant must not quarrel
Jas 4:15 you ought to say, "If it is the *L* will,

LORDING* (LORD†)
1Pe 5: 3 not *l* it over those entrusted to you,

LORD‡ (LORD'S‡)
Ge 2: 4 When the *L* God made the earth
2: 7 the *L* God formed the man
3:21 The *L* God made garments of skin
7:16 Then the *L* shut him in.
15: 6 Abram believed the *L*,
18:14 Is anything too hard for the *L*?
31:49 "May the *L* keep watch
Ex 3: 2 the angel of the *L* appeared to him
9:12 the *L* hardened Pharaoh's heart
14:30 That day the *L* saved Israel
20: 2 "I am the *L* your God, who
33:11 The *L* would speak to Moses face
40:34 glory of the *L* filled the tabernacle.
Lev 19: 2 'Be holy because I, the *L* your God,
Nu 8: 5 *L* said to Moses: "Take the Levites
14:21 glory of the *L* fills the whole earth,
Dt 2: 7 forty years the *L* your God has
5: 9 the *L* your God, am a jealous God,
6: 4 The *L* our God, the *L* is one.
6: 5 Love the *L* your God
6:16 Do not test the *L* your God
10:14 To the *L* your God belong
10:17 For the *L* your God is God of gods
11: 1 Love the *L* your God and keep his
28: 1 If you fully obey the *L* your God
30:16 today to love the *L* your God,
30:20 For the *L* is your life, and he will
31: 6 for the *L* your God goes with you;
Jos 22: 5 to love the *L* your God, to walk
24:15 my household, we will serve the *L*
1Sa 1:28 So now I give him to the *L*.
2: 2 "There is no one holy like the *L*;
7:12 "Thus far has the *L* helped us."
12:22 his great name the *L* will not reject
15:22 "Does the *L* delight
2Sa 22: 2 "The *L* is my rock, my fortress
1Ki 2: 3 and observe what the *L* your God
8:11 the glory of the *L* filled his temple.
8:61 fully committed to the *L* our God,
18:21 If the *L* is God, follow him;
2Ki 13:23 But the *L* was gracious to them
1Ch 16: 8 Give thanks to the *L*, call
16:23 Sing to the *L*, all the earth;
28: 9 for the *L* searches every heart
29:11 O *L*, is the greatness and the power
2Ch 5:14 the glory of the *L* filled the temple
16: 9 of the *L* range throughout the earth
19: 6 judging for man but for the *L*,
30: 9 for the *L* your God is gracious
Ne 1: 5 Then I said: "O *L*, God of heaven,
Job 1:21 *L* gave and the *L* has taken away;
38: 1 the *L* answered Job out
42: 9 and the *L* accepted Job's prayer.
Ps 1: 2 But his delight is in the law of the *L*
9: 9 The *L* is a refuge for the oppressed,
12: 6 And the words of the *L* are flawless
16: 8 I have set the *L* always before me.
18:30 the word of the *L* is flawless.
19: 7 The law of the *L* is perfect,
19:14 O *L*, my Rock and my Redeemer.
23: 1 The *L* is my shepherd, I shall not be
23: 6 I will dwell in the house of the *L*
27: 1 The *L* is my light and my salvation
27: 4 to gaze upon the beauty of the *L*
29: 1 Ascribe to the *L*, O mighty ones,
32: 2 whose sin the *L* does not count
33:12 is the nation whose God is the *L*,
33:18 But the eyes of the *L* are
34: 3 Glorify the *L* with me;
34: 7 The angel of the *L* encamps
34: 8 Taste and see that the *L* is good;
34:18 The *L* is close to the brokenhearted
37: 4 Delight yourself in the *L*
40: 1 I waited patiently for the *L*;
47: 2 How awesome is the *L* Most High,
48: 1 Great is the *L*, and most worthy
55:22 Cast your cares on the *L*
75: 8 In the hand of the *L* is a cup
84:11 For the *L* God is a sun and shield;
86:11 Teach me your way, O *L*,
89: 5 heavens praise your wonders, O *L*,
91: 2 I will say of the *L*, "He is my refuge
95: 1 Come, let us sing for joy to the *L*;
96: 1 Sing to the *L* a new song;
98: 4 Shout for joy to the *L*, all the earth,
100: 1 Shout for joy to the *L*, all the earth.
103: 1 Praise the *L*, O my soul;
103: 8 The *L* is compassionate
104: 1 O *L* my God, you are very great;
107: 8 to the *L* for his unfailing love
110: 1 The *L* says to my Lord:
113: 4 *L* is exalted over all the nations,
115: 1 Not to us, O *L*, not to us
116: 15 Precious in the sight of the *L*
118: 1 Give thanks to the *L*, for he is good
118: 24 This is the day the *L* has made;
121: 2 My help comes from the *L*,
121: 5 The *L* watches over you—
125: 2 so the *L* surrounds his people

‡This entry represents the translation of the Hebrew name for God. *Yahweh*, always indicated in the NIV by LORD. For Lord, see the concordance entries LORD† and LORD'S†.

Ps 127: 1 Unless the *L* builds the house,
127: 3 Sons are a heritage from the *L*,
130: 3 If you, O *L*, kept a record of sins,
135: 6 The *L* does whatever pleases him,
136: 1 Give thanks to the *L*, for he is good
139: 1 O *L*, you have searched me
144: 3 O *L*, what is man that you care
145: 3 Great is the *L* and most worthy
145: 18 The *L* is near to all who call on him
Pr 1: 7 The fear of the *L* is the beginning
3: 5 Trust in the *L* with all your heart
3: 9 Honor the *L* with your wealth,
3:12 the *L* disciplines those he loves,
3:19 By wisdom the *L* laid the earth's
5:21 are in full view of the *L*,
6:16 There are six things the *L* hates,
10:27 The fear of the *L* adds length to life
11: 1 The *L* abhors dishonest scales,
12:22 The *L* detests lying lips,
14:26 He who fears the *L* has a secure
15: 3 The eyes of the *L* are everywhere,
16: 2 but motives are weighed by the *L*.
16: 4 The *L* works out everything
16: 9 but the *L* determines his steps.
16:33 but its every decision is from the *L*.
18:10 The name of the *L* is a strong tower
18:22 and receives favor from the *L*.
19:14 but a prudent wife is from the *L*.
19:17 to the poor lends to the *L*,
21: 3 to the *L* than sacrifice.
21:30 that can succeed against the *L*.
21:31 but victory rests with the *L*.
22: 2 The *L* is the Maker of them all.
24:18 or the *L* will see and disapprove
31:30 a woman who fears the *L* is
Isa 6: 3 holy, holy is the *L* Almighty;
11: 2 The Spirit of the *L* will rest on him
11: 9 full of the knowledge of the *L*
12: 2 The *L*, the *L*, is my strength
24: 1 the *L* is going to lay waste the earth
25: 8 The Sovereign *L* will wipe away
29:15 to hide their plans from the *L*,
33: 6 the fear of the *L* is the key
35:10 the ransomed of the *L* will return.
40: 5 the glory of the *L* will be revealed,
40: 7 the breath of the *L* blows on them.
40:10 the Sovereign *L* comes with power,
40:28 The *L* is the everlasting God,
40:31 but those who hope in the *L*
Isa 42: 8 "I am the *L*; that is my name!
43:11 I, even I, am the *L*,
44:24 I am the *L*,
45: 5 I am the *L*, and there is no other;
45:21 Was it not I, the *L*?
51:11 The ransomed of the *L* will return.
53: 6 and the *L* has laid on him
53:10 and the will of the *L* will prosper
55: 6 Seek the *L* while he may be found;
58: 8 of the *L* will be your rear guard.
58:11 The *L* will guide you always;
59: 1 the arm of the *L* is not too short
61: 3 a planting of the *L*
61:10 I delight greatly in the *L*;
Jer 1: 9 Then the *L* reached out his hand
9:24 I am the *L*, who exercises kindness,
16:19 O *L*, my strength and my fortress,
17: 7 is the man who trusts in the *L*,
La 3:40 and let us return to the *L*.
Eze 1:28 of the likeness of the glory of the *L*.
Hos 1: 7 horsemen, but by the *L* their God."
3: 5 They will come trembling to the *L*
6: 1 "Come, let us return to the *L*.
Joel 2: 1 for the day of the *L* is coming.
2:11 The day of the *L* is great;
3:14 For the day of the *L* is near
Am 5:18 long for the day of the *L*?
Jnh 1: 3 But Jonah ran away from the *L*
Mic 4: 2 up to the mountain of the *L*,
6: 8 And what does the *L* require of you
Na 1: 2 The *L* takes vengeance on his foes
1: 3 The *L* is slow to anger
Hab 2:14 knowledge of the glory of the *L*,
2:20 But the *L* is in his holy temple;
Zep 3:17 The *L* your God is with you,
Zec 1:17 and the *L* will again comfort Zion
9:16 The *L* their God will save them
14: 5 Then the *L* my God will come,
14: 9 The *L* will be king
Mal 4: 5 and dreadful day of the *L* comes.

LORD'S‡ (LORD‡)

Ex 34:34 he entered the *L* presence
Nu 14:41 you disobeying the *L* command?
Dt 6:18 is right and good in the *L* sight,
32: 9 For the *L* portion is his people,
Jos 21:45 Not one of all the *L* good promises
Ps 24: 1 The earth is the *L*, and everything
32:10 but the *L* unfailing love
89: 1 of the *L* great love forever;
103: 17 *L* love is with those who fear him,
Pr 3:11 do not despise the *L* discipline
Isa 24:14 west they acclaim the *L* majesty.
Isa 62: 3 of splendor in the *L* hand,
Jer 48:10 lax in doing the *L* work!
La 3:22 of the *L* great love we are not
Mic 4: 1 of the *L* temple will be established

LOSE (LOSES LOSS LOST)

1Sa 17:32 "Let no one *l* heart on account
Mt 10:39 Whoever finds his life will *l* it,
Lk 9:25 and yet *l* or forfeit his very self?
Jn 6:39 that I shall *l* none of all that he has
Heb 12: 3 will not grow weary and *l* heart.
12: 5 do not *l* heart when he rebukes you

LOSES (LOSE)

Mt 5:13 But if the salt *l* its saltiness,
Lk 15: 4 you has a hundred sheep and *l* one
15: 8 has ten silver coins and *l* one.

LOSS (LOSE)

Ro 11:12 and their *l* means riches
1Co 3:15 he will suffer *l*; he himself will be
Php 3: 8 I consider everything a *l* compared

LOST (LOSE)

Ps 73: 2 I had nearly *l* my foothold.
Jer 50: 6 "My people have been *l* sheep;
Eze 34: 4 the strays or searched for the *l*.
34:16 for the *l* and bring back the strays.
Mt 18:14 any of these little ones should be *l*.
Lk 15: 4 go after the *l* sheep until he finds it?
15: 6 with me; I have found my *l* sheep.'
15: 9 with me; I have found my *l* coin.'
15:24 is alive again; he was *l* and is found
19:10 to seek and to save what was *l*."
Php 3: 8 for whose sake I have *l* all things.

LOT (LOTS)

Nephew of Abraham (Ge 11:27; 12:5). Chose to live in Sodom (Ge 13). Rescued from four kings (Ge 14). Rescued from Sodom (Ge 19:1-29; 2Pe 2:7). Fathered Moab and Ammon by his daughters (Ge 19:30-38).

Est 3: 7 the *l*) in the presence of Haman
9:24 the *l*) for their ruin and destruction.
Pr 16:33 The *l* is cast into the lap,
18:18 Casting the *l* settles disputes
Ecc 3:22 his work, because that is his *l*.
Ac 1:26 Then they drew lots, and the *l* fell

LOTS (LOT)

Ps 22:18 and cast *l* for my clothing.
Mt 27:35 divided up his clothes by casting *l*.

LOVE (BELOVED LOVED LOVELY LOVER LOVERS LOVES LOVING)

Ge 22: 2 your only son, Isaac, whom you *l*,
Ex 15:13 "In your unfailing *l* you will lead

Ex 20: 6 showing *l* to a thousand generations
20: 6 of those who *l* me
34: 6 abounding in *l* and faithfulness,
Lev 19:18 but *l* your neighbor as yourself.
19:34 *L* him as yourself,
Nu 14:18 abounding in *l* and forgiving sin
Dt 5:10 showing *l* to a thousand generations
5:10 of those who *l* me
6: 5 *L* the LORD your God
7:13 He will *l* you and bless you
10:12 to walk in all his ways, to *l* him,
11:13 to *l* the LORD your God
13: 6 wife you *l*, or your closest friend
30: 6 so that you may *l* him
Jos 22: 5 to *l* the LORD your God, to walk
1Ki 3: 3 Solomon showed his *l*
8:23 you who keep your covenant of *l*
2Ch 5:13 his *l* endures forever."
Ne 1: 5 covenant of *l* with those who *l* him
Ps 18: 1 I *l* you, O LORD, my strength.
23: 6 Surely goodness and *l* will follow
25: 6 O LORD, your great mercy and *l*,
31:16 save me in your unfailing *l*.
32:10 but the LORD's unfailing *l*
33: 5 the earth is full of his unfailing *l*.
33:18 whose hope is in his unfailing *l*,
36: 5 Your *l*, O LORD, reaches
36: 7 How priceless is your unfailing *l*!
45: 7 You *l* righteousness and hate
51: 1 according to your unfailing *l*;
57:10 For great is your *l*, reaching
63: 3 Because your *l* is better than life,
66:20 or withheld his *l* from me!
70: 4 may those who *l* your salvation
77: 8 Has his unfailing *l* vanished forever
85: 7 Show us your unfailing *l*, O LORD
85:10 *L* and faithfulness meet together;
86:13 For great is your *l* toward me;
89: 1 of the LORD's great *l* forever;
89:33 but I will not take my *l* from him,
92: 2 to proclaim your *l* in the morning
94:18 your *l*, O LORD, supported me.
100: 5 is good and his *l* endures forever;
101: 1 I will sing of your *l* and justice;
103: 4 crowns you with *l* and compassion.
103: 8 slow to anger, abounding in *l*.
103: 11 so great is his *l* for those who fear
107: 8 to the LORD for his unfailing *l*
108: 4 For great is your *l*, higher
116: 1 I *l* the LORD, for he heard my
118: 1 his *l* endures forever.
119: 47 because I *l* them.
119: 64 The earth is filled with your *l*,
Ps 119: 76 May your unfailing *l* be my
119: 97 Oh, how I *l* your law!
119:119 therefore I *l* your statutes.
119:124 your servant according to your *l*
119:132 to those who *l* your name.
119:159 O LORD, according to your *l*.
119:163 but I *l* your law.
119:165 peace have they who *l* your law,
122: 6 "May those who *l* you be secure.
130: 7 for with the LORD is unfailing *l*
136: 1 -26 *His l endures forever.*
143: 8 of your unfailing *l*,
145: 8 slow to anger and rich in *l*.
145: 20 over all who *l* him,
147: 11 who put their hope in his unfailing *l*
Pr 3: 3 Let *l* and faithfulness never leave
4: 6 *l* her, and she will watch over you.
5:19 you ever be captivated by her *l*.
8:17 I *l* those who *l* me,
9: 8 rebuke a wise man and he will *l* you
10:12 but *l* covers over all wrongs.
14:22 those who plan what is good find *l*
15:17 of vegetables where there is *l*
17: 9 over an offense promotes *l*,
19:22 What a man desires is unfailing *l*;
20: 6 claims to have unfailing *l*,
20:13 Do not *l* sleep or you will grow
20:28 through *l* his throne is made secure
21:21 who pursues righteousness and *l*
27: 5 rebuke than hidden *l*.
Ecc 9: 6 Their *l*, their hate
9: 9 life with your wife, whom you *l*,
SS 2: 4 and his banner over me is *l*.
8: 6 for *l* is as strong as death,
8: 7 Many waters cannot quench *l*;
8: 7 all the wealth of his house for *l*,
Isa 5: 1 I will sing for the one I *l*
16: 5 In *l* a throne will be established;
38:17 In your *l* you kept me
54:10 yet my unfailing *l* for you will not
55: 3 my faithful *l* promised to David.
61: 8 "For I, the LORD, *l* justice;
63: 9 In his *l* and mercy he redeemed
Jer 5:31 and my people *l* it this way.
31: 3 you with an everlasting *l*;
32:18 You show *l* to thousands
33:11 his *l* endures forever."
La 3:22 of the LORD's great *l* we are not
3:32 so great is his unfailing *l*.
Eze 33:32 more than one who sings *l* songs
Da 9: 4 covenant of *l* with all who *l* him
Hos 2:19 in *l* and compassion.
3: 1 Go, show your *l* to your wife again,
11: 4 with ties of *l*;
12: 6 maintain *l* and justice,
Joel 2:13 slow to anger and abounding in *l*,
Am 5:15 Hate evil, *l* good;
Mic 3: 2 you who hate good and *l* evil;
6: 8 To act justly and to *l* mercy
Zep 3:17 he will quiet you with his *l*,
Zec 8:19 Therefore *l* truth and peace."
Mt 3:17 "This is my Son, whom I *l*;
5:44 *L* your enemies and pray
6:24 he will hate the one and *l* the other,
17: 5 "This is my Son, whom I *l*;
19:19 and '*l* your neighbor as yourself.'"
22:37 "'*L* the Lord your God
Lk 6:32 Even 'sinners' *l* those who *l* them.
7:42 which of them will *l* him more?"
20:13 whom I *l*; perhaps they will respect
Jn 13:34 I give you: *L* one another.
13:35 disciples, if you *l* one another."
14:15 "If you *l* me, you will obey what I
15:13 Greater *l* has no one than this,
15:17 This is my command: *L* each other.
21:15 do you truly *l* me more than these
Ro 5: 5 because God has poured out his *l*
5: 8 God demonstrates his own *l* for us
8:28 for the good of those who *l* him,
8:35 us from the *l* of Christ?
8:39 us from the *l* of God that is
12: 9 *L* must be sincere.
12:10 to one another in brotherly *l*.
13: 8 continuing debt to *l* one another,
13: 9 "*L* your neighbor as yourself."
13:10 Therefore *l* is the fulfillment
13:10 *L* does no harm to its neighbor.
1Co 2: 9 prepared for those who *l* him"—
8: 1 Knowledge puffs up, but *l* builds up
13: 1 have not *l*, I am only a resounding
13: 2 but have not *l*, I am nothing.
13: 3 but have not *l*, I gain nothing.
13: 4 Love is patient, *l* is kind.
13: 4 *L* is patient, love is kind.
13: 6 *L* does not delight in evil
13: 8 *L* never fails.
13:13 But the greatest of these is *l*.
13:13 three remain: faith, hope and *l*.
14: 1 way of *l* and eagerly desire spiritual
16:14 Do everything in *l*.
2Co 5:14 For Christ's *l* compels us,
8: 8 sincerity of your *l* by comparing it
8:24 show these men the proof of your *l*
Gal 5: 6 is faith expressing itself through *l*.
5:13 rather, serve one another in *l*.
5:22 But the fruit of the Spirit is *l*, joy,
Eph 1: 4 In *l* he predestined us
2: 4 But because of his great *l* for us,
3:17 being rooted and established in *l*,
3:18 and high and deep is the *l* of Christ,
3:19 and to know this *l* that surpasses

Eph 4: 2 bearing with one another in *l*.
4:15 Instead, speaking the truth in *l*,
5: 2 loved children and live a life of *l*,
5:25 *l* your wives, just as Christ loved
5:28 husbands ought to *l* their wives
5:33 each one of you also must *l* his wife
Php 1: 9 that your *l* may abound more
2: 2 having the same *l*, being one
Col 1: 5 *l* that spring from the hope that is
2: 2 in heart and united in *l*,
3:14 And over all these virtues put on *l*,
3:19 *l* your wives and do not be harsh
1Th 1: 3 your labor prompted by *l*,
4: 9 taught by God to *l* each other.
5: 8 on faith and *l* as a breastplate,
2Th 3: 5 direct your hearts into God's *l*
1Ti 1: 5 The goal of this command is *l*,
2:15 *l* and holiness with propriety.
4:12 in life, in *l*, in faith and in purity.
6:10 For the *l* of money is a root
6:11 faith, *l*, endurance and gentleness.
2Ti 1: 7 of power, of *l* and of self-discipline.
2:22 and pursue righteousness, faith, *l*
3:10 faith, patience, *l*, endurance,
Tit 2: 4 women to *l* their husbands
Phm : 9 yet I appeal to you on the basis of *l*.
Heb 6:10 and the *l* you have shown him
10:24 may spur one another on toward *l*
13: 5 free from the *l* of money
Jas 1:12 promised to those who *l* him.
2: 5 he promised those who *l* him?
2: 8 "*L* your neighbor as yourself,"
1Pe 1:22 the truth so that you have sincere *l*
1:22 *l* one another deeply,
2:17 *L* the brotherhood of believers,
3: 8 be sympathetic, *l* as brothers,
3:10 "Whoever would *l* life
4: 8 Above all, *l* each other deeply,
4: 8 *l* covers over a multitude of sins.
5:14 Greet one another with a kiss of *l*.
2Pe 1: 7 and to brotherly kindness, *l*.
1:17 "This is my Son, whom I *l*;
1Jn 2: 5 God's *l* is truly made complete
2:15 Do not *l* the world or anything
3: 1 How great is the *l* the Father has
3:10 anyone who does not *l* his brother.
3:11 We should *l* one another.
3:14 Anyone who does not *l* remains
1Jn 3:16 This is how we know what *l* is:
3:18 let us not *l* with words or tongue
3:23 to *l* one another as he commanded
4: 7 Dear friends, let us *l* one another,
4: 7 for *l* comes from God.
4: 8 Whoever does not *l* does not know
4: 9 This is how God showed his *l*
4:10 This is *l*: not that we loved God,
4:11 we also ought to *l* one another.
4:12 and his *l* is made complete in us.
4:16 God is *l*.
4:16 Whoever lives in *l* lives in God,
4:17 *l* is made complete among us
4:18 But perfect *l* drives out fear,
4:19 We *l* because he first loved us.
4:20 If anyone says, "I *l* God,"
4:21 loves God must also *l* his brother.
5: 2 we know that we *l* the children
5: 3 This is *l* for God: to obey his
2Jn : 5 I ask that we *l* one another.
: 6 his command is that you walk in *l*.
: 6 this is *l*: that we walk in obedience
Jude :12 men are blemishes at your *l* feasts,
:21 Keep yourselves in God's *l*
Rev 2: 4 You have forsaken your first *l*.
3:19 Those whom I *l* I rebuke
12:11 they did not *l* their lives so much

LOVED (LOVE)
Ge 24:67 she became his wife, and he *l* her;
29:30 and he *l* Rachel more than Leah.
37: 3 Now Israel *l* Joseph more than any
Dt 7: 8 But it was because the LORD *l* you
1Sa 1: 5 a double portion because he *l* her,
20:17 because he *l* him as he *l* himself.
Ps 44: 3 light of your face, for you *l* them.
Jer 2: 2 how as a bride you *l* me
31: 3 "I have *l* you with an everlasting
Hos 2:23 to the one I called 'Not my *l* one.'
3: 1 though she is *l* by another
9:10 became as vile as the thing they *l*.
11: 1 "When Israel was a child, I *l* him,
Mal 1: 2 "But you ask, 'How have you *l* us?'
Mk 12: 6 left to send, a son, whom he *l*.
Jn 3:16 so *l* the world that he gave his one
3:19 but men *l* darkness instead of light
11: 5 Jesus *l* Martha and her sister
12:43 for they *l* praise from men more
13: 1 Having *l* his own who were
13:23 the disciple whom Jesus *l*,
13:34 As I have *l* you, so you must love
Jn 14:21 He who loves me will be *l*
15: 9 the Father has *l* me, so have I *l* you.
15:12 Love each other as I have *l* you.
19:26 the disciple whom he *l* standing
Ro 8:37 conquerors through him who *l* us.
9:13 "Jacob I *l*, but Esau I hated."
9:25 her 'my *l* one' who is not my *l* one,"
11:28 they are *l* on account
Gal 2:20 who *l* me and gave himself for me.
Eph 5: 2 as Christ *l* us and gave himself up
5:25 just as Christ *l* the church
2Th 2:16 who *l* us and by his grace gave us
2Ti 4:10 for Demas, because he *l* this world,
Heb 1: 9 You have *l* righteousness
1Jn 4:10 This is love: not that we *l* God,
4:11 Dear friends, since God so *l* us,
4:19 We love because he first *l* us.

LOVELY (LOVE)
Ps 84: 1 How *l* is your dwelling place,
SS 2:14 and your face is *l*.
5:16 he is altogether *l*.
Php 4: 8 whatever is *l*, whatever is

LOVER (LOVE)
SS 2:16 *Beloved* My *l* is mine and I am his;
7:10 I belong to my *l*,
1Ti 3: 3 not quarrelsome, not a *l* of money.

LOVERS (LOVE)
2Ti 3: 2 People will be *l* of themselves,
3: 3 without self-control, brutal, not *l*
3: 4 *l* of pleasure rather than *l* of God—

LOVES (LOVE)
Ps 11: 7 he *l* justice;
33: 5 The LORD *l* righteousness
34:12 Whoever of you *l* life
91:14 Because he *l* me," says the LORD,
127: 2 for he grants sleep to those he *l*.
Pr 3:12 the LORD disciplines those he *l*,
12: 1 Whoever *l* discipline *l* knowledge,
13:24 he who *l* him is careful
17:17 A friend *l* at all times,
17:19 He who *l* a quarrel *l* sin;
22:11 He who *l* a pure heart and whose
Ecc 5:10 whoever *l* wealth is never satisfied
Mt 10:37 anyone who *l* his son or daughter
Lk 7:47 has been forgiven little *l* little."
Jn 3:35 Father *l* the Son and has placed
10:17 reason my Father *l* me is that I lay
12:25 The man who *l* his life will lose it,
14:21 obeys them, he is the one who *l* me.
14:23 Jesus replied, "If anyone *l* me,
Ro 13: 8 for he who *l* his fellowman has

2Co 9: 7 for God *l* a cheerful giver.
Eph 5:28 He who *l* his wife *l* himself.
5:33 must love his wife as he *l* himself,
Heb 12: 6 the Lord disciplines those he *l*,
1Jn 2:10 Whoever *l* his brother lives
2:15 If anyone *l* the world, the love
4: 7 Everyone who *l* has been born
4:21 Whoever *l* God must also love his
5: 1 who *l* the father *l* his child
3Jn : 9 but Diotrephes, who *l* to be first,
Rev 1: 5 To him who *l* us and has freed us

LOVING (LOVE)
Ps 25:10 All the ways of the LORD are *l*
62:12 and that you, O Lord, are *l*.
145: 17 and *l* toward all he has made.
Heb 13: 1 Keep on *l* each other as brothers.
1Jn 5: 2 by *l* God and carrying out his

LOWLY
Job 5:11 The *l* he sets on high,
Pr 29:23 but a man of *l* spirit gains honor.
Isa 57:15 also with him who is contrite and *l*
Eze 21:26 *l* will be exalted and the exalted
1Co 1:28 He chose the *l* things of this world

LUKE*
Co-worker with Paul (Col 4:14; 2Ti 4:11; Phm 24).

LUKEWARM*
Rev 3:16 So, because you are *l*—neither hot

LUST
Pr 6:25 Do not *l* in your heart
Col 3: 5 sexual immorality, impurity, *l*,
1Th 4: 5 not in passionate *l* like the heathen,
1Jn 2:16 the *l* of his eyes and the boasting

LYING (LIE)
Pr 6:17 a *l* tongue,
26:28 A *l* tongue hates those it hurts,

MACEDONIA
Ac 16: 9 "Come over to *M* and help us."

MADE (MAKE)
Ge 1:16 He also *m* the stars.
1:25 God *m* the wild animals according
2:22 Then the LORD God *m* a woman
2Ki 19:15 You have *m* heaven and earth.
Ps 95: 5 The sea is his, for he *m* it,
100: 3 It is he who *m* us, and we are his;
118: 24 This is the day the LORD has *m*;
139: 14 I am fearfully and wonderfully *m*;
Ecc 3:11 He has *m* everything beautiful
Mk 2:27 "The Sabbath was *m* for man,
Jn 1: 3 Through him all things were *m*;
Ac 17:24 "The God who *m* the world
Heb 1: 2 through whom he *m* the universe.
Rev 14: 7 Worship him who *m* the heavens,

MAGI
Mt 2: 1 *M* from the east came to Jerusalem

MAGOG
Eze 38: 2 of the land of *M*, the chief prince
39: 6 I will send fire on *M*
Rev 20: 8 and *M*— to gather them for battle.

MAIDEN
Pr 30:19 and the way of a man with a *m*.
Isa 62: 5 As a young man marries a *m*,
Jer 2:32 Does a *m* forget her jewelry,

MAIMED
Mt 18: 8 It is better for you to enter life *m*

MAJESTIC (MAJESTY)
Ex 15: 6 was *m* in power.
15:11 *m* in holiness,
Ps 8: 1 how *m* is your name in all the earth
29: 4 the voice of the LORD is *m*.
111: 3 Glorious and *m* are his deeds,
SS 6:10 *m* as the stars in procession?
2Pe 1:17 came to him from the *M* Glory,

MAJESTY (MAJESTIC)
Ex 15: 7 In the greatness of your *m*
Dt 33:26 and on the clouds in his *m*.
1Ch 16:27 Splendor and *m* are before him;
Est 1: 4 the splendor and glory of his *m*.
Job 37:22 God comes in awesome *m*.
40:10 and clothe yourself in honor and *m*
Ps 45: 4 In your *m* ride forth victoriously
93: 1 The LORD reigns, he is robed in *m*
110: 3 Arrayed in holy *m*,
145: 5 of the glorious splendor of your *m*,
Isa 53: 2 or *m* to attract us to him,
Eze 31: 2 can be compared with you in *m*?
2Pe 1:16 but we were eyewitnesses of his *m*.
Jude :25 only God our Savior be glory, *m*,

MAKE (MADE MAKER MAKES MAKING)
Ge 1:26 "Let us *m* man in our image,
2:18 I will *m* a helper suitable for him."
12: 2 "I will *m* you into a great nation
Ex 22: 3 thief must certainly *m* restitution,
Nu 6:25 the LORD *m* his face shine
Ps 108: 1 *m* music with all my soul.
Isa 14:14 I will *m* myself like the Most High
29:16 "He did not *m* me"?
Jer 31:31 "when I will *m* a new covenant
Mt 3: 3 *m* straight paths for him.' "
28:19 and *m* disciples of all nations,
Mk 1:17 "and I will *m* you fishers of men."
Lk 13:24 "*M* every effort to enter
Lk 14:23 country lanes and *m* them come in,
Ro 14:19 *m* every effort to do what leads
2Co 5: 9 So we *m* it our goal to please him,
Eph 4: 3 *M* every effort to keep the unity
Col 4: 5 *m* the most of every opportunity.
1Th 4:11 *M* it your ambition
Heb 4:11 *m* every effort to enter that rest,
12:14 *M* every effort to live in peace
2Pe 1: 5 *m* every effort to add
3:14 *m* every effort to be found spotless,

MAKER (MAKE)
Job 4:17 Can a man be more pure than his *M*
36: 3 I will ascribe justice to my *M*.
Ps 95: 6 kneel before the LORD our *M*;
Pr 22: 2 The LORD is the *M* of them all.
Isa 45: 9 to him who quarrels with his *M*,
54: 5 For your *M* is your husband—
Jer 10:16 for he is the *M* of all things,

MAKES (MAKE)
1Co 3: 7 but only God, who *m* things grow.

MAKING (MAKE)
Ps 19: 7 *m* wise the simple.
Ecc 12:12 Of *m* many books there is no end,
Jn 5:18 *m* himself equal with God.
Eph 5:16 *m* the most of every opportunity,

MALE
Ge 1:27 *m* and female he created them.
Gal 3:28 slave nor free, *m* nor female,

MALICE (MALICIOUS)
Ro 1:29 murder, strife, deceit and *m*.
Col 3: 8 *m*, slander, and filthy language
1Pe 2: 1 rid yourselves of all *m*

MALICIOUS (MALICE)
Pr 26:24 A *m* man disguises himself
1Ti 3:11 not *m* talkers but temperate
6: 4 *m* talk, evil suspicions

MAN (MEN WOMAN WOMEN)
Ge 1:26 "Let us make *m* in our image,
2: 7 God formed the *m* from the dust
2:18 for the *m* to be alone
2:23 she was taken out of *m*.
9: 6 Whoever sheds the blood of *m*,
Dt 8: 3 *m* does not live on bread
1Sa 13:14 a *m* after his own heart
15:29 he is not a *m* that he
Job 14: 1 *M* born of woman is of few
14:14 If a *m* dies, will he live
Ps 1: 1 Blessed is the *m* who does
8: 4 what is *m* that you are
119: 9 can a young *m* keep his
127: 5 Blessed is the *m* whose quiver
Pr 14:12 that seems right to a *m*,
30:19 way of a *m* with a maiden.
Isa 53: 3 a *m* of sorrows,
Mt 19: 5 a *m* will leave his father
Mk 8:36 What good is it for a *m*

Lk 4: 4 '*M* does not live on bread
Ro 5:12 entered the world through one *m*
1Co 7: 2 each *m* should have his own
11: 3 head of every *m* is Christ,
11: 3 head of woman is *m*
13:11 When I became a *m*,
Php 2: 8 found in appearance as a *m*,
1Ti 2: 5 the *m* Christ Jesus,
2:11 have authority over a *m*;
Heb 9:27 as *m* is destined to die

MANAGE
Jer 12: 5 how will you *m* in the thickets
1Ti 3: 4 He must *m* his own family well
3:12 one wife and must *m* his children
5:14 to *m* their homes and to give

MANASSEH
1. Firstborn of Joseph (Ge 41:51; 46:20). Blessed (Ge 48).
2. Son of Hezekiah; king of Judah (2Ki 21:1-18; 2Ch 33:1-20).

MANGER
Lk 2:12 in strips of cloth and lying in a *m*."

MANNA
Ex 16:31 people of Israel called the bread *m*.
Dt 8:16 He gave you *m* to eat in the desert,
Jn 6:49 Your forefathers ate the *m*
Rev 2:17 I will give some of the hidden *m*.

MANNER
1Co 11:27 in an unworthy *m* will be guilty
Php 1:27 conduct yourselves in a *m* worthy

MARITAL* (MARRY)
Ex 21:10 of her food, clothing and *m* rights.
Mt 5:32 except for *m* unfaithfulness,
19: 9 except for *m* unfaithfulness,
1Co 7: 3 husband should fulfill his *m* duty

MARK (MARKS)
Cousin of Barnabas (Col 4:10; 2Ti 4:11; Phm 24; 1Pe 5:13), see JOHN.
Ge 4:15 Then the LORD put a *m* on Cain
Rev 13:16 to receive a *m* on his right hand

MARKS (MARK)
Jn 20:25 Unless I see the nail *m* in his hands
Gal 6:17 bear on my body the *m* of Jesus.

MARRED
Isa 52:14 his form *m* beyond human likeness

MARRIAGE (MARRY)
Mt 22:30 neither marry nor be given in *m*;
24:38 marrying and giving in *m*,
Ro 7: 2 she is released from the law of *m*.
Heb 13: 4 by all, and the *m* bed kept pure,

MARRIED (MARRY)
Ro 7: 2 by law a *m* woman is bound
1Co 7:27 Are you *m*? Do not seek a divorce.
7:33 But a *m* man is concerned about
7:36 They should get *m*.

MARRIES (MARRY)
Mt 5:32 and anyone who *m* the divorced
19: 9 and *m* another woman commits
Lk 16:18 the man who *m* a divorced woman

MARRY (INTERMARRY MARITAL MARRIAGE MARRIED MARRIES)
Mt 22:30 resurrection people will neither *m*
1Co 7: 1 It is good for a man not to *m*.
7: 9 control themselves, they should *m*,
1Ti 5:14 So I counsel younger widows to *m*,

MARTHA*
Sister of Mary and Lazarus (Lk 10:38-42; Jn 11; 12:2).

MARVELED
Lk 2:33 mother *m* at what was said about

MARY
1. Mother of Jesus (Mt 1:16-25; Lk 1:27-56; 2:1-40). With Jesus at temple (Lk 2:41-52), at the wedding in Cana (Jn 2:1-5), questioning his sanity (Mk 3:21), at the cross (Jn 19:25-27). Among disciples after Ascension (Ac 1:14).
2. Magdalene; former demoniac (Lk 8:2). Helped support Jesus' ministry (Lk 8:1-3). At the cross (Mt 27:56; Mk 15:40; Jn 19:25), burial (Mt 27:61; Mk 15:47). Saw angel after resurrection (Mt 28:1-10; Mk 16:1-9; Lk 24:1-12); also Jesus (Jn 20:1-18).
3. Sister of Martha and Lazarus (Jn 11). Washed Jesus' feet (Jn 12:1-8).

MASQUERADES*
2Co 11:14 for Satan himself *m* as an angel

MASTER (MASTERED MASTERS)
Mt 10:24 nor a servant above his *m*.
23: 8 for you have only one *M*
24:46 that servant whose *m* finds him
25:21 "His *m* replied, 'Well done,
Ro 6:14 For sin shall not be your *m*,
14: 4 To his own *m* he stands or falls.
2Ti 2:21 useful to the *M* and prepared

MASTERED* (MASTER)
1Co 6:12 but I will not be *m* by anything.
2Pe 2:19 a slave to whatever has *m* him.

MASTERS (MASTER)
Mt 6:24 "No one can serve two *m*.
Eph 6: 5 obey your earthly *m* with respect
6: 9 And *m*, treat your slaves
Tit 2: 9 subject to their *m* in everything,

MATTHEW*
Apostle; former tax collector (Mt 9:9-13; 10:3; Mk 3:18; Lk 6:15; Ac 1:13). Also called Levi (Mk 2:14-17; Lk 5:27-32).

MATURE (MATURITY)
Eph 4:13 of the Son of God and become *m*,
Php 3:15 of us who are *m* should take such
Heb 5:14 But solid food is for the *m*,
Jas 1: 4 work so that you may be *m*

MATURITY* (MATURE)
Heb 6: 1 about Christ and go on to *m*,

MEAL
Pr 15:17 Better a *m* of vegetables where
1Co 10:27 some unbeliever invites you to a *m*
Heb 12:16 for a single *m* sold his inheritance

MEANING
Ne 8: 8 and giving the *m* so that the people

MEANS
1Co 9:22 by all possible *m* I might save some

MEAT
Ro 14: 6 He who eats *m*, eats to the Lord,
14:21 It is better not to eat *m*

MEDIATOR
1Ti 2: 5 and one *m* between God and men,
Heb 8: 6 of which he is *m* is superior
9:15 For this reason Christ is the *m*
12:24 to Jesus the *m* of a new covenant,

MEDICINE*
Pr 17:22 A cheerful heart is good *m*,

MEDITATE (MEDITATES MEDITATION)
Jos 1: 8 from your mouth; *m* on it day
Ps 119: 15 I *m* on your precepts
119: 78 but I will *m* on your precepts.
119: 97 I *m* on it all day long.
145: 5 I will *m* on your wonderful works.

MEDITATES* (MEDITATE)
Ps 1: 2 and on his law he *m* day and night.

MEDITATION* (MEDITATE)
Ps 19:14 of my mouth and the *m* of my heart
104: 34 May my *m* be pleasing to him,

MEDIUM
Lev 20:27 " 'A man or woman who is a *m*

MEEK (MEEKNESS)
Ps 37:11 But the *m* will inherit the land
Mt 5: 5 Blessed are the *m*,

MEEKNESS* (MEEK)
2Co 10: 1 By the *m* and gentleness of Christ,

MEET (MEETING)
Ps 85:10 Love and faithfulness *m* together;
Am 4:12 prepare to *m* your God, O Israel."
1Th 4:17 them in the clouds to *m* the Lord

MEETING (MEET)
Heb 10:25 Let us not give up *m* together,

MELCHIZEDEK
Ge 14:18 *M* king of Salem brought out bread
Ps 110: 4 in the order of *M*."
Heb 7:11 in the order of *M*, not in the order

MELT
2Pe 3:12 and the elements will *m* in the heat.

MEMBERS
Mic 7: 6 a man's enemies are the *m*
Ro 7:23 law at work in the *m* of my body,
12: 4 of us has one body with many *m*,
1Co 6:15 not know that your bodies are *m*
12:24 But God has combined the *m*
Eph 4:25 for we are all *m* of one body.
Col 3:15 as *m* of one body you were called

MEN (MAN)
Mt 4:19 will make you fishers of *m*
5:16 your light shine before *m*
12:36 *m* will have to give account
Jn 12:32 will draw all *m* to myself
Ac 5:29 obey God rather than *m!*
Ro 1:27 indecent acts with other *m*,
5:12 death came to all *m*,
1Co 9:22 all things to all *m*
2Co 5:11 we try to persuade *m*.
1Ti 2: 4 wants all *m* to be saved
2Ti 2: 2 entrust to reliable *m*
2Pe 1:21 but *m* spoke from God

MENAHEM
King of Israel (2Ki 15:17-22).

MERCIFUL (MERCY)
Dt 4:31 the LORD your God is a *m* God;
Ne 9:31 for you are a gracious and *m* God.
Mt 5: 7 Blessed are the *m*,
Lk 6:36 Be *m*, just as your Father is *m*.
Heb 2:17 in order that he might become a *m*
Jude :22 Be *m* to those who doubt; snatch

MERCY (MERCIFUL)
Ex 33:19 *m* on whom I will have *m*,
Ps 25: 6 O LORD, your great *m* and love,
Isa 63: 9 and *m* he redeemed them;
Hos 6: 6 For I desire *m*, not sacrifice,
Mic 6: 8 To act justly and to love *m*
Hab 3: 2 in wrath remember *m*.
Mt 12: 7 'I desire *m*, not sacrifice,' you
23:23 justice, *m* and faithfulness.
Ro 9:15 "I will have *m* on whom I have *m*,
Eph 2: 4 who is rich in *m*, made us alive
Jas 2:13 *M* triumphs over judgment!
1Pe 1: 3 In his great *m* he has given us new

MESSAGE
Isa 53: 1 Who has believed our *m*
Jn 12:38 "Lord, who has believed our *m*
Ro 10:17 faith comes from hearing the *m*,
1Co 1:18 For the *m* of the cross is
2Co 5:19 to us the *m* of reconciliation.

MESSIAH*
Jn 1:41 "We have found the *M*" (that is,
4:25 "I know that *M*" (called Christ) "is

METHUSELAH
Ge 5:27 Altogether, *M* lived 969 years,

MICHAEL
Archangel (Jude 9); warrior in angelic realm, protector of Israel (Da 10:13, 21; 12:1; Rev 12:7).

MIDWIVES
Ex 1:17 The *m*, however, feared God

MIGHT (ALMIGHTY MIGHTY)
Jdg 16:30 Then he pushed with all his *m*,
2Sa 6:14 before the LORD with all his *m*,
Ps 21:13 we will sing and praise your *m*.
Zec 4: 6 'Not by *m* nor by power,
1Ti 6:16 To him be honor and *m* forever.

MIGHTY (MIGHT)
Ex 6: 1 of my *m* hand he will drive them
Dt 7: 8 he brought you out with a *m* hand
2Sa 1:19 How the *m* have fallen!
23: 8 the names of David's *m* men:
Ps 24: 8 The LORD strong and *m*,
50: 1 The *M* One, God, the LORD,
89: 8 You are *m*, O LORD,
136: 12 with a *m* hand and outstretched
147: 5 Great is our Lord and *m* in power;
Isa 9: 6 Wonderful Counselor, *M* God,
Zep 3:17 he is *m* to save.
Eph 6:10 in the Lord and in his *m* power.

MILE*
Mt 5:41 If someone forces you to go one *m*,

MILK
Ex 3: 8 a land flowing with *m* and honey—
Isa 55: 1 Come, buy wine and *m*
1Co 3: 2 I gave you *m*, not solid food,
Heb 5:12 You need *m*, not solid food!
1Pe 2: 2 babies, crave pure spiritual *m*,

MILLSTONE (STONE)
Lk 17: 2 sea with a *m* tied around his neck

MIND (DOUBLE-MINDED MINDFUL MINDS)
1Sa 15:29 Israel does not lie or change his *m;*
1Ch 28: 9 devotion and with a willing *m*,
Ps 26: 2 examine my heart and my *m;*
Isa 26: 3 him whose *m* is steadfast,
Mt 22:37 all your soul and with all your *m*.'
Ac 4:32 believers were one in heart and *m*.
Ro 7:25 I myself in my *m* am a slave
8: 7 the sinful *m* is hostile to God.
12: 2 by the renewing of your *m*.
1Co 2: 9 no *m* has conceived
14:14 spirit prays, but my *m* is unfruitful.
2Co 13:11 be of one *m*, live in peace.
Php 3:19 Their *m* is on earthly things.
1Th 4:11 to *m* your own business
Heb 7:21 and will not change his *m:*

MINDFUL* (MIND)
Ps 8: 4 what is man that you are *m* of him,
Lk 1:48 God my Savior, for he has been *m*
Heb 2: 6 What is man that you are *m* of him,

MINDS (MIND)
Ps 7: 9 who searches *m* and hearts,
Jer 31:33 "I will put my law in their *m*
Eph 4:23 new in the attitude of your *m;*
Col 3: 2 Set your *m* on things above,
Heb 8:10 I will put my laws in their *m*
Rev 2:23 I am he who searches hearts and *m*,

MINISTERING (MINISTRY)
Heb 1:14 Are not all angels *m* spirits sent

MINISTRY (MINISTERING)
Ac 6: 4 to prayer and the *m* of the word."
2Co 5:18 gave us the *m* of reconciliation:
2Ti 4: 5 discharge all the duties of your *m*.

MIRACLES (MIRACULOUS)
1Ch 16:12 his *m*, and the judgments he
Ps 77:14 You are the God who performs *m;*
Mt 11:20 most of his *m* had been performed,
11:21 If the *m* that were performed
24:24 and perform great signs and *m*
Mk 6: 2 does *m!* Isn't this the carpenter?
Jn 10:32 "I have shown you many great *m*
14:11 the evidence of the *m* themselves.
Ac 2:22 accredited by God to you by *m*,
19:11 God did extraordinary *m*
1Co 12:28 third teachers, then workers of *m*,
Heb 2: 4 it by signs, wonders and various *m*,

MIRACULOUS (MIRACLES)
Jn 3: 2 could perform the *m* signs you are
9:16 "How can a sinner do such *m* signs
20:30 Jesus did many other *m* signs
1Co 1:22 Jews demand *m* signs and Greeks

MIRE
Ps 40: 2 out of the mud and *m;*
Isa 57:20 whose waves cast up *m* and mud.

MIRIAM
Sister of Moses and Aaron (Nu 26:59). Led dancing at Red Sea (Ex 15:20-21). Struck with leprosy for criticizing Moses (Nu 12). Death (Nu 20:1).

MIRROR
Jas 1:23 a man who looks at his face in a *m*

MISERY
Ex 3: 7 "I have indeed seen the *m*
Jdg 10:16 he could bear Israel's *m* no longer.
Hos 5:15 in their *m* they will earnestly seek
Ro 3:16 ruin and *m* mark their ways,
Jas 5: 1 of the *m* that is coming upon you.

MISLED
1Co 15:33 Do not be *m:* "Bad company

MISS
Pr 19: 2 nor to be hasty and *m* the way.

MIST
Hos 6: 4 Your love is like the morning *m*,
Jas 4:14 You are a *m* that appears for a little

MISUSE*
Ex 20: 7 "You shall not *m* the name
Dt 5:11 "You shall not *m* the name
Ps 139: 20 your adversaries *m* your name.

MOCK (MOCKED MOCKER MOCKERS MOCKING)
Ps 22: 7 All who see me *m* me;
Pr 14: 9 Fools *m* at making amends for sin,
Mk 10:34 who will *m* him and spit on him,

MOCKED (MOCK)
Mt 27:29 knelt in front of him and *m* him.
27:41 of the law and the elders *m* him.
Gal 6: 7 not be deceived: God cannot be *m*.

MOCKER (MOCK)
Pr 9: 7 corrects a *m* invites insult;
9:12 if you are a *m*, you alone will suffer
20: 1 Wine is a *m* and beer a brawler;
22:10 Drive out the *m*, and out goes strife

MOCKERS (MOCK)
Ps 1: 1 or sit in the seat of *m*.

MOCKING (MOCK)
Isa 50: 6 face from *m* and spitting.

MODEL*
Eze 28:12 " 'You were the *m* of perfection,
1Th 1: 7 And so you became a *m*
2Th 3: 9 to make ourselves a *m* for you

MOMENT
Job 20: 5 the joy of the godless lasts but a *m*.
Ps 30: 5 For his anger lasts only a *m*,
Isa 66: 8 or a nation be brought forth in a *m*?
Gal 2: 5 We did not give in to them for a *m*,

MONEY
Ecc 5:10 Whoever loves *m* never has *m*
Isa 55: 1 and you who have no *m*,
Mt 6:24 You cannot serve both God and *M*.
Lk 9: 3 no bread, no *m*, no extra tunic.
1Co 16: 2 set aside a sum of *m* in keeping
1Ti 3: 3 not quarrelsome, not a lover of *m*.
6:10 For the love of *m* is a root
2Ti 3: 2 lovers of *m*, boastful, proud,
Heb 13: 5 free from the love of *m*
1Pe 5: 2 not greedy for *m*, but eager to serve

MOON
Ps 121: 6 nor the *m* by night.
Joel 2:31 and the *m* to blood
1Co 15:41 *m* another and the stars another;

MORNING
Ge 1: 5 and there was *m*— the first day.
Dt 28:67 In the *m* you will say, "If only it
Ps 5: 3 In the *m*, O LORD,
2Pe 1:19 and the *m* star rises in your hearts.
Rev 22:16 of David, and the bright *M* Star."

MORTAL
1Co 15:53 and the *m* with immortality.

MOSES
Levite; brother of Aaron (Ex 6:20; 1Ch 6:3). Put in basket into Nile; discovered and raised by Pharaoh's daughter (Ex 2:1-10). Fled to Midian after killing Egyptian (Ex 2:11-15). Married to Zipporah, fathered Gershom (Ex 2:16-22).

Called by the LORD to deliver Israel (Ex 3-4). Pharaoh's resistance (Ex 5). Ten plagues (Ex 7-11). Passover and Exodus (Ex 12-13). Led Israel through Red Sea (Ex 14). Song of deliverance (Ex 15:1-21). Brought water from rock (Ex 17:1-7). Raised hands to defeat Amalekites (Ex 17:8-16). Delegated judges (Ex 18; Dt 1:9-18).

Received Law at Sinai (Ex 19-23; 25-31; Jn 1:17). Announced Law to Israel (Ex 19:7-8; 24; 35). Broke tablets because of golden calf (Ex 32; Dt 9). Saw glory of the LORD (Ex 33-34). Supervised building of tabernacle (Ex 36-40). Set apart Aaron and priests (Lev 8-9). Numbered tribes (Nu 1-4; 26). Opposed by Aaron and Miriam (Nu 12). Sent spies into Canaan (Nu 13). Announced forty years of wandering for failure to enter land (Nu 14). Opposed by Korah (Nu 16). Forbidden to enter land for striking rock (Nu 20:1-13; Dt 1:37). Lifted bronze snake for healing (Nu 21:4-9; Jn 3:14). Final address to Israel (Dt 1-33). Succeeded by Joshua (Nu 27:12-23; Dt 34). Death (Dt 34:5-12).

"Law of Moses" (1Ki 2:3; Ezr 3:2; Mk 12:26; Lk 24:44). "Book of Moses" (2Ch 25:12; Ne 13:1). "Song of Moses" (Ex 15:1-21; Rev 15:3). "Prayer of Moses" (Ps 90).

MOTH
Mt 6:19 where *m* and rust destroy,

MOTHER (MOTHER'S)
Ge 2:24 and *m* and be united to his wife,
3:20 because she would become the *m*
Ex 20:12 "Honor your father and your *m*,
Lev 20: 9 " 'If anyone curses his father or *m*,
Dt 5:16 "Honor your father and your *m*,
21:18 who does not obey his father and *m*
27:16 who dishonors his father or his *m*."
1Sa 2:19 Each year his *m* made him a little
Ps 113: 9 as a happy *m* of children.
Pr 23:25 May your father and *m* be glad;
29:15 child left to himself disgraces his *m*.
31: 1 an oracle his *m* taught him:
Isa 49:15 "Can a *m* forget the baby
66:13 As a *m* comforts her child,
Mt 10:37 or *m* more than me is not worthy
15: 4 'Honor your father and *m*'
19: 5 and *m* and be united to his wife,
Mk 7:10 'Honor your father and your *m*,'
10:19 honor your father and *m*.' "
Jn 19:27 to the disciple, "Here is your *m*."

MOTHER'S (MOTHER)
Job 1:21 "Naked I came from my *m* womb,
Pr 1: 8 and do not forsake your *m* teaching

MOTIVES*
Pr 16: 2 but *m* are weighed by the LORD.
1Co 4: 5 will expose the *m* of men's hearts.
Php 1:18 whether from false *m* or true,
1Th 2: 3 spring from error or impure *m*,
Jas 4: 3 because you ask with wrong *m*,

MOUNTAIN (MOUNTAINS)
Mic 4: 2 let us go up to the *m* of the LORD,
Mt 17:20 say to this *m*, 'Move from here

MOUNTAINS (MOUNTAIN)
Isa 52: 7 How beautiful on the *m*
55:12 the *m* and hills
1Co 13: 2 if I have a faith that can move *m*,

MOURN (MOURNING)
Ecc 3: 4 a time to *m* and a time to dance,
Isa 61: 2 to comfort all who *m*,
Mt 5: 4 Blessed are those who *m*,
Ro 12:15 *m* with those who *m*.

MOURNING (MOURN)
Jer 31:13 I will turn their *m* into gladness;
Rev 21: 4 There will be no more death or *m*

MOUTH
Jos 1: 8 of the Law depart from your *m*;
Ps 19:14 May the words of my *m*
40: 3 He put a new song in my *m*,
119:103 sweeter than honey to my *m*!
Pr 16:23 A wise man's heart guides his *m*,
27: 2 praise you, and not your own *m*;
Isa 51:16 I have put my words in your *m*
Mt 12:34 overflow of the heart the *m* speaks.
15:11 into a man's *m* does not make him
Ro 10: 9 That if you confess with your *m*,

MUD
Ps 40: 2 out of the *m* and mire;
Isa 57:20 whose waves cast up mire and *m*.
2Pe 2:22 back to her wallowing in the *m*."

MULTITUDE (MULTITUDES)
Isa 31: 1 who trust in the *m* of their chariots
1Pe 4: 8 love covers over a *m* of sins.
Rev 7: 9 me was a great *m* that no one could

MULTITUDES (MULTITUDE)
Joel 3:14 *M*, *m* in the valley of decision!

MURDER (MURDERER MURDERERS)
Ex 20:13 "You shall not *m*.
Mt 15:19 *m*, adultery, sexual immorality,
Ro 13: 9 "Do not *m*," "Do not steal,"
Jas 2:11 adultery," also said, "Do not *m*."

MURDERER (MURDER)
Nu 35:16 he is a *m*; the *m* shall be put
Jn 8:44 He was a *m* from the beginning,

1Jn 3:15 who hates his brother is a *m,*

MURDERERS (MURDER)
1Ti 1: 9 for *m,* for adulterers and perverts,
Rev 21: 8 the *m,* the sexually immoral,

MUSIC
Jdg 5: 3 I will make *m* to the LORD,
Ps 27: 6 and make *m* to the LORD.
95: 2 and extol him with *m* and song.
98: 4 burst into jubilant song with *m;*
108: 1 make *m* with all my soul.
Eph 5:19 make *m* in your heart to the Lord,

MUSTARD
Mt 13:31 kingdom of heaven is like a *m* seed,
17:20 you have faith as small as a *m* seed,

MUZZLE
Dt 25: 4 Do not *m* an ox while it is treading
Ps 39: 1 I will put a *m* on my mouth
1Co 9: 9 "Do not *m* an ox while it is

MYRRH
Mt 2:11 of gold and of incense and of *m.*
Mk 15:23 offered him wine mixed with *m,*

MYSTERY
Ro 16:25 to the revelation of the *m* hidden
1Co 15:51 I tell you a *m:* We will not all sleep,
Eph 5:32 This is a profound *m*—
Col 1:26 the *m* that has been kept hidden
1Ti 3:16 the *m* of godliness is great:

MYTHS
1Ti 4: 7 Have nothing to do with godless *m*

NADAB
Son of Jeroboam I; king of Israel (1Ki 15:25-32).

NAIL* (NAILING)
Jn 20:25 "Unless I see the *n* marks

NAILING* (NAIL)
Ac 2:23 him to death by *n* him to the cross.
Col 2:14 he took it away, *n* it to the cross.

NAKED
Ge 2:25 The man and his wife were both *n,*
Job 1:21 *N* I came from my mother's womb,
Isa 58: 7 when you see the *n,* to clothe him,
2Co 5: 3 are clothed, we will not be found *n.*

NAME
Ex 3:15 This is my *n* forever, the *n*
20: 7 "You shall not misuse the *n*
Dt 5:11 "You shall not misuse the *n*
28:58 this glorious and awesome *n*—
1Ki 5: 5 will build the temple for my *N.'*
2Ch 7:14 my people, who are called by my *n,*
Ps 34: 3 let us exalt his *n* together.
103: 1 my inmost being, praise his holy *n.*
147: 4 and calls them each by *n.*
Pr 22: 1 A good *n* is more desirable
30: 4 What is his *n,* and the *n* of his son?
Isa 40:26 and calls them each by *n.*
57:15 who lives forever, whose *n* is holy:
Jer 14: 7 do something for the sake of your *n*
Da 12: 1 everyone whose *n* is found written
Joel 2:32 on the *n* of the LORD will be saved
Zec 14: 9 one LORD, and his *n* the only *n.*
Mt 1:21 and you are to give him the *n* Jesus,
6: 9 hallowed be your *n,*
18:20 or three come together in my *n,*
Jn 10: 3 He calls his own sheep by *n*
16:24 asked for anything in my *n.*
Ac 4:12 for there is no other *n*
Ro 10:13 "Everyone who calls on the *n*
Php 2: 9 him the *n* that is above every *n,*
Col 3:17 do it all in the *n* of the Lord Jesus,
Heb 1: 4 as the *n* he has inherited is superior
Rev 20:15 If anyone's *n* was not found written

NAOMI
Mother-in-law of Ruth (Ru 1). Advised Ruth to seek marriage with Boaz (Ru 2-4).

NARROW
Mt 7:13 "Enter through the *n* gate.

NATHANAEL
Apostle (Jn 1:45-49; 21:2). Probably also called Bartholomew (Mt 10:3).

NATION (NATIONS)
Ge 12: 2 "I will make you into a great *n*
Ps 33:12 Blessed is the *n* whose God is
Pr 14:34 Righteousness exalts a *n,*
Isa 65: 1 To a *n* that did not call on my name
1Pe 2: 9 a royal priesthood, a holy *n,*
Rev 7: 9 from every *n,* tribe, people

NATIONS (NATION)
Ge 17: 4 You will be the father of many *n.*
18:18 and all *n* on earth will be blessed
Ex 19: 5 of all *n* you will be my treasured
Ne 1: 8 I will scatter you among the *n,*
Ps 96: 3 Declare his glory among the *n,*
Isa 40:15 Surely the *n* are like a drop
Eze 36:23 *n* will know that I am the LORD,
Hag 2: 7 and the desired of all *n* will come,
Zec 8:23 *n* will take firm hold of one Jew
14: 2 I will gather all the *n* to Jerusalem
Mt 28:19 and make disciples of all *n,*
Rev 21:24 The *n* will walk by its light,

NATURAL (NATURE)
Ro 6:19 you are weak in your *n* selves.
1Co 15:44 If there is a *n* body, there is

NATURE (NATURAL)
Ro 8: 4 do not live according to the sinful *n*
8: 8 by the sinful *n* cannot please God.
Gal 5:19 The acts of the sinful *n* are obvious:
5:24 Jesus have crucified the sinful *n*
Php 2: 6 Who, being in very *n* God,

NAZARENE
Mt 2:23 prophets: "He will be called a *N."*

NAZIRITE
Jdg 13: 7 because the boy will be a *N* of God

NECESSARY
Ro 13: 5 it is *n* to submit to the authorities,

NEED (NEEDS NEEDY)
Ps 116: 6 when I was in great *n,* he saved me.
Mt 6: 8 for your Father knows what you *n*
Ro 12:13 with God's people who are in *n.*
1Co 12:21 say to the hand, "I don't *n* you!"
1Jn 3:17 sees his brother in *n* but has no pity

NEEDLE
Mt 19:24 go through the eye of a *n*

NEEDS (NEED)
Isa 58:11 he will satisfy your *n*
Php 4:19 God will meet all your *n* according

NEEDY (NEED)
Pr 14:21 blessed is he who is kind to the *n.*
14:31 to the *n* honors God.
31:20 and extends her hands to the *n.*
Mt 6: 2 "So when you give to the *n,*

NEGLECT (NEGLECTED)
Ne 10:39 We will not *n* the house of our God
Ps 119: 16 I will not *n* your word.
Ac 6: 2 for us to *n* the ministry of the word
1Ti 4:14 Do not *n* your gift, which was

NEGLECTED (NEGLECT)
Mt 23:23 But you have *n* the more important

NEHEMIAH
Cupbearer of Artaxerxes (Ne 2:1); governor of Israel (Ne 8:9). Returned to Jerusalem to rebuild walls (Ne 2-6). With Ezra, reestablished worship (Ne 8). Prayer confessing nation's sin (Ne 9). Dedicated wall (Ne 12).

NEIGHBOR (NEIGHBOR'S)
Ex 20:16 give false testimony against your *n.*
Lev 19:13 Do not defraud your *n* or rob him.
19:18 but love your *n* as yourself.
Pr 27:10 better a *n* nearby than a brother far
Mt 19:19 and 'love your *n* as yourself.' "
Lk 10:29 who is my *n?"* In reply Jesus said:
Ro 13:10 Love does no harm to its *n.*

NEIGHBOR'S (NEIGHBOR)
Ex 20:17 You shall not covet your *n* wife,
Dt 5:21 not set your desire on your *n* house
19:14 not move your *n* boundary stone

Pr 25:17 Seldom set foot in your *n* house—

NEW
Ps 40: 3 He put a *n* song in my mouth,
Ecc 1: 9 there is nothing *n* under the sun.
Isa 65:17 *n* heavens and a *n* earth.
Jer 31:31 "when I will make a *n* covenant
Eze 36:26 give you a *n* heart and put a *n* spirit
Mt 9:17 Neither do men pour *n* wine
Lk 22:20 "This cup is the *n* covenant
2Co 5:17 he is a *n* creation; the old has gone,
Eph 4:24 and to put on the *n* self, created
2Pe 3:13 to a *n* heaven and a *n* earth,
1Jn 2: 8 Yet I am writing you a *n* command;

NEWBORN (BEAR)
1Pe 2: 2 Like *n* babies, crave pure spiritual

NEWS
Isa 52: 7 the feet of those who bring good *n*,
Mk 1:15 Repent and believe the good *n*!"
16:15 preach the good *n* to all creation.
Lk 2:10 I bring you good *n*
Ac 5:42 proclaiming the good *n* that Jesus
17:18 preaching the good *n* about Jesus
Ro 10:15 feet of those who bring good *n*!"

NICODEMUS*
Pharisee who visted Jesus at night (Jn 3). Argued fair treatment of Jesus (Jn 7:50-52). With Joseph, prepared Jesus for burial (Jn 19:38-42).

NIGHT
Job 35:10 who gives songs in the *n*,
Ps 1: 2 on his law he meditates day and *n*.
91: 5 You will not fear the terror of *n*,
Jn 3: 2 He came to Jesus at *n* and said,
1Th 5: 2 Lord will come like a thief in the *n*.
5: 5 We do not belong to the *n*
Rev 21:25 for there will be no *n* there.

NOAH
Righteous man (Eze 14:14, 20) called to build ark (Ge 6-8; Heb 11:7; 1Pe 3:20; 2Pe 2:5). God's covenant with (Ge 9:1-17). Drunkenness of (Ge 9:18-23). Blessed sons, cursed Canaan (Ge 9:24-27).

NOBLE
Ru 3:11 you are a woman of *n* character.
Ps 45: 1 My heart is stirred by a *n* theme
Pr 12: 4 of *n* character is her husband's
31:10 A wife of *n* character who can find?
31:29 "Many women do *n* things,
Isa 32: 8 But the *n* man makes *n* plans,
Lk 8:15 good soil stands for those with a *n*
Ro 9:21 of clay some pottery for *n* purposes
Php 4: 8 whatever is *n*, whatever is right,
2Ti 2:20 some are for *n* purposes

NOTHING
Ne 9:21 in the desert; they lacked *n*,
Jer 32:17 *N* is too hard for you
Jn 15: 5 apart from me you can do *n*.

NULLIFY
Ro 3:31 Do we, then, *n* the law by this faith

OATH
Dt 7: 8 and kept the *o* he swore

OBEDIENCE (OBEY)
2Ch 31:21 in *o* to the law and the commands,
Pr 30:17 that scorns *o* to a mother,
Ro 1: 5 to the *o* that comes from faith.
6:16 to *o*, which leads to righteousness?
2Jn : 6 that we walk in *o* to his commands.

OBEDIENT (OBEY)
Lk 2:51 with them and was *o* to them.
Php 2: 8 and became *o* to death—
1Pe 1:14 As *o* children, do not conform

OBEY (OBEDIENCE OBEDIENT OBEYED)
Ex 12:24 "*O* these instructions as a lasting
Dt 6: 3 careful to *o* so that it may go well
13: 4 Keep his commands and *o* him;
21:18 son who does not *o* his father
30: 2 and *o* him with all your heart
32:46 children to *o* carefully all the words
1Sa 15:22 To *o* is better than sacrifice,
Ps 119: 34 and *o* it with all my heart.
Mt 28:20 to *o* everything I have commanded
Jn 14:23 loves me, he will *o* my teaching.
Ac 5:29 "We must *o* God rather than men!
Ro 6:16 slaves to the one whom you *o*—
Gal 5: 3 obligated to *o* the whole law.
Eph 6: 1 *o* your parents in the Lord,
6: 5 *o* your earthly masters with respect
Col 3:20 *o* your parents in everything,
1Ti 3: 4 and see that his children *o* him
Heb 13:17 *O* your leaders and submit
1Jn 5: 3 love for God: to *o* his commands.

OBEYED (OBEY)
Ps 119: 4 that are to be fully *o*.
Jnh 3: 3 Jonah *o* the word of the LORD
Jn 17: 6 and they have *o* your word.
Ro 6:17 you wholeheartedly *o* the form
Heb 11: 8 *o* and went, even though he did not
1Pe 3: 6 who *o* Abraham and called him her

OBLIGATED
Ro 1:14 I am *o* both to Greeks
Gal 5: 3 himself be circumcised that he is *o*

OBSCENITY
Eph 5: 4 Nor should there be *o*, foolish talk

OBSOLETE
Heb 8:13 he has made the first one *o*;

OBTAINED
Ro 9:30 not pursue righteousness, have *o* it,
Php 3:12 Not that I have already *o* all this,
Heb 9:12 having *o* eternal redemption.

OFFENDED (OFFENSE)
Pr 18:19 An *o* brother is more unyielding

OFFENSE (OFFENDED OFFENSIVE)
Pr 17: 9 over an *o* promotes love,
19:11 it is to his glory to overlook an *o*.

OFFENSIVE (OFFENSE)
Ps 139: 24 See if there is any *o* way in me,

OFFER (OFFERED OFFERING OFFERINGS)
Ro 12: 1 to *o* your bodies as living sacrifices,
Heb 13:15 therefore, let us continually *o*

OFFERED (OFFER)
Heb 7:27 once for all when he *o* himself.
11: 4 By faith Abel *o* God a better

OFFERING (OFFER)
Ge 22: 8 provide the lamb for the burnt *o*,
Ps 40: 6 Sacrifice and *o* you did not desire,
Isa 53:10 the LORD makes his life a guilt *o*,
Mt 5:23 if you are *o* your gift at the altar
Eph 5: 2 as a fragrant *o* and sacrifice to God.
Heb 10: 5 "Sacrifice and *o* you did not desire,

OFFERINGS (OFFER)
Mal 3: 8 do we rob you?' "In tithes and *o*.
Mk 12:33 is more important than all burnt *o*

OFFICER
2Ti 2: 4 wants to please his commanding *o*.

OFFSPRING
Ge 3:15 and between your *o* and hers;
12: 7 "To your *o* I will give this land."

OIL
Ps 23: 5 You anoint my head with *o*;
Isa 61: 3 the *o* of gladness
Heb 1: 9 by anointing you with the *o* of joy."

OLIVE (OLIVES)
Zec 4: 3 Also there are two *o* trees by it,
Ro 11:17 and you, though a wild *o* shoot,
Rev 11: 4 These are the two *o* trees

OLIVES (OLIVE)
Jas 3:12 a fig tree bear *o*, or a grapevine bear

OMEGA
Rev 1: 8 "I am the Alpha and the *O*,"

OMRI
King of Israel (1Ki 16:21-26).

OPINIONS*
1Ki 18:21 will you waver between two *o*?

Pr 18: 2 but delights in airing his own *o*.

OPPORTUNITY
Ro 7:11 seizing the *o* afforded
Gal 6:10 as we have *o*, let us do good
Eph 5:16 making the most of every *o*,
Col 4: 5 make the most of every *o*.
1Ti 5:14 to give the enemy no *o* for slander.

OPPOSES
Jas 4: 6 "God *o* the proud
1Pe 5: 5 because, "God *o* the proud

OPPRESS (OPPRESSED)
Ex 22:21 "Do not mistreat an alien or *o* him,
Zec 7:10 Do not *o* the widow

OPPRESSED (OPPRESS)
Ps 9: 9 The LORD is a refuge for the *o*,
Isa 53: 7 He was *o* and afflicted,
Zec 10: 2 *o* for lack of a shepherd.

ORDAINED
Ps 8: 2 you have *o* praise

ORDERLY
1Co 14:40 done in a fitting and *o* way.
Col 2: 5 and delight to see how *o* you are

ORGIES*
Ro 13:13 not in *o* and drunkenness,
Gal 5:21 drunkenness, *o*, and the like.
1Pe 4: 3 *o*, carousing and detestable

ORIGIN
2Pe 1:21 For prophecy never had its *o*

ORPHANS
Jn 14:18 will not leave you as *o*; I will come
Jas 1:27 to look after *o* and widows

OUTCOME
Heb 13: 7 Consider the *o* of their way of life
1Pe 4:17 what will the *o* be for those who do

OUTSIDERS*
Col 4: 5 wise in the way you act toward *o*;
1Th 4:12 daily life may win the respect of *o*
1Ti 3: 7 also have a good reputation with *o*,

OUTSTANDING
SS 5:10 *o* among ten thousand.
Ro 13: 8 no debt remain *o*,

OUTSTRETCHED
Ex 6: 6 and will redeem you with an *o* arm
Jer 27: 5 and *o* arm I made the earth
Eze 20:33 an *o* arm and with outpoured wrath

OUTWEIGHS
2Co 4:17 an eternal glory that far *o* them all.

OVERCOME (OVERCOMES)
Mt 16:18 and the gates of Hades will not *o* it.
Mk 9:24 I do believe; help me *o* my unbelief
Jn 16:33 But take heart! I have *o* the world."
Ro 12:21 Do not be *o* by evil, but *o* evil
1Jn 5: 4 is the victory that has *o* the world,
Rev 17:14 but the Lamb will *o* them

OVERCOMES* (OVERCOME)
1Jn 5: 4 born of God *o* the world.
5: 5 Who is it that *o* the world?
Rev 2: 7 To him who *o*, I will give the right
2:11 He who *o* will not be hurt at all
2:17 To him who *o*, I will give some
2:26 To him who *o* and does my will
3: 5 He who *o* will, like them, be
3:12 Him who *o* I will make a pillar
3:21 To him who *o*, I will give the right
21: 7 He who *o* will inherit all this,

OVERFLOW (OVERFLOWS)
Ps 119:171 May my lips *o* with praise,
Lk 6:45 out of the *o* of his heart his mouth
Ro 15:13 so that you may *o* with hope
2Co 4:15 to *o* to the glory of God.
1Th 3:12 *o* for each other and for everyone

OVERFLOWS* (OVERFLOW)
Ps 23: 5 my cup *o*.
2Co 1: 5 also through Christ our comfort *o*.

OVERJOYED* (JOY)
Da 6:23 The king was *o* and gave orders
Mt 2:10 they saw the star, they were *o*.
Jn 20:20 The disciples were *o*
Ac 12:14 she was so *o* she ran back
1Pe 4:13 so that you may be *o*

OVERSEER (OVERSEERS)
1Ti 3: 1 anyone sets his heart on being an *o*,
3: 2 Now the *o* must be above reproach,
Tit 1: 7 Since an *o* is entrusted

OVERSEERS* (OVERSEER)
Ac 20:28 the Holy Spirit has made you *o*.
Php 1: 1 together with the *o* and deacons:
1Pe 5: 2 as *o*— not because you must,

OVERWHELMED
Ps 38: 4 My guilt has *o* me
65: 3 When we were *o* by sins,
Mt 26:38 "My soul is *o* with sorrow
Mk 7:37 People were *o* with amazement.

OWE
Ro 13: 7 If you *o* taxes, pay taxes; if revenue
Phm :19 to mention that you *o* me your very

OX
Dt 25: 4 Do not muzzle an *o*
Isa 11: 7 and the lion will eat straw like the *o*
1Co 9: 9 "Do not muzzle an *o*

PAGANS
Mt 5:47 Do not even *p* do that? Be perfect,
1Pe 2:12 such good lives among the *p* that,

PAIN (PAINFUL)
Ge 3:16 with *p* you will give birth
Job 33:19 may be chastened on a bed of *p*
Jn 16:21 woman giving birth to a child has *p*

PAINFUL (PAIN)
Ge 3:17 through *p* toil you will eat of it
Heb 12:11 seems pleasant at the time, but *p*.
1Pe 4:12 at the *p* trial you are suffering,

PALMS
Isa 49:16 you on the *p* of my hands;

PANTS
Ps 42: 1 As the deer *p* for streams of water,

PARADISE*
Lk 23:43 today you will be with me in *p*."
2Co 12: 4 God knows—was caught up to *p*.
Rev 2: 7 of life, which is in the *p* of God.

PARALYTIC
Mk 2: 3 bringing to him a *p*, carried by four

PARDON (PARDONS)
Isa 55: 7 and to our God, for he will freely *p*.

PARDONS* (PARDON)
Mic 7:18 who *p* sin and forgives

PARENTS
Pr 17: 6 and *p* are the pride of their children
Lk 18:29 left home or wife or brothers or *p*
21:16 You will be betrayed even by *p*,
Ro 1:30 they disobey their *p*; they are
2Co 12:14 for their *p*, but *p* for their children.
Eph 6: 1 Children, obey your *p* in the Lord,
Col 3:20 obey your *p* in everything,
2Ti 3: 2 disobedient to their *p*, ungrateful,

PARTIALITY
Dt 10:17 who shows no *p* and accepts no
2Ch 19: 7 our God there is no injustice or *p*
Lk 20:21 and that you do not show *p*

PARTICIPATION
1Co 10:16 is not the bread that we break a *p*

PASS
Ex 12:13 and when I see the blood, I will *p*
La 1:12 to you, all you who *p* by?
Lk 21:33 Heaven and earth will *p* away,
1Co 13: 8 there is knowledge, it will *p* away.

PASSION (PASSIONS)
1Co 7: 9 better to marry than to burn with *p*.

PASSIONS (PASSION)
Gal 5:24 crucified the sinful nature with its *p*
Tit 2:12 to ungodliness and worldly *p*,

PASSOVER
Ex 12:11 Eat it in haste; it is the LORD's *P*.
Dt 16: 1 celebrate the *P* of the LORD your

1Co 5: 7 our *P* lamb, has been sacrificed.

PAST
Isa 43:18 do not dwell on the *p.*
Ro 15: 4 in the *p* was written to teach us,
Heb 1: 1 In the *p* God spoke

PASTORS*
Eph 4:11 and some to be *p* and teachers,

PASTURE (PASTURES)
Ps 37: 3 dwell in the land and enjoy safe *p.*
100: 3 we are his people, the sheep of his *p*
Jer 50: 7 against the LORD, their true *p,*
Eze 34:13 I will *p* them on the mountains
Jn 10: 9 come in and go out, and find *p.*

PASTURES (PASTURE)
Ps 23: 2 He makes me lie down in green *p,*

PATCH
Mt 9:16 No one sews a *p* of unshrunk cloth

PATH (PATHS)
Ps 27:11 lead me in a straight *p*
119:105 and a light for my *p.*
Pr 15:19 the *p* of the upright is a highway.
15:24 The *p* of life leads upward
Isa 26: 7 The *p* of the righteous is level;
Lk 1:79 to guide our feet into the *p* of peace
2Co 6: 3 no stumbling block in anyone's *p,*

PATHS (PATH)
Ps 23: 3 He guides me in *p* of righteousness
25: 4 teach me your *p;*
Pr 3: 6 and he will make your *p* straight.
Ro 11:33 and his *p* beyond tracing out!
Heb 12:13 "Make level *p* for your feet,"

PATIENCE (PATIENT)
Pr 19:11 A man's wisdom gives him *p;*
2Co 6: 6 understanding, *p* and kindness;
Gal 5:22 joy, peace, *p,* kindness, goodness,
Col 1:11 may have great endurance and *p,*
3:12 humility, gentleness and *p.*

PATIENT (PATIENCE PATIENTLY)
Pr 15:18 but a *p* man calms a quarrel.
Ro 12:12 Be joyful in hope, *p* in affliction,
1Co 13: 4 Love is *p,* love is kind.
Eph 4: 2 humble and gentle; be *p,*
1Th 5:14 help the weak, be *p* with everyone.

PATIENTLY (PATIENT)
Ps 40: 1 I waited *p* for the LORD;
Ro 8:25 we do not yet have, we wait for it *p.*

PATTERN
Ro 5:14 who was a *p* of the one to come.
12: 2 longer to the *p* of this world,
2Ti 1:13 keep as the *p* of sound teaching,

PAUL
Also called Saul (Ac 13:9). Pharisee from Tarsus (Ac 9:11; Php 3:5). Apostle (Gal 1). At stoning of Stephen (Ac 8:1). Persecuted Church (Ac 9:1-2; Gal 1:13). Vision of Jesus on road to Damascus (Ac 9:4-9; 26:12-18). In Arabia (Gal 1:17). Preached in Damascus; escaped death through the wall in a basket (Ac 9:19-25). In Jerusalem; sent back to Tarsus (Ac 9:26-30).

Brought to Antioch by Barnabas (Ac 11:22-26). First missionary journey to Cyprus and Galatia (Ac 13-14). Stoned at Lystra (Ac 14:19-20). At Jerusalem council (Ac 15). Split with Barnabas over Mark (Ac 15:36-41).

Second missionary journey with Silas (Ac 16-20). Called to Macedonia (Ac 16:6-10). Freed from prison in Philippi (Ac 16:16-40). In Thessalonica (Ac 17:1-9). Speech in Athens (Ac 17:16-33). In Corinth (Ac 18). In Ephesus (Ac 19). Return to Jerusalem (Ac 20). Farewell to Ephesian elders (Ac 20:13-38). Arrival in Jerusalem (Ac 21:1-26). Arrested (Ac 21:27-36). Addressed crowds (Ac 22), Sanhedrin (Ac 23:1-11). Transferred to Caesarea (Ac 23:12-35). Trial before Felix (Ac 24), Festus (Ac 25:1-12). Before Agrippa (Ac 25:13-26:32). Voyage to Rome; shipwreck (Ac 27). Arrival in Rome (Ac 28).

PAY (REPAID REPAY)
Lev 26:43 They will *p* for their sins
Pr 22:17 *P* attention and listen
Mt 22:17 Is it right to *p* taxes to Caesar
Ro 13: 6 This is also why you *p* taxes,
2Pe 1:19 you will do well to *p* attention to it,

PEACE (PEACEMAKERS)
Nu 6:26 and give you *p.*" '
Ps 34:14 seek *p* and pursue it.
85:10 righteousness and *p* kiss each other
119:165 Great *p* have they who love your
122: 6 Pray for the *p* of Jerusalem:
Pr 14:30 A heart at *p* gives life to the body,
17: 1 Better a dry crust with *p* and quiet
Isa 9: 6 Everlasting Father, Prince of *P.*
26: 3 You will keep in perfect *p*
48:22 "There is no *p,*" says the LORD,
Zec 9:10 He will proclaim *p* to the nations.
Mt 10:34 I did not come to bring *p,*
Lk 2:14 on earth *p* to men on whom his
Jn 14:27 *P* I leave with you; my *p*
16:33 so that in me you may have *p.*
Ro 5: 1 we have *p* with God
1Co 7:15 God has called us to live in *p.*
14:33 a God of disorder but of *p.*
Gal 5:22 joy, *p,* patience, kindness,
Eph 2:14 he himself is our *p,* who has made
Php 4: 7 the *p* of God, which transcends all
Col 1:20 by making *p* through his blood,
3:15 Let the *p* of Christ rule
1Th 5: 3 While people are saying, "*P*
2Th 3:16 the Lord of *p* himself give you *p*
2Ti 2:22 righteousness, faith, love and *p,*
1Pe 3:11 he must seek *p* and pursue it.
Rev 6: 4 power to take *p* from the earth

PEACEMAKERS* (PEACE)
Mt 5: 9 Blessed are the *p,*

Jas 3:18 *P* who sow in peace raise a harvest

PEARL* (PEARLS)
Rev 21:21 each gate made of a single *p.*

PEARLS (PEARL)
Mt 7: 6 do not throw your *p* to pigs.
13:45 like a merchant looking for fine *p.*
1Ti 2: 9 or gold or *p* or expensive clothes,
Rev 21:21 The twelve gates were twelve *p,*

PEKAH
King of Israel (2Ki 15:25-31; Isa 7:1).

PEKAHIAH*
Son of Menahem; king of Israel (2Ki 15:22-26).

PEN
Mt 5:18 letter, not the least stroke of a *p,*

PENTECOST
Ac 2: 1 of *P* came, they were all together

PEOPLE (PEOPLES)
Dt 32: 9 the LORD's portion is his *p,*
Ru 1:16 Your *p* will be my *p*
2Ch 7:14 if my *p,* who are called
Jer 24: 7 They will be my *p,*
Zec 2:11 and will become my *p.*
Lk 2:10 joy that will be for all the *p.*
Ac 15:14 from the Gentiles a *p.*
2Co 6:16 and they will be my *p.*"
Tit 2:14 a *p* that are his very own,
1Pe 2: 9 you are a chosen *p,*
Rev 21: 3 They will be his *p,*

PEOPLES (PEOPLE)
Da 7:14 all *p,* nations and men
Mic 4: 1 and *p* will stream to it.

PERCEIVING
Isa 6: 9 be ever seeing, but never *p.*'

PERFECT (PERFECTER PERFECTION)
SS 6: 9 but my dove, my *p* one, is unique,
Isa 26: 3 You will keep in *p* peace
Mt 5:48 as your heavenly Father is *p.*
Ro 12: 2 his good, pleasing and *p* will.
2Co 12: 9 for my power is made *p*
Col 1:28 so that we may present everyone *p*
3:14 binds them all together in *p* unity.
Heb 9:11 and more *p* tabernacle that is not
10:14 he has made *p* forever those who
Jas 1:17 Every good and *p* gift is from above
1:25 into the *p* law that gives freedom,
3: 2 he is a *p* man, able
1Jn 4:18 But *p* love drives out fear,

PERFECTER* (PERFECT)
Heb 12: 2 the author and *p* of our faith,

PERFECTION (PERFECT)
Ps 119: 96 To all *p* I see a limit;
2Co 13:11 Aim for *p,* listen to my appeal,
Heb 7:11 If *p* could have been attained

PERFORMS
Ps 77:14 You are the God who *p* miracles;

PERISH (PERISHABLE)
Ps 1: 6 but the way of the wicked will *p*.
102: 26 They will *p*, but you remain;
Lk 13: 3 unless you repent, you too will all *p*
Jn 10:28 eternal life, and they shall never *p*;
Col 2:22 These are all destined to *p* with use,
Heb 1:11 They will *p*, but you remain;
2Pe 3: 9 not wanting anyone to *p*,

PERISHABLE (PERISH)
1Co 15:42 The body that is sown is *p*,

PERJURERS
1Ti 1:10 for slave traders and liars and *p*—

PERMISSIBLE (PERMIT)
1Co 10:23 "Everything is *p*"— but not

PERMIT (PERMISSIBLE)
1Ti 2:12 I do not *p* a woman to teach

PERSECUTE (PERSECUTED PERSECUTION)
Mt 5:11 *p* you and falsely say all kinds
Jn 15:20 they persecuted me, they will *p* you
Ac 9: 4 why do you *p* me?" "Who are you,
Ro 12:14 Bless those who *p* you; bless

PERSECUTED (PERSECUTE)
1Co 4:12 when we are *p*, we endure it;
2Ti 3:12 life in Christ Jesus will be *p*,

PERSECUTION (PERSECUTE)
Ro 8:35 or hardship or *p* or famine

PERSEVERANCE (PERSEVERE)
Ro 5: 3 we know that suffering produces *p*;
5: 4 *p*, character; and character, hope.
Heb 12: 1 run with *p* the race marked out
Jas 1: 3 the testing of your faith develops *p*.
2Pe 1: 6 *p*; and to *p*, godliness;

PERSEVERE* (PERSEVERANCE PERSEVERED PERSEVERES)
1Ti 4:16 *P* in them, because if you do,
Heb 10:36 You need to *p* so that

PERSEVERED* (PERSEVERE)
Heb 11:27 he *p* because he saw him who is
Jas 5:11 consider blessed those who have *p*.
Rev 2: 3 You have *p* and have endured

PERSEVERES* (PERSEVERE)
1Co 13: 7 trusts, always hopes, always *p*.
Jas 1:12 Blessed is the man who *p*

PERSUADE
2Co 5:11 is to fear the Lord, we try to *p* men.

PERVERSION (PERVERT)
Lev 18:23 sexual relations with it; that is a *p*.
Jude : 7 up to sexual immorality and *p*.

PERVERT (PERVERSION PERVERTS)
Gal 1: 7 are trying to *p* the gospel of Christ.

PERVERTS* (PERVERT)
1Ti 1:10 for murderers, for adulterers and *p*,

PESTILENCE
Ps 91: 6 nor the *p* that stalks in the darkness

PETER
Apostle, brother of Andrew, also called Simon (Mt 10:2; Mk 3:16; Lk 6:14; Ac 1:13), and Cephas (Jn 1:42). Confession of Christ (Mt 16:13-20; Mk 8:27-30; Lk 9:18-27). At transfiguration (Mt 17:1-8; Mk 9:2-8; Lk 9:28-36; 2Pe 1:16-18). Caught fish with coin (Mt 17:24-27). Denial of Jesus predicted (Mt 26:31-35; Mk 14:27-31; Lk 22:31-34; Jn 13:31-38). Denied Jesus (Mt 26:69-75; Mk 14:66-72; Lk 22:54-62; Jn 18:15-27). Commissioned by Jesus to shepherd his flock (Jn 21:15-23).

Speech at Pentecost (Ac 2). Healed beggar (Ac 3:1-10). Speech at temple (Ac 3:11-26), before Sanhedrin (Ac 4:1-22). In Samaria (Ac 8:14-25). Sent by vision to Cornelius (Ac 10). Announced salvation of Gentiles in Jerusalem (Ac 11; 15). Freed from prison (Ac 12). Inconsistency at Antioch (Gal 2:11-21). At Jerusalem Council (Ac 15).

PHARISEES
Mt 5:20 surpasses that of the *P*

PHILIP
1. Apostle (Mt 10:3; Mk 3:18; Lk 6:14; Jn 1:43-48; 14:8; Ac 1:13).
2. Deacon (Ac 6:1-7); evangelist in Samaria (Ac 8:4-25), to Ethiopian (Ac 8:26-40).

PHILOSOPHY*
Col 2: 8 through hollow and deceptive *p*,

PHYLACTERIES*
Mt 23: 5 They make their *p* wide

PHYSICAL
1Ti 4: 8 For *p* training is of some value,
Jas 2:16 but does nothing about his *p* needs,

PIECES
Ge 15:17 and passed between the *p*.
Jer 34:18 and then walked between its *p*.

PIERCED
Ps 22:16 they have *p* my hands and my feet.
Isa 53: 5 But he was *p* for our transgressions,
Zec 12:10 look on me, the one they have *p*,
Jn 19:37 look on the one they have *p*."

PIGS
Mt 7: 6 do not throw your pearls to *p*.

PILATE
Governor of Judea. Questioned Jesus (Mt 27:1-26; Mk 15:15; Lk 22:66-23:25; Jn 18:28-19:16); sent him to Herod (Lk 23:6-12); consented to his crucifixion when crowds chose Barabbas (Mt 27:15-26; Mk 15:6-15; Lk 23:13-25; Jn 19:1-10).

PILLAR
Ge 19:26 and she became a *p* of salt.
Ex 13:21 ahead of them in a *p* of cloud
1Ti 3:15 the *p* and foundation of the truth.

PIT
Ps 40: 2 He lifted me out of the slimy *p*,
103: 4 who redeems your life from the *p*
Mt 15:14 a blind man, both will fall into a *p*."

PITIED
1Co 15:19 we are to be *p* more than all men.

PLAGUE
2Ch 6:28 "When famine or *p* comes

PLAIN
Ro 1:19 what may be known about God is *p*

PLAN (PLANNED PLANS)
Job 42: 2 no *p* of yours can be thwarted.
Pr 14:22 those who *p* what is good find love
Eph 1:11 predestined according to the *p*

PLANK
Mt 7: 3 attention to the *p* in your own eye?
Lk 6:41 attention to the *p* in your own eye?

PLANNED (PLAN)
Ps 40: 5 The things you *p* for us
Isa 46:11 what I have *p*, that will I do.
Heb 11:40 God had *p* something better for us

PLANS (PLAN)
Ps 20: 4 and make all your *p* succeed.
33:11 *p* of the LORD stand firm forever,
Pr 20:18 Make *p* by seeking advice;
Isa 32: 8 But the noble man makes noble *p*,

PLANTED (PLANTS)
Ps 1: 3 He is like a tree *p* by streams
Mt 15:13 Father has not *p* will be pulled
1Co 3: 6 I *p* the seed, Apollos watered it,

PLANTS (PLANTED)
1Co 3: 7 So neither he who *p* nor he who
9: 7 Who *p* a vineyard and does not eat

PLATTER
Mk 6:25 head of John the Baptist on a *p*."

PLAYED
Lk 7:32 " 'We *p* the flute for you,
1Co 14: 7 anyone know what tune is being *p*

PLEADED
2Co 12: 8 Three times I *p* with the Lord

PLEASANT (PLEASE)
Ps 16: 6 for me in *p* places;
133: 1 How good and *p* it is
147: 1 how *p* and fitting to praise him!
Heb 12:11 No discipline seems *p* at the time,

PLEASE (PLEASANT PLEASED PLEASES PLEASING PLEASURE PLEASURES)
Pr 20:23 and dishonest scales do not *p* him.
Jer 6:20 your sacrifices do not *p* me."
Jn 5:30 for I seek not to *p* myself
Ro 8: 8 by the sinful nature cannot *p* God.
15: 2 Each of us should *p* his neighbor
1Co 7:32 affairs—how he can *p* the Lord.

1Co 10:33 I try to *p* everybody in every way.
2Co 5: 9 So we make it our goal to *p* him,
Gal 1:10 or of God? Or am I trying to *p* men
1Th 4: 1 how to live in order to *p* God,
2Ti 2: 4 wants to *p* his commanding officer.
Heb 11: 6 faith it is impossible to *p* God,

PLEASED (PLEASE)
Mt 3:17 whom I love; with him I am well *p*
1Co 1:21 God was *p* through the foolishness
Col 1:19 For God was *p* to have all his
Heb 11: 5 commended as one who *p* God.
2Pe 1:17 whom I love; with him I am well *p*

PLEASES (PLEASE)
Ps 135: 6 The LORD does whatever *p* him,
Pr 15: 8 but the prayer of the upright *p* him.
Jn 3: 8 The wind blows wherever it *p*.
8:29 for I always do what *p* him."
Col 3:20 in everything, for this *p* the Lord.
1Ti 2: 3 This is good, and *p* God our Savior,
1Jn 3:22 his commands and do what *p* him.

PLEASING (PLEASE)
Ps 104: 34 May my meditation be *p* to him,
Ro 12: 1 *p* to God—which is your spiritual
Php 4:18 an acceptable sacrifice, *p* to God.
Heb 13:21 may he work in us what is *p* to him,

PLEASURE (PLEASE)
Ps 5: 4 You are not a God who takes *p*
147: 10 His *p* is not in the strength
Pr 21:17 He who loves *p* will become poor;
Eze 18:32 For I take no *p* in the death
Eph 1: 5 in accordance with his *p* and will—
1: 9 of his will according to his good *p*,
2Ti 3: 4 lovers of *p* rather than lovers

PLEASURES (PLEASE)
Ps 16:11 with eternal *p* at your right hand.
Heb 11:25 rather than to enjoy the *p* of sin
2Pe 2:13 reveling in their *p* while they feast

PLENTIFUL
Mt 9:37 harvest is *p* but the workers are

PLOW (PLOWSHARES)
Lk 9:62 "No one who puts his hand to the *p*

PLOWSHARES (PLOW)
Isa 2: 4 They will beat their swords into *p*
Joel 3:10 Beat your *p* into swords

PLUNDER
Ex 3:22 And so you will *p* the Egyptians."

POINT
Jas 2:10 yet stumbles at just one *p* is guilty

POISON
Mk 16:18 and when they drink deadly *p*,
Jas 3: 8 It is a restless evil, full of deadly *p*.

POLLUTE* (POLLUTED)
Nu 35:33 " 'Do not *p* the land where you are.
Jude : 8 these dreamers *p* their own bodies,

POLLUTED* (POLLUTE)
Ezr 9:11 entering to possess is a land *p*
Pr 25:26 Like a muddied spring or a *p* well
Ac 15:20 to abstain from food *p* by idols,
Jas 1:27 oneself from being *p* by the world.

PONDER
Ps 64: 9 and *p* what he has done.
119: 95 but I will *p* your statutes.

POOR (POVERTY)
Dt 15: 4 there should be no *p* among you,
15:11 There will always be *p* people
Ps 34: 6 This *p* man called, and the LORD
82: 3 maintain the rights of the *p*
112: 9 scattered abroad his gifts to the *p*,
Pr 10: 4 Lazy hands make a man *p*,
13: 7 to be *p*, yet has great wealth.
14:31 oppresses the *p* shows contempt
19: 1 Better a *p* man whose walk is
19:17 to the *p* lends to the LORD,
22: 2 Rich and *p* have this in common:
22: 9 for he shares his food with the *p*.
28: 6 Better a *p* man whose walk is
31:20 She opens her arms to the *p*
Isa 61: 1 me to preach good news to the *p*.
Mt 5: 3 saying: "Blessed are the *p* in spirit,
11: 5 the good news is preached to the *p*.
19:21 your possessions and give to the *p*,
26:11 The *p* you will always have
Mk 12:42 But a *p* widow came and put
Ac 10: 4 and gifts to the *p* have come up
1Co 13: 3 If I give all I possess to the *p*
2Co 8: 9 yet for your sakes he became *p*,
Jas 2: 2 and a *p* man in shabby clothes

PORTION
Dt 32: 9 For the LORD's *p* is his people,
2Ki 2: 9 "Let me inherit a double *p*
La 3:24 to myself, "The LORD is my *p*;

POSSESS (POSSESSING POSSESSION POSSESSIONS)
Nu 33:53 for I have given you the land to *p*.
Jn 5:39 that by them you *p* eternal life.

POSSESSING* (POSSESS)
2Co 6:10 nothing, and yet *p* everything.

POSSESSION (POSSESS)
Ge 15: 7 to give you this land to take *p* of it
Nu 13:30 "We should go up and take *p*
Eph 1:14 of those who are God's *p*—

POSSESSIONS (POSSESS)
Lk 12:15 consist in the abundance of his *p*."
2Co 12:14 what I want is not your *p* but you.
1Jn 3:17 If anyone has material *p*

POSSIBLE
Mt 19:26 but with God all things are *p*."
Mk 9:23 "Everything is *p* for him who
10:27 all things are *p* with God."
Ro 12:18 If it is *p*, as far as it depends on you,
1Co 9:22 by all *p* means I might save some.

POT (POTSHERD POTTER POTTERY)
2Ki 4:40 there is death in the *p*!"
Jer 18: 4 But the *p* he was shaping

POTSHERD (POT)
Isa 45: 9 a *p* among the potsherds

POTTER (POT)
Isa 29:16 Can the pot say of the *p*,
45: 9 Does the clay say to the *p*,
64: 8 We are the clay, you are the *p*;
Jer 18: 6 "Like clay in the hand of the *p*,
Ro 9:21 Does not the *p* have the right

POTTERY (POT)
Ro 9:21 of clay some *p* for noble purposes

POUR (POURED)
Ps 62: 8 *p* out your hearts to him,
Joel 2:28 I will *p* out my Spirit on all people.
Mal 3:10 *p* out so much blessing that you
Ac 2:17 I will *p* out my Spirit on all people.

POURED (POUR)
Ac 10:45 of the Holy Spirit had been *p* out
Ro 5: 5 because God has *p* out his love

POVERTY (POOR)
Pr 14:23 but mere talk leads only to *p*.
21: 5 as surely as haste leads to *p*.
30: 8 give me neither *p* nor riches,
Mk 12:44 out of her *p*, put in everything—
2Co 8: 2 and their extreme *p* welled up
8: 9 through his *p* might become rich.

POWER (POWERFUL POWERS)
1Ch 29:11 LORD, is the greatness and the *p*
2Ch 32: 7 for there is a greater *p* with us
Job 36:22 "God is exalted in his *p*.
Ps 63: 2 and beheld your *p* and your glory.
68:34 Proclaim the *p* of God,

Ps 147: 5 Great is our Lord and mighty in *p;*
Pr 24: 5 A wise man has great *p,*
Isa 40:10 the Sovereign LORD comes with *p*
Zec 4: 6 nor by *p,* but by my Spirit,'
Mt 22:29 do not know the Scriptures or the *p*
24:30 on the clouds of the sky, with *p*
Ac 1: 8 you will receive *p* when the Holy
4:33 With great *p* the apostles
10:38 with the Holy Spirit and *p,*
Ro 1:16 it is the *p* of God for the salvation
1Co 1:18 to us who are being saved it is the *p*
15:56 of death is sin, and the *p*
2Co 12: 9 for my *p* is made perfect
Eph 1:19 and his incomparably great *p*
Php 3:10 and the *p* of his resurrection
Col 1:11 strengthened with all *p* according
2Ti 1: 7 but a spirit of *p,* of love
Heb 7:16 of the *p* of an indestructible life.
Rev 4:11 to receive glory and honor and *p,*
19: 1 and glory and *p* belong to our God,
20: 6 The second death has no *p*

POWERFUL (POWER)
Ps 29: 4 The voice of the LORD is *p;*
Lk 24:19 *p* in word and deed before God
2Th 1: 7 in blazing fire with his *p* angels.
Heb 1: 3 sustaining all things by his *p* word.
Jas 5:16 The prayer of a righteous man is *p*

POWERLESS
Ro 5: 6 when we were still *p,* Christ died
8: 3 For what the law was *p* to do

POWERS (POWER)
Ro 8:38 nor any *p,* neither height nor depth
1Co 12:10 to another miraculous *p,*
Col 1:16 whether thrones or *p* or rulers
2:15 And having disarmed the *p*

PRACTICE
Lev 19:26 " 'Do not *p* divination or sorcery.
Mt 23: 3 for they do not *p* what they preach.
Lk 8:21 hear God's word and put it into *p.*"
Ro 12:13 *P* hospitality.
1Ti 5: 4 to put their religion into *p* by caring

PRAISE (PRAISED PRAISES PRAISING)
Ex 15: 2 He is my God, and I will *p* him,
Dt 32: 3 Oh, *p* the greatness of our God!
Ru 4:14 said to Naomi: "*P* be to the LORD,
2Sa 22:47 The LORD lives! *P* be to my Rock
1Ch 16:25 is the LORD and most worthy of *p;*
2Ch 20:21 and to *p* him for the splendor
Ps 8: 2 you have ordained *p*
33: 1 it is fitting for the upright to *p* him.
34: 1 his *p* will always be on my lips.
40: 3 a hymn of *p* to our God.
48: 1 the LORD, and most worthy of *p,*
68:19 *P* be to the Lord, to God our Savior
89: 5 The heavens *p* your wonders,
100: 4 and his courts with *p;*
105: 2 Sing to him, sing *p* to him;
106: 1 *P* the LORD.
119:175 Let me live that I may *p* you,
139: 14 I *p* you because I am fearfully
145: 21 Let every creature *p* his holy name
146: 1 *P* the LORD, O my soul.
150: 2 *p* him for his surpassing greatness.
150: 6 that has breath *p* the LORD.
Pr 27: 2 Let another *p* you, and not your
27:21 man is tested by the *p* he receives.
31:31 let her works bring her *p*
Mt 5:16 and *p* your Father in heaven.
21:16 you have ordained *p*'?"
Jn 12:43 for they loved *p* from men more
Eph 1: 6 to the *p* of his glorious grace,
1:12 might be for the *p* of his glory.
1:14 to the *p* of his glory.
Heb 13:15 offer to God a sacrifice of *p*—
Jas 5:13 happy? Let him sing songs of *p.*

PRAISED (PRAISE)
1Ch 29:10 David *p* the LORD in the presence
Ne 8: 6 Ezra *p* the LORD, the great God;
Da 2:19 Then Daniel *p* the God of heaven
Ro 9: 5 who is God over all, forever *p!*
1Pe 4:11 that in all things God may be *p*

PRAISES (PRAISE)
2Sa 22:50 I will sing *p* to your name.
Ps 47: 6 Sing *p* to God, sing *p;*
147: 1 How good it is to sing *p* to our God,
Pr 31:28 her husband also, and he *p* her:

PRAISING (PRAISE)
Ac 10:46 speaking in tongues and *p* God.
1Co 14:16 If you are *p* God with your spirit,

PRAY (PRAYED PRAYER PRAYERS PRAYING)
Dt 4: 7 is near us whenever we *p* to him?
1Sa 12:23 the LORD by failing to *p* for you.
2Ch 7:14 will humble themselves and *p*
Job 42: 8 My servant Job will *p* for you,
Ps 122: 6 *P* for the peace of Jerusalem:
Mt 5:44 and *p* for those who persecute you,
6: 5 "And when you *p,* do not be like
6: 9 "This, then, is how you should *p:*
26:36 Sit here while I go over there and *p*
Lk 6:28 *p* for those who mistreat you.
18: 1 them that they should always *p*
22:40 "*P* that you will not fall
Ro 8:26 do not know what we ought to *p,*
1Co 14:13 in a tongue should *p* that he may
1Th 5:17 Be joyful always; *p* continually;
Jas 5:13 one of you in trouble? He should *p.*
5:16 *p* for each other so that you may be

PRAYED (PRAY)
1Sa 1:27 I *p* for this child, and the LORD
Jnh 2: 1 From inside the fish Jonah *p*
Mk 14:35 *p* that if possible the hour might

PRAYER (PRAY)
2Ch 30:27 for their *p* reached heaven,
Ezr 8:23 about this, and he answered our *p.*
Ps 6: 9 the LORD accepts my *p.*
86: 6 Hear my *p,* O LORD;
Pr 15: 8 but the *p* of the upright pleases him
Isa 56: 7 a house of *p* for all nations."
Mt 21:13 house will be called a house of *p,*'
Mk 11:24 whatever you ask for in *p,*
Jn 17:15 My *p* is not that you take them out
Ac 6: 4 and will give our attention to *p*
Php 4: 6 but in everything, by *p* and petition
Jas 5:15 *p* offered in faith will make the sick
1Pe 3:12 and his ears are attentive to their *p,*

PRAYERS (PRAY)
1Ch 5:20 He answered their *p,* because they
Mk 12:40 and for a show make lengthy *p.*
1Pe 3: 7 so that nothing will hinder your *p.*
Rev 5: 8 which are the *p* of the saints.

PRAYING (PRAY)
Mk 11:25 And when you stand *p,*
Jn 17: 9 I am not *p* for the world,
Ac 16:25 and Silas were *p* and singing hymns
Eph 6:18 always keep on *p* for all the saints.

PREACH (PREACHED PREACHING)
Mt 23: 3 they do not practice what they *p.*
Mk 16:15 and *p* the good news to all creation.
Ac 9:20 At once he began to *p*
Ro 10:15 how can they *p* unless they are sent
15:20 to *p* the gospel where Christ was
1Co 1:17 to *p* the gospel—not with words
1:23 wisdom, but we *p* Christ crucified:
9:14 that those who *p* the gospel should
9:16 Woe to me if I do not *p* the gospel!
2Co 10:16 so that we can *p* the gospel
Gal 1: 8 from heaven should *p* a gospel
2Ti 4: 2 I give you this charge: *P* the Word;

PREACHED (PREACH)
Mk 13:10 And the gospel must first be *p*
Ac 8: 4 had been scattered *p* the word
1Co 9:27 so that after I have *p* to others,
15: 1 you of the gospel I *p* to you,
2Co 11: 4 other than the Jesus we *p*,
Gal 1: 8 other than the one we *p* to you,
Php 1:18 false motives or true, Christ is *p*.
1Ti 3:16 was *p* among the nations,

PREACHING (PREACH)
Ro 10:14 hear without someone *p* to them?
1Co 9:18 in *p* the gospel I may offer it free
1Ti 4:13 the public reading of Scripture, to *p*
5:17 especially those whose work is *p*

PRECEPTS
Ps 19: 8 The *p* of the LORD are right,
111: 7 all his *p* are trustworthy.
111: 10 who follow his *p* have good
119: 40 How I long for your *p!*
119: 69 I keep your *p* with all my heart.
119:104 I gain understanding from your *p;*
119:159 See how I love your *p;*

PRECIOUS
Ps 19:10 They are more *p* than gold,
116: 15 *P* in the sight of the LORD
Pr 8:11 for wisdom is more *p* than rubies,
Isa 28:16 a *p* cornerstone for a sure
1Pe 1:19 but with the *p* blood of Christ,
2: 6 a chosen and *p* cornerstone,
2Pe 1: 4 us his very great and *p* promises,

PREDESTINED* (DESTINY)
Ro 8:29 *p* to be conformed to the likeness
8:30 And those he *p*, he also called;
Eph 1: 5 In love he *p* us to be adopted
1:11 having been *p* according

PREDICTION*
Jer 28: 9 only if his *p* comes true."

PREPARE (PREPARED)
Ps 23: 5 You *p* a table before me
Am 4:12 *p* to meet your God, O Israel."
Jn 14: 2 there to *p* a place for you.
Eph 4:12 to *p* God's people for works

PREPARED (PREPARE)
Mt 25:34 the kingdom *p* for you
1Co 2: 9 what God has *p* for those who love
Eph 2:10 which God *p* in advance for us
2Ti 4: 2 be *p* in season and out of season;
1Pe 3:15 Always be *p* to give an answer

PRESENCE (PRESENT)
Ex 25:30 Put the bread of the *P* on this table
Ezr 9:15 one of us can stand in your *p*."
Ps 31:20 the shelter of your *p* you hide them
89:15 who walk in the light of your *p*,
Ps 90: 8 our secret sins in the light of your *p*
139: 7 Where can I flee from your *p?*
Jer 5:22 "Should you not tremble in my *p?*
Heb 9:24 now to appear for us in God's *p*.
Jude :24 before his glorious *p* without fault

PRESENT (PRESENCE)
2Co 11: 2 so that I might *p* you as a pure
Eph 5:27 and to *p* her to himself
2Ti 2:15 Do your best to *p* yourself to God

PRESERVES
Ps 1 19:50 Your promise *p* my life.

PRESS (PRESSED PRESSURE)
Php 3:14 I *p* on toward the goal

PRESSED (PRESS)
Lk 6:38 *p* down, shaken together

PRESSURE (PRESS)
2Co 1: 8 We were under great *p*, far
11:28 I face daily the *p* of my concern

PREVAILS
1Sa 2: 9 "It is not by strength that one *p;*

PRICE
Job 28:18 the *p* of wisdom is beyond rubies.
1Co 6:20 your own; you were bought at a *p*.
7:23 bought at a *p;* do not become slaves

PRIDE (PROUD)
Pr 8:13 I hate *p* and arrogance,
16:18 *P* goes before destruction,
Da 4:37 And those who walk in *p* he is able
Gal 6: 4 Then he can take *p* in himself,
Jas 1: 9 ought to take *p* in his high position.

PRIEST (PRIESTHOOD PRIESTS)
Heb 4:14 have a great high *p* who has gone
4:15 do not have a high *p* who is unable
7:26 Such a high *p* meets our need—
8: 1 We do have such a high *p*,

PRIESTHOOD (PRIEST)
Heb 7:24 lives forever, he has a permanent *p*.
1Pe 2: 5 into a spiritual house to be a holy *p*,
2: 9 you are a chosen people, a royal *p*,

PRIESTS (PRIEST)
Ex 19: 6 you will be for me a kingdom of *p*
Rev 5:10 to be a kingdom and *p*

PRINCE
Isa 9: 6 Everlasting Father, *P* of Peace.
Jn 12:31 now the *p* of this world will be
Ac 5:31 as *P* and Savior that he might give

PRISON (PRISONER)
Isa 42: 7 to free captives from *p*
Mt 25:36 I was in *p* and you came to visit me
1Pe 3:19 spirits in *p* who disobeyed long ago
Rev 20: 7 Satan will be released from his *p*

PRISONER (PRISON)
Ro 7:23 and making me a *p* of the law of sin
Gal 3:22 declares that the whole world is a *p*
Eph 3: 1 the *p* of Christ Jesus for the sake

PRIVILEGE*
2Co 8: 4 pleaded with us for the *p* of sharing

PRIZE
1Co 9:24 Run in such a way as to get the *p*.
Php 3:14 on toward the goal to win the *p*

PROCLAIM (PROCLAIMED PROCLAIMING)
1Ch 16:23 *p* his salvation day after day.
Ps 19: 1 the skies *p* the work of his hands.
50: 6 the heavens *p* his righteousness,
68:34 *P* the power of God,
118: 17 will *p* what the LORD has done.
Zec 9:10 He will *p* peace to the nations.
Ac 20:27 hesitated to *p* to you the whole will
1Co 11:26 you *p* the Lord's death

PROCLAIMED (PROCLAIM)
Ro 15:19 I have fully *p* the gospel of Christ.
Col 1:23 that has been *p* to every creature

PROCLAIMING (PROCLAIM)
Ro 10: 8 the word of faith we are *p:*

PRODUCE (PRODUCES)
Mt 3: 8 *P* fruit in keeping with repentance.
3:10 tree that does not *p* good fruit will

PRODUCES (PRODUCE)
Pr 30:33 so stirring up anger *p* strife."
Ro 5: 3 that suffering *p* perseverance;
Heb 12:11 it *p* a harvest of righteousness

PROFANE
Lev 22:32 Do not *p* my holy name.

PROFESS*
1Ti 2:10 for women who *p* to worship God.
Heb 4:14 let us hold firmly to the faith we *p*.
10:23 unswervingly to the hope we *p*,

PROMISE (PROMISED PROMISES)
1Ki 8:20 The LORD has kept the *p* he made
Ac 2:39 The *p* is for you and your children
Gal 3:14 that by faith we might receive the *p*
1Ti 4: 8 holding *p* for both the present life
2Pe 3: 9 Lord is not slow in keeping his *p*,

PROMISED (PROMISE)
Ex 3:17 And I have *p* to bring you up out
Dt 26:18 his treasured possession as he *p*,

Ps 119: 57 I have *p* to obey your words.
Ro 4:21 power to do what he had *p.*
Heb 10:23 for he who *p* is faithful.
2Pe 3: 4 "Where is this 'coming' he *p?*

PROMISES (PROMISE)
Jos 21:45 one of all the LORD's good *p*
Ro 9: 4 the temple worship and the *p.*
2Pe 1: 4 us his very great and precious *p,*

PROMPTED
1Th 1: 3 your labor *p* by love, and your
2Th 1:11 and every act *p* by your faith.

PROPHECIES (PROPHESY)
1Co 13: 8 where there are *p,* they will cease;
1Th 5:20 do not treat *p* with contempt.

PROPHECY (PROPHESY)
1Co 14: 1 gifts, especially the gift of *p.*
2Pe 1:20 you must understand that no *p*

PROPHESY (PROPHECIES PROPHECY PROPHESYING PROPHET PROPHETS)
Joel 2:28 Your sons and daughters will *p,*
Mt 7:22 Lord, did we not *p* in your name,
1Co 14:39 my brothers, be eager to *p,*

PROPHESYING (PROPHESY)
Ro 12: 6 If a man's gift is *p,* let him use it

PROPHET (PROPHESY)
Dt 18:18 up for them a *p* like you
Am 7:14 "I was neither a *p* nor a prophet's
Mt 10:41 Anyone who receives a *p*
Lk 4:24 "no *p* is accepted in his hometown.

PROPHETS (PROPHESY)
Ps 105: 15 do my *p* no harm."
Mt 5:17 come to abolish the Law or the *P;*
7:12 for this sums up the Law and the *P.*
24:24 false Christs and false *p* will appear
Lk 24:25 believe all that the *p* have spoken!
Ac 10:43 All the *p* testify about him that
1Co 12:28 second *p,* third teachers, then
14:32 The spirits of *p* are subject
Eph 2:20 foundation of the apostles and *p,*
Heb 1: 1 through the *p* at many times
1Pe 1:10 Concerning this salvation, the *p,*
2Pe 1:19 word of the *p* made more certain,

PROSPER (PROSPERITY PROSPERS)
Pr 28:25 he who trusts in the LORD will *p.*

PROSPERITY (PROSPER)
Ps 73: 3 when I saw the *p* of the wicked.
Pr 13:21 but *p* is the reward of the righteous.

PROSPERS (PROSPER)
Ps 1: 3 Whatever he does *p.*

PROSTITUTE (PROSTITUTES)
1Co 6:15 of Christ and unite them with a *p?*

PROSTITUTES (PROSTITUTE)
Lk 15:30 property with *p* comes home,
1Co 6: 9 male *p* nor homosexual offenders

PROSTRATE
Dt 9:18 again I fell *p* before the LORD

PROTECT (PROTECTS)
Ps 32: 7 you will *p* me from trouble
Pr 2:11 Discretion will *p* you,
Jn 17:11 *p* them by the power of your name

PROTECTS (PROTECT)
1Co 13: 7 It always *p,* always trusts,

PROUD (PRIDE)
Pr 16: 5 The LORD detests all the *p*
Ro 12:16 Do not be *p,* but be willing
1Co 13: 4 it does not boast, it is not *p.*

PROVE
Ac 26:20 *p* their repentance by their deeds.
1Co 4: 2 been given a trust must *p* faithful.

PROVIDE (PROVIDED PROVIDES)
Ge 22: 8 "God himself will *p* the lamb
Isa 43:20 because I *p* water in the desert
1Ti 5: 8 If anyone does not *p*

PROVIDED (PROVIDE)
Jnh 1:17 But the LORD *p* a great fish
4: 6 Then the LORD God *p* a vine
4: 7 dawn the next day God *p* a worm,
4: 8 God *p* a scorching east wind,

PROVIDES (PROVIDE)
1Ti 6:17 who richly *p* us with everything
1Pe 4:11 it with the strength God *p,*

PROVOKED
Ecc 7: 9 Do not be quickly *p* in your spirit,

PRUDENT
Pr 14:15 a *p* man gives thought to his steps.
19:14 but a *p* wife is from the LORD.
Am 5:13 Therefore the *p* man keeps quiet

PRUNING
Isa 2: 4 and their spears into *p* hooks.
Joel 3:10 and your *p* hooks into spears.

PSALMS
Eph 5:19 Speak to one another with *p,*
Col 3:16 and as you sing *p,* hymns

PUBLICLY
Ac 20:20 have taught you *p* and from house
1Ti 5:20 Those who sin are to be rebuked *p,*

PUFFS
1Co 8: 1 Knowledge *p* up, but love builds up

PULLING
2Co 10: 8 building you up rather than *p* you

PUNISH (PUNISHED PUNISHES)
Ex 32:34 I will *p* them for their sin."
Pr 23:13 if you *p* him with the rod, he will
Isa 13:11 I will *p* the world for its evil,
1Pe 2:14 by him to *p* those who do wrong

PUNISHED (PUNISH)
La 3:39 complain when *p* for his sins?
2Th 1: 9 be *p* with everlasting destruction
Heb 10:29 to be *p* who has trampled the Son

PUNISHES (PUNISH)
Heb 12: 6 and he *p* everyone he accepts

PURE (PURIFIES PURIFY PURITY)
2Sa 22:27 to the *p* you show yourself *p,*
Ps 24: 4 who has clean hands and a *p* heart,
51:10 Create in me a *p* heart, O God,
119: 9 can a young man keep his way *p?*
Pr 20: 9 can say, "I have kept my heart *p;*
Isa 52:11 Come out from it and be *p,*
Hab 1:13 Your eyes are too *p* to look on evil;
Mt 5: 8 Blessed are the *p* in heart,
2Co 11: 2 I might present you as a *p* virgin
Php 4: 8 whatever is *p,* whatever is lovely,
1Ti 5:22 Keep yourself *p.*
Tit 1:15 To the *p,* all things are *p,*
2: 5 to be self-controlled and *p,*
Heb 13: 4 and the marriage bed kept *p,*
1Jn 3: 3 him purifies himself, just as he is *p.*

PURGE
Pr 20:30 and beatings *p* the inmost being.

PURIFIES* (PURE)
1Jn 1: 7 of Jesus, his Son, *p* us from all sin.
3: 3 who has this hope in him *p* himself,

PURIFY (PURE)
Tit 2:14 to *p* for himself a people that are
1Jn 1: 9 and *p* us from all unrighteousness.

PURITY (PURE)
2Co 6: 6 in *p,* understanding, patience
1Ti 4:12 in life, in love, in faith and in *p.*

PURPOSE
Pr 19:21 but it is the LORD's *p* that prevails
Isa 55:11 and achieve the *p* for which I sent it
Ro 8:28 have been called according to his *p.*
Php 2: 2 love, being one in spirit and *p.*

PURSES
Lk 12:33 Provide *p* for yourselves that will

PURSUE
Ps 34:14 seek peace and *p* it.
2Ti 2:22 and *p* righteousness, faith,
1Pe 3:11 he must seek peace and *p* it.

QUALITIES (QUALITY)
2Pe 1: 8 For if you possess these *q*

QUALITY (QUALITIES)
1Co 3:13 and the fire will test the *q*

QUARREL (QUARRELSOME)
Pr 15:18 but a patient man calms a *q*.
17:14 Starting a *q* is like breaching a dam;
17:19 He who loves a *q* loves sin;
2Ti 2:24 And the Lord's servant must not *q*;

QUARRELSOME (QUARREL)
Pr 19:13 a *q* wife is like a constant dripping.
1Ti 3: 3 not violent but gentle, not *q*,

QUICK-TEMPERED
Tit 1: 7 not *q*, not given to drunkenness,

QUIET (QUIETNESS)
Ps 23: 2 he leads me beside *q* waters,
Zep 3:17 he will *q* you with his love,
Lk 19:40 he replied, "if they keep *q*,
1Ti 2: 2 we may live peaceful and *q* lives
1Pe 3: 4 beauty of a gentle and *q* spirit,

QUIETNESS (QUIET)
Isa 30:15 in *q* and trust is your strength,
32:17 the effect of righteousness will be *q*
1Ti 2:11 A woman should learn in *q*

QUIVER
Ps 127: 5 whose *q* is full of them.

RACE
Ecc 9:11 The *r* is not to the swift
1Co 9:24 that in a *r* all the runners run,
2Ti 4: 7 I have finished the *r*, I have kept
Heb 12: 1 perseverance the *r* marked out

RACHEL
Daughter of Laban (Ge 29:16); wife of Jacob (Ge 29:28); bore two sons (Ge 30:22-24; 35:16-24; 46:19).

RADIANCE (RADIANT)
Heb 1: 3 The Son is the *r* of God's glory

RADIANT (RADIANCE)
Ex 34:29 he was not aware that his face was *r*
Ps 34: 5 Those who look to him are *r*;
SS 5:10 *Beloved* My lover is *r* and ruddy,
Isa 60: 5 Then you will look and be *r*,
Eph 5:27 her to himself as a *r* church,

RAIN (RAINBOW)
Mt 5:45 and sends *r* on the righteous

RAINBOW (RAIN)
Ge 9:13 I have set my *r* in the clouds,

RAISED (RISE)
Ro 4:25 was *r* to life for our justification.
10: 9 in your heart that God *r* him
1Co 15: 4 that he was *r* on the third day

RAN (RUN)
Jnh 1: 3 But Jonah *r* away from the LORD

RANSOM
Mt 20:28 and to give his life as a *r* for many."
Heb 9:15 as a *r* to set them free

RAVENS
1Ki 17: 6 The *r* brought him bread
Lk 12:24 Consider the *r*: They do not sow

READ (READS)
Jos 8:34 Joshua *r* all the words of the law—
Ne 8: 8 They *r* from the Book of the Law
2Co 3: 2 known and *r* by everybody.

READS (READ)
Rev 1: 3 Blessed is the one who *r* the words

REAL (REALITY)
Jn 6:55 is *r* food and my blood is *r* drink.

REALITY* (REAL)
Col 2:17 the *r*, however, is found in Christ.

REAP (REAPS)
Job 4: 8 and those who sow trouble *r* it.
2Co 9: 6 generously will also *r* generously.

REAPS (REAP)
Gal 6: 7 A man *r* what he sows.

REASON
Isa 1:18 "Come now, let us *r* together,"
1Pe 3:15 to give the *r* for the hope that you

REBEKAH
Sister of Laban, secured as bride for Isaac (Ge 24). Mother of Esau and Jacob (Ge 25:19-26). Taken by Abimelech as sister of Isaac; returned (Ge 26:1-11). Encouraged Jacob to trick Isaac out of blessing (Ge 27:1-17).

REBEL
Mt 10:21 children will *r* against their parents

REBUKE (REBUKED REBUKING)
Pr 9: 8 *r* a wise man and he will love you.
27: 5 Better is open *r*
Lk 17: 3 "If your brother sins, *r* him,
2Ti 4: 2 correct, *r* and encourage—
Rev 3:19 Those whom I love I *r*

REBUKED (REBUKE)
1Ti 5:20 Those who sin are to be *r* publicly,

REBUKING (REBUKE)
2Ti 3:16 *r*, correcting and training

RECEIVE (RECEIVED RECEIVES)
Ac 1: 8 you will *r* power when the Holy
20:35 'It is more blessed to give than to *r*
2Co 6:17 and I will *r* you."
Rev 4:11 to *r* glory and honor and power,

RECEIVED (RECEIVE)
Mt 6: 2 they have *r* their reward in full.
10: 8 Freely you have *r*, freely give.
1Co 11:23 For I *r* from the Lord what I
Col 2: 6 just as you *r* Christ Jesus as Lord,
1Pe 4:10 should use whatever gift he has *r*

RECEIVES (RECEIVE)
Mt 7: 8 everyone who asks *r*; he who seeks
10:40 he who *r* me *r* the one who sent me.
Ac 10:43 believes in him *r* forgiveness of sins

RECKONING
Isa 10: 3 What will you do on the day of *r*,

RECOGNIZE (RECOGNIZED)
Mt 7:16 By their fruit you will *r* them.

RECOGNIZED (RECOGNIZE)
Mt 12:33 for a tree is *r* by its fruit.
Ro 7:13 in order that sin might be *r* as sin,

RECOMPENSE
Isa 40:10 and his *r* accompanies him.

RECONCILE (RECONCILED RECONCILIATION)
Eph 2:16 in this one body to *r* both of them

RECONCILED (RECONCILE)
Mt 5:24 First go and be *r* to your brother;
Ro 5:10 we were *r* to him through the death
2Co 5:18 who *r* us to himself through Christ

RECONCILIATION* (RECONCILE)
Ro 5:11 whom we have now received *r*.
11:15 For if their rejection is the *r*
2Co 5:18 and gave us the ministry of *r*:
5:19 committed to us the message of *r*.

RECORD
Ps 130: 3 If you, O LORD, kept a *r* of sins,

RED
Isa 1:18 though they are *r* as crimson,

REDEEM (KINSMAN-REDEEMER REDEEMED REDEEMER REDEMPTION)
2Sa 7:23 on earth that God went out to *r*
Ps 49: 7 No man can *r* the life of another
Gal 4: 5 under law, to *r* those under law,

REDEEMED (REDEEM)
Gal 3:13 Christ *r* us from the curse
1Pe 1:18 or gold that you were *r*

REDEEMER (REDEEM)
Job 19:25 I know that my *R* lives,

REDEMPTION (REDEEM)
Ps 130: 7 and with him is full *r*.
Lk 21:28 because your *r* is drawing near."
Ro 8:23 as sons, the *r* of our bodies.
Eph 1: 7 In him we have *r* through his blood
Col 1:14 in whom we have *r*, the forgiveness
Heb 9:12 having obtained eternal *r*.

REFLECT
2Co 3:18 unveiled faces all *r* the Lord's

REFUGE
Nu 35:11 towns to be your cities of *r*,
Dt 33:27 The eternal God is your *r*,
Ru 2:12 wings you have come to take *r*."

Ps 46: 1 God is our *r* and strength,
91: 2 "He is my *r* and my fortress,

REHOBOAM

Son of Solomon (1Ki 11:43; 1Ch 3:10). Harsh treatment of subjects caused divided kingdom (1Ki 12:1-24; 14:21-31; 2Ch 10-12).

REIGN

Ex 15:18 The LORD will *r*
Ro 6:12 Therefore do not let sin *r*
1Co 15:25 For he must *r* until he has put all
2Ti 2:12 we will also *r* with him.
Rev 20: 6 will *r* with him for a thousand years

REJECTED (REJECTS)

Ps 118: 22 The stone the builders *r*
Isa 53: 3 He was despised and *r* by men,
1Ti 4: 4 nothing is to be *r* if it is received
1Pe 2: 4 *r* by men but chosen by God
2: 7 "The stone the builders *r*

REJECTS (REJECTED)

Lk 10:16 but he who *r* me *r* him who sent me
Jn 3:36 whoever *r* the Son will not see life,

REJOICE (JOY)

Ps 2:11 and *r* with trembling.
66: 6 come, let us *r* in him.
118: 24 let us *r* and be glad in it.
Pr 5:18 may you *r* in the wife of your youth
Lk 10:20 but *r* that your names are written
15: 6 '*R* with me; I have found my lost
Ro 12:15 Rejoice with those who *r;* mourn
Php 4: 4 *R* in the Lord always.

REJOICES (JOY)

Isa 61:10 my soul *r* in my God.
Lk 1:47 and my spirit *r* in God my Savior,
1Co 12:26 if one part is honored, every part *r*
13: 6 delight in evil but *r* with the truth.

REJOICING (JOY)

Ps 30: 5 but *r* comes in the morning.
Lk 15: 7 in the same way there will be more *r*
Ac 5:41 *r* because they had been counted

RELIABLE

2Ti 2: 2 witnesses entrust to *r* men who will

RELIGION

1Ti 5: 4 all to put their *r* into practice
Jas 1:27 *R* that God our Father accepts

REMAIN (REMAINS)

Nu 33:55 allow to *r* will become barbs
Jn 15: 7 If you *r* in me and my words
Ro 13: 8 Let no debt *r* outstanding,
1Co 13:13 And now these three *r:* faith,
2Ti 2:13 he will *r* faithful,

REMAINS (REMAIN)

Ps 146: 6 the LORD, who *r* faithful forever.
Heb 7: 3 Son of God he *r* a priest forever.

REMEMBER (REMEMBERS REMEMBRANCE)

Ex 20: 8 "*R* the Sabbath day
1Ch 16:12 *R* the wonders he has done,
Ecc 12: 1 *R* your Creator
Jer 31:34 and will *r* their sins no more."
Gal 2:10 we should continue to *r* the poor,
Php 1: 3 I thank my God every time I *r* you.
Heb 8:12 and will *r* their sins no more."

REMEMBERS (REMEMBER)

Ps 103: 14 he *r* that we are dust.
111: 5 he *r* his covenant forever.
Isa 43:25 and *r* your sins no more.

REMEMBRANCE (REMEMBER)

1Co 11:24 which is for you; do this in *r* of me

REMIND

Jn 14:26 will *r* you of everything I have said

REMOVED

Ps 30:11 you *r* my sackcloth and clothed me
103: 12 so far has he *r* our transgressions
Jn 20: 1 and saw that the stone had been *r*

RENEW (RENEWED RENEWING)

Ps 51:10 and *r* a steadfast spirit within me.
Isa 40:31 will *r* their strength.

RENEWED (RENEW)

Ps 103: 5 that your youth is *r* like the eagle's.
2Co 4:16 yet inwardly we are being *r* day

RENEWING (RENEW)

Ro 12: 2 transformed by the *r* of your mind.

RENOUNCE (RENOUNCES)

Da 4:27 *R* your sins by doing what is right,

RENOUNCES (RENOUNCE)

Pr 28:13 confesses and *r* them finds

RENOWN

Isa 63:12 to gain for himself everlasting *r,*
Jer 32:20 have gained the *r* that is still yours.

REPAID (PAY)

Lk 14:14 you will be *r* at the resurrection
Col 3:25 Anyone who does wrong will be *r*

REPAY (PAY)

Dt 32:35 It is mine to avenge; I will *r.*
Ru 2:12 May the LORD *r* you
Ps 116: 12 How can I *r* the LORD
Ro 12:19 "It is mine to avenge; I will *r,*"
1Pe 3: 9 Do not *r* evil with evil

REPENT (REPENTANCE REPENTS)

Job 42: 6 and *r* in dust and ashes."
Jer 15:19 "If you *r,* I will restore you
Mt 4:17 "*R,* for the kingdom of heaven is
Lk 13: 3 unless you *r,* you too will all perish.
Ac 2:38 Peter replied, "*R* and be baptized,
17:30 all people everywhere to *r.*

REPENTANCE (REPENT)

Lk 3: 8 Produce fruit in keeping with *r.*
5:32 call the righteous, but sinners to *r.*"
Ac 26:20 and prove their *r* by their deeds.
2Co 7:10 Godly sorrow brings *r* that leads

REPENTS (REPENT)

Lk 15:10 of God over one sinner who *r.*"
17: 3 rebuke him, and if he *r,* forgive him

REPROACH

1Ti 3: 2 Now the overseer must be above *r,*

REPUTATION

1Ti 3: 7 also have a good *r* with outsiders,

REQUESTS

Ps 20: 5 May the LORD grant all your *r.*
Php 4: 6 with thanksgiving, present your *r*

REQUIRE

Mic 6: 8 And what does the LORD *r* of you

RESCUE (RESCUES)

Da 6:20 been able to *r* you from the lions?"
2Pe 2: 9 how to *r* godly men from trials

RESCUES (RESCUE)

1Th 1:10 who *r* us from the coming wrath.

RESIST

Jas 4: 7 *R* the devil, and he will flee
1Pe 5: 9 *R* him, standing firm in the faith,

RESOLVED

Ps 17: 3 I have *r* that my mouth will not sin.
Da 1: 8 But Daniel *r* not to defile himself
1Co 2: 2 For I *r* to know nothing while I was

RESPECT (RESPECTABLE)

Lev 19: 3 " 'Each of you must *r* his mother
19:32 show *r* for the elderly and revere
Pr 11:16 A kindhearted woman gains *r,*
Mal 1: 6 where is the *r* due me?" says
1Th 4:12 so that your daily life may win the *r*
5:12 to *r* those who work hard
1Ti 3: 4 children obey him with proper *r.*
1Pe 2:17 Show proper *r* to everyone:
3: 7 them with *r* as the weaker partner

RESPECTABLE* (RESPECT)

1Ti 3: 2 self-controlled, *r,* hospitable,

REST

Ex 31:15 the seventh day is a Sabbath of *r,*
Ps 91: 1 will *r* in the shadow
Jer 6:16 and you will find *r* for your souls.
Mt 11:28 and burdened, and I will give you *r.*

RESTITUTION

Ex 22: 3 "A thief must certainly make *r,*

Lev 6: 5 He must make *r* in full, add a fifth

RESTORE (RESTORES)
Ps 51:12 *R* to me the joy of your salvation
Gal 6: 1 are spiritual should *r* him gently.

RESTORES (RESTORE)
Ps 23: 3 he *r* my soul.

RESURRECTION
Mt 22:30 At the *r* people will neither marry
Lk 14:14 repaid at the *r* of the righteous."
Jn 11:25 Jesus said to her, "I am the *r*
Ro 1: 4 Son of God by his *r* from the dead:
1Co 15:12 some of you say that there is no *r*
Php 3:10 power of his *r* and the fellowship
Rev 20: 5 This is the first *r*.

RETRIBUTION
Jer 51:56 For the LORD is a God of *r*;

RETURN
2Ch 30: 9 If you *r* to the LORD, then your
Ne 1: 9 but if you *r* to me and obey my
Isa 55:11 It will not *r* to me empty,
Hos 6: 1 "Come, let us *r* to the LORD.
Joel 2:12 "*r* to me with all your heart,

REVEALED (REVELATION)
Dt 29:29 but the things *r* belong to us
Isa 40: 5 the glory of the LORD will be *r*,
Mt 11:25 and *r* them to little children.
Ro 1:17 a righteousness from God is *r*,
8:18 with the glory that will be *r* in us.

REVELATION (REVEALED)
Gal 1:12 I received it by *r* from Jesus Christ.
Rev 1: 1 *r* of Jesus Christ, which God gave

REVENGE (VENGEANCE)
Lev 19:18 " 'Do not seek *r* or bear a grudge
Ro 12:19 Do not take *r*, my friends,

REVERE (REVERENCE)
Ps 33: 8 let all the people of the world *r* him

REVERENCE (REVERE)
Lev 19:30 and have *r* for my sanctuary.
Ps 5: 7 in *r* will I bow down
Col 3:22 of heart and *r* for the Lord.
1Pe 3: 2 when they see the purity and *r*

REVIVE (REVIVING)
Ps 85: 6 Will you not *r* us again,
Isa 57:15 to *r* the spirit of the lowly

REVIVING (REVIVE)
Ps 19: 7 *r* the soul.

REWARD (REWARDED)
Ps 19:11 in keeping them there is great *r*.
127: 3 children a *r* from him.
Pr 19:17 he will *r* him for what he has done.
25:22 and the LORD will *r* you.
31:31 Give her the *r* she has earned,
Jer 17:10 to *r* a man according to his conduct
Mt 5:12 because great is your *r* in heaven,
6: 5 they have received their *r* in full.
16:27 and then he will *r* each person
1Co 3:14 built survives, he will receive his *r*.
Rev 22:12 I am coming soon! My *r* is with me

REWARDED (REWARD)
Ru 2:12 May you be richly *r* by the LORD,
Ps 18:24 The LORD has *r* me according
Pr 14:14 and the good man *r* for his.
1Co 3: 8 and each will be *r* according

RICH (RICHES)
Pr 23: 4 Do not wear yourself out to get *r*;
Jer 9:23 or the *r* man boast of his riches,
Mt 19:23 it is hard for a *r* man
2Co 6:10 yet making many *r*; having nothing
8: 9 he was *r*, yet for your sakes he
1Ti 6:17 Command those who are *r*

RICHES (RICH)
Ps 119: 14 as one rejoices in great *r*.
Pr 30: 8 give me neither poverty nor *r*,
Isa 10: 3 Where will you leave your *r*?
Ro 9:23 to make the *r* of his glory known
11:33 the depth of the *r* of the wisdom
Eph 2: 7 he might show the incomparable *r*
3: 8 to the Gentiles the unsearchable *r*
Col 1:27 among the Gentiles the glorious *r*

RID
Ge 21:10 "Get *r* of that slave woman
1Co 5: 7 Get *r* of the old yeast that you may
Gal 4:30 "Get *r* of the slave woman

RIGHT (RIGHTS)
Ge 18:25 the Judge of all the earth do *r*?"
Ex 15:26 and do what is *r* in his eyes,
Dt 5:32 do not turn aside to the *r*
Ps 16: 8 Because he is at my *r* hand,
19: 8 The precepts of the LORD are *r*,
63: 8 your *r* hand upholds me.
110: 1 "Sit at my *r* hand
Pr 4:27 Do not swerve to the *r* or the left;
14:12 There is a way that seems *r*
Isa 1:17 learn to do *r*!
Jer 23: 5 and do what is just and *r* in the land
Hos 14: 9 The ways of the LORD are *r*;
Mt 6: 3 know what your *r* hand is doing,
Jn 1:12 he gave the *r* to become children
Ro 9:21 Does not the potter have the *r*
12:17 careful to do what is *r* in the eyes
Eph 1:20 and seated him at his *r* hand
Php 4: 8 whatever is *r*, whatever is pure,
2Th 3:13 never tire of doing what is *r*.

RIGHTEOUS (RIGHTEOUSNESS)
Ps 34:15 The eyes of the LORD are on the *r*
37:25 yet I have never seen the *r* forsaken
119:137 *R* are you, O LORD,
143: 2 for no one living is *r* before you.
Pr 3:33 but he blesses the home of the *r*.
11:30 The fruit of the *r* is a tree of life,
18:10 the *r* run to it and are safe.
Isa 64: 6 and all our *r* acts are like filthy rags
Hab 2: 4 but the *r* will live by his faith—
Mt 5:45 rain on the *r* and the unrighteous.
9:13 For I have not come to call the *r*,
13:49 and separate the wicked from the *r*
25:46 to eternal punishment, but the *r*
Ro 1:17 as it is written: "The *r* will live
3:10 "There is no one *r*, not even one;
1Ti 1: 9 that law is made not for the *r*
1Pe 3:18 the *r* for the unrighteous,
1Jn 3: 7 does what is right is *r*, just as he is *r*.
Rev 19: 8 stands for the *r* acts of the saints.)

RIGHTEOUSNESS (RIGHTEOUS)
Ge 15: 6 and he credited it to him as *r*.
1Sa 26:23 LORD rewards every man for his *r*
Ps 9: 8 He will judge the world in *r*;
23: 3 He guides me in paths of *r*
45: 7 You love *r* and hate wickedness;
85:10 *r* and peace kiss each other.
89:14 *R* and justice are the foundation
111: 3 and his *r* endures forever.
Pr 14:34 *R* exalts a nation,
21:21 He who pursues *r* and love
Isa 5:16 will show himself holy by his *r*.
59:17 He put on *r* as his breastplate,
Eze 18:20 The *r* of the righteous man will be
Da 9:24 to bring in everlasting *r*,
12: 3 and those who lead many to *r*,
Mal 4: 2 the sun of *r* will rise with healing
Mt 5: 6 those who hunger and thirst for *r*,
5:20 unless your *r* surpasses that
6:33 But seek first his kingdom and his *r*
Ro 4: 3 and it was credited to him as *r*."
4: 9 faith was credited to him as *r*.
6:13 body to him as instruments of *r*.
2Co 5:21 that in him we might become the *r*
Gal 2:21 for if *r* could be gained
3: 6 and it was credited to him as *r*."
Eph 6:14 with the breastplate of *r* in place,
Php 3: 9 not having a *r* of my own that
2Ti 3:16 correcting and training in *r*,
4: 8 is in store for me the crown of *r*,
Heb 11: 7 became heir of the *r* that comes

2Pe 2:21 not to have known the way of *r*,

RIGHTS (RIGHT)
La 3:35 to deny a man his *r*
Gal 4: 5 that we might receive the full *r*

RISE (RAISED)
Isa 26:19 their bodies will *r*.
Mt 27:63 'After three days I will *r* again.'
Jn 5:29 those who have done good will *r*
1Th 4:16 and the dead in Christ will *r* first.

ROAD
Mt 7:13 and broad is the *r* that leads

ROBBERS
Jer 7:11 become a den of *r* to you?
Mk 15:27 They crucified two *r* with him,
Lk 19:46 but you have made it 'a den of *r*.' "
Jn 10: 8 came before me were thieves and *r*,

ROCK
Ps 18: 2 The LORD is my *r*, my fortress
40: 2 he set my feet on a *r*
Mt 7:24 man who built his house on the *r*.
16:18 and on this *r* I will build my church
Ro 9:33 and a *r* that makes them fall,
1Co 10: 4 the spiritual *r* that accompanied

ROD
Ps 23: 4 your *r* and your staff,
Pr 13:24 He who spares the *r* hates his son,
23:13 if you punish him with the *r*,

ROOM (ROOMS)
Mt 6: 6 But when you pray, go into your *r*,
Lk 2: 7 there was no *r* for them in the inn.
Jn 21:25 the whole world would not have *r*

ROOMS (ROOM)
Jn 14: 2 In my Father's house are many *r*;

ROOT
Isa 53: 2 and like a *r* out of dry ground.
1Ti 6:10 of money is a *r* of all kinds of evil.

ROYAL
Jas 2: 8 If you really keep the *r* law found
1Pe 2: 9 a *r* priesthood, a holy nation,

RUBBISH*
Php 3: 8 I consider them *r*, that I may gain

RUDE*
1Co 13: 5 It is not *r*, it is not self-seeking,

RUIN (RUINS)
Pr 18:24 many companions may come to *r*,
1Ti 6: 9 desires that plunge men into *r*

RUINS (RUIN)
Pr 19: 3 A man's own folly *r* his life,

2Ti 2:14 and only *r* those who listen.

RULE (RULER RULERS RULES)
1Sa 12:12 'No, we want a king to *r* over us'—
Ps 2: 9 You will *r* them with an iron
119:133 let no sin *r* over me.
Zec 9:10 His *r* will extend from sea to sea
Col 3:15 the peace of Christ *r* in your hearts,
Rev 2:27 He will *r* them with an iron scepter;

RULER (RULE)
Ps 8: 6 You made him *r* over the works
Eph 2: 2 of the *r* of the kingdom of the air,
1Ti 6:15 God, the blessed and only *R*,

RULERS (RULE)
Ps 2: 2 and the *r* gather together
Col 1:16 or powers or *r* or authorities;

RULES (RULE)
Ps 103: 19 and his kingdom *r* over all.
Lk 22:26 one who *r* like the one who serves.
2Ti 2: 5 he competes according to the *r*.

RUMORS
Mt 24: 6 You will hear of wars and *r* of wars,

RUN (RAN)
Isa 40:31 they will *r* and not grow weary,
1Co 9:24 *R* in such a way as to get the prize.
Heb 12: 1 let us *r* with perseverance the race

RUST
Mt 6:19 where moth and *r* destroy,

RUTH*
Moabitess; widow who went to Bethlehem with mother-in-law Naomi (Ru 1). Gleaned in field of Boaz; shown favor (Ru 2). Proposed marriage to Boaz (Ru 3). Married (Ru 4:1-12); bore Obed, ancestor of David (Ru 4:13-22), Jesus (Mt 1:5).

SABBATH
Ex 20: 8 "Remember the *S* day
Dt 5:12 "Observe the *S* day
Col 2:16 a New Moon celebration or a *S* day

SACKCLOTH
Mt 11:21 would have repented long ago in *s*

SACRED
Mt 7: 6 "Do not give dogs what is *s*;
1Co 3:17 for God's temple is *s*, and you are

SACRIFICE (SACRIFICED SACRIFICES)
Ge 22: 2 *S* him there as a burnt offering
Ex 12:27 'It is the Passover *s* to the LORD,
1Sa 15:22 To obey is better than *s*,
Hos 6: 6 For I desire mercy, not *s*,
Mt 9:13 this means: 'I desire mercy, not *s*.'
Heb 9:26 away with sin by the *s* of himself.
13:15 offer to God a *s* of praise—
1Jn 2: 2 He is the atoning *s* for our sins,

SACRIFICED (SACRIFICE)
1Co 5: 7 our Passover lamb, has been *s*.
1Co 8: 1 Now about food *s* to idols:
Heb 9:28 so Christ was *s* once

SACRIFICES (SACRIFICE)
Ps 51:17 The *s* of God are a broken spirit;
Ro 12: 1 to offer your bodies as living *s*,

SADDUCEES
Mk 12:18 *S*, who say there is no resurrection,

SAFE (SAVE)
Ps 37: 3 in the land and enjoy *s* pasture.
Pr 18:10 the righteous run to it and are *s*.

SAFETY (SAVE)
Ps 4: 8 make me dwell in *s*.
1Th 5: 3 people are saying, "Peace and *s*,"

SAINTS
Ps 116: 15 is the death of his *s*.
Ro 8:27 intercedes for the *s* in accordance
Eph 1:18 of his glorious inheritance in the *s*,
6:18 always keep on praying for all the *s*
Rev 5: 8 which are the prayers of the *s*.
19: 8 for the righteous acts of the *s*.)

SAKE
Ps 44:22 Yet for your *s* we face death all day
Php 3: 7 loss for the *s* of Christ.
Heb 11:26 He regarded disgrace for the *s*

SALT
Ge 19:26 and she became a pillar of *s*.
Mt 5:13 "You are the *s* of the earth.

SALVATION (SAVE)
Ex 15: 2 he has become my *s*.
1Ch 16:23 proclaim his *s* day after day.
Ps 27: 1 The LORD is my light and my *s*—
51:12 Restore to me the joy of your *s*
62: 2 He alone is my rock and my *s*;
85: 9 Surely his *s* is near those who fear
96: 2 proclaim his *s* day after day.
Isa 25: 9 let us rejoice and be glad in his *s*."
45:17 the LORD with an everlasting *s*;
51: 6 But my *s* will last forever,
59:17 and the helmet of *s* on his head;
61:10 me with garments of *s*
Jnh 2: 9 *S* comes from the LORD."
Zec 9: 9 righteous and having *s*,
Lk 2:30 For my eyes have seen your *s*,
Jn 4:22 for *s* is from the Jews.
Ac 4:12 *S* is found in no one else,
13:47 that you may bring *s* to the ends
Ro 11:11 *s* has come to the Gentiles
2Co 7:10 brings repentance that leads to *s*
Eph 6:17 Take the helmet of *s* and the sword
Php 2:12 to work out your *s* with fear
1Th 5: 8 and the hope of *s* as a helmet.
2Ti 3:15 wise for *s* through faith
Heb 2: 3 escape if we ignore such a great *s*?

Heb 6: 9 case—things that accompany *s.*
1Pe 1:10 Concerning this *s,* the prophets,
2: 2 by it you may grow up in your *s,*

SAMARITAN
Lk 10:33 But a *S,* as he traveled, came where

SAMSON
Danite judge. Birth promised (Jdg 13). Married to Philistine (Jdg 14). Vengeance on Philistines (Jdg 15). Betrayed by Delilah (Jdg 16:1-22). Death (Jdg 16:23-31). Feats of strength: killed lion (Jdg 14:6), 30 Philistines (Jdg 14:19), 1,000 Philistines with jawbone (Jdg 15:13-17), carried off gates of Gaza (Jdg 16:3), pushed down temple of Dagon (Jdg 16:25-30).

SAMUEL
Ephraimite judge and prophet (Heb 11:32). Birth prayed for (1Sa 1:10-18). Dedicated to temple by Hannah (1Sa 1:21-28). Raised by Eli (1Sa 2:11, 18-26). Called as prophet (1Sa 3). Led Israel to victory over Philistines (1Sa 7). Asked by Israel for a king (1Sa 8). Anointed Saul as king (1Sa 9-10). Farewell speech (1Sa 12). Rebuked Saul for sacrifice (1Sa 13). Announced rejection of Saul (1Sa 15). Anointed David as king (1Sa 16). Protected David from Saul (1Sa 19:18-24). Death (1Sa 25:1). Returned from dead to condemn Saul (1Sa 28).

SANCTIFIED (SANCTIFY)
Ac 20:32 among all those who are *s.*
Ro 15:16 to God, *s* by the Holy Spirit.
1Co 6:11 But you were washed, you were *s,*
7:14 and the unbelieving wife has been *s*
Heb 10:29 blood of the covenant that *s* him,

SANCTIFY (SANCTIFIED SANCTIFYING)
1Th 5:23 *s* you through and through.

SANCTIFYING (SANCTIFY)
2Th 2:13 through the *s* work of the Spirit

SANCTUARY
Ex 25: 8 "Then have them make a *s* for me,

SAND
Ge 22:17 and as the *s* on the seashore.
Mt 7:26 man who built his house on *s.*

SANDALS
Ex 3: 5 off your *s,* for the place where you
Jos 5:15 off your *s,* for the place where you

SANG (SING)
Job 38: 7 while the morning stars *s* together
Rev 5: 9 And they *s* a new song:

SARAH
. Wife of Abraham, originally named Sarai; barren (Ge 11:29-31; 1Pe 3:6). Taken by Pharaoh as Abraham's sister; returned (Ge 12:10-20). Gave Hagar to Abraham; sent her away in pregnancy (Ge 16). Name changed; Isaac promised (Ge 17:15-21; 18:10-15; Heb 11:11). Taken by Abimelech as Abraham's sister; returned (Ge 20). Isaac born; Hagar and Ishmael sent away (Ge 21:1-21; Gal 4:21-31). Death (Ge 23).

SATAN
Job 1: 6 and *S* also came with them.
Zec 3: 2 said to *S,* "The LORD rebuke you,
Mk 4:15 *S* comes and takes away the word
2Co 11:14 for *S* himself masquerades
12: 7 a messenger of *S,* to torment me.
Rev 12: 9 serpent called the devil, or *S,*
20: 2 or *S,* and bound him for a thousand
20: 7 *S* will be released from his prison

SATISFIED (SATISFY)
Isa 53:11 he will see the light ⌞of life⌟ and be *s*

SATISFIES (SATISFY)
Ps 103: 5 who *s* your desires with good things,

SATISFY (SATISFIED SATISFIES)
Isa 55: 2 and your labor on what does not *s?*

SAUL
1. Benjamite; anointed by Samuel as first king of Israel (1Sa 9-10). Defeated Ammonites (1Sa 11). Rebuked for offering sacrifice (1Sa 13:1-15). Defeated Philistines (1Sa 14). Rejected as king for failing to annihilate Amalekites (1Sa 15). Soothed from evil spirit by David (1Sa 16:14-23). Sent David against Goliath (1Sa 17). Jealousy and attempted murder of David (1Sa 18:1-11). Gave David Michal as wife (1Sa 18:12-30). Second attempt to kill David (1Sa 19). Anger at Jonathan (1Sa 20:26-34). Pursued David: killed priests at Nob (1Sa 22), went to Keilah and Ziph (1Sa 23), life spared by David at En Gedi (1Sa 24) and in his tent (1Sa 26). Rebuked by Samuel's spirit for consulting witch at Endor (1Sa 28). Wounded by Philistines; took his own life (1Sa 31; 1Ch 10).
2. See PAUL

SAVE (SAFE SAFETY SALVATION SAVED SAVIOR)
Isa 63: 1 mighty to *s.*"
Da 3:17 the God we serve is able to *s* us
Zep 3:17 he is mighty to *s.*
Mt 1:21 he will *s* his people from their sins
16:25 wants to *s* his life will lose it,
Lk 19:10 to seek and to *s* what was lost."
Jn 3:17 but to *s* the world through him.
1Ti 1:15 came into the world to *s* sinners—
Jas 5:20 of his way will *s* him from death

SAVED (SAVE)
Ps 34: 6 he *s* him out of all his troubles.
Isa 45:22 "Turn to me and be *s,*
Joel 2:32 on the name of the LORD will be *s;*
Mk 13:13 firm to the end will be *s.*
16:16 believes and is baptized will be *s,*
Jn 10: 9 enters through me will be *s.*
Ac 4:12 to men by which we must be *s.*"
16:30 do to be *s?*" They replied,
Ro 9:27 only the remnant will be *s.*
10: 9 him from the dead, you will be *s.*
1Co 3:15 will suffer loss; he himself will be *s,*
15: 2 By this gospel you are *s,*
Eph 2: 5 it is by grace you have been *s.*
2: 8 For it is by grace you have been *s,*
1Ti 2: 4 who wants all men to be *s*

SAVIOR (SAVE)
Ps 89:26 my God, the Rock my *S.*'
Isa 43:11 and apart from me there is no *s.*
Hos 13: 4 no *S* except me.
Lk 1:47 and my spirit rejoices in God my *S,*
2:11 of David a *S* has been born to you;
Jn 4:42 know that this man really is the *S*
Eph 5:23 his body, of which he is the *S.*
1Ti 4:10 who is the *S* of all men,
Tit 2:10 about God our *S* attractive.
2:13 appearing of our great God and *S,*
3: 4 and love of God our *S* appeared,
1Jn 4:14 Son to be the *S* of the world.
Jude :25 to the only God our *S* be glory,

SCALES
Lev 19:36 Use honest *s* and honest weights,
Da 5:27 You have been weighed on the *s*

SCAPEGOAT (GOAT)
Lev 16:10 by sending it into the desert as a *s.*

SCARLET
Isa 1:18 "Though your sins are like *s,*

SCATTERED
Jer 31:10 'He who *s* Israel will gather them
Ac 8: 4 who had been *s* preached the word

SCEPTER
Rev 19:15 "He will rule them with an iron *s.*"

SCHEMES
2Co 2:11 For we are not unaware of his *s.*
Eph 6:11 stand against the devil's *s.*

SCOFFERS
2Pe 3: 3 that in the last days *s* will come,

SCORPION
Rev 9: 5 sting of a *s* when it strikes a man.

SCRIPTURE (SCRIPTURES)
Jn 10:35 and the *S* cannot be broken—
1Ti 4:13 yourself to the public reading of *S,*
2Ti 3:16 All *S* is God-breathed
2Pe 1:20 that no prophecy of *S* came about

SCRIPTURES (SCRIPTURE)
Lk 24:27 said in all the *S* concerning himself.
Jn 5:39 These are the *S* that testify about
Ac 17:11 examined the *S* every day to see

SCROLL
Eze 3: 1 eat what is before you, eat this *s;*

SEA
Ex 14:16 go through the *s* on dry ground.
Isa 57:20 the wicked are like the tossing *s,*

Mic 7:19 iniquities into the depths of the *s.*
Jas 1: 6 who doubts is like a wave of the *s,*
Rev 13: 1 I saw a beast coming out of the *s.*

SEAL (SEALS)
Jn 6:27 God the Father has placed his *s*
2Co 1:22 set his *s* of ownership on us,
Eph 1:13 you were marked in him with a *s,*

SEALS (SEAL)
Rev 5: 2 "Who is worthy to break the *s*
6: 1 opened the first of the seven *s.*

SEARCH (SEARCHED SEARCHES SEARCHING)
Ps 4: 4 *s* your hearts and be silent.
139: 23 *S* me, O God, and know my heart;
Pr 2: 4 and *s* for it as for hidden treasure,
Jer 17:10 "I the LORD *s* the heart
Eze 34:16 I will *s* for the lost and bring back
Lk 15: 8 and *s* carefully until she finds it?

SEARCHED (SEARCH)
Ps 139: 1 O LORD, you have *s* me

SEARCHES (SEARCH)
Ro 8:27 And he who *s* our hearts knows
1Co 2:10 The Spirit *s* all things,

SEARCHING (SEARCH)
Am 8:12 *s* for the word of the LORD,

SEARED
1Ti 4: 2 whose consciences have been *s*

SEASON
2Ti 4: 2 be prepared in *s* and out of *s;*

SEAT (SEATED SEATS)
Ps 1: 1 or sit in the *s* of mockers.
Da 7: 9 and the Ancient of Days took his *s.*
2Co 5:10 before the judgment *s* of Christ,

SEATED (SEAT)
Ps 47: 8 God is *s* on his holy throne.
Isa 6: 1 I saw the Lord *s* on a throne,
Col 3: 1 where Christ is *s* at the right hand

SEATS (SEAT)
Lk 11:43 you love the most important *s*

SECRET (SECRETS)
Dt 29:29 The *s* things belong
Jdg 16: 6 Tell me the *s* of your great strength
Ps 90: 8 our *s* sins in the light
Pr 11:13 but a trustworthy man keeps a *s.*
Mt 6: 4 so that your giving may be in *s.*
2Co 4: 2 we have renounced *s* and shameful
Php 4:12 I have learned the *s*

SECRETS (SECRET)
Ps 44:21 since he knows the *s* of the heart?
1Co 14:25 the *s* of his heart will be laid bare.

SECURE (SECURITY)
Ps 112: 8 His heart is *s,* he will have no fear;
Heb 6:19 an anchor for the soul, firm and *s.*

SECURITY (SECURE)
Job 31:24 or said to pure gold, 'You are my *s,'*

SEED (SEEDS)
Lk 8:11 of the parable: The *s* is the word
1Co 3: 6 I planted the *s,* Apollos watered it,
2Co 9:10 he who supplies *s* to the sower
Gal 3:29 then you are Abraham's *s,*
1Pe 1:23 not of perishable *s,*

SEEDS (SEED)
Jn 12:24 But if it dies, it produces many *s.*
Gal 3:16 Scripture does not say "and to *s,"*

SEEK (SEEKS SELF-SEEKING)
Dt 4:29 if from there you *s* the LORD your
1Ch 28: 9 If you *s* him, he will be found
2Ch 7:14 themselves and pray and *s* my face
Ps 119: 10 I *s* you with all my heart;
Isa 55: 6 *S* the LORD while he may be
65: 1 found by those who did not *s* me.
Mt 6:33 But *s* first his kingdom
Lk 19:10 For the Son of Man came to *s*
Ro 10:20 found by those who did not *s* me;
1Co 7:27 you married? Do not *s* a divorce.

SEEKS (SEEK)
Jn 4:23 the kind of worshipers the Father *s.*

SEER
1Sa 9: 9 of today used to be called a *s.)*

SELF-CONTROL (CONTROL)
1Co 7: 5 you because of your lack of *s.*
Gal 5:23 faithfulness, gentleness and *s.*
2Pe 1: 6 and to knowledge, *s;* and to *s,*

SELF-CONTROLLED* (CONTROL)
1Th 5: 6 are asleep, but let us be alert and *s.*
5: 8 let us be *s,* putting on faith and love
1Ti 3: 2 *s,* respectable, hospitable,
Tit 1: 8 who is *s,* upright, holy
2: 2 worthy of respect, *s,* and sound
2: 5 to be *s* and pure, to be busy at home
2: 6 encourage the young men to be *s.*
2:12 to live *s,* upright and godly lives
1Pe 1:13 prepare your minds for action; be *s;*
4: 7 and *s* so that you can pray.
5: 8 Be *s* and alert.

SELF-INDULGENCE
Mt 23:25 inside they are full of greed and *s.*

SELF-SEEKING (SEEK)
1Co 13: 5 it is not *s,* it is not easily angered,

SELFISH*
Ps 119: 36 and not toward *s* gain.
Pr 18: 1 An unfriendly man pursues *s* ends;
Gal 5:20 fits of rage, *s* ambition, dissensions,
Php 1:17 preach Christ out of *s* ambition,
2: 3 Do nothing out of *s* ambition
Jas 3:14 and *s* ambition in your hearts,
3:16 you have envy and *s* ambition,

SEND (SENDING SENT)
Isa 6: 8 *S* me!" He said, "Go and tell this
Mt 9:38 to *s* out workers into his harvest
Jn 16: 7 but if I go, I will *s* him to you.

SENDING (SEND)
Jn 20:21 Father has sent me, I am *s* you."

SENSES*
Lk 15:17 "When he came to his *s,* he said,
1Co 15:34 Come back to your *s* as you ought,
2Ti 2:26 and that they will come to their *s*

SENSUAL
Col 2:23 value in restraining *s* indulgence.

SENT (SEND)
Isa 55:11 achieve the purpose for which I *s* it.
Mt 10:40 me receives the one who *s* me.
Jn 4:34 "is to do the will of him who *s* me
Ro 10:15 can they preach unless they are *s?*
1Jn 4:10 but that he loved us and *s* his Son

SEPARATE (SEPARATED SEPARATES)
Mt 19: 6 has joined together, let man not *s."*
Ro 8:35 Who shall *s* us from the love
1Co 7:10 wife must not *s* from her husband.
2Co 6:17 and be *s,* says the Lord.

SEPARATED (SEPARATE)
Isa 59: 2 But your iniquities have *s*

SEPARATES (SEPARATE)
Pr 16:28 and a gossip *s* close friends.

SERPENT
Ge 3: 1 the *s* was more crafty than any
Rev 12: 9 that ancient *s* called the devil

SERVANT (SERVANTS)
1Sa 3:10 "Speak, for your *s* is listening."
Mt 20:26 great among you must be your *s,*
25:21 'Well done, good and faithful *s!*
Lk 16:13 "No *s* can serve two masters.
Php 2: 7 taking the very nature of a *s,*
2Ti 2:24 And the Lord's *s* must not quarrel;

SERVANTS (SERVANT)
Lk 17:10 should say, 'We are unworthy *s;*

Jn 15:15 longer call you *s,* because a servant

SERVE (SERVICE SERVING)
Dt 10:12 to *s* the LORD your God
Jos 22: 5 and to *s* him with all your heart
24:15 this day whom you will *s,*
Mt 4:10 Lord your God, and *s* him only.' "
6:24 "No one can *s* two masters.
20:28 but to *s,* and to give his life
Eph 6: 7 *S* wholeheartedly,

SERVICE (SERVE)
1Co 12: 5 There are different kinds of *s,*
Eph 4:12 God's people for works of *s,*

SERVING (SERVE)
Ro 12:11 your spiritual fervor, *s* the Lord.
Eph 6: 7 as if you were *s* the Lord, not men,
Col 3:24 It is the Lord Christ you are *s.*
2Ti 2: 4 No one *s* as a soldier gets involved

SEVEN (SEVENTH)
Ge 7: 2 Take with you *s* of every kind
Jos 6: 4 march around the city *s* times,
1Ki 19:18 Yet I reserve *s* thousand in Israel—
Pr 6:16 *s* that are detestable to him:
24:16 a righteous man falls *s* times,
Isa 4: 1 In that day *s* women
Da 9:25 comes, there will be *s* 'sevens,'
Mt 18:21 Up to *s* times?" Jesus answered,
Lk 11:26 takes *s* other spirits more wicked
Ro 11: 4 for myself *s* thousand who have not
Rev 1: 4 To the *s* churches in the province
6: 1 opened the first of the *s* seals.
8: 2 and to them were given *s* trumpets.
10: 4 And when the *s* thunders spoke,
15: 7 to the *s* angels *s* golden bowls filled

SEVENTH (SEVEN)
Ge 2: 2 By the *s* day God had finished
Ex 23:12 but on the *s* day do not work,

SEXUAL (SEXUALLY)
1Co 6:13 body is not meant for *s* immorality,
6:18 Flee from *s* immorality.
10: 8 should not commit *s* immorality,
Eph 5: 3 even a hint of *s* immorality,
1Th 4: 3 that you should avoid *s* immorality

SEXUALLY (SEXUAL)
1Co 5: 9 to associate with *s* immoral people
6:18 he who sins *s* sins against his own

SHADOW
Ps 23: 4 through the valley of the *s* of death,
36: 7 find refuge in the *s* of your wings.
Heb 10: 1 The law is only a *s*

SHALLUM
King of Israel (2Ki 15:10-16).

SHAME (ASHAMED)
Ps 34: 5 their faces are never covered with *s*
Pr 13:18 discipline comes to poverty and *s,*
Heb 12: 2 endured the cross, scorning its *s,*

SHARE (SHARED)
Ge 21:10 that slave woman's son will never *s*
Lk 3:11 "The man with two tunics should *s*
Gal 4:30 the slave woman's son will never *s*
6: 6 in the word must *s* all good things
Eph 4:28 something to *s* with those in need.
1Ti 6:18 and to be generous and willing to *s.*
Heb 12:10 that we may *s* in his holiness.
13:16 to do good and to *s* with others,

SHARED (SHARE)
Heb 2:14 he too *s* in their humanity so that

SHARON
SS 2: 1 I am a rose of *S,*

SHARPER*
Heb 4:12 *S* than any double-edged sword,

SHED (SHEDDING)
Ge 9: 6 by man shall his blood be *s;*
Col 1:20 through his blood, *s* on the cross.

SHEDDING (SHED)
Heb 9:22 without the *s* of blood there is no

SHEEP
Ps 100: 3 we are his people, the *s*
119:176 I have strayed like a lost *s.*
Isa 53: 6 We all, like *s,* have gone astray,
Jer 50: 6 "My people have been lost *s;*
Eze 34:11 I myself will search for my *s*
Mt 9:36 helpless, like *s* without a shepherd.
Jn 10: 3 He calls his own *s* by name
10:15 and I lay down my life for the *s.*
10:27 My *s* listen to my voice; I know
21:17 Jesus said, "Feed my *s.*
1Pe 2:25 For you were like *s* going astray,

SHELTER
Ps 61: 4 take refuge in the *s* of your wings.
91: 1 in the *s* of the Most High

SHEM
Son of Noah (Ge 5:32; 6:10). Blessed (Ge 9:26). Descendants (Ge 10:21-31; 11:10-32).

SHEPHERD (SHEPHERDS)
Ps 23: 1 LORD is my *s,* I shall not be in want.
Isa 40:11 He tends his flock like a *s:*
Jer 31:10 will watch over his flock like a *s.'*
Eze 34:12 As a *s* looks after his scattered
Zec 11:17 "Woe to the worthless *s,*
Mt 9:36 and helpless, like sheep without a *s.*
Jn 10:11 The good *s* lays down his life
10:16 there shall be one flock and one *s.*
1Pe 5: 4 And when the Chief *S* appears,

SHEPHERDS (SHEPHERD)
Jer 23: 1 "Woe to the *s* who are destroying
Lk 2: 8 there were *s* living out in the fields
Ac 20:28 Be *s* of the church of God,
1Pe 5: 2 Be *s* of God's flock that is

SHIELD
Ps 28: 7 LORD is my strength and my *s;*
Eph 6:16 to all this, take up the *s* of faith,

SHINE (SHONE)
Ps 4: 6 Let the light of your face *s* upon us,
80: 1 between the cherubim, *s* forth
Isa 60: 1 "Arise, *s,* for your light has come,
Da 12: 3 are wise will *s* like the brightness
Mt 5:16 let your light *s* before men,
13:43 the righteous will *s* like the sun
2Co 4: 6 made his light *s* in our hearts
Eph 5:14 and Christ will *s* on you."

SHIPWRECKED*
2Co 11:25 I was stoned, three times I was *s,*
1Ti 1:19 and so have *s* their faith.

SHONE (SHINE)
Mt 17: 2 His face *s* like the sun,
Lk 2: 9 glory of the Lord *s* around them,
Rev 21:11 It *s* with the glory of God,

SHORT
Isa 59: 1 of the LORD is not too *s* to save,
Ro 3:23 and fall *s* of the glory of God,

SHOULDERS
Isa 9: 6 and the government will be on his *s*
Lk 15: 5 he joyfully puts it on his *s*

SHOWED
1Jn 4: 9 This is how God *s* his love

SHREWD
Mt 10:16 Therefore be as *s* as snakes and

SHUN*
Job 28:28 and to *s* evil is understanding.' "
Pr 3: 7 fear the LORD and *s* evil.

SICK
Pr 13:12 Hope deferred makes the heart *s,*
Mt 9:12 who need a doctor, but the *s.*
25:36 I was *s* and you looked after me,
Jas 5:14 of you *s?* He should call the elders

SICKLE
Joel 3:13 Swing the *s,*

SIDE
Ps 91: 7 A thousand may fall at your *s,*
124: 1 If the LORD had not been on our *s*
2Ti 4:17 But the Lord stood at my *s*

SIGHT
Ps 90: 4 For a thousand years in your *s*

Ps 116: 15 Precious in the *s* of the LORD
2Co 5: 7 We live by faith, not by *s.*
1Pe 3: 4 which is of great worth in God's *s.*

SIGN (SIGNS)
Isa 7:14 the Lord himself will give you a *s:*

SIGNS (SIGN)
Mk 16:17 these *s* will accompany those who
Jn 20:30 Jesus did many other miraculous *s*

SILENT
Pr 17:28 a fool is thought wise if he keeps *s,*
Isa 53: 7 as a sheep before her shearers is *s,*
Hab 2:20 let all the earth be *s* before him."
1Co 14:34 women should remain *s*
1Ti 2:12 over a man; she must be *s.*

SILVER
Pr 25:11 is like apples of gold in settings of *s.*
Hag 2: 8 'The *s* is mine and the gold is mine,'
1Co 3:12 *s,* costly stones, wood, hay or straw

SIMON
1. See PETER.
2. Apostle, called the Zealot (Mt 10:4; Mk 3:18; Lk 6:15; Ac 1:13).
3. Samaritan sorcerer (Ac 8:9-24).

SIN (SINFUL SINNED SINNER SINNERS SINNING SINS)
Nu 5: 7 and must confess the *s* he has
32:23 be sure that your *s* will find you
Dt 24:16 each is to die for his own *s.*
1Ki 8:46 for there is no one who does not *s*
2Ch 7:14 and will forgive their *s* and will heal
Ps 4: 4 In your anger do not *s;*
32: 2 whose *s* the LORD does not count
32: 5 Then I acknowledged my *s* to you
51: 2 and cleanse me from my *s.*
66:18 If I had cherished *s* in my heart,
119: 11 that I might not *s* against you.
119:133 let no *s* rule over me.
Isa 6: 7 is taken away and your *s* atoned
Mic 7:18 who pardons *s* and forgives
Mt 18: 6 little ones who believe in me to *s,*
Jn 1:29 who takes away the *s* of the world!
8:34 everyone who sins is a slave to *s.*
Ro 5:12 as *s* entered the world
5:20 where *s* increased, grace increased
6:11 count yourselves dead to *s*
6:23 For the wages of *s* is death,
14:23 that does not come from faith is *s.*
2Co 5:21 God made him who had no *s* to be *s*
Gal 6: 1 if someone is caught in a *s,*
Heb 9:26 to do away with *s* by the sacrifice
11:25 the pleasures of *s* for a short time.
12: 1 and the *s* that so easily entangles,
1Pe 2:22 "He committed no *s,*
1Jn 1: 8 If we claim to be without *s,*
3: 4 in fact, *s* is lawlessness.
3: 5 And in him is no *s.*
3: 9 born of God will continue to *s,*
5:18 born of God does not continue to *s;*

SINCERE
Ro 12: 9 Love must be *s.*
Heb 10:22 near to God with a *s* heart

SINFUL (SIN)
Ps 51: 5 Surely I was *s* at birth
51: 5 *s* from the time my mother
Ro 7: 5 we were controlled by the *s* nature,
8: 4 not live according to the *s* nature
8: 9 are controlled not by the *s* nature
Gal 5:19 The acts of the *s* nature are obvious
5:24 Jesus have crucified the *s* nature
1Pe 2:11 abstain from *s* desires, which war

SING (SANG SINGING SONG SONGS)
Ps 30: 4 *S* to the LORD, you saints of his;
47: 6 *S* praises to God, *s* praises;
59:16 But I will *s* of your strength,
89: 1 I will *s* of the LORD's great love
101: 1 I will *s* of your love and justice;
Eph 5:19 *S* and make music in your heart

SINGING (SING)
Ps 63: 5 with *s* lips my mouth will praise
Ac 16:25 Silas were praying and *s* hymns

SINNED (SIN)
2Sa 12:13 "I have *s* against the Lord."
Job 1: 5 "Perhaps my children have *s*
Ps 51: 4 Against you, you only, have I *s*
Da 9: 5 we have *s* and done wrong.
Mic 7: 9 Because I have *s* against him,
Lk 15:18 I have *s* against heaven
Ro 3:23 for all have *s* and fall short
1Jn 1:10 claim we have not *s,* we make him

SINNER (SIN)
Ecc 9:18 but one *s* destroys much good.
Lk 15: 7 in heaven over one *s* who repents
18:13 'God, have mercy on me, a *s.*'
1Co 14:24 convinced by all that he is a *s*
Jas 5:20 Whoever turns a *s* from the error
1Pe 4:18 become of the ungodly and the *s?"*

SINNERS (SIN)
Ps 1: 1 or stand in the way of *s*
Pr 23:17 Do not let your heart envy *s,*
Mt 9:13 come to call the righteous, but *s."*
Ro 5: 8 While we were still *s,* Christ died
1Ti 1:15 came into the world to save *s*—

SINNING (SIN)
Ex 20:20 be with you to keep you from *s."*
1Co 15:34 stop *s;* for there are some who are
Heb 10:26 If we deliberately keep on *s*
1Jn 3: 6 No one who lives in him keeps on *s*
3: 9 go on *s,* because he has been born

SINS (SIN)
2Ki 14: 6 each is to die for his own *s."*
Ezr 9: 6 our *s* are higher than our heads
Ps 19:13 your servant also from willful *s;*
32: 1 whose *s* are covered.
103: 3 who forgives all your *s*
130: 3 O LORD, kept a record of *s,*
Pr 28:13 who conceals his *s* does not
Isa 1:18 "Though your *s* are like scarlet,
43:25 and remembers your *s* no more.
59: 2 your *s* have hidden his face
Eze 18: 4 soul who *s* is the one who will die.
Mt 1:21 he will save his people from their *s*
18:15 "If your brother *s* against you,
Lk 11: 4 Forgive us our *s,*
17: 3 "If your brother *s,* rebuke him,
Ac 22:16 be baptized and wash your *s* away,
1Co 15: 3 died for our *s* according
Eph 2: 1 dead in your transgressions and *s,*
Col 2:13 us all our *s,* having canceled
Heb 1: 3 he had provided purification for *s,*
7:27 He sacrificed for their *s* once for all
8:12 and will remember their *s* no more
10:12 for all time one sacrifice for *s,*
Jas 4:17 ought to do and doesn't do it, *s.*
5:16 Therefore confess your *s*
5:20 and cover over a multitude of *s.*
1Pe 2:24 He himself bore our *s* in his body
3:18 For Christ died for *s* once for all,
1Jn 1: 9 If we confess our *s,* he is faithful
Rev 1: 5 has freed us from our *s* by his blood

SITS
Ps 99: 1 *s* enthroned between the cherubim,
Isa 40:22 He *s* enthroned above the circle
Mt 19:28 of Man *s* on his glorious throne,
Rev 4: 9 thanks to him who *s* on the throne

SKIN
Job 19:20 with only the *s* of my teeth.
19:26 And after my *s* has been destroyed,
Jer 13:23 Can the Ethiopian change his *s*

SLAIN (SLAY)
Rev 5:12 "Worthy is the Lamb, who was *s,*

SLANDER (SLANDERED SLANDERERS)
Lev 19:16 " 'Do not go about spreading *s*
1Ti 5:14 the enemy no opportunity for *s.*
Tit 3: 2 to *s* no one, to be peaceable

SLANDERED (SLANDER)
1Co 4:13 when we are *s,* we answer kindly.

SLANDERERS (SLANDER)
Ro 1:30 They are gossips, *s,* God-haters,
1Co 6:10 nor the greedy nor drunkards nor *s*
Tit 2: 3 not to be *s* or addicted

SLAUGHTER
Isa 53: 7 he was led like a lamb to the *s,*

SLAVE (SLAVERY SLAVES)
Ge 21:10 "Get rid of that *s* woman
Mt 20:27 wants to be first must be your *s*—
Jn 8:34 everyone who sins is a *s* to sin.
1Co 12:13 whether Jews or Greeks, *s* or free
Gal 3:28 *s* nor free, male nor female,
4:30 Get rid of the *s* woman and her son
2Pe 2:19 a man is a *s* to whatever has

SLAVERY (SLAVE)
Ro 6:19 parts of your body in *s* to impurity
Gal 4: 3 were in *s* under the basic principles

SLAVES (SLAVE)
Ro 6: 6 that we should no longer be *s* to sin
6:22 and have become *s* to God,

SLAY (SLAIN)
Job 13:15 Though he *s* me, yet will I hope

SLEEP (SLEEPING)
Ps 121: 4 will neither slumber nor *s.*
1Co 15:51 We will not all *s,* but we will all be

SLEEPING (SLEEP)
Mk 13:36 suddenly, do not let him find you *s.*

SLOW
Ex 34: 6 and gracious God, *s* to anger,
Jas 1:19 *s* to speak and *s* to become angry,
2Pe 3: 9 The Lord is not *s* in keeping his

SLUGGARD
Pr 6: 6 Go to the ant, you *s;*
20: 4 A *s* does not plow in season;

SLUMBER
Ps 121: 3 he who watches over you will not *s;*
Pr 6:10 A little sleep, a little *s,*
Ro 13:11 for you to wake up from your *s,*

SNAKE (SNAKES)
Nu 21: 8 "Make a *s* and put it up on a pole;
Pr 23:32 In the end it bites like a *s*
Jn 3:14 Moses lifted up the *s* in the desert,

SNAKES (SNAKE)
Mt 10:16 as shrewd as *s* and as innocent
Mk 16:18 they will pick up *s* with their hands;

SNATCH
Jn 10:28 no one can *s* them out of my hand.

Jude :23 *s* others from the fire and save

SNOW
Ps 51: 7 and I will be whiter than *s.*

SOAR
Isa 40:31 They will *s* on wings like eagles;

SODOM
Ge 19:24 rained down burning sulfur on *S*
Ro 9:29 we would have become like *S,*

SOIL
Ge 4: 2 kept flocks, and Cain worked the *s.*
Mt 13:23 on good *s* is the man who hears

SOLDIER
1Co 9: 7 as a *s* at his own expense?
2Ti 2: 3 with us like a good *s* of Christ Jesus

SOLE
Dt 28:65 place for the *s* of your foot.
Isa 1: 6 From the *s* of your foot to the top

SOLID
2Ti 2:19 God's *s* foundation stands firm,
Heb 5:12 You need milk, not *s* food!

SOLOMON
Son of David by Bathsheba; king of Judah (2Sa 12:24; 1Ch 3:5, 10). Appointed king by David (1Ki 1); adversaries Adonijah, Joab, Shimei killed by Benaiah (1Ki 2). Asked for wisdom (1Ki 3; 2Ch 1). Judged between two prostitutes (1Ki 3:16-28). Built temple (1Ki 5-7; 2Ch 2-5); prayer of dedication (1Ki 8; 2Ch 6). Visited by Queen of Sheba (1Ki 10; 2Ch 9). Wives turned his heart from God (1Ki 11:1-13). Jeroboam rebelled against (1Ki 11:26-40). Death (1Ki 11:41-43; 2Ch 9:29-31).
Proverbs of (1Ki 4:32; Pr 1:1; 10:1; 25:1); psalms of (Ps 72; 127); song of (SS 1:1).

SON (SONS)
Ge 22: 2 "Take your *s,* your only *s,* Isaac,
Ex 11: 5 Every firstborn *s* in Egypt will die,
Dt 21:18 rebellious *s* who does not obey his
Ps 2: 7 He said to me, "You are my *S;*
2:12 Kiss the *S,* lest he be angry
Pr 10: 1 A wise *s* brings joy to his father,
13:24 He who spares the rod hates his *s,*
29:17 Discipline your *s,* and he will give
Isa 7:14 with child and will give birth to a *s,*
Hos 11: 1 and out of Egypt I called my *s.*
Mt 2:15 "Out of Egypt I called my *s.*"
3:17 "This is my *S,* whom I love;
11:27 one knows the *S* except the Father,
16:16 "You are the Christ, the *S*
17: 5 "This is my *S,* whom I love;
20:18 and the *S* of Man will be betrayed
24:30 They will see the *S* of Man coming
24:44 the *S* of Man will come at an hour
27:54 "Surely he was the *S* of God!"
28:19 and of the *S* and of the Holy Spirit,
Mk 10:45 even the *S* of Man did not come
14:62 you will see the *S* of Man sitting
Lk 9:58 but the *S* of Man has no place
18: 8 when the *S* of Man comes,
19:10 For the *S* of Man came to seek
Jn 3:14 so the *S* of Man must be lifted up,
3:16 that he gave his one and only *S,*
17: 1 Glorify your *S,* that your *S* may
Ro 8:29 conformed to the likeness of his *S,*
8:32 He who did not spare his own *S,*
1Co 15:28 then the *S* himself will be made
Gal 4:30 rid of the slave woman and her *s,*
1Th 1:10 and to wait for his *S* from heaven,
Heb 1: 2 days he has spoken to us by his *S,*
10:29 punished who has trampled the *S*
1Jn 1: 7 his *S,* purifies us from all sin.
4: 9 only *S* into the world that we might
5: 5 he who believes that Jesus is the *S*
5:11 eternal life, and this life is in his *S.*

SONG (SING)
Ps 40: 3 He put a new *s* in my mouth,
96: 1 Sing to the LORD a new *s;*
149: 1 Sing to the LORD a new *s,*
Isa 49:13 burst into *s,* O mountains!
55:12 will burst into *s* before you,
Rev 5: 9 And they sang a new *s:*
15: 3 and sang the *s* of Moses the servant

SONGS (SING)
Job 35:10 who gives *s* in the night,
Ps 100: 2 come before him with joyful *s.*
Eph 5:19 with psalms, hymns and spiritual *s.*
Jas 5:13 Is anyone happy? Let him sing *s*

SONS (SON)
Joel 2:28 Your *s* and daughters will prophesy
Jn 12:36 so that you may become *s* of light."
Ro 8:14 by the Spirit of God are *s* of God.
2Co 6:18 and you will be my *s* and daughters
Gal 4: 5 we might receive the full rights of *s.*
Heb 12: 7 discipline; God is treating you as *s.*

SORROW (SORROWS)
Jer 31:12 and they will *s* no more.
Ro 9: 2 I have great *s* and unceasing
2Co 7:10 Godly *s* brings repentance that

SORROWS (SORROW)
Isa 53: 3 a man of *s,* and familiar

SOUL (SOULS)
Dt 6: 5 with all your *s* and with all your
10:12 all your heart and with all your *s,*

Jos 22: 5 with all your heart and all your *s*."
Ps 23: 3 he restores my *s*.
42: 1 so my *s* pants for you, O God.
42:11 Why are you downcast, O my *s*?
103: 1 Praise the LORD, O my *s*;
Pr 13:19 A longing fulfilled is sweet to the *s*,
Isa 55: 2 your *s* will delight in the richest
Mt 10:28 kill the body but cannot kill the *s*.
16:26 yet forfeits his *s*? Or what can
22:37 with all your *s* and with all your
Heb 4:12 even to dividing *s* and spirit,

SOULS (SOUL)
Pr 11:30 and he who wins *s* is wise.
Jer 6:16 and you will find rest for your *s*.
Mt 11:29 and you will find rest for your *s*.

SOUND
1Co 14: 8 if the trumpet does not *s* a clear call
15:52 the trumpet will *s*, the dead will
2Ti 4: 3 men will not put up with *s* doctrine.

SOVEREIGN
Da 4:25 that the Most High is *s*

SOW (SOWS)
Job 4: 8 and those who *s* trouble reap it.
Mt 6:26 they do not *s* or reap or store away
2Pe 2:22 and, "A *s* that is washed goes back

SOWS (SOW)
Pr 11:18 he who *s* righteousness reaps a sure
22: 8 He who *s* wickedness reaps trouble
2Co 9: 6 Whoever *s* sparingly will
Gal 6: 7 A man reaps what he *s*.

SPARE (SPARES)
Ro 8:32 He who did not *s* his own Son,
11:21 natural branches, he will not *s* you

SPARES (SPARE)
Pr 13:24 He who *s* the rod hates his son,

SPEARS
Isa 2: 4 and their *s* into pruning hooks.
Joel 3:10 and your pruning hooks into *s*.
Mic 4: 3 and their *s* into pruning hooks.

SPECTACLE
1Co 4: 9 We have been made a *s*
Col 2:15 he made a public *s* of them,

SPIN
Mt 6:28 They do not labor or *s*.

SPIRIT (SPIRIT'S SPIRITS SPIRITUAL SPIRITUALLY)
Ge 1: 2 and the *S* of God was hovering
6: 3 "My *S* will not contend
2Ki 2: 9 inherit a double portion of your *s*,"
Job 33: 4 The *S* of God has made me;
Ps 31: 5 Into your hands I commit my *s*;
51:10 and renew a steadfast *s* within me.
51:11 or take your Holy *S* from me.
51:17 sacrifices of God are a broken *s*;
139: 7 Where can I go from your *S*?
Isa 57:15 him who is contrite and lowly in *s*,
63:10 and grieved his Holy *S*.
Eze 11:19 an undivided heart and put a new *s*
36:26 you a new heart and put a new *s*
Joel 2:28 I will pour out my *S* on all people.
Zec 4: 6 but by my *S*,' says the LORD
Mt 1:18 to be with child through the Holy *S*
3:11 will baptize you with the Holy *S*
3:16 he saw the *S* of God descending
4: 1 led by the *S* into the desert
5: 3 saying: "Blessed are the poor in *s*,
26:41 *s* is willing, but the body is weak."
28:19 and of the Son and of the Holy *S*,
Lk 1:80 child grew and became strong in *s*;
11:13 Father in heaven give the Holy *S*
Jn 4:24 God is *s*, and his worshipers must
7:39 Up to that time the *S* had not been
14:26 But the Counselor, the Holy *S*,
16:13 But when he, the *S* of truth, comes,
20:22 and said, "Receive the Holy *S*.
Ac 1: 5 will be baptized with the Holy *S*."
2: 4 of them were filled with the Holy *S*
2:38 will receive the gift of the Holy *S*.
6: 3 who are known to be full of the *S*
19: 2 "Did you receive the Holy *S*
Ro 8: 9 And if anyone does not have the *S*
8:26 the *S* helps us in our weakness.
1Co 2:10 God has revealed it to us by his *S*.
2:14 man without the *S* does not accept
6:19 body is a temple of the Holy *S*,
12:13 baptized by one *S* into one body—
2Co 3: 6 the letter kills, but the *S* gives life.
5: 5 and has given us the *S* as a deposit,
Gal 5:16 by the *S*, and you will not gratify
5:22 But the fruit of the *S* is love, joy,
5:25 let us keep in step with the *S*.
Eph 1:13 with a seal, the promised Holy *S*,
4:30 do not grieve the Holy *S* of God,
5:18 Instead, be filled with the *S*.
6:17 of salvation and the sword of the *S*,
2Th 2:13 the sanctifying work of the *S*
Heb 4:12 even to dividing soul and *s*,
1Pe 3: 4 beauty of a gentle and quiet *s*,
2Pe 1:21 carried along by the Holy *S*.
1Jn 4: 1 Dear friends, do not believe every *s*

SPIRIT'S (SPIRIT)
1Th 5:19 not put out the *S* fire; do not treat

SPIRITS (SPIRIT)
1Co 12:10 to another distinguishing between *s*,
14:32 The *s* of prophets are subject
1Jn 4: 1 test the *s* to see whether they are

SPIRITUAL (SPIRIT)
Ro 12: 1 this is your *s* act of worship.
12:11 but keep your *s* fervor, serving
1Co 2:13 expressing *s* truths in *s* words.
3: 1 I could not address you as *s* but
12: 1 Now about *s* gifts, brothers,
14: 1 of love and eagerly desire *s* gifts,
15:44 a natural body, it is raised a *s* body.
Gal 6: 1 you who are *s* should restore him
Eph 1: 3 with every *s* blessing in Christ.
5:19 with psalms, hymns and *s* songs.
6:12 and against the *s* forces of evil
1Pe 2: 2 newborn babies, crave pure *s* milk,
2: 5 are being built into a *s* house

SPIRITUALLY (SPIRIT)
1Co 2:14 because they are *s* discerned.

SPLENDOR
1Ch 16:29 the LORD in the *s* of his holiness.
29:11 the glory and the majesty and the *s*,
Job 37:22 of the north he comes in golden *s*;
Ps 29: 2 in the *s* of his holiness.
45: 3 clothe yourself with *s* and majesty.
96: 6 *S* and majesty are before him;
96: 9 in the *s* of his holiness;
104: 1 you are clothed with *s* and majesty.
145: 5 of the glorious *s* of your majesty,
Isa 61: 3 the LORD for the display of his *s*.
63: 1 Who is this, robed in *s*,
Lk 9:31 appeared in glorious *s*, talking
2Th 2: 8 and destroy by the *s* of his coming.

SPOIL
Ps 119:162 like one who finds great *s*.

SPOTLESS
2Pe 3:14 make every effort to be found *s*,

SPREAD (SPREADING)
Ac 12:24 of God continued to increase and *s*.
19:20 the word of the Lord *s* widely

SPREADING (SPREAD)
1Th 3: 2 God's fellow worker in *s* the gospel

SPRING
Jer 2:13 the *s* of living water,

Jn 4:14 in him a *s* of water welling up
Jas 3:12 can a salt *s* produce fresh water.

SPUR*
Heb 10:24 how we may *s* one another

SPURNS*
Pr 15: 5 A fool *s* his father's discipline,

STAFF
Ps 23: 4 your rod and your *s*,

STAKES
Isa 54: 2 strengthen your *s*.

STAND (STANDING STANDS)
Ex 14:13 *S* firm and you will see
2Ch 20:17 *s* firm and see the deliverance
Ps 1: 5 Therefore the wicked will not *s*
40: 2 and gave me a firm place to *s*.
119:120 I *s* in awe of your laws.
Eze 22:30 *s* before me in the gap on behalf
Zec 14: 4 On that day his feet will *s*
Mt 12:25 divided against itself will not *s*.
Ro 14:10 we will all *s* before God's judgment
1Co 10:13 out so that you can *s* up under it.
15:58 Therefore, my dear brothers, *s* firm
Eph 6:14 *S* firm then, with the belt
2Th 2:15 *s* firm and hold to the teachings we
Jas 5: 8 You too, be patient and *s* firm,
Rev 3:20 Here I am! I *s* at the door

STANDING (STAND)
Ex 3: 5 where you are *s* is holy ground."
Jos 5:15 the place where you are *s* is holy."
1Pe 5: 9 Resist him, *s* firm in the faith,

STANDS (STAND)
Ps 89: 2 that your love *s* firm forever,
119: 89 it *s* firm in the heavens.
Mt 10:22 but he who *s* firm to the end will be
2Ti 2:19 God's solid foundation *s* firm,
1Pe 1:25 but the word of the Lord *s* forever

STAR (STARS)
Nu 24:17 A *s* will come out of Jacob;
Rev 22:16 and the bright Morning *S*."

STARS (STAR)
Da 12: 3 like the *s* for ever and ever.
Php 2:15 in which you shine like *s*

STATURE
Lk 2:52 And Jesus grew in wisdom and *s*,

STEADFAST
Ps 51:10 and renew a *s* spirit within me.
Isa 26: 3 him whose mind is *s*,
1Pe 5:10 and make you strong, firm and *s*.

STEAL
Ex 20:15 "You shall not *s*.
Mt 19:18 do not *s*, do not give false
Eph 4:28 has been stealing must *s* no longer,

STEP (STEPS)
Gal 5:25 let us keep in *s* with the Spirit.

STEPS (STEP)
Pr 16: 9 but the LORD determines his *s*.
Jer 10:23 it is not for man to direct his *s*.
1Pe 2:21 that you should follow in his *s*.

STICKS
Pr 18:24 there is a friend who *s* closer

STIFF-NECKED
Ex 34: 9 Although this is a *s* people,

STILL
Ps 46:10 "Be *s*, and know that I am God;
Zec 2:13 Be *s* before the LORD, all mankind

STIRS
Pr 6:19 and a man who *s* up dissension
10:12 Hatred *s* up dissension,
15: 1 but a harsh word *s* up anger.
15:18 hot-tempered man *s* up dissension,
16:28 A perverse man *s* up dissension,
28:25 A greedy man *s* up dissension,
29:22 An angry man *s* up dissension,

STONE (CAPSTONE CORNERSTONE MILLSTONE)
1Sa 17:50 the Philistine with a sling and a *s*;
Isa 8:14 a *s* that causes men to stumble
Eze 11:19 remove from them their heart of *s*
Mk 16: 3 "Who will roll the *s* away
Lk 4: 3 tell this *s* to become bread."
Jn 8: 7 the first to throw a *s* at her."
2Co 3: 3 not on tablets of *s* but on tablets

STOOP
2Sa 22:36 you *s* down to make me great.

STORE
Pr 10:14 Wise men *s* up knowledge,
Mt 6:19 not *s* up for yourselves treasures

STOREHOUSE (HOUSE)
Mal 3:10 Bring the whole tithe into the *s*,

STRAIGHT
Pr 3: 6 and he will make your paths *s*.
4:25 Let your eyes look *s* ahead,
15:21 of understanding keeps a *s* course.
Jn 1:23 'Make *s* the way for the Lord.' "

STRAIN
Mt 23:24 You *s* out a gnat but swallow

STRANGER (STRANGERS)
Mt 25:35 I was a *s* and you invited me in,
Jn 10: 5 But they will never follow a *s*;

STRANGERS (STRANGER)
1Pe 2:11 as aliens and *s* in the world,

STREAMS
Ps 1: 3 He is like a tree planted by *s*
46: 4 is a river whose *s* make glad
Ecc 1: 7 All *s* flow into the sea,
Jn 7:38 *s* of living water will flow

STRENGTH (STRONG)
Ex 15: 2 The LORD is my *s* and my song;
Dt 6: 5 all your soul and with all your *s*.
2Sa 22:33 It is God who arms me with *s*
Ne 8:10 for the joy of the LORD is your *s*."
Ps 28: 7 The LORD is my *s* and my shield;
46: 1 God is our refuge and *s*,
96: 7 ascribe to the LORD glory and *s*.
118: 14 The LORD is my *s* and my song;
147: 10 not in the *s* of the horse,
Isa 40:31 will renew their *s*.
Mk 12:30 all your mind and with all your *s*.'
1Co 1:25 of God is stronger than man's *s*.
Php 4:13 through him who gives me *s*.
1Pe 4:11 it with the *s* God provides,

STRENGTHEN (STRONG)
2Ch 16: 9 to *s* those whose hearts are fully
Ps 119: 28 *s* me according to your word.
Isa 35: 3 *S* the feeble hands,
41:10 I will *s* you and help you;
Eph 3:16 of his glorious riches he may *s* you
2Th 2:17 and *s* you in every good deed
Heb 12:12 *s* your feeble arms and weak knees.

STRENGTHENING (STRONG)
1Co 14:26 done for the *s* of the church.

STRIFE
Pr 20: 3 It is to a man's honor to avoid *s*,
22:10 out the mocker, and out goes *s*;

STRIKE (STRIKES)
Ge 3:15 and you will *s* his heel."
Zec 13: 7 "*S* the shepherd,
Mt 26:31 " 'I will *s* the shepherd,

STRIKES (STRIKE)
Mt 5:39 If someone *s* you on the right

STRONG (STRENGTH STRENGTHEN STRENGTHENING)
Dt 31: 6 Be *s* and courageous.
1Ki 2: 2 "So be *s*, show yourself a man,
Pr 18:10 The name of the LORD is a *s* tower
31:17 her arms are *s* for her tasks.
SS 8: 6 for love is as *s* as death,
Lk 2:40 And the child grew and became *s*;
Ro 15: 1 We who are *s* ought to bear
1Co 1:27 things of the world to shame the *s*.
16:13 in the faith; be men of courage; be *s*
2Co 12:10 For when I am weak, then I am *s*.
Eph 6:10 be *s* in the Lord and in his mighty

STRUGGLE
Ro 15:30 me in my *s* by praying to God

TABLE (TABLES)
Ps 23: 5 You prepare a *t* before me

TABLES (TABLE)
Ac 6: 2 word of God in order to wait on *t.*

TABLET (TABLETS)
Pr 3: 3 write them on the *t* of your heart.
7: 3 write them on the *t* of your heart.

TABLETS (TABLET)
Ex 31:18 he gave him the two *t*
Dt 10: 5 and put the *t* in the ark I had made,
2Co 3: 3 not on *t* of stone but on *t*

TAKE (TAKEN TAKES TAKING TOOK)
Dt 12:32 do not add to it or *t* away from it.
31:26 "*T* this Book of the Law
Job 23:10 But he knows the way that I *t;*
Ps 49:17 for he will *t* nothing with him
51:11 or *t* your Holy Spirit from me.
Mt 10:38 anyone who does not *t* his cross
11:29 *T* my yoke upon you and learn
16:24 deny himself and *t* up his cross

TAKEN (TAKE)
Lev 6: 4 must return what he has stolen or *t*
Isa 6: 7 your guilt is *t* away and your sin
Mt 24:40 one will be *t* and the other left.
Mk 16:19 he was *t* up into heaven
1Ti 3:16 was *t* up in glory.

TAKES (TAKE)
1Ki 20:11 should not boast like one who *t* it
Ps 5: 4 You are not a God who *t* pleasure
Jn 1:29 who *t* away the sin of the world!
Rev 22:19 And if anyone *t* words away

TAKING (TAKE)
Ac 15:14 by *t* from the Gentiles a people
Php 2: 7 *t* the very nature of a servant,

TALENT
Mt 25:15 to another one *t,* each according

TAME*
Jas 3: 8 but no man can *t* the tongue.

TASK
Mk 13:34 each with his assigned *t,*
Ac 20:24 complete the *t* the Lord Jesus has
1Co 3: 5 the Lord has assigned to each his *t.*
2Co 2:16 And who is equal to such a *t?*

TASTE (TASTED)
Ps 34: 8 *T* and see that the LORD is good;
Col 2:21 Do not *t!* Do not touch!"?
Heb 2: 9 the grace of God he might *t* death

TASTED (TASTE)
1Pe 2: 3 now that you have *t* that the Lord

TAUGHT (TEACH)
Mt 7:29 he *t* as one who had authority,
1Co 2:13 but in words *t* by the Spirit,
Gal 1:12 nor was I *t* it; rather, I received it

TAXES
Mt 22:17 Is it right to pay *t* to Caesar or not
Ro 13: 7 If you owe *t,* pay *t;* if revenue,

TEACH (TAUGHT TEACHER TEACHERS TEACHES TEACHING)
Ex 33:13 *t* me your ways so I may know you
Dt 4: 9 *T* them to your children
8: 3 to *t* you that man does not live
11:19 *T* them to your children, talking
1Sa 12:23 I will *t* you the way that is good
Ps 32: 8 *t* you in the way you should go;
51:13 I will *t* transgressors your ways,
90:12 *T* us to number our days aright,
143: 10 *T* me to do your will,
Jer 31:34 No longer will a man *t* his neighbor
Lk 11: 1 said to him, "Lord, *t* us to pray,
Jn 14:26 will *t* you all things and will remind
1Ti 2:12 I do not permit a woman to *t*
3: 2 respectable, hospitable, able to *t,*
Tit 2: 1 You must *t* what is in accord
Heb 8:11 No longer will a man *t* his neighbor
Jas 3: 1 know that we who *t* will be judged
1Jn 2:27 you do not need anyone to *t* you.

TEACHER (TEACH)
Mt 10:24 "A student is not above his *t,*
Jn 13:14 and *T,* have washed your feet,

TEACHERS (TEACH)
1Co 12:28 third *t,* then workers of miracles,
Eph 4:11 and some to be pastors and *t,*
Heb 5:12 by this time you ought to be *t,*

TEACHES (TEACH)
1Ti 6: 3 If anyone *t* false doctrines

TEACHING (TEACH)
Pr 1: 8 and do not forsake your mother's *t.*
Mt 28:20 *t* them to obey everything I have
Jn 7:17 whether my *t* comes from God or
14:23 loves me, he will obey my *t.*
1Ti 4:13 of Scripture, to preaching and to *t.*
2Ti 3:16 is God-breathed and is useful for *t,*
Tit 2: 7 In your *t* show integrity,

TEAR (TEARS)
Rev 7:17 God will wipe away every *t*

TEARS (TEAR)
Ps 126: 5 Those who sow in *t*
Php 3:18 and now say again even with *t,*

TEETH (TOOTH)
Mt 8:12 will be weeping and gnashing of *t.*"

TEMPERATE*
1Ti 3: 2 *t,* self-controlled, respectable,
3:11 not malicious talkers but *t*
Tit 2: 2 Teach the older men to be *t,*

TEMPEST
Ps 55: 8 far from the *t* and storm."

TEMPLE (TEMPLES)
1Ki 8:27 How much less this *t* I have built!
Hab 2:20 But the LORD is in his holy *t;*
1Co 3:16 that you yourselves are God's *t*
6:19 you not know that your body is a *t*
2Co 6:16 For we are the *t* of the living God.

TEMPLES (TEMPLE)
Ac 17:24 does not live in *t* built by hands.

TEMPT (TEMPTATION TEMPTED)
1Co 7: 5 again so that Satan will not *t* you

TEMPTATION (TEMPT)
Mt 6:13 And lead us not into *t,*
26:41 pray so that you will not fall into *t.*
1Co 10:13 No *t* has seized you except what is

TEMPTED (TEMPT)
Mt 4: 1 into the desert to be *t* by the devil.
1Co 10:13 he will not let you be *t*
Heb 2:18 he himself suffered when he was *t,*
4:15 but we have one who has been *t*
Jas 1:13 For God cannot be *t* by evil,

TEN (TENTH TITHE TITHES)
Ex 34:28 covenant—the *T* Commandments.
Ps 91: 7 *t* thousand at your right hand,
Mt 25:28 it to the one who has the *t* talents.
Lk 15: 8 suppose a woman has *t* silver coins

TENTH (TEN)
Dt 14:22 Be sure to set aside a *t*

TERRIBLE (TERROR)
2Ti 3: 1 There will be *t* times

TERROR (TERRIBLE)
Ps 91: 5 You will not fear the *t* of night,
Lk 21:26 Men will faint from *t,* apprehensive
Ro 13: 3 For rulers hold no *t*

TEST (TESTED TESTS)
Dt 6:16 Do not *t* the LORD your God
Ps 139: 23 *t* me and know my anxious
Ro 12: 2 Then you will be able to *t*
1Co 3:13 and the fire will *t* the quality
1Jn 4: 1 *t* the spirits to see whether they are

TESTED (TEST)
Ge 22: 1 Some time later God *t* Abraham.
Job 23:10 when he has *t* me, I will come forth
Pr 27:21 man is *t* by the praise he receives.

1Ti 3:10 They must first be *t;* and then

TESTIFY (TESTIMONY)
Jn 5:39 are the Scriptures that *t* about me,
2Ti 1: 8 ashamed to *t* about our Lord,

TESTIMONY (TESTIFY)
Isa 8:20 and to the *t!* If they do not speak
Lk 18:20 not give false *t,* honor your father

TESTS (TEST)
Pr 17: 3 but the LORD *t* the heart.
1Th 2: 4 but God, who *t* our hearts.

THADDAEUS
Apostle (Mt 10:3; Mk 3:18); probably also known as Judas son of James (Lk 6:16; Ac 1:13).

THANKFUL (THANKS)
Heb 12:28 let us be *t,* and so worship God

THANKS (THANKFUL THANKSGIVING)
1Ch 16: 8 Give *t* to the LORD, call
Ne 12:31 assigned two large choirs to give *t.*
Ps 100: 4 give *t* to him and praise his name.
1Co 15:57 *t* be to God! He gives us the victory
2Co 2:14 *t* be to God, who always leads us
9:15 *T* be to God for his indescribable
1Th 5:18 give *t* in all circumstances,

THANKSGIVING (THANKS)
Ps 95: 2 Let us come before him with *t*
100: 4 Enter his gates with *t*
Php 4: 6 by prayer and petition, with *t,*
1Ti 4: 3 created to be received with *t*

THIEF (THIEVES)
Ex 22: 3 A *t* must certainly make restitution
1Th 5: 2 day of the Lord will come like a *t*
Rev 16:15 I come like a *t!* Blessed is he who

THIEVES (THIEF)
1Co 6:10 nor homosexual offenders nor *t*

THINK (THOUGHT THOUGHTS)
Ro 12: 3 Do not *t* of yourself more highly
Php 4: 8 praiseworthy—*t* about such things

THIRST (THIRSTY)
Ps 69:21 and gave me vinegar for my *t.*
Mt 5: 6 Blessed are those who hunger and *t*
Jn 4:14 the water I give him will never *t.*

THIRSTY (THIRST)
Isa 55: 1 "Come, all you who are *t,*
Jn 7:37 "If anyone is *t,* let him come to me
Rev 22:17 Whoever is *t,* let him come;

THOMAS
Apostle (Mt 10:3; Mk 3:18; Lk 6:15; Jn 11:16; 14:5; 21:2; Ac 1:13). Doubted resurrection (Jn 20:24-28).

THONGS
Mk 1: 7 *t* of whose sandals I am not worthy

THORN (THORNS)
2Co 12: 7 there was given me a *t* in my flesh,

THORNS (THORN)
Nu 33:55 in your eyes and *t* in your sides.
Mt 27:29 then twisted together a crown of *t*
Heb 6: 8 But land that produces *t*

THOUGHT (THINK)
Pr 14:15 a prudent man gives *t* to his steps.
1Co 13:11 I talked like a child, I *t* like a child,

THOUGHTS (THINK)
Ps 94:11 The LORD knows the *t* of man;
139: 23 test me and know my anxious *t.*
Isa 55: 8 "For my *t* are not your *t,*
Heb 4:12 it judges the *t* and attitudes

THREE
Ecc 4:12 of *t* strands is not quickly broken.
Mt 12:40 *t* nights in the belly of a huge fish,
18:20 or *t* come together in my name,
27:63 'After *t* days I will rise again.'
1Co 13:13 And now these *t* remain: faith,
14:27 or at the most *t*— should speak,
2Co 13: 1 testimony of two or *t* witnesses."

THRESHING
2Sa 24:18 an altar to the LORD on the *t* floor

THRONE (ENTHRONED)
2Sa 7:16 your *t* will be established forever
Ps 45: 6 Your *t,* O God, will last for ever
47: 8 God is seated on his holy *t.*
Isa 6: 1 I saw the Lord seated on a *t,*
66: 1 "Heaven is my *t*
Heb 4:16 Let us then approach the *t* of grace
12: 2 at the right hand of the *t* of God.
Rev 4:10 They lay their crowns before the *t*
20:11 Then I saw a great white *t*
22: 3 *t* of God and of the Lamb will be

THROW
Jn 8: 7 the first to *t* a stone at her."
Heb 10:35 So do not *t* away your confidence;
12: 1 let us *t* off everything that hinders

THWART*
Isa 14:27 has purposed, and who can *t* him?

TIBNI
King of Israel (1Ki 16:21-22).

TIME (TIMES)
Est 4:14 come to royal position for such a *t*
Da 7:25 to him for a *t,* times and half a *t.*
Hos 10:12 for it is *t* to seek the LORD,
Ro 9: 9 "At the appointed *t* I will return,
Heb 9:28 and he will appear a second *t,*
10:12 for all *t* one sacrifice for sins,
1Pe 4:17 For it is *t* for judgment to begin

TIMES (TIME)
Ps 9: 9 a stronghold in *t* of trouble.
31:15 My *t* are in your hands;
62: 8 Trust in him at all *t,* O people;
Pr 17:17 A friend loves at all *t,*
Am 5:13 for the *t* are evil.
Mt 18:21 how many *t* shall I forgive my
Ac 1: 7 "It is not for you to know the *t*
Rev 12:14 *t* and half a time, out

TIMIDITY*
2Ti 1: 7 For God did not give us a spirit of *t*

TIMOTHY
Believer from Lystra (Ac 16:1). Joined Paul on second missionary journey (Ac 16-20). Sent to settle problems at Corinth (1Co 4:17; 16:10). Led church at Ephesus (1Ti 1:3). Co-writer with Paul (1Th 1:1; 2Th 1:1; Phm 1).

TIRE (TIRED)
2Th 3:13 never *t* of doing what is right.

TIRED (TIRE)
Ex 17:12 When Moses' hands grew *t,*
Isa 40:28 He will not grow *t* or weary,

TITHE (TEN)
Lev 27:30 " 'A *t* of everything from the land,
Dt 12:17 eat in your own towns the *t*
Mal 3:10 the whole *t* into the storehouse,

TITHES (TEN)
Mal 3: 8 'How do we rob you?' "In *t*

TITUS
Gentile co-worker of Paul (Gal 2:1-3; 2Ti 4:10); sent to Corinth (2Co 2:13; 7-8; 12:18), Crete (Tit 1:4-5).

TODAY
Mt 6:11 Give us *t* our daily bread.
Lk 23:43 *t* you will be with me in paradise."
Heb 3:13 daily, as long as it is called *T,*
13: 8 Christ is the same yesterday and *t*

TOIL
Ge 3:17 through painful *t* you will eat of it

TOLERATE
Hab 1:13 you cannot *t* wrong.
Rev 2: 2 that you cannot *t* wicked men,

TOMB
Mt 27:65 make the *t* as secure as you know
Lk 24: 2 the stone rolled away from the *t,*

TOMORROW
Pr 27: 1 Do not boast about *t,*
Isa 22:13 "for *t* we die!"
Mt 6:34 Therefore do not worry about *t,*
Jas 4:13 "Today or *t* we will go to this

TONGUE (TONGUES)
Ps 39: 1 and keep my *t* from sin;
Pr 12:18 but the *t* of the wise brings healing.

1Co 14: 2 speaks in a *t* does not speak to men
14: 4 He who speaks in a *t* edifies himself
14:13 in a *t* should pray that he may
14:19 than ten thousand words in a *t.*
Php 2:11 every *t* confess that Jesus Christ is
Jas 1:26 does not keep a tight rein on his *t,*
3: 8 but no man can tame the *t.*

TONGUES (TONGUE)
Isa 28:11 with foreign lips and strange *t*
66:18 and gather all nations and *t,*
Mk 16:17 in new *t;* they will pick up snakes
Ac 2: 4 and began to speak in other *t*
10:46 For they heard them speaking in *t*
19: 6 and they spoke in *t* and prophesied
1Co 12:30 Do all speak in *t?* Do all interpret?
14:18 speak in *t* more than all of you.
14:39 and do not forbid speaking in *t.*

TOOK (TAKE)
1Co 11:23 the night he was betrayed, *t* bread,
Php 3:12 for which Christ Jesus *t* hold of me.

TOOTH (TEETH)
Ex 21:24 eye for eye, *t* for *t,* hand for hand,
Mt 5:38 'Eye for eye, and *t* for *t.*'

TORMENTED
Rev 20:10 They will be *t* day and night

TORN
Gal 4:15 you would have *t* out your eyes
Php 1:23 I do not know! I am *t*

TOUCH (TOUCHED)
Ps 105: 15 "Do not *t* my anointed ones;
Lk 24:39 It is I myself! *T* me and see;
2Co 6:17 *T* no unclean thing,
Col 2:21 Do not taste! Do not *t!*"?

TOUCHED (TOUCH)
1Sa 10:26 men whose hearts God had *t.*
Mt 14:36 and all who *t* him were healed.

TOWER
Ge 11: 4 with a *t* that reaches to the heavens
Pr 18:10 of the LORD is a strong *t;*

TOWNS
Nu 35: 2 to give the Levites *t* to live
35:15 These six *t* will be a place of refuge

TRACING*
Ro 11:33 and his paths beyond *t* out!

TRADITION
Mt 15: 6 word of God for the sake of your *t.*
Col 2: 8 which depends on human *t*

TRAIN (TRAINING)
Pr 22: 6 *T* a child in the way he should go,
Eph 4: 8 he led captives in his *t*

TRAINING (TRAIN)
1Co 9:25 in the games goes into strict *t.*
2Ti 3:16 correcting and *t* in righteousness,

TRAMPLED
Lk 21:24 Jerusalem will be *t*
Heb 10:29 to be punished who has *t* the Son

TRANCE
Ac 10:10 was being prepared, he fell into a *t.*

TRANSCENDS*
Php 4: 7 which *t* all understanding,

TRANSFIGURED
Mt 17: 2 There he was *t* before them.

TRANSFORM* (TRANSFORMED)
Php 3:21 will *t* our lowly bodies

TRANSFORMED (TRANSFORM)
Ro 12: 2 be *t* by the renewing of your mind.
2Co 3:18 are being *t* into his likeness

TRANSGRESSION (TRANSGRESSIONS TRANSGRESSORS)
Isa 53: 8 for the *t* of my people he was
Ro 4:15 where there is no law there is no *t.*

TRANSGRESSIONS (TRANSGRESSION)
Ps 32: 1 whose *t* are forgiven,
51: 1 blot out my *t.*
103: 12 so far has he removed our *t* from us
Isa 53: 5 But he was pierced for our *t,*
Eph 2: 1 you were dead in your *t* and sins,

TRANSGRESSORS (TRANSGRESSION)
Ps 51:13 Then I will teach *t* your ways,
Isa 53:12 and made intercession for the *t.*
53:12 and was numbered with the *t.*

TREADING
Dt 25: 4 an ox while it is *t* out the grain.
1Co 9: 9 an ox while it is *t* out the grain."

TREASURE (TREASURED TREASURES)
Isa 33: 6 of the LORD is the key to this *t.*
Mt 6:21 For where your *t* is, there your
2Co 4: 7 But we have this *t* in jars of clay

TREASURED (TREASURE)
Dt 7: 6 to be his people, his *t* possession.
Lk 2:19 But Mary *t* up all these things

TREASURES (TREASURE)
Mt 6:19 up for yourselves *t* on earth,
Col 2: 3 in whom are hidden all the *t*
Heb 11:26 of greater value than the *t* of Egypt,

TREAT
Lev 22: 2 sons to *t* with respect the sacred
1Ti 5: 1 *T* younger men as brothers,
1Pe 3: 7 and *t* them with respect

TREATY
Dt 7: 2 Make no *t* with them, and show

TREE
Ge 2: 9 and the *t* of the knowledge of good
2: 9 of the garden were the *t* of life
Dt 21:23 hung on a *t* is under God's curse.
Ps 1: 3 He is like a *t* planted by streams
Mt 3:10 every *t* that does not produce good
12:33 for a *t* is recognized by its fruit.
Gal 3:13 is everyone who is hung on a *t.*"
Rev 22:14 they may have the right to the *t*

TREMBLE (TREMBLING)
1Ch 16:30 *T* before him, all the earth!
Ps 114: 7 *T,* O earth, at the presence

TREMBLING (TREMBLE)
Ps 2:11 and rejoice with *t.*
Php 2:12 out your salvation with fear and *t,*

TRESPASS
Ro 5:17 For if, by the *t* of the one man,

TRIALS
1Th 3: 3 one would be unsettled by these *t.*
Jas 1: 2 whenever you face *t* of many kinds,
2Pe 2: 9 how to rescue godly men from *t*

TRIBES
Ge 49:28 All these are the twelve *t* of Israel,
Mt 19:28 judging the twelve *t* of Israel.

TRIBULATION*
Rev 7:14 who have come out of the great *t;*

TRIUMPHAL* (TRIUMPHING)
Isa 60:11 their kings led in *t* procession.
2Co 2:14 us in *t* procession in Christ

TRIUMPHING* (TRIUMPHAL)
Col 2:15 of them, *t* over them by the cross.

TROUBLE (TROUBLED TROUBLES)
Job 14: 1 is of few days and full of *t.*
Ps 46: 1 an ever-present help in *t.*
107: 13 they cried to the LORD in their *t,*
Pr 11:29 He who brings *t* on his family will
24:10 If you falter in times of *t,*
Mt 6:34 Each day has enough *t* of its own.
Jn 16:33 In this world you will have *t.*
Ro 8:35 Shall *t* or hardship or persecution

TROUBLED (TROUBLE)
Jn 14: 1 "Do not let your hearts be *t.*
14:27 Do not let your hearts be *t*

TROUBLES (TROUBLE)
1Co 7:28 those who marry will face many *t*
2Co 1: 4 who comforts us in all our *t,*
4:17 and momentary *t* are achieving

TRUE (TRUTH)
Dt 18:22 does not take place or come *t,*

1Sa 9: 6 and everything he says comes *t.*
Ps 119:160 All your words are *t;*
Jn 17: 3 the only *t* God, and Jesus Christ,
Ro 3: 4 Let God be *t,* and every man a liar.
Php 4: 8 whatever is *t,* whatever is noble,
Rev 22: 6 These words are trustworthy and *t.*

TRUMPET
1Co 14: 8 if the *t* does not sound a clear call,
15:52 For the *t* will sound, the dead will

TRUST (ENTRUSTED TRUSTED TRUSTS TRUSTWORTHY)
Ps 20: 7 we *t* in the name of the LORD our
37: 3 *T* in the LORD and do good;
56: 4 in God I *t;* I will not be afraid.
119: 42 for I *t* in your word.
Pr 3: 5 *T* in the LORD with all your heart
Isa 30:15 in quietness and *t* is your strength,
Jn 14: 1 *T* in God; *t* also in me.
1Co 4: 2 been given a *t* must prove faithful.

TRUSTED (TRUST)
Ps 26: 1 I have *t* in the LORD
Isa 25: 9 we *t* in him, and he saved us.
Da 3:28 They *t* in him and defied the king's
Lk 16:10 *t* with very little can also be *t*

TRUSTS (TRUST)
Ps 32:10 surrounds the man who *t* in him.
Pr 11:28 Whoever *t* in his riches will fall,
28:26 He who *t* in himself is a fool,
Ro 9:33 one who *t* in him will never be put

TRUSTWORTHY (TRUST)
Ps 119:138 they are fully *t.*
Pr 11:13 but a *t* man keeps a secret.
Rev 22: 6 "These words are *t* and true.

TRUTH (TRUE TRUTHFUL TRUTHS)
Ps 51: 6 Surely you desire *t*
Isa 45:19 I, the LORD, speak the *t;*
Zec 8:16 are to do: Speak the *t* to each other,
Jn 4:23 worship the Father in spirit and *t,*
8:32 Then you will know the *t,*
8:32 and the *t* will set you free."
14: 6 I am the way and the *t* and the life.
16:13 comes, he will guide you into all *t.*
18:38 "What is *t?*" Pilate asked.
Ro 1:25 They exchanged the *t* of God
1Co 13: 6 in evil but rejoices with the *t.*
2Co 13: 8 against the *t,* but only for the *t.*
Eph 4:15 Instead, speaking the *t* in love,
6:14 with the belt of *t* buckled
2Th 2:10 because they refused to love the *t*
1Ti 2: 4 to come to a knowledge of the *t.*
3:15 the pillar and foundation of the *t.*
2Ti 2:15 correctly handles the word of *t.*
3: 7 never able to acknowledge the *t.*
Heb 10:26 received the knowledge of the *t,*
1Pe 1:22 by obeying the *t* so that you have
2Pe 2: 2 the way of *t* into disrepute.
1Jn 1: 6 we lie and do not live by the *t.*
1: 8 deceive ourselves and the *t* is not

TRUTHFUL (TRUTH)
Pr 12:22 but he delights in men who are *t.*
Jn 3:33 it has certified that God is *t.*

TRUTHS (TRUTH)
1Co 2:13 expressing spiritual *t*
1Ti 3: 9 hold of the deep *t* of the faith
Heb 5:12 to teach you the elementary *t*

TRY (TRYING)
Ps 26: 2 Test me, O LORD, and *t* me,
Isa 7:13 enough to *t* the patience of men?
1Co 14:12 *t* to excel in gifts that build up
2Co 5:11 is to fear the Lord, we *t*
1Th 5:15 always *t* to be kind to each other

TRYING (TRY)
2Co 5:12 We are not *t* to commend ourselves
1Th 2: 4 We are not *t* to please men but God

TUNIC
Lk 6:29 do not stop him from taking your *t.*

TURN (TURNED TURNS)
Ex 32:12 *T* from your fierce anger; relent
Dt 5:32 do not *t* aside to the right
28:14 Do not *t* aside from any
Jos 1: 7 do not *t* from it to the right
2Ch 7:14 and *t* from their wicked ways,
30: 9 He will not *t* his face from you
Ps 78: 6 they in *t* would tell their children.
Pr 22: 6 when he is old he will not *t* from it.
Isa 29:16 You *t* things upside down,
30:21 Whether you *t* to the right
45:22 "*T* to me and be saved,
55: 7 Let him *t* to the LORD,
Eze 33:11 *T! T* from your evil ways!
Mal 4: 6 He will *t* the hearts of the fathers
Mt 5:39 you on the right cheek, *t*
10:35 For I have come to *t*
Jn 12:40 nor *t*— and I would heal them."
Ac 3:19 Repent, then, and *t* to God,
26:18 and *t* them from darkness to light,
1Ti 6:20 *T* away from godless chatter
1Pe 3:11 He must *t* from evil and do good;

TURNED (TURN)
Ps 30:11 You *t* my wailing into dancing;
40: 1 he *t* to me and heard my cry.
Isa 53: 6 each of us has *t* to his own way;
Hos 7: 8 Ephraim is a flat cake not *t* over.
Joel 2:31 The sun will be *t* to darkness
Ro 3:12 All have *t* away,

TURNS (TURN)
2Sa 22:29 the LORD *t* my darkness into light
Pr 15: 1 A gentle answer *t* away wrath,
Isa 44:25 and *t* it into nonsense,
Jas 5:20 Whoever *t* a sinner from the error

TWELVE
Ge 49:28 All these are the *t* tribes of Israel,
Mt 10: 1 He called his *t* disciples to him

TWINKLING*
1Co 15:52 in a flash, in the *t* of an eye,

UNAPPROACHABLE*
1Ti 6:16 immortal and who lives in *u* light,

UNBELIEF (UNBELIEVER UNBELIEVERS UNBELIEVING)
Mk 9:24 help me overcome my *u!*"
Ro 11:20 they were broken off because of *u,*
Heb 3:19 able to enter, because of their *u.*

UNBELIEVER* (UNBELIEF)
1Co 7:15 But if the *u* leaves, let him do so.
10:27 If some *u* invites you to a meal
14:24 if an *u* or someone who does not
2Co 6:15 have in common with an *u?*
1Ti 5: 8 the faith and is worse than an *u.*

UNBELIEVERS (UNBELIEF)
1Co 6: 6 another—and this in front of *u!*
2Co 6:14 Do not be yoked together with *u.*

UNBELIEVING (UNBELIEF)
1Co 7:14 For the *u* husband has been
Rev 21: 8 But the cowardly, the *u,* the vile,

UNCERTAIN*
1Ti 6:17 which is so *u,* but to put their hope

UNCHANGEABLE*
Heb 6:18 by two *u* things in which it is

UNCIRCUMCISED
1Sa 17:26 Who is this *u* Philistine that he
Col 3:11 circumcised or *u,* barbarian,

UNCIRCUMCISION
1Co 7:19 is nothing and *u* is nothing.
Gal 5: 6 neither circumcision nor *u* has any

UNCLEAN
Isa 6: 5 ruined! For I am a man of *u* lips,
Ro 14:14 fully convinced that no food is *u*
2Co 6:17 Touch no *u* thing,

UNCONCERNED*
Eze 16:49 were arrogant, overfed and *u;*

UNCOVERED
Heb 4:13 Everything is *u* and laid bare

UNDERSTAND (UNDERSTANDING UNDERSTANDS)
Job 42: 3 Surely I spoke of things I did not *u,*
Ps 73:16 When I tried to *u* all this,
119:125 that I may *u* your statutes.
Lk 24:45 so they could *u* the Scriptures.
Ac 8:30 "Do you *u* what you are reading?"
Ro 7:15 I do not *u* what I do.
1Co 2:14 and he cannot *u* them,
Eph 5:17 but *u* what the Lord's will is.
2Pe 3:16 some things that are hard to *u,*

UNDERSTANDING (UNDERSTAND)
Ps 119:104 I gain *u* from your precepts;
147: 5 his *u* has no limit.
Pr 3: 5 and lean not on your own *u;*
4: 7 Though it cost all you have, get *u.*
10:23 but a man of *u* delights in wisdom.
11:12 but a man of *u* holds his tongue.
15:21 a man of *u* keeps a straight course.
15:32 whoever heeds correction gains *u.*
23:23 get wisdom, discipline and *u.*
Isa 40:28 and his *u* no one can fathom.
Da 5:12 a keen mind and knowledge and *u,*
Mk 4:12 and ever hearing but never *u;*
12:33 with all your *u* and with all your
Php 4: 7 of God, which transcends all *u,*

UNDERSTANDS (UNDERSTAND)
1Ch 28: 9 and *u* every motive
1Ti 6: 4 he is conceited and *u* nothing.

UNDIVIDED*
1Ch 12:33 to help David with *u* loyalty—
Ps 86:11 give me an *u* heart,
Eze 11:19 I will give them an *u* heart
1Co 7:35 way in *u* devotion to the Lord.

UNDOING
Pr 18: 7 A fool's mouth is his *u,*

UNDYING*
Eph 6:24 Lord Jesus Christ with an *u* love.

UNFADING*
1Pe 3: 4 the *u* beauty of a gentle

UNFAILING
Ps 33: 5 the earth is full of his *u* love.
119: 76 May your *u* love be my comfort,
143: 8 bring me word of your *u* love,
Pr 19:22 What a man desires is *u* love;
La 3:32 so great is his *u* love.

UNFAITHFUL (UNFAITHFULNESS)
Lev 6: 2 is *u* to the LORD by deceiving his
1Ch 10:13 because he was *u* to the LORD;
Pr 13:15 but the way of the *u* is hard.

UNFAITHFULNESS (UNFAITHFUL)
Mt 5:32 except for marital *u,* causes her
19: 9 for marital *u,* and marries another

UNFOLDING
Ps 119:130 the *u* of your words gives light;

UNGODLINESS
Tit 2:12 It teaches us to say "No" to *u*

UNIT
1Co 12:12 body is a *u,* though it is made up

UNITED (UNITY)
Ro 6: 5 If we have been *u* with him
Php 2: 1 from being *u* with Christ,
Col 2: 2 encouraged in heart and *u* in love,

UNITY (UNITED)
Ps 133: 1 is when brothers live together in *u!*
Ro 15: 5 a spirit of *u* among yourselves
Eph 4: 3 effort to keep the *u* of the Spirit
4:13 up until we all reach *u* in the faith
Col 3:14 them all together in perfect *u.*

UNIVERSE
Php 2:15 which you shine like stars in the *u*
Heb 1: 2 and through whom he made the *u.*

UNKNOWN
Ac 17:23 TO AN *U* GOD.

UNLEAVENED
Ex 12:17 "Celebrate the Feast of *U* Bread,

UNPROFITABLE
Tit 3: 9 because these are *u* and useless.

UNPUNISHED
Ex 34: 7 Yet he does not leave the guilty *u;*
Pr 19: 5 A false witness will not go *u,*

UNREPENTANT*
Ro 2: 5 stubbornness and your *u* heart,

UNRIGHTEOUS*
Zep 3: 5 yet the *u* know no shame.
Mt 5:45 rain on the righteous and the *u.*
1Pe 3:18 the righteous for the *u,* to bring you
2Pe 2: 9 and to hold the *u* for the day

UNSEARCHABLE
Ro 11:33 How *u* his judgments,
Eph 3: 8 preach to the Gentiles the *u* riches

UNSEEN
2Co 4:18 on what is seen, but on what is *u.*
4:18 temporary, but what is *u* is eternal.

UNSTABLE*
Jas 1: 8 he is a double-minded man, *u*
2Pe 2:14 they seduce the *u;* they are experts
3:16 ignorant and *u* people distort,

UNTHINKABLE*
Job 34:12 It is *u* that God would do wrong,

UNVEILED*
2Co 3:18 with *u* faces all reflect the Lord's

UNWORTHY
Job 40: 4 "I am *u*— how can I reply to you?
Lk 17:10 should say, 'We are *u* servants;

UPRIGHT
Job 1: 1 This man was blameless and *u;*
Pr 2: 7 He holds victory in store for the *u,*
15: 8 but the prayer of the *u* pleases him.
Tit 1: 8 who is self-controlled, *u,* holy
2:12 *u* and godly lives in this present

UPROOTED
Jude :12 without fruit and *u*— twice dead.

USEFUL
2Ti 2:21 *u* to the Master and prepared
3:16 Scripture is God-breathed and is *u*

USELESS
1Co 15:14 our preaching is *u*
Jas 2:20 faith without deeds is *u?*

USURY
Ne 5:10 But let the exacting of *u* stop!

UTTER
Ps 78: 2 I will *u* hidden things, things from of

UZZIAH
Son of Amaziah; king of Judah also known as Azariah (2Ki 15:1-7; 1Ch 6:24; 2Ch 26).

VAIN
Ps 33:17 A horse is a *v* hope for deliverance;
Isa 65:23 They will not toil in *v*
1Co 15: 2 Otherwise, you have believed in *v.*
15:58 labor in the Lord is not in *v.*
2Co 6: 1 not to receive God's grace in *v.*

VALLEY
Ps 23: 4 walk through the *v* of the shadow
Isa 40: 4 Every *v* shall be raised up,
Joel 3:14 multitudes in the *v* of decision!

VALUABLE (VALUE)
Lk 12:24 And how much more *v* you are

VALUE (VALUABLE)
Mt 13:46 When he found one of great *v,*
1Ti 4: 8 For physical training is of some *v,*
Heb 11:26 as of greater *v* than the treasures

VEIL
Ex 34:33 to them, he put a *v* over his face.
2Co 3:14 for to this day the same *v* remains

VENGEANCE (AVENGE REVENGE)
Isa 34: 8 For the LORD has a day of *v,*

VICTORIES (VICTORY)
Ps 18:50 He gives his king great *v;*

Ps 21: 1 great is his joy in the *v* you give!

VICTORIOUSLY* (VICTORY)
Ps 45: 4 In your majesty ride forth *v*

VICTORY (VICTORIES VICTORIOUSLY)
Ps 60:12 With God we will gain the *v*,
1Co 15:54 "Death has been swallowed up in *v*
15:57 He gives us the *v* through our Lord
1Jn 5: 4 This is the *v* that has overcome

VINDICATED
1Ti 3:16 was *v* by the Spirit,

VINE
Jn 15: 1 "I am the true *v*, and my Father is

VINEGAR
Mk 15:36 filled a sponge with wine *v*,

VIOLATION
Heb 2: 2 every *v* and disobedience received

VIOLENCE
Isa 60:18 No longer will *v* be heard
Eze 45: 9 Give up your *v* and oppression

VIPERS
Ro 3:13 "The poison of *v* is on their lips."

VIRGIN
Isa 7:14 The *v* will be with child
Mt 1:23 "The *v* will be with child
2Co 11: 2 that I might present you as a pure *v*

VIRTUES*
Col 3:14 And over all these *v* put on love,

VISION
Ac 26:19 disobedient to the *v* from heaven.

VOICE
Ps 95: 7 Today, if you hear his *v*,
Isa 30:21 your ears will hear a *v* behind you,
Jn 5:28 are in their graves will hear his *v*
10: 3 and the sheep listen to his *v*.
Heb 3: 7 "Today, if you hear his *v*,
Rev 3:20 If anyone hears my *v* and opens

VOMIT
Pr 26:11 As a dog returns to its *v*,
2Pe 2:22 "A dog returns to its *v*," and,

VOW
Nu 30: 2 When a man makes a *v*

WAGES
Lk 10: 7 for the worker deserves his *w*.
Ro 4: 4 his *w* are not credited to him
6:23 For the *w* of sin is death,

WAILING
Ps 30:11 You turned my *w* into dancing;

WAIST
2Ki 1: 8 with a leather belt around his *w*."
Mt 3: 4 he had a leather belt around his *w*.

WAIT (WAITED WAITS)
Ps 27:14 *W* for the LORD;
Ps 130: 5 I *w* for the LORD, my soul waits,
Isa 30:18 Blessed are all who *w* for him!
Ac 1: 4 *w* for the gift my Father promised,
Ro 8:23 as we *w* eagerly for our adoption
1Th 1:10 and to *w* for his Son from heaven,
Tit 2:13 while we *w* for the blessed hope—

WAITED (WAIT)
Ps 40: 1 I *w* patiently for the LORD;

WAITS (WAIT)
Ro 8:19 creation *w* in eager expectation

WALK (WALKED WALKS)
Dt 11:19 and when you *w* along the road,
Ps 1: 1 who does not *w* in the counsel
23: 4 Even though I *w*
89:15 who *w* in the light of your presence
Isa 2: 5 let us *w* in the light of the LORD.
30:21 saying, "This is the way; *w* in it."
40:31 they will *w* and not be faint.
Jer 6:16 ask where the good way is, and *w*
Da 4:37 And those who *w* in pride he is able
Am 3: 3 Do two *w* together
Mic 6: 8 and to *w* humbly with your God.
Mk 2: 9 'Get up, take your mat and *w*'?
Jn 8:12 Whoever follows me will never *w*
1Jn 1: 7 But if we *w* in the light,
2Jn : 6 his command is that you *w* in love.

WALKED (WALK)
Ge 5:24 Enoch *w* with God; then he was no
Jos 14: 9 which your feet have *w* will be your
Mt 14:29 *w* on the water and came toward

WALKS (WALK)
Pr 13:20 He who *w* with the wise grows wise

WALL
Jos 6:20 *w* collapsed; so every man charged
Ne 2:17 let us rebuild the *w* of Jerusalem,
Rev 21:12 It had a great, high *w*

WALLOWING
2Pe 2:22 back to her *w* in the mud."

WANT (WANTED WANTING WANTS)
1Sa 8:19 "We *w* a king over us.
Ps 23: 1 is my shepherd, I shall not be in *w*.
Lk 19:14 'We don't *w* this man to be our king
Ro 7:15 For what I *w* to do I do not do,
Php 3:10 I *w* to know Christ and the power

WANTED (WANT)
1Co 12:18 of them, just as he *w* them to be.

WANTING (WANT)
Da 5:27 weighed on the scales and found *w*.
2Pe 3: 9 with you, not *w* anyone to perish,

WANTS (WANT)
Mt 20:26 whoever *w* to become great
Mk 8:35 For whoever *w* to save his life will
Ro 9:18 he hardens whom he *w* to harden.
1Ti 2: 4 who *w* all men to be saved

WAR (WARS)
Isa 2: 4 nor will they train for *w* anymore.
Da 9:26 *W* will continue until the end,
2Co 10: 3 we do not wage *w* as the world does
Rev 19:11 With justice he judges and makes *w*

WARN (WARNED WARNINGS)
Eze 3:19 But if you do *w* the wicked man
33: 9 if you do *w* the wicked man to turn

WARNED (WARN)
Ps 19:11 By them is your servant *w*;

WARNINGS (WARN)
1Co 10:11 and were written down as *w* for us,

WARS (WAR)
Ps 46: 9 He makes *w* cease to the ends
Mt 24: 6 You will hear of *w* and rumors of *w*,

WASH (WASHED WASHING)
Ps 51: 7 *w* me, and I will be whiter
Jn 13: 5 and began to *w* his disciples' feet,
Ac 22:16 be baptized and *w* your sins away,
Rev 22:14 Blessed are those who *w* their robes

WASHED (WASH)
1Co 6:11 you were *w*, you were sanctified,
Rev 7:14 they have *w* their robes

WASHING (WASH)
Eph 5:26 cleansing her by the *w* with water
Tit 3: 5 us through the *w* of rebirth

WATCH (WATCHES WATCHING WATCHMAN)
Ge 31:49 "May the LORD keep *w*
Jer 31:10 will *w* over his flock like a shepherd
Mt 24:42 "Therefore keep *w*, because you do
26:41 *W* and pray so that you will not fall
Lk 2: 8 keeping *w* over their flocks at night
1Ti 4:16 *W* your life and doctrine closely.

WATCHES (WATCH)
Ps 1: 6 For the LORD *w* over the way
121: 3 he who *w* over you will not slumber

WATCHING (WATCH)
Lk 12:37 whose master finds them *w*

WATCHMAN (WATCH)
Eze 3:17 I have made you a *w* for the house

WATER (WATERED WATERS)
Ps 1: 3 like a tree planted by streams of *w*,
22:14 I am poured out like *w*,

Pr 25:21 if he is thirsty, give him *w* to drink.
Isa 49:10 and lead them beside springs of *w*.
Jer 2:13 broken cisterns that cannot hold *w*.
Zec 14: 8 On that day living *w* will flow out
Mk 9:41 anyone who gives you a cup of *w*
Jn 4:10 he would have given you living *w*."
7:38 streams of living *w* will flow
Eph 5:26 washing with *w* through the word,
1Pe 3:21 this *w* symbolizes baptism that now
Rev 21: 6 cost from the spring of the *w* of life.

WATERED (WATER)
1Co 3: 6 I planted the seed, Apollos *w* it,

WATERS (WATER)
Ps 23: 2 he leads me beside quiet *w*,
Ecc 11: 1 Cast your bread upon the *w*,
Isa 58:11 like a spring whose *w* never fail.
1Co 3: 7 plants nor he who *w* is anything,

WAVE (WAVES)
Jas 1: 6 he who doubts is like a *w* of the sea,

WAVES (WAVE)
Isa 57:20 whose *w* cast up mire and mud.
Mt 8:27 Even the winds and the *w* obey him
Eph 4:14 tossed back and forth by the *w*,

WAY (WAYS)
Dt 1:33 to show you the *w* you should go.
2Sa 22:31 "As for God, his *w* is perfect;
Job 23:10 But he knows the *w* that I take;
Ps 1: 1 or stand in the *w* of sinners
37: 5 Commit your *w* to the LORD;
119: 9 can a young man keep his *w* pure?
139: 24 See if there is any offensive *w* in me
Pr 14:12 There is a *w* that seems right
16:17 he who guards his *w* guards his life.
22: 6 Train a child in the *w* he should go,
Isa 30:21 saying, "This is the *w*; walk in it."
53: 6 each of us has turned to his own *w*;
55: 7 Let the wicked forsake his *w*
Mt 3: 3 'Prepare the *w* for the Lord,
Jn 14: 6 "I am the *w* and the truth
1Co 10:13 also provide a *w* out so that you can
12:31 will show you the most excellent *w*.
Heb 4:15 who has been tempted in every *w*,
9: 8 was showing by this that the *w*
10:20 and living *w* opened for us

WAYS (WAY)
Ex 33:13 teach me your *w* so I may know
Ps 25:10 All the *w* of the LORD are loving
51:13 I will teach transgressors your *w*,
Pr 3: 6 in all your *w* acknowledge him,
Isa 55: 8 neither are your *w* my *w*,"
Jas 3: 2 We all stumble in many *w*.

WEAK (WEAKER WEAKNESS)
Mt 26:41 spirit is willing, but the body is *w*."
Ro 14: 1 Accept him whose faith is *w*,
1Co 1:27 God chose the *w* things
8: 9 become a stumbling block to the *w*.
9:22 To the *w* I became *w*, to win the *w*.
2Co 12:10 For when I am *w*, then I am strong.
Heb 12:12 your feeble arms and *w* knees.

WEAKER (WEAK)
1Co 12:22 seem to be *w* are indispensable,
1Pe 3: 7 them with respect as the *w* partner

WEAKNESS (WEAK)
Ro 8:26 the Spirit helps us in our *w*.
1Co 1:25 and the *w* of God is stronger
2Co 12: 9 for my power is made perfect in *w*
Heb 5: 2 since he himself is subject to *w*.

WEALTH
Pr 3: 9 Honor the LORD with your *w*,
Mk 10:22 away sad, because he had great *w*.
Lk 15:13 and there squandered his *w*

WEAPONS
2Co 10: 4 The *w* we fight with are not

WEARIES (WEARY)
Ecc 12:12 and much study *w* the body.

WEARY (WEARIES)
Isa 40:31 they will run and not grow *w*,
Mt 11:28 all you who are *w* and burdened,
Gal 6: 9 Let us not become *w* in doing good,

WEDDING
Mt 22:11 who was not wearing *w* clothes.
Rev 19: 7 For the *w* of the Lamb has come,

WEEP (WEEPING WEPT)
Ecc 3: 4 a time to *w* and a time to laugh,
Lk 6:21 Blessed are you who *w* now,

WEEPING (WEEP)
Ps 30: 5 *w* may remain for a night,
126: 6 He who goes out *w*,
Mt 8:12 where there will be *w* and gnashing

WELCOMES
Mt 18: 5 whoever *w* a little child like this
2Jn :11 Anyone who *w* him shares

WELL
Lk 17:19 your faith has made you *w*."
Jas 5:15 in faith will make the sick person *w*

WEPT (WEEP)
Ps 137: 1 of Babylon we sat and *w*
Jn 11:35 Jesus *w*.

WEST
Ps 103: 12 as far as the east is from the *w*,

WHIRLWIND (WIND)
2Ki 2: 1 to take Elijah up to heaven in a *w*,
Hos 8: 7 and reap the *w*.
Na 1: 3 His way is in the *w* and the storm,

WHITE (WHITER)
Isa 1:18 they shall be as *w* as snow;
Da 7: 9 His clothing was as *w* as snow;
Rev 1:14 hair were *w* like wool, as *w* as snow,
3: 4 dressed in *w*, for they are worthy.
20:11 Then I saw a great *w* throne

WHITER (WHITE)
Ps 51: 7 and I will be *w* than snow.

WHOLE
Mt 16:26 for a man if he gains the *w* world,
24:14 will be preached in the *w* world
Jn 13:10 to wash his feet; his *w* body is clean
21:25 the *w* world would not have room
Ac 20:27 proclaim to you the *w* will of God.
Ro 3:19 and the *w* world held accountable
8:22 know that the *w* creation has been
Gal 3:22 declares that the *w* world is
5: 3 obligated to obey the *w* law.
Eph 4:13 attaining to the *w* measure
Jas 2:10 For whoever keeps the *w* law
1Jn 2: 2 but also for the sins of the *w* world.

WHOLEHEARTEDLY (HEART)
Dt 1:36 because he followed the LORD *w*
Eph 6: 7 Serve *w*, as if you were serving

WICKED (WICKEDNESS)
Ps 1: 1 walk in the counsel of the *w*
1: 5 Therefore the *w* will not stand
73: 3 when I saw the prosperity of the *w*.
Pr 10:20 the heart of the *w* is of little value.
11:21 The *w* will not go unpunished,
Isa 53: 9 He was assigned a grave with the *w*
55: 7 Let the *w* forsake his way
57:20 But the *w* are like the tossing sea,
Eze 3:18 that *w* man will die for his sin,
18:23 pleasure in the death of the *w*?
33:14 to the *w* man, 'You will surely die,'

WICKEDNESS (WICKED)
Eze 28:15 created till *w* was found in you.

WIDE
Isa 54: 2 stretch your tent curtains *w*,
Mt 7:13 For *w* is the gate and broad is
Eph 3:18 to grasp how *w* and long and high

WIDOW (WIDOWS)
Dt 10:18 cause of the fatherless and the *w*,
Lk 21: 2 saw a poor *w* put in two very small

WIDOWS (WIDOW)
Jas 1:27 look after orphans and *w*

WIFE (WIVES)
Ge 2:24 and mother and be united to his *w*,
24:67 she became his *w*, and he loved her;
Ex 20:17 shall not covet your neighbor's *w*,
Dt 5:21 shall not covet your neighbor's *w*.
Pr 5:18 in the *w* of your youth.
12: 4 *w* of noble character is her
18:22 He who finds a *w* finds what is
19:13 quarrelsome *w* is like a constant
31:10 *w* of noble character who can find?
Mt 19: 3 for a man to divorce his *w* for any
1Co 7: 2 each man should have his own *w*,
7:33 how he can please his *w*—
Eph 5:23 the husband is the head of the *w*
5:33 must love his *w* as he loves himself,
1Ti 3: 2 husband of but one *w*, temperate,
Rev 21: 9 I will show you the bride, the *w*

WILD
Lk 15:13 squandered his wealth in *w* living.
Ro 11:17 and you, though a *w* olive shoot,

WILL (WILLING WILLINGNESS)
Ps 40: 8 I desire to do your *w*, O my God;
143: 10 Teach me to do your *w*,
Isa 53:10 Yet it was the LORD's *w*
Mt 6:10 your *w* be done
26:39 Yet not as I *w*, but as you *w*."
Jn 7:17 If anyone chooses to do God's *w*,
Ac 20:27 to you the whole *w* of God.
Ro 12: 2 and approve what God's *w* is—
1Co 7:37 but has control over his own *w*,
Eph 5:17 understand what the Lord's *w* is.
Php 2:13 for it is God who works in you to *w*
1Th 4: 3 God's *w* that you should be
5:18 for this is God's *w* for you
Heb 9:16 In the case of a *w*, it is necessary
10: 7 I have come to do your *w*, O God
Jas 4:15 "If it is the Lord's *w*,
1Jn 5:14 we ask anything according to his *w*,
Rev 4:11 and by your *w* they were created

WILLING (WILL)
Ps 51:12 grant me a *w* spirit, to sustain me.
Da 3:28 were *w* to give up their lives rather
Mt 18:14 Father in heaven is not *w* that any
23:37 her wings, but you were not *w*.
26:41 The spirit is *w*, but the body is weak

WILLINGNESS (WILL)
2Co 8:12 For if the *w* is there, the gift is

WIN (WINS)
Php 3:14 on toward the goal to *w* the prize
1Th 4:12 your daily life may *w* the respect

WIND (WHIRLWIND)
Jas 1: 6 blown and tossed by the *w*.

WINE
Pr 20: 1 *W* is a mocker and beer a brawler;
Isa 55: 1 Come, buy *w* and milk
Mt 9:17 Neither do men pour new *w*
Lk 23:36 They offered him *w* vinegar
Ro 14:21 not to eat meat or drink *w*
Eph 5:18 on *w*, which leads to debauchery.

WINESKINS
Mt 9:17 do men pour new wine into old *w*.

WINGS
Ru 2:12 under whose *w* you have come
Ps 17: 8 hide me in the shadow of your *w*
Isa 40:31 They will soar on *w* like eagles;
Mal 4: 2 rise with healing in its *w*.
Lk 13:34 hen gathers her chicks under her *w*,

WINS (WIN)
Pr 11:30 and he who *w* souls is wise.

WIPE
Rev 7:17 God will *w* away every tear

WISDOM (WISE)
1Ki 4:29 God gave Solomon *w* and very
Ps 111: 10 of the LORD is the beginning of *w*;
Pr 31:26 She speaks with *w*,
Jer 10:12 he founded the world by his *w*
Mt 11:19 But *w* is proved right by her actions
Lk 2:52 And Jesus grew in *w* and stature,
Ro 11:33 the depth of the riches of the *w*
Col 2: 3 are hidden all the treasures of *w*
Jas 1: 5 of you lacks *w*, he should ask God,

WISE (WISDOM WISER)
1Ki 3:12 give you a *w* and discerning heart,
Job 5:13 He catches the *w* in their craftiness
Ps 19: 7 making *w* the simple.
Pr 3: 7 Do not be *w* in your own eyes;
9: 8 rebuke a *w* man and he will love
10: 1 A *w* son brings joy to his father,
11:30 and he who wins souls is *w*.
13:20 He who walks with the *w* grows *w*,
17:28 Even a fool is thought *w*
Da 12: 3 Those who are *w* will shine like
Mt 11:25 hidden these things from the *w*
1Co 1:27 things of the world to shame the *w*;
2Ti 3:15 able to make you *w* for salvation

WISER (WISE)
1Co 1:25 of God is *w* than man's wisdom,

WITHER (WITHERS)
Ps 1: 3 and whose leaf does not *w*.

WITHERS (WITHER)
Isa 40: 7 The grass *w* and the flowers fall,
1Pe 1:24 the grass *w* and the flowers fall,

WITHHOLD
Ps 84:11 no good thing does he *w*
Pr 23:13 Do not *w* discipline from a child;

WITNESS (WITNESSES)
Jn 1: 8 he came only as a *w* to the light.

WITNESSES (WITNESS)
Dt 19:15 by the testimony of two or three *w*.
Ac 1: 8 and you will be my *w* in Jerusalem,

WIVES (WIFE)
Eph 5:22 *W*, submit to your husbands
5:25 love your *w*, just as Christ loved
1Pe 3: 1 words by the behavior of their *w*,

WOE
Isa 6: 5 "*W* to me!" I cried.

WOLF
Isa 65:25 *w* and the lamb will feed together,

WOMAN (MAN)
Ge 2:22 God made a *w* from
3:15 between you and the *w*,
Lev 20:13 as one lies with a *w*,
Dt 22: 5 *w* must not wear men's
Ru 3:11 a *w* of noble character
Pr 31:30 a *w* who fears the LORD
Mt 5:28 looks at a *w* lustfully
Jn 8: 3 a *w* caught in adultery.
Ro 7: 2 a married *w* is bound to
1Co 11: 3 the head of the *w* is man,
11:13 a *w* to pray to God with
1Ti 2:11 A *w* should learn in

WOMEN (MAN)
Lk 1:42 Blessed are you among *w*,
1Co 14:34 *w* should remain silent in
1Ti 2: 9 want *w* to dress modestly
Tit 2: 3 teach the older *w* to be
1Pe 3: 5 the holy *w* of the past

WOMB
Job 1:21 Naked I came from my mother's *w*,
Jer 1: 5 you in the *w* I knew you,
Lk 1:44 the baby in my *w* leaped for joy.

WONDER (WONDERFUL WONDERS)
Ps 17: 7 Show the *w* of your great love,

WONDERFUL (WONDER)
Job 42: 3 things too *w* for me to know.
Ps 31:21 for he showed his *w* love to me
119: 18 *w* things in your law.
119:129 Your statutes are *w*;
139: 6 Such knowledge is too *w* for me,
Isa 9: 6 *W* Counselor, Mighty God,
1Pe 2: 9 out of darkness into his *w* light.

WONDERS (WONDER)
Job 37:14 stop and consider God's *w*.
Ps 119: 27 then I will meditate on your *w*.
Joel 2:30 I will show *w* in the heavens
Ac 2:19 I will show *w* in the heaven above

WOOD
Isa 44:19 Shall I bow down to a block of *w?*"
1Co 3:12 costly stones, *w,* hay or straw,

WORD (WORDS)
Dt 8: 3 but on every *w* that comes
2Sa 22:31 the *w* of the LORD is flawless.
Ps 119: 9 By living according to your *w.*
119: 11 I have hidden your *w* in my heart
119:105 Your *w* is a lamp to my feet
Pr 12:25 but a kind *w* cheers him up.
25:11 A *w* aptly spoken
30: 5 "Every *w* of God is flawless;
Isa 55:11 so is my *w* that goes out
Jn 1: 1 was the *W,* and the *W* was
1:14 The *W* became flesh and made his
2Co 2:17 we do not peddle the *w* of God
4: 2 nor do we distort the *w* of God.
Eph 6:17 of the Spirit, which is the *w* of God.
Php 2:16 as you hold out the *w* of life—
Col 3:16 Let the *w* of Christ dwell
2Ti 2:15 and who correctly handles the *w*
Heb 4:12 For the *w* of God is living
Jas 1:22 Do not merely listen to the *w,*
2Pe 1:19 And we have the *w* of the prophets

WORDS (WORD)
Dt 11:18 Fix these *w* of mine in your hearts
Ps 119:103 How sweet are your *w* to my taste
119:130 The unfolding of your *w* gives light;
119:160 All your *w* are true;
Pr 30: 6 Do not add to his *w,*
Jer 15:16 When your *w* came, I ate them;
Mt 24:35 but my *w* will never pass away.
Jn 6:68 You have the *w* of eternal life.
15: 7 in me and my *w* remain in you,
1Co 14:19 rather speak five intelligible *w*
Rev 22:19 And if anyone takes *w* away

WORK (WORKER WORKERS WORKING WORKMAN WORKMANSHIP WORKS)
Ex 23:12 "Six days do your *w,*
Nu 8:11 ready to do the *w* of the LORD.
Dt 5:14 On it you shall not do any *w,*
Ecc 5:19 his lot and be happy in his *w*—
Jer 48:10 lax in doing the LORD's *w!*
Jn 6:27 Do not *w* for food that spoils,
9: 4 we must do the *w* of him who sent
1Co 3:13 test the quality of each man's *w.*
Php 1: 6 that he who began a good *w*
2:12 continue to *w* out your salvation
Col 3:23 Whatever you do, *w* at it
1Th 5:12 to respect those who *w* hard
2Th 3:10 If a man will not *w,* he shall not eat
2Ti 3:17 equipped for every good *w.*
Heb 6:10 he will not forget your *w*

WORKER (WORK)
Lk 10: 7 for the *w* deserves his wages.
1Ti 5:18 and "The *w* deserves his wages."

WORKERS (WORK)
Mt 9:37 is plentiful but the *w* are few.
1Co 3: 9 For we are God's fellow *w;*

WORKING (WORK)
Col 3:23 as *w* for the Lord, not for men,

WORKMAN (WORK)
2Ti 2:15 a *w* who does not need

WORKMANSHIP* (WORK)
Eph 2:10 For we are God's *w,* created

WORKS (WORK)
Pr 31:31 let her *w* bring her praise
Ro 8:28 in all things God *w* for the good
Eph 2: 9 not by *w,* so that no one can boast.
4:12 to prepare God's people for *w*

WORLD (WORLDLY)
Ps 50:12 for the *w* is mine, and all that is in it
Isa 13:11 I will punish the *w* for its evil,
Mt 5:14 "You are the light of the *w.*
16:26 for a man if he gains the whole *w,*
Mk 16:15 into all the *w* and preach the good
Jn 1:29 who takes away the sin of the *w!*
3:16 so loved the *w* that he gave his one
8:12 he said, "I am the light of the *w.*
15:19 As it is, you do not belong to the *w,*
16:33 In this *w* you will have trouble.
18:36 "My kingdom is not of this *w.*
Ro 3:19 and the whole *w* held accountable
1Co 3:19 the wisdom of this *w* is foolishness
2Co 5:19 that God was reconciling the *w*
10: 3 For though we live in the *w,*
1Ti 6: 7 For we brought nothing into the *w,*
1Jn 2: 2 but also for the sins of the whole *w.*
2:15 not love the *w* or anything in the *w.*
Rev 13: 8 slain from the creation of the *w.*

WORLDLY (WORLD)
Tit 2:12 to ungodliness and *w* passions,

WORM
Mk 9:48 " 'their *w* does not die,

WORRY (WORRYING)
Mt 6:25 I tell you, do not *w* about your life,
10:19 do not *w* about what to say

WORRYING (WORRY)
Mt 6:27 of you by *w* can add a single hour

WORSHIP
1Ch 16:29 *w* the LORD in the splendor
Ps 95: 6 Come, let us bow down in *w,*
Mt 2: 2 and have come to *w* him."
Jn 4:24 and his worshipers must *w* in spirit
Ro 12: 1 this is your spiritual act of *w.*

WORTH (WORTHY)
Job 28:13 Man does not comprehend its *w;*
Pr 31:10 She is *w* far more than rubies.
Mt 10:31 are *w* more than many sparrows.
Ro 8:18 sufferings are not *w* comparing
1Pe 1: 7 of greater *w* than gold,
3: 4 which is of great *w* in God's sight.

WORTHLESS
Pr 11: 4 Wealth is *w* in the day of wrath,
Jas 1:26 himself and his religion is *w.*

WORTHY (WORTH)
1Ch 16:25 For great is the LORD and most *w*
Eph 4: 1 to live a life *w* of the calling you
Php 1:27 in a manner *w* of the gospel
3Jn : 6 on their way in a manner *w* of God.
Rev 5: 2 "Who is *w* to break the seals

WOUNDS
Pr 27: 6 *W* from a friend can be trusted,
Isa 53: 5 and by his *w* we are healed.
Zec 13: 6 'What are these *w* on your body?'
1Pe 2:24 by his *w* you have been healed.

WRATH
2Ch 36:16 scoffed at his prophets until the *w*
Ps 2: 5 and terrifies them in his *w,* saying,
76:10 Surely your *w* against men brings
Pr 15: 1 A gentle answer turns away *w,*
Jer 25:15 filled with the wine of my *w*
Ro 1:18 The *w* of God is being revealed
5: 9 saved from God's *w* through him!
1Th 5: 9 God did not appoint us to suffer *w*
Rev 6:16 and from the *w* of the Lamb!

WRESTLED
Ge 32:24 and a man *w* with him till daybreak

WRITE (WRITING WRITTEN)
Dt 6: 9 *W* them on the doorframes
Pr 7: 3 *w* them on the tablet of your heart.
Heb 8:10 and *w* them on their hearts.

WRITING (WRITE)
1Co 14:37 him acknowledge that what I am *w*

WRITTEN (WRITE)
Jos 1: 8 careful to do everything *w* in it.
Da 12: 1 everyone whose name is found *w*
Lk 10:20 but rejoice that your names are *w*
Jn 20:31 these are *w* that you may believe
1Co 4: 6 "Do not go beyond what is *w.*"
2Co 3: 3 *w* not with ink but with the Spirit

NOTES

NOTES

NOTES

NOTES